Register online at **www.oup.com/blackstones/criminal** for free online month
Blackstone's Briefing, a free regular newsletter. If you have any queries please co

Please visit www.oup.com/blackstones/criminal

BLACKSTONE'S

CRIMINAL PRACTICE

BLACKSTONE'S

CRIMINAL PRACTICE

2021

GENERAL EDITORS

DAVID ORMEROD QC (HON)

BARRISTER, BENCHER OF MIDDLE TEMPLE,
PROFESSOR OF CRIMINAL JUSTICE,
UNIVERSITY COLLEGE LONDON

DAVID PERRY QC

BARRISTER, 6KBW COLLEGE HILL

FOUNDING EDITOR

HIS HONOUR PETER MURPHY

CONTRIBUTORS

PARAMJIT AHLUWALIA, DUNCAN ATKINSON QC, ALEX BAILIN QC,
DIANE BIRCH OBE, HHJ JONATHAN COOPER, HHJ JOHANNAH CUTTS QC,
ANAND DOOBAY, ANTHONY EDWARDS, HHJ STEVEN EVERETT,
RUDI FORTSON QC, DANIEL GODDEN, HHJ MARTIN EDMUNDS QC,
KATHERINE HARDCASTLE, WILLIAM HAYS, MICHAEL HIRST,
LAURA C. H. HOYANO, PETER HUNGERFORD-WELCH, PAUL JARVIS,
ADRIAN KEANE, SALLY KYD, KARL LAIRD, MICHAEL LEREGO QC,
RICHARD MCMAHON QC, ALEXANDER MILLS, VALSAMIS MITSILEGAS,
TIM MOLONEY QC, REBECCA NIBLOCK, AMANDA PINTO QC,
HH PETER ROOK QC, RICHARD D. TAYLOR,
MARK TOPPING, MARTIN WASIK CBE

OXFORD
UNIVERSITY PRESS

OXFORD
UNIVERSITY PRESS

Great Clarendon Street, Oxford, OX2 6DP,
United Kingdom

Oxford University Press is a department of the University of Oxford.
It furthers the University's objective of excellence in research, scholarship,
and education by publishing worldwide. Oxford is a registered trade mark of
Oxford University Press in the UK and in certain other countries

First Edition published in 1991
Thirtieth Edition published in 2020

Impression: 1

Published in the United States of America by Oxford University Press
198 Madison Avenue, New York, NY 10016, United States of America

British Library Cataloguing in Publication Data
Data available

ISBN 978–0–19–886959–7

Printed in Italy by
L.E.G.O. S.p.A.

Preface

Writing in 1991 in the preface to the first edition of *Blackstone's Criminal Practice*, Peter Murphy noted that the book was the first wholly new work in criminal law since 1822 to deal 'as comprehensively as practicable with all the law of evidence and procedure practitioners need to know'. By 2017 *Blackstone's* had been recognised by the Judicial Executive Board as the standard criminal text to be provided in all criminal courts. It is a testament to the dedication of the team of authors and the publishing team at Oxford University Press that *Blackstone's* has secured such overwhelming trust and respect from practitioners and judges alike.

This 30th edition maintains the high standards for which *Blackstone's* has become renowned by combining, as it does, comprehensive coverage with rigorous analysis. It continues to provide the material necessary for work at all levels of the criminal courts, and is annually updated with writing 'of uncompromising and rigorous scholarly quality... meticulous attention to detail... and emphasis on the practice of the courts', as the preface to the first edition promised.

The last 12 months have created unprecedented challenges for the criminal justice system. *Blackstone's* has produced regular free supplements to deal with the relevant, and rapidly changing, Covid-19 regulations and the Coronavirus Act 2020 and their impact. We are especially grateful to the team who compiled those at such short notice and under other considerable pressures: Peter Hungerford-Welch, Karl Laird, and HHJ Lana Wood. The supplements are available from the Companion Website for *Blackstone's Criminal Practice 2021* and we do not duplicate that material in this main work.

One consequence of Covid-19, coupled with the political upheaval caused by Brexit and the 2019 General Election, has been that there are few new Acts of Parliament affecting criminal justice. We have dealt carefully with those which are relevant, including the Terrorist Offenders (Restriction of Early Release) Act 2020 as well as the numerous SIs including the Misuse of Drugs (Amendment) (England, Wales and Scotland) Regulations 2019 and the Money Laundering, Terrorist Financing and Transfer of Funds (Amendment) Regulations 2019. This edition also incorporates references to the new restatement of the CrimPR 2020 (replacing the 2015 Rules with some new numbering and additional content) as well as providing the text of the Rules in Supplement 1. Similarly, Supplement 1 contains the text of the Sentencing Council definitive guidelines complementing the referencing throughout the main work (this edition sees the inclusion of the new guideline on *Public Order Offences*).

Whilst Covid-19 has also impacted on the volume of appellate decisions handed down this year it has not affected the importance of the new cases examined, including: in the Supreme Court *Copeland* on explosive substances; in the Privy Council *Bain* on unrepresented defendants; in the Court of Appeal *A* on causation; *Mohamadi* and *Campenau* on intoxication; *Varley* on conspiracy to commit fraud; *Foy* on diminished responsibility; *DS* on modern slavery; *Jenkins v DPP* on firearms possession; *Lawrance* on deception and sexual offences, *KC* on 'sustained incident' in sentencing for sexual offences; *Richards* on voyeurism; *Barton* on dishonesty; *Pwr v DPP* on terrorism; *CB* on disclosure and mobile phones; *Reynolds* on summing up; *Thomas* on intermediaries; *PS* on sentencing and mental health; *Rashid* on evidence of gangs; *Nguyen* on hearsay and *Phillips* on identification from social media. In the Divisional Court *Pegram v DPP* on assaulting a police officer in the execution of his duty; *R (Jones) v Metropolitan Police Commissioner* on public assembly; *R (Chabloz) v CPS* on communications offences; *R (BBC) v Newcastle Crown Court* on search warrants; and *R (Chesterfield Poultry Ltd) v Sheffield Magistrates' Court* on judicial review.

The long-awaited Sentencing Code is before Parliament at the time of writing but is unlikely to receive Royal Assent before our publication date. We have however decided to refer to it as the Sentencing Act 2020 as the indications are that it will proceed with support from both government and opposition. To ensure that readers have an accurate statement of the current law at the time of publication, Part E in the main work does not reflect the Code. However an entirely new Part E will be published in Supplement 2 in advance of commencement. That material is vitally important because once the Code is in force, every individual convicted will be sentenced under the Code irrespective of the date of the commission of their offence. We are particularly grateful to Martin Wasik who has shouldered the burden of producing both these versions of Part E.

We express our enormous thanks as ever to the team of authors who have made such superb contributions to the 2021 edition. The team is joined this year by HHJ Steven Everett (the Hon Recorder of Chester) and HHJ Martin Edmunds QC (the Hon Recorder of Kensington and Chelsea) who bring a wealth of judicial experience, and Alexander Mills. Richard McMahon steps down after being solely responsible for Part C on road traffic and we extend our thanks for his meticulous care with that important Part over recent years. We are delighted that Professor Sally Kyd brings her considerable expertise to bear in succeeding him.

The team at Oxford University Press has undergone some significant changes with the departure of Peter Daniell after his many years managing the day to day operation of the book and we are grateful to him for his contribution to the success of *Blackstone's*. We are extremely fortunate in having Iona Jacob (Project Editor), Lucía Pérez (Senior Production Editor) and Nicola Freshwater (Editorial Coordinator) who have managed the production of this edition with great skill despite so many unforeseen challenges and disruptions to the working process.

David Perry would also like to express his thanks for the support of his colleagues at 21 College Hill.

Blackstone's strives to develop to meet the needs of users. We welcome constructive comments and suggestions from readers. Please continue to offer your feedback via the website at www.oup.com/blackstones/criminal. Alternatively, you can send us your comments by email at blackstonescriminal@oup.com.

We have endeavoured to state the law as at 31 July 2020.

Professor David Ormerod QC (Hon)

David Perry QC

Acknowledgements

Particular thanks are due to Nicola Freshwater for copy-editing and editorial coordination. Thanks are also due to Kim Harris for the index, Fiona Stables for the proofreading, Deborah Shelley for the tables, and Penny Dickman for her work on the Supplements.

The Code for Crown Prosecutors in Appendix 3 is reproduced with the kind permission of the Crown Prosecution Service.

The publishers are immensely grateful for detailed and invaluable assistance and for legal updates throughout the year from the research team of Alex Davidson, Niamh McEvoy, Gabriella Lewis, Rebecca Martin-Scott and Karl Laird.

For their thorough content review and insightful comments, we would like to thank Richard Whittam QC; 25 Bedford Row, particularly Nathaniel Rudolf, Emma Stuart-Smith and David Wood; and Doughty Street Chambers, particularly Katy Thorne QC, Christopher Sykes and Peter Finkill-Coombs.

Subscribers are invited to email (**blackstonescriminal@oup.com**) with any feedback or comments so that the service can continue to be developed and improved.

Abbreviations

The following abbreviations have been used in this edition:

ABCPA 2014	Anti-social Behaviour, Crime and Policing Act 2014
ABE	achieving best evidence
A-G	Attorney-General
A-G's Ref	Attorney-General's Reference
ASBA 2003	Anti-social Behaviour Act 2003
ASBO	anti-social behaviour order
A-TCSA 2001	Anti-terrorism, Crime and Security Act 2001
BA 1976	Bail Act 1976
CAA 1981	Criminal Attempts Act 1981
CAJA 2009	Coroners and Justice Act 2009
CBO	criminal behaviour order
CCA 2013	Crime and Courts Act 2013
CCRC	Criminal Cases Review Commission
CDA 1998	Crime and Disorder Act 1998
CJA	Criminal Justice Act (dates vary)
CJCA 2015	Criminal Justice and Courts Act 2015
CJEC	Court of Justice of the European Communities
CJEU	Court of Justice of the European Union
CJIA 2008	Criminal Justice and Immigration Act 2008
CJPA 2001	Criminal Justice and Police Act 2001
CJPO 1994	Criminal Justice and Public Order Act 1994
CLA	Criminal Law Act (dates vary)
CMCHA 2007	Corporate Manslaughter and Corporate Homicide Act 2007
CrimPD	Criminal Practice Directions
CPIA 1996	Criminal Procedure and Investigations Act 1996
CPN	community protection notice
CPS	Crown Prosecution Service
CRASBO	'post-conviction' ASBO
CrimPR	Criminal Procedure Rules 2020
C(S)A 1997	Crime (Sentences) Act 1997
CSO	community support officer
C-TA 2008	Counter-Terrorism Act 2008
C-TBSA 2019	Counter-Terrorism and Border Security Act 2019
C-TSA 2015	Counter-Terrorism and Security Act 2015
CYPA	Children and Young Persons Act (dates vary)
DPP	Director of Public Prosecutions
DVCVA 2004	Domestic Violence, Crime and Victims Act 2004
EAW	European Arrest Warrant
ECHR	European Convention on Human Rights
ECtHR	European Court of Human Rights
FA 1968	Firearms Act 1968
F(A)A	Firearms (Amendment) Act (dates vary)
FCA	Financial Conduct Authority
FSMA 2000	*Financial Services* and Markets Act 2000
HMRC	Her Majesty's Revenue and Customs
HRA 1998	Human Rights Act 1998
IPA 2016	Investigatory Powers Act 2016

IPP	imprisonment for public protection
KCPO	knife crime prevention order
LAA	Legal Aid Agency
LASPO 2012	Legal Aid, Sentencing and Punishment of Offenders Act 2012
MCA 1980	Magistrates' Courts Act 1980
MDA 1971	Misuse of Drugs Act 1971
NCA	National Crime Agency
OAPA 1861	Offences Against the Person Act 1861
ORA 2014	Offender Rehabilitation Act 2014
PACA 2009	Policing and Crime Act 2009
PACE 1984	Police and Criminal Evidence Act 1984
PCA 2017	Policing and Crime Act 2017
PCC(S)A 2000	Powers of Criminal Courts (Sentencing) Act 2000
PET	Preparation for Effective Trial
POA	Public Order Act (dates vary)
POCA 2002	Proceeds of Crime Act 2002
PRSRA 2011	Police Reform and Social Responsibility Act 2011
PSA 2016	Psychoactive Substances Act 2016
PSPO	public spaces protection order
PTPH	Plea and Trial Preparation Hearing
RCPO	Revenue and Customs Prosecutions Office
RIPA 2000	Regulation of Investigatory Powers Act 2000
RTA	Road Traffic Act (dates vary)
RTO	registered terrorist offender
RTOA 1988	Road Traffic Offenders Act 1988
RTRA	Road Traffic Regulation Act (dates vary)
SCA	Serious Crime Act (dates vary)
SCPO	serious crime prevention order
SFO	Serious Fraud Office
SGC	Sentencing Guidelines Council
SHPO	sexual harm prevention order
SMD	special measures direction
SOA	Sexual Offences Act (dates vary)
SOCA	Serious Organised Crime Agency
SOCPA 2005	Serious Organised Crime and Police Act 2005
SOPO	sexual offences prevention order
SPO	stalking protection order
STPO	slavery and trafficking prevention order
STRO	slavery and trafficking reparation/risk order
TA	Terrorism Act (dates vary)
TCDO	temporary class drug order
TPIM	terrorism prevention and investigation measures
UNCLOS	United Nations Convention on the Law of the Sea
VCRA 2006	Violent Crime Reduction Act 2006
VOO	violent offender order
YJCEA 1999	Youth Justice and Criminal Evidence Act 1999
YOT	youth offending team
YRO	youth rehabilitation order

Contributors

Paramjit Ahluwalia, Barrister
Lamb Building Chambers

Duncan Atkinson, QC, Barrister
6KBW College Hill, Senior Prosecuting Counsel for the Crown at the Central Criminal Court

Alex Bailin, QC, Barrister
Matrix Chambers, Recorder of the Crown Court, Deputy High Court Judge (Administrative Court)

Diane Birch, OBE, LLB
JC Smith Professor of Law, University of Nottingham

His Honour Judge Jonathan Cooper, MA, MPhil
Cambridge Crown Court; Honorary Professor, Nottingham Law School, Nottingham Trent University

The Hon. Mrs Justice Cutts
Judge of the Queen's Bench Division of the High Court

Anand Doobay, LLB, LLM, Solicitor
Partner, Boutique Law LLP

His Honour Judge Martin Edmunds, QC
Crown Court at Isleworth

Anthony Edwards, Non-practising solicitor
TV Edwards

His Honour Judge Steven Everett, BA (Hons)
The Honorary Recorder of Chester, Chester Crown Court

Rudi Fortson, QC, LLB, Barrister
25 Bedford Row, London
Visiting Professor of Law at Queen Mary University of London

Daniel Godden, Partner
Berkeley Square Solicitors

Katherine Hardcastle, MA (Hons), MPhil, Barrister
6KBW College Hill

William Hays, BA (Hons), Barrister
6KBW College Hill

Michael Hirst, LLB, LLM, FRSA
Emeritus Professor of Criminal Justice, Leicester De Montfort Law School

Laura C. H. Hoyano, BA, MA, JD, BCL, MA
Associate Professor of Law, University of Oxford; Senior Research Fellow in Law, Wadham College; Fellow of Middle Temple; Barrister, Red Lion Chambers

Peter Hungerford-Welch, LLB, FHEA, Barrister
Professor of Law and Associate Dean, The City Law School, City, University of London

Paul Jarvis, MA, Barrister
6KBW College Hill and Junior Prosecuting Counsel at the Central Criminal Court

Adrian Keane, LLB, Barrister
Emeritus Professor of Law, The City Law School, City, University of London

Sally Kyd, LLB, LLM, PhD
Professor of Law, Leicester Law School, University of Leicester

Karl Laird, LLB, BCL, Barrister
6KBW College Hill
Lecturer in Law, St Edmund Hall, Oxford

Michael Lerego, QC, MA, BCL, FCIArb (retired), FHEA
Visiting Lecturer, The University of Law

Richard McMahon, QC, LLB, LLM
The Deputy Bailiff of Guernsey

Alexander Mills, MA, MA, FHEA, Barrister
Associate Professor of Law, The City Law School, City, University of London

Valsamis Mitsilegas, LLB, LLM, PhD
Professor of European Criminal Law and Global Security and Director of the Criminal Justice Centre, Queen Mary University of London

Tim Moloney, QC, Barrister
Doughty Street Chambers

Rebecca Niblock, Partner
Kingsley Napley

Amanda Pinto, QC, MA, Barrister
33 Chancery Lane

His Honour Peter Rook, QC
Formerly Senior Circuit Judge sitting at the Central Criminal Court; Vice-Chair of the Parole Board of England and Wales

Richard D. Taylor, MA, LLM, Barrister
Professor of English Law, Lancashire Law School, University of Central Lancashire

Mark Topping, LLB, RD, Solicitor

Martin Wasik, CBE, LLB, MA, FRSA, Barrister
Recorder of the Crown Court; Emeritus Professor of Criminal Justice, Keele University

Summary of Contents

APPENDICES

Table of Cases

Aworinde [1996] RTR 66, 159 JP 618, [1995] Crim LR 825 . . . . . C4.18
Awoyemi [2016] 2 Cr App R 22 (303), [2016] EWCA Crim 668 . . . . . F13.7, F13.11, F13.49
Axen v Germany (1983) 6 EHRR 195 . . . . . A7.98
Axworthy [2012] EWCA Crim 2889 . . . . . E19.62
Aydin v Turkey (1998) 25 EHRR 251 . . . . . A7.33
Ayensu (1982) 4 Cr App R (S) 248, [1982] Crim LR 764 . . . . . D20.43, E19.66
Ayeva [2010] 2 Cr App R (S) 22 (143), [2009] EWCA Crim 2640 . . . . . B3.74
Ayhan [2012] 1 WLR 1775, [2012] 1 Cr App R 27 (391), [2012] 2 Cr App R (S) 37 (207), [2011] EWCA Crim 3184 . . . . . D23.58
Aylesbury Justices, ex parte Wisbey [1965] 1 WLR 339, [1965] 1 All ER 602, 129 JP 175, 109 SJ 173 . . . . . D5.15
Ayliffe v DPP [2006] QB 227, [2005] 3 WLR 628, [2005] 3 All ER 330, [2005] Crim LR 959, [2005] EWHC 684 (Admin) B13.45
Aylott [1996] 2 Cr App R 169, [1996] Crim LR 429 . . . . . D13.50, D19.77
Ayodeji [2001] 1 Cr App R (S) 106 (370) B11.202
Ayres [1984] AC 447, [1984] 2 WLR 257, [1984] 1 All ER 619, 78 Cr App R 232 . . . . D11.113, D11.115, D11.116
Ayu [1958] 1 WLR 1264, [1958] 3 All ER 636, 43 Cr App R 31, 123 JP 76 . . . . . E13.8
Azam v Epping Forest District Council [2009] EWHC 3177 (Admin) B16.63, D20.20, D21.19
Aziz [1996] AC 41, [1995] 3 WLR 53, [1995] 3 All ER 149, [1995] 2 Cr App R 478, 159 JP 669, [1995] Crim LR 897 . . . . . B19.67, D18.32, F14.1, F14.2, F14.3, F14.4, F14.11, F14.12, F14.15, F14.16, F14.17, F14.18, F14.19, F14.20, F18.94, F18.97
Aziz [2012] EWCA Crim 1063 . . . . . B19.10, B19.66, B19.104
Aziz [2017] 1 Cr App R (S) 28 (199), [2016] EWCA Crim 1945 . . . . . C3.38
Aziz [2019] EWCA Crim 1568 . . . . . D24.77, E3.12

B [2000] Crim LR 181 . . . . . F5.10
B [2001] 1 Cr App R (S) 89 (303), [2000] Crim LR 870 . . . . . E7.24
B [2004] 2 Cr App R 34 (570), [2004] EWCA Crim 1254 . . . . . D11.87
B [2004] EWCA Crim 1481 . . . . . F19.12
B [2006] Crim LR 54, [2005] EWCA Crim 805 . . . . . D4.9, F7.20
B [2007] 1 WLR 1567, [2007] 1 Cr App R 29 (388), [2006] EWCA Crim 2945 . . . . . B3.44, B3.51
B [2009] 1 Cr App R 19 (261), [2009] 1 WLR 1545, [2008] EWCA Crim 1997 . . . . . D12.8
B [2009] EWCA Crim 2113 . . . . . F18.5
B [2010] 1 Cr App R 16 (181), [2010] 2 All ER 728, [2009] EWCA Crim 2575 . . . . . B7.38
B [2011] EWCA Crim 2566 . . . . . B2.149
B [2013] 1 WLR 499, [2012] 2 Cr App R 15 (164), [2012] 3 All ER 1093, 176 JP 313, [2013] Crim LR 90, [2012] EWCA Crim 770 . . . . . C3.23, D12.11
B [2013] 2 Cr App R (S) 69 (443), [2013] Crim LR 614, [2013] EWCA Crim 291 . . . . . B11.179, E1.19
B [2017] 1 Cr App R 31 (457), [2017] EWCA Crim 35 . . . . . F13.39, F14
B (A Minor) v DPP [2000] 2 AC 428, [2000] 2 WLR 452, [2000] 1 All ER 833, [2000] 2 Cr App R 65 (HL); reversing [1999] 3 WLR 116, [1999] 4 All ER 265, [1999] 1 Cr App R 163 (DC) A2.18, A2.20, A2.30, A2.35, A3.6, A6.12, B2.138
B (A Minor) (Wardship: Medical Treatment), Re [1981] 1 WLR 1421, 80 LGR 107 . . . . . A1.21
B and R v DPP (2007) 171 JP 404, [2007] EWHC 739 (Admin) B4.70
B and S [2008] EWCA Crim 365 . . . . . F17.39
B (F) [2011] 1 WLR 844, [2010] 2 Cr App R 35 (422), [2011] Crim LR 81, [2010] EWCA Crim 1857 . . . . . D4.4, D4.10
B (JJ) [2012] 1 WLR 3133, [2012] EWCA Crim 1440 . . . . . D11.105, D11.107, D19.58
B (MA) [2013] 1 Cr App R 36 (481), [2013] EWCA Crim 3 . . . . . B3.37
B (MT) [2000] Crim LR 181 . . . . . F20.11
B, Re [2008] EWHC 3217 (Admin) E19.82
B (Restraint Order), Re [2009] 1 Cr App R 14 (203), [2008] EWCA Crim 1374 . . . . . D8.63
B (T) [2006] 2 Cr App R 3 (22), [2006] EWCA Crim 417 . . . . . F11.37, F11.39, F11.40
B v Auckland District Law Society [2003] 2 AC 736, [2003] 3 WLR 859, [2004] 4 All ER 269, (2003) UKPC 38 . . . . . F10.17
B v Austria (1991) 13 EHRR 20 . . . . . A7.73
B v Chief Constable of the Police Service of Northern Ireland [2015] EWHC 3691 (Admin) D1.25, D1.28
B v DPP (2008) 172 JP 449, [2008] EWHC 1655 (Admin) B2.45, B2.52, B4.73, B19.114, D1.13
B v DPP [2012] 1 WLR 2357, [2012] 2 Cr App R 2 (9), 176 JP 97, [2012] EWHC 72 (Admin) D25.29
B v Leathley [1979] Crim LR 314 . . . . . B4.84
B & Q plc [2005] EWCA Crim 2297 . . . . . D26.28
BBGP Managing General Partner Ltd v Babcock & Brown Global Partners [2011] Ch 296, [2011] 2 WLR 496, [2011] 2 All ER 297, [2010] EWHC 2176 (Ch) F10.36
BD [2018] EWCA Crim 154 . . . . . B2.102
BJ [2020] NICA 5 . . . . . F5.5, F5.9
BM [2018] EWCA Crim 560 . . . . . B2.16
BM v Republic of Ireland (No. 2) [2020] 4 WLR 70, [2020] EWHC 648 (Admin) D31.39
BR [2014] EWCA Crim 1311 . . . . . F13.64
BS v Court of First Instance Brussels (Belgium) [2017] EWHC 571 (Admin) D31.42
Baballa [2011] 1 Cr App R (S) 50 (329), [2010] EWCA Crim 1950 . . . . . B20.12
Babbs [2007] EWCA Crim 2737 . . . . . B11.153
Babiak [2017] 1 Cr App R (S) 52 (407), [2017] EWCA Crim 160 . . . . . E2.19
Backhouse [2010] EWCA Crim 1111 . . . . . C7.37
Backshall [1998] 1 WLR 1506, [1999] 1 Cr App R 35, [1998] RTR 423, [1999] Crim LR 662 . . . . . A3.50, C6.7
Badham [1987] Crim LR 202 . . . . . D1.140

Table of Statutes

Where a paragraph reference is underlined, this is the main entry for the relevant material, much of which is reproduced at that reference

OTHER JURISDICTIONS

Ireland

New Zealand

Table of Statutory Instruments

Where a paragraph reference is underlined much of the relevant material is reproduced at that reference

Table of Practice Directions

Where a paragraph reference is underlined the relevant material is reproduced at that reference but note that the full text of the Criminal Practice Directions is reproduced in the Supplement

Table of Codes of Conduct

Where a paragraph reference is underlined the relevant material is reproduced at that reference

Table of Guidelines

Where a paragraph reference is underlined the relevant material is reproduced at that reference

Table of Protocols and Circulars

Where a paragraph reference is underlined the relevant material is reproduced at that reference

Table of International Treaties and Conventions

Where a paragraph reference is underlined the relevant material is reproduced at that reference

Table of European Legislation

Where a paragraph reference is underlined the relevant material is reproduced at that reference

Section A1 *Actus Reus*: The External Elements of an Offence

INTRODUCTION

A1.1 It is customary to separate the essential elements of a crime into two main elements: (1) the prohibited act, omission or state of affairs, together with any specified consequence (the *actus reus*); and (2) any fault element, such as intent or recklessness, required in respect of it (the *mens rea*). *Smith, Hogan and Ormerod's Criminal Law* (15th edn, 2018, at p. 26) defines the *actus reus* as including 'all the elements in the definition of the crime except D's mental element or fault'. It thus represents the external manifestation of the offence.

THE NATURE OF AN *ACTUS REUS*

Conduct Crimes and Result Crimes

A1.2 The *actus reus* of an offence may be defined in such a way that D's conduct must cause or result in specified consequences. Homicide, for example, requires proof that D's conduct caused the death of another; and since assault requires the apprehension of imminent unlawful force, no assault is committed by D if a stone thrown at V flies past, unnoticed. Such offences may be referred to as 'result crimes'. In contrast, many offences are defined in such a way that the consequences, if any, of D's behaviour are irrelevant to liability. D's behaviour may amount to the complete *actus reus* of the offence, even if it fails to bring about the consequences intended or indeed any consequences at all. The *actus reus* of blackmail, for example, is complete as soon as D makes an unwarranted demand with menaces. A demand is 'made' as soon as it is uttered, and does not require successful communication to V (or anyone else). The mere posting of a letter containing such a demand is sufficient (*Treacy v DPP* [1971] AC 537). Blackmail, therefore, is a 'conduct crime' (*Pogmore* [2017] EWCA Crim 925, [2018] 2 Cr App R 2 (14)).

The classification of offences into 'conduct crimes' and 'result crimes' may sometimes seem awkward and unhelpful. Nevertheless, it is always necessary to identify the constituent elements of an offence, and use of this classification sometimes highlights key differences between offences. Thus, the offence of indecent exposure formerly contained within the Town Police Clauses Act 1847, s. 28, was a result crime, because it required proof that D's conduct caused residents or 'passengers' to be 'annoyed, obstructed or endangered'. In contrast, the offence of genital exposure created by the SOA 2003, s. 66, is a conduct crime, because it requires proof only that D exposed himself and intended this to cause alarm or distress. Nobody need actually have suffered alarm or distress. In theory, nobody need even have seen the offending act.

A1.3 **Jurisdictional Importance of Classification** The distinction between conduct crimes and result crimes was for many years crucial in determining jurisdiction over cross-frontier offences. Under the so-called 'terminatory' principle, jurisdiction over a conduct crime was held to depend on the relevant conduct occurring within England or Wales, whereas jurisdiction over a result crime ordinarily depended on at least some part of the proscribed result taking place there (see, e.g., *Secretary of State for Trade v Markus* [1976] AC 35, per Lord Diplock at p. 61, and *Harden* [1963] 1 QB 8); but a different rule now applies to any offences of fraud or dishonesty to which the CJA 1993, Part I, applies (see **A8.5**), and in *Smith (Wallace Duncan) (No. 4)* [2004]

EWCA Crim 631, [2004] QB 1418 the Court of Appeal effectively rejected the terminatory principle in favour of what has subsequently been referred to as the 'substantial measure principle' (see to similar effect *Sheppard* [2010] EWCA Crim 65, [2010] 2 All ER 850 and **A8.5**).

RELATIONSHIP BETWEEN *ACTUS REUS* AND *MENS REA*

General

A1.4 The general rule, expressed in the maxim *actus non facit reum nisi mens sit rea*, is that an offence can be committed only where criminal conduct is accompanied by some element of fault, the precise fault element required depending upon the particular offence involved. There are nevertheless many offences of strict liability, where it is not necessary to establish fault in relation to every element or where, in some cases, no fault element need be proved (see **A2**). In such cases, one can therefore have an *actus reus* without any corresponding *mens rea*.

In theory, there can be no criminal liability based on *mens rea* alone, but if the *actus reus* element of a crime is defined very widely (as is sometimes the case) a 'guilty mind' may turn an objectively innocent act into the *actus reus* of that offence. If D gives evidence without believing it to be true, this will be perjury, even if the evidence turns out to be true after all (see **B14.11**); and a shopper who openly selects goods in a self-service store, whilst secretly nursing a dishonest intention to avoid paying for them, is regarded as committing theft at the moment of selection, despite not having done anything objectively unlawful at that stage. The *actus reus* of perjury involves nothing more than giving material evidence in court; and the concept of appropriation, which lies at the heart of the *actus reus* of theft, has been defined so widely in cases such as *Gomez* [1993] AC 442 as to strip it of any special significance. Almost any form of dealing with another person's property, legitimate or otherwise, must now be regarded as an appropriation of it: the *actus reus* of theft (see generally **B4.34** *et seq.*).

D can meanwhile be guilty of a criminal attempt by doing an entirely lawful thing in the mistaken belief that it is something different, which would indeed have been criminal. If, for example, D imports a harmless vegetable powder mistakenly believing it to be heroin, D may be guilty of attempting to import a controlled drug, contrary to s. 1 of the CAA 1981. The objectively lawful importation of the powder becomes the *actus reus* of the criminal attempt (*Shivpuri* [1987] AC 1; see **A5.84**).

A Mental Element in the *Actus Reus*?

A1.5 The usual distinction between the mental element and the external manifestation of a crime can be difficult to apply in cases where the crime is one of 'possessing', 'permitting', 'keeping', 'appropriating', etc., because these terms simultaneously import both mental and physical elements. D may, for example, possess a controlled drug without realising what it is, but does not possess something which, unknown to D, has become stuck to the sole of D's shoe or the blade of D's penknife (*Warner v Metropolitan Police Commissioner* [1969] 2 AC 256; *Marriott* [1971] 1 All ER 595). It might therefore be argued that there is a mental element implicit in the *actus reus* of any offence of unlawful possession. From a strictly theoretical viewpoint, this cannot be correct. The correct analysis must be that the legal concept of possession involves both the *actus reus* element of physical possession and a state of mind, the *animus possidendi*, which can only be a part of the requisite *mens rea*. Nevertheless, it may be convenient in practice to treat the *animus possidendi* as if it were an *actus reus* element, because it must always be proved by the prosecution, even where, as in drug possession cases, the burden of proof in respect of other *mens rea* elements is placed on the defence (see **B19.27** *et seq.*).

Contemporaneity of *Actus Reus* and *Mens Rea*

A1.6 The general rule is that, to be guilty of a criminal offence requiring *mens rea*, D must possess that *mens rea* when performing the act or omission in question, and it must relate to that particular act or omission. If, for example, D accidentally kills his wife in a car crash on Monday, the fact that he was planning to cut her throat on Tuesday does not make him guilty of her murder, even if he is subsequently delighted to find that his wife has died. The general rule as to contemporaneity must nevertheless be qualified in certain respects.

Short-lived *Mens Rea* D's *mens rea* need not last beyond the moment at which D causes the *actus reus* to occur. After inflicting a fatal injury on V with murderous intent, D may repent and attempt to save V's life; but if V dies D will still be guilty of murder (*Jakeman* (1983) 76 Cr App R 223, per Wood J at p. 228). In *Jakeman,* D booked suitcases containing drugs onto a series of flights terminating in London. She abandoned them in Paris, allegedly because she no longer intended to import them, but the cases were sent on to London where the drugs were discovered. The Court of Appeal held that D's loss of *mens rea* came too late to prevent her being guilty of an importation offence. **A1.7**

Course of Conduct The *actus reus* of a crime may consist of an extended or ongoing course of conduct. Obvious examples are provided by crimes of unlawful possession. Where *mens rea* is a necessary element of such offences (as it must be in any offence of possession 'with intent...'), it will suffice if it accompanies the ongoing act of possession at any point. In *Styles* [2015] EWCA Crim 1619, D was charged with possessing a shotgun with intent to commit murder, contrary to the FA 1968, s. 18(1)). It sufficed in that case that D had such an intent at any moment 'within the timeframe of the indictment'. **A1.8**

Sexual intercourse is also an ongoing act, so even if D lacks *mens rea* for rape at the initial moment of penetration, that offence may yet be committed if D becomes aware of V's lack of consent at any point thereafter, and does not at once desist and withdraw (see *Kaitamaki v The Queen* [1985] AC 147 and the SOA 2003, s. 79(2)). Even where V does initially consent, V may withdraw consent thereafter (because it becomes painful, or for any other reason) and, if D is made aware that consent is withdrawn at any point, D must then desist at once to avoid committing rape.

A controversial example of the 'continuous act' principle can be found in *Fagan v Metropolitan Police Commissioner* [1969] 1 QB 439, where D was directed by a police officer to park his vehicle by the kerb, and drove it right onto the officer's foot. There was no proof that he did so deliberately, but he deliberately left it there after the officer told him what he had done. His conviction for assaulting the officer was upheld on the basis that there was an ongoing act, which became a criminal assault once D became aware of it. James J said:

> It is not necessary that *mens rea* should be present at the inception of the *actus reus*; it can be superimposed on an existing act. On the other hand, the subsequent inception of *mens rea* cannot convert an act which has been completed without *mens rea* into an assault.

Series of Actions The courts may extend the above principle by treating a series of different actions culminating in the *actus reus* of a crime as if they were a single, extended or continuous course of conduct. It will then be sufficient if D possessed the requisite *mens rea* at any point during that course of conduct. If, for example, D attempts to beat V to death, but actually kills V only by burying or dismembering what appears to be V's dead body, D will still be guilty of murder. As Lord Reid said in *Thabo Meli v The Queen* [1954] 1 All ER 373: **A1.9**

> It is much too refined a ground of judgment to say that, because the appellants were under a misapprehension at one stage and thought that their guilty purpose had been achieved before, in fact, it was achieved, therefore they are to escape the penalties of the law.

This principle has subsequently been applied, not only in cases where there was a prearranged plan, of which disposal of the body was a part (as in *Moore* [1975] Crim LR 229), but also in cases where there was no such plan. In *Church* [1966] 1 QB 59, D struck a woman and panicked because he mistakenly thought he had killed her. He threw her into a river, where she drowned. Edmund Davies J, giving the judgment of the Court of Criminal Appeal, held that 'if a killing by the first act would have been manslaughter, a later destruction of the supposed corpse should also be manslaughter'. *Church* was followed in *Le Brun* [1992] QB 61, where D struck his wife in the course of an argument outside their house, after she had refused to enter it with him. The blow left her unconscious. He then tried to drag her into the house. As he did so, her head struck the pavement, fracturing her skull and killing her. The case differed from *Church* in that the fatal impact was accidental, whereas Church's disposal of the 'body' was deliberate, but the Court of Appeal upheld a conviction for manslaughter by identifying a course of unlawful conduct. In attempting to drag his unconscious wife indoors, D was either trying to conceal his initial assault on her, or forcing her to enter the house against her wishes (this being the original reason for the assault). The trial judge had directed the jury to acquit if they concluded that D had been trying to aid or assist his wife when he attempted to move her, and the Court of Appeal agreed that this would have broken the essential nexus between the two halves of the incident.

A further difficulty arose in *A-G's Ref (No. 4 of 1980)* [1981] 2 All ER 617 where, in the course of a struggle, D pushed his girlfriend V over a landing rail onto the floor below and then, believing her dead, cut her throat and dismembered her in the bath so as to dispose of her body. It was impossible to establish whether V died in the original fall or whether D killed her (as in *Church*) by his subsequent actions. The Court of Appeal held that a manslaughter conviction was possible, despite uncertainty as to the actual cause of death, but only if it could be proved that each of D's acts was performed with the requisite *mens rea* for that offence. Since the initial fall may well have killed V, it would not suffice to establish *mens rea* (such as gross negligence) only in the subsequent act of disposal: the prosecution also had to disprove D's claim that he had merely pushed her away in a 'reflex action' when she dug her nails into him in the struggle on the upstairs landing.

VOLUNTARY AND INVOLUNTARY CONDUCT

Introduction

A1.10 The vast majority of criminal offences require acts or omissions on D's part, and these acts or omissions must ordinarily be willed or 'voluntary'. D does not therefore commit criminal damage if thrown from an upstairs window onto the roof of a car below. Nor is this merely because D lacks the requisite *mens rea* for that offence. It is because involuntary movements cannot ordinarily constitute the *actus reus* of any offence, not even one of strict liability. Involuntary conduct or events of this kind can best be understood not as anything *done* by D, but as something that *happens* to D.

Physical compulsion is merely one possible cause of involuntary conduct. Such conduct may also be caused by uncontrollable reflex actions or by a physical collapse brought on by injury or illness. If, for example, D suffers a sudden and unforeseen stroke or blackout whilst driving a car, which then careers through a red traffic light and collides with another vehicle, no offence is committed. The same rule would apply if D loses control of the car when suddenly attacked by a swarm of bees (an example suggested by Devlin J in *Hill v Baxter* [1958] 1 QB 277).

'Involuntary' conduct in this context does not include acts done by reason of duress, necessity or coercion (as to which, see **A3.34** *et seq.*) because such acts are still conscious, willed and rational; but it may include reflex acts and acts 'committed' by D when in a state of automatism, i.e. when not consciously in control of his or her own mind or body. A condition of automatism can arise where D is suffering from concussion, where D is a diabetic who suffers an attack of hypoglycaemia (very low blood sugar) after taking insulin (*Quick* [1973] QB 910) or, arguably, where D commits the *actus reus* whilst in a somnambulistic trance induced by hypnotism.

Limitations on the Defence of Automatism

A1.11 Although involuntariness or automatism is ordinarily a defence to any criminal charge, the use of that defence is limited by a number of considerations. These are more fully explained at

A3.12 *et seq*. It must suffice to note at this point that the defence may be rendered invalid where D was culpable for falling into such a condition, as for example by driving whilst suffering from exhaustion (*Kay v Butterworth* (1945) 173 LT 191) or by abusing alcohol or drugs (*Lipman* [1970] 1 QB 152; *Coley* [2013] EWCA Crim 223). It is also unavailable where the cause of the condition is a 'defect of reason arising from a disease of the mind', because this amounts in law to insanity. The term 'disease of the mind' embraces both organic and functional disorders of the mind, but excludes external causes, such as drugs, hypnosis or concussion. Epilepsy is in this sense a disease of the mind (*Sullivan* [1984] AC 156) as is a brain tumour (*Kemp* [1957] 1 QB 399) or even hyperglycaemia (excessive blood sugar) if this occurs naturally in a diabetic (*Hennessy* [1989] 2 All ER 9). Sleepwalking was regarded in *Bratty v A-G for Northern Ireland* [1963] AC 386 as a classic example of non-insane automatism, but sleep-associated automatism may be caused by functional disorders of the mind and in *Burgess* [1991] 2 QB 92 the Court of Appeal held that any such condition which manifests itself in violence must be treated as one of insanity. Finally, the defence of automatism appears to be unavailable where D has some, albeit impaired, control over his or her actions (*Broome v Perkins* [1987] Crim LR 271; *A-G's Ref (No. 2 of 1992)* [1994] QB 91; *Coley*); mere disinhibition is 'exactly *not* automatism' (*Coley* at [46]).

The Burden of Proof

Where the defence raise a defence of non-insane automatism, this must be disproved by the prosecution (in contrast to a defence of insanity or diminished responsibility, which must be proved by the defence) but there is always an evidential burden on the defence, which must produce some evidence of automatism before the prosecution can be required to address it (*Hill v Baxter* [1958] 1 QB 277; *Bratty v A-G for Northern Ireland* [1963] AC 386). See further **F3.42**. **A1.12**

Situational Liability

Voluntary conduct need not always be proved where D is charged with a strict liability offence in which the *actus reus* takes the form not of a prohibited act or omission but of a prohibited state of affairs. Authority can be found in *Larsonneur* (1933) 24 Cr App R 74 and *Winzar v Chief Constable of Kent* (1983) *The Times*, 28 March 1983. In the former case, D, a French citizen, visited the UK for the purpose of entering into a marriage of convenience. The police prevented this marriage and an order was served on her requiring her to leave and not re-enter the country. Instead of returning to France, D travelled to Ireland, whence she was deported and handed over to the British police in Holyhead. She was charged under the Aliens Order 1920 with 'being found in the United Kingdom' in breach of the original order excluding her. The fact that she had been returned to the UK under physical compulsion was held to be 'perfectly immaterial'. All that mattered was that she was found in the UK on the occasion in question. **A1.13**

In *Winzar*, the charge was one of being 'found drunk on a highway', contrary to the Licensing Act 1872, s. 12. D had been found drunk in a hospital and was asked to leave. When he failed to do so, police officers removed him to their patrol car, which was parked on the highway outside, and charged him with being found drunk there. Upholding his conviction, Goff LJ pointed out that a distinction would otherwise have to be drawn between a drunk who leaves a restaurant when asked to do so and one who is forcibly ejected after refusing to leave. If both are arrested in the street shortly afterwards, it would be wrong to regard the former as guilty and the latter as not; but the position would be different if the police were to drag a person out of bed and into the street before charging the person with being found drunk on a highway, because that would involve an abuse of process (see **D3.66**).

These cases were considered in *Robinson-Pierre* [2013] EWCA Crim 2396, [2014] 1 WLR 2638, in which it was accepted that 'the supremacy of Parliament embraces the power to create "state of affairs" offences in which no causative link between the prohibited state of affairs and the defendant need be established'. The question in any given case will be 'whether in any particular enactment Parliament intended to create one'. This is likely to require clear words to that effect, or a context in which the provision would otherwise be ineffective. In *Robinson-Pierre*, the Court of Appeal rejected submissions that this must have been Parliament's intent in enacting the Dangerous Dogs Act 1991, s. 3 (see **B20.5** and **B20.9**). That provision, as originally enacted, created a strict liability offence of owning or being in charge of a dog that is 'dangerously out of control in a public place' but it did not, said the Court, make such liability 'absolute in the sense that criminal liability may follow notwithstanding the absence of any act or omission of the defendant contributing to the prohibited state of affairs'.

OMISSION TO ACT

Introduction

A1.14 Most criminal offences require D to carry out some positive act before liability can be imposed. There can ordinarily be no liability for failure (or omission) to act, unless the law specifically imposes such a duty. The general rule is illustrated by this example from Stephen's *Digest of the Criminal Law* (3rd edn, 1887):

> A sees B drowning and is able to save him by holding out his hand. A abstains from doing so in order that B may be drowned, and B is drowned. A has committed no offence.

Despite failing to save B, A has done nothing to cause B's death. In some jurisdictions, A would always be under a duty to act in such a situation, at least where A does not have to endanger A's own life. Under English law, however, such a duty arises only in certain specific situations, and even then there are several offences which can be committed only through positive acts (see **A1.24**).

Where Statute Imposes a Specific Duty to Act

A1.15 There are many statutory provisions (mostly regulatory) which specifically impose duties on particular persons to act in particular ways and which impose criminal sanctions for failure or omission to act. Failure to keep proper accounts or business records, where these are required by law, may lead to criminal liability under the Companies Act 2006 or the Value Added Tax Act 1994. Road traffic law provides many further examples, including the offences of failing to stop after an accident and failing to provide a breath sample or a specimen for analysis.

Failure to Prevent or Report Criminal Conduct

A1.16 Failure to prevent or report the criminal activities of other persons is not ordinarily an offence. The offence of misprision of felony was abolished in 1967, but failure to report a known act of treason still amounts to misprision of treason and it also remains an offence at common law to refuse to assist a constable who calls for assistance in dealing with a breach of the peace (*Brown* (1841) Car & M 314; *Waugh* (1976) *The Times*, 1 October 1976). Modern legislation has added new offences of failure to disclose information relating to acts of terrorism or the funding of terrorism (see **B10.146** *et seq.*) and failure to disclose knowledge or suspicion of money laundering (see **B21.30**). As to the position of police officers who fail to act in accordance with their duty, see **A1.19**. As to the liability of parents etc., where a girl suffers genital mutilation, contrary to the Female Genital Mutilation Act 2003, s. 3A(1), see **B2.178**.

Duty Arising from Special Relationships

A1.17 **Care or Control of Children** If persons are in a close or special relationship to one another, the law may impose on one a duty to act on behalf of the other. Under the CYPA 1933, s. 1 (see **B2.145** *et seq.*), a parent or any other person over the age of 16 years who has responsibility for a child under that age may incur liability for any wilful neglect of that child that was likely to *cause unnecessary suffering or injury to health*. This specifically includes failure by a parent etc. to provide or obtain adequate food, clothing or medical care but could also include other forms of neglect, such as failure to rescue from drowning in circumstances of the kind described at **A1.14** or failure by a carer towards an elderly client or patient. Neglect leading to death may lead to liability for manslaughter by gross negligence (*Downes* (1875) 1 QBD 25; *Lowe* [1973] QB 702). The wilful neglect of a child contrary to s. 1 of the 1933 Act does not automatically give rise to liability for manslaughter merely because death results (*Lowe*), but it may sometimes do so if, for example, there is proof of an intent to harm the child through such neglect. Indeed, a parent who deliberately starves a child to death may be guilty of murder (*Gibbins* (1918) 13 Cr App R 134). As to the offence of causing or allowing the death of a child or vulnerable adult, see **B1.77**.

Assumption of Care for Another The CYPA 1933, s. 1, has no statutory counterpart in cases where the person in need of care or assistance is over the age of 16, but note the specific duties that may arise under the DVCVA 2004 in relation to both children and vulnerable adults (see **B1.90** and **B2.169**) and the duties imposed on care workers and care providers under the CJCA 2015, ss. 20 and 21 (see **B2.165**). In *Shepherd* (1862) 9 Cox CC 123 it was held that the parents of an 18-year-old and 'entirely emancipated' daughter were under no special duty to care for her. The common law nevertheless recognises that such a duty may arise in the context of a family relationship, as for example where a couple live together as husband and wife, or where a child continues to live with (and be dependent upon) parents even after becoming an adult (*Chattaway* (1922) 17 Cr App R 7). **A1.18**

If D voluntarily undertakes to care for another who is unable to do so as a result of age, illness or other infirmity, D may thereby incur a duty to discharge that undertaking, at least until such time as it can be handed over to someone else. In *Instan* [1893] 1 QB 450, D lived with her aunt, who was suddenly taken ill with gangrene in her leg and became unable either to feed herself or to call for help. D did not give her any food, nor did she call for medical help, even though she remained in the house and continued to eat her aunt's food. She was convicted of manslaughter. The principle laid down in *Instan* was applied and extended in *Stone* [1977] QB 354. Stone's sister, Fanny, came to live with him and his partner, Dobinson. Fanny was suffering from anorexia, but was initially able to look after herself. Gradually, however, her condition deteriorated, until she became bed-ridden. She needed medical help, but none was summoned and she eventually died in squalor, covered in bed sores and filth. Stone and Dobinson were each convicted of her manslaughter and the Court of Appeal upheld their convictions. Because they had taken Fanny into their home, they had assumed a duty of care for her and had been grossly negligent in the performance of that duty. The fact that Fanny was Stone's sister was merely incidental to this.

Official, Contractual or Public Duties D may in some cases incur criminal liability through failure to discharge official duties or contractual obligations. A typical example is provided by *Pittwood* (1902) 19 TLR 37, in which D was employed to operate a level-crossing on a railway but omitted to close the crossing gates when a train was signalled. A cart was crossing when the train struck it and killed one of the carters. D was convicted of manslaughter. In one sense this was based on his breach of contractual duty, but the carter was not, of course, a party to the contract, and D's liability can more accurately be based on the breach of a duty of care to users of the crossing, which the railway company paid D to discharge, and on which the users of the crossing relied. In the absence of such a duty, it is doubtful whether any criminal liability could have arisen, whatever D's contractual position with the railway company (cf. *Smith* (1869) 11 Cox CC 210). **A1.19**

Neglect of duty by a police officer was examined by the Court of Appeal in *Dytham* [1979] QB 722. D, whilst on duty, stood aside and watched as a man was beaten to death outside a nightclub. He then left the scene, without calling for assistance or summoning an ambulance. For this, he was convicted of the common-law offence of wilful misconduct in public office (see **B15.26**). Lord Widgery CJ said (at p. 727):

> The allegation was not one of mere non-feasance, but of deliberate failure and wilful neglect. This involves an element of culpability which is not restricted to corruption or dishonesty, but which must be of such a degree that the misconduct impugned is calculated to injure the public interest so as to call for condemnation and punishment.

Although D was not charged with manslaughter, it is submitted that a conviction for manslaughter might be possible on such facts, if it were proved that D's inaction was a factor contributing to the death of the deceased. It was not clear in *Dytham* that D could have saved the deceased even if he had tried to do so.

The new offence of corrupt or improper exercise of police powers (under the CJCA 2015, s. 26) may also take the form of a failure to act (see **B15.32**).

Duty to Avert a Danger of One's Own Making

A1.20 If D's error or misconduct creates or contributes to the creation of a dangerous situation, this may give rise to a duty to take reasonable steps to avert that danger, and D may therefore incur criminal liability for the consequences of a failure to do so. In *Miller* [1983] 2 AC 161, D was 'sleeping rough' in a building, and fell asleep on his mattress while smoking a cigarette. When he awoke, he saw that his mattress was smouldering but, instead of calling for help, he simply moved into another room, thereby allowing the fire to flare up and spread. He was convicted of arson, not for starting the fire but for failing to do anything about it. Lord Diplock said (at p. 176):

> . . . I see no rational ground for excluding from conduct capable of giving rise to criminal liability, conduct which consists of failing to take measures that lie within one's power to counteract a danger that one has oneself created, if at the time of such conduct one's state of mind is such as constitutes a necessary ingredient of the offence.

The *Miller* principle may also apply in cases of gross negligence manslaughter; as where D unlawfully supplies V with a dangerous drug and then fails to summon help when it is obvious that V has become dangerously ill as a result of ingesting it (*Evans* [2009] EWCA Crim 650, [2009] 1 All ER 13 at [21] and [31]). It must, however, be proved that this failure was a contributory cause of V's death. See also **B1.65**.

Failure to Provide Medical Treatment

A1.21 **Refusal of Consent to Treatment** Doctors and other healthcare professionals have a duty to provide medical care for their patients, and an omission to discharge that duty may sometimes involve criminal liability (e.g., for manslaughter or, in the case of a patient under 16, for wilful neglect under the CYPA 1933, s. 1), although this duty may be terminated if the patient refuses to accept medical treatment. If, for example, an adult hospital patient refuses consent to a life-saving amputation, the medical staff, far from being under a duty to provide that treatment, would ordinarily be acting unlawfully if they ignored the patient's objection (*Re C (Adult: Refusal of Treatment)* [1994] 1 All ER 819; *Re MB* [1997] 2 FLR 426).

Refusal of consent is not always decisive in such cases. Where children are concerned, the High Court may exercise its wardship jurisdiction and override parental refusal of consent (*Re B (A Minor) (Wardship: Medical Treatment)* [1981] 1 WLR 1421). In acute emergencies, healthcare professionals may have to act without consent.

Even in respect of adults, a refusal of consent to treatment may be vitiated by lack of capacity (within the meaning of the Mental Capacity Act 2005, s. 2) or by undue influence (*Re T (Adult: Refusal of Treatment)* [1993] Fam 95). Healthcare professionals must then provide appropriate treatment, in accordance with the patient's best interests. There is a presumption of capacity to choose, even if the patient's choice appears unwise. As to the effect of advance directives or 'living wills', see the Mental Capacity Act 2005, s. 26.

A1.22 **Withholding Treatment in the Best Interests of the Patient** If a patient is incapable of communicating wishes, a healthcare professional's normal duty is to do everything reasonably possible to keep that patient alive. In certain circumstances, however, a doctor may be absolved of this duty, even to the extent of being allowed to withhold essential clinically assisted nutrition and hydration (CANH). In *Airedale NHS Trust v Bland* [1993] AC 789, the patient had been left in a 'persistent vegetative state' after suffering irreversible brain damage. He continued to breathe normally, but was kept alive only by CANH. The Trust sought a declaration that it might lawfully discontinue this treatment and allow him to die with dignity and with minimum distress.

The House of Lords held that treatment could properly be withdrawn, because the best interests of the patient did not involve him being kept alive at all costs. Lord Goff nevertheless drew a fundamental distinction between acts and omissions in this context (at p. 865):

> ... the law draws a crucial distinction between cases in which a doctor decides not to provide, or to continue to provide, for his patient treatment or care which could or might prolong his life, and those in which he decides, for example by administering a lethal drug, actively to bring his patient's life to an end ... the former may be lawful, either because the doctor is giving effect to his patient's wishes ... or even in certain circumstances in which ... the patient is incapacitated from stating whether or not he gives his consent. But it is not lawful for a doctor to administer a drug to his patient to bring about his death, even though that course is prompted by a humanitarian desire to end his suffering, however great that suffering may be: see *Cox* (unreported) 18 September 1992.

See also *Frenchay Healthcare NHS Trust v S* [1994] 2 All ER 403 and *R (Nicklinson) v Ministry of Justice* [2014] UKSC 38, [2015] AC 657. Similar issues can arise in respect of the very elderly or babies born with very severe mental or physical disability, especially where major (and possibly repeated) surgery would be needed to keep them alive (*Re J* [1991] 3 All ER 930).

The question whether the consent of the court should be secured before CANH is withdrawn was considered by the Supreme Court in *An NHS Trust v Y* [2018] UKSC 46, [2018] 3 WLR 751. Having referred to English and ECtHR case law, including *Bland, Nicklinson, R (Burke) v General Medical Council* [2005] EWCA Civ 1003, [2006] QB 273, *Lambert v France* (2016) 62 EHRR 2 (57) and *Burke v UK* (2006) Appln. 19807/06, 11 July 2006, together with relevant provisions of the Mental Capacity Act 2005, Lady Black, giving the unanimous judgment of the Court, said (at [125]–[126]:

> If at the end of the medical process, it is apparent that the way forward is finely balanced, or there is a difference of medical opinion, or a lack of agreement to a proposed course of action from those with an interest in the patient's welfare, a court application can and should be made. As the decisions of the ECtHR underline, this possibility of approaching a court in the event of doubts as to the best interests of the patient is an essential part of the protection of human rights. The assessments, evaluations and opinions assembled as part of the medical process will then form the core of the material available to the judge, together with such further expert and other evidence as may need to be placed before the court at that stage.
>
> ... I do not consider that it has been established that the common law or the ECHR, in combination or separately, give rise to the mandatory requirement, for which the Official Solicitor contends, to involve the court to decide upon the best interests of every patient with a prolonged disorder of consciousness before CANH can be withdrawn. If the provisions of the MCA 2005 are followed and the relevant guidance observed, and if there is agreement upon what is in the best interests of the patient, the patient may be treated in accordance with that agreement without application to the court.

Practical and Financial Considerations Even apart from the question of whether treatment would be in the patient's best interests, it is recognised that financial or manpower constraints on the health service must come into consideration. It is clearly not practicable for the NHS to provide intensive forms of medical care (such as major surgery) to every patient whose life might possibly be prolonged by it; nor does a patient have the right to demand treatment that doctors consider to be clinically inappropriate (*R (Burke) v General Medical Council* [2005] EWCA Civ 100, [2006] QB 273 at [50]). **A1.23**

Offences for which Omissions Cannot be the Basis of Liability

Some offences are capable of commission only by positive acts. The offence of acting with intent to prevent the apprehension of an offender, contrary to the CLA 1967, s. 4, is an example (see **B14.58** *et seq.*). Crimes of assault or battery arguably come into this category. This was at least the view of the Divisional Court in *Fagan v Metropolitan Police Commissioner* [1969] 1 QB 439 (see **A1.8**), although D's conviction was upheld on the basis that his conduct amounted to a continuing act, rather than an innocent act followed by a deliberate omission to rectify it. **A1.24**

It has also been held that omissions cannot be the basis of liability for 'doing acts' likely to interfere with the peace and comfort of a residential occupier, contrary to the Protection from Eviction Act 1977 (*Ahmad* (1987) 84 Cr App R 64; and see **B13.17**) but the courts have not been consistent in interpreting references to 'acts' as necessarily excluding omissions. In *Speck* [1977] 2 All ER 859, for example, it was held that an omission could amount to an 'act' of gross indecency with a child, contrary to the Indecency with Children Act 1960, s. 1 (now repealed). See also *Yuthiwattana* (1984) 80 Cr App R 55, in which it was held that a landlord's omission to replace a lost key could be an 'act' of harassment against a tenant. As to constructive manslaughter, see *Lowe* [1973] QB 702 and **B1.50**.

CAUSATION

Introduction

A1.25 Causation issues may arise in respect of any 'result crime'. In order to establish whether D can be guilty of a given result crime, one must first establish a factual link between D's conduct and the result which it is alleged to have caused (as to proof of this, see **A1.40**). Once factual causation has been established, a second and more difficult question must be considered, namely whether D's conduct was a sufficient cause in law. This is a question of 'imputability' or 'legal causation'. It involves issues of value-judgment and the allocation of responsibility for what has occurred; but as Lord Hughes and Lord Toulson warned in *Hughes* [2013] UKSC 56, [2013] 4 All ER 613:

> The meaning of causation is heavily context-specific... Parliament (or in some cases the courts) may apply different legal rules of causation in different situations. Accordingly it is not always safe to suppose that there is a settled or 'stable' concept of causation which can be applied in every case.

Factual Causation

A1.26 The importance of proving factual causation is illustrated by *White* [1910] 2 KB 124. D put potassium cyanide in his mother's bedtime drink. When she was found dead the next morning, he was charged with her murder, but it was eventually established that his mother had consumed very little of the poison. She had died, coincidentally, of natural causes. D's conduct had not in any sense contributed to this. He was therefore guilty only of attempting to murder her.

It may also be necessary to prove a link between the proscribed result and a particular aspect of D's conduct, such as negligence. In *Dalloway* (1847) 2 Cox CC 273, D was charged with manslaughter when his cart struck and killed a girl who ran out in front of him. D was not holding the horse's reins at the time, but Erle J directed the jury that they could convict D of manslaughter only if they were satisfied that D could have avoided the accident had he been holding the reins correctly.

Factual causation is sometimes referred to as 'but for' (or *sine qua non*) causation, because it can be established only where the alleged result would not have occurred, or would not have occurred at the time or in the way it did, 'but for' D's act or culpable omission. The only qualification to this basic rule involves cases of complicity or joint venture, under which D may incur liability for encouraging or assisting the principal offender, even where it is proved that D's conduct made no difference to the outcome. Procuring appears to be the only form of secondary participation that requires a causal link between the participation and the crime. See **A4.1**.

Legal or Imputable Causation

A1.27 Legal causation is a narrower and more subjective concept than factual causation. Not every cause in fact is a cause in law. To be so, it must be adjudged an 'operating and substantial' cause of the consequence in issue (*Smith* [1959] 2 QB 35) albeit that it does not have to be the only or even the principal such cause. The isolation of a legal cause from amongst a possible multitude of factual causes is a process involving subjective common sense rather than objectively measurable criteria, but when seeking to apportion possible criminal responsibility in this way, one must in practice look for some kind of abnormal and culpable behaviour. The logic behind such reasoning is explained by Hart and Honoré, *Causation in the Law* (2nd edn, 1985):

> The notion that a cause is essentially something which interferes with or intervenes in the course of events which would normally take place, is central to our common-sense concept of cause...

> In distinguishing between causes and conditions, two contrasts are of prime importance. These are the contrasts between what is abnormal and what is normal in relation to any given thing or subject-matter, and between a free deliberate human action and all other conditions...
>
> In the case of a building destroyed by fire, 'mere conditions' will be factors such as the oxygen in the air, the presence of combustible material or the dryness of the building... which are present alike both... where such accidents occur and... where they do not... Such factors do not 'make the difference' between disaster and normal functioning, as... the dropping of a lighted cigarette does....

Multiple Causes and Multiple Blame

D may be guilty of causing something to happen even if D's conduct was not the only legal cause of it and even that conduct could not, on its own, have sufficed to make it happen (*Warburton* [2006] EWCA Crim 627). In *Hennigan* [1971] 3 All ER 133, D argued that he was not guilty of causing death by dangerous driving, because another driver was more to blame than him. The Court of Appeal replied that, as long as D's contribution was substantial, he could be held accountable. Without purporting to lay down any precise limits, the Court suggested that, even if just 20 per cent of the blame could be attributed to him, that would suffice. *Hennigan* was followed in *Notman* [1994] Crim LR 518, where it was stated that anything more than a *de minimis* contribution could suffice. In cases of causing death by driving when uninsured, etc. (RTA 1988, s. 3ZB), the Supreme Court in *Hughes* [2013] UKSC 56, [2013] 4 All ER 613 held that to be guilty D must be proved to have done something more than merely drive a vehicle on the road so that it was there to be involved in a fatal accident. It must be proved that D did or omitted to do something else that contributed in a more than minimal way to the death. There must in other words be something more than mere 'but for' causation (at [33]): **A1.28**

> Juries should thus be directed that it is not necessary for the Crown to prove careless or inconsiderate driving, but that there must be something open to proper criticism in the driving of the defendant, beyond the mere presence of the vehicle on the road, and which contributed in some more than minimal way to the death. How much this offence will in practice add to the other offences of causing death by driving will have to be worked out as factual scenarios present themselves; it may be that it will add relatively little.

The same approach has been adopted in respect of aggravated vehicle taking under the Theft Act 1968, s. 12A. In *Taylor* [2016] UKSC 5, [2016] 1 WLR 500, D was charged with taking a truck without consent, and that 'owing to the driving of the vehicle, an accident occurred by which [death] was caused'. But although the truck was involved in a fatal collision with a scooter while D was driving it, the fault was entirely that of the scooter rider, so D could not be said to have 'caused' the latter's death. The phrases 'caused the death of another person by driving a motor vehicle on a road' (s. 3ZB of the 1988 Act) and 'owing to the driving of the vehicle, an accident occurred by which injury was caused to any person' (s. 12A(2)(b) of the 1968 Act) both posit a direct causal connection between the driving and the injury. But in *Wilson* [2018] EWCA Crim 1184, [2019] 1 WLR 3916, the Court of Appeal held that guilt under s. 3ZB may be established if it is proved that D's driving at the critical time was such as significantly or materially to increase the risk of death. The Crown did not have to prove that the pedestrian who ran out in front of D's vehicle would have survived if D had driven carefully and within the prevailing 30 mph speed limit.

See further **B4.132**.

Indirect Causation

Although legal causation must be 'operative and substantial', it need not necessarily be a direct cause of the proscribed result. In *McKechnie* (1992) 94 Cr App R 51, D inflicted serious head injuries on V. These were not in themselves fatal, but they prevented doctors from operating on V's duodenal ulcer, and V died when the ulcer burst. D was held to have caused his death. Not all indirect causes will be sufficiently proximate to the result; questions of fact and degree may be crucial, and it is therefore impossible to formulate any universal rule in such cases. Indirect causation may also be the basis of liability in cases involving crimes other than homicide. See, e.g., *Roberts* (1971) 56 Cr App R 95 (see **A1.35**) and *Miller* (1992) 95 Cr App R 421. **A1.29**

The 'Eggshell Skull' Rule

A1.30 D must ordinarily 'take his victim as he finds him'. If, for example, the victim of D's assault is unusually vulnerable to physical injury as a result of an existing medical condition or old age, D must accept liability for any unusually serious consequences which result. In *Hayward* (1908) 21 Cox CC 692, D chased his wife into the road, threatening her with violence. She then collapsed and died as a result of a long-standing heart condition and D was held liable for her manslaughter. This principle was extended in *Blaue* [1975] 3 All ER 446. D stabbed a woman. A blood transfusion would have saved her life, but as a Jehovah's Witness she refused it. D was convicted of manslaughter (on grounds of diminished responsibility) and this verdict was upheld on appeal. Lawton LJ said (at p. 1415):

> It has long been the policy of the law that those who use violence on other people must take their victims as they find them. This in our judgment means the whole man, not just the physical man. It does not lie in the mouth of the assailant to say that the victim's religious beliefs which inhibited him from accepting certain kinds of treatment were unreasonable.

One possible qualification to this general rule may need to be noted. Where the victim of a crime dies of heart failure etc., resulting from stress or fright, the charge is likely to be one of manslaughter, and it must then be proved that D's unlawful conduct was obviously dangerous, in the sense of being likely to cause some injury. Where blows are struck, this is unlikely to be a problem, but what of cases in which V proved unusually vulnerable to injury caused by fear or stress? In *Dawson* (1985) 81 Cr App R 150 the Court of Appeal quashed D's conviction for the manslaughter of V, a 60-year-old petrol station attendant, who died of a heart attack after being threatened with a replica gun. The Court held that the trial judge had misdirected the jury by inviting them to take account of V's heart condition when deciding whether D's conduct had been obviously dangerous. D could not have known of this condition at the time. At first sight, *Dawson* may seem inconsistent with the eggshell skull rule, but it merely decides that it was unfair to judge the dangerousness of D's conduct as if V's heart defect was already obvious to everyone concerned. It is submitted that the jury should instead have been directed to consider whether the act of threatening an elderly man (of unknown health) with a replica gun involved an obvious risk of harming him. The answer to that question might well have been 'yes', and the eggshell skull rule would then have been applied. See also *Watson* [1989] 2 All ER 865, discussed at **B1.55**, *Carey* [2006] EWCA Crim 17 and *M (J)* [2012] EWCA Crim 2293, [2013] 1 WLR 1083.

NOVUS ACTUS INTERVENIENS

Introduction

A1.31 D will not be regarded as having caused a given consequence if there was a *novus actus interveniens* (or new intervening act) sufficient to break the chain of causation between D's original action and the consequence in question. Although the original act may remain a factual cause, 'but for which' the consequence would never have occurred, the intervening act may supplant it as the imputable or legal cause for the purpose of criminal liability. This intervening act may be the act of a third party, an act of the victim, or an unforeseeable natural event, sometimes called an 'act of God'. These three variants will be considered in turn, but one general point may be made at the outset: no intervening act can break the chain of causation if it merely complements or aggravates the effects of D's initial conduct. Suppose, for example, that D attacks V, inflicting serious injuries, and that V later suffers further harm, caused by E's act, by some natural disaster, or by V's failure to seek medical treatment. If V dies of such *cumulative* effects, there can be no question of the chain of causation being broken. The chain of causation is broken only where the effect of the intervening act is so overwhelming that any initial injuries are relegated to the status of mere background. The detailed application of this principle will be explored in the specific contexts within which it may arise, but the principle is the same in each case.

If poor or inadequate treatment of injuries cannot break the chain of causation, then *a fortiori* an omission to treat those initial injuries cannot do so, even if such neglect results in relatively minor injuries becoming fatal (*Holland* (1841) 2 Mood & R 351). As Lawton LJ said in *Blaue* [1975] 3 All ER 446, where V refused a life-saving blood transfusion on religious grounds:

> The question for decision is what caused [V's] death. The answer is the stab wound. The fact that [V] refused to stop this end coming about did not break the causal connection between the act and death.

It can make no difference whether the omission is that of V (as in *Blaue*) or of a third party, such as a doctor. It may even be the result of an unforeseen natural event, such as a flood which prevents medical assistance from reaching V.

Acts of Third Parties

Deliberate and Informed Interventions The subsequent intervention of a third party will ordinarily break the chain of causation if it is free, deliberate and informed (whether reasonably foreseeable or not), and provides the immediate cause of the event in question (*Pagett* (1983) 76 Cr App R 279; *Latif* [1996] 1 All ER 353). Another way of stating this principle is that D's voluntary act will usually be taken to be the cause of an act or omission where it was the last human conduct before the result that is said to have been caused. But even an accidental or unintended intervention may break the chain of causation if it was not reasonably forseeable in the circumstances (*Girdler* [2009] EWCA Crim 2666). This does not mean that the exact form of any such intervention must have been foreseeable at the time of the original assault etc. in order for the chain of causation to remain unbroken. If the general form and risk of further harm was reasonably foreseeable, it may not then matter if the specific manner in which it occurred was entirely unpredictable (*Wallace* [2018] EWCA Crim 690, [2018] 2 Cr App R 22 (325) at [84], citing *Maybin* 2012 SCC 24 (SC Canada)). See also *A* [2020] EWCA Crim 407, in which this analysis was approved (at [33]). The Court of Appeal held that the judge in that case had been wrong to withdraw a charge of causing death by dangerous driving from the jury in a case where D had pulled over onto the hard shoulder of a motorway in the dark, leaving her car parked without lights, and had then been hit, with fatal consequences, by a vehicle that had swerved off the main carriageway. Simon LJ said (at [35]): A1.32

> What had to be sensibly anticipated was that another vehicle might leave the carriageway and collide with the respondent's parked car. It would not be necessary for the jury to be sure that the particular circumstances of the collision or 'the exact form' of the subsequent act was reasonably foreseeable.

In *Latif*, D1 and D2 were involved in a plan to smuggle heroin into Britain. The heroin was delivered by D2 to a supposed accomplice in Pakistan, who was in fact an undercover operative of the US Drug Enforcement Agency. It was then flown into Britain by a British customs officer, technically without lawful authority, whilst D1 and D2 were lured to a meeting in London, where they were arrested. It was held that the importation by the customs officer, whilst unlawful, was a deliberate third-party act for which D2 was not responsible, although D2 could still be convicted of being concerned in an *attempt* to import it, contrary to the Customs and Excise Management Act 1979, s. 170(2) (see **B16.39** ***et seq.***). In contrast, the actions of an innocent agent, who is unaware of the true facts, cannot break the chain of causation. Had the case containing the heroin been forwarded by airline officials as lost luggage (as in *Jakeman* (1983) 76 Cr App R 223: see **A1.7**), D2 would have been held responsible for their actions.

In *Pagett*, D forcibly used his pregnant girlfriend, V, as a 'human shield' in a shoot-out with police officers. V was killed by bullets from officers returning his fire. D was convicted of her manslaughter. The Court of Appeal reasoned that the officers had acted 'involuntarily' in taking reasonable measures for the purpose of self-preservation and in the performance of their legal duty to apprehend D, and there was of course no suggestion that they shot V deliberately. Whether the police indeed acted 'reasonably' may be open to question; but this would make no difference to the outcome. Even if the police officers were at fault, their conduct was not free, deliberate and informed. D created a situation in which V's life was inevitably endangered, and what happened was a natural and foreseeable consequence of that behaviour. A1.33

In a controversial ruling that remains difficult to reconcile with *Latif*, the House of Lords held in *Environment Agency v Empress Car Co. (Abertillery) Ltd* [1999] 2 AC 22 that the operator of an installation from which diesel fuel escaped into a watercourse could be convicted of 'causing' that pollution, contrary to the Water Resources Act 1991, s. 85(1), as then in force, even though the immediate cause of the disaster was an act of vandalism by an unknown third party, who had opened the tap on a fuel storage tank during the night. Significantly, the defendant company had no measures in place to prevent such vandalism, or to restrict the subsequent escape of any fuel leaking from the tap. Lord Hoffmann reasoned that 'there may be different answers to questions about causation when attributing responsibility to different people under different rules' or even 'when attributing responsibility to different people under the same rule'. Looking at the policy behind the provision in question, he continued:

> Strict liability is imposed in the interests of protecting controlled waters from pollution.... Clearly, therefore, the fact that a deliberate act of a third party, caused the pollution does not in itself mean that the defendant's creation of a situation in which the third party could so act did not also cause the pollution for the purposes of section 85(1).

Lord Hoffmann added that it remained necessary to consider whether the third party's act was a 'normal fact of life or something extraordinary':

> If it was in the general run of things a matter of ordinary occurrence, it will not negative the causal effect of the defendant's acts, even if it was not foreseeable that it would happen to that particular defendant or take that particular form.... The distinction between ordinary and extraordinary is one of fact and degree to which the [court] must apply common sense and knowledge of what happens in the area.

The principles applied in *Empress* are not, however, of general application and were not even mentioned in *Hughes* [2013] UKSC 56, [2013] 4 All ER 613 (see **A1.28**). In *Kennedy (No. 2)* [2007] UKHL 38, [2008] 1 AC 269 the House of Lords explained (at [15]) that:

> [It] was not [in *Empress*] purporting to lay down general rules governing causation in criminal law. It was construing, with reference to the facts of the case before it, a statutory provision imposing strict criminal liability on those who cause pollution of controlled waters.

The company in *Empress* might reasonably have been expected to protect its tank against commonplace acts of vandalism, but liability did not turn on proof of default or neglect in that respect. See also *L* [2008] EWCA Crim 1970, [2009] 1 All ER 786 and *R (Natural England) v Day* [2014] EWCA Crim 2683, [2015] 1 Cr App R (S) 53 (364). In that case, Lord Thomas CJ noted (*obiter*) that he could see 'strong arguments for following the approach in *Empress*' in relation to liability for prohibited actions under the Wildlife and Countryside Act 1981, ss. 28E(1) and 28P(1), although on the facts of that case the apparent causation issue did not need to be resolved.

A1.34 **Medical Intervention** It is foreseeable that the victim of an attack or accident may require medical treatment, but it is also foreseeable that injuries may be misdiagnosed or that treatment may not be performed correctly. This is one reason why incorrect medical treatment is hardly ever categorised by the courts as amounting to a *novus actus interveniens*. An equally valid reason, in many cases, is that failure to provide proper treatment for an initial injury rarely amounts to an independent cause of death or injury: it is far more likely that such failure will merely aggravate the original injury, or that it will allow the original injury to take its natural course. In particular, the 'switching off' of a life support system, even if wrongful, will never break the chain of causation flowing from the original injury (*Malcherek* [1981] 2 All ER 422). Even where incorrect treatment leads to death or more serious injury, it will only break the chain of causation if it is (a) unforeseeably bad, and (b) the sole significant cause of the death (or more serious injury) with which D is charged.

An exceptional case in which palpably wrong medical treatment was held to have broken the chain of causation was *Jordan* (1956) 40 Cr App R 152. D stabbed V, who was taken to hospital, where he died. D was initially convicted of V's murder, but on appeal new evidence was admitted. This showed that at the time of V's death his wound had almost totally healed and that he had died as a result of a mix-up in which he was given antibiotics to which he had already proved highly allergic. The Court of Criminal Appeal concluded that, if the jury had heard this new evidence, they would have concluded that it was the medical treatment which had caused death and not the stab wound.

Smith [1959] 2 QB 35 is clearly distinguishable from *Jordan*. D stabbed his fellow soldier, V, with a bayonet during a brawl. Other soldiers carried V to a medical centre, dropping him twice on the way. An overworked doctor failed to notice that one of V's lungs had been pierced and the treatment V received 'might well have affected his chances of recovery'. This did not, however, break the chain of causation. According to the Courts-Martial Appeals Court:

> If at the time of death the original wound is still an operating cause and a substantial cause, then the death can properly be said to be the result of the wound, albeit that some other cause of death is also operating. Only if it can be said that the original wounding is merely the setting in which another cause operates can it be said that the death did not result from the wound ... only if the second cause is so overwhelming as to make the original wound merely part of the history can it be said that the death does not flow from the wound.

V's death could still be attributed to the wound inflicted by D. In contrast, the wound inflicted in *Jordan* had largely healed, and medical negligence was in effect the sole cause of death. Furthermore, the negligent mistreatment was so bizarre as to be unforeseeable. Had V died from the first dose of antibiotics, D's murder conviction would almost certainly have been upheld. This is apparent from the later case of *Cheshire* [1991] 3 All ER 670, in which D shot V, who later died as a result of medical complications arising from a tracheotomy he had undergone as part of his emergency treatment. The gunshot wounds had healed at the time of death, but D's conviction was upheld on the grounds that the complications were still a natural consequence of his acts. After careful consideration of existing authorities, including *Jordan, Smith* and *Malcherek*, Beldam LJ concluded (at pp. 851–2):

> ... when the victim of a criminal act is treated for wounds or injuries by a doctor or other medical staff attempting to repair the harm done, it will only be in the most extraordinary and unusual case that such treatment can be said to be so independent of the acts of the defendant that it could be regarded in law as a cause of the victim's death to the exclusion of the defendant's acts ...
>
> Even though negligence in the treatment of the victim was the immediate cause of his death, the jury should not regard it as excluding the responsibility of the accused unless the negligent treatment was so independent of his acts, and in itself so potent in causing death, that they regard the contribution made by his acts as insignificant.

Cheshire was followed in *Mellor* [1996] 2 Cr App R 245; see also *Gowans* [2003] EWCA Crim 3935 and *Wallace* [2018] EWCA Crim 690, [2018] 2 Cr App R 22 (325) (see **A1.38**).

Conduct of the Victim

In many cases, the *actus reus* of a crime is completed, not by an act of the offender, but by an act of the victim, as where the victim of a criminal deception is tricked into making a payment into the deceiver's account. Another is where V is injured in a fall whilst attempting to escape from an attack by D: the latter may be regarded as having caused that injury. Thus, in *Roberts* (1971) 56 Cr App R 95, D was convicted of assault occasioning actual bodily harm to a young woman who was injured jumping from his moving car after he had assaulted her in that car; and in *Corbett* [1996] Crim LR 594, D was convicted of manslaughter when a man he was assaulting was struck and killed by a car as he attempted to escape. See also *DPP v Daley* [1980] AC 237 and *Mackie* (1973) 57 Cr App R 453. A clear direction on causation is essential in such cases. In *Williams* [1992] 2 All ER 183, it was held that the question is whether V's reaction was 'within a range of responses which might be anticipated from a victim in his situation', or whether it was 'so daft as to make it his own voluntary act which amounted to a *novus actus interveniens*'. The jury should not, in this context, be invited to make any allowance for D's youth or inexperience (*Marjoram* [2000] Crim LR 372). D's inability to foresee V's reaction may be relevant to the question of *mens rea*, but as far as causation is concerned, the only subjective element relates to V. As Stuart-Smith LJ pointed out in *Williams*, the jury must be directed 'to bear in mind any particular characteristic of the victim and the fact that, in the agony of the moment, a victim may act without thought and deliberation'. **A1.35**

Conversely, D cannot be held responsible for 'causing' the voluntary and deliberate acts of V, merely because they were foreseeable responses to D's actions. The supplier of a controlled drug does not ordinarily 'cause' his client to take or ingest that drug, even if such conduct is both foreseeable and expected (*Dalby* [1982] 1 All ER 916; *Armstrong* [1989] Crim LR 149; *Kennedy (No. 2)* [2007] UKHL 38, [2008] 1 AC 269). The distinction between such cases and *Roberts* is that the drug supplier does not force the customers to do anything. They exercise informed free will and harm themselves by their own voluntary acts.

A1.36 **Drug-dealing Cases** This is not to suggest that a drug dealer can never be guilty of manslaughter if a customer dies after taking the drugs supplied. Where D supplies contaminated drugs, or supplies a drug such as heroin to a child, who is unable to make an informed decision concerning the dangers involved, D may well be considered to have 'caused' any harm that then results, just as if D had left the child a loaded gun to play with. Liability may also arise under the *Miller* principle (*Miller* [1983] 2 AC 161: see **A1.20**) where D fails to summon help when it is obvious that V has become dangerously ill as a result of ingesting drugs that D has supplied. See *Evans* [2009] EWCA Crim 650, [2009] 2 Cr App R 10 (156) and **B1.65**.

There may also be cases in which D and V can each be said to have jointly administered the drug. If the drug is held to be a noxious substance (as for example heroin would be), this might suffice to make D guilty of an offence under the OAPA 1861, s. 23, and of manslaughter if death results. See *Burgess* [2008] EWCA Crim 516 and **B1.60**. In *Rogers* [2003] EWCA Crim 945, [2003] 1 WLR 1374 it was held to suffice that D applied a tourniquet to V's arm as V self-injected; but in *Kennedy (No. 2)* the House of Lords disagreed (at [20]):

> There is, clearly, a difficult borderline between contributory acts which may properly be regarded as administering a noxious thing and acts which may not. But the crucial question is not whether the defendant facilitated or contributed to administration of the noxious thing, but whether he went further and administered it. What matters ... is whether the injection itself was the result of a voluntary and informed decision by the person injecting himself. In *R v Rogers*, as in the present case, it was. That case was, therefore, wrongly decided....

The House of Lords also overruled *Finlay* [2003] EWCA Crim 3868 and reversed the Court of Appeal's ruling in *Kennedy (No. 2)* [2005] EWCA Crim 685, [2005] 4 All ER 1083. The Court of Appeal in *Kennedy* had in effect followed *Rogers*; whereas in *Finlay* it had reasoned (following *Environment Agency v Empress Car Co. (Abertillery) Ltd* [1999] 2 AC 22) that V's voluntary but fatal act of self-injection with a syringe prepared by D did not necessarily break the chain of causation. As explained at **A1.33**, however, the House of Lords in *Kennedy* did not consider the *Empress* approach to causation to be applicable to cases of this kind.

A1.37 **Victim's Aggravation or Neglect** As explained at **A1.31**, a victim's aggravation or neglect of injuries is unlikely to affect the chain of causation. Thus, in *Wall* (1802) 28 St Tr 51, D was found guilty of murdering a soldier, V, whom he had subjected to an illegal flogging, notwithstanding that V subsequently aggravated his condition by drinking spirits to ease the pain. In *Dear* [1996] Crim LR 595, D appealed against his conviction for murder, arguing that V, whom he had repeatedly slashed with a knife, subsequently aggravated his own wounds so that they reopened, with fatal results. D's conviction was nevertheless upheld. Rose LJ said in *Dear* that the cause of death was bleeding from the artery which D had severed. Whether or not the resumption or continuation of that bleeding was deliberately caused by V, the jury were entitled to find that D's conduct made an operative and significant contribution to the death.

A1.38 **Suicide and Euthanasia** The Court of Appeal in *Dhaliwal* [2006] EWCA Crim 1139, [2006] 2 Cr App R 24 (348) held that, where D inflicts physical and/or psychological abuse on V and thereby causes V some kind of recognised psychiatric illness (i.e. injury amounting in law to actual or grievous bodily harm for the purposes of the OAPA 1861, s. 47 or s. 20) that conduct may give rise to liability for manslaughter (i.e. constructive manslaughter) should the illness in turn cause V to commit suicide. Conditions such as post-traumatic stress disorder, battered wife syndrome or reactive depression were identified as potential causes. In *Dhaliwal*, however, the prosecution could not prove that V had suffered any such psychiatric injury. The infliction of mere psychological harm would not suffice.

The Court of Appeal left open the possibility that a manslaughter conviction might sometimes be supportable on a somewhat different basis, which had been suggested by the trial judge but disavowed by the prosecution, namely that 'where a decision to commit suicide has been triggered by a physical assault which represents the culmination of a course of abusive conduct, it would be possible ... to argue that the final assault played a significant part in causing the victim's death'.

In *Wallace* [2018] EWCA Crim 690, [2018] 2 Cr App R 22 (325), D threw acid over V's face and body, inflicting horrific injuries that left him permanently maimed, disfigured, paralysed and in terrible, incurable pain. Unable even to take his own life, V was moved to Belgium, where doctors agreed to his request for voluntary euthanasia in accordance with Belgian law. The issue on appeal was whether this medical intervention broke the chain of causation, or whether a charge of murder could properly be left to the jury. The Court of Appeal held that it would be open to a jury to find that V's decision to ask for euthanasia, and the Belgian doctors' acts in carrying it out, were not only direct and foreseeable results of the injuries that D had inflicted upon him, but decisions that were far from being truly free and voluntary, and thus clearly distinguishable from the scenario the House of Lords was concerned with in *Kennedy* (No. 2). Giving the judgment of the court, Sharp LJ said (at [61]):

> [V's] request to the doctors, and the act of euthanasia itself carried out in accordance with his wishes, were not discrete acts or events independent of the defendant's conduct, nor were they voluntary, if by this is meant they were the product of the sort of free and unfettered volition presupposed by the *novus actus* rule. Instead they were a direct response to the inflicted injuries and to the circumstances created by them for which the defendant was responsible.

The doctors who carried out the euthanasia procedure were not obliged under Belgian law to participate in it, so in that sense their actions were entirely voluntary, but the Court of Appeal did not consider this to be a crucial distinction (at [85]):

> It would ... seem an odd result, if a defendant who paralysed one victim but not another in identical circumstances (so the second could take their own life, but the first could only do so through the intervention of a third party) would be legally responsible for the death of the second victim but not the first. In the event we consider that the jury could conclude on the facts as they were here that the acts of V and the doctors were not sensibly divisible; that the doctors' (lawful) conduct in carrying out with their hands what he could not carry out with his own was but one link in the chain of events instigated by the defendant and ... in the light of the decision in Dear the seeking of death ... as a response to horrific injuries does not preclude the jury finding that the defendant's conduct made a significant contribution to [V's] death.

The jury subsequently convicted D of throwing a corrosive substance with intent to maim, etc., but acquitted her of murder.

Exceptional Natural Events

An 'act of God' or other exceptional natural event may break the chain of causation leading from D's initial act, if it was the sole immediate cause of the consequence in question. Such an event must be 'of so powerful a nature that the conduct of the defendant was not a cause at all, but was merely a part of the surrounding circumstances' (*Southern Water Authority v Pegrum* [1989] Crim LR 442). If D attacks V and leaves him slowly dying of the injuries, the chain of causation may be broken if V is ultimately killed by a lightning bolt or a falling tree, rather than by the original injuries. In contrast, routine hazards, such as seasonal rain or cold winter nights, would not have such an effect (*Alphacell Ltd v Woodward* [1972] AC 824). Such things are more readily foreseeable, but as Lord Hoffmann said in *Environment Agency v Empress Car Co. (Abertillery) Ltd* [1999] 2 AC 22 at pp. 34–5 (see **A1.33**): **A1.39**

> The true common sense distinction is, in my view, between acts and events which, although not necessarily foreseeable in the particular case, are in the generality a normal and familiar fact of life, and acts or events which are abnormal and extraordinary....
>
> ... In the context of natural events, this distinction between normal and extraordinary events emerges in the decision of this House in *Alphacell Ltd v Woodward*.

Causation Issues and Alternative Explanations

A1.40 The court or jury must be satisfied that D caused the event which is the subject of the charge. If there is a plausible alternative explanation that cannot be disproved, D must be acquitted (*Kimel* [2016] EWCA Crim 1456). At a trial for, e.g., manslaughter by gross medical negligence, the prosecution must be able to prove that V would not have died as and when V did, but for D's negligence. Proof that D's negligence or neglect deprived V of an excellent chance of survival cannot suffice (*Morby* (1882) 8 QBD 571; *Misra* [2004] EWCA Crim 2375, [2005] 1 Cr App R 21 (328); *Sellu* [2016] EWCA Crim 1716, [2017] 1 Cr App R 24 (349); *Bawa-Garba* [2016] EWCA Crim 1841).

Difficulties may arise where the evidence suggests that D might have caused the *actus reus* in one of two or more different ways. The court or jury must be able to agree, not just on their verdict but on the basis for it, and must be directed accordingly. As Otton LJ explained in *Boreman* [2000] 1 All ER 307, 'where the two possible means by which the [offence] is effected comprise completely different acts, happening at different times ... the jury ought to be unanimous on which act leads them to the decision to convict'. See also *Brown* (1983) 79 Cr App R 115 at **D18.44**. This does not mean, however, that a court or jury must always be able to agree on how exactly D committed the crime. It will suffice if they can agree that D must, one way or another, have committed it. Thus, if six jurors believe that D committed murder by personally killing V (or, if not, by hiring an assassin to do the job) and the other six believe that D committed that same murder by hiring an assassin (or, if not, by personally killing V) they may still be able to convict D of that offence, because they can all agree that D was implicated in one way or another (*Giannetto* [1997] 1 Cr App R 1). Alternatively, the jury may have no idea as to how or when D committed the offence, and yet be able to agree that D must have done so, in one way or another (*A-G's Ref (No. 4 of 1980)* [1981] 2 All ER 617: see **A1.9**). In *Boreman*, however, V was beaten up by the appellants and later died in a fire at his home. There was some evidence that the beating had contributed to his death. There was also some evidence that the appellants had started the fire; but it did not follow that they must have killed V in one way or the other. It would not therefore suffice if some jurors thought they were guilty only on the first basis and some only on the second.

Section A2 *Mens Rea*

THE MENTAL ELEMENT GENERALLY

A2.1 In addition to proving that D satisfied the definition of the *actus reus* of the particular crime charged, the prosecution must also prove *mens rea*, i.e. that D had the necessary mental state or degree of fault at the relevant time. Lord Hailsham of St Marylebone said in *DPP v Morgan* [1976] AC 182 at p. 213: 'The beginning of wisdom in all the "*mens rea*" cases ... is, as was pointed out by Stephen J in *Tolson* (1889) 23 QBD 168 at p. 185, that "*mens rea*" means a number of quite different things in relation to different crimes.' Thus one must turn to the definition of particular crimes to ascertain the precise *mens rea* required for specific offences. Nevertheless, there are a number of recurrent concepts (such as intention, recklessness etc.) which can usefully be examined here. There are some general points that ought to be borne in mind when looking at the definition of any individual crime. Some of these general points (such as the question of transferred *mens rea*) are best looked at after examining the meaning of particular concepts such as intention etc., but by way of introduction it is useful to point out the varied ways in which the individual concepts may be used.

Criminal offences vary in that some may require intention as the *mens rea*, some require only recklessness or some other state of mind and some are even satisfied by negligence. The variety in fact goes considerably further than this in that not only do different offences make use of different types of mental element, but also they utilise those elements in different ways. Compare, for example, assault occasioning actual bodily harm (OAPA 1861, s. 47) and criminal damage contrary to the Criminal Damage Act 1971, s. 1(1). Both are in one sense crimes of recklessness (see *Venna* [1976] QB 421 for assault, and the Criminal Damage Act 1971, s. 1(1), itself for criminal damage) but the *extent* to which they apply this concept is quite different. It has been confirmed that the mental element in assault occasioning actual bodily harm only extends to the element of 'assault' and not to the element of 'occasioning actual bodily harm'. In *Roberts* (1971) 56 Cr App R 95, D was liable even though he did not intend or foresee any actual bodily harm and this case was approved by the House of Lords in *Savage* [1992] 1 AC 699. In contrast, in relation to damaging any property belonging to another, the mental element applies not only to the elements of 'damaging' and 'property' but also to the element of 'belonging to another'. So in *Smith* [1974] QB 354, D was not guilty because he intended to damage only property he believed to be his own, and did not intend, nor was he reckless, as to damaging property belonging to another. Thus the *range of application* of the concept of recklessness has been wider in relation to criminal damage, in the sense that it applies to all the elements of the *actus reus*, than in relation to assault occasioning actual bodily harm, where it applies only to the element of assault and not harm.

A2.2 This 'range of application' should be contrasted with the scope of meaning of recklessness which has, on a number of occasions, undergone radical change. The House of Lords' decision in *Metropolitan Police Commissioner v Caldwell* [1982] AC 341 *formerly* gave recklessness a so-called objective interpretation in relation to offences of criminal damage so as to include those who had failed to consider an obvious risk. In contrast, in relation to offences against the person, recklessness was understood in a more subjective sense to include only those who were actually aware of the relevant risk (*Spratt* [1990] 1 WLR 1073). Thus recklessness differed in both its range (of application) and its scope (of meaning) as between assault and criminal damage. This led to further distinctions between the meaning of recklessness in the offence of criminal damage and its meaning in rape (*S (Satnam)* (1983) 78 Cr App R 149), including the notion or attitude of 'couldn't care less', although the SOA 2003 has since redefined rape in such a way that the meaning of recklessness is no longer the crucial issue.

Quite apart from the disappearance of recklessness from the definition of rape, much greater consistency of meaning as between criminal damage and offences against the person was restored by the decision of the House of Lords in *G* [2003] UKHL 50, [2004] 1 AC 1034, which overruled *Caldwell* and reasserted a subjective test requiring actual awareness of risk in cases of criminal damage. However, it is clear from both Lord Bingham's opinion at [28] and from Lord Rodger's at [69] that it is still perfectly *possible* that recklessness could have different meanings in relation to different offences.

Lord Rodger, in agreeing that the subjective meaning of recklessness was the correct one under the Criminal Damage Act 1971, nevertheless recognised that:

> ... there is much to be said for the view that, if the law is to operate with the concept of recklessness, then it may properly treat as reckless the man who acts without even troubling to give his mind to a risk that would have been obvious to him if he had thought about it. This approach may be better suited to some offences than to others ... the opposing view, that only advertent risk-taking should ever be included within the concept of recklessness in criminal law, seems to be based, at least in part, on the kind of thinking that the late Professor Hart demolished in his classic essay, 'Negligence, *Mens Rea* and Criminal Responsibility' (1961), reprinted in HLA Hart *Punishment and Responsibility* (1968), pp. 136–157.

It therefore remains true to say that, in considering the mental element of any particular crime one has to consider not only the *scope* (of meaning) of that element and its *range* (of application — i.e. which of the elements of the *actus reus* it applies to) but also the *context* of its use which may itself influence the scope of meaning to be adopted.

A2.3 The position of the word expressly requiring the mental element may be significant, as can be seen in the House of Lords' decision in *Wings Ltd v Ellis* [1985] AC 272, which turned on the interpretation of the Trade Descriptions Act 1968, s. 14(1) (now repealed):

> It shall be an offence for any person in the course of any trade or business—
>
> (a) to make a statement which he knows to be false; or
>
> (b) recklessly to make a statement which is false.

The House was concerned with s. 14(1)(a) and held that the requirement of knowledge applied only to the element of the falsity of the statement and not to the act of making the statement in the first place. Thus Wings Ltd was convicted in relation to a statement in a brochure which was initially made innocently and which the company attempted to withdraw as soon as its falsity was realised. The statement was regarded as being made when a customer read it and booked a holiday and Wings Ltd was liable since by then the statement was known to the company to be false even though it was not known that the statement was being made. The decision is not beyond criticism but the contrast in wording between paras. (a) and (b) of s. 14(1) and the respective positioning of the words requiring *mens rea* help to explain the decision. The adverb 'recklessly' is right at the start of para. (b) so that it can naturally refer to both the act of making a statement and the requirement of its falsity whereas para. (a), instead of referring to 'knowingly making a false statement', which would be more consistent with para. (b), merely refers to making 'a statement which he knows to be false'. Thus the *range* of application of the concept of knowledge was restricted by the *position* of the word in the section.

INTENTION

A2.4 'Intention' is a word that is usually used in relation to consequences. D clearly intends a consequence if it is D's purpose that the consequence should follow from D's action. This is so whether the consequence is very likely or very unlikely to result. Thus D who shoots at V with the purpose of killing V, intends to kill whether V is 2 metres away and an easy target or whether V is 200 metres away and it would have taken an exceptionally good shot to hit V. In either case, even if D misses, D will be liable for a crime requiring intention to kill, such as attempted murder.

The meaning of 'intention' is not restricted to consequences which it is D's purpose to cause (sometimes referred to as 'direct' intent) but includes consequences which D might not want to follow but which D knows are virtually certain to do so (sometimes referred to as 'oblique' or 'indirect' intent). At one point it seemed that there was support in the House of Lords for a very wide view of oblique intent, i.e. that it included a state of not wanting a consequence to occur while knowing that it was 'highly probable' or even just 'probable' or 'likely' (*Hyam v DPP* [1975] AC 55 and see also per Lord Diplock in *Lemon* [1979] AC 617 at p. 638). This was regarded as too wide by the Court of Appeal in *Mohan* [1976] QB 1 in relation to attempt and in *Belfon* [1976] 3 All ER 46 in relation to wounding with intent to cause grievous bodily harm under the OAPA 1861, s. 18. It seemed that intention might mean different things in different offences but much of the uncertainty appeared to have been resolved by the decisions of the House of Lords in *Moloney* [1985] AC 905 and *Hancock* [1986] AC 455, although further refinements were added by another House of Lords case, *Woollin* [1999] AC 82.

The most important principles to emerge from *Moloney* were that (a) intention should have the same meaning throughout the criminal law (see per Lord Bridge of Harwich at p. 920F), although Lord Steyn appeared to cast some doubt upon this in *Woollin*, and (b) the foresight of the probability of a consequence does not of itself amount to intention but may be evidence of it (see *Jogee* [2016] UKSC 8, [2017] AC 387, discussed at **A4.10**, for emphasis that the same proposition is true for the *mens rea* of an accessory to murder where intention is also required). Unfortunately the guidelines laid down in *Moloney* for directing a jury on this issue (essentially that the jury could, but would not be obliged to, infer that D intended a consequence if D foresaw it as a 'natural' consequence of the action) were subsequently found by the House of Lords in *Hancock* to be 'unsafe and misleading'. Lord Scarman said ([1986] AC 455 at p. 473): **A2.5**

> [The guidelines] require a reference to probability. They also require an explanation that the greater the probability of a consequence the more likely it is that the consequence was foreseen and that if that consequence was foreseen the greater the probability is that that consequence was also intended. But juries also require to be reminded that the decision is theirs to be reached upon a consideration of all the evidence.

The result seemed to be that:

(a) Where there is clear evidence that D desired the consequence to occur, the question of whether D intended that consequence can be left to the jury without further elaboration.
(b) Where D may not have desired the consequence but may have foreseen it as a by-product of the action, a more detailed direction may be necessary.
(c) Such a direction would emphasise that 'the probability, however high, of a consequence is only a factor, though it may in some cases be a very significant factor, to be considered with all the other evidence in determining whether the accused intended to bring it about' (Lord Scarman in *Hancock* at p. 474).

The first two principles (paras. (a) and (b)) continue to apply following *Woollin*, whether the charge be murder or any other offence requiring intention. In the light of *Woollin*, para. (c) now seems potentially too broad, in relation to murder at least, since only foresight of a virtual certainty entitles a jury to find intention (in the absence of desire) on a murder charge (see further **B1.12** and **B1.14**). Given the statement of Lord Steyn in *Woollin* (at p. 96) that 'it does not follow that "intent" necessarily has precisely the same meaning in every context in the criminal law', it remains possible that lower levels of foresight could still be a sufficient basis for a legitimate inference in relation to other offences requiring intention. In either case, the effect of (c) seems to be that a discretion is conferred on the jury because the core notion of intention which they are inferring is left undefined (even after *Woollin*, in which Lord Steyn confirmed that 'the decision is for the jury upon a consideration of all the evidence in the case', and see also *Mathews* [2003] EWCA Crim 192, [2003] 2 Cr App R 30 (461)). For more detail on intent in relation to murder, see **B1.12** and **B1.14**; in relation to wounding with intent to cause grievous bodily harm, see *Bowden* [1993] Crim LR 379, which reiterates that foresight of 'virtual certainty' or at least 'a very high degree of probability' is required.

RECKLESSNESS

Recklessness Generally

A2.6 Essentially concerned with unjustified risk-taking, the precise meaning of the term 'recklessness' has been the subject of great controversy and will no doubt continue to be so. The reason for this is that recklessness has come to be the touchstone of criminal responsibility for a large number of criminal offences. For many offences, the precise boundaries of the concept of intention are not in themselves crucial as recklessness constitutes an alternative and sufficient *mens rea* and one which it is easier to prove. For example, under the Criminal Damage Act 1971, s. 1(1), a person has the requisite *mens rea* if that person acts 'intending to destroy or damage any property or being reckless as to whether any property would be destroyed or damaged'. If D threw a stone which damaged X's window and is charged under s. 1(1), D may plausibly be able to say, for example, that the aim was to hit the dog in front of the window and that there was no *intention* to damage the window. There would be little point here trying to argue that D realised that the probability was that the stone would miss the dog and break the window from which the jury should infer an intention to break the window. There would be a much greater chance of success in relying on recklessness which equally suffices for liability. The issue of foresight of probability as intention need only be explained in crimes such as murder or attempt where intention alone suffices for liability.

The relationship between intention and recklessness (in relation to consequences), and indeed the debate about the scope of recklessness itself, can be seen more clearly from the following list:

(a) Consequence aimed at (i.e. D acts in order to cause that consequence): intention.
(b) Consequence foreseen as virtually certain: intention *may* be found.
(c) Consequence foreseen as probable: typically (if risk unreasonable) recklessness (subjective).
(d) Consequence foreseen as possible: typically (if risk unreasonable) recklessness (subjective).
(e) Consequence not foreseen but ought to have been: negligence (objective recklessness).
(f) Consequence not foreseen which even a reasonable person would not foresee: strict liability.

The central case of intention is situation (a) although the jury may still find intention in situation (b) and possibly, although not in murder cases, even in (c). However, (b) and (c) are more appropriately and easily dealt with as recklessness where this will suffice for liability. Situation (d) is also capable of being within recklessness as is category (e). The difference between (d) and (e) essentially represents the distinction between the narrower subjective '*Cunningham*' recklessness (*Cunningham* [1957] 2 QB 396) and the wider objective '*Caldwell*' recklessness (*Metropolitan Police Commissioner v Caldwell* [1982] AC 341) favoured for two decades by the House of Lords but rejected, for criminal damage at least, in *G* [2003] UKHL 50, [2004] 1 AC 1034. Category (f), of course, is not a culpable state of mind and would not normally give rise to criminal responsibility except in relation to crimes of strict liability.

'Subjective' *Cunningham* Recklessness

A2.7 Following the decision of the House of Lords in *G* [2003] UKHL 50, [2004] 1 AC 1034, this type of recklessness can perhaps now be referred to as 'standard' recklessness, but it has in the past often been referred to as *Cunningham* recklessness (*Cunningham* [1957] 2 QB 396).

It covers categories (b), (c) and (d) (most typically the latter two) in the list at **A2.6**. These states of mind, of course, equally qualified as recklessness under the *Caldwell* test (*Metropolitan Police Commissioner v Caldwell* [1982] AC 341), *Caldwell* merely adding category (e) to the scope of recklessness. The spread over categories (b), (c) and (d) emphasises the point that the degree of foresight of risk that constitutes subjective recklessness is not fixed but variable.

As Lord Bingham formulated it in *G* in relation to criminal damage, adopting the Law Commission's Draft Criminal Code (Law Com. No. 177):

> A person acts recklessly ... with respect to—
> (i) a circumstance when he is aware of a risk that it exists or will exist;
> (ii) a result when he is aware of a risk that it will occur;
> and it is, in the circumstances known to him, unreasonable to take the risk.

The degree of foreseen risk which would make one reckless depends therefore on the reasonableness or otherwise of the risk. At one end of the scale, a surgeon operating on a critically ill patient may knowingly run a very high risk of the patient's death, but if the patient is even more likely to die if the operation is not attempted then it would be a reasonable risk to run and no one would describe the operation as reckless. There is a very strong justification which makes the operation reasonable. On the other hand, if one offers another a chocolate from a box containing 50, just one of which the offeror knows to contain arsenic, the offeror is clearly acting recklessly. The risk is a relatively low one (one in 50, or 2 per cent) but, since there is no justification for running the risk, it is an unreasonable one to take and the offeror is reckless. Thus in some circumstances, to run a very high risk may not be reckless and yet in others it may be reckless to run a relatively low risk. In the context of alleged criminal offences there will often be no plausible justification for running the risk (e.g., of wounding someone) and so often the foresight of *any* degree of risk, of the mere possibility of injury, may be sufficient. The greater the justification for running a risk, the higher the degree of *foreseen* risk which will be required to constitute recklessness.

Subjective Awareness of an Unreasonable Risk

Awareness of Risk Following *G* [2003] UKHL 50, [2004] 1 AC 1034, the emphasis is on the degree of risk that is actually foreseen by D or of which D is aware. It is to that extent that the test is subjective. The jury will *normally* assess this by reference to what they themselves would have foreseen in the circumstances which is why in many cases there will be little difference in outcome whether they are directed to consider a test of what D actually appreciated or the alternative (under the previous test in *Metropolitan Police Commissioner v Caldwell* [1982] AC 341) of whether the risk would have been obvious to a reasonable person. Focusing on D's actual awareness clearly may, however, make a difference where there is reason to suppose that D did not appreciate what the reasonable person would have appreciated. This is likely to be the case where D differs from the reasonable person in some relevant way, for example, because of age (the accused were 11 and 12 in *G*) or because of mental disorder (*Stephenson* [1979] QB 695, one of a number of decisions which as a result of *G* must be regarded as rehabilitated, where D was incapable of appreciating the risk of lighting a small fire in a straw stack in order to keep warm). The list of situations where the jury will find a difference between D's appreciation of risk (or lack of it) and what the reasonable person would have realised is not closed. Any reason why D did not in fact appreciate the risk seems at first sight, in principle, to be admissible except for, it still seems clear, voluntary intoxication through drink or drugs — see Lord Bingham's reference in *G* at [32] to *DPP v Majewski* [1977] AC 443 (see **A3.17**) **A2.8**

On the other hand, as Lord Bingham stated in *G* at [39]:

> There is no reason to doubt the common sense which tribunals of fact bring to their task. In a contested case based on intention, the defendant rarely admits intending the injurious result in question, but the tribunal of fact will readily infer such an intention, in a proper case,

> from all the circumstances and probabilities and evidence of what the defendant did and said at the time. Similarly with recklessness: it is not to be supposed that the tribunal of fact will accept a defendant's assertion that he never thought of a certain risk when all the circumstances and probabilities and evidence of what he did and said at the time show that he did or must have done.

Whilst this may be true, the question of what D was actually aware of must be left to the jury and, if it is not, any conviction may be quashed, as happened in *Briggs* [1977] 1 All ER 475, a pre-*Caldwell* case where D claimed that it did not occur to him that he might damage the handle of another person's car which he was trying forcibly to open in order to move the car out of the way of his garage door. *Westlake v CPS* [2016] EWHC 825 (Admin) provides a similar example of a conviction (for assault) being quashed because the magistrates had convicted on the basis of recklessness consisting of a 'failure to see the risk of injury' which D 'ought to have foreseen'. See also *R (Pinkney) v DPP* [2017] EWHC 854 (Admin). If, however, the correct subjective question is asked, it may well be that a jury (or magistrates) will not be sympathetic to a claim that D, acting in bad temper or for some other unattractive motive, did not appreciate an obvious risk and will conclude that D was in fact aware of it. Furthermore, Lord Bingham in *G* seemed quite happy (at [14]) with the approach in *Parker* [1977] 2 All ER 37 whereby, when D is fully aware of all the circumstances, including the degree of force used, closing one's mind to an obvious risk is regarded as equivalent to conscious awareness of the risk and:

> ... a man certainly cannot escape the consequences of his action in this particular set of circumstances by saying, 'I never directed my mind to the obvious consequences because I was in a self-induced state of temper.' (Geoffrey Lane LJ in *Parker* [1977] 1 WLR 600 at p. 604.)

One can explain this on the basis of the argument (referred to by Lord Bingham) that to close your mind to a risk you have first to realise that there is one (in which case it adds little to the requirement of awareness of risk) or alternatively on the basis that we all act in the light of a combination of explicit and implicit items of knowledge. I am aware in one sense (the implicit sense) that if I drive too fast I may cause an accident. I do not consciously think about this (at least most of the time) when driving as I am habituated to drive at a sensible speed. If I am late or angry or frustrated when driving, I may impulsively drive faster than is advisable. I may be aware of the risks in so doing but on occasions I may also truthfully be able to say I was so intent on getting to an appointment in time that the increased risk I ran did not consciously occur to me. But if I am aware of the speed I was doing, I do know (implicitly) of the increased risk even though my preoccupation with something else means I did not specifically think about it at the time. One can call this closing one's mind to the obvious or one can classify the case as one of implicit knowledge sufficient to satisfy a subjective test. In comparison, a child or mentally disordered person may lack even the implicit knowledge about the dangers of speed (or, as in *G*, about how fire can spread) and cannot in any sense be said to be aware of the risk. This was of no avail to the 'tipsy' defendant in *Booth v CPS* [2006] EWHC 192 (Admin), where the Divisional Court upheld a finding in effect that a pedestrian who steps out into the path of a car and is aware of the risk of a collision is implicitly aware of the risk of damaging the car. As Hallet LJ put it at [20]: 'The magistrates were entitled to find ... that if he was aware of the risk of a collision, inherent in that risk of a collision was not only the risk of personal injury but the risk of damage to property.'

A2.9 **Reasonableness of Running that Risk** Whatever the route to concluding that D is aware of a risk, which is the ultimate issue for the jury, even subjective recklessness then imposes an objective test of reasonableness as to whether it was reckless to run *that* risk (which is just one reason why labels of 'objective' or 'subjective' recklessness can be misleading or over simplistic). A very small risk may be unreasonable in many situations. For example, in *Chief Constable of Avon and Somerset Constabulary v Shimmen* (1986) 84 Cr App R 7, showing off one's martial arts skills to friends did not justify the small risk of which D was aware (despite his pride in his own skill) that he might misjudge matters and break the window he was shadow kicking.

Nor would it avail D to say that personally he regarded the running of such a (low) risk to be justifiable or reasonable. D's awareness is only relevant as to the level of the risk, not as to its reasonableness. It is the court's assessment of reasonableness that counts (albeit looking at the level of risk perceived by D).

In many other situations, however, running certain levels of risk is an inherent and accepted part of ordinary life. Driving a car carries a risk of damaging other vehicles but the degree of risk involved in driving with due care and attention is reasonable in the light of the overall balance as perceived in the current social consensus. Lighting a bonfire on Bonfire Night on one's own land inevitably carries *some* risk of fire spreading to adjoining land but, if reasonable precautions are taken so that the risk is sufficiently and suitably low, it would not be regarded as reckless to run that low risk of damage to another's property. But in the context in which many prosecutions are brought, there will be very little if any arguable justification for taking a risk (or for taking the degree of risk which was in fact taken) and the question will simply be whether D was aware of that risk.

'Objective' *Caldwell* Recklessness

The *Caldwell* test of recklessness (*Metropolitan Police Commissioner v Caldwell* [1982] AC 341), now abandoned even for offences under the Criminal Damage Act 1971, was encapsulated in the following model direction given by Lord Diplock in *Caldwell* at p. 354: **A2.10**

> ... a person charged with an offence under section 1(1) of the Criminal Damage Act 1971 is 'reckless as to whether any such property would be destroyed or damaged' if (1) he does an act which in fact creates an obvious risk that property will be destroyed or damaged and (2) when he does the act he either has not given any thought to the possibility of there being any such risk or has recognised that there was some risk involved and has nonetheless gone on to do it.

Although initially the same basic approach was simultaneously applied by the House of Lords in *Lawrence* [1982] AC 510 to the now defunct offence of causing death by reckless driving and thereafter for a time to manslaughter, the Criminal Damage Act 1971 was the last remaining arena in which the *Caldwell* test held any real sway. It is difficult to see now that there are any remaining offences of any significance to which this version of recklessness applies, whereby D may be 'reckless' on the basis of failure to consider an obvious risk if D cannot be said to be aware of the risk (even in the sense explained above of closing his or her mind to a risk).

Following the House of Lords' decision in *G* [2003] UKHL 50, [2004] 1 AC 1034, questionable assertions by apparently culpable defendants that they were not aware of the risks inherent in their conduct can be left to the jury to resolve in the light of common-sense inferences from the facts, aided perhaps by the response that closing one's mind to an obvious risk is equivalent to awareness of it. Judges no longer have to tell juries to their own and the jury's obvious discomfort, as the trial judge was compelled to in *G*, that D can be guilty of an offence of recklessness where the risk is one that D would not have appreciated even after thinking about it. This was the aspect of *Caldwell* as interpreted that was most problematic — the rejection of the conditionally subjective test for determining whether a risk is obvious (i.e. the rejection of the idea that the risk had to be one which would have been obvious to the particular individual if that person had actually stopped to think about it). But, if the purely subjective approach to awareness of risk ever throws up its own problems, a modified form of *Caldwell* recklessness, where the risk must be one which the particular D could have appreciated, may yet resurface at some time in the future, in relation to some offences at least. In truth there may be very little if any difference between a *Caldwell* test of recklessness moderated by a conditionally subjective test of 'obvious risk' and a 'subjective' awareness test of recklessness bolstered by a robust attitude to risks of which D is implicitly or subliminally aware or to which D may be regarded as having closed his or her mind. The idea that a purely subjective test of conscious awareness of risk at the time of acting can adequately deal with all the situations likely to arise has proved naïve in **A2.11** the past and a full reading of *G* reveals that the House of Lords was itself conscious of the risks of too simplistic an approach to complex issues.

MALICE

A2.12 Many provisions of the OAPA 1861, notably ss. 18, 20, 23 and 24, define offences in terms of 'maliciously' performing an act and it is now well established that this word is not to be understood in the sense of 'wickedly' or 'with ill will' but as requiring either actual intention to cause the relevant harm or at least foresight of the risk of causing the particular type of harm. The classic formulation was given by the Court of Appeal in *Cunningham* [1957] 2 QB 396 where it was said:

> ... malice must be taken ... as requiring either (1) An actual intention to do the ... harm ...; or (2) recklessness as to whether such harm should occur or not (i.e., the accused has foreseen that the particular type of harm might be done and yet has gone on to take the risk of it).

The case of *W (A Minor) v Dolbey* (1983) 88 Cr App R 1 made it clear (as had Lord Diplock himself in *Metropolitan Police Commissioner v Caldwell* [1982] AC 341) that this meaning of malice 'as a term of art' was unaffected by the *Caldwell* definition of recklessness. In *W (A Minor) v Dolbey*, the magistrates had convicted D of malicious wounding. D was a minor and had fired at his friend an air rifle, which he believed not to be loaded. This was on the basis of *Caldwell* recklessness (though arguably he was not even *Caldwell* reckless if he had consciously ruled out any risk of causing harm). The Divisional Court quashed the conviction since D did not foresee the risk of any harm to his friend. The Court of Appeal adopted a similar approach in quashing a conviction in *Morrison* (1988) 89 Cr App R 17, which was certainly not a case of ruling out the risk but of D not thinking about the risk to others in seeking to avoid arrest. The subjective meaning of malice was confirmed by the House of Lords in *Savage* [1992] 1 AC 699 (see **B2.37**). It is, however, sufficient for D to foresee that the harm 'might' or 'may' occur; it is not necessary that D foresees that it definitely would occur (*Rushworth* (1992) 95 Cr App R 252; *DPP v A* [2001] Crim LR 140).

WILFULLY

A2.13 'Wilfully', which has some similarities with 'malice' since it dates from an earlier legislative vocabulary, should not be understood merely in its most obvious or literal sense of 'deliberately' or 'voluntarily'. It is now taken as a composite word to cover both intention and recklessness (and trial judges ought to give a direction as to its meaning: *JD* [2008] EWCA Crim 2360). Until recently, it arguably differed from malice in that it may not have been restricted to subjective recklessness but appeared to include *Caldwell* recklessness or something very similar to it. This appearance arose from *Sheppard* [1981] AC 394, which in many ways was the precursor of the decision in *Metropolitan Police Commissioner v Caldwell* [1982] AC 341. In *Sheppard*, Lord Diplock provided a model direction as follows:

> ... on a charge of wilful neglect of a child under section 1 of the Children and Young Persons Act 1933 by failing to provide adequate medical aid, ... the jury must be satisfied (1) that the child did in fact need medical aid at the time at which the parent is charged with failing to provide it (the *actus reus*) and (2) either that the parent was aware at that time that the child's health might be at risk if it were not provided with medical aid, or that the parent's unawareness of this fact was due to his not caring whether his child's health were at risk or not (the *mens rea*).

As Lord Diplock himself commented, this last state of mind 'imports the concept of recklessness which is a common concept in *mens rea* in the criminal law' and the model direction, though not identical, is remarkably similar in structure and effect to that subsequently laid down for recklessness in *Caldwell*.

It now seems, however, that the meaning of recklessness imported by the term 'wilful' is the same subjective one adopted in *G* [2003] UKHL 50, [2004] 1 AC 1034 in preference to the *Caldwell* test. In *A-G's Ref (No. 3 of 2003)* [2004] EWCA Crim 868, [2005] QB 73, Pill LJ said in relation to the offence of misconduct in a public office (at [26] and [27]):

> Whether *Sheppard*, which was not cited in *Caldwell* and in which Lord Edmund-Davies did not, as in *Caldwell* a few months later, dissent, is consistent with *Cunningham* (not cited in *Sheppard*) and *G*, may be arguable, though, for present purposes, we greatly doubt whether there is any material difference. Lord Diplock is likely to have taken the view that the expression 'wilful neglect', in section 1 of the 1933 Act, required a subjective element not required in his view in *Caldwell* but, with the demise of *Caldwell*, the distinction is immaterial.
>
> . . . We do not accept the submission that *Sheppard* imposes a lower duty on the prosecution than does *G*. Indeed, we do not accept the submission that, in the present context, there is any material difference between them and, in our view, the approach to recklessness in *G* can be incorporated into a direction on wilfulness in relation to this offence.

Thus it would seem that 'wilfully' now means intentionally or recklessly and the meaning of recklessness is the same subjective meaning which is discussed at **A2.7**. Any objective tendencies detectable in Lord Diplock's model direction in *Sheppard* can be regarded as having been discarded along with the rejection of his approach in *Caldwell*. The subjective aspect of the meaning of 'wilfully' can be seen to have been confirmed in *W* [2006] EWCA Crim 2723, although the case turned on knowledge rather than recklessness. Sir Igor Judge P (at [38]) quoted with approval Lord Keith's observation in *Sheppard* that 'a parent who has genuinely failed to appreciate that his child needs medical care, through personal inadequacy or stupidity or both, is not guilty'. The subjective nature of the test was also stressed in *Turbill* [2013] EWCA Crim 1422, [2014] 1 Cr App R 7 (62). Although the trial judge had used the word 'recklessness', he had not made it clear to the jury that this imported a subjective test and had also used expressions such as 'grossly careless' and 'couldn't care less' which detracted from the essential subjective nature of the test for wilfulness.

KNOWLEDGE

'Knowledge' can be seen in many ways as playing the same role in relation to circumstances as intention plays in relation to consequences. One knows something if one is absolutely sure that it is so (quoted in *Godir* [2018] EWCA Crim 2294 at [15]), although, unlike intention, it is of no relevance whether one wants or desires the thing to be so. Since it is difficult ever to be absolutely certain of anything, it has to be accepted that a person who feels 'virtually certain' about something can equally be regarded as knowing it. See *Dunne* (1998) 162 JP 399 for confirmation of this approach. On the other hand, one may feel entirely sure and yet be proved wrong, in which case it is difficult to say that one 'knew'. For example, perjury involves making a statement in a judicial proceeding which, *inter alia*, one knows to be false. If D gave evidence which D felt absolutely sure was false but it turns out that D inadvertently told the truth, it cannot accurately be said that D 'knew' that the evidence was false. In fact, D can still be convicted of perjury since the offence also applies to statements which one does not believe to be true. However, where it is specifically knowledge that is required, as in statutory conspiracy, 'knowledge means true belief' (*Saik* [2006] UKHL 18, [2007] 1 AC 18 at [26]). See further **A5.59** and *Thomas* [2014] EWCA Crim 1958. **A2.14**

BELIEF

The concept of belief could be interpreted as differing from knowledge merely in the respect adumbrated in **A2.14**, i.e. that beliefs can turn out to be mistaken whereas knowledge implies correctness of belief. The degree of certainty or conviction required to be experienced by D would on this view be the same for both belief and knowledge. This is almost, in effect, how belief has been interpreted in the context of handling stolen goods under the Theft Act 1968, **A2.15**

s. 22, where the courts have stressed the need to distinguish belief from recklessness or suspicion and have held that it is not of itself sufficient that D believed it to be more probable than not that the goods were stolen. However, it has also been said that:

> Belief, of course, is something short of knowledge. It may be said to be the state of mind of a person who says to himself: 'I cannot say I know for certain that these goods are stolen, but there can be no other reasonable conclusion in the light of all the circumstances, in the light of all that I have heard and seen'. (Boreham J in *Hall* (1985) 81 Cr App R 260 at p. 264.)

The problem with this approach is that, even in the absence of the word 'belief', a court would no doubt hold that someone who felt that the only reasonable conclusion was that the goods were stolen, where the goods did indeed turn out to be stolen, could be said to know that fact. One is left therefore with the impression that the concept of belief adds little in this context to the requirement of knowledge.

Wilful blindness (deliberately shutting one's eyes to the truth) is sometimes said to be equivalent to knowledge (see per Lord Reid in *Warner v Metropolitan Police Commissioners* [1969] 2 AC 256 at p. 279G) but where an offence expressly requires knowledge or belief the better view seems to be that this may merely be regarded as evidence from which knowledge or belief may be inferred but should not be automatically equated with it (*Griffiths* (1974) 60 Cr App R 14).

NEGLIGENCE

A2.16 Some would exclude negligence from a discussion of *mens rea* on semantic grounds, i.e. on the basis that *mens rea* is concerned with states of mind and negligence is not a state of mind but is rather a failure to comply with the standards of the reasonable person. However, *mens rea* is here being used in the wider sense of the fault element required for liability, and although the required fault is, at least as regards the more serious offences, usually defined in terms of a state of mind, it is not exclusively so. Indeed, for the majority of criminal offences (the less serious ones), proof of *mens rea* in the sense of proof of a state of mind in relation to all the elements of the *actus reus* would be difficult to justify. One alternative to requiring a mental state to be proved is to abandon the requirement of fault altogether and say that the only concern is whether D's conduct actually satisfies the *actus reus* of the offence charged. This is the solution of strict liability (see **A2.20**). To base liability on negligence is a less extreme and, to many, a more attractive solution which switches attention away from D's state of mind towards whether D has complied with the standards of the reasonable person.

Despite the potential appeal of the compromise of negligence, offences are rarely defined expressly in terms of negligence. Manslaughter is the one exception at common law but here the negligence has to be 'gross' (see **B1.61** ***et seq.***). While statutory offences do not themselves normally expressly employ the words 'negligence' or 'negligently' (but see *Price* [2014] EWCA Crim 229, [2014] 3 All ER 208 for the interpretation of 'negligently' performing a duty contrary to the Armed Forces Act 2006, s. 15(2)), they do in effect often impose liability for negligence (i.e. for failure to comply with the standards of the reasonable person) through the following mechanisms.

A2.17 *By express use of words equivalent to 'negligence' in the definition of the offence.* The most obvious example is driving without due care and attention under the RTA 1988, s. 3 (see **C6.1** to **C6.12**). Perhaps a less well-known illustration is provided by the Wireless Telegraphy Act 2006, s. 37(1), which is as follows:

> A person who is in charge of premises that are used for unlawful broadcasting commits an offence if—
>
> (a) he knowingly causes or permits the premises to be so used; or
>
> (b) he has reasonable cause to believe that the premises are being so used but fails to take such steps as are reasonable in the circumstances of the case to prevent them from being so used.

The minimum fault element required by this offence is 'reasonable cause to believe' and failure to take 'such steps as are reasonable'. It matters not what D actually believes, it is what the reasonable person in the circumstances would have believed that counts. Similarly, it is not a question of what steps D thinks are needed but what steps the reasonable person would take and therefore on both issues, the minimum basis of liability is negligence.

See also *R (Gray) v Aylesbury Crown Court* [2013] EWHC 500 (Admin), [2013] 3 All ER 346 for a slightly different example of the imposition of negligence liability by means of the phrase 'knew or ought reasonably to have known' under the Animal Welfare Act 2006 (see **B20.23**). A further example, relating to the funding of terrorism, was discussed in *Lane* [2018] UKSC 36, [2018] 1 WLR 3647, construing the TA 2000, s. 17, which creates an offence where D 'knows or has reasonable cause to suspect that [funding] will or may be used for the purposes of terrorism'. The Supreme Court held that this clearly did not require actual suspicion but, rather, objectively assessed reasonable cause for suspicion. It was also pointed out (at [24]) that, unlike an offence of strict liability, D's state of mind was not irrelevant as 'objectively assessed cause for suspicion focuses attention on what information the accused had'. *Lane* is to be distinguished from *Saik* [2006] UKHL 18, [2007] 1 AC 18, where a similar phrase, 'reasonable grounds to suspect', did implicitly require actual suspicion, given the context of the offence and its overall wording (*Lane*, at [14]–[17]).

By judicial decision that the offence is still committed if the accused has made an unreasonable mistake of fact (see, e.g., *King* [1964] 1 QB 285, unreasonable mistake that first marriage void no defence to bigamy; *Phekoo* [1981] 3 All ER 84, mistake under Protection from Eviction Act 1977 (harassment of residential occupiers) required to be reasonable). D is convicted despite an innocent state of mind because D is negligent in believing that the facts are such that no offence is being committed. The reasonable person would not have made the same mistake. Negligence is not here expressly made part of the definition of the offence but is introduced as a limit on what might otherwise be a defence with similar effect. Following the decision of the House of Lords in *B (A Minor) v DPP* [2000] 2 AC 428, it would appear that the courts will be much less ready to require mistakes to be reasonable (see further **A3.6**). **A2.18**

By Parliament expressly requiring a belief to be reasonable as it has now done with an offence as serious as rape in the SOA 2003, s. 1(1). The offence remains one requiring intention as far as the act of penetration is concerned but given penetration by A and lack of consent by B, 'a person (A) commits an offence if… (c) A does not reasonably believe that B consents'. Thus the offence is effectively one of negligence in relation to the element of consent. **A2.19**

Other statutes provide 'no-negligence' defences of not dissimilar effect by means of different formulations, often putting the burden of proof on D, e.g., the MDA 1971, s. 28(2) ('it shall be a defence for the accused to prove that he neither knew of nor suspected nor had reason to suspect the existence of some fact alleged by the prosecution which it is necessary for the prosecution to prove').

It is worth reiterating at this stage the point made earlier about the range of application of fault concepts to different elements of the *actus reus*. As has already been seen with the offence of rape, the fact that an offence is effectively satisfied by negligence as to one element does not mean that negligence will suffice for all the other elements. To return to the example of the Trade Descriptions Act 1968, s. 14(1) (now repealed), and *Wings Ltd v Ellis* [1985] AC 272 discussed in **A2.3**, that offence expressly required knowledge as to the falsity of the statement but, as a result of the no-negligence defence in the Trade Descriptions Act 1968, s. 24 (on which the accused in *Wings Ltd v Ellis* chose not to rely), it was an offence satisfied by negligence in other respects, for example, as to whether a particular statement is being made.

STRICT LIABILITY

The point just made is particularly important in connection with offences of so-called strict liability. The term 'strict liability' is sometimes loosely explained as meaning 'liability without fault' but this is misleading insofar as it suggests that no mental or fault element whatsoever is required. Strict liability offences are normally those where no fault element is required in relation to one (perhaps crucial) element of the *actus reus* but where *mens rea* is required in relation to other aspects. The classic example is *Prince* (1875) LR 2 CCR 154 where D was convicted of **A2.20** taking a girl under the age of 16 out of the possession and against the will of her father. D's reasonable belief that she was over 16 was no defence, so even negligence was not required in relation to the element of her being over the age of 16. However, *mens rea* was required in relation to other elements of the offence, e.g., in relation to whether the taking was against the will of the father. As Bramwell B put it: 'If the taker believed he had the father's consent, though wrongly, he would have no *mens rea*.' (See Brooke LJ in *B (A Minor) v DPP* [2000] 2 AC 428 for a critical analysis of the influence of the decision in *Prince*, an influence drastically reduced following the House of Lords' decisions in that case and in *K* [2001] UKHL 41, [2002] 1 AC 462.) The influence of these two House of Lords' decisions (see **A3.6** for further discussion) was illustrated in the Court of Appeal's decision in *Kumar* [2004] EWCA Crim 3207, [2005] 1 WLR 1352 in which it was held that the offence of buggery under the SOA 1956, s. 12 (now replaced by the SOA 2003), was not a strict liability offence in respect of the other person's age. Thus an honest belief that the other person was over 16 was a valid defence. Although, by virtue of the SOA 2003, equivalent beliefs in this particular context are now required to be reasonable, the principle stated by the House of Lords, that, in the absence of strict liability, the normal inference of *mens rea* involves that there is a defence of honest belief that an aspect of the *actus reus* was not present, was reaffirmed in *CPS v M* [2009] EWCA Crim 2615, [2010] 4 All ER 51 (see **A2.23**).

A2.21 **Elements where Liability is Strict** Rather than talking of an offence as a whole being one of strict liability, it is more accurate to speak of it being an offence of strict liability with respect to a particular element or elements. Of course, the element in respect of which liability is strict may be the only element which has any possible criminal connotation, the remaining elements as to which some mental element is required being by contrast mundane and, in themselves, non-criminal in character. For example, in *Parker v Alder* [1899] 1 QB 20, D was convicted of selling adulterated milk when the adulteration took place after the milk had left his control and was en route by rail to the purchaser. The offence was therefore of strict liability as regards the milk being adulterated and the only element left was the act of selling. To say that the offence requires *mens rea* in respect of this element, that it requires 'an intention to sell milk', has a hollow ring about it since that is not an intention which is in any way culpable. By contrast with *Prince* then, this is an example of an offence where the imposition of strict liability in relation to the one significant aspect of the *actus reus* effectively means that the offence did indeed give rise to liability without fault. At the other end of the scale, assault occasioning actual bodily harm could be regarded as an offence of strict liability as far as relates to the requirement of actual bodily harm since the only *mens rea* required relates to the assault and not to the element of actual bodily harm. However, a person who intends to assault is clearly culpable and no one would describe this offence as giving rise to liability without fault, thus it is not normally thought of as an offence of strict liability but rather as an example of constructive liability (which amounts to much the same thing).

Traditional Attitude to Regulatory Offences

A2.22 A large number of regulatory offences are traditionally referred to as strict liability offences since, as with the case of *Parker v Alder* [1899] 1 QB 20 discussed at **A2.21**, no fault or mental element is required in respect of those features of the *actus reus* which give the offence its criminal character. The circumstances under which the courts will impose strict liability in respect of a particular statutory offence are difficult to predict and regard must be had to the authority (if any) on the individual statutory provision in question.

The Imposition of Strict Liability

A2.23 As Lord Reid emphasised in *Sweet v Parsley* [1970] AC 132, in cases where Parliament has not made it clear that strict liability is intended, the courts, in construing criminal legislation, start from the presumption that Parliament did not intend to punish a blameless individual and therefore that words importing *mens rea* must be read into the statute. The force of this presumption and its status as a matter of 'constitutional principle', especially in cases of offences carrying potentially serious sentences of imprisonment, was powerfully reasserted in *CPS v M* [2009] EWCA Crim 2615, [2010] 4 All ER 51 (bringing a prohibited article into prison under the Prison Act 1952, s. 40C(1)(a), not an offence of strict liability). Therefore, in line with the highly significant decisions of the House of Lords in *B (A Minor) v DPP* [2000] 2 AC 428 and *K* [2001] UKHL 41, [2002] 1 AC 462, it was held in *CPS v M* that the prosecution had to be able to prove the absence of an honest belief on D's part that he was not bringing the article in question with him when he entered the prison. On the other hand, strict liability is often applied to a so-called class of quasi-criminal offences, those referred to by Wright J in *Sherras v De Rutzen* [1895] 1 QB 918 as acts which are not criminal in the real sense but which are prohibited, by a penalty, in the public interest. The question even in this context is whether the danger to be guarded against is of such importance that strict liability is required (*Kirkland v Robinson* (1987) 151 JP 377) and whether the imposition of strict liability would promote the objects of the legislation (*Lim Chin Aik v The Queen* [1963] AC 160). Thus, in *Gammon (Hong Kong) Ltd v A-G of Hong Kong* [1985] AC 1, a case involving breaches of building regulations, the Privy Council stressed that the matter was one of social concern, and that strict liability could be shown to promote the objects of the statute and, in particular, greater vigilance in the carrying out of works. In *Matudi* [2003] EWCA Crim 697 the offence of importation of animal products contrary to the Products of Animal Origin (Import and Export) Regulations (SI 1996 No. 3124) was held to be one of strict liability; the Court of Appeal remarked that the unmonitored importation of animal products was of public concern because it posed hazards to human and animal health and possible economic consequences from an outbreak of, for example, foot and mouth disease. The social risk was great and the imposition of strict liability was likely to deter importers from acting improperly. Similarly, in *Highbury Poultry Farm Produce Ltd v CPS* [2018] EWHC 3122 (Admin), the factors of social concern and promotion of the objects of the statute were called in aid in rebutting the presumption. The case arose under the Welfare of Animals at the Time of Killing (England) Regulations 2015 (SI 2015 No. 1782), reg. 30(1)(g), the Divisional Court holding (at [79]) that 'the objects of this legislation are furthered, and greater vigilance engendered, by insisting on strict compliance ... not least because the greater the assiduity and efforts of the business operator in this regard, the more probable it will be that animals are spared avoidable suffering'. The case is currently on appeal to the Supreme Court, heard on 25 June 2020.

Significance of Penalty The circumstance that the likely penalty is pecuniary is more compatible with the imposition of strict liability (*Customs and Excise Commissioners, ex parte Claus* (1987) 86 Cr App R 189). This applies even though the maximum fine may be heavy (*Gammon (Hong Kong) Ltd v A-G of Hong Kong*). This is not an absolute principle: some offences bearing a heavy pecuniary penalty and even in theory a penalty of imprisonment attract strict liability (*Pharmaceutical Society of Great Britain v Storkwain Ltd* [1986] 2 All ER 635; *Blake* [1997] 1 All ER 963; *Harrow London Borough Council v Shah* [1999] 3 All ER 302). Allied to this is the mode of trial: where, as in *Ex parte Claus*, the offence is triable only summarily, strict liability will be more readily inferred than if the offence is triable either way or on indictment. In regulatory offences courts continue to give weight to the nature of the social danger involved, the limited applicability and reach of the legislation as regulating a particular trade or business, and the exigencies of successful enforcement. See further *Nurse v Republic of Trinidad and Tobago* [2019] UKPC 43, [2020] 2 WLR 131 (offences of false customs declarations and importing prohibited goods being strict liability despite potentially heavy penalties as directed primarily at persons who could take steps to ensure compliance). A2.24

Absence or Use of Particular Words The use of words importing *mens rea* elsewhere in a statute regulating a trade, profession or industry may be treated as an indication that an offence which uses no such words is intended to convey strict liability (*Pharmaceutical Society of Great Britain v Storkwain Ltd*; *Gammon (Hong Kong) Ltd v A-G (Hong Kong)*; *Kirkland v Robinson* (1987) 151 JP 377; *Jackson* [2006] EWCA Crim 2380, [2007] 1 WLR 1035; *R (Thames Water Utilities Ltd) v Bromley Magistrates' Court (No. 2)* [2013] EWHC 472 (Admin), [2013] 1 WLR 3641 (contrasting 'deposit' with 'knowingly cause or knowingly permit') — but contrast the approach in the non-regulatory context of *CPS v M* where such considerations were given little weight). In this context, it should be noted that whilst some words such as 'intentionally' always convey *mens rea*, other words, referable to knowledge rather than to purpose, sometimes do not do so. In general, such words as 'permitting' convey the need to prove *mens rea* (*Sweet v Parsley*; *Reynolds* A2.25

v GH Austin & Sons Ltd [1951] 2 KB 135). On some occasions they have been held not to do so (*Browning v JWH Watson (Rochester) Ltd* [1953] 2 All ER 775). The context in which a word is used may be significant and so too may be the use of the passive voice (*Cheshire County Council v Clegg* (1991) 89 LGR 600; *Cheshire County Council Trading Standards Department, ex parte Alan Helliwell & Sons (Bolton) Ltd* [1991] Crim LR 210). 'Causing' is relatively neutral as to whether *mens rea* is required and it was not so required in the leading case of *Alphacell Ltd v Woodward* [1972] AC 824 where the imperative of preventing pollution of rivers was a strong factor in the decision of the House of Lords that the company could be liable for causing polluted matter to enter a river irrespective of the lack of knowledge or negligence on the company's part. In contrast, however, in relation to causing an accident within the offence of aggravated vehicle-taking under the Theft Act 1968, s. 12A (see **B4.132**), the Supreme Court held in *Taylor* [2016] UKSC 5, [2016] 1 WLR 500 that there must be 'some element of fault . . . which contributes in some more than minimal way to the death' for it to be regarded as being 'owing to', i.e. caused by, the driving of the vehicle under s. 12A(2)(b). Lord Sumption considered that strict liability was not appropriate in relation to this aspect of the offence, *inter alia*, because the offence was in no sense a regulatory offence, given it had a maximum sentence of 14 years' imprisonment where death is caused and, even where only damage to property is caused, a maximum of two years.

A2.26 **Social Dangers** Dangerous drugs and offensive weapons are other areas where the social danger being guarded against has led to restrictive interpretations of *mens rea* and of the meaning of the term 'possession'. In relation to possession of drugs, in *Warner v Metropolitan Police Commissioner* [1969] 2 AC 256, Lords Pearce, Wilberforce and Reid (dissenting) sought a construction which would require the prosecution to prove some element of knowledge of the thing in possession, but not so particular a degree of knowledge as to stultify enforcement of the legislation. In the context of offensive weapons, this means that, in contrast to the introduction since *Warner* of a statutory defence under the Misuse of Drugs Act 1971, it is not a defence for D to show that D did not know and could not be expected to know that the article was an offensive weapon (*Bradish* [1990] 1 QB 981; now emphatically confirmed in *Deyemi* [2007] EWCA Crim 2060, [2008] 1 Cr App R 25 (345), which also confirmed that strict liability is not inconsistent with the ECHR, Article 6 or 7).

A2.27 **Statutory Defences** Where a statutory due-diligence or no-negligence defence is provided in relation to a prohibition otherwise apparently cast in absolute terms, the courts are likely to hold that the offence is, the statutory defence apart, one of strict liability (*Wings Ltd v Ellis* [1985] AC 272; *Kirkland v Robinson* (1987) 151 JP 377; *Bradish* [1990] 1 QB 981; *Harrow London Borough Council v Shah* [1999] 3 All ER 302). The absence of such a defence does not, however, necessarily imply that *mens rea* is to be presumed (*Alphacell Ltd v Woodward* [1972] AC 824).

In relation to such statutory defences, D may sometimes have to satisfy a legal burden but in other cases the provision will be interpreted only to impose an evidential burden. A legal burden makes inroads into the presumption of innocence protected by the ECHR, Article 6(2), and the HRA 1998 (see **F3.18**). Such a provision may, however, be valid provided that it is objectively justified and proportionate (*Johnstone* [2003] UKHL 28, [2003] 3 All ER 884 at p. 1749 per Lord Nicholls; *Sheldrake v DPP* [2003] EWHC 273 (Admin), [2004] QB 487; *Matthews* [2003] EWCA Crim 192, [2003] 2 Cr App R 30 (461)). If, however, a legal burden is found to be incompatible with Article 6(2), the provision may be 'read down' so as only to impose an evidential burden rendering it compatible with Article 6(2) (see *Lambert* [2001] UKHL 37, [2002] 2 AC 545 at **F3.19**).

Human Rights Compatibility

A2.28 Strict liability is not in itself incompatible with the HRA 1998 (*Muhamad* [2002] EWCA Crim 1856, [2003] QB 1031; *Barnfather v Islington Education Authority* [2003] EWHC 418 (Admin), [2003] 1 WLR 2318) and its imposition is not incompatible with the presumption of innocence enshrined in the ECHR, Article 6(2), even in relation to serious sexual offences such as the offence of rape of a child under 13 contrary to the SOA 2003, s. 5. That offence requires an intentional penetration with the penis but does not require knowledge that the child is under 13 and does not permit any defence of reasonable mistake as to age. The House of Lords in *G* [2008] UKHL 37, [2009] 1 AC 92 (see also **B3.86**) confirmed this interpretation of the offence and also the more general proposition that Article 6(2) does not affect the substance of the matters which may be legitimately proscribed by the content of the criminal law (provided that the burden of proving the matters selected for proscription is on the prosecution). The irony is that Article 6(2) can limit the nature of the burden put on D to establish a statutory defence but it has no impact on the more restrictive decision not to provide any such defence at all. The decision in *G* was approved in *G v UK* (2011) 53 EHRR SE25 (237) and the approach was further underlined by the Supreme Court in *Brown* [2013] UKSC 43, [2013] 4 All ER 860, where the offence of unlawful carnal knowledge of a girl under the age of 14 years, contrary to the Criminal Law Amendment Acts (Northern Ireland) 1885–1923, s. 4, was also confirmed as an offence of strict liability in relation to which the presumption of *mens rea* was displaced.

General Defences

As far as general defences to crime are concerned, it must be remembered that liability is normally strict, not absolute, and that many general defences to crime will equally apply to strict liability offences (including insanity, see *Loake v CPS* [2017] EWHC 2855 (Admin), [2018] QB 998). Thus strict liability offences normally involve proof that the accused voluntarily acted or omitted to act. This requirement may exceptionally be displaced by the words of the statute. In *Larsonneur* (1933) 24 Cr App R 74, a French citizen who was deported from the Irish Free State to the UK against her will was convicted of being an alien 'found within' the UK in breach of immigration legislation. In *Winzar v Chief Constable of Kent* (1983) *The Times*, 28 March 1983, D was convicted of being found drunk on a highway even though his presence there was attributable to the police who took him from a hospital corridor to the highway. Although these instances may be explicable on the basis of some prior fault on D's part, it is generally regarded as surprising that a requirement of voluntariness was not implied in the legislation in these cases. See now *Robinson-Pierre* [2013] EWCA Crim 2396, [2014] 1 WLR 2638 (discussed at **A1.13**). **A2.29**

Act of God It does, however, seem both from *Alphacell Ltd v Woodward* [1972] AC 824 and from *Southern Water Authority v Pegrum* [1989] Crim LR 442 that act of God can amount to a defence. So too will automatism, provided that the degree of impairment is virtually absolute (*A-G's Ref (No. 2 of 1992)* [1994] QB 91). Duress by threats and duress of circumstances should apply to offences of strict liability since they represent independent circumstances of excuse. Mistake, on the other hand, will not serve as a defence to the extent that its effect is to negate *mens rea* which, *ex hypothesi*, is not applicable here (contrast the House of Lords' decisions in *B (A Minor) v DPP* [2000] 2 AC 428 and *K* [2001] UKHL 41, [2002] 1 AC 462 discussed at **A3.6**) where the availability of the defence of genuine mistake was the logical consequence of the presumption of *mens rea* and of the offence *not* being one of strict liability. **A2.30**

TRANSFERRED *MENS REA*

Transferred *mens rea* (an expression now acknowledged as 'a better description' by the Supreme Court in *Gnango* [2011] UKSC 59, [2012] 1 AC 827 (at [16])) has traditionally been referred to as 'transferred malice' since the principal illustration was to be found in the case of *Latimer* (1886) 17 QBD 359, which was concerned with malicious wounding under the OAPA 1861, s. 20. D struck with his belt at C but missed and accidentally cut open the face of R. The Court for Crown Cases Reserved upheld the conviction. Lord Coleridge CJ pointed out that the section referred to wounding 'any other person'. This underlines the point that it is a question of interpreting the particular mental element required for the particular offence. The identity of the victim is not a material detail as far as most offences against the person are concerned, and therefore D's intention to injure A can be transferred so as to make D liable for an injury accidentally inflicted on B. The principle was applied to the offence of manslaughter in **A2.31**

Mitchell [1983] QB 741 where D assaulted A, aged 72, causing him to fall on to the even more elderly B (aged 89), ultimately causing her death. The Court of Appeal upheld the conviction for her manslaughter, Staughton J saying: 'We can see no reason of policy for holding that an act calculated to harm A cannot be manslaughter if it in fact kills B.'

A more restrictive approach to the doctrine of transferred malice was taken by the House of Lords in *A-G's Ref (No. 3 of 1994)* [1998] AC 245. Lord Mustill (at p. 261) recognised the doctrine only as an '"arbitrary exception to general principles"... useful enough to yield rough justice in particular cases... [which] could sensibly be retained not withstanding its lack of any sound intellectual basis'. However, it could not be extended to create liability for murder from an intentional infliction of grievous bodily harm on a pregnant woman which later resulted in the death of the child *in utero* subsequent to it having been born alive. Such a situation could give rise to liability for manslaughter, apparently without the need of the doctrine of transferred malice, but it was not murder. The decision seems to be influenced as much by the desire not to build any further on the grievous bodily harm/murder rule as by any deficiency in the transferred *mens rea* rule explained above. The logic of the decision would not necessarily preclude liability for murder of the child where the initial attack on the mother was with intent to *kill* her. More difficult would be the case where the attack was done with intent to destroy the foetus which resulted in a live birth followed by death. This would appear to be attempted child destruction (and possibly manslaughter) rather than murder.

Transfer within the Same Offence

A2.32 The last point is further exemplified by the rule that the *mens rea* for one offence cannot be transferred so as to make D liable for a different offence even if the two offences happen to share similar terminology in their definition. This is illustrated by the case of *Pembliton* (1874) LR 2 CCR 119 where D threw a stone at a crowd of people but missed and broke a glass window behind them. The jury found that he intended to hit the people but not the window. Although he could have been convicted of malicious wounding, had he injured someone, the Court for Crown Cases Reserved quashed his conviction for malicious damage since that was a separate offence with its own separate *mens rea* requiring foresight of damage to property rather than foresight of injury to a person. Lord Coleridge CJ observed that it would have been different if 'the jury had found that the prisoner had been guilty of throwing the stone recklessly, knowing that there was a window near which it might probably hit' for then he would have had the separate *mens rea* of the independent offence of malicious damage. If two separate offences have *precisely* the same *mens rea* then the problem disappears. Proof of the *mens rea* of one automatically involves proof of the *mens rea* of the other. This principle was applied in *Ellis* (1986) 84 Cr App R 235, in which it was held that an intention to import a prohibited substance is the *mens rea* sufficient both for importing a controlled drug of Class A and also for the separate offence (cf. *Courtie* [1984] AC 463) of importing a controlled drug of Class B. Thus if D believed that the drug imported was a Class B drug but it was in fact a Class A drug, D can be convicted of the latter offence since D had the necessary *mens rea* of an intention to import a prohibited substance. D's mistake might be relevant in determining the sentence. Similarly, D could be convicted of importing a controlled drug even if D believed that the material imported was prohibited under some other enactment, such as pornographic material.

Accessories

A2.33 The issue ultimately hinges on precisely what is required by the *mens rea* of the particular offence charged. This is an important point in relation to the liability of accessories (see A4.5), for D2 must intend, at least conditionally, to encourage or assist D1 to commit the principal offence, and if D1 does something outside the scope of that intention, D2 will not be liable. Thus if D2 encourages violence against a *particular* victim and D1 *deliberately* chooses another victim not intended by D2, D2 will not be liable (*Saunders* (1573) 2 Plow 473). However, if D1 tries to carry out the agreed plan but it accidentally misfires and victim B rather than victim A is injured, then the doctrine of transferred intention applies to D2 too and D2 will remain liable because D1 has at least tried to do what D2 intended: D1's acts, although perhaps not their consequences, are in accordance with D2's intention. This is neatly illustrated by *Grant* [2014] EWCA Crim 143, where the Court of Appeal applied the transferred *mens rea* principle to the conviction of a principal and two accessories in an attempted murder by shooting which also resulted in grievous bodily harm to two innocent bystanders. A finding of an intent to kill a specific individual forming the basis of the conviction on the attempted murder count was found inevitably to encompass within it an intent to cause grievous bodily harm, which could be the basis also of a conviction or convictions for causing grievous bodily harm to the bystanders under the OAPA 1861, s. 18, using the transferred *mens rea* rule. The argument that the intent to kill for attempted murder and the intent to cause grievous bodily harm for s. 18 were mutually exclusive or inconsistent with one another was roundly rejected — the former included the latter and conviction for the attempted killing of A plus conviction for the grievous bodily harm caused to B and C when the plan miscarried was perfectly proper for all three defendants. The application of the principle of transferred *mens rea* to accessories is also starkly illustrated by the strikingly unusual facts of *Gnango* [2011] UKSC 59, [2012] 1 AC 827, where D2 took part in a shoot-out with D1. D2 was found to have encouraged D1 to shoot at D2 with intent to kill and D2 was found liable, on the basis of transferred *mens rea*, for the death of the innocent passer-by who was shot by D1 in attempting to kill D2 himself.

PROOF OF *MENS REA*

The various mental states discussed in this section undeniably present courts and juries with difficult practical problems since, even when one is clear about the precise meaning of the mental state to be proved, it is not easy to be sure whether that corresponds to what actually went on in D's mind. Even in apparently clear cases, D's denial may raise a doubt in the minds of the jury. If D shoots someone at point-blank range with a revolver it may seem easy to infer that D intended to kill or at least injure that person but D may seek to deny this by asserting a belief that the revolver was not loaded or was merely a harmless imitation. In the absence of such an explanation, of course, a jury will doubtless infer that D intended the natural and probable result of the action, i.e. death or injury to the other. Apart from D's admissions, this is indeed the most obvious way to ascertain D's state of mind. Thus juries will probably infer that D intended or at least foresaw the natural and probable consequences of the actions. This is unexceptionable as a purely factual inference. Problems have arisen, however, when courts have sought to elevate such an inference to the status of an irrebuttable presumption. In the light of one such decision, *DPP v Smith* [1961] AC 290, Parliament intervened to ensure that it remains open to the jury to find that D did not intend or foresee the consequences (see also *Frankland v The Queen* [1987] AC 576). The CJA 1967, s. 8, provides: A2.34

> A court or jury, in determining whether a person has committed an offence,—
>
> (a) shall not be bound in law to infer that he intended or foresaw a result of his actions by reason only of its being a natural and probable consequence of those actions; but
>
> (b) shall decide whether he did intend or foresee that result by reference to all the evidence, drawing such inferences from the evidence as appear proper in the circumstances.

Although s. 8 makes it clear that there is no irrebuttable presumption, the concluding words of para. (b) equally mean that a jury *may* infer that D intended or foresaw the natural and probable consequences of the actions if this seems appropriate on all the evidence, e.g., in the absence of any evidence explaining why D did not intend or foresee that consequence. (For further discussion of s. 8 and the relationship between foresight and intention in murder, see **B1.12** and **B1.14**.) Section 33(8) of the CJCA 2015 enacts (arguably unnecessarily) a very similar rule to s. 8 of the CJA 1967 in relation to the question of whether a person intends to cause distress by the disclosure of a private sexual photograph or film (see **B18.31**). Part of the thinking behind s. 33(8) may be that s. 8 might be limited to intention or foresight in relation to 'results' that actually have occurred whereas s. 33(8) is concerned with an ulterior intent to cause distress, which consequence is not actually required as part of the *actus reus* of the offence.

The CJA 1967, s. 8, can apply only where the prosecution are seeking to prove that D intended or foresaw something. Therefore whilst it can apply to the proof of intention in murder or to the proof of foresight in, for example, crimes of malice or subjective recklessness, it cannot apply where the definition of the offence does not require intention or foresight. Thus it is of no relevance to the element of manslaughter that requires D's act to be likely to cause bodily harm since that is a purely objective element which does not require any intent or foresight on D's part (*Lipman* [1970] 1 QB 152).

A2.35 Section 8 is concerned with proof of intention and foresight in relation to consequences but a similar problem arises in relation to circumstances. Again, a reasonable prima facie rule is to assume that D was aware of facts of which the reasonable person would have been aware provided one is prepared to adjust that conclusion in the face of credible evidence as to why D was not actually aware of it. This will often take the form of a defence of mistake. The former requirement that such mistakes had always, as a matter of law, to be based on reasonable grounds was, in effect, an irrebuttable presumption that D was aware of facts of which the reasonable person would be aware. The House of Lords in *DPP v Morgan* [1976] AC 182, in abandoning this rule for crimes requiring subjective *mens rea*, performed a similar function in this area to that performed by the CJA 1967, s. 8, in relation to foresight of consequences. The reasonableness or otherwise of a mistake is certainly an important factor in deciding whether D actually made that mistake but the court must look at all the evidence in order to decide on D's actual state of mind.

The *Morgan* principle applies only to crimes for which a genuine mistake is inconsistent with the *mens rea* and does not apply to crimes which are in effect satisfied by negligence in this respect, e.g., bigamy (see the comments of the Law Lords on *Tolson* (1889) 23 QBD 168 in *DPP v Morgan* itself, but see also the approach now taken by the House of Lords in *B (A Minor) v DPP* [2000] 2 AC 428 and *K* [2001] UKHL 41, [2002] 1 AC 462, which seems to make the *Tolson* approach much less likely). Paradoxically, the *Morgan* principle no longer applies to the offence of rape as the SOA 2003 now expressly requires a belief in consent to be reasonable.

Section A3 General Defences

CATEGORIES OF GENERAL DEFENCE

This section deals with defences which are available in relation to a range of offences rather than those which are available only in relation to a particular crime. Particular defences to particular crimes (such as diminished responsibility in relation to murder) are dealt with in the section of this work dealing with the particular offence. The expression 'general defences' suggests something positive that must be put forward on behalf of the accused, but in truth it is more accurate to regard these defences as circumstances where the prosecution have been unable to prove all the requirements of liability beyond reasonable doubt. This is most obviously true of defences that consist of denying the existence of the mental element of the offence charged (as with the defence of mistake) but it is also true of defences such as duress where the burden is not on D to show affirmatively that D was acting under duress but rather on the prosecution (once there is evidence before the court capable of supporting duress) to prove that D was not acting under duress. Nevertheless, it is still possible and helpful to divide general defences into two categories: **A3.1**

(a) those which involve a denial of the basic requirements of *mens rea* and voluntary conduct (the defences of mistake and automatism are best regarded in this way), and
(b) those which do not deny these basic requirements but which rely on other circumstances of excuse or justification, as in the defences of duress and self-defence.

These two categories will be examined in turn.

DEFENCES DENYING BASIC ELEMENTS OF LIABILITY

Mistake and Inadvertence: Offences Requiring Intention or Foresight

Because the defences of mistake and inadvertence consist of a denial of the *mens rea* of the particular crime charged, the nature and the availability of the defences will vary from offence to offence but it is possible to identify categories of offences for which consistent principles can be formulated. The first category consists of offences requiring subjective fault (e.g., crimes requiring intention or subjective recklessness). For this category of offences it is clear that either a mistake (i.e. a positive belief) that a particular ingredient of the offence charged is lacking or, alternatively, a simple failure to appreciate the presence of the same ingredient will operate as a defence. For example, D, out in open country, shoots V dead with a crossbow at a range of 200 metres. There is a 'defence' if D thinks that V is a scarecrow (mistake) or, alternatively, if it has never occurred to D that V or anybody else might be so foolish as to traverse that part of the countryside selected by D to practise archery (inadvertence). In either case D would lack the necessary *mens rea* for murder, the intention to kill or cause grievous bodily harm, although D may well be liable for other offences. Similarly, the offence of malicious wounding (OAPA 1861, s. 20) requires subjective awareness at least of the risk of wounding, and either mistake or inadvertence will suffice for a defence. See, e.g., *W (A Minor) v Dolbey* (1983) 88 Cr App R 1, in which the Divisional Court held that D's belief that his air rifle was unloaded was a defence to a charge under s. 20. (This case also illustrates the artificiality and difficulty in many cases of distinguishing between mistake and inadvertence since D was also described **A3.2** as ignoring the risk that the gun might be unloaded. Fortunately, at least in this category of offences, it is not a distinction which needs to be made, a defence of lack of *mens rea* being present in either case.) See also *Morrison* (1988) 89 Cr App R 17.

It should be stressed that, because this category of offences requires subjective fault, the test of mistake (and of inadvertence) is also a subjective one; there is no requirement that the mistake be one which a reasonable person would have made (or that a reasonable person would have failed to appreciate that which D failed to appreciate). The previously traditional requirement that, as a matter of law, mistakes have to be reasonable was emphatically refuted by the House of Lords in *DPP v Morgan* [1976] AC 182, although it will naturally be more difficult to persuade a jury to accept that D genuinely made an unreasonable mistake. (The House of Lords upheld the convictions in *DPP v Morgan* itself on the basis that D had not actually held any mistaken belief.)

The important point is that the courts regard the rule that mistakes do not have to be reasonable in this context as a logical one which flows from the nature of the mental element required for this category of offences (see especially the speech of Lord Hailsham of St Marylebone in *DPP v Morgan*). Thus one can generalise that wherever an offence requires subjective awareness of a particular element, a genuine mistake that such an element is absent will be a defence.

A3.3 The logic of this rule is unassailable as applied to proof of intention. If D believes D is shooting only at an inanimate object such as a scarecrow, D cannot at the same time by that very act intend to kill. The same is true where knowledge is required. A person who believes that the goods bought are not stolen cannot at the same time know (or even believe) that the goods are stolen — the two states of mind are logically inconsistent with one another. However, with crimes satisfied by foresight or awareness of risk (i.e. crimes satisfied by malice or subjective recklessness) the logic is somewhat flawed. One can believe that the stone one throws in the open country is not going to injure someone whilst still recognising that there is a risk that someone lying out of sight might be injured. The point is that beliefs are not usually absolute and are not inconsistent with the recognition of the possibility of a contrary state of affairs (whereas a belief *is* inconsistent with *knowledge* of a contrary state of affairs). Of course, in most cases the belief will be sufficiently strong to leave only the faintest possibility (if any at all) in the believer's mind that he or she may be wrong and this small degree of possibility would not be sufficient to amount to recklessness or malice. It does, however, depend on what one means by 'belief' and also on what the jury understand by that term.

Mistake and Inadvertence: Implications of the Demise of Objective Recklessness

A3.4 It is clear that inadvertence is no defence to an offence satisfied by objective recklessness even should that concept survive or resurface anywhere in the criminal law following the overruling of *Metropolitan Police Commissioner v Caldwell* [1982] AC 341. It ought to be equally clear that a positive mistake can be a defence even to objective recklessness. The question of mistake in relation to consequences came to be considered under the heading of 'ruling out the risk' and the leading case was *Chief Constable of Avon and Somerset Constabulary v Shimmen* (1986) 84 Cr App R 7, where D claimed to have ruled out the risk of causing damage to a window when he aimed a martial-art-style kick in its direction, basing his view on his faith in his own prowess as an exponent of the Korean art of self-defence. In other words, he claimed to believe that no damage would result from his action (the subsequent shattering of the window revealing this belief to be a sadly mistaken one). The Divisional Court remitted the case to the magistrates with a direction to convict since the evidence did not show that D had ruled out all the risk (hence he was still reckless in consciously running a small risk). But the Court also expressly left open the possibility that D who mistakenly rules out any risk would not be objectively reckless (since D has neither failed to consider the risk nor consciously run it). The interesting point is the requirement that the risk has to be totally ruled out, which is akin to saying that mistaken beliefs have to be held with a degree of conviction equal to certainty and admitting of no doubts.

Logically the same argument should apply in a case like *Shimmen* even following the reversal of *Caldwell* as *Shimmen* was not based on D's failure to consider a risk but on his appreciation that there remained a small but unjustified risk.

The overall point to note is that the treatment of mistakes should not vary as between subjective and objective recklessness since the latter merely extended the former to include failure to think and D who acts under a mistaken belief has not failed to think — the only question can be whether D is subjectively reckless. The mistake is either inconsistent with the required awareness of an unreasonable risk, in which case D is not subjectively reckless, or, despite the mistake, D is still aware of an unreasonable level of risk — in which case, in principle, D may still be reckless. In general though, cases such as *Shimmen* apart, the courts seem to assume that, where D is treated as acting under a mistaken belief, that indicates that D is not at the same time conscious of any remaining risk that could be regarded as unreasonable.

Mistake and Inadvertence: Offences Satisfied by Negligence

It is clear that inadvertence is no defence to a crime of negligence. (This assumes that the risk of which D was unaware was one of which a reasonable person would have been aware. Strictly speaking, of course, inadvertence is wide enough to cover failure to consider non-obvious risks but the normal context of the use of the word 'inadvertence' is one whereby it is assumed that the risk is one of which a reasonable person would have been aware.) **A3.5**

Equally clearly, mistake can be a defence to crimes of negligence subject to the important qualification that the mistake must be a reasonable one since an unreasonable mistake itself supplies the negligence which is the sufficient basis of liability. The House of Lords in *DPP v Morgan* [1976] AC 182 specifically stated that the old requirement of reasonableness still applies to offences not requiring full *mens rea* but deliberately refrained from overruling *Tolson* (1889) 23 QBD 168, which required a mistaken belief in the death of a spouse in the offence of bigamy to be based on reasonable grounds. As Lord Fraser of Tullybelton put it ([1976] AC 182 at p. 238):

> ... bigamy was an absolute offence, except for one defence set out in a proviso, and it is clear that the mental element in bigamy is quite different from that in rape. In particular, bigamy does not involve any intention except the intention to go through a marriage ceremony, unlike rape in which I have already considered the mental element. So, if a defendant charged with bigamy believes that his spouse is dead, his belief does not involve the absence of any intent which forms an essential ingredient in the offence.

Thus, the logical argument that even an unreasonable mistake must deny the mental element, and so be a defence, does not apply to bigamy, and the offence is in effect interpreted as one satisfied by negligence as to whether the spouse is still alive. The courts sometimes adopt this approach in relation to other statutory offences as, for example, in *Phekoo* [1981] 3 All ER 84 in relation to the offence of harassment of a residential occupier under the Protection from Eviction Act 1977, s. 1(3). The Court of Appeal held that a belief that a person was not a residential occupier had to be reasonable to afford a defence. This is entirely consistent with the House of Lords' comments on *Tolson* in *DPP v Morgan*.

Treating an offence as one of negligence is at least a less draconian approach than imposing strict liability (whereby even a reasonable mistake would be no defence) and again is in line with the sentiments expressed by Lord Diplock in *Sweet v Parsley* [1970] AC 132 where he said (at pp. 163–4): **A3.6**

> ... had the significance of *Tolson* been appreciated here, as it was in the High Court of Australia, our courts, too, would have been less ready to infer an intention of Parliament to create offences for which an honest and reasonable mistake was no excuse.

When the Court of Appeal considered the case of *B (A Minor) v DPP* [2000] 2 AC 428, Brooke LJ clearly felt uneasy in holding that the offence under the Indecency with Children Act 1961, s. 1(1) (inciting a girl under 14 to commit an act of gross indecency), was one of strict liability in respect of the age of the girl. However, the House of Lords overturned the decision (also at [2000] 2 AC 428), holding not only that the offence was not one of strict liability but that D's honest belief that the girl was over 14 need not be based on reasonable grounds. Lord Nicholls indicated that 'as a matter of principle, the honest belief approach must be preferable' and that Lord Diplock's dictum in *Sweet v Parsley* referring to 'the absence of a belief, held honestly and upon reasonable grounds in the existence of facts which if true would make the act innocent' had in future to be read as though the reference to reasonable grounds were omitted. In *K* [2001] UKHL 41, [2002] 1 AC 462, the House of Lords held that D's honest belief that a girl was over 16 would be a defence to indecent assault under the Sexual Offences Act 1956, s. 14. Once again, as in *B (A Minor)*, their lordships held that the prosecution has to prove the absence of a belief in excusing circumstances and that such a defence of mistaken belief ought not to be tempered by a requirement that the belief be a reasonable one. Subjectivists welcomed these developments but it would be a pity if the courts regarded themselves as being confronted by a stark choice between full *mens rea* and strict liability and felt obliged to opt for strict liability in circumstances where the middle way of a defence of reasonable mistake and hence liability for negligence might better serve the social purposes of the legislation. The offences considered in these two decisions of the House of Lords have now been replaced by the SOA 2003 and, where the child has in fact reached the age of 13, the half-way house of a defence of reasonable belief in age of 16 or over, has been adopted.

A3.7 The case of *Lamb* [1967] 2 QB 981 provides an unusual example of a defence of mistake succeeding in relation to an offence involving negligence (manslaughter). D had 'jokingly' pointed and fired a revolver containing two live bullets at his best friend, thereby killing him. His mistake was in believing that, because the bullets were not in the firing position, the gun could not fire when in fact, unknown to him, pulling the trigger caused the cylinder to rotate and, in this case, placed one of the bullets in the firing position. The trial judge in effect directed the jury that D's beliefs were irrelevant, as was the evidence called on his behalf to show that this was a mistake that the ordinary person might make. The Court of Appeal quashed the conviction commenting (at p. 990):

> ... it would, of course, have been fully open to a jury, if properly directed, to find the defendant guilty because they considered his view as to there being no danger was formed in a criminally negligent way. But he was entitled to a direction that the jury should take into account the fact that he had undisputedly formed that view and that there was expert evidence as to this being an understandable view.

Thus an 'understandable' (reasonable) mistake could be a defence but a criminally negligent (unreasonable) one would not be.

Mistake and Inadvertence: Offences of Strict Liability

A3.8 Even a reasonable mistake is no defence to an offence of strict liability (see **A2.20**), although many so-called offences of strict liability now have statutory defences available based on particular types of reasonable mistake, the burden of proof of such defences being put on the accused. Such provisions may need to be read, in the light of the ECHR, Article 6, as imposing only an evidential burden. See, e.g., the Misuse of Drugs Act 1971, s. 28, at **B19.104**. As to burden of proof generally, see **F3.1** *et seq*.

Mistake of Law and Similar Defences

A3.9 Whilst the maxim 'Ignorance of the law is no excuse' generally holds good in English law, it is no more than a broad generalisation and is subject to exceptions. These exceptions are really no more than an illustration of the general theme already expounded — that where D lacks the *mens rea* required for the offence charged, D has a defence. Since *mens rea* generally relates to facts, it is mistake or ignorance of facts that is usually the basis of a denial of *mens rea*. However, in some offences the requirement of *mens rea* includes legal concepts and a mistake about that legal concept can mean that D lacks *mens rea*. Thus in *Smith* [1974] QB 354, D's conviction for criminal damage was quashed on the basis of a mistaken belief that the property damaged was still his own property and was therefore not property 'belonging to another'. It was D's ignorance of the civil law on the question of when property belongs to another (in particular, the law relating to a landlord's fixtures) which caused him to believe mistakenly that the property did not belong to the landlord. He thus lacked the *mens rea* of the offence because of his ignorance of law, and this was relevant because the offence required *mens rea* in relation to the civil-law concept of ownership (belonging to another).

It should be stressed that the mistake must be one of civil law rather than about the ambit or meaning of a criminal provision. This precludes not only defences such as 'I didn't think burglary included breaking into houses during the day' but also, for example, a defence to theft of a wild creature based on a belief that a wild creature is not 'property'. The Theft Act 1968, s. 4(4), specifically states that wild creatures are property for the purpose of theft (although there are restrictions on the circumstances when they can be the subject of a charge of theft) and this is a matter of the criminal law rather than whether wild creatures are property in any other branch of the law. Similarly, on a charge of handling stolen goods, it would be no defence to say that one did not know that goods obtained by fraud count as 'stolen' since this too is a matter of criminal rather than civil law (Theft Act 1968, s. 24(4)). The point can be further illustrated by reference to *Johnson v Youden* [1950] 1 KB 544. It was an offence under the Building Materials and Housing Act 1945, s. 7, to sell a house in excess of the prescribed price. The defendant solicitor knew that an extra £250 was being paid to the builder in a separate account to be spent on possible future work which might be done to the house by the builder. Even if the solicitor genuinely believed that this was not part of the price under the Act, his mistake was merely one of criminal law since s. 7(5) specifically stated that associated transactions had to be included in calculating the price.

Some offences expressly make D's beliefs about the legality of D's action relevant and in these cases there can be no question that a mistake of law can be relevant. The most obvious example is the Theft Act 1968, s. 2(1), under which a person is not to be regarded as dishonest: '(a) if he appropriates the property in the belief that he has in law the right to deprive the other of it'. A less obvious example is provided by *Secretary of State for Trade and Industry v Hart* [1982] 1 All ER 817 which concerned the statutory offence of acting as auditor of a company 'at a time when he knows that he is disqualified'. As a director of the company Hart was disqualified but he did not know of the quite separate statutory provision which so provided. Thus, although he knew the facts (that he was a director of the company), he did not know that he was disqualified (as the offence specifically required). Contrast *A-G's Ref (No. 1 of 1995)* [1996] 4 All ER 21, where the offence did not require any specific knowledge that deposit-taking had to be licensed by the Bank of England. See also *Lee* [2001] 1 Cr App R 19 (293) — mistake of law that arrest unlawful not capable of negating an intent to resist lawful arrest. **A3.10**

By the Statutory Instruments Act 1946, s. 3, it is a defence to prove that a relevant statutory instrument had not been issued at the time of the alleged offence although it is open to the Crown to prove that reasonable steps had been taken to bring it to the attention of relevant persons. However, it should be remembered that the *ultra vires* and unlawful nature of subordinate legislation or administrative decisions may be raised as a defence to a criminal charge (*Boddington v British Transport Police* [1999] 2 AC 143). **A3.11**

It has been a question of statutory interpretation for the trial judge whether a defence based on EU law is permitted (*Re Searby Ltd* [2003] EWCA Crim 1910, confirming the right of a citizen faced with a criminal charge to defend him or herself with any plea open, particularly the invalidity of the instrument under which he or she was charged). Provisions of UK criminal law, or its application in a particular instance, have been resisted on the ground of incompatibility with EU law, relying on either the general principles of EU law such as free movement rights (Case 34/79 *Henn and Darby* [1979] ECR 3795) or directly applicable legal instruments. See, e.g., the unsuccessful challenge to the ban on hunting under the Hunting Act 2004 as incompatible with specific provisions of the EC Treaty in *R (Countryside Alliance) v A-G* [2007] UKHL 52, [2008] 1 AC 719. The precise extent to which the scope for such challenges will be reduced, once the transitional period in the EU-UK Withdrawal Agreement has expired, remains to be seen. For a full discussion of EU law and its influence on domestic criminal law, see **A9**.

Automatism

A3.12 The defence of automatism arises where D's conduct lacks the basic requirement of being voluntary (see **A1.10** and **A1.11**).

The defence is limited to cases where there is a total destruction of voluntary control; impaired or reduced control is not enough (*A-G's Ref (No. 2 of 1992)* [1994] QB 91, a view confirmed in *Coley* [2013] EWCA Crim 223 (at [22]), where it was said that the question is not whether D is acting consciously or not but whether there is a 'complete destruction of voluntary control'). Where D is conscious, automatism will be rare but possible (e.g., reflex actions when startled by a sudden loud noise or when stung by a swarm of bees while driving: see *Hill v Baxter* [1958] 1 QB 277 and *Burns v Bidder* [1967] 2 QB 227 at p. 240). Contrast the mistaken pressing of the accelerator rather than the brake in *A-G's Ref (No. 4 of 2000)* [2001] EWCA Crim 780, [2001] 2 Cr App R 22 (417), which was held not to be a case of automatism. Where D has acted in a state of total unconsciousness, it is easier to conclude that D could not have acted otherwise, and in principle D should have the defence of automatism. The law imposes serious restrictions on such a defence, however, through the rules on voluntary intoxication and insanity to be discussed in **A3.16** to **A3.33**. The question which remains for discussion here is the extent to which, even where the automatism is not caused by insanity or voluntary intoxication, there is some further restriction or requirement that the automatism should not be self-induced.

A3.13 Such a requirement was first suggested by the Court of Appeal in *Quick* [1973] QB 910, even though in that case it quashed D's conviction for assault. The alleged assault had taken place whilst D (a diabetic) had been in a state of hypoglycaemia (low blood sugar) which the trial judge had (wrongly, in the view of the Court of Appeal) ruled amounted to insanity. The defence of (non-insane) automatism was thus never put to the jury, but Lawton LJ had the following to say (at pp. 922–3) about such a defence:

> A self-induced incapacity will not excuse... nor will one which could have been reasonably foreseen as a result of either doing, or omitting to do something, as, for example, taking alcohol against medical advice after using certain prescribed drugs, or failing to have regular meals while taking insulin...
>
> Had the defence of automatism been left to the jury, a number of questions of fact would have had to be answered... to what extent had he brought about his condition by not following his doctor's instructions about taking regular meals? Did he know that he was getting into a hypoglycaemic episode? If yes, why did he not use the antidote of eating a lump of sugar as he had been advised to do? On the evidence which was before the jury Quick might have had difficulty in answering these questions in a manner which would have relieved him of responsibility for his act.

It thus appeared after *Quick* that, even where automatism was not caught by the rules on insanity and intoxication, it was not available if it could be said to be self-induced. Thus in *Bailey* [1983] 2 All ER 503, a similar defence based on automatism caused by hypoglycaemia was held by the trial judge to be unavailable (on charges under the OAPA 1861, ss. 18 and 20) since it was self-induced. The Court of Appeal (whilst dismissing the appeal on the basis that no miscarriage of justice had actually occurred) held that this was too absolute a rule:

> In our judgment, self-induced automatism, other than that due to intoxication from alcohol or drugs, may provide a defence to crimes of basic intent. The question in each case will be whether the prosecution have provided the necessary element of recklessness. In cases of assault, if the accused knows that his actions or inaction are likely to make him aggressive, unpredictable or uncontrolled with the result that he may cause some injury to others and he persists in the action or takes no remedial action when he knows it is required, it will be open to the jury to find that he was reckless.

A3.14 The result of these authorities would seem to be that the fact that automatism is self-induced is a bar to the defence only if D was at fault (to the degree required by the particular offence charged). In

Bailey, Griffiths LJ took the view that a diabetic falling into a state of hypoglycaemia is not inevitably at fault since it is not common knowledge, even among diabetics, that a failure to take food after an insulin injection may lead to aggressive, unpredictable and uncontrolled conduct. (Whether that is still empirically true today may be open to debate.) Furthermore, the Court of Appeal held that the limitation on self-induced automatism as a defence could not apply at all to the offence under the OAPA 1861, s. 18, since even self-induced intoxication by drink or drugs would be a defence to such a charge, the offence being one, as will be seen, of specific intent. (Another way of looking at this would be to say that since *intent* to cause grievous bodily harm is required for this offence, D would have to *intend* to become violent through failure to take food in order to be deprived of the defence of automatism, cf. the Dutch courage rule in relation to intoxication discussed at **A3.22**.) The distinction, so clearly drawn in *Bailey*, between offences of basic and specific intent, appears to have been lost sight of in both *Coley* [2013] EWCA Crim 223 and *McKay* [2015] EWCA Crim 2098, [2016] 2 Cr App R 1 (1), where it was assumed, in relation to offences of specific intent, that automatism through voluntary intoxication was precluded because the automatism was self-induced. In both cases, the comments can be regarded as clearly *obiter* and if taken literally would be totally contrary to the rule in *DPP v Majewski* [1977] AC 443, discussed at **A3.17**.

Intoxication: General Rule

Intoxication is not a defence as such. It is, for example, no defence to say (as is undoubtedly true in many cases) that D would not have acted in the particular way but for the fact that D's inhibitions were reduced due to the consumption of alcohol. On the contrary, intoxication operates so as to restrict what would otherwise be valid defences of mistake, inadvertence or automatism. However, intoxication provides very credible evidence of the fact that D did in fact make the mistake claimed or that D did in fact fail to foresee the obvious risk being run or that D was indeed in a state of automatism. The restrictions which the law imposes on defences caused by voluntary intoxication are a response to the evidential power of intoxication in supporting such defences and to the frequency and ease with which such defences could be put forward. **A3.15**

Intoxication: Voluntary and Involuntary

The restrictive rules apply only where D's intoxication is voluntary. This is satisfied if D knowingly takes alcohol or other intoxicating drugs (save under medical supervision or direction) and it is immaterial that D may have misjudged the degree of intoxication that would be caused (*Allen* [1988] Crim LR 698). On the other hand, D drinking what is believed to be only orange juice, which was in fact orange juice spiked with quantities of vodka, would not be regarded as being voluntarily intoxicated and would have any defence that D's resultant state of mind warranted on ordinary principles (e.g., lack of *mens rea*). However, just as with voluntary intoxication, if despite or because of the involuntary intoxication D forms the necessary *mens rea* for the crime, there is no separate defence of involuntary intoxication recognised by the law — see the fully reasoned decision of the House of Lords in *Kingston* [1995] 2 AC 355, which reversed the decision of the Court of Appeal and restored the trial judge's ruling that involuntary intoxication provided no defence where D (with the necessary *mens rea*) indecently assaulted a boy pursuant to an intent induced by the influence of drugs administered secretly to D by a third party. Thus, the only advantage of a finding that the intoxication was involuntary is that it avoids the application of the restrictive rules discussed at **A3.17**. **A3.16**

What counts as an intoxicating drug for the purposes of the restrictive rules governing voluntary intoxication has been discussed by the courts in two cases, *Bailey* [1983] 2 All ER 503 and *Hardie* [1984] 3 All ER 848. In *Bailey*, the Court of Appeal talked about the intoxication rules being applicable to 'dangerous drugs', i.e. those where it is 'common knowledge' that the taker 'may become aggressive or do dangerous or unpredictable things' (amphetamines and LSD being obvious examples). In the second case the Court had to consider D, charged with an offence under the Criminal Damage Act 1971, s. 1(2), who had taken a number of Valium tablets (which were prescribed for someone else) and held that this did not necessarily amount to voluntary intoxication.

> [Valium is] wholly different in kind from drugs which are liable to cause unpredictability or aggressiveness ... if the effect of a drug is merely soporific or sedative the taking of it, even in some excessive quantity, cannot in the ordinary way raise a *conclusive* presumption against the admission of proof of intoxication for the purpose of disproving *mens rea* ...
>
> [The jury] should have been directed that if they came to the conclusion that, as a result of the Valium, the appellant was, at the time, unable to appreciate the risks to property and persons from his actions they should then consider whether the taking of the Valium was itself reckless.

Thus it would seem that there are two categories of drugs: 'dangerous' and 'non-dangerous', LSD being an obvious example of the former category and Valium being an example of the latter. Knowingly taking a 'dangerous' drug counts as voluntary intoxication whereas taking a 'non-dangerous' drug is governed by a similar rule to that discussed in relation to self-induced automatism (see **A3.12**) and depends on the subjective appreciation by D of the likely effects of the drug.

The common-law rules on intoxication have generally been taken only to apply to cases where the alcohol or drug in question is still present in D's body. In *Taj* [2018] EWCA Crim 1743, [2019] QB 655, a case on mistaken belief in self-defence 'attributable to intoxication' within the CJIA 2008, s. 76(5) (see **A3.61**), it was said that they apply equally to 'a mistaken state of mind immediately and proximately consequent upon earlier drink or drug taking... even though the person concerned is not drunk or intoxicated at the time' (at [60]). Although the Court was careful to distinguish this from 'long term mental illness precipitated (perhaps over a considerable period) by alcohol or drug misuse', this potentially represents a significant extension of the *Majewski* rule if applied beyond the self-defence context (as the Court seemed to envisage). It is arguable that different policy considerations apply to intoxicated self-defence (where the difference between basic and specific intent is also not relevant), and that *Taj* can be regarded as *obiter* in the present context of lack of *mens rea* due to being intoxicated.

Intoxication: Specific and Basic Intent

A3.17 The principal restriction imposed on defences based on intoxication is that voluntary intoxication can only give rise to a defence to crimes of specific rather than basic intent. The precise nature of the distinction between these two categories of offence has been shrouded in obscurity ever since Lord Birkenhead used the phrase 'specific intent' in *DPP v Beard* [1920] AC 479. Matters are a little clearer today, notwithstanding the *obiter* comments of the Court of Appeal in *Heard* [2007] EWCA Crim 125, [2008] QB 43. Prior to this decision, the view seemed to have emerged that any offence for which only intention will suffice as the mental element can be regarded as an offence of specific intent, whereas crimes satisfied by recklessness are to that extent crimes of basic intent (basic *mens rea* might be a better expression since the whole point is that intention as opposed to recklessness is *not* required). Thus murder, theft, robbery, wounding with intent, burglary under the Theft Act 1968, s. 9(1)(a), and any offence of attempt would all appear to be crimes requiring a specific intent and it is open to D to adduce evidence of a lack of the specific intent required by these offences due to voluntary intoxication. There is no doubt that these offences remain offences which require a specific intent.

However, the Court of Appeal in *Heard* took the view that the offence of sexual assault under the SOA 2003, s. 3, even though it required an intentional rather than reckless touching, was not in this respect an offence of specific intent, and evidence of intoxication could not be used to show that the touching was not intentional. (This was *obiter* since the Court of Appeal clearly indicated that the appeal could be dismissed on the basis that on the facts the intoxication did not negate D's intent.) Rather than a distinction between intention and recklessness, Hughes LJ (at [31]) preferred the distinction referred to by Lord Simon in *DPP v Majewski* [1977] AC 443 (who was quoting from Fauteux J in the Canadian case of *George* (1960) 128 CCC 289 at p. 301) 'between (i) intention as applied to acts considered in relation to their purposes and (ii) intention as applied to acts apart from their purposes'. It is the first category which is regarded as specific intent and this appears to include not only cases of so-called ulterior intent, i.e. an intent to do something beyond the *actus reus*, as with wounding with intent to cause grievous bodily harm, but also intent to cause a consequence in result crimes such as murder, the consequence being death (or grievous bodily harm). Intention to touch seems to be regarded as an example of the second category, i.e. intention as applied to acts apart from their purposes, and thus as not being a specific intent. The problem with this approach, however, is that it all depends how narrowly or broadly one describes the 'act'. If the act is described simply as moving one's hand with the result that it touches another, it would be an intentional act of moving with the specific intent (purpose) that it results in a touching. If, however, one describes it simply as an act of 'touching', as the Court of Appeal sees it, it is simply an intentional act of touching, the purpose of causing a touching having been subsumed within the description of the act as a 'touching' which requires only a basic and not a specific intent. Conversely, murder which looks like doing an act (e.g., stabbing) with a purpose (e.g., of causing a consequence — death) could equally be described as a 'killing', which term subsumes the purpose and could therefore be regarded simply as an intentional act of killing without any express reference to purpose and thus as not involving a specific intent but only a basic intent to do the act of killing, which is clearly not the law.

Notwithstanding the Court of Appeal's observations in *Heard,* which do not appear to have been applied in any subsequent cases, it is clear that certain other offences which do not specifically require intention but which require other special mental states, such as dishonesty, are to be treated as offences of specific intent, e.g., handling stolen goods (*Durante* [1972] 3 All ER 962). So too with criminal damage where the indictment restricts the allegation to intention as opposed to recklessness (*Metropolitan Police Commissioner v Caldwell* [1982] AC 341 at p. 356). The view was previously taken in this work that aggravated criminal damage under s. 1(2) of the 1971 Act was not a crime requiring specific intent (unless restricted to an allegation of committing it intentionally) since it could be committed recklessly, but the Court of Appeal in *Heard* was of the view (clearly *obiter*, as expressly acknowledged by Hughes LJ himself in *Coley* [2013] EWCA Crim 223 at [57]) that the requirement of being reckless as to endangering life is a specific intent since it goes beyond the *actus reus* of causing damage and thus voluntary intoxication could be relevant to show that there was no recklessness as to the endangerment of life. This basis of specific intent is at least intelligible and does not depend on the narrowness or otherwise of the definition of the act, since it is based on the notion of ulterior intent, or rather ulterior *mens rea*, i.e. a *mens rea* going beyond the *actus reus* of the offence as defined. It also works well in policy terms since it allows D a possible defence to the more serious offence under s. 1(2) but liability would remain for the less serious basic intent offence under s. 1(1) of reckless criminal damage. **A3.18**

All offences other than those requiring specific intent can be regarded as crimes of basic intent and the defence will not be allowed to show that D lacked the *mens rea* or was in a state of automatism due to voluntary intoxication. Crimes requiring only basic intent clearly include manslaughter, malicious wounding, all forms of assault (except those requiring a specific intent such as assault with intent to rob), and taking a conveyance contrary to the Theft Act 1968, s. 12. Thus, in these cases, even the fact that D has 'completely blacked out', as was alleged in the House of Lords case of *DPP v Majewski*, will provide no defence, nor will the fact that D is hallucinating that he is fighting snakes at the centre of the earth, as was alleged in the Court of Appeal case of *Lipman* [1970] 1 QB 152. The rule applies not only to D who is so intoxicated as to be unable to remember anything of the offence (as in *Woods* (1981) 74 Cr App R 312) but also where D makes a mistake about a particular aspect of D's actions as in *Fotheringham* (1988) 88 Cr App R 206. However, where a defence of honest mistake is specifically provided in a statute, then it appears that even an intoxicated mistake may sometimes suffice despite the offence being one of basic intent. In *Jaggard v Dickinson* [1981] QB 527, the Divisional Court held that the defence of honest belief in the owner's consent under the Criminal Damage Act 1971, s. 5(2), was still available even though D was drunk. The decision is today regarded as anomalous and unlikely to be extended to other provisions. Certainly the Court of Appeal was not prepared to allow, in relation to self-defence, a drunken mistake that D was being attacked

(*O'Grady* [1987] QB 995: see further **A3.60**). Furthermore, *Jaggard v Dickinson* was doubted and expressly distinguished in *Magee v CPS* [2014] EWHC 4089 (Admin), where an intoxicated mistake that no accident had occurred was held to be no defence to a charge of failing to stop after an accident.

A3.19 Various justifications for the basic intent rule have been put forward but not all have been persuasive and the Australian courts refused to adopt it (*O'Connor* (1980) 146 CLR 64). At root the rule seems to be one of legal policy — that a voluntarily intoxicated offender should have a potential defence to the most serious offences such as murder or wounding with intent but should remain liable for an appropriate lesser offence of basic intent such as manslaughter or malicious wounding. Although a Law Commission Consultation Paper in 1993 proposed abolition of the basic intent rule, the subsequent report (No. 229, 1995) reverted to recommending the retention of the rule in codified form; somewhat less complex proposals for achieving a similar end were contained in the Commission's Report, *Intoxication and Criminal Liability* (Law Com No. 314, 2009) but these were rejected by the government.

A3.20 **Applying the Basic Intent Rule** Although the policy behind the basic intent rule is clear, the precise manner of its application is less so. Early editions of this work, in common with many other commentators, followed the words of Lord Elwyn Jones in *DPP v Majewski* [1977] AC 443, which stated that evidence of intoxication 'supplies the evidence of *mens rea*, of guilty mind, certainly sufficiently for crimes of basic intent' and therefore suggested that to proffer such evidence would seem to discharge the prosecution from the burden of showing that D had the *mens rea* or was acting voluntarily in relation to basic intent crimes.

The alternative and better view is that evidence of intoxication is simply irrelevant and has to be ignored on the question of whether D has the *mens rea* of a basic intent crime but that the jury have to answer the hypothetical question of whether D would have had the *mens rea* if, contrary to the facts, D had not been intoxicated. This was the approach favoured by the Court of Appeal in *Richardson* [1999] 1 Cr App R 392 but it is an approach not without difficulties, especially in cases where the intoxication has reduced D to a state of automatism or something close to it. In most cases of course, either approach will yield the same result since, in the absence of any other special factor apart from intoxication, the jury will assume that D would have foreseen the natural and probable consequence of the actions if not intoxicated. The decision to quash the convictions in *Richardson* was perhaps a little generous since the only other factor mentioned by the Court of Appeal was the fact that the appellants 'were not hypothetical reasonable men, but university students' (who nevertheless are surely able to appreciate the natural and probable consequences of their actions, at least when sober) and the Court had previously stated that the 'reason they did not [appreciate the risk] was the amount of drink they had consumed'. Despite this, *Richardson* usefully suggests an opportunity for the defence to raise the issue that there was some exculpatory or innocent cause of D's mistake or inadvertence, other than voluntary intoxication, and the convictions were quashed on the facts because the jury had never been asked to consider this question.

A3.21 In relation to specific intent crimes, where evidence of intoxication is legally relevant, the question arises as to whether and how the jury should be specifically directed in relation to the effect of the intoxication on D's intent. The leading case for many years has been *Sheehan* (1974) 60 Cr App R 308, where the trial judge was found to be in error in directing the jury that the question was whether D was 'incapable of forming the intention' whereas the correct question was whether D did in fact form the requisite intention.

Geoffrey Lane LJ then gave guidance (at p. 312) as to how a jury should be directed 'where drunkenness and its possible effect on the defendant's *mens rea* is an issue'. This has come to be known as a *Sheehan* direction:

> ... the proper direction to a jury is, first, to warn them that the mere fact that the defendant's mind was affected by drink so that he acted in a way in which he would not have done had he been sober does not assist him at all, provided that the necessary intention was there. A drunken intent is nevertheless an intent. Secondly, and subject to this, the jury should merely be instructed to have

regard to all the evidence, including that relating to drink, to draw such inferences as they think proper from the evidence, and on that basis to ask themselves whether they feel sure that at the material time the defendant had the requisite intent.

The validity and correctness of the above direction is uncontested but issues have arisen as to the circumstances in which it needs to be given. It was found unnecessary on the facts in *McKnight* (2000) *The Times*, 5 May 2000 even though D had approximately 300 microgrammes of alcohol per 100 millilitres of blood at the time of the killing. In contrast, *Bennett* [1995] Crim LR 877 provides an example of failure to give a *Sheehan* direction in an appropriate case resulting in the conviction (for arson with intent to endanger life) being quashed. There were many other cases on either side of the line but in *Alden* [2001] EWCA Crim 3041 the argument that there were two divergent lines of authority was rejected and it was emphasised that the precondition for a *Sheehan* direction was evidence on the facts that D had not formed the requisite intention due to intoxication. *Alden* was followed in *Campenau* [2020] EWCA Crim 362, where again it was stressed that 'for a *Sheehan* direction to be necessary there must be a proper factual or evidential basis for it' (at [22]). This approach is also to be found in the *Crown Court Compendium* (July 2020), ch. 9:

9. A direction about the effect of intoxication by alcohol and/or drugs on D's state of mind will be necessary only if:
   (1) D claims not to have formed the required state of mind (*mens rea*) because he/she was intoxicated by such substances; and
   (2) there is evidence that D may have consumed such substances in such a quantity that D may not have formed that state of mind.
10. The need for and form of any such direction should be discussed with the advocates in the absence of the jury before closing speeches.

Mohamadi [2020] EWCA Crim 327 provides an example of where a *Sheehan* direction should have been given but, on the facts, its absence did not make the conviction unsafe. D was charged along with several others with rape, and a possible view of the evidence that the jury might have taken was that his only involvement was as spectator to the rapes carried out by others and that he was an accessory by intentional encouragement. There was also evidence that he was drunk and being young may have been particularly affected by the drink so there was a factual basis on which the jury might have concluded that in his intoxicated state he did not intend to encourage the others by his presence. Leggatt LJ therefore found that it would have been preferable if a *Sheehan* direction had been given but pointed out that such a direction is in two parts, the first of which — to the effect that a drunken intent is still an intent — is not favourable to the defence. The second part, which may be helpful to the defence, is 'little more than a direction to draw such inferences as to intention which the jury think proper from the evidence. The only additional content which the direction has is to remind the jury that part of the evidence is evidence relating to drink' (at [42]). Furthermore (at [44]), 'the direction which the appellant contends that the judge should have given was not a direction on a matter of law but a direction about how the jury should approach their fact finding task. Whilst such a direction might have been helpful to them, it went beyond the essential role of the judge.'

Notwithstanding these latter observations and the upholding of the conviction in *Mohamadi*, a *Sheehan* direction about the impact of intoxication clearly ought to be given (as envisaged in the *Crown Court Compendium*, following discussion with counsel) in cases where the evidential foundation is laid. Not only will it be helpful to the jury but its absence will potentially, unlike on the facts of *Mohamadi*, render the conviction unsafe (e.g. as in *Bennett*).

Intoxication: the Dutch Courage Rule

The so-called Dutch courage rule is more important in principle than in practice. A person who deliberately becomes intoxicated in order to commit a crime cannot raise a defence based on such intoxication, even to a crime of specific intent (*A-G for Northern Ireland v Gallagher* [1963] AC 349, per Lord Denning). The rule is eminently sensible but not necessarily applicable even to the facts of *A-G for Northern Ireland v Gallagher* itself and there seem to be no reported cases of it being applied since. The principle, however, is effectively the same as that laid down by the **A3.22** courts in relation to 'non-dangerous' drugs (see **A3.16**) — that if D has the fault element of the offence in becoming intoxicated, the lack of the fault element at the time of the offence due to such intoxication is irrelevant.

Insanity: General Principles: the M'Naghten Rules

A3.23 The defence of insanity is still governed by the M'Naghten rules (*M'Naghten's Case* (1843) 10 Cl & F 200), which today operate largely as a restriction on what might otherwise be a complete defence based on lack of *mens rea* or automatism. Only where D falls under that limb of the rules which requires D not to 'know he was doing what was wrong' do the rules provide any defence additional to that which would be available under the above general principles. The relationship between insanity and defences based not on lack of *mens rea* or voluntariness, such as self-defence, was discussed in *Oye* [2013] EWCA Crim 1725, [2014] 1 All ER 902, where D suffered from insane delusions that he was being confronted by 'evil spirits' intent on harming him. On the facts it was not necessary to decide, and the question was left open, whether self-defence could be put to the jury before insanity even though the belief in the need for self-defence was based on an insane delusion. In principle, where D's lack of responsibility is caused by insanity rather than any other factor, it would seem logical that the defence should be confined to, and classified as, insanity irrespective of whether the lack of responsibility takes the form of no *mens rea*/automatism or a belief in a justifying defence (see also the cases discussed at **A3.63**).

The 'special verdict' of 'not guilty by reason of insanity' is provided for in the Trial of Lunatics Act 1883, s. 2, and is one that is required to be returned by a jury rather than simply as a result of D's plea (*Crown Court at Maidstone, ex parte Harrow London Borough Council* [1999] 3 All ER 542). However, the Court of Appeal has power to substitute special verdicts under the Criminal Appeal Act 1968, s. 6, as was done in *Oye*. Where a special verdict is returned, under the Criminal Procedure (Insanity) Act 1964, s. 5, the court has a range of orders from which to choose (see **D12.16**). These include a hospital order (with or without a restriction order), a supervision order, and even an absolute discharge. The range of available orders does not apply where the offence to which the special verdict relates is murder or any other offence for which the sentence is fixed by law; in such a case the court must make a hospital order with a restriction order.

Whilst the burden of proving insanity is on D on the balance of probabilities (see **A3.26**), for a special verdict to be returned the prosecution must prove that D 'did the act or made the omission charged' (Trial of Lunatics Act 1883, s. 2(1)), otherwise D is entitled to a complete acquittal on the ground of lack of an *actus reus*, despite any insanity. It was confirmed in *A-G's Ref (No. 3 of 1998)* [2000] QB 401 that this does not involve proving *mens rea* but did require proof of 'the ingredients which constitute the *actus reus* of the crime' which seems to include the circumstances (other than *mens rea*) whose presence or absence render the act or omission criminally unlawful (such as, for example, on appropriate facts, the absence of legitimate grounds for self-defence). For a creative interpretation of the concept of the 'act ... charged against him as the offence' in the context of unfitness to plead, see *MB* [2012] EWCA Crim 770, [2012] 3 All ER 1093, and see more generally **D12.11**.

Even though the disincentives to plead insanity were reduced in 1991 by expanding the range of possible disposals, the scope of the M'Naghten rules remains important. Once the defence puts D's state of mind in issue, it is open to the prosecution to argue (see Lord Denning in *Bratty v A-G for Northern Ireland* [1963] AC 386) and to the trial judge to rule (see, e.g., *Sullivan* [1984] AC 156) that the defence really amounts to insanity (see also the Criminal Procedure (Insanity) Act 1964, s. 6). The rules in effect mark out one boundary of the defences of automatism (as in *Sullivan*) or lack of *mens rea* (see, e.g., *Clarke* [1972] 1 All ER 219 where, however, D was found on appeal not to be within the M'Naghten rules and thus had a complete defence of lack of *mens rea*).

A3.24 It should be noted that the above discussion relates to trials on indictment and that s. 2 of the Trial of Lunatics Act 1883 is inapplicable to trial in magistrates' courts. That the defence of insanity is available in magistrates' courts and that it leads to a complete acquittal rather than the special verdict was confirmed by the Divisional Court in *Horseferry Road Magistrates' Court, ex parte K*

[1997] QB 23 and reiterated in *R (Singh) v Stratford Magistrates' Court* [2007] EWHC 1582 (Admin), [2007] 4 All ER 407. While magistrates have a power to make a hospital order under the Mental Health Act 1983, s. 37(3), even though D is not convicted, there is no power to commit to the Crown Court for a restriction order to be made under s. 41 of that Act. The availability of the insanity plea in magistrates' courts was also for a number of years subject to the frequently criticised ruling in *DPP v H* [1997] 1 WLR 1406, to the effect that insanity could be a defence only in relation to crimes requiring *mens rea* or where *mens rea* was in issue. The Divisional Court in *Loake v CPS* [2017] EWHC 2855 (Admin), [2018] QB 998, however, decided that *DPP v H* should no longer be followed as it was based on a mistaken assumption about the scope of the M'Naghten rules and ignored the fact that the second limb of the rules, referring to whether D knew the act was 'wrong', clearly went beyond whether D had *mens rea*. One might add that it also ignores the fact that insanity may extend to automatism, i.e. a denial of voluntariness (which is normally a requirement even of crimes of strict liability). The judgment does, however, conclude (at [63]) with some words of caution about the use of the defence in cases such as that with which the Court was dealing under the Protection from Harassment Act 1997:

> Although in this judgment we have held that the M'Naghten Rules apply to the offence of harassment contrary to Section 2 of the PFHA just as they do to all other criminal offences, this should not be regarded as any encouragement to frequent recourse to a plea of insanity.... In the absence of cogent psychiatric evidence about the specific relevant aspects of a defendant's mental state throughout his alleged course of conduct, we would expect magistrates and judges to deal robustly with claimed defences of insanity.

The status of the M'Naghten rules in terms of the doctrine of precedent is somewhat anomalous but they have long been treated as authoritative, a treatment confirmed by the House of Lords in *Sullivan* in 1983. In *M'Naghten's Case* (1843) 10 Cl & F 200, the crucial passage (at p. 210) in the response given by Tindal CJ (on behalf of all the other judges save Maule J) reads as follows: **A3.25**

> ... the jurors ought to be told in all cases that *every man is to be presumed to be sane*, and to possess a sufficient degree of reason to be responsible for his crimes, *until the contrary be proved to their satisfaction*; and that to establish a defence on the ground of insanity, it must be clearly proved that, *at the time of the committing of the act*, the party accused was labouring under such *a defect of reason, from disease of the mind, as not to know the nature and quality of the act he was doing; or*, if he did know it, *that he did not know he was doing what was wrong.*

The emphases have been added and each emphasised phrase will now be explained in turn.

'... every man is to be presumed to be sane ... until the contrary be proved to [the jury's] satisfaction' **A3.26** This is the basis on which, exceptionally, the burden of proof in establishing the defence is placed on D but it is established that the proof need only be on the balance of probabilities (*Sodeman v The King* [1936] 2 All ER 1138, and see **F3.8**). This exception to the general rule on burden of proof is particularly problematical where D puts forward both insanity and non-insane automatism, as in *Bratty v A-G for Northern Ireland* [1963] AC 386. The solution seems to lie in remembering that, just as with intoxication, the principal utility of evidence of insanity to D is that the insanity is itself explanatory evidence of why D was not conscious of the actions (or of their obvious results). Other evidence of automatism, such as, for example, a blow on the head causing concussion, need only raise a doubt in the minds of the jury as to whether D's act was involuntary, but insofar as the evidence consists of evidence of insanity, the jury must be convinced on a balance of probabilities that the act was involuntary. The result may be, as was possibly the case in *Bratty*, that a jury convict even though they entertain some doubt as to whether D's act was voluntary because the only evidence causing that doubt is evidence of insanity and it is not sufficiently strong to convince them on a balance of probabilities. This may appear to be anomalous but it should be noted that in *Woolmington v DPP* [1935] AC 462, Lord Sankey said 'it is the duty of the prosecution to prove the prisoner's guilt *subject to what I have already said as to the defence of insanity*' (emphasis added).

'... at the time of the committing of the act' The M'Naghten rules, in common with the other defences discussed in this section, are concerned with D's state of mind at the time of the alleged offence. The sanity or otherwise of D at other times may be relevant in other ways, not by way of defence but, for example, in relation to whether D is fit to plead (see **D12.3** *et seq.*) **A3.27**

or in relation to the type of sentence or order to be passed. Such issues relating to the sanity of D at the time of the trial or the time of sentencing can arise whether or not D was sane or not at the time of the alleged offence.

A3.28 **'... a defect of reason'** This is a central notion in the rules even though it is not the concept around which most of the case law turns. It is the basic reason why irresistible impulse and other emotional or volitional defects or disorders are not within the rules, since they are not defects of reason. Rationality is the litmus test of criminal responsibility, and defects of will are regarded either as non-existent or as irrelevant. In this respect, the defence of diminished responsibility is potentially much more liberal. However, given the way in which insanity can operate as a restriction on other defences, the requirement of a defect of reason may sometimes come to D's aid. See *Clarke* [1972] 1 All ER 219, where the Court of Appeal held that even if the other elements of the rules were satisfied, there was no *defect* of reason but at most a mere absent-minded failure to use the powers of reasoning that D undoubtedly still possessed, and thus D was entitled to have the simple defence of lack of *mens rea* considered by the jury rather than the defence of insanity.

A3.29 **'... from disease of the mind'** The defect of reason must be caused by a disease of the mind (rather than by, for example, intoxication, which is probably the best explanation for the decision in *Thomas* [1995] Crim LR 314). It is the meaning of this concept around which most of the recent case law turns as it is this which primarily distinguishes insane automatism (a defence of insanity leading to the special verdict) from non-insane automatism (a defence of simple automatism leading to a complete acquittal).

The meaning of 'disease of the mind' is a legal question for the judge to decide rather than a medical one, even though the evidence of at least two registered medical practitioners is required by the Criminal Procedure (Insanity and Unfitness to Plead) Act 1991, s. 1. In *Sullivan* [1984] AC 156, two medical experts in the course of their testimony stated that they would not regard something as a disease of the mind unless it produced a disorder of brain functions for a prolonged period — in the case of one witness for more than a day and in the case of the other for more than a month. It was therefore argued that the relatively short period over which an epileptic seizure takes place meant that epilepsy was not a disease of the mind. Lord Diplock emphatically rejected this argument, noting (at p. 172) that:

> The nomenclature adopted by the medical profession may change from time to time... But the meaning of the expression 'disease of the mind' as the cause of 'a defect of reason' remains unchanged for the purposes of the application of the M'Naghten rules... 'mind' in the M'Naghten rules is used in the ordinary sense of the mental faculties of reason, memory and understanding. If the effect of a disease is to impair these faculties so severely as to have either of the consequences referred to in the latter part of the rules, it matters not whether the aetiology of the impairment is organic, as in epilepsy, or functional, or whether the impairment itself is permanent or is transient and intermittent, provided that it subsisted at the time of commission of the act.

A3.30 The relevance of the medical evidence seems to be limited to showing that the impairment of the mental faculties did in fact take place and what in fact was the cause. The classification of that impairment and its cause (whether or not it is a defect of reason from disease of the mind), is then purely a matter of law for the judge. It can also be seen that to a large extent, whether something is a disease *of the mind* depends on the consequences it produces — impairment of the faculties of reason, memory and understanding. The disease certainly need not be one primarily located in the brain if it produces the relevant consequences there. Thus arteriosclerosis (hardening of the arteries) causing temporary loss of consciousness is a disease of the mind for these purposes even though it is of physical rather than mental origin (per Devlin J in *Kemp* [1957] 1 QB 399 at p. 408).

However, not every cause of an impairment of these mental faculties is a *disease* of the mind. A disease is something *internal* to the accused and so:

> A malfunctioning of the mind of transitory effect caused by the application to the body of some *external* factor such as violence, drugs, including anaesthetics, alcohol and hypnotic influences cannot fairly be said to be due to disease (per Lawton LJ in *Quick* [1973] QB 910 at p. 922, emphasis added).

Quick's condition of hypoglycaemia was held not to have been due to a disease of the mind since it was attributable to an external factor — his use of insulin prescribed by his doctor:

> Such malfunctioning of his mind as there was, was caused by an external factor and not by a bodily disorder in the nature of a disease which disturbed the working of his mind (ibid. at pp. 922–3).

Treating the insulin, rather than the diabetes which necessitated the insulin, as the cause of the malfunctioning enabled the Court in *Quick* to keep the case outside the M'Naghten rules. However, this course was not available in *Hennessy* [1989] 2 All ER 9, which again concerned a diabetic, this time suffering from the opposite condition of hyperglycaemia (excessive blood sugar) which is directly caused by the diabetes when uncorrected by the administration of insulin. It was thus the *absence* of an external factor which allowed the disease of diabetes to produce the malfunctioning and, given this effect of the disease, the Court of Appeal felt constrained to classify it as a disease of the mind. See also *Bingham* [1991] Crim LR 433.

The Court of Appeal in *Hennessy* also rejected the argument that D's anxiety and depression due to marital problems constituted an external factor (even though there was medical evidence that anxiety and depression could contribute to an increased blood-sugar level). See also the Canadian case of *Rabey* (1977) 79 DLR (3d) 414, in which the Ontario Court of Appeal said (at p. 435) that 'the ordinary stresses and disappointments of life which are the common lot of mankind do not constitute an external cause'. This was subsequently approved by the English Court of Appeal in *Burgess* [1991] 2 QB 92. In this case, the Court held that violence whilst sleepwalking or 'sleep associated automatism' was due to an internal factor and was therefore within the M'Naghten rules. Where there is a combination of internal and external factors, it would appear from *Roach* [2001] EWCA Crim 2698 that, if the jury might conclude that it is the external factors which are operative, a defence of non-insane automatism (which it is for the prosecution to disprove) should be left to them notwithstanding that the defence psychiatrists had described it as 'insane automatism' (where the burden is on the accused). **A3.31**

In *Coley* [2013] EWCA Crim 223, D, having taken quantities of cannabis, perpetrated a violent knife attack on a man in his neighbour's bedroom. D's conviction for attempted murder was upheld; the Court of Appeal dismissed the argument that insanity should have been left to the jury on the grounds that there was a temporary defect of reason within the M'Naghten rules. To the extent that D was in a psychotic state, it was caused by an external factor, the cannabis, and was thus, applying *Quick* [1973] QB 910, not due to a disease of the mind but rather to voluntary intoxication. Neither was it necessary for (non-insane) automatism to be separately left to the jury since they had been told to consider whether D had the specific intent to kill and, having found against him on that score, there was no room on the facts for finding that he had acted with intent but involuntarily. The Court, however, was careful to say that in some cases, e.g., short-lived actions where intent may be inferred from the action, the question of automatism (i.e. whether the action was completely involuntary) ought to be separately put. For further observations on the internal/external distinction, see Mackay and Reuber, [2007] Crim LR 782 at pp. 791–3. It should be remembered, however, that, once one is in the realm of non-insane automatism, the question of prior fault may become relevant and the defence might fail altogether, at least in relation to basic intent crimes, a restriction in *Bailey* [1983] 2 All ER 503 that certain comments in *Coley* appear to overlook (comments which unfortunately appear to have been picked up in *McKay* [2015] EWCA Crim 2098, [2016] 2 Cr App R 1 (1): see **A3.14**).

'... as not to know the nature and quality of the act he was doing' This refers to the physical rather than moral quality of the act (per Lord Reading CJ in *Codere* (1916) 12 Cr App R 21) and according to Lord Diplock in *Sullivan* [1984] AC 156 at p. 173: 'Addressed to an audience of jurors in the 1980s it might more aptly be expressed as "He did not know what he was doing"'. Clearly this would be satisfied if D was unconscious at the time or, even if conscious, thought, to adopt an example quoted by Lord Denning in another context, that he was throwing a log rather than the baby on the fire. Equally clearly, D would have a defence of automatism or lack of *mens rea* respectively **A3.32**

in these two situations, and this underlines the point previously made that the M'Naghten rules generally merely qualify what would otherwise be a complete defence.

A3.33 **'... or ... that he did not know he was doing what was wrong'** This is an alternative to not knowing the nature and quality of the act and is the only sense in which an insane person is given a defence where none would be available to the sane (knowledge of moral or legal wrongness, as opposed to knowledge of the facts which render it wrong, being generally irrelevant to criminal responsibility). The major question debated here is whether 'wrong' means legally wrong or morally wrong. It is suggested that the key to a proper understanding of this question is to recognise that the question is a negative one. If D *does* know *either* that the act is *morally* wrong (according to the ordinary standard adopted by reasonable men, per Lord Reading in *Codere* (1916) 12 Cr App R 21) *or* that it is *legally* wrong then it cannot be said that D 'does *not* know he was doing what was wrong'. In two leading decisions on the matter (*Codere* and *Windle* [1952] 2 QB 826), it was only necessary to hold that it was correct to tell the jury that D could not rely on the defence if D knew that the act was legally wrong. Both were murder cases and it was not seriously suggested in either that D did not know the act was legally wrong and yet knew that it was morally wrong. (On the contrary, Windle thought he was morally right to kill his suicidal wife and yet knew it was legally wrong since he said, 'I suppose they will hang me for this'.) The ruling in *Windle* that '"wrong" means contrary to law' has now also been applied in *Johnson* [2007] EWCA Crim 1978 to a case where there was some evidence that D did not know that his act was morally wrong; it was held that this could not avail him as it was agreed that he knew that it was legally wrong. A converse case would be that of D who does not appreciate that the act is legally wrong but who does realise that it is morally wrong, where arguably the defence would again not be made out.

DEFENCES INVOLVING OTHER EXCUSES AND JUSTIFICATIONS

Introduction

A3.34 To treat certain defences as excuses or justifications and to deal with them separately from defences which deny the basic elements of liability is in one sense artificial since it can be pointed out, for example, that no one commits any offence unless acting unlawfully and, if D has a defence of justification available, then D has not acted unlawfully and one of the basic elements of liability is missing. Equally, it can be pointed out that the defences treated here as a denial of the elements of liability, such as mistake of fact, may be also properly classified as excuses. In the end all classifications are somewhat artificial and are really made for convenience and ease of understanding and exposition. On these grounds it seems sensible to separate out defences where it is admitted that D has voluntarily committed what is prima facie a crime with the state of mind normally sufficient for that offence but at the same time some *special* circumstances are put forward which D claims excuse or justify the actions. As Lord Wilberforce said of duress in *DPP for Northern Ireland v Lynch* [1975] AC 653 (at pp. 679–80):

> [It] is something which is superimposed upon the other ingredients which by themselves would make up an offence, i.e., upon act and intention.... the victim completes the act and knows that he is doing so; but the addition of the element of duress prevents the law from treating what he has done as a crime.

Duress by Threats: General Principles

A3.35 There has been a great deal of development since the 1960s in the defence of duress by threats. Its basis seems to be excuse rather than justification; an analysis confirmed by the House of Lords in *Hasan* [2005] UKHL 22, [2005] 2 AC 467 at [18]. The details of the defence can conveniently be considered under three headings: the type of threat necessary, the required cogency of the threat, and the offences and persons excluded from the defence. For the closely related defence of duress of circumstances, see **A3.50** to **A3.52**.

The Type of Threat Required All the decisions recognising duress as a defence have concerned threats of death or grievous bodily harm although in *Steane* [1947] KB 997, Lord Goddard CJ, *obiter*, included fear of imprisonment. While this has not been definitively ruled out by subsequent authorities, in *Dao* [2012] EWCA Crim 1717 the Court of Appeal, *obiter*, gave a number of reasons for its provisional view that duress should be regarded as confined to threats of death or serious injury and that a threat of false imprisonment should not of itself suffice. It would seem from *Baker* [1997] Crim LR 497 that a threat of serious psychological injury will not suffice and in *Quayle* [2005] EWCA Crim 1415, [2006] 1 All ER 988 it was said that an 'imminent danger of physical injury' was required. A threat of rape would also clearly be included (*Hammond* [2013] EWCA Crim 2709 (at [12])). Another question is whether the threat has to be directed at D or whether threats to third parties, especially close relatives, can suffice. In principle, threats to third parties should be *capable* of constituting duress since even the bravest persons may be prepared to risk their own neck whilst flinching at subjecting loved ones to serious peril. In *Ortiz* (1986) 83 Cr App R 173, threats to D's wife or family appear to have been considered to be sufficient and the suggestion in the 2003 Judicial Studies Board specimen direction that the threat can be directed to D or a member of D's immediate family or alternatively 'to a person for whose safety the defendant would reasonably regard himself as responsible' commended itself to Lord Bingham in *Hasan* [2005] UKHL 22, [2005] 2 AC 467 as being 'if strictly applied... consistent with the rationale of the duress exception'. A3.36

The Cogency of the Threat The fact that D believes that a threat of death or grievous bodily harm will be carried out if D does not commit the offence is not of itself sufficient 'if a person of reasonable firmness sharing the characteristics of the defendant would not have given way to the threats' (third certified question in *Howe* [1987] AC 417). In other words, the threat is only sufficiently cogent, and D will only be excused, if a person of reasonable firmness might have yielded to the threat. This objective approach was most clearly articulated by Lord Lane CJ in *Graham* [1982] 1 All ER 801 in a suggested direction (at p. 300) later approved by the House of Lords in *Howe*: A3.37

> (1) Was the defendant, or may he have been, impelled to act as he did because, as a result of what he reasonably believed [the threatener] had said or done, he had good cause to fear that if he did not so act [the threatener] would kill him or... cause him serious physical injury? (2) If so, have the prosecution made the jury sure that a sober person of reasonable firmness, sharing the characteristics of the defendant, would not have responded to whatever he reasonably believed [the threatener] said or did by taking part [in the offence].

Although the requirement of reasonableness, in relation to D's belief as to the facts, has been questioned by, amongst others, the Law Commission (whose subjective approach in its 1993 Report, *Legislating the Criminal Code*, continued to be preferred by Baroness Hale in *Hasan* [2005] UKHL 22, [2005] 2 AC 467 and has been the subject of some vacillation in the Court of Appeal: *DPP v Rogers* [1998] Crim LR 202; *Cairns* [1999] 2 Cr App R 137; *Martin* [2000] 2 Cr App R 42; *Safi* [2003] EWCA Crim 1809, [2004] 1 Cr App R 14 (157)), Lord Bingham, with whose speech the majority concurred in *Hasan*, was clear that 'there is no warrant for relaxing the requirement that the belief must be reasonable as well as genuine'.

Turning from reasonableness of belief to the reasonableness of D's response in committing the offence, the extent to which a person of reasonable firmness shares D's characteristics is a moot point. In *Bowen* [1996] 4 All ER 837, Stuart-Smith LJ, in denying the relevance of low IQ, derived a number of principles from the case law of which the seventh and last was as follows (at p. 380): A3.38

> In the absence of some direction from the judge as to what characteristics are capable of being regarded as relevant, we think that the direction approved in [*Graham*] without more will not be as helpful as it might be, since the jury may be tempted, especially if there is evidence, as there was in this case, relating to suggestibility and vulnerability, to think that these are relevant. *In most cases it is probably only the age and sex of the defendant that is capable of being relevant. If so, the judge should... confine the characteristics in question to these.* (emphasis added)

For the majority of cases, this is, it is respectfully suggested, a useful working rule, and confirms earlier cases such as *Horne* [1994] Crim LR 584 and *Hegarty* [1994] Crim LR 353, which excluded psychiatric or medical evidence to the effect that D was unusually pliable or vulnerable to pressure or emotionally unstable or in a 'grossly elevated neurotic state'. There remains the difficult question of what characteristics other than age and sex can exceptionally be relevant. In *Bowen* Stuart-Smith LJ gave some examples in his second principle (at p. 379) whereby:

> ... the defendant may be in a category of persons who the jury may think less able to resist pressure than people not within that category. Obvious examples are age, where a young person may well not be so robust as a mature one; possibly sex, though many women would doubtless consider they had as much moral courage to resist pressure as men; pregnancy, where there is added fear for the unborn child; serious physical disability, which may inhibit self protection; recognised mental illness or psychiatric condition, such as post traumatic stress disorder leading to learned helplessness.

A3.39 Putting aside age, the true relevance of most of these, it is submitted, lies in the fact that they increase the gravity of the threat rather than reducing the courage or steadfastness of the accused. A threat of physical violence to a pregnant woman is much more serious because of the vulnerability of the child in the womb. Similarly, physical violence to a physically disabled person is more serious and likely to result in more serious harm if there is reduced ability to defend oneself or ward off blows. On this basis, the mention of 'recognised mental illness or psychiatric condition, such as post traumatic stress disorder', which seems to refer to conditions rendering sufferers 'more susceptible to pressure and threats' (see the fifth principle described in the judgment of Stuart-Smith LJ at p. 379) may be thought problematic since it conflicts with the basic premise of the objective test of a person of reasonable firmness. However, it is clear that the courts will accept post-traumatic stress disorder as a relevant characteristic (*Sewell* [2004] EWCA Crim 2322) and in *Antar* (2004) *The Times*, 4 November 2004 the evidence of a psychologist as to D's level of suggestibility should, in the Court of Appeal's view, have been put before the jury since it was not merely put 'on the basis of [D's] very low IQ, but on the basis of the psychologist's opinion that he functioned cognitively at a significantly impaired level; that he had a moderate (now a mild) learning disability; and importantly, that he had a level of suggestibility sufficiently higher than that of the general population'. The decision in *Antar* seems to be a fairly generous application of the fifth principle in *Bowen*, which is as follows ([1996] 4 All ER 837 at p. 844):

> Psychiatric evidence may be admissible to show that the defendant is suffering from some mental illness, mental impairment or recognised psychiatric condition provided persons generally suffering from such condition may be more susceptible to pressure and threats and thus to assist the jury in deciding whether a reasonable person suffering from such a condition might have been impelled to act as the defendant did. It is not admissible simply to show that in the doctor's opinion an accused, who is not suffering from such illness or condition, is especially timid, suggestible or vulnerable to pressure and threats....

Vulnerability to pressure and threats is not of itself relevant unless, it seems, D belongs to a particular category of persons recognised as so vulnerable and this inevitably puts pressure on the criteria for recognising such a category, whether they be medical or otherwise.

The reference to a 'sober' person of reasonable firmness makes it plain that intoxication cannot be a relevant characteristic. Intoxication is of course normally self-induced (*quaere* whether involuntary intoxication might be relevant) and in *Flatt* [1996] Crim LR 576 it was held that other self-induced conditions, such as being a drug addict, are excluded.

A3.40 The immediacy of the threat and the possibility of seeking official protection are matters which the Court of Appeal said, in *Hurst* [1995] 1 Cr App R 82, require more attention to be paid to them. These matters had been considered in *Hudson* [1971] 2 QB 202 where the Court of Appeal (at p. 207) had taken what is now regarded as too liberal a view that:

> In the present case [of perjury] the threats ... were likely to be no less compelling, because their execution could not be effected in the court room, if they could be carried out in the streets of Salford the same night.

Whether D could be expected to take any opportunity of rendering the threat ineffective in the meantime by, for example, seeking police protection was a matter for the jury and:

> In deciding whether such an opportunity was reasonably open to the accused the jury should have regard to his age and circumstances, and to any risks to him which may be involved.

In *Hasan* at [27], Lord Bingham attributed to the decision in *Hudson*:

> ... the unfortunate effect of weakening the requirement that execution of a threat must be reasonably believed to be imminent and immediate if it is to support a plea of duress ... I can understand that the Court of Appeal [in *Hudson*] had sympathy with the predicament of the young appellants but I cannot, consistently with principle, accept that a witness testifying in the Crown Court at Manchester has no opportunity to avoid complying with a threat incapable of execution then or there.

For the future, Lord Bingham thought (at [28]) that it should:

> ... be made clear to juries that if the retribution threatened against the defendant or his family or a person for whom he reasonably feels responsible is not such as he reasonably expects to follow immediately or almost immediately on his failure to comply with the threat, there may be little if any room for doubt that he could have taken evasive action, whether by going to the police or in some other way, to avoid committing the crime with which he is charged.

Increasingly, the issue is resulting in the defence not even being put to the jury. In *Hammond* [2013] EWCA Crim 2709, the defence of duress was found to have been correctly withdrawn from the jury because the evidence could not satisfy the requirement that 'the threat must be imminent or immediate and have been operating on the actions which constituted the criminal conduct, namely the escape from prison'. Similarly, in *Batchelor* [2013] EWCA Crim 2638, the Court of Appeal relied heavily on Lord Bingham's views in *Hasan* and held that the defence was correctly withheld from the jury where D could have gone to the police at any time over a period of two and a half years and, notwithstanding the serious nature of the alleged threat, 'he could not reasonably believe that the execution of the threat was imminent and immediate'.

In *Brandford* [2016] EWCA Crim 1794, [2017] 1 Cr App R 14 (197), the question of immediacy again ultimately justified the trial judge's withdrawal of the defence from the jury, but the reason given by the judge for withdrawing the defence, that the threat was only indirectly relayed to D, was disapproved. There is no specific requirement that the threat be conveyed directly to D. However, the fact that a threat is indirectly conveyed may be a factor in deciding whether it constitutes duress and such a threat might or might not satisfy the restrictive tests for duress depending on all the circumstances, as Gross LJ explained (at [39]):

> It is very likely that the more directly a threat is conveyed, the more it will be capable of founding a defence of duress: e.g., the telling example of the loaded pistol in the back, given by Lord Simon of Glaisdale in *DPP for Northern Ireland v Lynch* [1975] AC 653, at p. 687. Conversely, the more indirectly the threat is relayed the more, all other things being equal, a defendant will struggle to satisfy the requirements of the defence, or (put in burden of proof terms) the more readily the prosecution will disprove it.

The focus should be on 'the reasonableness of the belief in the potency, imminence and immediacy of the threat — rather than the precise means by which it was conveyed'. The conviction was upheld because the test in *Bianco* [2001] EWCA Crim 2516 of whether 'no reasonable jury properly directed could fail to find the defence disproved' was satisfied. 'The threats simply lacked the immediacy to preclude [D] taking evasive action, most obviously by going to the police' (at [46]).

It is worth noting that Gross LJ (at [45]) considered that the defence was not required to be put to the jury due to factors going to limb (1) of the test in *Graham* (see **A3.37**), so that limb 2, the test of the sober person of reasonable firmness, was never reached. If there had been evidence capable of satisfying limb 1, so that limb 2 was reached, it would seem that the defence should then have been left to the jury. Although, as a matter of logic, the questions of the immediacy of the threat and of any opportunity to render it ineffective could equally well be subsumed under the second question in *Graham* of whether a person of reasonable firmness would have responded to the threat by committing the offence, Lord Bingham specifically warned (in *Hasan* at [24]) against collapsing these questions together and the approach in *Brandford* may show why.

Duress by Threats: Excluded Offences and Persons

Although duress has now been recognised as available on a wide range of charges, including strict liability offences (*Eden District Council v Braid* [1999] RTR 329), and is available in contempt **A3.41** proceedings (*K* (1983) 78 Cr App R 82), and is to that extent a general defence, there have always been doubts about whether it extends to murder or certain types of treason.

A3.42 **Murder** In *Howe* [1987] AC 417, the House of Lords unequivocally held that the defence of duress is *not* available on a murder charge either to D1 or D2, and in so doing declined to follow its own previous decision in *DPP for Northern Ireland v Lynch* [1975] AC 653. Singling out murder in this way does itself raise some anomalies, particularly in that duress appears still to be a defence to wounding with intent under the OAPA 1861, whereas if V should die the intent to cause grievous bodily harm is sufficient to found a murder charge and the defence suddenly becomes unavailable. The exclusion of duress applies equally on a charge of attempted murder (*Gotts* [1992] 2 AC 412) but the exclusion would not appear to apply to conspiracy to murder (*Ness* [2011] EWCA Crim 3105, [2012] 2 Cr App R (S) 39 (228)). There is thus no defence in law on a charge of murder available, even to a 13-year-old complying with instructions from his father which he was too frightened to disobey (*Wilson* [2007] EWCA Crim 1251, [2007] 2 Cr App R 31 (411)).

The Law Commission recommended in its report, *Murder, Manslaughter and Infanticide* (Law Com No. 304, 2006), that duress should be a defence to murder but with the legal burden on the accused.

A3.43 **Treason** Duress, or something akin to it, seems to have been recognised as a defence to certain forms of treason both as long ago as 1419 (*Oldcastle's Case* (1419) 1 Hale PC 50) and as relatively recently as 1945 in *Purdy* (1945) 10 JCL 182 (although see per Lord Goddard CJ in *Steane* [1947] KB 997 at p. 1005). Writers such as Hale and Stephen have doubted whether duress applies to the more serious forms of treason and the judges have traditionally reserved their opinion as to the extent to which duress is available (see, e.g., Lord Brandon in *Howe* [1987] AC 417 at p. 438). Given the decision in *Howe*, the courts may well be unwilling to allow a plea of duress where the particular act of treason would inevitably lead to the deaths of identifiable individuals, even if it would be difficult or impossible to bring a murder charge in relation to those deaths.

A3.44 **Excluded Persons** It is now clear that D cannot rely on the defence of duress if D has voluntarily by association with others been exposed to the risk of such duress (e.g., by joining a criminal organisation or gang). One of the earlier illustrations of this principle was in the Northern Ireland case of *Fitzpatrick* [1977] NI 20 where D had voluntarily joined the IRA and was therefore unable to plead duress based on threats from that organisation as a defence to, *inter alia*, armed robbery carried out on its behalf. The restriction on the defence was supported by dicta of members of the House of Lords in *DPP for Northern Ireland v Lynch* [1975] AC 653 and by provisions of various Commonwealth codes and was then applied by the English Court of Appeal in *Sharp* [1987] QB 853. D was a member of a gang which had carried out a series of armed robberies and sought to plead duress as a defence to manslaughter when a sub-postmaster was shot dead by the gang leader during the course of the last robbery. D alleged that he had sought to withdraw from this robbery when he saw the guns being put into the car but that a gun had then been pointed at him and a threat made 'to blow his head off' if he did not participate. Lord Lane CJ said (at p. 861):

> ... where a person has voluntarily, and with knowledge of its nature, joined a criminal organisation or gang which he knew might bring pressure on him to commit an offence and was an active member when he was put under such pressure, he cannot avail himself of the defence of duress.

It seemed clear from this statement that the organisation or gang had to be one likely to exercise duress and D had to be aware of this at the time of joining. In *Shepherd* (1987) 86 Cr App R 47, D, a member of a shoplifting gang, claimed that he found the experience unnerving and that he had only taken part in a subsequent burglary because of threats of violence to himself and his family. The Court of Appeal quashed the conviction for burglary as the trial judge had wrongly withdrawn the defence of duress from the jury purely on the basis that D had voluntarily joined a criminal organisation. Mustill LJ said (at p. 51):

> ... the concerted shoplifting enterprise did not involve violence to the victim either in anticipation or in the way it was actually put into effect. The members of the jury have had to ask themselves

whether the appellant could be said to have taken the risk of P's violence simply by joining a shoplifting gang.

A3.45 The precise ambit of D's knowledge was at issue in a number of conflicting Court of Appeal cases between 1999 and 2003, most of them cases involving duress exercised in furtherance of debts run up for the illegal supply of drugs. The last of these cases, *Z* [2003] EWCA Crim 191, [2003] 1 WLR 1489 (although not in itself a drugs case) *appeared* to settle the conflict and held that the proper question related to the risk of compulsion to commit 'offences of the type charged'. Thus on the facts of *Z*, D's participation in a prostitution racket may not have been thought by the jury to lay him open to an offence as serious as aggravated burglary. However, *Z* went to the House of Lords under the name of *Hasan* [2005] UKHL 22, [2005] 2 AC 467 and was reversed and D's conviction restored. The certified question was as follows:

> Whether the defence of duress is excluded when as a result of the accused's voluntary association with others:
> (i) he foresaw (or possibly should have foreseen) the risk of being subjected to any compulsion by threats of violence, or
> (ii) only when he foresaw (or should have foreseen) the risk of being subjected to compulsion to commit criminal offences, and, if the latter,
> (iii) only if the offences foreseen (or which should have been foreseen) were of the same type (or possibly of the same type and gravity) as that ultimately committed.

In a speech, which generally took a deliberately restrictive approach to the ambit of the defence of duress (see **A3.40**), Lord Bingham effectively selected option (i), which is of course the widest possible limitation on the defence. Not only that, it was the wider more objective form of option (i) which was approved, whereby it was enough that the risk of compulsion *ought* to have been foreseen rather than that it must have been *actually* foreseen by D. Option (i) means that not only do the foreseeable consequences of the compulsion not need to include offences of the same type as those with which D has actually been charged but there is not even any *requirement* that the foreseeable compulsion be related to the commission of any offences at all. The implications of this can be illustrated by reference to *Heath* [2000] Crim LR 109, where it was enough that D knew that in the drugs world violence is used to enforce debts and therefore, when his debt was enforced by means of requiring him to commit offences, he could not rely on duress. This point has been reinforced by *Mullally* [2012] EWCA Crim 687, where the Court of Appeal indicated that not only will the defence of duress not be available but that the threats will not be likely to have any significant impact on sentence.

A3.46 Although it was Lord Bingham's speech with which the majority agreed, Baroness Hale, in agreeing with the decision to allow the Crown's appeal, answered the certified question in a slightly different fashion and chose option (ii) (again with, it would seem, the objective variant of 'should have foreseen'). Baroness Hale also indicated a need to put a limitation on the exclusion of duress, by means of further explanation of the requirement of 'voluntary association' with the duressor, referring back also to the Law Commission's requirement that the exposure to the risk of duress should be 'without reasonable excuse', so as to cater for 'battered wives' or 'others in close personal or family relationships with their duressors and their associates, such as their mothers, brothers or children'. She prefaced this by saying (at [78]):

> It is one thing to deny the defence to people who choose to become members of illegal organisations, join criminal gangs, or engage with others in drug-related criminality. It is another thing to deny it to someone who has a quite different reason for becoming associated with the duressor and then finds it difficult to escape.

See also *C (GA)* [2013] EWCA Crim 1472 as to the possibility of duress arising from Battered Woman's Syndrome. The width of the exclusion of duress on the grounds of voluntary association is further illustrated by *Ali* [2008] EWCA Crim 716, where it was said not to be essential (for the exclusion to apply) to be associating with persons engaged in criminal activity so long as they were persons from whom threats of violence could reasonably be foreseen.

Necessity

A3.47 It has long been unclear whether a general defence of necessity exists in English law. The courts have now recognised a defence of duress of circumstances that achieves many of the same results. It is first necessary to examine the nature of, and the authorities concerning, necessity in order to appreciate the more recent cases on duress of circumstances.

Necessity differs from duress in that it is generally conceived of not as a concession to human frailty, i.e. as an excuse, but rather as a *justified* choice between two evils — the evil represented by committing the offence is outweighed by the greater evil which would ensue if the offence were not to be committed. This difference is often lost sight of because cases where necessity is raised also tend to be cases where there is an arguable case for excusing D.

A3.48 The leading case of *Dudley* (1884) 14 QBD 273 is a good example which is complicated by the fact that it was a murder charge (and involved cannibalism). (As with duress, the courts are reluctant to widen the range of available defences in such cases.) The two accused had found themselves adrift in a small boat on the high seas with another man and the young cabin boy. They had had virtually no food or water for 20 days and had been reduced, for example, to drinking their own urine. Finally they killed and ate the cabin-boy who was likely anyway to have been the first to die and without this deed they would probably themselves not have survived the further four days which elapsed before they were rescued. In rejecting any defence of necessity on these facts, Lord Coleridge CJ constantly switched from the language of justification to that of excuse, but it was the notion of justification which appears to have been dominant. On that basis, the defence was probably doomed on the facts since the jury had found that there was no greater necessity for killing the boy than any of the others. Although *Dudley* was distinguished by Brooke LJ in *Re A (Children) (conjoined twins: surgical separation)* [2001] Fam 147, ruling to be lawful an operation which would save one conjoined twin but kill the other; the earlier case set the tone whereby English courts have generally rejected a defence of necessity even where the balance of evils points much more clearly in favour of committing the offence. Thus in *Buckoke v Greater London Council* [1971] Ch 655 (a civil case concerning the legality of instructions issued to drivers of fire-engines), Lord Denning MR (at p. 668) accepted as correct the proposition that a driver would have no defence for having proceeded through a red light to save a man in imminent peril in a blaze 200 yards away (regulations passed since would now permit this), 'nevertheless such a man should not be prosecuted. He should be congratulated.' The defence is denied in law but the realities are recognised in practice by exercising discretion in prosecuting or sentencing. (The two accused in *Dudley* were sentenced to death but their sentences were later commuted to six months' imprisonment.)

Necessity was also found not to be available as a defence to murder or assisted suicide in cases of voluntary euthanasia or assisted dying by the Court of Appeal (Civil Division) in *R (Nicklinson) v Ministry of Justice* [2013] EWCA Civ 961, [2014] 2 All ER 32.

A3.49 So it seems that necessity as a justification is rarely recognised by English law (but see the dicta of Lord Brandon and Lord Goff in *F v West Berkshire Health Authority* [1990] 2 AC 1) as a general defence although *particular* offences may be defined in such a way as to make such a defence available. For example, the presence of the word 'unlawfully' in the OAPA 1861, s. 58, was used in *Bourne* [1939] 1 KB 687 to show that some abortions must be lawful and that that included one performed in good faith for the purpose of preserving the life of the mother (see now the Abortion Act 1967). Other statutes have more obvious specific defences such as that of lawful excuse in the Criminal Damage Act 1971 (see **B8.12**). The reluctance of the courts to recognise a *general* defence of necessity (as a justification) perhaps reflects sentiments similar to those expressed by Dickson J in the Supreme Court of Canada in *Perka* (1984) 13 DLR (4th) 1 where he said (at p. 14):

> It is still my opinion that, 'No system of positive law can recognise any principle which would entitle a person to violate the law because on his view the law conflicted with some higher social value' [*Morgentaler v The Queen* (1985) 53 DLR (3d) 161 at p. 209]. The Criminal Code has specified a

> number of identifiable situations in which an actor is justified in committing what would otherwise be a criminal offence. To go beyond that and hold that ostensibly illegal acts can be validated on the basis of their expediency, would import an undue subjectivity into the criminal law. It would invite the courts to second-guess the legislature and to assess the relative merits of social policies underlying criminal prohibitions.

Similar considerations influenced the Law Commission in once recommending (Law Com. No. 83 — but see now Law Com. No. 218, para. 35.7) that any general defence of necessity that might exist should be abolished. This proposal would have presented the apparent anomaly that a person who committed an offence in response to threats would have the defence of duress whereas if the pressure were created by some natural emergency or surrounding circumstances, no defence would be available. As will be seen in **A3.50**, the courts (and indeed the Law Commission — see Law Com. No. 218, para. 35.1) are now addressing this anomaly by recognising, as an excuse rather than as a justification, the defence of duress of circumstances which, again in the words of Dickson J in *Perka* is:

> ... much less open to criticism. It rests on a realistic assessment of human weakness, recognising that a liberal and humane criminal law cannot hold people to the strict obedience of laws in emergency situations where normal human instincts, whether of self-preservation or of altruism, overwhelmingly impel disobedience. The objectivity of the criminal law is preserved; such acts are still wrongful, but in the circumstances they are excusable. Praise is indeed not bestowed, but pardon is, when one does a wrongful act under pressure.

Duress of Circumstances

The early authorities on the defence of duress of circumstances were a series of cases dealing with road traffic offences, but in *Pommell* [1995] 2 Cr App R 607 the Court of Appeal confirmed that the defence applies to all crimes except murder, attempted murder and some forms of treason. The first case was *Willer* (1986) 83 Cr App R 225, where D drove his car on to the pavement and into (and back out of) a shopping precinct to escape from a gang of youths bent on attacking himself and his passengers. At his trial for reckless driving, the judge refused to put the defence of necessity to the jury, but the Court of Appeal thought that 'a very different defence', that of duress, should have been available. According to Watkins LJ (at p. 227, emphasis added) the question then would be: **A3.50**

> ... whether or not upon the outward or the return journey, or both, the appellant was wholly driven *by force of circumstance* into doing what he did and did not drive the car otherwise than under that form of compulsion.

It should be noted that although there were, in a sense, threats to D in this case, it was not a case of duress *by threats* as traditionally understood since in such a case D commits in order to *comply* with the threatener's demands rather than merely to *escape* from the threats. On the distinction between the two types of duress, see *Cole* [1994] Crim LR 582.

Willer was followed and applied in *Conway* [1989] QB 290, another reckless driving case, in which the Court of Appeal quashed the conviction, saying (at p. 297) 'it is still not clear whether there is a general defence of necessity' and 'necessity can only be a defence to a charge of reckless driving where the facts establish "duress of circumstances" '. See also *DPP v Harris* [1995] 1 Cr App R 170 for discussion of whether 'necessity of circumstances' can be a defence to a charge of driving without due care and attention for a police driver going through a red light. In *Backshall* [1998] 1 WLR 1506 the Court of Appeal confirmed that the defence is indeed available on a charge of driving without due care, a conclusion consistent with that in *Pommell* that the defence is of general application.

In *Martin* [1989] 1 All ER 652, duress of circumstances was recognised as a potential defence to driving while disqualified. According to Simon Brown J, it could arise from 'objective dangers threatening the accused or others' but 'the defence is available only if, from an objective standpoint, the accused can be said to be acting reasonably and proportionately in order to avoid a **A3.51** threat of death or serious injury'. The questions for the jury would then be virtually identical to that in relation to duress by threats (see **A3.35** to **A3.40**):

> ... first, was the accused, or may he have been, impelled to act as he did because as a result of what he reasonably believed to be the situation he had good cause to fear that otherwise death or serious physical injury would result; second, if so, would a sober person of reasonable firmness, sharing the characteristics of the accused, have responded to that situation by acting as the accused acted?

Since these are jury questions, a submission of no case to answer at the close of the prosecution case will not succeed unless the evidence is such that no reasonable jury, properly directed, could find that the defence has been disproved. This is illustrated by *Petgrave* [2018] EWCA Crim 1397, where the two questions were correctly put to the jury (who convicted) even though the judge thought it possible that in the circumstances it might have been reasonable to drive on the pavement, resulting in serious injuries to two pedestrians.

The reference to the sober person of reasonable firmness shows that, as with duress by threats, the crucial question is not so much whether D was justified as whether D can be excused on the grounds that a reasonable person would have felt impelled to act in the same way.

The circumstances impelling D to act must be external to D, so that the suicidal thoughts of life sentence prisoners could not of themselves amount to relevant circumstances excusing the offence of prison breaking according to the Court of Appeal in *Rodger* [1998] 1 Cr App R 143. The suicidal thoughts were 'a purely subjective element' as is the pain from which the cultivators of cannabis may wish to seek relief (*Quayle* [2005] EWCA Crim 1415, [2006] 1 All ER 988).

A3.52 Duress of circumstances has also been allowed by the Divisional Court on a charge of driving with excess alcohol in *DPP v Bell* [1992] RTR 335, where D, because of his terror of his pursuers, ran back to his car and drove off some distance down the road. The fact he did not continue to drive all the way home supported the finding that he was driving because of his fear and not because of any prior intention to use his car to get home even if intoxicated. This contrasted with the earlier case of *DPP v Jones* [1990] RTR 33 where a similar defence failed because D drove the two miles home without even bothering to check whether he was still being pursued. *DPP v Davis* [1994] Crim LR 600 was to similar effect and reflected an increasingly restrictive attitude to both types of duress, which has since been explicitly articulated in *Hasan* [2005] UKHL 22, [2005] 2 AC 467 (discussed at **A3.40** and **A3.45**) and applied in *Quayle* to deny the defence in relation to the production etc. of cannabis. *Quayle* was followed in *Altham* [2006] EWCA Crim 7, [2006] 1 WLR 3287, where the ECHR, Article 3, was unsuccessfully invoked by the appellant. *Quayle* was also referred to in *S (C)* [2012] EWCA Crim 389, [2012] 1 Cr App R 31 (429), where duress of circumstances (or necessity) was ruled not to be available in relation to the offence of removing a child from England and Wales contrary to the Child Abduction Act 1984. *DPP v Mullally* [2006] EWHC 3448 (Admin) further illustrates the increasingly restrictive attitude to duress and its failure in a motoring case; D continued to drive despite having been informed that the police had arrived to deal with the threat of violence. However, as to the difficulties in ruling out the defence at the stage of a preliminary hearing, see *S Ltd* [2009] EWCA Crim 85, [2009] 2 Cr App R 11 (171). It should also be noted that there is no requirement that the threat being avoided should be 'life threatening', a threat of either death or serious injury being sufficient (*Pipe v DPP* [2012] EWHC 1821 (Admin)).

Coercion and Compulsion

A3.53 At common law there was a rebuttable presumption that a wife who committed an offence (except murder or treason) in the presence of her husband did so under coercion and that she should be acquitted. The presumption was abolished by the CJA 1925, s. 47, which nevertheless went on to provide that:

> ... on a charge against a wife for any offence other than treason or murder it shall be a good defence to prove that the offence was committed in the presence of, and under the coercion of, the husband.

The defence preserved by the 1925 Act was finally abolished by the ABCPA 2014, s. 177, in relation to offences committed on or after 13 May 2014.

An increasingly more relevant concept today, however, is the coercion or compulsion to which victims of trafficking are subject. There is no separate defence of 'coercion' applicable to such victims but they may be entitled to a defence of duress on ordinary principles, whether it be as a defence to immigration offences or other offences which they are coerced into committing; see *O* [2008] EWCA Crim 2835; *N* [2012] EWCA Crim 189, [2013] QB 379 and *L* [2013] EWCA Crim 991, [2014] 1 All ER 113 for the protocols for dealing with offences committed by trafficked victims and other offences committed by young persons who may have been trafficked (further discussed in *Joseph (VS)* [2017] EWCA Crim 36, [2017] 1 Cr App R 33 (486)).

Section 45(1) of the Modern Slavery Act 2015 (in force from 31 July 2015: see SI 2015 No. 1476) introduced, for adult victims of slavery or trafficking, a defence of compulsion attributable to slavery or to relevant exploitation (i.e. exploitation, within the meaning of s. 3 of the Act, that is attributable to the exploited person being, or having been, a victim of human trafficking). An analogous defence for persons under 18 is also introduced by s. 45(4) under which the question is not one of 'compulsion' but whether the person does the act 'as a direct consequence of the person being, or having been, a victim of slavery or a victim of relevant exploitation'. In *Joseph (VS)*, the argument was rejected that the limits of the common-law defence of duress should be extended to cater for offences committed before the commencement of the 2015 Act by trafficked victims. The Act was not retrospective and the protocols relating to prosecution provided the appropriate framework. As to the question of granting leave out of time for convictions under the earlier, less generous versions of the protocols, see *GB* [2020] EWCA Crim 2 where the conviction was unsafe and, due to the impact of the conviction on D's future immigration status, the substantial injustice test was satisfied. See also *O* [2019] EWCA Crim 1389 to similar effect. Compare *GS* [2018] EWCA Crim 1824, [2019] 1 Cr App R 7 (84), where the conviction was not regarded as unsafe because the prosecution would have been appropriate even under the later protocols as the trafficking on the facts did not extinguish the culpability, given the seriousness of the offence and the options to avoid the compulsion. There was thus no question of there being substantial injustice in this case.

Modern Slavery Act 2015, s. 45 **A3.54**

(1) A person is not guilty of an offence if—
  (a) the person is aged 18 or over when the person does the act which constitutes the offence,
  (b) the person does that act because the person is compelled to do it,
  (c) the compulsion is attributable to slavery or to relevant exploitation, and
  (d) a reasonable person in the same situation as the person and having the person's relevant characteristics would have no realistic alternative to doing that act.
(2) A person may be compelled to do something by another person or by the person's circumstances.
(3) Compulsion is attributable to slavery or to relevant exploitation only if—
  (a) it is, or is part of, conduct which constitutes an offence under section 1 or conduct which constitutes relevant exploitation, or
  (b) it is a direct consequence of a person being, or having been, a victim of slavery or a victim of relevant exploitation.
(4) A person is not guilty of an offence if—
  (a) the person is under the age of 18 when the person does the act which constitutes the offence,
  (b) the person does that act as a direct consequence of the person being, or having been, a victim of slavery or a victim of relevant exploitation, and
  (c) a reasonable person in the same situation as the person and having the person's relevant characteristics would do that act.
(5) For the purposes of this section—
  'relevant characteristics' means age, sex and any physical or mental illness or disability;
  'relevant exploitation' is exploitation (within the meaning of section 3) that is attributable to the exploited person being, or having been, a victim of human trafficking.
(6) In this section references to an act include an omission.
(7) Subsections (1) and (4) do not apply to an offence listed in Schedule 4.

As to the burden of proof, Lord Burnett CJ in *MK* [2018] EWCA Crim 667, [2019] QB 86 (at [45]) made a clear ruling that s. 45 'does not implicitly require the defendant to bear the legal or persuasive burden of proof of any element of the defence. The burden on a defendant is evidential. It is for the defendant to raise evidence of each of those elements and for the prosecution to disprove one or more of them to the criminal standard in the usual way.'

These defences are nevertheless subject to very significant limitations because of the long list of offences specified in sch. 4 to which s. 45 does not apply. Schedule 4 specifies, *inter alia*, false imprisonment, kidnapping, manslaughter, murder, piracy, offences under the OAPA 1861, ss. 4, 16, 18, 20, 21, 22, 23, 27 to 32, 35, 37 and 38, offences under the Explosives Substances Act 1883, cruelty to children, certain firearm offences, robbery, burglary, blackmail, hostage-taking, hijacking and other offences endangering aircraft safety, terrorism offences and sexual offences.

See also the discussion at **B22.24** *et seq*.

Self-defence, Prevention of Crime and Related Defences Generally

A3.55 These defences are generally regarded as matters of justification rather than excuse. They are normally available only as defences to crimes committed by the use of force (*Renouf* [1986] 2 All ER 449, where reckless driving was regarded as involving force where the only relevant evidence of reckless driving was the 'forcing' of another car off the road. See also *Riddell* [2017] EWCA Crim 413, [2017] 2 Cr App R 3 (22), applying the same reasoning to confirm that self-defence can in principle be a defence to dangerous (or careless) driving where it involves the use of force). Nevertheless, they are undoubtedly available to a wide range of offences. In *Oraki v DPP* [2018] EWHC 115 (Admin), [2018] QB 1086, the Divisional Court recognised and upheld the availability of (mistaken) self-defence, including defence of another as it was on the facts, on a charge of obstructing a constable in the execution of his duty under the Police Act 1996, s. 89(2), (as well as on a charge of assaulting a constable in execution of his duty under s. 89(1)). (Contrast *Wheeldon v CPS* [2018] EWHC 249 (Admin) where there was no evidence of a relevant mistake of fact.)

Where there is evidence 'which if accepted could raise a prima facie case of self-defence, this should be left to the jury even if the accused has not formally relied upon self-defence' (*DPP (Jamaica) v Bailey* [1995] 1 Cr App R 257). See also *Hayes* [2011] EWCA Crim 2680 as to the importance of giving a full and careful direction on self-defence tailored to the circumstances of the case and, where relevant, tailored in relation to each count charged. Where self-defence is not available because the offence charged does not involve the use of force, duress of circumstances may equally be available (*Symonds* [1998] Crim LR 280).

Self-defence, defence of property and defence of another (sometimes referred to collectively as 'private defence') are still defences at common law (notwithstanding the impact of the CJIA 2008, s. 76: see **A3.58**) whereas the law on the use of force in the prevention of crime and in lawful arrest has for many years been statutory and is to be found in the CLA 1967, s. 3(1).

Criminal Law Act 1967, s. 3

(1) A person may use such force as is reasonable in the circumstances in the prevention of crime, or in effecting or assisting in the lawful arrest of offenders or suspected offenders or of persons unlawfully at large.

A3.56 **Prevention of Crime** Where D is relying on the prevention of crime, within the meaning of the CLA 1967, s. 3, as the justification for the use of reasonable force, the crime being sought to be prevented must not already have been completed. This is illustrated by *Attwater* [2010] EWCA Crim 2399, [2011] RTR 12 (173) (dangerous driving to force another car to stop some time after an alleged accident could not be justified as preventing the crime of failing to stop after an accident since any offence of failure to stop was already by then complete: see **C6.53**). *Williams* [2020] EWCA Crim 193 provides a further illustration; D had chased V who, having come to a house party uninvited with a large group of other youths, had stabbed D in the arm and taken the silver chain from round D's neck before fleeing. When D eventually caught and fatally stabbed V 'he was not defending his property, nor was he preventing the commission of a robbery which had been completed sometime earlier. He was engaged in an act of retaliation or revenge' (at [19]). Contrast *Morris* [2013] EWCA Crim 436, [2014] 1 WLR 16 (see **B5.44**), where D may have honestly believed that an offence of making off was in the course of being committed. The mistake in this case was one of fact as to the intentions of the taxi driver's passengers. A mistake of law, however, will not suffice, as in *Wilkinson* [2018] EWCA Crim 2154 where a taxi driver wrongly thought that his passenger's conduct constituted an offence.

The term 'crime' here means a crime under the law of England and Wales and this does not include a crime such as 'aggression', which is recognised only in customary international law (*Jones* [2006] UKHL 16, [2007] 1 AC 136). More generally, in relation to 'direct action protesters' who claim 'to be justified in doing acts which would otherwise be criminal', Lord Hoffmann had the following to say (at [94]):

> In a case in which the defence requires that the acts of the defendant should in all the circumstances have been reasonable, his acts must be considered in the context of a functioning state in which legal disputes can be peacefully submitted to the courts and disputes over what should be law or government policy can be submitted to the arbitrament of the democratic process. In such circumstances, the apprehension, however honest or reasonable, of acts which are thought to be unlawful or contrary to the public interest, cannot justify the commission of criminal acts and the issue of justification should be withdrawn from the jury. Evidence to support the opinions of the protesters as to the legality of the acts in question is irrelevant and inadmissible, disclosure going to this issue should not be ordered and the services of international lawyers are not required.

In *R (DPP) v Stratford Magistrates' Court* [2017] EWHC 1794 (Admin), [2017] 2 Cr App R 32 (467) the Divisional Court decided that prevention of crime was not available as a defence to protesters charged with obstructing the highway under the Highways Act 1980, s. 139, by lying down in the path of vehicles approaching a Defence and Security Equipment International Exhibition. There was insufficient nexus between their actions and the prevention of any imminent and immediate crime of which the appellants could be said to have any direct knowledge. Also, the defence generally only applies to the direct application of force and although the force did not have to be applied directly to a person (thus it would include, e.g., not only directly attacking a driver but also chaining oneself to the driver's vehicle), it did not apply to blocking access by lying down in the road or chaining oneself to gates. The Court also referred approvingly to Lord Hoffman's speech in *Jones* [2006] UKHL 16, [2007] 1 AC 136 as showing a 'clear and focussed review of the issues which arise in this type of case' (at [17]).

Consistency of Defences Based on Use of 'reasonable force' The criterion in the CLA 1967, s. 3, of 'such force as is reasonable in the circumstances' differs slightly from traditional formulations of the common-law rule for self-defence, which usually also include some reference to necessity. See, e.g., per Lord Lane CJ in *Williams* [1987] 3 All ER 411 at p. 414: 'the exercise of any necessary and reasonable force to protect himself'. **A3.57**

Some of the restrictive rules that applied at common law could be attributed to this reference to necessity but the modern trend seems to be to adopt a more flexible approach (as with the former so-called duty to retreat which has now been abandoned as such). Given the fact that in most cases where D is acting in self-defence D will also be acting to prevent a crime being committed by the aggressor, it would seem sensible for the tests for self-defence and prevention of crime to be identical. Even though the courts have not always formulated the test for self-defence in the exact words used in the CLA 1967, s. 3, for prevention of crime, there is no evidence from any of the cases that any such differences are matters of substance. Indeed in *Beckford v The Queen* [1988] AC 130, Lord Griffiths said (at p. 145) that: 'the test to be applied for self-defence is that a person may use such force as is reasonable in the circumstances as he honestly believes them to be in the defence of himself or another'. Whilst his lordship was primarily concerned with the question of mistaken belief in this case, his dictum closely echoes s. 3 and supports the view that the common-law rules governing the use of force in self-defence and the rules applicable to prevention of crime are now identical (see also *Clegg* [1995] 1 AC 482). The same view underpins the 'clarificatory' provisions of the CJIA 2008, s. 76, which, subject to one exception changing the formulation of the law relating to householders, applies in identical terms to both defences. Accordingly, the law can in general terms be formulated quite simply and neatly along the following lines:

A person may use such force as is reasonable in the circumstances as the person believes them to be for the purposes of:

(a) self-defence (and defence of another),
(b) defence of property,
(c) prevention of crime, or
(d) lawful arrest.

Although (a) and (b) above remain common-law defences, as distinct from (c) and (d) which are governed by the CLA 1967, s. 3, the meaning and interpretation of 'reasonable force' is now, for all of them, subject to statutory provision under the CJIA 2008, s. 76. Initially, this provision was intended solely 'to clarify' the operation of the common law but since the amendments to it made by the CCA 2013, s. 43, it now has to be seen as intending to change the law to some extent, but in relation to self-defence only, and only in 'householder cases'. It remains true, however, that even in such 'householder cases' the test is one of reasonable force and it is merely the interpretation of what force is 'not to be regarded as reasonable' which is subject to a different test (one of 'grossly disproportionate' as opposed to simply 'disproportionate' in the circumstances: see *R (Collins) v Secretary of State for Justice* [2016] EWHC 33 (Admin), [2016] QB 862, discussed further at **A3.64**). It is convenient to set out s. 76 at this point; its various provisions are commented on further in subsequent paragraphs where appropriate.

A3.58 **Criminal Justice and Immigration Act 2008, s. 76**

(1) This section applies where in proceedings for an offence—
 (a) an issue arises as to whether a person charged with the offence ('D') is entitled to rely on a defence within subsection (2), and
 (b) the question arises whether the degree of force used by D against a person ('V') was reasonable in the circumstances.

(2) The defences are—
 (a) the common law defence of self-defence;
 (aa) the common law defence of defence of property; and
 (b) the defences provided by section 3(1) of the Criminal Law Act 1967 or section 3(1) of the Criminal Law Act (Northern Ireland) 1967 (use of force in prevention of crime or making arrest).

(3) The question whether the degree of force used by D was reasonable in the circumstances is to be decided by reference to the circumstances as D believed them to be, and subsections (4) to (8) also apply in connection with deciding that question.

(4) If D claims to have held a particular belief as regards the existence of any circumstances—
 (a) the reasonableness or otherwise of that belief is relevant to the question whether D genuinely held it; but
 (b) if it is determined that D did genuinely hold it, D is entitled to rely on it for the purposes of subsection (3), whether or not—
  (i) it was mistaken, or
  (ii) (if it was mistaken) the mistake was a reasonable one to have made.

(5) But subsection (4)(b) does not enable D to rely on any mistaken belief attributable to intoxication that was voluntarily induced.

(5A) In a householder case, the degree of force used by D is not to be regarded as having been reasonable in the circumstances as D believed them to be if it was grossly disproportionate in those circumstances.

(6) In a case other than a householder case, the degree of force used by D is not to be regarded as having been reasonable in the circumstances as D believed them to be if it was disproportionate in those circumstances.

(6A) In deciding the question mentioned in subsection (3), a possibility that D could have retreated is to be considered (so far as relevant) as a factor to be taken into account, rather than as giving rise to a duty to retreat.

(7) In deciding the question mentioned in subsection (3) the following considerations are to be taken into account (so far as relevant in the circumstances of the case)—
 (a) that a person acting for a legitimate purpose may not be able to weigh to a nicety the exact measure of any necessary action; and
 (b) that evidence of a person's having only done what the person honestly and instinctively thought was necessary for a legitimate purpose constitutes strong evidence that only reasonable action was taken by that person for that purpose.

(8) Subsections (6A) and (7) are not to be read as preventing other matters from being taken into account where they are relevant to deciding the question mentioned in subsection (3).

(8A) For the purposes of this section 'a householder case' is a case where—
 (a) the defence concerned is the common law defence of self-defence,
 (b) the force concerned is force used by D while in or partly in a building, or part of a building, that is a dwelling or is forces accommodation (or is both),
 (c) D is not a trespasser at the time the force is used, and
 (d) at that time D believed V to be in, or entering, the building or part as a trespasser.

(8B) Where—
 (a) a part of a building is a dwelling where D dwells,
 (b) another part of the building is a place of work for D or another person who dwells in the first part, and
 (c) that other part is internally accessible from the first part,

that other part, and any internal means of access between the two parts, are each treated for the purposes of subsection (8A) as a part of a building that is a dwelling.

(8C) Where—
 (a) a part of a building is forces accommodation that is living or sleeping accommodation for D,
 (b) another part of the building is a place of work for D or another person for whom the first part is living or sleeping accommodation, and
 (c) that other part is internally accessible from the first part,

that other part, and any internal means of access between the two parts, are each treated for the purposes of subsection (8A) as a part of a building that is forces accommodation.

(8D) Subsections (4) and (5) apply for the purposes of subsection (8A)(d) as they apply for the purposes of subsection (3).

(8E) The fact that a person derives title from a trespasser, or has the permission of a trespasser, does not prevent the person from being a trespasser for the purposes of subsection (8A).

(8F) In subsections (8A) to (8C)—
'building' includes a vehicle or vessel, and
'forces accommodation' means service living accommodation for the purposes of Part 3 of the Armed Forces Act 2006 by virtue of section 96(1)(a) or (b) of that Act.

(9) This section, except so far as making different provision for householder cases, is intended to clarify the operation of the existing defences mentioned in subsection (2).

(10) In this section—
 (a) 'legitimate purpose' means—
  (i) the purpose of self-defence under the common law, ...
  [(ia) the purpose of defence of property under the common law, or]
  (ii) the prevention of crime or effecting or assisting in the lawful arrest of persons mentioned in the provisions referred to in subsection (2)(b);
 (b) references to self-defence include acting in defence of another person; and
 (c) references to the degree of force used are to the type and amount of force used.

The Subjective Question and the Objective Question in Defences Based on the Use of 'reasonable force' It has become axiomatic that there are two basic questions to be answered in relation to self-defence, prevention of crime and related defences. First, were the facts (as D believed them to be) such that the use of force was necessary (for the purpose claimed, e.g., for the purpose of self-defence). Secondly, was the degree of force used reasonable for that purpose in the light of those perceived facts. The first question is clearly, from the terms in which it is put, a subjective matter in that D is judged on the basis of the facts as D genuinely believed them to be. The second question is essentially an objective question in that how much force is reasonable in the perceived circumstances is ultimately a matter for the jury and not primarily dependent on D's own evaluation. These two basic questions will be examined in turn, starting with the subjective question. **A3.59**

A3.60 **The Subjective Question: The Circumstances as the Accused Believes Them to Be** Although the previous common-law rule, that D's belief had to be reasonable, remains true for the purpose of defending civil law claims for battery (*Ashley v Chief Constable of Sussex Police (Sherwood intervening)* [2008] UKHL 25, [2008] 1 AC 962), for the purposes of the criminal law, the Court of Appeal rescinded this requirement in the landmark decision in *Williams* [1987] 3 All ER 411, by analogy with the House of Lords' decision in *DPP v Morgan* [1976] AC 182. The Criminal Law Revision Committee's recommendation that a person may use such force as is reasonable in the circumstances *as he believes them to be* was adopted by Lord Lane CJ as representing the law. This approach was approved and followed by the Privy Council in *Beckford v The Queen* [1988] AC 130, where the appeal was allowed, as in *Williams*, because the trial judge had directed the jury that a reasonable belief was required. This subjective test for mistakes of fact is confirmed by the CJIA 2008, s. 76(3) and (4) (see **A3.58**), and the difference from the objective test for civil law purposes was reiterated in *R (Duggan) v HM Assistant Deputy Coroner* [2017] EWCA Civ 142, [2017] 1 WLR 2199.

It had been argued that under the ECHR, Article 2, a more demanding standard of honest belief 'for good reasons' may be required — especially as far as trained law enforcement officers are concerned (*Andronicou v Cyprus* (1998) 25 EHRR 491). However, the CJIA 2008, s. 76 (3) and (4), effectively confirm that the subjective test still holds sway and in *Duggan* Sir Brian Leveson P in the Divisional Court ([2014] EWHC 3343 (Admin), [2016] 1 WLR 525) noted that even in the ECtHR in relation to potential breaches of Article 2, notwithstanding the ambiguous use of the phrase 'for good reasons', 'the focus has been on whether the state actor responsible for a death honestly believed that he faced a threat which called for the use of lethal force'. The Grand Chamber of the ECtHR subsequently confirmed that the subjective, honest and genuine belief approach of the common law is compatible with Article 2 of the ECHR in *Da Silva v UK* (2016) 63 EHRR 12 (589), good reasons and reasonableness being nonetheless evidentially relevant to the question of whether the belief was indeed genuinely held. In *Shaw v The Queen* [2001] UKPC 26, [2001] 1 WLR 1519, the subjective test was interpreted to apply not only to D's belief as to the circumstances but also to D's belief as to the danger involved in those circumstances, an approach also endorsed in *Harvey* [2009] EWCA Crim 469. Of course, as is pointed out in s. 76(4), the reasonableness of a belief can be a factor in whether a jury believes it is genuinely held, but if it is found to be so held, it can be relied on irrespective of whether or not it is reasonable.

In *Duggan* the Court of Appeal (Civil Division) rejected the argument that there was any requirement for the Coroner (and even less for a judge in a criminal trial) to expressly tell the jury that, in assessing whether a belief was honestly and genuinely held, they needed to consider the reasonableness or otherwise of the belief. Indeed it was considered desirable in most cases not to give such a direction about the evidential relevance of the reasonableness of the belief as it was capable of confusing rather than helping a jury, given the quite separate substantive requirement of reasonableness as to the degree of force permitted.

Even where the main defence is that D was *actually* under attack, the judge may be under a duty to direct the jury on the possibility of a defence based on mistaken belief if there is evidence capable of supporting this (*Oatridge* (1991) 94 Cr App R 367). However, in *Keane* [2010] EWCA Crim 2514, Hughes LJ commented (at [39]) that there are many cases where the question of mistake is irrelevant because there is no suggestion that, if D may be telling the truth, D was not actually under attack. In such cases, it is not necessary or desirable to direct the jury about mistaken belief and to do so may distract the jury from the real question of whether they are sure that D was not in fact under attack. See also *Mohammed Ibrahim* [2014] EWCA Crim 121, where late medical evidence about the state of D's mind was held to have been rightly excluded, *inter alia*, because the case essentially turned on the factual question of whether D had been the sole aggressor. In that case, the Court of Appeal also noted that the case before it was not a case:

> ... in which the defendant suffered from a psychiatric condition that caused him to believe in a state of affairs which did not exist. In such case, as the authorities show, expert medical evidence is admissible in relation to the first limb of the defence of self-defence in order to establish what state of affairs the defendant genuinely believed to exist.

The Subjective Question: Effect of Voluntary Intoxication on Mistaken Belief The subjective approach to mistake does not apply where D's mistake was due to voluntary intoxication (*O'Grady* [1987] QB 995). Although the actual conviction in *O'Grady* was for manslaughter (a basic intent offence), the Court of Appeal seemed clear in the view that an intoxicated mistake could not be relied upon even in relation to a crime of specific intent such as murder. Lord Lane CJ said (at p. 999): A3.61

> We do not consider that any distinction should be drawn on this aspect of the matter between offences involving what is called specific intent, such as murder, and offences of so-called basic intent, such as manslaughter... the question of mistake can and ought to be considered separately from the question of intent.

O'Grady was followed in *O'Connor* [1991] Crim LR 135, although in that case the conviction was reduced to manslaughter on the separate ground that the intoxication might have prevented the formation of the specific intention to cause grievous bodily harm. *O'Grady* and *O'Connor* have been reaffirmed by the Court of Appeal in *Hatton* [2005] EWCA Crim 2951, [2006] 1 Cr App R 16 (247) and by the CJIA 2008, s. 76(5), which provides: 'subsection (4)(b) does not enable D to rely on any mistaken belief attributable to intoxication that was voluntarily induced'. Whether the offence is one of specific intent or not is therefore immaterial as far as defences of self-defence and prevention of crime are concerned and D cannot rely on a mistake about the existence or degree of an attack which is due to self-induced intoxication. 'Mistaken belief attributable to intoxication' includes a person whose mistake is due to the after-effects of immediately previous and proximate intoxication, but who is not actually currently intoxicated in the sense of drugs or alcohol still being present in the body (*Taj* [2018] EWCA Crim 1743, [2019] QB 655).

The Objective Question: The Degree of Force Permitted It is for the jury to determine whether the force was reasonable in the circumstances as D believed them to be, as is illustrated by *Owino* [1996] 2 Cr App R 128 and numerous other cases. However, the courts have generally applied the rule in a manner which attempts to take account of D's motives and situation and which is not totally and unreservedly objective. Thus in *Palmer v The Queen* [1971] AC 814, Lord Morris of Borth-y-Gest said (at p. 832): A3.62

> ... it will be recognised that a person defending himself cannot weigh to a nicety the exact measure of his necessary defensive action. If a jury thought that in a moment of unexpected anguish a person attacked had only done what he honestly and instinctively thought was necessary that would be most potent evidence that only reasonable defensive action had been taken. A jury will be told that the defence of self-defence, where the evidence makes its raising possible, will only fail if the prosecution show beyond doubt that what the accused did was not by way of self-defence.

This passage is echoed and indeed quoted almost verbatim in the CJIA 2008, s. 76(7). Section 76(8) goes on to make it clear that other considerations may also be taken into account where relevant.

The approach in *Palmer* (now reiterated in s. 76(7)) was described by Ormrod LJ in *Shannon* (1980) 71 Cr App R 192 at p. 194 as:

> ... a bridge between what is sometimes referred to as 'the objective test', that is what is reasonable judged from the viewpoint of an outsider looking at a situation quite dispassionately, and 'the subjective test', that is the viewpoint of the accused himself with the intellectual capabilities of which he may in fact be possessed and with all the emotional strains and stresses to which at the moment he may be subjected.

The Court of Appeal in this case quashed the conviction because the judge had ignored the subjective aspect of the question and put the question to the jury purely as: 'Did the appellant use more force than was necessary in the circumstances?' whereas the real question, according to Ormrod LJ (at p. 197), was:

> Was this stabbing within the conception of necessary self-defence judged by the standards of common sense, bearing in mind the position of the appellant at the moment of the stabbing, or was it a case of angry retaliation or pure aggression on his part?

A3.63 It is nevertheless clear from *Owino* and *DPP v Braun* [1999] Crim LR 416 that the test of unreasonable force remains an essentially objective test. Furthermore, in *Martin* [2001] EWCA Crim 2245, [2003] QB 1, a highly publicised case of a reclusive farmer using lethal and unreasonable force to defend his property, on appeal D tried to use the fact that, in relation to the objective condition in provocation, the House of Lords in *Smith* [2001] 1 AC 146 had, at that time, allowed evidence of D's subjective psychiatric condition to be considered relevant. The Court of Appeal in *Martin*, however, said that self-defence was a distinct and complete defence and subject to different considerations. Whilst D's physical characteristics might be relevant (e.g., one presumes, to explain why a physically weaker individual used a weapon rather than physical force in self-defence), it would not be appropriate 'except in exceptional circumstances which would make the evidence especially probative, in deciding whether excessive force has been used to take into account whether the defendant is suffering from some psychiatric condition'.

This raises the question of what will count as 'exceptional circumstances' making such evidence 'especially probative'. In *Oye* [2013] EWCA Crim 1725, [2014] 1 All ER 902, the Court of Appeal found it difficult to see in what circumstances, even exceptionally, a psychiatric condition could (or on policy grounds, ought to) be relevant to the question of excessive force (contrast its possible relevance to the question of subjective belief in the facts: see *Mohammed Ibrahim* [2014] EWCA Crim 121 and **A3.59**). Reference was made to the earlier case of *Canns* [2005] EWCA Crim 2264 where three highly experienced members of the Court of Appeal had also found it 'impossible to identify the sort of exceptional circumstances in which it would be appropriate to take a psychiatric condition from which a defendant is suffering into account'. However, in *Press* [2013] EWCA Crim 1849 there was evidence that D's post-traumatic stress disorder (a consequence of military service in Afghanistan) may have caused him to react oversensitively to perceived threats. The trial judge was found to have been correct to invite the jury to consider the psychiatric evidence when resolving the question whether D did only what he honestly believed was necessary in the circumstances, which under *Palmer v The Queen* [1971] AC 814, at common law, and now by statute under the CJIA 2008, s. 76(7)(b), 'constitutes strong evidence that only reasonable action was taken'. The jury nevertheless convicted and the conviction was upheld since 'strong evidence is not conclusive evidence and it was for the jury, not the defendant, to resolve the ultimate and objective question of whether the degree of force used was reasonable'.

A3.64 **The Objective Question: Force which is not Reasonable within the Meaning of the CJIA 2008, s. 76, and Householder Cases** The CJIA 2008, s. 76 (see **A3.58**), in addressing the essentially objective meaning of reasonableness, somewhat impenetrably provides in s. 76(6) that '[t]he degree of force used by D is not to be regarded as having been reasonable in the circumstances as D believed them to be if it was disproportionate in those circumstances'. To bring in the concept of 'disproportionate' as a (negative) gloss to 'reasonable in the circumstances' is not helpful since it simply explains one open-textured evaluative question in terms of another. In *Keane* [2010] EWCA Crim 2514, Hughes LJ helpfully confirmed that the statutory formulation of some of the rules relating to self-defence and related defences in the CJIA 2008, s. 76, did not alter the law as it had been for many years and expressed the view that to ask whether force is *reasonable* in all the circumstances or whether it is *proportionate* in all the circumstances is to ask the same question, as these expressions mean the same thing. However, the explanation of what is not reasonable in terms of it being disproportionate took on a new significance as from 25 April 2013 and the coming into force of the CCA 2013, s. 43, which inserted s. 76(5A):

> In a householder case, the degree of force used by D is not to be regarded as having been reasonable in the circumstances as D believed them to be if it was grossly disproportionate in those circumstances.

By s. 76(8A) a case is 'a householder case' only where the defence concerned is the common law of self-defence. There are also requirements that the force is used by D while in a building or part of a building which is a dwelling or forces accommodation, that D is not a trespasser at the time and that D believed V to be a trespasser (typically V will have entered as such but this is not essential, it is enough that D believes V has become a trespasser at the time D uses force; see *Cheeseman* [2019] EWCA Crim 149). Thus it seems now that householders who use what is in fact regarded as disproportionate (as opposed to grossly disproportionate) force in self-defence may be found nevertheless to have used reasonable force in the circumstances as they believed them to be. It should also be noted, however, that s. 76(5A) does not actually dictate this result in every case; it simply says that grossly disproportionate force is *not* reasonable, rather than saying that disproportionate force (falling short of grossly disproportionate) *is* automatically reasonable. The fundamental test still remains that in s. 76(1)(b), i.e. whether the force used was 'reasonable in the circumstances'. The new provision merely affects the interpretation of '(un)reasonable in the circumstances' so that force is not by law automatically unreasonable in householder cases simply because it is disproportionate, provided it is not grossly disproportionate.

The last sentence of the previous paragraph was quoted with approval by the Divisional Court in *R (Collins) v Secretary of State for Justice* [2016] EWHC 33 (Admin), [2016] QB 862, where the Court also adopted the view that the fundamental question remains whether the force used was reasonable in the circumstances and that thus the law remained compliant with the ECHR, Article 2, 'even after the minor qualification of s. 76(5)A'. A five-member Court of Appeal in *Ray* [2017] EWCA Crim 1391, [2018] QB 948 subsequently fully approved the Divisional Court decision in dismissing an appeal against conviction for murder. Lord Thomas CJ construed the Act as follows:

25. In determining the question of whether the degree of force used is reasonable ... the effect of s. 76(5A) is that the jury must first determine whether it was grossly disproportionate. If it was, the degree of force was not reasonable and the defence of self-defence is not made out.
26. If the degree of force was not grossly disproportionate, ... the jury must consider whether that degree of force was reasonable taking into account all the circumstances of the case as the defendant believed them to be. The use of disproportionate force which is short of grossly disproportionate is not, on the wording of the section, of itself necessarily the use of reasonable force. The jury are in such a case, where the defendant is a householder, entitled to form the view, taking into account all the other circumstances (as the defendant believed them to be), that the degree of force used was either reasonable or not reasonable.
27. The terms of the 2013 Act have therefore, in a householder case, slightly refined the common law in that a degree of force used that is disproportionate may nevertheless be reasonable.
28. As subsection (6) makes clear, in a non-householder case the position is different; in such a case the degree of force used is not to be regarded as reasonable if it was disproportionate
29. Thus in our judgment the amendments to s. 76 put the householder relying on self-defence in a position different from all others relying on the defence. This is clear on the language of the Act. But it is narrow and not of the wide-ranging effect for which the appellant contended. We accordingly reject the contention that provided the degree of force used by a householder is not grossly disproportionate then it is necessarily reasonable.

The extra leeway which s. 76(5A) is designed to give to householders (and the public signal that they should not be afraid of, or at risk of, prosecution for using reasonable force in self-defence against burglars, arguably already signalled, e.g., by s. 76(7) and the honest and instinctive test) is at the cost of considerable and arguably unnecessary complexity. The complexity includes the fact that a householder whose use of force is sought to be justified on the separate grounds of self-defence and defence of property is subject to different statements (in s. 76(5A) and s. 76(6)) of what is automatically unreasonable in relation to the two separate defences, which may not prove to be an easy matter to explain to a jury. The provision is arguably unnecessary in that s. 76(7) (and the common law which it reproduces) already provided considerations which could be used to mitigate the objective nature of the test in the context of the dilemma faced by a householder confronted by a trespasser in the home. Indeed it would seem that a curious overall effect of s. 76, contrary to the rhetoric with which it was introduced, has been to stipulate cases where force is deemed by law to be not reasonable rather than to produce any broadening of the existing perfectly sensible test of reasonableness, whether it be in relation to householder cases or otherwise.

For the separate common-law defence, distinct from self-defence, available to an occupier of property to use reasonable force to make a trespasser leave, see *Day (Edina)* [2015] EWCA Crim 1646.

A3.65 **The Objective Question: Self-defence: Complete Defence which Succeeds or Fails in its Entirety** Where the charge is murder, there is no common-law rule whereby, if self-defence fails because of the use of excessive force, it can have the effect of reducing the conviction to manslaughter (*McInnes* [1971] 3 All ER 295, confirmed in *Clegg* [1995] 1 AC 482) unless, for example, as in *Martin* [2001] EWCA Crim 2245, [2003] QB 1, the psychiatric evidence rejected as irrelevant to self-defence can be used as the basis for diminished responsibility. Perhaps a more significant example of how the use of excessive force in self-defence might nevertheless result in a manslaughter rather than murder conviction arises from the creation of the new partial defence of loss of control in the CAJA 2009, s. 54, which applies, *inter alia*, where D has lost self-control as a result of 'a fear of serious violence' (see **B1.26**). There is by no means any automatic requirement that such an alternative partial defence be put to the jury by the trial judge. It was stressed in *Martin* [2017] EWCA Crim 1359 that a rigorous evaluation of the evidence supporting each of the elements of the partial defence would be required before the issue of loss of control could be left to the jury, and there was no real evidence of loss of control on the facts.

A3.66 **Trespassers outside the Home** Whilst it has long been recognised that an occupier (and arguably an occupier's guest — see *Day (Edina)* [2015] EWCA Crim 1646) is entitled to use reasonable force to remove a trespasser from the occupier's land or home (either as part of, or by analogy with, the right to defend one's property), this right does not apply so clearly to removing someone from one's car, especially when the person was originally invited into the car and has only subsequently become a trespasser and the trespass can be more appropriately ended by returning the person to the place where originally invited into the car (*Burns* [2010] EWCA Crim 1023, [2010] 1 WLR 2694). See also *Francis* [2011] EWCA Crim 877, as to the right to eject passengers from a bus.

A3.67 **Self-defence and Pre-emptive Strikes** A person can use force to ward off an anticipated attack provided that it is anticipated as 'imminent' (*Chisam* (1963) 47 Cr App R 130). Any other rule would leave little room in which the mistaken belief rule could operate. In *Beckford v The Queen* [1988] AC 130, Lord Griffiths said (at p. 144), 'a man about to be attacked does not have to wait for his assailant to strike the first blow or fire the first shot; circumstances may justify a pre-emptive strike'. However, if a threat of force may be expected to deter the attacker, it may be difficult to convince the jury that it was reasonable to use actual force (cf. *Cousins* [1982] QB 526).

A3.68 **Scope of Defence of Another** Given the overlap already referred to between, for example, self-defence and prevention of crime, the precise boundaries of the individual defences are not always clear. Thus it is unclear whether defence of another is restricted to defence of a relative (and if so, how close) or extends to anyone with a sufficient nexus with the defender (*Devlin v Armstrong* [1971] NI 13) or to anyone at all. In *Duffy* [1967] 1 QB 63 the Court of Appeal found it unnecessary to decide whether defence of another extended to defence of a sister since what was done could be justified on the alternative basis of prevention of crime. The only case where this might not be so would be where D knows that the attacker is, for example, insane or under age, so that it cannot be said that D is acting 'in the prevention of crime' (cf. the reasoning of Ward LJ in *Re A (Children) (conjoined twins: surgical separation)* [2001] Fam 147). In such a case one would need to determine whether the person being attacked has a sufficient nexus with the defender to be within the scope of defence of another. In order to prevent anomalies, the better view is surely that no such nexus should be required and that one can act in defence of any other person (as recommended by the Criminal Law Revision Committee (14th Report)) provided, as always, that the use of force is reasonable in the circumstances.

A3.69 **Scope of Defence of Property** As with defence of another, it is unclear to what extent defending property of other persons is a justification for committing a crime, but the arguments in favour of having no restrictions are the same. In *DPP v Bayer* [2003] EWHC 2567 (Admin), [2004] 1 WLR 2856, it was emphasised that D must be acting to ward off an 'unlawful or criminal act'. Therefore defence of property did not arise in relation to opposing the lawful sowing of GM seed. In relation to defence of one's own home, it should be noted that the statement approved in *Hussey* (1924) 18 Cr App R 160 that: 'In defence of a man's house, the owner or his family may kill a trespasser who would forcibly dispossess him of it' is of debatable authority today. Forceful resistance would no doubt be in order (which might unintentionally cause death) but deliberate killing would normally be hard to justify. See also *Burns* [2010] EWCA Crim 1023, [2010] 1 WLR 2694 at **A3.66**.

No Duty to Retreat *per se* and the Position of the Initial Aggressor The statement approved in *Hussey* (1924) 18 Cr App R 160 and quoted in **A3.69** went on to say of the defender that 'in defending his home he need not retreat, as in other cases of self-defence, for that would be giving up his house to his adversary'. There is no longer any duty to retreat in any category of private defence. The duty was first watered down in *Julien* [1969] 2 All ER 856 where it was said (at p. 843) that 'what is necessary is that he should demonstrate by his actions that he does not want to fight'. Even this was subsequently held, in *Bird* [1985] 2 All ER 513, to be too restrictive. It is not 'necessary' to demonstrate by one's actions an unwillingness to fight. That is merely one way of negativing any suggestion that the defendant was the attacker or was acting out of motives of retaliation or revenge rather than self-defence, but it is by no means the only method of doing that. As Edmund Davies LJ said in *McInnes* [1971] 3 All ER 295 at p. 1607: 'We prefer the view expressed by the Full Court of [South] Australia [in *Howe* [1958] SASR 95] that a failure to retreat is only an *element* in the consideration upon which the reasonableness of an accused's conduct is to be judged'. The CJIA 2008, s. 76(6A) (see **A3.58**), inserted by the LASPO 2012, s. 148, effectively confirms this approach by providing that 'a possibility that D could have retreated is to be considered (so far as relevant) as a factor to be taken into account, rather than as giving rise to a duty to retreat'. **A3.70**

Similarly, there is no hard and fast rule that a person who initiates a confrontation cannot rely on self-defence (*Balogun* [1999] EWCA Crim 2120) nor that it cannot be used against an assailant who is known to be a police officer (*Burley* [2000] Crim LR 843). Although the appeal was dismissed on the facts, the Court of Appeal in *Rashford* [2005] EWCA Crim 3377 re-emphasised that the fact that D is the initial aggressor does not automatically mean that D cannot be acting in self-defence. Dyson LJ approved the Scottish decision in *Burns v HM Advocate* 1995 SLT 1090 as an important decision which should be more widely known wherein (at p. 1093H) it was said that the question: **A3.71**

> ... depends upon whether the violence offered by the victim was so out of proportion to the accused's own actings as to give rise to the reasonable apprehension that he was in an immediate danger from which he had no other means of escape, and whether the violence which he then used was no more than was necessary to preserve his own life or protect himself from serious injury.

The reference to 'reasonable' apprehension is not in line with English law in relation to the subjective approach to mistaken belief. *Rashford* was followed and considered in *Harvey* [2009] EWCA Crim 469, where it was however acknowledged that, in principle, it is not a question of reasonable apprehension of danger but of D's 'perception of the events and of the danger he believes he faces'. In *Keane* [2010] EWCA Crim 2514, Hughes LJ also followed *Rashford* and commented favourably on the decision in *Harvey*, including the use of the homely expression whether 'the tables had been turned' as being suitable for many cases subject to the following point. Just because the tables have been turned in the sense that the original aggressor finds himself getting the worst of it, merely because the original victim is defending himself reasonably, does not reverse the roles and turn the original victim into the aggressor and justify force used in response by the original aggressor. The Court of Appeal in *Keane* also rejected the argument that, if D succeeds in verbally provoking V into striking a blow at D which is not itself lawful, D is entitled to respond with force simply because of the fact that D is responding to unlawful force by V. D's use of force is not reasonable because the opportunity to use it has been unreasonably engineered by D and this would merely be one of many situations where the parties to voluntary fights are both using unlawful force. It would be different if D set out only to provoke a punch but V unexpectedly and disproportionately used a knife in response. In that case D could be entitled to use force in self-defence against the unexpected and disproportionate force confronting D, provided the force used was reasonable in all the circumstances.

Unknown Circumstances Justifying Force in Self-defence etc.

A3.72 The converse of mistaken belief in the need for self-defence etc. is the use of force in circumstances where, unknown to D, the facts would in fact justify the use of force. The case of *Dadson* (1850) 2 Den CC 35 has long been thought to hold that no defence is available in these circumstances. Dadson shot and wounded a fleeing thief, but this degree of force was only permissible, even at that time, in the prevention of crime if the offence being committed amounted to a felony. The particular form of theft involved was only a felony if the thief had two previous convictions for the offence. Although this condition was in fact satisfied in this case, Dadson was unaware of this fact when he shot. His conviction was upheld. Although this case may be taken to lay down the general principle, it may seem to be modified in relation to force used to effect an arrest by the PACE 1984, s. 24. It may be argued that since, under s. 24, an arrest of a person is lawful if *in fact* the person is, for example, 'in the act of committing an offence' (s. 24(1)(b)), the use of force in such circumstances is also lawful under the CLA 1967, s. 3. This argument could apply only to force used in effecting arrest, not self-defence or prevention of crime. However, s. 3 itself only permits 'such force as is reasonable in the circumstances'. If the circumstances include D's state of mind (cf. *Williams* [1987] 3 All ER 411) it could be said that it is not *reasonable* to use force where D lacks any knowledge of the lawfulness of the arrest. Since an arrest can be effected without any force at all being used, the fact that the arrest itself is lawful under the PACE 1984 does not automatically validate the use of force, the reasonableness of which is a distinct question.

Infancy

A3.73 Prior to the CDA 1998, s. 34, children fell into one of three age groups for the purposes of criminal responsibility. Once a child has reached the age of 14, no special defence based on age was or is available. Children aged under ten were (and still are) irrebuttably presumed to be incapable of criminal responsibility (*doli incapax*) by virtue of the CYPA 1933, s. 50, but in relation to children aged ten, 11, 12 or 13 there was formerly a rebuttable presumption of *doli incapax* which could be rebutted if the prosecution proved that the child had 'mischievous discretion', i.e. knew that the act was 'seriously' wrong, not just naughty or mischievous (*JM v Runeckles* (1984) 79 Cr App R 255). In *C (A Minor) v DPP* [1996] AC 1 the Divisional Court had boldly decided that the rebuttable presumption no longer formed part of English law since it had become outdated in the changed conditions of society; this decision had, however, been promptly reversed in the House of Lords (also [1996] AC 1), where it was held that such a change could only be made by statute. Section 34 of the CDA 1998 effected that change by declaring that the 'rebuttable presumption of criminal law that a child aged ten or over is incapable of committing an offence is hereby abolished'. It is only children under ten therefore who are now specifically exempted from the criminal law on account of their age, the irrebuttable presumption in their case being unaffected, thus producing a clear line with responsibility commencing at the relatively young age of ten.

As far as children between ten and 14 are concerned, s. 34 leaves them to be treated as equally responsible as adults since the *via media* of reversing rather than abolishing the presumption, which would have expressly permitted the defence to prove that the child did not understand that the act was seriously wrong, was argued for in Parliament but not accepted by the government. Although the brief wording of s. 34 only expressly abolishes the rebuttable presumption in favour of the child, any arguments that s. 34 should be treated as having merely reversed the burden of proof, or that the concept of *doli incapax* survives in any other way for those who have reached the age of ten, were finally laid to rest by the House of Lords in *JTB* [2009] UKHL 20, [2009] 1 AC 1310. (The concept is of course still applicable to subsequent trials of offences alleged to have been committed prior to the coming into force of s. 34 (30 September 1998) by persons aged between ten and 14 at the time of the offence. *PF* [2017] EWCA Crim 983 provides a reminder that in such cases, not only must the prosecution prove that D knew that the act was seriously wrong but there must also be clear positive evidence to that effect distinct from the doing of the act itself, irrespective of however obviously wrong that act might be.)

A3.74 D's age, whether over or under 14, is clearly a factor to be taken into account in assessing the reasonableness of D's conduct under the defences of loss of control (see **B1.24**), duress (*Bowen* [1996] 4 All ER 837 at **A3.38**) and arguably self-defence (see **A3.62**). In crimes requiring subjective recklessness and *a fortiori* intention, D's age may also be a relevant factor in assessing whether D did in fact foresee what might seem to be (to an adult) the obvious consequences of D's actions or whether D was aware of the relevant circumstances. Such considerations were perhaps less acute under the old law since children who lacked an understanding of the likely consequences or full circumstances of their actions were likely to argue first that the prosecution had not discharged the burden of rebutting the presumption of *doli incapax* but, in the absence of the rebuttable presumption, arguments based on lack of *mens rea* may need to be pressed into service more often. Similarly, if a child can be shown by the defence not to be of normal development for the child's age (proving normal development was previously a common means for the prosecution to reverse the presumption of *doli incapax*), this might possibly be brought within the partial defence of diminished responsibility on a murder charge (but see the discussion of 'developmental immaturity' at **B1.19**). Arguments such as these will turn on the precise *mens rea* to be proved for the individual offence or the terms of a particular defence.

Section A4 Parties to Offences

LIABILITY OF PRINCIPALS AND ACCESSORIES GENERALLY

A4.1 Responsibility for a criminal offence may be incurred either as a principal offender or as an accessory. Liability as an accessory applies to all offences (including statutory ones) unless it is expressly excluded by statute (*Jefferson* [1994] 1 All ER 270). See s. 73 of the SOA 2003 at **B3.79** for an example of partial exclusion. A principal offender is the actual perpetrator of the offence, the person whose individual conduct satisfied the definition of the particular offence in question, whilst an accessory is one who aids, abets, counsels or procures the commission of the offence. For indictable offences, the Accessories and Abettors Act 1861, s. 8, provides that such an accessory 'shall be liable to be tried, indicted, and punished as a principal offender'. The MCA 1980, s. 44(1), is of similar effect as far as summary offences are concerned.

The distinction between an accessory and a principal offender is thus in many cases of little importance. Indeed D charged as a principal may be convicted even though the real case was that D was an accessory, although it is preferable that the particulars of the offence be drawn 'in such a way as to disclose with greater clarity the real nature of the case that the accused has to answer' (per Lord Hailsham of St Marylebone in *DPP for Northern Ireland v Maxwell* [1978] 3 All ER 1140 at p. 1357D). If this is not done and if the prosecution do not make plain in presenting the case to the jury that liability as an accessory is one of the alleged bases of liability, it may be a misdirection for the judge to introduce it in summing-up (*Taylor* [1998] Crim LR 582; contrast *Montague* [2013] EWCA Crim 1781 where, on the particular facts of the case, such a misdirection was not significant). However, as *Giannetto* [1997] 1 Cr App R 1 demonstrates, if the jury are unsure as to whether D was an accessory or the principal, they can still convict (of murder) provided that they are all agreed that D was responsible on one basis or, if not, on the other (and thus had ruled out any third possibility by which D was not responsible on either basis) (see also **A1.40** and *Morton* [2003] EWCA Crim 1501, but contrast *Banfield* [2013] EWCA Crim 1394 where it was not clear whether A or B was the perpetrator and whilst it was possible the other was an accessory it could not be ruled out that one of them was acting alone and therefore neither could be convicted of murder). See **B1.77** for how this problem is dealt with in the context of causing death or serious physical harm to children or vulnerable adults in a domestic context.

A4.2 The phrase 'aid, abet, counsel and procure' may be, and generally is, used as a whole even though D's conduct may be properly described only by one of the four constituent words (*Re Smith* (1858) 3 H & N 227). Partly for this reason, the precise meaning of each constituent word has not been authoritatively determined, but putting procuring on one side for a moment, the modern approach is to say that assistance or encouragement is what is required to bring a person within the meaning of the ancient formula — see, e.g., *Stringer* [2011] EWCA Crim 1396, [2012] QB 160 and *Jogee* [2016] UKSC 8, [2017] AC 387 at [6]. Individual words are occasionally the subject of judicial discussion, as in *A-G's Ref (No. 1 of*

1975) [1975] QB 773, where D had laced the drinks of a friend with alcohol knowing that he would soon be driving home. As a result, the friend drove with an excess quantity of alcohol in his body and was convicted as principal. D was then charged with aiding, abetting, counselling and procuring that offence but the trial judge took the view that, since there was not the usual shared intention or meeting of minds between the principal and alleged accessory, D could not be said to be an accessory. The Court of Appeal took the view that, whilst that might be right for aiding, abetting and counselling, procuring did not require any sort of conspiracy or common purpose and therefore D could properly have been convicted. The Court said (at p. 779F): 'To procure means to produce by endeavour' and added at p. 780B: 'You cannot procure an offence unless there is a causal link between what you do and the commission of the offence.'

The reference to causation can, however, be misleading and it is the element of endeavour, intentionally trying (successfully) to bring about the offence, which is arguably more important even in procuring. Certainly, other modes of complicity such as counselling do not require such a clear causal link (*Calhaem* [1985] QB 808, followed in *Luffman* [2008] EWCA Crim 1739 and approved in *Jogee*); as long as the advice or encouragement of the accessory (D2) comes to the attention of D1 (the principal), it does not matter that D1 would have committed the offence anyway, even if not encouraged by D2 (*A-G v Able* [1984] QB 795 at p. 812). In relation to what came to be known as joint enterprise, comments by the Court of Appeal in *Mendez* [2010] EWCA Crim 516, [2011] QB 876 suggesting a stronger role for causation were subsequently explained in *Stringer* [2011] EWCA Crim 1396, [2012] QB 160, where it was reiterated that 'but-for' causation is not required although there must be a connection between D2's actions and D1's acts. The use of the term joint enterprise became fraught with difficulty and capable of causing misunderstanding (*Jogee* at [77]) and is probably now best avoided. More generally, in terms of the connection between D2's encouragement or assistance and the principal offence committed by D1, the relevant principles were succinctly summarised by the Supreme Court in *Jogee* (at [12]) where it said 'the prosecution does not have to go so far as to prove that it had a positive effect on D1's conduct or the outcome ... Ultimately it is a question of fact and degree whether D2's conduct was so distanced in time, place or circumstances from the conduct of D1 that it would not be realistic to regard D1's offence as encouraged or assisted by it.' **A4.3**

While the Accessories and Abettors Act 1861 makes the accessory's liability equal to that of the principal, the availability of duress on a murder charge used to depend on whether the accused was in truth a principal or merely an accessory, but that anomalous rule did not survive the House of Lords' decision in *Howe* [1987] AC 417. The distinction between conduct constituting that of a principal and that of (at most) an accessory has, however, resurfaced in another, but somewhat different, context in homicide. An example is where D assists a drug abuser to self-administer an injection resulting in fatal (but unintended) consequences — see the cases discussed at **B1.58** culminating in *Kennedy (No. 2)* [2007] UKHL 38, [2008] 1 AC 269. If D's role (such as performing or taking part in the act of injection) can be classified as a cause of death, D is guilty of manslaughter as a principal; if merely assisting or encouraging the act causing death (as it is now recognised is all that is involved in preparing and supplying a loaded syringe), D will not be guilty of manslaughter. The fact that the voluntary and informed act of another normally breaks the chain of causation and prevents a previous actor from being the principal is one of the main reasons that accessory liability is so important and significant (and forensically useful) in treating those who assisted or encouraged the offence as being equally guilty of it as the principal. Thus it *often* does not matter or need to be proved whether a person is principal or accessory, but it does matter in the *Kennedy* type scenario where it is only an offence for D to do something to *another* (D negligently causes V's death, D is guilty of manslaughter as **A4.4** principal) but not for that other to do it *to himself* (assisted or encouraged by D, V freely chooses to do an act which negligently causes V's *own* death, V commits not even the *actus reus* of an offence and there is therefore no offence to which D can be accessory). Aside from relatively unusual situations such as that outlined above (and see *Ferguson v Weaving* [1951] 1 KB 814 for a difference between principals and accessories in the quite different context of vicarious liability), the most important general distinction which remains between accessories and principals lies in the mental element required of an accessory.

THE MENTAL ELEMENT FOR ACCESSORIES

A4.5 The *actus reus* of D2 involves two concepts: (a) aiding, abetting, counselling and procuring (b) an offence. The *mens rea* can also be expected to relate to these two concepts. The mental element for D2 is generally considerably narrower and more demanding than that required for D1 in that intention or knowledge rather than recklessness or negligence or any other less culpable state of mind is required. The classic statement of the *mens rea* for D2 is that of Lord Goddard CJ in *Johnson v Youden* [1950] 1 KB 544 at p. 546 that: 'Before a person can be convicted of aiding and abetting the commission of an offence, he must at least know the essential matters which constitute that offence.' As the facts of the case demonstrate, in accordance with general principles, it is knowledge of the facts that counts, not knowledge of the law, as was reiterated in *O'Neil v Gale* [2013] EWCA Civ 1554, where knowledge of the legislation which renders those facts criminal was not required. *Chapman* [2015] EWCA Crim 539, [2015] QB 883 is a further example relating to aiding and abetting misconduct in public office. As will be seen, the emphasis in *Johnson v Youden* on knowledge of the facts is not the whole story and the concept of intention is an equally if not more important component of the *mens rea* for D2. This was emphasised by the Supreme Court in *Jogee* [2016] UKSC 8, [2017] AC 387, where it was said (at [9]) that 'the mental element in assisting or encouraging is an intention to assist or encourage the commission of the crime and this requires knowledge of any existing facts necessary for it to be criminal.... If the crime requires a particular intent, D2 must intend to assist or encourage D1 to act with such intent.' Before turning to the requirement of intent, however, the issue of knowledge of the facts will first be dealt with.

The Requirement of Knowledge

A4.6 The requirement of knowledge of the facts applies even where the principal offence is one of strict liability as in *Callow v Tillstone* (1900) 83 LT 411 where a vet negligently certified meat as sound and fit for sale, and a butcher was convicted of the strict-liability offence of exposing for sale meat which was unsound and unfit for human consumption. The vet's conviction for aiding and abetting was quashed since negligence was not sufficient for this form of liability even though the butcher's liability as principal offender was not dependent on proof of any degree of fault whatsoever.

The importance of this principle can be further seen in *Smith v Mellors* (1987) 84 Cr App R 279 where Mellors and Soar were both charged under the RTA 1972, s. 6(1)(a) (driving with excess alcohol, now the RTA 1988, s. 5(1)(a)). The prosecution were unable to prove who was the driver and who was the passenger. Nor could they prove that each defendant was aware that the other was over the limit. The magistrates ruled that there was no case to answer. The Divisional Court affirmed their decision whilst pointing out that, in the light of the MCA 1980, s. 44 (see A4.1), it was not always necessary to determine who was the accessory and who the principal. However, it was necessary where, as in this case, there was a material difference between the liability of the principal and the accessory. The RTA 1972, s. 6(1)(a), created an offence of strict liability for the principal but the accessory could be liable only if aware of the facts. Only if both knew that the other was over the limit could both be convicted without proof of who was driving. Presumably, if it is proved that A had the requisite knowledge, A, though not B, could be convicted since in that case A would be liable whether or not A was the driver. Croom-Johnson LJ stated (at p. 284): 'It might be that an aider and abettor would be an aider and abettor if he was simply reckless as to whether or not the driver had the requisite amount of alcohol in his blood. 'Whilst this statement might at one time have found some support in the earlier case of *Carter v Richardson* [1974] RTR 314, it is now clear that recklessness is not sufficient. In *Giorgianni v The Queen* (1985) 156 CLR 473, the Australian High Court, having discussed at length the English authorities, held that recklessness was not sufficient for an accessory to an offence of causing death by culpable (reckless) driving. The owner of a lorry involved in a fatal crash was not guilty as accessory unless he knew or was wilfully blind to the brake defect in the lorry. In the light of *Jogee* [2016] UKSC 8, [2017] AC 387, discussed at **A4.10**, it is now absolutely clear that recklessness cannot be sufficient.

The above discussion relates to the requirement of knowledge of existing facts. The question of knowledge or 'contemplation' of future facts is discussed at **A4.10**, but first it is necessary to discuss the separate requirement of intention to aid.

Intention to Aid

Lord Goddard's statement in *Johnson v Youden* [1950] 1 KB 544 (see **A4.5**) that the accessory 'must at least know the essential matters which constitute the offence' is not, and does not purport to be, a complete definition of the mental element because, *inter alia*, it relates only to part (b) of the *actus reus* as set out in **A4.5**, i.e. the principal offence. It says nothing about the intention to 'aid, abet, counsel and procure'. As Devlin J put it in *National Coal Board v Gamble* [1959] 1 QB 11 (at p. 20): **A4.7**

> ... aiding and abetting is a crime that requires proof of *mens rea*, that is to say, of intention to aid as well as of knowledge of the circumstances.

However, as Devlin J went on to point out, at p. 23, intention to aid does not require that the accused's purpose or motive must be that the principal offence should be committed:

> If one man deliberately sells to another a gun to be used for murdering a third, he may be indifferent about whether the third man lives or dies and interested only in the cash profit to be made out of the sale, but he can still be an aider and abettor. To hold otherwise would be to negative the rule that *mens rea* is a matter of intent only and does not depend on desire or motive.

Thus in *DPP for Northern Ireland v Lynch* [1975] AC 653, D2's alleged opposition to the principal offence did not preclude a finding that he intended to aid. It is generally accepted that the question of intention to aid is (and should be) governed by the general law on intention discussed at **A2.4** and that where D2 does not act in order to assist or encourage the commission of an offence, but knows that D2's actions are extremely likely or virtually certain to have that result, then the question is one for the jury to infer whether or not D2 has the requisite intent. *Gillick v West Norfolk and Wisbech Area Health Authority* [1986] AC 112 is an example of a type of case where the uncertainties of the precise meaning of intention effectively confer a perhaps welcome discretion on whether to impose responsibility. That case concerned, *inter alia*, the question of whether a doctor giving contraceptive advice or treatment to a girl under the age of 16 could be liable as accessory to a subsequent offence of unlawful sexual intercourse committed by the girl's sexual partner. The House of Lords held that generally this would not be the case (the action was a civil one for a declaration) since the doctor would lack the necessary intention (even though the doctor realised that the advice or treatment would facilitate such intercourse). One rationale for the decision would be that a jury would not infer intention in such circumstances if they thought that the doctor was acting in what the doctor considered to be the girl's best interests (such situations are now expressly catered for in the SOA 2003, s. 73). **A4.8**

Similar reasoning could be applied to a troublesome group of cases involving the supply of articles for use in crime which the recipient already has some sort of civil right to receive. The general position seems to be that this is not aiding and abetting (see, e.g., *Lomas* (1913) 9 Cr App R 220 concerning the return of a jemmy to its owner) because D2 does not intend to aid the offence but rather merely to comply with D2's supposed civil-law duties. Critics of this general position rightly point out that it can hardly apply to a person returning a revolver to its owner knowing that the owner is then going to use it to carry out a murder. But here a jury probably would infer intention to aid from D2's knowledge of the effects of the act, and the flexibility of the notion of intention enables an appropriate solution to be found to situations for which it is difficult to formulate precise rules in advance.

A4.9 It is particularly important to stress the need for an intention to aid where D2 may not personally appreciate the natural and probable consequences of the act, as in *Clarkson* [1971] 3 All ER 344 where there was 'at least the possibility that a drunken man with his self-discipline loosened by drink ... might not intend that his presence should offer encouragement to rapers; ... he might not realise that he was giving encouragement' (at p. 1406). The reference to intoxication underlines the fact that complicity requires intention rather than recklessness (*Blakely v DPP* [1991] Crim LR 763) and that, for the purposes of the *Majewski* rule (*DPP v Majewski* [1977] AC 443: see **A3.17**), complicity can be regarded as requiring specific intent.

The foregoing discussion was quoted approvingly in *Bryce* [2004] EWCA Crim 1231, [2004] 2 Cr App R 35 (592) at [63], where the Court of Appeal confirmed that an intention to assist (in the sense explained above) is required (although in many cases, as on the facts of *Bryce*, such an intention may be readily inferred from the voluntary performance of acts which obviously do in fact assist D1, in the absence of a credible explanation from D2 as to why this was not D2's intention — see *Bryce* at [101]). The decision of the Supreme Court in *Gnango* [2011] UKSC 59, [2012] 1 AC 827 provides a further example of an (indirect) intention to aid and abet being sufficient, notwithstanding it not being D2's purpose that the offence should successfully be carried out. D2's actions in shooting at D1, in pursuance of an agreement to shoot and be shot at, had the foreseen (virtually certain) effect of encouraging D1 to attempt to kill D2 even though D2 had no wish to be killed. Therefore D2 was guilty of encouraging the shots fired at himself and could be liable as accessory to the murder by D1 of a passer-by who was accidentally shot by a bullet intended for D2.

THE SCOPE OF THE (INTENDED) JOINT VENTURE

A4.10 The test of 'knowledge of the essential matters constituting the offence', as has already been intimated, needs some further elucidation since a strict requirement of knowledge is inappropriate or unworkable in certain situations, notably where the offence is to be committed in the future or by a person of whose precise intentions D2 cannot be certain in advance. A relatively simple case is where D2 knows that, for example, a burglary is to be committed and provides equipment to be used in the burglary. D2 is guilty even if unaware of the precise time, date or place of the proposed offence. Provided that D2 knows the type of crime, i.e. that it will be a burglary, it does not matter that D2 does not know the details of the particular crime in the sense of a particular date at particular premises (*Bainbridge* [1960] 1 QB 129 esp. at pp. 133–4). In some cases D2 may be convicted even though unsure whether the offence is to be burglary or some other type of crime such as handling or robbery. In *Maxwell* [1978] 1 WLR 1363, D2 had driven his car so as to guide a following car out to a remote public house into which a bomb was thrown from the second car. He argued that since he did not know exactly what type of offence was to be committed (it was obviously a terrorist attack of some sort but it was unclear whether it was to be a bombing or a shooting) he did not know the essential matters constituting the offences with which he was charged (under the Explosive

Substances Act 1883). Nevertheless, Lowry CJ upheld the conviction of D2 in relation to the bombing, saying (at pp. 1374–5):

> His guilt springs from the fact that he contemplates the commission of one (or more) of a number of crimes by the principal and he intentionally lends his assistance in order that such a crime will be committed . . .
>
> The relevant crime must be within the contemplation of the accomplice and only exceptionally would evidence be found to support the allegation that the accomplice had given the principal a completely blank cheque.
>
> [He] must . . . have contemplated the bombing of the Crosskeys Inn as not the only possibility but one of the most obvious possibilities among the jobs which the principals were likely to be undertaking.

Thus the test in this sort of case is not so much knowledge (D2 cannot 'know' things in advance) as contemplation. It is capable of application in a wide range of situations including:

> . . . that of two persons who agree to rob a bank on the understanding, either express or implied from conduct (such as the carrying of a loaded gun by one person with the knowledge of the other), that violence *may* be resorted to. The accomplice knows, not that the principal *will* shoot the cashier, but that he may do so; and if the principal does shoot him, the accomplice will be guilty of murder. (Ibid.)

The judgment of Lowry CJ (given in the Court of Criminal Appeal in Northern Ireland) was unanimously approved by the House of Lords ([1978] 1 WLR 1350). The decision was also referred to approvingly by the Supreme Court in *Jogee* [2016] UKSC 8, [2017] AC 387, but the emphasis in *Jogee* is not so much on contemplation but on intention (*Jogee* at [15]); D2 'did not know the precise form of attack that they were intending to carry out (which was in fact an explosion), but it was held to be enough that he knew that they were intending to carry out a violent attack on the inn and that he intended to assist them to do so'.

In the light of *Jogee* it may be better to see *Maxwell* as a case of conditional intention. D2 intended to assist the principals *if* the offence they went on to commit was one of the ones he contemplated. The contemplation is not in itself sufficient; D2 must intend to assist them by driving them, knowing that this was one of the offences they might commit. D2's intent to assist an offence was conditional in the sense that it required the condition to be fulfilled that the principals chose to go on to commit an offence from the list which D2 contemplated — and such a conditional intention, as opposed to mere contemplation, is sufficient.

Fundamental Restatement in *Jogee* and the Change of Emphasis from Foresight to Intention

The principles underlying the scope of the 'joint venture', or the 'intended venture', and indeed the precise formulation of the *mens rea* of an accessory for a crime committed by the principal, were fundamentally restated by the Supreme Court in *Jogee* [2016] UKSC 8, [2017] AC 387. Virtually all the previous cases on the mental element of an accessory must now be read in the light of *Jogee*, which means that most of them can no longer be relied upon without qualification, especially in relation to liability for murder. **A4.11**

The Supreme Court in *Jogee* decided that the law took a wrong turning in *Chan Wing-Siu* [1985] AC 168 in allowing foresight of the offence committed by D1 to be sufficient *mens rea in itself* for the liability of D2 for that offence, under what came to be known as parasitic accessory liability. It was also acknowledged that much of the case law since then, including House of Lords' decisions in *Powell* [1999] 1 AC 1 and *Rahman* [2008] UKHL 45, [2009] 1 AC 129, has proceeded on a wrong basis and the law ought to return to the correct principle, based on intent; i.e. D2 must intend to encourage or assist D1 to commit the offence and intend that D1 will have the *mens rea* required for that offence. Foresight may be evidence of that intent but it is not equivalent to intent. The intent may be conditional (e.g., that D1 would intentionally use serious violence if necessary) and intention needs to be distinguished from desire or purpose.

The return in *Jogee* to a requirement of intention was applied in *Noble* [2016] EWCA Crim 2219 in dismissing an appeal against conviction for murder. The judge had given what was described by the Court of Appeal (at [96]) as 'an entirely correct description of the requisite intent for accessory liability' when she said:

> ... if a person joins another who he realises is out to cause at least really serious injury, and a jury concludes that he intended [to encourage] or assist the deliberate intention of serious injury and that person acts with intent to cause really serious injury and death results, both will be guilty of murder.

This direction closely reflects *Jogee* itself (at [95]) but the appeal was based on another passage in the direction given by the trial judge referring to 'a common purpose to unlawfully assault a victim, in the knowledge that one of them had a weapon (a firearm) which he knew could be used to kill or cause serious bodily injury'. The use of the word 'could' rather than 'would' was said to amount to equating foresight with intention, contrary to *Jogee*. This argument was dismissed as this passage did not set out the test for intention but described the functionality of the weapon that the appellant knew about, i.e. 'a loaded gun, which, as is obvious, "could be used to kill or cause serious bodily injury"'. This did not equate foresight with intent but was a reference to evidence from which intent could be inferred.

The difficulties inherent in this area are, however, illustrated by the Court of Appeal's comment (at [99]) that the route to verdict provided to the jury correctly addressed the issue of intent as follows:

> Are you ... sure that the defendant ... either
> a) fired the shot with the intention that another should die or suffer really serious injury; or
> b) assist[ed] or encourage[d] the one who fired the shot with the intention that another should die or suffer serious injury?

It is far from clear that this is satisfactory. The first part of alternative (b) merely describes the *actus reus* of D2, the acts of assistance or encouragement. The intention in the second part of alternative (b) most naturally refers to the intention of D1. It fails to specify clearly the intention required of the accessory in accordance with *Jogee*, i.e. that D2 (i) intended to encourage or assist D1 to commit the offence and (ii) intended that D1 will have the *mens rea* (where the offence requires a particular intent). It is suggested that alternative (b) dealing with D2's liability ought to be on the following lines if it is to be consistent with *Jogee*:

> (b) intentionally assisted or encouraged the one who fired the shot, intending that such person would do so with the intention that another should die or suffer really serious injury (such person who fired the shot also in fact having that intention to kill or cause really serious injury)?

More generally, even though the basic shift from foresight (in its own right) to intent (possibly evidenced by foresight), including conditional intent, may not, in many cases, make any difference to the conclusion reached by the jury (and, in the light of *Anwar* [2016] EWCA Crim 551, [2016] 2 Cr App R 23 (315), will be even less likely to make any difference to whether there is a case to answer), in the light of the radical revision of the applicable principles, it is necessary to quote some of the key paragraphs where the judgment sets out the proper approach:

> [94] If the jury is satisfied that there was an agreed common purpose to commit crime A, and if it is satisfied also that D2 must have foreseen that, in the course of committing crime A, D1 might well commit crime B, it may in appropriate cases be justified in drawing the conclusion that D2 had the necessary conditional intent that crime B should be committed, if the occasion arose; or in other words that it was within the scope of the plan to which D2 gave his assent and intentional support. *But that will be a question of fact for the jury in all the circumstances.* [emphasis added]

That paragraph from *Jogee* was quoted in *Anwar* at [21]–[22], where it was observed that 'the same facts which would previously have been used to support the inference of *mens rea* before the decision in *Jogee* will equally be used now... the evidential requirements justifying a decision that there is a case to answer are likely to be the same even if, applying the facts to the different directions in law, the jury might reach a different conclusion'. Returning to the judgment in *Jogee*, the Supreme Court went on to illustrate a case where the jury would continue to infer the necessary intent:

> [95]...If D2 joins with a group which he realises is out to cause serious injury, the jury may well infer that he intended to encourage or assist the deliberate infliction of serious bodily injury and/or intended that that should happen if necessary. In that case, if D1 acts with intent to cause serious bodily injury and death results, D1 and D2 will each be guilty of murder.

The Court was keen to stress that, even where the requirement of intent means that D2 is not liable for the offence actually committed by D1, that does not mean that D2 will escape liability altogether. So, in the example at [95], if D2 does not have the necessary intent to assist or encourage the intentional infliction of serious bodily injury, D2 will not be guilty of the offence of murder for which D2 does not have the *mens rea* but may be guilty of unlawful act manslaughter. **A4.12**

> [96] If a person is a party to a violent attack on another, without an intent to assist in the causing of death or really serious harm, but the violence escalates and results in death, he will be not guilty of murder but guilty of manslaughter. So also if he participates by encouragement or assistance in any other unlawful act which all sober and reasonable people would realise carried the risk of some harm (not necessarily serious) to another, and death in fact results... [that too will be manslaughter].

Dreszer [2018] EWCA Crim 454 provides an example of a conviction for murder being quashed because of a pre-*Jogee* direction on foresight as an alternative to intention, but the accused being guilty of at least manslaughter.

Manslaughter is not, however, the inevitable verdict in all such cases, as is recognised at [97]:

> The qualification to this... is that it is possible for death to be caused by some overwhelming supervening act by the perpetrator which nobody in the defendant's shoes could have contemplated might happen and is of such a character as to relegate his acts to history; in that case the defendant will bear no criminal responsibility for the death.

That statement deals with and severely curtails the significance of the former 'fundamental difference' rule based on *English* [1997] 4 All ER 545, whereby there is no liability if the weapon used is fundamentally different to that contemplated by D2. This can be seen in *Jogee* at [98]:

> This type of case apart, there will normally be no occasion to consider the concept of 'fundamental departure' as derived from *English*. What matters is whether D2 encouraged or assisted the crime, whether it be murder or some other offence. He need not encourage or assist a particular way of committing it, although he may sometimes do so. In particular, his intention to assist in a crime of violence is not determined only by whether he knows what kind of weapon D1 has in his possession. The tendency which has developed in the application of the rule in *Chan Wing-Siu* to focus on what D2 knew of what weapon D1 was carrying can and should give way to an examination of whether D2 intended to assist in the crime charged. If that crime is murder, then the question is whether he intended to assist the intentional infliction of grievous bodily harm at least, which question will often, as set out above, be answered by asking simply whether he himself intended grievous bodily harm at least. Very often he may intend to assist in violence using whatever weapon may come to hand. In other cases he may think that D1 has an iron bar whereas he turns out to have a knife, but the difference may not at all affect his intention to assist, if necessary, in the causing of grievous bodily harm at least. Knowledge or ignorance that weapons generally, or a particular weapon, is carried by D1 will be evidence going to what the intention of D2 was, and may be irresistible evidence one way or the other, but it is evidence and no more.

The demise under *Jogee* of the former fundamental difference approach based on knowledge of the nature of the weapon used by D1 is illustrated in *Brown* [2017] EWCA Crim 1870. In upholding convictions of the secondary parties for unlawful wounding (where D1 was convicted of wounding with intent), Hallet LJ (Vice President) said (at [29]–[30]):

> ...the judge on the facts of this case was not obliged to direct the jury they could only convict a secondary party of either a section 18 offence or a section 20 offence if they were sure that the

> secondary party knew that the principal had a knife ... the judge correctly directed the jury to focus on the extent of the joint enterprise and then on the intent of the individual defendants.

A further illustration is provided by *Harper* [2019] EWCA Crim 343, [2019] 4 WLR 39. D2 was convicted of a murder where D1 inflicted the fatal wounds by means of a knife of which D2 said she was unaware. It was argued on appeal that 'the jury ought to have been directed in this case that they first had to be sure that Harper knew of the presence of the knife before they could consider the further elements of the offence' (at [27]). Sir Brian Leveson P emphatically rejected this argument, which he pointed out would ignore 'the thrust of *Jogee*'. The related argument that the use of the knife by D1 was an 'overwhelming supervening event' was also rejected. The Court also referred to *Tas* [2018] EWCA Crim 2603, [2019] 1 Cr App R 26 (343), where D2's liability was for manslaughter rather than murder; as to which see **A4.14**.

A4.13 **Divergence of *Mens Rea*—Residual Liability for Manslaughter (or Lesser Offence)** Difficult questions have arisen in the past where D2 intends to assist the act done by D1 but does not intend that it be done with the *mens rea* (e.g., intention to cause grievous bodily harm or to kill) with which D1 acts. D2 is not liable for the offence committed by D1 (e.g., murder), as has also been recognised in *Jogee*, but the question has been 'does the accessory remain liable for the consequences of the principal's act by means of a lesser crime according to his own *mens rea* (e.g., manslaughter)?' The fundamental question has been whether what was done by D1 is within the scope of the intended joint venture contemplated by D2. The issue arose in the Court of Appeal in Northern Ireland in *Gilmour* [2000] 2 Cr App R 407, where the following hypothetical (posed in this work since the 1996 edition) was cited with approval by Sir Robert Carswell CJ (at p. 414):

> Suppose P and A agree that P will post a specific incendiary device to V, A contemplating only superficial injuries to V when he opens it but P foreseeing and hoping that the injuries will be serious or fatal. If V is killed as a result, P will clearly be guilty of murder, A is clearly not guilty of murder as an accessory but should be guilty of manslaughter because the act done by P is precisely what was envisaged. The fact that P happens also to have the *mens rea* of murder is irrelevant because it does not change the nature of the act that he does or the manner in which he does it.

A4.14 The Court of Appeal decided that this was the correct principle to apply in *Gilmour*, where D2 drove the principals to a housing estate where they threw a petrol bomb into a house causing a fierce fire in which three young boys died. Although the principals were guilty of murder as they had an intention to kill, unknown to D2 who, in the view of the Court of Appeal, did not even contemplate an intention to cause grievous bodily harm, D2 could nevertheless be guilty of manslaughter since he knew about the petrol bomb and the principals had 'carried out the very deed' contemplated (or as it would now be, post-*Jogee*, intended) by him. The same result, it is submitted, will continue to apply following *Jogee*, especially given the remarks in the Supreme Court, discussed at **A4.12**, about the availability of a residual verdict of manslaughter where D2 does not intend D1 to act with the *mens rea* for murder but nonetheless can be regarded as party to the actions carried out by D1.

Carpenter [2011] EWCA Crim 2568, [2012] QB 722 is another pre-*Jogee* example of where it was right to leave the alternative verdict of manslaughter to the jury, and the availability of an alternative verdict of manslaughter was clearly a significant factor in the Supreme Court's decision in *Jogee* to reassert the primacy of the requirement of intention in relation to the liability of D2 for the offence of murder. As has been seen, the limitation on this residual liability for manslaughter following *Jogee* no longer turns on the question of whether D1's act is 'fundamentally different' from the one contemplated by D2. Rather, the limiting principle is where death is 'caused by some overwhelming supervening act by the perpetrator which nobody in the defendant's shoes could have contemplated might happen' (*Jogee* at [97]). In such a case, it cannot be regarded as within the scope of the intended joint venture.

In *Tas* [2018] EWCA Crim 2603, [2019] 1 Cr App R 26 (343), it was confirmed that the fact that D2 was unaware that D1 had a particular weapon (a knife in this case) does not, by any means, necessarily mean that D2 is not liable for manslaughter if D2 intends that unlawful force be used, even if D1 uses the knife with intent to cause serious injury and is guilty of murder. On the facts, the trial judge was entitled to reject the prosecution argument that he should leave the possibility of overwhelming supervening act to the jury. Sir Brian Leveson P stated (at [40]–[41]:

> ...the question can be asked whether the judge was entitled to conclude that there was insufficient evidence to leave to the jury ... [whether] the production of a knife is a wholly supervening event rather than a simple escalation...
>
> ...in the light of the relegation of knowledge of the weapon as going to proof of intent, it cannot be that the law brings back that knowledge as a pre-requisite for manslaughter. In our judgment, whether there is an evidential basis for overwhelming supervening event which is of such a character as could relegate into history matters which would otherwise be looked on as causative (or, indeed, withdrawal from a joint enterprise) rather than mere escalation which remained part of the joint enterprise is very much for the judge who has heard the evidence and is in a far better position than this court to reach a conclusion as to evidential sufficiency.

Impact of *Jogee* on Previous Convictions

The Supreme Court in *Jogee* [2016] UKSC 8, [2017] AC 387 emphasised that the correction of the previous error in the law — 'equating foresight with intent to assist rather than treating the first as evidence of the second' — did not mean that previous convictions under the old law were necessarily invalid. The error, though important as a matter of legal principle, may not have been important on the facts to the outcome of a particular trial or to the safety of a particular conviction. **A4.15**

> [100] ... Moreover, where a conviction has been arrived at by faithfully applying the law as it stood at the time, it can be set aside only by seeking exceptional leave to appeal to the Court of Appeal out of time. That court has power to grant such leave, and may do so if substantial injustice be demonstrated, but it will not do so simply because the law applied has now been declared to have been mistaken. This principle has been consistently applied for many years.

In the event, decisions in the Court of Appeal since *Jogee* have indicated that there will be very little impact on previous convictions. In *Johnson* [2016] EWCA Crim 1613, [2017] 1 Cr App R 12 (136) a strongly constituted Court of Appeal heard a group of 13 cases, in none of which was the appellant successful in challenging a conviction. Indeed (in respect of the appeals of Burton and Terrelonge at [82]) the Court observed that 'the prosecution case could be said to be stronger post-*Jogee*: knowledge of the precise weapon is no longer required but, if proved, may lead to an inference of intention'. (See *Noble* [2016] EWCA Crim 2219, at **A4.11**, for an example of this, and see now *Daley* [2019] EWCA Crim 627 for an example of no substantial injustice following a CCRC reference.) A number of the cases considered also illustrate the importance post-*Jogee* of the concept of conditional intention which may be inferred from knowledge or foresight. Although many of the cases were applications out of time and thus had to overcome the test of whether 'substantial injustice' had been done before the question of whether the conviction was unsafe could arise, in virtually all the cases the Court considered that the verdicts were in any event safe, or at least that there was no injustice, let alone substantial injustice. Subsequently, in *Garwood* [2017] EWCA Crim 59, [2017] 1 Cr App R 30 (451), some of the appellants in *Johnson* sought a certificate from the Court of Appeal that a point of law of general public importance was involved in its approach to the test of substantial injustice so that it could be challenged in the Supreme Court. However, the Court of Appeal declined to grant a certificate as it considered that it had no jurisdiction to do so in relation to a refusal of leave to appeal. *Jogee* will therefore continue to have very little effect on previous convictions, and it should be noted that even the successful appellant in *Jogee* itself was, at his retrial, convicted of manslaughter rather than murder. Similarly, in *Crilly* [2018] EWCA Crim 168, [2018] 2 Cr App R 12 (159), a rare case where exceptional leave was actually given, a plea of guilty to manslaughter rather than murder was subsequently accepted at the retrial. The original case was 'to all intent and purposes a case about his foresight' and the evidence against him 'was not so strong that we can safely and fairly infer the jury would have found the requisite intent to cause really serious bodily harm had the issue been left to them' (per Hallett LJ at [42]).

Notwithstanding the granting of leave in *Crilly, Varley* [2017] EWCA Crim 268 provides yet another example, in addition to those in *Johnson*, of the 'high threshold' for substantial injustice not being crossed in a case where a conviction for murder (prior to *Jogee*) had been based on foresight but where the Court of Appeal considered that on the evidence an inference of intent would have been fully justified.

In *Agera* [2017] EWCA Crim 740, [2017] 2 Cr App R 22 (277), leave to amend grounds of appeal out of time was refused as no substantial injustice had been shown, and the argument that the case should be dealt with differently from those in *Johnson* [2016] EWCA Crim 1613, [2017] 1 Cr App R 12 (136), on the grounds that the joint venture was on the spur of the moment, was rejected. In *Quinn* [2017] EWCA Crim 1071, leave to amend grounds of appeal out of time to include *Jogee* grounds, even where the in-time grounds of appeal had not yet been determined, was also refused on the grounds of no substantial injustice. In *Grant-Murray* [2017] EWCA Crim 1228, applications for leave out of time were refused on the basis that there were no grounds on which it could be contended that there was a substantial injustice or that the jury would have reached a different conclusion if they had been directed in accordance with *Jogee*. *White (Lindsey)* [2017] NICA 49 is to similar effect.

In *R (Davies) v CCRC* [2018] EWHC 3080 (Admin), the substantial injustice test in *Johnson* [2016] EWCA Crim 1613, [2017] 1 Cr App R 12 (136) was confirmed as applying equally to decisions of the CCRC whether to refer a conviction to the Court of Appeal (Criminal Division). *Towers* [2019] EWCA Crim 198 provides an example of a case where a conviction for murder was referred but, in upholding the conviction, the Court of Appeal was again clear that the high threshold of 'substantial injustice' was not satisfied. The Court emphasised the difference, in such an out of time/change of law case, between the substantial injustice test and the less demanding 'safety of the conviction test' normally applied to criminal appeals. Sir Brian Leveson P again referred (at [59]) to the following key passage in *Johnson* at [21]:

> In determining whether that high threshold has been met, the court will primarily and ordinarily have regard to the strength of the case advanced that the change in the law would, in fact, have made a difference. If crime A is a crime of violence which the jury concluded must have involved the use of a weapon so that the inference of participation with an intention to cause really serious harm is strong, that is likely to be very difficult. At the other end of the spectrum, if crime A is a different crime, not involving intended violence or use of force, it may well be easier to demonstrate substantial injustice.

LIABILITY OF ACCESSORY WHERE THERE IS NO PRINCIPAL

A4.16 A person can be liable as an accessory even though D1 cannot be identified or has been acquitted in a previous trial (*Hui Chi-ming* [1992] 1 AC 34) or even earlier in the same trial (*Hughes* (1860) Bell CC 242), although in this latter case such a result would only be justified where there was evidence admissible against D2 but not against D1 (*Humphreys* [1965] 3 All ER 689). See also *Petch* [2005] EWCA Crim 1883, [2005] 2 Cr App R 40 (657), where D1 was allowed to plead to a lesser offence in a subsequent trial. Where the same evidence is admissible against both it would normally be inconsistent for the same jury to acquit D1 and yet convict D2 of a crime which it has already found has not been committed by D1.

Liability where Principal has Complete Defence

A4.17 In a number of cases the Court of Appeal has upheld convictions of accessories whilst recognising that D1 would have a valid defence. Thus in *Bourne* (1952) 36 Cr App R 125, a husband's conviction for aiding and abetting his wife to commit buggery with a dog was upheld even though it was recognised that the wife could not have been convicted as principal (she was not in fact charged) since she was acting under duress from her husband. In *Cogan* [1976] QB 217, Leak's terrified wife had intercourse with Cogan (who had allegedly been told by Leak that she would consent) because of her fear of her husband. Cogan's conviction for rape was quashed because the jury had been told, contrary to the law at the time, that his alleged belief that Mrs Leak was consenting had to be reasonable whereas it was possible that his belief was genuinely held, but Leak's conviction as accessory was upheld. The Court of Appeal pointed out (at p. 223) that:

> ... one fact is clear — the wife had been raped. Cogan had had sexual intercourse with her without her consent. The fact that Cogan was innocent of rape because he believed that she was consenting does not affect the position that she was raped.

The Court then pointed out (at pp. 223–4) that Leak could have been guilty as a principal acting through an innocent agent:

> Had Leak been indicted as a principal offender, the case against him would have been clear beyond argument. Should he be allowed to go free because he was charged with 'being aider and abettor to the same offence'? If we are right in our opinion that the wife had been raped (and no one outside a court of law would say that she had not been), then the particulars of offence accurately stated what Leak had done, namely, he had procured Cogan to commit the offence.

A4.18 There has been some debate over the precise principle involved in these cases but everyone agrees that the result is just. To say that the liability is really that of a principal acting through an innocent agent can cause problems where the accused lacks some characteristic essential for liability as a principal, e.g., if in *Cogan* it had been a woman, rather than Mrs Leak's husband, who had terrorised her into submitting to intercourse. (See the discussion in *Varley* [2019] EWCA Crim 1074, at [99], accepting this limitation on innocent agency.) The definition of rape, even in the SOA 2003, s. 1, still requires it in effect to be committed by a man, whereas there is no problem in convicting a person as accessory to an offence which he or she cannot commit as principal (*Ram* (1893) 17 Cox CC 609, woman as accessory to rape). Thus it is probably preferable to adopt the principle that D2 can be liable provided that there is the *actus reus* of the principal offence even if D1 is entitled to be acquitted because of some personal defence.

It may well be, however, that this principle is limited to cases where D2 has procured the *actus reus* (i.e. has caused it to be committed as was the case in both *Bourne* and *Cogan*). This would also be consistent with the proposition that procuring does not need a common intention between D2 and D1 whereas other forms of aiding and abetting generally do. If D1 lacks the *mens rea* of the offence there can hardly be a common intention that it should be committed, but this is not required for procuring.

The above two paragraphs were specifically approved by the Court of Appeal in *Millward* [1994] Crim LR 527 as correctly stating the law. D2 in that case was convicted on the basis of procuring the offence of causing death by reckless driving even though the actual driver (his employee) did not know of the defect in the vehicle and was not therefore personally reckless. The case is not an easy one in which to apply the current principles because of the peculiar difficulties in defining the *actus reus* of (causing death by) reckless driving which was nevertheless, in the view of the Court of Appeal, to be found in 'the taking of the vehicle in the defective condition on to the road so as to cause the death of the little boy'; D2, 'being aware of the defects, ... had procured the offence by the giving of instructions to ... his employee'. *Millward* was approved in *Wheelhouse* [1994] Crim LR 756 and was followed in *DPP v K and B* [1997] 1 Cr App R 36, where two girls were convicted of procuring the rape of another teenage girl by an unknown boy even though the boy may not have had the *mens rea* of rape and in any event had to be assumed not to be responsible under the rebuttable presumption of *doli incapax* (now abolished by the CDA 1998, s. 34). It would apparently have been different if the boy had been shown to be under the age of ten, although the logic behind this last conclusion is not particularly compelling. For further support for the *Cogan* principle as being consistent with the principles now applicable to encouraging or assisting under the SCA 2007 (esp. s. 47(5)(a)(iii): see **A5.13**), see *Watkins* [2010] EWCA Crim 2349 where, however, the principle could not be applicable on the facts on any reasonable reading of the evidence.

A4.19 If not even the *actus reus* is committed there can be no liability for aiding and abetting. See *Kenning* [2008] EWCA Crim 1534, [2009] QB 221 for a simple illustration and confirmation of this basic proposition and of the related rule that there can be no liability for attempting (or it seems, conspiring) to aid and abet. As regards *Millward*, the situation would now be governed by the offence of causing death by dangerous rather than reckless driving, as is illustrated by *Loukes* [1996] 1 Cr App R 444. Under the relevant version of that offence the test of whether a person is driving dangerously is satisfied if 'it would be obvious to a competent and careful driver that driving the vehicle in its current state would be dangerous' (RTA 1988, s. 2A(2)). If it would not be so obvious *to the driver*, and the driver is acquitted on that ground (as in *Loukes*) then, according to the Court of Appeal in that case, there is not even the *actus reus* as no one has driven the vehicle dangerously. Therefore, the person responsible for maintaining the vehicle and sending it out on the road cannot be liable even as an accessory, a result described by the Court of Appeal as an 'injustice'.

The situation in *Thornton v Mitchell* [1940] 1 All ER 339, in which a bus driver was acquitted of driving without due care and attention, was somewhat simpler and clearer. The driver had had to rely on signals from his conductor in reversing the bus. Because of the conductor's negligence, two pedestrians were injured, one of them fatally. The conductor's conviction for aiding and abetting had to be quashed because clearly there was no principal offence of driving without due care to which he could be accessory. The driver had driven *with* due care rather than without it, so there was not even the *actus reus* of that offence. On the other hand, there was the *actus reus* of homicide (the causing of the death of the pedestrian). It may be that the conductor could have been liable for manslaughter if his negligence were sufficiently gross, though only on the basis that the conductor was the principal (whose own conduct caused the death) since liability as an accessory requires subjective fault rather than negligence (see **A4.6**).

Liability where Principal Liable Only for Lesser Offence

A4.20 An analogous problem to that described in **A4.17** arises where there are two or more offences which share the same *actus reus*, e.g., murder and manslaughter, or the offences under the OAPA 1861, ss. 18 and 20. If D1 commits the *actus reus* but with only the *mens rea* for the less serious of the two possible offences, can D2 nonetheless be convicted of the more serious offence if D2 has sufficient *mens rea*? The Court of Appeal in *Richards* [1974] QB 776 appeared to make the answer depend on whether D2 was present at the scene of the crime. However, this case almost certainly no longer represents the law following the House of Lords' decision in *Howe* [1987] AC 417, where it was indicated that *Richards* should not be followed (see at pp. 436B and 457–8) and having regard to *Millward*, where it was immaterial that the procurer was not present. The issue cannot be regarded as finally settled as the question certified for the House in *Howe* was in the following terms:

> Can one who incites or procures by duress another to kill or to be a party to a killing be convicted of murder if that other is acquitted by reason of duress?

This differs from the *Richards* question in that (a) D1 is not guilty of *any* crime and (b) D1's defence is duress rather than lack of *mens rea*. In fact, the certified question in *Howe* really raises the same question as in *Bourne* (1952) 36 Cr App R 125 (contrast the situation in *Dang* [2014] EWCA Crim 348, [2014] 1 WLR 3797) and the affirmative answer given by the House of Lords to the question can be regarded as confirmation of that decision. It would be extremely odd if D2 could be convicted where D1 is acquitted altogether but could not be convicted if D1 happens to be guilty of some lesser offence. *Richards* can perhaps safely be regarded as no longer stating the law. However, just as with the principle following from *Bourne* and *Cogan*, it may be that D2's *mens rea* can only be linked with D1's *actus reus* where D2 can be said to have procured the *actus reus*.

Such a limitation, however, would not apply to the Homicide Act 1957, s. 2(4), whereby, 'The fact that one party to a killing is by virtue of this section [diminished responsibility] not liable to be convicted of murder shall not affect the question whether the killing amounted to murder in the case of any other party to it'. In other words, D2 with sufficient *mens rea* can be convicted of murder even though D1 is convicted only of manslaughter because of diminished responsibility or, by virtue of the CAJA 2009, s. 54(8), because of loss of control.

MISCELLANEOUS ISSUES

Presence at the Scene of the Crime: Omissions

Neither mere presence at the scene of a crime nor a failure to prevent an offence will generally give rise to liability. However, presence at the scene of a crime is *capable* of constituting encouragement (see *Jefferson* [1994] 1 All ER 270 for an example and contrast *Coney* (1882) 8 QBD 534 — spectators at illegal prize fight, conviction quashed since jury directed that presence was *conclusive* evidence of encouragement—and similarly see *L v CPS* [2013] EWHC 4127 (Admin)). If D2 is present in pursuance of a prior agreement with D1, that will normally amount to aiding and abetting, but if D2 is present only accidentally then D2 must know that this presence is actually encouraging D1 (*Allan* [1965] 1 QB 130, in which it was held that a secret intention to join in if required was not of itself sufficient); there must be both actual encouragement and also awareness of that fact (*Allan* and *Tate* [1993] Crim LR 538). *Wilcox v Jeffery* [1951] 1 All ER 464 was a case where there was ample evidence to draw the inference of intentional encouragement from the presence of a spectator at an illegal saxophone performance (by an American forbidden to take employment in this country). D2 had not only paid for a ticket at the performance (thus his presence was not accidental) but had reported the arrival of the American at the airport in his magazine, *Jazz Illustrated*, and subsequently wrote a laudatory review of the concert. In contrast, in *Willett* [2010] EWCA Crim 1620, mere presence in a car which was deliberately driven over a person blocking its route was not of itself sufficient to constitute encouragement by the passenger of the murder committed by the driver. The Privy Council in *Robinson v The Queen* [2011] UKPC 3 reiterated (at [14]) the importance of making it clear to juries 'that mere approval of (ie "assent" to, or "concurrence" in) the offence by a bystander who gives no assistance, does not without more amount to aiding... [and] that the communication of willingness to give active assistance is a minimum requirement'. The requirement of an intention to help or encourage was again emphasised in *N* [2019] EWCA Crim 2280, [2020] 4 WLR 64, where D may have been one of the individuals who got out of a car and repeatedly stabbed the victim or he may have been one of those present in the car. If D was not the attacker but one of those present in the car, knowledge that there was going to be an attack was not sufficient to render him liable. He would have to 'intend by his presence to help or encourage the others to commit the crime by either giving moral support to another or by contributing simply to the force of numbers involved' (at [11]). This latter concept of 'contributing by force of numbers' was upheld in the Court of Appeal by reference to *Jogee* [2016] UKSC 8, [2017] AC 387, where it was said (at [89]) that the Supreme Court made clear that the act of assisting or encouraging 'may take many forms' and 'may include providing support by contributing to the force of numbers in a hostile confrontation'. It should be noted however that the contribution by force of numbers is simply the *actus reus* of D2's participation and there must also be the intention to encourage or assist D1 by such means. A4.21

A4.22 Where D2 is present and has both the right and ability to control D1, the failure to exercise that right of control may make D2 liable as an accomplice. Thus in *Rubie v Faulkner* [1940] 1 KB 571 a learner driver was convicted of driving without due care and attention in that he overtook on a bend, and D2 who was supervising him was convicted of aiding and abetting him by failing to exercise his right of control. Similarly, in *Tuck v Robson* [1970] 1 All ER 1171, a publican was held liable for aiding and abetting his customers to commit the offence of drinking after hours by failing to collect the customers' glasses or to eject them from the premises. See also *National Coal Board v Gamble* [1959] 1 QB 11, in which Slade J said: 'Mere passive acquiescence is sufficient only, I think, where the alleged aider and abettor has the power to control the offender *and is actually present when the offence is committed*' (emphasis added). Presence in this sort of case is arguably significant not only as evidence of encouragement but also as evidence that D2 has the knowledge that the offence is being committed and the opportunity to exercise control. In *JF Alford Transport Ltd* [1997] 2 Cr App R 326, the convictions of managers of a company for the offence of aiding and abetting the making of false tachograph records by the company's drivers were quashed because there was no evidence of knowledge in relation to any specific count. If such knowledge could have been proved, irrespective it was said of whether D2 was present when the offence was committed, the ability to control the action of D1 coupled with a decision to refrain from doing so would have been sufficient. Proof of encouragement and of knowledge of the facts may, however, be difficult to achieve where D2 is not present.

Withdrawal

A4.23 There is often an interval between D2's act and the completion of the offence by D1. In some circumstances, a change of heart by D2 coupled with steps to withdraw from participation in the offence can remove D2's responsibility for the completed offence (although D2 may remain liable for inchoate offences). Precisely what is required for an effective withdrawal will vary from case to case. It may depend on how imminent the completed offence is at the time of the attempted withdrawal by D2 and also on the nature of assistance and encouragement already given by D2. Thus in *Becerra* (1975) 62 Cr App R 212, D2 gave D1 a knife to use if they were disturbed during the course of a burglary. When D2 heard the tenant coming he called to D1: 'There's a bloke coming. Let's go' and jumped out of a window and fled. D1, however, stabbed and killed the tenant. Both D1 and D2 were convicted of murder. D2's application for leave to appeal was refused since, according to Roskill LJ at p. 219 (emphasis added):

> ... if [he] wanted to withdraw *at that stage*, he would have to 'countermand', to use the word that is used in some of the cases or 'repent' to use another word so used, in some manner vastly different and vastly more effective than merely to say 'Come on, let's go' and go out through the window.

Similarly, leave to appeal against a conviction for murder was refused in *Baker* [1994] Crim LR 444, where D2 inflicted three knife wounds, passed the knife to another, saying 'I'm not doing it', moved a few feet away and turned his back whilst others inflicted further wounds: the Court of Appeal considered that this constituted far from unequivocal notice that D2 was wholly disassociating himself from the entire enterprise. The words were quite capable of meaning no more than 'I will not myself strike any more blows'.

In *Becerra*, the Court left open the question whether it was necessary to take all reasonable steps to prevent the commission of the crime which D2 had agreed the others should commit. As a minimum, however, D2 must communicate the intention to withdraw to the other parties; it is not sufficient merely to fail to turn up as arranged (*Rook* [1993] 2 All ER 955). Such communication was found to be a sufficient withdrawal from a proposed burglary on the facts of *Whitefield* (1983) 79 Cr App R 36. The failure of the trial judge to put the defence of withdrawal to the jury was one of the grounds for the Court of Appeal quashing the conviction of Derek Bentley for murder, 45 years after he was hanged, following a reference by the CCRC (*Bentley* [2001] 1 Cr App R 21 (307)).

In *Mitchell* (1999) 163 JP 75, the Court of Appeal drew a distinction between pre-planned and spontaneous violence. With the latter, the issue was not whether there had been communication of withdrawal but whether the original joint venture was still continuing at the time of D1's act. *Mitchell* was followed in *O'Flaherty* [2004] EWCA Crim 526, [2004] 2 Cr App R 20 (315), where the question was 'whether a particular defendant disengaged before the fatal injury or injuries were caused'. Further illustrations and discussion of these principles, whereby continuing participation in a joint venture is found not to have been curtailed and thus extends to subsequent fatal assaults committed by others, can be found in *Mitchell* [2008] EWCA Crim 2552, [2009] 1 Cr App R 31 (438); *Campbell* [2009] EWCA Crim 50 and *Rajakumar* [2013] EWCA Crim 1512, [2014] 1 Cr App R 12 (168). **A4.24**

Victims Not Regarded as Accessories

Where a statutory offence is designed to protect a particular class of persons, a member of that class, i.e. a 'victim' of the offence, cannot be convicted as accessory even though the offence takes place with V's voluntary assistance. The principle is most likely to arise in the context of sexual offences where the offence takes place despite V's consent. The classic illustration is *Tyrrell* [1894] 1 QB 710, in which it was held that a girl under 16 could not be guilty of aiding and abetting an offence of unlawful carnal knowledge of her since the offence was created for the protection of the girl (see the SOA 2003, s. 9, for the modern offence). The principle can sometimes rebound so that it results in the acquittal of some other party who is not a victim, as in *Whitehouse* [1977] QB 868, where a father was acquitted of inciting his 15-year-old daughter to commit incest with him. The girl was regarded as within the class of persons the offence was designed to protect and if the girl herself could not be liable, even as an accessory, her father could not be liable for inciting her to do something which was not a crime. A special offence of incitement in these particular circumstances was subsequently created by the CLA 1977, s. 54 (see now the SOA 2003, s. 26, at **B3.169**). The exempted 'victim' rule is based on the implied intention of Parliament where legislation is designed for the protection of a particular class of persons. The Supreme Court in *Gnango* [2011] UKSC 59, [2012] 1 AC 827 held that there was no warrant for a common-law extension of the rule so as to exempt victims in any wider sense and that the principle certainly had no application so as to exempt from accessory liability a putative 'victim' who had encouraged the principal offender to shoot at him where the bullet had hit and killed an innocent third party. **A4.25**

Section A5 Inchoate Offences

INCITEMENT

Abolition of the Common-law Offence

A5.1 The common-law offence of incitement was abolished by the SCA 2007, s. 59, with effect from 1 October 2008 and supplanted by offences created by that Act. See **A5.3** ***et seq.*** A number of statutory offences of incitement or solicitation nevertheless survive, notably under the OAPA 1861, s. 4 (solicitation of murder: see **B1.135**); the Official Secrets Act 1920, s. 7 (see, e.g., **B9.10**); and the MDA 1971, s. 19 (incitement of drugs offences: see **B19.103**). As to the common-law offence, see the 2009 edition of this work at A5.1 *et seq.*, and *Jones* [2010] EWCA Crim 925, [2010] 3 All ER 1186.

References to 'incitement' in a number of older statutes such as the CJA 1993 and the Sexual Offences (Conspiracy and Incitement) Act 1996 must now be construed as references to the new offences which have replaced it (SCA 2007, s. 63(1)), but this is true only if the statute in question is one of those listed in sch. 6, part. 1. Further consequential amendments are contained in sch. 6, part 2.

Transitional Arrangements

A5.2 Prosecutions may still be brought at common law in respect of any acts of incitement committed 'wholly or partly' before 1 October 2008 (SCA 2007, sch. 13, para. 5). Where it is impossible to prove whether conduct inciting or encouraging the commission of an offence occurred before or after 1 October 2008, sch. 13, para. 6 provides that it must be presumed to have occurred *before* that date.

ENCOURAGING OR ASSISTING CRIME: SERIOUS CRIME ACT 2007

General

A5.3 The SCA 2007 creates three inchoate offences: intentionally encouraging or assisting an offence (s. 44); encouraging or assisting an offence, believing it will be committed (s. 45); and encouraging or assisting offences, believing one or more will be committed (s. 46). These share certain common elements. They overlap with, but do not supplant, some older statutory offences and with the rules governing secondary participation in substantive offences (see **A4**). There is a further overlap with the new offence of participating in the criminal activities of an organised crime group (SCA 2015, s. 45: see **A5.39**).

Actus Reus Elements Common to Offences under Part 2

In respect of each offence under the SCA 2007, Part 2, D must do an act that is *capable* of encouraging or assisting the commission of an offence (or in the case of s. 46, one or more offences) by another person or persons. It does not matter for this purpose whether any 'anticipated offence' is ever committed by the other person(s) (s. 49(1)) nor does it matter whether anyone was in fact assisted or encouraged by D's act. If the anticipated offence is indeed committed, a more appropriate charge against D may well be one of complicity in that offence (see **A4**). **A5.4**

By s. 65, D's act may take a number of different forms, including a course of conduct or a failure to discharge a duty; and it may also involve making threats (cf. *Race Relations Board v Applin* [1973] QB 815; *Evans* [1986] Crim LR 470). By s. 52 and sch. 4, an act committed abroad may suffice if certain jurisdictional requirements are satisfied, as may an act that is capable of encouraging or assisting the commission of an offence abroad (see **A5.33**); and a single act may give rise to liability under more than one of the three offence-creating provisions (s. 49(3)).

Serious Crime Act 2007, ss. 65 to 67 **A5.5**

65.—(1) A reference in this Part to a person's doing an act that is capable of encouraging the commission of an offence includes a reference to his doing so by threatening another person or otherwise putting pressure on another person to commit the offence.

(2) A reference in this Part to a person's doing an act that is capable of encouraging or assisting the commission of an offence includes a reference to his doing so by—

(a) taking steps to reduce the possibility of criminal proceedings being brought in respect of that offence;

(b) failing to take reasonable steps to discharge a duty.

(3) But a person is not to be regarded as doing an act that is capable of encouraging or assisting the commission of an offence merely because he fails to respond to a constable's request for assistance in preventing a breach of the peace.

66. If a person (D1) arranges for a person (D2) to do an act that is capable of encouraging or assisting the commission of an offence, and D2 does the act, D1 is also to be treated for the purposes of this Part as having done it.

67. A reference in this Part to an act includes a reference to a course of conduct, and a reference to doing an act is to be read accordingly.

Whether D's act was or was not 'capable' of encouraging or assisting E to commit a crime must ordinarily be a question of fact for the court or jury. At common law D could not 'incite' E unless E was aware of D's words or acts (*Ransford* (1874) 13 Cox CC 9; *Krause* (1902) 66 JP 121), but there is no such requirement in respect of offences under ss. 44 to 46 (see s. 65). Many inadvertent acts or omissions are capable of encouraging or assisting the commission of an offence, but *mens rea* must also be proved. No offence will be committed by an employee who genuinely forgets to set a burglar alarm when locking up for the night. **A5.6**

Impossibility The 'impossibility defence', which in 1981 was expunged from the law relating to statutory conspiracy and attempt (see **A5.60** and **A5.84**), survived in respect of incitement and now survives in the SCA 2007. If D's act is incapable of providing encouragement or assistance to E, D cannot be guilty even if D intended to provide such encouragement, etc. If for example D provides E with the wrong keys to F's house, this cannot assist E to commit a planned burglary at F's house. D might, however, be guilty of *attempting* to do an act that would have been capable of assisting E (i.e. providing the right keys) because impossibility is no defence to a charge of criminal attempt. Similarly, if D encourages E to steal, thinking E to be ten years old, when E is in fact below the age of criminal responsibility, D's act is incapable of encouraging E to commit a crime, but D may once again be guilty of attempting to do such an act. **A5.7**

Impossibility is heavily fact dependent. If D mistakes a police officer for a drug dealer, and seeks to buy heroin, D could still be guilty of encouraging the officer to supply heroin, because it would not be impossible for the officer to do so (cf. *DPP v Armstrong* [2000] Crim LR 379).

INTENTIONALLY ENCOURAGING OR ASSISTING AN OFFENCE

A5.8 **Serious Crime Act 2007, s. 44**

(1) A person commits an offence if—
   (a) he does an act capable of encouraging or assisting the commission of an offence; and
   (b) he intends to encourage or assist its commission.
(2) But he is not to be taken to have intended to encourage or assist the commission of an offence merely because such encouragement or assistance was a foreseeable consequence of his act.

Jurisdiction and Procedure

A5.9 The mode of trial for an offence under the SCA 2007, s. 44, is to be determined as if D had been charged with committing the 'anticipated offence'. If this was an offence triable either way, the s. 44 offence is thus triable either way (s. 55(1)). If tried on indictment, it is a class 3 offence. As to restrictions on the institution of proceedings in certain cases, see **A5.35**. As to alternative verdicts, see **A5.37**. As to acts done wholly or partly abroad, or with a view to encouraging or assisting the commission of offences abroad, see **A5.33**.

Indictment

A5.10 *Statement of Offence*

Intentionally [encouraging or] assisting an offence, contrary to section 44(1) of the Serious Crime Act 2007.

Particulars of Offence

A on or about the ... day of ... supplied B with keys to a house belong to C with the intention of assisting B to commit a burglary of that house.

Sentencing

A5.11 The penalties for offences under the SCA 2007, ss. 44 to 46, are laid down by s. 58. See **A5.38**.

Elements

A5.12 Section 44 of the SCA 2007 appears to create a single offence, and not separate offences of assistance and encouragement. By s. 49(2), however, 'If a person's act is capable of encouraging or assisting the commission of a number of offences, section 44 applies separately in relation to each offence that he intends to encourage or assist to be committed'. As to the *actus reus*, see also **A5.4** to **A5.7**.

The *mens rea* elements are more complex. The first (which distinguishes the s. 44 offence from that created by s. 45) is that D must specifically intend to encourage or assist in the commission of the 'anticipated offence'. That is not, however, the same thing as an intent that the offence should be committed by the person encouraged, etc. By s. 47, recklessness as to this may suffice: see **A5.13**. Section 44(2) states that a consequence is not intended merely because it was foreseeable; but that is trite law, since the CJA 1967, s. 8, has for many years laid down such a rule (see **A2.34**). The explanatory notes to s. 44 suggest that s. 44(2) (and s. 47(7)(b)) were meant to distinguish between direct intent (aim or purpose) on the one hand and oblique intent on the other, only the former sufficing for liability; but arguably they state a different rule. Some kind of oblique intent might therefore suffice; but if D's intent is unclear it would probably be easier to charge D under s. 45 or s. 46.

A5.13 **Proof of *Mens Rea*** Sections 44 to 46 must be read in accordance with s. 47, which lays down various rules as to proof of *mens rea*.

Serious Crime Act 2007, s. 47

(1) ...
(2) If it is alleged under section 44(1)(b) that a person (D) intended to encourage or assist the commission of an offence, it is sufficient to prove that he intended to encourage or assist the doing of an act which would amount to the commission of that offence.
(3) [See **A5.22**]
(4) [See **A5.29**]
(5) In proving for the purposes of this section whether an act is one which, if done, would amount to the commission of an offence—
  (a) if the offence is one requiring proof of fault, it must be proved that—
    (i) D believed that, were the act to be done, it would be done with that fault;
    (ii) D was reckless as to whether or not it would be done with that fault; or
    (iii) D's state of mind was such that, were he to do it, it would be done with that fault;
  and
  (b) if the offence is one requiring proof of particular circumstances or consequences (or both), it must be proved that—
    (i) D believed that, were the act to be done, it would be done in those circumstances or with those consequences; or
    (ii) D was reckless as to whether or not it would be done in those circumstances or with those consequences.
(6) For the purposes of subsection (5)(a)(iii), D is to be assumed to be able to do the act in question.
(7) In the case of an offence under section 44—
  (a) subsection (5)(b)(i) is to be read as if the reference to 'D believed' were a reference to 'D intended or believed'; but
  (b) D is not to be taken to have intended that an act would be done in particular circumstances or with particular consequences merely because its being done in those circumstances or with those consequences was a foreseeable consequence of his act of encouragement or assistance.
(8) Reference in this section to the doing of an act includes reference to—
  (a) a failure to act;
  (b) the continuation of an act that has already begun;
  (c) an attempt to do an act (except an act amounting to the commission of the offence of attempting to commit another offence).
(9) ...

By s. 47(2), D need not 'intend' that the act encouraged or assisted should be committed in circumstances that render it criminal, or that it should result in consequences that render it criminal; but to be guilty of any of the offences in Part 2 D must believe or be reckless as to those matters (s. 47(5)(b)). D does not, for example, encourage E to rape V unless D is at least reckless as to the possibility that sex would occur without V's consent; and D cannot be guilty of assisting E to commit murder if it never occurs to D that E might unlawfully kill someone. But ignorance of the law cannot be a defence, so it does not matter whether D knew that the act encouraged was, in the circumstances, an offence. **A5.14**

Section 47(5)(a) represents a departure from the law governing incitement. At common law, D did not incite E to commit an offence if D's plan was merely to use E as an innocent agent (this was the point that the Court of Appeal intended to make in *Curr* [1968] 2 QB 944 under the old law) but under s. 47(5)(a)(iii) it may suffice that D has *mens rea*, even if D knows that E has none. Section 47(6) ensures that D's own capacity to commit the 'anticipated offence' is not an issue. If, for example, D encourages E, a company director, to publish a materially false statement on behalf of E's company, D may be guilty of encouraging the commission by E of an offence under the Theft Act 1968, s. 19 (see **B6.15**), if D knows the statement to be false and seeks to deceive company creditors, etc.. It would not matter that E honestly believed the statement to be true or that D (not being an officer of the company) was personally incapable of committing the s. 19 offence.

The new law may apply less strictly to those who plan to commit an offence than to those who merely offer assistance or encouragement. If, for example, D1 declares an intention to burn down V's house, and D2 hands over some matches for that purpose, D2 will at once become guilty of encouraging or assisting an offence; but in the absence of a conspiracy D1 will not at that stage be guilty of any offence; and must do something more to incur any criminal liability.

This statement must, however, be qualified in one respect. If D1 *intentionally* encourages D2 to provide assistance or encouragement (e.g., by requesting or demanding help or support) D1 may personally commit an offence under s. 44 of the Act. As explained at **A5.32**, however, any 'doubly inchoate' offence must be committed with intent: such liability cannot arise under s. 45 or 46.

Defence of 'Acting Reasonably'

A5.15 Serious Crime Act 2007, s. 50

(1) A person is not guilty of an offence under this Part if he proves—
  (a) that he knew certain circumstances existed; and
  (b) that it was reasonable for him to act as he did in those circumstances.
(2) A person is not guilty of an offence under this Part if he proves—
  (a) that he believed certain circumstances to exist;
  (b) that his belief was reasonable; and
  (c) that it was reasonable for him to act as he did in the circumstances as he believed them to be.
(3) Factors to be considered in determining whether it was reasonable for a person to act as he did include—
  (a) the seriousness of the anticipated offence (or, in the case of an offence under section 46, the offences specified in the indictment);
  (b) any purpose for which he claims to have been acting;
  (c) any authority by which he claims to have been acting.

No indication is given in the Act or notes for guidance as to what conduct is likely to fit within the s. 50 defence. The Law Commission's original proposal was that the defence would not be open to those charged under s. 44, but only to those whose behaviour might unintentionally encourage others to break the law. For example, a TV crew covering a riot may become aware that their presence is encouraging some rioters to intensify their actions. The Commission proposed that the TV crew would avoid liability for this if they could prove that their actions were reasonable. As it is, it may be open to D to argue that it was 'reasonable' for D to encourage E to commit a serious crime with the intent that E should commit it. A possible beneficiary of this defence might be an undercover journalist or member of the security service engaged in entrapping and unmasking an offender, although s. 50 would not prevent such a person incurring liability as a secondary party to any crime actually committed by the person entrapped. See *Hardwicke* [2001] Crim LR 220; and in the context of corruption see also *Smith* [1960] 2 QB 423.

There may be argument as to whether the reverse burden of proof imposed by s. 50 is compliant with the ECHR, Article 6. If there is no doubt that 'certain circumstances existed' and the court would be minded to consider D's actions wholly reasonable in those circumstances, ought there to be any risk of the defence failing merely because it is not clear whether D actually knew of those circumstances? Arguably D deserves the benefit of any reasonable doubt in such a case; but s. 50 denies this.

Potential Victims of 'Protective Offences'

A5.16 Serious Crime Act 2007, s. 51

(1) In the case of protective offences, a person does not commit an offence under this Part by reference to such an offence if—
  (a) he falls within the protected category; and
  (b) he is the person in respect of whom the protective offence was committed or would have been if it had been committed.
(2) 'Protective offence' means an offence that exists (wholly or in part) for the protection of a particular category of persons ('the protected category').

As the notes for guidance make clear, this provision is designed to give effect to the so-called '*Tyrell* principle' which also applies in respect of conspiracy and secondary participation, although its exact limits in those contexts are not wholly clear (*Gnango* [2011] UKSC 59, [2012] 1 AC 827 at [49]). Underage children clearly fall within a protected category in respect of sex offences that may be committed against them. Similarly, D commits no offence under s. 44 by begging E for help in committing suicide, even though D is thereby encouraging E to commit an offence under the Suicide Act 1961, s. 2 (see **B1.140**).

ENCOURAGING OR ASSISTING AN OFFENCE BELIEVING IT WILL BE COMMITTED

Serious Crime Act 2007, s. 45 **A5.17**

A person commits an offence if—
(a) he does an act capable of encouraging or assisting the commission of an offence; and
(b) he believes—
   (i) that the offence will be committed; and
   (ii) that his act will encourage or assist its commission.

Jurisdiction and Procedure

The mode of trial for an offence under the SCA 2007, s. 45, is to be determined as if D had been charged with committing the 'anticipated offence'. If this was an offence triable either way, the s. 45 offence is triable either way (s. 55). If tried on indictment, it is a class 3 offence. As to restrictions on the institution of proceedings in certain cases, see **A5.35**. As to alternative verdicts, see **A5.37**. As to acts done wholly or partly abroad, or with a view to encouraging or assisting the commission of offences abroad, see **A5.33**. **A5.18**

Indictment

Statement of Offence **A5.19**

[Encouraging or] assisting an offence, believing it will be committed, contrary to section 45 of the Serious Crime Act 2007.

Particulars of Offence

A on or about the ... day of ... supplied B with keys to a house belong to C believing that B would commit a burglary of that house and that the keys would assist him to do so.

Sentencing

The penalties for offences under the SCA 2007, ss. 44 to 46, are laid down by s. 58. See **A5.38**. **A5.20**

Elements

Section 45 of the SCA 2007 apparently creates a single offence, not separate offences of assistance and encouragement. By s. 49(2)(b), however, s. 45 'applies separately in relation to each offence that [D] believes will be encouraged or assisted to be committed'. As to the *actus reus*, see **A5.4** to **A5.7**. **A5.21**

Mens Rea Section 47(5) and (6) of the SCA 2007 apply to offences under s. 45 as they apply to offences under s. 44 (see **A5.13**); but s. 47(3) applies in place of s. 47(2). **A5.22**

Serious Crime Act 2007, s. 47

(3) If it is alleged under section 45(b) that a person (D) believed that an offence would be committed and that his act would encourage or assist its commission, it is sufficient to prove that he believed—
   (a) that an act would be done which would amount to the commission of that offence; and
   (b) that his act would encourage or assist the doing of that act.

Section 45 does not make it an offence for D to do something, fearing or suspecting that it may possibly assist or encourage another person (or persons) to commit an offence. To be guilty under s. 45, D must positively believe that the conduct in question will indeed be committed, or that it will be committed if certain conditions are met (s. 49(7)). If D has this positive belief and if D's conduct is capable of providing such encouragement or assistance, it does not then matter if there was never any likelihood of the offence being committed by the person encouraged or assisted. But s. 47(5) applies as it does to a s. 44 offence, so recklessness on D's part as to the circumstances or consequences of the act in question, or of the fault element required for it, may still suffice (see **A5.13**).

Defences etc.

A5.23 The SCA 2007, s. 50, creates a defence of 'acting reasonably' (see **A5.15**) and the potential victims of 'protective offences' are also exempt from liability by virtue of s. 51 (see **A5.16**).

ENCOURAGING OR ASSISTING OFFENCES BELIEVING ONE OR MORE WILL BE COMMITTED

A5.24 **Serious Crime Act 2007, s. 46**

(1) A person commits an offence if—
  (a) he does an act capable of encouraging or assisting the commission of one or more of a number of offences; and
  (b) he believes—
    (i) that one or more of those offences will be committed (but has no belief as to which); and
    (ii) that his act will encourage or assist the commission of one or more of them.
(2) It is immaterial for the purposes of subsection (1)(b)(ii) whether the person has any belief as to which offence will be encouraged or assisted.
(3) If a person is charged with an offence under subsection (1)—
  (a) the indictment must specify the offences alleged to be the 'number of offences' mentioned in paragraph (a) of that subsection; but
  (b) nothing in paragraph (a) requires all the offences potentially comprised in that number to be specified.
(4) In relation to an offence under this section, reference in this Part to the offences specified in the indictment is to the offences specified by virtue of subsection (3)(a).

Jurisdiction and Procedure

A5.25 An offence under the SCA 2007, s. 46, is triable on indictment (s. 55(2)). It is a class 3 offence. As to restrictions on the institution of proceedings in certain cases, see **A5.35**. As to alternative verdicts, see **A5.37**. As to jurisdiction over acts done wholly or partly abroad, or with a view to encouraging or assisting the commission of offences abroad, see **A5.33**.

Indictment

A5.26 *Statement of Offence*

Intentionally assisting offences, believing one or more will be committed, contrary to section 46(1) of the Serious Crime Act 2007.

Particulars of Offence

A ... between the ... day of ... and the ... day of ..., supplied an ex-army bayonet to X, such supply being capable of assisting two or more possible offences by X, namely robbery, assault with intent to rob, or malicious wounding, believing that at least one such offence would be committed by X and that the bayonet supplied would assist him in its commission.

The indictment above follows *Sadique* [2013] EWCA Crim 1150, [2013] 4 All ER 924, in which the Court of Appeal revised its guidance as to the drafting of indictments for offences under the SCA 2007, s. 46(1). In particular, the Court accepted academic criticism of guidance previously given in *S* [2011] EWCA Crim 2872, [2012] 2 All ER 793 (see the 2013 edition of this work). This called for separate counts for each allegedly contemplated offence to which

s. 46 might apply. Separate counts were said to be necessary in order to avoid challenges based on uncertainty of scope that might otherwise be brought under the ECHR, Article 7, but this made it difficult to see what s. 46 usefully added to the offence created by s. 45 of the Act. Moreover, the guidance given in *S* was arguably in conflict with s. 46 itself, because a conviction on any one count was said to be possible only if D was proved to have believed that the offence in question *would* be committed, whereas an express element of the s. 46 offence is that D 'has no belief as to which' of the contemplated offences will actually be committed.

The Court in *Sadique* considered that the guidance in *S* was *obiter* and not strictly binding upon them. Lord Judge CJ noted that s. 46 was intended to cover the kind of scenario that featured in *DPP for Northern Ireland v Maxwell* [1978] 3 All ER 1140 (see **A4.1**) and added (at [34]):

> In our judgment the ingredients of the s. 46 offence, and the ancillary provisions, and s. 58(4)–(7) in particular, underline that an indictment charging a s. 46 offence by reference to one or more offences is permissible, and covers the precise situation for which the legislation provides.

Such an indictment is not bad for duplicity, nor defective for uncertainty. It achieves the objective of every count in any indictment, i.e. to give sufficient indication to D of the criminal conduct alleged (*Sadique* at [36]).

Where there is an issue as to whether D believed that only one of the specified offences would be committed (e.g., the less serious of the two) it may be helpful to combine a count under s. 46 with two or more counts under s. 45 (*Sadique* at [39]).

Sentencing

The penalties for offences under the SCA 2007, ss. 44 to 46, are laid down by s. 58. See **A5.38**. **A5.27**

Elements

As the Court of Appeal noted in *Sadique* [2013] EWCA Crim 1150, [2013] 4 All ER 924, s. 46 **A5.28**
provides for the 'relatively common case' where D contemplates that one of a range of offences might be committed as a result of D's encouragement or assistance. It apparently creates a single offence, not separate offences of assistance and encouragement. By s. 49(2)(b), however, s. 45 'applies separately in relation to each offence that [D] believes will be encouraged or assisted to be committed'. As to the *actus reus*, see **A5.4** to **A5.7**. In *S* [2012] EWCA Crim 2872, [2012] 2 All ER 793 and again in *Sadique* the Court of Appeal rejected submissions that the offence created by s. 46 is too vague and uncertain to be compatible with the ECHR, Article 6 or 7.

Mens Rea Section 47(5) and (6) of the SCA 2007 apply to offences under s. 46 as they apply to **A5.29**
offences under s. 44 (see **A5.13**); but s. 47(4) applies in place of s. 47(2); and s. 48 makes further provision as to what must be proved in order to establish a s. 46 offence.

Serious Crime Act 2007, ss. 47 and 48

47.—(4) If it is alleged under section 46(1)(b) that a person (D) believed that one or more of a number of offences would be committed and that his act would encourage or assist the commission of one or more of them, it is sufficient to prove that he believed—
- (a) that one or more of a number of acts would be done which would amount to the commission of one or more of those offences; and
- (b) that his act would encourage or assist the doing of one or more of those acts.

48.—(1) This section makes further provision about the application of section 47 to an offence under section 46.
- (2) It is sufficient to prove the matters mentioned in section 47(5) by reference to one offence only.
- (3) The offence or offences by reference to which those matters are proved must be one of the offences specified in the indictment.
- (4) Subsection (3) does not affect any enactment or rule of law under which a person charged with one offence may be convicted of another and is subject to section 57.

A5.30 By s. 46, if D, for example, supplies a gun requested by E, believing that E must need it either to commit a robbery or to commit a murder, but has no idea which of those offences E is considering, D can still be convicted of encouraging or assisting E to commit one of those offences. Moreover, D's punishment may then be determined by reference to the more serious of those offences. D may thus be guilty of assisting murder even though that is not really the offence that E had in mind. Indeed, it makes no difference if it transpires, to D's surprise, that E never had any intention of committing either offence.

Section 46 does not make it an offence for D to do something, merely fearing or suspecting that it may possibly encourage or assist another person (or persons) to commit offences. To be guilty under s. 46, D must positively (if perhaps wrongly) believe that some such offence will indeed be committed, or will be committed if certain conditions are met (s. 49(7)).

ENCOURAGING OR ASSISTING ANOTHER PERSON TO COMMIT AN INCHOATE OFFENCE

A5.31 **Serious Crime Act 2007, s. 49**

(4) In reckoning whether—
  (a) for the purposes of section 45, an act is capable of encouraging or assisting the commission of an offence; or
  (b) for the purposes of section 46, an act is capable of encouraging or assisting the commission of one or more of a number of offences;

offences under this Part and listed offences are to be disregarded.

(5) 'Listed offence' means—
  (a) in England and Wales, an offence listed in Part 1, 2 or 3 of Schedule 3 ...

A5.32 The offences listed in sch. 3, parts 1 to 3, include those under the OAPA 1861, s. 4; the Official Secrets Act 1920, s. 7; the MDA 1971, ss. 19 and 20; the Immigration Act 1971, ss. 25 and 25B; the Computer Misuse Act 1990, s. 3A(1), (2) and (3); the Terrorism Act 2000, s. 59; the Terrorism Act 2006, ss. 1(2), 2(1), 5, 6(1) and (2); the Perjury Act 1911, s. 7(2); the CLA 1967, ss. 4(1) and 5(1); the CLA 1977, ss. 1(1), 5(2) and (3); the CAA 1981, s. 1(1); the Public Order Act 1986, ss. 12(6), 13(9) and 14(6); the Cluster Munitions (Prohibitions) Act 2010, s. 2 and the SCA 2015, s. 45. Also covered are offences of attempt under special statutory provisions (see the CAA 1981, s. 3).

The SCA 2007, s. 49(4), ensures that it is not an offence to do an act that may encourage or assist another person to commit some other inchoate offence unless the original act is committed with the specific intention of encouraging or assisting its commission. Encouraging or assisting the commission of an inchoate offence may thus be prosecuted under s. 44 (which requires proof of such intent) but not under s. 45 or 46.

Under s. 44, D may incur liability by (for example) intentionally encouraging E to solicit F to commit murder (contrary to the OAPA 1861, s. 4) or by asking G to assist D in committing an offence. Inviting H to join a criminal conspiracy would also suffice.

JURISDICTION AND PROCEDURE

Offences with Foreign Elements

A5.33 **Serious Crime Act 2007, s. 52**

(1) If a person (D) knows or believes that what he anticipates might take place wholly or partly in England or Wales, he may be guilty of an offence under section 44, 45 or 46 no matter where he was at any relevant time.

(2) If it is not proved that D knows or believes that what he anticipates might take place wholly or partly in England or Wales, he is not guilty of an offence under section 44, 45 or 46 unless paragraph 1, 2 or 3 of schedule 4 applies.

(3) A reference in this section (and in any of those paragraphs) to what D anticipates is to be read as follows—
(a) in relation to an offence under section 44 or 45, it refers to the act which would amount to the commission of the anticipated offence;
(b) in relation to an offence under section 46, it refers to an act which would amount to the commission of any of the offences specified in the indictment.
(4) [Northern Ireland.]
(5) Nothing in this section or Schedule 4 restricts the operation of any enactment by virtue of which an act constituting an offence under this Part is triable under the law of England and Wales...

Where s. 52(1) applies, the position is relatively simple. D's conduct anywhere in the world may amount to an offence under English law, if D intends or believes that an act 'which would amount to the commission of the anticipated offence' (or offences) *will* be committed (as is required by ss. 44 to 46) and that it *might* be committed wholly or partly in England and Wales. In all other cases, s. 52(2) requires reference to be made to sch. 4. **A5.34**

Schedule 4, para. 1, applies where D acts wholly or partly within England and Wales, and the act D anticipates would still be punishable as an offence under English law, even if committed abroad (e.g., D encourages E, a British citizen, to commit murder on land outside the UK: a murder punishable under English law by virtue of the OAPA 1861, s. 9). If para. 1 does not apply, para. 2 applies where D acts wholly or partly within England and Wales and, although what D anticipates might take place outside England and Wales, it would be an offence under the law applicable in that place. If D wishes to argue that the anticipated offence was *not* punishable under local law, the issue must be raised for determination by the judge in accordance with the procedure set out in para. 2(2) to (4). Failing this, criminality under local law will be presumed. Finally, sch. 4, para. 3, applies where there may be no proven connection with England and Wales, but D would be liable to prosecution for an extraterritorial offence under English law if D were to commit the anticipated offence in the place or country in question.

Where the offence is punishable only by virtue of sch. 4, proceedings may not be instituted except by or with the consent of the A-G (s. 53) but, since the Bribery Act 2010 came into force on 1 July 2011 (see **B15.1**), this does not apply to offences of encouraging or assisting bribery (as to which see the SCA 2007, s. 54(1) and (2) (see **A5.35**) and the Bribery Act 2010, sch. 1, para. 13).

Institution of Proceedings etc.

Serious Crime Act 2007, s. 54 **A5.35**

(1) Any provision to which this section applies has effect with respect to an offence under this Part as it has effect with respect to the anticipated offence.
(2) This section applies to provisions made by or under an enactment (whenever passed or made) that—
(a) provide that proceedings may not be instituted or carried on otherwise than by, or on behalf or with the consent of, any person (including any provision which also makes exceptions to the prohibition);
(b) confer power to institute proceedings;
(c) confer power to seize and detain property;
(d) confer a power of forfeiture, including any power to deal with anything liable to be forfeited.
(3) In relation to an offence under section 46—
(a) the reference in subsection (1) to the anticipated offence is to be read as a reference to any offence specified in the indictment; and
(b) each of the offences specified in the indictment must be an offence in respect of which the prosecutor has power to institute proceedings.
(4) Any consent to proceedings required as a result of this section is in addition to any consent required by section 53.
(5) No proceedings for an offence under this Part are to be instituted against a person providing information society services who is established in an EEA State other than the United Kingdom unless the derogation condition is satisfied.
(6) The derogation condition is satisfied where the institution of proceedings—
(a) is necessary to pursue the public interest objective;

(b) relates to an information society service that prejudices that objective or presents a serious and grave risk of prejudice to it; and
(c) is proportionate to that objective.
(7) The public interest objective is public policy.
(8) In this section 'information society services' has the same meaning as in section 34, and subsection (7) of that section applies for the purposes of this section as it applies for the purposes of that section.

Section 54(5) to (8) give effect to the EC E-Commerce Directive (2000/31/EC [2000] OJ L178/1), which governs the circumstances in which an internet (or 'information society') service provider may be prosecuted for offences in a State other than the one in which it is established.

Persons who may be Perpetrators or Encouragers etc.

A5.36 **Serious Crime Act 2007, s. 56**

(1) In proceedings for an offence under this Part ('the inchoate offence') the defendant may be convicted if—
(a) it is proved that he must have committed the inchoate offence or the anticipated offence; but
(b) it is not proved which of those offences he committed.
(2) For the purposes of this section, a person is not to be treated as having committed the anticipated offence merely because he aided, abetted, counselled or procured its commission.
(3) In relation to an offence under section 46, a reference in this section to the anticipated offence is to be read as a reference to an offence specified in the indictment.

This provision enables D to be convicted on a charge of committing an inchoate offence under ss. 44 to 46 even if it is not clear whether D assisted or encouraged the anticipated offence, on the one hand, or actually committed it, on the other. As to the position where D must be guilty either of committing an offence or of aiding, abetting, counselling or procuring it, see *Giannetto* [1997] 1 Cr App R 1 and **A4.1**.

Alternative Verdicts and Guilty Pleas

A5.37 **Serious Crime Act 2007, s. 57**

(1) If in proceedings on indictment for an offence under section 44 or 45 a person is not found guilty of that offence by reference to the specified offence, he may be found guilty of that offence by reference to an alternative offence.
(2) If in proceedings for an offence under section 46 a person is not found guilty of that offence by reference to any specified offence, he may be found guilty of that offence by reference to one or more alternative offences.
(3) If in proceedings for an offence under section 46 a person is found guilty of the offence by reference to one or more specified offences, he may also be found guilty of it by reference to one or more other alternative offences.
(4) For the purposes of this section, an offence is an alternative offence if—
(a) it is an offence of which, on a trial on indictment for the specified offence, an accused may be found guilty; or
(b) it is an indictable offence, or one to which section 40 of the Criminal Justice Act 1988 applies (power to include count for common assault etc. in indictment), and the condition in subsection (5) is satisfied.
(5) The condition is that the allegations in the indictment charging the person with the offence under this Part amount to or include (expressly or by implication) an allegation of that offence by reference to it.
(6) Subsection (4)(b) does not apply if the specified offence, or any of the specified offences, is murder or treason.
(7) In the application of subsection (5) to proceedings for an offence under section 44, the allegations in the indictment are to be taken to include an allegation of that offence by reference to the offence of attempting to commit the specified offence.
(8) Section 49(4) applies to an offence which is an alternative offence in relation to a specified offence as it applies to that specified offence.
(9) In this section—
(a) in relation to a person charged with an offence under section 44 or 45, 'the specified offence' means the offence specified in the indictment as the one alleged to be the anticipated offence;

(b) in relation to a person charged with an offence under section 46, 'specified offence' means an offence specified in the indictment (within the meaning of subsection (4) of that section), and related expressions are to be read accordingly.

(10) A person arraigned on an indictment for an offence under this Part may plead guilty to an offence of which he could be found guilty under this section on that indictment.

(11) This section applies to an indictment containing more than one count as if each count were a separate indictment.

(12) This section is without prejudice to—

(a) section 6(1)(b) and (3) of the Criminal Law Act 1967 . . .

Section 57 makes similar provision in relation to alternative verdicts to that which would apply in respect of the anticipated offences (see generally **D19.41** *et seq*.), subject in the case of an alleged inchoate offence under s. 45 or s. 46 to the restriction imposed by s. 49(4) (as to which see **A5.31**). If, for example, D tells E where E's enemy, V, is hiding, and is charged under s. 45 with assisting or encouraging E, believing E would murder V, the jury might perhaps not be satisfied that D believed E would go as far as to commit murder, but it would then be open to them to convict D instead of providing assistance in the belief that E would cause V grievous bodily harm with intent.

Penalties and Sentencing

Serious Crime Act 2007, s. 58 **A5.38**

(1) Subsections (2) and (3) apply if—

(a) a person is convicted of an offence under section 44 or 45; or

(b) a person is convicted of an offence under section 46 by reference to only one offence ('the reference offence').

(2) If the anticipated or reference offence is murder, he is liable to imprisonment for life.

(3) In any other case he is liable to any penalty for which he would be liable on conviction of the anticipated or reference offence.

(4) Subsections (5) to (7) apply if a person is convicted of an offence under section 46 by reference to more than one offence ('the reference offences').

(5) If one of the reference offences is murder, he is liable to imprisonment for life.

(6) If none of the reference offences is murder but one or more of them is punishable with imprisonment, he is liable—

(a) to imprisonment for a term not exceeding the maximum term provided for any one of those offences (taking the longer or the longest term as the limit for the purposes of this paragraph where the terms provided differ); or

(b) to a fine.

(7) In any other case he is liable to a fine.

(8) Subsections (3), (6) and (7) are subject to any contrary provision made by or under—

(a) an Act; . . .

(9) In the case of an offence triable either way, the reference in subsection (6) to the maximum term provided for that offence is a reference to the maximum term so provided on conviction on indictment.

There are no published sentencing guidelines directly applicable to these offences, but in *Watling* [2012] EWCA Crim 2894, [2013] 2 Cr App R (S) 37 (256), the Court of Appeal said:

> Parliament has . . . specifically provided that those who . . . are guilty of offences under section 44 and 45 . . ., are liable to the maximum sentence available for the full anticipated offence if it had been committed (see section 58(1)). It is therefore highly relevant to consider the potential scale of those anticipated offences.

In *Hall* [2013] EWCA Crim 2499, [2014] Cr App R (S) 20 (136), the Court of Appeal could see no reason why that should not apply equally to s. 46, and added:

> It is important to emphasise what was involved in the offences of which these appellants were convicted: the doing of an act which was capable of assisting in the supply of Class A drugs, and the belief that one or more such offences would be committed and that the act would assist in its commission. When those ingredients of the section 46 offence are proved or admitted, it seems to us that the appropriate sentence generally will not differ significantly, and may perhaps not differ at all, from the sentence which would have been appropriate for the anticipated offence or for conspiracy to commit the anticipated offence.

See to similar effect *Woodford* [2013] EWCA Crim 1098, [2014] 1 Cr App R (S) 32 (194).

In *Blackshaw* [2011] EWCA Crim 2312, [2012] 1 WLR 1126, one of the appellants had pleaded guilty to a s. 46 offence after using Facebook to encourage or assist the commission of offences of riot, burglary and criminal damage, and another had pleaded guilty to a s. 44 offence in which he had used Facebook to invite 400 contacts to meet up for the purpose of starting public disorder. Sentences of four years' imprisonment were upheld in each case.

PARTICIPATING IN ORGANISED CRIME

Introduction

A5.39 The SCA 2015, s. 45 (see **A5.40**), created an offence of 'participating in the criminal activities of an organised crime group'. For detailed analysis, see P Jarvis and R Earis, 'Participating in the activities of an organised crime group: the new offence' [2015] Crim LR 766.

'Participation' is defined by s. 45(2) in such a way as to include not only participation in actual criminal activities, but also participation in activities that D knows or believes may aid the group in the commission of future offences. In that sense it may operate as an inchoate offence, but the new offence also overlaps to some extent with the rules governing secondary liability in respect of substantive offences (as to which see generally **A4**).

'Criminal activities' for the purposes of s. 45 are those which carry a maximum sentence of at least seven years (if committed within England and Wales) and must be carried on by an organised crime group of three or more persons with a view to obtaining (directly or indirectly) any gain or benefit, although not necessarily a financial one. The group might, for example, be concerned with the organised sexual abuse of children, rather than with material profit.

If carried on outside England and Wales, the activities of the group must satisfy a double criminality test (i.e. they must be of a kind that would be punishable by imprisonment for at least seven years if committed in England and Wales, as well as being punishable under local law). The offence is not, however, an extra-territorial one, because D's own participation in such criminal activities must (by s. 45(7)(b)) include at least one act or omission in England and Wales.

Definition

A5.40 **Serious Crime Act 2015, s. 45**

(1) A person who participates in the criminal activities of an organised crime group commits an offence.
(2) For this purpose, a person participates in the criminal activities of an organised crime group if the person takes part in any activities that the person knows or reasonably suspects—
  (a) are criminal activities of an organised crime group, or
  (b) will help an organised crime group to carry on criminal activities.
(3) 'Criminal activities' are activities within subsection (4) or (5) that are carried on with a view to obtaining (directly or indirectly) any gain or benefit.
(4) Activities are within this subsection if—
  (a) they are carried on in England or Wales, and
  (b) they constitute an offence in England and Wales punishable on conviction on indictment with imprisonment for a term of 7 years or more.
(5) Activities are within this subsection if—
  (a) they are carried on outside England and Wales,
  (b) they constitute an offence under the law in force of the country where they are carried on, and
  (c) they would constitute an offence in England and Wales of the kind mentioned in subsection (4)(b) if the activities were carried on in England and Wales.
(6) 'Organised crime group' means a group that—
  (a) has as its purpose, or as one of its purposes, the carrying on of criminal activities, and
  (b) consists of three or more persons who act, or agree to act, together to further that purpose.
(7) For a person to be guilty of an offence under this section it is not necessary—
  (a) for the person to know any of the persons who are members of the organised crime group,

(b) for all of the acts or omissions comprising participation in the group's criminal activities to take place in England and Wales (so long as at least one of them does), or
(c) for the gain or benefit referred to in subsection (3) to be financial in nature.

Defence

Serious Crime Act 2015, s. 45 **A5.41**

(8) It is a defence for a person charged with an offence under this section to prove that the person's participation was necessary for a purpose related to the prevention or detection of crime.

The specific defence provided by s. 45(8), which carries a reverse burden of proof, is additional to any general defences (such as duress) that might be available.

Sentence and Procedure

Offences under the SCA 2015, s. 45, are triable only on indictment, and are punishable by up to five years' imprisonment (s. 45(9)). There is no definitive sentencing guideline, but in *Crimes* [2019] EWCA Crim 1108, Holroyde LJ said (at [26]): **A5.42**

> Participating in the criminal activities of an organised crime group is by its nature a serious offence. With regard to the five purposes of sentencing identified in section 142 of the Criminal Justice Act 2003, sentencers dealing with such offences will, in our view, generally wish to focus on punishment, protection of the public and the reduction of crime by deterrence. The offence is by its nature an adjunct to other criminal activity; but that does not mean that the offender necessarily plays only a minor role in the commission of the offence.

In *Crimes*, D stole cars for use by professional criminals. He did not necessarily know what they were to be used for, but one was then used in connection with a shooting. The seriousness of the offence therefore went beyond the seriousness of stealing cars for their financial value and a sentence of 30 months was held to be within the appropriate range for such an offence. D also destroyed the vehicle used in the shooting with intent to impede the police investigation of that offence, and this was held to be more serious than a comparable case in which an offender destroys evidence relating to his own crime. A consecutive sentence based on a starting point of four years was held to be only slightly excessive in the circumstances.

CONSPIRACY GENERALLY

Common Law and Statutory Conspiracies

There are at least three distinct forms of conspiracy under English law, namely conspiracy to defraud at common law, conspiracy to commit a criminal offence contrary to the CLA 1977, s. 1, and conspiracy to commit abroad an offence under foreign law (to which the CLA 1977, s. 1, applies by virtue of s. 1A). The first two forms overlap because a conspiracy to defraud may also involve a statutory conspiracy, in which case the CJA 1987, s. 12, allows the prosecution to charge either offence (see **A5.65**). The Court of Appeal referred in *Dosanjh* [2013] EWCA Crim 2366, [2014] 1 WLR 1780 to a 'common law conspiracy to cheat the public revenue', but clearly meant a conspiracy under s. 1 to commit the common-law offence of cheating the revenue. **A5.43**

Two other forms of common-law conspiracy require brief consideration, namely conspiracy to corrupt public morals and conspiracy to outrage public decency; but their survival as separate forms of conspiracy is extremely doubtful. Section 5(3) of the 1977 Act purports to preserve such conspiracies as common-law offences, but only:

> ... if and in so far as [they] may be committed by entering into an agreement to engage in conduct which—
> (a) tends to corrupt public morals or outrages public decency; but
> (b) would not amount to or involve the commission of an offence if carried out by a single person otherwise than in pursuance of an agreement.

If, in other words, a conspiracy to outrage public decency involves an agreement to commit a substantive criminal offence, it can be charged *only* as a conspiracy under s. 1 of the Act. No overlap with the common-law offence is possible. When the 1977 Act was drafted, it was considered unclear whether any substantive offences of outraging public decency or corrupting public morals existed, and s. 5(3) was intended to preserve the effect of the notorious decisions of the House of Lords in *Shaw v DPP* [1962] AC 220 and *Knuller (Publishing, Printing and Promotions) Ltd v DPP* [1973] AC 435, lest statutory conspiracy failed to cover conduct of the kind dealt with in those cases. It is now clear that outraging public decency is indeed a substantive offence at common law (see **B3.350** *et seq.*). Agreements to do acts amounting to that offence must accordingly be charged as statutory conspiracies.

Authority in respect of corrupting public morals is sparse, but the Court of Criminal Appeal in *Shaw* held that it did indeed exist as a substantive common-law offence, and the House of Lords did not reject that view (although it did not form part of their *ratio decidendi*). It seems probable, therefore, that this form of common-law conspiracy has also been subsumed within the statutory offence, and that nothing at all has been preserved by s. 5(3). In any event, there has been no reported prosecution for this form of conspiracy since the 1977 Act came into force, and it does not warrant further discussion.

STATUTORY CONSPIRACY

Definition

A5.44 **Criminal Law Act 1977, s. 1**

(1) Subject to the following provisions of this Part of this Act, if a person agrees with any other person or persons that a course of conduct will be pursued which, if the agreement is carried out in accordance with their intentions, either—
  (a) will necessarily amount to or involve the commission of any offence or offences by one or more of the parties to the agreement; or
  (b) would do so but for the existence of facts which render the commission of the offence or any of the offences impossible,

  he is guilty of conspiracy to commit the offence or offences in question.

(2) Where liability for any offence may be incurred without knowledge on the part of the person committing it of any particular fact or circumstance necessary for the commission of the offence, a person shall nevertheless not be guilty of conspiracy to commit that offence by virtue of subsection (1) above unless he and at least one other party to the agreement intend or know that the fact or circumstance shall or will exist at the time when the conduct constituting the offence is to take place.

(3) [Repealed.]

(4) In this Part of this Act 'offence' means an offence triable in England and Wales.

Agreements relating to acts involving summary offences not punishable by imprisonment must be disregarded if the acts are to be done in contemplation or furtherance of a trade dispute (Trade Union and Labour Relations (Consolidation) Act 1992, s. 242).

Indictment

A5.45 *Statement of Offence*

Conspiracy to commit criminal damage contrary to section 1(2) of the Criminal Law Act 1977.

Particulars of Offence

A [and B] on or about the ... day of ... conspired together [and/or with persons unknown] to damage heavy goods vehicles belonging to V plc, with intent to endanger life, contrary to s. 1(2) of the Criminal Damage Act 1971.

A single agreement (and a single count of conspiracy) may embrace conduct involving several offences, without being bad for duplicity (*Roberts* [1998] 1 Cr App R 441; *Greenfield* [1973] 3 All ER 1050; *Taylor* [2001] EWCA Crim 1044, [2002] Crim LR 205; see also **D11.35**). It may in some cases be good practice to use two or more separate counts (*Cooke* [1986] AC 909) but, as the Court of

Appeal noted in *Shillam* [2013] EWCA Crim 160 at [19] and reiterated in *SFO v Papachristos* [2014] EWCA Crim 1863 at [57], this might sometimes be an unnecessary complication:

> The evidence may prove the existence of a conspiracy of narrower scope and involving fewer people than the prosecution originally alleged, in which case it is not intrinsically wrong for the jury to return guilty verdicts accordingly, but it is always necessary that for two or more persons to be convicted of a single conspiracy each of them must be proved to have shared a common purpose or design.

In *Ali* [2011] EWCA Crim 1260, [2011] 3 All ER 1071, the indictment at the initial trial of eight alleged Islamist terrorists was amended to include counts both for conspiracy to murder persons unknown and for conspiracy to commit such murders through the destruction of trans-atlantic airliners. This was because an issue arose as to whether some of the defendants might only have agreed to commit murder on a smaller scale and by different methods, albeit that the proposed substantive offence (murder of persons unknown) would be the same in each case. The Court of Appeal held (at [37]): **A5.46**

> It is not permissible to put into an indictment an alternative factual basis which makes no difference to the offence committed whether it is for the purpose of enabling a jury to decide an issue of fact or for any other purpose. The judge must resolve the factual issues which are material to sentencing if the offences are the same; in limited circumstances, the judge may ask the jury a specific question.

The Court was nevertheless satisfied (at [52]) that the indictment in this case addressed two 'distinctly different agreements as to the method and scale of the murder to be carried out' which meant that the inclusion of multiple counts was entirely lawful, albeit not essential.

Whether an indictment for conspiracy alleges one ulterior offence or several, it is important that it properly identifies the individual offences in question, in accordance with the Indictments Act 1915, s. 3(1), and what is now CrimPR 10.2 (*Roberts* [1998] 1 Cr App R 441 at pp. 449–50, and see Supplement, **R10.2**). Where, for example, an indictment charges a conspiracy to commit criminal damage, it should make it clear whether this refers to the basic offence (contrary to the Criminal Damage Act 1971, s. 1(1)) or to the aggravated offence (contrary to s. 1(2)). See also *Booth* [1999] Crim LR 144 (criminal damage or arson) and *Griffin* [2018] EWCA Crim 2538, [2019] 1 Cr App R (S) 37 (250) (simple burglary or domestic burglary). As to 'either/or' conspiracies, in which the parties agree to a course of conduct which will clearly involve the commission of some offence but cannot be certain which offence this will be, see *Hussain* [2002] EWCA Crim 6; *Singh* [2003] EWCA Crim 3712 (although *Singh* was overruled on other grounds in *Saik* [2006] UKHL 18, [2007] 1 AC 18) and *Suchedina* [2006] EWCA Crim 2543, [2007] 1 Cr App R 23 (305).

An indictment for conspiracy must not be misleading. An indictment alleging that the defendants conspired to supply drugs to 'another' cannot sensibly apply to a case in which the intended recipient was one of the conspirators (*Jackson* (1999) *The Times*, 13 May 1999; *Drew* [2000] 1 Cr App R 91). **A5.47**

A conspiracy count may be joined to substantive counts in an indictment where the facts warrant it and the interests of justice demand it, but as the Court of Appeal warned in *Shillam* [2013] EWCA Crim 160 (at [25]):

> ... the prosecution should always think carefully, before making use of the law of conspiracy, how to formulate the conspiracy charge or charges and whether a substantive offence or offences would be more appropriate.

As to the selection of charges generally, see P Jarvis and M Bisgrove, 'The use and abuse of conspiracy' [2014] Crim LR 261. See also CrimPD II, para. 10A.3 (see Supplement, **CPD.10A**), and **D11.96** generally.

Procedure and Sentencing

Conspiracy is triable only on indictment, even where it relates to a summary offence; but under the CLA 1977, s. 4(1), proceedings for conspiracy to commit summary offences may not be instituted except by or with the consent of the DPP. Where a prosecution for a substantive offence may only be brought by or with leave of the DPP or A-G, this is also required in **A5.48** respect of a charge of conspiracy to commit it (s. 4(2) and (3)). As to consent to proceedings brought by virtue of s. 1A, see s. 4(5) and **A5.61**. As to the form and timing of consent and the consequences of failure to comply with a s. 4 requirement, see *Welsh* [2015] EWCA Crim 906, [2016] 1 Cr App R 8 (113); *Welsh* [2015] EWCA Crim 1516, [2016] 1 Cr App R 9 (123), and **D2.17**. Where the time-limit for prosecuting a summary offence has expired, s. 4(4) provides that a prosecution for conspiracy is also barred, but this rule applies only where the substantive offence has been committed. As to the power of local authorities to prosecute for conspiracy, see *Jarrett* [1997] Crim LR 517 and *Richards* [1999] Crim LR 598.

Conspiracy to commit an offence punishable by life imprisonment (or for which the penalty is at large) is itself punishable by life imprisonment, but even in cases of conspiracy to murder, a life sentence is only discretionary (s. 3(2)). For the relevant principles relating to sentencing for conspiracy to murder, see *McNee* [2007] EWCA Crim 1529, [2008] 1 Cr App R (S) 24 (108) and *Barot* [2007] EWCA Crim 1119, [2008] 1 Cr App R (S) 31 (156).

In other cases, the maximum term of imprisonment may not exceed that for the relevant offence (or for whichever of two or more relevant offences carries the highest maximum) (s. 3(3)). Where a relevant offence is not punishable by imprisonment, a conspiracy is punishable by a fine (s. 3(1)(b)).

In *Cooke* [2017] EWCA Crim 1272, the Court of Appeal readily accepted that Sentencing Council guidelines in respect of the relevant offence must be taken into account when sentencing for conspiracy, but stated (at [15]) that where:

> ... a conspiracy rather than a substantive offence is alleged it will be important for a court to analyse carefully the position of an individual offender, if it is sentencing in those circumstances. Those involved in a conspiracy can play different roles or be involved in different ways and the court must be astute to avoid a one-size-fits-all approach to the guideline.

A conspiracy involving the actual completion of multiple offences may merit a sentence higher than that indicated in guidelines for any one substantive offence (*Hanrahan* [2017] EWCA Crim 1256) but cannot exceed the maximum for the most serious relevant offence.

In particularly grave cases of revenue fraud, it may, however, be proper to charge the alleged offenders with conspiracy to cheat the revenue (for which the maximum penalty is at large) rather than with conspiracy to commit individual offences under the Fraud Act 2006 (*Dosanjh* [2013] EWCA Crim 2366, [2014] 1 WLR 1780).

Agreement

A5.49 Agreement is the essence of conspiracy. There is no conspiracy if negotiations fail to result in agreement (*Walker* [1962] Crim LR 458) nor is there a conspiracy between A and B merely because each has conspired separately with C (*Griffiths* [1966] 1 QB 589). As Toulson LJ explained in *Shillam* [2013] EWCA Crim 160 (at [19]–[20]):

> ... for two or more persons to be convicted of a single conspiracy each of them must be proved to have a shared common purpose or design ... there must be a shared criminal purpose or design in which all have joined, rather than merely similar or parallel ones.

See also *SFO v Papachristos* [2014] EWCA Crim 1863 and *Johnson* [2020] EWCA Crim 482. It is possible, however, to have conspiracies in which some parties never meet others. These include 'chain' and 'wheel' conspiracies. In a chain conspiracy, A agrees with B, B agrees with C, C agrees with D, etc. In a wheel conspiracy, A, at the 'hub', recruits B, C and D to A's scheme (*Ardalan* [1972] 2 All ER 257). In either case, however, the alleged conspirators must each be shown to be party to a common design, and they must be aware that there is a larger scheme to which they are attaching themselves (*Meyrick* (1929) 21 Cr App R 94; *Chrastny* [1992] 1 All ER 189; *Barratt* [1996] Crim LR 495; *D* [2009] EWCA Crim 584). If B and C each believe they have their own individual agreements with A, there are two separate conspiracies, and a single count will not be valid, even if B and C are aware that A is making similar agreements with others (*Griffiths*).

Where a series of offences is committed by a group of persons over a long period, the prosecution may be tempted to proceed on the basis of a single conspiracy count, in preference to several substantive counts; but this tactic may be misconceived, because such offences are more likely to be the product of a series of agreements, and a single conspiracy may be impossible to prove (*Mehtab* [2015] EWCA Crim 1665). As to the drafting of indictments in cases involving agreements within agreements, see *Ali* [2011] EWCA Crim 1260, [2011] 3 All ER 1071 at **A5.46**.

Parties to Conspiracies and Acquittal of Other Alleged Conspirators

At least two persons must agree in order for there to be a conspiracy, although a single accused **A5.50**
may be charged and convicted, even if the identities of the fellow conspirators remain unknown. Furthermore, the CLA 1977, s. 5(8), confirms the principle established in *DPP v Shannon* [1975] AC 717, namely that acquittal of the only other alleged parties to a conspiracy (whether in the current trial or at a previous trial) need not prevent the conviction of the remaining accused, 'unless under all the circumstances of the case his conviction is inconsistent with the acquittal of the other person or persons in question'. Conviction of A and acquittal of B would be inconsistent if B is acquitted on the basis of a defence which, if true, must exonerate both, or if the evidence against each is the same (*Longman* (1980) 72 Cr App R 121); but it may be permissible to convict A on the basis of a pre-trial confession or other evidence which is not admissible against B or which does not incriminate B (cf. *Roberts* (1983) 78 Cr App R 41; *Testouri* [2003] EWCA Crim 3735, [2004] 2 Cr App R 4 (26); *Elkins* [2005] EWCA Crim 2711). It is likewise possible for A and B to be tried for conspiring with C, who has been acquitted at an earlier trial, even though it requires the prosecution to impugn or contradict the verdict at the earlier trial (*Austin* [2011] EWCA Crim 345, [2012] 1 Cr App R 24 (320)). But where D is charged with conspiring with persons who remain unidentified, proof that those other persons acted with the requisite intent may be difficult (*Thompson* [2018] EWCA Crim 2082).

As to the position where only one conspirator actually intended the agreed crime to be committed, see **A5.57**.

One or more corporations may be a party to a conspiracy (*ICR Haulage Ltd* [1944] KB 551), **A5.51**
but a company and its sole director cannot be the only parties to it because there can be no meeting of minds in such circumstances (*McDonnell* [1966] 1 QB 233). More than one human mind must be involved for there to be a conspiracy at all; but if other conspirators are involved, evidence establishing the guilty mind of a director who can be 'identified' as the directing mind and will of a corporation may still be probative of the guilt of that corporation (see *A Ltd, X, Y* [2016] EWCA Crim 1469, [2017] 1 Cr App R 1 (1) and **A6.2**), whether or not the directing mind and will is indicted as a co-conspirator or otherwise available to give evidence at trial (*Alstom Network UK Ltd* [2019] EWCA Crim 1318, [2019] 2 Cr App R 34 (417)).

Certain other combinations are excluded under s. 2(2): D cannot be guilty of statutory conspiracy if the only person(s) with whom D agrees (initially and during the currency of the agreement) are (a) D's lawful spouse or civil partner; (b) one or more children under the age of ten; and/or (c) intended victims of the relevant offences. If, however, a husband and wife conspire with a third person who does not fall within categories (b) or (c), all three may be guilty (*Chrastny* [1992] 1 All ER 189; cf. *Lovick* [1993] Crim LR 890). Moreover, s. 2(2) has no application to so-called 'common-law' marriages (*Pearce* [2001] EWCA Crim 2834, [2002] 1 WLR 1553; *Suski* [2016] EWCA Crim 24, [2016] 2 Cr App R 3 (32)) or cases in which the marriage or partnership is not valid under English law (*Bala* [2016] EWCA Crim 560, [2017] QB 430).

Intended victims are exempt from liability for statutory conspiracy (s. 2(1)). This appears designed to apply the principle established in *Tyrell* [1894] 1 QB 710 in respect of laws prohibiting sexual activity with underage children, etc. (see **A4.25**), and may perhaps be confined (as in the SCA 2007, s. 51) to cases in which the 'victim' is one of a class that the relevant offence is intended to protect (*Gnango* [2011] UKSC 59, [2012] 1 AC 827, *obiter* at [49]). But where D is legally incapable of committing the substantive offence, this does not preclude liability for conspiracy with E, if they agree that E will commit it (*Duguid* (1906) 21 Cox CC 200; *Burns* (1984) 79 Cr App R 173; *Sherry* [1993] Crim LR 536).

Agreement to Engage in Criminal Conduct

A5.52 To amount to a conspiracy under the CLA 1977, s. 1, an agreement must propose that a course of conduct be pursued which would necessarily involve the commission, by one or more of the parties, of a substantive offence which would itself be triable in England and Wales. Some substantive offences may be triable in England and Wales even if committed abroad, but conspiracies in England or Wales to commit acts abroad which are punishable *only* under the relevant foreign law must be dealt with by invoking s. 1A. See further **A5.61**.

To be the subject of a conspiracy, the course of conduct proposed must be something that will be done by one or more of the parties to the agreement, or by an innocent agent (*Varley* [2019] EWCA Crim 1074 at [89] *et seq*). An agreement to arrange for the commission of a murder by a third party (e.g., to hire a 'hit-man') is thus best charged as a conspiracy to commit the statutory offence of solicitation to murder (contrary to the OAPA 1861, s. 4), unless the hit-man has become a party to the conspiracy, in which case it becomes a conspiracy to murder.

A conspiracy to aid and abet an offence is clearly not an offence under the CLA 1977 (*Hollinshead* [1985] 1 All ER 850 (CA); *Kenning* [2008] EWCA Crim 1534, [2009] QB 221; *Varley*). Whether this is also true of a conspiracy to *procure* the commission of an offence is however open to argument, because when *Hollinshead* reached the House of Lords, that point was left open, and it was not in issue in *Kenning* or *Varley*. In *Varley*, the Court of Appeal inclined to the view that an agreement to procure an offence should be treated no differently from an agreement to aid and abet it, but 'reached no decision on it'. As Gross LJ explained (at [115]):

> The question of whether procuring is different from aiding and abetting, so that *Kenning* is not binding, is not necessarily straightforward. It best awaits a case where the outcome turns on it...

The appellants in *Hollinshead* conspired to market devices for use by third parties, which would falsify electricity meter readings and enable users to avoid paying for electricity used. The Court held that this could not amount to a conspiracy to commit offences under the Theft Act 1978, s. 2, even though any users would commit such offences. (Such conduct would now give rise to liability under the Fraud Act 2006, s. 7: see **B5.25**.) *Kenning* was distinguished in *Dang* [2014] EWCA Crim 348, [2014] 1 WLR 3797, where the defendants were held to have been properly convicted under the CLA 1977, s. 1, of conspiracy to be concerned in the production of a controlled drug in contravention of the MDA 1971, s. 4(2)(b), by agreeing to supply hydroponic and other products and equipment for the purpose of assisting others to grow cannabis plants. The defendants might not have been guilty of conspiracy actually to produce a controlled drug (the offence under the MDA 1971, s. 4(2)(a)) but the substantive offence under s. 4(2)(b) is much broader and does not require involvement in any particular process of production.

Conditional Agreements and Contingencies

A5.53 Problems may also arise where agreements could be carried out without committing the alleged substantive offence, or where the parties recognise that it might not prove necessary to carry out the agreement itself. On the face of it, the first kind of agreement falls outside the definition of a conspiracy. In *Reed* [1982] Crim LR 819, the Court of Appeal stated that, if A and B agree to drive from London to Edinburgh in a time which might or might not be achievable without breaking speed limits, depending on the traffic conditions, they do not thereby agree that they will *necessarily* commit any offence and are not therefore guilty of conspiracy. The Court of Appeal subsequently approved this dictum in *Jackson* [1985] Crim LR 442, whilst purporting to distinguish it on the facts. The appellants in *Jackson* agreed with one W, who was on trial for burglary, that he would be shot in the leg so as to induce the court to treat him leniently, should he be convicted. They were charged with conspiracy to pervert the course of justice, but argued that, when the agreement was made, it was not known whether W would be convicted. Thus, the planned shooting would not necessarily have interfered with the course of justice. Rejecting this argument, the Court replied that 'contingency planning' could amount to conspiracy:

> 'Necessarily' is not to be held to mean that there must inevitably be the carrying out of an offence, it means, if the agreement is carried out in accordance with the plan, there must be the commission of the offence referred to in the conspiracy count.

With respect, the agreed course of conduct (the shooting of W) was not contingent on the outcome of the trial: indeed, it was carried out before the trial ended. It was the effect of that conduct on the future course of justice that was uncertain. The convictions in *Jackson* can better be justified on the basis that the appellants conspired (unconditionally) to commit an act which was intended (conditionally on the outcome of the trial) to pervert the course of justice; and an act committed with such an intent is sufficient to amount to the substantive offence of perverting the course of justice (see **B14.38**). If, however, planning for a contingency may indeed amount to conspiracy (and *O'Hadhmaill* [1996] Crim LR 509 is clear authority that it may), motorists who agree to break speed limits, if necessary, in order to get to Edinburgh on time must after all be guilty, and robbers who agree to 'shoot to kill' if challenged must equally be guilty of conspiracy to murder. This was acknowledged by the House of Lords in *Saik* [2006] UKHL 18, [2007] 1 AC 18; but their lordships distinguished such cases from that in which A and B agree to launder money or other property that they suspect may *possibly* represent the proceeds of crime. If they do not know or intend this to be the case (as is required by the CLA 1977, s. 1(2); see **A5.58**), they are not guilty of conspiracy, even though it may transpire that their suspicions are well founded (in which case they may end up committing a substantive money laundering offence).

Agreement is the basis of liability in conspiracy. Abandonment of the agreement cannot affect such liability once it has been incurred (*Bolton* (1991) 94 Cr App R 74).

Agreement without Real Intent

If the *actus reus* of conspiracy is agreement, the *mens rea* is harder to identify. The concept of agreement does not necessarily import an intent by each party to carry out that agreement, but such an intent was (and still is) required in respect of conspiracy at common law (*Thomson* (1965) 50 Cr App R 1; *Yip Chieu-Chung v The Queen* [1995] 1 AC 111) whilst there are references in the CLA 1977, s. 1(1) and (4), to agreements being carried out in accordance with the intentions of the parties. The issue of intent may become problematic where one or more of the parties does not intend to keep to the agreement, as where a hired assassin agrees to commit a murder but intends only to make off with the advance fee, or where the supposed assassin is working undercover for the police, and intends only to collect evidence against those who did the hiring. Is the dishonest assassin or undercover officer guilty of conspiracy to murder? If not, where does that leave the other parties to the supposed agreement? **A5.54**

The House of Lords touched upon such questions in *Anderson* [1986] AC 27. D was charged with conspiracy to effect a convicted prisoner's escape from jail. He had agreed to such a plan and had supplied the other conspirators with diamond cutting wire in furtherance of it, but claimed that he had never believed the jailbreak could succeed, and was concerned only to obtain the money he had been promised for the wire. The Court of Appeal held that this amounted to an admission of complicity in the conspiracy as a secondary party, but the House of Lords preferred to categorise D as a principal offender. Lord Bridge, with whom the other members of the House agreed, said: **A5.55**

> I ... reject any construction of the statutory language which would require the prosecution to prove an intention on the part of each conspirator that the criminal offence or offences ... should in fact be committed.

> ... [B]eyond the mere fact of agreement, the necessary *mens rea* ... is ... established if, and only if ... the accused ... intended to play some part in the agreed course of conduct in furtherance of the criminal purpose which the agreed course of conduct was intended to achieve. Nothing less will suffice; nothing more is required.

Lord Bridge went on to emphasise that an undercover agent, 'ostensibly agreeing [but] with the purpose of exposing and frustrating the purpose of the other parties' cannot be guilty of conspiracy. This must be correct, but the earlier excerpts from his speech are problematic, and much of what he said is now widely considered to have been wrong. In particular, his ruling that a conspirator need not intend the offence in question to be committed does violence to the wording of the CLA 1977, s. 1(1), and is difficult to reconcile with s. 1(2) (see **A5.58**). Elsewhere, however, Lord Bridge refers to 'the criminal purpose which the agreed course of conduct was *intended* to achieve', adding, '[it] is, of course, necessary that any party to the agreement shall have assented to play his part ... knowing that the part to be played by one or more of the others will amount to or involve the commission of an offence'.

On that basis, the fraudulent hit-man who intends only to make off with the advance fee cannot after all be guilty of conspiracy to murder, because he knows that without him the plan must fail. Similarly, fraudulent drug dealers who intend to supply their customers with harmless powder cannot be regarded as having conspired to supply drugs. Their plan is in fact to obtain property from the customers by deception. This interpretation makes far more sense and appears to have been accepted by the Court of Appeal in *Edwards* [1991] Crim LR 352 and by the Northern Ireland Court of Appeal in *McPhillips* (1990 unreported). See also *Yip Chieu-Chung v The Queen* [1995] 1 AC 111 (see **A5.57**).

Where an apparent agreement to commit an offence is nothing more than fantasy, in that none of the parties seriously intend to put it into execution, the position is clear: a shared fantasy is not a conspiracy; and if the prosecution evidence is so equivocal that no reasonable jury, properly directed, could be sure the agreement was anything more than mere fantasy, there can be no case to answer. There must in other words, be some credible evidence of 'executory intent'. See *Goddard* [2012] EWCA Crim 1756.

Active and Passive Conspirators

A5.56 A second problem with Lord Bridge's ruling in *Anderson* [1986] AC 27 is that it appears to require each conspirator to intend playing some active part in furtherance of the conspiracy. If so, it is a proposition for which there is no basis in the CLA 1977 or in any cases decided before or after it. In *Siracusa* (1989) 90 Cr App R 340, the Court concluded that Lord Bridge could not have meant what he said. 'He cannot have been intending that the organiser of a crime, who recruited others to carry it out, would not himself be guilty of conspiracy ... Participation in a conspiracy is infinitely variable: it can be active or passive.'

Where Only One Conspirator is Genuine

A5.57 A cannot be guilty of conspiracy if B (the only other party to the supposed agreement) intends to frustrate or sabotage it. This issue did not arise in *Anderson* [1986] AC 27, but the Privy Council was required to consider it in *Yip Chieu-Chung v The Queen* [1995] 1 AC 111, where N, the appellant's only fellow conspirator in a plan to smuggle heroin out of Hong Kong, was an undercover agent working with the knowledge of the authorities. The Privy Council held that, if N's purpose had been to prevent the heroin being smuggled, no conspiracy would have existed. Lord Griffiths said:

> The crime of conspiracy requires an agreement between two or more persons to commit an unlawful act with the intention of carrying it out. It is the intention to carry out the crime that constitutes the necessary *mens rea* for the offence. As Lord Bridge pointed out [in *Anderson*] an undercover agent who has no intention of committing the crime lacks the necessary *mens rea* to be a conspirator.

Conspiracy under Hong Kong law was still a common-law offence, but Lord Griffiths did not seek to distinguish in this respect between common-law and statutory conspiracy. He was, however, able to uphold the appellant's conviction on the basis that N had intended to smuggle the heroin out of Hong Kong as agreed. The trap was to be sprung later, when the heroin arrived in Australia. The fact that the Hong Kong authorities acquiesced in this plan did not prevent it from being a criminal act. Both parties were therefore guilty, albeit that N would never be prosecuted. But see *Rafiq* [2008] EWCA Crim 1518, in which the Court doubted whether in such circumstances the undercover officer would be guilty of any offence in English law.

Mens Rea as to Circumstances

At common law, D could be guilty of conspiracy only if D and at least one other conspirator knew of any relevant circumstances necessary for the commission of the offence (*Churchill v Walton* [1967] 2 AC 224). The CLA 1977, s. 1(2) (see **A5.44**), maintains this rule in relation to statutory conspiracies. Conspiracy to commit an offence for which strict liability, negligence or recklessness would suffice cannot be established by proof of such negligence or recklessness, or on the basis of strict liability. Conspiracy is a full *mens rea* offence for which nothing less than knowledge of (or intent as to) all constituent facts or circumstances will suffice. As the House of Lords noted in *Saik* [2006] UKHL 18, [2007] 1 AC 18, any other interpretation would be absurd. On the other hand, knowledge of the relevant law which makes the proposed conduct illegal need not be proved, because ignorance of the law is generally no defence (*Broad* [1997] Crim LR 666), and even where an indictment wrongly includes reference to negligence or recklessness, etc., a conviction may still be considered safe on appeal if, on the evidence, the jury must inevitably have concluded that the conspirators knew exactly what they were doing (*Ali (Arie)* [2019] EWCA Crim 2448, [2020] 1 Cr App R 21 (371)). **A5.58**

Despite s. 1(2), an indictment may properly charge conspiracy to commit criminal damage or arson 'being reckless as to whether the life of another person would thereby be endangered', because actual endangerment is not 'a fact or circumstance necessary for the commission of the offence' under the Criminal Damage Act 1971, s. 1(2). It is necessary only that the conspirators realise that their plan *may*, if carried out, endanger life. See *Mir* (22 April 1994 unreported), *Browning* (6 November 1998 unreported), *Ryan* (1999) 163 JP 849, and *Saik*, per Lord Nicholls at [4].

In cases of conspiracy to commit money laundering offences under the POCA 2002, Part 7 (see **B21**), prosecutors sometimes appear to confuse the *mens rea* of the substantive offences (which may involve mere suspicion as to the criminal character of the property being laundered) with that required by the CLA 1977, s. 1(2), in respect of any conspiracy. As Davis LJ explained in *Thomas* [2014] EWCA Crim 1958 at [15]–[16]: **A5.59**

> It has authoritatively been decided … in the case of *Saik* [2007] 1 AC 18 that the *mens rea* applicable to the offence of conspiring to launder criminal proceeds is not to be equated with the *mens rea* applicable for the substantive offence. Further, so far as the *actus reus* of the substantive offence is concerned it is required that the property must in fact be the proceeds of crime.
>
> Consequently, in a case of conspiracy in this context an alleged conspirator must be proved … to have known that the proceeds were criminal proceeds where such proceeds existed, or to have intended that they be such proceeds, where the position was looking to the future. Suspicion alone would not suffice.

D cannot strictly speaking 'know' something to be true unless it is in fact true. A positive but mistaken belief in certain facts may nevertheless trigger liability for conspiring (or attempting) to commit an 'impossible' offence. See **A5.60** and (in respects of analogous charges of attempt) *Pace* [2014] EWCA Crim 186, [2014] 1 WLR 2687 and **A5.84**.

The CLA 1977, s. 1(2), seriously compromises the Crown's ability to use a single 'umbrella' conspiracy count in preference to multiple charges alleging a series of substantive money laundering transactions. The price for using such a charge is the need to prove knowledge or intent as to the criminal character of the property in question, where proof of well-founded suspicion would generally suffice for the substantive offences. But *Saik* makes clear that where a conspiracy count looks to future transactions there can be no question of having to prove that the property in question is in fact of illicit origin, for *ex hypothesi* it is as yet unidentified. What matters is the intent of the conspirators. See also *Suchedina* [2006] EWCA Crim 2543, [2007] 1 Cr App R 23 (305) at [18]–[20].

Impossibility

A5.60 At common law it was a defence to a charge of conspiracy that the object of the conspiracy was impossible to achieve. One could not, for example, be guilty of a conspiracy to extract cocaine from a substance which proved not to contain any cocaine (*DPP v Nock* [1978] AC 979). The CLA 1977, s. 1(1), was amended by the CAA 1981, so as largely to eliminate defences based on impossibility. If A and B wrongly believe that cocaine can be extracted from a given substance, they may now commit an indictable conspiracy or attempt to do so. They may also enter into an indictable conspiracy to murder someone who turns out to be dead already or to handle goods which they wrongly but firmly believe to have been stolen. In contrast, unfounded suspicion, even if based on strong evidence, cannot give rise to such liability, because suspicion as to circumstances cannot suffice for that purpose even where it proves well founded, or even where suspicion would suffice for the substantive offence (*Thomas* [2014] EWCA Crim 1958).

An agreement to pursue a course of conduct which the parties wrongly believe to be criminal, because they have misunderstood the law, cannot be indictable as a conspiracy (cf. *Taaffe* [1984] AC 539).

Jurisdiction over Statutory Conspiracy

A5.61 Conspiracy under the CLA 1977, s. 1, must involve an agreement to commit an offence triable under English law (s. 1(4)) and this usually means an offence which is to be committed within England and Wales or aboard a British ship or aircraft. A number of offences can however be tried under English law even if committed abroad (e.g., offences under the Aviation Security Act 1982 (see **B10.225** ***et seq.***) or murder/manslaughter committed by a British citizen on land outside the UK). Persons who conspire anywhere to commit such crimes abroad are therefore indictable under s. 1 (*Bow Street Metropolitan Stipendiary Magistrate, ex parte Pinochet Ugarte (No. 3)* [2000] 1 AC 147).

Persons who conspire in England and Wales to commit acts outside England and Wales, which are not offences under English law but are punishable under the law of the country or territory in question and would be punishable under English law if committed in England or Wales, may be charged with conspiracy by virtue of the CLA 1977, s. 1A. Such proceedings may however be instituted only by or with the consent of the A-G (CLA 1977, s. 4(5)). In *Patel* [2009] EWCA Crim 67, [2009] 2 Cr App R (S) 67 (475), the object of the agreement was illegal entry to the USA, contrary to US federal law. This fell within the ambit of s. 1A, the equivalent offence in English law being that under the Immigration Act 1971, s. 25 (see **B22.42**). In such a case, Part I of the 1977 Act (ss. 1 to 5) 'has effect in relation to the agreement' on the same basis as it applies to conspiracies that fall within s. 1(1) itself (see s. 1A(1)). In other words, s. 1A is not a stand-alone provision, but operates as an extension to the s. 1 offence.

A s. 1A conspiracy is committed if a party to the agreement, or the party's agent, did anything in England and Wales in relation to the agreement before its formation, or if a party joined it there (in person or through an agent), or if a party (or agent) did or omitted anything there in pursuance of the agreement (s. 1A(5)).

A5.62 Conspiracy to commit a 'cross frontier' offence of fraud or dishonesty which would itself be triable in England and Wales as a Group A offence under Part I of the CJA 1993 should be indicted under the CLA 1977, s. 1, without reference to s. 1A. A person may be guilty of conspiracy to commit such an offence whether or not any act or omission in relation to that offence occurred in England or Wales (*CJA 1993*, s. 3(2); and see further **A8.10** ***et seq.***).

Even in cases not covered by the CJA 1993, conspirators who, whilst abroad, plot the commission of a crime within England or Wales, may be indicted under English law, even if none of them enter the jurisdiction or trigger any consequences here. See *Liangsiriprasert v USA* [1991] 1 AC 225; *Sansom* (1991) 92 Cr App R 115; *Manning* [1998] 2 Cr App R 461; *R (Al-Fawwaz) v Governor of Brixton Prison* [2002] UKHL 69, [2002] 1 AC 556.

Evidential Issues

There are no special evidential rules peculiar to conspiracy. In *Murphy* (1837) 8 C & P 297, proof of conspiracy was said to be generally 'a matter of inference deduced from certain criminal acts of the parties accused', but there is no actual need for any such acts, and conspiracies may also be proved, *inter alia*, by direct testimony, secret recordings or confessions, subject only to the proviso that A's pre-trial confession cannot ordinarily be evidence against B. The acts and statements of one conspirator may be given in evidence against all the conspirators, provided they were done or said in furtherance of their common purpose, but that rule is not confined to conspiracies. See further **F17.66** ***et seq***. **A5.63**

CONSPIRACY TO DEFRAUD

Definition

The common-law offence of conspiracy to defraud was expressly preserved by the CLA 1977, s. 5(2). As Hickinbottom J explained in *Evans* [2014] 1 WLR 2817 (in a passage subsequently endorsed by the Court of Appeal in *Barton* [2020] EWCA Crim 575, at [121]), there are two principal variants of this offence, although these are not mutually exclusive. In either case the conspiracy must incorporate some unlawfulness, either in its object or in its means, although it need not necessarily include the commission of a substantive offence if carried out. But an agreement to achieve a lawful object by lawful means cannot amount to a conspiracy to defraud, however dishonourable or unscrupulous the object or means might be (*Evans* at [141]). The first variant is defined in the leading case of *Scott v Metropolitan Police Commissioner* [1975] AC 819, where Viscount Dilhorne said: **A5.64**

> ... an agreement by two or more [persons] by dishonesty to deprive a person of something which is his or to which he is or would be or might be entitled [or] an agreement by two or more by dishonesty to injure some proprietary right of his suffices to constitute the offence...

There may or may not be an intent to deceive in such cases, and there may or may not be an intent to cause economic or financial loss to the proposed victim or victims, but it is necessary that a proprietary right or interest of the potential victim is actually or potentially injured or put at risk (see also *Goldshield Group plc* [2008] UKHL 17, [2009] 1 Cr App R 33 (491); see **A5.66**).

In the second variant there must be a dishonest agreement to deceive another person into acting contrary to that person's duty. There is some doubt as to the exact scope of this offence. It was suggested (*obiter*) in *DPP v Withers* [1975] AC 842 that the person deceived must be a public official, and this was also the view of Lord Diplock in *Scott*, but the opinion of the Privy Council in *Wai Yu-tsang v The Queen* [1992] AC 269 was that it suffices if any person is deceived into acting contrary to the duty owed to clients or employers. The Privy Council approved and adopted the concept of 'intent to defraud' previously expounded by Lord Denning and Lord Radcliffe in *Welham v DPP* [1961] AC 103, which is that to defraud means 'to practise a fraud' and this need not necessarily involve any form of economic loss or prejudice.

Either variant of conspiracy to defraud is capable of overlapping with the offence of statutory conspiracy (see **A5.44** ***et seq***.). Such overlap will occur wherever the course of action agreed on would necessarily involve the commission of any offence or offences by one or more of the parties to the conspiracy if carried out in accordance with their intentions and would also involve a fraud being practised on another person. In such circumstances, the prosecution have a choice as to which kind of charge to prefer (CJA 1987, s. 12(1)). Under **A5.65** guidelines issued by the A-G in 2007 (see **appendix 2**), however, a charge of statutory conspiracy (or a charge alleging a substantive offence) should be brought in preference to a charge of conspiracy to defraud unless there are good reasons for doing otherwise. A charge of conspiracy to defraud may be appropriate where no charge of statutory conspiracy (or of a substantive offence) could properly reflect the gravity of the offence, and/or where such charges might require a large number of separate counts, severed trials, etc. There may also be cases in which the identification of specific target offences would be problematic.

Indictment and Procedure

A5.66 Conspiracy to defraud is triable only on indictment. It is punishable by up to ten years' imprisonment or a fine or both (CJA 1987, s. 12(3)). For trial purposes, it is a class 3 offence. An indictment for conspiracy to defraud should not lack particularity and should enable the defence and the judge to know precisely the nature of the prosecution's case (*Landy* [1981] 1 All ER 1172). This prevents the prosecution from shifting their ground during the trial, unless they obtain leave of the judge and amend the indictment itself (*Landy*). In *Goldshield Group plc* [2008] UKHL 17, [2009] 1 Cr App R 33 (491), it was held that an indictment for conspiracy to defraud by means of a price-fixing cartel required amendment insofar as it failed to specify how this practice (which was not criminal *per se*) operated to the detriment of the Department of Health, which was thereby deceived into paying over the odds for NHS medicines.

A single count of conspiracy to defraud may be founded on evidence of several fraudulent transactions if it can be shown that those transactions were each effected pursuant to a single agreement (*Mba* [2006] EWCA Crim 624).

In *K* [2004] EWCA Crim 2685, [2005] 1 Cr App R 25 (408), the Court of Appeal considered *Landy* and added this guidance as to the drafting of indictments for conspiracy to defraud:

> [The indictment] should identify the agreement alleged with the specificity necessary in the circumstances of each case; if the agreement alleged is complex, then details of that may be needed and those details will . . . form part of what must be proved. If this course is followed, it should then be clear what the prosecution must prove and the matters on which the jury must be unanimous: see *Bennett* [1999] EWCA Crim 1486. Further particulars should be given where it is necessary for the defendants to have further general information as to the nature of the charge and for the other purposes identified by Lawton LJ in *Landy*. Such further particulars form no part of the ingredients of the offence and on these the jury do not have to be unanimous, as this court correctly decided in *Hancock*.

Statement of Offence

Conspiracy to defraud contrary to common law.

Particulars of Offence

A on days between . . . and . . . conspired together and with B and C to defraud V by dishonestly exploiting their position to control or obtain money or proprietary rights belonging to V, for the benefit of A, B, C and/or their businesses, to which A, B, C and/or their businesses were not entitled

As to the power of local authorities to prosecute for conspiracy to defraud (e.g., in consumer protection cases), see *Jarrett* [1997] Crim LR 517 and *Richards* [1999] Crim LR 598. As to the A-G's guidelines on prosecutions for conspiracy to defraud, see **A5.65** and **appendix 2**.

Sentence

A5.67 The definitive sentencing guideline, *Fraud, Bribery and Money Laundering Offences* (see Supplement, **SG26-1** ***et seq.***), includes guidance on sentencing for conspiracy to defraud. The guideline applies to individual offenders aged 18 and over and organisations. It applies to all offenders sentenced on or after 1 October 2014 regardless of the date of the offence. There is a separate part of the guideline applicable to corporate offenders.

Actus Reus

As in cases of statutory conspiracy, there must always be an agreement. Two or more similar but separate agreements cannot be charged as a single conspiracy to defraud (see *Mehta* [2012] EWCA Crim 2824 and **A5.49**). The agreement may, however, be wider in certain respects than that required in respect of the statutory offence. It need not be an agreement that would necessarily involve the commission of a substantive offence if carried out (*Scott v Metropolitan Police Commissioner* [1975] AC 819; *Cooke* [1986] AC 909) and it need not necessarily be envisaged that the fraud will be perpetrated by the conspirators themselves. In *Hollinshead* [1985] AC 975, the appellants agreed to market devices designed to falsify gas or electricity meters, which would enable customers (who were not themselves party to the conspiracy) to defraud their gas and electricity suppliers. The appellants had no intention of using the devices themselves, but they were nevertheless guilty of conspiracy to defraud. In such circumstances a charge under the Fraud Act 2006, s. 7 (see **B5.26**), would now be more appropriate (see **A5.65** and the A-G's guidelines on prosecutions for conspiracy to defraud in **appendix 2**). **A5.68**

Other reported illustrations of agreements amounting to conspiracy to defraud include: agreement to conceal a bank's losses or liabilities from its shareholders, creditors and depositors (*Wai Yu-tsang v The Queen* [1992] AC 269); agreement by company directors to conceal secret profits from the company, where the company would be entitled to demand that the profits be accounted for (*Adams v The Queen* [1995] 1 WLR 52); agreement by British Rail catering staff to sell their own refreshments to customers whilst on duty, thereby depriving British Rail of profits from legitimate sales (*Cooke* [1986] AC 909); agreement to falsify hire-purchase or credit applications, so as to induce credit companies or other lenders to make loans they might not otherwise be willing to make (*Allsop* (1976) 64 Cr App R 29); and agreement to make pirate copies of films, etc., thereby depriving the makers and distributors of legitimate profits (*Scott v Metropolitan Police Commissioner*). As in cases of statutory conspiracy (see **A5.50**), it may be possible in some cases for one of two alleged conspirators to be convicted while the other is acquitted; but this would only be possible where there is evidence admissible against one but not the other (*Testouri* [2003] EWCA Crim 3735, [2004] 2 Cr App R 4 (26); *Elkins* [2005] EWCA Crim 2711).

As to the position where only one of the supposed conspirators really intends to proceed with or carry out the conduct agreed upon, see **A5.57**.

Mens Rea

To be guilty of conspiracy to defraud, D must be dishonest, and there must be a shared intent to defraud the proposed victim, in one or other of the senses explained at **A5.64**. Dishonesty in this context must now bear the same meaning as that adopted by the Supreme Court in *Ivey v Genting Casinos (UK) Ltd* [2017] UKSC 67, [2018] AC 391 and by the Court of Appeal in *Barton* [2020] EWCA Crim 575 (see **B4.55**) rather than the one previously stated in *Ghosh* [1982] QB 1053. The partial statutory definition of dishonesty that applies in theft cases (Theft Act 1968, s. 2) does not apply in cases of fraud or of conspiracy to defraud. A belief in one's legal entitlement to any property involved is not in this context an absolute bar to a finding of dishonesty, as it would be in a theft case by virtue of s. 2(1)(a). Nor, following the abrogation of the second limb of the *Ghosh* test, are a jury necessarily required to acquit those who did not realise that the conduct or proposed conduct agreed to would be considered dishonest by 'ordinary honest people'. **A5.69**

Under the *Ivey* test, however, a court or jury must still judge the honesty or dishonesty of the agreement in question on the basis of the facts or circumstances as the alleged conspirators (subjectively) understood them to be at the time. A belief in a claim of legal entitlement cannot be irrelevant to the question of dishonesty, merely because s. 2(1)(a) does not apply.

Moreover, as in theft cases, ignorance of the law may sometimes provide a good defence, in much the same way as a mistake of fact, because an intent to defraud V presupposes some knowledge or understanding of V's legal entitlement or of D's own duty (cf. *Bush* [2019] EWCA Crim 29). D cannot, for example, intend to deprive V of some right that D does not realise V possesses in the first place. But how exactly the revised test for dishonesty affects conspiracy to defraud was never addressed in *Ivey* and its impact has yet to be seen. See **A6.2** in relation to corporate liability, and as to dishonesty in fraud cases generally, see **B5.11**.

An intention to act unlawfully is not of itself sufficient, and this must be made clear to the jury (*Cassell v The Queen (Montserrat)* [2016] UKPC 19, [2017] 1 WLR 2738); but an intent to deceive is necessary only in respect of the second of the two variants of the offence. In *A-G's Ref (No. 1 of 1982)* [1983] QB 751, it was held that there can be no conspiracy to defraud where the defrauding would be a mere side-effect (rather than the 'true object') of the scheme agreed to, but this is now generally thought to be wrong, and has not been followed in subsequent cases. The correct position must be that D intends to defraud V wherever D is aware that the successful implementation of the plan will result in V being defrauded (cf. *McPherson* [1985] Crim LR 508).

Jurisdiction over Conspiracy to Defraud

A5.70 In *Board of Trade v Owen* [1957] AC 602, the House of Lords held that jurisdiction over conspiracy to defraud was governed by the same principles as conspiracy to commit a crime. In other words, a conspiracy abroad to defraud V within England and Wales may be indictable here, but no indictment will lie where V is to be defrauded abroad. Lord Tucker said:

> A conspiracy to commit a crime abroad is not indictable in this country unless the contemplated crime is one for which an indictment would lie here ... It necessarily follows that a conspiracy of the nature of that charged in count 3 [i.e. a conspiracy to defraud a West German government department] — which in my view was a conspiracy to attain a lawful object by unlawful means, rather than to commit a crime — is not triable in this country, since the unlawful means and the ultimate object were both outside the jurisdiction.

See also *A-G's Ref (No. 1 of 1982)* [1983] QB 751 and *Naini* [1999] 2 Cr App R 398, and **A8**. The position is now different in respect of things done on or after 1 June 1999. Section 5(3) of the CJA 1993 provides that various acts done or omitted within England and Wales, whether by a conspirator or by someone acting as an agent of a conspirator, may bring all the conspirators within English jurisdiction, even if the defrauding was intended to occur abroad. Conspirators may even be liable on the basis of acts previously done in England and Wales, before the conspiracy was formed.

Impossibility

A5.71 The abolition of the defence of impossibility in respect of attempts and statutory conspiracies has not affected the operation of that defence in the context of conspiracy to defraud nor did it affect the common-law offence of incitement. As to impossibility in offences under the SCA 2007, Part 2, see **A5.7**.

ATTEMPT

Definition

A5.72 The law relating to attempts is primarily governed by the CAA 1981.

Criminal Attempts Act 1981, s. 1

> (1) If, with intent to commit an offence to which this section applies, a person does an act which is more than merely preparatory to the commission of the offence, he is guilty of attempting to commit the offence.
>
> [(1A) and (1B) deal with attempts in England or Wales to commit acts abroad which would amount to offences of computer misuse (see **B17.18**) if committed in England and Wales.]

(2) A person may be guilty of attempting to commit an offence to which this section applies even though the facts are such that the commission of the offence is impossible.

(3) In any case where—
 (a) apart from this subsection a person's intention would not be regarded as having amounted to an intent to commit an offence; but
 (b) if the facts of the case had been as he believed them to be, his intention would be so regarded,
then for the purpose of subsection (1) above, he shall be regarded as having had an intent to commit that offence.

(4) This section applies to any offence which, if it were completed, would be triable in England and Wales as an indictable offence, other than—
 (a) conspiracy (at common law or under section 1 of the Criminal Law Act 1977);
 (b) aiding, abetting, counselling, procuring or suborning the commission of an offence;
 (c) offences under section 4(1) (assisting offenders) or 5(1) (accepting or agreeing to accept consideration for not disclosing information about a relevant offence) of the Criminal Law Act 1967.

(5) This section also applies to low-value shoplifting (which is defined in, and is triable only summarily by virtue of, section 22A of the Magistrates' Courts Act 1980).

An offence such as common assault is not 'triable in England and Wales as an indictable offence' merely because it can be included in a wider indictment by virtue of the CJA 1988, s. 40. Dicta to the contrary in *Nelson* [2013] EWCA Crim 30, [2013] 1 Cr App R 30 (405) must be disregarded as erroneous, because they overlook the Interpretation Act 1978, sch. 1, which is explicit on that point. In contrast, s. 1(5) ensures that attempts to commit low value shoplifting do fall within the scope of the offence (see *Chamberlin* [2017] EWCA Crim 39, [2017] 1 Cr App R (S) 46 (369) and **D6.29**). As to low value criminal damage (also within the scope of s. 1), see *Bristol Justices, ex parte E* [1999] 3 All ER 798 and **B8.2**.

Although a purely summary offence cannot be the object of a criminal attempt under the CAA 1981, s. 1, provisions creating summary offences sometimes create matching offences of attempt: see, e.g., the Road Traffic Act 1988, ss. 4 and 5, which create summary offences of driving *or attempting to drive* when unfit through drink or drugs or when over the prescribed limit for alcohol (see **C5.33** and **C5.58**). The CAA 1981, s. 3, provides that 'attempts under special statutory provisions' shall be governed by rules which mirror those in s. 1(1) to (3).

Section 1(4)(b) does not preclude charges of attempt in relation to substantive offences of 'procuring'; nor does anything in s. 1(4) preclude a charge of attempting to incite the commission of a criminal offence, or of attempting to commit a preparatory offence such as that under the SOA 2003, s. 14 (*Robson* [2008] EWCA Crim 619, [2009] 1 WLR 713).

Indictment

Statement of Offence **A5.73**

Attempted murder contrary to section 1(1) of the Criminal Attempts Act 1981.

Particulars of Offence

A on or about the ... day of ... attempted to murder V.

A person charged on indictment with an attempt to commit an offence can be convicted on that charge, notwithstanding any evidence proving that the person has committed the substantive offence (CLA 1967, s. 6(4)). The same rule applies to summary trials. See *Webley v Buxton* [1977] QB 481. This rule is unaltered by the CAA 1981.

Evidence, Procedure and Sentencing

Criminal Attempts Act 1981, s. 2 **A5.74**

(1) Any provision to which this section applies shall have effect with respect to an offence under section 1 above of attempting to commit an offence as it has effect with respect to the offence attempted.

(2) This section applies to provisions of any of the following descriptions made by or under any enactment (whenever passed)—
(a) provisions whereby proceedings may not be instituted or carried on otherwise than by, or on behalf or with the consent of, any person (including any provisions which also make other exceptions to the prohibition);
(b) provisions conferring power to institute proceedings;
(c) provisions as to the venue of proceedings;
(d) provisions whereby proceedings may not be instituted after the expiration of a time limit;
(e) provisions conferring a power of arrest or search;
(f) provisions conferring a power of seizure and detention of property;
(g) provisions whereby a person may not be convicted or committed for trial on the uncorroborated evidence of one witness (including any provision requiring the evidence of not less than two credible witnesses);
(h) provisions conferring a power of forfeiture, including any power to deal with anything liable to be forfeited;
(i) provisions whereby, if an offence committed by a body corporate is proved to have been committed with the consent or connivance of another person, that person also is guilty of the offence.

An attempt to commit an offence which is triable only on indictment is itself triable only on indictment, whilst an attempt to commit an offence triable either way is triable either way (CAA 1981, s. 4(1)).

A5.75 By s. 4, the maximum penalty for attempted murder is life imprisonment. Other indictable offences are subject to the same maximum as applies on conviction on indictment for the offence attempted, and if the offence is triable either way (or is low value shoplifting as defined by the MCA 1980, s. 22A) the maximum penalty on summary conviction is the same as the maximum penalty available for that offence tried summarily. The Court of Appeal in *Robson* (1974) CSP A1–4B01 indicated that it would be 'at least unusual that an attempt should be visited with punishment to the maximum extent that the law permits in respect of a completed offence'. It is submitted that the sentence for a given attempt should almost always be less than the sentence which would have been imposed if that offence had been completed, but much will depend on the stage at which the attempt failed, and the reason(s) for its non-completion. Clearly, some examples of attempt may merit more severe punishment than some examples of the completed offence. In *A-G's Ref (No. 92 of 2015) (Silva)* [2015] EWCA Crim 1965, a very serious case of attempted rape in which V had been subjected to a prolonged and violent intruder attack in her own home, the judge adopted a starting point of eight years' imprisonment from which he deducted two years to reflect the inchoate nature of the offence. The Court of Appeal considered this two-year 'discount' to be very generous in the circumstances, but not wrong in principle. The proper approach to sentencing for attempted murder is set out in the definitive sentencing guideline, *Attempted Murder* (see Supplement, **SG13-1**).

Actus Reus

A5.76 The CAA 1981, s. 1(1), requires D to have committed an act which is 'more than merely preparatory' to the offence attempted. A mere omission cannot suffice, even where accompanied by the requisite *mens rea*. A refusal to call an ambulance for a person who is gravely ill cannot, for example, amount to attempted murder; but in *Nevard* [2006] EWCA Crim 2896 the Court arguably erred in ruling that the same was true of D's attempt to deceive and put off the emergency services following a 999 call made by V. This surely was a positive act, and would, if successful, have resulted in V's death. Where trial is on indictment, it is for the judge to determine whether there is evidence on which a jury could properly find that D's actions did go beyond mere preparation, but it is then for the jury to decide that question as one of fact (s. 4(3); and see also *DPP v Stonehouse* [1978] AC 55).

At common law, acts amounting to attempts were distinguished from mere preparatory acts by the concept of 'proximity'. An example of the proximity test was provided in *Robinson* [1915] 2 KB 342, in which a jeweller clumsily faked a robbery at his premises with a view to making a fraudulent insurance claim in respect of his supposed loss. It was held that his conviction for attempting to obtain money from his insurers by false pretences could not stand, because he had been arrested before he could send any claim to his insurers. As it was not a decision under the 1981 Act, *Robinson* cannot be a binding authority on its interpretation, but it is unlikely that such a case would be decided differently under the Act. Indeed, a similar approach was adopted in *Campbell* [1991] Crim LR 268, where D armed himself with an imitation gun, approached to within a yard of a post office which he intended to rob, but never drew his weapon; it was held that there was no evidence on which the jury could properly have concluded that his acts went beyond mere preparation. See also *Widdowson* (1985) 82 Cr App R 314. In *Gullefer* [1990] 3 All ER 882, Lord Lane CJ stated that the crucial question was whether D had 'embarked upon the crime proper', but that it was not necessary, as some earlier cases had suggested, that D should have reached a 'point of no return' in respect of the full offence.

A Part A Criminal Law

This view was echoed in *A-G's Ref (No. 1 of 1992)* [1993] Crim LR 274, in which it was held that attempted rape may be committed without D having physically attempted to penetrate his victim. In practice, however, it may be difficult to prove attempted rape in the absence of either an attempt to penetrate or a confession by D. A conviction for sexual assault may be easier to secure (*Beaney* [2010] EWCA Crim 2551; *Ferriter* [2012] EWCA Crim 2211).

In *Jones* [1990] 3 All ER 886, D was charged with attempted murder. He climbed into V's car and drew a loaded gun with the intention of killing him, but was disarmed in a struggle that followed. The Court of Appeal held that it was open to the jury to regard this as attempted murder and in his judgment Taylor LJ provided useful guidance as to the distinction between preparation and attempts: **A5.77**

> The question for the judge in the present case was whether there was evidence from which a reasonable jury, properly directed, could conclude that [V] had done acts which were more than merely preparatory. Clearly his actions in obtaining the gun, in shortening it, in loading it, in putting on his disguise and going to the [ambush point] could only be regarded as preparatory acts. But ... once he had got into the car, taken out the loaded gun and pointed it at [V] with the intention of killing him, there was sufficient evidence for the consideration of the jury on the charge of attempted murder. It was a matter for them to decide whether they were sure those acts were more than merely preparatory.

Similar reasoning was applied in *Geddes* [1996] Crim LR 894, in which D was found trespassing in the lavatory block of a school, armed with a large knife and lengths of rope and tape. It appears that he had intended to kidnap a child, but his conviction for attempted false imprisonment was quashed on appeal. Citing *Campbell* with approval, Lord Bingham CJ held that no jury could properly have concluded that D's acts had gone beyond the stage of mere preparation. He may have equipped himself, and put himself in a position to commit the crime when the opportunity arose, but it could not be said that he had actually tried or started to commit it. Similarly, in *Mason v DPP* [2009] EWHC 2198 (Admin), [2010] RTR 11 (120), it was held that D could not be said to have 'attempted to drive' when over the legal limit for alcohol since he was prevented from even getting into his vehicle; attempting to open the car door was not enough. But contrast *Moore v DPP* [2010] EWHC 1822 (Admin), [2010] RTR 36 (429), in which D started his car on private property and was stopped by an officer a few metres from the public road towards which he was heading; on those facts, it was held that a court was fully entitled to find that he had attempted to drive on a public road.

The question will often be one of fact and degree, and the answer may not always be obvious. In *Tosti* [1997] Crim LR 746 the appellants had provided themselves with cutting equipment, driven **A5.78** to the scene, concealed the cutting equipment nearby, and approached the door of the premises they intended to break into. They were disturbed as they examined the padlock, and were arrested shortly afterwards. On those facts, it was held that a jury *was* entitled to convict of attempted burglary. *Campbell* is perhaps distinguishable on those facts, but the contrast with *Geddes* is less obvious. See also *Toothill* [1998] Crim LR 876; *K* [2009] EWCA Crim 1931 and *R* [2008] EWCA Crim 619, [2009] 1 WLR 713.

It may be necessary to identify the essential elements of the crime allegedly attempted, in order to determine whether D got beyond mere preparation. In *Nash* [1999] Crim LR 308, the Court of Appeal construed 'attempting to procure an act of gross indecency' as if it meant '*inciting* an act of gross indecency'; but procuring requires the commission of the offence procured (*Johnson* [1964] 2 QB 404) and it would seem, with respect, that the wrong test was applied.

Mens Rea

A5.79 Intent is the essence of any crime of attempt under the CAA 1981, as it was at common law (*Pearman* (1984) 80 Cr App R 259). The prosecution must ordinarily prove that D acted with a specific intent to commit the particular crime attempted, even if the full offence is one of strict liability, or one in which the *mens rea* required falls short of the *actus reus* (*Boyton* [2005] EWCA Crim 2979). Thus, although murder may be committed by someone who intends only to cause grievous bodily harm, attempted murder requires nothing less than an intent to kill (*Whybrow* (1951) 35 Cr App R 141).

'Intent' in this context bears the meaning laid down in *Moloney* [1985] AC 905 (see **A2.4**) and *Nedrick* [1986] 3 All ER 1. In most cases, however, a full *Nedrick* direction (see **B1.14**) would be unnecessary and potentially confusing. On a charge of attempted murder by shooting, for example, it may suffice to direct the jury to decide: (a) whether D shot V deliberately; and (b) if so, whether D was 'shooting to kill' (*Fallon* [1994] Crim LR 519).

In *Walker* (1989) 90 Cr App R 226, the defendants were convicted of attempted murder. They had hurled V from a third-floor balcony, but he somehow survived the fall. After correctly directing the jury to decide whether the defendants were 'trying to kill him', the trial judge elaborated by suggesting that such an intent may sometimes be inferred in cases where there is a 'very high degree of probability' that death will result. The Court of Appeal upheld the convictions, but doubted whether any such elaboration was called for on the facts of the case. There was a danger of confusing the jury into thinking that foresight of high probability could be equated with intention.

Mens Rea as to Circumstances

A5.80 Although the CAA 1981, s. 1(1), specifies that D must act 'with intent to commit an offence to which this section applies', there is authority to the effect that something less may suffice in respect of any relevant circumstances. In *Khan* [1990] 2 All ER 783, it was held that, since recklessness as to the victim's lack of consent then sufficed in relation to the full offence of rape, the offence of attempted rape was committed where D intended (but failed) to have intercourse with a woman and was reckless as to her lack of consent. In *A-G's Ref (No. 3 of 1992)* [1994] 2 All ER 121, the Court of Appeal likewise held that an attempt to commit an offence is committed where D has one of the states of mind required to commit the full offence and tries hard to supply what is missing from the completion of the full offence. If this is correct, then if D attempts to set fire to property, being reckless as to whether life would be endangered, D would then be guilty of an attempt to commit an offence under the Criminal Damage Act 1971, s. 1(2).

In *Pace* [2014] EWCA Crim 186, [2014] 1 WLR 2687, however, the Court of Appeal rejected the argument that, on a charge of attempting to commit an offence of converting criminal property, contrary to the POCA 2002, s. 327(1)(c), it would be sufficient for the prosecution to prove that D merely suspected the property in question to be criminal property. Suspicion of this kind suffices for the substantive offence (as it does for all such offences under ss. 327 to 329) but it cannot, said the Court, suffice for an attempt.

The Court suggested that *Khan* and *A-G's Ref (No. 3 of 1992)* could be distinguished (it had no power to overrule either of those cases) but its preferred view appears to have been that the same intent or knowledge as to the circumstances should be required for attempt as it is (under the CLA 1977, s. 1(2)) for conspiracy (see **A5.58**). One problem with that view is that Parliament could easily have inserted a similar provision into the CAA 1981, but chose not to do so. *Pace* was a case on 'attempting the impossible' (see further **A5.84**). This may be the best way to understand it, and the best way to distinguish it from *Khan*.

Pace was applied in *Wheeler* [2014] EWCA Crim 2706, where the Court of Appeal noted that cases were being charged (ineffectively) on the basis of suspicion, when the evidence was capable of proving much more:

> Wilfully shutting eyes to the obvious may constitute evidence connoting knowledge or belief; and it need not necessarily be assumed in all cases that suspicion is all that can safely be inferred from the relevant facts.

'Knowledge' cannot of course be alleged where (as in *Pace* or *Wheeler*) D has been tricked into buying or dealing with property and wrongly assumes it to be the proceeds of theft or some other offence; but a positive, mistaken belief (amounting to more than mere suspicion) may suffice instead. As to attempting the impossible, see **A5.84**.

Conditional Intent

Problems of conditional intent in attempts seldom arise otherwise than in relation to theft and **A5.81** related offences. A would-be thief may not know what will be found when searching through another person's property, and may not even be sure what to hope to find. In *Husseyn* (1978) 67 Cr App R 131, D1 and D2 dishonestly opened the door of a van, but were challenged just as they were about to examine a holdall lying inside the van. The holdall contained valuable scuba-diving equipment, but it was held that they could not be convicted on an indictment alleging that they attempted to steal that equipment. They did not even know what the holdall contained. A properly drafted indictment would have avoided this problem. Had it merely alleged that they 'attempted to steal from' the holdall or van, it would not have mattered whether the holdall or van contained anything which they might actually want to steal, or indeed any property at all.

Attempts with a Foreign Element

The CAA 1981, s. 1(4) (see **A5.72**), restates the common-law rule that conduct cannot amount **A5.82** to a criminal attempt under English law unless it is directed towards the commission of a substantive offence which would itself be indictable under English law. An attempt in England and Wales to publish an obscene article in Scotland is not, for example, indictable under English law, because the ulterior offence would not be. Attempts to commit offences of fraud or dishonesty are now covered by Part I of the CJA 1993 (see **A8.10**). An attempt in England and Wales to commit a 'Group A' offence (such as theft, forgery, etc.) abroad would be triable under the CAA 1981, s. 1, because a Group A offence is triable under English law where any 'relevant event' concerning it takes place in England or Wales.

The CJA 1993 inserted s. 1A into the CAA 1981, supposedly to cover cases where D in England and Wales attempts to commit abroad something which *would* be a Group A offence, but for the fact that it is not triable under English law. This provision is fundamentally at odds with itself. If a Group A offence is instigated by conduct within England and Wales, that offence will inevitably be triable under English law.

Where an attempt to commit an offence within England and Wales is instigated from abroad, the general rule is that such conduct does amount to an offence under s. 1. This has long been true where the attempt is furthered by consequences occurring within the jurisdiction (*Baxter* [1972] 1 QB 1; *DPP v Stonehouse* [1978] AC 55); but it is now clear that (as in conspiracy) such consequences are unnecessary (*Latif* [1996] 1 All ER 353). As to attempts made abroad to commit Group A offences wholly or partly in England and Wales, see the CJA 1993, s. 3(3).

Withdrawal

A5.83 There is no recognised defence of voluntary withdrawal in English law. If D has not progressed beyond the stage of mere preparatory acts (see **A5.76**) D can avoid incurring liability by refraining from further acts but, once beyond that stage, withdrawal will be irrelevant as far as D's liability for attempt is concerned.

Impossibility

A5.84 At common law, no offence of attempt could be committed where it would have been impossible (even in theory) for D to succeed in committing the substantive offence. D could not be guilty of attempting to steal from a bag or pocket which was empty, and could not be guilty of attempting to handle stolen goods if the goods in question had been recovered by the police and had accordingly ceased to be stolen (*Haughton v Smith* [1975] AC 476). This rule was abrogated by the CAA 1981, s. 1(2) and (3), but the precise effect of those provisions was for a time uncertain. In *Anderton v Ryan* [1985] AC 560, the House of Lords held that a distinction had to be drawn between the person who attempts to commit a crime but fails because the crime is impossible (the 'empty pocket' kind of case) and the person who succeeds in doing an 'objectively innocent' act but labours under a mistaken view of the facts or circumstances, and wrongly believes that an offence has been committed.

Anderton v Ryan was thought to be an example of the latter type of case. D bought a video recorder in suspicious circumstances, firmly believing it to be stolen. There was, however, no evidence to prove that it was stolen, and the House of Lords held that she could not be guilty even of an attempt to handle stolen goods. The decision was much criticised, and in *Shivpuri* [1987] AC 1 the House of Lords acknowledged that its earlier decision was wrong. Lord Bridge said:

> I am satisfied ... that the concept of 'objective innocence' is incapable of sensible application in relation to the law of criminal attempts ... Any attempt to commit an offence which ... for any reason fails, so that in the event no offence is committed must, *ex hypothesi*, from the point of view of the criminal law, be objectively innocent. What turns what would otherwise ... be an innocent act into a crime is the intent of the actor to commit an offence.

In *Shivpuri*, D was charged with an attempt to commit an offence under the MDA 1971, s. 3(1). He confessed to acting as a recipient and distributor of what he assumed to be an illegally imported drug. It transpired (to his surprise) that the substance was not a drug at all, but in accordance with the CAA 1981, s. 1(3), his liability for attempting to commit that offence was assessed on the basis of the facts as he believed them to be. See also *Jones* [2007] EWCA Crim 1118, [2008] QB 460.

Section 1(3) does not enable D to be convicted of attempting to commit an offence where D merely suspects the existence of facts that (if true) would make D guilty of the substantive offence (*Pace* [2014] EWCA Crim 186, [2014] 1 WLR 2687 at [61]). The defendants in *Pace* could not therefore be convicted of attempting to convert criminal property that was not in fact criminal property at all, 'because the Crown's case had been put not on the basis of belief but on the basis of suspicion'. See also *Wheeler* [2014] EWCA Crim 2706 and **A5.80**.

If D is not mistaken as to the facts, but wrongly believes that the actions amount to a criminal offence (i.e. as a result of D's mistaken view of the law), this mistake cannot make D guilty of any criminal attempt. Section 1(2) does not apply in such cases (cf. *Taaffe* [1984] AC 539).

Attempts and Alternative Offences

In many cases, there are substantive offences that could be charged as alternatives to a charge of attempt. Some cases of attempted robbery, for example, might instead be prosecuted as offences of assault with intent to rob (Theft Act 1968, s. 8(2)). If D throws acid at V, but misses or fails to cause any injury, a charge of casting or throwing corrosive fluid with intent to burn, maim, disfigure, disable or do grievous bodily harm (OAPA 1861, s. 29) carries the same maximum penalty as a charge of attempting to commit an offence under s. 18 of that Act (see **B12.246**). Where D is seen interfering with a vehicle or trailer, it is often difficult to prove which of a number of possible offences D is attempting to commit, but that difficulty no longer matters if D is charged instead with vehicle interference, contrary to the CAA 1981, s. 9 (see **B4.136** ***et seq.***). **A5.85**

Section A6 Corporate Liability

LIABILITY OF COMPANY

A6.1 Although in many ways a company enjoys the same rights and is bound by the same duties as an individual, there are also marked differences in the application of the criminal law to it. The essence of a limited liability company is that it has a separate legal personality distinct from its shareholders, and indeed its directors and officers, so it enjoys rights and is subject to duties in its own right like an individual person. It is a distinct legal entity, capable of owning and dealing with property, suing and being sued and contracting on its own behalf. It is equally capable of committing crimes. Who owns the shares and in what proportion is irrelevant. The company's acts are not the shareholders' acts, even if one of them also has sole control of its affairs (*Salomon v A Salomon & Co Ltd* [1897] AC 22). The way in which criminal liability attaches to a limited company depends on the appropriate rule of attribution as determined by the particular statutory provision and the interpretation of the courts; to establish whether a company is criminally liable, it is necessary to ascertain which rule of attribution applies.

A company can commit most offences. A requirement of *mens rea* is no bar to a company's guilt. The only crimes it cannot commit as a principal are murder and treason (because the punishment is necessarily incapable of being imposed on a company). Although a company could not factually be a principal offender in offences such as rape or bigamy, it could, just like a human person, be liable as an accessory (as indeed it could be to murder). For example, a company might procure girls for underage sex. Proof of *mens rea* is, of course, required for liability as an accessory but this is no bar to corporate liability; a company was convicted of aiding and abetting causing death by dangerous driving in *Robert Millar (Contractors) Ltd* [1970] 2 QB 54, the mental element being proved through a director with whom the company was identified.

RULES OF ATTRIBUTION: PRINCIPLE OF IDENTIFICATION

A6.2 For most crimes which require proof of a mental element (such as 'dishonestly', 'wilfully' or 'recklessly') the identification principle will be the appropriate rule of attribution. A company is fixed with criminal liability through the acts or omissions of its 'directing mind'; a corporation can be convicted of a criminal offence requiring proof of *mens rea* if the natural person who committed the offence is identified with the company. The ambit of those who fall into this category is both limited and uncertain, save to say that the officers of the company and the main board are likely to be included. It is important to observe that the person identified with the company who commits the offence is acting *as* the company not *for* it.

A company can act only within the terms of its memorandum and articles of association. These two instruments are important so far as corporate criminal liability is concerned because they represent the starting point in determining whose acts may be identified as those of the corporation itself. Lord Diplock (in *Tesco Supermarkets Ltd v Nattrass* [1972] AC 153 at p. 199) regarded them as paramount:

> . . . a corporation . . . owes its corporate personality and its powers to its constitution, the memorandum and articles of association. The obvious and the only place to discover by what natural persons its powers are exercisable, is in its constitution . . .

> In my view, therefore, the question: 'what natural persons are to be treated in law as being the company for the purposes of acts done in the course of its business' ... is to be found by identifying those natural persons who by the memorandum and articles of association or as a result of action taken by the directors, or by the company in general meeting pursuant to the articles, are entrusted with the exercise of the powers of the company.

Lord Reid said (at p. 170) that:

> It must be a question of law whether, once the facts have been ascertained, a person in doing particular things is to be regarded as the company or merely as the company's servant or agent.

This principle was reaffirmed in *A-G's Ref (No. 2 of 1999)* [2000] QB 796. A prosecution for manslaughter was brought against Great Western Trains as a result of the Southall rail disaster. To the question the A-G referred to the Court of Appeal: 'Can a non-human defendant be convicted of the crime of manslaughter by gross negligence in the absence of evidence establishing the guilt of an identified human individual for the same crime?' the answer was 'No'. Rose LJ stated:

> In our judgment, unless an identified individual's conduct, characterisable as gross criminal negligence, can be attributed to the company, the company is not, in the present state of the common law, liable for manslaughter.

The 'identified individual' being referred to by the Court was a single person identified as the embodiment of the company itself. *Tesco Supermarkets Ltd v Nattrass* continues to provide the relevant test for attributing criminal culpability to a corporation, subject to some qualification (per Davis LJ in *SFO v Barclays plc* [2018] EWHC 3055 (QB) at [66]). The distinction between civil and criminal law is important because, whereas civil law focuses on *liability*, crime focuses on *culpability* (at [67]). *SFO v Barclays plc* helpfully sets out four further over-arching propositions:

(a) criminal liability can still attach to a company when it is the victim of the acts of the individuals representing its directing mind and will;
(b) the knowledge and approval of one director is not necessarily to be regarded as the knowledge and approval of the board of directors (and thereby of the company);
(c) a company may delegate its powers and responsibilities to a committee of individuals that will apply the acts and mental state of that committee to the company under the identification doctrine. Although the doctrine as set out in *Tesco Supermarkets Ltd v Nattrass* may be that larger companies are more readily absolved from criminal responsibility than smaller companies, it would be quite wrong to presume that such devolved structures are put in place as a device to avoid corporate responsibility;
(d) recognising the limitations of the primary rules of attribution, it is, of course, open to Parliament to draft statutory offences with the position of corporations in mind.

Evidence of the guilt of a directing mind is relevant and admissible against the company, even when the individual is not prosecuted, so diary entries written by a director were admissible, direct evidence against the company even when the director was not in the trial. In *A Ltd, X, Y* [2016] EWCA Crim 1469, [2017] 1 Cr App R 1 (1), the Court of Appeal said (at [36]):

> ... a corporation can only operate through its directing mind or minds and [the director's] knowledge is, and must remain, the knowledge of the corporation. The presence or otherwise of a directing mind at the trial is irrelevant. Were it otherwise, as the judge observed, had the directing mind died, become incapacitated (as well as one whose attendance at trial could not be secured, perhaps because he had deliberately absented himself), it would not be possible to prosecute the relevant corporation however egregious the conduct.

Therefore, 'Proof of the guilt of the directing mind and will (BK) was probative of the guilt of the corporation (A Ltd). Thus, insofar as the diary entries of BK were probative of his guilty state of mind at the relevant time, they were relevant and admissible also to prove the guilt of A Ltd' (at [33]). This proposition was reaffirmed in *Alstom Network UK Ltd* [2019] EWCA Crim 1318, [2019] 2 Cr App R 34 (417).

It is noteworthy that in *SFO v Tesco Stores Ltd* (10 April 2017 unreported, Southwark Crown Court), when agreeing to a deferred prosecution agreement (DPA) (see **A6.22**), the company accepted that it was guilty of false accounting because senior managers knew the company had provided financial data to its listed parent company that led to the latter making false or misleading financial statements to the markets. The parent company had not committed an offence, despite being the company making the report, because its directing mind and will did not have the requisite *mens rea.*

Ivey v Genting Casinos (UK) Ltd [2017] UKSC 67, [2018] AC 391 rejected the second limb of the test for dishonesty determined in *Ghosh* [1982] QB 1053 (see **B4.55**). This was reaffirmed in *Barton* [2020] EWCA Crim 575. Despite suggestions to the contrary, this does not mean that the doctrine of identification is obsolete in dishonesty cases. When dishonesty is in question in respect of a corporate defendant, the fact-finding tribunal has first to ascertain, subjectively, the actual state of the directing mind's knowledge or belief as to the facts ('the question is whether [the belief] is genuinely held': *Ivey* at [74]). Reasonableness of that belief is a matter of evidence going to whether the directing mind genuinely held the belief (but the belief did not need to be reasonable). Once the directing mind's state of mind is established, the question whether the conduct was honest or dishonest is to be determined by applying the objective standards of ordinary decent people. In terms of the directing mind test in dishonesty cases, the relationship with what must be proved against an individual of sufficient capacity to be identified with the company has not changed.

Seniority and Identification

A6.3 The day-to-day management of a relatively substantial company will typically be delegated by the board to a managing director or directors. Whether a person is sufficiently senior to be identified with the company has been tested in court with apparently inconsistent results. In *Tesco Supermarkets Ltd v Nattrass* [1972] AC 153, a store manager was not sufficiently senior to be identified with the nationwide company, but was regarded as a third person (thus providing Tesco with a statutory defence to the charge); equally in *John Henshall (Quarries) Ltd v Harvey* [1965] 2 QB 233, a weighbridge operator was not identified with the company. In *Tesco v Nattrass,* Lord Reid said (at p. 175) that:

> ... the board never delegated any part of their functions. They set up a chain of command through regional and district supervisors, but they remained in control. The shop managers had to obey their general directions and also take orders from their superiors. The acts or omissions of shop managers were not acts of the company itself.

On the other hand, where the agreement and intention of the managing director were regarded as those of the company, even though the mental element is central to proof of the offence of conspiracy to defraud, the company was guilty (*ICR Haulage Ltd* [1944] KB 551). For a case at the other extreme, see *Redfern and Dunlop Ltd (Aircraft Division)* [1993] Crim LR 43.

Scope of Office

A6.4 Although there seems to be no decision directly in point, it is generally accepted that a company would only be identified with an act done by one of its officers within 'the scope of his office', to use the expression adopted in the Law Commission's Draft Criminal Code (Law Com No. 177), cl. 30(2). For example, if a director driving to a board meeting causes death by dangerous driving, the company would not be liable for the statutory offence, or for manslaughter, since the director was not exercising managerial functions whilst driving, even though on the way to a place where those functions would be exercised. On the other hand, if the acts done are within the scope of the office, as with the false purchase tax returns made by the company secretary in *Moore v I Bresler Ltd* [1944] 2 All ER 515, it does not matter that they are done to conceal a fraud on the company.

Conspiracy

A6.5 A company cannot be guilty of a conspiracy with just one of its own directors because at least two separate minds are required (*McDonnell* [1966] 1 QB 233, affirmed in *A Ltd, X, Y* [2016]

EWCA Crim 1469, [2017] 1 Cr App R 1 (1)). (There were several other named conspirators in *ICR Haulage Ltd* [1944] KB 551.) Nonetheless, the acts or omissions of several persons who might be identified with the company cannot be aggregated to attribute the company with criminal conduct — there must be a sole person whose act or omission is criminal and who can be identified with the company for it to be liable.

SPECIAL RULES OF ATTRIBUTION: STATUTORY CONSTRUCTION

The practical result of the decision of the House of Lords in *Tesco Supermarkets Ltd v Nattrass* [1972] AC 153 (see **A6.2**) was a narrow interpretation of corporate criminal liability. As a result of difficulties in pinning criminal responsibility on a corporation for offences with a mental element, a further theory of liability was expounded, the so-called 'rules of attribution'. **A6.6**

According to Lord Hoffmann in *Meridian Global Funds Management Asia Ltd v Securities Commission* [1995] 2 AC 500, the articles of association provide only the 'primary rules of attribution'. Through the primary and general rules of attribution, the acts of an employee or agent can count as the acts of the company. In the context of any particular criminal offence, it is necessary to determine whether the act of any particular agent of a company can be attributed to the company. In these circumstances (at p. 507):

> ... the court must fashion a *special* rule of attribution for the particular substantive rule ... By applying the usual canons of interpretation, taking into account the language of the statutory provision, its content and policy, it is possible for the court to ascertain whose act (or knowledge or state of mind) was for this purpose intended to count as the act etc. of the company.

Meridian decided that the policy behind legislation ought to determine who fixed a company with the *actus reus* and the *mens rea* of an offence. For offences involving consumer protection, the courts are likely to adopt a wide interpretation of the category of individuals through whom a company is saddled with liability. On trial on indictment it is for the judge to determine as a matter of law whether the criminal act and/or state of mind of the officer, servant or agent of the company is to be treated as that of the company itself.

The decisions in the following cases can be explained by reference to the public interest in the objective of the legislation being achieved. In *Alphacell Ltd v Woodward* [1972] AC 824, a company had its conviction, for causing polluting matter to enter a stream contrary to the Rivers (Prevention of Pollution) Act 1951, upheld by the House of Lords. Similarly, in *Atkinson v Sir Alfred McAlpine & Son Ltd* (1974) 16 KIR 220, a company was held liable for failure to give written notice or provide protective clothing as required by the Asbestos Regulations 1969 (SI 1969 No. 690). In *Tesco Stores Ltd v Brent London Borough Council* [1993] 2 All ER 718, the knowledge of, and information available to, a sales assistant (as to whether a video purchaser was underage) was sufficient to prove the offence against the company and prevent it from relying on the defence in the Video Recordings Act 1984, s. 11(2), because to allow it to do so would have defeated the aim of the legislation. **A6.7**

The interaction between *Tesco* and *Meridian* was considered in *St Regis Paper Co. Ltd* [2011] EWCA Crim 2527, [2012] 1 Cr App R 14 (177). Moses LJ characterised the question of statutory construction in terms of whether the provision justified 'a departure from the normal rule of attribution of liability of a corporation' (i.e. the identification principle as set out in *Tesco*). It was held that where the regulatory scheme provided liability for some offences of strict liability and others requiring *mens rea*, the legislation was not emasculated by limiting corporate liability for the *mens rea* offences via that small category of persons who could properly be described as the directing mind or will of the company.

Companies may be liable for acts done by individual employees to the same extent as human employers where the definition of the offence is equally capable of applying to the employer as to the employee. See *Green v Burnett* [1955] 1 QB 78, where the employer limited company was convicted of 'using' a vehicle being driven by its employee.

Under the common law, it was the case that a company could be convicted of the offence of manslaughter (*A-G's Ref (No. 2 of 1999)* [2000] QB 796 arising out of the Southall rail crash). However, because it depended on the identification principle it was practically impossible to prove except in relation to the smallest companies (in effect one-man bands) such as the one in *Mark* [2004] EWCA Crim 2490. This practical problem led to the enactment of the CMCHA 2007 (see **B1.69** ***et seq.***).

Nonetheless, the overarching position is that *Tesco Supermarkets Ltd v Nattrass* [1972] AC 153 remains binding, as Davis LJ set out in *SFO v Barclays plc* [2018] EWHC 3055 (QB). The 'key issue is whether the alleged criminal acts of individual officers of Barclays are to be attributed to Barclays so as to make it too criminally culpable'. That was a not a matter of evaluation or discretion but of law (at [14]–[15]). Although the consequence was that larger companies might be more readily absolved from criminal liability than smaller companies, devolution and delegation in large companies was a practical necessity and should not be presumed to be a device to avoid corporate responsibility (at [101]).

Increasingly, statutes provide particular routes to corporate liability. Frustratingly, however, the tests are not uniform. For example, the CMCHA 2007 provides for a test predicated on gross breach of a relevant duty of care in the way in which its activities are managed or organised; a company can no longer be convicted of involuntary manslaughter at common law (see **B1.69** ***et seq.***). The Bribery Act 2010, s. 7 (failure to prevent bribery: see **B15.20**), provides another test and the CJCA 2015, s. 21 (ill-treatment or neglect by a care provider: see **B2.168**) yet another. Most recently, the Criminal Finances Act 2017 extended corporate liability for failure to prevent the facilitation of UK (s. 45) and foreign (s. 46) tax evasion offences by a person associated with a company. An associated person is defined as an employee, an agent, or any other person who performs services for or on behalf of the company who is acting in the capacity of a person performing such services (s. 44(4)).

For the s. 46 offence, the company must either be incorporated or carry on business or part of a business in the UK. For both s. 45 and s. 46 offences, it is a defence for the company to prove that, when the tax evasion facilitation offence was committed, (a) it had in place such prevention procedures as were reasonable in all the circumstances, or (b) it was not reasonable in all the circumstances to expect it to have any prevention procedures in place. A comparison with the terms of the Bribery Act 2010 (see **B15.20**) demonstrates that the extension of liability under this statute is different, albeit that, like the Bribery Act 2010, the government must publish guidance about prevention procedures before the offences come into force.

Tests such as that of gross negligence, expressed in terms of the way the company is managed, are now used to criminalise corporate conduct and systems.

As to the possibility of a company being liable for perjury, see the Court of Appeal (Civil Division) decision in *Odyssey Re (London) Ltd v OIC Run-Off Ltd* (2000) *The Times*, 17 March 2000.

It currently seems unlikely that a general crime of failing to prevent economic crime will be added to the statute book in the very near future, despite many, including the Director of the SFO, calling for that change.

Vicarious and Personal Liability

A6.8 'In general, criminal liability only results from personal fault. We do not punish people in criminal courts for the misdeeds of others' (per Lord Morris in *Tesco Supermarkets Ltd v Nattrass [1972] AC 153* at p. 179). This basic tenet of English law applies to liability whether corporate or not, but vicarious liability must not be confused with personal liability. It is suggested that vicarious liability has no significant place in English criminal law, in contrast to English civil law or criminal law in the USA.

> Prima facie a master is not to be made criminally responsible for the acts of his servant to which the master is not party. But it may be the intention of the Legislature in order to guard against the happening of the forbidden thing, to impose a liability upon a principal even though he does not know of, and is not party to, the forbidden act done by his servant. Many statutes are passed with this object. (Viscount Reading CJ in *Mousell Bros v London & North West Railway Co.* [1917] 2 KB 836, at p. 844.)

It is necessary to distinguish this from liability for the acts of another (true vicarious liability). As Lord Sumption said in (the civil case) *Bilta (UK) Ltd v Nazir (No. 2)* [2015] UKSC 23, [2016] AC 1 at [90]: 'Vicarious liability does not involve any attribution of wrongdoing to the principal. It is merely a rule of law under which a principal may be held strictly liable for the wrongdoing of someone else.' In personal liability, although the offending act may be committed by an employee, it is the employer's own failure to prevent the harm that renders the employer liable.

Other than where D has aided, abetted, counselled or procured the act of another, the general principle is that one cannot be held criminally responsible as a result of the act of another. At common law, public nuisance and criminal libel (now abolished) were the only exceptions. An acknowledgement of this principle is *R (Craik, Chief Constable of Northumbria Police) v Newcastle upon Tyne Magistrates' Court* [2010] EWHC 935 (Admin). There are, however, two further exceptions to this principle in relation to statutory offences involving strict liability (see also **A2.20**): **A6.9**

(a) where the words of the statute are apt to describe not only the physical perpetrator of an act but also some other person, typically the perpetrator's employer;
(b) where the statute casts some special duty on a person, typically a licensee of a public house, which is delegated to another (the delegation principle: see **A6.14**).

There is a distinction between liability for the acts of another (true vicarious liability) and liability for breach of a personal duty. In the latter category, although the act may be committed by an employee, it is the employer's own failure to prevent the harm that renders the employer liable. The person committing the act does not personally commit the offence because it can only be committed by the person fixed with the duty. Such duties have been described as non-delegable, not because the person fixed with the duty must carry it out personally (impossible in the case of a corporation), but because the responsibility cannot be delegated.

An example of a personal duty is to be found in the Merchant Shipping Act 1995, s. 100(1), which imposes on the 'owner of a ship' a duty 'to take all reasonable steps to secure that the ship is operated in a safe manner'. The Divisional Court has held that although s. 31 (the section under the predecessor Merchant Shipping Act 1988, in respect of which the case was decided) excludes *mens rea* because of the public interest in protecting life and property at sea, it did not follow that ship owners are vicariously liable for the actions of all employees, however lowly. A ship owner was criminally liable only in respect of the failure to take such steps as it was reasonable to take in the circumstances (*Seaboard Offshore Ltd v Secretary of State for Transport* [1994] 2 All ER 99).

Whether the duty imposed by statute is vicarious or personal depends upon 'the object of the statute, the words used, the nature of the duty laid down, the person upon whom it is imposed, the person by whom it would in ordinary circumstances be performed, and the person upon whom the penalty is imposed' (per Atkin J in *Mousell Bros Ltd v London and North-Western Railway Co.* [1917] 2 KB 836 at p. 845).

Not all offences of strict liability also involve vicarious liability (e.g., some driving offences may be strict in the sense that they require no *mens rea*, but do not invoke vicarious liability of the employer). On the other hand, where a statute imposes a strict duty, an employer or principal may well be liable for the acts of employees or agents whether authorised or not. See *Chisholm v Doulton* (1889) 22 QBD 736, per Cave J at p. 741: **A6.10**

> A master is not criminally responsible for a death caused by his servant's negligence, and still less for an offence depending on the servant's malice; nor can a master be held liable for the guilt of his servant in receiving goods knowing them to be stolen. And this principle of common law applies also to statutory offences, with this difference, that it is in the power of the Legislature, if it so

> pleases, to enact ... that a man may be convicted and punished for an offence although there was no blameworthy condition of mind about him.

See also *Coppen v Moore (No. 2)* [1898] 2 QB 306. In these circumstances a corporation can properly be convicted for a breach of duty it did not encourage and may even have taken steps to prevent.

In *Coppen v Moore (No. 2)*, the shop owner, Mr Coppen, had given a clear written order forbidding staff from misdescribing goods for sale; nonetheless Lord Russell CJ stated:

> ... having regard to the language, scope, and object of those Acts, the Legislature intended to fix criminal responsibility upon the master for acts done by his servant in the course of his employment, although such acts were not authorized by the master, and might even have been expressly prohibited by him.

In effect, the courts have and will continue to interpret legislation to enable the desired result to follow in ordinary circumstances, much as propounded by Lord Hoffmann in *Meridian Global Funds Management Asia Ltd v Securities Commission* [1995] 2 AC 500.

A6.11 Although many offences which attract vicarious liability are strict, it is not true to say that vicarious liability attaches *only* to offences where there is no fault as to one or more elements. By way of example, the offence of selling videos to an underage person, where the person at the till must consider the age of the purchaser, has been held to be an offence of vicarious liability for the company selling the video, despite the fact that those identified with the company had no part to play in the transaction. To interpret the requirement otherwise would have defeated the aim of the legislation (*Tesco Supermarkets Ltd v Brent London Borough Council* [1993] 2 All ER 718). Where the purpose of a statutory provision would be inoperable without it, the courts will read in such an interpretation.

Strict Liability

A6.12 Given the presumption that some criminal state of mind, even in offences typically committed by a company, is required to prove a criminal offence (*Woolmington v DPP* [1935] AC 462 at p. 481), when considering whether an offence is one of strict liability, one must first determine whether it requires proof of *mens rea*. The court will presume that *mens rea* is an element of an offence unless Parliament has clearly indicated to the contrary, either expressly or by necessary implication (see *B (A Minor) v DPP* [2000] 2 AC 428; *K* [2001] UKHL 41, [2002] 1 AC 462 and **A2.20**). The presumption can be displaced by the wording of the offence-creating section and frequently is displaced in the case of the types of offences for which companies are most often prosecuted. As Lord Bingham CJ said in *Milford Haven Port Authority* [2000] 2 Cr App R (S) 423 at p. 432:

> Parliament creates an offence of strict liability because it regards the doing or not doing of a particular thing as itself so undesirable as to merit the imposition of criminal punishment on anyone who does or does not do that thing irrespective of that party's knowledge, state of mind, belief or intention. This involves a departure from the prevailing canons of the criminal law because of the importance which is attached to achieving the result which Parliament seeks to achieve.

This 'departure from the prevailing canons' is also necessary because without such liability many provisions are likely to be ineffective.

Strict liability offences do not offend the HRA 1988 unless disproportionate (see **A2.23**), but the courts have tended to distinguish between 'real' and 'quasi-crimes' in this regard. Clearly, the more serious the crime, the less likely it is, in the absence of powerful policy considerations, that an offence of strict liability will be proportionate. An example of the importance of public policy to crimes of strict liability is to be found in *Highbury Poultry Farm Produce Ltd v CPS* [2018] EWHC 3122 (Admin) in which the Administrative Court held that no proof of *mens rea*, culpable act or omission on the part of the business operator was necessary to make out an offence of failing to comply with a specified EU Regulation, which required business operators to ensure that animals should be spared avoidable pain, distress or suffering during their killing and related operations.

A6.13 Where a statutory duty is expressed as requiring the achievement/prevention of a particular result, the prosecution have to prove only that the identified result was not achieved or prevented. They need not identify the acts or omissions by which the breach of duty is alleged. The Crown must prove the breach of duty; how it proves the breach of duty will vary; the detail of the particulars need only be sufficient to give the defence proper notice of the breach alleged in the circumstances (*Chargot Ltd* [2008] UKHL 73, [2009] 1 WLR 1). Where the prosecution can prove an essential ingredient of the offence, but in a variety of ways, the jury must agree on at least one of them (*Brown* (1983) 79 Cr App R 115 (fraudulently inducing the investment of money by false statements), discussed at **D18.44**). Where the prosecution must prove the result (e.g., breach of duty), the jury need *not* be agreed on the way in which the Crown proves that result.

Delegation

The principle of delegation imposes a duty on a particular class of person, making breach of that duty an offence. Again, this is a personal liability arising in particular areas of operation such as licensing, where the offences have an element of *mens rea*. The crime can be committed only by the office holder, even if the act or omission is that of another person. The person under the duty can be convicted where that person has delegated the duty to another and that other does the prohibited act and has the appropriate state of mind. The *mens rea* of the delegate will be imputed to the office holder. In *St Regis Paper Co. Ltd* [2011] EWCA Crim 2527, [2012] 1 Cr App R 14 (177) Moses LJ reiterated (at [28]–[29]) the very rare circumstances in which delegation arises, and the fact that it must not be confused with vicarious liability. **A6.14**

PARTNERSHIPS AND OTHER UNINCORPORATED BODIES

Partnerships

Unlike companies, partnerships and other unincorporated bodies cannot themselves be liable for common-law offences since such bodies are not legal persons at common law. In an ordinary partnership, each partner is personally liable for all debts of the firm, whereas the members of an incorporated company have no individual liability to the company's creditors; their liability is only to the company and it is satisfied if they pay the calls properly made upon them by the company or its liquidator. However, for statutory offences enacted since 1889, it appears that the effect of the Interpretation Act 1889, s. 19 (and sch. 1 to the Interpretation Act 1978), is that 'person' includes a body of persons 'unincorporate'. This applies 'unless the contrary intention appears' (s. 5 of the 1978 Act). Woolf J seemed to think that such a contrary intention applied to statutory offences when he commented in passing that there could be no question of the Voluntary Euthanasia Society being liable for aiding and abetting suicide under the Suicide Act 1961 in *A-G v Able* [1984] QB 795. In *W. Stevenson & Sons (a Partnership)* [2008] EWCA Crim 273, [2008] 2 Cr App R 14 (187), Lord Phillips CJ stated (at [28]): **A6.15**

> ... whether or not the context permits one to read 'person' in a criminal statute as including a partnership may depend critically upon whether there is some restriction upon the assets that will properly be available to meet any penalty imposed.

His lordship had in mind the danger of an individual partner who was not personally at fault or responsible in any way for the offence becoming liable for personal assets to be seized as a result of the conviction of the partnership. A number of statutes now provide expressly that an offence can be committed by a partnership or unincorporated body but generally this is not seen as problematic since, in most cases, the statute restricts recovery of any fine to partnership assets or funds (e.g., the Health Act 2006, s. 77(5) and (6); for other examples see those listed in *Stevenson*, to which can now be added the CMCHA 2007, s. 14(3)). The problem that arose in *Stevenson* was that the particular offence-creating provision (a Sea Fishing Order) did not expressly limit recovery to partnership assets, but Lord Phillips was clear that such a limitation was implicit in the overall design of the order which permitted liability of an individual for the offence committed by the partnership only if it was 'committed with his consent, connivance or due to his neglect' (at [31]). In the context of a solicitors' firm being liable for breaches of rules made by the Financial Services Authority (prior to its replacement by the FCA) under the FSMA 2000, the Court of Appeal clearly considered the assets of the partnership to include one partner's hidden payments which, upon discovery, were accountable to the partnership to be properly taken into account when considering the profits of the firm (*Financial Services Authority v Fox Hayes (a firm)* [2009] EWCA Civ 76).

Although called partnerships, Limited Liability Partnerships or LLPs have more of the characteristics of corporations. They are creatures of statute under the Limited Liability Partnerships Act 2000. Section 1(2) of that Act provides that an LLP is:

> ... a body corporate (with legal personality separate from that of its members) which is formed by being incorporated under this Act; and—
> (a) in the following provisions of this Act (except in the phrase 'oversea limited liability partnership'), and
> (b) in any other enactment (except where provision is made to the contrary or the context otherwise requires),
>
> references to a limited liability partnership are to such a body corporate.

As an LLP explicitly has a separate legal personality from its members, it appears that criminal liability would attach for *mens rea* crimes in the same manner as it does to a corporation, principally via the doctrine of identification. Problems concerning the seniority of those capable of being identified with the LLP (similar to the problems arising in relation to corporations) are likely to arise. It is, for example, presently unresolved whether an equity partner would be of sufficient seniority in a large LLP to be identified with it or whether only managing partners actually running the business will suffice. Various provisions of the Companies Act 2006 specifically apply to an LLP through the Limited Liability Partnerships (Application of Companies Act 2006) Regulations 2009 (SI 2009 No. 1804), e.g., s. 993 on fraudulent trading.

Other Unincorporated Bodies

A6.16 The liability of unincorporated bodies other than partnerships was considered in *L* [2008] EWCA Crim 1970, [2009] 1 All ER 786, a prosecution under the Water Resources Act 1991, s. 85, brought against the chairman and treasurer of a golf club. The club's oil heating pipe was the source of a polluting escape. The absence of any specific statutory procedural provisions governing any aspect of the alleged responsibility of the unincorporated body did not amount to a contrary intention against such responsibility arising. Accordingly, the trial judge had been correct in ruling that the golf club itself could have been prosecuted. It was recognised that different considerations might well apply to statutory offences requiring *mens rea* as in *A-G v Able* [1984] QB 795. More worryingly perhaps, the absence of any officers' liability clause restricting the liability of members to offences in which they consented or connived etc., allowed for individual liability of all or any of the 900 members of the golf club, including the two defendants, and the trial judge had been wrong to rule they could not be prosecuted. (However, given that it was recognised that the club could itself be prosecuted and it was agreed that this was the appropriate choice to be made, the acquittal of the individual officers was directed.) In *Riley v CPS* [2016] EWHC 2531 (Admin), [2017] 1 WLR 505, the question of partnership liability was considered in respect of an offence which required proof of *mens rea*. Where there was no suggestion of a system failure on the part of the partnership or participation in the offence by absent individual partners, the CPS case against the partnership failed.

CORPORATIONS AND HUMAN RIGHTS

A6.17 Somewhat counter-intuitively, companies benefit from the ECHR and the HRA 1998, much as individual defendants do (see A7 for human rights generally). A company is entitled to a fair trial under Article 6, and many other provisions, such as Article 10 (right to freedom of expression) and Protocol 1 (right to property), also apply. Although the right to a fair trial is absolute, the constituent rights are not; other rights are balanced against the rights of others and public interest considerations. One can glean a distinction between where the balance is struck in the case of an individual, as opposed to a corporation, in the application of the concept of proportionality. The courts have consistently made decisions with reference to proportionality (e.g., *Bank Mellat v HM Treasury (No. 2)* [2013] UKSC 39, [2014] AC 700 on Protocol 1, Article 1 and *Sinclair Collis Ltd v Secretary of State for Health* [2010] EWHC 3112 (Admin), determining that a ban on the sale of tobacco from automatic vending machines was a necessary and proportionate response to public health concerns). Strict liability offences, many of which affect corporations, do not offend the presumption of innocence (see **A2.20**); neither do reverse burdens in appropriate circumstances (see **F3.18** ***et seq.***): the seriousness of the criminal charge, the risks to the public and the ability of the defendant to raise the defence are all matters considered relevant to Article 6 compliance.

DEFENCES TO CORPORATE CRIMES

Many statutory provisions, especially for strict liability offences, provide a statutory defence, most of which include a reverse burden. They mitigate against the severity of strict liability offences on the basis that, normally, D should be guilty of a criminal offence only where there is some element of fault by D, not another person. These defences may be phrased in terms of 'all reasonable steps', 'so far as reasonably practicable' or 'due diligence', proof of which usually lies with D. Even where the burden on D is a legal and not merely an evidential one, it may be HRA compliant. This reverse burden has frequently been tested in the courts and generally found to be proportionate in cases with corporate defendants. The test is whether the modification or limitation on the right to a fair trial (under the ECHR, Article 6(2)) pursues a legitimate aim and whether it satisfies the principle of proportionality in *Ashingdane v UK* (1985) 7 EHRR 528. See further **F3.18** ***et seq.*** **A6.18**

'All reasonable steps'

This gives rise to a duty that cannot be delegated to a third party or independent contractor. In *DEFRA v Keam* [2005] EWHC 1582 (Admin), the principle was stated: **A6.19**

> In a case where the keeper defendant employs an independent contractor to take care of his animals and nothing more, whether in these circumstances he has taken all reasonable steps is a matter for the trial court. In many cases if not in most, one would expect the keeper (a) to have ensured his independent contractor was indeed competent and (b) to take steps to ensure that his independent contractor was doing that which ought to be done in caring for the animals. In many if not most cases, simply to appoint an independent contractor... to care for his animals may well not amount to the taking of all reasonable steps. Conversely the fact that an independent contractor fails to take all reasonable steps does not of itself involve criminal liability on the part of the person... who has employed the independent contractor, if that [person] has taken all reasonable steps to ensure that [the regulations are complied with], that is to say, there is no vicarious liability for the default of the independent contractor in circumstances in which the keeper can show that he himself did take all reasonable steps.

As the defence states, D must show that *all* reasonable steps were taken and not just some; if D could have taken more, or other, reasonable steps which objectively would have prevented the offence, the defence will not have been proved. On the other hand, D need not show that all steps possible were taken, only those which are reasonable.

'So far as reasonably practicable'

Again, this is a personal duty. In *Associated Octel Co Ltd* [1996] 4 All ER 846, the House of Lords emphasised that engaging an independent contractor to do work and omitting to stipulate for 'whatever conditions are needed to avoid those [offending] risks and [which] are reasonably practicable' would not entitle D to rely on the defence. In *Gateway Foodmarkets Ltd* [1997] 3 All ER 78, the Court of Appeal indicated that: **A6.20**

> ... the duty... is broken if the specified consequences occur, but only if 'so far as is reasonably practicable' they have not been guarded against. So the company is in breach of duty unless all reasonable

precautions have been taken and we would interpret this as meaning 'taken by the company or on its behalf'. In other words ... the company is liable in the event that there is a failure to ensure the [duty is undertaken] unless all reasonable precautions have been taken ... by the company or on its behalf.

If the event was wholly unknown or unexpected, it would be unreasonable to require the accused to take measures against it and thus the defence could pertain (*Austin Rover Group Ltd v Inspector of Factories* [1990] 1 AC 619). Latham LJ in *HTM Ltd* [2006] EWCA Crim 1156, [2007] 2 All ER 665 stated (at [22]): 'Foreseeability is merely a tool with which to assess the likelihood of a risk eventuating. It is not a means of permitting a defendant to bring concepts of fault appropriate to civil proceedings into the equation by the back door.'

From a string of cases concerning the Health and Safety at Work etc. Act 1974, the following principles can be gleaned: health and safety offences are concerned primarily with exposure to risk; the law does not aim to create an environment which is risk-free, only one in which there is no material (as opposed to trivial, fanciful or hypothetical) risk to health and safety, i.e. risks 'which any reasonable person would appreciate and take steps to guard against' per Lord Hope in *Chargot Ltd* [2008] UKHL 73, [2009] 1 WLR 1 at [27]. This has an impact on whether there was a risk of harm at all, and on whether a defence of guarding against a risk so far as reasonably practicable had been raised or discharged; foreseeability of danger (and thus risk) is relevant to the question whether a risk to safety exists; but the principal relevance of foreseeability is to the defence of whether all reasonable precautions have been taken (*Tangerine Confectionery Ltd* [2011] EWCA Crim 2015 at [36]; *Porter* [2008] EWCA Crim 1271; *EGS Ltd* [2009] EWCA Crim 1942). In *Baker v Quantum Group Ltd* [2011] UKSC 17, [2011] 4 All ER 223, the Supreme Court, in a civil case relating to the Factories Act 1961, considered that compliance with acceptable standards at the time or 'recognized and established practice' was relevant to the issue of negligence. This reasoning was followed in the criminal case of *Tangerine Confectionery*.

'Due diligence'

A6.21 A number of permutations of the due diligence defence exist, with corresponding differences in application. Some offences require 'due diligence' whilst others require 'all due diligence' and yet others 'all due diligence and taken all reasonable steps'. They should not be considered to have identical effect; indeed, clearly the standard D has to meet is higher if 'all due diligence' is specified. What is sufficient to amount to due diligence is an objective fact and may not be based on ignorance of the law (*Renaissance Accountancy Services Ltd v Revenue and Customs Commissioners* [2012] UKFTT 83 (TC)). Acting in accordance with a relevant code of practice may be evidence of due diligence but need not be; the opposite will almost inevitably indicate a failure so to act. The phrase 'with all due diligence' consists of ordinary words; to add a further gloss, such as negligence and a reprehensible state of mind to prove guilt runs the risk of importing a mental element which is inappropriate (*Croydon London Borough Council v Pinch a Pound (UK) Ltd* [2010] EWHC 3283 (Admin), [2011] 1 WLR 1189). A company cannot rely on the defence if it has delegated its responsibilities to another because the defence, like the obligation, is personal (*Seaboard Offshore Ltd v Secretary of State for Transport* [1994] 2 All ER 99). But, as long as the company has put in place procedures, or relied upon another in such a manner that it amounts to evidence that it has done (all) due diligence, the defence will be available. In the seminal case of *Tesco Supermarkets Ltd v Nattrass* [1972] AC 153, the magistrates heard a considerable body of evidence and found as a fact that Tesco had fulfilled the defence of taking all reasonable precautions and had exercised all due diligence. It was emphasised in the Court of Appeal that such evidence is necessary if the defence is to be made out; if D calls no evidence whatsoever, the defence will inevitably fail (*Associated Octel Co Ltd* [1996] 4 All ER 846).

SENTENCING CORPORATE CRIMES

A6.22 Sentencing corporations convicted of crime brings its own specific challenges. Many of the guideline cases relate to health and safety and environmental legislation. The guideline case of *F Howe &*

Son (Engineers) Ltd [1999] 2 All ER 249 (see **E15.19**) provides a number of factors relevant to sentence which the parties should address and the court should take into account. These factors were largely replicated and enhanced in the guideline published by the Sentencing Council entitled *Corporate offenders: fraud, bribery and money laundering* (see Supplement, **SG26-33**), with effect from 1 October 2014. The case of *Thames Water Utilities Ltd* [2015] EWCA Crim 960, [2015] 1 WLR 4411 makes the following points on sentencing corporate defendants: first, the importance of adhering strictly to CrimPD VII Sentencing B and CrimPR 24.11 and 25.16 (see Supplement, **CPD.VII.B**, **R24.11** and **R25.16**) in terms of provision of information for the tribunal; secondly, following the stepped approach to sentencing set out in the guideline; and thirdly, where a company has acted negligently or worse and caused harm and its turnover greatly exceeds the threshold set out in the guideline, it will be necessary to set the fine at such a level as 'to bring the appropriate message home to the directors and shareholders and to punish them' (at [42]).

Further sentencing guidelines on financial penalties for health and safety, corporate manslaughter and food safety and hygiene offences came into force in February 2016 (see Supplement, **SG28-1**). Significantly, they followed the earlier guideline in requiring a court that has taken steps to determine culpability and harm to consider the overall level of appropriate fines and adjust them down or up, depending on the future safe and legal conduct of the business and, conversely, the level of corporate profit so that the fines will 'have a real economic impact'. It is likely that this approach to sentencing will be replicated for other corporate crimes.

A company may now be subject to a DPA pursuant to the CCA 2013, s. 45 and sch. 17 (see **D12.106**). The first DPA was approved in *SFO v Standard Bank plc* [2016] Lloyd's Rep FC 91 in November 2015. Since then, increasingly the Court has approved DPAs with a 50 per cent reduction in the level of the fine (*SFO v Sarclad Ltd* [2016] Lloyd's Rep FC 509; *SFO v Rolls Royce* [2017] Lloyd's Rep FC 249; *SFO v Tesco Stores Ltd* (10 April 2017 unreported, Southwark Crown Court); *SFO v Serco Geografix Ltd* [2019] Lloyd's Rep FC 5018). In *Rolls Royce*, Leveson P did so, even though there had been no self-report, because the level of cooperation was 'extraordinary'. At the present time, as a matter of fact, most DPAs have been agreed with larger companies. The SFO has stated a desire that DPAs be increasingly considered for SMEs.

The *Serco Geografix Ltd* case is important because it is the first DPA where undertakings as to future conduct were provided by the parent company as part of the DPA made with its subsidiary.

A corporate defendant is just as liable to confiscation proceedings as an individual defendant (see **E19**). However, the fact that a director is convicted of a crime does not mean that a non-defendant company's assets are caught by the director's confiscation order, even when the offence of which the director is convicted concerns the corporation. Concealment or evasion through the corporate structure were required where the corporate assets were to be caught by the officer's confiscation order: 'The Crown Court had no inherent jurisdiction of its own and the [POCA 2002] itself contained no provision purporting to sanction a departure from ordinary principles of company law. It followed that Crown Courts in confiscation cases should treat with a degree of circumspection, when an issue of lifting or piercing the corporate veil had been raised, tempting invitations to adopt a "robust" or "broad brush" approach and to avoid being distracted by "niceties"' (*Boyle Transport (Northern Ireland) Ltd* [2016] EWCA Crim 19, [2016] 2 Cr App R (S) 11 (43) at [91]–[94]).

DIRECTOR'S DUTIES AND CRIMES

Separate Identity of Company

Because a company is a separate person from its officers, the officers will not necessarily be guilty of a crime just because the company is. Conversely, since a company may be fixed with criminal liability through the acts or omissions of its 'directing mind', the way for criminal liability to be proved may, **A6.23** depending on the relevant rule of attribution, be by identifying the criminal acts of one of its officers; in those circumstances both the individual officer and the company may be guilty. In appropriate circumstances, both the company and its officers may be charged with a criminal offence and/or with aiding and abetting an employee to commit a crime (*JF Alford Transport Ltd* [1997] 2 Cr App R 326). On the other hand, it is no defence to a charge properly brought, that a person was acting in the course of employment or committing crime on behalf of an employer (*Standard Chartered Bank v Pakistan National Shipping Corporation (Nos. 2 and 4)* [2002] UKHL 43, [2003] 1 AC 959). Despite the separate identity of the company, a director cannot conspire with the company alone, the essence of conspiracy being an agreement between at least two separate persons (see **A6.5**).

Consent, Connivance and Neglect

A6.24 The liability of a company for an offence does not preclude the liability of an individual employee, but the fact that the company is liable may also have the effect of casting the net of individual responsibility more widely. This is because many statutes now contain a section imposing liability on any 'director, manager, secretary or other similar officer' with whose 'consent or connivance' the offence has been committed or to whose 'neglect' it is attributable (see, e.g., the Trade Descriptions Act 1968, s. 20). In order for any person to be successfully prosecuted under these provisions, the prosecution must prove that the company is guilty of an offence, although it need not be convicted nor on trial. In many cases such a person would be liable on normal principles as an accessory. However, the reference to 'neglect' means liability is wider than that for accessories for whom negligence is not normally sufficient (see **A4.5**). Neglect does not necessarily require actual knowledge if the circumstances were such that they should have put the officer on inquiry (*P* [2007] EWCA Crim 1937, a case under the Health and Safety at Work etc. Act 1974, s. 37). The approach in *P* was subsequently approved in the House of Lords in *Chargot Ltd* [2008] UKHL 73, [2009] 1 WLR 1, upholding a director's conviction for corporate offences under s. 37 arising from the death of a dumper-truck driver who had been working for the companies of which the appellant was a director. Lord Hope expressly referred to the issue of whether the officer 'should have been put on inquiry so as to have taken steps to determine whether or not the appropriate safety procedures were in place'. His lordship also commented that:

> ... no fixed rule can be laid down as to what the prosecution must identify and prove in order to establish that the officer's state of mind was such as to amount to consent, connivance or neglect. In some cases, as where the officer's place of activity was remote from the workplace or what was done there was not under his immediate direction and control, this may require the leading of quite detailed evidence of which fair notice may have to be given. In others, where the officer was in day to day contact with what was done there, very little more may be needed.

On the other hand, an officer of the company must hold a position of real authority with both the power and responsibility to decide corporate policy. The officer must perform a governing role in respect of the affairs of the company rather than merely a day-to-day management function (*Boal* [1992] QB 591).

There is no need for the Crown to prove specific knowledge of each allegation. In *Hutchins* [2011] EWCA Crim 1056, Rix LJ stated (at [25]):

> ... the nature of these regulatory statutes with their provisions for secondary liability by directors and managers in accordance with their consent, connivance or neglect is to ensure that they are held to proper standards of supervision and that the size of the company and the distance of directors and managers from the coal face of individual acts should not, where there is consent, connivance or neglect, afford directors or managers with the necessary knowledge a defence.

A6.25 In some statutes, the reference to 'neglect' is omitted (see, e.g., the Theft Act 1968, s. 18; Public Order Act 1986, s. 28; Copyright, Designs and Patents Act 1988, s. 110) and the prosecution must rely on connivance or consent, both of which would appear to require the same degree of knowledge as aiding and abetting. Even here, though, the liability is potentially wider than that of an accessory since a positive act of aiding and abetting is not necessarily required. A conscious failure to prevent or report a fellow director committing an offence would seem to be enough, even though there is not a sufficiently clear or immediate right of control over the fellow director to give rise to liability as an accessory.

INVESTIGATING CORPORATE WRONG-DOING

With the rise in regulatory and criminal sanctions for corporates has come a significant growth in internal investigations or investigations conducted on behalf of the corporate by external professionals. Two decisions impact on investigations into corporate crime, particularly cross-border crime. In *R (KBR Inc.) v Director of the SFO* [2018] EWHC 2368 (Admin), [2019] 2 WLR 267, the Administrative Court ruled that where there is a sufficient connection between the company and the jurisdiction, the SFO can serve a notice under the CJA 1987, s. 2(3), requiring material held outside the UK from a foreign company. Nonetheless, merely being the parent company was an insufficient connection. In *Director of the SFO v Eurasian Natural Resources Corporation Ltd* [2018] EWCA Civ 2006, [2019] 1 WLR 791, the Court of Appeal (Civil Division) decided that for litigation privilege to attach: (i) litigation must be in progress or contemplation; (ii) protected communications must be made for the sole or dominant purpose of conducting that litigation; and (iii) adversarial litigation applies to criminal investigations as well as civil proceedings and can include a SFO investigation being on the horizon. Although it was unnecessary to rule on legal advice privilege, the Court of Appeal stated that the decision in *Three Rivers District Council v Governor and Company of the Bank of England (No. 5)* [2003] EWCA Civ 474, [2003] QB 1556 was, in the Court's view, wrong and ripe for review. **A6.26**

The Crime (Overseas Production Orders) Act 2019, enacted on 12 February 2019, allows judges in England and Wales to grant an overseas production order requiring the named overseas service provider to produce or allow access to stored electronic information, for the purposes of investigating or prosecuting serious crime, which would compel the overseas company to produce electronic data. By s. 4 there must, *inter alia*, be reasonable grounds for believing that an indictable offence has been committed, and that the data is likely to be of substantial value to the investigation, likely to be relevant evidence (the latter being a necessary requirement for all but terrorism offences) and likely to be in the public interest. The order may be served (e.g. electronically) directly on the foreign company that holds the data, replacing the more cumbersome route of mutual legal assistance.

Section A7 Human Rights

INTRODUCTION

A7.1 The European Convention for the Protection of Human Rights and Fundamental Freedoms (Cm. 8969) (the ECHR) is an international treaty of the Council of Europe. It was adopted in 1950, ratified by the UK in 1951 and entered into force in 1953. The unusual feature of the Convention, as an international human rights instrument, is that it provides a mechanism for individuals to enforce their Convention rights against States Parties.

The Convention has been amplified by a number of Protocols. One of the most important is Protocol 11, which abolished the European Commission of Human Rights. As a result, the Convention is now administered by two bodies: the European Court of Human Rights (ECtHR) and the Committee of Ministers of the Council of Europe. The great majority of the judgments of the Court are given by Chambers, but a Grand Chamber of the Court, composed of 17 judges, deals with cases that raise a serious question of interpretation or application of the Convention, or a serious issue of general importance.

The HRA 1998 is designed 'to give further effect to the rights and freedoms guaranteed under the European Convention on Human Rights' (see the long title). It is intended to 'give people in the United Kingdom opportunities to enforce their rights under the European Convention in British courts rather than having to incur the cost and delay of taking a case to the European Human Rights... Court in Strasbourg' (Prime Minister's preface to the White Paper, *Bringing Rights Home*, Cm. 3782).

Convention Rights

A7.2 The rights protected by the HRA 1998 are called 'Convention rights' (s. 1(1)). They are set out in sch. 1 to the HRA 1998.

In the HRA 1998, 'the Convention rights' means the rights and fundamental freedoms set out in: (a) Articles 2 to 12 and 14 of the ECHR, (b) Articles 1 to 3 of the First Protocol, and (c) Article 1 of the Thirteenth Protocol (s. 1(1)).

The subject-matter of these rights is as follows:

Article 2:	The right to life
Article 3:	Prohibition on torture
Article 4:	Prohibition on slavery and forced labour
Article 5:	Right to liberty and security
Article 6:	Right to a fair trial
Article 7:	No punishment without law
Article 8:	Right to respect for private and family life
Article 9:	Freedom of thought, conscience and religion
Article 10:	Freedom of expression
Article 11:	Freedom of assembly and association

Article 12: Right to marry
Article 14: Prohibition on discrimination
Article 1, Protocol 1: Protection of property
Article 2, Protocol 1: Right to education
Article 3, Protocol 1: Right to free elections
Article 1, Protocol 13: Abolition of the death penalty

These rights are to be read with Article 16 (restrictions on political activities of aliens), Article 17 (prohibition of abuse of rights) and Article 18 (limitation on use of restrictions on rights) of the ECHR (s. 1(1)).

The Legality of Restrictions on Convention Rights

Any restriction on Convention rights must be lawful. In some places, such as Article 5, the word 'lawful' itself is used. In others, such as Articles 8 and 9, phrases such as 'in accordance with law' or 'prescribed by law' are used. Even where no express provision is made (e.g., in Protocol 1, Article 1), any restriction on Convention rights must nonetheless be 'lawful'. **A7.3**

Under the ECHR the term 'lawful' has a special meaning. A restriction on Convention rights will be 'lawful' only if: (a) there is an established legal basis in domestic law for the restriction: e.g., where it is provided for by legislation or special rules; (b) the provision in question is 'accessible': i.e. those likely to be affected by it can find out what it says; and (c) the provision in question is 'foreseeable': i.e. it is formulated with sufficient clarity to enable those likely to be affected by it to understand it and to regulate their conduct accordingly.

The Legitimacy of Restrictions on Convention Rights

Any restriction on Convention rights must be legitimate. For qualified rights, so long as a restriction genuinely pursues one of the aims set out in the article itself, it will be legitimate. The aims set out in Articles 8 to 11 include: national security, public safety, the prevention of disorder or crime and the protection of the rights and freedoms of others. **A7.4**

The Necessity and Proportionality of Restrictions on Convention Rights

Any restriction on Convention rights must be necessary and proportionate. For qualified rights, this requirement flows from the use of the phrase 'necessary in a democratic society' in Articles 8 to 11. **A7.5**

Necessary The word 'necessary' in the ECHR is not synonymous with 'reasonable'. In *Handyside v UK* (1979–80) 1 EHRR 737, the ECtHR said (at [48]): **A7.6**

> ... whilst the adjective 'necessary', within the meaning of Article 10(2), is not synonymous with 'indispensable', neither has it the flexibility of such expressions as 'admissible', 'ordinary', 'useful', 'reasonable', or 'desirable'.

Nor will a restriction be necessary just because the majority are in favour of it (*Chassagnou v France* (2000) 29 EHRR 615 at [112]).

Proportionality A restriction will be proportionate only if the objective behind the restriction justifies interference with a Convention right, there is a rational connection between the objective and the restriction in question, and the means employed are not more than is necessary to achieve the objective. **A7.7**

In making this assessment, the following factors are relevant: (a) whether relevant and sufficient reasons have been advanced for the restriction; (b) whether there was a less restrictive, but equally effective, way of achieving the same objective; (c) whether sufficient regard has been paid to the rights and interests of those affected (in some cases, e.g., in family cases, those affected should be consulted); (d) whether safeguards exist to guard against error or abuse (e.g., in secret surveillance cases); and (e) whether the restriction in question destroys the very essence of the Convention right in issue.

Positive Obligations

A7.8 The ECHR safeguards Convention rights by limiting the circumstances in which they can be restricted (if at all). Public authorities are under a duty to refrain from restricting Convention rights in any other circumstances.

The ECHR also safeguards Convention rights by imposing an obligation on public authorities to adopt positive measures to protect the Convention rights of individuals. In *Plattform Ärzte für das Leben v Austria* (1991) 13 EHRR 204, the ECtHR said (at [32]):

> Genuine, effective freedom of peaceful assembly cannot . . . be reduced to a mere duty on the part of the state not to interfere; a purely negative conception would not be compatible with the object and purpose of Article 11. Like Article 8, Article 11 sometimes requires positive measures to be taken, even in the sphere of relations between individuals, if need be.

The extent of this obligation will vary according to such factors as the nature of the Convention right in issue, the importance of the right for the individual and the nature of the activities involved in the case.

A7.9 The most onerous positive obligations arise where, by very definition, a Convention right requires the provision of resources: e.g., the right to free legal assistance in criminal cases under Article 6(3)(c). However, the doctrine of positive obligations under the ECHR is not restricted to the provision of resources in such circumstances. It includes a duty on the relevant authorities to put in place a legal framework which provides effective protection for Convention rights (*X and Y v Netherlands* (1986) 8 EHRR 235 at [27]). In *A v UK* (1999) 27 EHRR 611, the ECtHR held that the defence of 'reasonable chastisement' to an alleged offence of assaulting a child was so wide that the child's rights under Article 3 (the prohibition on ill-treatment) were not respected.

Prohibition on Abuse of Rights under Article 17

A7.10 **European Convention on Human Rights, Article 17**

> Nothing in this Convention may be interpreted as implying for any State, group or person any right to engage in any activity or perform any act aimed at the destruction of any of the rights and freedoms set forth herein or at their limitation to a greater extent than is provided for in this Convention.

The purpose of Article 17 is to prevent extremists using the ECHR to destroy the rights of others (*Lawless v Ireland (No. 3)* (1979–80) 1 EHRR 15 at [7]).

Article 17 can be applied only to those rights which are capable of being exercised so as to destroy the rights of others: it cannot be used to restrict rights designed to protect the individual such as those in Articles 5 and 6 (*Lawless v Ireland (No. 3)* at [7]; *Glimmerveen and Hagenbeek v Netherlands* (1979) 18 DR 187 at p. 195). Furthermore, any measure taken under Article 17 must be strictly proportionate to the threat to the rights of others (*De Becker v Belgium* (1961) Series B, No. 4, Appln. 214/56 at [279]; *Lehideux and Isorni v France* (2000) 30 EHRR 665). Article 17 was relied on in *DPP v Collins* [2006] UKHL 40, [2006] 4 All ER 602 when interpreting the Communications Act 2003, s. 127.

The Interpretation of Convention Rights

A7.11 A number of general principles have emerged from the case law of the ECtHR and the Commission of Human Rights about the way in which Convention rights should be interpreted.

A7.12 **Object and Purpose** Convention rights should be interpreted in light of their object and purpose: i.e. to protect individual rights, maintain the rule of law and uphold the ideas and values of a democratic society (*Golder v UK* (1979–80) 1 EHRR 524 at [34]; *Soering v UK* (1989) 11 EHRR 439 at [87]).

Practical and Effective Convention rights should be interpreted in such a way as to make them 'practical and effective'. In *Soering v UK* (1989) 11 EHRR 439, the ECtHR held (at [87]): A7.13

> In interpreting the Convention regard must be had to its special character as a treaty for the collective enforcement of human rights and fundamental freedoms... Thus, the object and purpose of the Convention as a living instrument for the protection of individual human beings require that its provisions be interpreted and applied so as to make its safeguards practical and effective.

Autonomous Meaning Words and phrases in the ECHR are to be given an autonomous meaning, i.e. the meaning ascribed by the ECtHR, not (necessarily) the meaning ascribed in the domestic law of the Contracting States. This is to prevent States undermining the efficacy of the ECHR (*Chassagnou v France* (2000) 29 EHRR 615 at [100]). A7.14

Living Instrument The ECHR is a 'living instrument' requiring a dynamic, evolving interpretation. For example, when considering what conduct might offend Article 3, the ECtHR held in the case of *Selmouni v France* (2000) 29 EHRR 365 (at [101]): A7.15

> The Court has previously examined cases in which it concluded that there had been treatment which could only be described as torture... However, having regard to the fact that the Convention is a 'living instrument' which must be interpreted in the light of present-day conditions... the Court considers that certain acts which were classified in the past as 'inhuman and degrading treatment' as opposed to 'torture' could be classified differently in future. It takes the view that the increasingly high standard being required in the area of the protection of human rights and fundamental liberties correspondingly and inevitably requires greater firmness in assessing breaches of the fundamental values of democratic societies.

Generous and Purposive Construction A generous and purposive construction is to be given to Convention rights under the HRA 1998 suitable to give to individuals the full measure of the fundamental rights and freedoms to which all persons in the State are to be entitled (*DPP, ex parte Kebilene* [2000] 2 AC 326, Lord Hope at p. 998E–F; for the general principle, see *Minister of Home Affairs v Fisher* [1980] AC 319 at p. 328). A7.16

Burden and Standard of Proving a Breach of Convention Rights

It is for the complainant to show that his Convention rights have been infringed, but for the relevant public authority to justify any infringement established (*Jersild v Denmark* (1995) 19 EHRR 1 at [31]). Where absolute rights are at stake, the standard of proof is high: beyond reasonable doubt. However, this can be established by the coexistence of sufficiently strong, clear and concordant inferences or similar unrebutted presumptions of fact. For example, in *Aksoy v Turkey* (1997) 23 EHRR 553, the ECtHR held (at [61]): A7.17

> ... where an individual is taken into police custody in good health but is found to be injured at the time of release, it is incumbent on the State to provide a plausible explanation as to the causing of the injury, failing which a clear issue arises under Article 3 of the Convention.

Failure of the relevant authority to furnish information may also lead to adverse inferences being drawn (*Timurtas v Turkey* (2000) Appln. 23531/94, 13 June 2000 at [66]).

Waiver of Convention Rights

Convention rights can be waived only in limited circumstances and waiver must be established in an unequivocal manner (*Zana v Turkey* (1999) 27 EHRR 671 at [70]). In *Pfeifer and Plankl v Austria* (1992) 14 EHRR 692, the ECtHR held (at [37]): A7.18

> According to the Court's case law, the waiver of a right guaranteed by the Convention — in so far as it is permissible — must be established in an unequivocal manner. Moreover... in the case of procedural rights a waiver, in order to be effective for Convention purposes, requires minimum guarantees commensurate with its importance.

Failure to raise an issue cannot be automatically equated with waiver (*McGonnell v UK* (2000) 30 EHRR 289 at [44]–[46], in the context of a fair trial).

Certain Convention rights probably cannot be waived at all: e.g., absolute rights such as the right to life and the prohibition on torture and slavery, and perhaps also fair trial rights under Article 6 (*Pfeifer and Plankl v Austria* (1992) 14 EHRR 692 at [39]). In *Jones* [2002] UKHL 5, [2003] 1 AC 1, the House of Lords held that D had waived his right to legal representation when he absconded at trial, both at common law and under the ECHR.

THE INTERPRETATION OF LEGISLATION

Primary Legislation

A7.19 **Human Rights Act 1998, s. 3**

(1) So far as it is possible to do so, primary legislation and subordinate legislation must be read and given effect in a way which is compatible with Convention rights.

The use of the word 'possible' is intended to convey a stronger interpretative requirement than 'reasonable' (Home Secretary, *Hansard*, HC vol. 313, col. 421 (3 June 1998)).

A7.20 The scope of the approach to interpretation authorised by s. 3 has been considered in a number of cases at the highest level. The House of Lords in *Ghaidan v Ghodin-Mendoza* [2004] UKHL 30, [2004] 2 AC 557 held that 'excessive concentration on the linguistic features of the [statute to be interpreted]', should be substituted in favour of a 'purposive' approach concentrating on 'the importance of the fundamental right involved'. As Lord Nicholls pointed out, if it is accepted that s. 3 was intended to supersede the pre-HRA principle that legislation had to be ambiguous before it was 'possible' to interpret it compatibly with the ECHR, Parliament cannot have intended the courts to 'depend critically upon the particular form of words adopted by the parliamentary draftsman' in the legislation in question without making the application of s. 3 'something of a semantic lottery' (*Ghaidan v Ghodin-Mendoza* at [31]).

In *Ali (Humza)* [2018] EWCA Crim 547, [2018] 1 WLR 6105, D argued in the Court of Appeal that the TA 2006, s. 2, should be read down so as to protect his rights to freedom of expression under Article 10. In particular he argued that where s. 2 referred to 'acts of terrorism' the jury should have been directed that that expression meant 'criminal offences'. The Court rejected that submission. The terms of s. 2 do not prevent a person from holding offensive views or personally supporting a terrorist cause or communicating the fact that the person supports such a cause. What s. 2 prohibits is the intentional or reckless dissemination of a terrorist publication where the effect of D's conduct is a direct or indirect encouragement to the commission, preparation or instigation of acts of terrorism. It followed that the aim of s. 2 was clearly lawful, proportionate and necessary and its terms did not need to be read down in order to ensure its compatibility with D's Convention rights. Nevertheless, when directing juries as to the elements of the offence it was important that judges 'did sufficient to protect the defendant's rights of expression so that he was not in danger of being convicted for conduct which fell short of the statute and represented a legitimate exercise of his rights' (at [17]). In *Ali (Humza)* the summing-up adequately protected D's right to freedom of expression and so his conviction was safe.

Nothing in the HRA 1998 affects the validity, continuing operation or enforcement of primary legislation which is incompatible with Convention rights (s. 3(2)(b)). But in certain circumstances a 'declaration of incompatibility' can be made.

Declarations of Incompatibility

A7.21 Under the HRA 1998, certain courts are given the power to make declarations of incompatibility if they determine that a provision in primary legislation is incompatible with Convention rights (s. 4(2)). The relevant courts for England and Wales are the Supreme Court, the Court of Appeal, the High Court and the Courts-Martial Appeal Court (s. 4(5)). A declaration of incompatibility is intended to operate as a signal to Parliament that an incompatibility has been found and to prompt remedial action. It does not affect the validity, continuing operation or enforcement of the provision in question (s. 4(6)(a)).

If a court is considering whether or not to make a declaration of incompatibility, the Crown has a right to be notified and can intervene (s. 5(1) and (2)). In criminal proceedings, if any application is to be made to the Court of Appeal for a declaration of incompatibility or any issue is to be raised which may have that effect, the procedure set out in CrimPR 36.12 (see Supplement, **R36.12**) must be followed.

Subordinate Legislation

So far as it is possible to do so, subordinate legislation must be read and given effect in a way which is compatible with Convention rights (HRA 1998, s. 3(1)). As with primary legislation, this rule of interpretation applies whenever the subordinate legislation in question was enacted (s. 3(2)(a)). But, unlike the position in relation to primary legislation, where subordinate legislation cannot be read and given effect in a way which is compatible with Convention rights, this *does* affect its validity, continuing operation and enforcement (s. 3(2)(b) and (c)) and it can be quashed or declared invalid by reason of incompatibility (s. 10(4)). The only exception is where primary legislation prevents the removal of any incompatibility (s. 3(1)(c)). In such circumstances, a declaration of incompatibility can be made (s. 4(4)). **A7.22**

The Relevance of Strasbourg Jurisprudence

A court or tribunal determining a question which has arisen in connection with a Convention right must take into account judgments of the ECtHR and Commission of Human Rights and decisions of the Commission and the Committee of Ministers (HRA 1998, s. 2(1)). But such judgments and decisions are not binding. **A7.23**

In *R (Hicks) v Metropolitan Police Commissioner* [2014] EWCA Civ 3, [2014] 1 WLR 2152 at [80], the Court of Appeal reviewed the relevant authorities and extracted the following principles:

(1) It is the duty of the national courts to enforce domestically enacted Convention rights.
(2) The ECtHR is the court that, ultimately, must interpret the meaning of the Convention.
(3) The UK courts will be bound to follow an interpretation of a provision of the Convention if given by the Grand Chamber as authoritative, unless it is apparent that it has misunderstood or overlooked some significant feature of English law or practice which, properly explained, would lead to that interpretation being reviewed by the ECtHR when its interpretation was being applied to English circumstances.
(4) The same principle and qualification applies to a 'clear and consistent' line of decisions of the ECtHR other than one of the Grand Chamber.
(5) Convention rights have to be given effect in the light of the domestic law which implements in detail the 'high level' rights set out in the ECHR.
(6) Where there are 'mixed messages' in the existing Strasbourg case law, a 'real judicial choice' will have to be made about the scope and application of the relevant provision of the Convention.

In the Supreme Court, no doubt was cast on the principles extracted by the Court of Appeal and set out above (*R (Hicks) v Metropolitan Police Commissioner* [2017] UKSC 9, [2017] AC 256). In *Metropolitan Police Commissioner v DSD* [2018] UKSC 11, [2018] 2 WLR 895, the Supreme Court considered a number of issues in relation to the general duty imposed by the HRA 1998 to investigate ill-treatment that amounts to a violation of the ECHR, Article 3 (see **A7.33**). One of those issues was whether the general duty was owed to the public or to individual victims of the breach of Article 3, even in circumstances where the person who caused the ill-treatment was not an agent of the State. Lord Kerr reviewed the Strasbourg case law and concluded (at [48]) that it provided 'clear and constant' authority for the proposition that the State is obliged under Article 3 to conduct an effective investigation into crimes which involve serious violence to persons, whether that has been carried out by State agents or individual criminals. In doing so he referred to *R (Ullah) v Special Adjudicator* [2004] UKHL 26, [2004] 2 AC 323, where Lord Bingham of Cornhill observed (at [20]) that in the absence of special circumstances the courts should follow any clear and constant jurisprudence of the Strasbourg Court. Lord Kerr referred to Lord Bingham's statement as the 'so-called "mirror principle"' (at [76]) whereby pronouncements by national courts on Convention rights should precisely match those of Strasbourg. In Lord Kerr's opinion, the statement from Lord Bingham in *Ullah* had been used in subsequent judgments to support the proposition that the content of domestic rights under the HRA 1998 should not, as a matter of principle, differ from that pronounced by Strasbourg and, moreover, that where the Strasbourg Court has not given clear guidance on the nature and content of a particular Convention right the national courts should decline to recognise 'the substance of a claimed entitlement under ECHR'. Lord Kerr observed that more recent cases have marked a departure from the mirror principle. In particular, in *Moohan v Lord Advocate* [2014] UKSC 67, [2015] AC 901, Lord Wilson held (at [105]) that where there is no directly relevant decision of the Strasbourg Court with which it would be possible to keep pace, the national courts can and must do more by determining for themselves the existence or otherwise of an alleged Convention right. In the view of Lord Kerr in *DSD*, the opinion of Lord Wilson in *Moohan* was 'inescapably correct' (at [78]) and so reticence by the UK courts in deciding whether a Convention right has been violated could be an abnegation of their statutory obligation under the HRA 1998, s. 6. Accordingly, even if there had been no clear and constant line of authority in support of the interpretation of Article 3 urged upon the Court by the respondents, Lord Kerr would have firmly rejected the suggestion that the decision whether the respondents enjoy a right under the HRA 1998 to claim compensation against the appellant should be influenced, much less inhibited, by any perceived absence of authoritative guidance from Strasbourg (at [79]). In his separate judgment, Lord Mance also referred to the statement of Lord Bingham in *Ullah*. He noted that the general aim of the HRA 1998 was to align domestic law with Strasbourg law and so domestic courts should not normally refuse to follow Strasbourg authority. He recognised that circumstances can exist where it is appropriate for domestic courts to depart from the Strasbourg authorities, but in such a situation 'a healthy dialogue may then ensue' (at [152]), as occurred in the appeal of *Horncastle* [2009] UKSC 14, [2010] 2 AC 373. Lord Mance went on to express the converse view that domestic courts should not, at least by way of interpretation of the Convention rights as they apply domestically, forge ahead without good reason, but where good reasons exist then 'the English courts can and should, as a matter of domestic law, go with confidence beyond existing Strasbourg authority' (at [153]). It followed, in his view, that where the existence or otherwise of a Convention right is unclear, it may be appropriate for domestic courts to make up their own minds whether the Convention rights should or should not be understood to embrace it.

A7.24 One example of a 'healthy dialogue' took place in *A-G's Ref (No. 69 of 2013) (McLoughlin)* [2014] EWCA Crim 188, [2014] 3 All ER 73, where the Court of Appeal declined to follow the view of the Grand Chamber in *Vinter v UK* (2016) 63 EHRR 1 (1) that an order for a convicted defendant to serve the remainder of his life in prison was irreducible and therefore in violation of Article 3. Lord Thomas CJ said (at [30]) that the Grand Chamber had attached too much significance to the wording of a policy document (the Lifer Manual) and thereby ignored the true scope of the powers of the Secretary of State under the Crime (Sentences) Act 1997, s. 30. In *Hutchinson v UK* (2015) 69 EHRR 13 (393) (a Fourth Section Chamber judgment), the ECtHR heard an appeal from another prisoner who had been sentenced to a whole life order. He prayed in aid the decision of the Grand Chamber in *Vinter* in order to show that his rights under Article 3 had been breached. The ECtHR considered, however, that the judgment of Lord Thomas CJ in *A-G's Ref (No. 69 of 2013)* had addressed the concerns raised in *Vinter* such that the Court was now satisfied that the regime for imposing whole life orders did not infringe Article 3. When the case of *Hutchinson* came before the Grand Chamber ([2017] ECHR 65), the Court held by a majority of 14 to three that whole life orders were not incompatible with the

Convention rights of a convicted murderer for the reasons given by the lower court and by the Court of Appeal.

The UK's obligations under Article 46 do not automatically require domestic courts to quash the conviction in any case where the ECtHR finds a breach of the ECHR (*Lyons* [2002] UKHL 44, [2003] 1 AC 976). In *Abdurahman* [2019] EWCA Crim 2239, [2020] 1 Cr App R 27 (439), D had been convicted in 2008 of assisting an offender and failing to give information about acts of terrorism. The Court of Appeal dismissed his appeal against conviction. D appealed to the ECtHR. The Fourth Section held the appeal was admissible but it concluded there had been no violation of D's Article 6 rights. On appeal to the Grand Chamber, D's appeal was allowed and the Court held that his Article 6 rights had been violated by the admission into evidence at the trial of a witness statement D gave to the police at a time when D should have been cautioned and provided with access to free and independent legal advice, but where the police did not take either step. Following the Grand Chamber ruling, the CCRC referred D's case back to the Court of Appeal, which dismissed the appeal against conviction. In so doing the Court held that the issues before the Grand Chambers on the one hand and the Court of Appeal on the other were different. The Grand Chamber was concerned to decide whether D's Convention rights had been infringed but the Court of Appeal was solely concerned with the safety of D's convictions. The Grand Chamber's conclusion that D's Article 6 rights had been infringed rested on the presumption that the denial of legal advice to D had caused irredeemable prejudice to D's case at trial, and that was a significant development in the jurisprudence of the ECtHR, which the domestic courts were not obliged to follow. Even if the Grand Chamber had been correct in its conclusions about an infringement of D's Article 6 rights, aside from the witness statement, the evidence against D was devastating and so putting that one piece of evidence aside did not undermine the safety of the convictions.

PUBLIC AUTHORITIES

The HRA 1998, s. 6, makes it unlawful for a public authority to act in a way which is incompatible with Convention rights, unless required to do so to give effect to primary legislation. **A7.25**

Human Rights Act 1998, s. 6

(1) It is unlawful for a public authority to act in a way which is incompatible with a Convention right.
(2) Subsection (1) does not apply to an act if—
  (a) as the result of one or more provisions of primary legislation, the authority could not have acted differently; or
  (b) in the case of one or more provisions of, or made under, primary legislation which cannot be read or given effect in a way which is compatible with the Convention rights, the authority was acting so as to give effect to or enforce those provisions.

In this context, 'act' includes a failure to act; but does not include a failure to legislate or make remedial orders (s. 6(6)).

Definition of a Public Authority

The HRA 1998 does not fully define a 'public authority', but s. 6(3) does include within its meaning: (a) courts and tribunals; and (b) any person certain of whose functions are functions of a public nature. The inclusion of 'any person certain of whose functions are functions of a public nature' is intended to expand, not restrict, the definition of public authority (Lord Chancellor, *Hansard*, HL vol. 583, col. 811 (24 November 1997)). **A7.26**

Remedies

A person who claims that a public authority has acted (or proposes to act) in a way that is incompatible with Convention rights may either bring proceedings against the authority in the appropriate court or tribunal; or rely on Convention rights in any legal proceedings **A7.27**

(HRA 1998, s. 7(1)). Legal proceedings in this context include proceedings brought by or at the instigation of a public authority, and any appeal against the decision of a court or tribunal (s. 7(6)).

Proceedings against a public authority can be brought only by an individual who is (or would be) a victim within the meaning of the ECHR, Article 34; likewise, only victims can rely on their Convention rights in legal proceedings (s. 6(1) and (7)).

In relation to any act (or proposed act) of a public authority which the court finds is (or would be) unlawful, it may grant such relief or remedy, or make such order, within its powers as it considers just and appropriate (s. 8(1)). But damages for breach of the HRA 1998 may be awarded only by a court which has power to award damages or to order the payment of compensation in civil proceedings (s. 8(2)). The level of damages will be assessed in accordance with the principles applied by the ECtHR (*R (Greenfield) v Secretary of State for the Home Department* [2005] UKHL 14, [2005] 2 All ER 240).

Judicial Acts

A7.28 Where individuals claim that their Convention rights have been infringed by a judicial act, they must bring their claim by way of an appeal or in such other forum as may be prescribed by rules (HRA 1998, s. 9(1): no rules have yet been made for England and Wales). But this does not expand the scope for judicial review of courts (s. 9(2)). The term 'judicial act' in this context includes the acts of members of tribunals, justices of the peace, clerks and other officers entitled to exercise the jurisdiction of the court (s. 9(5)). It also includes acts done on the instructions, or on behalf, of such individuals (HRA 1998, s. 9(5)).

In respect of a judicial act done in good faith, damages may not be awarded otherwise than to compensate a person to the extent required by the ECHR, Article 5(5) (s. 9(3)). An award of damages in respect of a judicial act done in good faith is to be made against the Crown, but only if the minister responsible for the court concerned, or nominated person or government department, is joined as a party (s. 9(4) and (5)).

Retrospectivity

A7.29 Proceedings against a public authority for breach of Convention rights can be brought only in relation to acts or omissions occurring after 2 October 2000 (HRA 1998, s. 22(4)). The same applies where an individual otherwise seeks to rely on Convention rights in legal proceedings, save where proceedings are brought by or at the instigation of a public authority — in which case a breach of Convention rights can be relied upon whenever the breach took place (s. 22(4)). In *Janowiec v Russia* (2014) 58 EHRR 30 (792), the Grand Chamber held that where agents of the State committed acts — in that case a massacre of thousands of Polish prisoners in 1940 (the triggering event) — before the State became a signatory to the ECHR — which, in Russia's case, occurred only in 1998 (the critical date) — the failure of the State properly to investigate those acts could engage Article 2 of the ECHR if there was a 'genuine connection' between the triggering event and the critical date. Such a connection could exist where (i) the lapse in time between the triggering event and the critical date was no more than ten years and (ii) a major part of the investigation into the triggering event occurred or should have occurred after the critical date because, for example, new material came to light that had not been available earlier. The Court of Appeal in *Keyu v Secretary of State for Foreign and Commonwealth Affairs* [2014] EWCA Civ 412, [2015] QB 57 held (at [66]) that the Grand Chamber's decision in *Janowiec* now stands as 'the definitive exposition of the relevant principles' under the ECHR. The Supreme Court did not demur from that statement when *Keyu* came before it on appeal (*Keyu v Secretary of State for Foreign and Commonwealth Affairs* [2015] UKSC 69, [2016] AC 1355).

Derogations and Reservations

Convention rights under the HRA 1998 are subject to designated derogations (HRA 1998, s. 1(2)). Designated derogations cease to have effect after five years, unless renewed (s. 16). A7.30

Convention rights under the HRA 1998 are also subject to designated reservations (s. 1(2)). The UK has one reservation in place concerning the right to education under Protocol 1, Article 2. The terms of this derogation are set out in the HRA 1998, sch. 3, part II.

Substantive Challenges to the Criminal Law

Subject to the ECHR, Article 7, and the procedural requirements of Articles 5 and 6, Parliament is free, in principle, to apply the criminal law to acts which are not carried out in the normal exercise of one of the rights protected under the Convention (*Engel v Netherlands* (1979–80) 1 EHRR 647; *Salabiaku v France* (1991) 13 EHRR 379 at [27]). A7.31

In *G* [2008] UKHL 37, [2009] 1 AC 92, the House of Lords reiterated that Article 6 was concerned with the procedural fairness of the system for the administration of justice in the Contracting States, not with the substantive content of domestic law. Lord Hope stated that when Article 6(2) used the words 'innocent' and 'guilty' it was dealing with the burden of proof regarding the elements of the offence and any defence to it; it was not dealing with what those elements were or what defences ought to be available.

Different considerations may apply where criminal offences overlap with Convention rights; particularly those contained in Articles 8 to 11. In such cases, the Strasbourg institutions will require any interference with a Convention right to be 'necessary in a democratic society' in pursuit of a legitimate aim. The tensions between sexual activity classified as criminal in Convention States and the Convention-protected right of privacy provides a classic example. In *G v UK* (2011) 53 EHRR SE25 (237), the ECtHR confirmed that the strict liability aspect of the SOA 2003, s. 5, with which G's case was concerned, was an acceptable such interference.

In *Suski* [2016] EWCA Crim 24, [2016] 2 Cr App R 3 (32), D argued that his convictions for conspiracy to handle stolen goods and conspiracy to transfer and convert criminal property were unsafe because D's co-conspirator was his long-term cohabiting partner and, as such, applying Articles 8 and 14, she was the equivalent of a spouse or civil partner such that D was entitled to the benefit of s. 2 of the CLA 1977 ('A person shall not be guilty [of a statutory conspiracy] if the only other person or persons with whom he agrees' are, *inter alia*, his spouse or civil partner). The Court of Appeal rejected this argument and upheld the convictions on the basis that Articles 8 and 14 did not require the words 'spouse or civil partner' to be read down to include long-term cohabiting partners. A7.32

Articles 9 and 10 have also been invoked to challenge substantive criminal law provisions. Where D has a statutory defence of reasonable excuse or lawful authority it is possible to argue that the exercise of D's Convention rights at the time of the offence provide such an excuse or authority. In *DPP v Ziegler* [2019] EWHC 71 (Admin), the defendants were charged with obstruction of the highway, contrary to the Highways Act 1980, s. 137, after they disrupted access to the Excel Centre in East London for those wishing to attend an arms fair. At trial the respondents argued that they had a lawful excuse for their conduct, which required the magistrates' court to consider whether the actions of the respondents had been reasonable in all the circumstances. The district judge found all of the respondents to be not guilty and the prosecution appealed by way of case stated. The Divisional Court recognised that the prosecution engaged the respondents' rights to freedom of expression under Article 10 and freedom of peaceful assembly under Article 11. In the Court's view it was perfectly possible to interpret s. 137 of the 1980 Act in a way that is compatible with those articles. The Court held that the usual approach would be for the trial court to ask itself the following questions:

(1) Is what D did in exercise of one of the rights in Articles 10 or 11?
(2) If so, is there an interference by a public authority with that right?
(3) If there is an interference, is it 'prescribed by law'?
(4) If so, is the interference in pursuit of a legitimate aim as set out in Article 10(2) or Article 11(2), for example the protection of the rights of others?
(5) If so, is the interference 'necessary in a democratic society' to achieve that legitimate aim?

If, in the final analysis, there has been no violation of D's Convention rights then D will not have a lawful excuse. In the circumstances of this case, and apart from a separate jurisdictional issue that arose in relation to two of the respondents, the appeals were allowed because the district judge had failed to strike a fair balance between the rights of the respondents to protest and the general interests of the community to be permitted to travel along a public highway. The Supreme Court has allowed an application for permission to appeal from the decision of the Divisional Court.

THE INVESTIGATION OF CRIME

Duty to Investigate Crime Effectively

A7.33 In certain circumstances, the ECHR obliges law enforcement bodies, such as the police, to carry out effective and prompt investigations where serious human rights issues arise (see, e.g., *Aydin v Turkey* (1998) 25 EHRR 251 at [103]; *Labita v Italy* (2008) 46 EHRR 50 (1228) at [131]; *McDonnell v UK* [2014] ECHR 1370; *Al Nashiri v Poland* (2015) 60 EHRR 16 (393)). When individuals have been killed as a result of the use of force by agents of the State or where an individual makes a credible assertion of having suffered ill-treatment at the hands of State officials or, in the absence of an express complaint, there are clear indications that torture or some form of ill-treatment *may* have occurred, an effective investigation should be held. However, where an individual is released from State custody and dies some time later in circumstances where (a) the State does not control the territory where the individual died, and (b) the State cannot be held directly or indirectly responsible for the death, no obligation to investigate arises under Article 2. The argument that the investigative obligation arose as a consequence of the State releasing the individual into territory controlled by a third party where there was a real risk of death or mistreatment at the hands of that third party was rejected by the Court (*Hassan v UK* [2014] ECHR 1162).

Examples where the ECtHR has found that there has been a failure to conduct a thorough and effective investigation include: (a) failing to ascertain the identity of possible eye-witnesses; (b) failing to question suspects at an early stage; (c) failing to search for corroborating evidence; (d) the adoption of an over-deferential attitude to those in authority; (e) failing to follow up proper complaints; (f) ignoring obvious evidence; (g) failing to carry out a proper autopsy; and (h) failing to test gunpowder traces (see, e.g., *Aksoy v Turkey* (1997) 23 EHRR 553; *Aydin v Turkey* (1998) 25 EHRR 251; *Kurt v Turkey* (1999) 27 EHRR 373; *Labita v Italy* (2008) 46 EHRR 50 (1228)). In *Metropolitan Police Commissioner v DSD* [2018] UKSC 11, [2018] 2 WLR 895 (at **A7.23**) the majority of the Supreme Court held that the ECHR, Article 3, establishes that the State is obliged to conduct an investigation into crimes which involve serious violence to persons, whether that has been carried out by State agents or individual criminals, and that in order for that right to be practical and effective, an individual who has suffered ill-treatment contrary to Article 3 should have a right to claim compensation against the State where there has been a failure by State authorities to conduct an effective investigation into the crime. The majority (Lady Hale and Lords Kerr, Neuberger and Mance) favoured the view that a claimant need only establish a serious defect in the investigation into the particular case, irrespective of whether there were systemic failures. Lord Hughes, in contrast, held that a claimant will have to establish serious failings of a systemic nature and that failings of a purely operational nature will not suffice, at least where the perpetrator was not an agent of the State. See also *Michael v Chief Constable of South Wales Police* [2015] UKSC 2, [2015] AC 1732 (at [96]).

In *Armani da Silva v UK* (2016) 63 EHRR 12 (589), the applicant challenged the adequacy of the investigation into the death of Jean Charles De Menezes under Article 2 on the basis, *inter alia*, that the prosecutorial system had failed to hold to account those responsible for his death. The Grand Chamber held that the obligation in Article 2 did not carry with it any right to expect that an investigation would lead to a prosecution, even less to a conviction (at [238]). This is because the obligation is one of means and not results. There was not an example the Grand Chamber could recount where it had found fault with a prosecutorial decision either way following the completion of an Article 2 compliant investigation (at [259]). The threshold evidential test applied by the CPS is within the UK's margin of appreciation and so its existence could not be described as an institutional deficiency or failing on the part of the domestic prosecutorial system that would preclude those who killed Jean Charles De Menezes from being held accountable for his death (at [276]). Accordingly, there was no breach of Article 2. See also *MLIA v Chief Constable of Hampshire* [2017] EWHC 292 (QB).

In *Tomanovic v Foreign and Commonwealth Office* [2019] EWHC 3350 (QB), [2020] 4 WLR 5, the Divisional Court reiterated that the reference to 'jurisdiction' in Article 1 of the ECHR is not limited to territorial jurisdiction and can, in certain circumstances, extend to land beyond the borders of a particular Contracting Party.

Surveillance

Secret surveillance amounts to a serious interference with an individual's private life under Article 8 (*Kopp v Switzerland* (1999) 27 EHRR 91). Therefore it must be 'prescribed by law': i.e. the applicable legal rules must be accessible and formulated with sufficient precision to enable citizens to foresee — if need be with appropriate advice — the consequences of their actions (see, e.g., *Amann v Switzerland* (2000) 30 EHRR 843). Since intercepting telephone calls constitutes a serious interference with private life, particular precision in the law is required, including the rules applicable in prisons (*Doerga v Netherlands* (2004) 41 EHRR 4 (45)). **A7.34**

Surveillance must also be necessary and proportionate: police surveillance should be restricted to that which is strictly necessary to achieve the required objective. What is legitimate for the prevention and detection of serious crime may not be legitimate for less serious crime. Secret surveillance is tolerable under the Convention only insofar as it is strictly necessary for the protection of national security or the prevention of disorder or crime (*Klass v Germany* (1979–80) 2 EHRR 214).

Article 8 can be engaged where telephone calls (or other communications) are intercepted at work, even where they take place on private or internal telecommunications systems. In *Halford v UK* (1997) 24 EHRR 523, the ECtHR held (at [46]): **A7.35**

> ... telephone calls made from business premises as well as from the home may be covered by the notions of 'private life' and 'correspondence' within the meaning of Article 8(1).

The law on secret surveillance must be particularly precise and provide effective safeguards against abuse. Although there is no requirement that individuals be given prior notice of surveillance (because in most cases that would defeat its purpose), the law governing powers of secret surveillance must be clear enough to give citizens an adequate indication of the circumstances in which, and the conditions upon which, public authorities are entitled to resort to the use of such powers (*Halford v UK* (1997) 24 EHRR 523; *Malone v UK* (1985) 7 EHRR 14; *Khan v UK* (2001) 31 EHRR 45 (1016); *Elahi v UK* (2007) 44 EHRR 30 (645)).

The RIPA 2000 was designed to ensure that surveillance carried out within the framework it provides is compatible with Article 8. In *Kennedy v UK* (2011) 52 EHRR 4 (207), the ECtHR found that the domestic law, together with the clarifications brought by the Code published under the Act, indicated with sufficient clarity the procedures for authorisation and processing of interception warrants as well as processing, communication and destruction of intercept material; there was no evidence of any significant shortcomings in the application and operation of the UK surveillance regime.

Informers and Undercover Police Officers

A7.36 So long as informers and undercover officers do not actively instigate criminal offences, the fact that they carry out private surveillance does not *in itself* breach the ECHR, Article 8, because those who engage in serious crime cannot have any reasonable expectation that their activities will not be observed. As the ECtHR observed in *Ludi v Switzerland* (1993) 15 EHRR 173 (at [40]):

> ... the use of an undercover agent did not, either alone or in combination with the telephone interception, affect private life within the meaning of Article 8 ... [the applicant] must ... have been aware ... that he was engaged in a criminal act ... and that consequently he was running the risk of encountering an undercover police officer whose task would in fact be to expose him.

However, the law governing the use of undercover agents must be clear and precise; it must also provide safeguards against abuse (*Teixeira de Castro v Portugal* (1999) 28 EHRR 101). Where informers/undercover officers go beyond observation and actively incite the commission of an offence, issues of fairness under Article 6 will arise.

Entrapment

A7.37 It is unfair under the ECHR, Article 6, to prosecute an individual for a criminal offence incited by undercover agents, which, but for the incitement, would probably not have been committed. Even the public interest in the detection of serious crime cannot justify the instigation of criminal offences by undercover agents (*Teixeira de Castro v Portugal* (1999) 28 EHRR 101 at [39]). However, so long as informers and/or undercover officers keep within the reasonable limits of passive surveillance, no issue arises under Article 6 (fair trial); nor does any privacy issue arise under Article 8 (*Ludi v Switzerland* (1993) 15 EHRR 173). In *A-G's Ref (No. 3 of 2000) (Looseley)* [2001] UKHL 53, [2001] 1 WLR 2060 (see **F2.21**), the House of Lords held that the approach of the domestic courts to entrapment was no different to the approach taken in *Teixeira de Castro v Portugal*. The decision in *Teixeira* was distinguished in *Shannon v UK (Admissibility)* [2005] Crim LR 133 and *Kuzmickaja v Lithuania (Admissibility)* (2008) 47 EHRR SE21 (257), but in *Palmer* [2014] EWCA Crim 1681, the Court of Appeal referred to *Teixeira* with approval and observed, at [65], that 'English law does not in any way conflict with [that] decision'. What matters is whether the conduct complained of on the part of the authorities crosses the line between what is proper and what is improper. In *Furcht v Germany* (2015) 61 EHRR 25 (704), the ECtHR followed *Teixeira* and observed (at [48]) that: 'Police incitement occurs where the officers involved do not confine themselves to investigating criminal activity in an essentially passive manner, but exert such an influence on the subject as to incite the commission of an offence that would otherwise not have been committed'. For a case considering entrapment in the context of undercover police operations, see *Syed (Haroon Ali)* [2018] EWCA Crim 2809, [2019] 1 Cr App R 21 (267) and for a case considering entrapment by private individuals rather than by State authorities, see *TL* [2018] EWCA Crim 1821, [2018] 1 WLR 6037.

Searching Individuals

A7.38 Whereas in *R (Gillan) v Metropolitan Police Commissioner* [2006] UKHL 12, [2006] 2 AC 307 the House of Lords held that superficial search of the individual and the opening of bags, etc., using powers available under the TA 2000, ss. 44 and 45 (since repealed in that form), would probably not engage Article 8, in *Gillan v UK* (2010) 50 EHRR 45 (1105) the ECtHR held that the use of the coercive powers conferred by the TA 2000 to require an individual to submit to a detailed search of his or her person, clothing and personal belongings amounted to a clear interference with the right to respect for private life. Such an interference could be justified under Article 8(2) only if it was, among other things, in accordance with the law. The law had to indicate with sufficient clarity the scope of any such discretion conferred on the competent authorities and the manner of its exercise.

The power in question in the instant case had a basis in domestic law, namely ss. 44 to 47 of the 2000 Act, but the safeguards provided by domestic law had not been demonstrated to constitute a real curb on the wide powers afforded to the executive so as to offer the individual adequate protection against arbitrary interference. Of particular concern was the breadth of the discretion conferred on the individual police officer. The officer's decision to stop and search would be based exclusively on professional intuition. Not only was it unnecessary to demonstrate the existence of any reasonable suspicion, the officer was not required even subjectively to suspect anything about the person stopped and searched. There was a clear risk of arbitrariness in the grant of such a broad discretion to the police officer. The powers were not therefore in accordance with the law and it followed that there had been a violation of Article 8. In the context of powers under para. 2(1) of sch. 7 to the 2000 Act to question and recover items from a person in order to determine whether that person appears to be a terrorist, the Divisional Court in *R (Miranda) v Secretary of State for the Home Department* [2014] EWHC 255 (Admin), [2014] 1 WLR 3140 held, *inter alia*, that those powers were prescribed by law, for the purposes of Article 10(2), and so their exercise to seize items in the hands of a partner of a journalist who was in transit from one country to another did not infringe his right to freedom of expression. The decision of the Divisional Court in *Miranda* went on appeal to the Court of Appeal ([2016] EWCA Civ 6, [2016] 1 WLR 1505). That Court held, *inter alia*, that the power under sch. 7 to the 2000 Act was incompatible with Article 10 in relation to journalistic material because it does not provide adequate safeguards against the arbitrary exercise of the power to search for and confiscate such material. See also *R (Roberts) v Metropolitan Police Commissioner* [2015] UKSC 79, [2016] 1 Cr App R 19 (272).

Searching Premises and Vehicles

Search and seizure interfere with the right to private and family life, home and correspondence protected by the ECHR, Article 8. Therefore such measures must be justified in accordance with Article 8(2). Judicial authorisation is a highly relevant factor, but not determinative of the lawfulness of search and seizure under the ECHR. **A7.39**

Where there has been no judicial authorisation for a search, courts should be particularly vigilant to ensure that other safeguards exist to protect individuals from unnecessary intrusion into their privacy. At the very least, a proper legal framework with very strict limits on search powers will be required (*Camenzind v Switzerland* (1999) 28 EHRR 458 at [45]). Furthermore, where the police retain a discretion whether to enter premises, that discretion must be properly exercised (*McLeod v UK* (1999) 27 EHRR 493 at [54]–[57]). See *R (M) v Chief Constable of Hampshire* [2014] EWCA Civ 1615, [2015] 1 WLR 1176.

Any warrant authorising search and seizure must be clear, specific and contain safeguards against abuse. If a warrant is drawn in very broad terms or gives too much discretion to those executing it, it is likely to breach Article 8 (*Funke v France* (1993) 16 EHRR 297 at [56] and [57]). For example, the ECtHR has held that a warrant which authorised a search for 'documents' without any limitation is too broad for compliance with Article 8 (*Niemietz v Germany* (1993) 16 EHRR 97). The notion of an individual's private life under Article 8 can be extended to business and commercial premises (*Niemietz v Germany* (1993) 16 EHRR 97; *Sallinen v Finland* (2005) 44 EHRR 18 (358)). Therefore warrants to search business premises should comply with Article 8. Although lawyers' premises are not immune from search, professional confidentiality must be respected. In *Niemietz v Germany*, the ECtHR found a breach of Article 8 where a lawyer's offices were searched by the police acting on a court warrant in order to obtain information about the identity and whereabouts of a third party who was the subject of a criminal investigation. In *R (Haralambous) v Crown Court at St Albans* [2018] UKSC 1, [2018] 2 WLR 357, the UK Supreme Court considered a number of significant issues regarding the procedures whereby magistrates may issue warrants to enter and search premises and seize property under the PACE 1984, s. 8, and Crown Courts may order the retention by the police of unlawfully seized material under the CJPA 2001, s. 59, and how third parties affected by those decisions can challenge them. The Court held that on such applications magistrates and

Crown Court judges can rely on material that is not, and cannot, be disclosed to those affected by the applications. Moreover, there is no rule of law that requires the 'gist' of the undisclosed material to be given to an affected person in every case. The Strasbourg authorities recognise that there may be circumstances where it is in the public interest to withhold even the gist of the material relied on. The relevant authorities were analysed by the UK Supreme Court in *Tariq v Home Office* [2011] UKSC 45, [2012] 1 AC 452 at [27]–[37]. Where a person who is affected by one of these decisions seeks to challenge that decision by way of judicial review, the principle in *Al-Rawi v Security Service* [2011] UKSC 34, [2012] 1 AC 531 (that in the absence of express Parliamentary authorisation to conduct a closed material procedure the court cannot have regard to information that, on public interest grounds, has been withheld from the person affected by the decision) is displaced and so the Divisional Court can consider that undisclosed material when determining the lawfulness of the impugned decision that was based, in part at least, on that material. A departure from the *Al-Rawi* principle was justified because it would be 'self-evidently unsatisfactory, risk injustice and in some cases be absurd' (at [57]) if the High Court on judicial review was bound to address the matter on a different basis from the magistrates' court and the Crown Court.

Fingerprints and Other Samples

A7.40 Measures such as taking personal details, photographs and samples all engage the ECHR, Article 8, and must be justified (*Murray v UK* (1995) 19 EHRR 193). The prevention of crime can justify such measures, but only where they are prescribed by law, necessary and proportionate. In some cases, the collection of personal data from those who are not under suspicion can be justified, but only in very limited circumstances: e.g., where individuals are stopped crossing a national border and the purpose of the measures in question is the prevention of terrorism (*McVeigh, O'Neill and Evans v UK* (1983) 5 EHRR 71). In *R (R) v A Chief Constable* [2013] EWHC 2864 (Admin), [2014] 1 Cr App R 16 (222), a claimant with previous criminal convictions unsuccessfully argued that the decision of the police to require him to attend a police station in order that a non-intimate sample could be taken from him, pursuant to the PACE 1984, s. 63(3B)(a) and (3BA)(a), infringed his rights under Article 8. Pitchford LJ held that the interference with the claimant's Article 8 rights was justified as a proportionate response to the need to detect crime.

The retention of personal data is different from its collection and must be separately justified (*X v Germany* 9 Coll Dec 53; Appln. 1307/61). The prevention of terrorism (or other serious offences) can justify the retention of personal data, but only for so long as it serves that purpose (*McVeigh, O'Neill and Evans v UK*). In *R (Catt) v Association of Chief Police Officers* [2015] UKSC 9, [2015] AC 1065, the Supreme Court held, by a majority, that the practices of the police governing the retention of electronic data about individuals (which consisted entirely of records of what those individuals had done in public places) did not infringe Article 8 because there was a sufficiently intensive regime of statutory and administrative regulation, in particular under the Data Protection Act 1998.

In *S and Marper v UK* (2009) 48 EHRR 50 (1169), the ECtHR held that the 'blanket and indiscriminate' power to retain biometric data indefinitely, provided for by the PACE 1984, was not proportionate under Article 8(2). The Supreme Court confirmed in *R (GC) v Metropolitan Police Commissioner* [2011] UKSC 21, [2011] 3 All ER 859 that, in light of the decision in *S and Marper*, the retention of the DNA samples of two acquitted defendants by the Commissioner pursuant to ACPO guidelines was an unjustified interference with their Article 8(1) rights. The Protection of Freedoms Act 2012, ss. 1 to 25, provide a scheme for the regulation of biometric data and take account of the ECtHR judgment in *R (GC)*.

International Co-operation in the Investigation of Crime

A7.41 The ECHR is relevant to questions of international co-operation in the investigation of crime. Law enforcement officers from the UK who carry out their functions in other countries remain subject to the ECHR. It will therefore be possible for a suspect arrested and detained abroad by UK law enforcement officers to claim a breach of Convention rights (*Reinette v France* (1989) 63 DR 189). It would breach the ECHR if international co-operation in the investigation of crime exposed an individual to the risk of torture or ill-treatment contrary to Article 3, or interfered with the individual's right to life under Article 2 (e.g., through extradition or deportation). However, although there is no absolute rule that Contracting States to the ECHR should not co-operate with non-Contracting States merely because they do not comply with the standards set out in Article 6 (fair trial), unless there has been, or is likely to be, a flagrant denial of justice, co-operation should be refused (*Drozd and Janousek v France and Spain* (1992) 14 EHRR 745 at [110]).

In *R (Al-Skeini) v Secretary of State for Defence* [2007] UKHL 26, [2008] 1 AC 153 the House of Lords held that s. 6 of the HRA 1998 was capable of applying to acts of UK public authorities which took place outside the territory of the UK. Whether or not any such act was unlawful would then depend on whether it was within the 'jurisdiction' of the UK within the meaning of Article 1. On that basis, s. 6 applied to the acts of UK soldiers who held an individual in their custody in Iraq. See also *Smith v Oxfordshire Assistant Deputy Coroner* [2010] UKSC 29, [2011] 1 AC 1.

ARREST AND PRE-TRIAL DETENTION

Reasonable Suspicion

Article 5(1)(c) of the ECHR authorises arrest on 'reasonable suspicion' that an individual has committed an offence. Such suspicion requires objective justification. The honesty and good faith of a suspicion constitute indispensable elements of its reasonableness, but honest belief alone is not enough. There must be an objective basis justifying arrest and/or detention (*Fox, Campbell and Hartley v UK* (1991) 13 EHRR 157 at [32]). A reasonable suspicion can be based on information obtained from anonymous informers; but if challenged the authorities must furnish at least some evidence capable of satisfying a court under Article 5(3) (*O'Hara v UK* (2002) 34 EHRR 32 (812)). An arrest for failing to supply a name and address must be proportionate. In *Vasileva v Denmark* (2003) 40 EHRR 27 (681), a breach of Article 5 was found where a 67-year-old woman was detained for 13 hours because she refused to give her name and address. A7.42

In *Ostendorf v Germany* [2013] ECHR 197, the ECtHR held that there had been no infringement of Article 5 in circumstances where D had been arrested and detained at a police station for four hours before being released because the police suspected that he might otherwise have engaged in acts of crowd violence at a football match. Article 5(1)(c) did not provide a justification for his detention but Article 5(1)(b) did because there was a specific and imminent risk that in the absence of detention D would commit a criminal offence. In *R (Hicks) v Metropolitan Police Commissioner* [2014] EWCA Civ 3, [2014] 1 WLR 2152, a case concerned with the arrest and detention of protestors during the Royal Wedding on 29 April 2011, the Court of Appeal doubted the ECtHR's interpretation of Article 5(1)(c) in *Ostendorf* and in the event declined to follow it because it did not represent a 'clear and consistent' line of authority from the Strasbourg Court. In the Court of Appeal's view, the arrest and detention of the protestors was justified under Article 5(1)(c) and may also have been justified under Article 5(1)(b). The Supreme Court dismissed the appeals, holding that while Article 5(1)(b) was not applicable on the facts of this case, Article 5(1)(c) was (*R (Hicks) v Metropolitan Police Commissioner* [2017] UKSC 9, [2017] AC 256).

Article 5(1) must be interpreted in a manner which takes into account the specific context in which police techniques are deployed as well as the responsibilities of the police to fulfil their duties of maintaining order and protecting the public (*Austin v UK* (2012) 55 EHRR 14 (359)); the practice of 'kettling' in the particular circumstances of the case did not involve a deprivation of liberty and Article 5(1) was not engaged.

Reasons

A7.43 Article 5(2) of the ECHR requires that anyone arrested 'be informed promptly, in a language which he understands, of the reasons for his arrest and of any charge against him'. The promptness of reasons is to be assessed in light of all the circumstances of the case. Giving reasons within a few hours might suffice where terrorist offences are suspected (*Fox, Campbell and Hartley v UK* (1991) 13 EHRR 157; *Murray v UK* (1995) 19 EHRR 193 at [40]).

The purpose of giving reasons for an arrest is to enable anyone arrested to challenge the lawfulness of the detention (*Fox, Campbell and Hartley v UK*; *Murray v UK*). But reasons need not be in writing (*X v Netherlands* (1966) 9 Yearbook 474; *X v Germany* (1974) 14 Yearbook 250). Merely informing an individual that the detention is under emergency legislation is insufficient (*Ireland v UK* (1979–80) 2 EHRR 25).

Access to a Lawyer

A7.44 The right to a fair trial under the ECHR, Article 6, normally requires that a suspect have access to a lawyer at the initial stages of a police investigation, particularly where steps may be taken which will impact on the defence (*Imbroscia v Switzerland* (1994) 17 EHRR 441 at [36]; *Murray (John) v UK* (1996) 22 EHRR 29 at [63], [65] and [66]). However, the actual requirements of Article 6 at the pre-trial stage will vary according to the circumstances (see, e.g., *Zachar v Slovenia* [2015] ECHR 721 on the ineffectiveness of the waiver of the right to see a lawyer when the full seriousness of potential charges had not been revealed). In *Imbroscia v Switzerland* (1994) 17 EHRR 4411, the ECtHR held (at [36]):

> ... the manner in which Article 6(1) and 3(c) is to be applied during the preliminary investigation depends on the special features of the proceedings involved and the circumstances of the case; in order to determine whether the aim of Article 6 — a fair trial — has been achieved, regard must be had to the entirety of the proceedings conducted in the case.

To deny access to a lawyer for a long period in a situation where the rights of the defence were irretrievably prejudiced is, whatever the justification, likely to be incompatible with Article 6 (*Magee v UK* (2001) 31 EHRR 35 (822); *Averill v UK* (2001) 31 EHRR 36 (839)). But see *Brennan v UK* (2002) 34 EHRR 18 (507), where no breach was found where denial of access to a lawyer was in good faith and on reasonable grounds.

Communications between suspect and lawyer should be confidential. In *Ocalan v Turkey* (2005) 41 EHRR 45 (985), the ECtHR stated (at [146]) that 'an accused's right to communicate with his legal representative out of hearing of a third person is part of the basic requirements of fair trial in a democratic society and follows from Article 6(3)(c)'. The Court went on to acknowledge that the right of confidential communication was not an absolute right and may be subject to restrictions. However, the mere fact that a number of lawyers are co-ordinating their defence strategy cannot justify interference with lawyer/client confidentiality (*S v Switzerland* (1992) 14 EHRR 670). In *Ocalan v Turkey* [2014] ECHR 286, the ECtHR held, *inter alia*, that during the course of D's detention following his conviction, there had been no violation of Article 3 where D's conversations with his lawyers had been recorded and conducted in the presence of an observer. Turkey had been entitled to impose 'legitimate restrictions' on prisoners convicted of terrorist activities insofar as they were strictly necessary to protect society against violence.

In *Ibrahim v UK* [2016] ECHR 750, the Grand Chamber considered the case of those convicted of their involvement in the London bombings of 21 July 2005. The Court found that in respect of three of the defendants there had been no violation of their rights under Article 6 by the decision of the authorities to question them in 'safety' interviews in the absence of their lawyers and the subsequent use of the content of those interviews as evidence against them in their trial. The Court found that the urgent need to question the defendants presented a compelling reason for denying them access to legal advice before the interviews. In the case of the fourth defendant, there had been a violation of his rights under Article 6 because unlike the others he had not been cautioned and so he had not been told about his right to remain silent. For a case considering *Ibrahim*, see *Beuze v Belgium* (2019) 69 EHRR 1 (1). In *Simeonovi v Bulgaria* (2018) 66 EHRR 2 (47), the Grand Chamber reiterated that 'restrictions on access to legal advice were permitted only in exceptional circumstances, must be of a temporary nature and must be based on an individual assessment of the particular circumstances of the case' (at [117]). Compelling reasons to withhold access to legal advice can exist where there is an urgent need 'to avert serious adverse consequences to life, liberty or physical integrity', but the absence of compelling reasons does not necessarily mean there has been a violation of the fair trial requirements in Article 6.

Access to Others

Suspects in custody should normally be allowed access to their families. In *McVeigh, O'Neill and Evans v UK* (1983) 5 EHRR 71, the European Commission held (at [239]): **A7.45**

> Unless there is a danger of accomplices being warned, a failure to allow persons so detained to make contact with their families cannot be justified under Article 8(2) as being necessary for the prevention of crime etc.

See also *Ocalan v Turkey* [2014] ECHR 286 at **A7.44**.

Right to Silence

The ECHR recognises a right to remain silent during police questioning. In *Murray (John) v UK* (1996) 22 EHRR 29, the ECtHR held (at [20]): **A7.46**

> ... although not specifically mentioned in Article 6 of the Convention, there can be no doubt that the right to remain silent under police questioning and the privilege against self-incrimination are generally recognised international standards which lie at the heart of the notion of a fair procedure under Article 6.

That does not mean that adverse inference cannot be drawn from silence. The fairness of drawing such inferences is a matter to be determined at trial in light of all the evidence (see **F19**). But it does mean that the introduction into evidence in a criminal trial for the purpose of incriminating the accused of transcripts of statements made under compulsion (e.g., to non-prosecutorial inspectors) will breach Article 6 (*Saunders v UK* (1997) 23 EHRR 313; see also *Shannon v UK* (2005) Appln. 6563/03, 4 October 2005). The same applies where the authorities seek to compel a suspect to hand over incriminating documentation (*Funke v France* (1993) 16 EHRR 297). Incriminating answers obtained by the questioning of a suspect during incommunicado detention require very close scrutiny (*G v UK* (1984) 34 DR 75). See also *Beghal v DPP* [2015] UKSC 49, [2016] AC 88.

Right to be Brought Promptly before a Court

Everyone arrested for a criminal offence has the right to be brought promptly before a judge or other officer authorised by law to exercise judicial power. **A7.47**

European Convention on Human Rights, Article 5

> (3) Everyone arrested or detained in accordance with the provisions of paragraph 1(c) of this Article shall be brought promptly before a judge or other officer authorised by law to exercise judicial power and shall be entitled to trial within a reasonable time or to release pending trial. Release may be conditioned by guarantees to appear for trial.

Article 5(3) does not depend on the detainee making an application for the case to be heard; it requires automatic consideration of the case by the court. It also requires provisional release once detention ceases to be reasonable (*TW v Malta; Aquilina v Malta* (2000) 29 EHRR 185). Although authorised by law to review detention, a commanding officer is not sufficiently independent and impartial to satisfy the requirements of Article 5(4) in court-martial cases (*Hood v UK* (2000) 29 EHRR 365; *Jordan v UK* (2001) 31 EHRR 6 (201)).

When determining whether an arrested person has been brought promptly before a judge or judicial officer, the scope for flexibility in interpreting and applying the notion of 'promptness' is very limited. In *Brogan v UK* (1989) 11 EHRR 117, the ECtHR held (at [62]) that a delay of four days and six hours was too long, even when an arrest is made under prevention of terrorism legislation.

Bail

A7.48 Despite its wording, the ECHR, Article 5(3), does not provide for trial within a reasonable period *or* release pending trial *as alternatives*: D is entitled to trial within a reasonable period *and* release pending trial unless the prosecuting authorities advance relevant and sufficient reasons for refusing bail (*Wemhoff v Germany* (1979–80) 1 EHRR 55).

Grounds for refusing bail which have been approved by the ECtHR include: (a) fear of absconding (*Stogmuller v Austria* (1979–80) 1 EHRR 155; *Neumeister v Austria* (1979–80) 1 EHRR 91); (b) interference with the course of justice (*Wemhoff v Germany*; *Letellier v France* (1992) 14 EHRR 83); (c) prevention of further offences (*Matznetter v Austria* (1979–80) 1 EHRR 198; (d) the preservation of public order (*Letellier v France*); and (e) the protection of the defendant (*IA v France* (1998) Appln. 28213/95, 23 September 1998). The mere fact that there are reasonable grounds for suspecting that a person has committed an offence is not enough (*Letellier v France*).

A7.49 Conditional bail is permitted under the ECHR and should be granted as an alternative to pre-trial detention where objections to bail can be met with conditions (*Wemhoff v Germany*). Permissible conditions of bail include a requirement to surrender travel documents (*Stogmuller v Austria*), the imposition of a residence requirement (*Schmid v Austria* (1985) 44 DR 195) and the provision of a surety — which must be assessed by reference to the means of the accused (*Wemhoff v Germany*; *Neumeister v Austria*; *Schertenleib v Switzerland* (1980) 23 DR 137). The task of assessing appropriate bail conditions is as exacting as the task of deciding whether to grant bail at all (*Iwanczuk v Poland* (2004) 38 EHRR 8 (148)). Bail proceedings must be fair and there must be equality of arms between the prosecution and the defence. In the domestic context, in *R (KS) v Northampton Crown Court* [2010] EWHC 723 (Admin), [2010] 2 Cr App R 23 (175) the Administrative Court held that a special advocate should have been appointed where a judge refused bail having already had sight of material relating to jury tampering when deciding that the defendant should be tried by judge alone.

FAIR TRIAL IN CRIMINAL PROCEEDINGS

Meaning of 'criminal proceedings' under Article 6

A7.50 The fair trial requirements of the ECHR, Article 6, distinguish between criminal and civil proceedings. Whether proceedings are criminal or civil is to be determined according to three criteria: (a) the classification in domestic law — if classified as criminal, this is determinative; if classified as civil, this is a starting point, but not determinative; (b) the nature of the conduct in question — sanctions which apply to the population as a whole, rather than to an identifiable sub-class, point toward a criminal classification; (c) the severity of any possible penalty — severe penalties (including those with imprisonment in default) and penalties intended to deter are pointers towards a criminal classification of proceedings (*Engel v Netherlands (No. 1)* (1979–80) 1 EHRR 647; *Benham v UK* (1996) 22 EHRR 293). The second and third criteria are alternative, not cumulative (*Lauko v Slovakia* (2001) 33 EHRR 40 (994) at [57]). In *R (Wilson) v Independent Adjudicator* [2016] EWHC 176 (Admin), [2016] 4 WLR 27, the Divisional Court assumed (without deciding the point) that Article 6 applies to matters of prison discipline that are brought before a prison adjudicator but this does not mean that the adjudicator is required to apply principles of *substantive* criminal law, such as the defence of duress.

In *Steel v UK* (1999) 28 EHRR 603, the ECtHR held that although 'breach of the peace' is not classified as a criminal offence under English law, it is nonetheless to be considered an 'offence' within the meaning of Article 6(1) (at [54]–[55]). On the other hand, in *Escoubet v Belgium* (2001) 31 EHRR 46 (1034), the ECtHR found that a procedure whereby a driving licence could be withdrawn for 15 days on the direction of a Crown prosecutor where a driver was drunk did not amount to the determination of a criminal charge under Article 6. Similarly, in *Benjafield* [2002] UKHL 2, [2003] 1 AC 1099, the House of Lords held that confiscation proceedings were part of the sentencing process and did not involve a fresh criminal charge; accordingly Article 6(2) was not applicable to such proceedings. In *Briggs-Price* [2009] UKSC 19, [2009] 1 AC 1026, the House of Lords held that, where the prosecution sought to rely on criminal offending other than a conviction to prove the existence of benefit and the usual statutory assumptions had not been applied, Article 6(1) required that a statutory provision which required proof to the civil standard should be read as requiring proof to the criminal standard. **A7.51**

Right to be Informed of Charge

European Convention on Human Rights, Article 6 **A7.52**

(3) Everyone charged with a criminal offence has the following minimum rights:
  (a) to be informed promptly, in a language which he understands and in detail, of the nature and cause of the accusation against him;

  ...

The purpose of this provision is to enable the individual to begin preparing a defence (*GSM v Austria* (1983) 34 DR 119).

Where the offence is fairly specific, it may be enough to provide a brief description of the offence, the date, place and alleged victim (*Brozicek v Italy* (1990) 12 EHRR 371). Otherwise, the information provided should be detailed (*Pelisser and Sassi v France* (2000) 30 EHRR 715).

Right to Adequate Time and Facilities to Prepare a Defence

European Convention on Human Rights, Article 6 **A7.53**

(3) Everyone charged with a criminal offence has the following minimum rights:

  ...

  (b) to have adequate time and facilities for the preparation of his defence.

The adequate time requirement inevitably depends on the nature and complexity of the case; it cannot be determined in the abstract but only by reference to the circumstances of each case (*X and Y v Austria* (1979) 15 DR 160). Where there is a late change of lawyer, an adjournment may be necessary. Where it is obvious that a lawyer has not had adequate time to prepare the defence properly, the court should consider adjourning the case on its own motion (*Goddi v Italy* (1984) 6 EHRR 457).

Disclosure

Under the ECHR, a disclosure requirement is based on: (a) the requirement that there be equality of arms between prosecution and defence (*Jespers v Belgium* (1981) 27 DR 61); (b) D's right to adequate time and facilities to prepare a defence under the ECHR, Article 6(3)(b) (*Edwards v UK* (1993) 15 EHRR 417); and (c) the requirement in Article 6(3)(d) that there be parity of conditions for the examination of witnesses (*Edwards v UK* (1993) 15 EHRR 417, Commission Report). In *Rowe and Davis v UK* (2000) 30 EHRR 1 (see **D9.60**), the ECtHR held (at [60]): **A7.54**

> It is a fundamental aspect of the right to a fair trial that criminal proceedings, including the elements of such proceedings which relate to procedure, should be adversarial and that there should be equality of arms between the prosecution and defence. The right to an adversarial trial means, in a criminal case, that both prosecution and defence must be given an opportunity to have knowledge of and comment on the observations filed and the evidence adduced by the other party... In

> addition Article 6(1) requires ... that the prosecution authorities should disclose to the defence all material evidence in their possession for or against the accused ...
>
> The requirement in Article 6(3)(d) that there be parity of conditions for the examination of witnesses requires disclosure of any material relevant to the testimony of the witnesses, including their credibility (*Edwards v UK* (1993) 15 EHRR 417, Commission Report).

A7.55 The privacy rights of complainants may require notice to be given to them, along with an opportunity to make representations, when, for example, a witness summons is directed to a hospital to produce its medical records (*R (B) v Stafford Crown Court* [2006] EWHC 1645 (Admin), [2007] 1 All ER 102).

In *HM Advocate v Murtagh* [2009] UKPC 36, [2011] 1 AC 731, a case arising on the duty of disclosure in Scotland, it was held that the ECHR, Article 6, does not require disclosure of *all* of the previous convictions of the prosecution witnesses. A balance had to be struck between D's Article 6 right and the witness's Article 8 right. It would be wrong for the Crown to withhold all aspects of a witness's criminal history to which objection could possibly be taken for not being relevant. A generous approach was therefore to be taken to what might be relevant, but there were limits to that approach, bearing in mind the witness's Article 8 right. A rule that the entire criminal history of a witness must be disclosed went too far. See also **D9.15**.

Public Interest Immunity

A7.56 There may be circumstances under the ECHR in which material need not be disclosed to the defence on grounds of public interest immunity; but they must be subject to strict control by the courts. In *Rowe and Davis v UK* (2000) 30 EHRR 1, the ECtHR held (at [61]):

> ... the entitlement to disclosure of relevant evidence is not an absolute right. In any criminal proceedings there may be competing interests, such as national security or the need to protect witnesses at risk of reprisals or keep secret police methods of investigation of crime, which must be weighed against the rights of the accused ... In some cases it may be necessary to withhold certain evidence from the defence so as to preserve the fundamental rights of another individual or to safeguard an important public interest. However, only such measures restricting the rights of the defence which are strictly necessary are permissible under Article 6(1) ... Moreover, in order to ensure that the accused receives a fair trial, any difficulties caused to the defence by a limitation on its rights must be sufficiently counterbalanced by the procedures followed by the judicial authorities.

Public interest immunity hearings on an *ex parte* basis do not necessarily breach Article 6 (*Jasper v UK* (2000) 30 EHRR 97; *Fitt v UK* (2000) 30 EHRR 223; *Botmeh v UK* (2008) 46 EHRR 31 (659)). However, where material should have been disclosed to the trial judge but was not, an *ex parte* hearing at the appeal stage is unlikely to be sufficient under Article 6 (see, e.g., *Atlan v UK* (2002) 34 EHRR 33 (833)).

There is an important distinction between material that is, and material that is not, actually deployed against the accused. In *Edwards v UK* (2005) 40 EHRR 24 (593), the ECtHR found a breach of Article 6 where the material relevant to an issue to be decided by the judge rather than the jury (entrapment) was not disclosed on grounds of public interest immunity. In *McKeown v UK* (2012) 54 EHRR 7 (165), the ECtHR noted this problem does not arise under the system of Diplock courts in Northern Ireland where a separate disclosure judge is appointed.

A7.57 In *Twomey* [2011] EWCA Crim 8, [2011] 1 Cr App R 29 (356), the Court of Appeal held that trial by jury was not a right which was protected by the Convention nor did its removal for certain cases (by the CJA 2003, s. 44) involve interference with the rights to liberty or property or fair process protected by the Convention. It was not a pre-condition to the fairness of the trial that the procedural steps which resulted in that trial should proceed on the basis of material which was disclosed to the accused. The approach to disclosure to be adopted by domestic courts was spelt out by the House of Lords in *H* [2004] UKHL 3, [2004] 2 AC 134, where the earlier case of *Smith* [2001] 1 WLR 1031 was overruled as being incompatible with the ECHR.

Right to an Independent and Impartial Tribunal

The ECHR, Article 6(1), provides that: 'In the determination of... any criminal charge against him, everyone is entitled to a fair and public hearing by an independent and impartial tribunal established by law'. Independence must be institutional and functional; but does not require trial by jury (*X and Y v Ireland* (1981) 22 DR 51). **A7.58**

Relevant to the question of independence will be: (a) the manner of appointment and duration of office (*Le Compte, van Leuven and De Meyere v Belgium* (1982) 4 EHRR 1), but the mere fact that the executive appoint judges is not automatically a breach of Article 6 (*Campbell and Fell v UK* (1985) 7 EHRR 165); (b) protection from external influences (*Piersack v Belgium* (1983) 5 EHRR 169); (c) an appearance of independence (*Delcourt v Belgium* (1979–80) 1 EHRR 355 at [31]; *Campbell and Fell v UK* at [78]). For a case on the use of clerks in the Scottish district courts, see *Clark (Procurator Fiscal) v Kelly* [2003] UKPC D 1, [2004] 1 AC 681.

On the question of impartiality, the ECtHR has adopted a dual test: (a) first assessing whether there is any evidence of actual bias; here impartiality is presumed unless there is proof to the contrary; (b) then assessing the circumstances alleged to give rise to a risk of bias; here the question is whether there are 'ascertainable facts which may raise doubts' about the court's impartiality (*Piersack v Belgium* (1983) 5 EHRR 169; *Hauschildt v Denmark* (1990) 12 EHRR 266). The behaviour of a judge towards counsel can raise issues of impartiality (e.g., where the judge frequently interrupts counsel) and there may be a breach of Article 6 where the behaviour in question prevents counsel from pursuing a line of argument or otherwise renders the trial unfair (*CG v UK* (2002) 34 EHRR 31 (789)). Judges are free to criticise developments in the law, but they should refrain from criticism (or praise) which by its nature and language gives rise to legitimate concerns about their impartiality (*Hoekstra v HM Advocate* [2000] HRLR 410, where the judge in question had criticised the ECHR in very strong terms).

Where a judge has taken key decisions before trial, issues of impartiality may arise. But the mere fact that a judge has previously decided a bail decision based on suspicion that D has committed an offence will not automatically preclude that judge's participation in the trial. In *Hauschildt v Denmark* (1990) 12 EHRR 266, the ECtHR held (at [50]): **A7.59**

> ... the questions which the judge has to answer when taking... pre-trial decisions are not the same as those which are decisive for his final judgment... Suspicion and a formal finding of guilt are not to be treated as being the same... therefore, the mere fact that a trial judge or an appeal judge... has also made pre-trial decisions in the case, including those concerning detention on remand, cannot be held as in itself justifying fears as to his impartiality.

Nor will the fact that a judge has dealt with D on a previous occasion; the key issue will be the nature and character of the previous decision (*Hauschildt v Denmark*, breach where trial judge previously refused bail on a high threshold test; cf. *Brown v UK* (1986) 8 EHRR 272, no breach where appeal court judge refusing leave had previously been involved in restraint proceedings, and *Depiets v France* (2006) 43 EHRR 55 (1206), where one member of the court had conducted ancillary pre-trial hearings).

Allegations of impartiality must be properly investigated, unless they are manifestly devoid of merit (*Remli v France* (1996) 22 EHRR 253 at [48]; *Gregory v UK* (1998) 25 EHRR 577 at [44]). In some circumstances, the nature of the alleged bias or impartiality will require decisive action; directions to the jury to try the case on the evidence may not suffice (*Sander v UK* (2001) 31 EHRR 44 (1003), where a juror had made racist jokes and comments and the judge declined to discharge the jury, but instead directed the jury to come to a verdict without prejudice). The limits of any inquiry about the deliberations of the jury were considered by the House of Lords in *Mirza* [2004] UKHL 2, [2004] 1 AC 1118 (see **D19.31**). In *Abdroikov* [2007] UKHL 37, [2008] 1 All ER 315, the House of Lords observed that there is no difference between the common law and **A7.60**

Article 6 in the requirements of an independent and impartial court and as to the importance of justice not only being done, but that it should 'manifestly and undoubtedly be seen to be done'. Applying those principles, appeals were allowed in two cases where a police officer on the jury shared the same service background with a key police officer witness, and a CPS lawyer sat on the jury in a case being brought by the CPS. In the third case the mere fact that a police officer sat on the jury did not offend either the common law or Article 6 (see also *Pintori* [2007] EWCA Crim 1700). In *Hanif v UK* (2012) 55 EHRR 16 (424), on the other hand, the ECtHR found a violation of Article 6(1) where there was a conflict regarding police evidence and a member of the jury was both a police officer and acquaintance of one of the officers who had given evidence; jury directions and judicial warnings were insufficient to guard against the risk that the juror may favour the evidence of the police. *Hanif* was considered in *Armstrong v UK* [2014] ECHR 1368, where the Court found no violation of Article 6. As to complaints on a retrial about pre-trial publicity arising from reports of the original trial, see *Ali v UK* (2016) 62 EHRR 7 (274).

In *Slomka v Poland* (2020) 70 EHRR 7 (165), there had been a breach of the impartiality requirement in Article 6(1) where the same bench of judges dealt with D summarily after he had jumped behind the judges and shouted loud protests against the judgment they were about to deliver. The judges were the object of D's actions, rather than the justice system more generally.

Right to a Public Hearing

A7.61 **European Convention on Human Rights, Article 6**

(1) In the determination of... any criminal charge against him, everyone is entitled to a fair and public hearing by an independent and impartial tribunal established by law. Judgment shall be pronounced publicly but the press and public may be excluded from all or part of the trial in the interest of morals, public order or national security in a democratic society, where the interests of juveniles or the protection of the private life of the parties so require, or to the extent strictly necessary in the opinion of the court in special circumstances where publicity would prejudice the interests of justice.

There is a presumption that ordinary criminal proceedings should be public, even where they involve dangerous individuals (*Campbell and Fell v UK* (1985) 7 EHRR 165 at [87]; see also *Hummatov v Azerbaijan* (2009) 49 EHRR 36 (960), where the importance of providing information to the public and press about hearings was emphasised). A less strict approach has, on occasion, been taken to the requirement that 'judgment shall be pronounced publicly' (*Pretto v Italy* (1984) 6 EHRR 182). The principle of open justice was considered by the Court of Appeal in *Re Guardian News and Media Ltd* [2016] EWCA Crim 11, [2016] 1 WLR 1767. Gross LJ said (at [10]):

> Open justice is both a fundamental principle of the common law and a means of ensuring public confidence in our legal system; exceptions are rare and must be justified on the facts. Any such exceptions must be necessary and proportionate. No more than the minimum departure from open justice will be countenanced.

He acknowledged that a tension can exist between the principle of open justice and national security. He suggested that this tension could be resolved by taking the following approach. First, considerations of national security will not by *themselves* justify a departure from open justice (at [16]). Secondly, 'open justice must, however, give way to the yet more fundamental principle that the paramount object of the court is to *do* justice' (at [17]). Thirdly, the question of whether to give effect to a Ministerial Certificate (asserting, e.g., the need for privacy) is for the court and not for the Minister (at [19]). As to the second step, Gross LJ said (at [18]):

> ... where there is a *serious possibility* that an insistence on open justice in the national security context would frustrate the administration of justice, for example, by deterring the Crown from prosecuting a case where it otherwise should do so, a departure from open justice may be justified.

The *Re Guardian News* case related to the trial of Erol Incedal, who was charged with committing terrorism offences. Following his acquittal, the media applied to the trial judge, Nicol J, for permission to publish extracts of the evidence that had been heard in private and in the absence of accredited journalists. Nicol J refused permission and Guardian News appealed. In *Re Guardian News and Media Ltd* [2016] EWCA Crim 11, [2016] 1 WLR 1767, the Court of Appeal dismissed the appeal. Lord Thomas CJ said that the nature of the evidence (set out in a closed annex to the judgment) necessitated a departure from the principles of open justice and that necessity continued to exist. The Court acknowledged the difficulties that can arise when, as here, both Nicol J and the Court of Appeal were required to produce open and closed judgments.

In *R (Yam) v Central Criminal Court* [2015] UKSC 76, [2016] AC 771, the Supreme Court held that the judge at the Central Criminal Court had been correct to refuse D permission to put in camera evidence before the ECtHR as part of his appeal. In the related case of *Yam v UK* [2020] ECHR 41, the First Section of the ECtHR dismissed D's case that by holding part of the trial in camera, D's Article 6 rights had been infringed. The ECtHR held that the public character of judicial proceedings, as required by Article 6, 'protects litigants against the administration of justice in secret with no public scrutiny' (at [52]), and added that there is a high expectation that criminal proceedings will be conducted in public. However, Article 6 does not prohibit the court from restricting the public's access to criminal proceedings where special features of the case justify taking that course. Those special features will include the maintenance of public order and the protection of national security, for example. Any such restriction should be no more than is strictly necessary to achieve the stated purpose of the restriction. In D's case the decision of the Crown Court judge to hold part of the trial in camera was taken on the grounds of national security. The ECtHR reviewed the circumstances in which that decision had been taken and concluded that it was the result of a thorough and independent review of the relevant material. D's argument that the inability to place the in camera evidence before the ECtHR unfairly prejudiced the appeal was noted, but in the event the ECtHR was satisfied that as D had seen that material in the original proceedings, and as no complaint was made by D about the overall fairness of those proceedings, the absence of that material did not undermine the conclusion that there had been no violation of Article 6.

Legal Aid and Legal Representation

European Convention on Human Rights, Article 6 **A7.62**

(3) Everyone charged with a criminal offence has the following minimum rights:

...

(c) to defend himself in person or through legal assistance of his own choosing or, if he has not sufficient means to pay for legal assistance, to be given it free when the interests of justice so require.

Relevant to the 'interests of justice' test are: (a) the complexity of the case; (b) the ability of D to understand and present the relevant arguments without assistance; and (c) the severity of the possible penalty (*Benham v UK* (1996) 22 EHRR 293; *Granger v UK* (1990) 12 EHRR 469; *Quaranta v Switzerland* (1991) Appln. 12744/87, 24 May 1991). Where deprivation of liberty is at stake, the interests of justice, in principle, call for legal aid and any refusal of legal aid should be kept under review (*Benham v UK*; *Granger v UK*; *Perks v UK* (2000) 30 EHRR 33). Rules that do not permit legal aid whatever the circumstances will invariably breach Article 6 (*Beet v UK* (2005) 41 EHRR 23 (441); *Lloyd v UK* (2005) Appln. 29798/96, 1 March 2005).

Merely allocating a lawyer to the accused is not enough under Article 6(3)(c) if that lawyer is manifestly unable to provide effective representation. In *Artico v Italy* (1981) 3 EHRR 1, where D's nominated legal aid lawyer refused to represent him in an appeal against a fraud conviction and he was unable to secure the services of another lawyer, the ECtHR held (at [33] and [36]): **A7.63**

> Article 6(3) speaks of 'assistance' and not of 'nomination'... [M]ere nomination does not ensure effective assistance, since the lawyer appointed for legal aid purposes may die, fall seriously ill, be

> prevented for a protracted period from acting or shirk his duties. If they are notified of the situation, the authorities must either replace him or cause him to fulfil his obligations ... Admittedly, a State cannot be held responsible for every shortcoming on the part of a lawyer appointed for legal aid purposes, but, in the particular circumstances, it was for the ... authorities to take steps to ensure that the applicant enjoyed effectively the right to which they had recognised he was entitled.

In *Daud v Portugal* (2000) 30 EHRR 400, the ECtHR held that there had been a breach of Article 6 where defence counsel had not had sufficient time to prepare the case. Even though defence counsel made no application to adjourn the case, the court should have done so itself.

A7.64 The right to be legally represented does not give D an absolute right to determine how the defence will be conducted: D cannot require counsel to disregard basic principles of professional duty in the presentation of D's defence (*X v UK* (1980) 21 DR 126 at [6]).

In legal aid cases, D does not have an unqualified right to counsel of D's choosing. In *Croissant v Germany* (1993) 16 EHRR 135, the ECtHR held (at [29]):

> [Article 6(3)(c)] is necessarily subject to certain limitations where free legal aid is concerned and ... it is for the courts to decide whether the interests of justice require that the accused be defended by counsel appointed by them. When appointing defence counsel the national courts must certainly have regard to the defendant's wishes ... However, they can override those wishes when there are relevant and sufficient grounds for holding that this is necessary in the interests of justice.

See also *Mayzit v Russia* (2006) 43 EHRR 38 (805).

Rules requiring D to be represented by a lawyer where sexual offences are alleged will not necessarily breach Article 6(3)(c) (*Baegen v Netherlands* (Series A/327-B) (1995) at [77]).

Where a sanction such as the deprivation of liberty is at stake, the interests of justice require not only that a lawyer be appointed, but also that that lawyer be given an opportunity to make representations; see *Hooper v UK* (2005) 41 EHRR 1 (1), where D was bound over for 28 days for causing a disturbance in court without his lawyer having been heard on the matter (see also *Aerts v Belgium* (2000) 29 EHRR 50).

Right to be Present at Trial

A7.65 As a general rule, D has a right to be present at trial (*Ekbetani v Sweden* (1991) 13 EHRR 504 at [25]) and adducing important evidence in D's absence will usually be unfair (*Barbera, Messegue and Jabardo v Spain* (1989) 11 EHRR 360 at [89]). Consequently the authorities are under a duty to notify all accused about the proceedings against them (*Goddi v Italy* (1984) 6 EHRR 457). However, the right to be present at trial is not an absolute right. For example, D can be excluded for causing disruption to the proceedings, refusing to come to court, or making him or herself too ill to attend, provided that D's interests are protected, e.g., because D's lawyer is present (*Ensslin v Germany* (1978) 14 DR 64 at [21] and [22], where the applicants were unable to attend trial because of ill-health induced by hunger strike). But special care is needed where D is ill (*Romanov v Russia* (2007) 44 EHRR 23 (479)).

D may waive the right to be present either expressly or impliedly by failing to attend the hearing having been given effective notice (*C v Italy* (1988) 56 DR 40). But waiver must be clear and unequivocal (*Colozza v Italy* (1985) 7 EHRR 516; *Brozicek v Italy* (1990) 12 EHRR 371; *Poitrimol v France* (1994) 18 EHRR 130; *Lala v Netherlands* (1994) 18 EHRR 856; *Pelladoah v Netherlands* (1995) 19 EHRR 81). There may be circumstances where an absent D is entitled to a rehearing on subsequently emerging (*Colozza v Italy*). Moreover, where D chooses to be absent, counsel must nonetheless be permitted to attend the trial (*Poitrimol v France* (1994) 18 EHRR 130; *Geyseghem v Belgium* (2001) 32 EHRR 24 (554)). For consideration of the issue by the House of Lords, see *Jones* [2002] UKHL 5, [2003] 1 AC 1 (see **D15.85**), where a trial in D's absence was held not to have violated D's Article 6 rights.

Right to Participate in the Trial

A7.66 All accused have a right to participate effectively in the proceedings. In *Stanford v UK* (1994) Series A, No. 282 (at [26]) and in *V v UK* (2000) 30 EHRR 121 (at [85]), the ECtHR held:

> ... Article 6, read as a whole, guarantees the right of an accused to participate effectively in a criminal trial. In general this includes, inter alia, not only his right to be present, but also to hear and follow the proceedings.

Particular account must be taken of factors such as D's age and ability to comprehend the proceedings. In respect of a young child charged with a grave offence attracting high levels of media and public interest, it is necessary to conduct the hearing in such a way as to reduce as far as possible any feelings of intimidation and inhibition (*V v UK* at [86] and [87]; *Practice Direction (Crown Court: Young Defendants)* [2000] 1 WLR 659 was made as a result). In *SC v UK* (2005) 40 EHRR 10 (226), the ECtHR found a breach of Article 6(1) where D, aged 11 and with limited intellectual ability, was unable to understand the criminal proceedings brought against him for robbery in the Crown Court. The ECtHR held that it was essential in such circumstances that D be tried in a specialist tribunal.

Right to an Interpreter and Translation

A7.67

European Convention on Human Rights, Article 6

> (3) Everyone charged with a criminal offence has the following minimum rights:
>
> ...
>
> (e) to have the free assistance of an interpreter if he cannot understand or speak the language used in court.

This right is not subject to qualification, even if D is subsequently convicted; hence a convicted person cannot be ordered to pay the costs of an interpreter (*Luedicke, Delkasam and Koc v Germany* (1979–80) 2 EHRR 149 at [42] and [46]; *Ozturk v Germany* (1984) 6 EHRR 409).

The right to interpretation extends to all documentary material disclosed before trial; but this does not necessarily mean that all translations must be in written form; in limited circumstances, some oral translation is acceptable (*Luedicke, Delkasam and Koc v Germany*; *Kamasinski v Austria* (1991) 13 EHRR 36). The court has an obligation to ensure the quality of interpretation (*Kamasinski v Austria* at [74]). Responsibility for ensuring that a defendant who needs an interpreter gets appropriate assistance rests with the judge, not counsel. In *Cuscani v UK* (2003) 36 EHRR 2 (11), the ECtHR found a breach of Article 6 where the judge acceded to counsel's suggestion that D's brother could translate for him at the sentencing phase.

Article 6(3)(e) applies only where D does not understand or speak the language used in court; it does not provide a right to conduct proceedings in the language of D's choice (*K v France* (1984) 35 DR 203 at [8] — D who understood French wanted to conduct his defence in the Breton language). For a detailed analysis of the issues that can arise on appeal where D argues that inadequate translation services were provided during the trial, see the decision of the Canadian Supreme Court in *Tran* 2010 SCC 58.

Pre-trial Publicity

A7.68 Since pre-trial publicity can prejudice D's prospects of a fair trial, it can be restricted without necessarily breaching the ECHR, Article 10. In *Hodgson, Woolf Productions and the NUJ v UK* (1988) 10 EHRR 503, the European Commission held (at p. 509):

> ... the need to ensure a fair trial and to protect members of the jury from exposure to prejudicial influences corresponds to a pressing social need ... where there is a real risk of prejudice the appropriate response ... is one which must lie, in principle, with the person responsible for ensuring the fairness of the trial, namely, the trial judge.

This was reinforced by the ECtHR in *Krone Verlag GmbH & Co KG v Austria* (2003) 36 EHRR 57 (1059), which held (at [56]) that 'the limits of permissible comment on pending criminal proceedings may not extend to statements which are likely to prejudice, whether intentionally or not, the chances of a person receiving a fair trial or to undermine the confidence of the public in the role of the courts in the administration of justice'.

A7.69 Prejudice will be harder to establish in a case tried by a judge than in a case tried by a jury (*Crociani v Italy* (1980) 22 DR 147 at [20]; see also *Ensslin v Germany* (1978) 14 DR 64 at [15]) and a proper balance between fair trial and press freedom must be maintained. In *Worm v Austria* (1998) 25 EHRR 454, the ECtHR held (at [50]):

> There is a general recognition of the fact that the courts cannot operate in a vacuum. Whilst the courts are the forum for the determination of a person's guilt or innocence on a criminal charge, this does not mean that there can be no prior or contemporaneous discussion of the subject-matter of criminal trials elsewhere, be it in specialised journals, in the general press or amongst the public at large... Provided that it does not overstep the bounds imposed in the interests of the proper administration of justice, reporting, including comment, on courts proceedings contributes to their publicity and is thus perfectly consonant with the requirement under Article 6(1) of the Convention that hearings be public. Not only do the media have the task of imparting such information and ideas; the public has a right to hear them.

Equality of Arms

A7.70 The principle that there should be equality of arms between the parties before the court is fundamental to the notion of a fair trial under the ECHR, Article 6. In particular, each party must know the case being made against him or her, have an effective opportunity to challenge it and an effective opportunity to advance the party's own case. See also *Roberts v Parole Board* [2005] UKHL 45, [2005] 2 AC 738 and see further **A7.53**.

Right to an Adversarial Hearing

A7.71 All evidence and submissions should be made in D's presence and in circumstances in which D has an opportunity to comment upon them. The right to an adversarial trial means the opportunity for the parties to have knowledge of and comment on the observations filed or evidence adduced by the other party (*Ruiz Mateos v Spain* (1993) 16 EHRR 505 at [63]; see also *Krcmar v Czech Republic* (2001) 31 EHRR 41 (953) at [40]). This applies even where submissions are made by an independent party — such as an *amicus* lawyer — and are wholly objective (*Van Orshoven v Belgium* (1998) 26 EHRR 55 at [39]–[42]).

Reasons

A7.72 Article 6(1) of the ECHR obliges courts to give reasons for their judgments. In *Hiro Balani v Spain* (1995) 19 EHRR 566, the ECtHR held (at [27]):

> The Court reiterates that Article 6(1) obliges the courts to give reasons for their judgments, but cannot be understood as requiring a detailed answer to every argument. The extent to which this duty to give reasons applies may vary according to the nature of the decision. It is moreover necessary to take account, *inter alia*, of the diversity of the submissions that a litigant may bring before the courts and the differences existing in the Contracting States with regard to statutory provisions, customary rules, legal opinion and the presentation and drafting of judgments.

In *Inner London Crown Court, ex parte London Borough of Lambeth* [2000] Crim LR 303, the Divisional Court held that the Crown Court is as much under a duty to give reasons for its decision when it allows an appeal against conviction as when it dismisses one.

In the context of jury trial, in *Taxquet v Belgium* (2012) 54 EHRR 26 (933) the Grand Chamber held:

> ... the Convention does not require jurors to give reasons for their decision and... Article 6 does not preclude a defendant from being tried by a lay jury even where reasons are not given for the verdict. Nevertheless, for the requirements of a fair trial to be satisfied, the accused, and indeed the public, must be able to understand the verdict that has been given; this is a vital safeguard against arbitrariness.

Article 6 required sufficient safeguards to avoid any risk of arbitrariness. In the case of jury trial, these might include procedural safeguards such as directions or guidance provided by the judge to the jurors on legal issues arising or the evidence adduced; precise, unequivocal questions put to the jury by the judge, forming a framework on which the verdict is based; and any avenues of appeal open to the accused.

Trial within a Reasonable Period

The right to trial within a reasonable period is guaranteed under the ECHR, Article 5(3), for those in pre-trial detention (see **A7.47**) and more generally for anyone facing criminal proceedings under Article 6(1). Since it is primarily concerned with those in pre-trial detention, the standards under Article 5(3) are more exacting than those under Article 6(1) (*Abdoella v Netherlands* (1995) 20 EHRR 585). **A7.73**

Time begins to run under both Article 5(3) and Article 6(1) when an individual is 'charged'. This may stretch back to arrest, rather than formal charge (*Eckle v Germany* (1983) 5 EHRR 1 at [73]; *Ewing v UK* (1988) 10 EHRR 141 at p. 143). In *A-G's Ref (No. 2 of 2001)* [2003] UKHL 68, [2004] 2 AC 72, the House of Lords held that in England and Wales time will usually run from the time that an individual is formally charged or served with a summons. In *Burns v HM Advocate* [2008] UKPC 63, [2009] 1 AC 720, where D had been arrested, interviewed and bailed in England but a warrant to appear before a sheriff was not issued until nearly two years later in Scotland, the Privy Council held that the reasonable time requirement was to be interpreted generously so as to provide practical and effective safeguards. The term 'charge' was to be understood, having regard to the substance of the procedure in question rather than its appearance, as connoting the official notification given by the competent authority to an individual of an allegation that the individual had committed a criminal offence, and the relevant period began when the individual was first officially alerted to the likelihood of criminal proceedings.

Time ends for Article 5(3) purposes with the finding of guilt or innocence (*B v Austria* (1991) 13 EHRR 20); time ends for Article 6(1) purposes when the proceedings are over, including any appeal. In *Minshall v UK* (2012) 55 EHRR 36 (1058), the ECtHR found that there had been a breach of the requirement where four years and seven months had elapsed between the grant of leave to appeal against a confiscation order and the determination of the appeal.

Neither the court nor the prosecution is responsible for delays attributable to D or D's lawyers (*Konig v Germany* (1979–80) 2 EHRR 170). However, D is perfectly entitled to take legitimate points, if necessary, by way of appeal (*Ledonne (No. 1) v Italy* [1999] ECHR 25 at [25], where D twice sought adjournment and twice challenged the validity of summons issued against him, but the prosecuting authorities could not provide good reason for two periods of delay totalling two years and ten months and on that basis breach of Article 6(1) was found).

Periods spent at large are discounted (*Girolami v Italy* (1991) A/196-E). The workload of the court is not a good reason for delay — and, in any event, should be supported with evidence of steps taken to alleviate the position (*Majaric v Slovenia* (2000) Appln. 28400/95, 8 February 2000 at [39]) — nor is a shortage of resources. Article 6(1) imposes on Contracting States the duty to organise their judicial system in such a way that their courts can meet their requirement to hear a case within a reasonable time (*Ledonne (No. 2) v Italy* [1999] ECHR 26 at [23]). **A7.74**

The remedy in domestic law for a breach of the requirement that there be trial within a reasonable period has been considered at the highest level on several occasions. In *Mills v HM Advocate* [2002] UKPC 2, [2004] 1 AC 441, the Privy Council held that quashing a conviction was a possible, but exceptional, remedy. In the subsequent case of *A-G's Ref (No. 2 of 2001)* [2003] UKHL 68, [2004] 2 AC 74, a nine-judge House of Lords held that, where criminal proceedings are not dealt with in a reasonable period, there is necessarily a breach of Article 6(1), but the remedy to be afforded will depend on all the circumstances of the case. See also *Crawley* [2014] EWCA Crim 1028, [2014] 2 Cr App R 16 (214). In *O'Neill v UK* (2017) 64 EHRR 16 (856), the ECtHR held that while a delay of some nine years was in breach of the right to a fair trial, the court's finding of a violation was adequate satisfaction without the need to award damages.

Retroactive Offences

A7.75 **European Convention on Human Rights, Article 7**

(1) No one shall be held guilty of any criminal offence on account of any act or omission which did not constitute a criminal offence under national or international law at the time when it was committed. Nor shall a heavier penalty be imposed than the one that was applicable at the time the criminal offence was committed.

(2) This Article shall not prejudice the trial and punishment of any person for any act or omission which, at the time it was committed, was criminal according to the general principles of law recognised by civilised nations.

Article 7 prohibits not only the creation of retroactive offences by legislation, but also the retroactive application of existing criminal offences through the development of the common law (*Custers v Denmark* (2008) 47 EHRR 28 (665); *X Ltd and Y v UK* (1982) 28 DR 77; *SW v UK* (1996) 21 EHRR 363). But it does not apply to the enforcement of penalties (*Grava v Italy* (2003) Appln. 43522/98, 10 July 2003).

Double Jeopardy

A7.76 Double jeopardy is dealt with in Protocol 7 to the ECHR. The UK has not ratified this yet. Limited protection from double jeopardy may also be provided for under Article 6 (*X v Austria* (1970) 35 EHRR CD 151; *S v Germany* (1983) 39 DR 43). For double jeopardy generally, see **D12.20** ***et seq.***

Costs

A7.77 There is no right to costs for D under the ECHR (*Lutz v Germany* (1988) 10 EHRR 182 at [59], where a court refused to reimburse costs after proceedings against D for road traffic offences were discontinued). However, where the court has a discretion to order costs, it must respect the presumption of innocence (*Minelli v Switzerland* (1983) 5 EHRR 554 at [37]). The presumption of innocence will not necessarily be infringed where costs are not awarded in a case where, by not disclosing his defence, D prolonged the proceedings against him (*Byrne v UK* [1998] EHRLR 626). In *R (Henderson) v Crown Court at Kingston upon Thames* [2015] EWHC 130 (Admin), [2015] 1 Cr App R 29 (440), D argued that the Prosecution of Offences Act 1985, s. 16A, was incompatible with Article 6 because it precluded him from recovering his privately incurred costs from central funds. The Divisional Court held that a failure to reimburse the legal costs of an acquitted defendant cannot amount to a violation of Article 6, relying on *Masson and Van Zon v Netherlands* (1996) 22 EHRR 491, *Hussain v UK* (2006) 43 EHRR 22 (437) and *Ashendon v UK* (2012) 54 EHRR 13 (433).

EVIDENCE

The Burden of Proof and the Presumption of Innocence

A7.78 As a general rule the presumption of innocence imposes the burden of proving guilt on the prosecution. In *Barbera, Messegue and Jabardo* (1989) 11 EHRR 360, the ECtHR held (at [77]):

> [Article 6(2)] embodies the principle of the presumption of innocence. It requires, *inter alia*, that when carrying out their duties, the members of a court should not start with the preconceived idea that the accused has committed the offence charged; the burden of proof is on the prosecution …

(see also *Austria v Italy* (1963) 6 Yearbook 740, at p. 782).

However, where the prosecution have proved an offence, the burden of avoiding criminal liability can, within reasonable limits, pass to D (*Lingens v Austria* (1981) 26 DR 171, at [4], which was a criminal prosecution of journalists for writing a defamatory article about a senior politician in which there was a burden on the accused to prove the truth of the statement which was the subject of the complaint as part of the defence).

Similarly, not all presumptions of law and/or fact will offend the presumption of innocence: the question is whether such presumptions remain within reasonable limits. In *Salabiaku v France* (1991) 13 EHRR 379, the ECtHR held (at [28]):

> Presumptions of fact or of law operate in every legal system. Clearly, the Convention does not prohibit such presumptions in principle. It does, however, require ... States to remain within certain limits ... Article 6(2) does not ... regard presumptions of fact or of law provided for in the criminal law with indifference. It requires States to confine them within reasonable limits which take into account the importance of what is at stake and maintain the rights of the defence.

The relevant factors to be taken into account when assessing whether presumptions of fact or law are confined within reasonable limits were considered by the House of Lords in *Lambert* [2001] UKHL 37, [2002] 2 AC 545 and *Johnstone* [2003] UKHL 28, [2003] 3 All ER 884 (see also *Sheldrake v DPP* [2004] UKHL 43, [2005] 1 AC 264). The relevant principles are fully discussed at **F3.18** ***et seq.***

Standard of Proof

Any doubt in criminal cases must be resolved in favour of the accused (*Austria v Italy* (1963) 6 Yearbook 740 at p. 784; *Barbera, Messegue and Jabardo* (1989) 11 EHRR 360). **A7.79**

Right to Call and Examine Witnesses

European Convention on Human Rights, Article 6 **A7.80**

(3) Everyone charged with a criminal offence has the following minimum rights:

...

(d) to examine or have examined witnesses against him and to obtain the attendance and examination of witnesses on his behalf under the same conditions as witnesses against him.

This rule has not been applied inflexibly and there are certain circumstances in which hearsay evidence is permitted under the ECHR (see **A7.81**). Nonetheless, Article 6(3)(d) does embody the principle that there should be equality of arms between the parties before the court and this includes the right to advance and to challenge evidence in court. In *Krcmar v Czech Republic* (2001) 31 EHRR 41 (953), the ECtHR held (at [40]):

> ... the concept of a fair hearing also implies the right to adversarial proceedings, according to which the parties must have the opportunity not only to make known any evidence needed for their claims to succeed, but also to have knowledge of, and comment on, all evidence adduced or observations filed, with a view to influencing the courts' decision ...

In addition, Article 6 can require positive steps to be taken to ensure that D can confront and call witnesses (*Barbera, Messegue and Jabardo* (1989) 11 EHRR 360 at [78]).

Steps legitimately taken to protect witnesses will not breach Article 6, for example, where special measures are taken to protect child witnesses (*R (D) v Camberwell Green Youth Court* [2005] UKHL 4, [2005] 1 All ER 999).

Hearsay Evidence

As a general rule, under the ECHR, all the evidence should be produced in D's presence at a public hearing and D has a right to examine and have examined the witnesses against him or her. Reliance on 'hearsay' evidence does not necessarily breach the ECHR: e.g., where there is some opportunity to challenge the evidence at an earlier committal hearing (*Kostovski v Netherlands* **A7.81**

(1990) 12 EHRR 434 at [41]; *Trivedi v UK* (1997) EHRLR 521). But hearsay evidence must be kept within strict limits, 'having regard to the place that the right to a fair administration of justice holds in a democratic society, any measures restricting the rights of the defence should be strictly necessary. If a less restrictive measure can suffice then that measure should be applied' (*Van Mechelen v Netherlands* (1998) 25 EHRR 647 at [59]). The question in each case is whether there has been overall fairness (*Unterpertinger v Austria* (1991) 13 EHRR 175; *Kostovski v Netherlands*).

A7.82 In *Horncastle* [2009] UKSC 14, [2010] 2 AC 373 (see **A7.24**) the Supreme Court found that the common law had, by the hearsay rule, addressed the aspect of a fair trial that Article 6(3)(d) was designed to ensure, long before the Convention came into force. Parliament had enacted exceptions to the hearsay rule that were required in the interests of justice. The exceptions were not subject to a 'sole or decisive' rule, since the regime enacted by Parliament contained safeguards which rendered that rule unnecessary. In particular, the CJA 2003 contained a code intended to ensure that hearsay evidence was admitted only when it was fair that it should be. Hearsay was not made generally admissible by the code, but it made provision for a limited number of categories of admissible hearsay, and established special stipulations to which hearsay evidence was subject. Article 6(3)(d) did not deal with the appropriate procedure where compliance was impossible.

In *Al-Khawaja and Tahery v UK* (2012) 54 EHRR 23 (807), a Grand Chamber of the ECtHR held that convictions based solely or decisively on statements from absent witnesses which were read out at trial will not automatically result in a breach of Article 6(1) in conjunction with Article 6(3)(d). As long as there are sufficient counterbalancing factors to compensate for the difficulties of admitting hearsay evidence, including strong procedural safeguards to ensure a fair trial, there will be no breach.

Where a hearsay statement is the sole or decisive evidence against D, its admission as evidence will not automatically result in a breach of Article 6(1). At the same time, where a conviction is based solely or decisively on the evidence of absent witnesses, a court must subject the proceedings to the most searching scrutiny. Because of the dangers of the admission of such evidence, it will constitute a very important factor to balance in the scales, and one which will require sufficient counterbalancing factors, including the existence of strong procedural safeguards. The question in each case is whether there are sufficient counterbalancing factors, including measures that permit a fair and proper assessment of the reliability of that evidence to take place. This will permit a conviction to be based on such evidence only if it is sufficiently reliable given its importance in the case. The safeguards contained in the CJA 1988 and the CJA 2003 regulating the admission of hearsay, supported by those contained in the PACE 1984, s. 78, and the common law, are, in principle, strong safeguards designed to ensure fairness. The ECtHR concluded that there was no breach of Article 6(1) in Al-Khawaja's case because of the presence of adequate safeguards, but that there was a violation of Article 6(1) in Tahery's case.

In *Ibrahim* [2012] EWCA Crim 837, [2012] 4 All ER 225, the Court of Appeal further criticised the attempt of the Grand Chamber to clarify the sole and decisive test, and suggested an alternative test as to the admission of hearsay evidence. In *Riat* [2012] EWCA Crim 1509, [2013] 1 All ER 349, the approach was further refined; the CJA 2003 did not require that a hearsay statement had to be wholly verified from an independent source before it could be admissible in evidence or left to the jury. The task of the judge was to ensure that the hearsay evidence could safely be held to be reliable; that involved looking at its strengths and weaknesses, at the tools available to the jury for testing it, and at its importance to the case as a whole.

In *Horncastle v UK* (2015) 60 EHRR 31 (1331), the ECtHR considered a number of appeals including an appeal from the decision of the Supreme Court in *Horncastle* itself. The ECtHR noted the view of Lord Phillips in *Horncastle* that the safeguards in the CJA 2003 pertaining to the admission of hearsay evidence meant that there could be no breach of Article 6(3)(d) even if a conviction was based solely or to a decisive extent on absent witness-evidence (at [87]). The ECtHR confirmed (at [130]) that 'the admissibility of evidence is primarily a matter for regulation by national law' and that the ECtHR's function was to determine whether the proceedings *as a whole* were fair. Referring to the decision of the Grand Chamber in *Al-Khawaja and Tahery*, the ECtHR held (at [138]) that the admission of hearsay evidence that is the sole or decisive evidence against D will not automatically breach Article 6 and will not do so where there are counterbalancing measures that permit a fair and proper assessment of the reliability of the hearsay evidence. With that in mind, the ECtHR went on to find that in none of the cases before it had there been a violation of Article 6. See also **F17.20** and **F17.89**. In the subsequent case of *Seton v UK* [2016] Crim LR 653, the ECtHR found that the reception of hearsay evidence from an absent witness did not infringe Article 6.

Anonymous Witnesses

Evidence from anonymous witnesses should be treated with caution under the ECHR, Article 6. In *Kostovski v Netherlands* (1990) 12 EHRR 434, the ECtHR held (at [42] and [44]): **A7.83**

> If the defence is unaware of the identity of the person it seeks to question, it may be deprived of the very particulars enabling it to demonstrate that he or she is prejudiced, hostile or unreliable. Testimony or other declarations inculpating an accused may well be designedly untruthful or simply erroneous and the defence will scarcely be able to bring this to light if it lacks the information permitting it to test the author's reliability or cast doubt on his credibility ... Although the growth in organised crime doubtless demands the introduction of appropriate measures, the Government's submissions appear ... to lay insufficient weight on ... 'the interest of everybody in a civilised society in a controllable and fair judicial procedure.' The right to a fair administration of justice holds so prominent a place in a democratic society that it cannot be sacrificed to expediency. The Convention does not preclude reliance at the investigation stage of criminal proceedings, on sources such as anonymous informants. However, the subsequent use of anonymous statements as sufficient evidence to found a conviction ... is a different matter.

But evidence from anonymous witnesses can be relied upon, where justified, so long as there are counterbalancing factors to protect D (*Doorson v Netherlands* (1996) 22 EHRR 330). Cogent and specific evidence will be needed before anonymous evidence from law enforcement officers can be relied upon (*Van Mechelen v Netherlands* (1998) 25 EHRR 647 at [61]). In *Davis* [2008] UKHL 36, [2008] 1 AC 1128, the House of Lords reviewed the use of anonymous witnesses in domestic law, quashing D's conviction; that judgment led to the passing of the witness anonymity provisions now in the CAJA 2009 (see **D14.72**). See also *Re Guardian News and Media Ltd* [2016] EWCA Crim 11, [2016] 1 WLR 1767 at **A7.61**.

Accomplice Evidence

Reliance on the evidence of an accomplice is not prohibited under the ECHR (*X v Austria* (1962) Appln. 1599/62) but it may put in doubt the fairness of the proceedings if there are insufficient safeguards to protect D. Close scrutiny and control is called for. In *Baragiola v Switzerland* (1993) 75 DR 76, the European Commission held (at p. 118): **A7.84**

> ... the sentences imposed on the co-defendants who had given evidence for the prosecution were considerably reduced and alleviated ... As they ran the risk of losing the advantages they had been given if they went back on their previous statements or retracted their confessions, their statements were open to question. It was therefore necessary for the ... courts to adopt a critical approach in assessing the statements.

Effective cross-examination is a minimum requirement (*MH v UK* [1997] EHRLR 279 at pp. 279–80: in that case D had been unable to cross-examine a former accomplice witness on his guilty plea which had been admitted in evidence against him).

Evidence of Informers and Undercover Officers

Reliance on the evidence of informers and undercover officers is not prohibited under the ECHR, but safeguards are necessary to protect the rights of the defence (*Ludi v Switzerland* (1993) 15 EHRR 173, see also *X v Germany* (1989) 11 EHRR 84, where evidence was obtained **A7.85** by a ruse when an undercover officer posed as a remand prisoner). The defence must have the opportunity to challenge the evidence (*Ludi v Switzerland* at [49]). Moreover, the proceedings as a whole will be unfair if the informer or undercover officer incited the commission of an offence which would not otherwise have been committed (see **A7.37** and **F2.17**).

Unlawfully Obtained Evidence

A7.86 Evidence obtained in breach of absolute rights (such as rights under the ECHR, Article 3) should always be excluded from trial (*Ludi v Switzerland* (1993) 15 EHRR 173) (on the approach to be taken by domestic courts to evidence that may have been obtained by oppression, see the House of Lords' decision in *Mushtaq* [2005] UKHL 25, [2005] 3 All ER 885). Evidence obtained by torture is inadmissible in any legal proceedings (*A v Secretary of State for the Home Department (No. 2)* [2005] UKHL 71, [2006] 2 AC 221); for the approach of the ECtHR to such evidence, see *Jalloh v Germany* (2007) 44 EHRR 32 (667) and *Harutyunyan v Austria* (2009) 49 EHRR 9 (202). Otherwise, the mere fact that evidence has been obtained in breach of qualified rights under the ECHR does not automatically lead to its exclusion. In *Khan v UK* (2001) 31 EHRR 45 (1016), the ECtHR adopted the following approach (at [34]):

> The question which must be answered is whether the proceedings as a whole, including the way in which the evidence was obtained, were fair. This involves an examination of the 'unlawfulness' in question and, where violation of another Convention right is concerned, the nature of the violation found.

The central question under Article 6 is therefore overall fairness. Relevant to that assessment will be whether the breach of Convention rights was in good faith or not — and whether there was any element of entrapment or inducement. Whether the unlawfully obtained evidence is the only evidence against D will also be relevant, but not determinative (*Khan v UK* (2001) 31 EHRR 45 (1016) at [36]).

Where evidence has been obtained unlawfully during the course of a criminal investigation, and the police are invited to disclose it to a regulator acting in accordance with its statutory functions to regulate the defendant's professional activities, the police must consider Article 8 as part of the process of deciding whether to disclose that evidence (*R (Nakash) v Metropolitan Police Service* [2014] EWHC 3810 (Admin)).

The Protection against Self-incrimination

A7.87 The right to a fair trial includes 'the right of anyone charged with a criminal offence ... to remain silent and not to contribute to incriminating himself' (*Funke v France* (1993) 16 EHRR 297). In *Saunders v UK* (1997) 23 EHRR 313, the ECtHR explained (at [68]) that:

> ... although not specifically mentioned in Article 6 of the Convention, the right to silence and the right not to incriminate oneself, are generally recognised international standards which lie at the heart of the notion of a fair procedure under Article 6. Their rationale lies, *inter alia*, in the protection of the accused against improper compulsion by the authorities thereby contributing to the avoidance of miscarriages of justice and to the fulfilment of the aims of Article 6. The right not to incriminate oneself, in particular, presupposes that the prosecution in a criminal case seek to prove their case against the accused without resort to evidence obtained through methods of coercion or oppression in defiance of the will of the accused. In this sense the right is closely linked to the presumption of innocence contained in Article 6(2).

The protection against self-incrimination applies to criminal proceedings in respect of all types of criminal cases without distinction from the most simple to the most complex (*Saunders v UK* at [74]). It is not confined to statements of admission of wrongdoing or to remarks which are directly incriminating (*Saunders v UK*; see also *Heaney and McGuiness v Ireland* (2001) 33 EHRR 12 (264), where failure by the applicants to account for their movements attracted adverse inferences). However, it does not protect individuals from taking the oath, which is designed to ensure that statements made are truthful (*Serves v France* (1999) 28 EHRR 267).

The mere fact that the police place a police informant in a cell with an accused prisoner in the hope that the prisoner may say something to self-incriminate will not necessarily breach Article 6. But if that individual induces D to self-incriminate by persistent questioning at the insistence of the police, Article 6 will be breached (*Allan v UK* (2003) 36 EHRR 12 (143)).

However, the protection from self-incrimination is not absolute (see the comments of the ECtHR in *Saunders v UK* at [74]). A presumption that the owner of a car is responsible for speeding and parking offences does not necessarily breach the protection against self-incrimination (*Tora Tolmos v Spain* (1995) Appln. 23816/94, 17 May 1995; *DN v Netherlands* (1975) Appln. 6170/73; *JP, KR and GG v Austria* (1989) Appln. 15135/89, 5 September 1989). In *Brown v Stott* [2003] 1 AC 681, the Privy Council found no violation of Article 6 where the statement made by D under the RTA 1988, s. 172, was used by the prosecution against her (see **F10.11**). That decision was considered by the Grand Chamber of the ECtHR in *O'Halloran v UK* (2008) 46 EHRR 21 (397) and found to be compatible with Article 6. The ECtHR held that, in order to determine whether the essence of those rights was infringed, it was necessary to focus on the nature and degree of compulsion used to obtain the evidence, the existence of any relevant safeguards in the procedure, and the use to which any material so obtained was put. Where D was questioned as a witness when he should have been questioned as a suspect, there was no violation of Article 6 when the answers he gave were subsequently admitted in evidence against him (*Ibrahim v UK* (2015) 61 EHRR 9 (264) and [2016] ECHR 750: see also **B10.18**). **A7.88**

It is not the compulsory questioning as such that infringes the ECHR: it is the use in criminal proceedings of answers elicited as a result of criminal proceedings to incriminate D (*Saunders v UK* at [67]; *Abas v Netherlands* (1997) Appln. 27943/95, 26 February 1997). Permitting the court to draw adverse inferences from silence does not equate with compulsory questioning and is permitted within limits (*Murray (John) v UK* (1996) 22 EHRR 29 at [46]–[52]; *Condron v UK* (2001) 31 EHRR 1 (1)). But where inferences can be drawn from D's silence during police interview, it is essential that D should have access to a lawyer before interview (*Murray (John) v UK* at [66]) and, furthermore, it is essential that the trial judge give due weight to the explanation advanced for that silence (*Beckles v UK* (2003) 36 EHRR 13 (162), where the trial judge failed to direct the jury properly when D remained silent on his solicitor's advice).

Intimate Samples

The protection against self-incrimination does not prevent the use in criminal proceedings of intimate body samples obtained by compulsion. In *Saunders v UK* (1997) 23 EHRR 313, the ECtHR held (at [69]): **A7.89**

> ... [the right not to incriminate oneself] does not extend to the use in criminal proceedings of material which may be obtained from the accused through the use of compulsory powers but which has an existence independent of the will of the suspect such as, inter alia, documents acquired pursuant to a warrant, breath, blood and urine samples and bodily tissues for the purpose of DNA testing.

Referring to *Saunders v UK*, the Divisional Court held in *R (River East Supplies Ltd) v Crown Court at Nottingham* [2017] EWHC 1942 (Admin), [2017] 2 Cr App R 27 (384), that the common-law privilege against self-incrimination does not extend to material that came into existence independently of the person claiming the privilege and at a time before any compulsory discovery process was commenced.

Expert Evidence

The principle that there must be equality between prosecution and defence applies in relation to expert witnesses (*Bonisch v Austria* (1987) 9 EHRR 191). But the mere fact that a court-appointed expert works at the same institute as the expert relied upon by the prosecution does not automatically breach the ECHR, Article 6 (*Brandstetter v Austria* (1993) 15 EHRR 378). **A7.90**

SENTENCE

Fair Trial Guarantees in Sentencing

A7.91 The fair trial requirements of the ECHR, Article 6, do not cease to apply at the sentencing stage, but the requirements do not apply in the same way. The presumption of innocence ceases to apply (*Engel v Netherlands* (1979–80) 1 EHRR 647 at [90]). For a similar approach under the Canadian Charter of Rights, see *R v Gardiner* (1982) 2 SCR 368.

Retroactive Penalties

A7.92 Article 7 of the ECHR, which protects individuals from being convicted of criminal offences which did not exist at the time the act was committed, also prohibits the imposition of a more severe penalty for an offence than that which applied at the time the offence was committed. The concept of a 'penalty' is autonomous: to render the protection offered by Article 7 effective, courts must be free to go behind appearances and assess for themselves whether a particular measure amounts in substance to a penalty (*Welch v UK* (1995) 20 EHRR 247).

Where the law changes between the date of D's conviction and the date of the sentencing hearing, Article 7 requires the sentencing court to apply the most favourable of the two sentencing regimes (pre-change or post-change) to the defendant when passing sentence ('*lex mitior*') (*Docherty* [2014] EWCA Crim 1197, [2014] 2 Cr App R (S) 76 (601) (at [39])). The Court of Appeal referred to the decision of the Grand Chamber in *Scoppola v Italy (No. 2)* (2010) 51 EHRR 12 (323), where the Strasbourg Court said (at [108] and [109]):

> ... it is consistent with the principle of the rule of law, of which Article 7 forms an essential part, to expect a trial court to apply to each punishable act the penalty which the legislator considers appropriate. Inflicting a heavier penalty for the sole reason that it was prescribed at the time of the commission of the offence would mean applying to the defendant's detriment the rules governing the succession of criminal laws in time. In addition, it would amount to disregarding any legislative change favourable to the accused which might have come in before the conviction and continuing to impose penalties which the State — and the community it represents — now consider excessive. The Court notes that the obligation to apply, from among several criminal laws, the one whose provisions are the most favourable to the accused is a clarification of the rules on the succession of criminal laws, which is in accord with another essential element of Article 7, namely the foreseeability of penalties.
>
> In the light of the foregoing considerations, the Court takes the view that ... where there are differences between the criminal law in force at the time of the commission of the offence and subsequent criminal laws enacted before a final judgment is rendered, the courts must apply the law whose provisions are most favourable to the defendant.

The Court of Appeal in *Docherty* concluded that it should follow the *Scoppola* interpretation of Article 7 but on the facts the Court held that '*lex mitior*' was not engaged. The Supreme Court confirmed that D should be sentenced according to the law and practice prevailing at the date of sentence subject to not exceeding the maximum sentence permissible at the time the offence was committed. It was not appropriate to examine the sentencing regimes that may have existed between the date of commission and the date of sentence and choose the one most favourable to D (*Docherty* [2016] UKSC 62, [2017] 1 WLR 181). In *Knights (Secretary of State for Justice intervening)* [2017] EWCA Crim 1052, [2017] 2 Cr App R (S) 33 (288), D's case was referred back to the Court of Appeal by the CCRC. In 2008 D was sentenced to imprisonment for public protection (IPP) with a minimum term of eight months. Some 16 days after D was sentenced, the law changed so that an IPP could only be imposed where the minimum term was for two years or more. The basis of his appeal was that the ECHR, Article 7, and the principle of *lex mitior* meant that D should have the benefit of this change in the law and so D's IPP sentence should be quashed. D sought to distinguish *Docherty* but the Court held that it was bound by that decision. *Lex mitior* in its ordinary form (namely that D could not receive a higher sentence than the maximum available for the offence at the time it was committed) was a part of Article 7 and the common law but the principle in its wider form (namely that D is entitled to the benefit of any subsequent change in the law) was not.

In *Bell* [2015] EWCA Crim 1926, [2016] 1 WLR 1, the Court of Appeal held that, in a case where the maximum sentence available both at the date of commission (2000) and at the date of sentence (2014) was a discretionary term of life imprisonment, Article 7 does not require a sentencing court to determine what sentence it would have imposed on D in 2000 and then compare that to the sentence it would have imposed if the offence had been committed in 2014 and impose the lesser of the two. Instead, Article 7 directs the court to consider whether a heavier penalty is available in 2014 for the offence committed in 2000 than would have been available in 2000 had D been convicted then. In this case, the same maximum sentence was available in both 2000 and 2014 (life imprisonment) and so the question of which one was 'heavier' did not arise. Accordingly, the sentencing court was bound to apply *H* [2011] EWCA Crim 2753, [2012] 2 Cr App R (S) 21 (88) and sentence D according to the practice in force in 2014. If this resulted in D receiving a longer minimum term than would have been imposed had D been convicted and sentenced in 2000, that penalty did not infringe Article 7. In *Forbes* [2016] EWCA Crim 1388, [2017] 1 WLR 53, the Court of Appeal held that, even in circumstances where the maximum sentence at the time of commission of the offence was a term of imprisonment but on account of D's circumstances at that time (in particular, youth) such a sentence would not have been available then it would be contrary to Article 7 and common-law notions of fairness to impose a custodial sentence now. In *L* [2017] EWCA Crim 43, [2017] 1 Cr App R (S) 51 (402), the Court of Appeal affirmed the decision in *Forbes* and held that provided a term of detention of any length would have been available as a sentence for D at the time the offence was committed that was sufficient to enable the court to impose a custodial term at the time of sentencing without infringing Article 7 or the common law principles of fairness.

Proportionality in Sentencing

Where an individual is sentenced for conduct protected as a qualified right under the ECHR, any punishment must be proportionate (*Arrowsmith v UK* (1978) 19 DR 5). In *Price v UK* (2002) 34 EHRR 53 (1285), the ECtHR held that to detain a severely disabled person in conditions where she was dangerously cold, ill and unable to use the toilet constituted degrading treatment under Article 3. See also *Mouisel v France* (2004) 38 EHRR 34 (735), where the ECtHR found a breach of Article 3 where the relevant authorities failed to take sufficient care of the conditions in which D, a prisoner suffering from leukaemia, was transferred to and from hospital. By contrast, in *Khan* [2016] EWCA Crim 1292, [2016] 2 Cr App R (S) 42 (458), the Court of Appeal rejected a claim that sentences of 12 months' imprisonment on a couple suffering from (less serious) medical conditions were compatible with Article 3. **A7.93**

Preventative Sentences

European Convention on Human Rights, Article 5 **A7.94**

(4) Everyone who is deprived of his liberty by arrest or detention shall be entitled to take proceedings by which the lawfulness of his detention shall be decided speedily by a court and his release ordered if the detention is not lawful.

Where individuals are sentenced solely for the purposes of retribution, deterrence or protection of the public, Article 5(4) will be engaged as soon as the punitive part of the sentence is served and the preventative component begins. The key question at that stage is whether the prisoner's dangerousness continues to justify the detention.

In *James v UK* (2013) 56 EHRR 12 (399), the ECtHR found that, in circumstances where a government sought to rely solely on the risk posed by offenders to the public in order to justify continued detention, regard must be had to the need to encourage the rehabilitation of offenders. In the applicants' cases this meant that they were required to be provided with reasonable opportunities to undertake courses aimed at helping them to address their offending behaviour and the risks they posed. There was, however, no violation of Article 5(4) as the applicants had failed to establish that the combination of Parole Board and judicial review proceedings could not have resulted in an order for their release. In *Brown v Parole Board for Scotland* [2017] UKSC 69, [2018] AC 1, the Supreme Court held that it was appropriate now to adopt the same approach to the interpretation of the ECHR, Article 5(1)(a), as has been followed by the Strasbourg Court since *James v UK*. Accordingly, there will only be a breach of Article 5 where the prisoner's detention has become arbitrary. Where the prison authorities had failed to provide courses to the prisoner, the satisfactory completion of which would have enabled him to prove that he was no longer a danger to the public, that failure did not entitle the prisoner to be released immediately. If the failure rendered his continued detention unlawful under Article 5 there were other remedies available to the prisoner, including monetary compensation. In *Stott v Secretary of State for Justice* [2018] UKSC 59, [2018] 3 WLR 1831, the Supreme Court held that the difference in treatment between a life sentence prisoner and an extended determinate sentence prisoner was proportionate and so did not amount to an unjustified interference with Articles 5 and 14.

APPEALS

Fair Trial Guarantees at the Appeal Stage

A7.95 There is no requirement under the ECHR to set up an appeal procedure. Limitations can therefore be placed on the right to appeal, including time-limits, so long as they are reasonable and proportionate (*Bricmont v Belgium* (1986) 48 DR 106, at p. 151). If time-limits for appealing are imposed, the relevant authorities are under a duty to inform D of these limits (*Vacher v France* (1997) 24 EHRR 482 at [28]).

Although there is no requirement under the ECHR to set up an appeal procedure, where such an appeal procedure is set up, it must conform to Article 6 principles (*Delcourt v Belgium* (1979–80) 1 EHRR 335 at [25]). Inevitably, the way in which these principles are applied will not be the same as at trial and will depend upon the special features of appeal proceedings. In *Monnell v UK* (1988) 10 EHRR 205, the ECtHR held (at [56]):

> The manner in which paragraph 1, as well as paragraph 3(c), of Article 6 is to be applied in relation to appellate or cassation courts depends upon the special features of the proceedings involved. Account must be taken of the entirety of the proceedings conducted in the domestic legal order and of the role of the appellate or cassation court therein.

Where a court, including a court of appeal, has power to substitute a conviction for an offence other than that with which an individual is actually charged, the defence must be afforded an opportunity to deal with the alternative charge (*Pelissier v France* (2000) 30 EHRR 715, substitution of aiding and abetting for principal offence by the court of appeal). This is particularly so where it is conceivable that the defence would have been different.

Leave to Appeal

A7.96 Article 6 of the ECHR applies to leave proceedings since these constitute part of the determination of the criminal charge (*Monnell v UK* (1988) 10 EHRR 205, at [54]). However, the limited nature of proceedings for leave to appeal may not require a full public hearing (*Monnell v UK* at [57] and [58]). Similarly, full reasons may not be needed at the leave stage (*Webb v UK* (1997) 24 EHRR CD 73 at p. 74).

Legal Aid and Legal Representation

A7.97 The interests of justice require that D be granted legal aid where the case is a complex one and/or there are serious consequences at stake. D's ability to understand the proceedings and effectively participate will be relevant in determining whether D requires legal assistance (*Granger v UK* (1990) 12 EHRR 469 at [46] and [47] — refusal of legal aid in appeal against conviction for perjury).

The more severe the potential penalty if the appeal is unsuccessful, the greater the need for representation (*Maxwell v UK* (1995) 19 EHRR 97 at [38]–[40]). But the prospects of success are important (*Monnell v UK* (1988) 10 EHRR 205 at [67]). Decisions about legal aid should be kept under review (*Granger v UK* at [46]).

Right to a Hearing

A7.98 The right to a public hearing does not automatically extend to every stage of the proceedings provided the process viewed as a whole has been fair. The nature of the appellate stage will determine whether a hearing is required. Where the appeal court is merely required to assess points of law which do not require oral argument, the need for a rehearing can be dispensed with (*Axen v Germany* (1984) 6 EHRR 195 at [28]). In contrast, where the court is having to determine D's guilt or innocence based upon examination of law and the facts, there is a greater need for a full hearing (*Ekbatani v Sweden* (1991) 13 EHRR 504 at [32]).

Right to be Present

A7.99 There is no absolute rule that D must be present during appellate proceedings: it depends what issues are being considered. Where on appeal the court is simply reviewing the findings of fact below, no new facts are adduced and there is no prospect of the sentence being increased, there is no duty on the authorities to ensure that D is present, particularly where D is represented (*Prinz v Austria* (2001) 31 EHRR 12 (357) at [34]; see also *Belziuk v Poland* (2000) 30 EHRR 614). But where an assessment of the facts, or more particularly D's mental state, are in issue, D should be present (*Cooke v Austria* (2001) 31 EHRR 11 (338) at [42]; since D's sentence could have been increased and the determination of this issue involved a fresh assessment of his mental state at the time of the killing, D's presence was essential; see also *Kamasinski v Austria* (1991) 13 EHRR 36 at [106]–[107]). Even where the sentence cannot be increased, D's attendance may be required if the appeal court is likely to consider the motive for the offence and/or D's personality and character (*Pobornikoff v Austria* (2003) 36 EHRR 25 (418)).

Penalties for Appealing

A7.100 Loss of time as a penalty for appealing will not necessarily breach the ECHR (*Monnell v UK* (1988) 10 EHRR 205 at [46]). Nor will an increase in sentence which reflects an appeal court's re-assessment of the facts of the offence and any aggravating features necessarily breach the ECHR (*De Salvador Torres v Spain* (1997) 23 EHRR 601).

Extent to which Appeal Court May Remedy Trial Defects

A7.101 As a general rule, the whole of the proceedings, including any appeal, are relevant to an assessment of fairness under the ECHR, Article 6 (*Edwards v UK* (1993) 15 EHRR 417, non-disclosure at first instance). However, in some respects, an appeal court will not be able to rectify fairness problems that arose at trial: e.g., where a trial judge misdirects the jury on the question of adverse inferences (*Condron v UK* (2001) 31 EHRR 1 (1) at [63]). Nor can an appeal court provide the required scrutiny in cases where material is not disclosed on grounds of public interest immunity (*Rowe and Davis v UK* (2000) 30 EHRR 1 at [65]).

Reasons in Appeal Cases

A7.102 As a general rule, reasons should be given in an appeal hearing. However, full reasons need not necessarily be given at the leave stage (*Webb v UK* (1997) 24 EHRR CD 73; *X v Germany* (1981) 25 DR 240).

Section A8 Territorial and Extra-territorial Jurisdiction

INTRODUCTION

A8.1 A distinction must be drawn between the ambit of English criminal law, on the one hand, and 'venue', or the jurisdiction of particular courts, on the other. Things done beyond the ambit of English law cannot amount to offences under that law. Whether English law applies in a given case is therefore a question of substantive law, rather than one of procedure; but where English law does apply there are no longer any territorial restrictions on the jurisdiction of particular courts to try the alleged offence.

By the Senior Courts Act 1981, s. 46(1), the Crown Court has jurisdiction in proceedings on indictment for offences wherever committed, and in particular proceedings on indictment for offences within the jurisdiction of the Admiralty of England.

By the MCA 1980, s. 2(1), magistrates' courts are similarly free of territorial limitations on their criminal jurisdiction. Jurisdiction over summary offences was previously limited (with some exceptions) to offences committed within a court's own commission area, or within 500 yards of the boundary between that and another commission area, but this limitation was removed by the Courts Act 2003, s. 44.

Conduct that amounts to an offence under English law may also amount to an offence under the laws of one or more other States, especially where it involves acts or consequences in more than one jurisdiction. Within the EU, Council Framework Decision 2009/948/JHA seeks to ensure that Member States co-operate and exchange information etc. in such a way as to avoid the instigation of 'parallel proceedings' in two or more jurisdictions. The UK government (and some others) decided that the practices it embodies were already well established in domestic law and saw no need to implement it (see **A9.25**). A person charged in England and Wales who has already been convicted or acquitted of that same offence or its equivalent anywhere abroad, may however enter a plea of autrefois acquit or autrefois convict on the same basis as if previously convicted or acquitted under English law (see *Aughet* (1919) 13 Cr App R 101 and **D12.25**).

TERRITORIAL JURISDICTION

The General Rule

A8.2 English criminal law applies throughout the realm of England and Wales and over all persons who come within the realm. Even though some such persons (e.g., foreign diplomats) may enjoy immunity from prosecution, they are nevertheless required to obey the law, and diplomatic immunity may in some cases be waived (see **A8.25**).

In contrast, English criminal law does not ordinarily extend to things done outside the realm, *even when done by British citizens* (*Harden* [1963] 1 QB 8). Specific statutory provision is required before any part of English criminal law can apply to conduct abroad or indeed to things done in other parts of the UK, which have their own jurisdiction over crime. The common law had no extra-territorial ambit, and in the absence of such provision, a statutory offence is presumed subject to similar constraints. As Viscount Simonds said in *Cox v Army Council* [1963] AC 48, at p. 67:

> Apart from those exceptional cases in which specific provision is made in respect of acts committed abroad, the whole body of the criminal law of England deals only with acts committed in England.

Parliament may give an offence whatever extra-territorial application it thinks fit, but must do so expressly. Lord Morris of Borth-y-Gest explained the position in *Treacy v DPP* [1971] AC 537 (at pp. 552–3):

> In general, ... acts committed out of England, even though they are committed by British subjects, are not punishable under the criminal law of this country. But, as Parliament is supreme, it is open to Parliament to pass an enactment in relation to such acts. It is, however, a general rule of construction that unless there is something which points to a contrary intention a statute will be taken to apply only to the UK. It would be open to Parliament to enact that if a British subject committed anywhere an act designated as blackmail he would commit an offence punishable in England. Such an enactment would, however, have to be in clear and express terms: specific provision would have to be made with regard to acts committed abroad ...

The territorial or extra-territorial ambit of an offence must be distinguished from the 'territorial extent' of the legislation creating it. The Outer Space Act 1986, for example, 'extends to England and Wales, Scotland and Northern Ireland' (so is law in all three parts of the UK), but by s. 1 of that Act it *applies* to specified activities 'whether carried on in the United Kingdom or elsewhere ... [including] any activity in outer space'. **A8.3**

Even where a statute extends to Scotland or Northern Ireland, as well as to England and Wales, the commission of an offence in one part of the UK is not ordinarily punishable in another. An exception is created by the C-TA 2008, s. 28 (see **B10.1**).

Where the laws of British overseas territories, or of the Channel Islands, incorporate elements of English criminal law, this does not make misconduct there punishable in England. An offence committed in Jersey, for example, is ordinarily punishable only in Jersey.

The Territorial Limits

The realm (which marks the limit of criminal jurisdiction at common law) comprises the land territory of England and Wales and the airspace above it. It now includes the English section of the Channel Tunnel system (Channel Tunnel Act 1987, s. 10). The seaward boundary of the realm is in most cases the water's edge, but the realm includes such internal waters (bays, harbours, etc.) as lie within county boundaries. **A8.4**

By the Territorial Waters Jurisdiction Act 1878, ss. 2 and 7, English criminal law also applies (in respect of offences triable on indictment) to things done on the open sea within territorial limits. This ordinarily means within 12 nautical miles of the low water mark around the coast, or of a line drawn across the mouth of a designated bay or estuary (Territorial Sea (Baselines) Order 2014 (SI 2014 No. 1353); Territorial Sea Act 1987). The limits of the territorial sea derived from these baselines are now shown on Admiralty Charts published by the UK Hydrographic Office and obtainable from Admiralty Chart agents. A person who is not a British subject (as to which see **A8.20**) may not ordinarily be prosecuted under that Act for a crime committed aboard a foreign ship, unless a Principal Secretary of State certifies that the institution of such proceedings is expedient (see s. 3 of the 1878 Act), but note that this does not apply to prosecutions for drug trafficking offences under the Criminal Justice (International Co-operation) Act 1990, s. 19. Waters adjacent to Scotland are part of Scotland (Scotland Act 1998, s. 126) and thus outwith English jurisdiction.

By the Criminal Jurisdiction (Offshore Activities) Order 1987 (SI 1987 No. 2198) and the Petroleum Act 1998, s. 10, English criminal law also extends to things done on (or within 500 metres of) platforms in designated areas of the continental shelf within which the UK claims rights to the seabed and natural resources. As to restrictions on prosecutions for certain offences, see the Petroleum Act 1998, s. 12.

CROSS-FRONTIER OFFENCES

The General Rule

A8.5 An offence may be committed within England and Wales even where some elements or consequences occur abroad. This is undoubtedly the case where the last essential constituent element of the offence takes place (i.e. the offence is completed) within England and Wales (*Harden* [1963] 1 QB 8; *Treacy v DPP* [1971] AC 537). In the case of a conduct crime, such as blackmail, the offence is complete upon the commission of the conduct in question, which in the case of blackmail is the 'making' of the unwarranted demand. If this occurs within the jurisdiction, it matters not whether the intended consequences occur abroad, or indeed whether they occur at all (*Treacy*; *Pogmore* [2017] EWCA Crim 925, [2018] 2 Cr App R 2 (14) (but see further **B5.53**)). In the case of a result crime, jurisdiction is established upon the occurrence of any specified result within England and Wales (*Secretary of State for Trade v Markus* [1976] AC 35). If the victim of an act of violence abroad subsequently dies in an English hospital, it might seem odd to regard this as a case of murder or manslaughter 'committed in England', but such a conclusion appears unavoidable, given that the principle is firmly established in English law.

The position was previously less clear where some essential elements took place within the jurisdiction, but completion of the offence occurred elsewhere. The traditional approach in English law was that in the absence of specific statutory provision (such as may be found in the CJA 1993, Part 1: see **A8.10**), a crime was deemed to be committed *only* where it was completed. This was known as the 'terminatory' approach to jurisdiction. See, e.g., *Harden* [1963] 1 QB 8, *DPP v Stonehouse* [1978] AC 55, *Nanayakkara* [1987] 1 All ER 650 and *Manning* [1998] 2 Cr App R 461. In *Smith (Wallace Duncan) (No. 4)* [2004] EWCA Crim 631, [2004] QB 1418, however, the Court of Appeal held that a crime may be regarded as committed within the jurisdiction if 'a substantial part of the offence' was committed in England and Wales, even if the last constituent element took place abroad. This 'inclusive' approach eschews the petty legal technicalities that dogged the terminatory approach and, although initially hard to justify on the basis of precedent, it was endorsed (*obiter*) by Lord Hope in *R (Purdy) v DPP* [2009] UKHL 45, [2010] 1 AC 345 and has consistently been endorsed or applied by the Court of Appeal, notably in *Sheppard* [2010] EWCA Crim 65, [2010] 2 All ER 850; *AIL* [2016] EWCA Crim 2, [2016] QB 763 and *Burns* [2017] EWCA Crim 1466.

The Court of Appeal also purported to apply principles derived from *Smith (No. 4)* in *Rogers* [2014] EWCA Crim 1680, [2015] 1 WLR 1017, in upholding D's conviction for a money laundering offence under the POCA 2002, s. 327(1)(c). The alleged offence involved converting in Spain criminal property which was derived from frauds against victims in England and Wales, but which was already in Spain by the time D came to launder it. The problem here was that *no* element of the offence charged had occurred within the jurisdiction, making the analogy with *Smith* unsound. The reasoning in *Rogers* was also flawed in that it was supposed that the POCA 2002, s. 340(11)(d), provided an extra-territorial ambit to the various money laundering offences, whereas it refers only to acts that '*would* constitute an offence ... *if* done in the United Kingdom'. It contemplates, in other words, that an act of 'money laundering' may fail to constitute an offence precisely because it takes place abroad.

A8.6 The terminatory approach was capable of leading to the conviction under English law of a foreigner in respect of conduct abroad that only indirectly produced a proscribed result within the jurisdiction. In *Perrin* [2002] EWCA Crim 747, for example, a French citizen was convicted in England of an offence under the Obscene Publications Act 1959, s. 2(1), merely because the contents of his foreign-based web site were downloaded (and thus 'published') by a police officer in England. No evidence was adduced as to whether this material was illegal in the country from which it was uploaded. Such an outcome may perhaps be less likely under the more flexible approach adopted in *Smith,* but jurisdiction might still be asserted over foreigners in respect of acts abroad where what happened in England was a direct consequence of their actions and forms a 'substantial part' of the offence. There is no requirement of 'double-criminality' in such cases.

Inchoate and Secondary Liability

As to the rules governing inchoate offences of a cross-frontier kind, see **A5.33** (assistance or encouragement under the SCA 2007, Part 2); **B1.135** (solicitation of murder); **B10.82** (incitement of terrorism abroad); **A5.61** (statutory conspiracy); **A5.70** (conspiracy to defraud) and **A5.82** (criminal attempts). **A8.7**

In respect of secondary offenders, the general rule is that if (but only if) D commits an offence in England, E may be liable as a secondary party to that offence, even if E has personally done nothing within the jurisdiction. In *Robert Millar (Contractors) Ltd* [1970] 2 QB 54, a fatal road accident occurred on a motorway in England when a visibly worn and defective front tyre on a lorry blew out at speed. The driver admitted causing death by dangerous driving, and the appellants, a Scottish haulage company and its managing director, were convicted as secondary parties, on the basis that they knew of the defect when they despatched the lorry from its Glasgow depot. The Court of Appeal rejected an argument that the appellants had done nothing in England. Fenton Atkinson LJ said:

> The offence of causing death by dangerous driving was committed in England... but the appellants are guilty of participating in that crime and not of some self-subsisting crime on their own account and, therefore, they are in the same position as the principal offender and they are liable to be tried in this country.

In *R (Purdy) v DPP* [2009] UKHL 45, [2010] 1 AC 345, the House of Lords considered (but ultimately declined to resolve) the argument that in the converse kind of case, where D in England aids, counsels or procures an act by E that is committed abroad, no offence is committed in England. The case concerned the Suicide Act 1961, s. 2 (see **B1.140**), which (prior to its amendment by the CAJA 2009) created a substantive offence of secondary participation in the suicide or attempted suicide of another person, but the principles applicable appear to be similar in most respects to those governing cases of secondary participation in the crime of another. **A8.8**

Lord Hope was minded to reject the argument, preferring the more inclusive approach to jurisdiction advanced in *Smith (Wallace Duncan) (No. 4)* [2004] EWCA Crim 631, [2004] QB 1418 (see **A8.5**). The majority view, however, was that the principal issue in the case could and should be decided without deciding the jurisdiction issue, which had initially been overlooked and on which no oral argument had been heard.

Statutory Provisions

A number of statutory provisions create special jurisdictional rules for specific offences or classes of offence. These include the OAPA 1861, s. 10 (see **B1.10**), which makes special provision for offences of murder or manslaughter in which an unlawful wound etc. in England leads to death abroad (or vice versa) and the Perjury Act 1911, s. 1(4) and (5) (see **B14.1** *et seq.*), which deal with statements made abroad for the purpose of proceedings within the jurisdiction (and vice versa). **A8.9**

More recent provisions include the CJA 1993, Part 1, which makes special provision for specified offences of cross-frontier fraud, blackmail or dishonesty; the Computer Misuse Act 1990, ss. 4 to 7 (see **B17.16** to **B17.18**); and the Female Genital Mutilation Act 2003 (see **B2.178**).

Criminal Justice Act 1993

Faced with modern forms of international fraud and dishonesty, the traditional 'terminatory' approach to identifying the *locus* of a crime (see **A8.5**) was manifestly inadequate. As Buxton LJ pointed out in *Manning* [1998] 2 Cr App R 461, strict application of that principle would all too often mean that 'plainly dishonest conduct with a strong connection **A8.10** with this country [could not] be tried here'. The CJA 1993, Part 1, which did not come into force until 1 June 1999, addressed this problem by introducing special rules in respect of designated offences, which are then divided into substantive 'Group A offences' and inchoate 'Group B offences'.

The Group A offences listed in s. 1 now comprise:

- offences under the Theft Act 1968, ss. 1 (theft), 17 (false accounting), 19 (false statements by company directors, etc.), 21 (blackmail), 22 (handling stolen goods) and 24A (retaining credits from dishonest sources, etc.);
- offences under the Fraud Act 2006, ss. 1 (fraud), 6 (possession etc. of articles for use in frauds), 7 (making or supplying articles for use in frauds), 9 (participating in fraudulent business carried on by sole trader, etc.) and 11 (obtaining services dishonestly);
- offences under the Forgery and Counterfeiting Act 1981, ss. 1 (forgery), 2 (copying a false instrument), 3 (using a false instrument), 4 (using a copy of a false instrument), 5 (offences relating to money orders, share certificates, passports, etc.), 14 (counterfeiting notes and coins), 15 (passing etc. counterfeit notes and coins), 16 (custody or control of counterfeit notes and coins), 17 (making or custody or control of counterfeiting materials, etc.), 20 (importation of counterfeit notes and coins) and 21 (exportation of counterfeit notes and coins);
- offences under the Identity Documents Act 2010, ss. 4 to 6; and
- cheating the public revenue.

The Group B offences are: conspiracy to commit a Group A offence (see **A5.61**); conspiracy to defraud (see **A5.70**); attempting to commit a Group A offence (see **A5.82**); and relevant offences under the SCA 2007, Part 2 (SCA 2007, s. 63 and sch. 6).

A8.11 Prior to 15 January 2007, the Group A list included offences of deception under the Theft Act 1968, ss. 15, 15A, 16, 17 and 20(2), and under the Theft Act 1978, ss. 1 and 2. These offences were all repealed on that date by the Fraud Act 2006 but, under transitional provisions in that Act (see sch. 2, para. 3), this repeal 'does not affect any liability, investigation, legal proceeding or penalty for or in respect of any [deception] offence partly committed before commencement'.

No transitional arrangements were ever made in respect of the jurisdiction provisions in the CJA 1993, but in light of the subsequent decision of the Court of Appeal in *Smith (Wallace Duncan) (No. 4)* [2004] EWCA Crim 631, [2004] QB 1418 (see **A8.5**), this is probably of no real consequence. Indeed, the perceived necessity for that Act largely disappeared once the 'inclusionary principle' of jurisdiction was adopted by the courts.

Relevant Events under the Criminal Justice Act 1993

A8.12 The key to establishing jurisdiction under the CJA 1993 is the occurrence of a 'relevant event' within England and Wales. Where such an event occurs, it is irrelevant whether D was a British citizen or was at any material time in England and Wales (s. 3(1)). A relevant event is defined for most purposes as any event that is an essential element of the offence in question. That must mean an *actus reus* element (because *mens rea* is not an event). It is not sufficient that some preparatory event occurred in England if that event is not itself a definitional element of the offence charged. Nor in a case such as *Atakpu* [1994] QB 69 (see **B4.34**), is there any relevant act of theft in England where D steals a car abroad and (having already completed that theft) brings the stolen car into England.

A8.13 Special provision is made in s. 2(1A) for the new offence of fraud. Fraud is a conduct crime in which the actual making of a gain or the causing of a loss to another forms no part of the offence at all. But for s. 2(1A), a fraud successfully practised from abroad on a victim in England would not necessarily fall within English jurisdiction. See further **B5.13**.

Criminal Justice Act 1993, s. 2

(1) For the purposes of this Part, 'relevant event', in relation to any Group A offence, means (subject to subsection (1A)) any act or omission or other event (including any result of one or more acts or omissions) proof of which is required for conviction of the offence.

(1A) In relation to an offence under section 1 of the Fraud Act 2006 (fraud), 'relevant event' includes—
 (a) if the fraud involved an intention to make a gain and the gain occurred, that occurrence;
 (b) if the fraud involved an intention to cause a loss or to expose another to a risk of loss and the loss occurred, that occurrence.

(2) For the purpose of determining whether or not a particular event is a relevant event in relation to a Group A offence, any question as to where it occurred is to be disregarded.

(3) A person may be guilty of a Group A offence if any of the events which are relevant events in relation to the offence occurred in England and Wales.

The CJA 1993, s. 4, attempts to provide guidance as to what may constitute the occurrence of an event in England and Wales. **A8.14**

Criminal Justice Act 1993, s. 4

In relation to a Group A or Group B offence—
(a) there is an obtaining of property in England and Wales if the property is either despatched from or received at a place in England and Wales; and
(b) there is a communication in England and Wales of any information, instruction, request, demand or other matter if it is sent by any means:
 (i) from a place in England and Wales to a place elsewhere; or
 (ii) from a place elsewhere to a place in England and Wales.

The wording of s. 4 is unfortunate because, in contrast to s. 2(1A), it fails to provide that such events are necessarily 'relevant events'. The 'communication' of a blackmail demand is not a 'relevant event' for the purposes of the offence of blackmail, because a blackmail demand can be 'made' under the Theft Act 1968, s. 21, without ever being communicated (*Treacy v DPP* [1971] AC 537), but the purpose of the provision was clearly to ensure that jurisdiction over blackmail would arise in either of the circumstances listed in s. 4(b)(i) and (ii) and that is how it was interpreted in *Pogmore* [2017] EWCA Crim 925, [2018] 2 Cr App R 2 (14) (see further **B5.53**).

OFFENCES ABOARD SHIPS OR AIRCRAFT

Offences aboard British or UK Ships

British ships (as defined in the Merchant Shipping Act 1995, s. 1) are not properly described as 'floating territory', but do sail under Admiralty jurisdiction when on the high seas (a term which in this context includes berths in foreign or Commonwealth ports (*Anderson* (1868) XI Cox CC 198; *Liverpool Justices, ex parte Molyneux* [1972] 2 QB 384). Admiralty jurisdiction over indictable offences is now exercised by the ordinary criminal courts (see **A8.1**). **A8.15**

A British ship registered in the UK is a 'United Kingdom ship' for the purposes of the Merchant Shipping Acts. (A wider definition, extending to unregistered British-owned vessels, applies for the purposes of the Policing and Crime Act 2017 (Maritime Enforcement Powers: Code of Practice) Regulations 2018 (SI 2018 No. 229).) By the Merchant Shipping Act 1995, s. 281, English courts have jurisdiction over any person charged with committing an offence aboard a UK ship on the high seas, 'as if it had been committed on board a UK ship within the limits of its ordinary jurisdiction'. This includes jurisdiction over summary offences. Although s. 281 confusingly refers only to 'offences under this Act', the MCA 1980, s. 3A, and the Senior Courts Act 1981, s. 46A, ensure that it is in fact of general application.

Ships include some small craft, but jet skis or other 'personal water craft' that are designed and used only for recreational purposes, rather than for navigation, are not currently considered to be ships at all, even if they have been registered as such in the UK (*Goodwin* [2005] EWCA Crim 3184, [2006] 1 Cr App R 22 (354)).

Her Majesty's Ships and Vessels are not 'British ships' within the meaning of the Merchant Shipping Act 1995, but are subject to Admiralty jurisdiction (*Devon Justices, ex parte DPP* [1924] 1 KB 503). As to the position of civilians aboard Her Majesty's ships (or any other ships used for the purposes of any of Her Majesty's forces) see the Armed Forces Act 2006, sch. 15, para. 2.

As to the status of offshore oil and gas platforms, see **A8.4**. As to offences committed by a master or seaman from a UK ship (including offences committed after the loss of such a ship), see **A8.22**.

Offences aboard Foreign Ships, etc.

A8.16 English criminal law does not ordinarily apply to things done on foreign ships outside English territorial limits but, by virtue of the Merchant Shipping Act 1995, s. 281 (see **A8.15**), a British citizen may be prosecuted under English law for an offence committed in a foreign port or harbour or aboard a foreign ship to which the British citizen does not belong, 'as if it had been committed on board a UK ship within the limits of its ordinary jurisdiction to try the offence'.

In *Kelly* [1982] AC 665, the House of Lords held that the Merchant Shipping Act 1894, s. 686(1) (from which the current s. 281 is derived), was not merely a 'venue' provision, dealing with the jurisdiction of particular courts (see **A8.1**), but instead made the ordinary rules of English criminal law applicable to things done by British passengers on foreign ships. See also *Cumberworth* (1989) 89 Cr App R 187, in which what is now s. 282 was held to apply even where the foreign ship in question was docked (with its loading ramp lowered) in a foreign port.

A 'foreign ship' is defined by the Merchant Shipping Act 1995, s. 313, as one that is neither a UK ship nor a small unregistered British ship; but the term, 'foreign port or harbour' is narrower in that it excludes ports or harbours in the Republic of Ireland or in any Commonwealth country (*Liverpool Justices, ex parte Molyneux* [1972] 2 QB 384).

As to offences committed aboard ships of 'Convention countries' within the meaning of the Suppression of Terrorism Act 1978 (see **A8.23**), see s. 4(7) of that Act.

As to piracy *iure gentium* and offences under the Aviation and Maritime Security Act 1990, see **B10.209**, **B10.243** *et seq.* and **B10.213**.

Offences Committed in UK Airspace or on board Aircraft in Flight Elsewhere

A8.17 At common law, land includes the airspace above it, and accordingly it is assumed that English criminal law automatically applies to things done in English airspace; but it does not apply to conduct in the skies over Scotland or Northern Ireland, even if it takes place aboard a British controlled aircraft. Jurisdiction over things done in flight elsewhere is governed by the Civil Aviation Act 1982, s. 92.

Civil Aviation Act 1982, s. 92

(1) Any act or omission taking place on board a British-controlled aircraft or (subject to subsection (1A) below) a foreign aircraft while in flight elsewhere than in or over the UK which, if taking place in, or in a part of, the United Kingdom, would constitute an offence under the law in force in, or in that part of, the United Kingdom shall constitute that offence; but this subsection shall not apply to any act or omission which is expressly or impliedly authorised by or under that law when taking place outside the United Kingdom.

(1A) Subsection (1) above shall only apply to an act or omission which takes place on board a foreign aircraft where—

(a) the next landing of the aircraft is in the United Kingdom, and

(b) in the case of an aircraft registered in a country other than the United Kingdom, the act or omission would, if taking place there, also constitute an offence under the law in force in that country.

(1B) Any act or omission punishable under the law in force in any country is an offence under that law for the purposes of subsection (1A) above, however it is described in that law.

'British-controlled aircraft' are defined in s. 92(5). The consent of the DPP is required in respect of any prosecutions brought in England under s. 92 (see s. 92(2)(a)).

No express provision has been made by legislation for criminal jurisdiction to extend to things done in the airspace above English territorial waters. Waters adjacent to England and Wales are not strictly part of England and Wales (in contrast to Scottish waters, which are now part of Scotland). By the Civil Aviation Act 1982, s. 106, references to the UK are deemed to include airspace above such waters; but this merely serves to *prevent* any possible reliance on s. 92 of the 1982 Act where aircraft are in flight above English waters. The only solution would be for the Territorial Waters Jurisdiction Act 1878 to be construed as extending by implication to such airspace. **A8.18**

As to offences committed in flight aboard aircraft of 'Convention countries' within the meaning of the Suppression of Terrorism Act 1978 (see **A8.23**), see s. 4(7) of that Act.

As to terrorist offences and offences under the Aviation Security Act 1982, see **B10** and in particular **B10.225** ***et seq***.

EXTRA-TERRITORIAL JURISDICTION

Extra-territorial jurisdiction in English criminal law invariably has a statutory basis. Some statutory provisions extend the ambit of English criminal law generally (or substantial parts thereof) to specified classes of person. Persons subject to extra-territorial English criminal jurisdiction of this type include: Crown servants acting or purporting to act in the course of their employment (CJA 1948, s. 31(1)); masters or seamen from UK ships (Merchant Shipping Act 1995, s. 282); and members of the British armed forces or anyone else who is for the time being subject to service law. Such persons may be held liable under English law for extra-territorially committed crimes such as theft, assault or even dangerous driving (as in *Cox v Army Council* [1963] AC 48) which would otherwise have no extra-territorial ambit at all. **A8.19**

Legislation may alternatively provide an extra-territorial ambit to specific offences, as for example it has done in respect of murder or manslaughter on land outside the UK (see **B1.9**), sexual offences committed against children under the age of 18 (see **B3.315**), bribery (see **B15.24**) and a wide range of offences involving terrorism, hijacking or piracy (see generally **B10**). As to conspiracy, see **A5.61** and **A5.70**; as to criminal attempts, see **A5.82**.

Extra-territorial jurisdiction is ordinarily limited to things done or omitted by persons who hold some form of British nationality or domicile. There is little consistency in the exact form of British nationality required. Modern statutes typically restrict any extra-territorial application to British citizens (as does the Merchant Shipping Act 1995) or to UK nationals or residents (as does the International Criminal Court Act 2001). Some refer instead to 'United Kingdom persons', a term which includes Scottish partnerships and bodies incorporated in the UK. References in older statutes imposing criminal jurisdiction over 'British subjects', 'subjects of her Majesty' or 'citizens of the United Kingdom and colonies' for things done in foreign or Commonwealth countries or in Ireland must now be construed as references to British citizens, British overseas territories citizens, British overseas citizens, and British nationals (overseas): see the British Nationality Act 1948, s. 3(1), read in conjunction with the British Nationality Act 1981, s. 51. **A8.20**

There is a strong presumption that a provision creating extra-territorial criminal liability will not apply to things done or omitted by foreigners abroad (*Jameson* [1896] 2 QB 425; *Air India v Wiggins* [1980] 2 All ER 593). In exceptional cases, however, a wider basis of jurisdiction may be specified in accordance with customary international law or specific treaty obligations. This may involve 'universal jurisdiction' over crimes (e.g., piracy, hijacking of aircraft and other offences against aviation security) that are recognised internationally as meriting or demanding such treatment, or it may involve (on a reciprocal convention basis) the assertion of jurisdiction over things done by persons in specified countries or things done elsewhere by nationals of specified countries. See, e.g., the Suppression of Terrorism Act 1978, s. 4 (at **A8.23**).

Persons Subject to Armed Service Discipline

A8.21 Where a member of the British armed forces (or a civilian subject to service discipline) is guilty of conduct anywhere that would in England and Wales have amounted to an offence under English law, that person may be charged with an offence under the Armed Forces Act 2006, s. 42. This provision (read in conjunction with ss. 43 to 48) supplants three earlier provisions, namely the Army Act 1955, s. 70, the Air Force Act 1955, s. 70, and the Naval Discipline Act 1957, s. 42.

The relationship between an offence under s. 42 of the 2006 Act and a corresponding offence under the civilian law of England is essentially the same as that under the 1955 legislation, and was explained in that context by Lord Rodger of Earlsferry in *Spear* [2002] UKHL 31, [2002] 3 All ER 1074 (at p. 1088):

> Where anyone who is subject to military law is guilty of an act or omission in England that would be punishable by the law of England, he is also guilty of an offence under [the Army Act 1955] s. 70. Similarly, anyone who is guilty of an act or omission that would be punishable by the law of England if committed in England is guilty of an offence under s. 70 wherever he commits it, whether in some other part of the UK or elsewhere in the world: *Cox v Army Council*. So, for instance, a soldier or airman who possesses cocaine in England is guilty not only of an offence under s. 5(1) of the Misuse of Drugs Act 1971, but also of an offence against s. 70 of the Army Act or the Air Force Act, as the case may be, although he can, of course, be prosecuted for only one of them. If he possesses cocaine while on duty in Afghanistan, on the other hand, he does not commit an offence under s. 5(1) of the 1971 Act since the legislation does not apply there, but he is guilty of an offence under s. 70 of the relevant 1955 Act, because he would have been guilty of a contravention of s. 5(1) if he had been in possession of the drug in England. Offences of this kind, which mirror offences under English criminal law, are referred to as 'civil' offences (s. 70(2)). As s. 70(3) makes clear, these civil offences are triable by court-martial.

By the Armed Forces Act 2006, s. 51, certain offences committed abroad by civilians subject to service discipline (including some offences under s. 42 of the 2006 Act) may be tried by 'service civilian courts', but this does not extend to offences that would be triable only on indictment if committed within England and Wales.

Masters or Seamen from UK Ships

A8.22 **Merchant Shipping Act 1995, s. 282**

(1) Any act in relation to property or person done in or at any place (ashore or afloat) outside the United Kingdom by any master or seaman who at the time is employed in a United Kingdom ship, which, if done in any part of the United Kingdom, would be an offence under the law of any part of the United Kingdom, shall—
 (a) be an offence under that law, and
 (b) be treated for the purposes of jurisdiction and trial as if it had been done within the jurisdiction of the Admiralty of England.
(2) Subsection (1) above also applies in relation to a person who had been so employed within the period of three months expiring with the time when the act was done.
(3) Subsections (1) and (2) above apply to omissions as they apply to acts.

This provision is not expressly limited to British citizens or UK nationals, but such a limitation must arguably be inferred (see **A8.20**). Nor is it expressly limited to offences triable on indictment, but such a limitation is impliedly imposed by the fact that such offences are triable, 'as if committed within the jurisdiction of the Admiralty of England', because Admiralty jurisdiction does not extend over summary offences.

Section 282 is derived from the Merchant Shipping Act 1854, s. 267, which was the basis upon which jurisdiction was asserted over the shipwrecked cannibals in *Dudley and Stephens* (1884) 24 QBD 273. Note, however, that it has no application to things done by persons from British *ships that are not registered in the* UK, or to things done by passengers etc. from any ship. If D, a passenger from a sunk or sinking British vessel kills V in the sea in order to seize V's lifejacket or raft, D will commit no offence under English law unless within territorial waters at the time.

Offences Committed in 'Convention Countries' or by Nationals of Convention Countries

The Suppression of Terrorism Act 1978, s. 4(1), creates no new offences of its own (*Venclovas* [2013] EWCA Crim 2182) but extends the ambit of a number of existing offences under English criminal law so that they can apply to things done in 'Convention countries' by persons of any nationality. Section 4(1) meanwhile provides an even wider ambit for murder, manslaughter and certain offences under the Explosive Substances Act 1883. **A8.23**

Suppression of Terrorism Act 1978, s. 4

(1) If a person, whether a citizen of the United Kingdom and Colonies or not, does in a Convention country any act which, if he had done it in a part of the United Kingdom, would have made him guilty in that part of the United Kingdom of—
(a) an offence mentioned in paragraph 1, 2, 4, 5, 10, 11, 11B, 12, 13, 14 or 15 of Schedule 1 to this Act; or
(b) an offence of attempting to commit any offence so mentioned,
he shall, in that part of the United Kingdom, be guilty of the offence or offences aforesaid of which the act would have made him guilty if he had done it there.

...

(3) If a person who is a national of a Convention country but not a citizen of the United Kingdom and Colonies does outside the United Kingdom and that Convention country any act which makes him in that Convention country guilty of an offence and which, if he had been a citizen of the United Kingdom and Colonies, would have made him in any part of the United Kingdom guilty of an offence mentioned in paragraph 1, 2 or 13 of Schedule 1 to this Act, he shall, in any part of the United Kingdom, be guilty of the offence or offences aforesaid of which the act would have made him guilty if he had been such a citizen.

As to offences committed aboard ships or aircraft of Convention countries, see s. 4(7).

Countries and Offences to which s. 4 Applies 'Convention countries' are those designated by the Secretary of State as Parties to the 1977 European Convention on the Suppression of Terrorism, namely: Albania, Austria, Belgium, Bulgaria, Croatia, Cyprus, Czech Republic, Denmark, Estonia, Finland, France, Georgia, Germany, Greece, Hungary, Iceland, Italy, Latvia, Liechtenstein, Lithuania, Luxembourg, Malta, Moldova, the Netherlands, Norway, Poland, Portugal, Republic of Ireland, Romania, Russian Federation, San Marino, Serbia and Montenegro, Slovakia, Slovenia, Spain, Sweden, Switzerland, Turkey and Ukraine. The UK, although a Party to the Convention, has not designated itself as a Convention country, which means that s. 4 gives English law no jurisdiction over things done in Scotland or Northern Ireland (or vice versa). An 'application of provisions order' made under s. 5 (see SI 1993 No. 2533) treats India for most purposes as if it were a Convention country; but an application of provisions order relating to the USA deals only with extradition, and excludes any jurisdiction under s. 4. **A8.24**

The offences to which s. 4(1)(a) applies (excluding offences under Scots law or Northern Irish law) are murder, manslaughter, kidnapping and false imprisonment, together with offences under the Child Abduction Act 1984, s. 2, the OAPA 1861, ss. 28, 29 and 30, the Explosive Substances Act 1883, ss. 2 and 3, and the Firearms Act 1968, ss. 16 and 17(1). Section 4(1)(b) adds attempts to commit such offences (see, e.g., *Kalinowski v Poland* [2019] EWHC 3734 (Admin)), but not conspiracies. In other circumstances, it might be arguable that a conspiracy abroad to commit a substantive extraterritorial offence is itself an extraterritorial offence (*Bow Street Metropolitan Stipendiary Magistrate, ex parte Pinochet Ugarte (No. 3)* [2000] 1 AC 147, per Lord Hope at pp. 237 to 238) but the wording of s. 4(1) appears to exclude that possibility (if only by implication) in cases brought under that provision.

The only offences in English law to which s. 4(3) of the 1978 Act applies are murder, manslaughter and offences under the Explosive Substances Act 1883, ss. 2 and 3. No inchoate offences are included.

Prosecutions brought by virtue of s. 4(1) or (3) need not have anything to do with terrorism. By s. 4(4), such prosecutions require the consent of the A-G. This provides 'a possible check on the inappropriately wide use of the provision', as the Court of Appeal noted in *Venclovas* [2013] EWCA Crim 2182, but such consent was readily given in that case even though it had no terrorist connection whatever. The victim in *Venclovas* was D's estranged wife, V. He had abducted her in England and her body was later found in Poland. It was not clear whether V had been murdered in England or in Poland or indeed in one of the Convention countries through which D had driven en route to Poland, but the offence in each case was the same, namely murder at common law, so there was no need to prove where exactly it had been committed. Note, however, that the position would have been quite different if V's body had been found in Scotland or Northern Ireland. Neither s. 4, nor the OAPA 1861, s. 9, could be of any help in such a case.

JURISDICTIONAL IMMUNITIES

Diplomatic Immunity

A8.25 Diplomatic immunity under English law is governed in the case of members of permanent diplomatic missions by the Diplomatic Privileges Act 1964, which incorporates certain provisions of the Vienna Convention on Diplomatic Relations 1961. See generally *Reyes v Al-Malki* [2017] UKSC 61, [2017] 3 WLR 923. These provisions include Article 29, by which, 'the person of a diplomatic agent shall ... not be liable to any form of arrest or detention', and Article 31(1), by which, 'a diplomatic agent shall enjoy immunity from the criminal jurisdiction of the receiving State'. By Article 37, the same privileges and immunities extend to 'the members of the family of a diplomatic agent forming part of his household ..., if they are not nationals of the receiving State' and to 'members of the administrative and technical staff of the mission, together with members of their families forming part of their respective households ..., if they are not nationals of or permanently resident in the receiving State'; but members of the service staff enjoy such immunity only in respect of acts performed in the course of their duties, and the private servants of members of the mission have no immunities from the criminal law other than those (if any) admitted by the receiving State.

By Article 39(2), the immunities of a diplomat 'shall normally cease when he leaves the country, or on expiry of a reasonable period in which to do so, but ...with respect to acts performed ... in the exercise of his functions as a member of the mission, immunity shall continue to subsist'. As to the rationale behind this rule, see *Bow Street Metropolitan Stipendiary Magistrate, ex parte Pinochet Ugarte (No. 3)* [2000] 1 AC 147, per Lord Browne-Wilkinson at p. 202.

Immunity from prosecution does not involve immunity from the duty to comply with the law. See, e.g., the Vienna Convention on Diplomatic Relations 1961, Article 41: 'It is the duty of all persons enjoying such privileges and immunities to respect the laws and regulations of the receiving state'. A foreign diplomat in England has no right or licence to ignore the rules of English law. A diplomat committing an offence under English law may be prosecuted for it, but only if diplomatic immunity is waived by the sending State. If immunity is not waived, other persons who are complicit in the offence may still face prosecution.

The Vienna Convention (and thus the 1964 Act) has no application to members of ad hoc or 'special' diplomatic missions, but similar immunity arises at common law (through the adoption or incorporation of customary international law) provided that the diplomatic status of that mission (and of the individual in question) is recognised by the Foreign and Commonwealth Office on behalf of HM Government (*R (Freedom and Justice Party) v Secretary of State for Foreign and Commonwealth Affairs* [2018] EWCA Civ 1719, [2019] 2 WLR 578). A certificate to (or against) that effect issued by the FCO must be treated as conclusive on that issue (*Governor of Pentonville Prison, ex parte Teja* [1971] 2 QB 274; *Bat v Investigating Judge of the Federal Court, Germany* [2011] EWHC 2029 (Admin), [2013] QB 349). Special missions have performed the role of *ad hoc* diplomats for many years and cannot be expected to perform that role without the protection of core diplomatic immunities.

Consular Immunity

Consular immunity is more limited than diplomatic immunity, and for most purposes excludes immunity from criminal prosecution, save in respect of acts performed in the course of consular duties. See generally the Consular Relations Act 1968. **A8.26**

Persons Connected with International Organisations

In respect of an international organisation of which the UK is a member, the International Organisations Act 1968, s. 1, enables certain immunities to be granted to its officers or representatives. The exact terms of such immunities vary from one case to another. See, e.g., the United Nations and International Court of Justice (Immunities and Privileges) Order 1974 (SI 1974 No. 1261), the European Court of Human Rights (Immunities and Privileges) Order 2000 (SI 2000 No. 1817) and the International Maritime Organisation (Immunities and Privileges) Order 2002 (SI 2002 No. 1826). As with diplomatic immunities, these immunities may be waived by the organisation in question. **A8.27**

The Commonwealth Secretariat Act 1966 makes provision for immunities of officers of the Secretariat.

Foreign Heads of State and Government Ministers

By the State Immunity Act 1978, s. 20, the Diplomatic Privileges Act 1964 applies (with appropriate modifications) to foreign sovereigns or heads of State, their households and private servants, as it applies to heads of diplomatic missions, to members of their family forming part of their household and to their private servants. **A8.28**

Certain other high ranking officials, such as foreign ministers, may also be able to claim State immunity from criminal liability or process, but the right to claim immunity in criminal or extradition cases is far more limited than it is in civil cases (*Bat v Investigating Judge of the Federal Court, Germany* [2011] EWHC 2029 (Admin), [2013] QB 349).

Former heads of State, like former diplomats, are entitled to immunity from prosecution only in respect of acts done by them (or on their orders) in connection with their former office; and there are certain offences (such as torture committed by agents of a State or de facto rebel government) to which even this immunity cannot attach (*Bow Street Metropolitan Stipendiary Magistrate, ex parte Pinochet Ugarte (No. 3)* [2000] 1 AC 147).

Visiting Forces

When foreign or Commonwealth armed forces are stationed on British soil, criminal jurisdiction over their personnel and families etc. is ceded in some circumstances to their own authorities. See the Visiting Forces Act 1952, s. 3. Foreign naval vessels are immune from local jurisdiction, even in respect of offences committed within English ports or harbours. **A8.29**

Offences Committed on or within Diplomatic Premises

The premises of diplomatic missions in England and Wales are not in any sense foreign territory, although such premises may not be entered by the police or by any other agents of the UK government except with the consent of the ambassador or head of the mission (Diplomatic Privileges Act 1964, s. 2(1) and sch. 3). **A8.30**

Subject to any individual claims to diplomatic immunity etc., offences committed on or within such premises are accordingly triable in England and Wales under the ordinary territorial principles of English law: see *Nejad* (1981 unreported) in which acts committed by terrorists who seized the Iranian embassy in London were held to be justiciable under English law; and see also *Radwan v Radwan* [1972] 3 All ER 967.

Section A9 European Union Law

THE RELEVANCE OF EU LAW FOR DOMESTIC CRIMINAL LAW

A9.1 EU criminal law is perhaps the fastest growing area of EU law. A number of EU criminal law measures have been adopted under the 'old' third pillar of the EU Treaties. The entry into force of the Treaty of Lisbon in December 2009 created a fresh momentum towards the adoption of new EU measures in the field. The adoption of criminal law at the level of the EU has significant consequences for domestic criminal justice systems.

While the UK has now exited the European Union, EU law continues to apply at the time of writing by virtue of the EU-UK Withdrawal Agreement, which entered into force on 1 February 2020. The applicability of key measures of EU criminal law to the UK is confirmed in Title V of the Withdrawal Agreement (Articles 62 to 65). Of particular relevance to the criminal justice system is the continuous applicability of the EU Mutual Legal Assistance Convention and of a series of EU mutual recognition instruments including the Framework Decisions on the EAW and on the mutual recognition of freezing and confiscation orders, of financial penalties, of orders imposing custodial sentences, on taking into account previous convictions, and on bail (Article 62(1)). Article 62(1) of the Withdrawal Agreement also extends the applicability of EU measures on the exchange of information in criminal records and on the European Criminal Records Information System (ECRIS), as well as of Directive 2011/99/EU on the European protection order ([2011] OJ L338/2) and Directive 2014/41/EU regarding the European investigation order in criminal matters ([2014] OJ L130/1). All these measures apply for requests received before the end of the transitional period envisaged in the Withdrawal Agreement. Article 65 provides that the provisions of Directive 2010/64/EU on the right to interpretation and translation in criminal proceedings ([2010] OJ L280/1) and Directive 2012/13/EU on the right to information in criminal proceedings ([2012] OJ L142/1) will continue to apply in the context of EAW proceedings.

The Court of Justice of the European Union (CJEU) will continue to have jurisdiction to give preliminary rulings on requests from courts and tribunals of the UK made before the end of the transition period (Withdrawal Agreement, Article 86(2)). The expiry of the Withdrawal Agreement (at the time of writing set for the end of 2020) will give rise to a new landscape in EU-UK relations in the field of criminal justice, with the negotiating positions of both the UK and the EU revealing the ambition of future close alignment, including in the fields of extradition and mutual legal assistance.

Despite the UK's exit, EU law continues to have considerable impact on domestic criminal law. The principal impact of EU criminal law on domestic criminal law post-Brexit can be viewed primarily at three levels:

(a) at the level of aligning domestic law with EU law — a close future relationship will be based on a degree of legislative alignment and commonly accepted benchmarks of protection of fundamental rights;

(b) at the level of the development of criminal law principles: in the absence of detailed EU legislation in the field, the CJEU has developed principles in the field of criminal justice — the interpretation of the principle of *ne bis in idem* (double jeopardy) is a prime example;
(c) at the level of interpreting domestic criminal law: courts in EU Member States are called to interpret domestic law in the light of any EU criminal law measures it is designed to implement and in the light of general principles of EU law; in this context, ensuring the effective enforcement of EU law in the domestic legal order is of paramount importance since the entry into force of the Lisbon Treaty.

This section examines the impact of EU criminal law on the domestic legal system by focusing on three aspects:

(a) an overview of the institutional framework for the adoption of EU criminal law, explaining the differences between the 'old' third pillar and the Lisbon Treaty in order to clarify the differences in the nature and legal effects of EU criminal law legal instruments post-Lisbon;
(b) an overview of the applicability of general principles of EU law in the field, and their impact on the conduct of domestic criminal proceedings; and
(c) an overview of the principal EU criminal law measures and principles, focusing on measures related to judicial co-operation in criminal matters and measures with a cross-border dimension.

INSTITUTIONAL BACKGROUND AND LEGAL INSTRUMENTS

There are two main stages in the development of the institutional framework of EU criminal law: (i) the 'third pillar' stage and (ii) the Lisbon Treaty stage. **A9.2**

The third pillar was abolished by the Lisbon Treaty. However, it is important to consider it because:

(a) under the Protocol on transitional provisions agreed under the Lisbon Treaty, measures adopted under the third pillar continued to have the same 'old' third pillar effects (unless amended or repealed) until 30 November 2014;
(b) the majority of EU criminal law measures (including legislation on the EAW) have taken the form of third pillar instruments (namely Framework Decisions) so, to the extent that these instruments have not been amended, they continue to have the 'old' third pillar effects.

The so-called third pillar was introduced in EU law by the Treaty of Maastricht, and was amended by the Treaty of Amsterdam to include provisions on EU action on police and judicial co-operation in criminal matters. It was one of the two more 'intergovernmental' pillars of the EU Treaty, to be contrasted with the more 'supranational' first pillar, which consisted of provisions of traditional Community (EC) law. Placing EU action in criminal matters under the third pillar (and not under the first, Community, pillar) meant that Member States would retain their sovereignty in the field by limiting the application of Community law principles in criminal law. Under the third pillar, the control of EU institutions (such as the European Commission, the European Parliament and the CJEU) over EU criminal law was limited; the general principles of EC law did not apply to EU criminal law fully; and the effects of third pillar legal instruments were less far-reaching than those of traditional EC law. Under the 'old' third pillar (Article 34(2) of the Treaty on the European Union (TEU)) binding EU criminal law mainly took the form of Framework Decisions, Conventions and Decisions. The majority of EU criminal law instruments in the third pillar have taken the form of Framework Decisions which, similarly to first pillar Directives, are binding upon the Member States as to the result to be achieved but leave to the national authorities the choice of form and methods. However, unlike Directives, Framework Decisions do not entail direct effect.

A9.3 The Lisbon Treaty abolished the old third pillar and subsumed EU action in criminal matters under the full control of the EU institutions. A key change involves the form of EU legislative action in criminal matters. Following the Lisbon Treaty, Framework Decisions are no longer made. The normalisation of EU criminal law under Lisbon means that legislation in the field now takes the form of Regulations, Directives and Decisions. As regards the two main instruments, Article 288 of the Treaty on the Functioning of the European Union (TFEU) reiterates that:

- a Regulation has general application and is binding in its entirety and directly applicable in all Member States: this means that Regulations are applicable from the date of their publication in the Official Journal of the European Union to all Member States, without the need of further domestic implementation; and
- a Directive is binding as to the result to be achieved upon each Member State to which it is addressed, but leaves to the national authorities the choice of form and methods: this means that Member States will have to transpose the text of a Directive into their domestic legal system, normally by the adoption of implementing legislation.

General principles of EU law, such as direct effect, apply to EU criminal law adopted post-Lisbon and EU institutions now assume their full powers of control. In this context, it is important to note that the CJEU extends its full jurisdiction to criminal matters; in particular, it is granted jurisdiction to give preliminary rulings (Article 267 TFEU) and to rule on infringement proceedings brought against Member States by the European Commission for failing to fulfil their obligations under EU law (Articles 258 and 260 TFEU). Infringement proceedings may thus be instituted in cases where Member States are deemed not to have implemented EU criminal law fully. However, it must be emphasised that for EU law adopted under the old third pillar the Lisbon effects do not come into effect automatically. EU institutions assumed full powers over third pillar law on 1 December 2014.

EU LAW PRINCIPLES IN DOMESTIC COURTS

Fundamental Rights

A9.4 Respect for fundamental rights has been a long-standing general principle of EU law (Case C-11/70 *Internationale Handelsgesellschaft* [1970] ECR 1125). The Lisbon Treaty confirms that fundamental rights, as guaranteed by the ECHR and as they result from the constitutional traditions common to the Member States 'constitute general principles of Union law' (Article 6(3) TEU). It also recognises the provisions of the Charter of Fundamental Rights which, according to Article 6(1) TEU, has the same legal value as the EU Treaties. The opening provision of the Treaty chapter on the Area of Freedom, Security and Justice (Title V) also stresses respect for fundamental rights (Article 67(1) TFEU). EU criminal law measures and their implementation at the domestic level must be interpreted in accordance with fundamental rights. The obligation to respect fundamental rights in the context of executing a EAW (see **A9.12**) was expressly highlighted by the CJEU (see Case C-303/05 *Advocaten voor de Wereld* [2007] ECR I-3633 at **A9.13**). Key Charter provisions are those in Chapter VI, on the right to an effective remedy and fair trial, the presumption of innocence and rights of defence, the principle of legality and proportionality in criminal offences and penalties, and the principle of *ne bis in idem* (Articles 47 to 50 respectively). The CJEU has confirmed that the principle that criminal penalties must have a proper legal basis, which is enshrined in Article 49(1) of the Charter, would prohibit the imposition of criminal penalties even if the national rule were contrary to EU law (Case C-7/11 *Fabio Caronna* [2012] All ER (D) 49 (Sep)).

The CJEU has confirmed the broad application of the Charter with regard to national law. In the leading judgment in Case C-617/10 *Åklagaren v Åkerberg Fransson* [2013] 2 CMLR 46 (1273) (see **A9.23**), the Court confirmed that the Charter applies in national law even if the latter has not been enacted specifically to implement Union law. In Case C-206/13 *Siragusa v*

Regione Sicilia [2014] 3 CMLR 13 (251), the Court produced a series of criteria to establish when Member States implement Union law in accordance with Article 51 of the Charter. The Court confirmed (at [24]) that the concept of 'implementing Union law' requires a certain degree of connection above and beyond the matters covered being closely related or one of those matters having an indirect impact on the other. Some of the points to be determined are whether the legislation is intended to implement a provision of EU law; the nature of that legislation and whether it pursues objectives other than those covered by EU law, even if it is capable of indirectly affecting EU law; and also whether there are specific rules of EU law on the matter or capable of affecting it (at [25]).

Direct Effect

The principle of direct effect lies at the heart of the decentralised enforcement of EU law. It allows an individual to invoke and rely upon EU law provisions directly in *national* courts (Case 26/62 *Van Gend en Loos* [1963] ECR 13) if EU law has not been implemented or properly implemented in Member States. The principle is not absolute — EU law must be clear, unconditional and sufficiently precise to be invoked in national courts. However, the principle is of immense importance to ensure the full effectiveness of EU law and particularly relevant in measures which confer rights on individuals. Direct effect can be used in domestic courts to claim that an individual derives rights directly from EU law in cases where it is thought that EU law has not been implemented fully or properly in the UK. Framework Decisions do not currently entail direct effect. EU criminal law Directives adopted post-Lisbon can have direct effect if the relevant conditions (i.e. that the EU provision is clear, unconditional and sufficiently precise) are met. In Case C-105/14 *Taricco* [2016] 1 CMLR 21 (749), the Court confirmed (at [51]) that Articles 325(1) and (2) TFEU, placing obligations upon the EU and Member States to counter fraud against the budget of the EU effectively, entail direct effect. In Case C-544/14 *Ognyanov* [2017] QB 732, the Grand Chamber found that Articles 17(1) and (2) of Framework Decision 2008/909/JHA on the application of the principle of mutual recognition to custodial sentences or measures involving deprivation of liberty ([2008] OJ L327/27) do not have direct effect. **A9.5**

Interpretative Obligation — Indirect Effect

Under the principle of indirect effect, national courts are under a duty to interpret domestic law as far as possible in conformity with EU law. The principle has been developed by the CJEU in order to ensure the effective enforcement of EU law in particular in cases where EU measures were deemed not to entail direct effect. As with direct effect, indirect effect is a principle relying on national courts to give effect to EU law. **A9.6**

The principle of indirect effect was applicable in EU criminal law before the entry into force of the Lisbon Treaty. The CJEU in Case C-105/03 *Pupino* [2005] ECR I-5285 extended the application of the principle to the third pillar. *Pupino* is applicable by analogy to ensure the effective implementation of the EAW (Case C-579/15 *Poplawski* [2017] 4 WLR 173). The interpretative obligation of national courts is, however, limited by general principles of law, such as legal certainty and non-retroactivity: those principles prevent that obligation from leading to the criminal liability of persons who contravene the provisions of a Framework Decision from being judged or punished on the basis of a Framework Decision alone, independently of an implementing law (Case C-403/02 *Berlusconi* [2005] ECR I-3565). Indirect effect cannot serve as the basis for an interpretation of domestic law *contra legem* (i.e. which is inconsistent with the precise wording of a statutory provision or other rule of law), but the national court must consider the whole of domestic law in order to assess how far it can be applied in such a way as not to produce a result contrary to that envisaged by the Framework Decision. The obligation to interpret domestic law in conformity with EU law under *Pupino* has been cited repeatedly by the House of Lords in its case law on the implementation of the EAW Framework Decision (*Dabas v High Court of Justice, Madrid* [2007] UKHL 6, [2007] 2 AC 31; *Pilecki v Circuit Court of Legnica, Poland* [2008] UKHL 7, [2008] 4 All ER 445; *Caldarelli v Court of Naples* [2008] UKHL 51, [2009] 1 All ER 1). In *Assange v Swedish Prosecution Authority*

[2012] UKSC 22, [2012] 2 AC 471, the Supreme Court found that although the Supreme Court is not bound to apply *Pupino* to the Extradition Act 2003, it should nonetheless do so.

Primacy

A9.7 The CJEU proclaimed the primacy of EU law over domestic law in the 1960s (Case 6/64 *Costa v Enel* [1964] ECR 585). The principle has been accepted by the UK courts (*Factortame Ltd v Secretary of State for Transport (No. 2)* [1991] 1 AC 603; *Equal Opportunities Commission v Secretary of State for Employment* [1994] 2 All ER 121; *Thoburn v Sunderland City Council* [2002] EWHC 195 (Admin), [2003] QB 151). The Treaty on the European Union and the CJEU were silent as to the applicability of primacy to third pillar law. The entry into force of the Lisbon Treaty means that EU criminal law adopted post-Lisbon (and old third pillar law from December 2014) has primacy over domestic law. This finding has been confirmed by the CJEU (Case C-399/11 *Melloni v Ministerio Fiscal* [2013] QB 1067 at [55]–[59]). The CJEU has also confirmed that Article 325(1) and (2) TFEU have primacy over national law and have the effect of rendering automatically inapplicable, merely by their entering into force, any conflicting provision of national law. It follows that national courts are under the obligation to disapply any conflicting national provisions (Case C-105/14 *Taricco* (CJEU, 8 September 2015) at [51]–[52]). In its follow-up judgment in *'Taricco II'* (Case C-42/17 *MAS* [2018] 2 CMLR 15 (355)), the CJEU confirmed that obligation to disapply conflicting national provisions unless to do so would entail 'a breach of the principle that offences and penalties must be defined by law because of the lack of precision of the applicable law or because of the retroactive application of legislation imposing conditions of criminal liability stricter than those in force at the time the infringement was committed' (at [64]). In Case C-554/14 *Ognyanov* [2017] QB 732, the Grand Chamber confirmed that in order to give a Framework Decision full effect, a national court must disapply of its own motion any conflicting provision of national law including the obligation to alter established case law, where necessary, if that is based on an interpretation of national law that is incompatible with EU law (at [34] and [35]). In Case C-579/15 *Poplawski v Openbaar Ministerie* [2017] 4 WLR 173, the CJEU ruled that the principle of primacy does not entail the disapplication by a national court of a provision of national law which is incompatible with the provisions of a Framework Decision if the latter provisions do not entail direct effect. National courts retain however the duty to interpret national law to the extent possible in conformity with EU law (principle of indirect effect).

State Liability for Damages

A9.8 A key move towards the effective enforcement of EU law has been the development by the CJEU of the principle of State liability for damages (Joined Cases C-6/90 and C-9/90 *Francovich* [1991] ECR I-5357), which obliges States to award compensation for harm caused to individuals by breaches of EU law for which they can be held responsible. The principle of State liability for damages is central to the enforcement and implementation of EU law. It applies not only to the executive, but also to courts. Under certain conditions, failure by national courts to refer to the CJEU questions related to the interpretation of EU law may trigger State liability for damages.

In particular, in Case C-224/01 *Köbler* [2003] ECR I-10239, the CJEU held that State liability is applicable where the alleged infringement of EU law stems from a decision of a court adjudicating at last instance where the rule of EU law infringed is intended to confer rights on individuals, the breach is sufficiently serious and there is a direct causal link between that breach and the loss or damage suffered by the injured parties. Determining factors include non-compliance by the court in question with its obligation to make a reference for a preliminary ruling (*Köbler* at [55]).

References for Preliminary Rulings

A9.9 The extension of State liability in Case C-224/01 *Köbler* [2003] ECR I-10239 is of particular relevance in the light of the fact that national courts against whose decisions there is no judicial remedy under domestic law are under the duty to send questions on the validity or interpretation of post-Lisbon EU criminal law raised before them to the CJEU (Article 267(3) TFEU). The Lisbon Treaty extends the option of sending questions for preliminary rulings regarding EU criminal law adopted post-Lisbon to lower courts where the court considers that a decision on the question is necessary to enable it to give judgment (Article 267(2) TFEU). During the transitional period set out by the EU-UK Withdrawal Agreement, domestic courts continue to be empowered to send preliminary references to the CJEU even after the UK's exit from the EU (Withdrawal Agreement, Article 86(2)).

Sending references for preliminary rulings to the CJEU is a key tool for clarifying issues where the interpretation of domestic law in the light of EU criminal law or in the light of general principles of EU law is unclear. A request for a preliminary ruling may be necessary when the domestic court is called upon to rule on a provision implementing EU criminal law (e.g., the EAW Framework Decision) or on EU criminal law principles (e.g., the cross-border double jeopardy principle enshrined in Article 54 of the Schengen Implementing Convention).

Requests for preliminary rulings are of particular relevance in view of the development by the CJEU of autonomous concepts in the field of EU criminal justice. The CJEU has assigned an autonomous EU meaning to a number of terms included in the EAW Framework Decision (Case C-66/08 *Kozlowski* [2008] ECR I-6041 on residence and stay; Case C-60/12 *Balaz* [2014] RTR 7 (61) on the concept of judicial authority; Case C-452/16 PPU *Poltorak* [2017] 4 WLR 8; Case C-453/16 PPU *Özçelik* [2017] 4 WLR 9 and Case C-477/16 PPU *Kovalkovas* [2017] 4 WLR 10 on the concepts of judicial decision and judicial authority—see **A9.21**; Case C-108/16 PPU *Dworzecki* (CJEU, 24 May 2016) on the concepts of 'summoned in person' and 'by other means actually received official information of the scheduled date and place of that trial in such a manner that it was unequivocally established that he or she was aware of the scheduled trial'; Case C-294/16 PPU *JZ* (CJEU, 28 July 2016) on the concept of detention). In particular, a reference to the CJEU is necessary where there is no EU law precedent on the point. The preliminary rulings mechanism provides a first class avenue of co-operation between the CJEU and national courts. In order to benefit fully from this mechanism, awareness of EU law, and of the fact that domestic legislation is actually intended to implement EU law, is key.

Detailed guidance on how to send references for preliminary rulings is included in a series of Recommendations produced by the CJEU ([2016] OJ C439/1): **A9.10**

(1) A court or tribunal against whose ruling there is no judicial remedy under domestic law must refer questions on the interpretation of EU law to the CJEU unless there is already well established case law on the point or unless the correct interpretation of the rule of law in question admits of no reasonable doubt (para. 6).
(2) A court or tribunal against whose decision there is a judicial remedy may refer a question on interpretation if it considers that it is necessary to do so in order to resolve a dispute brought before it. A reference for preliminary ruling may prove particularly useful when there is a new question of interpretation of general interest for the uniform application of EU law in all the Member States, or where the existing case law does not appear to be applicable to a new set of facts (para. 5).
(3) A national court or tribunal may refer a question to the CJEU for a preliminary ruling as soon as it finds that a ruling on the point of validity or interpretation is necessary to enable it to give judgment. It is desirable that a decision to seek a preliminary ruling should be taken when the national proceedings have reached a stage at which the national court is able to define the factual and legal context of the question, so that the CJEU has available to it all the information necessary to check that EU law applies to the main proceedings. In the interests of the proper administration of justice, it may also be desirable for the reference to be made only after both sides have been heard (paras. 12 and 13).
(4) The lodging of a request for a preliminary ruling calls for the national proceedings to be stayed until the CJEU has given its ruling (para. 23).

According to Article 267(4) TFEU, if a question is raised in a case pending before a court or tribunal of a Member State with regard to a person in custody, the CJEU must act with the minimum of delay. Moreover, an urgent preliminary reference procedure has been established by the Rules of Procedure of the Court of Justice ([2012] OJ L265/1) and by the Protocol on the Statute of the Court of Justice annexed to the Lisbon Treaty (Article 23a). According to the Rules of Procedure, a national court or tribunal may request that a reference for a preliminary ruling which raises questions in the areas covered by Title V of the TFEU (on the Area of Freedom, Security and Justice, including EU criminal law) is dealt with under an urgent procedure. Detailed rules are set out in the Rules of Procedure (Articles 107 to 114) and in the Information Note on references for a preliminary ruling (paras. 38 to 41).

See **D30.6** for the text of Article 267 and domestic case law.

UK PARTICIPATION IN EU CRIMINAL LAW

A9.11 Protocol 21 to the Lisbon Treaty extended the right of the UK not to participate in EU law to the whole of Title V TFEU, including criminal law measures. The right not to participate also extends to legislation amending existing measures which are binding upon the UK. The government decides on its participation in post-Lisbon measures on a case-by-case basis. As regards old third pillar law, the Protocol on Transitional Provisions granted the UK, upon the expiry on 30 November 2014 of the five-year transitional period from the entry into force of the Lisbon Treaty, the right not to accept the full powers of the EU institutions in third pillar law. Where the UK decided not to accept these powers, such legislation ceased to apply to the UK. The UK notified the Presidency of the EU that, pursuant to Article 10(4) of Protocol 36, it did not accept the powers of the EU institutions; accordingly, those acts ceased to apply in the UK from 1 December 2014 (Council doc. 12750/13). However, the UK also indicated that it would seek to opt back into 35 of these measures including the EAW Framework Decision, and the continuation of the applicability of these 35 measures to the UK has been confirmed. Third pillar law continues to apply to the UK vis-à-vis the vast majority of measures applying the principle of mutual recognition in criminal matters (including the EAW Framework Decision) and a number of other key measures including legislation establishing Europol and Eurojust and legislation on joint investigation teams and criminal records (see Annex to Decision 2014/836/EU, [2014] OJ L343/11). Third pillar law which has ceased to apply to the UK following the expiry of the transitional period includes, *inter alia*, a number of measures on substantive criminal law, the Council Framework Decision on prevention and settlement of conflicts of jurisdiction and, from the mutual recognition *acquis*, the Framework Decision on the mutual recognition of probation decisions (Notice 430/03 [2014] OJ C430/17).

In Case C-327/18 PPU *Minister for Justice and Equality v RO* [2019] 1 WLR 1095, the CJEU considered the impact of the UK leaving the EU in relation to EAWs. The CJEU held that notification of an intention to withdraw from the EU does not mean that in the interim EU law does not apply. There is no evidence that individuals subject to the EAW are at risk of being deprived of their fundamental rights, even after the UK leaves the EU.

MUTUAL RECOGNITION

A9.12 Under the principle of mutual recognition, judicial authorities in one Member State are under the duty to recognise and execute judgments and orders issued by judicial authorities in other Member States on the basis of mutual trust and with a minimum of formality. Scrutiny of the judicial decision by the issuing authority is limited. In the majority of EU mutual recognition instruments, verification of dual criminality for an extensive list of categories of serious offences has been abolished; dual criminality means that the conduct for which a EAW (or another judicial decision falling under the mutual recognition principle) has been issued constitutes an offence under both the national law of the authority issuing the EAW and the national law of the authority in the executing Member State. Moreover, the grounds available to the judicial authority in the executing State to refuse the recognition and execution of the decision by the issuing State are limited and mostly procedural (for detailed analysis see V Mitsilegas, *EU Criminal Law* (2009), ch. 3).

The mutual recognition principle applies to a wide range of elements of the criminal justice process, from the pre-trial to the post-trial stage. Mutual recognition is applicable to judgments in the following fields.

Arrest and Surrender

The EU Council Framework Decision on the European Arrest Warrant and the surrender procedures between Member States (2002/584/JHA, [2002] OJ L190/1) was implemented by the Extradition Act 2003 (see **D31.2**). The EAW system and its innovations continue to apply to the UK during the transition period set out in the EU-UK Withdrawal Agreement, though one difference to the status quo ante has been that three EU Member States (Germany, Austria and Slovenia) have declared that they will cease to extradite their nationals to the UK during the transition period (Council doc. XT 21011/20). **A9.13**

The CJEU has been called upon to interpret a number of aspects of the EAW Framework Decision. Its rulings are of relevance as regards the interpretation of these legal issues in domestic proceedings concerning EAWs. In Case C-303/05 *Advocaten voor de Wereld* [2007] ECR I-3633 the CJEU held (at [53]) that the abolition of dual criminality in the Framework Decision is not a breach of the legality principle as:

> ... the definition of those offences and of the penalties applicable continue to be matters determined by the law of the issuing Member State which, as is, moreover, stated in Article 1(3) of the Framework Decision, must respect fundamental rights and fundamental legal principles as enshrined in Article 6 EU and, consequently, the principle of the legality of criminal offences and penalties.

In assessing whether the offence for which the EAW has been issued falls within the scope of Article 2(2) of the Framework Decision (and the verification of dual criminality is no longer required) the executing authority must take into account the law of the issuing State in the version applicable to the facts giving rise to the case in which the EAW was issued (Case C-717/18 *X* (CJEU, 3 March 2020)). The verification of dual criminality in cases where requirement to verify has not been abolished by the Framework Decision must be narrowly construed (Case 289/15 *Grundza* [2017] 4 WLR 66).

In Case C-306/09 *IB* [2011] 1 WLR 2227, the CJEU found that the execution of a EAW issued for the purposes of execution of a sentence imposed *in absentia* within the meaning of Article 5(1) may be subject to the condition that the person concerned should be returned to the executing State in order to serve the sentence there, following a new trial organised in the person's presence in the issuing State. In Case C-388/08 *Leymann and Pustovarov* [2008] ECR I-8993, the CJEU found that, to establish specialty under Article 27(2) of the Framework Decision, it must be ascertained whether the constituent elements of the offence are those in respect of which the person was surrendered and whether there is a sufficient correspondence between the information given in the arrest warrant and that contained in the later procedural document.

Two cases address the issue of the compatibility of the EAW with fundamental rights in cases involving judgments *in absentia*. In Case C-396/11 *Criminal proceedings against Radu* [2013] QB 1031, the CJEU found that the EAW Framework Decision, as amended by Framework Decision 2009/299/JHA on judgments *in absentia* ([2009] OJ L81/24), must be interpreted as meaning that the executing judicial authorities cannot refuse to execute a EAW issued for the purposes of conducting a criminal prosecution on the ground that the requested person was not heard in the issuing Member State before that arrest warrant was issued. In Case C-399/11 *Melloni v Ministerio Fiscal* [2013] QB 1067, the CJEU found that Article 4a(1) of the Framework Decision, as amended by the 2009 Framework Decision, precludes the executing authorities from making the execution of the warrant issued for the purposes of executing a sentence conditional upon the conviction rendered *in absentia* being open to review in the issuing Member State. The Court found that Article 4a(1) is compatible with the requirements under Articles 47 and 48(2) of the Charter of Fundamental Rights.

In Joined Cases C-404/15 and C-659/15 *Aranyosi* [2016] QB 921, the CJEU considered the EAW and claims of deficiencies in detention conditions in the issuing Member State which raise a real risk of inhuman or degrading treatment. The Court ruled (at [104]):

> where there is objective, reliable, specific and properly updated evidence with respect to detention conditions in the issuing Member State that demonstrates that there are deficiencies, which may be systemic or generalised, or which may affect certain groups of people, or which may affect certain places of detention, the executing judicial authority must determine, specifically and precisely, whether there are substantial grounds to believe that the individual concerned ... will be exposed, because of the conditions for his detention in the issuing Member State, to a real risk of inhuman or degrading treatment, within the meaning of Article 4 of the Charter, in the event of his surrender to that Member State. To that end, the executing judicial authority must request that supplementary information be provided by the issuing judicial authority, which ... must send that information within the time limit specified in the request. The executing judicial authority must postpone its decision on the surrender of the individual concerned until it obtains the supplementary information that allows it to discount the existence of such a risk. If the existence of that risk cannot be discounted within a reasonable time, the executing judicial authority must decide whether the surrender procedure should be brought to an end.

The CJEU clarified the parameters of this dialogue between issuing and executing authority in Cases C-220/18 PPU *ML* [2019] 1 WLR 1052 and C-128/18 *Dorobantu* [2020] 2 CMLR 5. The CJEU also held that the *Aranyosi* test is applicable in cases concerning questions regarding the right to a fair trial stemming from concerns related to judicial independence and the rule of law in the issuing Member State (Case C-216/18 PPU *Minister for Justice and Equality v LM* [2019] 1 WLR 1004). See also **D31.34**.

With regard to the application of the principle of proportionality in the execution of EAWs, the Commission Handbook on the EAW recommends that proportionality issues are examined in the issuing, and not in the executing, Member State ([2017] OJ C335/1, para. 2.4). A similar approach has been adopted by Article 6(1) of Directive 2014/41/EU on the European Investigation Order. The amendment of the Extradition Act 2003, however, treats breach of the principle of proportionality as a ground of refusal to execute a EAW, to be considered by the executing authority (ABCPA 2014, s. 157, amended the Extradition Act 2003, s. 21A, to treat lack of proportionality as a ground for refusal (s. 21A(1)(b)).

Another issue dealt with by the CJEU is the need to issue a national arrest warrant, distinct from the EAW, in line with Article 8(1) of the EAW Framework Decision, and whether the lack of it constitutes an implicit ground for refusal to execute the EAW. In Case C-241/15 *Bob-Dogi* [2016] 1 WLR 4583, the Court found that a national arrest warrant forms the basis of the EAW and its lack must in principle result in the executing judicial authority refusing to give effect to the EAW (at [54]), but the executing judicial authority must request the issuing judicial authority to furnish all necessary supplementary information as a matter of urgency (at [65]–[67]). As for the time-frame for the effective surrender of a requested person, in Case C-640/15 *Vilkas* [2017] 4 WLR 69 the Court opined that an expiration of the time-limits set out in Article 23 of the EAW Framework Decision, due to repeated resistance of the requested person, does not relieve the executing Member State of its obligation to carry on with the procedure for executing a EAW and to surrender the requested person; therefore, agreeing on a new surrender date is the way forward (at [70]–[72]).

With regard to a refusal to execute a EAW on grounds of age of criminal responsibility, the CJEU *held that Article 3(3) of the EAW Framework Decision* means that the executing Member State should only refuse to surrender minors who are the subject of a EAW who, under the law of that State, have not yet reached the age at which they are regarded as criminally responsible. In deciding whether a minor is to be surrendered, the executing authority must simply verify whether the person concerned has reached the minimum age required for criminal responsibility under the law of the executing State, without having to consider any additional conditions (Case C-367/16 *Piotrowski* [2018] 4 WLR 72).

Evidence

The Framework Decision on the mutual recognition of orders freezing property or evidence ([2003] OJ L196/45) and the Framework Decision on the European Evidence Warrant ([2008] OJ L350/72) have replaced some elements of the current system of Mutual Legal Assistance co-operation. The freezing orders Framework Decision was implemented partly by the Crime (International Co-operation) Act 2003, ss. 7 to 28. However, the European Evidence Warrant Framework Decision has not been implemented by many Member States in view of the fact that a new, post-Lisbon Directive on mutual recognition of evidence is currently being negotiated in Brussels. The Directive on the European Investigation Order has replaced the mutual legal assistance instruments as regards the relations between EU Member States. The European Investigation Order has established a system for the mutual recognition of requests for evidence across the EU. The UK has opted into the European Investigation Order Directive (see the Criminal Justice (European Investigation Order) Regulations 2017 (SI 2017 No. 730)). According to the CJEU, Article 5(1) of the European Investigation Order Directive, read in conjunction with Section J of the form set out in Annex A to that Directive, must be interpreted as meaning that the judicial authority of a Member State does not, when issuing a European Investigation Order, have to include in that section a description of the legal remedies, if any, which are provided for in its Member State against the issuing of such an order (Case C-324/17 *Gavanozov* [2019] 4 WLR 159). **A9.14**

Financial Penalties

The Framework Decision on the mutual recognition of judgments imposing financial penalties ([2005] OJ L76/16), implemented by the CJIA 2008, ss. 80 to 92 and schs. 18 and 19, applies. The CJEU has held that Articles 7(2)(g) and 20(3) of Council Framework Decision 2005/214/JHA ([2005] OJ L76/16) as amended by Council Framework Decision 2009/299/JHA ([2009]) OJ L81/24), must be interpreted as meaning that where a decision requiring payment of a financial penalty has been notified in accordance with the national legislation of the issuing Member State, indicating the right to contest the case and the time limit for such a legal remedy, the authority of the Member State of execution may not refuse to recognise and execute that decision provided that the person concerned has had sufficient time to contest that decision, which is for the national court to verify, and the fact that the procedure imposing the financial penalty in question is administrative in nature is not relevant in that regard. Moreover, Article 20(3) of Framework Decision 2005/214/JHA, as amended by Framework Decision 2009/299/JHA, must be interpreted as meaning that the competent authority of the Member State of execution may not refuse to recognise and execute a decision requiring payment of a financial penalty in respect of road traffic offences where such a penalty has been imposed on the person in whose name the vehicle in question is registered on the basis of a presumption of liability laid down in the national legislation of the issuing Member State, provided that that presumption may be rebutted (Case C-671/18 *CJIB* (CJEU, 5 December 2019)). **A9.15**

Confiscation

The Framework Decision on the mutual recognition of confiscation orders ([2006] OJ L328/59) applies (see **E19.87**). However, the UK is not bound by the two EU instruments harmonising confiscation law at EU level: Council Framework Decision 2005/212/JHA of 24 February 2005 on Confiscation of Crime-related Proceeds, Instrumentalities and Property ([2005] OJ L68/49) and Directive 2014/42/EU of 3 April 2014 on the freezing and confiscation of instrumentalities and proceeds of crime in the European Union ([2014] OJ L127/39). The Preamble to the latter states that the UK is to be bound by that Directive only in respect of the offences covered by the instruments by which it is bound (recital 32). **A9.16**

Regulation (EU) 2018/1805 on the mutual recognition of freezing and confiscation orders ([2018] OJ L303/1) has been adopted. It will replace Framework Decisions 2003/577/JHA ([2003] OJ L196/45) and 2006/783/JHA ([2006] OJ L328/59) and will complement Directive 2014/42/EU. The UK has opted into the Regulation.

The CJEU held that Council Framework Decision 2005/212/JHA does not preclude national legislation which allows confiscation on the basis of a procedure which does not require the finding of the existence of a criminal offence or the conviction of the individuals presumed to have committed this offence (Case C-234/18 *'AGRO IN 2001'* (CJEU, 19 March 2020)).

Supervision Measures

A9.17 The Framework Decision on the mutual recognition of decisions on supervision measures as alternatives to provisional detention ([2009] OJ L294/20) and the Framework Decision on the application of the principle of mutual recognition to judgments and probation decisions with a view to the supervision of probation measures and alternative sanctions ([2008] OJ L337/102) apply.

Transfer of Sentenced Persons

A9.18 The Framework Decision on the transfer of custodial sentences (sentenced persons) ([2008] OJ L327/27) applies. As regards the applicable national law, in Case C-544/14 *Ognyanov* (CJEU, 8 November 2016) the Grand Chamber clarified that with respect to the part of the custodial sentence served by the prisoner on the territory of the issuing Member State until transfer to the executing Member State, only the law of the former applies, not least to the question of any grant of a reduction in sentence. Consequently, the law of the executing Member State can apply only to the part of the sentence that remains to be served on its territory and it cannot substitute its own rules with respect to the part which has already been served in the issuing Member State. In Case C-582/15 *van Vemde* [2017] 4 WLR 50 the Court clarified that Article 28(2) of that Framework Decision only covers judgments that became final by 5 December 2011 at the latest (at [30]–[31]).

Examination of Effect of Recognising and Executing Judicial Decision

A9.19 Important guidance on the issue of the extent to which executing authorities should examine the substance of the legal system of the issuing State when deciding whether to recognise and execute a judicial decision was given in Case C-411/10 *R (NS) v Secretary of State for the Home Department* [2013] QB 102. While the case involved the application of EU asylum law (the Dublin Regulation), its key finding that there is no conclusive presumption that fundamental rights are respected in Member States does apply to the operation of mutual recognition in criminal matters as well. *NS* precludes automaticity in the execution of mutual recognition requests and obliges national judicial authorities to examine the impact of execution on the fundamental rights of the affected individuals on a case-by-case basis. The Court confirmed in *NS* that the Charter of Fundamental Rights (with the exception of its Chapter IV) is applicable to the UK (at [116]–[122]).

Similar questions have arisen in domestic courts. In *Assange v Swedish Prosecution Authority* [2011] EWHC 2849 (Admin), the Divisional Court interpreted the Extradition Act 2003 to a great extent in accordance with the EAW Framework Decision which it was designed to implement as far as surrender to EU Member States was concerned. The need to interpret the Extradition Act 2003 in conformity with the EAW Framework Decision was highlighted from the outset, referring to leading judgments in both the CJEU (Case C-105/03 *Pupino* [2005] ECR I-5285) and the House of Lords (*Dabas v High Court of Justice, Madrid* [2007] UKHL 6, [2007] 2 AC 31). *Assange* confirms that 'it is now well established that Part I of the 2003 Act must be read in the context of the Framework Decision and that the national courts of the Member States should construe national laws so far as possible to attain the results sought to be achieved by the Framework Decision' (at [9]). The need to take into account the aims of the Framework Decision under the principle of mutual recognition does not, however, negate any scrutiny of EAWs by domestic courts (at [17]): the intensity of such scrutiny increases in cases where a EAW is issued by a judicial authority who is not a judge (at [19]). However, the Divisional Court did examine the substance of the defendant's claims.

AUTONOMOUS CONCEPTS OF EU LAW

See also **A9.9** in relation to requests for preliminary rulings. **A9.20**

Judicial Authority

The CJEU has granted an autonomous EU meaning to the term 'court having jurisdiction in particular in criminal matters'. The term must be interpreted as covering any court or tribunal which applies a procedure that satisfies the essential characteristics of criminal procedure (Case C-60/12 *Balaz* [2014] RTR 7 (61)). Police services of a Member State are excluded (Case C-452/16 PPU *Poltorak* [2017] 4 WLR 8) and the public prosecutor's office constitutes a national authority responsible for administering criminal justice (Case C-453/16 PPU *Özçelik* [2017] 4 WLR 9). Furthermore, an organ of the executive, such as the Ministry of Justice, must not be designated as a 'judicial authority' (Case C-477/16 PPU *Kovalkovas* [2017] 4 WLR 10). **A9.21**

The CJEU elaborated further on the concept of judicial authority in subsequent case law concerning the functions of the German public prosecutor. The Court found that the concept of judicial authority is capable of including authorities which, although not necessarily judges or courts, participate in the administration of criminal justice — with public prosecutor's offices being capable of being regarded as participating in the administration of criminal justice (Joined Cases C-508/18 and C-82/19 PPU *OG (Public Prosecutor's Office of Lübeck)* (CJEU, 27 May 2019)). There are two constituent elements which must apply cumulatively for the autonomous concept of judicial authority for the purposes of issuing a EAW to be established:

(a) Independence: the issuing authority under Article 6(1) of the EAW Framework Decision must be capable of exercising its responsibilities objectively without being exposed to the risk that its decision-making power be subject to external directions or instructions in particular from the executive, so that it is beyond doubt that the decision to issue a EAW lies with that authority and not, ultimately, with the executive.
(b) Remedy: there must be an effective remedy against the decision to issue a EAW, including reviewing the proportionality of such a decision.

These two elements apply cumulatively (Case C-509/18 *PF* [2019] 4 WLR 125). The CJEU found that while the Lithuanian Prosecutor General could be considered a 'judicial authority' for the purposes of the operation of the EAW, this was not the case regarding the German Prosecutor. In subsequent case law, the Court found that the French Public Prosecutor's Office, the Swedish Prosecution Authority and the Belgian Public Prosecutor's Office all fell within the autonomous EU law concept of judicial authority for the purposes of the EAW (Joined Cases C-556/19 PPU and C-626/19 PPU, Case C-625/19 PPU and Case C-627/19 PPU (CJEU, 12 December 2019)).

In the domestic context, in *Assange v Swedish Prosecution Authority* [2012] UKSC 22, [2012] 2 AC 471, the Supreme Court found that the meaning of the term 'judicial authority' is identical in the EAW Framework Decision and in the Extradition Act 2003 and that the term encompasses prosecutors. In *Ministry of Justice, Republic of Lithuania v Bucnys* [2013] UKSC 71, [2014] AC 480 the Supreme Court confirmed (at [43]–[45]) that the term 'judicial authority' for the purposes of the operation of the EAW Framework Decision is an autonomous European concept which must be interpreted in a teleological and contextual manner. See also **D31.13**.

Trial Resulting in a Decision in Judgments *in absentia*

A9.22 In Case C-271/17 PPU *Zdziaszek* [2017] 4 WLR 189, the CJEU considered the concept of 'trial resulting in the decision' within the meaning of Article 4a(1) of the EAW Framework Decision as amended by Council Framework Decision 2009/299/JHA on trials *in absentia*. The Court found that the phrase must be interpreted as referring not only to proceedings which gave rise to the decision on appeal, where that decision, after a fresh examination of the case on the merits, finally determined the guilt of the person concerned, but also to subsequent proceedings, at the end of which the decision that finally amended the level of the initial sentence was handed down, inasmuch as the authority which adopted the latter decision enjoyed a certain discretion in that regard. In Case C-270/17 PPU *Tupikas* [2017] 4 WLR 188, the CJEU held that the concept of 'trial resulting in the decision' must be interpreted as relating only to the instance at the end of which the decision is handed down which finally rules on the guilt of the person concerned and imposes a penalty, such as a custodial sentence, following a re-examination, in fact and in law, of the merits of the case. Where a party has appeared in person in criminal proceedings that result in a judicial decision which finds the party guilty of an offence and imposes a custodial sentence the execution of which is subsequently suspended, the concept of 'trial resulting in the decision' must be interpreted as not including subsequent proceedings in which that suspension is revoked on the grounds of infringement of those conditions during the probationary period, provided that the revocation does not change the nature or the level of the sentence initially imposed (Case C-571/17 PPU *Ardic* (CJEU, 22 December 2017)).

DOUBLE JEOPARDY

A9.23 Domestic courts are obliged to respect the principle of double jeopardy or *ne bis in idem*, which was introduced into EU law via the incorporation of the Schengen *acquis* in the EU legal order. It forms part of the *acquis* which is binding on the UK. Article 54 of the Schengen Implementing Convention (CISA) sets out the principle as follows:

> A person whose trial has been finally disposed of in one Contracting Party may not be prosecuted in another Contracting Party for the same acts provided that, if a penalty has been imposed, it has been enforced, is actually in the process of being enforced or can no longer be enforced under the laws of the sentencing Contracting Party.

Article 54 CISA has thus established a cross-border double jeopardy principle. The principle applies to cross-border cases involving the UK and another EU Member State and is of relevance in cases where it is thought that a defendant in domestic criminal proceedings has already been subject to criminal proceedings which have been finally disposed of in another EU Member State. The scope of the principle in EU law is broad (it applies to the same acts, and not to the same offences) and it has been extended further by the CJEU to protect the defendant. See **D12.20** ***et seq.*** for more detailed discussion of double jeopardy and its application in practice.

Ne bis in idem is also recognised as a fundamental right in Article 50 of the Charter of Fundamental Rights. The question has thus arisen whether Article 50 is applicable beyond cross-border cases as envisaged by Article 54 CISA, in purely domestic cases involving the implementation of EU law. The CJEU found in Case C-617/10 *Äklagaren v Äkerberg Fransson* [2013] 2 CMLR 46 (1273) that the Charter is applicable even in cases where national law has not been adopted to transpose an EU Directive, as long as a direct link is established between domestic law and the obligation of Member States to ensure the effectiveness of Union law (at [16]–[31]). The *ne bis in idem* principle applies in a domestic law context involving the imposition of criminal law and administrative law penalties only if the administrative penalties are criminal in nature. The criteria for the purposes of addressing whether administrative penalties (tax penalties in *Fransson*) are criminal are the legal classification of the offence under national law, the nature of the offence and the nature and degree of the severity of the penalty (at [34] and [35]).

TAKING ACCOUNT OF PREVIOUS CONVICTIONS

A system of taking account of previous convictions was established by Framework Decision 2008/675/JHA ([2008] OJ L220/2). It places Member States under a duty to ensure that in the course of criminal proceedings against a person, previous convictions handed down against the same person for different facts in other Member States are taken into account to the extent that previous domestic convictions are taken into account, and that equivalent legal effects are attached to them as to previous domestic convictions, in accordance with domestic law (Article 3(1)). Where, in the course of criminal proceedings in a Member State, information is available on a previous conviction in another Member State, as far as possible the person concerned should not be treated less favourably than if the previous conviction had been a domestic conviction (Preamble, recital 8). The CJEU found in Case C-171/16 *Beshkov* (CJEU, 21 September 2017) that Framework Decision 2008/675/JHA is applicable to a national procedure that is concerned with the imposition, for the purposes of execution, of an overall custodial sentence that takes into account the sentence imposed on that person by a national court and also that imposed following a previous conviction handed down by a court of another Member State against the same person for different facts. Article 3(3) of Framework Decision 2008/675/JHA precludes national legislation which provides that a national court, seised of an application for the imposition, for the purposes of execution, of an overall custodial sentence that takes into account, *inter alia*, the sentence imposed following a previous conviction handed down by a court of another Member State, may alter for that purpose the arrangements for execution of the latter sentence. Domestic implementation has taken place via the CAJA 2009, s. 144 and sch. 17 (see **F12.1** *et seq.*, **F13.5** and **F13.36**). **A9.24**

CONFLICTS OF JURISDICTION

An attempt to establish a system to prevent and settle conflicts of jurisdiction was made by Framework Decision 2009/948/JHA ([2009] OJ L328/42). The Framework Decision aims at encouraging direct contact between competent national authorities for this purpose. In October 2013, it was indicated in Parliament that the UK government 'do not currently intend to take any steps to implement this Framework Decision' on the basis that the practices it embodies are already well established in the UK. **A9.25**

The Framework Decision establishes an obligation to contact when there are reasonable grounds to believe that parallel proceedings are being conducted in another Member State (Article 5) and a corresponding obligation to reply (Article 6). It also imposes a duty to enter into direct consultations when it is established that parallel proceedings exist, with the aim of reaching consensus on 'any effective solution aimed at avoiding the adverse consequences arising from such parallel proceedings, which may, where appropriate, lead to the concentration of the criminal proceedings in one Member State' (Article 10(1)). The Framework Decision thus does not in itself impose an obligation on a Member State to prosecute or to refrain from prosecution in cases of conflicts of jurisdiction. It also does not set out a series of binding criteria which must be taken into account when deciding on conflicts of jurisdiction. The Preamble refers to relevant criteria developed by Eurojust as possible criteria to be taken into account (recital 9). However, these criteria are not binding and not hierarchical. See **A8** for jurisdiction generally.

DEFENCE RIGHTS

The Lisbon Treaty has granted the EU competence to adopt minimum standards on defence rights to the extent necessary to facilitate mutual recognition (Article 82(2) TFEU). Secondary EU law on defence rights will flesh out protection established in general human rights instruments such as that under the ECHR, Article 6. Moreover, the EU Charter of Fundamental Rights (binding upon Member States after the entry into force of the Lisbon Treaty) includes **A9.26** a general provision on the right to a fair trial (Article 47) and a specific provision guaranteeing respect for the rights of the defence of anyone who has been charged (Article 48(2)). Any secondary EU law in the field must be interpreted in the light of these provisions.

The first EU measure on defence rights to be adopted was Directive 2010/64/EU on the right to interpretation and translation in criminal proceedings ([2010] OJ L280/1). It applies to both criminal proceedings and proceedings for the execution of a EAW (Article 1(1)). It grants a right to interpretation 'without delay' (Article 2(1)) and a right to translation within a reasonable period of time of all documents which are essential to ensure that D is able to exercise the right of defence and to safeguard the fairness of the proceedings (Article 3(1)). Essential documents include any decision depriving a person of liberty, any charge or indictment, and any judgment (Article 3(2)). In proceedings for the execution of a EAW, the competent authorities must provide a written translation of it (Article 3(6)). The Directive contains a non-regression clause with regard to the ECHR, the EU Charter of Fundamental Rights, international law and domestic law which provides a higher level of protection (Article 8). In Case C-216/14 *Covaci* (CJEU, 15 October 2015) the Court found that Articles 1 to 3 of Directive 2010/64/EU must be interpreted as not precluding national legislation which, in criminal proceedings, does not permit the individual against whom a penalty order has been made to lodge an objection in writing against that order in a language other than that of the proceedings, even though that individual does not have a command of the language of the proceedings, provided that the competent authorities do not consider, in accordance with Article 3(3) of that Directive, that, in the light of the proceedings concerned and the circumstances of the case, such an objection constitutes an essential document. In Case C-278/16 *Sleutjes* (CJEU, 12 October 2017), the Court found that Article 3 of Directive 2010/64/EU must be interpreted as meaning that a measure, such as an order provided for by national law for imposing sanctions in relation to minor offences and delivered by a judge following a simplified unilateral procedure, constitutes a 'document which is essential' within the meaning of Article 3(1) of the Directive. The UK has opted into the Directive and PACE Code C implements it (see **D1.91**).

Directive 2012/13/EU on the right to information in criminal proceedings ([2012] OJ L142/1), to which the UK has opted in, grants suspects and accused persons a right to be informed about their rights (Articles 3, 4 and 5), a right to information about the accusation (Article 6) and a right of access to the materials of the case (Article 7). The CJEU found in *Covaci* that Articles 2, 3(1)(c) and 6(1) and (3) of Directive 2012/13/EU must be interpreted as not precluding legislation of a Member State which, in criminal proceedings, makes it mandatory for D not residing in that Member State to appoint a person authorised to accept service of a penalty order concerning D, provided that D does in fact have the benefit of the whole of the prescribed period for lodging an objection against that order. The CJEU held in Case C-612/15 *Kolev* (CJEU, 5 June 2018) that Article 7(3) of the Directive must be interpreted as meaning that it is for the national court to be satisfied that the defence has been granted a genuine opportunity to have access to the case materials.

The UK has not opted into Directive 2013/48/EU on the right of access to a lawyer in criminal proceedings ([2013] OJ L294/1), which contains measures that are key in safeguarding fundamental rights in EU criminal law. Since they were adopted post-Lisbon and confer rights on individuals, provisions on defence rights are highly likely to have direct effect, and thus can be invoked in domestic courts in cases of perceived inadequate implementation.

Directive 2016/343/EU on the strengthening of certain aspects of the presumption of innocence and of the right to be present at the trial in criminal proceedings ([2016] OJ L65/1) is intended to complement the legal framework provided by the ECHR and the EU Charter of Fundamental Rights. The UK has not opted into this Directive. Its aim is to strengthen mutual trust and confidence between the judicial authorities of the Member States and facilitate mutual recognition of decisions in criminal matters. The Directive provides two rights linked to this principle: the right to remain silent and the right not to incriminate oneself. In addition, Member States will have to respect the following related obligations: before the final judgment, the authorities should abstain from giving the impression that suspects and accused persons are guilty by using measures of physical restraint or presenting them wearing prison clothes, and the burden of proof is on the prosecution while any reasonable doubts as to guilt should benefit the accused. The right to be present at one's trial is also addressed, while Member States must ensure that suspects and accused persons have an effective remedy if their rights under this Directive are breached.

Even though the deadline for implementation of this Directive was April 2018, in its first judgment in Case C-439/16 PPU *Milev* [2017] 2 CMLR 5 (141), the CJEU found that the opinion issued by the Bulgarian Special Court for criminal matters, according to which the national law governing criminal procedure was contrary to ECHR case law, was not liable to seriously compromise the attainment of the aim of the Directive, as the opinion in question leaves national courts free to apply the ECHR provisions, or those of national criminal procedural law (at [40]). In Case C-310/18 PPU *Milev* (CJEU, 19 September 2018), the CJEU held that the Directive does not preclude the adoption of preliminary decisions of a procedural nature, such as a decision taken by a judicial authority that pre-trial detention should continue, which are based on suspicion or on incriminating evidence, provided that such decisions do not refer to the person in custody as being guilty.

The UK has not opted into Directive 2016/800/EU on procedural safeguards for children who are suspects or accused persons in criminal proceedings ([2016] OJ L132/1). Its aim is to set out minimum rules to ensure that suspected or accused children are able to understand and follow criminal proceedings. In this respect, its main innovation involves the role of lawyers who must assist children where necessary, by providing legal aid, unless assistance by a lawyer is not proportionate in light of the circumstances of the case. Rights to information, to an individual assessment, to a medical examination and to audio-visual recording of questioning are also envisaged, as well as specific safeguards for children deprived of their liberty, in particular during pre- and post-trial detention.

The UK has not opted into Directive 2016/1919/EU on legal aid for suspects and accused persons in criminal proceedings and for requested persons in European arrest warrant proceedings ([2016] OJ L297/1). This instrument lays down minimum rules concerning the right to legal aid for suspects or accused persons in criminal proceedings who are deprived of liberty, and in certain other situations. It also ensures that legal aid is made available in EAW proceedings, upon the arrest of the requested person in the executing State. The scope of application of the Directive includes a right to ordinary legal aid, rather than a provisional one, at all stages of the criminal justice process. It includes a means test (whether the person lacks sufficient resources to pay for legal assistance) and a merits test (whether the provision of legal aid would be in the interests of justice in the light of the circumstances of the case), which may be used to determine whether a person is eligible for legal aid.

DATA PROTECTION

Article 8 of the EU-UK Withdrawal Agreement states that UK access to EU networks, information systems and databases will cease at the end of the transition period, unless otherwise provided. Under Article 62(2) the UK will be entitled to use, for no longer than one year after the end of the transition period and only as strictly necessary, the Secure Information Exchange Network Application (SIENA) to exchange information within joint investigation teams. Article 63 provides for continuing participation of the UK in a number of EU policing and law enforcement instruments, including Directive (EU) 2016/681 on the use of passenger name record data ([2016] OJ L119/132) and Schengen and police co-operation measures. See the Law Enforcement and Security (Amendment) (EU Exit) Regulations 2019 (SI 2019 No. 742). **A9.27**

A key pre-condition for a close EU-UK relationship in the field of data exchange after the expiry of the Withdrawal Agreement is the adequacy of UK data protection law, or its essential equivalence with EU law (Case C-362/14 *Schrems v Data Protection Commissioner* [2016] QB 527). Directive 2016/680/EU on the protection of individuals with regard to the processing of personal data by competent authorities for the purposes of prevention, investigation, detection or prosecution of criminal offences or the execution of criminal penalties, and the free movement of such data ([2016] OJ L119/89) repeals Council Framework Decision 2008/977/JHA on data protection in the field of law enforcement co-operation ([2008] OJ L350/60). The Directive introduces detailed rules on data processing, the rights of the data subject, transfers of personal data to third countries, the establishment of independent supervisory authorities in Member States, and provisions on remedies for affected individuals. Two important caveats exist regarding the applicability of the Directive. The specific provisions for the protection of personal data in acts of the EU adopted in the field of judicial co-operation in criminal matters and police co-operation prior to the adoption of this Directive and the access of designated authorities of Member States to information systems will remain unaffected (Article 60). This covers instruments such as the 'Prüm' Decisions, which establish a system whereby police forces of EU Member States are able automatically to share DNA, fingerprint and vehicle registration data (Decision 2008/615/JHA and Decision 2008/616/JHA). The UK opted back into these Decisions in January 2016 (Council document 5650/16). Moreover, the UK is not bound by the Directive when carrying out activities in the field of police and judicial co-operation in criminal matters where it is not bound by the underlying rules governing the forms of judicial co-operation in criminal matters or police co-operation which require compliance with the data protection provisions (recital 99).

Directive 2016/681/EU on the use of passenger name record data requires air carriers to retain and transfer PNR data to specified units that will be established in each Member State as a means of assisting in the fight against terrorism and other serious criminal offences. The UK has decided to opt into this Directive.

Joined Cases C-203/15 and C-698/15 *Tele2 Sverige* [2017] QB 771 considered the interpretation of Directive 2002/58/EC (the 'ePrivacy Directive', [2002] OJ L201/37) concerning the retention of telecommunication data for criminal law purposes. Following the line of reasoning in Joined Cases C-293/12 and C-594/12 *Digital Rights Ireland* [2015] 1 QB 127, the CJEU found that EU law precludes national legislation which, for the purpose of fighting crime, provides for general and indiscriminate retention of all traffic and location data of all subscribers and registered users relating to all means of electronic communication. Furthermore, access to the retained data must be restricted solely to fighting serious crime, must be subject to prior review by a court or an independent administrative authority, and the data should be retained within the EU.

EXTERNAL RELATIONS

A9.28 In a case involving a request for extradition of an Estonian national by Latvian authorities to Russia (Case C-182/15 *Petruhhin* [2017] QB 299) the Grand Chamber ruled that in order to prevent the risk of impunity, a Member State is not required to grant every EU citizen who has moved within its territory the same protection against extradition as that granted to its own nationals. Nevertheless, before extraditing the citizen, the Member State concerned must prioritise the exchange of information with the Member State of origin and allow that State to request the citizen's surrender for the purposes of prosecution. The CJEU applied aspects of *Petruhhin* in cases where an extradition agreement between the EU and a third State has been adopted (Case C-191/16 *Pisciotti v Germany* [2019] QB 104) and in cases involving extradition for the purpose of enforcing a custodial sentence (Case C-247/17 *Raugevicius* [2019] 2 CMLR 3 (73)).

Section B1 Homicide and Related Offences

MURDER

Definition

Murder is when a [person] ... unlawfully killeth ... any reasonable creature *in rerum natura* under the Queen's peace, with malice aforethought ... (Derived from *Coke's Institutes*, 3 Co Inst 47) **B1.1**

Procedure

Murder is triable only on indictment. It is a class 1A offence. **B1.2**

Indictment

Statement of Offence **B1.3**

Murder

Particulars of Offence

A on or about the ... day of ... murdered V

Alternative Verdicts

Criminal Law Act 1967, s. 6 **B1.4**

(2) On an indictment for murder a person found not guilty of murder may be found guilty—
   (a) of manslaughter, or of causing grievous bodily harm with intent to do so; or
   (b) of any offence of which he may be found guilty under an enactment specifically so providing, or under section 4(2) of this Act [assisting offenders]; or
   (c) of an attempt to commit murder, or of an attempt to commit any other offence of which he might be found guilty;

but may not be found guilty of any offence not included above.

The major enactments specifically providing for an alternative verdict within s. 6(2)(b) are as follows:

(a) Suicide Act 1961, s. 2(2) (encouraging or assisting suicide: see **B1.140**);
(b) Infant Life (Preservation) Act 1929, s. 2(2) (child destruction: see **B1.102** to **B1.110**);
(c) Infanticide Act 1938, s. 2(2) (infanticide: see **B1.92** to **B1.101**).

To these alternative verdicts must be added:

(d) manslaughter;
(e) wounding with intent (under the CLA 1967, s. 6(2)(a));

(f) assisting (contrary to the CLA 1967, s. 4(1)) anyone guilty of any of the above offences; and
(g) attempting to commit any of the above offences.

Murder is specifically excluded from the general rule on alternative verdicts laid down in the CLA 1967, s. 6(3) (see **D19.42**).

Although s. 6(2)(a) refers to a person being 'found not guilty of murder', a person can still, under the common law, irrespective of s. 2, be found guilty of manslaughter as an alternative verdict where the jury are unable to agree and are discharged by the judge from returning a verdict on the charge of murder (*Saunders* [1988] AC 148). As to when it is necessary for a judge to leave an alternative verdict of manslaughter to a jury, see *Coutts* [2006] UKHL 39, [2007] 1 Cr App R 6 (60), discussed at **D19.63**; see also *Barre* [2016] EWCA Crim 216 for an illustration of where the trial judge is not obliged to leave the alternative verdict to the jury. *Braithwaite* [2019] EWCA Crim 597 is an example of where the alternative verdict of unlawful act manslaughter was left to the jury on the basis of lack of intent to cause grievous bodily harm but the judge was correct in not leaving it also on another 'artificial and unreal' factual basis contended for by the appellant. See also *JB* [2013] EWCA Crim 256 on the effect of the decision to discharge the jury from returning a verdict on the murder charge and to take the alternative verdict of manslaughter, i.e. that there can be no subsequent retrial for murder.

It is permissible to include other counts in an indictment for murder (*Connelly v DPP* [1964] AC 1254; as to joinder of counts generally, see **D11.63** ***et seq.***).

Sentence

B1.5 The penalty for murder is as follows:

> Murder: Life imprisonment (mandatory sentence) (Murder (Abolition of Death Penalty) Act 1965, s. 1(1)).
>
> Murder by a person aged 18 but under 21: Custody for life (mandatory sentence) (PCC(S)A 2000, s. 93).
>
> Murder by person aged under 18 at the time of the offence: Detention at Her Majesty's pleasure (mandatory sentence) (PCC(S)A 2000, s. 90).

The CJA 2003, ss. 269 to 277 and schs. 21 and 22, provide the statutory scheme for the setting of minimum terms in all murder cases. There is no offence-specific guideline but the Sentencing Council's *General Guideline: Overarching Principles* (see Supplement, **SG2-1**) is used for all offenders sentenced on or after 1 October 2019. As to mandatory life sentences generally, see **E3**. As to the determination of the minimum term under the CJA 2003, sch. 21, see **E3.3**. For reduction in sentence in a murder case following a plea of guilty, the Sentencing Council definitive guideline, *Reduction in Sentence for a Guilty Plea* (see Supplement, **SG5-1**), applies.

For sentencing for attempted murder, see the definitive sentencing guideline, *Attempted Murder* (see Supplement, **SG13-1**). It should be noted that this is a Sentencing Guidelines Council guideline (one of the few not superseded by a Sentencing Council guideline) and the ranges and starting points are based upon an adult 'first time offender' aged 18 or over who is convicted after a trial. The Court of Appeal in *Jolie* [2010] EWCA Crim 1816, [2011] 1 Cr App R (S) 87 (527) said that the guideline was relevant in a case of conspiracy to murder where the facts might well have amounted to attempted murder. In *Terry* [2012] EWCA Crim 1411, [2013] 1 Cr App R (S) 51 (285), where the offender struck the victim in the face many times with a claw hammer causing multiple skull fractures, an extended sentence with a custodial term of 18 years and an extension period of five years imposed after a trial was upheld on appeal. The Court of Appeal reviewed the sentencing guidelines in detail in *Barnaby* [2012] EWCA Crim 1327, [2013] 1 Cr App R (S) 53 (302) and found that a sentence of imprisonment for public protection with a minimum term of 11 years after a trial was appropriate where the offender stabbed the victim twice causing life-threatening injuries. The guideline makes comparison with the starting points set out in sch. 21 appropriate to fixing the minimum term in a murder case, and in *Barnaby* it was said to be right for a judge sentencing a case of attempted murder involving use of a knife to have regard to para. 5A in that schedule (25-year starting point where offender takes a knife or other weapon to the scene). *Hardy* [2012] EWCA Crim 2671, [2013] 2 Cr App R (S) 24 (164), where a husband attempted to murder his wife by hitting her on the head with a lump hammer, causing physical and psychological injury, was considered to be a level 2 offence with a starting point of 15 years, reduced to ten years to reflect a plea of guilty. An exceptional case is *Wade* [2012] EWCA Crim 2605, [2013] 2 Cr App R (S) 12 (52), where the offender briefly tried to suffocate his partner who was ill and whose behaviour had become very difficult to cope with; the Court of Appeal reduced the sentence to 16 months' imprisonment.

Elements

The definition set out at **B1.1** is often condensed to the form 'unlawful killing with malice aforethought', to be contrasted with those forms of manslaughter which consist of unlawful killing without malice aforethought. This contrast emphasises the point that the principal distinguishing feature of murder is malice aforethought, the *mens rea*, which can now be confidently stated to be an intention to kill or to cause grievous bodily harm. Since the *actus reus* of murder also governs both manslaughter and infanticide and affects certain other offences too, it is especially important to clarify the longer definition given by Coke. **B1.6**

Unlawful Killing The word 'unlawfully' can be taken to exclude killings for which the accused has a complete and valid justification, such as killing (reasonably) in self-defence (see **A3.55** to **A3.72**). See also *Airedale NHS Trust v Bland* [1993] AC 789 for the distinction between (lawful) withdrawal of treatment supporting life and (unlawful) active termination of a patient's life. This distinction was reiterated in *Inglis* [2010] EWCA Crim 2637, [2011] 2 Cr App R (S) 13 (66) by Lord Judge CJ in upholding the conviction for murder of a mother who had deliberately killed her son in his hospital bed with a carefully planned injection of heroin. She regarded it as an act of mercy but mercy killing remains unlawful and constitutes murder in the absence of, e.g., diminished responsibility or some other partial defence. Similarly it was confirmed in *R (Nicklinson) v Ministry of Justice* [2012] EWHC 2381 (Admin) that voluntary euthanasia cannot provide a defence to murder by way of necessity and that the ECHR, Article 8, does not require the recognition of any such defence; that view was affirmed by the Court of Appeal ([2013] EWCA Civ 961, [2014] 2 All ER 32), whose decision on this point was clearly accepted as correct by the Supreme Court ([2014] UKSC 38, [2015] AC 657: see, e.g., Lord Neuberger at [130]). **B1.7**

'Killeth' or 'kills' means 'causes the death of', and reference should be made to the discussion of causation in **A1.25** to **A1.40** (most of the cases there discussed being homicide cases). It should also be noted that murder is a result crime for the purposes of the rule laid down by the House of Lords in *Miller* [1983] 2 AC 161 in relation to the duty to act in the face of a danger one has created oneself (see **A1.20**).

Any Reasonable Creature *in Rerum Natura* This can be safely shortened to 'any human being' which includes a conjoined twin totally dependent on its twin for oxygenated blood (*Re A (Children) (Conjoined twins: surgical separation)* [2001] 4 All ER 961), provided that expression is understood as being limited to one who is born alive, i.e. when it is fully expelled from its mother's body (*Poulton* (1832) 5 C & P 329) with an existence independent of its mother. Although there are difficulties about identifying the precise time at which this occurs (Criminal Law Revision Committee, 14th Report, paras. 33–37), if death is caused before the child has an existence independent of its mother, the jury can convict of the offence of child destruction (see **B1.102** to **B1.110**). The accused's act may take place before the birth of the victim if it causes the victim to die after having been born alive but liability for murder or manslaughter will depend on the precise intention with which the act is done. The House of Lords decided in *A-G's Ref (No. 3 of 1994)* [1998] AC 245 that the child *in utero* is not simply a part of its mother as the Court of Appeal ([1996] QB 581) had held but that they are distinct organisms between which, however, the doctrine of transferred *mens rea* does not fully apply (see **A2.31**). An intention to **B1.8**

inflict grievous bodily harm on the mother cannot ground liability for murder in respect of the subsequent live-birth-then-death of the child (although this can be manslaughter). It may, however, still be the case that there could be liability for the murder of the child if the intention was to kill the mother and certainly if it was intended to cause the child to die after having been born alive. The fact that the House of Lords in *A-G's Ref (No. 3 of 1994)* recognised that there could be liability for manslaughter, in relation to a child that was injured *in utero* and died after being born alive, is a result of the rules about causation in homicide and does not affect the proposition also recognised by the House that the child prior to its birth was not a legal person while still a foetus in the womb—see *Criminal Injuries Compensation Authority v First-Tier Tribunal (Social Entitlement Chamber)* [2014] EWCA Civ 1554, [2015] QB 459 concerning whether a foetus in the womb could be 'another person' for the purposes of an offence under the OAPA 1861, s. 23 (administering poison etc.: see **B2.89**).

B1.9 **Under the Queen's Peace** The original significance of this expression is somewhat unclear (*Page* [1954] 1 QB 170), but it was, in part at least, concerned with matters of jurisdiction now provided for by statute, although it may also still have a continuing role, in terms of excluding from the definition of murder, the killing of an enemy alien or persons rebelling against the Crown. It certainly does not operate so as to exonerate a *defendant* who claims to be at war with the Queen, an argument roundly dismissed as 'completely hopeless' by Lord Thomas CJ in *Adebelajo* [2014] EWCA Crim 2779, [2015] 4 All ER 194 at [33], where he went on to say:

> The reference to 'the Queen's peace', as originally dealt with in the cases to which we have referred, went essentially to jurisdiction. Although the Queen's Peace may play some part still in the elements that have to be proved for murder as regards the status of the victim (and it is not necessary to examine or define the ambit of that), it can only go to the status of the victim; it has nothing whatsoever to do with the status of the killer.

Subject to the point about excluding the killing of rebels, or enemy aliens in wartime, the killing of anyone, whether British subject or not and whether within the jurisdiction or outside it, by a British subject can amount to murder (or manslaughter) and is triable in England. Any doubts about the precise position in Coke's time in relation to killings taking place outside the jurisdiction (*Page* [1954] 1 QB 170) were resolved by the OAPA 1861, s. 9 (murder or manslaughter abroad), which provides as follows:

B1.10 **Offences against the Person Act 1861, s. 9**

> Where any murder or manslaughter shall be committed on land out of the United Kingdom, whether within the Queen's dominions or without, and whether the person killed were a subject of Her Majesty or not, every offence committed by any subject of Her Majesty in respect of any such case, whether the same shall amount to the offence of murder or manslaughter,... may be dealt with, inquired of, tried, determined, and punished... in England or Ireland.

Section 9 deals with the case where the whole of the *actus reus* takes place abroad, i.e. both the act causing death and the death itself. There is nevertheless liability because the perpetrator is a British subject. Section 10 by contrast imposes liability whether or not the perpetrator is a British subject, where one of these two elements of the *actus reus* takes place inside the jurisdiction, even though the other takes place outside it:

Offences against the Person Act 1861, s. 10

> Where any person being criminally stricken, poisoned, or otherwise hurt upon the sea, or at any place out of England or Ireland, shall die of such stroke, poisoning, or hurt in England or Ireland, or, being criminally stricken, poisoned or otherwise hurt in any place in England or Ireland, shall die of such stroke, poisoning, or hurt upon the sea, or at any place out of England or Ireland, every offence committed in respect of any such case, whether the same shall amount to the offence of murder or of manslaughter,... may be dealt with, inquired of, tried, determined, and punished... in England or Ireland.

In *Lewis* (1857) Dears & B 182, it was held that the predecessor of s. 10 (9 Geo. IV c. 34 s. 8) did not apply to a blow struck out of the jurisdiction by a foreigner which resulted in death within the jurisdiction. Even if *Lewis* were still to be regarded as authoritative, s. 10 would still apply to a foreigner inflicting injury in this country which results in death abroad.

The effect of all the above is that the killing of *anyone* by a British subject anywhere in the world (except, it would seem, in Scotland or Northern Ireland—see M Hirst at [1995] CLJ 488 and the words 'on land out of the United Kingdom' in s. 9) is triable here, and the killing of anyone by an alien is also triable here, if at least the accused's act, even if not the actual death, took place within the jurisdiction. This was succinctly summed up by Lord Thomas CJ in *Adebelajo* at [33] as follows:

> The law is now clear. An offender can generally be tried for murder wherever committed if he is a British subject, or, if not a British subject, the murder was committed within England and Wales.

By way of exception to all this, under the War Crimes Act 1991, certain killings in Germany or German Occupied Territory during the Second World War can be prosecuted in the UK irrespective of the nationality of the accused at the time of the alleged offence (*Sawoniuk* [2000] 2 Cr App R 220, discussed at **F13.35**). (For offences committed on a British ship or aircraft, terrorist offences and jurisdictional questions generally, see **A8**.)

Abolition of Death within a Year and a Day Rule The former limitation that death had to occur within a year and a day of the infliction of injury was abolished, in relation to acts or omissions on or after 17 June 1996, by s. 1 of the Law Reform (Year and a Day Rule) Act 1996. The abolition is 'for all purposes' and thus affects not only murder and manslaughter but also infanticide, encouraging and assisting suicide, a coroner's verdict of suicide and any statutory offences of causing death such as causing death by dangerous driving. **B1.11**

However, by s. 2 of the 1996 Act, the A-G's consent is required before proceedings can be instituted for a 'fatal offence' where either:

(a) the injury alleged to have caused the death was sustained more than three years before the death occurred, or
(b) the person has previously been convicted of an offence committed in circumstances alleged to be connected with the death.

It may be noted that the three-year period is expressed to run from the date that the injury is sustained rather than the date of the accused's act or omission, which may in some cases be earlier.

Malice Aforethought Malice aforethought, the *mens rea* for murder, is now considerably clearer and rather narrower than it has been in the past; the major remaining uncertainty relating to precisely how or when a jury should infer intention from foresight (see **A2.4**), a problem which is not confined to the offence of murder. Contrary to what may be suggested by the ancient term itself, neither ill will nor premeditation is *required*, and malice aforethought is satisfied by either: **B1.12**

(a) an intention to kill; or
(b) an intention to cause grievous bodily harm.

Care must be taken when referring to any cases prior to 1957, since before s. 1 of the Homicide Act of that year, an intention to further any felony was also sufficient (the so-called felony-murder or constructive malice rule). Although it was clear that constructive malice was abolished by that Act, it has taken six House of Lords' decisions, and further statutory intervention, to establish the following propositions:

(a) Murder requires intention, and nothing less (e.g., wicked recklessness as in Scotland) will suffice, i.e. it is a crime requiring specific intent, and, while foresight of virtual certainty may be evidence of intention, it is not to be equated with it (*Moloney* [1985] AC 905, explaining *Hyam v DPP* [1975] AC 55; see further **A2.4**). It is clear following the landmark ruling in *Jogee* [2016] UKSC 8, [2017] AC 387 (see **A4.11**) that the same requirement of intention, and the same distinction between foresight and intent, apply to a person charged as accessory to murder.

(b) Grievous bodily harm should be given its ordinary and natural meaning, i.e. really serious bodily harm (*DPP v Smith* [1961] AC 290), and is not restricted to harm likely to endanger life (*Cunningham* [1982] AC 566). As Lord Edmund-Davies commented in that case (at pp. 582–3), 'I find it passing strange that a person can be convicted of murder if death results from, say, his intentional breaking of another's arm, an action, which, while calling for severe punishment, would in most cases be unlikely to kill'. His lordship went on to recognise, however, that any change in the law on this matter was a task for Parliament. Whilst omission of the word 'really' before 'serious bodily harm' will not necessarily be fatal to a direction (see *Janjua* [1999] 1 Cr App R 91), the use of the full expression 'really serious' is preferable and avoids confusion of the sort that arose in *Sidhu* [1999] EWCA Crim 1034.

(c) Murder, like any other crime requiring proof of intention, involves proof of a subjective state of mind on the part of the accused.

Criminal Justice Act 1967, s. 8

> A court or jury, in determining whether a person has committed an offence,—
> (a) shall not be bound in law to infer that he intended or foresaw a result of his actions by reason only of its being a natural and probable consequence of those actions; but
> (b) shall decide whether he did intend or foresee that result by reference to all the evidence, drawing such inferences from the evidence as appear proper in the circumstances.

(This reversed the effect of *DPP v Smith* [1961] AC 290, which had appeared to lay down an irrebuttable presumption that 'a man intends the natural and probable consequences of his actions', but had subsequently been said by the Privy Council in *Frankland v The Queen* [1987] AC 576 never to have accurately represented the common law of England.)

B1.13 Thus, where an accused, as in *DPP v Smith* itself, does something of which the natural and probable result is death or grievous bodily harm (e.g., as in that case, driving at high speed in an erratic manner with a police officer clinging to the car), the logical processes available to the jury would appear to be as follows:

(a) They may, but do not have to, infer that death or grievous bodily harm was *intended* (CJA 1967, s. 8).

(b) They may, but do not have to, infer that death or grievous bodily harm was *foreseen* (CJA 1967, s. 8) *from which* they may, but do not have to, infer that death or grievous bodily harm was *intended* (*Moloney* [1985] AC 905, *Nedrick* [1986] 3 All ER 1 and *Woollin* [1999] AC 82, and see **A2.4**).

(c) They may, in the light of all the evidence, decide not to draw the inferences in (a) or (b) above, and conclude that the accused lacked the *mens rea* for murder.

The difference between (a) and (b) is that in (a) the inference of intention is made directly, whereas in (b) it is made indirectly via foresight (of a virtual certainty, see *Nedrick* and *Woollin* at **B1.14**). Process (a) seems to be where the jury conclude from all the evidence that D intended death etc., in the sense that it was D's purpose to cause it, and process (b) appears to be where a jury conclude that D intended death etc., even though it was not necessarily D's purpose to cause it.

B1.14 **Direction on Foresight Rarely Needed** It is well established that, normally, there will be no necessity to refer expressly to D's foresight (see *Fallon* [1994] Crim LR 519 for an example of a direction being needlessly complicated and *R (Charles) v CCRC* [2017] EWHC 1219 (Admin), [2017] 2 Cr App R 14 (175) (at [57]) for reiteration of the point that 'save very exceptionally, a judge directing a jury in a case of murder ought not to elaborate on what is meant by intent'). In the words of Lord Lane CJ in *Nedrick* [1986] 3 All ER 1 at pp. 1027–8:

> [The jury] simply has to decide whether the defendant intended to kill or do serious bodily harm. In order to reach that decision the jury must pay regard to all the relevant circumstances, including what the defendant himself said and did.
>
> In the great majority of cases a direction to that effect will be enough, particularly where the defendant's actions amounted to a direct attack upon his victim, because in such cases the evidence relating to the

> defendant's desire or motive will be clear and his intent will have been the same as his desire or motive. But in some cases, of which this is one, the defendant does an act which is manifestly dangerous and as a result someone dies. The primary desire or motive of the defendant may not have been to harm that person, or indeed anyone. In that situation what further directions should a jury be given?...
>
> Where the charge is murder and in the rare cases where the simple direction is not enough, the jury should be directed that they are not entitled to infer the necessary intention, unless they feel sure that death or serious bodily harm was a virtual certainty (barring some unforeseen intervention) as a result of the defendant's actions and that the defendant appreciated that such was the case.

Lord Lane CJ used the words 'virtual certainty', but in *Walker* (1990) 90 Cr App R 226, the Court of Appeal, while obviously preferring this phrase, held that it was not a misdirection to instruct a jury in terms of 'a very high degree of probability'. This was permissible provided that the dividing line between intention and recklessness was not blurred as the House of Lords held had occurred in *Woollin* [1999] AC 82 through reference to foresight of 'a substantial risk'. Lord Steyn emphasised that the *Nedrick* direction was a 'tried and tested formula' which trial judges should continue to use. This was subject to, apparently for the purposes of clarity, the substitution of the words 'to find' for the words 'to infer'.

It is instructive to look at the facts of *Nedrick*, where the appellant poured paraffin through the front door of a house and set it alight, claiming that he wished to frighten the occupant but had no desire to kill or inflict grievous bodily harm. These facts are to all intents and purposes identical with those in *Hyam v DPP* [1975] AC 55, and in each case the death or deaths of child occupants were caused. Whereas the House of Lords in *Hyam v DPP* upheld a conviction for murder based on a direction that equated foresight of a high probability with intent, the same direction was held to be a misdirection in *Nedrick*. The conviction for murder was quashed and a verdict of manslaughter substituted. **B1.15**

Murder is often the initial charge in these types of case but if the jury accept D's evidence of not wanting to cause death or grievous bodily harm, they would only be *entitled* to convict (and even then they would not be *compelled* to do so: see *Scalley* [1995] Crim LR 504 and the final observation of Lord Steyn in *Woollin*) if they felt sure that D foresaw death or grievous bodily harm as a 'virtual certainty'. In *Mathews* [2003] EWCA Crim 192, [2003] 2 Cr App R 30 (461), the Court of Appeal confirmed that there was still a discretion left to the jury as to the inference of intention from foresight of virtual certainty. This discretion was regarded as 'a strength and not a weakness' by the Law Commission in its *Report on Murder, Manslaughter and Infanticide* (Law Com No. 304 at para. 3.27); the Commission succinctly summarised the existing law:

> (1) A person should be taken to intend a result if he or she acts in order to bring it about.
> (2) In cases where the judge believes that justice may not be done unless an expanded understanding of intention is given, the jury should be directed as follows: an intention to bring about a result may be found if it is shown that the defendant thought that the result was a virtually certain consequence of his or her action.

Partial Defences Generally

There are three partial defences to murder—loss of control (replacing the common-law defence of provocation), diminished responsibility, and killing in pursuance of a suicide pact. All three defences reduce the offence from murder to manslaughter rather than leading to an outright acquittal, and the last two are still governed by the Homicide Act 1957 as amended by the CAJA 2009, ss. 52 to 56. Those amendments came into force on 4 October 2010 (SI 2010 No. 816). For offences committed from that date, the common-law defence of provocation (which was also previously partly governed by s. 3 of the 1957 Act) was abolished, s. 3 repealed and provocation replaced by the new purely statutory defence of 'loss of control' (contained in the CAJA 2009, ss. 54 and 55). Diminished responsibility remains a statutory defence contained in the Homicide Act 1957, s. 2, but the amendments under the CAJA 2009 made significant changes to its constituent elements as from 4 October 2010. Killing in pursuance of a suicide pact remains the creation of s. 4 of the 1957 Act, and was not amended by the CAJA 2009. Although **B1.16** for some considerable time after 4 October 2010 some homicide trials will relate to offences alleged to have been committed 'wholly or partly' (see the CAJA 2009, sch. 22, para. 7) before that date, these will be increasingly rare and, where they do arise, reference should be made to the 2013 and earlier editions of this work. The law set out in the remainder of this section is the law applicable to offences committed wholly on or after 4 October 2010, incorporating the changes made by the CAJA 2009.

B1.17 The three partial defences are needed principally because the mandatory life sentence for murder does not leave any discretion to the judge in sentencing whereby account can be taken of mitigating factors, as would normally be the case on lesser charges where the sentence is not fixed by law. There is, however, a view that, even if the mandatory penalty were to be abolished, these defences should be retained as serving 'the valuable function of removing certain specific categories of acts from the stigma attaching to a conviction for murder and of ensuring that the facts were determined after a proper hearing before a jury' (House of Lords Select Committee on Murder and Life Imprisonment 1989, para. 82).

Before turning to the three partial defences in more detail, it should also be noted that the offence of infanticide (see **B1.92** to **B1.101**) also reduces the stigma and introduces discretion as to sentence in relation to what would otherwise be murder. The difference is, however, that infanticide is an independent offence, which can be charged from the outset, whereas manslaughter on the basis of a partial defence such as diminished responsibility arises only by way of defence to an initial charge of murder. Infanticide is, however, an alternative verdict to murder (as, of course, is manslaughter) (see **B1.4**).

The defences of diminished responsibility and loss of control often arise in the context of domestic abuse. The relevance of the theory of coercive control (see **B2.175** for the separate offence of controlling or coercive behaviour) to partial defences to murder was discussed in *Challen* [2019] EWCA Crim 916, a fresh psychiatric evidence appeal from a conviction for murder originally returned in 2011 under the law prior to the CAJA 2009. Hallet LJ commented that 'it is important to remember that coercive control as such is not a defence to murder'. The important issue, however, which led to the quashing of the murder conviction and an order for a retrial (and ultimately an accepted plea of guilty of manslaughter) was that the psychiatric evidence about two potential disorders (borderline personality disorder and severe mood disorder) and the impact on the defendant of an abusive relationship had not been explored at the trial and they may have supported a partial defence of diminished responsibility or (at the time) provocation (now loss of control).

DIMINISHED RESPONSIBILITY

Basis of Defence

B1.18 This defence is purely statutory, having been introduced for the first time into English law (it had long been known to the Scottish courts) by the Homicide Act 1957, s. 2.

Homicide Act 1957, s. 2 (as amended by the CAJA 2009, s. 52)

(1) A person ('D') who kills or is a party to the killing of another is not to be convicted of murder if D was suffering from an abnormality of mental functioning which—
  (a) arose from a recognised medical condition,
  (b) substantially impaired D's ability to do one or more of the things mentioned in subsection (1A), and
  (c) provides an explanation for D's acts and omissions in doing or being a party to the killing.

(1A) Those things are—
  (a) to understand the nature of D's conduct;
  (b) to form a rational judgment;
  (c) to exercise self-control.

(1B) For the purposes of subsection (1)(c), an abnormality of mental functioning provides an explanation for D's conduct if it causes, or is a significant contributory factor in causing, D to carry out that conduct.

(2) On a charge of murder, it shall be for the defence to prove that the person charged is by virtue of this section not liable to be convicted of murder.

(3) A person who but for this section would be liable, whether as principal or as accessory, to be convicted of murder shall be liable instead to be convicted of manslaughter.

(4) The fact that one party to a killing is by virtue of this section not liable to be convicted of murder shall not affect the question whether the killing amounted to murder in the case of any other party to it.

Section 2(1) is the only subsection affected by the CAJA 2009, but it contains the most important definitional provisions. Section 2(2) is unaffected and has always put the burden of proof on the defence, although this burden is only required to be on the balance of probabilities rather than beyond reasonable doubt (*Dunbar* [1958] 1 QB 1, and see generally **F3.9** and **F3.54**). The placing of the burden on the defence does not breach the ECHR, Article 6, and is therefore unaffected by the HRA 1998 (*Lambert* [2001] 1 All ER 1014, confirmed in *Foye* [2013] EWCA Crim 475 where the issue was thoroughly rehearsed and the legal burden was emphatically confirmed as justified and necessary). This was unequivocally confirmed still to be the case following the 2009 Act amendments in *Wilcocks* [2016] EWCA Crim 2043, [2017] 1 Cr App R 23 (338). The prosecution are themselves allowed to allege diminished responsibility where D puts forward a defence of insanity (Criminal Procedure (Insanity) Act 1964, s. 6), and in such a case (which it is difficult to imagine arising very often, but see *Nott* (1958) 43 Cr App R 8) the prosecution must satisfy the normal burden of proof beyond a reasonable doubt.

The defence of diminished responsibility has largely replaced the insanity defence in murder cases. However, it is not available on a charge of attempted murder (*Campbell* [1997] Crim LR 495) nor under the Criminal Procedure (Insanity) Act 1964, s. 4A(2), following a finding of unfitness to plead (*Antoine* [2001] 1 AC 340). The courts have interpreted and applied the defence in a fairly flexible manner to enable it to reduce a wide range of killings, where there are compelling mitigating circumstances, from murder to manslaughter, provided that there was some supporting medical evidence to enable the court to be satisfied of the required ingredients.

Abnormality of Mental Functioning The phrase 'abnormality of mental functioning' replaces the original concept of 'abnormality of mind' (a concept defined in the leading case of *Byrne* [1960] 2 QB 396 as much wider than 'defect of reason' within the M'Naghten Rules (see **A3.28**) and as 'wide enough to cover the mind's activities in all its aspects' (Lord Parker CJ at p. 403)). **B1.19**

The change to 'abnormality of mental functioning' is not intended to have major effects in practice but is part of the attempt to use language and concepts which more accurately or appropriately focus directly on how medical conditions can affect D's control and understanding of D's behaviour and thus to be more susceptible to relevant and coherent medical evidence consistent with up-to-date medical knowledge. Focusing on mental functioning avoids impenetrable philosophical questions about the nature of 'mind' and addresses directly the issue of how normally or abnormally did D's mental processes of function.

The abnormality of mental functioning must have arisen 'from a recognised medical condition'. This is a more substantial change and replaces the rather vague list of permissible causes of the abnormality in the original s. 2(1) with a concept that seems at first sight rather more precise. However, the Court of Appeal in *Dowds* [2012] EWCA Crim 281, [2012] 1 Cr App R 34 (455) ruled that the presence of a recognised medical condition is 'a necessary, but not always sufficient, condition to raise the issue of diminished responsibility'. In particular, the inclusion of 'acute intoxication' and 'alcohol intoxication' as disorders in the international classification systems, ICD-10 and DSM-V respectively, does not alter the previous rule that voluntary intoxication (unclouded by alcoholism or dependence) does not give rise to the defence. The same considerations ruled out a drug-induced psychosis (arising from voluntary drug taking) in *Lindo* [2016] EWCA Crim 1940 (and the possible combination of such a psychosis with a prodromal state was also doubted). Hughes LJ also pointed out (in *Dowds* at [31]) other listed conditions which the courts are likely to be reluctant to recognise as giving rise to an abnormality of mental functioning within the section including 'unhappiness', 'irritability and anger' and 'paedophilia'. In discussing the broader question of temporary or transient conditions, Hughes LJ (at [39]) perhaps gave a clue as to the type of conditions which will qualify:

> ... there may be *genuine mental conditions, in no sense the fault of the defendant and well recognised by doctors*, which although temporary may indeed be within the ambit of the Act. Whether concussion, for example, is such a condition is a question which does not arise for decision in this case. (emphasis added)

Since it is a necessary even if not a sufficient condition, medical evidence will clearly be essential to show that the abnormality arose from a recognised medical condition. The 'practical necessity' that there should be medical evidence adduced by D was emphasised in *Bunch* [2013] EWCA Crim 2498, where it was also stressed that this evidence must be capable of discharging the burden on the accused to show on the balance of probabilities that each ingredient of the defence is made out. Thus, the very limited indirect evidence given of alcohol dependency, even if it could establish that medical condition, provided 'no evidence on which the jury could find that the applicant was suffering from an abnormality of mental functioning which arose from that medical condition and which substantially impaired one of the three capacities mentioned in the Act' (at [10]).

Although the Law Commission recommendations from which the new definition was devised included, in addition to abnormality of mental functioning, 'developmental immaturity' as a permissible alternative or supplementary explanation for the killing (Law Com No. 304, para. 5.125), this was rejected by the government as going too far and is not included in the Act. The view was taken that there was sufficient protection for appropriate cases which would qualify under the heading of a 'recognised medical condition', learning disabilities and autistic spectrum disorders being given as examples that could qualify in this way (Ministry of Justice Response to Consultation CP(R) 19/08, paras. 97 to 103). In *Conroy* [2017] EWCA Crim 81, [2017] 2 Cr App R 26 (371), a case concerning autistic spectrum disorder, Davis LJ (at [37]) warned against unduly glossing the elements of the Homicide Act 1957, s. 2, in summing up to the jury: 'in the context of assessing [the] ability to form a rational judgment, it is likely to be over-refined to divorce... a defendant's thinking processes from the actual outcome'. However (at [32]) he also said that 'the jury may properly assess all relevant circumstances preceding, and perhaps preceding over a very long period, the killing as well as any relevant circumstances following the killing'. Thus, the assessment could in an appropriate case 'involve an appraisal of the impact of any abnormality of mental functioning both on a defendant's decision-making generally and also on the particular decision to kill the victim specifically'.

Davis LJ also made similar remarks, in a case concerning paranoid personality disorder, about the relevance of periods of time 'going back over many years and even sometimes to a particular defendant's childhood' (*Squelch* [2017] EWCA Crim 204 at [44]).

B1.20 **Substantial Impairment** Notwithstanding the retention of the word 'responsibility' in the title of the defence, the thing to be substantially impaired is no longer explicitly (and somewhat obscurely) stated as D's 'mental responsibility' but instead it is D's 'ability' to do one or more of the things listed in s. 2(1A) (which to a large extent echo Lord Parker's explication of abnormality of mind under the old law in *Parker* [1960] 2 QB 396), i.e. the ability to understand the nature of D's conduct, to form a rational judgement, to exercise self-control.

Medical evidence continues to be highly relevant (a 'practical necessity'—see *Bunch* [2013] EWCA Crim 2498 at **B1.19**) as to whether D's ability to do these things was or could have been impaired by D's abnormality of mental functioning, and medical witnesses do no doubt feel more comfortable testifying directly about such matters rather than relating their evidence to the non-medical concept of responsibility. However, whilst the question of whether and to what extent such abilities actually were impaired may be a medical question on which the medical evidence may in most cases be effectively determinative, the evaluation of whether a particular degree of impairment should be characterised as sufficiently 'substantial' to enable the defence to succeed is still ultimately a question of fact and degree for the jury. In *Golds* [2016] UKSC 61, [2017] 1 Cr App R 18 (273), a number of earlier cases on the meaning of the word substantial were reviewed. The Supreme Court, in dismissing the appeal, held (at [27]) that 'substantial' did not have the narrow meaning simply of 'having some substance' or 'anything more than merely trivial' but rather required something 'important or weighty'. As Lord Hughes put it (at [36]), 'it is appropriate, as it always has been, for the reduction to the lesser offence to be occasioned where there is a weighty reason for it and not merely a reason which just passes the trivial'. It was, however, not normally appropriate to try to define the concept for the jury. His lordship provided guidance (at [43]) in answering the certified questions as follows:

1. Ordinarily in a murder trial where diminished responsibility is in issue the judge need not direct the jury beyond the terms of the statute and should not attempt to define the meaning of 'substantially'. Experience has shown that the issue of its correct interpretation is unlikely to arise in many cases. The jury should normally be given to understand that the expression is an ordinary English word, that it imports a question of degree, and that whether in the case before it the impairment can properly be described as substantial is for it to resolve.
2. If, however, the jury has been introduced to the question of whether any impairment beyond the merely trivial will suffice, or if it has been introduced to the concept of a spectrum between the greater than trivial and the total, the judge should explain that whilst the impairment must indeed pass the merely trivial before it need be considered, it is not the law that any impairment beyond the trivial will suffice. The judge should likewise make this clear if a risk arises that the jury might misunderstand the import of the expression; whether this risk arises or not is a judgment to be arrived at by the trial judge who is charged with overseeing the dynamics of the trial ... Illustrative expressions of the sense of the word may be employed so long as the jury is given clearly to understand that no single synonym is to be substituted for the statutory word...

Lord Hughes also commented on *Brennan* [2014] EWCA Crim 2387, [2015] 1 Cr App R 14 (161), in which the Court of Appeal had said that the charge of murder should not have been put to the jury where the partial defence of diminished responsibility was unequivocally supported by reputable expert evidence which is not contradicted by any prosecution expert evidence. While not disapproving of the result in *Brennan*, his lordship advised caution in withdrawing the defence from the jury at the close of evidence. Amongst the reasons for this was the burden of proof, since (at [50]–[51]):

> The *Galbraith* process is generally a conclusion that no jury, properly directed, could be satisfied that the Crown has proved the relevant offence so that it is sure. In the context of diminished responsibility, murder can only be withdrawn from the jury if the judge is satisfied that no jury could fail to find that the defendant has proved it... a finding of diminished responsibility is not a single-issue matter; it requires the defendant to prove that the answer to each of the four questions ... is 'yes'...
>
> Where, however, in a diminished responsibility trial the medical evidence supports the plea and is uncontradicted, the judge needs to ensure that the Crown explains the basis on which it is inviting the jury to reject that evidence. He needs to ensure that the basis advanced is one which the jury can properly adopt... [The trial judge] needs to make it clear to the jury that, if there is a proper basis for rejecting the expert evidence, the decision is theirs—that trial is by jury and not by expert—it will also ordinarily be wise to advise the jury against attempting to make themselves amateur psychiatrists, and that if there is undisputed expert evidence the jury will probably wish to accept it, unless there is some identified reason for not doing so. To this extent, the approach of the court in *Brennan* is to be endorsed.

In *Blackman* [2017] EWCA Crim 190, a strongly constituted Court Martial Appeal Court (sitting as a panel of five including Lord Thomas CJ) summarised the position following *Brennan* and *Golds* as follows (at [43]):

> ... it will be a rare case where the judge will exercise the power to withdraw a charge of murder from the jury when the prosecution do not accept that the evidence gives rise to the defence of diminished responsibility.

The Court went on to say (at [45]) that the case in front of it was 'clearly not one of those rare cases where we should simply follow the views of the psychiatrists, even though they are agreed and are highly persuasive. The prosecution is plainly entitled to put its case that the partial defence did not arise.' A similar approach was taken in *Hussain* [2019] EWCA Crim 666 where the Court reiterated that it was not the law that a trial judge should withdraw a charge of murder from the jury simply on the basis that the medical evidence points one way.

B1.21 **Providing an Explanation for Acts and Omissions** Under the old law, the issue of 'substantial impairment' provided the main focus for the evaluative question which ultimately the jury had to decide. The new definition appears to add, in s. 2(1)(c), another evaluative component: whether the abnormality 'provides an explanation for D's acts and omissions in doing or being a party to the killing'. This phrase originates with the Law Commission which referred to an 'appropriate connection' between the abnormality and the killing (Law Com No. 304, para. 5.124) in terms of 'mitigation' rather than committing itself to a potentially problematic requirement of strict causation. However, the government was insistent that there must be an explicit causal requirement and thus s. 2(1B) was added to spell out that an abnormality of mental functioning provides an explanation within s. 2(1)(c) 'if it causes, or is a significant contributory factor in causing, D to carry out' the offence. Whether s. 2(1B) achieves its desired effect may be questioned since it could be interpreted as simply giving a common, or the most common, illustration of where the abnormality will provide an explanation but does not exclude other cases where the abnormality should be regarded as fulfilling an explanatory and mitigatory role even though it may not be possible to prove even a contributory causal effect. After all, s. 2(1B) does not say 'if, but only if' and, if it was to be read in that way, why have the primary concept of providing 'an explanation' in s. 2(1)(c) in the first place if it is to be exhaustively defined in s. 2(1B) as requiring causation? If that was the intention, it would have been perfectly possible, and simpler and clearer, to insert the causal requirement directly into s. 2(1)(c) without using the misleading mediating concept of 'provides an explanation'.

B1.22 Whether s. 2(1B) is treated as a partial or exhaustive definition of providing 'an explanation', it is clear that it does not require the abnormality to be the sole cause of the killing; it can be a contributory cause, although this must be a significant rather than trivial contribution. How one measures and proves the degree of causation of human behaviour may well throw up some difficulties but no doubt these will be matters for the jury to evaluate. It is in this context that the difficulties the courts experienced under the old law, relating to the influence of alcohol and drugs (*Dietschmann* [2003] UKHL 10, [2003] 1 AC 1209) and how to deal with conditions such as alcohol dependency syndrome (*Tandy* [1989] 1 All ER 267; *Wood* [2008] EWCA Crim 1305, [2008] 2 Cr App R 34 (507); *Stewart* [2009] EWCA Crim 593, [2009] 2 Cr App R 30 (500)), are likely to resurface. Indeed, in *Kay* [2017] EWCA Crim 647, [2017] 2 Cr App R 16 (201), the Court of Appeal approved of the continued application of the approach in *Stewart* and the previous cases. This approach was confirmed and applied in *Foy* [2020] EWCA Crim 270, where the defence was found to be unavailable on the facts, even if an application to adduce new evidence were to have been granted (which it was not). The fresh psychiatric evidence was not capable of giving rise to a viable defence on the balance of probabilities as it was not capable, 'excluding the involvement of the voluntarily ingested alcohol and cocaine', of establishing the required 'abnormality of mental functioning arising from a recognised medical condition which *substantially* impaired the appellant's ability in the relevant respects and which provided an *explanation* (in the sense of the statute) for his acts' (at [95]). It is submitted that the relevant questions therefore continue to include the following:

(1) What abnormality of mental functioning arose from the recognised medical condition (i.e. not from other causes such as voluntary intoxication)?

(2) Did *that* abnormality of mental functioning substantially impair D's ability to do the things mentioned in s. 2(1A)?

(3) Did *that* abnormality of mental functioning provide an explanation for D's acts and omissions in doing or being a party to the killing as required by s. 2(1)(c)?

In relation to question (3), the fact that D may not have killed had D not been drunk should not automatically deprive D of the defence if the abnormality could also have influenced the decision to do the acts or omissions constituting the offence. On the other hand, if D would still have killed anyway, even without the abnormality of mental functioning, the exhaustive interpretation of s. 2(1B) would say that (there being no significant contributory cause, according to the Ministry of Justice Response to Consultation) there would be no defence. The partial definition interpretation of s. 2(1B), on the other hand, would say that there is still a question to be asked as to whether the abnormality provides a satisfactory (mitigatory) explanation other than a causal one (which is perhaps most likely to be relevant where the ability substantially impaired under s. 2(1A) was D's ability to form a rational judgement rather than to exercise self-control).

Accepting Plea of Diminished Responsibility

B1.23 It has already been noted that one cannot initially charge manslaughter on the basis of diminished responsibility, and so D has to be indicted for murder no matter how clearly D appears to come within the terms of the Homicide Act 1957, s. 2(1). In a large number of cases the prosecution have been able to accept a plea of manslaughter to an indictment for murder. In *Cox* [1968] 1 All ER 386, Winn LJ said (at p. 310):

> ... that there are cases where, on an indictment for murder, it is perfectly proper, where the medical evidence is plainly to this effect, to treat the case as one of substantially diminished responsibility and accept, if it be tendered, a plea to manslaughter on that ground, and avoid a trial for murder.

Notwithstanding the discussion in *Brennan* [2014] EWCA Crim 2387, [2015] 1 Cr App R 14 (161) and *Golds* [2016] UKSC 61, [2017] 1 Cr App R 18 (273) (see **B1.20**) about the rare occasions justifying withdrawing a murder charge from the jury during the trial (where the prosecution are opposed to that course), if the prosecution are willing to accept a plea of manslaughter at the outset, that quite common practice is still clearly justified under the defence as now formulated, provided it is clear that all the elements of the defence of diminished responsibility are unequivocally supported by uncontradicted reputable expert evidence.

However, it will still be necessary to remember that, as the Court of Appeal in *Vinagre* (1979) 69 Cr App R 104 warned (in the context of the acceptance of a plea based on the 'Othello syndrome'):

> ... it was never intended that pleas should be accepted on flimsy grounds [but only] when there is clear evidence of mental imbalance. We do not consider that in this case there was clear evidence of mental imbalance. There was clear evidence of killing by a jealous husband which, until modern times, no one would have thought was anything else but murder. (per Lawton LJ, at pp. 106–7)

Thus, in a novel or borderline sort of case, the plea ought not to be accepted but the evidence presented to a jury for their determination. The public interest may demand this in a notorious case such as that of the 'Yorkshire Ripper' (*The Times*, 23 May 1981). This was a striking case, in the sense that the prosecution were prepared to accept the plea in the light of unanimous psychiatric reports that the accused, Sutcliffe, was a paranoid schizophrenic, but the judge insisted that there should be a trial before a jury who convicted of murder. The nub of the problem is that, as emphasised in *Golds*, however unanimous the medical witnesses may be about there being an abnormality of mental functioning, whether that abnormality '*substantially* impaired D's ability' within the meaning of s. 2(1)(b) and provided an explanation for the killing within s. 2(1)(c) are ultimately questions for the jury to determine in the light of the medical evidence (and any other evidence) actually given. Thus, as a general rule, the prosecution should accept a plea (and the judge should approve that acceptance) only where there is clear and persuasive evidence of each of the required elements of diminished responsibility. Lord Hughes in *Golds* (at [48]) acknowledged the frequency and propriety of accepting a plea to manslaughter in these circumstances, just as he had previously observed in *Robinson v State (Trinidad and Tobago)* [2015] UKPC 34 (at [29]) that there are very many cases in practice where it is appropriate to accept a plea, though he also noted that it:

> ... remains of great importance that pleas are accepted only in cases where it is proper to do so. Generally that means cases where there is no significant material dispute either of underlying fact or of medical analysis, and moreover it is clear that the defendant's mental responsibility for the killing can properly be described as substantially impaired.

In *Blackman* [2017] EWCA Crim 190 the Court Martial Appeal Court noted (at [79]) Lord Hughes' dictum in *Robinson* that decisions about accepting pleas are 'facilitated by the usually ready availability of full medical reports from experienced forensic psychiatrists' and commented that 'it is the experience of members of this court that in cases before the ordinary courts, the routine practice of the prosecution in obtaining reports is no longer followed... [which] is particularly unfortunate in any case involving conduct which is entirely inconsistent with the prior character and conduct of the defendant'.

LOSS OF CONTROL

B1.24 The statutory partial defence of loss of control, created by the CAJA 2009, ss. 54 and 55, came into force on 4 October 2010 (SI 2010 No. 816). Section 56 abolished the common-law defence of provocation in relation to killings from that date. The Court of Appeal has stressed on a number of occasions, most emphatically in *Gurpinar* [2015] EWCA Crim 178, [2015] 1 Cr App R 31 (464), that it 'should rarely be necessary to look at cases decided under the old law of provocation. When it is necessary, the cases must be considered in the light of the fact that the defence of loss of control is a defence different to provocation and is fully encompassed within the statutory provisions.'

Coroners and Justice Act 2009, ss. 54 and 55

54.—(1) Where a person ('D') kills or is a party to the killing of another ('V'), D is not to be convicted of murder if—
(a) D's acts and omissions in doing or being a party to the killing resulted from D's loss of self-control,
(b) the loss of self-control had a qualifying trigger, and
(c) a person of D's sex and age, with a normal degree of tolerance and self-restraint and in the circumstances of D, might have reacted in the same or in a similar way to D.

(2) For the purposes of subsection (1)(a), it does not matter whether or not the loss of control was sudden.

(3) In subsection (1)(c) the reference to 'the circumstances of D' is a reference to all of D's circumstances other than those whose only relevance to D's conduct is that they bear on D's general capacity for tolerance or self-restraint.

(4) Subsection (1) does not apply if, in doing or being a party to the killing, D acted in a considered desire for revenge.

(5) On a charge of murder, if sufficient evidence is adduced to raise an issue with respect to the defence under subsection (1), the jury must assume that the defence is satisfied unless the prosecution proves beyond reasonable doubt that it is not.

(6) For the purposes of subsection (5), sufficient evidence is adduced to raise an issue with respect to the defence if evidence is adduced on which, in the opinion of the trial judge, a jury, properly directed, could reasonably conclude that the defence might apply.

(7) A person who, but for this section, would be liable to be convicted of murder is liable instead to be convicted of manslaughter.

(8) The fact that one party to a killing is by virtue of this section not liable to be convicted of murder does not affect the question whether the killing amounted to murder in the case of any other party to it.

55.—(1) This section applies for the purposes of section 54.
(2) A loss of self-control had a qualifying trigger if subsection (3), (4) or (5) applies.
(3) This subsection applies if D's loss of self-control was attributable to D's fear of serious violence from V against D or another identified person.
(4) This subsection applies if D's loss of self-control was attributable to a thing or things done or said (or both) which—
(a) constituted circumstances of an extremely grave character, and
(b) caused D to have a justifiable sense of being seriously wronged.
(5) This subsection applies if D's loss of self-control was attributable to a combination of the matters mentioned in subsections (3) and (4).
(6) In determining whether a loss of self-control had a qualifying trigger—
(a) D's fear of serious violence is to be disregarded to the extent that it was caused by a thing which D incited to be done or said for the purpose of providing an excuse to use violence;
(b) a sense of being seriously wronged by a thing done or said is not justifiable if D incited the thing to be done or said for the purpose of providing an excuse to use violence;
(c) the fact that a thing done or said constituted sexual infidelity is to be disregarded.
(7) In this section references to 'D' and 'V' are to be construed in accordance with section 54.

The Elements of the Defence

Killing Resulting from Loss of Self-control The first of the three requirements for the defence under s. 54(1) is that 'the killing resulted from D's loss of self-control'. This apparently simple but rather elusive requirement can be thought of as analogous to the subjective condition in the old law of provocation but of course there are differences. In particular, s. 54(2) provides that the loss of self-control need not be sudden, a limitation which the common law of provocation had not quite managed formally to shed even though, certainly since *Ahluwalia* [1992] 4 All ER 889, it had been effectively recognised that 'sudden' did not necessarily connote 'immediately' and that a delayed but sudden reaction could come within the defence. Nevertheless, the formal removal of the suddenness requirement should be a further step in opening up the defence to the victims of domestic violence and abuse in relation to whose delayed reactions the requirement of suddenness under the old law could seem a problematic or inhibitory factor. The legitimate concern that underlay the requirement of suddenness was that partial defences should not apply to killings motivated by revenge and s. 54(4) goes directly to this point by excluding from the defence cases where D 'acted in a considered desire for revenge'. In *Clinton* [2012] EWCA Crim 2, [2013] QB 1 Lord Judge CJ (at [128]) approved a direction which included the statement that 'a considered act of revenge, whether performed calmly or in anger, is not a loss of self control'. There is a danger that the effect of this may be to diminish the impact of the removal of 'suddenness' insofar as a delayed but angry reaction is treated as considered revenge and not loss of control. See also *Jewell* [2014] EWCA Crim 414, where the trial judge was found to be correct not to have left the defence to the jury in a case described by the Court of Appeal as a 'planned execution'. *Nixon* [2020] EWCA Crim 336 also shows that acting in anger is not of itself sufficient to establish loss of self-control. The Court of Appeal refused leave to appeal and agreed that D 'may well have lost his temper and reacted aggressively to what may well have been violence from the deceased, but that is a long way from evidence that he had lost his self-control' (evidence of which was singularly lacking on the facts). The meaning of loss of self-control was also discussed in *Gurpinar* [2015] EWCA Crim 178, [2015] 1 Cr App R 31 (464) at [18]–[21] where a number of questions were canvassed, including 'whether the loss of self-control had to be a total loss or whether some loss of self-control was sufficient'. The Court of Appeal found it unnecessary to resolve these issues which it observed were fact-sensitive and not required to be decided on the particular facts of the cases under consideration. B1.25

Qualifying Triggers The new statutory defence differs from the previous common law in that the broad concept of 'provocation' (which was thought too readily to indulge predominantly male 'anger') is abandoned in favour of more specifically limited 'qualifying triggers' for loss of control. The trigger which most closely relates to the former defence of provocation B1.26

(in the CAJA 2009, s. 55(4), 'attributable to a thing or things done or said') is designed to be *much* more limited in also requiring both 'circumstances of an extremely grave character' and the causing of 'a justifiable sense of being seriously wronged'. See *Dawes* [2013] EWCA Crim 322, [2013] 2 Cr App R 3 (24) for examples (in the cases of appellants Hatter and Bowyer) of situations which clearly do not satisfy the new more stringent trigger and see also *Meanza* [2017] EWCA Crim 445 where emphasis was placed on the word 'justifiable'. These essentially objective limitations indicate a shift in philosophy from what might primarily have been seen as one of 'partial excuse' underpinning the defence of provocation to the new defence being primarily based on 'partial justification'. Similarly, the other qualifying trigger (s. 55(3)), 'fear of serious violence from V', is clearly related to the justificatory defence of self-defence but is only a partial justification because D has not acted proportionately and has lost control and has, implicitly, used excessive force. This qualifying trigger, in contrast to the 'things done or said' trigger, does of course broaden the scope of the available partial defences to murder. It is in particular designed to accommodate more readily the dilemma faced by those, most typically women afraid of a violent partner (often as the result of violent and abusive conduct over an extended period of time), for whom the sudden and temporary requirement of the common law of provocation had frequently been a stumbling block. Furthermore, s. 55(5) makes it clear that D can rely on a combination of the two triggers as causing D's loss of self-control.

B1.27 The partially justificatory aspect of the qualifying triggers is also evident in s. 55(6)(c) providing that the fact that 'a thing said or done constituted sexual infidelity' is to be disregarded when determining whether a loss of self-control has a qualifying trigger. The inclusion of this sub-paragraph was insisted upon by the government, despite attempts in Parliament to remove it, as being necessary to ensure that violent men could no longer hope to rely on sexual infidelity as a ground for a partial defence to murder. It was acknowledged that the thing 'said or done' may still be relevant to whether there is a qualifying trigger for reasons other than its character as sexual infidelity. Thus, for example, finding one's partner having incestuous sex or having sex with a minor might still be capable of being a qualifying trigger not because it constitutes sexual infidelity but because of the nature of the sexual activity involved. The 'formidable' difficulties of interpretation of s. 55(6)(c) were extensively discussed by Lord Judge CJ in *Clinton* [2012] EWCA Crim 2, [2013] QB 1, where the prohibition on having regard to sexual infidelity was held to apply only where sexual infidelity is the sole potential qualifying trigger. Where, however, as will often be the case, there are other matters which may potentially give rise to a qualifying trigger (e.g., as was the case in *Clinton*, the taunting of D as to his lack of courage to commit the suicide which he had contemplated) and sexual infidelity is integral to and forms an essential part of the context in which to make a just evaluation of whether those other matters are grave or serious enough to constitute a qualifying trigger, the sexual infidelity is not excluded. As to the precise meaning of sexual infidelity in terms of 'things done', it was acknowledged that there will be difficult cases at the margins in terms of what counts as infidelity (how long or strong does a relationship have to be before one can be unfaithful in it) and in terms of what sort of conduct is sufficiently 'sexual'. However, it was clarified (at [26]) that things 'said' constituting sexual infidelity include 'admissions of sexual infidelity (even if untrue) as well as reports (by others) of sexual infidelity'.

Section 55(6)(a) and (b) further limit the scope of the triggers and together have the effect of excluding from the ambit of either trigger, things 'incited…for the purpose of providing an excuse to use violence'. The new statutory limitation applies only where D acts for the 'purpose' of providing an excuse as opposed to situations where D's blameworthy conduct has in fact prompted the provocation even though that was not D's purpose. See *Dawes* [2013] EWCA *Crim 322, [2013] 2 Cr App R 3 (24)*, where the Court of Appeal found that there was not sufficient evidence of such 'purpose'; the judge was therefore wrong to withdraw the defence from the jury on this ground (s. 55(6)(a) or (b)).

Normal Degree of Tolerance and Self-restraint Section 54(1)(c) of the CAJA 2009 addresses the question previously characterised in the common law as the objective question of how the reasonable person would have reacted, although it is in truth a mixture of subjective and objective considerations. It is similarly subjective as the former test laid down in the cases of *DPP v Camplin* [1978] AC 705 and *A-G for Jersey v Holley* [2005] UKPC 23, [2005] 2 AC 580 in that it concerns how a person of the age and sex of D would react and is similarly objective insofar as it assumes the 'normal degree of tolerance and self-restraint' of a person of that age and sex. Like the *Camplin/Holley* test it also recognises a further limited subjective aspect but it is formulated quite differently. Instead of asking whether D's characteristics would affect the gravity of the trigger for the loss of self-control (formerly the gravity of the provocation question), the statute now directs attention specifically to how a person (of normal tolerance and self-restraint) '*in the circumstances of D*' might have reacted. This may potentially open up a broader range of subjective considerations than under the *Camplin/Holley* test, notwithstanding that, rather like the old law, s. 54(3) effectively excludes circumstances 'whose only relevance to D's conduct is that they bear on D's general capacity for tolerance or self-restraint'. The difference is, however, that, while roughly the same sorts of things are *excluded*, there is now no positive requirement that, to be *included*, D's individual circumstances must affect the gravity of the triggering conduct. Instead, all D's circumstances are included, provided that they are not only relevant as bearing on D's general capacity for tolerance or self-restraint. Although this may be thought to be a somewhat subtle change, it is a sensible and desirable one in that juries were often baffled by the gravity of the provocation/powers of self-control dichotomy. It is more straightforward to take into account D's circumstances (such as having been the victim of a long-term abusive relationship), even though it was in principle possible to bring this in as a factor affecting the gravity of the provocation. It is no longer explicitly necessary to make this connection with gravity (although in practice the vast majority of admissible circumstances will be those which do in fact have relevance to the gravity of the qualifying trigger). B1.28

The application of the CAJA 2009, s. 54(3), to personality disorders was one of the issues in *Wilcocks* [2016] EWCA Crim 2043, [2017] 1 Cr App R 23 (338) where the Court of Appeal approved the following direction (at [40]) on the question of whether a disorder should be included 'in the circumstances of D':

> ... a personality disorder which made him unusually likely to become angry and aggressive at the slightest provocation, that would of course be relevant to diminished responsibility but it could not assist him in relation to loss of control. But if you thought that a personality disorder had caused him to attempt suicide, then you would have been entitled to take into account as one of his circumstances the effect on him of being taunted that he should have killed himself.

In *Rejmanski* [2017] EWCA Crim 2061, [2018] 1 Cr App R 18 (267), post-traumatic stress disorder attributable to military service in Afghanistan was found to not 'only' have relevance as bearing on the capacity for tolerance or self-restraint, because it also affected the gravity of the qualifying trigger which consisted of taunts about that service. It was not therefore excluded by s. 54(3). However, the Court of Appeal stressed that the fact that the post-traumatic stress disorder was included in the circumstances of D within s. 54(1)(c) (in terms of the impact of the taunts on him) did not mean that, having been let in, it could then also be taken into account in relation to the degree of tolerance and self-restraint expected. Hallet LJ emphasised (at [25]) that although mental disorders may form part of 'the circumstances of D' in the CAJA 2009, s. 54(1)(c), they cannot be used to reduce the normal degree of tolerance and self-restraint to be expected:

> ... the wording of s. 54(1)(c) is clear: ... the defendant is to be judged against the standard of a person with a normal degree, and not an abnormal degree, of tolerance and self-restraint. If, and in so far as, a personality disorder reduced the defendant's general capacity for tolerance or self-restraint, that would not be a relevant consideration.

In contrast to the appeal of *Rejmanski*, the conjoined appeal of *Gassman* [2017] EWCA Crim 2061, [2018] 1 Cr App R 18 (267) provides an illustration of a disorder (emotionally unstable personality disorder) which on the facts *was* regarded as *only* having relevance as bearing on D's general capacity for tolerance or self-restraint and which was thus excluded by s. 54(3) from 'the circumstances of D'. The Court also rejected the 'ingenious' argument that an effect on D's ability to exercise tolerance or self-restraint on a particular day could be distinguished from the effect on D's *general* capacity for tolerance or self-restraint. The trial judge had therefore correctly told the jury not to take the disorder into account at all in relation to the s. 54(1)(c) question. The effect of *Rejmanksi* and *Gassman* together seems to be that the safest course will be for all D's arguably relevant circumstances (except those such as emotionally unstable personality disorder which are taken *only* to bear on the general capacity for tolerance or self-restraint) to be put before the jury who should be told to take account of them in so far as they are relevant (i) in assessing gravity in relation to the qualifying trigger under s. 55(4), and also (ii) under s. 54(1)(c) in relation to the question of how a person of normal tolerance and self-restraint might have reacted in those (grave) circumstances, but (iii) not in relation to the question of the degree of tolerance and self-restraint expected of that normal person, as to which latter prohibition the judge should specifically instruct the jury.

B1.29 **Significance of the Concept of Tolerance** The presence of the word 'or' after 'tolerance' is important in the CAJA 2009, s. 54(3). It shows that tolerance is a distinct concept from self-restraint (contrast the word 'and' in s. 54(1)(c) which confirms nevertheless that both qualities are required). Self-restraint is very similar to the old concept of self-control in the abolished provocation defence but 'tolerance' is now added as a separate, additional component of the objective criterion. Tolerance is also apt to exclude those who are bigoted or prejudiced against individuals from minority, vulnerable or protected groups in society or who are unacceptably intolerant in other ways, e.g., because of unacceptable attitudes such as those underpinning so-called 'honour killings' or because of excessive jealousy or sexual possessiveness. The term 'tolerance' can thus be seen to be relevant to Lord Hoffmann's concern (under the old law) in *Smith (Morgan)* [2001] 1 AC 146 at p. 169 that 'male possessiveness and jealousy should not today be an acceptable reason for loss of self-control leading to homicide'. In *Clinton* [2012] EWCA Crim 2, [2013] QB 1, the Court of Appeal ruled that the restriction on the relevance of sexual infidelity in s. 55(6) in relation to it being a qualifying trigger does not restrict the meaning of 'the circumstances of D' in s. 54(3) and that sexual infidelity can be taken into account in deciding whether a person with an ordinary degree of tolerance and self-restraint might have reacted in a similar way. The effect would seem to be that the jury will have to weigh the impact of the sexual infidelity (and other triggering conduct) against the ordinary degree of tolerance (and the ordinary degree of self-restraint) which they would expect to be shown and make a judgement. This seems a more nuanced and appropriate way of dealing with sexual infidelity, insisting on an ordinary degree of 'tolerance' from the accused in the face of it, rather than artificially insisting that it should be ignored altogether. It also should be remembered that the question of what a person with an ordinary degree of tolerance and self-restraint might have done, in the case of the things 'done or said' trigger, does not really arise unless there is evidence that those things done or said satisfied the test of being 'extremely grave' and caused a 'justifiable sense of being seriously wronged'. In other words, and this applies whether or not sexual infidelity is involved, there is quite a high objective test to be surmounted in the test for the qualifying trigger in s. 55(4) before one gets on to the objective aspects of the test of tolerance and self-restraint under s. 54(1)(c).

B1.30 **Intoxication** Although the Act does not specifically mention intoxication, it was always likely, given the general approach to intoxication in defences, as exemplified in *Dowds* [2012] EWCA Crim 281, [2012] 1 Cr App R 34 (455) in relation to diminished responsibility, that the effects of voluntary intoxication would not be found to be relevant to the question of whether the person of normal tolerance and self-restraint might have reacted in a similar way to D. In *Asmelash* [2013] EWCA Crim 157, [2014] QB 103 the Court of Appeal, not unexpectedly, confirmed that, in considering the question under s. 54(1)(c) of whether 'a person of D's sex and age, with a normal degree of tolerance and self-restraint and in the circumstances of D, might have reacted in the same or similar way to D', the fact that D had voluntarily consumed alcohol was not to be included in D's circumstances. Lord Judge CJ upheld the following direction from the trial judge: 'Are you sure that a person of [D's] sex and age with a normal degree of tolerance and self-restraint and in the same circumstances, *but unaffected by alcohol*, would not have reacted in the same or similar way?' (emphasis added). His lordship went on to point out (at [25]) that this:

> ...does not mean that the defendant who has been drinking is deprived of any possible loss of control defence...If a sober individual in the defendant's circumstances, with normal levels of tolerance and self-restraint might have behaved in the same way as the defendant confronted by the relevant qualifying trigger, he would not be deprived of the loss of control defence just because he was not sober.

It was also acknowledged that different considerations would apply to the quite different situation of a person mercilessly taunted about a severe alcohol or drug problem which would then form part of the circumstances. The decision about the irrelevance of the voluntary intoxication has also to be read in the light of the fact that it was not suggested in this case that D's intoxication:

> ...caused him to be mistaken about anything that was going on at the relevant time, or about what he was doing. Accordingly, the only relevance of the drunkenness was that it affected the appellant's self-restraint and caused him to act in a way in which he would not have acted if sober (at [19]).

The fact that *Asmelash* was not a case of intoxicated mistake and was purely about intoxication affecting self-restraint may be important. Insofar as intoxication simply diminishes D's tolerance or self-restraint, it is clearly excluded anyway by s. 54(3). However, s. 54(3) only excludes a circumstance if that is its 'only' relevance; so if D can point to some other relevance of the intoxication to D's conduct (e.g., that it caused a relevant mistake), D might be able to bring it into consideration, although it is difficult to envisage how this would add much to the defences already available such as lack of specific intent. If the mistake was one whereby D exaggerated the nature of the triggering conduct, the issue might then be whether there is in fact a qualifying trigger in the first place and the extent to which a mistaken belief, drunken or otherwise, in the existence of a trigger can give rise to a defence under the statute. In relation to the 'things done or said' trigger, the requirement of a justifiable sense of being seriously wronged might be used to counter any such argument but, in relation to the other trigger, D's fear of serious violence seems to be a subjective matter which would in principle have to take account of D's mistaken view of the facts, just as with self-defence. However, this analogy might also suggest that no account will be taken of such mistakes due to intoxication notwithstanding that murder is a crime of specific intent (*Hatton* [2005] EWCA Crim 2951, [2006] 1 Cr App R 16 (247), discussed at **A3.61**). **B1.31**

Burden of Proof and Role of Jury

As under the previous defence of provocation, once there is evidence capable of supporting the defence, the burden of disproving it rests with the prosecution to the usual standard of beyond reasonable doubt. The CAJA 2009, s. 54(5), refers to 'sufficient evidence...to raise an issue with respect to the defence'. This is then explained in s. 54(6) as being sufficient evidence 'on which, in the opinion of the trial judge, a jury, properly directed, could reasonably conclude that the defence might apply'. This clearly means that there must be sufficient evidence to raise an issue as to each of the three elements of the defence as defined in s. 54(1). This was the approach adopted in *Gurpinar* [2015] EWCA Crim 178, [2015] 1 Cr App R 31 (464) where it was made clear that, if there is not 'sufficient' evidence on **B1.32** any one of the three elements, the defence should not be put to the jury. This approach was also applied in *McDonald* [2016] EWCA Crim 1529 where the trial judge was held to have been entitled to withdraw the defence from the jury on the basis that while the first element of the defence, actual loss of control, might legitimately be accepted by the jury, there was not a sufficient evidential basis for the second and third elements. The circumstances were not of an extremely grave character or ones which could give rise to a justifiable sense of being seriously wronged and a jury could also not reasonably conclude that a person of the appellant's age and sex with a normal degree of tolerance and self-restraint might have reacted in a similar way. Conversely, in *Martin* [2017] EWCA Crim 1359 (where the appellant relied on self-defence) the trial judge was found to have rightly not put the defence of loss of control to the jury because there was not a sufficient evidential basis for the first element, i.e. that D had suffered a loss of control. The point was made that 'the fact that there may, on the evidence, be a qualifying trigger does not necessarily indicate that a loss of control had thereby been caused' (at [44]). It does, however, continue to be incumbent on the trial judge to leave the defence to the jury where the evidence given in the case *is* capable of satisfying the test in s. 54(6) even if the defence have not for tactical or other reasons themselves sought to rely on loss of control as a defence. That this approach continues to be the correct one was confirmed by Lord Judge CJ in *Dawes* [2013] EWCA Crim 322, [2013] 2 Cr App R 3 (24) at [53] in the course of a wide-ranging judgment commenting on a number of aspects of the defence and again by Lord Thomas CJ in *Gurpinar*. In the latter case his lordship commented (at [15]) that:

> . . . a judge must be assisted by the advocates. It is generally desirable that the possibility of such an issue arising should be notified to the judge as early as possible in the management of the case, even though it may not form part of the defence case. If, at the conclusion of the evidence, there is a possibility that the judge should leave the issue to the jury when it is not part of the defence case, the judge must receive written submissions from the advocates so that he can carefully consider whether the evidence is such that the statutory test is met.

Goodwin [2018] EWCA Crim 2287, [2019] 1 Cr App R 9 (107) is another example of a case where the main defence put forward was self-defence and the judge was found to have been correct on the facts in not putting loss of control to the jury as an alternative. There must be a 'rigorous evaluation' of the evidence before there can be found to be sufficient evidence on each of the three components of the defence to leave the defence to the jury. There was no room 'for what may be called a "defensive" summing up on such an issue' and 'a trial judge should not "clutter up" a jury's deliberations by inviting them to consider issues which do not arise on the evidence' (at [35]). In *Islam* [2019] EWCA Crim 2419, there was simply insufficient evidence of loss of control. *Goodwin* was followed and the Court of Appeal noted (at [32]) that it is often difficult 'to rely both on the defence of self-defence and on the partial defence of loss of control'.

For an example of a case where the defence actually did seek to rely on the defence but which might not actually have needed to be left to the jury under the more demanding tests laid down in the new law, see the comments of Lord Judge CJ in *Clinton* [2012] EWCA Crim 2, [2013] QB 1 at [75] and [105] in considering the facts affecting the appellant Parker. See also the comments of Lord Judge in *Dawes* at [66] (concerning the appellant Bowyer, a self-confessed burglar claiming to have a justifiable sense of being seriously wronged by the entirely reasonable response of the householder).

KILLING IN PURSUANCE OF SUICIDE PACT

B1.33 **Homicide Act 1957, s. 4**

> (1) It shall be manslaughter, and shall not be murder, for a person acting in pursuance of a suicide pact between him and another to kill the other or be a party to the other being killed by a third person.

The burden of proof that D was acting in pursuance of a suicide pact is placed on D by s. 4(2). This is a reverse legal burden on the balance of probabilities and is compatible with the ECHR,

Article 6(2) (*A-G's Ref (No. 1 of 2004)* [2004] EWCA Crim 1025, [2004] 2 Cr App R 27 (424) at [130]–[132]).

'Suicide pact' is defined in s. 4(3) as:

> ... a common agreement between two or more persons having for its object the death of all of them, whether or not each is to take his own life, but nothing done by a person who enters into a suicide pact shall be treated as done by him in pursuance of the pact unless it is done while he has the settled intention of dying in pursuance of the pact.

Thus the burden of proof on D involves not only proof that there was in fact a suicide pact, but also that at the time of the killing D still had the intention of dying.

Killing in pursuance of a suicide pact is closely related to the offence of assisting and encouraging suicide under the Suicide Act 1961, s. 2(1) (see **B1.140**). Section 2(2) provides that, if on an indictment for murder or manslaughter it is proved that D committed an offence under s. 2(1) (complicity in suicide), the jury may find D guilty of that offence. If D assisted or encouraged a killing by a third person, that is still potentially murder, but will be reduced to manslaughter under the Homicide Act 1957, s. 4, if it was done in pursuance of a suicide pact.

MANSLAUGHTER GENERALLY

Voluntary and Involuntary Manslaughter

Manslaughter can be classified as either voluntary or involuntary. Voluntary manslaughter has in effect already been considered, since it consists of those killings which would be murder (because D has the relevant *mens rea*—hence the label *voluntary* manslaughter) but which are reduced to manslaughter because of one of the three partial defences, discussed at **B1.16** to **B1.33**. Voluntary manslaughter is not an offence one can be indicted for, but rather is a verdict which can result from an initial indictment for murder. The actual verdict, however, will be simply 'manslaughter' without the label of 'voluntary'. **B1.34**

Involuntary manslaughter, on the other hand, refers to those types of manslaughter which can be charged in their own right and where D lacks the *mens rea* for murder, although equally they can result from an indictment for murder where the prosecution fail to prove the *mens rea*. **B1.35**

The fact that a verdict of manslaughter can reflect a number of different views of the facts taken by the jury (or by different members of the same jury) can lead to difficulties in sentencing and in relation to the normal rule requiring unanimity of verdicts (cf. **D18.44**). It was said by the Court of Criminal Appeal in *Larkin* [1943] KB 174 that it was 'most undesirable' that the jury should be asked to explain the basis of their verdict. However, in *Matheson* [1958] 2 All ER 87 the Court of Criminal Appeal said (at p. 480) that if diminished responsibility and some other ground such as provocation (now, loss of control) are left to the jury, the judge may, and generally should, ask the jury whether the verdict was based on diminished responsibility, or on the other ground or on both. This matter was further considered in *Jones* (1999) *The Times*, 17 February 1999 (where neither of the above cases was referred to). The Court of Appeal made it clear that there is no obligation on the judge to ask any such question (of which advance warning should in any event be given), it being 'a matter entirely for him or her in the exercise of his or her discretion'. Neither is there any obligation on the jury to give an answer if asked, any such answer being merely additional information to help with sentence:

> ... provided that the jury are agreed that the defendant is guilty of manslaughter, in the sense that they are sure that he perpetrated an unlawful act which caused the death of the accused, it is unnecessary that there be any unanimity by the jury as to the route by which that verdict is achieved.

This seems right on the facts of the case and for those cases (the majority) where the offence is at least manslaughter and may be murder if malice aforethought can be established and if loss of control and diminished responsibility (if in issue) can be negated. The prosecution have to prove causation and the unlawful act (such as an intentional assault), and negate complete defences such as self-defence if in issue, but the different possible reasons for an offence being manslaughter rather than murder are negative ones (reasonable doubt by the jury as to whether malice aforethought has been proved or whether diminished responsibility or loss of control has been negated). It is not a question of the prosecution having to prove any of these things for manslaughter; manslaughter is merely the residual verdict for any one of these reasons. It is submitted, however, that it would be different if manslaughter is alleged on two fundamentally separate grounds: unlawful act and gross negligence. It arguably should not be sufficient that six jurors thought that D's act causing death was unlawful but not grossly negligent and the other six thought it was grossly negligent but not unlawful. Here the prosecution have not proved either of the two forms of manslaughter beyond reasonable doubt; it is quite different from a case where what would otherwise be murder has been proved and the jurors merely differ as to the reason for *reducing* the offence to manslaughter (see RD Taylor, 'Jury Unanimity in Homicide' [2001] Crim LR 283 and HH Judge Clarke, 'Jury Unanimity—A Practitioner's Problem' [2001] Crim LR 301).

Definition of Involuntary Manslaughter

B1.36 Superficially, this is the same as the definition for murder (see **B1.1**) without the requirement of malice aforethought. This is only helpful in that it emphasises that requirements such as that the victim be a fully born human being are equally part of the offence of manslaughter. It is more common to refer to manslaughter as 'unlawful killing without malice aforethought', but this is not particularly helpful, because it does not indicate which killings will be regarded as unlawful in the absence of malice aforethought. In fact there now appear to be at least two main categories of killing without malice aforethought which are regarded as unlawful and hence amount to manslaughter:

(a) killing by an unlawful act likely to cause bodily harm—often called 'unlawful act manslaughter' or 'constructive manslaughter'; and
(b) killing grossly negligently.

There is also some authority (*Lidar* (11 November 1999 unreported)) for a third category of involuntary manslaughter, killing by subjective recklessness as to serious injury or death. It is arguable that such a category is not appropriate or necessary given the existence of unlawful act manslaughter, since any killing done with such recklessness would almost inevitably involve a sufficient unlawful act under the OAPA 1861 and, even if exceptionally for some reason it did not (e.g., because it was an omission rather than an act), it would be likely to come under gross negligence manslaughter (and see **B1.61** ***et seq.*** for how recklessness has historically been tangled up in the development of the test for gross negligence). Although gross negligence has come to be limited to circumstances where there is a risk of death as opposed to serious injury, it is arguable that the same limitation should also now apply to any residual category, if there is one, of killing by subjective recklessness, but this is as yet a matter awaiting explicit judicial determination. In *Hussain* [2012] EWCA Crim 188, [2012] 2 Cr App R (S) 75 (427), a case (like *Lidar*) arising out of the use of a motor vehicle, the Crown's case had been put not on the basis of unlawful act manslaughter or gross negligence but on the basis of recklessness as to death or grievous bodily harm. In an appeal against sentence only, this was not adversely commented on. The fact that the appellant knew the child victim was under the car and knowingly took the risk, by driving on, of killing him or causing him serious injury was an aggravating factor in sentencing but it seems clear that the appellant's conviction could have been perfectly well established either under unlawful act manslaughter (e.g., based on an unlawful act under the OAPA 1861, s. 20) or gross negligence manslaughter (there being an obvious risk of death). For further discussion of whether there is a separate category of reckless manslaughter (albeit arguing that the law should be reformed), see F Stark, 'Reckless Manslaughter' [2017] Crim LR 763.

Procedure

Manslaughter is triable only on indictment. It is a class 1A offence. It is a distinct offence from murder and attracts its own custody time-limit (*R (Wardle) v Crown Court at Leeds* [2001] UKHL 12, [2002] 1 AC 754). **B1.37**

Indictment

Statement of Offence **B1.38**

Manslaughter

Particulars of Offence

A on or about the . . . day of . . ., unlawfully killed V

Alternative Verdicts

These include: **B1.39**

(a) child destruction (Infant Life (Preservation) Act 1929, s. 2(2)), see **B1.102** to **B1.110**;
(b) abortion (Infant Life (Preservation) Act 1929, s. 2(3)), see **B1.111** to **B1.121**;
(c) complicity in suicide (Suicide Act 1961, s. 2(2)), see **B1.140** to **B1.146**;
(d) assisting an offender (CLA 1967, s. 4(2), see **B14.58**).

By way of exception to the general rule, there appears to be no such verdict as attempted manslaughter (*Bruzas* [1972] Crim LR 367; *Campbell* [1997] Crim LR 495).

Sentencing Guidelines: Diminished Responsibility

The maximum penalty is life imprisonment (OAPA 1861, s. 5). The Sentencing Council definitive guideline, *Manslaughter* (see Supplement, **SG25-5**), applies to individual offenders aged 18 and over sentenced for manslaughter by reason of diminished responsibility on or after 1 November 2018, irrespective of the date of the offence. In a press release published on 31 July 2018 the Sentencing Council said that the guideline on manslaughter by diminished responsibility 'ensures comprehensive guidance where previously it was very limited' but that 'overall the guideline is unlikely to change sentence levels'. The guideline indicates a single level of harm and requires the court to determine the degree of responsibility retained by the offender at the time of the offence (whether high, medium or lower). The guideline requires consideration of the issue of dangerousness at Step 3 (see **E4**), consideration of disposals under the Mental Health Act 1983 at Step 4 (see **E22**), and a further review at Step 5 to see whether 'the sentence as a whole meets the objectives of punishment, rehabilitation and protection of the public in a fair and proportionate way'; relevant matters at this stage to include are the psychiatric evidence and the regime on release. The Court of Appeal in *Fisher* [2019] EWCA Crim 1066 considered the application of the guideline in a case where the defendant had killed his mother by a single stab wound but, in light of psychiatric evidence that he was suffering from paranoid schizophrenia, a plea of guilty to manslaughter was accepted. The Court noted that the guideline substantially reflected the approach taken in the pre-guideline case of *Edwards* [2018] EWCA Crim 595, [2018] 2 Cr App R (S) 17 (120) (see **E22.14**), and *Fisher* itself provides a valuable review of the available sentencing options. While the judge's approach in relation to Steps 1 to 3 in the guideline was said to be unimpeachable, the Court, noting that the defendant's level of retained responsibility fell into the lowest category and he had no previous convictions, quashed a life sentence with a minimum term of two years coupled with a s. 45A hospital and limitation direction, and substituted a hospital order with a restriction order. **B1.40**

Although the sentencing guideline supersedes earlier case law, the hitherto leading case of *Wood* [2009] EWCA Crim 651, [2010] 1 Cr App R (S) 2 (6) may still be of value. In that case a **B1.41** five-member Court of Appeal said that subject to the specific element of reduced culpability in diminished responsibility cases, which in some cases could be small and in others very significant indeed, there plainly was a link to the principles set out in the CJA 2003, sch. 21, relating to sentencing for murder. A five-member Court of Appeal in *Blackman* [2017] EWCA Crim 325 endorsed the sentencing approach laid down in *Wood*. Further, in *Dantes* [2016] EWCA Crim 733, [2016] 2 Cr App R (S) 25 (212) the offender had stabbed his parents to death. The offender had a background of mental health problems, exacerbated by drug use. The medical evidence was that he was suffering from a psychotic illness and had delusional beliefs at the time of the offence which would have affected his judgement and ability to exercise self-control. A life sentence with a s. 45A and s. 45B direction and a minimum term of 19 years was upheld by the Court of Appeal. Hallett LJ said that a 'nuanced approach' to the scheme in sch. 21 was appropriate, but that the greater the offender's residual culpability the greater the relevance of that schedule.

Sentencing Guidelines: Loss of Control

B1.42 The Sentencing Council definitive guideline, *Manslaughter* (see Supplement, **SG25-4**), applies to individual offenders aged 18 and over sentenced for manslaughter by reason of loss of control on or after 1 November 2018, irrespective of the date of the offence. In a press release published on 31 July 2018 the Sentencing Council said that the guideline on manslaughter by reason of loss of control 'is unlikely to change sentence levels'. The earlier definitive guideline, *Manslaughter by Reason of Provocation*, no longer applies. The new guideline indicates a single level of harm and requires the court to determine the degree of culpability attaching to the offender's conduct (whether high, medium or lower).

The court 'should balance these characteristics to reach a fair assessment of the offender's overall culpability' and 'should avoid an overly mechanistic application of these factors'.

Sentencing Guidelines: Killing in Pursuance of Suicide Pact

B1.43 The maximum penalty is life imprisonment (OAPA 1861, s. 5). There is no offence-specific guideline but the Sentencing Council's *General Guideline: Overarching Principles* (see Supplement, **SG2-1**) is used for all offenders sentenced on or after 1 October 2019.

The offender in *Sweeney* (1986) 8 Cr App R (S) 419 pleaded guilty to the manslaughter of his wife. He was prone to depression and had married the deceased when she was suffering from advanced muscular dystrophy. They decided to commit suicide together by taking tablets and then setting fire to their car when they were inside it. Once the fire started both tried to escape, but the wife was killed. The offender suffered serious burns. The Court of Appeal reduced a four-year prison term to one of two years, that being 'sufficient, in our judgment, to mark the seriousness of this matter'. See also *England* (1990) 12 Cr App R (S) 98.

Sentencing Guidelines: Constructive/Unlawful Act Manslaughter

B1.44 The maximum penalty is life imprisonment (OAPA 1861, s. 5). The Sentencing Council definitive guideline, *Manslaughter* (see Supplement, **SG25-2**), applies to individual offenders aged 18 and over sentenced for constructive/unlawful act manslaughter on or after 1 November 2018, irrespective of the date of the offence. In a press release published on 31 July 2018 the Sentencing Council said that the guideline on unlawful act manslaughter 'is unlikely to change sentence levels'. The guideline indicates a single level of harm and requires the court to determine the degree of culpability attaching to the offender's conduct (whether very high, high, medium or lower). The court 'should balance these characteristics to reach a fair assessment of the offender's overall culpability' and 'should avoid an overly mechanistic application of these factors'.

In two of the early cases to reach the Court of Appeal, the trial judge's approach to sentence was criticised for failing to follow the two-step approach to sentence that is set out in the guideline. Step 1 is to assess culpability and Step 2 is to address aggravating and mitigating features. In

Bailey [2019] EWCA Crim 731, [2019] 2 Cr App R (S) 36 (262) it was said that the judge failed to have proper regard to the background of self-defence when coming to an initial categorisation of the offence in Step 1. In that case the offender had to respond to an assault on himself by an assailant wielding a heavy wooden ornament. Having been knocked to the floor of a balcony the offender then stabbed his assailant repeatedly in the legs and chest, fleeing and discarding the knife as his assailant lay dying. Charged with murder, he claimed self-defence but was convicted of unlawful act manslaughter. The judge found that the defendant acted in a way that carried a high risk of death or grievous bodily harm which ought to have been obvious to the defendant, and at the time of the killing he was well beyond self-defence. He therefore excluded self-defence from his consideration at Step 1, dealing with it only as a mitigating factor at Step 2 which might reduce the sentence within the category range. The Court of Appeal noted the wide disparity in starting points for the various categories and indicated that the sentencing judge had to reach a fair starting point—whether those set out in the guideline or, depending on individual circumstances, 'somewhere in between'. However, the initial consideration had always to incorporate consideration of self-defence, one in the exhaustive list of factors set out in the criteria for culpability at Step 1. On the facts of the case it should have fallen into Category B, at least in principle, and absent the feature of self-defence would have had a starting point of 12 years. Given that the element of self-defence had real significance, it would have been appropriate to adjust the starting point very significantly to six years and only then to consider matters of mitigation and aggravation. Here the significant aggravating features were that the offence was committed when the defendant was under the influence of heroin, he took steps to conceal and dispose of the weapon, and his poor criminal record. The sentence of six years was unduly lenient and a sentence of eight years' imprisonment was imposed in its place. A similar point was made in *Harris* [2019] EWCA Crim 2008, [2020] 4 WLR 32 in which a sentencing judge dealing with a woman convicted of manslaughter for stabbing to death her partner after a history of domestic violence, had failed to reach any initial conclusion on the category of culpability under the guideline. The Court of Appeal re-emphasised that a category and starting point should be decided before consideration of the aggravating and mitigating factors.

Public Disorder and Fights Although the sentencing guideline supersedes earlier case law, the hitherto leading case of *A-G's Ref (No. 60 of 2009) (Appleby)* [2009] EWCA Crim 2693, [2010] 2 Cr App R (S) 46 (311), where a five-member Court of Appeal reviewed a large number of cases where the victim had been killed as a result of violence in which no weapon had been used and in which, but for the death of the victim, the offence would have been an assault under the OAPA 1861, s. 47 or s. 20, may still be of value. The Court said that what is now required, without diminishing the importance of the offender's culpability, is for greater weight to be given to the consequences of those actions. On the other hand, where death was occasioned by no more than a push, causing the intoxicated victim to fall down some stairs, culpability was 'very low' and, even in the light of the general increase in sentence signalled in *Appleby*, the sentence was reduced from three and a half years to two years in *Bebbington* [2011] EWCA Crim 2163, [2012] 1 Cr App R (S) 99 (606). In *Maling* [2016] EWCA Crim 1740, [2017] 1 Cr App R (S) 14 (94), the Court of Appeal confirmed that where the killing results from a campaign of domestic violence, it is a seriously aggravating feature that must be properly reflected in the sentence imposed. On the facts, the Court considered a sentence of ten years' imprisonment unduly lenient and substituted a term of 15 years. **B1.45**

Weapons Although the sentencing guideline supersedes earlier case law, in *A-G's Ref (No. 36 of 2015) (Nicholles)* [2015] EWCA Crim 1174, the Court of Appeal said (at [16]): **B1.46**

> It is abundantly clear by now that the decision of this court in *Appleby* signals a clear change to the approach to sentence in unlawful act manslaughter cases. There is to be an upward movement in sentences to reflect the new focus on harm under section 143 of the Criminal Justice Act 2003, the sentencing regime for offences of murder contained in Schedule 21 to the Act, and the sterner approach to sentencing in cases involving the carrying of knives and other weapons ...

It is submitted that the Sentencing Council guideline must be read as having incorporated that change in approach.

Twelve years following a trial was upheld in *Bishop* [2011] EWCA Crim 1225, [2012] 1 Cr App R (S) 13 (60) where the offender had sought out a man who had been harassing his girlfriend and stabbed him seven times. In *Huggins* [2016] EWCA Crim 1715, [2017] 1 Cr App R (S) 21 (147), the Court of Appeal provided guidance in sentencing cases where culpability was at, or approaching, the highest level for involuntary manslaughter due to the use of knives for causing injury together with premeditation and a high foreseeable risk of death. On the facts, the Court considered a sentence of nine years' detention unduly lenient and substituted a term of 15 years.

B1.47 **Course of Commission of Another Offence** Although the sentencing guideline supersedes earlier case law, in *Jumah* [2010] EWCA Crim 2900, [2011] 2 Cr App R (S) 32 (200), applying *A-G's Ref (No. 60 of 2009) (Appleby)* [2009] EWCA Crim 2693, [2010] 2 Cr App R (S) 46 (311), an offender who planned and organised a robbery and was present at the scene when another offender stabbed and killed the store manager had his sentence increased from 14 years to 18 years' imprisonment. Clearly, much depends on the precise circumstances of the killing. In *A-G's Ref (Nos. 38, 39 and 40 of 2007)* [2007] EWCA Crim 1692, [2008] 1 Cr App R (S) 56 (319), the Court of Appeal considered sentence in a case of manslaughter committed in the course of a robbery in the victim's home. The 67-year-old victim was threatened with an iron bar and punched once. He died a week later, a scan showing that blood had collected in his skull and compressed the brain. All three offenders pleaded guilty to robbery and the second offender pleaded guilty to manslaughter. The Court of Appeal had regard to the definitive sentencing guideline on robbery (see Supplement, **SG30-1**), and inferred that, following a trial, the appropriate range for a person without previous convictions who was convicted of manslaughter in such circumstances was eight to nine years' imprisonment. The sentence of three years and six months was increased to five years, having regard to the guilty plea, the element of double jeopardy, and other matters. A number of earlier similar appeals were reviewed in this case. *A-G's Ref (No. 133 of 2006)* [2007] EWCA Crim 809, [2007] 2 Cr App R (S) 91 (594) was a case of manslaughter committed in the course of arson, where an 18-year-old offender of previous good character had assisted an older man in deliberately starting a fire in a family's home late in the evening. In *Mahmood* [2012] EWCA Crim 400, [2012] 2 Cr App R (S) 63 (373), where a fire was deliberately started in a family's home and three deaths resulted, a sentence of 17 years' detention in a young offender institution after a trial was upheld on an 18-year-old offender, who had assisted his brother in the offence.

B1.48 **Manslaughter of Child** Although the sentencing guideline supersedes earlier case law, in *A-G's Ref (No. 125 of 2010)* [2011] EWCA Crim 577, [2011] 2 Cr App R (S) 97 (534) the offender, a man of previous good character, pleaded guilty to the manslaughter of his four-month-old baby son. The offender forcefully shook and/or threw the baby, causing serious brain damage. The child died three weeks later. A sentence of three and a half years' imprisonment was increased by the Court of Appeal to five years. The Court stressed that the higher sentencing levels now applicable to other forms of manslaughter indicated in *A-G's Ref (No. 60 of 2009) (Appleby)* [2009] EWCA Crim 2693, [2010] 2 Cr App R (S) 46 (311) (see **B1.45**) also applied in the present context. It is submitted that the Sentencing Council guideline must be read as having incorporated that change in approach.

Sentencing Guidelines: Gross Negligence Manslaughter

B1.49 The Sentencing Council definitive guideline, *Manslaughter* (see Supplement, **SG25-3**), applies to individual offenders aged 18 and over sentenced for gross negligence manslaughter on or after 1 November 2018, irrespective of the date of the offence. In a press release published on 31 July 2018 the Sentencing Council said that the guideline in relation to manslaughter 'is unlikely to change sentence levels but it is expected that in some gross negligence cases sentences will increase where, for example, an employer's long-standing and serious disregard for the safety of employees, motivated by cost-cutting, has led to someone being killed'. The guideline indicates a single level of harm and requires the court to determine the degree of culpability attaching to the offender's conduct (whether very high, high, medium or lower). The court 'should balance these characteristics to reach a fair assessment of the offender's overall culpability' and 'should avoid an overly mechanistic application of these factors'. The gross negligence manslaughter guideline also states that 'where an offender's acts or omissions would also constitute another offence, the sentencer should have regard to any guideline relevant to the other offence to ensure that the sentence for manslaughter does not fall below what would be imposed under that guideline'.

In *Broadhurst* [2019] EWCA Crim 2026 the appellant and victim, both intoxicated, engaged in sexual activity. At the victim's request, the appellant struck the victim and inserted a carpet cleaner bottle into her vagina, which become lodged. On removal, the bottle broke, which caused the victim's vagina to bleed. The appellant then went to bed, without seeking assistance. The victim died shortly thereafter. The appellant pleaded guilty to gross negligence manslaughter and was sentenced to three years and eight months' imprisonment. The Court of Appeal held that the case was properly placed towards the upper end of category C of the gross negligence manslaughter guidelines. While it could not be said that the applicant had shown a blatant disregard for a very high risk of death, he had shown a blatant disregard for the victim's obvious injuries, to which he had contributed, and for the obvious need to summon medical assistance. The sentence was upheld.

In common with other areas of manslaughter, the Court of Appeal in the pre-guideline case of *Barrass* [2011] EWCA Crim 2629, [2012] 1 Cr App R (S) 80 (450) said that, following the decision in *A-G's Ref (No. 60 of 2009) (Appleby)* [2009] EWCA Crim 2693, [2010] 2 Cr App R (S) 46 (311), greater importance should now be focused on the consequences of the offence. It is submitted that the Sentencing Council guideline must be read as having incorporated that change in approach.

CONSTRUCTIVE MANSLAUGHTER (KILLING BY AN UNLAWFUL ACT LIKELY TO CAUSE BODILY HARM)

The Unlawful Act

The accused's act must be unlawful, in that it constitutes a criminal offence in its own right (independently of the fact that it has caused death). See *Franklin* (1883) 15 Cox CC 163, where the fact that D had committed a tort did not make D's act an unlawful one for the purposes of manslaughter, although it should be noted that D was nonetheless convicted on the ground of gross negligence. Typically the unlawful act will be an assault (see, e.g., *Larkin* [1943] KB 174) or some other offence against the person such as administering a noxious thing under the OAPA 1861, s. 23. **B1.50**

It now seems clear that the offence need not be directed against the person; an offence of arson or criminal damage can supply the required element of unlawfulness (*Goodfellow* (1986) 83 Cr App R 23; *F (J)* [2015] EWCA Crim 167, [2015] 2 Cr App R (S) 5 (64)). However, being a participant in the public order offence of affray will not suffice except insofar as the accused individually commits or is party to an assault perpetrated on the victim as part of the affray (*Carey* [2006] EWCA Crim 17).

The unlawful act must be an act which is unlawful in itself rather than one which is unlawful because of the negligent manner of its performance. Thus, driving without due care and attention does not count as an unlawful act for these purposes (*Andrews v DPP* [1937] AC 576, per Lord Atkin at p. 585), otherwise unlawful act manslaughter would swallow up both the **B1.51** statutory offence of causing death by dangerous driving and also killing by gross negligence in the context of road traffic deaths. Perhaps a better way of excluding driving without due care and attention would be to say that the unlawful act must be an offence which requires the proof of full *mens rea* in the sense of intention or recklessness or some equally culpable state of mind. This would have the merit of also clearly excluding offences of strict liability (e.g., under health and safety legislation) which happen to result in death. Such situations should only be capable of amounting to manslaughter (and are only so treated) if they come within the gross negligence head discussed at **B1.61** to **B1.67**. Unfortunately, in *Andrews* [2002] EWCA Crim 3021, [2003] Crim LR 477, the Court of Appeal treated the strict liability offence under the Medicines Act 1968 of administering a prescription only medicine (in this case insulin, in order to give someone a 'rush') as a sufficient unlawful act. The main point at issue was whether consent could be a defence by rendering the act lawful, which it clearly could not. However, the charge of administering a noxious thing contrary to the OAPA 1861, s. 23, (which had been left to lie on the file), would have been a much more appropriate offence on which to base the unlawful act.

B1.52 The type of offence sufficient for an unlawful act may also be thought to have been somewhat stretched in *Meeking* [2012] EWCA Crim 641, [2012] 1 WLR 3349, where the Court of Appeal upheld a conviction for constructive manslaughter based on an unlawful act contrary to the RTA 1988, s. 22A(1)(b). The specific unlawful act involved the accused pulling on the handbrake while her husband was driving their car at 60 mph, resulting in an accident which caused his death. The Court confirmed that such conduct amounts to an offence under s. 22A in that she 'interferes with a motor vehicle … in such circumstances that it would be obvious to a reasonable person that to do so would be dangerous'. The main argument raised in the Court of Appeal was whether the statutory offence should be limited to acts of interference with a vehicle prior to it being driven (see **C3.66**) but it was also argued that, even though the statutory offence was committed, it was not an appropriate unlawful act for the purposes of constructive manslaughter given that the offence is essentially one based on negligence and that, therefore, in line with *Andrews v DPP* [1937] AC 576, it should not count as an unlawful act for these purposes. Toulson LJ adverted to this issue (at [14]) and noted that the case might more naturally have been put forward on the basis of gross negligence and that, if it had been, it was impossible to conclude that the jury would not have convicted on that ground. One might add that it is arguable that cases such as this should *only* be prosecuted under gross negligence and that the category of unlawful acts should not be stretched to include offences which do not require full *mens rea* and which are defined in terms of negligence as to a significant element. The issue would of course be most critical if a case arose, such as the type about which Toulson LJ himself would have some concerns, 'which was essentially one of negligence, but arguably negligence falling short of gross negligence'.

The phrase 'unlawful act' has been taken to require an act as opposed to an omission since *Lowe* [1973] QB 702, where wilful neglect of a child under the CYPA 1933, s. 1, was held not to supply the unlawful act required. However *Lowe* was decided when wilful neglect did not require any *mens rea* as to consequences (which was subsequently held to be wrong in *Sheppard* [1981] AC 394). This absence of *mens rea* was arguably the real reason for the reluctance to convict in *Lowe*, so that decision should not therefore be taken to preclude, in a case with appropriate *mens rea*, a relevant unlawful act in manslaughter being committed by omission (see R Taylor, 'The contours of involuntary manslaughter' [2019] Crim LR 205).

Mens Rea of the Unlawful Act

B1.53 Although a person accused of manslaughter by definition lacks the *mens rea* for murder, the prosecution must normally prove that D has the *mens rea* appropriate to the unlawful act which caused the victim's death, a point well illustrated by the case of *Lamb* [1967] 2 QB 981, where D 'in jest' pointed a loaded revolver at his friend and pulled the trigger, believing that it was safe to do so because neither of the two bullets in the gun was in a chamber opposite the barrel. What neither D nor his friend (who was similarly treating the incident as a joke) appreciated was that pulling the trigger rotated the cylinder so as to place one of the bullets opposite the barrel, and hence in the firing position. On appeal, the conviction for manslaughter was quashed on the ground that 'the element of intent without which there can be no assault' was not proved. It would have been different had Lamb intended to frighten his friend (for then he would have had the *mens rea* of an unlawful act)—see *Ball* [1989] Crim LR 730. Since the decision in *Lamb* [1967] 2 QB 981, it has been confirmed that recklessness is sufficient *mens rea* for assault (*Venna* [1976] QB 421). However, it is subjective recklessness which applies (*Spratt* [1990] 1 WLR 1073) so Lamb would still lack the necessary *mens rea*. See also *Slingsby* [1995] Crim LR 570, where vigorous consensual sexual activity did not amount to a battery or other unlawful act since there was no intention to cause, or foresight of, harm.

D cannot, however, rely on lack of *mens rea* induced by voluntary intoxication, as manslaughter is a crime of basic intent (*Lipman* [1970] 1 QB 152). This was an extreme case in many ways, in which D killed his girlfriend whilst suffering LSD-induced hallucinations that he was at the centre of the earth being attacked by snakes. If the unlawful act alleged were to be a crime of specific intent, then D's intoxication *should* be relevant, but such situations are likely to be rare (see, however, *Watson* [1989] 2 All ER 865, burglary with intent to steal).

Likely to Cause Bodily Harm

The Objective Nature of the Test The classic formulation of this requirement, sometimes referred to as the requirement that the unlawful act be 'dangerous', is that of Edmund Davies J in *Church* [1966] 1 QB 59, where he said (at p. 70): **B1.54**

> ... the unlawful act must be such as all sober and reasonable people would inevitably recognise must subject the other person to, at least, the risk of some harm resulting therefrom, albeit not serious harm.

This formulation has the merit that it emphasises that the test is an objective one, which depends not on D's appreciation of likely harm but on what the sober and reasonable person would appreciate. The objective nature of the test was confirmed by the House of Lords in *DPP v Newbury* [1977] AC 500, where two youths pushed a paving stone off the parapet of a bridge into the path of an approaching train, thereby killing the guard. The House of Lords upheld the convictions for manslaughter and answered yes to the certified question, 'Can a defendant be properly convicted of manslaughter, when his mind is not affected by drink or drugs, if he did not foresee harm to another?'

On the other hand, D's foresight of harm may be relevant to the separate question of whether D has the *mens rea* of the unlawful act if the unlawful act is an offence against the person. The House of Lords in *DPP v Newbury* [1977] AC 500 did not make it clear what the unlawful act was, and indeed appeared to be rather dismissive of the requirement of *mens rea* for the unlawful act. However, it now seems clear in the light of *Goodfellow* (1986) 83 Cr App R 23 and *F (J)* [2015] EWCA Crim 167, [2015] 2 Cr App R (S) 5 (64) (see **B1.50**) that criminal damage would be the obvious and sufficient unlawful act in *Newbury*, and that the two accused were probably reckless as to criminal damage, so that they did have the *mens rea* for an unlawful act even if they did not foresee harm to another. Even where the unlawful act is an assault, the *mens rea* need not relate to harm; an intention to put in fear is sufficient. Thus the following dictum of Lord Denning MR in *Gray v Barr* [1971] 2 QB 554, at p. 568, on which doubt was cast by Lord Salmon in *Newbury*, is perfectly sound in the context of a case where the unlawful act is an assault: 'the accused must do a dangerous act with the *intention* of frightening or harming someone, or with the *realisation* that it is likely to frighten or harm someone'. Lord Denning was not casting doubt on the requirement that the act be *objectively* likely to cause bodily harm (he refers to a 'dangerous' act), but was making the important and separate point that D must be shown to have the *mens rea* for whatever is alleged to be the unlawful act. See also *Jennings* [1990] Crim LR 588 and *Scarlett* [1993] 4 All ER 629.

B1.55 **Physical Harm Not Mere Emotional Disturbance** The harm *likely* to result from the act must be physical harm. Emotional disturbance will not suffice, even though physical harm (and death) does in fact result from the foreseeable emotional disturbance: see *Dawson* (1985) 81 Cr App R 150, where the fact that a robbery of a petrol station was likely to cause emotional disturbance to the 60-year-old attendant was held not to be sufficient, even though the attendant, who had a weak heart, suffered a heart attack and died. The heart attack did constitute physical harm but the reasonable person would not have *foreseen* physical harm as likely to result. The reasonable person is to be regarded as having the knowledge of facts that the accused has, and the accused in this case did not know that the attendant had a weak heart. A similar approach was taken in *Carey* [2006] EWCA Crim 17, where the Court of Appeal regarded it as an even clearer case than *Watson* in that the sober and reasonable bystander would not have recognised a risk of shock leading to a heart attack in the case of an apparently healthy 15-year-old girl. In *Johnston* [2007] EWCA Crim 3133, insults and spittle directed at an apparently healthy and active 67-year-old were similarly not 'dangerous acts' nor likely to give rise to a foreseeable injury. Since, however, they could not be ruled out in the light of the medical evidence as in fact the sole cause of a fatal heart attack, the later throwing of stones which struck the victim's head, whilst clearly a dangerous act, could not be proved to be a significant cause of death on which a manslaughter verdict could be sustained. However, as is shown by *M (J)* [2012] EWCA Crim 2293, [2013] 1 Cr App R 10 (144), provided that there is a risk of physical harm that any sober and reasonable person would recognise, the actual death does not need to result from that sort of harm, if D's unlawful act did indeed cause the death. Thus an affray which was likely to cause bodily harm (e.g., through the direct effects of physical violence) could potentially give rise to unlawful act manslaughter even though the actual cause of death might be the effects of shock caused by the affray leading to the rupture of an aneurysm which would not have been foreseen by anyone in an apparently healthy 40-year-old.

In *Watson* [1989] 2 All ER 865, the unlawful act was burglary under the Theft Act 1968, s. 9(1)(a), which allegedly caused the elderly occupier (again with a weak heart) to suffer a heart attack and die. The Court of Appeal held (at p. 867) that, although the appellant did not know the age or physical condition of the occupier at the point of entry:

> ... the jury were entitled to ascribe to the bystander the knowledge which the appellant gained during the whole of his stay in the house ... The unlawful act in the present circumstances comprised the whole of the burglarious intrusion and did not come to an end on the appellant's foot crossing the threshold ...

The statement about the duration of the unlawful act seems, with respect, to stretch the definition of the offence under s. 9(1)(a) and can be regarded as *obiter*, since the conviction was quashed on another ground. However, the case is a useful illustration of the proposition that if D knows of the victim's susceptibility to physical harm, then that knowledge can be ascribed to the reasonable person and the accused's act can be regarded as 'likely to cause bodily harm'. See *Bristow* [2013] EWCA Crim 1540 for another example where the known features of the particular burglary were such that it was objectively likely to cause some harm.

On the other hand, the reasonable person does not share D's mistaken beliefs. In *Ball* [1989] Crim LR 730, D mistakenly believed he had loaded the gun with blank cartridges but the reasonable bystander, not sharing that belief, would have considered the act of firing the gun dangerous.

B1.56 **The Nature of the Causal Link** A further limitation on the type of harm required was suggested in *Dalby* [1982] 1 All ER 916, where the Court of Appeal quashed a conviction for manslaughter based on D unlawfully supplying his friend with drugs, which his friend subsequently *injected into himself with fatal consequences.* Waller LJ said that the act had to be 'directed at the victim and likely to cause *immediate* injury, however slight' (emphasis added). The harm (or injury) in this case was caused by the deceased's own act of injecting the drugs. The mere supply of the drug was not dangerous in the sense that it was likely to cause *immediate* injury. The qualification suggested in *Dalby* was capable of restricting the scope of constructive manslaughter in a number of ways but it was quickly distinguished in subsequent cases including *Mitchell* [1983] QB 741 and *Pagett* (1983) 76 Cr App R 279.

The decision in *Goodfellow* (1986) 83 Cr App R 23 moved more clearly away from the limitation suggested in *Dalby*. D, wishing to be rehoused, set fire to his council house. The fire spread more rapidly than he had anticipated, and his wife and child and another woman were killed in the blaze. The Court of Appeal upheld the conviction for manslaughter, even though D's acts were not directed at a victim but rather against property. Lord Lane CJ said (at p. 27) that all that had been intended to be said in *Dalby* was that 'there must be no fresh intervening cause between the act and the death'. His lordship went on: **B1.57**

> The questions which the jury have to decide on the charge of manslaughter of this nature are: (1) Was the act intentional? (2) Was it unlawful? (3) Was it an act which any reasonable person would realise was bound to subject some other human being to the risk of physical harm, albeit not necessarily serious harm? (4) Was that act the cause of death?

It should be noted that, in a case such as *Lamb* [1967] 2 QB 981 (see **B1.53**), Lord Lane's second question for the jury would need to be amplified in order to stress that an act is only unlawful if D has the *mens rea* for the particular unlawful act alleged. To ask, 'Was the act intentional?' is not sufficient, since that can be interpreted merely as referring to voluntariness, e.g., on the facts of *Lamb*, as asking 'Did D intend to pull the trigger?' rather than 'Did D intend to assault his friend?' On the facts of *Goodfellow* (1986) 83 Cr App R 23, the problem does not really arise, because D clearly had the *mens rea* for criminal damage.

Drug-related Deaths, Causation and 'jointly administering' The essential requirement from *Dalby* [1982] 1 All ER 916 that 'there must be no intervening cause' between D's act and the victim's death has come into focus as a result of a number of decisions starting with *Kennedy* [1999] Crim LR 65, which was subsequently referred to the Court of Appeal by the CCRC, only for the conviction to be upheld a second time in the Court of Appeal in *Kennedy (No. 2)* [2005] EWCA Crim 685, [2005] 2 Cr App R 23 (348) before finally being quashed in the House of Lords in *Kennedy (No. 2)* [2007] UKHL 38, [2008] 1 AC 269. The facts of *Kennedy* involved D supplying a prepared syringe of heroin with which the deceased voluntarily injected himself; that injection caused the victim's death for which D was (initially) held responsible. Precisely how the accused could be responsible for the consequences of a free and voluntary act done by the victim was never very clear. Basing his liability on the act of supply was contrary to *Dalby* (which on its facts has never been doubted) since the supply, as opposed to the injection, was clearly not the cause of death. The subsequent case of *Dias* [2001] EWCA Crim 2986, [2002] 2 Cr App R 5 (96) demonstrated that it could not be based on aiding and abetting the act of the victim since the act of self-injection by the victim was not unlawful, there being no offence of self-manslaughter. **B1.58**

The House of Lords' decision in *Kennedy (No. 2)* shows that there was no valid ground for upholding the conviction and emphatically reasserted the principle that 'D is not to be treated as causing V to act in a certain way if V makes a voluntary and informed decision to act in that way rather than another' (Lord Bingham at [14]). Such a decision by V to do an act means that he is the cause of the consequences of that act and not some other person. On the facts it was clear that, whilst the syringe was prepared by D, it was V's choice to inject it and the act of injection was his alone. Kennedy had therefore not caused the injection or the death and his conviction had to be quashed and other analogous cases (such as *Finlay* [2003] EWCA Crim 3868) were disapproved of. **B1.59**

Even a case such as *Rogers* [2003] EWCA Crim 945, [2003] 2 Cr App R 10 (160), where D had held the tourniquet and had been convicted on the basis of jointly administering a noxious thing contrary to the OAPA 1861, s. 23, did not escape. Lord Bingham recognised (at [20]) that there is:

> ... a difficult borderline between contributory acts which may properly be regarded as administering a noxious thing and acts which may not ... the crucial question is not whether the defendant facilitated or contributed to administration of the noxious thing but whether he went further and administered it. What matters, in a case such as *R v Rogers* and the present, is whether the injection itself was the result of a voluntary and informed decision by the person injecting himself. In *R v Rogers*, as in the present case, it was. That case was, therefore, wrongly decided.

B1.60 Although *Rogers* is not to be treated as an instance of joint administration, Lord Bingham accepted (at [24]) that it is 'possible to imagine factual scenarios in which two people could properly be regarded as acting together to administer an injection' and this possibility was further discussed in *Burgess* [2008] EWCA Crim 516, where Sir Igor Judge considered (at [12]) that the accused:

> ... is not automatically entitled to be acquitted if the deceased rather than the defendant physically operated the plunger on the syringe and caused the drug to enter his body. In the present case there was evidence which might reasonably have led a jury to conclude that this appellant had indeed jointly participated in the administration of the fatal dose of heroin. From the interviews as they developed, it emerged that he supplied the deceased with the heroin, which he, the appellant, drew into the syringe ... He did not hand the syringe to the deceased but he took it and the needle to the deceased's arm, where he found an appropriate vein. He laid the tip of the needle against the skin of the deceased above that vein. It is not clear from the interview that he ever in fact let go of the syringe, but on his account the deceased depressed the plunger. Having done so, the appellant assisted in the physical withdrawal of the plunger from the deceased's arm.

His lordship considered that it would have been open to the jury to convict on the basis of a joint administration on these facts but a retrial was not in fact ordered for other reasons (D having originally pleaded guilty on a different and false basis prior to the House of Lords' decision in *Kennedy (No. 2)* and now having already served his sentence).

For an illustration of how drug-related deaths can give rise to convictions for gross negligence manslaughter based on a duty of care, see *Evans* [2009] EWCA Crim 650, [2009] 2 Cr App R 10 (156) at **B1.65**.

MANSLAUGHTER BY GROSS NEGLIGENCE

Establishment of the *Adomako* Formula of Gross Breach of a Duty of Care

B1.61 Manslaughter has traditionally been the one offence at common law in which negligence is expressly recognised as a sufficient basis of liability, but even here the negligence has to be 'gross'. Defining the precise degree of negligence required has always been problematical, and ultimately the question, being one of degree, has been one for the jury. This is evident from the following test laid down by Lord Hewart CJ in *Bateman* (1925) 19 Cr App R 8, at pp. 11 to 12:

> ... the facts must be such that, in the opinion of the jury, the negligence of the accused went beyond a mere matter of compensation between subjects and showed such disregard for the life and safety of others as to amount to a crime against the State and conduct deserving punishment.

For many years, judges often used the word 'reckless', which at the time had no settled legal meaning, to sum up to the jury the high degree of fault required. This led to serious problems in the decade after the apparently authoritative (but now overturned) House of Lords' decisions on the objective meaning of recklessness in *Metropolitan Police Commissioner v Caldwell* [1982] AC 341 and *Lawrence* [1982] AC 510. Indeed, following the decision of the House of Lords in *Seymour* [1983] 2 AC 493, it appeared that the objective version of recklessness may have replaced negligence as the primary test for manslaughter, at least in relation to cases of motor manslaughter, and the decision of the Privy Council in *Kong Cheuk Kwan v The Queen* (1985)

82 Cr App R 18 suggested that objective recklessness may have become the primary test more generally.

However, in the landmark decision of *Adomako* [1995] 1 AC 171 the House of Lords restored gross negligence rather than recklessness as the essential basis of liability and reasserted that the *Bateman* gross negligence test was of general application and that there should be no separate test based on recklessness for motor manslaughter.

Lord Mackay set out what he regarded as the essentials of gross negligence (at p. 187):

> ... in my opinion the ordinary principles of the law of negligence apply to ascertain whether or not the defendant has been in breach of a duty of care towards the victim who has died. If such a breach of duty is established the next question is whether that breach of duty caused the death of the victim. If so, the jury must go on to consider whether that breach of duty should be characterised as gross negligence and therefore as a crime. This will depend on the seriousness of the breach of duty committed by the defendant in all the circumstances in which the defendant was placed when it occurred...
>
> ... The essence of the matter which is supremely a jury question is whether, having regard to the risk of death involved, the conduct of the defendant was so bad in all the circumstances as to amount in their judgment to a criminal act or omission.

The proof of breach of duty was discussed in *Zaman* [2017] EWCA Crim 1783, [2018] 1 Cr App R (S) 26 (177) where the appellant's negligence was characterised by the Court of Appeal as 'not just gross' but his behaviour as 'appalling' (at [81]). The argument was rejected that a *Brown* direction (on unanimity as to particular facts constituting the breach of duty) ought to have been given. Hickinbottom J stated (at [46]):

> The prosecution case was ... based upon a single alleged breach of duty by the Appellant, i.e. that he had failed to take reasonable steps to avoid injury to customers who had a declared allergy. It was never the prosecution case that individual acts or omissions of the Appellant upon which it relied, including the Appellant's failure to have taken steps that Mr Blacklock and the prosecution expert Dr Chan said could and should have been in place, each constituted a discrete breach of duty.

The 'truly exceptionally bad' Test for Grossness

The appellate courts have recently taken a more explicit stand on how bad negligence has to be **B1.62**
in order to be characterised as gross, giving their express approval to a form of direction that had become common but not universal at trial court level. In *R (Oliver) v DPP* [2016] EWHC 1771 (Admin), Davis LJ, in reviewing a decision not to prosecute, referred approvingly to *Misra* [2004] EWCA Crim 2375, [2005] 1 Cr App R 21 (328), saying (at [11]):

> Mistakes, even very serious mistakes, and errors of judgment, even very serious errors of judgment, will not of themselves suffice. A proper direction to the jury on the issue of gross negligence was held in that case to be that they should be sure that the conduct in question was something 'truly exceptionally bad and which showed such indifference to an obviously serious risk to life and which showed such a departure from the standard to be expected' so as to constitute the very serious crime of manslaughter. The bar is thus set high: perhaps unsurprisingly so, given that such cases ordinarily involve no criminal intent.

In *Sellu* [2016] EWCA Crim 1716, [2017] 1 Cr App R 24 (349), the Court of Appeal, in quashing a conviction, further underlined the importance of explaining to the jury the seriousness of the departure from ordinary standards required by the concept of gross negligence. The question of whether the negligence is gross is a matter ultimately for the jury rather than the experts, although expert evidence is, of course, important for identifying in what respects the conduct of D fell below that to be expected. It is not sufficient, however, simply to leave to the jury the question of whether the departure was gross or severe. What is required (at [152], per Sir Brian Leveson P) is:

> ... that the jury are assisted sufficiently to understand how to approach their task of identifying the line that separates even serious or very serious mistakes or lapses, from conduct which ... was 'truly exceptionally bad and was such a departure from that standard [of a reasonably competent doctor] that it consequently amounted to being criminal'.

In *Bawa-Garba* [2016] EWCA Crim 1841 a conviction for gross negligence manslaughter was upheld partly because in this case 'the judge had correctly directed the jury that the prosecution had to show that what a defendant did or didn't do was "truly exceptionally bad"...this jury was (and all juries considering this offence should be) left in no doubt as to the truly exceptional degree of negligence which must be established if it is to be made out' (at [36]).

No Requirement for Subjective Foresight of Risk

B1.63 Lord Mackay in *Adomako* [1995] 1 AC 171 emphasised that, while a judge may feel it appropriate to use the word 'reckless' as indicating the extent to which D's conduct must deviate from a proper standard of care, it would not be right 'to require that this should be done and certainly not right that it should incorporate the full detail required in *Lawrence*'. Furthermore, in *A-G's Ref (No. 2 of 1999)* [2000] QB 796, the Court of Appeal held that proof of gross negligence does not require proof of any particular state of mind and does not require evidence of D's state of mind. Although one can agree that a specific state of mind such as recklessness is not required, it is difficult to see how one can avoid looking into what facts D either knew (and failed to take adequate precautions for) or did not know about (but should have done). Either way, this surely requires evidence of D's state of mind. In *R (Rowley) v DPP* [2003] EWHC 693 (Admin), the absence of evidence of subjective recklessness was held to be an appropriate factor to take into account in a decision not to prosecute. However, it was confirmed in *Misra* [2004] EWCA Crim 2375, [2005] 1 Cr App R 21 (328) that the fault element that the prosecution have to prove remains gross negligence and, despite the rehabilitation of subjective recklessness in *G* [2003] UKHL 50, [2004] 1 AC 1034 in relation to criminal damage, there is no warrant for replacing gross negligence in manslaughter with a requirement to prove subjective recklessness. Judge LJ noted in *Misra* (at [55]) that, in his speech in *G*, Lord Bingham emphasised that 'he was not addressing the meaning of "reckless" in any other statutory or common law context than section 1(1) and (2) of the Criminal Damage Act 1971'. In *Mark* [2004] EWCA Crim 2490, Scott Baker LJ made the same point in coming to the same conclusion that it is gross negligence and not subjective recklessness that has to be proved. Thus the trial judge was correct in telling the jury in relation to the facts of that case that 'actual foresight or perception of the risk is not a prerequisite of the crime of gross negligence' and that D could be guilty of gross negligence simply on the basis of a complete failure to advert to what is an obvious and important matter, i.e. an obvious and serious risk of death. The objective nature of the test was further underlined in *S* [2015] EWCA Crim 558, [2015] 2 Cr App R (S) 29 (260) where a conviction was upheld notwithstanding D's subjective belief that the gun he was handling was unloaded. D's state of belief as to the gun being unloaded was one of the factors to be taken into account but the ultimate question was 'whether a reasonably prudent person, in [D's] position, would have taken all obvious and necessary steps to ensure that a gun, fitted with a magazine, and being left with him along with other loose bullets by the dangerous acquaintance, was not loaded before he pointed it at [the deceased] and pulled the trigger' (at [20]).

Legal Certainty

B1.64 The Court of Appeal in *Misra* [2004] EWCA Crim 2375, [2005] 1 Cr App R 21 (328) rejected the argument that gross negligence manslaughter offends against the principle of legal certainty inherent in the ECHR, Article 7. In the Court's view (Judge LJ at [48]):

> The decision of the House of Lords in *Adomako* clearly identified the ingredients of manslaughter by gross negligence. In very brief summary, confirming *Andrews v DPP* [1937] AC 576, the offence requires first, death resulting from a negligent breach of the duty of care owed by the defendant to the deceased, second, that in negligent breach of that duty, the victim was exposed by the defendant to the risk of death, and third, that the circumstances were so reprehensible as to amount to gross negligence.

His lordship reiterated (at [64]) that:

> ...the law is clear. The ingredients of the offence have been clearly defined, and the principles decided in the House of Lords in *Adomako*. They involve no uncertainty. The hypothetical citizen,

seeking to know his position, would be advised that, assuming he owed a duty of care to the deceased which he had negligently broken, and that death resulted, he would be liable to conviction for manslaughter if, on the available evidence, the jury was satisfied that his negligence was gross. A doctor would be told that grossly negligent treatment of a patient which exposed him or her to the risk of death, and caused it, would constitute manslaughter.

Existence of a Duty of Care

The reintroduction of the ordinary principles of negligence to decide whether there is a breach of a duty of care is not necessarily a simple matter, especially if the factual situation is one where, if it were a civil claim, policy factors might impinge. Certainly the maxim '*ex turpi causa*' has no applicability in this context, as is illustrated by *Wacker* [2002] EWCA Crim 1944, [2003] QB 1207, where the Court of Appeal confirmed that a duty of care could be owed by a lorry driver to illegal immigrants whom he had concealed in the back of his lorry. The policy factors here were clearly in favour of responsibility although in other situations they might point in the opposite direction. Nevertheless, in *Winter* [2010] EWCA Crim 1474, [2011] 1 Cr App R (S) 78 (476), a duty of care was still found to be owed to a civilian filming fire fighters who were responding to a massive fireworks fire and explosion caused by the negligence of the defendants, even though the civilian may have disobeyed instructions in being so close. **B1.65**

The issue of who decides whether there was a duty of care was clarified by Lord Judge CJ in *Evans* [2009] EWCA Crim 650, [2009] 2 Cr App R 10 (156), a case involving a breach of duty to take reasonable steps to summon obviously needed medical help for a heroin overdose victim for whom the appellant had procured the drug. In accordance with normal principles, the question of whether there is a duty of care (given certain facts) is a matter of law for the trial judge although it is for the jury to decide whether any contingent facts (which the trial judge has identified the duty to depend upon) are established.

The Need for a Serious and Obvious Risk of Death

As to what type of risk must be foreseeable on which the duty of care is based, various formulations have been used in the past including a risk to health and welfare, a risk of serious injury and a risk of death. *Singh* [1999] Crim LR 582 explicitly confined it to a risk of death whereby 'the circumstances must be such that a reasonably prudent person would have foreseen a serious and obvious risk not merely of injury, even serious injury, but of death' and in *Misra* [2004] EWCA Crim 2375, [2005] 1 Cr App R 21 (328), the Court of Appeal confirmed this approach as being in line with *Adomako* [1995] 1 AC 171 (and Lord Mackay's reference to 'having regard to the risk of death involved'). The Court was emphatic, in the face of a challenge to the compatibility of gross negligence manslaughter with the principle of legal certainty inherent in the ECHR, Article 7, that it was now quite clear that a (foreseeable) risk of death was required and the point was also made that this was consistent with the offence being one designed to protect the right to life: 'In short, the offence requires gross negligence in circumstances where what is at risk is the life of an individual to whom the defendant owes a duty of care. As such it serves to protect his or her right to life' (Judge LJ at [52]). References to risks to 'safety', or indeed to any other consequence except death, are now superfluous and should be avoided (*Yaqoob* [2005] EWCA Crim 2169). **B1.66**

That the risk of death must be an obvious and serious one at the time of the breach of duty was emphasised in *Rudling* [2016] EWCA Crim 741. It was subsequently decided in *Rose* [2017] EWCA Crim 1168, [2018] QB 328 that 'in assessing reasonable foreseeability of serious and obvious risk of death, it is not appropriate to take into account what the defendant would have known but for his breach of duty' (at [94]). So an optometrist who, in breach of her explicit statutory duty to properly examine the eye of the patient, did not see the life threatening papilloedema, could not — on the specific facts including the routine nature of the eye examination in the absence of knowledge of the presence of the rare papilloedema — be expected to have reasonably foreseen an obvious and serious risk of death at the time of the breach of the statutory duty. Sir Brian Leveson

P pointed out (at [77]) that a 'mere possibility that an assessment might reveal something life-threatening is not the same as an obvious risk of death: an obvious risk is a present risk which is clear and unambiguous, not one which might become apparent on further investigation'. While the decision may seem at first glance to give the defendant the benefit of her own failure to spot what she should have spotted, the requirement of an obvious and serious risk of death is an aspect of the restriction of gross negligence manslaughter to the worst cases of negligence causing death. The factual matrix was said to be crucial; the eye test was not primarily concerned with diagnosing life-threatening conditions and in different circumstances an optometrist might be guilty of gross negligence manslaughter. One might say that there is a difference between the statutory duty imposed on the optometrist and the duty of care which might be imposed on D, relevant to gross negligence, dependent on there being an obvious and serious risk of death at the time of the acts or omissions complained of. *Rose* was distinguished in *Winterton* [2018] EWCA Crim 2435, [2019] 2 Cr App R 12 (101) where a construction site manager was convicted in relation to a death resulting from the collapse of a steep-sided trench. He ought to have known (and arguably did know) that it was dangerously dug and 'the warning signs and serious and obvious risk of death were there' for all to see (at [29]). However, in *Kuddus* [2019] EWCA Crim 837, [2019] 2 Cr App R 16 (145), *Rose* was followed in quashing the conviction of a restaurant owner who prepared part of a meal which caused a fatal allergic reaction but who did not know of the allergy and who would therefore not have foreseen a serious and obvious risk of death.

The Corporate Manslaughter and Corporate Homicide Act 2007, s. 20, abolished the common-law offence of manslaughter by gross negligence insofar as it concerns corporations or other organisations to which s. 1 of that Act applies (see **B1.69**).

Sentencing Guidelines

B1.67 See **B1.49**.

MOTOR MANSLAUGHTER AND ROAD TRAFFIC ACT OFFENCES

B1.68 Until the coming into force of the Road Traffic Act 1991, s. 1, there appeared to be a complete overlap between common-law motor manslaughter and the statutory offence of causing death by reckless driving (*Seymour* [1983] 2 AC 493). The 1991 Act replaced the offence of causing death by reckless driving in the Road Traffic Act 1988, s. 1, by the offence of causing death by dangerous driving and s. 2A of the 1988 Act defines the meaning of dangerous driving in a way which has echoes of the (objective) *Lawrence* definition of recklessness (now overruled) but is not identical with it; indeed it is somewhat wider in its scope. There thus ceased to be, as from 1991, the complete overlap with motor manslaughter previously envisaged in *Seymour* (and there was even less overlap after the decision of the House of Lords in *Adomako* [1995] 1 AC 1710). It is therefore even clearer today that common-law manslaughter should be reserved for the very worst cases (see, e.g., *Dobby* [2017] EWCA Crim 775, [2017] 2 Cr App R (S) 27 (216)). If a charge of manslaughter is being considered rather than the statutory offence, it should be borne in mind that causing death by dangerous driving is an alternative verdict to manslaughter in connection with the driving of a mechanically propelled motor vehicle (RTOA 1988, s. 24(A1), inserted by the Road Safety Act 2006, s. 33). (See further **C3.1** ***et seq.***)

CORPORATE MANSLAUGHTER

B1.69 The Corporate Manslaughter and Corporate Homicide Act (CMCHA) 2007 abolished the common-law offence of manslaughter by gross negligence in its application to corporations (s. 20) and in doing so replaced the 'identification principle' (see **A6.2**) with an offence based on a qualified aggregation principle whereby the fault of a number of individuals may be relevant to a management or organisational failure causing death, and the organisation can be liable provided that the contribution of 'senior management' is a 'substantial element' in the breach of duty. Only corporations and certain other organisations (including partnerships that are employers, public bodies and government departments) can commit the new offence. Individual directors and managers cannot be guilty under the Act although their own potential liability at common law for their own acts and omissions still, in principle, remains. The Act does not operate as a principle of attribution of criminal responsibility for an existing offence to corporations, rather it creates a criminal offence which can be committed only by corporations and similar bodies. The offence is called corporate manslaughter in England, Wales and Northern Ireland and corporate homicide in Scotland (s. 1(5)).

Definition

Corporate Manslaughter and Corporate Homicide Act 2007, s. 1 **B1.70**

(1) An organisation to which this section applies is guilty of an offence if the way in which its activities are managed or organised—
  (a) causes a person's death, and
  (b) amounts to a gross breach of a relevant duty of care owed by the organisation to the deceased.
(2) The organisations to which this section applies are—
  (a) a corporation;
  (b) a department or other body listed in Schedule 1;
  (c) a police force;
  (d) a partnership, or a trade union or employers' association, that is an employer.
(3) An organisation is guilty of an offence under this section only if the way in which its activities are managed or organised by its senior management is a substantial element in the breach referred to in subsection (1).

Procedure and Sentence

The offence of corporate manslaughter is triable only on indictment. Proceedings may not be instituted without the consent of the DPP (CMCHA 2007, s. 17). **B1.71**

The penalty available on conviction is a fine (s. 1(6)). The court may also, on the application of the prosecution, make a 'remedial order' under s. 9 requiring the organisation to take specified steps and, under s. 10, the court is now empowered to make a 'publicity order', i.e. an order for the conviction and specified particulars to be publicised. The definitive sentencing guideline, *Health and safety offences, corporate manslaughter and food safety and hygiene offences* (see Supplement, **SG28-1**, for relevant extracts), is applicable to organisations sentenced on or after 1 February 2016, irrespective of the date of the offence. The offence range is a fine of £180,000 to £20 million.

Relevant Duty of Care

Corporate Manslaughter and Corporate Homicide Act 2007, s. 2 **B1.72**

(1) A 'relevant duty of care', in relation to an organisation, means any of the following duties owed by it under the law of negligence—
  (a) a duty owed to its employees or to other persons working for the organisation or performing services for it;
  (b) a duty owed as occupier of premises;
  (c) a duty owed in connection with—
    (i) the supply by the organisation of goods or services (whether for consideration or not),
    (ii) the carrying on by the organisation of any construction or maintenance operations,
    (iii) the carrying on by the organisation of any other activity on a commercial basis, or
    (iv) the use or keeping by the organisation of any plant, vehicle or other thing;
  (d) a duty owed to a person who, by reason of being a person within subsection (2), is someone for whose safety the organisation is responsible.

(2) A person is within this subsection if—
(a) he is detained at a custodial institution or in a custody area at a court or police station;
(aa) he is detained in service custody premises;
(b) he is detained at a removal centre or short-term holding facility;
(c) he is being transported in a vehicle, or being held in any premises, in pursuance of prison escort arrangements or immigration escort arrangements;
(d) he is living in secure accommodation in which he has been placed;
(e) he is a detained patient;
(3) Subsection (1) is subject to sections 3 to 7.
(4) A reference in subsection (1) to a duty owed under the law of negligence includes a reference to a duty that would be owed under the law of negligence but for any statutory provision under which liability is imposed in place of liability under that law.
(5) For the purposes of this Act, whether a particular organisation owes a duty of care to a particular individual is a question of law.
The judge must make any findings of fact necessary to decide that question.
(6) For the purposes of this Act there is to be disregarded—
(a) any rule of the common law that has the effect of preventing a duty of care from being owed by one person to another by reason of the fact that they are jointly engaged in unlawful conduct;
(b) any such rule that has the effect of preventing a duty of care from being owed to a person by reason of his acceptance of a risk of harm.

B1.73 There are some very significant limitations to the above, fairly broad, meaning of 'relevant duty of care'. These are to be found in ss. 3 to 7. Sections 4, 5, 6 and 7 exclude or limit the relevant duty of care in certain specific areas of activity (i.e. military activities (s. 4), policing and law enforcement (s. 5), responses to emergency situations (s. 6) and child protection and probation functions (s. 7)). Two distinct methods of exclusion or limitation are utilised. First, duties in relation to certain activities are simply excluded as in the case of certain types of military activities or operations within s. 4. Secondly, duties as to certain other activities are not a relevant duty of care unless the duty falls within para. (a) or (b) of s. 2(1) (i.e. unless they are duties owed to employees etc. or as an occupier). This technique is used in s. 6 in relation to responses to emergency situations so that, for example, a fire and rescue authority will not be liable (e.g., to those being rescued or to bystanders) for the way it responds to an emergency but it can be liable to its own employees for breach of its duty towards them or to visitors for breach of its duty as an occupier of premises. The same applies to an NHS body responding to an emergency, although s. 6(3) and (4) further qualify this by saying that such a body can nevertheless be liable for the way in which medical treatment is carried out or is decided to be carried out, but not for decisions as to the order in which persons are to be given such treatment.

Both of the techniques of exclusion referred to above are used in s. 5, whereby some police operations are simply excluded (essentially where they deal with terrorism, civil unrest or serious disorder and officers come under attack or threat of attack or violent resistance), whereas any other activities can give rise to a relevant duty of care but only under s. 2(1)(a) or (b) (as employer or occupier). While ss. 4 to 7 limit the meaning of 'relevant duty of care' in relation to certain specific types of activity, s. 3 is of potentially more general application. The broadest exclusion comes in s. 3(1), which excludes 'any duty of care owed by a public authority in respect of a decision as to matters of public policy (including in particular the allocation of public resources or the weighing of competing public interests)'. Arguments that a person's death is due to a government decision not to allocate appropriate resources to a particular service carried out by a public authority are thus not to be countenanced.

B1.74 A second exclusion comes in s. 3(2) in relation to things done 'in the exercise of an exclusively public function', although in this instance the duty of care as employer or occupier under s. 2(1)(a) or (b) still survives. The phrase 'exclusively public function' is defined in s. 3(4) as referring to a function falling under the Crown prerogative or by nature exercisable only with authority conferred by the exercise of the prerogative or by or under a statutory provision. This exclusion is not limited to public authorities but could, for example, include a private sector organisation given statutory powers (e.g., licensing powers or power to detain in custody as in the case of privatised prisons). More naturally, it will apply to public authorities, including HM Prison Service, but it should be remembered that the duty as employer or occupier still survives.

Overall, the provisions of ss. 3 to 7 significantly limit the effect of the expansion in s. 1(1) of the scope of the offence beyond corporations to government departments and other public bodies. To a large extent they also reflect some of the policy issues that at common law would come into play in deciding against a duty of care in tort and answer the question fairly directly as to how and to what extent the duty of care for the purposes of the criminal law should be limited by analogous considerations even though their precise scope and interpretation remain to be determined.

Gross Breach

Corporate Manslaughter and Corporate Homicide Act 2007, s. 8 **B1.75**

(1) This section applies where—
  (a) it is established that an organisation owed a relevant duty of care to a person, and
  (b) it falls to the jury to decide whether there was a gross breach of that duty.
(2) The jury must consider whether the evidence shows that the organisation failed to comply with any health and safety legislation that relates to the alleged breach, and if so—
  (a) how serious that failure was;
  (b) how much of a risk of death it posed.
(3) The jury may also—
  (a) consider the extent to which the evidence shows that there were attitudes, policies, systems or accepted practices within the organisation that were likely to have encouraged any such failure as is mentioned in subsection (2), or to have produced tolerance of it;
  (b) have regard to any health and safety guidance that relates to the alleged breach.
(4) This section does not prevent the jury from having regard to any other matters they consider relevant.

For a discussion in the first decided case under the Act of the potential impact of the reverse burden of proof under health and safety legislation on the burden of proof for corporate manslaughter as a result of s. 8 and the mention therein of failure to comply with health and safety legislation, see *Cotswold Geotechnical Holdings Ltd* [2011] EWCA Crim 1337, [2012] 1 Cr App R (S) 26 (153), commentary by Dobson at [2012] Crim LR 200, and, on the Act more generally, Wells [2014] Crim LR 849.

Related Offences

The offence cannot be committed by an individual nor can an individual be guilty of aiding, abetting, counselling or procuring the commission of an offence of corporate manslaughter (CMCHA 2007, s. 18(1)). The same principle applies in respect of assisting and encouraging crime in Part 2 of the SCA 2007, s. 62 of which inserted s. 18(1A) into the CMCHA 2007. **B1.76**

Section 19 makes provision as to the relationship between corporate manslaughter and health and safety offences.

Corporate Manslaughter and Corporate Homicide Act 2007, s. 19

(1) Where in the same proceedings there is—
  (a) a charge of corporate manslaughter or corporate homicide arising out of a particular set of circumstances, and
  (b) a charge against the same defendant of a health and safety offence arising out of some or all of those circumstances, the jury may, if the interests of justice so require, be invited to return a verdict on each charge.
(2) An organisation that has been convicted of corporate manslaughter or corporate homicide arising out of a particular set of circumstances may, if the interests of justice so require, be charged with a health and safety offence arising out of some or all of those circumstances.

CAUSING OR ALLOWING THE DEATH OF A CHILD OR VULNERABLE ADULT

Definition

B1.77 **Domestic Violence, Crime and Victims Act 2004, s. 5**

(1) A person ('D') is guilty of an offence if—
(a) a child or vulnerable adult ('V') dies or suffers serious physical harm as a result of the unlawful act of a person who—
(i) was a member of the same household as V, and
(ii) had frequent contact with him,
(b) D was such a person at the time of that act,
(c) at that time there was a significant risk of serious physical harm being caused to V by the unlawful act of such a person, and
(d) either D was the person whose act caused the death or serious physical harm or—
(i) D was, or ought to have been, aware of the risk mentioned in paragraph (c),
(ii) D failed to take such steps as he could reasonably have been expected to take to protect V from the risk, and
(iii) the act occurred in circumstances of the kind that D foresaw or ought to have foreseen.
(2) The prosecution does not have to prove whether it is the first alternative in subsection (1)(d) or the second (sub-paragraphs (i) to (iii)) that applies.

The Domestic Violence, Crime and Victims (Amendment) Act 2012 amended s. 5 and related provisions so as to extend their application to cases involving a child or vulnerable adult suffering serious physical harm. For the offence and sentence for the offence related to such harm, see **B2.169**. Notwithstanding the new non-fatal version of the offence, the procedural provisions still clearly envisage that the fatal version of the offence remains a distinct offence with its own rules.

Procedure

B1.78 The offence is triable only on indictment and is a class 1A offence if a fatality has resulted and a class 2A offence in any other case (CrimPD XIII, para. B: see Supplement, **CPD.XIII.B**).

The DVCVA 2004, s. 6(5), expressly provides for an offence of causing or allowing a person's death under s. 5 to be treated as an offence of homicide for the purposes of:

(a) the MCA 1980, ss. 24 and 25, relating to mode of trial of a child or young person;
(b) the CDA 1998, s. 51A, relating to sending cases to the Crown Court in relation to children and young persons;
(c) the PCC(S)A 2000, s. 8, relating to the remittal of young offenders to youth courts for sentence.

The offence of causing or allowing a person's death is a 'fatal offence' for the purposes of the Law Reform (Year and a Day Rule) Act 1996, s. 2, thereby requiring the A-G's consent to a prosecution in certain circumstances, including where the death occurs more than three years after the injury alleged to have caused it (DVCVA 2004, sch. 10, para. 33).

B1.79 More controversially, under s. 6(1), 'where a person is charged in the same proceedings with an offence of murder or manslaughter and with an offence under section 5 in respect of the same death', s. 6(2), (3) and (4) affect the evidence and procedure applicable to the offence of murder or manslaughter in three different but related ways:

(a) under s. 6(2), where by virtue of the CJPO 1994, s. 35(3), inferences may be drawn in relation to the s. 5 offence from D's failure to give evidence or refusal to answer a question, the court or jury may also draw such inferences in determining whether D is guilty of murder or manslaughter (or any alternative verdict offence on those charges) even if there would otherwise be no case for D to answer in relation to murder or manslaughter (or the alternative verdict offence);

(b) under s. 6(3), unless the s. 5 offence is itself dismissed, the charge of murder or manslaughter is not to be dismissed on an application to the Crown Court under the CDA 1998, sch. 3, para. 2;

(c) under s. 6(4), the question of whether there is a case for D to answer on the charge of murder or manslaughter is not to be considered before the close of all the evidence (unless D has already ceased to be charged with the s. 5 offence).

Domestic Violence, Crime and Victims Act 2004, s. 6 **B1.80**

(1) Subsections (2) to (4) apply where a person ('the defendant') is charged in the same proceedings with an offence of murder or manslaughter and with an offence under section 5 in respect of the same death ('the section 5 offence').

(2) Where by virtue of section 35(3) of the Criminal Justice and Public Order Act 1994 a court or jury is permitted, in relation to the section 5 offence, to draw such inferences as appear proper from the defendant's failure to give evidence or refusal to answer a question, the court or jury may also draw such inferences in determining whether he is guilty—
  (a) of murder or manslaughter, or
  (b) of any other offence of which he could lawfully be convicted on the charge of murder or manslaughter, even if there would otherwise be no case for him to answer in relation to that offence.

(3) The charge of murder or manslaughter is not to be dismissed under paragraph 2 of Schedule 3 to the Crime and Disorder Act 1998 (unless the section 5 offence is dismissed).

(4) At the defendant's trial the question whether there is a case for the defendant to answer on the charge of murder or manslaughter is not to be considered before the close of all the evidence (or, if at some earlier time he ceases to be charged with the section 5 offence, before that earlier time).

These provisions clearly contemplate proceedings for murder or manslaughter being brought where a child or vulnerable adult dies in A's (and often B's) household and there is evidence that A (and/or B) may have been guilty of an offence under s. 5 but there is not yet a prima facie case for murder or manslaughter against A or B (the problem in *Lane* (1986) 82 Cr App R 5). Proceedings for murder or manslaughter against A (and/or B), if instituted, cannot now be dismissed in advance by means of an application to dismiss in the Crown Court nor can the charges be dismissed at trial by a submission of no case to answer (the *Lane* problem) before the close of *all* the evidence, by when it will be known if and to what extent A has given evidence (and by when there may be other evidence incriminating A given by B in B's own defence). In addition, A can actually be convicted of murder or manslaughter on the basis of inferences drawn from A's failure to testify or refusal to answer questions at trial, even though without those inferences there would not be a case for A to answer in relation to murder or manslaughter. The fact that there would 'otherwise be no case for A to answer' does not necessarily mean that A is at risk of being convicted 'solely' on the basis of an inference from silence, since one would expect there to be other evidence, albeit not sufficient on its own to amount to a prima facie case, but there is a clear risk that it might amount to a conviction based 'mainly' on an inference from silence and, as such, it is highly likely to be subject to challenge under the ECHR, Article 6 (see **F20.49** and *Murray v UK* (1996) 22 EHRR 29). It should be stressed that these provisions modify the evidential and procedural rules only in relation to offences of murder and manslaughter charged in the same proceedings as a s. 5 offence and do not affect the s. 5 offence itself, which is subject to the normal rules on no case to answer and adverse inferences and the like. **B1.81**

Indictment

Statement of Offence **B1.82**

Causing or allowing the death of a child [or vulnerable adult] contrary to section 5 of the Domestic Violence, Crime and Victims Act 2004.

Particulars of Offence

A, on or about the...day of..., being a member of the same household as a child [or vulnerable adult] V and having frequent contact with him, fell into one or other of the following alternatives, it being immaterial, and unnecessary to prove, which one it was, that is to say that

either he caused the death of V as a result of his (A's) own unlawful act which carried a significant risk of serious physical harm being caused to V,

or, alternatively, he failed to take such steps as he could reasonably have been expected to take to protect V from the significant risk of serious physical harm from the unlawful act which caused V's death, the unlawful act having been committed in this alternative not by A but by another person who was a member of the same household as V and who had frequent contact with V, the significant risk in this alternative being one which A was aware of or ought to have been aware of and the other's unlawful act occurring in circumstances of the kind which A foresaw or ought to have foreseen.

Alternative Verdicts

B1.83 There are no alternative verdicts specifically provided for and the offence is not itself an alternative verdict to murder or manslaughter, but note the procedural and evidential links to murder and manslaughter (see **B1.78** ***et seq.***). The offence is in a sense, within itself, one self-contained alternative verdict in that D is guilty provided that it can be proved that D must have satisfied one or other of the two alternatives even though it cannot be proved which particular one. Given the problems of proof underlying the creation of the offence, it is inappropriate for a special verdict, as to whether a particular defendant actually caused as opposed to allowed the death, to be sought (*Hopkinson* [2013] EWCA Crim 795, [2014] 1 Cr App R 3 (22)).

Sentence

B1.84 The maximum penalty for an offence under the DVCVA 2004, s. 5, where death is involved is 14 years' imprisonment (s. 5(7)). The Sentencing Council definitive guideline, *Child Cruelty* (see Supplement, **SG20-1**), includes this offence, but only where the victim of the offence is a child aged 15 or under. It applies to offenders aged 18 and over who are sentenced on or after 1 January 2019, irrespective of the date of the offence. There is one level of harm and three levels of culpability (high, medium and lesser). The guideline supersedes earlier case law on causing or allowing a child to die, but does not cover causing or allowing the death of a vulnerable adult, for which the Sentencing Council's *General Guideline: Overarching Principles* (see Supplement, **SG2-1**) is used for all offenders sentenced on or after 1 October 2019.

Earlier case law will continue to be relevant in vulnerable adult cases. In *Ikram* [2008] EWCA Crim 586, [2008] 2 Cr App R 24 (347), the Court of Appeal indicated that the general approach to sentencing in manslaughter cases was applicable to s. 5 offences. Following *A-G's Ref (No. 60 of 2009) (Appleby)* [2009] EWCA Crim 2693, [2010] 2 Cr App R (S) 46 (311) (see **B1.45**), sentence levels were generally increased in unlawful act manslaughter cases. In *Wiltshire* [2017] EWCA Crim 1686, [2018] 1 Cr App R (S) 22 (149), it was held that there was no reason to confine that authority to unlawful act rather than gross negligence manslaughter, and that the new levels must also apply to the s. 5 offence. The Court of Appeal went on to observe that when it comes to criminal liability the statute makes no distinction between actual and constructive knowledge of a risk, but when it comes to an assessment of culpability the distinction was potentially important. The Court cautioned that the distinction was not unitary and was always a matter of degree, but the principle was applied to reduce sentences for each of two defendants from 11 to ten years' imprisonment on the basis that although they should have been aware of the relevant risks posed to their deceased daughter, they were genuinely unaware of them.

The distinction between causing and allowing a death was considered in *Mills* [2017] EWCA Crim 559, [2017] 2 Cr App R (S) 7 (38), in which three offenders were convicted of allowing the death of a vulnerable adult (a man with significant learning difficulties) who was living with them. They were all aware of violence being inflicted on the victim by the son of one of the offenders, but did nothing to assist the victim; they fed him painkillers to keep him sedated.

Eventually, a further assault caused his death. The perpetrator was convicted of murder. The Court of Appeal said that the offence under s. 5 was serious and in some cases as serious as the worst offence of manslaughter. When sentencing, culpability had to be assessed very carefully, including the nature of the relationship between the parties and the nature of the breach of duty, though each of those elements might be equally relevant. 'Allowing' a child or vulnerable adult to die (as in this case) was not necessarily less culpable than 'causing' that outcome. Sentences of eight years, five years, and three years were appropriate.

Elements

The offence is a response to the problems exemplified in *Lane* (1986) Cr App R 5 and discussed in Law Com No. 282, *Children: Their Non-Accidental Death or Serious Injury (Criminal Trials)*. It goes beyond the Law Commission proposals by including vulnerable adults (defined in the DVCVA 2004, s. 5(6), as 'a person aged 16 or over whose ability to protect himself from violence, abuse or neglect is significantly impaired through physical or mental disability or illness, through old age or otherwise'. In *Uddin* [2017] EWCA Crim 1072, [2017] 2 Cr App R 31 (454), this definition of vulnerable adult was given a broad interpretation. It was decided that the words 'or otherwise' are not limited to categories similar to the preceding two (disability/illness and old age) but incorporate a different third category which could be defined as a 'cause (other than physical or mental disability or illness or old age) which has the effect on the victim of significantly impairing his ability to protect himself from violence, abuse or neglect' (at [37]). The cause of the impaired ability to protect oneself under this third category could be intrinsic or external and could be 'physical, psychological and/or arise from the victim's circumstances' but they were not limited to cases of 'utter dependency' as postulated in *Khan* [2009] EWCA Crim 2, [2009] 1 Cr App R 28 (370): 'A victim of sexual or domestic abuse or modern slavery, for instance, might find himself in a vulnerable position, having suffered long term physical and mental abuse leaving them scared, cowed and with a significantly impaired ability to protect themselves' (at [40]). **B1.85**

As can be seen from the draft indictment (see **B1.82**) there are two ways of committing the offence (it being unnecessary to prove which one it is). The first can be compared with unlawful act manslaughter and the second with gross negligence manslaughter, but there are significant differences in each case. Unlawful act manslaughter requires only that the unlawful act carry a risk of 'some harm resulting therefrom, albeit not serious harm', whereas under s. 5(1)(c) there has to be a 'significant risk of *serious* physical harm', which is defined in s. 5(6) as 'harm that amounts to grievous bodily harm for the purposes of the Offences Against the Person Act 1861'. The risk must also be a 'significant' one; 'significant' is an ordinary English word which should not be further defined for the jury and it is incorrect to tell the jury that it means 'more than minimal' (*Stephens* [2007] EWCA Crim 1249, [2007] 2 Cr App R 26 (330)). Comparing the second limb of the offence with gross negligence manslaughter reveals that there is no requirement under s. 5(1)(d)(ii) that the failure 'to take such steps as he reasonably could have been expected to take' has to be gross, but, on the other hand, it should be noted that as a result of s. 5(1)(a), the death must occur as a result of the unlawful act of *someone* (in the same household etc.), even if it is not the unlawful act of the accused. This introduces an element of unlawfulness that is not required for gross negligence manslaughter.

Unlawful Act An unlawful act is defined in s. 5(5) as one that: **B1.86**

(a) constitutes an offence, or
(b) would constitute an offence but for being the act of—
  (i) a person under the age of ten, or
  (ii) a person entitled to rely on a defence of insanity.

Paragraph (b) does not apply to an act of D.

As with unlawful act manslaughter, it might frequently be an assault or some other offence against the person that is constituted by the unlawful act but it will only constitute an offence if the person who committed it had the *mens rea* required for that offence. This requirement is also implicit in subsection (5)(b) which specifically provides that an act is still unlawful for these purposes even if the person who committed it is under the age of ten or can rely on the defence of insanity. There is no provision for the act to be unlawful even if the person who committed it lacks *mens rea*. Proving this when one is not sure whether it is D's act or the act of another person that caused death may cause problems, although it is enough to show that whoever committed the unlawful act must have done so with the relevant *mens rea* of that unlawful act. As far as the first limb of the offence is concerned, i.e. where it is D's unlawful act that has caused death, as opposed to it being the unlawful act of some other person, s. 5(5) is stated not to apply for the obvious reason that infancy or insanity would be defences available to D in any event.

B1.87 **Relationship of Offence with Child Cruelty** Where it is a child who has died, the unlawful act might constitute an offence of child cruelty under the CYPA 1933 (see **B2.145**). An aggravated offence of child cruelty where death occurs was part of the Law Commission's proposed mechanisms for dealing with the problems in this area (see Law Com No. 282, para. 6.2). Child cruelty can itself be committed in many different ways (see **B2.146** and **B2.152**), and note that an 'act' for the purposes of the DVCVA 2004, s. 5, 'includes a course of conduct and also includes omission' (s. 5(6)). Provided the other requirements of s. 5 are satisfied, one can envisage a successful prosecution based on s. 5 where it can be proved that a child must have died as a result of child cruelty by one or the other of the two (or more) members of the child's household. Although the offence of child cruelty requires the accused to have 'responsibility' for the child, this is not required under s. 5, whereby it is enough that the accused was a member of the same household and had frequent contact with the child.

B1.88 **Member of Same Household** Section 5(4) explains further the concepts of 'member' and 'the same household as V'.

Domestic Violence, Crime and Victims Act 2004, s. 5

(4) For the purposes of this section—
   (a) a person is to be regarded as a 'member' of a particular household, even if he does not live in that household, if he visits it so often and for such periods of time that it is reasonable to regard him as a member of it;
   (b) where V lived in different households at different times, 'the same household as V' refers to the household in which V was living at the time of the act that caused the death or serious physical harm.

Section 5(4)(a) focuses on *D's* membership of a household and makes it clear that D does not have to live in it to be a member whereas s. 5(4)(b) focuses on V (the child or vulnerable adult) and makes it clear that it is the household that V 'lives in' at the time of the act in question that is important. In focusing on the household V 'lives in' (as opposed to households of which V is a member), s. 5(4)(b) seems to ignore the possibility that V might be a member of different households during the period in which a course of conduct (see the definition of 'act' in s. 5(6)) took place.

It should be noted that in addition to being a member of the same household as V, D is also required to have had frequent contact with V at the time of the act (s. 5(1)(a)(ii)), an issue which in *Khan* [2009] EWCA Crim 2, [2009] 1 Cr App R 28 (370) was said to be free-standing and independent of the question of whether D ought to have been aware of the risk to V.

B1.89 **Liability of Persons Aged under 16** Although in principle a sibling, or other person, who is under 16 could be guilty of an offence under s. 5 (as unlike child cruelty, D does not have to have responsibility for the child or vulnerable adult), s. 5(3) effectively excludes this possibility:

...if D was not the mother or father of V—
   (a) D may not be charged with an offence under this section if he was under the age of 16 at the time of the act that caused the death or serious physical harm...

So a child sibling cannot be charged, but an under-age parent can be. Section 5(3)(b) goes on to provide that, other than for parents of V, a person cannot be held responsible for failures to take reasonable steps under s. 5(1)(d)(ii) prior to reaching the age of 16.

Failure to Take Steps In relation to the second alternative manner of commission of the offence, failing 'to take such steps as he could reasonably have been expected to take to protect V from the risk', whilst this is clearly an objective test, it is one that focuses on the steps that D could have been expected to take, not the steps that some paradigmatic reasonable person might have taken. This may be very important given that potential accused persons may themselves have been at risk of abuse from other members of the household, and focusing on the steps that the particular accused could have been reasonably expected to take was used in the Parliamentary debates to ward off suggestions that victims of domestic violence should be specifically exempted from the scope of the offence. Account can be taken of their situation through consideration of what steps they, in their situation, could reasonably be expected to take, an approach which was also endorsed by Lord Judge CJ in *Khan* [2009] EWCA Crim 2, [2009] 1 Cr App R 28 (370), although on the facts it was not necessary for the judge to speculate on such matters. **B1.90**

Directions on Offence The offence is designed to combat difficulties of proof, but it will be a challenging task to explain to juries precisely what it is that they must be satisfied of (see **B1.82**). Essentially, the jury must be satisfied that D (being a member of the same household etc.) *either* caused the victim's death by D's own unlawful act (carrying a significant risk of serious physical harm) *or, if not,* that D failed to take steps that D could reasonably have been expected to take to protect V from the risk of such harm from an unlawful act by another member of the same household and D ought to have both been aware of the significant risk and to have foreseen the circumstances in which the unlawful act occurred. The circumstances need only be of the same kind as, and need not be identical to, those which should have been foreseen (*Khan* [2009] EWCA Crim 2, [2009] 1 Cr App R 28 (370), where it was also said (at [36]) that 'generally speaking a direction framed in accordance with the statute pre-empts any criticism'). See also *Ikram* [2008] EWCA Crim 586, [2008] 2 Cr App R 24 (347) at [62] for an example of 'a helpful way of directing a jury about the ingredients of the offence'. **B1.91**

INFANTICIDE

Definition

Infanticide Act 1938, s. 1 **B1.92**

(1) Where a woman by any wilful act or omission causes the death of her child being a child under the age of 12 months, but at the time of the act or omission the balance of her mind was disturbed by reason of her not having fully recovered from the effect of giving birth to the child or by reason of the effect of lactation consequent upon the birth of the child, then, [if] the circumstances were such that but for this Act the offence would have amounted to murder [or manslaughter], she shall be guilty of [an offence], to wit of infanticide, and may for such offence be dealt with and punished as if she had been guilty of the offence of manslaughter of the child.

Procedure

Infanticide is triable only on indictment. It is a class 1A offence. **B1.93**

Indictment

Statement of Offence **B1.94**

Infanticide contrary to section 1(1) of the Infanticide Act 1938

Particulars of Offence

A on or about the... day of... did cause the death of her child V aged under 12 months by a wilful act [or omission], namely, smothering him with a pillow [failing to...], but at a time when the balance of her mind was disturbed by reason of the fact that she had not fully recovered from the effect of giving birth to V [and/or from the effect of lactation consequent on giving birth to V]

Alternative Verdicts

Child destruction (Infant Life (Preservation) Act 1929, s. 2(2)), see **B1.102**. **B1.95**

Sentence

B1.96 The maximum sentence is life imprisonment (Infanticide Act 1938, s. 1). There is no offence-specific guideline but the Sentencing Council's *General Guideline: Overarching Principles* (see Supplement, **SG2-1**) is used for all offenders sentenced on or after 1 October 2019.

The approach for sentencing in cases of infanticide was considered by the Court of Appeal in *Sainsbury* (1989) 11 Cr App R (S) 533. The offender had become pregnant at the age of 15. She did not tell anyone, and gave birth to the baby without medical assistance. The baby was then wrapped in a blanket, taken some distance away and drowned in a river. The sentencer accepted that the balance of the offender's mind was disturbed by the effect of giving birth, but did not accept that her responsibility was removed altogether. He imposed a sentence of 12 months' detention in a young offender institution. The Court of Appeal, having regard to statistics which indicated that in 59 cases of infanticide dealt with over the previous ten years there had been no custodial sentences, all offenders having been dealt with by way of probation, supervision or hospital orders, decided that although the offence was serious the mitigating factors were overwhelming, and varied the sentence to probation. See also *Lewis* (1989) 11 Cr App R (S) 457.

Elements Generally

B1.97 The offence predates the introduction of the defence of diminished responsibility, and is designed to serve a similar role in relation to killings of very young children by their mothers in circumstances where the mothers are not fully responsible for their actions. It differs from diminished responsibility (and thus has survived the introduction of that defence) in that it can be charged from the outset and can be used to avoid charging a woman with the offence of murder (or now manslaughter) in relation to her own child. Under s. 1(2) of the Infanticide Act 1938, it can also be returned as an alternative verdict to murder (or, it would now appear, as an alternative verdict to manslaughter with effect from 4 October 2010 as a result of the CAJA 2009, s. 57), although s. 1(3) makes it clear that that is without prejudice to the jury's power on an indictment for murder to return a verdict of manslaughter or not guilty by reason of insanity. The offence covers a narrower range of circumstances than diminished responsibility, as the disturbance of the mother's mind must be due either to 'her not having fully recovered from the effect of giving birth' or to 'the effect of lactation consequent upon the birth of the child', criteria now regarded as outdated and unduly narrow. However, notwithstanding Judge LJ's statement in *Kai-Whitewind* [2005] EWCA Crim 1092, [2005] 2 Cr App R 31 (457) at [134] that 'no other circumstances are relevant', it is now clear following *Tunstill* [2018] EWCA Crim 1696, [2018] 2 Cr App R 31 (499) that this does not require the causes specified in the definition to be the sole cause of the balance of mind being disturbed. Treacy LJ stated (at [31]):

> ...as long as a failure to recover from the effects of birth is an operative or substantial cause of the disturbance of balance of mind that should be sufficient, even if there are other underlying mental problems (perhaps falling short of diminished responsibility) which are part of the overall picture.

Any broadening of the scope for an infanticide verdict is advantageous where the prosecution are alleging murder since a legal burden of proof is placed on the defence in a case of diminished responsibility whereas if there is evidence capable of showing it is infanticide, the burden of proving that it is not a case of infanticide remains on the prosecution. Nevertheless the comment in *Kai-Whitewind* at [140] that 'the law relating to infanticide is unsatisfactory and outdated' remains true. See further Law Com No. 304 (November 2006), paras. 8.44 to 8.59, for a discussion of possible procedural reforms (distinct from the change actually effected by the CAJA 2009, s. 57).

Mens Rea

The *mens rea* for infanticide was reviewed in the case of *Gore* [2007] EWCA Crim 2789. The case was a tragic one where the accused had herself died since her conviction following a guilty plea. The case had been referred by the CCRC to the Court of Appeal on the basis that she may not have had the *mens rea* for murder, which it was said was a prerequisite to a charge of infanticide (as seemed to have been assumed in *Smith* [1983] Crim LR 789). The Court of Appeal was of the opinion that proof of an intention to cause death or grievous bodily harm was not an integral part of the crime. The words in s. 1(1), as in force at the time, 'notwithstanding that the circumstances were such that but for this Act the offence would have amounted to murder', simply had their natural meaning of 'even if' and should not be artificially read as 'provided that'. The *mens rea* was to be found in the opening words of s. 1(1), 'by any wilful act or omission', and this had the beneficial effect in the court's view that: **B1.98**

> ... the offence of infanticide covers a wider range of cases ... A distressed young mother in a similar position to this appellant is not forced to confront what may be the stark truth that, for whatever reason, however disturbed she may have been at the time, she killed her child intending to kill or cause really serious bodily harm ... a mother in this position, often a woman in severe distress, is not required to acknowledge that she has murdered her child before she can benefit from a charge of infanticide. (Hallet LJ at [35].)

The Court did not explain in detail what precisely is required for a 'wilful' act or omission and simply said 'the prosecution must prove that the defendant acted or omitted to act wilfully', but references in the judgment to *Sheppard* [1981] AC 394 and wilful neglect under the CYPA 1933, s. 1 (see **A2.13** and **B2.155**), suggest that the Court may have had a similar interpretation in mind. Despite this involving a subjective test, it is very considerably wider than the *mens rea* for murder or even manslaughter; not only does it encompass recklessness rather than intention but the recklessness can relate simply to the child's health being at risk rather than to death or serious injury. The resultant breadth of the offence is seen by the Court as a good thing insofar as it avoids detailed examination or rehearsal of the often tragic circumstances where a distressed mother kills her young child. The amendments to s. 1 of the Infanticide Act 1938 effected by the CAJA 2009, s. 57 (in force from 4 October 2010), have the effect of confirming *Gore* insofar as the killing would not be required to have otherwise amounted to murder but narrow it in that the offence would otherwise have had to amount to at least manslaughter.

Act or Omission which Causes Death

See **A1.14** to **A1.24** for liability for omissions. See **A1.17** for the duty of parents to preserve the life of their children; essentially, parents have a duty to take any reasonable steps lying within their power to prevent harm to their child. See **A1.25** *et seq.* for the principles of causation. **B1.99**

'Of Her Child under the Age of 12 Months'

If the mother kills the child of another, even if it is in the course of killing her own child, then the killing of that other cannot amount to infanticide. If the mother intended to kill or cause grievous bodily harm, it would prima facie be murder but might be brought within the defence of diminished responsibility. Strictly speaking, the same principles apply if the mother kills, say, her own 11-month-old child as a result of giving birth to another child later in the same year, since the disturbance of her mind has to be due to the effects of the birth of the child which is killed. **B1.100**

The offence cannot apply once the child has reached the age of 12 months, but again, diminished responsibility would be the appropriate defence to consider. If, at the other end of the scale, the child has not been fully born before the mother kills it, the offence is not infanticide but child destruction (see **B1.102** to **B1.110**) and, by virtue of the Infant Life (Preservation) Act 1929, s. 2(2), child destruction is an alternative verdict to infanticide.

Complicity and Attempt

B1.101 Where a mother aids and abets the killing of her child by another (e.g., the father) but cannot be said to cause its death, it would appear that infanticide is inapplicable, and again, diminished responsibility would have to be relied on. If a third person (including, e.g., the father) aids and abets the mother to commit what is (for her) only infanticide, it would seem likely that, by analogy with the Homicide Act 1957, s. 2(4) (see **B1.18**), that third person should still be guilty of murder if he has the appropriate *mens rea*.

Some doubts have been expressed whether attempted infanticide is an offence known to the law, but such an indictment was approved in *Smith* [1983] Crim LR 789.

CHILD DESTRUCTION

Definition

B1.102 **Infant Life (Preservation) Act 1929, s. 1**

(1) Subject as hereinafter in this subsection provided, any person who, with intent to destroy the life of a child capable of being born alive, by any wilful act causes a child to die before it has an existence independent of its mother, shall be guilty of [an offence], to wit, of child destruction, and shall be liable on conviction thereof on indictment to life imprisonment:
Provided that no person shall be found guilty of an offence under this section unless it is proved that the act which caused the death of the child was not done in good faith for the purpose only of preserving the life of the mother.

Procedure

B1.103 Child destruction is triable only on indictment. It is a class 1A offence.

Indictment

B1.104 *Statement of Offence*

Child destruction contrary to section 1(1) of the Infant Life (Preservation) Act 1929

Particulars of Offence

A on or about the... day of..., with intent to destroy the life of a child capable of being born alive, did cause the death of the child of V, before it had an existence independent of the said V, by means of a wilful act, namely...

Alternative Verdict

B1.105 Abortion contrary to the OAPA 1861, s. 58 (Infant Life (Preservation) Act 1929, s. 2(3)).

Sentence

B1.106 The maximum sentence is life imprisonment (Infant Life (Preservation) Act 1929, s. 1). There is no offence-specific guideline but the Sentencing Council's *General Guideline: Overarching Principles* (see Supplement, **SG2-1**) is used for all offenders sentenced on or after 1 October 2019. In *Wilson* [2016] EWCA Crim 1555, [2017] 1 Cr App R (S) 7 (35) the offender, aged 22 and with no convictions, together with another man attacked the pregnant girlfriend of the offender, kicking and stamping on her stomach in a deliberate attempt to abort the child. The woman was 32 weeks pregnant at the time; the child was delivered stillborn following an emergency Caesarean section and the victim required life-saving surgery. The offender was convicted of causing grievous bodily harm with intent and child destruction. He received a life sentence with a minimum term of 16 years. Although allowing the appeal and reducing the minimum term to 14 years, the Court of Appeal said that individually the offences would have merited determinate sentences of 18 years and, in the case of child destruction, possibly longer.

Relationship with Other Offences

This offence was created to fill the gap between murder (which, as noted at **B1.1** and **B1.8**, requires a live birth) and abortion (which requires an attempt to procure a miscarriage, see **B1.111** to **B1.121**). A child killed in the process of being born would not be murdered, because there would be no live birth, and it would not be abortion since there was no miscarriage. The offence, however, overlaps with abortion, as it is not restricted to acts done while the child is in the process of being born and also covers the causing of miscarriage of a child 'capable of being born alive'. Abortion is an alternative verdict to child destruction (Infant Life (Preservation) Act 1929, s. 2(3)). **B1.107**

Meaning of 'Capable of Being Born Alive'

Infant Life (Preservation) Act 1929, s. 1 **B1.108**

(2) For the purposes of this Act, evidence that a woman had at any material time been pregnant for a period of 28 weeks or more shall be prima facie proof that she was at that time pregnant of a child capable of being born alive.

In addition to this statutory presumption, it is open to the prosecution to try to prove that a particular child was capable of being born alive even though it has not reached the relevant number of weeks' gestation. In a civil case, *C v S* [1988] QB 135, the Court of Appeal held that a child between 18 and 21 weeks was not capable of being born alive, as it could not breathe. On the other hand, in *Rance v Mid-Downs Health Authority* [1991] 1 QB 587, Brooke J held that a child of 26 or 27 weeks' gestation, who could have breathed unaided for two to three hours at least, was capable of being born alive.

Meaning of 'Wilful Act'

In contrast to the offence of infanticide discussed at **B1.92** to **B1.101**, the definition requires a positive act and an omission will not suffice. 'Wilful' seems here to mean merely 'voluntary', as the *mens rea* of an 'intent to destroy the life of a child capable of being born alive' is separately stated. For the meaning of wilfulness generally, see **A2.13**. Recklessness is clearly insufficient in this context. **B1.109**

Special Defences

Under the proviso to the Infant Life (Preservation) Act 1929, s. 1(1), 'no person shall be found guilty... unless it is proved that the act which caused the death of the child was not done in good faith for the purpose only of preserving the life of the mother'. **B1.110**

Thus, the burden is on the prosecution to negate this defence, whether or not, it would seem, the accused adduces any evidence to raise the issue. The only cases relating to the scope of this defence are first instance rulings of trial judges, and even these were prosecutions for abortion under the OAPA 1861, s. 58, where the court implied a similar defence by analogy with the proviso currently under discussion. A fairly flexible view of the meaning of 'preserving the life of the mother' was taken in these cases. In *Bourne* [1939] 1 KB 687, at p. 694, Macnaghten J took the view that the jury could properly conclude that D was acting in good faith to preserve the life of the mother if D believed 'that the probable consequence of the continuance of the pregnancy will be to make the woman a physical or mental wreck'. In *Newton* [1958] Crim LR

469, Ashworth J referred to 'preserving the life or health of the woman... not only her physical health but also her mental health'.

The Abortion Act 1967, s. 5(1), provides a defence to a charge of child destruction as follows:

> No offence under the Infant Life (Preservation) Act 1929 shall be committed by a registered medical practitioner who terminates a pregnancy in accordance with the provisions of this Act.

The offence of child destruction and the presumption that a child is capable of being born alive at 28 weeks' gestation no longer therefore represent one of the limits on the lawfulness of abortions under the 1967 Act. If the provisions of the 1967 Act (see **B1.119**) are complied with, an act is neither abortion nor child destruction.

ABORTION

Definition

B1.111 **Offences against the Person Act 1861, s. 58**

> Every woman, being with child, who, with intent to procure her own miscarriage, shall unlawfully administer to herself any poison or other noxious thing, or shall unlawfully use any instrument or other means whatsoever with the like intent, and whosoever, with intent to procure the miscarriage of any woman, whether she be or be not with child, shall unlawfully administer to her or cause to be taken by her any poison or other noxious thing, or shall unlawfully use any instrument or other means whatsoever with the like intent, shall be guilty of [an offence], and being convicted thereof shall be liable to [imprisonment] for life.

Procedure

B1.112 Abortion is triable only on indictment. It is a class 1A offence.

Indictment

B1.113 *Statement of Offence (1)*

Administering poison with intent to procure miscarriage contrary to section 58 of the Offences against the Person Act 1861

Particulars of Offence

A on or about the... day of... did unlawfully administer [or cause to be administered] to V a poison or other noxious thing, namely..., with intent to procure her miscarriage

Statement of Offence (2)

Using an instrument or other means with intent to procure miscarriage contrary to section 58 of the Offences against the Person Act 1861

Particulars of Offence

A on or about the... day of... did unlawfully use the following means, namely..., with intent to procure the miscarriage of V

Sentence

B1.114 The maximum penalty is life imprisonment (OAPA 1861, s. 58). There is no offence-specific guideline but the Sentencing Council's *General Guideline: Overarching Principles* (see Supplement, **SG2-1**) is used for all offenders sentenced on or after 1 October 2019.

Sentences of three years' imprisonment were upheld on offenders in *Scrimaglia* (1971) 55 Cr App R 280 who pleaded guilty to using an instrument to procure a miscarriage. Lord Parker CJ endorsed the trial judge's comment that: 'Now that abortions can be performed legally either under the National Health Service or at the patient's own expense, operations such as yours, carried out at a cut price and in disgraceful, insanitary and even dangerous conditions, are totally unnecessary apart from being against the law'. The offender in *Catt* [2013] EWCA Crim 1187, [2014] 1 Cr App R (S) 35 (210) was a 36-year-old woman, married with two young children. She induced her own miscarriage when 40 weeks' pregnant by taking a drug which she had obtained over the internet. A sentence of eight years' imprisonment was reduced to three and a half years on appeal.

Elements Generally

Given the large number of abortions now carried out legally under the provisions of the Abortion Act 1967 (see **B1.119**), the offence is comparatively rarely prosecuted. There are two peculiar features to note about the definition of the offence. First, it is in the nature of a statutory attempt. The *actus reus* does not require the actual procuring of a miscarriage, but rather an act done with the intention of procuring that result. Secondly, the requirements of the offence differ according to whether it is the (pregnant) woman herself or another person who is charged. In the case of the woman herself she must indeed be pregnant, whereas in the case of others, it is sufficient if she is believed to be pregnant and there is thus an intention to procure her miscarriage. This latter distinction is now almost redundant, because: **B1.115**

(a) if a non-pregnant woman is helped by another, she can be convicted either of encouraging and assisting (*Sockett* (1908) 1 Cr App R 101) or conspiring with (*Whitchurch* (1890) 24 QBD 42) that other; and
(b) even if she is acting alone, she would appear to be guilty of an attempt to commit the offence under s. 58 as a result of the CAA 1981, s. 1(2) (see **A5.72** *et seq*.).

In practice, the woman herself is rarely prosecuted today, and the offence is aimed principally at third parties operating outside the terms of what is permitted under the Abortion Act 1967 and exploiting the woman's predicament for financial gain.

Intention to Procure Miscarriage

For the meaning of 'intention', see **A2.4**. What stage of a pregnancy has to be reached before it is possible to 'miscarry' is a matter of some controversy. Is it as soon as the ovum is fertilised, or only when the fertilised ovum is implanted in the womb some ten days later? If it were the former, then some types of so-called contraceptives, such as 'the morning-after' pill, would be technically illegal under the OAPA 1861, s. 58. However, in *R (Smeaton) v Secretary of State for Health* [2002] EWHC 610 (Admin), [2002] Crim LR 664, Munby J ruled that 'miscarriage' means the termination of an established pregnancy and that there is no established pregnancy prior to implantation. Hence the prescription of the morning-after pill is not a criminal offence. **B1.116**

'Poison or other Noxious Thing...Instrument or Other Means'

If the indictment alleges the administration of a poison or noxious thing, it must either be a 'recognised poison' or, to be a noxious thing, some substance which is either harmful in itself or administered in such a quantity as to be harmful (*Cramp* (1880) 5 QBD 307) though not necessarily abortifacient (*Marlow* (1964) 49 Cr App R 49). However, it may be that a practical way out of the difficulty, if there is any doubt about whether the substance administered constitutes a poison or noxious thing, would be to utilise that form of the offence that can be committed by 'any means whatsoever', and to frame the indictment accordingly as in Statement of Offence (2) at **B1.113**. **B1.117**

Special Defences

It was held in *Bourne* [1939] 1 KB 687 that, by analogy to the proviso to the Infant Life (Preservation) Act 1929, s. 1(1), an act was not unlawful within s. 58 of the 1861 Act if it was **B1.118** done in good faith for the purpose only of preserving the life of the mother. This defence now seems to be entirely supplanted by the provision in the Abortion Act 1967, s. 5, that anything done with intent to procure a woman's miscarriage is unlawfully done unless authorised by s. 1 of the 1967 Act (see **B1.119**).

Abortion Act 1967, ss. 1 and 5

B1.119 **Abortion Act 1967, ss. 1 and 5**

1.—(1) Subject to the provisions of this section, a person shall not be guilty of an offence under the law relating to abortion when a pregnancy is terminated by a registered medical practitioner if two registered medical practitioners are of the opinion, formed in good faith—

(a) that the pregnancy has not exceeded its twenty-fourth week and that the continuance of the pregnancy would involve risk, greater than if the pregnancy were terminated, of injury to the physical or mental health of the pregnant woman or any existing children of her family; or

(b) that the termination is necessary to prevent grave permanent injury to the physical or mental health of the pregnant woman; or

(c) that the continuance of the pregnancy would involve risk to the life of the pregnant woman, greater than if the pregnancy were terminated; or

(d) that there is a substantial risk that if the child were born it would suffer from such physical or mental abnormalities as to be seriously handicapped.

(2) In determining whether the continuance of a pregnancy would involve such risk of injury to health as is mentioned in paragraph (a) or (b) of subsection (1) of this section, account may be taken of the pregnant woman's actual or reasonably foreseeable environment.

(3) Except as provided by subsection (4) of this section, any treatment for the termination of pregnancy must be carried out in a hospital vested in the Secretary of State for the purposes of his functions under the National Health Service Act 2006 or the National Health Service (Scotland) Act 1978 or in a hospital vested in a National Health Service trust established under section 18 of the National Health Service (Wales) Act 2006 or the National Health Service (Scotland) Act 1978 or an NHS foundation trust or in a place approved for the purposes of this section by the Secretary of State.

(3A) The power under subsection (3) of this section to approve a place includes power, in relation to treatment consisting primarily in the use of such medicines as may be specified in the approval and carried out in such manner as may be so specified, to approve a class of places.

(4) Subsection (3) of this section, and so much of subsection (1) as relates to the opinion of two registered medical practitioners, shall not apply to the termination of a pregnancy by a registered medical practitioner in a case where he is of the opinion, formed in good faith, that the termination is immediately necessary to save the life or to prevent grave permanent injury to the physical or mental health of the pregnant woman.

5.—(1) No offence under the Infant Life (Preservation) Act 1929 shall be committed by a registered medical practitioner who terminates a pregnancy in accordance with the provisions of this Act.

(2) For the purposes of the law relating to abortion, anything done with intent to procure a woman's miscarriage (or, in the case of a woman carrying more than one foetus, her miscarriage of any foetus) is unlawfully done unless authorised by section 1 of this Act and, in the case of a woman carrying more than one foetus, anything done with intent to procure her miscarriage of any foetus is authorised by that section if—

(a) the ground for termination of the pregnancy specified in subsection (1)(d) of that section applies in relation to any foetus and the thing is done for the purpose of procuring the miscarriage of the foetus, or

(b) any of the other grounds for termination of the pregnancy specified in that section applies.

Since under s. 5(1) of the 1967 Act, as amended by the Human Fertilisation and Embryology *Act 1990, s. 37, compliance with* the provisions of the 1967 Act is also a defence to a charge of child destruction under the Infant Life (Preservation) Act 1929 (see **B1.108**), the upper time-limits for legal abortions now are 24 weeks (see *R (British Pregnancy Advisory Service) v Secretary of State* [2020] EWCA Civ 355 for the precise point at which this occurs, taking account of day 0 as the first day of the pregnancy) for abortions under s. 1(1)(a) of the 1967 Act, and right up to the point of live birth under s. 1(1)(b), (c) or (d). Section 1(3A) is intended to cater for drugs such as RU 486 (mifepristone) being used in places other than National Health Service hospitals or approved nursing homes. Section 5(2) makes it clear that selective reduction (procuring the miscarriage of one or more, but not all, of the foetuses in a multiple pregnancy) may in appropriate cases be authorised by s. 1.

Section 1 was considered by the House of Lords in *Royal College of Nursing of the UK v Department of Health and Social Security* [1981] AC 800, in which Lord Diplock said (at p. 828): **B1.120**

> Subsection 1 although it is expressed to apply only 'when a pregnancy is terminated by a registered medical practitioner'... also appears to contemplate treatment that is in the nature of a team effort and to extend its protection to all those who play a part in it.

Thus, methods of abortion, such as induction of premature delivery by means of prostaglandin drip, which involve nurses (or others) playing a substantial role, are covered, and all the participants are exempted provided that a registered medical practitioner accepts (at p. 828):

> ... responsibility for all stages of the treatment for the termination of the pregnancy. The particular method to be used should be decided by the doctor in charge of the treatment for termination of the pregnancy; he should carry out any physical acts, forming part of the treatment, that in accordance with accepted medical practice are done only by qualified medical practitioners, and should give specific instructions as to the carrying out of such parts of the treatment as in accordance with accepted medical practice are carried out by nurses or other members of the hospital staff without medical qualifications. To each of them, the doctor, or his substitute, should be available to be consulted or called on for assistance from beginning to end of the treatment.

Although s. 1 refers to when 'a pregnancy *is* terminated', its protection also extends to cases where the attempt to terminate is unsuccessful (at p. 828), a not insignificant point, since the offence under the OAPA 1861, s. 58, is committed irrespective of whether a miscarriage is actually procured.

Medical Practitioners' Opinion The precise scope of the grounds for abortion enumerated in s. 1 are likely to continue to escape detailed interpretation by the courts, since the question is not whether these grounds actually exist but whether 'two registered medical practitioners are of the opinion, formed in good faith' that they exist. It was said in *Smith* [1973] 1 All ER 376 that a conviction of a doctor without evidence as to professional practice and the medical probabilities was likely to be unsafe, but it was stressed that the question of good faith is a matter for the jury to be determined by reference to all the evidence (and the appeal in that case was dismissed). **B1.121**

Although under the Abortion Act 1967, s. 1(3), the termination must normally be carried out in a National Health Service hospital or an approved clinic, under s. 1(4) this requirement does not apply if just one registered medical practitioner 'is of the opinion, formed in good faith, that the termination is immediately necessary to save the life or to prevent grave permanent injury to the physical or mental health of the pregnant woman'. Although, as noted at **B1.118**, s. 5 makes compliance with the Act the sole test of unlawfulness for the purposes of the law of abortion, it is possible that this does not exclude a general defence such as duress of circumstances (see **A3.50** and also the Canadian case of *Morgentaler v The Queen* (1975) 53 DLR (3d) 161), e.g., where a competent medical student, rather than a registered medical practitioner, is faced with the sort of emergency situation outlined in s. 1(4).

Regulations have been made under s. 2(1) of the 1967 Act relating to the form of certificates of opinions, requiring notifications etc. of terminations and prohibiting disclosure of information in such notifications etc. Under s. 2(3) of the Act, contravention of the regulations is a summary offence, but would not appear to render an abortion illegal if the provisions of s. 1 of the Act are complied with. However, absence of the proper certificates may make it more difficult to show that the relevant opinion(s) had indeed been formed in good faith.

SUPPLYING OR PROCURING THE PHYSICAL MEANS FOR ABORTION

Definition

B1.122 **Offences against the Person Act 1861, s. 59**

> Whoever shall unlawfully supply or procure any poison or other noxious thing, or any instrument or thing whatsoever, knowing that the same is intended to be unlawfully used or employed with intent to procure the miscarriage of any woman, whether she be or be not with child, shall be guilty of [an offence], and being convicted thereof shall be liable... to imprisonment... for any term not exceeding five years.

Procedure

B1.123 Supplying or procuring the physical means for abortion is triable only on indictment. It is normally a class 3 offence, but see CrimPD XIII, para. B (see Supplement, **CPD.XIII.B**), for the additional factors that the court considers on allocation.

Indictment

B1.124 *Statement of Offence*

> Supplying [or procuring] the physical means to procure a miscarriage contrary to section 59 of the Offences against the Person Act 1861

Particulars of Offence

> A on or about the... day of... unlawfully supplied [or procured] a poison or other noxious thing, namely..., knowing that it was intended to be unlawfully used with intent to procure the miscarriage of V

Sentence

B1.125 The maximum sentence is five years' imprisonment (OAPA 1861, s. 59). There is no offence-specific guideline but the Sentencing Council's *General Guideline: Overarching Principles* (see Supplement, SG2-1) is used for all offenders sentenced on or after 1 October 2019.

Elements

B1.126 'Supply' obviously means supply to another, and conversely 'procure' (any poison etc.) means procure *from* another, i.e. 'get possession of something of which you do not have possession already' (*Mills* [1963] 1 QB 522). Thus, the offence is not committed merely by producing the instrument or noxious thing etc. from one's cupboard (although the offence clearly is committed if it is then supplied, with the necessary knowledge, to another). In *Ahmed* [2010] EWCA Crim 1949, [2011] QB 512, where the appellant had tried to trick his wife into undergoing an abortion procedure at a clinic, the Court of Appeal ruled that he did not fall within the section as the means or 'thing' supplied or procured must be 'some sort of article or object rather than something such as a medical procedure which has no physical existence'. The words 'or thing whatsoever' in the OAPA 1861, s. 59, were contrasted with the phrase 'any means whatsoever' in s. 58. The latter might be apt to refer to a procedure as well as to a physical thing but 'thing' in s. 59 had a narrower meaning and was in effect interpreted *sui generis* with 'poison', 'noxious thing' and 'instrument'—all of which are physical objects.

Although s. 59 refers to the accused's *knowledge* of the intentions of others, such old authorities as there are interpret this in effect as *belief* that the others intend unlawfully to use the poison etc. with intent to procure a miscarriage (*Hillman* (1863) Le & Ca 343; *Titley* (1880) 14 Cox CC 502)—i.e. the accused can be convicted even if in actual fact the other or others do not intend so to use it unlawfully. The effect of the CAA 1981, s. 1(3) (see **A5.72** ***et seq.***), is probably that, quite apart from these decisions, the accused could now be convicted of attempt in these circumstances.

Special Defences

The exemption from liability provided by the Abortion Act 1967, s. 1, is equally applicable to this offence, as s. 6 of the Act defines 'the law relating to abortion' as meaning, 'sections 58 and 59 of the OAPA 1861 and any rule of law relating to the procurement of abortion'. **B1.127**

CONCEALMENT OF BIRTH

Definition

Offences against the Person Act 1861, s. 60 **B1.128**

> If any woman shall be delivered of a child, every person who shall, by any secret disposition of the dead body of the said child, whether such child died before, at, or after its birth, endeavour to conceal the birth thereof, shall be guilty of [an offence], and being convicted thereof shall be liable, at the discretion of the court, to be imprisoned for any term not exceeding two years.

Procedure

Concealing the birth of a child is triable either way. When tried on indictment it is normally a class 3 offence, but see CrimPD XIII, para. B (see Supplement, **CPD.XIII.B**), for the additional factors that the court considers on allocation. **B1.129**

Indictment

Statement of Offence **B1.130**

> Endeavouring to conceal birth contrary to section 60 of the Offences against the Person Act 1861

Particulars of Offence

> A on or about the... day of... endeavoured to conceal the birth of a child of which V had been delivered by a secret disposition of the dead body of that child

Alternative Verdicts

There are no alternative verdicts. It should also be noted that as a result of the CLA 1967, sch. 2, it is no longer possible to convict of this offence on an indictment for murder, infanticide or child destruction. Other offences which should be borne in mind include the common-law misdemeanours of disposing of or destroying a dead body with intent to prevent an inquest being held (*Stephenson* (1884) 13 QBD 331) and preventing the burial of a body (*Hunter* [1974] QB 95). See also **B14.56**. **B1.131**

Sentence

The maximum penalty is two years' imprisonment (OAPA 1861, s. 60). There is no offence-specific guideline but the Sentencing Council's *General Guideline: Overarching Principles* (see Supplement, **SG2-1**) is used for all offenders sentenced on or after 1 October 2019. **B1.132**

Meaning of 'Child'

In *Berriman* (1854) 6 Cox CC 388, Erle J said (at p. 390) that the child must have: **B1.133**

> ...arrived at that stage of maturity at the time of birth, that it might have been a living child.... No specific limit can be assigned to the period when the chance of life begins, but it may, perhaps, be safely assumed that under seven months the great probability is that the child would not be born alive.

However, in *Colmer* (1864) 9 Cox CC 506, a child of just four or five months' gestational age, about the length of a man's finger, was said by Martin B at first instance to be within the definition. The decision has been doubted, and indeed the jury acquitted. The meaning given to 'child' in *Berriman* is probably preferable and would make the offence consistent with that of child destruction. The qualifying words 'capable of being born alive' in the Infant Life (Preservation) Act 1929 (see **B1.102**), although in one sense somewhat otiose if 'child' itself is given the more limited *Berriman* meaning, could be regarded as clarifying the ambiguity already demonstrated in these cases.

Secret Disposition

B1.134 This is satisfied by putting the dead body in a place where it is unlikely to be found, even though the body is not concealed in the sense that it is completely hidden from view (*Brown* (1870) LR 1 CCR 244). Conversely, hiding the body from view is not sufficient if it is in such a manner that the body is nevertheless likely to be found (*George* (1868) 11 Cox CC 41). The accused's act must be done in relation to a dead body, so that the offence is not committed where the accused conceals a living child which later dies (*May* (1867) 10 Cox CC 448). However, there is almost certain to be liability for murder or manslaughter in this situation (or at least for attempt to commit an offence under the OAPA 1861, s. 60, where the accused believes the child is already dead). In *Hughes* (1850) 4 Cox CC 447, the accused concealed a living child, returned and found it dead, and replaced the covers which were concealing it. This was held to be an offence within a predecessor of s. 60 (9 Geo. 4 c. 31, s. 14), and to be a disposition of the dead body. An alternative and more appropriate charge would appear to be some form of homicide in relation to the initial act of concealing the living child which led to its death.

SOLICITATION OF MURDER

Definition

B1.135

Offences against the Person Act 1861, s. 4

Whosoever shall solicit, encourage, persuade or endeavour to persuade, or shall propose to any person, to murder any other person, whether he be a subject of Her Majesty or not, and whether he be within the Queen's dominions or not, shall be guilty of [an offence], and being convicted thereof shall be liable to imprisonment for life.

Procedure

B1.136 Solicitation of murder is triable only on indictment. It is a class 1A offence.

Indictment

B1.137

Statement of Offence

Soliciting to commit murder contrary to section 4 of the Offences against the Person Act 1861

Particulars of Offence

A on or about the . . . day of . . ., solicited [or encouraged etc.] X to murder V

Sentence

B1.138 The maximum penalty is life imprisonment (OAPA 1861, s. 4). There is no offence-specific guideline but the Sentencing Council's *General Guideline: Overarching Principles* (see *Supplement*, **SG2-1**) is used for all offenders sentenced on or after 1 October 2019. It is submitted that there will be cases where the definitive sentencing guideline, *Attempted Murder* (see Supplement, **SG13-1**), may be of some assistance.

An extended sentence for soliciting murder, with a custodial term of 12 years' imprisonment and an extension period of five years, was upheld in *Ahmad* [2012] EWCA Crim 959, [2014] 1 Cr App R (S) 17 (89), where the offender published material on a website encouraging the murder of Members of Parliament and providing their personal details. In *Hunter* [2007] EWCA Crim 3424, [2008] 2 Cr App R (S) 40 (226) eight years' imprisonment was upheld in the case of a woman who incited her partner to arrange the murder of a former partner and his new wife by a contract killer. She was convicted of incitement to solicit murder. The Court of Appeal said that the increase in sentences for murder since the coming into force of the CJA 2003, sch. 21, was relevant to related offences such as this. For similar comments see *Da Costa* [2009] EWCA Crim 482, [2009] 2 Cr App R (S) 98 (647).

Elements

Although the soliciting must be done from within the jurisdiction, the phrase 'whether he be a subject of Her Majesty or not, and whether he be within the Queen's dominions or not' has now in effect been interpreted so that it applies not only to the person to be murdered but also to the person being solicited. Thus in *Abu Hamza* [2006] EWCA Crim 2918, [2007] QB 659 it was no defence that the persons being solicited were of various nationalities and the murders were to take place abroad and that it was not proved that any of those solicited to murder were British nationals. The encouragement does not in any event have to be directed to a particular individual—see *Most* (1881) 7 QBD 244, where the offence was committed by means of a newspaper article. See also *El-Faisal* [2004] EWCA Crim 456, a case involving solicitation to indiscriminate killing which was recorded on tape, the defence of limitation to self-defence on the battlefield not being made out. **B1.139**

The offence is not complete until someone is in receipt of the solicitation, although the act of sending it can constitute an attempt (*Krause* (1902) 66 JP 121). It does not matter that the recipient is not in fact influenced, although in this case it might be prudent to allege an 'endeavour to persuade' in the particulars. Encouraging a pregnant woman to kill her child in the future, after it shall have been born alive, is an offence within the section (*Shephard* [1919] 2 KB 125). See *Tait* [1990] 1 QB 290 and **B1.151**. The wording of the offence is wide enough to include soliciting someone to participate in murder as a secondary party, as in *Winter* [2007] EWCA Crim 3493 (e.g., by encouraging someone to provide access to the intended venue of the killing).

ENCOURAGING OR ASSISTING SUICIDE

Definition

Suicide Act 1961, ss. 2 and 2A **B1.140**

2.—(1) A person ('D') commits an offence if—
(a) D does an act capable of encouraging or assisting the suicide or attempted suicide of another person, and
(b) D's act was intended to encourage or assist suicide or an attempt at suicide.

(1A) The person referred to in subsection (1)(a) need not be a specific person (or class of persons) known to, or identified by, D.

(1B) D may commit an offence under this section whether or not a suicide, or an attempt at suicide, occurs.

(1C) An offence under this section is triable on indictment and a person convicted of such an offence is liable to imprisonment for a term not exceeding 14 years.

(2) If on the trial of an indictment for murder or manslaughter of a person it is proved that the deceased person committed suicide, and the accused committed an offence under subsection (1) in relation to that suicide, the jury may find the accused guilty of the offence under subsection (1)

2A.—(1) If D arranges for a person ('D2') to do an act that is capable of encouraging or assisting the suicide or attempted suicide of another person and D2 does that act, D is also to be treated for the purposes of this Act as having done it.

(2) Where the facts are such that an act is not capable of encouraging or assisting suicide or attempted suicide, for the purposes of this Act it is to be treated as so capable if the act would have been so capable had the facts been as D believed them to be at the time of the act or had subsequent events happened in the manner D believed they would happen (or both).

(3) A reference in this Act to a person ('P') doing an act that is capable of encouraging the suicide or attempted suicide of another person includes a reference to P doing so by threatening another person or otherwise putting pressure on another person to commit or attempt suicide.

Procedure

B1.141 Encouraging or assisting suicide is triable only on indictment. It is a class 1A offence. The consent of the DPP is required to initiate proceedings for this offence (Suicide Act 1961, s. 2(4)). The House of Lords has held that the DPP cannot be required, nor does the DPP have the power, to give an undertaking to withhold consent to prosecution in advance of a contemplated assisted suicide (*R (Pretty) v DPP* [2001] UKHL 61, [2002] 1 AC 800), notwithstanding the compassionate factors of the particular case where the contemplated assistance would involve assistance in travelling to a country where assisted suicide is lawful. However, as regards the separate question of whether the offence in such circumstances interferes with the right to respect for private life under the ECHR, Article 8(1), the House of Lords in *R (Purdy) v DPP* [2009] UKHL 45, [2010] 1 AC 345 revised its own approach in *Pretty* (which was to the effect that Article 8 was not engaged) and followed the approach of the ECtHR in *Pretty v UK* (2002) 35 EHRR 1 (1) in holding that Article 8 is indeed engaged in that choices about the closing moments of life are part of the act of living. Furthermore, for the interference to be 'in accordance with the law' within Article 8(2), the House of Lords in *Purdy* concluded that there was a legal requirement for the DPP 'to promulgate an offence-specific policy identifying the facts and circumstances which he will take into account in deciding, in a case such as that which Ms Purdy's case exemplifies, whether or not to consent to a prosecution under section 2(1) of the 1961 Act'. The DPP policy on prosecuting cases of assisted suicide can be found at tinyurl.com/ycz8j36y and 'applies when the act that constitutes the encouragement or assistance is committed in England and Wales; any suicide or attempted suicide as a result of that encouragement or assistance may take place anywhere in the world, including in England and Wales'. In *R (Nicklinson) v Ministry of Justice* [2013] EWCA Civ 961, [2014] 2 All ER 32, the Court of Appeal held (with Lord Judge CJ dissenting) that the DPP had not done all that was required of him in *R (Purdy) v DPP* [2009] UKHL 45, [2010] 1 AC 345 in publishing a policy as to the facts and circumstances that would be taken into account in deciding whether to consent to a prosecution. However, in the Supreme Court ([2014] UKSC 38, [2015] AC 657), the DPP's appeal was unanimously allowed on this point, the content of the policy being constitutionally a matter for the DPP. In the course of the proceedings in the Supreme Court, counsel for the DPP indicated that the DPP agreed with Lord Judge's interpretation (given in the Court of Appeal) of factor 14 in para. 43 of the Policy, i.e. that factor 14 tending in favour of prosecution was concerned only with professionals who abused a position of trust arising from their professional relationship with the patient, e.g. by bringing undue influence to bear. It would thus not extend to a 'professional carer who, with no earlier responsibility for the care of the victim, comes in from outside to help'. On 16 October 2014 the DPP amended para. 43.14 of the policy (perfectly legally: see *R (Kenward) v DPP* [2015] EWHC 3508 (Admin), [2016] 1 Cr App R 16 (226)) in order to make this clear, by emphasising, in bold, its concluding words, and by adding a footnote to explain the role of those concluding words, so that it now is presented as saying that a prosecution is more likely to be required if:

> ... the suspect was acting in his or her capacity as a medical doctor, nurse, other healthcare professional, a professional carer [whether for payment or not], or as a person in authority, such as a prison officer, and the victim was in his or her care; [1]
>
> Footnote [1]: For the avoidance of doubt the words 'and the victim was in his or her care' qualify all of the preceding parts of this paragraph. This factor does not apply merely because someone was acting in a capacity described within it: it applies only where there was, in addition, a relationship of care between the suspect and the victims such that it will be necessary to consider whether the suspect may have exerted some influence on the victim.

The Supreme Court in *Nicklinson* also confirmed that the general prohibition created by s. 2 engages the ECHR, Article 8, and that the Court has jurisdiction to decide whether it is justified under Article 8(2) or incompatible under the HRA 1998. However, the majority considered that the matter was either in principle or, for the moment at least, one more appropriate for Parliament to resolve. In *R (Conway) v Secretary of State for Justice* [2017] EWHC 2447 (Admin), [2020] QB 1, the Divisional Court held that it was free to consider on its merits an application for a declaration that the Suicide Act 1961, s. 2, was incompatible with the domestically interpreted Article 8 rights of the applicant who was terminally ill with motor neurone disease. Nevertheless, following detailed consideration, the interference with the right to respect for the private life of the applicant caused by the blanket prohibition in s. 2 was found to be objectively justified under Article 8(2). The decision and reasoning of the Divisional Court was upheld by the Court of Appeal in *R (Conway) v Secretary of State for Justice* [2018] EWCA Civ 1431, [2020] QB 1.

Indictment

Statement of Offence **B1.142**

> Doing an act capable of encouraging or assisting suicide contrary to section 2(1) of the Suicide Act 1961

Particulars of Offence

> A on or about the ... day ... did an act, namely ..., capable of encouraging or assisting the commission of suicide or attempted suicide, intending thereby to encourage or assist suicide or attempted suicide

Alternative Verdicts

There are no alternative verdicts specifically provided for. The offence is itself an alternative verdict to murder or manslaughter (Suicide Act 1961, s. 2(2)). **B1.143**

Sentence

The maximum penalty is 14 years' imprisonment (Suicide Act 1961, s. 2). There is no offence-specific guideline but the Sentencing Council's *General Guideline: Overarching Principles* (see Supplement, **SG2-1**) is used for all offenders sentenced on or after 1 October 2019. **B1.144**

The Court of Appeal reviewed the relevant sentencing considerations for offences of encouraging or assisting suicide or attempted suicide in *Howe* [2014] EWCA Crim 114, [2014] 2 Cr App R (S) 38 (311). Treacy LJ referred to cases involving 'face to face' encouragement, rather than 'remote' encouragement over the internet. On degrees of harm involved, the most serious cases were those where death resulted, then those where serious harm resulted. Harm may be psychological as well as physical, and the effects on others as well as the victim should be taken into account. At the lower end of the harm range will be cases where, despite the encouragement of the offender, the victim does not go on to attempt suicide, or where a substance is provided but it turns out to be harmless. Turning to culpability, the court will have to consider issues of premeditation, persistence, and extent of the encouragement. Motivation may be important, with compassion at one end of the range and malice or prospect of gain at the other. There may also be breach of a duty of care or trust. The court should also consider whether the victim had a settled, voluntary and informed intention to commit suicide or not, whether the victim sought assistance from the offender, the victim's capacity to choose and the offender's knowledge of the extent of the vulnerability of the victim. Evidence of threats, pressure or persuasion applied to the victim will also be relevant. In those cases where the custodial threshold is crossed, the likely sentencing range is three years' imprisonment to 12 years or more after a trial. If the victim has not attempted suicide, there may be cases where custody is not required, but the range of general aggravating and mitigating factors will apply and the particular facts in each case must be examined with care. The Court found no reason to disapprove sentences imposed in the few earlier reported cases, such as *McGranaghan* [1987] 9 Cr App R (S) 447 and *A-G's Ref (No. 85 of 2006) (Workman)* [2006] EWCA Crim 2623, [2007] 1 Cr App R (S) 104 (637). On the facts of *Howe* itself, the 19-year-old offender, immature but with no previous convictions, was a close friend of the victim who suffered from mental health problems and had threatened in the past to take his own life. After spending much of the day drinking together, the offender drove to a petrol station to buy petrol and a cigarette lighter and returned to the victim's home. The victim then poured petrol on himself and set himself on fire, causing 95 per cent burns. Death did not result but the victim was grievously injured. The Court reduced a sentence of 12 years' detention in a young offender institution, imposed after a trial, to ten years' imprisonment. The Court said that the Sentencing Council guideline on offences under the OAPA 1861, s. 18, was not of assistance when sentencing an offence of assisting suicide.

Elements

B1.145 This special statutory offence was created because the substantive offence of suicide was abolished by the Suicide Act 1961, s. 1, and it originally used the traditional language of complicity expressed in terms of aiding, abetting counselling or procuring suicide. Changes to s. 2 made by the CAJA 2009, s. 59, having effect from 1 February 2010, were designed to state the existing law more clearly and unambiguously rather than to make any particular changes and are designed to bring the offence into line with, and to make use of the terminology in, Part 2 of the SCA 2007 relating to the inchoate offence of (intentionally) encouraging and assisting crime (see **A5.3** *et seq.*). Since there is in law no offence of suicide which can be encouraged or assisted, s. 2 makes the conduct which is capable of encouraging or assisting suicide an offence in its own right, just as under the previous formulation the aider and abettor of suicide was the principal offender as there was in law no principal offence of suicide to aid and abet. An inchoate basis of liability is in this sense somewhat more appropriate than one based on aiding and abetting which normally presupposes the commission of the principal offence which has been aided and abetted. The explicitly inchoate nature of the new formulation of the offence (spelled out in the new s. 2(1B)) also removes the former need to rely on a prosecution under the CAA 1981 for attempt to assist suicide where no one as a result of the encouragement actually commits or attempts to commit suicide. The full inchoate offence under s. 2(1) is committed by doing an act capable of encouraging or assisting suicide whether or not any suicide is committed or attempted and the law of attempt does not come into it (indeed the CAJA 2009, sch. 21, para. 58, excludes the operation of the CAA 1981 in relation to offences under s. 2 of the Suicide Act 1961). Section 2(1A) makes it explicit that one can be liable for doing acts capable of encouraging or assisting persons unknown to commit suicide. One example of this would be by means of material on a web site.

B1.146 *The accused must, of course, intend that someone* commit or attempt to commit suicide (*A-G v Able* [1984] 1 QB 795 under the old law and see now s. 2(1)(b)) but it is unnecessary for the accused to know or believe that the person encouraged had been intending or contemplating suicide (*S* [2005] EWCA Crim 819). Despite the confusion over whether there can generally be a conspiracy to aid and abet (see **A5.52**), there could be liability for conspiracy to aid and abet under s. 2(1) (*Reed* [1982] Crim LR 819) and there is no reason why the position should be any different under the new version of the offence.

Section 2A also makes it clear (a) that the offence can be committed through an intermediary, (b) that there is no defence of impossibility, and (c) that encouragement by threats or other forms of pressure is covered. Section 2B clarifies that D's liability need not be based on an individual act but may be based on a course of conduct over a period of time.

THREATS TO KILL

Definition

Offences against the Person Act 1861, s. 16 **B1.147**

A person who without lawful excuse makes to another a threat, intending that that other would fear it would be carried out, to kill that other or a third person shall be guilty of an offence and liable on conviction on indictment to imprisonment for a term not exceeding 10 years.

Procedure

Threatening to kill is triable either way. When tried on indictment this is normally a class 3 offence, but see CrimPD XIII, para. B (see Supplement, **CPD.XIII.B**), for the additional factors that the court considers on allocation. **B1.148**

Indictment

Statement of Offence **B1.149**

Making a threat to kill contrary to section 16 of the Offences against the Person Act 1861

Particulars of Offence

A on or about the... day of..., without lawful excuse, threatened V that he would kill him [or that he would kill X] intending that V would fear that the said threat would be carried out

Sentence

The maximum penalty is ten years' imprisonment (CLA 1977, sch. 12, replacing OAPA 1861, s. 16). The Sentencing Council definitive guideline, *Intimidatory Offences* (see Supplement, **SG27-1**) applies in respect of offenders aged 18 and over, sentenced on or after 1 October 2018, irrespective of the date of the offence. Prior to the guideline coming into effect, factors relevant to sentencing this offence were identified by Lord Bingham CJ in *A-G's Ref (No. 84 of 1999) (Jennison)* [2000] 2 Cr App R (S) 213. His lordship said that it may be relevant whether the threat is uttered in a state of sobriety or of drunkenness and whether there is repetition of the threat, and it is relevant to have regard to the vulnerability of the party threatened. Most important, however, in any case of this kind, is the reality of the threat: the likelihood, in the view of V, that the threat will be carried out and the extent to which V is put in genuine fear. It is relevant to consider whether D is known to be violent, and whether D is known to have some grudge or animus or grievance which may cause D to act in the manner threatened. **B1.150**

Elements

The words 'without lawful excuse' in the OAPA 1861, s. 16, would exempt, for example, a threat made reasonably in self-defence to deter an apprehended attack or to prevent crime (*Cousins* **B1.151**

[1982] QB 526). An implied threat will suffice (see the facts of *Solanke* [1970] 3 All ER 1383), as will a threat that is only to be carried out at some time in the future, although it would seem that it has to be one that will be carried out by D, or at least under D's instructions. V must be intended to fear that the threat will be carried out against V or another so it is the person to whom the threat is made, rather than the person to be killed (if different), who must be intended to fear that the threat will be carried out (for an illustration, see *Donovan* [2009] EWCA Crim 1258). A threat to a pregnant woman in respect of her unborn child is not sufficient if the threat is to kill it before its birth but if it is a threat to kill the child after its birth, then that would appear to be within s. 16 (*Tait* [1990] 1 QB 290). Alleging more than one threat in a single count may make it duplicitous but this will not necessarily result in any injustice so as to justify quashing a conviction (*Marchese* [2008] EWCA Crim 389, [2008] 2 Cr App R 12 (147)).

Section B2 Non-fatal Offences Against the Person

ASSAULT AND BATTERY

Definition

Assault and battery (or assault by beating) are separate and distinct summary offences. An assault is committed when D intentionally or recklessly causes another to apprehend immediate and unlawful violence. A battery is committed when D intentionally or recklessly inflicts unlawful force. A battery may, but does not inevitably, follow an assault. Despite this technical difference, the term 'assault', or 'common assault', has been generally used, both in cases (*Fagan v Metropolitan Police Commissioner* [1969] 1 QB 439) and in statutes (OAPA 1861, ss. 38, 42, 47), to cover either an assault or a battery. **B2.1**

It is now at least preferable to be more specific when laying an information. The Divisional Court in *DPP v Taylor* [1992] QB 645 held that all common assaults and batteries are offences contrary to what is now the CJA 1988, s. 39(1), and that the information must include a reference to that section. An information would be bad for duplicity if the phrase 'assault and battery' were used; the Court suggested that 'assault by beating' was the appropriate wording to use in cases of battery. As to the relationship between the two offences and the importance of charging them correctly, see *R (Kracher) v Leicester Magistrates' Court* [2013] EWHC 4627 (Admin), although in *R (Ward) v Black Country Magistrates' Court* [2020] EWHC 680 (Admin), [2020] 2 Cr App R 6 (88), it was suggested (*obiter*) that a charge of 'common assault' may be valid in respect of actual violence, as long as it is made clear that this is what D is accused of.

The CDA 1998, s. 29(1)(c), created a racially or religiously aggravated form of common assault or battery which carries a higher maximum penalty. For the meaning of 'racially or religiously aggravated', see **B11.145**.

By the CJA 1988, s. 39(2), s. 39(1) is now also subject to the Assaults on Emergency Workers (Offences) Act 2018, s. 1 of which makes provision for increased sentencing powers for offences of common assault and battery committed against an emergency worker acting in the exercise of functions as such a worker. See further **B2.43** *et seq.*

Procedure

B2.2 Common assault is generally triable only summarily (CJA 1988, s. 39), although the racially or religiously aggravated form created by the CDA 1998, s. 29(1)(c), is triable either way. A count for the basic summary offence may be included in an indictment in the circumstances prescribed by the CJA 1988, s. 40 (see *Walton* [2011] EWCA Crim 2832 and **D11.20**), but this does not make it an indictable offence (e.g., for the purposes of the CAA 1981, s. 1). See the Interpretation Act 1978, sch. 1, which was overlooked in *Nelson* [2013] EWCA Crim 30, [2013] 1 WLR 2861. As to the procedure on charging both the basic and aggravated offence, see *Henderson v DPP* [2016] EWHC 464 (Admin), [2016] 1 WLR 1990, discussed at **B11.46.**

Common assault under s. 40 has the ordinary everyday meaning of that word, including battery (*Lynsey* [1995] 3 All ER 654). Furthermore, a jury may convict D of common assault on an indictment for an offence such as assault occasioning actual bodily harm (CLA 1967, s. 6(3A)). In *Nelson* it was held that s. 6(3A) does not enable a jury to convict of common assault on a count alleging assault by beating, because a battery can be committed on someone who never saw the blow coming, but with respect this overlooks *Metropolitan Police Commissioner v Wilson* [1984] AC 242 and the numerous cases that have followed it (see **D19.48**), none of which were cited to or by the court in *Nelson.*

Sentence (Basic Offence)

B2.3 The maximum penalties for common assault or battery other than in the racially or religiously aggravated form (see **B2.4**) are six months' imprisonment, an unlimited fine, or both (CJA 1988, s. 39). Note the definitive sentencing guideline, *Assault* (see Supplement, **SG12-7**), and the guideline and notes derived therefrom in the *Magistrates' Court Sentencing Guidelines.* Where the offence occurs in a domestic setting the definitive sentencing guideline, *Domestic Abuse,* is applicable (see Supplement, **SG6-1**).

In *Fenton* (1994) 15 Cr App R (S) 682, the offender pleaded guilty to common assault (charges of assault occasioning actual bodily harm and dangerous driving were not proceeded with). In the course of an altercation between two motorists, the offender pushed the victim in the chest. The Court of Appeal said that almost all cases of violence between motorists would be so serious that only custody could be justified. The appropriate sentence was seven days' imprisonment. In *Peet* [2014] EWCA Crim 2800, [2015] 1 Cr App R (S) 48 (344), concurrent sentences of two months' imprisonment were appropriate for the offender, who twice spat into the faces of security officers while in custody at a magistrates' court.

Racial or religious aggravation cannot normally be taken into account by the sentencer when sentencing for the basic offence of common assault, given the availability of the racially aggravated form of the offence. To do so would infringe the principle that offenders must not be sentenced for an alternative offence for which they have not been charged and convicted (*McGillivray* [2005] EWCA Crim 604, [2005] 2 Cr App R (S) 60 (366); *Kentsch* [2005] EWCA Crim 2851, [2006] 1 Cr App R (S) 126 (737)). See, however, *O'Leary* [2015] EWCA Crim 1306, [2016] 1 Cr App R (S) 11 (66), a case involving unlawful wounding, where the Court of Appeal upheld the judge's view that the basic offence was religiously aggravated by the offender's comment at the time of the offence that he wanted to 'kill a Muslim', even though the racially aggravated form of the offence had not been charged. It was held that the approach was justified on the facts, where the judge had presided over the trial and had been entitled to conclude, to the criminal standard, that the assault was racially aggravated.

Sentence (Racially or Religiously Aggravated Form of Offence)

B2.4 The maximum penalty for the aggravated form of common assault is two years, a fine or both on indictment; six months, an unlimited fine or both summarily (CDA 1998, s. 29(3)). Note the definitive sentencing guideline, *Assault* (see Supplement, **SG12-7**), and the guideline and notes derived therefrom in the *Magistrates' Court Sentencing Guidelines.*

The definitive sentencing guideline gives the same offence range for the aggravated offence as for the basic offence, namely up to 26 weeks' imprisonment, but states that 'the court should determine the appropriate sentence for the offence without taking account of the element of aggravation and then make an addition to the sentence, considering the level of aggravation involved. It may be appropriate to move outside the identified category range, taking into account the increased statutory maximum', i.e. to two years' imprisonment. Since the maximum sentence for the basic offence is six months' imprisonment (from which credit will be deducted where there is a plea) this begs the question as to the appropriate proportionate uplift, about which there is no explicit guidance. The pre-guideline case of *Kelly* [2001] EWCA Crim 170, [2001] 2 Cr App R (S) 73 (341) nevertheless set out a series of relevant factors to consider in assessing the extent of the racial aggravation (see **B2.34**), and cases involving a 100 per cent uplift of the basic sentence have repeatedly been upheld. For example, in *Johnson* [2010] EWCA Crim 3077, [2011] 2 Cr App R (S) 29 (164) the Court of Appeal quashed a sentence of 18 months on a guilty plea in a case where the offender had acted aggressively towards a pregnant woman and called her a 'stupid white bitch'. The sentence was reduced because the judge had expressly taken 15 months as the starting point for the basic offence, whereas the maximum is only six months, and was varied to nine months, of which half was for the basic offence and half for the racial aggravation. In *Niewulis* [2013] EWCA Crim 556, [2013] 2 Cr App R (S) 83 (534), a sentence of six months after a trial, comprising three months for the basic offence and three months uplift for the racial element, was appropriate for an unpleasant but relatively minor offence committed by an offender with a record of racially motivated offending.

Actus Reus of Assault

Actions and Words An assault requires conduct which causes V 'to apprehend the imminent application of unlawful force upon her' (*Ireland* [1998] AC 147, per Lord Steyn at p. 161). A fear or apprehension of *possible* violence may suffice (*Ireland*) and it may also suffice where V is unsure as to when exactly the threatened attack may occur; but as the Court of Appeal pointed out in *Constanza* [1997] 2 Cr App R 492, the conduct in question must at least provoke some apprehension of violence 'at some time not excluding the immediate future'. A threat of violence only in the more distant future cannot suffice. As to what may amount to unlawful force, see **B2.9** and **B2.13** to **B2.21**. An omission to act arguably cannot amount to an assault, or indeed a battery, but see **B2.10**. **B2.5**

The relevant conduct in cases of assault may take the form of threatening acts or gestures, as for example where D brandishes a weapon at V or fires a shot in his direction; but it may also take the form of threatening words, or it may involve acts and words together. It may even involve a series of acts (*Cox* [1998] Crim LR 810). It was at one time thought that words alone, whether written or spoken, could never amount to an assault (*Meade and Belt* (1823) 1 Lew CC 184; *Russell on Crime*, 4th edn, 1865) but this view has now been rejected, both by the Court of Appeal in *Constanza* (a case involving the sending of threatening letters) and by the House of Lords in *Ireland* (a case involving telephone calls). Giving the judgment of the House of Lords in *Ireland*, Lord Steyn said:

> The proposition that a gesture may amount to an assault, but that words can never suffice, is unrealistic and indefensible. A thing said is also a thing done. There is no reason why something said should be incapable of causing an apprehension of immediate personal violence... I would, therefore, reject the proposition that an assault can never be committed by words.

In *Ireland* D made 'silent' telephone calls to a number of women, and it was held that such conduct could amount to the *actus reus* of assault if it caused victims to fear that physical violence might be used against them in the immediate future. It may suffice for this purpose if it causes V to fear the mere *possibility* of imminent violence, but it cannot suffice if V fears only the prospect of receiving further calls (*Ireland*, per Lord Hope at p. 166), nor can it suffice if it is clear to V that D or D's friends can do nothing to harm V in the immediate future. **B2.6**

The concept of immediacy has nevertheless been interpreted with some flexibility, and there have been a number of cases in which 'stalkers' have been prosecuted for assault on that basis. In *Smith v Chief Superintendent, Woking Police Station* (1983) 76 Cr App R 234, the Divisional

Court held that a threat of violence could be considered immediate, even though D was still outside V's home, looking in at her through a window, and would have needed to force an entry before he could attack her. In *Ireland*, the House of Lords adopted an even more flexible approach, stating (at p. 162) that 'there is no reason why a telephone caller who says to a woman in a menacing way, "I will be at your door in a minute or two" may not be guilty of an assault'. Such conduct may alternatively, and perhaps more appropriately, be prosecuted under the Protection from Harassment Act 1997 (see **B2.181**).

B2.7 **Negated and Conditional Threats** Words used by the accused may indicate that no attack is threatened, even where the circumstances might otherwise suggest that one is. Thus, in *Tuberville v Savage* (1669) 1 Mod 3, T, in the course of a quarrel with S, placed his hand on the hilt of his sword (an act which might ordinarily have been construed as an assault) and exclaimed, 'If it were not assize time, I would not take such language from you'. This was held to be no assault, 'for the declaration of [T] was that he would not assault [S], the judges being in town'.

A 'conditional' threat of unlawful violence may amount to an assault, even though V is told that violence may be avoided by complying with D's conditions. Thus, in the civil case of *Read v Coker* (1853) 13 CB 850, the plaintiff successfully sued for assault on the basis that D and his men had surrounded him and threatened to 'break his neck' if he refused to leave D's premises. See also *Ansell v Thomas* [1974] Crim LR 31.

B2.8 **Result Crime** Although an assault may take the form of a 'failed battery', as where D's blow fails to connect with V, assault is always a result crime (see **A1.2**). No assault can be committed unless the threats are actually perceived by V. There is no assault if a stone thrown by D sails past V's head without V noticing (although D may have attempted to commit an offence under the OAPA 1861, s. 47). If, however, D threatens V with an imitation firearm, this will indeed amount to an assault, unless V knows that the weapon cannot fire (*Logdon v DPP* [1976] Crim LR 121). If V does apprehend the threat of imminent violence, it does not matter whether V is frightened by it. V may even relish the opportunity to teach D a lesson, and yet still be regarded as the victim of D's assault.

Actus Reus of Battery

B2.9 A battery requires the unlawful application of force upon the victim. It cannot include the circumstances of a telephone caller who thereby causes V's psychiatric injury (*Ireland* [1998] AC 147 at p. 161); but as to assault, see **B2.5**; as to liability under the Protection from Harassment Act 1997, see **B2.181**.

Battery need not necessarily be preceded by any assault. A blow may, for example, be struck from behind, without warning. Nor need a battery involve any serious violence. Any unlawful touching of another may be classed as a battery (*Afolabi v CPS* [2017] EWHC 2960 (Admin)). As Goff LJ stated in *Collins v Wilcock* [1984] 3 All ER 374 (at p. 378), 'everybody is protected, not only against physical injury, but against any form of physical molestation'.

B2.10 **Direct and Indirect Application of Force** There is authority that a battery must take the form of a positive act, rather than a mere omission, and must involve a *direct* application of force. V might, for example, suffer pain or injury by slipping on a patch of oil that D has previously spilled and omitted to clear up, but arguably that is no battery, even if the spillage was deliberate. The need for a positive act was emphasised in *Fagan v Metropolitan Police Commissioner* [1969] 1 QB 439 (as to which, see **A1.8**). If *Fagan* is correct, there is no room in assault or battery cases for application of the *Miller* principle (see **A1.20**) because one cannot beat another person through mere inaction.

The question whether a battery must involve a direct application of unlawful force to V is however unclear. In *Metropolitan Police Commissioner v Wilson* [1984] AC 242, the House of

Lords held (albeit by implication) that *indirect* violence, such as the setting of a trap into which V falls, may not amount to a battery, even if it involves the unlawful 'infliction' of harm, for the purpose of liability under the OAPA 1861, s. 20, and that view was reiterated in *Savage* [1992] 1 AC 699 and in *Ireland* [1998] AC 147 at p. 160. *Martin* (1881) 8 QBD 54 merely decided that M's conduct in barring the doors to a theatre and putting out the lights could lead to the 'infliction' of grievous bodily harm on persons who were crushed in the ensuing panic. It says nothing about assault.

Two cases do support the concept of indirect battery. In *DPP v K* [1990] 1 All ER 331, the Divisional Court held that K, a schoolboy, was guilty of an offence under the OAPA 1861, s. 47, when he poured acid into a warm-air drier in his school cloakroom, causing injury to the next pupil who used it. No account was taken of *Fagan* or *Wilson*. The point was expressly left undecided in *Haystead v Chief Constable of Derbyshire* [2000] 3 All ER 890, but *DPP v K* was followed in *DPP v Santa-Bermudez* [2003] EWHC 2908 (Admin) in which D was held to have committed a battery against a police officer when he falsely assured her that he had no 'sharps' in his possession, and thus caused her to stab herself on a hypodermic needle as she searched him. However, none of the conflicting authorities or dicta was cited in that case.

The administering of a poison or noxious substance can amount to a battery (e.g., where it is sprayed directly into V's face, as in *Gillard* (1988) 87 Cr App R 189: see **B2.89**) and setting a dog on another person clearly involves a direct use of force, because the dog is used as a weapon. The same is true where D strikes P, causing her to drop and injure her child, Q. In *Haystead v Chief Constable of Derbyshire*, this was held to be a battery against both P and Q. There must also be a battery where D attacks P by pushing over a ladder on which P is standing, or by striking P's horse, so that it rears and throws P off. **B2.11**

Setting a spring gun or trap with intent to cause serious injury to any person may more appropriately be prosecuted under the OAPA 1861, s. 31, which may apply even if no injury is caused (*Cockburn* [2008] EWCA Crim 316, [2008] 2 All ER 1153; but contrast *Munks* [1963] 3 All ER 757, where a device designed to inflict an electric shock was held not to be 'a mantrap or other engine' within the meaning of s. 31).

Mens Rea of Assault or Battery

An assault or battery must be committed intentionally or recklessly: i.e., recklessness as to the risk of assault if the charge is one of assault; or recklessness as to the risk of battery if the charge is one of battery (*Afolabi v CPS* [2017] EWHC 2960 (Admin)). Recklessness, in this context, means subjective or *Cunningham* recklessness (*Savage* [1992] 1 AC 699). This is true both of common assault and of aggravated assaults under the OAPA 1861, s. 47, or the Police Act 1996, s. 89; but D's subjective state of mind may in some cases be inferred from the circumstances or (as in *Afolabi*) from video footage, even if there is no other evidence to establish it. Evidence of voluntary intoxication cannot, however, assist the defence in respect of such offences because they do not require 'specific intent' (see **A3.17**). **B2.12**

Lawful and Unlawful Force

Assault or battery must involve the use or threat of unlawful force. The use or threat of force is not always unlawful. In particular, it may be justified on the basis of actual or implied consent; on the basis of self-defence, crime prevention or crowd control; or on the basis that it involved the lawful correction of a child. **B2.13**

A mere technical battery is unlikely to be prosecuted; but difficulties have sometimes arisen where persons are touched by police officers against their will, because even a trivial technical assault or battery by a police officer takes that officer outside the scope of his duty, and prevents the officer from qualifying as the victim of any offence under the Police Act 1996, s. 89 (see **B2.45**).

Self-defence and related justifications for the use or threat of force are considered in **A3** and in particular at **A3.55**. Consent and lawful correction are considered at **B2.14** and **B2.20**.

B2.14 **Consent** Where consent is in issue, the burden of disproving it is on the prosecution (*Donovan* [1934] 2 KB 498). The two principal questions that may arise in this context are: (1) Did the complainant in fact consent (expressly or by implication) to what was done; and (2) if so, do public policy considerations invalidate that consent?

Whether consent was given is usually a simple question of fact, but we are all 'deemed' to consent to various harmless or unavoidable everyday contacts with our fellow citizens, which for that reason cannot be unlawful (*Wilson v Pringle* [1986] 2 All ER 440). Participants in contact sports such as football are meanwhile deemed to consent to the risk of clumsy or mistimed tackles or challenges; but this does not include tackles that are deliberately late or intended to cause harm. As Lord Woolf CJ pointed out in *Barnes* [2004] EWCA Crim 3246, [2005] 2 All ER 113, a jury should be told the importance of the distinction between D going for the ball, albeit late, and 'going for' an opponent. Some jobs notoriously involve the risk of being subjected to violence, but that has nothing to do with consent and no proper analogy can be drawn with implied consent in contact sports (*H v CPS* [2010] EWHC 1374 (Admin), [2010] 4 All ER 264).

B2.15 A person must ordinarily understand what is being consented to, if that person's consent to a physical procedure or intervention is to be effective (*Burrell v Harmer* [1967] Crim LR 169; *D* [1984] AC 778). It does not necessarily follow, however, that fraud or deception will invalidate consent. As the Court of Appeal explained in *Melin* [2019] EWCA Crim 557, [2019] QB 1063 (at [29]):

> Plainly it would be undesirable for the law to treat all false or fraudulent representations as vitiating consent because that would lead to, at least potentially, trivial lies about the person or the conduct, treatment or activity as giving rise to criminal liability.

To vitiate consent, the fraud or deception in question must instead relate *either* to the nature or quality of the act, *or* to the identity of the person performing it.

Fraud or deception as to identity may include for this purpose deception as to D's professional status or qualification, but only if that is, in the circumstances, 'integral' to D's identity, and crucial to V's consent. If, for example, V consents to undergo a medical procedure that should be performed only by a qualified surgeon, D's lack of any such qualification may invalidate V's consent (*Melin*, at [31]).

Difficult questions may, however, arise as to whether a given qualification or status is indeed sufficiently relevant or important to be 'integral' to D's identity. In *Richardson* [1999] QB 444, which was distinguished in *Melin*, D, a qualified dentist, recently suspended by her regulatory body, was not guilty of assault when she continued to treat her patients, without warning them of her suspension. Her suspension did not, said Otton LJ, alter or undermine her essential identity, even though her conduct was 'clearly reprehensible and may well found the basis of a civil claim in damages' (at p. 450).

In *Melin* itself, serious harm was caused to two of D's patients as a result of reactions to Botox injections. D had allegedly claimed to be a qualified medical practitioner, but Botox injections may be administered quite lawfully by persons who are not so qualified. The complainants, however, alleged that they had consented to treatment by D *only* because of his claim, and in one case there was sufficient evidence of this to support the guilty verdict returned by the jury. D's conviction for maliciously inflicting grievous bodily harm on that one count was accordingly upheld.

Fraud as to the nature or quality of the act or procedure is illustrated by *Tabassum* [2000] 2 *Cr App R 328, in which several women allowed D to examine their breasts on the basis of his* false representation that he was medically qualified and conducting a survey into breast cancer. Upholding D's conviction for indecent assault, Rose LJ said, '[t]hey were consenting to touching for medical purposes, and not to indecent behaviour, that is, there was consent to the nature of the act, but not its quality' (at p. 337). By the same token, in *Richardson*, D would clearly have been guilty had she drilled healthy teeth for fraudulent financial reasons.

In cases where it is alleged that D recklessly infected a partner with a sexually transmitted disease, *Clarence* (1888) 22 QBD 23 can no longer be considered good law. *Dica* [2004] EWCA Crim 1103, [2004] QB 1257 and *Konzani* [2005] EWCA Crim 706, [2005] 2 Cr App R 14 (198) now establish that D commits no offence if there is informed consent by D's partner, V, to the risk of sexually transmitted infection, but there will be no such informed consent if D is aware of the infection but has concealed it from V. As Judge LJ observed in *Konzani* (at [41]):

> There is a critical distinction between taking a risk of the various, potentially adverse and possibly problematic consequences of sexual intercourse, and giving an informed consent to the risk of infection with a fatal disease.

See also the CPS statement on policy for prosecuting the intentional or reckless sexual transmission of infection at tinyurl.com/ycdsneas. This was considered in the context of a prosecution under the OAPA 1861, s. 20, in *Golding* [2014] EWCA Crim 889.

Invalid Consent Where actual bodily harm (or worse) is deliberately inflicted, consent to it will ordinarily be deemed invalid on grounds of public policy, even if V knows exactly what is being consented to. In *Brown* [1994] 1 AC 212, the House of Lords upheld convictions for offences under the OAPA 1861, ss. 20 and 47, in respect of a group of homosexual sado-masochists, who had engaged in acts of consensual torture with each other for the purpose of sexual gratification. Lord Templeman said (at pp. 231, 234 and 236): **B2.16**

> In some circumstances violence is not punishable under the criminal law. When no actual bodily harm is caused, the consent of the person affected precludes him from complaining. There can be no conviction for the summary offence of common assault if the victim has consented...Even when violence is intentionally inflicted and results in...wounding or serious bodily harm the accused is entitled to be acquitted if the injury was a foreseeable incident of a lawful activity in which the person injured was participating. Surgery...is a lawful activity ...ritual [male] circumcision, tattooing, ear piercing and violent sports including boxing are lawful activities.
>
> ...The question whether the defence of consent should be extended to the consequences of sado-masochistic encounters can only be decided by consideration of policy and public interest....
>
> I am not prepared to invent a defence of consent for sado-masochistic encounters which breed and glorify cruelty and result in offences under sections 47 and 20 of the Act of 1861.

The appellants in *Brown* sought redress from the ECtHR (*Laskey v UK* (1997) 24 EHRR 39), but the Court ruled that State interference in this aspect of their private lives could be justified on the basis of 'protection of health'.

The approach adopted in *Brown* is consistent with earlier decisions such as *Donovan* [1934] 2 KB 498 (17-year-old girl could not validly consent to sado-masochistic caning) and *A-G's Ref (No. 6 of 1980)* [1981] QB 715 (not in the public interest to allow a defence of consent in the context of a fist-fight where actual bodily harm was intended and/or caused for no good reason, 'minor struggles' being excepted). It was followed in *BM* [2018] EWCA Crim 560, [2019] QB 1, in which the Court of Appeal rejected the submission that valid consent could be given by adults to acts of 'body modification' such as tongue splitting, ear removal or nipple excision, performed without anaesthetic by a tattooist with no medical training. Lord Burnett CJ noted that, whereas tattooing and piercing are (like boxing) long-accepted practices, 'deeply embedded in our law and general culture', body modifications of the kind under consideration are not, and such extreme and dangerous operations, which can easily lead to infections, cannot properly be considered analogous to mere tattooing.

Even were the general rule to be revisited by Parliament or the Supreme Court and a different line drawn which allows consent to act as a defence to causing actual bodily harm and wounding, body modification causes really serious harm. Moreover (at [41]):

> New exceptions should not be recognised on a case by case basis, save perhaps where there is a close analogy with an existing exception to the general rule established in the *Brown* case. The recognition of an entirely new exception would involve a value judgement which is policy laden, and on which there may be powerful conflicting views in society. The criminal trial process is inapt to enable a wide-ranging inquiry into the underlying policy issues, which are much better explored in the political environment.

B2.17 Lord Burnett CJ did not, however, challenge the correctness of *Wilson* [1997] QB 47, in which it was held that nothing said in *Brown* prevented a wife from validly consenting to her husband branding his initials on her buttocks using a hot knife. This was considered analogous to tattooing. Moreover, 'consensual activity between husband and wife in the privacy of the matrimonial home is not... normally a proper matter for criminal investigation, let alone criminal prosecution' (at p. 50).

Wilson must, however, be contrasted with *Emmett* (1999) *The Times*, 15 October 1999, in which it was held that dangerous and damaging sado-masochistic games (involving suffocation and burning) were not exempted by the *Wilson* principle, even where carried out consensually in a domestic relationship.

B2.18 **Consensual Risk-taking** One must distinguish between consent to the deliberate infliction of injury and consent to a lawful (if dangerous) activity in which injury is accidentally caused (*Slingsby* [1995] Crim LR 571). It is clear that persons may ordinarily consent to sexual or other activities that involve a significant risk of injury, even where they could not validly consent to the deliberate infliction of such injury. In *Dica* [2004] EWCA Crim 1103, [2004] QB 1257 Judge LJ explained (at [51]) why this is so:

> The problems of criminalising the consensual taking of risks... include the sheer impracticability of enforcement and the haphazard nature of its impact. The process would undermine the general understanding of the community that sexual relationships are pre-eminently private and essentially personal to the individuals involved in them. And if adults were to be liable to prosecution for the consequences of taking known risks with their health, it would seem odd that this should be confined to risks taken in the context of sexual intercourse, while they are nevertheless permitted to take the risks inherent in so many other aspects of everyday life...

See also *Meachen* [2006] EWCA Crim 2414. Another example of consensual risk-taking concerns 'rough and undisciplined horseplay'. In *Jones* (1986) 83 Cr App R 375, D and others tossed other youths into the air and let them fall to the ground. One of the victims suffered a ruptured spleen and another suffered a broken arm. The trial judge refused to allow the issue of consent to be raised, owing to the serious nature of the injuries, but the Court of Appeal held that the defence should (for what it was worth) have been left to the jury. This ruling was approved in *Brown* and followed in *Aitken* [1992] 4 All ER 541, but its proper limits must be understood. Individuals may lawfully engage in rough horseplay only where there is at least a genuine belief that V is consenting, and then only where no injury is intended. It is not a 'bully's charter'.

In *A-G's Ref (No. 6 of 1980)* [1981] QB 715, Lord Lane CJ also identified an exception covering 'dangerous exhibitions', although the extent of that exception has never been explored.

B2.19 **Medical Treatment** The law concerning the limits and effectiveness of consent to medical treatment is a highly specialised subject which cannot be covered in detail here; but the basic issues are examined at **A1.21**.

B2.20 **Lawful Correction or Chastisement** At common law, a parent or any other person acting *in loco parentis* may administer reasonable corporal punishment to control the behaviour of children in his or her care. Concepts of reasonableness have narrowed over the years, as the

Court of Appeal recognised in *H (Assault of child: Reasonable chastisement)* [2001] EWCA Crim 1024, [2002] 1 Cr App R 7 (59), and are strongly influenced by human rights issues. Caning, for example, was condemned by Strasbourg as 'inhuman and degrading treatment' (*A v UK* (1999) 27 EHRR 611) and must now be considered unlawful.

This is reflected in the Children Act 2004, s. 58, which clarifies the scope of reasonable correction or chastisement.

Children Act 2004, s. 58

(1) In relation to any offence specified in subsection (2), battery of a child cannot be justified on the ground that it constituted reasonable punishment.
(2) The offences referred to in subsection (1) are—
  (a) an offence under section 18 or 20 of the Offences against the Person Act 1861 (wounding and causing grievous bodily harm);
  (b) an offence under section 47 of that Act (assault occasioning actual bodily harm);
  (c) an offence under section 1 of the Children and Young Persons Act 1933 (cruelty to persons under 16).

Physical punishment is thus an offence if it causes any harm or injury such as bruising (see **B2.35**) and see also the CYPA 1933, s. 1 (see **B2.145**). Moreover, smacking a very young child for failing to understand something that child cannot be expected to understand might well be considered 'unreasonable' at common law, even if it causes no injury. **B2.21**

Under the Education Act 1996, s. 548, teachers and other staff (even at private schools) no longer have any right to administer corporal punishment 'by virtue of their position' but retain the right to avert an immediate danger of personal injury or damage to property (s. 548(5)). Staff may use reasonable force to prevent a pupil from committing any offence, causing personal injury to, or damage to the property of, any person (including the pupil himself), or prejudicing the maintenance of good order and discipline at the school or among any pupils receiving education there, whether during a teaching session or otherwise (Education and Inspections Act 2006, s. 93).

ASSAULT WITH INTENT TO RESIST OR PREVENT ARREST

Definition

Offences against the Person Act 1861, s. 38 **B2.22**

Whosoever . . . shall assault any person with intent to resist or prevent the lawful apprehension or detainer of himself or of any other person for any offence, shall be guilty of [an offence], . . .

Procedure

Assault with intent to resist or prevent arrest is triable either way. When tried on indictment this is normally a class 3 offence, but see CrimPD XIII, para. B (see Supplement, **CPD.XIII.B**) for the additional factors that the court considers on allocation. **B2.23**

Indictment

Statement of Offence **B2.24**

Assault with intent to resist arrest, contrary to section 38 of the Offences against the Person Act 1861

Particulars of Offence

A on or about the . . . day of . . . assaulted X with intent to resist or prevent the lawful apprehension of A [or another] for the commission of an offence

Sentence

The maximum penalty is two years (OAPA 1861, s. 38) on indictment; six months, or an unlimited fine, or both, summarily. Note the definitive sentencing guideline, *Assault* (see Supplement, **B2.25**

SG12-5), which gives an offence range up to 51 weeks' custody, and the guideline and notes derived therefrom in the *Magistrates' Court Sentencing Guidelines*.

Elements

B2.26 On a literal reading of s. 38, the only *actus reus* required is that of common assault (see B2.5), whereas the *mens rea* is that of common assault, coupled with an intent to resist or prevent one's own, or another person's, lawful arrest or detention, etc. Nevertheless, it is firmly established that the arrest or detention in question must in fact be lawful (*Self* [1992] 3 All ER 476; *Lee* [2001] 1 Cr App R 19 (293)) and this must accordingly be treated as a further essential *actus reus* element. The victim need not be a police officer, but may be a private citizen assisting such an officer, or a private citizen or store detective making a 'citizen's arrest'. In *Lee*, Rose LJ appears to have assumed that the victim must be the person seeking to make the lawful arrest; but this was *obiter* and (with respect) mistaken. There is no good reason why s. 38 should not extend to assaults on hapless citizens who unwittingly obstruct D's attempt to escape from pursuing officers. As to the contrast between the powers of arrest given to police officers and the more restricted powers given to private citizens, see *Self* and **D1.29**.

The *mens rea* requirement in s. 38 may be negatived by D's mistaken view of the facts, e.g., where D mistakes plain-clothed police officers for rival gangsters, and believes that an arrest is actually an abduction. In such a case D would have no intent to resist lawful arrest. Indeed, D would not even have the *mens rea* of assault (*Kenlin v Gardiner* [1967] 2 QB 510; *Williams* [1987] 3 All ER 411; *Brightling* [1991] Crim LR 364). The mistake would not have to be a reasonable one (*Williams; Lee; Blackburn v Bowering* [1994] 3 All ER 380). In contrast, D has no defence if the mistake is merely one of law, e.g., where D does not appreciate that a citizen has a power of arrest, or where D assumes that an arrest is unlawful merely because D is (or believes that he or she is) innocent of the offence in question. As Rose LJ said in *Lee*:

> Whether or not an offence has actually been committed or is believed by the defendant not to have been committed is irrelevant. We reach this conclusion without regret. Neither public order nor the clarity of the criminal law would be improved if juries were required to consider in relation to s. 38 offences the impact of a defendant's belief as to the lawfulness of his arrest in cases where a lawful arrest is being properly attempted on reasonable grounds.

ASSAULT OCCASIONING ACTUAL BODILY HARM

Definition

B2.27 **Offences against the Person Act 1861, s. 47**

> Whosoever shall be convicted upon an indictment of any assault occasioning actual bodily harm shall be liable... to [imprisonment for five years].

The CDA 1998, s. 29(1)(b), creates a racially or religiously aggravated form of this offence which carries a higher maximum penalty. For the meaning of 'racially or religiously aggravated', see **B11.145**.

Procedure

B2.28 Assault occasioning actual bodily harm (whether in its aggravated form or not) is triable either way. When tried on indictment this is normally a class 3 offence, but see CrimPD XIII, para. B (see Supplement, **CPD.XIII.B**) for the additional factors that the court considers on allocation. See the *Magistrates' Court Sentencing Guidelines* for indications as to when a case should be sent to the Crown Court. As to the procedure on charging both the basic and aggravated offence, see *Henderson v DPP* [2016] EWHC 464 (Admin), [2016] 1 WLR 1990, discussed at **B11.46**.

Indictments

Basic Offence B2.29

Statement of Offence

Assault occasioning actual bodily harm, contrary to section 47 of the Offences against the Person Act 1861

Particulars of Offence

A on or about the... day of... assaulted V by beating him, thereby causing him actual bodily harm

Aggravated Offence B2.30

Statement of Offence

Racially aggravated assault occasioning actual bodily harm, contrary to section 29(1)(b) of the Crime and Disorder Act 1998

Particulars of Offence

A on or about the... day of... assaulted V thereby causing him actual bodily harm and at the time or shortly after demonstrated to V hostility based on his membership of a racial group, by calling him a 'bloody paki'

Sentence (Basic Offence)

The maximum penalty for the offence other than in the racially or religiously aggravated form (see **B2.34**) is five years (OAPA 1861, s. 47) on indictment; six months, or an unlimited fine, or both, summarily. Note the definitive sentencing guideline, *Assault* (see Supplement, **SG12-4**), which sets out three categories for sentencing purposes with starting points of a medium level community order, 26 weeks' imprisonment and one year six months' imprisonment with an overall offence range up to three years' imprisonment. Particularly serious offending may justify a sentence outside that range. Note also the guideline and notes derived therefrom in the *Magistrates' Court Sentencing Guidelines*. **B2.31**

Where the offence occurs in a domestic setting the definitive sentencing guideline, *Domestic Abuse*, is applicable (see Supplement, **SG6-1**).

As with all current sentencing guidelines a combination of high harm and culpability will lead to categorisation in the highest sentence category. In *Ridgewell* [2018] EWCA Crim 1154, [2018] 2 Cr App R (S) 38 (332) the Court of Appeal held that a laceration to the face or head would be serious in the context of a s. 47 offence and justify designation as 'serious harm'.

In *Halane* [2014] EWCA Crim 477, [2014] 2 Cr App R (S) 46 (375) the 27-year-old offender, with minor previous convictions none of which involved violence, had been drinking with a friend when he came into contact with the victim, who was very intoxicated. The incident began when the victim punched the offender in the face, cutting his mouth. The offender then launched a 'ferocious' attack on the victim, knocking him to the ground and then kicking him repeatedly and jumping or stamping on his head twice. A sentence of 16 months' imprisonment for what was a serious example of a category 1 offence was 'stiff' but not manifestly excessive. The judge had been entitled to treat the intoxicated victim as 'vulnerable' for the purposes of the guideline, despite being the original aggressor. There was strong personal mitigation but it was very fortunate that much more serious harm had not been caused. The case was too serious for a custodial sentence to be suspended. By contrast, in *Broadbent* [2018] EWCA Crim 1495 one of the participants in an unprovoked, drink-fuelled joint attack punched a stranger and then joined with others in knocking him to the ground, where he lost consciousness. Ultimately, however, although suffering ongoing anxiety, the victim sustained no more than soft-tissue injuries to his face. The case was appropriately sentenced as category 2. The starting point of six months had to be raised to reflect significant aggravating features including location and timing, the intake of alcohol and the ongoing effect on the victim but these were offset to some extent by good character. The sentence after trial would have been nine months' imprisonment but would be reduced to six months for plea. Once again, the sentence could not be suspended.

B2.32 Heavier custodial sentences will be imposed where the assault was committed against a public servant. Nine months' imprisonment was upheld on a guilty plea in the pre-guideline case of *Broyd* [2001] EWCA Crim 1437, [2002] 1 Cr App R (S) 47 (197), where the offender head-butted a person he knew to be an officer who was trying to arrest him, causing a split lip and a chipped tooth. Six months' imprisonment was appropriate in *McNally* [2000] 1 Cr App R (S) 535, where a relative of a hospital patient became abusive with medical staff and struck a doctor in the face. The victim suffered bruising and bleeding in the ear which caused a hearing loss. In *McDermott* [2006] EWCA Crim 1899, [2007] 1 Cr App R (S) 28 (145), a sentence of 15 months' imprisonment was upheld on a man who, while under the influence of drink, had punched an ambulance attendant to the head. Although the offender pleaded guilty he had relevant previous convictions and the offence fell into a pattern of alcohol-related violence. In *Byrne* [2000] 1 Cr App R (S) 282, where a schoolteacher was assaulted by a parent who forced his way into the staff room, 15 months' imprisonment was reduced to nine months. There is no reason to treat an assault committed by one motorist upon another after a road accident or dispute as any less serious than an assault committed in other circumstances (*Arnold* [1996] 1 Cr App R (S) 115, where six months' imprisonment was upheld for head-butting the victim, causing a broken nose).

Racial or religious aggravation cannot normally be taken into account by the sentencer when sentencing for the basic offence of assault occasioning actual bodily harm, given the availability of the racially aggravated offence (although see *O'Leary* [2015] EWCA Crim 1306, [2016] 1 Cr App R (S) 11 (66) at **B2.3**).

B2.33 **Sentences above the Range** Serious cases may be sentenced outside the offence range and in an exceptional case a maximum sentence may be justified. In *DH* [2017] EWCA Crim 2503, [2018] 2 Cr App R (S) 2 (8) the sentencer started at five years' imprisonment (the statutory maximum), reduced the sentence by only 20 per cent for plea, on the grounds that the evidence was compelling, and arrived at a custodial element of four years to which, since the offender was deemed to be dangerous (see **E.4**), a year of extended licence was added. The resulting sentence of five years as an extended determinate sentence did not exceed the maximum for the offence and was upheld on appeal. The offending involved a sustained and brutal attack on a terrified mother in the presence of three young children by a professional boxer with numerous previous convictions, some for serious violence. In upholding the appeal, the Court of Appeal said that maximum sentences were not confined to the worst cases conceivable. (For a comparable approach in a case of wounding under the OAPA 1861, s. 20, see *Saxton* [2018] EWCA Crim 1976 at **B2.65**.)

Sentence (Racially or Religiously Aggravated Form of Offence)

B2.34 The maximum penalty for the aggravated form of the offence is seven years, a fine or both on indictment; six months, an unlimited fine or both summarily (CDA 1998, s. 29(2)). Note the definitive sentencing guideline, *Assault* (see Supplement, **SG12-4**), and the guideline and notes derived therefrom in the *Magistrates' Court Sentencing Guidelines*.

The relevance of racial aggravation as a factor in sentencing has been the subject of guidance from the Court of Appeal in *Saunders* [2000] 1 Cr App R 458 and in *Kelly* [2001] EWCA Crim 170, [2001] 2 Cr App R (S) 73 (341), both cases of assault occasioning actual bodily harm. The Court established that the sentencer should indicate what the appropriate sentence would have been for the offence in the absence of racial aggravation and then add a further term to reflect the racial element, so that the total sentence would reflect the overall criminality. Even if the basic offence would not have crossed the custody threshold, the aggravation may mean that it did so. This guidance is reflected in the current definitive sentencing guideline. In *Saunders*, Rose LJ referred to a number of relevant features of such cases, such as the nature of the racial hostility, its duration and locality. In *Kelly*, matters said to aggravate the racial element were: where the racist element was a planned part of the offence; the offence was part of a pattern of racist offending;

the offender was part of a group promoting racist activities; and the deliberate setting up of the victim to humiliate or offend. The impact on the victim was also important, such as where the offence took place in or near the victim's home; where the victim was particularly vulnerable, or was providing a service to the public; where the timing or location of the offence was such as to maximise the harm or distress it caused; if expressions of racial hostility were repeated or prolonged; if fear and distress throughout a particular community resulted from the offence; or if particular distress was caused to the victim or the victim's family.

Actus Reus

An offence under the OAPA 1861, s. 47, must involve an assault or battery (as to which see **B2.5**) and it must be established that this assault or battery occasioned (i.e. caused) the victim actual bodily harm. The intentional infliction of such injury cannot ordinarily be consented to (see **B2.14**). As to the position where bodily harm results from the cumulative effect of a series of separate incidents, see *Cox* [1998] Crim LR 810. As long as there was a direct assault or battery, it does not matter if the bodily harm was suffered indirectly. In *Roberts* (1971) 56 Cr App R 95, R assaulted a young woman in his car, and frightened her to the extent that she leaped from it to escape whilst it was still in motion; she suffered injuries as a result. R was convicted of a s. 47 offence. Stephenson LJ said: **B2.35**

> The test is: was [her injury] the natural result of what [R] said and did, in the sense that it was something that could reasonably have been foreseen as the consequence of what he was saying or doing.

'Actual bodily harm' has been defined as any injury which is 'calculated to interfere with the health or comfort of the [victim]' (*Miller* [1954] 2 QB 282, per Lynskey J at p. 292). Minor cuts and bruises may in theory satisfy this test; and in *R (T) v DPP* [2003] EWHC 266 (Admin), [2003] Crim LR 622, it was held that a momentary loss of consciousness by V, following a kick to the head, could properly be regarded as actual bodily harm even where there was no other discernible evidence of injury. The CPS guidance (incorporating the Charging Standard) does not, however, encourage the bringing of s. 47 charges in the absence of some relatively serious injury, of a kind that has permanent effects and/or requires medical intervention.

It was held in *DPP v Smith* [2006] EWHC 94 (Admin), [2006] 2 All ER 16 that the cutting of a substantial part of V's hair in the course of an assault may involve actual bodily harm, even though no pain or other injury may be involved, as may putting paint on it or some unpleasant substance which marks or damages it. Sir Igor Judge P said (at [18]): **B2.36**

> Even if, medically and scientifically speaking, the hair above the surface of the scalp is no more than dead tissue, it remains part of the body and is attached to it. While it is so attached ... it falls within the meaning of 'bodily' in the phrase 'actual bodily harm'. It is concerned with the body of the individual victim.

See, to similar effect, *Stefanski* [2019] EWCA Crim 831, in which the Court of Appeal regarded D's forcible cutting of his wife's hair as an injury and an abuse of power, but not a serious injury.

A recognisable psychiatric illness may amount to actual or grievous bodily harm (*Chan-Fook* [1994] 2 All ER 552; *Ireland* [1998] AC 147). Where such illness or injury is alleged, it must be proved by expert psychiatric evidence (*Chan-Fook*) and there must also be expert evidence to prove that D's conduct was the cause of that injury. For the purposes of s. 47, this conduct must involve an assault or battery. In the absence of expert evidence, there may be no case to leave to the jury (*Morris* [1998] 1 Cr App R 386). Distress, grief, anxiety or other psychological harm, not amounting to any recognisable psychiatric illness, is not bodily harm for the purposes of the 1861 Act (*Dhaliwal* [2006] EWCA Crim 1139, [2006] 2 Cr App R 24 (348)).

Mens Rea

The *mens rea* of a s. 47 offence is no different from that required in respect of a common assault or battery (see **B2.12**). Although the causing of actual bodily harm is an additional *actus reus* element, no *mens rea* as to it is required. If injury is caused, it need not even be proved that the injury was foreseeable, because this element of the offence is one of strict liability. This is clear **B2.37** from the decision of the House of Lords in *Savage* [1992] 1 AC 699, in which S aimed to throw the contents of a beer glass over B, but inadvertently allowed the glass to slip from her hand and break, with the result that B was injured by it. It was held that a conviction for malicious wounding could not be sustained in the absence of proof that S had at least foreseen the possibility of injury to B, but a conviction for an offence under s. 47 could be substituted, because throwing beer over B was an intentional assault (indeed a battery) and that same assault had resulted in B's injury. Similarly, in a case such as *Ireland* [1998] AC 147, where threats are made by letter or by telephone etc., *mens rea* for a s. 47 offence can be established if D intends or foresees that they may cause V to apprehend immediate violence. D need not intend or foresee (nor even have any reason to foresee) that V will suffer psychiatric injury.

ASSAULTS ON CONSTABLES AND EMERGENCY WORKERS

Assaults on Emergency Workers

B2.38 **Assaults on Emergency Workers (Offences) Act 2018, ss. 1 and 3**

1 (1) This section applies to an offence of common assault, or battery, that is committed against an emergency worker acting in the exercise of functions as such a worker.

(2) A person guilty of an offence to which this section applies is liable—

(a) on summary conviction, to imprisonment for a term not exceeding [six] months, or to a fine, or to both;

(b) on conviction on indictment, to imprisonment for a term not exceeding 12 months, or to a fine, or to both.

(3) For the purposes of subsection (1), the circumstances in which an offence is to be taken as committed against a person acting in the exercise of functions as an emergency worker include circumstances where the offence takes place at a time when the person is not at work but is carrying out functions which, if done in work time, would have been in the exercise of functions as an emergency worker.

3 (1) In sections 1 and 2, 'emergency worker' means—

(a) a constable;

(b) a person (other than a constable) who has the powers of a constable or is otherwise employed for police purposes or is engaged to provide services for police purposes;

(c) a National Crime Agency officer;

(d) a prison officer;

(e) a person (other than a prison officer) employed or engaged to carry out functions in a custodial institution of a corresponding kind to those carried out by a prison officer;

(f) a prisoner custody officer, so far as relating to the exercise of escort functions;

(g) a custody officer, so far as relating to the exercise of escort functions;

(h) a person employed for the purposes of providing, or engaged to provide, fire services or fire and rescue services;

(i) a person employed for the purposes of providing, or engaged to provide, search services or rescue services (or both);

(j) a person employed for the purposes of providing, or engaged to provide—

(i) NHS health services, or

(ii) services in the support of the provision of NHS health services,

and whose general activities in doing so involve face to face interaction with individuals receiving the services or with other members of the public.

(2) It is immaterial for the purposes of subsection (1) whether the employment or engagement is paid or unpaid.

Custodial institutions, custody and prisoner custody officers, escort functions and NHS Health services are further defined in s. 3(3)).

B2.39 **Procedure** Assaulting an emergency worker is triable either way. When tried on indictment, it *is normally a class 3 offence, but see* CrimPD XIII, para. B (see Supplement, **CPD.XIII.B**) for the additional factors that the court considers on allocation.

The wording of s. 1 is such that it does not simply create a free-standing offence, as for example does the OAPA 1861, s. 47. Instead, it creates aggravated versions of the existing offences of common assault and common battery, and such offences should accordingly be charged as 'contrary to the CJA 1988, s. 39(2), and the Assaults on Emergency Workers (Offences) Act 2018, s. 1(2)'.

Selection of Charges CPS guidelines suggest that the new offence should ordinarily be charged in preference to the summary offence of assaulting a constable in the execution of his duty, contrary to the Police Act 1964, s. 89. The guideline describes the s. 89 offence as 'superseded', but it remains in force, as do a number of analogous provisions relating to traffic officers, immigration officers, etc., some of whom would not necessarily qualify as emergency workers for the purposes of the 2018 Act. The more serious offence of assault with intent to resist or prevent arrest also survives (see **B2.22**). Moreover, s. 89 may apply where the person assaulted was merely a civilian assisting a constable, and there is no equivalent provision in the 2018 Act. **B2.40**

As with the s. 89 offence, there may be circumstances in which it is prudent to include an alternative charge of common assault or battery, notably where there may be some doubt or issue as to the status or role of the complainant. This would be particularly important where the case is to be tried summarily and an alternative verdict cannot be returned on the main charge (cf. *Dixon v CPS* [2018] EWHC 3154 (Admin), [2019] 1 Cr App R 20 (255)).

If any significant injury has been caused by an assault on an emergency worker exercising functions as such, a charge under the OAPA 1861, ss. 18, 20 or 47 (or one of attempting to commit such an offence) may be more appropriate and will permit a more severe sentence. By s. 2 of the 2018 Act, if the victim of such an offence is an emergency worker acting in that capacity at the time, this must be treated (and referred to) as an aggravating factor that increases the seriousness of the offence for sentencing purposes.

Sentence The maximum penalty for an assault or battery against an emergency worker on conviction on indictment is 12 months' imprisonment, or an unlimited fine or both. The Act requires a court to consider any offence committed against an emergency worker acting in the course of functions as such a worker as an aggravating factor in sentencing for any offence set out at s. 2(3) of the 2018 Act, namely: OAPA 1861, ss. 16 (threats to kill), 18 (wounding with intent to cause grievous bodily harm), 20 (malicious wounding), 23 (administering poison etc.), 28 (causing bodily injury by gunpowder etc.), 29 (using explosive substances etc. with intent to cause grievous bodily harm), 47 (assault occasioning actual bodily harm), Sexual Offences Act 2003, s. 3 (sexual assault), manslaughter, kidnapping, and any offence ancillary thereto. In such cases the court is to regard the offending as more serious, meriting an increased sentence within the maximum for the offence, a matter which must be declared in the course of the sentencing remarks. **B2.41**

In *McGarrick* [2019] EWCA Crim 530, [2019] 2 Cr App R (S) 31 (231) the Court of Appeal considered whether existing guidelines for assault were of assistance when sentencing for this offence. The appellant was sentenced to four months' imprisonment, having pleaded guilty to one count of assault by beating of an emergency worker (consecutive to a nine-month sentence for fraud by false representation, which was not criticised on appeal). Submitting that the four-month sentence on a plea for a relatively low-level assault was manifestly excessive, the appellant invited the Court to have regard to the definitive guideline, *Assault* (see Supplement, **SG12-1** ***et seq.***), arguing that the Court should be limited in practice to a six-month maximum. Dismissing the appeal, the Court stated that neither the common assault guideline (where the offence maximum is six months) nor the resisting arrest guideline (where the offence maximum is two years) provided a useful analogy. Whether or not this would have been a low-level offence of assault by beating in other circumstances, it had elements of greater harm and higher culpability when considered as an assault on an emergency worker. There was a clear legislative intent that assaults on public servants doing their work as part of the emergency services should be sentenced more severely than previously. Sentencers should not be limited by the maximum sentence available for a different, and less serious, offence. In *Whelan* [2020] EWCA Crim 195, the Court of Appeal reiterated the comments in *McGarrick*, confirming that sentences of immediate custody may well be appropriate even for a reckless rather than an intentional assault. However in that case a reckless and unpremeditated kick with a shod foot had resulted in minimal harm, so the appropriate sentence after a trial was one month's imprisonment, not three.

B2.42 **Elements** Any conduct that falls within the ambit of s. 1 of the 2018 Act must previously have been punishable as common assault or battery, and might additionally have been punishable as an assault on a constable, or one of the many analogous offences noted at **B2.45**. Such conduct may indeed still be dealt with in one of those ways, but if it is to be triable either way, as provided for by s. 1, the new element that must be proved is that it was committed against an emergency worker 'acting in the exercise of functions as such a worker'. Whether this additional element can be proved in a given case must largely be a question of fact. It is clear from the wording of ss. 1(3) and 3(1) and (2) that s. 1 extends to assaults on unpaid volunteers, such as special constables, or on off-duty emergency personnel (such as off-duty doctors or paramedics) who have stepped in to help in an emergency, but it does not appear to extend to retired or unemployed doctors, or nurses etc., or those from another country, even if they do exactly the same thing.

It is moreover not yet clear whether constables who act unlawfully, and thus inconsistently with their duty, can ever be said to be acting 'in the exercise of his functions' for the purposes of the 2018 Act. Can some honest mistakes or misunderstandings on the part of a constable be disregarded for these purposes, even though they would have been fatal to a prosecution under the Police Act 1964, s. 89? On the other hand, the new offence clearly cannot apply unless the constable (or other emergency worker) was at least attempting to do the job ('exercise his functions') at the time. This could not be said, for example, of a constable caught planting evidence or otherwise acting in deliberate violation of duty.

Assaulting a Constable in the Execution of his Duty

B2.43 **Police Act 1996, s. 89**

> Any person who assaults a constable in the execution of his duty, or a person assisting a constable in the execution of his duty, shall be guilty of an offence ...

By the Prison Act 1952, s. 8, every prison officer while acting as such shall have all the powers, authority, protection and privileges of a constable.

B2.44 **Procedure and Sentence** This offence is triable only summarily. This may be a consideration when deciding whether to charge under s. 89 or under the Assaults on Emergency Workers (Offences) Act 2018, s. 1, which overlaps it, and is triable either way. CPS guidance suggests that the latter offence should now usually be preferred, but s. 89 remains fully in force.

The maximum penalties are six months' imprisonment, an unlimited fine, or both (Police Act 1996, s. 89(1)). Note the definitive sentencing guideline, *Assault* (see Supplement, **SG12-6**), and the guideline and notes derived therefrom in the *Magistrates' Court Sentencing Guidelines*.

See also the sentencing considerations for assault occasioning actual bodily harm, at **B2.31**.

B2.45 *Actus Reus* An offence under s. 89(1) must involve an assault or battery (as defined in **B2.5**) and it must be proved that V was a police or prison officer (of any rank) acting in the execution of his duty, or a person assisting such an officer.

Police and community support officers (CSOs) are not protected by s. 89 unless assisting a constable at the time, but as to assaults etc. on CSOs or other 'designated or accredited persons' see the Police Reform Act 2002, s. 46. As to assaults on members of international joint investigation teams, see the Police Act 1996, s. 89(4), and the SOCPA 2005, s. 57. As to assaults on persons carrying out surveillance in England and Wales under the RIPA 2000, s. 76A, see the Crime (International Co-operation) Act 2003, s. 84. As to assaults on traffic officers, see the Traffic Management Act 2004, s. 10(1); as to assaults on revenue and customs officers, see the Commissioners for Revenue and Customs Act 2005, s. 32; as to assaults on NCA officers designated as having the powers of constables, see the CCA 2013, s. 10 and sch. 5, para. 22; as to assaults on immigration officers, see the UK Borders Act 2007, ss. 22 and 23; as to assaults on accredited financial investigators exercising powers under the POCA 2002, see s. 453A of that Act; as to assaults on officers of the SFO, see the POCA 2002, s. 453B; as to assaults on secure college custody officers, see the CJCA 2015, sch. 10, paras. 10 and 14. Many (but not all) of the above would also be protected by the Assaults on Emergency Workers (Offences) Act 2018, s. 1. See **B2.38**.

An off-duty police officer may act in the course of duty if a breach of the peace or other incident occurs which justifies immediate action on that officer's part (*Albert v Lavin* [1982] AC 546) but it is essential in all cases that the officer is shown to have been acting lawfully, because even a minor, technical act of unlawfulness will mean that the officer cannot have been acting in the execution of his duty (*Riley v DPP* (1989) 91 Cr App R 14; *Kerr v DPP* [1995] Crim LR 394). A violent assault in response to a trivial act of unlawfulness on the part of a police officer may be punishable on some other basis (e.g., as a common assault or battery, or as assault occasioning actual bodily harm), but although common assault is necessarily included within any s. 89 assault, courts of summary jurisdiction have no power to convict of included offences, and it may therefore be desirable to draft alternative charges in cases where the legality of the officer's conduct is in doubt (see *Bentley v Brudzinski* (1982) 75 Cr App R 217; *Dixon v CPS* [2018] EWHC 3154 (Admin), [2019] 1 Cr App R 20 (255) and **D1.173** *et seq.*).

Neither legislation, nor judicial scrutiny and precedent, can prescribe everything that an officer may lawfully do in the execution of duty. It is clear, however, that a police officer may be acting lawfully, even when doing more than the minimum which the law requires (*Waterfield* [1964] 1 QB 164; *Coffin v Smith* (1980) 71 Cr App R 221). It is also clear that any action amounting to assault, battery, unlawful arrest or trespass to property takes the officer concerned outside the lawful course of duty (*Davis v Lisle* [1936] 2 KB 434) but another officer who then tries to protect him from injury etc. may be acting lawfully in accordance with his duty (*Dixon v CPS* [2018] EWHC 3154 (Admin), [2019] 1 Cr App R 20 (255)). **B2.46**

Even where an officer has no legal right to remain on private property when required to leave, offensive remarks telling the officer to 'go away' will not necessarily suffice to withdraw any implied permission to enter or remain, and the officer must in any event be given a reasonable opportunity to leave once such permission has effectively been withdrawn (*R (Fullard) v Woking Magistrates' Court* [2005] EWHC 2922 (Admin)).

Moreover, an error that leads an officer to arrest on the wrong charge will not ordinarily make the arrest unlawful (*McCann v CPS* [2015] EWHC 2461 (Admin), [2016] 1 Cr App R 6 (82)); nor will an officer act unlawfully if acting in the genuine and reasonable belief that arresting an individual for breaching an injunction is authorised by court order, even if the court order itself proves to be unlawful or defective. Officers cannot be expected to check the validity of apparently lawful court orders (*Ahmed v CPS* [2017] EWHC 1272 (Admin)). Some of the most difficult cases in this area concern the power of a police officer to touch or take hold of an individual (without making an arrest) in order to speak with or restrain that individual. In *Donnelly v Jackman* [1970] 1 All ER 987, it was held that it is not every interference with a citizen's liberty which will amount to a course of conduct sufficient to take the officer out of the execution of his duty; but how far an officer may go in attracting or retaining the citizen's attention appears to be largely a question of fact and degree. In *Mepstead v DPP* (1996) 160 JP 475, it was held to be lawful for a police officer to take hold of D's arm in order to attract D's attention and calm him down, and in *Pegram v DPP* [2019] EWHC 2673 (Admin), the Administrative Court held that an officer was justified in continuing to hold D's arm for long enough to deliver a warning as to his conduct, which was in danger of amounting to a public order offence, adding (at [36]) that a 'civilian member of the public might have done as much, for [D's] own sake'; but in *Collins v Wilcock* [1984] 3 All ER 374, a police officer was held to have acted unlawfully when, without purporting to exercise any lawful power of arrest, she held a woman by the arm in order to question her. See also *Kenlin v Gardiner* [1967] 2 QB 510; *Wood v DPP* [2008] EWHC 1056 (Admin); *B v DPP* [2008] EWHC 1655 (Admin) and *Elkington v DPP* [2012] EWHC 3398 (Admin). As to the powers of CSOs, see the Police Reform Act 2002, sch. 4, and *D v DPP* [2010] EWHC 3400 (Admin), [2011] 1 WLR 882. Police powers are more fully examined in **D1**.

B2.47 *Mens Rea* The *mens rea* required in respect of this offence is no different from that required in respect of common assault or battery. D need not know, or even have reason to suspect, that the victim is a police officer or that the officer is acting in the execution of his duty (*Forbes* (1865) 10 Cox CC 362; *Blackburn v Bowering* [1994] 3 All ER 380). In this respect, the offence is one of strict liability. In *Albert v Lavin* [1982] AC 546, D unlawfully assaulted a man who attempted to prevent him from causing a breach of the peace. He claimed not to know that this man was a police officer, but the House of Lords held that his alleged mistake was irrelevant. He would have been guilty of an assault or battery even if the man had not been a police officer, because the officer had been doing only what any citizen would have had the right to do in the circumstances. If however D honestly believes that D is being attacked or kidnapped by criminals, or assaulted by police officers who are acting unlawfully, and uses force to resist them, D will not be guilty of any s. 89 offence, because in accordance with the general principles governing self-defence, D must be judged on the basis of the facts as D honestly believed them to be. D's honest belief in the need to act in self-defence would (unless triggered by self-induced intoxication) negative any *mens rea* for assault (*Kenlin v Gardiner* [1967] 2 QB 510; *Wheeldon v CPS* [2018] EWHC 249 (Admin); *Dixon v CPS* [2018] EWHC 3154 (Admin), [2019] 1 Cr App R 20 (255) and see generally **A3.60**).

RESISTING OR WILFULLY OBSTRUCTING A CONSTABLE, ETC.

Definition

B2.48 **Police Act 1996, s. 89**

(2) Any person who resists or wilfully obstructs a constable in the execution of his duty, or a person assisting a constable in the execution of his duty, shall be guilty of an offence ...

Procedure

B2.49 This offence is triable only summarily (Police Act 1996, s. 89(2)). As to powers of arrest, see **D1.14**.

Sentence

B2.50 The maximum penalty is one month's imprisonment, a fine not exceeding level 3, or both (Police Act 1996, s. 89(2)). The *Magistrates' Court Sentencing Guidelines* (see Supplement, **SG10-119**) provide guidance for this offence.

Elements

B2.51 D obstructs a police constable by making it more difficult for the constable to carry out his duty (*Hinchcliffe v Sheldon* [1955] 3 All ER 406, *obiter*). While 'resisting' implies some physical action, no physical act is necessary to constitute obstruction. Simple refusal to answer questions does not constitute an obstruction (*Rice v Connolly* [1966] 2 QB 414), neither does advising another person not to answer (*Green v DPP* (1991) 155 JP 816). Answering questions incorrectly may, however, amount to obstruction, although the distinction is not always clear (*Ledger v DPP* [1991] Crim LR 439).

D may obstruct an officer by omission, but only if under an initial duty to act (*Lunt v DPP* [1993] Crim LR 534). There is also a little-used common law offence of refusing to aid a constable who is attempting to prevent or to quell a breach of the peace and who calls for assistance (see *Waugh* (1986) *The Times*, 1 October 1986).

B2.52 In *Green v Moore* [1982] QB 1044 the Divisional Court held that a tip-off to persons who were preparing to commit an offence, and who as a result of the tip-off decided not to commit such an offence, could amount to an obstruction. Police could still be said to be acting in execution of their duty even if only making general inquiries before an offence was committed.

The Court admitted that this was a difficult situation, but liability would depend on D's intent. If it was simply to prevent the commission of a crime, no offence would be committed.

If, however, D's intent was to enable the potential offender to commit that crime (or a similar crime) at a more opportune moment, this would amount to obstruction.

The same intent issue may arise in cases where motorists are seen warning other road users of speed traps ahead, but it will also be necessary in such a case to prove that those warned were already speeding or were likely to do so at the location of the speed trap. Otherwise the police cannot have been obstructed in fact and there can be no *actus reus*. See *R (DPP) v Glendinning* [2005] EWHC 2333 (Admin).

As in the offence of assaulting a constable (see **B2.45**), no offence under s. 89(2) can be committed if the officer is acting unlawfully (*Edwards v DPP* (1993) 97 Cr App R 301; *B v DPP* [2008] EWHC 1655 (Admin)). An error that leads an officer to arrest on the wrong charge will not ordinarily make that arrest unlawful (*McCann v CPS* [2015] EWHC 2461 (Admin), [2016] 1 Cr App R 6 (82)), but an honest belief in the need for self-defence (or defence of another) may still in appropriate cases be relied upon in answer to a charge of resisting or obstructing an officer, whether or not this resistance or obstruction involves any use of force (*Oraki v CPS* [2018] EWHC 115 (Admin), [2018] QB 1086). Police powers are examined in **D1**.

If obstruction (rather than resistance) is alleged, it must be proved to have been wilful. D cannot be guilty of wilful obstruction by trying to help the police, even if this actually makes their job more difficult (*Wilmott v Atack* [1977] QB 498) nor can D be guilty if unaware of obstructing police officers at all (*Ostler v Elliott* [1980] Crim LR 584), but if D deliberately obstructs the police, it will be no defence to argue that this was merely an attempt to prevent the arrest of a person D believed to be innocent (*Lewis v Cox* [1985] QB 509). As to the obstruction of international joint investigation teams, see the Police Act 1996, s. 89(4), and the SOCPA 2005, s. 57. As to the obstruction of traffic officers, see the Traffic Management Act 2004, s. 10(2); as to the obstruction of revenue and customs officers, see the Commissioners for Revenue and Customs Act 2005, s. 31; as to resisting or wilfully obstructing NCA officers designated as having the powers of constables, see the CCA 2013, s. 10 and sch. 5, para. 21; as to the obstruction or hindrance of emergency workers or persons assisting such workers, see the Emergency Workers (Obstruction) Act 2006, ss. 1 to 4; as to resisting or wilfully obstructing an accredited financial investigator exercising powers under the POCA 2002, see s. 453A of that Act; as to resisting or wilfully obstructing officers of the SFO, see s. 453B; and as to resisting or obstructing immigration officers in the exercise of relevant powers, see s. 453C. **B2.53**

WOUNDING OR INFLICTING GRIEVOUS BODILY HARM

Definition

Offences against the Person Act 1861, s. 20 **B2.54**

> Whosoever shall unlawfully and maliciously wound or inflict any grievous bodily harm upon any other person, either with or without any weapon or instrument, shall be guilty of [an offence] ...

The CDA 1998, s. 29(1)(a), creates a racially or religiously aggravated form of this offence which carries a higher maximum penalty. For the meaning of 'racially or religiously aggravated', see **B11.145**.

Procedure

Both forms of the offence are triable either way. When tried on indictment this is normally a class 3 offence, but see CrimPD XIII, para. B (see Supplement, **CPD.XIII.B**) for the additional factors that the court considers on allocation. See the *Magistrates' Court Sentencing Guidelines* for indications as to when a case should be sent to the Crown Court. As to the procedure on charging both the basic and aggravated offence, see *Henderson v CPS* [2016] EWHC 464 (Admin), [2016] 1 WLR 1990, discussed at **B11.46**. **B2.55**

Indictments

B2.56 **Basic Offence: Inflicting Grievous Bodily Harm**

Statement of Offence

Unlawfully inflicting grievous bodily harm, contrary to section 20 of the Offences against the Person Act 1861

Particulars of Offence

A on or about the ... day of ... unlawfully and maliciously inflicted grievous bodily harm on V

B2.57 **Aggravated Offence: Wounding**

Statement of Offence

Racially aggravated wounding, contrary to section 29 (1)(a) of the Crime and Disorder Act 1998

Particulars of Offence

A on or about the ... day of ... maliciously wounded V and was wholly or partly motivated to do so by hostility to V's racial group, namely Arabs

Alternative Verdicts

B2.58 A verdict of assault occasioning actual bodily harm under the OAPA 1861, s. 47, can be returned (see the CLA 1967, s. 6(3)).

Sentence (Basic Offence)

B2.59 The maximum penalty for the offence other than in the racially or religiously aggravated form (see **B2.66**) is five years (OAPA 1861, s. 20) on indictment; six months, an unlimited fine, or both, summarily. Note the definitive sentencing guideline, *Assault* (see Supplement, **SG12-3**), and the guideline and notes derived therefrom in the *Magistrates' Court Sentencing Guidelines*. Where the offence occurs in a domestic setting the definitive sentencing guideline, *Domestic Abuse*, is applicable (see Supplement, **SG6-1**).

In *Heggarty* [2017] EWCA Crim 988, [2017] 2 Cr App R (S) 48 (409) the Court of Appeal said that although the *Assault* guideline requires a court to consider when sentencing a category 3 case whether the custodial threshold has been passed, whether a custodial sentence is inevitable and, if so, whether the sentence can be suspended, the guideline was not intended to entirely exclude the possibility of a suspended sentence in a category 2 case. Where, exceptionally, that possibility arose in a category 2 case the judge should apply the guideline on *Imposition of Community and Custodial Sentences* (see Supplement, **SG9-1**). See also *Tharmaratnam* [2017] EWCA Crim 887, [2017] 2 Cr App R (S) 36 (318).

In *Mercer* [2017] EWCA Crim 228, the Court of Appeal upheld a sentence of three years and four months where the offender kicked an unconscious victim in the head, wandered off, then returned and kicked the victim in the head again. The Court held that the conduct amounted to a repeated attack on a vulnerable victim and therefore fell into category 1. In *Jonsyn* [2013] EWCA Crim 1655, [2014] 1 Cr App R (S) 67 (438) the 19-year-old offender was abusive and aggressive to the police at the time of his arrest. In a cell at the police station he punched a police officer in the face, fracturing his eye socket, which required surgery. The Court of Appeal said that this was a category 2 offence (greater harm, lower culpability) with several aggravating features — the assault was on a police officer, the offender had a poor record for violence and resisting arrest, and he was on police bail at the time. On the other hand, the offender was young, and this would be his first taste of custody. A starting point of 30 months' detention in a young offender institution was reduced to 20 months to reflect the guilty plea. In *Peet* [2014] EWCA Crim 2800, [2015] 1 Cr App R (S) 48 (344) the offender, while in the dock in a magistrates' court, grabbed the hand of the dock custody officer and deliberately broke his finger; the offence was at the top of category 2 or the bottom of category 1, with a starting point of three years' imprisonment, reduced to two years to reflect the guilty plea. In *Lawrence* [2011] EWCA Crim 3129, [2012] 2 Cr App R (S) 42 (243) the offender punched the victim in the face during a brawl in a Sunday League soccer match. The victim received facial fractures and a metal plate had to be inserted. The offender was sentenced to nine months' imprisonment following a trial. The Court of Appeal agreed with the judge that the case fell within category 2 rather than category 3, since the harm was serious in the context of the offence. Upholding the sentence, Pitchford LJ said that assessment of seriousness of injury in context was a matter of judicial knowledge and experience. In *McIntosh* [2014] EWCA Crim 1003, [2014] 2 Cr App R (S) 64 (503) the Court of Appeal found that the injuries sustained by the victim (a fractured ankle and torn knee ligaments) were not injuries constituting 'greater harm' within the meaning of the guideline. In *Williams* [2019] EWCA Crim 741 the appellant, who had shot the victim in the head with an air rifle causing cuts and grazes, accepted responsibility for the offence and expressed remorse. The sentencing judge considered this to be a category 1 case. The Court of Appeal considered that the injuries were not serious in the context of a s. 20 wounding, even though the risk of such injury was evident, and the case should have been located in category 2. The sentence was reduced from two-and-a-half years to two years' imprisonment.

Use of Weapon The use of a weapon is an important aggravating feature which may result in a significantly enhanced sentence for the assault. It may also, without double counting, result in a consecutive sentence for the separate offence of simple possession of the weapon in public. In *Majeed* [2019] EWCA Crim 516, [2019] 2 Cr App R (S) 29 (220), D brought a machete to his ex-partner's house and used it to attack V. The Court indicated that the repeated use of the machete had aggravated the s. 20 wounding, so a sentence of four years' imprisonment after a late plea could not be called into question. However the possession of the machete and carrying it through the streets and bringing it to the house was separate and serious offending from the use of the machete in the count of unlawful wounding. That element had not already been taken into account and thus the separate consecutive sentence of 15 months was not wrong in principle or double-counted. **B2.60**

In *Morrison* [2012] EWCA Crim 796, [2012] 2 Cr App R (S) 101 (594) the offender struck the victim on the head with a bottle. The bottle broke, and the victim received several fractures to the skull and eye socket which required an operation. The offender pleaded guilty on the day of the trial. The judge found this to be a category 1 case, and took a starting point of four and a half years. The Court of Appeal said that there was clearly greater harm, but in terms of culpability the use of the weapon had to be set against lack of premeditation. Whether one took the case as falling within category 1 or on the cusp between categories 1 and 2, the combination of aggravating and mitigating factors took the case to a starting point of three and a half years. The final sentence, allowing for the late plea, was three years' imprisonment. In *Marsh* [2011] EWCA Crim 3190, [2012] 2 Cr App R (S) 31 (178) the female offenders became involved in a fight with a 16-year-old girl. One held the girl's arms behind her back while the second cut the girl's face with a key, causing a 4 cm laceration which would leave a permanent scar. The Court of Appeal agreed with the judge that this was a category 1 case, given that this was a cold-blooded attack which caused physical and psychological damage. Coulson J said that it was important that all the various factors in the guideline were looked at in the round. Sentences of two years' imprisonment and 20 months' detention in a young offender institution were upheld.

Glassing Pre-guideline cases involving 'glassing' include *Robertson* [1998] 1 Cr App R (S) 21, where the Court of Appeal noted that, in the light of earlier authorities, any sentence of more than two years' imprisonment for unlawful wounding required careful scrutiny to see if it was justified on the facts. In that case the offender had been drinking in a public house and had thrust a beer glass into another man's face, causing wounds to his face. A sentence of 30 months was reduced to two years. In *Marsden* (1993) 15 Cr App R (S) 177, the offender became involved in an argument in a public house and, after having been asked to leave, threw a glass across the room. It hit the victim and caused a cut to the head which required hospital treatment. A sentence of 12 months' imprisonment was upheld. These two decisions were considered in *McGhee* [2008] EWCA Crim 25, [2008] 2 Cr App R (S) 53 (330), where the victim was struck twice with a glass and then kicked on the ground. A sentence of 27 months' imprisonment was appropriate on a plea of guilty. See also **B2.78**. **B2.61**

B2.62 **Corrosive Substances** In 2017 the Sentencing Council published observations in relation to sentencing for assault involving the use of acid or other corrosive substances, noting that use of a corrosive substance is a factor indicating high culpability. The use of acid as a weapon is specifically mentioned in the assault guideline. All guidelines of course also consider harm to the victim, whether physical or psychological. Note that mere possession of a corrosive substance in public is now a specific offence under the Offensive Weapons Act 2019 (see **B12.227** ***et seq.***), with a presumptive minimum sentence of six months' imprisonment and a maximum of four years.

B2.63 **Racial or Religious Aggravation in Basic Offence** Racial or religious aggravation cannot normally be taken into account by the sentencer when sentencing for the basic offence of wounding or inflicting grievous bodily harm (see **B2.3**), although in *O'Leary* [2015] EWCA Crim 1306, [2016] 1 Cr App R (S) 11 (66), the Court of Appeal upheld the judge's view that the basic offence of unlawful wounding was religiously aggravated by the offender's comment at the time of the offence that he wanted to 'kill a Muslim', even though the racially aggravated form of the offence had not been charged. It was held that the approach was justified on the facts, where the judge had presided over the trial and had been entitled to conclude, to the criminal standard, that the assault was racially aggravated.

B2.64 **Malicious Transmission of Sexually Transmitted Disease** In *P (SJ)* [2006] EWCA Crim 2599, the offender had unprotected sexual relations with a man, without informing him that she had been diagnosed as HIV positive. When he became infected, she led him to believe, to his great distress, that he had infected her. She eventually pleaded guilty to the malicious infliction of grievous bodily harm, and a sentence of 32 months' imprisonment was upheld on appeal. The Court of Appeal received representations from the Terrence Higgins Trust to the effect that deterrent sentences in cases such as this had adverse effects on the willingness of suspected HIV sufferers to seek treatment or to undergo testing, but concluded that the courts had a duty to deter those who knew that they were HIV positive from recklessly transmitting the virus (see also *Rowe* [2018] EWCA Crim 2688, [2019] 1 Cr App R (S) 38 (256), in which the offender engaged in a campaign to infect others with HIV and was sentenced for offences contrary to s. 18, at **B2.82**).

B2.65 **Sentences above the Range** Serious cases may be sentenced outside the offence range and in an exceptional case a maximum sentence may be justified. In *Saxton* [2018] EWCA Crim 1976 a starting point at the statutory maximum of five years was upheld for a prison assault by an offender with 90 previous convictions. The attack left the victim in an induced coma for several days although he was subsequently able to make a full physical recovery. Giving a discount of 20 per cent for a late plea, the sentencer arrived at four years' imprisonment for an offender deemed to be dangerous, and then added the longest period of extended licence available, namely one year. The resulting sentence of five years as an extended determinate sentence did not exceed the maximum for the offence. Giving detailed reasons for upholding the sentence, Cheema-Grubb J. said (at [12]–[13]):

> The starting point in the guideline is three years' custody and the category range for a Category 1 offence is two-and-a-half years to four years' custody. Accordingly, and not unusually, the top of the range for the most serious category in a sentencing guideline is nonetheless less than the statutory maximum for that offence. Plainly sentencing must be fact-specific and sentences greater than the top end of the top category in a Sentencing Council Guideline are available to a judge when a case requires a departure from the guideline. It is well established that the maximum sentence permitted by Statute is reserved not for the worst possible case which can realistically be conceived, but for cases which are truly identified as being of the utmost gravity. This can be because of one single stand out feature or a series of features.
>
> Where the maximum sentence allowed by statute is relatively low there may indeed be a broad range of cases that require sentences at or approaching the maximum permitted. The range of factual circumstances in which a judge may have to pass a sentence for [an] offence contrary to section 20 of the Offences Against the Person Act 1861 is very broad indeed and there is some head room beyond the top of the guideline Category 1 to accommodate what may be a proportionately significant number of cases.

This approach to the maximum sentence substantially mirrors that taken in *DH* [2017] EWCA Crim 2503, [2018] 2 Cr App R (S) 2 (8), a case concerning an assault contrary to the OAPA 1861, s. 47 (see **B2.33**). In *Dodds* [2013] EWCA Crim 22, [2013] 2 Cr App R (S) 54 (358) a sentence of three years following a guilty plea was upheld where the offender had struck the victim a single blow to the face causing him to fall and strike his head. The victim incurred very serious head injuries leaving him with long-term disability and disfigurement. The Court of Appeal said that the judge had been entitled to take a starting point of four and a half years before reduction for plea even though the top of the offence range is four years. Apart from the very serious harm incurred, the offender had a record of an escalating pattern of violence and the offence involved violence in the street at night. A further stark example of a sentence well outside the range is *Whittet* [2017] EWCA Crim 2516, a case in which the offender knocked his victim, a peacemaker in a developing pub fracas, unconscious with a single blow. The sentencer explained that with higher harm but lesser culpability the case would have been in category 2, with a starting point of 18 months' imprisonment, but she chose a starting point of four years' imprisonment instead, the top of the range for category 1. The reason for this enhancement was that the victim had not regained consciousness and was unlikely ever to do so. The factor 'ongoing effect on the victim' is an element of aggravation rather than a factor that defines the initial category (on this point, see the discussion of *Williams* [2018] EWCA Crim 740, [2018] 2 Cr App R (S) 20 (192) at **B2.75**) and in this case it had to be reflected in a category 2 sentence that was very significantly above the category range. The resultant sentence of 32 months' imprisonment (including two months' imprisonment imposed consecutively for related minor assaults) took into account good character, remorse and guilty plea. On appeal, the Court said that the sentence could not be faulted.

Sentence (Racially or Religiously Aggravated Form of Offence)

The maximum penalty for the aggravated form of wounding or inflicting grievous bodily harm is seven years, a fine or both on indictment; six months, an unlimited fine or both summarily (CDA 1998, s. 29(2)). Note the definitive sentencing guideline, *Assault* (see Supplement, **SG12-3**), and the guideline and notes derived therefrom in the *Magistrates' Court Sentencing Guidelines*. **B2.66**

The definitive guideline states that 'the court should determine the appropriate sentence for the offence without taking account of the element of aggravation and then make an addition to the sentence, considering the level of aggravation involved. It may be appropriate to move outside the identified category range, taking into account the increased statutory maximum', thus reflecting the Court of Appeal judgment in *Saunders* [2000] 1 Cr App R 458, as elaborated in *Kelly* [2001] EWCA Crim 170, [2001] 2 Cr App R (S) 73 (341). See further **B2.34**. In an early post-guideline case under s. 29 a sentence of 30 months' detention in a young offender institution, comprising 22 months for the basic offence and eight months for the racial aggravation, was appropriate for an unprovoked attack by an 18-year-old on a 61-year-old man where the attack was accompanied by words of racial abuse (*Sweet* [2011] EWCA Crim 1208, [2012] 1 Cr App R (S) 8 (35)).

Elements

The *actus reus* of an offence under the OAPA 1861, s. 20, may involve either unlawful wounding or the unlawful infliction of grievous bodily harm. Deliberate injury cannot ordinarily be consented to, but the risk of it occurring accidentally often can be. See **B2.14** *et seq*. Wounding requires the breaking of the continuity of the whole of the skin (dermis and epidermis) or the breaking of the inner skin within the cheek, lip or urethra (*Smith* (1837) 8 C & P 173; *Waltham* (1849) 3 Cox 442). It does not include the rupturing of internal blood vessels (*JJC (A Minor) v Eisenhower* [1983] 3 All ER 230). In theory, even trivial wounds may qualify, but the guidance (incorporating the Charging Standard) suggests that minor injuries are charged as common assault and that the s. 20 offence should be reserved for wounds that are really serious. Where, however, there is evidence of a serious wound, this ought generally to be charged as wounding, rather than as inflicting grievous bodily harm (*McReady* [1978] 3 All ER 967). **B2.67**

The penalty is five years or a fine or both on indictment, six months, an unlimited fine, or both, summarily.

Grievous bodily harm means really serious harm (*DPP v Smith* [1961] AC 290; *Cunningham* [1982] AC 566). It may be physical or psychiatric (*Ireland* [1998] AC 147) but not merely psychological (*Dhaliwal* [2006] EWCA Crim 1139, [2006] 2 Cr App R 24 (348)). It may also result from infection, but need not be permanent or dangerous (*Ashman* (1858) 1 F & F 88) and in determining its seriousness account must be taken of its effect on the individual victim (*Golding* [2014] EWCA Crim 889; *Bollom* [2003] EWCA Crim 2846, [2004] 2 Cr App R 6 (50)). Injury to a finger could thus be grievous bodily harm where V is a professional musician. A number of individually minor injuries may collectively be considered grievous (*Birmingham* [2002] EWCA Crim 2608). Expert evidence may be required, and will certainly be required (as to both cause and effect) in cases of alleged psychiatric injury, as in cases brought under s. 47 (see **B2.36**).

A direction equating grievous bodily harm with 'serious injury' may sometimes suffice (see, e.g., *Saunders* [1985] Crim LR 230) but in other cases such a direction might fail sufficiently to express the gravity of what is meant by grievous bodily harm (*Janjua* [1999] 1 Cr App R 91; *Sidhu* [2019] EWCA Crim 1034, [2019] 2 Cr App R (S) 34 (247)). Judges should distinguish where necessary between 'really serious injury' and 'serious injury falling short of grievous bodily harm'.

Whether an injury is 'really serious' is ultimately a question for the court or jury, subject to the judge's duty to withdraw the issue in the absence of evidence sufficient to support a conviction (*Golding*).

B2.68 **Infliction** Section 20 refers to the 'infliction' of grievous bodily harm. The meaning of this term was once a matter of some uncertainty and debate, but appears to have been largely resolved by the decision of the House of Lords in *Ireland* [1998] AC 147, where Lord Steyn, in giving the majority judgment, held (at p. 160) that harm could be inflicted without the need for an assault, and that in the context of the 1861 Act, there was no radical divergence between the meanings of the words 'cause' and 'inflict' (see also *Salisbury* [1976] VR 452; *Metropolitan Police Commissioner v Wilson* [1984] AC 242). Grievous bodily harm within the meaning of s. 20 could thus be inflicted by means of menacing telephone calls which gave rise to serious psychiatric injury, whether or not the injury was caused by fear of imminent physical attack.

On the other hand, Lord Steyn denied that the words 'cause' and 'inflict' were exactly synonymous, and this point was developed by Lord Hope, who said that, although there was no real practical difference between the two words, the word 'inflict' invariably implies detriment to the victim of some kind. Lord Steyn and Lord Hope both appear to have stopped just short of overruling the authority of *Clarence* (1888) 22 QBD 23, in which it was held that grievous bodily harm was caused, *but not inflicted*, where C enjoyed consensual sexual intercourse with his wife, without warning her that he was infected with a venereal disease, which she then contracted. The authority and rationale of *Clarence* were nevertheless gravely damaged by what was said and decided in *Ireland*, and in *Dica* [2004] EWCA Crim 1103, [2004] QB 1257 (see **B2.15**) the Court of Appeal concluded that it should no longer be followed. Judge LJ said:

> The effect of this judgment in relation to s. 20 is to remove some of the outdated restrictions against the successful prosecution of those who, knowing that they are suffering HIV or some other serious sexual disease, recklessly transmit it through consensual sexual intercourse, and inflict grievous bodily harm on a person from whom the risk is concealed and who is not consenting to it. In this context, *Clarence* has no continuing relevance. Moreover, to the extent that *Clarence* suggested that consensual sexual intercourse of itself was to be regarded as consent to the risk of consequent disease, again, it is no longer authoritative. If however, the victim consents to the risk, this continues to provide a defence under s 20 ...

See also *Golding* [2014] EWCA Crim 889. The injury in question must be inflicted (directly or indirectly) by some deliberate, non-accidental conduct on D's part. This may be deliberate or recklessly dangerous and/or drunken driving (*Kaeppner* [2012] EWCA Crim 158, [2012] 2 Cr App R (S) 47 (276); *Horwood* [2012] EWCA Crim 253) although the use of s. 20 in dangerous driving cases will no doubt decline now that the offence of causing serious injury by dangerous driving (see **C3.33**) is in force. In *Brady* [2006] EWCA Crim 2413, D had consumed a significant quantity of alcohol at a nightclub. As he sat down on a low railing on the first-floor gallery above the dance floor, he lost his balance and fell, landing on V and crippling her. The Court of Appeal opined (*obiter*) that although the fall may have been accidental, the act of perching drunkenly on the rail was not. Hallett LJ said (at [25]):

> This deliberate act, on any view, led almost immediately and directly to the fall over the railing and to the infliction of grievous bodily harm. It was a substantial cause of the infliction of those injuries. We would not be inclined to accept, therefore, [counsel's] submission that, because it was the unintentional fall rather than the deliberate act which, in fact, caused [the victim's] injuries, this broke the chain of causation. The one led inevitably to the other.

D's apparent lack of *mens rea* could then be addressed under the *Majewski* rule (as to which see **A3.17**). His appeal against his conviction was however allowed on other grounds.

Maliciously A s. 20 offence must be committed 'maliciously'. Maliciousness requires *either* an intent to do some kind of bodily harm to another person *or* recklessness (in the subjective or *Cunningham* sense) as to whether any such harm might be caused (*DPP v W* [2006] EWHC 92 (Admin)). The harm intended or foreseen by D need not amount to a wound or grievous bodily harm: an intent to cause minor injury, which inadvertently results in the infliction of a wound or serious injury, is sufficient to found liability under s. 20 (*Mowatt* [1968] 1 QB 421; *Sullivan* [1981] Crim LR 46; *DPP v W*). On the other hand, there cannot ordinarily be liability under s. 20 if D was unaware that the conduct might cause any injury at all (*Savage* [1992] 1 AC 699; *Meachen* [2006] EWCA Crim 2414). The only qualification to this rule concerns cases of voluntary intoxication: such intoxication cannot be relied upon by a defendant in order to negate *mens rea* under s. 20, because it is not a crime of 'specific intent' (*Brady* [2006] EWCA Crim 2413 at **B2.68** and see also **A3.17**). **B2.69**

In *Barnes* [2004] EWCA Crim 3246, [2005] 2 All ER 113, Lord Woolf CJ suggested (at [17]) that recklessness in this context 'means no more than the defendant foresaw the risk that some bodily harm (however slight) might result from what he was going to do and yet, ignoring that risk, he went on to commit the offending act'. If that were indeed so, most tackles committed in contact sports such as football would (as Lord Woolf concedes) be deemed 'malicious'. With respect, however, such conduct is not reckless at all unless the risk-taking in question can be described as unreasonable or unjustified in the circumstances. This is required by *Cunningham* recklessness (see **A2.7**), which, according to Judge P in *DPP v W*, is the only form of recklessness relevant to the s. 20 offence. In most cases falling within the scope of s. 20, however, there will be no question of any risk-taking being 'reasonable'. Even if D foresees only that D's punch might possibly leave V with a bruise or a cut lip, that will be enough to make the punch malicious. No direction as to reasonableness would be required in such a case.

The Court of Appeal held in *Beeson* [1994] Crim LR 190 that it was unnecessary to direct the jury on the meaning of the word 'maliciously'; but whilst such an omission may have been unimportant on the facts of that particular case (where the only real issue was self-defence), there will be many cases in which careful guidance on its meaning must be vital. The concept of maliciousness is further explained at **A2.12**.

WOUNDING OR CAUSING GRIEVOUS BODILY HARM WITH INTENT

Definition

Offences against the Person Act 1861, s. 18 **B2.70**

> Whosoever shall unlawfully and maliciously by any means whatsoever wound or cause any grievous bodily harm to any person with intent to do some grievous bodily harm to any person, or with intent to resist or prevent the lawful apprehension or detainer of any person, shall be guilty of [an offence] ...

Procedure

Wounding or causing grievous bodily harm with intent is triable on indictment only. It is normally a class 3 offence, but see CrimPD XIII, para. B (see Supplement, **CPD.XIII.B**) for the additional factors that the court considers on allocation. **B2.71**

Indictment

B2.72

Statement of Offence

Wounding [or causing grievous bodily harm] with intent, contrary to section 18 of the Offences against the Person Act 1861

Particulars of Offence

A on or about the ... day of ... unlawfully and maliciously wounded [or caused grievous bodily harm to] V with intent to do him grievous bodily harm [or to prevent the lawful apprehension of X]

As to the proper form of indictment in a 'transferred malice' case, where it is alleged that D wounded V whilst intending to do grievous bodily harm to another, see *Monger* [1973] Crim LR 301 and *Slimmings* [1999] Crim LR 69. An indictment for a s. 18 offence does not become invalid merely because it refers to the 'infliction' (rather than the 'causing') of grievous bodily harm, or because it omits any reference to the specific intent required (*Hodgson* [2008] EWCA Crim 895, [2008] 2 Cr App R 35 (521)).

Alternative Verdicts

B2.73 Where wounding is alleged in a count under the OAPA 1861, s. 18, then wounding under s. 20 and s. 47 assault are possible alternative verdicts. See generally **D19.41**. *Lahaye* [2005] EWCA Crim 2847, [2006] 1 Cr App R 11 (205) confirms that on a charge of wounding with intent to do grievous bodily harm, a conviction for malicious wounding is available even if not expressly charged. The Court of Appeal nevertheless recommended that it would be preferable, in such cases, for the lesser offence to be included on the face of the indictment.

B2.74 If, however, the s. 18 count alleges the causing of grievous bodily harm only, the situation is more complex. The House of Lords in *Mandair* [1995] 1 AC 208 held that a judge is entitled under the CLA 1967, s. 6(3), to leave s. 20 as an alternative to s. 18 because the term 'causing' is wide enough to include 'inflicting' (*Metropolitan Police Commissioner v Wilson* [1984] AC 242). Even though in *Mandair* the word 'inflicting' was not used, the meaning is clear given the context of the direction in the case and the wording of the verdict. A verdict of 'causing grievous bodily harm contrary to s. 20' can only mean causing grievous bodily harm by inflicting it, as that is the particular method referred to in s. 20. *Mandair* was applied in *White* [1995] Crim LR 393.

Although an alternative verdict can be considered following an oral direction, the House of Lords in *Mandair* re-affirmed that it is preferable to include an alternative count using the correct wording of the statute. Moreover, failure to direct the jury on an alternative verdict that might otherwise have been open to them (notably where the alleged injury might arguably have been inflicted by D without the specific intent required under s. 18) may render a s. 18 conviction unsafe, because the jury might merely have been unwilling to acquit D outright. See *Brown* [2014] EWCA Crim 2176 and *Hodson* [2009] EWCA Crim 1590 (see **D19.58**).

If D is acquitted under s. 18 without an alternative indictment under s. 20, a later prosecution under s. 20 cannot be brought, unless D was for some reason not in jeopardy of a s. 20 conviction at the first trial. See *Old Street Magistrates' Court, ex parte Davies* [1995] Crim LR 629, and *Brookes* [1995] Crim LR 630, where the initial charge was under s. 20, and the subsequent charge was under s. 18.

Sentence

B2.75 The maximum penalty for an offence under the OAPA 1861, s. 18, is life imprisonment. The definitive sentencing guideline, *Assault* (see Supplement, **SG12-2**), sets out three categories with starting points of four, six and 12 years' imprisonment respectively, and an offence range between three and 16 years, although very serious offending will justify a sentence outside that range (see **B2.82**). The guideline does not formally apply to the offence of wounding with intent to resist arrest, chargeable under the same section, but a judge will not be criticised for having regard to it in assessing culpability and harm (*Smith (Craig William)* [2018] EWCA Crim 2393, [2019] 1 Cr App R (S) 30 (203)). The maximum penalty of life imprisonment also applies for the related offences of attempting to choke, suffocate or strangle with intent (OAPA 1861, s. 21) and throwing corrosive fluid (s. 29), neither of which has a definitive guideline. For guidance on sentencing an offence under s. 21 see *Woolridge* [2018] EWCA Crim 1537 where assistance was gleaned from guidelines for robbery and attempted murder. For cases of acid attacks see **B2.83** and **B12.269**. Where the offence occurs in a domestic setting the definitive sentencing guideline, *Domestic Abuse* (see Supplement, **SG6-1**), is applicable.

As with all current sentencing guidelines a combination of high harm and culpability will lead to categorisation in the highest sentence category. The wide margin in the definitive sentencing guideline between the starting points for category 1 and 2 (12 years and six years) has provoked close scrutiny of the individual factors that would be required to justify findings of greater harm and greater culpability. The question of harm which is 'serious in the context of the offence' was considered in *Smith (Christopher Grant)* [2015] EWCA Crim 1482, [2016] 1 Cr App R (S) 8 (49), in which it was held that 'greater harm' must be significantly above the serious level of harm which is normal for the offence. However, in *Sowter* [2018] EWCA Crim 1332, the Court of Appeal recalled that the guideline refers to harm *intended* as well as harm actually sustained, and in *Williams* [2018] EWCA Crim 740, [2018] 2 Cr App R (S) 20 (192) the Court held that where the victim suffered life-threatening injuries there was no need to demonstrate that the harm amounted to permanent injury or disability. The Court said that it would be counter-intuitive to exclude from 'serious harm' a case where the victim was left at death's door but was saved by expert intervention, and noted that 'ongoing effect upon the victim', often cited as a factor at Step One, was included in the guideline only as an aggravating factor at Step Two, to be considered once the initial categorisation had been determined. (For a stark example of this point in relation to s. 20 assault, see *Whittet* [2017] EWCA Crim 2516, at **B2.65**.) The question of 'sustained or repeated assault' was also considered in *Smith (Christopher Grant)* and was taken to require some degree of 'persistent repetition', otherwise almost all cases would be classified in the higher level, an approach reflected in *O'Doherty* [2018] EWCA Crim 1638. In that case the offender and victim were involved in a long fracas culminating only at its conclusion in the offender using a bottle to hit his victim. The Court of Appeal concluded that it would be hard to say the s. 18 assault itself was repeated or sustained.

The six-year margin between starting points in the two higher categories has in practice led the Court of Appeal to endorse a pragmatic approach to cases that fall on the cusp between the two, such as *Collis* [2012] EWCA Crim 1335. In that case, the victim forced his way into the offender's flat and attacked the offender's wife in a dispute over drugs. The offender stabbed him in the neck with a knife, pleading guilty on the basis that he had not armed himself in advance. The Court said this was a case of greater harm having regard to the life-threatening nature of the injury to the victim but was at the borderline of higher and lower culpability. The case overall was therefore at the borderline of categories 1 and 2, requiring a starting point of nine years' imprisonment. After reduction for plea, the final sentence was six years.

Knives An example of sentencing at the very top of the range is provided by *Duesbury* [2019] EWCA Crim 1555, in which the Court of Appeal upheld an extended sentence of 23 years (with a custodial term of 18 years) following an incident in which the offender first severely slashed his former girlfriend in the face and then stabbed her new boyfriend through the hand when he tried to intervene to protect her. The offender had 16 previous convictions for 39 offences, including serious assaults and woundings, and was clearly a danger to the public. The Court identified as further aggravating factors his status on bail, his intent to cause more serious harm to his victim than he actually caused, the fact the attacks were in a street in daylight, and that there were two victims who suffered severe injuries. **B2.76**

In *Fadeiro* [2012] EWCA Crim 1292, [2013] 1 Cr App R (S) 66 (366), the 19-year-old offender stabbed a 17-year-old youth in the face with a knife, causing a deep penetrating injury close to his eye. By great good fortune, no permanent or serious damage was done. The judge selected a starting point at the lower end of category 1 (greater harm and higher culpability). The Court of Appeal upheld the sentence of 11 years' detention in a young offender institution, but preferred to say that it was category 2 on the basis that greater harm (in the context of the offence) had not been caused, although culpability was high because of the use of the knife and also the aggravating factor that the offender had a previous conviction for robbery in which a knife had been produced. In *Karakas* [2012] EWCA Crim 1245, [2013] 1 Cr App R (S) 46 (261), the offender, a man of previous good character, stabbed the victim four times following a series of disputes. The femoral artery was severed, there were injuries to bladder and bowel, and the victim lost five pints of blood and was in hospital for two months. Following a guilty plea, the judge passed a sentence of ten years' imprisonment based on a starting point of 15 years. The Court of Appeal agreed that this was a category 1 case but, in light of personal mitigation, the sentence was reduced to eight years.

B2.77 **Other Weapons** The use of other weapons will attract comparable sentences, depending upon the extent of the injuries, taken together with relevant mitigating and aggravating factors. In *Lashley* [2017] EWCA Crim 260, [2017] 2 Cr App R (S) 4 (14), 12 years' imprisonment was appropriate where the offender took a car without consent and used it as a weapon by driving into the victim and reversing over the victim's legs. A similar starting point was taken in *Talbot* [2012] EWCA Crim 2322, [2013] 2 Cr App R (S) 6 (29), resulting in eight years' imprisonment after a plea, where the offender caused grievous bodily harm to a police officer with intent to resist arrest. He ran his car into the victim, knocking him down, and then drove over him, fracturing the officer's leg. In *Crawford* [2017] EWCA Crim 1891 an offender who pleaded guilty to using his car as a weapon by driving at a group including his girlfriend, trapping her beneath the vehicle and breaking her ankle, should have been sentenced as a category 2 case with a starting point of six years' imprisonment. The Court of Appeal considered that culpability was high but there was no really serious harm, even if that was purely a matter of chance.

B2.78 **Glassing** The Court of Appeal has considered many cases where a broken bottle or glass has been used as a weapon. On application of the current guidelines, nine years' imprisonment following a trial was upheld in *Burtenshaw* [2012] EWCA Crim 3058, [2013] 2 Cr App R (S) 41 (277), where the offender smashed a glass and struck a man twice in the face with it, causing serious cuts which required 30 stitches and produced long-term psychological effects and permanent scarring. The Court of Appeal said that the case was on the borderline between categories 1 and 2. Six years' imprisonment was upheld in *Anani* [2013] EWCA Crim 65, [2013] 2 Cr App R (S) 57 (370) where the offender pleaded guilty to two s. 18 offences. After a drunken argument, he struck the first victim with a broken bottle, causing serious injury to his face, and then used the bottle to stab a second man in the arm. The Court of Appeal said the case was either a category 1 case or on the borderline with category 2, and was aggravated by its commission under the influence of alcohol in a public place. In *Foster* [2015] EWCA Crim 916, [2015] 2 Cr App R (S) 45 (348), where the offender used a broken bottle to stab his victim three times in the back in quick succession, the Court of Appeal said that this was a case of higher culpability (because of the repeated use of the weapon) but did not amount to greater harm and, in particular, could not be described as a 'sustained' assault. The judge's starting point of seven years' imprisonment within category 2 was therefore excessive, and the final sentence should have been four years allowing full credit for a guilty plea.

B2.79 **Weapon Equivalents** In *A-G's Ref (No. 6 of 2015) (Voisey)* [2015] EWCA Crim 625, [2015] 2 Cr App R (S) 24 (223) a sentence of 30 months' imprisonment was increased to 54 months where the offender had used his teeth as a 'weapon equivalent' in biting off the ear of a door supervisor at a bar, causing permanent disfigurement. The starting point should have been five years and then adjusted for a late guilty plea. In *Thompson* [2015] EWCA Crim 1575, [2016] 1 Cr App R (S) 26 (162) the offender bit away a portion of flesh from the victim's eyebrow, an injury which required plastic surgery to repair. The Court of Appeal upheld a sentence of seven years' imprisonment after a trial, saying that although this was a category 2 offence, in that it fell short of injury 'which is serious in the context of the offence', it carried higher culpability because teeth had been used as a weapon. In *A-G's Ref. (JDL)* [2018] EWCA Crim 1766, [2018] 2 Cr App R (S) 45 (376), the offender's knee was characterised as a weapon equivalent, leading to a finding of higher culpability. He had held the victim's head and brought his knee up into her face up to ten times with the intention of inflicting grievous bodily harm.

Kicking or Stamping It is clear that where an offender causes grievous bodily harm by kicking or stamping on the victim's head while the latter is on the ground, a substantial custodial term should be imposed. In *Cripps* [2012] EWCA Crim 806, [2013] 1 Cr App R (S) 7 (43) a sentence of nine years' imprisonment was upheld where the offender had attacked a man, punched him unconscious, and then kicked his head while he lay on the floor. The victim sustained extensive fractures to the jaw, cheekbones, eye sockets and nose. His face and eye socket were reconstructed surgically. The judge regarded this as a category 1 case. The Court of Appeal said that it lay on the cusp between category 1 and category 2. Greater harm was clearly present, but in respect of culpability the lack of premeditation had to be set against the use of the shod foot as a weapon. In any event, the sentence was in no way excessive. Further, in *Truskowski* [2017] EWCA Crim 1869, the Court said that an offender who uses a weapon (in this case a shod foot) is undoubtedly more culpable, even if the bulk of the injury is caused by a different means (such as punching). In *Henning* [2015] EWCA Crim 879, [2015] 2 Cr App R (S) 37 (302) the Court of Appeal refused to distinguish between a foot shod in trainers from other footwear, saying that trainers can still cause terrible harm. **B2.80**

Corrosive Fluid See also **B12.269** (acid attacks). In *Midmore* [2017] EWCA Crim 533, [2017] 2 Cr App R 8 (73), two defendants were sentenced to 15 years' (with an extension period of five years) and nine years' imprisonment respectively (the latter after a guilty plea) for throwing sulphuric acid at the victim's face. In *Isaac* [2016] EWCA Crim 1907, sentences of ten and six years' detention were imposed on two young offenders, respectively, who had been convicted under the OAPA 1861, s. 29 (see also *Riley* [2017] EWCA Crim 243). On 27 July 2017 the Sentencing Council published observations about the use of acid or other corrosive substances, emphasising their use is already a guideline factor indicating high culpability. In *Ardic* [2019] EWCA Crim 1836, [2020] 1 Cr App R (S) 59 (457), two offenders involved in an attack in which V was sprayed in the face with a corrosive substance, were found guilty of s. 29 offences and sentenced to custodial terms of 14 and 14½ years, extended in each case by three years. A third offender, who had brought the substance to the scene, had sprayed members of the public indiscriminately during the course of the attack and had been involved in earlier disorder, was sentenced to 17 years with a similar extension period. The trial judge had been right to use the factors within the s. 18 guideline to assess culpability and harm. However, in view of the length of the custodial element of the sentences there was no need for these admittedly dangerous offenders to receive extended sentences. Determinate sentences of 12, 14 and 16 years' imprisonment were substituted. **B2.81**

Sentences above the Range Cases involving multiple or very serious offending may be sentenced outside the range. In *Wilson* [2016] EWCA Crim 1555, [2017] 1 Cr App R (S) 7 (35), the defendant was convicted of grievous bodily harm under the OAPA 1861, s. 18, and child destruction following a staged attack with an accomplice, each disguised with crash helmets, on a woman 32 weeks pregnant with his child. They repeatedly targeted blows and kicks at her abdomen, intending to destroy the unborn baby. The results were catastrophic for the child, which was delivered still-born by emergency surgery, and were life-threatening for the mother. The offender was sentenced to life imprisonment as a dangerous offender, but the Court of Appeal said that aside from the dangerousness regime, if the s. 18 offence had stood alone it would have merited 18 years as a determinate sentence and may well have fallen into the rare category justifying a discretionary life sentence. Similarly, in a case involving multiple and very serious offending by a doctor maliciously performing brutal mutilating operations on 17 patients (*A-G's Ref (Paterson)* [2017] EWCA Crim 1625, (2018) 1 Cr App R (S) 14 (79)) the harm and culpability factors were exceptionally high and a sentence outside the range was inevitable, resulting in an increase from 15 years' imprisonment to 20. In *Rowe* [2018] EWCA Crim 2688, [2019] 1 Cr App R (S) 38 (256), the offender was convicted of engaging in a campaign of infecting sexual partners with HIV. The lifelong impact on his ten victims was very severe. He was found to be dangerous and was sentenced to life imprisonment with a minimum term of 12 years' imprisonment before he could apply for parole. A sentencer considering an extended sentence will usually require reports as to the offender's dangerousness. Where there is already a sound evidential basis for such a finding and the question of obtaining reports has been carefully **B2.82**

considered, the failure to obtain a pre-sentence report will not invalidate an extended sentence (*Allen* [2019] EWCA Crim 1772).

Elements

B2.83 An offence under the OAPA 1861, s. 18, may take one of four different forms, namely:

(a) wounding with intent to do grievous bodily harm;
(b) causing grievous bodily harm with intent to do so;
(c) maliciously wounding with intent to resist or prevent the lawful apprehension etc. of any person; or
(d) maliciously causing grievous bodily harm with intent to resist or prevent lawful apprehension etc. of any person.

As to the meaning of the terms 'wound' and 'grievous bodily harm', see **B2.67**. Following the decision of the House of Lords in *Ireland* [1998] AC 147, it now seems unlikely that anything of significance turns on the supposed difference between 'causing' injury in cases under s. 18 and 'inflicting' injury in cases under s. 20. This means that the *actus reus* elements of the two offences are for most purposes the same. The difference lies in the specific intent required under s. 18. Where it is alleged that D acted with intent to cause grievous bodily harm, the jury should be directed along the following or similar lines: 'You must feel sure that [D] intended to cause [really] serious bodily harm to [V]. You can only decide what his intention was by considering all the relevant circumstances and in particular what he did and what he said about it' (*Purcell* (1986) 83 Cr App R 45).

If D is alleged to have acted with intent to do grievous bodily harm, the concept of maliciousness is rendered otiose and need not be examined (*Mowatt* [1968] 1 QB 421). Where, in contrast, it is alleged that D merely intended to resist arrest etc., it must be proved that D was malicious. If, for example, D tries to pull free from the arresting officer and quite unforeseeably injures the officer in the process, D commits no offence under s. 18. If, however, D intends or foresees even minor injury, D is malicious.

Where it is alleged that D acted with intent to resist the lawful apprehension of any person, whether D or another, the lawfulness of that arrest, etc., must be proved by the prosecution (*Howarth* (1828) 1 Mood 207). In a case such as *Kenlin v Gardiner* [1967] 2 QB 510, where D mistook arresting officers for kidnappers, mistaken self-defence may be raised in accordance with the principles established in *Williams* [1987] 3 All ER 411 and now embodied in the CJIA 2008, s. 76 (see **A3.64**). See generally **A3.55**.

Where serious injury is caused or attempted by means of an acid attack, D may be charged with committing or attempting to commit a s. 18 offence, but consideration may also be given to the OAPA 1861, s. 29 (casting or throwing corrosive fluid with intent to burn, maim, disfigure, disable or do grievous bodily harm: see **B12.267**).

ADMINISTERING POISON ETC. SO AS TO ENDANGER LIFE ETC.

Definition

B2.84 **Offences against the Person Act 1861, s. 23**

> Whosoever shall unlawfully and maliciously administer to or cause to be administered to or taken by any other person any poison or other destructive or noxious thing, so as thereby to endanger the life of such person, or so as thereby to inflict upon such person any grievous bodily harm, shall be guilty of [an offence] ...

Note also the A-TCSA 2001, s. 113 (see **B10.173**).

Procedure

An offence under the OAPA 1861, s. 23, is triable only on indictment. It is normally a class 3 offence, but see CrimPD XIII, para. B (see Supplement, **CPD.XIII.B**) for the additional factors that the court considers on allocation. **B2.85**

Indictment

Statement of Offence **B2.86**

Administering poison so as to endanger life [or so as to cause grievous bodily harm], contrary to section 23 of the Offences against the Person Act 1861

Particulars of Offence

A on or about the ... day of ... unlawfully and maliciously administered to V a poison, namely ..., so as thereby to endanger the life of the said V [or so as to inflict on the said V grievous bodily harm]

Alternative Verdicts

Under the OAPA 1861, s. 25, if a jury are not satisfied that a person charged under s. 23 is guilty of that offence but they are satisfied that the person is guilty of an offence under s. 24 (see **B2.93** to **B2.98**), they can acquit under s. 23 and return a verdict of guilty under s. 24, and D will be sentenced as if tried on indictment under s. 24. **B2.87**

B

Part B Offences

Sentence

The maximum penalty is ten years' imprisonment (OAPA 1861, s. 23). There is no offence-specific guideline but the Sentencing Council's *General Guideline: Overarching Principles* (see Supplement, **SG2-1**) is used for all offenders sentenced on or after 1 October 2019. **B2.88**

In *MK* [2008] EWCA Crim 425, [2008] 2 Cr App R (S) 78 (437) the 23-year-old offender pleaded guilty to the offence under s. 23 in circumstances where he had given a three-year-old child in his care a teaspoonful of methadone. The offender planned to obtain a urine sample from the child, which would be free from Class A drugs but positive for methadone. The child suffered a life-threatening illness as a result. The offender did not admit to the doctors treating the child what he had done, so the child's suffering was prolonged. A sentence of four and a half years' imprisonment was upheld on appeal.

Actus Reus

In *Kennedy (No. 2)* [2007] UKHL 38, [2008] 1 AC 269, the House of Lords held that s. 23 creates three distinct offences. The first is committed where D administers the noxious thing directly to V, as by injecting V with the noxious thing, holding a glass containing the noxious thing to V's lips, or (as in *Gillard* (1988) 87 Cr App R 189) spraying a noxious thing (e.g., CS gas or ammonia) in V's face. See also *A-G's Ref (No. 69 of 2005)* [2005] EWCA Crim 3050, [2006] 1 Cr App R (S) 130 (756) (dousing victims in petrol and threatening to light it). **B2.89**

The second is typically committed where D does not directly administer the noxious thing to V but causes an innocent third party (T) to administer it to V. If D, knowing a syringe to be filled with poison, instructs T to inject V, when T believes the syringe to contain a legitimate therapeutic substance, D would commit this offence.

The third covers the situation where the noxious thing is not administered to V but is taken by V, provided D causes the noxious thing to be taken by V and V does not make a voluntary and informed decision to take it. If D puts a noxious thing in food which V is about to eat and V, ignorant of the presence of the noxious thing, eats it, D commits the offence (see also *Harley* (1830) 4 C & P 369).

In each case, the administration must endanger the life of a person or inflict grievous bodily harm on a person. A foetus is not a 'person' and cannot be the victim of such an offence

(*Criminal Injuries Compensation Authority v First-Tier Tribunal (Social Entitlement Chamber)* [2014] EWCA Civ 1554, [2015] QB 459). If the poison etc. is not consumed and does not come into contact with any potential victim's body in a way that may cause harm, there can, at most, be an attempt to administer it (*Dale* (1852) 6 Cox CC 14).

The administering must be unlawful. Consent will normally negate unlawfulness, but not where it is procured by deception or where considerations of public policy invalidate that consent. A person cannot, for example, validly consent to being injected with a dangerous drug, such as heroin, unless this is done for bona fide medical reasons (*Cato* [1976] 1 All ER 260).

B2.90 In some cases D might be said to have administered the drug to V, even though V helped D to do it. Joint administration would suffice to make D guilty of an offence under s. 23 (and of manslaughter if death results). See *Burgess* [2008] EWCA Crim 516 at [12]. In *Rogers* [2003] EWCA Crim 945, [2003] 1 WLR 1374, D applied a tourniquet to V's arm as V self-injected. The Court of Appeal held that this made D guilty of (jointly) administering it; but in *Kennedy* (at [20]) the House of Lords disagreed:

> There is, clearly, a difficult borderline between contributory acts which may properly be regarded as administering a noxious thing and acts which may not. But the crucial question is not whether the defendant facilitated or contributed to administration of the noxious thing, but whether he went further and administered it. What matters ... is whether the injection itself was the result of a voluntary and informed decision by the person injecting himself. In *R v Rogers*, as in the present case, it was. That case was, therefore, wrongly decided ...

If D had injected V while V applied the tourniquet to his own arm, the House of Lords would presumably have approved the decision. The House of Lords also reversed *Kennedy (No. 2)* [2005] EWCA Crim 685, [2005] 4 All ER 1083, in which it had been held that D may be guilty of administering a noxious drug to V on the basis of a joint venture or agreement, even though V alone performs the physical act of injection.

B2.91 Whether a substance is a poison, etc. is largely a question of fact, but the meaning of the term 'noxious' was examined in *Marcus* [1981] 2 All ER 833, where M put sleeping pills into her neighbour's milk. Were sleeping pills a noxious substance? The question was held to be one of both quantity and quality. Something which is harmless in small doses may be noxious in larger doses or when taken at the wrong time. Its effect on V is what is important. The Court of Appeal referred to the dictionary definition of 'noxious' as 'injurious, hurtful, harmful, unwholesome' and held that it could also apply to objectionable or obnoxious substances, although the potential of such a wide definition is greater in s. 24, where no dangerous or harmful consequence is required. See also *Hill* (1986) 83 Cr App R 386; *Gantz* [2004] EWCA Crim 2862, [2005] 1 Cr App R (S) 104 (587) and *Veysey* [2019] EWCA Crim 1332, [2019] 2 Cr App R 29 (327) (see **B2.98**).

Mens Rea

B2.92 The *mens rea* required under s. 23 is maliciousness, which has the same meaning as it does under s. 20 (see **B2.69**). This means that D must act either with intent or with subjective recklessness; but this *mens rea* requirement applies only to the act of administering or causing the administration of the noxious substance. It does not extend to the consequences of that administration, which are governed by strict or constructive liability. D may therefore be guilty even if D did not intend or foresee that the action would cause grievous bodily harm or endanger life. See *Cato* [1976] 1 All ER 260.

ADMINISTERING POISON ETC. WITH INTENT

Definition

B2.93 **Offences against the Person Act 1861, s. 24**

> Whosoever shall unlawfully and maliciously administer to or cause to be administered to or taken by any other person any poison or other destructive or noxious thing, with intent to injure, aggrieve, or annoy such person, shall be guilty of [an offence] ...

Procedure

Administering poison etc. with intent is triable only on indictment. It is normally a class 3 offence, but see CrimPD XIII, para. B (see Supplement, **CPD.XIII.B**) for the additional factors that the court considers on allocation. **B2.94**

Indictment

Statement of Offence **B2.95**

Administering a noxious thing with intent, contrary to section 24 of the Offences against the Person Act 1861

Particulars of Offence

D on or about the ... day of ... unlawfully and maliciously administered to V a noxious thing, namely by throwing urine in V's face, with intent to aggrieve or annoy the said V

Alternative Verdicts

See **B2.87**. **B2.96**

Sentence

The maximum penalty is five years' imprisonment (OAPA 1861, s. 24). There is no offence-specific guideline but the Sentencing Council's *General Guideline: Overarching Principles* (see Supplement, **SG2-1**) is used for all offenders sentenced on or after 1 October 2019. **B2.97**

In *Veysey* [2019] EWCA Crim 1332, [2019] 2 Cr App R 29 (327) the Court of Appeal offered this guidance (at [44]) on sentencing serving prisoners who throw urine or faeces into the faces of prison officers:

> It is wholly unrealistic to treat offences of this nature as if they were no more than a common assault, or a minor offence of assault occasioning minimal bodily harm. Nor is it realistic to suggest that a case of this nature, properly prosecuted before the criminal courts and liable to a maximum sentence of five years' imprisonment, should be sentenced in a way which is not much different from the limited range of penalties available under the Prison Rules. Section 24 offences of this kind are serious offences which are intended or likely to undermine discipline and good order in prisons and which add significantly to the burdens already faced by those charged with assisting prisoners and maintaining discipline. The need to punish and deter makes it necessary to impose severe punishment. In our judgment, offences of this nature will generally attract a starting point after trial in the range of two to three years' imprisonment, with offences involving urine falling at the lower end of that range and offences involving faeces at the upper end.

In *Jones* (1990) 12 Cr App R (S) 233, Glidewell LJ accepted that the appropriate sentencing bracket for this offence was equivalent to that for an offence of wounding or inflicting grievous bodily harm under the OAPA 1861, s. 20 (see **B2.59**), or a serious example of an offence of assault occasioning actual bodily harm under the OAPA 1861, s. 47 (see **B2.31**), on the basis that the maximum penalty available for each of the three offences is five years. Nine months' imprisonment was said to be the correct sentence in *Hogan* (1994) 15 Cr App R (S) 834, where the offender gave to a woman a drink which contained a large quantity of a Class C drug. It caused her to fall into a deep sleep for a day. Two years was appropriate in *Liles* [2000] 1 Cr App R (S) 31, where the offender allowed two young boys to inhale isobutyle nitrate so that they became dizzy and unwell. Thirty months after a trial was upheld in *Bryan* [2011] EWCA Crim 316, [2011] 2 Cr App R (S) 70 (407), where the offender threw liquid containing a mixture of chilli, black pepper and turmeric into the face of the victim, causing non-permanent damage to her eyes.

Elements

The *actus reus* of the OAPA 1861, s. 24, is similar to that of s. 23, save that no consequential harm or endangerment is required. It is a conduct crime. For that reason, where D deliberately coughs or spits over V while infected with the Covid-19 virus, a charge under s. 24 may be much **B2.98**

Part B Offences

B

easier to establish than one under s. 23, where, even if V later contracts the disease, causation may well be impossible to prove.

As with s. 23, D must act maliciously in administering the noxious thing, but there is a further or ulterior intent, namely to injure, aggrieve or annoy, which must additionally be proved. This means that s. 24 — the lesser offence — is one of specific intent for the purposes of the *Majewski* rule (see **A3.17**), whereas the more serious s. 23 offence is one of basic intent.

In *Veysey* [2019] EWCA Crim 1332, [2019] 2 Cr App R 29 (327) the Court of Appeal considered three appeals from serving prisoners who had been convicted, *inter alia*, of offences under the OAPA 1861, s. 24, for conduct colloquially referred to in the prisons system as 'potting': i.e., throwing at a prison officer, or smearing a prison officer with, urine, faeces or a mixture of the two. One of the issues in each case was whether urine or faeces could properly be categorised as noxious substances for the purpose of the s. 24 offence. The Court held, following *Marcus* [1981] 2 All ER 833, that it is at least open to a jury to hold (on the facts) that they are. Holroyde LJ said (at [25]–[26]):

> In our view, the matter is concluded by the decision of this court in *Marcus* [in which] ... the court plainly accepted the dictionary definition of 'noxious' which extends to a substance which is 'unwholesome'.
>
> In our judgment, where an issue arises as to whether a substance is a noxious thing for the purpose of section 24 of the 1861 Act, it will be for the judge to rule as a matter of law whether the substance concerned, in the quantity and manner in which it is shown by the evidence to have been administered, could properly be found by the jury to be injurious, hurtful, harmful or unwholesome. If it can be properly so regarded, it will be a matter for the jury whether they are satisfied that it was a noxious thing within that definition. In the present case, the judges below were entitled to find that a cupful of human urine, from an unknown source, thrown at the face of a victim is capable of being regarded as an unwholesome, and therefore a noxious, thing. It follows that they were correct to dismiss the applications made, and that the jury were entitled to conclude that Veysey had on three occasions administered a noxious thing to prison officers.

Section 24 has been used successfully to prosecute defendants who 'spike' their victims' drinks with drugs such as ecstasy (*Gantz* [2004] EWCA Crim 2862, [2005] 1 Cr App R (S) 104 (587)) or who ply children with such drugs for improper purposes. The 'overstimulation' of a victim's metabolism that such action is intended to cause can be viewed as a type of injury. In *Hill* (1986) 83 Cr App R 386, H administered slimming pills to young boys in order to keep them awake. The House of Lords held that he had been properly convicted under s. 24. Lord Griffiths said:

> The defence conceded that the tablets were a noxious thing and that the respondent had unlawfully administered them to the boys. In these circumstances the only issue that the jury had to determine was whether he did so with the intent to injure them ... Here was a man who admitted being sexually attracted to young boys plying them with a drug which he knew would overstimulate and excite them and doing so with a reckless disregard for what might be the safe dosage and, in fact, giving them a gross overdose. The only reasonable inference to draw from such conduct was an intention that the drug should injure the boys in the sense of causing harm to the metabolism of their bodies by overstimulation with the motive of either ingratiating himself with them or, more probably, rendering them susceptible to homosexual advances.

FALSE IMPRISONMENT

Definition

B2.99 False imprisonment is a common-law offence but is more common as a civil action in tort. The overlap with kidnapping (see **B2.105**) and child abduction (see **B2.112**) means that those offences may often represent more suitable charges than simple false imprisonment.

The case of *Rahman* (1985) 81 Cr App R 349 provides the following definition (at p. 353): 'False imprisonment consists in the unlawful and intentional or reckless restraint of a victim's freedom of movement from a particular place.'

Procedure

False imprisonment is triable only on indictment. It may be classified in class 2A, 2B or 3; see CrimPD XIII, para. B (see Supplement, **CPD.XIII.B**) for the additional factors that the court considers on allocation. **B2.100**

Indictment

Statement of Offence **B2.101**

False imprisonment

Particulars of Offence

D between the ... day of ... and the ... day of ... falsely imprisoned V and detained the said V against his will

Sentence

The maximum penalty is at large (common-law offence). There is no offence-specific guideline but the Sentencing Council's *General Guideline: Overarching Principles* (see Supplement, **SG2-1**) is used for all offenders sentenced on or after 1 October 2019. **B2.102**

In *A-G's Ref (Nos. 92 and 93 of 2014)* [2014] EWCA Crim 2713, [2015] 1 Cr App R (S) 44 (323) Treacy LJ said (at [19]) that relevant sentencing factors will include:

> the length of detention; the circumstances of detention, including location and any method of restraint; the extent of any violence used; the involvement of weapons; whether demands were made of others; whether threats were made to others; the effect on the victim and others; the extent of planning; the number of offenders involved; the use of torture or humiliation; whether what was done arose from or was in furtherance of previous criminal behaviour, and any particular vulnerability of the victim whether by reason of age or otherwise.

In *BD* [2018] EWCA Crim 154, [2018] 1 Cr App R (S) 50 (384) a sentence, after a plea, of three years and eight months' imprisonment for the false imprisonment of two young children following a domestic dispute which led to a stand-off with police was described as severe but not manifestly excessive. See also the authorities referred to at **B2.108**.

Actus Reus

This consists of preventing V's freedom of movement. V may be restrained physically or by deliberate intimidation (*James* (1997) *The Times*, 2 October 1997). V might be detained in a building or vehicle, or simply prevented from going on his way. In *Bird v Jones* (1845) 7 QB 742, a civil case, V was prevented from going in one particular direction in which he wished to go, but there was an alternative route available to him; this did not constitute a false imprisonment. **B2.103**

The *actus reus* is the imprisoning without lawful excuse, and there seems no logical reason for requiring that V realise this is the case. No such realisation is necessary in the tort of false imprisonment (*Meering v Grahame White Aviation Co. Ltd* (1919) 122 LT 44).

The imprisonment must be unlawful. Two main situations arise where this can be problematic. One is in respect of a parent restraining a child. In *Rahman* (1985) 81 Cr App R 349 the question arose of the limits of a parent's right to lawfully restrain a child. D had taken his 15-year-old daughter from her foster parents against her will. He was convicted and appealed. The Court of Appeal held that it was a question of fact in each case whether a parent had overstepped the limits of lawful correction and restraint. Whether the child's lack of consent was relevant must also be a question of fact depending on the circumstances of a particular case. In this case D had overstepped his right as a parent to exercise normal parental control. (See also kidnapping at **B2.105** and child abduction at **B2.112**.)

The other main situation in which false imprisonment can arise is where an arrest is carried out, by either a constable or a private citizen, which turns out to be unlawful. The lawfulness of an arrest is to be decided by reference to the general law, including the PACE 1984, s. 24. See, as to lawful and unlawful arrests, **D1.14**. If the arrest is unlawful, the *actus reus* of the offence will have been committed.

Mens Rea

B2.104 *Rahman* (1985) 81 Cr App R 349 states that the *mens rea* for false imprisonment is intention or recklessness. Recklessness here means subjective or *Cunningham* recklessness (*James* (1997) *The Times*, 2 October 1997).

The offence is one of basic intent, and therefore evidence of D's voluntary intoxication is irrelevant. This was confirmed in *Hutchins* [1988] Crim LR 379, which also emphasised the overlap and analogy with kidnapping. In that case D, having taken drugs at a party, took a neighbour hostage. He was charged with both kidnapping and false imprisonment. It was confirmed that his intoxication was irrelevant, and the Court of Appeal took the opportunity to define both 'false imprisonment' and 'kidnapping'. It emphasised that in kidnapping the taking must be by force or fraud, and that the definition was in terms of 'taking or carrying away' rather than a mere detaining, which would suffice for false imprisonment.

KIDNAPPING

Definition

B2.105 Kidnapping is a common-law offence. It overlaps partly with false imprisonment (see **B2.99**) and partly with child abduction (see **B2.112**).

The offence consists of the taking or carrying away of one person by another by force or fraud, without the consent of that person and without lawful excuse.

Procedure

B2.106 Kidnapping is triable only on indictment. It may be classified in class 2A, 2B or 3; see CrimPD XIII, para. B (see Supplement, **CPD.XIII.B**) for the additional factors that the court considers on allocation.

Indictment

B2.107

Statement of Offence

Kidnapping

Particulars of Offence

A on or about the ... day of ... unlawfully took and carried away V against his will

Despite the acknowledged overlap between the offences of kidnapping and statutory abduction, an indictment should not contain counts for both offences (*C* (1990) *The Times*, 9 November 1990).

Sentence

B2.108 The maximum penalty is at large (common-law offence). There is no offence-specific guideline but the Sentencing Council's *General Guideline: Overarching Principles* (see Supplement, SG2-1) is used for all offenders sentenced on or after 1 October 2019. At the top end of the sentencing scale for this offence, cases involving hostage-taking, torture and demands for ransom generally attract sentences close to 16 years before reduction for plea. The leading authorities were reviewed in *Osei* [2018] EWCA Crim 2728, in which a kidnapping related to drug dealing required a sentence of eight years' imprisonment. The Court of Appeal stressed the fact-specific nature of such offences, noting the seriousness factors identified in *A-G's Ref (No. 92 of 2014) (Gibney)* [2014] EWCA Crim 2713, [2015] 1 Cr App R (S) 44 (323) at [19]:

> ... the length of detention; the circumstances of detention, including location and any method of restraint; the extent of any violence used; the involvement of weapons; whether demands were

made of others; whether threats were made to others; the effect on the victim and others; the extent of planning; the number of offenders involved; the use of torture or humiliation; whether what was done arose from or was in furtherance of previous criminal behaviour, and any particular vulnerability of the victim whether by reason of age or otherwise.

In *A-G's Ref (Nos. 102 and 103 of 2014) (Perkins)* [2014] EWCA Crim 2922, [2015] 1 Cr App R (S) 55 (389) the victim was repeatedly punched and kicked by the two offenders, both of whom had records of violence. He was then tied up and blindfolded before being tortured, burned with an iron and partly suffocated by repeated immersion of his head in water. The Court of Appeal said that an extended sentence of 13 years, with a custodial term of ten years with an extended licence period of three years, was appropriate following a trial. See also *Mahmood* [2015] EWCA Crim 441, [2015] 2 Cr App R (S) 18 (182) and *Hussain* [2012] EWCA Crim 2093, [2013] 1 Cr App R (S) 112 (580).

In *Jones* [2019] EWCA Crim 2050, sentences with a starting point before plea of seven and five years respectively were upheld on appeal in a case where the two offenders (father and son) pleaded guilty to the violent kidnapping of a man who had escaped from the caravan in which he was being kept. The kidnapping lasted about 24 hours before the victim was rescued by the police. He had suffered a severe beating and was traumatised. Both men had bad criminal records and there was no mitigation other than a small discount for late guilty pleas.

In *Ashworth* [2009] EWCA Crim 1028, [2010] 1 Cr App R (S) 15 (84), a sentence of two years was appropriate for a brief period of false imprisonment of a father by his 24-year-old son after a domestic argument, and 12 months was upheld for false imprisonment in *Saker* [2011] EWCA Crim 1196, [2012] 1 Cr App R (S) 16 (87) where a mother was involved in tying up and imprisoning her daughter for a short time in the hope of preventing drug use by the daughter. In *Clarke* [2018] EWCA Crim 1845, [2019] 1 Cr App R (S) 15 (108) sentences of four years and eight months' detention in a young offender institution were not unduly lenient. Two young offenders with very bad records had pleaded guilty to a sustained kidnap of a 16-year-old victim who was taken to woods and threatened at knifepoint. The sentences (which were components of sentences totalling up to seven years' detention for related offences of aggravated burglary) could have been longer but the appropriate reduction on account of the offenders' youth would be more than minimal and so on this basis the sentences, though lenient, were not unduly so.

Actus Reus

The *actus reus* of kidnapping (as defined at **B2.105**) is similar to that of false imprisonment (see **B2.99**) insofar as it involves the unlawful deprivation of V's liberty; but it differs from false imprisonment in that it also requires V to be taken or carried away, either by force (including the threat of force: *Archer* [2011] EWCA Crim 2252) or by fraud. V need not be carried far: in *Wellard* [1978] 3 All ER 161, D impersonated a constable and thereby tricked or coerced V into walking a few yards to his car in order to submit to a 'drugs search'. This was held to be a sufficient 'taking'. **B2.109**

In *D* [1984] AC 778, the House of Lords held that a parent who took custody of his own child in contravention of a court order could be guilty of kidnapping, and a majority held that the rule was more general, and that parents could be acting without lawful excuse in some circumstances by taking their children even where there was no court order. It will be a question of fact whether or not a parent has a lawful excuse to exercise such physical control over the whereabouts of the child.

Kidnapping must be committed without the valid consent of the victim. Consent or compliance procured by force or fear is not true consent (*Greenhalgh* [2001] EWCA Crim 1367). Very young children may be incapable of giving such consent (*D* [1984] AC 778); but it may sometimes prove difficult to show force or fraud if a child is simply picked up and taken. In such circumstances, a charge under the Child Abduction Act 1984 may be easier to prove, although in the most serious cases the higher maximum penalty that may be imposed for kidnapping may warrant consideration (*Kayani* [2011] EWCA Crim 2871, [2012] 2 All ER 641). If a person initially consents to being taken away, the offence will be committed if that consent is later withdrawn and force is used to maintain a kidnapping (*Lewis* (22 March 1993 unreported)).

B2.110 As to the need for a deprivation of liberty, this appears to have been overlooked in *Cort* [2003] EWCA Crim 2149, [2004] QB 388, in which D tricked his 'victims' into riding in his car by deceiving them into thinking that their bus had broken down. This was held to be sufficient for an offence of kidnapping, even though there was no evidence to suggest that D made any attempt to detain them against their will. But *Cort* is inconsistent with *Wellard* and was doubted in *Hendy-Freegard* [2007] EWCA Crim 1236, [2008] QB 57, where Lord Phillips CJ said (at [55]):

> We cannot see that there was justification for extending the offence of kidnapping to cover the situation in which the driver of the car has no intention of detaining his passenger against her will nor of doing other than taking her to the destination to which she wishes to go, simply because in some such circumstances the driver may have an objectionable ulterior motive. The consequence of the decision in *Cort* would seem to be that the mini-cab driver, who obtains a fare by falsely pretending to be an authorised taxi, will be guilty of kidnapping.

In *Hendy-Freegard*, D tricked his victims into making certain journeys they would not otherwise have made; but these journeys were made independently, and D did not even accompany them. The Court of Appeal held that this could not amount to kidnapping, for otherwise, as Lord Phillips CJ pointed out at [57]:

> … the bigamist who induces a woman to travel to the church for a wedding ceremony might be guilty not merely of bigamy but also of kidnapping. Such a submission transforms the offence of kidnapping in a manner that cannot be justified, even on the basis of the decision in *Cort*.

Mens Rea

B2.111 The *mens rea* is not specifically discussed in *D* [1984] AC 778, but the Court of Appeal in *Hutchins* [1988] Crim LR 379 pointed out the close analogy between false imprisonment and kidnapping, the differences being in the *actus reus*. This indicates that the *mens rea* is likely to be the same as that for false imprisonment (see **B2.104**).

CHILD ABDUCTION

Abduction by Person Connected with Child

B2.112 Definition

Child Abduction Act 1984, s. 1

(1) Subject to subsections (5) and (8) below, a person connected with a child under the age of 16 commits an offence if he takes or sends the child out of the United Kingdom without the appropriate consent.

(2) A person is connected with a child for the purposes of this section if—
  (a) he is a parent of the child; or
  (b) in the case of a child whose parents were not married to, or civil partners of, each other at the time of his birth, there are reasonable grounds for believing that he is the father of the child; or
  (c) he is a guardian of the child; or
  (ca) he is a special guardian of the child; or
  (d) he is a person named in a child arrangements order as a person with whom the child is to live; or
  (e) he has custody of the child.

(3) In this section 'the appropriate consent', in relation to a child, means—
  (a) the consent of each of the following—
    (i) the child's mother;
    (ii) the child's father, if he has parental responsibility for him;
    (iii) any guardian of the child;
    (iiia) any special guardian of the child;
    (iv) any person named in a child arrangements order as a person with whom the child is to live;
    (v) any person who has custody of the child; or
  (b) the leave of the court granted under or by virtue of any provision of Part II of the Children Act 1989; or
  (c) if any person has custody of the child, the leave of the court which awarded custody to him.

(4) A person does not commit an offence under this section by taking or sending a child out of the United Kingdom without obtaining the appropriate consent if—
(a) he is a person named in a child arrangements order as a person with whom the child is to live and he takes or sends him out of the United Kingdom for a period of less than one month; or
(b) he is a special guardian of the child and he takes or sends the child out of the United Kingdom for a period of less than three months.
(4A) Subsection (4) above does not apply if the person taking or sending the child out of the United Kingdom does so in breach of an order under Part II of the Children Act 1989.
(5) A person does not commit an offence under this section by doing anything without the consent of another person whose consent is required under the foregoing provisions if—
(a) he does it in the belief that the other person—
(i) has consented; or
(ii) would consent if he was aware of all the relevant circumstances; or
(b) he has taken all reasonable steps to communicate with the other person but has been unable to communicate with him; or
(c) the other person has unreasonably refused to consent.
(5A) Subsection (5)(c) above does not apply if—
(a) the person who refused to consent is a person—
(i) named in a child arrangements order as a person with whom the child is to live;
(ia) who is a special guardian of the child; or
(ii) who has custody of the child; or
(b) the person taking or sending the child out of the United Kingdom is, by so acting, in breach of an order made by a court in the United Kingdom.
(6) Where, in proceedings for an offence under this section, there is sufficient evidence to raise an issue as to the application of subsection (5) above, it shall be for the prosecution to prove that that subsection does not apply.
(7) For the purposes of this section—
(a) 'guardian of a child', 'special guardian' 'child arrangements' and 'parental responsibility' have the same meaning as in the Children Act 1989; and
(b) a person shall be treated as having custody of a child if there is in force an order of a court in the United Kingdom awarding him (whether solely or jointly with another person) custody, legal custody or care and control of the child.
(8) This section shall have effect subject to the provisions of the schedule to this Act in relation to a child who is in the care of a local authority, detained in a place of safety, remanded to local authority accommodation or the subject of proceedings or an order relating to adoption.

Procedure The consent of the DPP is required before a prosecution under s. 1 of the Act can be brought (Child Abduction Act 1984, s. 4(2)). The offence is triable either way (s. 4(1)). When tried on indictment this is normally a class 3 offence, but see CrimPD XIII, para. B (see Supplement, **CPD.XIII.B**) for the additional factors that the court considers on allocation. **B2.113**

Indictment **B2.114**

Statement of Offence

Child abduction by person connected with child contrary to section 1 of the Child Abduction Act 1984

Particulars of Offence

A on or about the ... day of ..., being a parent of V, a child under the age of 16 years, unlawfully took the said V out of the United Kingdom, to Dallas, Texas, in the United States of America, without the consent of ...

Sentence The maximum penalty is seven years' imprisonment (Child Abduction Act 1984, s. 4(1)) on indictment; six months, an unlimited fine or both, summarily. There is no offence-specific guideline but the Sentencing Council's *General Guideline: Overarching Principles* (see Supplement, **SG2-1**) is used for all offenders sentenced on or after 1 October 2019. In *RH* [2016] EWCA Crim 1754, [2017] 1 Cr App R (S) 23 (165) the Court of Appeal gave guidance on sentencing in cases of child abduction. **B2.115**

(i) The most serious class of case would involve a high level of harm exemplified by a very lengthy period of abduction or detention, a serious effect on the child or serious damage to or severance of a loving relationship with a parent, siblings or other relevant person. High culpability might be exemplified by persistent non-disclosure or concealment of the place of abduction, significant and sophisticated planning, breach of a court order or disregard of the court process, an intention to sever the relationship between the child and another relevant person, or abduction for a criminal purpose. Where there was both a high level of harm and a high level of culpability, the sentence should be five to seven years after a trial (see, e.g., *Kayani* [2011] EWCA Crim 2871, [2012] 2 Cr App R (S) 38 (214)).

(ii) Cases at the lower end of the spectrum of harm would include situations where there had been a brief period of abduction or detention, minimal effect on the child, or minimal effect on the relationship between the child and the other affected party. There would be lesser culpability where the abduction or detention was impulsive or spontaneous or where there had been prompt subsequent disclosure of the place of abduction, enabling effective action to be taken by the authorities. Cases at this level would be particularly fact-sensitive. A range between a high-level community order and 18 months' imprisonment was appropriate where low-level harm and culpability factors were in play. Some of the more minor cases might in fact be dealt with by the Family Court by way of contempt proceedings.

(iii) Where there was a combination of high culpability and low harm or vice versa, the case would fall into an intermediate sentencing range of 18 months to five years. That range was necessarily wide to reflect a multiplicity of circumstances. There might be combinations of high and low harm and culpability factors. A sentence in that range might also be based on medium-level harm factors and/or medium-level culpability factors. Medium-level harm would occur, for example, where there had been some emotional or other effect on the child or where there was some harmful effect on the relationship between the child and the adult from whose custody or control he had been taken. A medium level of culpability would arise where some degree of planning was involved. In considering where to place a case within a range, the court would also need to have regard to aggravating and mitigating factors in the usual way.

(iv) Features common to all offences such as previous good or bad character would play their part. Offence-related aggravating factors would include exposing the child to a risk of harm, the abduction of an already vulnerable child, group action, the use of significant force, abduction to a non-Hague Convention country, abduction to a place with which the child had no prior links and, in cases under the Child Abduction Act 1984, s. 2, removal from the jurisdiction. Mitigating factors would include enabling prompt contact to take place with the adult deprived of custody or control, compliance with court orders and co-operation with the authorities. In addition, the court could take into account the effect of a sentence on a child where the offending person was the sole carer for the child abducted or other children. That was not a matter of mitigation personal to the offender; rather, it arose from the need for the court to have regard to the interests of the child or children affected.

As to the applications before the court, a sentence of 20 months' imprisonment had been rightly imposed on a mother who had pleaded guilty to child abduction after taking her daughter, in defiance of a court order and in furtherance of a plan to prevent contact with the father, out of the country for over three months. As to the second application, a sentence of 30 months' imprisonment would be reduced to one of 15 months in the case of a grandfather who had pleaded guilty to child abduction after forcibly abducting his grandson for a short period in the context of a dispute about whether the child should live with his mother or father.

B2.116 *Actus Reus* The offence can be committed only by a person 'connected with' the child, and this is defined in the Child Abduction Act 1984, s. 1(2) (see **B2.112**).

Such a person must either take, or be responsible for sending, the child out of the UK himself. This offence is not committed by holding the child within the jurisdiction, or by failing to return a child who has previously been taken abroad (*R (Nicolaou) v Redbridge Magistrates' Court*

[2012] EWHC 1647 (Admin), [2012] 2 Cr App R 23 (290)). The meanings of 'taking' and of 'sending' are set out in s. 3 of the Act, and include causing a child to be taken, inducing a child to accompany D or any other person, and causing a child to be sent.

Lack of appropriate consent is a necessary circumstance which must be established. Consent of each of the persons mentioned in s. 1(3)(a) is required, or if there is a relevant court order in force the court's permission must be sought. Alternatively, the leave of the court under Part II of the Children Act 1989 will suffice. In contrast to kidnapping, however, the offence may be committed notwithstanding the consent of the child in question (see *Kayani* [2011] EWCA Crim 2871, [2012] 2 All ER 641 and **B2.109**).

Mens Rea No *mens rea* is specified in the definition of the offence, but it can be deduced from the 'defences' available under the Child Abduction Act 1984, s. 1(5), at least in respect of the circumstance of lack of appropriate consent (see **B2.118**). **B2.117**

Defences Under the Child Abduction Act 1984, s. 1(5), D will not be liable if D acts in the belief that the appropriate person has consented, or would have done so if that person had known the relevant circumstances. There is no requirement that such belief be reasonable, and the test is therefore subjective. **B2.118**

There is an additional objectively based defence if either D has taken all reasonable steps to communicate with the appropriate person, or if the consent has been unreasonably withheld. The issue of reasonableness is one of fact. If the consent needed is that of the court, then, under s. 1(5A), the provision concerning unreasonably withheld consent does not apply.

Once D provides prima facie evidence of any such defence, then the burden is on the prosecution to disprove it. The scheme of the legislation leaves no scope for any wider defence of necessity (*S* [2012] EWCA Crim 2872, [2012] 2 All ER 793).

B
Part B Offences

Abduction of Child by Other Persons

Definition The Child Abduction Act 1984, s. 2(1), creates two further offences covering cases in which someone other than a parent or other person connected to the child takes or detains a child under the age of 16. They may apply to the child's father where he was not married to the mother at the time of the child's birth, but note the defence provided by s. 2(3), discussed at **B2.124**. **B2.119**

Child Abduction Act 1984, s. 2

(1) Subject to subsection (3) below, a person, other than one mentioned in subsection (2) below, commits an offence if, without lawful authority or reasonable excuse, he takes or detains a child under the age of 16—
   (a) so as to remove him from the lawful control of any person having lawful control of the child; or
   (b) so as to keep him out of the lawful control of any person entitled to lawful control of the child.
(2) The persons are—
   (a) where the father and mother of the child in question were married to, or civil partners of, each other at the time of his birth, the child's father and mother;
   (b) where the father and mother of the child in question were not married to, or civil partners of, each other at the time of his birth, the child's mother; and
   (c) any other person mentioned in section 1(2)(c) to (e) above.
(3) In proceedings against any person for an offence under this section, it shall be a defence for that person to prove—
   (a) where the father and mother of the child in question were not married to, or civil partners of, each other at the time of his birth—
      (i) that he is the child's father; or
      (ii) that, at the time of the alleged offence, he believed, on reasonable grounds, that he was the child's father; or
   (b) that, at the time of the alleged offence, he believed that the child had attained the age of sixteen.

Procedure Offences under s. 2(1) are triable either way. When tried on indictment they are normally class 3 offences, but see CrimPD XIII, para. B (see Supplement, **CPD.XIII.B**) for the **B2.120**

additional factors that the court considers on allocation. In contrast to alleged s. 1 offences committed by persons connected with the child, prosecutions under the Child Abduction Act 1984, s. 2, do not require the consent of the DPP.

B2.121 **Indictment**

Statement of Offence

Child abduction contrary to section 2(1)(b) of the Child Abduction Act 1984

Particulars of Offence

A on or about the ... day of ... without lawful authority or reasonable excuse detained V, a child under the age of 16 years, so as to keep him out of the lawful control of X, a person entitled to lawful control of V

B2.122 **Sentence** The maximum penalty is seven years' imprisonment (Child Abduction Act 1984, s. 4(1)) on indictment; six months, an unlimited fine or both, summarily. The Court of Appeal gave guidance on sentencing for this offence in *RH* [2016] EWCA Crim 1754, [2017] 1 Cr App R (S) 23 (165). The guidance (which also applies to the offence under s. 1) is summarised at **B2.115**.

B2.123 **Elements** Section 2(1) of the Child Abduction Act 1984 requires an intentional or reckless taking or detention of a child under the age of 16, the effect or objective consequence of which is to remove or to keep that child within the meaning of s. 2(1)(a) or (b) — each of which creates a separate and distinct offence (*Foster v DPP* [2004] EWHC 2955 (Admin), [2005] 1 WLR 1400). 'Detaining' is defined in s. 3 so as to include causing the child to be detained or inducing the child to remain with D or another person. 'Taking' is defined in s. 3 so as to include causing or inducing the child to accompany D or any other person or causing the child to be taken. A child can be removed from lawful control without necessarily being taken to another place. It may suffice if the child is deflected into some unauthorised activity induced by D (see *Leather* (1993) 98 Cr App R 179, where children were persuaded by D to go with him to look for a 'missing bicycle'). Nor need D's conduct be the sole cause of the abduction, as long as it was more than merely peripheral. It is no defence that another cause may be the child's own decision or state of mind (*A* [2000] 2 All ER 177). Thus in *Shepherd v CPS* [2017] EWHC 2566 (Admin) D's conviction for an offence contrary to s. 2(1)(b) was upheld on the basis that, knowing of a child abduction warning notice that prohibited contact or communication with a named 14-year-old child, he allowed that child to enter his house and remain with him for some hours, thereby keeping her out of the lawful control of her mother. The fact that the child visited D and remained with him willingly was no defence.

The words, 'so as to' do not import any further *mens rea*; an offence may therefore be committed whether or not D intends to interfere with another person's lawful control or entitlement (*Foster v DPP*; *Hunter* [2015] EWCA Crim 372). Insofar as *Re Owens* [2000] 1 Cr App R 195 suggests otherwise, it is inconsistent with *Leather* and was not followed in *Foster v DPP* or in *Pringle* [2019] EWCA Crim 1722. The consent of that other person would amount to 'lawful authority', but the consent of the child is irrelevant. This distinguishes the offence from that of kidnapping, as does the absence of any requirement of force or fraud (see **B2.106**).

B2.124 **Defences** Section 2(3)(a) of the Child Abduction Act 1984 provides a defence only if the parents of the child were not married at the time the child was born and D is, or reasonably believes himself to be, the father of that particular child. It does not apply where D mistakenly takes the wrong child from a nursery, thinking it to be his daughter, although it is just possible that D may in such circumstances be able to advance a defence of reasonable excuse under s. 2(1) (*Berry* [1996] 2 Cr App R 226). The burden of proving that such a taking or detention was committed without lawful authority or reasonable excuse rests with the Crown (*Berry*).

TAKING OF HOSTAGES

Definition

Taking of Hostages Act 1982, s. 1 **B2.125**

(1) A person, whatever his nationality, who, in the United Kingdom or elsewhere—
  (a) detains any other person ('the hostage'), and
  (b) in order to compel a State, international governmental organisation, or person to do or abstain from doing any act, threatens to kill, injure or continue to detain the hostage,
commits an offence.

Procedure

The consent of the A-G is required before a prosecution can be brought under the Taking of Hostages Act 1982, s. 1. Taking hostages is triable only on indictment. It is a class 1B offence. **B2.126**

Indictment

Statement of Offence **B2.127**

Hostage taking contrary to section 1 of the Taking of Hostages Act 1982

Particulars of Offence

A between the ... day of ... and the ... day of ..., unlawfully detained V, and in order to compel the Government of the United Kingdom to release from prison certain convicted offenders, threatened during that period to kill the said V

Sentence

The maximum penalty is life imprisonment (Taking of Hostages Act 1982, s. 1(2)). There is no offence-specific guideline but the Sentencing Council's *General Guideline: Overarching Principles* (see Supplement, SG2-1) is used for all offenders sentenced on or after 1 October 2019. **B2.128**

Elements

The *actus reus* consists of detaining any person, and making threats to kill, injure or continue to detain that person. **B2.129**

The *mens rea* defined is in terms of the purpose for which the act and threat take place, and in that respect D's motive is relevant. The offence could therefore be seen as one of further or ulterior intent to cause the doing or abstaining from any act, and such intent or purpose must be proved, although it does not have to be achieved.

BIGAMY

Definition

Offences against the Person Act 1861, s. 57 **B2.130**

Whosoever, being married, shall marry any other person during the life of the former husband or wife, whether the second marriage shall have taken place in England or Ireland or elsewhere, shall be guilty of [an offence], and being convicted thereof shall be liable to [imprisonment] for any term not exceeding seven years ...: Provided, that nothing in this section contained shall extend to any second marriage contracted elsewhere than in England and Ireland by any other than a subject of Her Majesty, or to any person marrying a second time whose husband or wife shall have been continually absent from such person for the space of seven years then last past, and shall not have been known by such person to be living within that time, or shall extend to any person who, at the time of such second marriage, shall have been divorced from the bond of the first marriage, or to any person whose former marriage shall have been declared void by the sentence of any court of competent jurisdiction.

Procedure

B2.131 Bigamy is triable either way (MCA 1980, s. 17 and sch. 1). When tried on indictment this is normally a class 3 offence, but see CrimPD XIII, para. B (see Supplement, **CPD.XIII.B**) for the additional factors that the court considers on allocation.

Indictment

B2.132

Statement of Offence

Bigamy contrary to section 57 of the Offences against the Person Act 1861

Particulars of Offence

A on or about the ... day of ... married V during the life of his wife, W

Sentence

B2.133 The maximum penalty is seven years, a fine, or both, on indictment (OAPA 1861, s. 57); six months, an unlimited fine or both, summarily. There is no offence-specific guideline but the Sentencing Council's *General Guideline: Overarching Principles* (see Supplement, **SG2-1**) is used for all offenders sentenced on or after 1 October 2019.

There are very few Court of Appeal decisions on the proper approach to sentencing for this offence. According to Waller LJ in *Crowhurst* (1978) CSP B9–43A01:

> It appears to this court that the sentence for bigamy must vary very much with the particular circumstances of the case. In many cases of bigamy it is possible to deal with the case by some sentence which does not involve deprivation of liberty. In other cases there may be a clear deception which has resulted in some injury to the woman concerned; in which an immediate custodial sentence must be passed, and the length of that sentence must depend greatly on the seriousness of the injury that has been done.

On the facts of the particular case, where the marriage was not consummated and lasted only a week, but where the woman's evidence was that she would not have married the offender had she known that he was still married, a short custodial sentence was held to be proper. The Court of Appeal reduced an 18-month sentence, which was 'wholly out of proportion to the gravity of this offence', to one of four months. *Crowhurst* was followed and applied in *Smith* (1994) 15 Cr App R (S) 407. Three months' imprisonment was appropriate in *Ballard* [2007] EWCA Crim 751, [2007] 2 Cr App R (S) 94 (608), where the offender was convicted of bigamy after a trial.

This offence has also arisen in the context of bogus marriages designed to avoid immigration controls. In *Khan* [2004] EWCA Crim 3316, [2005] 2 Cr App R (S) 45 (273), the offender, who was lawfully married and of previous good character, went through two further marriage ceremonies with Bangladeshi nationals with intent to assist them in avoiding immigration controls. The Court of Appeal upheld sentences totalling 27 months on the offender, who pleaded guilty, and 18 months on her co-defendant, for aiding and abetting one of the offences. See also *Cairns* [1997] 1 Cr App R (S) 118.

Actus Reus

B2.134 The *actus reus* of bigamy is committed where D 'marries' another person whilst still lawfully married to a surviving spouse. No offence is committed, however, where D's original spouse has been missing for seven years or more (see **B2.139**); nor is any offence committed under English law where a foreigner commits bigamy abroad, even if the original marriage was registered in England. If, however, D is a British (or British overseas, etc.) citizen, it is irrelevant where the bigamous marriage takes place, because bigamy is punishable in England and Wales (or in Northern Ireland) if committed by such a person anywhere in the world (*Earl Russell* [1901] AC 446). This includes bigamy committed in Scotland, even though s. 57 is not applicable under Scots law (*Topping* (1856) Dears 647).

The Act of 'Marrying' Although the OAPA 1861, s. 57, uses the term 'marry', a bigamous marriage must inevitably be void under English law. Section 57 is accordingly construed as criminalising the act of bigamously *purporting* to marry (*Allen* (1872) LR 1 CCR 367). **B2.135**

The existence of other reasons for invalidity of the second 'marriage', such as the second spouse's lack of age or capacity, is no defence on a charge of bigamy (*Allen*). D must, however, go through a ceremony of marriage that purports to be legally binding. D does not commit bigamy by, for example, contracting an unregistered Islamic marriage in England without disclosing the existence of a subsisting marriage (*Al-Mudaris v Al-Mudaris* [2001] 2 FLR 6).

'Being Married' The burden is on the prosecution to prove both that D was validly married on an earlier occasion *and* that this marriage was still subsisting at the time of the second ceremony. The validity of the original marriage cannot be presumed, as it might be presumed in civil cases, but may be proved by adducing a certified copy of the relevant entry in the Register of Marriages (see **F8.24** and **F17.47**) together with evidence of the identity of the parties to the marriage (*Tolson* (1864) 4 F & F 103; *Birtles* (1911) 6 Cr App R 177). In the case of a marriage celebrated abroad, expert evidence of local marriage law may be required (*Sussex Peerage Case* (1844) 11 Cl & F 85; and see **F11.27**). **B2.136**

If D alleges that the earlier marriage is invalid for a particular reason, D need do no more than raise the issue, and the burden will then be on the prosecution to establish its validity (*Kay* (1887) 16 Cox CC 292). An admission by D as to the validity of the earlier marriage may suffice, but not where the marriage was celebrated abroad (*Naguib* [1917] 1 KB 359; *Flaherty* (1847) 2 Car & Kir 782).

Polygamous Marriages A British citizen who practises polygamy abroad in accordance with local law commits no offence under s. 57. This is not because such conduct is lawful where it takes place. It is because, as far as the English law of bigamy is concerned, polygamous or even potentially polygamous marriages have never been considered to be marriages at all, even though they may be recognised as valid by the civil courts in accordance with the rules of private international law. **B2.137**

Nevertheless, a marriage registered in the UK is necessarily monogamous, and precludes any subsequent polygamy by either party to it; and if D is domiciled in England and Wales (or in any other country that prohibits polygamy), D cannot lawfully practise polygamy abroad. An overseas marriage contracted by someone with English domicile must accordingly be considered monogamous.

A potentially polygamous foreign marriage may become monogamous in certain circumstances, notably where the party who might otherwise have been entitled to take a second spouse subsequently acquires a domicile of choice in a country that does not permit polygamy. This may happen, for example, where D settles permanently in England and Wales, thereby acquiring an English domicile. If D were then to contract a further marriage in England and Wales, D would thereby commit bigamy (*Sagoo* [1975] QB 885). If D also acquires British citizenship, s. 57 would equally apply to any second marriage subsequently entered into abroad.

Mens Rea

There is no specific mention of the requisite *mens rea* for the offence in the OAPA 1861, s. 57. This is unlikely to cause any problems in respect of the intent to go through a ceremony of marriage, but what if D mistakenly believes the first spouse to be dead or mistakenly believes himself to be lawfully divorced? In other sections of the 1861 Act strict liability was once applied to certain circumstances of an offence (*Prince* (1875) LR 2 CCR 154), and the absence of the word 'malicious' from s. 57, in contrast to its presence in other sections, was at one time taken to suggest that strict liability applied under s. 57. **B2.138**

The leading case on the *mens rea* for bigamy has for many years been *Tolson* (1889) 23 QBD 168. D had remarried, reasonably, but mistakenly, believing that her first husband was dead. It was held that a mistake of this kind was a good defence to the charge, as long as it was a reasonable one. The same argument would also apply where D believed that she was divorced, or that her first marriage was void, etc. The situation has always been different as regards the proviso in s. 57, relating to seven years' absence of the first spouse, because this may provide a defence, even where D suspects that the spouse is still alive (see **B2.139**).

Tolson was followed by the Court of Appeal in *Gould* [1968] 2 QB 65, and confirmed, *obiter*, by the House of Lords in *DPP v Morgan* [1976] AC 182, but its authority has been undermined by the House of Lords in *B (a minor) v DPP* [2000] 2 AC 428 in which it was held that, where *mens rea* may be ousted by an honest but mistaken belief, it is as well ousted by an unreasonable belief as by a reasonable one. It is accordingly submitted that the same principles must apply to mistake in bigamy cases as to mistake in other crimes. The reasonableness or otherwise of any alleged mistake should now be considered irrelevant, except when assessing its credibility.

Continual Absence of First Spouse for Seven Years

B2.139 Under the proviso to the OAPA 1861, s. 57, D has a defence to a charge of bigamy if D's husband or wife 'shall have been continually absent … for the space of seven years then last past, and shall not have been known [by D] to have been living within that time'. The scope and limitations of this proviso must be noted. First, it does nothing to relieve the prosecution from its duty to prove that the first spouse was indeed alive at the time of the second ceremony. Even if D remarried just a few months after the first spouse's disappearance, a prosecution for bigamy would still fail in the absence of such proof. Secondly, if D honestly believed the spouse to be dead after a shorter period than seven years (see **B2.138**) the proviso defence is not necessary. On the other hand, if the conditions of the proviso are satisfied, it does not matter whether D really believed the first spouse to be dead at all. The spouse's continuous absence (combined with the absence of any news of the spouse being alive) is a sufficient defence in itself.

To establish the defence, D must adduce evidence of continual absence for the requisite seven-year period. The prosecution must then prove either that there was no such continual absence, or that D knew the spouse to be alive at some time during that period (*Curgerwen* (1865) LR 1 CCR 1). Actual knowledge would have to be proved. D need not even have attempted to contact the spouse or ascertain whether the spouse was alive (*Jones* (1842) C & Mar 614; *Briggs* (1856) Dears & B 98). If s. 57 had been intended to impose any such duty on D, it would surely have stipulated this expressly.

FORCED MARRIAGE

Offences Relating to Non-consensual Marriage

B2.140 The ABCPA 2014 created three offences in connection with forced or non-consensual marriage, with effect from 16 June 2014 (SI 2014 No. 949). The first relates to breach of a forced marriage protection order made under the Family Law Act 1996. Previously, such a breach was punishable only as a contempt of court, but the ABCPA 2014, s. 120, added s. 63CA to that Act, under which a person who without reasonable excuse does anything prohibited by such an order commits an offence triable either way and is punishable following conviction on indictment by up to five years' imprisonment, or a fine, or both. Such conduct may still be punishable as contempt, but not both as an offence and as contempt (s. 63CA(3) and (4)).

The second offence (created by s. 121(1)) involves the use of violence, threats or other coercion for the purpose of forcing another person into a marriage. This extends (by s. 121(2)) to any other conduct intended to cause a person to marry when lacking the capacity to give valid consent to such a marriage.

The third offence (created by s. 121(3)) involves the practice of deception with intent to lure the victim into a forced marriage abroad.

Coercion or Deception for the Purpose of Marriage

Anti-social Behaviour, Crime and Policing Act 2014, s. 121 **B2.141**

(1) A person commits an offence under the law of England and Wales if he or she—
  (a) uses violence, threats or any other form of coercion for the purpose of causing another person to enter into a marriage, and
  (b) believes, or ought reasonably to believe, that the conduct may cause the other person to enter into the marriage without free and full consent.

(2) In relation to a victim who lacks capacity to consent to marriage, the offence under subsection (1) is capable of being committed by any conduct carried out for the purpose of causing the victim to enter into a marriage (whether or not the conduct amounts to violence, threats or any other form coercion).

(3) A person commits an offence under the law of England and Wales if he or she—
  (a) practises any form of deception with the intention of causing another person to leave the United Kingdom, and
  (b) intends the other person to be subjected to conduct outside the United Kingdom that is an offence under subsection (1) or would be an offence under that subsection if the victim were in England or Wales.

(4) 'Marriage' means any religious or civil ceremony of marriage (whether or not legally binding).

(5) 'Lacks capacity' means lacks capacity within the meaning of the Mental Capacity Act 2005.

(6) It is irrelevant whether the conduct mentioned in paragraph (a) of subsection (1) is directed at the victim of the offence under that subsection or another person.

Procedure Offences under the ABCPA 2014, s. 121(1) or (3), are triable either way. When tried on indictment they are normally class 3 offences, but see CrimPD XIII, para. B (see Supplement, **CPD.XIII.B**), for the additional factors that the court considers on allocation. **B2.142**

Sentence The maximum penalty following conviction on indictment is seven years' imprisonment or a fine or both (ABCPA 2014, s. 121(9)(a)). The maximum penalty on summary conviction is imprisonment for a term not exceeding six months or a fine, or both (s. 121(9)(b) and (10)). There is no offence-specific guideline but the Sentencing Council's *General Guideline: Overarching Principles* (see Supplement, **SG2-1**) is used for all offenders sentenced on or after 1 October 2019. The Sentencing Council definitive guideline, *Domestic Abuse* (see Supplement, **SG6-1**) may be of assistance when sentencing for this offence. Paragraph 2 of the guideline cites the government's definition of domestic abuse, which includes 'forced marriage'. **B2.143**

Elements The offence created by the ABCPA 2014, s. 121(1), may be committed either by the use of coercion or (in cases involving a victim who lacks the capacity to give valid consent) by any other conduct, which might include deceptive conduct; but in either case the offence is a 'conduct crime'. The purpose specified in s. 121(1) and (2) is clearly a form of ulterior intent and the substantive offence may be committed even where no marriage takes place or when the threats etc. prove wholly ineffectual. **B2.144**

In most cases the offending conduct will involve the coercion or attempted coercion of the very person who is to be forcibly married, but this is not essential. The coercion etc. may instead be directed towards a third party, such as a parent or sibling.

The *mens rea* requirement in s. 121(1)(b) is unlikely to be problematic in cases falling within s. 121(1)(a), but may be harder to establish in some cases falling within s. 121(2), where D may claim to have been unaware of any lack of capacity and therefore unaware of any lack of consent.

The offence under s. 121(3) requires the practising of a deception but does not in terms require that any person be actually deceived, and it would be consistent with the scheme of s. 121 to read this as a conduct crime, as in s. 121(1). The deceptive conduct must be directed not to the proposed marriage itself, but to causing the person who is to be forcibly married (V) to leave the UK. The person D seeks to deceive may or may not be V but in any event it is not enough that D lies about the real purpose of a proposed travel; D must do so 'intending' that there will be a forced marriage abroad, or at least that someone will be subject to coercion etc. abroad for that purpose. 'Intent' here must be a wider concept than 'purpose', as used in s. 121(1), so D may be found to intend that V will be coerced abroad if D knows or believes it will happen in the normal course of events, even if D would prefer that it did not happen at all.

ILL-TREATMENT OR NEGLECT OF CHILDREN

Definition

B2.145

Children and Young Persons Act 1933, s. 1

(1) If any person who has attained the age of sixteen years and has responsibility for any child or young person under that age, wilfully assaults, ill-treats, (whether physically or otherwise) neglects, abandons, or exposes him, or causes or procures him to be assaulted, ill-treated (whether physically or otherwise), neglected, abandoned, or exposed, in a manner likely to cause him unnecessary suffering or injury to health (whether the suffering or injury is of a physical or a psychological nature), that person shall be guilty of an offence ...

(2) For the purposes of this section—

(a) a parent or other person legally liable to maintain a child or young person or the legal guardian of a child or young person shall be deemed to have neglected him in a manner likely to cause injury to his health if he has failed to provide adequate food, clothing, medical aid or lodging for him, or if, having been unable otherwise to provide such food, clothing, medical aid or lodging, he has failed to take steps to procure it to be provided under the enactments applicable in that behalf;

(b) where it is proved that the death of an infant under three years of age was caused by suffocation (not being suffocation caused by disease or the presence of any foreign body in the throat or air passages of the infant) while the infant was in bed with some other person who has attained the age of sixteen years, that other person shall, if he was, when he went to bed, or at any later time before the suffocation, under the influence of drink or a prohibited drug, be deemed to have neglected the infant in a manner likely to cause injury to its health.

(2A) The reference in subsection (2)(b) to the infant being 'in bed' with another ('the adult') includes a reference to the infant lying next to the adult in or on any kind of furniture or surface being used by the adult for the purpose of sleeping (and the reference to the time when the adult 'went to bed' is to be read accordingly).

(2B) A drug is a prohibited drug for the purposes of subsection (2)(b) in relation to a person if the person's possession of the drug immediately before taking it constituted an offence under section 5(2) of the Misuse of Drugs Act 1971.

(3) A person may be convicted of an offence under this section—

(a) notwithstanding that actual suffering or injury to health, or the likelihood of actual suffering or injury to health, was obviated by the action of another person;

(b) notwithstanding the death of the child or young person in question.

Indictment

B2.146

Statement of Offence

Cruelty to a person under the age of 16, contrary to s. 1(1) of the Children and Young Persons Act 1933

Particulars of Offence

A, between the ... day of ... and the ... day of ..., being a person who had attained the age of 16 and having responsibility for V, a child under that age, wilfully neglected the said V in a manner likely to cause her unnecessary suffering or injury to her health by failing to provide medical aid for her

The drafting of indictments for offences under s. 1 may be complicated by the fact that the offence can be committed in several different ways. As to the importance of identifying the appropriate form of allegation in a given case, see *Hayles* [1969] 1 QB 364; *Beard* (1987) 85 Cr App R 395 and *Cooper* [2019] EWCA Crim 43.

Procedure

An offence under this provision is triable either way. When tried on indictment, this is normally a class 2A offence, but see CrimPD XIII, para. B (see Supplement, **CPD.XIII.B**) for the additional factors that the court considers on allocation. Where an alleged offence is tried summarily, the CYPA 1933, s. 14, has effect. See the Sentencing Council's definitive guideline, *Child Cruelty* (see Supplement, **SG20.1** ***et seq.***) for indications as to when a case should be sent to the Crown Court. **B2.147**

Children and Young Persons Act 1933, s. 14

(1) Where a person is charged with committing any of the offences mentioned in the first Schedule to this Act in respect of two or more children or young persons, the same information or summons may charge the offence in respect of all or any of them, but the person charged shall not, if he is summarily convicted, be liable to a separate penalty in respect of each child or young person except upon separate informations.

(2) The same information or summons may charge him with the offence of assault, ill-treatment, neglect, abandonment, or exposure, together or separately, and may charge him with committing all or any of those offences in a manner likely to cause unnecessary suffering or injury to health, alternatively or together, but when those offences are charged together, the person charged shall not, if he is summarily convicted, be liable to a separate penalty for each.

Sentence

The maximum penalty on conviction on indictment is ten years' imprisonment; the maximum penalty on summary conviction is six months' imprisonment, or an unlimited fine or both (CYPA 1933, s. 1(1)). The Sentencing Council definitive guideline, *Child Cruelty* (see Supplement, **SG20-1**), applies in respect of offenders aged 18 and over, sentenced on or after 1 January 2019, irrespective of the date of the offence. The guideline sets out three broad sentencing categories with a range of starting points from community order to six years' imprisonment with a range up to eight years' imprisonment. As with all current guidelines the categorisation of the case depends on harm and culpability factors. The guidelines address some matters particular to cases involving child victims, including, for example, the question whether to impose custody in cases where the offender has parental responsibility and is sole or primary carer for the victim or other children. Cases charged as assaults on children are outside the ambit of the new guideline, and for these, the 2008 definitive sentencing guideline, *Overarching Principles: Assaults on Children and Cruelty to a Child*, will continue to have relevance, together with any other offence-specific guideline that may be applicable. **B2.148**

Establishing the Basis of Sentence It is particularly important to establish the basis of sentence in child cruelty cases, a principle illustrated by *FW* [2019] EWCA Crim 275 where a mother was sentenced on the basis that she had not called medical assistance for her sick child, and the sentencer was significantly influenced by matters that post-dated the emergency call that was eventually made. The resulting sentence was reduced from 12 months' to six months' imprisonment. The principle is of particular importance where two defendants blame each other for cruelty. In such a case the sentencer must either resolve the conflict by hearing evidence, or accept the mitigation, sentencing each defendant on the basis of that defendant's plea (*J* [2004] EWCA Crim 2002, [2005] 1 Cr App R (S) 63 (284)). In *Lindsay* [2018] EWCA Crim 2171 a sentence was suspended to reflect the specific factual basis of the defendant's plea, and her responsibilities (applying *Petherick* [2012] EWCA Crim 2214, [2013] 1 Cr App R (S) 116 (598)) in relation to her remaining children who were not considered at risk. The defendant's seven-week old baby died during the night after, unknown to her, it had been brought by her partner to their bed. The plea was on the limited basis that during the preceding evening she had left the baby in the care of her partner, a man whom she knew could not cope with the baby. **B2.149**

Cases sentenced before the 2019 guideline generally drew a distinction between those cases where there had been deliberate infliction of serious injury, perhaps on more than one occasion, where a lengthy custodial sentence would be upheld, and one-off cases of less serious injury taking place in a context of very considerable economic or domestic pressure, where a rather lower custodial sentence was the norm. These distinctions are now reflected, on a more structured basis, in the 2019 guideline ranges.

In *GG* [2018] EWCA Crim 1161 consecutive sentences leading to a custodial term of 12 years' imprisonment with a five-year extension period were upheld for a 'calculating, controlling and violent individual who posed a real danger to anyone within his family'. He had subjected his two young children to a range of violent and humiliating behaviours. The sentences were rightly consecutive because they reflected the separate harm caused to separate victims. There was no double-counting in taking account of the assault on the daughter and the separate cruelty of making the son watch because both suffered harm thereby and both were victims.

B [2011] EWCA Crim 2566 is another 2008 guideline case in which the offender maltreated four fostered children in his care, all of whom had special needs in various different forms. A total sentence of 18 months' imprisonment was upheld on a guilty plea. The case was said to fall on the borderline between the two lower levels in the guideline. Relevant aggravating factors were the number of children harmed, the duration of the ill-treatment (ten months), and the particular breach of trust involved in the harming of such vulnerable children by a person entrusted by the State with their care. There was some mitigation in the offender's inability to cope with such challenging children, but the Court of Appeal said that help was available to the offender and he had failed to access it. A community rehabilitation order with a programme in parenting skills was held not to be unduly lenient in *A-G's Ref (No. 105 of 2004)* [2004] EWCA Crim 3295, [2005] 2 Cr App R (S) 42 (250), where the 41-year-old offender pleaded guilty to using excessive chastisement on three of his children, aged eight, ten and 13. The Court of Appeal said the offences arose from a distorted view of what was appropriate, rather than from cruelty for its own sake.

In *S* [2008] EWCA Crim 1662, [2009] 1 Cr App R (S) 40 (220) the offender subjected his five-year-old stepdaughter to a harsh regime of discipline, by sending her to her room for long periods of time, but did not inflict any significant violence. A sentence of 30 months' imprisonment was varied to a community order on appeal. The Court of Appeal found the 2008 sentencing guideline unhelpful in this case, and said that on its facts this case should have been regarded as falling within the lowest category of seriousness. Nor were the 2008 guidelines really applicable in *MB* [2013] EWCA Crim 910, [2014] 1 Cr App R (S) 29 (173), where the Court reduced a sentence of ten months' imprisonment (following a trial) to four months where the offender was a Nigerian woman who was in the country illegally because she had overstayed her right to remain. She failed to seek medical treatment for her baby son after she had arranged for an unqualified person to carry out circumcision. While there had been 'real neglect', there was significant personal mitigation.

B2.150 **Cruelty or Neglect** Most of the reported cases on cruelty or neglect (as opposed to infliction of an injury) arise from the offender's culpable failure to summon medical assistance for a child. In the pre-2008 guideline case of *Taggart* [1999] 2 Cr App R (S) 68 the offender's child aged three and a half suffered severe scalding while in the bath. It was accepted that the scalding had been accidental, but the offender pleaded guilty to cruelty on the basis of his failure to summon medical attention until more than 24 hours later. The appropriate sentence was 30 months' imprisonment.

In *Mason* [2013] EWCA Crim 1666, [2014] 1 Cr App R (S) 78 (482) the offender's young son (aged 22 months) had fallen from a worktop and struck his head. When the child showed signs of fitting the offender called an ambulance, but did not tell the paramedics or the doctors what had happened. The child died, and the offender pleaded guilty on the basis that he might have been saved if the truth had been told at once. A sentence of 15 months' imprisonment was reduced to ten months, but the Court of Appeal declined to suspend it.

Another category of neglect is where injury has been inflicted upon the offender's child by another person with the offender's knowledge. Sentences totalling five years' imprisonment were upheld in *Creed* [2000] 1 Cr App R (S) 304, where a woman had failed to protect her child from sustained violence over a period of seven months from the man with whom she was living.

By contrast, in *Tilby* [2019] EWCA Crim 1623, a sentence of two years and four months' imprisonment for child cruelty imposed (on a guilty plea) following the death of the offender's four-week-old baby was held to be manifestly excessive. The incident involved a single evening of drunken neglect and the baby had otherwise been well cared for. CCTV footage showed the offender and her sister partying drunkenly at a campsite bar while holding the baby and handling him in ways that were clearly dangerous. She then went to bed with the baby and rolled on top of him in her sleep. When discovered underneath her, the baby could not be roused. The offender was not charged with manslaughter because (said the Crown) sudden infant death syndrome could not be ruled out. In terms of the applicable sentencing guideline, the Court of Appeal ruled that it was a category 2B offence, rather than one at the top end of category 2A, as determined by the sentencing judge. The correct sentence would ordinarily have been one of two years' imprisonment but would be reduced to take account of the strong mitigation, including the devastating impact of the child's death on the offender herself, and her guilty plea. The final sentence was one of 16 months, suspended for 12 months.

Actus Reus

Age and Responsibility To be guilty of an offence under the CYPA 1933, s. 1, D must have been 16 or over at the time of the offence, and must have 'had responsibility' for the child or young person in question. If proof of D's or the victim's ages is an issue, reference may be made to the CYPA 1933, s. 99, which provides (s. 99(2)) that, where in such a case the person by or in respect of whom the offence was allegedly committed 'appears to the court to have been at the date of the alleged offence a child or young person or to have been under or to have attained a particular age, as the case may be, he shall ... be presumed to have been under or to have attained that age, as the case may be, unless the contrary is proved'. Where this presumption applies, the defence may have the burden of proving that the young person in question was in fact 16 or over (s. 99(4)). **B2.151**

'Responsibility' in this context may be shared by more than one person, and it may involve questions both of fact and law (*Liverpool Society for the Prevention of Cruelty to Children v Jones* [1914] 3 KB 813). Any person who has parental responsibility or who has any other legal liability to maintain a child or young person will be 'presumed' to have responsibility for him under the Act and 'shall not be taken to have ceased to be responsible for him by reason of the fact that he does not have care of him' (CYPA 1933, s. 17(1)(a) and (2)); but other persons, such as baby-sitters or teachers, may also have responsibility whilst a child or young person is in their care (s. 17(1)(b)).

Conduct Although the CYPA 1933, s. 1, creates just one offence, it may take a number of different forms (*Hayles* [1969] 1 QB 364; *Harding* [1997] Crim LR 815). It may take the form of positive abuse (assault, ill-treatment, abandonment or exposure) or of mere neglect, or it may take the form of causing or procuring abuse or neglect, but humiliation is not a form of conduct listed in s. 1 and it would be wrong to focus on this, either in an indictment or in the presentation or summing up of the prosecution case (*Cooper* [2019] EWCA Crim 43). The abuse or neglect in question must be committed 'in a manner likely to cause unnecessary suffering or injury to health' (as to which see s. 1(1)); but the offence is essentially a conduct crime rather than a result crime. It need not therefore be shown that any such injury was caused, and indeed it is no defence to show that any suffering of or danger to V was obviated by the action of another person (s. 1(3)(a)). **B2.152**

'Assault' in this context will usually mean assault by beating, or battery as to which see **B2.9** ***et seq***. Ill-treatment is self-explanatory in the context of the requirement that it must be likely to cause unnecessary suffering or injury (see **B2.154**). In *Boulden* (1957) 41 Cr App R 105, the Court of Criminal Appeal considered a case of abandonment in which a father of five children had left them and travelled to Scotland. Although the evidence was somewhat contradictory, the Court found sufficient evidence to show that he had 'washed his hands' of his children, and had 'left them to their fate'; this was sufficient proof of abandonment.

The offence of exposing a child in a manner likely to cause unnecessary suffering or injury has had little consideration in case law. Exposure to bad weather in itself would not be enough, given the second limb of the *actus reus* (*Williams* (1910) 4 Cr App R 89, a case concerning the Children Act 1908).

B2.153 **Neglect** Cases of neglect have received frequent attention in the courts. The requisite neglect will be deemed to have occurred, and therefore need not be proved, in the circumstances set out in s. 1(2)(a) and (b), although the Court of Appeal in *Wills* [1990] Crim LR 714 stressed that even where neglect is deemed the *mens rea* element of the offence must be proved (see **B2.155**). Where s. 1(2)(a) applies, it may be the basis for proving neglect; in any event, it gives a general indication of what constitutes neglect. For example, a relative who was not the legal guardian of, or legally liable to maintain, a child, but who was looking after the child for several weeks, might be under a duty to act (see **A1.17**). Such a person would then be expected to provide care of the kind mentioned in s. 2(1)(a).

B2.154 The Court of Appeal in *S and M* [1995] Crim LR 486 explained 'neglecting' in the context of failing to obtain medical help. Either S the parent or M the boyfriend assaulted the child, who had bruising to the spine and buttocks. There was then further neglect in the failure to get medical help. The argument that there was no neglect because there was nothing a doctor could have done was rejected. The Court of Appeal held that S or M had neglected the child within the meaning of the statute by refraining from seeking medical help, being reckless as to whether the child might need such help. There are difficulties not addressed in this case concerning the burden of proof, given that it was clear that one party had committed the assault but it was not clear which. However, there is clearly an argument that both were liable for neglect, both being under a duty to act.

The Court of Appeal in *Wills* was concerned with the meaning of the phrase 'in a manner likely to cause unnecessary suffering or injury to health' and more particularly the exact meaning of the word 'likely'. The trial judge had relied on remarks of Lord Diplock in *Sheppard* [1981] AC 394, that 'likely' was simply meant to exclude what was highly unlikely. Although the Court of Appeal agreed that these remarks were *obiter dicta*, it found that Lord Diplock had properly construed the word in the context of this statute, given the difficulties for parents in deciding how serious an injury is, and the possible grave consequences of lack of treatment. The Court went on to point out, however, that, because of the 'deeming' provision under s. 1(2)(a) of the Act, it was unnecessary for the Court to come to a decision about the meaning of the word, and these remarks too were *obiter*. In the context of interpreting s. 1(2)(a), it was held that medical aid included medical supervision or medical care in the sense of observation to discover the gravity of any particular injury. The deeming provision was also relevant in *Sheppard* and was explained by Lord Diplock as follows:

> Did the parents fail to provide ... in the period before [the child's] death medical aid that was in fact adequate in view of his actual state of health at the relevant time? This, as it seems to me, is a pure question of objective fact to be determined in the light of what has become known by *the date of the trial* to have been the child's actual state of health at the relevant time. It does not depend upon whether a reasonably careful parent, with knowledge of those facts only which such a parent might reasonably be expected to observe for himself, would have thought it prudent to have recourse to medical aid.

The requisite *mens rea* must still be proved, even when the deeming provisions apply.

Mens Rea

The *mens rea* of this offence is defined as 'wilfully' carrying out any of the various modes of the *actus reus*. *Sheppard* [1981] AC 394 is the leading case on the interpretation of the word in this context, and although it was decided in the context of cruelty by neglect, it is now clear that it bears the same meaning wherever it is used in the CYPA 1933, s. 1 (*D* [2008] EWCA Crim 2360). **B2.155**

In *Sheppard*, a child aged 16 months died of hypothermia following severe gastroenteritis. The parents were poor and of low intelligence, and had not appreciated the seriousness of his condition. They were convicted under s. 1 on the basis of an objective test. The House of Lords in *Sheppard* allowed their appeals, and Lord Diplock explained the *mens rea* requirement as follows:

> The proper direction to be given to a jury on a charge of wilful neglect of a child under section 1 of the Children and Young Persons Act 1933 by failing to provide adequate medical aid, is that the jury must be satisfied (1) that the child did in fact need medical aid at the time at which the parent is charged with failing to provide it (the *actus reus*) and (2) either that the parent was aware at the time that the child's health might be at risk if it were not provided with medical aid, or that the parent's unawareness of this fact was due to his not caring whether the child's health was at risk or not (the *mens rea*).

This passage was formerly interpreted by some commentators as conveying *Caldwell* recklessness; but this was always difficult to reconcile with the concept of 'not caring', or with Lord Diplock's observation in *Sheppard* that the concept of what the reasonable parent would observe and understand has no part to play in the *mens rea* of this offence. In *W (Emma)* [2006] EWCA Crim 2723 it was held that D may be guilty of wilful neglect where D knows that the child needs medical care, but deliberately refrains from obtaining it, or fails to obtain it because D does not care whether it is needed or not. But if, whether through personal inadequacy or stupidity or both, D genuinely fails to appreciate that the child needs medical care, D does not act wilfully and is not guilty of the offence.

General

D can be charged under the CYPA 1933, s. 1, even if death occurs (s. 1(3)(b)) and in such circumstances the charge is often coupled with a charge of murder or manslaughter brought against that defendant and/or a co-defendant. Note also the DVCVA 2004, s. 5 (see **B1.79** and **B2.169**). **B2.156**

As to a parent or school staff's rights to use force, see **B2.20**.

ILL-TREATMENT OR NEGLECT OF MENTAL PATIENTS OR PERSONS WHO LACK CAPACITY

Ill-treatment or Neglect of Mental Patients

Mental Health Act 1983, s. 127 **B2.157**

(1) It shall be an offence for any person who is an officer on the staff of or otherwise employed in, or who is one of the managers of, a hospital, independent hospital or care home—
  (a) to ill-treat or wilfully to neglect a patient for the time being receiving treatment for mental disorder as an in-patient in that hospital or home; or
  (b) to ill-treat or wilfully to neglect, on the premises of which the hospital or home forms part, a patient for the time being receiving such treatment there as an out-patient.

(2) It shall be an offence for any individual to ill-treat or wilfully to neglect a mentally disordered patient who is for the time being subject to his guardianship under this Act or otherwise in his custody or care (whether by virtue of any legal or moral obligation or otherwise).

B2.158 **Procedure** Offences under s. 127 are triable either way. When tried on indictment they are normally class 3 offences, but see CrimPD XIII, para. B (see Supplement, **CPD.XIII.B**) for the additional factors that the court considers on allocation. No proceedings may be instituted except by or with the consent of the DPP (s. 127(4)).

B2.159 **Sentence** The maximum penalty following conviction on indictment is five years' imprisonment and/or a fine (s. 127(3)(b)). The maximum penalty on summary conviction is imprisonment for a term not exceeding six months and/or an unlimited fine. There is no offence-specific guideline but the Sentencing Council's *General Guideline: Overarching Principles* (see Supplement, **SG2-1**) is used for all offenders sentenced on or after 1 October 2019.

B2.160 **Elements** Ill-treatment and wilful neglect, which are separate offences (*Newington* (1990) 91 Cr App R 247), have the same meanings as under the CYPA 1933, s. 1 (see **B2.152** and *Sheppard* [1981] AC 394). It follows that neglect arising from a genuine mistake is not enough (*Morrell* [2002] EWCA Crim 2547).

'Mental disorder' is defined in the Mental Health Act 1983, s. 1, as 'any disorder of disability of the mind', which includes in this context any learning disability, but not dependence on alcohol or drugs (Mental Health Act 1983, s. 1(2A) to (3)).

Ill-treatment or Neglect of Persons who Lack Capacity

B2.161 **Mental Capacity Act 2005, s. 44**

(1) Subsection (2) applies if a person ('D')—
  (a) has the care of a person ('P') who lacks, or whom D reasonably believes to lack, capacity,
  (b) is the donee of a lasting power of attorney, or an enduring power of attorney (within the meaning of Schedule 4), created by P, or
  (c) is a deputy appointed by the court for P.

(2) D is guilty of an offence if he ill-treats or wilfully neglects P.

Although P's lack of capacity (or D's reasonable belief that P lacks capacity) is mentioned only in s. 44(1)(a), the same 'incapacity requirement' must also be proved in a prosecution brought under s. 44(1)(b) or (c); but it is not necessary for an enduring power of attorney to have been registered in accordance with the Act. The wording of s. 44(1)(b) imposes no such requirement (*Kurtz* [2018] EWCA Crim 2743, [2019] 1 Cr App R 19 (237)).

B2.162 **Procedure** Offences under s. 44 are triable either way. When tried on indictment they are normally class 3 offences, but see CrimPD XIII, para. B (see Supplement, **CPD.XIII.B**) for the additional factors that the court considers on allocation.

B2.163 **Sentence** The maximum penalty following conviction on indictment is imprisonment for five years or a fine or both. The maximum penalty on summary conviction is imprisonment for six months or an unlimited fine or both (s. 44(3)). A sentence of eight months' imprisonment was upheld in *Kenyon* [2013] EWCA Crim 2123, [2014] 1 Cr App R (S) 71 (455) where a care assistant at a residential home for the elderly left eight vulnerable residents sitting in their own urine and faeces for several hours. The offender had been passed over for promotion, and she wilfully neglected her patients in this manner over a single shift. She was of previous good character and had a very good record of care. The case was said to be worse than *Heaney* [2011] EWCA Crim 2682, where a senior carer fed one resident a drink containing vinegar and slapped another around the head. Nine months' imprisonment was reduced to six months in that case.

B2.164 **Elements** Ill-treatment and wilful neglect have the same meanings as under the CYPA 1933, s. 1 (see **B2.152** and *Sheppard* [1981] AC 394). Mere carelessness or negligence cannot therefore be equated with wilful neglect (*Turbill* [2013] EWCA Crim 1422, [2014] 1 Cr App R 7 (62)). But, in contrast to the CYPA 1933, s. 1, the offence under the Mental Capacity Act 2005, s. 44, does not include the qualifying words 'in a manner likely to cause unnecessary suffering or injury to health'. In *Patel* [2013] EWCA Crim 965 the Court of Appeal therefore held that it could be no defence to show that a patient who was wrongly denied CPR when she stopped breathing would have died even if that treatment had been provided. 'Lack of capacity' is defined for purposes of the Mental Capacity Act 2005 in s. 2: 'a person lacks capacity in relation to a matter if at the material time he is unable to make a decision for himself in relation to the matter because of an impairment of, or a disturbance in the functioning of, the mind or brain'. This may be proved on a mere balance of probabilities and it 'does not matter whether the impairment or disturbance is permanent or temporary'. This definition is supplemented by s. 3, which provides an elaborate diagnostic test for identifying the circumstances in which an individual is to be found to be unable to make decisions for himself. But in the context of a prosecution for ill-treatment or wilful neglect it may not always be necessary or appropriate for a jury to be directed in terms of this diagnostic test. See *Dunn* [2010] EWCA Crim 2935, [2011] 1 Cr App R 34 (425). In *Nursing* [2012] EWCA Crim 2521, [2013] 1 All ER 1139 the Court of Appeal considered the extent to which a person of limited mental capacity might nevertheless have, or be believed to have, the capacity to decide what care or treatment should be received, and noted that, in areas where an individual has such capacity, the individual's autonomy should be respected. Lord Judge CJ said (at [18]):

> ... section 44 did not create an absolute offence. Therefore, actions or omissions, or a combination of both, which reflect or are believed to reflect the protected autonomy of the individual needing care do not constitute wilful neglect.

ILL-TREATMENT OR NEGLECT BY CARE WORKERS AND CARE PROVIDERS

Care Worker Offence

The CJCA 2015, s. 20, creates an offence in cases where an individual who has the care of another individual by virtue of being a care worker ill-treats or wilfully neglects that other individual. Corporate bodies or unincorporated associations acting as care providers are not subject to this offence, but negligence or neglect on their part (or on the part of an individual who provides such care and employs, or has otherwise made arrangements with, other persons to assist in providing such care) may in such cases be the subject of prosecutions under s. 21 (see **B2.168**). **B2.165**

Definition

Criminal Justice and Courts Act 2015, s. 20 **B2.166**

(1) It is an offence for an individual who has the care of another individual by virtue of being a care worker to ill-treat or wilfully to neglect that individual.

(2) [Sentencing.]

(3) 'Care worker' means an individual who, as paid work, provides—
  (a) health care for an adult or child, other than excluded health care, or
  (b) social care for an adult,

including an individual who, as paid work, supervises or manages individuals providing such care or is a director or similar officer of an organisation which provides such care.

(4) An individual does something as 'paid work' if he or she receives or is entitled to payment for doing it other than—
  (a) payment in respect of the individual's reasonable expenses,
  (b) payment to which the individual is entitled as a foster parent,
  (c) a benefit under social security legislation, or
  (d) a payment made under arrangements under section 2 of the Employment and Training Act 1973 (arrangements to assist people to select, train for, obtain and retain employment).

(5) 'Health care' includes—
  (a) all forms of health care provided for individuals, including health care relating to physical health or mental health and health care provided for or in connection with the protection or improvement of public health, and

(b) procedures that are similar to forms of medical or surgical care but are not provided in connection with a medical condition,

and 'excluded health care' has the meaning given in Schedule 4.

(6) 'Social care' includes all forms of personal care and other practical assistance provided for individuals who are in need of such care or assistance by reason of age, illness, disability, pregnancy, childbirth, dependence on alcohol or drugs or any other similar circumstances.

(7) References in this section to a person providing health care or social care do not include a person whose provision of such care is merely incidental to the carrying out of other activities by the person.

(8) In this section—

'adult' means an individual aged 18 or over;

'child' means an individual aged under 18;

'foster parent' means—

(a) a local authority foster parent within the meaning of the Children Act 1989,

(b) a person with whom a child has been placed by a voluntary organisation under section 59(1)(a) of that Act, or

(c) a private foster parent within the meaning of section 53 of the Safeguarding Vulnerable Groups Act 2006.

Health care in a range of children's services and settings (including schools, academies, day care centres and children's homes) is excluded by sch. 4 on the basis that sufficient laws already exist to protect children in those settings. The provision of social care for children is meanwhile excluded by the terms of s. 20(3).

Sentence and Procedure

B2.167 Offences under the CJCA 2015, s. 20, are triable either way. They are punishable on indictment by up to five years' imprisonment and a fine, or both, and on summary conviction by six months' imprisonment and an unlimited fine, or both. There is no offence-specific guideline but the Sentencing Council's *General Guideline: Overarching Principles* (see Supplement, **SG2-1**) is used for all offenders sentenced on or after 1 October 2019. In *McNulty* [2019] EWCA Crim 2081, a starting point after trial of four years' imprisonment for two offences comprising 19 physical assaults against two adults in care, one with Down's syndrome and one with autism, was manifestly excessive. D, of previous good character, with long service, significant remorse, and personal mental health difficulties, had pleaded guilty at the first opportunity. The sentences were rightly consecutive to one another, but in view of the extensive mitigation would be reduced to a proper starting point of three years. Taking account of the plea, two years would suffice, but appropriate punishment could only be achieved by immediate imprisonment.

Care Provider Offence

B2.168 The CJCA 2015, s. 21, addresses the potential liability of a 'care provider'. This may be an individual, a corporation or an unincorporated association that provides or arranges the provision of health or adult social care. Hospitals, medical practices and care homes are typical examples. By s. 21(1) such liability may arise where:

(a) an individual who has the care of another individual by virtue of being part of the care provider's arrangements ill-treats or wilfully neglects that individual,

(b) the care provider's activities are managed or organised in a way which amounts to a gross breach of a relevant duty of care owed by the care provider to the individual who is ill-treated or neglected, and

(c) in the absence of the breach, the ill-treatment or wilful neglect would not have occurred or would have been less likely to occur.

In dealing with the liability of corporations and associations, s. 21 draws on the approach adopted in respect of corporate liability for manslaughter by the CMCHA 2007 (see **B1.71** ***et seq.***).

Provisions relating to penalties, remedial orders and publicity orders are set out in s. 23. Section 22 limits the scope of the offence in various ways, notably by providing that local authorities and other bodies undertaking functions on their behalf will not be considered 'care providers' for such purposes to the extent that they provide non-health children's services (e.g., children's social care).

CAUSING OR ALLOWING A CHILD OR VULNERABLE ADULT TO SUFFER SERIOUS PHYSICAL HARM

The Domestic Violence, Crime and Victims (Amendment) Act 2012 amended the DVCVA 2004, s. 5 (causing or allowing the death of a child or vulnerable adult: see **B1.79**), and related provisions so as to extend their application to cases involving a child or vulnerable adult suffering serious physical harm. **B2.169**

Procedure and Evidence

The offence is triable only on indictment and is normally a class 1A or 2A offence (see CrimPD XIII, para. B (see Supplement, **CPD.XIII.B**) for the additional factors that the court considers on allocation). **B2.170**

Where D is charged in the same proceedings with an offence under the OAPA 1861, s. 18 or 20, or with attempted murder as well as with an offence under the DVCVA 2004, s. 5 (as amended), in respect of the same harm, s. 6A(3) to (5) affect the evidence and procedure applicable in three different but related ways:

(a) under s. 6A(3), where by virtue of the CJPO 1994, s. 35(3), inferences may be drawn in relation to the s. 5 offence from D's failure to give evidence or refusal to answer a question, the court or jury may also draw such inferences in determining whether D is guilty of the offence under the OAPA 1861 or attempted murder, even if there would otherwise be no case for D to answer in relation to those offences;
(b) under s. 6A(4), unless the s. 5 offence is itself dismissed, the charge of the offence under the OAPA 1861 or attempted murder is not to be dismissed on an application to the Crown Court under the CDA 1998, sch. 3, para. 2;
(c) under s. 6A(5), the question of whether there is a case for D to answer on the charge of the offence under the OAPA 1861 or attempted murder is not to be considered before the close of all the evidence (unless D has already ceased to be charged with the s. 5 offence).

Domestic Violence, Crime and Victims Act 2004, s. 6A **B2.171**

(1) Subsections (3) to (5) apply where a person ('the defendant') is charged in the same proceedings with a relevant offence and with an offence under section 5 in respect of the same harm ('the section 5 offence').
(2) In this section 'relevant offence' means—
 (a) an offence under section 18 or 20 of the Offences against the Person Act 1861 (grievous bodily harm etc);
 (b) an offence under section 1 of the Criminal Attempts Act 1981 of attempting to commit murder.
(3) Where by virtue of section 35(3) of the Criminal Justice and Public Order Act 1994 a court or jury is permitted, in relation to the section 5 offence, to draw such inferences as appear proper from the defendant's failure to give evidence or refusal to answer a question, the court or jury may also draw such inferences in determining whether the defendant is guilty of a relevant offence, even if there would otherwise be no case for the defendant to answer in relation to that offence.
(4) The charge of the relevant offence is not to be dismissed under paragraph 2 of Schedule 3 to the Crime and Disorder Act 1998 (unless the section 5 offence is dismissed).
(5) At the defendant's trial the question whether there is a case for the defendant to answer on the charge of the relevant offence is not to be considered before the close of all the evidence (or, if at some earlier time the defendant ceases to be charged with the section 5 offence, before that earlier time).

Alternative Verdicts

There are no alternative verdicts specifically provided for and the offence is not itself an alternative verdict to an offence under the OAPA 1861, s. 18 or 20, or to an offence of attempted **B2.172** murder. It does however allow for a guilty verdict in cases where the exact nature of D's misconduct is unclear.

Sentence

B2.173 The maximum penalty for an offence under the DVCVA 2004, s. 5, where serious physical harm is involved, is ten years' imprisonment (s. 5(8)). The Sentencing Council definitive guideline, *Child Cruelty* (see Supplement, **SG20-1**), applies in respect of offenders aged 18 and over, sentenced on or after 1 January 2019, irrespective of the date of the offence. The guideline sets out an offence range between community order and nine years' imprisonment.

Elements

B2.174 As to the meaning of the terms 'vulnerable adult' and 'unlawful act', see *Uddin* [2017] EWCA Crim 1072, [2017] 2 Cr App R 31 (454) and **B1.87**. As to 'member of the same household', liability of persons aged under 16 and 'failure to take steps', see **B1.88** ***et seq.***

Where it is a child who has suffered serious physical harm, the unlawful act might constitute an offence of child cruelty under the CYPA 1933 (see **B2.145**). Where a vulnerable adult is the victim, there may in some cases be an offence of ill-treatment of mental patients or persons who lack capacity (see **B2.157** ***et seq.***).

CONTROLLING OR COERCIVE DOMESTIC ABUSE

General

B2.175 The SCA 2015, s. 76(1), creates an offence of 'controlling or coercive behaviour' in intimate or family relationships, other than parent-child or analogous relationships. Such behaviour must be either repeated or continuous and must have a 'serious effect' on V, but need not necessarily involve any assault or the threat or infliction of any physical harm or violence. The offence targets 'psychological abuse' or 'mental cruelty' in which one partner to a relationship coerces and controls the life of the other, without necessarily or frequently resorting to threats or violence. A 'serious effect' on V need not be intended but, if it cannot be proved that D knew it was being caused, it must at least be proved that D ought to have known it (s. 76(4)).

A specific defence (additional to any general defences that might be available) may be invoked in the limited circumstances provided for by s. 76(8) to (10).

Serious Crime Act 2015, s. 76

(1) A person (A) commits an offence if—
  (a) A repeatedly or continuously engages in behaviour towards another person (B) that is controlling or coercive,
  (b) at the time of the behaviour, A and B are personally connected,
  (c) the behaviour has a serious effect on B, and
  (d) A knows or ought to know that the behaviour will have a serious effect on B.
(2) A and B are 'personally connected' if—
  (a) A is in an intimate personal relationship with B, or
  (b) A and B live together and—
    (i) they are members of the same family, or
    (ii) they have previously been in an intimate personal relationship with each other.
(3) But A does not commit an offence under this section if at the time of the behaviour in question—
  (a) A has responsibility for B, for the purposes of Part 1 of the Children and Young Persons Act 1933 (see section 17 of that Act), and
  (b) B is under 16.
(4) A's behaviour has a 'serious effect' on B if—
  (a) it causes B to fear, on at least two occasions, that violence will be used against B, or

(b) it causes B serious alarm or distress which has a substantial adverse effect on B's usual day-to-day activities.

(5) For the purposes of subsection (1)(d) A 'ought to know' that which a reasonable person in possession of the same information would know.

(6) For the purposes of subsection (2)(b)(i) A and B are members of the same family if—
(a) they are, or have been, married to each other;
(b) they are, or have been, civil partners of each other;
(c) they are relatives;
(d) they have agreed to marry one another (whether or not the agreement has been terminated);
(e) they have entered into a civil partnership agreement (whether or not the agreement has been terminated);
(f) they are both parents of the same child;
(g) they have, or have had, parental responsibility for the same child.

(7) In subsection (6)—
'civil partnership agreement' has the meaning given by section 73 of the Civil Partnership Act 2004;
'child' means a person under the age of 18 years;
'parental responsibility' has the same meaning as in the Children Act 1989;
'relative' has the meaning given by section 63(1) of the Family Law Act 1996.

Sentence

The maximum penalty for an offence under the SCA 2015, s. 76, is five years' imprisonment and/or a fine on indictment and six months and/or an unlimited fine summarily (ss. 76(11) and 86(14)). The Sentencing Council definitive guideline, *Intimidatory Offences* (see Supplement, **SG27-1**), applies in respect of offenders aged 18 and over, sentenced on or after 1 October 2018, irrespective of the date of the offence. The guideline sets out offence categories with starting points from community order to 30 months' imprisonment and an offence range up to four years' imprisonment. **B2.176**

In *Katira* [2020] EWCA Crim 89, the offender pleaded guilty to an offence under the SCA 2015, s. 76(1). His plea was on the basis of admissions to five specific incidents of coercive and violent conduct towards his wife over a nine-month period. He appealed against a sentence of 22 months' immediate imprisonment based on the judge's categorisation of the offending in the most serious sentencing category, 1A. The Court of Appeal made some observations of general importance in relation to sentencing for such offences. First, as to culpability, the higher category A should be reserved for those cases with behaviour exceeding the five incidents pleaded to in this case, bearing in mind the offence is not made out at all until two such occasions are present. Five occasions, as here, each of relatively short duration, should not take the offending into higher culpability. Secondly, good character will be of little weight in the circumstances of this case, bearing in mind behaviour outside the home may have little relevance to bullying and aggressive behaviour within it. Indeed, as reflected in para. M2 of the Sentencing Council's Table of Expanded Explanations for Factors Reducing Seriousness or Reflecting Personal Mitigation, where an offender has used good character or status to facilitate or conceal the offending it could be treated as an aggravating factor.

In the pre-guideline case of *Vidgen* [2018] EWCA Crim 2385 the defendant's behaviour towards his wife was described as being 'nasty, dominating and bullying'. As well as a period of coercive behaviour there was a separate and discrete incident of violence. The Court of Appeal upheld consecutive sentences of 13 months' imprisonment for coercive behaviour and nine months' imprisonment for an assault occasioning actual bodily harm. The Court looked carefully at the decision to impose the sentences consecutively and found nothing wrong, noting that there was no overlap in time, or in the nature of each allegation. 'Had there been but one count of coercive behaviour, to cover all aspects of the appellant's behaviour including violence, the starting point would have been significantly longer than the 10 months used … in this case and would have resulted in a total sentence in the region of 21 months after credit for plea in any event' (at [24]). In *Barratt* [2017] EWCA Crim 1631, offending which involved prolonged and serious aggression by the appellant towards his former partner fully justified a sentence of 30 months' imprisonment which, once again, was imposed consecutively to other sentences.

Defence

B2.177 **Serious Crime Act 2015, s. 76**

(8) In proceedings for an offence under this section it is a defence for A to show that—
(a) in engaging in the behaviour in question, A believed that he or she was acting in B's best interests, and
(b) the behaviour was in all the circumstances reasonable.
(9) A is to be taken to have shown the facts mentioned in subsection (8) if—
(a) sufficient evidence of the facts is adduced to raise an issue with respect to them, and
(b) the contrary is not proved beyond reasonable doubt.
(10) The defence in subsection (8) is not available to A in relation to behaviour that causes B to fear that violence will be used against B.

FEMALE GENITAL MUTILATION

Principal Offences and Defences

B2.178 **Female Genital Mutilation Act 2003, ss. 1 to 4**

1.—(1) A person is guilty of an offence if he excises, infibulates or otherwise mutilates the whole or any part of a girl's labia majora, labia minora or clitoris.
(2) But no offence is committed by an approved person who performs—
(a) a surgical operation on a girl which is necessary for her physical or mental health, or
(b) a surgical operation on a girl who is in any stage of labour, or has just given birth, for purposes connected with the labour or birth.
(3) The following are approved persons—
(a) in relation to an operation falling within subsection (2)(a), a registered medical practitioner,
(b) in relation to an operation falling within subsection (2)(b), a registered medical practitioner, a registered midwife or a person undergoing a course of training with a view to becoming such a practitioner or midwife.
(4) There is also no offence committed by a person who—
(a) performs a surgical operation falling within subsection (2)(a) or (b) outside the United Kingdom, and
(b) in relation to such an operation exercises functions corresponding to those of an approved person.
(5) For the purpose of determining whether an operation is necessary for the mental health of a girl it is immaterial whether she or any other person believes that the operation is required as a matter of custom or ritual.

2. A person is guilty of an offence if he aids, abets, counsels or procures a girl to excise, infibulate or otherwise mutilate the whole or any part of her own labia majora, labia minora or clitoris.

3.—(1) A person is guilty of an offence if he aids, abets, counsels or procures a person who is not a United Kingdom national or United Kingdom resident to do a relevant act of female genital mutilation outside the United Kingdom.
(2) An act is a relevant act of female genital mutilation if—
(a) it is done in relation to a United Kingdom national or permanent United Kingdom resident, and
(b) it would, if done by such a person, constitute an offence under section 1.
(3) But no offence is committed if the relevant act of female genital mutilation—
(a) is a surgical operation falling within section 1(2)(a) or (b), and
(b) is performed by a person who, in relation to such an operation, is an approved person or exercises functions corresponding to those of an approved person.

3A.—(1) If a genital mutilation offence is committed against a girl under the age of 16, each person who is responsible for the girl at the relevant time is guilty of an offence.
This is subject to subsection (5).

(2) For the purposes of this section a person is 'responsible' for a girl in the following two cases.
(3) The first case is where the person—
(a) has parental responsibility for the girl, and
(b) has frequent contact with her.
(4) The second case is where the person—
(a) is aged 18 or over, and
(b) has assumed (and not relinquished) responsibility for caring for the girl in the manner of a parent.
(5) It is a defence for the defendant to show that—
(a) at the relevant time, the defendant did not think that there was a significant risk of a genital mutilation offence being committed against the girl, and could not reasonably have been expected to be aware that there was any such risk, or
(b) the defendant took such steps as he or she could reasonably have been expected to take to protect the girl from being the victim of a genital mutilation offence.
(6) A person is taken to have shown the fact mentioned in subsection (5)(a) or (b) if—
(a) sufficient evidence of the fact is adduced to raise an issue with respect to it, and
(b) the contrary is not proved beyond reasonable doubt.
(7) For the purposes of subsection (3)(b), where a person has frequent contact with a girl which is interrupted by her going to stay somewhere temporarily, that contact is treated as continuing during her stay there.
(8) In this section—
'genital mutilation offence' means an offence under section 1, 2 or 3 (and for the purposes of subsection (1) the prosecution does not have to prove which section it is);
'parental responsibility'—
(a) in England Wales, has the same meaning as in the Children Act 1989;
...
'the relevant time' means the time when the mutilation takes place.

4.—(1) Sections 1 to 3A extend to any acts or omissions done outside the United Kingdom by a United Kingdom national or United Kingdom resident.
(2) If an offence under this Act is committed outside the United Kingdom—
(a) proceedings may be taken, and
(b) the offence may for incidental purposes be treated as having been committed,
in any place in England and Wales or Northern Ireland.

In this Act (other than for the purposes of s. 3A), a 'girl' includes a woman (s. 6(1)). An adult woman cannot therefore give valid consent to any procedure that would involve an offence committed against her under ss. 1, 2 or 3 of the Act.

The principal provisions extend to acts done outside the UK by UK nationals or habitual UK residents (s. 4); and this includes aiding, abetting, counselling or procuring a person who is not a UK national or resident to do a relevant act of female genital mutilation outside the UK (s. 3); aiding, abetting, counselling or procuring a girl or woman to mutilate herself (s. 2); and failing to protect a girl from risk of genital mutilation (s. 3A).

Procedure and Sentence

For CPS policy on the prosecution of such cases, see tinyurl.com/ycguys9w. Offences under ss. 1 to 3A are triable either way. By s. 5, the maximum penalty following conviction on indictment for offences under ss. 1 to 3 is imprisonment for 14 years or a fine or both; and on summary conviction imprisonment for up to six months or an unlimited fine or both. There is no offence-specific guideline but the Sentencing Council's *General Guideline: Overarching Principles* (see Supplement, **SG2-1**) is used for all offenders sentenced on or after 1 October 2019. **B2.179**

The first conviction for an offence under this section was *N (Female Genital Mutilation)* (8 March 2019 unreported, Central Criminal Court). D claimed her three-year-old daughter's injuries were caused when she fell from a kitchen counter onto an open, metal-lined cupboard door. The jury rejected her account. D was sentenced to 11 years' imprisonment, the sentencer describing her conduct as 'barbaric' and 'sickening' and 'a form of child abuse'. The s. 3A offence of failing to protect a girl from the risk of genital mutilation carries a maximum penalty of seven years. The Sentencing Council definitive guideline, *Child Cruelty* (see Supplement, **SG20-1**), applies in respect of this offence, setting out an offence range up to six years' imprisonment. It applies to those aged 18 and over, sentenced on or after 1 January 2019, irrespective of the date of the offence. The definitive guideline, *Domestic Abuse* (see Supplement, **SG6-1**) may also be of assistance when sentencing for this offence. Paragraph 2 of the guideline cites the government's definition of domestic abuse, which includes 'female genital mutilation'.

Related Orders and Offences

B2.180 The Female Genital Mutilation Act 2003, s. 5A and sch. 2, enable the High Court or a family court to make female genital mutilation protection orders. See *Secretary of State for the Home Department v Suffolk County Council* [2020] EWCA Civ 731. Breach of such an order is triable either way and punishable on indictment by up to five years' imprisonment. Breach of such an order is alternatively be punishable as a contempt of court, in which case the maximum penalty is two years' imprisonment.

OFFENCES OF HARASSMENT

B2.181 **Protection from Harassment Act 1997, ss. 1 and 2**

1.—(1) A person must not pursue a course of conduct—
(a) which amounts to harassment of another, and
(b) which he knows or ought to know amounts to harassment of the other.

(1A) A person must not pursue a course of conduct—
(a) which involves harassment of two or more persons, and
(b) which he knows or ought to know involves harassment of those persons, and
(c) by which he intends to persuade any person (whether or not one of those mentioned above)—
(i) not to do something that he is entitled or required to do, or
(ii) to do something that he is not under any obligation to do.

2.—(1) A person who pursues a course of conduct in breach of section 1(1) or (1A) is guilty of an offence.

The CDA 1998, s. 32, creates a racially or religiously aggravated form of this offence. For the meaning of 'racially or religiously aggravated', see **B11.145**.

Procedure and Alternative Verdicts

B2.182 The basic offence is triable summarily (Protection from Harassment Act 1997, s. 2(2)). The aggravated form of the offence is triable either way. As to the procedure on charging both the basic and aggravated offence, see *Henderson v CPS* [2016] EWHC 464 (Admin), [2016] 1 WLR 1990, discussed at **B11.46**.

A judge who rules that there is no case to answer on an indictment alleging an offence under s. 4 of the Act (see **B2.197**) may allow the jury to consider an alternative verdict of harassment, contrary to s. 2 (*Livesey* [2006] EWCA Crim 3344, [2007] 1 Cr App R 35 (462), applying *Carson* (1990) 92 Cr App R 236).

Where there is a continuing offence, it is possible to take into account events occurring outside the six-month limitation period imposed by the MCA 1980, s. 127, provided that at least one of the incidents occurred within that time period (*DPP v Baker* [2004] EWHC 2782 (Admin).

Sentence (Basic Offence)

B2.183 The maximum penalty is imprisonment for six months, an unlimited fine, or both (Protection from Harassment Act 1997, s. 2(2)). As to the imposition of restraining orders, see **E21.32**. The Sentencing Council definitive guideline, *Intimidatory Offences* (see Supplement, **SG27-1**) applies in respect of offenders aged 18 and over, sentenced on or after 1 October 2018, irrespective of the date of the offence. The Sentencing Council definitive guideline, *Domestic Abuse* (see Supplement, **SG6-1**) may be of assistance when sentencing for this offence. In respect of breach of a restraining order, the Sentencing Council definitive guideline, *Breach Offences* (see Supplement, **SG15-6**) applies to all offenders aged 18 and over sentenced on or after 1 October 2018, irrespective of the date of the offence.

Racial or religious aggravation cannot normally be taken into account by the sentencer when sentencing for the basic offence of harassment (see **B2.3**). See **E1.19** for increase in sentence, under the CJA 2003, s. 146, for aggravation relating to disability, sexual orientation or transgender identity.

Sentence (Racially or Religiously Aggravated Form of Offence)

The maximum penalty is two years, a fine or both on indictment; six months, an unlimited fine or both, summarily (CDA 1998, s. 32(3)). As to the imposition of restraining orders, see **E21.32**. **B2.184**

The Sentencing Council definitive guideline, *Intimidatory Offences* (see Supplement, **SG27-1**) applies in respect of offenders aged 18 and over, sentenced on or after 1 October 2018, irrespective of the date of the offence. The guideline confirms earlier practice that when sentencing for the racially aggravated form of an offence the sentencer should indicate the appropriate sentence for the offence in the absence of racial aggravation and then determine the appropriate uplift for the racial or religious aggravation.

Elements

Course of Conduct **B2.185**

Protection from Harassment Act 1997, s. 7

(3) A 'course of conduct' must involve—
 (a) in the case of conduct in relation to a single person (see section 1(1)), conduct on at least two occasions in relation to that person, or
 (b) in the case of conduct in relation to two or more persons (see section 1(1A)), conduct on at least one occasion in relation to each of those persons.

(3A) A person's conduct on any occasion shall be taken, if aided, abetted, counselled or procured by another—
 (a) to be conduct on that occasion of the other (as well as conduct of the person whose conduct it is); and
 (b) to be conduct in relation to which the other's knowledge and purpose, and what he ought to have known, are the same as they were in relation to what was contemplated or reasonably foreseeable at the time of the aiding, abetting, counselling or procuring.

(4) 'Conduct' includes speech.

Establishing a course of conduct, rather than a series of unrelated acts, is crucial to the success of any prosecution for harassment, and 'it is the course of conduct which has to have the quality of amounting to harassment, rather than individual instances of conduct' (*Iqbal v Dean Manson (Solicitors)* [2011] EWCA Civ 123 per Rix LJ at [45]). The matters said to constitute the course of conduct amounting to harassment must be properly particularised in the information laid or the indictment (*C v CPS* [2008] EWHC 148 (Admin)) and must be so connected in type and in context as to justify the conclusion that they amount to a course of conduct (*Patel* [2004] EWCA Crim 3284, [2005] 1 Cr App R 27 (440); *Pratt v DPP* [2001] EWHC Admin 483; *C v CPS*). The fewer and further apart the incidents, the less likely it is that they will be so regarded, but circumstances can be conceived 'where incidents, as far apart as a year, could constitute a course of conduct' (*Lau v DPP* [2000] Crim LR 580). See also *Hills* [2001] 1 FLR 580 and *Sahin* [2009] EWCA Crim 2616. In *Baron v CPS* (13 June 2000 unreported), two letters sent some four and a half months apart were capable of constituting a course of conduct amounting to harassment. At the other end of the scale, it was held in *Kelly v DPP* [2002] EWHC 1428 (Admin) that three telephone calls made over a space of five minutes could amount to a 'course of conduct', taking into account the separate and distinct nature of the calls.

A course of conduct that may initially take the form of a legitimate inquiry or complaint may descend into harassment if unreasonably prolonged or persisted in, as in *DPP v Hardy* [2008] EWHC 2874 (Admin), where D made 95 telephone calls over a 90-minute period and threatened to keep calling all night. See also *James v CPS* [2009] EWHC 2925 (Admin). In *R (Taffurelli) v DPP* [2004] EWHC 2791 (Admin), it was accepted that deliberate failure to control dogs following a number of complaints could constitute 'conduct'.

B2.186 **Two or More Persons Harassed** The problems previously caused where D's course of conduct harassed two or more persons separately (as in *Caurti v DPP* [2001] EWHC Admin 867, [2002] Crim LR 131) are resolved by the introduction of a specific statutory solution in the Protection from Harassment Act 1997, s. 1(1A). But s. 2 remains the offence-creating provision.

B2.187 **Indirect Awareness of Victim** A person may become aware of a course of conduct, or parts of it, indirectly. So, the offence was complete when V knew of the relevant telephone calls made by D, even though that knowledge came from being informed by a third party, provided there was evidence on the basis of which the court can properly conclude that D was pursuing a course of conduct with the necessary *mens rea* (*Kellett v DPP* [2001] EWHC Admin 107).

Definition of Harassment

B2.188 **Protection from Harassment Act 1997, s. 7**

(2) References to harassing a person include alarming the person or causing the person distress.

...

(5) References to a person, in the context of the harassment of a person, are references to a person who is an individual.

The definition provided by s. 7 is clearly inclusive and not exhaustive (*DPP v Ramsdale* [2001] EWHC Admin 106). 'Harassment' is generally understood to involve improper oppressive and unreasonable conduct that is targeted at an individual and calculated to produce the consequences described in s. 7. By s. 1(3) of the Act (see **B2.191**), reasonable and/or lawful courses of conduct may be excluded (see *N(Z)* [2016] EWCA Crim 92, [2016] 2 Cr App R 10 (112) at [38] (where this summary is endorsed) and *Tan* [2017] EWCA Crim 493 at [18]). The practice of stalking is arguably the prime example of harassment (*Curtis* [2010] EWCA Crim 123, [2010] 1 Cr App R (S) 31 (193)) but a wide range of other actions could, if persisted in, be so categorised. A course of conduct which is unattractive and unreasonable does not of itself necessarily constitute harassment; it must be unacceptable and oppressive conduct such that it should sustain criminal liability. See *Majrowski v Guy's and St Thomas's NHS Trust* [2006] UKHL 34, [2007] 1 AC 224, per Lord Nicholls at [30]. Harassment includes negative emotion by repeated molestation, annoyance or worry. The words 'alarm and distress' are to be taken disjunctively and not conjunctively, but there is a minimum level of alarm or distress which must be suffered in order to constitute harassment.

The courts, in view of the individual's right to protest and demonstrate about issues of public interest, will resist attempts to interpret the statute widely (*Huntingdon Life Sciences Ltd v Curtin* (1997) *The Times*, 11 December 1997). However, 'whatever may have been the purpose behind [the Act], its words are clear, and it can cover harassment of any sort' (*DPP v Selvanayagam* (1999) *The Times*, 23 June 1999, per Collins J). In *Iqbal v Dean Manson (Solicitors)* [2011] EWCA Civ 123 it was held (in the context of a civil action) that a series of letters written by one litigant to another (and copied to the court), attacking the personal and professional integrity of the second litigant's solicitor, could potentially be seen as harassment of that solicitor under s. 1. Similarly, in *Plavelil v DPP* [2014] EWHC 736 (Admin), it was held that the repeated making of false and malicious assertions against a doctor in connection with an investigation by the General Medical Council could amount to harassment; they could be oppressive even if they could easily be rebutted.

Publication by Press as Harassment It was held in *Thomas v News Group Newspapers Ltd* [2001] EWCA Civ 1233, that the publication of press articles is, in law, capable of amounting to harassment, although only in very rare circumstances. Whether conduct is reasonable depends upon the circumstances of the particular case. It was common ground between the parties that, before press publications are capable of constituting harassment, they must be attended by some exceptional circumstances which justify sanctions and the restriction on the freedom of expression (under the ECHR, Article 10) that they involve. An example of such conduct amounting to harassment which was agreed by the parties to that case was the publication of press articles calculated to incite racial hatred of an individual. **B2.189**

Mens Rea

The *mens rea* for this offence, as defined in s. 1(1)(b), is that D knows or ought to know that the course of conduct amounts to harassment of the other. Assistance in determining when D ought to know this is provided by s. 1(2). **B2.190**

Protection from Harassment Act 1997, s. 1

(2) For the purposes of this section or section 2A(2)(c), the person whose course of conduct is in question ought to know that it amounts to or involves harassment of another if a reasonable person in possession of the same information would think the course of conduct amounted to or involved harassment of the other.

This is an objective test, and no allowance can be made for conditions such as paranoid schizophrenia that may affect D's perception (*Colohan* [2001] EWCA Crim 1251) unless they are such as to enable D to raise a defence of insanity (see *Loake v CPS* [2017] EWHC 2855 (Admin), [2018] QB 998 and **A3.23**). Furthermore, nothing that involves cultural or racial differences should be taken into account, unless it is relevant and supported by proper evidence (*C v CPS* [2008] EWHC 148 (Admin)). But where D actually intends to cause alarm or distress and actually does so, that is likely to meet the requirements of s. 1(1)(b). In *Lang v CPS* [2017] EWHC 3639 (Admin) a magistrates' court found that D's conduct in sending a series of text messages to his estranged wife, in order to attempt to embarrass, alarm and distress her, was oppressive and unreasonable. They recorded no finding that D either knew or ought to have known that this amounted to harassment, but the Divisional Court held that this could be inferred from the other findings.

Lawful Courses of Conduct

Protection from Harassment Act 1997, s. 1 **B2.191**

(3) Subsection (1) or (1A) does not apply to a course of conduct if the person who pursued it shows—
   (a) that it was pursued for the purpose of preventing or detecting crime;
   (b) that it was pursued under any enactment or rule of law or to comply with any condition or requirement imposed by any person under any enactment, or
   (c) that in the particular circumstances the pursuit of the course of conduct was reasonable.

In *Hayes v Willoughby* [2013] UKSC 17, [2013] 2 All ER 405, the Supreme Court held that s. 1(3)(a) may be relied upon by both law enforcement agencies and private individuals, whether or not D can prove that the behaviour was objectively reasonable. Their lordships rejected (*obiter*) the Court of Appeal's view that such a purpose must be D's sole purpose. But as Lord Sumption explained (at [15]):

> Before an alleged harasser can be said to have had the purpose of preventing or detecting crime, he must have sufficiently applied his mind to the matter. He must have thought rationally about the material suggesting the possibility of criminality and formed the view that the conduct said to constitute harassment was appropriate for the purpose of preventing or detecting it ... If, on the other hand, he has not engaged in these minimum mental processes necessary to acquire the relevant state of mind ... two consequences will follow. The first is that the law will not regard him as having had the relevant purpose at all. He has simply not taken the necessary steps to form one. The second is that the causal connection which section 1(3)(a) posits between the purpose of the alleged harasser and the conduct constituting the harassment, will not exist.

Section 1(3)(b) protects, *inter alia*, the right to free speech. The requirement in s. 1(3)(c) poses an objective test, namely whether D's conduct is, in the judgement of the jury or magistrates, reasonable; there is no warrant for attaching to the word 'reasonable' or via the words 'particular circumstances' the standards or characteristics of D himself (*Colohan* [2001] EWCA Crim 1251; *C v CPS* [2008] EWHC 148 (Admin)). The imposition of a legal burden upon D may be open to challenge in the light of the human rights cases on the 'reverse burden' (see **F3.7**).

B2.192 In *DPP v Selvanayagam* (1999) *The Times*, 23 June 1999, the Divisional Court considered the relevance of an injunction to the question of whether a course of conduct pursued by M and S was reasonable. The injunction was in force against S (and others), but not against M. The terms of the injunction were crucial: they endeavoured to prevent harassment (defined as in the 1997 Act) of H and his family. The Court found it difficult to see how a course of conduct in contravention of the injunction and amounting to harassment could be reasonable. There might be circumstances in which it was necessary for those covered by the injunction to go on to the other's land, but to make this of relevance they would have to explain away a course of conduct and not merely one emergency entry on to that land. In the case of M, it was not sufficient to be aware of the existence of the injunction. M would have to be aware of its specific terms. M was not sufficiently aware, and so the defence of reasonableness of the course of conduct was open for consideration. In the balancing exercise to determine reasonableness, the existence, in general terms, of the injunction would be relevant, though it would have little impact. On a more general level, when engaging in the balancing of different interests (such as the right of peaceful protest and the right to quiet enjoyment of property) the courts may have to get involved in the same sort of exercise as occurs when considering the exercise of the police powers to prevent a breach of the peace. It does not follow that it is always the first party's rights that are protected (e.g., to process). They may, in effect, be held responsible for the reaction of the other party. Priority will, however, always be given, where possible, to lawful activity that is not (deliberately) provocative. For consideration of this problem, see *Redmond-Bate v DPP* (1999) 163 JP 789.

For the special defence relating to national security etc., see s. 12 at **B2.204**.

Related Offence

B2.193 Where the High Court or the county court has granted an injunction under the Protection from Harassment Act 1997, s. 3(3)(a), to restrain D from conduct which amounts to harassment, it is by s. 3(6) an offence for D, without reasonable excuse, to do anything prohibited by that injunction. Such conduct is not punishable as a contempt of court (s. 3(7)) nor can a person be convicted of this offence for any conduct which has been punished as a contempt of court (s. 3(8)). A person guilty of this offence is liable, on conviction on indictment, to imprisonment for a term not exceeding five years or a fine or both; and, on summary conviction, to imprisonment for a term not exceeding six months or an unlimited fine or both (s. 3(9)).

OFFENCE OF STALKING

Protection from Harassment Act 1997, s. 2A **B2.194**

(1) A person is guilty of an offence if—
  (a) the person pursues a course of conduct in breach of section 1(1), and
  (b) the course of conduct amounts to stalking.
(2) For the purposes of subsection (1)(b) (and section 4A(1)(a)) a person's course of conduct amounts to stalking of another person if—
  (a) it amounts to harassment of that person,
  (b) the acts or omissions involved are ones associated with stalking, and
  (c) the person whose course of conduct it is knows or ought to know that the course of conduct amounts to harassment of the other person.
(3) The following are examples of acts or omissions which, in particular circumstances, are ones associated with stalking—
  (a) following a person,
  (b) contacting, or attempting to contact, a person by any means,
  (c) publishing any statement or other material—
    (i) relating or purporting to relate to a person, or
    (ii) purporting to originate from a person,
  (d) monitoring the use by a person of the internet, email or any other form of electronic communication,
  (e) loitering in any place (whether public or private),
  (f) interfering with any property in the possession of a person,
  (g) watching or spying on a person. …
(6) This section is without prejudice to the generality of section 2.

The CDA 1998, s. 32, has been amended to create a racially or religiously aggravated form of this offence. For the meaning of 'racially or religiously aggravated', see **B11.145**.

Procedure and Sentence

B2.195 The offence is triable summarily only. The maximum penalty is imprisonment for six months, an unlimited fine or both (Protection from Harassment Act 1997, s. 2A(4) and (5)). The Sentencing Council definitive guideline, *Intimidatory Offences* (see Supplement, **SG27-1**) applies in respect of offenders aged 18 and over, sentenced on or after 1 October 2018, irrespective of the date of the offence. The Sentencing Council definitive guideline, *Domestic Abuse* (see Supplement, **SG6-1**), may be of assistance when sentencing for this offence. In respect of breach of a restraining order, the Sentencing Council definitive guideline, *Breach Offences* (see Supplement, **SG15-6**) applies to all offenders aged 18 and over sentenced on or after 1 October 2018, irrespective of the date of the offence. As to the procedure on charging both the basic and aggravated offence, see *Henderson v CPS* [2016] EWHC 464 (Admin), [2016] 1 WLR 1990, discussed at **B11.46**. Earlier guidance on sentencing for this offence can be found in *Redman* [2016] EWCA Crim 225.

Elements

B2.196 Behaviour prior to the commencement of the Protection of Freedoms Act 2012, s. 111, cannot found an offence under the Protection from Harassment Act 1997, s. 2A, but may still constitute harassment under s. 2 since the stalking offence is nothing more than the existing offence of harassment within the meaning of s. 1(1) with the added requirement that the harassment in question takes the form of stalking. The penalties are the same. To put it another way, anything that would amount to an offence of stalking on or after commencement could equally be charged as harassment either before or after commencement. But the various forms of stalking listed in s. 2A(3) are at least identified as potential forms of harassment.

For the meaning of 'course of conduct' for the purposes of s. 2A(1), see s. 7(3) and (4) at **B2.185**. For the definition of harassment, see s. 7(2) and (5) of the 1997 Act at **B2.188**. As to the specific *mens rea* required by virtue of s. 2A(2), note that s. 1(2) also applies in respect of s. 2A (see **B2.190**). The acts or omissions mentioned in s. 2A(3) are referred to as examples and thus do not exclude, *inter alia*, newly developing forms of behaviour such as electronic tracking of an individual.

As to criminal breaches of stalking protection orders or interim orders made under the Stalking Protection Act 2019, s. 1, see s. 8 of that Act and **D25.90**.

PUTTING PEOPLE IN FEAR OF VIOLENCE

B2.197 **Protection from Harassment Act 1997, s. 4**

> (1) A person whose course of conduct causes another to fear, on at least two occasions, that violence will be used against him is guilty of an offence if he knows or ought to know that his course of conduct will cause the other so to fear on each of those occasions.

The CDA 1998, s. 32, creates a racially or religiously aggravated form of this offence. For the meaning of 'racially or religiously aggravated', see **B11.145**.

Procedure and Alternative Verdicts

B2.198 The basic and aggravated offences are each triable either way (Protection from Harassment Act, s. 4(4); CDA 1998, s. 32(4)). When tried on indictment, they are normally class 3 offences, but see CrimPD XIII, para. B (see Supplement, **CPD.XIII.B**) for the additional factors that the court considers on allocation. If a jury acquit D of racially aggravated harassment, they may convict D of the basic offence (s. 32(6)). As to the procedure on charging both the basic and aggravated offence, see *Henderson v CPS* [2016] EWHC 464 (Admin), [2016] 1 WLR 1990, discussed at **B11.46**.

The Protection from Harassment Act 1997, s. 4(5), provides that if D is tried on indictment for the s. 4 offence the jury may instead convict D of the offence under s. 2 or s. 2A (see **B2.181** and **B2.194**). If they do so, the Crown Court has the same powers and duties as a magistrates' court would have on convicting D of an offence under s. 2 or 2A (s. 4(6)). Similarly, a judge who rules that there is no case to answer on an indictment alleging an offence under s. 4 may allow the jury to consider an alternative verdict of harassment contrary to s. 2 (*Livesey* [2006] EWCA Crim 3344, [2007] 1 Cr App R 35 (462), applying *Carson* (1990) 92 Cr App R 236) or the offence of stalking under s. 2A.

The *Magistrates' Court Sentencing Guidelines* indicate that, where the nature of the activity involves sexual threats or the targeting of a vulnerable person, Crown Court trial is appropriate.

Sentence (Basic Offence)

B2.199 The maximum penalty is ten years, a fine or both on indictment; six months, an unlimited fine or both, summarily (Protection from Harassment Act 1997, s. 4(4)). As to the imposition of restraining orders, see **E21.32**.

The Sentencing Council definitive guideline, *Intimidatory Offences* (see Supplement, **SG27-1**) applies in respect of offenders aged 18 and over, sentenced on or after 1 October 2018, irrespective of the date of the offence. The Sentencing Council definitive guideline, *Domestic Abuse* (see Supplement, **SG6-1**) may be of assistance when sentencing for this offence. In respect of breach of a restraining order, the Sentencing Council definitive guideline, *Breach Offences* (see Supplement, **SG15-6**) applies to all offenders aged 18 and over sentenced on or after 1 October 2018, irrespective of the date of the offence.

Racial or religious aggravation cannot normally be taken into account by the sentencer when sentencing for the basic offence of harassment (see **B2.3**). See **E1.19** for increase in sentence, under the CJA 2003, s. 146, for aggravation relating to disability, sexual orientation or transgender identity.

Sentence (Racially or Religiously Aggravated Form of Offence)

The maximum penalty is 14 years, a fine or both on indictment; six months, an unlimited fine or both, summarily (CDA 1998, s. 32(4)). As to the imposition of restraining orders, see **E21.32**. **B2.200**

The Sentencing Council definitive guideline, *Intimidatory Offences* (see Supplement, **SG27-1**) applies in respect of offenders aged 18 and over, sentenced on or after 1 October 2018, irrespective of the date of the offence. The guideline confirms earlier practice that, when sentencing for the racially aggravated form of an offence, the sentencer should indicate the appropriate sentence for the offence in the absence of racial aggravation and then determine the appropriate uplift for the racial or religious aggravation.

Course of Conduct Causing Fear on at least Two Occasions

As to the meaning of 'course of conduct', see **B2.185**. In *R (A) v DPP* [2004] EWHC 2454 (Admin), it was confirmed that there must be at least two occasions involving threats or other conduct giving rise to the fear of violence. On the other hand, it would be sufficient for this to be a fear of violence on separate and later occasions, as where D tells V, 'I'll come back and get you' (*Qosja* [2016] EWCA Crim 1543, [2017] 1 Cr App R 17 (264) at [34]). **B2.201**

Other Elements of the Offence

'Violence' is not defined in the Act. As to the similar, though not identical, concept defined for the purposes of the POA 1986, see **B11.22** and **B11.42**. **B2.202**

D's conduct must cause the complainant to fear that violence will be used; it is not sufficient for it to frighten the complainant as to what *might* happen (*Henley* [2000] Crim LR 582; *Caurti v DPP* [2001] EWHC Admin 867, [2002] Crim LR 131; *Qosja* [2016] EWCA Crim 1543, [2017] 1 Cr App R 17 (264)). It is always a question of fact (*Caurti*; *R (Simon Howard) v DPP* [2001] EWHC Admin 17) and, whilst it can sometimes be inferred from the evidence, there should, if possible, be direct evidence from the complainant (*R (Simon Howard) v DPP*; *Caurti*).

The s. 4 offence does not in terms require proof of harassment, but it has been interpreted as if it did (*Curtis* [2010] EWCA Crim 123, [2010] 1 Cr App R 31 (457); *Widdows* [2011] EWCA Crim 1500; *Haque* [2011] EWCA Crim 1871, [2012] 1 Cr App R 5 (48)). The prosecution must prove that the conduct in question was targeted at an individual, that it was calculated to produce the consequences described in s. 7 of the Act (alarming the person or causing the person distress) and that it was both oppressive and unreasonable (*Haque* at [70]–[73]). A prosecution under s. 4 is not normally appropriate for use as a means of criminalising conduct, not charged as violence, during incidents in a long and predominantly affectionate relationship in which both parties persisted and wanted to continue (*Widdows* at [29]).

Mens Rea

Protection from Harassment Act 1997, s. 4 **B2.203**

(2) For the purposes of this section, the person whose course of conduct is in question ought to know that it will cause another to fear that violence will be used against him on any occasion if a reasonable person in possession of the same information would think the course of conduct would cause the other so to fear on that occasion.

A direction under s. 4(2) should be routinely given (*Henley* [2000] Crim LR 582). The effect of s. 4(2) is that fear must have been caused on each occasion within the course of conduct (*Kelly v DPP* [2002] EWHC 1428 (Admin)).

Defences

B2.204 **Protection from Harassment Act 1997, ss. 4 and 12**

4.—(3) It is a defence for a person charged with an offence under this section to show that—
(a) his course of conduct was pursued for the purpose of preventing or detecting crime,
(b) his course of conduct was pursued under any enactment or rule of law or to comply with any condition or requirement imposed by any person under any enactment, or
(c) the pursuit of his course of conduct was reasonable for the protection of himself or another or for the protection of his or another's property.

12.—(1) If the Secretary of State certifies that in his opinion anything done by a specified person on a specified occasion related to—
(a) national security,
(b) the economic well-being of the United Kingdom, or
(c) the prevention or detection of serious crime,
and was done on behalf of the Crown, the certificate is conclusive evidence that this Act does not apply to any conduct of that person on that occasion.

In s. 12, 'specified' means specified in the certificate in question (s. 12(2)). A document purporting to be such a certificate is to be received in evidence and, unless the contrary is proved, treated as being such a certificate (s. 12(3)). For consideration of when the course of conduct may be reasonable, see *Kellett v DPP* [2001] EWHC Admin 107 and **B2.191**. The imposition of a legal burden upon D may be open to challenge in the light of the human rights cases on the 'reverse burden' (see **F3.7**).

OFFENCE OF STALKING INVOLVING FEAR OF VIOLENCE OR SERIOUS ALARM OR DISTRESS

B2.205 **Protection from Harassment Act 1997, s. 4A**

(1) A person ('A') whose course of conduct—
(a) amounts to stalking, and
(b) either—
(i) causes another ('B') to fear, on at least two occasions, that violence will be used against B, or
(ii) causes B serious alarm or distress which has a substantial adverse effect on B's usual day-to-day activities is guilty of an offence if A knows or ought to know that A's course of conduct will cause B so to fear on each of those occasions or (as the case may be) will cause such alarm or distress.

(2) For the purposes of this section A ought to know that A's course of conduct will cause B to fear that violence will be used against B on any occasion if a reasonable person in possession of the same information would think the course of conduct would cause B so to fear on that occasion.

(3) For the purposes of this section A ought to know that A's course of conduct will cause B serious alarm or distress which has a substantial adverse effect on B's usual day-to-day activities if a reasonable person in possession of the same information would think the course of conduct would cause B such alarm or distress.

The CDA 1998, s. 32, has been amended to create a racially or religiously aggravated form of this offence. For the meaning of 'racially or religiously aggravated', see **B11.145**.

Procedure and *Alternative* Verdicts

B2.206 The basic offence is triable either way (Protection from Harassment Act 1997, s. 4A(5)). The aggravated form of the offence is triable either way. As to the procedure on charging both the basic and aggravated offence, see *Henderson v CPS* [2016] EWHC 464 (Admin), [2016] 1 WLR 1990, discussed at **B11.46**.

By virtue of s. 4A(7), on trial on indictment, if the jury find D not guilty of the offence under s. 4A, they may find D guilty of an offence under s. 2 or 2A (see **B2.181** and **B2.194**).

Sentence (Basic Offence)

The maximum penalty is ten years, a fine or both on indictment; six months, an unlimited fine or both, summarily (Protection from Harassment Act 1997, s. 4A(5) and (6)). As to the imposition of restraining orders, see **E21.32**. The Sentencing Council definitive guideline, *Intimidatory Offences* (see Supplement, **SG27-1**) applies in respect of offenders aged 18 and over, sentenced on or after 1 October 2018, irrespective of the date of the offence. In respect of breach of a restraining order, the Sentencing Council definitive guideline, *Breach Offences* (see Supplement, **SG15-6**) applies to all offenders aged 18 and over sentenced on or after 1 October 2018, irrespective of the date of the offence. The Sentencing Council definitive guideline, *Domestic Abuse* (see Supplement, **SG6-1**), may be of assistance when sentencing for this offence. **B2.207**

Racial or religious aggravation cannot normally be taken into account by the sentencer when sentencing for the basic offence of harassment (see **B2.3**). See **E1.19** for increase in sentence, under the CJA 2003, s. 146, for aggravation relating to disability, sexual orientation or transgender identity.

In *McNeill* [2019] EWCA Crim 1566, the Court of Appeal dismissed D's appeal against her sentence of nine years' imprisonment for a number of offences, including four grave s. 4A offences and breaches of numerous restraining orders. The Court agreed (at [14]) with the trial judge that D's conduct amounted to 'one of the most serious cases of stalking in breach of a restraining order that there can be'. D (aged 74) subjected her various victims to a vicious and prolonged course of harassment and lies, which included publishing and circulating unfounded allegations of depraved child abuse. The Court quoted (at [9]) this passage from the judge's sentencing remarks:

> The direct consequence of your actions is that for the four families concerned in counts 1 to 4 you have ruined all normal family life. Their children have been unable to attend school normally, and are either home-schooled, or have to carry tracking devices and alarms. The families have escape routes planned in case of attack. Mothers have slept on the floors of their children's bedrooms to protect them. They have had to move home. They have had businesses ruined as a result of being unable to have an online profile. As if that is not bad enough, for the children they will never, as things stand at the moment, be able to go online and put their own names in online without seeing the vile filth that you have peddled over a period of years.

Sentence (Racially or Religiously Aggravated Form of Offence)

The Sentencing Council definitive guideline, *Intimidatory Offences* (see Supplement, SG27-1) applies in respect of offenders aged 18 and over, sentenced on or after 1 October 2018, irrespective of the date of the offence. The guideline confirms earlier practice that, when sentencing for the racially aggravated form of an offence, the sentencer should indicate the appropriate sentence for the offence in the absence of racial aggravation and then determine the appropriate uplift for the racial or religious aggravation. **B2.208**

Elements

For the meaning of 'course of conduct' for the purposes of s. 4A(1), see s. 7(3) and (4) at **B2.185**. As to fear of violence on at least two occasions, see **B2.201** *et seq.*; *Qosja* [2016] EWCA Crim 1543, [2017] 1 Cr App R 17 (264) and *Pendlebury v DPP* [2018] EWHC 3567 (Admin), in which Irwin J said (at [29]): 'It is not enough to establish that conditions existed which might reasonably have engendered a fear of violence… The [court or jury] must be sure that such a fear was actually engendered.' **B2.209**

Some of the criticism that may be levelled against the offence under s. 2A (see **B2.196**) applies equally to the s. 4A offence. In large part, it is merely the existing s. 4 offence with the added requirement of stalking. But s. 4A(1)(b)(ii) is significant, and may sometimes enable the s. 4A offence to be proved where the s. 4 offence could not be.

Defence

B2.210 **Protection from Harassment Act 1997, s. 4A**

(4) It is a defence for A to show that—
 (a) A's course of conduct was pursued for the purpose of preventing or detecting crime,
 (b) A's course of conduct was pursued under any enactment or rule of law or to comply with any condition or requirement imposed by any person under any enactment, or
 (c) the pursuit of A's course of conduct was reasonable for the protection of A or another or for the protection of A's or another's property.

HARASSMENT OF A PERSON IN HIS HOME

Definition

B2.211 **Criminal Justice and Police Act 2001, s. 42A**

(1) A person commits an offence if—
 (a) that person is present outside or in the vicinity of any premises that are used by any individual ('the resident') as his dwelling;
 (b) that person is present there for the purpose (by his presence or otherwise) of representing to the resident or another individual (whether or not one who uses the premises as his dwelling), or of persuading the resident or such another individual—
  (i) that he should not do something that he is entitled or required to do; or
  (ii) that he should do something that he is not under any obligation to do;
 (c) that person—
  (i) intends his presence to amount to the harassment of, or to cause alarm or distress to, the resident; or
  (ii) knows or ought to know that his presence is likely to result in the harassment of, or to cause alarm or distress to, the resident; and
 (d) the presence of that person—
  (i) amounts to the harassment of, or causes alarm or distress to, any person falling within subsection (2); or
  (ii) is likely to result in the harassment of, or to cause alarm or distress to, any such person.
(2) A person falls within this subsection if he is—
 (a) the resident,
 (b) a person in the resident's dwelling, or
 (c) a person in another dwelling in the vicinity of the resident's dwelling.
(3) The references in subsection (1)(c) and (d) to a person's presence are references to his presence either alone or together with that of any other persons who are also present.

'Dwelling' has the same meaning as in the POA 1986, Part 1 (s. 42A(7)). D ought to know that D's presence is likely to result in the harassment of, or to cause alarm or distress to, a resident if a reasonable person in possession of the same information would think that D's presence was likely to have that effect (s. 42A(4)).

Procedure and Sentence

B2.212 Offences under s. 42A are triable summarily (CJPA 2001, s. 42A(4)). The maximum penalty is imprisonment for six months, or an unlimited fine or both. There is no offence-specific guideline but the Sentencing Council's *General Guideline: Overarching Principles* (see Supplement, SG2-1) is used for all offenders sentenced on or after 1 October 2019.

Section B3 Sexual Offences

INTRODUCTION

The SOA 2003 represented the most important overhaul of the law governing sexual offences since at least Victorian times. Some offences were swept away, others were redefined and many new ones were created. Part 1 of the Act created over 50 offences. Some carry different sentences depending upon the precise factual ingredients proved, which in accordance with the decision in *Courtie* [1984] AC 463 means they actually create even more offences. The Sexual Offences Act 2003 (Commencement Order) 2004 (SI 2004 No. 874) brought the Act fully into force on 1 May 2004. **B3.1**

Section 141 empowered the Secretary of State to make transitional provisions, but no such provisions have been made. It followed that, where there was doubt as to whether an offence of rape occurred before or after the coming into force of the SOA 2003, the prosecution failed because it could not be proved whether a statutory offence was committed under the old or the new law (*A (Prosecutor's Appeal)* [2005] EWCA Crim 3533, [2006] 1 Cr App R 28 (433); *Newbon* [2005] Crim LR 738; *F* [2008] EWCA Crim 994). The lacuna was addressed in the VCRA 2006, s. 55. This deeming provision covers the situation where D is charged in respect of the same conduct both with an offence under the SOA 2003 and an offence under the old law, and the only thing preventing D being found guilty of the 2003 Act offence or the offence under the old law is the fact that it has not been proved beyond a reasonable doubt that the time when the conduct took place was either after the coming into force of the SOA 2003 or before the repeal of the old law. In such circumstances, for the purpose of determining guilt, it will be conclusively presumed that the time when the conduct took place was when the old law applied if the offence attracted a lesser maximum penalty; otherwise it will be presumed the conduct took place after the implementation of the new law. Where the evidence is likely to be unclear as to whether the offence should be charged under the old or new law, in order to rely upon s. 55 each offence should be charged in the alternative under the new regime and the old (*Chaney* [2009] EWCA Crim 21, [2009] 1 Cr App R 35 (512); *F* [2008] EWCA Crim 994). Adopting a procedural device with the particulars of an offence under both the old and new law in the same count is not an appropriate solution. Such a count would be duplicitous and would impede the proper working of s. 55; directions to the jury would be difficult, if not impossible (*Marshall* (2 December 2009 unreported, Woolwich Crown Court)).

In *Stocker* [2013] EWCA Crim 1993, [2014] 1 Cr App R 18 (247) D was convicted under the wrong statute in that the statement of offence of rape referred to the SOA 1956, s. 1(1), when the offence was committed in 2008 and the SOA 2003 applied. The Court of Appeal treated this mistake as a purely technical defect. From the beginning to the end of the process the charge was, in substance, one of rape under the SOA 2003. For helpful discussion as to the implications of drafting errors in a sexual offence case, see *AD* [2016] EWCA Crim 454, [2016] 2 Cr App R 18 (241). See also *Coatman* [2017] EWCA Crim 392, [2018] 1 Cr App R 19 (289) where the Court of Appeal found a serious error of substance which fundamentally undermined both counts upon which D was convicted. For further discussion in respect of indictment errors see **B3.392**.

B3.2 For the old law, which continues to apply to offences committed before 1 May 2004, see **B3.372** and the 2004 edition of this work.

SENTENCING UNDER THE SEXUAL OFFENCES ACT 2003

Adults

B3.3 The Sentencing Council's definitive guideline, *Sexual Offences*, applies in respect of the sentencing of offenders aged 18 and older convicted of sexual offences who are sentenced on or after 1 April 2014 (see Supplement, **SG31-1**). It follows that the guideline applies to sexual offences committed before the implementation of the SOA 2003. For sentencing in respect of historic sexual offences see **B3.373**.

The guideline focuses on the extent of the harm to the victim rather than on the nature of the particular physical activity. It uses a number of models for addressing harm and culpability, each different from the model used in the previous guideline. The model used for the majority of offences, including rape and sexual assault, has a lowest level (a baseline) where inherent harm and culpability are assumed.

As to sentences of imprisonment, discretionary life sentences, sentences of detention for life, automatic life sentences and extended sentences, see **E4** and **E5**.

The Sentencing Council took the view that the guideline is concerned with sentencing levels for a single offence, adopting a different approach from the previous SGC guideline which placed repeated rape of the same victim *or* rape involving multiple victims in the category with the highest starting point. However, for cases involving a campaign of rape see **B3.24**.

B3.4 **Dangers of Double Counting** *Forbes* [2016] EWCA Crim 1388, [2017] 1 WLR 53 provides guidance in respect of the use of the guidelines in sexual offences generally. The Court of Appeal stressed that when aggravating features come to be considered, it is essential that the court avoids double counting by bearing in mind that the starting points will reflect the essential gravity of the offence in question.

Assessment of Harm Caused

B3.5 To determine the degree of harm, reference should be made only to the factors set out in the harm table in the guideline. The Court of Appeal has provided further guidance in respect of some of these factors.

B3.6 **Existence of Extreme Category 2 Factors** The guideline relating to offences of rape states that the extreme nature of one or more category 2 factors or the extreme impact caused by a combination of category 2 factors may elevate a case to category 1. Category 2 factors include prolonged detention, sustained incident, violence or threats of violence beyond that which is inherent in the offence as well as forced uninvited entry into V's home. All these factors existed in *Mamaliga* [2018] EWCA Crim 515, which involved a planned sexual attack by two brothers on a woman who lived on a narrowboat. The Court of Appeal concluded that in view of the extreme nature of the category 2 factors, the case should have been categorised in category 1.

Sustained Incident The concept of 'sustained incident' is found throughout the sentencing guidelines as an indicator of the measure of harm. It is relevant to all offences covered by the SOA 2003, ss. 1 to 8. In *KC* [2019] EWCA Crim 1632, [2020] 1 Cr App R (S) 41 (296) the Court of Appeal considered the meaning of 'sustained incident' when deciding that the trial judge had been wrong to decide that three separate assaults by penetration of a child aged seven to eight, contrary to the SOA 2003, s. 6, with significant time elapsing between each assault, amounted to a sustained incident. The Court observed that the guidelines refer to an 'incident', and not 'incidents'. An incident can refer to a single episode set in its surrounding circumstances or to a single episode of some duration within which one assault might take place, such as in *Mamaliga*. The Court concluded that the facts that over a period of years D remained in a position of trust in relation to V and was sharing the same home with him were not sufficient, individually or collectively, without more, to create the continued linkage needed to make the three assaults a single incident. This was to be contrasted with *Mamaliga* where the defendants were convicted of multiple violent rapes and assaults in an episode lasting about 25 minutes, leading the Court on an A-G's reference to describe that incident as 'sustained'. In *KC* the Court also drew support for its conclusion from the fact that the expression 'sustained incident' appears in the guidelines as part of the expression 'prolonged detention/sustained incident' and the two phrases are clearly intended to be similar or analogous. **B3.7**

Severe Psychological or Physical Harm In *Forbes* [2016] EWCA Crim 1388, [2016] 2 Cr App R (S) 44 (472), Lord Thomas CJ observed (at [25]) that a judge who has heard evidence from the victims will be well placed to make an assessment of the effect of the offending upon them. It follows that it is not essential for there to be a psychiatric or psychological report before the court for a judge to find severe psychological harm. **B3.8**

However, while acknowledging that the effect of such offending can be devastating upon victims, the Court made it clear that it must be borne in mind, so that double counting is avoided, that the starting points and sentencing ranges provide for the effect upon the victim which is the inevitable effect of this type of serious criminal behaviour. There must be significantly more before harm is taken into account as a distinct and further aggravating factor and/or before a judge makes a finding of extremely severe psychological or physical harm so as to justify placing the offence in the top category of harm.

In *Chall* [2019] EWCA Crim 865, [2019] 2 Cr App R (S) 44 (344), the Court of Appeal considered five otherwise unconnected cases which raised a common issue as to the approach a sentencing judge should take when assessing, for the purposes of a relevant sentencing guideline, whether a victim of crime has suffered severe psychological harm. The Court confirmed that expert evidence is not an essential precondition of a finding that a victim has suffered severe psychological harm. A judge may assess that such harm has been suffered on the basis of evidence from the victim, including evidence contained in a victim personal statement, and may rely on observation of the victim while giving evidence. Whether a victim personal statement provides evidence which is sufficient for a finding of severe psychological harm depends on the circumstances of the particular case. The Court accepted the submission that, in assessing whether the psychological harm in a particular sexual case is severe, a judge must keep in mind that the levels of sentence which the definitive guidelines set out already take into account the psychological harm that is inherent in the offence.

It is clear from *Nasir* [2015] EWCA Crim 1604 that the harm can be aggravated by the impact upon V and V's family within the particular community. That does not mean that offences are aggravated by reason of V's ethnic and religious origins.

Victim is Particularly Vulnerable Due to Personal Circumstances In *A-G's Ref (No. 51 of 2015) (Whitmore)* [2015] EWCA Crim 1699, the Court of Appeal explained the potential width of the category 2 factor which features in all non-consensual sexual offences ('victim is particularly vulnerable due to personal circumstances') in that it is not qualified by a requirement of something such as permanent disability. It includes temporary circumstances such as a young female who is alone at night and very intoxicated. See, e.g., *Sepulvida-Gomez* [2019] EWCA **B3.9**

Crim 2174, [2020] 4 WLR 11, where the Court of Appeal held that the judge had been right to find that the complainant was 'particularly vulnerable due to personal circumstances' where she had drunk a half bottle of wine, was asleep in her boyfriend's room and therefore defenceless. It followed that the case was correctly placed in category 2B harm in respect of assault by penetration and sexual assault, although when compared to some cases in category B it would be at the lower end of the category. See also *A-G's Ref (No. 122 of 2015) (Patton)* [2016] EWCA Crim 392, where the Court made it clear that the fact that D may have been so drunk as to be unable to recognise that V was incapable of giving consent does not provide any mitigation. For an example of the Court of Appeal distinguishing between a victim who was *vulnerable* but not *particularly vulnerable* as contemplated by the harm aspect of the guideline, see *GK* [2020] EWCA Crim 197.

Assessment of Culpability

B3.10 Similarly, to assess the culpability level reference should only be made to the exhaustive list of factors set out in the table in the guideline. Again the Court of Appeal has provided guidance on some of these factors.

B3.11 **Significant Degree of Planning** A finding of a significant degree of planning is a category A factor. Context is all-important when determining whether there was a significant degree of planning as determinative of culpability.

While each case is fact-specific, it is clear that there does not need to be an element of sophistication in D's conduct for there to have been a significant degree of planning. In *Teklu* [2017] EWCA Crim 1477, [2018] 1 Cr App R (S) 12 (64) the Court of Appeal held that 'significant' is not an absolute concept. In the context of sexual assault, which could be committed without 'implements' or tools or any sophisticated planning, the Court considered that lying in wait in a position designed to prey on lone young women on their way home from a night out did involve a significant degree of planning. In contrast, in *Dogra* [2019] EWCA Crim 145 the Court of Appeal was not convinced that the case could be categorised by the factor 'a *significant* degree of planning' as determinative of culpability even though D had embarked upon a calculated and protracted pursuit of V. Accordingly, the case fell in the culpability B category. D had been convicted of one offence of rape, two offences of assault by penetration and one offence of causing a person to engage in sexual activity without consent, all arising from the same incident. He received an extended sentence of 15 years' imprisonment, comprising a 13-year term and a two-year extension period. D pursued his victim for three-quarters of a mile after seeing her at the railway station. He then attacked her, dragging her to some nearby woodland. He threatened to stab her if she did not comply with his directions and then committed the offences. However, the Court was influenced by the fact that there was no evidence that, before D saw V, D was thinking in terms of carrying out a sexual attack. It concluded that the case fell in culpability category B. Nevertheless, in the light of the lengthy and determined pursuit and the terrifying attack, the sentence imposed by the judge was not manifestly excessive.

B3.12 **Abuse of Trust** Taking advantage of a relationship to commit an offence may have already been taken into account in the selection of a starting point; the Court of Appeal in *Forbes* [2016] EWCA Crim 1388, [2017] 1 WLR 53 explained that something more is therefore required to establish abuse of trust as a separate aggravating factor or to justify placing the offence in a particular category of culpability. What is necessary is a close examination of the facts and clear justification given if abuse of trust is to be found. While acknowledging that in the colloquial sense the children's parents would have trusted a cousin, other relation or a neighbour, as in *Forbes* and *Farlow* (conjoined appeal), to behave properly towards their young children, the Court stressed that the phrase 'abuse of trust', as used in the guideline, connotes something more than that. The mere fact of association or the fact that one sibling is older than another does not necessarily amount to breach of trust in this context. The phrase plainly includes teachers, priests and scoutmasters who have children in their charge. The Court indicated that it may also include parental or quasi-parental relationships or arise from an *ad hoc* situation, e.g., where a late night taxi driver takes a lone female fare.

For instance, in *W* [2018] EWCA Crim 2657, a reference by the Solicitor General, the Court of Appeal observed that while the mere fact of a familial relationship will not necessarily impose a position of trust, on the facts of the case it undoubtedly did arise. D was the 33-year-old uncle and carer of V who was then aged eight. V's parents trusted D to look after V when she visited his house or other members of the family. By way of contrast, in *A-G's Ref (D)* [2017] EWCA Crim 2509, [2018] 1 Cr App R (S) 47 (356) D had committed numerous sexual offences, including rape, against his cousins over a number of years when aged 18 to 26 and while living in the family home, being treated like a brother and a son. At the reference hearing, the A-G accepted that the Recorder had fallen into error in that the offences could not properly be described as involving an element of breach of trust, given that familial sexual offences by an older member of the family against a younger member did not, for that reason alone, involve a breach of trust.

AH [2017] EWCA Crim 117 is a good illustration of a case where the Court of Appeal, adopting the approach of Lord Thomas CJ in *Forbes* [2016] EWCA Crim 1388, [2017] 1 WLR 53 (see **B3.4** ***et seq.***), concluded that a case could not be characterised as one where there was 'a very clear' breach of trust. D pleaded guilty to one count of inciting a child to engage in sexual activity, contrary to the SOA 2003, s. 10. V was D's niece. When she was aged 13, D sent her a Facebook message requesting a picture of her breasts and making suggestive remarks. He desisted and apologised when V stated that he was asking for 'too much information'. When dealing with the issue of breach of trust, Hadden-Cave J, giving the judgment of the Court, stated that care needs to be taken to distinguish between three different situations: (a) being placed in a specific position of trust vis-à-vis a child (and exploiting that situation); (b) being generally 'trusted' by a child because of a particular familial or other relationship (and exploiting that relationship); and (c) simply using the opportunity for association with a child that a familial or other relationship affords. In *AH*, close examination of the facts did not suggest that the familial relationship played a significant role in the abuse, save simply to give D the opportunity to initiate an inappropriate conversation with V on Facebook, she having invited him to join as a friend (i.e. situation (c) above).

In *O (D)* [2014] EWCA Crim 2202, [2015] 1 Cr App R (S) 41 (299) the Court of Appeal considered whether the broad nature of the term abuse of trust required that a rape within a relationship would automatically constitute an abuse of trust such as to bring the case within culpability category A. It was held that the term could include circumstances where D may not hold a formal position in relation to V, but had abused the trust engendered by status and/or standing. However, in *O (D)*, the fact that the rape took place within a relationship was not sufficient for the offence to represent an abuse of trust, albeit it did constitute a gross betrayal which was itself an aggravating factor.

Good Character and/or Exemplary Conduct While this factor features in the guideline as a mitigating factor, it is subject to two forms of explanatory wording providing guidance as to how judges should reflect good character in sentence. Where the offence carries a statutory maximum under 14 years, the guideline states: **B3.13**

> Previous good character/ exemplary conduct is different from having no previous convictions. The more serious the offence, the less the weight should normally be attributed to this factor. Where previous good character / exemplary conduct has been used to facilitate the offence, the mitigation should not normally be allowed and such conduct may constitute an aggravating factor.

This would include a defendant who misuses his celebrity status so as to be in a position to commit the offences (*A-G's Ref (No. 38 of 2013) (Hall)* [2013] EWCA Crim 1450, [2014] 1 Cr App R (S) 61 (394)).

Furthermore, where the offence carries a statutory maximum of 14 years or more, 'good character/exemplary conduct should not normally be given any significant weight and will not normally justify a substantial reduction in what would otherwise be the appropriate sentence'.

These principles cannot be avoided by enhancing the value of good character as a mitigating factor by combining it with the courage shown by D pleading guilty (*A-G's Ref (No. 115 of 2014)* [2015] EWCA Crim 200).

B3.14 **Advanced Age as a Mitigating Factor** The increased number of prosecutions for historic sexual offending has led to offenders of advanced age coming before the courts. In *Clarke* [2017] EWCA Crim 393, [2017] 2 Cr App R (S) 18 (140) the Court of Appeal considered two otherwise unconnected cases where offenders aged 101 and 96 with health problems had fallen to be sentenced for sexual offences committed at a time when they were much younger. In each case D was relatively fit for a man of his chronological age.

While acknowledging that old age is a material mitigating consideration, the Court concluded that the focus of the court should be on the extent to which a custodial sentence would be more onerous when compared to a younger, fitter offender. Old age and extreme old age are both relevant aspects of that consideration even in the absence of specific health considerations. However, there was no warrant for treating the aged as akin to terminally ill individuals. Sentencing had to be done on a case-by-case basis with the court requiring evidence and information specific to the particular offender. Furthermore, it would be necessary for D to provide firm evidence that the prison estate was not capable of making adequate provision for elderly offenders.

It is a well-established principle that sentence should not be calculated by reference to early release provisions. D's diminished life expectancy, age, health and the prospect of dying in prison were factors legitimately to be taken into account in passing sentence, but they had to be balanced against the gravity of the offending and the public interest in setting appropriate punishment for very serious crimes. Although courts should make allowance for the factors of extreme old age and health, and although they should give the most anxious scrutiny to those factors, the approach of taking them into account in a limited way was the correct one. While such a conclusion left open the possibility that offenders might die in prison, the Court drew attention to the CJA 2003, s. 248, which granted the Secretary of State power to release a prisoner on compassionate grounds where exceptional circumstances exist to justify it.

Children and Young People

B3.15 The definitive guideline, *Sentencing Children and Young People* (see Supplement, **SG8-1**), applies to all offenders under the age of 18 who are sentenced on or after 1 June 2017, regardless of the date of the offence. It supersedes part 7 of the original 2007 guideline. It considers background factors that may have played a part in leading a child or young person to commit a sexual offence (at p. 36). These may assist in respect of the assessment of the offender's maturity, as opposed to chronological age, at Step One (at p. 37), the seriousness of the offending in respect of non-exhaustive mitigating factors at Step Two (at p. 38), or personal mitigation at Step Three (at p. 39). At Step Five, the court must review the sentence to ensure it is the most appropriate one for the child or young person. This will include an assessment of the likelihood of reoffending and the risk of causing serious harm.

Even in grave cases the court should consider whether the totality of the sentence reflects sufficient allowance for D's youth. For a 15-year-old a long sentence will inevitably have a heavier impact than it would for an older person. In *Taylor* [2016] EWCA Crim 2044 the Court of Appeal allowed appeals against sentence of two youths who had been convicted of the rapes of girls aged 11 to 15. D1 (aged 15/16 at the time of the offences) had been sentenced to an extended sentence comprising an 11-year custodial term and a five-year licence period, for one offence of rape and one offence of rape of a child. D2 (aged 14/15 at the time of the offences) had received an extended sentence comprising nine years' detention and five years on licence, for four offences of rape. The appellants were friends and had committed the offences over a ten-month period employing behaviour which ranged from pestering to violence. D1's offences represented a sustained pattern of offending with violence accompanying two of the rapes he perpetrated. The pre-sentence report prepared upon him indicated that he treated females with contempt and as objects for his sexual gratification. His behaviour had been shocking and of the utmost gravity and there had been ample evidence to support the judge's finding that D1 was dangerous. However, the Court also took the view that the totality of the sentence was too burdensome for someone of D1's youth. The sentence was reduced to nine years in detention together with an extended licence of five years. In respect of D2, the Court observed that he had shown a total lack of empathy or remorse and he viewed women in a derogatory fashion. A had committed a terrible catalogue of crime and, as with D1, there had been ample evidence that he was dangerous. However, the judge had also paid insufficient regard to his age. The sentence was reduced to seven years in detention together with an extended licence of five years.

In *PS* [2019] EWCA Crim 2286, [2020] 2 Cr App R (S) 9 (56), the Court of Appeal considered three cases, otherwise unconnected, which raised issues about the proper approach to sentencing offenders who suffer from autism or other mental health conditions or disorders. When giving judgment, Lord Burnett of Maldon CJ referred to the guideline, *Overarching Principles: Sentencing Children and Young People* (see Supplement, **SG8-3**) and the offence-specific guideline, *Sexual Offences* (see Supplement, **SG8-10**), which make it clear that, when sentencing offenders aged under 18, a number of considerations come into play that differ from those relating to adults. Both guidelines required a careful assessment of CF as a young offender with particular difficulties including mental health concerns and learning disabilities. The Court stated that it was inappropriate in CF's case to assess the length of sentence largely by reference to an adult offence-specific guideline for an offence which can only be committed against a child under 13 where the sentencing levels take into account the inevitable difference in age between adult offender and child victim.

Section 13 of the SOA 2003 (which has the effect that for offences contrary to ss. 9 to 12, the maximum sentence for a young offender is limited to five years' custody, rather than the 14 and ten-year maxima applicable to adult offenders) represents statutory recognition that when dealing with sexual offending, the court must be careful not to treat the young offender as simply a reduced-size version of an adult offender committing similar offences.

CF provides a highly instructive illustration as to how a young offender's mental disorder, as well as developmental age and maturity, may be important factors when assessing culpability for sexual offending. The Court of Appeal considered that CF's mental health significantly reduced his culpability. CF had pleaded guilty to seven sexual offences committed when he was aged 15 or 16 against three other children who, although a few years younger than him, were his friends. The Court took the view that the nature of the offending was suggestive of inappropriate sexual experimentation by an immature and vulnerable offender. The expert view that CF's behaviour fitted a diagnosis of Autism Spectrum Disorder, his vulnerability and his intellectual limitations were important factors in relation to culpability. Insufficient weight had been given to CF's mental disorder and intellectual problems in determining the length of sentence. Even after the decision had been properly reached that a custodial sentence was unavoidable, the evidence of CF's mental disorder was an important factor which made it necessary to give less weight to the guidelines appropriate for adult offenders and more weight to the individual circumstances of the young offender's case. Moreover, CF's developmental age and maturity were important factors. Accordingly, a total sentence of five years' detention pursuant to the PCC(S)A 2000, s. 91, was reduced to two and a half years' detention. See **B3.102** for greater detail in respect of the offences to which s.13 applies and **B3.124** for explanation of the SOA 2003, s. 13.

Presumptions and Alternative Verdicts

In relation to rape (SOA 2003, s. 1), assault by penetration (s. 2), sexual assault (s. 3) and causing a person to engage in sexual activity without consent (s. 4), presumptions as to consent and/or reasonable belief as to consent may apply. They do not apply to inchoate offences. However, the evidential presumptions about consent (s. 75) arise very rarely in practice as in most cases it is likely that sufficient evidence will be adduced, from whatever source, to raise an issue as to consent and reasonable belief as to consent. A s. 75 presumption must not be elevated into a conclusive presumption (*Shanjil Zhang* [2007] EWCA Crim 2018; *White* [2010] EWCA Crim 1929). In contrast, s. 76 creates conclusive presumptions. However, essentially the s. 76 presumptions replicate the previous common law (with some limited extension) as to deception as to the nature or **B3.16** purpose of the act, and impersonation, and so will rarely be triggered (see *Jheeta* [2007] EWCA Crim 1699, [2007] 2 Cr App R 34 (477), *Bingham* [2013] EWCA Crim 823, [2013] 2 Cr App R 29 (307) and *Devonald* [2008] EWCA Crim 527 at **B3.45** ***et seq.***). These presumptions are dealt with fully in relation to rape and cross-referenced in respect of the other offences to which they apply. Beyond the limited type of case where s. 76 arises, and assuming that s. 75 has no application, the issue of consent has to be addressed in the context of s. 74 (see **B3.29**).

The issue of alternative offences and included offences is covered at **B3.355** and referred to throughout the text. If the jury are not sure that there was penile penetration, they may nevertheless return a verdict of guilty of attempted rape if D's conduct amounted to more than mere preparation and he had the requisite intent (*A-G's Ref (No. 1 of 1992)* [1993] 2 All ER 190). Nor is it necessary that D should have done an act of an unequivocally sexual nature (*Patnaik* [2000] 3 Arch News 2, CA). See also *Beaney* [2010] EWCA Crim 2551, where the Court of Appeal substituted a conviction for attempted sexual assault, and *Ferriter* [2012] EWCA Crim 2211, where the Court of Appeal substituted a conviction for sexual assault which had been an alternative on the indictment.

Evidence will often be consistent with both attempted rape and attempted sexual assault. The critical question is whether the evidence, taken at its highest, is capable of sustaining the conviction for the offence charged, and not whether it is consistent with a lesser charge (*Bryan* [2015] EWCA Crim 548).

RAPE

B3.17 Rape is a statutory offence which can be committed by a man upon a woman or another man. It consists of non-consensual vaginal, anal or oral intercourse.

Sexual Offences Act 2003, s. 1

(1) A person (A) commits an offence if—
  (a) he intentionally penetrates the vagina, anus or mouth of another person (B) with his penis,
  (b) B does not consent to the penetration, and
  (c) A does not reasonably believe that B consents.
(2) Whether a belief is reasonable is to be determined having regard to all the circumstances, including any steps A has taken to ascertain whether B consents.
(3) Sections 75 and 76 apply to an offence under this section. Sections 75 and 76 deal with presumptions as to consent.

Procedure

B3.18 Rape is triable only on indictment. As to the classification of the offence for the purpose of listing, see CrimPD XIII, para. B (see Supplement, **CPD.XIII.B**). The presumption that a boy under the age of 14 was incapable of sexual intercourse was abolished by the SOA 1993, s. 1, and does not apply where penetration occurred after 20 September 1993. It continues to apply to rape cases where the offence is alleged to have occurred before that date (*JOC* [2012] EWCA Crim 2458). Where B was under 18 at the time of the offence, the extended jurisdiction provisions of s. 72 apply (see **B3.315**).

The DPP has published guidelines which are designed to set out the approach that prosecutors should take when dealing with child sexual abuse cases (see tinyurl.com/y9pzft7s). For the special protections relating to complainants in sexual cases, see **F7.26**; for special measures, see **D14**.

See **B3.355** for alternative verdicts.

B3.19 Indictment

Statement of Offence

Rape, contrary to section 1 of the Sexual Offences Act 2003.

Particulars of Offence

A, on or about the . . . day of . . . penetrated the [vagina] [anus] [mouth] of V with his penis without her consent and not reasonably believing that V did consent.

Sentencing Guidelines

The maximum penalty for rape, and attempted rape, is life imprisonment (SOA 2003, s. 1(4)). The definitive sentencing guideline, *Sexual Offences* (see Supplement, **SG31-3**), applies to all offenders aged 18 and older, who are sentenced on or after 1 April 2014. The definitive guideline, *Sentencing Children and Young People* (see Supplement, **SG8-3**), applies to all offenders under the age of 18 who are sentenced on or after 1 June 2017, regardless of the date of the offence. It supersedes part 7 of the original 2007 guideline. **B3.20**

The guideline recognises that all rape is extremely harmful to the victim by assuming there is always a baseline of harm. This is reflected in the fact that category 3 harm, the least serious category of rape, reflecting that assumed baseline with none of the stipulated harm and culpability factors present, is five years with a category range of four to seven years (see harm category 3, culpability category B). At the other end of the scale, where the extreme nature or impact of one or more category 2 harm factors has elevated the case into category 1, and this is combined with the presence of one or more culpability A factors, the starting point is 15 years with a category range of 13 to 19 years.

Aggravating and mitigating factors are set out in the guideline, but these are additional to those set out in the *General Guideline: Overarching Principles* (see Supplement, **SG2-4**).

For an example of the application of the sentencing guideline to an offence of rape and the dangers of double counting, see *Carroll* [2014] EWCA Crim 2818, [2015] 1 Cr App R (S) 54 (381).

Form of Penetration and Sex of the Victim Guidance on sentencing in respect of the offences of rape, following the change of definition of that offence in the SOA 2003, was provided by the Court of Appeal in *A-G's Ref (No. 104 of 2004) (Garvey)* [2004] EWCA Crim 2672, [2005] 1 Cr App R (S) 117 (666). The Court stated that the starting point for an adult for rape should be the same, whether the penetration was of the vagina, anus or mouth, and whether the victim was male or female. In *Ismail* [2005] EWCA Crim 397, [2005] 2 Cr App R (S) 88 (542), a case of forcible oral sex, the Court of Appeal stressed that for the purposes of sentencing offences of rape under the SOA 2003 no distinction is to be drawn between oral rape and other forms of the offence. **B3.21**

In certain circumstances, the fact that there was no actual penetration will provide little or no mitigation. See, e.g., *Collier* [2013] EWCA Crim 1038, where the overall circumstances included attempted oral and attempted vaginal rape so no allowance was appropriate for the fact that the offences were attempts. However, save where it can exceptionally be said that the attempt is virtually indistinguishable from the full offence or where the nature of the circumstances mean that as much harm was caused as would usually be the case for the full offence, some reduction is normally appropriate to reflect the fact that the offence was an attempt, as the level of sentence is dependent upon harm done (*Cooper* [2014] EWCA Crim 946, where the Court of Appeal observed that typically less harm is done by the attempt than the full offence). See also *Woodland* [2015] EWCA Crim 629, supporting the view that, where A has a positive change of mind and consciously draws back from committing the full offence, a reduction is appropriate, and *C (RA)* [2015] EWCA Crim 1856.

Relationship between Victim and Offender *Millberry* [2002] EWCA Crim 2891, [2003] 2 All ER 939 established the fundamental principle that the same starting point applies for 'relationship rape' or 'acquaintance rape' as for 'stranger rape'. Any rape is a traumatic and humiliating **B3.22**

experience and, although the particular circumstances in which the rape takes place may affect the sentence imposed, the starting point for sentencing should be the same. This principle applies to all non-consensual offences. It follows that marital rape is as serious as other forms of rape. See *Benney* [2010] EWCA Crim 1288 where the Court of Appeal, having acknowledged this principle, went on to reduce the sentence for marital rape on the very specific basis accepted by the prosecution. In *MA* [2012] EWCA Crim 1646 the Court of Appeal, presided over by Lord Judge CJ, roundly rejected a submission that a man who raped his wife should be treated less severely if he came from a culture which instilled in him a belief that he had a right to do so.

B3.23 **Previous Consensual Activity** Previous sexual activity between A and B is not included as a mitigating factor in the non-exhaustive list set out at Step Two. Cases under the old guideline suggest that it may amount to mitigation, but only if there was some level of consensual activity on the same occasion or immediately before the rape. However, the seriousness of the non-consensual act may overwhelm any other consideration. It is important to focus upon the circumstances in which the rape was committed. In *A-G's Ref (No. 77 of 2012)* [2013] EWCA Crim 202, leave to refer a sentence of two years' imprisonment for the rape of the offender's wife was refused. The Court of Appeal described the offence as one occasion of unwanted sexual intercourse during a period of consensual sexual relations. After the offence, and when the offence was known, continuing consensual relations continued over a not inconsiderable period. This case should be treated with care; the Court noted the exceptional circumstances in that there was no evidence of psychological harm nor anger. In *O'Brien* [2006] EWCA Crim 1419, [2007] 1 Cr App R (S) 35 (189) a sentence of six years' imprisonment for anal rape following consensual vaginal sex was reduced to four and a half years on the basis that it was a case of consensual sex which went too far. See also *A-G's Ref (No. 96 of 2006) (Miles)* [2006] EWCA Crim 3251, [2007] 2 Cr App R (S) 30 (170) for a case where intercourse was consensual at the outset.

B3.24 **Highest Suggested Starting Points and Cases More Serious than Envisaged in the Guidelines** Although the top of the category range for a category 1, culpability A single offence of rape is 19 years, the sentencing guideline acknowledges that offences may be of such severity, for example involving a campaign of rape, that sentences of 20 years and above may be appropriate. It is important to remember that this rubric is not confined to 'campaign cases'. For instance, it may apply to very serious offences against a very young victim which are repeated. In *JH* [2015] EWCA Crim 54, [2015] 1 Cr App R (S) 59 (409), the offender had been convicted of five offences of rape and three of indecent assault committed upon his own daughter when she was aged between 11 and 15. The Court of Appeal said that an overall sentence of 22 years' imprisonment was not too long for this series of offences; it was important to focus upon the rubric.

Sentences higher than envisaged in the old guideline have been held by the Court of Appeal to have been appropriate in a number of very grave cases. In *DJ* [2015] EWCA Crim 563, [2015] 2 Cr App R (S) 16 (164) the Court of Appeal reviewed the appropriate level of sentence for campaigns of rape and offending of extreme severity. The earlier decisions in *Watkins* [2013] EWCA Crim 734, [2014] 1 Cr App R (S) 6 (41) and *P (P)* [2009] EWCA Crim 1048 were described as representing cases at the extreme end of the spectrum of offending. Treacy LJ stated that care needs to be taken in relying on phrases such as 'the depths of depravity' as if that established a particular category of offence. He explained that a case may reach the level of utmost seriousness by a variety of routes and the attaching of labels is not a particularly good guide.

In *Bassam Karrar* [2015] EWCA Crim 850, the 'Oxford grooming' case, notional minimum terms significantly above the guideline were upheld by the Court of Appeal; Hallett LJ described the case as one of the worst sexual exploitation cases to come before the courts with men operating in gangs deliberately targeting and grooming vulnerable children both for their own self-gratification and for brutal and humiliating sexual exploitation by others. She saw considerable force in the Crown's submission that this was one of those cases for which the guidelines were not intended and previous decisions would only be of limited assistance.

However, as the Sentencing Council does not provide any additional guidance in respect of what constitutes 'a campaign of rape', the Court of Appeal in *Daniels* [2019] EWCA Crim 948 was invited to bear in mind examples of cases such as *Watkins*; *DJ* [2015] EWCA Crim 563, [2015] 1 Cr App R (S) 16 (164) and *Falder* [2018] EWCA Crim 2514, [2019] 1 Cr App R (S) 46 (309) even though they were not guideline cases and were fact-specific. Furthermore, it was accepted that it would have been helpful if the trial judge had been referred to the cases.

D had been sentenced in October 2017 to an extended determinate sentence consisting of a custodial period of 12 years and an extension period of five years. In December 2018, when D was aged 70, he pleaded guilty to 78 counts in relation to the serious sexual assault of 20 victims. 35 of those counts were multiple incidents. These counts were the subject matter of the reference.

D was a committed paedophile who took advantage of the trust placed in him by parents, systematically abusing 20 children from 13 families over a period of nearly ten years. Most of the children were under ten. He repeatedly raped six of the children vaginally and anally. While there was no challenge to the trial judge's imposition of a life sentence or his general approach, the Court of Appeal found that the minimum term of nine years' imprisonment was unduly lenient in the light of the gravity of the offending, the number of victims and the abundance of aggravating features. When giving her reasoning, Hallett VP observed that as the sentence stood the punitive element was limited to nine years, and then the sole consideration for the Parole Board would be one of dangerousness. Yet under the extended determinate term D had received in October 2017 he would have served just one year less before becoming eligible for parole. An extremely unfortunate anomaly arose because of the different release on licence regimes combined with the fact that the judge had not been able to sentence for the entirety of the offending at the same time. In effect, he would have served an additional two years for an additional 78 offences against 20 child victims.

For further examples of sentences well above the sentencing range in the first bracket of the rape guideline upheld by the Court of Appeal, see *A-G's Ref (No. 27 of 2013) (Burinskas)* [2014] EWCA Crim 334, [2014] 1 WLR 4209 (considering the conjoined case of *C*, involving countless rapes of a step-daughter over a ten-year period) and *A-G's Refs (Nos. 14 and 15 of 2006) (French and Webster)* [2006] EWCA Crim 1335, [2007] 1 All ER 718 (where the Court of Appeal held that the extraordinary and abhorrent features of the case went beyond those envisaged in the guideline cases, combining aggravating features of repeated rape of a victim over a period of time, breach of trust, and the most vulnerable victim possible — a baby).

Life Imprisonment: Automatic and Discretionary Life Sentences Following the implementation of the LASPO 2012, discretionary life sentences and sentences of detention for life remain available for an offender convicted of a serious offence, where the court is of the opinion the offender is dangerous, the offence carries life imprisonment as a possible sentence, and the court considers that the seriousness of the offence, or the offence and one or more offences associated with it, is such as to justify the imposition of a sentence of imprisonment (or detention) for life. See *Saunders* [2013] EWCA Crim 1027, [2014] 1 Cr App R (S) 45 (258), for an explanation from Lord Judge CJ of the impact of the removal of IPP as a sentencing option, and *A-G's Ref (No. 27 of 2013) (Burinskas)* [2014] EWCA Crim 334, [2014] 1 WLR 4209, in which Lord Thomas CJ observed that it was inevitable that the application of the CJA 2003, s. 225, would lead to the imposition of life sentences in circumstances where previously the sentence would have been one of IPP. It is what Parliament intended and also ensures (as Parliament also intended), so far as is possible, the effective protection of the public. There will be cases where an extended sentence which requires an offender's release at the end of the custodial term will not adequately protect the public. *Burinskas* provides an example of a serious rape involving a sustained attack by a very dangerous man on a vulnerable woman at night where the Court of Appeal decided an extended sentence would not provide adequate protection of the public. Even assuming there would be long-term work done in prison, it was not possible to say with any confidence that the offender B3.25

would no longer be dangerous after the custodial term of an extended sentence. The conjoined appeal of *Phillips* provides a further example where the Court upheld a life sentence in respect of a rape upon a former partner which was part of a planned sustained campaign of violence designed to take revenge upon her; with a background of previous and violent offending, the Court decided that an extended sentence would not adequately protect the public. In *Arifin* [2018] EWCA Crim 145 the Court of Appeal upheld discretionary life sentences in respect of rapes of two vulnerable victims by a 33-year-old appellant of previous good character. The appellant was also convicted of a sexual assault upon a vulnerable work colleague committed before the rapes. One of the rapes was accompanied by violence over and above that inherent in the offence and it caused severe psychological damage. The appellant also took steps to stop the victim reporting the rape. It fell in category 1B. In addition the Court observed that there was the stark feature of the continuing danger the appellant posed to women and the uncertain duration of that risk. The appellant had been undeterred by the fact that he was on bail for the first rape when he committed the second rape. The trial judge had taken the view that in the light of the defendant's persistent predatory behaviour women could only be protected by a discretionary life sentence. She had been correct to reject the option of an extended sentence.

The Court in *Burinskas* went on to consider the retrospective availability of the 'new' extended sentence under s. 226A for sexual offences in respect of persons aged 18 or over. The extension must be necessary for the period of licence which the court considers necessary for the purpose of protecting the public from serious harm subject to a maximum of eight years for a specified sexual offence. In the conjoined appeal of *C*, it was confirmed that the effect of s. 226A(11) is that the 'new' extended sentence is available provided the necessary conditions are met, even where the offence was committed before 4 April 2005.

In *Saunders* the Court of Appeal held that a life sentence was correctly imposed even though at that time the option of IPP or an extended sentence had been available to the judge. The offender, a photography student aged 23, was sentenced to life imprisonment with a minimum term of eight years for a rape of a child under 13, contrary to the SOA 2003, s. 5. He was given concurrent sentences for various other sexual offences. He had committed truly grave offences against two girls aged eight and six respectively when 'baby sitting' and was plainly dangerous in that he had an entrenched pattern of offending against children.

B3.26 Normally a minimum term should be specified (*Burke* [2008] EWCA Crim 1077). Whole life sentences (no minimum term) are reserved for rare and exceptional cases, and the sentence must be justified by the extreme seriousness of the offence as opposed to the dangerousness of the offender (*Hogg* [2007] EWCA Crim 1357, [2008] 1 Cr App R (S) 22 (99)). That category is most unlikely to include sexual cases, however serious they may be, unless they are combined with homicide. This was confirmed in *Oakes* [2012] EWCA Crim 2435, [2013] QB 979. Researches had revealed that, among the cases where a whole life order had been imposed, none could be found in the context of sexual crime where one or more of the victims had not been murdered. This is well illustrated by the conjoined appeal of *Roberts* where (at [102]) a whole life order was quashed and life with a minimum of 25 years was substituted. *Roberts* was a case of the utmost depravity where women, living alone and no longer young, had been attacked and raped in their own homes. As a result an entire community in South London had been terrified and the last years of the victims' lives had been blighted. It was accepted that this was an extremely serious series of offences in which the interests of public safety amply justified the imposition of a life sentence, but it was successfully argued that the whole life order was inappropriate and wrong in principle.

B3.27 **Automatic Life Sentences** Under the CJA 2003, s. 224A, an automatic life sentence applies to an adult offender convicted of an offence listed in the CJA 2003, sch. 15B, part 1, where the offence was committed after 3 December 2012, and where the sentence condition and the previous offence conditions are met. The offences listed in sch. 15B include many sexual offences. See **E5** for further details.

Actus Reus

Rape, as a principal, can be committed only by a man. A woman who encourages or assists a man to penetrate another person, not reasonably believing the other person is consenting, may be convicted of aiding and abetting rape (*Cogan* [1976] QB 217). B3.28

Section 1 of the SOA 2003 makes clear that the vital ingredients of the *actus reus* consist of penetration by the penis of the vagina, anus or mouth of the complainant, together with the absence of consent of the complainant. 'Vagina' is to be taken as including the vulva (s. 79(9)). The slightest penetration is sufficient. In respect of penetration of the vagina, it is not necessary to show the hymen was ruptured. Whether the defendant ejaculates or not is irrelevant.

A count alleging that A committed rape by penetrating B vaginally or anally is not duplicitous. A jury need to be sure that one of the proscribed orifices has been penetrated. They do not need to be satisfied as to which (*K* [2008] EWCA Crim 1900, [2009] 1 Cr App R 9 (331)).

References to the parts of the body specified above include references to a part surgically constructed (in particular through gender reassignment surgery) (s. 79(3)). The offence thus protects transsexuals but also means that a person who has a surgically constructed penis can commit the offence of rape.

Under the SOA 2003, penile penetration of the mouth without consent constitutes rape, whereas formerly it amounted only to indecent assault.

Penetration is a continuing act from entry to withdrawal (s. 79(2)). It follows that if there is no longer consent to penetration, the man must withdraw (*Kaitamaki v The Queen* [1985] AC 147; *Tarmohammed* [1997] Crim LR 458). If the man is aware that a person has ceased to consent to penetration, he cannot claim that there was a consent to its continuation (*Cooper* [1994] Crim LR 531). In the event of a claim of a mistaken belief that consent persisted, A will be guilty of rape if he did not reasonably believe, having regard to all the circumstances, that B continued to consent (s. 1(2)).

Absence of Consent

Section 74 of the 2003 Act defines consent to the extent that it provides: 'For the purposes of this part, a person consents if he or she agrees by choice and has the freedom and capacity to make that choice'. The definition, with its emphasis on free agreement, is designed to focus upon the complainant's autonomy. It highlights the fact that if a complainant simply freezes with no protest or resistance, this may nevertheless not amount to consent. Violence or the threat of violence is not a necessary ingredient. To have the freedom to make a choice a person must be free from physical pressure, but it remains a matter of fact for a jury as to what degree of coercion has to be exercised upon a person's mind before that person is not agreeing by choice with the freedom to make that choice. Context is all-important. *C* [2012] EWCA Crim 2034 provides a good illustration. It was alleged that the accused had sexually abused the complainant for many years during her childhood. It was also alleged that he raped her in later years, including when she was at university. The complainant's actions in respect of the later counts were consistent with apparent consent. Lord Judge CJ observed that the reality of the case could not be understood without reference to the long years of the complainant's childhood when she was the victim of repeated abuse by the appellant. Evidence of prolonged grooming and potential corruption of the complainant when she was a child provided the context in which the evidence of apparent consent should be examined and assessed. It reflected upon the accused's apparent dominance and control over the complainant. The Court of Appeal approved the judge's direction that the jury could take into account the history of sexual abuse in relation to the later counts if they were sure of the history of sexual abuse. Another instructive case is *Kirk* [2008] EWCA Crim 434 where a vulnerable and destitute 14-year-old girl submitted to sexual intercourse with the appellant accused for money so as to buy food. The accused had abused her in the past. A rape B3.29

conviction (under the 1956 Act) was upheld by the Court of Appeal even though there was no evidence of pressure, threats or deception at the time of the rape. Clearly the result would have been the same under the SOA 2003.

Evidence of grooming may be an important part of the overall context and is likely to be of great relevance as to whether there may have been a genuine consent. In *Robinson* [2011] EWCA Crim 916, also under the old law, the Court of Appeal held that a jury had been entitled to find that a 12-year-old's immaturity, coupled with the evidence of her acquiescence rather than enthusiastic consent (particularly in the context of what could be perceived as grooming), meant that there was no proper consent.

In *Ali (Yasir)* [2015] EWCA Crim 813, [2015] 2 Cr App R (S) 33 (457) the Court of Appeal considered the potential relevance of grooming to the issue of consent in a case where it was alleged that the defendants had targeted vulnerable young teenage girls for the purposes of sexual exploitation; as a result the girls had become sexually compliant and any apparent consent on their part was not genuine or real. The defence contended in respect of one of the complainants, who had not at any stage asserted that she had not consented, that there was clear evidence of consent and that no reasonable jury could conclude that the complainant had not consented, still less that the accused did not reasonably believe she consented. Fulford LJ, in rejecting the defence submissions, commented that, in these circumstances, compliance can mask true lack of consent on the part of the victim. He continued (at [58]):

> Although, as Elias LJ observed [in *Robinson* [2011] EWCA Crim 1916 at [21]], grooming does not necessarily vitiate consent, it starkly raises the possibility that a vulnerable or immature individual may have been placed in a position in which he or she is led merely to acquiesce rather than to give proper and real consent. One of the consequences of grooming is that it has a tendency to limit or subvert the alleged victim's capacity to make free decisions, and it creates the risk that he or she simply submitted because of the environment of dependency created by those responsible for treating the alleged victim in this way. Indeed, the individual may have been manipulated to the extent that he or she is unaware of, or confused about, the distinction between acquiescence and genuine agreement at the time the incident occurred.

Fulford LJ explained that, where grooming is alleged, the question of whether real or proper consent was given will usually be for the jury unless the evidence clearly indicates that proper consent was given. Evidence must be considered in the round and cases should not be withdrawn from the jury because the judge is led artificially to focus on limited areas of the evidence.

B3.30 Consent covers a range of behaviour from whole-hearted enthusiastic agreement to reluctant acquiescence. Context is critical. Where the prosecution allegation of absence of consent is based on lack of agreement without evidence of violence or threats of violence, there will be circumstances, particularly where there has been a consensual sexual relationship between the parties, where a jury will require assistance with distinguishing lack of consent from reluctant but free exercise of choice. A direction along the lines of the direction of Pill J approved in *Zafar* (18 June 1993 unreported, CA: see the *Crown Court Compendium* (July 2020), ch. 20-4, para. 4) may well be appropriate in such circumstances.

In making the distinction care must be used in choice of language. Submission to a demand that a complainant feels unable to resist may in certain circumstances be consistent with reluctant acquiescence (*Watson* [2015] EWCA Crim 559). Similarly, in *Dunbar* [2017] EWCA Crim 469 the trial judge in a rape case had directed the jury that submission by the complainant's own free choice to a demand made physically or in words is not the same as consent. The prosecution case was that the defendant had not listened to the complainant's refusal. She was scared that the defendant would have sex with her forcibly and gave in to his demands. She did not consent at any stage. The defence case was that in response to her request to do so, they had had consensual sex after she had voluntarily undressed. The Court of Appeal took the view that the direction given was unfortunately phrased, but it was used in the sense that the complainant's free choice was overborne, i.e. she did not have a free choice.

Where the prosecution and defence cases are diametrically opposed, e.g., where the prosecution allege a violent rape and the defence case is free agreement without any coercion, such a direction will not be necessary provided the distinction between the respective cases is made clear. In these cases, there is no half-way position. In *Doyle* [2010] EWCA Crim 119, the Court of Appeal described the distinction between (i) reluctant but free exercise of choice, especially in a long-term loving relationship, and (ii) unwilling submission due to fear of worse consequences. The Court upheld a conviction for a violent rape of an ex-girlfriend where the defence case was free agreement and no coercion after the parties had made up. The relationship had been volatile with periods of violence by the accused followed by periods of making up. In his summing up, the judge had distinguished between consent as defined in s. 74 and 'mere submission to something she did not want'. It was argued on appeal that 'submission' was only appropriate in pre-2003 cases and the judge should have given more assistance in the context of a consensual sexual relationship, and he had failed to give any further explanation as to the distinction between 'submission' and consent freely given by choice. The Court rejected these submissions, holding that the judge's directions had made a clear distinction between the prosecution and defence cases. The directions were appropriate in the context of the case and there was no possibility that he might have given the jury the wrong impression or that the jury had convicted the accused on the basis of a misunderstanding between consent and submission.

Capacity to Consent

'Capacity' is an integral part of the definition of consent. A valid consent can be given only by a person who has the capacity to give it. The SOA 2003 does not define capacity. Common-law principles that developed under the old law suggest that a complainant will not have had capacity to agree by choice where her understanding and knowledge were so limited that she was not in a position to decide whether or not to agree (*Howard* (1965) 50 Cr App R 56). This may arise in a variety of different circumstances; for instance, when a complainant is suffering from some forms of mental disorder, very young or intoxicated by alcohol or drugs. These principles still apply under the SOA 2003. **B3.31**

Lack of Capacity Owing to Mental Disorder There is a clear overlap between offences under ss. 30 to 33 (see **B3.180**) and offences under ss. 1 to 4. A person who is 'unable to refuse because of or for a reason related to mental disorder' is likely not to have the capacity to agree by choice, enabling prosecutors to charge a non-consensual offence and rely on s. 74. The narrow interpretation of ss. 30 to 33 by the Court of Appeal in *C* [2008] EWCA Crim 1155, [2009] 1 Cr App R 15 (211) left prosecutors in a position where they might have preferred the option of proceeding under ss. 1 to 4, but the decision in *Cooper* [2009] UKHL 35, [2009] 4 All ER 33 has given a wider interpretation to ss. 30 to 33 (see **B3.181**) and, in any event, the accused's mental element will be easier to prove (see Baroness Hale at [32]). However, there will be cases where a person with a mental disorder either did not have the capacity to agree or may have had the capacity to agree, but, nevertheless, did not freely agree within the meaning of s. 74. In such a case, the prosecution may prefer the option of charging under ss. 1 to 4 (at the very least in the alternative to s. 30). The House of Lords' decision in *Cooper* has not clarified the appropriate direction on capacity in respect of a person with mental disorder charged under s. 1 as the case concerned s. 30. Before *Cooper* it had been thought that where the issue is whether a person with a mental disorder had the capacity to agree by choice, the jury need to consider whether the complainant did not have sufficient knowledge or understanding to comprehend that what was proposed to be done was the physical fact of the penetration of her body by the male organ or, if that is not proved, the sexual nature of the act. See the decision of the Supreme Court of Victoria in *Morgan* [1970] VR 337 as approved by Munby J in *X City Council v MB* [2006] EWHC 168 (Fam) and the Court of Appeal in *Cooper*. In her judgment in the House of Lords in *Cooper*, Baroness Hale did not accept Munby J's line of reasoning (at [24]). Clearly with the definition of capacity in the Mental Capacity Act 2005, ss. 2(1) and 3(1), in mind, she stressed that in order to be able to make a decision a person (a) must be able to understand the information relevant to making it and (b) must be able to weigh that information in the balance to arrive at a choice. A mentally **B3.32**

disordered person might appreciate the sexual nature of the act but not be able to weigh the information in the balance so as to be able to arrive at a choice.

In *IM v LM* [2014] EWCA Civ 37, [2015] Fam 61, the Court of Appeal (Civil Division) explained the apparent different approaches, stating that Munby J was not saying that consideration of the ability to 'weigh' up relevant information had no place in determining capacity to consent to sexual relations. Sir Brian Leveson P also explained the distinction between the general *capacity* to give or withhold consent to sexual relations, which is the necessary forward-looking focus of the Court of Protection, and the person-specific, time and place-specific occasion when that capacity is actually deployed and consent is either given or withheld, which is the focus of criminal law.

In *IM* the Court of Appeal shed light on how the ability to weigh up information should be approached when determining capacity. Section 1(4) of the Mental Capacity Act 2005 provides that a person is not to be treated as unable to make a decision merely because the decision made is unwise. This led Sir Brian Leveson P to observe that the ability to use and weigh information is unlikely to loom large in the evaluation of capacity to consent to sexual relations. He continued:

> It is not an irrelevant consideration; indeed (as we have emphasised) the statute mandates that it be taken into account, but the notional process of using and weighing information attributed to the protected person should not involve a refined analysis of the sort which does not typically inform the decision to consent to sexual relations made by a person of full capacity.

In *JB* [2020] EWCA Civ 735, the Court of Appeal, when dealing with an appeal from the Court of Protection, identified the requirement that in order to have capacity to decide to have sexual relations under the 2005 Act, a person needs to understand that the other person must at all times be consenting to sexual relations.

In most cases where an accused is charged with raping a severely mentally disordered complainant, the test of capacity set out in *Howard* (1965) 50 Cr App R 56 is appropriate (i.e. with no real understanding of what was involved or such limited awareness or understanding as to be in no position to agree, the complainant will have lacked capacity). Where a more refined test is necessary, assistance can be derived from *Avanzi* [2014] EWCA Crim 299, [2014] 2 Cr App R 5 (73), where the Court of Appeal expressed the view that civil and criminal jurisdictions should apply the same test for capacity to consent to sexual relations. The approach should be informed by the definition and guidance contained in the Mental Capacity Act 2005, ss. 2 and 3. That is not to say that a jury will need to be directed in strict accordance with the language used by, and steps to be adopted in accordance with, proceedings brought pursuant to the Mental Capacity Act 2005. Macur LJ adopted the approach in *IM*:

> The question relating to the understanding of reasonable foreseeable consequences obviously should not become divorced from the actual decision-making process carried out in that regard on a daily basis by persons of full capacity. . . . this process is 'largely visceral rather than cerebral, and owes more to instinct and emotion rather than to analysis.'

B3.33 **Capacity Affected by Alcohol and/or Drugs** When summing up the judge should give the jury some assistance with the meaning of 'capacity' in circumstances where a complainant was significantly affected by voluntarily induced intoxication through drink or drugs. The judge should also assist the jury on the issue of whether, and to what extent, they could take that voluntary intoxication into account in deciding whether the complainant had consented. See *Bree* [2007] EWCA Crim 804, [2008] QB 131 and *Coates* [2007] EWCA Crim 1471, [2008] 1 Cr App R 3 (52) at [44] per Sir Igor Judge P. The following points may need to be addressed in the summing-up.

(a) Consumption of alcohol or drugs may cause someone to become disinhibited and behave differently. If she is aware of what is happening, but the consumption of alcohol or drugs has caused her to consent to activity which she would ordinarily refuse, then she has consented despite any later regrets. The fact that a person makes an unwise choice does not connote a lack of capacity to make it. A drunken consent is still a consent if a person has the capacity to make the decision whether to agree by choice.

(b) However, if a complainant becomes so intoxicated as to no longer have the capacity to agree, there will be no consent. Clearly the complainant will not have the capacity to agree by choice when so intoxicated through drink or drugs that her understanding and knowledge are so limited that she was not in a position to decide whether or not to agree. (This relates to understanding and knowledge of what is going on, as opposed to the quality of the decision-making.)
(c) A person may reach such a state without losing consciousness. For instance, a person may not want to take part in any sexual activity with someone, but be incapable of saying so. Alternatively, the person may have been affected to such a degree that, whilst having some limited awareness of what is happening, the person is incapable of making any decision at all.
(d) A person who is asleep or has lost consciousness through drink or drugs cannot consent, and that is so even though the person's body responds to the accused's advances.

See also *Kamki* [2013] EWCA Crim 2335, where the Court of Appeal approved this approach and held that the issues had been correctly addressed in the summing-up.

It remains unnecessary to give a direction on 'capacity' where the complainant's and accused's respective accounts are completely at odds and the issue does not arise from the evidence. In *Wright* [2007] EWCA Crim 3473 the trial judge was held to have correctly summed up the case on the basis that the jury had a stark choice, namely, that either (i) the complainant had been unconscious at the time of sexual intercourse, in which case she had not consented and, if the accused had known of her unconscious state, he would be guilty; or (ii) the complainant had been affected by her own voluntarily induced intoxication, but that she had nevertheless remained capable of choosing whether or not to have intercourse and, in drink, had agreed to do so, in which case the accused would not be guilty.

Hysa [2007] EWCA Crim 2056, a prosecution appeal from a terminating ruling, is a highly instructive example of the principles in operation. A 16-year-old complainant got into a car with three strangers after heavy drinking, and alleged that she was then raped. In the car, the accused asked her for sex. She could not remember her replies, but recalled her jeans being removed and the accused having sex with her. She thought she tried or might have tried to tell him to get off. She did not want to have sex with the accused, did not think she did so willingly and did not think she would have consented to having intercourse in such circumstances. She could not remember what she said to the accused, as she was drunk. When he had finished, one of the other men asked if it was his turn and she said 'No'. In *Hysa* the trial judge acceded to a defence submission of no case to answer, stating that the evidence of the complainant's drunkenness was insufficient to allow a jury to conclude that she lacked the capacity to consent. There was evidence that she had demonstrated capacity to agree or disagree by choice in relation to advances from other men. The evidence of her friends was that, although she was very drunk, she was capable of expressing herself clearly and insisting on doing what she wanted. As to whether she had in fact consented, the complainant's evidence at its highest was that she did not think that she would have done. The prosecution had accepted that she could not say that she had not said 'Yes'. When allowing the appeal and remitting the case back to the Crown Court for the trial to continue, Hallett LJ said (at [34]):

> Issues of consent and capacity to consent to intercourse in cases of alleged rape should normally be left to the jury to determine. It would be a rare case indeed where it would be appropriate for a judge to stop a case in which, on one view, a 16-year-old girl, alone at night and vulnerable through drink, is picked up by a stranger who has sex with her within minutes of meeting her and she says repeatedly she would not have consented in these circumstances.

In an important comment, Hallett LJ stated (at [31]) that it was not fatal to the prosecution case that the complainant did not say 'No' at the moment of initial penetration. There is no requirement that absence of consent has to be demonstrated or communicated to the accused (*Malone* [1998] 2 Cr App R 447). Furthermore, the fact that a complainant cannot remember whether she has consented or not need not be fatal to the prosecution. For an example, see *Tambedou (Seedy)*

[2014] EWCA Crim 954, where the complainant had no recollection whatsoever of having sexual intercourse.

There is also no requirement that the complainant should be incapable of putting up some physical resistance or actually did put up some resistance. A jury is entitled to bear in mind any lies by an accused as to whether or not he had sex with the complainant.

B3.34 Capacity should not be left to the jury when it is not a live issue in the case. For an example of a conviction still being held to be safe even though the judge summed up in relation to capacity when it was not in issue, see *S* [2011] EWCA Crim 2427. When directing a jury as to capacity, there is no obligation to use the words 'a drunken consent is still a consent', provided the critical points have been addressed (*Evans (Chedwyn)* [2012] EWCA Crim 2559).

B3.35 The anachronism that a woman could not in law refuse sexual intercourse with her husband was ended by the House of Lords in *R* [1992] 1 AC 599. The Court of Appeal has since held that a man may properly be convicted of raping his wife even though the offence was committed over 20 years before the final demise of the marital exemption (*C* [2004] EWCA Crim 292, [2004] 1 WLR 2098).

Mens Rea

B3.36 First, the prosecution must prove that the accused intended to penetrate the vagina, anus or mouth of another. Following the reasoning in *Heard* [2007] EWCA Crim 125, [2008] QB 43 in respect of sexual assault, this would seem to be no more than a requirement that the penetration be deliberate (meaning simply voluntarily willed movement), and self-induced intoxication does not provide a defence. In any event, in the vast majority of cases, if penetration is proved there will be no issue as to whether it was intentional. If a defendant is unconscious through sleep, penetration would not be deliberate; however, a jury are likely to have difficulty in accepting that an accused may have been an unconscious participant when penetration has occurred (*F* [2014] EWCA Crim 878, a case under s. 9). Secondly, by virtue of the SOA 2003, s. 1(1)(c), the prosecution must also prove that the accused did not reasonably believe that the complainant was consenting at the time of penetration. Whilst this section reverses the decision in *DPP v Morgan* [1976] AC 182 and abolishes the wholly subjective test for the mental element, the Act does not adopt a test based on what a reasonable man would have believed. The provision focuses upon the belief of the particular accused. Since s. 1(2) provides that regard is to be had to 'all the circumstances, including any steps A has taken to ascertain whether B consents' in determining whether an accused had a reasonable belief, it is clear that a jury may take into account relevant characteristics of the accused, such as extreme youth and a learning disability.

B3.37 In *B (MA)* [2013] EWCA Crim 3, [2013] 1 Cr App R 36 (481) the Court of Appeal has, to some extent, clarified whether a mental disorder that might affect a person's capacity to understand the true nature of a situation may be a relevant characteristic. Delusional thinking, psychotic or otherwise, can never be considered to be reasonable. Such a permissive construction would fly in the face of the legislative intention to reverse the decision of *DPP v Morgan*. The Court of Appeal concluded that, unless and until the state of mind of an accused amounts to insanity in law, beliefs in consent arising from conditions such as delusional psychotic illness or personality disorders must be judged by objective standards of reasonableness and not by taking into account a mental disorder which induced a belief which could not reasonably arise without it. Once a belief could be judged reasonable only by a process which labelled a plainly irrational belief as reasonable, it cannot be open to a jury to conclude that it was reasonable without straying outside the SOA 2003.

The Court did, however, acknowledge that there may be cases in which the personality and abilities of the accused may be relevant to whether the accused's positive belief in consent was reasonable. Cases could arise in which the reasonableness of such belief depends on the reading by the accused of subtle social signals, and in which an impaired ability to do so is relevant. The Court did not attempt exhaustively to foresee the circumstances which might arise in which a belief might be held which is not in any sense irrational even though most people would not have had it.

The Court illustrated the difficulty in identifying the dividing line in such cases. It gave the example of an accused of less than ordinary intelligence or with a demonstrated inability to recognise behavioural cues as possibly such a case. The Court felt that it is possible that beliefs generated by such factors may not properly be described as irrational and might be judged by a jury not to be unreasonable on the particular facts. This has left open the relevance of conditions such as autism spectrum and Asperger's Syndrome, which might lead to an impaired or distorted perception of a complainant's behaviour.

Section 1(2) does not positively require an accused to have taken steps to ascertain whether the complainant consents. However, this is something the jury will consider when considering the reasonableness of the accused's belief. More steps are likely to be expected where there is no established relationship. **B3.38**

Under the old law, rape was held to be a crime of basic intent and self-induced intoxication could not be used as the basis of a denial of *mens rea*. In *Woods* (1982) 74 Cr App R 312, the Court of Appeal held that 'reasonable grounds' under the Sexual Offences (Amendment) Act 1976, s. 1(2), were grounds that would have been reasonable had the accused been sober. See also *Fotheringham* (1989) 88 Cr App R 206. Whilst s. 1(2) does stipulate that whether a person's belief is reasonable is to be determined having regard to all the circumstances, given that the new test has become more objective it is clear that the Court of Appeal's reasoning under the old law continues to apply. Whilst self-induced intoxication may be relevant as to whether an accused may have had a genuine belief that the complainant was consenting, and a drunk person may make a reasonable mistake, it is not a relevant factor when considering whether such a belief may have been reasonable. This approach was confirmed by the Court of Appeal in *Grewal* [2010] EWCA Crim 2448.

In *A-G's Ref (No. 79 of 2006)* [2006] EWCA Crim 2626, [2007] 1 Cr App R (S) 122 (752), the Court of Appeal, when dealing with an application to make a reference, expressed the view that it had doubts about the ruling of the trial judge that it is not a defence to a charge under ss. 1 or 2 of the SOA 2003 if the accused has made a mistake, however reasonable, as to the identity of the person to whom the sexual activity is directed. The judge had felt that he must adopt the narrow view in that the offences related to a named complainant (B), and the requirement in s. 1(2) cannot widen the scope of such consideration so as to allow for the accused's state of mind in relation to any third party. The Court observed that a possible alternative way of dealing with such a very rare set of circumstances would be to hold that the offence is committed if a reasonable (therefore sober) person would have realised that the person being penetrated or sexually touched was not the person whom the accused thought he was consensually penetrating. **B3.39**

A direction upon absence of reasonable belief falls to be given by the judge when, but only when, there is material on which a jury might come to the conclusion that (a) the complainant did not in fact consent, but (b) the accused thought she was consenting. Such a direction is not necessary where prosecution and defence cases on consent are diametrically opposed and there is simply no scope, in the case of either party, for any misunderstanding by the accused as to presence of consent (*Taran* [2006] EWCA Crim 1498).

Where there is a specific allegation of anal rape, and there is a live issue as to whether the penetration of the anus was intentional, the trial judge should direct the jury that the prosecution must establish deliberate penetration of the anus. (Contrast a case where the allegation is that the rape was committed by penetrating the complainant vaginally or anally; see **B3.28**.) In *Gabbai* [2019] EWCA Crim 2287, there was a count alleging anal rape and it was the appellant's case that there had been no anal penetration. However, in evidence the appellant stated that during consensual sexual activity he had intended vaginal penetration, but conceded that he could not entirely exclude the possibility of accidental anal penetration. Accidental penetration could not have formed the basis of a proper conviction and yet when summing up the trial judge failed to include the requirement of intentional anal penetration in the route to verdict. The Court of Appeal concluded that the jury may have missed the importance of the requirement of intentional anal penetration. Furthermore, the omission was of particular significance where the appellant had been acquitted of other counts alleging vaginal rape where the issue was consent.

Evidential Presumptions about Consent

B3.40 The SOA 2003 creates evidential presumptions and conclusive presumptions as to consent and reasonable belief in consent.

B3.41 **Evidential Presumptions** Section 75 of the SOA 2003 lists circumstances in which the complainant is taken not to have consented to the relevant act *unless* sufficient evidence is adduced to raise an issue as to whether the complainant consented. Also the accused is to be taken not to have reasonably believed that the complainant consented *unless* sufficient evidence is adduced to raise an issue as to whether he reasonably believed it (s. 75(1)).

There must be some foundation in the evidence, and it must not be merely speculative or fanciful for there to be sufficient evidence. However, it is vital to understand that if the trial judge decides (presumably at the close of the evidence) that there is sufficient evidence to raise an issue as to whether the complainant consented and/or the accused reasonably believed the complainant was consenting, then the judge will put the issues to the jury in accordance with the key sections (i.e. ss. 74 and 1(2)), and the s. 75 route is barred. In the relatively rare cases where the judge decides that there is not sufficient evidence on one or both of the issues, a s. 75 direction must be given on that issue. The above summary was expressly endorsed by Goldring LJ in *White* [2010] EWCA Crim 1929 at [10].

Section 75 must not be elevated into an irrebuttable presumption (*Kapezi* [2013] EWCA Crim 560). To find absence of consent and/or absence of reasonable belief, the jury have to be sure of three matters: (i) that the accused did the relevant act (in the case of rape, it is the intentional penile penetration of the complainant's vagina, anus or mouth: s. 77) (s. 75(1)(a)); (ii) any of the s. 75(2) circumstances existed; and (iii) the accused knew those circumstances existed (s. 75(1)(c)). It should be noted that where a s. 75 evidential presumption arises there is no question of the issue being removed from the jury. In *Mba* [2012] EWCA Crim 2773 the Court of Appeal upheld a conviction where the trial judge had given both a s. 74 and a s. 75 direction. The Court was not approving a hybrid direction; rather it was considering the safety of the conviction on its own special facts. It follows that trial judges should continue to follow the approach set out in this paragraph as endorsed in *White*.

There will be cases where even though technically s. 75 does not arise, directions following the wording of s. 75 may accurately reflect the reality of the factual dispute the jury have to resolve when deciding between the complainant's and defendant's evidence where they have given two wholly different and conflicting accounts. In *H* [2019] EWCA Crim 1042, the trial judge had directed the jury in line with s. 75(2)(b) on the basis that a person is to be presumed not to be consenting, if at the time of the sexual activity or immediately before it began, the defendant was using violence or was acting in a way that caused the person to fear immediate violence. On appeal it was contended by A that a s. 75 evidential presumption should not have arisen as in both his interview and his evidence A had stated that there was no violence at the time of the sexual activity and that B had consented to all such activity. It followed that sufficient evidence had been adduced to raise an issue as to whether B consented within the meaning of s. 75(1). Furthermore, it was submitted that the presumption had been wrongly elevated by the judge from a rebuttable presumption to an irrebuttable one. The Court of Appeal examined the directions on the law which reflected the stark difference between the prosecution and defence cases, and concluded that the directions were adequate and realistic and tailored to the true issues arising where the prosecution and defence cases had been diametrically opposed. The judge had made it clear to the jury that the issue whether A had used violence towards B immediately before the penetration and threatened her with violence were matters the jury needed to consider, and so he had not elevated the presumption to an irrebuttable presumption. As the judge had explained to the jury it was no part of A's case that if the jury believed B, and therefore disbelieved him, he would be arguing that notwithstanding the violence B still consented. It followed that the issue was not a live one and there was no need to direct the jury on a hypothetical matter.

See *Ciccarelli* [2011] EWCA Crim 2665, [2012] 1 Cr App R 15 (190), for a classic example of a s. 75 presumption arising where there was insufficient evidence that the accused's belief that the complainant was consenting was reasonable. There must be evidence that a belief is reasonable. It follows that an accused's asserted belief may not be sufficient to raise an issue.

The circumstances in which evidential presumptions about consent apply are set out in s. 75(2)(a) to (f). **B3.42**

Sexual Offences Act 2003, s. 75

(2) The circumstances are that—
   (a) any person was, at the time of the relevant act or immediately before it began, using violence against the complainant or causing the complainant to fear that immediate violence would be used against him;
   (b) any person was, at the time of the relevant act or immediately before it began, causing the complainant to fear that violence was being used, or that immediate violence would be used, against another person;
   (c) the complainant was, and the defendant was not, unlawfully detained at the time of the relevant act;
   (d) the complainant was asleep or otherwise unconscious at the time of the relevant act;
   (e) because of the complainant's physical disability, the complainant would not have been able at the time of the relevant act to communicate to the defendant whether the complainant consented;
   (f) any person had administered to or caused to be taken by the complainant, without the complainant's consent, a substance which, having regard to when it was administered or taken, was capable of causing or enabling the complainant to be stupefied or overpowered at the time of the relevant act.

The circumstances set out in s. 75(2) are not exhaustive of the cases where consent will be absent. The categories of threats and behaviour capable of negating consent are wider than the categories to which the presumptions apply. For example, the evidential presumptions under (a) and (b) do not deal with the situation where a complainant fears future as opposed to 'immediate violence' although in such circumstances the complainant may well not be consenting within the definition in s. 74.

Section 75(3) provides that in s. 75(2)(a) and (b) the reference to the time immediately before the relevant act began is, in the case of an act which is one of a continuous series of sexual activities, a reference to the time immediately before the first sexual activity began.

Conclusive Presumptions about Consent In contrast to the rebuttable presumptions of s. 75 of the SOA 2003, s. 76 creates conclusive presumptions. **B3.43**

Sexual Offences Act 2003, s. 76

(1) If in proceedings for an offence to which this section applies it is proved that the defendant did the relevant act and that any of the circumstances specified in subsection (2) existed, it is to be conclusively presumed—
   (a) that the complainant did not consent to the relevant act, and
   (b) that the defendant did not believe that the complainant consented to the relevant act.
(2) The circumstances are that—
   (a) the defendant intentionally deceived the complainant as to the nature or purpose of the relevant act;
   (b) the defendant intentionally induced the complainant to consent to the relevant act by impersonating a person known personally to the complainant.

Section 76 essentially replicates the common law, although both limbs of s. 76(2) in some respects go further. Where the prosecution are able to prove that the accused did the relevant act (in the case of rape, the intentional penile penetration of the complainant's vagina, anus or mouth: s. 77), and either of the circumstances set out in s. 76(2) existed, it is conclusively presumed that the complainant did not consent to the relevant act and that the accused did not believe that the complainant consented to the relevant act. The jury should be directed to convict if they find either of these matters proved. For the presumption to arise, the deception or impersonation must be shown to have operated upon the mind of the complainant so as to induce consent (see J Temkin and A Ashworth, [2004] Crim LR 328 at p. 335).

B3.44 Section 76(2)(a) follows the common law, which established that in the comparatively rare cases where the complainant has been induced to consent on the basis of fraudulent misrepresentations as to the nature of the act there was no consent (*Williams* [1923] 1 KB 340; *Flattery* [1877] 2 QB 410). Arguably the inclusion of the word 'purpose' extends the pre-existing law which had evolved to the extent that deceptions as to the purpose of the physical act were sufficient to vitiate consent (*Tabassum* [2000] 2 Cr App R 328; *Green* [2002] EWCA Crim 1501). However, as was stressed by the Court of Appeal in *Jheeta* [2007] EWCA Crim 1699, [2007] 2 Cr App R 34 (477), s. 76(2)(a) does not address the 'quality' of the act, but confines itself to its 'purpose'. It follows that deception by representing a false medical purpose may be sufficient to trigger s. 76, but not if consent is induced by a bogus ceremony of marriage or false promise of payment (see the facts of *Linekar* [1995] 2 Cr App R 49 as considered in *Jheeta* at [25]). In the Australian case of *Papadimitropoulos* (1957) 98 CLR 249 the High Court refused to find that a deception arising from a bogus ceremony of marriage invalidated a woman's consent. However, s. 76(2)(a) might apply on such facts as arguably there is a deception as to the purpose of the act, the consummation of marriage.

B3.45 In *Jheeta* the Court of Appeal held that no conclusive presumptions arose merely because the complainant had been deceived in some way by disingenuous blandishments from or the lies of the accused. The creation of a bizarre fantasy which had pressurised the complainant into having sexual intercourse with the accused more frequently than she otherwise would have done was not a deception as to the nature or purpose of sexual intercourse. Such conduct might be deceptive or persuasive, but would rarely go to the nature or purpose of intercourse. In many cases, notwithstanding deceptive conduct, the accused's motivation will be sexual gratification and so there will have been no relevant deception as to purpose operating upon the complainant's mind. In *Bingham* [2013] EWCA Crim 823, [2013] 2 Cr App R 29 (307) (seven counts of causing his girlfriend to engage in sexual activity without consent under s. 4), D, using pseudonyms, established an online Facebook relationship with his girlfriend so as to persuade and then blackmail her into providing him with photographs of her engaging in sexual activity. The Court of Appeal held that reliance at trial upon s. 76 was misplaced. The motive behind the conduct was sexual gratification, and there was no deception as to that. The prosecution would have had a forceful argument under s. 74 on the basis that she only complied because she was blackmailed. In the light of s. 76(2), it would appear that deception as to the identity of the recipient would not be sufficient as it was the impersonation of a person unknown to the complainant. Contrast *Devonald* [2008] EWCA Crim 527 for a case under s. 4 where the Court of Appeal held that s. 76 applied: it was open to the jury to conclude that the complainant was deceived into believing he was masturbating for the gratification of a 20-year-old girl via a webcam when in fact he was doing it for the father of a former girlfriend who was teaching him a lesson. Here 'purpose' has been given a wide meaning in that the deception was not as to sexual purpose, rather it was as to the purpose of the act of masturbation. For a clear example of deception as to purpose, see *Matt* [2015] EWCA Crim 162 where a plumber, posing as a film maker, deceived the complainant into believing she was undergoing a casting process and induced her to carry out sexual acts with him. The Court of Appeal had no difficulty in finding that there was a deception as to purpose falling within s. 76(2)(a) in that the ostensible purpose of the activity was not sexual pleasure but simulated sexual pleasure for commercial purposes.

Section 76(2)(b) extends the law by widening the categories of impersonation sufficient to vitiate consent beyond the complainant's husband or regular sexual partner to 'a person known personally to the complainant'.

Consent in Absence of Presumption In most cases neither the evidential nor conclusive presumptions will arise, and the jury must determine whether the prosecution have established absence of consent and/or absence of reasonable belief in accordance with the key definitions in ss. 74 and 1(2). Section 76 replicates and extends the common law. It simply identifies the relatively rare situations in which conclusive presumptions arise. It was designed to buttress s. 74, not to limit it. The conclusive presumptions are concerned with proof of absence of consent rather than its definition. Whilst deceptions by the accused as to purely peripheral circumstances will not vitiate consent, it does not follow from the existence of s. 76 that lesser deceptions which do not trigger the conclusive presumptions cannot ever do so. B3.46

In *Assange v Swedish Prosecution Authority* [2011] EWHC 2849 (Admin), the Divisional Court suggested that s. 76 should be given a stringent construction because it provides for a conclusive presumption. The question of consent, and the issue of the materiality of the use of a condom, fell to be determined by reference to s. 74. It would be open to a jury to hold that, if the complainant had made clear that she would consent to sexual intercourse only if the appellant used a condom, then there would be no consent if, without her consent, he did not use a condom, or removed or tore the condom without her consent.

If conduct is not within s. 76, that does not preclude reliance upon s. 74. Section 76 deals simply with a conclusive presumption in the very limited circumstances to which it applies. The Court rejected the argument that if the deception was not a deception within s. 76 (a deception as to the nature and quality of the act or a case of impersonation) then the deception could not be taken into account for the purposes of s. 74. Sir John Thomas P stated (at [88]): 'It would, in our view, have been extraordinary if Parliament had legislated in terms that, if conduct that was not deceptive could be taken into account for the purposes of s. 74, conduct that was deceptive could not be.'

Following the reasoning in *Assange* the Divisional Court in *R (F) v DPP* [2013] EWHC 945 (Admin), [2014] QB 581 allowed judicial review of a decision by the DPP not to prosecute a man for rape. Ejaculation without consent could transform an incident of consensual intercourse into rape where there was evidence that the man had deliberately ignored the crucial feature upon which the claimant's original consent to penetration was based as a manifestation of his control over her. In *McNally* [2013] EWCA Crim 1051, [2014] QB 593 the Court of Appeal, when considering deception in the context of offences of assault by penetration under the SOA 2003, s. 2, concluded that deliberate deception as to gender could vitiate consent.

> ...while, in a physical sense, the acts of assault by penetration of the vagina are the same whether perpetrated by a male or a female, the sexual nature of the acts is, on any common sense view, different where the complainant is deliberately deceived by a defendant into believing that the latter is a male. Assuming the facts to be proved as alleged, M chose to have sexual encounters with a boy and her preference (her freedom to choose whether or not to have a sexual encounter with a girl) was removed by the appellant's deception.

McNally confirms by implication that only an active deception (as opposed to a failure to disclose) falls within the scope of s. 74. However, it did not provide a guiding principle enabling the identification of deceptions capable of vitiating consent. Considerable assistance as to the appropriate approach is now to be found in *R (Monica) v DPP* [2018] EWHC 3508 (Admin), [2019] 1 Cr App R 28 (363), which provided a clear analysis of the law governing consent and deception when rejecting an application for judicial review of a decision of the DPP confirming an earlier decision not to prosecute a former undercover police officer for the offences of rape, indecent assault, procurement of sexual intercourse and misconduct in public office. Between April and October 1997, the claimant, an environmental activist involved in a protest movement, and the undercover officer were sexual partners. The undercover officer had infiltrated that movement on the orders of his superiors in the police service and had befriended the claimant who was unaware of his real identity. The relationship began at the instigation of the claimant with the officer successfully maintaining his cover throughout this period. Following media reports 14 years later the claimant discovered the true position. The claimant's evidence was accepted that under no circumstances would she have entered into any sort of relationship with the officer had she known that he was not a genuine environmental activist.

While the issue in the proceedings was whether the DPP's decision was legally flawed in public law terms, determining that issue necessitated a comprehensive review of the authorities relating to consent both before and after implementation of the 2003 Act. The Court concluded that consent had only ever been held to be vitiated by deceptions which are closely connected to the performance of the sexual act, or are intrinsically so fundamental, owing to that connection, that they can be treated as cases of impersonation. The Court rejected the claimant's submission that on a proper analysis *Olugboja* [1982] QB 320 had represented a change in the law in respect of deception and fraud by freeing the interpretation of 'consent' from any earlier restrictions by reducing the issue of consent in all cases of rape to a straightforward examination of the victim's state of mind at the critical time. The Court observed that in *Olugboja* the critical issue had been whether the sort of coerced acquiescence exemplified in that case amounted to consent. The facts had had nothing to do with fraud. The directions recommended by Dunn LJ in *Olugboja* were crafted for that type of case and not with deception about status, underlying beliefs or philosophy etc. in mind. The Court observed (at [49]) that there is a consistent line of authority under common law and the SOA 1956 supporting the proposition that 'only two frauds are capable of vitiating consent', namely fraud as to the nature of the sexual act and fraud as to the identity of the perpetrator (impersonation of husband or partner), and there is no authority which indicates or suggests otherwise.

The Court then reviewed the post-2003 authorities in which deceptions falling short of s. 76 deceptions have been held to be capable of vitiating consent. It derived from *Assange* the proposition that a deception which is closely connected with 'the nature or purpose of the act', because it relates to sexual intercourse itself rather than the broad circumstances surrounding it, is capable of negating a complainant's free exercise of choice for the purposes of s. 74 of the 2003 Act. This was consistent with *R (F) v DPP* and *McNally.*

In *Lawrance* [2020] EWCA Crim 971, the Court of Appeal applied this proposition when considering whether a lie about fertility could negate consent. As in *Monica*, a deception about something central to the complainant's choice still did not vitiate consent for the purposes of sexual offending. The 'but for' test was insufficient of itself to vitiate consent. The appellant had been convicted of two counts of rape on the basis that his false representation to the complainant that he had had a vasectomy vitiated her consent in that she had only agreed to unprotected sex as a result of that representation. Otherwise she would have insisted on his wearing a condom. Burnett CJ distinguished a lie about fertility from a lie about whether a condom would be worn (*Assange*) or engaging in intercourse not intending to withdraw having promised to do so (*R (F)*) or misrepresenting gender (*McNally*.) The complainant in *Lawrance* had agreed to sexual intercourse with the appellant without imposing any physical restrictions. She had agreed to both the penetration of her vagina and to ejaculation without the protection of a condom. She was deceived about the nature and quality of the ejaculate. The deception did not relate to the physical performance of the sexual act but the risks and consequences associated with it. It made no difference where there was an express deception. The issue was whether the appellant's lie was sufficiently closely connected to the performance of the sexual act rather than the broad circumstances surrounding it.

In *Monica* the Court had acknowledged that the present law apparent from these decisions, i.e. that deceptions closely associated with the nature or purpose of the sexual act can vitiate consent, *may represent a relatively modest extension* of the way in which the law examines 'consent' in the context of sexual offending. However, the Court rejected the submission that the authorities post-*Olugboja* reveal a profound change in the test for ascertaining absence of consent and deception. The Court observed (at [84]) that it had not been shown any admissible aids to construction to support the expansive construction of the definition of consent sought by the claimant, and no existing authority provided any support for that construction. Furthermore, such a test would necessarily include the fundamental deception by a person entering a bigamous marriage. It regarded such a step as one that could only be achieved by Parliament.

As to the parameters of consent where there has been no deception, the SOA 2003 leaves juries to grapple with such concepts as freedom, choice and capacity. It remains for the jury to resolve such questions as whether the degree of coercion and/or abuse of power or authority exercised upon a complainant's mind was such that she did not agree by choice with the freedom to make that choice. It may well be, for example, that a threat to expose a woman's previous sexual conduct to her family will negate consent, particularly if the woman comes from a milieu in which such a revelation might pose the danger of physical harm or even death (*Sharif* [2004] EWCA Crim 3386). **B3.47**

In *Doody* [2008] EWCA Crim 2394 the Court of Appeal considered the extent of permissible judicial comment as to the mental state of rape complainants. The Court held that a judge is entitled to make comments as to the way evidence is to be approached, particularly in areas where there is a danger of a jury coming to an unjustified conclusion without an appropriate warning, but any comment should be uncontroversial. The fact that the trauma of rape can cause feelings of shame and guilt which might inhibit a woman from making a complaint is sufficiently well known to justify a comment to that effect. The Court approved an example in general terms of an appropriate direction in such circumstances which covers the following points: (i) experience shows that people react differently to the trauma of a serious sexual assault, that there is no one classic response; (ii) some may complain immediately whilst others feel shame and shock and do not complain for some time; and (iii) a late complaint does not necessarily mean it is a false complaint. A judge is entitled to add mention of the particular feelings of shame and embarrassment which may arise when the allegation is of sexual assault by a partner. This general approach was attacked unsuccessfully in *Miller* [2010] EWCA Crim 1578, where it was argued that the judge's directions in a child rape case were not properly based on evidence that was adduced before the jury and that they offended the common-law principle that judicial notice can be taken only of facts of particular notoriety or common knowledge. The Court of Appeal gave short shrift to these submissions, pointing out that that was precisely what dealing with these generalisations was intended to do. In *Andreous* [2014] EWCA Crim 2886, where a dentist was on trial for a sexual offence, the Court of Appeal approved a direction given to the jury that they should proceed on the basis that an individual is not more or less likely to have committed an offence because of culture, age, class or profession. For examples of further directions to juries to guard against false assumptions, see the *Crown Court Compendium* (July 2020), ch. 20-1. As with all directions to the jury, such directions should be couched firmly in the context of the factual matrix of the case in hand (*Smith* [2012] EWCA Crim 404). **B3.48**

Given the development of permissible neutral judicial warnings to guard against false assumptions, there is limited scope for generic expert evidence as to the possible impact of sexual offences upon victims. In *ER* [2010] EWCA Crim 2522 the Court of Appeal, when holding that the evidence of a psychotherapist should not have been admitted, took a highly restrictive approach as to the circumstances in which expert evidence may be given in this area. Hughes LJ stated that such evidence should not be given unless it is directed to something which is quite outside the experience of the jury and the ability of a judge to explain common understanding and common patterns of behaviour. **B3.49**

Non-disclosure of STDs and Consent At common law a man who had consensual intercourse with another person, knowing but not disclosing that he suffers from a sexually transmitted illness, could not be convicted of rape. In *Dica (Mohammed)* [2004] EWCA Crim 1103, [2004] QB 1257, the Court of Appeal, referring to the old law, stated that consent to sexual intercourse defeated **B3.50**

liability for rape. A failure to disclose any sexually transmitted disease (STD) is not a deception as to the nature or purpose of the act, and accordingly the conclusive presumption under s. 76(2)(a) does not arise. In *B* [2006] EWCA Crim 2945, [2007] 1 WLR 1567, it was held that an accused's failure to disclose his HIV status did not affect the issue of consent in rape where there had been no allegations that the accused had deceived the complainant. Latham LJ stated (at [17]):

> Where one party to sexual activity has a sexually transmissible disease which is not disclosed to the other party any consent that may have been given to that activity by the other party is not thereby vitiated. The act remains a consensual act. However, the party suffering from the sexual transmissible disease will not have any defence to any charge which may result from harm created by that sexual activity, merely by virtue of that consent, because such consent did not include consent to infection by the disease.

Ignorance defeats consent under the OAPA 1861, s. 20, where the illness is life-threatening (*Konzani* [2005] EWCA Crim 706, [2005] 2 Cr App R 14 (198): see **B2.15**).

B3.51 In *McNally* [2013] EWCA Crim 1051, [2014] QB 593 (see **B3.46**), the Court of Appeal observed (at [24]) that *B* was not authority for the proposition that concealment of, or deception about, HIV status could not vitiate consent. *B* had left the issue open as to whether concealment or deception could vitiate consent if, for example, a complainant had been positively assured that the accused was not HIV positive. However, in *Lawrance* [2020] EWCA Crim 971, Lord Burnett CJ explained that the transmission of disease through sexual intercourse is not part of the performance of the sexual act. It is a consequence. It followed that such a deception, whether express or involving concealment, was not sufficiently closely connected to vitiate consent under s. 74. The Court saw force in the analogy between a lie about fertility and a lie about being HIV positive. Neither lie altered the position that the complainant consented to every aspect of the physical act itself, namely penile penetration and usually ejaculation. For further discussion of *Lawrance* see **B3.46**.

See also the CPS guidance 'Policy for prosecuting cases involving the intentional or reckless sexual transmission of infection' (15 July 2011).

Attempted Rape and Conspiracy to Rape

B3.52 Attempted rape is governed by the principles of the law of attempts generally (see **A5.72**). Attempted rape may be charged as such, or may be an alternative verdict on a charge of rape where the evidence does not disclose that the accused achieved sexual intercourse with the victim.

Following the approach adopted by the Court of Appeal in *Pace* [2014] EWCA Crim 186, [2014] 1 WLR 2867, a case involving an allegation of an impossible attempt under the POCA 2002, s. 327 (see **A5.80**), it may be argued that the prosecution must prove that the accused intended each and every aspect of the *actus reus*, i.e. an intention to penetrate and an intention that the penetration be without consent. However, in the context of attempted rape, it is likely that the courts will continue to follow the reasoning under the old law in *Khan* [1990] 2 All ER 783 and rely upon the distinction between consequences and circumstances, taking the view that the mental element in attempted rape is the same as that required for the full offence, namely an intention to penetrate (the conduct/consequences) and the absence of reasonable belief (the circumstances).

It is not necessary to prove that the accused had gone so far as to attempt physical penetration of the vagina, anus or mouth. It suffices if acts be proved which the jury could regard as more than merely preparatory (*A-G's Ref (No.1 of 1992)* [1993] 2 All ER 190).

To establish a conspiracy to rape, the prosecution must prove not only an agreement to rape but also an actual intention to carry out that agreement (*Hedgecock* [2007] EWCA Crim 3486; *G* [2012] EWCA Crim 1756); see also **A5.57**.

ASSAULT BY PENETRATION

This offence was created in response to the recommendation by the Sexual Offences Review, which recognised that non-consensual penetration by objects or parts of the body other than the penis can be as serious in their impact on the victim as rape. It also recommended that the offence should be defined in a way that would enable it to be used where there was doubt as to the nature of the penetration (e.g., where a child knows it was penetrated but cannot say whether it was by a penis, finger or another object). **B3.53**

Sexual Offences Act 2003, s. 2

(1) A person (A) commits an offence if—
   (a) he intentionally penetrates the vagina or anus of another person with a part of his body or anything else,
   (b) the penetration is sexual,
   (c) B does not consent to the penetration, and
   (d) A does not reasonably believe that B consents.
(2) Whether a belief is reasonable is to be determined having regard to all the circumstances, including any steps A has taken to ascertain whether B consents.
(3) Sections 75 and 76 apply to an offence under this section.

Procedure

Assault by penetration is triable only on indictment. As to the classification of the offence for the purpose of listing, see CrimPD XIII, para. B (see Supplement, **CPD.XIII.B**). The extended jurisdiction provisions of s. 72 (see **B3.315**) apply where B was under 18 at the time of the offence. **B3.54**

See **B3.355** for alternative verdicts.

Sentence

The maximum penalty for assault by penetration is life imprisonment (SOA 2003, s. 2(4)). The definitive sentencing guideline, *Sexual Offences* (see Supplement, **SG31-4**) applies to sex offenders aged 18 or over who are sentenced on or after 1 April 2014 (see **B3.3**). The guideline reflects the fact that the types of penetration that may be involved in assault by penetration are wider than in relation to rape, and range from acts as severe as the highest category rape (e.g., a violent sexual attack involving penetration of the victim with an object likely or intended to cause significant injury to the victim) to an activity that, whilst involving severe violation of the victim, is more akin to a serious sex assault (e.g., momentary penetration with fingers). Under the previous guideline, a lower sentence would be given for penetration with a body part, such as a finger or a tongue, where no physical harm was sustained; a higher sentence would be given for penetration with an object (the larger or more dangerous the object, the higher the sentence would be) or penetration combined with abduction, detention, abuse of trust or more than one offender acting together. **B3.55**

The Council agreed with the conclusions of public research that, generally, where penetration of the genitals has occurred, the public felt that this was akin to rape regardless of what had been used to penetrate due to the inherent level of violation. The Council therefore adopted the approach that such assaults should generally be treated in very similar terms to rape in terms of harm caused with only two differences in the harm factors specified in the guidelines in relation to the two offences. The factor relating to pregnancy or an STI occurring as a consequence of the offence is not included in the guideline for assault by penetration but 'penetration using large or dangerous object(s)' is included as a harm factor in relation to assault by penetration because, whilst it is acknowledged that psychological harm results whatever the means of penetration, the Council was of the view that where a large or dangerous object is used, this increases the physical consequences of the attack and also the psychological harm, and so should increase the starting point for sentence.

The guideline adopts a similar model as in rape in that it recognises that all examples of this offence are extremely harmful to the victim by assuming there is *always* a baseline of harm. This is reflected in offence category 3, which covers offences in which harm factors identified in category 2 are not present. The extreme nature of one or more category 2 factors or the extreme impact caused by a combination of category 2 factors may elevate the case to category 1. Having identified the offence category, the court should then determine whether any culpability A factors are present in order to ascertain the starting point. There is an assumed baseline of culpability reflected in category B. The starting points and sentence ranges are the same as for rape, representing an increase from the levels recommended in the previous guideline. In respect of categories 2 and 3, sentencing levels are lower than for rape, but there is a discernible upwards shift. In a case involving the lowest level of harm (category 3) and lower culpability (category A), where there is sufficient prospect of rehabilitation, a community order with a sex offender treatment programme requirement can be a proper alternative to a short or moderate length custodial sentence.

Where there are counts of digital penetration alleged to have taken place in the course of an incident of rape, the totality principle will apply. In *A-G's Ref (Nos. 12 and 13 of 2015) (McClaren and Whitelaw)* [2015] EWCA Crim 1223 the Court of Appeal declined to interfere with sentences of nine years' imprisonment for rape. The concurrent sentence imposed for assault by penetration could not be categorised as wrong in principle, and the judge was entitled to regard the sentence as appropriate for the total of both the penile and digital anal penetration.

The definitive guideline, *Sentencing Children and Young People* (see Supplement, **SG8-1**), applies to all offenders under the age of 18 who are sentenced on or after 1 June 2017, regardless of the date of the offence. It supersedes part 7 of the original 2007 guideline.

The offence is a qualifying offence for an automatic life sentence under the CJA 2003, sch. 15B (see **B3.25** and **E4**).

In every case the court should consider a sexual harm prevention order (see **E21.22**). There is a notification requirement under the SOA 2003, s. 80 and sch. 3 (see **E23**).

Indictment

B3.56 *Statement of Offence*

Assault by penetration contrary to section 2(1) of the Sexual Offences Act 2003.

Particulars of Offence

A, on or about the... day of... penetrated the [vagina] [anus] of V with [] without [her][his] consent and did not reasonably believe that V was consenting.

Actus Reus

B3.57 The essence of the offence is penetration of the vagina or anus of another person. The penetration may be penetration with a part of the offender's body, e.g., a finger or a fist, or with anything else, e.g., a dildo or a sharp object. The term 'anything else' will include an animal or other living organism. As with rape, references to a vagina include a surgically constructed vagina (SOA 2003, s. 79(3)). The penetration is a continuing act from entry to withdrawal (s. 79(2)).

Penetration must be 'sexual' in character. The requirement that conduct (penetration, touching etc.) is 'sexual' recurs in a number of offences. Section 78 seeks to explain the approach to be adopted when considering whether particular conduct is 'sexual' for the purposes of the Act.

Sexual Offences Act 2003, s. 78

For the purposes of this Part (except sections 15A and section 71) penetration, touching or any other activity is sexual if a reasonable person would consider that—

(a) whatever its circumstances or any person's purpose in relation to it, it is because of its nature sexual, or

(b) because of its nature it may be sexual and because of its circumstances or the purpose of any person in relation to it (or both) it is sexual.

Section 78 was amended by the Serious Crime Act 2015, s. 85 and sch. 4, para. 63, with effect from 3 April 2017.

Section 78(a) covers conduct where the nature of the activity is unambiguously sexual. To determine whether the conduct is 'sexual' it should be considered without reference to its circumstances or the purpose of the accused. For example, in respect of penile penetration or oral sex, the activity is sexual whatever the accused's purpose. It follows that it will not be a defence to a charge under s. 2 to claim that penetration was performed not for sexual gratification but as an assertion of dominance.

The correct approach to the application of s. 78(b) where the nature of the activity is ambiguous and 'may' be sexual, was set out by the Court of Appeal in *H* [2005] EWCA Crim 732, [2005] 1 WLR 2005. The Court said that the provision contains two distinct questions for the jury: first, whether they, as 12 reasonable people, considered that, because of its nature, the touching *might* be sexual: and, if so, secondly, whether, in view of the circumstances and/or the purpose of any person in relation to it, the touching *was* in fact sexual. These are two distinct questions which must be considered separately. The nature of the touching refers to the actual touching that took place and, therefore, in considering whether the touching, because of its nature, might be sexual, the jury are not concerned with the circumstances before or after the touching or the purpose of the accused in relation to it. In *H*, there was evidence that before pulling the complainant's tracksuit bottoms, the accused had said to her 'Do you fancy a shag?' At trial, it was submitted on behalf of the accused that the touching that had occurred could not be regarded by a reasonable person as 'sexual' within the meaning of the Act. The trial judge took the view that there were clearly circumstances, including the words allegedly spoken beforehand, which could make what had occurred sexual. The Court of Appeal said that the judge had not adopted the required two-stage approach to s. 78(b) but had looked at the matter as a whole. The problem with that was that, in a borderline case, a person's intention could make a touching sexual, even though the nature of the touching could not be sexual. That, said the Court, is not an appropriate approach, even though in the great majority of cases the result will be the same. B3.58

The Court in *H* disapproved the decision in *George* [1956] Crim LR 52, an allegation of indecent assault in which it was held that a shoe fetishist's act in removing a woman's shoe was not capable of being indecent. *George* was expressly approved in *Court* [1989] AC 28, where the House of Lords set out the meaning of 'indecency' in the offence of indecent assault and the reasoning in *Court* is essentially reproduced in the definition of 'sexual' in s. 78. The potentially wide scope of the application of s. 78(b) is highlighted by the Court's discussion of *George* in *H*. A wide variety of conduct is capable of being regarded by a reasonable person as possibly being 'sexual', albeit the vast majority of people would regard it as objectively innocuous.

Section 78(b) will have the effect of making an intimate medical examination involving digital examination of the vagina or anus 'sexual' where the examination is not a bona fide examination and the doctor's purpose is sexual gratification. Arguably, even where a doctor conducts a properly required intimate medical examination, if it was conducted in an inappropriate manner, it may be concluded that the activity was 'sexual' if it can be established that the doctor had an ulterior purpose of sexual gratification. See the facts of *Bolduc and Bird* (1967) 63 DLR (2d) 82, where a doctor carried out a necessary examination but allowed a friend to be present for his sexual gratification. B3.59

It is instructive to consider examples of activities which are not unambiguously 'sexual' but may be 'sexual' following the approach outlined in s. 78(b) as interpreted in *H*. For example, a slap on an athlete's buttocks by her coach is capable of being considered 'sexual' but may not be so where the occasion, filing off a field after a game, is not obviously sexual and where no words or gestures connote a sexual purpose (*Gauthier* Can Cr L. Digest 42887 and see also *J (BJ)* (1996) 193 AR 151 (Alta SC)). Stroking the legs of another is certainly capable of being sexual (*Price* [2003] EWCA Crim 2405, [2004] 1 Cr App R 12 (145)). The accused's admission in that case that he had done it because he was a shoe fetishist would be admissible under the second question in s. 78(b).

B3.60 As with all the non-consensual sexual offences, it is a fundamental requirement of the offence that the prosecution can establish the complainant's absence of consent (see **B3.40** ***et seq.***).

For consent and public policy, and, in particular, where an accused deliberately inflicts injury upon a complainant, see *Meachen* [2006] EWCA Crim 2414 and see **B2.14** ***et seq.***

In appropriate circumstances the presumptions in ss. 75 and 76 will apply. See **B3.40** ***et seq.***

Mens Rea

B3.61 The accused must intend to penetrate the vagina or anus of another person. On a natural reading of the section, the prosecution need not prove that the accused intended the penetration should be 'sexual'.

As with rape, the prosecution must prove that the accused did not reasonably believe that the complainant was consenting (see **B3.41**). In appropriate circumstances, the presumptions in ss. 75 and 76 as to consent and/or reasonable belief as to consent will apply. The 'relevant act' under s. 77 is 'the defendant intentionally penetrating, with a part of his body or anything else, the vagina or anus of another person, where the penetration is sexual'.

SEXUAL ASSAULT

B3.62 Sexual Offences Act 2003, s. 3

(1) A person (A) commits an offence if—
  (a) he intentionally touches another person (B),
  (b) the touching is sexual,
  (c) B does not consent to the touching, and
  (d) A does not reasonably believe that B consents.
(2) Whether a belief is reasonable is to be determined having regard to all the circumstances, including any steps A has taken to ascertain whether B consents.
(3) Sections 75 and 76 apply to an offence under this section.

Sections 75 and 76 relate to the presumptions as to consent (see **B3.40** ***et seq.***).

Procedure

B3.63 Sexual assault is triable either way. As to the classification of the offence for the purpose of listing, see CrimPD XIII, para. B (see Supplement, **CPD.XIII.B**). The extended jurisdiction provisions of s. 72 (see **B3.315**) apply to this offence where the victim was under 18 at the time of the offence.

See **B3.355** for alternative verdicts.

Indictment

B3.64 *Statement of Offence*

Sexual assault contrary to section 3(1) of the Sexual Offences Act 2003.

Particulars of Offence

A on or about the... day of... sexually touched V without [his] [her] consent not reasonably believing that V was consenting.

Sentence

The maximum sentence for an offence under the SOA 2003, s. 3, on conviction on indictment is ten years' imprisonment. On summary conviction, the maximum sentence is imprisonment for a term not exceeding six months and/or an unlimited fine (s. 3(4)). **B3.65**

The definitive sentencing guideline, *Sexual Offences* (see Supplement, **SG31-5**), applies to all sex offenders aged 18 or over who are sentenced on or after 1 April 2014 (see **B3.3**). The previous guideline categorised the offence of sexual assault purely by reference to the type of touching involved. The current guideline is intended to reflect fully the psychological and physical harm caused by the offence.

Four of the factors in category 2 in respect of rape and assault by penetration are placed in category 1 in respect of sexual assault: severe psychological harm, abduction, violence or threats of violence, and forced/uninvited entry into victim's home. This is because the Sentencing Council considered that category 1 sexual assaults will never be as severe as category 1 rapes or assaults by penetration, as reflected in the lower statutory maximum (ten years' imprisonment rather than life).

As with rape and assault by penetration, category 3 does not list any factors in order to reflect the fact that there is an inherent degree of harm caused by any sexual assault.

In the draft guideline the first factor in category 2 did not distinguish between clothed and naked genitalia on the basis that the type of activity does not necessarily reflect the type of harm caused. In the face of mixed responses to the consultation document on this issue, the Council amended the factor to 'touching of naked genitalia or naked breasts'. As a result, touching of clothed genitalia or breasts, without more, will fall within category 3. However, often the context of the offence will involve other factors in the harm categories.

A case of particular gravity, reflected by multiple features of culpability or harm, could merit upward adjustment from the starting point before further adjustment for aggravating or mitigating features. In respect of the most serious category (category 1, culpability A), the recommended starting point is four years' custody with a range of three to seven years. In respect of appropriate category 2 or 3 offences where there is a sufficient prospect of rehabilitation, a community order with a sex offender treatment programme requirement can be a proper alternative to a short or moderate length custodial sentence. The court should also consider whether the custodial threshold has been passed, and, if so, whether if a custodial sentence is unavoidable, it should be suspended.

The definitive guideline, *Sentencing Children and Young People* (see Supplement, **SG8-1**), applies to all offenders under the age of 18 who are sentenced on or after 1 June 2017, regardless of the date of the offence. It supersedes part 7 of the original 2007 guideline.

In every case the court should consider a sexual harm prevention order (see **E21.22**). There is a notification requirement under the SOA 2003, s. 80 and sch. 3, subject to the age of the offender and the sentence imposed (see **E23**). The *Magistrates' Court Sentencing Guidelines* apply when sentencing in a magistrates' court.

Range of Sexual Assaults The offence of sexual assault covers many activities formerly within the offence of indecent assault, although the most serious offences within that former category will now be prosecuted as rape, assault by penetration or a child sex offence. Sexual assault covers all forms of non-consensual sexual touching, but mainly applies to the lesser forms of assault. **B3.66**

Young Offenders The guideline on sexual offences applies only to offenders aged 18 and older. General principles to be considered in sentencing of youths are found in the definitive guideline, *Sentencing Children and Young People* (see Supplement, **SG8-1**). See *Sharp* [2008] **B3.67**

EWCA Crim 1059, [2009] 1 Cr App R (S) 16 (86) for an example of the Court of Appeal dealing with a young offender. The Court substituted a supervision order with elements of treatment and participation in a sexual offender programme for a sentence of four years' detention in respect of a sexual assault upon a 75-year-old woman by a boy aged nearly 13.

Elements

B3.68 The *actus reus* may simply be defined as touching where the touching is 'sexual' in character. There is no requirement of force or violence: the lightest touching will suffice. Nor is any element of 'hostility' required as was held to be the case in one line of indecent assault authorities. Section 79(8) provides that touching includes touching with any part of the body, with anything else, and through anything. In particular, it includes touching amounting to penetration. Touching a person through that person's clothing clearly amounts to a touching for the purposes of this offence, so too does touching the victim's clothing even though the person of the victim is not touched through clothing (*H* [2005] EWCA Crim 732, [2005] 2 All ER 859 at [26]). The victim need not be aware of being touched. See *Bounekhla* [2006] EWCA Crim 1217 where the accused surreptitiously took his penis out of his trousers and ejaculated onto a woman's clothing when pressed up against her dancing at a nightclub. In one area, sexual assault is narrower than indecent assault which could be committed if the accused caused the complainant to apprehend that she was about to be touched indecently (cf. *Rolfe* (1952) 36 Cr App R 4). If touching does not occur, the offence is not completed, although the circumstances may amount to an attempt. Nevertheless, it remains arguable that ejaculation onto a victim without contact with any part of an accused's body still constitutes a touching.

Section 78, which provides when a touching or other activity is 'sexual', is considered at **B3.57**. If the act itself is objectively equivocal, the purpose of the accused may be a relevant consideration as provided by s. 78(b), and that must be a reference to his own (subjective) purpose.

The prosecution must establish that the complainant did not consent to the touching (see **B3.29**).

B3.69 The mental element consists of an intentional touching coupled with an absence of reasonable belief that the complainant was consenting. In *Heard* [2007] EWCA Crim 125, [2008] QB 43, the Court of Appeal confirmed that the prosecution must prove that the touching was deliberate, and a reckless touching is not sufficient. Voluntary intoxication cannot be relied upon as defeating intentional touching. However, if the touching is an unintended accident, such as a consequence of impairment of control of the limbs, no offence under s. 3 is committed. A drunken accident is still an accident. See **B3.34**.

In appropriate circumstances, the evidential and conclusive presumptions about consent in ss. 75 and 76 (see **B3.40** ***et seq.***) may apply to this offence (s. 77).

CAUSING A PERSON TO ENGAGE IN SEXUAL ACTIVITY WITHOUT CONSENT

B3.70 **Sexual Offences Act 2003, s. 4**

(1) A person (A) commits an offence if—
 (a) he intentionally causes another person (B) to engage in an activity,
 (b) the activity is sexual,
 (c) B does not consent to engaging in the activity, and
 (d) A does not reasonably believe that B consents.
(2) Whether a belief is reasonable is to be determined having regard to all the circumstances, including any steps A has taken to ascertain whether B consents.
(3) Sections 75 and 76 apply to an offence under this section.

Procedure

Causing a person to engage in sexual activity is triable either way unless penetration is involved. As to the classification of the offence for the purpose of listing, see CrimPD XIII, para. B (see Supplement, **CPD.XIII.B**). The extended jurisdiction provisions of the SOA 2003, s. 72 (see **B3.315**), apply to this offence where B was under 18. **B3.71**

See **B3.355** for alternative verdicts.

Indictment

Statement of Offence **B3.72**

Causing a person to engage in sexual activity without consent contrary to section 4(1) of the Sexual Offences Act 2003.

Particulars of Offence

A, on or about the... day of... caused V to engage in a sexual activity without her [his] consent, namely, to allow her vagina [anus] [mouth] to be penetrated by [the penis of] another [or — to penetrate the anus or vagina of another by [V's body] [an object] or — to penetrate the mouth of another by V's penis] not reasonably believing that V was consenting.

B

Part B Offences

Sentence

The maximum punishment varies according to the activity concerned and is set out in the SOA 2003, s. 4(4) and (5). **B3.73**

Sexual Offences Act 2003, s. 4

(4) A person guilty of an offence under this section, if the activity caused involved—
  (a) penetration of B's anus or vagina,
  (b) penetration of B's mouth with a person's penis,
  (c) penetration of a person's anus or vagina with a part of B's body or by B with anything else, or
  (d) penetration of a person's mouth with B's penis,
  is liable, on conviction on indictment, to imprisonment for life.

(5) Unless subsection (4) applies, a person guilty of an offence under this section is liable—
  (a) on summary conviction, to imprisonment for a term not exceeding six months or to [an unlimited fine] or both;
  (b) on conviction on indictment, for a term not exceeding 10 years.

The definitive sentencing guideline, *Sexual Offences* (see Supplement, **SG31-6**), applies to sex offenders aged 18 or over who are sentenced on or after 1 April 2014 (see **B3.3**). In respect of s. 4 offences, the guideline adopts the same approach and sentencing levels as those specified for (i) the offence of assault by penetration (where the offence involved penetration) and (ii) the offence of sexual assault (where the offence did not involve penetration).

There is a baseline of assumed harm where no category 2 harm factors are present (category 1). The extreme nature or impact of one or more category 2 factors may elevate the case into category 1. Similarly, there is a baseline of assumed culpability (category B). One or more category A culpability factors will take the case into culpability category A. The categorisation of harm and culpability enables the court to identify the starting point and category range. Then the court should consider whether the presence of aggravating or mitigating factors should result in upward or downward adjustment from the starting point or an imposition of a sentence outside the category range. The guideline provides a non-exhaustive list of such factors. In particular, relevant convictions are likely to result in an upward adjustment. When sentencing appropriate category 2 or 3 offences, the court should also consider whether the custody threshold has been passed; if so, whether a custodial sentence is unavoidable; and if it is, whether that sentence can be suspended.

The previous guideline expressly stated that the same degree of seriousness and the same starting points apply whether an offender causes an act to take place, incites an act that actually takes place, or incites an act that does not take place only because it is prevented by factors beyond the control of the offender, though some reduction will generally be appropriate when the incited activity does not, in fact, take place. It is likely that the same principles will be followed in respect of the current guideline. In every case the court should consider a disqualification from working with children (see **E21.17** and **E21.21**) and a sexual offences prevention order (see **E21.22**). There is a notification requirement under the SOA 2003, s. 80 and sch. 3 (see **E23**). The offence is a qualifying offence for an automatic life sentence under the CJA 2003, sch. 15B, if the offender is liable on conviction on indictment to imprisonment for life (see **B3.25**).

B3.74 An offender causing his victim to masturbate him with her hand does not fall in the higher category which includes acts involving contact between naked genitalia or causing a victim to masturbate himself or herself (*Ayeva* [2009] EWCA Crim 2640, [2010] 2 Cr App R (S) 22 (143)).

For an example of a case where there were serious aggravating features, see *H* [2008] EWCA Crim 1202. The visibly mentally disabled victim was forced (i) to take a dog's penis in his mouth and (ii) to be penetrated in the anus by the dog. The two accused filmed the incident on their mobile phones and the footage was extensively circulated and placed on the internet. A sentence of seven years' detention was upheld in respect of a 17-year-old. The Court of Appeal noted that s. 4(4)(b) does not apply to penetration by a dog's penis and so the PCC(S)A 2000, s. 91, could not apply. Section 4(4)(c) does, however, cover penetration of the anus by a dog's penis. For an example of sentencing in a case where very grave sexual offending included offences under the SOA 2003, s. 4, see *Gorringe* [2019] EWCA Crim 552, where a total extended sentence of 32 years comprising a custodial term of 24 years plus an eight-year extended licence made up from a series of consecutive sentences was held not to be excessive in light of the seriousness of the various prolonged offences against two teenagers. The Recorder had correctly described the appellant as a predatory manipulative sexual deviant whose taste extended to humiliation and depravity.

The definitive guideline, *Sentencing Children and Young People* (see Supplement, **SG8-1**), applies to all offenders under the age of 18 who are sentenced on or after 1 June 2017, regardless of the date of the offence. It supersedes part 7 of the original 2007 guideline.

Elements

B3.75 *Actus Reus* The offence covers the situation where A causes B to engage in sexual activity without B's consent, whether or not A also engages in it and whether or not A is present. The term 'activity' is not defined, and is capable of being given a wide interpretation, although it must actually have taken place. The activity which B is caused to engage in may involve B alone such as where A forces B to masturbate himself or herself, or it may be with A, or with a third person (whether or not the third person consents) or even an animal. It would include causing a person to act as a prostitute. The activity must be 'sexual' in accordance with s. 78 (see **B3.57**). It can include engaging A in a conversation of a sexual nature (*Grout* [2011] EWCA Crim 299, [2011] 1 Cr App R 38 (472)). The word 'causes' is not defined and so any causative conduct may suffice, including threats of violence, inducements or persuasion. The prosecution must establish that B did not consent to engaging in the activity (see **B3.29**).

This complicated offence overlaps partly with rape which is also cast in terms of vaginal, anal or oral penetration. The offence is wider than rape, in that rape can be committed only by a man, as a principal, and does not involve penetration with an object. This offence can be committed by and against persons of either sex and includes cases of 'female rape', i.e. where A causes B to penetrate her vagina with his penis. Furthermore, the offence makes A criminally liable for causing B to engage in sexual activity where B cannot himself be convicted of any offence because he has a defence such as duress or is under the age of criminal responsibility (see the discussion at [2004] Crim LR 328 at p. 330).

The aggravated form of the offence covers all the activities mentioned in s. 4(4). All involve some form of penetration, either penetration of the anus or vagina with a penis or with anything else *or* the penetration of the mouth with a penis. This attracts a maximum penalty of life imprisonment. There is a residual category of sexual activities, which do not involve any of the above penetrations, which attract the lower penalty. This category is wider than sexual assault, not least because it covers the case where A forces B to take an active role in touching a third party such as coercing the victim to masturbate another or coercing B to masturbate himself. Following the principle in *Courtie* [1984] AC 463, since different factual ingredients attract different punishments, separate offences are created and this must be reflected in the indictment (see *Grout*).

Mens Rea The accused must *intend* to cause another person to enter into the activity in the sense that it must have been deliberate. However, following the reasoning in *Heard* [2007] EWCA Crim 125, [2008] QB 43, an accused's state of voluntary intoxication at the time of the causing is not a relevant factor when deciding whether the accused had this intent. Furthermore, the prosecution do not have to prove that the accused intended the activity to be 'sexual'. **B3.76**

As with all non-consensual offences, the prosecution must prove that the accused did not reasonably believe the complainant (B) was consenting (see **B3.29**). This would appear to apply to the time when the complainant engaged in the activity.

Presumptions In appropriate circumstances, the SOA 2003, ss. 75 and 76 (evidential presumptions and conclusive presumptions about consent), will apply to this offence (see **B3.40 *et seq.***, especially *Bingham* [2013] EWCA Crim 823, [2013] 2 Cr App R 29 (307) and the discussion of *Devonald* [2008] EWCA Crim 527, a case where the Court of Appeal held that the conclusive presumption under s. 76 applied). **B3.77**

RAPE AND OTHER OFFENCES AGAINST CHILDREN AGED UNDER 13

Sections 5 to 8 of the SOA 2003 mirror the non-consensual offences in ss. 1 to 4 of the Act but apply specifically to cases where the child is under 13. In respect of each section, any apparent consent is irrelevant for the purposes of proving the offence as is any mistake as to the child's age. The offences are gender neutral. **B3.78**

Exceptions to Aiding, Abetting and Counselling

Sexual Offences Act 2003, s. 73 **B3.79**

(1) A person is not guilty of aiding, abetting or counselling the commission against a child of an offence to which this section applies if he acts for the purpose of—
- (a) protecting the child from sexually transmitted infection,
- (b) protecting the physical safety of the child,
- (c) preventing the child from becoming pregnant, or
- (d) promoting the child's emotional well-being by the giving of advice,

and not for the purpose of obtaining sexual gratification or for the purpose of causing or encouraging the activity constituting the offence or the child's participation in it.

(2) This section applies to—
- (a) an offence under any of sections 5 to 7 (offences against children under 13);
- (b) an offence under section 9 (sexual activity with a child);
- (c) an offence under section 13 which would be an offence under section 9 if the offender were aged 18;
- (d) an offence under any of sections 16, 25, 30, 34 and 38 (sexual activity) against a person under 16.

(3) This section does not affect any other enactment or any rule of law restricting the circumstances in which a person is guilty of aiding, abetting or counselling an offence under this part.

Section 73 exempts a person from liability for aiding, abetting, or counselling the commission of an offence against a child in circumstances where the person acts for the purposes specified in the section and not for sexual gratification. Section 73 applies to a number of offences dealt with in the remainder of this section. Section 73 would not apply if an offender was charged with encouraging or assisting any such offence under the SCA 2007, s. 44 (see **A5.3**).

Rape of a Child under 13

B3.80 Sexual Offences Act 2003, s. 5

(1) A person commits an offence if—
(a) he intentionally penetrates the vagina, anus or mouth of another person with his penis, and
(b) the other person is under 13.

B3.81 **Procedure** An allegation of an offence contrary to s. 5 is triable only on indictment. As to the classification of the offence for the purpose of listing, see CrimPD XIII, para. B (see Supplement, **CPD.XIII.B**). It is also an offence to which the extra-territorial jurisdiction provisions of s. 72 apply (see **B3.315**).

See **B3.355** for alternative verdicts.

B3.82 **Indictment**

Statement of Offence

Rape of a child under 13 contrary to section 5 of the Sexual Offences Act 2003.

Particulars of Offence

A, on or about the…day of…penetrated the [vagina][anus][mouth] of V a child then under the age of 13 years with his penis.

B3.83 **Sentence** The maximum sentence is imprisonment for life (s. 5(2)).

There is a notification requirement under the SOA 2003, s. 80 and sch. 3 (see **E23**). The offence is a qualifying offence for an automatic life sentence under the CJA 2003, sch. 15B (see **B3.25**). The provisions of the CJA 2003, s. 236A (offenders of particular concern: see **E4.31**), apply to this offence. The court should consider a sexual harm prevention order (see **E21.22**).

The definitive sentencing guideline, *Sexual Offences* (see Supplement, **SG31-7**), applies to all sex offenders aged 18 or over who are sentenced on or after 1 April 2014 (see **B3.3**). The Council issued separate guidelines for the under-13 offences. That approach reflects the belief that there are issues and sensitivities unique to offences against children under 13 that require a separate guideline to ensure clarity for sentencers as to the factors to be taken into account and to provide a transparent process for others concerned with these cases.

Cases where a child under 13 has been groomed into acquiescence are to be treated equally for sentencing purposes with cases of forced non-consensual activity. That is so because of the evidence that younger children are increasingly at risk of sexual exploitation. In the exceptional case of a non-exploitative relationship, the Council considered that such cases should be sentenced outside the guideline. The Council stated that:

> When dealing with the statutory offence of rape of a child under 13, the court may be faced with a wide range of offending behaviour. Sentencers should have particular regard to the fact that these offences are not only committed through force or fear of force but may include exploitative behaviour towards a child which should be considered to indicate high culpability.
>
> Offences may be of such severity, for example involving a campaign of rape, that sentences of 20 years and above may be appropriate.
>
> This guideline is designed to deal with the majority of offending behaviour which deserves a significant custodial sentence; the starting points and ranges reflect the fact that such offending merits such an approach. There may also be exceptional cases, where a lengthy community order with a

> requirement to participate in a sex offender treatment programme may be the best way of changing the offender's behaviour and of protecting the public by preventing any repetition of the offence. This guideline may not be appropriate where the sentencer is satisfied that on the available evidence, and in the absence of exploitation, a young or particularly immature defendant genuinely believed, on reasonable grounds, that the victim was aged 16 or over and that they were engaging in lawful sexual activity.
>
> Sentencers are reminded that if sentencing outside the guideline they must be satisfied that it would be contrary to the interests of justice to follow the guideline.

The Court of Appeal considered the application of the sentencing guideline to a s. 5 offence in *A-G's Ref (No. 105 of 2014) (Musa Harrak)* [2014] EWCA Crim 2751, [2015] 1 Cr App R (S) 45 (330). Treacy LJ addressed the relevance of *Corran* [2005] EWCA Crim 192, [2005] 2 Cr App R (S) 73 (253):

> That was a case decided at a time prior to any guideline for this class of offending.... Accordingly, as a relevant sentencing authority *Corran* has limited value as sentencing practice has moved on. However, we observe that... the court remarked in relation to the section 5 offence of rape of a child under 13:
>
> There will be very few cases in which immediate custody is not called for, even in relation to a young offender, because the purpose of the legislation is to protect children under 13 from themselves, as well as from others minded to prey upon them.
>
> Those observations hold good today

Applying the guideline, the Court overturned a non-custodial sentence and imposed a total sentence of two and a half years for an offender aged 18 at the time of his offending when the victim was a 12-year-old girl. Although full sex had not taken place between the two, she had performed oral sex on him and masturbated him. He had touched her breast under her clothing.

Treacy LJ observed (at [24]):

> This class of case will, as the guideline observes, involve a wide range of offending behaviour. Care must be taken to approach the matter on a case-specific basis especially in the case of a young defendant. However, the type of truly exceptional case identified at page 28 of the section 5 guideline, concerning a particularly immature offender, who genuinely believes on reasonable grounds that the victim was 16 or over and that he was engaging in lawful sexual activity does not arise here. This offender was aware that S was under age. He thought she was 14 or 15. That no doubt is why he told her to keep matters secret. The reports available to us show he is not lacking in intelligence.

For examples of the application of the guideline, see *A-G's Ref (No. 142 of 2015) (Brown)* [2016] EWCA Crim 80, [2016] 1 Cr App R (S) 68 (503) and *H* [2015] EWCA Crim 1579, [2016] 1 Cr App R (S) 13 (94).

In *KC* [2019] EWCA Crim 1632, [2020] 1 Cr App R (S) 41 (296) at [42] the Court of Appeal was reluctant to express a firm view as to what is meant by 'extreme youth' in the guidelines, but, given that the concept takes its starting-point as a child under 13, it tended towards the view that it had to be seen as referring to children who were exceptionally young. The Court did not accept that a child aged seven or eight was on the border of 'extreme youth'. In *PS* [2019] EWCA Crim 2286, [2020] 2 Cr App R (S) 9 (56), Lord Burnett CJ observed (at [75]) that in the context of offences where an offence can only be committed against a child under 13, the Court did not regard the ages of five or six as being 'extreme youth'.

The definitive guideline, *Sentencing Children and Young People* (see Supplement, **SG8-1**), applies to all offenders under the age of 18 who are sentenced on or after 1 June 2017, regardless of the date of the offence. It supersedes part 7 of the original 2007 guideline.

In *A-G's Ref (Nos. 11 and 12 of 2012)* [2012] EWCA Crim 1119, [2013] 1 Cr App R (S) 43 (237), **B3.84**
the Court of Appeal had earlier said that careful analysis of the circumstances of an offence under s. 5 is always required and a *Newton* hearing may be necessary when the claim is made that the victim was consenting in fact and/or that the offender believed the victim to be significantly older

than in actual fact. The prosecutor bears a burden of responsibility to ensure that factual concessions to a basis of plea or mitigation of the offence are made only when justified and that, if made, the precise import of the concession is understood by the offender and the court. See also *KC* [2019] EWCA Crim 2311, where the Court of Appeal quashed an extended sentence imposed on the appellant and substituted a determinate sentence as sufficient to meet the sentencing needs of the case.

B3.85 **Elements** Save for the issue of consent, the elements of the offence are the same as those for rape and reference should therefore be made to **B3.28** to **B3.52**.

In contrast to rape of an adult, consent is no defence and so there is no requirement on the prosecution to prove that the accused did not reasonably believe that the victim was consenting. The position in respect of a child close to her 13th birthday where the accused maintains that the sex was consensual has caused some difficulties in practice. Strictly speaking, so far as it is relevant, the issue of consent is for the trial judge in a *Newton* hearing and CPS policy is simply to charge an accused with the s. 5 offence. But some judges have resisted depriving a jury of the opportunity of deciding such an important issue and encouraged the prosecution to charge rape under s. 1 with the s. 5 offence as an alternative. Plainly, this does not appear to have been the Parliamentary intention.

B3.86 In respect of ss. 5 to 8, it is necessary to prove that the complainant was under the age of 13, but ss. 5 to 8 do not require the prosecution to prove that the accused knew or suspected that the child was under that age. In *G* [2008] UKHL 37, [2009] 1 AC 92, a 15-year-old boy had pleaded guilty to an offence under s. 5 committed in respect of a 12-year-old girl. The plea was entered on an accepted basis that the complainant consented and that the accused thought she was aged 15. The Court of Appeal (*G* [2006] EWCA Crim 821, [2006] 1 WLR 2052) rejected his appeal based on submissions that s. 5 was incompatible with the ECHR, Articles 6 and 8. The House of Lords also dismissed his subsequent appeal. Their lordships were unanimous in holding that s. 5 was not incompatible with Article 6; in essence, it was held that it is a matter for Contracting States to define the essential elements of the offence with which a person has been charged. By a majority of three to two, the House also rejected the argument based on the incompatibility of s. 5 with Article 8. The majority (Lord Hoffmann, Baroness Hale and Lord Mance) held that the prosecution of D under s. 5 did not engage his Article 8 rights but, even if it did, the prosecution was 'both rational and proportionate in pursuit of the legitimate aims of the protection of health and morals and of the rights and freedoms of others' (Baroness Hale at [55]). The minority (Lords Hope and Carswell) expressed the view that the sanctions that can be imposed under s. 13 for mutual sexual activity by a person under 18 with a child aged under 13 provide all that is needed by way of punishment that is proportionate to the offence. Section 5 is designed for a much more serious situation, with a maximum sentence of life imprisonment and the description of the offence as rape (with all the consequences that go with that description), and a prosecution is entirely appropriate where the offence has been committed by a person over the age of 18 against a child under the age of 13. It may also be appropriate where the offender is younger than 18 but the younger the offender, the less appropriate it is (Lord Hope at [39]). As the offence committed by D fell within the ambit of s. 13, to continue to prosecute him under s. 5 was disproportionate and incompatible with his Article 8 right. Despite being in the minority, Lord Hope suggested (at [40]) that there was a lesson to be learnt from the instant case which he hoped would be taken into account in future cases of this kind. In *G v UK* [2011] ECHR 1308 the majority view of the House of Lords was supported by the ECtHR. In *Brown* [2013] UKSC 43, [2013] 4 All ER 860, the Supreme Court held that the Northern Irish offence of having unlawful carnal knowledge with a girl under the age of 14 did not require proof that the accused did not honestly believe that the girl was over the age of 14.

Tolhurst v DPP [2008] EWHC 2976 (Admin) was an unsuccessful application for judicial review of a decision by the CPS to prosecute an accused under s. 5 rather than s. 9 (see **B3.103**) or s. 13 (see **B3.124**). A further unsuccessful attempt to revive the defence arguments advanced in *G* was seen in *Delahaye-Bryan* [2015] EWCA Crim 1987.

The provisions of s. 73 apply to this offence (see **B3.79**).

Assault of a Child under 13 by Penetration

Sexual Offences Act 2003, s. 6 B3.87

(1) A person commits an offence if—
- (a) he intentionally penetrates the vagina or anus of another person with a part of his body or anything else,
- (b) the penetration is sexual, and
- (c) the other person is under 13.

Procedure An allegation of an offence contrary to s. 6 is triable only on indictment. As to the classification of the offence for the purpose of listing, see CrimPD XIII, para. B (see Supplement, **CPD.XIII.B**). It is an offence to which the extra-territorial jurisdiction provisions of s. 72 apply (see **B3.315**). B3.88

See **B3.355** for alternative verdicts.

Indictment B3.89

Statement of Offence

Assault of a child under 13 by penetration contrary to section 6 of the Sexual Offences Act 2003.

Particulars of Offence

A, on or about the... day of... penetrated the vagina [anus] of V a child then under the age of 13 years.

Sentence The maximum sentence is imprisonment for life (s. 6(2)). B3.90

The definitive sentencing guideline, *Sexual Offences* (see Supplement, **SG31-4**), applies to all sex offenders aged 18 or over who are sentenced on or after 1 April 2014 (see **B3.3**). The Council has issued separate guidelines for the under-13 offences (see Supplement, **SG31-8**). The definitive guideline, *Sentencing Children and Young People* (see Supplement, **SG8-1**), applies to all offenders under the age of 18 who are sentenced on or after 1 June 2017, regardless of the date of the offence. It supersedes part 7 of the original 2007 guideline.

There is a notification requirement under the SOA 2003, s. 80 and sch. 3 (see **E23**).

The offence is a qualifying offence for an automatic life sentence under the CJA 2003, sch. 15B (see **B3.25**). The provisions of the CJA 2003, s. 236A (offenders of particular concern: see **E4.31**), apply to this offence. The court should consider a sexual harm prevention order (see **E21.22**).

Elements The basic elements of the offence are the same as those governing such an assault on an adult and reference should therefore be made to **B3.53** to **B3.61**. However, consent is no defence and so there is no requirement on the prosecution to prove that the accused did not reasonably believe that the victim was consenting. It is necessary to prove that the victim was under the age of 13 at the time of the offence, but as with s. 5, it is not necessary to show that the accused knew or suspected that to be the case (see **B3.85**). B3.91

Section 73 applies to this offence (see **B3.79**).

Sexual Assault of a Child under 13

Sexual Offences Act 2003, s. 7 B3.92

(1) A person commits an offence if—
- (a) he intentionally touches another person,
- (b) the touching is sexual, and
- (c) the other person is under 13.

Procedure An allegation of an offence contrary to s. 7 is triable either way. As to the classification of the offence for the purpose of listing, see CrimPD XIII, para. B (see Supplement, **CPD.XIII.B**). The extra-territorial jurisdiction provisions of s. 72 apply (see **B3.315**). B3.93

See **B3.355** for alternative verdicts.

B3.94 Indictment

Statement of Offence

Sexual assault of a child under 13 contrary to section 7 of the Sexual Offences Act 2003

Particulars of Offence

A, on or about the . . . day of . . . sexually touched V, then a child under the age of 13 years.

B3.95 Sentence The maximum sentence for an offence under the SOA 2003, s. 7, on conviction on indictment is 14 years' imprisonment. On summary conviction, the maximum sentence is imprisonment for a term not exceeding six months and/or an unlimited fine.

The definitive sentencing guideline, *Sexual Offences* (see Supplement, **SG31-5**), applies to all sex offenders aged 18 or over who are sentenced on or after 1 April 2014 (see **B3.3**). The Council has issued separate guidelines for the under-13 offences (see Supplement, **SG31-9**). The definitive guideline, *Sentencing Children and Young People* (see Supplement, **SG8-1**), applies to all offenders under the age of 18 who are sentenced on or after 1 June 2017, regardless of the date of the offence. It supersedes part 7 of the original 2007 guideline.

There is a notification requirement under the SOA 2003, s. 80 and sch. 3, if the offender was aged 18 or over or was sentenced to at least 12 months' imprisonment (see **E23**). The court should consider a sexual harm prevention order (see **E21.22**).

The *Magistrates' Court Sentencing Guidelines* apply when sentencing in a magistrates' court. For an example of the application of the guideline, see *Nasir* [2015] EWCA Crim 1604.

The offence is a qualifying offence for an automatic life sentence under the CJA 2003, sch. 15B (see **B3.25**).

B3.96 Elements The elements of this offence are the same as for the adult offence (see **B3.68**) save that consent is not a defence. It is submitted that there is a necessary implication that this offence is one of strict liability as to age (see by analogy *K* [2001] UKHL 41, [2002] 1 AC 462).

In respect of aiding, abetting and counselling, the SOA 2003, s. 73, applies to this offence (see B3.79).

Causing or Inciting a Child under 13 to Engage in Sexual Activity

B3.97 **Sexual Offences Act 2003, s. 8**

(1) A person commits an offence if—
- (a) he intentionally causes or incites another person (B) to engage in an activity,
- (b) the activity is sexual, and
- (c) B is under 13.

B3.98 Procedure An allegation of an offence contrary to s. 8 is triable either way, except where the activity involved is penetrative when the allegation is triable on indictment only. As to the classification of the offence for the purpose of listing, see CrimPD XIII, para. B (see Supplement, **CPD.XIII.B**). The extra-territorial jurisdiction provisions of s. 72 apply (see B3.315).

See **B3.355** for alternative verdicts.

B3.99 Indictment

Statement of Offence

Causing or inciting a child under 13 to engage in sexual activity contrary to section 8 of the Sexual Offences Act 2003.

Particulars of Offence

A, on or about the... day of... caused V, then a child under the age of 13 years, to engage in sexual activity consisting of the penetration of V's [anus] [vagina] [mouth] with a part of V's body [an object].

Sentence The maximum sentence for an offence under the SOA 2003, s. 8, varies according to the type of activity involved. **B3.100**

Sexual Offences Act 2003, s. 8

(2) A person guilty of an offence under this section, if the activity caused or incited involved—
  (a) penetration of B's anus or vagina,
  (b) penetration of B's mouth with a person's penis,
  (c) penetration of a person's anus or vagina with a part of B's body or by B with anything else, or
  (d) penetration of a person's mouth with B's penis
  is liable, on conviction on indictment, to imprisonment for life.

(3) Unless subsection (2) applies, a person guilty of an offence under this section is liable—
  (a) on summary conviction, to imprisonment for a term not exceeding 6 months or to [an unlimited fine] or both;
  (b) on conviction on indictment, to imprisonment for a term not exceeding 14 years.

The definitive sentencing guideline, *Sexual Offences* (see Supplement, **SG31-10**), applies to all sex offenders aged 18 or over who are sentenced on or after 1 April 2014 (see **B3.3**). The definitive guideline, *Sentencing Children and Young People* (see Supplement, **SG8-1**), applies to all offenders under the age of 18 who are sentenced on or after 1 June 2017, regardless of the date of the offence. It supersedes part 7 of the original 2007 guideline.

There is a notification requirement under the SOA 2003, s. 80 and sch. 3 (see **E23**). The court should consider a sexual harm prevention order (see **E21.22**).

The offence is a qualifying offence for an automatic life sentence under the CJA 2003, sch. 15B (see **B3.25**).

Elements The basic elements of the offence of causing a child to engage in sexual activity are the same as those relating to the corresponding offence in relation to an adult and reference should therefore be made to **B3.70** to **B3.77**. In contrast to a similar offence against an adult, consent is no defence and so there is no requirement on the prosecution to prove that the accused did not reasonably believe that the victim was consenting. It is necessary to prove that the victim was under the age of 13 at the time of the offence. **B3.101**

In *Walker* [2006] EWCA Crim 1907, the Court of Appeal held that the essence of the offence of incitement was the encouragement of a person under the age of 13 to engage in the activity. It is that encouragement that must be intentional or deliberate. It is not necessary to prove that the accused intended that the encouraged sexual activity should actually happen. On the face of it, that is at odds with the general position in relation to common-law incitement that a person had to intend that the activity incited actually take place. In *Jones* [2007] EWCA Crim 1118, [2008] QB 460, the Court of Appeal held that the gravamen of the offence is the incitement of children under the age of 13 to engage in sexual activity; it is not concerned with the effect on a particular child. The criminality at which the offence is aimed is the incitement and it matters not if this is directed at a particular child or a very large group of children, or whether the child or children can be identified.

In *Grout* [2011] EWCA Crim 299, [2011] 1 Cr App R (S) 38 (472) the Court of Appeal emphasised (as pointed out by the authors of *Rook and Ward on Sexual Offences: Law and Practice* (4th edn, 2010) at para. 3.92, and (5th edn, 2016) at paras. 3.132 to 3.133) that because there are higher maximum punishments for offences committed under s. 8(2) of the SOA 2003, the effect of the House of Lords' decision in *Courtie* [1984] AC 463 is that, in practice, it creates four different offences. Each of those offences must be carried out intentionally. The first offence is causing penetrative sexual activity, the second is inciting such activity, the third is causing non-penetrative sexual activity and the fourth is inciting such activity. It is therefore important that the charge or indictment specifies which of these offences is being alleged.

For the meaning of 'sexual', see **B3.57**.

SEX OFFENCES AGAINST CHILDREN AGED 13 TO 15

B3.102 The child sex offences under the SOA 2003 which protect children under the age of 16 are contained in ss. 9 to 15 of the Act. In contrast to ss. 5 to 8, a reasonable mistaken belief as to the child's age will be capable of founding a defence but only if the child is 13 years of age or older. The offences are all gender neutral.

The Court Service is under an obligation to give priority to cases involving vulnerable witnesses, including child witnesses, and the prosecution and defence should remind the court of the need for priority listing. This point is specifically addressed in the *Witness Charter: Standards of care for witnesses in the Criminal Justice System* (December 2013).

Sexual Activity with a Child

B3.103

Sexual Offences Act 2003, s. 9

(1) A person aged 18 or over (A) commits an offence if—
   (a) he intentionally touches another person (B),
   (b) the touching is sexual, and
   (c) either—
      (i) B is under 16 and A does not reasonably believe that B is 16 or over, or
      (ii) B is under 13.

B3.104 **Procedure** An allegation of an offence contrary to s. 9 is triable either way unless the sexual activity involves penetration, in which case it is triable only on indictment. As to the classification of the offence for the purpose of listing, see CrimPD XIII, para. B (see Supplement, **CPD.XIII.B**). The extra-territorial jurisdiction provisions of s. 72 apply (see **B3.315**).

See **B3.355** for alternative verdicts.

An issue may arise as to whether D is 18 or over at the time of the offence. Under s. 9, unless the jury were sure that D was over 18, he would be not guilty of the charge. In respect of an alternative count under s. 13 (see **B3.124**), the same jury may not be sure that D was under 18 at the relevant time. Should D be acquitted of both charges? Whilst there is a degree of ambiguity in the relationship between ss. 9 and 13, it is submitted that D should not be acquitted of both counts. The essence of the offence alleged in both sections is sexual touching. The age of the offender is not determinative of whether an offence has taken place. Rather, the age of the offender is only decisive of the maximum penalty which may be imposed upon conviction (14 years' imprisonment for an offender aged 18 or over, five years' imprisonment for an offender under the age of 18). It would be absurd and unjust if a jury were to find that D had committed an offence against V but D had to be acquitted because they could not decide if he was under or over 18 at the time of the offence. In such circumstances, it is submitted that the benefit of any doubt should manifest itself in the maximum sentence which might be imposed. Thus, it is submitted that the court should seek to establish at an early stage of the proceedings whether any such issue exists. If such an issue does exist, or even if the issue emerges during the course of evidence, an alternative count alleging an offence under s. 13 should be added to the indictment. Upon retirement, the jury should be asked to consider, first, whether sexual touching occurred. If the answer to that is in the affirmative, they should next ask whether they were sure that the accused was aged 18 or over at the time of the offence. If they were sure of that there would be no need for them to consider the s. 13 count and they should then go on to consider the remaining relevant considerations under s. 9. If they were not sure that D was 18 or over at the relevant time, the appropriate verdict should be not guilty of s. 9. The jury should then go on to consider the remaining elements of the s. 13 count.

Indictment B3.105

Statement of Offence

Sexual activity with a child contrary to section 9(1) of the Sexual Offences Act 2003.

Particulars of Offence

A, on or about the... day of..., being then a person aged 18 or over, intentionally sexually touched V, then a child under the age of [16] [13] years

or

A, on or about the... day of..., being then a person aged 18 or over, intentionally sexually touched V, then a child under the age of [16] [13] years, by penetrating V's [anus] [vagina] with a part of A's body, namely... [an object].

Sentence The maximum sentence for an offence under the SOA 2003, s. 9, varies according to the activity involved. B3.106

For important guidance as to sentencing for this offence see *PS* [2019] EWCA Crim 2286, [2020] 2 Cr App R (S) 9 (56) at **B3.15**.

Sexual Offences Act 2003, s. 9

(2) A person guilty of an offence under this section, if the touching involved—
  (a) penetration of B's anus or vagina with a part of A's body or anything else,
  (b) penetration of B's mouth with A's penis,
  (c) penetration of A's anus or vagina with a part of B's body, or
  (d) penetration of A's mouth with B's penis,
  is liable, on conviction on indictment, to imprisonment for a term not exceeding 14 years.

(3) Unless subsection (2) applies, a person guilty of an offence under this section is liable—
  (a) on summary conviction, to imprisonment for a term not exceeding 6 months or to [an unlimited fine] or both;
  (b) on conviction on indictment, to imprisonment for a term not exceeding 14 years.

The maximum penalty also varies with A's age; if A is aged under 18, the maximum penalty is five years (see **B3.126**).

The definitive sentencing guideline, *Sexual Offences* (see Supplement, **SG31-11**), applies to all sex offenders aged 18 or over who are sentenced on or after 1 April 2014 (see **B3.3**).

For an example of the application of the guideline that demonstrates the seriousness with which the Court of Appeal views the grooming of children under the age of 16, especially in the context of an abuse of a position of trust, see *A-G's Ref (No. 106 of 2014) (Burns)* [2015] EWCA Crim 379. The Court took a similarly firm approach in *A-G's Ref (No. 124 of 2014) (Broni)* [2015] EWCA Crim 103 and *Spragg* [2017] EWCA Crim 263. In *TF* [2019] EWCA Crim 1785 (concerning offences under the SOA 2003, ss. 9 and 10), the Court of Appeal re-emphasised that the mere fact of the existence of a family relationship does not amount to a breach of trust and, absent planning or grooming, a 12-month suspended sentence was sufficient where consensual oral and vaginal intercourse took place between the appellant aged 19 and the complainant aged 14.

For the relationship between the guidelines relevant to offences under ss. 9 and 10, see *A-G's Ref (No. 94 of 2014)* [2014] EWCA Crim 2752, [2016] 4 WLR 121 (see **B3.112**).

There is a notification requirement under the SOA 2003, s. 80 and sch. 3 (see **E23**). The court should consider a sexual harm prevention order (see **E21.22**).

The offence is a qualifying offence for an automatic life sentence under the CJA 2003, sch. 15B (see **B3.25**).

A suspended sentence of 12 months' imprisonment for a 40-year-old woman who had had regular sexual intercourse with a boy of 14 was varied so as to be immediate in *A-G's Ref (No. 67 of 2008) (SE)* [2009] EWCA Crim 132, [2009] 2 Cr App R (S) 60 (428). Lord Judge CJ emphasised that the then guideline provided that there should be no distinction in sentence on the grounds of B3.107

the gender of the offender, save in specified circumstances where a distinction is justified on the basis of the nature of the offence. For an example of the use of the guideline when sentencing for offences of sexual assault of a child pre-dating the 2003 Act, see *Millar* [2009] EWCA Crim 74.

In *Howard* [2016] EWCA Crim 1511, [2017] 1 Cr App R (S) 8 (44), the Court of Appeal formed the view that an offender's severe learning difficulties, low IQ, low emotional maturity and vulnerability were relevant to culpability when it dealt with an A-G's reference relating to three offences under s. 9 of the SOA 2003 committed by a 26-year-old man against a 14-year-old girl. The offender had been sentenced to two years' imprisonment, suspended for two years for his offending. He was of previous good character and the girl and he had sexual intercourse at his flat on three occasions. There was no dispute that the offending fell into category 1 for harm. The issue before the Crown Court was in respect of the level of culpability and that centred on the age disparity between the offender and the girl. The judge considered the mental ages to be much closer than their chronological ages. Accordingly, culpability was assessed as somewhere between category 1A and 1B.

Upon reference to the Court of Appeal, the A-G submitted that the offender's learning difficulties should have been taken into account at Step Two (i.e. after the offences had been placed in the relevant category) so that the culpability should have been category 1A. The Court rejected that argument and refused permission, deciding that there was a link between the offender's learning difficulties and the true significance, in terms of culpability, of the disparity in age.

B3.108 **Elements** The basic elements of the offence are the same as those in respect of such an assault on an adult and reference should therefore be made to **B3.62** to **B3.69**.

As to 'sexual', see **B3.57**. For 'touching', see **B3.68**.

It is a defence if, even though the complainant was under 16, the accused reasonably believed the complainant to be 16 years old or older. The defence is not available if the child is under 13.

The provisions of s. 73 apply to this offence (see **B3.79**).

Causing or Inciting a Child to Engage in Sexual Activity

B3.109 **Sexual Offences Act 2003, s. 10**

(1) A person aged 18 or over (A) commits an offence if—
  (a) he intentionally causes or incites another person (B) to engage in an activity,
  (b) the activity is sexual, and
  (c) either—
    (i) B is under 16 and A does not reasonably believe that B is 16 or over, or
    (ii) B is under 13.

B3.110 **Procedure** An allegation of an offence contrary to s. 10 is ordinarily triable either way but, where the activity involves penetration, it is indictable only. As to the classification of the offence for the purpose of listing, see CrimPD XIII, para. B (see Supplement, **CPD.XIII.B**). The extra-territorial jurisdiction provisions of s. 72 apply (see **B3.315**).

See **B3.355** for alternative verdicts.

B3.111 **Indictment**

Statement of Offence

Intentionally causing or inciting a child to engage in a sexual activity contrary to section 10(1) of the Sexual Offences Act 2003.

Particulars of Offence

A, on or about the ... day of ... [being then a person aged 18 or over] intentionally caused or incited V, then a child under [16] [13] years of age, to engage in a sexual activity, namely ...

or

A, on or about the...day of... [being then a person aged 18 years or over] intentionally caused or incited V, then a child under the age of [16] [13] years, to engage in sexual activity, namely the penetration of V's [anus] [vagina] by another.

Sentence The maximum sentence for an offence under the SOA 2003, s. 10, varies according to the activity concerned. Section 10(2) and (3) indicate the maximum sentence which applies and in terms almost identical to s. 9(2) and (3) (see **B3.106**). The maximum penalty also varies with the age of the offender; if the offender is aged under 18, the maximum penalty is five years (see **B3.126**). **B3.112**

The definitive sentencing guideline, *Sexual Offences* (see Supplement, **SG31-11**), applies to all sex offenders aged 18 or over who are sentenced on or after 1 April 2014 (see **B3.3**). For an example of the application of the adult guideline, see *Petrie* [2014] EWCA Crim 2912. There is a notification requirement under the SOA 2003, s. 80 and sch. 3 (see **E23**). The court should consider a sexual harm prevention order (see **E21.22**).

The Court of Appeal considered whether a sentence of 180 days' imprisonment was unduly lenient in *A-G's Ref (No. 94 of 2014) (Baker)* [2014] EWCA Crim 2752, [2016] 4 WLR 121. The 34-year-old offender had invited a 13-year-old girl to perform oral sex on him in exchange for him buying her an iPhone. He was of previous good character and effectively pleaded guilty at the first opportunity. The A-G submitted that his offending fell into category 1A of the guideline, offending with a starting point of five years, but the application was refused. Sir Brian Leveson P observed that the question was whether incitement of the victim in the way admitted, which did not involve anything more, fell within the same category of harm as either penetration of the vagina or anus (using a body or object) or penile penetration of the mouth, deserving of similar sanction subject to culpability and such aggravating and mitigating circumstances as might otherwise exist. He continued (at [30]–[34]):

> On this basis, such incitement, which does not involve physical contact or exposure of any sort is more serious than a category 2 offence which involves touching or exposure of naked genitalia or naked breasts by or of the victim. To provide colour to this example, if the analysis is correct, it is more serious to incite a child as this offender did than had he actually persuaded her to undress before a web camera and expose to him her breasts or genitalia. It would equally be more serious than persuading a boy to masturbate in front of a web camera. In our judgment, that simply cannot be right.
>
> ...
>
> The answer however is to recognise that this guideline covers very different offending and that the language used within it must be construed by particular reference to the offence then under consideration. Thus, if over a web camera, a female child is incited to insert an object into her vagina and she does so, a category 1 offence is committed; if a child is persuaded to touch or expose his or her naked genitalia and does so, that is a category 2 offence. Similarly, if a child is incited to persuade someone else (whether or not the offender) actually to behave in that manner, the offence is correctly characterised as category 1 or 2 respectively. The harm is the impact on the victim of behaving as he or she has done, whether in the presence of the offender or remotely or on line.
>
> To that extent, the offence of causing sexual activity is potentially more serious than inciting such activity because the actual activity is a necessary part of the offence. Incitement can lead to actual activity which can be categorised accordingly. But where the incitement does not lead the child to behave in the manner incited, although the culpability is likely to be identical, the harm is necessarily less: the same is so in relation to attempts.
>
> In our judgment, what happened here did not fall within category 1 at all. In the circumstances, because the offending did not proceed beyond incitement, it was 'other sexual activity' within category 3. That accords not only with the judge's rejection of the suggestion that the offender's behaviour justified a starting point of five years but also provides appropriate headroom between the sexual suggestion and any actual activity without necessarily engaging upon the exceptional basis for departing from the Guideline.

In *Johnson* [2019] EWCA Crim 1537, the Court of Appeal dealt with an appeal against a sentence of 16 months' detention in a young offender institution for an offence contrary to the SOA 2003, s. 10(1). The appellant had developed a relationship with a 14-year-old girl when he was 17 but close to his 18th birthday. The girl's parents tried to discourage the relationship. He had recently reached the age of 18 when he sent her a series of text messages encouraging her to have full sexual intercourse with him. The sentencing judge assessed the offending as falling into category 1B. That has a sentencing range of a high level community order to two years' custody with a starting point of 12 months' custody. The judge indicated that he would have sentenced the appellant to two years' imprisonment after trial, and with full credit for a guilty plea reduced the sentence to one of 16 months. On appeal it was contended that the learned judge had taken too high a starting point for sentence; he did not have sufficient regard for the age of the applicant; he did not have sufficient regard for the personal mitigation relating to the applicant's background and psychological issues; and there was an appropriate alternative to custody available which should have been pursued. So far as the starting point was concerned, the Court referred to what appears to be a void between the sentencing ranges for category 1A offending and 1B offending, observing:

> 17. Although it does not appear explicitly from the sentencing remarks, we suspect that the judge's decision to settle on 2 years before discount for plea was influenced by the submission that this was in fact a category 1A case because of the possible element of grooming to which we have referred. It is an unusual feature of this particular guideline that there is a 'void' between the category ranges for category 1A, 4 to 10 years, and category B, community order to 2 years. That void poses a potential difficulty where, as here, a case may be said not to fall entirely happily into one category or the other and the court settles on the lower category.
>
> 18. This was undoubtedly a serious case such that all agreed that it fell within category 1. But once the judge settled on category 1B it is not clear from the sentencing remarks what features were relied upon to justify a one hundred per cent increase from the starting point of 1 year unless it was intended simply to be recognition of the worrying features of the case to which we have referred.

The Court also saw force in the appellant's other submissions and substituted a sentence of 12 months' imprisonment.

For important guidance as to sentencing for this offence see *PS* [2019] EWCA Crim 2286, [2020] 2 Cr App R (S) 9 (56) at **B3.15**. For an example of a successful reference of an unduly lenient sentence for offences contrary to the SOA 2003, s. 10, see *FS* [2019] EWCA Crim 2389.

In *Gustafsson* [2017] EWCA Crim 1078 (subsequently approved in Cook [2018] EWCA Crim 530, [2018] 2 Cr App R (S) 16 (117) and *Liddiard* [2019] EWCA Crim 1819), the Court of Appeal held that where the offending arises out the offender's efforts to incite penetrative sex but no such activity occurs and there is no communication with an actual child (merely a fictional child), that will only constitute category 3 harm. The Court thus followed the lead set in *Baker*.

The approach to be taken in offences charged under the SOA 2003, ss. 9 and 10 may in future be different to that taken in respect of offences under s. 14 (see *Privett* [2020] EWCA Crim 557 at **B3.131**). In *Manning* [2020] EWCA Crim 592, [2020] 4 WLR 77 (where the judgment was delivered by Lord Maldon CJ the day after judgment was delivered by Fulford V-P in *Privett*), the Solicitor-General sought to challenge as unduly lenient a suspended sentence order of 12 months' duration imposed on an offender for offences under ss. 9 and 10. The offender had pleaded guilty to four counts of sexual activity with a child, contrary to s. 9(1) (counts 1 to 4), and to one count of causing or inciting a child to engage in sexual activity, contrary to s. 10(1) (count 5). The 49-year-old offender and 14-year-old complainant met on a number of occasions and the sexual activity between them included kissing, the touching of the complainant's breast through her clothes and the placing of the complainant's hand on the offender's erect penis over his clothes. The incitement count related to text messages sent by the offender which referred to the possibility of penetrative sex. It had been argued by the prosecution before the sentencing judge that because the sexual activity incited was penetrative sex, the offence should be located within category 1 for harm. There was no issue but that the culpability fell within category A and, in those circumstances, the prosecution contended that the starting point for the incitement count was five years' custody, with a category range of four to ten years' custody. The fact that no penetrative sex had occurred should be treated only as a mitigating factor. The judge rejected that argument and concluded that the case fell within category 3 harm, namely, 'other sexual activity'. When linked with culpability at level A, the starting point was one of 26 weeks' custody, with a category range of a high-level community order to three years' custody. The first and principal argument by the Solicitor-General on the reference was that the categorisation of harm as category 3 was in error and, despite the fact that no penetrative activity had taken place, the case should have been located within category 1 harm. Following a review of the relevant authorities, including Baker and Cook, the Court of Appeal said (at [11]):

> [Counsel] who appears on behalf of the Solicitor General, realistically recognises that in the face of the weight of that authority, the first and principal argument advanced on behalf of the Solicitor General in the Final Reference cannot be sustained.

The Court of Appeal allowed the reference to the extent of substituting for the custodial term of 12 months a custodial term of 24 months. The sentence remained a suspended sentence.

The offence is a qualifying offence for an automatic life sentence under the CJA 2003, sch. 15B (see **B3.25**).

Elements The offender must be at least 18 years of age. Plainly, when the victim is under the age of 13, the offence will be covered by s. 8. A reasonable belief that the victim was at least 16 years of age affords a defence unless the victim was under 13. **B3.113**

In *Mumford* (11 November 2014 unreported) the Court of Appeal reversed a terminating ruling relating to the trial of an offence under the SOA 2003, s. 10, where D had handed a note to a 13-year-old girl which read 'Between me and you your beautiful and have a nice bum lol. Come round for some fun if you want at 12. Please keep it quiet tho. If you don't that's fine. Come round the back if you do. X.' The trial judge had ruled that the communication did not amount to incitement. The Court of Appeal disagreed, ruling:

> ...we have no doubt that the words used are capable of amounting to an incitement to engage in sexual activity. It is certainly a proposal or request. It seeks to influence the mind of the girl whom he propositioned by reference to the flattering description of her body and the prospect of having fun. In those circumstances, it is certainly open to the jury to conclude that he was inciting sexual activity in that he was proposing, seeking to instigate and stimulating it. Neither is this inconsistent with it being an invitation which the girl was at liberty to refuse. It is a perfectly legitimate inference that he wanted her to accept otherwise why proposition her?

For the meaning of 'sexual', see **B3.57**.

Engaging in Sexual Activity in the Presence of a Child

Sexual Offences Act 2003, s. 11 **B3.114**

(1) A person aged 18 or over (A) commits an offence if—
  (a) he intentionally engages in an activity,
  (b) the activity is sexual,
  (c) for the purpose of obtaining sexual gratification, he engages in it—
    (i) when another person (B) is present or is in a place from which A can be observed, and
    (ii) knowing or believing that B is aware, or intending that B should be aware, that he is engaging in it, and
  (d) either—
    (i) B is under 16 and A does not reasonably believe that B is 16 or over, or
    (ii) B is under 13.

Procedure An allegation of an offence contrary to s. 11 is triable either way. As to the classification of the offence for the purpose of listing, see CrimPD XIII, para. B (see Supplement, **CPD.XIII.B**). The extra-territorial jurisdiction provisions of s. 72 apply (see **B3.315**). **B3.115**

See **B3.355** for alternative verdicts.

B3.116 **Indictment**

Statement of Offence

Intentionally engaging in sexual activity in the presence of a child contrary to section 11(1) of the Sexual Offences Act 2003.

Particulars of Offence

A, on or about the... day of... [being then a person aged 18 years or over] intentionally engaged in a sexual activity for the purpose of obtaining sexual gratification from knowing that V, then a child under the age of [16] [13] years was present or was in a place from which he could observe A and knew [believed] that V was aware that he was engaging in it [intending that V should be aware that he was engaging in it].

B3.117 **Sentence** The maximum sentence for an offence under the SOA 2003, s. 11, on indictment is ten years' imprisonment. The maximum penalty varies with the age of the offender; if the offender is aged under 18, the maximum penalty is five years (see **B3.126**). On summary conviction, the maximum sentence is six months and/or an unlimited fine (s. 11(2)).

The definitive sentencing guideline, *Sexual Offences* (see Supplement, **SG31-13**), applies to all sex offenders aged 18 or over who are sentenced on or after 1 April 2014 (see **B3.3**).

For important guidance as to sentencing for this offence see *PS* [2019] EWCA Crim 2286, [2020] 2 Cr App R (S) 9 (56) at **B3.15**.

There is a notification requirement under the SOA 2003, s. 80 and sch. 3 (see **E23**). The court should consider a sexual harm prevention order (see **E21.22**).
The offence is a qualifying offence for an automatic life sentence under the CJA 2003, sch. 15B (see **B3.25**).

B3.118 **Elements** The offender must be aged 18 or over and must intentionally engage in sexual activity with a person other than the victim.

It is a defence that the alleged offender reasonably believed the victim to be aged at least 16 unless the victim is under 13.

For 'sexual gratification', see **B3.123**. In *B* [2018] EWCA Crim 1439, the Court of Appeal decided that the offender must gain sexual gratification from the presence of the child. It is not enough that the offender engages in sexual conduct bringing sexual gratification while knowing that a child is present. Giving the judgment of the Court, Hallett V-P said (at [29]):

> ... the ordinary and natural meaning of the section and the intention of the legislature is that the offence is committed if a person (A)
> i. intentionally engages in an activity that is sexual,
> ii. in the presence or under the observation of a child (B),
> iii. A does so for the purpose of A's obtaining (some) sexual gratification from B's presence or observation,
> iv. A knew or believed that B was aware of the activity or intended that B should be aware of the activity, and
> v. the child B was under 16 and A did not reasonably believe that B was 16 or over or B was under 13.

For the meaning of 'sexual', see **B3.57**.

Causing a Child to Watch a Sex Act

B3.119 **Sexual Offences Act 2003, s. 12**

(1) A person aged 18 or over (A) commits an offence if—
 (a) for the purpose of obtaining sexual gratification, he intentionally causes another person (B) to watch a third person engaging in an activity, or to look at an image of any person engaging in an activity,
 (b) the activity is sexual, and
 (c) either—
  (i) B is under 16 and A does not reasonably believe that B is 16 or over, or
  (ii) B is under 13.

Procedure An allegation of an offence contrary to s. 12 is triable either way. As to the classification of the offence for the purpose of listing, see CrimPD XIII, para. B (see Supplement, **CPD.XIII.B**). The extra-territorial jurisdiction provisions of s. 72 apply (see **B3.315**). **B3.120**

See **B3.355** for alternative verdicts.

Indictment **B3.121**

Statement of Offence

Causing a child to watch a sexual act contrary to section 12(1) of the Sexual Offences Act 2003.

Particulars of Offence

A, on or about the... day of... [being then a person aged 18 years or over] for the purpose of obtaining sexual gratification for himself intentionally caused V a child under the age of [16] [13] years to watch a third person engaging in [or][look at an image of another person engaging in], a sexual activity, the said A not reasonably believing that V was aged 16 or over.

Sentence The maximum sentence for an offence under the SOA 2003, s. 12 on conviction on indictment is ten years' imprisonment. On summary conviction the maximum sentence is six months and/or an unlimited fine (s. 12(2)). The maximum penalty also varies with the age of the offender; if the offender is aged under 18, the maximum penalty is five years (see **B3.126**). **B3.122**

The definitive sentencing guideline, *Sexual Offences* (see Supplement, **SG31-13**), applies to sex offenders aged 18 or over who are sentenced on or after 1 April 2014 (see **B3.3**).

For important guidance as to sentencing for this offence see *PS* [2019] EWCA Crim 2286, [2020] 2 Cr App R (S) 9 (56) at **B3.15**.

There is a notification requirement under the SOA 2003, s. 80 and sch. 3 (see **E23**). The court should consider a sexual harm prevention order (see **E21.22**).

The offence is a qualifying offence for an automatic life sentence under the CJA 2003, sch. 15B (see **B3.25**).

Elements The offender must be aged 18 or over and must intentionally engage in sexual activity with a person other than the victim. **B3.123**

It is a defence that the alleged offender reasonably believed the victim to be aged at least 16 unless the victim was under 13.

For the meaning of 'sexual', see **B3.57**.

In *Abdullahi* [2006] EWCA Crim 2060, [2007] 1 WLR 225, the Court of Appeal considered whether it was necessary for the purposes of s. 12 for the sexual gratification to be simultaneous or contemporaneous or synchronised with the watching of the sexual activity or image. The Court ruled that there was nothing in the language of s. 12 to suggest that that was the case and consequently the gratification could be deferred until much later. (For commentary on this case by Professor David Ormerod, see [2007] Crim LR 184.)

The offence has a 'bolted on intent' in that the intentional act must be 'for the purpose of obtaining sexual gratification'. It is therefore an offence of specific intent and, consequently, voluntary intoxication may negate the intent required for the offence (*Heard* [2007] EWCA Crim 125, [2008] QB 43).

For consideration of the acts necessary to constitute an attempt to commit an offence contrary to s. 12 see *K* [2009] EWCA Crim 1931.

Child Sex Offences Committed by Children or Young Persons

Sexual Offences Act 2003, s. 13 **B3.124**

(1) A person under 18 commits an offence if he does anything which would be an offence under any of sections 9 to 12 if he were aged 18.

(2) A person guilty of an offence under this section is liable—
(a) on summary conviction, to imprisonment for a term not exceeding 6 months or [an unlimited fine] or both;
(b) on conviction on indictment, to imprisonment for a term not exceeding 5 years.

B3.125 **Procedure** An allegation of an offence contrary to s. 13 is triable either way. As to the classification of the offence for the purpose of listing, see CrimPD XIII, para. B (see Supplement, **CPD.XIII.B**). The extra-territorial jurisdiction provisions of s. 72 apply (see **B3.315**).

See **B3.355** for alternative verdicts.

For discussion as to the appropriate course to take when there is an issue as to whether D was aged 18 or over at the time of the offence, see **B3.104**.

B3.126 **Sentence** The maximum sentence for an offence under the SOA 2003, s. 13, on conviction on indictment is five years' imprisonment. On summary conviction, the maximum is six months and/or an unlimited fine (s. 13(2)).

The definitive guideline, *Sentencing Children and Young People* (see Supplement, **SG8-1**), applies to all offenders under the age of 18 who are sentenced on or after 1 June 2017, regardless of the date of the offence. It supersedes part 7 of the original 2007 guideline.

There is a notification requirement under the SOA 2003, s. 80 and sch. 3, if the offender was sentenced to at least 12 months' imprisonment (see **E23**). The court should consider a sexual harm prevention order (see **E21.22**).

B3.127 **Elements** For the elements of the offences contrary to ss. 9 to 12, see **B3.108**, **B3.113**, **B3.118** and **B3.123**. For an example of potential difficulties that may be encountered in summing up a case concerning s. 13 see *JAS* [2015] EWCA Crim 2254.

If the offence charged under s. 13 would amount to an offence under s. 9 if the offender was aged 18, then the provisions of s. 73 apply (see **B3.79**).

Arranging or Facilitating Commission of a Child Sex Offence

B3.128 **Sexual Offences Act 2003, s. 14**

(1) A person commits an offence if—
(a) he intentionally arranges or facilitates something that he intends to do, intends another person to do, or believes that another person will do, in any part of the world, and
(b) doing it will involve the commission of an offence under any of sections 9 to 13.
(2) A person does not commit an offence under this section if—
(a) he arranges or facilitates something that he believes another person will do, but that he does not intend to do or intend another person to do, and
(b) any offence within subsection (1)(b) would be an offence against a child for whose protection he acts.
(3) For the purposes of subsection (2), a person acts for the protection of a child if he acts for the purpose of—
(a) protecting the child from sexually transmitted infection,
(b) protecting the physical safety of the child,
(c) preventing the child from becoming pregnant, or
(d) promoting the child's emotional well-being by the giving of advice,
and not for the purpose of obtaining sexual gratification or for the purpose of causing or encouraging the activity constituting the offence within subsection (1)(b) or the child's participation in it.

B3.129 **Procedure** An allegation of an offence contrary to s. 14 is triable either way. As to the classification of the offence for the purpose of listing, see CrimPD XIII, para. B (see Supplement, **CPD.XIII.B**). The extra-territorial jurisdiction provisions of s. 72 apply (see **B3.315**).

See **B3.355** for alternative verdicts.

Indictment B3.130

Statement of Offence

Arranging or facilitating commission of a child sex offence contrary to section 14(1) of the Sexual Offences Act 2003.

Particulars of Offence

A, on [or about] the...day of...intentionally arranged the doing or facilitating of an act [intending that it be done] [by himself] [by another] [believing that it would be done by another] [in any part of the world] and knowing that the doing of it will involve [sexual activity with a child under 16 years of age] [causing or inciting a child under the age of 16 to engage in sexual activity] [causing or inciting a child under 16 years of age to engage in sexual activity] [engaging in sexual activity in the presence of a child under 16 years of age] [causing a child under 16 years of age to watch a sexual act].

Sentence The maximum sentence for an offence under the SOA 2003, s. 14, on conviction on indictment is 14 years' imprisonment. On summary conviction, the maximum sentence is six months and/or an unlimited fine (s. 14(4)). B3.131

The definitive sentencing guideline, *Sexual Offences* (see Supplement, **SG31-14**), applies to all sex offenders aged 18 or over who are sentenced on or after 1 April 2014 (see **B3.3**). The definitive guideline, *Sentencing Children and Young People* (see Supplement, **SG8-1**), applies to all offenders under the age of 18 who are sentenced on or after 1 June 2017, regardless of the date of the offence. It supersedes part 7 of the original 2007 guideline.

For examples of the application of the adult guideline to offences contrary to s. 14, see *Haldane* [2015] EWCA Crim 1991, *Collins* [2015] EWCA Crim 915, [2015] 2 Cr App R (S) 50 (368), *Lewis* [2016] EWCA Crim 304 and *Robinson* [2016] EWCA Crim 1546.

In *Privett* [2020] EWCA Crim 557, the Court of Appeal deal with four otherwise unrelated appeals together in order to address sentencing practice for offences under s. 14. The common feature was that when the individual defendants arranged, via the internet, to commit a sexual offence with a child, they were unaware they were in contact with a police officer. After a comprehensive review of occasionally apparently inconsistent, relevant authorities, Fulford V-P, giving the judgment of the Court, said (at [67]):

> Focusing on the particular issue raised in these appeals, we consider that for a section 14 offence, the position under the Guideline is clear: the judge should, first, identify the category of harm on the basis of the sexual activity the defendant intended ('the level of harm should be determined by reference to the type of activity arranged or facilitated'), and, second, adjust the sentence in order to ensure it is 'commensurate' with, or proportionate to, the applicable starting point and range if no sexual activity had occurred (including because the victim was fictional) ('sentences commensurate with the applicable starting point and range will ordinarily be appropriate').

The Court distinguished the approach taken in *A-G's Ref (No. 94 of 2014) (Baker)* [2014] EWCA Crim 2752, [2016] 4 WLR 121 (see **B3.112**), on the basis that it was dealing with a different offence and, at least to an extent, different circumstances. The Court said that it was unable to accept the submission that *Baker* requires that s. 14 offences in which there is no real child must always be treated as category 3A offences under the guideline. The Court also recognised that aspects of the decision in *Baker* may well need to be revisited in the light of its judgment, but emphasised that it was dealing with offences under s. 14 and not offences under ss. 9 and 10. Consequently, the Court disapproved the approach taken in the s. 14 cases of *Allington* [2019] EWCA Crim 1430, [2020] 1 Cr App R (S) 16 (134) and *Stillwell* [2016] EWCA Crim 1375. The Court concluded (at [69]):

> Sentencers in future with section 14 offences in these circumstances should follow the Sentencing Guideline in the way we have described above at [67]. This may lead to the result that a defendant who arranges the rape of a fictional 6-year-old is punished more severely than a defendant who facilitates a comparatively minor sexual assault on a real 15-year-old. In our view, there is nothing necessarily wrong in principle with that result. The sentence should be commensurate with the applicable starting point and range, and in cases where the child is a fiction this will usually involve some reduction...to reflect the lack of harm.

The argument in *Privett* was heard on 25 February 2020 and judgment was delivered on 29 April 2020. On 30 April 2020, Lord Maldon CJ delivered the judgment in *Manning* [2020] EWCA Crim 592, [2020] 4 WLR 77 (see **B3.112**), a case concerning ss. 9 and 10, in which the prosecution conceded that, in the light of authority, its first and principal argument (to the effect that if penetrative sex was incited the harm should be viewed as category 1 and the fact that no penetrative sex had occurred should be treated only as a mitigating factor) could not be sustained.

There is a notification requirement under the SOA 2003, s. 80 and sch. 3, if the offender was aged 18 or over or was sentenced to at least 12 months' imprisonment (see **E23**). The court should consider a sexual harm prevention order (see **E21.22**).

The offence is a qualifying offence for an automatic life sentence under the CJA 2003, sch. 15B (see **B3.25**).

B3.132 **Elements** The elements of offences under the SOA 2003, ss. 9 to 13, are set out at **B3.108**, **B3.113**, **B3.118**, **B3.123** and **B3.127**.

The defence set out in s. 14(2) would cover such acts for the physical and emotional well-being of a child as the provision of contraceptives and the giving of advice as an 'agony aunt'.

R [2008] EWCA Crim 619, [2009] 1 WLR 713 concerned an appeal against a terminating ruling in respect of an allegation of an offence contrary to s. 14. The accused was a regular client of the principal prosecution witness, a prostitute, and asked her repeatedly whether she knew of any young girls aged 12 or 13 who were working as prostitutes. The witness did not make any inquiries and reported the matter to the police when she received two text messages reading 'Heard owt of 12 lass, let me know' and, on the following day, 'you got the 12 year old sorted yet?' The trial judge ruled that the facts as alleged could not amount to an offence under s. 14, nor an attempt to commit such an offence. The Court of Appeal, in an extempore ruling from Moses LJ, varied that ruling in concluding that the request could amount to an attempt to commit an offence under s. 14, as the acts of preparation criminalised by s. 14 comprise a substantive offence and not an attempt. The purpose of the imposition of criminal liability in that way (as with other sections of the 2003 Act) was to prevent the risk of children being subjected to sexual abuse. The jury were entitled to take the view that what the accused did in making the request was an attempt and not the mere preparation to make the arrangement. The request was the final thing he needed to do to make the arrangement and if the request had been accepted the full offence would have been committed. The Court of Appeal confined itself to whether the facts could establish an attempt to commit such an offence and specifically stated that it did not need to decide whether in merely making the request the accused could properly be said to have committed the full offence. Indeed, Moses LJ said that nothing the Court had said was designed to indicate that what was alleged might not indeed constitute the full offence under s. 14.

When the case returned to the Crown Court, D was convicted of an attempt to commit an offence contrary to s. 14 and sentenced to three years' imprisonment. His conviction was later quashed because of a separate judicial misdirection (*JR* [2008] EWCA Crim 2912).

Meeting a Child following Sexual Grooming

B3.133 **Sexual Offences Act 2003, s. 15**

(1) A person aged 18 or over (A) commits an offence if—
   (a) A has met or communicated with another person (B) on one or more occasions and subsequently—
      (i) A intentionally meets B,
      (ii) A travels with the intention of meeting B in any part of the world or arranges to meet B in any part of the world, or
      (iii) B travels with the intention of meeting A in any part of the world,
   (b) A intends to do anything to or in respect of B, during or after the meeting mentioned in paragraph (a)(i) to (iii) and in any part of the world, which if done will involve the commission by A of a relevant offence,

(c) B is under 16, and
(d) A does not reasonably believe that B is 16 or over.
(2) In subsection (1)—
(a) the reference to A having met or communicated with B is a reference to A having met B in any part of the world or having communicated with B by any means from, to or in any part of the world;
(b) 'relevant offence' means—
(i) an offence under this part,
(ii) an offence within any of paragraphs 61 to 92 of Schedule 3, or
(iii) anything done outside England and Wales and Northern Ireland which is not an offence within sub-paragraph (i) or (ii) but would be an offence within sub-paragraph (i) if done in England and Wales.

Procedure An allegation of an offence contrary to s. 15 is triable either way. As to the classification of the offence for the purpose of listing, see CrimPD XIII, para. B (see Supplement, **CPD.XIII.B**). The extra-territorial jurisdiction provisions of s. 72 apply (see **B3.315**). **B3.134**

See **B3.355** for alternative verdicts.

Indictment **B3.135**

Statement of Offence

Meeting a child following sexual grooming contrary to section 15(1) of the Sexual Offences Act 2003.

Particulars of Offence

A, on or about the... day of... having met or communicated with V a child under the age of 16 years on two earlier occasions intentionally met V [travelled with the intention of meeting V] and with intent to [specify facts constituting relevant offence].

Sentence The maximum sentence for an offence under the SOA 2003, s. 15, on conviction on indictment is ten years' imprisonment. On summary conviction, the maximum is six months and/or an unlimited fine (s. 15(4)). **B3.136**

The definitive sentencing guideline, *Sexual Offences* (see Supplement, **SG31-15**) applies to sex offenders aged 18 or over who are sentenced on or after 1 April 2014 (see **B3.3**). There is a notification requirement under the SOA 2003, s. 80 and sch. 3 (see **E23**). The court should consider a sexual harm prevention order (see **E21.22**).

In *Solanki* [2017] EWCA Crim 1282, [2018] 1 Cr App R (S) 34 (243), the Court of Appeal observed (at [26]) that in a case where the appellant went to the meeting place intending penetrative activity with an underage girl, an immediate custodial term was appropriate even in the case of a man of good character.

For an example of the application of the definitive guideline to the sentencing of a female teaching assistant at a school for children with special needs see *Beattie-Milligan* [2019] EWCA Crim 2367.

The offence is a qualifying offence for an automatic life sentence under the CJA 2003, sch. 15B (see **B3.25**).

Elements The offender must be aged 18 or over and a reasonable belief that the victim was 16 or over constitutes a defence. **B3.137**

A relevant offence is defined under s. 15(2) as being any offence under part 1 or paras. 61 to 92 of sch. 3 to the SOA 2003. Part 1 is comprised of ss. 1 to 79; the sch. 3 paragraphs referred to identify sexual offences under the law of Northern Ireland.

In *G* [2010] EWCA Crim 1693 the Court of Appeal explained that there is absolutely no requirement that any communication which forms part of the grooming be sexual in nature. The only requirement prior to the intentional meeting during which A (over 18) intends to do anything to B (under 16) which, if carried out, would involve the commission by A of a relevant offence is that they have met or communicated 'on at least two occasions'.

Section 36(1) of the CJCA 2015 amended s. 15(1)(a) with effect from 13 April 2015 by requiring that A has met B on 'one or more occasions' rather than on 'at least two occasions', as had been the previous wording. Section 36(2) of the CJCA 2015 makes clear that, in a case in which person A met or communicated with person B only once before the event mentioned in s. 15(1)(a)(i) to (iii), an offence under s. 15 is committed only if the meeting or communication took place after s. 36 came into force.

Sexual Communication with a Child

B3.138 **Sexual Offences Act 2003, s. 15A**

(1) A person aged 18 or over (A) commits an offence if—
   (a) for the purpose of obtaining sexual gratification, A intentionally communicates with another person (B),
   (b) the communication is sexual or is intended to encourage B to make (whether to A or to another) a communication that is sexual, and
   (c) B is under 16 and A does not reasonably believe that B is 16 or over.
(2) For the purposes of this section, a communication is sexual if—
   (a) any part of it relates to sexual activity, or
   (b) a reasonable person would, in all the circumstances but regardless of any person's purpose, consider any part of the communication to be sexual;

and in paragraph (a) 'sexual activity' means an activity that a reasonable person would, in all the circumstances but regardless of any person's purpose, consider to be sexual.

Section 15A was inserted by the SCA 2015, s. 67, in force from 3 April 2017 (SI 2017 No. 451).

B3.139 **Procedure** The offence is triable either way.

B3.140 **Sentence** The maximum penalty is six months' imprisonment and/or an unlimited fine on summary conviction, and two years' imprisonment on conviction on indictment (s. 15A(3)). In *Stephenson* [2019] EWCA Crim 2418, the Court of Appeal quashed a sentence of 12 months' imprisonment and substituted a suspended sentence of six months where a 63-year-old offender of previous good character chatted online with a person he believed to be a 12-year-old girl (but who was in fact a police officer) and ended the conversation voluntarily.

B3.141 **Elements** Note that the term 'sexual' is to be interpreted in accordance with s. 15A(2); the definition of the term in s. 78 of the SOA 2003 does not apply (SCA 2015, sch. 4, para. 63).

ABUSE OF A POSITION OF TRUST

B3.142 Offences involving abuse of a position of trust are contained in ss. 16 to 19 of the SOA 2003. The conditions giving rise to a position of trust between A and B are set out in s. 21.

The offences set out in ss. 16 to 19 essentially correspond to the offences under ss. 9 to 12 but with the added element of the breach of trust and some other minor differences.

Section 22 provides further definitions relevant to the operation of ss. 16 to 19.

Sections 23 and 24 make specific provision for defences to charges under ss. 16 to 19. Section 23 provides a defence to such a charge if B is aged 16 or over and A and B are either lawfully married or civil partners of each other. Section 24 provides a defence if a lawful sexual relationship existed between A and B before the formation of a relationship between them of the type referred to in s. 21.

The defences provided for by ss. 23 and 24 must be proved by the accused. It is submitted that the burden is evidential.

Sexual Offences Act 2003, ss. 21 to 24 B3.143

21.—(1) For the purposes of sections 16 to 19, a person (A) is in a position of trust in relation to another person (B) if—
(a) any of the following subsections applies, or
(b) any condition specified in an order made by the Secretary of State is met.
(2) This subsection applies if A looks after persons under 18 who are detained in an institution by virtue of a court order or under an enactment, and B is so detained in that institution.
(3) This subsection applies if A looks after persons under 18 who are resident in a home or other place in which—
(a) accommodation and maintenance are provided by an authority in accordance with section 22C(6) of the Children Act 1989 or section 81(6) of the Social Services and Well-being (Wales) Act 2014, or
(b) accommodation is provided by a voluntary organisation under section 59(1) of the Children Act 1989,
and B is resident, and is so provided with accommodation and maintenance or accommodation, in that place.
(4) This subsection applies if A looks after persons under 18 who are accommodated and cared for in one of the following institutions—
(a) a hospital,
(b) in Wales, an independent clinic,
(c) a care home,
(d) a community home, voluntary home or children's home, or
(e) a home provided under section 82(5) of the Children Act 1989,
(f) [repealed]
(g) a place in Wales at which a care home service is provided,
(h) premises in Wales at which a secure accommodation service is provided,
and B is accommodated and cared for in that institution.
(5) This subsection applies if A looks after persons under 18 who are receiving education at an educational institution and B is receiving, and A is not receiving, education at that institution.
(6) [Repealed.]
(7) This subsection applies if A is engaged in the provision of services under, or pursuant to anything done under—
(a) sections 8 to 10 of the Employment and Training Act 1973, or
(b) section 68, 70(1)(b) or 74 of the Education and Skills Act 2008,
and, in that capacity, looks after B on an individual basis.
(8) This subsection applies if A regularly has unsupervised contact with B (whether face to face or by any other means)—
(a) in the exercise of functions of a local authority under section 20 or 21 of the Children Act 1989 or section 76 or 77 of the Social Services and Well-being (Wales) Act 2014.
(b) [repealed].
(9) This subsection applies if A, as a person who is to report to the court under section 7 of the Children Act 1989 on matters relating to the welfare of B, regularly has unsupervised contact with B (whether face to face or by any other means).
(10) This subsection applies if A is a personal adviser appointed for B under—
(a) section 23B(2) of, or paragraph 19C of Schedule 2 to, the Children Act 1989, or
(aa) section 106(1) of the Social Services and Well-being (Wales) Act 2014 in respect of category 1 or 2 young persons within the meaning of that Act,
(b) [repealed]
and, in that capacity, looks after B on an individual basis.
(11) This subsection applies if—
(a) B is subject to a care order, a supervision order or an education supervision order, and
(b) in the exercise of functions conferred by virtue of the order on an authorised person or the authority designated by the order, A looks after B on an individual basis.
(12) This subsection applies if A—
(a) is an officer of the Service or Welsh family proceedings officer (within the meaning given by section 35 of the Children Act 2004) appointed for B under section 41(1) of the Children Act 1989,
(b) is appointed a children's guardian of B under rule 6 or rule 18 of the Adoption Rules 1984 (SI 1984/265),

(c) is appointed to be the guardian ad litem of B under rule 9.5 of the Family Proceedings Rules 1991 (SI 1991/1247), or
(d) is appointed to be the children's guardian of B under rule 59 of the Family Procedure (Adoption) Rules 2005 (SI 2005/2795) or rule 16.3(1)(ii) or rule 16.4 of the Family Procedure Rules 2010 (SI 2010/2955),

and, in that capacity, regularly has unsupervised contact with B (whether face to face or by any other means).

(13) This subsection applies if—
(a) B is subject to requirements imposed by or under an enactment on his release from detention for a criminal offence, or is subject to requirements imposed by a court order made in criminal proceedings, and
(b) A looks after B on an individual basis in pursuance of the requirements.

22.—(1) The following provisions apply for the purposes of section 21.
(2) Subject to subsection (3), a person looks after persons under 18 if he is regularly involved in caring for, training, supervising or being in sole charge of such persons.
(3) A person (A) looks after another person (B) on an individual basis if—
(a) A is regularly involved in caring for, training or supervising B, and
(b) in the course of his involvement, A regularly has unsupervised contact with B (whether face to face or by any other means).
(4) A person receives education at an educational institution if—
(a) he is registered or otherwise enrolled as a pupil or student at the institution, or
(b) he receives education at the institution under arrangements with another educational institution at which he is so registered or otherwise enrolled.
(5) [Contains various definitions.]
(6) [Lists services referred to in the definition of hospital in subsection (5).]

23.—(1) Conduct by a person (A) which would otherwise be an offence under any of sections 16 to 19 against another person (B) is not an offence under that section if at the time—
(a) B is 16 or over, and
(b) A and B are lawfully married or civil partners of each other.
(2) In proceedings for such an offence it is for the defendant to prove that A and B were at the time lawfully married or civil partners of each other.

24.—(1) Conduct by a person (A) which would otherwise be an offence under any of sections 16 to 19 against another person (B) is not an offence under that section if, immediately before the position of trust arose, a sexual relationship existed between A and B.
(2) Subsection (1) does not apply if at that time sexual intercourse between A and B would have been unlawful.
(3) In proceedings for an offence under any of sections 16 to 19 it is for the defendant to prove that such a relationship existed at that time.

Section 22(5) provides that 'authority' in relation to England and Wales means a local authority and contains definitions of a wide range of other terms used in s. 21.

Abuse of Position of Trust: Sexual Activity with a Child

B3.144 **Sexual Offences Act 2003, s. 16**

(1) A person aged 18 or over (A) commits an offence if—
(a) he intentionally touches another person (B),
(b) the touching is sexual,
(c) A is in a position of trust in relation to B,
(d) where subsection (2) applies, A knows or could reasonably be expected to know of the circumstances by virtue of which he is in a position of trust in relation to B, and
(e) either—
(i) B is under 18 and A does not reasonably believe that B is 18 or over, or
(ii) B is under 13.

(2) This subsection applies where A—
(a) is in a position of trust in relation to B by virtue of circumstances within section 21(2), (3), (4) or (5), and
(b) is not in such a position of trust by virtue of other circumstances.

(3) Where in proceedings for an offence under this section it is proved that the other person was under 18, the defendant is to be taken not to have reasonably believed that that person was 18 or over unless sufficient evidence is adduced to raise an issue as to whether he reasonably believed it.

(4) Where in proceedings for an offence under this section—

(a) it is proved that the defendant was in a position of trust in relation to the other person by virtue of circumstances within section 21(2), (3), (4) or (5), and

(b) it is not proved that he was in such a position of trust by virtue of other circumstances,

it is to be taken that the defendant knew or could reasonably have been expected to know of the circumstances by virtue of which he was in such a position of trust unless sufficient evidence is adduced to raise an issue as to whether he knew or could reasonably have been expected to know of those circumstances.

Procedure An allegation of an offence contrary to s. 16 is triable either way. As to the classification of the offence for the purpose of listing, see CrimPD XIII, para. B (see Supplement, **CPD.XIII.B**). The extra-territorial jurisdiction provisions of s. 72 apply (see **B3.315**). **B3.145**

See **B3.355** for alternative verdicts.

Indictment **B3.146**

Statement of Offence

Sexual activity with a child by a person in a position of trust contrary to section 16(1) of the Sexual Offences Act 2003.

Particulars of Offence

A, on or about the . . . day of . . . being then a person in a position of trust towards V a child under the age of [18] [13] sexually touched V.

Sentence The maximum sentence for an offence under the SOA 2003, s. 16, on conviction on indictment is five years' imprisonment. On summary conviction, the maximum sentence is six months and/or an unlimited fine (s. 16(5)). **B3.147**

The definitive sentencing guideline, *Sexual Offences* (see Supplement, **SG31-16**), applies to sex offenders aged 18 or over who are sentenced on or after 1 April 2014 (see **B3.3**). There is a notification requirement under the SOA 2003, s. 80 and sch. 3, if the offender is imprisoned, detained in a hospital or receives a community sentence of at least 12 months (see **E23**). The court should consider a sexual harm prevention order (see **E21.22**).

Elements The basic elements of the offence are the same as required in s. 9 (see **B3.108**). In addition, A must be in a position of trust and B may be as old as 17. **B3.148**

It is a defence if the accused reasonably believes that the victim is 18 or over when in fact he is not, unless the child is under 13 in which case that defence is not available.

There are two rebuttable presumptions under the SOA 2003, s. 16, which impose an evidential burden on the accused. Under s. 16(3), if it is proved that the victim was under the age of 18, the accused is taken to have not reasonably believed the victim to be over 18 unless sufficient evidence is adduced to raise an issue as to whether the accused did in fact have that reasonable belief. It is then for the prosecution to prove to the criminal standard that he did not have that reasonable belief.

Under s. 16(4), if it is proved that the accused is in a position of trust in relation to the alleged victim by virtue of circumstances within s. 21(2), (3), (4) or (5) and it is not proved that the position of trust arose because of other circumstances, then it is taken that the accused either knew or could reasonably have been expected to know of the circumstances placing him in a position of trust unless sufficient evidence is adduced to raise an issue as to whether he did in fact know or could have reasonably been expected to know of the circumstances founding the position of trust. Once sufficient evidence has been adduced then, as with s. 16(3), it is for the prosecution to prove the contrary to the criminal standard.

The provisions of s. 73 apply to this offence (see **B3.79**).

Abuse of Position of Trust: Causing or Inciting a Child to Engage in Sexual Activity

B3.149 Sexual Offences Act 2003, s. 17

(1) A person aged 18 or over (A) commits an offence if—
- (a) he intentionally causes or incites another person (B) to engage in an activity,
- (b) the activity is sexual,
- (c) A is in a position of trust in relation to B,
- (d) where subsection (2) applies, A knows or could reasonably be expected to know of the circumstances by virtue of which he is in a position of trust in relation to B, and
- (e) either—
  - (i) B is under 18 and A does not reasonably believe that B is 18 or over, or
  - (ii) B is under 13.

B3.150 **Procedure** An allegation of an offence contrary to s. 17 is triable either way. As to the classification of the offence for the purpose of listing, see CrimPD XIII, para. B (see Supplement, CPD.XIII.B). The extra-territorial provisions of s. 72 apply (see **B3.315**).

See **B3.355** for alternative verdicts.

B3.151 **Indictment**

Statement of Offence

Causing or inciting a child by a person in a position of trust to engage in sexual activity contrary to section 17(1) of the Sexual Offences Act 2003.

Particulars of Offence

A, on or about the... day of... being then in a position of trust towards V a child under the age of [18][13] caused or incited V to engage in a sexual activity.

B3.152 **Sentence** The maximum sentence for an offence under the SOA 2003, s. 17, is the same as that for a s. 16 offence (see **B3.147**).

The definitive sentencing guideline, *Sexual Offences* (see Supplement, **SG31-16**), applies to sex offenders aged 18 or over who are sentenced on or after 1 April 2014 (see **B3.3**). There is a notification requirement under the SOA 2003, s. 80 and sch. 3, if the offender is imprisoned, detained in a hospital or receives a community sentence of at least 12 months (see **E23**). The court should consider a sexual harm prevention order (see **E21.22**).

B3.153 **Elements** The basic elements of an offence contrary to s. 17 are the same as those under s. 10 (see **B3.113**) but there are some differences: A must be in a position of trust and B may be as old as 17. The same assumptions apply as under s. 16 (see **B3.148**).

Abuse of Position of Trust: Sexual Activity in Presence of Child

B3.154 Sexual Offences Act 2003, s. 18

(1) A person aged 18 or over (A) commits an offence if—
- (a) he intentionally engages in an activity,
- (b) the activity is sexual,
- (c) for the purpose of obtaining sexual gratification, he engages in it—
  - (i) when another person (B) is present or is in a place from which A can be observed, and
  - (ii) knowing or believing that B is aware, or intending that B should be aware, that he is engaging in it,
- (d) A is in a position of trust in relation to B,
- (e) where subsection (2) applies, A knows or could reasonably be expected to know of the circumstances by virtue of which he is in a position of trust in relation to B, and

(f) either—
(i) B is under 18 and A does not reasonably believe that B is 18 or over, or
(ii) B is under 13.

Procedure An allegation of an offence contrary to s. 18 is triable either way. As to the classification of the offence for the purpose of listing, see CrimPD XIII, para. B (see Supplement, **CPD.XIII.B**). The extra-territorial jurisdiction provisions of s. 72 apply (see **B3.315**). **B3.155**

See **B3.355** for alternative verdicts.

Sentence The maximum sentence for an offence under the SOA 2003, s. 18, is the same as that for a s. 16 offence (see **B3.147**). The definitive sentencing guideline, *Sexual Offences* (see Supplement, **SG31-17**), applies to sex offenders aged 18 or over who are sentenced on or after 1 April 2014 (see **B3.3**). **B3.156**

There is a notification requirement under the SOA 2003, s. 80 and sch. 3, if D is imprisoned, detained in a hospital or receives a community sentence of at least 12 months (see **E23**). The court should consider a sexual harm prevention order (see **E21.22**).

Elements The basic elements of an offence contrary to s. 18 are the same as those under s. 11 (see **B3.118**) but there are some differences. The differences are that A must be in a position of trust and B may be as old as 17. The same assumptions apply as under s. 16 (see **B3.148**). **B3.157**

For 'gratification', see **B3.123**.

Abuse of Position of Trust: Causing a Child to Watch a Sexual Act

Sexual Offences Act 2003, s. 19 **B3.158**

(1) A person aged 18 or over (A) commits an offence if—
(a) for the purpose of obtaining sexual gratification, he intentionally causes another person (B) to watch a third person engaging in an activity, or to look at an image of any person engaging in an activity,
(b) the activity is sexual,
(c) A is in a position of trust in relation to B,
(d) where subsection (2) applies, A knows or could reasonably be expected to know of the circumstances by virtue of which he is in a position of trust in relation to B, and
(e) either—
(i) B is under 18 and A does not reasonably believe that B is 18 or over, or
(ii) B is under 13.

Procedure An allegation of an offence contrary to s. 19 is triable either way. As to the classification of the offence for the purpose of listing, see CrimPD XIII, para. B (see Supplement, **CPD.XIII.B**). The extra-territorial jurisdiction provisions of s. 72 apply (see **B3.315**). **B3.159**

See **B3.355** for alternative verdicts.

Sentence The maximum sentence for an offence under the SOA 2003, s. 19, is the same as that for an offence under s. 16 (see **B3.147**). **B3.160**

The definitive sentencing guideline, *Sexual Offences* (see Supplement, **SG31-17**), applies to sex offenders aged 18 or over who are sentenced on or after 1 April 2014 (see **B3.3**). There is a notification requirement under the SOA 2003, s. 80 and sch. 3, if the offender is imprisoned, detained in a hospital or receives a community sentence of at least 12 months (see **E23**). The court should consider a sexual harm prevention order (see **E21.22**).

Elements The basic elements of an offence contrary to s. 19 are the same as those under s. 12 (see **B3.123**) but there are some differences. The differences are that A must be in a position of trust and B may be as old as 17. The same assumptions apply as under s. 16 (see **B3.148**). **B3.161**

For 'gratification', see **B3.123**.

FAMILIAL CHILD SEX OFFENCES

B3.162 In ss. 25 and 26, the SOA 2003 creates two gender-neutral offences which are designed to counter the sexual abuse and exploitation of children within the 'family unit'. Section 25 creates an offence of sexual activity with a child family member and s. 26 creates an offence of inciting a child family member to engage in sexual activity. There are common features of each offence governed by ss. 27, 28 and 29. Section 27 defines which relationships between A and B are relevant for the purposes of those sections. Section 28 provides a defence to a charge under s. 25 or s. 26 if B is aged 16 or over and A and B are either lawfully married or civil partners of each other. Section 29 provides a defence if a lawful sexual relationship existed between A and B before the formation of a relationship between them of the type referred to in s. 27(3), (4) or (5). If the relationship is one referred to in s. 27(2) (see below), or would fall within that subsection if B had not been adopted by another, then the defence is not available.

The defences provided for by ss. 28 and 29 must be proved by the accused. It is submitted that the burden is evidential.

B3.163 **Sexual Offences Act 2003, ss. 27 to 29**

27.—(1) The relation of one person (A) to another (B) is within this section if—

(a) it is within any of subsections (2) to (4), or

(b) it would be within one of those subsections but for section 39 of the Adoption Act 1976 or section 67 of the Adoption and Children Act 2002 (status conferred by adoption).

(2) The relation of A to B is within this subsection if—

(a) one of them is the other's parent, grandparent, brother, sister, half-brother, half-sister, aunt or uncle, or

(b) A is or has been B's foster parent.

(3) The relation of A to B is within this subsection if A and B live or have lived in the same household, or A is or has been regularly involved in caring for, training, supervising or being in sole charge of B, and—

(a) one of them is or has been the other's step-parent,

(b) A and B are cousins,

(c) one of them is or has been the other's stepbrother or stepsister, or

(d) the parent or present or former foster parent of one of them is or has been the other's foster parent.

(4) The relation of A to B is within this subsection if—

(a) A and B live in the same household, and

(b) A is regularly involved in caring for, training, supervising or being in sole charge of B.

(5) For the purposes of this section—

(a) 'aunt' means the sister or half-sister of a person's parent, and 'uncle' has a corresponding meaning;

(b) 'cousin' means the child of an aunt or uncle;

(c) a person is a child's foster parent if—

(i) he is a person with whom the child has been placed under section 23(2)(a) or 59(1)(a) of the Children Act 1989 in a placement falling within subsection (6)(a) or (b) of that section (placement with local authority foster parent),

(ia) he is a person with whom the child has been placed under section 59(1)(a) of that Act (placement by voluntary organisation), or

(ii) he fosters the child privately, within the meaning given by section 66(1)(b) of that Act;

(d) a person is another's partner (whether they are of different sexes or the same sex) if they live together as partners in an enduring family relationship;

(e) 'step-parent' includes a parent's partner and 'stepbrother' and 'stepsister' include the child of a parent's partner.

28.—(1) *Conduct by a person* (A) which would otherwise be an offence under section 25 or 26 against another person (B) is not an offence under that section if at the time—

(a) B is 16 or over, and

(b) A and B are lawfully married or civil partners of each other.

(2) In proceedings for such an offence it is for the defendant to prove that A and B were at the time lawfully married or civil partners of each other.

29.—(1) Conduct by a person (A) which would otherwise be an offence under section 25 or 26 against another person (B) is not an offence under that section if—
(a) the relation of A to B is not within subsection (2) of section 27,
(b) it would not be within that subsection if section 39 of the Adoption Act 1976 or section 67 of the Adoption and Children Act 2002 did not apply, and
(c) immediately before the relation of A to B first became such as to fall within section 27, a sexual relationship existed between A and B.

(2) Subsection (1) does not apply if at the time referred to in subsection (1)(c) sexual intercourse between A and B would have been unlawful.

(3) In proceedings for an offence under section 25 or 26 it is for the defendant to prove the matters mentioned in subsection (1)(a) to (c).

Sexual Activity with a Child Family Member

Sexual Offences Act 2003, s. 25 **B3.164**

(1) A person (A) commits an offence if—
(a) he intentionally touches another person (B),
(b) the touching is sexual,
(c) the relation of A to B is within section 27,
(d) A knows or could reasonably be expected to know that his relation to B is of a description falling within that section, and
(e) either—
(i) B is under 18 and A does not reasonably believe that B is 18 or over, or
(ii) B is under 13.

(2) Where in proceedings for an offence under this section it is proved that the other person was under 18, the defendant is to be taken not to have reasonably believed that that person was 18 or over unless sufficient evidence is adduced to raise an issue as to whether he reasonably believed it.

(3) Where in proceedings for an offence under this section it is proved that the relation of the defendant to the other person was of a description falling within section 27, it is to be taken that the defendant knew or could reasonably have been expected to know that his relation to the other person was of that description unless sufficient evidence is adduced to raise an issue as to whether he knew or could reasonably have been expected to know that it was.

Procedure An allegation of an offence contrary to s. 25 is triable either way unless the alleged offender is 18 or over at the time of the offence and penetration is involved, in which case the allegation is triable on indictment only. As to the classification of the offence for the purpose of listing, see CrimPD XIII, para. B (see Supplement, **CPD.XIII.B**). The extra-territoriality provisions of s. 72 apply (see **B3.315**). **B3.165**

See **B3.355** for alternative verdicts.

Indictment **B3.166**

Statement of Offence

Sexual activity with a child family member contrary to section 25(1) of the Sexual Offences Act 2003.

Particulars of Offence

A on or about the... day of... being then in a family relationship to V, a child then under the age of [18] [13] years sexually touched V

or

A, on or about the... day of... being then in a family relationship to V, a child then under the age of [18] [13] years, sexually touched V by penetrating V's [anus] [vagina] with a part of his body [an object] or [by penetrating V's mouth with his penis]

or

A, on or about the ... day of ... being then in a family relationship to V, a child then under the age of [18] [13] years, sexually touched V by allowing V to penetrate A's [anus] [vagina] with a part of V's body [an object] or [by allowing V to penetrate A's mouth with his penis].

B3.167 **Sentence** Where A is over 18 and the activity involved penetration, the maximum penalty for an offence under the SOA 2003, s. 25, is 14 years' imprisonment. In the case of any other activity and where A is aged 18 or over, the maximum penalty on conviction on indictment remains 14 years but, on summary conviction, it is six months and/or an unlimited fine. The maximum penalty where A is aged under 18 is five years on conviction on indictment and, on summary conviction, it is six months or an unlimited fine, or both (s. 25(4) to (6)).

The definitive sentencing guideline, *Sexual Offences* (see Supplement, **SG31-12**), applies to sex offenders aged 18 or over who are sentenced on or after 1 April 2014 (see **B3.3**). There is a notification requirement under the SOA 2003, s. 80 and sch. 3, if the offender is imprisoned, detained in a hospital or receives a community sentence of at least 12 months (see **E23**). The court should consider a sexual harm prevention order (see **E21.22**).

For an example of exceptional circumstances justifying the imposition of a non-custodial sentence, see *SG* [2010] EWCA Crim 1250.

The offence is a qualifying offence for an automatic life sentence under the CJA 2003, sch. 15B, if A is aged 18 or over at the time of the offence (see **B3.25**).

B3.168 **Elements** The basic elements of the offence are the same as those in s. 9 (see **B3.108**) but with the additional necessity of the existence of a relationship between the parties of the kind encompassed by s. 27.

For 'sexual', see **B3.57**. As to 'touching', see **B3.68**.

The provisions of s. 73 apply (see **B3.79**) where the alleged victim is less than 16 years old.

Inciting a Child Family Member to Engage in Sexual Activity

B3.169 Sexual Offences Act 2003, s. 26

(1) A person (A) commits an offence if—
  (a) he intentionally incites another person (B) to touch, or allow himself to be touched by, A,
  (b) the touching is sexual,
  (c) the relation of A to B is within section 27,
  (d) A knows or could reasonably be expected to know that his relation to B is of a description falling within that section, and
  (e) either—
    (i) B is under 18 and A does not reasonably believe that B is 18 or over, or
    (ii) B is under 13.

B3.170 **Procedure** An allegation of an offence contrary to s. 26 is triable either way unless A is aged 18 or over at the time of the offence and penetration is involved, in which case the allegation is triable on indictment only. As to the classification of the offence for the purpose of listing, see CrimPD XIII, para. B (see Supplement, **CPD.XIII.B**). The extra-territorial jurisdiction provisions of s. 72 apply (see **B3.315**).

See **B3.355** for alternative verdicts.

B3.171 **Indictment**

Statement of Offence

Inciting a child family member to engage in sexual activity contrary to section 26 of the Sexual Offences Act 2003.

Particulars of Offence

A, on or about the ... day of ... being then in a family relationship to V, a child under the age of [18] [13] years incited V [to touch A sexually] [to allow himself to be touched by A sexually].

Sentence The provisions as to penalties for an offence under the SOA 2003, s. 26, are contained in s. 26(4) to (6) and are in identical terms to s. 25(4) to (6) (see **B3.167**). B3.172

The definitive sentencing guideline, *Sexual Offences* (see Supplement, **SG31-12**), applies to sex offenders aged 18 or over who are sentenced on or after 1 April 2014 (see **B3.3**). There is a notification requirement under the SOA 2003, s. 80 and sch. 3, if A was aged 18 or over or was sentenced to at least 12 months' imprisonment (see **E23**). The court should consider a sexual harm prevention order (see **E21.22**).

The offence is a qualifying offence for an automatic life sentence under the CJA 2003, sch. 15B, if A is aged 18 or over at the time of the offence (see **B3.25**).

Elements The elements of this offence are similar to those in respect of a s. 10 offence (see **B3.113**) but the offence is much more limited in scope, being restricted to incitement and applying only to sexual touching. B3.173

For 'incitement', see **B3.101**. For 'sexual', see **B3.57**. For 'touching', see **B3.68**.

OFFENCES AGAINST PERSONS WITH A MENTAL DISORDER IMPEDING CHOICE

Sections 30 to 41 of the SOA 2003 cover a wide range of offences designed to protect persons of either gender who suffer from a mental disorder. By virtue of s. 79(6), 'mental disorder' is as defined in s. 1 of the Mental Health Act 1983, and so a person with a learning difficulty finds protection in the Act. In addition, activities prohibited by the Act extend beyond sexual intercourse and indecent assault to sexual touching of a mentally disordered person, the causing or inciting of sexual activity by a mentally disordered person, engaging in sexual activity in the presence of a mentally disordered person and causing a mentally disordered person to watch sexual activity. B3.174

Sections 30 to 33 govern offences arising out of sexual activity with persons with a mental disorder which impedes their capacity for choice.

Sexual Activity with a Person with a Mental Disorder Impeding Choice

Sexual Offences Act 2003, s. 30 B3.175

(1) A person (A) commits an offence if—
  (a) he intentionally touches another person (B),
  (b) the touching is sexual,
  (c) B is unable to refuse because of or for a reason related to a mental disorder, and
  (d) A knows or could reasonably be expected to know that B has a mental disorder and that because of it or for a reason related to it B is likely to be unable to refuse.
(2) B is unable to refuse if—
  (a) he lacks the capacity to choose whether to agree to the touching (whether because he lacks sufficient understanding of the nature or reasonably foreseeable consequences of what is being done, or for any other reason), or
  (b) he is unable to communicate such a choice to A.

Procedure An allegation of an offence contrary to s. 30 is triable either way unless the conduct involves penetration, in which case it is triable only on indictment. As to the classification of the offence for the purpose of listing, see CrimPD XIII, para. B (see Supplement, **CPD.XIII.B**). The extra-territorial jurisdiction provisions of s. 72 apply when B was under 18 at the time of the offence (see **B3.315**). B3.176

See **B3.355** for alternative verdicts.

B3.177 Indictment

Statement of Offence

Sexual touching of a person who was then unable to refuse because of a reason relating to a mental disorder contrary to section 30(1) of the Sexual Offences Act 2003.

Particulars of Offence

A, on or about the... day of... intentionally sexually touched V a person who he knew [ought reasonably to have known] was unable to refuse to be touched by reason of a mental disorder

or

A, on or about the... day of... sexually touched V, a person who he knew [ought reasonably to have known] was unable to refuse to be touched by reason of a mental disorder by penetrating V's [anus] [vagina] with a part of his, A's, body [an object]

or

A, on or about the... day of... sexually touched V, a person who he knew [ought reasonably to have known] was unable to refuse to be touched by reason of a mental disorder by allowing V to penetrate A's [anus] [vagina] with a part of his, V's, body [to penetrate A's mouth with his, V's, penis].

B3.178 Sentence The maximum penalty applicable is determined by the nature of the activity.

Sexual Offences Act 2003, s. 30

(3) A person guilty of an offence under this section, if the touching involved—
  (a) penetration of B's anus or vagina with a part of A's body or anything else,
  (b) penetration of B's mouth with A's penis,
  (c) penetration of A's anus or vagina with a part of B's body, or
  (d) penetration of A's mouth with B's penis, is liable, on conviction on indictment, to imprisonment for life.

(4) Unless subsection (3) applies, a person guilty of an offence under this section is liable—
  (a) on summary conviction, to imprisonment for a term not exceeding 6 months or to [an unlimited fine];
  (b) on conviction on indictment, to imprisonment for a term not exceeding 14 years.

It is a curiosity of the section that in the case of penetration by touching, the maximum penalty is enhanced where A commits the offence by penetration by a part of the body or by an object, but where the essence of the offence is allowing B to penetrate A's anus or vagina, penetration by an object is not comprehended. Penetration enhances the maximum penalty where it is with a part of B's body.

The definitive sentencing guideline, *Sexual Offences* (see Supplement, **SG31-24**), applies to sex offenders aged 18 or over who are sentenced on or after 1 April 2014 (see **B3.3**). There is a notification requirement under the SOA 2003, s. 80 and sch. 3 (see **E23**). The court should consider a sexual harm prevention order (see **E21.22**).

The offence is a qualifying offence for an automatic life sentence under the CJA 2003, sch. 15B, if A is liable on conviction to imprisonment for life (see **B3.25**).

B3.179 In *P* [2015] EWCA Crim 753, [2015] 2 Cr App R (S) 28 (257), the 69-year-old offender had been sentenced to 13 years' imprisonment. The victim had suffered severe brain damage following a medical operation during the course of which her brain had been starved of oxygen. She had profound physical as well as mental disabilities and had been assessed as being unable to consent to sexual activity. D and his co-defendant (the victim's step-father) perpetrated serious sexual assaults and told the victim not to tell anybody or they would get into trouble. One ground of appeal was that no regard was had to the fact that the victim had said in her recorded interview that she had enjoyed what had occurred. The Court of Appeal rejected that argument. She had been medically assessed and found unable to genuinely consent to such activity. What she said was therefore of limited significance, if any. The Court also emphasised that in a case of such seriousness, character and age barely signify as mitigating factors.

Elements The elements of the offence are essentially the same as those required for an offence under s. 9 (see **B3.108**) but with the additional elements concerning B's mental disorder (see s. 30(1)(c)) and the *mens rea* of A (see s. 30(1)(d)). **B3.180**

In *Hulme v DPP* [2006] EWHC 1347 (Admin), a woman with cerebral palsy and a mental age well below her actual age of 27 could not communicate her feelings as to sexual acts in a way that a person of her age without her disabilities would be able to. The evidence was that when the offender touched her private parts she did not know what to do or say but it made her sad, hurt and upset. She was therefore unable to communicate her choice within the meaning of s. 30 because of or for a reason related to a mental disorder and thus 'unable to refuse'.

The House of Lords considered the ambit of the phrases 'capacity to choose' and 'unable to communicate' in ss. 30 to 33 of the Act in *Cooper* [2009] UKHL 35, [2009] 4 All ER 33. Their lordships held that the Court of Appeal had been wrong in holding that a lack of capacity to choose cannot be person or situation specific and had been wrong in holding that an irrational fear that prevents the exercise of choice cannot be equated with a lack of capacity to choose. Moreover, s. 30(2)(b) did not require that a complainant was physically unable to communicate by reason of her mental disorder. In a speech with which the other Law Lords agreed, Baroness Hale observed that it was not necessary to decide whether the reasoning of Munby J contained in family law cases which had underpinned the judgment of the Court of Appeal was correct (see **B3.31**); the SOA 2003 made the position clear. Under s. 30(2)(a), a person is unable to refuse if that person lacks the capacity to choose whether to agree to the touching, whether because of a lack of sufficient understanding of the nature or reasonably foreseeable consequences of what is being done, 'or for any other reason'. Provided that the inability to refuse is, under s. 30(2)(c) 'because of or for a reason related to a mental disorder', and the other ingredients of the offence are proved, the perpetrator is guilty. Baroness Hale said that the words 'for any other reason' are plainly capable of encompassing a wide range of circumstances in which a person's mental disorder may lead to an inability to make an autonomous choice, even though the person may have sufficient understanding of the information relevant to making it. These could include the kind of compulsion which drives a person with anorexia to refuse food or the phobia (or irrational fear) which drives a person to refuse a life-saving injection. Moreover, the capacity to choose can be situation or person specific. The SOA 2003 refers to 'the' touching and is therefore concerned with the specific act of touching with which the accused is charged. Once it is accepted that choice is an exercise of free will and that the mental disorder may rob the person of such free will, then a mentally disordered person may be quite capable of refusing touching in one situation rather than another. Whilst the complainant was unable to refuse in the vulnerable and terrifying circumstances in which the accused had placed her, she might well have been able to refuse a person who had not placed her in a situation of that nature: 'One does not consent to sex in general. One consents to this act of sex with this person at this time and in this place' (at [27]). Such an approach is in keeping with the concept of autonomy in matters of private life guaranteed by the ECHR, Article 8. There is no justification for limiting the requisite inability to communicate to physical inability. Baroness Hale observed that an offence under s. 1 or s. 34 could have been proceeded with in these circumstances (see **B3.31**). **B3.181**

The provisions of s. 73 apply to this offence (see **B3.79**) when B is less than 16 years old.

Causing or Inciting a Person with a Mental Disorder Impeding Choice to Engage in Sexual Activity

Sexual Offences Act 2003, s. 31 **B3.182**

(1) A person (A) commits an offence if—
  (a) he intentionally causes or incites another person (B) to engage in an activity,
  (b) the activity is sexual,
  (c) B is unable to refuse because of or for a reason related to a mental disorder, and
  (d) A knows or could reasonably be expected to know that B has a mental disorder and that because of it or for a reason related to it B is likely to be unable to refuse.

(2) B is unable to refuse if—
(a) he lacks the capacity to choose whether to agree to engaging in the activity caused or incited (whether because he lacks sufficient understanding of the nature or reasonably foreseeable consequences of the activity, or for any other reason), or
(b) he is unable to communicate such a choice to A.

B3.183 **Procedure** An allegation of an offence contrary to s. 31 is triable either way unless the conduct involves penetration, in which case it is triable only on indictment. As to the classification of the offence for the purpose of listing, see CrimPD XIII, para. B (see Supplement, **CPD.XIII.B**). The extra-territorial jurisdiction provisions of s. 72 apply (see **B3.315**).

See **B3.355** for alternative verdicts.

B3.184 **Indictment**

Statement of Offence

Causing or inciting a person who was then unable to refuse because of a mental disorder impeding choice to engage in sexual activity contrary to section 31(1) of the Sexual Offences Act 2003.

Particulars of Offence

A, on or about the... day of... intentionally caused or incited V a person who he knew [ought reasonably to have known] was unable to refuse consent to the said activity by reason of mental disorder to engage in a sexual activity

or

A, on or about the... day of... intentionally caused or incited V, a person who he knew [ought reasonably to have known] was unable to refuse consent to the said activity by reason of mental disorder, to engage in a sexual activity, namely, causing or inciting the penetration of V's [anus] [vagina] or [V's mouth with the penis of another]

B3.185 **Sentence** The provisions as to the maximum sentence for an offence under s. 31 are the same as those which apply in respect of an offence under s. 30 (see **B3.178**).

The definitive sentencing guideline, *Sexual Offences* (see Supplement, **SG31-24**), applies to sex offenders aged 18 or over who are sentenced on or after 1 April 2014 (see **B3.3**). There is a notification requirement under the SOA 2003, s. 80 and sch. 3 (see **E23**). The court should consider a sexual harm prevention order (see **E21.22**).

The offence is a qualifying offence for an automatic life sentence under the CJA 2003, sch. 15B, if A is liable on conviction to imprisonment for life (see **B3.25**).

B3.186 **Elements** The elements of the offence are essentially the same as those required for an offence under s. 10 (see **B3.113**), but with the additional elements concerning B's mental disorder (see s. 31(1)(c)) and A's *mens rea* (see s. 31(1)(d)).

Engaging in Sexual Activity in the Presence of a Person with a Mental Disorder

B3.187 **Sexual Offences Act 2003, s. 32**

(1) A person (A) commits an offence if—
(a) he intentionally engages in an activity,
(b) the activity is sexual,
(c) for the purpose of obtaining sexual gratification, he engages in it—
(i) when another person (B) is present or is in a place from which A can be observed, and
(ii) knowing or believing that B is aware, or intending that B should be aware, that he is engaging in it,
(d) B is unable to refuse because of or for a reason related to a mental disorder, and
(e) A knows or could reasonably be expected to know that B has a mental disorder and that *because of it or for a reason related to it* B is likely to be unable to refuse.

(2) B is unable to refuse if—

(a) he lacks the capacity to choose whether to agree to being present (whether because he lacks sufficient understanding of the nature of the activity, or for any other reason), or
(b) he is unable to communicate such a choice to A.

Procedure An allegation of an offence contrary to s. 32 is triable either way. As to the classification of the offence for the purpose of listing, see CrimPD XIII, para. B (see Supplement, **CPD.XIII.B**). The extra-territorial jurisdiction provisions of s. 72 apply where B was aged under 18 at the time of the offence (see **B3.315**). **B3.188**

See **B3.355** for alternative verdicts.

Sentence The maximum sentence for an offence under the SOA 2003, s. 32, on conviction on indictment is ten years' imprisonment. On summary conviction, the maximum sentence is six months and/or an unlimited fine (s. 32(3)). **B3.189**

The definitive sentencing guideline, *Sexual Offences* (see Supplement, **SG31-25**), applies to sex offenders aged 18 or over who are sentenced on or after 1 April 2014 (see **B3.3**). There is a notification requirement under the SOA 2003, s. 80 and sch. 3 (see **E23**). The court should consider a sexual harm prevention order (see **E21.22**).

Elements The elements of the offence are essentially the same as those required for an offence under s. 11 (see **B3.118**) but with the additional elements concerning B's mental disorder (see s. 3(1)(c)) and A's *mens rea* (see s. 32(1)(d)). **B3.190**

For 'gratification', see **B3.123**.

Causing a Person with a Mental Disorder Impeding Choice to Watch a Sexual Act

Sexual Offences Act 2003, s. 33 **B3.191**

(1) A person (A) commits an offence if—
(a) for the purpose of obtaining sexual gratification, he intentionally causes another person (B) to watch a third person engaging in an activity, or to look at an image of any person engaging in an activity,
(b) the activity is sexual,
(c) B is unable to refuse because of or for a reason related to a mental disorder, and
(d) A knows or could reasonably be expected to know that B has a mental disorder and that because of it or for a reason related to it B is likely to be unable to refuse.
(2) B is unable to refuse if—
(a) he lacks the capacity to choose whether to agree to watching or looking (whether because he lacks sufficient understanding of the nature of the activity, or for any other reason), or
(b) he is unable to communicate such a choice to A.

Procedure An allegation of an offence contrary to s. 33 is triable either way. As to the classification of the offence for the purpose of listing, see CrimPD XIII, para. B (see Supplement, **CPD.XIII.B**). The extra-territorial jurisdiction provisions of s. 72 apply where B was aged under 18 at the time of the offence (see **B3.315**). **B3.192**

See **B3.355** for alternative verdicts.

Sentence The maximum sentence for an offence under the SOA 2003, s. 33, on conviction on indictment is ten years' imprisonment. On summary conviction, the maximum is six months and/or an unlimited fine (s. 33(3)). **B3.193**

The definitive sentencing guideline, *Sexual Offences* (see Supplement, **SG31-25**), applies to sex offenders aged 18 or over who are sentenced on or after 1 April 2014 (see **B3.3**). There is a notification requirement under the SOA 2003, s. 80 and sch. 3 (see **E23**). The court should consider a sexual harm prevention order (see **E21.22**).

B3.194 **Elements** The elements of the offence are essentially the same as those required for an offence under s. 12 (see **B3.123**) but with the additional elements concerning B's mental disorder (see s. 33(1)(c)) and A's *mens rea* (see s. 33(1)(d)).

For 'gratification', see **B3.123**.

INDUCEMENTS TO PERSONS WITH A MENTAL DISORDER

B3.195 Sections 34 to 37 cover sexual activity in relation to a mentally disordered victim where agreement is obtained by inducement, threat or deception.

Inducement, Threat or Deception to Procure Sexual Activity with a Person

B3.196 **Sexual Offences Act 2003, s. 34**

(1) A person (A) commits an offence if—
- (a) with the agreement of another person (B) he intentionally touches that person,
- (b) the touching is sexual,
- (c) A obtains B's agreement by means of an inducement offered or given, a threat made or a deception practised by A for that purpose,
- (d) B has a mental disorder, and
- (e) A knows or could reasonably be expected to know that B has a mental disorder.

B3.197 **Procedure** An allegation of an offence contrary to s. 34 is triable either way unless the conduct involves penetration, in which case it is triable only on indictment. As to the classification of the offence for the purpose of listing, see CrimPD XIII, para. B (see Supplement, **CPD.XIII.B**). The extra-territorial jurisdiction provisions of s. 72 apply where B was aged under 18 at the time of the offence (see **B3.315**).

See **B3.355** for alternative verdicts.

B3.198 **Indictment**

Statement of Offence

Intentionally sexually touching a person suffering from mental disorder by agreement procured by inducement, threat or deception contrary to section 34(1) of the Sexual Offences Act 2003.

Particulars of Offence

A, on or about the... day of... sexually touched V *[by penetration... by procuring penetration]* a person who he then knew or ought reasonably to have known suffered from a mental disorder by agreement procured by an inducement offered or given, a threat made or a deception practised on V.

B3.199 **Sentence** The maximum sentence varies according to the nature of the activity involved.

Sexual Offences Act 2003, s. 34

(2) A person guilty of an offence under this section, if the touching involved—
- (a) penetration of B's anus or vagina with a part of A's body or anything else,
- (b) penetration of B's mouth with A's penis,
- (c) penetration of A's anus or vagina with a part of B's body, or
- (d) penetration of A's mouth with B's penis,

is liable, on conviction on indictment, to imprisonment for life.

(3) Unless subsection (2) applies, a person guilty of an offence under this section is liable—
- (a) on summary conviction, to imprisonment for a term not exceeding 6 months or [an unlimited fine] or both;
- (b) on conviction on indictment, to imprisonment for a term not exceeding 14 years.

Note that where B penetrates A, the penalty is only enhanced where penetration is by part of B's body.

The definitive sentencing guideline, *Sexual Offences* (see Supplement, **SG31-26**), applies to sex offenders aged 18 or over who are sentenced on or after 1 April 2014 (see **B3.3**). There is a notification requirement under the SOA 2003, s. 80 and sch. 3 (see **E23**). The court should consider a sexual harm prevention order (see **E21.22**).

The offence is a qualifying offence for an automatic life sentence under the CJA 2003, sch. 15B, if A is liable on conviction to imprisonment for life (see **B3.25**).

Elements The elements of the offence are essentially the same as those under s. 9 (see **B3.108**) but also include additional features relating to the agreement obtained by means of an inducement, threat or deception, B's mental disorder and A's *mens rea*. The Home Office Explanatory Notes to the 2003 Act give examples of what might be sufficient to constitute an inducement, threat or deception. An inducement might be the promise of anything from sweets to a holiday; a threat might be a statement by the offender that he would hurt a member of the victim's family; and a deception might be a statement by the offender that the victim will get into trouble if he does not engage in sexual activity. **B3.200**

The provisions of s. 73 apply (see **B3.79**) when B is under 16 years of age.

Causing a Person with a Mental Disorder to Engage in or Agree to Engage in Sexual Activity by Inducement, Threat or Deception

Sexual Offences Act 2003, s. 35 **B3.201**

(1) A person (A) commits an offence if—
  (a) by means of an inducement offered or given, a threat made or a deception practised by him for this purpose, he intentionally causes another person (B) to engage in, or to agree to engage in, an activity,
  (b) the activity is sexual,
  (c) B has a mental disorder, and
  (d) A knows or could reasonably be expected to know that B has a mental disorder.

Procedure An allegation of an offence contrary to s. 35 is triable either way unless the conduct involves penetration, in which case it is triable only on indictment. As to the classification of the offence for the purpose of listing, see CrimPD XIII, para. B (see Supplement, **CPD.XIII.B**). The extra-territorial jurisdiction provisions of s. 72 apply where B was aged under 18 at the time of the offence (see **B3.315**). **B3.202**

See **B3.355** for alternative verdicts.

Sentence Where the activity concerned consists of anal, vaginal or oral penetration, the maximum penalty is life imprisonment. Otherwise, on indictment, it is 14 years' imprisonment or, on summary conviction, six months or and/or an unlimited fine (s. 35(2) and (3)). **B3.203**

The definitive sentencing guideline, *Sexual Offences* (see Supplement, **SG31-26**), applies to sex offenders aged 18 or over who are sentenced on or after 1 April 2014 (see **B3.3**). There is a notification requirement under the SOA 2003, s. 80 and sch. 3 (see **E23**). The court should consider a sexual harm prevention order (see **E21.22**).

The offence is a qualifying offence for an automatic life sentence under the CJA 2003, sch. 15B, if A is liable on conviction to imprisonment for life (see **B3.25**).

Elements The elements of the offence are essentially the same as those under s. 10 (see **B3.113**) but also include the additional features relating to the agreement obtained by means of an inducement, threat or deception, B's mental disorder and A's *mens rea*. It should also be noted that the scope of s. 35 is limited to causing sexual activity and unlike s. 10 does not include inciting. For examples of inducement, threat and deception, see **B3.200**. **B3.204**

Engaging in Sexual Activity in the Presence, Procured by Inducement, Threat or Deception, of a Person with a Mental Disorder

B3.205 **Sexual Offences Act 2003, s. 36**

(1) A person (A) commits an offence if—
(a) he intentionally engages in an activity,
(b) the activity is sexual,
(c) for the purpose of obtaining sexual gratification, he engages in it—
(i) when another person (B) is present or is in a place from which A can be observed, and
(ii) knowing or believing that B is aware, or intending that B should be aware, that he is engaging in it,
(d) B agrees to be present or in the place referred to in paragraph (c)(i) because of an inducement offered or given, a threat made or a deception practised by A for the purpose of obtaining that agreement,
(e) B has a mental disorder, and
(f) A knows or could reasonably be expected to know that B has a mental disorder.

B3.206 **Procedure** An allegation of an offence contrary to s. 36 is triable either way. As to the classification of the offence for the purpose of listing, see CrimPD XIII, para. B (see Supplement, CPD.XIII.B). The extra-territorial jurisdiction provisions of s. 72 apply where B was aged under 18 at the time of the offence (see **B3.315**).

See **B3.355** for alternative verdicts.

B3.207 **Sentence** The maximum sentence for an offence under the SOA 2003, s. 36, on conviction on indictment is ten years' imprisonment. On summary conviction, the maximum penalty is six months and/or an unlimited fine (s. 36(2)).

The definitive sentencing guideline, *Sexual Offences* (see Supplement, **SG31-27**), applies to sex offenders aged 18 or over who are sentenced on or after 1 April 2014 (see **B3.3**). There is a notification requirement under the SOA 2003, s. 80 and sch. 3 (see **E23**). The court should consider a sexual harm prevention order (see **E21.22**).

B3.208 **Elements** The elements of the offence are essentially the same as those under s. 11 (see **B3.118**) but also include the additional features relating to the agreement obtained by means of an inducement, threat or deception, B's mental disorder and A's *mens rea*. For examples of inducement, threat and deception, see **B3.200**.

For 'gratification', see **B3.123**.

Causing a Person with a Mental Disorder to Watch a Sexual Act by Inducement, Threat or Deception

B3.209 **Sexual Offences Act 2003, s. 37**

(1) A person (A) commits an offence if—
(a) for the purpose of obtaining sexual gratification, he intentionally causes another person (B) to watch a third person engaging in an activity, or to look at an image of any person engaging in an activity,
(b) the activity is sexual,
(c) B agrees to watch or look because of an inducement offered or given, a threat made or a deception practised by A for the purpose of obtaining that agreement,
(d) B has a mental disorder, and
(e) A knows or could reasonably be expected to know that B has a mental disorder.

B3.210 **Procedure** An allegation of an offence contrary to s. 37 is triable either way. As to the classification of the offence for the purpose of listing, see CrimPD XIII, para. B (see Supplement, CPD.XIII.B). The extra-territorial jurisdiction provisions of s. 72 apply where B was aged under 18 at the time of the offence (see **B3.315**).

See **B3.355** for alternative verdicts.

Sentence The maximum sentence for an offence under the SOA 2003, s. 37, on conviction on indictment is ten years' imprisonment. On summary conviction, the maximum penalty is six months and/or an unlimited fine (s. 37(2)). **B3.211**

The definitive sentencing guideline, *Sexual Offences* (see Supplement, SG31-27), applies to sex offenders aged 18 or over who are sentenced on or after 1 April 2014 (see **B3.3**). There is a notification requirement under the SOA 2003, s. 80 and sch. 3 (see **E23**). The court should consider a sexual harm prevention order (see **E21.22**).

Elements The elements of the offence are essentially the same as those under s. 12 (see **B3.123**) but also include the additional features relating to the agreement obtained by means of an inducement, threat or deception, B's mental disorder and A's *mens rea*. For examples of inducement, threat and deception, see **B3.200**. **B3.212**

For 'gratification', see **B3.123**.

CARE WORKERS FOR PERSONS WITH A MENTAL DISORDER

Sections 38 to 41 govern offences committed by care workers against people with a mental disorder in their care. Section 42 defines a care worker for the purposes of these sections. Sections 43 and 44 provide for defences analogous to those set out in ss. 23 and 24 (see **B3.143**). **B3.213**

Sexual Offences Act 2003, ss. 42 to 44

42.—(1) For the purposes of sections 38 to 41, a person (A) is involved in the care of another person (B) in a way that falls within this section if any of subsections (2) to (4) applies.

(2) This subsection applies if—

(a) B is accommodated and cared for in a care home, community home, voluntary home, children's home, or premises in Wales at which a secure accommodation service is provided, and

(b) A has functions to perform in the home in the course of employment which have brought him or are likely to bring him into regular face to face contact with B.

(3) This subsection applies if B is a patient for whom services are provided—

(a) by a National Health Service body or an independent medical agency; or

(b) in an independent hospital;

(c) in Wales, in an independent clinic,

and A has functions to perform for the body or agency or in the hospital or clinic in the course of employment which have brought A or are likely to bring A into regular face to face contact with B.

(4) This subsection applies if A—

(a) is, whether or not in the course of employment, a provider of care, assistance or services to B in connection with B's mental disorder, and

(b) as such, has had or is likely to have regular face to face contact with B.

(5) [Definition of terms used in the section.]

(6) [Definition of terms used in the section.]

43.—(1) Conduct by a person (A) which would otherwise be an offence under any of sections 38 to 41 against another person (B) is not an offence under that section if at the time—

(a) B is 16 or over, and

(b) A and B are lawfully married or civil partners of each other.

(2) In proceedings for such an offence it is for the defendant to prove that A and B were at the time lawfully married or civil partners of each other.

44.—(1) Conduct by a person (A) which would otherwise be an offence under any of sections 38 to 41 against another person (B) is not an offence under that section if, immediately before A became involved in B's care in a way that falls within section 42, a sexual relationship existed between A and B.

(2) Subsection (1) does not apply if at that time sexual intercourse between A and B would have been unlawful.
(3) In proceedings for an offence under any of sections 38 to 41 it is for the defendant to prove that such a relationship existed at that time.

Care Workers: Sexual Activity with a Person with a Mental Disorder

B3.214 **Sexual Offences Act 2003, s. 38**

(1) A person (A) commits an offence if—
(a) he intentionally touches another person (B),
(b) the touching is sexual,
(c) B has a mental disorder,
(d) A knows or could reasonably be expected to know that B has a mental disorder, and
(e) A is involved in B's care in a way that falls within section 42.

(2) Where in proceedings for an offence under this section it is proved that the other person had a mental disorder, it is to be taken that the defendant knew or could reasonably have been expected to know that that person had a mental disorder unless sufficient evidence is adduced to raise an issue as to whether he knew or could reasonably have been expected to know it.

B3.215 **Procedure** An allegation of an offence contrary to s. 38 is triable either way unless the conduct involves penetration, in which case it is triable only on indictment. As to the classification of the offence for the purpose of listing, see CrimPD XIII, para. B (see Supplement, **CPD.XIII.B**). The extra-territorial jurisdiction provisions of s. 72 apply where B was aged under 18 at the time of the offence (see **B3.315**).

See **B3.355** for alternative verdicts.

B3.216 **Indictment**

Statement of Offence

Sexual touching of a mentally disordered person by a person involved in the care of that person contrary to section 38(1) of the Sexual Offences Act 2003.

Particulars of Offence

A, on or about the... day of... being then involved in V's care, knowing that V had a mental disorder or in circumstances where he could reasonably be expected to know that V had a mental disorder, intentionally sexually touched V *[namely, by penetration...]*.

B3.217 **Sentence** The maximum sentence for an offence under the SOA 2003, s. 38, varies depending on the sexual activity concerned. Where the touching amounts to penetration the maximum penalty on indictment is 14 years. For these purposes penetration of B's anus or vagina may be with a part of A's body or anything else. Where B penetrates A, the higher penalty applies to bodily penetration of A's anus or vagina or mouth with B's penis. It does not extend to penetration of A's sexual organs or mouth with anything else. Where touching does not amount to penetration, the maximum penalty on indictment is ten years, and on summary conviction is six months and/or an unlimited fine (s. 38(3) and (4)).

The definitive sentencing guideline, *Sexual Offences* (see Supplement, **SG31-28**), applies to sex offenders aged 18 or over who are sentenced on or after 1 April 2014 (see **B3.3**). For an example of the application of the guideline, see *Taylor* [2015] EWCA Crim 322. There is a notification requirement under the SOA 2003, s. 80 and sch. 3, subject to A's age and the sentence imposed (see **E23**). The court should consider a sexual harm prevention order (see E21.22).

See *Jones* [2009] EWCA Crim 237, [2009] 2 Cr App R (S) 76 (523) and *Watts* [2010] EWCA Crim 1824 for examples of sentencing under the old guideline.

B3.218 **Elements** The elements of the offence are essentially the same as those under s. 9 (see **B3.108**) but also include the additional features relating to A's position as a care worker, B's mental disorder and A's *mens rea*. As a good illustration of the way in which the SOA 2003 has widened protection for persons who are vulnerable because of their mental state, proceedings have been brought successfully under s. 38 where a social worker had sexual intercourse with the complainant when she was suffering from post-natal depression (*Bradford* [2006] EWCA Crim 2629).

The provisions of s. 73 apply (see **B3.79**) when B is less than 16 years old.

Care Workers: Causing or Inciting Sexual Activity

Sexual Offences Act 2003, s. 39 **B3.219**

(1) A person (A) commits an offence if—
  (a) he intentionally causes or incites another person (B) to engage in an activity,
  (b) the activity is sexual,
  (c) B has a mental disorder,
  (d) A knows or could reasonably be expected to know that B has a mental disorder, and
  (e) A is involved in B's care in a way that falls within section 42.
(2) Where in proceedings for an offence under this section it is proved that the other person had a mental disorder, it is to be taken that the defendant knew or could reasonably have been expected to know that that person had a mental disorder unless sufficient evidence is adduced to raise an issue as to whether he knew or could reasonably have been expected to know it.

Procedure An allegation of an offence contrary to s. 39 is triable either way unless the conduct involves penetration, in which case it is triable only on indictment. As to the classification of the offence for the purpose of listing, see CrimPD XIII, para. B (see Supplement, **CPD.XIII.B**). The extra-territorial jurisdiction provisions of s. 72 apply where B was aged under 18 at the time of the offence (see **B3.315**). **B3.220**

See **B3.355** for alternative verdicts.

Indictment **B3.221**

Statement of Offence

Causing or inciting a mentally disordered person to engage in a sexual activity by a care worker for whose care he was responsible contrary to section 39(1) of the Sexual Offences Act 2003.

Particulars of Offence

A, on or about the... day of... being then involved in V's care knowing that V had a mental disorder or in circumstances where he could reasonably be expected to have known that V had a mental disorder intentionally caused or incited V, to engage in a sexual activity *[namely, by penetration...]*.

Sentence Where penetration is concerned, the maximum penalty on indictment is 14 years' imprisonment. Otherwise it is ten years on conviction on indictment or, on summary conviction, six months and/or an unlimited fine (s. 39(3) and (4)). Note that for these purposes penetration attracting the higher penalty may be of B's anus or vagina seemingly by any part of A's body or an object, or B's mouth with a person's penis. Where, however, it is B who penetrates another's anus or vagina such penetration may be by any part of B's body or anything else or by penetration of another's mouth by B's penis. **B3.222**

The definitive sentencing guideline, *Sexual Offences* (see Supplement, **SG31-29**), applies to sex offenders aged 18 or over who are sentenced on or after 1 April 2014 (see **B3.3**). There is a notification requirement under the SOA 2003, s. 80 and sch. 3, subject to A's age and the sentence imposed (see **E23**). The court should consider a sexual harm prevention order (see **E21.22**).

Elements The elements of the offence are essentially the same as those under s. 10 (see **B3.113**) but also include the additional features relating to A's position as a care worker, B's mental disorder and A's *mens rea*. **B3.223**

Care Workers: Sexual Activity in the Presence of a Person with a Mental Disorder

B3.224 **Sexual Offences Act 2003, s. 40**

(1) A person (A) commits an offence if—
  (a) he intentionally engages in an activity,
  (b) the activity is sexual,
  (c) for the purpose of obtaining sexual gratification, he engages in it—
    (i) when another person (B) is present or is in a place from which A can be observed, and
    (ii) knowing or believing that B is aware, or intending that B should be aware, that he is engaging in it,
  (d) B has a mental disorder,
  (e) A knows or could reasonably be expected to know that B has a mental disorder, and
  (f) A is involved in B's care in a way that falls within section 42.

(2) Where in proceedings for an offence under this section it is proved that the other person had a mental disorder, it is to be taken that the defendant knew or could reasonably have been expected to know that that person had a mental disorder unless sufficient evidence is adduced to raise an issue as to whether he knew or could reasonably have been expected to know it.

B3.225 **Procedure** An allegation of an offence contrary to s. 40 is triable either way. As to the classification of the offence for the purpose of listing, see CrimPD XIII, para. B (see Supplement, CPD.XIII.B). The extra-territorial jurisdiction provisions of s. 72 apply where B was aged under 18 at the time of the offence (see **B3.315**).

See **B3.355** for alternative verdicts.

B3.226 **Sentence** The maximum sentence for an offence under the SOA 2003, s. 40, on conviction on indictment is seven years' imprisonment. On summary conviction, the maximum is six months and/or an unlimited fine.

The definitive sentencing guideline, *Sexual Offences* (see Supplement, **SG31-29**), applies to sex offenders aged 18 or over who are sentenced on or after 1 April 2014 (see **B3.3**). There is a notification requirement under the SOA 2003, s. 80 and sch. 3, subject to A's age and the sentence imposed (see **E23**). The court should consider a sexual harm prevention order (see **E21.22**).

B3.227 **Elements** The elements of the offence are essentially the same as those under s. 11 (see **B3.118**) but also include the additional features relating to A's position as a care worker, B's mental disorder and A's *mens rea*.

For 'gratification', see **B3.123**.

Care Workers: Causing a Person with a Mental Disorder to Watch a Sexual Act

B3.228 **Sexual Offences Act 2003, s. 41**

(1) A person (A) commits an offence if—
  (a) for the purpose of obtaining sexual gratification, he intentionally causes another person (B) to watch a third person engaging in an activity, or to look at an image of any person engaging in an activity,
  (b) the activity is sexual,
  (c) B has a mental disorder,
  (d) A knows or could reasonably be expected to know that B has a mental disorder, and
  (e) A is involved in B's care in a way that falls within section 42.

(2) Where in proceedings for an offence under this section it is proved that the other person had a mental disorder, it is to be taken that the defendant knew or could reasonably have been expected to know that that person had a mental disorder unless sufficient evidence is adduced to raise an issue as to whether he knew or could reasonably have been expected to know it.

Procedure An allegation of an offence contrary to s. 41 is triable either way. As to the classification of the offence for the purpose of listing, see CrimPD XIII, para. B (see Supplement, **CPD.XIII.B**). The extra-territorial jurisdiction provisions of s. 72 apply (see **B3.315**). **B3.229**

See **B3.355** for alternative verdicts.

Sentence The maximum penalties for an offence under the SOA 2003, s. 41, are the same as for an offence under s. 40 (see **B3.226**). **B3.230**

The definitive sentencing guideline, *Sexual Offences* (see Supplement, **SG31-29**), applies to sex offenders aged 18 or over who are sentenced on or after 1 April 2014 (see **B3.3**). There is a notification requirement under the SOA 2003, s. 80 and sch. 3, subject to A's age and the sentence imposed (see **E23**). The court should consider a sexual harm prevention order (see **E21.22**).

Elements The elements of the offence are essentially the same as those under s. 12 (see **B3.123**) but also include the additional features relating to A's position as a care worker, B's mental disorder and A's *mens rea*. The offence under s. 41 is also limited to 'causing' whilst s. 12 prohibits both causing and inciting. **B3.231**

For 'gratification', see **B3.123**.

ABUSE OF CHILDREN THROUGH SEXUAL EXPLOITATION AND PORNOGRAPHY

Sections 47 to 50 govern offences involving sexual exploitation of children. Prior to the implementation of the SCA 2015, s. 68, on 3 May 2015, the offences referred to involving children in prostitution or pornography. Section 51 is a definitional section of common application to each of ss. 47 to 50. It is set out below as amended by the SCA 2015, s. 68(6). **B3.232**

Sexual Offences Act 2003, s. 51

(1) [Repealed.]
(2) For the purposes of sections 48 to 50, a person (B) is sexually exploited if—
  (a) on at least one occasion and whether or not compelled to do so, B offers or provides sexual services to another person in return for payment or a promise of payment to B or a third person, or
  (b) an indecent image of B is recorded [or streamed or otherwise transmitted]; and 'sexual exploitation' is to be interpreted accordingly.
(3) In subsection (2), 'payment' means any financial advantage, including the discharge of an obligation to pay or the provision of goods or services (including sexual services) gratuitously or at a discount.

Sexual Exploitation of Children

Sexual Offences Act 2003, s. 47 **B3.233**

(1) A person (A) commits an offence if—
  (a) he intentionally obtains for himself the sexual services of another person (B),
  (b) before obtaining those services, he has made or promised payment for those services to B or a third person, or knows that another person has made or promised such a payment, and
  (c) either—
    (i) B is under 18, and A does not reasonably believe that B is 18 or over, or
    (ii) B is under 13.
(2) In this section, 'payment' means any financial advantage, including the discharge of an obligation to pay or the provision of goods or services (including sexual services) gratuitously or at a discount.

B3.234 **Procedure** An allegation of an offence contrary to s. 47 is triable either way unless the conduct involves penetration, in which case it is triable only on indictment. As to the classification of the offence for the purpose of listing, see CrimPD XIII, para. B (see Supplement, **CPD.XIII.B**). The extra-territorial jurisdiction provisions of s. 72 apply (see **B3.315**).

See **B3.355** for alternative verdicts.

B3.235 **Indictment**

Statement of Offence

Intentionally obtaining the sexual services of a person under the age of 18 years by prior payment or promise of payment to that person or another person contrary to section 47(1) of the Sexual Offences Act 2003.

Particulars of Offence

A, on or about the... day of... intentionally obtained the sexual services of V then a child under the age of 18 [13] years then knowing that V was under the age of 18 years or not believing on reasonable grounds that V was over the age of 18 years by making or promising payment for such services to V or to another person before obtaining those services.

B3.236 **Sentence** The maximum penalty for an offence under the SOA 2003, s. 47, varies according to the age of the child and whether or not the offence involved penetration.

Sexual Offences Act 2003, s. 47

(3) A person guilty of an offence under this section against a person under 13, where subsection (6) applies, is liable on conviction on indictment to imprisonment for life.
(4) Unless subsection (3) applies, a person guilty of an offence under this section against a person under 16 is liable—
 (a) where subsection (6) applies, on conviction on indictment, to imprisonment for a term not exceeding 14 years;
 (b) in any other case—
  (i) on summary conviction, to imprisonment for a term not exceeding 6 months or [an unlimited fine] or both;
  (ii) on conviction on indictment, to imprisonment for a term not exceeding 14 years.
(5) Unless subsection (3) or (4) applies, a person guilty of an offence under this section is liable—
 (a) on summary conviction, to imprisonment for a term not exceeding 6 months or [an unlimited fine] or both;
 (b) on conviction on indictment, to imprisonment for a term not exceeding 7 years.
(6) This subsection applies where the offence involved—
 (a) penetration of B's anus or vagina with a part of A's body or anything else,
 (b) penetration of B's mouth with A's penis,
 (c) penetration of A's anus or vagina with a part of B's body or by B with anything else, or
 (d) penetration of A's mouth with B's penis.

The definitive sentencing guideline, *Sexual Offences* (see Supplement, **SG31-22**), applies to sex offenders aged 18 or over who are sentenced on or after 1 April 2014 (see **B3.3**). There is a notification requirement under the SOA 2003, s. 80 and sch. 3, where B was under 16 and A was aged 18 or over or was sentenced to at least 12 months' imprisonment (see **E23**). The court should consider a sexual harm prevention order (see **E21.22**).

The offence is a qualifying offence for an automatic life sentence under the CJA 2003, sch. 15B (see **B3.25**).

B3.237 **Elements** The offender (A) must intentionally obtain the sexual services of a person under the age of 18 (B). Before doing so A must have either made or promised payment to the child or a third party or must be aware that such a payment has been made or promised.
Section 47(2) contains a very broad definition of payment.

It is a defence for A to have reasonably believed that B was aged 18 or over, but the defence does not apply if B was aged under 13 at the material time.

Causing or Inciting Sexual Exploitation of a Child

Sexual Offences Act 2003, s. 48 **B3.238**

(1) A person (A) commits an offence if—
 (a) he intentionally causes or incites another person (B) to be sexually exploited in any part of the world, and
 (b) either—
  (i) B is under 18, and A does not reasonably believe that B is 18 or over, or
  (ii) B is under 13.

Procedure An allegation of an offence contrary to s. 48 is triable either way. As to the classification of the offence for the purpose of listing, see CrimPD XIII, para. B (see Supplement, **CPD.XIII.B**). The extra-territorial jurisdiction provisions of s. 72 apply (see **B3.315**). **B3.239**

See **B3.355** for alternative verdicts.

Indictment **B3.240**

Statement of Offence

Intentionally causing or inciting a child under the age of 18 years to be sexually exploited in any part of the world contrary to section 48(1) of the Sexual Offences Act 2003

Particulars of Offence

A, on or about the . . . day of . . . being then a person aged 18 or over, intentionally caused or incited V, then a child under the age of [18, knowing that V was under the age of 18 or not believing on reasonable grounds that V was aged 18 or over,] [13] to be sexually exploited [by V offering or providing sexual services to another in return for payment or promise of payment to V or a third party] [by recording an indecent image of V]

Sentence The maximum sentence for an offence under the SOA 2003, s. 48, on conviction on indictment is 14 years' imprisonment. On summary conviction, the maximum sentence is six months and/or an unlimited fine (s. 48(2)). **B3.241**

The definitive sentencing guideline, *Sexual Offences* (see Supplement, **SG31-21**), applies to sex offenders aged 18 or over who are sentenced on or after 1 April 2014 (see **B3.3**).

The offence is a qualifying offence for an automatic life sentence under the CJA 2003, sch. 15B (see **B3.25**). The court should consider a sexual harm prevention order (see **E21.22**).

Elements The offender (A) must intentionally cause or incite a person under the age of 18 (B) to be sexually exploited. For the meaning of 'sexual exploitation', see **B3.232**. **B3.242**

It is a defence for A to have reasonably believed that B was not under 18 years of age even though B was actually under 18. However, if B was under 13 at the material time then no such defence is available.

Controlling a Child in Relation to Sexual Exploitation

Sexual Offences Act 2003, s. 49 **B3.243**

(1) A person (A) commits an offence if—
 (a) he intentionally controls any of the activities of another person (B) relating to B's sexual exploitation in any part of the world, and
 (b) either—
  (i) B is under 18, and A does not reasonably believe that B is 18 or over, or
  (ii) B is under 13.

Procedure An allegation of an offence contrary to s. 49 is triable either way. As to the classification of the offence for the purpose of listing, see CrimPD XIII, para. B (see Supplement, **CPD.XIII.B**). The extra-territorial jurisdiction provisions of s. 72 apply (see **B3.315**). **B3.244**

See **B3.355** for alternative verdicts.

B3.245 **Indictment**

Statement of Offence

Intentionally controlling the activities of another person under the age of 18 years relating to that person's sexual exploitation in any part of the world contrary to section 49 of the Sexual Offences Act 2003.

Particulars of Offence

A, on or about the... day of... intentionally controlled activities of V, then a child under the age of [18, knowing that V was under the age of 18 or not believing on reasonable grounds that V was aged 18 or over,] [13] relating to V's sexual exploitation.

B3.246 **Sentence** The maximum sentence for an offence under the SOA 2003, s. 49, on conviction on indictment is 14 years' imprisonment. On summary conviction, the maximum sentence is six months and/or an unlimited fine (s. 49(2)).

The definitive sentencing guideline, *Sexual Offences* (see Supplement, **SG31-21**), applies to sex offenders aged 18 or over who are sentenced on or after 1 April 2014 (see **B3.3**). The court should consider a sexual harm prevention order (see **E21.22**).

The offence is a qualifying offence for an automatic life sentence under the CJA 2003, sch. 15B (see **B3.25**).

B3.247 **Elements** The essence of the offence is that A must intentionally control the sexual exploitation of a child. For the meaning of 'sexual exploitation', see **B3.232**. For 'control' see **B3.261**.

It is a defence for A to have reasonably believed that B was aged 18 or over, but the defence does not apply if B was aged under 13 at the material time.

Arranging or Facilitating Sexual Exploitation of a Child

B3.248 **Sexual Offences Act 2003, s. 50**

(1) A person (A) commits an offence if—
(a) he intentionally arranges or facilitates the sexual exploitation in any part of the world of another person (B), and
(b) either—
(i) B is under 18, and A does not reasonably believe that B is 18 or over, or
(ii) B is under 13.

B3.249 **Procedure** An allegation of an offence contrary to s. 50 is triable either way. As to the classification of the offence for the purpose of listing, see CrimPD XIII, para. B (see Supplement, **CPD.XIII.B**). The extra-territorial jurisdiction provisions of s. 72 apply (see **B3.315**).

See **B3.355** for alternative verdicts.

B3.250 **Sentence** The maximum sentence for an offence under the SOA 2003, s. 50, on conviction on indictment is 14 years' imprisonment. On summary conviction, the maximum sentence is six months and/or an unlimited fine (s. 50(2)).

The definitive sentencing guideline, *Sexual Offences* (see Supplement, **SG31-21**), applies to sex offenders aged 18 or over who are sentenced on or after 1 April 2014 (see **B3.3**). The court should consider a sexual harm prevention order (see **E21.22**).

The offence is a qualifying offence for an automatic life sentence under the CJA 2003, sch. 15B (see **B3.25**).

B3.251 **Elements** The offender (A) must intentionally arrange or facilitate the sexual exploitation of a person under the age of 18 (B). For the meaning of 'sexual exploitation', see **B3.232**.

It is a defence for A to have reasonably believed that B was aged 18 or over, but the defence does not apply if B was aged under 13 at the material time.

EXPLOITATION OF PROSTITUTION

Offences concerning Exploitation of Prostitution

Sections 52 to 53A of the SOA 2003 concern the exploitation of prostitution. Common interpretation provisions in s. 54 apply to them. B3.252

Sexual Offences Act 2003, s. 54

(1) In sections 52, 53 and 53A, 'gain' means—
  (a) any financial advantage, including the discharge of an obligation to pay or the provision of goods or services (including sexual services) gratuitously or at a discount; or
  (b) the goodwill of any person which is or appears likely, in time, to bring financial advantage.
(2) In sections 51A, 52, 53 and 53A 'prostitute' means a person (A) who, on at least one occasion and whether or not compelled to do so, offers or provides sexual services to another person in return for payment or a promise of payment to A or a third person; and 'prostitution' is to be interpreted accordingly.
(3) In subsection (2) and section 53A, 'payment' means any financial advantage, including the discharge of an obligation to pay or the provision of goods or services (including sexual services) gratuitously or at a discount.

Gain is expressed in terms of either financial advantage or good will which appears likely to bring financial advantage in the future. Financial advantage is widely defined by s. 54(1).

The extra-territorial jurisdiction provisions of s. 72 do not apply to these offences and therefore the acts constituting the offence must be committed in England and Wales.

Causing or Inciting Prostitution for Gain

Sexual Offences Act 2003, s. 52 B3.253

(1) A person commits an offence if—
  (a) he intentionally causes or incites another person to become a prostitute in any part of the world, and
  (b) he does so for or in the expectation of gain for himself or a third person.

Procedure An allegation of an offence contrary to s. 52 is triable either way. As to the classification of the offence for the purpose of listing, see CrimPD XIII, para. B (see Supplement, **CPD.XIII.B**). B3.254

See **B3.355** for alternative verdicts.

Indictment B3.255

Statement of Offence

Intentionally causing or inciting a person to become a prostitute in any part of the world in the expectation of gain contrary to section 52(1) of the Sexual Offences Act 2003.

Particulars of Offence

A, on or about the... day of... intentionally and in the expectation of gain to himself or another caused [incited] V to become a prostitute in any part of the world.

Sentence The maximum penalty for an offence under the SOA 2003, s. 52, on conviction on indictment is seven years' imprisonment. On summary conviction, the maximum is six months and/or an unlimited fine (s. 52(2)). B3.256

The definitive sentencing guideline, *Sexual Offences* (see Supplement, **SG31-19**), applies to sex offenders aged 18 or over who are sentenced on or after 1 April 2014 (see **B3.3**). The court should consider a sexual harm prevention order (see **E21.22**).

B3.257 **Elements** The essence of the offence is that the accused must intentionally cause or incite another person to become a prostitute in any part of the world. The person's acts must, however, have been done in England and Wales as the extra-territorial jurisdiction provisions of s. 72 do not apply. Plainly, the person incited need not in fact have engaged in an act of prostitution. A must act in the expectation of gain for A or a third person.

The wide definition of 'prostitute' contained in s. 51(2) applies to this offence by virtue of s. 54(2) (see **B3.252**). CPS guidance suggests that the provision of accommodation in return for sex is capable of amounting to an offence under s. 52 of causing or inciting a person to become a prostitute, especially when a vulnerable person is persuaded to enter into an arrangement.

Controlling Prostitution for Gain

B3.258

Sexual Offences Act 2003, s. 53

(1) A person commits an offence if—
(a) he intentionally controls any of the activities of another person relating to that person's prostitution in any part of the world, and
(b) he does so for or in the expectation of gain for himself or a third person.

B3.259 **Procedure** An allegation of an offence contrary to s. 53 is triable either way. As to the classification of the offence for the purpose of listing, see CrimPD XIII, para. B (see Supplement, **CPD.XIII.B**).

See **B3.355** for alternative verdicts.

B3.260 **Sentence** The maximum penalty for an offence under the SOA 2003, s. 53, on conviction on indictment is seven years' imprisonment. On summary conviction, the maximum is six months and/or an unlimited fine (s. 53(2)).

The definitive sentencing guideline, *Sexual Offences* (see Supplement, **SG31-19**), applies to sex offenders aged 18 or over who are sentenced on or after 1 April 2014 (see **B3.3**).

B3.261 **Elements** The essence of the offence is that A must intentionally control any of the activities of another person relating to that person's prostitution in any part of the world. Such control may be direct or through an intermediary.

The meaning of 'control' in s. 53 was considered in *Massey* [2007] EWCA Crim 2664, [2008] 1 WLR 937. In dismissing M's appeal against conviction, the Court of Appeal said 'control' includes but is not limited to one who forces another to carry out an activity. The Court saw no need to lay down a comprehensive definition of an ordinary English word, it is enough that a person instructs or directs another to carry out a particular activity or do it in a particular way. There is a wide variety of possible reasons why a person may do as instructed. It may be, for example, because of the use or threat of physical violence, or it may be because of emotional blackmail, or the lure of gain. There is no necessity for the victim to have acted without free will.

B3.262 In *LM* [2010] EWCA Crim 2327, [2011] 1 Cr App R 12 (135), the Court of Appeal considered the applicability of the Council of Europe Convention on Action against Trafficking in Human Beings 2005 to proceedings concerned with controlling prostitution for gain contrary to s. 53. Article 26 of the Convention provides for the possibility of not imposing penalties on victims for their involvement in unlawful activities to the extent that they had been compelled to be involved. Under Article 10, a number of agencies were established and charged with the identification of persons who had reasonable grounds for being treated as a victim of trafficking.

Moreover, guidelines issued by the CPS required prosecutors to consider whether the public interest was best served in continuing a relevant prosecution. The accused were prosecuted for offences contrary to s. 53. The Crown's case against them had been that they had initially been victims of trafficking, but they had subsequently become controllers of prostitution by others. At a late stage, the Crown accepted pleas of guilty entered on the basis that the accused had been trafficked, beaten and coerced into prostitution themselves and that anything that had amounted to controlling prostitution had been done under pressure which fell short of duress. The Court of Appeal quashed the convictions on the basis that the Article 26 duty was ignored at the point when the factual basis changed. If the duty had been discharged, the Crown should have offered no evidence or an application to stay should have been successful on the basis that any decision to continue to prosecute was one which no reasonable prosecutor could make. The Court also observed that, whilst any breach of Article 10 is deplorable, such a breach is not sufficient simply of itself to render a prosecution unlawful or amenable to stay. In any case where trafficking was an obvious possibility, the police should inquire into it. In this case they did so by raising it with the accused in interview and formed the view that the accused probably had been trafficked. The accused ought then to have been referred to the referral agencies, because other possible measures apart from decisions about prosecution might have followed. If an accused was legally represented then, unless there was something unusual about the case, it was not desirable for the police to be required to refer people to the agencies against their wishes and following legal advice. The police fulfilled their duties by reminding the solicitors of the availability of the relevant agencies. So far as an unrepresented offender was concerned, the situation might well be different. It had initially been the Crown's case on a fair assessment of the evidence available that, although previously victims of trafficking, the accused had become voluntary abusers of others. That assessment justified a decision to prosecute. The Crown's case might or might not have been made out, but it was not unreasonable to decide to pursue it. See the defence provided by the Modern Slavery Act 2015, s. 45 (in force from 31 July 2015: see **A3.54** and **B22.24**).

Because the extra-territorial jurisdiction provisions of s. 72 do not apply, A's acts must be done in or from England and Wales. Here too 'prostitution' bears the wide protective meaning in s. 54(2) (see **B3.252**). Thus, controlling an activity relating to a single act of prostitution is sufficient to bring A within the section.

A must act with an expectation of gain for A or a third party. 'Gain' is defined in terms of financial advantage (see s. 54(1) at **B3.252**).

CPS guidance suggests that the provision of accommodation in return for sex is capable of amounting to an offence under s. 53 of controlling prostitution for gain, even when victims are apparently acting of their own free will.

Paying for Sexual Services of a Prostitute Subjected to Exploitative Conduct

Sexual Offences Act 2003, s. 53A **B3.263**

(1) A person (A) commits an offence if—
   (a) A makes or promises payment for the sexual services of a prostitute (B),
   (b) a third person (C) has engaged in exploitative conduct of a kind likely to induce or encourage B to provide the sexual services for which A has made or promised payment, and
   (c) C engaged in that conduct for or in the expectation of gain for C or another person (apart from A or B).

(2) The following are irrelevant—
   (a) where in the world the sexual services are to be provided and whether those services are provided,
   (b) whether A is, or ought to be, aware that C has engaged in exploitative conduct.

(3) C engages in exploitative conduct if—
   (a) C uses force, threats (whether or not relating to violence) or any other form of coercion, or
   (b) C practises any form of deception.

Procedure The offence is summary only. **B3.264**

B3.265 **Sentence** The offence is punishable by a fine not exceeding level 3 on the standard scale (SOA 2003, s. 53A(4)). The Sentencing Council guidelines on sexual offences (see **B3.3**) do not refer to this offence.

B3.266 **Elements** It is of note that, by virtue of s. 53A(2), it is deemed to be irrelevant whether A was, or ought to have been, aware that B had been exploited. Moreover, by virtue of s. 53A(3)(b), it appears that A may be guilty even if B is not aware of having been exploited due to deception. As to the meaning of 'prostitute' and 'payment', see **B3.252**.

TRAFFICKING

B3.267 The Protection of Freedoms Act 2012, s. 109, which came into force on 6 April 2013, repealed the SOA 2003, ss. 57 to 59, substantially amended s. 60 and inserted s. 59A (see **B3.268**). The Protection of Freedoms Act 2012 (Commencement No. 5 and Saving and Transitional Provision) Order 2013 (SI 2013 No. 470) provides that the amendments and repeals made by s. 109 do not have effect in relation to offences committed wholly or partly before 6 April 2013 (art. 3) but also provides that, where D is charged under both the SOA 2003, s. 59A, and any of ss. 57 to 59, and it cannot be proved whether the conduct in question came before or after 6 April 2013, it shall be conclusively presumed that the offence was committed before that date. The Modern Slavery Act 2015, in force from 31 July 2015, repeals and replaces the SOA 2003, ss. 59A to 60C, with new provisions applicable, *inter alia*, to all kinds of trafficking (see **B22.5**).

For the now repealed ss. 57 to 59, see the 2014 edition of this work.

Trafficking People for Sexual Exploitation

B3.268 **Sexual Offences Act 2003, s. 59A**

(1) A person ('A') commits an offence if A intentionally arranges or facilitates—
  (a) the arrival in, or entry into, the United Kingdom or another country of another person ('B'),
  (b) the travel of B within the United Kingdom or another country, or
  (c) the departure of B from the United Kingdom or another country, with a view to the sexual exploitation of B.

(2) For the purposes of subsection (1)(a) and (c) A's arranging or facilitating is with a view to the sexual exploitation of B if, and only if—
  (a) A intends to do anything to or in respect of B, after B's arrival, entry or (as the case may be) departure but in any part of the world, which if done will involve the commission of a relevant offence, or
  (b) A believes that another person is likely to do something to or in respect of B, after B's arrival, entry or (as the case may be) departure but in any part of the world, which if done will involve the commission of a relevant offence.

(3) For the purposes of subsection (1)(b) A's arranging or facilitating is with a view to the sexual exploitation of B if, and only if—
  (a) A intends to do anything to or in respect of B, during or after the journey and in any part of the world, which if done will involve the commission of a relevant offence, or
  (b) A believes that another person is likely to do something to or in respect of B, during or after the journey and in any part of the world, which if done will involve the commission of a relevant offence.

(4) A person who is a UK national commits an offence under this section regardless of—
  (a) where the arranging or facilitating takes place, or
  (b) which country is the country of arrival, entry, travel or (as the case may be) departure.

(5) A person who is not a UK national commits an offence under this section if—
  (a) any part of the arranging or facilitating takes place in the United Kingdom, or
  (b) the United Kingdom is the country of arrival, entry, travel or (as the case may be) departure.

With effect from *31 July 2015*, s. 59A is repealed and replaced by offences under the Modern Slavery Act 2015 (see **B22.5**).

Procedure and Sentence An allegation of an offence contrary to s. 59A is triable either way. As to the classification of the offence for the purpose of listing, see CrimPD XIII, para. B (see Supplement, **CPD.XIII.B**). The maximum penalty on conviction on indictment is 14 years' imprisonment. On summary conviction, the maximum penalty is six months and/or an unlimited fine (s. 59A(6)). **B3.269**

The definitive sentencing guideline, *Sexual Offences* (see Supplement, **SG31-23**), applies to sex offenders aged 18 or over who are sentenced on or after 1 April 2014 (see **B3.3**). For powers of forfeiture relating to land, vehicles, ships and aircraft used in commission of an offence under the SOA 2003, s. 59A, see s. 60A.

Elements A relevant offence is defined by s. 60(1), as substituted by the Protection of Freedoms Act 2012, s. 109(3), to mean (a) any offence under the law of England and Wales which is an offence under the SOA 2003, Part 1, or under the Protection of Children Act 1978, s. 1(1)(a), or (b) anything done outside England and Wales which is not an offence within (a) but would be if done in England and Wales. **B3.270**

PREPARATORY OFFENCES

Administering a Substance with Intent

Sexual Offences Act 2003, s. 61 **B3.271**

(1) A person commits an offence if he intentionally administers a substance to, or causes a substance to be taken by, another person (B)—
  (a) knowing that B does not consent, and
  (b) with the intention of stupefying or overpowering B, so as to enable any person to engage in a sexual activity that involves B.

Procedure An allegation of an offence contrary to s. 61 is triable either way. As to the classification of the offence for the purpose of listing, see CrimPD XIII, para. B (see Supplement, **CPD.XIII.B**). The extra-territorial jurisdiction provisions of s. 72 apply (see **B3.315**) if B was under the age of 18 at the time of the alleged offence. **B3.272**

See **B3.355** for alternative verdicts.

Indictment **B3.273**

Statement of Offence

Intentionally administering a substance to or causing a substance to be taken by another with the intention of stupefying or overpowering that other in order to enable another person to engage in sexual activity with that person contrary to section 61(1) of the Sexual Offences Act 2003.

Particulars of Offence

A, on or about the... day of... intentionally administered a substance to [caused a substance to be taken by] V knowing that V did not consent and with the intention of stupefying or overpowering V so as to enable himself or another to engage in a sexual activity involving V.

Sentence The maximum penalty for an offence under the SOA 2003, s. 61, on conviction on indictment is ten years' imprisonment. On summary conviction, the maximum is six months and/or an unlimited fine. **B3.274**

The definitive sentencing guideline, *Sexual Offences* (see Supplement, **SG31-33**), applies to sex offenders aged 18 or over who are sentenced on or after 1 April 2014 (see **B3.3**).

There is a notification requirement under the SOA 2003, s. 80 and sch. 3 (see **E23**).

B3.275 **Elements** The Home Office Explanatory Notes to the 2003 Act suggest that the substance may be administered to B in any way, e.g., in a drink, by injection or by covering B's face with a cloth impregnated with the substance. The offence is made out both where A administers the substance to B, or A persuades a third party, C, to administer the substance because C knows B and so is more easily able to do so. The intended sexual activity need not involve A but instead it may be planned that a third party have sex with B.

For the meaning of consent, see **B3.29**.

For the meaning of 'sexual', see **B3.57**.

Committing an Offence with Intent to Commit a Sexual Offence

B3.276 **Sexual Offences Act 2003, s. 62**

(1) A person commits an offence under this section if he commits any offence with the intention of committing a relevant sexual offence.
(2) In this section, 'relevant sexual offence' means any offence under this Part (including an offence of aiding, abetting, counselling or procuring such an offence).

B3.277 **Procedure** An allegation of an offence contrary to s. 62 is triable either way unless the offence alleged is one of either kidnapping or false imprisonment. In such a case, the alleged offence is triable on indictment only. As to the classification of the offence for the purpose of listing, see CrimPD XIII, para. B (see Supplement, **CPD.XIII.B**). If B was under 18 years of age at the time of the offence, the extra-territorial jurisdiction provisions of s. 72 apply (see **B3.315**).

See **B3.355** for alternative verdicts.

B3.278 **Indictment**

Statement of Offence

Committing an offence with intent to commit a sexual offence contrary to section 62(1) of the Sexual Offences Act 2003.

Particulars of Offence

A, on or about the... day of... [e.g., unlawfully had in his possession a controlled drug of class B with intent to administer the same] with the intention of committing a relevant sexual offence, namely [specify relevant sexual offence e.g., under s. 61(1) of the Sexual Offences Act 2003].

B3.279 **Sentence** The maximum penalty on conviction on indictment is ten years' imprisonment. However, where the offence is committed by kidnapping or false imprisonment, the maximum penalty is imprisonment for life. On summary conviction, the maximum penalty is six months and/or an unlimited fine (s. 62(3) and (4)).

The definitive sentencing guideline, *Sexual Offences* (see Supplement, **SG31-34**), applies to sex offenders aged 18 or over who are sentenced on or after 1 April 2014 (see **B3.3**). Essentially, it states that the starting point for any sentence should be commensurate with that for the preparatory offence actually committed but enhanced to reflect the nature and severity of the intended sexual offence. Two years' imprisonment is suggested to be a suitable enhancement where the intent was to commit rape or assault by penetration.

The offence is a qualifying offence for an automatic life sentence under the CJA 2003, sch. 15B, if the offender is liable on conviction to imprisonment for life (see **B3.25**). There is a notification requirement under the SOA 2003, s. 80 and sch. 3, subject to the age of the offender and the sentence passed and subject to the age of the victim (see **E23**).

In *A-G's Ref (No. 133 of 2015) (Senussi)* [2016] EWCA Crim 38, [2016] 1 Cr App R (S) 70 (518) the Court of Appeal increased concurrent sentences of two years' imprisonment to concurrent sentences of five years for an offence contrary to s. 62 and an offence of sexual assault. The Court rejected a submission that the offence was not Category 1A because the acquittal of the co-accused meant that the offender had not 'acted together with others to commit the offence', observing (at [26]) that the wording of the guideline 'has to be read both objectively and sensibly. From the point of view of the victim, if another or others are present at the relevant time and acting with the offender, a degree of menace or force or assistance is conveyed.'

Elements An offence 'under this part' means any within the SOA 2003, ss. 1 to 79. **B3.280**

As to the necessity for the prosecution to prove the nature of the relevant offence intended, see **B3.285**. It is submitted that the same conclusion must be reached in respect of an offence under s. 62 as in respect of an offence under s. 63.

Trespass with Intent to Commit a Sexual Offence

Sexual Offences Act 2003, s. 63 **B3.281**

(1) A person commits an offence if—
  (a) he is a trespasser on any premises,
  (b) he intends to commit a relevant sexual offence on the premises, and
  (c) he knows that, or is reckless as to whether, he is a trespasser.
(2) In this section—
  'premises' includes a structure or part of a structure;
  'relevant sexual offence' has the same meaning as in section 62;
  'structure' includes a tent, vehicle or vessel or other temporary or movable structure.

Procedure An allegation of an offence contrary to s. 63 is triable either way. As to the classification of the offence for the purpose of listing, see CrimPD XIII, para. B (see Supplement, **CPD.XIII.B**). The extra-territorial jurisdiction provisions of s. 72 apply (see **B3.315**) if the victim was under the age of 18 at the time of the alleged offence. **B3.282**

See **B3.355** for alternative verdicts.

Indictment **B3.283**

Statement of Offence

Trespass with intent to commit a sexual offence contrary to section 63(1) of the Sexual Offences Act 2003.

Particulars of Offence

A, on or about the... day of... being a trespasser on premises and knowing that, or being reckless as to whether he was, a trespasser, intended to commit a relevant sexual offence on the premises, namely [here specify the relevant offence].

Sentence The maximum penalty for an offence under the SOA 2003, s. 63, on conviction on indictment is ten years' imprisonment. On summary conviction, the maximum is six months and/or an unlimited fine. **B3.284**

The definitive sentencing guideline, *Sexual Offences* (see Supplement, **SG31-35**), applies to sex offenders aged 18 or over who are sentenced on or after 1 April 2014 (see **B3.3**). There is a notification requirement under the SOA 2003, s. 80 and sch. 3, subject to the age of the offender and the sentence passed and subject to the age of the victim (see **E23**).

Elements The offender must be at least reckless as to whether he is trespassing. In *Pacurar* [2016] EWCA Crim 569, [2016] 1 WLR 3913 it was held that Parliament must have intended the SOA 2003, s. 63, to cover circumstances where it was obvious that the accused intended to commit a sexual offence, but it was not possible to specify precisely which one and upon whom. Therefore a count was not bad for lack of particularity when it merely stated that D had 'intended to commit a relevant sexual offence'. The Court of Appeal also considered that, as the prosecution had narrowed down the possible offences to those under ss. 1 to 3 and 5 to 7 of the SOA 2003 as against specified individuals at an identified time and place, there was less **B3.285**

difficulty than if they had put their case on the basis that D intended to commit any offence in Part 1 of the SOA 2003 against any of the people in the local area. The Court, however, went on to observe that prosecutors may wish to put more details into the particulars in future. The Court also held that a *Brown* direction (see **D18.44**) was not necessary in such circumstances; it would not matter that some jurors were satisfied that D intended to commit one offence and others a different offence provided that they were all satisfied that he had trespassed with intent to commit a sexual offence.

SEX WITH AN ADULT RELATIVE

Sex with an Adult Relative: Penetration

B3.286 Sexual Offences Act 2003, s. 64

(1) A person aged 16 or over (A) (subject to subsection (3A)) commits an offence if—
  (a) he intentionally penetrates another person's vagina or anus with a part of his body or anything else, or penetrates another person's mouth with his penis,
  (b) the penetration is sexual,
  (c) the other person (B) is aged 18 or over,
  (d) A is related to B in a way mentioned in subsection (2), and
  (e) A knows or could reasonably be expected to know that he is related to B in that way.

(2) The ways that A may be related to B are as parent, grandparent, child, grandchild, brother, sister, half-brother, half-sister, uncle, aunt, nephew or niece.

(3) In subsection (2)—
  (za) 'parent' includes an adoptive parent;
  (zb) 'child' includes an adopted person within the meaning of Chapter 4 of Part 1 of the Adoption and Children Act 2002;
  (a) 'uncle' means the brother of a person's parent, and 'aunt' has a corresponding meaning;
  (b) 'nephew' means the child of a person's brother or sister, and 'niece' has a corresponding meaning.

(3A) Where subsection (1) applies in a case where A is related to B as B's child by virtue of subsection (3)(zb), A does not commit an offence under this section unless A is 18 or over.

(4) Where in proceedings for an offence under this section it is proved that the defendant was related to the other person in any of those ways, it is to be taken that the defendant knew or could reasonably have been expected to know that he was related in that way unless sufficient evidence is adduced to raise an issue as to whether he knew or could reasonably have been expected to know that he was.

Any reference to an adoptive relationship is to be read as including a reference to the corresponding relationship arising by virtue of a parental order under the Human Fertilisation and Embryology Act 2008 (Human Fertilisation and Embryology (Parental Orders) Regulations 2010 (SI 2010 No. 985), sch. 4).

B3.287 **Procedure** An allegation of an offence contrary to s. 64 is triable either way. As to the classification of the offence for the purpose of listing, see CrimPD XIII, para. B (see Supplement, **CPD.XIII.B**).

See **B3.355** for alternative verdicts.

B3.288 **Sentence** The maximum penalty for an offence under the SOA 2003, s. 64, on conviction on indictment is two years' imprisonment. On summary conviction, the maximum is six months and/or an unlimited fine (s. 64(5)).

The definitive sentencing guideline, *Sexual Offences* (see Supplement, **SG31-32**), applies to sex offenders aged 18 or over who are sentenced on or after 1 April 2014 (see **B3.3**). There is a notification requirement under the SOA 2003, s. 80 and sch. 3, subject to the age of the offender and the sentence imposed (see **E23**).

Elements Section 64 of the SOA 2003 contains a rebuttable presumption as to the accused's *mens rea* in respect of the relationship between the accused and the person penetrated. If the prosecution prove that the relationship is a relevant one for the purposes of s. 64 then the accused is taken to have either known of that relationship, or could reasonably have been expected to know of it, unless sufficient evidence is adduced so as to raise an issue as to whether the accused knew or could reasonably have known of that relationship. The burden is evidential and once sufficient evidence is raised the prosecution has the usual burden of proving the contrary to the criminal standard. **B3.289**

Sex with an Adult Relative: Consenting to Penetration

Sexual Offences Act 2003, s. 65 **B3.290**

(1) A person aged 16 or over (A) (subject to subsection (3A)) commits an offence if—
- (a) another person (B) penetrates A's vagina or anus with a part of B's body or anything else, or penetrates A's mouth with B's penis,
- (b) A consents to the penetration,
- (c) the penetration is sexual,
- (d) B is aged 18 or over,
- (e) A is related to B in a way mentioned in subsection (2), and
- (f) A knows or could reasonably be expected to know that he is related to B in that way.

Section 65(2) to (4) and (6) are in identical terms to s. 64(2) to (4) and (6) (see **B3.286**).

Any reference to an adoptive relationship is to be read as including a reference to the corresponding relationship arising by virtue of a parental order under the Human Fertilisation and Embryology Act 2008 (Human Fertilisation and Embryology (Parental Orders) Regulations 2010 (SI 2010 No. 985), sch. 4).

Procedure An allegation of an offence contrary to s. 65 is triable either way. As to the classification of the offence for the purpose of listing, see CrimPD XIII, para. B (see Supplement, **CPD.XIII.B**). **B3.291**

See **B3.355** for alternative verdicts.

Indictment **B3.292**

Statement of Offence

Consenting to the penetration of his body by a related person contrary to section 65(1) of the Sexual Offences Act 2003.

Particulars of Offence

A on or about the . . . day of . . . being then a person aged 16 years or over permitted V a person related to her and over the age of 18 years sexually to penetrate [her vagina or anus] [his anus] [with his penis, fingers,] [with a part of her body, namely her fingers].

Sentence The maximum sentence for an offence under the SOA 2003, s. 65, on conviction on indictment is two years. On summary conviction, the maximum is six months and/or an unlimited fine (s. 65(5)). **B3.293**

The definitive sentencing guideline, *Sexual Offences* (see Supplement, **SG31-32**), applies to sex offenders aged 18 or over who are sentenced on or after 1 April 2014 (see **B3.3**). There is a notification requirement under the SOA 2003, s. 80 and sch. 3, subject to the age of the offender and the sentence imposed (see **E23**).

Elements Section 65 contains a rebuttable presumption as to the accused's *mens rea* in respect of the relationship between the accused and the person penetrated. The provision is identical to that contained within s. 64 and reference should therefore be had to **B3.289** for its nature and effect. **B3.294**

OTHER OFFENCES

Exposure

B3.295 **Sexual Offences Act 2003, s. 66**

(1) A person commits an offence if—
- (a) he intentionally exposes his genitals, and
- (b) he intends that someone will see them and be caused alarm or distress.

B3.296 **Procedure** An allegation of an offence contrary to s. 66 is triable either way. As to the classification of the offence for the purpose of listing, see CrimPD XIII, para. B (see Supplement, **CPD.XIII.B**).

See **B3.355** for alternative verdicts.

B3.297 **Sentence** The maximum penalty for an offence under the SOA 2003, s. 66, on conviction on indictment is two years' imprisonment. On summary conviction, the maximum is six months and/or an unlimited fine.

The definitive sentencing guideline, *Sexual Offences* (see Supplement, **SG31-30**), applies to sex offenders aged 18 or over who are sentenced on or after 1 April 2014 (see **B3.3**).

The Court of Appeal reduced sentences totalling four years and six months to a total of four years following guilty pleas to five offences of exposure in *Nicholson* [2014] EWCA Crim 2710. The offender was a young man with a learning disability who had committed a number of serious offences of exposure prior to the offending with which the Court was concerned. He had previously received custodial sentences for those offences. He had refused to receive treatment to deal with his offending. The offences dealt with by the Court had all taken place while he was an inmate at Aylesbury YOI and were directed at female prison officers. The Court recognised that the offender was dangerous but an extended sentence could not be imposed for the offence of exposure. Thus, although the Court reduced the sentences imposed to a limited extent, it observed that the judge was entitled to pass a sentence which considerably exceeded the maximum for a single offence. For a further example of a successful appeal against a sentence imposed for offending contrary to s. 66, see *Morrison* [2019] EWCA Crim 1343.

There is a notification requirement under the SOA 2003, s. 80 and sch. 3, subject to the age of the offender, the age of the victim, and the sentence imposed (see **E23**). The court should consider a sexual harm prevention order (see **E21.22**).

B3.298 **Elements** The essence of the offence is that the accused intentionally exposes his genitals and intends that another person see them and is thereby caused alarm or distress. The offence thus has a 'bolted on intent' and is therefore one of specific intent. Consequently, voluntary intoxication may negate the intent required for the offence (*Heard* [2007] EWCA Crim 125, [2008] QB 43).

Voyeurism

B3.299 **Sexual Offences Act 2003, ss. 67, 67A and 68**

67.—(1) A person commits an offence if—
- (a) for the purpose of obtaining sexual gratification, he observes another person doing a private act, and
- (b) he knows that the other person does not consent to being observed for his sexual gratification.

(2) A person commits an offence if—
- (a) he operates equipment with the intention of enabling another person to observe, for the purpose of obtaining sexual gratification, a third person (B) doing a private act, and
- (b) he knows that B does not consent to his operating equipment with that intention.

(3) A person commits an offence if—
(a) he records another person (B) doing a private act,
(b) he does so with the intention that he or a third person will, for the purpose of obtaining sexual gratification, look at an image of B doing the act, and
(c) he knows that B does not consent to his recording the act with that intention.
(4) A person commits an offence if he instals equipment, or constructs or adapts a structure or part of a structure, with the intention of enabling himself or another person to commit an offence under subsection (1).

67A.—(1) A person (A) commits an offence if—
(a) A operates equipment beneath the clothing of another person (B),
(b) A does so with the intention of enabling A or another person (C), for a purpose mentioned in subsection (3), to observe—
(i) B's genitals or buttocks (whether exposed or covered with underwear), or
(ii) the underwear covering B's genitals or buttocks, in circumstances where the genitals, buttocks or underwear would not otherwise be visible, and
(c) A does so—
(i) without B's consent, and
(ii) without reasonably believing that B consents.
(2) A person (A) commits an offence if—
(a) A records an image beneath the clothing of another person (B),
(b) the image is of—
(i) B's genitals or buttocks (whether exposed or covered with underwear), or
(ii) the underwear covering B's genitals or buttocks, in circumstances where the genitals, buttocks or underwear would not otherwise be visible,
(c) A does so with the intention that A or another person (C) will look at the image for a purpose mentioned in subsection (3), and
(d) A does so—
(i) without B's consent, and
(ii) without reasonably believing that B consents.
(3) The purposes referred to in subsections (1) and (2) are—
(a) obtaining sexual gratification (whether for A or C);
(b) humiliating, alarming or distressing B.

68.—(1) for the purposes of section 67, a person is doing a private act if the person is in a place which, in the circumstances, would reasonably be expected to provide privacy, and—
(a) the person's genitals, buttocks or breasts are exposed or covered only with underwear,
(b) the person is using a lavatory, or
(c) the person is doing a sexual act that is not of a kind ordinarily done in public.
(1A) For the purposes of sections 67 and 67A, operating equipment includes enabling or securing its activation by another person without that person's knowledge.
(2) In section 67, 'structure' includes a tent, vehicle or vessel or other temporary or movable structure.

Procedure An allegation of an offence contrary to s. 67 or 67A is triable either way. As to the classification of the offence for the purpose of listing, see CrimPD XIII, para. B (see Supplement, **CPD.XIII.B**). **B3.300**

See **B3.355** for alternative verdicts.

Indictment **B3.301**

Statement of Offence

Operating equipment with the intention of enabling another person to observe a private act for the purposes of sexual gratification contrary to section 67(2) of the Sexual Offences Act 2003.

Particulars of Offence

A, on or about the . . . day of . . . knowing that V did not consent thereto operated equipment with the intention of enabling another person to observe V doing a private act.

Statement of Offence

Operating equipment beneath the clothing of another person with the intention of enabling another person to view [genitals or buttocks or the underwear covering the genitals or buttocks] for the purposes of [sexual gratification/ humiliation] contrary to section 67A of the Sexual Offences Act 2003.

Particulars of Offence

A, on or about the ... day of ... knowing that V did not consent thereto operated equipment beneath the clothing of V with the intention of enabling another person of viewing the genitals or buttocks of V

B3.302 **Sentence** The maximum penalty for an offence under the SOA 2003, s. 67 or 67A, on conviction on indictment is two years' imprisonment. On summary conviction, the maximum is six months and/or an unlimited fine (s. 67(5)).

The definitive sentencing guideline, *Sexual Offences* (see Supplement, **SG31-31**), applies to sex offenders aged 18 or over who are sentenced on or after 1 April 2014 (see **B3.3**).

There is a notification requirement under the SOA 2003, s. 80 and sch. 3, subject to A's age and the sentence imposed (see **E23**). The court should consider a sexual harm prevention order (see E21.22).

B3.303 **Elements** As to 'gratification', see **B3.123**. For 'consent', see **B3.29**. 'Private act' is defined in s. 68 (see **B3.299**).

In *Bassett* [2008] EWCA Crim 1174, [2009] 1 WLR 1032, the appellant had been convicted of voyeurism after using a concealed camera to film a man wearing swimming trunks in the showers of a public swimming pool. The Court of Appeal quashed the conviction on the basis that s. 68(1)(a) related only to the breasts of women and not men. The issue also arose as to whether the complainant was doing a private act at the time of the offence. The fact that the showers were open plan was not inevitably fatal to the conviction as a person may have a reasonable expectation of privacy from the type of observation which occurred whilst in the shower area. That issue of reasonable expectation of privacy is one for the jury. For commentary on *Bassett*, see [2008] Crim LR 998.

In *Richards* [2020] EWCA Crim 95 the Court of Appeal considered the appeal of an offender convicted of two counts of voyeurism who was sentenced to concurrent nine-month terms of imprisonment. The two complainants (SD and JW) were prostitutes and the appellant had filmed them without their consent having sex with him. The evidence of SD was that she enjoyed being filmed but charged extra for that service and did not consent to being filmed with the appellant. JW said she had not consented and would not have done so. The appellant's case was that he had been charged a higher price for filming the sexual encounters. An unsuccessful submission of no case to answer had been made on the basis that an offence of voyeurism contrary to the SOA 2003, s. 67, could not be committed by a participant in a private act.

Upon appeal against conviction, it was argued by the appellant that the kind of activity the section is aimed at capturing is a voyeur who will necessarily be observing or recording another's private act. It was submitted that, for the purposes of s. 67(3), an offender could never be a participant in an act that was being recorded and it was therefore not a private act.

The Crown argued that the absence of consent for the filming by the two complainants created a reasonable expectation of privacy. Whether there was, in fact, a reasonable expectation of privacy was intended by Parliament to be considered by a jury and it is a matter of fact and degree depending on the kind of observation that occurred. For example, where a doctor examines a patient's genitalia or breasts for medical examination, the expectation is that they will be viewed once. If the doctor covertly filmed the examination it would be open to the jury to conclude there was a reasonable expectation of privacy against the secret filming for the purposes of the doctor's subsequent sexual gratification.

On behalf of an intervener (who was a party to judicial review proceedings which would be significantly affected by the outcome of the appeal) it was submitted that the purpose of s. 67 is to protect those who suffer nuisance and distress from being observed or filmed in the course of an intimate act. The intervener emphasised the centrality of Article 8 of the ECHR to the consideration of whether there is a reasonable expectation of privacy, and it was submitted that *Reklos v Greece* [2009] EMLR 16, for example, demonstrated that one's image and control of it is a chief attribute of privacy.

The Court concluded that where there is deliberate and covert filming of consensual intercourse, it necessary to consider whether the recording met the specific circumstances of s. 67(3). It was clear in the instant case that sexual gratification had occurred and the issue of whether there was a reasonable expectation of privacy was for the jury to resolve. Detailed consideration was necessary as to whether the appellant had recorded a private act given he was one of participants. The Court found assistance in that question from the approach in *Bassett* [2008] EWCA Crim 1174, [2009] 1 Cr App R 7 (90) which explained that the reasonable expectation of privacy depends on context. What occurred in the appellant's and complainants' case was a private act where they were the only people who witnessed what occurred. There was a case for the jury to consider that there would have been an expectation that there would have been no publicity or display of that private act, nor any secret observation or recording. The presence of the appellant would not lessen the expectation of privacy; the expectation being that what occurred would not be available for later viewing, even if only by the appellant. The Court remarked that it may be an unexpected decision; that one can be guilty of voyeurism in respect of an act in which one participates. But the Court emphasised that it is clear that the behaviour under consideration was of the type that s. 67(3) was created to address.

Section 67A and consequent amendments to s. 68 were inserted into the SOA 2003 by the Voyeurism (Offences) Act 2019 and came into force on 12 April 2019. They are designed to deal with 'upskirting' and apply only in England and Wales. The amendment of s. 68, with the insertion of s. 68(1A) confirms that operating equipment includes enabling or securing its activation by another person without that person's knowledge. An example would be the use of a camera that is activated by someone entering a room.

Intercourse with an Animal

Sexual Offences Act 2003, s. 69 **B3.304**

(1) A person commits an offence if—
  (a) he intentionally performs an act of penetration with his penis,
  (b) what is penetrated is the vagina or anus of a living animal, and
  (c) he knows that, or is reckless as to whether, that is what is penetrated.
(2) A person (A) commits an offence if—
  (a) A intentionally causes, or allows, A's vagina or anus to be penetrated,
  (b) the penetration is by the penis of a living animal, and
  (c) A knows that, or is reckless as to whether, that is what A is being penetrated by.

Procedure An allegation of an offence contrary to s. 69 is triable either way. As to the classification of the offence for the purpose of listing, see CrimPD XIII, para. B (see Supplement, **CPD.XIII.B**). **B3.305**

See **B3.355** for alternative verdicts.

Sentence The maximum penalty for an offence under the SOA 2003, s. 69, on conviction on indictment is two years' imprisonment. On summary conviction, the maximum is six months and/or an unlimited fine (s. 69(3)). **B3.306**

The definitive sentencing guideline, *Sexual Offences* (see **B3.3**), does not cover this offence. There is a notification requirement under the SOA 2003, s. 80 and sch. 3, subject to A's age and the sentence imposed (see **E23**). The court should consider a sexual harm prevention order (see **E21.22**).

B3.307 **Elements** The essence of the offence under the SOA 2003, s. 69(1), is an intentional act of penetration by the penis and so it can be committed only by a male person. Penetration must be of the vagina or anus of a living animal. 'Vagina' or 'anus' is defined in s. 79(10) to include references to any similar part. A must know or be reckless as to whether that is what is penetrated.

By contrast, the offence under s. 69(2) can be committed by a male or female person as the essence of it is that A intentionally allows his or her anus or her vagina to be penetrated by the penis of a living animal. A must know or be reckless that it is the anus or vagina that is being penetrated.

See **B3.344** for explanation of the circumstances in which possession of an image of intercourse or oral sex with an animal is capable of constituting an offence.

Sexual Penetration of a Corpse

B3.308 Sexual Offences Act 2003, s. 70

(1) A person commits an offence if—
- (a) he intentionally performs an act of penetration with a part of his body or anything else,
- (b) what is penetrated is a part of the body of a dead person,
- (c) he knows that, or is reckless as to whether, that is what is penetrated, and
- (d) the penetration is sexual.

B3.309 **Procedure** An allegation of an offence contrary to s. 67 is triable either way. As to the classification of the offence for the purpose of listing, see CrimPD XIII, para. B (see Supplement, **CPD.XIII.B**).
See **B3.355** for alternative verdicts.

B3.310 **Sentence** The maximum penalty for an offence under the SOA 2003, s. 70, on conviction on indictment is two years' imprisonment. On summary conviction, the maximum is six months and/or an unlimited fine (s. 70(2)). The definitive sentencing guideline, *Sexual Offences* (see **B3.3**), does not cover this offence.

B3.311 **Elements** The essence of the offence is the intentional penetration of the body of a dead person. That penetration can be by means of either a part of the body or an object. The accused must know that or be reckless as to whether he is penetrating a part of the body of a dead person and the penetration must be sexual. For 'sexual', see **B3.57**.

Sexual Activity in a Public Lavatory

B3.312 Sexual Offences Act 2003, s. 71

(1) A person commits an offence if—
- (a) he is in a lavatory to which the public or a section of the public has or is permitted to have access, whether on payment or otherwise,
- (b) he intentionally engages in an activity, and,
- (c) the activity is sexual.

(2) For the purposes of this section, an activity is sexual if a reasonable person would, in all the circumstances but regardless of any person's purpose, consider it to be sexual.

B3.313 **Procedure and Sentence** An allegation of an offence contrary to s. 71 is triable summarily only.

The maximum penalty upon conviction is six months' imprisonment and/or a fine not exceeding level 5 on the standard scale (s. 71(3)).

The definitive sentencing guideline, *Sexual Offences* (see **B3.3**), does not cover this offence but the *Magistrates' Court Sentencing Guidelines* (see Supplement, **SG10-131**) apply in respect of the sentencing of offenders aged 18 and older who are sentenced on or after 24 April 2017 in relation to s. 71.

Elements An offender must intentionally engage in sexual activity in a lavatory to which the public, or a section of the public, is permitted access either by payment or otherwise. The definition of 'sexual' is objective for the purposes of s. 71. **B3.314**

TERRITORIAL AND EXTRA-TERRITORIAL JURISDICTION

Extra-territorial jurisdiction is provided for in respect of many offences under the SOA 2003 by s. 72. **B3.315**

Sexual Offences Act 2003, s. 72

(1) If—
 (a) a United Kingdom national does an act in a country outside the United Kingdom, and
 (b) the act, if done in England and Wales, would constitute a sexual offence to which this section applies, the United Kingdom national is guilty in England and Wales of that sexual offence.

(2) If—
 (a) a United Kingdom resident does an act in a country outside the United Kingdom,
 (b) the act constitutes an offence under the law in force in that country, and
 (c) the act, if done in England and Wales, would constitute a sexual offence to which this section applies,

 the United Kingdom resident is guilty in England and Wales of that sexual offence.

(3) If—
 (a) a person does an act in a country outside the United Kingdom at a time when the person was not a United Kingdom national or a United Kingdom resident,
 (b) the act constituted an offence under the law in force in that country,
 (c) the act, if done in England and Wales, would have constituted a sexual offence to which this section applies, and
 (d) the person meets the residence or nationality condition at the relevant time,

 proceedings may be brought against the person in England and Wales for that sexual offence as if the person had done the act there.

(4) The person meets the residence or nationality condition at the relevant time if the person is a United Kingdom national or a United Kingdom resident at the time when the proceedings are brought.

(5) An act punishable under the law in force in any country constitutes an offence under that law for the purposes of subsections (2) and (3) however it is described in that law.

(6) The condition in subsection (2)(b) or (3)(b) is to be taken to be met unless, not later than rules of court may provide, the defendant serves on the prosecution a notice—
 (a) stating that, on the facts as alleged with respect to the act in question, the condition is not in the defendant's opinion met,
 (b) showing the grounds for that opinion, and
 (c) requiring the prosecution to prove that it is met.

(7) But the court, if it thinks fit, may permit the defendant to require the prosecution to prove that the condition is met without service of a notice under subsection (6).

(8) In the Crown Court the question whether the condition is met is to be decided by the judge alone.

(9) In this section—

 'country' includes territory;

 'United Kingdom national' means an individual who is—
 (a) a *British* citizen, a British overseas territories citizen, a British National (Overseas) or a British Overseas citizen;
 (b) a person who under the British Nationality Act 1981 is a British subject; or
 (c) a British protected person within the meaning of that Act;

 'United Kingdom resident' means an individual who is resident in the United Kingdom.

(10) Schedule 2 lists the sexual offences to which this section applies.

Schedule 2, para. 1, applies to England and Wales.

Sexual Offences Act 2003, sch. 2, para. 1

In relation to England and Wales, the following are sexual offences to which section 72 applies—

(a) an offence under any of sections 5 to 19, 25 and 26 and 47 to 50;
(b) an offence under any of sections 1 to 4, 30 to 41 and 61 where the victim of the offence was under 18 at the time of the offence;
(c) an offence under section 62 or 63 where the intended offence was an offence against a person under 18;
(d) an offence under—
  (i) section 1 of the Protection of Children Act 1978 (indecent photographs of children), or
  (ii) section 160 of the Criminal Justice Act 1988 (possession of indecent photograph of child).

Section 72 was substituted by the CJIA 2008, s. 72, with effect from 14 July 2008. It is no longer confined to offences against children under the age of 16. In respect of non-consensual offences such as rape, or offences involving child prostitution or breach of trust, the limit is now set at 18. More controversially, by virtue of s. 72(1) (and in contrast to UK residents and others coming under s. 72(2) and (3)), UK nationals are deprived of any defence based on lack of dual criminality. Thus a UK national who engages in consensual sexual activity with a child aged 15 in a country outside the UK may incur criminal liability even if he is not resident in the UK and the activity is perfectly lawful in the country in which it takes place.

SOLICITING

B3.316 **Street Offences Act 1959, s. 1**

(1) It shall be an offence for a person aged 18 or over (whether male or female) persistently to loiter or solicit in a street or public place for the purpose of prostitution.
(2) A person guilty of an offence under this section shall be liable on summary conviction to a fine of an amount not exceeding level 2 on the standard scale or, for an offence committed after a previous conviction, to a fine of an amount not exceeding level 3 on that scale.
(3) [Repealed by the SOCPA 2005, schs. 7 and 17.]
(4) For the purposes of this section—
  (a) conduct is persistent if it takes place on two or more occasions in any period of three months;
  (b) any reference to a person loitering or soliciting for the purposes of prostitution is a reference to a person loitering or soliciting for the purposes of offering services as a prostitute;
  (c) 'street' includes any bridge, road, lane, footway, subway, square, court, alley or passage, whether a thoroughfare, or not, which is for the time being open to the public; and the doorways and entrances of premises abutting on a street (as hereinbefore defined), and any ground adjoining and open to a street, shall be treated as forming part of the street.

Sexual Offences Act 2003, s. 51A

(1) It is an offence for a person in a street or public place to solicit another (B) for the purpose of obtaining B's sexual services as a prostitute.
(2) The reference to a person in a street or public place includes a person in a vehicle in a street or public place.

Procedure

B3.317 An allegation of an offence contrary to s. 1 of the Street Offences Act 1959 or s. 51A of the SOA 2003 is triable summarily only.

Sentence

B3.318 The maximum penalty for the offence of loitering for the purposes of prostitution under the Street Offences Act 1959 is a fine not exceeding level 2 on the standard scale; for an offence committed after a previous conviction, the maximum penalty is a fine not exceeding level 3 (Street Offences Act 1959, s. 1(2)). Soliciting contrary to the SOA 2003, s. 51A, carries a maximum penalty of a fine not exceeding level 3.

The Policing and Crime Act 2009, s. 17, amended the Street Offences Act 1959, s. 1, so as to provide new sentencing powers relating to offences under s. 1, namely orders requiring attendance at meetings to assist the offender to address the causes of the conduct constituting the offence.

Elements

Soliciting can be carried out by either a male or female, the essence of the offence being the solicitation of another to engage in prostitution (*DPP v Bull* [1995] QB 88). The person soliciting need not be in a public place provided the solicitation extends into a public place (*Behrendt v Burridge* [1977] 3 All ER 285). 'Loitering' is simply lingering with no intent to move on either on foot or in a vehicle (*Bridge v Campbell* (1947) 177 LT 444). There is no definition of public place and any issue will be resolved as a matter of fact and degree (*Glynn v Simmonds* [1952] 2 All ER 57; *Elkins v Cartlidge* [1947] 1 All ER 829). B3.319

A person is in a street or public place for the purposes of s. 51A if in a vehicle in that street or public place. The term 'street' has the same meaning under s. 51A as under the Street Offences Act 1959, s. 1 (SOA 2003, s. 51A(4)).

INDECENT PHOTOGRAPHS OF CHILDREN, ETC.

The Protection of Children Act 1978 and the CJA 1988 govern the making, possession, publication and distribution of indecent images of children with offenders being punished with up to ten years' imprisonment. These provisions are dealt with in detail below. B3.320

Protection of Children Act 1978, ss. 1 and 1A

1.—(1) Subject to section 1A and 1B, it is an offence for a person—
- (a) to take, or permit to be taken or to make, any indecent photograph or pseudo-photograph of a child; or
- (b) to distribute or show such indecent photographs or pseudo-photographs; or
- (c) to have in his possession such indecent photographs or pseudo-photographs, with a view to their being distributed or shown by himself or others; or
- (d) to publish or cause to be published any advertisement likely to be understood as conveying that the advertiser distributes or shows such indecent photographs or pseudo-photographs, or intends to do so.

1A.—(1) This section applies where, in proceedings for an offence under section 1(1)(a) of taking or making an indecent photograph or pseudo-photograph of a child, or for an offence under section 1(1)(b) or (c) relating to an indecent photograph or pseudo-photograph of a child, the defendant proves that the photograph or pseudo-photograph was of the child aged 16 or over, and that at the time of the offence charged the child and he—
- (a) were married or civil partners of each other, or
- (b) lived together as partners in an enduring family relationship.

(2) Subsections (5) and (6) also apply where, in proceedings for an offence under section 1(1)(b) or (c) relating to an indecent photograph or pseudo-photograph of a child, the defendant proves that the photograph or pseudo-photograph was of the child aged 16 or over, and that at the time when he obtained it the child and he—
- (a) were married or civil partners of each other, or
- (b) lived together as partners in an enduring family relationship.

(3) This section applies whether the photograph or pseudo-photograph showed the child alone or with the defendant, but not if it showed any other person.

(4) In the case of an offence under section 1(1)(a), if sufficient evidence is adduced to raise an issue as to whether the child consented to the photograph or pseudo-photograph being taken or made, or as to whether the defendant reasonably believed that the child

so consented, the defendant is not guilty of the offence unless it is proved that the child did not so consent and that the defendant did not reasonably believe that the child so consented.

(5) In the case of an offence under section 1(1)(b), the defendant is not guilty of the offence unless it is proved that the showing or distributing was to a person other than the child.

(6) In the case of an offence under section 1(1)(c), if sufficient evidence is adduced to raise an issue both—

(a) as to whether the child consented to the photograph or pseudo-photograph being in the defendant's possession, or as to whether the defendant reasonably believed that the child so consented, and

(b) as to whether the defendant had the photograph or pseudo-photograph in his possession with a view to its being distributed or shown to anyone other than the child,

the defendant is not guilty of the offence unless it is proved either that the child did not so consent and that the defendant did not reasonably believe that the child so consented, or that the defendant had the photograph or pseudo-photograph in his possession with a view to its being distributed or shown to a person other than the child.

B3.321 **Criminal Justice Act 1988, ss. 160 and 160A**

160.—(1) Subject to section 160A, it is an offence for a person to have any indecent photograph or pseudo-photograph of a child in his possession.

(2) Where a person is charged with an offence under subsection (1) above, it shall be a defence for him to prove—

(a) that he had a legitimate reason for having the photograph or pseudo-photograph in his possession; or

(b) that he had not himself seen the photograph or pseudo-photograph and did not know, nor had any cause to suspect, it to be indecent; or

(c) that the photograph or pseudo-photograph was sent to him without any prior request made by him or on his behalf and that he did not keep it for an unreasonable time.

160A.—(1) This section applies where, in proceedings for an offence under section 160 relating to an indecent photograph or pseudo-photograph of a child, the defendant proves that the photograph or pseudo-photograph was of the child aged 16 or over, and that at the time of the offence charged the child and he—

(a) were married or civil partners of each other, or

(b) lived together as partners in an enduring family relationship.

(2) This section also applies where, in proceedings for an offence under section 160 relating to an indecent photograph or pseudo-photograph of a child, the defendant proves that the photograph or pseudo-photograph was of the child aged 16 or over, and that at the time when he obtained it the child and he—

(a) were married or civil partners of each other, or

(b) lived together as partners in an enduring family relationship.

(3) This section applies whether the photograph or pseudo-photograph showed the child alone or with the defendant, but not if it showed any other person.

(4) If sufficient evidence is adduced to raise an issue as to whether the child consented to the photograph or pseudo-photograph being in the defendant's possession, or as to whether the defendant reasonably believed that the child so consented, the defendant is not guilty of the offence unless it is proved that the child did not so consent and that the defendant did not reasonably believe that the child so consented.

Procedure

B3.322 An allegation of an offence contrary to s. 1 of the Protection of Children Act 1978 is triable either way. An allegation of an offence contrary to s. 160(1) of the CJA 1988 is similarly triable either way. As to the classification of the offences for the purpose of listing, see CrimPD XIII, para. B (see *Supplement*, **CPD.XIII.B**). Proceedings in relation to either offence may not be instituted without the consent of the DPP. The extra-territorial jurisdiction provisions of the SOA 2003, s. 72 (see **B3.315**) apply.

Indictment

In *Thompson* [2004] EWCA Crim 669, [2004] 2 Cr App R 16 (262), the Court of Appeal gave guidance as to the drafting of an indictment where a case involves possession of a large number of photographs under the CJA 1988, s. 160. It is submitted that the same guidance will apply to prosecutions under the 1978 Act. The following principles were set out in *Thompson*: **B3.323**

(1) In addition to the specific counts, a comprehensive count should be included to cover the remainder.
(2) The photographs used in the specific counts should, if practicable, be selected so as to be broadly representative of the images in the comprehensive count. If agreement can be reached as to the number of photographs to be included at each level (*Oliver* [2002] EWCA Crim 2766, [2003] 1 Cr App R 28 (463)), the need for the judge to view the entirety of the offending material may be avoided. It is submitted that this principle will apply in the same way to the levels of images set out in the 2014 Sentencing Council definitive guideline (see **B3.325**).
(3) Where it is impracticable to present the court with specific counts that are agreed to be representative of the comprehensive count, there must be available to the court an approximate breakdown of the number of images at each of the five levels (*Oliver*). It is submitted that the counts settled should now be representative of the three levels identified in the 2014 Sentencing Council definitive guideline (see **B3.325**). That may best be achieved by the prosecution providing the defence with a schedule setting out the information and ensuring that the defence have an opportunity, well in advance of the sentencing hearing, of viewing the images and checking the accuracy of the schedule.
(4) The specific counts should make it clear whether the image in question is a real image or a pseudo-image: the same count should not charge both. There might be a significant difference between the two and, where there was a dispute, there should be alternative counts.
(5) Each image charged in a specific count should be identified by its 'jpg' or other reference so that it is clear with which image the specific count is dealing.
(6) The estimated age range of the child shown in each of the images should, where possible, be provided to the court.

In *Pinkerton* [2017] EWCA Crim 38, [2017] 1 Cr App R (S) 47 (375), the Court of Appeal said that it would only be in the most exceptional circumstances, or where there was serious dispute as to the categorisation of images, that it would be necessary for a judge to view the materials which were the subject-matter of the indictment. If the categorisation process is carried out properly, it should obviate the need for a sentencing judge to do so. Moreover, if a single judge grants leave to appeal, it should normally not be necessary for the Court of Appeal to view the material.

Sentence

The maximum penalty for an offence under the Protection of Children Act 1978, s. 1, is ten years on indictment and six months and/or an unlimited fine on summary conviction (Protection of Children Act 1978, s. 8; Criminal Justice and Court Services Act 2000, s. 41). The maximum penalty for an offence under the CJA 1988, s. 160, is five years on indictment and six months and/or an unlimited fine on summary conviction (2000 Act, s. 41). **B3.324**

The definitive sentencing guideline, *Sexual Offences* (see Supplement, **SG31-18**), applies to all sex offenders aged 18 or over who are sentenced on or after 1 April 2014 (see **B3.3**). The definitive guideline, *Sentencing Children and Young People* (see Supplement, **SG8-1**), applies to all offenders under the age of 18 who are sentenced on or after 1 June 2017, regardless of the date of the offence. It supersedes part 7 of the original 2007 guideline in respect of an offence under s. 1 of the 1978 Act or the CJA 1988, s. 160.

B3.325 The *Sexual Offences* guideline has radically altered the approach to be taken by courts. The approach to sentencing in respect of the relevant offences is also different to that taken in respect of other offences covered by the guideline. That different approach is necessary because the 'harm and culpability' model employed in relation to other offences is not so readily applicable to these offences. The Council focuses on the role of the offender as the starting point for the assessment of culpability. The three roles are:

- Possession. An offender falls within this category if he possesses images but there is no evidence of distributing, possession with a view to distributing, or involvement in the production of the image.
- Distribution. This category includes both actual distribution and possession of images with a view to distributing them, showing them or sharing them with others.
- Production/taking. This category includes involvement in the actual taking or making of an image at source, i.e. involvement in its production, and is the highest category for sentencing purposes.

B3.326 The role of the offender then must be viewed in the context of the type of images upon which the offending is centred. The Council identified three levels (in contrast to the previous *Oliver* scale). The three levels are:

- Category A: 'Images involving penetrative sexual activity' and 'images involving sexual activity with an animal or sadism'.
- Category B: 'Images involving non-penetrative sexual activity'.
- Category C: 'Other indecent images not falling within categories A or B'.

The collections of many offenders contain images at a mix of levels. In respect of 'mixed collections' the Council has decided that the appropriate starting point and range should initially be determined by the highest category of image level present in the collection. But if those images are unrepresentative of the offender's conduct, a lower category may be appropriate. Nevertheless, a lower category will not be appropriate if the offender has produced or taken images of a higher category. It should be noted that the quantity of material possessed is no longer used to determine the offence category (see tinyurl.com/ydfj5cp7).

B3.327 The Court of Appeal provided significant additional guidance as to sentencing for offences under s. 1 of the 1978 Act in *Pinkerton* [2017] EWCA Crim 38, [2017] 1 Cr App R (S) 47 (375). Following early guilty pleas, D had been sentenced to a total of 32 months' imprisonment in respect of three counts concerning child pornography and one count concerning images of sexual intercourse with animals. In passing sentence, the judge indicated that he was going to sentence outside the relevant guideline. The judge did not justify going above the guideline range by reference to quantity, but instead said it was justifiable to do so because the images he had seen were exceptionally depraved.

While the Court of Appeal ultimately upheld the sentence, it had a number of observations to make as to the sentencing process. Giving the judgment of the Court, Treacy LJ said that it was not appropriate for the judge to have used his assessment of the particular depravity of one of the films to justify moving outside the guideline. The guideline was created after extensive research and consultation and simplified matters for investigators, lawyers and judges. The court can consider the content of images by including as aggravating features the age and/or vulnerability of the child, discernible pain or distress suffered by the child and depiction of an intoxicated or drugged child as part of Step Two of the guideline. If prosecutors wish to rely on such aggravating features, that must be done by reference to the categories and aggravating factors identified in the guideline. The Court said that the Child Abuse Image Database (CAID) is a mechanism which may assist in this process, and observed that the CPS has issued guidance on its use (see tinyurl.com/ydfj5cp7). The Court was of the view that the judge in this case was not entitled to go outside the category range based on his assessment of the depravity of one film which was not shown to be representative of the collection. Moreover, the Court said that it would only be in the most exceptional circumstances, or where there is serious dispute as to the categorisation of images, where it would be necessary for a judge to view the materials. And if a single judge grants leave to appeal, it should normally not be necessary for the Court of Appeal to view the material.

The Court rejected criticism of the judge for placing emphasis on the harm committed by this sort of offending. Reliance had been placed by D on *Terrell* [2007] EWCA Crim 3079, [2008] 2 All ER 1065 (see **E4.21**) where it was held that the lack of proximity between the offending and the risk of future harm meant that the dangerousness threshold was not met. The Court observed that that will not necessarily always be the case and further explained that *Terrell* is not authority for the proposition that the offending in question does not cause harm, nor is it authority for the proposition that a judge cannot take that harm into account when sentencing. Indirect harm is caused by downloading which helps to perpetuate the market for such material and thus leads to further abuse of children. Even though such harm will ordinarily be reflected in the sentencing level resulting from application of the guideline, the judge was entitled to refer to this harm and had not placed undue weight on it. For a recent example of an unsuccessful appeal against a sentence imposed for making and distributing indecent photographs of children, see *Grumitt* [2019] EWCA Crim 2437.

Elements of the 1978 Act Offence

A person's intention in making photographs of children may be relevant to *mens rea* but it is not relevant to the question of whether they are indecent for the purposes of s. 1(1)(a) (*Smethurst* [2001] EWCA Crim 772, [2002] 1 Cr App R 6 (50)). 'Making' can be comprised of simply copying an indecent photograph (*Atkins v DPP* [2000] 2 All ER 425). If a person intentionally opens an attachment to an e-mail and knows that it contains an indecent photograph of a child or is likely to contain such a photograph, then that person is guilty of making a photograph for the purposes of the Act (*Smith* [2002] EWCA Crim 683, [2003] 1 Cr App R 13 (212)). In *WP* [2016] EWCA Crim 745, [2016] 2 Cr App R 27 (351) the Court of Appeal ruled that where the making of an indecent image takes place through the more direct action of photographing or filming, the offence under s. 1(1)(a) is made out by the deliberate act of photographing or filming without more. **B3.328**

In *Harrison* [2007] EWCA Crim 2976, [2008] 1 Cr App R 29 (387), it was held that a person who accesses an adult pornographic web site knowing that indecent images of children will automatically be generated as 'pop-ups' on the screen is guilty of 'making' an image each time that it appears. The person is equally guilty of making an image if aware that it will be automatically saved to the computer's hard drive, and the person possesses the image as long as it remains there. In *Dodd* [2013] EWCA Crim 660, where the errors in the trial were such as to undermine the safety of the conviction, the Court of Appeal did not need to decide what it described as the interesting question of whether images which are on their face innocuous can be rendered indecent by their context; in *Dodd* that context was text which surrounded the images. In *M (A)* [2015] EWCA Crim 353, [2015] 2 Cr App R 22 (307), the Court of Appeal re-emphasised that the question of whether the images admitted into evidence are indecent or not is one for the jury.

In *Fox* [2009] EWCA Crim 653 D had been convicted of, *inter alia*, two counts of taking indecent photographs of a child contrary to s. 1(1)(a). Two photographs had been specified in the particulars of the indictment as sample counts. In relation to each count, the jury were provided with a bundle of photographs relating to that count. The trial judge directed the jury that they could convict provided they were sure that at least one in each bundle was indecent. The Court of Appeal quashed the convictions. The jury should have been directed that in order to convict on either count they had to be sure that either of the photographs specified in the indictment was indecent. The way the trial judge had directed the jury allowed for the possibility that different jurors might have different views on which photograph they considered indecent and it may have been that the jury did not consider the photograph specified in the indictment to be indecent.

B3.329 The Court of Appeal rejected an argument that s. 1A(4) should be interpreted so as to apply to a 'one night stand' in *DM* [2011] EWCA Crim 2752. It was submitted that s. 1A should be interpreted so as to apply to a casual encounter of the type which occurred. Such an interpretation was said to be compatible with the ECHR, Articles 8 and 10. Unmarried and non-cohabiting 16 or 17-year-olds are able to consent to sexual intercourse but not the taking of an indecent photograph whilst their married or cohabiting counterparts are able to consent to both. The legislation therefore failed to make allowance for sexually active 16 or 17-year-olds living with their parents and violated their rights under Articles 8 and 10. The Court held that the 1978 Act was drafted and interpreted so as to provide effective protection of children whilst balancing rights under Article 8. A defence which included a 'brief sexual relationship' would diminish the protection provided. The Act strikes the balance between keeping interference by the State in the private lives of individuals to the minimum and maintaining under the law maximum protection for children from sexual abuse and exploitation.

Section 2(3) provides that a person is to be taken as having been a child at any material time if it appears, from the evidence as a whole, that the person was then under the age of 18.

For the purposes of the Protection of Children Act 1978, a child is a person under the age of 18 (s. 7(6)).

The offence is not incompatible with the ECHR, Article 10 (*Graham-Kerr* (1989) 88 Cr App R 302).

The offence of showing an indecent photograph of a child is not made out where the accused proposes to show it only to himself. This is also true of the offence of possession with intent to show (*ET* (1999) 163 JP 349). Similarly, the phrase 'with a view to' distribution of indecent photographs or pseudo-photographs in the Protection of Children Act 1978, s. 1(1)(c), requires that the distribution or showing must be at least one of the accused's purposes, but not necessarily the primary purpose. Thus in *Dooley* [2005] EWCA Crim 3093, [2006] 1 WLR 775, D did not intend to show or distribute indecent images when he downloaded pornography with a view to placing it in a secure file but did not have time to remove it from a shared file before others could look at it. If an offender provides another person with a password to access a computer in order to view relevant images, that is sufficient to amount to 'showing' (*Fellows* [1997] 1 Cr App R 244). In *Price* [2006] EWCA Crim 3363, the Court of Appeal held that the offence under s. 1(1)(b) is one of strict liability, subject only to the defence in s. 1(4).

Under s. 1(4), it is a defence to a charge of distribution or possession if the accused proves that there was a legitimate reason for either possessing, showing or distributing such photographs or he had not seen the photographs and did not know or have reason to suspect that they were indecent. In *Toure* [2019] EWCA Crim 1961, [2020] 1 Cr App R 24 (400), a woman had sent a video depicting sexual abuse of a young child to three people. Her defence was that she sent it as a warning about how sexual abuse could occur. The Court of Appeal held that the judge had correctly directed the jury that there were two separate questions to consider. The first was whether her reason for holding and distributing the video was a genuine and truthful one and, if so, the second was whether that reason was legitimate. Moreover, the judge had been right to make it clear that the genuineness of her reason for holding and distributing the video was irrelevant when considering the second question of whether that reason was objectively legitimate.

If the photograph or pseudo-photograph is made pursuant to an appropriate authorisation given by a relevant authority for the purposes of the prevention, detection or investigation of crime or criminal proceedings, then the making is exempt from criminal proceedings under s. 1B.

B3.330 Photograph and pseudo-photograph are defined in detail in s. 7

Protection of Children Act 1978, s. 7

(1) The following subsections apply for the interpretation of this Act.
(2) References to an indecent photograph include an indecent film, a copy of an indecent photograph or film, and an indecent photograph comprised in a film.
(3) Photographs (including those comprised in a film) shall, if they show children and are indecent, be treated for all purposes of this Act as indecent photographs of children and so as respects pseudo-photographs.
(4) References to a photograph include—
 (a) the negative as well as the positive version; and
 (b) data stored on a computer disc or by other electronic means which is capable of conversion into a photograph.
(4A) References to a photograph also include—
 (a) a tracing or other image, whether made by electronic or other means (of whatever nature)—
  (i) which is not itself a photograph or pseudo-photograph, but
  (ii) which is derived from the whole or part of a photograph or pseudo-photograph (or a combination of either or both); and
 (b) data stored on a computer disc or by other electronic means which is capable of conversion into an image within paragraph (a);
and subsection (8) applies in relation to such an image as it applies in relation to a pseudo-photograph.
(5) 'Film' includes any form of video-recording.
(6) 'Child', subject to subsection (8), means a person under the age of 18.
(7) 'Pseudo-photograph' means an image, whether made by computer-graphics or otherwise howsoever, which appears to be a photograph.
(8) If the impression conveyed by a pseudo-photograph is that the person shown is a child, the pseudo-photograph shall be treated for all purposes of this Act as showing a child and so shall a pseudo-photograph where the predominant impression conveyed is that the person shown is a child notwithstanding that some of the physical characteristics shown are those of an adult.
(9) References to an indecent pseudo-photograph include—
 (a) a copy of an indecent pseudo-photograph; and
 (b) data stored on a computer disc or by other electronic means which is capable of conversion into an indecent pseudo-photograph.

Elements of the 1988 Act Offence

Under the CJA 1988, s. 160, simple possession of a relevant photograph or pseudo-photograph may constitute an offence. **B3.331**

In *Porter* [2006] EWCA Crim 560, [2006] 2 Cr App R 25 (359), it was held that the offence of possession required that the accused had possession or control of the images. If the images had been deleted from his computer then it would be a question of fact as to whether he had control of them. That question could be answered by reference to whether he had the expertise and equipment to retrieve the images. *Porter* was applied in *Rowe* [2008] EWCA Crim 2712 and in *Leonard* [2012] EWCA Crim 277, [2012] 2 Cr App R 12 (138).

The defence set out in s. 160(2) is available if the accused did not have cause to suspect that the photograph was an indecent photograph of a child (*Collier* [2004] EWCA Crim 1411, [2005] 1 WLR 843), albeit the accused suspected that the image was of an indecent nature.

In *Okoro (No. 3)* [2018] EWCA Crim 1929, [2019] 1 Cr App R 2 (15) the Court of Appeal further considered the meaning of possession for the purposes of the CJA 1988, s. 160, and the CJIA 2008, s. 63 (see **B3.344**). The Court observed that in neither statute is possession defined; that the legal requirements for possession are the same for both statutory provisions; that the statutory defences in the CJIA 2008, s. 65, are materially the same as those under the CJA 1988, s. 160(2); and reviewed the authorities that have considered the meaning of possession in both statutes. The Court remarked that if a defendant had intentionally downloaded material, possession was proved provided that the material was within the defendant's custody or control. Any question of whether the defendant was ignorant of the critical contents of the material could be resolved by reference to the statutory defences. The Court then went on to specifically address the meaning of possession when an intentional download of material was in dispute, such as when the accused asserted that it was sent by others without invitation. Giving the judgment of the Court, Irwin LJ said:

> 43 It cannot be the law that a defendant must be shown to be aware of all the relevant content of a digital file on his device. If that were necessary, then the statutory defences in s. 160(2) CJA 1988 would be redundant. The question is whether it is enough that the accused should know that digital files had been sent to him, say, as an attachment to an email, or perhaps more likely as an encrypted file by one of the many apps by which digital content may be transmitted. Can possession be established by demonstrating that material is contained in an attachment to an unopened email in an inbox? Or, as claimed here, where the information was transmitted through WhatsApp without any invitation from the accused, and without him viewing any or all of the material.
>
> 44 There is such a volume of information in the memory of modern devices that proof of knowledge of all transmitted content would be impossible. For commercial reasons, many of the great internet business corporations collect and store information on phone and computer memories, individual to the user, but quite unknown and indeed inaccessible to the user.
>
> 45 We are clear that the statute requires proof by the Crown of possession of the pornography or images of child abuse, as a preliminary step before the burden of proof shifts to the accused, to establish the statutory defences. An accused cannot be convicted in relation to material of which he was genuinely totally unaware. Nor could a defendant be said to be in possession of a digital file if it was in practical terms impossible for him to access that file. However, for these statutory purposes we are clear that possession is established if the accused can be shown to have been aware of a relevant digital file or package of files which he has the capacity to access, even if he cannot be shown to have opened or scrutinised the material. That represents the closest possible parallel to the test laid down in the authorities set out above, and appears to us to be consistent with the criminal law of possession in other fields, such as unlawful possession of drugs.

Photograph and pseudo-photograph have the same meaning as in s. 7 of the Protection of Children Act 1978 (s. 160(4)).

POSSESSION OF PROHIBITED IMAGES OF CHILDREN

B3.332 The CAJA 2009, ss. 62 to 68, govern offences of possession of prohibited images of children, associated defences and ancillary provisions.

Coroners and Justice Act 2009, s. 62

(1) It is an offence for a person to be in possession of a prohibited image of a child.

(2) A prohibited image is an image which—
  (a) is pornographic,
  (b) falls within subsection (6), and
  (c) is grossly offensive, disgusting or otherwise of an obscene character.

(3) An image is 'pornographic' if it is of such a nature that it must reasonably be assumed to have been produced solely or principally for the purpose of sexual arousal.

(4) Where (as found in the person's possession) an image forms part of a series of images, the question whether the image is of such a nature as is mentioned in subsection (3) is to be determined by reference to—
  (a) the image itself, and
  (b) (if the series of images is such as to be capable of providing a context for the image) the context in which it occurs in the series of images.

(5) So, for example, where—
  (a) an image forms an integral part of a narrative constituted by a series of images, and
  (b) having regard to those images as a whole, they are not of such a nature that they must reasonably be assumed to have been produced solely or principally for the purpose of sexual arousal,

the image may, by virtue of being part of that narrative, be found not to be pornographic, even though it might have been found to be pornographic if taken by itself.

(6) An image falls within this subsection if it—
  (a) is an image which focuses solely or principally on a child's genitals or anal region, or
  (b) portrays any of the acts mentioned in subsection (7).

(7) Those acts are—
  (a) the performance by a person of an act of intercourse or oral sex with or in the presence of a child;
  (b) an act of masturbation by, of, involving or in the presence of a child;
  (c) an act which involves penetration of the vagina or anus of a child with a part of a person's body or with anything else;
  (d) an act of penetration, in the presence of a child, of the vagina or anus of a person with a part of a person's body or with anything else;
  (e) the performance by a child of an act of intercourse or oral sex with an animal (whether dead or alive or imaginary);
  (f) the performance by a person of an act of intercourse or oral sex with an animal (whether dead or alive or imaginary) in the presence of a child.

(8) For the purposes of subsection (7), penetration is a continuing act from entry to withdrawal.

Indictment

Statement of Offence **B3.333**

Possession of a prohibited image contrary to section 62 of the Coroners and Justice Act 2009

Particulars of Offence

A, on or about the . . . day of . . . possessed a prohibited image of a child which focused principally on the child's genitals

Procedure

The offence is triable either way. Proceedings under the CAJA 2009, s. 62, may not be instituted without the consent of the DPP. **B3.334**

Sentence

The maximum penalty on conviction on indictment is three years' imprisonment or a fine or both. On summary conviction, the maximum penalty is six months' imprisonment and/or an unlimited fine (CAJA 2009, s. 66 and sch. 22, para. 12). The court should consider a sexual harm prevention order (see **E21.22**). **B3.335**

Elements

An image is 'pornographic' for the purposes of the CAJA 2009 if it must reasonably be assumed to have been produced solely or principally for the purpose of sexual arousal (CAJA 2009, s. 62(3)). Its potential pornographic nature is to be considered in the context of the whole where it forms part of a series of images found in D's possession (s. 62(4)). 'Image' is defined to include a moving or still image produced by any means; or data stored by any means which is capable of conversion into a moving or still image but does not include an indecent photograph or indecent pseudo-photograph of a child (s. 65(2) and (3)). **B3.336**

'Child' means a person under the age of 18 (s. 65(5)).

An image is to be treated as an image of a child if the impression created is that the person shown is a child, or the predominant impression conveyed is that the person shown is a child despite the fact that some of the physical characteristics shown are not those of a child (s. 65(6)).

Section 63 defines 'excluded images' to which s. 62 does not apply. Broadly speaking, excluded images are those contained within a classified work. Classified work is work which has been given a classification certificate by a designation certificate (whenever issued). All images contained within a classified work are, however, not necessarily exempt from s. 62. Section 63(3) states that an image or images extracted from a classified work solely or principally for the purposes of sexual arousal will not be excluded.

Defences

B3.337 Under the CAJA 2009, s. 64(1), it is a defence for a person charged under s. 62(1) to prove any of the following matters.

(a) that the person had a legitimate reason for being in possession of the image concerned;
(b) that the person had not seen the image concerned and did not know, nor had any cause to suspect, it to be a prohibited image;
(c) that the person—
  (i) was sent the image concerned without any prior request having been made by or on behalf of the person, and
  (ii) did not keep it for an unreasonable time.

It is submitted that the burden on the accused is evidential.

Section 68 and sch. 13 make special provision for persons providing information society services.

POSSESSION OF A PAEDOPHILE MANUAL

B3.338 The SCA 2015, s. 69, in force from 3 May 2015 (SI 2015 No. 820), makes it an offence to possess a paedophile manual.

Serious Crime Act 2015, s. 69

(1) It is an offence to be in possession of any item that contains advice or guidance about abusing children sexually.

Indictment

B3.339

Statement of Offence

Possession of a paedophile manual contrary to section 68 of the Serious Crime Act 2015.

Particulars of Offence

A, on or about the... day of... had in his possession an item [entitled...] that contained advice or guidance as to how to abuse children sexually.

Procedure

B3.340 The offence is triable either way. Any prosecution under s. 69 requires the consent of the DPP.

Sentence

B3.341 The maximum penalty on summary conviction is six months' imprisonment and/or a fine; on conviction on indictment, the maximum is three years' imprisonment. The court should consider a sexual harm prevention order (see **E21.22**).

Elements

B3.342 A paedophile manual is any item that contains advice or guidance about abusing children sexually. The term 'abusing children sexually' is defined in s. 69(8) to include any offence under the SOA 2003, Part 1, against a person aged under 16; any offence under the Protection of Children Act 1978, s. 1, involving indecent photographs (but not pseudo-photographs); and an offence under the Modern Slavery Act 2015, s. 2 (human trafficking: see **B22.6**), with a view to sexual exploitation. It also includes any equivalent offence under Northern Ireland legislation. The definition goes on to include 'doing anything outside England and Wales or Northern Ireland that would constitute such an offence if done in England and Wales or Northern Ireland'. An 'item' includes anything in which information of any description is recorded.

By virtue of s. 69(5), the Protection of Children Act 1978, s. 4 (relating to search and seizure), and the schedule to that Act (forfeiture of indecent photographs) apply to prohibited items under s. 69 as they would apply to indecent photographs. Schedule 3 to the SCA 2015 makes special provision for persons providing information society services.

Defences

Three specific defences are contained within the SCA 2015, s. 69(2). Each must be proved by the accused. It is submitted that they therefore impose a persuasive burden to the civil standard. **B3.343**

Serious Crime Act 2015, s. 69

(2) It is a defence for a person (D) charged with an offence under this section—
 (a) to prove that D had a legitimate reason for being in possession of the item;
 (b) to prove that—
  (i) D had not read, viewed or (as appropriate) listened to the item, and
  (ii) D did not know, and had no reason to suspect, that it contained advice or guidance about abusing children sexually; or
 (c) to prove that—
  (i) the item was sent to D without any request made by D or on D's behalf, and
  (ii) D did not keep it for an unreasonable time.

EXTREME PORNOGRAPHIC IMAGES

In contrast to the relevant provisions of the Protection of Children Act 1978 and the CJA 1988 (see **B3.320** and **B3.321**), the images prohibited by the CJIA 2008, s. 63, are not only those of children but may also include adults and animals. **B3.344**

Criminal Justice and Immigration Act 2008, s. 63

(1) It is an offence for a person to be in possession of an extreme pornographic image.
(2) An 'extreme pornographic image' is an image which is both—
 (a) pornographic, and
 (b) an extreme image.
(3) An image is 'pornographic' if it is of such a nature that it must reasonably be assumed to have been produced solely or principally for the purpose of sexual arousal.
(4) Where (as found in the person's possession) an image forms part of a series of images, the question whether the image is of such a nature as is mentioned in subsection (3) is to be determined by reference to—
 (a) the image itself, and
 (b) (if the series of images is such as to be capable of providing a context for the image) the context in which it occurs in the series of images.
(5) So, for example, where—
 (a) an image forms an integral part of a narrative constituted by a series of images, and
 (b) having regard to those images as a whole, they are not of such a nature that they must reasonably be assumed to have been produced solely or principally for the purpose of sexual arousal,
 the image may, by virtue of being part of that narrative, be found not to be pornographic, even though it might have been found to be pornographic if taken by itself.
(5A) In relation to possession of an image in England and Wales, an 'extreme image' is an image which—
 (a) falls within subsection (7) or (7A), and
 (b) is grossly offensive, disgusting or otherwise of an obscene character.
(6) [Northern Ireland.]

(7) An image falls within this subsection if it portrays, in an explicit and realistic way, any of the following—
(a) an act which threatens a person's life,
(b) an act which results, or is likely to result, in serious injury to a person's anus, breasts or genitals,
(c) an act which involves sexual interference with a human corpse, or
(d) a person performing an act of intercourse or oral sex with an animal (whether dead or alive),
and a reasonable person looking at the image would think that any such person or animal was real.

(7A) An image falls within this subsection if it portrays, in an explicit and realistic way, either of the following—
(a) an act which involves the non-consensual penetration of a person's vagina, anus or mouth by another with the other person's penis, or
(b) an act which involves the non-consensual sexual penetration of a person's vagina or anus by another with a part of the other person's body or anything else,
and a reasonable person looking at the image would think that the persons were real.

(7B) For the purposes of subsection (7A)—
(a) penetration is a continuing act from entry to withdrawal;
(b) 'vagina' includes vulva.

(8) In this section 'image' means—
(a) a moving or still image (produced by any means); or
(b) data (stored by any means) which is capable of conversion into an image within paragraph (a).

(9) In this section references to a part of the body include references to a part surgically constructed (in particular through gender reassignment surgery).

Indictment

B3.345 *Statement of Offence*

Possession of an extreme pornographic image contrary to section 63 of the Criminal Justice and Immigration Act 2008

Particulars of Offence

A, on or about the... day of... possessed an extreme pornographic image namely an image...

Procedure

B3.346 An allegation of an offence of possession of extreme pornographic images is triable either way. As to the classification of the offence for the purpose of listing, see CrimPD XIII, para. B (see Supplement, **CPD.XIII.B**). Proceedings for an offence under the CJIA 2008, s. 63, may not be instituted except by or with the consent of the DPP (s. 63(10)).

Sentence

B3.347 By virtue of the CJIA 2008, s. 67, if the offending image portrays any act within s. 63(7)(a) or (b) or 7A(a) or (b), the maximum sentence on summary conviction is six months' imprisonment and/or an unlimited fine. On conviction on indictment, the maximum sentence is three years' imprisonment and/or a fine. If the image does not portray an act within s. 63(7)(a) or (b) or 7A(a) or (b), the maximum sentence on summary conviction is six months' imprisonment and/or an unlimited fine; on conviction on indictment, the maximum sentence is two years' imprisonment and/or a fine. The court should consider a sexual harm prevention order (see **E21.22**).

The Sentencing Council's guidelines for sexual offences (see **B3.3**) do not cover this offence.

In *Oliver* [2011] EWCA Crim 3114, [2012] 2 Cr App R (S) 45 (269) the Court expressed the view that the public would be surprised if the seriousness of possession of adult images under s. 63(1) should be equated with those involving images of children. The need to protect children enables the courts to pass deterrent sentences when images of children are involved and on principle no narrow comparison is to be made between images of children and adults. In that case

D had downloaded extreme pornographic images before their possession became illegal under s. 63(1). An aggravating feature of his offending was that he subsequently downloaded a software program called 'Team Viewer' which enabled others to access the images by taking remote control of his computer, but he was a 54-year-old man of previous positive good character with substantial personal mitigation. The Court reduced a sentence of six months' imprisonment to one of two months.

In *Lewis* [2012] EWCA Crim 1071, [2013] 1 Cr App R (S) 23 (121), the Court of Appeal upheld a sentence of 12 months' imprisonment following guilty pleas to two offences under s. 63(1). The Court observed that the offence under s. 63 is not a victimless crime and women photographed in such extreme pornographic images are often trafficked or forced into their involvement.

In *L* [2013] EWCA Crim 1600 the Court of Appeal reduced the sentence for an offender who had pleaded guilty to three offences of possessing extreme pornographic images from a total of 14 months' imprisonment to four months. D had a large number of still and moving images on his laptop of horses and dogs penetrating women. He admitted the offences immediately upon police officers arriving at his home. The Court decided that, even though the number of extreme images involved was large and D had deliberately sought them out, since he had no previous convictions, was of good character and had demonstrated remorse for his actions and there were no other aggravating features in his case and the personal mitigation was extremely strong, an element of leniency was justified.

Elements

An image is 'pornographic' for the purposes of the CJIA 2008 if it must reasonably be assumed to have been produced solely or principally for the purpose of sexual arousal (s. 63(3)). Its potential pornographic nature is to be considered in the context of the whole where it forms part of a series of images found in D's possession (s. 63(4)). 'Image' is defined to include a moving or still image produced by any means; or data stored by any means which is capable of conversion into a moving or still image (s. 63(8)). **B3.348**

In *DB* [2016] EWCA Crim 474, [2016] 2 Cr App R 25 (333), the Court of Appeal considered s. 63(3) and rejected a submission that the relevant purpose had to be that of the person who sent the image to the person possessing it rather than that of the photographer or photographers who took the original images. D had received the images as part of a series of 'WhatsApp' messages. The forensic examiner formed the view that they were part of a collection of assumed humorous messages. McCombe LJ explained (at [15]):

> Subsection (3) asks what is reasonably to be assumed that the purpose of the production of the image was: was it solely or principally for the purpose of sexual arousal. In other words, in our judgment, it means simply was it produced (and by whom is utterly immaterial) for the purpose of sexual arousal of anyone who comes to have it, be that the producer himself, a distributor or ultimate recipient. The section is obviously designed to prevent the possession of such images by whomsoever that may be. For that purpose the section has to define the images. It does so in subsections (2) in subsection (3). That is all that the subsections do. These definition provisions are only telling us what images it is an offence to possess; they are not there to draw subtle distinctions between photographer, sender and any ultimate recipient of images. The circumstances in which the images are received are immaterial.

Section 64 defines 'excluded images' to which s. 63 does not apply. Broadly speaking, excluded images are those contained within a classified work. Classified work is work which has been given a classification certificate by a designation certificate (whenever issued). All images contained within a classified work are, however, not necessarily exempt from s. 63. Section 64 states that an image or images extracted from a classified work solely or principally for the purposes of sexual arousal will not be excluded.

For possession, see *Pin Chen Cheung* [2009] EWCA Crim 2963 (discussed at **B3.349**), *Okoro (No. 3)* [2018] EWCA Crim 1929, [2019] 1 Cr App R 2 (15) (discussed at **B3.331**) and the various cases relating to drugs at **B19.27** *et seq.*, especially **B19.34**.

Defences

B3.349 Under the CJIA 2008, s. 65(1), it is a defence for a person charged under s. 63 to prove any of the matters set out in s. 65(2).

Criminal Justice and Immigration Act 2008, s. 65

(2) The matters are—
- (a) that the person had a legitimate reason for being in possession of the image concerned;
- (b) that the person had not seen the image concerned and did not know, nor had any cause to suspect, it to be an extreme pornographic image;
- (c) that the person—
  - (i) was sent the image concerned without any prior request having been made by or on behalf of the person, and
  - (ii) did not keep it for an unreasonable time.

The nature of possession for the purposes of s. 63 and the nature of the burden on the accused in establishing a defence under s. 65(2) was considered in *Pin Chen Cheung* [2009] EWCA Crim 2963. The Court of Appeal made clear that the burden on the accused in establishing a defence under s. 65(2) is not simply evidential. Drawing on cases dealing with possession of drugs under the Misuse of Drugs Act 1971, the Court of Appeal ruled that, in order for the Crown to prove possession under s. 63, it was not enough that D simply had custody or control of them. Before the defence under s. 65(2) became relevant, the prosecution had to show that D had knowledge of the 'things' that gave rise to liability. But the prosecution did not need to go so far as to prove that D knew that the 'things' knowingly in D's custody or control contained extreme pornographic images. If that were the case, the defence under s. 65(2)(b) would be otiose. If D may have believed that the items were of a wholly different nature to the subject matter of the allegations, such as floor-tiles, then D would not be guilty. The question of what amounted to items of a wholly different nature was one of fact and degree for a jury. Once possession had been established, the onus shifted to D to establish the defence under s. 65(2) on the balance of probabilities.

There are further defences available to a person charged with possessing an image which comes within s. 63(7)(a) to (c) or (7A) but does not portray an act within s. 63(7)(d). In the case of any such image, it is a defence that D participated in any of the acts portrayed and that the act or acts did not involve the infliction of any non-consensual harm on any person, provided (i) that, in respect of an image within s. 63(7)(c), what is portrayed as a human corpse was not in fact a corpse and (ii) in respect of an image within s. 67(7A), what is portrayed as non-consensual was in fact consensual. For the purposes of s. 66, harm is 'non-consensual' if the harm is of such a nature that the person cannot in law consent to it being inflicted on him or herself; or, where the person can in law consent to it being so inflicted, that person does not in fact consent (s. 66(3)).

Thus no defence is available under s. 66 when the image portrays, in an explicit and realistic way, an act of intercourse or oral sex with an animal.

OUTRAGING PUBLIC DECENCY

B3.350 At common law it is an offence to outrage public decency, to expose the person or to engage in or simulate a sexual act in public. As to the offence of outraging public decency by way of obscene publication, see **B18.1**.

Procedure

The offence is triable either way; see **B3.355** for alternative verdicts. **B3.351**

Indictment

Statement of Offence **B3.352**

Outraging public decency.

Particulars of Offence

A on or about the ... day of ... outraged public decency, namely by publicly, to wit in the street at ..., having sexual intercourse with X, within the sight and to the outrage of other persons then present.

Sentence

The maximum penalty for the common-law offence on conviction on indictment is imprisonment and/or a fine at large. On summary conviction, the maximum is six months and/or an unlimited fine. See further **B3.297**. The Sentencing Council guidelines for sexual offences (see **B3.3**) do not cover this offence. **B3.353**

In *Ferguson* [2008] EWCA Crim 2940, [2009] 2 Cr App R (S) 8 (39), D had pleaded guilty to offences of outraging public decency, exposure and harassment. A further 19 offences of exposure were taken into consideration. He was 43 years of age with a number of previous convictions including 13 for indecency in the USA. He was sentenced to concurrent terms of 21 months' imprisonment for the offences of outraging public decency and exposure and a further six months concurrent for the offence of harassment. It was argued that the sentence was manifestly excessive because the maxima for the offences of exposure and harassment were 24 and six months respectively. The Court of Appeal rejected the argument, observing that the sentence for outraging public decency is at large. The judge could therefore have passed shorter consecutive sentences for the three offences to which D had pleaded guilty or could have imposed shorter concurrent sentences to the one of 21 months for outraging public decency. See also *Cosco* [2005] EWCA Crim 207, [2005] 2 Cr App R (S) 66 (405) and *Vaiculevicius* [2013] EWCA Crim 185, [2013] 2 Cr App R (S) 55 (362) in which both *Ferguson* and *Cosco* are cited. A total sentence of three years' imprisonment following guilty pleas and committal for sentence in respect of three offences of outraging public decency and one of sexual assault was upheld in *Heywood* [2019] EWCA Crim 2181.

An extended sentence may not be imposed for such an offence (*Chevron* [2005] EWCA Crim 303).

Elements

The act must be lewd, obscene or disgusting and must be of such a nature as to outrage minimum standards of public decency as judged by a jury in contemporary society (*Knuller (Publishing, Printing and Promotions) Ltd v DPP* [1973] AC 435) but it is not necessary that any particular member of the public is outraged (*Mayling* [1963] 3 QB 717; *Choi* [1999] EWCA Crim 1279). **B3.354**

The public element to the offence is satisfied if at least two persons are present and could see the act even if they do not. In *Hamilton* [2007] EWCA Crim 2062, [2008] QB 224, H had used a camera concealed in a rucksack to film up the skirts of women who were shopping. Nobody had ever noticed what he was doing but when his home was searched films produced from the activity were found. It was accepted at trial that there was a clear line of sight shown in the films, so it was contended by the prosecution (and disputed by the defence) that the camera lens must have been visible. The trial judge directed the jury that it was sufficient for the offence to be made out that there was a real possibility that when H was filming at least two people would have been able to see the act. In dismissing the appeal after a comprehensive review of the authorities, the Court of Appeal held that for the public element to be satisfied it was not necessary that two people actually see or hear the act. It is sufficient if at least two people are present and the accused's acts are capable of being seen. Whether the actions were capable of being seen was a question of fact for the jury. See also *Rose v DPP* [2006] EWHC 852 (Admin), [2006] 1 WLR 2626 and *F* [2010] EWCA Crim 2243.

The act need not take place in a public place, it is sufficient that members of the public are able to see the act (*Wellard* (1884–85) LR 14 QBD 63).

For the offence under the SOA 2003, s. 67A, in respect of upskirting see **B3.299** ***et seq.***

ALTERNATIVE VERDICTS

B3.355 Plainly, there is a degree of overlap between many of the offences contained within the SOA 2003 and thus an offender may sometimes be found guilty of a lesser charge than that on the indictment (see **D19.41** ***et seq.*** for the applicable general principles). In the case of an allegation of rape, it is possible that the accused could be alternatively found guilty of attempted rape, assault by penetration, sexual assault, sexual activity with a child, sexual activity with a child family member, sexual activity with a person having a mental disorder impeding choice, sexual activity by a care worker or sex with an adult relative. In respect of rape of a child, an accused may alternatively be found guilty of attempted rape, assault by penetration, sexual assault of a child contrary to s. 7 or sexual assault of a child contrary to s. 9.

BROTHELS AND DISORDERLY HOUSES

Keeping a Brothel

B3.356 **Sexual Offences Act 1956, ss. 33 and 33A**

33. It is an offence for a person to keep a brothel, or to manage, or act or assist in the management of, a brothel.

33A.—(1) It is an offence for a person to keep, or to manage, or act or assist in the management of a brothel to which people resort for practices involving prostitution (whether or not also for other practices).

(2) In this section 'prostitution' has the meaning given by section 51(2) of the Sexual Offences Act 2003.

Sexual Offences Act 1967, s. 6

Premises shall be treated for purposes of sections 33 to 35 of the Act of 1956 as a brothel if people resort to it for the purpose of lewd homosexual practices in circumstances in which resort thereto for lewd heterosexual practices would have led to its being treated as a brothel for the purposes of those sections.

B3.357 **Procedure** The offence contrary to s. 33 of the SOA 1956 is triable summarily. The offence contrary to s. 33A is triable either way.

B3.358 **Sentence** Under s. 33 of the SOA 1956, for an offence committed after a previous conviction for the same or a related offence, the maximum penalty is six months or a fine not exceeding level 4 on the standard scale, or both; otherwise three months or a fine not exceeding level 3 on the standard scale, or both (SOA 1956, s. 37 and sch. 2). For an offence under s. 33A, the maximum penalty is seven years' imprisonment; on summary conviction, it is six months and/or an unlimited fine.

The definitive sentencing guideline, *Sexual Offences* (see Supplement, **SG31-20**), applies to all sex offenders aged 18 or over who are sentenced on or after 1 April 2014 (see **B3.3**). The definitive guideline, *Sentencing Children and Young People* (see Supplement, **SG8-1**), applies to all offenders under the age of 18 who are sentenced on or after 1 June 2017, regardless of the date of the offence. It supersedes part 7 of the original 2007 guideline in respect of an offence under s. 33A.

Elements A brothel is essentially a place where people are allowed to engage in unlawful sexual intercourse. For specific elaborations upon that general definition, regard should be had to *Kelly v Purvis* [1983] AC 663, *Stevens v Christy* (1987) 85 Cr App R 249, *Donovan v Gavin* [1965] 2 QB 648, and *Korie* [1966] 1 All ER 50. By virtue of s. 6 of the SOA 1967, homosexual activity is as capable as heterosexual activity of founding the existence of a brothel. **B3.359**

The nature and extent of the activities which comprise management or assisting in the management of a brothel have been considered in a number of cases, including *Stevens v Christy* (1987) 85 Cr App R 249, *DPP v Curley* [1991] COD 186, *Abbott v Smith* [1965] 2 QB 662 and *Jones v DPP* (1992) 96 Cr App R 130.

A person does not keep a brothel unless that person is aware that the premises are to be used by more than one prostitute for the purposes of prostitution.

Landlord Letting Premises as a Brothel

Sexual Offences Act 1956, s. 34 **B3.360**

> It is an offence for the lessor or landlord of any premises or his agent to let the whole or part of the premises with the knowledge that it is to be used, in whole or in part, as a brothel, or, where the whole or part of the premises is used as a brothel, to be wilfully a party to that use continuing.

Procedure The offence contrary to s. 34 of the SOA 1956 is triable summarily. **B3.361**

Sentence Under s. 34 of the SOA 1956, for an offence committed after a previous conviction for the same or a related offence, the maximum penalty is six months or a fine not exceeding level 4 on the standard scale, or both; otherwise three months or a fine not exceeding level 3 on the standard scale, or both (SOA 1956, s. 37 and sch. 2). The Sentencing Council guidelines for sexual offences (see **B3.3**) do not cover this offence. **B3.362**

Elements The offence under the SOA 1956, s. 34, requires the landlord to know that the premises are to be used as a brothel or are being used as a brothel. **B3.363**

Tenant Permitting Premises to be Used as a Brothel or for Prostitution

Sexual Offences Act 1956, ss. 35 and 36 **B3.364**

> 35.—(1) It is an offence for the tenant or occupier, or person in charge, of any premises knowingly to permit the whole or part of the premises to be used as a brothel.
>
> (2) Where the tenant or occupier of any premises is convicted of knowingly permitting the whole or part of the premises to be used as a brothel, the first Schedule to this Act shall apply to enlarge the rights of the lessor or landlord with respect to the assignment or determination of the lease or other contract under which the premises are held by the person convicted.
>
> (3) Where the tenant or occupier of any premises is so convicted . . . and either—
>
> (a) the lessor or landlord, after having the conviction brought to his notice, fails or failed to exercise his statutory rights in relation to the lease or contract under which the premises are or were held by the person convicted; or
>
> (b) the lessor or landlord, after exercising his statutory rights so as to determine that lease or contract, grants or granted a new lease or enters or entered into a new contract of tenancy of the premises to, with or for the benefit of the same person, without having all reasonable provisions to prevent the recurrence of the offence inserted in the new lease or contract;
>
> then, if subsequently an offence under this section is committed in respect of the premises during the subsistence of the lease or contract referred to in paragraph (a) of this subsection or (where paragraph (b) applies) during the subsistence of the new lease or contract, the lessor or landlord shall be deemed to be a party to that offence unless he shows that he took all reasonable steps to prevent the recurrence of the offence.

References in this subsection to the statutory rights of a lessor or landlord refer to his rights under the First Schedule to this Act.

36. It is an offence for the tenant or occupier of any premises knowingly to permit the whole or part of the premises to be used for the purposes of habitual prostitution (whether any prostitute involved is male or female).

B3.365 **Procedure** An offence contrary to s. 34 or 35 of the SOA 1956 is triable summarily.

B3.366 **Sentence** Under ss. 35 and 36 of the SOA 1956, for an offence committed after a previous conviction for the same or a related offence, the maximum penalty is six months or a fine not exceeding level 4 on the standard scale, or both; otherwise three months or a fine not exceeding level 3 on the standard scale, or both (SOA 1956, s. 37 and sch. 2).

The Sentencing Council guidelines for sexual offences (see **B3.3**) do not cover this offence.

B3.367 **Elements** The offence under s. 35 of the SOA 1956 applies to tenants who sublet their premises or simply allow the premises to be used as a brothel. If a tenant or occupier is convicted of allowing premises to be used as a brothel then the landlord of those premises has increased powers of eviction in relation to that tenancy under s. 35(2). If the landlord fails to exercise those powers or grants a new lease or licence to the offender, and the tenant or occupier repeats the offence, the landlord will be liable as a party to the offence unless the landlord shows that all reasonable steps were taken to prevent the recurrence of the offence (s. 35(3)).

In contrast to those sections of the SOA 1956 dealing with brothels, the offence under s. 36 can be committed if only one prostitute engages in prostitution in the premises.

Keeping a Disorderly House

B3.368 It is an offence at common law for a person to keep a disorderly house.

B3.369 **Procedure** This common-law offence is triable either way.

B3.370 **Sentence** As a common-law offence, punishment is at large by imprisonment or fine, or both. The Sentencing Council guidelines (see **B3.3**) do not cover this offence.

B3.371 **Elements** The elements of the common-law offence of keeping a disorderly house were set out in *Tan* [1983] QB 1053:

(a) there must be some element of keeping open house;
(b) the house must not be regulated by the restraints of morality, or must be unchaste or of bad repute;
(c) it must be so conducted as to violate law and good order.

In *Moores v DPP* [1992] QB 125, it was held that D must also be aware that the house was used in that way. The requisite disorderliness of the house is not confined to sexual behaviour (*Berg* (1927) 20 Cr App R 38).

In *Court* [2012] EWCA Crim 133, [2012] 1 WLR 2260, following a review of the authorities, the Court of Appeal (presided over by Lord Judge CJ) quashed convictions for the offence. The evidence relied on at trial by the prosecution was very limited. Two unremarkable advertisements had been placed in the personal section of a local newspaper. No addresses were given but when the mobile numbers advertised were contacted by the officers they were offered sexual services. Those services went no further than normal sexual intercourse. Officers visited the premises. At one address, a woman wearing not much clothing was seen; at the other, no one was found. At both addresses, a large number of condoms were found and at one of the addresses a vibrator was recovered. There had been no complaints about the house from any of the neighbouring houses. The Court of Appeal observed that the judgment in *Tan* had proceeded on the basis that the provision of straightforward sexual intercourse could not be sufficient to constitute the offence. Therefore, taken at their highest, the circumstances of the case were not capable of falling within the common-law offence.

PROSECUTION OF HISTORIC SEXUAL OFFENCES

The SOA 2003 swept away many offences that had been part of the legal landscape for many generations, including incest, indecent assault, buggery, bestiality and gross indecency between men. Many were replaced by new offences that are essentially modernised versions of the old ones. In the light of the major increase in prosecutions for sexual offences committed before the implementation of the SOA 2003, this chapter now includes some coverage of the main sexual offences that existed before 1 May 2004, and the law that must be applied in respect of the prosecution of these offences. **B3.372**

In the main, the old law governing sexual offences is contained in the SOA 1956 (which was in itself a consolidating Act). It is important to note that the SOA 1956 was amended at various times before it was repealed by the SOA 2003. In particular, a number of maximum sentences were increased.

A comprehensive table setting out the effective dates and maximum sentences of all the historic offences can be found in the *Sexual Offences* definitive guideline (see Supplement, **SG31-38**). Those conducting historic cases need to be careful not to overlook (i) time limits, (ii) requisite consents and (iii) the continued existence of presumptions before their abolition.

Sentencing in Historic Sexual Cases

The *Sexual Offences-Historic* definitive sentencing guideline (see Supplement, **SG31-37**) sets out the appropriate approach to sentencing historic sexual offences. This was clarified by the Court of Appeal in *H* [2011] EWCA Crim 2753, [2012] 2 All ER 340. Having reviewed a large body of earlier judicial decisions, some of which were impossible to reconcile, Lord Judge CJ summarised the following principles. He suggested (at [46]) that reference to earlier decisions is unlikely to be helpful, and is to be discouraged, and that the following considerations should be treated as guidance (at [47]). **B3.373**

(a) Sentence will be imposed at the date of the sentencing hearing, on the basis of the legislative provisions then current, and by measured reference to any definitive sentencing guidelines relevant to the situation revealed by the established facts.
(b) Although sentence must be limited to the maximum sentence at the date when the offence was committed, it is wholly unrealistic to attempt an assessment of sentence by seeking to identify [at the time of sentencing] what the sentence for the individual offence was likely to have been if the offence had come to light at or shortly after the date when it was committed.
(c) As always, the particular circumstances in which the offence was committed and its seriousness must be the main focus. Due allowance for passage of time may be appropriate. The date may have a considerable bearing on the offender's culpability. If, for example, the offender was very young and immature at the time when the case was committed, that remains a continuing feature of the sentencing decision. Similarly if the allegations had come to light many years earlier, and when confronted with them, the defendant had admitted them but, for whatever reason, the complaint had not been drawn to the attention of, or investigated by, the police, or had been investigated and not then pursued to trial, these too would be relevant features.
(d) In some cases it may be safe to assume that the fact that, notwithstanding the passage of years, the victim has chosen spontaneously to report what happened during childhood or younger years would be an indication of continuing inner turmoil. However the circumstances in which the facts come to light varies, and careful judgment of the harm done to the victim is always a critical feature of the sentencing decision. Simultaneously, equal care needs to be taken to assess the true extent of the defendant's criminality by reference to what was actually done and the circumstances in which it was done.
(e) The passing of years may demonstrate aggravating features if, for example, the defendant has continued to commit sexual crime or represents a continuing risk to the public. On the other hand, mitigation may be found in an unblemished life over the years since the offences were committed, particularly if accompanied by evidence of positive good character.

(f) Early admissions and a guilty plea are of particular importance in historic cases. Just because they relate to facts which are long passed, the defendant will inevitably be tempted to escape the allegations by lying. It is greatly to the defendant's credit to make early admissions. Even more powerful mitigation is available to an offender who out of a sense of guilt and remorse reports him or herself to the authorities. Considerations like these provide the victim with vindication, often a feature of great importance.

For examples of the application of *H*, see *Clarke* [2012] EWCA Crim 9, *Wheller* [2012] EWCA Crim 84, and *D* [2012] EWCA Crim 2370, [2013] 1 Cr App R (S) 127 (674) where the Court of Appeal upheld a life sentence in respect of an historic case where D had broken into his grandmother's home and raped her in 1983. The Court concluded that the pre-conditions for a discretionary life sentence in a pre-CJA 2003 case which were laid down in *Hodgson* (1968) 52 Cr App R 113 were satisfied. The offence was grave enough to require a very long sentence, and it appeared from the nature of the offence and from D's history that he was a person of unstable character likely to commit such offences in the future; if such offences were committed, the consequences to others might be especially injurious. The Court re-emphasised how seriously offences of rape committed on a lone woman in her home at night after a forced entry into the house by an offender are now regarded. The case is of significance in that D would have been unlikely to have received a life sentence if he had been sentenced at the time of the offence. For another example of a pre-CJA 2003 case where a discretionary life sentence was upheld for a brutal rape of an elderly woman after forced entry into her own home, see *Baker* [2014] EWCA Crim 242. In *Clifford* [2014] EWCA Crim 2245, [2015] 1 Cr App R (S) 32 (242) the Court of Appeal made it clear that the gravity of offending by modern standards can be reflected by passing consecutive sentences in respect of old offences where sentencing powers are limited provided the overall sentence is consistent with the principle of totality.

In *Forbes* [2016] EWCA Crim 1388, [2017] 1 WLR 53, the Court of Appeal described the *Sexual Offences - Historic* definitive sentencing guideline as a convenient statement of the applicable principles which a court should apply without the need to refer to *H* or other cases. The Court then went on to clarify and elaborate upon the guidance in important ways.

B3.374 **Immaturity** In *Forbes* there was one important qualification of the *Sexual Offences - Historic* guideline. Whereas para. 9 of the guideline provides that if the offender was very young and immature at the time of the offence, then depending upon the circumstances of the offence, this may be regarded as personal mitigation, in *H* the view was expressed that immaturity goes to culpability. The Court of Appeal considered the approach in *H* to accord better with principle than the guidance given at para. 9.

In *Forbes* [2016] EWCA Crim 1388, [2017] 1 WLR 53 the Court of Appeal observed that when sentencing an adult offender, the then Youth Guidelines and part 7 of the original SGC *Sexual Offences* guideline (in relation to sentencing young offenders for offences with a lower statutory maximum sentence under the 2003 Act) would not generally be applicable as they are predicated on the basis of an offender who is still a youth. Their relevance in these circumstances was confined to the emphasis placed in each on the significance of immaturity at the time of the offending to the assessment of culpability. *GB* [2015] EWCA Crim 1501, [2016] 1 Cr App R (S) 17 (127) should not be followed.

In the light of the Court's identification of the relevance of guidelines in respect of sentencing children or young persons when sentencing an adult offender for offences committed when under 18, the definitive guideline, *Sentencing Children and Young People*, which was published after *Forbes* (effective from 1 June 2017 — see Supplement, **SG8-1**), may assist with the assessment of the offender's maturity at the time. It is observed (at p. 36) that children and young people are less emotionally developed than adults; offending can arise through inappropriate experimentation, gang or peer group pressure to engage in sexual activity, or a lack of understanding regarding consent, exploitation, coercion and appropriate sexual behaviour. The guideline then sets out a non-exhaustive list of factors that illustrate the type of background factors that may have played a part in leading a child or a young person to commit an offence of this kind. These matters, if relevant, may have some bearing on both culpability and personal mitigating factors. Reference to this guideline on that limited basis will not be inconsistent with *Forbes*.

In *Goldfinch* [2019] EWCA Crim 878, the Court of Appeal, applying the principles in *Forbes* [2016] EWCA Crim 1388, [2017] 1 WLR 53 and *H* [2011] EWCA Crim 2753, [2012] 2 All ER 340, allowed an appeal against sentence of six and a half years where D had been a mature adult in his thirties when he was sentenced following conviction for an offence of indecent assault under the SOA 1956, s. 15, which he had committed upon a child aged four when he had been 16. While D had put his penis into a young child's mouth and there was a breach of trust, the recorder had explicitly recognised that D was not a predatory offender. Lord Burnett CJ, substituting a sentence of three years' imprisonment, observed that the recorder had failed to attach sufficient weight to two significant factors. First, that although the equivalent offences under the 2003 Act carry a maximum sentence of life imprisonment, the maximum available for the offence for which D was convicted was ten years' imprisonment. Secondly, that the culpability in this case was that of a 16-year-old boy whose single offence was the result of teenage experimentation. Each of these features individually would result in significant reduction from any notional starting-point for a recent adult offender. For an application of the principles in *Forbes* in a grooming case see the appeal of AY in *KK* [2020] EWCA Crim 1643, at [159]. The Court of Appeal reduced a sentence of seven and a half years to five and a half years for indecent assault under the SOA 1956, s. 14(1) (penile penetration of the mouth which would now be styled as rape), observing that it was influenced by the fact that there had been a ten-year maximum for indecent assault under s. 14 while the modern guideline is geared to offences where the maximum is life.

Measured Reference The offender must be sentenced in accordance with the regime applicable at the date of sentence. However, the Court of Appeal held that a court should, in assessing the appropriate sentence in any case, have regard to the maximum sentence applicable to the offence and not simply apply in a mechanistic way guidelines premised on higher maximum sentences. The CAJA 2009, s. 125(1)(a), which imposes the duty to follow the guidelines, only applies to offences committed after that Act came into force on 6 April 2010. The phrase 'have regard to' (which was intended to have the same meaning as 'by measured reference to') was intended to make clear that the judge should not simply apply the relevant guideline applicable at the date of sentence, subject to any lower statutory maximum sentence applicable at the date the offence was committed, but should use the guideline in a measured and reflective manner to arrive at the appropriate sentence. **B3.375**

Selection of Modern Equivalent Offence The sentencing judge should guard against too mechanistic an approach, either in terms of selecting the modern equivalent offence or in adopting the figures in the guideline without having regard to the fact that generally higher maxima are provided for some modern offences. However, the judge should go no further and not attempt an alternative notional sentencing guideline as the judge mistakenly did in *A-G's Ref (No. 27 of 2015)* [2015] EWCA Crim 1538. **B3.376**

There will be cases where it will be helpful to consider more than one guideline. The Court of Appeal selected *Warren* (one of the conjoined appeals in *Forbes* [2016] EWCA Crim 1388, [2017] 1 WLR 53) as a helpful example. Warren procured scouts in his charge to inflict sadomasochistic sexual assaults on him; he pleaded guilty to charges of indecency with a child contrary to the Indecency with Children Act 1960, s. 1(1). The judge had selected as the modern equivalent the offence under the SOA 2003, ss. 16 and 17, which was intended to cover cases of 16 to 18-year-old youths who consent to the sexual activity but whose consent is vitiated by the relationship of trust with the adult in question. This was not the correct choice as all the children were below the age of consent (half under 13 and the others 13); the two relevant guidelines were those under s. 8 of the 2003 Act (for those under the age 13) and s. 9 (for those who were 13), but it was necessary to have regard to the fact that the maximum sentences greatly exceeded the maximum for the offences committed.

Another example of cases where sentencers should consider more than one guideline can be found in historic cases where there has been penile penetration of the mouth of a child under 13. This would be rape under the SOA 2003, s. 5, where the maximum is life, whereas if the offence was committed before 1 May 2014 it would be charged under the SOA 1956, s. 15(1), where the maximum was ten years. While s. 5 is the equivalent modern offence, the court should take into account the significantly higher maximum. In those circumstances it can be helpful to make some reference to the starting points for sexual assault or sexual activity with a child under 13 (*Rouse*, one of the conjoined appeals in *Forbes*, at ([125]–[152]). See also *Clifford* [2014] EWCA Crim 2245, [2015] 1 Cr App R (S) 32 (242).

B3.377 **ECHR, Article 7** Although the court is not concerned to ascertain what sentence would have been passed apart from consideration of the statutory maximum, the Court of Appeal acknowledged the existence of one rare exception. In the conjoined appeal of *BD* (*Forbes* [2016] EWCA Crim 1388, [2017] 1 WLR 53 at [13], [110]–[121]), D was under 14 when he committed some of the indecent assaults and so, at the relevant time, he could not have been sentenced to a custodial sentence because of his age. Taking into account the ECHR, Article 7, and the common-law requirement of fairness, the Court held that it would not be right to impose any custodial sentence for those offences. The Court contrasted *BD* with the appeal of *Rouse* (at [144]) where, although D was only a little older than *BD* when he committed the offences, a custodial sentence would have been available. In particular the Court was at pains to stress that the rare circumstances of the appeal of *BD* should not operate as an encouragement or licence to courts to consider a similar exercise in any other situation. Furthermore in any event, in *AM* [2018] EWCA Crim 279, in a reference by the A-G, the Court of Appeal, without determining the issue, expressed the view that it saw some force in the argument that two potential custodial options (a remand home or approved school) were available for *BD* at the time he committed the offences. This had not been brought to the attention of the Court in *Forbes*.

B3.378 For the impact of advanced age as a mitigating factor see *Clarke* [2017] EWCA Crim 393, [2017] 2 Cr App R (S) 18 (140). For a non-exhaustive list of circumstances to be considered when sentencing a defendant for historic offences of a similar character and date as offences for which the defendant has already been sentenced and/or served a sentence see *Green* [2019] EWCA Crim 196, [2019] 4 WLR 37 at [18]. See also *Cosburn* [2013] EWCA Crim 1815.

Rape

B3.379
- SOA 1956, s. 1(1): 1 January 1957 until 21 December 1976. Maximum sentence life.
- SOA 1956, s. 1(1), as amended by the Sexual Offences (Amendment) Act 1976: 22 December 1976 until 30 April 2004. Maximum sentence life.

B3.380 **Definition of Rape** The SOA 1956, s. 1(1), as originally enacted, simply provided 'It is a felony for a man to rape a woman'. Rape was defined, however, at common law as unlawful sexual intercourse with a woman without her consent, by force, fear or fraud (1 Hale 626; East PC 434). This definition was potentially misleading as the essence of rape is the absence of the complainant's consent. In 1976, after the recommendation of the Heilbron Committee in response to public concern following the House of Lords' decision in *DPP v Morgan* [1976] AC 182, the definition of rape was for the first time declared in statutory form. Section 1(1) of the Sexual Offences (Amendment) Act 1976 provided:

> A man commits rape if—
> (a) he has unlawful sexual intercourse with a woman who at the time of the intercourse does not consent to it; and
> (b) at the time he knows that she does not consent to the intercourse or he is reckless as to whether she consents to it.

B3.381 **Sexual Intercourse** To prove sexual intercourse took place, the prosecution must prove that the defendant's penis penetrated the victim's vagina. By s. 142 of the CJPO 1994, Parliament altered the basis of the offence of rape by enacting that rape included penetration of the anus, with the result that a man as well as a woman could be the victim of rape.

Until that time rape was confined to non-consensual penetration of a woman's vagina. Penile penetration of the anus (whether of a man or a woman) was charged as buggery under the SOA 1956, s. 12(1). This was amended by the SOA 1967, which provided that homosexual acts in private between consenting adults (which included those that would otherwise constitute the offence of buggery or gross indecency) were no longer an offence.

Before the widening of the definition of rape in the SOA 2003 to include non-consensual penile penetration of the mouth, such acts would be charged as indecent assault.

Unlawful Sexual Intercourse 'Unlawful sexual intercourse' was construed as meaning outside marriage. Marital immunity from rape was gradually eroded by judicial decisions until, finally, the anachronism that a woman could not in law refuse sexual intercourse with her husband unless the law had placed some barrier between them was finally swept away in *R* [1992] 1 AC 599. Shortly afterwards, s. 142 of the CJPO 1994 removed the word 'unlawful' from the then statutory definition of rape, thereby confirming that rape may occur within marriage. Following the decision of the ECtHR in *SW v UK* (1996) 21 EHRR 363 and the Court of Appeal in *C* [2004] EWCA Crim 292, [2004] 1 WLR 2098, it is clear that a man may be properly convicted of raping his wife even though it occurred well before the final demise of the marital exemption. **B3.382**

Absence of Consent Until the SOA 2003, s. 74, there was no statutory definition of 'consent' in respect of the law governing sexual offences. In the majority of cases the approach to consent will be the same whether the allegation relates to conduct before or after the implementation of the SOA 2003 on 1 May 2004. The definition of consent in s. 74 in terms of 'free agreement' is not inconsistent with the appropriate approach to consent in historic cases. Both before and after the implementation of s. 74, consent would necessarily involve a free and genuine agreement. Simply to comply or to submit is not necessarily to consent. Consent must be freely given. Furthermore, as before, absence of protest, resistance or injury does not necessarily mean the complainant consented (*Malone* (1998) 2 Cr App R 447). **B3.383**

The leading pre-2003 Act authority of *Olugboja* [1982] QB 320 left the parameters of absence of consent undefined. However, in *R (Monica) v DPP* [2018] EWHC 3508 (Admin), [2019] 1 Cr App R 28 (363) the Divisional Court observed that Dunn LJ in *Olugboja* was dealing with directions when the allegation is that intercourse was by force, the fear of force, or at least by threats not involving violence (see **B3.46**). It follows that *Olugboja* did not address the issue of deception or fraud vitiating consent and the law under the pre-2003 Act remained that only those as to the nature of the sexual act or fraud as to the identity of the perpetrator (impersonation of husband or partner) were capable of vitiating consent. In *Monica* the Divisional Court observed that there is no decided case which holds in terms that the 2003 Act has made no difference to the notion of 'consent'. In fact there is a compelling argument that the SOA 2003, s. 74, as applied in subsequent decisions such as *Assange v Swedish Prosecution Authority* [2011] EWHC 2849 (Admin), has added to the categories of deception that are capable of vitiating consent. These are categorised in *Monica* as being those deceptions that are so closely connected to the performance of the sexual act *or* are intrinsically so fundamental, owing to that connection, that they can be treated as cases of impersonation. For example, Sir John Thomas (as he then was) stated in *Assange* (at [86]) that Mr Assange's conduct in having sexual intercourse without a condom in circumstances where his partner had made clear that she would only have intercourse if he used one would amount to an offence under the 2003 Act, 'whatever the position may have been prior to that Act'. He added (at [88]) that it would, in the Court's view, 'have been extraordinary if Parliament had legislated in terms that, if conduct that was not deceptive could be taken into account for the purposes of s. 74, conduct that was deceptive could not be'. Furthermore, as was recognised in *Monica,* there must at least be room for the argument that the abolition of the offence of procurement under the SOA 1956, s. 3, may have widened the scope of the offence of rape.

While the presumptions under the SOA 2003, ss. 75 and 76, will not apply to historic allegations of non-consensual offences, under the common law if a complainant was induced to consent to sexual intercourse upon the basis of a fraudulent misrepresentation as to the nature of the act, there would have been no consent (*Flattery* (1877) 1 QBD 410; *Williams* [1923] 1 KB 340).

B3.384 **Mental Element** However, the SOA 2003 did bring about a major change in the mental element required in order to establish rape. Under s. 1(1)(b) of the Sexual Offences Amendment Act 1976, the mental element in rape was (a) an intention to have unlawful sexual intercourse with a woman, and (b) either knowledge on the part of the defendant that the woman was not consenting or recklessness as to whether she was consenting. The mental element was entirely subjective. In *Morgan v DPP* [1976] AC 182 the House of Lords decided that if at the time of intercourse the defendant had a mistaken belief that the woman was consenting, he cannot be convicted of rape even if he had no reasonable grounds for such a belief. In *Taylor* (1985) 80 Cr App R 327 Lord Lane CJ explained (at p. 332) that in rape the defendant is reckless if he does not believe that the woman is consenting and could not care less whether she is consenting or not but presses on regardless.

B3.385 **Attempted Rape** The maximum sentence was seven years' imprisonment until 1985 when it was increased to life by the SOA 1985, ss. 3 and 5(5).

This lower maximum can lead to difficulty where a court has to sentence an offender for attempted rape committed before 1985 where a sentence higher than seven years would have otherwise been entirely appropriate (*H* [2011] EWCA Crim 2753, [2012] 2 Cr App R (S) 21 (88)).

Incest

B3.386
- SOA 1956, s. 10. Incest by a male person. Maximum sentence life if victim aged under 13; otherwise seven years' imprisonment.
- SOA 1956, s. 11. Incest by a female person. Maximum sentence seven years' imprisonment.
- CLA 1977, s. 54. Incitement of a girl under 16 to commit incest (from 8 September 1977). Maximum sentence two years' imprisonment.

The SOA 2003, s. 10(1), provided:

> It is an offence for a man to have sexual intercourse with a woman he knows to be his granddaughter, daughter, sister or mother.

The SOA 2003, s. 11(1), provided:

> It is an offence for a woman of the age of sixteen or over to permit a man whom she knows to be her grandfather, father, brother or son to have sexual intercourse with her by her consent.

Unlike the new offences created by the SOA 2003 (sexual activity with child family members and sex with an adult relative), the existence of a blood relationship was a vital component of the old offence of incest. Furthermore, under the old law of incest, the proscribed sexual behaviour was limited to vaginal sexual intercourse.

A prosecution, whether for the full offence under s. 10 or s. 11 or an attempt, may not be commenced without the sanction of the A-G, except by or on behalf of the DPP (SOA 1956, s. 37(1), 2 and sch. 2, para. 14(a)).

Apart from the separate offence of incest for men and women, there was an additional offence under s. 54(1) of the CLA 1977 of inciting a girl under the age of 16 to have incestuous intercourse. This was enacted because of the lacuna exposed in *Whitehouse* [1977] QB 868 where it had been held that since the girl was under the age of 16 and could not commit the offence of incest, her father could not be guilty of the common-law offence of inciting her to commit that offence with him. Nor could he be guilty of inciting the girl to aid and abet him in the commission of the crime of incest, as she herself was to be the victim of the crime and therefore could not be an accessory to it (*Tyrell* [1894] 1 QB 710).

Indecent Assault

- SOA 1956, s. 14. Indecent assault on a woman. 1 November 1957 until 30 April 2004. Maximum sentence for offences committed before 16 September 1985 was two years' imprisonment, or five years after 1 January 1961 if the complainant was a girl under 13 and that fact was averred in the indictment (SOA 1956, s. 37 and sch. 2, as amended by the Indecency with Children Act 1960). Maximum sentence for offences committed on or after 16 September 1985 was ten years' imprisonment regardless of the age of the victim (SOA 1956, s. 37 and sch. 2, as amended by the SOA 1985, s. 3). **B3.387**
- SOA 1956, s. 15. Indecent assault on a man. 1 November 1957 until 30 April 2004. Maximum sentence ten years' imprisonment.

Indecent assault includes conduct which after the implementation of the SOA 2003 would be prosecuted as rape (penetration of the complainant's mouth by the defendant's penis) or assault by penetration (digital penetration of the vagina).

'indecent' The precise manner in which the issue of indecency should be left to a jury was considered by the House of Lords in *Court* [1989] AC 28. A jury must decide whether 'right-minded persons' would consider the conduct indecent or not. If the assault is either inherently indecent or rendered indecent by its accompanying circumstances, the element of indecency can be established simply by proving the facts constituting the assault, and the defendant's motive will be irrelevant. If the assault is incapable of being considered indecent, the prosecution cannot secure a conviction by adducing that a defendant had a secret indecent motive. However, if the assault is at most capable of being considered indecent, a defendant's sexual motive is admissible both to show the assault was, in fact, indecent and he had intended it to be so. **B3.388**

Absence of Consent This is an essential ingredient of indecent assault. By virtue of the SOA 1956, s. 14(2) and s. 15(2) respectively, if the victim is a girl or boy under 16 consent is no defence. **B3.389**

There is a significant difference between indecent assault under the SOA 1956 and sexual assault under the SOA 2003. Sexual assault is confined to cases where an actual touching takes place and so does not extend to cases where a victim is put in fear of being touched. However, while a sexual assault must be deliberate, there need be no hostile intent. In *Fairclough v Whipp* (1951) 35 Cr App R 138, the Divisional Court decided that an invitation by a man to a girl to touch his penis could not amount to an assault on the girl. This led to Parliament enacting the Indecency with Children Act 1960. This apparent acceptance that *Fairclough v Whipp* was correctly decided means that there will be no indecent assault without some form of threat or show of force to the victim. This led to the Court of Appeal in *Dunn* [2015] EWCA Crim 724, [2015] 2 Cr App R 13 (210) quashing a conviction for indecent assault between March 1999 and March 2000 upon a 15-year-old girl by the offender causing her to masturbate him. This revealed a lacuna in the pre-SOA 2003 law in that a charge under s. 1(1) of the Indecency with Children Act 1960 would not have been appropriate either as it was not until 2001 that the protection of that provision was extended to children aged 14 and 15.

Mental Element The prosecution must prove either that the defendant knew the complainant was not consenting or was reckless as to whether the complainant consented. In this context a defendant is reckless if he did not care less whether the complainant was consenting (*Kimber* [1983] 1 WLR 1118). **B3.390**

Sexual Intercourse with Girl under 13/ Girl under 16

- SOA 1956, s. 5. Sexual intercourse with a girl under 13. Maximum sentence life (attempt seven years' imprisonment). **B3.391**
- SOA 1956, s. 6. Sexual intercourse with a girl under 16. Maximum sentence two years' imprisonment.

By virtue of the SOA 1956, s. 37 and sch. 2, a prosecution under s. 6 of the 1956 Act, or for an attempt to commit the offence, could not be brought more than 12 months after the offence was committed. As a result the offence can no longer be charged as inevitably the prosecution will be out of time. The House of Lords decided in 2004 that the problem cannot be overcome by charging indecent assault after the expiry of the 12-month time limit (*J* [2004] UKHL 42, [2005] 1 AC 562). See also *Hessey* [2020] EWCA Crim 467, for application of this rule. The allegation, which related to 1996 to 1998, would have been charged as unlawful sexual intercourse with a girl under 16 contrary to the SOA 1956, s. 6(1), when the complainant was 14 or 15. That was why s. 14(1) had been charged. The Court of Appeal observed that, in the circumstances, the time restriction precluded the Crown from charging s. 14(1). The change in the law effected by the decision in *J* will not necessarily give rise to a meritorious ground of appeal in respect of pre-*J* convictions as it is unlikely that substantial injustice will have arisen (*Cottrell* [2007] EWCA Crim 2016, [2007] 1 WLR 3262; *Johnson* [2016] EWCA Crim 1613, [2017] 1 Cr App R 12 (136)). The prohibition in *J* relates to the institution of proceedings rather than the alternative verdict to rape under s. 6(3) of the CLA 1967. If rape has been properly charged in respect of a complainant under the age of 16, a jury could, in appropriate circumstances, still reach an alternative verdict of indecent assault. There was no equivalent offence of unlawful sexual intercourse with a boy under the age of 16 under the 1956 Act and so no statutory time bar if a woman is prosecuted under s. 15 for indecent assault on a boy in respect of an act of sexual intercourse with him (*Perrett* [2019] EWCA Crim 685).

Gross Indecency with a Child

B3.392 • Indecency with Children Act 1960, s. 1. Gross indecency with a child. Until 30 September 1997 the offence could be committed only in relation to a child under 14 and the maximum sentence was two years' imprisonment. From 1 October 1997 the maximum was ten years. From 21 January 2001 the offence was extended to cover gross indecency with children under 16.

The Indecency with Children Act 1960, s. 1(1), rendered liable to conviction 'Any person who commits an act of gross indecency with or towards a child under the age of fourteen, or who incites a child under that age to such an act with him or another'.

A charge of gross indecency laid contrary to the SOA 1956, s. 13, as opposed to the correct charge under s. 1(1) of the Indecency with Children Act 1960, will be time barred by reason of the SOA 1956, s. 7(1) and (2)(a). The repeal of s. 7 when the SOA 2003 came into force did not have retrospective effect (*Silverwood* [2015] EWCA Crim 2401 and see also the conjoined appeal of *Warren* in *Forbes* [2016] EWCA Crim 1388, [2017] 1 WLR 53 at [56]). Where an indictment is defective for this reason, consideration should be given as to whether the defect is one of form or substance (*AD* [2016] EWCA Crim 454, [2016] 2 Cr App R 18 (241)).

English courts have declined to define the concept of 'gross indecency'. Clearly it is conduct which represents a marked departure from decent conduct. It appears that simply doing nothing can, in an appropriate case, amount to an 'act' for the purposes of s. 1(1). For instance, in *Speck* [1977] 2 All ER 859 an eight-year-old girl had placed her hand on the appellant's penis outside his trousers and left it there for approximately five minutes. As a consequence of the girl's conduct the appellant had an erection. The Court of Appeal held that his inactivity was capable of amounting to an invitation to the child to act or continue to act in a particular way and it was open for the jury to find that such conduct amounted to gross indecency.

Presumptions that Apply to Historic Offences if the Offence was Committed before the Date of Abolition

B3.393 The rebuttable presumption at common law that a child of not less than ten but under 14 years of age was *doli incapax* (i.e. incapable of committing a crime) still applies to historic abuse cases relating to events that preceded the presumption's abolition on 30 September 1998 (*Fethney* [2010] EWCA Crim 3096; *Bevan* [2011] EWCA Crim 654). In *PF* [2017] EWCA Crim 983 the Court of Appeal confirmed that in historic cases involving defendants in respect of acts done when they were children aged between ten and 14 where the rebuttable presumption still applies, the prosecution must establish that the child knew that the alleged act was seriously wrong by clear positive evidence to that effect distinct from the doing of the alleged act itself. McCombe LJ said (at [28]): 'It seems to us in a case where such sexual conduct of a nature of childish experimentation is admitted, it is particularly important to focus the jury's attention upon the evidence said to be properly capable of demonstrating that the particular defendant must have known that his conduct went well beyond the mere "rude or naughty" and to direct them that they must be satisfied by that evidence that the defendant knew that what he did was seriously wrong in the relevant sense.' See also *AM* [2018] EWCA Crim 279 where the trial judge failed to assist the jury by expressly directing that they must look for evidence other than the offending itself. In *AM* the Court commended the *Crown Court Compendium*, ch. 7-1, which provides a form of words and a set of directions that show how the jury could and should have been helped to focus on the extremely difficult issue of establishing what an 11-year-old boy knew over 50 years ago (see also **A3.73**).

In *RP v The Queen* [2016] HCA 53 the High Court of Australia shed light on how this presumption should be approached. The fact that a child's conduct had gone well beyond ordinary childish experimentation does not carry with it a conclusion that the child understood the conduct was seriously wrong in a moral sense as distinct from it being rude or naughty. Statements such as the nearer a child is to the age of 14, the less strong need the evidence be to rebut the presumption, ignore the fact that children do not mature at a uniform rate. Rebutting the presumption directs attention to the intellectual and moral development of the particular child.

The anomalous common-law presumption that a boy under the age of 14 was incapable of vaginal or anal intercourse was abolished by the SOA 1993, s. 1, which came into force on 20 September 1993. However it was not abolished retrospectively. It follows that, whatever the circumstances, a defendant cannot be convicted of rape where the relevant penetration occurred before 20 September 1993, and at that time the defendant was under the age of 14 (*JOC* [2012] EWCA Crim 2458). The issue arose in *AM* as to whether the irrebuttable presumption applies to attempted rape. While the Court of Appeal did not determine the issue, it gave a provisional view that it could see no reason to depart from the view of Lord Hailsham in *Smith (Roger Daniel)* [1975] AC 476 that a boy could not commit the offence of attempted rape when he was incapable of the full offence. **B3.394**

Section B4 Theft, Handling Stolen Goods and Related Offences

THEFT

Definition

B4.1 **Theft Act 1968, s. 1**

(1) A person is guilty of theft if he dishonestly appropriates property belonging to another with the intention of permanently depriving the other of it; and 'thief' and 'steal' shall be construed accordingly.

Procedure

B4.2 With one exception, theft is triable either way (MCA 1980, s. 17 and sch. 1, para. 28). Low-value shoplifting, as defined by s. 22A(3) (see **D6.27**), is said to be triable only summarily (s. 22A(1)) but an accused aged 18 or over may elect Crown Court trial (s. 22A(2)) and s. 22A then ceases to apply (*Chamberlin* [2017] EWCA Crim 39, [2017] 1 Cr App R (S) 46 (369)). Any such election must now be notified to the Crown Court in accordance with CrimPR 9.5 (see Supplement, **R9.5**). In all shoplifting cases, the value of any property allegedly stolen must also be stated, if known, in the particulars of any summons, warrant or charge, so as to indicate whether it is a low-value case to which s. 22A may apply (CrimPR 7.3(1): see Supplement, **R7.3**). Low-value shoplifting is deemed to remain an indictable offence for the purposes of the law of attempt etc., but is not an offence to which the CJA 1988, s. 40, applies, so unless D makes an election under s. 22A(2) such a charge cannot be added to an indictment for other offences (*McDermott-Mullane* [2016] EWCA Crim 223, [2017] 4 WLR 127; *Maxwell* [2017] EWCA Crim 1233, [2018] 1 Cr App R 5 (76); *Yeo* [2019] EWCA Crim 2460).

When tried on indictment, theft is normally a class 3 offence, but see CrimPD XIII, para. B (see Supplement, **CPD.XIII.B**) for the additional factors that the court considers on allocation. It is a Group A offence for jurisdiction purposes under the CJA 1993, Part I (see **A8.10**). See the *Magistrates' Court Sentencing Guidelines* (see Supplement, **SG10-90**) for indications as to when a case should be sent to the Crown Court.

Where the property in question belonged to D's spouse or civil partner, a prosecution for theft (or criminal damage, or inchoate versions of those offences) may be instituted against D only by or with the consent of the DPP (Theft Act 1968, s. 30(4)). See *Withers* [1975] Crim LR 647. This restriction must also apply to charges of robbery or of burglary by stealing, etc., but does not apply to other persons charged with committing the offence jointly with D; nor does it apply where the parties are separated by judicial decree or order or under no obligation to cohabit (s. 30(4)(a)).

Indictment

Statement of Offence B4.3

Theft contrary to section 1(1) of the Theft Act 1968.

Particulars of Offence

A on or about the... day of... stole a pearl necklace belonging to V.

It is proper to allege in a single count the theft of an aggregate sum of money or items of property where the evidence does not disclose the precise dates and amounts of each individual transaction, provided that D's conduct amounted to a continuous offence over a period of time. Such an allegation is usually referred to as theft of a 'general deficiency'. Thus it would be proper to indict for theft of the total sum missing on a day on which D was bound to account for it, even though D took it in instalments (*Balls* (1871) LR 1 CCR 328) or theft of all items stolen from a department store on one day, even though the various articles emanated from different departments of the store (*Wilson* (1979) 69 Cr App R 83; *Heaton v Costello* (1984) 148 JP 688). A count drafted in this way is not bad for duplicity. This principle also applies where 'money' was in different forms and it could not be said whether what was stolen was a debt, cash drawn from a bank account or cash disposed of otherwise and representing funds provided by clients of financial advisers (*Hallam* [1995] Crim LR 323). The elements of the offence must exist throughout; otherwise there would be a lack of coincidence (see **B4.25**). As to indictments for continuous offences generally, see *DPP v Merriman* [1973] AC 584 and **D11.32** ***et seq.***

Not all the items mentioned in an information or count must be proved to have been stolen (*Machent v Quinn* [1970] 2 All ER 255), provided it is proved that D stole at least one of them. However, there will be cases where the prosecution should not include in a single count more than one allegation of theft, for example where several items are alleged to have been stolen from an employer on different days (*Jackson* (1991) *The Guardian*, 20 November 1991). Some property must be specified in the indictment or information.

As to the relevance of conditional intention in drafting an indictment, see **B4.64**. As to the relationship between theft and handling, see **B4.175**.

Alternative Verdicts

In addition to the general power under the CLA 1967, s. 6(3), the Theft Act 1968, s. 12(4), provides that, as an alternative to a conviction of theft, the jury may on a trial on indictment for theft find D guilty of an offence under s. 12(1) (taking a motor vehicle or other conveyance without authority etc.; see **B4.116** to **B4.126**). B4.4

Sentence

The maximum penalty is seven years (Theft Act 1968, s. 7) on indictment; six months or an unlimited fine, or both, summarily. Under the Penalties for Disorderly Behaviour (Amount of Penalty) Order 2002 (SI 2002 No. 1837), as amended, this offence is a penalty offence and the amount payable by persons aged 18 and over is £90. B4.5

Offences of Theft Generally The definitive sentencing guideline, *Theft* (see Supplement, **SG33-1**), applies to adult offenders sentenced on or after 1 February 2016, irrespective of the date of the offence. The guideline covers (i) general theft (including theft from the person, theft in a dwelling, theft in breach of trust, theft from a motor vehicle, theft of a motor vehicle and theft of a pedal cycle, and (ii) theft from a shop or stall (see **B4.7**). General theft has an offence range of discharge to six years' custody. B4.6

Shoplifting The definitive sentencing guideline, *Theft* (see Supplement, **SG33-1**), applies to adult offenders sentenced on or after 1 February 2016, irrespective of the date of the offence. Theft from a shop or stall is a distinct category of theft dealt with in the guideline, with an offence range of discharge to three years' custody. *Chamberlin* [2017] EWCA Crim 39, [2017] 1 Cr App R (S) 46 (369) is a useful authority in relation to sentencing offenders who have a long history of similar offending. See **E1.14**. B4.7

B4.8 **Theft from the Person** The definitive sentencing guideline, *Theft* (see Supplement, **SG33-1**), applies to adult offenders sentenced on or after 1 February 2016, irrespective of the date of the offence. Theft from the person is no longer a distinct category within the guideline. In *Fothergill* [2019] EWCA Crim 2236 sentences with starting points of two years and six months' imprisonment on two men who had stolen money from a blind busker were not manifestly excessive. The sentencing judge had been entitled, in the interests of justice, to depart from the sentencing guideline because of the offenders' serious and extensive criminal records.

B4.9 **Theft in Breach of Trust** The definitive sentencing guideline, *Theft* (see Supplement, **SG33-1**), applies to adult offenders sentenced on or after 1 February 2016, irrespective of the date of the offence. Theft in breach of trust is no longer a distinct category within the guideline but breach of trust is a factor adding to culpability. The Court of Appeal in *Green* [2017] EWCA Crim 1204, [2018] 1 Cr App R (S) 4 (24) upheld an immediate sentence of six months on D who was a carer for an 88-year-old woman with severe physical disabilities, from whom she stole £900. The sentence was upheld despite very strong personal mitigation.

The Five Elements of Theft

B4.10 By the Theft Act 1968, s. 1(1), theft consists of five elements: (i) dishonest (ii) appropriation (iii) of property (iv) belonging to another (v) with the intention of permanently depriving the other of it. Those five elements are amplified (but not fully defined) in ss. 2 to 6. It is usually said that the first and last elements constitute the *mens rea* of the offence, whereas the second, third and fourth constitute the *actus reus*; but this is an oversimplification, because appropriation necessarily involves a mental element (see **B4.35**).

Section 1(1) does not expressly require that the appropriation in question must be the means whereby D intends to deprive V of V's property. It does not, in other words, say that D must appropriate the property 'with the intention *thereby* of permanently depriving V'. One might suppose that on a purposive reading of s. 1(1) such a requirement would be implied, but the House of Lords in *Morris* [1984] AC 320 held otherwise. If D does something to V's property that amounts to a dishonest appropriation, but intends to deprive V only by some later act (which the first appropriation may perhaps be intended to facilitate) then D has already stolen V's property (even though V may still have it); and because D cannot ordinarily re-steal property he has already stolen, the later act which actually deprives V may not then amount to theft at all. See further **B4.34** ***et seq.***

'Property'

B4.11 **Theft Act 1968, s. 4**

(1) 'Property' includes money and all other property, real or personal, including things in action and other intangible property.

(2) A person cannot steal land, or things forming part of land and severed from it by him or by his directions, except in the following cases, that is to say—

(a) when he is a trustee or personal representative, or is authorised by power of attorney, or as liquidator of a company, or otherwise, to sell or dispose of land belonging to another, and he appropriates the land or anything forming part of it by dealing with it in breach of the confidence reposed in him; or

(b) when he is not in possession of the land and appropriates anything forming part of the land by severing it or causing it to be severed, or after it has been severed; or

(c) when, being in possession of the land under a tenancy, he appropriates the whole or part of any fixture or structure let to be used with the land.

For purposes of this subsection 'land' does not include incorporeal hereditaments; 'tenancy' means a tenancy for years or any less period and includes an agreement for such a tenancy, but a person who after the end of a tenancy remains in possession as statutory tenant or otherwise is to be treated as having possession under the tenancy, and 'let' shall be construed accordingly.

(3) A person who picks mushrooms growing wild on any land, or who picks flowers, fruit or foliage from a plant growing wild on any land, does not (although not in possession of the land) steal what he picks, unless he does it for reward or for sale or other commercial purpose.

For purposes of this subsection 'mushroom' includes any fungus, and 'plant' includes any shrub or tree.

(4) Wild creatures, tamed or untamed, shall be regarded as property; but a person cannot steal a wild creature not tamed nor ordinarily kept in captivity, or the carcase of any such creature, unless either it has been reduced into possession by or on behalf of another person and possession of it has not since been lost or abandoned, or another person is in course of reducing it into possession.

Money Coins and banknotes are property (*Davis* (1988) 88 Cr App R 347). 'Money' does not include cheques or credit balances held in bank or building society accounts, but see **B4.15** and **B4.16**. **B4.12**

Real Property and Wild Plants etc. Special rules apply to land, buildings, fixtures, and other things that form part of the land (including crops, plants, etc.). These can be the subject of a theft charge only in limited circumstances specified by s. 4(2). **B4.13**

Trustees and other persons falling within the scope of s. 4(2)(a) may commit theft by dishonestly appropriating any such property in a deliberate breach of their fiduciary duties, assuming all other elements of theft can be established. This provision must, however, be construed strictly. D must actually *be* a trustee or personal representative, or *be* authorised by power of attorney, or *be* a liquidator, etc., before it can apply. The provision cannot be read so as to apply to those who merely purport to so act, or mistakenly believe themselves to be so authorised (*Gimbert* [2018] EWCA Crim 2190, [2019] 1 Cr App R 14 (189)). If D acts dishonestly, D may, however, still be guilty of fraud, or (where mistaken as to status) of attempted theft, based on the facts as D believed them to be.

Under s. 4(2)(b), persons who are not in possession of land may commit theft in a variety of ways, notably by severing fixtures, plants, topsoil, etc., from the land or by appropriating such property after it has been severed. This would not however, for example, include a person who dishonestly moves a boundary fence so as to appropriate some part of a neighbouring property.

Nor does s. 4(2)(b) apply to tenants or to persons in possession of land under a licence or tenancy. The appropriation of fixtures by tenants (as defined at the end of s. 4(2)) is governed by s. 4(2)(c), but by what appears to be an oversight this does not extend to mere licensees. So, whereas a tenant who dishonestly sells a valuable fireplace or greenhouse forming part of the property falls squarely within s. 4(2)(c), even if it has not yet been severed or removed, a licensee doing exactly the same thing would not be caught by that provision. Nor in such a case would the licensee be caught by s. 4(2)(b) or indeed be guilty of theft at all.

Whether a particular object forms part of the land may be a difficult question. Under the law of real property, an article that was a chattel may become annexed to the land if it is attached to the land (or building etc.) in order to improve or facilitate the use of the land or building, but not where it is attached only to facilitate its own use as a chattel (*Elitestone Ltd v Morris* [1997] 2 All ER 513). **B4.14**

The restrictions imposed by s. 4(2) do not apply to incorporeal hereditaments (or intangible real property) such as easements, profits à prendre and rentcharges.

Where charges of theft are problematic because of the nature of the property involved, the dishonest obtaining of land or fixtures may in some cases be more easily prosecuted as an offence of fraud or (where it occurred before 15 January 2007) under the Theft Act 1968, s. 15 (see **B5.1**).

Section 4(3) is clumsily expressed, but is designed to ensure that persons who pick wild mushrooms, flowers or berries for non-commercial purposes cannot be guilty of theft, even if they trespass on private land when so doing. Commercial pickers may be guilty of theft in such circumstances, but only if all other elements of theft are established. The picking, destruction or uprooting of wild plants protected under the Wildlife and Countryside Act 1981, sch. 8, or the uprooting of any wild plant, may be an offence under s. 13 of that Act.

B4.15 **Personal Property** Personal property includes tangible personal property, which might also be described as 'things (or choses) in possession', 'chattels' or 'goods'. A cheque, bill of exchange or other valuable security (or even an uncompleted cheque form or cheque book) is personal property capable of being appropriated (*Arnold* [1997] 4 All ER 1; *Clark* [2001] EWCA Crim 884, [2002] 1 Cr App R 14 (141)) but see *Preddy* [1996] AC 815. Personal property also includes things (or choses) in action and other intangible property.

A debt for a liquidated, or known, sum is a common form of thing in action, as are shares in a company. In *Marshall* [1998] 2 Cr App R 282, the Court of Appeal, stated, *obiter*, that, because the issuing of an underground train ticket resulted in the creation of a contract between the customer and the train operator, the contractual rights arising were enforceable by action:

> Therefore it is arguable, we suppose, that by the transaction each party has acquired a chose in action. On the side of the purchaser it is represented by a right to use the ticket to the extent which it allows travel on the underground system. On the side of [the operator] it encompasses the right to insist that the ticket is used by no one other than the purchaser. It is that right which is disregarded when the ticket is acquired by the appellant and sold on.

'Other intangible property' includes patents (Patents Act 1977, s. 30), copyright (Copyright, Designs and Patents Act 1988, s. 1) and design rights (Copyright, Designs and Patents Act 1988, s. 213), although a mere breach of copyright is not theft. See also *A-G of Hong Kong v Nai-Keung* [1987] 1 WLR 1339 (export quotas held to be intangible property). However, confidential information is not a form of property. Thus in *Oxford v Moss* (1978) 68 Cr App R 183, D, an undergraduate, committed no theft by dishonestly copying questions from an examination paper he was due to sit. It would seem to follow that no theft can be committed in cases of 'industrial espionage' where D dishonestly acquires trade secrets from V, unless D also appropriates documents etc., on which such information is recorded, and does so with the requisite *mens rea*.

B4.16 **Bank Accounts** A credit balance in a bank or a building society account provides the holder with a thing in action. The relationship of debtor and creditor exists between the bank and the customer. This debt cannot be physically possessed, but may be enforced by legal action and is capable of being stolen (*Kohn* (1979) 69 Cr App R 395 at p. 404; see also *Chan Man-sin v The Queen* [1988] 1 All ER 1; *Wille* (1987) 86 Cr App R 296; *Preddy* [1996] AC 815 at p. 825).

Where an account is overdrawn the bank remains obliged to honour cheques as long as the account remains within agreed overdraft limits. This again is a thing in action and capable of being stolen (see *Kohn* at p. 407; *Chan Man-sin* at p. 198E); but as Cranston J explained in *Adamczewski v District Court in Jelenia Gora, Poland* [2014] EWHC 2958 (Admin) (at [14]):

> A basic feature of our law is that if parties make payments from their bank account without funds in the account, or without an agreed overdraft, that constitutes a request to the bank to provide overdraft facilities sufficient to meet the payment instruction. The bank has the option whether or not to comply with that request (see *Barclays Bank v WJ Simms & Cook Southern Ltd* [1981] QB 677).

It is thus difficult to envisage a case in which an account holder could steal from his bank by excessive spending on his account. Where, however, D attempts to use a forged cheque or other instrument to withdraw funds from P's account, this may amount to theft or attempted theft from the bank (cf. *Hendricks* [2003] EWCA Crim 1040) and D may be guilty of fraud or of offences under the Forgery and Counterfeiting Act 1981, regardless of the state of the account in question.

B4.17 **Wild Creatures** *Section 4(4)* restricts the circumstances in which wild creatures are covered by the law of theft. Wild creatures that are neither tamed nor kept in captivity cannot be stolen unless they have already been reduced into possession by another or are in the process of being so reduced (cf. *Cresswell v DPP* [2006] EWHC 3379 (Admin)), although an escaped creature can be stolen if ordinarily kept in captivity. The poaching of wild animals, birds or fish may be punishable under a number of statutes, including the Night Poaching Act 1828 and the Game Act 1831 (see **B13.91**). The intentional killing or taking of such creatures may also be punishable under the Wildlife and Countryside Act 1981, Part 1.

Other Forms of Property Electricity cannot be stolen (*Low v Blease* [1975] Crim LR 513) but it is an offence to abstract electricity contrary to the Theft Act 1968, s. 13 (see **B4.140** ***et seq.***). **B4.18**

Human bodies are not ordinarily anyone's property, but bodies or body parts are capable of being stolen 'if they have acquired different attributes by virtue of the application of skill, such as dissection or preservation techniques, for exhibition or teaching purposes' (*Kelly* [1999] QB 621 at p. 632, following *Doodeward v Spence* (1907) 6 CLR 406 and *Dobson v North Tyneside Health Authority* [1997] 4 All ER 474). An Egyptian mummy, for example, may be the property of a museum. In *Kelly* the Court of Appeal said, at p. 632:

> It may be that if . . . the question arises, the courts will hold that human body parts are capable of being property for the purposes of the [Theft Act 1968, s. 4], even without the acquisition of different attributes, if they have a use or significance beyond their mere existence. This may be so if, for example, they are intended for use in an organ transplant operation, for the extraction of DNA or, for that matter, as an exhibit in a trial.

As to theft of forensic human tissue samples, see *Welsh* [1974] RTR 478. As to sperm stored by fertility clinics for future use on behalf of the donor, see *Yearworth v North Bristol NHS Trust* [2009] EWCA Civ 37, [2009] 2 All ER 986. The Human Tissue Act 2004, s. 5, creates specific offences in relation to the improper and unauthorised use, storage or removal of human bodies, organs and other tissue. As to embryos etc., see also the Human Fertilisation and Embryology Act 1990, s. 41.

As to unlawfully possessed drugs or other contraband, see *Smith* [2011] EWCA Crim 66, [2011] 1 Cr App R 30 (379) and **B4.20**.

'Belonging to Another'

Theft Act 1968, s. 5 **B4.19**

> (1) Property shall be regarded as belonging to any person having possession or control of it, or having in it any proprietary right or interest (not being an equitable interest arising only from an agreement to transfer or grant an interest).
> (2) Where property is subject to a trust, the persons to whom it belongs shall be regarded as including any person having a right to enforce the trust, and an intention to defeat the trust shall be regarded accordingly as an intention to deprive of the property any person having that right.
> (3) Where a person receives property from or on account of another, and is under an obligation to the other to retain and deal with that property or its proceeds in a particular way, the property or proceeds shall be regarded (as against him) as belonging to the other.
> (4) Where a person gets property by another's mistake, and is under an obligation to make restoration (in whole or in part) of the property or its proceeds or of the value thereof, then to the extent of that obligation the property or proceeds shall be regarded (as against him) as belonging to the person entitled to restoration, and an intention not to make restoration shall be regarded accordingly as an intention to deprive that person of the property or proceeds.
> (5) Property of a corporation sole shall be regarded as belonging to the corporation notwithstanding a vacancy in the corporation.

The identity of the owner is generally irrelevant, provided that someone other than D has a property right or interest in the property in question. In *Sullivan* [2002] Crim LR 758, a trial judge decided that money found on a dead drug dealer did not belong to anyone and could not be stolen. With respect, however, it must have belonged to someone. It may have belonged to the deceased's estate or to the Crown as bona vacantia.

Ownership, Possession or Control Theft is usually perpetrated against the owner of the property, who may or may not also be in possession of it (*Hancock* [1990] 2 QB 242) but can equally be perpetrated against persons with lesser interests, as s. 5(1) makes clear. A person may be in **B4.20**

control of property, even though unaware of its presence, since the general principle is that control of a site by excluding others from it gives prima facie control of articles on the site (*Woodman* [1974] QB 754 at p. 758; *Waverley BC v Fletcher* [1996] QB 334). The 'owner' may even be in possession of the property unlawfully. Property may thus be stolen by one thief from another, and a drug dealer may be the victim of robbery if the dealer's stock is taken by force; the criminal law is concerned with keeping the Queen's peace, not with protecting private property rights (*Smith* [2011] EWCA Crim 66, [2011] 1 Cr App R 30 (379)).

B4.21 If the interest of a person satisfies s. 5(1), the property belongs to that person for the purposes of the Act. In *Turner (No. 2)* [1971] 2 All ER 441, the Court of Appeal held that an owner of property can steal that property from someone else with a sufficient interest, including mere possession through a bailment. On that basis, the Court upheld D's conviction for stealing his own car from V who had been undertaking repairs on it. D had dishonestly removed the car from V's premises during the night, apparently with the intention of evading his duty to pay for the repairs. The trial judge had directed the jury to decide the case without reference to any repairer's lien that V might have had over the car, and the Court therefore had to decide whether the conviction could be upheld even if there had been no such lien. With respect, however, it is hard to see how D's removal of the car could ever have been categorised as dishonest had he not been aware of that lien. But for V's lien, D would have had a legal right to reclaim his car (see s. 2(1)(a)). Contrast *Meredith* [1973] Crim LR 253.

The person to whom the property belongs need not be an individual. A corporation may own property which can be stolen from it, even by persons who are in total control of it by reason of shareholding and directorships (*A-G's Ref (No. 2 of 1982)* [1984] QB 624; *Philippou* (1989) 89 Cr App R 290: see **B4.45**).

Under the Treasure Act 1996, s. 4(1), when treasure is found, it vests, subject to prior interests and rights, in the franchisee (if there is one) and otherwise (and more usually) in the Crown. 'Treasure' is defined in s. 1 of that Act; 'prior interests or rights' is defined in s. 2; and 'franchisee' is defined in s. 5. Property (other than treasure) found buried on land will ordinarily belong to the owner of the land in priority to the finder, even if the public were permitted access to that land (*Waverley BC v Fletcher* [1996] QB 334).

B4.22 **Proprietary Rights or Interests** For the purposes of the Theft Act 1968, property 'belongs' to any person who has any proprietary right or interest in it other than an equitable interest arising only from an agreement to transfer or grant an interest (s. 5(1)). A partner, who has a proprietary interest in partnership property, may steal it, as the co-partners also have such an interest (*Bonner* [1970] 2 All ER 97). In *Marshall* [1998] 2 Cr App R 282, D acquired London Underground tickets and travel cards that had not been fully used up and sold them to other travellers. The Court of Appeal held that the tickets 'belonged to London Underground'. Although the tickets had previously been issued to travellers, London Underground retained a sufficient proprietary right or interest in the tickets for the purposes of s. 5(1).

B4.23 Trust property 'belongs' to the trustee who has legal title to it, but also to 'any person having a right to enforce the trust' (s. 5(2)); that is, any beneficiary or, in the case of a charitable trust, the A-G (Charities Act 1993, s. 33). A trustee who appropriates trust property with the intention of defeating the trust is to be regarded as intending to deprive the person who has the right to enforce the trust of property (s. 5(2)).

However, secret profits which become subject to a constructive trust do not thereby 'belong', for the purposes of the Act, to the person for whose benefit the trust was imposed. In *A-G's Ref (No. 1 of 1985)* [1986] QB 491, D, a publican, sold his own beer in a tied house, keeping the profit for himself. A constructive trust arose in respect of the profits; but the Court of Appeal took the view that s. 5(2) does not result in this profit 'belonging' to the brewery for the purposes of the law of theft. Behaviour which had previously not been considered to be criminal would otherwise have been criminalised and clearer words were needed to make such a major change. There was in any event no identifiable trust property which could form the subject-matter of a theft charge. D's only obligation was to account for the profit being made, until, if ever, that profit was identified as a separate piece of property, which then could provide the basis for a theft charge. See also *Governor of Pentonville Prison, ex parte Tarling* (1978) 70 Cr App R 77. Similarly, a bribe received by an employee does not 'belong' to the employer and the employee does not commit theft by keeping it (*Powell v MacRae* [1977] Crim LR 571).

A-G's Ref (No. 1 of 1985) was distinguished in *Re Holmes* [2004] EWHC 2020 (Admin), [2005] 1 All ER 490 in which it was held that where property is fraudulently obtained from V, the proceeds of that fraud (e.g., funds credited to a bank account) may become subject to a constructive trust in V's favour and will then 'belong' to V for the purposes of s. 5(2).

Equitable Proprietary Interests Where A transfers legal ownership of property to B, but retains an equitable proprietary interest in that property, it may still be said to 'belong' to A for the purposes of s. 5(1) and (2). If B dishonestly appropriates the property (e.g., by disposing of it in a way that prejudices A's interest), B may then be guilty of stealing it from A (*Clowes (No. 2)* [1994] 2 All ER 316; *Wain* [1995] 2 Cr App R 660). It is not strictly necessary to invoke s. 5(3) or (4) in such cases. The latter provisions (which are examined at **B4.27** and **B4.31**) *may* still be used, but are unlikely to offer any real advantages to prosecutors. In *Hallam* [1995] Crim LR 323, the Court of Appeal held that the clients of financial advisers, having paid cheques in the expectation that investments would be made on their behalf, retained an equitable interest in the cheques, their proceeds and any balance in accounts operated by D or the company through which they operated to which the payment could be traced. It was immaterial whether the property belonged to the clients within the meaning of s. 5(1) or whether it was merely deemed to belong to them under s. 5(3). See also *Governor of Brixton Prison, ex parte Levin* [1997] AC 741. **B4.24**

An equitable proprietary interest may also be retained by A where property is got by B on the basis of A's mistake (*Chase Manhattan Bank NA v Israel-British Bank (London) Ltd* [1981] Ch 105). Where this is the case, reliance on s. 5(4) will not strictly be necessary. In *Shadrokh-Cigari* [1988] Crim LR 465, a child's bank account in England was mistakenly credited by an American bank with £286,000 instead of £286. Realising the error, D, her guardian, dishonestly appropriated all but £21,000 of this for his own use. It was held (applying *Chase Manhattan*) that the bank retained an equitable interest in the transferred funds, although the Court of Appeal accepted that an argument based on s. 5(4) would also succeed. *Chase Manhattan* has been criticised in subsequent civil cases (*Re Goldcorp Exchange Ltd* [1995] 1 AC 74; *Westdeutsche Landesbank Girozentrale v Islington London Borough Council* [1996] AC 669), but *Shadrokh-Cigari* was followed in *Webster* [2006] EWCA Crim 2894. In *Webster* D, a soldier, was charged with stealing a medal 'belonging to the Secretary of State' by selling it on the internet. His captain (C) had been issued with two of the medals by mistake, and had passed the duplicate to D. The Court of Appeal held that the Secretary of State 'clearly' retained a proprietary interest in it for the purposes of s. 5(1), and it was not open to C to permit its sale (as D claimed C had done).

Property Must Belong to Another when Appropriated Property cannot be stolen unless it belonged to another at the moment of appropriation. There can be no theft where D decides not to pay for a meal only after eating it (*Corcoran v Whent* [1977] Crim LR 52) or for petrol only after refuelling a car (*Edwards v Ddin* [1976] 1 WLR 942). **B4.25**

This principle can easily give rise to difficulty where intangible property is involved, as *Preddy* [1996] AC 815 demonstrated in the context of dishonestly obtained mortgage loans, although many of the difficulties of the kind that arose in *Preddy* can be avoided where the facts permit a charge of fraud instead (see **B5.4 *et seq.***).

Questions of ownership in relation to property (and the passing of property) are essentially questions of civil law. In *Morris* [1984] AC 320 Lord Roskill opined that difficult questions of whether contracts were void or voidable on the ground of mistake or fraud or whether any mistake is sufficiently fundamental to vitiate a contract should, so far as possible, be confined to those fields of law to which they are immediately relevant and should not be dragged into the law of theft. This view was quoted with approval by Parker LJ in *Dobson v General Accident Fire and Life Assurance Corporation plc* [1990] 1 QB 274 and later approved by Lord Keith in *Gomez* [1993] AC 442. The intricacies of the civil law cannot, however, be ignored where they determine proprietary rights. In *Walker* [1984] Crim LR 112, D sold a video recorder to C who then returned it as faulty. D resold it to E and was charged with stealing it from C. D's defence was that under the law on sale of goods, the customer had rejected the recorder (so that ownership of it had reverted to him). Dunn LJ, giving the judgment of the Court of Appeal, rightly observed that 'a careful direction as to the law relating to the passing of property and rejection of goods under the provisions of the Sale of Goods Act was plainly required' and that on this issue 'there is no distinction between the civil law and the criminal law'. See also *Wheeler* (1991) 92 Cr App R 279; *Davies v Leighton* (1978) 68 Cr App R 4.

An example of the difficulties which may be created by failure to pay due regard to the civil law is presented by *Hinks* [2001] 2 AC 241 (see **B4.39**) in which the House of Lords contrived to hold that a person who acquires an indefeasible title to property under the civil law may still, if considered dishonest, be convicted of thereby stealing that property. On the facts of *Hinks*, D's title to the property might perhaps have been challenged on the basis of undue influence, but that was not the basis for the ruling.

B4.26 **Abandoned Goods** Where property has been abandoned by A, it cannot be stolen from A (*Small* (1988) 86 Cr App R 170; *White* (1912) 7 Cr App R 266; *Ellerman's Wilson Line Ltd v Webster* [1952] 1 Lloyd's Rep 179). But A does not abandon property by leaving it outside a charity shop, or in a collection bag outside the front door, with a view in either case to it being collected on behalf of the charity (*R (Ricketts) v Basildon Magistrates' Court* [2011] EWHC 2358 (Admin), [2011] 1 Cr App R 15 (202); *Toleikis* [2013] EWCA Crim 600) or by setting it aside for disposal or destruction by B. Abandonment suggests that A has no further interest in what may become of it or who may then appropriate it. If, for example, A puts some unwanted property in a bag labelled 'confidential waste for incineration' and some in a box labelled, 'help yourselves', A may have abandoned the latter, but not the former; and if B has been tasked with disposal or destruction, B may now have rights over the former property (cf. *Williams v Phillips* (1957) 41 Cr App R 5). D's mistaken belief that A has abandoned the property, or D's failure to appreciate that B has already acquired rights to property that A has abandoned, may however mean that D lacks the requisite *mens rea* for theft (*Small* (1988) 86 Cr App R 170; *White* (1912) 7 Cr App R 266; *Ellerman's Wilson Line Ltd v Webster* [1952] 1 Lloyd's Rep 179).

Property is not abandoned merely because it has been lost (*Hibbert v McKiernan* [1948] 2 KB 142) or because the owner is not currently able to recover it. Thus, golf balls lying at the bottom of a lake within a golf club may still belong to the club, even if it has no immediate plans to dredge the lake for them (*Rostron* [2003] EWCA Crim 2206).

B4.27 **Obligation to Retain and Deal with Property or Proceeds** Section 5(3) (see **B4.19**) provides that property received by D from or on account of V shall be 'regarded' (as against D) as belonging to V if D has an obligation to deal with it or its proceeds in a particular way. What this means, in practice, is that D may be found to have stolen such property by (for example) disposing of it (or its proceeds) in such a way as to deprive V of V's entitlement, and this may be the case whether or not V actually has any legal or equitable interest in that property such as would make V an owner of it for the purposes of s. 5(1) or (2). It is thus a 'deeming' provision so that, where D is under the specified obligation, the property may for the purposes of the law of theft be treated as if it belonged at least partly to V. In *Adams* [2003] EWCA Crim 3620, for example, s. 5(3) was applied to ensure that cheques made payable to D and belonging only to D nevertheless could be regarded as property belonging to V because their creation was a part of a process whereby D managed an investment account on V's behalf.

The obligation in s. 5(3) must be a legal one. A moral or social obligation is not sufficient (*Hall* [1973] QB 126; *Wakeman v Farrar* [1974] Crim LR 136). But D need not have been under any obligation to retain or hand over the particular monies or property received: it may suffice that D is obliged to set aside and hand over an equivalent sum (*Wain* [1995] 2 Cr App R 660).

In *Hall*, D, a travel agent, received money from customers as deposits and payments for flights which were never provided. The business became insolvent and none of the money was refunded. But in the absence of special contractual arrangements to the contrary (of which there was no evidence) D's only obligation was as a debtor to the customers; he was not obliged to retain and deal with the deposits in any particular way, but was entitled to pay the proceeds into his general trading account. By failing to provide the tickets he was in breach of contract, but nothing more.

Whether an agent is obliged to keep the principal's money or property separate from the agent's own or whether the relationship is merely that of creditor and debtor will depend upon their intentions and on the type of transaction involved. Had the travel agent in *Hall* been a solicitor who received deposits from purchasers in connection with property transactions, the position would clearly have been different. *Hall* was similarly distinguished in *Hallam* [1995] Crim LR 323.

It is necessary to identify the person to whom the obligation is owed. If the only such person is V, an indictment charging D with theft from X will be defective (*Dyke* [2001] EWCA Crim 2184, [2002] 1 Cr App R 30 (404)). An obligation under s. 5(3) will normally arise where a person receives money for onward transmission to a charity (e.g., from donors or sponsors), either because the charity imposes such an obligation as a condition of involvement or because the sponsors impose such an obligation, at least implicitly, in handing over their money (*Wain* [1995] 2 Cr App R 660). In *Dyke* it was held that the 'collector of money from the public receives that money subject to the charitable trust and shall treat the money as belonging to the beneficiaries of that charity'; there is in other words an obligation within the meaning of s. 5(3), but it is owed to the charity and its beneficiaries and not to the donors who contributed the money in question. On the other hand, it would be no defence to a charge brought under s. 5(3) in such a case that liability would in any event arise under s. 5(1) or (2). **B4.28**

In *Klineberg* [1999] 1 Cr App R 427 the allegation was that money was stolen from intending purchasers of timeshares rather than from the company established to sell the timeshares. This meant that the necessary obligation had to be established with regard to each of the intending purchasers. This could be established on the facts (taking particular account of the element of the scheme whereby investors' money would be safeguarded by a trusteeship pending completion of the purchase) and, since it was established that the money had not been used properly, theft convictions were upheld.

It is not sufficient that a duty to account arises (*Powell v MacRae* [1977] Crim LR 571). Section 5(3) does not therefore apply to the secret profit scenario illustrated by *A-G's Ref (No. 1 of 1985)* [1986] QB 491 (see **B4.23**). As Lord Lane CJ explained in that case: **B4.29**

> [D] received the money on his own account as a result of his private venture. No doubt... he is under an obligation to account to the employers at least for the profit he has made out of his venture, but that is a different matter. The fact that A may have to account to B for money he has received from X does not mean necessarily that he received the money on account of B.

Since D's obligation must be a legal one, one might suppose that it must also be legally enforceable. Two cases cause problems with regard to this requirement and must each be regarded as questionable on that basis. In *Cullen* (1974 unreported) V gave D, his partner, £20 to buy food and pay certain domestic debts, but she spent it on herself. Parties to domestic housekeeping arrangements do not ordinarily intend to create legally enforceable obligations (*Balfour v Balfour* [1919] 2 KB 571) and yet the court ruled that D's obligation to deal with the money as V directed did not cease to be a legal obligation simply because she was his mistress. She was guilty of theft by virtue of s. 5(3). The other problem case is *Meech* [1974] QB 549, where V fraudulently obtained a cheque from a finance company and D undertook to cash it for him. Having discovered V's fraud, D then arranged for some accomplices to stage a fake robbery in which the proceeds of the cheque (withdrawn by D from his own account) were supposedly taken. Because of his own fraud, V could not have enforced D's undertaking to pay him the proceeds, but D was nevertheless convicted on the basis of s. 5(3).

B4.30 The courts have made clear that whether an obligation sufficient to satisfy s. 5(3) arises depends upon the particular facts of the case (*Hall* [1973] QB 126; *McHugh* (1993) 97 Cr App R 335). The functions of judge and jury were described in *Mainwaring* (1981) 74 Cr App R 99 at p. 107 in a passage later approved in *Dubar* [1994] 1 All ER 781 and *Breaks* [1998] Crim LR 349):

> Whether or not an obligation arises is a matter of law, because an obligation must be a legal obligation. But a legal obligation arises only in certain circumstances, and in many cases the circumstances cannot be known until the facts have been established. It is for the jury, not the judge, to establish the facts, if they are in dispute.
>
> What, in our judgment, a judge ought to do is this: if the facts relied upon by the prosecution are in dispute he should direct the jury to make their findings on the facts, and then say to them: 'If you find the facts to be such-and-such, then I direct you as a matter of law that a legal obligation arose to which section 5(3) applies'.

If however the facts are not in dispute, it may be appropriate for the judge to direct the jury that an obligation had been undertaken by the person receiving the property.

Liability under s. 5(3) can be established only by proof that D had direct knowledge of the relevant obligation. Knowledge of an agent cannot be imputed to the principal for the purposes of the criminal law, whatever may be the position in civil law (*Wills* (1991) 92 Cr App R 297) and in any event, D's dishonesty must be almost impossible to establish without proof of such knowledge.

B4.31 **Obligation to Make Restoration of Property** Section 5(4) deals with the case where ownership in property is passed by mistake to another who is under an obligation to return the property or its proceeds. The property is regarded, as against the recipient, as belonging to the person entitled to restoration.

As the Court of Appeal recognised in *Gilks* [1972] 3 All ER 280, s. 5(4) was enacted to deal with the mischief of the decision in *Moynes v Cooper* [1956] 1 QB 439, in which D was overpaid in his weekly wages, having received an advance payment which was not then deducted from his pay packet at the end of the week. D committed no offence under the Larceny Act 1916 by keeping this money because, *inter alia*, he was held to be the only person with a legal interest in it. Section 5(4) would now apply to such a case: D clearly 'got' property in the form of coins and notes, and this would be deemed (as against him) to belong to his employer.

In *A-G's Ref (No. 1 of 1983)* [1985] QB 182, s. 5(4) was applied to intangible property. A policewoman was mistakenly credited with wages and overtime for a day which she had not worked. Her bank account was credited by credit transfer with £74.74. The Court of Appeal was satisfied that she had got property, since she had acquired a thing in action against her bank. This is clearly a form of property (see **B4.16**). See also *Stalham* [1993] Crim LR 310.

Not only does 'property' have a wide meaning, but so also does the word 'got'. It is about as wide a word as could possibly have been adopted (*A-G's Ref (No. 1 of 1983)*). Consequently, it would not only cover the handing over of coins and notes as in *Moynes v Cooper*, but also the crediting of a bank account by credit transfer.

Section 5(4) applies only where some error has been made by the giver of the property which amounts to a mistake. In *Moynes v Cooper* the mistake was the error of the wages clerk in believing that M was entitled to his full wages, whereas he should have deducted the money received in advance. In *A-G's Ref (No. 1 of 1983)* the mistake was the belief that the policewoman had worked on a particular day and was entitled to wages and overtime, when in fact she had not so worked.

Section 5(4) does not apply unless the obligation to make restoration is a legal obligation (*Gilks* [1972] 1 WLR 1341). In *Gilks* D placed a bet on a horse called Flying Scot. The race was won by Flying Taff. The relief manager paid out to D as if D had backed the winning horse and so D was overpaid by £106.63. D knew that a mistake had been made, but decided to keep the money. The Court of Appeal held that D did not owe a legal obligation to return the money because the bookmaker could not have sued on a gaming transaction (*Morgan v Ashcroft* [1938] 1 KB 490). Nor did s. 5(4) apply to D's moral or social obligation to return the money. **B4.32**

In *A-G's Ref (No. 1 of 1983)* [1985] QB 182 the Court of Appeal decided that 'restoration' has the same meaning as 'restitution'. Consequently, it has to be established that the recipient of the property is under an obligation within the general principles of restitution. The Court went on to say that a recipient of property is obliged to pay for a benefit received when it has been given under a mistake on the part of the giver about a material fact. The mistake has to be about a fundamental or essential fact and the payment must have been induced by the mistaken fact (*Norwich Union Fire Insurance Society Ltd v Wm H Price Ltd* [1934] AC 455). Consequently, not everyone who receives property under a mistake sufficient to satisfy the first element of s. 5(4) will, as a result of that mistake, be under an obligation to make restoration. **B4.33**

In *Davis* (1988) 88 Cr App R 347 the Court of Appeal indicated that the 'language of quasi-contract and of other parts of the civil law' are 'unwelcome visitors to a statute which is supposed to furnish lay juries with tests which they can readily grasp and apply'. It is submitted that the solution must be not a refusal to make use of the law of quasi-contract or restitution, but rather that care should be taken in directions given to juries such that the jury are clear that if they find certain facts then an obligation to restore has been established. This approach is consistent with that to be used when directing juries with regard to s. 5(3) as laid down in *Mainwaring* (1981) 74 Cr App R 99 (see **B4.30**).

'Appropriation'

Theft Act 1968, s. 3 **B4.34**

(1) Any assumption by a person of the rights of an owner amounts to an appropriation, and this includes, where he has come by the property (innocently or not) without stealing it, any later assumption of a right to it by keeping or dealing with it as owner.

(2) Where property or a right or interest in property is or purports to be transferred for value to a person acting in good faith, no later assumption by him of rights which he believed himself to be acquiring shall, by reason of any defect in the transferor's title, amount to theft of the property.

The meaning of 'appropriation' has been considered in four House of Lords cases (*Lawrence v Metropolitan Police Commissioner* [1972] AC 626; *Morris* [1984] AC 320; *Gomez* [1993] AC 442; *Hinks* [2001] 2 AC 24) as well as by numerous decisions of the Court of Appeal. Most commentators are highly critical of these House of Lords cases, which have distorted the concept of appropriation by giving it a much wider meaning than that which was intended by Parliament. But we are obliged to live with these decisions. We must accordingly accept that an appropriation of property belonging to another (which if committed with dishonest intent, etc., will amount to theft) may be committed:

- whether or not the act is unlawful as a matter of civil law (there need be no misappropriation);
- with or without the consent or authority of the owner;
- by the assumption of any one right of ownership or of all;
- with or without any physical taking or obtaining; and even
- by receipt of a valid gift from the lawful owner.

In many everyday instances, the only difference between lawful appropriation and theft will be the presence or absence of dishonesty.

Section 3(1) itself provides that D may appropriate (and steal) property belonging to another even where D has already 'come by' that property without stealing it, but the courts have decided that D cannot be guilty of repeated thefts of property that D has already stolen, even if the original stealing was committed abroad and beyond the reach of English criminal law (see *Atakpu* [1994] QB 69 at **B4.42**). But D may be guilty of theft from V by dishonestly receiving or dealing with property originally stolen by E. The fact that D may more obviously be guilty of handling stolen goods does not mean D cannot also be guilty of theft (see **B4.42**).

B4.35 **The Mental Element in Appropriation** In *Gomez*, Lord Browne-Wilkinson said (at p. 495) that appropriation is an 'objective description of the act done irrespective of the mental state of either the owner or the accused'; but (with respect) an appropriation must involve some kind of mental element, sometimes referred to as *'animus appropriendi'*. If D picks up a shopping bag, D does not thereby appropriate property that E has placed in the bag without D's knowledge. D cannot be said to assume rights of ownership over property of which D knows nothing.

If it can be proved that D acted dishonestly and with intent permanently to deprive V, proof of D's intention to appropriate is unlikely to be an issue. But, as explained at **B4.36**, it is possible for D to be charged with appropriating V's property by one act, with the intention of depriving V by some subsequent act, which may or may not have taken place as intended. The prosecution might conceivably find itself able to prove D's ulterior intent, but not that D performed any act with the requisite *'animus appropriendi'* and in such a case there can be no conviction for theft.

It is also possible for D to appropriate property already in D's possession or control by 'keeping or dealing with it as owner', and there can surely be no question of an 'appropriation by keeping' in this context unless the keeping is accompanied by intent.

B4.36 **Assumption of Just One of the Rights of an Owner** In *Gomez* [1993] AC 442 the House of Lords held, approving *Morris* [1984] AC 320 on this point, that it is sufficient for the prosecution to prove the assumption by D of any one of the rights of the owner. It followed that 'the removal of an article from the shelf [of a supermarket] and the changing of the price label on it constituted an assumption of one of the rights of the owner and hence an appropriation'. Lord Keith stated in *Gomez* that 'the switching of price labels on the article is in itself an assumption of one of the rights of the owner, whether or not it is accompanied by some other act such as removing the article from the shelf and placing it in a basket or trolley' because 'no one but the owner has the right to remove a price label from an article or to place a price label upon it'.

With respect, s. 3(1) expressly refers to an assumption of the owner's rights (plural), and it is hard to see how interference with just one of the owner's rights can be equated with an assumption of ownership generally. In the label switching scenario, D replaces one of V's labels with another and then offers to buy the item from V at the lower price. This may be dishonest, but is hardly consistent with an assumption of ownership, and is not even the means by which D intends to deprive V of the item in question (but see **B4.10**).

B4.37 **Consent or Authority of Owner** The House of Lords in *Gomez* [1993] AC 442 (following *Lawrence v Metropolitan Police Commissioner* [1972] AC 626 rather than *Morris* [1984] AC 320 on this point) held that an appropriation of property (even one amounting to theft) can be committed by an act that has the consent of the owner. In *Lawrence* the House rejected an argument that s. 1(1) must be construed as though it contained the words, 'without the consent of the owner'. Viscount Dilhorne said (at pp. 631–2):

> I see no ground for concluding that the omission of the words 'without the consent of the owner' was inadvertent and not deliberate, and to read the subsection as if they were included is, in my opinion, wholly unwarranted. Parliament by the omission of these words has relieved the prosecution

of the burden of establishing that the taking was without the owner's consent. That is no longer an ingredient of the offence.

In *Lawrence* D was a taxi-driver who picked up V, who spoke little English, at an airport. The proper fare for the journey was less than £1. V offered D £1, but D said it was not enough. V then offered his wallet, and D took from it another £6. As the House of Lords acknowledged, it was far from clear on these facts that V's lack of resistance amounted to consent, but consent was not in doubt in *Gomez*, where D, an assistant manager of an electrical shop, obtained the consent or authorisation of the manager for goods to be delivered to D's accomplices against two building society cheques which D knew to be worthless. D's conviction for theft was upheld. The obvious charge on those facts was one of obtaining (or enabling others to obtain) property by deception, contrary to the Theft Act 1968, s. 15. In respect of things done on or after 15 January 2007, the obvious charge would now be one of fraud (see **B5.1**). But in *Gomez* only Lord Lowry (dissenting) was prepared to consider the Eighth Report of the Criminal Law Revision Committee (1966) Cmnd. 2977, which clearly showed that a fraud of that kind was not meant to be included within the concept of theft.

The majority in *Gomez* held (at p. 460) that no 'sensible distinction can be made in this context between consent and authorisation' and they approved both *Lawrence* and *Dobson v General Accident Fire and Life Assurance Corporation plc* [1990] 1 QB 274. Contrary dicta in *Morris* were rejected as erroneous and decisions of the Court of Appeal in *Skipp* [1975] Crim LR 114 and *Fritschy* [1985] Crim LR 745 were overruled. In *Fritschy* D had been contracted to collect gold coins in London and deliver them to a bank in Switzerland. He collected them as instructed, but appears to have acted all along with the dishonest intention of disposing of them elsewhere. The question was whether he appropriated (and stole) the coins (a) as soon as he collected them, or (b) only when he acted on his plan and took them to Italy instead of Switzerland. The Court of Appeal's answer was (b), according to which D committed no offence in England (see **A8.2**), but in *Gomez* the correct answer was said to have been (a). D accordingly stole the coins as soon as he collected them — even though he had not at that stage done anything other than what he had been hired to do. The problem with this approach is that it can reduce theft to little more than a thought crime. An objectively innocent act may become theft because of a dishonest intent that D has not yet put into operation. In *Fritschy* D would on that basis have stolen the coins on collection even if he later changed his mind and delivered them as contracted to the Swiss bank. **B4.38**

Several other cases require reconsideration following *Gomez*. These include *Meech* [1974] QB 549, *Hircock* (1978) 67 Cr App R 278, *Eddy v Niman* (1981) 73 Cr App R 237, and *McPherson* [1973] Crim LR 191.

Appropriation and the Civil Law *Hinks* [2001] 2 AC 241 is the hardest to defend of the House of Lords theft cases. It was held that D may be guilty of theft by receiving a valid and indefeasible gift of property from V, provided that D acted dishonestly in receiving it. The House rejected an argument, deriving from *Mazo* [1997] 2 Cr App R 518, that a distinction should be drawn between cases (such as *Gomez* [1993] AC 442) in which V's consent was obtained by fraud or deception and cases in which that consent was untainted by such factors. Consent obtained by deception may be voidable and it would not necessarily create a conflict with the civil law if D were to be held guilty of theft in such a case. The same might be said of cases in which V's gift is procured by the exercise of undue influence, but although there was some evidence of that in *Hinks* (where V, a naïve and vulnerable man, was persuaded by D, his carer, to give her £60,000 from his savings account), the basis of the decision was that D could be convicted if the jury considered her to have acted dishonestly in accepting the gift — regardless of its legal validity. **B4.39**

Despite *Hinks*, it seems that the recipient of a legally valid and binding gift can rarely be categorised as guilty of theft because D will seldom be dishonest within the meaning of the Theft Act 1968, s. 2(1) (see **B4.51**), even if properly described as greedy and unscrupulous. Even if dishonesty can be proved, it remains necessary to prove that the property in question was appropriated when it still 'belonged to another'. That other person would not necessarily have to be the donor and it might belong to that person only in one of the extended senses provided for by s. 5 (see **B4.20**) but D cannot commit theft by appropriating property that has already become entirely D's own (*Briggs* [2003] EWCA Crim 3662, [2004] 1 Cr App R 34 (451)).

Hinks is not concerned only with gifts. The question posed for consideration by the House of Lords in that case (and answered in the affirmative) was 'whether the acquisition of an indefeasible title to property is capable of amounting to an appropriation of property belonging to another for the purposes of s. 1(1)'. It may now be possible, following *Hinks*, for an allegation of theft to be made where D acts unscrupulously in receiving payment or other consideration under a valid contractual agreement. D may perhaps be able to escape conviction on such facts by claiming that the conduct is not dishonest under s. 2(1)(a), but D cannot simply rely on the fact that a valid legal title to the object in question was acquired. To that extent, *Hinks* again puts the criminal law potentially at odds with the civil.

B4.40 **Appropriation of Property Previously Acquired, but Not Stolen** D may appropriate or otherwise 'come by' property belonging to V without initially stealing it. D may do so by means of an unlawful appropriation (e.g., by taking it without V's consent) or lawfully (e.g., by borrowing it *with* V's consent) but in either case any later assumption of a right to it by keeping it or dealing with it as owner will amount to an appropriation (s. 3(1)); and if committed with the requisite *mens rea*, such appropriation may constitute theft.

For this rule to operate, D must originally have 'come by the property...without stealing it'. The rule does not address the problem of successive appropriations of property that has already been stolen; but see on this **B4.42**.

In order to have appropriated property of which D already has possession, D must 'keep or deal with it as owner'. There may be little difficulty in determining that D has 'dealt with' borrowed property as owner if D attempts to sell it as his or her own. However, it may not be so easy to establish that D has merely kept property as owner (see e.g., *Broom v Crowther* (1984) 148 JP 592).

B4.41 **Appropriation by Purchaser in Good Faith of Stolen Goods** Ordinarily a person who has previously gained possession of property appropriates (and potentially steals) that property if that person then keeps or deals with it as owner (s. 3(1); see **B4.40**). However, s. 3(2) (see **B4.34**) provides an exception in cases where D acquired the property in good faith and for value.

A typical example would be where D innocently purchases a used car only to discover later that it is a stolen vehicle. D commits no theft in this scenario merely by retaining the car after discovering the truth. But s. 3(2) does not prevent the stolen property from being reclaimed, nor does it mean that D would act lawfully in attempting to sell it on to E. Such an act could not amount to theft of the property, and nor would it amount to an offence of handling stolen goods (see *Bloxham* [1983] 1 AC 109, and **B4.174**) but it would almost inevitably involve fraud, unless D has warned E of the defective title.

As regards the words 'rights which he believed himself to be acquiring', the relevant time at which D's belief must be held is the moment when D purchased for value (*Adams* [1993] Crim LR 72).

B4.42 **Property Stolen Abroad and Brought into England** The Theft Acts apply to England and Wales but ordinarily have no application to things done abroad (or even in other parts of the UK). For exceptions to this rule see generally **A8**. Unless some such exception applies, an act abroad that amounts to theft or stealing under local law is not therefore an offence of theft under English law.

If property stolen abroad is then brought into England, it ordinarily remains the property of the original owner, but it was held in *Atakpu* [1994] QB 69 that it cannot be stolen again by the original thief or thieves. Anyone else who dishonestly receives or otherwise handles that property may, however, be guilty of handling (see **B4.159**) or indeed of theft, because a dishonest receiver of stolen goods will ordinarily appropriate them with the requisite *mens rea* for theft (see *Stapylton v O'Callaghan* [1973] 2 All ER 782 and **B4.176**). The original thief cannot be guilty of theft or handling, but may now be guilty of offences under the POCA 2002, Part 7 (see **B21**).

There may sometimes be room for argument as to whether D stole V's property in England or abroad. In *Ascroft* [2003] EWCA Crim 2365, [2004] 1 Cr App R (S) 56 (326), D, who ran a road haulage firm, challenged a confiscation order imposed following his conviction for conspiracy to steal goods from shipping containers carried on his lorries. The prosecution proved that sealed containers were regularly opened by his accomplices, without breaking the seals, and that parts of each consignment (typically cases of spirits) were then removed before the containers were closed up again. This appears to have occurred in each case at or near the company's depot in England. Counsel for D nevertheless argued that in 17 of the 25 acts of theft to which this count of conspiracy related the goods in question had already been stolen even before the containers were opened—when the sealed containers were first loaded onto D's lorries in Scotland.

The Court of Appeal acknowledged that a charge of conspiracy to steal under English law cannot be based on an agreement to steal goods in Scotland. The question, therefore, was whether the contents of the containers in question were dishonestly appropriated (i.e. stolen) when first collected in Scotland, or whether the appropriation occurred in England, when the containers were improperly opened and the selected goods removed. The Court of Appeal preferred the latter view. Scott Baker LJ said (at [43]–[45]): **B4.43**

> We do not believe that *Gomez* was ever intended to apply to the sort of situation that obtains in this case. The reality seems to us to be that there was a conspiracy to steal goods being conveyed in the appellant's company's lorries as and when appropriate opportunities occurred, with the actual operation to achieve their removal from the lorries (which, we would add, requires some effort and subtlety) taking place at or near the appellant's premises. If the appellant's argument is correct, the theft involves not only those goods that the conspirators subsequently stole but also those that they left in the lorry.
>
> . . . In our judgment there never was in any ordinary sense of the word an appropriation of the stolen goods until the conspirators removed them from the containers.

The Court of Appeal's view of appropriation in *Ascroft* is a sensible and realistic one, but with respect it is not entirely easy to reconcile with the overruling of *Fritschy* [1985] Crim LR 745 in *Gomez* [1993] AC 442. The only significant difference is that the thieves in *Ascroft* needed to separate the goods they were taking from the rest of the consignment.

Appropriation as a Continuing or Ongoing Act In *Atakpu* [1994] QB 69, the Court of Appeal recognised (*obiter*) that appropriation might sometimes take the form of a continuous or ongoing course of action. It would thus be open to a jury to find, in a given case, that the appropriation (or act of theft) was ongoing for as long as the thief (or robber, burglar etc.) could properly be regarded as 'on the job'. This possibility is more directly supported by *Hale* (1978) 68 Cr App R 415, *Gregory* (1981) 77 Cr App R 41 and *Lockley* [1995] Crim LR 656 and is particularly relevant in cases of alleged robbery where force is used only after the initial act of appropriation. **B4.44**

In *Hale*, the Court of Appeal held that 'it is a matter for the jury to decide whether or not the act of appropriation has finished'. It was open to the jury in that case to decide that D's theft of a jewellery box did not finish with the initial seizure, even though the offence was complete by that point. The jury was entitled to find that the offence was ongoing as D attempted to make his getaway from the house. Force used or threatened by D in order to facilitate that getaway could then turn the theft into robbery.

B4.45 **Appropriation of Company Property by Directors** A corporation, such as a registered company, has legal personality and may own property in its own right. Directors, managers and other officers may exercise control over the company and its property, and consent on its behalf to things being done to it, but if they dishonestly appropriate its property they may thereby commit theft. This remains possible even where the directors concerned are also the sole mangers of the company's affairs and/or the sole owners of its shares. As Lord Browne-Wilkinson explained in *Gomez* [1993] AC 442 (at p. 496), the presence of absence of consent in such a case is not decisive, and is irrelevant to the question whether there has been an appropriation:

> Whether or not those controlling the company consented or purported to consent to the abstraction of the company's property by the accused, he will have appropriated the property of the company. The question will be whether the other necessary elements are present, viz. was such appropriation dishonest and was it done with the intention of permanently depriving the company of such property?

Lord Browne-Wilkinson approved *A-G's Ref (No. 2 of 1982)* [1984] QB 624 and *Philippou* (1989) 89 Cr App R 290. See also *R (A) v Snaresbrook Crown Court* [2001] EWHC Admin 456.

B4.46 **Appropriation without Real Loss to V** Since an appropriation may occur even though not all the rights of an owner are assumed, it follows that the owner need not necessarily lose the property, even for a moment. In *Chan Man-sin v The Queen* [1988] 1 All ER 1, D, an accountant, forged company cheques to his own benefit. The company lost nothing, since it was always entitled to have the initial debit to its account reversed, but it was held that D had appropriated the company's credit balance. An intention permanently to deprive is ordinarily required before an appropriation can amount to theft, but since D intended to dispose of the credit balance regardless of the company's rights (see **B4.58**) this requirement was deemed to be satisfied and D's conviction for theft was upheld. See also *Wille* (1989) 86 Cr App R 296, where Woolf LJ said (at p. 302):

> When what the appellant did in this case is considered, it is hard to see what more he could do to assume the rights of the owner in respect of the account at Barclays Bank to the extent of the amount for which the cheques were drawn, than to draw a cheque, issue the cheque, and then take steps which were designed to achieve that the account of the company at the bank was debited with the amount of the cheque... The fact that the company may still have rights against the bank for the amounts of those cheques is... irrelevant to the issues with which the jury were concerned.

In both *Wille* and *Chan Man-sin v The Queen*, the cheques were honoured by the banks, but D might in each case have been guilty even if the cheques had not been honoured (*Wheatley v Commissioner of Police of the British Virgin Islands* [2006] UKPC 24, [2006] 1 WLR 1683).

A complete offence of theft may be committed by an act that D would regard as a failed attempt. In *Corcoran v Anderton* (1980) 71 Cr App R 104, for example, D tugged at V's handbag, causing her to drop it, but never obtained control over the bag and escaped empty-handed. This was a sufficient appropriation to make D guilty of robbery. He would indeed have committed that offence, even if V never released her hold on the bag.

B4.47 **Appropriation by Destruction** V's property can be appropriated by D even though D never attempts to make use of or profit from that property. Dishonestly causing the destruction of such property can itself be theft (*Kohn* (1979) 69 Cr App R 395). This was confirmed in *Graham* [1997] 1 Cr App R 302, where Lord Bingham CJ said:

> We wish to make it clear that nothing we said was intended to cast doubt upon the principle that theft of a chose in action may be committed when a chose in action belonging to another is destroyed by the defendant's act of appropriation as defined by section 3(1) of the Act.

This does not make theft an appropriate charge where D merely smashes V's car window by throwing a brick though it. Criminal damage would be the only appropriate charge on such facts. But a charge of theft might be a reasonable option where D takes and ignites V's fireworks, thereby destroying them. Theft might indeed be seen as a more appropriate charge on those facts than one of arson.

Cheques, Credit Balances and Money Transfers Where an alleged theft involves a thing in action such as the credit balance in V's bank account, or the right to payment on a cheque, it can sometimes be particularly difficult to identify the crucial act of appropriation, even where it seems clear that D has been dishonestly enriched at V's expense. **B4.48**

In most such cases, the prosecution would be well advised to use charges other than theft: advice which the Court of Appeal endorsed in *Darroux* [2018] EWCA Crim 1009, [2019] QB 33. Alternative charges to consider might (depending on the facts) include fraud, forgery or using a false instrument. But if for some reason a charge of theft is brought, the following principles may require consideration.

Where V is deceived into drawing a cheque in favour of D, as payee, D thereby acquires a thing in action (the payee's right to enforce the cheque) but this thing in action is created for D and has never belonged to anyone else, so D cannot steal it (*Preddy* [1996] AC 815; *Graham* [1997] 1 Cr App R 302; and see also *Darroux*, at [37]). Nor can D steal funds that are credited to D's account under a bank transfer, because here again the thing in action is property that has only ever belonged to D.

A solution of sorts was adopted in *Williams* [2001] 1 Cr App R 23 (362). D dishonestly tricked elderly customers into overpaying him by cheque for building services supposedly rendered. He was convicted of theft: not theft of the cheques themselves, nor theft of the moneys which were credited to his account, but theft of the credit balances in the bank accounts of his victims. By causing the cheques to be paid and credited to his own account he was held to have 'appropriated' their property by reducing the sizes of their bank balances. It made no difference that this appropriation took place with their consent, as long as his conduct could be described as dishonest. Once he 'banked' the cheques they would be collected and paid more or less automatically and any human involvement in that process would be the acts of innocent agents. As to the precise moment at which theft would be committed in such a case, see *Governor of Pentonville Prison, ex parte Osman* [1990] 3 All ER 701 and *Ngan* [1998] 1 Cr App R 331 (discussed in *Smith's Law of Theft* (9th edn, 2007) at paras. 2.80 *et seq.*). **B4.49**

In *Naviede* [1997] Crim LR 662, however, the Court rejected the argument that D could appropriate property in V's account by deceiving V or V's agent into consciously making a transfer or withdrawal from that account:

> We are not satisfied that a misrepresentation which persuades the account holder to direct payment out of his account is an assumption of the rights of the account holder as owner such as to amount to an appropriation of his rights within section 3(1) of the 1968 Act.

The decisions in these cases were accepted as correct in *Darroux* [2018] EWCA Crim 1009, [2019] QB 33, as was the decision, if not the whole of the reasoning, in *Briggs* [2003] EWCA Crim 3662, [2004] 1 Cr App R 34 (451), where D deceived elderly relatives into authorising a transfer of £49,500 from the proceeds of their house sale into a bank account controlled by her. It was held, as in *Naviede*, that the transfer was not an act of appropriation by D, even though her dishonest intent was not in doubt. In *Darroux* itself, D, the manager of a housing association, was accused of defrauding that association of nearly £50,000 by submitting falsely inflated overtime/on-call claims and claims in lieu of holiday entitlement, which the association's agents had paid by bank transfer into her account. This, said the Court of Appeal, was a paradigm case of fraud; but the charge, unfortunately, was theft. The Court could find no appropriation by D of property belonging to another. Those who made the payments were **B4.50** not the agents of D, but her dupes. The case was analogous to *Naviede* or *Briggs*, rather than *Williams*. D's conviction had to be quashed.

Where D draws a cheque on V's account for an improper purpose, or forges V's cheque or purports to issue instructions to V's bank, an appropriation may be relatively easy to identify, because such acts involve misuse by D of the 'key' to V's account. See, e.g., *Hilton* [1997] 2 Cr App R 445, in which D, the chairman of a charity, abused his position by instructing the bank (in two cases by fax and in another by cheque) to make payments from the charity's account which were used to settle his personal debts. D's conviction for theft was upheld.

Davis LJ, giving the judgment of the Court in *Darroux*, added two observations (at [64]), neither of which need cause any concern if the misuse of theft charges in such cases is avoided:

> (1) While the above cited statement in *Naviede*, as restated in *Briggs*, may in general terms frequently represent the correct position, . . . we do not think that such statement should be taken as an inflexible statement of principle of invariable application. . . . There may be cases where a deceptive representation inducing an account holder to make payment out of his bank account could constitute an appropriation (within the meaning of the 1968 Act). It would depend on the circumstances.
>
> (2) It has been suggested, most notably by Professor Sir John Smith [[1997] Crim LR 662, at p. 666], that cases where a cheque is dishonestly obtained and presented are different from cases where payment out of an account is procured in circumstances where the bank uses electronic or automated means. In common with the court in *Hilton*, we have some difficulty with that. It is at all events hard to see how or why . . . the latter scenario may give rise to a break in the chain of causation but the former not. That said, . . . we do not regard the causative impact of a deception as of itself determinative of whether there has been an appropriation by a defendant with regard to a bank account in any particular case.

'Dishonesty'

B4.51 Dishonesty is not fully defined in the Theft Act 1968. In theft cases (and thus also in prosecutions for offences such as robbery that involve theft) a partial definition can, however, be found in s. 2 of the Act, and this is supplement by judicial definition, as to which see **B4.54** *et seq*.

Theft Act 1968, s. 2

(1) A person's appropriation of property belonging to another is not to be regarded as dishonest—
  (a) if he appropriates the property in the belief that he has in law the right to deprive the other of it, on behalf of himself or a third person; or
  (b) if he appropriates the property in the belief that he would have the other's consent if the other knew of the appropriation and the circumstances of it; or
  (c) (except where the property came to him as trustee or personal representative) if he appropriates the property in the belief that the person to whom the property belongs cannot be discovered by taking reasonable steps.

(2) A person's appropriation of property belonging to another may be dishonest notwithstanding that he is willing to pay for the property.

Where D has acted with any of the three states of mind listed in s. 2(1), D's actions cannot be considered dishonest, but the converse is not true. In other words, it does not follow that D's conduct *must* be considered dishonest just because it falls outwith any of the s. 2(1) categories. The test to be applied in cases where dishonesty is in issue and s. 2(1) does not provide the answer is examined at **B4.54**, and see also the *Crown Court Compendium* (July 2020), ch. 8-6.

There is no requirement in s. 2(1) that D's belief must be based on reasonable grounds, but the reasonableness or otherwise of D's supposed belief may be relevant to its credibility (*Holden* [1991] Crim LR 478).

Section 2(1)(a) requires only that D genuinely believed he was entitled to take the property in question. D need not necessarily have believed he was entitled to take it in the way he did

(*Robinson* [1977] Crim LR 173) although the use of improper methods (trespass to property, threats, violence, etc.) may give rise to other forms of civil or criminal liability.

The importance of drawing the jury's attention in appropriate cases to the provisions of s. 2(1)(a) was emphasised by the Court of Appeal in *Falconer-Atlee* (1973) 58 Cr App R 348. The Court of Appeal held in *Wootton* [1990] Crim LR 201 that a jury must be directed on s. 2(1)(a) whenever a claim of right is raised. See also *Forrester* [1992] Crim LR 793. In *Barton* [2020] EWCA Crim 575 however, it was held that although a direction on s. 2(1) might properly have been given, it sufficed that the jury were directed to consider D's claim that the 'gifts' he had received from his elderly and vulnerable clients had been freely given to him by people of capacity, and were straightforward gifts which he neither procured nor accepted dishonestly. By convicting D, the jury clearly rejected that claim, and found him to have acted dishonestly.

What then if D acts unscrupulously and knowingly takes advantage of V's evident vulnerability, but still believes that, as a matter of law, V's gift provides D with a valid title to the property, and thus a legal right to deprive V of it? In such a case, a charge of fraud by abuse of position (see **B5.22**) might (at least in a case such as *Barton*) enable a court or jury to concentrate on the wider issue of dishonesty, without having to identify a dishonest appropriation of the property in question.

The Court of Appeal considered s. 2(1)(a) and (b) in *A-G's Ref (No. 2 of 1982)* [1984] QB 624. **B4.52** It was held that where the directors of a company appropriate assets belonging to the company they cannot rely on s. 2(1)(b) to negate dishonesty if the only consent they believe they would have is their own consent, given on behalf of the company. Whether they could succeed under s. 2(1)(a) would depend on whether they honestly believed they were entitled to do what they did. The Court rejected arguments that, when all the members and directors of a company agree to such action, they cannot be held to have acted dishonestly. The appropriation of company assets may prejudice the wider interests of the company and its creditors, even if its own members are not prejudiced.

As to s. 2(1)(c), this appears to cover not only cases in which D believes the owner cannot reasonably be identified but also cases in which D believes that the owner (although known to D) cannot reasonably be traced or located. An example given in *Smith's Law of Theft* (9th edn, 2007) at para. 2.285 is that D may have agreed to store V's furniture. V moves away and fails to keep in touch. Needing the space and being genuinely convinced that V cannot be found, D eventually disposes of V's furniture. This would not be theft.

Dishonesty Notwithstanding Willingness to Pay Although under s. 2(2) D's appropriation **B4.53** of V's property may sometimes be considered dishonest even though willing to pay for it (notably where D knows that V is not willing to sell), D's willingness to pay a fair price may in other circumstances be powerful evidence of honesty (*Boggeln v Williams* [1978] 2 All ER 1061). To put it another way, it is often D's evident intent to *avoid* paying that most clearly demonstrates dishonesty.

Judicial Definition of Dishonesty The failure of the Theft Act 1968 to provide anything more **B4.54** than the partial definition of dishonesty found in s. 2(1) led to a long period of uncertainty and to a series of conflicting decisions as to the correct test to apply in cases where s. 2 does not provide the answer. This uncertainty affected all offences of dishonesty, but appeared to have been resolved when the Court of Appeal in *Ghosh* [1982] QB 1053 (a case involving the old offence of dishonestly obtaining property by deception) established a precise two-limbed definition ('the *Ghosh* test') which, although often criticised, was consistently applied for the next 35 years. This has now, however, been partially rejected by the Supreme Court in *Ivey v Genting Casinos (UK) Ltd* [2017] UKSC 67, [2018] AC 391 and by the Court of Appeal in *Barton* [2020] EWCA Crim 575 (see **B4.55**).

The first part of the old *Ghosh* test remains good law, even after *Ivey* and *Barton*. A jury in any case where dishonesty is in issue must still be directed to decide whether 'according to the ordinary standards of reasonable and honest people what was done was dishonest'. This test is an objective one (save that D's honesty must still be judged on the basis of the facts as D believed them to be), and the standards are those of ordinary honest people (as presumably reflected in the standards of the court or jury itself). The test should not be distorted so as reflect instead the peculiar ethics of D's environment or profession. If, for example, D is charged with theft by pilfering, and argues that 'everyone I know does the same thing', the question for the court or jury is not whether that is indeed how D's fellow workers or acquaintances behave, but whether such behaviour is considered acceptable, rather than dishonest, by honest and reasonable people generally. Honest and reasonable people might perhaps be quicker to condemn pilfering by bank staff than they would the behaviour of a teenager who takes some coins found down the back of an armchair in the family home, but it is always the standards of the ordinary honest person that must be applied.

In *Hayes* [2015] EWCA Crim 1944, [2016] 1 Cr App R (S) 63 (449) (a case of conspiracy to defraud), the Court of Appeal rejected a submission that the jury ought to have been directed instead to determine and apply the ethical standards of the market or business in which D was operating, namely the international inter-bank market in commercial loans. Lord Thomas CJ said (at [32]):

> Not only is there is no authority for the proposition that objective standards of honesty are to be set by a market, but such a principle would gravely affect the proper conduct of business.... From time to time, markets adopt patterns of behaviour which are dishonest by the standards of honest and reasonable people; in such cases, the market has simply abandoned ordinary standards of honesty. Each member of this court has seen such cases and the damage caused when a market determines its own standards of honesty in this way.

B4.55 **The New Test of Dishonesty** The second limb of the *Ghosh* test was focused on D's own *mens rea*. If (but only if) D's conduct was considered objectively dishonest under the text outlined above, juries were directed to consider a second question, namely, whether D must have realised that the conduct was (by the standards of reasonable and honest people) dishonest.

The Court of Appeal in *Ghosh* acknowledged that in practice this question would only rarely arise (at p. 1064E–G): 'In most cases, where the actions are obviously dishonest by ordinary standards, there will be no doubt about it. It will be obvious that the defendant himself knew that he was acting dishonestly.' Even so, this part of the test was widely criticised. Lord Hughes argued in *Ivey v Genting Casinos (UK) Ltd* [2017] UKSC 67, [2018] AC 391 (at [59]):

> There is no reason why the law should excuse those who make a mistake about what contemporary standards of honesty are, whether in the context of insurance claims, high finance, market manipulation or tax evasion. The law does not, in principle, excuse those whose standards are criminal by the benchmarks set by society, nor ought it to do so.

The *Ghosh* test was also different from the essentially objective one adopted by the civil courts. In *Barlow Clowes International Ltd v Eurotrust International Ltd* [2005] UKPC 37, [2006] 1 WLR 1476, for example, Lord Hoffman said (at pp. 1479–1480) that in a civil case: 'The standard by which the law determines... [dishonesty] is objective. If by ordinary standards a defendant's mental state would be characterised as dishonest, it is irrelevant that the defendant judges by different standards.'

See also *Royal Brunei Airlines Sdn Bhd v Tan* [1995] 2 AC 378. Lord Hughes in *Ivey* (at [63]) attached great importance to this conflict: 'Dishonesty is a simple, if occasionally imprecise, English word. It would be an affront to the law if its meaning differed according to the kind of proceedings in which it arose.' The addition of a subjective element in criminal cases did, however, ensure that D could not be a thief unless D at least knew that to be so. There could thus be no question of D being properly convicted where D had no idea of having done anything that would be considered wrong.

As previously noted, this second limb of the *Ghosh* was rejected in *Ivey*, and is now of little more than historical interest. Lord Hughes, giving the unanimous judgment of the court, ruled that this limb of the *Ghosh* test 'should no longer be followed by civil or criminal courts or included in directions to juries'. He concluded (at [74]):

> The test of dishonesty is as set out by Lord Nicholls in *Royal Brunei Airlines Sdn Bhd v Tan* and by Lord Hoffmann in *Barlow Clowes*. When dishonesty is in question the fact-finding tribunal must first ascertain (subjectively) the actual state of the individual's knowledge or belief as to the facts. The reasonableness or otherwise of his belief is a matter of evidence (often in practice determinative) going to whether he held the belief, but it is not an additional requirement that his belief must be reasonable; the question is whether it is genuinely held. When once his actual state of mind as to knowledge or belief as to facts is established, the question whether his conduct was honest or dishonest is to be determined by the fact-finder by applying the (objective) standards of ordinary decent people. There is no requirement that the defendant must appreciate that what he has done is, by those standards, dishonest.

Strictly speaking, what was said about *Ghosh* was *obiter* on the facts of *Ivey*, which was not even a criminal case, but in practice it was inevitable that the criminal courts would follow the Supreme Court, and this was confirmed in *Barton* [2020] EWCA Crim 575, in which Lord Burnett CJ said (at [104]):

> Where the Supreme Court itself directs that an otherwise binding decision of the Court of Appeal should no longer be followed and proposes an alternative test that it says must be adopted, the Court of Appeal is bound to follow what amounts to a direction from the Supreme Court even though it is strictly obiter. To that limited extent the ordinary rules of precedent (or stare decisis) have been modified. We emphasise that this limited modification is confined to cases in which all the judges in the appeal in question in the Supreme Court agree that to be the effect of the decision.

Implications of *Ivey* The abrogation of the subjective limb of the *Ghosh* test clearly simplifies both the law and the task of a jury faced with an issue of dishonesty. By bringing the criminal test for dishonesty into line with the civil, it also reduces (but cannot eliminate) the possibility that civil and criminal courts will reach different verdicts as to dishonesty in cases based on the very same facts. It may also, incidentally, affect the outcomes of some professional disciplinary cases. In *General Medical Council v Krishnan* [2017] EWHC 2892 (Admin), for example, a Medical Practitioners Tribunal ruling that a doctor had not acted dishonestly on the basis of the *Ghosh* test was remitted to the tribunal to reconsider on the basis of the more objective *Ivey* test (and see also *Wingate v Solicitors Regulation Authority* [2018] EWCA Civ 366, [2018] 1 WLR 3969). **B4.56**

It is clear that, under the test adopted in *Ivey*, any factual misunderstanding or ignorance on D's part may be relevant to the question of dishonesty. D must be judged on the basis of the facts or circumstances as D believed them to be, taking account, where relevant, of D's experience and intelligence (see *Barton*, at [108]). What then of a mistake concerning *legal* rights or powers? This is not addressed in either *Ivey* or *Barton*. The general rule of course is that ignorance of the law is no defence to a criminal charge, but where the Theft Act 1968, s. 2(1)(a), applies, such ignorance clearly can give rise to a defence, even if it is not a defence in its own right. Is there a wider principle to this effect that could apply where s. 2 cannot (e.g., in cases of alleged fraud)? There are dicta in *Clowes (No. 2)* [1994] 2 All ER 316 and *Lightfoot* (1992) 97 Cr App R 24 to the effect that, for the purposes of the *Ghosh* test, D's knowledge of the civil or criminal law is irrelevant. With respect, however, it is surely more likely (even applying a largely objective test in accordance with *Ivey*) that a jury would consider D to have behaved dishonestly if D clearly knew the actions to be unlawful, than it would be if D thought he was exercising legal rights.

Intention Permanently to Deprive

On a charge of theft, the prosecution must prove that D had an intention permanently to deprive the owner of the property in question when appropriating it. If this can be proved, it is no defence that D subsequently had a change of heart and returned the property (*McHugh* (1993) 97 Cr App R 335). If, **B4.57** however, no such intent is proved, there can be no conviction either for theft or for any other offence (such as robbery) that involves theft or requires an intention to steal (*Warner* (1970) 55 Cr App R 93; *Cocks* (1976) 63 Cr App R 79). Even a violent carjacking cannot amount to robbery of the car if D intends only to use that car for a getaway before abandoning it (*Mitchell* [2008] EWCA Crim 850). The Theft Act 1968, s. 6, (see **B4.58**), may sometimes assist in establishing whether the requisite intention can be established, but it does not purport to define the concept and should be referred to 'in exceptional cases only' (*Lloyd* [1985] QB 829; *Coffey* [1987] Crim LR 498).

What actually amounts to 'permanent deprivation' is largely a question of fact, but may also involve questions of law. See, e.g., the discussion of *Duru* [1974] 3 All ER 715 and *Preddy* [1996] AC 815.

Intention to Treat Property as One's Own to Dispose of

B4.58 Section 6 does not fully define what is meant by an intention to permanently deprive, but stretches the meaning of that phrase by providing that in some cases an intent to cause something less than outright or permanent deprivation will suffice.

Theft Act 1968, s. 6

(1) A person appropriating property belonging to another without meaning the other permanently to lose the thing itself is nevertheless to be regarded as having the intention of permanently depriving the other of it if his intention is to treat the thing as his own to dispose of regardless of the other's rights; and a borrowing or lending of it may amount to so treating it if, but only if, the borrowing or lending is for a period and in circumstances making it equivalent to an outright taking or disposal.

(2) Without prejudice to the generality of subsection (1) above, where a person, having possession or control (lawfully or not) of property belonging to another, parts with the property under a condition as to its return which he may not be able to perform, this (if done for purposes of his own and without the other's authority) amounts to treating the property as his own to dispose of regardless of the other's rights.

B4.59 Section 6 is essentially a 'deeming' provision. It enables a court to find in appropriate cases that D intended permanently to deprive V of certain property, even though D may have intended that V would eventually regain that property. For s. 6 to apply, D must intend to treat the property as D's own to 'dispose' of it regardless of V's rights. Section 6(2) identifies one way in which such a disposal may be made. The 'second limb' of s. 6(1) identifies another. But what else may suffice? An example suggested by the Court of Appeal in *Lloyd* [1985] QB 829 at p. 836 was:

> ... the sort of case where [D] takes things and then offers them back to the owner for the owner to buy if he wishes. If [D] intends to return them to the owner only upon such payment, then, on the wording of section 6(1), that is deemed to amount to the necessary intention permanently to deprive.

See, e.g., *Raphael* [2008] EWCA Crim 1014 (where the charge was one of conspiracy to steal). Other kinds of behaviour might also suffice, notably where it involves the 'disposal' of V's property. There is much to be said for Sir John Smith's argument that a disposal of property must involve getting rid of it or expending it (e.g., by selling it). This was accepted by the Court of Appeal in *Cahill* [1993] Crim LR 141 but *Cahill* was overlooked in *DPP v Lavender* [1994] Crim LR 297, where D had without authority taken doors from one council house and installed them in another house owned by the very same council. The Divisional Court held on these facts that s. 6(1) clearly applied, so that D was guilty of theft; but with respect, this decision must be open to question. D had no right to relocate the doors, but never intended to dispose of them in such a way as to deprive the council of them.

The Court of Appeal in *Lloyd* interpreted s. 6 restrictively, 'in such a way as to ensure that nothing is construed as an intention permanently to deprive which would not prior to the 1968 Act have been so construed'. See also *Warner* (1970) 55 Cr App R 93. In contrast, the court in *Downes* (1983) 77 Cr App R 260 preferred to give the words of s. 6 their normal meaning, without reference to the technicalities of the law prior to 1968, and this now appears to be the preferred approach. See *Duru* [1974] 3 All ER 715, *Bagshaw* [1988] Crim LR 321, *Governor of Pentonville Prison, ex parte Osman* [1990] 3 All ER 701, *Fernandes* [1996] 1 Cr App R 175 and *Raphael*. In *Vinall* [2011] EWCA Crim 2652, [2012] 1 Cr App R 29 (400), Pitchford LJ said (at [16]):

> What section 6(1) requires is a state of mind in the defendant which Parliament regards as the equivalent of an intention permanently to deprive... [It] does not require that the thing has been disposed of, nor does it require that the defendant intends to dispose of the thing in any particular way. No doubt evidence of a particular disposal or a particular intention to dispose of the thing will constitute evidence of the defendant's state of mind but it is, in our view, for the jury to decide upon the circumstances proved whether the defendant harboured the statutory intention.

In *Chan Man-sin v The Queen* [1988] 1 All ER 1, D forged cheques from two companies for which he worked and paid them into his own account. The companies' credit balances at their banks were reduced each time, and H was charged with stealing those balances. He may perhaps have known that once the fraud was discovered the companies' accounts would have to be reimbursed and that the companies would ultimately lose nothing, but the Privy Council referred to the Hong Kong equivalent of s. 6(1) and ruled that, even if D expected this to happen, he was still on these facts 'purporting to deal with the companies' property without regard to their rights' and could be deemed to have the requisite intention. **B4.60**

Another example is provided by *Marshall* [1998] 2 Cr App R 282 in which D acquired unexpired London Underground tickets from travellers who no longer needed them and then dishonestly resold these tickets to other travellers. It was assumed (perhaps wrongly) that on expiry the tickets would eventually be returned to or retained by London Underground, but the Court of Appeal held that D would nevertheless remain guilty of theft by virtue of s. 6(1). By acquiring and reselling the tickets, D had 'an intention to treat [them] as his own to dispose of regardless of London Underground Limited's rights' (at p. 287). But if this approach is correct it should also be possible to apply s. 6(1) in a case such as *Preddy* [1996] AC 815—a possibility that does not appear to have been properly examined in that case.

Borrowing or Lending as Equivalent to Outright Taking In *Lloyd* [1985] QB 829, D, a cinema projectionist, clandestinely removed feature films due to be shown in the cinema where he worked. His co-defendants copied them onto video tape and they sold many such 'pirate' copies; but the original films were returned in perfect working order and continued to attract audiences to the cinema. On such facts there was clearly no theft. Copyright offences had been committed, and there was a criminal conspiracy, but there was no intent to deprive the owners of any films even under the second limb of s. 6(1). For it to apply to a 'borrowing' case, said the Court of Appeal, D's intention must be to return the thing in question 'in such a changed state that it can truly be said that all its goodness or virtue has gone' (at p. 836). This might include taking a season ticket until the end of the season, or using V's (non-rechargeable) torch battery until it is discharged and 'flat'. See also *Coffey* [1987] Crim LR 498, *Bagshaw* [1988] Crim LR 321 and *Waters* [2015] EWCA Crim 402. **B4.61**

Despite what was said in *Lloyd*, it may perhaps be argued that D commits theft by dishonestly 'borrowing' V's season ticket with the intention of returning it halfway through the season. This would be equivalent to the outright taking of half of a complete series of individual tickets, which is what a season ticket represents. If this is correct, borrowing the season ticket for just *one* afternoon must also suffice to trigger s. 6(1). That afternoon's events will never be repeated and to that extent V's deprivation is not just temporary.

In *Velumyl* [1989] Crim LR 299, the Court of Appeal rejected an argument that if D 'borrows' money from his employer expecting to return an equivalent sum he has no intention permanently to deprive his employer of that money. That would be true only if D intended to return the very same notes or coins, and in practice that is most improbable. Section 6 accordingly has no application on such facts.

B4.62 **Parting with Property on a Condition which D May Not be Able to Perform** Section 6(2) covers such instances as D pawning V's property, hoping to redeem the property at the appropriate time, but not knowing whether that will be possible.

B4.63 **Intention to Deprive under s. 5** In relation to trust property, s. 5(2) (see **B4.19**) provides that 'an intention to defeat the trust shall be regarded as an intention to deprive of the property any person having that right'. The right referred to is the right to enforce the trust and 'that person' is the person to whom the trust property belongs (see **B4.24**). Section 5(2) states only that an intention to defeat the trust is an intention to deprive. An intention to deprive permanently must still be established.

In respect of property got by another's mistake (see **B4.31**), s. 5(4) provides that 'an intention not to make restoration shall be regarded accordingly as an intention to deprive that person of the property or proceeds'. 'That person' is the person who is entitled to restoration. Section 5(4) states only that the intention not to make restoration is an intention to deprive. It must still be established whether there was an intention to deprive permanently.

B4.64 **Conditional Intention** Problems have arisen in relation to cases of theft or attempted theft where D has been caught interfering with V's property but claims merely to be ascertaining whether there is anything worth stealing. In *Easom* [1971] 2 QB 315 the Court of Appeal said that 'a conditional appropriation will not do'. So rummaging through V's handbag with that intention was not sufficient. In *Husseyn* (1977) 67 Cr App R 131, the Court of Appeal followed *Easom* and so held that D was not guilty of attempted theft of some sub-aqua equipment from a holdall, because D had not yet looked into the bag or decided whether there was anything worth stealing. A solution to this problem can usually be found in careful drafting of the charge or indictment. In a case such as *Easom* or *Husseyn*, D may be charged with attempting to steal some or all of the contents of the handbag or the holdall. There is then no need to prove that D intended to steal any of the specific items found within the bag or holdall, but simply that D intended to steal anything worth stealing (*A-G's Ref (Nos. 1 and 2 of 1979)* [1980] QB 180).

Where D takes a specific item from V with a view to ascertaining whether it is valuable, or can profitably be disposed of, it is no defence to argue that D was planning to return it unless it proved valuable. D is thereby treating that item as D's own to dispose of, regardless of V's rights. See **B4.58**.

Theft of Mails within the British Postal Area

B4.65 For most purposes, the Theft Acts apply only to things done within England and Wales or (notably where the CJA 1993, Part I, applies) to things done partly in England and partly abroad (see generally **A8**); but the Theft Act 1968, s. 14, creates a special rule in respect of mail in transit within any part of the British Postal Area.

Theft Act 1968, s. 14

(1) Where a person—
  (a) steals or attempts to steal any mailbag or postal packet in the course of transmission as such between places in different jurisdictions in the British postal area, or any of the contents of such a mailbag or postal packet, or
  (b) in stealing or with intent to steal any such mailbag or postal packet or any of its contents, commits any robbery, attempted robbery or assault with intent to rob;

then, notwithstanding that he does so outside England and Wales, he shall be guilty of committing or attempting to commit the offence against this Act as if he had done so in England or Wales, and he shall accordingly be liable to be prosecuted, tried and punished in England and Wales without proof that the offence was committed there.

(2) In subsection (1) above the reference to different jurisdictions in the British postal area is to be construed as referring to the several jurisdictions of England and Wales, of Scotland, of Northern Ireland, of the Isle of Man and of the Channel Islands.

There are specific offences concerned with mail thefts: it is an offence, contrary to the Postal Services Act 2000, s. 83, for a postal operator to interfere with the mail; and it is an offence, contrary to s. 84, for any person to interfere with the mail. For other offences, see ss. 85 to 88. Section 125 of that Act defines 'mail bag' and 'postal packet'.

ROBBERY AND ASSAULT WITH INTENT TO ROB

Definition

Theft Act 1968, s. 8 B4.66

(1) A person is guilty of robbery if he steals, and immediately before or at the time of doing so, and in order to do so, he uses force on any person or puts or seeks to put any person in fear of being then and there subjected to force.

(2) A person guilty of robbery, or of an assault with intent to rob, shall on conviction on indictment be liable to imprisonment for life.

Procedure

Robbery and assault with intent to rob are triable only on indictment; they are normally class 3 offences, but see CrimPD XIII, para. B (see Supplement, **CPD.XIII.B**) for the additional factors that the court considers on allocation. B4.67

Indictment

Statement of Offence B4.68

Robbery contrary to section 8(1) of the Theft Act 1968.

Particulars of Offence

A on the... day of... robbed V of a gold watch.

As to the practice of including (where relevant) a count for an offence contrary to the Firearms Act 1968, see *French* (1982) 75 Cr App R 1 per Lord Lane CJ.

Alternative Verdicts

Theft is the obvious alternative verdict by the application of the CLA 1967, s. 6(3). The House of Lords in *Maxwell* [1990] 1 All ER 801 has held that the trial judge is only obliged to leave such a lesser alternative verdict to the jury if necessary in the interests of justice, for example, if the question of force was in doubt but there was substantial evidence of theft. B4.69

The decision in *Tennant* [1976] Crim LR 133, that it is not possible under the CLA 1967, s. 6(3), to convict a person of an assault on a charge of robbery, needs to be reconsidered in the light of *Metropolitan Police Commissioner v Wilson* [1984] AC 242. An allegation of robbery may in many cases impliedly include an allegation of an assault, because most uses of force will involve an assault, even though it is not possible exactly to assimilate 'force' as required for robbery with 'assault'.

Sentence

The maximum penalty for robbery or assault with intent to rob is life imprisonment (s. 8(2)). The combination of violence and theft makes robbery the most serious of the common offences of dishonesty. The great majority of offenders convicted of robbery receive custodial sentences. B4.70

The definitive sentencing guideline, *Robbery* (see Supplement, **SG30-1**), applies to all offences of robbery committed by an adult offender irrespective of the date of the offence. For all offenders aged under 18 who are sentenced for robbery, irrespective of the date of the offence, the court must refer instead to the guideline, *Sentencing Children and Young People* (see Supplement, **SG8-1**), which, as well as setting out the overarching principles for sentencing young offenders, contains offence-specific guidelines for robbery. That guideline does not provide sentencing ranges and starting points in the same style as the respective adult guideline. At Step One it provides *examples* of the type of culpability and harm factors that may indicate that a particular sentencing threshold has been crossed. Step Two deals with aggravating and mitigating factors, and Step Three deals with personal mitigation, before adjustment for a guilty plea at Step Four and a 'review of the sentence' at Step Five 'to ensure it is the most appropriate one for the child or young person', taking into account a report from the youth offending team. Although throughout the new guideline the Sentencing Council stresses the importance of the different principles which apply when sentencing those aged under 18, and the need for an individualistic approach, the revised robbery guideline applicable to offenders under the age of 18 ends with the observation that where a custodial sentence is unavoidable the court may wish to consider the equivalent adult guideline, and 'apply a sentence broadly within the region of half to two thirds of the appropriate sentence for those aged 15–17 and allow a greater reduction for those aged under 15'. The Council stresses that 'this must not be applied mechanistically' and 'the individual factors relating to the offence and the child or young person are of the greatest importance and may present good reason to impose a sentence outside of this range'.

B4.71 The adult guideline applies to *all* forms of robbery, in contrast to the earlier guideline which excluded professionally planned commercial robberies and violent personal robberies in the home. The guideline is broken down into three categories: (i) street robbery and less sophisticated commercial robbery, (ii) professionally planned commercial robbery, and (iii) robbery in a dwelling. Inevitably there will be cases on the borderline between (i) and (ii), which have very different ranges and starting points. No doubt the judge will consider submissions from counsel as to which category applies. The point arose in *Khan* [2017] EWCA Crim 48, [2017] 2 Cr App R (S) 19 (157), where the Court of Appeal upheld the judge's assessment that the offenders had committed a 'professionally planned commercial robbery' where, armed with knives, they had raided a bank and slashed the faces of two members of staff. The robbers failed to gain access to the tills, left empty-handed and were soon arrested. The Court referred to the issue of planning, relevant to both categories of the offence, and said that the guideline encompassed a spectrum of degrees of sophistication and organisation. The judge was correct to find that the current case was at the lower end of the range of the more serious category, and a starting point of 12 years reduced by one third to reflect the guilty plea, was upheld. By contrast, in *Noel* [2017] EWCA Crim 782, [2018] 1 Cr App R (S) 5 (27), where the offender had alerted others to a work colleague leaving business premises carrying £3,000 in cash in a bag, and the bag was snatched from her in the street with limited violence and no use of weapons, the Court of Appeal said that the case fell between categories (i) and (ii), indicating a starting point in the offender's case of five years before reduction for guilty plea. While it will normally be clear if the court is dealing with a 'robbery in a dwelling', there can be cases where the robbery naturally falls into the 'less sophisticated commercial robbery' category, but the victim lives 'over the shop'. The 'less sophisticated commercial robbery' category recognises that point, by including 'location of the offence (including cases where the location of the offence is the victim's residence)' as a possible aggravating factor.

In *Mayers* [2018] EWCA Crim 1552, [2019] 1 Cr App R (S) 1 (1), a case of conspiracy to rob where a large group of armed men wearing disguises had targeted and attacked a travellers' site in the expectation of finding large sums of money there, and where victims were assaulted and tied up, the appropriate guideline was robbery in a dwelling rather than professionally planned commercial robbery. The Court of Appeal said that the former guideline is well capable of providing for an offence which is sophisticated and organised in nature and involves targeting or obtaining very high-value goods in circumstances where physical injury or psychological harm is caused to the victim. Determinate sentences ranging from nine to 18 years were appropriate. In *Mahon* [2018] EWCA Crim 959 D, aged 48, admitted three offences of robbery and two of house burglary, all involving encounters with elderly occupants in their own homes. Some incidents involved significant violence and threats with a weapon, forcing victims to hand over money and other property. Entry to the homes was gained by deception, including pretending to be a police officer. D had a long history of offending in the same way, and he began committing these offences just three days after release on licence. The Court of Appeal upheld an appropriate custodial sentence after trial of 22½ years for this apparently compulsive offender, resulting after credit for plea in sentences of 20 years (custodial term 15 years, extension period five years) in respect of each of the robberies, with concurrent sentences for the burglaries. Edis J said that the case was highly unusual, D appeared to be incapable of reform, and the guidelines did not provide directly for cases as extreme as this one.

Actus Reus

Robbery requires theft. In *Robinson* [1977] Crim LR 173 it was held that where D uses or threatens force in order to appropriate property to which D believes he is entitled, this cannot be either theft or robbery, even if D knows the force to be unlawful. Threats of force in such circumstances might however amount to blackmail. If theft is intended but not committed (e.g., because V escapes or has nothing for D to steal), a charge of assault with intent to rob under the Theft Act 1968, s. 8(2), or a charge of attempted robbery under the CAA 1981, s. 1 (see **A5.72**), may still be possible. If D has at least committed an assault, a charge under s. 8(2) may be preferable in that it avoids the uncertainties that can beset a prosecution for attempt. **B4.72**

To be guilty of robbery, D must either use force or put another person in fear of being then and there subjected to force, and must do this in order to steal. In *Shendley* [1970] Crim LR 49 the trial judge clearly erred by directing the jury that 'if the violence was unconnected with the stealing but you are satisfied there was a stealing it . . . would be open to you to find [D] guilty of robbery . . . without violence'. The Court of Appeal quashed D's conviction for robbery and substituted a conviction for theft. It would not matter, however, if D also had some additional motive for using or threatening force.

In *Dawson* (1976) 64 Cr App R 170 the Court of Appeal held that 'force' is a word in ordinary use, which juries understand. The jury in that case were entitled to find that force was used where the defendants stood around the victim, one of them nudged him and his wallet was stolen. In such cases, an implicit threat of force may suffice, as where a gang surround V in order to steal. It does not then matter whether V is actually put in fear or not: it is the intention of the perpetrator that matters (*B v DPP* [2008] EWHC 1655 (Admin)). **B4.73**

Whether force has been used on a person is a question for the jury to consider, and it appears that they may conclude that force has been used when it is used indirectly. In *Clouden* [1987] Crim LR 56 the Court dismissed an appeal against a conviction for robbery when D had wrenched the victim's shopping basket from her hand and run off with it. Indeed, it should not matter in such a case that V's grip on her bag is too strong for D to break: by grabbing the bag with intent, D has appropriated it and the theft (and robbery) is complete. See also *Corcoran v Anderton* (1980) 71 Cr App R 104, but contrast *P v DPP* [2012] EWHC 1657 (Admin), [2013] 1 WLR 2337, where snatching a cigarette away from V's hand, without making any contact with V, was akin to picking V's pocket and could not therefore be robbery.

Force must be used or threatened immediately before or at the time of stealing. Consequently, it is important to know whether D had already finished committing the theft when the force or threat was used (see **B4.44**, *Vinall* [2011] EWCA Crim 2652, [2012] 1 Cr App R 29 (400) and *James* [1997] Crim LR 598).

Mens Rea

Robbery and assault with intent to rob each require the *mens rea* elements of theft, namely dishonesty (see **B4.51** to **B4.56**) and intention permanently to deprive (see **B4.57** to **B4.64**) as well as the intention to appropriate the property in question (*Zerei* [2012] EWCA Crim 1114). There must also be intention or at least recklessness as to the use of force. The accidental use of force during the course of an ordinary theft would not suffice since D must use the force in order to steal. Similarly, D does not commit robbery merely when interrupted by V in the course of a theft or burglary and V momentarily fears an attack by D. **B4.74**

BURGLARY

Definition

B4.75

Theft Act 1968, s. 9

(1) A person is guilty of burglary if—
(a) he enters any building or part of a building as a trespasser and with intent to commit any such offence as is mentioned in subsection (2) below; or
(b) having entered any building or part of a building as a trespasser he steals or attempts to steal anything in the building or that part of it or inflicts or attempts to inflict on any person therein any grievous bodily harm.
(2) The offences referred to in subsection (1)(a) above are offences of stealing anything in the building or part of a building in question, of inflicting on any person therein any grievous bodily harm, and of doing unlawful damage to the building or anything therein.

Section 9 creates two groups of offences: one of entering a building (or part of a building) as a trespasser with the requisite intent, contrary to s. 9(1)(a); the other of having entered a building (or part of a building) as a trespasser and committing a specified offence, contrary to s. 9(1)(b). In each case there are now (by s. 9(4) as amended) two offences dependent upon whether the building is or is not a dwelling. The different sentence provisions applicable (see **B4.80**) mean that, under *Courtie* [1984] AC 463, burglary of a dwelling is now a distinct offence from burglary of any other type of building.

Procedure

B4.76 By virtue of the MCA 1980, s. 17 and sch. 1, para. 28, most forms of burglary are triable either way. When tried on indictment, it is normally a class 3 offence, but see CrimPD XIII, para. B (see Supplement, **CPD.XIII.B**) for the additional factors that the court considers on allocation. However:

(a) if the burglary comprises the commission of, or an intention to commit, an offence which is triable only on indictment, then the burglary is also triable only on indictment (sch. 1, para. 28(b));
(b) if the burglary is in a dwelling-house and any person in the dwelling was subjected to violence or the threat of violence, the offence is triable only on indictment (sch. 1, para. 28(c)) (the violence need not have been used as part of effecting the burglary: *McGrath* [2003] EWCA Crim 2062, [2004] 1 Cr App R 15 (173));
(c) if the burglary is a domestic burglary and the accused, who is now aged 18 or over, has two previous separate convictions for domestic burglary in respect of offences committed after 30 November 1999, the offence is triable only on indictment (PCC(S)A 2000, s. 111(4)).

B4.77 See the *Magistrates' Court Sentencing Guidelines* for indications as to when a case should be sent to the Crown Court.

Indictment

B4.78

Statement of Offence

Burglary of a dwelling with intent contrary to section 9(1)(a) of the Theft Act 1968.

Particulars of Offence

A, on or about the... day of... entered a dwelling [or part of a dwelling, or a building or part of a building], namely..., as a trespasser with intent to steal therein [or inflict grievous bodily harm upon a person therein, or to do unlawful damage to the building or anything therein].

Statement of Offence

Burglary of a dwelling contrary to section 9(1)(b) of the Theft Act 1968.

Particulars of Offence

A on or about the... day of..., having entered a dwelling [or part of a dwelling, or a building or part of a building], namely..., as a trespasser, stole therein [or attempted to steal therein, or inflicted grievous bodily harm upon... therein].

In *Machent v Quinn* [1970] 2 All ER 255 the Divisional Court decided that it is unnecessary for the prosecution to prove that all the articles mentioned in an information or an indictment have been stolen. Proof that D stole any one of those articles is sufficient.

Alternative Verdicts

By virtue of the CLA 1967, s. 6(3), on an indictment for burglary contrary to the Theft Act 1968, s. 9(1)(b), D may alternatively be convicted of the underlying offence that D is alleged to have committed after entering the building (*Lillis* [1972] 2 QB 236). In *Metropolitan Police Commissioner v Wilson* [1984] AC 242, the House of Lords ruled that by virtue of s. 6(3) a conviction under the OAPA 1861, s. 47, may also be available as an alternative verdict on a charge of burglary by inflicting grievous bodily harm under s. 9(1)(b), just as it may be on an indictment alleging the commission of an offence under the OAPA 1861, s. 20. See **D19.47**. **B4.79**

The approach in *Wilson* has been applied in *Whiting* (1987) 85 Cr App R 78. The Court of Appeal decided that it is possible that a person may be found guilty of burglary under s. 9(1)(a) on a charge of burglary under s. 9(1)(b), because s. 9(1)(b) impliedly includes an allegation of an offence contrary to s. 9(1)(a). Such an alternative verdict can be arrived at in some, but not all cases, since these two offences are essentially different in certain respects (see **B4.83**, **B4.89** and **B4.94**).

Sentence

The maximum penalty for dwelling burglary (i.e. burglary of a building or part of a building which is a dwelling) is 14 years' imprisonment or a fine, or both, on indictment; six months or an unlimited fine, or both, summarily (s. 9(3)). The maximum custodial penalty for any other form of burglary is ten years' imprisonment, with financial and summary penalties unchanged. **B4.80**

The definitive guideline, *Burglary Offences* (see Supplement, **SG19-1** *et seq.*), which covers domestic and non-domestic burglary, applies to all offenders aged 18 and over sentenced on or after 16 January 2012, irrespective of the date of the offence. The offence range for domestic burglary is a community order to six years' custody, and for non-domestic burglary it is a fine to five years' custody. In a 'three-strikes' domestic burglary case the guideline should always be considered first (see **E5.6**).

The question whether the burgled building was a dwelling or not cannot be resolved by a *Newton* hearing at sentencing. It should be settled by a jury after the insertion of alternative counts in the indictment, or by an appropriate guilty plea (*Flack* [2013] EWCA Crim 115, [2013] 2 Cr App R (S) 56 (366)) on an indictment that clearly sets out the Crown's allegation that the property in question was a dwelling. In *Griffin* [2018] EWCA Crim 2538, [2019] 1 Cr App R (S) 37 (250) two defendants pleaded guilty to conspiracy to burgle, an offence encompassing 22 burglaries in a two-month period, 20 of which were dwellings. The Court of Appeal held that those responsible for drafting indictments must be astute to the point that in order to attract the higher maximum sentence of 14 years' imprisonment the indictment must make express reference to the nature of the buildings involved. In this case the offence was charged simply as 'conspiracy to burgle' and despite the true nature of the substantive offending, the maximum sentence could only be ten years' imprisonment.

A minimum custodial sentence of three years must be imposed by the court where an offender aged 18 or over is convicted of a third qualifying 'domestic burglary', where all three of the offences were committed after 30 November 1999, and where there are no particular circumstances relating to any of the offences, or the offender, such that the imposition of a custodial sentence of at least three years would be unjust in all the circumstances (PCC(S)A 2000, s. 111, and see **E5.4**). The statutory test should be applied literally, and if it is felt that imposition would be unjust it is incumbent on the sentencer to spell out clearly the reasons for such a conclusion. It is not enough simply to say that imposition of the minimum term is 'inappropriate': see *Buckland* [2019] EWCA Crim 952, a case in which a suspended sentence order was considered unduly lenient and replaced with a term that would have been four years after trial, reduced for guilty plea to two years, eight months' imprisonment. For a similar case in which the decision of the sentencer not to impose the mandatory minimum sentence was unduly lenient, see *Fearn* [2019] EWCA Crim 1232. Describing the proper approach, the Court of Appeal said (at [23]):

> The object of that statutory provision is to require courts to impose a sentence of not less than the prescribed minimum term in circumstances where but for the section the courts would not or might not do so: see *R v McInerney and Keating* [2002] EWCA Crim 3003, [2003] 2 Cr App R (S) 39 at [16]. The correct approach is to apply the Definitive Guideline for burglary offences in the usual way and then to check that the resulting provisional sentence does not infringe the minimum term provisions. If it does, the court must then consider whether there are particular circumstances relating to the offence or to the offender which make it unjust to impose the minimum sentence: see *Leonard* [2018] EWCA Crim 870. The length of time which has elapsed between the qualifying offences is a matter to be taken into account but is not in itself a factor which makes it unjust to impose the minimum sentence: see *Attorney General's Reference, R v Marland* [2018] EWCA Crim 1770, [2018] 2 Cr App R (S) 51 at [24]. Although the effect of applying the minimum term provisions may in some circumstances seem harsh, the courts must not treat perfectly normal circumstances as being 'particular circumstances' in order to circumvent the statute: see *Lucas* [2011] EWCA Crim 2806, [2012] 2 Cr App R (S) 14 at [14] and *Marland* at [24].

Where the offence triggering the minimum term is to be sentenced with other offending, the minimum sentence should be imposed consecutively to any other term (*Haddock* [2018] EWCA Crim 2860, [2019] 1 Cr App R (S) 45 (304)).

B4.81 **Burglary from Dwellings** For a domestic burglary falling within category 1 (greater harm and higher culpability) the starting point is three years within a range of two to six years; for category 2 (greater harm and lower culpability or lesser harm and higher culpability) the starting point is one year within a range of high level community order to two years, and for category 3 (lesser harm and lower culpability) the starting point is a high level community order within a range of low level community order to 26 weeks. The guideline stresses that relevant recent convictions are likely to result in an upward movement. Appropriate reduction should be made for a guilty plea. According to *Blaydes* [2014] EWCA Crim 798, [2014] 2 Cr App R (S) 55 (447), whether or not two offenders constitute a 'group or gang' for guideline purposes, the involvement of more than one offender is always an aggravating factor in burglary.

Sentences outside the offence range will sometimes be justified. In *Airey* [2017] EWCA Crim 1440 a single serious house burglary committed by a man with an appalling record for burglary justified a starting point of nine years. In *Griffin* [2018] EWCA Crim 2538, [2019] 1 Cr App R (S) 37 (250) (see **B4.80**) the Court of Appeal upheld an appropriate sentence after trial of ten years' imprisonment (the statutory maximum) for two defendants who pleaded guilty to a conspiracy to burgle which involved 22 burglaries in a two-month period. By contrast, in *Brinkley* [2013] EWCA Crim 760 a persistent house burglar, whose latest offence fell within category 3 of the guideline, did not merit a sentence of 40 months after a guilty plea to reflect his very poor record. The Court of Appeal substituted a sentence of two years and five months (based on the PCC(S)A 2000, s. 111, less the limited statutory discount for plea).

Distraction burglary of the elderly or otherwise vulnerable is a category of burglary that has always attracted lengthy custodial sentences. The Court of Appeal in *Dance* [2014] EWCA Crim 1412, [2014] 1 Cr App R (S) 51 (304) said that in such cases a sentence above the offence range in the guidelines may be appropriate, particularly if there is a pattern of repeat offending. In *Brooker* [2011] EWCA Crim 1836, [2012] 1 Cr App R (S) 70 (298) the Court of Appeal upheld sentences totalling six years for a series of distraction burglaries committed at the homes of elderly people, by a man with a long record of drug-related property offences. In *Cash* [2012] EWCA Crim 201, [2012] 2 Cr App R (S) 65 (381), a sentence of five years on a plea of guilty in respect of three distraction burglaries at the homes of people aged over 80 was 'severe' but not excessive according to the Court of Appeal. In *Roberts* [2012] EWCA Crim 2729, [2013] 2 Cr App R (S) 19 (84) a sentence of six years was appropriate after a guilty plea for D who went to the home of an elderly woman, pretended to be from the council, and stole her handbag and bank books. D had a very long record of dishonesty, including burglary of the elderly. The Court of Appeal said that this was a category 1 case and it was right to take a starting point above the offence range. In *Hanrahan* [2017] EWCA Crim 1256 a conspiracy to commit multiple distraction burglaries justified a sentence above the indicated range for a single substantive offence. See also *Mahon* [2018] EWCA Crim 959, summarised at **B4.71**.

Burglary from Non-dwelling Burglary committed in relation to premises other than a dwelling is regarded as somewhat less serious than the previous category. The maximum penalty for burglary other than from a dwelling is ten years' imprisonment on indictment, six months or a fine not exceeding the statutory maximum, or both, summarily (Theft Act 1968, s. 9(3)). In respect of burglary from a non-dwelling, the definitive sentencing guideline, *Burglary Offences*, applies. For a non-domestic burglary falling within category 1 (greater harm and higher culpability) the starting point is two years within a range of one to five years; for category 2 (greater harm and lower culpability or lesser harm and higher culpability) the starting point is 18 weeks within a range of low level community order to 51 weeks; and for category 3 (lesser harm and lower culpability) the starting point is a medium level community order within a range of Band B fine order to 18 weeks. The guideline stresses that relevant recent convictions are likely to result in an upward movement. Appropriate reduction should be made for a guilty plea. In *Rye* [2012] EWCA Crim 2792, [2013] 2 Cr App R (S) 11 (50) the offenders had committed night-time attacks on electricity sub-stations connected with the rail network to steal copper. About £8,000 worth of damage was done. The Court of Appeal said that the case fell into category 1 of the guideline, and sentences of three and a half years would have been appropriate following a trial. **B4.82**

Cases of so-called 'ram-raiding' are likely to attract severe sentences. In the pre-guideline case of *Delaney* [2010] EWCA Crim 988, [2011] 1 Cr App R (S) 16 (117) the Court of Appeal said that sentences totalling ten years were appropriate after a trial for two 'professionally executed' offences in which D (an 'accomplished and ruthless criminal') had used a JCB digger to remove a cash dispenser from buildings. A total of £98,000 was stolen and damage was done to the fabric of the buildings. The two offences were separated by three months. Appropriate sentences of three and seven years' imprisonment were rightly made consecutive. See also *Lawlor* [2012] EWCA Crim 1870, [2013] 1 Cr App R (S) 102 (532).

Elements Common to Both s. 9(1)(a) and (b)

Although the Theft Act 1968, s. 9(1)(a) and (b) create separate offences, some elements are common to both. A 'building or part of a building' must be or have been 'entered' as 'a trespasser' in order for burglary to have been committed. The trespassory entry requirement demands a consideration not only of whether the entry was trespassory, but also whether D knew that it was trespassory, or was reckless as to that. The difference lies in s. 9(1)(a) with the need for an intention to commit certain offences and in s. 9(1)(b) with the need to do certain things in the building (see, e.g., *O'Leary* (1986) 82 Cr App R 341 at p. 343). **B4.83**

Meaning of 'Building' and 'Dwelling' The Theft Act 1968 does not define a 'building', other than by providing that inhabited vehicles or vessels are deemed to be buildings. Whether a given thing can be called a building is not always straightforward and may be context-dependent. The best-known judicial definition is that provided by Byles J in *Stevens v Gourley* (1859) CBNS 99 at p. 112: 'a structure of considerable size and intended to be permanent or at least to endure for a considerable period'. Such structures need not be inhabited, nor need they have doors, windows or foundations. A garden shed, a multi-storey car park and a portakabin office might each be regarded as a building, although the status of a tent is doubtful. In *B v Leathley* [1979] Crim LR 314, it was held that a freezer container in a farmyard was a building. The freezer was 25 feet long with 7 feet square cross-section, weighing about three tons and had been in place for two or three years. In *Norfolk Constabulary v Seekings* [1986] Crim LR 167, however, a disconnected freezer trailer was held not to be a building. In *Manning* (1871) LR 1 CCR 338 it was decided **B4.84**

that a building does not have to be complete. In that case the building was a house which was very nearly complete, but the Court was satisfied that less complete structures could also be 'buildings'.

Section 9(4) provides:

> References in subsections (1) and (2) above to a building, and the reference in subsection (3) above to a dwelling, shall apply also to an inhabited vehicle or vessel, and shall apply to any such vehicle or vessel at times when the person having a habitation in it is not there as well as at times when he is.

'Inhabited vehicles' include caravans and motor homes (or even derelict vehicles) that are used for habitation at the relevant time. It is submitted that a caravan is not 'inhabited' when laid up unoccupied for the winter, even if it is fully stocked and furnished. Some HGVs now provide a sleeping area in the cab for long-distance drivers to rest in; but it seems unlikely that a sleeping HGV driver could properly be said to 'inhabit' the lorry, unless the driver has nowhere else to live at the time.

Inhabited vessels include occupied houseboats and ships on which at least some members of the crew can be said to 'live', rather than merely work. A cruise ship is also 'inhabited' by its passengers during the cruise. If, in order to steal, etc., D boards such a ship or enters a cabin or compartment on a ship knowing this is not permitted, D will accordingly commit burglary, provided that D is at the time subject to English law (as to which see **A8.15** *et seq.*).

B4.85 Since D need enter only a part of a building as a trespasser to be a burglar, it is possible to become a burglar by entering a particular room or area of the building (such as a private office) to which entry is restricted. In *Walkington* [1979] 2 All ER 716, it was held that a jury may have to decide whether an area is sufficiently segregated to amount to a distinct 'part of a building'. In this case, D had gone behind the sales counter in a large store. The counter was moveable, but occupied a clearly identified area. In the circumstances, the Court took the view that there was evidence on which the jury could conclude that there was a separate part of the building identified by the counter area, since there was a physical partition and the management impliedly prohibited customers from entering the area.

For the reasons given at **B4.80**, it may be important to determine whether the building in question is a 'dwelling'. In many cases, the facts will be plain. A building (or caravan etc.) in which someone has a home must be a dwelling, whereas a shop, warehouse or factory will not be. Difficulties may, however, arise in the case of a hotel or time-shared holiday home. Most hotel guests do not use the hotel as their dwelling, but some may do so, as may some of the hotel staff; and difficulties may also arise in respect of a building (or part of a building) that has been constructed or adapted to serve as a dwelling (and perhaps furnished for that purpose) but is not currently occupied as such. In *Hudson v CPS* [2017] EWHC 841 (Admin), [2017] 2 Cr App R 21 (269) the Divisional Court held that in such cases the status of the building or part of a building must be determined as a question of fact and degree. In contrast, the Public Order Act 1986, s. 8 (see **B11.54**) and the Terrorism Act 2000, s. 121, each define a dwelling as a building etc. that is currently occupied or used as a dwelling; but in *Hudson* the Court considered the contexts of those statutes to be 'so different that they did not assist' in burglary cases. See also *Flack* [2013] EWCA Crim 115, in which it was said that alternative counts for domestic and non-domestic burglary should be included in any indictment where the issue is likely to arise, and the jury left to decide.

It is submitted that in reaching a decision on the facts, a court or jury should consider the reasons for distinguishing between dwellings and other premises. If a new house that is burgled is still unoccupied and still owned by the building contractors, no resident occupier will be distressed, *violated or endangered by that burglary,* which is in effect no different from a burglary of commercial premises. The same might be said in respect of rental property that has long been unoccupied (*Sticklen* [2013] EWCA Crim 615). But where a house has been purchased and furnished as a home, and is burgled shortly before the new owners move in, there is a strong case for treating this as burglary of a dwelling. In *Hudson*, the burgled property was a furnished house that had recently been vacated by tenants. The Divisional Court held that a district judge was fully entitled to rule that this was a burglary of a dwelling, even though new tenants had yet to be found.

Meaning of 'Entry' In *Collins* [1973] QB 100, the Court of Appeal decided (at p. 106) that D has to make 'an effective and substantial entry into' a building or part of a building. This phrase was considered by the Court of Appeal in *Brown* [1985] Crim LR 212 and it took the view that the important point was whether the entry was 'effective'. A person could, therefore, enter a building when only part of the body is actually within it, so D had entered where the top half of his body was leaning into a shop window. The prosecution does not have to prove that the person was capable of stealing when only partially in a building. The issue is whether the partial entry was capable of constituting entry, as it was where D was stuck in an open window; the matter is then for the tribunal of fact to decide (*Ryan* (1996) 160 JP 610). **B4.86**

It was said in *Collins* that entry must be 'deliberate'. Consequently, it cannot be shown that this element of the crime has been satisfied if the entry is accidental, which it might be, for example, if boundaries of private land are unclear or obstructed by snow.

It is not clear whether a person who boards an inhabited vessel, but fails to get inside, can be said to have 'entered' the vessel. Arguably the person has not, and is in the same position as someone who climbs onto the roof of a building. There may be an attempted burglary on such facts, but nothing more.

Meaning of 'as a Trespasser' It is important that at the time D entered the building, the entry was as a trespasser (*Laing* [1995] Crim LR 395). A trespasser is someone who does not have permission, express or implied, to be on the premises. Since this is an aspect of the criminal law, it must be shown that there was a trespassory entry, and also that the person entered with *mens rea* (i.e. knew that the entry was as a trespasser or was reckless as to whether this was so). **B4.87**

Adequate permission can be given by someone other than the householder. In *Collins* [1973] QB 100, D climbed up a ladder to look into a girl's bedroom. As he reached the window, she woke up and, thinking D was her boyfriend, invited him in. There was some doubt as to whether he had already entered at that point. They had sexual intercourse before she realised her mistake. D was initially convicted of burglary with intent to rape (a variant now replaced by a new offence under the Sexual Offences Act 2003, s. 63). His appeal against that conviction succeeded because the jury had not been asked to consider whether he had entered the building as a trespasser and whether he knew or was reckless as to whether he was entering as a trespasser. It was held that the girl's invitation would have sufficed to make the entry non-trespassory but only if D was still outside the building at that time.

As to *mens rea* the Court of Appeal said (at p. 105E): **B4.88**

> ... there cannot be a conviction for entering premises 'as a trespasser' within the meaning of section 9 ... unless the person entering does so knowing that he is a trespasser and nevertheless deliberately enters, or, at the very least, is reckless as to whether or not he is entering the premises of another without the other party's consent.

The matter will not always be a simple one of deciding whether at the time D entered, permission had been granted. Permission, specific or general, may be exceeded. It is then to be determined whether that makes the entry trespassory. In *Jones* [1976] 3 All ER 54, D and E dishonestly entered a house belonging to D's father and there stole two television sets. The question for the Court was whether they had entered as trespassers for the purposes of s. 9. The Court said:

> ... a person is a trespasser for the purpose of section 9(1)(b) ... if he enters premises of another knowing that he is entering in excess of the permission that has been given to him, or being reckless as to whether he is entering in excess of the permission that has been given to him to enter. Provided the facts are known to the accused which enable him to realise that he is acting in excess of the permission given or that he is acting recklessly as to whether he exceeds that permission, then that is sufficient for the jury to decide that he is in fact a trespasser.

Since the jury were satisfied that D and E acted outside the scope of any permission they might otherwise have had, their convictions were upheld.

It is essential, therefore, for the person entering to know that entry is prohibited, or at least be advertently reckless as to the prohibition. In *Walkington* [1979] 2 All ER 716 (see **B4.85**) the Court of Appeal emphasised that it was necessary in order for a conviction to be sustained that D knew the counter area should not be entered.

The common-law doctrine of trespass *ab initio* has no application to burglary (*Collins* [1973] QB 100 at p. 107). If, having lawfully entered a building or part of a building, D then commits a theft inside it, this does not amount to burglary.

Burglary with Intent (s. 9(1)(a)): Proof of Intent

B4.89 On a charge of burglary with intent contrary to s. 9(1)(a), it must be shown that, at the time of the entry (not before and not after), D intended to commit the offences listed in s. 9(2). As to intention generally, see **A2.4**.

B4.90 **Intent to Commit an Offence of Stealing** 'Stealing' is defined in the Theft Act 1968, s. 1; see **B4.1**. It is not burglary to enter a building with intent to abstract electricity because abstracting electricity is not stealing (*Low v Blease* [1975] Crim LR 513). In *Gregory* (1981) 77 Cr App R 41, the Court of Appeal said (at p. 46):

> In a case of burglary of a dwelling-house and before any property is removed from it, it may consist of a continuing process and involve either a single appropriation by one or more persons or a number of appropriations of the property in the house by several persons at different times during the same incident... Thus a person who may have more the appearance of a handler than the thief can nevertheless still be convicted of theft, and thus of burglary, if the jury are satisfied that with the requisite dishonest intent he appropriated, or took part in the appropriation, of another person's goods.

As to the question whether, in theft and therefore burglary, an appropriation is instantaneous or continuing, see **B4.44**.

B4.91 **Intent to Commit an Offence of Inflicting Grievous Bodily Harm** In order to prove an intention to commit grievous bodily harm on a charge of burglary with intent it is unnecessary to prove an assault (*Metropolitan Police Commissioner v Wilson* [1984] AC 242). As to the meaning of 'grievous bodily harm', see generally **B2.67**.

In *O'Neill* (1986) *The Times*, 17 October 1986 the Court of Appeal appears to have decided, presumably on the facts of the particular case in question, that charges of burglary by entering a building with intent to inflict grievous bodily harm should not have been left to the jury because there was no specific express evidence of such intent. No weapons had been carried and no grievous bodily harm had been committed, even though two persons on the premises had been assaulted. The offence is committed by intending, at the time of entering premises as a trespasser, to inflict grievous bodily harm, and the fact that no grievous bodily harm is actually inflicted does not affect liability, though it may make it very difficult to prove the intent.

B4.92 **Intent to Commit an Offence of Doing Unlawful Damage** It is to be presumed that this phrase refers to what is now criminal damage (see **B8.1** to **B8.30**).

B4.93 **Conditional Intent** At one stage it was thought that a 'burglar's charter' had been created by the case of *Husseyn* (1977) 67 Cr App R 131. The argument was that if D only intended to steal that which was worth stealing, there would then be no settled intention to steal, since any intent was conditional on finding something of value. An answer was found in *Walkington* [1979] 2 All ER 716 and adopted in *A-G's Refs (Nos. 1 and 2 of 1979)* [1980] QB 180: if the indictment makes no reference to the intended theft of any specific items, D can be said to intend to steal anything in the building, and the fact that there was nothing in the building worth stealing is then immaterial. The problem is identical to that which may arise on a charge of theft (see **B4.64**).

Burglary (s. 9(1)(b)): Proof of Stealing or Grievous Bodily Harm

On a charge of burglary contrary to s. 9(1)(b), the prosecution must establish that D either stole or attempted to steal in the building or part of a building, or inflicted or attempted to inflict on any person in the building or part of a building any grievous bodily harm. For the meaning of 'steal' and 'inflict grievous bodily harm', see **B4.1** and **B2.67**. For the law of attempts, see **A5.72** ***et seq.*** It is not burglary under s. 9(1)(b) to cause unlawful damage, though intent to cause such damage is relevant to burglary with intent contrary to s. 9(1)(a). **B4.94**

Related Offence

An offence that might be considered as an alternative to burglary is that contrary to the Vagrancy Act 1824, s. 4(1), by which (i) every person wandering abroad and lodging in any barn or outhouse, or in any deserted or unoccupied building, or in the open air, or under a tent, or in any cart or wagon, and not giving a good account of himself; (ii) every person being found in or upon any dwelling house, warehouse, coach-house, stable, or outhouse, or in any enclosed yard, garden, or area, for any unlawful purpose; commits an offence. The maximum penalty is three months' imprisonment. If the CJA 2003, sch. 32, para. 146, is brought into force, the maximum penalty for an offence in category (i) will be a fine on level 1 of the standard scale and for an offence in category (ii) it will be a level 3 fine. As to the restricted meaning of 'enclosed yard... or area', see *Akhurst v DPP* [2009] EWHC 806 (Admin), in which it was held that this does not include a university campus or buildings. The phrase 'for an unlawful purpose' means for the purpose of committing an offence, such as burglary. Hiding from the police is not such a purpose (*L v CPS* [2007] EWHC 1843 (Admin), [2008] 1 Cr App R 8 (131)). **B4.95**

AGGRAVATED BURGLARY

Definition

Theft Act 1968, s. 10 **B4.96**

(1) A person is guilty of aggravated burglary if he commits any burglary and at the time has with him any firearm or imitation firearm, any weapon of offence, or any explosive.

Procedure

Aggravated burglary is triable only on indictment. It is normally a class 3 offence, but see CrimPD XIII, para. B (see Supplement, **CPD.XIII.B**) for the additional factors that the court considers on allocation. **B4.97**

Indictment

Statement of Offence **B4.98**

Aggravated burglary contrary to section 10(1) of the Theft Act 1968.

Particulars of Offence

A on or about the... day of... having entered a dwelling [or part of a dwelling, or a building or part of a building], namely..., as a trespasser stole therein [or attempted to steal therein, or inflicted grievous bodily harm upon... therein] and at the time had with him a firearm [or an imitation firearm, or a weapon of offence or an explosive], namely...

See also **B4.78**.

Alternative Verdicts

Burglary contrary to either s. 9(1)(a) or s. 9(1)(b) of the Theft Act 1968 (by virtue of the CLA 1967, s. 6(3)). See also **B4.79**. **B4.99**

Sentence

B4.100 The maximum penalty is life imprisonment (Theft Act 1968, s. 10(2)). In respect of aggravated burglary the definitive sentencing guideline, *Burglary Offences*, provides that for an offence falling within category 1 (greater harm and higher culpability) the starting point is ten years within a range of nine to 13 years; for category 2 (greater harm and lower culpability or lesser harm and higher culpability), the starting point is six years within a range of four to nine years, and for category 3 (lesser harm and lower culpability), the starting point is two years within a range of one to four years. The guideline stresses that relevant recent convictions are likely to result in an upward movement. Appropriate reduction should be made for a guilty plea.

Of the more important pre-guideline cases, towards the top of the scale of seriousness is *O'Driscoll* (1986) 8 Cr App R (S) 121, where D gained access to the home of an elderly man and struck him a number of blows with a hammer. V was also threatened with a lighted gas poker, tied up with wire and gagged. A sentence of 15 years was upheld. Subsequent decisions which treated *O'Driscoll* as a guideline case included *A-G's Refs (Nos. 32 and 33 of 1995)* [1996] 2 Cr App R (S) 345 and *Eastap* [1997] 2 Cr App R (S) 55. However, in the post-guideline case of *Smith* [2018] EWCA Crim 761, a similar sentence of 15 years' imprisonment was reduced to 13 years by the Court of Appeal. The victim of the offences was an 87-year-old jeweller who still undertook work at his home. The offenders broke into the house with sledge hammers, threatened him and locked him in his bedroom before stealing £150,000 worth of jewellery. D had a bad record, but the Court of Appeal noted that no actual violence had been used, and a sentence at the top of the category range was sufficient to meet the gravity of the offending. In *Ndaliki* [2018] EWCA Crim 1250, [2018] 2 Cr App R (S) 40 (343), consecutive sentences totalling 16 years' imprisonment for two offences of aggravated burglary, incorporating a small discount for a late plea, were upheld as severe but not manifestly excessive. D, with an accomplice, had committed two offences within days, first targeting a person in her home who was likely to have goods of high value, and then a person working alone in a pizza takeaway shop. In each case the victim was subjected to serious threats with a weapon, some actual violence and an extended ordeal.

Meaning of 'Firearm', 'Imitation Firearm', 'Weapon of Offence', 'Explosive'

B4.101 **Theft Act 1968, s. 10**

(1) ...and for this purpose—
  (a) 'firearm' includes an airgun or air pistol, and 'imitation firearm' means anything which has the appearance of being a firearm, whether capable of being discharged or not, and
  (b) 'weapon of offence' means any article made or adapted for use for causing injury to or incapacitating a person, or intended by the person having it with him for such use; and
  (c) 'explosive' means any article manufactured for the purpose of producing a practical effect by explosion, or intended by the person having it with him for that purpose.

B4.102 **Paragraph (a)** Whilst a definition of 'imitation firearm' is provided, there is no definition of 'firearm', except to make clear that it includes airguns and air pistols. It may be that the general definition of 'firearm' in the FA 1968 is appropriate (see **B12.8**).

B4.103 **Paragraph (b)** In *Stones* [1989] 1 WLR 156, approved in *Kelly* (1992) 97 Cr App R 245, the Court of Appeal said (at p. 160):

> It is not necessary to prove the intention to use the [weapon] to cause injury etc. during the course of the burglary.
>
> ...The mischief at which the section is clearly aimed is that if a burglar has a weapon which he intends to use to injure some person unconnected with the premises burgled [as in the instant case], he may nevertheless be tempted to use it if challenged during the course of the burglary and put under sufficient pressure.

The Court also drew attention to the similarity between para. (b) and the provisions of the Prevention of Crime Act 1953, s. 1, concerned with the possession of offensive weapons. Whilst the two provisions are not identical since the phrase 'incapacitating a person' does not appear in s. 1 of the 1953 Act, some assistance may be obtained from the cases concerned with possession of offensive weapons. In the case of something (such as a bottle or screw-driver) that is a weapon only because D 'has it with him for such use', D must intend to use it to injure or incapacitate, or to do so if the need arises, and not merely intend to frighten (*Kelly* at p. 251).

The defence of lawful authority or reasonable excuse for the possession of an offensive weapon (see **B12.168** to **B12.170**) does not appear to apply to aggravated burglary.

Paragraph (c) The definition of 'explosive' for the purposes of aggravated burglary is narrower than that to be found in the Explosive Substances Act 1883, but that Act may be of assistance in determining the meaning of s. 10(1)(c). **B4.104**

Meaning of 'Has with Him'

There is a requirement for a degree of immediate control of the weapon of offence or other article (*Kelt* [1977] 3 All ER 1099; *Pawlicki* [1992] 3 All ER 902). Indeed, 'the word will normally mean "carrying"' (*Kelt* and *Klass* [1998] 1 Cr App R 453). Since a dictum in *Stones* [1989] 1 WLR 156 at p. 160, it has been unclear whether the prosecution must prove that D knew he had a weapon of offence with him or whether it suffices that D knew he had something with him which was, in fact, a weapon of offence. It is submitted that the latter interpretation is to be preferred, being more consistent with the general approach to this type of offence. Such at least is the approach adopted under the FA 1968, ss. 19 (see **B12.110**) and 1 (see **B12.36**). As to knowledge of possession in drugs cases, see **B19.29**. This issue has also arisen for decision under the Prevention of Crime Act 1953, s. 1 where the matter is controversial (see **B12.162**). The offence contrary to the FA 1968, s. 18, explicitly requires knowledge (see **B12.107**). **B4.105**

Relevant Time

The gravamen of the aggravated offence of burglary with intent is entry into a building with a weapon. Therefore, at least one of the entrants to the building must have a weapon with him at that time (*Klass* [1998] 1 Cr App R 453). If, however, D is charged, as in *O'Leary* (1986) 82 Cr App R 341, with aggravated burglary by stealing *after* entry, under ss. 10 and 9(1)(b), it follows that, according to the Court of Appeal in that case (at p. 343): **B4.106**

> . . . the time at which [D] must be proved to have had with him a weapon of offence to make him guilty of aggravated burglary was the time at which he actually stole . . .

In *O'Leary* D entered a building as a trespasser, armed himself with a knife from the kitchen, and confronted the occupiers to demand their cash and jewellery. This was an act of theft, and since D at that point had the kitchen knife in his hand it became aggravated burglary, even though D may have entered the building unarmed. See also *Kelly* (1992) 97 Cr App R 245. Cases decided under the Prevention of Crime Act 1953, s. 1 (such as *Ohlson v Hylton* [1975] 2 All ER 490), are of no assistance here because of the different purposes of the two provisions (*Kelly* (1992) 97 Cr App R 245).

No s. 10 offence was proved in *Chevannes* [2009] EWCA Crim 2725. D's accomplice carried a weapon when he and D assaulted V at the door of his caravan and when they chased him from it, but there was no evidence that D carried any weapon when he went on to burgle the caravan.

REMOVAL OF ARTICLES FROM PLACES OPEN TO THE PUBLIC

Definition

B4.107

Theft Act 1968, s. 11

(1) Subject to subsections (2) and (3) below, where the public have access to a building in order to view the building or part of it, or a collection or part of a collection housed in it, any person who without lawful authority removes from the building or its grounds the whole or part of any article displayed or kept for display to the public in the building or that part of it or in its grounds shall be guilty of an offence.

Procedure

B4.108 Removal of an article from a place open to the public is triable either way (MCA 1980, s. 17 and sch. 1, para. 28). When tried on indictment it is normally a class 3 offence, but see CrimPD XIII, para. B (see Supplement, **CPD.XIII.B**) for the additional factors that the court considers on allocation.

Indictment

B4.109

Statement of Offence

Removing an article from a place open to the public contrary to section 11 of the Theft Act 1968.

Particulars of Offence

A on or about the... day of... without lawful authority removed from the V art gallery, being a place to which the public then had access in order to view an art collection therein, a painting, namely *Portrait of the Madonna* by von Klomp.

Sentence

B4.110 The maximum penalty is five years on indictment (s. 11(4)); six months and/or an unlimited fine summarily. There is no offence-specific guideline but the Sentencing Council's *General Guideline: Overarching Principles* (see Supplement, **SG2-1**) is used for all offenders sentenced on or after 1 October 2019.

Purpose for which the Public Have Access

B4.111 An offence under s. 11(1), can be committed only in relation to a building to which the public have access for the purpose of viewing the building (or a part of it) or a collection (or part of a collection). It is the purpose of the inviter in granting access that matters (*Barr* [1978] Crim LR 244).

Meaning of 'Collection'

B4.112

Theft Act 1968, s. 11

(1) For this purpose, 'collection' includes a collection got together for a temporary purpose, but references in this section to a collection do not apply to a collection made or exhibited for the purpose of effecting sales or other commercial dealings.

Time of Public Access

B4.113

Theft Act 1968, s. 11

(2) It is immaterial for purposes of subsection (1) above, that the public's access to a building is limited to a particular period or particular occasion; but where anything removed from a building or its grounds is there otherwise than as forming part of, or being on loan for exhibition with, a collection intended for permanent exhibition to the public, the person removing it does not thereby commit an offence under this section unless he removes it on a day when the public have access to the building as mentioned in subsection (1) above.

If an art gallery, for example, is usually open it is possible for an offence under s. 11(1) to be committed on a day when the gallery is closed by removing an item which is part of a collection intended for permanent exhibition, whether it is actually on display or kept in store and exhibited on a rota basis (*Durkin* [1973] QB 786).

Meaning of 'Displayed or Kept for Display'

Whether an article is displayed, or kept for display, depends upon the intention of the person setting out the articles. For example, in *Barr* [1978] Crim LR 244 it was found that a cross and ewer in a church were not on display but were intended to be aids to worship and devotion. **B4.114**

Belief in Lawful Authority

Theft Act 1968, s. 11 **B4.115**

(3) A person does not commit an offence under this section if he believes that he has lawful authority for the removal of the thing in question or that he would have it if the person entitled to give it knew of the removal and the circumstances of it.

It is submitted that, if the defence raise the issue of belief in lawful authority, it is then for the prosecution to prove beyond reasonable doubt that D had no such belief (compare the position under s. 12 of the Act, see **B4.124**). As to the defence of mistake generally, see **A3.2** to **A3.11**.

TAKING CONVEYANCE WITHOUT AUTHORITY

Definition

Theft Act 1968, s. 12 **B4.116**

(1) Subject to subsections (5) and (6) below, a person shall be guilty of an offence if, without having the consent of the owner or other lawful authority, he takes any conveyance for his own or another's use or, knowing that any conveyance has been taken without such authority, drives it or allows himself to be carried in or on it.

Procedure

An offence under s. 12(1), is triable only summarily. However, a count for such an offence may be included in an indictment for another offence in the circumstances set out in the CJA 1988, s. 40 (see **D11.18**). On the trial of an indictment for theft, the jury may find the accused guilty of an offence under s. 12(1) as an alternative verdict (s. 12(4)). **B4.117**

Proceedings for the offence (unless they fall within s. 12(4)) in relation to a mechanically propelled vehicle (a) shall not be commenced after the end of the period of three years beginning with the day on which the offence was committed, but (b) subject to that, may be commenced at any time within the period of six months beginning with the relevant day (s. 12(4A)). 'The relevant day' means:

(a) in the case of a prosecution for an offence under s. 12(1) by a public prosecutor, the day on which sufficient evidence to justify the proceedings came to the knowledge of any person responsible for deciding whether to commence any such proceedings;
(b) in the case of a prosecution for an offence under s. 12(1), which is commenced by a person other than a public prosecutor after the discontinuance of a prosecution falling within s. 12(4B)(a) and relates to the same facts, the day on which sufficient evidence to justify the proceedings came to the knowledge of the person who has decided to commence the prosecution or (if later) the discontinuance of the other prosecution;
(c) in the case of any other prosecution for an offence under s. 12(1), the day on which sufficient evidence to justify the proceedings came to the knowledge of the person who has decided to commence the prosecution (s. 12(4B)).

For the purposes of s. 12(4A)(b), a certificate of a person responsible for deciding whether to commence a prosecution of a kind mentioned in s. 12(4B)(a) as to the date on which such evidence as is mentioned in the certificate came to the knowledge of any person responsible for deciding whether to commence any such prosecution shall be conclusive evidence of that fact (s. 12(4C)).

Sentencing Guidelines

B4.118 The maximum penalty for taking a conveyance without authority is six months and/or an unlimited fine (s. 12(2)). Additionally, for the offence or an attempt to commit it in respect of a motor vehicle, there is discretionary disqualification (RTOA 1988, sch. 2). The same maximum penalty and liability for disqualification applies in relation to the offence of driving or allowing oneself to be carried in or on a conveyance taken without authority.

The *Magistrates' Court Sentencing Guidelines* provide guidelines for this offence (see Supplement, SG10-151).

Meaning of 'Conveyance'

B4.119 Whilst the marginal note to s. 12 uses the phrase 'motor vehicle or other conveyance', the section itself refers only to a 'conveyance'. A definition of 'conveyance' is to be found in s. 12(7)(a):

> 'conveyance' means any conveyance constructed or adapted for the carriage of a person or persons whether by land, water or air, except that it does not include a conveyance constructed or adapted for use only under the control of a person not carried in or on it, and 'drive' shall be construed accordingly.

This definition would ordinarily include a pedal cycle, but for s. 12(5), which creates a separate offence (see **B4.135**), and makes clear that the offence under s. 12(1) does not apply in relation to pedal cycles. An electrically assisted (or pedelec) cycle arguably falls within s. 12(1). In *Neal v Gribble* (1978) 68 Cr App R 9, the Divisional Court had to consider whether a horse was a conveyance within the meaning of s. 12. The Court was of the view that it was not such a conveyance, since the definition in s. 12(7)(a) 'seems to be directed towards artefacts rather than towards animals'.

Taking for his Own or Another's Use

B4.120 It is essential that a conveyance be moved in order for it to be taken, however small that movement may be. Merely trying to start the engine of a motor vehicle without moving the vehicle does not amount to taking it (*Bogacki* [1973] QB 832). Attempt is not available as an alternative offence (CAA 1981, s. 1(1) and (4)). On a charge of taking it is not necessary that D used the conveyance to convey himself, merely that D 'took' it. In *Pearce* [1973] Crim LR 321 an appeal against conviction was dismissed where D placed an inflatable rubber dinghy on a trailer and drove away with it.

On a charge of taking, the prosecution must prove that D took the conveyance 'for his own or another's use'. In *Bow* (1976) 64 Cr App R 54, it was argued that D had not taken the conveyance 'for his own use' when he got into a Land Rover which was obstructing his way and released its handbrake and let it coast for about 200 yards. The Court of Appeal said (at p. 58):

> The short answer . . . is that where as here, a conveyance is taken and moved in a way which necessarily involves its use as a conveyance, the taker cannot be heard to say that the taking was not for that use. If he has in fact taken the conveyance and used it as such, his motive in so doing is . . . quite immaterial.

B4.121 In *Stokes* [1983] RTR 59, D pushed a car round a corner as a practical joke. The conviction could not be upheld because the judge failed specifically to emphasise the importance of establishing that it was being taken for use as a conveyance, rather than merely that it was 'taken'.

Pearce, Bow and *Stokes* were further explained by the Court of Appeal in *Marchant* (1984) 80 Cr App R 361. Robert Goff LJ, giving the judgment of the Court, stated that 'to be guilty of the offence, D must have both taken the vehicle, i.e. have taken control of it and caused it to be moved, and must have done so for his own or another's use'. That phrase requires that it be taken *for use as* a conveyance, which is satisfied provided that is why it was taken, even if it was never so used. For example, if D takes a car by pushing it around a corner and leaving it, this satisfies the first element of the requirement. If D intends to drive it later, or allow a friend to drive it, the full offence is committed by the initial act of moving it. In *Pearce* the dinghy was clearly taken and D's purpose was to use it as a dinghy, that is, as a conveyance. In *Bow* D actually used the Land Rover as a conveyance whilst taking it. In *Stokes* D did take the conveyance, but his purpose was not to use it as a conveyance and so the offence was not committed.

Having once taken a conveyance, D does not commit a further offence each time it is used, but if D then abandons it, and E finds and takes it afresh, E may be guilty of a separate s. 12 offence (*DPP v Spriggs* [1994] RTR 1).

Without the Consent of the Owner or Other Lawful Authority

On a charge of taking a conveyance without authority, the prosecution must prove that the **B4.122**
taking was actually without the owner's consent or other lawful authority (*Ambler* [1979] RTR 217; *Sturrock v DPP* [1996] RTR 216). 'Owner' is defined by s. 12(7)(b) of the Theft Act 1968, in relation to a conveyance which is the subject of a hiring agreement or hire-purchase agreement, as meaning the person in possession of the conveyance under that agreement.

In *Whittaker v Campbell* [1984] QB 318 the two defendants, neither of whom had a driving licence, had come by Dunn's licence. They hired a van, using that acquired licence by pretending that one of them was Dunn. They paid the appropriate hire charge and drove the van away. The Divisional Court was asked to consider the effect of the false representation on the consent that was obtained as a consequence. It stated that there is no general principle of law that fraud vitiates consent. The Court took the view that where force is used, it is possible to distinguish between consent and mere submission, but that when the factor being exercised was fraud and not force, no such sensible distinction can be drawn. In common-sense terms, the owner has consented and, despite the fraud, that means that no offence is committed.

In *Peart* [1970] 2 QB 672, the Court of Appeal quashed a conviction where D had falsely **B4.123**
represented to the owner of a car that he needed it to drive from Bedlington to Alnwick to sign a contract. The owner let him have the vehicle, provided he returned it that day. As D always intended, he drove the car instead to Burnley in the evening. The Court reserved the question whether a fundamental misrepresentation can vitiate consent (according to *Whittaker v Campbell* it would appear that it does not), but decided that the sort of false pretence in the particular case did not vitiate the consent, and the activity involved was not the type of activity with which s. 12 was concerned.

In *Phipps* (1970) 54 Cr App R 300 the Court of Appeal approved a direction by the trial judge that if, after a lawful purpose had been fulfilled, D then did not return the car but drove it off on his own business, the offence was committed. It is not clear whether a deception was practised upon the owner, and the decision of the Court of Appeal does not raise the issue of such a deception. It may, therefore, be that this case can be regarded as consistent with *Peart* and *Whittaker v Campbell* since in *Phipps* there may well have been no question of consent obtained by fraud or a false representation. Rather it seems that it was a case of D going beyond the limits of the consent that had been given by the owner of the car (see also *McKnight v Davies* [1974] RTR 4).

Mens Rea of Offence of Taking

There are two aspects to the mental element of the offence. **B4.124**

First, the taking must be intentional. In *Blayney v Knight* (1974) 60 Cr App R 269, Lord Widgery CJ stated, 'I do not see how anybody could be charged with taking a motor car because of the fact that the car accidentally moves forward'.

Secondly, the Theft Act 1968, s. 12(6), provides:

> A person does not commit an offence under this section by anything done in the belief that he has lawful authority to do it or that he would have the owner's consent if the owner knew of his doing it and the circumstances of it.

It is essential that this belief exist at the time of the taking. It is not enough if the owner says, later, that he would have consented had he known (*Ambler* [1979] RTR 217). This question is one for the court to decide, and the court may well take into account factors such as whether D was insured to drive it (*Clotworthy* [1981] RTR 477).

The onus of proof of this matter lies on the prosecution (*MacPherson* [1973] RTR 157; *Gannon* (1987) 87 Cr App R 254) but before that stage is reached, it is for the defence to raise the issue by adducing or identifying evidence that tends to indicate such belief (*Gannon*).

The offence is one of basic intent for the purposes of any defence involving voluntary intoxication (*Gannon, MacPherson*). As to basic and specific intent generally, see **A3.17** to **A3.22**.

Driving or Allowing Himself to be Carried

B4.125 Section 12(7)(a) of the Theft Act 1968 indicates that 'drive' is to be construed in accordance with the meaning of 'conveyance' (see **B4.119**) and therefore includes 'driving' not only motor vehicles, but any land, water or air conveyance. The meaning of 'drives' is considered generally at **C1.2**.

On a charge of allowing himself to be carried in or on a conveyance taken without authority, it is not enough for the prosecution to prove that D was in or on the conveyance; there must have been some movement of the conveyance (*Miller* [1976] Crim LR 417). If, having taken a motor vehicle, D's friend offers D a lift and D gets in, D then commits no offence until the vehicle moves off (*Diggin* (1980) 72 Cr App R 204).

Mens Rea of Offence of Driving or Allowing Himself to be Carried

B4.126 On a charge of driving or allowing himself to be carried in or on a conveyance taken without authority, it must be proved that D knew that the conveyance had been taken without lawful authority (*Diggin* (1980) 72 Cr App R 204; *Boldizsar v Knight* [1980] Crim LR 653). As to the meaning of these terms, see **B4.119** to **B4.124**. Mere suspicion is not enough, but wilful blindness must suffice, as where D chooses not to inquire as to how a penniless friend with numerous convictions for s. 12 offences could legitimately be in possession of a new and expensive car. As to knowledge generally, see **A2.14**.

Section 12(6) of the Theft Act 1968 applies to the offence of driving or allowing oneself to be carried in or on a conveyance taken without consent (see **B4.125**).

AGGRAVATED VEHICLE-TAKING

B4.127 The Theft Act 1968, s. 12A (inserted by the Aggravated Vehicle-Taking Act 1992), creates aggravated forms of the basic s. 12 offence.

Theft Act 1968, s. 12A

(1) Subject to subsection (3) below, a person is guilty of aggravated taking of a vehicle if—
  (a) he commits an offence under section 12(1) above (in this section referred to as a 'basic offence') in relation to a mechanically propelled vehicle; and
  (b) it is proved that, at any time after the vehicle was unlawfully taken (whether by him or another) and before it was recovered, the vehicle was driven, or injury or damage was caused, in one or more of the circumstances set out in paragraphs (a) to (d) of subsection (2) below.

(2) The circumstances referred to in subsection (1)(b) above are—
(a) that the vehicle was driven dangerously on a road or other public place;
(b) that, owing to the driving of the vehicle, an accident occurred by which injury was caused to any person;
(c) that, owing to the driving of the vehicle, an accident occurred by which damage was caused to any property, other than the vehicle;
(d) that damage was caused to the vehicle.

Since the maximum penalty is greater where death is caused (see **B4.130**), s. 12A(1) and (2)(b) create two offences (*Sherwood* [1995] RTR 60, following *Courtie* [1984] AC 403). Where, however, there is clear evidence of causing death by dangerous driving (see **C3.7**) following the unauthorised taking of a motor vehicle, that offence should ordinarily be charged in preference to a charge under s. 12A (*Roberts* [2013] EWCA Crim 785, [2013] RTR 32 (436)).

Procedure

The offences are triable either way. When tried on indictment they are normally class 3 offences, but see CrimPD XIII, para. B (see Supplement, **CPD.XIII.B**) for the additional factors that the court considers on allocation. **B4.128**

D has no right to elect trial on indictment where the only allegation is of damage to the vehicle or other property or both and the total value of the damage alleged to have been caused is less than the 'relevant sum' (i.e. £5,000) (MCA 1980, ss. 22 and 33 and sch. 2: see **D6.26**).

See the *Magistrates' Court Sentencing Guidelines* (see Supplement, **SG10-149**) for indications as to when a case should be sent to the Crown Court.

Alternative Verdict

Under the Theft Act 1968, s. 12A(5), where D is acquitted of an aggravated offence, D may be convicted instead of the basic summary offence, contrary to s. 12(1) (see **B4.116** ***et seq.*** and **D19.55**). The Crown Court in such a case has the same powers and duties as a magistrates' court would have had on convicting D of such an offence (s. 12A(6)) (see **B4.118**). **B4.129**

Sentence

The maximum penalty is, on indictment, two years or a fine or both. The maximum penalty, on indictment, is increased to 14 years where it is proved that, in circumstances falling within the Theft Act 1968, s. 12A(2)(b), the accident caused the death of the person concerned (s. 12A(4)). **B4.130**

The maximum penalty on summary conviction is six months and/or an unlimited fine. The limit on penalties imposed by the MCA 1980, s. 33(1), with regard to an offence tried summarily in pursuance of the MCA 1980, s. 22, does not apply where the offence is aggravated vehicle-taking (MCA 1980, s. 33(3)).

By virtue of the RTOA 1988, ss. 28, 96 and 97 and sch. 2, part II, where a person is convicted of aggravated vehicle-taking, disqualification from driving is obligatory, endorsement of licence is obligatory and the penalty points which may be imposed for the offence are 3 to 11. As to disqualification, endorsement of licence and penalty points, see **C7**. The fact that D did not drive the vehicle at any particular time or at all is not a special reason to avoid obligatory disqualification (RTOA 1988, s. 34).

The *Magistrates' Court Sentencing Guidelines* provide guidelines for this offence when dealt with summarily (see Supplement, **SG10-149**). There is no offence-specific guideline but the Sentencing Council's *General Guideline: Overarching Principles* (see Supplement, **SG2-1**) is used for all offenders sentenced on or after 1 October 2019.

In *Clifford* [2007] EWCA Crim 2442, [2008] 1 Cr App R (S) 100 (593) D pleaded guilty to aggravated vehicle-taking resulting in death. D had taken his partner's car for a drive but was not authorised to do so since he had only a provisional licence. A seven-year-old boy was killed when **B4.131** he stepped into the path of the car. It was accepted by the prosecution that D, who had no prior driving convictions, had not been speeding nor had he consumed alcohol, and that D could not have seen the boy and avoided the accident. D initially left the scene but shortly afterwards went to the police station. A sentence of two years' imprisonment was reduced to six months.

Actus Reus

B4.132 An offence of aggravated vehicle-taking can be committed only if an offence under the Theft Act 1968, s. 12(1), is committed in respect of a mechanically propelled vehicle (s. 12A(1)(a)). In the RTA 1988, s. 185, the following are defined and are all mechanically propelled vehicles: heavy locomotive, heavy motor car, invalid carriage, light locomotive, motor car, motor cycle, motor tractor, and motor vehicle. This excludes electrically assisted (pedelec) cycles, aircraft or boats. Secondly, the prosecution must prove that, at any time after the vehicle was taken and before it was recovered, one or more of the circumstances in s. 12A(2)(a) to (d) occurred (s. 12A(1)(b)). All that the prosecution must prove is that the circumstances occurred; they do not have to prove that D was the cause of them (*Dawes v DPP* [1995] 1 Cr App R 65); it is for D to prove one of the specific defences in order to avoid conviction (see **B4.134**).

The circumstances of aggravation in s. 12A(2) are listed at **B4.127**. The phrase 'driven dangerously', which occurs in s. 12A(2)(a), is defined in s. 12A(7) in identical terms to the definition which applies to the offence of dangerous driving (see **C3.10**). Whilst the vehicle must be driven dangerously for s. 12A(2)(a) to apply, there is no such express requirement in s. 12A(2)(b) or (c), and in *Marsh* [1997] 1 Cr App R 67 it was held that the simple fact that the vehicle was being driven, even without fault, sufficed for the purposes of liability under s. 12A(2)(b); but *Marsh* was overruled by the Supreme Court in *Taylor* [2016] UKSC 5, [2016] 1 WLR 500, in which Lord Sumption, giving the judgment of the Court, said:

> [29]...Of the four aggravating circumstances identified in subsection (2), (a) expressly imports a requirement of fault (the car must have been driven dangerously), while (b), (c) and (d) contain nothing which expressly excludes such a requirement. As Lord Reid explained in *Sweet v Parsley* [1970] AC 132 this difference cannot itself be enough to make (b), (c) and (d) operate independent of fault. On the contrary, in the case of (b) and (c), it is implicit in the requirement that the accident must have occurred 'owing to the driving of the vehicle', that there will have been something wrong with the driving. As this court pointed out in *Hughes* [2013] 1 WLR 2461, the driving cannot be said to have caused the accident if it merely explained how the vehicle came to be in the place where the accident occurred.
>
> ...
>
> [32] I would express the test applicable in this case in the same terms as Lord Hughes and Lord Toulson expressed it in *Hughes* at para [36]. There must be 'at least some act or omission in the control of the car, which involves some element of fault, whether amounting to careless/inconsiderate driving or not, and which contributes in some more than minimal way to the death'.

If, however, damage or injury is indeed caused by the driving of a motor vehicle that D has taken unlawfully, D may be convicted even if not proved to have been in or near to the vehicle at the time. To avoid this, D may however seek to establish a defence under s. 12A(3) (see **B4.134**).

None of the other phrases used in s. 12A(2) are specifically defined. For 'damage', see **B8.6**; for 'driving', see **C1.2**; for 'accident', see **C1.1** and *Branchflower* [2004] EWCA Crim 2042, [2005] 1 Cr App R 10 (140), where it was decided that 'accident' in this offence is perfectly capable of applying to an untoward occurrence that has adverse physical results, notwithstanding that one event in the chain of events which led to the untoward occurrence was a deliberate act on the part of some mischievous person.

An offence under s. 12A may be committed only in the period after the vehicle is taken and before it is recovered. A vehicle is recovered when it is restored to its owner or other lawful possession or custody (s. 12A(8)); a similar concept is used in the offence of handling stolen goods, see **B4.169**. 'Owner' has the same meaning as in s. 12 (s. 12A(8)) (see **B4.123**).

Mens Rea

Mens rea must be established with regard to the first element of an offence of aggravated vehicle-taking, i.e. the *mens rea* of the basic offence (see **B4.124** and **B4.126**). No *mens rea* need be shown with regard to the second element, the circumstances of aggravation: the offences are offences of strict liability in that regard. **B4.133**

Specific Defence

Theft Act 1968, s. 12A **B4.134**

(3) A person is not guilty of an offence under this section if he proves that, as regards any such proven driving, injury or damage as is referred to in subsection (1)(b) above, either—
 (a) the driving, accident or damage referred to in subsection (2) above occurred before he committed the basic offence; or
 (b) he was neither in nor in the immediate vicinity of the vehicle when that driving, accident or damage occurred.

TAKING OR RIDING A PEDAL CYCLE WITHOUT AUTHORITY

It is an offence, contrary to the Theft Act 1968, s. 12(5), and subject to s. 12(6) (see **B4.124**), for a person, without having the consent of the owner or other lawful authority, to take a pedal cycle for his own or another's use, or ride a pedal cycle knowing it to have been taken without such authority. In *Sturrock v DPP* [1996] RTR 216, it was held that it is not necessary to have a formal statement of ownership from the owner of a cycle where the primary facts permit the inference that the cycle had not been abandoned and had an owner. The offence is punishable on summary conviction with a fine not exceeding level 3 on the standard scale. **B4.135**

INTERFERENCE WITH VEHICLES

Definition

Criminal Attempts Act 1981, s. 9 **B4.136**

(1) A person is guilty of the offence of vehicle interference if he interferes with a motor vehicle or trailer or with anything carried in or on a motor vehicle or trailer with the intention that an offence specified in subsection (2) below shall be committed by himself or some other person.
(2) The offences mentioned in subsection (1) above are—
 (a) theft of the motor vehicle or trailer or part of it;
 (b) theft of anything carried in or on the motor vehicle or trailer; and
 (c) an offence under section 12(1) of the Theft Act 1968 (taking and driving away without consent);
 and, if it is shown that a person accused of an offence under this section intended that one of those offences should be committed, it is immaterial that it cannot be shown which it was.

Procedure

The offence is triable summarily only (CAA 1981, s. 9(3)). **B4.137**

Sentence

The maximum penalty is imprisonment for a term not exceeding three months or a fine not exceeding level 4 on the standard scale or both (CAA 1981, s. 9(3)). **B4.138**

The *Magistrates' Court Sentencing Guidelines* provide guidelines for this offence (see Supplement, SG10-147).

Elements

B4.139 As to theft, see **B4.1** ***et seq***. As to offences under the Theft Act 1968, s. 12(1), see **B4.116** ***et seq***.

There is no definition of 'interference'. Clearly there has to be interference as well as intention. Merely looking into cars is probably not an act of interference whereas opening doors and putting pressure on the door handles is an act of interference. However, whether placing a hand on a door handle is an act of interference is not clear, nor was it clarified in the Crown Court case of *Reynolds and Warren v Metropolitan Police* [1982] Crim LR 831.

'Motor vehicle' and 'trailer', by virtue of s. 9(5), have the same meaning as in the RTA 1988, s. 185(1):

> 'motor vehicle' means, subject to section 20 of the Chronically Sick and Disabled Persons Act 1970 (which makes special provision about invalid carriages, within the meaning of that Act), a mechanically propelled vehicle intended or adapted for use on roads, and 'trailer' means a vehicle drawn by a motor vehicle.

ABSTRACTING ELECTRICITY

Definition

B4.140 **Theft Act 1968, s. 13**

> A person who dishonestly uses without due authority, or dishonestly causes to be wasted or diverted, any electricity shall on conviction on indictment be liable to imprisonment for a term not exceeding five years.

Procedure

B4.141 Abstracting electricity is triable either way (MCA 1980, s. 17 and sch. 1, para. 28). When tried on indictment it is normally a class 3 offence, but see CrimPD XIII, para. B (see Supplement, **CPD.XIII.B**) for the additional factors that the court considers on allocation.

Indictment

B4.142 *Statement of Offence*

> Abstracting electricity contrary to section 13 of the Theft Act 1968.

Particulars of Offence

> A on or about the... day of... dishonestly and without due authority used [or dishonestly caused to be wasted or diverted] a quantity of electricity.

Sentencing Guidelines

B4.143 The maximum penalty on indictment is five years; six months or an unlimited fine, or both, summarily. The definitive sentencing guideline *Theft* (see Supplement, **SG33-6**) applies to adult offenders sentenced on or after 1 February 2016.

The *Magistrates' Court Sentencing Guidelines* provide guidelines for this offence when tried summarily.

Actus Reus

B4.144 Electricity cannot be property and so when electricity is 'obtained' the only available offence is the present one (*Low v Blease* [1975] Crim LR 513). Any use, waste or diversion of electricity will suffice (*Low v Blease*), so a meter does not have to be tampered with (*McCreadie* (1992) 96 Cr App R 143). Electricity is abstracted where the electricity supply to a house is reconnected without the consent of the electricity supplier (*Boggeln v Williams* [1978] 2 All ER 1061). It is also abstracted where the electricity supply to a house is caused not to be registered by the meter

(*Collins v DPP* (1987) *The Times*, 20 October 1987). It may well be an abstraction of electricity to make a call from a telephone belonging to another person (*Low v Blease*).

Mens Rea

Abstracting electricity is an offence of dishonesty which must now be given the largely objective meaning adopted by the Supreme Court in *Ivey v Genting Casinos* [2017] UKSC 67, [2018] AC 391 (see **B4.54**). This must be so even though the Court of Appeal in *Boggeln v Williams* [1978] 2 All ER 1061 took the view that 'dishonesty' was to be approached as a subjective concept in s. 13. **B4.145**

DISHONEST USE OF TELECOMMUNICATION SYSTEMS AND DISHONEST RECEIPT OF PROGRAMMES

Electronic Communications Service

It is an offence, contrary to the Communications Act 2003, s. 125(1), dishonestly to obtain an electronic communications service with intent to avoid payment of a charge applicable to the provision of that service. Section 125(2) makes it clear that it is not an offence under s. 125 to obtain a service mentioned in the Copyright, Designs and Patents Act 1988, s. 297(1) (see **B4.147**). The offence is triable either way, and the maximum penalty is, on conviction on indictment, imprisonment for a term not exceeding five years or a fine or both; on summary conviction, imprisonment for a term not exceeding six months or an unlimited fine or both (s. 125(3)). It is also an offence, contrary to s. 126(1), for D to have in his possession or under his control anything which may be used for obtaining an electronic communications service, provided D has the requisite intention (which is defined in s. 126(3)). It is also an offence, contrary to s. 126(2), to supply or offer to supply anything which may be so used, where D knows or believes that the intentions of the person supplied or offered fall within s. 126(3). Both offences under s. 126 are triable either way and the maximum penalty, on conviction on indictment, is a term of imprisonment not exceeding five years, a fine or both; on summary conviction, a term of imprisonment not exceeding six months, an unlimited fine or both (s. 126(5)). For neither of these offences will an intention fall within s. 126(3) if it relates exclusively to the obtaining of a service mentioned in the Copyright, Designs and Patents Act 1988, s. 297(1) (s. 126(4)). For the definition of relevant terms, see s. 126(6) and s. 151. **B4.146**

Broadcast or Cable Service

It is a summary offence, contrary to the Copyright, Designs and Patents Act 1988, s. 297(1), dishonestly to receive a programme included in a broadcasting or cable programme service provided from a place in the UK with intent to avoid payment of any charge applicable to the reception of the programme. Section 297A of the 1988 Act (inserted by the Conditional Access (Unauthorised Decoders) Regulations 2000 (SI 2000 No. 1175) creates an offence triable either way concerned with certain commercial activities in relation to unauthorised decoders (i.e. apparatus to enable receipt of encrypted transmissions). **B4.147**

Mobile Telephone Re-programming

The Mobile Telephones (Re-programming) Act 2002 creates four offences concerned with the re-programming of mobile telephones: changing a unique device identifier (s. 1(1)(a)); interfering with a unique device identifier's operation (s. 1(1)(b)); offering or agreeing to change, or interfere with the operation of, a unique device identifier (s. 1(1)(c)); and offering or agreeing to arrange for another person to do so (s. 1(1)(d)). **B4.148**

A unique device identifier is an electronic equipment identifier which is unique to a mobile wireless communications device (s. 1(2) and s. 2(4)); a SIM card is an obvious example. D does not commit an offence if D is the device manufacturer or does the act with the written consent of the manufacturer (s. 1(2)). The maximum penalty is, on indictment, five years' imprisonment or a fine or both, and summarily, six months' imprisonment or an unlimited fine or both (s. 1(4)). The Act also creates three offences concerned with the possession or supply of things for such programming. D commits such an offence by: (1) having in his custody or under his control anything which may be used for the purpose of changing or interfering with a unique device identifier's operation where D has the intention to use the thing unlawfully for that purpose or to allow it to be used unlawfully for that purpose (s. 2(1)); (2) supplying anything which may be used for the purpose of changing or interfering with a unique device identifier's operation where D knows or believes that the person to whom it is supplied intends to use it unlawfully for that purpose or to allow it to be used unlawfully for that purpose (s. 2(2)); (3) offering to supply anything which may be used for the purpose of changing or interfering with a unique device identifier's operation where D knows or believes that the person to whom it is offered intends, if it is supplied to him, to use it unlawfully for that purpose or to allow it to be used unlawfully for that purpose (s. 2(3)). The maximum penalty, on indictment, is five years' imprisonment or a fine or both; on summary conviction, six months' imprisonment or an unlimited fine or both (s. 2(6)).

Sentence

B4.149 In *Nadig* (1993) 14 Cr App R (S) 49 D was convicted of fraudulent use of a telecommunications system. He used a tone-dialling device to make calls from a telephone box without paying. A suspended sentence was held to be wrong in principle for an isolated offence. Auld J, in the Court of Appeal, said that the preferred sentence was a fine, and that comparison between sentencing for this offence and sentencing for abstracting electricity (see **B4.143**) would be helpful only where the fraudulent use of the telephone had taken place over a period of time. See also *Adewale* (1994) 15 Cr App R (S) 790 and *Aslam* [1996] 2 Cr App R 377.

GOING EQUIPPED

Definition

B4.150 Theft Act 1968, s. 25

(1) A person shall be guilty of an offence if, when not at his place of abode, he has with him any article for use in the course of or in connection with any burglary or theft.
(2) A person guilty of an offence under this section shall on conviction on indictment be liable to imprisonment for a term not exceeding three years.
(3) Where a person is charged with an offence under this section, proof that he had with him any article made or adapted for use in committing a burglary or theft shall be evidence that he had it with him for such use.
(4) [Repealed.]
(5) For purposes of this section an offence under section 12(1) of this Act of taking a conveyance shall be treated as theft.

As to offences of possessing, making or supplying articles for use in frauds, see **B5.22** and **B5.25**.

Procedure

B4.151 Going equipped for stealing is triable either way (MCA 1980, s. 17 and sch. 1, para. 28). When tried on indictment it is normally a class 3 offence, but see CrimPD XIII, para. B (see Supplement, **CPD.XIII.B**) for the additional factors that the court considers on allocation.

Indictment

B4.152 *Statement of Offence*

Going equipped for burglary contrary to section 25 of the Theft Act 1968.

Particulars of Offence

A on or about the... day of..., not being at his place of abode, had with him articles, namely a jemmy and a kitchen knife, for use in the course of or in connection with burglary.

Sentence

The maximum penalty is three years (s. 25(2)) on indictment; six months or an unlimited fine, or both, summarily. If committed with reference to the theft or taking of motor vehicles, disqualification is discretionary (RTOA 1988, sch. 2). The definitive sentencing guideline *Theft* (see Supplement, **SG33-5**) applies to adult offenders sentenced on or after 1 February 2016. The offence range is discharge to 18 months' custody. The *Magistrates' Court Sentencing Guidelines* provide guidelines for this offence when tried summarily. **B4.153**

Pre-guideline authorities which may still be of some assistance are *Flack* [2011] EWCA Crim 1112, *Shariff* [2012] EWCA Crim 768 and *Hodgkins* [2016] EWCA Crim 360, [2016] 2 Cr App R (S) 13 (95).

Relation to Other Offences

It is not an offence under the Theft Act 1968, s. 25, to keep or possess articles intended for use in theft, burglary etc. as long as those articles are kept at home. An individual who has been found to possess a jemmy or similar implement at home may, however, be charged under the Criminal Damage Act 1971, s. 3, if it appears that the thing in question might be used to damage windows, locks etc. in the course of forcing an entry for the purpose of theft or burglary. Firearms or imitation firearms kept for the purpose of a robbery or aggravated burglary come within the scope of s. 25, but more obviously come within the provisions of the FA 1968. **B4.154**

When Not at his Place of Abode

'Place of abode' is not defined in the Theft Act 1968. It could include a caravan or motor vehicle, but in *Bundy* [1977] 2 All ER 382 the Court of Appeal held that a vehicle is not to be regarded as a place of abode unless parked at a site where D abides or intends to abide. A traveller who keeps housebreaking tools in a vehicle ordinarily kept at such a site, may therefore commit an offence under s. 25 by driving the vehicle away from that site. **B4.155**

Meaning of 'Has with Him'

This phrase must bear a broadly similar meaning in s. 25 to the one it bears in s. 10 of the Act (see **B4.105**) and implies a degree of immediate control (*Kelt* [1977] 3 All ER 1099), but is not confined to cases of 'carrying'. It may suffice if D had the article available for use in his car or bag, or at his place of work; but it is submitted that, as in cases involving firearms and other weapons, there must be some close geographical, temporal or purposive link between D and the item in question (*Henderson* [2016] EWCA Crim 965, [2017] 1 Cr App R 4 (29)). In *Re McAngus* [1994] Crim LR 602 the Divisional Court held, in relation to extradition proceedings, that a s. 25 offence could be made out where D showed undercover agents counterfeit shirts stored in a bonded warehouse. **B4.156**

Any Article for Use in the Course of or in Connection with any Burglary or Theft

The connection between the articles and the proposed theft etc. must not be too remote. In *Mansfield* [1975] Crim LR 101, D was charged under the Theft Act 1968, s. 25, with possessing another person's driving licence, with intent to use this to obtain employment, in the course of which D would have an opportunity to steal. Not surprisingly, the Court of Appeal quashed the conviction. **B4.157**

As to the offences which may be intended, see s. 25(5). Although the taking of pedal cycles contrary to s. 12(5) of the Act is not one of those offences, the possession of bolt-cutters etc. for cutting cycle locks could readily be interpreted as intended for use in theft. Burglary includes burglary with intent to inflict grievous bodily harm etc. under s. 9(1)(a) and theft includes theft with force which would amount to robbery.

The most ordinary of articles, including footwear and clothing, could be used in the course of such crimes, but in practice s. 25 is used only in connection with articles which seem intended to play a prominent or obvious role: something which D would not have with him if not intending to commit such a crime. Coshes, masks, jemmies, glass-cutters and skeleton keys are obvious examples; less obvious perhaps are credit cards stolen or illicitly borrowed from their real owners (see also *Re McAngus* [1994] Crim LR 602: counterfeit clothing). This does not mean that apparently innocuous articles cannot be within the scope of the section. Bottles of wine were found to constitute such articles in *Doukas* [1978] 1 All ER 1071, where D had apparently brought the wine to the hotel where he worked as a waiter in order dishonestly to sell it to his employer's customers, who would be deceived (contrary to s. 15 of the Act) into thinking that they were buying wine from the employer. A charge under the Fraud Act 2006, s. 6 (see **B5.22**), would now be more appropriate on such facts.

B4.158 The article need not be intended for use that day, nor for use by D himself, but it must be intended for *future* use. The possession of articles that *have been used* in theft etc. with a view only to disposing of them is not an offence under s. 25, although a charge under the CLA 1967, s. 4, may sometimes be appropriate (*Ellames* [1974] 3 All ER 130).

In the absence of a confession or other self-incriminating behaviour by D, it may sometimes be difficult to prove that the article was indeed intended for use in the course of or in connection with burglary or theft, and proof of intent is needed: it is not sufficient to show that D merely contemplated possible use (*Hargreaves* [1985] Crim LR 243). Section 25(3) is of very limited use in this respect, since it only states the obvious. If D was found to be carrying a jemmy or a bunch of skeleton keys, a court or jury would in any case consider this to be evidence (and possibly sufficient proof) of intent to commit burglary. Possession of a torch or screwdriver would be less likely to be considered evidence of such intent, and here s. 25(3) is of no help at all (*Harrison* [1970] Crim LR 415).

HANDLING STOLEN GOODS

Definition

B4.159 **Theft Act 1968, s. 22**

(1) A person handles stolen goods if (otherwise than in the course of the stealing) knowing or believing them to be stolen goods he dishonestly receives the goods, or dishonestly undertakes or assists in their retention, removal, disposal or realisation by or for the benefit of another person, or if he arranges to do so.

Procedure

B4.160 Handling stolen goods is triable either way (MCA 1980, s. 17 and sch. 1, para. 28). When tried on indictment it is normally a class 3 offence, but see CrimPD XIII, para. B (see Supplement, **CPD.XIII.B**) for the additional factors that the court considers on allocation. It is a Group A offence for jurisdiction purposes under the CJA 1993, Part I (see **A8.10**).

See the *Magistrates' Court Sentencing Guidelines* for indications as to when a case should be sent to the Crown Court.

Indictment

B4.161 **First Count**

Statement of Offence

Handling stolen goods contrary to section 22(1) of the Theft Act 1968.

Particulars of Offence

A on or about the . . . day of . . . dishonestly received stolen goods, namely a pearl necklace belonging to V, knowing or believing the same to be stolen goods.

Second Count

Statement of Offence

Handling stolen goods contrary to section 22(1) of the Theft Act 1968.

Particulars of Offence

A on or about the... day of... dishonestly undertook or assisted in the retention, removal, disposal or realisation of stolen goods, namely a pearl necklace belonging to V, by or for the benefit of B, or dishonestly arranged to do so, knowing or believing the same to be stolen goods.

It may be prudent to include both counts unless there is clear evidence of one particular form of handling and the prosecution intend to present the case exclusively in those terms. See further *Deakin* [1972] 3 All ER 803.

The general deficiency principle applies to counts for handling stolen goods (for the application of this principle to theft, see **B4.3**, and for the drafting of counts for continuous offences generally, see **D11.32**). It is, therefore, proper to indict for the handling of a total amount of money if the evidence does not precisely disclose the date or amount of each dishonest transaction but the transactions are so closely linked as to be, in effect, a continuous transaction (*Cain* [1983] Crim LR 802). However, if D is charged with handling items of property which are clearly the proceeds of different thefts, burglaries or robberies, and which are received or dealt with on separate occasions, there should be a separate count of handling for each occasion (*Smythe* (1980) 72 Cr App R 8). **B4.162**

Theft Act 1968, s. 27

(1) Any number of persons may be charged in one indictment, with reference to the same theft, with having at different times or at the same time handled all or any of the stolen goods, and the persons so charged may be tried together.

(2) On the trial of two or more persons indicted for jointly handling any stolen goods the jury may find any of the accused guilty if the jury are satisfied that he handled all or any of the stolen goods, whether or not he did so jointly with the other accused or any of them.

Section 27(2), arguably goes further than the general rule, established in *DPP v Merriman* [1973] AC 584, that a person jointly indicted for an offence may be convicted of committing it independently of the others. It also covers cases in which two co-accused handle goods on separate occasions (*French* [1973] Crim LR 632).

Sentence

The maximum penalty is 14 years (Theft Act 1968, s. 22(2)) on indictment; six months or an unlimited fine, or both, summarily. The definitive sentencing guideline *Theft* (see Supplement, **SG33-4**) applies to adult offenders sentenced on or after 1 February 2016. **B4.163**

The *Magistrates' Court Sentencing Guidelines* provide guidelines for this offence when tried summarily. The old guideline case of *Webbe* [2001] EWCA Crim 1217, [2002] 1 Cr App R (S) 22 (82) is superseded.

Meaning of 'Goods', 'Stolen Goods', 'Theft' etc.

Sections 22 to 24 of the Theft Act 1968 deal with what are referred to therein as 'stolen goods' but the combined effect of ss. 24 and 34(2)(b) ensures that the provisions apply to a wider range of property than the ordinary meaning of that term might suggest. **B4.164**

Theft Act 1968, s. 34(2)(b)

'goods', except insofar as the context otherwise requires, includes money and every other description of property except land, and includes things severed from the land by stealing.

A credit balance in a bank account might be regarded as stolen goods if it directly or indirectly represents the proceeds of theft etc. (s. 24(2); *Forsyth* [1997] 2 Cr App R 299: but see **B4.187**). As to things severed from land, see **B4.13**.

The concept of stolen goods has an extended meaning by statute.

Theft Act 1968, ss. 24 and 24A

24.—(1) The provisions of this Act relating to goods which have been stolen shall apply whether the stealing occurred in England or Wales or elsewhere, and whether it occurred before or after the commencement of this Act, provided that the stealing (if not an offence under this Act) amounted to an offence where and at the time when the goods were stolen; and references to stolen goods shall be construed accordingly.

(2) For purposes of those provisions references to stolen goods shall include, in addition to the goods originally stolen and parts of them (whether in their original state or not),—
   (a) any other goods which directly or indirectly represent or have at any time represented the stolen goods in the hands of the thief as being the proceeds of any disposal or realisation of the whole or part of the goods stolen or of goods so representing the stolen goods; and
   (b) any other goods which directly or indirectly represent or have at any time represented the stolen goods in the hands of a handler of the stolen goods or any part of them as being the proceeds of any disposal or realisation of the whole or part of the stolen goods handled by him or of goods so representing them.

(3) But no goods shall be regarded as having continued to be stolen goods after they have been restored to the person from whom they were stolen or to other lawful possession or custody, or after that person and any other person claiming through him have otherwise ceased as regards those goods to have any right to restitution in respect of the theft.

(4) For purposes of the provisions of this Act relating to goods which have been stolen (including subsections (1) to (3) above) goods obtained in England or Wales or elsewhere either by blackmail or, subject to subsection (5) below, by fraud (within the meaning of the Fraud Act 2006) shall be regarded as stolen; and 'steal', 'theft' and 'thief' shall be construed accordingly.

(5) Subsection (1) above applies in relation to goods obtained by fraud as if—
   (a) the reference to the commencement of this Act were a reference to the commencement of the Fraud Act 2006, and
   (b) the reference to an offence under this Act were a reference to an offence under section 1 of that Act.

24A.—(8) References to stolen goods include money which is dishonestly withdrawn from an account to which a wrongful credit has been made, but only to the extent that the money derives from the credit.

If the property in question appears to represent the proceeds of an offence that falls outside the scope of s. 24 or s. 24A(8) it may be possible to consider charges under the 'money laundering' provisions (as to which, see **B21**). These provisions overlap significantly with the offence of handling, and, even where the goods concerned are stolen, the prosecution may in some cases find it easier to charge one or more of the offences they create in preference to handling. As to the handling of dishonestly obtained money transfers, see s. 24A, discussed at **B4.184** ***et seq.***

B4.165 **Goods Obtained by Blackmail or Fraud** Section 24(4) governs s. 24(1) to (3) and extends the meaning of 'stolen goods' to cover the fruits or proceeds of fraud offences and offences under s. 21 (blackmail). No mention of burglary or robbery is needed, because any property obtained by such means must necessarily have been obtained by theft.

B4.166 **Goods Stolen outside England and Wales** Theft Act 1968 offences (other than theft of mails under s. 14 and offences on British ships etc.) do not ordinarily apply to conduct taking place outside England or Wales (see generally **B4.65** and **A8**) but s. 24(1), read in conjunction with s. 24(4), ensures that property obtained outside the jurisdiction, by what would in England have been regarded as theft, blackmail or fraud, will be regarded as stolen property within the jurisdiction if either:

(a) the stealing etc. was (exceptionally) punishable as an extra-territorial offence under English law (e.g., where D was a British citizen aboard a foreign ship to which D did not belong: Merchant Shipping Act 1995, s. 281); or
(b) the stealing was punishable under the law then in force where it took place.

Thus, if a thief stole property in Spain, and D received it (or its proceeds) in England, knowing of the circumstances, D may be guilty of handling under s. 22, but it must be proved that the conduct of the thief was, at the time of the theft, punishable under Spanish law. It is not possible to rely on any presumption that foreign law will be similar to English law, nor can judicial notice be taken of foreign law for such a purpose (*Ofori* (1994) 99 Cr App R 219). See also **F11.27** for the general rules on evidence of foreign law.

Fruits and Proceeds of Stolen Goods Although wide-ranging, s. 24(2) is significantly narrower than the corresponding provision in the Larceny Act 1916, which it replaced. The old law failed to distinguish between the proceeds of stolen goods in the hands of a thief or receiver of stolen goods, and such proceeds in the hands of an innocent person. Thus, anything purchased with, or exchanged for, stolen goods or the proceeds thereof would itself become categorised as stolen goods, even if it had never itself been possessed by either the thief or a receiver. In theory, the potential spread of the contagion was almost limitless. **B4.167**

The present position is that property is categorised as stolen only if it is the original property stolen, or something that has at some time represented the proceeds thereof in the hands of the original thief or of a dishonest handler. For example, if D innocently acquires a stolen bicycle and then (still innocently) part-exchanges it for a new one, the new cycle cannot be categorised as stolen goods; but it would be otherwise if D knew the original one was stolen.

It may be difficult to determine whether property subsequently acquired by the thief or by an alleged handler represents the proceeds of a disposal of the original stolen goods. Classification may be particularly problematic where bank accounts are involved. D may for example pay into a bank account both legitimately obtained moneys (such as salary) and the proceeds of thefts. D may then buy goods with funds drawn from that account, or arrange for funds to be transferred to other accounts. In *A-G's Ref (No. 4 of 1979)* [1981] 1 All ER 1193, the Court of Appeal held that in such a case any credit balance in D's account constitutes, in part, stolen goods and that funds withdrawn from that account by D may also constitute stolen goods, to the extent that they derive from the thefts, etc. If the withdrawal involves a sum greater than the amount covered by 'legitimate' funds in the account, it must necessarily represent (at least in part) the proceeds of theft; but in other cases, it must be proved that D intended the withdrawal to represent such proceeds, as where D's intention is to settle up with an accomplice to whom D 'owes' part of the proceeds. Note that it is D's intention which matters. The recipient's belief that this is what the withdrawal represents cannot suffice (*A-G's Ref (No. 4 of 1979)*). **B4.168**

If D withdraws money (i.e. cash) from the account, and hands this to E as E's share of the proceeds of theft, E undoubtedly receives stolen goods (s. 24A(8): see **B4.164**). If, however, D arranges for funds to be transferred from the account to an account operated by E, then, for reasons which are explained in **B4.187**, E cannot be guilty of handling the chose in action thereby created in E's favour. The proper charge would be one of dishonestly retaining a wrongful credit, contrary to s. 24A (see **B4.184** ***et seq.***) or one of knowingly acquiring or possessing the proceeds of criminal conduct, contrary to the POCA 2002, s. 329 (see **B4.189** and **B21.22**).

Goods Restored to Owner etc. As to what amounts to restoration to lawful possession, see *Haughton v Smith* [1975] AC 476 and *A-G's Ref (No. 1 of 1974)* [1974] QB 744. In the latter case, a police officer immobilised a parked car he suspected to contain stolen goods, and apprehended D when he attempted to start it. The question arose whether D could be guilty of handling at the time of his arrest, or whether the goods had already been taken into lawful police custody. It was held by the Court of Appeal that, if the police officer had already resolved to prevent the removal of the goods under any circumstances, they would indeed have ceased to be stolen; but if he had remained in doubt, and had resolved only to seek a satisfactory explanation before deciding whether or not to take charge of them, then they would remain stolen. **B4.169**

On somewhat different facts, it was held in *Metropolitan Police Commissioner v Streeter* (1980) 71 Cr App R 113 that stolen goods were not taken into lawful custody merely because they had been marked for later identification and followed in the thief's possession to a rendezvous with the handler.

If there is any doubt about the status of such property when received, it may sometimes be desirable to charge theft (since receiving will usually amount to appropriation of property belonging to another), or it may be easier to prove that D arranged to receive the goods before they ceased to be stolen. Other possibilities are attempt (now that *Haughton v Smith* is no longer good law) and conspiracy.

B4.170 'Loss of right to restitution' is a matter determined by the civil law. Briefly, this right will be lost where a stolen cheque or other negotiable instrument is acquired by a person who can establish title to it as a holder in due course (Bills of Exchange Act 1882, s. 29). See also the Factors Act 1889, s. 2 (theft by mercantile agent and sale to bona fide purchaser) and the Hire Purchase Act 1964, s. 27.

Goods which are 'stolen' in the sense of being the proceeds of fraud or deception, rather than theft, may have become in law the property of the fraudster, albeit subject to the victim's right to rescind for fraud. In such a case, any bona fide purchaser may acquire good title to them (Sale of Goods Act 1979, s. 23). Property obtained by blackmail will sometimes give the blackmailer voidable title (as with fraud or deception); but since some kinds of blackmail are analogous to robbery, there will be cases in which no title passes, because the victim never 'consented' to parting with it. Loss to right to restitution of the original property need not usually prevent any proceeds from continuing to be classed as stolen goods.

Actus Reus: Goods must be Stolen

B4.171 However dishonest D may be, there can be no offence of handling stolen goods unless the goods in question were in fact stolen goods at the time of the alleged handling. See **B4.176**. However, a person who has done an act which would be a sufficient act of handling, intended to handle, was dishonest and believed the goods to be stolen will be liable for an attempt to handle if the goods were not stolen (CAA 1981, s. 1(2) and (3); *Shivpuri* [1987] AC 1; see generally **A5.84**). The cases of *Haughton v Smith* [1975] AC 476 and *Anderton v Ryan* [1985] AC 560, which were formerly authority for the contrary proposition, are no longer good law.

Proof that handled goods were stolen may be facilitated by the Theft Act 1968, s. 27(4), which provides for the use, in theft or handling cases, of statutory declarations by witnesses to loss of goods in transit where D is notified and does not require personal attendance of the witnesses.

Theft Act 1968, s. 27

(4) In any proceedings for the theft of anything in the course of transmission (whether by post or otherwise), or for handling stolen goods from such a theft, a statutory declaration made by any person that he dispatched or received or failed to receive any goods or postal packet, or that any goods or postal packet when dispatched or received by him were in a particular state or condition, shall be admissible as evidence of the facts stated in the declaration, subject to the following conditions:—

(a) a statutory declaration shall only be admissible where and to the extent to which oral evidence to the like effect would have been admissible in the proceedings; and

(b) a statutory declaration shall only be admissible if at least seven days before the hearing or trial a copy of it has been given to the person charged, and he has not, at least three days before the hearing or trial or within such further time as the court may in special circumstances allow, given the prosecutor written notice requiring the attendance at the hearing or trial of the person making the declaration.

(4A) Where the proceedings mentioned in subsection (4) above are proceedings before a magistrates' court inquiring into an offence as examining justices that subsection shall have effect with the omission of the words from 'subject to the following conditions' to the end of the subsection.

(5) This section is to be construed in accordance with section 24 of this Act; and in subsection (3)(b) above the reference to handling stolen goods shall include any corresponding offence committed before the commencement of this Act.

Actus Reus: The Forms of Handling

The Theft Act 1968, s. 22, must be read in conjunction with s. 24 (see **B4.164**). The term 'handling' is a form of shorthand embracing the several forms of dealing in the property specified in s. 22(1). In *Bloxham* [1983] 1 AC 109, Lord Bridge of Harwich stated, *obiter*, that s. 22 creates two distinct offences: receiving (or arranging to receive) being one and the various other forms being different variants of the other; but as most commentators have been quick to point out, this is, strictly speaking, incorrect. There is only one offence (*Griffiths v Freeman* [1970] 1 All ER 1117), and an indictment alleging 'handling' without specifying the form is not therefore bad for duplicity (*Nicklin* [1977] 2 All ER 444). On the other hand, Lord Bridge's dictum has been accepted as a good indication of proper practice. An indictment should indicate which of the two main forms of handling is alleged, and if both are alleged there should be separate counts. A person cannot be accused of one and convicted on the basis of the other (*Nicklin*). **B4.172**

Except in cases of receiving or arranging to receive, it must be both alleged and proved that D assisted, or acted for the benefit of, another person: this is the main difference between receiving etc. and the other variants of the offence.

Receiving and Arranging to Receive

The Theft Act 1968 does not define 'receiving', but cases on receiving decided under the Larceny Act 1916, s. 33, defined it as involving the taking of possession or control of property, either jointly, or exclusively (*Frost* (1964) 48 Cr App R 284). Possession does not necessarily require physical handling, nor indeed would such handling suffice in the absence of any intent to possess or control the goods (*Hobson v Impett* (1957) 41 Cr App R 138). It is sufficient that the goods were handled by D's agents on D's behalf (*Miller* (1854) 6 Cox CC 353). Things in action, which are not capable of physical handling, can certainly be received, as where the proceeds of a stolen cheque are credited to a bank account. **B4.173**

Arranging to receive is a substantive offence which may consist of the kind of preparatory arrangements that would fall short of constituting an attempt to receive, or of arrangements with an innocent party, so that there would be no conspiracy. It is not enough, however, for arrangements to be made for receipt of goods that have yet to be stolen. This might be conspiracy to steal and to handle stolen goods, but cannot be a full s. 22 offence (*Park* (1987) 87 Cr App R 164).

Undertaking or Assisting in Retention, Removal, Disposal or Realisation by or for the Benefit of Another Person

In *Bloxham* [1983] 1 AC 109, D innocently purchased a car which he later came to realise must have been stolen. He sold it to an unidentified person at a knockdown price, and it was alleged that this amounted to realisation for the benefit of that unidentified purchaser. The House of Lords disagreed, on the basis that the sale (realisation) was for the benefit of D himself, and Lord Bridge of Harwich added (at pp. 113–14): **B4.174**

> The offence can be committed in relation to any one of [four named] activities in one or other of two ways. First, the offender may himself undertake the activity *for the benefit of* another person. Secondly, the activity may be undertaken *by* another person and the offender may assist him... the category of other persons contemplated by the subsection is subject to the same limitations in whichever way the offence is committed. Accordingly, a purchaser, as such, of stolen goods, cannot... be 'another person' within the subsection, since his act of purchase could not sensibly be described as a disposal or realisation of the stolen goods *by* him... therefore, even if the sale to him could be described as a disposal or realisation for his benefit, the transaction is not... within the ambit of the subsection.

See also *Gingell* (1999) 163 JP 648, *Tokeley-Parry* [1999] Crim LR 578 and *Toleikis* [2013] EWCA Crim 600 (although there is nothing in the judgment in that case to explain why it could be assumed that D acted for the benefit of anyone other than himself).

Assisting in the retention of stolen goods requires active assistance to be given to the other person. Accommodating or banking the stolen property would suffice (*Pitchley* (1972) 57 Cr App R 30); but mere failure to co-operate with the police during a search for stolen goods would not (*Brown* [1970] 1 QB 105). It is not necessary that the assistance should be successful; an attempt to deceive the police during such a search will amount to the complete offence under the Theft Act 1968, s. 22 (*Kanwar* [1982] 2 All ER 528).

Disposing of or assisting in the disposal or realisation of stolen goods typically means moving the property from one place to another or converting it from one form into another (*Forsyth* [1997] 2 Cr App R 299 at p. 317). This may be a continuing offence and may be committed in England even where much of the relevant conduct occurs abroad (*Forsyth*). Because handling is a group A offence for the purposes of the CJA 1993, Part I, it would now suffice for any 'relevant event' to occur within the jurisdiction. Cases of 'money laundering', in which arrangements are made for the transfer, concealment or investment, etc., of criminal property (including stolen goods) may also involve offences under the POCA 2002, ss. 327 to 329. Such offences will in many cases be easier to prove than handling, and carry the same maximum penalties: see **B21.27**.

Relationship between Handling and other Offences

B4.175 The Theft Act 1968, s. 22, stipulates that the offence of handling may only be committed 'otherwise than in the course of the stealing'. The stealing referred to is the crime whereby the goods become 'stolen' in the first place. (This may, under s. 24(4), take the form of blackmail or fraud: see **B4.166**). The stipulation prevents thieves or blackmailers etc. becoming handlers whilst still participating in the original offence, which may take the form of a continuous or on-going series of acts (see **B4.44**). Where, for example, burglar A passes the items he steals to his accomplice, burglar B, who carries them to the get-away car, B might otherwise become a handler through 'receiving' stolen goods. It may therefore be necessary for the prosecution to prove, in appropriate cases, that the stealing had been completed prior to the alleged act of handling and was not still in progress at the time. This was the issue in *Pitham* (1976) 65 Cr App R 45, where the appellants were invited by one M to pay him for furniture belonging to another man, who was in prison at the time. They agreed a price with M and removed the furniture, and were indicted on those facts with alternative counts of burglary and handling. (As to the joinder of 'mutually destructive' counts within a single indictment, see *Bellman* [1989] AC 836 and **D11.67**.) They were convicted of handling and their convictions were upheld on appeal; Lawton LJ took the view that the jury were fully justified in finding that the appellants had dealt with the furniture only after M had stolen it by assuming the right to dispose of it.

B4.176 The prosecution need not affirmatively prove every alleged handler to be innocent of the original theft, blackmail or deception. The courts have refused to place such a burden on the prosecution where there is no evidence to suggest that D was anything other than a handler (*Cash* [1985] QB 801). Problems may, however, arise where the evidence is ambiguous, as where property that has been stolen in a burglary is discovered a day later, hidden in D's attic. Under the doctrine of recent possession (see **F3.63**), the court or jury may legitimately infer, in the absence of any alternative explanation, that D must either have been the burglar or have dishonestly received the property knowing it to be stolen; but unless there is some further evidence to indicate which of the two offences D committed, it would appear to be impossible for them to draw one inference rather than the other.

The problem in such cases would not be solved merely by treating the words 'otherwise than in the course of the stealing' as a proviso or qualification to the general words of s. 22, and thus as a matter to be raised and proved by the defence under the rule as to the burden of proof which was affirmed by the House of Lords in *Hunt* [1987] AC 352 (see **F3.16**). The prosecution would still have to prove that D 'received the goods, knowing or believing them to be stolen'; this would not be the case if D was the original burglar. Nor is it permissible for the court or jury to convict

D of whichever offence appears, on balance, to be the more likely possibility. They must be sure that D is guilty of the specific offence of which D is convicted (*A-G of Hong Kong v Yip Kai-foon* [1988] AC 642; cf. *Bellman* [1989] AC 836, per Lord Griffiths at p. 838).

It does not follow that D must be acquitted in such circumstances. The courts have recognised two possible solutions to the problem, each of which enables a conviction to be recorded. The first, and preferable, solution is for the prosecution to compromise by seeking a conviction for theft. Although a thief or burglar cannot become guilty of handling in the course of the original stealing, the offences of theft and handling are not mutually exclusive. Receiving property stolen or obtained in an earlier, completed theft must invariably involve a further appropriation of it, and it follows that a dishonest receiver of such goods must also be a thief (*Stapylton v O'Callaghan* [1973] 2 All ER 782). It is accordingly open to the prosecution to include within the indictment a count for theft, drawn sufficiently widely to cover an appropriation of the property on any date between that of the original theft or burglary etc. and the date on which the property was found in D's possession (*More* [1987] 3 All ER 825). This count may be additional to more specific counts, such as for handling or burglary, or it may stand alone; but the prosecution should in either case be able to prove that D stole the property at some point, and it need not matter if they cannot prove whether it was theft by burglary or theft by receiving (*Shelton* (1986) 83 Cr App R 379).

In *Shelton* the Court of Appeal offered the following advice (at pp. 384–5). **B4.177**

> As we have been asked by counsel to do so, for the guidance of judges and counsel we make the following comments. First that the long-established practice of charging theft and handling as alternatives should continue whenever there is a real possibility, not a fanciful one, that at trial the evidence might support one rather than the other. Secondly, that there is a danger that juries may be confused by reference to second or later appropriations since the issue in every case is whether the defendant has in fact appropriated property belonging to another. If he has done so, it is irrelevant how he came to make the appropriation provided it was in the course of theft. Thirdly, that a jury should be told that a handler can be a thief, but he cannot be convicted of being both a thief and a handler. Fourthly, that handling is the more serious offence, carrying a heavier penalty because those who knowingly have dealings with thieves encourage stealing. Fifthly, in the unlikely event of the jury not agreeing amongst themselves whether theft or handling has been proved, they should be discharged. Finally, and perhaps most importantly, both judges and counsel when directing and addressing juries should avoid intellectual subtleties which some jurors may have difficulty in grasping; the golden rule should be 'Keep it short and simple'.

The second possible solution to the problem has the support of the Privy Council in *A-G of Hong Kong v Yip Kai-foon* [1988] AC 642 and that of the Court of Appeal in *Foreman* [1991] Crim LR 702, but is, with respect, based on doubtful logic. In *Yip Kai-foon*, the Privy Council took the view that, where the evidence was equally consistent with robbery or handling, and the jury were accordingly unable to convict D of robbery, it would then be open to them to rely upon D's 'innocence' of that offence as proof that it must have been handling. This is objectionable, in that it can lead to a conviction for handling being recorded when the jury think it more likely that D committed robbery, burglary or simple theft (see Sir John Smith's commentary on *Ryan v DPP* [1994] Crim LR 457). It is accordingly submitted that a widely drawn count for theft offers a more logical solution to cases in which it is unclear how D acquired the stolen property.

A third possible solution would be for charges to be laid instead under Part 7 of the POCA 2002. Section 327 of that Act (see **B21.12**) creates offences of concealing, disguising, converting or transferring abroad 'criminal property' (as defined in s. 340). Section 329 (see **B21.22**) creates offences of acquiring, using or possessing such property. This includes property that directly or indirectly represents any person's benefit from criminal conduct (including D's own conduct). Dishonesty need not be proved, and mere suspicion as to the provenance of the property may suffice, although mere suspicion will *not* suffice where the alleged offence is one of attempt (*Pace* [2014] EWCA Crim 186, [2014] 1 WLR 2867; *Wheeler* [2014] EWCA Crim 2706 and see **A5.80**). If misused, charges brought under the POCA 2002 (which was intended to deal with money laundering) may enable prosecutors to sidestep basic *mens rea* requirements in what would otherwise be routine cases of handling, and there are dicta (notably in *GH* [2015] UKSC 24, [2015] 1 WLR 2126 at [49]) by which such tactics are discouraged. As to the overlap between these offences and handling stolen goods see **B21.27**.

See also the offences under the Scrap Metal Dealers Act 1964, as amended by the LASPO 2012, s. 146 (which inserts the offence of buying scrap metal for cash).

Mens Rea

B4.178 **Dishonesty** The meaning of dishonesty is examined at **B4.54**. The *Ivey* test (see **B4.55**) must be applied; but the Theft Act 1968, s. 2, is relevant only to the extent that it may bear on whether the property in question was originally stolen or not. As to the possible relationship between knowledge and dishonesty, see **B4.179**.

B4.179 **Knowledge or Belief that the Goods are Stolen** On a charge of handling stolen goods, it must be proved that D actually knew that the goods were stolen, or correctly believed that they were. This knowledge or belief must correspond in time with the *actus reus* (*Williams* [1994] Crim LR 934). In cases of handling by receiving, this means the moment of receipt or acquisition. If D only later becomes aware that the goods are stolen, this will not suffice, even if D's retention of them is clearly dishonest (*Brook* [1993] Crim LR 455). On the other hand, dishonest retention in such circumstances may sometimes amount to theft (subject to the Theft Act 1968, s. 3(2), which precludes such liability in cases where the property was acquired bona fide and for value); or it may amount to an offence under the POCA 2002, s. 329 (see **B21.22**).

Knowledge of the circumstances which make the goods stolen will generally suffice for liability in cases of alleged handling whether or not D appreciated the legal consequences of those circumstances. An accused's belief that the proceeds of blackmail are something different from stolen goods will accordingly be no defence; nor should it be any defence that D believed the goods to be the proceeds of theft when they are in fact the proceeds of blackmail, fraud or deception. In either event, the goods are stolen, and D's belief is not incorrect in any material sense.

Another immaterial error would be one about the precise identity of the goods. It would be no defence that D thought a container held stolen whisky when in fact it contained stolen cigars (*McCullum* (1973) 57 Cr App R 645).

D's ignorance of the law may prevent D from being considered dishonest, even after *Ivey* [2017] UKSC 67, [2018] AC 391. For example, D may know that certain property indirectly represents the proceeds of the sale, by a thief or handler, of the original stolen goods, but may not realise that these proceeds are accordingly 'stolen goods' within the meaning of the Theft Act 1968, s. 24. Not realising the legal position, D is perhaps less likely to be adjudged dishonest by a court or jury, applying the standards of reasonable and honest people. In contrast, a money-laundering charge brought under the POCA 2002 would involve no such complication.

B4.180 Belief that goods are stolen is an alternative *mens rea* to knowledge of that fact. It is not of course an alternative to the goods actually *being* stolen (*Haughton v Smith* [1975] AC 485 at p. 503). If the goods are not in fact stolen, there may be an attempt to handle stolen goods (see **B4.171**) or D may actually steal them, but cannot be guilty of handling.

The distinction between knowledge and belief is not crucial in this context, since either state of mind may suffice for liability. In *Hall* (1985) 81 Cr App R 260, the Court of Appeal nevertheless attempted to distinguish between the two concepts by suggesting that D 'knows' goods are stolen if someone with first-hand knowledge (such as the thief) has told D so; and 'believes' that fact if, despite lacking such knowledge, D realises that there is no other reasonable explanation. With respect, however, D cannot properly be said to 'know' a fact merely on the basis of received hearsay. D can know a fact only on the basis of first-hand knowledge of it, as for example by witnessing the theft taking place (cf. *Overington* [1978] Crim LR 692; *Hulbert* (1979) 69 Cr App

R 243). Failing this, D can at most 'believe' the goods to be stolen, but since belief is sufficient *mens rea*, the point may be largely academic in this context.

The critical distinction in handling cases is that between knowledge or belief, on the one hand, and mere suspicion, on the other, because it has been held on many occasions that suspicion, even grave suspicion accompanied by dishonesty and failure to make reasonable inquiries, cannot suffice for liability (*Griffiths* (1974) 60 Cr App R 14; *Pethick* [1980] Crim LR 242; *Moys* (1984) 79 Cr App R 72; *Forsyth* [1997] 2 Cr App R 299). The Court of Appeal in *Hall* suggested that D may believe goods to be stolen where D 'refuses to believe what his brain tells him is obvious', but this suggestion has rightly been rejected as potentially confusing (*Forsyth*). A person cannot sensibly be said to believe what he or she refuses to believe, and the test must be a subjective one, rather than an objective test based on what D ought to have realised. In *Forsyth*, the Court of Appeal defined belief as 'the mental acceptance of a fact as true or existing', and suggested that juries might be directed in the following terms, as previously suggested by Lord Lane CJ in *Moys*:

> ... it must be proved that the defendant was aware of the theft or that he believed the goods to be stolen. Suspicion that they were stolen, even coupled with the fact that he shut his eyes to the circumstances, is not enough, although these matters may be taken into account ... in deciding whether or not the necessary knowledge or belief existed.

This is certainly preferable to the definition attempted in *Hall*, but the definition of belief remains imprecise. Does belief on balance of probabilities suffice, or must D have felt sure of it, beyond reasonable doubt? In *Forsyth*, the Court of Appeal merely observed, rather unhelpfully, that 'between suspicion and belief there may be a range of awareness' and it would therefore be safer to assume that the stricter concept of belief applies. In other words, D believes that goods are stolen only if harbouring no serious or substantial doubt as to that fact.

If D receives or deals with property merely suspecting it to have been stolen, this suspicion cannot suffice as *mens rea* for handling, but may leave D open to conviction for an offence under Part 7 of the POCA 2002 which requires neither positive belief nor dishonesty (see **B21**). Where however D realises that the property in question *must* almost certainly be stolen (e.g., because the serial number has been removed from an item offered at a knock-down price), failure to ask awkward questions, or turning a blind eye to the facts, 'can be capable, depending on the circumstances, of providing evidence going to prove knowledge or belief' on a charge of handling (*Pace* [2014] EWCA Crim 186, [2014] 1 WLR 2687, per Davis LJ at [81]). See also *Griffiths* (1974) 60 Cr App R 14 and **F3.62**. **B4.181**

As to the position where D wrongly concludes that the property in question is stolen (e.g., because D is caught in a police 'sting' operation where undercover officers pretend to be thieves), see **A5.84**.

Previous Convictions as Evidence On a charge of handling, the Theft Act 1968, s. 27(3) (which remains in force despite the enactment of the 'bad character' provisions of the CJA 2003), makes evidence of D's previous convictions for theft or handling, or of D's previous dealings in stolen goods, admissible in certain circumstances for the limited purpose of proving D's knowledge or belief that the goods were stolen on the present occasion. Section 27(3), and its relationship to the regime laid down by the CJA 2003, is examined at **F13.92** *et seq*. **B4.182**

Effect of Conviction or Acquittal of the Alleged Thief

A conviction for handling stolen goods does not depend on the conviction of the alleged thief (or blackmailer etc.), nor is it even necessary to identify that person in every case. It follows that there is nothing necessarily inconsistent in the acquittal of the alleged thief and the conviction at the same trial of the alleged handler. It may be, for example, that the handler is convicted on the basis of a confession that is not admissible against the co-accused. Acquittal of the alleged thief may in other circumstances be fatal to conviction of the alleged handler. A court or jury must be satisfied that the goods are stolen, and this would not, for example, be consistent with **B4.183** a finding that the alleged thief was under the age of criminal responsibility (cf. *Walters v Lunt* [1951] 2 All ER 645).

At D's trial for handling stolen goods, E's conviction for theft of those same goods by a court in the UK or EU, or by a Service court outside the UK is admissible evidence that E committed the theft in question, and will be presumed to be correct. If the defence claim that E did not steal them, that claim must be proved on a balance of probabilities (PACE 1984, s. 74; *Barnes* [1991] Crim LR 132 and **F12.6**). Conviction of the alleged thief by any other foreign court is not, however, admissible as evidence of the theft. This may hamper the use of the Theft Act 1968, s. 24(1) (see **B4.164**), although it does not preclude expert evidence that an act would have been an offence under foreign law.

DISHONESTLY RETAINING A WRONGFUL CREDIT

Definition

B4.184 Theft Act 1968, s. 24A

(1) A person is guilty of an offence if—
   (a) a wrongful credit has been made to an account kept by him or in respect of which he has any right or interest;
   (b) he knows or believes that the credit is wrongful; and
   (c) he dishonestly fails to take such steps as are reasonable in the circumstances to secure that the credit is cancelled.
(2) References to a credit are to a credit of an amount of money.
(2A) A credit to an account is wrongful to the extent that it derives from—
   (a) theft;
   (b) blackmail; or
   (c) fraud (contrary to the Fraud Act 2006); or
   (d) stolen goods.
(3) [Repealed—see below and **B4.187**.]
(4) [Repealed—see below and **B4.187**.]
(5) In determining whether a credit to an account is wrongful, it is immaterial (in particular) whether the account is overdrawn before or after the credit is made.
(6) A person guilty of an offence under this section shall be liable on conviction on indictment to imprisonment for a term not exceeding ten years.
(7) Subsection (8) below applies for purposes of provisions of this Act relating to stolen goods (including subsection (2A) above).
(8) References to stolen goods include money which is dishonestly withdrawn from an account to which a wrongful credit has been made, but only to the extent that the money derives from the credit.
(9) 'Account' means an account kept with—
   (a) a bank;
   (b) a person carrying on a business which falls within subsection (10) below; or
   (c) a person falling within any of paragraphs (a) to (j) of the definition of 'electronic money issuer' in regulation 2(1) of the Electronic Money Regulations 2011.
(10) A business falls within this subsection if—
   (a) in the course of the business money received by way of deposit is lent to others; or
   (b) any other activity of the business is financed, wholly or to any material extent, out of the capital of or the interest on money received by way of deposit.
(11) References in subsection (10) above to a deposit must be read with—
   (a) section 22 of the Financial Services and Markets Act 2000;
   (b) any relevant order under that section; and
   (c) Schedule 2 to that Act;
   but any restriction on the meaning of deposit which arises from the identity of the person making it is to be disregarded.
(12) For the purposes of subsection (10) above—
   (a) all the activities which a person carries on by way of business shall be regarded as a single business carried on by him; and
   (b) 'money' includes money expressed in a currency other than sterling.

Section 24A is shown as amended by the Fraud Act 2006, sch. 1, para. 7, but these amendments do not affect its operation in relation to credits falling within s. 24A(3) or (4) and made before 15 January 2007 (Fraud Act 2006, sch. 2, para. 5). This means that s. 24A will continue to apply where a credit represents or is derived from a money transfer obtained before that date, contrary to the Theft Act 1968, s. 15A. See **B4.187**.

Procedure and Sentence

An offence under s. 24A is triable either way (MCA 1980, s. 17 and sch. 1, para. 28). When tried on indictment, it is normally a class 3 offence, but see CrimPD XIII, para. B (see Supplement, **CPD.XIII.B**) for the additional factors that the court considers on allocation. It is a Group A offence for jurisdiction purposes under the CJA 1993, Part I (see **A8.10**). **B4.185**

The maximum penalty is ten years' imprisonment (Theft Act 1968, s. 24A(6)) on indictment; six months and/or an unlimited fine on summary conviction. There is no offence-specific guideline but the Sentencing Council's *General Guideline: Overarching Principles* (see Supplement, **SG2-1**) is used for all offenders sentenced on or after 1 October 2019.

Indictment

Statement of Offence **B4.186**

Dishonestly retaining a wrongful credit, contrary to section 24A(1) of the Theft Act 1968.

Particulars of Offence

A between the . . . day of . . . and the . . . day of . . . knowing or believing that a wrongful credit, namely a transfer of £20,000 obtained by B from Nationwide Building Society, contrary to section 1 of the Fraud Act 2006, had been made to a current account (no. . . .) kept jointly by A and B at Barclays Bank plc, dishonestly failed to take such steps as were reasonable in the circumstances to secure that the credit was cancelled.

Wrongful Credits and Stolen Goods

One (at least arguable) side-effect of the decision of the House of Lords in *Preddy* [1996] AC 815 was that, where D dishonestly obtained a money transfer from V, the sum thereby credited to D's account could no longer be categorised as stolen goods. This indeed was the view of the Law Commission when reviewing the impact of *Preddy*. To some extent, this is now addressed by the enactment of the Fraud Act 2006 and the consequential amendment of the Theft Act 1968, s. 24, so as to classify the proceeds of fraud as stolen goods; but this assists only in respect of frauds committed on or after 15 January 2007. Furthermore, even where A pays stolen bank notes directly into an account, the proceeds of a subsequent transfer from that account to an account held by B cannot be classed as stolen goods, because any credit balance thereby created in B's account is an entirely different chose in action from the credit balance which previously represented the stolen money in A's account. B's credit balance admittedly represents the proceeds of A's original crime, but it has never done so in the hands of the original thief, and any argument that it does so in the hands of a handler of the stolen property (i.e. B) is circular, because that presupposes the very point it seeks to establish, namely that the funds in B's account are stolen goods. In *A-G's Ref (No. 4 of 1979)* [1981] 1 All ER 1193, it was held that B may be guilty of handling in such circumstances; but this cannot stand with *Preddy* on that particular issue. **B4.187**

Section 24A addresses the problem by ensuring (originally through subsections (3) and (4) and now through subsection (2A)) that D commits an offence by dishonestly retaining a credit which D knows or correctly believes represents or is derived from theft, blackmail, s. 15A deception (prior to 15 January 2007), fraud (contrary to the Fraud Act 2006, s. 1) or stolen goods. If, for example, A pays stolen money into a bank account and transfers the funds from that account to an account owned by B, a wrongful credit is thereby made to B's account, and B may commit a s. 24A offence by dishonestly retaining it, knowing or believing it to be derived from one or other of those offences. Section 24A(8), meanwhile, provides that any *money* dishonestly withdrawn from an account to which a wrongful credit has been made can be classed as stolen goods, subject to the principles explained in **B4.167** in respect of withdrawals from accounts into which both 'clean' and 'dirty' money has been paid. It may seem strange that the proceeds of A's original theft can be classed as stolen goods when paid into A's own bank account, cease to be so classified when effectively 'transferred' to B's account, and yet revert to being stolen goods when dishonestly withdrawn as cash by B; but such is the law.

Dishonesty, Omissions and Bona Fide Purchasers

B4.188 The offence created by s. 24A(1) is one of dishonest omission. Dishonesty must bear its usual meaning (see **B4.54**), but knowledge in this context cannot always be equated with dishonesty. A may discover that her spouse, B, has caused the payment of a wrongful credit into their joint account. It may be difficult for A to insist on the cancellation of this credit, unless she is prepared to inform on B, but would a court or jury necessarily categorise her inactivity as dishonest? Similarly, although the bona fide purchaser of a credit is not exempted from liability under s. 24A where he retains the credit after belatedly discovering it to have been a wrongful one (contrast the Theft Act 1968, s. 3(2)) it may be very difficult to persuade a jury that such a person acted dishonestly.

The word 'cancelled' as used in s. 24A(1)(c) means cancelling the original credit so as to achieve the same effect as if it had not been made in the first place. In many cases that will be achieved by a corresponding debit reversing the original entry in the account (*Lee* [2006] EWCA Crim 156, per Moore-Bick LJ at [24]).

Wrongful Credits and the Proceeds of Criminal Conduct

B4.189 The POCA 2002, s. 327 (see **B21.12**), creates offences of concealing, disguising, converting or transferring abroad 'criminal property' (as defined in s. 340 of the Act). Section 329 (see **B21.22**) creates offences of acquiring, using or possessing such property. This includes property that directly or indirectly represents any person's benefit from criminal conduct. Dishonesty need not be proved, and mere suspicion as to the provenance of the property may suffice. These offences nevertheless carry higher maximum penalties than offences under the Theft Act 1968, s. 24A.

Where a money transfer is made, for example, from the thief's account to an account held by D, what is credited to D's account represents the benefit to the thief of the original crime, and (in contrast to the position under the Theft Act 1968, s. 22) it does not matter for this purpose that this credit was never held by the thief. *Preddy* [1996] AC 815 does not apply to or affect the operation of money laundering offences.

Section 24A applies only to wrongful credits made on or after 18 December 1996 (Theft (Amendment) Act 1996, s. 2(2)), whereas criminal property may, for the purposes of the POCA 2002, derive from more ancient crimes.

ADVERTISING REWARDS FOR RETURN OF GOODS STOLEN OR LOST

Definition

B4.190 Theft Act 1968, s. 23

Where any *public advertisement* of a reward for the return of any goods which have been stolen or lost uses any words to the effect that no questions will be asked, or that the person producing the goods will be safe from apprehension or inquiry, or that any money paid for the purchase of the goods or advanced by way of loan on them will be repaid, the person advertising the reward and any person who prints or publishes the advertisement shall on summary conviction be liable to a fine not exceeding level 3 on the standard scale.

Elements

Section 23 does not necessarily forbid the offering of rewards for the return of stolen goods, nor does it necessarily prohibit advertisements promising that 'no questions will be asked'. What it prohibits are public advertisements which *combine* an offer of a reward with a promise that no questions will be asked or that immunity will be granted. It does not matter if the advertiser is uncertain whether the goods were lost or stolen; the advertiser may even be confident that they were only lost. **B4.191**

The printing or publishing of an offending advertisement is an offence of strict liability (*Denham v Scott* (1984) 77 Cr App R 210).

For the meaning of 'goods', 'stolen goods', 'theft' etc., see **B4.164** ***et seq.***

UNLAWFUL DEALING IN CULTURAL OBJECTS

The Dealing in Cultural Objects (Offences) Act 2003, s. 1, creates an offence of acquiring, disposing of, importing or exporting tainted cultural objects, or agreeing or arranging to do so. **B4.192**

By ss. 1 and 2 of the Act, a 'tainted cultural object' is one that has been criminally removed from a building or structure of historical, architectural or archaeological interest where the object has at any time formed part of the building or structure, or from a monument of such interest. This removal may have been criminal under UK law or 'under the law of any other country or territory', but the offence of dealing itself (extensively defined in s. 3) has not been given any extra-territorial ambit.

By s. 4, proceedings for an offence relating to the dealing in a tainted cultural object may be instituted by the DPP or by order of the Commissioners of HM Revenue and Customs if it appears to either of them that the offence has involved the importation or exportation of such an object.

The maximum penalty is seven years' imprisonment and/or a fine on indictment and six months and/or an unlimited fine summarily (s. 1(3)). There is no offence-specific guideline but the Sentencing Council's *General Guideline: Overarching Principles* (see Supplement, **SG2-1**) is used for all offenders sentenced on or after 1 October 2019.

The Cultural Property (Armed Conflicts) Act 2017, s. 17(1), adds an offence of dealing in 'unlawfully exported cultural property' (s. 16), knowing or having reason to suspect that it has been unlawfully exported. It does not extend to property imported into the UK before the Act came into force on 12 December 2017.

The Act enables the UK to implement the Hague Convention for the Protection of Cultural Property in the Event of Armed Conflict of 1954 and the Protocols to that Convention of 1954 and 1999, which, *inter alia*, prohibit the theft, pillage or misappropriation during armed conflicts of cultural property protected under the Convention. Conduct of that kind (involving serious violations of the Second Protocol) committed by UK nationals or servicemen in armed conflicts or in occupied territories may be punishable under s. 3 of the Act.

Section B5 Fraud and Blackmail

DECEPTION AND FRAUD: THE OLD AND NEW LAW

B5.1 The Theft Acts 1968 and 1978 created several deception offences covering situations in which something was dishonestly obtained, secured or procured, or in which liability was evaded, by the deception of another person.

The offences in the Theft Act 1968 were those created by s. 15 (obtaining property), s. 15A (obtaining a money transfer), s. 16 (obtaining a pecuniary advantage) and s. 20(2) (procuring the execution of a valuable security). The Theft Act 1978 added offences of obtaining services (s. 1), securing remission of an existing liability (s. 2(1)(a)), inducing a creditor to wait for or forgo payment (s. 2(1)(b)) and obtaining exemption from, or abatement of, liability to make a payment (s. 2(1)(c)).

These offences were repealed by the Fraud Act 2006, s. 14 and sch. 1, on 15 January 2007 (Fraud Act 2006 (Commencement) Order 2006 (SI 2006 No. 3200)); they were replaced on that date:

(1) by a general offence of fraud (Fraud Act 2006, s. 1) that may be committed:
   (a) by dishonestly making a false (i.e. untrue or misleading) representation with a view to gain or with intent to cause loss or to expose to a risk of loss (s. 2);
   (b) by dishonestly (and with a view to gain or with intent to cause loss etc.) failing to disclose information when under a legal duty to disclose it (s. 3); or
   (c) by dishonest abuse of a position, with a view to gain or with intent to cause loss etc. (s. 4); and

(2) by an offence of obtaining services dishonestly (s. 11).

The Fraud Act (largely based on proposals made by the Law Commission in 2002 (Cm 5560)) also creates offences of possessing or making articles for use in frauds (e.g., false identity documents, counterfeit goods or stolen credit cards) (see **B5.22** *et seq.*) but does not, as was originally proposed, abrogate the common-law offence of conspiracy to defraud (see **A5.64**).

Because the Fraud Act has no retrospective effect, it remains necessary to rely upon the old law when prosecuting frauds that predate the commencement of that Act (*Goldsmith* [2009] EWCA Crim 1840). Some cases that involve both pre- and post-commencement elements may also fall to be prosecuted under the old law (see **B5.2**). For coverage of the old law, see the 2013 edition of this work at B5.54 *et seq*.

Transitional Provisions and Pre-commencement Offences

B5.2 The repeal of the deception offences by the Fraud Act 2006, sch. 1, para. 1, 'does not affect any liability, investigation, legal proceeding or penalty for or in respect of any offence partly committed before' commencement (i.e. 15 January 2007) (sch. 2, para. 3(1)). An offence will be deemed to have been partly committed before that date if a 'relevant event' (i.e. any act, omission or other event, including any result of one or more acts or omissions, proof of which is required for conviction of the offence) occurs before it, and another event occurs on or after it (sch. 2, para. 3(2) and (3)).

Where frauds are committed over a long period of time, but involve false representations etc. committed *only* prior to 15 January 2007, the old law must continue to be relied upon, even if any gain or obtaining takes place well after commencement. Whereas the old law is given transitional application under sch. 2, para. 3 (above), the new offence of fraud has no retrospective effect, and creates a conduct crime rather than a result crime. The obtaining of property in 2008 as a result of a fraudulent representation made in 2005 would not therefore satisfy the *actus reus* of the new fraud offence. If, however, fraudulent acts or omissions can be identified both before and after 15 January 2007 (and that might include a single but ongoing or repeated representation), a prosecutor might be in a position to choose between proceeding under the old law and proceeding under the new. Similarly, the new offence of obtaining services dishonestly (s. 11), which is a result crime, may perhaps result from a pre-commencement deception although no deception is strictly necessary under that section. Here again, the old and new offences may overlap so that the prosecutor can choose under which to proceed.

B

Part B Offences

Two transitional scenarios remain problematic. **B5.3**

(a) If it is unclear whether a 'relevant event' occurred before or after commencement, the Crown may put alternative counts on the indictment (i.e. one under the 2006 Act and one under the repealed legislation). This is permissible under the principles established in *Bellman* [1989] AC 836 (see **D11.67**), but will not help unless the correct date and charge become clear during the course of the trial. Unless one of the transitional provisions applies, evidence that D must have committed either a deception offence or a Fraud Act offence will not enable D to be convicted of either.
(b) No transitional provisions have been made in respect of the jurisdiction provisions in the CJA 1993, Part I (see **A8.11**). As of 15 January 2007, the deception offences ceased to be Group A offences under that Act, and are replaced in that role by Fraud Act offences (Fraud Act 2006, sch. 1, para. 24). No express provision is made in that context for deception offences partly committed before commencement. None of the transitional provisions in sch. 2 purport to qualify sch. 1, para. 24. Parliament may have assumed that this problem was covered by sch. 2, para. 3, but that provision deals only with the repeal of the deception offences by sch. 1, para. 3, whereas the jurisdiction problem referred to here arises from amendments made to the CJA 1993.

As pointed out at **A8.11**, *Smith (Wallace Duncan) (No. 4)* [2004] EWCA Crim 631, [2004] QB 1418 arguably provides a solution to the latter problem, but only at the expense of rendering the provisions of the CJA 1993, Part I, largely otiose. Alternatively, a court or prosecutor might possibly seek to draw an analogy with *C* [2007] EWCA Crim 2581, [2008] 1 WLR 966, in which the Court of Appeal adopted a flexible approach to a broadly similar (but not identical) transitional difficulty in connection with changes to the laws governing sexual offences (see **F7.26**).

THE OFFENCE OF FRAUD

Fraud Act 2006, s. 1 **B5.4**

(1) A person is guilty of fraud if he is in breach of any of the sections listed in subsection (2) (which provide for three different ways of committing the offence).
(2) The sections are—
  (a) section 2 (fraud by false representation),
  (b) section 3 (fraud by failing to disclose information), and
  (c) section 4 (fraud by abuse of position).

These are reproduced and examined at **B5.14** ***et seq.***

In all three variants of the offence, the focus is on proscribed conduct and ulterior intent. The consequences of that conduct are not legally significant. Fraud is, in other words, a conduct crime, in which causation issues cannot arise in respect of the *actus reus* and in which unsuccessful 'attempts' to defraud (or even communicate with) V may in law amount to a complete or substantive offence. Indeed, it is difficult (as with blackmail) to envisage conduct that could give rise to liability for an attempt to commit it, save where D tries to make a false representation, but stammers helplessly, or mistakenly tells the truth (*Deller* (1952) 36 Cr App R 184; *Cornelius* [2012] EWCA Crim 500 at [36]), or intends to withhold information, but unwittingly discloses it.

Procedure and Jurisdiction

B5.5 Fraud is triable either way. When tried on indictment, it is normally a class 3 offence, but see CrimPD XIII, para. B (see Supplement, **CPD.XIII.B**) for the additional factors that the court considers on allocation. It is a Group A offence for jurisdiction purposes under the CJA 1993, Part I (see **A8.10**). Company officers may be proceeded against and punished for any such offence committed by the company with their consent or connivance (Fraud Act 2006, s. 12(2)). As to the position where a body corporate is managed by its members, see s. 12(3).

Indictment

B5.6 *Statement of Offence*

Fraud, contrary to the Fraud Act 2006, section 1.

Particulars of Offence

A on or about the . . . day of . . . 2007, dishonestly made a false representation to B, namely, . . . knowing this to be [might be] untrue [misleading] and intending thereby to make a gain for himself [expose B to a risk of loss].

Sentencing for Fraud Offences Generally

B5.7 The maximum sentence for fraud, whether committed in breach of the Fraud Act 2006, s. 2, 3, or 4, is (i) on summary conviction, six months' imprisonment or an unlimited fine or both, (ii) on conviction on indictment, ten years' imprisonment or a fine, or both (s. 1(3)).

The definitive sentencing guideline, *Fraud, Bribery and Money Laundering Offences* (see Supplement, **SG26-1**) is applicable. The guideline applies to all individual offenders aged 18 and over and to organisations sentenced on or after 1 October 2014 regardless of the date of the offence. The part of the guideline on fraud is applicable to fraud by false representation (see **B5.14**), fraud by failing to disclose information (see **B5.19**), fraud by abuse of position (see **B5.21**), conspiracy to defraud, and false accounting. A separate part of the guideline applies to possessing, making or supplying articles for use in fraud, a third applies to revenue fraud, and a fourth to benefit fraud. A further separate part of the guideline applies to corporate offenders.

The guideline is structured differently to others. The assessment of culpability reflects approaches elsewhere, including such features as role, sophistication, planning, sustained offending and targeting of the vulnerable. Harm is assessed in a two stage process. 'Harm A' is the actual, intended or risked loss arising from the offence expressed in monetary terms, and 'Harm B' relates to the impact of the loss on the victim. Medium impact will have the effect of raising the level of sentence within the relevant category, while high impact will raise the case into a higher category. Features of high victim impact include serious detrimental effect on V whether financial or otherwise, for example substantial damage to credit rating, as well as the particular vulnerability of V including as a result of age, financial circumstances or mental capacity.

Vulnerability, a feature that is often present in fraud, may feature in two distinct respects in the assessment of sentence. An argument that vulnerability had been double counted was successful in

Churchill [2017] EWCA Crim 841, [2017] 2 Cr App R (S) 34 (305), an approach firmly rebuffed in *Collins* [2018] EWCA Crim 1713, [2019] 1 Cr App R (S) 7 (53), in which Treacy LJ said that the sentence guideline reflected a proper focus on the two concepts of culpability and harm, each separately and distinctly requiring a consideration of vulnerability. The Court held that any views to the contrary expressed in *Churchill* were wrong and the case should not be followed.

Conspiracy In *Samuriwo* [2016] EWCA Crim 1948, [2017] 1 Cr App R (S) 30 (226) the Court of Appeal gave guidance as to the operation of the guideline, particularly in relation to conspiracy cases. The Court said that the guideline applied to offences of conspiracy to defraud at common law, which clearly indicated that it was intended to apply to group offending that might be charged as conspiracy. The trial judge's view that he was entitled not to follow the guideline rigidly was therefore incorrect: he was required to follow the guideline and could not avoid doing so simply because the case was charged as conspiracy. The culpability assessment for a group of offenders might not be the same for each offender. In deciding on culpability in a conspiracy case, it was appropriate to look not only at what the particular appellant did, but at what the agreement that he joined was collectively trying to do. For this reason, conspiracy offences might be more serious than a series of substantive offences, and it might be difficult to put a precise financial value on the harm that the conspiracy intended to cause. The Court was entitled not simply to look at the events on one day of the conspiracy period and sentence on the basis that this resolved the harm category into which the offence was to be placed; indeed, it would be an error to do so. Where a sophisticated system of fraud had been set up, there was no reason to suppose that the offenders did not intend to carry on using this as long as they could. The loss intended, even if it could not be precisely quantified, had to be taken into account. Where the harm could not be quantified, the appropriate course was to move the case up to the corresponding point in the next category above the level of harm that had been quantified. **B5.8**

These points were illustrated in *Jones* [2018] EWCA Crim 2885, in which Lady Justice Hallett VP prefaced a judgment in which sentences were upheld in relation to each defendant as follows (at [46]):

> First, we make one general but important observation: a judge in sentencing for a conspiracy or conspiracies must attempt to make a fair assessment of the overall offending. The judge is not obliged to limit their assessment of the seriousness of the offending to the specific sums that have been obtained. The major flaw in the arguments advanced before us today is to focus on those amounts and to ignore the extent of the conspiracies generally and the applicants' and the appellant's participation in them.

Substantive Offences By contrast, where D acts alone it is necessary to identify the direct results of the offending. In *Green* [2016] EWCA Crim 1888, [2017] 1 Cr App R (S) 22 (161) D, a solicitor, had written cheques to the value of £25,000 from the firm that employed her to a bogus company which she had formed, also having created false clients in order to further the fraud. None of the money was recovered. A victim personal statement from the firm indicated that in consequence of the offending they had to pay over £180,000 to the Legal Aid Authority and incurred their own costs of £30,000. The judge placed the offence in culpability category A and harm category 2 based on a starting point of £300,000. The sentence was three years. The Court of Appeal said that the judge had erred because it had not been established to the criminal standard that the consequential losses were the direct result of the offence. The case fell within 3A rather than 2A, and the sentence was reduced to two years. Despite personal mitigation, immediate custody was inevitable. **B5.9**

In *Hussain* [2019] EWCA Crim 1534, D pleaded guilty to five 'sophisticated and systematic' offences of fraud by false representation and two of possessing an article for use in fraud. The false representations were made in respect of used but unroadworthy cars that he sold to members of the public, whose complaints he then ignored or responded to with threats. The articles in question were false documents and service stamps used to make the cars look more valuable and roadworthy than they really were. When examined, they were found to have been used in many of his fraudulent sales. He had recent convictions for fraud and tax evasion in respect of his business activities. The judge placed the frauds into category 3A of the definitive guideline,

Fraud, Bribery and Money Laundering Offences (see Supplement, **SG26-1**), with a starting point of three years' imprisonment, which he increased to 42 months on the basis of D's criminal record, before making a 15 per cent reduction for the late plea, leaving 35 months, to which he added 24 months consecutive for possession of the articles, giving a total of 59 months. On appeal, it was argued that consecutive sentences were wrong, given the close relationship between the fraud offences and the possession offences.

The Court of Appeal 'favoured the view' that consecutive sentences were inappropriate on the facts, but declined to interfere with the overall sentence. It did not necessarily matter, said Gross LJ at [29], how the judge had structured the sentence, but only whether the total sentence was manifestly excessive, and in this case it was not bearing in mind D's conduct towards the victims, its impact, and the fact the articles would have been available for use in further frauds.

The definitive sentencing guideline on *Fraud, Bribery and Money-laundering Offences* was also considered in *Marijeni* [2019] EWCA Crim 1655, a case involving a conspiracy to defraud the Department for Work and Pensions (see **A5.67**) and again in *Pike* [2019] EWCA Crim 1951, in which D appealed against a sentence of 30 months' imprisonment for using a stolen and falsified passport to obtain employment that he held for several years. It was argued in *Pike* that D's offence could have been prosecuted under the Identity Documents Act 2010, s. 4, and that sentencing for the fraud offence should reflect the significantly lower range of sentences appropriate to such cases when prosecuted under the 2010 Act (as to which see **B22.75**, and *Ovieriakhi* [2009] EWCA Crim 452) instead of the definitive guideline itself. The Court of Appeal rejected that argument and upheld D's sentence. Simler LJ said:

> 9. The appellant was charged and convicted of fraud. His gain in this case was the obtaining of employment and the wages he was paid in that employment by the use of a forged passport. In addition to the lengthy employment and the wages he obtained, there were other aggravating features. For example, he applied to renew the passport when it expired and at a certain point obtained a copy birth certificate.
>
> 10. We share the judge's view that this is a difficult case to fit neatly within the Fraud Guideline but we are in no doubt that the judge was required to follow that Guideline unless it was contrary to the interests of justice to do so. We can see no basis for concluding that it was.

An offence of possession of articles for use in fraud merited a total sentence of 18 months after a trial in *Bouferache* [2015] EWCA Crim 1611, [2016] 1 Cr App R (S) 25 (158). D had obtained refunds from Oyster Cards loaded with credit from cloned or false credit cards. The scheme was sophisticated, but could net only quite small sums of money (£15 from each card). The Court of Appeal observed that exploitation of a weakness in the Oyster Card system did not amount to targeting a vulnerable victim within the terms of the guideline.

Cases decided under the previous guideline are now generally of no relevance, but the various sentencing factors identified in *Yates* [2010] EWCA Crim 1028, [2011] 1 Cr App R (S) 15 (112) in relation to mortgage fraud may still be of some assistance, as may *Graduiara* [2012] EWCA Crim 1312, [2013] 1 Cr App R (S) 50 (282) in relation to possession of an article for use in fraud (a 'Lebanese loop').

B5.10 **Benefit Fraud etc.** Most cases involving the dishonest obtaining of social security benefits or payments are dealt with summarily under the Social Security Administration Act 1992, s.111A (see **B16.59**). More serious cases will be prosecuted under the Fraud Act 2006. The relevant definitive sentencing guideline is *Fraud, Bribery and Money Laundering* (see Supplement, **SG26-1**), which is applicable to all individual offenders aged 18 or over and to organisations sentenced on or after 1 October 2014, regardless of the date of the offence.

Dishonesty in Fraud Cases

B5.11 The concept of dishonesty in fraud cases is broadly similar to that which applies to offences of dishonesty under the Theft Act 1968 (see **B4.51** *et seq.* and the *Crown Court Compendium* (July 2020), ch. 8-6), subject to the caveat that the Theft Act 1968, s. 2, is not directly applicable to any offence that does not involve either theft or an intent to steal. The test for dishonesty in fraud cases (or cases of conspiracy to defraud) is thus the largely objective one laid down by the Supreme Court in *Ivey v Genting Casinos (UK) Ltd* [2017] UKSC 67, [2018] AC 391 and followed by the Court of Appeal in *Barton* [2020] EWCA Crim 575, as to which see **B4.54** ***et seq.***; and as in theft cases, there will often be no issue as to whether what is alleged would, if proved, be considered dishonest. See *Nyonyintono* [2020] EWCA Crim 454.

The rejection of the second limb of the old *Ghosh* test in *Ivey* and *Barton* may perhaps be felt more acutely in some fraud cases than in cases to which the Theft Act 1968, s. 2(1), applies. According to *Wootton* [1990] Crim LR 201 a trial judge in a theft case must always direct the jury as to s. 2(1)(a) if a claim of right is raised by the defence; but if instead of simply appropriating property etc. that D believes himself entitled to, D resorts to lies or false representations in an attempt to persuade V to give or return it, and is charged with fraud, s. 2 cannot apply, and the subjective second limb of the *Ghosh* test (which arguably served a similar function) has now been rejected as well. Had this rejection been foreseen, it is likely that a provision analogous to s. 2(1) would have been included in the Fraud Act itself. Unfortunately, the wording of the Fraud Act 2006 may encourage a court or jury to focus on the honesty or dishonesty of D's methods, rather than on the honesty or dishonesty of D's ulterior purpose, which ought to be more important. Section 2 of that Act, for example, deals with fraud by *dishonestly making a false representation* with a view to making a gain etc., rather than making a false representation with a view to *dishonestly making a gain*, etc.

In *Clarke* [1996] Crim LR 824, however, it was held that D's lies concerning his experience and background did not *ipso facto* make him guilty of obtaining a pecuniary advantage (through employment) by deception, contrary to the Theft Act 1968, s. 16, because the jury should also have been directed to consider D's argument that he could do the job properly and intended to do so. It is submitted that a similarly broad approach should still be adopted in cases of fraud. In considering whether D's conduct was objectively dishonest, a jury should be directed to take account not only of D's false representations, etc., but also of any belief D may claim to have had to have been entitled to whatever it was that D sought to gain. If, for example, the alleged dishonesty involves a company director covering up or failing to disclose false or misleading accounting practices within the company, it may be necessary to prove that the director was aware not only of the practices complained of, but also of their unlawfulness (*Bush* [2019] EWCA Crim 29).

In a widely reported incident, a woman in Bristol whose bicycle had been stolen found that someone was advertising it for sale. When the police proved unhelpful, she approached the 'vendor' and used false representations to secure a 'test ride', upon which she rode off at top speed and safely recovered her property. If charged with theft, she would clearly have had a good defence under the Theft Act 1968, s. 2(1)(a). If charged instead with fraud by false representation, s. 2(1) would no longer apply, but it would be absurd if the outcome were any different.

Intent to Gain or Cause Loss

Another *mens rea* element common to all variants of the fraud offence is that D must act *either* with intent to gain for himself or another *or* with intent to cause loss to another or expose another to a risk of loss. The intent in each case is ulterior. It does not matter whether any gain, loss or exposure actually occurs, but if the prosecution case is presented exclusively on the basis of D's alleged intent to gain, a submission of no case may properly be addressed on that same basis, even if there is some evidence of intent to expose P to a risk of loss (*Bush* [2019] EWCA Crim 29 at [134]). **B5.12**

Fraud Act 2006, s. 5

(1) The references to gain and loss in sections 2 to 4 are to be read in accordance with this section.
(2) 'Gain' and 'loss'—
 (a) extend only to gain or loss in money or other property;
 (b) include any such gain or loss whether temporary or permanent;
 and 'property' means any property whether real or personal (including things in action and other intangible property).

(3) 'Gain' includes a gain by keeping what one has, as well as a gain by getting what one does not have.
(4) 'Loss' includes a loss by not getting what one might get, as well as a loss by parting with what one has.

It has been held in cases decided under the Theft Act 1968, s. 34(2)(a), that D may act with 'intent to gain' even where merely seeking to acquire property that is owing to D (*A-G's Ref (No. 1 of 2001)* [2002] EWCA Crim 1768, [2002] 3 All ER 849), although in the context of a fraud charge D would doubtless argue that it would not have been possible to have acted dishonestly in such circumstances (see **B5.11**). In *Eden* (1971) 55 Cr App R 193, a false-accounting case, it was emphasised that an intent to gain or lose on a temporary basis may suffice under s. 34(2)(a); but in *Golechha* [1989] 3 All ER 908, it was held that the falsification of bills of exchange with intent to postpone the enforcement of a debt owing to a bank was not made with a view to gain, because it was designed simply to postpone the enforcement of an obligation. *Golechha* is widely considered to be wrongly decided, because clearly one purpose of the falsification in that case was to enable D to keep (if only temporarily) property that would otherwise have had to be expended in meeting his obligations. See also *Lee Cheung Wing v The Queen* (1992) 94 Cr App R 355 (**B6.13**). In *Gilbert* [2012] EWCA Crim 2392, the issue was whether an offence of fraud by false representation could be committed on the basis of lies told when opening a bank account. Such an account is not of itself 'money or other property', but it was argued that there was a possibility of gains arising from future legitimate property developments, using the account. In the Court of Appeal's view, however, the link between the false representation and any such prospective gain was simply too vague and tenuous to base a conviction upon it.

B5.13 **Jurisdictional Issues** One consequence of fraud offences being 'conduct crimes' (see **B5.4**) is that where D is guilty of fraudulent conduct abroad, with intent to deceive a victim within England and Wales, or with intent to gain or cause loss etc. within England and Wales, no constituent element of fraud is necessarily committed in England and Wales. The offence may be completed (and thus committed) entirely abroad. The CJA 1993, Part I, applies English criminal law to transnational offences of fraud or dishonesty if, but only if, a 'relevant event' takes place within the jurisdiction — and the fraudulent obtaining of property etc. following a false representation or abuse of position etc. is not itself a 'relevant event' (see **A8.5** and **A8.12** ***et seq.***).

The Fraud Act 2006, sch. 1, para. 25, addresses this point (if only in part) by inserting s. 2(1A) into the CJA 1993. This provides that, in relation to an offence of fraud, a 'relevant event' includes:

(a) if the fraud involved an intention to make a gain *and the gain occurred*, that occurrence; and
(b) if the fraud involved an intention to cause a loss or to expose another to a risk of loss *and the loss occurred*, that occurrence. [emphasis added]

Clearly, however, this will not assist the prosecution in cases where D intended by conduct abroad to make a gain or cause a loss within England and Wales, but failed to do so; nor does it assist even where D actually succeeds in exposing V to a risk of loss in England. This omission is curious, because it conflicts with a strong trend towards the assumption of jurisdiction over acts such as conspiracies abroad that are intended to cause, but fail to cause, harm within the jurisdiction. See *Liangsiriprasert v USA* [1991] 1 AC 225 and **A5.61**.

FRAUD BY FALSE REPRESENTATION

B5.14 **Fraud Act 2006, s. 2**

(1) A person is in breach of this section if he—
 (a) dishonestly makes a false representation, and
 (b) intends, by making the representation—
  (i) to make a gain for himself or another, or
  (ii) to cause loss to another or to expose another to a risk of loss.
(2) A representation is false if—
 (a) it is untrue or misleading, and
 (b) the person making it knows that it is, or might be, untrue or misleading.

(3) 'Representation' means any representation as to fact or law, including a representation as to the state of mind of—
   (a) the person making the representation, or
   (b) any other person.
(4) A representation may be express or implied.
(5) For the purposes of this section a representation may be regarded as made if it (or anything implying it) is submitted in any form to any system or device designed to receive, convey or respond to communications (with or without human intervention).

Elements

This provision must be read in conjunction with s. 1 of the Act (**B5.4**) because it creates a variant of the basic fraud offence, not an offence in its own right. Intent to gain and intent to cause loss are examined in **B5.12**. Dishonesty is examined at **B5.11**. **B5.15**

The *actus reus* of a fraud of this kind consists solely of making a false representation, either to another person or (by subsection (5)) to a 'system or device'. No deception need result from such a representation, and no gain or loss need result. Because it is a conduct crime, the offence may be complete even if the representation is rejected out of hand, or treated with derision by those to whom it is addressed. Indeed, as with a blackmail demand, a false representation is presumably 'made' as soon as it is uttered. If that is so, there is no need for it even to be communicated to the intended recipients. An offence under s. 1 may then be complete even if (for example) the letter containing the offending representation is lost or intercepted in the post, or the person to whom it is directed fails to hear or understand it (*Treacy v DPP* [1971] AC 537 (see **B5.53**); and see also *DPP v Collins* [2006] UKHL 40, [2006] 4 All ER 602).

B
Part B Offences

Section 2 defines the elements that make up a false representation. By s. 2(2) a statement that is literally true may be treated as false if it is misleading, although this is complicated by the introduction in s. 2(2)(b) of what is in effect a *mens rea* requirement masquerading as part of the *actus reus*. This ensures that an honest mistake by D cannot give rise to a 'false' representation within the meaning of s. 2, but as Gross LJ noted in *Varley* [2019] EWCA Crim 1074 (at [108]):

> The *actus reus*, the conduct element of the offence, is the making of an objectively untrue or misleading representation. The *mens rea*, or mental element is made up of the requisite knowledge, dishonesty and intention. The *actus reus* is therefore contained in s.2(2)(a), with the *mens rea* found in s. 2(2)(b), s. 2(1)(a) and s. 2(1)(b).

It follows that the doctrine of innocent agency (see **A1.32**) is capable of applying to s. 2(2), because an innocent agent, when performing the external elements of the offence, need not know that the representation is or might be untrue or misleading.

By s. 2(3), a representation may concern matters of fact or of law, and these must no doubt be matters of existing fact or law. A promise does not become a false representation merely because it is later broken; but (as was the case under the law governing deception) a representation may be considered false if it misrepresents the current intentions or state of mind of the person making it or anyone else, so a promise involves a false representation if D never intended to keep that promise in the first place.

Where D dishonestly tenders a stolen or forged credit or debit card to pay for goods or services, or shows another person's season ticket or bus pass in order to use facilities or services to which D is not entitled, it is clear that this amounts to a false representation. Even if D says nothing, the impression is given that the card or season ticket is genuine, that D is the authorised user, and is entitled to use it. The same may be true (under subsection (5)) where D enters a security code, password and/or PIN so as to represent to a 'system or device' that D is authorised to access an account or use a facility where that is not in fact the case. **B5.16**

Another classic example of an implied representation is that made by a customer who dines in a restaurant or stays in a hotel. The customer does not need to state that the food and service will be paid for at the end, because an inference to that effect will in any case arise from the customer's behaviour (cf. *DPP v Ray* [1974] AC 370).

The making of a false representation may itself be proved by inference. Where a vulnerable person has paid D vastly more for a job or product (such as gardening work) than it was worth, it may be open to a court or jury to infer that D must dishonestly have misrepresented the value of that job or product, even if there is no direct evidence of any such misrepresentation (*Greig* [2010] EWCA Crim 1183).

Where an unidentified imposter prepared to take a driving test in D's name it could be inferred that D was complicit in any false representations made by that person with a view to gaining a pass certificate in D's name (*Idrees v DPP* [2011] EWHC 624 (Admin)).

B5.17 **False Representations in Cheques** Tendering a forged or stolen cheque (or one drawn on a defunct account) will inevitably involve the making of a false representation; but where D tenders a genuine cheque in payment for goods or services, the position would appear to be much the same as it was under the law relating to deception. It is tempting to suggest that, by tendering the cheque, D represents that it will be paid by the bank in due course; but this cannot suffice as a false representation, under either the old law or the new, because it is a representation or promise concerning future events.

As the Court of Appeal pointed out in *Gilmartin* [1983] QB 953, one must identify a false representation as to an existing fact. Clearly D represents that the account is active and genuine. But it cannot be said that merely by drawing the cheque D makes any representation as to whether the account currently contains adequate funds to meet it. When tendering a cheque, D may know that the account is badly overdrawn; but expect it to be refreshed the next day by new funds. The solution adopted in *Gilmartin* was that:

> . . . by the simple giving of a cheque, whether postdated or not, the drawer impliedly represents that the state of facts existing at the date of delivery of the cheque is such that in the ordinary course the cheque will on presentation for payment on or after the date specified in the cheque, be met.

Arguably this differs only in phrasing from a promise that the cheque will be honoured on presentation, but such is the law. What is clear is that account may be taken of existing expectations, such as salaries due to be credited, standing orders due to be debited, and perhaps D's credit rating with the bank on which it is drawn.

The representations usually associated with issuing a cheque may sometimes be overridden by express words. D may, for example, admit uncertainty about the state of the current account, but assure V that there will be indemnification in the event of any dishonour. Each case must thus be judged on its own facts. Thus, in *United Arab Emirates v Allen* [2012] EWHC 1712 (Admin), [2012] 1 WLR 3419, the Administrative Court refused to infer that a mortgagor who issued a cheque for the full amount of the loan by way of additional security for that loan thereby represented that it would 'in the ordinary course' be honoured on presentation; if she had funds of that kind at her disposal, she would not have needed the loan in the first place.

There will not ordinarily be any fraud if D genuinely expects sufficient funds to be credited to the account in time to meet the cheque on presentation; but in *Greenstein* [1975] 1 All ER 1 the appellants drew cheques for sums vastly exceeding their credit limits in order to subscribe for the largest possible number of shares in oversubscribed company flotations. They relied on being allocated only a small percentage of the shares applied for, and on the issuing houses' refund cheques arriving in time to ensure their own cheques would be honoured. They had been warned that such tactics were considered improper, and in some cases had given an express undertaking that their cheques would be honoured on first presentation (something of which they could not in fact be sure and which did not always happen). In those circumstances they were held to have committed offences under the Theft Act 1968, s. 15. Arguably, they would now be considered guilty of fraud by false representation.

Representations Made to Systems or Devices An important difference between the old and new law concerns untrue or misleading representations that are intended to operate on ATMs, 'chip and pin' card readers, computer systems or other devices. Section 2(5) of the Fraud Act 2006 enables the offence of fraud to apply in such cases. The old law on deception was generally thought to be inapplicable in such cases on the basis that 'a machine cannot be deceived'. The Fraud Act does not of course state that a machine *can* be deceived, but only that it may be an offence dishonestly to supply a system or device with false information. **B5.18**

Section 2(5) also provides that the submission of a representation to an appropriate system or device, etc., may be treated as a 'making' of that representation. In the case of an 'online' fraud, the representation is presumably (and by analogy with the making of a blackmail demand; see **B5.53**) made only when transmitted, and not when merely saved onto an application form that has yet to be completed. If transmitted, however, it may not matter that the system to which it is sent fails to process or receive it.

FRAUD BY FAILING TO DISCLOSE INFORMATION

Fraud Act 2006, s. 3 **B5.19**

A person is in breach of this section if he—
(a) dishonestly fails to disclose to another person information which he is under a legal duty to disclose, and
(b) intends, by failing to disclose the information—
  (i) to make a gain for himself or another, or
  (ii) to cause loss to another or to expose another to a risk of loss.

This is not an offence in its own right, but another variant of the offence of fraud under s. 1 (see **B5.4** *et seq*.). Intent to gain and intent to cause loss are examined in **B5.12**. Dishonesty is examined at **B5.11**.

Under the Theft Acts, liability for deception offences could be incurred in some cases through dishonest omissions to provide correct information (*Firth* (1989) 91 Cr App R 217). The Fraud Act 2006, s. 3, introduces a potentially broader concept of fraud through non-disclosure, but only in cases where there is a legal duty to disclose. 'Legal duty' is not defined in the Act, but the Law Commission provided this explanation in its Report (Cm. 5560, 2002) at paras. 7.28 and 7.29:

> Such a duty may derive from statute (such as the provisions governing company prospectuses), from the fact that the transaction in question is one of the utmost good faith (such as a contract of insurance), from the express or implied terms of a contract, from the custom of a particular trade or market, or from the existence of a fiduciary relationship between the parties (such as that of agent and principal).
>
> For this purpose there is a legal duty to disclose information not only if the defendant's failure to disclose it gives the victim a cause of action for damages, but also if the law gives the victim a right to set aside any change in his or her legal position to which he or she may consent as a result of the non-disclosure. For example, a person in a fiduciary position has a duty to disclose material information when entering into a contract with his or her beneficiary, in the sense that a failure to make such disclosure will entitle the beneficiary to rescind the contract and to reclaim any property transferred under it.

Whether such a duty arises on any given set of facts (assuming the jury are satisfied as to those facts) must ordinarily be for the judge to decide as a question of law. In *D* [2019] EWCA Crim 209 the Court of Appeal noted that, in the case of a person who may be liable to pay council tax, the Local Government Finance Act 1992 does not create any express legal duty to notify the local authority of any facts giving rise to such liability; and nor was the Court willing to find that such a duty arose by implication. A local authority, said Davis LJ at [27], 'is in a good position to get the information which it needs'. It can also rely on civil remedies for non-payment, whether or not the taxpayer has acted dishonestly.

Where a duty to disclose arises, s. 3 does not state that D must be aware of it, but proof of such awareness will ordinarily be necessary before there can be any finding of dishonesty. If, however, such knowledge is proved or admitted, a direction on dishonesty (see **B5.11**) will often be unnecessary (see, e.g., *Razoq* [2012] EWCA Crim 674).

Non-disclosure and Misrepresentation

B5.20 If D took advantage of V's misunderstanding, but was under no legal duty to disclose information to correct the misunderstanding, it may still be possible to argue that D is guilty of fraud by false (implied) representation (see **B5.16**). In *Rai* [2000] 1 Cr App R 233, D failed to inform his local authority that his disabled mother had died, lest he should lose the benefit of a home improvement grant that he had recently obtained on the basis of her needs. By saying nothing he impliedly represented that her needs were unchanged. But where a recipient of benefits dishonestly fails to disclose income, etc. when under a legal obligation to disclose it, as in *El Mashta* [2010] EWCA Crim 2595, fraud by failure to disclose may be a more appropriate charge.

FRAUD BY ABUSE OF POSITION

B5.21 **Fraud Act 2006, s. 4**

(1) A person is in breach of this section if he—
 (a) occupies a position in which he is expected to safeguard, or not to act against, the financial interests of another person,
 (b) dishonestly abuses that position, and
 (c) intends, by means of the abuse of that position—
  (i) to make a gain for himself or another, or
  (ii) to cause loss to another or to expose another to a risk of loss.

(2) A person may be regarded as having abused his position even though his conduct consisted of an omission rather than an act.

This is a variant of the offence of fraud under s. 1; not an offence in its own right. Intent to gain and intent to cause loss are examined at **B5.12**. Dishonesty is examined at **B5.11**.

Section 4 is in theory broader than the Law Commission's proposed offence of fraud by 'dishonest *and secret* abuse of position', but in practice nothing is likely to turn on this, because such abuse is most unlikely to take place openly.

The clear intention of the provision is to cover the dishonest abuse of a position of financial trust or responsibility, including that of a trustee, company director or executor, but it is not confined to such fiduciary relationships and would extend to frauds committed by employees, including acts that could not be prosecuted as theft; e.g., where a cinema projectionist copies newly released films for private profit (cf. *Scott v Metropolitan Police Commissioner* [1975] AC 819), where an officer or employee of a company or business clones software or leaks confidential client information to a rival business, or where hotel or catering staff supply (and retain the profits from) their own food or drink, thereby depriving their employer of profits that would otherwise have been made from such sales (cf. *Cooke* [1986] AC 909; *Doukas* [1978] 1 All ER 1071). As to potential overlap with offences of bribery (on the basis that any officer, employee or agent accepting or soliciting a bribe may thereby be dishonestly abusing his position with a view to gain), see *Kensington International Ltd v Republic of Congo* [2007] EWCA Civ 1128, [2008] 1 WLR 1144 and **F10.8**.

In *Valujevs* [2014] EWCA Crim 2888, [2015] QB 745 there was evidence that the defendant gangmasters had assumed control of collecting the wages of vulnerable migrant workers or controlled those wages at the moment they were paid over. The Court of Appeal held (allowing a prosecution appeal against a terminating ruling) that the defendants could arguably have been under a duty to avoid acting against the interests of those workers, so that a dishonest breach of that duty would bring them within the ambit of the offence.

Liability for an omission might arise where, for example, a company director or employee dishonestly fails to secure or negotiate for a contract, lease or other business opportunity for the company, with the object of later securing it for himself. Whether given behaviour amounts to an abuse of D's position must largely be a question of fact for a jury, but it would be proper in many cases for a judge to make rulings or give directions as to the existence of fiduciary duties or other relationships. The abuse of information etc. legitimately acquired in connection with a *former* position of trust appears not to be covered by s. 4.

Where D has abused his position by dishonestly appropriating V's property, a charge of theft may sometimes be easier to establish than a charge of fraud. In *Hinks* [2001] 2 AC 241, for example, D's liability for theft did not depend on whether her position as V's carer was one in which she was 'expected to safeguard or not to act against' V's financial interests; and indeed it seems doubtful whether it was such a position.

POSSESSION OR CONTROL OF ARTICLES FOR USE IN FRAUD

Fraud Act 2006, s. 6 **B5.22**

(1) A person is guilty of an offence if he has in his possession or under his control any article for use in the course of or in connection with any fraud.

Possession and control are not defined in the Act but in *Tarley* [2012] EWCA Crim 464 the Court of Appeal observed that case law on possession of drugs or firearms may assist, and that liability may arise on the basis of participation in a fraudulent joint enterprise involving the article in question, even where D lacks physical possession or control of it. See to similar effect *Montague* [2013] EWCA Crim 1781. An 'article' includes for this purpose (or for the purposes of the PACE 1984, s. 1(7)(b)) any program or data held in electronic form (Fraud Act 2006, s. 8(1)). This addresses the importance of computer technology in the perpetration of frauds. This offence complements the offence of having custody or control of a false instrument with intent (Forgery and Counterfeiting Act 1981, s. 5; see **B6.51**) and to some extent supplants the offence of 'going equipped' under the Theft Act 1968, s. 25 (see **B4.150**). The latter provision is amended by the Fraud Act so that it no longer applies to the possession of articles intended for use in a 'cheat'. In its application to offences of fraud, the new offence has a much wider ambit than s. 25, which did not (and in its application to burglary or theft still does not) apply to articles possessed by D at his place of abode. Moreover, the only kind of 'cheat' to which it related was an offence under the Theft Act 1968, s. 15, whereas the new offence may apply to the possession, anywhere, of articles of any description that are intended for use in respect of any fraud offence. On the other hand, the possession of articles that have *previously* been used for such purposes does not fall within the scope of this offence (*Sakalauskas* [2013] EWCA Crim 2278, [2014] 1 All ER 1231; see also *Ellames* [1974] 3 All ER 130 and **B4.158**) but the Court of Appeal held in *Smith (Andrew)* [2020] EWCA Crim 38, [2020] 1 Cr App R 23 (390) (at [29]) that such cases should be distinguished from one in which D creates a false document in order to conceal or disguise a fraud already committed:

> There is nothing in those authorities which holds that the relevant fraud cannot be one which has already been committed in the past. What they do decide is that the defendant must intend to use the article either then or in the future in connection with fraud. As those authorities make clear, it will not suffice that it is an article which has been used in the past in connection with fraud.

Procedure and Jurisdiction

An offence under s. 6 is triable either way. When tried on indictment, it is normally a class 3 offence, but see CrimPD XIII, para. B (see Supplement, **CPD.XIII.B**) for the additional factors that the court considers on allocation. It is a Group A offence for jurisdiction purposes under the CJA 1993, Part I (see **A8.10**). Company officers may be proceeded against and punished for any such offence committed by the company with their consent or connivance (Fraud Act 2006, s. 12(2)). As to the position where a body corporate is managed by its members, see s. 12(3). **B5.23**

Sentence

B5.24 The maximum penalty on conviction on indictment is five years' imprisonment; on summary conviction, it is six months and/or an unlimited fine (s. 6(2)). The relevant definitive sentencing guideline is *Fraud, Bribery and Money Laundering* (see Supplement, **SG26-1**), which is applicable to all offenders aged 18 or over sentenced on or after 1 October 2014. There is a separate part of the guideline for corporate offenders.

MAKING OR SUPPLYING ARTICLES FOR USE IN FRAUD

B5.25 Fraud Act 2006, s. 7

(1) A person is guilty of an offence if he makes, adapts, supplies or offers to supply any article—
  (a) knowing that it is designed or adapted for use in the course of or in connection with fraud, or
  (b) intending it to be used to commit, or assist in the commission of, fraud.

As to the meaning of the term, 'article', see the Fraud Act 2006, s. 8(1) and **B5.22**. The offence created by s. 7(1) overlaps substantially with offences such as forgery or copying a false instrument (see **B6.36** and **B6.41**) but could also be used to prosecute persons who make, adapt, advertise or supply devices such as 'black boxes' for the purpose of falsifying readings on electricity meters.

Procedure and Jurisdiction

B5.26 An offence under s. 7 is triable either way. When tried on indictment, it is normally a class 3 offence, but see CrimPD XIII, para. B (see Supplement, **CPD.XIII.B**) for the additional factors that the court considers on allocation. It is a Group A offence for jurisdiction purposes under the CJA 1993, Part I (see **A8.10**). Company officers may be proceeded against and punished for any such offence committed by the company with their consent or connivance (Fraud Act 2006, s. 12(2)). As to the position where a body corporate is managed by its members, see s. 12(3).

Sentence

B5.27 The maximum penalty on conviction on indictment is ten years' imprisonment; on summary conviction, it is six months and/or an unlimited fine (s. 7(2)). The relevant definitive sentencing guideline is *Fraud, Bribery and Money Laundering* (see Supplement, **SG26-1**), which is applicable to all offenders aged 18 or over sentenced on or after 1 October 2014. In *Allsopp* [2019] EWCA Crim 95, immediate sentences of eight and 12 months' detention were required for two participants, aged 18 and 20 respectively, who pleaded guilty to their roles in a hacking operation against TalkTalk. Had they been responsible for the initial attack the sentences would have been significantly more severe.

The guideline gives a sentence category range up to seven years. However, in *Kalinins* [2019] EWCA Crim 1973, [2020] 1 Cr App R (S) 28 (217), a theoretical nine years' imprisonment after trial was an appropriate starting point where D was found with tens of thousands of items for use in what was obviously a sophisticated operation to create false identity documents to order on an industrial scale. There is a separate part of the guideline for corporate offenders.

PARTICIPATING IN FRAUDULENT BUSINESS CARRIED ON BY SOLE TRADER ETC.

B5.28 Fraud Act 2006, s. 9

(1) A person is guilty of an offence if he is knowingly a party to the carrying on of a business to which this section applies.
(2) This section applies to a business which is carried on—
  (a) by a person who is outside the reach of section 993 of the Companies Act 2006 (offence of fraudulent trading), and
  (b) with intent to defraud creditors of any person or for any other fraudulent purpose.

(3) The following are within the reach of that section —
  (a) a company (as defined in section 1(1) of the Companies Act 2006);
  (b) a person to whom that section applies (with or without adaptations or modifications) as if the person were a company;
  (c) a person exempted from the application of that section.
(4) [Applies only to Northern Ireland.]
(5) 'Fraudulent purpose' has the same meaning as in that section.

Procedure and Jurisdiction

An offence under s. 9 is triable either way. When tried on indictment, it is normally a class 3 offence, but see CrimPD XIII, para. B (see Supplement, **CPD.XIII.B**) for the additional factors that the court considers on allocation. It is a Group A offence for jurisdiction purposes under the CJA 1993, Part I (see **A8.10**), whereas fraudulent trading under the Companies Act 2006 is not. **B5.29**

Sentence

The maximum penalty on conviction on indictment is ten years' imprisonment; on summary conviction, it is six months and/or an unlimited fine (s. 9(6)). The maximum penalty of ten years' imprisonment is higher than that formerly applicable to fraudulent trading by companies, but the Fraud Act 2006, s. 10, increases the penalty for that offence, so the two offences now carry identical penalties. There is no offence-specific guideline but the Sentencing Council's *General Guideline: Overarching Principles* (see Supplement, **SG2-1**) is used for all offenders sentenced on or after 1 October 2019. **B5.30**

Elements

The offence of fraudulent trading by registered companies or by other legal persons to which the Companies Act 2006, s. 993 applies (including limited liability partnerships) is dealt with at **B7.7** *et seq.* **B5.31**

The Fraud Act 2006, s. 9, gives effect to a recommendation of the Law Commission in its Report on Multiple Offending (Cm 5609, 2002) by adopting the Companies Act offence and applying it to fraudulent trading committed by unincorporated businesses such as those operated by sole traders or partnership firms, or by persons (such as employees) connected with such businesses.

As to the carrying on of a business, see **B7.11**. As to intent to defraud creditors and other fraudulent purposes, see **B7.13**.

OBTAINING SERVICES DISHONESTLY

Fraud Act 2006, s. 11 **B5.32**

(1) A person is guilty of an offence under this section if he obtains services for himself or another—
  (a) by a dishonest act, and
  (b) in breach of subsection (2).
(2) A person obtains services in breach of this subsection if—
  (a) they are made available on the basis that payment has been, is being or will be made for or in respect of them,
  (b) he obtains them without any payment having been made for or in respect of them or without payment having been made in full, and
  (c) when he obtains them, he knows—
    (i) that they are being made available on the basis described in paragraph (a), or
    (ii) that they might be, but intends that payment will not be made, or will not be made in full.

Indictment

Statement of Offence **B5.33**

Obtaining services dishonestly, contrary to the Fraud Act 2006, section 11(1).

Particulars of Offence

A on or about the ... day of ... 2007, dishonestly entered the ... Cinema in ... without paying the required entrance fee, and viewed [a part of] the film then being screened, knowing that payment was required and intending that such payment would not be made.

Procedure and Jurisdiction

B5.34 An offence under s. 11 is triable either way. When tried on indictment, it is normally a class 3 offence, but see CrimPD XIII, para. B (see Supplement, **CPD.XIII.B**) for the additional factors that the court considers on allocation. It is a Group A offence for jurisdiction purposes under the CJA 1993, Part I (see **A8.10**). Company officers may be proceeded against and punished for any such offence committed by the company with their consent or connivance (Fraud Act 2006, s. 12(2)). As to the position where a body corporate is managed by its members, see s. 12(3).

Sentence

B5.35 The maximum penalty on conviction on indictment is five years' imprisonment; on summary conviction, it is six months and/or an unlimited fine (s. 11(3)). This offence may be committed in circumstances that otherwise could be charged as an offence contrary to s. 1 or may be more akin to making off without payment. If the former, the court should apply the appropriate fraud guideline (see **B5.7**); if the latter, the guideline for that offence in the *Magistrates' Court Sentencing Guidelines* should be used.

Elements

B5.36 This offence differs in several respects from fraud itself, and is in part derived from the offence of obtaining services by deception contrary to the Theft Act 1978, s. 1, which it replaces. It resembles the old offence in that it requires the dishonest obtaining of services, and is therefore a 'result crime', in contrast to fraud itself, which is a conduct crime. It also resembles the old offence in that it has no application to the obtaining of services other than those that are provided in return for payment.

In most other respects, however, the new offence is broader than the old. It does not require any deception, nor indeed does it require any fraudulent representation. If, for example, D sneaks into a cinema to watch a film without paying, this would suffice for liability, assuming D's conduct is dishonest and that D succeeds in viewing part at least of the film.

B5.37 **Obtaining Services** The terms 'services' and 'obtaining' are not defined in the Fraud Act 2006, but must bear a similar meaning to that given in the Theft Act 1978, s. 1(2), in which an obtaining of services was defined as the conferring of a benefit by doing an act or permitting an act to be done. As under the old law, the provision of gratuitous services is excluded, even if the whole basis of the fraud is that D is entitled to receive them free of charge, when D is not.

Also excluded is the taking by D of a benefit that V has no intention of providing to anyone. If, for example, D sneaks aboard a lorry or freight train, and obtains a free ride, this would not amount to an offence under s. 11, because the haulage company or freight train operator does not provide such rides, even for payment. What is not excluded is the provision of a service in return for a payment that could not be enforced in a court of law. It may not be rape dishonestly to secure the services of a prostitute without intending to pay, and D cannot even be guilty of making off without payment if he 'does a runner' afterwards (see **B5.43**), but such conduct would give rise to liability under the Fraud Act 2006, s. 11.

B5.38 Where D resorts to false representations in order to obtain (or attempt to obtain) a service, it might sometimes be more appropriate to consider a charge of fraud. According to the explanatory notes accompanying the Act, the offence under s. 11 may be committed where D uses false credit card details or other false personal information in order to obtain access to a subscription service on the internet. With respect, reliance on such a charge might cause difficulty because the prosecution would have to prove full payment was not made and that D 'intended that payment would not be made, or would not be made in full'. D might argue that the plan was for the service to be paid for — not by D, of course, but by the lawful holder of the credit card or by the bank which issued it. Indeed, payment may already have been made in that way by the time the service was provided. It might accordingly be safer in such a case to charge D with fraud on the basis of a false representation (namely the implied representation that D was entitled to use the credit card). Proving an intent to gain or cause loss should not be difficult in such a case, because D certainly intends to avoid paying in person and must realise that someone else will suffer a corresponding loss. It does not matter whether D knows (or cares) who that loser will be.

In *Halai* [1983] Crim LR 624, the Court of Appeal held that a building society had not provided services merely by allowing D to open a savings account because building societies do not charge any fees for such accounts. The position would be different if D dishonestly opens a current or credit card account with a bank which applies charges to such accounts (*Shortland* [1995] Crim LR 893; *Sofroniou* [2003] EWCA Crim 3681, [2004] QB 1218). It was also held in *Halai* that a mortgage advance falls outside the definition of 'services', but this ruling was abrogated (in respect of matters occurring on or after 18 December 1996) by the Theft (Amendment) Act 1996, s. 4. Even in respect of matters occurring before that date, it was held on several occasions that *Halai* should no longer be followed (see, e.g., *Graham* [1997] 1 Cr App R 302, and *Smith (Wallace Duncan) (No. 4)* [2004] EWCA Crim 631, [2004] QB 1418).

In one respect, the new offence is actually narrower than the old. Under the Theft Act 1978, s. 1, the deception practised by D did not have to concern the issue of payment. If D, not being eligible for a service (e.g., one available only to members of an exclusive club, etc.) dishonestly obtained, but nevertheless paid for, that service, such conduct could give rise to liability under the old law. Under the new law, however, D can be guilty *only* by intending that payment will not be made, or will not be made in full.

MAKING OFF WITHOUT PAYMENT

Definition

Theft Act 1978, s. 3 **B5.39**

(1) Subject to subsection (3) below, a person who, knowing that payment on the spot for any goods supplied or service done is required or expected from him, dishonestly makes off without having paid as required or expected and with intent to avoid payment of the amount due shall be guilty of an offence.
(2) For purposes of this section 'payment on the spot' includes payment at the time of collecting goods on which work has been done or in respect of which service has been provided.
(3) Subsection (1) above shall not apply where the supply of the goods or the doing of the service is contrary to law, or where the service done is such that payment is not legally enforceable.

Procedure

Making off without payment is triable either way (s. 4(1)). When tried on indictment it is normally a class 3 offence, but see CrimPD XIII, para. B (see Supplement, **CPD.XIII.B**) for the additional factors that the court considers on allocation. **B5.40**

Indictment

Statement of Offence **B5.41**

Making off without payment contrary to section 3(1) of the Theft Act 1978.

Particulars of Offence

A on or about the... day of..., knowing that payment on the spot of £... was required of him for petrol supplied to him by V, dishonestly made off without having paid the amount due as so required and with intent to avoid payment thereof.

Sentence

B5.42 The maximum penalty is two years (Theft Act 1978, s. 4(2)(b)) on indictment; six months, an unlimited fine, or both, summarily. The definitive sentencing guideline *Theft* (see Supplement, SG33-1) applies to adult offenders sentenced on or after 1 February 2016. The offence range is discharge to two years' custody. The *Magistrates' Court Sentencing Guidelines* provide guidelines for this offence when tried summarily.

Overlap with Other Offences

B5.43 Because of the relative ease with which the offence of making off without payment can be proved, it may be charged in circumstances where a more serious charge such as theft might otherwise have been pressed. If, for example, D dishonestly makes off without paying for a meal, the Theft Act 1978, s. 3, provides the obvious charge. It may be that D never intended to pay, and therefore committed fraud by ordering the meal, or theft by consuming it, but this will be far harder to prove in the absence of a confession or other evidence of D's state of mind at the time of the original obtaining.

There may also be some overlap between the offence of making off without payment under s. 3 and that of obtaining services dishonestly (**B5.32**), e.g., where D tricks a taxi driver and then makes off. If, however, D deceives V into accepting a worthless cheque in payment, or into allowing D to 'put a cheque in the post' the following day, one of the other charges must be preferred, because D now leaves with V's consent and V no longer expects payment on the spot when D 'makes off' (*Hammond* [1982] Crim LR 611; *Vincent* [2001] EWCA Crim 295; [2001] 1 WLR 1172). In *Morris* [2013] EWCA Crim 436, [2014] 1 WLR 16, Leveson LJ said:

> If a passenger were to explain (honestly) to the taxi driver that he had to enter his house in order to obtain the fare, the moment for payment would be deferred for him to do so. A decision not to return to the taxi would mean that, from that moment, the passenger is making off without payment.

With respect, failing to return cannot properly be called 'making off' unless it involves continued movement away from the place where payment is expected. Hiding behind a wall is not 'making off'. But the offence may indeed be committed if, having been allowed to leave the cab to fetch payment, D changes his mind and runs off down the road. Payment at the cab is still expected in such a case, even if the driver agreed to defer it for a few minutes (*Vincent* at [12]).

Payment on the Spot for Goods Supplied or Service Done

B5.44 The phrase 'payment on the spot' used in the Theft Act 1978, s. 3(1), is partially explained in s. 3(2). The 'spot' in question is the place where payment is required, and this will usually be the premises where the transaction takes place, but it may sometimes mean something narrower (see **B5.45**).

Under the Theft Act 1978, s. 5(2), 'goods' in s. 3(1) is to be interpreted in accordance with the Theft Act 1968, s. 34(2)(b), and it can be assumed that 'service' bears the same meaning as in s. 1 of the 1978 Act.

The required payment must be one which is legally enforceable (Theft Act 1978, s. 3(3)). It may be possible to commit an offence of dishonestly obtaining services by tricking another person into entering into a legally unenforceable transaction; but the evasion of an unenforceable obligation, whether by deception or by making off, cannot be an offence.

Meaning of 'Making Off'

B5.45 In *Brooks* (1982) 76 Cr App R 66, it was held that the words 'dishonestly makes off' are easily understandable by a jury, and ordinarily require no elaboration in a summing-up; but such elaboration may be needed in some cases. If D practises a deception, as a result of which V allows D to leave without paying, this cannot be an offence under s. 3, and a jury must be directed accordingly. As Pill LJ explained in *Vincent* [2001] EWCA Crim 295; [2001] 1 WLR 1172: 'If the expectation [of payment on the spot] is defeated by an agreement, it cannot be said to exist. The fact that the agreement is obtained dishonestly does not re-instate the expectation.' A charge of fraud may be more appropriate here (cf. *Hammond* [1982] Crim LR 611).

'Making off' ordinarily means leaving the premises concerned, and if D is stopped at the exit it will usually amount only to an attempt (*McDavitt* [1981] Crim LR 843), but this must be a question of fact. If, for example, D slips away from the top-floor restaurant in a department store, without paying for a meal at the counter, and is caught on the ground floor before leaving the building, there can be little doubt that D has made off (i.e. from the restaurant) within the meaning of s. 3 (cf. *Brooks* (1982) 76 Cr App R 66). If D hires a taxi but then makes off without paying, the relevant 'spot' is the place where the taxi is standing (*Aziz* [1993] Crim LR 708). In *Morris* [2013] EWCA Crim 436, [2014] 1 WLR 16, Leveson LJ suggested that this may not always be the case (see **B5.43**). If D travels on a public transport system without a ticket and dishonestly makes off when required to produce one, it will be no defence to argue that payment should have been made before the journey began (*Moberley v Alsop* (1991) 156 JP 514). An honest passenger inadvertently travelling without a ticket would of course be expected to pay during or after the journey.

Mens Rea: Dishonesty and Intent to Avoid Payment

On a charge of making off without payment the prosecution must prove that D intended to make permanent default (*Allen* [1985] AC 1029). If D makes off, but intends to pay later, this cannot suffice for liability. **B5.46**

As to the meaning of 'dishonesty', see *Ivey v Genting Casinos (UK) Ltd* [2017] UKSC 67, [2018] AC 391 and **B4.54**. The issue of dishonesty may, for example, arise where D claims to have walked out of a restaurant only in protest at poor service or poor food. If the court or jury (as ordinary honest citizens) consider this conduct to have been justified, or at least excusable, they may properly decline to convict D of any such offence.

BLACKMAIL

Definition

Theft Act 1968, s. 21 **B5.47**

(1) A person is guilty of blackmail if, with a view to gain for himself or another or with intent to cause loss to another, he makes any unwarranted demand with menaces; and for this purpose a demand with menaces is unwarranted unless the person making it does so in the belief—
 (a) that he has reasonable grounds for making the demand; and
 (b) that the use of the menaces is a proper means of reinforcing the demand.

(2) The nature of the act or omission demanded is immaterial, and it is also immaterial whether the menaces relate to action to be taken by the person making the demand.

Procedure and Jurisdiction

Blackmail is triable only on indictment (MCA 1980, s. 17 and sch. 1, para. 28). It is normally a class 3 offence, but see CrimPD XIII, para. B (see Supplement, **CPD.XIII.B**) for the additional factors that the court considers on allocation. It is a Group A offence for jurisdiction purposes under the CJA 1993, Part I (see **A8.10**). **B5.48**

Indictment **B5.49**

Statement of Offence

Blackmail contrary to section 21(1) of the Theft Act 1968.

Particulars of Offence

A on or about the... day of..., with a view to gain for himself, made an unwarranted demand for £1,000 from V with menaces.

Sentencing Guidelines

B5.50 The maximum penalty is 14 years (s. 21(3)).

There is no offence-specific guideline but the Sentencing Council's *General Guideline: Overarching Principles* (see Supplement, **SG2-1**) is used for all offenders sentenced on or after 1 October 2019.

In *Roberts* [2019] EWCA Crim 1931, [2020] 1 Cr App R (S) 53 (399), the Court of Appeal noted the absence of any offence-specific guideline for blackmail, and offered some general observations on the proper approach to sentencing such cases. Simon LJ said:

> It has been repeatedly said in judgments of this court that blackmail is an ugly and vicious crime. In *Hadjou* (1989) 11 Cr App R(S) 30, Lord Lane CJ ... characterised the offence in a striking phrase as 'an attempted murder of the soul', and one for which the courts always impose severe, deterrent sentences. Part of the reason is that the threat to disclose discreditable information, or information that the victim does not wish to be disclosed, creates 'enduring fear, ever present anxiety and fear of discovery which gnaws away at him for long periods': see *Greer* [2005] EWCA Crim 2185 at [8]. However, ...the reported cases are generally fact specific: see *Ford* [2015] EWCA Crim 561, at [15].

In *Roberts* itself, D had repeatedly lied to her victim about being pregnant by him, and about the supposed birth, illness and death of what he believed to be his child. She used these lies, backed by threats to inform his family and partner, to obtain one payment after another from him over a period of a year, until his entire life savings of nearly £30,000 were gone and he was driven to rely on payday loans. She persistently applied 'maximum pressure' and intentionally caused him distress, which had consequences not just for him but for his family. This called, said the Court, for a starting point in the order of five years' imprisonment.

Previous cases have discussed the applicability of other guidelines. In *Hutchinson* [2018] EWCA Crim 631, [2018] 2 Cr App R (S) 5 (26) the Court of Appeal said that the judge was entitled to treat the Sentencing Council guideline on fraud as some indicator of the proper approach to culpability, but that blackmail, demanding money with menaces, was likely to be more serious than an attempt to obtain the same amount by fraud alone. In that case a former dentist, struck off after being reported by his colleagues, later came into possession of photographs of two nurses posing naked at the surgery. He demanded £250,000 for the photographs, threatening to publish them if no money was paid. He was sentenced to six years' imprisonment. In *Ford* [2015] EWCA Crim 561, [2015] 2 Cr App R (S) 17 (177) the Court of Appeal said that the guideline for robbery was unhelpful, at least in the context of that offence. The offender had extracted £12,000 by threats made to the victim and his family over a period of seven months, but no actual violence was used. The offender had many previous convictions, including harassment and threatening behaviour. Treacy LJ said that important sentencing factors were the amount of money demanded and the psychological harm done, or intended to be done, to the victim. This was a 'very bad case', and a sentence of seven years' imprisonment was appropriate after a trial. In *Murphy* [2019] EWCA Crim 438, [2019] 2 Cr App R (S) 13 (101) the Court of Appeal doubted that the guideline on threats to kill was persuasive even where the blackmail consisted of such a threat. In that case the blackmail consisted of threats in a single phone call by an offender who confessed soon afterwards. A starting point of four years' imprisonment was appropriate.

Earlier cases may continue to have relevance, not least for examples of the different ways in which the offence may be committed. In *Read* [2018] EWCA Crim 2186 D was an IT officer for a tech company and, having been tasked to manage a cyber-attack on the firm, he took it over, distributing pornographic images and threats to individual company workers, and demanding money in the form of bitcoins from the company itself. The sentence of six years' imprisonment after a late plea was upheld. In *Ablewhite* [2007] EWCA Crim 832, [2007] 2 Cr App R (S) 93 (604),

12 years' imprisonment for conspiracy to commit blackmail was upheld, where the offenders had been involved in a six-year campaign against a company engaged in breeding guinea pigs for medical research. The campaign was calculated to cause maximum fear and disruption. Three years' imprisonment was said to be appropriate in *Stone* (1989) 11 Cr App R (S) 176, where D took part in homosexual activities with V and then demanded sums of money under the threat of disclosing V's behaviour to the police. The offenders in *Taberer* [2011] EWCA Crim 1186, [2011] 2 Cr App R (S) 105 (603) made phone calls to a wealthy businessman demanding payment of £1 million under the threat of kidnapping members of V's family. The Court of Appeal said that four years' imprisonment was the proper sentence following a guilty plea. In *Havell* [2006] EWCA Crim 735, [2006] 2 Cr App R (S) 97 (633), sentences of three years' and two years' imprisonment were appropriate for offenders convicted of seven counts of blackmail. They ran an illicit wheel-clamping business. Motorists who stopped their cars on land for a short period found that they were clamped and prevented from driving away until they had paid a sum of money between £45 and £95. The offenders behaved in a hostile manner. In *A-G's Ref (No. 67 of 2007) (W)* [2007] EWCA Crim 2878, [2008] 1 Cr App R (S) 92 (549), D, aged 45 and of previous good character, blackmailed his elderly uncle, V, by threatening to reveal that he had previously sexually abused D. V committed suicide as a result of the threat. The Court of Appeal substituted a sentence of four years' imprisonment for the 12-month suspended sentence originally imposed. The Court of Appeal in *Arshad* [2014] EWCA Crim 2485 said that custody 'was close to being inevitable' in a case where D, aged 18, sent a message to a 14-year-old girl via a social media site demanding £50 as the price for not showing a topless photograph of the girl to her brother. In fact D did not have such a picture, and the money was not paid. D, who had no previous convictions, was convicted after a trial. Custody for 12 months, although 'tough', was upheld.

B
Part B Offences

View to Gain or Intent to Cause Loss

Demands reinforced by improper threats do not necessarily constitute blackmail, which can only be committed 'with a view to gain ... or intent to cause loss' (s. 21(1)). The concepts of gain and loss are defined for this purpose in s. 34(2)(a) of the Act: **B5.51**

Theft Act 1968, s. 34

(2) ...
- (a) 'gain' and 'loss' are to be construed as extending only to gain or loss in money or other property, but as extending to any such gain or loss whether temporary or permanent; and—
  - (i) 'gain' includes a gain by keeping what one has, as well as a gain by getting what one has not; and
  - (ii) 'loss' includes a loss by not getting what one might get, as well as a loss by parting with what one has.

It is possible to commit blackmail by using improper menaces in the course of demanding money or other property to which one is legally entitled (*Lawrence* (1971) 57 Cr App R 64); but merely seeking sexual favours or political advantage is not blackmail, though procuring sexual intercourse by threats etc. may amount to rape if V is found to have submitted without genuinely consenting (see **B3.40** ***et seq.***).

A blackmailer need not be seeking any kind of material profit. In *Bevans* (1987) 87 Cr App R 64, D used menaces in order to obtain a pain-killing injection from a doctor; this was held to be blackmail as the drug involved was a form of property.

Meaning of 'Making a Demand'

The definition of the offence of blackmail in the Theft Act 1968, s. 21, is deliberately drafted in such a way as to penalise the making of the blackmail demand, rather than the obtaining of property or the intimidation of V. In other words, it is a 'conduct crime', in which the consequences or success of D's behaviour form no constituent part of the offence (*Pogmore* [2017] EWCA Crim 925, [2018] 2 Cr App R 2 (14) at [30]). **B5.52**

'Demands' are not defined in the Act. A demand need not be expressed openly. As was pointed out in *Studer* (1915) 85 LJ KB 1017, 'it may be in language only a request'; and indeed it need not even be that, if the context makes the blackmailer's meaning clear. A demand may even be made by one who poses as the victim (*Lambert* [2009] EWCA Crim 2860, [2010] 1 Cr App R 21 (299)).

The kidnapper who writes to the child's parents, asking them whether they regard the child as being worth £10,000, would clearly be regarded as having 'demanded' that sum. Similarly, there would be a demand where D offers to sell V 'protection' while D's friends demonstrate their willingness to wreck V's premises in the event of the offer being declined (*Colister* (1955) 39 Cr App R 100).

B5.53 The earlier authorities did not provide any definite answer to the question whether a demand could be 'made' without successful communication to the intended recipient; but the question came before the House of Lords in *Treacy v DPP* [1971] AC 537, where D had posted his blackmail demand from England to V in Germany. If receipt of the demand was regarded as an essential part of its 'making' then the blackmail would have been completed (and thus committed, for jurisdictional purposes) in Germany, beyond the territorial ambit of the Theft Act 1968; but it was held that the demand was made earlier, and within the jurisdiction, when the letter was posted.

Following *Treacy*, the successful communication of the demand cannot properly be described as an element of the offence of blackmail, and it was accordingly doubted whether the receipt of a demand by V in England could render a 'cross-frontier' blackmailer liable for any offence under English law. The point was left open in *Treacy*, although it was suggested (*obiter*) in that case that the concept of a 'continuing demand' might constitute a basis for jurisdiction. The CJA 1993, Part I (see **A8.10**), was intended to clarify the position. By s. 4(b)(i) of that Act, there is now deemed to be a 'communication' of a demand within the jurisdiction if it is sent from England and Wales to a place elsewhere, and by s. 4(b)(ii) when it is sent from elsewhere to a place in England and Wales. This wording is unfortunate, because communication is not a 'relevant event' for the purposes of that Act, as the Court of Appeal conceded in *Pogmore* [2017] EWCA Crim 925, [2018] 2 Cr App R 2 (14). What s. 4(b) ought to have said is that there will be '*making*' of a demand in England and Wales in either of those circumstances, but (as predicted in previous editions of this work) the Court adopted a purposive interpretation of the provision. Clearly, Parliament did not intend it to be more restrictive than the House of Lords had been in *Treacy*:

> 50. Section 4...was intended to resolve the jurisdictional questions raised in *Treacy* and did so by adopting both sets of views as to how jurisdiction was established. So far as blackmail was concerned, the communication of a demand founded jurisdiction if it were sent either (a) from a place in England and Wales to a place elsewhere, or (b) from a place elsewhere to a place in England and Wales.
>
> 55...Parliament's intent was that jurisdiction was to be founded in each of the cases described in s. 4(b)(i) and (ii).

Attempted Blackmail

B5.54 It follows from the way blackmail is defined that offences of attempted blackmail must be unlikely occurrences. One could perhaps have such an offence where a telephone call is cut off just as the caller is starting to present the demand, or where a letter containing demands is seized just as the demander is about to post it; but in other circumstances it would seem that either the full offence is committed or only preparatory acts, which would not suffice for liability under the CAA 1981.

Meaning of 'Menaces'

B5.55 In drafting the proposals which later became incorporated into the Theft Act 1968, s. 21, the Criminal Law Revision Committee adopted the term 'menaces' in preference to 'threats', on the basis that the latter term might possibly be too wide. As the Court of Appeal later said in *Clear [1968] 1 QB 670:*

> Words or conduct which would not intimidate or influence anyone to respond to the demand would not be menaces..., but threats and conduct of such a nature and extent that the mind of an

ordinary person of normal stability and courage might be influenced or made apprehensive so as to accede unwillingly to the demand would be sufficient for a jury's consideration.

Menaces are therefore serious or significant threats; but since blackmail cases rarely involve any dispute about whether the alleged threats, if proved, were serious, there is generally no need for a trial judge to define the term for the jury. (See *Lawrence* (1971) 57 Cr App R 64; and *Garwood* [1987] 1 All ER 1032, in which it was said, somewhat questionably, that the term 'menaces' is an ordinary English word which any jury can be expected to understand.)

Nevertheless, there are at least two situations in which it is recognised that the jury may need guidance:

(a) A threat which one person would find trivial may be one which another would find terrifying. Some people are more timid than others, and fear is not always rational, even in people who may otherwise be very brave. If D knows that V suffers from arachnophobia, the threat to drop a large spider down V's back would obviously be calculated to have at least the same impact as a threat of serious violence. In *Garwood* [1987] 1 All ER 1032, it was recognised that V's 'unusual timidity' could be taken into account, provided D knew of it; and it is submitted that it should suffice if D merely hoped to discover such weakness (e.g., where D mistakenly believed V suffers from such a phobia).
(b) In the converse situation, where an apparently serious threat failed to intimidate V at all (perhaps because V knew something D did not), the jury should be told that liability may still be incurred (*Clear* [1968] 1 QB 670).

Meaning of 'Unwarranted Demands'

A demand with menaces will be unwarranted unless D genuinely believes both that there are reasonable grounds for making the demand, and that it is proper to reinforce it with those particular menaces. Note that D need not have reasonable grounds for the belief: it is a subjective test of what D thinks is reasonable and proper. Once the issue is raised, the prosecution will have the burden of proving that D had no such belief (*Ashiq* [2015] EWCA Crim 1617). **B5.56**

A menace may be considered improper without necessarily being a threat to do anything improper. Publicising a person's scandalous behaviour may in itself be perfectly legitimate: threatening that person with such publicity in order to extract money would clearly be a classic case of blackmail.

In *Harvey* (1980) 72 Cr App R 139, the Court of Appeal stated that one cannot believe a threat to be proper if one knows it would be unlawful (i.e. criminal) to carry it out. This seemingly conflicts with the later pronouncement of the Court of Appeal in *Cousins* [1982] QB 526 that a threat to kill might sometimes be lawful where the killing threatened would not be; but the dicta in *Harvey* clearly indicate a link between legality and propriety. A fanatic might believe that killing or threatening to kill could be justified for the sake of the cause, but cannot realistically claim to believe such threats are *proper* when it is obvious that what is threatened would be criminal (*Harvey* (1980) 72 Cr App R 139 at p. 142).

In this respect, blackmail can be contrasted with robbery. If D repossesses property borrowed by V, believing (rightly or wrongly) that such repossession is justified by law, this cannot amount to theft, so cannot amount to robbery even where D threatens V with serious violence in order to recover it; but since D can hardly believe such threats are lawful or proper, this must almost certainly amount to blackmail (*Lawrence* (1971) 57 Cr App R 64; *Harvey* (1980) 72 Cr App R 139).

HARASSMENT OF DEBTORS

Administration of Justice Act 1970, s. 40 **B5.57**

(1) A person commits an offence if, with the object of coercing another person to pay money claimed from the other as a debt due under a contract, he—

(a) harasses the other with demands for payment which, in respect of their frequency or the manner or occasion of making any such demand, or of any threat or publicity by which any demand is accompanied, are calculated to subject him or members of his family or household to alarm, distress or humiliation;
(b) falsely represents, in relation to the money claimed, that criminal proceedings lie for failure to pay it;
(c) falsely represents himself to be authorised in some official capacity to claim or enforce payment; or
(d) utters a document falsely represented by him to have some official character or purporting to have some official character which he knows it has not.

(2) A person may be guilty of an offence by virtue of subsection (1)(a) above if he concerts with others in the taking of such action as is described in that paragraph, notwithstanding that his own course of conduct does not by itself amount to harassment.

(3) Subsection (1) (a) above does not apply to anything done by a person which is reasonable (and otherwise permissible in law) for the purpose—
(a) of securing the discharge of an obligation due, or believed by him to be due, to himself or to persons for whom he acts, or protecting himself or them from future loss; or
(b) of the enforcement of any liability by legal process.

(3A) Subsection (1) above does not apply to anything done by a person to another in circumstances where what is done is a commercial practice within the meaning of the Consumer Protection from Unfair Trading Regulations 2008 and the other is a consumer in relation to that practice.

(4) A person guilty of an offence under this section shall be liable on summary conviction to [an unlimited fine].

The overlap between this summary offence and blackmail is clearly significant. If D acts for the purpose of coercing V into paying money, this necessarily involves 'a view to gain', and some at least of the tactics proscribed by s. 40(1)(a) to (d) could well amount to the use of menaces.

OTHER OFFENCES INVOLVING THREATS OR DEMANDS

B5.58 Threats to kill, whether or not amounting to blackmail, may be punishable under the OAPA 1861, s. 16 (see **B1.147** to **B1.151**). Threats of immediate violence may be punished as assault (see **B2.5**) or under the POA 1986 (see **B11**); and if done for the purposes of theft may amount to robbery or assault with intent to rob (see **B4.66** ***et seq.***). If they are part of a course of conduct, the making of threats may amount to harassment, or to an offence under the Protection from Harassment Act 1997, s. 4 (see **B2.197**).

Threats to damage property may be covered by the Criminal Damage Act 1971, s. 2 (see **B8.31** to **B8.35**). Threats of violence for the purpose of securing entry to premises may be covered by the CLA 1977, s. 6(1) (see **B13.24**). The CLA 1977, s. 51, deals with bomb hoaxes (see **B11.92**), which may or may not be made with a view to gain etc. Contamination of goods (often connected with blackmail of the manufacturers or suppliers) is punishable under the POA 1986, s. 38 (see **B11.98**).

Threatening letters, messages or electronic communications are covered by the Malicious Communications Act 1988, s. 1 (see **B18.30**). As to menacing messages etc. (whether containing demands or not) posted or sent on public electronic communications networks, see the Communications Act 2003, s. 127 (see **B18.27**).

Section B6 Falsification, Forgery and Counterfeiting

FALSIFICATION, FORGERY AND FRAUD

There is a significant overlap between the offences covered in this section and the offences of fraud and deception covered in **B5**. Offences of falsification, false accounting or forgery committed on or after 15 January 2007 will often involve conduct amounting equally to fraud within the meaning of the Fraud Act 2006, s. 1 (see **B5.4** ***et seq.***), although dishonesty, which is an essential element of any fraud or false accounting offence, need not be proved in cases charged under the Forgery and Counterfeiting Act 1981, the Trade Marks Act 1994 or the offences arising under the regulations governing unfair commercial practice or misleading advertising. **B6.1**

FALSIFICATION, FALSE STATEMENTS AND FALSE INSTRUMENTS

The concept of falsity, as applied to documents or instruments, is not always the same as that of falsity in statements. A lie is a false statement, but documents containing lies or false statements are not always regarded as false instruments. **B6.2**

As far as offences under the Forgery and Counterfeiting Act 1981 are concerned, an instrument is only false if it purports to be something it is not, or if it 'tells a lie' about its own authorship, origins or history. Conversely, such an instrument might be false in one or more of those respects, despite being a true and accurate statement of the matters with which it deals (as where an exact copy of a genuine document purports to be the original). See further, s. 9 of the Act (see **B6.28** to **B6.31**), which provides an exhaustive definition of falsity for those purposes.

For most purposes a document is not regarded as 'falsified' unless it has been fraudulently altered or interfered with. Such a document will usually be rendered 'false' for the purposes of the Forgery and Counterfeiting Act 1981, even if falsified by the same person who made it in the first place (s. 9(1)(g) of the Act); but the concept of falsification would not necessarily extend to the inclusion of false statements in an original document or record. For example, the offence of falsification by a bankrupt of his papers (Insolvency Act 1986, s. 355(2)(b)) would not be committed where the bankrupt merely enters incorrect details when drawing up accounts; the correct charge would be one of making false entries, contrary to s. 355(2)(c) (see **B7.62**).

There are few decided cases on the meaning of 'falsification', but the issue arose in *Edwards v Toombs* [1983] Crim LR 43, where it was held that an act which interferes with a mechanical (or presumably electronic) recording device (in that case a turnstile meter at a soccer stadium) can amount to falsification of the record, for the purpose of liability under the Theft Act 1968, s. 17(1)(a).

Falsification is 'deemed' to bear a further meaning in s. 17, by virtue of s. 17(2), but this has no wider application, and is therefore dealt with in the analysis of that provision at **B6.10** and **B6.11**.

FALSE ACCOUNTING

B6.3 Theft Act 1968, s. 17

(1) Where a person dishonestly, with a view to gain for himself or another or with intent to cause loss to another,—
(a) destroys, defaces, conceals or falsifies any account or any record or document made or required for any accounting purpose; or
(b) in furnishing information for any purpose produces or makes use of any account, or any such record or document as aforesaid, which to his knowledge is or may be misleading, false or deceptive in a material particular; he shall, on conviction on indictment, be liable to imprisonment for a term not exceeding seven years.

(2) For purposes of this section a person who makes or concurs in making in an account or other document an entry which is or may be misleading, false or deceptive in a material particular, or who omits or concurs in omitting a material particular from an account or other document, is to be treated as falsifying the account or document.

Procedure and Jurisdiction

B6.4 False accounting is triable either way (MCA 1980, s. 17 and sch. 1, para. 28). When tried on indictment it is normally a class 3 offence, but see CrimPD XIII, para. B (see Supplement, **CPD.XIII.B**) for the additional factors that the court considers on allocation. It is a Group A offence for jurisdiction purposes under the CJA 1993, Part I (see **A8.10**).

For the liability of officers of a company for an offence committed by the company, see the Theft Act 1968, s. 18, **B6.14** and **A6.23**.

Indictment

B6.5 *Statement of Offence*

False accounting contrary to section 17(1)(a) of the Theft Act 1968.

Particulars of Offence

A on or about the... day of... dishonestly and with a view to gain for himself [or for X] [or with intent to cause loss to Y] falsified a document required for an accounting purpose, namely a ledger, by making therein an entry which was misleading, false or deceptive in a material particular in that it falsely purported to show that A had received the sum of £10,000 from Z in payment for services rendered.

Sentence

B6.6 The maximum penalty is seven years (s. 17(1)) on indictment; six months, an unlimited fine, or both, summarily. The definitive sentencing guideline, *Fraud, Bribery and Money Laundering* (see Supplement, **SG26-1**), is applicable to all individual offenders aged 18 or over and organisations sentenced on or after 1 October 2014 regardless of the date of the offence. There is a separate part of the guideline for corporate offenders. The offence of false accounting may be the relevant offence in relation to the guideline on fraud, revenue fraud or benefit fraud.

In the pre-guideline case of *Chaytor* [2011] EWCA Crim 929, [2011] 2 Cr App R (S) 114 (653), where a serving MP admitted three counts of false accounting relating to Parliamentary expenses, the Court of Appeal upheld a sentence of 18 months' imprisonment. The offence involved 'serious dishonesty' and had damaged the reputation of Parliament.

Scope of Offence

Section 17 creates two distinct offences: destruction, concealment or falsification etc. (s. 17(1)(a)) and using false or misleading documents etc. in furnishing information (s. 17(1)(b)). The user of falsified accounts may well be the person who falsified them, but this is not necessarily so. D does not, however, commit an offence under s. 17(1)(b) unless D knows of the misleading, false or deceptive nature of the documents in question. Section 17(2) seems incapable of applying to s. 17(1)(b) because it deals only with falsification — the subject-matter of s. 17(1)(a). **B6.7**

Relationship to Other Offences

There are potential overlaps between the offence under s. 17(1)(a) and forgery; and between the s. 17(1)(b) offence and using a false instrument (see **B6.26** ***et seq.***). Nevertheless it would be wrong to assume that any case of false accounting must necessarily involve forgery (*Dodge* [1972] 1 QB 416). As explained in **B6.2**, the concept of falsity in the 1981 Act is a narrow one, and does not generally extend to the making of false or misleading entries when compiling a document, or to the destruction (as opposed to the falsification) of documents or records. **B6.8**

A further area of significant overlap involves documents relating to the affairs of companies or bankrupts. See the Companies Act 1985, s. 450 and the Insolvency Act 1986, ss. 209 and 355(2) (see **B7.15**, **B7.50** and **B7.62**).

Cases of false accounting are often closely associated with various other offences of dishonesty. The falsification or concealment may be a cover for past, contemporaneous or future offences of theft or fraud and it is not unusual for an indictment to include counts for both false accounting and theft. In *Eden* (1971) 55 Cr App R 193, the Court of Appeal expressed the view that the inclusion of parallel counts of this kind should be discouraged if they would both stand or fall by the same evidence; but the inclusion of both counts was at the same time recognised as prudent in a situation where (as in *Eden* itself) theft might be harder to prove.

False accounting and theft are not always clearly distinguishable from each other. The courts appear prone at times to confuse the appropriation of money or things in action (such as debts) with the falsification or misuse of documents or records relating to them. *Monaghan* [1979] Crim LR 673 is an example of this. D's dishonest failure to record a payment of £3.99 on the supermarket till she was operating, with a view to taking an equivalent sum from the till later in the day, was held to amount to theft, even though the cash was properly placed in the till, where it belonged, and even though D would no doubt have taken different notes and coins anyway. Even after *Gomez* [1993] AC 442 (see **B4.34** ***et seq.***), the better view must be that she had done nothing more than falsify the till roll; but if *Monaghan* is indeed correct, the overlap between s. 17(2) and theft must be very substantial.

Accounts, Records and Documents

The word 'account' must be given the meaning it bears in normal English usage (*Scot-Simmonds* [1994] Crim LR 933). A record or account need not necessarily be a document. In *Edwards v Toombs* [1983] Crim LR 43 it was held that a turnstile meter at a soccer stadium was a record, and thus within **B6.9** the scope of the section. See also *Solomons* [1909] 2 KB 980 (taxi meter). Conversely, a document or record need not be an account, as long as it is made or required for an accounting purpose, either by D or by another person. This purpose need not be anything more than a secondary or incidental one; thus in *A-G's Ref (No. 1 of 1980)* [1981] 1 All ER 366 it was held that loan proposal forms, which would eventually be used by the loan company for an accounting purpose, could be the subject of an offence under s. 17 (see also *Cummings-John* [1997] Crim LR 660). Whether a document is one required for an accounting purpose is a question of fact and may need to be proved by the prosecution. See *Okanta* [1997] Crim LR 451, *Osinuga v DPP* [1998] Crim LR 216, *Sundhers* [1998] Crim LR 497 and *Manning* [1998] 2 Cr App R 461, but in some cases this may be self-evident. As Hooper LJ explained in *O* [2010] EWCA Crim 2233, [2011] 2 Cr App R 33 (487) at [49]:

> Without any further direct evidence of the accounting practices of the lender, a jury is entitled to come to the conclusion that an application for a mortgage or a loan made to a commercial institution is a document required for an accounting purpose.

Extended Meaning of Falsification under Theft Act 1968, s. 17(2)

B6.10 Section 17(2) gives 'falsification' a specially extended meaning for the purposes of s. 17(1)(a). It clearly embraces the preparation of false accounts as well as the falsification of existing ones (*Scot-Simmonds* [1994] Crim LR 933). It does not, however, purport to provide an exhaustive definition of the concept, and it was held in *Edwards v Toombs* [1983] Crim LR 43 that anything amounting to falsification within the ordinary meaning of the term (see **B6.2**) would equally amount to falsification for s. 17 purposes.

Falsification by Omission

B6.11 Section 17(2) expressly provides that the omission of material information from a document etc. can have the effect of falsifying it. In *Shama* [1990] 2 All ER 602 the Court of Appeal upheld the conviction of a telephone operator who had failed even to start filling out standard forms provided by his employer for the recording of international calls. He was held to have falsified the forms by leaving them unmarked. See also *Neil* [2008] EWCA Crim 478, [2008] 2 Cr App R (S) 76 (425). A statement or record with material omissions may be misleading for purposes of s. 17(1)(b) even if it contains no outright lies; there is authority to the effect that such statements may also be regarded as being 'false in a material particular' (*Lord Kylsant* [1932] 1 KB 442) but it would not be necessary to rely thereon.

Meaning of 'Material'

B6.12 Falsity etc. is not a basis of liability under the Theft Act 1968, s. 17, unless it is falsity 'in a material particular'. The meaning of this concept was examined in *Mallett* [1978] 3 All ER 10, where the Court of Appeal rejected the argument that the falsity etc. must be material in the sense of being directly connected with the accuracy etc. of an accounting process. D had furnished false information to a finance company concerning the status of a potential customer. The falsity was material to the company's decision to finance the transaction, and the form containing the false information was required for accounting purposes. It was held that D had been rightly convicted even though no accounts had been rendered inaccurate by his supply of false information.

An omission is 'material' only if it makes the document misleading in a way that is significant (or in some way that 'matters'); the omission of information required by an application form does not necessarily amount to the omission of a material particular (*Lancaster* [2010] EWCA Crim 370, [2010] 3 All ER 402).

Mens Rea

B6.13 In false accounting there need be no proof of any intent to permanently deprive another person of that person's property. What is needed is dishonesty (as redefined by the Supreme Court in *Ivey v Genting Casinos (UK) Ltd* [2017] UKSC 67, [2018] AC 391, and by the

Court of Appeal in *Barton* [2020] EWCA Crim 575: see **B4.55**) coupled with a 'view to gain' or 'intent to cause loss'; and in *Eden* (1971) 55 Cr App R 193 it was said that this might involve nothing more than an intent to gain or avoid loss on a temporary basis, perhaps in order to play for time, whilst losses caused by honest incompetence are made good. In *Lee Cheung Wing v The Queen* (1992) 94 Cr App R 355, falsified documents were used by securities dealers to mask withdrawals of unauthorised profits from accounts they had kept secret from their employers. The Privy Council held that the falsification of these documents had been made with a view to gain and constituted an offence under equivalent legislation in Hong Kong.

Proof of dishonesty in complex false accounting cases may be problematic in the absence of evidence that D understood not only what the relevant accounting practices were, but also that they were unlawful. This is especially likely to be true in cases where D is not alleged to be directly responsible for the practice, but only for a failure to disclose or correct it (*Bush* [2019] EWCA Crim 29).

As to the meaning of 'gain' and 'loss' in this context, see the Theft Act 1968, s. 34(2)(a), *Golechha* [1989] 3 All ER 908 and *A-G's Ref (No. 1 of 2001)* [2002] EWCA Crim 1768, [2002] 3 All ER 840 (see **B5.12** and **B5.51**).

B

Part B Offences

Liability of Company Officers for Offences Committed by the Company

Theft Act 1968, s. 18 **B6.14**

(1) Where an offence committed by a body corporate under section 17 of this Act is proved to have been committed with the consent or connivance of any director, manager, secretary or other similar officer of the body corporate, or any person who was purporting to act in any such capacity, he as well as the body corporate shall be guilty of that offence, and shall be liable to be proceeded against and punished accordingly.

(2) Where the affairs of a body corporate are managed by its members, this section shall apply in relation to the acts and defaults of a member in connection with his functions of management as if he were a director of the body corporate.

In respect of things done wholly or partly prior to 15 January 2007, s.18 also applies to offences under ss. 15 and 16 and to offences under the Theft Act 1978, ss. 1 and 2 (Theft Act 1978, s. 5(1); Fraud Act 2006, sch. 2, para. 3).

As to the limitations on the scope of s. 18, see the discussion of *Boal* [1992] 1 QB 591 at **A6.24**. Offences to which it applies can be committed by corporations only if the persons who control them possess the requisite *mens rea*, which can then be imputed to the corporation. Such persons will necessarily be guilty as joint perpetrators or as accessories under the general law governing complicity in offences, without any need for reference to s. 18. A junior manager or officer who knowingly assists in the commission of such an offence by the company will similarly incur secondary liability.

This leaves s. 18 with one significant function. It may apply to senior officers or directors who knowingly consent to the commission of relevant offences, without themselves doing any acts that could result in liability as accessories under the general law (see further **A6.24**).

FALSE STATEMENTS BY OFFICERS OF COMPANY OR ASSOCIATION

Theft Act 1968, s. 19 **B6.15**

(1) Where an officer of a body corporate or unincorporated association (or person purporting to act as such), with intent to deceive members or creditors of the body corporate or association about its affairs, publishes or concurs in publishing a written statement or account which to

his knowledge is or may be misleading, false or deceptive in a material particular, he shall on conviction on indictment be liable to imprisonment for a term not exceeding seven years.

(2) For purposes of this section a person who has entered into a security for the benefit of a body corporate or association is to be treated as a creditor of it.

(3) Where the affairs of a body corporate or association are managed by its members, this section shall apply to any statement which a member publishes or concurs in publishing in connection with his functions of management as if he were an officer of the body corporate or association.

Procedure and Jurisdiction

B6.16 An offence under s. 19 is triable either way (MCA 1980, s. 17 and sch. 1, para. 28). When tried on indictment it is normally a class 3 offence, but see CrimPD XIII, para. B (see Supplement, **CPD.XIII.B**) for the additional factors that the court considers on allocation. It is a Group A offence for jurisdiction purposes under the CJA 1993, Part I (see **A8.10**).

Indictment

B6.17

Statement of Offence

Publishing a false statement contrary to section 19(1) of the Theft Act 1968.

Particulars of Offence

A on or about the... day of..., being a director of a body corporate, namely X plc, with intent to deceive the members or creditors or the said X plc, published a written statement about the affairs of the said X plc which to his knowledge was misleading, false or deceptive in a material particular in that it falsely stated that X plc then had no contingent liabilities.

Sentence

B6.18 The maximum penalty is seven years (s. 19(1)) on indictment; six months, an unlimited fine, or both, summarily. There is no guideline judgment reported for an offence under s. 19(1). There is no offence-specific guideline but the Sentencing Council's *General Guideline: Overarching Principles* (see Supplement, **SG2-1**) is used for all offenders sentenced on or after 1 October 2019. For sentencing guidelines for offences of fraud generally, see **B5.7**. For sentencing guidelines for theft offences, see **B4.5** to **B4.9**.

Relationship to Other Offences

B6.19 The commission of an offence under the Theft Act 1968, s. 19(1), by a company director may be in circumstances in which the company itself commits an offence under s. 17 or possibly ss. 15 or 16 for which the director may be liable under s. 18. There is clearly some overlap between such liability and possible liability under s. 19(1), subject to the consideration that under s. 19(1) there need be no successful deception, no proof of dishonesty and no need for the statement to be made or required for any accounting purpose, but, insofar as the s. 19 offence can be committed by officers of an unincorporated association, its scope is nevertheless wider than that of s. 18.

'Officer of a Body Corporate or Unincorporated Association'

B6.20 In relation to a body corporate, the term 'officer' includes a director, manager or secretary (Companies Act 1985, s. 744; Companies Act 2006, s. 1121), and an auditor may also be considered to be an officer (*Shacter* [1960] 2 QB 252). As to the meaning of manager, see **A6.24**.

In relation to unincorporated associations, treasurers, secretaries and chairmen would be considered to be officers; as would any partner publishing or concurring in the publication of an offending statement in connection with the firm's affairs. Where the affairs of a company or association are managed by its members, a member may commit this offence (s. 19(3)).

Intent to Deceive Members or Creditors

A statement published with intent to deceive only prospective members or creditors would not appear to come within the ambit of this offence, but would be likely to fall within the Financial Services Act 2012, ss. 89 or 90 (see **B7.25**) or amount to an offence under the Insolvency Act 1986 (see **B7.40** ***et seq.***). The Theft Act 1968, s. 19(2), provides that for the purposes of s. 19, a person who has entered into a security for the benefit of a body corporate or association is to be treated as a creditor of it. This seems to refer to a guarantor, though the precise scope of the subsection is unclear. **B6.21**

SUPPRESSION OF DOCUMENTS

Definition

Theft Act 1968, s. 20(1) **B6.22**

> A person who dishonestly, with a view to gain for himself or another or with intent to cause loss to another, destroys, defaces or conceals any valuable security, any will or other testamentary document or any original document of or belonging to, or filed or deposited in, any court of justice or any government department shall on conviction on indictment be liable to imprisonment for a term not exceeding seven years.

Procedure

This offence is triable either way (MCA 1980, s. 17 and sch. 1). When tried on indictment it is normally a class 3 offence, but see CrimPD XIII, para. B (see Supplement, **CPD.XIII.B**) for the additional factors that the court considers on allocation. **B6.23**

Sentence

The maximum penalty is seven years (s. 20(1)) on indictment; six months, an unlimited fine, or both, summarily. There is no offence-specific guideline but the Sentencing Council's *General Guideline: Overarching Principles* (see Supplement, **SG2-1**) is used for all offenders sentenced on or after 1 October 2019. There is no guideline judgment reported for an offence under s. 20(1). For sentencing guidelines for theft offences, see **B4.5** to **B4.9**. **B6.24**

Elements

Section 20(1) is little used, perhaps because offences involving the destruction or concealment of wills etc. are difficult to detect. The defacing of such instruments may sometimes amount to forgery if intended to deceive, and destruction etc. might in many cases be charged as theft or criminal damage. **B6.25**

Most of the terms used in this provision have been discussed elsewhere. The meaning of 'dishonesty' is discussed in **B4.51** ***et seq.*** and **B5.11**. The definition of 'view to gain' etc. in s. 34(2)(a) is discussed at **B5.51**. 'Valuable security' is defined in s. 20(3).

FORGERY AND KINDRED OFFENCES: GENERAL CONSIDERATIONS

Offences and Penalties under Part I of the Forgery and Counterfeiting Act 1981

The Forgery and Counterfeiting Act 1981, Part 1 (ss. 1 to 13) created the following offences: **B6.26**

(a) making a false instrument (s. 1);
(b) copying a false instrument (s. 2);
(c) using a false instrument (s. 3);

(d) using a copy of a false instrument (s. 4);
(e) having custody or control of specified kinds of false instrument (s. 5(1)); and
(f) making or having custody etc. of machines, paper etc. for making false instruments of that kind (s. 5(3)).

These offences all require proof of an 'intention to induce somebody to accept the instrument as genuine' (or as a copy of a genuine instrument) and 'by reason of so accepting it to do or not to do some act to his own or any other person's prejudice'. They are punishable following conviction on indictment with up to ten years' imprisonment under s. 6(2) and (3) of the Act.

In addition, s. 5(2) and (4) create two further, less serious, offences, which do not require proof of this ulterior intent, but which are otherwise comparable to the offences created by s. 5(1) and (3) respectively. These are punishable with up to two years' imprisonment under s. 6(4).

On summary conviction, all eight offences attract up to six months' imprisonment and/or an unlimited fine (s. 6(1)).

The above offences all use certain key terms, the meaning of which is defined in ss. 8 to 10 of the Act.

Meaning of 'Instrument'

B6.27 **Forgery and Counterfeiting Act 1981, s. 8**

(1) Subject to subsection (2) below, in this Part of this Act 'instrument' means—
   (a) any document, whether of a formal or informal character;
   (b) any stamp issued or sold by a postal operator;
   (c) any Inland Revenue stamp; and
   (d) any disc, tape, soundtrack or other device on or in which information is recorded or stored by mechanical, electronic or other means.
(2) A currency note within the meaning of Part II of this Act is not an instrument for the purposes of this Part of this Act.
(3) A mark denoting payment of postage which a postal operator authorises to be used instead of an adhesive stamp is to be treated for the purposes of this Part of this Act as if it were a stamp issued by the postal operator concerned.

It had been recognised that one of the many difficulties surrounding the old Forgery Act 1913 was uncertainty about what kinds of article fell within the scope of the offences it created. The fact that it referred to 'documents', without providing any definition of that term, meant, *inter alia*, that doubts surrounded things such as wrappers on goods or the signatures on paintings or other works of art (*Closs* (1857) Dears & B 460; *Smith* (1858) Dears & B 566; *Douce* [1972] Crim LR 105). In proposing the new legislation, the Law Commission advocated the adoption of the term 'instrument' instead, on the basis that forgery and its kindred offences should apply only to those documents, such as cheques, which create rights and duties, or which give directions that are to be accepted and acted upon. This proposal was seemingly rejected; the term 'instrument' has indeed been adopted in the Act, but it has been defined in such a way that it includes any document (still without defining that term!) and several things that might not otherwise have been thought of as documents at all. The only documents excluded are currency notes, which are covered by the counterfeiting offences in Part II of the Act.

Electronic impulses representing passwords for accessing computers are too ephemeral to be instruments (*Gold* [1988] AC 1063) though the misuse of such a password may be an offence under the Computer Misuse Act 1990 (see **B17**).

Meaning of 'False' and 'Making'

B6.28 **Forgery and Counterfeiting Act 1981, s. 9**

(1) An instrument is false for the purposes of this Part of this Act—
   (a) if it purports to have been made in the form in which it is made by a person who did not in fact make it in that form; or

(b) if it purports to have been made in the form in which it is made on the authority of a person who did not in fact authorise its making in that form; or
(c) if it purports to have been made in the terms in which it is made by a person who did not in fact make it in those terms; or
(d) if it purports to have been made in the terms in which it is made on the authority of a person who did not in fact authorise its making in those terms; or
(e) if it purports to have been altered in any respect by a person who did not in fact alter it in that respect; or
(f) if it purports to have been altered in any respect on the authority of a person who did not in fact authorise the alteration in that respect; or
(g) if it purports to have been made or altered on a date on which, or at a place at which, or otherwise in circumstances in which, it was not in fact made or altered; or
(h) if it purports to have been made or altered by an existing person but he did not in fact exist.

(2) A person is to be treated for the purposes of this Part of this Act as making a false instrument if he alters an instrument so as to make it false in any respect (whether or not it is false in some other respect apart from that alteration).

As was the position at common law and under the earlier legislation, a false statement in a document or instrument does not ordinarily make that instrument a forgery; a false instrument is one which purports to be something which it is not (*Re Windsor* (1865) 10 Cox CC 118; *Warneford* [1994] Crim LR 753).

Section 9(1) lists the ways in which an instrument may be false. It is an exhaustive list: an instrument cannot be regarded as false on any alternative basis. On the other hand, an indictment does not need to specify the exact ground on which an instrument is alleged to be false.

Falsity as to Authorship or Authority (s. 9(1)(a), (c), (d) or (h)) An instrument will be false if the supposed maker did not make it at all, or if it has been altered since that person made it. The obvious example of such falsity would be where D forges another's signature on a cheque (*Lack* (1986) 84 Cr App R 342). **B6.29**

The concept might appear to be a simple one, but is not always so. In *Macer* [1979] Crim LR 659, decided under earlier, but essentially similar, provisions, it was held *not* to be forgery to sign one's own name on a cheque, but with a different signature from normal, with a view to later denying its authenticity. It was said that the cheque did not 'purport' to have been signed by any other person.

Another difficulty concerns the use of assumed names. There is generally no law against the use of assumed names. An instrument signed in a false name is not necessarily a forgery, even if the false name has been used for dishonest purposes (*More* [1987] 3 All ER 825). However, assuming the name of another person in the pretence of being that other person may constitute forgery. In *More*, D stole a cheque and paid it into a building society account opened in the same name as the payee. He later withdrew the proceeds, using withdrawal forms signed in that same name, and was charged, *inter alia*, with forgery of those forms. The House of Lords held that the forms were not forgeries: they purported to have been signed by the person who had opened the account, as indeed they had been, and (crucially) did not refer back to the original cheque.

More was distinguished in *Atunwa* [2006] EWCA Crim 673, in which D was found in possession of cheques purporting to have been signed on behalf of registered companies, but bearing the signatures of unknown individuals who (if they existed at all) had no connection with those companies. His convictions for possessing false instruments with intent (see **B6.51**) were upheld. Dyson LJ said (at [8]):

> If A signs a cheque on behalf of X Limited in the name of B, and B is authorised to sign cheques on behalf of X Limited, A commits the offence; he purports to make an instrument 'in the terms in which it is made on the authority of a person who did not in fact authorise its making in those terms'... But the offence may also be committed if A purports to sign a cheque on behalf of X Limited in his own name where he is not an authorised signatory. In this situation too, A purports

to make an instrument in the terms in which it is made on the authority of a person who did not in fact authorise its making in those terms. In both cases the cheque tells a lie about itself, namely that it is a cheque duly signed by a person authorised to sign the cheque on behalf of the company.

B6.30 **Falsification by Alteration (s. 9(1)(e))** Alteration of an instrument so as to change its value or terms would come within s. 9(1)(c) if the alteration is intended to pass undetected. Section 9(1)(e) covers alterations which purport to be those of someone other than the person who made, or authorised the making of, the instrument, even an alteration which purports to be unauthorised (done, for example, for the purpose of falsely accusing someone else of forgery). If the person purportedly responsible for the alteration did not really exist then the instrument would be false by virtue of s. 9(1)(h).

B6.31 **Falsity as to Date, Place or Circumstances (s. 9(1)(g))** An instrument which is dated otherwise than with the date on which it is made is not necessarily false, because in some cases it is recognised that the date indicates, not the date of making, but the date at which the instrument becomes enforceable (as with a postdated cheque).

The final part of s. 9(1)(g) is a 'sweeping-up' provision, which is potentially very wide ranging. In some circumstances, the concept of falsity can be hard to distinguish from that of mere false statements which fall outside the scope of the Act (see **B6.2**).

In *Donnelly* [1984] 1 WLR 1017, the Court of Appeal held that a jeweller's certificate purporting to value jewellery that did not really exist was a forgery. This must be correct. The certificate was not merely an inflated valuation; it purported to be something it was not: a valuation based on an inspection of real jewellery.

Donnelly was followed in *Jeraj* [1994] Crim LR 595 and *A-G's Ref (No. 1 of 2000)* [2001] 1 WLR 331. In the latter case, Lord Woolf CJ noted that a document which tells lies about the circumstances under which it is made becomes a forgery if, but only if, those circumstances need to exist before the document can properly be made. One cannot, for example, produce a valuation of jewellery unless the jewellery in question exists; nor can one issue a genuine receipt for a security that has not in fact been received (as in *Jeraj*).

Meaning of 'Prejudice' and 'Induce'

B6.32 **Forgery and Counterfeiting Act 1981, s. 10**

(1) Subject to subsections (2) and (4) below, for the purposes of this Part of this Act an act or omission intended to be induced is to a person's prejudice if, and only if, it is one which if it occurs—
 (a) will result—
  (i) in his temporary or permanent loss of property; or
  (ii) in his being deprived of an opportunity to earn remuneration or greater remuneration; or
  (iii) in his being deprived of an opportunity to gain a financial advantage otherwise than by way of remuneration; or
 (b) will result in somebody being given an opportunity—
  (i) to earn remuneration or greater remuneration from him; or
  (ii) to gain a financial advantage from him otherwise than by way of remuneration; or
 (c) will be the result of his having accepted a false instrument as genuine, or a copy of a false instrument as a copy of a genuine one, in connection with his performance of any duty.
(2) An act which a person has an enforceable duty to do and an omission to do an act which a person is not entitled to do shall be disregarded for the purposes of this Part of this Act.
(3) In this Part of this Act references to inducing somebody to accept a false instrument as genuine, or a copy of a false instrument as a copy of a genuine one, include references to inducing a machine to respond to the instrument or copy as if it were a genuine instrument or, as the case may be, a copy of a genuine one.
(4) Where subsection (3) above applies, the act or omission intended to be induced by the machine responding to the instrument or copy shall be treated as an act or omission to a person's prejudice.
(5) In this section 'loss' includes not getting what one might get as well as parting with what one has.

Section 10 provides an exhaustive definition of the concept of 'prejudice' for the purposes of the six offences which require an intent to induce another person to act or omit to act to that person's or another's prejudice (see **B6.32**). 'Inducing' is only defined to the extent that it applies to machines.

To be guilty of one of these offences, D need not have induced any reaction at all: it is a matter of ulterior intent, rather than of *actus reus* (*Ondhia* [1998] 2 Cr App R 150). It would not, however, suffice that D was merely aware that prejudice might result (*Garcia* [1988] Crim LR 115).

Section 10(1)(a) covers situations in which acceptance of a false instrument would result in loss, or loss of potential profit; s. 10(1)(b) covers situations where actual loss might be difficult to identify, but where someone might be able to obtain a pecuniary advantage from the person induced; and the broad scope of s. 10(1)(c) is illustrated by *Campbell* (1984) 80 Cr App R 47, in which it was held that a bank would be prejudiced if it was induced to pay or collect payment on a forged cheque, whether or not it suffered financially by so doing, and whether or not anyone profited thereby. Another illustration is provided by *Utting* [1987] 1 WLR 1375, where, but for a defective indictment, D might have been convicted of forging an instrument in order to induce the police to act to their prejudice by not prosecuting him. See also *A-G's Ref (No. 1 of 2001)* [2002] EWCA Crim 1768, [2002] 3 All ER 840. **B6.33**

The effect of s. 10(2) is that it cannot be an offence under the Act to make or use a false instrument in order to secure or protect one's lawful rights against anyone it is intended to deceive; but it cannot provide any defence to a charge under s. 5(2) or (4) (see **B6.51**) and, if a benefit etc. is payable only if and when supported by genuine documentation, s. 10(2) may similarly be ineffective (*Winston* [1999] 1 Cr App R 337; *Knock* [2014] EWCA Crim 1986). **B6.34**

Section 10(3) and (4) ensure, *inter alia*, that the use of a forged card in an automatic service till could be an offence under s. 3, and making such a forged card could be an offence under s. 1. Similar provision is made by the Fraud Act 2006 (see **B5.18**). In contrast, the obtaining of cash using such a device was not regarded as a deception offence under the Theft Acts, which lacked any provisions akin to these. The correct charge in such a case was theft. Section 10(3) and (4) would also apply where forged identification cards are used in computers etc., but not where hackers merely transmit or key in false user identification numbers, these being too ephemeral to constitute 'instruments' under s. 8 (*Gold* [1988] AC 1063). Similar considerations would apply to the misuse of another person's card and personal identification number in a bank automatic service till. Misuse of a user identification may, however, be an offence under the Computer Misuse Act 1990 (see **B17**). **B6.35**

FORGERY

Forgery and Counterfeiting Act 1981, s. 1 **B6.36**

> A person is guilty of forgery if he makes a false instrument, with the intention that he or another shall use it to induce somebody to accept it as genuine, and by reason of so accepting it to do or not to do some act to his own or any other person's prejudice.

Procedure and Jurisdiction

Forgery is triable either way (Forgery and Counterfeiting Act 1981, s. 6). When tried on indictment it is normally a class 3 offence, but see CrimPD XIII, para. B (see Supplement, **CPD.XIII.B**) for the additional factors that the court considers on allocation. It is a Group A offence for jurisdiction purposes under the CJA 1993, Part I (see **A8.10**). **B6.37**

Indictment

Statement of Offence **B6.38**

Forgery contrary to section 1 of the Forgery and Counterfeiting Act 1981.

Particulars of Offence

A on or about the... day of... made a false instrument, namely a document purporting to be the will of X, with the intention of using it to induce Y to accept it as genuine and by reason of so accepting to give A a Ming vase forming part of the estate of X to the prejudice of the beneficiaries under the true will of X.

Sentence

B6.39 The maximum sentence is ten years on indictment; six months or an unlimited fine or both summarily (Forgery and Counterfeiting Act 1981, s. 6). There is no offence-specific guideline but the Sentencing Council's *General Guideline: Overarching Principles* (see Supplement, **SG2-1**) is used for all offenders sentenced on or after 1 October 2019. In *Cano-Uribe* [2015] EWCA Crim 1824, [2016] 1 Cr App R (S) 36 (210) the Court of Appeal said that the guideline on *Fraud, Bribery and Money Laundering* was of limited assistance.

In *Mussa* [2012] EWCA Crim 693, [2012] 2 Cr App R (S) 99 (585) the Court of Appeal dealt with a case in which the offenders admitted conspiracy to produce large numbers of false French identity documents. The forged documents were of high quality and would have enabled false bank accounts to be set up, driving penalties to be avoided, and facilitated illegal entry and residence in the UK. Cranston J said that the key considerations in sentencing such a case were the role of the offender in the operation, its scale and sophistication, the type of documents being produced, the damage caused and the income generated. The scale in this case was 'vast', and sentences of six and half years' imprisonment on a guilty plea were upheld. In *Belkaid* [2018] EWCA Crim 2488 a runner for a Belgian false identity card operation acted as the UK agent, transmitting passport style photographs back to Belgium and supplying the finished products to UK customers. He pleaded guilty to conspiracy to make a false instrument, albeit on a limited basis. An appropriate sentence after conviction would have been four years' imprisonment.

Elements

B6.40 Most of the key terms used in s. 1 are considered in **B6.27** to **B6.32**. By virtue of s. 9(2), 'making' a false instrument includes falsifying an existing one; but however it is made, it must be proved that it was made with the specified 'double intention': it must be proved that D intended both that the instrument would be accepted as genuine and that someone would therefore act to his own or another's prejudice. It is a specific intent; recklessness or foresight will not suffice (*Garcia* [1988] Crim LR 115). In *Ondhia* [1998] 2 Cr App R 150, D created a false 'copy bill of lading', not for the purpose of using it directly to deceive any other person, but for the purpose of feeding it into his fax machine, so that the recipient of his call would receive the facsimile copy thereby created. This was held to amount to an offence of forgery under s. 1. No doubt D would also have been guilty of copying a false instrument, contrary to s. 2 of the Act, but overlapping offences are common in English law, and there is nothing artificial or unnatural in the argument that a person who faxes a forged document to another 'uses' that document for the purpose of inducing that other (or indeed a third party) to accept it as genuine. A person who relies upon a facsimile of a bill of lading will recognise it to be a facsimile; and if deceived by the facsimile, is deceived by the original from which it was made.

On the other hand, dishonesty is not an essential ingredient in this or any other offences under the Act (*Campbell* (1984) 80 Cr App R 47; *Winston* [1999] 1 Cr App R 337), and the intent is ulterior, so that actual inducement or prejudice need not be proved, and need not even be intended to take place within the jurisdiction (cf. *Treacy v DPP* [1971] AC 537; *Berry* [1985] AC 246).

COPYING A FALSE INSTRUMENT

Definition

B6.41 **Forgery and Counterfeiting Act 1981, s. 2**

It is an offence for a person to make a copy of an instrument which is, and which he knows or believes to be, a false instrument, with the intention that he or another shall use it to induce somebody to accept it as a copy of a genuine instrument, and by reason of so accepting it to do or not to do some act to his own or any other person's prejudice.

Procedure and Jurisdiction

The offence is triable either way (s. 6). When tried on indictment it is normally a class 3 offence, but see CrimPD XIII, para. B (see Supplement, **CPD.XIII.B**) for the additional factors that the court considers on allocation. It is a Group A offence for jurisdiction purposes under the CJA 1993, Part I (see **A8.10**). **B6.42**

Indictment

Statement of Offence **B6.43**

Copying a false instrument contrary to section 2 of the Forgery and Counterfeiting Act 1981.

Particulars of Offence

A on or about the... day of... made a copy of an instrument, namely a document purporting to be the will of X, which was and which he knew to be a false instrument, with the intention of using it to induce Y to accept it as genuine and by reason of so accepting to give A a Ming vase forming part of the estate of X to the prejudice of the beneficiaries under the true will of X.

Sentence

The maximum sentence is ten years on indictment; six months or an unlimited fine or both summarily (s. 6). There is no offence-specific guideline but the Sentencing Council's *General Guideline: Overarching Principles* (see Supplement, **SG2-1**) is used for all offenders sentenced on or after 1 October 2019. **B6.44**

Elements

Section 2 does not deal with copies which are intended to be passed off as originals, even if they are themselves copies of copies, nor does it deal with instruments which purport to be copies of originals which do not in fact exist. (The correct charge for making such copies is one of forgery under s. 1.) This provision aims instead at copies (particularly photocopies) which purport to be true copies of original instruments, but which are not, either because the original has been falsified prior to photocopying etc., or because the original was a complete forgery from the start. **B6.45**

It might be argued that there is really no need for such a provision, since a document which purports to be a photocopy of a genuine instrument, but which is in fact a copy of a forgery, would *ipso facto* be false under s. 9(1)(g) (and see *Utting* [1987] 1 WLR 1375). This might be true where the original is a total forgery; but difficulties could arise in other circumstances. If, for example, a copy of an individual's birth certificate is required, and the individual takes a photocopy for that purpose, knowing that the original was falsified in some way by someone else ten years before, it could be argued that the photocopy is a true copy of the certificate, and thus not false within s. 9 at all. Section 2, however, would clearly apply in such circumstances.

USING A FALSE INSTRUMENT; USING A COPY OF A FALSE INSTRUMENT

Forgery and Counterfeiting Act 1981, ss. 3 and 4 **B6.46**

3. It is an offence for a person to use an instrument which is, and which he knows or believes to be, false, with the intention of inducing somebody to accept it as genuine, and by reason of so accepting it to do or not to do some act to his own or any other person's prejudice.
4. It is an offence for a person to use a copy of an instrument which is, and which he knows or believes to be, a false instrument, with the intention of inducing somebody to accept it as a copy

of a genuine instrument, and by reason of so accepting it to do or not to do some act to his own or any other person's prejudice.

Procedure and Jurisdiction

B6.47 Both offences are triable either way (s. 6). When tried on indictment they are normally class 3 offences, but see CrimPD XIII, para. B (see Supplement, **CPD.XIII.B**) for the additional factors that the court considers on allocation. It is a Group A offence for jurisdiction purposes under the CJA 1993, Part I (see **A8.10**).

Indictment

B6.48

Statement of Offence

Using a false instrument contrary to section 3 of the Forgery and Counterfeiting Act 1981.

Particulars of Offence

A on or about the . . . day of . . . used an instrument, namely a document purporting to be the will of X, which was and which he knew to be false, with the intention of inducing Y to accept it as genuine and by reason of so accepting to give A a Ming vase forming part of the estate of X to the prejudice of the beneficiaries under the true will of X.

This form may easily be adapted for a charge under s. 4.

Sentence

B6.49 The maximum sentence is ten years on indictment; six months or an unlimited fine or both summarily (s. 6). There is no offence-specific guideline but the Sentencing Council's *General Guideline: Overarching Principles* (see Supplement, **SG2-1**) is used for all offenders sentenced on or after 1 October 2019.

In *Singh* [1999] 1 Cr App R (S) 490, the Court of Appeal upheld a sentence of eight months' imprisonment on an offender who had pleaded guilty to an offence under s. 3, in that he had attempted to use a false British passport at Gatwick Airport in order to travel to Canada. After reviewing a number of authorities involving the misuse of passports, Rose LJ explained that a deterrent custodial sentence within the range of six to nine months would usually be merited. A guilty plea would always attract an appropriate discount, but previous good character and personal mitigation were of very limited value. *Singh* was revisited by the Court of Appeal in *Kolawole* [2004] EWCA Crim 3047, [2005] 2 Cr App R (S) 14 (71), where Rose LJ said that sentences at a higher level had become necessary and that in such a case as *Singh* the appropriate sentence, even on a guilty plea by a person of good character, should usually be in the range of 12 to 18 months.

Elements

B6.50 Whereas s. 1 penalises the making of a false instrument, even if it is never used for its intended purpose or intended for use outside the jurisdiction, s. 3 strikes at the use of such an instrument, even if it was not originally made to be used in a way prohibited by s. 3, or made outside the jurisdiction. The same 'double intention' is required as in s. 1: see **B6.40** and *Tobierre* [1986] 1 All ER 346.

Section 4 relates to s. 2 as s. 3 relates to s. 1. Like s. 2 it does not apply to copies which purport to be originals; and like s. 3 it does not matter who made the copy, or for what purpose it was made.

'Using' is not defined in the Act. Previous legislation used the term 'uttering', and using was the principal form of uttering (*Harris* [1966] 1 QB 184). 'Use' must presumably bear its ordinary meaning: 'Take, hold, or deploy (something) as a means of accomplishing or achieving something; employ' (*Oxford Dictionaries Online*). However, the use need not be successful: the full offence may be committed even if the instrument is at once recognised as a forgery.

OFFENCES RELATING TO STAMPS, SHARE CERTIFICATES ETC.

Forgery and Counterfeiting Act 1981, s. 5 **B6.51**

(1) It is an offence for a person to have in his custody or under his control an instrument to which this section applies which is, and which he knows or believes to be, false, with the intention that he or another shall use it to induce somebody to accept it as genuine, and by reason of so accepting it to do or not to do some act to his own or any other person's prejudice.
(2) It is an offence for a person to have in his custody or under his control, without lawful authority or excuse, an instrument to which this section applies which is, and which he knows or believes to be, false.
(3) It is an offence for a person to make or to have in his custody or under his control a machine or implement, or paper or any other material, which to his knowledge is or has been specially designed or adapted for the making of an instrument to which this section applies, with the intention that he or another shall make an instrument to which this section applies which is false and that he or another shall use the instrument to induce somebody to accept it as genuine, and by reason of so accepting it to do or not to do some act to his own or any other person's prejudice.
(4) It is an offence for a person to make or to have in his custody or under his control any such machine, implement, paper or material, without lawful authority or excuse.
(5) The instruments to which this section applies are—
(a) money orders;
(b) postal orders;
(c) United Kingdom postage stamps;
(d) Inland Revenue stamps;
(e) share certificates;
(f) [repealed];
(fa) [repealed];
(g) cheques and other bills of exchange;
(h) travellers' cheques;
(ha) bankers' drafts;
(hb) promissory notes;
(j) cheque cards;
(ja) debit cards;
(k) credit cards;
(l) certified copies relating to an entry in a register of births, adoptions, marriages, civil partnerships or deaths and issued by the Registrar-General, the Registrar-General for Northern Ireland, a registration officer or a person lawfully authorised to issue certified copies relating to such entries; and
(m) certificates relating to entries in such registers.
(6) In subsection (5)(e) above 'share certificate' means an instrument entitling or evidencing the title of a person to a share or interest—
(a) in any public stock, annuity, fund or debt of any government or State, including a State which forms part of another State; or
(b) in any stock, fund or debt of a body (whether corporate or unincorporated) established in the United Kingdom or elsewhere.
(6A) In subsection (5)(l) above, 'conversion' means the conversion of a civil partnership into a marriage under section 9 of the Marriage (Same Sex Couples) Act 2013 and regulations made under that section.
(7) An instrument is also an instrument to which this section applies if it is a monetary instrument specified for the purposes of this section by an order made by the Secretary of State.

Procedure and Jurisdiction

Offences under the Forgery and Counterfeiting Act 1981, s. 5(1) and (3), are triable either way (Forgery and Counterfeiting Act 1981, s. 6). When tried on indictment they are normally class 3 offences, but see CrimPD XIII, para. B (see Supplement, **CPD.XIII.B**) for the additional **B6.52** factors that the court considers on allocation. They are Group A offences for jurisdiction purposes under the CJA 1993, Part I (see **A8.10**).

Alternative Verdicts

B6.53 Based on the usual principles of law governing alternative verdicts (CLA 1967, s. 6(3): see **D19.41** *et seq.*), it is submitted that on an indictment for an offence under the Forgery and Counterfeiting Act 1981, s. 5(1), the jury may return a verdict of guilty of an offence under s. 5(2); and that on an indictment for an offence under s. 5(3) the jury may return a verdict of guilty under s. 5(4). It may, nevertheless, be prudent to add alternative counts.

Sentence

B6.54 The maximum sentence for an offence under s. 5(1) or (3) is ten years on indictment; six months or an unlimited fine or both summarily (Forgery and Counterfeiting Act 1981, s. 6).

The maximum sentence for an offence under s. 5(2) or (4) of the Forgery and Counterfeiting Act 1981 is two years on indictment; six months or an unlimited fine or both summarily (Forgery and Counterfeiting Act 1981, s. 6). There are no offence-specific guidelines for these offences but the Sentencing Council's *General Guideline: Overarching Principles* (see Supplement, **SG2-1**) is used for all offenders sentenced on or after 1 October 2019.

Elements

B6.55 It is not generally an offence merely to have custody or control of false instruments, or materials etc. for making them, even if the instruments or materials are intended for some unlawful purpose. The instruments listed in the Forgery and Counterfeiting Act 1981, s. 5(5), have been singled out for protection, as have those to which the Mental Health Act 1983, s. 126, applies (specified documents relating to mental health).

Most of the terms used in the Forgery and Counterfeiting Act 1981, s. 5, are considered in **B6.27** to **B6.32**, but the concepts of 'custody or control' and 'lawful authority or excuse' require some comment.

B6.56 **Custody or Control** The offences in the Forgery and Counterfeiting Act 1981, s. 5, are not limited to having the offending items on one's person, or even 'with' one in the sense required for liability under comparable legislation dealing with offensive weapons or theft etc. (e.g., Theft Act 1968, ss. 10 and 25; see **B4.105** and **B4.156**). It will suffice if they are kept in one's home, garage, car or workplace. Problems of liability based on 'innocent possession', such as sometimes arise in other offences (e.g., possession of drugs or firearms) should not be a problem, because the prosecution must prove D's knowledge of the falsity and, in cases under s. 5(1) or (3), D's ulterior intent. One might perhaps know of the falsity etc. without knowing one had custody or control (cf. *Wings Ltd v Ellis* [1985] AC 272), but such a case would be most unusual, and it is doubtful whether strict liability would be imposed even then.

B6.57 **Lawful Authority or Excuse** In the absence of any definition in the Forgery and Counterfeiting Act 1981 itself, the concept of lawful excuse must presumably extend to any recognised general defences, and would also cover possession with intent to hand the relevant items to the police or other authorities at the first reasonable opportunity (*Wuyts* [1969] 2 QB 474; *Sunman* [1995] Crim LR 569). While the cases on reasonable excuse in the context of weapons are generally of little assistance, the approach on forgetfulness may be relevant (see, e.g., *Glidewell* [1999] EWCA Crim 1221 at **B12.173**) as may be the approach in *Densu* [1998] 1 Cr App R 400 on ignorance of the nature of the object in question (see **B12.170**). It would seem that the burden of proving lawful authority or excuse must only be evidential: contrast s. 17(4) of the Act (making or having implements etc. for counterfeiting protected coins), where the legal burden of proof is expressly placed on the defence. If this is correct, then once D raises the issue of lawful authority or excuse, the prosecution must disprove it beyond reasonable doubt. (As to the legal and evidential burdens of proof generally, see **F3.1** *et seq*. and **F3.54**.)

OFFENCES UNDER THE IDENTITY DOCUMENTS ACT 2010

Offences under the Identity Documents Act 2010 are dealt with at **B22.71** *et seq*. For the statutory defences under the Immigration and Asylum Act 1999, s. 31, and the Modern Slavery Act 2015, s. 45, see **B22.86** and **B22.24**. **B6.58**

Identity documents to which the 2010 Act applies include not only passports (originally covered by the Forgery and Counterfeiting Act 1981, s. 5) and immigration documents, but also driving licences whether issued in the UK or abroad.

SUPPLYING SPECIALIST PRINTING EQUIPMENT FOR CRIMINAL PURPOSES

Persons who supply specialist printing equipment or materials in the knowledge that they are to be used for the purposes of creating false identity documents, false instruments or counterfeit currency, etc., may thereby be guilty of encouraging or assisting crime (see **A5.3**) and if the materials are then used as anticipated the supplier may become a secondary party to a substantive offence such as forgery or offences under applicable foreign laws. It was nevertheless considered that the prosecution and punishment of such suppliers under English law would be aided by the creation of a specific 'targeted' offence; and such an offence was accordingly created by the Specialist Printing Equipment and Materials (Offences) Act 2015. **B6.59**

Definition

Specialist Printing Equipment and Materials (Offences) Act 2015, s. 1 **B6.60**

(1) A person commits an offence if—
   (a) the person supplies any specialist printing equipment, and
   (b) in making the supply, the person knows that the equipment will be or is intended to be used for the purposes of criminal conduct.
(2) 'Criminal conduct' means conduct which constitutes—
   (a) an offence under the law of England and Wales, or
   (b) an offence under the law of a country outside England and Wales which, if it took place in England and Wales, would constitute an offence in England and Wales.

'Specialist printing equipment' is defined in s. 2(1) as any equipment (defined in s. 2(6) as including any device, machinery or apparatus and any wire or cable, together with any software used with it) which is designed or adapted for, or is otherwise capable of being used for, the making of relevant documents, including any material or article that is used in the making of such documents; and by s. 2(2) 'relevant documents' are those that are or purport to be: passports and other identity documents (as defined in s. 2(3)); travel or entry documents (defined in s. 2(4) and (5) as including travel and event tickets, driving licences, disabled user badges and security passes); documents used for verifying the holder's age or national insurance number; currency notes and protected coins; debit and credit cards; and any other instrument to which the Forgery and Counterfeiting Act 1981, s. 5, applies.

Procedure and Sentence

B6.61 The offence under s. 1 is triable only on indictment and is punishable by a maximum of ten years' imprisonment and/or a fine. There are no offence-specific guidelines for these offences but the Sentencing Council's *General Guideline: Overarching Principles* (see Supplement, **SG2-1**) is used for all offenders sentenced on or after 1 October 2019. Section 3 makes provision for the liability of bodies corporate and partnerships: a body (corporate or not) is to be treated as knowing a fact about a supply of equipment if a person who has responsibility within the body for the supply knows of the fact; and where an offence is committed by a body corporate with the consent or connivance of a director, manager or other officer, or committed through neglect on the part of such an officer (which by s. 3(9) means the officer ought reasonably to have known of it), that officer may also be prosecuted for and convicted of the offence. Similarly, where an offence is committed by a partnership through the consent, connivance or neglect of a partner, that partner may also be prosecuted and convicted of the offence.

Defence

B6.62 By s. 1(5) it is a defence for a person charged under s. 1 to prove that the conduct was necessary for a purpose related to the prevention or detection of crime. This does not preclude the use of other defences such as duress, where they arise on the facts.

FORGERY, FALSIFICATION ETC. OF REGISTERS, CERTIFICATES OR CERTIFIED COPIES

Forgery Act 1861

B6.63 Under the Forgery Act 1861, ss. 36 and 37, it is an offence, punishable with a maximum penalty of life imprisonment, unlawfully to destroy, deface, injure etc. any register of births, baptisms, marriages, deaths or burials; to cause or permit such damage; or knowingly to make, sign or permit the making of false entries or insertions in such registers or in copies thereof, or knowingly to issue false certificates or copies. These provisions overlap with those of the Forgery and Counterfeiting Act 1981, but deal with acts of damage and destruction as well as with falsification.

Other Provisions Relating to Registers and Certificates

B6.64 As to the falsification of birth or death certificates, see the Births and Deaths Registration Act 1953, s. 37. As to the making of false statements and the use of false certificates in connection with births and deaths, see the Perjury Act 1911, s. 4 (see **B14.23**). Various non-parochial registers deposited with the Registrar-General are protected under the Non-parochial Registers Act 1840, s. 8.

As to dishonestly inducing another to alter entries under the Land Registration Act 2002, see s. 124 of that Act. See also s. 123 of that Act (suppression of information).

The falsification of any pedigree upon which title to land (or some interest therein) depends, with intent to defraud a purchaser who might thereby be induced to accept the title offered, is punishable with up to two years' imprisonment and/or a fine under the Law of Property Act 1925, s. 183. The A-G must give leave before any prosecution is commenced.

As to falsification of entries in the register of trade marks, see the Trade Marks Act 1994, s. 94. As to forgery of a county court summons or other process of the county court, see the County Courts Act 1984, s. 135.

COUNTERFEITING MONEY AND KINDRED OFFENCES

Introduction

The counterfeiting of currency notes and 'protected coins' is dealt with in Part II (ss. 14 to 28) of the Forgery and Counterfeiting Act 1981; the counterfeiting of hallmarks and dies etc. is protected under the Hallmarking Act 1973, s. 6; as to 'counterfeit goods' to which false trade marks are applied, so as to imitate the products of leading manufacturers, see the Trade Marks Act 1994, ss. 92 and 97 (see **B6.100** to **B6.106**). **B6.65**

Scope of Offences under Part II of the Forgery and Counterfeiting Act 1981

Part II of the Forgery and Counterfeiting Act 1981 applies only in respect of currency notes and protected coins, as defined in s. 27. British and Irish notes come within this definition even if no longer customarily used as money (s. 27(1)(a)); but foreign or Commonwealth notes must be in current use (s. 27(1)(b)). Neither kind need ever have been legal tender: Scottish notes, for example, are not legal tender even in Scotland. **B6.66**

Coins must either be in current use or be specified by the Treasury for the purpose of this Act. The following coins have been so specified: sovereigns, half-sovereigns, krugerrands, coins which are denominated in fractions of krugerrands, Maria-Theresa thalers dated 1780 and euro-coins (Forgery and Counterfeiting (Protected Coins) Orders 1981 and 1999 (SI 1981 No. 1505 and SI 1999 No. 2095)). The counterfeiting of ancient coins *not* specified for these purposes cannot be an offence under this Act, however dishonest the motives.

Meaning of 'Counterfeit'

Forgery and Counterfeiting Act 1981, s. 28 **B6.67**

(1) For the purposes of this Part of this Act a thing is a counterfeit of a currency note or of a protected coin—
  (a) if it is not a currency note or a protected coin but resembles a currency note or protected coin (whether on one side only or on both) to such an extent that it is reasonably capable of passing for a currency note or protected coin of that description: or
  (b) if it is a currency note or protected coin which has been so altered that it is reasonably capable of passing for a currency note or protected coin of some other description.
(2) For the purposes of this Part of this Act—
  (a) a thing consisting of one side only of a currency note, with or without the addition of other material, is a counterfeit of such a note:
  (b) a thing consisting—
    (i) of parts of two or more currency notes: or
    (ii) of parts of a currency note, or of parts of two or more currency notes, with the addition of other material,

  is capable of being a counterfeit of a currency note.
(3) References in this Part of this Act to passing or tendering a counterfeit of a currency note or a protected coin are not to be construed as confined to passing or tendering it as legal tender.

It is not possible to argue that a one-sided note or coin is *ipso facto* incapable of passing for a genuine one, but in other respects the question of what kind of imitation can amount to a counterfeit is one of fact. An incompetent counterfeiter whose notes would fool nobody can be guilty of an attempt to counterfeit or of an offence under s. 17 of the Act (making or having custody of materials etc. for counterfeiting; see **B6.92** to **B6.97**).

Section 19 of the Act (imitation coins produced for promotional purposes) appears to assume that a coin may imitate a British coin in size, shape and substance, without necessarily being a counterfeit. Since any such coins could, in some circumstances, be confused with the real thing (e.g., when mixed in a handful of change in poor light), it would seem that a counterfeit must be 'reasonably capable' of bearing some direct scrutiny, if not perhaps close or careful scrutiny.

Sentencing Guidelines

B6.68 The maximum penalties for the various offences are set out in the sections dealing with them below. There are no offence-specific guidelines for these offences but the Sentencing Council's *General Guideline: Overarching Principles* (see Supplement, **SG2-1**) is used for all offenders sentenced on or after 1 October 2019.

In *Crick* (1981) 3 Cr App R (S) 275, Mustill J made the following general remarks about the offences of counterfeiting notes or coinage:

> Coining is a serious offence. It was rightly treated as such by the learned judge, who correctly took the view that it called for an immediate custodial sentence. It must, however, be recognised that not all such offences are of the same gravity. At one extreme is the professional forger, with carefully prepared plates, and elaborate machinery, who manufactures large quantities of banknotes and puts them into circulation. A long sentence of imprisonment is appropriate in such a case. Here the offence is at the other end of the scale. The tools used to make the blanks were primitive, and were not acquired specially for the purpose; the techniques used were amateurish, and there was little real attempt to make the blanks a facsimile of a 50 pence piece. The coins were not, and could not have been, put into general circulation.

A three-year sentence was reduced to one of nine months.

B6.69 **Banknote Production** Longer sentences will be upheld for *production* of banknotes, but much depends on the sophistication of the enterprise and the success of the offenders. Sentences of ten years and eight months were appropriate in *Hartley* [2011] EWCA Crim 1957, [2012] 1 Cr App R (S) 76 (429), for two offences involving the production of counterfeit currency, with a total value in excess of £790,000. In *Allen* [2010] EWCA Crim 846, [2011] 1 Cr App R (S) 10 (92) six years' imprisonment was upheld for an offender who pleaded guilty to conspiracy to produce counterfeit currency. He had purchased specialist equipment for the production of counterfeit notes, and forged currency with a face value of about £15,000 was seized from his home. He admitted to producing currency with a face value of up to £250,000. See also *Allyson* (1989) 11 Cr App R (S) 60, *Britton* (1994) 15 Cr App R (S) 482, and *Dossiter* [1999] 2 Cr App R (S) 248.

B6.70 **Passing of Banknotes** In *Edirin-Etareri* [2014] EWCA Crim 1536, [2014] 2 Cr App R (S) 82 (641) D pleaded guilty to custody of seven counterfeit £20 notes. A sentence of 12 months' imprisonment following a one-third reduction for guilty plea was upheld, the Court of Appeal commenting that imprisonment was almost inevitable in such a case, because of the potential harm to the country's financial well-being through corruption of its currency. The Court considered and approved *Miller* [2010] EWCA Crim 257, [2010] 2 Cr App R (S) 62 (413). In that case D, who had a long history of offending, tendered two £20 notes for drinks at a bar and it was noticed that the notes had the same serial number. Three more such notes were found at D's home. The Court of Appeal said that a sentence of 15 months' imprisonment was appropriate on a guilty plea. See also *Forde* [2013] EWCA Crim 2548.

COUNTERFEITING NOTES OR COINS

B6.71 **Forgery and Counterfeiting Act 1981, s. 14**

> (1) It is an offence for a person to make a counterfeit of a currency note or of a protected coin, intending that he or another shall pass or tender it as genuine.
> (2) It is an offence for a person to make a counterfeit of a currency note or of a protected coin without lawful authority or excuse.

Procedure

B6.72 Offences under s. 14(1) are, by s. 22 of the Act, triable either way. When tried on indictment they are normally a class 3 offence, but see CrimPD XIII, para. B (see Supplement, **CPD.XIII.B**), for the additional factors that the court considers on allocation. They are Group A offences for jurisdiction purposes under the CJA 1993, Part I (see **A8.10**).

Indictment

Statement of Offence B6.73

Counterfeiting contrary to section 14(1) of the Forgery and Counterfeiting Act 1981.

Particulars of Offence

A on or about the... day of... made a counterfeit of a currency note, namely a Bank of England £5 note, intending to pass or tender the same as genuine.

Alternative Verdicts

It is submitted that, on an indictment for an offence under s. 14(1) it is open to the jury to return a verdict of guilty of the offence under s. 14(2) (see generally the CLA 1967, s. 6(3), and **D19.41** ***et seq.***). It may, however, be prudent to add an alternative count. B6.74

Sentence

The Forgery and Counterfeiting Act 1981, s. 22, prescribes the maximum penalties: for an offence under s. 14(1), the maximum penalty is ten years and/or a fine on indictment; six months and/or an unlimited fine summarily; for an offence under s. 14(2), it is two years and/or a fine on indictment; six months and/or an unlimited fine summarily. There is no offence-specific guideline but the Sentencing Council's *General Guideline: Overarching Principles* (see Supplement, **SG2-1**) is used for all offenders sentenced on or after 1 October 2019. For sentencing cases, see **B6.68**. B6.75

Elements

In s. 14, a distinction is drawn (as in s. 5 of the Act: see **B6.51** to **B6.57**) between cases in which there is proof of an intent that the fake item shall be passed as genuine (s. 14(1)) and cases in which there is not (s. 14(2)). In the latter kind of case counterfeiting is still an offence (albeit a less serious one), unless the maker has lawful authority or excuse. The reason for this is that even the honest manufacture of realistic fakes carries risks of confusion or subsequent misuse. See *Heron* [1982] 1 All ER 993, decided under the Coinage Offences Act 1936, in which the making of counterfeit coins was held to be an offence without proof of any intent to deceive; see also *Selby v DPP* [1972] AC 515. B6.76

The intent specified in s. 14(1) is ulterior. The actual passing of the counterfeit need never happen, and it would suffice even if it was intended to happen outside the jurisdiction, as long as the counterfeiting itself was committed within it. In contrast to ss. 1 to 4 and s. 5(1) of the Act, there is no need to prove an intent to induce someone to act to his own or another's prejudice.

PASSING, TENDERING OR DELIVERING COUNTERFEIT NOTES OR COINS

Forgery and Counterfeiting Act 1981, s. 15 B6.77

(1) It is an offence for a person—
  (a) to pass or tender as genuine any thing which is, and which he knows or believes to be, a counterfeit of a currency note or of a protected coin; or
  (b) to deliver to another any thing which is, and which he knows or believes to be, such a counterfeit, intending that the person to whom it is delivered or another shall pass or tender it as genuine.

(2) It is an offence for a person to deliver to another, without lawful authority or excuse, any thing which is, and which he knows or believes to be, a counterfeit of a currency note or of a protected coin.

Procedure

B6.78 Offences under s. 15 are, by s. 22 of the Act, triable either way. When tried on indictment they are normally class 3 offences, but see CrimPD XIII, para. B (see Supplement, **CPD.XIII.B**) for the additional factors that the court considers on allocation. They are Group A offences for jurisdiction purposes under the CJA 1993, Part I (see **A8.10**).

Alternative Verdicts

B6.79 It is submitted that, on an indictment for an offence under s. 15(1)(b), it is open to the jury to return a verdict of guilty of the offence under s. 15(2) (see generally the CLA 1967, s. 6(3), and **D19.41** *et seq.*). It may, however, be prudent to add an alternative count.

Sentence

B6.80 Section 22 of the Act, prescribes the maximum penalties: for an offence under s. 15(1)(a) or (b), the maximum penalty is ten years and/or a fine on indictment; six months and/or an unlimited fine summarily; for an offence under s. 15(2), it is two years and/or a fine on indictment; six months and/or an unlimited fine summarily. There is no offence-specific guideline but the Sentencing Council's *General Guideline: Overarching Principles* (see Supplement, **SG2-1**) is used for all offenders sentenced on or after 1 October 2019. For sentencing cases, see **B6.68**.

Scope of Offence

B6.81 Section 15 follows the same pattern as s. 14 (see **B6.71** to **B6.76**), in that it distinguishes between cases in which a counterfeit is passed as genuine or delivered to another with intent that it should be so passed, and cases in which it is merely 'delivered', perhaps expressly described as a reproduction (*Selby v DPP* [1972] AC 515). The latter kind of case attracts less serious penalties, but is still regarded as dangerous and undesirable.

Meaning of 'Passing' and 'Tendering'

B6.82 'Passing' suggests acceptance by the person to whom the thing is given, but a counterfeit may be *tendered* as genuine, even if it is at once rejected, and an offence may be committed even where the item in question is not passed or tendered as legal tender (s. 28(3)). Many forms of notes etc. used as money are not legal tender (e.g., Scottish notes), and many protected coins have a collectors' value exceeding any nominal value as currency.

Knowledge and Belief

B6.83 It would not be an offence under s. 15 to pass or tender a note etc. which one suspects *may* be a counterfeit, even if the suspicion is a strong one. The section requires knowledge or belief, as in handling stolen goods under the Theft Act 1968, s. 22 (see **B4.159**), and those terms must presumably bear the same meanings as under that provision.

Meaning of 'Delivering'

B6.84 'Delivering', in s. 15(1)(b) and (2) of the 1981 Act need not involve any intent to deceive as to the nature of the thing delivered, but the more serious offence under s. 15(1)(b) may be committed if it is intended that the counterfeits should eventually be tendered as genuine, by the recipient or some other person.

Lawful Authority or Excuse

B6.85 An obvious example of lawful delivery, which would not be an offence under s. 15(2), would be where the counterfeits are handed over to the police; but lawful excuse could extend to general defences, such as mistake or duress. In view of the contrast with s. 17(4) (see **B6.97**), in which the legal burden of proof is expressly placed on the defence, it seems clear that the defence have only an evidential burden to discharge under s. 15(2). If the issue is raised by evidence, the prosecution must disprove the existence of lawful authority or excuse (see generally **F3.1** *et seq*. and **F3.18** *et seq*.), but if there is no evidence capable of supporting such a defence, the judge need not leave it to the jury (*Sunman* [1995] Crim LR 569).

CUSTODY OR CONTROL OF COUNTERFEIT NOTES OR COINS

Forgery and Counterfeiting Act 1981, s. 16 **B6.86**

(1) It is an offence for a person to have in his custody or under his control any thing which is, and which he knows or believes to be, a counterfeit of a currency note or of a protected coin, intending either to pass or tender it as genuine or to deliver it to another with the intention that he or another shall pass or tender it as genuine.

(2) It is an offence for a person to have in his custody or under his control, without lawful authority or excuse, any thing which is, and which he knows or believes to be, a counterfeit of a currency note or of a protected coin.

(3) It is immaterial for the purposes of subsections (1) and (2) above that a coin or note is not in a fit state to be passed or tendered or that the making or counterfeiting of a coin or note has not been finished or perfected.

Procedure

Offences under s. 16(1) are, by s. 22 of the Act, triable either way. When tried on indictment they are normally class 3 offences, but see CrimPD XIII, para. B (see Supplement, **CPD.XIII.B**) for the additional factors that the court considers on allocation. They are Group A offences for jurisdiction purposes under the CJA 1993, Part I (see **A8.10**). **B6.87**

Indictment

Statement of Offence **B6.88**

Having custody or control of a counterfeit note contrary to section 16(1) of the Forgery and Counterfeiting Act 1981.

Particulars of Offence

A on or about the... day of... had in his custody or under his control a counterfeit of a currency note, namely a Bank of England £5 note, knowing or believing the same to be counterfeit and intending to pass or tender it as genuine [or to deliver it to X with the intention that X should pass or tender it as genuine].

Alternative Verdicts

It is submitted that on an indictment for an offence under s. 16(1), it is open to the jury to return a verdict of guilty of the offence under s. 16(2) (see generally the CLA 1967, s. 6(3), and **D19.41** *et seq*.). It may, however, be prudent to add an alternative count. **B6.89**

Sentence

Section 22 of the Act prescribes the maximum penalties: for an offence under s. 16(1), the maximum penalty is ten years and/or a fine on indictment; six months and/or an unlimited fine summarily; for an offence under s. 16(2), it is two years and/or a fine on indictment; six months and/or an unlimited fine summarily. There is no offence-specific guideline but the Sentencing Council's *General Guideline: Overarching Principles* (see Supplement, **SG2-1**) is used for all offenders sentenced on or after 1 October 2019. For sentencing cases, see **B6.68**. **B6.90**

Elements

B6.91 Section 16 follows the same format as ss. 14 and 15 (see **B6.71** to **B6.85**). Section 16 serves the same kind of function as that served by s. 5(1) and (2) in relation to forgery offences (see **B6.51** to **B6.57**). As to the meaning of 'custody and control' in this context, see the discussion of s. 5 at **B6.56**.

OFFENCES RELATING TO MATERIALS AND IMPLEMENTS FOR COUNTERFEITING

Definitions

B6.92 **Forgery and Counterfeiting Act 1981, s. 17**

(1) It is an offence for a person to make, or to have in his custody or under his control, any thing which he intends to use, or permit any other person to use, for the purpose of making a counterfeit of a currency note or of a protected coin with the intention that it be passed or tendered as genuine.

(2) It is an offence for a person without lawful authority or excuse—

(a) to make; or

(b) to have in his custody or under his control,

any thing which, to his knowledge, is or has been specially designed or adapted for the making of a counterfeit of a currency note.

(3) Subject to subsection (4) below, it is an offence for a person to make, or to have in his custody or under his control, any implement which, to his knowledge, is capable of imparting to any thing a resemblance—

(a) to the whole or part of either side of a protected coin: or

(b) to the whole or part of the reverse of the image on either side of a protected coin.

(4) It shall be a defence for a person charged with an offence under subsection (3) above to show—

(a) that he made the implement or, as the case may be, had it in his custody or under his control, with the written consent of the Treasury; or

(b) that he had lawful authority otherwise than by virtue of paragraph (a) above, or a lawful excuse, for making it or having it in his custody or under his control.

Procedure

B6.93 Both offences under s. 17 are, by s. 22 of the Act, triable either way. When tried on indictment they are normally class 3 offences, but see CrimPD XIII, para. B (see Supplement, **CPD.XIII.B**) for the additional factors that the court considers on allocation. They are Group A offences for jurisdiction purposes under the CJA 1993, Part I (see **A8.10**).

Indictment

B6.94 *Statement of Offence*

Having custody or control of thing intended for use in making a counterfeit, with intent, contrary to section 17(1) of the Forgery and Counterfeiting Act 1981.

Particulars of Offence

A on or about the... day of... had in his custody or under his control a press and a quantity of inks intending to use the same to make a counterfeit of a currency note, namely a Bank of England £5 note, with the intention that such note be passed or tendered as genuine.

Sentence

B6.95 Section 22 prescribes the maximum penalties: for an offence under s. 17(1), the maximum penalty is ten years and/or a fine on indictment; six months and/or an unlimited fine summarily; for an offence under s. 17(2) or (3), it is two years and/or a fine on indictment; six months and/or an unlimited fine summarily. There is no offence-specific guideline but the Sentencing Council's *General Guideline: Overarching Principles* (see Supplement, **SG2-1**) is used for all offenders sentenced on or after 1 October 2019. For sentencing cases, see **B6.68**.

Scope of Offence

Section 17 serves the same kind of function as that served by s. 5(3) and (4) of the Act in relation to forgery offences (see **B6.51** to **B6.57**), and it follows s. 5 in distinguishing between cases where there is proof of an intent to pass false items as genuine and cases where there is not. Subsection (1) of s. 17 deals with the more serious kind of case; subsections (2) and (3) deal with the less serious kind. Either subsection may apply, not only to essential counterfeiting materials such as inks, but also to optional 'quality-control' devices such as chromolins (*Maltman* [1995] 1 Cr App R 239). **B6.96**

Lawful Authority or Excuse

Section 17(3) is subject to subsection (4), which expressly places the burden of proving lawful authority or excuse on the defence. However, subsection (2) is not subject to subsection (4). This indicates that the legal burden lies on the prosecution to disprove beyond reasonable doubt defences of lawful excuse etc. under s. 17(2), and indeed under all other provisions in the Act except s. 17(3). See generally **F3.1** *et seq*. and **F3.18** *et seq*. **B6.97**

IMPORTATION AND EXPORTATION OF COUNTERFEIT NOTES OR COINS

The Forgery and Counterfeiting Act 1981, ss. 20 and 21, impose prohibitions on the importation, exportation, landing or unloading of counterfeit currency notes or counterfeits of protected coins without the consent of the Treasury (this includes exportation to the Isle of Man), but these are not themselves offence-creating provisions. The relevant offences are those created under the Customs and Excise Management Act 1979, ss. 50 and 68 (see **B16.27** and **B16.34**). Any such offences involving breaches of ss. 20 or 21 are Group A offences for jurisdiction purposes under the CJA 1993, Part I (see **A8.10**). **B6.98**

POWERS OF SEARCH, SEIZURE AND FORFEITURE

Powers of search and seizure in relation to false instruments and the means of their production are contained in the Forgery and Counterfeiting Act 1981, s. 7(1). Broadly similar powers in relation to counterfeiting are contained in s. 24(1) of that Act. **B6.99**

An order for the forfeiture, destruction or disposal of such objects may be obtained from a magistrates' court, if it is satisfied that the order is conducive to the public interest; but anyone claiming a proprietary right or other interest in the objects concerned must be given the opportunity to 'show cause why the order should not be made' (ss. 7(4) and 24(4)). Where convictions are imposed under the Act, the court concerned may order the destruction or forfeiture of any object which has been shown to relate to the offence, or it may order it to be dealt with in such other manner as it thinks fit (ss. 7(3) and 24(3)). Any applicant claiming an interest in the object concerned must be given the opportunity to oppose the order under s. 7(4) or 24(4).

FALSE APPLICATION OR USE OF TRADE MARKS

Trade Marks Act 1994, s. 92 **B6.100**

(1) A person commits an offence who with a view to gain for himself or another, or with intent to cause loss to another, and without the consent of the proprietor—

(a) applies to goods or their packaging a sign identical to, or likely to be mistaken for, a registered trade mark, or
(b) sells or lets for hire, offers or exposes for sale or hire or distributes goods which bear, or the packaging of which bears, such a sign, or
(c) has in his possession, custody or control in the course of a business any such goods with a view to the doing of anything, by himself or another, which would be an offence under paragraph (b).

(2) A person commits an offence who with a view to gain for himself or another, or with intent to cause loss to another, and without the consent of the proprietor—
(a) applies a sign identical to, or likely to be mistaken for, a registered trade mark to material intended to be used—
(i) for labelling or packaging goods,
(ii) as a business paper in relation to goods, or
(iii) for advertising goods, or
(b) uses in the course of a business material bearing such a sign for labelling or packaging goods, as a business paper in relation to goods, or for advertising goods, or
(c) has in his possession, custody or control in the course of a business any such material with a view to the doing of anything, by himself or another, which would be an offence under paragraph (b).

(3) A person commits an offence who with a view to gain for himself or another, or with intent to cause loss to another, and without the consent of the proprietor—
(a) makes an article specifically designed or adapted for making copies of a sign identical to, or likely to be mistaken for, a registered trade mark, or
(b) has such an article in his possession, custody or control in the course of a business, knowing or having reason to believe that it has been, or is to be, used to produce goods, or material for labelling or packaging goods, as a business paper in relation to goods, or for advertising goods.

Sentence and Procedure

B6.101 Offences under s. 92 are punishable on indictment with a fine and/or a maximum of ten years' imprisonment; on summary conviction with imprisonment for six months and/or an unlimited fine (s. 92(6)). When tried on indictment they are normally class 3 offences, but see CrimPD XIII, para. B (see Supplement, **CPD.XIII.B**), for the additional factors that the court considers on allocation. The offence is covered in the *Magistrates' Court Sentencing Guidelines* (see Supplement, **SG10-139**). In the Crown Court there is no definitive guideline for this offence but the *General Guideline: Overarching Principles* (see Supplement, **SG2-1**) is used for all offenders sentenced on or after 1 October 2019.

The principles were considered by the Court of Appeal in *Demir* [2018] EWCA Crim 1116 in which it was said that the court should take account of the sophistication of the operation, the length of time the offending lasted and the profits procured. The defendants were found guilty of counterfeiting designer clothes. The products, made to order in Turkey, were marketed through a boutique shop which passed them off as genuine bespoke pieces. The defendants received nearly £600,000, most of which was found to come from illegal dealing in counterfeit goods. The Court of Appeal upheld sentences starting at 24 months' imprisonment, but which were discounted slightly for personal mitigation.

In *Manders* [2012] EWCA Crim 908, [2013] 1 Cr App R (S) 13 (73) the Court of Appeal had reviewed a number of earlier authorities before upholding a sentence of two years' imprisonment on an offender who pleaded guilty on the day of trial to manufacturing counterfeit DVDs on a commercial scale. The first level of his house was given over to the production of these, and 32,000 counterfeit discs were found together with computer hard drives, DVD writing machines, printers and scanners. The offender was well aware of the illegality of his operation, and had even downloaded sentencing decisions in comparable cases from the internet.

The use of related sentencing guidelines was considered in *Alshateri* [2016] EWCA Crim 1266, [2017] 1 Cr App R (S) 3 (11). D was a shop owner selling counterfeit tobacco products. It was held that the sentencing judge's direct application of the sentencing guideline for revenue fraud led to an unduly high starting point of four years' imprisonment. The guideline related specifically to the loss to the Revenue, which in this case was unclear. A starting point of three years was appropriate, which after credit for an early plea resulted in a sentence of 24 months.

In *Clements* [2019] EWCA Crim 2253, the Court of Appeal upheld D's suspended sentence of two years' imprisonment coupled with a five-year disqualification pursuant to the Company Directors Disqualification Act 1986, s. 2, imposed for a single offence of unauthorised use of a trade mark contrary to s. 92. D had been acquitted of a second count of fraud. D (aged 70) had sold over £300,000 worth of offending merchandise. He complained that he had been sentenced as if for an offence of dishonesty. The Court of Appeal rejected that complaint. D had deliberately committed the offence and although it did not in terms require proof of dishonesty, the jury must have been sure that D used false trade marks with a view to gain for himself or another, or with an intent to cause loss to another, and without the consent of the proprietor. This is not defined in the legislation as an act of 'dishonesty' but did assume 'a degree of deliberate wrongdoing for financial gain' (at [16]). The Court cited *Gill* [2010] EWCA Crim 324:

> Offending of this type and on this scale is serious. Legitimate businesses are cheated of the profit to which they are entitled having invested in design and marketing. The manufactured items are passed off as high quality when they are not. Investigation and prosecution is time-consuming and expensive.

Proceedings for offences committed by partnerships must be brought against the partnership in the name of the firm, and not that of the partners (s. 101(1)). As to the liability of individual partners, see **B6.105**.

Local weights and measures authorities are responsible for the enforcement of s. 92, and for this purpose are vested with the same powers to make test purchases, enter premises, seize goods and documents, etc., as under the Trade Descriptions Act 1968 or the new regulations that have largely replaced that Act (see **B6.107** ***et seq.***) (Trade Marks Act 1994, s. 93).

Requirement for Specific Offence

Although commercial activities involving trade in counterfeit goods will often involve the commission of offences under the Consumer Protection from Unfair Trading Regulations 2008 (see **B6.107** ***et seq.***), and in some cases offences under the Theft Act 1968, it was felt that a set of specific offences should exist to combat this trade. The Trade Marks Act 1994, s. 92, creates such offences. **B6.102**

Scope of Offences under Trade Marks Act 1994, s. 92

The offences created by s. 92(1) to (3) deal only with the infringement, etc., of registered trade marks in respect of goods. A trade mark is currently defined in s. 1 of the 1994 Act as any sign capable of being represented graphically which is capable of distinguishing goods or services of one undertaking from those of other undertakings. It may consist of words, names, designs, letters, numerals or the shape of goods or their packaging. This definition was amended as of 14 January 2019, so as, *inter alia*, to remove the need for a trade mark to be capable of graphical representation (Trade Mark Regulations 2018 (SI 2018 No. 825), reg. 3). Registration gives the owner a property right in it, which is protected under the 1994 Act (s. 2). Section 92 does not, however, apply to infringement of trade marks in respect of services. Furthermore, s. 92(4) provides that no offence can be committed under s. 92 unless the goods involved are goods in respect of which the trade mark has been registered, or the use of the counterfeit mark, etc., would take unfair advantage of, or be detrimental to the distinctive character or reputation of, a trade mark that has a reputation in the UK. **B6.103**

An offence under s. 92(1), (2) or (3), can be committed only when the offending sign is used as an indication or badge of trade origin. This involves a question of fact in each case, namely whether the sign would be so perceived by the average customer of the type of goods in question (*Johnstone* [2003] UKHL 28, [2003] 3 All ER 884; *Thompson* [2006] EWCA Crim 3058). But it is no defence to argue that the quality of counterfeiting is so poor that a buyer is unlikely to be deceived (*Boulter* [2008] EWCA Crim 2375).

A 'bootleg' recording of music by artists such as the Rolling Stones, if it does not purport to be anything *other* than a bootleg recording, does not offend under s. 92, even though the name 'Rolling Stones' is a registered trade mark. It would be otherwise if the disc purported to be (or would be perceived by customers as) a work released *by* the Rolling Stones, because the use of the trade mark under those circumstances would indeed purport to indicate the trade origin of the disc itself, and not merely serve to identify the artists. It is not, however, a defence for a maker or supplier to inform the immediate client that the goods are counterfeit: the focus must be on the appearance of the goods themselves, and how they might later be perceived by consumers (*Morgan* [2006] EWCA Crim 1742).

An offence under s. 92(1)(b) or (c) may, however, be committed in respect of branded goods that are not outright counterfeits, but which are being sold or marketed without the authority of the copyright proprietor (*M* [2017] UKSC 58, [2017] 2 Cr App R 30 (446)). Such goods (often referred to as 'grey goods') may include: goods representing part of an order placed with an authorised manufacturer by the trade mark proprietor but then cancelled; goods forming part of a batch whose manufacture had been authorised but which, after manufacture, were rejected as not being of sufficient standard ('seconds'); goods manufactured, pursuant to an order, with authority, but in excess of the required amount, or even goods imported and marketed outside the normal distribution channels by persons who have no authorised relationship with the manufacturer ('grey imports'). But, as Lord Hughes pointed out in *M* (at [15]), the offence does not extend to the resale of goods which a proprietor has voluntarily put into the European single market with the trade mark still attached:

> Section 12 of the 1994 Act, transposing article 7 of Directive 89/104/EEC, has the effect that further objection to the use of the mark is limited to special cases, such as changes or impairments to the goods.... Where it applies, this concept of exhaustion means that there is no infringement of the mark as a matter of civil law, and thus no criminal offence.

As to the scope of s. 92(1)(c), see *Kousar* [2009] EWCA Crim 139, [2009] 2 Cr App R 5 (88), in which it was held that a market trader's wife did not have possession, custody or control of his stock merely because he kept it at their home and that, even if she did possess it, she could commit no offence under s. 92(1)(c) unless she was involved in the business as a participant.

Mens Rea and Defences

B6.104 D must in all cases be shown to have acted with a view to gain or with an intent to cause loss to another. This is the same ulterior intent that is required under the Theft Act 1968, ss. 17 and 21, and it must have the same meaning as it bears there (see **B5.51**). This is not defined in the legislation as an act of 'dishonesty' but, by its terms, it assumes a degree of deliberate wrongdoing for financial gain (*Clements* [2019] EWCA Crim 2253, at [16]).

Under s. 92(5), it is a defence for D to prove a belief on reasonable grounds that the use or proposed use of the offending sign concerned was not an infringement of the registered trade mark. This applies both to cases in which D reasonably believes there is no such registered trade mark and to cases in which D is aware of the trade mark but unaware that it is being infringed (*Johnstone* [2003] UKHL 28, [2003] 3 All ER 884). The burdens imposed here are persuasive and not merely evidential (*Johnstone*).

It does not follow that someone who is simply ignorant of the existence of a registered trade mark, or who has not paid any attention to it, still less someone who has been reckless of its existence, has a defence under s. 92(5) (*McCrudden* [2005] EWCA Crim 466).

By s. 101(4), 'Where a partnership is guilty of an offence under this Act, every partner, other than a partner who is proved to have been ignorant of or to have attempted to prevent the commission of the offence, is also guilty of the offence and liable to be proceeded against and punished accordingly'. This does not require the prior conviction of the firm. It merely requires the court to be satisfied that the firm (which may no longer exist) is or was guilty of such an offence (*Wakefield* [2004] EWCA Crim 2278).

Offences Committed by Bodies Corporate

Directors, managers or other officers of a body corporate who connive at or consent to the commission of an offence by that body will be guilty of the same offence (s. 101(5)). As to the meaning of the term 'manager', see **A6.24**. **B6.105**

Forfeiture Provisions

The Trade Marks Act 1994, s. 97, provides for the making of forfeiture orders in relation to counterfeit goods or packaging (or articles used in their production, etc.) seized in connection with the investigation or prosecution of an offence under s. 92, an offence under the Consumer Protection from Unfair Trading Regulations 2008 or the Business Protection from Misleading Marketing Regulations 2008, or an offence of dishonesty or deception. Such orders may be sought either from the court before which relevant criminal proceedings have been brought or, where no such application has been made, by way of complaint to a magistrates' court (s. 97(2)). **B6.106**

If satisfied on a balance of probabilities that a relevant offence has been committed in relation to the goods, etc. (or other goods which are representative of them), the court may order that they be destroyed in accordance with its directions, or that they be released to a specified person, on condition (a) that offending signs are removed or obliterated and (b) that any order against that person to pay costs in those proceedings is complied with (s. 97(7)). It is not necessary in such cases that anyone has been charged or convicted of a relevant offence. Nor does the trial and acquittal of a defendant bar the making of such an order, which is made against the offending goods, and not against any particular person (*R (Drain) v Birmingham Crown Court* [2018] EWHC 1255 (Admin)).

UNFAIR COMMERCIAL PRACTICES, MISLEADING ADVERTISEMENTS ETC.

The Consumer Protection from Unfair Trading Regulations 2008 (SI 2008 No. 1277) implement Directive 2005/29/EC of the European Parliament and of the Council concerning unfair business-to-consumer commercial practices ([2005] OJ L149/22) together with Article 6.2 of Directive 1999/44/EC of the European Parliament and of the Council on certain aspects of the sale of consumer goods and associated guarantees ([1999] OJ L171/12). **B6.107**

They are supplemented by the Business Protection from Misleading Marketing Regulations 2008 (SI 2008 No. 1276) which implement Directive 2006/114/EC of the European Parliament and of the Council concerning misleading and comparative advertising ([2006] OJ L376/21).

Unfair Commercial Practices

The Consumer Protection from Unfair Trading Regulations, reg. 3(1), prohibits (but does not itself criminalise) a range of 'unfair commercial practices'. Such practices are not confined to those that involve misleading acts or omissions. A commercial practice is defined in **B6.108** reg. 2 as an act, omission, course of conduct, representation or commercial communication (including advertising and marketing) by a trader, which is directly connected with the promotion, sale or supply of a product to or from consumers, whether occurring before, during or after a commercial transaction (if any) in relation to a product. This definition was considered by the Court of Appeal in *X Ltd* [2013] EWCA Crim 818, [2013] 2 Cr App R 15 (159) where it was held that an unfair commercial practice could take the form of an isolated act and was not confined to courses of repeated malpractice. 'A commercial practice' said Leveson LJ, 'can be derived from a single incident. It will depend on the circumstances.' Moreover, there need be no actual sale or transaction, as the words 'if any' make clear. If there has been such a transaction the unfair practice may come later, as where a trader misleads a customer as to rights or duties under that transaction.

The concept was further explored in *Warwickshire County Council v Halfords Autocentres Ltd* [2018] EWHC 3007 (Admin), [2019] 2 All ER 69, in which it was held that a test purchase carried out by a trading standards officer merely purporting to be a consumer could still properly be described as a commercial practice within the meaning of the consumer protection regulations. Hickinbottom LJ said (at [41]):

> A commercial practice for the purposes of article 2(d) of the Directive (and thus regulation 2(1) of the 2008 Regulations) may be constituted by or derived from a test purchase made of a product (including a service) that is generally promoted to and intended for purchase by consumers, even where the purchaser may not himself be a consumer. Specifically, the giving to the test purchaser of an invoice or other document incorporating false information as to a main characteristic of the product (including the execution of a service) that would mislead the average consumer into paying for services that he has not received (which he would not otherwise have done) is a commercial practice which is a misleading action for the purposes of regulations 5 and 9 of the 2008 Regulations, being 'directly connected with the promotion, sale or supply of a product to … consumers'.

By reg. 3(3), a commercial practice is deemed unfair if (a) it contravenes the requirements of 'professional diligence' (skill and care commensurate with honest market practice or good faith); and (b) it materially distorts or is likely to materially distort the economic behaviour of the 'average consumer' with regard to the product. These concepts are further defined in reg. 2.

By reg. 3(4), a commercial practice is also deemed unfair if (a) it is a misleading action under the provisions of reg. 5; (b) it is a misleading omission under the provisions of reg. 6; (c) it is aggressive under the provisions of reg. 7; or (d) it is listed in sch. 1.

B6.109 Regulations 5 and 6 define misleading actions and omissions. By reg. 7(1) (which should be read in conjunction with reg. 7(2) and (3)), a commercial practice is 'aggressive' if in its factual context, taking account of all of its features and circumstances:

(a) it significantly impairs or is likely significantly to impair the average consumer's freedom of choice or conduct in relation to the product concerned through the use of harassment, coercion or undue influence; and
(b) it thereby causes or is likely to cause the consumer to take a transactional decision that would not otherwise have been taken.

Schedule 1 lists over 30 commercial practices that are deemed inherently (and 'in all circumstances') unfair. Many of the practices involve false or misleading statements, and most but not all give rise to criminal liability under reg. 12 (see **B6.110**).

Offences Relating to Unfair Commercial Practices

B6.110 By regs. 8 to 12, a trader (defined in reg. 2 as any person who in relation to a commercial practice is acting for purposes relating to that person's business, and anyone acting in the name of or on behalf of a trader) may incur criminal liability for engaging in specified unfair commercial practices. An illustrative sentencing case is *Ahmed* [2017] EWCA Crim 1281, where the Court of Appeal said that, even in the absence of dishonesty, consecutive sentences of six months' immediate imprisonment were appropriate for offences of engaging in unfair and aggressive commercial practices by operating a travel company that took over £40,000 from customers whose tickets and hotels were never booked. Complaints were then dismissed or ignored. Goss J observed (at [19]): 'Although this was a case of neglect and failure to monitor staff, it must have been apparent to the appellant that regulatory offences were being committed when the business should not have been operating at all, let alone in the way that it was.' The Court then considered mitigating circumstances which had not been made known to the trial judge, and suspended the custodial term.

Consumer Protection from Unfair Trading Regulations 2008, regs. 8 to 12

8.—(1) A trader is guilty of an offence if—
(a) he knowingly or recklessly engages in a commercial practice which contravenes the requirements of professional diligence under regulation 3(3)(a); and
(b) the practice materially distorts or is likely to materially distort the economic behaviour of the average consumer with regard to the product under regulation 3(3)(b).
(2) For the purposes of paragraph (1)(a) a trader who engages in a commercial practice without regard to whether the practice contravenes the requirements of professional diligence shall be deemed recklessly to engage in the practice, whether or not the trader has reason for believing that the practice might contravene those requirements.

9. A trader is guilty of an offence if he engages in a commercial practice which is a misleading action under regulation 5 otherwise than by reason of the commercial practice satisfying the condition in regulation 5(3)(b).

10. A trader is guilty of an offence if he engages in a commercial practice which is a misleading omission under regulation 6.

11. A trader is guilty of an offence if he engages in a commercial practice which is aggressive under regulation 7.

12. A trader is guilty of an offence if he engages in a commercial practice set out in any of paragraphs 1 to 10, 12 to 27 and 29 to 31 of schedule 1.

Strict liability is applicable to offences under regs. 9 to 12, subject to defences of due diligence (reg. 17) or innocent publication of an offending advertisement (reg. 18), but the reg. 8 offence requires proof of knowledge or recklessness, which is given an extended and objective meaning under reg. 8(2). **B6.111**

Persons other than traders may incur liability under reg. 16 where their acts or defaults cause traders to commit offences under regs. 9 to 12, or acts, etc., that would have involved offences but for the availability of defences under regs. 17 or 18. As to offences by corporations or Scottish partnerships, see reg. 15.

Enforcement and Procedure

Enforcement of the regulations depends in England and Wales on the Competition and Markets Authority, and on local weights and measures authorities. Their duties and powers of investigation and enforcement are set out in the Consumer Rights Act 2015, sch. 5. By reg. 13 of the 2008 Regulations, all offences under regs. 8 to 12 are triable either way and punishable on indictment by a fine and/or imprisonment for a term not exceeding two years. Following summary conviction, the maximum penalty is an unlimited fine. There is also a summary offence of obstructing authorised officers (reg. 23), also punishable by a fine. As to the power of local authorities to prosecute for conspiracy to defraud, see **A5.66**. **B6.112**

By reg. 14(1), no proceedings for an offence under the regulations may be commenced after the end of the period of three years beginning with the date of the commission of the offence, or the end of the period of one year beginning with the date of discovery of the offence by the prosecutor, whichever is earlier. A certificate signed by or on behalf of the prosecutor and stating the date on which the offence was discovered shall be conclusive evidence of that fact and a certificate stating that matter and purporting to be so signed shall be treated as so signed unless the contrary is proved (reg. 14(2)). Any such certificate must no doubt comply strictly with these requirements before it can be relied upon (cf. *RSPCA v King* [2010] EWHC 637 (Admin) (see **B20.20**) concerning a similarly worded provision in the Animal Welfare Act 2006).

Notwithstanding anything in the MCA 1980, s. 127(1), an information relating to an offence under the Regulations which is triable by a magistrates' court in England and Wales may be so tried if it is laid at any time before the end of the period of 12 months beginning with the date of the commission of the offence (reg. 14(3)).

Misleading Business to Business Advertising

B6.113 The Business Protection from Misleading Marketing Regulations 2008 prohibit misleading business-to-business advertising and set out the conditions under which comparative advertisements (which is any advertisement which identifies a competitor or a competitor's product) are permitted.

The Business Protection Regulations broadly follow the pattern of the Consumer Protection from Unfair Trading Regulations. A 'misleading' advertisement (defined as one which deceives or is likely to deceive the traders to whom it is addressed or whom it reaches; and by reason of its deceptive nature is likely to affect their economic behaviour; or which for those reasons, injures or is likely to injure a competitor), is prohibited under reg. 3. By reg. 6, a trader who engages in such advertising commits a criminal offence, subject to any 'due diligence' or 'innocent publications' defences under regs. 11 and 12. In contrast, breaches of the rules relating to comparative advertising (reg. 4) are criminalised only if the advertisement thereby becomes misleading under regs. 3 and 6.

Persons other than traders may incur liability under reg. 9 where their acts or defaults cause traders to commit offences under reg. 6, or acts that would have been offences but for defences under regs. 11 or 12. As to offences by corporations or Scottish partnerships, see reg. 8.

Civil or criminal enforcement of the Regulations is entrusted in England and Wales to the Competition and Markets Authority, and to local weights and measures authorities. Their powers of investigation and enforcement remain governed by Part 3 of the Regulations, but investigatory powers are now set out in the Consumer Rights Act 2015, sch. 5.

By reg. 7 of the 2008 Regulations, an offence under reg. 6 is triable either way and punishable on indictment by a fine and/or imprisonment for a term not exceeding two years. Following summary conviction, the maximum penalty is an unlimited fine. There is also a summary offence of obstructing authorised officers (reg. 25), also punishable by a fine. As to the power of local authorities to prosecute for conspiracy to defraud, see **A5.66**.

Regulation 10 deals with time-limits on prosecutions. These are similar to those that apply under the Consumer Protection from Unfair Trading Regulations 2008, reg. 14 (see **B6.112**).

Property Misdescriptions and Holiday Accommodation Contracts

B6.114 Misleading statements or representations concerning residential or commercial property sales or lettings fall within the ambit of the Consumer Protection from Unfair Trading Regulations or the Business Protection from Misleading Marketing Regulations but, prior to 1 October 2013, were more specifically dealt with under the Property Misdescriptions Act 1991, s. 1. The existence of largely duplicated offences in this area was however considered to be 'burdensome and confusing', and the 1991 Act was accordingly repealed on 1 October 2013 by the Property Misdescriptions Act 1991 (Repeal) Order 2013 (SI 2013 No. 1575).

Offences under the Consumer Protection from Unfair Trading Regulations committed in connection with timeshares and other regulated holiday accommodation contracts may alternatively be prosecuted under the Timeshare, Holiday Products, Resale and Exchange Contracts Regulations 2010 (SI 2010 No. 2960), regs. 27 to 31. As to the power of local authorities to prosecute for conspiracy to defraud, see **A5.66**.

Providing False Information as to Health Services or Adult Social Care

The Care Act 2014, s. 92(1), enacted in response to issues identified by the Francis report into the Mid-Staffordshire NHS foundation trust scandal, creates an offence in cases where a 'Care Provider' as defined in s. 92(3) supplies, publishes or otherwise makes available information of a specified description that is required under an enactment or other legal obligation, but which is false or misleading in a material respect. **B6.115**

The False or Misleading Information (Specified Care Providers and Specified Information) Regulations 2015 (SI 2015 No. 988) specify the information to which s. 92 applies and the full range of care providers that will be subject to it, but s. 92 applies to any public body which provides health services or adult social care in England and to those that provide such care pursuant to arrangements made with such a public body, thus including NHS trusts and local authorities.

Liability is strict, subject to a due diligence defence provided by s. 91(2). The maximum penalty is a fine on summary conviction, or imprisonment for up to two years and a fine (or both) following conviction on indictment (s. 93(1)).

Remedial orders (requiring the provider to take specified steps to remedy any matter or deficiency) and/or publicity orders (requiring the provider to publicise in a specified manner details of the offence and conviction etc.) may be made instead of or in addition to such penalties in accordance with s. 93(3) to (7). Failure to comply with such an order is an offence (s. 93(8)).

Section B7 Company, Commercial and Insolvency Offences

OFFENCES UNDER THE COMPANIES ACTS: GENERAL

Scope of the Companies Acts

B7.1 The bulk of the legislation affecting companies is contained in the Companies Act 2006. A small number of the provisions of the Companies Act 1985 (principally under Part XIV relating to company investigations) remain in force. This section adopts the definition of 'the Companies Acts' in s. 2 of the Companies Act 2006 as meaning Parts 1 to 39 (ss. 1 to 1181) of that Act, the provisions of the Companies Act 1985 which remain in force, and Part 2 of the Companies (Audit, Investigations and Community Enterprise) Act 2004.

The Companies Acts contain over 150 offence-creating provisions, many of which must be read in conjunction with other provisions which do not themselves create offences. Some provisions create summary offences relating to comparatively minor defaults, typically involving failure to notify the Registrar of Companies of matters affecting the company and its constitution or to provide information to shareholders. But other provisions create serious crimes, many of which involve fraud. The distinction is not, however, clear-cut. Minor defaults and irregularities will often be associated with more serious crime, for example where improperly maintained accounts or records are used to conceal fraudulent trading or unlawful dealings with directors. In such cases, an indictment may include counts alleging fraud offences and counts alleging lesser defaults and irregularities, some of which are triable either way.

A general work on criminal law cannot attempt to cover all offences under the Companies Acts or to discuss the relationship between the offence-creating provisions and the rest of this massive Act. Readers requiring fuller coverage must therefore refer to specialist works on company law.

Offences Punishable with Imprisonment under the Companies Acts

B7.2 The more serious offences under the Companies Acts, punishable with imprisonment, are listed below. Each of the listed offences is triable either way. The maximum penalty on indictment for each of these offences is a term of imprisonment not exceeding two years and/or a fine, except for (i) fraudulent trading (see **B7.7**), for which the maximum sentence is ten years' imprisonment and/or a fine, and (ii) the aggravated offences under ss. 1006 to 1007 of the Companies Act 2006 and the offences under ss. 450 to 451 of the Companies Act 1985, for which the maximum sentence is seven years and/or a fine. On summary conviction each of the offences listed is punishable with imprisonment not exceeding six months (s. 1131) and/or an unlimited fine. The offence under s. 980 of the Companies Act 2006 also carries a daily default fine (currently £100 per day).

Section of Act creating offence	General nature of offence
Companies Act 2006	
119, 747 & 814	Making a misleading, false or deceptive statement in a request to inspect the register of members' names, register of debenture holders or register of interests disclosed; or disclosing for an improper purpose information obtained by a request.
350	Making a misleading, false or deceptive statement to an independent assessor appointed to report on a poll taken at a general meeting of a quoted company.
387 & 389	Failing to keep and preserve accounting records.
418	Making a false statement as to audit information in a directors' report.
458	Wrongful use of tax information disclosed for the revision of defective company accounts.
460	Wrongful disclosure of information obtained under compulsory powers in connection with the revision of defective company accounts.
501	Making false, misleading or deceptive statement to an auditor.
572	Inclusion of misleading, false or deceptive matter in a directors' statement disapplying pre-emption rights.
643	Making a solvency statement without having reasonable grounds for the opinion expressed in it.
658	Company acquiring its own shares.
680	Financial assistance by a public company for the acquisition of its own shares or shares in its private holding company (see **B7.19**).
715	Directors' statement for the redemption or purchase of a private company's own shares without reasonable grounds for the opinion expressed in the statement.
795	Failing to comply with a notice requiring information about interests in shares in a public company or making a false statement in compliance with such a notice.
949	Wrongful disclosure of information provided to the Takeover Panel.
980	Failure to send a copy of a notice to buy out a minority shareholder and a statutory declaration to the company or making a false declaration.
993	Being a party to carrying on company's business with intent to defraud creditors, or for any fraudulent purpose (see **B7.7**).
1006 & 1007	Failure to send a copy of an application for voluntary striking off to members, creditors, employees, etc. with intent to conceal the making of the application (aggravated offence).
1112	Making a misleading, false or deceptive statement to the Registrar of Companies.
1153	Making a misleading, false or deceptive statement to a person carrying out an independent valuation and report required in connection with the allotment or transfer of shares.
1250	Furnishing misleading, false or deceptive information for the purposes of or in connection with an application under Part 42 (auditors) or in purported compliance with a requirement under that part.
Companies Act 1985	
444(3)	Failure to give the Secretary of State, when required to do so, information about interests in shares, etc.; giving false information.
449(6)	Wrongful disclosure of information obtained under statutory powers.
450	Destroying or mutilating company documents; falsifying such documents or making false entries; parting with such documents or altering them or making omissions (see **B7.15**).
451	Providing false information in purported compliance with a requirement to provide documents and information.

Ambit of the Companies Acts

B7.3 The Companies Acts are primarily concerned with registered companies as defined in ss. 1 and 1171 of the Companies Act 2006 (i.e. those registered under that Act and former Companies Acts). Some of the provisions have a wider ambit. Unregistered companies are relatively uncommon, but the Unregistered Companies Regulations 2009 (SI 2009 No. 2436) apply some provisions of the Companies Acts to them. More importantly, many provisions of Part XIV of the Companies Act 1985 (ss. 431 to 457: company investigations) apply also to companies incorporated outside Great Britain which are or have been carrying on business in Great Britain (s. 453). The 2006 Act extends to the whole of the UK. The Overseas Companies Regulations 2009 (SI 2009 No. 1801) impose a duty on companies incorporated outside the UK which open an establishment in the UK to deliver a return and documents to the Registrar of Companies. By s. 1054 of the 2006 Act and reg. 11, failure to comply with any of the regulations is an offence punishable by a fine not exceeding level 3 on the standard scale and a daily default fine not exceeding one tenth of level 3.

Liability of Officers in Default

B7.4 **Companies Act 2006, s. 1121**

(1) This section has effect for the purposes of any provision of the Companies Acts to the effect that, in the event of a contravention of an enactment in relation to a company, an offence is committed by every officer of the company who is in default.
(2) For this purpose 'officer' includes—
  (a) any director, manager or secretary, and
  (b) any person who is to be treated as an officer of the company for the purposes of the provision in question.
(3) An officer is 'in default' for the purposes of the provision if he authorises or permits, participates in, or fails to take all reasonable steps to prevent, the contravention.

By virtue of the Companies Act 2006, s. 250, 'director' includes 'any person occupying the position of director, by whatever name called'. Section 1123 contains provisions applying s. 1121 to bodies other than companies.

When the Small Business, Enterprise and Employment Act 2015, s. 87, is brought into force, it will insert ss. 156A to 156C into the Companies Act 2006, requiring that, subject to exceptions, all company directors must be natural persons.

Consents for Prosecutions

B7.5 Consent is required for certain prosecutions by s. 1126(2) of the Companies Act 2006. No proceedings are to be brought under ss. 458, 460, 949, 953 or 1122 of the 2006 Act or under ss. 448 to 451 or 453A of the 1985 Act except by or with the consent of the Secretary of State or the DPP. Proceedings under s. 798 of, or sch. 13, para. 5 or 6, to, the 2006 Act or s. 455 of the 1985 Act require the consent of the Secretary of State.

Summary Offences: General Provisions

B7.6 **Companies Act 2006, ss. 1125, 1127 and 1128**

1125.—(1) This section defines what is meant in the Companies Acts where it is provided that a person guilty of an offence is liable on summary conviction to a fine not exceeding a specified amount 'and, for continued contravention, a daily default fine' not exceeding a specified amount.
(2) This means that the person is liable on a second or subsequent summary conviction of the offence to a fine not exceeding the latter amount for each day on which the contravention is continued (instead of being liable to a fine not exceeding the former amount).

...

1127.—(1) Summary proceedings for any offence under the Companies Acts may be taken—
  (a) against a body corporate, at any place at which the body has a place of business, and
  (b) against any other person, at any place at which he is for the time being.
(2) This is without prejudice to any jurisdiction exercisable apart from this section.

1128.—(1) An information relating to an offence under the Companies Acts that is triable by a magistrates' court in England and Wales may be so tried if it is laid—
(a) at any time within three years after the commission of the offence, and
(b) within twelve months after the date on which evidence sufficient in the opinion of the Director of Public Prosecutions or the Secretary of State (as the case may be) to justify the proceedings comes to his knowledge.
(2) and (3) [Apply only to Scotland and Northern Ireland.]
(4) For purposes of this section a certificate of the Director of Public Prosecutions ... or the Secretary of State (as the case may be) as to the date on which such evidence as is referred to above came to his knowledge is conclusive evidence.

Section 1128(1) has no effect in relation to the summary trial of offences triable either way (*Thames Metropolitan Stipendiary Magistrate, ex parte Horgan* [1998] QB 719).

FRAUDULENT TRADING

Companies Act 2006, s. 993 B7.7

(1) If any business of a company is carried on with intent to defraud creditors of the company or creditors of any other person, or for any fraudulent purpose, every person who is knowingly a party to the carrying on of the business in that manner commits an offence.
(2) This applies whether or not the company has been, or is in the course of being, wound up.

The Fraud Act 2006, s. 9, makes fraudulent trading by sole traders and other non-corporate entities a criminal offence (see **B5.28**).

Procedure and Sentence

For procedural provisions see **B7.5** and **B7.6**. For disqualification orders, see **E21.8**. B7.8

On conviction on indictment, the maximum sentence is ten years' imprisonment and/or a fine; on summary conviction, the maximum sentence is six months' imprisonment and/or an unlimited fine (ss. 993(3) and 1131).

The definitive sentencing guideline, *Fraud, Bribery and Money Laundering Offences* (see Supplement, **SG26-1**), does not apply to an offence under s. 993 but it was held under the previous guideline that a judge is entitled to pay regard to such a guideline where the fraudulent trading bears similarities to an offence to which the guideline does apply (*McCrae* [2012] EWCA Crim 976, [2013] 1 Cr App R (S) 1 (1) at [16]). See also *Mackey* [2012] EWCA Crim 2205, [2013] 1 Cr App R (S) 100 (522). In *Ali (Mohammed)* [2019] EWCA Crim 1263 the Court of Appeal dismissed appeals against sentence where the judge had taken the same approach to the current guideline.

Before the issue of sentencing guidelines, the Court of Appeal in *Smith (Colin John)* [1997] 2 Cr App R (S) 167 (at p. 170) had commented that, broadly speaking, a charge of fraudulent trading resulting in a deficiency to creditors is less seriously regarded than a charge of theft or fraud of the same amount. In *Freeman* [2011] EWCA Crim 2534, [2012] Cr App R (S) 105 (629), D carried out an investment fraud involving losses of £14 million to 335 victims. He pleaded guilty to fraudulent trading. The Court of Appeal reduced the sentence for fraudulent trading to six years' imprisonment with a further 12 months consecutive for bankruptcy offences.

Civil Liability of Parties

Earlier legislation contained provisions imposing criminal and civil liability for fraudulent trading within the same section (Companies Act 1948, s. 332). Those provisions were separated as part of the reforms to company and insolvency legislation in 1985 to 1986. The Insolvency Act 1986, s. 213, now provides that persons who were knowingly parties to such conduct may be required to contribute to the assets of the company concerned. Unlike criminal liability, s. 213 B7.9

and its predecessor, s. 332(1) of the Companies Act 1948, has and had no application unless the company is in liquidation.

In *Bilta (UK) Ltd v Nazir (No. 2)* [2015] UKSC 23, [2016] AC 1, the Supreme Court decided that s. 213 has extra-territorial effect and extends to persons outside the jurisdiction.

Indictment

B7.10 *Statement of Offence*

Fraudulent trading contrary to section 993 of the Companies Act 2006

Particulars of Offence

A between the … day of … and the … day of … was knowingly a party to the carrying on of certain business of a company called … with intent to defraud creditors of the said company [or with intent to defraud creditors of …] [or for a fraudulent purpose, namely …]

Carrying on the Business of the Company

B7.11 The meaning of the words 'any business of the company has been carried on with intent to defraud creditors' has been considered in cases under the Insolvency Act 1986, s. 213. In *Morphitis v Bernasconi* [2003] EWCA Civ 289, [2003] Ch 552 (at [42]–[49]) the Court of Appeal considered that the legislation is aimed at the carrying on of a business and not the execution of individual transactions in the course of carrying on that business. Thus not every fraud perpetrated on a customer amounts to fraudulent trading. But circumstances can arise, as in *Re Gerald Cooper Chemicals Ltd* [1978] Ch 262, in which a single transaction in which only one creditor is defrauded will suffice (see also *Lockwood* [1986] Crim LR 244). In *Philippou* (1989) 89 Cr App R 290, it was held that the fraudulent obtaining of an air travel organiser's licence from the Civil Aviation Authority involved carrying on a business for a fraudulent purpose, as the licence was essential to that business.

Intent to Defraud and Knowledge

B7.12 Dishonesty is an essential element in fraudulent trading (*Cox* (1982) 75 Cr App R 291). For the meaning of dishonesty, see **B4.54**, *Ivey v Genting Casinos (UK) Ltd* [2017] UKSC 67, [2018] AC 391 and *Barton* [2020] EWCA Crim 575, especially at [84] and [105].

As in other cases involving fraud, there need not be any intent to cause financial loss to another person (see **A5.64** and **A5.68**). Deliberately and dishonestly putting another person's property or financial interests in jeopardy may suffice (*Allsop* (1977) 64 Cr App R 29; *Wai Yu-Tsang v The Queen* [1992] 1 AC 269), whether or not there is any deception (*Scott v Metropolitan Police Commissioner* [1975] AC 819). It may be fraud to deceive public officers into failing to perform their duty (see *Welham v DPP* [1961] AC 103; *Philippou* (1989) 89 Cr App R 290 at **B7.11**).

In *Bank of India v Morris* [2005] EWCA Civ 693, [2005] BCC 739 at [14] the Court of Appeal held (albeit on a concession) that knowledge includes 'blind-eye' knowledge, namely a firmly grounded suspicion of specific facts and a deliberate decision to avoid confirming that they exist.

Frauds on Creditors and Other Fraudulent Purposes

B7.13 The word 'creditors' in the Companies Act 2006, s. 993, denotes people to whom money is owed. But it is immaterial whether the debt can presently be sued for; creditors who come into existence after the fraudulent trading has begun are within the scope of s. 993 (*Smith (Wallace Duncan)* [1996] 2 Cr App R 1).

A typical example of fraudulent trading involves a company which has lapsed into insolvency, but which continues to obtain credit in circumstances where its directors know that there can be little if any chance of the creditors being paid. It would probably not be considered dishonest for debts to be incurred in the expectation that they could be repaid shortly after they fall due, but a jury may well consider it dishonest for debts to be incurred when they could at best be repaid months late (*Grantham* [1984] QB 675).

The argument that the words 'any fraudulent purpose' should be given a limited construction and that defrauding customers should not be regarded as falling within the scope of this provision, was rejected in *Kemp* [1988] QB 645; the Court of Appeal held that the mischief aimed at is fraudulent trading generally, and not just insofar as it affects creditors. In *Philippou* (1989) 89 Cr App R 290, the fraudulent obtaining of an air travel organiser's licence was held to have involved fraudulent trading. This perhaps stretches the meaning of 'purpose', because the licence was obtained as a means to an end, rather than as an end in itself; but it signals a clear rejection of any attempt to restrict the offence to frauds on existing or potential creditors.

In civil proceedings it was decided that the mere preference of one creditor over another did not amount to fraudulent trading (*Re Sarflax Ltd* [1979] Ch 592). In *HM Advocate v Withy* [2017] HCJAC 47, 2017 SCL 657 an allegation that those in control of Rangers Football Club plc had caused it to pay some of the company's debts, but not others, was held by the High Court of Justiciary (at [36]) to be insufficient to sustain a charge of fraudulent trading.

It is not necessarily fraudulent trading for a holding company to issue letters of comfort in respect of a subsidiary which it later allows to go into insolvent liquidation, though it would largely depend on whether the holding company was sincere at the time the letters were issued (*Re Augustus Barnett & Son Ltd* [1986] BCLC 170).

Persons who May be Liable for Fraudulent Trading

The Court of Appeal held in *Miles* [1992] Crim LR 657 that the offence of fraudulent trading **B7.14** can be committed only by persons who exercise some kind of controlling or managerial function within the company. But employees who exercise no such function (including junior managers and managers of local branches) might, despite this narrow interpretation, incur liability as secondary parties to offences committed by the company's directors or senior managers. And persons holding no formal position within the company, such as shadow directors, could incur liability for fraudulent trading if they exercise de facto managerial powers.

In *Maidstone Buildings Provisions Ltd* [1971] 3 All ER 363, it was said that some positive action on the part of a company secretary, rather than inertia, was required to make a person holding that office liable. Passivity on the part of an executive director might be different, but *mens rea* would be needed in any event.

See also **A6** on corporate liability generally.

DESTRUCTION, MUTILATION OR FALSIFICATION OF COMPANY DOCUMENTS

Companies Act 1985, s. 450 **B7.15**

(1) An officer of a company, who—
  (a) destroys, mutilates or falsifies, or is privy to the destruction, mutilation or falsification of a document affecting or relating to the company's property or affairs, or
  (b) makes, or is privy to the making of, a false entry in such a document, is guilty of an offence, unless he proves that he had no intention to conceal the state of affairs of the company or to defeat the law.

(1A) Subsection (1) applies to an officer of an authorised insurance company which is not a body corporate as it applies to an officer of a company.

(2) Such a person as above mentioned who fraudulently either parts with, alters or makes an omission in any such document or is privy to fraudulent parting with, fraudulent altering or fraudulent making of an omission in, any such document, is guilty of an offence.

By s. 450(5), 'document' includes information recorded in any form.

Procedure and Sentence No proceedings for an offence under s. 450 are to be brought **B7.16** except by or with the consent of the Secretary of State or the DPP (Companies Act 2006, s. 1126(2): see **B7.5**). For procedural provisions, see **B7.6**.

On conviction on indictment, the maximum sentence is seven years' imprisonment and/or a fine; on summary conviction, the maximum sentence is six months' imprisonment and/or an unlimited fine (ss. 450(3) and 1131). In *Dane* (15 August 2000 unreported, CA) the Court of Appeal upheld a sentence of nine months' immediate imprisonment on a 65-year-old offender of previous good character who had been convicted after a trial of destroying company property. The involvement by him of staff in the cover-up was treated as an aggravating factor.

This is one of the most serious offences under the Companies Acts. Such conduct is often designed to remove evidence of serious fraud. It may also be designed to frustrate or hinder an investigation into the company's affairs under Part XIV (ss. 431 to 453) of the Companies Act 1985; but the offence may be committed whether or not any such investigation is in prospect.

B7.17 **Burden of Proof** The wording of the offence is similar to the Insolvency Act 1986, s. 206(1)(c) and (d) and (4)(b) (see **B7.45**). It follows from *A-G's Ref (No. 1 of 2004)* [2004] EWCA Crim 1025, [2004] 4 All ER 457 (at [80]–[84]) and other cases on the incidence of burden of proof (see **F3.18** ***et seq.***, particularly **F3.26**) that the imposition of the full persuasive burden on the accused is compatible with the ECHR, Article 6.

FINANCIAL ASSISTANCE PROVIDED BY COMPANIES IN CONNECTION WITH THE ACQUISITION OF THEIR OWN SHARES

B7.18 The provision by a company of financial assistance in connection with the acquisition of its own shares may in some circumstances be unobjectionable, but in other instances company funds may be improperly depleted by loans for the purchase of its own shares and the loans never repaid. Following particularly scandalous instances of asset-stripping of companies with cash or other liquid assets (described in *Re VGM Holdings Ltd* [1942] Ch 235 at p. 239), widely drawn legislation was enacted in 1929; but this rendered criminal many harmless transactions, while providing wholly inadequate penalties for serious fraud. The legislation was recast in a more complex form in 1981. The mischief to which it is directed is that the resources of the company and its subsidiaries should not be used directly or indirectly to assist the purchaser financially to make the acquisition, because this may prejudice the interests of creditors of the company or group and the interests of shareholders other than those whose shares are bought (*Chaston v SWP Group plc* [2002] EWCA Civ 1999, [2003] 3 BCC 140 at [31]).

The current legislation is contained in ss. 677 to 683 of the Companies Act 2006 and applies only to public companies.

B7.19 **Companies Act 2006, s. 680**

(1) If a company contravenes section 678(1) or (3) or section 679(1) or (3) (prohibited financial assistance) an offence is committed by—
   (a) the company, and
   (b) every officer of the company who is in default.

On conviction on indictment, the maximum sentence is two years' imprisonment and/or a fine; on summary conviction, the maximum sentence is six months' imprisonment and/or an unlimited fine (ss. 680(2) and 1131).

B7.20 For procedural provisions, see **B7.5** and **B7.6**. Although the only penalty expressly provided for breach of s. 678 (and its predecessors) is criminal, the civil courts held, after initial hesitation, that breaches of the prohibition also give rise to civil remedies. Readers are referred to specialist works on company law for discussions of the substantial body of case law in civil litigation on the interpretation of these provisions.

FINANCIAL SERVICES OFFENCES

Introduction

The Financial Services and Markets Act 2000, as amended by the Financial Services Act 2012, makes provision for the regulation of financial services and markets. Section 19 contains a 'general prohibition' against carrying on a regulated activity in the UK, unless authorised or exempt. Regulated activities are specified in the Financial Services and Markets Act 2000 (Regulated Activities) Order 2001 (SI 2001 No. 544), which is regularly amended. **B7.21**

Under the FSMA 2000, ss. 1B to 1H, the Financial Conduct Authority (FCA) has the strategic objective of ensuring that financial markets, markets for regulated financial services and markets for services carrying on regulated activities function well. The FCA also has three operational objectives, namely, consumer protection, integrity and competition (s. 1B(3)). The Prudential Regulation Authority (PRA) regulates deposit-takers, insurers and designated investment firms (ss. 2A to 2P).

The FSMA 2000 creates a relatively small number of criminal offences. Breaches of the Act and rules are mainly enforced by remedies in civil courts or disciplinary procedures. Where the Act creates offences, proceedings can be instituted only by the appropriate regulator, the Secretary of State or the DPP, or with the consent of the DPP (s. 401). For the role of the FCA in prosecuting, see *R (Uberoi) v City of Westminster Magistrates' Court* [2008] EWHC 3191 (Admin), [2009] 1 WLR 1905, and for the power to prosecute offences beyond the Act, see s. 402 and *Rollins* [2010] UKSC 39, [2010] 4 All ER 880.

Summary proceedings may be taken against a company or unincorporated association at any place where it has a place of business and against an individual at any place where that individual is for the time being (s. 403(5)). Where an offence committed by a body corporate is proved to have been committed with the consent or connivance of a director or other officer, or is attributable to neglect, that person may also be prosecuted for that offence (s. 400(1)).

Contravention of the General Prohibition

By the FSMA 2000, s. 23(1), contravention of the general prohibition is punishable, on indictment, with a maximum penalty of two years' imprisonment or a fine, or both; on summary conviction, the maximum penalty is six months' imprisonment or a fine of the statutory maximum, or both. By s. 23(3), it is a defence for D to show that all reasonable precautions were taken and all due diligence exercised to avoid committing the offence. In relation to aiding the commission of an offence under s. 23(1), see *O'Neil v Gale* [2013] EWCA Civ 1554 (at [10]–[22]). **B7.22**

In *Epton* [2009] EWCA Crim 515, [2009] 2 Cr App R (S) 96 (639) a sentence of 15 months' imprisonment for contravening the general prohibition was upheld, plus nine months consecutive for transferring criminal property. In *Dowse* [2017] EWCA Crim 598, [2017] 2 Cr App R (S) 26 (208) sentences of 15 months' imprisonment were also imposed, on pleas of guilty, for engaging over two years in a money-lending business, a regulated activity, when not authorised or exempt. In *Cooper* [2013] EWCA Crim 2703 a sentence of three months' immediate imprisonment was upheld for contravening the general prohibition by advising without being authorised to do so, plus six months consecutive for dishonestly concealing a material fact.

By s. 23(1A) to (1G), an authorised person who carries on a credit-regulated activity otherwise than in accordance with permission commits an offence, punishable in the same way as an offence under s. 23(1).

False Claims to be Authorised or Exempt

Section 24 of the FSMA 2000 creates a summary offence of making false claims to be authorised or exempt, punishable by a maximum of six months' imprisonment and/or an unlimited fine. **B7.23**

Where the offence involves or includes the public display of any material, the maximum fine is multiplied by the number of days of any public display. Again it is a defence for D to show that all reasonable precautions were taken and all due diligence exercised to avoid committing the offence.

Section 333 of the FSMA 2000 creates a similar offence of making a false claim to be a person to whom the general prohibition does not apply.

Breach of Restrictions on Financial Promotion

B7.24 Section 25 of the FSMA 2000 and the Financial Services and Markets Act 2000 (Financial Promotion) Order 2005 (SI 2005 No. 1529) impose restrictions on financial promotion (communication of an invitation or inducement to engage in investment activity) in the course of business. By s. 25, breach of the restrictions on financial promotion is an offence. It is punishable on indictment with a maximum penalty of two years' imprisonment and/or a fine; on summary conviction, the maximum penalty is six months' imprisonment and/or an unlimited fine (s. 25(1)). It is a defence for D to show a belief on reasonable grounds that the content of the communication was prepared, or approved for the purposes of s. 21, by an authorised person or that D took all reasonable precautions and exercised all due diligence to avoid committing the offence (s. 25(2)).

In *Powell* [2008] EWCA Crim 1214, [2009] 1 Cr App R (S) 30 (158) sentences of 15 months' imprisonment were upheld for offences under s. 25 where the offenders had participated in an investment scam.

Misleading Statements and Impressions

B7.25 Part X1 of the Financial Services Act 2012 contains three sections creating offences concerning false or misleading statements or impressions relating to agreements, investments or benchmarks of types specified by Order made by the Treasury. The offence under s. 89 is knowingly or recklessly making a false or misleading statement or dishonestly concealing material facts in relation to an agreement or investment. The offence under s. 90 is acting or engaging in a course of conduct which creates a false or misleading impression as to the market in, or price or value of, an investment. The offence under s. 91 is knowingly or recklessly making a false or misleading statement in the course of arrangements to set an index, rate or price (a 'benchmark') or acting or engaging in a course of conduct which creates a false or misleading impression as to the price or value of an investment or interest rate. Each section needs to be read with definitions contained in s. 93.

The legislation is set out below as subsequently amended. The Financial Services and Markets Act 2000 (Market Abuse) Regulations 2016 (SI 2016 No. 680), reg. 3, gave effect to Regulation (EU) No. 596/2014 on market abuse ([2014] OJ L173/1) so as to make UK law compatible with that regulation. The wording of s. 93(8B) is substituted with effect from 31 December 2020 by the Bank of England (Amendment) (EU Exit) Regulations 2018 (SI 2018 No. 1297), reg. 8(5) and the European Union (Withdrawal Agreement) Act 2020, s. 39(1) and sch. 5, para. 1.

Financial Services Act 2012, ss. 89 to 91 and 93

89.—(1) Subsection (2) applies to a person ('P') who—

(a) makes a statement which P knows to be false or misleading in a material respect,

(b) makes a statement which is false or misleading in a material respect, being reckless as to whether it is, or

(c) dishonestly conceals any material facts whether in connection with a statement made by P or otherwise.

(2) P commits an offence if P makes the statement or conceals the facts with the intention of inducing, or is reckless as to whether making it or concealing them may induce, another person (whether or not the person to whom the statement is made)—

(a) to enter into or offer to enter into, or to refrain from entering or offering to enter into, a relevant agreement, or

(b) to exercise, or refrain from exercising, any rights conferred by a relevant investment.

(3) In proceedings for an offence under subsection (2) brought against a person to whom that subsection applies as a result of paragraph (a) of subsection (1), it is a defence for the person charged ('D') to show that the statement was made in conformity with—
(a) price stabilising rules,
(b) control of information rules, or
(c) the relevant provisions of Article 5 (exemption for buy-back programmes and stabilisation) of the market abuse regulation.
(4) Subsections (1) and (2) do not apply unless—
(a) the statement is made in or from, or the facts are concealed in or from, the United Kingdom or arrangements are made in or from the United Kingdom for the statement to be made or the facts to be concealed,
(b) the person on whom the inducement is intended to or may have effect is in the United Kingdom, or
(c) the agreement is or would be entered into or the rights are or would be exercised in the United Kingdom.

90.—(1) A person ('P') who does any act or engages in any course of conduct which creates a false or misleading impression as to the market in or the price or value of any relevant investments commits an offence if—
(a) P intends to create the impression, and
(b) the case falls within subsection (2) or (3) (or both).
(2) The case falls within this subsection if P intends, by creating the impression, to induce another person to acquire, dispose of, subscribe for or underwrite the investments or to refrain from doing so or to exercise or refrain from exercising any rights conferred by the investments.
(3) The case falls within this subsection if—
(a) P knows that the impression is false or misleading or is reckless as to whether it is, and
(b) P intends by creating the impression to produce any of the results in subsection (4) or is aware that creating the impression is likely to produce any of the results in that subsection.
(4) Those results are—
(a) the making of a gain for P or another, or
(b) the causing of loss to another person or the exposing of another person to the risk of loss.
(5) References in subsection (4) to gain or loss are to be read in accordance with subsections (6) to (8).
(6) 'Gain' and 'loss'—
(a) extend only to gain or loss in money or other property of any kind;
(b) include such gain or loss whether temporary or permanent.
(7) 'Gain' includes a gain by keeping what one has, as well as a gain by getting what one does not have.
(8) 'Loss' includes a loss by not getting what one might get, as well as a loss by parting with what one has.
(9) In proceedings brought against any person ('D') for an offence under subsection (1) it is a defence for D to show—
(a) to the extent that the offence results from subsection (2), that D reasonably believed that D's conduct would not create an impression that was false or misleading as to the matters mentioned in subsection (1),
(b) that D acted or engaged in the conduct—
(i) for the purpose of stabilising the price of investments, and
(ii) in conformity with price stabilising rules,
(c) that D acted or engaged in the conduct in conformity with control of information rules, or
(d) that D acted or engaged in the conduct in conformity with the relevant provisions of Article 5 (exemption for buy-back programmes and stabilisation) of the market abuse regulation.
(10) This section does not apply unless—
(a) the act is done, or the course of conduct is engaged in, in the United Kingdom, or
(b) the false or misleading impression is created there.
(11) See section 137Q(3) of FSMA 2000 regarding the power of the FCA to make rules for the purposes of subsection (9)(d).

91.—(1) A person ('A') who makes to another person ('B') a false or misleading statement commits an offence if—
(a) A makes the statement in the course of arrangements for the setting of a relevant benchmark,
(b) A intends that the statement should be used by B for the purpose of the setting of a relevant benchmark, and
(c) A knows that the statement is false or misleading or is reckless as to whether it is.

(2) A person ('C') who does any act or engages in any course of conduct which creates a false or misleading impression as to the price or value of any investment or as to the interest rate appropriate to any transaction commits an offence if—
(a) C intends to create the impression,
(b) the impression may affect the setting of a relevant benchmark,
(c) C knows that the impression is false or misleading or is reckless as to whether it is, and
(d) C knows that the impression may affect the setting of a relevant benchmark.
(3) In proceedings for an offence under subsection (1), it is a defence for the person charged ('D') to show that the statement was made in conformity with —
(a) [repealed,]
(b) control of information rules, or
(c) the relevant provisions of Article 5 (exemption for buy-back programmes and stabilisation) of the market abuse regulation.
(4) In proceedings brought against any person ('D') for an offence under subsection (2) it is a defence for D to show—
(a) that D acted or engaged in the conduct—
(i) for the purpose of stabilising the price of investments, and
(ii) in conformity with price stabilising rules,
(b) that D acted or engaged in the conduct in conformity with control of information rules, or
(c) that D acted or engaged in the conduct in conformity with the relevant provisions of Article 5 (exemption for buy-back programmes and stabilisation) of the market abuse regulation.
(5) Subsection (1) does not apply unless the statement is made in or from the United Kingdom or to a person in the United Kingdom.
(6) Subsection (2) does not apply unless—
(a) the act is done, or the course of conduct is engaged in, in the United Kingdom, or
(b) the false or misleading impression is created there.
(7) See section 137Q(3) of FSMA 2000 regarding the power of the FCA to make rules for the purposes of subsection (4)(c).

...

93.—(1) This section has effect for the interpretation of this part.
(2) 'Investment' includes any asset, right or interest.
(3) 'Relevant agreement' means an agreement—
(a) the entering into or performance of which by either party constitutes an activity of a kind specified in an order made by the Treasury, and
(b) which relates to a relevant investment.
(4) 'Relevant benchmark' means a benchmark of a kind specified in an order made by the Treasury.
(5) 'Relevant investment' means an investment of a kind specified in an order made by the Treasury.
(6) Schedule 2 to FSMA 2000 (except paragraphs 25 and 26) applies for the purposes of subsections (3) and (5) with references to section 22 of that Act being read as references to each of those subsections.
(7) Nothing in Schedule 2 to FSMA 2000, as applied by subsection (6), limits the power conferred by subsection (3) or (5).
(8) 'Price stabilising rules' and 'control of information rules' have the same meaning as in FSMA 2000.
(8A) 'Market abuse regulation' means Regulation (EU) No 596/2014 of the European Parliament and of the Council of 16 April 2014 on market abuse (market abuse regulation) and repealing Directive 2003/6/EC of the European Parliament and of the Council and Commission Directives 2003/124/EC, 2003/125/EC and 2004/72/EC.
(8B) References to Article 5 of the market abuse regulation include—
(a) any EU regulation originally made under that Article, which is retained direct EU legislation, and
(b) any subordinate legislation (within the meaning of the Interpretation Act 1978) made under that Article on or after exit day.
(9) In this section 'benchmark' has the meaning given in section 22(6) of FSMA 2000.

Schedule 2 to the FSMA 2000 identifies activities which may be regulated under s. 22 of the Act.

By the FSMA 2000, s. 22(6), 'benchmark' means an index, rate or price that (a) is determined from time to time by reference to the state of the market, (b) is made available to the public (whether free of charge or on payment), and (c) is used for reference for purposes that include one or more of the following: (i) determining the interest payable, or other sums due, under loan agreements or under other contracts relating to investments; (ii) determining the price at which investments may be bought or sold or the value of investments; (iii) measuring the performance of investments.

'Price stabilising rules' means rules made by the FCA under the FSMA 2000, s. 137Q. 'Control of information rules' means rules made by either regulator under s. 137P.

Sentence

B7.26 Offences under the Financial Services Act 2012, ss. 89 to 91, are punishable on indictment by a maximum of seven years' imprisonment and/or a fine; on summary conviction by up to six months' imprisonment and/or an unlimited fine (s. 92).

In *Hayes* [2015] EWCA Crim 1944, [2016] 1 Cr App R (S) 63 (449), a case of conspiracy to defraud by the manipulation of LIBOR (London Interbank Offered Rates), rather than breach of a statutory offence, the Court of Appeal stated (at [98]) that those who act dishonestly in financial markets must receive severe sentences to deter others from criminality that is often hard to detect and has such a damaging effect on markets and the general prosperity of the State. The Court added (at [109]) that conduct involving the fraudulent manipulation of markets would result in severe sentences of considerable length.

In *Von Badlo* [2015] EWCA Crim 1236, a case of making a misleading, false or deceptive statement or forecast, the Court of Appeal said (at [15]–[16]) that judges should consider (i) the degree of recklessness involved; (ii) the financial context in which the statement was made; (iii) the financial consequences of the statement; (iv) the purpose behind the FSMA 2000 of protecting investors by reinforcing openness and transparency; and (v) the personal responsibility of the offender. A sentence of two years' imprisonment following a guilty plea was upheld for recklessly introducing and reassuring investors in a scheme that promised high rewards, but was making heavy losses.

Sections 89 to 91 replaced the FSMA 2000, s. 397, which was also punishable by a maximum of seven years' imprisonment. The following cases were decided under this and previous legislation. In *Feld* [1999] 1 Cr App R (S) 1, sentences totalling six years were approved after a trial for raising in excess of £20 million by false statements relating to the financial position of a company (see also *Chauhan* [2000] 2 Cr App R (S) 230). In *Bailey* [2005] EWCA Crim 3487, [2006] 2 Cr App R (S) 36 (250), offenders were convicted, after a trial, of recklessly (rather than knowingly) making the relevant statement. In light of personal mitigation, sentences were reduced to nine months and 18 months' imprisonment. Similarly, 18 months' imprisonment was upheld in *O'Hanlon* [2007] EWCA Crim 3074, [2008] 2 Cr App R (S) 16 (96), where the misrepresentations had been 'comparatively spontaneous'. In *Hipwell* [2006] EWCA Crim 736, [2006] 2 Cr App R (S) 98 (636) six months' imprisonment was upheld on a financial journalist who had tipped companies in which he had bought shares.

Elements

B7.27 A false or misleading promise must be one which is false or misleading when made (e.g., because the speaker never has any intention or expectation that it will ever be kept). Under previous legislation it was held that material facts include D's present intention (*R (Young) v Central Criminal Court* [2002] EWHC 548 (Admin), [2002] 2 Cr App R 12 (178) at [34]). It is not enough to prove that a promise was broken (cf. *Re Augustus Barnett & Son Ltd* [1986] BCLC 170, discussed at **B7.13**).

Likewise it was held that where several false or misleading statements are alleged, they may be included in a single count (*Linnell* [1969] 3 All ER 849), but the judge must warn the jury that they cannot convict merely because some jurors are satisfied as to the falsity of one statement and the others are satisfied as to the falsity of another (*Brown* (1983) 79 Cr App R 115: see **D18.44**).

Other Financial Services Offences

B7.28 Other offences created by the FSMA 2000 are listed in the table below. As with most of the Companies Acts offences (see B7.2), offences that are punishable on indictment with imprisonment carry a maximum term of imprisonment of two years.

Section	General nature of offence	Mode of prosecution	Punishment
55P(10)	Releasing or dealing with trust assets subject to an assets requirement without the consent of a regulator	Summary	An unlimited fine
56(4)	Breach of a prohibition order	Summary	An unlimited fine
85(3)	Dealing in transferable securities without an approved prospectus	1. On indictment 2. Summary	2 years and/or a fine; 3 months and/or an unlimited fine
131L(3)	Breach of short selling regulation	1. On indictment 2. Summary	2 years and/or a fine 3 months and/or an unlimited fine
133B(2)(a)	Refusal to attend tribunal or to give evidence	Summary	An unlimited fine
133B(2)(b)	Alter, suppress, conceal, destroy or refuse to produce a document for tribunal proceedings	1. On indictment 2. Summary	2 years and/or a fine 3 months and/or an unlimited fine
177(3)	Falsify, conceal, destroy or dispose of a document relevant to an investigation under Part XI	1. On indictment 2. Summary	2 years and/or a fine; 6 months and/or an unlimited fine
177(4)	Provide false or misleading information in connection with an investigation	1. On indictment 2. Summary	2 years and/or a fine; 6 months and/or an unlimited fine
177(6)	Obstruction of entry and search warrant in connection with an investigation	Summary	3 months and/or an unlimited fine
191F(1)	Failure to comply with an obligation to notify a regulator of change in control of a UK authorised person	1. On indictment 2. Summary	A fine An unlimited fine
191F(2)	Acquisition before the expiry of an assessment period	1. On indictment 2. Summary	A fine An unlimited fine
191F(3)	Contravention of a condition in a warning or decision notice	1. On indictment 2. Summary	A fine An unlimited fine
191F(4)	Acquisition in contravention of a notice	1. On indictment 2. Summary	2 years and/or a fine An unlimited fine
191F(4A)	Failure to comply with a direction given by the Bank of England	1. On indictment 2. Summary	2 years and/or a fine; An unlimited fine
191F(5)	Acquisition after approval ceased to be effective	1. On indictment 2. Summary	A fine An unlimited fine
191F(6)	Providing false information to a regulator	1. On indictment 2. Summary	A fine An unlimited fine
191F(7)	Breach of a direction in a restriction notice	1. On indictment 2. Summary	A fine An unlimited fine
301L(1)	Failure to comply with an obligation to notify the FCA of acquisition or increased control over a recognised investment exchange	1. On indictment 2. Summary	A fine An unlimited fine
301L(2)	Acquisition before the expiry of an assessment period	1. On indictment 2. Summary	A fine An unlimited fine

Section	General nature of offence	Mode of prosecution	Punishment
301L(3)	Acquisition in contravention of a notice	1. On indictment 2. Summary	2 years and/or a fine; 3 months and/or an unlimited fine
301L(4)	Acquisition after approval ceased to be effective	1. On indictment 2. Summary	A fine An unlimited fine
301L(5)	Providing false information to a regulator	1. On indictment 2. Summary	An unlimited fine An unlimited fine
301L(6)	Breach of a direction in a restriction notice	1. On indictment 2. Summary	A fine An unlimited fine
346(1)	Provision of false or misleading information to an auditor or actuary	1. On indictment 2. Summary	2 years and/or a fine; 6 months and/or an unlimited fine
352(1)	Disclosure of confidential information	1. On indictment 2. Summary	2 years and/or a fine; 3 months and/or an unlimited fine
352(3) & (4)	Use of confidential information in contravention of regulations or s. 350(4)	Summary	3 months and/or an unlimited fine
366(2)	Failure to notify the PRA of resolution to wind up voluntarily insurer of long term contracts of insurance	Summary	An unlimited fine
398(1)	Misleading the FCA or PRA	1. On indictment 2. Summary	A fine An unlimited fine
399	Misleading the Competition and Markets Authority	1. On indictment 2. Summary	A fine An unlimited fine

INSIDER DEALING

Part V of the Criminal Justice Act 1993 contains the offence of insider dealing. The offence is set out in s. 52 and is subject to defences set out in s. 53, which refers to further special defences set out in sch. 1. Section 62 contains territorial limits to the scope of the offence, linking it to the UK. **B7.29**

This is a complex area of law. For a full explanation and discussion readers are referred to S Clarke, *Insider Dealing Law and Practice* (2nd edn, 2019). The Supreme Court has decided that, where two people conspire to commit an offence of insider dealing, and pursuant to their agreement one transfers money to the other for the purchase of shares, but the purchase does not take place, that payment is recoverable by the payer in civil proceedings (*Patel v Mirza* [2016] UKSC 42, [2017] AC 467).

Criminal Justice Act 1993, ss. 52 and 53 **B7.30**

52.—(1) An individual who has information as an insider is guilty of insider dealing if, in the circumstances mentioned in subsection (3), he deals in securities that are price-affected securities in relation to the information.

(2) An individual who has information as an insider is also guilty of insider dealing if—

(a) he encourages another person to deal in securities that are (whether or not that other knows it) price-affected securities in relation to the information, knowing or having reasonable cause to believe that the dealing would take place in the circumstances mentioned in subsection (3); or

(b) he discloses the information, otherwise than in the proper performance of the functions of his employment, office or profession, to another person.

(3) The circumstances referred to above are that the acquisition or disposal in question occurs on a regulated market, or that the person dealing relies on a professional intermediary or is himself acting as a professional intermediary.

(4) This section has effect subject to section 53.

53.—(1) An individual is not guilty of insider dealing by virtue of dealing in securities if he shows—
(a) that he did not at the time expect the dealing to result in a profit attributable to the fact that the information in question was price-sensitive information in relation to the securities, or
(b) that at the time he believed on reasonable grounds that the information had been disclosed widely enough to ensure that none of those taking part in the dealing would be prejudiced by not having the information, or
(c) that he would have done what he did even if he had not had the information.

(2) An individual is not guilty of insider dealing by virtue of encouraging another person to deal in securities if he shows—
(a) that he did not at the time expect the dealing to result in a profit attributable to the fact that the information in question was price-sensitive information in relation to the securities, or
(b) that at the time he believed on reasonable grounds that the information had been or would be disclosed widely enough to ensure that none of those taking part in the dealing would be prejudiced by not having the information, or
(c) that he would have done what he did even if he had not had the information.

(3) An individual is not guilty of insider dealing by virtue of a disclosure of information if he shows—
(a) that he did not at the time expect any person, because of the disclosure, to deal in securities in the circumstances mentioned in subsection (3) of section 52; or
(b) that, although he had such an expectation at the time, he did not expect the dealing to result in a profit attributable to the fact that the information was price-sensitive information in relation to the securities.

...

(6) In this section references to a profit include references to the avoidance of a loss.

Section 52 does not apply to anything done by an individual acting on behalf of a public sector body in pursuit of monetary policies or policies with respect to exchange rates or the management of public debt or foreign exchange reserves (s. 63(1)).

Procedure

B7.31 The offence is triable either way (CJA 1993, s. 61(1)). Proceedings cannot be instituted except by or with the consent of the Secretary of State or the DPP (s. 61(2)). The FCA has power to prosecute an offence under s. 52 (FSMA 2000, s. 402(1), and see *Rollins* [2010] UKSC 39, [2010] 4 All ER 880).

Summary proceedings may be brought against an individual at any place at which the individual is for the time being (s. 61A(1)). If tried summarily, the information must be laid within three years after the commission of the offence and within 12 months after the date on which evidence sufficient in the opinion of the DPP or the Secretary of State (as the case may be) to justify the proceedings comes to that person's knowledge (s. 61A(2)).

Sentence

B7.32 When tried on indictment the maximum penalty is seven years' imprisonment and/or a fine. When tried summarily, the maximum penalty is six months and/or an unlimited fine (CJA 1993, s. 61(1)).

In *McQuoid* [2009] EWCA Crim 1301, [2010] 1 Cr App R(S) 43 (269) at [14] the Court of Appeal stated that the sentencing considerations for insider dealing are (1) the nature of D's employment or retainer, or involvement in the arrangements which enabled D to participate in the insider dealing of which D is guilty; (2) the circumstances in which D came into possession of confidential information and the use D made of it; (3) whether D behaved recklessly or acted deliberately, and almost inevitably therefore, dishonestly; (4) the level of planning and sophistication involved in the activity, as well as the period of trading and the number of individual trades; (5) whether D acted alone or with others and, if so, D's relative culpability; (6) the amount of anticipated or intended financial benefit or loss avoided, as well as the actual benefit or loss avoided; (7) although the absence of any identified victim is not normally a matter going to mitigation, the impact, if any, on any individual victim; (8) the impact of the offence on overall confidence in the integrity of the market; because of its impact on public confidence, an offence committed jointly by more than one person trusted with confidential information will be more damaging to public confidence than an offence committed in isolation by one person acting alone; (9) age and a guilty plea; (10) good character, but it is often the case that a person is trusted with confidential information because that person is of good character and by misusing the information that trust has been breached. The Court added that valuable assistance was also to be found in the Sentencing Council's then guideline on *Theft in Breach of Trust* under ch. E. Theft in breach of trust is now included under General Theft in the current Sentencing Council guideline, *Theft Offences* (see Supplement, **SG33-2**).

In *Butt* [2006] EWCA Crim 137, [2006] 2 Cr App R (S) 44 (295) D was the compliance officer at an investment bank who originated, and (with others) ran over a three-year period a scheme based on inside information which produced a profit of £287,000. The Court of Appeal reduced D's sentence for conspiracy to commit insider dealing from five years' imprisonment to four years.

Elements

Sections 54 to 60 of the CJA 1993 contain definitions of the terms used in ss. 52 and 53. **B7.33**
'Securities' to which the provisions apply are defined in sch. 2. In summary, they consist of shares, debt securities, warrants, depositary receipts, options, futures and contracts for differences. 'Dealing' is defined in s. 55 and, again in summary, involves acquisition or disposal. Sections 56 and 57 define 'inside information' and 'insiders'.

Criminal Justice Act 1993, ss. 56 and 57 **B7.34**

56.—(1) For the purposes of this section and section 57, 'inside information' means information which—

(a) relates to particular securities or to a particular issuer of securities or to particular issuers of securities and not to securities generally or to issuers of securities generally;
(b) is specific or precise;
(c) has not been made public; and
(d) if it were made public would be likely to have a significant effect on the price of any securities.

(2) For the purposes of this Part, securities are 'price-affected securities' in relation to inside information, and inside information is 'price-sensitive information' in relation to securities, if and only if the information would, if made public, be likely to have a significant effect on the price of the securities.

(3) For the purposes of this section 'price' includes value.

57.—(1) For the purposes of this Part, a person has information as an insider if and only if—

(a) it is, and he knows that it is, inside information, and
(b) he has it, and knows that he has it, from an inside source.

(2) For the purposes of subsection (1), a person has information from an inside source if and only if—

(a) he has it through—
  (i) being a director, employee or shareholder of an issuer of securities; or
  (ii) having access to the information by virtue of his employment, office or profession; or
(b) the direct or indirect source of his information is a person within paragraph (a).

Section 58 contains a non-exhaustive definition of 'made public' and s. 59 defines 'professional intermediary'.

Defences

In addition to the defences provided by the CJA 1993, s. 53(1) to (3) (see **B7.30**), sch. 1 to the **B7.35**
Act provides special defences relating to market makers (para. 1), market information (paras. 2 to 4) and price stabilisation (para. 5).

THE CARTEL OFFENCE

B7.36 At common law price fixing was not an offence (*Norris v Government of the USA* [2008] UKHL 16, [2008] 1 AC 920). Sections 188 to 189 of the Enterprise Act 2002, as amended by the Enterprise and Regulatory Reform Act 2013, s. 47, create a cartel offence, aimed at arrangements between undertakings which affect the price, supply or production of products or services in the UK. The amendments removed the requirement for the prosecution to prove dishonesty. But no offence is committed if the arrangement is not concealed from customers or the Competition and Markets Authority.

As with revenue and customs offences (see **B16.2**), this criminal sanction co-exists with civil remedies and sanctions, particularly those under the Competition Act 1998.

B7.37 **Enterprise Act 2002, ss. 188 to 189**

188.—(1) An individual is guilty of an offence if he agrees with one or more other persons to make or implement, or to cause to be made or implemented, arrangements of the following kind relating to at least two undertakings (A and B).

(2) The arrangements must be ones which, if operating as the parties to the agreement intend, would—

(a) directly or indirectly fix a price for the supply by A in the United Kingdom (otherwise than to B) of a product or service,

(b) limit or prevent supply by A in the United Kingdom of a product or service,

(c) limit or prevent production by A in the United Kingdom of a product,

(d) divide between A and B the supply in the United Kingdom of a product or service to a customer or customers,

(e) divide between A and B customers for the supply in the United Kingdom of a product or service, or

(f) be bid-rigging arrangements.

(3) Unless subsection (2)(d), (e) or (f) applies, the arrangements must also be ones which, if operating as the parties to the agreement intend, would—

(a) directly or indirectly fix a price for the supply by B in the United Kingdom (otherwise than to A) of a product or service,

(b) limit or prevent supply by B in the United Kingdom of a product or service, or

(c) limit or prevent production by B in the United Kingdom of a product.

(4) In subsections (2)(a) to (d) and (3), references to supply or production are to supply or production in the appropriate circumstances (for which see section 189).

(5) 'Bid-rigging arrangements' are arrangements under which, in response to a request for bids for the supply of a product or service in the United Kingdom, or for the production of a product in the United Kingdom—

(a) A but not B may make a bid, or

(b) A and B may each make a bid but, in one case or both, only a bid arrived at in accordance with the arrangements.

(6) [Repealed.]

(7) 'Undertaking' has the same meaning as in Part 1 of the Competition Act 1998.

(8) This section is subject to section 188A.

188A.—(1) An individual does not commit an offence under section 188(1) if, under the arrangements—

(a) in a case where the arrangements would (operating as the parties intend) affect the supply in the United Kingdom of a product or service, customers would be given relevant information about the arrangements before they enter into agreements for the supply to them of the product or service so affected,

(b) in the case of bid-rigging arrangements, the person requesting bids would be given relevant information about them at or before the time when a bid is made, or

(c) in any case, relevant information about the arrangements would be published, before the arrangements are implemented, in the manner specified at the time of the making of the agreement in an order made by the Secretary of State.

(2) In subsection (1), 'relevant information' means—

(a) the names of the undertakings to which the arrangements relate,

(b) a description of the nature of the arrangements which is sufficient to show why they are or might be arrangements of the kind to which section 188(1) applies,
(c) the products or services to which they relate, and
(d) such other information as may be specified in an order made by the Secretary of State.

(3) An individual does not commit an offence under section 188(1) if the agreement is made in order to comply with a legal requirement.
(4) In subsection (3), 'legal requirement' has the same meaning as in paragraph 5 of Schedule 3 to the Competition Act 1998.
(5) and (6) [Order-making powers and procedure.]

188B.—(1) In a case where the arrangements would (operating as the parties intend) affect the supply in the United Kingdom of a product or service, it is a defence for an individual charged with an offence under section 188(1) to show that, at the time of the making of the agreement, he or she did not intend that the nature of the arrangements would be concealed from customers at all times before they enter into agreements for the supply to them of the product or service.
(2) It is a defence for an individual charged with an offence under section 188(1) to show that, at the time of the making of the agreement, he or she did not intend that the nature of the arrangements would be concealed from the Competition and Markets Authority.
(3) It is a defence for an individual charged with an offence under section 188(1) to show that, before the making of the agreement, he or she took reasonable steps to ensure that the nature of the arrangements would be disclosed to professional legal advisers for the purposes of obtaining advice about them before their making or (as the case may be) their implementation.

189.—(1) For section 188(2)(a), the appropriate circumstances are that A's supply of the product or service would be at a level in the supply chain at which the product or service would at the same time be supplied by B in the United Kingdom.
(2) For section 188(2)(b), the appropriate circumstances are that A's supply of the product or service would be at a level in the supply chain—
(a) at which the product or service would at the same time be supplied by B in the United Kingdom, or
(b) at which supply by B in the United Kingdom of the product or service would be limited or prevented by the arrangements.

(3) For section 188(2)(c), the appropriate circumstances are that A's production of the product would be at a level in the production chain—
(a) at which the product would at the same time be produced by B in the United Kingdom, or
(b) at which production by B in the United Kingdom of the product would be limited or prevented by the arrangements.

(4) For section 188(2)(d), the appropriate circumstances are that A's supply of the product or service would be at the same level in the supply chain as B's.
(5) For section 188(3)(a), the appropriate circumstances are that B's supply of the product or service would be at a level in the supply chain at which the product or service would at the same time be supplied by A in the United Kingdom.
(6) For section 188(3)(b), the appropriate circumstances are that B's supply of the product or service would be at a level in the supply chain—
(a) at which the product or service would at the same time be supplied by A in the United Kingdom, or
(b) at which supply by A in the United Kingdom of the product or service would be limited or prevented by the arrangements.

(7) For section 188(3)(c), the appropriate circumstances are that B's production of the product would be at a level in the production chain—
(a) at which the product would at the same time be produced by A in the United Kingdom, or
(b) at which production by A in the United Kingdom of the product would be limited or prevented by the arrangements.

Procedure

The offence is triable either way (Enterprise Act 2002, s. 190(1)). Proceedings may be instituted **B7.38**
only by the Director of the SFO or by or with the consent of the Competition and Markets Authority (s. 190(2)). No proceedings can be brought in respect of an agreement outside

the UK, unless it has been implemented in whole or in part in the UK (s. 190(3)). In order to encourage co-operation and admissions, s. 190(4) enables the Competition and Markets Authority to give a written notice that no proceedings will be taken for an offence under s. 188.

In *B* [2009] EWCA Crim 2575, [2010] 1 Cr App R 16 (181) the jurisdiction of the Crown Court to try an indictment alleging an offence under s. 188 was unsuccessfully challenged as contrary to EU law.

Sentence

B7.39 When tried on indictment the maximum penalty is five years' imprisonment and/or a fine. When tried summarily the maximum penalty is six months and/or an unlimited fine (Enterprise Act 2002, s. 190(1)(a)).

INSOLVENCY OFFENCES: GENERAL

B7.40 The legislation relating to personal and corporate insolvency is contained in the Insolvency Act 1986, a consolidating Act, but with subsequent amendments. The principal offences under the Act are contained in Part IV, ch. X (in relation to company insolvency), and Part IX, ch. VI (in respect of bankruptcy of individuals). Six offences were created by the Insolvency (England and Wales) Rules 2016 (SI 2016 No. 1024). These are listed in sch. 3 to the Rules.

The scale, complexity and specialised subject-matter of this legislation again precludes comprehensive coverage of its offences within a general work on criminal law. This section accordingly covers only the principal offences.

Penalties

B7.41 Penalties for offences under the Insolvency Act 1986, together with brief descriptions of the offences and details of modes of trial, are set out in sch. 10. The more serious offences, punishable with imprisonment, are listed at **B7.75**.

OFFENCES CONCERNING COMPANY INSOLVENCY AND LIQUIDATION

Procedure in Summary Proceedings

B7.42 **Insolvency Act 1986, s. 431**

(1) Summary proceedings for any offence under any of Parts I to VII of this Act may (without prejudice to any jurisdiction exercisable apart from this subsection) be taken against a body corporate at any place at which the body has a place of business, and against any other person at any place at which he is for the time being.

(2) Notwithstanding anything in section 127(1) of the Magistrates' Courts Act 1980, an information relating to such an offence which is triable by a magistrates' court in England and Wales may be so tried if it is laid at any time within 3 years after the commission of the offence and within 12 months after the date on which evidence sufficient in the opinion of the Director of Public Prosecutions or the Secretary of State (as the case may be) to justify the proceedings comes to his knowledge.

(3) [Applies only to Scotland.]

(4) For purposes of this section, a certificate of the Director of Public Prosecutions, the Lord Advocate or the Secretary of State (as the case may be) as to the date on which such evidence as is referred to above came to his knowledge is conclusive evidence.

The court is not entitled to go behind the face of a certificate under the Insolvency Act 1986, s. 431(4) (*Roberts v Procurator Fiscal, Kilmarnock* [2019] SAC (Crim) 10). But see *R (Chesterfield Poultry Ltd) v Sheffield Magistrates' Court* [2019] EWHC 2953 (Admin), [2020] 1 Cr App R 26 (419) (at **B16.64**) for the limited circumstances in which such a certificate might be challenged.

Insolvency and Winding Up

A company can be wound up by an order of the High Court or (if its paid up share capital does not exceed £120,000) by an order of the county court (Insolvency Act 1986, s. 117). This is called a compulsory winding up. A company can also be wound up voluntarily if the company passes a resolution for voluntary winding up under s. 84. A company that is being wound up is referred to as being in liquidation. Companies in liquidation are not always insolvent, and the offences contained within the Insolvency Act 1986 are often capable of applying to the winding up of solvent companies. In practice, however, prosecutions under the Act usually concern the winding up of insolvent companies. **B7.43**

The date at which winding up commences can be crucial to the application of the relevant law. This is because some offences, e.g. under the Insolvency Act 1986, s. 206 (see **B7.45**), are defined by reference to events occurring within the 12 months immediately preceding the commencement of the winding up (*Druzyc* [2019] EWCA Crim 1076). A voluntary winding up commences when the resolution for winding up is passed by the company (s. 86) and, under s. 129, this remains the relevant date even when a winding-up order is later made in respect of that company. In compulsory winding up, the relevant date is the date on which the winding-up petition was presented (s. 129(2)).

As an alternative to being wound up, a company may seek to enter into a voluntary arrangement with its creditors under Part I of the Insolvency Act 1986. For the offence of fraud in connection with such an arrangement, see **B7.72** and **B7.75**.

As to the application of the Insolvency Act 1986 to limited liability partnerships, see the Limited Liability Partnerships Regulations 2001 (SI 2001 No. 1090), reg. 5.

False Declarations of Solvency in Voluntary Liquidations

Insolvency Act 1986, s. 89 **B7.44**

(1) Where it is proposed to wind up a company voluntarily, the directors (or, in the case of a company having more than two directors, the majority of them) may at a directors' meeting make a statutory declaration to the effect that they have made a full inquiry into the company's affairs and that, having done so, they have formed the opinion that the company will be able to pay its debts in full, together with interest at the official rate (as defined in section 251), within such period, not exceeding 12 months from the commencement of the winding up, as may be specified in the declaration

...

(4) A director making a declaration under this section without having reasonable grounds for the opinion that the company will be able to pay its debts in full, together with interest at the official rate, within the period specified is liable to imprisonment or a fine, or both.

(5) If the company is wound up in pursuance of a resolution passed within 5 weeks after the making of the declaration, and its debts (together with interest at the official rate) are not paid or provided for in full within the period specified, it is to be presumed (unless the contrary is shown) that the director did not have reasonable grounds for his opinion.

Section 89 also applies, subject to modifications, to friendly societies (Friendly Societies Act 1992, s. 23 and sch. 10).

For procedural provisions, see **B7.42**; for sentencing provisions, see **B7.75** and **B7.76**.

The importance of the declaration is that it determines whether the winding up will be a members' voluntary winding up or a creditors' voluntary winding up (s. 90). In the latter, the company has to call a creditors' meeting (s. 98) and the creditors' nomination of the liquidator takes precedence over the members' nomination (s. 100).

In a creditors' voluntary winding up it is an offence under s. 166, punishable by a fine, for any liquidator nominated by the members to dispose of company property (except perishables and other goods likely to diminish in value) unless and until the liquidator's status is confirmed by a creditors' meeting. This prohibits the once prevalent practice of selling assets of insolvent companies to directors or others associated with the company at knock-down prices without the creditors being warned or consulted (This was known, in the jargon of company lawyers, as 'centrebinding' after the case of *Re Centrebind Ltd* [1967] 3 All ER 889, in which it was held that the members' nomination of a liquidator was effective.)

Fraud etc. in Anticipation of Winding Up

B7.45 Insolvency Act 1986, s. 206

(1) When a company is ordered to be wound up by the court, or passes a resolution for voluntary winding up, any person, being a past or present officer of the company, is deemed to have committed an offence if, within the 12 months immediately preceding the commencement of the winding up, he has—
- (a) concealed any part of the company's property to the value of £500 or more, or concealed any debt due to or from the company, or
- (b) fraudulently removed any part of the company's property to the value of £500 or more, or
- (c) concealed, destroyed, mutilated or falsified any book or paper affecting or relating to the company's property or affairs, or
- (d) made any false entry in any book or paper affecting or relating to the company's property or affairs, or
- (e) fraudulently parted with, altered or made any omission in any document affecting or relating to the company's property or affairs, or
- (f) pawned, pledged or disposed of any property of the company which has been obtained on credit and has not been paid for (unless the pawning, pledging or disposal was in the ordinary way of the company's business).

(2) Such a person is deemed to have committed an offence if within the period above mentioned he has been privy to the doing by others of any of the things mentioned in paragraphs (c), (d) and (e) of subsection (1); and he commits an offence if, at any time after the commencement of the winding up, he does any of the things mentioned in paragraph (a) to (f) of that subsection, or is privy to the doing by others of any of the things mentioned in paragraphs (c) to (e) of it.

(3) For purposes of this section, 'officer' includes a shadow director.

(4) It is a defence—
- (a) for a person charged under paragraph (a) or (f) of subsection (1) (or under subsection (2) in respect of the things mentioned in either of those two paragraphs) to prove that he had no intent to defraud, and
- (b) for a person charged under paragraph (c) or (d) of subsection (1) (or under subsection (2) in respect of the things mentioned in either of those two paragraphs) to prove that he had no intent to conceal the state of affairs of the company or to defeat the law.

(5) Where a person pawns, pledges or disposes of any property in circumstances which amount to an offence under subsection (1)(f), every person who takes in pawn or pledge, or otherwise receives, the property knowing it to be pawned, pledged or disposed of in such circumstances, is guilty of an offence.

For procedural provisions, see **B7.42**; for sentencing provisions, see **B7.75** and **B7.76**.

Fraud is a definitional element in the offences under s. 206(1)(b) and (e), and must therefore be proved by the prosecution. In the case of other offences under s. 206(1), liability is strict, unless D is able to rely on the defence provided by s. 206(4). The burden placed on D under this provision is the full persuasive burden. This does not infringe the ECHR, Article 6 (*A-G's Ref (No. 1 of 2004)* [2004] EWCA Crim 1025, [2004] 4 All ER 457 at [83]–[84] and *Sheldrake v DPP* [2004] UKHL 43, [2005] 1 AC 624 at [32]: see **F3.26** and **F3.27**).

The words 'book or paper' in s. 206(1)(d) include records kept on computer (*Taylor* [2011] EWCA Crim 728, [2011] 1 WLR 1809). By s. 251, 'books or papers' include writing and, by s. 436B, a thing in writing includes that thing in electronic form.

The combined effect of s. 206(1) and (2) is that offences can be committed before or after commencement of winding up. Offences under s. 206(1)(c) to (e) can be committed by officers who are 'privy' to the acts of others; these others need not themselves be officers nor need they be *guilty of any offence.*

Subsections (1) and (2) create separate offences; a charge cannot be brought under s. 206(1) in respect of things done after the commencement of the winding up. As the wording of that subsection makes clear, it penalises acts done within the 12 months immediately preceding the commencement of the winding up (see *Druzyc* [2019] EWCA Crim 1076 at **B7.43** for the importance of identifying correctly when the winding up commenced).

Fraudulent Conduct and Intent to Defraud References to fraudulent conduct in the Insolvency Act 1986, s. 206(1), and to 'intent to defraud' in s. 206(4)(a), must be concerned with the same concept (for further discussion of this in the context of fraudulent trading, see **B7.12**). It must, in other words, involve dishonesty, but need not involve deceit. **B7.46**

Receipt of Property Disposed of Contrary to s. 206(1)(f) etc. The wording of the Insolvency Act 1986, s. 206(5), seems open to two possible interpretations. One possibility is that the recipient need know only of the circumstances specified in s. 206(1)(f), and that knowledge of whether the person disposing of the property could establish a defence under s. 206(4) is irrelevant; fraud is not, after all, a definitional element in an offence under s. 206(1)(f). The other possibility is that the prosecution must prove the recipient's knowledge of the disposer's guilt, and that that guilt arises only where the disposer is unable to prove a defence under s. 206(4); the recipient would therefore need to know that no such defence could be established (in other words, the recipient must be shown to know that the disposer is acting fraudulently). It is submitted that the latter interpretation is the correct one; the former could lead to cases in which the recipient is convicted despite the acquittal of the disposer and would be in marked contrast to the position under the corresponding bankruptcy provision (Insolvency Act 1986, s. 359 — see **B7.66**). In contrast, there is nothing illogical in a rule under which conviction of the disposer is made easier than conviction of the recipient. **B7.47**

For the approach to disposal otherwise than in the ordinary course of business, see *Countrywide Banking Corporation Ltd v Dean* [1998] AC 338. A transfer of all property to a close relative is clearly not in the ordinary course of business (*Thomas* (1870) 22 LT 138).

Transactions in Fraud of Creditors

Insolvency Act 1986, s. 207 **B7.48**

(1) When a company is ordered to be wound up by the court or passes a resolution for voluntary winding up, a person is deemed to have committed an offence if he, being at the time an officer of the company—
  (a) has made or caused to be made any gift or transfer of, or charge on, or has caused or connived at the levying of any execution against, the company's property, or
  (b) has concealed or removed any part of the company's property since, or within 2 months before, the date of any unsatisfied judgment or order for the payment of money obtained against the company.

(2) A person is not guilty of an offence under this section—
  (a) by reason of conduct constituting an offence under subsection (1)(a) which occurred more than 5 years before the commencement of the winding up, or
  (b) if he proves that, at the time of the conduct constituting the offence, he had no intent to defraud the company's creditors.

For procedural provisions, see **B7.42**; for sentencing provisions, see **B7.75** and **B7.76**.

Although s. 207(1)(a) is widely expressed, its effect is heavily curtailed by s. 207(2). Because of the decision of the Court of Appeal on the similarly worded bankruptcy provision, s. 357 (see **B7.64**), the burden placed on D under s. 207(2)(b) would appear to be merely an evidential burden (*A-G's Ref (No. 1 of 2004)* [2004] EWCA Crim 1025, [2004] 4 All ER 457 at [85]–[92] and see **F3.26**).

It would seem that 'creditors' should be given the same meaning in s. 207(2)(b) as in the similar wording in the Companies Act 2006, s. 993 (see **B7.13**). Old authority under the Debtors Act 1869, s. 13 (see **B7.64**), to the effect that any intent to defraud creditors must refer to creditors at the time of the action concerned (*Hopkins* [1896] 1 QB 652) seems doubtful on principle. It would produce very unsatisfactory results where the company has a long-term debt problem, but a series of short-term creditors. More recent case law, particularly *Seillon* [1982] Crim LR 676, *Kemp* [1988] QB 645 and *Smith (Wallace Duncan)* [1996] 2 Cr App R 1, supports a wider interpretation.

A person 'causes' a thing to be done when the person orders or directs it to be done (*Houston v Buchanan* [1940] 2 All ER 179).

Misconduct in the Course of Winding Up

B7.49 **Insolvency Act 1986, s. 208**

(1) When a company is being wound up, whether by the court or voluntarily, any person, being a past or present officer of the company, commits an offence if he—
  (a) does not to the best of his knowledge and belief fully and truly discover to the liquidator all the company's property, and how and to whom and for what consideration and when the company disposed of any part of that property (except such part as has been disposed of in the ordinary way of the company's business), or
  (b) does not deliver up to the liquidator (or as he directs) all such part of the company's property as is in his custody or under his control, and which he is required by law to deliver up, or
  (c) does not deliver up to the liquidator (or as he directs) all books and papers in his custody or under his control belonging to the company and which he is required by law to deliver up, or
  (d) knowing or believing that a false debt has been proved by any person in the winding up, fails to inform the liquidator as soon as practicable, or
  (e) after the commencement of the winding up, prevents the production of any book or paper affecting or relating to the company's property or affairs.

(2) Such a person commits an offence if after the commencement of the winding up he attempts to account for any part of the company's property by fictitious losses or expenses; and he is deemed to have committed that offence if he has so attempted in connection with any qualifying decision procedure or deemed consent procedure of the company's creditors within the 12 months immediately preceding the commencement of the winding up.

(3) For the purposes of this section, 'officer' includes a shadow director.

(4) It is a defence—
  (a) for a person charged under paragraph (a), (b) or (c) of subsection (1) to prove that he had no intent to defraud, and
  (b) for a person charged under paragraph (e) of that subsection to prove that he had no intent to conceal the state of affairs of the company or to defeat the law.

In s. 208(2) the words 'in connection with any qualifying decision procedure or deemed consent procedure' replaced the words 'at any meeting' with effect from 6 April 2017 (Small Business, Enterprise and Employment Act 2015, sch. 9, para. 52, and SI 2016 No. 1020, reg. 4(e)). Provisions requiring meetings were replaced by more flexible procedures in ss. 246ZE and 246ZF of the Insolvency Act 1986 from that date.

For procedural provisions, see **B7.42**; for sentencing provisions, see **B7.75** and **B7.76**.

This is an important section, because the reason for appointing the liquidator is to ensure that the winding up is conducted by an independent person. That purpose would be defeated if the liquidator was unable to obtain access to, and control of, the company's property and records. The burden imposed on the defence by s. 208(4) is the full persuasive burden of proof (*R (Griffin) v Richmond Magistrates' Court* [2008] EWHC 84 (Admin), [2008] 3 All ER 274 and **F3.27**).

It is not necessary for the liquidator to have demanded the specific property in question. There is accordingly a continuing duty to disclose and deliver any valuable items of which the liquidator may be unaware (*McCredie* [2000] BCC 617). In *McCredie* the words 'books and papers' in s. 208(1)(c) were treated as including records on floppy disks. This was considered to be correct in *Taylor* [2011] EWCA Crim 728, [2011] 1 WLR 1809 at [24] (see also **B7.45**).

No special defences are available to the offences in s. 208(1)(d) and (2). Under s. 208(2), full and frank disclosure to the liquidator does not excuse previous lies told to creditors, and under s. 208(1)(d) mere hesitation in disclosing a false claim may be sufficient.

Falsification of Company Books

Insolvency Act 1986, s. 209 B7.50

(1) When a company is being wound up, an officer or contributory of the company commits an offence if he destroys, mutilates, alters or falsifies any books, papers or securities, or makes or is privy to the making of any false or fraudulent entry in any register, book of account or document belonging to the company with intent to defraud or deceive any person.

For procedural provisions, see **B7.42**; for sentencing provisions, see **B7.75** and **B7.76**.

Section 209(1) is not clearly worded. It is not clear whether the words 'belonging to the company' govern only the immediately preceding words 'register, book of account or document' or whether they also govern the words 'any books, papers or securities' earlier in the subsection. But the phrase 'with intent to defraud or deceive any person' appears to apply to each of the ways in which the offence can be committed.

The term 'documents' is defined in s. 436 as including computer records and other non-documentary records. This means, for example, that the fraudulent insertion of false entries on a company computer record would be an offence under s. 209(1) if the insertion is made with intent to defraud or deceive.

Material Omissions from Statements Relating to the Company's Affairs

Insolvency Act 1986, s. 210 B7.51

(1) When a company is being wound up, whether by the court or voluntarily, any person, being a past or present officer of the company, commits an offence if he makes any material omission in any statement relating to the company's affairs.
(2) When a company has been ordered to be wound up by the court, or has passed a resolution for voluntary winding up, any such person is deemed to have committed that offence if, prior to the winding up, he has made any material omission in any such statement.
(3) For the purposes of this section, 'officer' includes a shadow director.
(4) It is a defence for a person charged under this section to prove that he had no intent to defraud.

For procedural provisions, see **B7.42**; for sentencing provisions, see **B7.75** and **B7.76**.

The width of this provision is limited by the defence in s. 210(4). Unlike the equivalent provision in respect of bankruptcy (s. 356(1); see **B7.63**), it is not necessary that the material omission be made in a statement under any provision of the Act, such as the statutory statement of affairs under s. 131 in compulsory winding up; any statement, oral or written, would seem to be within its scope, whether made during winding up or prior to it. If a material omission was understandable in the circumstances (as where the statement was informal and unrehearsed), it would be difficult to conclude that there was any intent to defraud.

False Representations to Creditors

Insolvency Act 1986, s. 211 B7.52

(1) When a company is being wound up, whether by the court or voluntarily, any person, being a past or present officer of the company—
   (a) commits an offence if he makes any false representation or commits any other fraud for the purpose of obtaining the consent of the company's creditors or any of them to an agreement with reference to the company's affairs or to the winding up, and
   (b) is deemed to have committed that offence if, prior to the winding up, he has made any false representation, or committed any other fraud, for that purpose.
(2) For purposes of this section, 'officer' includes a shadow director.

For procedural provisions, see **B7.42**; for sentencing provisions, see **B7.75** and **B7.76**.

In view of the fact that s. 211 makes no provision for D to prove that there was no fraudulent intent, and in view of the references to false representations 'or any other fraud', it is submitted that the offence of making false representations should be construed as requiring the prosecution to prove fraud. This interpretation gains some support from *Cherry* (1871) 12 Cox 32, in which it was said (in relation to bankruptcy provisions) that, in this context, 'false' means 'fraudulent'.

Re-use of Company Names

B7.53 **Insolvency Act 1986, s. 216**

(1) This section applies to a person where a company ('the liquidating company') has gone into insolvent liquidation on or after the appointed day and he was a director or shadow director of the company at any time in the period of 12 months ending with the day before it went into liquidation.

(2) For the purposes of this section, a name is a prohibited name in relation to such a person if—
(a) it is a name by which the liquidating company was known at any time in that period of 12 months, or
(b) it is a name which is so similar to a name falling within paragraph (a) as to suggest an association with that company.

(3) Except with leave of the court or in such circumstances as may be prescribed, a person to whom this section applies shall not at any time in the period of 5 years beginning with the day on which the liquidating company went into liquidation—
(a) be a director of any other company that is known by a prohibited name, or
(b) in any way, whether directly or indirectly, be concerned or take part in the promotion, formation or management of any such company, or
(c) in any way, whether directly or indirectly, be concerned or take part in the carrying on of a business carried on (otherwise than by a company) under a prohibited name.

For procedural provisions, see **B7.42**; for sentencing provisions, see **B7.75** and **B7.76**.

Section 216 deals with one aspect of 'Phoenix companies', where companies in insolvent liquidation would re-appear, with almost identical names, businesses and directors, a few months later. The re-born companies would in law be new enterprises, unfettered by the unpaid debts of the previous ones, but would, to outside appearances, be the same as before. For an example, see *R (Griffin) v Richmond Magistrates' Court* [2008] EWHC 84 (Admin), [2008] 3 All ER 274 at [2]–[9]. However, s. 216 is not limited to such cases (*Ricketts v Ad Valorem Factors Ltd* [2003] EWCA Civ 1706, [2004] 1 All ER 894; *First Independent Factors and Finance Ltd v Mountford* [2008] EWHC 835 (Ch), [2008] BCC 598).

The court which may give leave under s. 216(3) is the court having jurisdiction to wind up companies, and a company is regarded as going into insolvent liquidation if its assets are insufficient to meet its liabilities and the expenses of the winding up (s. 216(5) and (7)). Circumstances prescribed as exceptions from the prohibition in s. 216 are set out in Part 22 of the Insolvency Rules 2016. Section 216 does not apply where a partnership (other than a limited liability partnership) has been wound up (*Re Newtons Coaches Ltd* [2016] EWHC 3068 (Ch), [2017] BCC 34). References, in relation to any time, to a name by which a company is known, are to the name of the company at that time or to any name under which the company carries on business at that time (s. 216(6)).

Contravention of s. 216 may involve civil liability under s. 217 as well as the criminal penalties prescribed in sch. 10. The offence created by s. 216 is one of strict liability (*Cole* [1998] BCC 87; *Doring* [2002] EWCA Crim 1695, [2003] 1 Cr App R 9 (143)).

In *Weintroub* [2011] EWCA Crim 2167 the Court of Appeal decided that where directors had traded under a prohibited company name, the amount of benefit they had received for the purposes of the POCA 2002 was the full amount that they had received as directors and not just the proportion of that sum attributable to the prohibited name. See also *Neuberg (No. 2)* [2016] EWCA Crim 1927, [2017] 4 WLR 58.

Offence in Relation to Inspection of Documents

B7.54 **Insolvency (England and Wales) Rules 2016, r. 1.56**

(1) It is an offence for a person who does not have the right under these Rules to inspect a relevant document falsely to claim to be a creditor, a member of a company or a contributory of a company with the intention of gaining sight of the document.

(2) A relevant document is one which is on the court file, the bankruptcy file or held by the office-holder or any other person and which a creditor, a member of a company or a contributory of a company has the right to inspect under these Rules.

This offence replaced the similar offence under r. 12.18 of the Insolvency Rules 1986 with effect from 6 April 2017. It is triable either way. On conviction on indictment, the maximum penalty is two years' imprisonment and/or a fine; on summary conviction, it is six months' imprisonment and/or an unlimited fine.

BANKRUPTCY OFFENCES

The provisions of the Insolvency Act 1986, Part IX, ch. VI, deal with the principal bankruptcy offences and are in many respects similar, but not identical, to the provisions dealing with company insolvency and liquidation offences. An individual is made bankrupt if the court makes a bankruptcy order against that individual on the petition of a creditor in respect of a debt or debts of £5,000 or more (ss. 264 to 267) or if an adjudicator makes a bankruptcy order against an individual on the individual's own bankruptcy application (ss. 263H to 263M). In individual insolvency the trustee in bankruptcy performs a role similar to that of a liquidator in company liquidation. **B7.55**

Like companies (see **B7.43**), an individual may seek to enter into a voluntary arrangement with creditors under Part VIII of the Insolvency Act 1986 (see **B7.72**). In addition, an individual whose debts do not exceed £20,000, whose monthly surplus income does not exceed £50 and whose property does not exceed £1,000 in value may apply for a debt relief order under Part VIIA of the Insolvency Act 1986 These monetary conditions for a debt relief order are set out in the Insolvency Proceedings (Monetary Limits) Order 1986 (SI 1986 No. 1996), sch. 1. For an explanation of debt relief orders, see *R (Cooper) v Secretary of State for Work and Pensions* [2011] UKSC 60, [2012] 2 AC 1 at [7]–[11].

Scheme of Individual Insolvency Offences

Insolvency Act 1986, s. 350 **B7.56**

(1) Subject to section 360(3) below, this chapter applies:
  (a) where an adjudicator has made a bankruptcy order as a result of a bankruptcy application, or
  (b) where the court has made a bankruptcy order on a bankruptcy petition.

(2) This chapter applies whether or not the bankruptcy order is annulled, but proceedings for an offence under this chapter shall not be instituted after the annulment.

(3) Without prejudice to his liability in respect of a subsequent bankruptcy, the bankrupt is not guilty of an offence under this chapter in respect of anything done after his discharge; but nothing in this group of parts prevents the institution of proceedings against a discharged bankrupt for an offence committed before his discharge.

(3A) Subsection (3) is without prejudice to any provision of this chapter which applies to a person in respect of whom a bankruptcy restrictions order is in force.

(4) It is not a defence in proceedings for an offence under this chapter that anything relied on, in whole or in part, as constituting that offence was done outside England and Wales.

(5) Proceedings for an offence under this chapter or under the rules shall not be instituted except by the Secretary of State or by or with the consent of the Director of Public Prosecutions.

(6) A person guilty of any offence under this chapter is liable to imprisonment or a fine, or both.

Penalties for offences under ch. VI (ss. 353 to 362) are prescribed by sch. 10, the relevant parts of which are printed at **B7.75**.

Section 360(3) (see **B7.67**) creates an offence by a person whose estate has been sequestrated in Scotland or adjudged bankrupt in Northern Ireland of doing anything in England and Wales which would be an offence under s. 360(1) if that person had been adjudicated bankrupt under Part IX of the Act and not been discharged from bankruptcy.

Sections 251O to 251S create offences in connection with debt relief orders. As with other individual insolvency offences, proceedings for these offences can only be instituted by the Secretary of State or by or with the consent of the DPP (s. 251T).

Definitions

B7.57 **Insolvency Act 1986, ss. 351 and 381**

351.—(1) In the following provisions of this chapter—

(a) references to property comprised in the bankrupt's estate or to property possession of which is required to be delivered up to the official receiver or the trustee of the bankrupt's estate include any property which would be such property if a notice in respect of it were given under section 307 (after-acquired property), section 308 (personal property and effects of bankrupt having more than replacement value) or section 308A (vesting in trustee of certain tenancies);

(b) 'the initial period' means the period between the making of the bankruptcy application or (as the case may be) the presentation of the bankruptcy petition and the commencement of the bankruptcy.

381.—(1) 'Bankrupt' means an individual who has been made bankrupt, and, in relation to a bankruptcy order, it means the individual made bankrupt by that order.

(1A) 'Bankruptcy application' means an application to an adjudicator for a bankruptcy order.

(2) 'Bankruptcy order' means an order making an individual bankrupt.

(3) 'Bankruptcy petition' means a petition to the court for a bankruptcy order.

Under s. 306 the bankrupt's estate vests in the trustee in bankruptcy. Under s. 307, the bankrupt's trustee may by notice in writing claim for the estate property acquired or devolved upon the bankrupt since commencement of the bankruptcy.

Further definitions are to be found in ss. 382 to 385.

Powers of the Bankruptcy Court

B7.58 The criminal penalties discussed here exist alongside the powers of the bankruptcy court. By s. 363(1) every bankruptcy is under the control of that court. In cases of absconding, removal of goods and concealment or destruction of goods or documents, the bankruptcy court can make an order under s. 364 for the arrest of an undischarged bankrupt or a debtor against whom a bankruptcy petition has been issued and the seizure of documents or goods in that person's possession. For the procedure to be followed, see rr. 12.6 to 12.13 and r. 12.54 of the Insolvency (England and Wales) Rules 2016 (SI 2016 No. 1024) and *Hickling v Baker* [2007] EWCA Civ 287, [2007] 4 All ER 390. Breaches of orders of the bankruptcy court without reasonable excuse (s. 363(3)) and failure to comply with many of the obligations imposed on a bankrupt by the Insolvency Act 1986 without reasonable excuse are contempts of court and punishable accordingly. The procedure to be followed in applying for committal for contempt in such cases is discussed in *Simmonds v Pearce* [2017] EWHC 3126 (Admin), [2018] 1 WLR 1849. In that case a sentence of 12 months' imprisonment was imposed on a bankrupt for serious and deliberate breaches involving concealing assets ([2017] EWHC 3641 (Admin)).

Defence of Innocent Intention

B7.59 **Insolvency Act 1986, s. 352**

Where in the case of an offence under any provision of this chapter it is stated that this section applies, a person is not guilty of the offence if he proves that, at the time of the conduct constituting the offence, he had no intent to defraud or to conceal the state of his affairs.

The reasons for the imposition of a reverse burden of proof in insolvency cases are set out in *A-G's Ref (No. 1 of 2004)* [2004] EWCA Crim 1025, [2004] 4 All ER 457 at [80]–[82] (see **F3.26**). At [92] Lord Woolf CJ said that in appropriate cases s. 352 could be read down as imposing no more than an evidential burden of proof and that its effect within ch. VI of the Insolvency Act 1986 depends on the context of its application. See further **B7.60** and **B7.64**.

Offences of Non-disclosure

Insolvency Act 1986, s. 353 **B7.60**

(1) The bankrupt is guilty of an offence if—
  (a) he does not to the best of his knowledge and belief disclose all the property comprised in his estate to the official receiver or the trustee, or
  (b) he does not inform the official receiver or the trustee of any disposal of any property which but for the disposal would be so comprised, stating how, when, to whom and for what consideration the property was disposed of.
(2) Subsection (1)(b) does not apply to any disposal in the ordinary course of a business carried on by the bankrupt or to any payment of the ordinary expenses of the bankrupt or his family.
(3) Section 352 applies to this offence.

For procedural provisions, see **B7.56**; for sentencing provisions, see **B7.75** and **B7.76**. As to the meaning of 'property' see **B7.57**. Section 353(1)(b) is primarily concerned with property which the bankrupt has had at some time and which the trustee might be able to trace and reclaim through exercise of powers under the Act.

As to what might or might not amount to disposal 'in the ordinary course of business', see **B7.47** and *Countrywide Banking Corporation Ltd v Dean* [1998] AC 338.

The burden of proof placed on D by s. 352 in a charge under s. 353(1) is a legal burden of proof and does not infringe the EHCR, Article 6(2) (*A-G's Ref (No. 1 of 2004)*) [2004] EWCA Crim 1025, [2004] 4 All ER 457 at [93]–[95] and [99]; see **F3.26**).

Section 251O(1), (2) and (4), create offences of knowingly or recklessly making any false representation or omission in connection with a debt relief order.

Concealment of Property and Failure to Account for Losses

Insolvency Act 1986, s. 354 **B7.61**

(1) The bankrupt is guilty of an offence, if—
  (a) he does not deliver up possession to the official receiver or trustee, or as the official receiver or trustee may direct, of such part of the property comprised in his estate as is in his possession or under his control, and possession of which he is required by law so to deliver up,
  (b) he conceals any debt due to or from him or conceals any property the value of which is not less than the prescribed amount and possession of which he is required to deliver up to the official receiver or trustee, or
  (c) in the 12 months before the making of the bankruptcy application or (as the case may be) the presentation of the bankruptcy petition, or in the initial period, he did anything which would have been an offence under paragraph (b) above if the bankruptcy order had been made immediately before he did it.

  Section 352 applies to this offence.
(2) The bankrupt is guilty of an offence if he removes, or in the initial period removed, any property the value of which was not less than the prescribed amount and possession of which he has or would have been required to deliver up to the official receiver or the trustee.

  Section 352 applies to this offence.
(3) The bankrupt is guilty of an offence if he without reasonable excuse fails, on being required to do so by the official receiver, the trustee or the court—
  (a) to account for the loss of any substantial part of his property incurred in the 12 months before the making of the bankruptcy application or (as the case may be) the presentation of the bankruptcy petition or in the initial period, or
  (b) to give a satisfactory explanation of the manner in which such a loss was incurred.

For procedural provisions, see **B7.56**; for sentencing provisions, see **B7.75** and **B7.76**. For the defence under s. 352 (defence of innocent intention), see **B7.59**. The 'prescribed amount' for the purposes of s. 354 is fixed by the Insolvency Proceedings (Monetary Limits) Order 1986 (SI 1986 No. 1996) at £1,000.

The offence contained within s. 354(3) differs from those contained within the preceding subsections in that it is absolute, and does not allow for any possible defence under s. 352. For the jury direction in relation to a similarly worded offence under the Bankruptcy Act 1914, see *Salter* [1968] 2 QB 793 at p. 798. An explanation, if clear and true, need not also be 'satisfactory' in the sense of clearing the bankrupt of blame. If, for example, the explanation reveals heavy gambling losses, this may still be satisfactory for the purposes of s. 354.

The offence under s. 354(3)(a) is compatible with the accused's right to silence and not to self-incriminate (*Kearns* [2002] EWCA Crim 748, [2002] 1 WLR 2815).

Concealment or Falsification of Books and Papers

B7.62 **Insolvency Act 1986, s. 355**

(1) The bankrupt is guilty of an offence if he does not deliver up possession to the official receiver or the trustee, or as the official receiver or trustee may direct, of all books, papers and other records of which he has possession or control and which relate to his estate or his affairs.
Section 352 applies to this offence.

(2) The bankrupt is guilty of an offence if—
  (a) he prevents, or in the initial period prevented, the production of any books, papers or records relating to his estate or affairs;
  (b) he conceals, destroys, mutilates or falsifies, or causes or permits the concealment, destruction, mutilation or falsification of, any books, papers or other records relating to his estate or affairs;
  (c) he makes or causes or permits the making of, any false entries in any book, document or record relating to his estate or affairs; or
  (d) in the 12 months before the making of the bankruptcy application or (as the case may be) the presentation of the bankruptcy petition, or in the initial period, he did anything which would have been an offence, under paragraph (b) or (c) above if the bankruptcy order had been made before he did it.
Section 352 applies to this offence.

(3) The bankrupt is guilty of an offence if—
  (a) he disposes of, or alters or makes any omission in, or causes or permits the disposal, altering or making of any omission in, any book, document or record relating to his estate or affairs, or
  (b) in the 12 months before the making of the bankruptcy application or (as the case may be) the presentation of the bankruptcy petition, or in the initial period, he did anything which would have been an offence under paragraph (a) if the bankruptcy order had been made before he did it.

(4) In their application to a trading record subsections (2)(d) and (3)(b) shall have effect as if the reference to 12 months were a reference to two years.

(5) In subsection (4) 'trading record' means a book, document or record which shows or explains the transactions or financial position of a person's business, including—
  (a) a periodic record of cash paid and received,
  (b) a statement of periodic stock-taking, and
  (c) except in the case of goods sold by way of retail trade, a record of goods sold and purchased which identifies the buyer and seller or enables them to be identified.
Section 352 applies to this offence.

For procedural provisions, see **B7.56**; for sentencing provisions, see **B7.75** and **B7.76**. For the meaning of 'the initial period', see **B7.57**. For the defence under s. 352 (lack of fraudulent intent), see **B7.59**. Section 251P creates similar offences by a person in respect of whom a debt relief order is made.

'Causing' an act means ordering or directing it, and 'permitting' it means allowing it to happen (*Houston v Buchanan* [1940] 2 All ER 179). It is not clear whether D must be proved to know the circumstances which make the act criminal, although, in this context, it is unlikely that such proof would be required. Where D has, for example, permitted an assistant to clear out old files, and it transpires that these included papers relating to D's estate or affairs, it is submitted that the only defence to a charge under s. 355(2)(b) would be that provided by s. 352.

The point which was argued unsuccessfully in *Taylor* [2011] EWCA Crim 728, [2011] 1 WLR 1809 (see **B7.45**) about company records kept on computer could not have arisen in relation to individual bankruptcy as s. 355 expressly extends to records other than books or papers.

The offences under s. 355(2) and (3) overlap with the Theft Act 1968, s. 17 (see **B6.3**), and the Forgery and Counterfeiting Act 1981, s. 1 (see **B6.36**).

False Statements

Insolvency Act 1986, s. 356 **B7.63**

(1) The bankrupt is guilty of an offence if he makes or has made any material omission in any statement made under any provision in this group of parts and relating to his affairs.
Section 352 applies to this offence.

(2) The bankrupt is guilty of an offence if—
(a) knowing or believing that a false debt has been proved by any person under the bankruptcy, he fails to inform the trustee as soon as practicable; or
(b) he attempts to account for any part of his property by fictitious losses or expenses; or
(c) in connection with any creditors' decision procedure or deemed consent procedure in the 12 months before the making of the bankruptcy application or (as the case may be) the presentation of the bankruptcy petition or (whether or not in connection with such a procedure) at any time in the initial period, he did anything which would have been an offence under paragraph (b) if the bankruptcy order had been made before he did it; or
(d) he is, or at any time has been, guilty of any false representation or other fraud for the purpose of obtaining the consent of his creditors, or any of them, to an agreement with reference to his affairs or to his bankruptcy.

For procedural provisions, see **B7.56**; for sentencing provisions, see **B7.75** and **B7.76**. For the defence under s. 352 (lack of fraudulent intent), see **B7.59**.

A charge under s. 356 remains appropriate even where the bankrupt's false statement was made prior to bankruptcy (*Edwards* [2010] EWCA Crim 1682). Section 356(1) differs from the equivalent company liquidation offence (s. 210) in that the statement concerned must be one made under relevant provisions of the Act. This might be a 'statement of affairs' under s. 288 or a statement made in purported compliance with s. 333 or any other relevant provision.

Where the alleged material omission is a failure to disclose creditors, it is not necessary for the prosecution to identify who those creditors were or for the jury all to agree who the creditors were. No *Brown* direction (see **D18.44**) is required (*Aviss* [2014] EWCA Crim 2210 at [14]–[17]).

The defence under s. 352 applies only to s. 356(1); the offences under s. 356(2) require proof of knowledge or belief. Thus, proof of the inaccuracy of a bankrupt's account would not suffice to prove an offence under s. 366(2)(b): it must also be proved to be fictitious (i.e. that the inaccuracy is deliberate). In respect of s. 356(2)(d), fraud must be proved (see the discussion of the equivalent provision in s. 211 at **B7.52**). In respect of the other offences under s. 356(2), the requisite *mens rea* need not necessarily involve fraud, which thus becomes wholly irrelevant to the issue of guilt: the prosecution need not prove it, and it will not avail the defence to prove its absence.

Section 251O(1), (2) and (4), create offences of knowingly or recklessly making any false representation or omission in connection with a debt relief order.

Fraudulent Disposal or Concealment of Property

Insolvency Act 1986, s. 357 **B7.64**

(1) The bankrupt is guilty of an offence if he makes or causes to be made, or has in the period of 5 years ending with the commencement of the bankruptcy made or caused to be made, any gift or transfer of, or any charge on, his property.
Section 352 applies to this offence.

(2) The reference to making a transfer of or charge on any property includes causing or conniving at the levying of any execution against the property.
(3) The bankrupt is guilty of an offence if he conceals or removes, or has at any time before the commencement of the bankruptcy concealed or removed, any part of his property after, or within 2 months before, the date on which a judgment or order for the payment of money has been obtained against him, being a judgment or order which was not satisfied before the commencement of the bankruptcy.
Section 352 applies to this offence.

For procedural provisions, see **B7.56**; for sentencing provisions, see **B7.75** and **B7.76**; for definitions, see **B7.57**.

Section 357(1) is similar to the companies offence contained within s. 207 (see **B7.48**) and, like s. 207, would be of very wide application but for the defence provided under s. 352 (see **B7.59**). The burden of proof placed on a defendant by s. 352 in a charge under s. 357 is to be read down so as to impose merely an evidential burden on the defendant (*A-G's Ref (No. 1 of 2004)* [2004] EWCA Crim 1025, [2004] 4 All ER 457 at [85]–[92] and [99]; see **F3.26**).

Section 251Q creates a similar offence to that under s. 357(1) in relation to the fraudulent disposal of property by a person in respect of whom a debt relief order is made, but in that case the period starts two years before the application for the debt relief order is made.

A bankrupt who commits an offence under s. 357 can expect to receive a custodial sentence, even if of previous good character (*Mungroo* [1998] BPIR 784; see also *Ferguson* [2013] EWCA Crim 1089).

The Debtors Act 1869, s. 13(2) and (3), create offences similar in form to the Insolvency Act 1986, s. 357(1) and (3), but do not require there to be a bankruptcy, and place the burden of proving fraud on the prosecution. The meaning of 'creditors' in s. 13(2) was interpreted in *Hopkins* [1896] 1 QB 652 as excluding a claimant in an action to recover unliquidated damages. But this decision seems out of line with the interpretation of 'creditors' in other legislation (see **B7.13** and **B7.48**).

Absconding with Property

B7.65 **Insolvency Act 1986, s. 358**

The bankrupt is guilty of an offence if—
(a) he leaves, or attempts or makes preparations to leave, England and Wales with any property the value of which is not less than the prescribed amount and possession of which he is required to deliver up to the official receiver or the trustee, or
(b) in the 6 months before the making of the bankruptcy application or (as the case may be) the presentation of the bankruptcy petition, or in the initial period, he did anything which would have been an offence under paragraph (a) if the bankruptcy order had been made immediately before he did it.
Section 352 applies to this offence.

For procedural provisions, see **B7.56**; for sentencing provisions, see **B7.75** and **B7.76**; for definitions, see **B7.57**. The 'prescribed amount' is fixed by the Insolvency Proceedings (Monetary Limits) Order 1986 (SI 1986 No. 1996) at £1,000.

If the bankrupt has done nothing worse than travel abroad with property (e.g. driving a car) and has returned with that property, it may well be easy for the bankrupt to show an absence of intent to defraud and thus take advantage of the defence under s. 352 (see **B7.59**).

Fraudulent Dealing with Property Obtained on Credit

B7.66 **Insolvency Act 1986, s. 359**

(1) The bankrupt is guilty of an offence if, in the 12 months before the making of the bankruptcy application or (as the case may be) the presentation of the bankruptcy petition, or in the initial

period, he disposed of any property which he had obtained on credit and, at the time he disposed of it, had not paid for.
Section 352 applies to this offence.

(2) A person is guilty of an offence if, in the 12 months before the making of the bankruptcy application or (as the case may be) the presentation of the bankruptcy petition or in the initial period, he acquired or received property from the bankrupt knowing or believing—
(a) that the bankrupt owed money in respect of the property, and
(b) that the bankrupt did not intend, or was unlikely to be able, to pay the money he so owed.

(3) A person is not guilty of an offence under subsection (1) or (2) if the disposal, acquisition or receipt of the property was in the ordinary course of a business carried on by the bankrupt at the time of the disposal, acquisition or receipt.

(4) In determining for the purposes of this section whether any property is disposed of, acquired or received in the ordinary course of a business carried on by the bankrupt, regard may be had, in particular, to the price paid for the property.

(5) In this section references to disposing of property include pawning or pledging it; and references to acquiring or receiving property shall be read accordingly.

For procedural provisions, see **B7.56**; for sentencing provisions, see **B7.75** and **B7.76**. For definitions, see **B7.57**. For the defence of no intent under s. 352, see **B7.59**. Section 251R(1) and (2) creates similar offences in relation to the disposal of property by a person in respect of whom a debt relief order has been made where the property was obtained on credit and has not been paid for.

The mischief against which s. 359 strikes is that of obtaining goods on credit, and then selling or otherwise disposing of them, often on disadvantageous terms or for inadequate consideration, as a method of raising cash which may be unobtainable by more conventional means. Such methods are generally resorted to only by persons who are already in serious financial difficulties, and prejudice the interests of the unpaid suppliers.

As to what may amount to disposal 'otherwise than in the ordinary course of business', see **B7.47**.

Obtaining Credit: Engaging in Business

Insolvency Act 1986, s. 360 **B7.67**

(1) The bankrupt is guilty of an offence if—
(a) either alone or jointly with any other person, he obtains credit to the extent of the prescribed amount or more without giving the person from whom he obtains it the relevant information about his status; or
(b) he engages (whether directly or indirectly) in any business under a name other than that in which he was adjudged bankrupt without disclosing to all persons with whom he enters into any business transaction the name in which he was so made.

(2) The reference to the bankrupt obtaining credit includes the following cases—
(a) where goods are bailed to him under a hire-purchase agreement, or agreed to be sold to him under a conditional sale agreement, and
(b) where he is paid in advance (whether in money or otherwise) for the supply of goods or services.

(3) A person whose estate has been sequestrated in Scotland, or who has been adjudged bankrupt in Northern Ireland, is guilty of an offence if, before his discharge, he does anything in England and Wales which would be an offence under subsection (1) if he were an undischarged bankrupt and the sequestration of his estate or the adjudication in Northern Ireland were an adjudication under this part.

(4) For the purposes of subsection (1)(a), the relevant information about the status of the person in question is the information that he is an undischarged bankrupt or, as the case may be, that his estate has been sequestrated in Scotland and that he has not been discharged.

(5) This section applies to the bankrupt after discharge while a bankruptcy restrictions order is in force in respect of him.

(6) For the purposes of subsection (1)(a) as it applies by virtue of subsection (5), the relevant information about the status of the person in question is the information that a bankruptcy restrictions order is in force in respect of him.

For procedural provisions, see **B7.56**; for sentencing provisions, see **B7.75** and **B7.76**. Section 251S creates similar offences by a person in respect of whom a debt relief order is made.

Section 360 is not subject to the defence of innocent intention under s. 352. The offences re-enacted in s. 360 have always been regarded as absolute. Thus, in *Duke of Leinster* [1924] 1 KB 311, it was held that D committed the offence even though D's agent had been instructed to inform the creditor of D's status and had failed to do so. See also *Dyson* [1894] 2 QB 176.

B7.68 **Credit to the Extent of the Prescribed Amount** The amount prescribed by the Insolvency Proceedings (Monetary Limits) Order 1986 (SI 1986 No. 1996) is £500. This limit governs the aggregate of the credit obtained, and it cannot be circumvented merely by ensuring that no one transaction exceeds the limit (*Juby* (1886) 16 Cox 160; *Hartley* [1972] 2 QB 1). It seems to have been assumed in *Hartley* that the prescribed amount nevertheless refers to the aggregate obtained from any one creditor. If this is correct, it would be no offence for a bankrupt to obtain £499 worth of credit from each of four different persons without admitting to being a bankrupt. This proposition is of doubtful validity, for, although the section refers to 'the person' from whom credit is obtained, the general principle is that the singular includes the plural (Interpretation Act 1978, s. 6(c)) and the risk of loss to each creditor is increased by the increase in the aggregate of the bankrupt's debt.

B7.69 **Obtaining** Any obtaining must be of credit given to the bankrupt. The agreement to provide credit does not have to be enforceable (*Roder Ltd v West* [2011] EWCA Civ 1126, [2012] QB 752 at [17]). Credit given to the bankrupt jointly with another is expressly included, but cases where credit is obtained by the bankrupt as agent for another person to whom the creditor looks for payment would not be covered (*Godwin* (1980) 71 Cr App R 97). 'Obtaining' has a narrower meaning for the purposes of s. 360 than it has, for example, in respect of insider dealing; it must involve 'some conduct, either by words or otherwise ... which amounts to an obtaining' (*Hayat* (1976) 63 Cr App R 181). There may not necessarily have been any 'obtaining' in this sense where the bankrupt's bank account becomes overdrawn as a result of the dishonouring of certain incoming cheques and the honouring of certain cheques drawn on that account; it will be a question of fact for the jury (*Hayat*). There is no obtaining of credit where the bankrupt defaults on an existing hire-purchase obligation and thereby becomes liable to pay the arrears (*Miller* [1977] 3 All ER 986) nor where funds are received from a business partner in the course of a joint venture. It makes no difference if the bankrupt intends to default on the bargain: 'It is the nature of the agreement which determines whether or not credit has been obtained, not the intention of the defendant' (*Ramzan* [1998] 2 Cr App R 328 at p. 334).

Credit is 'obtained' where any goods or monies concerned are received (*Ellis* [1899] 1 QB 230), but the Insolvency Act 1986, s. 350(4) (see **B7.56**), ensures that the provisions of ch. VI have extra-territorial effect, and so it will be no defence to argue that credit was obtained abroad.

B7.70 **Engaging in Business** A bankrupt may engage in business without necessarily disclosing that status, but the bankrupt cannot become a company director, manager or promoter without leave of the court (see the Company Directors Disqualification Act 1986, ss. 11 and 13, at **B7.73**). The bankrupt must not hide the bankruptcy by using a different name. The reference in the Insolvency Act 1986, s. 360(1)(b), to indirectly engaging in business is designed to deal with bankrupts who procure some other persons to 'front' businesses effectively controlled by themselves.

FALSE REPRESENTATIONS AND OMISSIONS IN CONNECTION WITH A BANKRUPTCY APPLICATION

Section 263O creates offences in connection with bankruptcy applications. This section, which came into force on 6 April 2016, is consequential on changes in bankruptcy procedure under which a debtor now applies to an adjudicator for a bankruptcy order to be made, rather than, as before, presenting the debtor's own petition to the court for a bankruptcy order. **B7.71**

Insolvency Act 1986, 263O

(1) It is an offence knowingly or recklessly to make any false representation or omission in—
 (a) making a bankruptcy application to an adjudicator, or
 (b) providing any information to an adjudicator in connection with a bankruptcy application.
(2) It is an offence knowingly or recklessly to fail to notify an adjudicator of a matter in accordance with a requirement imposed by or under this Part.
(3) It is immaterial for the purposes of an offence under this section whether or not a bankruptcy order is made as a result of the application.
(4) It is not a defence in proceedings for an offence under this section that anything relied on, in whole or in part, as constituting the offence was done outside England and Wales.
(5) Proceedings for an offence under this section may only be instituted—
 (a) by the Secretary of State, or
 (b) by or with the consent of the Director of Public Prosecutions.

For sentencing provisions, see **B7.75**.

FRAUD IN RESPECT OF VOLUNTARY ARRANGEMENTS

As explained at **B7.43** and **B7.55**, Parts I and VIII of the Insolvency Act 1986 make provision for voluntary arrangements by agreement with creditors for the satisfaction of debts or a scheme of arrangement. Sections 6A and 262A create offences, in similar terms, in relation to false representations and frauds for the purpose of obtaining approval to such a proposal. Section 6A relates to company voluntary arrangements and s. 262A relates to individual voluntary arrangements. **B7.72**

Insolvency Act 1986, ss. 6A and 262A

6A.—(1) If, for the purpose of obtaining the approval of the members or creditors of a company to a proposal for a voluntary arrangement, a person who is an officer of the company—
 (a) makes any false representation, or
 (b) fraudulently does, or omits to do, anything,
 he commits an offence.
(2) Subsection (1) applies even if the proposal is not approved.
(3) For purposes of this section 'officer' includes a shadow director.

262A.—(1) If, for the purpose of obtaining the approval of his creditors to a proposal for a voluntary arrangement, the debtor—
 (a) makes any false representation, or
 (b) fraudulently does, or omits to do, anything, he commits an offence.
(2) Subsection (1) applies even if the proposal is not approved.

These offences are punishable on indictment by a maximum of seven years' imprisonment. For other sentencing provisions, see **B7.75** and **B7.76**.

OFFENCES RELATING TO DISQUALIFICATION

Disqualification from Company Management etc.

The Company Directors Disqualification Act 1986, s. 11, makes it an offence for an undischarged bankrupt, or other person subject to Insolvency Act orders listed in s. 11(2), to act as **B7.73** a company director or to take part in the promotion, formation or management of a company without the leave of the bankruptcy court.

Company Directors Disqualification Act 1986, ss. 11 and 13

11.—(1) It is an offence for a person to act as director of a company or directly or indirectly to take part in or be concerned in the promotion, formation or management of a company, without the leave of the court, at a time when any of the circumstances mentioned in subsection (2) apply to the person.

(2) The circumstances are—

(a) the person is an undischarged bankrupt—

(i) in England and Wales or Scotland, or

(ii) in Northern Ireland,

(b) a bankruptcy restrictions order or undertaking is in force in respect of the person under—

(i) the Bankruptcy (Scotland) Act 1985 or the Insolvency Act 1986, or

(ii) the Insolvency (Northern Ireland) Order 1989,

(c) a debt relief restrictions order or undertaking is in force in respect of the person under—

(i) the Insolvency Act 1986, or

(ii) the Insolvency (Northern Ireland) Order 1989,

(d) a moratorium period under a debt relief order applies in relation to the person under—

(i) the Insolvency Act 1986, or

(ii) the Insolvency (Northern Ireland) Order 1989.

(2A) In subsection (1) 'the court' means—

(a) for the purposes of subsection (2)(a)(i)—

(i) the court by which the bankruptcy order was made or (if the order was not made by a court) the court to which a debtor may appeal against a refusal to make a bankruptcy order, or

(ii) in Scotland, the court by which sequestration of the person's estate was awarded or, if awarded other than by the court, the court which would have jurisdiction in respect of sequestration of the person's estate,

(b) for the purposes of subsection (2)(b)(i)—

(i) the court which made the order,

(ii) in Scotland, if the order has been made other than by the court, the court to which the person may appeal against the order, or

(iii) the court to which the person may make an application for annulment of the undertaking,

(c) for the purposes of subsection (2)(c)(i)—

(i) the court which made the order, or

(ii) the court to which the person may make an application for annulment of the undertaking,

(d) for the purposes of subsection (2)(d)(i), the court to which the person would make an application under section 251M(1) of the Insolvency Act 1986 (if the person were dissatisfied as mentioned there),

(e) for the purposes of paragraphs (a)(ii), (b)(ii), (c)(ii) and (d)(ii) of subsection (2), the High Court of Northern Ireland.

(3) In England and Wales, the leave of the court shall not be given unless notice of intention to apply for it has been served on the official receiver; and it is the latter's duty, if he is of opinion that it is contrary to the public interest that the application should be granted, to attend on the hearing of the application and oppose it.

(4) In this section 'company' includes a company incorporated outside Great Britain that has an established place of business in Great Britain.

13. If a person acts in contravention of a disqualification order or disqualification undertaking or in contravention of section 12(2), 12A or 12B, or is guilty of an offence under section 11, he is liable—

(a) on conviction on indictment, to imprisonment for not more than 2 years or a fine, or both; and

(b) on summary conviction, to imprisonment for not more than 6 months or a fine not exceeding the statutory maximum, or both.

Liability under s.11 is strict; it is no defence that D honestly believed that the bankruptcy had been discharged at the relevant time (*Brockley* [1994] Crim LR 671). The scope of the prohibition is illustrated by *Campbell* (1983) 78 Cr App R 95, where it was held under the previous legislation that a disqualified person could be concerned or take part in the management of a company by advising on financial matters and on company restructuring as a 'management consultant'.

For disqualification orders by criminal courts, see **E21.8** to **E21.10**.

Under ss. 3, 4 and 6, a disqualification order may also be made against a person by a court with jurisdiction to wind up companies (see **B7.43**) (i) for persistent breaches of companies legislation; (ii) if, in the course of winding up a company, it appears that the person has been guilty of fraudulent trading (see **B7.7**) or any fraud or breach of duty as an officer, liquidator or receiver of the company; or (iii) the person's conduct as a director makes that person unfit to be concerned in the management of a company. A person against whom an application is made may give a disqualification undertaking under s. 1A. By s. 10, a disqualification order can be made against a person liable to contribute to the company's assets following fraudulent or wrongful trading.

Disqualification is to be taken seriously and is enforced strictly. In *Cowley-Hurlock* [2014] EWCA Crim 1702, Foskett J stated (at [21]) that there was:

> ... a spectrum of activity that constitutes an offence of this nature, which will lead to differing sentencing results within the rather narrow band afforded by a maximum sentence of two years' imprisonment ... there is plainly a difference between a relatively short period of inadvertent breach of a disqualification order or undertaking and a prolonged period of obvious, deliberate and cynical breach aggravated by a past history of similar activity.

For other sentencing decisions, see **B7.76**. For confiscation orders following convictions under the Company Directors Disqualification Act 1986, see *Seager* [2009] EWCA Crim 1303, [2010] 1 WLR 815.

Disqualification under the Insolvency Act 1986

It is an offence under the Insolvency Act 1986, s. 31, for a bankrupt who is undischarged **B7.74** or subject to a bankruptcy restrictions order to act as a receiver or manager on behalf of debenture holders, unless appointed by the court, and since such a person is also disqualified from acting as an insolvency practitioner (Insolvency Act 1986, s. 390(4) and (5)), it follows that the person commits an offence under s. 389 by acting as a liquidator, administrator, or trustee in bankruptcy.

SCHEDULE OF OFFENCES UNDER THE INSOLVENCY ACT 1986

Section 430 and sch. 10 set out the way in which offences under the Insolvency Act 1986 are **B7.75** punishable on conviction. The offences introduced into that Act by way of amendments made by the Tribunals, Courts and Enforcement Act 2007 and the Small Business, Enterprise and Employment Act 2015 are stated in the schedule to be punishable on summary conviction by a maximum of 12 months' imprisonment. But it is respectfully suggested that the effect of the PCC(S)A 2000, s. 78(2) (see **D23.14**), is to reduce the maximum length of imprisonment on summary conviction for one of those offences to six months. The more serious offences, punishable with imprisonment, are listed in the table.

Insolvency Act 1986, sch. 10, Abridged

Section	General nature of offence	Mode of prosecution	Punishment
6A(1)	False representation or fraud for purpose of obtaining members' or creditors' approval of proposed voluntary arrangement.	1. On indictment. 2. Summary.	7 years or a fine, or both. 6 months or [an unlimited fine]; or both.
31	Bankrupt or person in respect of whom a debt relief order is made acting as receiver or manager.	1. On indictment. 2. Summary.	2 years or a fine, or both. 6 months or [an unlimited fine], or both.
89(4)	Director making statutory declaration of company's solvency without reasonable grounds for his opinion.	1. On indictment. 2. Summary.	2 years or a fine, or both. 6 months or [an unlimited fine], or both.
206(1)	Fraud, etc. in anticipation of winding up.	1. On indictment. 2. Summary.	7 years or a fine, or both. 6 months [an unlimited fine], or both.
206(2)	Privity to fraud in anticipation of winding up; fraud, or privity to fraud, after commencement of winding up.	1. On indictment. 2. Summary.	7 years or a fine, or both. 6 months or [an unlimited fine], or both.
206(5)	Knowingly taking in pawn or pledge, or otherwise receiving, company property.	1. On indictment. 2. Summary.	7 years or a fine, or both. 6 months or [an unlimited fine], or both.
207	Officer of company entering into transaction in fraud of company's creditors.	1. On indictment. 2. Summary.	2 years or a fine, or both. 6 months or [an unlimited fine], or both.
208	Officer of company misconducting himself in course of winding up.	1. On indictment. 2. Summary.	7 years or a fine, or both. 6 months or [an unlimited fine], or both.
209	Officer or contributory destroying, falsifying, etc. company's books.	1. On indictment. 2. Summary.	7 years or a fine, or both. 6 months or [an unlimited fine], or both.
210	Officer of company making material omission from statement relating to company's affairs.	1. On indictment. 2. Summary.	7 years or a fine, or both. 6 months or [an unlimited fine], or both.
211	False representation or fraud for purposes of obtaining creditors' consent to an agreement in connection with winding up.	1. On indictment. 2. Summary.	7 years or a fine, or both. 6 months or [an unlimited fine], or both.
216(4)	Contravening restrictions on re-use of name of company in insolvent liquidation.	1. On indictment. 2. Summary.	2 years or a fine, or both. 6 months or [an unlimited fine], or both.
251O(1)	False representations or omissions in making an application for a debt relief order.	1. On indictment. 2. Summary.	7 years or a fine, or both. 12 months or [an unlimited fine], or both.
251O(2)(a)	Failing to comply with duty in connection with an application for a debt relief order.	1. On indictment. 2. Summary.	2 years or a fine, or both. 12 months or [an unlimited fine], or both.
251O(2)(b)	False representations or omissions in connection with duty in relation to an application for a debt relief order.	1. On indictment. 2. Summary.	7 years or a fine, or both. 12 months or [an unlimited fine], or both.
251O(4)(a)	Failing to comply with duty in connection with a debt relief order.	1. On indictment. 2. Summary.	2 years or a fine, or both. 12 months or [an unlimited fine], or both.

Section	General nature of offence	Mode of prosecution	Punishment
251O(4)(b)	False representations or omissions in connection with a duty in relation to a debt relief order.	1. On indictment. 2. Summary.	7 years or a fine, or both. 12 months or [an unlimited fine], or both.
251P(1)	Failing to deliver books, records and papers to official receiver, concealing or destroying them or making false entries in them by person in respect of whom a debt relief order is made.	1. On indictment. 2. Summary.	7 years or a fine, or both. 12 months or [an unlimited fine], or both.
251P(2)	Person in respect of whom debt relief order is made doing anything falling within paragraphs (c) to (e) of section 251P(1) during the period of 12 months ending with the application date or doing anything falling within paragraphs (b) to (e) of section 251P(1) after that date but before the effective date.	1. On indictment. 2. Summary.	7 years or a fine, or both. 12 months or [an unlimited fine], or both.
251Q(1)	Fraudulent disposal of property by person in respect of whom a debt relief order is made.	1. On indictment. 2. Summary.	2 years or a fine, or both. 12 months or [an unlimited fine], or both.
251R(1)	Disposal of property that is not paid for by person in respect of whom a debt relief order is made.	1. On indictment. 2. Summary.	7 years or a fine, or both. 12 months or [an unlimited fine], or both.
251R(2)	Obtaining property in respect of which money is owed by a person in respect of whom a debt relief order is made.	1. On indictment. 2. Summary.	7 years or a fine, or both. 12 months or [an unlimited fine], or both.
251S(1)	Person in respect of whom a debt relief order is made obtaining credit or engaging in business without disclosing his status or name.	1. On indictment. 2. Summary.	2 years or a fine, or both. 12 months or [an unlimited fine], or both.
262A(1)	False representation or fraud for purposes of obtaining creditors' approval of proposed voluntary arrangement.	1. On indictment. 2. Summary.	7 years or a fine, or both. 6 months or [an unlimited fine], or both.
263O	False representations or omissions in connection with a bankruptcy application	1. On indictment. 2. Summary.	7 years or a fine, or both. 12 months or [an unlimited fine], or both.
353(1)	Bankrupt failing to disclose property or disposals to official receiver or trustee.	1. On indictment. 2. Summary.	7 years or a fine, or both. 6 months or [an unlimited fine], or both.
354(1)	Bankrupt failing to deliver property to, or concealing property from, official receiver or trustee.	1. On indictment. 2. Summary.	7 years or a fine, or both. 6 months or [an unlimited fine], or both.
354(2)	Bankrupt removing property which he is required to deliver to official receiver or trustee.	1. On indictment. 2. Summary.	7 years or a fine, or both. 6 months or [an unlimited fine], or both.
354(3)	Bankrupt failing to account for loss of substantial part of property.	1. On indictment. 2. Summary.	2 years or a fine, or both. 6 months or [an unlimited fine], or both.
355(1)	Bankrupt failing to deliver books, papers and records to official receiver or trustee.	1. On indictment. 2. Summary.	7 years or a fine, or both. 6 months or [an unlimited fine], or both.

Section	General nature of offence	Mode of prosecution	Punishment
355(2)	Bankrupt concealing, destroying etc. books, papers or records, or making false entries in them.	1. On indictment. 2. Summary.	7 years or a fine, or both. 6 months or [an unlimited fine], or both.
355(3)	Bankrupt disposing of, or altering, books, papers or records relating to his estate or affairs.	1. On indictment. 2. Summary.	7 years or a fine, or both. 6 months or [an unlimited fine], or both.
356(1)	Bankrupt making material omission in statement relating to his affairs.	1. On indictment. 2. Summary.	7 years or a fine, or both. 6 months or [an unlimited fine], or both.
356(2)	Bankrupt making false statement, or failing to inform trustee, where false debt proved.	1. On indictment. 2. Summary.	7 years or a fine, or both. 6 months or [an unlimited fine], or both.
357	Bankrupt fraudulently disposing of property.	1. On indictment. 2. Summary.	2 years or a fine, or both. 6 months or [an unlimited fine], or both.
358	Bankrupt absconding with property he is required to deliver to official receiver or trustee.	1. On indictment. 2. Summary.	2 years or a fine, or both. 6 months or [an unlimited fine], or both.
359(1)	Bankrupt disposing of property obtained on credit and not paid for.	1. On indictment. 2. Summary.	7 years or a fine, or both. 6 months or [an unlimited fine], or both.
359(2)	Obtaining property in respect of which money is owed by a bankrupt	1. On indictment. 2. Summary.	7 years or a fine, or both. 6 months or [an unlimited fine], or both.
360(1)	Bankrupt obtaining credit or engaging in business without disclosing his status or name in which he was made bankrupt	1. On indictment. 2. Summary.	2 years or a fine, or both. 6 months or [an unlimited fine], or both.
360(3)	Person made bankrupt in Scotland or Northern Ireland obtaining credit, etc. in England and Wales.	1. On indictment. 2. Summary.	2 years or a fine, or both. 6 months or [an unlimited fine], or both.
389	Acting as insolvency practitioner when not qualified.	1. On indictment. 2. Summary.	2 years or a fine, or both. 6 months or [an unlimited fine], or both.
429(5)	Contravening s. 429 in respect of disabilities imposed by county court on revocation of administration.	1. On indictment. 2. Summary.	2 years or a fine, or both. 6 months or [an unlimited fine], or both.
Sch. A1, para. 9(2)	Directors failing to notify nominee of beginning of moratorium	1. On indictment. 2. Summary.	2 years or a fine, or both. 6 months or [an unlimited fine], or both.
Sch. A1, para. 17(3)(b)	Obtaining credit for company without disclosing existence of moratorium	1. On indictment. 2. Summary.	2 years or a fine, or both. 6 months or [an unlimited fine], or both.
Sch. A1, para. 18(3)(b)	Authorising or permitting disposal of company property without approval during moratorium	1. On indictment. 2. Summary.	2 years or a fine, or both. 6 months or [an unlimited fine], or both.
Sch. A1, para. 19(3)(b)	Authorising or permitting a payment in respect of a liability existing before beginning of moratorium	1. On indictment. 2. Summary.	2 years or a fine, or both. 6 months or [an unlimited fine], or both.
Sch. A1, para. 22(2)	Authorising or permitting disposal of charged property during moratorium	1. On indictment. 2. Summary.	2 years or a fine, or both. 6 months or [an unlimited fine], or both.

Section	General nature of offence	Mode of prosecution	Punishment
Sch. A1, para. 23(1)(b)	Authorising or permitting company to enter market contract during moratorium	1. On indictment. 2. Summary.	2 years or a fine, or both. 6 months or [an unlimited fine], or both.
Sch. A1, para. 41(2)	Fraud or privy to fraud in anticipation of moratorium	1. On indictment. 2. Summary.	7 years or a fine, or both. 6 months or [an unlimited fine], or both.
Sch. A1, para. 41(3)	Fraud or privy to fraud during moratorium	1. On indictment. 2. Summary.	7 years or a fine, or both. 6 months or [an unlimited fine], or both.
Sch. A1, para. 41(7)	Knowingly taking in pawn or pledge or otherwise receiving company property during moratorium	1. On indictment. 2. Summary.	7 years or a fine, or both. 6 months or [an unlimited fine], or both.
Sch. A1, para. 42(1)	False representation or fraud for purpose of obtaining or extending moratorium	1. On indictment. 2. Summary.	7 years or a fine, or both. 6 months or [an unlimited fine],
Sch. B1, para. 18(7)	Making false statement in statutory declaration where administrator appointed by holder of floating charge	1. On indictment. 2. Summary.	2 years or a fine, or both. 6 months or [an unlimited fine],
Sch. B1, para. 20	Holder of floating charge failing to notify administrator or others of commencement of appointment	1. On indictment. 2. Summary.	2 years or a fine, or both. 6 months or [an unlimited fine],
Sch. B1, para. 27(4)	Making false statement in statutory declaration where appointment of administrator proposed by company or directors	1. On indictment. 2. Summary.	2 years or a fine, or both. 6 months or [an unlimited fine],
Sch. B1, para. 29(7)	Making false statement in statutory declaration where administrator appointed by company or directors	1. On indictment. 2. Summary.	2 years or a fine, or both. 6 months or [an unlimited fine],
Sch. B1, para. 32	Company or directors failing to notify administrator or others of commencement of appointment	1. On indictment. 2. Summary.	2 years or a fine, or both. 6 months or [an unlimited fine],

SENTENCING: INSOLVENCY AND BANKRUPTCY OFFENCES

In *Vanderwell* [1998] 1 Cr App R (S) 439, D pleaded guilty to two counts of being concerned in the management of a company while an undischarged bankrupt, one count of obtaining credit as a bankrupt, one of obtaining by deception, one of failing to keep proper business accounts and one of concealment of debts. He had been made bankrupt in 1978 and in 1986, sentenced to imprisonment in 1990 and disqualified from acting as a company director. On his release he again started trading and accumulated debts of £25,000. The Court of Appeal regarded him as thoroughly dishonest, and upheld a total prison sentence of four years and three months, together with a company director disqualification for 15 years. **B7.76**

In contrast, many who commit insolvency and bankruptcy offences have no previous convictions. In *Mungroo* [1998] BPIR 784, the Court of Appeal stated that a bankrupt offender, against whom a judgment debt had been entered, who concealed assets and used them to pay personal debts, could expect to receive a custodial sentence, even if of previous exemplary character. In *Bevis* [2001] EWCA Crim 9, [2001] 2 Cr App R (S) 49 (257), D was 53 years old and of previous good character. The Court of Appeal reduced a sentence for failing to disclose company property and details of its disposal contrary to the Insolvency Act 1986, s. 208(1)(a), from 18 months' imprisonment to nine months. In *Taylor* [2011] EWCA Crim 728, [2011] 1 WLR 1809 D, again of good character, pleaded guilty to acting as a director of a company while an undischarged bankrupt and was convicted of falsifying books or papers relating to the company's affairs and making a material omission in a statement relating to the company's affairs. He had effectively stolen £23,000 from the company's creditors and used three of the company's vehicles for himself. The Court of Appeal upheld a total sentence of 16 months' imprisonment. See also *Hussain* [2014] EWCA Crim 2243, [2014] 2 Cr App R (S) 15 (114) (six months' imprisonment imposed on a bankrupt for making a false statement and fraudulent concealment of property), *Brownlees* [2005] EWCA Crim 532, and *Simmonds v Pearce* [2017] EWHC 3126 (Admin), [2018] 1 WLR 1849 and [2017] EWHC 3641 (Admin) (see **B7.58**).

Confiscation orders under the POCA 2002 may also be made (see *Lowe* [2009] EWCA Crim 194, [2009] 2 Cr App R (S) 81 (544) and *Weintroub* [2011] EWCA Crim 2167 at **B7.53**).

Because no specific sentencing guideline applies to insolvency and bankruptcy offences, the Sentencing Council's *General Guideline: Overarching Principles* (see Supplement, **SG2-1** ***et seq.***) applies to sentencing for these offences.

Section B8 Damage to Property

SIMPLE CRIMINAL DAMAGE

Criminal Damage Act 1971, s. 1 **B8.1**

(1) A person who without lawful excuse destroys or damages any property belonging to another intending to destroy or damage any such property or being reckless as to whether any such property would be destroyed or damaged shall be guilty of an offence.

The CDA 1998, s. 30, creates a racially or religiously aggravated form of this offence which carries a higher maximum penalty (see **B8.43**). For the meaning of racially or religiously aggravated, see **B11.145** ***et seq.***

Procedure

Criminal damage is generally triable either way (MCA 1980, s. 17 and sch. 1, para. 29). When tried on indictment it is normally a class 3 offence, but see CrimPD XIII, para. B (see Supplement, **CPD.XIII.B**), for the additional factors that the court considers on allocation. However, where the value of the property alleged to have been destroyed or the value of the alleged damage is not more than £5,000 (unless the destruction or damage was by fire and thus constitutes arson, see **B8.25** to **B8.30**), criminal damage (unless charged in the racially aggravated form) is treated as if it were triable only summarily (MCA 1980, s. 22 and sch. 2). This does not convert it into a summary offence for all purposes and thus there can still be an attempt to commit low value criminal damage even though only an attempt to commit an indictable offence is caught by the CAA 1981, s. 1(4) (*Bristol Justices, ex parte E* [1999] 3 All ER 798). For consideration of the mode of trial for criminal damage, including the method of determining the value involved, see **D6**. Even if the value involved is not more than £5,000, a count for criminal damage may be included in an indictment for another offence in the circumstances set out in the CJA 1988, s. 40 (see **D11**). However if D has pleaded guilty in the magistrates' court, it would seem there is no power to commit to the Crown Court for sentence for such an offence under the Powers of Criminal Courts (Sentencing) Act 2000, s. 6(4) (see *Bangar* [2019] EWCA Crim 1533, on the basis that once the offence is treated as summary only it is no longer an offence triable either way for the purposes of s. 6(4)(b)). **B8.2**

See the *Magistrates' Court Sentencing Guidelines* which indicate that, where the value of the damage exceeds £10,000, Crown Court trial may be appropriate. **B8.3**

The aggravated form of the offence is triable either way, irrespective of the value of the damage. Even if the value is not more than £5,000, simple criminal damage is available on indictment as an alternative verdict if the aggravated element is not made out (*Fennell* [2000] 1 WLR 2011).

As to the procedure on charging both the basic and aggravated offence, see *Henderson v DPP* [2016] EWHC 464 (Admin), [2016] 1 WLR 1990, discussed at **B11.46**.

Indictment

Statement of Offence **B8.4**

Criminal damage contrary to section 1(1) of the Criminal Damage Act 1971.

Particulars of Offence

A on or about the... day of... did without lawful excuse damage [or destroy] a glass window, having a value of £120, belonging to V intending to damage [or destroy] such property or being reckless as to whether such property would be damaged [or destroyed].

Sentence

B8.5 For the maximum penalty and for sentencing guidelines, see **B8.41** to **B8.46**.

Meaning of 'Damage'

B8.6 'Damage' is left undefined in the Criminal Damage Act 1971. The courts have construed the term liberally. Criminal damage is not limited to permanent damage, so smearing mud on the walls of a police cell may be criminal damage. See *Roe v Kingerlee* [1986] Crim LR 735, where it was also said that: 'What constitutes criminal damage is a matter of fact and degree and it is for the justices, applying their common sense, to decide whether what occurred was damage or not.' In *Fiak* [2005] EWCA Crim 2381, where a blanket was soaked (but not soiled) with water from a toilet in a police cell and three cell floors were flooded, a conclusion that the blanket and floor were not damaged (even though the damage was remediable) 'would have been incomprehensible'.

Older (persuasive) authorities under pre-1971 enactments further illustrate the breadth of the notion of damage: see, e.g., *Roper v Knott* [1898] 1 QB 868 (milk damaged by adulteration with water) and *Tacey* (1821) Russ & Ry 452 (machine damaged by removal of essential part, although if the constituent part or parts are not themselves damaged it is important to charge damage to the machine, i.e. to the whole rather than to the parts — see *Woolcock* [1977] Crim LR 104 and 161). *Hardman v Chief Constable of Avon and Somerset* [1986] Crim LR 330 is a more modern illustration of the scope of the meaning of 'damage', in which water-soluble pavement paintings were held to constitute damage to the pavement.

The damage need not be tangible or visible if it affects the value or performance of the property (*Cox v Riley* (1986) 83 Cr App R 54, where a plastic circuit card for controlling a computerised saw was held to have been damaged by the erasure of the programs electronically written on it). Nor did it matter that the damage was not permanent in that it could be remedied, as restoring the programs necessitated 'time, labour and expense'. See now *Whiteley* (1991) 93 Cr App R 25, where a computer disk was held to be damaged by the addition and deletion of files. The interference with the disk amounted to an 'impairment of the value or usefulness of the disk to the owner'. These two decisions remain significant for the general meaning of damage but are overtaken as regards their own particular facts by the Computer Misuse Act 1990, s. 3 (see further **B17.11**).

Meaning of 'Property'

B8.7 **Criminal Damage Act 1971, s. 10**

(1) In this Act 'property' means property of a tangible nature, whether real or personal, including money and—
 (a) including wild creatures which have been tamed or are ordinarily kept in captivity...; but
 (b) not including mushrooms growing wild on any land or flowers, fruit or foliage or a plant growing wild on any land.

This definition of property is wider than that in the Theft Act 1968, s. 4 (see **B4.11** to **B4.18**), in that it lacks the restrictions on stealing land in that section, but, on the other hand, is narrower in that it does not include 'things in action and other intangible property'. Thus, land can be damaged by, e.g., dumping on it, even though it cannot be stolen (see discussion in *Cox* *v Riley* (1986) 83 Cr App 54 and **B8.6**). However, a copyright cannot be damaged by infringing it (contrast the offences under the Copyright, Designs and Patents Act 1988, s. 107), even though it can in theory be stolen. In *Cox v Riley*, even though the erased program might be said to be 'intangible property', the property alleged to be damaged was the circuit card and not the erased program itself. See also *Whiteley* (1991) 93 Cr App R 25, discussed at **B8.6**. (Note that both *Whiteley* and *Cox v Riley* have now to be read in the light of the Computer Misuse Act 1990, s. 3; see **B17.11**.)

Meaning of 'Belonging to Another'

Criminal Damage Act 1971, s. 10 **B8.8**

(2) Property shall be treated for the purposes of this Act as belonging to any person—
 (a) having the custody or control of it;
 (b) having in it any proprietary right or interest (not being an equitable interest arising only from an agreement to transfer or grant an interest); or
 (c) having a charge on it.

The effect of this provision (as with theft, see **B4.19** to **B4.27**) is that D can be guilty of criminal damage to D's own property if at the same time it belongs to someone else within the extended meaning of s. 10. This also means that D will be guilty even if D has a mistaken belief of owning the property if D also believes another has a proprietary interest in it (*Seray-Wurie v DPP* [2012] EWHC 208 (Admin)). A genuine belief in that person's consent might then be a defence under s. 5(2)(a) (see **B8.12**) but such a belief does not appear to have been argued on the facts in *Seray-Wurie*.

Mens Rea

This is satisfied by either intention or recklessness, and it is the latter, wider concept which **B8.9** has proved crucial. It seemed to be the case for 20 years following *Metropolitan Police Commissioner v Caldwell* [1982] AC 341 that recklessness in this context did not require subjective appreciation of the risk of causing damage, but was also satisfied by a failure to consider an obvious risk.

However, in *G* [2003] UKHL 50, [2004] 1 AC 1034, the House of Lords overruled its own previous decision in *Caldwell* and restored a subjective test to the meaning of recklessness for the purposes of the Criminal Damage Act 1971 as it ruled that this had always been Parliament's intention.

Lord Bingham adopted the meaning of recklessness given in the Law Commission's Draft Criminal Code (Law Com. No. 177) to the effect that:

A person acts recklessly . . . with respect to—
(i) a circumstance when he is aware of a risk that it exists or will exist;
(ii) a result when he is aware of a risk that it will occur;
(iii) and it is, in the circumstances known to him, unreasonable to take the risk.

For a more detailed analysis of the meaning of recklessness, see **A2.7** to **A2.11**. In the absence **B8.10** of a credible explanation, juries will normally conclude in relation to most if not all obvious risks that D was actually aware of the risk and thus liable even under a subjective test. The notion of closing one's mind to an obvious risk is also available where, as in the case of *Parker* [1977] 2 All ER 37, referred to seemingly approvingly by Lord Bingham as a case of conscious awareness of risk, D claims not to have been aware of a risk because of anger or another unsympathetic emotion. The concept of closing one's mind was referred to in the quite remarkable case of *Booth v CPS* [2006] EWHC 192 (Admin), which concerned the damage caused by a pedestrian to the bonnet of a vehicle into the path of which he suddenly stepped out. The Divisional Court upheld the findings of magistrates that the accused pedestrian was aware:

> ... of the risks associated with running into the road, namely the risk of a collision and the damage to property. Aware of those risks, he then deliberately put them out of his mind and, for reasons of his own, ran out into the path of a car.

One might have thought that the more obvious risk in such a case, as argued by the defence, is one of risk of injury to the pedestrian but the Court was not sympathetic to arguments which it regarded as, in effect, inviting it to characterise the particular findings of the magistrates as perverse.

Where D lacks the ability to appreciate an obvious risk (e.g., as in *G* itself, because of youth, or as in *Stephenson* [1979] QB 695, because of mental illness), the subjective test has clearly made a major difference and the courts are no longer compelled to convict because of what D ought to have been aware of had D had the degree of awareness of the standard reasonable person (see *Elliot v C* and *R (Stephen Malcolm)*, both of which can be regarded as overruled along with *Caldwell*).

B8.11 It will be noted that the test of recklessness refers to both circumstances and consequences. In criminal damage cases it will normally be the awareness of risk of a consequence — damage to property — which will be relevant. In this connection it appears from *G* that it is the awareness of the risk of damage to the property named in the charge that is relevant, in that case damage to the building rather than simply to the wheelie bins (given that Lord Bingham said (at [33]) that 'they would have had little defence' to a charge of recklessly damaging the wheelie bins). On the other hand it would not be necessary to foresee the extent of the damage (i.e. in *G*, £1 million worth of damage to the building). Nor is it necessary (whether for the purposes of recklessness or intention) that D realises that what is done to the property legally constitutes damage (e.g., where D writes on a notice with a black marker pen: see *Seray-Wurie v DPP* [2012] EWHC 208 (Admin)).

Awareness of risk of circumstances can also be relevant however, the circumstance being that the property was 'belonging to another'. If D decides to destroy all the papers in D's filing cabinet but is aware of the risk that some of D's flat-mate's valuable papers may also be in the cabinet and may also be destroyed, D is aware of the risk of a circumstance, that some of the property belongs to another. However, if D is not aware of any such risk and believes the property destroyed is D's own, D is not guilty under a subjective test (*Smith* [1974] QB 354 for an analogous example where the mistake was one of law).

Meaning of 'Without Lawful Excuse'

B8.12 The meaning of 'lawful excuse' is specially provided for in relation to this offence in the Criminal Damage Act 1971, s. 5 (which, however, is not applicable to the aggravated offence of criminal damage under s. 1(2) — see **B8.16** to **B8.24**).

Criminal Damage Act 1971, s. 5

(2) A person charged with an offence to which this section applies shall, whether or not he would be treated for the purposes of this Act as having a lawful excuse apart from this subsection, be treated for those purposes as having a lawful excuse—

(a) if at the time of the act or acts alleged to constitute the offence he believed that the person or persons whom he believed to be entitled to consent to the destruction of or damage to the property in question had so consented, or would have so consented to it if he or they had known of the destruction or damage and its circumstances; or

(b) if he destroyed or damaged or threatened to destroy or damage the property in question or, *in the case of a charge of an offence under section 3 above, intended to use or cause or* permit the use of something to destroy or damage it, in order to protect property belonging to himself or another or a right or interest in property which was or which he believed to be vested in himself or another, and at the time of the act or acts alleged to constitute the offence he believed—

(i) that the property, right or interest was in immediate need of protection; and
(ii) that the means of protection adopted or proposed to be adopted were or would be reasonable having regard to all the circumstances.

(3) For the purposes of this section it is immaterial whether a belief is justified or not if it is honestly held.
(4) For the purposes of subsection (2) above a right or interest in property includes any right or privilege in or over land, whether created by grant, licence or otherwise.
(5) This section shall not be construed as casting doubt on any defence recognised by law as a defence to criminal charges.

The words in s. 5(2), 'whether or not he would be treated for the purposes of this Act as having a lawful excuse apart from this subsection', together with s. 5(5), indicate that the section is not intended to be an exhaustive account of the circumstances of lawful excuse. Thus, general defences such as duress or prevention of crime are not excluded (cf. *Baker* [1997] Crim LR 497) but they do require D to be acting reasonably, and damaging perimeter fencing in order to challenge the lawful storage of nuclear weapons was held not to be reasonable by the Divisional Court in *Hutchinson v DPP* (2000) *Independent*, 20 November 2000. A motorist who damages a wheel clamp to free his car, having parked on another's property knowing of the risk of being clamped, does not have a lawful excuse (*Lloyd v DPP* [1992] 1 All ER 982: contrast the entirely different approach to wheel clamping in the Scottish case *Black v Carmichael* (1992) *The Times*, 25 June 1992, and see now the Protection of Freedoms Act 2012, s. 54). **B8.13**

Section 5 specifically covers two alternative types of belief which are outlined in more detail in s. 5(2):

(a) belief in consent; or
(b) belief in the immediate necessity to protect property.

Subjective Nature of Belief Section 5(3) emphasises that the question is the purely subjective one of whether the belief is honestly held, not whether it is justified or reasonable. In *Jaggard v Dickinson* [1981] QB 527, D, due to intoxication, mistakenly believed she would have had the owner's consent to breaking a window in order to gain access to a house (unfortunately she tried to break into the wrong house). The Divisional Court quashed her conviction, saying (per Mustill J, at pp. 531–2), 'the court is required by section 5(3) to focus on the existence of the belief, not its intellectual soundness; and a belief can be just as much honestly held if it is induced by intoxication, as if it stems from stupidity, forgetfulness or inattention'. **B8.14**

Although the test under s. 5(2)(b)(ii) is clearly *subjective* and the question is not whether the D's action is *in fact* reasonable (contrast *Hutchinson v DPP* (2000) *Independent*, 20 November 2000 at **B8.13**) but whether D *believed* it to be reasonable, whether D is acting 'in order to protect property' under s. 5(2)(b) does seem to have an objective aspect. In *Hunt* (1977) 66 Cr App R 105, D set fire to bedding to draw attention to a defective fire alarm in old people's accommodation which the court ruled was not 'in order to protect property', despite D's belief that it would ultimately have that effect. See further *Hill* (1988) 89 Cr App R 74, where D's beliefs about the ultimate effects of damaging perimeter fencing at a US naval base were held not to amount to a purpose of protecting property, or to a belief that property was in *imminent* need of protection under s. 5(2)(b)(i). See, however, *Chamberlain v Lindon* [1998] 2 All ER 538 for a case where these two requirements were satisfied. There is no requirement that the threat to property believed to be in need of protection is a threat of *unlawful* damage (*Jones* [2004] EWCA Crim 1981, [2005] QB 259).

If D does hold a belief provided for in s. 5, it is immaterial as far as D's liability for criminal damage is concerned that D has some ulterior fraudulent or criminal purpose. Thus, in *Denton* [1981] 1 All ER 65, D set fire to the cotton mill where he worked, because he believed he had been asked to do so by his employer with a view to gaining the insurance money on the property. The Court of Appeal quashed his conviction for criminal damage, pointing out that if the owner **B8.15** himself had caused the damage he would have committed no offence (under s. 1(1), though other charges might be possible), since he was not damaging property 'belonging to another', and hence D, who believed he was acting on behalf of the owner and with his consent, should be in no worse position. In fact, the 'employer' (an individual) in this case was not strictly the owner of the property, which legally belonged to the company, a separate legal entity. This did not particularly matter on the facts, since it was conceded that D honestly believed that his 'employer' was the person 'entitled to consent' within s. 5(2)(a). Contrast *Appleyard* (1985) 81 Cr App R 319, where a managing director was convicted of destroying the company's store, and was not allowed to claim that he himself was the person entitled to consent to the damage. It would seem, therefore, that the belief under s. 5(2)(a) must relate to some other person having the right to consent and not to D personally. If D mistakenly believes D is the actual owner (as opposed to being merely the person entitled to consent), then D has a defence, not under s. 5(2) but because D lacks *mens rea* (*Smith* [1974] QB 354).

AGGRAVATED CRIMINAL DAMAGE

B8.16 **Criminal Damage Act 1971, s. 1**

(2) A person who without lawful excuse destroys or damages any property, whether belonging to himself or another—

(a) intending to destroy or damage any property or being reckless as to whether any property would be destroyed or damaged; and

(b) intending by the destruction or damage to endanger the life of another or being reckless as to whether the life of another would be thereby endangered;

shall be guilty of an offence.

Procedure

B8.17 Aggravated criminal damage is triable only on indictment. It is normally a class 3 offence, but see CrimPD XIII, para. B (see Supplement, **CPD.XIII.B**), for the additional factors that the court considers on allocation.

Indictment

B8.18 *Statement of Offence*

Destroying [or damaging] property with intent to endanger life [or being reckless as to whether life would be endangered] contrary to section 1(2) of the Criminal Damage Act 1971.

Particulars of Offence

A on or about the... day of... did without lawful excuse damage [or destroy] a motor vehicle belonging to V, intending to damage [or destroy] such vehicle or being reckless as to whether such vehicle would be damaged [or destroyed] and intending by such damage [or destruction] to endanger the life of V or being reckless as to whether the life of V would be thereby endangered.

Alternative Verdicts

B8.19 It is submitted that in some cases, on an indictment for aggravated criminal damage, it may be possible for the jury to return an alternative verdict of simple criminal damage, pursuant to the Criminal Law Act 1967, s. 6(3) (see **D19.41** ***et seq.***). However, this is problematic in that it will be possible only where:

(a) it is specifically alleged that the property in question belonged not to D but to another (which is not an essential averment under the Criminal Damage Act 1971, s. 1(2), but is under s. 1(1)); and

(b) there is no issue as to lawful excuse (the meaning of which differs as between the two offences, inasmuch as the provisions of the Criminal Damage Act 1971, s. 5, do not apply to offences under s. 1(2)).

It is therefore always appropriate to add an alternative count (which may be done even where the value of the property is less than £5,000 — see the CJA 1988, s. 40, and **D11.18**). In the absence of such an alternative count, trial judges may be reluctant to leave the alternative to the jury (see generally **D19.58** *et seq*.).

Sentence

For the maximum penalty and for sentencing guidelines, see **B8.41** to **B8.44**. **B8.20**

Relationship to Simple Criminal Damage

Aggravated criminal damage is identical with the offence under the Criminal Damage Act 1971, s. 1(1), as far as it relates to the meaning of damage and property (see **B8.6** and **B8.7**), but differs in three main respects: **B8.21**

(a) The presence of the aggravating ulterior *mens rea* of intention to endanger life or recklessness as to whether life would be endangered.
(b) The fact that the offence can be committed irrespective of whether the property 'belongs to another'.
(c) The inapplicability of s. 5 of the Act to the meaning of 'lawful excuse'.

Mens Rea In accordance with the subjective meaning of recklessness endorsed in *G* [2003] UKHL 50, [2004] 1 AC 1034, D must be subjectively aware of both the risk of damaging property and the risk of endangering the life of another. Again, the more obvious the risk of endangering life, the more likely that the jury will conclude that D was aware of the risk unless D gives some plausible explanation of why the obvious risk would not have been appreciated. According to the Court of Appeal in *Heard* [2007] EWCA Crim 125, [2008] QB 43 (see **A3.17**), recklessness as to endangering life is not a basic intent but is a specific (ulterior) intent and it would thus seem that voluntary intoxication can be admitted in order to show that D did not appreciate the risk of endangering life (but see also *Coley* [2013] EWCA Crim 223 at **A3.18**). **B8.22**

In the case of attempt to commit an offence under the Criminal Damage Act 1971, s. 1(2), recklessness as to life being endangered will suffice even though a specific intent to cause damage is also required (*A-G's Ref (No. 3 of 1992)* [1994] 2 All ER 121). See, however, *Pace* [2014] EWCA Crim 186; [2014] 1 WLR 2867 and the discussion at **A5.80**.

Requirement that Danger to Life Result from Damage Intended D must be at least reckless as to causing damage, as to endangering life and also as to whether life would be endangered *as a result of the damage*. The offence was thus not made out in *Steer* [1988] AC 111, where D shot through a window behind which two people were standing. Although D was reckless as to whether life would be endangered, the danger to life was not due to the damage to the window but due to the bullet itself. Compare *Webster* [1995] 2 All ER 168, where damaging the windscreen of a moving car or ramming the car was held to be capable of endangering life as a result of the damage. Furthermore, it is the damage which D intended, or as to which D was reckless, that is relevant, rather than the actual damage that happens to be caused. See *Dudley* [1989] Crim LR 57, where only trivial damage, not likely to endanger life, was *actually* caused, but D's conviction was upheld since D created a *risk* of much more serious damage which was capable of endangering life. *Steer* was considered in *Wenton* [2010] EWCA Crim 2361 where the case was even plainer in that the offence as charged was not made out since the act charged as causing the damage (breaking a window by throwing a brick) was a quite separate act from the act creating the risk to life (throwing through the window a petrol canister which in the event did not ignite). Although the appeals against conviction based on the first act of throwing the brick clearly had to be allowed, it seems that the facts could have been successfully dealt with by charging the *second* act of throwing the canister as an attempt to cause damage by fire, being reckless as to whether that *intended* damage by fire would endanger life. **B8.23**

B8.24 **Meaning of 'Without Lawful Excuse'** The partial definition of 'lawful excuse' in the Criminal Damage Act 1971, s. 5, is not applicable, because belief in the owner's consent or the immediate need to protect *property* cannot justify the endangering of human life. However, 'without lawful excuse' in any other sense remains part of the definition of the offence so that, e.g., damaging property in lawful self-defence would not be criminal even if it endangers the aggressor's (or possibly even a third party's) life, provided that it was reasonable to do so.

ARSON

B8.25 **Criminal Damage Act 1971, s. 1**

(3) An offence committed under this section by destroying or damaging property by fire shall be charged as arson.

Procedure

B8.26 Simple arson contrary to the Criminal Damage Act 1971, s. 1(1) and (3), is triable either way (MCA 1980, s. 17 and sch. 1, para. 29). When tried on indictment it is normally a class 3 offence, but see CrimPD XIII, para. B (see Supplement, **CPD.XIII.B**), for the additional factors that the court considers on allocation. The value involved in simple arson does not cause the MCA 1980, s. 22, to restrict the mode of trial because arson is, by sch. 2 to the MCA 1980, not an offence to which s. 22 applies.

Aggravated arson contrary to the Criminal Damage Act 1971, s. 1(2) and (3), is triable only on indictment. It is a class 2A offence.

Indictment

B8.27 The wording of the Criminal Damage Act 1971, s. 1(3) (see **B8.25**), has been held to be mandatory in the Crown Court, and a charge of criminal damage 'contrary to s. 1(1) plus (3) of the Act' was held to be a nullity in *Booth* [1999] Crim LR 144. However, *Booth* was distinguished in *Drayton* [2005] EWCA Crim 2013 in the context of a charge in a magistrates' court. The charge of damage by fire under s. 1(1), (3) and (4), was held to be a valid one to which D could lawfully plead guilty and on which D could be lawfully committed for sentence. The important issue was that the allegation was at least identified as 'damage *by fire*' rather than by the use of the specific word 'arson' with which it was synonymous, although it would be preferable to use the word 'arson'. Hedley J said (at [11]) that:

> ... the essence of section 1(3), the mischief which it is designed to address, is that the defendant shall know that he is facing an allegation of damage by fire, because by section 1(4) the penalties in relation to damage by fire are different and significantly potentially more severe than those of simple criminal damage by other means.

In *Booth*, the charge in the Crown Court was conspiracy to incite a variety of forms of criminal damage including damage by fire but it appears that the indictment whilst mentioning s. 1(3) did not specifically mention either 'arson' or 'damage *by fire*'. The focus in *Drayton* was on damage by fire and nothing else and, in describing the offence alleged in ordinary language avoiding technical terms like arson and giving reasonable information as to the nature of the charge, it complied with the requirements of the rules (now CrimPR 7.2; see Supplement, **R7.2**). Hedley J left open the position in the Crown Court saying (at [10]):

> Clearly on indictment where the rules require both a statement of offence and particulars of offence *it is desirable that the word arson should continue to be used in the statement of offence.* Whether the absence of that word arson from a count that plainly alleges damage by fire and nothing else invalidates the count must await decision as and when that point arises.

Statement of Offence

Arson contrary to section 1(1) and (3) of the Criminal Damage Act 1971.

Particulars of Offence

A on or about the... day of... did without lawful excuse damage by fire a motor vehicle, having a value of £3,500, belonging to V intending to damage such vehicle by fire or being reckless as to whether such vehicle would be damaged by fire.

An offence under s. 1(2) by fire must also be charged as arson. In such a case there should be separate counts of arson with intent to endanger life and arson being reckless as to whether life would be endangered (*Hoof* (1980) 72 Cr App 126; *sed quaere*, the two forms of *mens rea* do not mean that the section creates two offences, and, of course, the maximum penalty is the same).

First Count

Statement of Offence

Arson contrary to section 1(2) and (3) of the Criminal Damage Act 1971.

Particulars of Offence

A on or about the... day of... did without lawful excuse damage by fire a motor vehicle, having a value of £3,500, belonging to V intending to damage such vehicle by fire and intending by such damage to endanger the life of V.

Second Count

As above, but alleging instead of the intent to endanger life: '... and being reckless as to whether the life of V would thereby be endangered'.

Alternative Verdicts

See **B8.19**. On indictment for arson under the Criminal Damage Act 1971, s. 1(1) and (3) or s. 1(2) and (3), it is submitted that the jury should not be invited to return an alternative verdict of guilty of criminal damage other than by fire, even under the corresponding subsection of s. 1, because of the different nature of the *actus reus*. In the unlikely event of doubt as to the method of causing the damage, an alternative count should be added. **B8.28**

Sentence

For the maximum penalty and for sentencing guidelines, see **B8.41** to **B8.46**. **B8.29**

Elements

Arson differs from simple or aggravated criminal damage only in that the destruction or damage to the property must be 'by fire'. *Quaere* whether this might extend to damage caused, for example, by water in saving the property from imminent destruction by the fire, or by a fall resulting from the collapse due to fire of a structure on which the property had stood. **B8.30**

THREATS TO DESTROY OR DAMAGE PROPERTY

Criminal Damage Act 1971, s. 2 **B8.31**

A person who without lawful excuse makes to another a threat, intending that that other would fear it would be carried out,—

(a) to destroy or damage any property belonging to that other or a third person; or

(b) to destroy or damage his own property in a way which he knows is likely to endanger the life of that other or a third person;

shall be guilty of an offence.

Procedure

A threat to destroy or damage property is triable either way (MCA 1980, s. 17 and sch. 1, para. 29). When tried on indictment it is normally a class 3 offence, but see CrimPD XIII, para. B (see Supplement, **CPD.XIII.B**), for the additional factors that the court considers on allocation. **B8.32**

Indictment

B8.33 *Statement of Offence*

Threatening to destroy property contrary to section 2(a) of the Criminal Damage Act 1971.

Particulars of Offence

A on or about the... day of... did without lawful excuse make a threat to V to destroy a motor vehicle belonging to V [or X] intending that V would fear that the threat would be carried out.

Sentence

B8.34 For the maximum penalty and sentencing guideline see **B8.47**.

Elements

B8.35 For the meaning of 'without lawful excuse', see **B8.12**, but note that by virtue of the Criminal Damage Act 1971, s. 5(1), the partial definition of 'lawful excuse' does not apply where D knows that the threatened damage is likely to endanger life. This is no doubt for the same sorts of reasons that s. 5 does not apply to aggravated criminal damage under s. 1(2).

There is no requirement that the threat be carried out or be capable of being carried out immediately, or that D intended to carry it out or that the person threatened *actually* fears that it will be carried out, provided that D *intends* that there should be such fear. Although in *Ankerson* [2015] EWCA Crim 549, a conviction was upheld following a direction that D need only intend that the person threatened would fear that the threat *might* (as opposed to *would*) be carried out, Elias LJ advised that 'a judge summing-up with respect to this offence in future would be wise simply to use the language of the statute'. A threat to set oneself on fire may come within s. 2(a) if, objectively considered, it constitutes a threat to destroy or damage another's property as a consequence (*Cakmak* [2002] EWCA Crim 500, [2002] 2 Cr App R 10 (158)).

POSSESSION WITH INTENT TO DESTROY OR DAMAGE PROPERTY

B8.36 **Criminal Damage Act 1971, s. 3**

A person who has anything in his custody or under his control intending without lawful excuse to use it or cause or permit another to use it—

(a) to destroy or damage any property belonging to some other person; or

(b) to destroy or damage his own or the user's property in a way which he knows is likely to endanger the life of some other person;

shall be guilty of an offence.

Procedure

B8.37 Possession of an article with intent to destroy or damage property is triable either way (MCA 1980, s. 17 and sch. 1, para. 29). When tried on indictment it is normally a class 3 offence, but see CrimPD XIII, para. B (see Supplement, **CPD.XIII.B**), for the additional factors that the court considers on allocation.

Indictment

B8.38 *Statement of Offence*

Possession of an article with intent to destroy [or damage] property contrary to section 3 of the Criminal Damage Act 1971.

Particulars of Offence

A on or about the... day of... did have in his custody [or under his control] a can of spray paint intending without lawful excuse to use it [or cause or permit X to use it] to damage a motor vehicle belonging to V.

Sentence

For the maximum penalty, see **B8.41**. **B8.39**

Elements

The essence of the offence is the intention to use *any article*, or to cause or permit it to be used, to cause damage. A conditional intention to so use it if given circumstances arise will suffice (*Buckingham* (1976) 63 Cr App R 159). **B8.40**

The partial definition of 'lawful excuse' in the Criminal Damage Act 1971, s. 5, is applicable only to the form of the offence in s. 3(a) and not to that in s. 3(b), although it is still open to D to put forward a lawful excuse independently of s. 5.

The Criminal Damage Act 1971, s. 6, enables the police to search for articles used, or intended to be used, to cause criminal damage.

Criminal Damage Act 1971, s. 6

(1) If it is made to appear by information on oath before a justice of the peace that there is reasonable cause to believe that any person has in his custody or under his control or on his premises anything which there is reasonable cause to believe has been used or is intended for use without lawful excuse—
  (a) to destroy or damage property belonging to another; or
  (b) to destroy or damage any property in a way likely to endanger the life of another,
  the justice may grant a warrant authorising any constable to search for and seize that thing.
(2) A constable who is authorised under this section to search premises for anything, may enter (if need be by force) and search the premises accordingly and may seize anything which he believes to have been used or to be intended to be used as aforesaid.
(3) The Police (Property) Act 1897 (disposal of property in the possession of the police) shall apply to property which has come into the possession of the police under this section as it applies to property which has come into the possession of the police in the circumstances mentioned in that Act.

SENTENCING: OFFENCES INVOLVING DAMAGE TO PROPERTY

Maximum Penalties

Criminal damage, with intent to endanger life or being reckless whether life is endangered: life imprisonment (Criminal Damage Act 1971, s. 4(1)). **B8.41**

Criminal damage: ten years (s. 4(2)) on indictment; six months and/or an unlimited fine summarily. If, however, damage is quantified at less than £5,000, so that the offence is treated as triable summarily only: three months, a fine not exceeding level 4 on the standard scale, or both. In *Gilheaney* [2016] EWCA Crim 2059 the defendant stabbed and killed a pet dog. The offence was charged as simple criminal damage, with no evidence of the dog's value. The sentence of six months imposed by the judge was therefore unlawful and was reduced to two months on appeal.

Racially or religiously aggravated criminal damage: 14 years on indictment (CDA 1998, s. 30(2)); six months and/or an unlimited fine summarily.

Arson (where either of the above offences is committed by fire): life imprisonment (Criminal Damage Act 1971, s. 4(1)) on indictment; where criminal damage by fire, but not criminal damage with intent or recklessness whether life is endangered, six months and/or an unlimited fine summarily.

Threat to destroy or damage property: ten years (s. 4(2)) on indictment; six months and/or an unlimited fine summarily.

Possessing article with intent to destroy or damage property: ten years (s. 4(2)) on indictment; six months and/or an unlimited fine summarily.

Sentencing Guidelines (All Offences)

B8.42 The definitive sentencing guidelines which cover arson and criminal damage offences apply to all offenders aged 18 and over sentenced on or after 1 October 2019 regardless of the date of the offence (see Supplement, **SG11-1** *et seq.*). Individual guidelines cover simple criminal damage valued above and below £5,000 (including racially aggravated offending); simple arson; arson or criminal damage being reckless whether life is endangered or with intent to endanger life; and threats to cause criminal damage. Offence ranges extend from discharge in a very low level simple criminal damage case to 12 years' imprisonment for an offence involving arson or other criminal damage with intent to endanger life, or indeed longer given the express provision within that guideline to exceed the top of the offence range in cases where there are exceptional features.

The guidelines for the various offences have much in common in their structure and content. They identify broadly common elements of culpability, including attacks motivated by revenge, careful planning, and an intention to cause a high risk of injury or very serious damage to property. Assessment of harm starts with the severity of the damage, but also considers serious physical and/or psychological harm to the victim and others, as well as any wider economic impacts or social impacts of the offending. In the latter category, the guidelines acknowledge the wider impact of harm when damage is caused to heritage sites such as churches and historic buildings as well as civic facilities such as community halls.

Sentencing Guidelines: Criminal Damage Other than by Fire, under £5,000 /over £5,000

B8.43 There are separate guidelines for this offence depending on value, both effective from 1 October 2019 (see Supplement, **SG11-4** and **SG11-3**). The maximum sentence for the simple offence of criminal damage under £5,000 is three months' imprisonment, and the guidelines set out an offence range from discharge to three months' imprisonment or a level 4 fine. A count of criminal damage added to an indictment is punishable by up to ten years' imprisonment, whatever its value. In low-value cases sentencers should have regard to the 'under £5,000' guideline. For simple offences of criminal damage over £5,000, the maximum custodial sentence is ten years' imprisonment, with an offence range from discharge to four years' imprisonment.

By virtue of the Penalties for Disorderly Behaviour (Amount of Penalty) Order 2002 (SI 2002 No. 1837), the offence under the Criminal Damage Act 1971, s. 1(1), is a fixed penalty offence and attracts a penalty of £90 for persons aged 18 or over.

Some pre-guideline cases that illustrate the sentencing issues that arise in this type of case include *Brzezinski* [2012] EWCA Crim 198, [2012] 2 Cr App R (S) 62 (364), in which a sentence of 18 months' imprisonment together with an ASBO was upheld on a 23-year-old man who admitted eight counts of criminal damage, all involving the writing of graffiti in railway carriages.

Racial or religious aggravation cannot be taken into account by the sentencer when sentencing for the basic offence of criminal damage. To do so would infringe the principle that offenders must not be sentenced for an offence for which they have not been charged and convicted (*McGillivray* [2005] EWCA Crim 604, [2005] 2 Cr App R (S) 60 (366)). Where there is evidence that racial or religious aggravation was present, the aggravated form of the offence should be charged.

Sentencing Guidelines: Racially or Religiously Aggravated Criminal Damage

B8.44 The maximum sentence for the racially or religiously aggravated offence is 14 years' imprisonment, but these offences must be assessed by reference to the relevant 'value' guideline, based on the harm of the underlying offence. Sentencers should declare the sentence which would have been imposed without the racial aggravation and then the uplift that has been applied because of the impact of the aggravation. In a case of high impact, an otherwise non-custodial case may be deemed to have crossed the custody threshold. A case already worth immediate custody may have the length of the sentence increased. Beyond these indications there is no guidance as to the extent of the uplift but pre-guideline authorities illustrate a broadly consistent approach to the proportionate uplift. In *Johnston* [2005] EWCA Crim 2737, [2006] 1 Cr App R (S) 115 (665), a sentence of six years' detention in a young offender institution was upheld for racially aggravated criminal damage in the form of damaging headstones in a Jewish cemetery, combined with other racially aggravated offences. Sixty-two headstones had been smashed or pushed over, with damage estimated at £100,000. The judge indicated that the sentence for the basic offence would have been three years, with a further three years to reflect the racial element. The Court of Appeal noted that the case contained a number of high-level aggravating features and had clearly been calculated to cause maximum distress to the families of those whose graves had been targeted.

Sentencing Guideline: Simple Arson (Criminal Damage by Fire)

The maximum sentence for arson is life imprisonment. The guideline (see Supplement, SG11-1 *et seq.*), effective from 1 October 2019, indicates that for an offence falling within the highest category (greater harm and higher culpability) the starting point is four years with a range from two to eight years, although longer sentences may be imposed for exceptional offences in this category. For the most minor offences, such as an impulsive act causing negligible harm by an offender whose responsibility is substantially reduced by a mental disorder or learning disability, the starting point is a community order and the range includes a discharge. The guideline advises sentencers to consider requesting a report from liaison and diversion services, a psychiatrist or other medical practitioner, to ascertain whether the offence is linked to a mental disorder or learning disability (to assist in the assessment of culpability) and also as to whether any mental health disposal should be considered. **B8.45**

Sentencing Guidelines: Arson, or Other Criminal Damage, Being Reckless Whether Life is Endangered or with Intent to Endanger Life

The maximum sentence is life imprisonment. The guideline (see Supplement, SG11-6 *et seq.*), effective from 1 October 2019, refers to the common harm factors which apply in other guidelines, but the categories of culpability now focus on the two possible mental states — namely recklessness or intent. For an offence falling within the highest category (greater harm and an intention to endanger life) the starting point is eight years' imprisonment with a range up to 12 years, although for exceptional offences in this category, sentences beyond the upper range may be imposed. **B8.46**

The guideline advises sentencers to consider requesting a report from liaison and diversion services, a psychiatrist or other medical practitioner, to ascertain whether the offence is linked to a mental disorder or learning disability (to assist in the assessment of culpability) and also as to whether any mental health disposal should be considered.

Pre-guideline cases illustrating the issues that can arise in sentencing for offences of arson being reckless whether life was endangered or with intent to endanger life include *Finnemore* [2019] EWCA Crim 1585 where a sentence of five years' imprisonment for two offences of arson being reckless as to whether life was endangered and one offence of arson with intent to endanger life was found to be unduly lenient. Given the offences were premeditated, carried out in revenge, with the reckless offences committed in order to distract the fire brigade from the intentional fire setting near a block of flats, which was done at night when D would have known that the occupants were asleep, the Court concluded that ten years' imprisonment reflected more accurately the seriousness of the offending. In *Cox* [2017] EWCA Crim 1366, [2018] 1 Cr App R (S) 3 (15) the A-G referred to the Court of Appeal as unduly lenient a sentence of four-and-a-half years' imprisonment for a conviction for arson, being reckless as to whether life was endangered. D had been a passenger on a commercial flight. He had been drinking heavily and, while smoking in the plane's toilet, had started a fire in the waste paper bin. The fire was extinguished and D given a warning by the captain. An hour later, a second fire was discovered, and although it was extinguished, it forced an emergency landing. The Court found that the sentence was unduly lenient considering the level of culpability and potential harm. Starting a fire and not ensuring that it was fully extinguished should be dealt with as though it were deliberate fire setting. The potential for catastrophic loss of life ought to have been obvious. D had been warned previously and took no notice. The appropriate starting point was 11 years' imprisonment, not five. Three years following a plea of guilty was appropriate in *Keates* [2017] EWCA Crim 309, where the 21-year-old offender of previous good character, heavily intoxicated and angry with his ex-partner, pushed burning paper through her door in an act of revenge. There was no significant planning, no accelerant was used and, because the occupants were woken by the noise and quickly put out the fire, only minor damage was caused.

Pre-guideline cases illustrating the issues that can arise in sentencing for non-arson criminal damage endangering life include *C* [2009] EWCA Crim 1441, [2010] 1 Cr App R (S) 55 (347), in which terms of detention of four years, three years and two years were upheld on young persons aged 16, 15 and 13 who threw stones and bricks at vehicles travelling on a busy road. Eleven vehicles were damaged. An accident then occurred in which two of the cars collided and the driver of one was killed. In *Dodd* [1997] 1 Cr App R (S) 127, D pleaded guilty to damaging property being reckless whether life was endangered, and to driving while disqualified. He had driven his car at between 35 and 40mph through the glass-fronted doors of Plymouth Magistrates' Court and through inner doors, the car coming to rest against the rear wall of the building, causing £34,000 worth of damage. Nobody was injured. A sentence of four years' imprisonment for the criminal damage offence was upheld by the Court of Appeal.

Sentencing Guideline: Threatening to Commit Criminal Damage

B8.47 The maximum sentence for threatening criminal damage is ten years' imprisonment. The guideline (see Supplement, **SG11-7** ***et seq.***), effective from 1 October 2019, indicates that for an offence falling into the highest category the starting point is 18 months' imprisonment. The offence range is from discharge to four years' imprisonment.

Section B9 Offences Affecting Security

ACTS PREJUDICIAL TO SAFETY OR INTERESTS OF STATE ('SPYING')

Official Secrets Act 1911, s. 1 **B9.1**

(1) If any person for any purpose prejudicial to the safety or interests of the State—
  (a) approaches, inspects, passes over or is in the neighbourhood of, or enters any prohibited place within the meaning of this Act, or
  (b) makes any sketch, plan, model, or note which is calculated to be or might be or is intended to be directly or indirectly useful to an enemy; or
  (c) obtains, collects, records, or publishes, or communicates to any other person any secret official code word or pass word, or any sketch, plan, model, article, or note, or other document or information which is calculated to be or might be or is intended to be directly or indirectly useful to an enemy;

he shall be guilty of [an offence].

Procedure

This offence is triable only on indictment. It is a class 1B offence. **B9.2**

Official Secrets Act 1911, s. 8

A prosecution for an offence under this Act shall not be instituted except by or with the consent of the Attorney-General.

By virtue of the Official Secrets Act 1911, s. 10(1) and (2), and the Official Secrets Act 1920, s. 8(3), a competent British court in the place where the offence was committed has jurisdiction to try a person, and a court in England has jurisdiction to try a person alleged to have committed the instant offence, even though the offence was committed elsewhere. As to territorial jurisdiction generally, see **A8**.

In addition to general powers (see **D3.122** ***et seq.***), the Official Secrets Act 1920, s. 8(4), permits the court, on the application of the prosecution, on grounds of national safety to exclude all or some of the public from a trial, except during any sentencing hearing. This power applies to all offences under the 1911, 1920 and 1989 Acts, except those created by s. 8 of the 1989 Act. The ambit of s. 8(4) was considered in *A-G v Leveller Magazine Ltd* [1979] AC 440, in relation to the granting of anonymity to a prosecution witness. The judge's wide discretion in this area was upheld. Likewise, the restrictive trial arrangements in *Shayler* [2003] EWCA Crim 2218 (which included screens and anonymity for security services witnesses and a requirement of prior notice by D in relation to any questions or evidence relating to security or intelligence on penalty of contempt) were upheld, albeit in circumstances where D refused to give any assurance that he would not attempt to raise a 'public interest' defence (which the House of Lords had already ruled was unavailable to him). The procedure for applications under s. 8 is set out in CrimPR 6.6 (see **D3.124**). *In camera* proceedings should not result in both anonymity for D and a sealed indictment but if there is a serious possibility that the prosecution could not proceed in open court because of well-founded national security concerns, a substantial portion of the trial may have the public excluded (*Re Guardian News and Media Ltd* [2014] EWCA Crim 1861, [2015] 1 Cr App R 4 (36), applied in *Re Guardian News and Media Ltd* [2016] EWCA Crim 11, [2016] 1 WLR 1767).

Indictment

B9.3 *Statement of Offence*

Entering a prohibited place contrary to section 1(1)(a) of the Official Secrets Act 1911.

Particulars of Offence

A on or about the...day of..., for a purpose prejudicial to the safety or interests of the State, namely..., entered a prohibited place, namely...

Sentence

B9.4 A person guilty of an offence under the Official Secrets Act 1911, s. 1, is liable to imprisonment for a term not exceeding 14 years (Official Secrets Act 1920, s. 8(1)). There is no offence-specific guideline but the Sentencing Council's *General Guideline: Overarching Principles* (see Supplement, **SG2-1**) is used for all offenders sentenced on or after 1 October 2019.

Offences committed under the Official Secrets Act 1911, s. 1, will inevitably attract a lengthy custodial sentence. In *Prime* (1983) 5 Cr App R (S) 127, D pleaded guilty to seven offences against the Official Secrets Acts. Having been employed for nine years in the Government Communications Service, with access to highly sensitive intelligence information of importance to national security, he had passed on such information to the Soviet Union. He received consecutive terms of 14, 14, and seven years' imprisonment, which were upheld on appeal. In *Schulze* (1986) 8 Cr App R (S) 463, the offenders' home was found to contain a variety of spying equipment and documents and related equipment. They were convicted of doing acts preparatory to the commission of an offence under s. 1 of the Act. Sentences of ten years were upheld in each case. In *James* [2009] EWCA Crim 1261, [2010] 1 Cr App R (S) 57 (362) the Court of Appeal reviewed the relevant sentencing authorities and upheld a deterrent sentence of ten years' imprisonment following a conviction under s. 1 of the Act imposed on an interpreter for NATO forces in Afghanistan for spying on behalf of Iran. Lord Judge CJ emphasised that a deterrent element would necessarily govern every sentencing decision in cases of treachery. Although allied military relationships were not jeopardised by D's actions, it was an aggravating feature that they might have been. The fact that the spying occurred in a war zone and that material was passed to a hostile State also increased the gravity of the offence. In *Devenney* (12 December 2012 unreported, Central Criminal Court), D received a total of eight years' imprisonment (concurrent) having pleaded guilty to one offence under s. 1 and one offence of misconduct in public office. He was a Royal Navy petty officer who, over a period of four months, covertly passed details of a secret code to MI5 officers whom he believed to be Russian agents. His motive was retribution; he considered the Royal Navy had treated him badly, and he was depressed at the time. Saunders J considered that a deterrent sentence was required even though D had actually achieved nothing by his actions. Following the introduction of the definitive sentencing guideline, *Terrorism Offences* (see Supplement, **SG32-1**), from 27 April 2018, the sentencer may treat the fact that an offence had a terrorist connection as a non-statutory aggravating factor.

Offence Not Limited to 'Spying'

B9.5 The Official Secrets Act 1911, s. 1, is stated in the marginal note as being concerned with 'penalties for spying', but it is not limited to 'spying' and extends to sabotage and temporary sabotage (*Chandler v DPP* [1964] AC 763).

Mens Rea: Purpose Prejudicial to the Safety or Interests of the State

An offence under the Official Secrets Act 1911, s. 1(1), may be committed in a number of ways, which must be considered separately. However, the *mens rea* requirement that a person act with a 'purpose prejudicial to the safety or interests of the State' is common to each paragraph of s. 1(1). The House of Lords in *Chandler v DPP* [1964] AC 763 held that it is not necessary to establish an overt act on D's part evidencing the requisite purpose — circumstantial evidence will suffice. It is to be presumed that a sketch, plan, model etc. made etc. by a person not acting under lawful authority is made etc. for a purpose prejudicial to the interests of the State until the contrary is proved. Furthermore, 'prejudicial to the safety or interests of the State' does not refer to the government or the executive, or UK residents. 'The country' or 'the realm' are good synonyms as are 'the organised community' or 'the organs of government of a national community'. Whether a person's purpose is prejudicial to the safety or interests of the State is a matter for the jury to decide on the basis that it is for the Crown to decide what is for the safety or interests of the State and that decision of the Crown is not challengeable. Thus, D's opinion as to what is for the safety or interests of the State is irrelevant (*Bettaney* [1985] Crim LR 104). Similarly, in a prosecution under related regulations in *M* (1916) 11 Cr App R 207, it was held that the information provided to the enemy need not be correct provided that D intended to inform the enemy. See further **B9.67**. **B9.6**

Approaching, etc. Prohibited Place

'Prohibited place' is defined by the Official Secrets Act 1911, s. 3. **B9.7**

Official Secrets Act 1911, ss. 3 and 12

3. For the purposes of this Act, the expression 'prohibited place' means—
   (a) any work of a defence, arsenal, naval or air force establishment or station, factory, dockyard, mine, minefield, camp, ship, or aircraft belonging to or occupied by or on behalf of His Majesty, or any telegraph, telephone, wireless or signal station, or office so belonging or occupied, and any place belonging to or occupied by or on behalf of His Majesty and used for the purpose of building, repairing, making, or storing any munitions of war, or any sketches, plans, models, or documents relating thereto, or for the purpose of getting any metals, oil, or minerals of use in time of war;
   (b) any place not belonging to His Majesty where any munitions of war, or any sketches, models, plans or documents relating thereto, are being made, repaired, gotten or stored under contract with, or with any person on behalf of, His Majesty, or otherwise on behalf of His Majesty; and
   (c) any place belonging to or used for the purposes of His Majesty which is for the time being declared by order of a Secretary of State to be a prohibited place for the purposes of this section on the ground that information with respect thereto, or damage thereto, would be useful to an enemy; and
   (d) any railway, road, way, or channel, or other means of communication by land or water (including any works or structures being part thereof or connected therewith), or any place used for gas, water, or electricity works or other works for purposes of a public character, or any place where any munitions of war, or any sketches, models, plans or documents relating thereto, are being made, repaired, or stored otherwise than on behalf of His Majesty, which is for the time being declared by order of a Secretary of State to be a prohibited place for the purposes of this section, on the ground that information with respect thereto, or the destruction or obstruction thereof, or interference therewith, would be useful to an enemy.

12. In this Act, unless the context otherwise requires,—
   Any reference to a place belonging to His Majesty includes a place belonging to any department of the Government . . . whether the place is or is not actually vested in His Majesty; . . .
   The expression 'document' includes part of a document;
   The expression 'model' includes design, pattern and specimen;
   The expression 'sketch' includes any photograph or other mode of representing any place or thing;
   The expression 'munitions of war' includes the whole or any part of any ship, submarine, aircraft, tank or similar engine, arms and ammunition, torpedo, or mine, intended or adapted for use in war, and any other article, material, or device, whether actual or proposed, intended for such use;

The Official Secrets (Prohibited Places) Order 1994 (SI 1994 No. 968), made under s. 3(c), provides that the works and offices of the UKAEA at Dounreay, the BNF sites at Sellafield and

Capenhurst, the Urenco site at Capenhurst and the UKAEA sites at Harwell and Windscale are prohibited places. Further, any place used by the Civil Aviation Authority is a place belonging to Her Majesty under s. 3(c) (Civil Aviation Act 1982, s. 18(2) to (4)); and any electronic communications station or office belonging to, or occupied by, the provider of a public electronic communications service is a prohibited place (Communications Act 2003, sch. 17, para. 2).

Making Sketches etc. Useful to Enemy

B9.8 For the definitions of 'sketch' and 'model' in the Official Secrets Act 1911, s. 12, see **B9.7**.

As to the meaning of the word 'enemy', the Court of Appeal in *Parrott* (1913) 8 Cr App R 186 held that 'it does not mean necessarily someone with whom this country is at war, but a potential enemy with whom we might some day be at war'.

Obtaining or Communicating Sketches etc. Useful to Enemy

B9.9 A partial definition of the words 'obtains' and 'communicates' is provided by the Official Secrets Act 1911, s. 12:

Official Secrets Act 1911, s. 12

> Expressions referring to communicating include any communicating, whether in whole or in part, and whether the sketch, plan, model, article, note, document, or information itself or the substance, effect, or description thereof only be communicated; expressions referring to obtaining or retaining any sketch, plan, model, article, note, or document, include the copying or causing to be copied the whole or any part of any sketch, plan, model, article, note, or document, and expressions referring to the communication of any sketch, plan, model, article, note or document include the transfer or transmissions of the sketch, plan, model, article, note or document.

For the definitions of 'sketch', 'model' and 'enemy', see **B9.7** and **B9.8**.

The Official Secrets Act 1920, s. 2(1), provides that communication with a foreign agent is to be evidence that D has obtained or communicated information useful to an enemy with a purpose prejudicial to the safety or interests of the State. Section 2(2)(a) lays down the circumstances in which a person is deemed to have been in communication with a foreign agent, unless the contrary is proved. They are:

> (i) he has, either within or without the United Kingdom, visited the address of a foreign agent or consorted or associated with a foreign agent; or
> (ii) either within or without the United Kingdom, the name or address of, or any other information regarding a foreign agent has been found in his possession, or has been supplied by him to any other person, or has been obtained by him from any other person.

'Foreign agent' is defined by s. 2(2)(b) as including any person who is, or has been, or is reasonably suspected of being or having been employed by a foreign power either directly or indirectly for the purpose of committing an act, either within or without the UK, prejudicial to the safety or interests of the State, or who has, or is reasonably suspected of having, either within or without the UK, committed, or attempted to commit, such an act in the interests of a foreign power.

Finally, s. 2(2)(c) provides that an address, whether or not in the UK, is deemed to be the address of a foreign agent, and communications to that address deemed to be communications with a foreign agent, if the address is reasonably suspected of being an address for the receipt of communications or where the agent resides, or resorts for giving or receiving communications or carries on a business. The relevance of the activities of a foreign agent in proving the above requirements was considered in *Kent* (1943) 28 Cr App R 23.

Related Offences

B9.10 (a) A duty to give information about the commission of an offence under the Official Secrets Act 1911, s. 1(1), may be imposed by a chief officer of police acting under the Official Secrets Act 1920, s. 6. It is an offence to fail to provide such information. A person guilty of this offence is liable, on conviction on indictment, to imprisonment for a term not exceeding two years or a fine, or both or, on summary conviction, to a term of imprisonment not exceeding three months or a fine not exceeding the prescribed sum or both (Official Secrets Act 1920, s. 8(2)).

(b) The Official Secrets Act 1920, s. 7, makes it an offence to attempt, solicit or endeavour to persuade, or to aid and abet or do an act preparatory to, an offence under the Official Secrets Act 1911, s. 1(1), or the Official Secrets Act 1920, s. 6. The penalty for this offence is the same as for the substantive offence.

(c) It is an offence, contrary to the Official Secrets Act 1989, s. 5(6), for a person to disclose any information, document or other article which that person knows, or has reasonable cause to believe, to have come into his possession as a result of a contravention of the Official Secrets Act 1911, s. 1.

HARBOURING 'SPIES'

Official Secrets Act 1911, s. 7 B9.11

If any person knowingly harbours any person whom he knows, or has reasonable grounds for supposing, to be a person who is about to commit or who has committed an offence under this Act, or knowingly permits to meet or assemble in any premises in his occupation or under his control any such persons, or if any person having harboured any such person, or permitted to meet or assemble in any premises in his occupation or under his control any such persons, wilfully omits or refuses to disclose to a superintendent of police any information which it is in his power to give in relation to any such person he shall be guilty of [an offence].

Procedure

As to prosecutions requiring the consent of the A-G, see **B9.2**. B9.12

The offence is triable either way, subject to the proviso to the Official Secrets Act 1920, s. 8(2), which provides that the offence may be dealt with summarily only with the consent of the A-G. When tried on indictment it is a class 1B offence.

As to the special provisions relating to place of trial, territorial jurisdiction, excluding the public from the trial and offences tried outside the UK, see **B9.2**.

Indictment

Statement of Offence B9.13

Harbouring an offender contrary to section 7 of the Official Secrets Act 1911.

Particulars of Offence

A on or about the...day of...harboured O whom he knew or had reasonable grounds for supposing was about to commit [or had committed] an offence under the Official Secrets Act 1911, namely [state the offence].

Sentence

The maximum penalty is: on conviction on indictment, imprisonment for a term not exceeding two years and/or a fine; on summary conviction, a term of imprisonment not exceeding three months and/or an unlimited fine (Official Secrets Act 1920, s. 8(2)). There is no offence-specific guideline but the Sentencing Council's *General Guideline: Overarching Principles* (see Supplement, **SG2-1**) is used for all offenders sentenced on or after 1 October 2019. B9.14

Offence Not Limited to Harbouring 'Spies'

The offence is not limited to harbouring 'spies', since the person being harboured must simply have committed an 'offence under this Act', which means any act, omission, or other thing which is punishable under the 1911 Act (Official Secrets Act 1911, s. 12). B9.15

Meaning of 'Superintendent of Police'

B9.16 **Official Secrets Act 1911, s. 12**

In this Act, unless the context otherwise requires,—

...

The expression 'superintendent of police' includes any police officer of a like or superior rank and any person upon whom the powers of a superintendent of police are for the purposes of this Act conferred by a Secretary of State.

Related Offences

B9.17 The Official Secrets Act 1920, s. 7, makes it an offence to attempt, solicit or endeavour to persuade, or to aid and abet or do an act preparatory to, an offence under the Official Secrets Act 1911, s. 7.

GAINING ACCESS TO PROHIBITED PLACES

B9.18 **Official Secrets Act 1920, s. 1**

(1) If any person for the purpose of gaining admission, or of assisting, any other person to gain admission, to a prohibited place, within the meaning of the Official Secrets Act 1911 . . ., or for any other purpose prejudicial to the safety or interests of the State within the meaning of the said Act—

(a) uses or wears, without lawful authority, any naval, military, air-force, police, or other official uniform, or any uniform so nearly resembling the same as to be calculated to deceive, or falsely represents himself to be a person who is or has been entitled to use or wear any such uniform; or

(b) orally, or in writing in any declaration or application, or in any document signed by him or on his behalf, knowingly makes or connives at the making of any false statement or any omission; or

(c) tampers with any passport or naval, military, air-force, police, or other official pass, permit, certificate, licence, or other document of a similar character (hereinafter in this section referred to as an official document), or has in his possession any forged, altered, or irregular official document; or

(d) personates, or falsely represents himself to be a person holding, or in the employment of a person holding office under His Majesty, or to be or not to be a person to whom an official document or secret official code word or pass word has been duly issued or communicated, or with intent to obtain an official document, secret official code word or pass word, whether for himself or any other person, knowingly makes any false statement; or

(e) uses, or has in his possession or under his control, without the authority of the Government Department or the authority concerned, any die, seal, or stamp of or belonging to, or used, made or provided by any Government Department, or by any diplomatic, naval, military, or air force authority appointed by or acting under the authority of His Majesty, or any die, seal or stamp so nearly resembling any such die, seal or stamp as to be calculated to deceive, or counterfeits any such die, seal or stamp, or uses, or has in his possession, or under his control, any such counterfeited die, seal or stamp;

he shall be guilty of [an offence].

Procedure

B9.19 As to prosecutions requiring the consent of the A-G, see **B9.2**.

The offence is triable either way, subject to the proviso to the Official Secrets Act 1920, s. 8(2), which provides that the offence may be dealt with summarily only with the consent of the A-G. *When tried on indictment* it is a class 1B offence.

As to the special provisions relating to place of trial, territorial jurisdiction, excluding the public from the trial and offences tried outside the UK, see **B9.2**.

Indictment

Statement of Offence B9.20

Unlawfully wearing a uniform for the purpose of gaining access to a prohibited place contrary to section 1(1) of the Official Secrets Act 1920.

Particulars of Offence

A on or about the . . . day of . . ., for the purpose of gaining admission to a prohibited place, namely . . ., wore a naval [or military etc.] uniform without lawful authority.

Sentence

The maximum penalty is: on conviction on indictment, imprisonment for a term not exceeding two years and/or a fine; on summary conviction, a term of imprisonment not exceeding three months and/or an unlimited fine (Official Secrets Act 1920, s. 8(2)). There is no offence-specific guideline but the Sentencing Council's *General Guideline: Overarching Principles* (see Supplement, **SG2-1**) is used for all offenders sentenced on or after 1 October 2019. B9.21

Elements

For the meaning of 'prohibited place', see **B9.7**. For the meaning of 'purpose prejudicial to the safety or interests of the State', see **B9.6**. B9.22

By virtue of the Official Secrets Act 1911, s. 12, 'office under His Majesty' includes any office or employment in or under any department of the government of the UK or of any British possession. A police officer is in employment under Her Majesty (*Lewis v Cattle* [1938] 2 KB 454).

Related Offences

The Official Secrets Act 1920, s. 7, makes it an offence to attempt, solicit or endeavour to persuade, or to aid and abet or do an act preparatory to, an offence under the Official Secrets Act 1920, s. 1(1). The mental element for the s. 7 offence was considered in *Bingham* [1973] QB 870. B9.23

RETENTION AND POSSESSION OF OFFICIAL DOCUMENTS ETC.

Official Secrets Act 1920, s. 1 B9.24

(2) If any person—

(a) retains for any purpose prejudicial to the safety or interests of the State any official document, whether or not completed or issued for use, when he has no right to retain it, or when it is contrary to his duty to retain it, or fails to comply with any directions issued by any government department or any person authorised by such department with regard to the return or disposal thereof, or

(b) allows any other person to have possession of any official document issued for his use alone, or communicates any secret official code word or pass word so issued, or, without lawful authority or excuse, has in his possession any official document or secret official code word or pass word issued for the use of some person other than himself, or on obtaining possession of any official document by finding or otherwise, neglects or fails to restore it to the person or authority by whom or for whose use it was issued, or to a police constable; or

(c) without lawful authority or excuse, manufactures or sells, or has in his possession for sale any such die, seal or stamp as aforesaid;

he shall be guilty of [an offence].

Procedure

As to prosecutions requiring the consent of the A-G, see **B9.2**. B9.25

The offence is triable either way, subject to the proviso to the Official Secrets Act 1920, s. 8(2), which provides that the offence may be dealt with summarily only with the consent of the A-G. When tried on indictment it is a class 1B offence.

As to the special provisions relating to place of trial, territorial jurisdiction, excluding the public from the trial and offences tried outside the UK, see **B9.2**.

Indictment

B9.26 *Statement of Offence*

Retaining an official document contrary to section 1(2) of the Official Secrets Act 1920.

Particulars of Offence

A on or about the... day of..., for a purpose prejudicial to the safety or interests of the State, namely..., retained an official document, namely..., when he had no right to retain it [or when it was contrary to his duty to retain it].

Sentence

B9.27 The maximum penalty is: on conviction on indictment, imprisonment for a term not exceeding two years and/or a fine; on summary conviction, a term of imprisonment not exceeding three months and/or an unlimited fine (Official Secrets Act 1920, s. 8(2)). There is no offence-specific guideline but the Sentencing Council's *General Guideline: Overarching Principles* (see Supplement, **SG2-1**) is used for all offenders sentenced on or after 1 October 2019.

Elements

B9.28 For the meaning of 'official document', see the Official Secrets Act 1920, s. 1(1)(c), at **B9.18**. For the meaning of 'die, seal or stamp', see s. 1(1)(e) of that Act. For the meaning of 'communicate', see **B9.9**.

For the meaning of 'purpose prejudicial to the safety or interests of the State', see **B9.6**.

Related Offences

B9.29 The Official Secrets Act 1920, s. 7, makes it an offence to attempt, solicit or endeavour to persuade, or to aid and abet or do an act preparatory to, an offence under the Official Secrets Act 1920, s. 1(2).

INTERFERING WITH OFFICERS OF POLICE OR MEMBERS OF ARMED FORCES IN VICINITY OF PROHIBITED PLACE

B9.30 **Official Secrets Act 1920, s. 3**

No person in the vicinity of any prohibited place shall obstruct, knowingly mislead or otherwise interfere with or impede, the chief officer or a superintendent or other officer of police, or any member of His Majesty's forces engaged on guard, sentry, patrol, or other similar duty in relation to the prohibited place, and, if any person acts in contravention of, or fails to comply with, this provision, he shall be guilty of [an offence].

Procedure

B9.31 As to the restriction on prosecutions requiring the consent of the A-G, see **B9.2**.

This offence is triable either way, subject to the proviso to the Official Secrets Act 1920, s. 8(2), which provides that the offence may be dealt with summarily only with the consent of the A-G. When tried on indictment it is a class 1B offence.

As to the special provisions relating to territorial jurisdiction, excluding the public from the trial and offences tried outside the UK, see **B9.2**.

Sentence

B9.32 The maximum penalty is: on conviction on indictment, imprisonment for a term not exceeding two years and/or a fine; on summary conviction, a term of imprisonment not exceeding three months and/or an unlimited fine (Official Secrets Act 1920, s. 8(2)). There is no offence-specific guideline but the Sentencing Council's *General Guideline: Overarching Principles* (see Supplement, **SG2-1**) is used for all offenders sentenced on or after 1 October 2019.

Elements

For the meaning of 'prohibited place', see **B9.7**. **B9.33**

In *Adler v George* [1964] 2 QB 7, it was held that the phrase 'in the vicinity of' in the Official Secrets Act 1920, s. 3, is to be interpreted as 'in or in the vicinity of' so that obstruction of someone at an airbase could constitute an offence under the section.

The word 'obstruct' presumably has the same meaning as in the offence of obstruction of a police officer in the execution of his duty (see **B2.48** to **B2.53**). The meaning of 'superintendent' is considered at **B9.16**. For the meaning of 'chief officer of police', see the Police Act 1996, s. 101.

Related Offences

The Official Secrets Act 1920, s. 7, makes it an offence to attempt, solicit or endeavour to persuade, or to aid and abet or do an act preparatory to, an offence under the Official Secrets Act 1920, s. 3. As to the offences of assaulting and obstructing a police officer in the execution of his duty, see **B2.43** to **B2.53**. **B9.34**

DISCLOSURE OF SECURITY AND INTELLIGENCE INFORMATION

Official Secrets Act 1989, s. 1 **B9.35**

(1) A person who is or has been—
  (a) a member of the security and intelligence services; or
  (b) a person notified that he is subject to the provisions of this subsection,
shall be guilty of an offence if without lawful authority he discloses any information, document or other article relating to security or intelligence which is or has been in his possession by virtue of his position as a member of any of those services or in the course of his work while the notification is or was in force.

Procedure and Extra-territoriality

Official Secrets Act 1989, ss. 9, 11, and 15 **B9.36**

9.—(1) Subject to subsection (2) below, no prosecution for an offence under this Act shall be instituted in England and Wales or in Northern Ireland except by or with the consent of the Attorney-General or, as the case may be, the Attorney-General for Northern Ireland.

(2) Subsection (1) above does not apply to an offence in respect of any such information, document or article as is mentioned in section 4(2) above but no prosecution for such an offence shall be instituted in England and Wales or in Northern Ireland except by or with the consent of the Director of Public Prosecutions or, as the case may be, the Director of Public Prosecutions for Northern Ireland.

11.—(5) Proceedings for an offence under this Act may be taken in any place in the United Kingdom.

15.—(1) Any act—
  (a) done by a British citizen or Crown servant; or
  (b) done by any person in any of the Channel Islands or the Isle of Man or any colony,
shall, if it would be an offence by that person under any provision of this Act other than section 8(1), (4) or (5) when done by him in the United Kingdom, be an offence under that provision.

This offence is triable either way (Official Secrets Act 1989, s. 10(1)). When tried on indictment it is a class 1B offence.

The power to exclude the public under the Official Secrets Act 1920, s. 8(4), applies to the instant offence by virtue of the Official Secrets Act 1989, s. 11(4) (see **B9.2**).

Indictment

B9.37 *Statement of Offence*

Unlawful disclosure of information contrary to section 1(1) of the Official Secrets Act 1989.

Particulars of Offence

A on or about the... day of..., being a person notified that he was subject to the provisions of section 1 of the Official Secrets Act 1989, without lawful authority disclosed to P a document, namely..., which related to security or intelligence and which the said A had in his possession in the course of his work while the said notification was in force.

Sentence

B9.38 The maximum penalty is: on conviction on indictment, imprisonment for a term not exceeding two years and/or a fine; on summary conviction, imprisonment for a term not exceeding six months and/or an unlimited fine (Official Secrets Act 1989, s. 10(1)). There is no offence-specific guideline but the Sentencing Council's *General Guideline: Overarching Principles* (see Supplement, SG2-1) is used for all offenders sentenced on or after 1 October 2019. In *Shayler* [2002] UKHL 11, [2003] 1 AC 247, a former member of the security service received a total of six months' imprisonment for offences under s. 1, following a contested trial. In 2010 Daniel Houghton, a former MI6 agent, pleaded guilty to attempting to sell classified material to Dutch Intelligence and received a total of 12 months for two offences under s. 1.

Persons who Can Commit Offence

B9.39 An offence under the Official Secrets Act 1989, s. 1(1), can be committed by either a person who is or has been a member of the security and intelligence services, or someone who is or has been a notified person (i.e. notified that he or she is subject to s. 1 of the Act).

Official Secrets Act 1989, s. 1

(6) Notification that a person is subject to subsection (1) above shall be effected by a notice in writing served on him by a Minister of the Crown; and such a notice may be served if, in the Minister's opinion, the work undertaken by the person in question is or includes work connected with the security and intelligence services and its nature is such that the interests of national security require that he should be subject to the provisions of that subsection.

(7) Subject to subsection (8) below, a notification for the purposes of subsection (1) above shall be in force for the period of five years beginning with the day on which it is served but may be renewed by further notices under subsection (6) above for periods of five years at a time.

(8) A notification for the purposes of subsection (1) above may at any time be revoked by a further notice in writing served by the Minister on the person concerned; and the Minister shall serve such a further notice as soon as, in his opinion, the work undertaken by that person ceases to be such as is mentioned in subsection (6) above.

Meaning of 'Security' and 'Intelligence'

B9.40 **Official Secrets Act 1989, s. 1**

(9) In this section 'security or intelligence' means the work of, or in support of, the security and intelligence services or any part of them, and references to information relating to security or intelligence include references to information held or transmitted by those services or by persons in support of, or of any part of, them.

The security service has now been placed on a statutory basis (see the Security Service Act 1989), as has the Secret Intelligence Service (Intelligence Services Act 1994).

Disclosure of Information

B9.41 **Official Secrets Act 1989, ss. 1 and 13**

1.—(2) The reference in subsection (1) above to disclosing information relating to security or intelligence includes a reference to making any statement which purports to be a disclosure of such information or is intended to be taken by those to whom it is addressed as being such a disclosure.

13.—(1) In this Act—
'disclose' and 'disclosure', in relation to a document or other article, include parting with possession of it.

'Disclose' is not defined merely as 'make public', for example. This is capable of causing difficulties in relation to the absolute right of D to provide legal advisers with instructions relating to D's defence. It is possible to do so only if provision of the instructions would not involve the commission of a further offence by such disclosure to the lawyers. In cases where, for example, the alleged disclosure was not widely publicised, D's lawyers may need to seek authorisation under s. 7 before they can even view the subject-matter of the indictment. Undoubtedly there is likely to be an application for such trials to be held in camera. Although Lord Bingham in *Shayler* [2002] UKHL 11, [2003] 1 AC 247 suggested a special advocate solution (at [34]), this related only to a judicial review of a refusal to authorise disclosure, not criminal proceedings in which D seeks to provide lawyers with instructions/material relevant to D's defence. In *M v Netherlands* (2018) 67 EHRR 3 (50), the ECtHR held that it was a violation of Article 6 where an interpreter employed by the Dutch intelligence and security services was impeded in the instructions he could give to his criminal defence counsel; such restrictions being imposed in order to avoid criminal liability for further disclosures to non-authorised persons.

The issue of prior publication is relevant to whether the disclosure in question is damaging but not decisive of it: see the White Paper, *Reform of Section 2 of the Official Secrets Act 1911* (1988) Cm. 408 at paras. 62 to 63. The White Paper recommendations 'bear directly on the interpretation of the Act' (*Shayler* [2002] UKHL 11, [2003] 1 AC 247 at [11]; *R (Bancoult) v Secretary of State for Foreign and Commonwealth Affairs (No. 3)* [2014] EWCA Civ 708, [2014] 1 WLR 2921 at [69]–[73]).

Meaning of 'Without Lawful Authority'

The Official Secrets Act 1989, s. 1(1), applies only to unauthorised disclosures. Section 7 provides for the only circumstances in which a disclosure may be made 'with lawful authority'. Only s. 7(1) applies to s. 1(1), since the offence applies only to the limited range of Crown servants who work for the security and intelligence services, or who are notified as being covered by the provisions of s. 1(1). **B9.42**

Official Secrets Act 1989, s. 7

(1) For the purposes of this Act a disclosure by—
(a) a Crown servant; or
(b) a person, not being a Crown servant or government contractor, in whose case a notification for the purposes of section 1(1) above is in force,
is made with lawful authority if, and only if, it is made in accordance with his official duty.

As to the broader provisions relating, generally, to authorised disclosures, see **B9.54**; as to defences, see **B9.43**.

Defences

Official Secrets Act 1989, ss. 1 and 7 **B9.43**

1.—(5) It is a defence for a person charged with an offence under this section to prove that at the time of the alleged offence he did not know, and had no reasonable cause to believe, that the information, document or article in question related to security or intelligence.

7.—(4) It is a defence for a person charged with an offence under any of the foregoing provisions of this Act to prove that at the time of the alleged offence he believed that he had lawful authority to make the disclosure in question and had no reasonable cause to believe otherwise.

Although the legal burden appears to lie upon the accused, it is likely that only an evidential burden would be compatible with the ECHR, Article 6 (see *Keogh* [2007] EWCA Crim 528, [2007] 3 All ER 789 and **F3.18** *et seq.*). The rationale given in the White Paper, *Reform of Section 2 of the Official Secrets Act 1911* for the reversal of the burden of proof (that a Crown servant or government contractor can be expected to appreciate the consequences of disclosure and that it is reasonable to expect them to demonstrate that this was not the case) was insufficient justification for the imposition of a legal burden.

B9.44 According to the House of Lords in *Shayler* [2002] UKHL 11, [2003] 1 AC 247, there is no additional defence of a disclosure being in the national or public interest, the offence contrary to the Official Secrets Act 1989, s. 1(1), or the offence contrary to s. 4(1). The House held that the blanket ban on disclosures by members of the security services nevertheless satisfied the requirements of the ECHR, Article 10(2). The intention to counter terrorism, criminal activity, hostile activity and subversion was a sufficient purpose to satisfy Article 10(2), and the restrictions were clear, and so prescribed by law. The restrictions were also necessary in a democratic society because of the defences that existed (which vary from offence to offence): the two means of gaining authorisation for a disclosure under s. 7 and the possibility of challenging an adverse decision under judicial review (with a suitably rigorous and intensive form of review for the alleged breach of a Convention right). Moreover, no prosecution would take place without the consent of the A-G. In *A v B* [2009] UKSC 12, [2010] 2 AC 1 the Supreme Court held that the RIPA 2000, s. 65, conferred on the Investigatory Powers Tribunal exclusive jurisdiction to hear claims, including a challenge to a refusal to permit disclosure (under the HRA 1998, s. 7(1)(a)) against any of the intelligence services. In *R (Privacy International) v Investigatory Powers Tribunal* [2019] UKSC 22 the Supreme Court held (by a majority) that the RIPA 2000, s. 67(8), did not have the effect of ousting judicial review of the Investigatory Powers Tribunal in relation to decisions of the Tribunal which were vitiated by an error of law (jurisdictional or otherwise). In *R v Coltman* [2018] EWCA Crim 2059, in the context of prosecution for an offence under s.1(1) of the Computer Misuse Act 1990 (unauthorised access to a program or data held on a computer), the Court of Appeal held that the HRA 1998 does not require the reading into statute of a public interest defence.

'Public interest', however, remains relevant to whether any particular disclosure is damaging (i.e. for *all* offences except those under s. 1(1) and s. 4 of the Act): see White Paper, *Reform of Section 2 of the Official Secrets Act 1911*, at para. 61. For offences requiring damaging disclosure, it is necessary for the prosecution to prove not only that the disclosure is damaging but also that the person making the disclosure knows or has reasonable grounds to believe that it would be damaging (in the sense that it is likely to have that effect). It is insufficient for the prosecution to prove that there were reasonable grounds to believe that the disclosure might be damaging, or that this was merely a possibility.

B9.45 Although in *Shayler* the House of Lords held that Shayler himself was not 'within measurable distance' of the defence of necessity (as to which, see further **A3.47**), necessity remains available as a defence to *all* offences under the 1989 Act. The potential width of the defence is illustrated by one of the prosecution's stated reasons for not proceeding with the case against Katharine Gun, namely that it could not rebut her defence of necessity. She was a GCHQ employee who, in 2004, was charged with s. 1 disclosure of the US request for the UK to spy on the UN in the run-up to the Iraq war. Her publicly stated defence was a desire to prevent a war without a lawfully obtained second UN resolution.

Related Offences

B9.46 It is an offence, contrary to the Official Secrets Act 1989, s. 1(3), for a Crown servant or government contractor to make a damaging disclosure of security or intelligence information (see **B9.47** to **B9.56**).

DAMAGING DISCLOSURE OF SECURITY AND INTELLIGENCE INFORMATION

B9.47 **Official Secrets Act 1989, s. 1**

(3) A person who is or has been a Crown servant or government contractor shall be guilty of an offence if without lawful authority he makes a damaging disclosure of any information, document or other article relating to security or intelligence which is or has been in his possession by virtue of his position as such but otherwise than as mentioned in subsection (1) above.

Procedure

B9.48 As to the requirement of consent of the A-G, see the Official Secrets Act 1989, s. 9(1), and **B9.36**.

The offence is triable either way (s. 10(1)). When tried on indictment it is a class 1B offence.

As to provisions relating to place of trial, territorial jurisdiction and excluding the public from the trial, see **B9.36**.

Indictment

Statement of Offence **B9.49**

Unlawfully making a damaging disclosure of information relating to security [or intelligence] contrary to section 1(3) of the Official Secrets Act 1989.

Particulars of Offence

A on or about the... day of..., being then [or having been] a Crown servant [or government contractor], without lawful authority disclosed to P information relating to security [or intelligence], namely..., which was in his possession by virtue of his position as a Crown servant [or government contractor], which disclosure caused [or disclosure of which would have been likely to cause] damage to the work of the security and intelligence services [or the work of..., being part of the security and intelligence services].

Sentence

The maximum penalty is: on conviction on indictment, imprisonment for a term not exceeding two years and/or a fine; on summary conviction, imprisonment for a term not exceeding six months and/or an unlimited fine (Official Secrets Act 1989, s. 10(1)). There is no offence-specific guideline but the Sentencing Council's *General Guideline: Overarching Principles* (see Supplement, **SG2-1**) is used for all offenders sentenced on or after 1 October 2019. **B9.50**

Meaning of 'Security', 'Intelligence', 'Disclosure', 'Damaging Disclosure'

For the meaning of 'security' and 'intelligence', see **B9.40**. For the meaning of 'disclosure', see **B9.41**. The words 'damaging disclosure' are defined by the Official Secrets Act 1989, s. 1(4). **B9.51**

Official Secrets Act 1989, s. 1

(4) For the purposes of subsection (3) above a disclosure is damaging if—
- (a) it causes damage to the work of, or of any part of, the security and intelligence services; or
- (b) it is of information or a document or other article which is such that its unauthorised disclosure would be likely to cause such damage or which falls within a class or description of information, documents or articles the unauthorised disclosure of which would be likely to have that effect.

This offence is committed whether or not the information disclosed was secret or confidential, and whether or not the disclosure was damaging to national interests (*A-G v Blake* [1997] Ch 84, per Sir Richard Scott (*obiter*)). 'Public interest' is relevant to whether the disclosure is damaging, see **B9.44**.

Meaning of 'Crown Servant'

Official Secrets Act 1989, s. 12 **B9.52**

(1) In this Act 'Crown servant' means—
- (a) a Minister of the Crown;
- (aa) a member of the Scottish Executive or a junior Scottish minister;
- (ab) the First Minister of Wales, a Welsh Minister appointed under section 48 of the Government of Wales Act 2006, the Counsel General to the Welsh Assembly Government or a Deputy Welsh Minister;
- (b) [repealed]
- (c) any person employed in the civil service of the Crown, including Her Majesty's Diplomatic Service, Her Majesty's Overseas Civil Service, the civil service of Northern Ireland and the Northern Ireland Court Service;
- (d) any member of the naval, military or air forces of the Crown, including any person employed by an association established for the purposes of Part XI of the Reserve Forces Act 1996;

B
Part B Offences

(e) any constable and any other person employed or appointed in or for the purposes of any police force (including the Police Service of Northern Ireland and the Police Service of Northern Ireland Reserve) or an NCA special (within the meaning of Part 1 of the Crime and Courts Act 2013);
(f) any person who is a member or employee of a prescribed body or a body of a prescribed class and either is prescribed for the purposes of this paragraph or belongs to a prescribed class of members or employees of any such body;
(g) any person who is the holder of a prescribed office or who is an employee of such a holder and either is prescribed for the purposes of this paragraph or belongs to a prescribed class of such employees.

The Official Secrets Act 1989 (Prescription) Order 1990 (SI 1990 No. 200), art. 2 and sch. 1, prescribe classes of members or employees of certain bodies (and classes of bodies) as 'Crown servants' for the purpose of s. 12(1)(f); art. 3 and sch. 2 prescribe classes of members or employees as 'Crown servants' for the purposes of s. 12(1)(g).

The 1989 Act applies to the First Minister and deputy First Minister in Northern Ireland and Northern Ireland Ministers and junior Ministers in the same way as it applies to Crown servants (Official Secrets Act 1989, s. 12(5)).

Meaning of 'Government Contractor'

B9.53 **Official Secrets Act 1989, ss. 12 and 13**

12.—(2) In this Act 'government contractor' means, subject to subsection (3) below, any person who is not a Crown servant but who provides, or is employed in the provision of, goods or services—
(a) for the purposes of any Minister of the Crown or person mentioned in paragraph (a), (ab) or (b) of subsection (1) above, of any of the services, forces or bodies mentioned in that subsection or of the holder of any office prescribed under that subsection; or
(b) under an agreement or arrangement certified by the Secretary of State as being one to which the government of a State other than the United Kingdom or an international organisation is a party or which is subordinate to, or made for the purposes of implementing, any such agreement or arrangement.

(3) Where an employee or class of employees of any body, or of any holder of an office, is prescribed by an order made for the purposes of subsection (1) above—
(a) any employee of that body, or the holder of that office who is not prescribed or is not within the prescribed class; and
(b) any person who does not provide, or is not employed in the provision of, goods or services for the purposes of the performance of those functions of the body or the holder of the office in connection with which the employee or prescribed class of employees is engaged,

shall not be a government contractor for the purposes of this Act.

13.—(1) In this Act—

. . .

'international organisation' means, subject to subsections (2) and (3) below, an organisation of which only States are members and includes a reference to any organ of such an organisation;

. . .

'State' includes the government of a State and any organ of its government and references to a State other than the United Kingdom include references to any territory outside the United Kingdom.

(2) In section 12(2)(b) above the reference to an international organisation includes a reference to any such organisation whether or not one of which only States are members and includes a commercial organisation.
(3) In determining for the purposes of subsection (1) above whether only States are members of an organisation, any member which is itself an organisation of which only States are members, or which is an organ of such an organisation, shall be treated as a State.

'Without Lawful Authority'

B9.54 An offence under the Official Secrets Act 1989, s. 1(3), is committed only if the disclosure is 'without lawful authority'. The only circumstances in which a disclosure is made with lawful authority are to be found in s. 7.

Official Secrets Act 1989, s. 7

(1) For the purposes of this Act a disclosure by—
(a) a Crown servant; or
(b) a person, not being a Crown servant or government contractor, in whose case a notification for the purposes of section 1(1) above is in force,
is made with lawful authority if, and only if, it is made in accordance with his official duty.
(2) For the purposes of this Act a disclosure by a government contractor is made with lawful authority if, and only if, it is made—
(a) in accordance with an official authorisation; or
(b) for the purposes of the functions by virtue of which he is a government contractor and without contravening an official restriction.
(3) For the purposes of this Act a disclosure made by any other person is made with lawful authority if, and only if, it is made—
(a) to a Crown servant for the purposes of his functions as such; or
(b) in accordance with an official authorisation.
...
(5) In this section 'official authorisation' and 'official restriction' mean, subject to subsection (6) below, an authorisation or restriction duly given or imposed by a Crown servant or government contractor or by or on behalf of a prescribed body or a body of a prescribed class.

The Civil Aviation Authority and the Investigatory Powers Tribunal were prescribed by the Official Secrets Act 1989 (Prescription) Order 1990, art. 4 and sch. 3, for the purpose of s. 7(5) so as to enable them to give official authorisations or restrictions.

Specific Defences

The defence of having no knowledge or reasonable cause to believe that information related to security or intelligence, created by the Official Secrets Act 1989, s. 1(5), and the defence that D believed there was lawful authority for disclosure, apply to this offence. There is no defence of disclosure in the public or national interest for an offence under s. 1(1) (*Shayler* [2002] UKHL 11, [2003] 1 AC 247), but 'public interest' is relevant to whether the disclosure is damaging. The defences are considered at **B9.43**. **B9.55**

Related Offences

It is an offence, contrary to the Official Secrets Act 1989, s. 1(1), for a present or past member of the security and intelligence services or a notified person to make a disclosure of security or intelligence information (see **B9.35** to **B9.46**). **B9.56**

DAMAGING DISCLOSURE OF DEFENCE INFORMATION

Official Secrets Act 1989, s. 2 **B9.57**

(1) A person who is or has been a Crown servant or government contractor shall be guilty of an offence if without lawful authority he makes a damaging disclosure of any information, document or other article relating to defence which is or has been in his possession by virtue of his position as such.

Procedure

As to the requirement of consent of the A-G, see **B9.36**. The offence is triable either way (Official Secrets Act 1989, s. 10(1)). When tried on indictment it is a class 1B offence. **B9.58**

As to provisions relating to place of trial, territorial jurisdiction and excluding the public from the trial, see **B9.36**.

Indictment

Statement of Offence **B9.59**

Unlawfully making a damaging disclosure of information relating to defence contrary to section 2(1) of the Official Secrets Act 1989.

Particulars of Offence

A on or about the ... day of ..., being then [or having been] a Crown servant [or government contractor], without lawful authority disclosed to P information relating to defence, namely ..., which was in his possession by virtue of his position as a Crown servant [or government contractor], which disclosure prejudiced [or disclosure of which would have been likely to prejudice] the capability of the armed forces of the Crown to carry out their tasks [or other form of damage specified in s. 2(2): see **B9.61**].

Sentence

B9.60 The maximum penalty is: on conviction on indictment, imprisonment for a term not exceeding two years and/or a fine; on summary conviction, imprisonment for a term not exceeding six months and/or an unlimited fine. There is no offence-specific guideline but the Sentencing Council's *General Guideline: Overarching Principles* (see Supplement, **SG2-1**) is used for all offenders sentenced on or after 1 October 2019.

Elements

B9.61 The meaning of 'disclosure' is considered at **B9.41**.

Official Secrets Act 1989, s. 2

(2) For the purposes of subsection (1) above a disclosure is damaging if—
- (a) it prejudices the capability of, or any part of, the armed forces of the Crown to carry out their tasks or leads to loss of life or injury to members of those forces or serious damage to the equipment or installations of those forces; or
- (b) otherwise than in paragraph (a) above, it endangers the interests of the United Kingdom abroad, seriously obstructs the promotion or protection by the United Kingdom of those interests or endangers the safety of British citizens abroad; or
- (c) it is of information or of a document or article which is such that its unauthorised disclosure would be likely to have any of those effects.

...

(4) In this section 'defence' means—
- (a) the size, shape, organisation, logistics, order of battle, deployment, operations, state of readiness and training of the armed forces of the Crown;
- (b) the weapons, stores or other equipment of those forces and the invention, development, production and operation of such equipment and research relating to it;
- (c) defence policy and strategy and military planning and intelligence;
- (d) plans and measures for the maintenance of essential supplies and services that are or would be needed in time of war.

The meanings of 'Crown servant' and 'government contractor' are considered at **B9.52** and **B9.53**. As to the meaning of 'without lawful authority', see s. 7 of the Act, at **B9.54**. As to the only circumstances in which a disclosure is made with lawful authority, see **B9.54**.

Specific Defences

B9.62 **Official Secrets Act 1989, s. 2**

(3) It is a defence for a person charged with an offence under this section to prove that at the time of the alleged offence he did not know, and had no reasonable cause to believe, that the information, document or article in question related to defence or that its disclosure would be damaging within the meaning of subsection (1) above.

To ensure compliance with the ECHR, Article 6, D has only an evidential burden as regards proving this defence (*Keogh* [2007] EWCA Crim 528, [2007] 3 All ER 789: cf. the Terrorism Act 2000, s. 118 at **B10.31** and see further **F3.18** *et seq.*).

The defence that D believed that there was lawful authority for disclosure, created by the Official Secrets Act 1989, s. 7(4), also applies to this offence, and is considered at **B9.43** together with other defences.

DAMAGING DISCLOSURE OF INTERNATIONAL RELATIONS INFORMATION

Official Secrets Act 1989, s. 3 **B9.63**

(1) A person who is or has been a Crown servant or government contractor shall be guilty of an offence if without lawful authority he makes a damaging disclosure of—
  (a) any information, document or other article relating to international relations; or
  (b) any confidential information, document or other article which was obtained from a State other than the United Kingdom or an international organisation,

being information or a document or article which is or has been in his possession by virtue of his position as a Crown servant or government contractor.

Procedure

As to the requirement of the A-G's consent, see **B9.36**. The offence is triable either way (Official Secrets Act 1989, s. 10(1)). When tried on indictment it is a class 1B offence. **B9.64**

As to provisions relating to place of trial, territorial jurisdiction and excluding the public from the trial, see **B9.36**.

Indictment

Statement of Offence **B9.65**

Unlawfully making a damaging disclosure of information relating to international relations contrary to section 3(1) of the Official Secrets Act 1989.

Particulars of Offence

A on or about the . . . day of . . ., being then [or having been] a Crown servant [or government contractor], without lawful authority disclosed to P information relating to international relations, namely . . ., which was in his possession by virtue of his position as a Crown servant [or government contractor], which disclosure endangered [or disclosure of which would have been likely to endanger] the interests of the United Kingdom abroad [or other form of damage specified in s. 3(2): see **B9.67**].

Sentence

The maximum penalty is: on conviction on indictment, imprisonment for a term not exceeding two years and/or a fine; on summary conviction, imprisonment for a term not exceeding six months and/or an unlimited fine (Official Secrets Act 1989, s. 10(1)). There is no offence-specific guideline but the Sentencing Council's *General Guideline: Overarching Principles* (see Supplement, **SG2-1**) is used for all offenders sentenced on or after 1 October 2019. **B9.66**

Elements

The meaning of 'disclosure' is considered at **B9.41**. The phrases 'damaging disclosure', 'international relations' and 'confidential information' are defined by the Official Secrets Act 1989, s. 3. **B9.67**

Official Secrets Act 1989, s. 3

(2) For the purposes of subsection (1) above a disclosure is damaging if—
  (a) it endangers the interests of the United Kingdom abroad, seriously obstructs the promotion or protection by the United Kingdom of those interests or endangers the safety of British citizens abroad; or
  (b) it is of information or of a document or article which is such that its unauthorised disclosure would be likely to have any of those effects.

(3) In the case of information or a document or article within subsection (1) above—
  (a) the fact that it is confidential, or
  (b) its nature or contents,

may be sufficient to establish for the purposes of subsection (2)(b) above that the information, document or article is such that its unauthorised disclosure would be likely to have any of the effects there mentioned.

. . .

(5) In this section 'international relations' means the relations between States, between international organisations or between one or more States and one or more such organisations and includes any matter relating to a State other than the United Kingdom or to an international organisation which is capable of affecting the relations of the United Kingdom with another State or with an international organisation.

(6) For the purposes of this section any information, document or article obtained from a State or organisation is confidential at any time while the terms on which it was obtained require it to be held in confidence or while the circumstances in which it was obtained make it reasonable for the State or organisation to expect that it would be so held.

Section 13 of the Act defines 'State and international organisation' (see **B9.53**). The meanings of 'Crown servant' and 'government contractor' are considered at **B9.52** and **B9.53**. The phrase 'without lawful authority' is defined by s. 7 of the Act (see **B9.54**). The Act does not define the 'interests of the United Kingdom abroad'. This is an inchoate concept which raises important and difficult issues of interpretation. There is some first instance authority for the proposition that the concept of the national interest is to be treated as synonymous with the interests of the government of the day. On the other hand, it is axiomatic that the interests of any particular political party, or of any individual public official, are not to be equated with the interests of the UK as a whole. A good indication of the kind of harm contemplated by s. 3 is set out in the White Paper, *Reform of Section 2 of the Official Secrets Act 1911* at para. 27.

Specific Defences

B9.68 **Official Secrets Act 1989, s. 3**

(4) It is a defence for a person charged with an offence under this section to prove that at the time of the alleged offence he did not know, and had no reasonable cause to believe, that the information, document or article in question was such as is mentioned in subsection (1) above or that its disclosure would be damaging within the meaning of that subsection.

To ensure compliance with the ECHR, Article 6, D has only an evidential burden as regards proving this defence (*Keogh* [2007] EWCA Crim 528, [2007] 3 All ER 789: cf. the Terrorism Act 2000, s. 118 and see further **F3.18** *et seq.*).

The defence that D believed that there was lawful authority for disclosure also applies to this offence. For defences generally, see **B9.43**.

DISCLOSURE OF INFORMATION RELEVANT TO CRIMINAL INVESTIGATIONS

B9.69 **Official Secrets Act 1989, s. 4**

(1) A person who is or has been a Crown servant or government contractor is guilty of an offence if without lawful authority he discloses any information, document or other article to which this section applies and which is or has been in his possession by virtue of his position as such.

As to the materials referred to, see s. 4(2) and (3) at **B9.73**.

Procedure

B9.70 As to the requirement of the consent of the A-G, see **B9.36**. This offence is triable either way (Official Secrets Act 1989, s. 10(1)). When tried on indictment it is a class 1B offence.

As to provisions relating to the place of trial, territorial jurisdiction and excluding the public from the trial, see **B9.36**.

Indictment

B9.71 *Statement of Offence*

Unlawful disclosure of information resulting in the commission of an offence contrary to section 4(1) of the Official Secrets Act 1989.

Particulars of Offence

A on or about the . . . day of . . ., being then [or having been] a Crown servant [or government contractor], without lawful authority disclosed to P information, which was such that its unauthorised disclosure resulted in the commission of an offence, namely . . .

Sentence

The maximum penalty is: on conviction on indictment, imprisonment for a term not exceeding two years and/or a fine or both; on summary conviction, imprisonment for a term not exceeding six months and/or an unlimited fine (Official Secrets Act 1989, s. 10(1)). There is no offence-specific guideline but the Sentencing Council's *General Guideline: Overarching Principles* (see Supplement, **SG2-1**) is used for all offenders sentenced on or after 1 October 2019. **B9.72**

Elements

Official Secrets Act 1989, s. 4 **B9.73**

(2) This section applies to any information, document or other article—
(a) the disclosure of which—
(i) results in the commission of an offence; or
(ii) facilitates an escape from legal custody or the doing of any other act prejudicial to the safekeeping of persons in legal custody; or
(iii) impedes the prevention or detection of offences or the apprehension or prosecution of suspected offenders; or
(b) which is such that its unauthorised disclosure would be likely to have any of those effects.

(3) This section also applies to—
(a) any information obtained by reason of the interception of any communication in obedience to a warrant issued under section 2 of the Interception of Communications Act 1985 or under the authority of an interception warrant under section 5 of the Regulation of Investigatory Powers Act 2000, any information relating to the obtaining of information by reason of any such interception and any document or other article which is or has been used or held for use in, or has been obtained by reason of, any such interception; and
(b) any information obtained by reason of action authorised by a warrant issued under section 3 of the Security Service Act 1989, any information relating to the obtaining of information by reason of any such action and any document or other article which is or has been used or held for use in, or has been obtained by reason of, any such action; and
(c) any information obtained under a warrant under Chapter 1 of Part 2 or Chapter 1 of Part 6 of the Investigatory Powers Act 2016, any information relating to the obtaining of information under such a warrant and any document or other article which is or has been used or held for use in, or has been obtained by reason of, the obtaining of information under such a warrant.

. . .

(6) In this section 'legal custody' includes detention in pursuance of any enactment or any instrument made under an enactment.

The meaning of 'discloses' is considered at **B9.41**. With regard to the meaning of 'without lawful authority', see s. 7 of the Act, at **B9.54**.

Specific Defences

Official Secrets Act 1989, s. 4 **B9.74**

(4) It is a defence for a person charged with an offence under this section in respect of a disclosure falling within subsection (2)(a) above to prove that at the time of the alleged offence he did not know, and had no reasonable cause to believe, that the disclosure would have any of the effects there mentioned.

(5) It is a defence for a person charged with an offence under this section in respect of any other disclosure to prove that at the time of the alleged offence he did not know, and had no reasonable cause to believe, that the information, document or article in question was information or a document or article to which this section applies.

Although the accused appears to have the legal burden of proving these defences, it is likely that only an evidential burden would be compatible with the ECHR, Article 6 (see *Keogh* [2007] EWCA Crim 528, [2007] 3 All ER 789 and **F3.18** *et seq*.).

The defence that D believed that there was lawful authority for disclosure also applies to this offence (see **B9.43** for all defences). There is no defence of disclosure in the public or national interest (*Shayler* [2002] UKHL 11, [2003] 1 AC 247; see **B9.44**).

OTHER OFFENCES RELATING TO UNAUTHORISED DISCLOSURE OF INFORMATION

B9.75 Other offences dealing with the unauthorised disclosure of information are listed below. They are subject to the same procedural rules governing consent for commencement of proceedings, mode of trial, place of trial, territorial jurisdiction and exclusion of the public from the trial as the offence under s. 1(1) of the Act (see the Official Secrets Act 1989, ss. 9, 11 and 15, and **B9.36**). As to sentence, see s. 10 of the Act.

The terms 'disclose', 'Crown servant', 'government contractor', 'State', 'international organisation' and 'without lawful authority' have the same meanings as elsewhere in the Act (see **B9.41**, **B9.52**, **B9.53** and **B9.54**).

The other offences created by the Official Secrets Act 1989 are:

(a) Disclosure of information resulting from unauthorised disclosures or entrusted in confidence (s. 5(1) and (2)). This offence provides additional protection for information 'protected against disclosure' (for the meaning of which, see s. 5(5)). Under the 1989 Act, it is not an offence merely to be the recipient of unsolicited information where the disclosure of that information involves the commission of an offence under the Act by the person who provides the information. However, the effect of s. 5 is that, where a third party comes into possession of information either directly or indirectly as a result of an unauthorised disclosure, that third party may be guilty of an offence in the event of further disclosure. Section 5 applies to any information, document or other article which is protected against disclosure by ss. 1 to 4.

(b) Disclosure of information possessed in contravention of the Official Secrets Act 1911, s. 1 (Official Secrets Act 1989, s. 5(6)). For s. 1 of the 1911 Act, see **B9.1** to **B9.10**.

(c) Disclosure of information entrusted in confidence to other states or an international organisation (Official Secrets Act 1989, s. 6(1) and (2)). Under this provision, a disclosure is to be regarded as 'damaging' if it would be so regarded in relation to an offence under ss. 1(3), 2(1) or 3(1) (s. 6(4)). For the meaning of 'damaging disclosure' under those provisions, see **B9.51**, **B9.61** and **B9.67** and the White Paper, *Reform of Section 2 of the Official Secrets Act 1911* at para. 28.

(d) Disclosure of official information which can be used for gaining access to protected information (Official Secrets Act 1989, s. 8(6)). For the meaning of 'disclosure of official information', see s. 8(7).

B9.76 The CJA 1991, s. 91, creates an offence of wrongful disclosure of information by a person employed in pursuance of prison escort arrangements. The offence is triable either way. On conviction on indictment, the maximum penalty is imprisonment for a term not exceeding two years and/or a fine; on summary conviction, the maximum penalty is imprisonment for a term not exceeding six months and/or an unlimited fine. The CJPO 1994, s. 14, creates a similar offence in respect of the wrongful disclosure of information relating to offenders in youth detention accommodation.

Section 69 of the SCA 2007 creates an offence of wrongful further disclosure of protected information which has been disclosed to the recipient by a public authority which is a 'specified anti-fraud organisation' (as designated by the Secretary of State under SI 2014 No. 1608 but subject to s. 68(8)).

A number of offences concern nuclear energy and uranium. The Atomic Energy Act 1946, s. 11, makes it an offence for a person to disclose information related to atomic energy plants without authority. Section 13 of the 1946 Act also criminalises the unauthorised disclosure of information obtained through powers granted by the Act. The A-TCSA 2001, s. 79, criminalises the unauthorised disclosure of information that relates to nuclear security. Regulations made in accordance with the A-TCSA 2001, s. 80, criminalise the unauthorised disclosure of specified categories of information relating to uranium enrichment technology (SI 2004 No. 1818). The Nuclear Industries Security Regulations 2003 (SI 2003 No. 403) create an offence of failing to safeguard sensitive nuclear information.

Disclosure of information which is not protected by the Official Secrets Acts or other specific enactments by a person holding public office may amount to the common-law offence of misconduct in a public office (see **B15.26**).

The Data Protection Act 1998 (now repealed by the Data Protection Act 2018) includes a public interest defence to an offence of unlawfully obtaining/disclosing personal data. In *Shepherd v Information Commissioner* [2019] EWCA Crim 2 the Court of Appeal held that the defence under the Data Protection Act 1998, s. 55(2), imposes no more than an evidential burden.

FAILURE TO SAFEGUARD INFORMATION

The Official Secrets Act 1989, s. 8, creates three offences concerned with failure to safeguard information: **B9.77**

(a) Section 8(1) makes it an offence for a Crown servant or government contractor to fail to safeguard certain information.
(b) Section 8(4) makes it an offence for a person with information as a consequence of an unauthorised disclosure or entrusted in confidence to fail to safeguard it.
(c) Section 8(5) makes it an offence for a person with information entrusted in confidence to States or international organisations to fail to comply with official directions for its return or disposal.

Official Secrets Act 1989, s. 8

(1) Where a Crown servant or government contractor, by virtue of his position as such, has in his possession or under his control any document or other article which it would be an offence under any of the foregoing provisions of this Act for him to disclose without lawful authority he shall be guilty of an offence if—
 (a) being a Crown servant, he retains the document or article contrary to his official duty; or
 (b) being a government contractor, he fails to comply with an official direction for the return or disposal of the document or article,
 or if he fails to take such care to prevent the unauthorised disclosure of the document or article as a person in his position may reasonably be expected to take.

. . .

(4) Where a person has in his possession or under his control any document or other article which it would be an offence under section 5 above for him to disclose without lawful authority, he shall be guilty of an offence if—
 (a) he fails to comply with an official direction for its return or disposal; or
 (b) where he obtained it from a Crown servant or government contractor on terms requiring it to be held in confidence or in circumstances in which that servant or contractor could reasonably expect that it would be so held, he fails to take such care to prevent its unauthorised disclosure as a person in his position may reasonably be expected to take.

(5) Where a person has in his possession or under his control any document or other article which it would be an offence under section 6 above for him to disclose without lawful authority, he shall be guilty of an offence if he fails to comply with an official direction for its return or disposal.

Procedure

As to the requirement of consent of the A-G, see **B9.36**. These offences are triable summarily only (Official Secrets Act 1989, s. 10(2)). Section 11(5) (place of trial) applies to these offences (see **B9.36**). **B9.78**

Sentence

B9.79 The maximum penalty on summary conviction is imprisonment for a term not exceeding three months and/or an unlimited fine (Official Secrets Act 1989, s. 10(2)). There is no offence-specific guideline but the Sentencing Council's *General Guideline: Overarching Principles* (see Supplement, **SG2-1**) is used for all offenders sentenced on or after 1 October 2019. In October 2008 a senior Whitehall official who pleaded guilty to leaving highly classified intelligence documents about Al-Qa'ida and the capabilities of the Iraqi security forces on a train was fined £2,500 by a magistrates' court for the offence. In December 2017, a senior counter-terrorism officer who left operational documents in the boot of his car while on holiday was fined £3,500 and subsequently dismissed from the force after pleading guilty to offences under s. 10 (*R (Beale) v West Midlands Special Case Panel* [2018] EWHC 759 (Admin)).

Common Elements

B9.80 Certain elements are common to all three offences:

The terms 'possession' and 'control' are not defined by the Act, but 'possession' appears as an essential requirement in a number of criminal offences, and, it is submitted, should be interpreted in the same way as in relation to, e.g., dangerous drugs (see **B19.17** *et seq.*). The meaning of the word 'disclose' is considered at **B9.41**.

As to the meaning of 'official direction', the Official Secrets Act 1989, s. 8(9), provides that 'official direction' means a direction duly given by a Crown servant or government contractor or by or on behalf of a prescribed body or a body of a prescribed class. The Official Secrets Act 1989 (Prescription) Order, art. 4 and sch. 3, specify the bodies which have the power to impose official restrictions for the purpose of s. 8(9); the Civil Aviation Authority and the Investigatory Powers Tribunal have such power.

As to the only circumstances in which a disclosure is made with lawful authority, see s. 7 of the Act and **B9.54**.

Elements Specific to s. 8(1) and (4)

B9.81 The meanings of 'Crown servant' and 'government contractor' are considered at **B9.52** and **B9.53**. However, for the purposes of this offence, the Official Secrets Act 1989, s. 8(3), provides that 'Crown servant' includes a person notified within the meaning of s. 1(1), who is not otherwise either a Crown servant or a government contractor (see **B9.39**).

Elements Specific to s. 8(5)

B9.82 The information protected by this offence is that which it would be an offence to disclose under s. 6 of the Act (see **B9.75**). As to such information, see s. 6(1).

Specific Defences

B9.83 D's belief that there was lawful authority for the disclosure is a defence to all three charges under the Official Secrets Act 1989, s. 8. As to this and other defences, see **B9.43**.

In relation to the offence under s. 8(1) only, the Official Secrets Act 1989, s. 8(2), provides that it is a defence for a Crown servant to prove that at the time of the alleged offence he believed that he was acting in accordance with his official duty and had no reasonable cause to believe otherwise. Although the legal burden of proving this defence appears to lie on D, it is likely that only an evidential burden would be compatible with the ECHR, Article 6 (see *Keogh* [2007] EWCA Crim 528, [2007] 3 All ER 789 and **F3.18** *et seq.*).

UNLAWFUL INTERCEPTION OF COMMUNICATIONS BY PUBLIC AND PRIVATE SYSTEMS

The IPA 2016 created two criminal offences relating to the unlawful interception of communications by public and private systems. Section 3 creates a criminal offence of intentional interception of a communication in the course of its transmission by means of (i) a public telecommunications system, (ii) a private telecommunications system or (iii) a public postal service. Section 11 creates an offence (for those holding specified public authority roles listed in sch. 4) of unauthorised obtaining of communications data. **B9.84**

The IPA 2016 repealed the whole of Part I of the RIPA 2000 and created new interception of communications offences. Previously, the RIPA 2000, s. 1, contained two interception offences. One (s. 1(1)) was concerned with the interception of communications transmitted by either public postal or public telecommunications systems; the other offence (s. 1(2)) was concerned with the interception of communications transmitted by private telecommunications systems.

The new IPA 2016, s. 3, offence was brought into force on 27 June 2018 by the Investigatory Powers Act 2016 (Commencement No. 5 and Transitional and Savings Provisions) Regulations 2018 (SI 2018 No. 652); and the s. 11 offence was brought into force on 5 February 2019 by the Investigatory Powers Act 2016 (Commencement No. 11) Regulations 2019 (SI 2019 No. 174). A detailed commentary on the provisions of the IPA 2016 and the Act's legislative background is set out in S McKay, *Blackstone's Guide to the Investigatory Powers Act 2016* (2017). The offences contained within the RIPA 2000, s. 1, continue to apply to conduct taking place before 27 June 2018 (SI 2018 No. 652, reg. 19). Commentary on the provisions of the RIPA 2000 can be found in earlier editions of this work.

Unlawful Interception: Definition

Investigatory Powers Act 2016, s. 3 **B9.85**

(1) A person commits an offence if—
  (a) the person intentionally intercepts a communication in the course of its transmission by means of—
    (i) a public telecommunication system,
    (ii) a private telecommunication system, or
    (iii) a public postal service,
  (b) the interception is carried out in the United Kingdom, and
  (c) the person does not have lawful authority to carry out the interception.
(2) But it is not an offence under subsection (1) for a person to intercept a communication in the course of its transmission by means of a private telecommunication system if the person—
  (a) is a person with a right to control the operation or use of the system, or
  (b) has the express or implied consent of such a person to carry out the interception.
(3) Sections 4 and 5 contain provision about—
  (a) the meaning of 'interception', and
  (b) when interception is to be regarded as carried out in the United Kingdom.
(4) Section 6 contains provision about when a person has lawful authority to carry out an interception.
(5) For the meaning of the terms used in subsection (1)(a)(i) to (iii), see sections 261 and 262.
(6) A person who is guilty of an offence under subsection (1) is liable—
  (a) on summary conviction in England and Wales, to a fine;
  (b) on summary conviction in Scotland or Northern Ireland, to a fine not exceeding the statutory maximum;
  (c) on conviction on indictment, to imprisonment for a term not exceeding 2 years or to a fine, or to both.
(7) No proceedings for any offence which is an offence by virtue of this section may be instituted—
  (a) in England and Wales, except by or with the consent of the Director of Public Prosecutions;
  (b) in Northern Ireland, except by or with the consent of the Director of Public Prosecutions for Northern Ireland.

Procedure

B9.86 The offence is triable either way (IPA 2016, s. 3(6)). Proceedings for an offence cannot be instituted except, in England and Wales, with the consent of the DPP (s. 3(7)(a)).

Sentence

B9.87 The maximum punishment is: on conviction on indictment, imprisonment for a term not exceeding two years and/or a fine; on summary conviction, an unlimited fine (IPA 2016, s. 3(6)). There is no offence-specific guideline but the Sentencing Council's *General Guideline: Overarching Principles* (see Supplement, SG2-1) is used for all offenders sentenced on or after 1 October 2019.

Elements of the Offence: Telecommunications Systems and Postal Service

B9.88 Sections 261 and 262 of the IPA 2016 define various terms.

'Public telecommunication system' means a telecommunication system located in the UK by means of which any public telecommunications service is provided, or which consists of parts of any other telecommunication system by means of which any such service is provided.

'Telecommunication system' means any system (including the apparatus comprised in it) that exists (whether wholly or partly in the UK or elsewhere) for the purpose of facilitating the transmission of communications by any means involving the use of electrical or electromagnetic energy.

'Public telecommunications service' means any telecommunications service which is offered or provided to, or to a substantial section of, the public in any one or more parts of the UK.

'Telecommunications service' means any service that consists in the provision of access to, and of facilities for making use of, any telecommunication system (whether or not one provided by the person providing the service), and includes any case where a service consists in or includes facilitating the creation, management or storage of communications transmitted, or that may be transmitted, by means of such a system.

'Private telecommunication system' means any telecommunication system which, not being a public telecommunication system, is a system that satisfies certain conditions: (a) it is attached, directly or indirectly and whether or not for the purpose of the communication in question, to a public telecommunication system; and (b) there is apparatus comprised in the system which is both located in the UK and used (with or without other apparatus) for making the attachment to the public telecommunication system.

'Public postal service' means any postal service which is offered to or provided to, or to a substantial section of, the public in one or more parts of the UK. 'Postal service' means any service which (a) consists in the following, or in any one or more of them, namely, the collection, sorting, conveyance, distribution and delivery (whether in the UK or elsewhere) of postal items; and (b) is offered or provided as a service the main purpose of which, or one of the main purposes of which, is to make available, or to facilitate, a means of transmission from place to place of postal items containing communications.

General terms such as 'apparatus' and 'communication' and related terms are defined in the IPA 2016, s. 263.

Interception

B9.89 Section 4(1) of the IPA 2016 defines 'interception' for the purposes of the Act. A person intercepts a communication in the course of its transmission by means of a telecommunication system if, and only if, the person (a) does a relevant act in relation to the system, and (b) the effect of the relevant act is to make any content of the communication available, at a relevant time, to a person who is not the sender or intended recipient of the communication.

A relevant act means (a) modifying, or interfering with the system or its operation, (b) monitoring transmissions made by means of the system, or (c) monitoring transmissions made by wireless telegraphy to or from apparatus that is part of the system (s. 4(2)).

Modification of a telecommunication system includes references to the attachment of any apparatus to, or other modification of or interference with (a) any part of the system, or (b) any wireless telegraphy apparatus used for making transmissions to or from apparatus comprised in the system (s. 4(3)).

The relevant time at which the communication must be made available to the person other than the sender or intended recipient of the communication is (a) any time when the communication is being transmitted, and (b) any time, whether before or after its transmission, when the communication is stored in or by the system (s. 4(4)).

References to the interception of a communication do not include reference to the interception of any communication broadcast for general reception (s. 5(1)).

An interception is carried out in the UK if, and only if, both (a) the relevant act or interception is carried out by conduct within the UK; and (b) the communication is intercepted in the course of its transmission by means of a public telecommunication system or a public postal service or in the course of a transmission by means of a private telecommunication system in a case in which the sender or intended recipient of the communication is in the UK (s. 4(8)).

The relevant time at which a communication is made available to another person includes any time when the communication is diverted or recorded at a relevant time so as to make any content of the communication available to a person (not merely the intended recipient) after that time (s. 4(5); cf. *Coulson* [2013] EWCA Crim 1026, [2014] 1 WLR 1119). In relation to the previous RIPA 2000, s. 2(8), the tape recording of a telephone call by one party to it, without the knowledge of the other party, does not amount to interception of a communication within s. 2 (*Hardy* [2002] EWCA Crim 3012, [2003] 1 Cr App R 30 (494)). Nor did a recording of what one person said on the telephone, picked up by a surveillance device placed in his car which did not record any speech by the other party (*E* [2004] EWCA Crim 1243, [2004] 1 WLR 3279; *Allsopp* [2005] EWCA Crim 703). The compatibility of interception (and surveillance) which has been authorised under the RIPA 2000 with the ECHR, Article 8, was confirmed in *Kennedy v UK* (2011) 52 EHRR 4 (207).

'Postal item' means any letter, postcard or other such thing in writing as may be used by the sender for imparting information to the recipient, or any packet or parcel (s. 262(5)).

Postal Data The exception in relation to postal data is limited to interception by means of a postal service and provides that references to the interception of a communication in the course of its transmission by means of a postal service do not include reference to (a) any conduct that takes place in relation only to so much of the communication as consists in any postal data comprised in, included as part of, attached to, or logically associated with a communication (whether by the sender or otherwise) for the purposes of any postal service by means of which it is being or may be transmitted; or (b) any such conduct, in connection with conduct falling within paragraph (a), as gives a person who is neither the sender nor the intended recipient only so much access to a communication as is necessary for the purpose of identifying postal data so comprised or attached (s. 5(2)). 'Postal data' is defined in s. 262(4). Under the RIPA 2000 data of this kind was referred to as 'Traffic data'. **B9.90**

'Data' in this context includes anything written on the outside of the item (s. 262(4)).

Lawful Authority

Investigatory Powers Act 2016, ss. 6, 44 to 52 **B9.91**

6.—(1) For the purposes of this Act, a person has lawful authority to carry out an interception if, and only if—

(a) the interception is carried out in accordance with—

(i) a targeted interception warrant or mutual assistance warrant under Chapter 1 of Part 2, or

(ii) a bulk interception warrant under Chapter 1 of Part 6,

(b) the interception is authorised by any of sections 44 to 52, or
(c) in the case of a communication stored in or by a telecommunication system, the interception—
(i) is carried out in accordance with a targeted equipment interference warrant under Part 5 or a bulk equipment interference warrant under Chapter 3 of Part 6,
(ii) is in the exercise of any statutory power that is exercised for the purpose of obtaining information or taking possession of any document or other property, or
(iii) is carried out in accordance with a court order made for that purpose.

(2) Conduct which has lawful authority for the purposes of this Act by virtue of subsection (1)(a) or (b) is to be treated as lawful for all other purposes.

(3) Any other conduct which—
(a) is carried out in accordance with a warrant under Chapter 1 of Part 2 or a bulk interception warrant, or
(b) is authorised by any of sections 44 to 52,
is to be treated as lawful for all purposes.

44.—(1) The interception of a communication is authorised by this section if the sender and the intended recipient of the communication have each consented to its interception.

(2) The interception of a communication is authorised by this section if—
(a) the communication is one sent by, or intended for, a person who has consented to the interception, and
(b) surveillance by means of that interception has been authorised under—
(i) Part 2 of the Regulation of Investigatory Powers Act 2000, or
(ii) the Regulation of Investigatory Powers (Scotland) Act 2000 (2000 asp 11).

45.—(1) The interception of a communication is authorised by this section if the interception is carried out—
(a) by, or on behalf of, a person who provides a postal service or a telecommunications service, and
(b) for any of the purposes in subsection (2).

(2) The purposes referred to in subsection (1) are—
(a) purposes relating to the provision or operation of the service;
(b) purposes relating to the enforcement, in relation to the service, of any enactment relating to—
(i) the use of postal or telecommunications services, or
(ii) the content of communications transmitted by means of such services;
(c) purposes relating to the provision of services or facilities aimed at preventing or restricting the viewing or publication of the content of communications transmitted by means of postal or telecommunications services.

(3) A reference in this section to anything carried out for purposes relating to the provision or operation of a telecommunications service includes, among other things, a reference to anything done for the purposes of identifying, combating or preventing anything which could affect—
(a) any telecommunication system by means of which the service is provided, or
(b) any apparatus attached to such a system.

46.—(1) Conduct is authorised by this section if it is authorised by regulations made under subsection (2).

(2) The Secretary of State may by regulations authorise conduct of a description specified in the regulations if that conduct appears to the Secretary of State to constitute a legitimate practice reasonably required for the purpose, in connection with the carrying on of any relevant activities (see subsection (4)), of monitoring or keeping a record of—
(a) communications by means of which transactions are entered into in the course of the relevant activities, or
(b) other communications relating to the relevant activities or taking place in the course of the carrying on of those activities.

(3) But nothing in any regulations under subsection (2) may authorise the interception of any communication except in the course of its transmission using apparatus or services provided by or to the person carrying on the relevant activities for use (whether wholly or partly) in connection with those activities.

(4) In this section 'relevant activities' means—
(a) any business,
(b) any activities of a government department, the Welsh Government, a Northern Ireland department or any part of the Scottish Administration,
(c) any activities of a public authority, and

(d) any activities of any person or office holder on whom functions are conferred by or under any enactment.

47.—(1) The interception of a communication in the course of its transmission by means of a public postal service is authorised by this section if it is carried out by an officer of Revenue and Customs under section 159 of the Customs and Excise Management Act 1979, as applied by virtue of—

(a) section 105 of the Postal Services Act 2000 (power to open postal items etc.), or
(b) that section and another enactment.

(2) The interception of a communication in the course of its transmission by means of a public postal service is authorised by this section if it is carried out under paragraph 9 of Schedule 7 to the Terrorism Act 2000 (port and border controls).

48.—(1) Conduct falling within subsection (2) is authorised by this section if it is carried out by OFCOM for purposes connected with a relevant matter (see subsection (3)).

(2) The conduct referred to in subsection (1) is—

(a) the interception of a communication in the course of its transmission by means of a telecommunication system;
(b) the obtaining, by or in connection with the interception, of information about the sender or recipient, or intended recipient, of the communication (whether or not a person);
(c) the disclosure of anything obtained by conduct falling within paragraph (a) or (b).

(3) Each of the following is a relevant matter for the purposes of subsection (1)—

(a) the grant of wireless telegraphy licences under the Wireless Telegraphy Act 2006 ('the 2006 Act');
(b) the prevention or detection of anything which constitutes interference with wireless telegraphy;
(c) the enforcement of—
   (i) any provision of Part 2 (other than Chapter 2 and sections 27 to 31) or Part 3 of the 2006 Act, or
   (ii) any enactment not falling within sub-paragraph (i) that relates to interference with wireless telegraphy....

49.—(1) Conduct taking place in a prison is authorised by this section if it is conduct in exercise of any power conferred by or under prison rules.

(2) In this section 'prison rules' means any rules made under—

(a) section 47 of the Prison Act 1952,
(b) section 39 of the Prisons (Scotland) Act 1989, or
(c) section 13 of the Prison Act (Northern Ireland) 1953.

(3) In this section 'prison' means—

(a) any prison, young offender institution, young offenders centre, secure training centre, secure college or remand centre which—
   (i) is under the general superintendence of, or is provided by, the Secretary of State under the Prison Act 1952, or
   (ii) is under the general superintendence of, or is provided by, the Department of Justice in Northern Ireland under the Prison Act (Northern Ireland) 1953, or
(b) any prison, young offenders institution or remand centre which is under the general superintendence of the Scottish Ministers under the Prisons (Scotland) Act 1989, and includes any contracted out prison, within the meaning of Part 4 of the Criminal Justice Act 1991 or section 106(4) of the Criminal Justice and Public Order Act 1994, and any legalised police cells within the meaning of section 14 of the Prisons (Scotland) Act 1989.

50.—(1) Conduct is authorised by this section if—

(a) it takes place in any hospital premises where high security psychiatric services are provided, and
(b) it is conduct in pursuance of, and in accordance with, any relevant direction given to the body providing those services at those premises.

(2) 'Relevant direction' means—

(a) a direction under section 4(3A)(a) of the National Health Service Act 2006, or
(b) a direction under section 19 or 23 of the National Health Service (Wales) Act 2006.

(3) Conduct is authorised by this section if—

(a) it takes place in a state hospital, and
(b) it is conduct in pursuance of, and in accordance with, any direction given to the State Hospitals Board for Scotland under section 2(5) of the National Health Service

(Scotland) Act 1978 (regulations and directions as to the exercise of their functions by health boards).

The reference to section 2(5) of that Act is to that provision as applied by Article 5(1) of, and the Schedule to, the State Hospitals Board for Scotland Order 1995 (which applies certain provisions of that Act to the State Hospitals Board).

(4) Conduct is authorised by this section if it is conduct in exercise of any power conferred by or under—
   (a) section 281 of the Mental Health (Care and Treatment) (Scotland) Act 2003 (2003 asp 13) (power to withhold correspondence of certain persons detained in hospital), or
   (b) section 284 of that Act (powers relating to the use of telephones by certain persons detained in hospital).

(5) In this section—
'high security psychiatric services' has the same meaning as in section 4 of the National Health Service Act 2006;
'hospital premises' has the same meaning as in section 4(3) of that Act;
'state hospital' has the same meaning as in the National Health Service (Scotland) Act 1978.

51.—(1) Conduct taking place in immigration detention facilities is authorised by this section if it is conduct in exercise of any power conferred by or under relevant rules.

(2) In this section—
'immigration detention facilities' means any removal centre, short-term holding facility or pre-departure accommodation;
'removal centre', 'short-term holding facility' and 'pre-departure accommodation' have the meaning given by section 147 of the Immigration and Asylum Act 1999;
'relevant rules' means—
   (a) in the case of a removal centre, rules made under section 153 of that Act;
   (b) in the case of a short-term holding facility, rules made under, or having effect by virtue of, section 157 of that Act;
   (c) in the case of pre-departure accommodation, rules made under, or having effect by virtue of, section 157A of that Act.

52.—(1) The interception of a communication in the course of its transmission by means of a telecommunication system is authorised by this section if conditions A to D are met.

(2) Condition A is that the interception—
   (a) is carried out by or on behalf of a telecommunications operator, and
   (b) relates to the use of a telecommunications service provided by the telecommunications operator.

(3) Condition B is that the interception is carried out in response to a request made in accordance with a relevant international agreement by the competent authorities of a country or territory outside the United Kingdom.

In this subsection 'relevant international agreement' means an international agreement to which the United Kingdom is a party and which is designated as a relevant international agreement by regulations made by the Secretary of State, see further sections (6) and (7).

(4) Condition C is that the interception is carried out for the purpose of obtaining information about the communications of an individual—
   (a) who is outside the United Kingdom, or
   (b) who each of the following persons believes is outside the United Kingdom—
      (i) the person making the request;
      (ii) the person carrying out the interception.

(5) Condition D is that any further conditions specified in regulations made by the Secretary of State for the purposes of this section are met.

(6) Subsection (7) applies where an international agreement provides for requests for the interception of a communication to be made by the competent authorities of a country or territory, or of more than one country or territory, in which a person found guilty of a criminal offence may be sentenced to death for the offence under the general criminal law of the country or territory concerned.

Such an offence is referred to in subsection (7) as a 'death penalty offence'.

(7) Where this subsection applies, the Secretary of State may not designate the agreement as a relevant international agreement unless the Secretary of State has sought, in respect of each country or territory referred to in subsection (6), a written assurance, or written assurances, relating to the non-use of information obtained by virtue of the agreement in connection with proceedings for a death penalty offence in the country or territory.

The decision in *R (NTL Group Ltd) v Ipswich Crown Court* [2002] EWHC 1585 (Admin), [2003] QB 131 is given statutory effect in s. 6(1)(c)(ii) to (iii): where the interception is in the exercise of any statutory power or court order to take possession of any document or other property, that too will amount to lawful authority. As to the lawfulness of bulk interception in the context of the ECHR, Articles 8 and 10, see *R (Liberty) v Secretarys of State for the Home Department* [2019] EWHC 2057 (Admin), [2020] 1 WLR 243, where the High Court found that the provisions of the IPA 2016 are compatible with those rights. **B9.92**

The Investigatory Powers (Interception by Businesses etc. for Monitoring and Record-keeping Purposes) Regulations 2018 (SI 2018 No. 356), passed under the IPA 2016, s. 46(2), authorise certain lawful business practices. This is in substantially similar terms to the Telecommunications (Lawful Business Practice) (Interception of Communications) Regulations 2000 (SI 2000 No. 2699) made under the RIPA 2000. These authorisations do not exceed those permitted by Articles 5.2 and 15.1 of Directive 2002/58/EC ([2002] OJ L201/37). In particular, the Regulations specify that interceptions can only be authorised if the system controller has made all reasonable efforts to inform the users of the system that communications may be intercepted.

Previously, the Investigatory Powers (Consequential Amendments etc.) Regulations 2018 (SI 2018 No. 682), reg. 5, provided that the Convention on Mutual Assistance in Criminal Matters between the Member States of the European Union is a designated international agreement for the purposes of s. 52(3). However, that designation was subsequently revoked by force of the Law Enforcement and Security (Amendment) (EU Exit) Regulations 2019 (SI 2019 No. 742).

Probably the most important means of making an interception lawful will be through action taken under an interception warrant. The lawful interception of communications by warrant was previously provided for in six sections of the RIPA 2000. This number has more than quadrupled in the IPA 2016, and the provisions are found in ss. 15 to 43. Under the former regime, there was one type of interception warrant which could be issued under the RIPA 2000, s. 5. Section 15 of the IPA 2016 replaces the previous single interception warrant scheme and creates three types of warrants: targeted interception, targeted examination, and mutual assistance warrants. Part 6, chapter 1 of the IPA 2016 creates a fourth type of interception warrant: the bulk interception warrant.

There are extensive statutory procedures in relation to the issuing, exercising and oversight of such warrants (IPA 2016, Part 2, ch. 1; Part 6, ch. 1). Warrants must be approved by a Judicial Commissioner (ss. 23 to 24, 140). The First Section of the European Court of Human Rights held that the scheme of bulk data warrants under the previous s. 8(4) of the RIPA 2000 did not meet the 'quality of law' requirement of the ECHR, Article 8 (*Big Brother Watch v UK* (2018) Applns 58170/13, 62322/14 and 24960/15, 13 September 2018). However, the Court affirmed that the operation of a bulk telecommunications interception regime was, in principle, compatible with the ECHR. Therefore, the impact of the decision on the bulk data warrants scheme under the IPA 2016 is uncertain. The case has since been referred to the Grand Chamber.

The admissibility of foreign intercept evidence will often make it disclosable under the usual principles (*Koc* [2008] EWCA Crim 77).

Providers of relevant services, including persons outside the UK (IPA 2016, s. 253(8)), have an obligation to maintain an interception capability if required by the Secretary of State pursuant to a technical capability notice under s. 253. The power to give a 'notice requiring the person who is to be subject to the obligations to take all such steps as may be specified or described in the notice' was previously provided for in the RIPA 2000, s. 12. That provision was enacted by way of an amendment made in response to Joined Cases C-293/12 and C-594/12 *Digital Rights Ireland Ltd* [2015] QB 127, the status of which in English law was considered in *R (Davis) v Secretary of State for the Home Department* [2015] EWCA Civ 1185, [2017] 1 All ER 62 and *Secretary of State for the Home Department v Watson* [2018] EWCA Civ 70, [2018] QB 912.

Further, there is a provision providing a general saving for lawful conduct. **B9.93**

Investigatory Powers Act 2016, sch. 9, para. 10

Nothing in any of the provisions of this Act by virtue of which conduct of any description is or may be authorised by any warrant, authorisation or notice, or by virtue of which information may be obtained in any manner, is to be read—

(a) as making it unlawful to engage in any conduct of that description which is not otherwise unlawful under this Act and would not be unlawful apart from this Act,

(b) as otherwise requiring—

(i) the issue, grant or giving of such a warrant, authorisation or notice, or

(ii) the taking of any step for or towards obtaining the authority of such a warrant, authorisation or notice, before any such conduct of that description is engaged in, or

(c) as prejudicing any power to obtain information by any means not involving conduct that may be authorised under this Act.

As to the continuing validity of a warrant issued under the RIPA 2000, see the IPA 2016, s. 44(2). The Home Office has prepared draft codes of practice relating to interceptions of communications and bulk acquisitions of communications data under the IPA 2016, sch. 7. They have not yet come into force.

Private Telecommunications Interceptions: Defence

B9.94 A person's conduct is excluded from criminal liability for the offence contrary to the IPA 2016, s. 3, if that person has a right to control the operation or the use of the system; or has the express or implied consent of such a person to make the interception (s. 3(2)). In *Stanford* [2006] EWCA Crim 258, [2006] 1 WLR 1554, it was held that 'control' for the purposes of the previous s. 1(2) of the RIPA 2000 means 'authorise and forbid' and not the unrestricted ability physically to use and operate the system. Any other approach would contravene the purposes of the legislation. It is likely that 'control' for the purposes of s. 3(2) of the IPA 2016 will be found to have the same meaning.

Unlawful Obtaining of Communications Data: Definition

B9.95 **Investigatory Powers Act 2016, s. 11**

(1) A relevant person who, without lawful authority, knowingly or recklessly obtains communications data from a telecommunications operator or a postal operator is guilty of an offence.

(2) In this section 'relevant person' means a person who holds an office, rank or position with a relevant public authority (within the meaning of Part 3).

(3) Subsection (1) does not apply to a relevant person who shows that the person acted in the reasonable belief that the person had lawful authority to obtain the communications data.

(4) A person guilty of an offence under this section is liable—

(a) on summary conviction in England and Wales—

(i) to imprisonment for a term not exceeding 12 months (or 6 months, if the offence was committed before the commencement of section 154(1) of the Criminal Justice Act 2003), or

(ii) to a fine, or to both;

(b) on summary conviction in Scotland—

(i) to imprisonment for a term not exceeding 12 months, or

(ii) to a fine not exceeding the statutory maximum, or to both;

(c) on summary conviction in Northern Ireland—

(i) to imprisonment for a term not exceeding 6 months, or

(ii) to a fine not exceeding the statutory maximum, or to both;

(d) on conviction on indictment, to imprisonment for a term not exceeding 2 years or to a fine, or to both.

B9.96 **Procedure** The offence is triable either way (IPA 2016, s. 11(4)). Unlike the position in relation to the s. 3 offence, the commencement of a prosecution for the s. 11 offence does not require the consent of the DPP.

B9.97 **Sentence** The maximum punishment is: on conviction on indictment, imprisonment for a term not exceeding two years and/or a fine; on summary conviction, a fine or imprisonment for a term not exceeding 12 months, or, if in England and Wales and the offence was committed before the commencement of the CJA 2003, s. 154, for a term not exceeding six months (IPA 2016, s. 11(4)).

Elements The offence only applies to a 'relevant person', being a person holding an office, rank or position within a relevant public authority (s. 11(2)). The relevant public authorities are set out in sch. 4 to the IPA 2016. **B9.98**

The s. 11 offence applies to the acquisition only of communications data (s. 11(1)). 'Communications data', in relation to a telecommunications operator, service, or system, means three categories of entity or events data. The first is that which is to be, or is capable of being, held, or obtained by, or on behalf of, a telecommunications operator. This is subject to three qualifications: it is about an entity to which a telecommunications service is provided and relates to the provision of the service; is comprised in, included as part of, attached to, or logically associated with a communication, regardless of where it originates from or is going to, for the purposes of a telecommunications system by means of which the communication is being or may be transmitted; or does not fall within either of the first two qualifications but does relate to the use of a telecommunications service or system. The second is that which is available directly from a telecommunication system and falls within the parameters of the second qualification. The third is that which is, or would be capable of, being held or obtained by, or on behalf of, a telecommunications operator, is about the architecture of a telecommunication system, and is not about a specific person. In no circumstances can communications data include any content of a communication, or would-be content of a communication, other than systems data (s. 261(5)). Content for this purpose means any element of the communication, or any data attached to or logically associated with it, that reveals anything of what might reasonably be considered to be the meaning, if any, of the communication. This is subject to two exceptions: any meaning arising from the fact of the communication or from any data relating to the transmission of the communication is to be disregarded; and systems data (s. 261(6)).

Data is only 'communications data' if it is either entity data or events data. 'Entity data' means any data which (a) is about an entity, an association between a telecommunications service and an entity, or an association between any part of a telecommunication system and an entity; (b) consists of or includes data which identifies or describes the identity, whether by reference to its location or otherwise, and (c) is not events data. 'Events data' is any data which identifies or describes an event on, in or by means of a telecommunication system where the event consists of one or more entities engaging in a specific activity at a specific time.

The data must be obtained from a telecommunications officer or postal officer (s. 11(1)). A 'telecommunications operator' is a person who offers or provides a telecommunications service to persons in the UK, or who controls or provides a telecommunication system which is wholly or partly in the UK or controlled from the UK (s. 261(10)). A 'postal operator' means a person providing a postal service to persons in the UK (s. 262(6)).

The meaning of 'lawful authority' is considered at **B9.95** to **B9.96**.

The relevant mental element is knowledge or recklessness (s. 11(1)). A relevant person will have a defence to the s. 11 offence where the person acted in the reasonable belief that there was lawful authority to obtain the communications data (s. 11(3)). **B9.99**

INCITEMENT TO DISAFFECTION

Incitement to Disaffection Act 1934, ss. 1 and 2 **B9.100**

1. If any person maliciously and advisedly endeavours to seduce any member of His Majesty's forces from his duty or allegiance to His Majesty, he shall be guilty of an offence under this Act.

2.—(1) If any person, with intent to commit or to aid, abet, counsel, or procure the commission of an offence under section 1 of this Act, has in his possession or under his control any document of such a nature that the dissemination of copies thereof among members of His Majesty's forces would constitute such an offence, he shall be guilty of an offence under this Act.

Police Act 1996, s. 91

(1) Any person who causes, or attempts to cause, or does any act calculated to cause, disaffection amongst the members of any police force, or induces or attempts to induce, or does any act calculated to induce, any member of a police force to withhold his services, shall be guilty of an offence...

(2) This section applies in the case of—
(a) special constables appointed for a police area,
(b) members of the Civil Nuclear Constabulary, and
(c) members of the British Transport Police Force,
as it applies in the case of members of a police force.

There are like offences in relation to Ministry of Defence police (see the Ministry of Defence Police Act 1987, s. 6).

Procedure

B9.101 **Incitement to Disaffection Act 1934, s. 3**

(2) No prosecution in England under this Act shall take place without the consent of the Director of Public Prosecutions.

(3) Where a prosecution under this Act is being carried on by the Director of Public Prosecutions, a court of summary jurisdiction shall not deal with the case summarily without the consent of the Director.

The offences under the Incitement to Disaffection Act 1934 and the Police Act 1996 are triable either way. When tried on indictment they are class 1B offences.

Sentence

B9.102 The maximum penalties are:

Incitement to Disaffection Act 1934, s. 1: on indictment, two years and/or a fine; summarily, four months and/or an unlimited fine (s. 3(1)). There is no offence-specific guideline but the Sentencing Council's *General Guideline: Overarching Principles* (see Supplement, SG2-1) is used for all offenders sentenced on or after 1 October 2019. The court also has power to order the destruction or other disposal of any documents connected with the offence after D's conviction and after expiration of the time during which an appeal may be lodged (s. 3(4)).

Police Act 1996, s. 91: on indictment, two years and/or a fine; summarily, six months and/or an unlimited fine.

Elements

B9.103 It is not necessary to show that any particular individual was the object of the attempted seduction; members of the armed forces or a police force generally will suffice (*Bowman* (1912) 76 JP 271). Evidential and *mens rea* requirements were considered in *Fuller* (1797) 2 Leach 790. 'Allegiance' was considered in *Joyce v DPP* [1946] AC 347, and the correct form of the indictment was considered in *Arrowsmith* [1975] QB 678.

The method of attempted seduction, whether by written or oral communication, is irrelevant, though circumstances such as the offering of an inducement or the use of threats or blackmail will no doubt affect sentence.

Section B10 Terrorism, Piracy and Hijacking

TERRORISM: OVERVIEW

This section deals with the investigative anti-terrorist powers, the substantive offences relating to terrorism, the sentencing guidance relevant to those offences and the financial powers which aim to obstruct terrorist funding. TPIMs and the Terrorism Prevention and Investigation Measures Act 2011 are also considered. Offences related to nuclear and chemical weapons and piracy, hijacking and some other offences concerning maritime and air security are also covered. **B10.1**

In terms of investigation, the TA 2000 gave permanent effect to anti-terrorist powers for the first time. Those powers have since been supplemented by, *inter alia*, the Anti-terrorism, Crime and Security Act 2001 (A-TCSA 2001), the Terrorism Act 2006 (TA 2006), the Counter-Terrorism Act 2008 (C-TA 2008), the Counter-Terrorism and Security Act 2015 (C-TSA 2015) and the Counter-Terrorism and Border Security Act 2019 (C-TBSA 2019). The financial powers available to the authorities to stem the flow of funds to terrorist groups have become more extensive (see, e.g., the Terrorism Asset Freezing Act 2010).

Trials of terrorist offences are governed by CrimPD XIII, Annex 4 (see Supplement, **CPD.XIII.x4**). Annex 4 provides for administrative arrangements specific to terrorist cases and substitutes for the previous 'Terrorism Protocol'. The Unduly Lenient Sentence procedure (see **D28.1** to **D28.8**) can be applied to 42 of the offences covered by this section: 31 are terrorism offences—there are 11 others.

Some offences covered by this section have unusually wide jurisdiction provisions. By virtue of the C-TA 2008, s. 28, specified terrorist offences may be tried in any place in the UK, irrespective of where in the UK the offence was committed: the offence is treated as having been committed in the place where proceedings are taken.

Sections 62 to 63E of the TA 2000 provide extended jurisdiction for both terrorist and some other offences. Some apply only to UK nationals or UK residents committing offences abroad and some apply to people of any nationality who commit offences anywhere. Section 81 of the SCA 2015 includes offences contrary to ss. 5 and 6 of the TA 2006 within the scope of s. 17 of that Act and therefore preparation of terrorist acts or training abroad for terrorism can be prosecuted in a UK court.

Some offences relating to nuclear, biological and chemical devices, piracy, hijacking and aviation and maritime security matters can also be prosecuted in a UK court, even if not committed in the UK or by a UK national or resident.

Definition of Terrorism

B10.2 **Terrorism Act 2000, s. 1**

(1) In this Act 'terrorism' means the use or threat of action where—
   (a) the action falls within subsection (2),
   (b) the use or threat is designed to influence the government or an international governmental organisation or to intimidate the public or a section of the public, and
   (c) the use or threat is made for the purpose of advancing a political, religious, ideological, or racial cause.

(2) Action falls within this subsection if it—
   (a) involves serious violence against a person,
   (b) involves serious damage to property,
   (c) endangers a person's life, other than that of the person committing the action,
   (d) creates a serious risk to the health or safety of the public or a section of the public, or
   (e) is designed seriously to interfere with or seriously to disrupt an electronic system.

The definition of terrorism is widely drawn and, in essence, involves the use or threat of violence for political, religious, ideological or racial causes. Terms used in s. 1(1) and (2) are defined in s. 1(4) and (5). The references to action, person, public, property and government apply equally whether the action, person, public property or government is inside or outside the UK (s. 1(4)(a) to (d) and (5)). In *F* [2007] EWCA Crim 243, [2007] QB 960 it was held that the meaning of the phrase 'a country other than the United Kingdom' in s. 1(4)(d) is plain and the terrorist legislation applies equally in respect of undemocratic countries as it does in relation to democratic governments. In *Gul* [2012] EWCA Crim 280, [2012] 1 Cr App R 37 (504) the Court of Appeal held that there was nothing in international law that required the terms of s. 1 to be read down so as to exclude those perpetrating military attacks in a time of non-international armed conflict. The Supreme Court upheld that decision in *Gul* [2013] UKSC 64, [2014] AC 1260. The certified question was whether the definition of 'terrorism' in the TA 2000, s. 1, operated so as to include any or all military attacks by a non-State armed group against any or all State or inter-governmental organisation armed forces in the context of a non-international armed conflict. The Court concluded that, although it had concerns about the breadth of the definition (referring to the reports of the Independent Reviewer of Terrorism Legislation and the comments on this issue from David Anderson QC in particular), there was no basis in domestic law to restrict the statutory definition in the way advanced by the appellant, namely that:

(a) some provisions of the 2000 and 2006 Acts were enacted to give effect to the UK's treaty obligations concerned with the suppression of terrorism, and that 'terrorism' should accordingly be given a meaning which accords with the international law norm, consistent with the definition in the treaty to which effect is being given, and
(b) as the 2000 and 2006 Acts criminalise certain 'terrorist' actions committed outside the UK, the meaning of 'terrorism' in those statutes should not be wider than what is accepted as an international norm.

The Court noted the absence of any accepted norm in international law as to what constitutes terrorism, citing its decision in *Al-Sirri v Secretary of State for the Home Department* [2012] UKSC 54, [2013] 1 AC 745. It observed that, whilst some UN and other texts provided significant support for the argument that terrorism did not extend to the acts of insurgents or 'freedom fighters' in non-international armed conflicts, it was insufficient to demonstrate a rule of international law requiring the definition to be read down as being in conflict with the UK's ECHR or other international law obligations. It reiterated the point made in *Al-Sirri* that 'an attack on ISAF in Afghanistan is in principle capable of being an act contrary to the purposes and principles of the United Nations' and such an attack therefore can constitute 'terrorism'. The Court pointed to UN resolutions which referred to the activities of Al-Qa'ida and the Taliban as 'terrorism', even though their actions involved insurgents attacking forces of States and inter-governmental organisations in non-international armed conflict and noted that insurgents do not benefit from combatant immunity in non-international armed conflicts.

Next, the Court considered the argument that the TA 2000, ss. 62 to 64, and some provisions of the TA 2006, gave effect to the UK's obligations under international conventions, two of which exclude insurgent attacks on military forces in non-international armed conflicts from their definitions. However, the Court declined to read down the definition of terrorism because some of the activities which became offences under the TA 2000 were included in order to fulfil international law obligations; the UK can go beyond its international law obligations in criminalising conduct. And, even if the wide definition of terrorism in s. 1 had to be read down for the purposes of ss. 62 to 64, it did not have to be read down when interpreting the rest of the Act.

INVESTIGATIVE POWERS UNDER THE TERRORISM ACT 2000

Sections 32 to 39 of, and schs. 5 and 6 to the TA 2000 provide a plethora of powers to be deployed in terrorist investigations. They are dealt with below. The definition of a terrorist investigation is contained in s. 32. **B10.3**

Terrorism Act 2000, s. 32

(1) In this Act, 'terrorist investigation' means an investigation of—
   (a) the commission, preparation or instigation of acts of terrorism,
   (b) an act which appears to have been done for the purposes of terrorism,
   (c) the resources of a proscribed organisation,
   (d) the possibility of making an order under s. 3(3), or
   (e) the commission, preparation or instigation of an offence under this Act or under Part 1 of the Terrorism Act 2006 other than an offence under section 1 or 2 of that Act.

Cordons

Police officers, usually of the rank of at least superintendent, are empowered under ss. 33 and 34 of the TA 2000 to designate an area as a cordoned area for the purposes of a terrorist investigation. An order may be made only when it is considered expedient for the purposes of a terrorist investigation. The cordoned area must be demarcated by tape or in any other manner that the officer considers appropriate. Sections 35 and 36 provide for the duration of a cordon and the powers of a constable in relation to that cordon respectively. A failure to comply with the requirements of a constable in relation to the cordoned area is a summary offence punishable by up to three months' imprisonment. **B10.4**

Securing Information and Evidence: Search and Seizure Powers

Section 37 of the TA 2000 gives effect to sch. 5, which contains a number of provisions relating to the securing of information for the purposes of terrorist investigations. Any application in respect of sch. 5 is governed by CrimPR Part 47 (see Supplement, **R-47.1** *et seq.*). **B10.5**

Paragraph 1 of sch. 5 governs the procedure for search warrants. An application may be made to a justice of the peace for a warrant to search premises in order to seize material which a constable has reasonable grounds for believing is likely to be of substantial value to a terrorist investigation and must be seized in order to prevent it being concealed, lost, damaged or destroyed (para. 1(3)). By virtue of para. 1(2A), the premises to be searched may be specified (a 'specific premises warrant') or may concern all premises occupied or controlled by a person specified in the application (an 'all premises warrant'). A warrant cannot authorise the seizure of legally privileged material, nor may a constable executing the warrant require any person to remove any clothing in public other than headgear, footwear, an outer coat, jacket or gloves. The application may be granted if the justice of the peace is satisfied that the warrant is sought for the purposes of a terrorist investigation (para. 1(5)(a)), that the reasonable grounds for the belief held by the constable are made out and the material to be seized is not legally privileged (para. 1(5)(b)), that the warrant is likely to be necessary in the circumstances of the case (para. 1(5)(c)) and, in the case of an all premises warrant, that it is not reasonably practicable to specify all the premises owned or occupied by the person concerned (para. 1(5)(d)).

Paragraph 2 of sch. 5 concerns an application for a specified premises warrant for non-residential premises by an officer of at least the rank of superintendent. Even if the justice of the peace is not satisfied that the condition in para. 1(5)(c) is satisfied, the warrant may be granted provided that para. 1(5)(a) and (b) are made out. Such a warrant must be executed within 24 hours of it being issued.

B10.6 Officers of at least the rank of superintendent (or in urgent cases, officers of lesser rank) may themselves authorise the search of specified premises by virtue of para. 3 of sch. 5. Such authorisation may be given when the premises are within an area subject to a cordon created under the TA 2000, s. 33 (see **B10.4**). Paragraph 1(3) of sch. 5 (the authorising officer must have reasonable grounds for believing that the material has value, etc.) applies. No legally privileged material may be seized. Such a search may be authorised on any number of occasions during the period that the cordon is in existence. It is an offence punishable with up to three months' imprisonment and/or a fine to the level 4 maximum to obstruct such a search.

Paragraph 4 defines 'excluded material', 'items subject to legal professional privilege' and 'special procedure material' as having the meanings given to them by the PACE 1984, ss. 11, 10 and 14, respectively (see **D1.149**, **F10.33** and **D1.150**).

B10.7 Applications for warrants to search for excluded material or special procedure material must be made to a circuit judge under sch. 5, paras. 5 and 6.

Terrorism Act 2000, sch. 5, paras. 5 and 6

5.—(1) A constable may apply to a circuit judge for an order under this paragraph for the purposes of a terrorist investigation.

(2) An application for an order shall relate to particular material, or material of a particular description, which consists of or includes excluded material or special procedure material.

(3) An order under this paragraph may require a specified person—

(a) to produce to a constable within a specified period for seizure and retention any material which he has in his possession, custody or power and to which the application relates;

(b) to give a constable access to any material of the kind mentioned in paragraph (a) within a specified period;

(c) to state to the best of his knowledge and belief the location of material to which the application relates if it is not in, and it will not come into, his possession, custody or power within the period specified under paragraph (a) or (b).

(4) For the purposes of this paragraph—

(a) an order may specify a person only if he appears to the circuit judge to have in his possession, custody or power any of the material to which the application relates, and

(b) a period specified in an order shall be the period of seven days beginning with the date of the order unless it appears to the judge that a different period would be appropriate in the particular circumstances of the application.

(5) Where a circuit judge makes an order under sub-paragraph (3)(b) in relation to material on any premises, he may, on the application of a constable, order any person who appears to the judge to be entitled to grant entry to the premises to allow any constable to enter the premises to obtain access to the material.

6.—(1) A circuit judge may grant an application under paragraph 5 if satisfied—
(a) that the material to which the application relates consists of or includes excluded material or special procedure material,
(b) that it does not include items subject to legal privilege, and
(c) that the conditions in sub-paragraphs (2) and (3) are satisfied in respect of that material.
(2) The first condition is that—
(a) the order is sought for the purposes of a terrorist investigation, and
(b) there are reasonable grounds for believing that the material is likely to be of substantial value, whether by itself or together with other material, to a terrorist investigation.
(3) The second condition is that there are reasonable grounds for believing that it is in the public interest that the material should be produced or that access to it should be given having regard—
(a) to the benefit likely to accrue to a terrorist investigation if the material is obtained, and
(b) to the circumstances under which the person concerned has any of the material in his possession, custody or power.

By virtue of para. 7 an order under para. 5 may be made in relation to material which is expected to come into existence within 28 days of making the order. An order under para. 5 does not confer any rights of access or production in relation to legally privileged information and has effect notwithstanding any statutory restriction on disclosure. Where a para. 5 order relates to computer material, it shall have effect as an order to produce or give access to the material in a form which is visible and legible (para. 8). **B10.8**

An order under para. 5 may be made against a government department as defined by the Crown Proceedings Act 1947 (para. 9).

Paragraph 11 governs the procedure for making an application to a circuit judge by a constable for a specific premises warrant or any premises warrant, applying a similar scheme to that under para. 1. Under para. 12, a circuit judge may grant a specific premises warrant if satisfied that a para. 5 order relating to excluded or special procedure material at the premises has not been complied with (para. 12(1)), or (under para. 12(2)) there are reasonable grounds for believing that there is special procedure or excluded material (which is not legally privileged material) on the premises and the conditions in paras. 12(3) and (4) are met. The condition in para. 12(3) is that the warrant is for the purposes of a terrorist investigation and the material is likely to be of substantial value to a terrorist investigation. The condition in para. 12(4) is that it is not appropriate to make an order under para. 5 either because it is not practicable to communicate with any person entitled to produce or grant access to the material or grant entry to the relevant premises or because a terrorist investigation may be seriously prejudiced unless a constable can secure immediate access to the material. Under para. 12(2A), a circuit or district judge may grant an application for an all premises warrant if satisfied that an order under para. 5 has not been complied with and the person specified in the application is also specified in the order. An all premises warrant may also be granted by a circuit or district judge under para. 12(2B) if there are reasonable grounds for believing that there is excluded or special procedure material (which is not legally privileged material) in the premises in question and the conditions in para. 12(3) and (4) are met.

Schedule 5 also provides for a system of explanation orders requiring a person to provide an explanation for any material that is seized under para. 1 or 11 or produced or made available under para. 5. Paragraph 13 provides that a constable may apply to a circuit judge for such an order. A lawyer may be required to provide the name and address of a client (para. 13(3)) but is not required to disclose information that it would be possible to refuse to disclose on the grounds of legal professional privilege in proceedings in the High Court (para. 13(2)); statements in compliance with such an order may be made orally or in writing and may only be used in evidence against the maker for prosecution for an offence under para. 14 (para. 13(4)). Paragraph 14 creates an offence; it is an offence to make a statement in purported compliance with an order under para. 13 which the maker knows is false or misleading in relation to **B10.9** a material particular or recklessly to make a statement which is false or misleading in a material particular. Such an offence is triable either way and punishable summarily with imprisonment up to six months and/or an unlimited fine. On indictment, the maximum sentence is one of two years' imprisonment and/or a fine (para. 14(2)).

In circumstances where an officer of at least the rank of superintendent has reasonable grounds for believing that the case is one of great emergency and immediate action is necessary, para. 15 allows the officer to sign a written order giving a constable the authority to carry out a search which would be given by a warrant secured under para. 1 or para. 11 (para. 15(2)). If such a written order is signed, the particulars of the case must be notified to the Secretary of State as soon as is reasonably practicable. Any person wilfully obstructing such a search commits an offence punishable with up to three months' imprisonment and/or a fine up to level 4. Moreover, under para. 16, an officer of at least the rank of superintendent, if there are reasonable grounds for believing that the case is one of great emergency, may require by written notice a person to provide an explanation of any material seized in pursuance of an order under para. 15. A person commits an offence by failing to comply with such a notice, punishable with up to six months' imprisonment and/or an unlimited fine. It is a defence to the alleged offence that the person had a reasonable excuse for the failure to provide the explanation.

Financial Information

B10.10 Section 38 of the TA 2000 gives effect to sch. 6. An application for an order under sch. 6 must be made by a police officer of at least the rank of superintendent. A circuit judge should make the order only if satisfied that the order is sought for the purposes of a terrorist investigation, the tracing of terrorist property is desirable for the purposes of the investigation, and the order will enhance the effectiveness of the investigation (paras. 2, 3 and 5). Any application for an order pursuant to sch. 6 is governed by CrimPR Part 47 (see Supplement, R-47.1 *et seq.*).

Where a circuit judge has made the relevant supporting order, a named constable may require a financial institution to provide customer information for the purposes of a terrorist investigation (sch. 6, para. 1(1)). That information must be supplied in such a way and within such time as the constable specifies and notwithstanding any restriction on the disclosure of information imposed by statute or otherwise (para. 1(2)). It is a summary offence for the institution to fail to comply with the requirement (para. 1(3)), but it is a defence for the institution to prove that the information required was not in the institution's possession, or that it was not reasonably practicable for the institution to comply with the requirement (para. 1(4)). The penalty for the offence is an unlimited fine (para. 1(5)). If the offence was committed with the consent or connivance of an officer of the institution, or was attributable to neglect on the part of an officer of the institution, that officer, as well as the institution, is guilty of the offence (para. 8(1) and (2)). The maximum penalty is imprisonment for a term not exceeding six months, and/or an unlimited fine (para. 8(3)).

B10.11 **Customer Information and Business Relationship** 'Customer information' is defined in para. 7(1) and includes details of bank account numbers, start and end dates of accounts, past and present addresses and the identity of any person sharing the account.

A 'business relationship' exists between a financial institution and a person if (and only if) (a) there is an arrangement between them designed to facilitate the carrying out of frequent or regular transactions between them, and (b) the total amount of payments to be made in the course of the arrangement is neither known nor capable of being ascertained when the arrangement is made (para. 7(2)).

If a financial institution provides 'customer information', it is not admissible in evidence in criminal proceedings against the institution or any of its officers or employees (para. 9(1)), except in relation to proceedings for an offence contrary to para. 1(3) or para. 8.

Account Monitoring Orders

Account monitoring orders can be imposed on financial institutions in relation to accounts (whether all or particular) held by any person specified in an application by virtue of s. 38A of and sch. 6A to the TA 2000. Any application for such an order is governed by CrimPR Part 47 (see Supplement, **R-47.1** ***et seq.***). During a specified period the institution is required to provide information of a specified description to an appropriate officer (para. 2(4) and (5)). The order must be complied with irrespective of any legislative or other restriction on the disclosure of information (para. 6(2)). Ordinarily, a statement made by a financial institution in response to an account monitoring order may not be used in evidence against it in criminal proceedings. However, there are certain exceptions to that rule. The statement may be used: **B10.12**

(a) in the case of proceedings for contempt of court;
(b) in the case of proceedings under s. 23 (forfeiture) where the financial institution has been convicted of an offence under any of ss. 15 to 18 (terrorist property offences: see **B10.122** to **B10.145**); or
(c) on a prosecution for an offence where, in giving evidence, the financial institution makes a statement inconsistent with the first statement (but the statement may not be used against a financial institution unless evidence relating to it is adduced or a question relating to it is asked by or on behalf of the financial institution in the proceedings arising out of the prosecution (para. 7(1) to (3)).

Disclosure of and Interference with Information Offences

Terrorism Act 2000, s. 39 **B10.13**

(1) Subsection (2) applies where a person knows or has reasonable cause to suspect that a constable is conducting or proposes to conduct a terrorist investigation.
(2) The person commits an offence if he—
 (a) discloses to another anything which is likely to prejudice the investigation, or
 (b) interferes with material which is likely to be relevant to the investigation.
(3) Subsection (4) applies where a person knows or has reasonable cause to suspect that a disclosure has been or will be made under any of sections 19 to 21B or 38B.
(4) The person commits an offence if he—
 (a) discloses to another anything which is likely to prejudice an investigation resulting from the disclosure under that section, or
 (b) interferes with material which is likely to be relevant to an investigation resulting from the disclosure under that section.
(5) It is a defence for a person charged with an offence under subsection (2) or (4) to prove—
 (a) that he did not know and had no reasonable cause to suspect that the disclosure or interference was likely to affect a terrorist investigation, or
 (b) that he had a reasonable excuse for the disclosure or interference.
(6) Subsections (2) and (4) do not apply to a disclosure which is made by a professional legal adviser—
 (a) to his client or to his client's representative in connection with the provision of legal advice by the adviser to the client and not with a view to furthering a criminal purpose, or
 (b) to any person for the purpose of actual or contemplated legal proceedings and not with a view to furthering a criminal purpose.
(6A) Subsections (2) and (4) do not apply if—
 (a) the disclosure is of a matter within section 21D(2) or (3)(a) (terrorist property: tipping off), and
 (b) the information on which the disclosure is based came to the person in the course of a business in the regulated sector.
(7) A person guilty of an offence under this section shall be liable—
 (a) on conviction on indictment, to imprisonment for a term not exceeding five years, to a fine or to both, or
 (b) on summary conviction, to imprisonment for a term not exceeding six months, [an unlimited fine] or to both.

(8) For the purposes of this section—
 (a) a reference to conducting a terrorist investigation includes a reference to taking part in the conduct of, or assisting, a terrorist investigation, and
 (b) a person interferes with material if he falsifies it, conceals it, destroys it or disposes of it, or if he causes or permits another to do any of those things.
(9) The reference in subsection (6A) to a business in the regulated sector is to be construed in accordance with Schedule 3A.

There are two offences concerned with the disclosure of or interference with information linked to a terrorist investigation created by s. 39.

The defence provided for under s. 39(5)(a) is subject to the provisions of s. 118 of the TA 2000 (see **B10.31**), but the defence under s. 39(5)(b) is not. For the significance of the reverse burden, see **F3.18** *et seq.*

COUNTER-TERRORISM POWERS UNDER THE TERRORISM ACT 2000

Arrest without Warrant

B10.14 Section 41(1) of the TA 2000 provides that a constable may arrest without warrant any person reasonably suspected to be a terrorist. When a person is arrested under s. 41, that person must be taken as soon as is reasonably practicable to the police station which the arresting constable considers the most appropriate (sch. 8, para. 1(4)). PACE Code H (see **appendix 1**) applies to such detainees.

The detention provisions of the TA 2000 contain no provisions about bail. The effect is that neither a custody officer nor a court has power to bail a suspect detained under the TA 2000 powers before charge, either conditionally or otherwise. Consequently, at an application for a warrant for further detention (see **B10.22**) any submission that the detained person be bailed pending further inquiries is bound to fail. Moreover, a custody officer cannot grant bail after charge; only a court can do so. If a suspect is arrested on suspicion of a terrorism offence under the PACE 1984 and dealt with in accordance with that regime, the ordinary rules about detention apply, including provisions about grant of bail before or after charge.

Detention

B10.15 Where a person is arrested under the power provided by the TA 2000, s. 41, the provisions of sch. 8 apply to that person's detention, treatment, review of detention and extension of detention (s. 41(2)). A person detained under s. 41 may be detained (unless detained under any other power) for no longer than the period of 48 hours beginning (a) with the time of arrest, or (b) if detained under sch. 7 when arrested under s. 41, with the time when the examination under sch. 7 began (s. 41(3)). The C-TBSA 2019, s. 18, amends the TA 2000, s. 41 and sch. 7 (see **B10.27**), in respect of the time-limit for detention of terrorist suspects who are receiving medical treatment. Only the time during which a person is questioned counts towards the maximum period of detention. Any period of time the person is detained in hospital while not being questioned, or time spent travelling to and from the hospital, does not count towards the maximum period of detention. The amendments come into force on a day or days to be appointed by the Secretary of State. If a reviewing officer reviewing the person's detention under sch. 8, part II, does not authorise continued detention, the person must (unless detained in accordance with s. 41(5) or (6) or under any other power) be released (s. 41(4)). Where a police officer intends to make an application for a warrant of further detention under sch. 8, para. 29, the person may be detained pending the making of the application (s. 41(5)). Where an application has been made under sch. 8, para. 29 or 36, the person may be detained until the proceedings in relation to the application are concluded (s. 41(6)). If an application under sch. 8, para. 29 or 36, is refused, that does not prevent continued detention under s. 41, although the person must be released at the end of the relevant period.

As to post-charge questioning under the C-TA 2008, s. 22 (see **B10.22**).

Identification

An authorised person may take any steps that are reasonably necessary for (a) photographing, (b) measuring, or (c) identifying the detained person (TA 2000, sch. 8, para. 2(1)). **B10.16**

Detained Person's Rights

Informing a Named Person **B10.17**

Terrorism Act 2000, sch. 8, para. 6

(1) Subject to paragraph 8, a person detained under Schedule 7 or section 41 at a place in England, Wales or Northern Ireland shall be entitled, if he so requests, to have one named person informed as soon as is reasonably practicable that he is being detained there.
(2) The person named must be—
 (a) a friend of the detained person,
 (b) a relative, or
 (c) a person who is known to the detained person or who is likely to take an interest in his welfare.
(3) Where a detained person is transferred from one place to another, he shall be entitled to exercise the right under this paragraph in respect of the place to which he is transferred.

The exercise of this right may be delayed by an officer of at least the rank of superintendent if the officer believes that there will be interference with the investigation, evidence or a person, or that persons will be alerted and the prevention of crime or the recovery of a criminal benefit will be made more difficult (sch. 8, para. 8(1)(a), (4) and (5)). If authorisation for delay is given orally, it must be recorded in writing as soon as reasonably practicable (para. 8(6)). The reason for the delay must be communicated to the detained person and recorded as soon as reasonably practicable (para. 8(7)) and if the reason for the delay ceases to exist the detained person must be allowed to exercise the right without further delay (para. 8(8)). The detained person must be allowed to exercise the right to inform a named person of the detainee's whereabouts before the end of the period of detention under the TA 2000 (para. 8(2)).

The Terrorism Act 2000 (Code of Practice for Examining Officers and Review Officers) Order 2014 (SI 2014 No. 1838) applies.

Informing a Solicitor **B10.18**

Terrorism Act 2000, sch. 8, paras. 7 and 7A

7.—(1) Subject to paragraphs 8 and 9, a person detained under Schedule 7 or section 41 in England, Wales or Northern Ireland shall be entitled, if he so requests, to consult a solicitor as soon as is reasonably practicable, privately and at any time.
(2) Where a request is made under sub-paragraph (1), the request and the time at which it was made shall be recorded.

7A.—(1) This paragraph applies where a person detained under Schedule 7 requests to consult a solicitor.
(2) The examining officer may not question the detained person under paragraph 2 or 3 of Schedule 7 until the person has consulted a solicitor (or no longer wishes to do so).
(3) Sub-paragraph (2) does not apply if the examining officer reasonably believes that postponing the questioning until then would be likely to prejudice determination of the relevant matters.
(4) The powers given by paragraph 8 of Schedule 7 (search powers where a person is questioned under paragraph 2 of Schedule 7) may be used when questioning is postponed because of sub-paragraph (2).
(5) The detained person is entitled to consult a solicitor in person.
(6) Sub-paragraph (5) does not apply if the examining officer reasonably believes that the time it would take to consult a solicitor in person would be likely to prejudice determination of the relevant matters.
(7) In that case the examining officer may require any consultation to take place in another way.
(8) In this paragraph 'the relevant matters' means the matters the examining officer seeks to determine under paragraph 2 or 3 of Schedule 7.

In *Ibrahim* [2008] EWCA Crim 880, [2008] 4 All ER 208, the Court of Appeal dismissed an appeal that principally concerned the admission into evidence of police 'safety' interviews of terrorist suspects conducted in the absence of a solicitor. Such interviews are often carried out to try to establish whether there are any further devices or terrorists at large which might imperil the safety of members of the public. The Court of Appeal held that the trial judge had properly exercised his discretion in allowing the interviews to go before the jury and rejected a policy-based argument that to do so would discourage terrorist suspects from providing information which might lead to lives being saved. The case concerned those arrested for the attempted bombing of the London Transport network on 21 July 2005 and so the relevant Code of Practice governing the 'safety' interviews conducted was at that time Code C. It is submitted that the same principles discussed by the Court would govern the admission of safety interviews governed by Code H. The Court of Appeal remarked that if a suspect was given an undertaking by the police to the effect that the fruits of any safety interview would not be deployed in evidence then that would provide the basis for a powerful argument to exclude any interview at trial.

In *Ibrahim v UK* [2014] ECHR 1392 the Chamber of the ECtHR held that there had been no violation of the ECHR, Article 6(1) and (3)(c), by allowing the safety interviews to go to the jury, a decision upheld by the Grand Chamber in respect of safety interviews (*Ibrahim v UK* [2016] ECHR 750).

Schedule 8, para. 9, provides for a direction that a consultation with a solicitor be in the sight and hearing of a police officer.

Fingerprints and Intimate and Non-intimate Samples

B10.19 Schedule 8, para. 10, to the TA 2000 regulates the taking of fingerprints and other samples from a person detained under the TA 2000.

Terrorism Act 2000, sch. 8, para. 10

(1) This paragraph applies where a person is detained in England, Wales or Northern Ireland under Schedule 7 or section 41.

(2) Fingerprints may be taken from the detained person only if they are taken by a constable—
 (a) with the appropriate consent given in writing, or
 (b) without that consent under sub-paragraph (4).

(3) A non-intimate sample may be taken from the detained person only if it is taken by a constable—
 (a) with the appropriate consent given in writing, or
 (b) without that consent under sub-paragraph (4).

(4) Fingerprints or a non-intimate sample may be taken from the detained person without the appropriate consent only if—
 (a) he is detained at a police station and a police officer of at least the rank of superintendent authorises the fingerprints or sample to be taken, or
 (b) he has been convicted of a recordable offence and, where a non-intimate sample is to be taken, he was convicted of the offence on or after 10th April 1995 (or 29th July 1996 where the non-intimate sample is to be taken in Northern Ireland).

(5) An intimate sample may be taken from a person detained under section 41, but only if—
 (a) he is detained at a police station,
 (b) the appropriate consent is given in writing,
 (c) a police officer of at least the rank of superintendent authorises the sample to be taken, and
 (d) subject to paragraph 13(2) and (3), the sample is taken by a constable.

(6) Subject to sub-paragraph (6A) an officer may give an authorisation under sub-paragraph (4)(a) or (5)(c) only if—
 (a) in the case of a person detained under section 41, the officer reasonably suspects that the person has been involved in an offence under any of the provisions mentioned in section 40(1)(a), and the officer reasonably believes that the fingerprints or sample will tend to confirm or disprove his involvement, or
 (b) in any case in which an authorisation under that sub-paragraph may be given, the officer is satisfied that the taking of the fingerprints or sample from the person is necessary in order to assist in determining whether he falls within section 40(1)(b).

(6A) An officer may also give an authorisation under sub-paragraph (4)(a) for the taking of fingerprints if—
(a) he is satisfied that the fingerprints of the detained person will facilitate the ascertainment of that person's identity; and
(b) that person has refused to identify himself or the officer has reasonable grounds for suspecting that that person is not who he claims to be.
(6B) In this paragraph references to ascertaining a person's identity include references to showing that he is not a particular person.
(7) If an authorisation under sub-paragraph (4)(a) or (5)(c) is given orally, the person giving it shall confirm it in writing as soon as is reasonably practicable.

If the detained person refuses to consent to the giving of a sample, a court may be entitled to draw appropriate adverse inferences (see **F20**).

Any fingerprints or samples or information provided may be used only for the purpose of a terrorist investigation. A check cannot be made against such samples under the PACE 1984, s. 63A(1), except for the purpose of a terrorist investigation (TA 2000, sch. 8, para. 14(3)).

Review and Extension of Detention

The Protection of Freedoms Act 2012, s. 57, reduced the maximum period of detention to 14 days. Section 58 provides an emergency procedure whereby the limit may temporarily be increased to 28 days by the Home Secretary. **B10.20**

Parts II and III of sch. 8 to the TA 2000 contain detailed provisions on review and extension of detention.

Section 41 of the TA 2000 requires periodical review of the detention of a suspect. The first review must be carried out as soon as is reasonably practicable after the time of the detained person's arrest and any subsequent reviews must be carried out at intervals of not more than 12 hours (sch. 8, para. 21(1) to (3)). A review may be postponed if at the latest time when it should be carried out (a) the detained person is being questioned by a police officer and an officer is satisfied that an interruption of the questioning would prejudice the investigation, (b) no review officer is readily available, or (c) it is not practicable for any other reason to carry it out (sch. 8, para. 22(1)). If a review is postponed, a review must be carried out as soon as is reasonably practicable after the postponement (sch. 8, para. 22(2)).

The authorisation of continued detention is governed by sch. 8, para. 23. **B10.21**

Terrorism Act 2000, sch. 8, para. 23

(1) A review officer may authorise a person's continued detention only if satisfied that it is necessary—
(a) to obtain relevant evidence whether by questioning him or otherwise,
(b) to preserve relevant evidence,
(ba) pending the result of an examination or analysis of any relevant evidence or of anything the examination or analysis of which is to be or is being carried out with a view to obtaining relevant evidence,
(c) pending a decision whether to apply to the Secretary of State for a deportation notice to be served on the detained person,
(d) pending the making of an application for the Secretary of State for a deportation notice to be served on the detained person, or
(e) pending consideration by the Secretary of State whether to serve a deportation notice on the detained person, or
(f) pending a decision whether the detained person should be charged with an offence.

The review officer must not authorise continued detention unless the investigation or process for deportation is being conducted diligently and expeditiously (sch. 8, para. 23(2) and (3)). The detained person, or a solicitor representing the detained person who is available at the time of the review, must be given an opportunity to make oral or written representations about the detention before the review officer decides whether to authorise detention (para. 26(1) and (2)). The review officer may refuse oral representations by the person detained if the officer considers that the person is unfit because of the person's condition or behaviour (para. 26(3)). The detained person has the right to have a named person informed and to consult a solicitor (paras. 6 and 7: see **B10.17** and **B10.18**); when authorising continued detention, the review officer must inform the detained person of those rights where they have been exercised or inform the person that they have been delayed. Under para. 27(1) and (2), the review officer must also review the reasons for the delay under para. 8 (see **B10.17**).

It is not permissible to question a person for more than two hours unless detained. Moreover, any detained person must be released after a maximum of six hours (unless detained under another power).

B10.22 A warrant of further detention may be sought by a Crown Prosecutor or a police officer of at least the rank of superintendent. The application is made to a judicial authority (a specially designated district judge) (para. 29(1) and (4)). If a warrant is granted it authorises further detention of the person under s. 41 for a specified period. Information on which the applicant for extension intends to rely may be withheld from the detained person or anyone representing that person upon application to the district judge (para. 34(1)).

There may be extension or further extension of the specified period upon further application by an officer of at least the rank of superintendent (para. 36(1)). Where the application would extend the period to a time that is no more than 14 days after (in effect) arrival at the police station and no application has previously been made to a senior judge (i.e. a judge of the High Court), the application is heard by the judicial authority; in any other case, the application must be heard by a senior judge (para. 36(1A), (1B) and (7)). The decision of the High Court judge is not amenable to judicial review.

If at any time it appears to the police officer or other person in charge that any of the conditions under which the warrant of further detention was issued no longer apply, the officer must '(a) if he has custody of the detained person, release him immediately, and (b) if he does not, immediately inform the person who does have custody that those matters no longer apply' and that person must release the detained person immediately (para. 37(1) to (3)).

The C-TBSA 2019 amends the TA 2000, s. 41, in respect of the time-limit for detention of terrorist suspects who are receiving medical treatment. Only the time during which a person is questioned counts towards the maximum period of detention. Any period of time the person is detained in hospital while not being questioned, or time spent travelling to and from the hospital, does not count towards the maximum period of detention. The amendments come into force on a day or days to be appointed by the Secretary of State.

Detention under s. 41 and sch. 8 was held to be compatible with the ECHR, Article 5, in *R (I) v City of Westminster Magistrates' Court and Chief Constable of Greater Manchester Police* [2008] EWHC 2146 (Admin).

Post-charge questioning is permissible under the C-TA 2008, s. 22. Section 22 empowers a Crown Court judge to authorise questioning of a person about a terrorism offence (or an offence which appears to the judge to have a terrorist connection) after the person has been charged with it, or been officially informed of the possibility of being prosecuted for it, or even after the person has been sent for trial for the offence. Under s. 22(3), the judge must specify the period during which questioning is authorised, and may impose such conditions as appear to be necessary in the interests of justice, including conditions as to the place where the questioning is to be carried out. The period authorised for questioning must not exceed 48 hours and runs continuously from when questioning pursuant to the authorisation begins. However, s. 22 plainly envisages that further authorisations of up to 48 hours may be allowed as s. 22(4) states that the 48-hour limit is 'without prejudice to any application for a further authorisation under this section'. If a person is in prison or detained elsewhere then, under s. 22(5), the judge may authorise removal of the person to another place for questioning. Section 22(6) limits the circumstances under which a Crown Court judge may allow such questioning. It stipulates that a judge must not authorise questioning under s. 22 unless satisfied that three conditions are met:

(a) that further questioning of the person is necessary in the interests of justice;
(b) that the investigation for the purposes of which the further questioning is proposed is being conducted diligently and expeditiously; and
(c) that what is authorised will not interfere unduly with the preparation of the person's defence to the charge in question or any other criminal charge.

There is no requirement in s. 22 that the questioning be based on evidence which was not available before charge, though a judge granting permission could impose that limitation. The most important safeguard is that the person may be questioned under s. 22 only about the offence for which charges *have been* brought. A question may arise as to whether a person can be questioned about a more serious offence than the one charged, if it arises from the same facts.

Search of Premises for a Person

Powers of search are provided for under s. 42 of the TA 2000. Upon application by a constable, a magistrate may issue a warrant in relation to specified premises if satisfied that there are reasonable grounds for suspecting that a person whom the constable reasonably suspects to be a person falling within s. 40(1)(b) (i.e. a person who is or has been concerned in the commission, preparation or instigation of acts of terrorism) is to be found there (s. 42(1)). Any constable is thereby authorised to enter and search the specified premises for the purpose of arresting the person under s. 41 (s. 42(2)). **B10.23**

Search of Person and Vehicle

A constable may stop and search a person whom the constable reasonably suspects to be a terrorist to discover whether the person has in his possession anything that may constitute evidence of being a terrorist (TA 2000, s. 43(1)). In addition a constable may search a person arrested under s. 41 to discover whether he has in his possession anything that may constitute evidence of being a terrorist (s. 43(2)). **B10.24**

Stop and Search Power

Under the TA 2000, s. 47A and sch. 6B, if a senior officer reasonably suspects that an act of terrorism will take place and considers that the stop and search powers are necessary to prevent such an act of terrorism, the senior officer may authorise the use of those powers in an area within the officer's police force area no larger than necessary and for a period no longer than necessary for that purpose (and for a maximum of 14 days). Authorisations must be confirmed by the Secretary of State within 48 hours if they are to last beyond that period and the Secretary of State has the power to restrict the scope of authorisations. Where an authorisation is in place, an officer in uniform may stop and search a person or a vehicle to search for evidence that the person is a terrorist or that the vehicle is being used for purposes of terrorism, whether or not the officer reasonably suspects that such evidence will be present. An individual or vehicle may be detained whilst a search is carried out, but only at or near the place where the person or vehicle is stopped. Written records are required to be kept and provided to a person searched, or the owner of a vehicle, if requested. **B10.25**

Prohibiting or Restricting Parking

Under s. 48 of the TA 2000 authorisation may be given to prohibit or restrict the parking of vehicles on a specified road if the person authorising it considers it expedient for the prevention of acts of terrorism (s. 48(1) and (2)). The power may then be exercised by a constable placing a traffic sign on the road concerned (s. 49(1)). A constable exercising the power may suspend a parking place (s. 49(2)). **B10.26**

The period of authorisation must not exceed 28 days (s. 50(1) and (2)). An authorisation may be renewed in writing by the authoriser or by a person who could have authorised it; a renewed authorisation has effect as if it were a new authorisation (s. 50(3)). Section 51 penalises any person who contravenes any relevant restriction or prohibition but it is a defence to prove that there was a reasonable excuse for the act or omission in question (s. 51(3)). Under s. 51(4), possession of a current disabled person's badge does not of itself constitute a reasonable excuse. The offences under s. 51 are triable summarily only. For an offence contrary to s. 51(1), a person is liable to a fine not exceeding level 4 (s. 51(5)). For the offence contrary to s. 51(2), a person is liable to imprisonment for a term not exceeding three months, a fine not exceeding level 4 on the standard scale, or both (s. 51(6)).

The C-TBSA 2019, s. 15, amends the RTRA 1984 to deal with restrictions on parking imposed for the prevention of terrorism, with effect from 12 April 2019.

Port and Border Controls

B10.27 A number of port and border controls are made available by s. 53(1) of, and sch. 7 to, the TA 2000. The exercise of the powers created in sch. 7 is not affected by any of the rights conferred by s. 1 of the Immigration Act 1971 (general principles regulating entry into and stay in the UK). These border controls operate in respect of Northern Ireland (TA 2000, sch. 7, para. 4). The powers created include powers of search, controls on embarkation and disembarkation and powers to compel disclosure of passenger information. It is an offence (i) wilfully to fail to comply with a duty under sch. 7, (ii) wilfully to contravene a prohibition imposed under sch. 7, or (iii) wilfully to obstruct or seek to frustrate a search or examination under sch. 7. The maximum penalty for these summary offences is imprisonment for a term not exceeding three months, a fine not exceeding level 4 on the standard scale, or both (para. 18(2)).

In *Beghal v DPP* [2015] UKSC 49, [2016] AC 88, on appeal from the Divisional Court, the Supreme Court confirmed that the TA 2000, sch. 7, did not breach the ECHR, Articles 5, 6 or 8. The Court concluded that sch. 7 makes some intrusion upon Article 8 rights but it is a fair balance between the rights of individuals and the interests of community at large: it is 'comparatively light' and within the expectations of travellers. It is for the prevention and detection of terrorism, the importance of which 'can scarcely be overstated'. The power of detention falls within Article 5(1)(b) because it is done to secure a legal obligation, the reinforcement of the sch. 7 powers: it is not automatically justified and should be for no longer than needed to complete the process. As to privilege, self-incrimination and Article 6: the wording of sch. 7 excludes privilege against self-incrimination. The powers under sch. 7 would be ineffective if privilege applied. Port questioning and search is not a criminal investigation, so Article 6 has no application because the individual is not a person charged with an offence. Where appropriate, the PACE 1984, s. 78, may render such evidence inadmissible.

In *Miranda v Secretary of State for the Home Department* [2014] EWHC 255 (Admin), [2014] 1 WLR 3140 the Divisional Court ruled that sch. 7 is not incompatible with Article 10. Subsequently in *R (Miranda) v Secretary of State Home Department* [2016] EWCA Civ 6, [2016] 1 WLR 1505, the Court of Appeal (Civil Division) ruled that the stop power conferred by sch. 7, para. 2(1), is incompatible with Article 10 in relation to journalistic material, in that it is not subject to adequate safeguards against its arbitrary exercise. The Court distinguished *Beghal*, on the basis that the considerations were 'materially different' as that case did not involve a journalist, or someone carrying journalistic material. A certificate of incompatibility was made and the Court said that it would be for Parliament to establish safeguards; the most obvious form of which could be some judicial or other independent and impartial scrutiny conducted in such a way as to protect the confidentiality in the material.

B10.28 The C-TBSA 2019, s. 16, amends the TA 2000, sch. 7 (see **B10.27**), by inserting para. 5A to give effect to a recommendation made by David Anderson QC, then Independent Reviewer of

Terrorism Legislation, that 'there should be a statutory bar to the introduction of Schedule 7 admissions in a subsequent criminal trial'. Thus the answers given to questions asked in a sch. 7 port stop are inadmissible except in limited circumstances set out in para. 5A. Schedule 7 is also amended by s. 16 in respect of the time-limit for detention of terrorist suspects who are receiving medical treatment. Only the time during which a person is questioned counts towards the maximum period of detention. Any period of time the person is detained in hospital while not being questioned, or time spent travelling to and from the hospital, does not count towards the maximum period of detention. The amendments come into force on a day or days to be appointed by the Secretary of State.

The C-TSA 2015 provides, via sch. 1, power for police officers and some immigration, Border Force and customs officials to require the hand-over of passports and other travel documents by a traveller and to search for, seize and temporarily retain them, where a person is suspected of intending to leave Great Britain or the UK in connection with terrorism-related activity.

By virtue of para. 15(1), it is an offence for a person who is required to hand over all travel documents in the person's possession to fail to do so without reasonable excuse. A person also commits an offence by intentionally obstructing or seeking to frustrate a search. The offence is summary only and the maximum penalty is imprisonment for a term not exceeding six months and/or an unlimited fine.

Schedule 1 and the Code of Practice for Officers Exercising Functions under Schedule 1 to the Counter-Terrorism and Security Act 2015 in Connection with Seizing and Retaining Travel Documents (issued under SI 2015 No. 217) contain detailed rules about the operation of the powers.

The seizure and retention of documents is permitted where a police officer has reasonable grounds to suspect that a person at a port intends to leave Great Britain to become involved in terrorism-related activity outside the UK, or where an officer has reasonable grounds to suspect that a person at a port or in the border area in Northern Ireland intends to leave the UK for that purpose. The term 'in the border area' means 'within a mile of the border'. Therefore, the power may be exercised where a person travels within the UK from Great Britain to Northern Ireland for the purpose of involvement in terrorism outside the UK, but not where the person is travelling from Northern Ireland to Great Britain for that purpose. This provision is designed to deal with individuals who go to Northern Ireland in order then to travel via the Republic of Ireland to terrorism-related activity.

Any person who is required to hand over travel documents or who is searched must be informed of the suspicion held by the authorities. An immigration officer or customs official who has the passport or travel document, e.g. as a result of a routine passport check, may ask a police officer for a direction that the travel document should be handed to the police, and can retain it while waiting for an answer. However, it is important to note that it is the police officer who must have the requisite reasonable suspicion, as at present no other officials are trained and accredited to do so.

Schedule 1, supported by the Code, deals in detail with the steps required in respect of passports and travel documents, time-limits and court hearings.

Unless a document can be retained for use as evidence in criminal proceedings, or for deportation proceedings, para. 4 requires an officer to seek authorisation for retention of documents from an officer of at least the rank of superintendent as soon as possible. For that authorisation to be given, the senior officer must be satisfied that there are reasonable grounds for the suspicion that the person intends to leave Great Britain or the UK to become involved in terrorism-related activity outside the UK. If authorisation is not granted, the documents must be returned as soon as possible unless they can be retained under any other power (e.g. under immigration legislation). Where authorisation is granted, the document may be retained while possible cancellation of a passport or the possibility of charging an offence, or the obtaining of an order or **B10.29** measure (a 'TPIM') is considered. This decision must be reviewed within 72 hours by a more senior officer (of at least the rank of Chief Superintendent).

The initial period of retention for as long as the above reasons apply is 14 days; this can be extended to 30 days under para. 8 if an application is made to a district judge within the 14 days. The district judge must grant an extension if satisfied that the investigators have been acting diligently and expeditiously, but otherwise must refuse it. The individual must be allowed to make oral or written representations about the application, and is entitled to be legally represented at the hearing. However, the police may apply for information in the application to be withheld from the person to whom it relates and the person's legal representative, and dealt with *ex parte*. The district judge may so order for a variety of reasons, including risk to national security. One further application can be made for a second 30-day order.

But different time-limits apply where retention of a document under sch. 1 has been used on two or more occasions in the same person's case in the previous six months. In such a case, the 14-day period becomes five days. If there is an application for an extension under para. 8, the district judge must grant the extension if satisfied that the relevant persons have been acting diligently and expeditiously and there are exceptional circumstances justifying the further use of the power.

SUBSTANTIVE OFFENCES UNDER THE TERRORISM ACT 2000

B10.30 The TA 2000 created numerous offences designed to fill perceived gaps in the legislative scheme aimed at countering acts of terrorism and developed the system of proscribing organisations, first introduced in response to Irish terrorism in 1974.

Special Evidence Provisions

B10.31 **Terrorism Act 2000, s. 118**

(1) Subsection (2) applies where in accordance with a provision mentioned in subsection (5) it is a defence for a person charged with an offence to prove a particular matter.
(2) If the person adduces evidence which is sufficient to raise an issue with respect to the matter the court or jury shall assume that the defence is satisfied unless the prosecution proves beyond reasonable doubt that it is not.
(3) Subsection (4) applies where in accordance with a provision mentioned in subsection (5) a court—
 (a) may make an assumption in relation to a person charged with an offence unless a particular matter is proved, or
 (b) may accept a fact as sufficient evidence unless a particular matter is proved.
(4) If evidence is adduced which is sufficient to raise an issue with respect to the matter mentioned in subsection (3)(a) or (b) the court shall treat it as proved unless the prosecution disproves it beyond reasonable doubt.
(5) The provisions in respect of which subsections (2) and (4) apply are—
 (a) sections 12(4), 39(5)(a), 54, 57, 58, 58A, 77 and 103 of this Act, and
 (b) sections 13, 32 and 33 of the Northern Ireland (Emergency Provisions) Act 1996 (possession and information offences) as they have effect by virtue of Schedule 1 to this Act.

These special evidence provisions are concerned with many of the offences that impose a reverse burden on D and are designed to ensure that the legislation is not incompatible with the ECHR. (For analysis of the effect of reverse burdens, see **F3.18** ***et seq.***)

B10.32 **Documentary Evidence** There are special rules relating to documentary evidence set out in s. 120.

Terrorism Act 2000, s. 120

(1) A document which purports to be—
 (a) a notice or direction given or order made by the Secretary of State for the purposes of a provision of this Act, and
 (b) signed by him or on his behalf, shall be received in evidence and
shall, until the contrary is proved, be deemed to have been given or made by the Secretary of State.

(2) A document bearing a certificate which—
 (a) purports to be signed by or on behalf of the Secretary of State, and
 (b) states that the document is a true copy of a notice or direction given or order made by the Secretary of State for the purposes of a provision of this Act,

shall be evidence (or, in Scotland, sufficient evidence) of the document in legal proceedings.

(3) In subsections (1) and (2) a reference to an order does not include a reference to an order made by statutory instrument.

(4) The Documentary Evidence Act 1868 shall apply to an authorisation given in writing by the Secretary of State for the purposes of this Act as it applies to an order made by him.

Membership of a Proscribed Organisation

Terrorism Act 2000, s. 11 **B10.33**

(1) A person commits an offence if he belongs or professes to belong to a proscribed organisation.

Procedure and Jurisdiction The offence of belonging to a proscribed organisation is triable either way and when tried on indictment is normally a class 3 offence, but see CrimPD XIII, para. B (see Supplement, **CPD.XIII.B**), for the additional factors that the court considers on allocation. Under the TA 2000, s. 117(2), as amended by the C-TA 2008, s. 29, the consent of the DPP is generally required for proceedings to be instituted; if it appears to the DPP that the offence is committed outside the UK or for a purpose wholly or partly connected with the affairs of a country other than the UK, then the A-G's consent is required (s. 117(2A)). The A-G's consent must be obtained before any plea before venue proceedings (*Lambert* [2009] EWCA Crim 700, [2010] 1 WLR 898). **B10.34**

The procedure set out in the Proscribed Organisations (Applications for Deproscription) Regulations 2001 (SI 2001 No. 107) enables an application to be made for an organisation to be removed from the list contained in sch. 2. An appeal against a refusal to remove an organisation from the list may be made to the Proscribed Organisations Appeal Commission under the TA 2000, s. 5(1) and (2).

Under s. 10(1), the following evidence may not be called by the prosecution in proceedings for this offence:

(a) evidence of anything done in relation to an application under s. 4 to deproscribe the organisation;
(b) evidence of anything done in relation to proceedings before the Proscribed Organisations Appeal Commission under the TA 2000, s. 5, or the HRA 1998, s. 7(1);
(c) evidence of anything done in relation to a further appeal on a matter of law under the TA 2000, s. 6; and
(d) any document submitted for any of the above purposes.

However, s. 10(2) allows such evidence to be called by the defence. Under the TA 2006, s. 17 (see **B10.91**), if a person does anything outside the UK which would amount to an offence under s. 11(1) if done in any part of it, the person will be liable for the offence in that part of the UK (see **A8**).

Sentence The maximum penalty is: on conviction on indictment, imprisonment for a term not exceeding ten years and/or a fine; on summary conviction, imprisonment for a term not exceeding six months and/or an unlimited fine (TA 2000, s. 11(3)). The definitive guideline, *Terrorism Offences* (see Supplement, **SG32-6**), governing all sentences imposed after 27 April 2018, applies to this offence. **B10.35**

Examples of sentencing prior to the guideline include *Hundal* [2004] EWCA Crim 389, 2 Cr App R 19 (307), where the offenders were convicted of offences under s. 11, of belonging to the International Sikh Youth Federation. The offenders did not know that the organisation was proscribed in the UK. Sentences of 30 months' imprisonment were reduced to 12 months. See also *Ahmed* [2011] EWCA Crim 184 where concurrent sentences of two years' and nine years' imprisonment imposed after trial for offences of professing membership of Al-Qa'ida and membership of Al-Qa'ida respectively were upheld by the Court of Appeal.

The Sentencing Council has issued draft revised guidelines for consultation which include guidelines for this offence to reflect significant changes to terrorism legislation brought about by the C-TBSA 2019. The consultation ran until 3 December 2019. There is no date fixed for when the new guidelines will come into force.

When the Sentencing Act 2020 is enacted the maximum penalty for an offence under s. 11 will increase from ten to 14 years for any such offence committed on or after the day the Act comes into force.

B10.36 **Elements** Proscribed organisations are listed in the TA 2000, sch. 2, as amended. It is an offence to be a member of an organisation listed in sch. 2 or an organisation operating under the name of an organisation listed in sch. 2. The Secretary of State may amend sch. 2 by order (s. 3) and such orders are made regularly and have almost immediate effect.

Under s. 3(6), if the Secretary of State is of the belief that a proscribed organisation is operating under a different name than one listed in sch. 2 or is operating under a name that does not appear in sch. 2 but is to all intents and purposes the same organisation as one listed in sch. 2, the Secretary of State may direct that the name not specified shall be treated as the same as one listed in sch. 2. A number of such orders have been made.

In *Ahmed* [2011] EWCA Crim 184, the Court of Appeal observed that what amounts to membership of a proscribed organisation is likely to depend upon the nature of the organisation in question. Membership of a loose and unstructured organisation may not require any formal steps, whereas a more structured organisation may have an express process by which a person becomes a member. A criminal association is inherently more likely to lack formality than an innocent one. Deriving assistance from the analysis by Jack J of the organisation known as the Animal Liberation Front in *Smith Kline Beecham plc v Avery* [2009] EWHC 1488 (QB), the Court expressed the view that the core elements of membership were voluntary and knowing association with others with a view to furthering the aims of the proscribed organisation. In some cases, a trial judge directing a jury may need to make clear that unilateral sympathy with the aims of an organisation, even coupled with acts designed to promote similar objectives, will not always be sufficient. The jury may need to consider whether there is the necessary element of acceptance or reciprocity from the organisation which is involved in belonging.

If a person joins an organisation in a country where the organisation is not proscribed, the person nonetheless commits the offence by remaining a member of the organisation and travelling to this jurisdiction (*Hundal* [2004] EWCA Crim 389, [2004] 2 Cr App R 19 (307)).

B10.37 **Specific Defence**

Terrorism Act 2000, s. 11

(2) It is a defence for a person charged with an offence under subsection (1) above to prove—
- (a) that the organisation was not proscribed on the last (or only) occasion on which he became a member or began to profess to be a member, and
- (b) that he has not taken part in the activities of the organisation at any time while it was proscribed.

In *Sheldrake v DPP* [2004] UKHL 43, [2005] 1 AC 264 (see **F3.33**), the House of Lords read down s. 11(2) so as to interpret it as imposing only an evidential burden on D. See **F3.18**.

Supporting a Proscribed Organisation

B10.38 **Terrorism Act 2000, s. 12**

(1) A person commits an offence if—
- (a) he invites support for a proscribed organisation, and
- (b) the support is not, or is not restricted to, the provision of money or other property (within the meaning of section 15).

(1A) A person commits an offence if the person—
- (a) expresses an opinion or belief that is supportive of a proscribed organisation, and

(b) in doing so is reckless as to whether a person to whom the expression is directed will be encouraged to support a proscribed organisation.

(2) A person commits an offence if he arranges, manages or assists in arranging or managing a meeting which he knows is—
(a) to support a proscribed organisation,
(b) to further the activities of a proscribed organisation, or
(c) to be addressed by a person who belongs or professes to belong to a proscribed organisation.

(3) A person commits an offence if he addresses a meeting and the purpose of his address is to encourage support for a proscribed organisation or to further its activities.

Procedure An allegation of an offence contrary to the TA 2000, s. 12, is triable either way; when tried on indictment it is normally a class 3 offence, but see CrimPD XIII, para. B (see Supplement, **CPD.XIII.B**), for the additional factors that the court considers on allocation. For consent to prosecution, see **B10.34**. **B10.39**

Sentence The maximum penalty is: on conviction on indictment, imprisonment for a term not exceeding ten years and/or a fine; on summary conviction, imprisonment for a term not exceeding six months and/or an unlimited fine (TA 2000, s. 12(6)). The definitive guideline, *Terrorism Offences* (see Supplement, **SG32-7**), governing all sentences imposed after 27 April 2018, applies to this offence. **B10.40**

The Court of Appeal dealt with *Alamgir* [2018] EWCA Crim 21, [2018] 1 Cr App R (S) 49 (371) prior to the creation of the guideline. The Court observed that there was no sentencing guideline for terrorist offences at present, nor was there any guideline case decided by the Court in relation to s. 12 offences. It said that in those circumstances, a court should approach sentencing a s. 12 offence by reference to a consideration of seriousness, having regard to culpability and harm, as required by the CJA 2003. So far as culpability is concerned, a court should 'consider the position of the offender and whether they are in a position of authority or influence' (at [34]). The persistence of efforts to gain support will be relevant, as will the type of activity involved. When the offending involves addressing a live meeting, it will be necessary to consider the size and nature of the audience targeted. In relation to harm, a court should consider the extent of support gained or likely to be gained for the proscribed organisation.

The Sentencing Council has issued draft revised guidelines for consultation which include guidelines for this offence to reflect significant changes to terrorism legislation brought about by the C-TBSA 2019. The consultation ran until 3 December 2019. There is no date fixed for when the new guidelines will come into force.

When the Sentencing Act 2020 is enacted by Parliament the maximum penalty for an offence under s. 12 will increase from ten to 14 years for any such offence committed on or after the day the Act comes into force.

Elements For 'proscribed organisation', see **B10.36**. **B10.41**

A 'meeting' consists of a gathering of three or more people (TA 2000, s. 12(5)(a)). In *Choudary* [2016] EWCA Crim 1436, [2018] 1 WLR 695, the Court of Appeal provided guidance as to the proper interpretation of s. 12(1). The Court held that to secure a conviction under s. 12(1)(a), the prosecution must prove that the organisation was already proscribed for the purposes of the 2000 Act, that D used words which invited support for that organisation, and that D knew, when using those words, that D was inviting support for that organisation. The provision does not, however, prohibit the mere holding of opinions or beliefs supportive of a proscribed organisation; or even the expression of those opinions or beliefs (although a profession of membership may amount to an offence under s. 11: as to which see **B10.33**).

The Court also agreed with the judge's pre-trial ruling that, in its ordinary meaning, 'support' can encompass both practical or tangible assistance, including intellectual support: that is to say, agreement with and approval, approbation or endorsement of that which is supported.

The word 'invite' does not necessarily connote or imply that the maker of the invitation was already engaged in something or intended to do that thing, although such an implication might arise in ordinary conversation, depending on the context. While common sense suggests that a defendant charged under s. 12(1)(a) might provide support for the proscribed organisation, or intended to do so, and might want others to join in such activities, there was nothing in the language of the section to support the proposition that the prosecution had to prove that as part of the *actus reus* of the offence. The criminality lay in inviting support from third parties for the proscribed organisation, and not necessarily in inviting those third parties to join with the defendant in providing it.

Section 12(1A) was inserted by the C-TBSA 2019, s. 1. It provides that the offence may be committed by expressing an opinion or belief supportive of a proscribed organisation while being reckless as to whether the person to whom the expression is directed will be encouraged to support a prescribed organisation. The amendment applies only in a case where every act or other event, proof of which is required for conviction of the offence in question, takes place on or after 12 April 2019 (s. 25(1)).

B10.42 Specific Defence

Terrorism Act 2000, s. 12

(4) Where a person is charged with an offence under subsection (2)(c) in respect of a private meeting it is a defence for him to prove that he had no reasonable cause to believe that the address mentioned in subsection (2)(c) would support a proscribed organisation or further its activities.

The defence under s. 12(4) is subject to the provisions of s. 118 of the 2000 Act and thus an evidential burden is imposed on D.

Wearing a Uniform

B10.43 **Terrorism Act 2000, s. 13**

(1) A person in a public place commits an offence if he—
   (a) wears an item of clothing, or
   (b) wears, carries or displays an article,
   in such a way or in such circumstances as to arouse reasonable suspicion that he is a member or supporter of a proscribed organisation.

(1A) A person commits an offence if the person publishes an image of—
   (a) an item of clothing, or
   (b) any other article,
   in such a way or in such circumstances as to arouse reasonable suspicion that the person is a member or supporter of a proscribed organisation.

(1B) In subsection (1A) the reference to an image is a reference to a still or moving image (produced by any means).

B10.44 **Procedure** An allegation of an offence contrary to the TA 2000, s. 13, is triable summarily only. For consent to prosecution, see **B10.34**.

B10.45 **Sentence** The maximum penalty is imprisonment for a term not exceeding six months and/or an unlimited fine (TA 2000, s. 13(3)).

B10.46 **Elements** By virtue of the TA 2000, s. 121, an 'article' includes a substance or any other thing and a 'public place' is one to which the public have access, whether for payment or not.

The C-TBSA 2019, s. 2, inserted s. 13(1A) and (1B) so as to ensure that the offence is also now committed by publishing an image of an item of clothing or other article in such a way or in such circumstances as to arouse 'reasonable suspicion' that the writer is a member of or supports a proscribed organisation. Section 13 is also amended by the creation of a power under s. 13(4) to (6) to be used by a constable to seize an item of clothing or any other article if the constable reasonably suspects that it is evidence in relation to an offence under s. 13 and is satisfied that it is necessary to seize it in order to prevent the evidence being concealed, lost, altered or destroyed. When exercising the power a constable may require a person to remove the item of clothing or other article if the person is wearing it, but may not do so if the item of clothing is being worn next to the skin or immediately over a garment being worn as underwear. The section invites the question of whether a hat or cap may be seized for these purposes. The amendment applies only in a case where every act or other event, proof of which is required for conviction of the offence in question, takes place on or after 12 April 2019 (s. 25(1)).

In *Rankin v Murray* 2004 SLT 1164, D had worn jewellery which bore the initials 'UVF'. Even on the assumption that it was established that D had received the ring as a gift, regularly visited Northern Ireland, and was not a member or supporter of the said organisation, those facts did not negate the actual suspicion of the officers nor the objectively reasonable basis for that suspicion.

In *Pwr v DPP* [2020] EWHC 798 (Admin), the Divisional Court concluded that an offence under the TA 2000, s. 13, is one of strict liability. Giving the judgment of the Court, Holroyde LJ concluded that Parliament clearly intended to create an offence without *mens rea* when enacting s. 13 and it was not open to the Court to interpret the section as if it had been drafted in different terms (at [61]). Moreover, the Court found that s. 13 is compatible with the ECHR, Article 10 (at [73]).

For 'proscribed organisation' and deproscription, see **B10.36**.

For the related public order offence, see **B11.8**.

Information about Acts of Terrorism

Terrorism Act 2000, s. 38B **B10.47**

(1) This section applies where a person has information which he knows or believes might be of material assistance—
(a) in preventing the commission by another person of an act of terrorism, or
(b) in securing the apprehension, prosecution or conviction of another person,
in the United Kingdom, for an offence involving the commission, preparation or instigation of an act of terrorism.
(2) The person commits an offence if he does not disclose the information as soon as reasonably practicable in accordance with subsection (3).
(3) Disclosure is in accordance with this subsection if it is made—
(a) in England and Wales, to a constable...

Procedure An offence under s. 38B is triable either way; when tried on indictment it is normally a class 3 offence, but see CrimPD XIII, para. B (see Supplement, **CPD.XIII.B**), for the additional factors that the court considers on allocation. For consent to prosecution, see **B10.34**. **B10.48**

Sentence The maximum penalty is, on conviction on indictment, imprisonment for a term not exceeding ten years and/or a fine; on summary conviction, imprisonment for a term not exceeding six months and/or an unlimited fine (TA 2000, s. 38B(5)). The maximum term of imprisonment was increased from five years by the C-TBSA 2019, s. 7. The new maximum applies only in relation to an offence committed on or after 12 April 2019. The definitive guideline, *Terrorism Offences* (see Supplement, **SG32-9**), governing all sentences imposed after 27 April 2018, applies to this offence. **B10.49**

An example of a pre-guideline decision is *Sherif* [2008] EWCA Crim 2653, [2009] 2 Cr App R (S) 33 (235). The case concerned the failed 21/7 London Underground bombings. Many of the offenders had been sentenced to the maximum of five years for offences contrary to s. 38B; some had also received consecutive sentences for failure to disclose information both before and after the attempted bombings. The totality of the sentences ranged from three to 17 years. The following issues of principle were dealt with by the Court of Appeal:

(a) So far as offences contrary to s. 38B are concerned, in many cases it will be the seriousness of the terrorist activity about which an offender has failed to give information that will determine the level of criminality, rather than the extent of the information that could be provided, which will affect the sentence. The case being dealt with was so serious as to merit the imposition of the statutory maximum.
(b) There was nothing wrong in principle with imposing consecutive sentences where both limbs of s. 38B have been charged. The failure to give information before the act (said by the Court to be arguably the more serious offence) and failure to give information afterwards are entirely separate offences even though the failure may arise out of the same state of mind (e.g., misguided loyalty).

(c) There is always a place for exceptional personal mitigation, even in cases as grave as the one the Court was dealing with. There may be cases when the court may be able to show some understanding and even mercy when someone, if vulnerable either because of age or a particular relationship with an offender, mistakenly and misguidedly puts loyalty to a family or to a friend before duties to the public or before disclosing what that person knows to the police.

The principles set out in *Sherif* were subsequently applied in *Girma* [2009] EWCA Crim 912, [2010] 1 Cr App R (S) 28 (172).

The Sentencing Council has issued draft revised guidelines for consultation which include guidelines for this offence to reflect significant changes to terrorism legislation brought about by the C-TBSA 2019. The consultation ran until 3 December 2019. There is no date fixed for when the new guidelines will come into force.

B10.50 **Elements** Under the TA 2000, s. 38B(6), the offence may, for the purposes of the proceedings, be taken to have occurred in any place where D is or has been since D first knew or believed that the information might be of material assistance in the way referred to in s. 38B(1). The proceedings may also be taken in any such place.

B10.51 **Specific Defence** Section 38B(4) of the TA 2000 provides that it is a defence for D to prove a reasonable excuse for failing to make the required disclosure.

For the compatibility of the reverse burden with the ECHR, Article 6, see **F3.18** ***et seq.***

Weapons Training

B10.52 Terrorism Act 2000, s. 54

(1) A person commits an offence if he provides instruction or training in the making or use of—
(a) firearms,
(aa) radioactive material or weapons designed or adapted for the discharge of any radioactive material,
(b) explosives, or
(c) chemical, biological or nuclear weapons.

(2) A person commits an offence if he receives instruction or training in the making or use of—
(a) firearms,
(aa) radioactive material or weapons designed or adapted for the discharge of any radioactive material,
(b) explosives, or
(c) chemical, biological or nuclear weapons.

(3) A person commits an offence if he invites another to receive instruction or training and the receipt—
(a) would constitute an offence under subsection (2), or
(b) would constitute an offence under subsection (2) but for the fact that it is to take place outside the United Kingdom.

B10.53 **Procedure** An allegation of an offence contrary to the TA 2000, s. 54, is triable either way and if tried on indictment is normally a class 3 offence, but see CrimPD XIII, para. B (see Supplement, **CPD.XIII.B**), for the additional factors that the court considers on allocation. For consent to prosecution, see **B10.34**.

B10.54 **Sentence** The maximum penalty is: on conviction on indictment, life imprisonment (or, where committed prior to 13 April 2015, ten years' imprisonment) and/or a fine; on summary conviction, a sentence of imprisonment not exceeding six months and/or an unlimited fine (TA 2000, s. 54(6)). The court may also make a forfeiture order in accordance with s. 23A, as inserted by the C-TA 2008, s. 35 (see **B10.119**).

B10.55 **Elements** By virtue of the TA 2000, s. 54(4), the provision of, or invitation to, training referred to in s. 54(1) and (3) can be to specific persons or generally.

Section 55 of the Act provides definitions of most of the items referred to in s. 54(1). Thus:

'biological weapon' means a biological agent or toxin (within the meaning of the Biological Weapons Act 1974) in a form capable of use for hostile purposes or anything to which s. 1(1)(b) of that Act applies;

'chemical weapon' has the meaning given by s. 1 of the Chemical Weapons Act 1996;
'radioactive material' means radioactive material capable of endangering life or causing harm to human health;
a 'firearm' is defined in s. 121 as including an air gun or air pistol.

Under s. 17 of the TA 2006 (see **B10.91**) if a person does anything outside the UK which would amount to an offence under s. 54 if done in any part of the UK, the person will be liable for the offence in that part of the UK.

Specific Defence **B10.56**

Terrorism Act 2000, s. 54

(5) It is a defence for a person charged with an offence under this section in relation to instruction or training to prove that his action or involvement was wholly for a purpose other than assisting, preparing for or participating in terrorism.

The defence under s. 54(4) is subject to the provisions of s. 118 of the 2000 Act and thus imposes an evidential burden on D (see **B10.31**).

Directing a Terrorist Organisation

Terrorism Act 2000, s. 56 **B10.57**

(1) A person commits an offence if he directs, at any level, the activities of an organisation which is concerned in the commission of acts of terrorism.

Procedure An allegation of an offence contrary to the TA 2000, s. 56, is triable on indictment only and is normally a class 1B offence, but see CrimPD XIII, para. B (see Supplement, **CPD.XIII.B**), for the additional factors that the court considers on allocation. For consent to prosecution, see **B10.34**. **B10.58**

For the extended jurisdiction provisions in relation to this offence, see **B10.87**.

Sentence A person convicted of this offence is liable to imprisonment for life (TA 2000, s. 56(2)). Rangzieb Ahmed was convicted after trial and was sentenced to life imprisonment with a minimum term of ten years to be served for the offence; that sentence was not the subject of any appeal. For the outline facts of the offence, see *Ahmed* [2011] EWCA Crim 184. In passing sentence upon him in December 2008, Saunders J said he had to bear in mind that, while directing a terrorist organisation is a very serious offence, Ahmed had not been proved to be directly involved in any terrorist act. Moreover, while he was satisfied that at the time of his arrest Ahmed was planning something, he did not know what it was, how imminent it was, what were the chances of it succeeding or what (if any) loss of life it was likely to cause. **B10.59**

Elements For 'terrorism', see **B10.2**. **B10.60**

Possession of an Article for Terrorist Purposes

Terrorism Act 2000, s. 57 **B10.61**

(1) A person commits an offence if he possesses an article in circumstances which give rise to a reasonable suspicion that his possession is for a purpose connected with the commission, preparation or instigation of an act of terrorism.

Procedure An allegation of an offence contrary to the TA 2000, s. 57, is triable either way; if tried on indictment it is normally a class 3 offence, but see CrimPD XIII, para. B (see Supplement, **CPD.XIII.B**), for the additional factors that the court considers on allocation. For consent to prosecution, see **B10.34**. **B10.62**

For the extended jurisdiction provisions in relation to this offence, see **B10.87**.

Sentence The maximum penalty is: on conviction on indictment, imprisonment for a term not exceeding 15 years and/or a fine; on summary conviction, imprisonment for a term not **B10.63**

exceeding six months and/or an unlimited fine (TA 2000, s. 57(4)). The court may also make a forfeiture order in accordance with s. 23A (see **B10.119**). The definitive guideline, *Terrorism Offences* (see Supplement, **SG32-10**), governing all sentences imposed after 27 April 2018, applies to this offence.

B10.64 **Elements** Under the TA 2000, s. 57(3), if it is proved that an article was on any premises at the same time as D, or was on premises of which D was the occupier or which D habitually used otherwise than as a member of the public, the court may assume that D possessed the article unless D proves ignorance of the presence of the article on the premises or had no control over it. By virtue of s. 118, the burden on D is evidential (see **B10.31**).

In *Rowe* [2007] EWCA Crim 635, [2007] QB 975, the Court of Appeal held that a document or record was capable of constituting an article for the purposes of s. 57. The Court observed that ss. 57 and 58 (see **B10.65** ***et seq.***) deal with different aspects of activities relating to terrorism. Section 57 deals with possession of articles *for the purpose* of terrorist acts. Section 58 is concerned with the collecting or holding of information that *is of a kind likely to be useful* to those involved in acts of terrorism. Section 57 also includes a specific intention whilst s. 58 does not. Those differences between the two sections were said to be rational features of a statute whose aims included the prohibition of different types of support for, and involvement in, terrorism. There is thus no basis for any conclusion that Parliament intended to have a completely separate regime for documents and records from that which applies to other articles. In so holding, the Court found that the decision, on interlocutory appeal from a preparatory hearing, to the opposite effect in *M (No. 1)* [2007] EWCA Crim 218 was wrongly decided *per incuriam*. *Rowe* has since been followed in *M* [2007] EWCA Crim 970, [2007] 3 All ER 53, and in *G* [2009] UKHL 13, [2010] 1 AC 43 (see **B10.72**) the House of Lords said that the decision in *Rowe* was plainly correct.

The accused in *M* were subsequently convicted of offences contrary to s. 57 at the Central Criminal Court. Examination of their computers had revealed that they were in possession of radical Islamic material and other material such as a US military manual downloaded from the internet. They successfully appealed against conviction (*Zafar* [2008] EWCA Crim 184, [2008] QB 810). The Court of Appeal concluded (with Lord Phillips CJ giving the judgment of the Court) that, if s. 57 was to have the certainty of meaning that the law requires, it must be interpreted in a way that requires a direct connection between the object possessed and the act of terrorism. Section 57 should therefore be interpreted as if it reads that a person commits an offence by possessing an article in circumstances which give rise to a reasonable suspicion it is intended to be used for the purpose of the commission, preparation or instigation of an act of terrorism. Possessing a document for the purposes of inciting a person to commit an act of terrorism falls within the ambit of s. 57, as one synonym for 'instigation' is 'incitement'. In *G* it was made clear that the Crown does not have to prove what D's terrorist purpose actually is.

B10.65 **Specific Defence**

Terrorism Act 2000, s. 57

(2) It is a defence for a person charged with an offence under this section to prove that his possession of the article was not for a purpose connected with the commission, preparation or instigation of an act of terrorism.

The defence under s. 57(2) is subject to the provisions of s. 118 and thus imposes an evidential burden on D (see **B10.31**).

Collection of Information

B10.66

Terrorism Act 2000, s. 58

(1) A person commits an offence if—

(a) he collects or makes a record of information of a kind likely to be useful to a person committing or preparing an act of terrorism,

(b) he possesses a document or record containing information of that kind, or
(c) the person views, or otherwise accesses, by means of the internet a document or record containing information of that kind.

(1A) The cases in which a person collects or makes a record for the purposes of subsection (1)(a) include (but are not limited to) those in which the person does so by means of the internet (whether by downloading the record or otherwise).

Procedure An allegation of an offence contrary to the TA 2000, s. 58, is triable either way; if tried on indictment it is normally a class 3 offence, but see CrimPD XIII, para. B (see Supplement, **CPD.XIII.B**), for the additional factors that the court considers on allocation. For consent to prosecution, see **B10.34**. **B10.67**

For the extended jurisdiction provisions in relation to this offence, see **B10.87**.

Sentence The maximum penalty is: on conviction on indictment, a term of imprisonment not exceeding fifteen years and/or a fine; on summary conviction, a term of imprisonment not exceeding six months and/or an unlimited fine (TA 2000, s. 58(4)). The maximum term of imprisonment was increased from ten years by the C-TBSA 2019, s. 7. The new maximum applies only in relation to an offence committed on or after 12 April 2019. **B10.68**

The definitive guideline, *Terrorism Offences* (see Supplement, **SG32-11**), governing all sentences imposed after 27 April 2018, applies to this offence. The court may also make a forfeiture order in accordance with s. 23A (see **B10.119**).

The Sentencing Council has issued draft revised guidelines for consultation which include guidelines for this offence to reflect significant changes to terrorism legislation brought about by the C-TBSA 2019. The consultation ran until 3 December 2019. There is no date fixed for when the new guidelines will come into force.

Elements The first comprehensive guidance on the ambit of the TA 2000, s. 58, was set out by the Court of Appeal in *K* [2008] EWCA Crim 185, [2008] QB 827. Giving the judgment of the Court, Lord Phillips CJ explained that a document or record will fall within s. 58 only if it is of a kind that is likely to provide practical assistance to a person committing or preparing an act of terrorism. A document that simply encourages the commission of acts of terrorism does not fall within s. 58. The natural meaning of s. 58 requires that a document or record that infringes it must contain information of a nature likely to give rise to a reasonable suspicion that it is intended to be used to assist in the commission or preparation of an act of terrorism. Thus s. 58 places a burden on D to provide a reasonable excuse for possessing it (see **B10.72**). Extrinsic evidence may be adduced to explain the nature of the material but it is not legitimate to call extrinsic evidence to show that a document which is innocuous on its face is intended to be used for the preparation or commission of an act of terrorism. **B10.69**

In *G* [2009] UKHL 13, [2010] 1 AC 43, s. 58 was considered by the House of Lords. The cases were prosecution appeals against the application of the *ratio* of *K* by the Court of Appeal. Confirming the dictum in *K*, it was recognised that the aim of s. 58 was to catch information which would typically be of use to terrorists, as opposed to ordinary members of the public; the information collected or possessed must, of its very nature, be designed to provide practical assistance to a person committing or preparing an act of terrorism. It is not necessary that the information should be useful only to a person involved in an act of terrorism. For instance, information on where to obtain explosives is capable of falling within s. 58(1), even though an ordinary criminal planning a bank robbery might also find it useful. The House of Lords also confirmed the dictum in *K* that the role of extrinsic evidence is limited and provided further analysis and definition of the elements of the offence: **B10.70**

(a) the Crown must prove that D had control of a record which contained information that was likely to provide practical assistance to a person committing or preparing an act of terrorism;
(b) the Crown must prove that D was aware of having the record;
(c) the Crown must prove that D knew the kind of information which it contained, although it does not have to prove that D knew everything that was in the document or record.

The Crown must establish all three elements beyond reasonable doubt and, if it does so, it has proved its case.

G was applied in *Muhammed* [2010] EWCA Crim 227, [2010] 3 All ER 759, where it was argued that a document containing guidance as to how to maintain secrecy in respect of mobile phone and email usage, along with suggestions as how to avoid surveillance by the authorities and a suggested reading list, should not fall within s. 58. Giving the judgment of the Court of Appeal, Hooper LJ said (at [47]):

> Provided that the document containing the information is not one in every day use by ordinary members of the public (e.g. published timetables and maps) and provided that a reasonable jury could properly conclude that the document contains information of a kind likely to be useful to a person committing or preparing an act of terrorism, then it will be a matter for the jury whether they are sure that it contains such information. If so, and provided the defendant has the necessary *mens rea*, then the only issue will be whether the defendant has a reasonable excuse.

In *Brown* [2011] EWCA Crim 2751, [2012] 2 Cr App R (S) 10 (39) the Court of Appeal held that s. 58 constituted a proportionate restriction on freedom of expression under the ECHR and freedom of speech at common law.

The C-TBSA 2019, s. 3, amended s. 58(1) and inserted s. 58(1A) so as to include within its ambit the collection or making a record of information likely to be useful to a person committing or preparing an act of terrorism when the person views, or otherwise accesses, by means of the internet (whether by downloading the record or otherwise) a document or record containing information of that kind. The amendment applies only in a case where every act or other event, proof of which is required for conviction of the offence in question, takes place on or after 12 April 2019.

B10.71 Specific Defence

Terrorism Act 2000, s. 58

(3) It is a defence for a person charged with an offence under this section to prove that he had a reasonable excuse for his action or possession.

(3A) The cases in which a person has a reasonable excuse for the purposes of subsection (3) include (but are not limited to) those in which—

(a) at the time of the person's action or possession the person did not know, and had no reason to believe, that the document or record in question contained, or was likely to contain, information of a kind likely to be useful to a person committing or preparing an act of terrorism, or

(b) the person's action or possession was for the purposes of—

(i) carrying out work as a journalist, or

(ii) academic research.

The defence under s. 58(3) is subject to the provisions of s. 118 and thus imposes an evidential burden on D (see **B10.31**). Section 58(3A) was inserted by the C-TBSA 2019, s. 3, and came into force on 12 April 2019.

In *F* [2007] EWCA Crim 243, [2007] QB 960 it was held by the Court of Appeal that possession of documents as part of an effort to change an illegal or undemocratic regime could not constitute a reasonable excuse under s. 58(3). In the interlocutory appeal *Y (A)* [2010] EWCA Crim 762, [2010] 1 WLR 2644, D's case was that he possessed various documents in order to, amongst other things, assist Somali Muslims in self-defence against opposing forces. The Court of Appeal dismissed the Crown's appeal against a refusal by the trial judge to rule that the defence could not give rise to a reasonable excuse under s. 58(3).

B10.72 In *K* [2008] EWCA Crim 185, [2008] QB 827 (see **B10.69**), the Court of Appeal held that the nature of a reasonable excuse is simply an explanation that the document or record is possessed for a purpose other than to assist in the commission or preparation of an act of terrorism. It matters not that that purpose may infringe some other provision of the criminal or civil law. In *G* [2009] UKHL 13, [2010] 1 AC 43, the House of Lords overturned the definition of reasonable excuse set out in *K*. Lord Rodger said that the Court of Appeal went wrong in *K* when it interpreted the defence of reasonable excuse in the way that it did. Their lordships accepted the submission by the appellants that the Court of Appeal had, in effect, substituted for the defence of reasonable excuse enacted in s. 58(3) a quite different defence which was in effect a reproduction of the defence in s. 57(2) (see **B10.65**). Lord Rodger stated that the real issue under s. 58 is not whether D had a terrorist purpose. Whether D had such a purpose is neutral. Instead D has to show an objectively reasonable excuse for possessing the document or record which Parliament has made it prima facie a crime to possess because of its potential utility to terrorists. Possessing such a document or record for the purposes of carrying out a bank robbery is a purpose which is not connected with terrorism, but it is not a reasonable excuse. Unless a trial judge is satisfied that no reasonable jury could regard D's excuse as reasonable, the judge must leave the matter for the jury to decide. When doing so, the judge may indicate to the jury various factors that may be useful to them in determining the issue, such as D's age, associates, background and how long D possessed the item.

Eliciting, Publishing or Communicating Information About Members of Armed Forces etc.

Terrorism Act 2000, s. 58A **B10.73**

(1) A person commits an offence who—
- (a) elicits or attempts to elicit information about an individual who is or has been—
  - (i) a member of Her Majesty's forces,
  - (ii) a member of any of the intelligence services, or
  - (iii) a constable,

  which is of a kind likely to be useful to a person committing or preparing an act of terrorism, or
- (b) publishes or communicates any such information.

Procedure An allegation of an offence contrary to the TA 2000, s. 58A, is triable either way; if tried on indictment it is normally a class 3 offence, but see CrimPD XIII, para. B (see Supplement, **CPD.XIII.B**), for the additional factors that the court considers on allocation. For consent to prosecution, see **B10.34**. **B10.74**

For the extended jurisdiction provisions in relation to this offence, see **B10.87**.

Sentence The maximum penalty is: on conviction on indictment, a term of imprisonment not exceeding fifteen years and/or a fine; on summary conviction, a term of imprisonment not exceeding six months and/or an unlimited fine (TA 2000, s. 58A(3)). The maximum term of imprisonment was increased from ten years by the C-TBSA 2019, s. 7. The new maximum applies only in relation to an offence committed on or after 12 April 2019. The court may also make a forfeiture order in accordance with s. 23A (see **B10.119**). **B10.75**

Elements The scheme of s. 58A is very similar to that of s. 58 (see **B10.66**). Under s. 58, the information collected or possessed by D must, of its very nature, be designed to provide practical assistance to a person committing or preparing an act of terrorism. In argument in the House of Lords in *G* [2009] UKHL 13, [2010] 1 AC 43, the Crown asserted that Parliament could never have intended to criminalise the possession of information of a kind that is useful to people for all sorts of everyday purposes and that many members of the public regularly obtain or use, simply because that information could also be useful to someone who was preparing an act of terrorism. By contrast, under s. 58A, it is submitted that the information most likely to be of use to a terrorist is the home address of the member, or former member, of the armed services etc. That information is not of its very nature of the type designed to provide practical assistance to a terrorist. If *G* is to be applied in respect of s. 58A, it would seem to be enough for the Crown **B10.76**

to establish, for example, simply that D elicited the address, knew that this had been done and knew that the address elicited was that of a member of the armed forces etc. It would then be for D to establish a reasonable excuse under s. 58A(2).

B10.77 **Specific Defence**

Terrorism Act 2000, s. 58A

(2) It is a defence for a person charged with an offence under this section to prove that they had a reasonable excuse for their action.

The defence under s. 58A(2) is subject to the provisions of s. 118 and thus imposes an evidential burden on D (see **B10.31**).

Section 58A contains the defence of reasonable excuse and is in almost identical terms to that in s. 58 (see **B10.71**). It is submitted that the rationale for the definition of reasonable excuse contained within *G* [2009] UKHL 13, [2010] 1 AC 43 is more difficult to support in the context of s. 58A. It is submitted that the type of information covered by s. 58A is much more likely to be held and used by ordinary members of the public and much less demanding of an explanation than the information covered by s. 58.

Entering or Remaining in a Designated Area

B10.78 **Terrorism Act 2000, s. 58B**

(1) Subject to subsections (3) and (4), a person commits an offence if—
  (a) the person enters, or remains in, a designated area, and
  (b) the person is a United Kingdom national, or a United Kingdom resident, at the time of entering the area or at any time during which the person remains there.

(2) It is a defence for a person charged with an offence under this section to prove that the person had a reasonable excuse for entering, or remaining in, the designated area.

(3) A person does not commit an offence under this section of entering, or remaining in, a designated area if—
  (a) the person is already travelling to, or is already in, the area on the day on which it becomes a designated area, and
  (b) the person leaves the area before the end of the period of one month beginning with that day.

(4) A person does not commit an offence under this section of entering, or remaining in, a designated area if—
  (a) the person enters, or remains in, a designated area involuntarily, or
  (b) the person enters, or remains in, a designated area for or in connection with one or more of the purposes mentioned in subsection (5).

(5) The purposes are—
  (a) providing aid of a humanitarian nature;
  (b) satisfying an obligation to appear before a court or other body exercising judicial power;
  (c) carrying out work for the government of a country other than the United Kingdom (including service in or with the country's armed forces);
  (d) carrying out work for the United Nations or an agency of the United Nations;
  (e) carrying out work as a journalist;
  (f) attending the funeral of a relative or visiting a relative who is terminally ill;
  (g) providing care for a relative who is unable to care for themselves without such assistance.

(6) But a person does not commit an offence of entering or remaining in a designated area by virtue of subsection (4)(b) only if—
  (a) the person enters or remains in the area exclusively for or in connection with one or more of the purposes mentioned in subsection (5), or
  (b) in a case where the person enters or remains in the area for or in connection with any other purpose or purposes (in addition to one or more of the purposes mentioned in subsection (5)), the other purpose or purposes provide a reasonable excuse for doing so under subsection (2).

(7) The Secretary of State may by regulations add a purpose to or remove a purpose from subsection (5).

(8) For the purposes of subsection (5)—
  (a) the reference to the provision of aid of a humanitarian nature does not include the provision of aid in contravention of internationally recognised principles and standards applicable to the provision of humanitarian aid;
  (b) references to the carrying out of work do not include the carrying out of any act which constitutes an offence in a part of the United Kingdom or would do so if the act occurred in a part of the United Kingdom;
  (c) a person is 'terminally ill' at any time if at that time the person suffers from a progressive disease and the person's death in consequence of that disease can reasonably be expected within 6 months.

Procedure An allegation of an offence contrary to the TA 2000, s. 58B, is triable either way; if tried on indictment it is normally a class 3 offence, but see CrimPD XIII, para. B (see Supplement, **CPD.XIII.B**), for the additional factors that the court considers on allocation. For consent to prosecution, see **B10.34**. For the extended jurisdiction provisions in relation to this offence, see **B10.90**. **B10.79**

Sentence The maximum penalty is: on conviction on indictment, a term of imprisonment not exceeding ten years and/or a fine; on summary conviction, a term of imprisonment not exceeding six months and/or an unlimited fine (TA 2000, s. 58B(9)). **B10.80**

The court may also make a forfeiture order in accordance with s. 23A (see **B10.119**).

Elements Section 58B was inserted into the TA 2000 by the C-TBSA 2019, s. 4. The new offence, which is in force from 12 April 2019, is concerned with entering or remaining in a designated area. A person commits an offence if the person enters, or remains in, a designated area when a UK national or a UK resident. Section 58B(2) provides a 'reasonable excuse' defence to an allegation under s. 58B, and s. 58B(3) to (6) to explain circumstances in which a person may enter and remain in a designated area without committing an offence. Thus, under s. 58B(3) an offence is not committed if the person is already travelling to, or is already in, the area on the day on which it becomes a designated area, and the person leaves the area before the end of the period of one month beginning with that day. Under s. 58B(4), a person does not commit an offence if the person enters or remains in a designated area involuntarily, or remains in a designated area for or in connection with one or more of the purposes mentioned in s. 58B(5). **B10.81**

By virtue of s. 58B(6), a person only avoids liability under the section due to involvement in one of the purposes mentioned in s. 58B(5) if the person enters or remains in the area exclusively for or in connection with one or more of the purposes mentioned in s. 58B(5), or, where the person enters or remains in the area for or in connection with any other purpose or purposes (in addition to one or more of the purposes mentioned in s. 58B(5)), the other purpose or purposes provide a reasonable excuse for doing so under s. 58B(2).

Section 58B(8) defines 'aid of a humanitarian nature' and 'terminally ill' and s. 58B(10) defines 'relative', 'United Kingdom national' and 'United Kingdom resident' for the purposes of the Act. The offence is indictable only, carrying a maximum sentence of ten years' imprisonment and/or a fine. Section 58(12) provides an exemption to liability for servants or officers of the Crown.

Section 58C empowers the Secretary of State to designate an area outside the UK, if satisfied that it is necessary for the purpose of protecting members of the public from a risk of terrorism, to restrict UK nationals and UK residents from entering, or remaining in, the area.

TERRORISM OVERSEAS

Inciting Terrorism Overseas

Terrorism Act 2000, s. 59 **B10.82**

(1) A person commits an offence if—
  (a) he incites another person to commit an act of terrorism wholly or partly outside the United Kingdom, and

(b) the act would, if committed in England and Wales, constitute one of the offences listed in subsection (2).

(2) Those offences are—

(a) murder,

(b) an offence under section 18 of the Offences against the Person Act 1861 (wounding with intent),

(c) an offence under section 23 or 24 of that Act (poison),

(d) an offence under section 28 or 29 of that Act (explosions), and

(e) an offence under section 1(2) of the Criminal Damage Act 1971 (endangering life by damaging property).

(3) A person guilty of an offence under this section shall be liable to any penalty to which he would be liable on conviction of the offence listed in subsection (2) which corresponds to the act which he incites.

(4) For the purposes of subsection (1) it is immaterial whether or not the person incited is in the United Kingdom at the time of the incitement.

(5) Nothing in this section imposes criminal liability on any person acting on behalf of, or holding office under, the Crown.

B10.83 **Procedure** By virtue of the TA 2000, s. 59(3), an allegation of an offence contrary to s. 59 is triable in the same way that the substantive offence listed in s. 59(2) would be tried. As all of those offences are triable only on indictment, s. 59 is effectively indictable only. It is a class 1B offence. For consent to prosecution, see **B10.34**.

For the extended jurisdiction provisions in relation to this offence, see **B10.86**.

B10.84 **Sentence** The maximum penalty is that which would be available on conviction of the substantive offence (TA 2000, s. 59(3)). The court may also make a forfeiture order in accordance with s. 23A (see **B10.119**).

In *A-G's Ref (Nos. 85, 86 and 87 of 2007) (Tsouli)* [2007] EWCA Crim 3300, [2008] 2 Cr App R (S) 45 (247), sentences of between six and a half and ten years' imprisonment following guilty pleas during the course of the trial were increased to range between ten and 16 years having allowed for double jeopardy. The offenders had maintained web sites through which they incited murder, primarily in Iraq. In *S* (2 October 2015 unreported, Manchester Crown Court) Saunders J sentenced a 14-year-old boy to life imprisonment with a minimum term of five years' imprisonment for his part in a terrorist plot to murder police officers in Australia.

B10.85 **Elements** For murder, see **B1.1**; for the OAPA 1861, ss. 18, 23, 24, 28 and 29, see **B2.70, B2.84, B2.93, B12.263** and **B12.267** respectively; for the CDA 1971, s. 1(2), see **B8.16**.

Extended Jurisdiction: Terrorist Bombing Committed Abroad and Terrorist Financing Abroad

B10.86 **Terrorism Act 2000, ss. 62 and 63**

62.—(1) If—

(a) a person does anything outside the United Kingdom as an act of terrorism or for the purposes of terrorism, and

(b) his action would have constituted the commission of one of the offences listed in subsection (2) if it had been done in the United Kingdom,

he shall be guilty of the offence.

(2) The offences referred to in subsection (1)(b) are—

(a) an offence under section 2, 3 or 5 of the Explosive Substances Act 1883 (causing explosions, &c),

(b) an offence under section 1 of the Biological Weapons Act 1974 (biological weapons), and

(c) an offence under section 2 of the Chemical Weapons Act 1996 (chemical weapons).

63.—(1) If—

(a) a person does anything outside the United Kingdom, and

(b) his action would have constituted the commission of an offence under any of sections 15 to 18 if it had been done in the United Kingdom,

he shall be guilty of the offence.

(2) For the purposes of subsection (1)(b), section 18(1)(b) shall be read as if for 'the jurisdiction' there were substituted 'a jurisdiction'.

The 2000 Act provides for extended jurisdiction in relation to offences of terrorist bombing and terrorism finance committed outside the UK.

Extended Jurisdiction for Offences Committed Abroad for Terrorist Purposes

Terrorism Act 2000, ss. 63A to 63E **B10.87**

63A.—(1) If—
- (a) a United Kingdom national or a United Kingdom resident does anything outside the United Kingdom, and
- (b) his action, if done in any part of the United Kingdom, would have constituted an offence under any of sections 56 to 61,

he shall be guilty in that part of the United Kingdom of the offence.

(2) For the purposes of this section and sections 63B and 63C a 'United Kingdom national' means an individual who is—
- (a) a British citizen, a British overseas territories citizen, a British National (Overseas) or a British Overseas citizen,
- (b) a person who under the British Nationality Act 1981 is a British subject, or
- (c) a British protected person within the meaning of that Act.

(3) For the purposes of this section and sections 63B and 63C a 'United Kingdom resident' means an individual who is resident in the United Kingdom.

63B.—(1) If—
- (a) a United Kingdom national or a United Kingdom resident does anything outside the United Kingdom as an act of terrorism or for the purposes of terrorism, and
- (b) his action, if done in any part of the United Kingdom, would have constituted an offence listed in subsection (2),

he shall be guilty in that part of the United Kingdom of the offence.

(2) These are the offences—
- (a) murder, manslaughter, culpable homicide, rape, assault causing injury, assault to injury, kidnapping, abduction or false imprisonment,
- (b) an offence under section 4, 16, 18, 20, 21, 22, 23, 24, 28, 29, 30 or 64 of the Offences against the Person Act 1861,
- (c) an offence under any of sections 1 to 5 of the Forgery and Counterfeiting Act 1981,
- (d) the uttering of a forged document or an offence under section 46A of the Criminal Law (Consolidation) (Scotland) Act 1995,
- (e) an offence under section 1 or 2 of the Criminal Damage Act 1971,
- (f) an offence under article 3 or 4 of the Criminal Damage (Northern Ireland) Order 1977,
- (g) malicious mischief,
- (h) wilful fire-raising.

63C.—(1) If—
- (a) a person does anything outside the United Kingdom as an act of terrorism or for the purposes of terrorism,
- (b) his action is done to, or in relation to, a United Kingdom national, a United Kingdom resident or a protected person, and
- (c) his action, if done in any part of the United Kingdom, would have constituted an offence listed in subsection (2),

he shall be guilty in that part of the United Kingdom of the offence.

(2) These are the offences—
- (a) murder, manslaughter, culpable homicide, rape, assault causing injury, assault to injury, kidnapping, abduction or false imprisonment,
- (b) an offence under section 4, 16, 18, 20, 21, 22, 23, 24, 28, 29, 30 or 64 of the Offences against the Person Act 1861,
- (c) an offence under section 1, 2, 3, 4 or 5(1) or (3) of the Forgery and Counterfeiting Act 1981,
- (d) the uttering of a forged document or an offence under section 46A(1) of the Criminal Law (Consolidation) (Scotland) Act 1995.

(3) [Relates to the liability of protected persons].

63D.—(1) If—
(a) a person does anything outside the United Kingdom as an act of terrorism or for the purposes of terrorism,
(b) his action is done in connection with an attack on relevant premises or on a vehicle ordinarily used by a protected person,
(c) the attack is made when a protected person is on or in the premises or vehicle, and
(d) his action, if done in any part of the United Kingdom, would have constituted an offence listed in subsection (2),

he shall be guilty in that part of the United Kingdom of the offence.

(2) These are the offences—
(a) an offence under section 1 of the Criminal Damage Act 1971,
(b) an offence under article 3 of the Criminal Damage (Northern Ireland) Order 1977,
(c) malicious mischief,
(d) wilful fire-raising.

(3) If—
(a) a person does anything outside the United Kingdom as an act of terrorism or for the purposes of terrorism,
(b) his action consists of a threat of an attack on relevant premises or on a vehicle ordinarily used by a protected person,
(c) the attack is threatened to be made when a protected person is, or is likely to be, on or in the premises or vehicle, and
(d) his action, if done in any part of the United Kingdom, would have constituted an offence listed in subsection (4),

he shall be guilty in that part of the United Kingdom of the offence.

(4) These are the offences—
(a) an offence under section 2 of the Criminal Damage Act 1971,
(b) an offence under article 4 of the Criminal Damage (Northern Ireland) Order 1977,
(c) breach of the peace (in relation to Scotland only).

(5) [Definition of premises]

63E.—(1) Proceedings for an offence which (disregarding the Acts listed in subsection (2)) would not be an offence apart from section 63B, 63C or 63D are not to be started—
(a) in England and Wales, except by or with the consent of the Attorney General,
(b) in Northern Ireland, except by or with the consent of the Advocate General for Northern Ireland.

(2) These are the Acts—
(a) the Internationally Protected Persons Act 1978,
(b) the Suppression of Terrorism Act 1978,
(c) the Nuclear Material (Offences) Act 1983,
(d) the United Nations Personnel Act 1997.

(3) For the purposes of sections 63C and 63D it is immaterial whether a person knows that another person is a United Kingdom national, a United Kingdom resident or a protected person.

Sections 63A to 63E represent important provisions extending the jurisdiction of the courts of the UK to deal with offences committed outside it by and against persons associated with the UK.

SUBSTANTIVE OFFENCES UNDER THE TERRORISM ACT 2006

B10.88 The TA 2006 created a number of offences designed to counter the activities of terrorists which had not been previously addressed by legislation.

Encouragement of Terrorism

B10.89 **Terrorism Act 2006, s. 1**

(1) This section applies to a statement that is likely to be understood by a reasonable person to whom it is published as a direct or indirect encouragement or other inducement to some or all members of the public to the commission, preparation or instigation of acts of terrorism or Convention offences.

(2) A person commits an offence if—

(a) he publishes a statement to which this section applies or causes another to publish such a statement; and
(b) at the time he publishes it or causes it to be published, he—
    (i) intends members of the public to be directly or indirectly encouraged or otherwise induced by the statement to commit, prepare or instigate acts of terrorism or Convention offences; or
    (ii) is reckless as to whether members of the public will be directly or indirectly encouraged or otherwise induced by the statement to commit, prepare or instigate such acts or offences.

Procedure An allegation of an offence contrary to the TA 2006, s. 1, is triable either way (s. 1(7)); when tried on indictment it is normally a class 3 offence, but see CrimPD XIII, para. B (see Supplement, **CPD.XIII.B**), for the additional factors that the court considers on allocation. The consent of the DPP is necessary for the institution of proceedings under the TA 2006 (s. 19(1)) unless the offence is committed outside the UK or wholly or partly in connection with the affairs of a country outside the UK, in which case the consent of the A-G is required (s. 19(2) as amended by the CT-A 2008, s. 29). **B10.90**

Jurisdiction By virtue of the TA 2006, s. 17, the offence under s. 1 (and offences under ss. 5, 6, and 8 to 11 of the 2006 Act and ss. 11(1) and 54 of the 2000 Act) may be committed by any person of any nationality anywhere in the world. The courts of the UK therefore have universal jurisdiction in relation to the offence. If a person does anything outside the UK which would constitute an offence in any part of the UK, the person will be guilty of the offence in that part of the UK. Proceedings in respect of the offence may be taken anywhere in the UK and the offence may be treated for incidental purposes as having been committed in any such place (s. 17(4)). **B10.91**

Sentence The maximum penalty is: on conviction on indictment, imprisonment for a term not exceeding 15 years and/or a fine; and, on summary conviction, imprisonment for a term not exceeding six months and/or an unlimited fine (TA 2006, s. 1(7) and (8)). The maximum term of imprisonment was increased from seven years by the C-TBSA 2019, s. 7. The new maximum applies only in relation to an offence committed on or after 12 April 2019. The definitive guideline, *Terrorism Offences* (see Supplement, **SG32-5**), governing all sentences imposed after 27 April 2018, applies to this offence. **B10.92**

The Sentencing Council has issued draft revised guidelines for consultation which include guidelines for this offence to reflect significant changes to terrorism legislation brought about by the C-TBSA 2019. The consultation ran until 3 December 2019. There is no date fixed for when the new guidelines will come into force.

Elements By virtue of s. 1(3), the statements that are likely to be understood by a reasonable person as indirectly encouraging the commission or preparation of acts of terrorism or Convention offences include every statement which (a) glorifies the commission or preparation (whether in the past, in the future or generally) of such acts or offences; and (b) is a statement from which those members of the public could reasonably be expected to infer that what is being glorified is being glorified as conduct that should be emulated by them in existing circumstances. **B10.93**

'Terrorism' has the same definition as applies under the TA 2000 (see **B10.2**).

'Convention offence' in s. 1(1) means an offence listed in the TA 2006, sch. 1, or an equivalent offence under the law of a country or territory outside the UK.

The questions of how a statement is likely to be understood and what members of the public could reasonably be expected to infer from it must be determined having regard to both (a) the contents of the statement as a whole, and (b) the circumstances and manner of its publication (s. 1(4)).

'Glorification' is defined in s. 20(2) as including any form of praise or celebration, and cognate expressions are to be construed accordingly.

'Conduct that should be emulated in existing circumstances' includes conduct that is illustrative of a type of conduct that should be so emulated (s. 20(7)).

B10.94 By virtue of s. 20(3), references to 'the public' (a) are references to the public of any part of the UK or of a country or territory outside the UK, or any section of the public, and (b) except in s. 9(4), also include references to a meeting or other group of persons which is open to the public (whether unconditionally or on the making of a payment or the satisfaction of other conditions).

References to a person's publishing a statement are references to (a) publishing it in any manner to the public, (b) providing electronically any service by means of which the public have access to the statement, or (c) using a service provided to that person electronically by another so as to enable or to facilitate access by the public to the statement (s. 20(4)). This subsection does not apply to the references to a publication in s. 2 (see **B10.97**).

Under s. 20(5), 'providing a service' includes making a facility available.

References to 'a statement' are references to a communication of any description, including a communication without words consisting of sounds or images or both (s. 20(6)).

For the purposes of s. 1(1) to (3), it is irrelevant (a) whether anything mentioned in those subsections relates to the commission, instigation or preparation of one or more particular acts of terrorism or Convention offences, of acts of terrorism or Convention offences of a particular description, or of acts of terrorism or Convention offences generally, and (b) whether any person is in fact encouraged or induced by the statement to commit, prepare or instigate any such act or offence (s. 1(5)).

B10.95 Section 18 provides that, where an offence under Part 1 of the Act is committed by a body corporate and is proved to have been committed with the consent or connivance of a director, manager, secretary or other similar officer of the body corporate (or a person purporting to act in that capacity), that person (as well as the body corporate) is guilty of that offence and is liable to be proceeded against and punished accordingly. For the purposes of s. 18, where a body corporate is managed by its members, a member is a director.

For extended jurisdiction in respect of suppliers of information society services who are established in the UK where a relevant act occurs in the EEA, see the Electronic Commerce Directive (Terrorism Act 2006) Regulations 2007 (SI 2007 No. 1550). The Regulations also provide for special defences and limited liability where they apply.

With effect from 12 April 2019, s. 1 was amended by the C-TBSA 2019, s. 5, to apply to a reasonable person. It applies only in a case where every act or other event, proof of which is required for conviction of the offence in question, takes place on or after that date.

B10.96 **Specific Defence** Section 1(6) of the TA 2006 provides that, where it is not proved that D intended the statement directly or indirectly to encourage or otherwise induce the commission, preparation or instigation of acts of terrorism or Convention offences, it is a defence to show (a) that the statement neither expressed D's views nor had D's endorsement (whether by virtue of s. 3 or otherwise); and (b) that it was clear, in all the circumstances of the statement's publication, that it did not express D's views and (apart from the possibility of D's having been given and failed to comply with a notice under s. 3(3); see **B10.102**) did not have D's endorsement.

Dissemination of Terrorist Publications

B10.97 Terrorism Act 2006, s. 2

(1) *A person commits an offence* if he engages in conduct falling within subsection (2) and, at the time he does so—

(a) he intends an effect of his conduct to be a direct or indirect encouragement or other inducement to the commission, preparation or instigation of acts of terrorism;

(b) he intends an effect of his conduct to be the provision of assistance in the commission or preparation of such acts; or
(c) he is reckless as to whether his conduct has an effect mentioned in paragraph (a) or (b).

(2) For the purposes of this section a person engages in conduct falling within this subsection if he—
(a) distributes or circulates a terrorist publication;
(b) gives, sells or lends such a publication;
(c) offers such a publication for sale or loan;
(d) provides a service to others that enables them to obtain, read, listen to or look at such a publication, or to acquire it by means of a gift, sale or loan;
(e) transmits the contents of such a publication electronically; or
(f) has such a publication in his possession with a view to its becoming the subject of conduct falling within any of paragraphs (a) to (e).

Procedure An allegation of an offence contrary to s. 2 of the TA 2006 is triable either way (s. 2(11)); when tried on indictment it is normally a class 3 offence, but see CrimPD XIII, para. B (see Supplement, **CPD.XIII.B**), for the additional factors that the court considers on allocation. For consent to prosecution, see **B10.90**. **B10.98**

B

The provisions of s. 17 apply to this offence (see **B10.91**). For the liability of company directors, see **B10.95**.

Part B Offences

Sentence The maximum penalty is, on conviction on indictment, imprisonment for a term not exceeding 15 years and/or a fine and, on summary conviction, imprisonment for a term not exceeding six months and/or an unlimited fine (TA 2006, s. 2(11) and (12)). The maximum term of imprisonment was increased from seven years by the C-TBSA 2019, s. 7. The new maximum applies only in relation to an offence committed on or after 12 April 2019. **B10.99**

The definitive guideline, *Terrorism Offences* (see Supplement, **SG32-5**), governing all sentences imposed after 27 April 2018, applies to this offence. The court may also make a forfeiture order in accordance with s. 23A (see **B10.119**).

The Sentencing Council has issued draft revised guidelines for consultation which include guidelines for this offence to reflect significant changes to terrorism legislation brought about by the C-TBSA 2019. The consultation ran until 3 December 2019. There is no date fixed for when the new guidelines will come into force.

For sentencing guidance in respect of pre-guideline cases see *Rahman* [2008] EWCA Crim 1465, [2008] 4 All ER 661. Lord Phillips CJ stated that the seriousness of the offence could not be said to be largely measurable simply by reference to the quality and quantity of the material. Other matters should be given the importance they deserve. Whether D intended dissemination of terrorist publications to encourage the commission, preparation or instigation of acts of terrorism or was merely reckless as to such consequences is likely to be significant. The volume and content of the material disseminated will be relevant to the harm caused, intended or foreseeable. The Court specifically approved the dictum of Calvert-Smith J in sentencing *Yahya* (5 November 2007 unreported) for an offence under s. 58 (see **B10.68**) when he observed that the offence could be committed in an almost infinite variety of ways and the appropriate sentence for such an offence would need to reflect the particular facts and circumstances of the offence and offender. The Court observed that those words apply with particular force to offences under s. 2 and, if sentences are imposed which are more severe than the circumstances of the case warrant, that is likely to inflame rather than deter terrorism. The Court allowed Rahman's appeal to the extent that the six-year sentence was reduced to five years and six months for reasons primarily concerned with the *Goodyear* procedure adopted. The Court stated that, had the s. 2 offence stood alone, the sentence would have been significantly too high.

Elements The C-TBSA 2019, s. 5, amended s. 2 to refer to a reasonable person. The amendment applies only in a case where every act or other event, proof of which is required for conviction of the offence in question, takes place on or after 12 April 2019. **B10.100**

A publication is a terrorist publication, in relation to the conduct mentioned in the TA 2006, s. 2(2), if matter contained in it is likely (a) to be understood by a reasonable person as a direct or indirect encouragement or other inducement, to some or all of the persons to whom it is or may become available as a result of that conduct, to the commission, preparation or instigation of acts of terrorism; or (b) to be useful in the commission or preparation of such acts and to be understood, by some or all of those persons, as contained in the publication, or made available to them, wholly or mainly for the purpose of being so useful to them (s. 2(3)).

Matter that is likely to be understood by a reasonable person as indirectly encouraging the commission or preparation of acts of terrorism includes any matter which (a) glorifies the commission or preparation (whether in the past, in the future or generally) of such acts, and (b) is matter from which that person could reasonably be expected to infer that what is being glorified is being glorified as conduct that should be emulated in existing circumstances (s. 2(4)).

Whether a publication is a terrorist publication must be determined (a) as at the time of the conduct, and (b) having regard both to the contents of the publication as a whole and to the circumstances in which the conduct occurs (s. 2(5)).

References to the effect of a person's conduct in relation to a terrorist publication include references to an effect of the publication on one or more persons to whom it is or may become available as a consequence of that conduct (s. 2(6)).

Evidence of possession of a publication by known terrorists is admissible, if at all, only for the 'extremely limited purpose' of demonstrating that such persons may be among those who read it. It cannot prove that they were encouraged by it to commit or instigate terrorist offences; but there is an obvious risk that a jury may be prejudiced into condemning the publication purely by reason of its association with known terrorists, and if such evidence is properly admitted at all there must be a clear warning to the jury as to what it can and cannot be used to prove (*Faraz* [2012] EWCA Crim 2820, [2013] 1 WLR 2615).

It is irrelevant whether anything in s. 2(1) to (4) is in relation to the commission, preparation or instigation of one or more particular acts of terrorism, of acts of terrorism of a particular description or of acts of terrorism generally (s. 2(7)). It is also irrelevant whether any person is in fact encouraged or induced by the matter contained in any articles to commit, prepare or instigate acts of terrorism, or in fact makes use of it in the commission or preparation of such acts (s. 2(8)).

'Article' includes anything for storing data (s. 20(2)). 'Publication' means any article or record of any description that contains any of the following, or a combination of them: matter to be read, matter to be listened to, matter to be looked at or watched (s. 2(13)).

In *Brown* [2011] EWCA Crim 2571, [2012] 2 Cr App R (S) 10 (39) the Court of Appeal held that s. 2 constituted a proportionate restriction on the right to freedom of expression under the ECHR and freedom of speech at common law.

In *Iqbal* [2014] EWCA Crim 2650, the Court of Appeal noted that, in contrast to the decision of the trial judge, an individual's rights under the ECHR, Article 10, are engaged at the decision-to-prosecute stage. Any CPS decision to prosecute a person is a decision of a public authority, so the Convention rights of the person are potentially engaged. Nevertheless, the Court upheld the trial judge's decision on the substantive issue that D's rights had not been violated by the decision to prosecute having regard to Article 10(2). The Court reviewed *Brown* and *Faraz* and noted that the right to freedom of expression protected by Article 10 is qualified, not absolute. The freedom is subject to the restrictions and penalties prescribed by law and necessary in a democratic society in the interests of national security, public safety, for the prevention of disorder or crime and for the protection of the rights of others. All those interests are engaged by acts of terrorism, which violate the fundamental rights of others. As held in *Brown*, it is proportionate and legitimate to interfere with the right to freedom of expression in order to reduce, diminish or extinguish such acts. The Court noted that Parliament has determined that the dissemination of terrorist publications, for example through internet forums, either with the intention that they should directly or indirectly encourage acts of terrorism, or recklessly as to whether they will do so, should be penalised. For a case to similar effect, see *Ali (Humza)* [2018] EWCA Crim 547, [2018] 1 WLR 6105. In the case of recklessness only, it is a defence to show that the publication did not express D's views and was not endorsed by D. The Court considered that the issue of the compatibility of subjective recklessness with Article 10 had been addressed and answered explicitly and implicitly in *Brown* and *Faraz*.

Specific Defences The TA 2006 provides for two special defences to an allegation under s. 2. The first defence concerns D establishing that the views were not D's nor did D endorse them. **B10.101**

Terrorism Act 2006, s. 2

(9) In proceedings for an offence under this section against a person in respect of conduct to which subsection (10) applies, it is a defence for him to show—
  (a) that the matter by reference to which the publication in question was a terrorist publication neither expressed his views nor had his endorsement (whether by virtue of section 3 or otherwise); and
  (b) that it was clear, in all the circumstances of the conduct, that that matter did not express his views and (apart from the possibility of his having been given and failed to comply with a notice under [s. 3(3): see **B10.102**]) did not have his endorsement.

(10) This subsection applies to the conduct of a person to the extent that—
  (a) the publication to which his conduct related contained matter by reference to which it was a terrorist publication by virtue of [s. 2(3)(a)]; and
  (b) that person is not proved to have engaged in that conduct with the intention specified in [s. 2(1)(a)].

The second defence relates to internet activity and repeat statements.

Terrorism Act 2006, s. 3

(5) In proceedings against a person for an offence under section 1 or 2 the requirements of subsection (2)(a) to (c) are not, in his case, to be regarded as satisfied in relation to any time by virtue of subsection (4) if he shows that he—
  (a) has, before that time, taken every step he reasonably could to prevent a repeat statement from becoming available to the public and to ascertain whether it does; and
  (b) was, at that time, a person to whom subsection (6) applied.

(6) This subsection applies to a person at any time when he—
  (a) is not aware of the publication of the repeat statement; or
  (b) having become aware of its publication, has taken every step that he reasonably could to secure that it either ceased to be available to the public or was modified as mentioned in subsection (3)(b).

Internet Activity In relation to the TA 2006, ss. 1 and 2, s. 3 applies where a statement is published or caused to be published in the course of, or in connection with, the provision or use of a service provided electronically, or conduct falling within s. 2(2) was in the course of, or in connection with, the provision or use of such a service (s. 3(1)). The statement or article or record to which the conduct relates is to be regarded as having the endorsement of a person at any time more than two working days after a constable has given the person notice under s. 3(3) and the relevant person has failed, without reasonable excuse, to comply with the notice (s. 3(2)). **B10.102**

Section 3(7) sets out when a statement or an article or record is unlawfully terrorism-related.

Section 4 deals with the delivery of s. 3 notices.

For extended jurisdiction in respect of suppliers of information society services who are established in the UK where a relevant act occurs in the EEA, see the Electronic Commerce Directive (Terrorism Act 2006) Regulations 2007 (SI 2007 No. 1550). The Regulations also provide for special defences and limited liability where they apply.

B10.103 **Search Power** If a magistrate is satisfied that there are reasonable grounds for suspecting that articles likely to be the subject of conduct falling within s. 2(2)(a) to (e) and to be treated as a terrorist publication are likely to be found on any premises, the magistrate may issue a warrant authorising a constable (a) to enter and search the premises, and (b) to seize anything found there which the constable has reason to believe is such an article (TA 2006, s. 28(1) and (2)). The person searching may use such force as is reasonable in the circumstances for exercising the power (s. 28(3)).

Preparation of Terrorist Acts

B10.104 **Terrorism Act 2006, s. 5**

(1) A person commits an offence if, with the intention of—

(a) committing acts of terrorism, or

(b) assisting another to commit such acts,

he engages in any conduct in preparation for giving effect to his intention.

B10.105 **Procedure** The offence is indictable only (TA 2006, s. 5(1)) and is a class 1B offence. For consent to prosecution, see **B10.90**.

The provisions of s. 17 apply to this offence (see **B10.91**). For the liability of company directors, see **B10.95**.

In *Kahar* [2016] EWCA Crim 568, [2016] 1 WLR 3156, the Court of Appeal declined to say that prosecutors should only charge under s. 5 after consideration had been given to what other charges could appropriately be brought.

B10.106 **Sentence** The maximum penalty is life imprisonment (TA 2006, s. 5(3)). The court may also make a forfeiture order in accordance with s. 23A (see **B10.119**). The definitive guideline, *Terrorism Offences* (see Supplement, **SG32-3**), governing all sentences imposed after 27 April 2018, applies to this offence.

In *Ali (Khalid Mohamed)* [2019] EWCA Crim 1527, [2020] 1 Cr App R 1 (1) the Court of Appeal refused a renewed application for leave to appeal against sentence where the applicant had been sentenced to life imprisonment with a minimum term of 25 years for an offence contrary to the TA 2006, s. 5.

Substantial guidance in respect of sentencing pre-guideline cases was provided in *Kahar* [2016] EWCA Crim 568, [2016] 1 WLR 3156. The Court observed that, in relation to all terrorist offences and terrorist related offences, so-called 'just' or 'noble cause' terrorism is irrelevant to sentence and does not provide any mitigation.

The underlying principles relevant to sentencing in s. 5 cases were identified as follows:

- conduct threatening democratic government and the security of the State has a seriousness all of its own;
- the purpose of sentence in s. 5 cases is to punish, deter and incapacitate, and, except at the very bottom end of the scale, rehabilitation is unlikely to play a part;
- the CJA 2003, s. 143(1), requires the sentencer to consider D's culpability (likely to be extremely high), and any harm which the offence caused, was intended to cause or might foreseeably have caused;
- the starting point is the sentence that would have been imposed if the intended act(s) had been carried out — with the offence generally being more serious the closer D was to the completion of the intended act(s);
- when relevant, it is necessary to distinguish between a primary intention to endanger life and a primary intention to cause serious damage to property, with the most serious offences being those involving an intended threat to human life.

Moreover, the Court observed that an intention to assist one or more others to commit acts of terrorism may be just as serious as, or even more serious than, the offence of the person whom D assists (e.g., a mastermind who has no intention of carrying out the intended acts in person).

D's particular vulnerability and, if vulnerable, the extent to which D was groomed, and any voluntary disengagement, may be amongst the mitigating factors to be considered.

Depending on the seriousness of the offence, sentences may vary between a life sentence with a very long minimum term to a relatively short determinate sentence.

D's culpability is decided by looking at whether the intended acts were to be done in the near future, and the commitment to carry them out. Harm is assessed by examining the impact of the intended act(s), the intended number of acts, the direct impact intended on the immediate victims and the wider intended impact on the public in general if the act(s) had been successful.

The offence is a 'specified violent offence' (see **E4.4**), and the judge must consider whether to impose a life sentence (see **E4.5**) or an extended sentence (see **E4.10**). That involves an assessment as to the extent and depth of any radicalisation and/or extremism and the likelihood of its continuance. An offender who is in the grip of idealistic extremism is likely to pose a serious risk for an indefinite period.

The Court set six levels of offending. The range relates to the sentence (actual or notional) after trial. There is a degree of overlap between the levels, and aggravating and mitigating features may move the final sentence up or down within a level, or may move it to another level. Regard should be had to the full judgment in order to see examples of previous cases which the Court viewed as examples of the different levels.

Level 1: this is the highest level, where the offender has taken steps which amount to attempted multiple murder, or something near to it, or to a conspiracy to do so which is likely to lead to an attempt that is likely to succeed, but no physical harm has been caused. The definitive guideline relating to attempted murder is not directly applicable. For such an offence a sentence of life imprisonment with a minimum term of 30 to 40 years or more is appropriate.

Level 2: a little lower on the scale are those who are not fully prepared to act, or where the harm which may have been caused was not quite as serious. In such a case a life sentence will generally be called for with a minimum term in the range of 21 to 30 years or a very long determinate sentence and an extension period of five years.

Level 3: these are cases involving leadership, recruiting, planning killings and supplying equipment or funds for terrorist purposes. D will invariably be dangerous and the appropriate sentence will be a life sentence with a minimum term of 15 to 20 years or a long determinate sentence of 20 to 30 years or more with an extension period of five years.

Level 4: the typical case will be an offender who joins, or otherwise supports a terrorist organisation, usually engaged in a conflict overseas, and either participates on the periphery of the actual combat or trains for it (whether in the UK or abroad), with a plan to carry out acts in the UK in the future. Such an offender is likely to be dangerous, and a determinate sentence in the range of ten to 20 years or more with an extension period of five years is likely to be appropriate.

Level 5: a typical case will usually be in the lower realms of seriousness in the UK. Examples include an offender who sets out to join a terrorist organisation engaged in a conflict overseas but does not complete his journey, or who makes extensive preparations with a real commitment but does not travel far, or who does not make detailed preparations for an intended act. In such a case, where the offender is not dangerous, the range of a determinate sentence is likely to be five to ten years.

Level 6: the typical offender will be one who never sets out, or who sets out but is likely not to go far, or returns without going far, or who has a minor role in relation to intended acts at the lowest end of seriousness in the UK. Sentences in the range of 21 months to five years are likely to be appropriate.

In *Abdallah* [2016] EWCA Crim 1868, [2017] 1 Cr App R (S) 29 (204), the Court of Appeal, affirming the guidance in *Kahar* [2016] EWCA Crim 568, [2016] 1 WLR 3156, considered two further matters relating to sentencing for offences contrary to s. 5. First, attempts to contrast facts when determining the appropriate category of offending should not be made due to the highly fact-sensitive nature of cases. For the same reason, the descriptions of the guideline levels are not intended to be mechanistically applied. Second, when considering an extended sentence in the context of the CJA 2003, s. 226A(1)(b), although the territorial scope of 'the public' is not expressly defined, the phrase must be intended to include the public in other countries. Giving further guidance, the Court observed (at [87]):

> In assessing both the culpability and dangerousness of an offender who has engaged in preparatory conduct with the intention of committing terrorist acts, two dimensions of the offence need to be considered. One is the gravity of the intended acts. The other is how close the offender came to the commission of those acts.

B10.107 **Elements** By virtue of the TA 2006, s. 5(2), it is irrelevant whether the intention and preparation referred to in s. 5(1) relate to one or more particular acts of terrorism, acts of terrorism of a particular description, or acts of terrorism generally. The offence under s. 5 has been prosecuted relatively frequently. Its breadth has meant that prosecutors have not relied on the TA 2000, ss. 57 and 58, as often as they did prior to 2006.

In *Roddis* [2009] EWCA Crim 585, D was in possession of two of the three component ingredients of the primary explosive TATP, had made attempts to secure the final ingredient and had carried out research into bomb-making and explosives. It was submitted on appeal that the evidence did not amount to a case to answer as it did not go beyond mere possession. Allied with that was a further submission that the judge ought to have directed the jury that conduct in the context of this case meant, and meant only, acquisition and accordingly the only relevant time to look at D's intent was the time of acquisition of the material. The acquisition of the ingredients for TATP had been some 18 months before arrest and any subsequent intent ought to have been treated as irrelevant. So far as the first submission was concerned, the Court of Appeal observed that the Crown's case was one of successive acts of acquisition of knowledge and materials for bomb-making which amounted to a continuing process. There was ample evidence of that continuing process, a simple example of which was afforded by the attempts to buy the final ingredient for the TATP. In respect of the allied submission, the Court observed that the summing-up had made clear to the jury that the coincidence of conduct and intent was essential. The conduct in which D was alleged to have engaged was researching on the internet how to make home-made explosives and purchasing two of the ingredients to manufacture explosives and use them in an improvised explosive device along with the nails also purchased for that purpose and the fuse obtained from fireworks. It follows that the conduct left to the jury was not simply the acquisition of the ingredients, but extended to acquisition of knowledge, which was on the facts a continuing process. The real issue in the case was D's intent.

Training for Terrorism

B10.108 **Terrorism Act 2006, s. 6**

(1) A person commits an offence if—
 (a) he provides instruction or training in any of the skills mentioned in subsection (3); and
 (b) at the time he provides the instruction or training, he knows that a person receiving it intends to use the skills on which he is being instructed or trained—
  (i) for or in connection with the commission or preparation of acts of terrorism or Convention offences; or
  (ii) for assisting the commission or preparation by others of such acts or offences.

(2) A person commits an offence if—
 (a) he receives instruction or training in any of the skills mentioned in subsection (3); and
 (b) at the time of the instruction or training, he intends to use the skills which he is being instructed or trained—
  (i) for or in connection with the commission or preparation of acts of terrorism or Convention offences; or
  (ii) for assisting the commission or preparation by others of such acts or offences.

(3) The skills are—
(a) the making, handling or use of a noxious substance, or of substances of a description of such substances;
(b) the use of any method or technique for doing anything else that is capable of being done for the purposes of terrorism, in connection with the commission or preparation of an act of terrorism or Convention offence or in connection with assisting the commission or preparation by another of such an act or offence; and
(c) the design or adaptation for the purposes of terrorism, or in connection with the commission or preparation of acts of terrorism or Convention offences, of any method or technique for doing anything.

Procedure An allegation of an offence contrary to s. 6 of the TA 2006 is triable either way (s. 6(5)); when tried on indictment it is normally a class 3 offence, but see CrimPD XIII, para. B (see Supplement, **CPD.XIII.B**), for the additional factors that the court considers on allocation. For consent to prosecution, see **B10.90**. **B10.109**

The provisions of s. 17 apply to this offence (see **B10.91**). For the liability of company directors, see **B10.95**.

Sentence The maximum penalty is, on conviction on indictment, life imprisonment (or, where committed prior to 13 April 2015, ten years' imprisonment) and/or a fine; on summary conviction, a sentence of imprisonment not exceeding six months and/or an unlimited fine (TA 2006, s. 6(5) and (6)). The court may order the forfeiture of anything the court considers to have been in the person's possession for purposes connected with the offence (s. 7(1)). The court may also make a more wide-ranging forfeiture order in accordance with s. 23A (see **B10.119**). **B10.110**

Elements It is irrelevant (a) whether any instruction or training that is provided is provided to one or more particular persons or generally; (b) whether the acts or offences in relation to which a person intends to use such skills consist of one or more particular acts of terrorism or Convention offences, acts of terrorism or Convention offences of a particular description, or acts of terrorism or Convention offences generally; and (c) whether assistance that a person intends to provide to others is intended to be provided to one or more particular persons or to one or more persons whose identities are not yet known (TA 2006, s. 6(4)). **B10.111**

'Noxious substance' means (a) a dangerous substance within the meaning of the A-TCSA 2001, part 7, or (b) any other substance which is hazardous or noxious or which may be or become hazardous or noxious only in certain circumstances. 'Substance' includes any natural or artificial substance (whatever its origin or method of production and whether in solid or liquid form or in the form of a gas or vapour) and any mixture of substances (s. 6(7)).

Attendance at a Place for Terrorist Training

Terrorism Act 2006, s. 8 **B10.112**

(1) A person commits an offence if—
(a) he attends at any place, whether in the United Kingdom or elsewhere;
(b) while he is at that place, instruction or training of the type mentioned in section 6(1) of this Act or section 54(1) of the Terrorism Act 2000 is provided there;
(c) that instruction or training is provided there wholly or partly for purposes connected with the commission or preparation of acts of terrorism or Convention offences; and
(d) the requirements of subsection (2) are satisfied in relation to that person.
(2) The requirements of this subsection are satisfied in relation to a person if—
(a) he knows or believes that instruction or training is being provided there wholly or partly for purposes connected with the commission or preparation of acts of terrorism or Convention offences; or
(b) a person attending at that place throughout the period of that person's attendance could not reasonably have failed to understand that instruction or training was being provided there wholly or partly for such purposes.

B10.113 **Procedure** An allegation of an offence contrary to s. 8 of the TA 2006 is triable either way (s. 8(4)); when tried on indictment it is normally a class 3 offence, but see CrimPD XIII, para. B (see Supplement, **CPD.XIII.B**), for the additional factors that the court considers on allocation. For consent to prosecution, see **B10.90**.

The provisions of s. 17 apply to this offence (see **B10.91**). For the liability of company directors, see **B10.95**.

B10.114 **Sentence** The maximum penalty is, on conviction on indictment, imprisonment for a term not exceeding ten years and/or a fine, and, on summary conviction, imprisonment for a term not exceeding six months and/or an unlimited fine (TA 2006, s. 8(4) and (5)). In *Hamid* (26 February 2008 unreported), Pitchers J imposed sentences ranging between three and a half years' and four and a half years' imprisonment on offenders convicted of offences under s. 8. The judge took into account that each had come under the influence of the charismatic principal offenders.

When the Sentencing Act 2020 is enacted by Parliament the maximum penalty for an offence under s. 8 will increase from ten to 14 years for any such offence committed on or after the day the Act comes into force.

B10.115 **Elements** It is immaterial '(a) whether the person concerned receives the instruction or training himself; and (b) whether the instruction or training is provided for purposes connected with one or more particular acts of terrorism or Convention offences, acts of terrorism or Convention offences of a particular description, or acts of terrorism or Convention offences generally' (TA 2006, s. 8(3)). Under s. 8, and in contrast to s. 6(2) (see **B10.108**), the prosecution plainly do not have to prove that D intended to use the training received for terrorist purposes.

SENTENCING FOR OFFENCES COMMITTED IN A TERRORIST CONTEXT

B10.116 In *Barot* [2007] EWCA Crim 1119, [2008] 1 Cr App R (S) 31 (156), the Court of Appeal gave substantial guidance (at [33]–[62]) as to the sentencing of persons committing offences in a terrorist context. Lord Phillips CJ observed that a terrorist who is in the grip of idealistic extremism to the extent of plotting to commit murder of innocent citizens over a long period is likely to pose a serious risk to the public for an indefinite period if not confined. Thus, if the terrorist commits an offence that permits the court to impose an indeterminate sentence, that is likely to be the appropriate course. The Court considered *Taylor and Thomas* (1995) 16 Cr App R (S) 873, *Martin* [1999] 1 Cr App R (S) 477 and *Hindawi* (1988) 10 Cr App R (S) 104 in deciding how the appropriate minimum term of that indefinite sentence should be set. The guidelines in *Martin* required review as there had been a significant increase in the minimum terms imposed in serious murders since the implementation of the CJA 2003. Where mass murder flows from the actions of the offenders, whole life terms will be imposed. Other than in exceptional circumstances, a life sentence with a minimum of 40 years should represent the maximum sentence for a terrorist who sets out to achieve mass murder but is not successful in causing any physical harm. That sentence should be reserved for a terrorist convicted, after trial, of a serious and viable attempt to commit mass murder. If the offence charged is one of conspiracy and the plot falls short of an attempt, the sentence should be lower. Where a court is of the view that the conspiracy was likely to lead to an attempt which was likely to be successful, then it may be right to draw little distinction between the conspiracy and attempt. Where the court cannot be certain that the conspiracy would have been put into practice, or would have led to a successful attempt to murder, the sentence should be significantly lower than that imposed for an attempt. D's role in the plot will also be significant, with a leader being subject to a more severe sentence than a follower.

In *Khan (Usman)* [2013] EWCA Crim 468 the Court of Appeal set out principles for sentencing in terrorism cases which, the Court observed, come in many different forms. The Court did not provide guidelines because of 'the enormous breadth of potential offences and … the differing potential assessment of culpability and harm depending on the precise facts'. The principles to be applied are:

(a) an assessment of culpability and harm, as required by the CJA 2003, s. 143, is necessary: the Court of Appeal noted that 'in most ... terrorist offences, the former will be extremely high';
(b) 'the purpose of sentence for the most serious terrorist offences is to punish, deter and incapacitate. Rehabilitation will play little, if any part' (see *Martin*);
(c) 'the starting point for sentence for an inchoate offence is the sentence that would have been imposed if the objective had been achieved, with an attempt to commit the offence being more serious than a conspiracy' (see *Barot*);
(d) sentences based on *Martin* or other cases pre-dating implementation of the CJA 2003, sch. 21, are of historical interest only and do not provide any assistance as to the approach now.

In *Saleem* [2007] EWCA Crim 2692, [2008] 2 Cr App R (S) 12 (70), the Court of Appeal identified factors affecting the seriousness of an allegation of solicitation to murder in a terrorist context. The case concerned demonstrations against the publication in Denmark of cartoons depicting the Prophet Mohammed. The Court quashed sentences of six years' imprisonment imposed after trial and substituted sentences of four years. Giving the judgment of the Court, Lord Phillips CJ said (at [38] and [45]): **B10.117**

> These appeals relate to sentences for inchoate offences of the kind that can lead others to commit acts of terrorism. When considering the seriousness of such offences in the context of terrorism it is material to have regard to the period of time covered by the offending, the sophistication, skill and industry devoted to it, and the likelihood that the offending would lead others to commit acts of terrorism, or may even have done so. ...
>
> The offences with which we are concerned involved a one-off demonstration, mounted at short notice without sophisticated planning ... Insofar as this crude chanting and the messages on the placards solicited murder, we do not think that this was likely to persuade those who witnessed the demonstration in central London, or who saw the television broadcasts of it, to resort to killing, although one cannot be sure of the effect that it might have on those already inclined to terrorist activity.

The Court observed that the seriousness of the offending was less than that in *El-Faisal* [2004] EWCA Crim 465, [2004] 2 Cr App R (S) 80 (429) (seven years' imprisonment for solicitation to murder upheld on appeal) and *Abu Hamza* [2006] EWCA Crim 2918, [2007] QB 659 (no appeal against sentence of seven years' imprisonment imposed for solicitation to murder) which involved a persistent and protracted course of conduct aimed at indoctrinating young Muslims into committing terrorist murder.

In *Rahman* [2008] EWCA Crim 1465, [2008] 4 All ER 661, Lord Phillips CJ observed that sentences which are more severe than the circumstances of the case warrant are likely to inflame rather than deter terrorism.

In *Al Daour* [2011] EWCA Crim 2392 the Court of Appeal dealt with the question of whether a period of police detention under the TA 2000 should be taken into account, by virtue of the CJA 2003, s. 240, for the purposes of any subsequent sentence and determined that it should (see **E2.14**).

The Terrorism Offenders (Restriction of Early Release) Act 2020 came into force on 26 February 2020. It amends the CJA 2003 to make substantial changes to early release provisions for prisoners convicted of terrorism offences and offences committed in a terrorist context. It applies to all serving prisoners and will apply to all future serving prisoners.

Terrorism as an Aggravating Factor

By virtue of the C-TA 2008, s. 30, a judge considering the seriousness of an offence listed in sch. 2 to that Act (a list of offences which may have a terrorist connection) must determine **B10.118** whether the offence has a terrorist connection if there is material before the court which suggests that it may have such a connection. If the court decides that there is a terrorist connection to the offence, that much must be stated in open court and must be treated as an aggravating factor for the purposes of sentencing.

Forfeiture

B10.119 Under the TA 2000, ss. 23 to 23B (as inserted by the C-TA 2008, ss. 34 to 36), extensive powers of forfeiture are available to the court when sentencing for terrorist offences under ss. 15 to 18 of the TA 2000. In short, the court may order the forfeiture of any money or other property which an offender had possession or control of at the time of the offence and which had been used, or which an offender intended should be used, or had reasonable cause to suspect might be used for the purposes of terrorism. Forfeiture may be ordered if the court finds that the money or property will be used for the purposes of terrorism unless forfeited, or that it was received by any person as a payment or other reward in connection with the commission of the offence.

Notification Requirements

B10.120 A system of notification requirements for persons convicted of terrorist offences was created by the C-TA 2008, ss. 40 to 61. The scheme is similar in nature to that applying to sexual offenders (see **E23**). They apply to persons convicted of an offence on or after 1 October 2009 but also apply retrospectively to offenders who were either in custody or on licence in relation to a custodial sentence for a terrorist offence specified in s. 41(1) on that date (s. 43). The provisions apply only to terrorist offenders who are sentenced to a minimum of 12 months' imprisonment or made subject to a hospital order when charged with such an offence (s. 45). Sections 47 to 52 set out the procedure for notification and the details which the offender must provide. The C-TBSA 2019, s. 12, amended notification requirements under the C-TA 2008, ss. 47 and 48, with effect from 12 April 2019, creating a new s. 48A governing notification in respect of changes in financial information and identification documents.

The duration of any notification requirements will be determined by the length of sentence imposed on the offender (s. 53). Section 54 makes it an offence to fail to comply with a notification requirement. On summary conviction, the maximum penalty is six months' imprisonment and/or an unlimited fine. On conviction on indictment the maximum sentence is five years' imprisonment and/or a fine (s. 54(2)). Notification requirements can also be imposed on persons who have been convicted outside the UK in respect of a corresponding foreign offence (s. 57). The C-TBSA 2019, s. 13, inserted s. 56A into the C-TA 2008, with effect from 12 April 2019, which allows the police to enter and search the home address of a Registered Terrorist Offender ('RTO'). Section 56A enables a justice of the peace in England and Wales (or a sheriff in Scotland or a magistrate in Northern Ireland) to issue a warrant pursuant to an application by an officer of the rank of superintendent and above to allow a constable to enter and search the home of a RTO for the purposes of assessing the risks that the RTO may pose to the community. The warrant must be executed by a constable of the police force in whose area the premises are located.

Section 58 implements sch. 5 and provides for the making of foreign travel restriction orders prohibiting persons subject to notification orders from travelling outside the UK. See *Metropolitan Police Commissioner v Ahsan* [2015] EWHC 2354 (Admin), [2016] 1 WLR 654 for an example of the refusal of an application for a notification order in respect of a man who had recently returned to the UK after serving a sentence of imprisonment for a terrorism offence in the USA. The Divisional Court was mindful of the fact that once the requirements are imposed then (in accordance with the judgment in *R (Irfan) v Secretary of State for the Home Department* [2012] EWCA Civ 1471, [2013] QB 885) there is no review mechanism.

The PCA 2017, s. 68, creates an offence of breaching pre-charge bail conditions relating to travel. The section applies where a person is arrested in respect of an offence mentioned in the C-TA 2008, s. 41(1) and (2), and released without charge and on bail subject to a travel restriction. Section 69 defines words used in s. 68. The maximum penalty is: on conviction on indictment, imprisonment for a term not exceeding 12 months and/or a fine; on summary conviction, imprisonment for a term not exceeding 12 months and/or a fine.

FINANCIAL MEASURES TO COUNTER TERRORISM: GENERAL

Provisions designed to stem the flow of funds to terrorist groups have assumed increasing importance in the international fight against terrorism. The first substantive provisions emerged in the TA 2000, creating offences relating to the funding of terrorism, money laundering and the failure to provide information relating to terrorism finance during the course of employment. The A-TCSA 2001 supplemented those provisions, enabling the forfeiture of money connected to terrorism. In the wake of the Al-Qa'ida attacks on the World Trade Center, a number of UN resolutions designed to prohibit the provision of funds to named individuals and groups were incorporated into English law under the auspices of the United Nations Act 1946. The C-TA 2008 implemented a range of financial directions, found in sch. 7 to the Act. The Terrorism Asset Freezing Act 2010 added to those powers and amended sch. 7 to the C-TA 2008. **B10.121**

FINANCIAL MEASURES UNDER THE TERRORISM ACT 2000

Terrorist Fundraising

Terrorism Act 2000, s. 15 **B10.122**

(1) A person commits an offence if he—
(a) invites another to provide money or other property, and
(b) intends that it should be used, or has reasonable cause to suspect that it may be used, for the purposes of terrorism.
(2) A person commits an offence if he—
(a) receives money or other property, and
(b) intends that it should be used, or has reasonable cause to suspect that it may be used, for the purposes of terrorism.
(3) A person commits an offence if he—
(a) provides money or other property, and
(b) knows or has reasonable cause to suspect that it will or may be used for the purposes of terrorism.

Procedure An allegation of an offence contrary to the TA 2000, s. 15, is triable either way and when tried on indictment is normally a class 3 offence, but see CrimPD XIII, para. B (see Supplement, **CPD.XIII.B**), for the additional factors that the court considers on allocation. For consent to prosecution, see **B10.34**. **B10.123**

See **B10.87** for extended jurisdiction provisions in relation to this offence.

Sentence The maximum penalty is: on conviction on indictment, imprisonment for a term not exceeding 14 years and/or a fine; on summary conviction, imprisonment for a term not exceeding six months and/or an unlimited fine (TA 2000, s. 22). The definitive guideline, *Terrorism Offences* (see Supplement, **SG32-8**), governing all sentences imposed after 27 April 2018, applies to this offence. A court may also make a forfeiture order (s. 23 and sch. 4). See also **B10.119**. **B10.124**

Pre-guideline cases include *Saleem* [2009] EWCA Crim 920, where custodial sentences ranging from two to two and a half years for fund-raising in relation to Iraq were reduced on appeal by the Court of Appeal. In *Golamaully* [2017] EWCA Crim 898 D successfully challenged a 22-month immediate custodial sentence imposed following an early guilty plea to an offence contrary to the TA 2000, s. 15. She and her husband had been jointly responsible for sending a single payment of £219 to their nephew, an IS fighter in Syria. There was evidence that her husband had regularly read the nephew's online posts and stayed in contact with him. Her husband had been sentenced to 27 months' imprisonment following a guilty plea at the same stage as D. D had substantial personal mitigation and the imposition of the sentence of imprisonment upon both parents had significantly affected their four children who were aged between nine and 15. The Court was persuaded that there was insufficient difference between the sentence imposed on D and that imposed on her husband, whose culpability was significantly greater. The Court also heard the 'prayer for mercy' on her behalf and concluded that, exceptionally, it was an appropriate case in which to find that 'the more general need for deterrence does not drown out a requirement for compassion' (at [25]).

B10.125 **Elements** By virtue of the TA 2000, s. 121, 'property' includes property wherever situated and whether real or personal, heritable or moveable, things in action and other intangible or incorporeal property.

B10.126 **Specific Defences** Section 21 of the TA 2000 provides a number of specific defences to an allegation of an offence contrary to s. 15. Each of the defences involves co-operation with police officers.

(1) Under s. 21(1), no offence is committed if a person who is involved in any of the actions covered by s. 15 is acting with the express consent of a constable.
(2) By virtue of s. 21(2), if a person is involved in a transaction or arrangement relating to money or other property, no offence is committed if the person discloses to a constable (a) a suspicion or belief that the money or other property is terrorist property, and (b) the information on which that suspicion or belief is based. This defence applies only where a person makes a disclosure as soon as is reasonably practicable and on the person's own initiative after becoming concerned in the relevant transaction (s. 21(3)). By virtue of s. 21(4), if a constable forbids a person from continuing involvement in the transaction or arrangement in relation to which the disclosure was made but the person nevertheless continues, the defence does not apply. For 'terrorist property', see **B10.131**.
(3) For any person charged with an offence under s. 15(2) or (3), but not s. 15(1), the defence is open to prove that the person intended to make a disclosure of the kind mentioned in s. 21(2) and (3), but there is a reasonable excuse for failure to do so (s. 21(5)).

The TA 2000 makes special provision for employees where their employer has established a procedure for making any required disclosure. Under s. 21(6), in relation to all these defences, where a person is in employment and the employer has established a procedure for making disclosures, the duty of disclosure on the employee is to make disclosure in accordance with the procedure. 'Transaction or arrangement relating to money or other property' includes a reference to use or possession (s. 21(7)).

B10.127 The Terrorism Act 2000 and the Proceeds of Crime Act 2002 (Amendment) Regulations 2007 (SI 2007 No. 3398) inserted ss. 21ZA to 21ZC into the TA 2000, providing further specific defences to a charge under ss. 15 to 18. They relate to disclosure to authorised officers as opposed to constables.

An 'authorised officer' is an officer of the NCA.

For the compatibility of the reverse burden with the ECHR, Article 6, see **F3.18** ***et seq.***

Possession of Property

B10.128 **Terrorism Act 2000, s. 16**

(1) A person commits an offence if he uses money or other property for the purposes of terrorism.
(2) A person commits an offence if he—
    (a) possesses money or other property, and
    (b) intends that it should be used, or has reasonable cause to suspect that it may be used, for the purposes of terrorism.

Procedure An allegation of an offence contrary to the TA 2000, s. 16, is triable either way and when tried on indictment is normally a class 3 offence, but see CrimPD XIII, para. B (see Supplement, **CPD.XIII.B**), for the additional factors that the court considers on allocation. For consent to prosecution, see **B10.34**. **B10.129**

See **B10.87** for extended jurisdiction provisions in relation to this offence.

Sentence The maximum penalty is: on conviction on indictment, imprisonment for a term not exceeding 14 years and/or a fine; on summary conviction, imprisonment for a term not exceeding six months and/or an unlimited fine (TA 2000, s. 22). The definitive guideline, *Terrorism Offences* (see Supplement, **SG32-8**), governing all sentences imposed after 27 April 2018, applies to this offence. A court may also make a forfeiture order (s. 23 and sch. 4). See also **B10.119**. **B10.130**

Elements For 'terrorism', see **B10.2**. By virtue of s. 14(1) of the 2000 Act, 'terrorist property' means (a) money or other property which is likely to be used for the purposes of terrorism (including any resources of a proscribed organisation), (b) proceeds of the commission of acts of terrorism, and (c) proceeds of acts carried out for the purposes of terrorism. The 'proceeds' of an act include any property which, wholly or partly and directly or indirectly, represents the proceeds of the act (including payments or other rewards in connection with its commission). An organisation's resources include any money or other property which is applied or made available, or is to be applied or made available, for use by the organisation (s. 14(2)). For 'property', see **B10.125**. **B10.131**

In *O'Driscoll v Secretary of State for the Home Department* [2002] EWHC 2477 (QB), [2003] ACD 35 it was suggested that the offence is one of specific intent and is concerned with knowingly providing money or other property in support of a proscribed organisation. In the light of the ruling of the Court of Appeal in *AB* [2017] EWCA Crim 129 (see **B10.136**), it is clear that the offence may be committed other than with a specific intent.

Specific Defences The defences available to a person charged with an offence contrary to the TA 2000, s. 16, are the same as those available to a person charged with an offence contrary to s. 15 (see **B10.126**). **B10.132**

For the compatibility of the reverse burden with the ECHR, Article 6, see **F3.18** ***et seq***.

Funding Arrangements

Terrorism Act 2000, s. 17 **B10.133**

A person commits an offence if—

(a) he enters into or becomes concerned in an arrangement as a result of which money or other property is made available or is to be made available to another, and

(b) he knows or has reasonable cause to suspect that it will or may be used for the purposes of terrorism.

Procedure An allegation of an offence contrary to the TA 2000, s. 17, is triable either way and when tried on indictment is normally a class 3 offence, but see CrimPD XIII, para. B (see Supplement, **CPD.XIII.B**), for the additional factors that the court considers on allocation. For consent to prosecution, see **B10.34**. **B10.134**

See **B10.87** for extended jurisdiction provisions in relation to this offence.

Sentence The maximum penalty is: on conviction on indictment, imprisonment for a term not exceeding 14 years and/or a fine; on summary conviction, imprisonment for a term not exceeding six months and/or an unlimited fine (TA 2000, s. 22). The definitive guideline, *Terrorism Offences* (see Supplement, **SG32-8**), governing all sentences imposed after 27 April 2018, applies to this offence. A court may also make a forfeiture order (s. 23 and sch. 4). See also **B10.119**. **B10.135**

In *Wakil* [2019] EWCA Crim 1351, [2020] 1 Cr App R (S) 11 (92) the Court of Appeal considered the sentence of a man found guilty after trial of funding terrorism contrary to the TA

2000, s. 17. D was of previous good character, suffered from paranoid schizophrenia and had last been an in-patient in 2013. He had an IQ of 70 and was abnormally suggestible. He lived at home with his parents and a number of younger siblings. He had never had a relationship, had no real friends and had had no employment since his acute episode of illness in 2013. The Court observed that he 'was socially isolated and was, on any view, a vulnerable individual' (at [19]). His younger sister had been radicalised in her teens and had travelled to Syria when aged 16. The family opposed her actions and begged her to return. The Crown did not suggest that any of her family, including D, shared her beliefs. The family were in contact with the police and liaised with them at all times. They were all warned not to send money to her as it could be seen as terrorist funding. In December 2016, she asked D for money to pay people smugglers to get out. He agreed to send money to her, via an intermediary, at the end of January 2017. Four days later, he was expressly warned not to send her money. At the end of February 2017, he withdrew the necessary money and sent it to her. She then told him that the price demanded by the people smugglers had gone up and asked for more money. He did not send her any further amounts. In December 2017, he was arrested and charged. He was convicted of an offence contrary to the TA 2000, s. 17, on 15 January 2019 and sentenced on 8 February 2019.

Upon appeal against sentence, the Court observed that it is clear that sentencing for the offences created by the TA 2000, ss. 15 to 18, is especially fact-sensitive and there are clearly different underlying degrees of culpability. Guidelines 'do not create impermeable or hermitically sealed categories which place a straitjacket around a sentencing judge' (at [29]). The guideline relevant to an offence under s. 17 makes clear that there may be a range of factors that can result in a sentence moving significantly away from the starting point and indeed, if appropriate, outside the category range first considered. There is also a series of factors reducing seriousness or reflecting personal mitigation. Relevant to D was that his responsibility was substantially reduced by a learning disability, a lack of maturity and his suggestibility. The Court concluded that the underlying features of this offending and D's particular personal circumstances called for a greater reduction from the starting point. The offence was committed substantially as a result of D's suggestibility and his difficulties in resisting his sister's blandishments. The Court also thought it relevant that D's problems would make his life in custody more difficult than usual. Accordingly, the Court reduced the sentence from 30 months' to 20 months' imprisonment.

B10.136 **Elements** For 'terrorism', see **B10.2**.

In *Lane* [2018] UKSC 36, [2018] 2 Cr App R 35 (606), the Supreme Court confirmed the decision of the Court of Appeal in the interlocutory appeal of *AB* [2017] EWCA Crim 129 in respect of the *mens rea* of an offence under the TA 2000, s. 17. The Supreme Court ruled that the phrase 'has reasonable cause to suspect' was not equivalent in meaning to 'has reasonable suspicion'. Accordingly, D does not actually have to suspect that the money would or might be used for terrorist purposes. Instead the test is whether, objectively, there was 'reasonable cause to suspect' on the basis of the information of which D was aware. When the case subsequently returned to the Central Criminal Court for trial, the prosecution unsuccessfully argued before the trial judge that the defence of duress of circumstances (pleaded in the defence statements) should not be available to a charge under s. 17. The prosecution pursued an interlocutory appeal against the ruling of the Recorder of London. In *Lane* [2018] EWCA Crim 2602, the Court of Appeal refused the prosecution appeal. The prosecution had argued that the policy and scheme of the 2000 Act precluded the availability of the defence of duress and/or necessity. Reliance was placed on the wide compass of the offence and the obvious requirement for individuals to be vigilant not to commit it. It was further contended that the potential defence provided by the consent of a constable under s. 21 meant that permitting a defence of duress of circumstances to a charge under s. 17 would effectively allow an individual to go behind a constable's refusal and permit such a person to take the law into his or her own hands. In that way, the rationale for the provision would be undermined. The Court rejected the proposition that the structure of the legislation excludes any consideration of duress or necessity. The decision of the Court of Appeal arguably had a significant impact on the outcome of the trial. The defendants were convicted of the one count where the defence of duress of circumstances was not available to them. In respect of the remaining two counts where the defence was available, they were acquitted of one count and the jury could not reach a verdict in respect of the other.

Specific Defences The defences available to a person charged with an offence contrary to the TA 2000, s. 17, are the same as those available to a person charged with an offence contrary to s. 15 (see **B10.126**). **B10.137**

For the compatibility of the reverse burden with the ECHR, Article 6, see **F3.18** ***et seq.***

Insurance Payments for Terrorist Demands

The TA 2000, s. 17A, provides that an insurer commits an offence if it makes a payment under an insurance contract (or purportedly under it) for money or property which has been or is to be handed over in response to a demand made wholly or partly for the purposes of terrorism, when the insurer knows or has reasonable cause to suspect that the money has been, or is to be, handed over for that purpose. Section 17A(2) provides for individual liability for directors etc. where the offence is committed by a body corporate through that person's consent, connivance or neglect. **B10.138**

Procedure The offence is triable either way. For consent to prosecution, see **B10.34**. See **B10.87** for extended jurisdiction provisions in relation to this offence. **B10.139**

Sentence The maximum penalty for an offence under s. 17A is: on conviction on indictment, imprisonment for a term not exceeding 14 years and/or a fine; on summary conviction, imprisonment for a term not exceeding six months and/or an unlimited fine (TA 2000, s. 22). A court may also make a forfeiture order. **B10.140**

Money Laundering

Terrorism Act 2000, s. 18 **B10.141**

(1) A person commits an offence if he enters into or becomes concerned in an arrangement which facilitates the retention or control by or on behalf of another person of terrorist property—
  (a) by concealment,
  (b) by removal from the jurisdiction,
  (c) by transfer to nominees, or
  (d) in any other way.

Procedure An allegation of an offence contrary to s. 18 is triable either way and when tried on indictment is normally a class 3 offence, but see CrimPD XIII, para. B (see Supplement, **CPD.XIII.B**), for the additional factors that the court considers on allocation. For consent to prosecution, see **B10.34**. **B10.142**

See **B10.87** for extended jurisdiction provisions in relation to this offence.

Sentence The maximum penalty is: on conviction on indictment, imprisonment for a term not exceeding 14 years and/or a fine; on summary conviction, imprisonment for a term not exceeding six months and/or an unlimited fine (TA 2000, s. 22). The definitive guideline, *Terrorism Offences* (see Supplement, **SG32-8**), governing all sentences imposed after 27 April 2018, applies to this offence. A court may also make a forfeiture order (s. 23 and sch. 4). See also **B10.119**. **B10.143**

Elements For terrorism, see **B10.2**. For terrorist property, see **B10.131**. **B10.144**

Specific Defence **B10.145**

Terrorism Act 2000, s. 18

(2) It is a defence for a person charged with an offence under subsection (1) to prove that he did not know and had no reasonable cause to suspect that the arrangement related to terrorist property.

In addition to the defence set out in s. 18(2), the same defences available to a person charged with an offence contrary to s. 15 (see **B10.126**) are available to a person charged with an offence contrary to s. 18.

For the compatibility of the reverse burden with the ECHR, Article 6, see **F3.18** *et seq*.

FAILURE TO COMPLY WITH A DUTY OF DISCLOSURE

General Duty of Disclosure

B10.146 Terrorism Act 2000, s. 19

(1) This section applies where a person—
(a) believes or suspects that another person has committed an offence under any of sections 15 to 18, and
(b) bases his belief or suspicion on information which comes to his attention—
(i) in the course of a trade, profession or business, or
(ii) in the course of his employment (whether or not in the course of a trade, profession or business).

(1A) But this section does not apply if the information came to the person in the course of a business in the regulated sector.

(2) The person commits an offence if he does not disclose to a constable as soon as is reasonably practicable—
(a) his belief or suspicion, and
(b) the information on which it is based.

B10.147 **Procedure** An allegation of an offence contrary to the TA 2000, s. 19, is triable either way and when tried on indictment is normally a class 3 offence, but see CrimPD XIII, para. B (see Supplement, **CPD.XIII.B**), for the additional factors that the court considers on allocation. For consent to prosecution, see **B10.34**.

B10.148 **Sentence** The maximum penalty is: on conviction on indictment, imprisonment for a term not exceeding five years and/or a fine; on summary conviction, imprisonment for a term not exceeding six months and/or an unlimited fine (TA 2000, s. 19(8)).

B10.149 **Elements** For the offences under the TA 2000, ss. 15 to 18, see **B10.122** *et seq*.

By virtue of s. 19(7), a person is treated as having committed one of the offences in ss. 15 to 18 if '(a) he has taken an action or been in possession of a thing, and (b) he would have committed an offence under one of those sections if he had been in the United Kingdom at the time when he took the action or was in possession of the thing'.

The term 'a business in the regulated sector' must be construed in accordance with sch. 3A (s. 19(7A)). 'A constable' includes an officer of the NCA (s. 19(7B)).

B10.150 **Specific Defence**

Terrorism Act 2000, s. 19

(3) It is a defence for a person charged with an offence under subsection (2) to prove that he had a reasonable excuse for not making the disclosure.

(4) Where—
(a) a person is in employment,
(b) his employer has established a procedure for the making of disclosures of the matters specified in subsection (2), and
(c) he is charged with an offence under that subsection,
it is a defence for him to prove that he had disclosed the matters specified in that subsection in accordance with the procedure.

(5) Subsection (2) does not require disclosure by a professional legal adviser of—
(a) information which he obtains in privileged circumstances, or
(b) a belief or suspicion based on information which he obtains in privileged circumstances.

For the compatibility of the reverse burden with the ECHR, Article 6, see **F3.18** *et seq*.

Failure to Disclose: Regulated Sector

Terrorism Act 2000, s. 21A **B10.151**

(1) A person commits an offence if each of the following three conditions is satisfied.
(2) The first condition is that he—
(a) knows or suspects, or
(b) has reasonable grounds for knowing or suspecting,
that another person has committed or attempted to commit an offence under any of sections 15 to 18.
(3) The second condition is that the information or other matter—
(a) on which his knowledge or suspicion is based, or
(b) which gives reasonable grounds for such knowledge or suspicion,
came to him in the course of a business in the regulated sector.
(4) The third condition is that he does not disclose the information or other matter to a constable or nominated officer as soon as is practicable after it comes to him.

Procedure An allegation of an offence contrary to the TA 2000, s. 21A, is triable either way and when tried on indictment is normally a class 3 offence, but see CrimPD XIII, para. B (see Supplement, **CPD.XIII.B**), for the additional factors that the court considers on allocation. For consent to prosecution, see **B10.34**. **B10.152**

Sentence The maximum penalty is: on conviction on indictment, imprisonment for a term not exceeding five years and/or a fine; and, on summary conviction, imprisonment for a term not exceeding six months and/or an unlimited fine (TA 2000, s. 21A(12)). **B10.153**

Elements Section 21A(6) of the TA 2000 provides that, when a court is deciding whether a person has committed an offence under s. 21A, it must decide whether the person followed any relevant guidance issued by a supervisory authority or any other appropriate body approved by the Treasury and published in a manner that the Treasury thought appropriate in order to bring it to the attention of persons likely to be affected by it. **B10.154**

For the purposes of s. 21A(4), s. 21A(7) requires that disclosure is made to a nominated officer if it is made to a person nominated by D's employer to receive such disclosures.

By virtue of s. 21A(11), a person is taken to have committed an offence under s. 21A(2) if '(a) he has taken an action or been in possession of a thing and (b) he would have committed the offence if he had been in the United Kingdom at the time when he took the action or was in possession of the thing'.

The meanings of 'supervisory authority' and 'regulated sector' are to be found in sch. 3A to the 2000 Act (s. 21A(10)).

Specific Defences Section 21A(5) of the TA 2000 provides that a person does not commit an offence under the section if there is a reasonable excuse for not disclosing the information or other matter or the person is a professional legal adviser or relevant professional adviser and the information or matter was obtained in legally privileged circumstances. Section 21A(5A) provides that s. 21A(5) applies to a person if the person is employed by, or is in partnership with, a professional legal adviser or relevant professional adviser to provide the adviser with assistance or support, and the information or other matter comes to the person in connection with the provision of such assistance or support, and, finally, that the information or other matter came to the adviser in privileged circumstances. For legal professional privilege, see **F10.16** *et seq*. **B10.155**

Legally privileged circumstances are defined in s. 21A(8) as being when information is given to a legal adviser or relevant professional adviser by a client (or the client's representative) in connection with legal advice, by a person (or the person's representative) seeking legal advice or by any other person in connection with proceedings which are in progress or contemplated. Information or other material which is provided in furtherance of a criminal purpose is not covered by s. 21A(8) (s. 21A(9)).

By s. 21A(15), a relevant professional adviser means an accountant, auditor or tax adviser who is a member of a professional body which is established for accountants, auditors or tax advisers (as the case may be) and which makes provision for testing the competence of those seeking admission to membership of such a body as a condition for such admission and, finally, imposing and maintaining professional and ethical standards for its members, as well as imposing sanctions for non-compliance with those standards.

Under s. 21B, a disclosure is not to be taken to breach any restriction on the disclosure of information, however imposed, if it fulfils three conditions. The first is that the information or other matter disclosed came to the person in the course of a business in the regulated sector. The second is that the information or other matter causes the person to know or suspect, or gives reasonable grounds for knowing or suspecting, that another person has committed an offence under ss. 15 to 18 of the 2000 Act. Third, the person to whom the information or other matter has been given must inform a constable or nominated officer as soon as practicable after receiving it.

Tipping-off: Regulated Sector

B10.156 Terrorism Act 2000, s. 21D

(1) A person commits an offence if—
  (a) the person discloses any matter within subsection (2);
  (b) the disclosure is likely to prejudice any investigation that might be conducted following the disclosure referred to in that subsection; and
  (c) the information on which the disclosure is based came to the person in the course of a business in the regulated sector.

(2) The matters are that the person or another person has made a disclosure under a provision of this part—
  (a) to a constable,
  (b) in accordance with a procedure established by that person's employer for the making of disclosures under that provision,
  (c) to a nominated officer, or
  (d) to a National Crime Agency officer,

of information that came to that person in the course of a business in the regulated sector.

(3) A person commits an offence if—
  (a) the person discloses that an investigation into allegations that an offence under this Part has been committed is being contemplated or is being carried out;
  (b) the disclosure is likely to prejudice that investigation; and
  (c) the information on which the disclosure is based came to the person in the course of a business in the regulated sector.

B10.157 **Procedure** An allegation of an offence contrary to the TA 2000, s. 21A, is triable either way and when tried on indictment is normally a class 3 offence, but see CrimPD XIII, para. B (see Supplement, **CPD.XIII.B**), for the additional factors that the court considers on allocation. For consent to prosecution, see **B10.34**.

B10.158 **Sentence** The maximum penalty is, on conviction on indictment, imprisonment for a term not exceeding five years and/or a fine; and, on summary conviction, imprisonment for a term not exceeding six months and/or an unlimited fine (TA 2000, s. 21A(12)).

B10.159 **Elements** Section 21H defines terms used in ss. 21D to 21G. The references under ss. 21D to 21G to business in the regulated sector, and to a supervisory authority, are to be construed in accordance with sch. 3A.

B10.160 **Specific Defences** Sections 21E to 21F of the TA 2000 provide for defences relating to s. 21D.

(a) An employee, officer or partner of an undertaking does not commit an offence under s. 21D if the disclosure is to an employee, officer or partner of the same undertaking (s. 21E(1)).
(b) A person does not commit an offence under s. 21D in respect of a disclosure by a credit institution or a financial institution if the disclosure is to a credit institution or a financial institution which is situated in an EEA State or in a country or territory imposing

equivalent money laundering requirements and both the institution making the disclosure and the institution to whom it is made belong to the same group (s. 21E(2)).

(c) A professional legal adviser or a relevant professional adviser does not commit an offence under s. 21D if the disclosure is to a professional legal adviser or a relevant professional adviser, both the person making the disclosure and the person to whom it is made carry on business in an EEA State or in a country or territory imposing equivalent money laundering requirements, and those persons perform their professional activities within different undertakings that share common ownership, management or control (s. 21E(4)).

(d) Section 21F applies to a disclosure by one credit institution, financial institution, professional legal adviser or relevant professional adviser to another institution or adviser having that same status. No offence is committed where such a disclosure relates to a client or former client of the institution or adviser making the disclosure and the institution or adviser to whom it is made, a transaction involving them both, or the provision of a service involving them both, provided that the disclosure is to prevent an offence under Part III, and both institutions or advisers are situated in an EEA State or in a territory imposing equivalent money laundering requirements and equivalent duties of professional confidentiality with regard to the protection of personal data.

(e) Two further defences apply under s. 21G.

Terrorism Act 2000, s. 21G **B10.161**

(1) A person does not commit an offence under section 21D if the disclosure is—
  (a) to the authority that is the supervisory authority for that person by virtue of the Money Laundering Regulations 2007 [see **B21.35**]; or
  (b) for the purpose of—
    (i) the detection, investigation or prosecution of a criminal offence (whether in the United Kingdom or elsewhere),
    (ii) an investigation under the Proceeds of Crime Act 2002, or
    (iii) the enforcement of any order of a court under that Act.

(2) A professional legal adviser or a relevant professional adviser does not commit an offence under section 21D if the disclosure—
  (a) is to the adviser's client, and
  (b) is made for the purpose of dissuading the client from engaging in conduct amounting to an offence.

(3) A person does not commit an offence under section 21D(1) if the person does not know or suspect that the disclosure is likely to have the effect mentioned in section 21D(1)(b).

(4) A person does not commit an offence under section 21D(3) if the person does not know or suspect that the disclosure is likely to have the effect mentioned in section 21D(3)(b).

Section 21H defines terms used in ss. 21D to 21G. In those sections 'credit institution' has the same meaning as in sch. 3A and 'financial institution' means an undertaking that carries on a business in the regulated sector by virtue of any of para. 1(1)(b) to (i) thereof. References in ss. 21D to 21G to a disclosure by or to a credit institution or a financial institution include disclosure by or to an employee, officer or partner of the institution acting on its behalf. For the purposes of those sections, a country or territory imposes 'equivalent money laundering requirements' if it imposes requirements equivalent to those laid down in Directive 2005/60/EC on the prevention of the use of the financial system for the purpose of money laundering and terrorist financing. 'Relevant professional adviser' has the same meaning as in s. 21A (see **B10.155**).

FINANCIAL MEASURES UNDER THE ANTI-TERRORISM, CRIME AND SECURITY ACT 2001

Forfeiture of Cash

Powers to seize and forfeit cash which is intended to be used for terrorist purposes, represents **B10.162**
the resources of a proscribed organisation or represents property obtained through terrorist

activities are contained in sch. 1 to the A-TCSA 2001, as amended by the C-TA 2008, ss. 83 and 84. The powers are exercisable through civil proceedings in the magistrates' courts and, under s. 1(2), apply whether or not criminal proceedings have been instituted (A-TCSA 2001, s. 1(1)).

Freezing Orders

B10.163 Detailed provisions in relation to the making of freezing orders are set out in the A-TCSA 2001, ss. 4 to 8 and sch. 3. The procedure for making an order is set out in ss. 10 to 14.

Under s. 4, the Treasury may make such a freezing order, prohibiting any person from making funds available to a specified person or persons, if the Treasury reasonably believes:

(a) either (i) action to the detriment of the UK's economy (or part of it) has been or is likely to be taken by a person or persons, or (ii) action constituting a threat to the life or property of one or more nationals of the UK or residents of the UK has been or is likely to be taken by a person or persons; and
(b) if one person is believed to have taken or be likely to take the action, that the person is (i) the government of a country or territory outside the UK, or (ii) a resident of a country or territory outside the UK or, where two or more persons are believed to be involved, each of them falls within category (i) or (ii).

'National' and 'resident' are defined in s. 9.

The PCA 2017, s. 45, amends sch. 3 by increasing the maximum penalty in respect of failing to comply with a prohibition imposed by a freezing order under the A-TCSA 2001 to seven years' imprisonment on conviction on indictment.

By virtue of s. 62 of the C-TA 2008, any challenge to such a freezing order must be made by way of judicial review (see **B10.165**).

Disclosure by Public Authorities

B10.164 **Anti-terrorism, Crime and Security Act 2001, s. 17**

(1) This section applies to the provisions listed in Schedule 4, so far as they authorise the disclosure of information.
(2) Each of the provisions to which this section applies shall have effect, in relation to the disclosure of information by or on behalf of a public authority, as if the purposes for which the disclosure of information is authorised by that provision included each of the following—
   (a) the purposes of any criminal investigation whatever which is being or may be carried out, whether in the United Kingdom or elsewhere;
   (b) the purposes of any criminal proceedings whatever which have been or may be initiated, whether in the United Kingdom or elsewhere;
   (c) the purposes of the initiation or bringing to an end of any such investigation or proceedings;
   (d) the purpose of facilitating a determination of whether any such investigation or proceedings should be initiated or brought to an end.
(3) and (4) [Order-making powers and procedure.]
(5) No disclosure of information shall be made by virtue of this section unless the public authority by which the disclosure is made is satisfied that the making of the disclosure is proportionate to what is sought to be achieved by it.
(6) Nothing in this section shall be taken to prejudice any power to disclose information which exists apart from this section.
(7) The information that may be disclosed by virtue of this section includes information obtained before the commencement of this section.

The duties of disclosure of information by public bodies to investigators were significantly widened by s. 17. The provisions to which the extended disclosure duties relate are set out in sch. 4. Under s. 17(5), the public body must be satisfied that the disclosure is proportionate to the objectives of the request. Section 18 places limitations on disclosure of information for the purposes of proceedings overseas.

FINANCIAL POWERS UNDER THE COUNTER-TERRORISM ACT 2008

There is further provision for the use of financial powers against terrorism in the C-TA 2008. Section 62 and sch. 7 (as amended by the Terrorism Asset Freezing Act 2010 — see **B10.166**) confer wide powers on the Treasury to act against terrorist financing. The powers enable the Treasury to direct financial and credit institutions to take action in respect of business with persons in certain countries where there is concern about money laundering, terrorist financing or proliferation. Schedule 7 also provides for a supervisory regime, and for the imposition of civil and criminal penalties. Upon indictment, the maximum penalty for the breach of a direction from the Treasury is seven years' imprisonment. Section 63 creates a structure for the challenge of any decision made by the Treasury under sch. 7, or freezing orders under Part 2 of the A-TCSA 2001. Any person affected by any such decision may apply to the High Court to set it aside. The application will be determined by the court in accordance with the principles of judicial review and the court may give such relief as may be given in judicial proceedings. For an example of an unsuccessful judicial review pursuant to the C-TA 2008, s. 63, related to a freezing order under the Al-Qa'ida and Taliban (United Nations Measures Order) 2006 (SI 2006 No. 2952), see *R (K) v HM Treasury* [2009] EWHC 1643 (Admin). See also *Bank Mellat v HM Treasury* [2010] EWHC 1332 (QB). **B10.165**

Part 2 of the Terrorist Asset-Freezing Act 2010 amends sch. 7. It clarifies the persons to whom a direction may be given, broadens the definition of persons in relation to whom restrictions may be applied, and prohibits the circumvention of the requirements of a direction. Schedule 7 is also amended so as to remove some enforcement functions of the Department of Enterprise, Trade and Investment in Northern Ireland.

The PCA 2017, s. 145, further amends sch. 7 by increasing the maximum penalty in respect of failing to comply with a requirement imposed by a direction under the C-TA 2008 to seven years' imprisonment on conviction on indictment.

TERRORIST ASSET-FREEZING ACT 2010

The Terrorist Asset-Freezing Act 2010 gives effect in the UK to resolutions of the UN Security Council. Resolution 1373 (2001) was adopted by the Security Council on 28 September 2001 and relates to terrorism. Resolution 1452 (2002) was adopted on 20 December 2002 and relates to humanitarian exemptions. The Act also provides for enforcement of Regulation (EC) 2580/2001 on specific measures directed at certain persons and entities with a view to combating terrorism ([2001] OJ L344/70). **B10.166**

The Terrorist Asset-Freezing Act 2010 makes provision for imposing financial restrictions on persons believed or suspected to be involved in, or to have previously been involved in, terrorism. The Act allows for actions to be taken in respect of 'designated persons', as defined in s. 1. Under s. 2, two conditions must be fulfilled before the Treasury may make a final designation of a person. First, the Treasury must reasonably believe that the person is or has been involved in terrorist activity, that the person is owned or controlled directly or indirectly by such a person or that the person is acting on behalf of or at the direction of such a person. Secondly, the Treasury must consider it necessary that financial restrictions are placed on the person for purposes connected with protecting members of the public from terrorism. By virtue of s. 6, the Treasury may make an 'interim designation' of a person. Such a designation is permissible when the Treasury merely reasonably suspects that the conditions which justify a final designation are **B10.167** fulfilled. An interim designation expires after 30 days but may be replaced by a final designation during that period (s. 8). The Treasury may not make more than one interim designation against a person based on the same set of facts. A final designation has a maximum duration of one year but may be renewed. A renewed final designation expires after a further year but may be renewed again (s. 4). Under s. 26, any person who is designated may appeal against the decision to the High Court. Moreover, any decisions in relation to the making of the order are susceptible to judicial review (s. 27).

B10.168 Sections 11 to 15 of the Act prohibit particular actions in respect of designated persons. A person must not deal with the funds or economic resources of a designated person (s. 11), make funds or financial services available to a designated person (s. 12), make funds or financial services available for the benefit of a designated person (s. 13), make economic resources available to a designated person (s. 14), nor make economic resources available for the benefit of a designated person (s. 15). The relevant terms are defined in ss. 39 to 42. Any person who contravenes any of the prohibitions commits an offence. Section 16 provides for exceptions for certain institutions required to pay interest credits to frozen accounts and s. 17 allows the granting of licences by the Treasury to deal with frozen accounts. Section 18 makes it an offence intentionally to participate in activities knowing that the object of them is to circumvent any of the prohibitions in ss. 11 to 15 or to enable or facilitate the circumvention of any such prohibition. By virtue of s. 32, any person who commits an offence under ss. 11 to 15 or 18 is liable upon conviction on indictment to up to seven years' imprisonment and/or a fine; on summary conviction, the maximum penalty is six months' imprisonment and/or an unlimited fine.

Under s. 10, the Treasury may provide that certain information in connection with the making of a designation be kept confidential. Any person who breaches that confidentiality commits an offence. Section 17 makes it an offence to provide false details when applying for a licence. On conviction on indictment, the maximum penalty for either offence is two years' imprisonment and/or a fine; on summary conviction, the maximum penalty is six months' imprisonment and/or an unlimited fine (s. 32).

Under s. 19, institutions have an obligation to report to the Treasury any reasonable suspicion that they are dealing with a designated person. Section 22 creates an offence of failing to comply with a request for information from the Treasury. The offences under ss. 19 and 22 are summary only and are punishable by up to six months' imprisonment and/or an unlimited fine.

The provisions of the Act have extra-territorial effect (s. 33). By virtue of s. 37, the consent of the A-G must be secured for any prosecution under the Act.

BREACH OF TERRORISM PREVENTION AND INVESTIGATION MEASURES ('TPIMS')

B10.169 TPIMs were introduced by the Terrorism Prevention and Investigation Measures Act 2011 which came into force on 15 December 2011. They replaced the system of control orders created under the Prevention of Terrorism Act 2005. The Terrorism Prevention and Investigation Measures Act 2011 (Continuation) Order 2016 (SI 2016 No. 1166) continues the powers conferred by the Act for a further five years until 13 December 2021. It is an offence under s. 23 of the 2011 Act to breach any measure specified in the TPIM without reasonable excuse. The offence is triable either way. Upon summary conviction, the offence is punishable with up to six months' imprisonment and/or a fine. On conviction on indictment, the offence is punishable with up to five years' imprisonment and/or a fine.

Sections 16 to 20 of the C-TSA 2015, in force from 12 February 2015, amended the TPIM provisions, enabling 'measures' (conditions) to be imposed to regulate a subject's overnight place of residence, restrict a subject's travel outside the area of residence, prohibit a subject having firearms, offensive weapons or explosives, and to require a subject to meet with officials as part of the management of the measures. This enables some of the measures previously contained in the control order provisions to be imposed on an individual subject to an order.

FURTHER OFFENCES UNDER THE TERRORISM ACT 2006

The TA 2006 provides for offences relating to radioactive material and nuclear facilities. The offences concern 'Making and Possession of Radioactive Materials' (s. 9), 'Misuse of Radioactive Devices or Material and Misuse and Damage of Nuclear Facilities' (s. 10) and 'Terrorist Threats Relating to Radioactive Devices or Materials and Nuclear Facilities' (s. 11). Each offence is triable only on indictment. The maximum penalty for each of the offences is life imprisonment and a forfeiture order may also be made in accordance with s. 23A (see **B10.119**). **B10.170**

FURTHER OFFENCES UNDER THE ANTI-TERRORISM, CRIME AND SECURITY ACT 2001

The A-TCSA 2001 creates a number of offences to deal with weapons of mass destruction. Section 67 makes it an offence to fail to comply with any duty or direction in relation to the security of pathogens and toxins without reasonable excuse. In addition it is an offence for a person giving information under the Act knowingly or recklessly to make a statement which is false or misleading in any material particular. The offence is triable either way. On indictment it is punishable with up to five years' imprisonment and/or a fine; on summary conviction, the maximum penalty is six months' imprisonment and/or an unlimited fine. **B10.171**

Section 47 creates a number of offences relating to the use of nuclear weapons. The offences are triable on indictment only and are punishable with life imprisonment.

Section 79 makes it an offence to disclose information which might prejudice the safety of any nuclear facility or nuclear material if the disclosure is made either intending or being reckless as to whether such prejudice occurs. The offence is triable either way and on indictment is punishable with up to seven years' imprisonment and/or a fine; on summary conviction, the maximum penalty is six months' imprisonment and/or an unlimited fine.

Offences relating to noxious substances which have been the subject of prosecutions since coming into force are contained in ss. 113 and 114 of the Act. **B10.172**

Use or Threat of Use of Noxious Substances or Things to Cause Harm and Intimidate

Anti-terrorism, Crime and Security Act 2001, s. 113 **B10.173**

(1) A person who takes any action which—
 (a) involves the use of a noxious substance or other noxious thing;
 (b) has or is likely to have an effect falling within subsection (2); and
 (c) is designed to influence the government or an international governmental organisation or to intimidate the public or a section of the public,

is guilty of an offence.

(2) *Action* has an effect falling within this subsection if it—
 (a) causes serious violence against a person anywhere in the world;
 (b) causes serious damages to real or personal property anywhere in the world;
 (c) endangers human life or creates a serious risk to the health or safety of the public or a section of the public; or
 (d) induces in members of the public the fear that the action is likely to endanger their lives or create a serious risk to their health or safety;

but any effect on the person taking the action is to be disregarded.

(3) A person who—
(a) makes a threat that he or another will take any action which constitutes an offence under subsection (1); and
(b) intends thereby to induce in a person anywhere in the world the fear that the threat is likely to be carried out,

is guilty of an offence.

B10.174 **Procedure** An allegation of an offence contrary to the A-TCSA 2001, s. 113, is triable either way (s. 113(4)); when tried on indictment it is normally a class 3 offence, but see CrimPD XIII, para. B (see Supplement, **CPD.XIII.B**), for the additional factors that the court considers on allocation.

Conduct which occurs outside the UK will be covered by s. 113 provided two conditions are met (s. 113A). The first is that the conduct is done for the purpose of advancing a political, religious, ideological or racial cause. The second is that the conduct is (a) by a UK national or a UK resident, (b) by any person if done to, or in relation to, a UK national, a UK resident or a protected person, or (c) by any person if done in the circumstances which fall within the TA 2000, s. 63D(1)(b) and (c) or (3)(b) and (c) (s. 113A(2) and (3)). As to the TA 2000, s. 63D, see **B10.87**. 'United Kingdom national', 'United Kingdom resident', and 'protected person' have the same meaning as in the TA 2000, ss. 63C and 63D (s. 113A(4)). By virtue of s. 113A(5), it is immaterial whether a person knows that another is a UK national, UK resident or a protected person.

Section 113B(1) provides that the consent of the A-G is necessary for the institution of proceedings under s. 113, and s. 113B(2) provides for such proceedings to be taken, and the offence for incidental purposes to be treated as having been committed, in any part of the UK.

B10.175 **Sentence** The maximum penalty is, on indictment, 14 years' imprisonment and/or a fine; on summary conviction, six months' imprisonment and/or an unlimited fine (A-TCSA 2001, s. 113(4)).

B10.176 **Elements** For the meaning of 'noxious thing' in the OAPA 1861, see **B2.91**.

Under the A-TCSA 2001, s. 113(5), 'government' means the government of the UK or a part of the UK or of a country other than the UK. Under the same section, 'public' includes the public of a country other than the UK.

'Substance' includes any biological agent and any other natural or artificial substance (whatever its form, origin or method of production) (s. 115(1)).

For a person to be guilty of an offence under s. 113(3), 'it is not necessary for him to have any particular person in mind as the person in whom he intends to induce the belief in question' (s. 115(2)).

Hoaxes Involving Noxious Substances or Things

B10.177 **Anti-terrorism, Crime and Security Act 2001, s. 114**

(1) A person is guilty of an offence if he—
(a) places any substance or other thing in any place; or
(b) sends any substance or other thing from one place to another (by post, rail or any other means whatever);

with the intention of inducing in a person anywhere in the world a belief that it is likely to be (or contain) a noxious substance or other noxious thing and thereby endanger human life or create a serious risk to human health.

(2) A person is guilty of an offence if he communicates any information which he knows or believes to be false with the intention of inducing in a person anywhere in the world a belief that a noxious substance or other noxious thing is likely to be present (whether at the time the information is communicated or later) in any place and thereby endanger human life or create a serious risk to human health.

Procedure The offence is triable either way (A-TCSA 2001, s. 114(3)); when tried on indictment it is normally a class 3 offence, but see CrimPD XIII, para. B (see Supplement, **CPD.XIII.B**), for the additional factors that the court considers on allocation. **B10.178**

Sentence The maximum penalty is, on indictment, seven years' imprisonment and/or a fine; on summary conviction, six months' imprisonment and/or an unlimited fine (A-TCSA 2001, s. 114(3)). **B10.179**

Elements See **B10.176** for definitions of the elements of the offence. **B10.180**

For a person to be guilty of an offence under s. 114 'it is not necessary for him to have any particular person in mind as the person in whom he intends to induce the belief in question' (s. 115(2)).

OTHER OFFENCES RELATING TO CHEMICAL, BIOLOGICAL AND NUCLEAR WEAPONS

In addition to those offences provided for under the TA 2000, the A-TCSA 2001 and the TA 2006, there are legislative provisions relating to chemical, biological and nuclear weapons in the Biological Weapons Act 1974, the Chemical Weapons Act 1996 and the Nuclear Material (Offences) Act 1983. It is not necessary to prove that the actions were for terrorist purposes. Some actions in relation to biological or chemical material outside the UK may result in prosecution in any UK jurisdiction, but only if the suspect is a 'United Kingdom person', defined in the same way as in the TA 2000, s. 63A (see **B10.87**). But actions outside the UK by a person of any nationality in relation to, or by means of using nuclear material, can be tried in the UK if those actions would have made the person guilty of murder, manslaughter or numerous other offences in the UK. **B10.181**

Developing, Producing etc. Biological Agents, Toxins and Weapons

Biological Weapons Act 1974, s. 1 **B10.182**

(1) No person shall develop, produce, stockpile, acquire or retain—
   (a) any biological agent or toxin of a type and in quantity that has no justification for prophylactic, protective or other peaceful purposes; or
   (b) any weapon, equipment or means of delivery designed to use biological agents or toxins for hostile purposes or in armed conflict.

(1A) A person shall not—
   (a) transfer any biological agent or toxin to another person or enter into an agreement to do so, or
   (b) make arrangements under which another person transfers any biological agent or toxin or enters into an agreement with a third party to do so,

   if the biological agent is likely to be kept or used (whether by the transferee or any other person) otherwise than for prophylactic, protective or other peaceful purposes and he knows or has reason to believe that that is the case.

Procedure An allegation of an offence contrary to the Biological Weapons Act 1974, s. 1, is triable on indictment only (s. 1(3)). As to the classification of the offence for the purpose of listing, see CrimPD XIII, para. B (see Supplement, **CPD.XIII.B**). **B10.183**

If the requirements of s. 1B are met, then proceedings for the offence may be instituted by the DPP or by order of the Commissioners of Revenue and Customs.

Sentence The maximum penalty is imprisonment for life (Biological Weapons Act 1974, s. 1(3)). **B10.184**

Elements Under the Biological Weapons Act 1974, s. 1(2), 'biological agent' means any microbial or other biological agent and 'toxin' means any toxin, whatever its origin or method of production. **B10.185**

Use etc. of Chemical Weapons

B10.186 **Chemical Weapons Act 1996, s. 2**

(1) No person shall—
 (a) use a chemical weapon;
 (b) develop or produce a chemical weapon;
 (c) have a chemical weapon in his possession;
 (d) participate in the transfer of a chemical weapon;
 (e) engage in military preparations, or in preparations of a military nature, intending to use a chemical weapon

...

(8) A person contravening this section is guilty of an offence....

B10.187 **Procedure** An allegation of an offence contrary to the Chemical Weapons Act 1996, s. 2, is triable on indictment only (s. 2(8)). As to the classification of the offence for the purpose of listing, see CrimPD XIII, para. B (see Supplement, **CPD.XIII.B**). The consent of the A-G is required for the institution of proceedings under this section (s. 31(1)).

B10.188 **Sentence** The maximum penalty is imprisonment for life (Chemical Weapons Act 1996, s. 2(8)). As to the power of forfeiture, see s. 30.

B10.189 **Elements**

Chemical Weapons Act 1996, ss. 1 and 10

1.—(1) Chemical weapons are—
 (a) toxic chemicals and their precursors;
 (b) munitions and other devices designed to cause death or harm through the toxic properties of toxic chemicals released by them;
 (c) equipment designed for use in connection with munitions and devices falling with in paragraph (b).

(2) Subsection (1) is subject to sections 2(2) and (3), 10(1) and 11(2) (by virtue of which an object is not a chemical weapon if the use or intended use is only for permitted purposes).

(3) Permitted purposes are—
 (a) peaceful purposes;
 (b) purposes related to protection against toxic chemicals;
 (c) legitimate military purposes;
 (d) purposes of enforcing the law.

(4) Legitimate military purposes are all military purposes except those which depend on the use of the toxic properties of chemicals as a method of warfare in circumstances where the main object is to cause death, permanent harm or temporary incapacity to humans or animals.

(5) A toxic chemical is a chemical which through its chemical action on life processes can cause death, permanent harm or temporary incapacity to humans or animals; and the origin, method of production and place of production are immaterial.

(6) A precursor is a chemical reactant which takes part at any stage in the production (by whatever method) of a toxic chemical.

(7) References to an object include references to a substance.

10.—(1) If an object is in the possession of a person who intends that it will be used only for permitted purposes, it is not a chemical weapon for the purposes of sections 4(1) and (3) and 5(1) and (2); and in deciding whether permitted purposes are intended the types and quantities of objects shall be taken into account.

It should be noted that 's. 11(2)', referred to in s. 1(2) above, does not apply to this offence.

The specific provisions are as follows:

Chemical Weapons Act 1996, s. 2

(2) For the purposes of subsection (1)(a) an object is not a chemical weapon if the person uses the object only for permitted purposes; and in deciding whether permitted purposes are intended the types and quantities of objects shall be taken into account.

(3) For the purposes of subsection (1)(b), (c), (d) or (e) an object is not a chemical weapon if the person does the act there mentioned with the intention that the object will be used only for permitted purposes; and in deciding whether permitted purposes are intended the types and quantities of objects shall be taken into account.

Specific Defence Under the Chemical Weapons Act 1996, s. 2(6), it is a defence for D to prove '(a) that he neither knew nor suspected nor had reason to suspect that the object was a chemical weapon, or (b) that he knew or suspected it to be a chemical weapon and as soon as reasonably practicable after he first so knew or suspected he took all reasonable steps to inform the Secretary of State or a constable of his knowledge or suspicion'. By virtue of s. 2(7), the s. 2(6) defence does not prejudice any other defence which it is open to a person charged with this offence to raise. **B10.190**

Restrictive and Enforcement Powers under the Chemical Weapons Act 1996

Issuing of Notices in Relation to Suspicious Objects By virtue of s. 4 of the Chemical Weapons Act 1996, if the Secretary of State has grounds to suspect that an object is a chemical weapon and someone appears to be in possession of it or has a sufficient interest in it, a notice may be issued to that person which will state, *inter alia*, that destruction of the object is being considered and that the object must not be relinquished before a specified date. **B10.191**

Powers of Entry, Search and Seizure Section 5 of the Chemical Weapons Act 1996 gives powers of entry, search and seizure in relation to suspected involvement with chemical weapons. If the Secretary of State has reasonable cause to believe that, on premises to which the public have access or where the occupier consents to access, an object is on such premises and it is a chemical weapon, the Secretary of State may authorise entry and search of the premises (s. 5(1)). A magistrate may issue a warrant to enter premises of whatever nature if there is reasonable cause to believe that an object, which is a chemical weapon, is on the premises (s. 5(2)). The person issued with the warrant may take such people and equipment as are necessary, and objects found on the relevant premises may be seized and removed or immobilised and made safe (s. 5(3) to (7)). **B10.192**

Power to Destroy Removed Objects Section 6 of the Chemical Weapons Act 1996 provides for the destruction of objects removed under the power provided by virtue of s. 5. **B10.193**

Chemical Weapons Premises

Chemical Weapons Act 1996, s. 11 **B10.194**

(1) No person shall—
  (a) construct premises he intends to be used to produce chemical weapons;
  (b) alter premises in circumstances where he intends that they will be used to produce chemical weapons;
  (c) instal or construct equipment he intends to be used to produce chemical weapons;
  (d) alter equipment in circumstances where he intends that it will be used to produce chemical weapons;
  (e) permit the construction on land he occupies of premises he intends to be used to produce chemical weapons;
  (f) permit premises on land he occupies to be altered in circumstances where he intends that they will be used to produce chemical weapons;
  (g) permit the installation or construction on land he occupies of equipment he intends to be used to produce chemical weapons;
  (h) permit equipment on land he occupies to be altered in circumstances where he intends that it will be used to produce chemical weapons.

(2) For the purposes of subsection (1) an object is not a chemical weapon if the person intends that the object will be used only for permitted purposes; and in deciding whether permitted purposes are intended the types and quantities of objects shall be taken into account.

Procedure An allegation of an offence contrary to the Chemical Weapons Act 1996, s. 11, is triable on indictment only (s. 11(3)). It does not have an extended jurisdiction provision. **B10.195**

B10.196 **Sentence** The maximum sentence is one of imprisonment for life.

Chemicals Used for Permitted Purposes

B10.197 **Chemical Weapons Act 1996, s. 19**

(1) Subject to section 20 (which relates to licences) no person shall—
(a) use a Schedule 1 toxic chemical or precursor for a permitted purpose, or
(b) produce or have in his possession a Schedule 1 toxic chemical or precursor with the intention that it will be used for a permitted purpose.
(2) A Schedule 1 toxic chemical or precursor is a toxic chemical or precursor listed in Schedule 1 to the annex on chemicals to the Convention; and for ease of reference that Schedule is set out in the Schedule to this Act.
(3) A person contravening this section is guilty of an offence....

B10.198 **Procedure** An allegation of an offence contrary to the Chemical Weapons Act 1996, s. 19, is triable either way (s. 19(3)); when tried on indictment it is normally a class 3 offence, but see CrimPD XIII, para. B (see Supplement, **CPD.XIII.B**), for the additional factors that the court considers on allocation.

The consent of the Secretary of State is necessary for the institution of proceedings under the section (s. 31(2)). It does not have an extended jurisdiction provision.

B10.199 **Sentence** The maximum penalty, whether on summary conviction or indictment, is a fine (Chemical Weapons Act 1996, s. 19(3)).

Holding or Dealing with Nuclear Material

B10.200 **Nuclear Material (Offences) Act 1983, ss. 1, 1B and 1C**

1.—(1) If a person, whatever his nationality, does outside the United Kingdom, in relation to or by means of nuclear material, any act which, had he done it in any part of the United Kingdom, would have made him guilty of—
(a) the offence of murder, manslaughter, culpable homicide, assault to injury, malicious mischief or causing injury, or endangering the life of the lieges, by reckless conduct, or
(b) an offence under section 18 or 20 of the Offences against the Person Act 1861 or section 1 of the Criminal Damage Act 1971, or Article 3 of the Criminal Damage (Northern Ireland) Order 1977, or section 52 of the Criminal Law (Consolidation) (Scotland) Act 1995, or
(c) the offence of theft, embezzlement, robbery, assault with intent to rob, burglary or aggravated burglary, or
(d) the offence of fraud or extortion or an offence under section 21 of the Theft Act 1968 or section 20 of the Theft Act (Northern Ireland) 1969,

he shall in any part of the United Kingdom be guilty of such of the offences mentioned in paragraphs (a) to (d) above as are offences of which the act would have made him guilty had he done it in that part of the United Kingdom.

(1A) If—
(a) a person, whatever his nationality, does outside the United Kingdom an act directed at a nuclear facility, or which interferes with the operation of such a facility,
(b) the act causes death, injury or damage resulting from the emission of ionising radiation or the release of radioactive material, and
(c) had he done that act in any part of the United Kingdom, it would have made him guilty of an offence mentioned in subsection (1)(a) or (b) above,

the person shall in any part of the United Kingdom be guilty of such of the offences mentioned in subsection (1)(a) and (b) as are offences of which the act would have made him guilty had he done it in that part of the United Kingdom.

1B.—(1) If a person, whatever his nationality, in the United Kingdom or elsewhere contravenes *subsection (2) or (3) he is guilty of an offence.*
(2) A person contravenes this subsection if without lawful authority—
(a) he receives, holds or deals with nuclear material, and
(b) he does so either—

(i) intending to cause, or for the purpose of enabling another to cause, damage to the environment by means of that material, or
(ii) being reckless as to whether, as a result of his so receiving, holding or dealing with that material, damage would be caused to the environment by means of that material.

(3) A person contravenes this subsection if without lawful authority—
(a) he does an act directed at a nuclear facility, or which interferes with the operation of such a facility, and
(b) he does so either—
(i) intending to cause, or for the purpose of enabling another to cause, damage to the environment by means of the emission of ionising radiation or the release of radioactive material, or
(ii) being reckless as to whether, as a result of his act, damage would be caused to the environment by means of such an emission or release.

1C.—(1) If a person, whatever his nationality, outside the United Kingdom contravenes subsection (2) below he shall be guilty of an offence.

(2) A person contravenes this subsection if he is knowingly concerned in—
(a) the unlawful export or shipment as stores of nuclear material from one country to another, or
(b) the unlawful import of nuclear material into one country from another.

(3) For the purposes of subsection (2)—
(a) the export or shipment as stores of nuclear material from a country, or
(b) the import of nuclear material into a country,
is unlawful if it is contrary to any prohibition or restriction on the export, shipment as stores or import (as the case may be) of nuclear material having effect under or by virtue of the law of that country.

Procedure An allegation of an offence contrary to the Nuclear Material (Offences) Act 1983, s. 1, is triable on indictment only. As to the classification of the offence for the purpose of listing, see CrimPD XIII, para. B (see Supplement, **CPD.XIII.B**). Section 1D makes provision for the conduct of investigations relating to an offence under s. 1C. Proceedings for an offence which (disregarding the Internationally Protected Persons Act 1978, the Suppression of Terrorism Act 1978, the United Nations Personnel Act 1997 and the TA 2000) would not be an offence but for the Nuclear Materials (Offences) Act 1983 must have the consent of the A-G. **B10.201**

Sentence By virtue of s. 1A, life imprisonment is the maximum penalty for an offence under s. 1(1)(a) or (b) when the offence is committed by means of, or in relation to nuclear material and the act was directed at a nuclear facility and caused death, injury or damage as a result of the emission of nuclear material. Similarly, an offence under s. 1(1)(c) or (d) committed by means of, or in relation to, nuclear material is punishable by life imprisonment as is an offence under s. 1B. For an offence under s. 1C, the maximum penalty is 14 years' imprisonment. **B10.202**

Elements By virtue of the Nuclear Material (Offences) Act 1983, s. 6(1) and (5), references to 'nuclear material' relate to 'nuclear material used for peaceful purposes' within the meaning of the Convention on the Physical Protection of Nuclear Material and Nuclear Facilities. Under s. 6(2), any statement by the Secretary of State to the effect that the nuclear material either was or was not for peaceful purposes will be conclusive as to the issue. For the implications of such a provision reversing the burden of proof in the light of the ECHR, Article 6, see **F3.18** ***et seq***. Similarly for the purposes of s. 1C any statement by a foreign government that a shipment of material was contrary to a prohibition shall be conclusive unless the contrary is proved (s. 1C(4) and (5)). **B10.203**

Nuclear Material: Offences Involving Preparatory Acts and Threats

Nuclear Material (Offences) Act 1983, ss. 2 and 2A **B10.204**

2.—(1) If a person, whatever his nationality, in the United Kingdom or elsewhere contravenes subsection (2), (3), (4) or (7) he shall be guilty of an offence.

(2) A person contravenes this subsection if without lawful authority—
(a) he receives, holds or deals with nuclear material, and

(b) he does so either—
(i) intending to cause, or for the purpose of enabling another to cause, relevant injury or damage by means of that material, or
(ii) being reckless as to whether, as a result of his so receiving, holding or dealing with that material, relevant injury or damage would be caused by means of that material.

(3) A person contravenes this subsection if without lawful authority—
(a) he does an act directed at a nuclear facility, or which interferes with the operation of such a facility, and
(b) he does so either—
(i) intending to cause, or for the purpose of enabling another to cause, relevant injury or damage by means of the emission of ionising radiation or the release of radioactive material, or
(ii) being reckless as to whether, as a result of his act, relevant injury or damage would be caused by means of such an emission or release.

(4) A person contravenes this subsection if he—
(a) makes a threat of a kind falling within subsection (5), and
(b) intends that the person to whom the threat is made shall fear that it will be carried out.

(5) A threat falls within this subsection if it is a threat that the person making it or any other person will cause any of the consequences set out in subsection (6) either—
(a) by means of nuclear material, or
(b) by means of the emission of ionising radiation or the release of radioactive material resulting from an act which is directed at a nuclear facility, or which interferes with the operation of such a facility.

(6) The consequences mentioned in subsection (5) are—
(a) relevant injury or damage, or
(b) damage to the environment.

(7) A person contravenes this subsection if, in order to compel a State, international organisation or person to do, or abstain from doing, any act, he threatens that he or any other person will obtain nuclear material by an act which, whether by virtue of section 1(1) above or otherwise, is an offence mentioned in section 1(1)(c) above.

(8) A person guilty of an offence under this section shall be liable, on conviction on indictment, to imprisonment for life.

(9) In this section references to relevant injury or damage are references to death or to injury or damage of a type which constitutes an element of any offence mentioned in section 1(1)(a) or (b) above.

2A.—(1) If a person, whatever his nationality—
(a) does an act outside the United Kingdom, and
(b) his act, if done in any part of the United Kingdom, would constitute an offence falling within subsection (2),

he shall be guilty in that part of the United Kingdom of the offence.

(2) The offences are—
(a) attempting to commit a nuclear offence;
(b) conspiring to commit a nuclear offence;
(c) inciting the commission of a nuclear offence;
(d) aiding, abetting, counselling or procuring the commission of a nuclear offence.

B10.205 **Procedure** Proceedings for an offence contrary to s. 2 of the Nuclear Material (Offences) Act 1983 are triable on indictment only. The same conditions apply for the requirement of the consent of the A-G as pertain to s. 1 (see **B10.201**).

B10.206 **Sentence** The maximum sentence for an offence under s. 2 is life imprisonment (s. 2(8)).

B10.207 **Elements** Nuclear material has the same meaning as in s.1 (see **B10.203**). The term 'nuclear offence' is defined in s. 2A(3) and (4). In essence it is one of the offences listed in s. 1(1)(a) to (d) (see **B10.200**) or blackmail committed in a nuclear context, an offence contrary to s. 1B, *1C* or *2(1)* to *(3)*, or one of a number of offences under the Customs and Excise Management Act 1979.

OFFENCES RELATING TO SHIPS AND AIRCRAFT

Offences in or against ships and aircraft are often committed for terrorist purposes and can normally be prosecuted under the terrorism legislation, or they may be dealt with at sentencing as offences committed in a terrorist context (see **B10.116**). But actions in or against ships and aircraft and/or their occupants also often occur for non-terrorist reasons. The following paragraphs deal with actions against ships and aircraft; actions inside ships and aircraft by crew (e.g. mutiny) or passengers (e.g., violence or drunkenness); and actions relating to operation/navigation by crew. As with terrorism offences, many offences committed on or towards ships or aircraft have extended jurisdiction provisions. **B10.208**

PIRACY

Piracy has been a common-law offence in English law since the 16th century and is recognised internationally as being a crime of universal jurisdiction. The continued existence of the offence is confirmed by its modern statutory definition. **B10.209**

Merchant Shipping and Maritime Security Act 1997, s. 26

(1) For the avoidance of doubt it is hereby declared that for the purposes of any proceedings before a court in the United Kingdom in respect of piracy, the provisions of the United Nations Convention on the Law of the Sea 1982 that are set out in Schedule 5 shall be treated as constituting part of the law of nations.

(2) For the purposes of those provisions the high seas shall (in accordance with paragraph 2 of Article 58 of that Convention) be taken to include all waters beyond the territorial sea of the United Kingdom or of any other state.

Merchant Shipping and Maritime Security Act 1997, sch. 5

Article 101 Piracy consists of any of the following acts:

(a) any illegal acts of violence or detention, or any act of depredation, committed for private ends by the crew or the passengers of a private ship or a private aircraft, and directed—
  (i) on the high seas, against another ship or aircraft, or against persons or property on board such ship or aircraft;
  (ii) against a ship, aircraft, persons or property in a place outside the jurisdiction of any State;
(b) any act of voluntary participation in the operation of a ship or of an aircraft with knowledge of facts making it a pirate ship or aircraft;
(c) any act of inciting or of intentionally facilitating an act described in subparagraph (a) or (b).

Article 102 The acts of piracy, as defined in article 101, committed by a warship, government ship or government aircraft whose crew has mutinied and taken control of the ship or aircraft are assimilated to acts committed by a private ship or aircraft.

Article 103 A ship or aircraft is considered a pirate ship or aircraft if it is intended by the persons in dominant control to be used for the purpose of committing one of the acts referred to in article 101. The same applies if the ship or aircraft has been used to commit any such act, so long as it remains under the control of the persons guilty of that act.

Articles 101 to 103 are from the United Nations Convention on the Law of the Sea (UNCLOS).

There is no UK case law defining the terms contained within Article 101 of UNCLOS, but courts in the USA have had cause to consider the meaning of both 'private ends' (*Institute of Cetacean Research v Sea Shepherd Conservation Society*, Opinion of the Ninth Circuit Courts of Appeal, No. 12-35266) and 'the high seas' (*US v Ali*, US District Court, District of Columbia, No. 11-0106). In the *Sea Shepherd* case, which concerned tactics used by anti-whaling protesters who routinely used violence against whaling ships, the appellate court approved a previous decision saying that '[t]he law looks to [piracy] as an act of hostility... being committed by a vessel not commissioned and engaged in lawful warfare' and concluded that '"private ends" include those pursued on personal, moral or philosophical grounds, such as Sea Shepherd's professed environmental goals. That the perpetrators believe themselves to be serving the public good does not render their ends public.'

Procedure and Jurisdiction

B10.210 Piracy *iure gentium* is a class 1B offence and triable only on indictment.

The fact that D is a foreign national does not affect the jurisdiction of a court. However, the English courts will be slow to assume jurisdiction when the alleged offence has no real connection with England and Wales (*Republic of Bolivia v Indemnity Mutual Marine Assurance Co. Ltd* [1909] 1 KB 785). There is a potential problem about enforcement of this offence outside the territorial jurisdiction of England and Wales. The 1997 Act is silent as to powers of arrest and detention for acts of piracy, and Article 105 of UNCLOS, which provides for detention, is not incorporated into English law. There is no recent authority on the point. It is arguable that a common-law power to detain survives, and a Royal Navy officer detaining a piracy suspect may be said to do so under the Royal Prerogative, that being the basis for deployment of UK forces overseas. For a ruling of the ECtHR on the lawfulness of an extended detention at sea (in a drugs case), see *Medvedyev v France* (2010) 51 EHRR 39 (899).

Sentence

B10.211 **Piracy Act 1837, s. 2**

> Whosoever, with intent to commit or at the time of or immediately before or immediately after committing the crime of piracy in respect of any ship or vessel, shall assault, with intent to murder, any person being on board of or belonging to such ship or vessel, or shall stab, cut or wound any such person, or unlawfully do any act, by which the life of such person may be endangered, shall be guilty of [an offence], and being convicted thereof shall be liable to imprisonment for life.

An act of piracy *iure gentium* committed without the aggravating acts described within s. 2 is punishable by imprisonment and a fine at large at common law. Any specific offences committed during the piracy are punishable as if committed on land (Offences at Sea Act 1799).

Elements

B10.212 'Depredation' means an act of attacking or plundering. The offences created by Article 101 require that illegal acts are committed 'for private ends' so as to exclude actions taken during the course of an armed conflict or by law-enforcement officials. It arguably does not exclude offences committed for terrorist or political motives, as they are personal to those committing the acts. The offence defined by Article 101(a) requires an attack by a ship (or aircraft) on another ship (the 'two-ship rule'), so an act of violence etc. committed by the passengers or crew within a ship against others in the same ship would not be piracy.

Piracy cannot be committed in UK internal waters or territorial seas, or generally, in the internal waters or territorial seas of another State. The appropriate offence would be one contrary to domestic law, e.g., robbery.

HIJACKING OF SHIPS AND RELATED OFFENCES

Hijacking of Ships

B10.213 **Aviation and Maritime Security Act 1990, s. 9**

> (1) A person who unlawfully, by the use of force or threats of any kind, seizes a ship or exercises control of it, commits the offence of hijacking a ship, whatever his nationality and whether the ship is in the United Kingdom or elsewhere, but subject to subsection (2) below.

Procedure and Jurisdiction Under the Aviation and Maritime Security Act 1990, s. 9(1), the general rule is that a person can be found guilty of an offence contrary to s. 9 whatever the person's nationality and wherever the ship is at the time of the offence. There are exceptions in some circumstances for warships, naval auxiliary vessels and those in naval or customs service. **B10.214**

An allegation of an offence contrary to s. 9 is triable only on indictment and is normally a class 3 offence, but see CrimPD XIII, para. B (see Supplement, **CPD.XIII.B**), for the additional factors that the court considers on allocation.

Proceedings for an offence under s. 9 can be instituted only with the consent of the A-G (s. 16(1)).

Sentence The maximum penalty is life imprisonment (Aviation and Maritime Security Act 1990, s. 9(3)). **B10.215**

Elements For 'United Kingdom national', see **B10.228**. **B10.216**

In s. 17(1) of the Aviation and Maritime Security Act 1990, 'ship' is defined as meaning any vessel (including hovercraft, submersible craft and other floating craft) other than one which permanently rests on, or is permanently attached to, the seabed, or has been withdrawn from navigation or laid up.

'Naval service' includes military and air force service (s. 17(1)).

Other Maritime Security Offences

Further offences dealing with the safety of ships and fixed platforms are provided for under the Aviation and Maritime Security Act 1990 and the Merchant Shipping Act 1995. **B10.217**

Aviation and Maritime Security Act 1990, ss. 10 to 13

10.—(1) A person who unlawfully, by the use of force or by threats of any kind, seizes a fixed platform or exercises control of it, commits an offence, whatever his nationality and whether the fixed platform is in the United Kingdom or elsewhere.

(2) A person guilty of an offence under this section is liable on conviction on indictment to imprisonment for life.

11.—(1) Subject to subsection (5) below, a person commits an offence if he unlawfully and intentionally—

(a) destroys a ship or a fixed platform,

(b) damages a ship, its cargo or a fixed platform so as to endanger, or to be likely to endanger, the safe navigation of the ship, or as the case may be, the safety of the platform, or

(c) commits on board a ship or on a fixed platform an act of violence which is likely to endanger the safe navigation of the ship, or as the case may be, the safety of the platform.

(2) Subject to subsection (5) below, a person commits an offence if he unlawfully and intentionally places, or causes to be placed, on a ship or fixed platform any device or substance which—

(a) in the case of a ship, is likely to destroy the ship or is likely so to damage it or its cargo as to endanger its safe navigation, or

(b) in the case of a fixed platform, is likely to destroy the fixed platform or so to damage it as to endanger its safety.

(3) Nothing in subsection (2) above is to be construed as limiting the circumstances in which the commission of any act—

(a) may constitute an offence under subsection (1) above, or

(b) may constitute attempting or conspiring to commit, or aiding, abetting, counselling, procuring or inciting, or being art and part in, the commission of such an offence.

(4) Except as provided by subsection (5) below, subsections (1) and (2) above apply whether any such act as is mentioned in those subsections is committed in the United Kingdom or elsewhere and whatever the nationality of the person committing the act.

(5) Subsections (1) and (2) above do not apply in relation to any act committed in relation to a warship or any other ship used as a naval auxiliary or in customs or police service unless—

(a) the person committing the act is a United Kingdom national, or

(b) his act is committed in the United Kingdom, or
(c) the ship is used in the naval or customs service of the United Kingdom or in the service of any police force in the United Kingdom.

(6) A person guilty of an offence under this section is liable on conviction on indictment to imprisonment for life.

12.—(1) Subject to subsection (6) below, it is an offence for any person unlawfully and intentionally—
(a) to destroy or damage any property to which this subsection applies, or
(b) seriously to interfere with the operation of any such property,
where the destruction, damage or interference is likely to endanger the safe navigation of any ship.

(2) Subsection (1) above applies to any property used for the provision of maritime navigation facilities, including any land, building or ship so used, and including any apparatus or equipment so used, whether it is on board a ship or elsewhere.

(3) Subject to subsection (6) below, it is also an offence for any person intentionally to communicate any information which he knows to be false in a material particular, where the communication of the information endangers the safe navigation of any ship.

(4) It is a defence for a person charged with an offence under subsection (3) above to prove that, when he communicated the information, he was lawfully employed to perform duties which consisted of or included the communication of information and that he communicated the information in good faith in performance of those duties.

(5) Except as provided by subsection (6) below, subsections (1) and (3) above apply whether any such act as is mentioned in those subsections is committed in the United Kingdom or elsewhere and whatever the nationality of the person committing the act.

(6) For the purposes of subsections (1) and (3) above any danger, or likelihood of danger, to the safe navigation of a warship or any other ship used as a naval auxiliary or in customs or police service is to be disregarded unless—
(a) the person committing the act is a United Kingdom national, or
(b) his act is committed in the United Kingdom, or
(c) the ship is used in the naval or customs service of the United Kingdom or in the service of any police force in the United Kingdom.

(7) A person guilty of an offence under this section is liable on conviction on indictment to imprisonment for life.

13.—(1) A person commits an offence if—
(a) in order to compel any other person to do or abstain from doing any act, he threatens that he or some other person will do in relation to any ship or fixed platform an act which is an offence by virtue of section 11(1) of this Act, and
(b) the making of that threat is likely to endanger the safe navigation of the ship or, as the case may be, the safety of the fixed platform.

(2) Subject to subsection (4) below, a person commits an offence if—
(a) in order to compel any other person to do or abstain from doing any act, he threatens that he or some other person will do an act which is an offence by virtue of section 12(1) of this Act, and
(b) the making of that threat is likely to endanger the safe navigation of any ship.

(3) Except as provided by subsection (4) below, subsections (1) and (2) above apply whether any such act as is mentioned in those subsections is committed in the United Kingdom or elsewhere and whatever the nationality of the person committing the act.

(4) Section 12(6) of this Act applies for the purposes of subsection (2)(b) above as it applies for the purposes of section 12(1) and (3) of this Act.

B10.218 **Procedure** Each of the offences is triable only on indictment. Proceedings may be instituted only with the consent of the A-G.

B10.219 **Sentence** The maximum sentence for each offence is life imprisonment.

B10.220 **Elements** For 'act of violence', see **B10.232**. For 'unlawful', see **B10.232**. Hijacking a *ship is the act of unlawfully seizing a ship* or exercising control of it by the use of force or by threats. The offence can be committed in the territorial seas of the UK or any other State, or in UK internal waters, as well as on the high seas. It can be committed by individuals within a ship.

Related Offences and Powers

There are ancillary offences relevant to provisions within the Aviation and Maritime Security Act 1990 along with a power of delivery to a ship's master: **B10.221**

Ancillary Offences under s. 14(1): Section 14(1) and (2) of the Act provide that, where a person (of whatever nationality) does any act outside the UK which, if done in the UK, would constitute an offence of murder, attempted murder, manslaughter, culpable homicide or assault, or an offence under the OAPA 1861, ss. 18, 20, 21, 22, 23, 28 and 29, or an offence contrary to s. 2 of the Explosive Substances Act 1883, the act constitutes that offence if it is done in connection with an offence under the Aviation and Maritime Security Act 1990, ss. 9, 10, 11, or 12, committed or attempted by that person. These provisions are without prejudice to the jurisdiction clauses of the Merchant Shipping Act 1995, ss. 281 and 282, or the Petroleum Act 1998, s. 10 (Aviation and Maritime Security Act 1990, s. 14(3)).

Inducing or Assisting in Commission of Offences under s. 14(4): It is an offence for any person in the UK to induce or assist the commission outside the UK of any act which would, but for the Aviation and Maritime Security Act 1990, s. 9(2), be an offence under ss. 9, 11, 12 or 13 (offences involving threats). These offences can be committed against a Naval, Customs or police vessel as well as a civilian ship. The offences are triable on indictment only and the maximum penalty is life imprisonment (s. 14(5)).

Master's Power of Delivery: Section 15 of the Act provides the master of a ship with the power to deliver a person to an appropriate officer in the UK or any other Rome Convention country where the master has reasonable grounds to believe that that person has (a) committed an offence under s. 9, 11, 12 or 13, (b) attempted to commit such an offence, or (c) aided, abetted, counselled, procured or incited, been art and part in, the commission of such an offence.

Discipline The Merchant Shipping Act 1995, s. 58, creates offences relating to conduct on ships which causes danger, concerted disobedience and neglect of duty. These offences, which carry a maximum sentence of two years' imprisonment, provide a discipline system for those working or travelling in merchant ships. Section 58 applies not only to the master and crew of a UK ship, but to the master and crew of a foreign-registered ship when it is in a port in the UK or within UK waters while proceeding to or from any UK port. But if the foreign ship in question is travelling through UK territorial seas but not on passage to or from a UK port (e.g., passing through the English Channel from Belgium to Spain), the Act does not apply. Section 106 of the 1995 Act provides that, where a person goes to sea in a ship without the consent of the master or of any other person authorised to give it, ss. 58 and 59 apply as if the person were a seaman employed in the ship (s. 106 does not apply to fishing vessels). **B10.222**

Stowaways and Port and Harbour Security There are ancillary provisions within the Merchant Shipping Act 1995 which deal with persons not lawfully on board ships, and which give powers of detention to the master of a UK ship. **B10.223**

Section 103 deals with stowaways. A person who goes to sea or attempts to go to sea in a UK ship, without the consent of the master or of any other person authorised to give it, is guilty of a summary only offence with a maximum penalty of a fine not exceeding level 3 on the standard scale. Section 104 makes it an offence to go on board a UK ship or a ship registered in any other country in a port in the UK without the consent of the master or of any other persons authorised to give it; or to remain on board the ship after being requested to leave by the master, a constable, an officer authorised by the Secretary of State or an officer of customs and excise. This is a summary only offence with a maximum penalty of an unlimited fine.

Section 105 provides that the master of any UK ship may cause any person on board the ship to be put under restraint if and for so long as it appears to the master necessary or expedient in the interest of safety or for the preservation of good order or discipline on board the ship.

The Aviation and Maritime Security Act 1990, s. 39, makes it an offence to go into a restricted zone in a harbour without authorisation, or to remain there after being requested to leave by a competent authority or person. The offence is summary only and punishable with an unlimited fine. A constable or any person acting on behalf of the competent authority may use such force as is reasonable in the circumstances to remove from a restricted zone a person remaining in it in contravention of the section. Notices stating that the area concerned is a restricted zone must be posted so as to be readily seen and read by persons entering the restricted zone.

HIJACKING OF AIRCRAFT AND RELATED OFFENCES

B10.224 A number of offences relating to the safety of and security of aircraft are provided for by the Aviation Security Act 1982. Part II provides for the safety of aircraft, aerodromes and air navigation installations against acts of violence and Part III for the policing of airports. The Aviation and Maritime Security Act 1990, s. 1, creates the offence of endangering safety at airports.

Hijacking of Aircraft

B10.225 **Aviation Security Act 1982, s. 1**

(1) A person on board an aircraft in flight who unlawfully, by the use of force or by threats of any kind, seizes the aircraft or exercises control of it commits the offence of hijacking, whatever his nationality, whatever the State in which the aircraft is registered and whether the aircraft is in the United Kingdom or elsewhere but subject to subsection (2) below.

B10.226 **Procedure and Jurisdiction**

Aviation Security Act 1982, s. 5

(1) Any court in the United Kingdom having jurisdiction in respect of piracy committed on the high seas shall have jurisdiction in respect of piracy committed by or against an aircraft, wherever that piracy is committed.

Under s. 1(1), the general rule is that a person can be found guilty of an offence contrary to s. 1 whatever the person's nationality, wherever the aircraft is registered and wherever the aircraft is at the time of the offence. But, under s. 1(2), if the aircraft is used in military, police or customs service or both the place of take-off and landing are in the territory of the State where the plane is registered, s. 1(1) will not apply unless the alleged hijacker is a UK national or the act is committed in the UK or the aircraft is registered in the UK or is used in the military or customs service of the UK or the service of any police force in the UK.

An allegation of an offence contrary to s. 1 is triable only on indictment and is normally a class 3 offence, but see CrimPD XIII, para. B (see Supplement, **CPD.XIII.B**), for the additional factors that the court considers on allocation.

Proceedings for an offence under s. 1 can be instituted only with the consent of the A-G (s. 8(1)).

Section 37 of the Act makes similar provision for the liability of bodies corporate to that contained in s. 18 of the TA 2006 (see **B10.95**).

B10.227 **Sentence** The maximum penalty is life imprisonment (Aviation Security Act 1982, s. 1(3)).

B10.228 **Elements** 'In flight' is defined in s. 38(3)(a) of the Aviation Security Act 1982 as being from the point when all an aircraft's external doors are closed following embarkation until the point when one of those doors is opened for disembarkation. When a plane is forced to land, it is 'in flight' until the competent authorities take responsibility for the plane and its occupants and any property on board.

'Military service' is defined so as to include naval and air force service; 'United Kingdom national' is a person who is (a) a British citizen, a British Dependent Territories citizen or a

British overseas citizen, (b) a British subject under the British Nationality Act 1981, or (c) a British protected person (s. 38(1)).

Destroying, Damaging or Endangering the Safety of an Aircraft

Aviation Security Act 1982, s. 2 **B10.229**

(1) It shall, subject to subsection (4) below, be an offence for any person unlawfully and intentionally—
 (a) to destroy an aircraft in service or so to damage such an aircraft as to render it incapable of flight or as to be likely to endanger its safety in flight; or
 (b) to commit on board an aircraft in flight any act of violence which is likely to endanger the safety of the aircraft.

(2) It shall also, subject to subsection (4) below, be an offence for any person unlawfully and intentionally to place, or cause to be placed, on an aircraft in service any device or substance which is likely to destroy the aircraft, or is likely so to damage it, as to render it incapable of flight or as to be likely to endanger its safety in flight; but nothing in this subsection shall be construed as limiting the circumstances in which the commission of any act—
 (a) may constitute an offence under subsection (1) above, or
 (b) may constitute attempting or conspiring to commit, or aiding, abetting, counselling or procuring, or being art and part in, the commission of such an offence.

Procedure and Jurisdiction The Aviation Security Act 1982, s. 2(3) is in identical terms to s. 1(1) (see **B10.225**). **B10.230**

An allegation of an offence contrary to s. 2 is triable only on indictment and is normally a class 3 offence, but see CrimPD XIII, para. B (see Supplement, **CPD.XIII.B**), for the additional factors that the court considers on allocation.

Proceedings for an offence under s. 2 can be instituted only with the consent of the A-G (s. 8(1)).

Sentence The maximum penalty is life imprisonment (Aviation Security Act 1982, s. 2(5)). **B10.231**

Elements 'Unlawful' in relation to an act in the UK means that it constitutes an offence under the law of the part of the UK in which it is committed. In relation to an act outside the UK, 'unlawful' means that it would constitute an offence if it had been committed in England, Scotland or Wales (Aviation Security Act 1982, s. 2(6)). **B10.232**

'Act of violence' is any act in the UK that constitutes the offence of murder, manslaughter, culpable homicide or assault, an offence under any of ss. 18, 20, 21, 22, 23, 24, 28 or 29 of the OAPA 1861, or an offence under s. 2 of the Explosive Substances Act 1883. Outside the UK, it is any act that would constitute any of the offences mentioned above if it occurred in the UK (s. 2(7)).

'In service' is defined as the period from pre-flight preparation of the aircraft to a time 24 hours after it has landed following completion of the flight (s. 38(3)(b)). For 'in flight', see **B10.228**. For 'United Kingdom national', see **B10.228**.

Other Acts Endangering or Likely to Endanger the Safety of an Aircraft

Aviation Security Act 1982, s. 3 **B10.233**

(1) It shall, subject to subsections (5) and (6) below, be an offence for any person unlawfully and intentionally to destroy or damage any property to which this subsection applies, or to interfere with the operation of any such property, where the destruction, damage or interference is likely to endanger the safety of the aircraft in flight.

(2) Subsection (1) above applies to any property used for the provision of air navigation facilities, including any land, building or ship so used, and including any apparatus or equipment so used, whether it is on board an aircraft or elsewhere.

(3) It shall also, subject to subsections (4) and (5) below, be an offence for any person intentionally to communicate any information which is false, misleading or deceptive in a material particular, where the communication of the information endangers the safety of an aircraft in flight or is likely to endanger the safety of aircraft in flight.

B10.234 **Procedure and Jurisdiction** Provisions concerning jurisdiction are contained in the Aviation Security Act 1982, s. 3(5) and (6).

Aviation Security Act 1982, s. 3

(5) Subsections (1) and (3) above shall not apply to the commission of any act unless either the act is committed in the United Kingdom or, where it is committed outside the United Kingdom—

(a) the person committing it is a United Kingdom national; or

(b) the commission of the act endangers or is likely to endanger the safety in flight of civil aircraft registered in the United Kingdom or chartered by demise to a lessee whose principal place of business, or (if he has no place of business) whose permanent residence, is in the United Kingdom; or

(c) the act is committed on board a civil aircraft which is so registered or so chartered; or

(d) the act is committed on board a civil aircraft which lands in the United Kingdom with the person who committed the act still on board.

(6) Subsection (1) above shall also not apply to any act committed outside the United Kingdom and so committed in relation to property which is situated outside the United Kingdom and is not used for the provision of air navigation facilities in connection with international air navigation, unless the person committing the act is a United Kingdom national.

An allegation of an offence contrary to s. 3 is triable only on indictment and is normally a class 3 offence, but see CrimPD XIII, para. B (see Supplement, **CPD.XIII.B**), for the additional factors that the court considers on allocation.

Proceedings for an offence under s. 3 can be instituted only with the consent of the A-G (s. 8(1)).

B10.235 **Sentence** The maximum penalty is life imprisonment (Aviation Security Act 1982, s. 3(7)).

In *Voice* [2008] EWCA Crim 953, [2009] 1 Cr App R (S) 11 (54) the Court of Appeal quashed a sentence of four months' imprisonment imposed for recklessly endangering the safety of an aircraft and substituted a community sentence. D had shone a high-powered torch out of the window of his flat into the cockpit of a helicopter that was attempting to land, rendering the pilot unable to see any of the cockpit instruments. The pilot was therefore required to take evasive action. D had acquired the torch in order to deter groups of youths which had been congregating on the estate on which he lived. He had not directed the torch at the landing helicopter, and instead was directing it at youths, but accepted that he was reckless as to the danger his behaviour had caused. In substituting the community sentence, the Court of Appeal regarded as crucial the agreed basis of plea which included an express acceptance by the Crown that the torch was not shone directly or deliberately at the helicopter but was being shone out of the window for another reason altogether. By contrast, in *Hussain* [2008] EWCA Crim 1559, [2009] 1 Cr App R (S) 65 (373), the Court of Appeal held that sentences of six months' imprisonment and six months' detention in a young offender institution respectively for the two offenders were the least that could properly have been imposed following guilty pleas entered at the first opportunity. The pilot of a police helicopter was forced to take emergency action when the appellants had shone a green laser beam at the cockpit. The offenders had previous convictions but they were said by the Court to have little bearing on the decision it made. *Voice* could be distinguished on two bases. First, in *Voice* the torch was shone for a legitimate reason whereas in *Hussain* there was no legitimate reason for possession of the laser pen. Secondly, in *Voice*, the helicopter flew through and out of the beam of light and the beam was not aimed at the aircraft nor did it follow the aircraft. In this case, the beam was directed at the aircraft and followed the aircraft for several minutes.

B10.236 **Elements** 'Property' includes any land, buildings or work, any aircraft or vehicle and any baggage, cargo or any other article of any description (s. 38(1)).

'Civil aircraft' constitutes any aircraft other than an aircraft used in military, customs or police service (s. 3(8)).

For 'unlawful', see **B10.232**. For 'in flight', see **B10.228**. For 'United Kingdom national', see **B10.228**.

Specific Defence **B10.237**

Aviation Security Act 1982, s. 3

(4) It shall be a defence for a person charged with an offence under subsection (3) above to prove—
- (a) that he believed, and had reasonable grounds for believing, that the information was true; or
- (b) that, when he communicated the information, he was lawfully employed to perform duties which consisted of or included the communication of information and that he communicated the information in good faith in the performance of those duties.

See **F3.18** *et seq*. for the significance of the reverse burden within this defence.

Dangerous Articles

Aviation Security Act 1982, s. 4 **B10.238**

(1) It shall be an offence for any person without lawful authority or reasonable excuse (the proof of which shall lie on him) to have with him—
- (a) in any aircraft registered in the United Kingdom, whether at a time when the aircraft is in the United Kingdom or not, or
- (b) in any other aircraft at a time when it is in, or in flight over, the United Kingdom, or
- (c) in any part of an aerodrome in the United Kingdom, or
- (d) in any air navigation installation in the United Kingdom which does not form part of an aerodrome,

any article to which this section applies.

Procedure An allegation of an offence contrary to the Aviation and Maritime Security Act 1990, s. 4, is triable either way (s. 4(4)); when tried on indictment it is normally a class 3 offence, but see CrimPD XIII, para. B (see Supplement, **CPD.XIII.B**), for the additional factors that the court considers on allocation. **B10.239**

Sentence The maximum penalty on conviction on indictment is imprisonment for a term not exceeding five years and/or a fine; on summary conviction, it is imprisonment for a term not exceeding three months and/or an unlimited fine (Aviation Security Act 1982, s. 4(4)). **B10.240**

Elements **B10.241**

Aviation Security Act 1982, s. 4

(3) For the purposes of this section a person who is for the time being in an aircraft, or in part of an aerodrome, shall be treated as having with him in an aircraft, or in that part of the aerodrome, as the case may be, an article to which this section applies if—
- (a) where he is in an aircraft, the article, or an article in which it is contained, is in the aircraft and has been caused (whether by him or by any other person) to be brought there as being, or as forming part of, his baggage on a flight in the aircraft, or has been caused by him to be brought there as being, or as forming part of, any other property to be carried on such a flight, or
- (b) where he is in part of an aerodrome (otherwise than in an aircraft), the article, or an article in which it is contained, is in that or any other part of the aerodrome and has been caused (whether by him or by any other person) to be brought into the aerodrome as being, or as forming part of, his baggage on a flight from that aerodrome or has been caused by him to be brought there as being, or as forming part of, any other property to be carried on such a flight on which he is also to be carried,

notwithstanding that the circumstance may be such that (apart from this subsection) he would not be regarded as having the article with him in the aircraft or in a part of the aerodrome, as the case may be.

Section 4(2) sets out the articles to which s. 4 is relevant: **B10.242**

(a) any firearm, or any article having the appearance of being a firearm, whether capable of being discharged or not;

(b) any explosive, any article manufactured or adapted (whether in the form of a bomb, grenade or otherwise) so as to have the appearance of being an explosive, whether it is capable of producing a practical effect by explosion or not, or any article marked or labelled so as to indicate that it is or contains an explosive; and
(c) any article (not falling within either of the preceding paragraphs) made or adapted for use for causing injury to or incapacitating a person or for destroying or damaging property, or intended by the person having it with him for such use, whether by him or by any other person.

'Explosive' means any article manufactured for the purpose of producing a practical effect by explosion, or intended for that purpose by a person having the article with him. Firearm includes an airgun or air pistol (s. 38(1)).

'Have with him' receives some explanation in s. 4(3) but s. 4(5) provides that nothing in s. 4(3) shall be taken to limit the circumstances in which a person could be regarded as having an article with him.

For 'in flight', see **B10.228**. For 'United Kingdom national', see **B10.228**. For 'unlawfully', see B10.232.

'Air navigation installation' means any building, works, apparatus or equipment used wholly or mainly for the purpose of assisting air traffic control or as an aid to air navigation, together with any land contiguous or adjacent to any such building, works, apparatus or equipment and used wholly or mainly for purposes connected therewith (s. 38(1)).

Endangering Safety at Aerodromes

B10.243 **Aviation and Maritime Security Act 1990, s. 1**

(1) It is an offence for any person by means of any device, substance or weapon intentionally to commit at an aerodrome serving international civil aviation any act of violence which—
(a) causes or is likely to cause death or serious personal injury, and
(b) endangers or is likely to endanger the safe operation of the aerodrome or the safety of persons at the aerodrome.
(2) It is also, subject to subsection (4) below, an offence for any person by means of any device, substance or weapon unlawfully and intentionally—
(a) to destroy or seriously to damage—
(i) property used for the provision of any facilities at an aerodrome serving international civil aviation (including any apparatus or equipment so used), or
(ii) any aircraft which is at such aerodrome but is not in service, or
(b) to disrupt the services of such an aerodrome,
in such a way as to endanger or be likely to endanger the safe operation of the aerodrome or the safety of persons at the aerodrome.

B10.244 **Procedure and Jurisdiction** Under s. 1(3) of the Aviation and Maritime Security Act 1990, the general rule is that a person can be found guilty of an offence contrary to s. 2 whatever the person's nationality and wherever the aircraft is at the time of the offence. But, under s. 1(4), if the aircraft is used in military, police or customs service, s. 1(1) and (2) will not apply unless the alleged act is committed in the UK or, if the act is committed outside the UK, it is committed by a UK national.

An allegation of an offence contrary to s. 1 is triable only on indictment and is normally a class 3 offence, but see CrimPD XIII, para. B (see Supplement, **CPD.XIII.B**), for the additional factors that the court considers on allocation.

Proceedings for an offence under s. 1 can be instituted only with the consent of the A-G (s. 1(7)).

B10.245 **Sentence** The maximum penalty is life imprisonment (Aviation and Maritime Security Act 1990, s. 1(5)).

Elements 'Act of violence' is defined by the Aviation and Maritime Security Act 1990, s. 1(9), in terms identical to those used under the Aviation Security Act 1982, s. 2(7) (see **B10.232**). **B10.246**

'Aerodrome' means any area of land or water designed, equipped, set apart or commonly used for affording facilities for the landing and departure of aircraft. It includes any area or space, whether on the ground, on the roof of a building or elsewhere, which is designed, equipped or set apart for affording facilities for the landing and departure of aircraft capable of descending or climbing vertically (Civil Aviation Act 1982, s. 105(1)).

For 'unlawfully', see **B10.232**. For 'United Kingdom national', see **B10.228**. For 'in service', see **B10.232**.

The Air Navigation Order 2016 (SI 2016 No. 765) and the Rules of the Air Regulations 2015 (SI 2015 No. 840), which came into force on 25 August 2016, contain a vast number of offences and regulations about air operations, often referred to as the 'Rules of the Air'. All relevant conduct prior to 25 August 2016 is regulated by the Air Navigation Order 2009 (SI 2009 No. 3015) (see **B11.78**). The provisions of the Order were most recently amended by the Air Navigation Amendment Order 2018 (SI 2018 No. 623) with effect from 30 July 2018. The Air Navigation Order governs the manner in which aircraft may move or fly, provisions for securing the safety of aircraft in flight and in movement, and the safety of persons and property on land and sea. They may be used to deal with cases in which individuals seek to interfere with aircraft or aerodrome operation, e.g., users of lasers or flying drones near aircraft or aerodromes (see also the provisions of the Laser Misuse (Vehicles) Act 2018 at **B12.222**). A guide to the Order and Regulations is published as CAP 393 by the Civil Aviation Authority (tinyurl.com/yd5ycbyl). Under art. 240, a person must not recklessly or negligently act in a manner likely to endanger an aircraft, or any person in an aircraft; the maximum sentence on conviction on indictment is five years' imprisonment and a fine and, on summary conviction, is an unlimited fine (art. 265(8) and sch. 13, part 4). Two articles of the Air Navigation Order 2016 apply to operators of drones: arts. 94 (small unmanned aircraft) and 95 (small unmanned surveillance aircraft). Amendments to arts. 94 and 95 took effect from 30 July 2018 and create new categories of person for the purpose of the Order: the 'remote pilot' (defined as an individual who remotely operates the aircraft's flight controls, or who monitors its course while it is flying automatically and is able to intervene by operating the flight controls) and the 'SUA operator' (defined as the person who has the management of the aircraft) (art. 94G). Of particular note is a prohibition on causing or permitting a SUA to be used more than 400 feet above ground (art. 94A), or over or within 1km of a protected aerodrome at certain times (art. 94B), unless the required permission has been obtained. From 30 November 2019, there will also be new procedural requirements applying to SUAs with a mass of 250 grams or more. The remote pilot and SUA operator will need to register the SUA and the remote pilot will require an acknowledgement of competency (arts. 94C to 94F). **B10.247**

Air Navigation Order 2016, arts. 94 to 95 **B10.248**

94.—(1) A person must not cause or permit any article or animal (whether or not attached to a parachute) to be dropped from a small unmanned aircraft so as to endanger persons or property.

(2) The remote pilot of a small unmanned aircraft may only fly the aircraft if reasonably satisfied that the flight can safely be made.

(3) The remote pilot of a small unmanned aircraft must maintain direct, unaided visual contact with the aircraft sufficient to monitor its flight path in relation to other aircraft, persons, vehicles, vessels and structures for the purpose of avoiding collisions.

(4) If a small unmanned aircraft has a mass of more than 7kg excluding its fuel but including any articles or equipment installed in or attached to the aircraft at the commencement of its flight, the SUA operator must not cause or permit the aircraft to be flown, and the remote pilot in charge of the aircraft must not fly it:

(a) in Class A, C, D or E airspace unless the permission of the appropriate air traffic control unit has been obtained; or

(b) within an aerodrome traffic zone during the notified hours of watch of the air traffic control unit (if any) at that aerodrome unless the permission of any such air traffic control unit has been obtained.

(4A) Paragraph (4) does not apply to any flight within the flight restriction zone of a protected aerodrome (within the meaning given in article 94B).

(5) The SUA operator must not cause or permit a small unmanned aircraft to be flown for the purposes of commercial operations, and the remote pilot of a small unmanned aircraft must not fly it for the purposes of commercial operations, except in accordance with a permission granted by the CAA.

94A.—(1) The SUA operator must not cause or permit a small unmanned aircraft to be flown at a height of more than 400 feet above the surface, and the remote pilot of a small unmanned aircraft must not fly it at a height of more than 400 feet above the surface, unless the permission of the CAA has been obtained.

(2) This article does not apply to any flight within the flight restriction zone of a protected aerodrome (within the meaning given in article 94B).

94B.—(1) This article applies to a flight by a small unmanned aircraft within the flight restriction zone of a protected aerodrome.

(2) The 'flight restriction zone' of a protected aerodrome consists of the following two zones—
(a) the 'Inner Zone', which is the area within, and including, the boundary of the aerodrome;
(b) the 'Outer Zone', which is the area between—
(i) the boundary of the aerodrome, and
(ii) a line that is 1 km from the boundary of the aerodrome (the '1 km line').

(3) In the circumstances set out in an entry in column 1 of the following table—
(a) the SUA operator must not cause or permit the small unmanned aircraft to be flown in the Inner Zone or the Outer Zone, and
(b) the remote pilot of the small unmanned aircraft must not fly it in the Inner Zone or the Outer Zone, if the flight breaches a flight restriction set out in the entry in column 3 of the table which relates to that zone in those circumstances.

(4) The 1 km line is to be drawn so that the area which is bounded by it includes every location that is 1 km from the boundary of the aerodrome, measured in any direction from any point on the boundary.

(5) In this article, 'protected aerodrome' means—
(a) an EASA certified aerodrome,
(b) a Government aerodrome,
(c) a national licensed aerodrome, or
(d) an aerodrome that is prescribed or of a prescribed description.

95.—(1) The SUA operator must not cause or permit a small unmanned surveillance aircraft to be flown in any of the circumstances described in paragraph (2), and the remote pilot of a small unmanned surveillance aircraft must not fly it in any of those circumstances, except in accordance with a permission issued by the CAA.

(2) The circumstances referred to in paragraph (1) are—
(a) over or within 150 metres of any congested area;
(b) over or within 150 metres of an organised open-air assembly of more than 1,000 persons;
(c) within 50 metres of any vessel, vehicle or structure which is not under the control of the SUA operator or the remote pilot of the aircraft; or
(d) subject to paragraphs (3) and (4), within 50 metres of any person.

(3) Subject to paragraph (4), during take-off or landing, a small unmanned surveillance aircraft must not be flown within 30 metres of any person.

(4) Paragraphs (2)(d) and (3) do not apply to the remote pilot of the small unmanned surveillance aircraft or a person under the control of the remote pilot of the aircraft.

(5) In this article, 'a small unmanned surveillance aircraft' means a small unmanned aircraft which is equipped to undertake any form of surveillance or data acquisition.

B10.249 **Procedure and Jurisdiction** The offences are summary only. Some of these cases are prosecuted by CPS, and others by the Civil Aviation Authority.

B10.250 **Sentence** The maximum penalty is a fine not exceeding level 4 on the standard scale.

Section B11 Offences Affecting Public Order

INTRODUCTION

The POA 1986 abolished a number of common-law offences, including riot, unlawful assembly and affray, replacing them with statutory offences of riot, violent disorder, affray, threatening behaviour etc. and disorderly conduct. It extended controls over processions and created controls over open-air assemblies. It expanded the law relating to the stirring up of racial hatred and provided for the exclusion of certain offenders from sporting events, notably association football matches. It was further expanded by the Racial and Religious Hatred Act 2006, which inserted a number of new offences relating to the stirring up of religious hatred. The CJIA 2008, s. 74 and sch. 16, expanded it yet further by covering offences relating to hatred on the grounds of sexual orientation. **B11.1**

This section also deals with surviving offences under the POA 1936 and the common-law offence of public nuisance.

PROHIBITION OF QUASI-MILITARY ORGANISATIONS

Public Order Act 1936, s. 2 **B11.2**

(1) If the members or adherents of any association of persons, whether incorporated or not, are—
 (a) organised or trained or equipped for the purpose of enabling them to be employed in usurping the functions of the police or of the armed forces of the Crown; or

(b) organised and trained or organised and equipped either for the purpose of enabling them to be employed for the use or display of physical force in promoting any political object, or in such manner as to arouse reasonable apprehension that they are organised and either trained or equipped for that purpose;

then any person who takes part in the control or management of the association, or in so organising or training as aforesaid any members or adherents thereof, shall be guilty of an offence under this section.

Procedure

B11.3 Offences under the POA 1936, s. 2, are triable either way (POA 1936, s. 7(1)). When tried on indictment they are normally class 3 offences, but see CrimPD XIII, para. B (see Supplement, CPD.XIII.B) for the additional factors that the court considers on allocation. By virtue of s. 2(2), no prosecution shall be instituted without the consent of the A-G.

Public Order Act 1936, s. 2

(4) In any criminal or civil proceedings under this section proof of things done or of words written, spoken or published (whether or not in the presence of any party to the proceedings) by any person taking part in the control or management of an association or in organising, training or equipping members or adherents of an association shall be admissible as evidence of the purposes for which, or the manner in which, members or adherents of the association (whether those persons or others) were organised, or trained, or equipped.

Indictment

B11.4 *Statement of Offence*

Taking part in the control or management [or organising or training members or adherents] of an association contrary to section 2(1)(a) of the Public Order Act 1936.

Particulars of Offence

A between the . . . day of . . . and the . . . day of . . . took part in the management or control [or organising or training members or adherents] of an association, namely . . ., whose members or adherents were organised, trained or equipped for the purpose of enabling them to be employed in usurping the functions of the police or the armed forces of the Crown.

Sentence

B11.5 The maximum penalty is two years or a fine or both on indictment; six months or a fine not exceeding the prescribed sum or both summarily (POA 1936, s. 7(1)).

Specific Defences

B11.6 **Public Order Act 1936, s. 2**

Provided that in any proceedings against a person charged with the offence of taking part in the control or management of such an association as aforesaid it shall be a defence to that charge to prove that he neither consented to nor connived at the organisation, training, or equipment of members or adherents of the association in contravention of the provisions of this section.

Furthermore, s. 2(6) provides that s. 2 does not prohibit the employment of a reasonable number of people as stewards to assist in the preservation of order at a public meeting held on private premises, or the making of arrangements for that purpose or the instruction of people to be so employed in their lawful duties as such stewards, or their being furnished with badges or other distinguishing signs.

When the legal burden is on the accused, the standard required is proof on a balance of probabilities (see **F3.5** and **F3.53**). For a summary of the case law relating to 'reverse burden' challenges under the HRA 1998, see **F3.18** ***et seq.***

Powers of High Court in Relation to Quasi-military Organisations

Public Order Act 1936, s. 2 B11.7

(3) If upon application being made by the Attorney-General it appears to the High Court that any association is an association of which members or adherents are organised, trained, or equipped in contravention of the provisions of this section, the court may make such order as appears necessary to prevent any disposition without the leave of the court of property held by or for the association and in accordance with rules of court may direct an inquiry and report to be made as to any such property as aforesaid and as to the affairs of the association and make such further orders as appear to the court to be just and equitable for the application of such property in or towards the discharge of the liabilities of the association lawfully incurred before the date of the application or since that date with the approval of the court, in or towards the repayment of moneys to persons who became subscribers or contributors to the association in good faith and without knowledge of any such contravention as aforesaid, and in or towards any costs incurred in connection with any such inquiry and report as aforesaid or in winding-up or dissolving the association, and may order that any property which is not directed by the court to be so applied as aforesaid shall be forfeited to the Crown.

Under s. 2(5) a High Court judge may grant a search warrant with a view to seizing evidence of the commission of an offence under s. 2. The judge must be satisfied on information under oath that there is reasonable ground for believing that an offence under s. 2 has been committed, and that evidence of it may be found at the place specified in the information. Application must be made by a police officer of a rank not lower than inspector.

PROHIBITION OF UNIFORMS IN CONNECTION WITH POLITICAL OBJECTS

Public Order Act 1936, s. 1 B11.8

(1) Subject as hereinafter provided, any person who in any public place or at any public meeting wears uniform signifying his association with any political organisation or with the promotion of any political object is guilty of an offence:
Provided that, if the chief officer of police is satisfied that the wearing of any such uniform as aforesaid on any ceremonial, anniversary, or other special occasion will not be likely to involve risk of public disorder, he may, with the consent of a Secretary of State, by order permit the wearing of such uniform on that occasion either absolutely or subject to such conditions as may be specified in the order.

Procedure

An offence under the POA 1936, s. 1(1), is triable only summarily (POA 1936, s. 7(2)). By virtue of s. 1(2), no further proceedings after charge shall be instituted without the consent of the A-G. B11.9

Sentence

The maximum penalty is imprisonment for a term not exceeding three months or a fine not exceeding level 4 on the standard scale, or both (POA 1936, s. 7(2)). B11.10

Uniform Signifying Association with a Political Organisation etc.

In *O'Moran v DPP* [1975] QB 864 the Divisional Court held that D was wearing a uniform when wearing a black beret, because that beret was worn by each member of the group to signify that he was a member of a group in association with others. The Court took the view that the requirement of the POA 1936, s. 1, that the uniform should signify association with a political organisation could be satisfied either by proof that the uniform had previously been worn as a uniform of a recognised, although not necessarily specified, organisation, or by judging D's activities at the time D was seen wearing that uniform. B11.11

Meaning of 'Public Place' and 'Public Meeting'

B11.12 The concept of 'public place' in the POA 1936 was frequently litigated. All that litigation is relevant to the instant offence and also to the POA 1986, and probably also all other legislation in which a similar concept plays an important part.

Public Order Act 1936, s. 9

(1) In this Act the following expressions have the meanings hereby respectively assigned to them, that is to say:—

...

'Public place' includes any highway and any other premises or place to which at the material time the public have or are permitted to have access, whether on payment or otherwise.

This is an incomplete definition. The question of whether a particular place is a 'public place' depends upon a number of factors as decided by a series of cases on the since repealed s. 5 of the POA 1936. (See also **B12.167**.)

B11.13 Whether a place is a public place depends upon an assessment of the factual position at 'the material time'. For example, the Court of Appeal in *Edwards* (1978) 67 Cr App R 228 held that the front garden of a house was not a public place because members of the public only had access on an individual basis as lawful visitors.

Public Order Act 1936, s. 9

(1) In this Act the following expressions have the meanings hereby respectively assigned to them, that is to say:—

...

'Meeting' means a meeting held for the purpose of the discussion of matters of public interest or for the purpose of the expression of views on such matters;...

'Public meeting' includes any meeting in a public place and any meeting which the public or any section thereof are permitted to attend, whether on payment or otherwise.

Related Offence

B11.14 It is an offence, contrary to the Police Act 1996, s. 90(2), for someone who is not a police officer to wear any article of police uniform, which includes distinctive badges, marks and documents, where it gives that person an appearance so resembling a member of a police force that it is calculated to deceive. The offence is punishable on summary conviction with a fine not exceeding level 3.

For offences relating to the use of uniforms to gain access to prohibited places (Official Secrets Act 1920, s. 1(1)), see **B9.18** to **B9.23**.

RIOT

B11.15 **Public Order Act 1986, s. 1**

(1) Where 12 or more persons who are present together use or threaten unlawful violence for a common purpose and the conduct of them (taken together) is such as would cause a person of reasonable firmness present at the scene to fear for his personal safety, each of the persons using unlawful violence for the common purpose is guilty of riot.
(2) It is immaterial whether or not the 12 or more use or threaten unlawful violence simultaneously.
(3) The common purpose may be inferred from conduct.
(4) No person of reasonable firmness need actually be, or be likely to be, present at the scene.
(5) Riot may be committed in private as well as in public places.

Procedure

B11.16 *Riot is triable only on indictment* (POA 1986, s. 1(6)). It is a class 1C or 2A offence, depending on whether it is in the course of a serious civil disturbance (CrimPD XIII, para. B (see Supplement, **CPD.XIII.B**)). By s. 7(1), a prosecution for riot or incitement to riot may be commenced only by, or with the consent of, the DPP (the common-law offence of incitement has been abolished by the SCA 2007, s. 59, so the reference to incitement in s. 7(1) has effect as a reference to (or to conduct amounting to) the offences under Part 2 of that Act (see **A5**): SCA 2007, s. 63 and sch. 6, para. 13). See the CPS Legal Guidance on Public Disorder for the current charging criteria.

Indictment

Statement of Offence **B11.17**

Riot contrary to section 1 of the Public Order Act 1986.

Particulars of Offence

A on or about the . . . day of . . ., being one of 12 or more persons present together at . . . and using [or threatening] unlawful violence for a common purpose, namely . . ., used unlawful violence for the said common purpose by assaulting members of the public, the conduct of the 12 or more persons aforesaid, taken together, being such as would cause a person of reasonable firmness present at the scene to fear for his personal safety.

This form of indictment was approved by the Court of Appeal in *Tyler* (1992) 96 Cr App R 332 and *Jefferson* [1994] 1 All ER 270.

As to the importance of alleging the presence of the required 12 persons, see by analogy *Mahroof* (1989) 88 Cr App R 317 (a case concerned with violent disorder: see **B11.30** and **B11.33**). See also *Fleming* (1989) 153 JP 517; *Worton* (1989) 154 JP 201.

The POA 1986, s. 7(2), declares that for the purposes of the rules against charging more than one offence in the same count, each of ss. 1 to 5 of the Act creates one offence.

Alternative Verdicts

B11.18 The POA 1986, s. 7(3), provides for alternative verdicts on charges under the Act without mentioning s. 1. However, the CLA 1967, s. 6(3) (see **D19.42** ***et seq.***), would allow the jury on an indictment for riot to return an alternative verdict of guilty of violent disorder under the POA 1986, s. 2, or of affray under s. 3 (see also **B11.31**). It may, however, be prudent to add alternative counts.

Sentencing Guidelines

B11.19 The maximum penalty is ten years or a fine or both (POA 1986, s. 1(6)). Riot is a specified offence for the purposes of the public protection provisions in the CJA 2003 (see **E4**). The definitive sentencing guideline, *Public Order Offences* (see Supplement, **SG29-5**), applies from 1 January 2020. For riot, culpability will be 'A' if certain factors are present and 'B' if they are not. Culpability 'A' factors include the use or intended use of a petrol bomb or other incendiary device, a firearm or another 'highly dangerous weapon'. Whether a weapon is highly dangerous is a matter for the sentencing court but in order to qualify the dangerous nature of the weapon must be substantially above and beyond the legislative definition of an offensive weapon. Similarly, harm will be category 1 where there are 'multiple and extreme examples of' a number of listed factors and category 2 where those examples are absent. For a category 1A offence the starting point is seven years' custody with a range of six to nine years, for a category 1B offence or a category 2A offence the starting point is six years' custody with a range of four to seven years, and for a category 2B offence the starting point is five years' custody with a range of three to six years.

Twelve or More Persons Present Using or Threatening Violence for a Common Purpose

B11.20 It is immaterial whether or not the 12 or more use or threaten unlawful violence simultaneously (POA 1986, s. 1(2)). It is also immaterial (by s. 6(7)) whether all of the 12 or more intend to use violence or are aware that their conduct may be violent (the mental element in the offence of riot: see **B11.25**). In other words, a person may be guilty of riot even if some of the 12 or more co-rioters are not guilty of riot (or of violent disorder or affray) because of lack of *mens rea* (see **B11.33**). Common purpose may be inferred from the conduct of the rioters (POA 1986, s. 1(3)) together with such circumstances as the carrying of banners, shouting of slogans, threats and the like.

Accused Must Use Violence

B11.21 There must be 12 or more persons using or threatening violence but only those who actually use violence will be guilty of the offence of riot (*Jefferson* [1994] 1 All ER 270). In *Mitsui Sumitomo Insurance (Europe) Ltd v Mayor's Office for Policing and Crime* [2013] EWHC 2743 (Comm), [2014] 1 All ER 422 the claimants sued for damages under the Riot (Damages) Act 1886 following a fire at a warehouse that occurred during the civil disorder of August 2011. The claimants had to establish that there had been a riot within the meaning of the POA 1986, s. 1. It was not in dispute that a number of youths had been responsible for the fire but there was an issue as to whether the elements of riot were made out on the facts. Flaux J (at [69]) held that there had been a riot. He said:

> ... even if not all the gang were smashing down the door or throwing petrol bombs, the others by their presence were threatening unlawful violence, or, putting it another way, they were all engaged together in the joint enterprise of breaking into the premises and looting and destroying them, even the two twelve year olds [a witness] encountered outside.

The reasoning here is open to question and it should be noted that the case was presented as one of joint enterprise. It cannot be the case that because 12 or more persons are present together with a common purpose that *some* of their number should use or threaten violence that in the event all 12 have therefore used or threatened violence. If, on different facts, 12 persons had assembled with the common purpose that one of their number should start a fight in the street and that person did so while the others stood and watched, that could not be described as a riot. When the decision of Flaux J was appealed to the Court of Appeal (Civil Division) ([2014] EWCA Civ 682, [2015] QB 180), the finding that there had been a riot within the meaning of the POA 1986, s. 1, was not challenged (at [70]).

Meaning of 'Unlawful Violence'

B11.22 **Public Order Act 1986, s. 8**

> (1) In this part—
> ...
> 'violence' means any violent conduct, so that—
> (a) except in the context of affray, it includes violent conduct towards property as well as violent conduct towards persons, and
> (b) it is not restricted to conduct causing or intended to cause injury or damage but includes any other violent conduct (for example, throwing at or towards a person a missile of a kind capable of causing injury which does not hit or falls short).

As to the meaning of 'unlawful', see **B11.41**.

Consequences of the Use or Threat of Violence

B11.23 Under the POA 1986, s. 1(1), riot occurs where a person of reasonable firmness present at the scene *would* be caused, not *was* caused, to 'fear for his personal safety'. Further, s. 1(4) provides that: 'No person of reasonable firmness need actually be, or be likely to be, present at the scene' (see **B11.43**).

Place of Commission

B11.24 Riot may occur in private as well as in public places (POA 1986, s. 1(5)).

Mens Rea

A person is guilty of riot only if the person intends to use violence or is aware that the conduct may be violent (POA 1986, s. 6(1)). A direction as to *mens* rea must normally be given (*Blackwood* [2002] EWCA Crim 3102), and care must be taken to distinguish between principal offenders and aiders and abettors in that direction (see also A4). B11.25

Effect of Voluntary, Self-induced Intoxication on *Mens Rea*

The POA 1986, s. 6, deals with the problem of whether D's intoxication should be taken into account when determining that of which D was aware. Consequently, the problems encountered with the defence of self-induced intoxication (see **A3.16** to **A3.22**) and the effect of intoxication on mistakes which a person makes are of no direct concern in the offence of riot. B11.26

Public Order Act 1986, s. 6

(5) For the purposes of this section a person whose awareness is impaired by intoxication shall be taken to be aware of that of which he would be aware if not intoxicated, unless he shows either that his intoxication was not self-induced or that it was caused solely by the taking or administration of a substance in the course of medical treatment.
(6) In subsection (5) 'intoxication' means any intoxication, whether caused by drink, drugs or other means, or by a combination of means.

VIOLENT DISORDER

Public Order Act 1986, s. 2 B11.27

(1) Where three or more persons who are present together use or threaten unlawful violence and the conduct of them (taken together) is such as would cause a person of reasonable firmness present at the scene to fear for his personal safety, each of the persons using or threatening unlawful violence is guilty of violent disorder.
(2) It is immaterial whether or not the three or more use or threaten unlawful violence simultaneously.
(3) No person of reasonable firmness need actually be, or be likely to be, present at the scene.
(4) Violent disorder may be committed in private as well as in public places.

Procedure

Violent disorder is triable either way (POA 1986, s. 2(5)). For the procedure to be followed on determining mode of trial, see **D6.6**. When tried on indictment, violent disorder is normally a class 3 offence, but see CrimPD XIII, para. B (see Supplement, **CPD.XIII.B**) for the additional factors that the court considers on allocation. See the CPS Legal Guidance on Public Disorder for the current charging criteria. B11.28

Indictment

Statement of Offence B11.29

Violent disorder contrary to section 2(1) of the Public Order Act 1986.

Particulars of Offence

A on or about the...day of..., being one of three or more persons present together at...and using [or threatening] unlawful violence used [or threatened to use] unlawful violence by assaulting members of the public, the conduct of the three or more persons aforesaid, taken together, being such as would cause a person of reasonable firmness present at the scene to fear for his personal safety.

The POA 1986, s. 7(2), declares that for the purposes of the rules against charging more than one offence in the same count, each of ss. 1 to 5 of the Act creates one offence.

B11.30 Violent disorder is not committed unless there are three or more persons together. In *Mahroof* (1988) 88 Cr App R 317, the jury had acquitted two of the accused named in the indictment, but had convicted Mahroof. The Court of Appeal decided that there was a sufficient allegation in the indictment, even though no other persons were named, 'subject to two *very important* qualifications':

(a) 'that there is evidence before the jury that there were three people involved in the criminal behaviour, though not necessarily those named in the indictment' (see also *Lemon* [2002] EWCA Crim 1661), and
(b) 'that the defence are apprised of what it is they have to meet'.

The Court made clear that the best way, and generally the only way, of satisfying the second qualification is by putting it in the indictment. This could be done by adding the phrase, after naming certain individuals, 'and others', which could have been pursued in this case by the defence seeking particulars, which would have led to the provision of information about two other people who were known about. In *Mahroof*, qualification (b) was not satisfied. This decision was followed in *Fleming* (1989) 153 JP 517 and was followed and applied by the Court of Appeal in *Worton* (1989) 154 JP 201, although the Court seems to have been satisfied that the defence were sufficiently appraised of the matter. It seems unsatisfactory that qualification (b) should be satisfied by the evidence given by the prosecution at the trial, rather than information provided in advance of the trial.

If one or more of the accused may lack the *mens rea* for the offence, the determination of numbers is not affected (see **B11.33**). See also *Mechen* [2004] EWCA Crim 388, confirming that acquittal of a person on the grounds of self-defence removes that person from inclusion in the minimum number required for the offence.

Alternative Verdicts

B11.31 **Public Order Act 1986, s. 7**

(3) If on the trial on indictment of a person charged with violent disorder... the jury find him not guilty of the offence charged, they may (without prejudice to section 6(3) of the Criminal Law Act 1967) find him guilty of an offence under section 4.
(4) The Crown Court has the same powers and duties in relation to a person who is by virtue of subsection (3) convicted before it of an offence under section 4 as a magistrates' court would have on convicting him of the offence.

As to the operation of the POA 1986, s. 7(3), see *Mahroof* (1988) 88 Cr App R 317 and *Worton* (1989) 154 JP 201. Section 7(3) applies only where the jury have found D not guilty, whether as a result of their own deliberations or as a result of following the judge's proper direction (*Carson* (1990) 92 Cr App R 236). The CLA 1967, s. 6(3) (see **D19.42** ***et seq.***), may be resorted to where D on arraignment pleads not guilty to an offence contrary to the POA 1986, s. 2 or 3, but wishes to plead guilty to an offence contrary to s. 4 (*O'Brien* (1992) 156 JP 925). The operation of the 1967 Act is unaffected by the POA 1986, so, on a charge of violent disorder, it is possible, provided the elements of the offence are established, to substitute a conviction, for example, of affray under s. 3 (*Fleming* (1989) 153 JP 517). Particular attention must be paid to matters such as the different meanings of 'violence' in the offences (*McGuigan* [1991] Crim LR 719 and see **B11.33** and **B11.43**).

The same principles apply to finding a person guilty of an offence contrary to s. 4 in the alternative. However, if a judge decides to leave s. 4 as an alternative to the jury, the defence should be given an opportunity to address the jury (*Perrins* [1995] Crim LR 432; *Stanley* [1993] Crim LR 618). In *Mbagwu* [2007] EWCA Crim 1068 it was said to be improper to leave s. 4 in the alternative to the jury after they had been in retirement for over a day and had already acquitted eight other defendants. See also *Va Kun Hau* [1990] Crim LR 518, where s. 4 was not available because the act took place in a dwelling-house.

Sentencing Guidelines

The maximum penalty is five years and/or a fine on indictment (POA 1986, s. 2(5)); six months and/or an unlimited fine summarily. Violent disorder is a specified offence for the purposes of the public protection provisions in the CJA 2003 (see **E4**). The definitive sentencing guideline, *Public Order Offences* (see Supplement, **SG29-7**), applies from 1 January 2020. For violent disorder, culpability will be either 'A', 'B' or 'C', and harm will be either category 1, 2 or 3, depending on whether particular identified factors are present or not. For a case that falls into category 1A the starting point is four years' custody with a range of three years to four years and six months, whereas for category 3C the starting point is 26 weeks' custody with a range of a medium level community order to one year's custody. **B11.32**

Actus Reus

Three or More People Present Together Using or Threatening Violence It is immaterial whether or not the three or more use or threaten unlawful violence simultaneously (POA 1986, s. 2(2)). **B11.33**

As stated at **B11.30**, it is essential to establish that three or more people were present together using or threatening violence. In *NW* [2010] EWCA Crim 404, [2010] 1 WLR 1426, the Court of Appeal considered the meaning of the expression 'present together'. It held that it means no more than being in the same place at the same time. Moore-Bick LJ stated (at [19]) that:

> Three or more people using or threatening violence in the same place at the same time, whether for the same purpose or different purposes, are capable of creating a daunting prospect for those who may encounter them simply by reason of the fact that they represent a breakdown of law and order which has unpredictable consequences. We are unable to accept that the phrase requires any degree of co-operation between those who are using or threatening violence; all that is required is that they be present in the same place at the same time.

The Court of Appeal in *Church* (12 November 1999 unreported) felt that assistance can be derived from the decision of the Divisional Court in *Allen v Ireland* [1984] 1 WLR 903 where Kerr LJ stated (at p. 910) that 'a defendant's voluntary presence during an affray or as part of a crowd engaged in threatening behaviour is capable of raising a prima facie case of participation against the defendant...but that mere voluntary presence is not sufficient to convict a defendant unless the court is satisfied that he at least also gave some overt encouragement to the others who were directly involved in the affray or threatening behaviour'. Whether any particular defendant is involved is, then, a question of fact. In *Fleming* (1989) 153 JP 517, the Court of Appeal made it clear that a jury should be directed that 'if it cannot be sure that three or more of the defendants were using or threatening violence, then it should acquit every defendant, even if satisfied that one or more particular defendants were unlawfully fighting'. Usually, therefore, when only three are named in the indictment, the jury must acquit all three if they acquit one. This is not the case where the jury are satisfied that others not charged were taking part in the violent disorder, in which case the jury may convict (*Worton* (1989) 154 JP 201). Account can be taken of such others only if the requirements established in *Mahroof* (1988) 88 Cr App R 317 (see **B11.30**) are satisfied. Further, where one (or more) defendant is acquitted as a result of lack of *mens rea* (see **B11.35**), the determination of the number of persons is unaffected (POA 1986, s. 6(7)). Thus if one (or more) of the named defendants is found not guilty because of a lack of *mens rea*, the remaining defendants may be found guilty, even if there are only two of them.

Other Elements Unlike the offence of riot, it is not part of the definition of violent disorder that those present have a common purpose (see *NW* [2010] EWCA Crim 404, [2010] 1 WLR 1426 at **B11.33**). **B11.34**

For the elements of unlawful violence, producing fear in a person of reasonable firmness, and place of commission, see the discussion of those elements in the offence of riot at **B11.22** to **B11.24**.

Mens Rea

B11.35 **Public Order Act 1986, s. 6**

(2) A person is guilty of violent disorder... only if he intends to use or threaten violence or is aware that his conduct may be violent or threaten violence.

The *mens rea* is subjective, see **B11.75**. For the effect of voluntary, self-induced intoxication on *mens rea*, see the discussion in relation to the offence of riot at **B11.26**.

AFFRAY

B11.36 **Public Order Act 1986, s. 3**

(1) A person is guilty of affray if he uses or threatens unlawful violence towards another and his conduct is such as would cause a person of reasonable firmness present at the scene to fear for his personal safety.
(2) Where two or more persons use or threaten the unlawful violence, it is the conduct of them taken together that must be considered for the purposes of subsection (1).
(3) For the purposes of this section a threat cannot be made by the use of words alone.
(4) No person of reasonable firmness need actually be, or be likely to be, present at the scene.
(5) Affray may be committed in private as well as in public places.

Procedure

B11.37 Prosecutions for affray should be instituted only where the incident gives rise to serious disturbance to public order (Law Commission Report No. 123, para. 3.38, referred to in *Davison* [1992] Crim LR 31); it is thoroughly bad practice to charge what are straightforward assaults as public order offences (*Connor* (13 March 2000 unreported)). See the CPS Legal Guidance on Public Disorder for the current charging criteria.

Affray is triable either way (POA 1986, s. 3(7)). The *Magistrates' Court Sentencing Guidelines* (see **B11.40** for a summary) give guidance on offence seriousness. For the procedure to be followed on determining mode of trial, see **D6.6**. When tried on indictment, affray is normally a class 3 offence, but see CrimPD XIII, para. B (see Supplement, **CPD.XIII.B**), for the additional factors that the court considers on allocation.

Indictment

B11.38 *Statement of Offence*

Affray contrary to section 3(1) of the Public Order Act 1986.

Particulars of Offence

A on or about the... day of... used [or threatened] violence towards one V, the conduct of A being such as to cause a person of reasonable firmness present at the scene to fear for his personal safety.

The POA 1986, s. 7(2), declares that for the purpose of the rules against charging more than one offence in the same count, each of ss. 1 to 5 of the Act creates one offence.

Although affray is a continuing offence, it is better practice to charge separate offences where there are distinct incidents and not all defendants are alleged to be involved in each of them (*Flounders* [2002] EWCA Crim 1325). See also *Smith* [1997] 1 Cr App R 14 as to how to direct a jury when a continuous affray has separate parts to it.

Alternative Verdicts

B11.39 **Public Order Act 1986, s. 7**

(3) If on the trial on indictment of a person charged with... affray the jury find him not guilty of the offence charged, they may (without prejudice to section 6(3) of the Criminal Law Act 1967) find him guilty of an offence under section 4.

(4) The Crown Court has the same powers and duties in relation to a person who is by virtue of subsection (3) convicted before it of an offence under section 4 as a magistrates' court would have on convicting him of the offence.

It is important that the jury be properly directed as to the lesser offence, which they should consider only if it is unsure that affray has been committed (*Stanley* [1993] Crim LR 618). The differences between the offences may be crucial (*Va Kun Hau* [1990] Crim LR 518, where s. 4 was not available because the act took place in a dwelling-house).

As to the interrelationship between s. 7(3) and the CLA 1967, s. 6(3), see **B11.31**.

Sentencing Guidelines

The maximum penalty is three years and/or a fine on indictment (POA 1986, s. 3(7)); six months and/or an unlimited fine summarily. Affray is a specified offence for the purposes of the public protection provisions in the CJA 2003 (see E4). The definitive sentencing guideline, *Public Order Offences* (see Supplement, **SG29-2**), applies from 1 January 2020. For affray, culpability will be either 'A', 'B' or 'C', and harm will be either category 1, 2 or 3, depending on whether particular identified factors are present or not. For a case that falls into category 1A the starting point is two years' custody with a range of one year and six months to two years and nine months, whereas for category 3C the starting point is a medium level community order with a range of a band C fine to a high level community order. **B11.40**

Meaning of 'Threat' and 'Unlawful Violence'

The essential elements of affray, according to the Court of Appeal, are '(a) the use or threat of violence by the defendant; (b) to another person; which (c) would cause a third person to fear for his or her own safety' (*Thind* [1999] Crim LR 842). For (a) and (b), see below. For (c), see **B11.43**. Lord Bingham CJ has described affray in *Smith* [1997] 1 Cr App R 14 at p. 16: **B11.41**

> It typically involves a group of people who may well be shouting, struggling, threatening, waving weapons, throwing objects, exchanging and threatening blows and so on. Again, typically, it involves a continuous course of conduct, the criminal character of which depends on the general nature and effect of the conduct as a whole and not on particular incidents and events which may take place in the course of it. Where reliance is placed on such a continuous course of conduct, it is not necessary for the Crown to identify and prove particular incidents.

These 'typical activities' must amount to the use or threat of unlawful violence (POA 1986, s. 3(1)). The definition of 'violence' in affray is different from its definition for other purposes in the POA 1986. By s. 8, violence, for affray, does not include violent conduct towards property. It is, therefore, limited to violent conduct towards persons. Otherwise, s. 8 provides:

> 'violence' means any violent conduct, so that—
>
> . . .
>
> (b) it is not restricted to conduct causing or intended to cause injury or damage but includes any other violent conduct (for example, throwing at or towards a person a missile of a kind capable of causing injury which does not hit or falls short).

In *Rothwell* [1993] Crim LR 626, it was held that the word 'unlawful' is intended to ensure that defences such as self-defence apply to offences under the POA 1986.

Since a threat cannot be made by words alone (POA 1986, s. 3(3)), there must be conduct on the part of D (*Robinson* [1993] Crim LR 581). In *Dixon* [1993] Crim LR 579, ordering a dog to attack was sufficient to constitute a threat; because there was conduct, the dog being used as a weapon. **B11.42**

The words 'threatens unlawful violence' carry their ordinary and natural meaning so that the carrying of dangerous weapons, such as petrol bombs by a group of persons can, in some circumstances, constitute the threat of violence, without those weapons being waved or brandished towards another person (*I v DPP* [2001] UKHL 10, [2001] 2 All ER 583). Whether the carrying of weapons is sufficient in any given case is a matter for the tribunal of fact to decide. Unlawful violence must be used or threatened to another. That other must be present at the scene. As the only people proved to be present in *I v DPP* were the members of the gang possessing and brandishing petrol bombs, there was no 'another' to whom violence was used or threatened and so there was no affray.

The Test for Conduct Causing Fear

B11.43 The test, as for riot and violent disorder, is whether a person of reasonable firmness present at the scene *would* be caused, not *was* caused, to 'fear for his personal safety'. No person of reasonable firmness need actually be, or be likely to be, present at the scene (POA 1986, s. 3(4)).

In *Davison* [1992] Crim LR 31, the Court of Appeal, taking account of Law Commission Report No. 123, decided that the conduct to be considered is that of D. Its consequences are judged by an objective standard, i.e. whether the hypothetical bystander of reasonable firmness (not the person assaulted) would be put in fear for his personal safety if present. Account may be taken of the nature of the premises and scene where the incident took place, and of the fact that the violence was limited to those involved. Account may also be taken of the reactions of others who were present, whether those reactions showed fear (*Freeman v DPP* [2013] EWHC 610 (Admin)) or disinterest (*DPP v Cotcher* (1992) *The Times*, 29 December 1992), provided that the jury are directed that in considering their verdict only the reaction of the hypothetical bystander matters. In *Sanchez* (1996) 160 JP 321, the Divisional Court approved the commentary of Professor Sir John Smith to *Davison* as being the correct approach: 'the question in the present case was not whether a person of reasonable firmness in [V's] shoes would have feared for his personal safety but whether [the] hypothetical person, present in the room and seeing [D's] conduct towards [V] would have so feared... [The offence] is designed for the protection of the bystander. It is a public order offence. There are other offences for the protection of persons at whom the violence is aimed.' See also *Blinkhorn* [2006] EWCA Crim 1416. In *Leeson v DPP* [2010] EWHC 994 (Admin), the Administrative Court reviewed all the authorities in this area. Applying *Cotcher*, it found that the magistrates had been wrong to convict D of affray after she issued a drunken threat to kill her long-term partner whilst holding a knife, in a bathroom, in an otherwise unoccupied house. The Court found that there was no possibility of a hypothetical bystander fearing for his safety as the exchanges were personal and restricted to turbulence between the couple, and so could not have given rise to a fear of unlawful violence to anyone else.

Where the defendant is one of a number of people who use or threaten unlawful violence, in deciding whether the person of reasonable firmness present at the scene would be caused to fear for his personal safety, it is the conduct of the entire group taken as a whole that counts and so there is no need in such a situation for the court to attribute individual roles to the participants (*Dragjoshi v Croydon Magistrates' Courts* [2017] EWHC 2840 (QB)).

Mens Rea

B11.44 **Public Order Act 1986, s. 6**

(2) A person is guilty of... affray only if he intends to use or threaten violence or is aware that his conduct may be violent or threaten violence.

The *mens rea* is subjective, see **B11.75**. A direction about *mens rea* should normally be given (*Mann* [2002] EWCA Crim 3045). For the effect of voluntary, self-induced intoxication on *mens rea*, see the discussion in relation to the offence of riot at **B11.26**.

FEAR OR PROVOCATION OF VIOLENCE

Public Order Act 1986, s. 4 **B11.45**

(1) A person is guilty of an offence if he—
 (a) uses towards another person threatening, abusive or insulting words or behaviour, or
 (b) distributes or displays to another person any writing, sign or other visible representation which is threatening, abusive or insulting,

with intent to cause that person to believe that immediate unlawful violence will be used against him or another by any person, or to provoke the immediate use of unlawful violence by that person or another, or whereby that person is likely to believe that such violence will be used or it is likely that such violence will be provoked.

(2) An offence under this section may be committed in a public or a private place, except that no offence is committed where the words or behaviour are used, or the writing, sign or other visible representation is distributed or displayed, by a person inside a dwelling and the other person is also inside that or another dwelling.

The CDA 1998, s. 31, created a racially or religiously aggravated form of this offence. For the meaning of racially or religiously aggravated, see **B11.145**.

Procedure

An offence under the POA 1986, s. 4(1), is, by s. 4(4) of the Act, triable summarily only. The racially aggravated form of the offence is triable either way (CDA 1998, s. 31(4)). If, on trial on indictment, the jury find D not guilty of the racially aggravated form of the offence, they may find D guilty of the basic offence (s. 31(6)). It is not permissible for a magistrates' court to convict a person of both an offence under s. 4(1) and the racially aggravated form of the offence, where both offences arise out of the same facts. The charges are in the alternative and it is a basic principle of English justice that a person should be convicted only once for one wrong (*R (Dyer) v Watford Magistrates' Court* [2013] EWHC 547 (Admin): see also **D22.72**). In *Henderson v DPP* [2016] EWHC 464 (Admin), [2016] 1 WLR 1990, the Divisional Court held that, in a summary trial, where D is charged both with the racially aggravated offence and the underlying offence, and the court convicted D of the racially aggravated offence, the court should adjourn the trial of the underlying offence *sine die*. If D had previously indicated a plea of guilty to the underlying offence, that indication should be noted on the file but no plea taken. If, having been convicted of the aggravated offence, D appeals that conviction to the Crown Court, that court would still have the power to acquit D of the aggravated offence but convict D of the underlying offence. **B11.46**

The POA 1986, s. 7(2), declares that for the purposes of the rules against charging more than one offence in the same information, each of ss. 1 to 5 of the Act creates one offence. The offence under s. 4 may be committed in one of four ways (*Winn v DPP* (1992) 156 JP 881, and see **B11.50**). Care must be taken in formulating the charge so that the way of committing the offence reflects the facts of the case, otherwise there may be unjustifiable variance between the charge and the particulars alleged. More than one way of committing the offence may be included and amendment is possible if necessary (*Winn v DPP*; *Loade v DPP* [1990] 1 QB 1052: for amendment, see **D21.11**).

The person towards whom threatening, abusive or insulting words or behaviour are used can be held to perceive the threatening words or behaviour even when the person does not give evidence at the trial (*Swanston v DPP* (1997) 161 JP 203). Of course, there must be other evidence, as there was in *Swanston* in view of the small area in which the incidents took place, and the evidence of the police constable.

In a prosecution for an offence contrary to s. 4, the prosecution do not have to prove that the decision to prosecute is proportionate and, accordingly, that it does not amount to an infringement of the ECHR, Article 10. The 'necessary balance of proportionality is struck by the terms of the offence-creating provision, without more ado': per Ouseley J in *James v DPP* [2015] EWHC 3296 (Admin), [2016] 1 WLR 2118 at [35], disapproving *Dehal v CPS* [2005] EWHC 2154 (Admin) and approving *Bauer v DPP* [2013] EWHC 634 (Admin), [2013] 1 WLR 3617.

Sentencing Guidelines (Basic Offence)

B11.47 The maximum penalty is six months and/or an unlimited fine (POA 1986, s. 4(4)). The definitive sentencing guideline, *Public Order Offences* (see Supplement, **SG29-6**), applies from 1 January 2020. For s. 4, culpability will be 'A' and harm will be category 1 when certain identified factors are present and 'B' and category 2 when they are not. For a case that falls into category 1A the starting point is a high level community order with a range of a low level community order to 26 weeks' custody. For category 1B or category 2A the starting point is a medium level community order with a range of a band C fine to 12 weeks' custody, and for category 2B the starting point is a low level community order with a range of a discharge to a medium level community order.

Where D is made subject to a community order following conviction for an offence contrary to the POA 1986, s. 4, and D then breaches the order, a period of imprisonment for the breach is likely but the court should not jump straight to the maximum sentence for the offence when deciding the length of any custodial term (*Bywater* [2014] EWCA Crim 405).

B11.48 Racial or religious aggravation cannot be taken into account by the sentencer when sentencing for the basic offence of fear or provocation of violence. To do so would infringe the principle that D must not be sentenced for an offence for which D has not been charged and convicted (*McGillivray* [2005] EWCA Crim 604, [2005] 2 Cr App R (S) 60 (366)). Where there is evidence that racial aggravation was present, the aggravated form of the offence should be charged (*O'Callaghan* [2005] EWCA Crim 317, [2005] 2 Cr App R (S) 83 (514)). See **E1.19** for increase in sentence, under the CJA 2003, s. 146, for aggravation relating to disability, sexual orientation or transgender identity. Where the offence is committed in a domestic context, reference should be made to the definitive sentencing guideline, *Domestic Abuse* (see Supplement, **SG6-1**).

Sentencing Guidelines (Racially or Religiously Aggravated Form of Offence)

B11.49 The maximum penalty for the aggravated form of the offence is two years and/or a fine on indictment; six months and/or an unlimited fine summarily (CDA 1998, s. 31(4)). The definitive sentencing guideline, *Public Order Offences* (see Supplement, **SG29-6**), provides that for the aggravated form of the s. 4 offence the court should determine whether the racial or religious aggravation is at a high level, a medium level or a low level. Where at a high level, the court should increase the length of any custodial sentence or consider imposing a custodial sentence where a custodial sentence would not have been justified for the basic offence alone. Where at a medium level, the court should consider imposing a significantly more onerous penalty of the same type or consider a more severe type of sentence than for the basic offence. Where at a low level, the court should consider imposing a more onerous penalty of the same type identified for the basic offence.

The Four Ways of Committing an Offence under s. 4

B11.50 Common to all four ways of committing an offence under the POA 1986, s. 4, are (i) the use of threatening words or behaviour or the distribution or display of threatening, abusive or insulting writing etc. (see **B11.52** to **B11.54**) and (ii) the requirement as to *mens rea* in s. 6(3) (see **B11.55**). The four ways, as indicated in *Winn v DPP* (1992) 156 JP 881, are:

(a) D must 'intend the person against whom the conduct is directed to believe that immediate unlawful violence will be used against him or another by [any] person' — as McCowan LJ put it in *Swanston v DPP* (1997) 161 JP 203, 'It is a vital component of the offence that it does not have to be shown that the other person believed: it has to be shown that the [D]

had the intention to cause that person to believe' that immediate unlawful violence would be used against him;
(b) D must 'intend to provoke the immediate use of unlawful violence by that person or another';
(c) 'the person against whom [the words, behaviour, distribution or display] are directed is likely to believe that such violence will be used' (note that the person who must be caused to believe that violence will be used or threatened is the person to whom the words, behaviour, distribution or display are directed, see *Loade v DPP* [1990] 1 QB 1052 and *Horgle v DPP* [2015] EWHC 856 (Admin));
(d) 'it is likely that such violence will be provoked'.

In paragraphs (c) and (d) above, 'such violence' means 'immediate unlawful violence' (*Horseferry Road Metropolitan Stipendiary Magistrate, ex parte Siadatan* [1991] 1 QB 260).

Uses Towards

The Divisional Court in *Atkin v DPP* (1989) 89 Cr App R 199 held that the phrase 'uses towards' in the POA 1986, s. 4(1)(a), connotes the physical presence of the person to whom the words were used. That other person must 'perceive with his own senses' the threatening words or behaviour (see also **B11.43**). In *Atkin* the conviction had to be quashed, since the person outside the dwelling was only aware of the threat because it was relayed by a Customs and Excise officer. **B11.51**

Threatening, Abusive or Insulting

The phrase 'threatening, abusive or insulting words or behaviour' used in the POA 1986, s. 4(1)(a), is not defined in the Act. However, 'threatening, abusive or insulting' was used with reference to words or behaviour in the POA 1936, s. 5, and the Metropolitan Police Act 1839, s. 54(13), both of which have since been repealed. **B11.52**

The House of Lords in *Brutus v Cozens* [1973] AC 854 decided that 'insulting' is to be given its ordinary meaning and whether words or behaviour are insulting is a question of fact. The same approach is adopted with regard to the words 'threatening' and 'abusive' and the courts have adopted this approach in the interpretation of the 1986 Act (*DPP v Clarke* (1991) 94 Cr App R 359, a decision on s. 5). In *Ambrose* (1973) 57 Cr App R 538, the Court of Appeal said that rude or offensive words were not necessarily insulting. However, describing an Asian person as a 'fucking Islam' is almost undeniably abusive, if not insulting (*R (DPP) v Humphrey* [2005] EWHC 822 (Admin)).

Meaning of 'Writing' and 'Display'

'Writing' includes typing, printing, lithography, photography and other modes of representing or reproducing words in a visible form (Interpretation Act 1978, s. 5 and sch. 1). As to 'display', see **B11.71**. **B11.53**

Place of Commission

Public Order Act 1986, ss. 4 and 8 **B11.54**

4.—(2) An offence under this section may be committed in a public or a private place, except that no offence is committed where the words or behaviour are used, or the writing, sign or other visible representation is distributed or displayed, by a person inside a dwelling and the other person is also inside that or another dwelling.

8. In this part—
'dwelling' means any structure or part of a structure occupied as a person's home or as other living accommodation (whether the occupation is separate or shared with others) but does not include any part not so occupied, and for this purpose 'structure' includes a tent, caravan, vehicle, vessel or other temporary or movable structure.

'The other person' referred to in s. 4(2) is the same person as is referred to as 'another person' in s. 4(1)(a). Thus the offence is not committed in a dwelling if the only person to whom the words or behaviour are used, etc. (see **B11.51**) is also in that or another dwelling (*Atkin v DPP* (1989) 89 Cr App R 199). It appears to follow that the offence can be committed by the use of telephones, fax machines, e-mail and social media.

Where common parts (a communal landing) were the means of access to living accommodation, they were not part of a dwelling, even though access was via an entry phone system, and were not part of the living area or home (*Rukwira v DPP* [1993] Crim LR 882). Similarly, in *Le Vine v DPP* [2010] EWHC 1128 (Admin), the Administrative Court, applying *Rukwira*, found that a laundry room, commonly used by tenants in sheltered housing, did not form part of a dwelling. In *Francis* [2006] EWCA Crim 3323, [2007] 1 WLR 1021 it was held that a police cell is not living accommodation. For a case where the Court of Appeal reviewed a number of authorities in this area see *DPP v D* [2017] EWHC 2244 (Admin), [2017] 4 WLR 177.

Mens Rea

B11.55 The intention with which the defendant must act is to be found in s. 4(1) (see **B11.45**) as explained further at **B11.50**. Thus, the *mens rea* that must be proved is dependent upon which form of the offence is charged.

For all four forms of the offence, the following applies.

Public Order Act 1986, s. 6

(3) A person is guilty of an offence under section 4 only if he intends his words or behaviour, or the writing, sign or other visible representation, to be threatening, abusive or insulting, or is aware that it may be threatening, abusive or insulting.

B11.56 Whichever *mens rea* applies, the question of whether immediate unlawful violence was intended arises. In *DPP v Ramos* [2000] Crim LR 768 it was decided that it is V's state of mind that 'is crucial rather than the statistical risk of violence actually occurring within a very short space of time'. Thus, there was evidence on the basis of which the magistrate could infer the requisite intention as to V's belief since the letters that were sent contained a very serious threat, of a bombing campaign, and there was nothing to exclude the immediate future from the period when that violence would be used. This case demonstrates the importance of identifying whether there will be immediate violence. The Divisional Court in *Horseferry Road Metropolitan Stipendiary Magistrate, ex parte Siadatan* [1991] 1 QB 260 decided that it is not sufficient that the conduct was likely to lead to violence at some unspecified time in the future. However, it decided also that 'immediate' does not mean 'instantaneous', so a relatively short time interval may elapse between the act and the violence. The court also decided that 'immediate' connotes proximity in both time and causation, i.e. the violence must result within a relatively short period of time and without any intervening occurrence. Thus, as it was not contended that immediate unlawful violence would be provoked as a result of the publication of *The Satanic Verses*, the failure to issue a summons against Penguin Viking Books Ltd was not open to challenge. The Divisional Court held in *Valentine v DPP* [1997] COD 339 that the justices were entitled to find D guilty where his threats caused a woman to fear 'immediate' violence the next time her husband went to work, but only because he might have gone to work the same night that the threat was made. Assistance on this matter may also be found in the concept of immediacy in assault (see **B2.5**), referred to by the Divisional Court in *DPP v Ramos*. As to the definition of 'violence' in the POA 1986, s. 8, see **B11.22**.

Since the POA 1986, s. 6, deals with intoxication when determining that of which D was aware, the general problems encountered with self-induced intoxication (see **A3.16** to **A3.22**), and the effect of intoxication on mistakes, are of no direct concern in this offence.

INTENTIONALLY CAUSING HARASSMENT, ALARM OR DISTRESS

Public Order Act 1986, s. 4A **B11.57**

(1) A person is guilty of an offence if, with intent to cause a person harassment, alarm or distress, he—
(a) uses threatening, abusive or insulting words or behaviour, or disorderly behaviour, or
(b) displays any writing, sign or other visible representation which is threatening, abusive or insulting,
thereby causing that or another person harassment, alarm or distress.

The CDA 1998, s. 31, created a racially or religiously aggravated form of this offence. For the meaning of racially or religiously aggravated, see **B11.145** ***et seq.*** In *Valentine* [2017] EWCA Crim 207, the Court of Appeal held that where the racial hostility was directed at someone who was not the victim of the s. 4A offence, then, where the offence was said to have been racially aggravated under the CDA 1998, s. 28(1)(a), the elements of the racially aggravated form of the offence were not made out. In reaching this conclusion, the Court held that the victim of the s. 4A offence is the person who is caused harassment, alarm or distress and not the person the defendant intended to harass, alarm or distress, where those people are different.

Procedure and Sentencing Guidelines (Basic Offence)

The basic offence is triable summarily only (POA 1986, s. 4A(5)). The maximum penalty is a **B11.58**
term of imprisonment not exceeding six months and/or an unlimited fine (s. 4A(5)). For the charging criteria in cases that engage the ECHR, Article 10, see **B11.46**.

The definitive sentencing guideline, *Public Order Offences* (see Supplement, **SG29-3**), applies from 1 January 2020. For s. 4A, culpability will be 'A' and harm will be category 1 where certain identified factors are present and 'B' and category 2 respectively when those factors are absent. Category 1A has a starting point of a high level community order with a range of a low level community order to 26 weeks' custody. Category 1B and category 2A have starting points of a low level community order with a range of a band C fine to 12 weeks' custody. Category 2B has a starting point of a band C fine with a range of a discharge to a low level community order. Racial or religious aggravation cannot be taken into account by the sentencer when sentencing for the basic offence. See **B11.47**.

Procedure and Sentencing Guidelines (Racially or Religiously Aggravated Form of Offence)

The aggravated form of the offence is triable either way (CDA 1998, s. 31(4)). If, on trial on **B11.59**
indictment, the jury find D not guilty of the racially aggravated form of the offence, they may find D guilty of the basic offence (s. 31(6)). See also **B11.46**. The maximum penalty on indictment is a term of imprisonment for two years and/or a fine and, on summary trial, a term of imprisonment for six months, and/or an unlimited fine (s. 31(4)).

When sentencing for the aggravated form of the s. 4A offence, the definitive guideline provides that the aggravation should be assessed as being either high level, medium level or low level. High level aggravation should increase the length of any custodial sentence imposed or prompt the sentencing court to consider imposing a custodial sentence. Medium level aggravation generally merits a significantly more onerous penalty of the same type or a more severe type of sentence than for the basic offence. Where there is low level aggravation the court should consider imposing a more onerous penalty of the same type identified for the basic offence.

Meaning of 'Harassment, Alarm or Distress' etc.

B11.60 Harassment, alarm or distress have not been defined, but it is assumed that they are ordinary words of the English language unless and until a definition is provided. The guidance on these words under the POA 1986, s. 5, supports this approach, see **B11.74**. In *R (R) v DPP* [2006] EWHC 1375 (Admin), a prosecution under the POA 1986, s. 4A, the High Court described them as relatively strong words befitting an offence which may carry imprisonment or a substantial fine and held that the word 'distress' in this context requires emotional disturbance or upset.

For the meaning of the phrase 'threatening, abusive or insulting', see **B11.52.** For the meaning of 'disorderly behaviour', see **B11.70**. For the meaning of 'writing', see **B11.53**. For the meaning of 'display' in the POA 1986, s. 5, see **B11.71**.

There must be a causal connection between what D does and the other person's harassment, alarm or distress, as was emphasised in *Rogers v DPP* (22 July 1999 unreported). It was held that the causal connection was not broken where a cat breeder heard the noise of the crowd and was concerned by it and its cumulative increase, but watched the incident on security close circuit television. In *Steele v DPP* [2008] EWHC 438 (Admin), [2008] 1 WLR 2847 the Divisional Court held that the offence was made out even if the material that eventually caused the harassment, alarm or distress was no longer in the public domain at the time it caused that reaction. On the facts of that case, material displayed on an animal rights web site was preserved by police before it was removed by D and subsequently shown to V by the police.

Place of Commission of Offence

B11.61 **Public Order Act 1986, s. 4A**

(2) An offence under this section may be committed in a public or a private place, except that no offence is committed where the words or behaviour are used, or the writing, sign or other visible representation is displayed, by a person inside a dwelling and the person who is harassed, alarmed or distressed is also inside that or another dwelling.

As to the consideration of the similar provision in s. 5(2), see **B11.74**.

A police cell is not a place which a person occupies as living accommodation, and cannot be classified as a dwelling or living accommodation for the purposes of s. 4A (*Francis* [2006] EWCA Crim 3323, [2007] 1 WLR 1021).

Mens Rea

B11.62 This is an offence requiring proof of an intention to cause harassment, alarm or distress (POA 1986, s. 4A(1)). This is the fundamental question and it may be inferred where D's 'activities are committed in the context of a large crowd there to express disapproval of [the other's] activities and in the context of fence removal and penetration of the police line' even though there is no evidence that D knew that the other was present at the scene or could directly experience the disorderly behaviour (*Rogers v DPP* (22 July 1999 unreported)). It may also be inferred from the words used, though it does not necessarily follow that the requisite intention is established by the use of words such as 'black bastard' (*DPP v Weeks* (2000) *Independent*, 17 July 2000). As to the meaning of 'intention', see **A2.4**. For the effect of voluntary, self-induced intoxication on *mens rea*, see the discussion in relation to the offence of riot at **B11.26**.

Specific Defences

B11.63 **Public Order Act 1986, s. 4A**

(3) It is a defence for the accused to prove—
  (a) that he was inside a dwelling and had no reason to believe that the words or behaviour used, or the writing, sign or other visible representation displayed, would be heard or seen by a person outside that or any other dwelling; or
  (b) that his conduct was reasonable.

When the legal burden is on D, the standard required is proof on a balance of probabilities (see **F3.5** and **F3.53**). For a summary of the case law relating to 'reverse burden' challenges under the HRA 1998, see **F3.18** ***et seq.***

A person's conduct will be reasonable if the person is exercising ECHR rights in circumstances in which an interference with that exercise would not be justified under Articles 10(2) (the qualifications to the right to freedom of expression) and 9(2) (the qualifications to freedom of religion) (*Hammond v DPP* [2004] EWHC 69 (Admin), a case relating to the POA 1986, s. 5). See also *James v DPP* [2015] EWHC 3296 (Admin), [2016] 1 WLR 2118 at **B11.46**.

Alternative Offence

It is a summary offence, contrary to the CJA 1967, s. 91, where a person in any public place is, while drunk, guilty of disorderly behaviour (see **B11.198**). **B11.64**

HARASSMENT, ALARM OR DISTRESS

Public Order Act 1986, s. 5 **B11.65**

(1) A person is guilty of an offence if he—
(a) uses threatening or abusive words or behaviour, or disorderly behaviour, or
(b) displays any writing, sign or other visible representation which is threatening or abusive,
within the hearing or sight of a person likely to be caused harassment, alarm or distress thereby.
[(2) and (3) concern the place of commission of the offence and a specific defence: see **B11.74** and **B11.76**.]

The CDA 1998, s. 31, created a racially or religiously aggravated form of this offence. For the meaning of racially or religiously aggravated, see **B11.145** ***et seq.***; the definition has effect as if the person likely to be caused harassment, alarm or distress were the victim of the offence (s. 31(7)).

ECHR, Article 10 A prosecution under the POA 1986, s. 5, does not *per se* engage the ECHR, Article 10 (the right to freedom of expression): *Percy v DPP* [2001] EWHC 1125 (Admin) (but see the defence of 'reasonableness' at **B11.76**). In *Abdul v DPP* [2011] EWHC 247 (Admin) the five appellants were protestors who were convicted of offences under the POA 1986, s. 5. They attended a parade in Luton town centre the purpose of which was to celebrate the homecoming of the local Royal Anglian Regiment from its duties in Afghanistan and Iraq. They carried placards, chanted slogans such as 'British soldiers burn in hell', and called the soldiers murderers, rapists and baby-killers. One of the submissions made at the close of the prosecution case was that the prosecution itself was disproportionate bearing in mind the ECHR, Article 10. The Divisional Court found that the district judge was entitled to conclude that prosecution was a proportionate response. The principles governing the relationship between s. 5 and Article 10 could be summarised as follows: the starting point was the importance of the right to freedom of expression, but it was to be recognised that legitimate protest could be offensive, at least to some; the justification for interference had to be convincingly established and the restrictions in Article 10(2) were to be construed narrowly; the justification for invoking the criminal law was the threat to public order and was for the Crown to establish; in striking the right balance when determining whether speech was threatening, abusive or insulting, the focus on minority rights was not to result in overlooking the rights of the majority; if the line between legitimate freedom of expression and a threat to public order was crossed, freedom of speech would not be impaired by 'ruling out' threatening, abusive or insulting speech. (*Abdul* was heard prior to the amendment that removed 'insulting' from s. 5(1).) Finally, the decision was one for the judge and was not to be overturned unless shown to be plainly wrong. In *Campaign Against Anti-Semitism v DPP* [2019] EWHC 9 (Admin), a charitable organisation brought a claim for judicial review against the DPP's decision to take over and discontinue the organisation's private prosecution of D under s. 5 in circumstances where it was alleged that D had shouted anti-Semitic remarks during a public parade. Referring to *Abdul*, the Court held that there was **B11.66**

a line between legitimate freedom of expression on the one hand and a threat to public order on the other. There is not and cannot be any universal test for resolving when speech goes beyond legitimate protest, so attracting the sanction of the criminal law, but the context of the occasion will be of the first importance. See also **B11.46**.

See also the CPS Legal Guidance on Public Disorder for the current charging criteria.

Procedure

B11.67 The offence is, by s. 5(6) of the POA 1986, triable summarily only. The racially or religiously aggravated form of the offence is also triable only summarily.

The POA 1986, s. 7(2), declares that, for the purposes of the rules against charging more than one offence in the same information, each of ss. 1 to 5 of the Act creates one offence.

Sentencing Guidelines (Basic Offence)

B11.68 The maximum penalty is a fine not exceeding level 3 (POA 1986, s. 5(6)). Under the Penalties for Disorderly Behaviour (Amount of Penalty) Order 2002 (SI 2002 No. 1837), as amended, this offence is a penalty offence and the amount payable is £90. See the *Magistrates' Courts Sentencing Guidelines* (see Supplement, **SG10-66**). For s. 5, culpability will be 'A' and harm will be category 1 where certain identified factors are present and 'B' and category 2 respectively when those factors are absent. Category 1A has a starting point of a band C fine with a range of a band B fine to a band C fine. Categories 1B and 2A have starting points of a band B fine and a range of a band A fine to a band C fine. Category 2B has a starting point of a band A fine with a range of a discharge to a band B fine.

Racial or religious aggravation cannot be taken into account by the sentencer when sentencing for the basic offence (see **B11.47**); see **E1.19** for increase in sentence, under the CJA 2003, s. 146, for aggravation relating to disability, sexual orientation or transgender identity.

Sentencing Guidelines (Racially or Religiously Aggravated Form of Offence)

B11.69 The maximum penalty is a fine not exceeding level 4 (CDA 1998, s. 31(5)).

When sentencing for the aggravated form of the s. 5 offence, the definitive guideline provides that the aggravation should be assessed as being either high level, medium level or low level. Where there is high level aggravation, and the sentence for the basic offence was a fine, the court should multiply that fine by 2.5, and where the sentence for the basic offence was a discharge, the court should impose a fine at the top of the basic offence category range or for particularly severe cases move to sentence in the next basic offence category. Where there is medium level aggravation, and the sentence for the basic offence was a fine, the court should multiply that fine by two, and where the sentence for the basic offence was a discharge, the court should impose a fine at the mid to top of the basic offence category range. Where there is low level aggravation, and the sentence for the basic offence was a fine, the court should multiply that fine by 1.5, and where the sentence for the basic offence was a discharge, the court should impose a fine at the low to mid end of the basic offence category range. See further **B11.49** and **B2.34**.

Threatening or Abusive Words or Behaviour; Disorderly Behaviour; Writing

B11.70 For the meaning of the phrase 'threatening or abusive', see **B11.52**. This element of the offence and that of causing harassment, alarm or distress are separate and different; the two must not be equated. The approach in *Brutus v Cozens* [1973] AC 854 (i.e. that words should be given their ordinary meaning: see **B11.52**) should be adopted in considering the meaning of disorderly behaviour. The disorderly behaviour need not be threatening or abusive nor is it necessary to prove any feeling of insecurity in an apprehensive sense (*Chambers v DPP* [1995] Crim LR 896). The decision in *Hammond v DPP* [2004] EWHC 69 (Admin) that the traditional approach under *Brutus v Cozens* is to be followed, but also that full account must be taken of the ECHR, Article 10 (freedom of expression) (though the Divisional Court was then concerned with whether words or behaviour were insulting) may now be considered to apply in respect of threatening or abusive words or behaviour: see **B11.66**. For the meaning of 'writing', see **B11.53**.

Display

The Divisional Court in *Chappell v DPP* (1988) 89 Cr App R 82 held that magistrates were correct to decide that the posting of an envelope, with writing containing abusive or insulting words concealed inside it, through a letter box of someone's home could not amount to a 'display'. This approach might apply to envelopes containing threatening or abusive material even in public. **B11.71**

Within the Hearing or Sight of a Person Likely to be Caused Harassment, Alarm or Distress

Harassment, alarm and distress are alternatives. In *R (R) v DPP* [2006] EWHC 1375 (Admin), a prosecution under the POA 1986, s. 4A, the High Court described them as relatively strong words befitting an offence which may carry imprisonment or a substantial fine and held that the word 'distress' in this context requires emotional disturbance or upset. In *Southard v DPP* [2006] EWHC 3449 (Admin) it was held that distress, by its very nature, involves an element of emotional disturbance or upset, but harassment does not. However, the harassment must be real as opposed to trivial. 'Harassment' does not demand any element of apprehension about personal safety (*Chambers v DPP* [1995] Crim LR 896). **B11.72**

In *Taylor v DPP* [2006] EWHC 1202 (Admin), it was held that there must be evidence that there was someone *able* to hear or see D's conduct, and that the prosecution does not have to call evidence that the person did *actually* hear the words spoken or see the behaviour. In *Mladenov v Bulgaria* [2013] EWHC 903 (Admin), D, when in Bulgaria, had waved a newspaper in a police officer's face, shouted at him in a threatening tone and intimated that the officer would lose his job if he carried on telling D what to do. As to whether this conduct would amount to an offence under the POA 1986, s. 5, if it had occurred in England, Mitting J said this (at [21]):

> I have no doubt that a robust English magistrates' court would conclude that this was the sort of thing that police officers had to put up with day in, day out, and that their reaction, if not of boredom, would have been of resignation and a willingness to continue to perform their official duties without interruption. For a court to conclude that a police officer in Investigator Grigorov's position would be likely to be subjected to 'harassment' by this conduct would, in my judgment, be an erroneous conclusion which would not afford proper respect to the stoicism and fortitude of a policeman in the position of Investigator Grigorov.

In *Lodge v DPP* (1988) *The Times*, 26 October 1988, the Divisional Court decided that whether a person was likely to be caused harassment, alarm or distress is a matter of fact to be determined by the magistrates. The Court indicated that it is sufficient if the other person in question, in that case a police officer, feels alarm (or harassment or distress) for someone else, for example a child.

In *Southard v DPP* [2006] EWHC 3449 (Admin), the Divisional Court had stated that the words 'fuck you' or 'fuck off' were potentially abusive, whether they were addressed to a police officer or a member of the public and on the facts of the case the police officer was harassed by the use of those words directed at him by the appellant during an incident in which he was making it impossible for the officer to detain a suspect. In *Williams v CPS* [2018] EWHC 2869 (Admin), the Divisional Court re-emphasised that law enforcement officers are expected to show a certain degree of resilience to inappropriate language. **B11.73**

Place of Commission of Offence

B11.74 **Public Order Act 1986, s. 5**

(2) An offence under this section may be committed in a public or a private place, except that no offence is committed where the words or behaviour are used, or the writing, sign or other visible representation is displayed, by a person inside a dwelling and the other person is also inside that or another dwelling.

The Divisional Court in *Chappell v DPP* (1988) 89 Cr App R 82 held that the delivery of a letter to a person's own home, where the person reads it and is alarmed or distressed by its contents, cannot be an offence under s. 5. Such conduct would constitute an offence contrary to the Malicious Communications Act 1988, s. 1(1). See also **B11.61**. In *DPP v Distill* [2017] EWHC 2244 (Admin), [2017] 4 WLR 177, the Divisional Court held that a private garden was, generally, not part of a dwelling for the purposes of the POA 1986, s. 5(2), and so the offence in s. 5(1) could be committed where a person in a private garden directed harassing, alarming or distressing words to another person who was also in a private garden. The same reasoning will apply to offences contrary to ss. 4 and 4A.

Mens Rea

B11.75 **Public Order Act 1986, s. 6**

(4) A person is guilty of an offence under section 5 only if he intends his words or behaviour, or the writing, sign or other visible representation, to be threatening or abusive, or is aware that it may be threatening or abusive or (as the case may be) he intends his behaviour to be or is aware that it may be disorderly.

Whether D had the intention or awareness is to be tested subjectively in the light of the whole evidence, the burden of proof beyond a reasonable doubt lying upon the prosecution (*DPP v Clarke* (1991) 94 Cr App R 359). D must intend the behaviour to be disorderly or be aware that it might be disorderly (*Chambers v DPP* [1995] Crim LR 896). In *DPP v Smith* [2017] EWHC 3193 (Admin), the Divisional Court reiterated that the prosecution are not required to prove that D intended to cause harassment, alarm or distress. The mental element is set out in s. 6(4) and so it was not lawful for the magistrates to have acquitted D simply because an intention to cause harassment, alarm or distress was lacking on the evidence. The Court added that the elements of the s. 5 offence do not refer to offensiveness, and noted that '[n]ot everything which is offensive is distressing, although there is plainly a good deal of overlap between the two categories' (at [17]).

For the effect of voluntary, self-induced intoxication on *mens rea*, see the discussion in relation to the offence of riot at **B11.26**.

Specific Defences

B11.76 **Public Order Act 1986, s. 5**

(3) It is a defence for the accused to prove—
 (a) that he had no reason to believe that there was any person within hearing or sight who was likely to be caused harassment, alarm or distress, or
 (b) that he was inside a dwelling and had no reason to believe that the words or behaviour used, or the writing, sign or other visible representation displayed, would be heard or seen by a person outside that or any other dwelling, or
 (c) that his conduct was reasonable.

When the legal burden is on D, the standard required is proof on a balance of probabilities (see **F3.5** and **F3.53**). For a summary of the case law relating to 'reverse burden' challenges under the HRA 1998, see **F3.18** ***et seq.*** As to whether incompatibility with the ECHR arises in the context of the 'reverse burden' in the POA 1986, s. 5, see Auld LJ's comments in *Norwood v DPP* [2003] EWHC 1564 (Admin), [2003] Crim LR 888.

An objective test must be used to assess the conduct referred to in s. 5(3)(c) (*DPP v Clarke* (1991) 94 Cr App R 359). A person's conduct will be reasonable if exercising ECHR rights in circumstances in which an interference with that exercise would not be justified under Articles 10(2) (the qualifications to the right to freedom of expression) and 9(2) (the qualifications to freedom of religion) (*Percy v DPP* [2001] EWHC 1125 (Admin) and see **B11.46**).

In *Percy v DPP*, a protester who had for many years protested against the use of weapons of mass destruction and against US military policy defaced the American flag at a US air base by writing 'Stop Star Wars' across the stripes, stepped in front of a vehicle and placed the flag down in front of it and then stood on it. American service personnel and/or their families were distressed to varying degrees by her actions. On appeal to the Divisional Court, she argued that her conduct was reasonable within the meaning of s. 5(3)(c), relying on Article 10. Her conviction was quashed on the basis that insufficient weight had been given to the question of proportionality when considering whether her conduct was reasonable. By contrast in *Hammond v DPP* [2004] EWHC 69 (Admin), H, an Evangelical Christian preacher, had on more than one occasion carried a large double-sided sign with the words 'Stop Immorality! Stop Homosexuality! Stop Lesbianism!', whilst preaching in the centre of Bournemouth. This attracted a large crowd: some found the words on the placard insulting, others found them distressing, one person found them disgusting and annoying. The Divisional Court considered his actions in the context of Articles 10 and 11 and found that they were not reasonable within the meaning of s. 5(3)(c). Similarly, in *Norwood v DPP* [2003] EWHC 1564 (Admin), [2003] Crim LR 888, the action of a member of the BNP in placing a sign in window saying 'Islam out of Britain' and 'Protect the British people' was not considered reasonable. **B11.77**

Related Offence

It is an offence, contrary to the Air Navigation Order 2016 (SI 2016 No. 795), art. 245, (a) to use any threatening, abusive or insulting words towards an aircraft crew member, (b) to behave in a threatening, abusive, insulting or disorderly manner towards an aircraft crew member, or (c) to interfere intentionally with the performance by an aircraft crew member of the crew member's duties. The offences mentioned in (a) and (b) are triable summarily only; on conviction the maximum penalty is a fine not exceeding level 4 on the standard scale (art. 265(6) and sch. 13, part 2). The offence mentioned in (c) is triable either way; the maximum penalty on conviction on indictment is a term of imprisonment not exceeding two years and/or a fine; on summary conviction, the maximum penalty is an unlimited fine (art. 265(7) and sch. 13, part 3). See **B10.247** for the offence of recklessly or negligently acting in a manner likely to endanger an aircraft, or any person in an aircraft. **B11.78**

Alternative Offence

The summary offence of being drunk and disorderly (see **B11.198**) may be an appropriate alternative offence. **B11.79**

PUBLIC NUISANCE

Definition

The Court of Appeal has expressed approval of the following definitions of public nuisance: **B11.80**

> Public nuisance is an offence at common law. A person is guilty of a public nuisance (also known as a common nuisance) who (a) does an act not warranted by law, or (b) omits to discharge a legal duty, if the effect of the act or omission is to endanger the life, health, property, morals, or comfort of the public, or to obstruct the public in the exercise or enjoyment of rights common to all Her Majesty's subjects. (*Goldstein* [2003] EWCA Crim 3450, [2004] 2 All ER 589 at [3].)

A common nuisance is an act not warranted by law or an omission to discharge a legal duty, which act or omission obstructs or causes inconvenience or damage to the public in the exercise of rights common to all of His Majesty's subjects. (*Stephen's Digest of Criminal Law*, confirmed in *A-G v PYA Quarries Ltd* [1957] 2 QB 169, per Romer LJ, *Madden* [1975] 1 WLR 1379 and *Shorrock* [1994] QB 279.)

Nuisance, nocumentum, or annoyance, signifies anything that worketh hurt, inconvenience, or damage. And nuisances are of two kinds; public or common nuisances, which affect the public, and are an annoyance to all the King's subjects; for which reason we must refer them to the class of public wrongs, or crimes and misdemeanours; and private nuisances, which are the objects of our present consideration, and may be defined, anything done to the hurt or annoyance of the lands, tenements or hereditaments of another. (*Blackstone's Commentaries*, confirmed in *A-G v PYA Quarries Ltd* [1957] 2 QB 169 and quoted, with apparent approval, in *Shorrock* [1994] QB 279.)

Procedure and Limit on Prosecution

B11.81 It is a common-law offence, triable either way, for a person to cause a public nuisance. When tried on indictment, it is normally a class 3 offence, but see CrimPD XIII, para. B (see Supplement, **CPD.XIII.B**) for the additional factors that the court considers on allocation.

The House of Lords in *Rimmington* [2005] UKHL 63, [2006] 1 AC 459 made clear that this offence should not ordinarily be prosecuted where there is a statutory offence covering the relevant mischief. Lord Bingham said (at [30]):

It cannot in the ordinary way be a reason for resorting to the common law offence that the prosecutor is freed from mandatory time limits or restrictions on penalty. It must rather be assumed that Parliament imposed the restrictions which it did having considered and weighed up what the protection of the public reasonably demanded. I would not go to the length of holding that conduct may never be lawfully prosecuted as a generally expressed common law crime where it falls within the terms of a specific statutory provision, but good practice and respect for the primacy of statute do in my judgment require that conduct falling within the terms of a specific statutory provision should be prosecuted under that provision unless there is good reason for doing otherwise.

The statutory offences that may be prosecuted include the following (as identified by Lord Bingham in *Rimmington* at [29]): statutory nuisance under the Environmental Protection Act 1990, s. 79(1); dumping of waste under the Environmental Protection Act 1990, s. 33; wilfully obstructing the highway under the Highways Act 1980, s. 137; harassment under the Protection from Harassment Act 1997, ss. 1 and 4; racially or religiously aggravated offences under the CDA 1998, s. 32; dealing with raves, etc. under the CJPO 1994, s. 63; bomb hoaxes under the CLA 1977, s. 51; sending substances inducing someone to believe they are noxious under the Anti-terrorism, Crime and Security Act 2001, s. 114; sending by post matter that is obscene or indecent or is likely to injure a postal worker under the Postal Services Act 2000, s. 85; sending malicious etc. communications under the Malicious Communications Act 1988, s. 1; and improperly using a public electronic communications network under the Communications Act 2003, s. 127. In *Stockli* [2017] EWCA Crim 1410, [2018] 1 WLR 5609 the Court of Appeal allowed the prosecution's appeal against a terminatory ruling where the judge had found that it was an abuse of process for the prosecution to charge public nuisance when there were other statutory offences available under which provisions the defendants could have been prosecuted. The Court held that *Rimmington* had not created some free-ranging category of abuse that permitted the court to stop a case because in the court's view there was no good reason why the prosecution had charged the defendants with the common-law offence. On the facts, there had been no manipulation of the court process that could justify a stay of proceedings.

Sentence

B11.82 On conviction on indictment, the maximum sentence is at the discretion of the court. On summary conviction, the statutory maxima apply. In *Cleator* [2016] EWCA Crim 1361, the Court of Appeal remarked on the 'scant precedents' that exist for this offence. On the facts, a sentence of two years' imprisonment after a trial was appropriate for a defendant who, when in drink, climbed onto a protective cage covering a footpath over the M56 motorway and then acted in a way that distracted passing motorists, which resulted in the imposition of traffic restrictions for some considerable time while the police tried to coax him down.

In *Roberts* [2018] EWCA Crim 2739, [2019] 1 WLR 2577, the applicants were convicted of public nuisance arising out of their conduct in protesting against fracking during which one carriageway of the A583 had been blocked for several days. The Court of Appeal found that substantial disruption had been caused to thousands of people. They were sentenced to imprisonment for 16 months and 15 months respectively. On appeal, those sentences were replaced with community orders. In doing so, the Court rejected the submission that for the offence of public nuisance a custodial sentence could only be justified where the defendant had used violence against the person. Moreover, the Court found that there was nothing in the Strasbourg jurisprudence to support the proposition that detention is necessarily disproportionate in such circumstances. The Court recognised that there are 'a wide range of offences that may be committed in the course of peaceful protest of differing seriousness; and within the offending very different levels of harm may be suffered by individuals or groups of individuals' (at [32]). The Court added that the commission of non-violent crimes in the course of peaceful protest 'does not generally impute high levels of culpability'. The Court quoted from the speech of Lord Hoffmann in *Jones (Margaret)* [2006] UKHL 16, [2007] 1 AC 136 at [89]–[94] about the honourable history of civil disobedience and emphasised that the conscientious motives of protestors should be taken into account when they are sentenced. In the applicants' case their offending had not been so serious that only a custodial sentence could have been considered appropriate. In the Court's view a community sentence with punitive elements would have met the justice of the case.

Private and Public Nuisance

The torts and the crime are closely connected: 'public nuisance is defined by reference to private nuisance and as differing from private nuisance only in the range of its effect' (*Shorrock* [1994] QB 279). The idea that public nuisance could be committed by isolated acts or isolated acts in a series (which originated from Denning LJ's judgment in *A-G v PYA Quarries Ltd* [1957] 2 QB 169) was firmly rejected by the House of Lords in *Rimmington* [2005] UKHL 63, [2006] 1 AC 459 (at [37]): **B11.83**

> ... to permit a conviction of causing a public nuisance to rest on an injury caused to separate individuals rather than on an injury suffered by the community or a significant section of it as a whole was to contradict the rationale of the offence and pervert its nature.

See further **B11.87**.

Where someone suffers particular damage as a result of a public nuisance they may sue in tort for public nuisance.

Nuisance

There must be conduct by D which 'renders the enjoyment of life and property uncomfortable' (*White* (1775) 1 Burr 333, per Lord Mansfield) or 'materially affects the reasonable comfort and convenience of a class of Her Majesty's subjects' (*A-G v PYA Quarries Ltd* [1957] 2 QB 169, approved by the Court of Appeal in *Johnson* [1996] 2 Cr App R 434). Not all obstructions of the highway amount to a public nuisance (see, e.g., *Dwyer v Mansfield* [1946] KB 437 and *DPP v Jones* [1999] 2 AC 240). **B11.84**

Criminal convictions have, for example, been successful in the following circumstances:

(a) D was responsible for a house which was ruinous and likely to fall down thus endangering people using the highway (*Watts* (1757) 1 Salkeld 357);
(b) colliers had allowed industrial refuse to fall into a navigable river (*Stephens* (1866) LR 1 QB 702);

(c) D caused 30 houses and the highway to be affected by dust and noise from its quarry (*A-G v PYA Quarries Ltd* [1957] 2 QB 169);
(d) D sniffed glue in a school playground when staff and pupils were absent (*Sykes v Homes* [1985] Crim LR 791, holding that it was a nuisance within the Local Government (Miscellaneous Provisions) Act 1982, s. 40 — whether it would be a public nuisance would depend upon the public nature of the nuisance);
(e) D allowed a rave to take place in his field (*Shorrock* [1994] QB 279).

Act or Omission

B11.85 It is clear that a public nuisance may be caused by either an act (see, e.g., *Vantandillo* (1815) 4 M & S 73 and *A-G v PYA Quarries Ltd* [1957] 2 QB 169) or an omission (see, e.g., *Watts* (1757) 1 Salkeld 357 and *Shorrock* [1994] QB 279; see also *A-G v Tod Heatley* [1897] 1 Ch 560, where it was held that it was the duty of the owner of land to prevent it from being used as a dumping ground which caused a public nuisance).

The Public Nature of the Nuisance

B11.86 In order to establish that a crime has been committed, it is necessary to establish the essential public nature of the nuisance. It is clear that not all the public need be affected. But it must be established that the act or omission was sufficiently widespread or indiscriminate as to amount to a public rather than a private nuisance. In *A-G v PYA Quarries Ltd* [1957] 2 QB 169, Romer LJ stated:

> ... any nuisance is 'public' which materially affects the reasonable comfort and convenience of life of a class of Her Majesty's subjects. The sphere of the nuisance may be described generally as 'the neighbourhood'; but the question whether the local community within that sphere comprises sufficient number of persons to constitute a class of the public is a question of fact in every case. It is not necessary, in my judgment, to prove that every member of the class has been injuriously affected; it is sufficient to show that a representative cross-section of the class has been so affected for an injunction to issue.

In the same case, Denning LJ said, 'a public nuisance is a nuisance which is so widespread in its range or so indiscriminate in its effect that it would not be reasonable to expect one person to take proceedings on his own responsibility to put a stop to it, but that it should be taken on the responsibility of the community at large'. In that case, there was a public nuisance where 30 houses and the highway were affected by dust and noise from the workings of a quarry.

B11.87 In *Rimmington* [2005] UKHL 63, [2006] 1 AC 459, the House of Lords held (at [12]) that 'a common injury is a, perhaps the, distinguishing feature of this offence'. Further (at [36]) that what must be looked for is whether the act of omission contemplated by D 'was likely to inflict significant injury on a substantial section of the public exercising their ordinary rights as such'. In consequence, the House overruled the decision in *Johnson* [1996] 2 Cr App R 434, where the conviction had been upheld after D had made hundreds of telephone calls to at least 13 women in South Cumbria. The error was that this was a series of acts involving individual members of the public and could not constitute the necessary effect on the public or a significant section of the public for there to be a public nuisance. So, per Lord Nicholls at [42], a telephone hoax call might involve a public nuisance if it was a call that an explosive device had been left at a railway station as opposed to a call which would only inconvenience the recipient. R's conviction was quashed as he had sent offensive and racist messages to a series of individuals. G's conviction was quashed because of the lack of *mens rea*, but it was stated that, if the *mens rea* had been present, sending salt through the post anticipating that, if it leaked, it could be thought to be anthrax and its effect would be sufficiently serious to affect a section of the public could have been a public nuisance. Relying on *Rimmington*, the Divisional Court in *DPP v Fearon* [2010] EWHC 340 (Admin), [2010] 2 Cr App R 22 (169) held that D had not committed a public nuisance when, on a public highway, he solicited an undercover police officer for sex on one occasion. The prosecution had argued that D's actions should be seen in the context of similar conduct carried on by other men in that area at around the same time, and so it was their collective actions that lent a 'public' air to D's nuisance behaviour. Elias LJ rejected that argument in emphatic terms (at [13]).

Mens Rea

The 'requirement as to D's state of mind is the same whether the proceedings brought be civil or criminal. Actual knowledge of the nuisance need not be established'. The *mens rea*, therefore, is that D is 'guilty of the offence charged if either he knew or he ought to have known, in the sense that the means of knowledge were available to him, that there was a real risk that the consequences of the licence granted by [D] in respect of his field [on which a rave took place] would be to create the sort of nuisance that in fact occurred' (*Shorrock* [1994] QB 279, approved in *Rimmington* [2005] UKHL 63, [2006] 1 AC 459). **B11.88**

Vicarious Liability

For the ordinary rules relating to vicarious liability, see **A6.8**. However, a master may be liable for a public nuisance even if the act of the servant is contrary to the master's orders (see *Stephens* (1866) LR 1 QB 702 and *Smith and Hogan's Criminal Law* (15th edn, 2018), at p. 266). The decision in *Stephens* was doubted in *Chisholm v Doulton* (1889) 22 QBD 736. It remains to be seen whether such a rule will continue to apply and, if so, if it will apply consistently to all forms of public nuisance (a view the decision in *Shorrock* [1994] QB 279 may be interpreted as implicitly supporting). **B11.89**

Defences

Statutory authorisation is a defence to public nuisance, provided that the statute covers that which is done (*Hammersmith and City Railway Co. v Brand and Louisa* (1868) LR 4 QB 171; *Managers of the Metropolitan Asylum District v Hill* (1881) LR 6 AC 193; *London, Brighton and South Coast Railway v Truman* (1885) LR 11 AC 45; *Saunders v Holborn District Board of Works* [1895] 1 QB 64). **B11.90**

Compliance with the European Convention on Human Rights

The House of Lords in *Rimmington* [2005] UKHL 63, [2006] 1 AC 459 took the view that the offence of public nuisance did not breach the ECHR, Article 7 (the prohibition on retrospective criminal offences: see **A7.77**). It should be noted, first, that the House decided that it should be prosecuted rarely as it should be used only where there was no statutory nuisance that ordinarily ought to be prosecuted (see **B11.81**); secondly, the House emphasised the requirement of a sufficiently serious effect on the public or a section of it (see **B11.86**); finally, it confirmed the *mens rea* requirement (see **B11.88**). The standards that the House identified were, per Lord Bingham (at [35]) that the: **B11.91**

> ... offence must be clearly defined in law ... and a norm cannot be regarded as a law unless it is formulated with sufficient precision to enable the citizen to foresee, if need be with appropriate advice, the consequences which a given course of conduct may entail.... It is accepted that absolute certainty is unattainable, and might entail excessive rigidity since the law must be able to keep pace with changing circumstances, some degree of vagueness is inevitable and development of the law is a recognised feature of common law courts ... But the law-making function of the courts must remain within reasonable limits ... existing offences may not be extended to cover facts which did not previously constitute a criminal offence. The law may be clarified and adapted to new circumstances which can reasonably be brought under the original concept of the offence.... But any development must be consistent with the essence of the offence and be reasonably foreseeable ... and the criminal law must not be extensively construed to the detriment of an accused, for instance by analogy.

Lord Bingham took the view (at [36] and [37]) that these requirements would not have been met had the recent development moving the law away from the requirement for an effect on the public or a significant section of it not been re-emphasised.

BOMB HOAXES

B11.92 **Criminal Law Act 1977, s. 51**

(1) A person who—
   (a) places any article in any place whatever; or
   (b) dispatches any article by post, rail or any other means whatever of sending things from one place to another,

   with the intention (in either case) of inducing in some other person a belief that it is likely to explode or ignite and thereby cause personal injury or damage to property is guilty of an offence. In this subsection 'article' includes substance.

(2) A person who communicates any information which he knows or believes to be false to another person with the intention of inducing in him or any other person a false belief that a bomb or other thing liable to explode or ignite is present in any place or location whatever is guilty of an offence.

Procedure

B11.93 Offences under the CLA 1977, s. 51, are triable either way. When tried on indictment they are normally class 3 offences, but see CrimPD XIII, para. B (see Supplement, **CPD.XIII.B**), for the additional factors that the court considers on allocation.

Indictment

B11.94 **First Count**

Statement of Offence

Perpetrating bomb hoax contrary to section 51(1) of the Criminal Law Act 1977.

Particulars of Offence

A on or about the . . . day of . . . placed an article, namely a parcel, in [or: dispatched by post (or rail etc.) an article, namely a parcel, to] the Dead Parrot Public House at . . . with the intention of inducing in V, the manager of the said house, a belief that the said parcel was likely to explode or ignite and thereby cause personal injury or damage to property therein.

Second Count

Statement of Offence

Perpetrating bomb hoax contrary to section 51(2) of the Criminal Law Act 1977.

Particulars of Offence

A on or about the . . . day of . . . communicated to V the information that a parcel containing a bomb liable to explode or ignite was present on the premises of the Dead Parrot Public House at . . ., knowing or believing the said information to be false and with the intention of inducing in V the false belief that it was true.

Sentencing Guidelines

B11.95 The maximum penalty is seven years on indictment; six months and/or an unlimited fine summarily (CLA 1977, s. 51(4)).

In *Dunbar* (1987) 9 Cr App R (S) 393, the offenders pleaded guilty to communicating a bomb hoax. They telephoned the police to say that incendiary devices had been placed in various stores, apparently in order to cause financial loss to the stores. Sentences of 12 months' imprisonment were upheld by the Court of Appeal, Leggatt J commenting that:

> A bomb hoax of this kind, as this court has had occasion to say in the past, is a public nuisance, and it is important not to underrate the anxiety and apprehension that this kind of behaviour engenders. The public rightly expect judges to pass severe sentences as a mark of public disapprobation of this kind of offence.

In *Harris* [2005] EWCA Crim 775, [2005] 2 Cr App R (S) 103 (649), D manufactured two devices designed to look like bombs. D took one to a police station and one to a restaurant. The premises and surrounding area had to be evacuated. There was no evidence that D suffered from a treatable mental disorder. Bearing in mind that D's conduct had been more than a nuisance and had caused fear and disruption, a total sentence of three years' imprisonment was appropriate on a guilty plea.

In *Walter* [2012] EWCA Crim 3115, [2013] 2 Cr App R (S) 46 (302), D pleaded guilty to three offences of communicating false information with intent. On each occasion D called the emergency services to say that a bomb would detonate and kill the Queen. Concurrent sentences of three years' imprisonment were held to be manifestly excessive. Concurrent sentences of two years' imprisonment were substituted. In *Pinder* [2014] EWCA Crim 1710, D made four telephone calls and sent one text message to South Yorkshire Police, four days after the Boston Marathon bombings. During those calls and in that text, D said that she was going to detonate bombs at various police stations and kill all of the officers inside. Following an early guilty plea, the judge sentenced D to four years' imprisonment. The Court of Appeal reduced that sentence to 16 months' imprisonment.

Elements

A call stating 'there is a bomb' is sufficient to constitute the offence, even though there is no reference to a place or location (*Webb* (1995) *The Times*, 19 June 1995). **B11.96**

By the CLA 1977, s. 51(3), for a person to be guilty of an offence under s. 51(1) or (2), 'it is not necessary for him to have any particular person in mind as the person in whom he intend to induce the belief mentioned in [the relevant subsection]'.

Related Offence: False Alarm of Fire

It is an offence, contrary to the Fire and Rescue Services Act 2004, s. 49(1), if a person knowingly gives or causes to be given a false alarm of fire to a person acting on behalf of a fire and rescue authority. A person guilty of such an offence is liable, on summary conviction, to a fine not exceeding level 4 on the standard scale, or a term of imprisonment not exceeding three months, or to both (Fire and Rescue Services Act 2004, s. 49(2) and (3)). Under the Penalties for Disorderly Behaviour (Amount of Penalty) Order 2002 (SI 2002 No. 1837), sch. 1, part 1, this offence is a penalty offence and the amount payable is £90. **B11.97**

CONTAMINATION OF OR INTERFERENCE WITH GOODS

Public Order Act 1986, s. 38 **B11.98**

(1) It is an offence for a person, with the intention—
  (a) of causing public alarm or anxiety, or
  (b) of causing injury to members of the public consuming or using the goods, or
  (c) of causing economic loss to any person by reason of the goods being shunned by members of the public, or
  (d) of causing economic loss to any person by reason of steps taken to avoid such alarm or anxiety, injury or loss,

to contaminate or interfere with goods, or make it appear that goods have been contaminated or interfered with, or to place goods which have been contaminated or interfered with, or which appear to have been contaminated or interfered with, in a place where goods of that description are consumed, used, sold or otherwise supplied.

(2) It is also an offence for a person, with any such intention as is mentioned in paragraph (a), (c) or (d) of subsection (1), to threaten that he or another will do, or claim that he or another has done, any of the acts mentioned in that subsection.

(3) It is an offence for a person to be in possession of any of the following articles with a view to the commission of an offence under subsection (1)—
  (a) materials to be used for contaminating or interfering with goods or making it appear that goods have been contaminated or interfered with, or
  (b) goods which have been contaminated or interfered with, or which appear to have been contaminated or interfered with.

Procedure

B11.99 Offences under the POA 1986, s. 38, are triable either way (POA 1986, s. 38(4)). When tried on indictment they are normally class 3 offences, but see CrimPD XIII, para. B (see Supplement, CPD.XIII.B), for the additional factors that the court considers on allocation.

Indictment (for an Offence Contrary to s. 38(1)(a))

B11.100 *Statement of Offence*

Contamination of goods contrary to section 38(1)(a) of the Public Order Act 1986.

Particulars of Offence

A on or about the... day of... with the intention of causing public alarm or anxiety, placed certain goods, namely 100 jars of... brand honey which had been contaminated by the insertion of fragments of broken glass therein, in a place where goods of that description are sold to the public, namely V's department store,...

Sentence

B11.101 The maximum penalty is ten years and/or a fine on indictment (POA 1986, s. 38(4)); six months and/or an unlimited fine summarily. In *Cruickshank* [2001] EWCA Crim 98, [2001] 2 Cr App R (S) 57 (278), D pleaded guilty to contaminating food in a supermarket by inserting pins, needles or nails into various items. D persisted in this behaviour for three months, and some minor injuries were incurred by customers who bought the contaminated products. There was no logical explanation for D's behaviour, and no financial motive, but a medical disposal was not recommended. Three years' imprisonment was upheld by the Court of Appeal. Examples of cases involving *threats* to contaminate goods are *Witchelo* (1992) 13 Cr App R (S) 371 and *Smith* (1994) 15 Cr App R (S) 106.

Meaning of 'Goods'

B11.102 In the POA 1986, s. 38, 'goods' includes substances whether natural or manufactured and whether or not incorporated in or mixed with other goods (s. 38(5)).

Meaning of 'Claim' that Acts Have Been Committed

B11.103 The reference in the POA 1986, s. 38(2), to a person claiming that certain acts have been committed does not include a person who in good faith reports or warns that such acts have been, or appear to have been, committed (s. 38(6)).

PRISON MUTINY

B11.104 The Prison Security Act 1992 created the offence of prison mutiny. For offences relating to the escape of prisoners, see **B14.74** ***et seq.***

Prison Security Act 1992, s. 1

(1) Any prisoner who takes part in a prison mutiny shall be guilty of an offence and liable, on conviction on indictment, to imprisonment for a term not exceeding ten years or to a fine or to both.

(2) For the purposes of this section there is a prison mutiny where two or more prisoners, while on the premises of any prison, engage in conduct which is intended to further a common purpose of overthrowing lawful authority in that prison.

(3) For the purposes of this section the intentions and common purpose of prisoners may be inferred from the form and circumstances of their conduct and it shall be immaterial that conduct falling within subsection (2) above takes a different form in the case of different prisoners.

(4) Where there is a prison mutiny, a prisoner who has or is given a reasonable opportunity of submitting to lawful authority and fails, without reasonable excuse, to do so shall be regarded for the purposes of this section as taking part in the mutiny.

(5) Proceedings for an offence under this section shall not be brought except by or with the consent of the Director of Public Prosecutions.
(6) In this section—
'conduct' includes acts and omissions;
'prison' means any prison, young offender institution or remand centre which is under the general superintendence of, or is provided by, the Secretary of State under the Prison Act 1952, including a contracted out prison within the meaning of Part IV of the Criminal Justice Act 1991;
'prisoner' means any person for the time being in a prison as a result of any requirement imposed by a court or otherwise that he be detained in legal custody.

Sentence

Sentences of up to nine years' imprisonment were upheld in *Lambert* [2006] EWCA Crim 827, [2006] 2 Cr App R (S) 107 (699) for the instigators of a prison mutiny at Lincoln prison. During the riot, which lasted for several hours and spread to all parts of the prison, a prison officer was attacked and knocked unconscious, there were numerous other instances of violence, and damage in excess of £2 million was caused. The offenders were convicted after a trial which lasted for 13 weeks. In *Mitchell* (1995) 16 Cr App R (S) 924, custodial sentences of five years were upheld in respect of two offenders convicted of prison mutiny. They had taken a leading part in an incident involving 120 remand prisoners which had caused extensive damage at Reading prison. **B11.105**

Elements

The offence may be committed in one of two ways as found in s. 1(2) and (4). The offence in s. 1(2) is committed where there is a common purpose and that is aimed at overthrowing lawful authority in the prison. This latter requirement is a stronger word than 'subversion' and is not synonymous with 'widespread failure to follow lawful orders'; it is limited to serious disturbances and does not cover a mere defiance of, or challenge to, that lawful authority. The offence in s. 1(4) is committed on a deemed basis and is parasitic to the commission of the s. 1(2) offence. An indictment should make clear on which basis the offence is charged (*Mason* [2004] EWCA Crim 2173, [2005] 1 Cr App R 11 (145)). In *Barratt* [2018] EWCA Crim 1603, [2018] 4 WLR 127, the Court of Appeal held that so far as the 'deemed' basis of the offence is concerned in s. 1(4), the prosecution must prove that a mutiny had taken place but it was not necessary to prove that the person who failed to submit to a lawful authority shared the purpose of 'overthrowing lawful authority'. However, the prosecution must prove 'synchronicity' between the mutiny and the failure to submit to lawful authority. If the disturbance only 'ripened into mutiny' after the failure to submit to a lawful order, the failure would not be caught by s. 1(4). The Court went on to say that a reasonable opportunity of submitting to lawful authority did not require any order to have been given, although the fact that an order was given and not heeded by D may well be powerful evidence that D did in fact have a reasonable opportunity to submit to authority and failed to do so. **B11.106**

CONTROL OF PROCESSIONS, ASSEMBLIES AND MEETINGS

Advance Notice of Public Procession

It is an offence, contrary to the POA 1986, s. 11(7), for a person organising a public procession to fail to satisfy the requirements in s. 11 concerning the giving of notice of the procession to the police. By s. 11(2), notice is not required where the procession is one commonly or customarily held in the police area (or areas) in which it is proposed to be held or is a funeral procession organised by a funeral director acting in the normal course of business. A mass cycle ride, beginning at the same place and held at the same time each month but with no predetermined route, **B11.107** was, assuming s. 11 applied, a commonly or customarily held procession within the meaning of s. 11(2) and so no notice of it had to be given (*R (Kay) v Metropolitan Police Commissioner* [2008] UKHL 69, [2009] 2 All ER 935). Having given notice, an organiser commits an offence if the date when the procession is held, the time when it starts or its route differ from the date, time or route specified in the notice. The offence is triable only summarily and is punishable with a fine not exceeding level 3.

It is a defence, under s. 11(8), for D to prove that D did not know of, and neither suspected nor had reason to suspect, the failure to satisfy the requirements or (as the case may be) the difference of date, time or route. It is also a defence, under s. 11(9), when the offence turns on a difference of date, time or route, for D to prove that the difference arose from circumstances beyond D's control or from something done with the agreement of a police officer or by the officer's direction.

A constable in uniform cannot make a dispersal direction under the ABCPA 2014, Part 3 (see **B11.113**), if the person the constable wishes to disperse is one of a group of persons who are taking part in a public procession of the kind mentioned in the POA 1986, s. 11(1) (ABCPA 2014, s. 36(4)(b)).

Failure to Comply with Conditions Imposed on Public Procession

B11.108 Under the POA 1986, s. 12, conditions may be imposed on public processions. Conditions may be imposed either in advance or at the time of the procession by the senior police officer acting under s. 12(1) to (3). It is an offence, triable only summarily:

(a) for a person who organises a public procession knowingly to fail to comply with a condition (s. 12(4)) (*DPP v Baillie* [1995] Crim LR 426);
(b) for a person who takes part in such a procession knowingly to fail to comply with a condition (s. 12(5));
(c) for a person to incite another to commit an offence under s. 12(5) (s. 12(6)).

In *Jukes v DPP* [2013] EWHC 195 (Admin), an appeal by way of case stated, the question for the Divisional Court to answer was the circumstances in which conditions imposed under the POA 1986, s. 12, continue to apply to those who left the route designated by those conditions for the purposes of joining a different demonstration. The Court, upholding their convictions, found that leaving the agreed route was an offence if at that time those leaving were still participating in the public procession to which the conditions applied. In *Powlesland v DPP* [2013] EWHC 3846 (Admin), [2014] 1 WLR 2984, D was a participant in a Critical Mass Cycle Ride (CMCR) through London. The ride started at a certain location but there was no fixed route, end-time or destination. Before the ride started the senior police officer imposed a condition on the participants that they should not go north of the Thames. D went north of the Thames in breach of the condition. D was convicted and appealed by way of case stated. D argued that, as there was no fixed route for the ride, the senior police officer could not have had regard to its 'route or proposed route' (s. 12(1)) when making the condition and thus his exercise of the power under that subsection was unlawful. Ouseley J, giving the judgment of the Divisional Court, was not persuaded by that argument. All s. 12(1) states is that the senior police officer could consider the 'reasonably possible future routes of a procession' before making any direction that the procession should not take a particular route; there was nothing in s. 12(1) to suggest that a condition could only be imposed where the route the procession would take was known in advance.

In the case of the organiser's offence and the offence committed by a person taking part, it is a defence to prove that the failure to comply with a condition arose from circumstances beyond D's control.

The maximum penalty for the organiser's offence and the inciter's offence is imprisonment for a term not exceeding three months or a fine not exceeding level 4 or both (s. 12(10)).

A person who commits an offence by taking part in a procession is liable to a fine not exceeding level 3.

Contravening Prohibition of Public Procession

Under the POA 1986, s. 13, a public procession may be prohibited. Where the procession is to take place outside the City of London or the metropolitan police district, it is the district council, on application from the chief officer of police and with the approval of the Secretary of State, which may make a procession prohibition order (s. 13(1) to (3)). In the City of London or the metropolitan police district, it is the relevant Commissioner, with the approval of the Secretary of State, who may make a procession prohibition order (s. 13(4)). **B11.109**

It is an offence, triable only summarily:

(a) for a person to organise a public procession the holding of which the person knows to be prohibited (s. 13(7));
(b) for a person to take part in a public procession the holding of which the person knows to be prohibited (s. 13(8));
(c) for a person to incite another to commit an offence under s. 13(8) (s. 13(9)).

The maximum penalty for the organiser's offence and the inciter's offence is imprisonment for a term not exceeding three months or a fine not exceeding level 4 or both (s. 13(13)). A person who commits an offence by taking part in a procession is liable to a fine not exceeding level 3.

Failure to Comply with Conditions Imposed on Public Assembly

Under the POA 1986, s. 14, conditions may be imposed on a public assembly. Conditions may be imposed either in advance or at the time of the assembly by the senior police officer acting under s. 14(1) to (3). It is an offence, triable only summarily: **B11.110**

(a) for a person who organises a public assembly knowingly to fail to comply with a condition (s. 14(4)) (*DPP v Baillie* [1995] Crim LR 426);
(b) for a person who takes part in such an assembly knowingly to fail to comply with a condition (s. 14(5)) (*Broadwith v DPP* [2000] All ER (D) 225);
(c) for a person to incite another to commit an offence under s. 14(5) (s. 14(6)).

The term 'public assembly' means an assembly of two or more persons in a public place which is wholly or partly open to the air (s. 16). In *R (Jones) v Metropolitan Police Commissioner* [2019] EWHC 2957 (Admin), [2020] 1 WLR 519, the Divisional Court held that a 'public assembly' must be in a particular location to which the public or any section of the public has access, which is wholly or partly open to the air, and which can be fairly described as a 'scene' (at [67]). Separate gatherings, separated both in time and by many miles, even if co-ordinated under the umbrella of one body, are not one public assembly (at [72]). It followed that the Extinction Rebellion Autumn Uprising (XRAU) that was intended to take place at multiple locations between 7 and 19 October 2019 was not a 'public assembly' and so there was no power in s. 14 for the police to treat the XRAU as a public assembly and impose conditions on it.

In the case of the organiser's offence and the offence committed by a person taking part, it is a defence to prove that the failure to comply with a condition arose from circumstances beyond the defendant's control. The prosecution do not have to prove that the decision to prosecute is proportionate (*James v DPP* [2015] EWHC 3296 (Admin), [2016] 1 WLR 2118 and see **B11.46**).

The maximum penalty for the organiser's offence and the inciter's offence is imprisonment for a term not exceeding three months or a fine not exceeding level 4 or both (s. 14(10)). A person who commits an offence by taking part in an assembly is liable to a fine not exceeding level 3.

Contravention of Prohibition of Trespassory Assembly

B11.111 Under the POA 1986, s. 14A, the chief officer of police has the power, if the officer reasonably believes that it is intended to hold a trespassory assembly which may result in serious disruption to the life of the community or significant damage to the land, building or monument which is of historical, archaeological or scientific importance, to apply to the district council for an order prohibiting for a specified period the holding of all trespassory assemblies in the district or part of it, but the order must not last for more than four days and must not apply to an area greater than that represented by a circle of five miles radius from a specified centre. The council must receive the consent of the Secretary of State for the making of such an order. The Metropolitan Police Commissioner or the Commissioner of the City of London Police may make such an order with the consent of the Secretary of State.

It is an offence, triable only summarily:

(a) for a person to organise an assembly which the person knows is prohibited by an order under s. 14A (s. 14B(1));
(b) for a person to take part in an assembly which the person knows is prohibited by such an order (s. 14B(2));
(c) for a person to incite another to commit an offence under s. 14B(2) (s. 14B(3)).

An assembly is not trespassory where the user of the highway is reasonable, and it does not amount to a public or private nuisance or an obstruction of the highway unreasonably impeding the primary right of the general public to pass and repass (*DPP v Jones (Margaret)* [1999] 2 AC 240). In *DPP v Ziegler* [2019] EWHC 71 (Admin), [2020] QB 253, the Divisional Court held that the decision of the House of Lords in *Jones (Margaret)* should be approached with a degree of caution because that case was decided before the HRA 1998 came into force. In the view of Singh LJ, the lawful exercise of Convention rights under the HRA 1998 will not be unreasonable.

B11.112 The maximum penalty for the organiser's offence and the inciter's offence is imprisonment for a term not exceeding three months or a fine not exceeding level 4 on the standard scale or both (s. 14B(5) and (7)). A person who commits an offence by taking part is liable to a fine not exceeding level 3 on the standard scale (s. 14B(6)).

A constable in uniform has power, which may be exercised only within the area to which an order under s. 14A applies, to stop someone the constable reasonably believes to be on the way to an assembly prohibited by an order under s. 14A and to direct the person not to proceed in the direction of the assembly (s. 14C(1) and (2)). A person who knows that such a direction has been given and fails to comply with it commits a summary offence punishable with a fine not exceeding level 3 on the standard scale (s. 14C(3) and (5)).

Dispersal of Groups and Removal of Persons under 16 to their Place of Residence

B11.113 The ABCPA 2014, Part 3 (ss. 34 to 42), contains a number of dispersal powers. Under s. 34(1), a police officer of at least the rank of inspector may authorise the use in a specified locality, during a specified period of not more than 48 hours, of the powers conferred by s. 35. An officer may give such an authorisation only if satisfied on reasonable grounds that the use of the powers in the locality during that period may be necessary for the purpose of removing or reducing the likelihood of members of the public in the locality being harassed, alarmed or distressed or the occurrence in the locality of crime or disorder (s. 34(2)). In deciding whether to give such an authorisation, an officer must have particular regard to the rights of freedom of expression and freedom of assembly set out in the ECHR, Articles 10 and 11 (s. 34(3)). An authorisation must be in writing, must be signed by the officer giving it and must specify the grounds on which it is given (s. 34(4)).

Section 35(1) provides that, if the conditions in s. 35(2) and (3) are met and a s. 34 authorisation is in force, a constable in uniform may direct a person who is in a public place in the specified locality to leave the locality (or part of the locality) and not to return for the period specified in the direction ('the exclusion period'). A 'public place' means a place to which at the material time the public or a section of the public has access, on payment or otherwise, as of right or by virtue of express or implied permission (s. 35(10)). In deciding whether to give a direction, a constable must have particular regard to the rights of freedom of expression and freedom of assembly (s. 36(5)). The first condition is that the constable has reasonable grounds to suspect that the behaviour of the person in the locality has contributed to or is likely to contribute to the following events: (a) members of the public in the locality being harassed, alarmed or distressed, or (b) the occurrence in the locality of crime or disorder (s. 35(2)). The second condition is that the constable considers that giving a direction to the person is necessary for the purpose of removing or reducing the likelihood of such events (s. 35(3)). The exclusion period may not exceed 48 hours (s. 35(4)). A direction under s. 35(1) must be given in writing unless that is not reasonably practicable, must specify the area to which it relates and may impose requirements as to the time by which the person must leave the area and the manner in which the person must do so (including the route) (s. 35(5)). The constable must (unless it is not reasonably practicable) tell the person to whom the direction is given that failing without reasonable excuse to comply with the direction is an offence (s. 35(6)). If the constable reasonably believes that the person to whom the direction is given is under the age of 16, the constable may remove the person to a place where the person lives or a place of safety (s. 35(7)). Any constable may withdraw or vary a direction under s. 35; but a variation must not extend the duration of a direction beyond 48 hours from when it was first given (s. 35(8)). Notice of withdrawal or variation of a direction must be given to the person to whom the direction was given, unless that is not reasonably practicable and, if given, must be given in writing unless that is not reasonably practicable (s. 35(9)).

Within s. 36 are a number of restrictions that prevent a constable from giving a direction under s. 35 where (1) the person appears to the constable to be under the age of ten, (2) the direction would prevent the person to whom it is given from having access to a place where the person lives, (3) the direction would prevent the person to whom it is given from attending at a place where the person is (a) required to attend for the purposes of the person's employment, or a contract of services to which the person is a party, (b) required to attend by an obligation imposed by or under an enactment or by the order of a court or tribunal, or (c) expected to attend for the purposes of education or training or for the purposes of receiving medical treatment, at a time when the person is required or expected (as the case may be) to attend there, or (4) the person is one of a group of persons who are engaged in conduct that is lawful under the Trade Union and Labour Relations (Consolidation) Act 1992, s. 220 (peaceful picketing), or taking part in a public procession of the kind mentioned in the POA 1986, s. 11(1) (see **B11.107**), in respect of which written notice has been duly given or is not required to be given. **B11.114**

A constable who gives a person a direction under s. 35 may also direct the person to surrender to the constable any item in the person's possession or control that the constable reasonably believes has been used or is likely to be used in behaviour that harasses, alarms or distresses members of the public (s. 37(1)). A direction under s. 37(1) must be given in writing unless that is not reasonably practicable (s. 37(2)). A constable who gives a person a direction under s. 37 must (unless it is not reasonably practicable) tell the person that failing without reasonable excuse to comply with the direction is an offence, and give the person information in writing about when and how the person may recover the surrendered item (s. 37(3)). The surrendered item must not be returned to the person before the end of the exclusion period (s. 37(4)). If, after the end of the exclusion period, the person asks for the item to be returned, it must be returned (unless there is power to retain it under another enactment) (s. 37(5)). But if it appears to the constable that the person is under the age of 16 and is not accompanied by a parent or other responsible adult, the item may be retained until the person is so accompanied (s. 37(6)). If the person has not asked for the return of the item before the end of the period of 28 days beginning with the day on which the direction was given, the item may be destroyed or otherwise disposed of (s. 37(7)). Section 38 deals with the responsibilities of the constable to keep a record of any direction **B11.115** given under either s. 35 or s. 37. The offence-creating provision is s. 39. A person given a direction under s. 35 who fails without reasonable excuse to comply with it commits an offence (s. 39(1)) and will be liable on summary conviction to a period of imprisonment not exceeding three months or to a fine not exceeding level 4 on the standard scale (s. 39(2)). A person given a direction under s. 37 who fails without reasonable excuse to comply with it commits an offence (s. 39(3)) and will be liable on summary conviction to a fine not exceeding level 2 (s. 39(4)). *Statutory guidance for frontline professionals* was issued in July 2014 and part 2.4 of this guidance references the dispersal powers.

B11.116 **Meaning of 'Removal'** If a constable reasonably believes that the person to whom a direction under the ABCPA 2014, s. 35(1), is given is under the age of 16, the constable may remove the person to a place where the person lives or a place of safety (s. 35(7)). In *R (W) v Metropolitan Police Commissioner* [2006] EWCA Civ 458, [2006] 3 All ER 458 it was held that the word 'remove' in s. 30(6) of the ASBA 2003 naturally and compellingly means 'take away using reasonable force if necessary'. It was also held that s. 30(6) of the ASBA 2003, like s. 35(7) of the ABCPA 2014, does not have an illegitimate curfew effect. The constable is not free to act arbitrarily, but must act for the purpose for which the power was conferred. There is no power to remove a person under the age of 16 simply because the person is in the designated dispersal area. Further, the power should be exercised only if it is reasonable to do so and in so deciding constables must have regard to circumstances such as how young the child is, how late at night it is, whether the child is vulnerable or in distress, the child's explanation for his or her conduct and presence in the area, and the nature of the actual or imminently anticipated anti-social behaviour.

B11.117 **Protests** In *R (Singh) v Chief Constable of West Midlands Police* [2006] EWCA Civ 1118, [2007] 2 All ER 297, D challenged the use of a s. 30 authorisation under the ASBA 2003 which had been created to deal with New Year revelries when used to deal with disturbances outside a theatre which was showing a play to which many Sikhs objected. First, the Court of Appeal held that s. 30 can be applied to protests. Secondly, it held that its usage was not a breach of Article 9, 10 or 11 of the ECHR as, on the critical issue of proportionality, the evidence demonstrated that the police had considered the correct questions; these involved a recognition of the particular importance of the right to protest and the need to determine whether some alternative, less intrusive means could have been used. Thirdly, it held that there was no reason to restrict the use of the authorisation and bar its use in relation to matters that were not anticipated when it was originally made as that would be absurd and unworkable. The same approach is likely to be taken to the exercise of the dispersal powers under the ABCPA 2014, Part 3.

Controls on Activities in Parliament Square Garden and Adjoining Pavements

B11.118 The PRSRA 2011, part 3 (ss. 142 to 149), introduced controls on activities in Parliament Square Garden and adjoining pavements. The Court of Appeal has ruled that neither s. 143 nor s. 145 is incompatible with the ECHR, Articles 6, 10 or 11 (*R (Gallastegui) v Westminster City Council* [2013] EWCA Civ 28, [2013] 2 All ER 579).

See the CPS Legal Guidance on the charging criteria in such cases.

B11.119 **Prohibited Activities** The prohibited activities are: operating any amplified noise equipment in the controlled area; erecting or keeping erected a tent or any other structure that is designed, or adapted (solely or mainly) for the purpose of facilitating sleeping or staying in a place for any period in the controlled area; using any tent or other such structure in the controlled area for the purpose of sleeping or staying in that area; placing or keeping in place in the controlled area any sleeping equipment with a view to its use (whether or not by the person placing it or keeping it in place) for the purpose of sleeping overnight in that area; and using any sleeping equipment in the controlled area of Parliament Square or in the Palace of Westminster for the purpose of sleeping overnight in that area (PRSRA 2011, s. 143(2)).

Police Powers of Direction By s. 143(1) of the PRSRA 2011, 'a constable or authorised officer [as defined in s. 148] who has reasonable grounds for believing that a person is doing, or is about to do, a prohibited activity may direct the person (a) to cease doing that activity, or (b) (as the case may be) not to start doing that activity'. By s. 143(8), a person who fails without reasonable excuse to comply with a direction under s. 143(1) commits an offence and is liable on summary conviction to an unlimited fine. **B11.120**

Section 144 gives the relevant officer further powers of direction (a direction requiring a person to cease doing a prohibited activity may include a direction that the person does not start doing that activity again after having ceased it). Such a direction continues in force for a specified period of no more than 90 days or for 90 days from the day the direction was given (s. 144(2) and (3)). It may be given orally, may be given to any person individually or to two or more persons together, and may be withdrawn or varied by the person who gave it (s. 142(6)).

Police Powers to Seize Property Section 145 of the PRSRA 2011 gives the relevant officer power to seize and retain property, namely a prohibited item that is on any land in the controlled area of Parliament Square or the Palace of Westminster if it appears to that constable or officer that the item is being, or has been, used in connection with the commission of an offence under s. 143. There is also a power to seize and retain a prohibited item that is on any land outside the controlled area if it appears to the constable that the item has been used in connection with the commission of an offence under s. 143. By s. 143(4), a constable may use reasonable force, if necessary, in exercising a power of seizure. **B11.121**

Forfeiture The court has wide, additional powers upon conviction. These include (a) the power to make an order providing for the forfeiture of any item of a kind mentioned in the PRSRA 2011, s. 143(2), that was used in the commission of the offence and (b) the power to make such other order as the court considers appropriate for the purpose of preventing the defendant from engaging in any prohibited activity in the controlled area of Parliament Square or the Palace of Westminster (s. 146(1), including a requirement not to enter the controlled area of Parliament Square or the Palace of Westminster for such period as may be specified in the order (s. 146(2))). **B11.122**

Endeavouring to Break up a Public Meeting

It is an offence, contrary to the Public Meeting Act 1908, s. 1(1), for a person at a lawful public meeting to act in a disorderly manner for the purpose of preventing the transaction of the business for which the meeting was called together. The offence is triable summarily only. A person guilty of the offence is liable to imprisonment for a term not exceeding six months and/or an unlimited fine. **B11.123**

There is no definition of either 'meeting' or 'public meeting' in the Public Meeting Act 1908 though there is in the POA 1936, s. 9. The case law that exists is concerned with whether the public meeting is lawful or not and indicates that a lawful meeting may be held on a highway, even if it might amount to an obstruction of that highway (*Burden v Rigler* [1911] 1 KB 337). Further, a public meeting does not cease to be lawful just because there is disorderly opposition from other persons (*Beatty v Gillbanks* (1882) 9 QBD 308, the authority of which does not, on this point, seem to be doubted by the Divisional Court in *Duncan v Jones* [1936] 1 KB 218). See also *Laporte v Metropolitan Police Commissioner* [2014] EWHC 3574 (QB). It is an offence, contrary to the Public Meeting Act 1908, s. 1(2), to incite another person to commit an offence under s. 1; the offence is subject to similar punishment.

Failure to Comply with Constable's Request with Regard to Public Meeting

It is an offence, contrary to the Public Meeting Act 1908, s. 1(3), for a person to refuse or fail to declare his or her name and address when asked to do so by a constable who reasonably suspects the person of committing an offence under the Public Meeting Act 1908, s. 1(1) or (2) (see **B11.124**

B11.123) if the constable has been requested to ask for them by the chairman of the meeting. It is an offence to give a false name and address in such circumstances. A person guilty of the offence is liable to a fine not exceeding level 1.

Illegal Electoral Practice with Regard to Public Meeting

B11.125 It is one of the illegal electoral practices, contrary to the Representation of the People Act 1983, s. 97(1), for a person at a lawful public meeting to act, or incite others to act, in a disorderly manner for the purpose of preventing the transaction of the business for which the meeting was called together. The offence is triable summarily only. It is punishable on summary conviction with an unlimited fine.

'Lawful public meeting' in this offence means a political meeting held in any constituency between the date of the issue of the writ for the return of a Member of Parliament for the constituency and the date at which a return to the writ is made, or a meeting held with reference to a local government election in the electoral area for that election in the period beginning with the last date on which notice of the election may be published in accordance with the local government election rules and ending with the day of the election (Representation of the People Act 1983, s. 97(2)).

OFFENCES UNDER THE FOOTBALL (OFFENCES) ACT 1991

B11.126 The Football (Offences) Act 1991 creates three offences: throwing of missiles (s. 2), indecent or racialist chanting (s. 3) and going onto the playing area (s. 4).

Football (Offences) Act 1991, ss. 2, 3 and 4

2. It is an offence for a person at a designated football match to throw anything at or towards—
   (a) the playing area, or any area adjacent to the playing area to which spectators are not generally admitted, or
   (b) any area in which spectators or other persons are or may be present, without lawful authority or lawful excuse (which shall be for him to prove).

3.—(1) It is an offence to engage or take part in chanting of an indecent or racialist nature at a designated football match.
   (2) For this purpose—
   (a) 'chanting' means the repeated uttering of any words or sounds (whether alone or in concert with one or more others); and
   (b) 'of racialist nature' means consisting of or including matter which is threatening, abusive or insulting to a person by reason of his colour, race, nationality (including citizenship) or ethnic or national origins.

4. It is an offence for a person at a designated football match to go onto the playing area, or any area adjacent to the playing area to which spectators are not generally admitted, without lawful authority of lawful excuse (which shall be for him to prove).

Sentence and Procedure

B11.127 The offences are all triable summarily only.

The maximum penalty is a fine not exceeding level 3 on the standard scale (s. 5(2)). The *Magistrates' Court Sentencing Guidelines* for football related offences (see Supplement, **SG10-99**) were revised in 2017. Under these guidelines, sentencing for offences contrary to ss. 2 to 4 are considered together. The starting point for category 1 (higher culpability and greater harm) is a band C fine, with a sentencing range of a band B to a band C fine. The starting point for category 3 (lower culpability and lesser harm) is a band A fine with a range of a conditional discharge to a band B fine. Higher culpability factors include deliberate or flagrant action, disregard of warnings, commercial operation, incitement of others, possession of a large quantity of alcohol and targeted abuse. The greater harm factors are distress or alarm caused, actual injury or risk of injury, and significant financial loss to others. When sentencing for these offences the court must consider imposing a banning order as well.

Elements

A 'designated football match' is an association football match designated, or of a description designated, for the purposes of the Act by the Secretary of State. The Football (Offences) (Designation of Football Matches) Order 2004 (SI 2004 No. 2410), as amended, designates football matches for this purpose. **B11.128**

References to things done at a designated football match include anything done at the ground:

(a) within the period beginning two hours before the start of the match or (if earlier) two hours before the time at which it is advertised to start and ending one hour after the end of the match,
(b) where the match is advertised to start at a particular time on a particular day but does not take place, within the period beginning two hours before and ending one hour after the advertised starting time (s. 1(2)).

When the phrase 'you're just a town of Pakis' was used at a football match, that was a chant of a racist nature. The term 'Paki' was being used in a racially derogatory or insulting sense. It is possible that the context could make it non-racist, so each use would have to be considered on a case-by-case basis (*DPP v Stoke on Trent Magistrates' Court* [2003] EWHC 1593 (Admin), [2003] 3 All ER 1086).

OFFENCES UNDER THE FOOTBALL SPECTATORS ACT 1989

The Football Spectators Act 1989 was designed to control the admission of spectators at designated football matches and provided for the making of restriction orders on persons convicted of offences of violence or disorder at, or in connection with, such matches. In the light of the Taylor Report on the deaths which occurred at Hillsborough, many of its provisions, particularly those relating to a national football membership scheme, have not been, and are not likely to be, brought into force. However, the majority of the provisions relating to the grant of licences to admit spectators and the whole of Part II (which concerns football matches taking place outside England and Wales) are in force. **B11.129**

Under s. 9, it is an offence to admit spectators to watch a designated football match unless it is played at licensed premises. By virtue of s. 10(13), it is a summary offence for any responsible person to contravene any term or condition of a licence granted to admit spectators to any premises for the purpose of watching any designated football match played there. It is a defence, in accordance with s. 10(14), for D to prove that the contravention took place without D's consent and that D took all reasonable precautions and exercised all due diligence to avoid the commission of such an offence. The relevant licences are those issued by the Football Licensing Authority under the Football Spectators (Seating) Orders that are made annually. The Football Spectators (Prescription) Order 2004 (SI 2004 No. 2409), as amended, designates matches for the purposes of the Act.

As to banning orders and other powers to exclude persons from football matches, see E21.3.

TICKET TOUTS

Criminal Justice and Public Order Act 1994, s. 166 **B11.130**

(1) It is an offence for an unauthorised person to—
  (a) sell a ticket for a designated football match, or
  (b) otherwise to dispose of such a ticket to another person.

Sentence and Procedure

B11.131 The offence is triable summarily (CJPO 1994, s. 166(3)).

The maximum sentence is a fine (CJPO 1994, s. 166(3)). The starting points and category ranges for this offence are the same as for the offences contrary to the Football (Offences) Act 1991, ss. 2 to 4. See **B11.127**.

Elements

B11.132 A person is 'an unauthorised person' unless authorised in writing to sell or otherwise dispose of tickets for the match by the organisers of the match; 'ticket' means anything which purports to be a ticket; and 'selling' a ticket includes offering to sell it, exposing it for sale, making it available for sale by another; advertising that it is available for purchase; and giving it to a person who pays or agrees to pay for some other goods or services or offers to do so (CJPO 1994, s. 166(2)). For the meaning of 'designated football match', see the Ticket Touting (Designation of Football Matches) Order 2007 (SI 2007 No. 790).

Search of Person and Premises

B11.133 The PACE 1984, s. 32, has effect in relation to an offence under the CJPO 1994, s. 166, as if the power conferred on a constable to enter and search any vehicle extended to any vehicle which the constable has reasonable grounds for believing was being used for any purpose connected with the offence (s. 166(5)).

INTIMIDATION OR ANNOYANCE BY VIOLENCE OR OTHERWISE

B11.134 **Trade Union and Labour Relations (Consolidation) Act 1992, s. 241**

(1) A person commits an offence who, with a view to compelling another person to abstain from doing or to do any act which that person has a legal right to do or abstain from doing, wrongfully and without legal authority—
- (a) uses violence to or intimidates that person or his wife or children, or injures his property,
- (b) persistently follows that person about from place to place,
- (c) hides any tools, clothes or other property owned or used by that person, or deprives him of or hinders him in the use thereof,
- (d) watches or besets the house or other place where that person resides, works, carries on business or happens to be, or the approach to any such house or place, or
- (e) follows that person with two or more other persons in a disorderly manner in or through any street or road.

Sentence and Procedure

B11.135 An offence under the Trade Union and Labour Relations (Consolidation) Act 1992, s. 241, is triable summarily only.

The maximum penalty is six months and/or an unlimited fine (Trade Union and Labour Relations (Consolidation) Act 1992, s. 241(2)).

Elements

B11.136 It was made clear by the Divisional Court in *Todd v DPP* [1996] Crim LR 344 that the offence is not limited to trade disputes. It can, therefore, apply to someone engaged in an anti-roads protest (as in *Todd*) and might apply, for example, to stalking. The general elements of the offence are, first, the *mens rea*, which is dealt with below and, secondly, the requirements that the act be done 'wrongfully' and 'without lawful authority'. No special consideration has been given to the phrase 'without lawful authority' apart from the creation of a defence for trade unions acting in contemplation or furtherance of a dispute, which is treated as a defence, below.

Meaning of 'Wrongfully' Scott J in *Thomas v National Union of Mineworkers (South Wales Area)* [1986] Ch 20 decided that the authorities established that conduct must, in order to be an offence under what was, prior to consolidation, the Conspiracy, and Protection of Property Act 1875, s. 7, be tortious (at p. 61). This approach to the question of whether there is a wrongful act does indeed seem to be consistent with the existing case law. The Court of Appeal in *Ward, Lock & Co. Ltd v Operative Printers' Assistants' Society* (1906) 22 TLR 327 clearly took the view that s. 7 (now the Trade Union and Labour Relations (Consolidation) Act 1992, s. 241) was concerned only to provide a criminal remedy to what was already recognised as being a civil wrong. Thus in order for the criminal remedy to be available, it had to be established that what was done was a civil wrong, without reference to the provisions of the Act. **B11.137**

Intimidates The Court of Appeal in *Jones* (1974) 59 Cr App R 120, whilst not wishing to define 'intimidation' exhaustively, said that: **B11.138**

> ... 'intimidate' in this section includes putting persons in fear by the exhibition of force or violence or the threat of force or violence, and there is no limitation restricting the meaning to cases of violence or threats of violence to the person.

In *Connor v Kent* [1891] 2 QB 545, the Court also did not want to attempt an exhaustive definition of the word, preferring instead to make clear (at p. 559) that 'intimidate' is 'a word of common speech and everyday use; and it must receive, therefore, a reasonable and sensible interpretation according to the circumstances of the cases as they arise from time to time'. Further assistance may be gleaned from the decision of Stuart-Smith J in *News Group Newspapers Ltd v SOGAT 82 (No. 2)* [1987] ICR 181, at pp. 204–5, considering the related tort of intimidation.

Persistently Follows In *Smith v Thomasson* (1890) 62 LT 68, Hawkins J stated that: 'It is impossible to define generally what is "persistently following"'. However, it was held dogging of a workman's footsteps could amount to 'persistently following' him. See also *Elsey v Smith* 1982 SCCR 218. **B11.139**

Deprivation of Property The Court of Appeal in *Fowler v Kibble* [1922] 1 Ch 487 made clear the significance of the requirement that the activity must be wrongful separately from a consideration of the section creating the offence. Thus there could be no offence where a workman did not let miners who were not members of a particular union have safety lamps because such an act of deprivation was not unlawful. **B11.140**

Watches or Besets In general, it would seem that the words 'watch' and 'beset' are viewed as words of the ordinary English language (see, e.g., *J. Lyons & Sons v Wilkins* [1899] 1 Ch 811; *Ward, Lock & Co. Ltd v Operative Printers' Assistants' Society* (1906) 22 TLR 327). The High Court of Justiciary in *Galt v Philp* 1983 JC 51 took the view that the essence of the offence comprised preventing access to and egress from somewhere. Thus a sit-in satisfied this element of the offence. **B11.141**

The watching and besetting must be 'wrongful', that is, unlawful without reference to s. 241. Thus, for example, in *J. Lyons & Sons v Wilkins* [1899] 1 Ch 811, careful consideration was given to the question of whether the activity amounted to a nuisance and was therefore 'wrongful' and within the ambit of the section. The length of time the people were present was relevant, since that would help determine whether there was a nuisance. Consequently, lawful picketing is not 'watching and besetting' unless it amounts to a nuisance, or some other tort or other wrong such as obstruction of the highway (see, e.g., *News Group Newspapers Ltd v SOGAT 82 (No. 2)* [1987] ICR 181 and *Walters v Green* [1899] 2 Ch 696; see also *Bonsall* [1985] Crim LR 150).

In *Charnock v Court* [1899] 2 Ch 35 and *Farmer v Wilson* (1900) 69 LJ QB 496, it was made clear that the offence is committed when any place where the person happens to be is watched and beset, whether or not such persons are in the service or employment of any person. This latter point in *Farmer v Wilson* makes clear that the offence is not solely concerned with employment disputes.

B11.142 **Following in a Disorderly Manner** Whether the following is in a disorderly manner is a question of fact in each case, and therefore will depend upon D's conduct and all the circumstances of the particular case (*McKenzie* [1892] 2 QB 519; *Elsey v Smith* 1982 SCCR 218).

Mens Rea: With a View to Compel Any Other Person

B11.143 This is a *mens rea* requirement importing not motive but purpose according to the Divisional Court in *DPP v Fidler* [1992] 1 WLR 91, explaining *J. Lyons & Sons v Wilkins* [1899] 1 Ch 255. The Divisional Court stated that purpose is a more objective concept not concerned with the different motives with which members of the group might have joined, for example, a demonstration. The Court also decided that D's purpose must be one to compel and not merely to persuade (see also *Bonsall* [1985] Crim LR 150; *McKenzie* [1892] 2 QB 519). It is not necessary to show that the compulsion was in any way effective (*Agnew v Munro* (1891) 18 R (J) 22). The phrase 'such other person' refers back to the person whom D has a view to compel to abstain from doing or to do something (*J. Lyons & Sons v Wilkins* [1899] 1 Ch 811).

Application to Trade or Employment Disputes

B11.144 **Trade Union and Labour Relations (Consolidation) Act 1992, s. 220**

(1) It is lawful for a person in contemplation or furtherance of a trade dispute to attend—
 (a) at or near his own place of work, or
 (b) if he is an official of a trade union, at or near the place of work of a member of that union whom he is accompanying and whom he represents,
 for the purpose only of peacefully obtaining or communicating information, or peacefully persuading any person to work or abstain from working.
(2) If a person works or normally works—
 (a) otherwise than at any one place, or
 (b) at a place the location of which is such that attendance there for a purpose mentioned in subsection (1) above is impracticable,
 his place of work for the purposes of that subsection shall be any premises of his employer from which he works or from which his work is administered.
(3) In the case of a worker who is not in employment where—
 (a) his last employment was terminated in connection with a trade dispute, or
 (b) the termination of his employment was one of the circumstances giving rise to a trade dispute,
 in relation to that dispute his former place of work shall be treated for the purposes of subsection (1) as being his place of work.
(4) A person who is an official of a trade union by virtue only of having been elected or appointed to be a representative of some of the members of the union shall be regarded for the purposes of subsection (1) above as representing only those members; but otherwise an official of a trade union shall be regarded for those purposes as representing all its members.

RACIALLY OR RELIGIOUSLY AGGRAVATED OFFENCES

B11.145 The CDA 1998 introduced a series of racially aggravated offences, i.e. existing offences which are racially aggravated according to the definition in s. 28. These provisions were extended by the A-TCSA 2001, s. 39, so as to include religiously aggravated offences.

Crime and Disorder Act 1998, s. 28

(1) An offence is racially or religiously aggravated for the purposes of sections 29 to 32 below if—
 (a) at the time of committing the offence, or immediately before or after doing so, the offender demonstrates towards the victim of the offence hostility based on the victim's membership (or presumed membership) of a racial or religious group; or
 (b) the offence is motivated (wholly or partly) by hostility towards members of a racial or religious group based on their membership of that group.
(2) In subsection (1)(a) above—
 'membership', in relation to a racial or religious group, includes association with members of that group;
 'presumed' means presumed by the offender.

(3) It is immaterial for the purposes of paragraph (a) or (b) of subsection (1) above whether or not the offender's hostility is also based, to any extent, on any other factor not mentioned in that paragraph.
(4) In this section 'racial group' means a group of persons defined by reference to race, colour, nationality (including citizenship) or ethnic or national origins.
(5) In this section 'religious group' means a group of persons defined by reference to religious belief or lack of religious belief.

The offences which may be racially or religiously aggravated are an offence contrary to the OAPA 1861, ss. 20 and 47, and common assault (CDA 1998, s. 29: see **B2.1**, **B2.27** and **B2.54**), criminal damage (CDA 1998, s. 30: see **B8.1**), offences contrary to the POA 1986, ss. 4, 4A and 5 (CDA 1998, s. 31: see **B11.45**, **B11.57** and **B11.65**) and harassment and stalking etc. contrary to the Protection from Harassment Act 1997, ss. 2, 2A, 4 and 4A (CDA 1998, s. 32: see **B2.181** to **B2.210**). In each case, the court must first establish that the basic offence has been committed and then consider whether it was racially or religiously aggravated within the meaning of s. 28 (but see also **B11.46**). The racially or religiously aggravated form of each offence carries a higher maximum penalty than the ordinary form of the offence and this is reflected by significantly higher sentences in practice (*Kelly* [2001] EWCA Crim 170, [2001] 2 Cr App R (S) 73 (341); *Bridger* [2006] EWCA Crim 3169; *A-G's Ref (No. 52 of 2013)* [2013] EWCA Crim 1733; *Letchford* [2014] EWCA Crim 1474 and see **E1.19**). By way of illustration, where a person is convicted of an offence contrary to the Protection from Harassment Act 1997, s. 4A, the maximum sentence is five years' imprisonment, but upon conviction for the racially/religiously aggravated form of that offence, the maximum sentence is 14 years' imprisonment (CDA 1998, s. 32). See also **B11.49**.

If the offence is not one of those to which s. 28 applies, it is for the sentencer to decide whether it was racially aggravated and, if it was, to treat this as an aggravating factor in sentencing (CJA 2003, s. 145). See generally *Rogers* [2007] UKHL 8, [2007] 2 AC 62. Even where the offence is one to which s. 28 applies, but the prosecution chose not to charge the aggravated form of the offence, upon conviction for the underlying offence the court can, when sentencing, take into account racial or religious aggravation as a factor that increases the seriousness of the offence (*O'Leary* [2015] EWCA Crim 1306, [2016] 1 Cr App R (S) 11 (66); *Cooke* [2015] EWCA Crim 1414). In *Cooke*, the Court of Appeal commented that, even where the sentencing court could not be satisfied to the criminal standard that D's conduct was racially or religiously aggravated, if D deliberately chose to join with others who were committing racially or religiously aggravated offences that 'was a gravely aggravating feature'. The decision in *O'Leary* should not be taken to mean that prosecutors can routinely pursue the underlying offence alone even where there is clear evidence of racial or religious aggravation and then invite the court to take that evidence into account at the sentencing stage. Where there is evidence that supports the aggravated form of the underlying offence, a count to reflect the aggravated offence should be on the indictment (*Khan* [2009] EWCA Crim 389, [2010] 1 Cr App R (S) 1 (1)). If D is acquitted of the aggravated offence but convicted of the underlying offence, the court cannot sentence D on the basis that the underlying offence was racially or religiously aggravated because that would amount to an impermissible trespass on the jury's determination.

Racial or Religious Groups By the CDA 1998, s. 28(4), a 'racial group' means a group of persons defined by reference to race, colour, nationality (including citizenship) or ethnic or national origins. This definition is derived from that used in the Race Relations Act 1976 and is also used in the POA 1986, s. 17 (see **B11.158**). In *Mandla v Dowell Lee* [1983] 2 AC 548, it was necessary to determine whether the Sikhs are a 'racial group' for the purposes of the 1976 Act. The House of Lords was satisfied that it was necessary to determine whether Sikhs are a group defined by ethnic origins, since none of the other descriptions would distinguish them from at least some other groups of people. In holding that Sikhs are an ethnic group, Lord Fraser of Tullybelton said (at pp. 562D–563A): **B11.146**

> For a group to constitute an ethnic group in the sense of the Act of 1976, it must, in my opinion, regard itself, and be regarded by others, as a distinct community by virtue of certain characteristics. Some of these characteristics are essential; others are not essential but one or more of them

> will commonly be found and will help to distinguish the group from the surrounding community. The conditions which appear to me to be essential are these: (1) a long shared history, of which the group is conscious as distinguishing it from other groups, and the memory of which it keeps alive; (2) a cultural tradition of its own, including family and social customs and manners, often but not necessarily associated with religious observance. In addition to those two essential characteristics the following characteristics are, in my opinion, relevant; (3) either a common geographical origin, or descent from a small number of common ancestors; (4) a common language, not necessarily peculiar to the group; (5) a common literature peculiar to the group; (6) a common religion different from that of neighbouring groups or from the general community surrounding it; (7) being a minority or being an oppressed or a dominant group within a larger community, for example a conquered people (say the inhabitants shortly after the Norman conquest) and their conquerors might both be ethnic groups.
>
> A group defined by reference to enough of these characteristics would be capable of including converts, for example, people who marry into the group, and of excluding apostates. Provided a person who joins the group feels himself or herself to be a member of it, and is accepted by other members, then he is, for the purposes of the Act, a member. . . . In my opinion, it is possible for a person to fall into a particular racial group either by birth or by adherence, and it makes no difference, so far as the Act of 1976 is concerned, by which route he finds his way into the group.

Lord Templeman, taking a similar approach to that of Lord Fraser, said (at p. 569E):

> In my opinion, for the purposes of the Race Relations Act a group of persons defined by reference to ethnic origins must possess some of the characteristics of a race, namely group descent, a group of geographical origin and a group history.

Lord Fraser also approved the decision of the New Zealand Court of Appeal in *King-Ansell v Police* [1979] 2 NZLR 531 that Jews form a group with common ethnic origins within the New Zealand Race Relations Act 1971. In the course of his judgment, Richardson J said (at p. 543):

> . . . a group is identifiable in terms of its ethnic origins if it is a segment of the population distinguished from others by a sufficient combination of shared customs, beliefs, traditions and characteristics derived from a common or presumed common past, even if not drawn from what in biological terms is a common racial stock. It is that combination which gives them an historically determined social identity in their own eyes and in the eyes of those outside the group. They have a distinct social identity based not simply on group cohesion and solidarity but also on their belief as to their historical antecedents.

B11.147 Romany gypsies are recognised as a racial group on the basis of their ethnic origin (*Commission for Racial Equality v Dutton* [1989] QB 783). In more recent times and certainly since the first instance discrimination case of *O'Leary v Punch Retail* (HHJ Goldstein, Westminster County Court, 29 August 2000), Irish Travellers have also been considered an ethnic racial group. Following the test in *Mandla v Dowell Lee*, the Court of Appeal held that Rastafarians are not members of an ethnic group separate from the rest of the Afro-Caribbean community but nevertheless share beliefs that identify them as members of a religious group (*Crown Suppliers (Property Services Agency) v Dawkins* [1993] ICR 517).

In *White* [2001] EWCA Crim 216, [2001] 1 WLR 1352, the Court of Appeal, following *Mandla* and *Ealing London Borough Council v Race Relations Board* [1972] AC 342, noted that the statutory language is to be given a broad, non-technical meaning and that words are to be construed as generally used in England and Wales. In its judgment (at [17]), 'the word "African" does describe a "racial group" defined by reference to race. In ordinary speech, the word "African" denotes a limited group of people regarded as of common stock and regarded as one of the major divisions of humankind having in common distinct physical features. It denotes a person characteristic of the blacks of Africa.' On the other hand, the Court of Appeal took the view that the expression 'South American', in England and Wales, probably does not have a racial connotation.

Thus, a broad and non-technical approach has been adopted in the context of s. 28. In *Rogers* [2007] UKHL 8, [2007] 2 AC 62, the House of Lords was asked, 'Do those who are not of British origin constitute a racial group within s. 28(4)?' The unanimous answer was 'yes'.

'Foreigners' likewise constitute such a group; and of course it follows that those who are of British origin must enjoy the same legal protection as those who are not: each forms for these purposes a 'racial group', even though many more racial groups exist within them. See *White* [2001] EWCA Crim 216, [2001] 1 WLR 1352; *DPP v M* [2004] EWHC 1543, [2004] 1 WLR 2758; *A-G's Ref (No. 4 of 2004)* [2005] EWCA Crim 889, [2005] 1 WLR 2810 and *Kendall v DPP* [2008] EWHC 1848 (Admin).

Although in other contexts 'religion' has been interpreted as involving a belief in some kind of god or supernatural being (*Registrar General, ex parte Segerdal* [1970] 2 QB 697), a much broader approach is clearly required in the context of s. 28. It is clear from s. 28(5) that a 'religious group' may for these purposes include a group defined by its lack of religious beliefs. If, for example, D assaults V because V is an atheist or humanist who rejects religious beliefs, D must be guilty of a religiously aggravated offence. **B11.148**

Proof of Hostility A racially or religiously aggravated offence, may, but need not have been, committed for racial or religious motives. It suffices if D formed the view that V was a member of a racial or religious group and then said or did something that demonstrated hostility towards V based on membership of that group. This will usually involve racist words or gestures, but may in some cases be manifested in other ways (*Rogers* [2007] UKHL 8, [2007] 2 AC 62 per Baroness Hale at [13]). Whether, in general, words actually demonstrated racial hostility was a question of fact for the relevant tribunal (*Johnson v DPP* [2008] EWHC 509 (Admin); *DPP v Howard* [2008] EWHC 608 (Admin)). **B11.149**

To be guilty of an offence that is racially or religiously aggravated, it is not necessary that D be of a different racial, national or ethnic (or religious) group from V (*White* [2001] EWCA Crim 216, [2001] 1 WLR 1352). Section 28(2) specifically addresses the possibility that D's attack on V may be aggravated as a result of D's hostility to V's actual or supposed association with other groups. D may also be mistaken as to V's own race or religion.

In *DPP v Pal* [2000] Crim LR 756, Simon Brown LJ stated that, for the purposes of s. 28(1)(a), it will always be necessary for the prosecution to prove the demonstration of racial hostility, although the use of racially abusive insults will ordinarily be found sufficient. Following this, the Divisional Court in *DPP v McFarlane* [2002] EWHC 485 (Admin) decided that, where the expressions 'jungle bunny', 'black bastard' and 'wog' were used, the offence was properly made out as the words were used immediately before and at the time of the commission of the offence contrary to the POA 1986, s. 4 (see **B11.45 *et seq.***), those words were of a racial nature, and they were racial, threatening and abusive towards V. The decision in *Pal*, where the words 'white man's arse licker' and 'brown Englishman' were used, was to be limited to its own particular facts, notably that both parties were Asian. Even so, *DPP v Pal* appears hard to reconcile with s. 28(2), as Baroness Hale noted in *Rogers* at [15]. **B11.150**

The fact that D may have had some additional reason for the choice of words is immaterial (*McFarlane*; *DPP v Woods* [2002] EWHC 85 (Admin); *DPP v Green* [2004] EWHC 1225 (QB), (2004) *The Times*, 7 July 2004; *DPP v M*). Also irrelevant is V's perception of the incident and the fact that D's frame of mind was such that D would have abused any person standing where V was by reference to an obvious physical characteristic, such as obesity or baldness (*Woods*). D need not act for any racial or religious motive (*DPP v Green*). It would nevertheless be wrong for charges of aggravated offences to be brought where vulgar abuse has included racial epithets that did not, when all the relevant circumstances are considered, indicate hostility to V on account of V's race or religion (*Rogers* per Baroness Hale at [17]).

In *G v DPP* [2004] EWHC 183 (Admin), the Divisional Court considered the two routes to establishing racial aggravation of an offence. Section 28(1)(a) requires the prosecution to prove facts that indicate that D had demonstrated racial hostility at the time of committing the offence or immediately before or after doing so. This is not to prove D's state of mind, but what D did or said so as to demonstrate racial hostility towards V. The demonstration will often be by way **B11.151** of words, shouting, holding up a banner, etc. or by adherence to a group that is demonstrating racial hostility. Section 28(1)(b) is concerned with D's motivation, which does concern D's state of mind. Often the evidence establishing this will involve the kind of demonstration referred to in relation to s. 28(1)(a). The prosecution may base their case on both of s. 28(1)(a) and (b) and cases may arise where it is legitimate to require the prosecution to make clear the basis upon which they are proceeding. In *Taylor v DPP* [2006] EWHC 1202 (Admin), it was decided that use of phrases such as 'fucking nigger' and 'fucking coon bitch', patently not used in a jesting manner, must, in the circumstance of the case, have led any judge to find that the offence (in this case, the POA 1986, s. 5(1)(a)) was motivated, at least in part, by racial hostility as described in s. 28(1)(b). It is also clear that it is better that this matter be dealt with more explicitly, in particular that the two possible approaches in s. 28 be clearly identified and separated for the benefit of the jury. In relation to s. 28(1)(b), see also *DPP v Howard* [2008] EWHC 608 (Admin) and *DPP v Dykes* [2008] EWHC 2775 (Admin); in the latter the Administrative Court said the prosecutor ought to make it absolutely clear that s. 28(1)(b) is very much in play as part of the allegation made of racial aggravation in a summary trial so that the magistrates have in mind that it is not simply the abuse directed at V which is being alleged, but also a motivation based on racial hostility. In *R (Jones) v Bedfordshire and Mid-Bedfordshire Magistrates' Court* [2010] EWHC 523 (Admin), [2011] 1 WLR 833, the Administrative Court made plain that *Howard* was a case exclusively concerned with s. 28(1)(b) and subjective motivation of racial hostility did not have to be proved for each limb. Applying *G v DPP*, Ouseley J stated at [18] that:

> Even though the facts of a particular case may satisfy both limbs simultaneously, limb (a) involves no examination of subjective intent or motivation behind the demonstration of racial hostility for the victim. It merely requires the demonstration of racial hostility. It contains an objective test of whether the defendant demonstrated racial hostility to the victim. That makes particular sense where a victim is present towards whom such racial hostility is demonstrated. The offence is concerned with the objective view of whether racial hostility had been demonstrated, in part because of its effect upon the victim, rather than being concerned with a subjective motivation of the defendant. By contrast, limb (b) is examining the defendant's subjective motivation whether an individual victim is present or not. The former deals with what is demonstrated by the behaviour, the latter with the motivation behind it.

B11.152 The case of *SH* [2010] EWCA Crim 1931, [2011] 1 Cr App R 14 (182) demonstrates a misunderstanding by the lower courts of the difference between the CDA 1998, s. 28(1)(a) and s. 28(1)(b). The trial judge insisted on effectively ending the case at the close of the prosecution case. The prosecution appealed. As the Court of Appeal pointed out it is difficult to see how it could be suggested that repeated angry references to a Nigerian as a 'black monkey' or 'monkey' did not generate a prima facie case of an outward manifestation of racial hostility (s. 28(1)(a)). The Court found that the judge was quite wrong to conclude that, because the jury could not exclude vulgar abuse as a factor, there was no case to answer.

B11.153 **Timing of Demonstration of Hostility** The word 'immediately' in s. 28(1) qualifies both 'before' and 'after', and this means that the subsection deals with words uttered or acts done in the immediate context of the substantive offence, so it was not possible that the section was satisfied where D had quit the scene and used the relevant words when sitting in D's own house (which was the next door house) some 20 minutes after the criminal damage had been caused (*Parry v DPP* [2004] EWHC 3112 (Admin)). See also *Babbs* [2007] EWCA Crim 2737.

USING WORDS OR BEHAVIOUR OR DISPLAYING WRITTEN MATERIAL STIRRING UP RACIAL HATRED

B11.154 **Public Order Act 1986, s. 18**

(1) A person who uses threatening, abusive or insulting words or behaviour, or displays any written material which is threatening, abusive or insulting, is guilty of an offence if—
  (a) he intends thereby to stir up racial hatred, or
  (b) having regard to all the circumstances racial hatred is likely to be stirred up thereby.

Procedure

An offence under the POA 1986, s. 18, is triable either way. When tried on indictment it is normally a class 3 offence, but see CrimPD XIII, para. B (see Supplement, **CPD.XIII.B**), for the additional factors that the court considers on allocation. No proceeding may be instituted except by, or with the consent of, the A-G (POA 1986, s. 27(3)). **B11.155**

For the liability of corporate officers, see **B11.161**.

Indictment

Statement of Offence **B11.156**

Displaying threatening, abusive or insulting material with intent to stir up racial hatred contrary to section 18 of the Public Order Act 1986.

Particulars of Offence

A on or about the... day of... at... displayed certain threatening, abusive or insulting materials, namely a quantity of pamphlets entitled... with intent thereby to stir up racial hatred.

The POA 1986, s. 27(2), declares that for the purposes of the rules against charging more than one offence in the same count, each of ss. 18 to 23 of the Act creates one offence.

Sentencing Guidelines

The definitive guideline, *Public Order Offences* (see Supplement, **SG29-4**) covers this offence, as well as those created by the POA 1986, ss. 19 to 23 and 29B to 29G. The guideline applies to adults over the age of 18 who are sentenced on or after 1 January 2020. The maximum penalty is seven years' imprisonment and/or a fine on indictment (POA 1986, s. 27(3)); six months and/or an unlimited fine summarily. Culpability will be either high, medium or lesser. High culpability factors are where D uses a position of trust, authority or influence to stir up hatred, where D had an intention to incite serious violence and where D's actions were persistent. The only lesser culpability factor is that D was reckless as to whether hatred would be stirred up. If high and lesser culpability factors are missing, culpability will be medium. Harm will be category 1 where the statement, publication, performance or broadcast directly encouraged activity which threatened or endangered life or where it was disseminated widely. If those factors are missing, harm will be category 2. For a category 1A case the starting point is three years' custody with a range of two to six years. For a category 1B or 2A case that starting point is two years' custody with a range of one to four years. For a category 1C or 2B case the starting point is one year's custody with a range of six months to three years. For a category 2C case, the starting point is a high level community order with a range of a low level community order to one year's custody. **B11.157**

Public Order Act 1986, s. 25

(1) A court by or before which a person is convicted of—
   (a) an offence under section 18 relating to the display of written material, or
   (b) an offence under section 19, 21 or 23,
   shall order to be forfeited any written material... produced to the court and shown to its satisfaction to be written material... to which the offence relates.
(2) An order made under this section shall not take effect—
   (a) in the case of an order made in proceedings in England and Wales, until the expiry of the ordinary time within which an appeal may be instituted or, where an appeal is duly instituted, until it is finally decided or abandoned...
(3) For the purposes of subsection (2)(a)—
   (a) an application for a case stated or for leave to appeal shall be treated as the institution of an appeal, and
   (b) where a decision on appeal is subject to a further appeal, the appeal is not finally determined until the expiry of the ordinary time within which a further appeal may be instituted or, where a further appeal is duly instituted, until the further appeal is finally decided or abandoned.

Elements

B11.158 The essence of the offence under the POA 1986, s. 18, lies in the use of words or behaviour or the display of material either when D intends to stir up racial hatred (s. 18(1)(a)) or where racial hatred is, in the circumstances, likely to be stirred up (s. 18(1)(b)). The concept of 'racial hatred' is therefore central to the offence. It does not matter that D intends to stir up racial hatred in another country, or that in all the circumstances racial hatred is only likely to be stirred up in another country (*Burns* [2017] EWCA Crim 1466 (at [11])).

Public Order Act 1986, s. 17

In this Part [i.e. ss. 17 to 29] 'racial hatred' means hatred against a group of persons defined by reference to colour, race, nationality (including citizenship) or ethnic or national origins.

For the meaning of 'racial group', see **B11.146**.

For discussion of the phrase 'threatening, abusive or insulting', see **B11.52**.

In the POA 1986, ss. 17 to 29, 'written material' includes any sign or other visible representation (s. 29). This includes articles in electronic form, such as material disseminated via a web site (*Sheppard* [2010] EWCA Crim 65, [2010] 2 All ER 850). For the meaning of 'writing', see **B11.53**.

For the offence under the POA 1986, s. 18(1)(a), an intention to stir up racial hatred is required. The *mens rea* of the offence under s. 18(1)(b) is established by reference to s. 18(5):

A person who is not shown to have intended to stir up racial hatred is not guilty of an offence under this section if he did not intend his words or behaviour, or the written material, to be, and was not aware that it might be, threatening, abusive or insulting.

Place of Commission

B11.159 **Public Order Act 1986, s. 18**

(2) An offence under this section may be committed in a public or a private place, except that no offence is committed where the words or behaviour are used, or the written material is displayed, by a person inside a dwelling and are not heard or seen except by other persons in that or another dwelling.

...

(4) In proceedings for an offence under this section it is a defence for the accused to prove that he was inside a dwelling and had no reason to believe that the words or behaviour used, or the written material displayed, would be heard or seen by a person outside that or any other dwelling.

Section 29 provides that, in ss. 17 to 29:

'dwelling' means any structure or part of a structure occupied as a person's home or other living accommodation (whether the occupation is separate or shared with others) but does not include any part not so occupied; and for this purpose 'structure' includes a tent, caravan, vehicle, vessel or other temporary or movable structure.

Offence Does Not Apply to Broadcasts or Cable Programme Services

B11.160 The POA 1986, s. 18, does not (by s. 18(6)) apply to words or behaviour used, or written material displayed, solely for the purpose of being included in a programme service. Such activity is controlled by s. 22 of the Act, see **B11.172**.

Liability of Corporate Officers

B11.161 **Public Order Act 1986, s. 28**

(1) Where a body corporate is guilty of an offence under this Part and it is shown that the offence was committed with the consent or connivance of a director, manager, secretary or other similar officer of the body, or a person purporting to act in any such capacity, he as well as the body corporate is guilty of the offence and liable to be proceeded against and punished accordingly.

(2) Where the affairs of a body corporate are managed by its members, subsection (1) applies in relation to the acts and defaults of a member in connection with his functions of management as it applies to a director.

As to corporate liability generally, and the liability of corporate officers, see **A6.23**.

Defence for Reports of Parliamentary and Judicial Proceedings

Public Order Act 1986, s. 26 **B11.162**

(1) Nothing in this Part applies to a fair and accurate report of proceedings in Parliament or in the Scottish Parliament or in the National Assembly for Wales.
(2) Nothing in this Part applies to a fair and accurate report of proceedings publicly heard before a court or tribunal exercising judicial authority where the report is published contemporaneously with the proceedings or, if it is not reasonably practicable or would be unlawful to publish a report of them contemporaneously, as soon as publication is reasonably practicable and lawful.

This and the general defences (see **A3**) are the only defences available to D. The truth of material, or belief in its truth, is not a defence (*Birdwood* (11 April 1995 unreported)).

PUBLISHING OR DISTRIBUTING WRITTEN MATERIAL STIRRING UP RACIAL HATRED

Public Order Act 1986, s. 19 **B11.163**

(1) A person who publishes or distributes written material which is threatening, abusive or insulting is guilty of an offence if—
  (a) he intends thereby to stir up racial hatred, or
  (b) having regard to all the circumstances racial hatred is likely to be stirred up thereby.

Procedure

An offence under the POA 1986, s. 19, is triable either way (POA 1986, s. 27(3)). When tried on indictment it is normally a class 3 offence, but see CrimPD XIII, para. B (see Supplement, **CPD.XIII.B**), for the additional factors that the court considers on allocation. No proceeding may be instituted except by, or with the consent of, the A-G (POA 1986, s. 27(3)). Where D had produced racially inflammatory material and posted it on a web site hosted by a remote server in the USA, D could still be tried in England and Wales as the appropriate jurisdictional test was the 'substantial measure' test laid down in *Smith (Wallace Duncan) (No. 4)* [2004] EWCA Crim 631, [2004] QB 1418 (*Sheppard* [2010] EWCA Crim 65, [2010] 2 All ER 850 and *Burns* [2017] EWCA Crim 1466 (at [11]): see further **A8.5**). The POA 1986, s. 27(2), declares that for the purposes of the rules against charging more than one offence in the same count or information, each of ss. 18 to 23 of the Act creates one offence. **B11.164**

For the liability of corporate officers, see **B11.161**.

Sentence

See **B11.157**. **B11.165**

Meaning of Terms Used in Defining the Offence

For the meaning of 'racial hatred' see **B11.158**. For the meaning of 'threatening, abusive or insulting', see **B11.52**. The POA 1986, s. 29, states that 'written material includes any sign or other visible representation' (see **B11.158**). In *Sheppard* [2001] EWCA Crim 65, [2010] 2 All ER 850, the Court of Appeal held that the word 'includes' was plainly intended to widen the scope of the expression and the words were sufficiently wide to include articles in electronic form, such as material disseminated by a web site. 'Publication' does not require proof that anybody had actually read or heard the material (*Sheppard*). **B11.166**

References in the POA 1986, ss. 17 to 29, to the publication or distribution of written material are, by s. 19(3) of the Act, to the publication or distribution of that material to the public or a section of the public.

Defences

B11.167 In proceedings for an offence under the POA 1986, s. 19, it is, by virtue of s. 19(2), a defence for D who is not shown to have intended to stir up racial hatred to prove that D was not aware of the content of the material and did not suspect, and had no reason to suspect, that it was threatening, abusive or insulting. The burden of proof of this defence lies on D on the balance of probabilities (see generally **F3.5** and **F3.53**). For a summary of the case law relating to 'reverse burden' challenges under the HRA 1998, see **F3.18** ***et seq***. The defence in the POA 1986, s. 26 (savings for reports of parliamentary and judicial proceedings: see **B11.162**), applies to s. 19.

These and the general defences (see **A3**) are the only defences available to D. The truth of the material, or a belief in its truth, is not a defence (*Birdwood* (11 April 1995 unreported)).

PUBLIC PERFORMANCE, BROADCASTING AND POSSESSION OF MATERIALS STIRRING UP RACIAL HATRED

General Provisions

B11.168 Sections 20 to 23 of the POA 1986 deal with the public performance, broadcasting and possession of materials intended to, or likely to, stir up racial hatred. The offences are triable either way, and the following general provisions of Part III of the Act apply:

(a) Prosecution may only be by, or with the consent of, the A-G (s. 27(1)).
(b) Each section creates one offence (s. 27(2)).
(c) The maximum penalty is seven years' imprisonment and/or a fine, on indictment; six months' imprisonment and/or an unlimited fine (s. 27(3)) (see **B11.157**).
(d) There is a saving for fair and accurate reports of parliamentary or judicial proceedings (see **B11.162**).
(e) For the liability of corporate officers, see **B11.161**.

For the meaning of 'racial hatred' see **B11.158**. For the meaning of 'threatening, abusive or insulting', see **B11.52**. For the meaning of 'written material', see **B11.158**.

References in the POA 1986, ss. 17 to 29, to the publication or distribution of written material are, by s. 19(3) of the Act, to the publication or distribution of that material to the public or a section of the public. References to the distribution, showing or playing of a recording are, by s. 21(2), to the distribution, showing or playing of the recording to the public or a section of the public. 'Recording' means any record from which visual images or sounds may, by any means, be reproduced (s. 21(2)).

As to the limited defences available and that the truth of material, or a belief in its truth, is not a defence, see *Birdwood* (11 April 1995 unreported).

Public Performance of Play Stirring up Racial Hatred

B11.169 **Public Order Act 1986, s. 20**

(1) If a public performance of a play is given which involves the use of threatening, abusive or insulting words or behaviour, any person who presents or directs the performance is guilty of an offence if—
(a) he intends thereby to stir up racial hatred, or
(b) having regard to all the circumstances (and, in particular, taking the performance as a whole) racial hatred is likely to be stirred up thereby.

Section 20(5) of the POA 1986 provides that the words 'play' and 'public performance' in s. 20 have the same meaning as in the Theatres Act 1968, s. 18(1).

The meaning of 'public place' in the POA 1936 is considered at **B11.12**.

B11.170

Public Order Act 1986, s. 20

(2) If a person presenting or directing the performance is not shown to have intended to stir up racial hatred, it is a defence for him to prove—
   (a) that he did not know and had no reason to suspect that the performance would involve the use of the offending words or behaviour, or
   (b) that he did not know and had no reason to suspect that the offending words or behaviour were threatening, abusive or insulting, or
   (c) that he did not know and had no reason to suspect that the circumstances in which the performance would be given would be such that racial hatred would be likely to be stirred up.

(3) This section does not apply to a performance given solely or primarily for one or more of the following purposes—
   (a) rehearsal,
   (b) making a recording of the performance, or
   (c) enabling the performance to be included in a programme service,

   but if it is proved that the performance was attended by persons other than those directly concerned with the giving of the performance or the doing in relation to it of the things mentioned in paragraph (b) or (c), the performance shall, unless the contrary is shown, be taken not to have been given solely for the purposes mentioned above.

(4) For the purposes of this section—
   (a) a person shall not be treated as presenting a performance of a play by reason only of his taking part in it as a performer,
   (b) a person taking part as a performer in a performance directed by another shall be treated as a person who directed the performance if without reasonable excuse he performs otherwise than in accordance with that person's direction, and
   (c) a person shall be taken to have directed a performance of a play given under his direction notwithstanding that he was not present during the performance;

   and a person shall not be treated as aiding or abetting the commission of an offence under this section by reason only of his taking part in a performance as a performer.

Distributing, Showing or Playing a Recording Stirring up Racial Hatred

Public Order Act 1986, s. 21 **B11.171**

(1) A person who distributes, or shows or plays, a recording of visual images or sounds which are threatening, abusive or insulting is guilty of an offence if—
   (a) he intends thereby to stir up racial hatred, or
   (b) having regard to all the circumstances racial hatred is likely to be stirred up thereby.

(2) [See **B11.168**]

(3) In proceedings for an offence under this section it is a defence for an accused who is not shown to have intended to stir up racial hatred to prove that he was not aware of the content of the recording and did not suspect, and had no reason to suspect, that it was threatening, abusive or insulting.

(4) This section does not apply to the showing or playing of a recording solely for the purpose of enabling the recording to be included in a programme service.

Broadcasting Programme Stirring up Racial Hatred

Public Order Act 1986, s. 22 **B11.172**

(1) If a programme involving threatening, abusive or insulting visual images or sounds is included in a programme service, each of the persons mentioned in subsection (2) is guilty of an offence if—
   (a) he intends to stir up racial hatred, or
   (b) having regard to all the circumstances racial hatred is likely to be stirred up thereby.

(2) The persons are—
   (a) the person providing the programme service,
   (b) any person by whom the programme is produced or directed, and
   (c) any person by whom offending words or behaviour are used.

(3) If the person providing the service, or a person by whom the programme was produced or directed, is not shown to have intended to stir up racial hatred, it is a defence for him to prove that—
 (a) he did not know and had no reason to suspect that the programme would involve the offending material, and
 (b) having regard to the circumstances in which the programme was included in a programme service, it was not reasonably practicable for him to secure the removal of the material.

(4) It is a defence for a person by whom the programme was produced or directed who is not shown to have intended to stir up racial hatred to prove that he did not know and had no reason to suspect—
 (a) that the programme would be included in a programme service, or
 (b) that the circumstances in which the programme would be so included would be such that racial hatred would be likely to be stirred up.

(5) It is a defence for a person by whom offending words or behaviour were used and who is not shown to have intended to stir up racial hatred to prove that he did not know and had no reason to suspect—
 (a) that a programme involving the use of the offending material would be included in a programme service, or
 (b) that the circumstances in which a programme involving the use of the offending material would be so included, or in which a programme so included would involve the use of the offending material, would be such that racial hatred would be likely to be stirred up.

(6) A person who is not shown to have intended to stir up racial hatred is not guilty of an offence under this section if he did not know, and had no reason to suspect, that the offending material was threatening, abusive or insulting.

Possession of Written Material or Recording Stirring up Racial Hatred

B11.173 **Public Order Act 1986, s. 23**

(1) A person who has in his possession written material which is threatening, abusive or insulting, or a recording of visual images or sounds which are threatening, abusive or insulting, with a view to—
 (a) in the case of written material, its being displayed, published, distributed, or included in a programme service, whether by himself or another, or
 (b) in the case of a recording, its being distributed, shown, played, or included in a programme service, whether by himself or another, is guilty of an offence if he intends racial hatred to be stirred up thereby or, having regard to all the circumstances, racial hatred is likely to be stirred up thereby.

(2) For this purpose regard is to be had to such display, publication, distribution, showing, playing, or inclusion in a programme service as he has, or it may reasonably be inferred that he has, in view.

(3) In proceedings for an offence under this section it is a defence for an accused who is not shown to have intended to stir up racial hatred to prove that he was not aware of the content of the written material or recording and did not suspect, and had no reason to suspect, that it was threatening, abusive or insulting.

USING WORDS OR BEHAVIOUR OR DISPLAYING WRITTEN MATERIAL STIRRING UP HATRED ON RELIGIOUS GROUNDS OR ON GROUNDS OF SEXUAL ORIENTATION

B11.174 Part 3A of the POA 1986 contains a number offences that criminalise certain acts of hatred against persons on religious grounds or on grounds of sexual orientation.

Procedure

B11.175 Offences under the POA 1986, ss. 29B(1), 29C(1), 29D(1), 29E(1), 29F(1) and 29G(1), are triable either way (s. 29L(3)). When tried on indictment, they are normally class 3 offences, but see CrimPD XIII, para. B (see Supplement, **CPD.XIII.B**) for the additional factors that the court considers on allocation. No proceedings may be instituted except by or with the consent of the A-G (s. 29L(1)). For the purposes of rules against charging more than one offence in the same count or information, this section creates one offence (s. 29L(2)). For the liability of corporate offenders, see s. 29M, which is worded in the standard format.

Sentence

See **B11.157**. **B11.176**

In relation to the offences relating to the display of written material, the court has the following forfeiture power.

Public Order Act 1986, s. 29I

(1) A court by or before which a person is convicted of—
 (a) an offence under section 29B relating to the display of written material, or
 (b) an offence under section 29C, 29E or 29G,
 shall order to be forfeited any written material or recording produced to the court and shown to its satisfaction to be written material or a recording to which the offence relates.
(2) An order made under this section shall not take effect—
 (a) until the expiry of the ordinary time within which an appeal may be instituted or, where an appeal is duly instituted, until it is finally decided or abandoned.
 (b) [repealed]
(3) For the purposes of subsection (2)(a)—
 (a) an application for a case stated or for leave to appeal shall be treated as the institution of an appeal, and
 (b) where a decision on appeal is subject to a further appeal, the appeal is not finally determined until the expiry of the ordinary time within which a further appeal may be instituted or, where a further appeal is duly instituted, until the further appeal is finally decided or abandoned.

Definition of Offence

Public Order Act 1986, s. 29B **B11.177**

(1) A person who uses threatening words or behaviour, or displays any written material which is threatening, is guilty of an offence if he intends thereby to stir up religious hatred or hatred on the grounds of sexual orientation.

Elements

Key concepts are the meaning of 'religious hatred' and the meaning of hatred on the grounds of sexual orientation. **B11.178**

Public Order Act 1986, ss. 29A and 29AB

29A.—In this Part 'religious hatred' means hatred against a group of persons defined by reference to religious belief or lack of religious belief.

29AB.—In this Part 'hatred on the grounds of sexual orientation' means hatred against a group of person defined by reference to sexual orientation (whether towards persons of the same sex, the opposite sex or both).

It is possible that the meaning of 'religion' will play a part in considering the offence relating to 'religious hatred'. It is a notoriously difficult concept to define. For a consideration of this issue in the context of religiously aggravated offences, see **B11.146**. It is submitted that, utilising the jurisprudence under the ECHR, Article 9, regarding these words as ordinary words of the English language is the approach that will be adopted. The government, in the Explanatory Memorandum, provides a list of 'religions widely recognised in this country' and lists: Christianity, Islam, Hinduism, Judaism, Buddhism, Sikhism, Rastafarianism, Baha'ism, Zoroastrianism and Jainism. For those who lack a religious belief, the government lists groups such as atheists and humanists. These offences are, according to the government, 'based on the fact that members of the group do not share the particular religious beliefs of the perpetrator'.

B11.179 As for 'hatred on the grounds of sexual orientation', the Ministry of Justice Circular 2010/05, para. 7, expresses the view that the definition 'is expressly limited to orientation towards persons of the same sex, the opposite sex, or both. The term does not extend to orientation based on, for example, a preference for particular sexual acts or practices. It therefore covers only groups of people who are gay, lesbian, bisexual or heterosexual.' An offence was not motivated by, nor was there a demonstration of hostility towards, V's sexual orientation, where D believed that V was a paedophile (*B* [2013] EWCA Crim 291, [2013] 2 Cr App R (S) 69 (443)).

In order to meet many of the deep concerns that this kind of legislation would prevent what has been acceptable behaviour, particularly that of those wishing to convert people to their own religion or of comedians, entertainers and social commentators, and a feeling that the existence of the ECHR, Articles 9, 10 and 11, would not provide sufficient protection, the Act provides as follows.

Public Order Act 1986, ss. 29J and 29JA

29J.—Nothing in this Part shall be read or given effect in a way which prohibits or restricts discussion, criticism or expressions of antipathy, dislike, ridicule, insult or abuse of particular religions or the beliefs or practices of their adherents, or of any other belief system or the beliefs or practices of its adherents, or proselytising or urging adherents of a different religion or belief system to cease practising their religion or belief system.

29JA.—(1) In this part, for the avoidance of doubt, the discussion or criticism of sexual conduct or practices or the urging of persons to refrain from or modify such conduct or practices shall not be taken of itself to be threatening or intended to stir up hatred.

(2) In this Part, for the avoidance of doubt, any discussion or criticism of marriage which concerns the sex of the parties to marriage shall not be taken of itself to be threatening or intended to stir up hatred.

Ministry of Justice Circular 2010/05, para. 12, states: 'The offences are limited to threatening conduct or material which is intended to stir up hatred. Subject to those conditions, they do not prevent the telling of jokes or the preaching of religious doctrine. Hatred is a very strong emotion. Conduct or material which only stirs up ridicule or dislike, or which simply causes offence, would not meet that threshold. The offences are not intended to cover, for example, teenagers who call each other names in the playground where this is not threatening and there is no intention of stirring up hatred against a group.'

B11.180 The offence may be committed in a public or a private place, but no offence is committed where the words or behaviour are used or the written material is displayed by a person inside a dwelling and are not heard or seen except by other persons in that or another dwelling (s. 29B(2)). The offence does not apply to words or behaviour used or written material displayed solely for the purpose of being included in a programme service (s. 29B(5)). For the relevant offence that may be committed, see **B11.192**. 'Dwelling' means any structure or part of a structure occupied as a person's home or other living accommodation (whether the occupation is separate or shared with others) but does not include any part not so occupied, and 'structure' includes a tent, caravan, vehicle, vessel or other temporary or moveable structure (s. 29N).

For a discussion of 'threatening, abusive or insulting', see **B11.52**. 'Written material' includes any sign or other visible representation (s. 29N). This includes articles in electronic form, such as material disseminated via a web site (*Sheppard* [2010] EWCA Crim 65, [2010] 2 All ER 850).

D must have the relevant intention (s. 29B(1)).

There is a special saving for reports of parliamentary and judicial proceedings.

Public Order Act 1986, s. 29K

(1) Nothing in this Part applies to a fair and accurate report of proceedings in Parliament, in the Scottish Parliament or in the National Assembly for Wales.

(2) Nothing in this Part applies to a fair and accurate report of proceedings publicly heard before a court or tribunal exercising judicial authority where the report is published contemporaneously with the proceedings or, if it is not reasonably practicable or would be unlawful to publish a report of them contemporaneously, as soon as publication is reasonably practicable and lawful.

Defence

It is a defence for D to prove that D was inside the dwelling and had no reason to believe that the words or behaviour used or the written material displayed would be heard or seen by a person outside that or any other dwelling (POA 1986, s. 29B(4)). **B11.181**

Powers of Arrest

The citizen's power of arrest in the PACE 1984, s. 24A, does not apply to this offence (PACE 1984, s. 24A(5)). For arrest generally, see **D1.14** ***et seq.*** **B11.182**

PUBLISHING OR DISTRIBUTING WRITTEN MATERIAL STIRRING UP HATRED ON RELIGIOUS GROUNDS OR ON GROUNDS OF SEXUAL ORIENTATION

Public Order Act 1986, s. 29C **B11.183**

(1) A person who publishes or distributes written material which is threatening is guilty of an offence if he intends thereby to stir up religious hatred or hatred on the grounds of sexual orientation.

For procedure and sentence, see **B11.175** and **B11.157**.

Elements

As to the meaning of 'religious hatred' and the special provision on the protection of freedom of expression (POA 1986, ss. 29J and 29JA), see **B11.179**. As to the meaning of 'threatening', see **B11.52**, but note that it is only material that is threatening which forms this offence. **B11.184**

References to the publication or distribution of written material are to its publication or distribution to the public or a section of the public (s. 29C(2)).

D must have the relevant intention (s. 29C(1)).

For savings for reports of parliamentary and judicial proceedings under POA 1986, s. 29K, see **B11.180**.

PUBLIC PERFORMANCE OF PLAY STIRRING UP HATRED ON RELIGIOUS GROUNDS OR ON GROUNDS OF SEXUAL ORIENTATION

Public Order Act 1986, s. 29D **B11.185**

(1) If a public performance of a play is given which involves the use of threatening words or behaviour, any person who presents or directs the performance is guilty of an offence if he intends thereby to stir up religious hatred or hatred on the grounds of sexual orientation.

For procedure and sentence, see **B11.175** and **B11.157**.

Elements

As to the meaning of 'religious hatred' and 'hatred on the grounds of sexual orientation' and the special provision on the protection of freedom of expression, see **B11.180**. As to the meaning of 'threatening', see **B11.52**, but note that it is only material that is threatening which forms this offence. **B11.186**

The offence does not apply to certain performances.

Public Order Act 1986, s. 29D

(2) This section does not apply to a performance given solely or primarily for one or more of the following purposes—
(a) rehearsal,
(b) making a recording of the performance, or
(c) enabling the performance to be included in a programme service;
but if it is proved that the performance was attended by persons other than those directly connected with the giving of the performance or the doing in relation to it of the things mentioned in paragraph (b) or (c), the performance shall, unless the contrary is shown, be taken not to have been given solely or primarily for the purpose mentioned above.

As regards those who may or may not be directing a performance, the following provision applies.

Public Order Act 1986, s. 29D

(3) For the purposes of this section—
(a) a person shall not be treated as presenting a performance of a play by reason only of his taking part in it as a performer,
(b) a person taking part as a performer in a performance directed by another shall be treated as a person who directed the performance if without reasonable excuse he performs otherwise than in accordance with that person's direction, and
(c) a person shall be taken to have directed a performance of a play given under his direction notwithstanding that he was not present during the performance;
and a person shall not be treated as aiding or abetting the commission of an offence under this section by reason only of his taking part in a performance as a performer.

D must have the relevant intention (POA 1986, s. 29D(1)).

'Play' and 'public performance' have the same meaning as in the Theatres Act 1968 (s. 29D(4)). Further, the Theatres Act 1968, ss. 9 (script as evidence of what was performed), 10 (power to make copies of script) and 15 (powers of entry and inspection) apply to this offence (s. 29D(5)).

For savings for reports of parliamentary and judicial proceedings under s. 29K, see **B11.180**.

Power of Arrest

B11.187 The citizen's power of arrest in the PACE 1984, s. 24A, does not apply to this offence (PACE 1984, s. 24A(5)).

DISTRIBUTING, SHOWING OR PLAYING A RECORDING STIRRING UP HATRED ON RELIGIOUS GROUNDS OR ON GROUNDS OF SEXUAL ORIENTATION

B11.188 **Public Order Act 1986, s. 29E**

(1) A person who distributes, or shows or plays, a recording of visual images or sounds which are threatening is guilty of an offence if he intends thereby to stir up religious hatred or hatred on the grounds of sexual orientation.

For procedure and sentence, see **B11.175** and **B11.157**.

Elements

B11.189 As to the meaning of 'religious hatred' and 'hatred on the grounds of sexual orientation', and the special provision on the protection of freedom of expression, see **B11.180**. As to the meaning of 'threatening', see **B11.52**, but note that it is only material that is threatening which forms this offence. Section 29E defines 'recording'.

Public Order Act 1986, s. 29E

(2) In this Part 'recording' means any record from which visual images or sounds may, by any means, be reproduced; and references to the distribution, showing or playing of a recording are to its distribution, showing or playing to the public or a section of the public.

D must have the relevant intention (s. 29E(1)).

This offence does not apply to the showing or playing of a recording solely for the purpose of enabling it to be included in a programme service (s. 29E(3)). For the relevant offence, see **B11.192**.

For savings for reports of parliamentary and judicial proceedings under s. 29K, see **B11.180**.

Power of Arrest

The citizen's power of arrest in the PACE 1984, s. 24A, does not apply to this offence (PACE 1984, s. 24A(5)). **B11.190**

BROADCASTING OR INCLUDING PROGRAMME IN PROGRAMME SERVICE STIRRING UP HATRED ON RELIGIOUS GROUNDS OR ON GROUNDS OF SEXUAL ORIENTATION

Public Order Act 1986, s. 29F **B11.191**

(1) If a programme involving threatening visual images or sounds is included in a programme service, each of the persons mentioned in subsection (2) is guilty of an offence if he intends thereby to stir up religious hatred or hatred on the grounds of sexual orientation.
(2) The persons are—
   (a) the person providing the programme service,
   (b) any person by whom the programme is produced or directed, and
   (c) any person by whom offending words or behaviour are used.

For procedure and sentence, see **B11.175** and **B11.157**.

Elements

As to the meaning of 'religious hatred' and 'hatred on the grounds of sexual orientation', and the special provision on the protection of freedom of expression, see **B11.180**. As to the meaning of 'threatening', see **B11.52**, but note that it is only material that is threatening which forms this offence. **B11.192**

'Programme service' has the same meaning as in the Broadcasting Act 1990 (s. 29N). 'Programme' means any item which is included in a programme service (s. 29N).

D must have the relevant intention (s. 29F(1)).

For savings for reports of parliamentary and judicial proceedings under s. 29K, see **B11.180**.

Power of Arrest

The citizen's power of arrest in the PACE 1984, s. 24A, does not apply to this offence (PACE 1984, s. 24A(5)). **B11.193**

POSSESSION OF INFLAMMATORY MATERIAL

Public Order Act 1986, s. 29G **B11.194**

(1) A person who has in his possession written material which is threatening, or a recording of visual images or sounds which are threatening, with a view to—
   (a) in the case of written material, its being displayed, published, distributed, or included in a programme service whether by himself or another, or

(b) in the case of a recording, its being distributed, shown, played, or included in a programme service, whether by himself or another,

is guilty of an offence if he intends thereby to stir up religious hatred or hatred on the grounds of sexual orientation.

For procedure and sentence, see **B11.175** and **B11.157**.

Elements

B11.195 As to the meaning of 'religious hatred' and 'hatred on the grounds of sexual orientation', and the special provision on the protection of freedom of expression, see **B11.180**. As to the meaning of 'threatening', see **B11.52**, but note that it is only material that is threatening which forms this offence.

For this offence regard is had to such display, publication, distribution, showing, playing, or inclusion in a programme service as D has, or it may be reasonably be inferred that D has, in view (s. 29G(2)).

D must have the relevant intention (s. 29G(1)).

For savings for reports of parliamentary and judicial proceedings under s. 29K, see **B11.180**.

Power of Arrest

B11.196 The citizen's power of arrest in the PACE 1984, s. 24A, does not apply to this offence (PACE 1984, s. 24A(5)).

Entry and Search

B11.197

Public Order Act 1986, s. 29H

(1) If a justice of the peace is satisfied by information on oath laid by a constable that there are reasonable grounds for suspecting that a person has possession of written material or a recording in contravention of section 29G, the justice may issue a warrant under his hand authorising any constable to enter and search the premises where it is suspected the material or recording is situated.

(2) [repealed]

(3) A constable entering or searching premises in pursuance of a warrant issued under this section may use reasonable force if necessary.

(4) In this section 'premises' means any place and, in particular, includes—
  (a) any vehicle, vessel, aircraft or hovercraft,
  (b) any offshore installation as defined in section 12 of the Mineral Workings (Offshore Installations) Act 1971, and
  (c) any tent or movable structure.

DRUNK AND DISORDERLY

Offence, Procedure and Sentence

B11.198 It is a summary offence, contrary to the CJA 1967, s. 91(1), where 'Any person who in any public place is guilty, while drunk, of disorderly behaviour…'. The maximum penalty for the offence is a fine not exceeding level 3 on the standard scale. The revised *Magistrates' Court Sentencing Guidelines* (see Supplement, **SG10-76**) identify the starting point as being a band A fine with a sentencing range from a conditional discharge up to a band C fine.

Community rehabilitation orders and curfew orders are the only available community sentences for this offence.

Under the Penalties for Disorderly Behaviour (Amount of Penalty) Order 2002 (SI 2002 No. 1837), as amended, this offence is a penalty offence and the amount payable is £90.

Drunk

It was held by the Divisional Court in *Neale v RMJE (a minor)* (1984) 80 Cr App R 20 that the natural and ordinary meaning of the word 'drunk' in this statutory context is that it is limited to cases of drunkenness induced by alcohol. It is not, therefore, committed where D's state is a product of glue-sniffing. This decision was followed by the Divisional Court in *Lanham v Rickwood* (1984) 148 JP 737, a decision on the meaning of the word 'drunk' in the Licensing Act 1872, s. 12, which states: 'Every person found drunk in any highway or other public place, whether building or not, or on any licensed premises, shall be liable to a penalty'. **B11.199**

In *Lanham v Rickwood* it was also decided that the condition in which D was found does not have to be solely attributable to alcohol:

> In each case, the magistrates have to ask themselves, no doubt as a matter of simple common sense, whether a person's loss of self-control is attributable to his having indulged in an excessive consumption of intoxicating liquor. If the evidence before them is that he has indulged both in an excessive consumption of intoxicating liquor and also in some other form of activity, such as glue-sniffing, which may also have affected his self-control, they have to decide, as a matter of common sense, whether they are satisfied that, apart from the glue-sniffing, he has consumed intoxicating liquor to an extent which affects his steady self-control.

This decision is important not only on multiple causes of a condition, but also because it gives an indication of what is meant by 'drunk'. In *Neale v RMJE (a minor)* Robert Goff LJ made the same point about the meaning of drunkenness: 'the word "drunk", in ordinary common speech,...refers to someone who has taken intoxicating liquor to an extent which affects his steady self control'. Note that a person may be in a condition which can be described as 'drunk' but that need not be the same condition as that necessary to raise the defence of intoxication.

In *Carroll v DPP* [2009] EWHC 554 (Admin) the Divisional Court confirmed that this is one of the most basic offences in the calendar and that it requires proof of three elements, namely that (1) D was drunk; (2) D was in a public place; and (3) D was guilty of disorderly behaviour. As to the first element, approving *Neale*, it said that whether D was drunk is a simple question of fact in each case. If the voluntary consumption of alcohol results in D becoming drunk then the first element is proved.

Disorderly Behaviour

The words are to be given their ordinary and natural meaning; what is required is proof that objectively viewed D was guilty of disorderly behaviour — there is no *mens rea* requirement (*Carroll v DPP* [2009] EWHC 554 (Admin)). The disorderly conduct, though, must occur before D is arrested as the gravamen of the offence is disorderly conduct whilst being drunk (*R (H) v CPS* [2005] EWHC 2459 (Admin)). **B11.200**

Public Place

The CJA 1967, s. 91(4), provides that, in s. 91, '"public place" includes any highway and any other premises or place to which at the material time the public have or are permitted to have access, whether on payment or otherwise'. As to this definition, see *Williams v DPP* (1992) 95 Cr App R 415 and *Cleaver* [2011] EWCA Crim 983. **B11.201**

Related Offence: Drunk on an Aircraft

It is an offence, contrary to the Air Navigation Order 2016 (SI 2016 No. 765), art. 242, for a person to enter any aircraft when drunk or to be drunk in any aircraft. It is also an offence for a person, when acting as an aircraft crew member or being carried in any aircraft for the purpose of so acting, to be under the influence of drink or drugs to such an extent as to impair that person's capacity to act. Both offences are triable either way. The maximum penalty is: on conviction on indictment, two years' imprisonment and/or a fine; on summary conviction, an unlimited fine (art. 265(7) **B11.202** and sch. 13, part 3). A sentence of eight months for this offence was upheld in *Ayodeji* [2001] 1 Cr App R (S) 106 (370) (at that time the maximum sentence was five years on indictment). In *Ator* [2011] EWCA Crim 769, [2011] 2 Cr App R (S) 108 (618) D pleaded guilty to being drunk in an aircraft and received a sentence of six months' imprisonment. Shorter concurrent terms were imposed in relation to two offences of common assault and an offence of interfering with the performance of the duties of a crew member on an aircraft. The Court of Appeal (considering *Cooper* [2003] EWCA Crim 3277, [2004] 2 Cr App R (S) 16 (82) and *Matlach* [2005] EWCA Crim 2911, [2006] 2 Cr App R (S) 1 (1)) upheld the sentence, despite D being a man of previous good character with a series of 'impressive personal references from a number of sources'. The aggravating features identified were that this was a prolonged series of events whilst the aircraft was in the air, a number of passengers were upset and distressed by D's behaviour, D ignored numerous requests to calm down and behave, and in the course of his conduct D assaulted a passenger by biting him and also assaulted an attendant who was doing her job. See **B10.247** for the offence of recklessly or negligently acting in a manner likely to endanger an aircraft, or any person in an aircraft. See also *Cox* [2017] EWCA Crim 1366, [2018] 1 Cr App R (S) 3 (15).

ALCOHOL OFFENCES IN CONNECTION WITH SPORTING EVENTS

Alcohol on Coaches and Trains

B11.203 **Sporting Events (Control of Alcohol etc.) Act 1985, s. 1**

(2) A person who knowingly causes or permits alcohol to be carried on a vehicle to which this section applies is guilty of an offence—

(a) if the vehicle is a public service vehicle and he is the operator of the vehicle or the servant or agent of the operator, or

(b) if the vehicle is a hired vehicle and he is the person to whom it is hired or the servant or agent of that person.

(3) A person who has alcohol in his possession while on a vehicle to which this section applies is guilty of an offence.

(4) A person who is drunk on a vehicle to which this section applies is guilty of an offence.

B11.204 **Sentence and Procedure** Offences under the Sporting Events (Control of Alcohol etc.) Act 1985, s. 1, are, by s. 8 of the Act, triable summarily only and punishable:

(a) in the case of an offence under s. 1(2), a fine not exceeding level 4 on the standard scale;

(b) in the case of an offence under s. 1(3), a fine not exceeding level 3 on the standard scale or imprisonment for a term not exceeding three months, or both;

(c) in the case of an offence under s. 1(4), a fine not exceeding level 2 on the standard scale.

B11.205 **Meaning of 'Vehicle'**

Sporting Events (Control of Alcohol etc.) Act 1985, s. 1

(1) This section applies to a vehicle which—

(a) is a public service vehicle or railway passenger vehicle, and

(b) is being used for the principal purpose of carrying passengers for the whole or part of a journey to or from a designated sporting event.

(2) to (4) [see **B11.204**]

(5) In this section 'public service vehicle' and 'operator' have the same meaning as in the Public Passenger Vehicles Act 1981.

B11.206 **Meaning of 'Designated Sporting Event'**

Sporting Events (Control of Alcohol etc.) Act 1985, s. 9

(3) 'Designated sporting event'—

(a) means a sporting event or proposed sporting event for the time being designated, or of a class designated, by order made by the Secretary of State, and

(b) includes a designated sporting event within the meaning of Part II of the Criminal Law (Consolidation) (Scotland) Act 1995;

and an order under this subsection may apply to events or proposed events outside Great Britain as well as those in England and Wales.

See the Sports Grounds and Sporting Events (Designation Order) 2005 (SI 2005 No. 3204).

Alcohol on Other Vehicles

Sporting Events (Control of Alcohol etc.) Act 1985, s. 1A **B11.207**

(2) A person who knowingly causes or permits alcohol to be carried on a motor vehicle to which this section applies is guilty of an offence—
(a) if he is its driver, or
(b) if he is not its driver but is its keeper, the servant or agent of its keeper, a person to whom it is made available (by hire, loan or otherwise) by its keeper or the keeper's servant or agent, or the servant or agent of a person to whom it is so made available.

(3) A person who has alcohol in his possession while on a motor vehicle to which this section applies is guilty of an offence.

(4) A person who is drunk on a motor vehicle to which this section applies is guilty of an offence.

Sentence and Procedure Offences under the Sporting Events (Control of Alcohol etc.) Act 1985, s. 1A are, by s. 8, triable summarily only and punishable. **B11.208**

(a) in the case of an offence under s. 1A(2), a fine not exceeding level 4 on the standard scale;
(b) in the case of an offence under s. 1A(3), a fine not exceeding level 3 on the standard scale or imprisonment for a terms not exceeding three months, or both;
(c) in the case of an offence under s. 1A(4), a fine not exceeding level 2 on the standard scale.

Meaning of Terms **B11.209**

Sporting Events (Control of Alcohol etc.) Act 1985, s. 1A

(1) This section applies to a motor vehicle which—
(a) is not a public service vehicle but is adapted to carry more than 8 passengers, and
(b) is being used for the principal purpose of carrying two or more passengers for the whole or part of a journey to or from a designated sporting event.

. . .

(5) In this section—
'keeper', in relation to a vehicle, means the person having the duty to take out a licence for it under the Vehicle Excise and Registration Act 1994,
'motor vehicle' means a mechanically propelled vehicle intended or adapted for use on roads, and
'public service vehicle' has the same meaning as in the Public Passenger Vehicles Act 1981.

Containers etc. at Sports Grounds

Sporting Events (Control of Alcohol etc.) Act 1985, s. 2 **B11.210**

(1) A person who has alcohol or an article to which this section applies in his possession—
(a) at any time during the period of a designated sporting event when he is in any area of a designated sports ground from which the event may be directly viewed, or
(b) while entering or trying to enter a designated sports ground at any time during the period of a designated sporting event at that ground, is guilty of an offence.

(1A) Subsection (1)(a) above has effect subject to section 5A(1) of this Act.

(2) A person who is drunk in a designated sports ground at any time during the period of a designated sporting event at that ground or is drunk while entering or trying to enter such a ground at any time during the period of a designated sporting event at that ground is guilty of an offence.

Special provision is made by s. 5A(1) for private rooms from which the sporting event can be viewed; although prospectively repealed by the Licensing Act 2003, s. 198 and sch. 6, this provision remains in force.

B11.211 **Sentence and Procedure** Offences under the Sporting Events (Control of Alcohol etc.) Act 1985, s. 2, are, by s. 8 of the Act, triable summarily only and punishable:

(a) in the case of an offence under s. 2(1), a fine not exceeding level 3 on the standard scale or imprisonment for a term not exceeding three months, or both;
(b) in the case of an offence under s. 2(2), a fine not exceeding level 2 on the standard scale.

The *Magistrates' Court Sentencing Guidelines* (see Supplement, **SG10-99**) deal with a number of 'football ground offences' (offences under this section as well as those dealt with at **B11.126** and **B11.129**) all together. The culpability and harm factors are as set out at **B11.127**. The starting point for these offences for category 1 is a band C fine, with a sentencing range of a band C fine to a high level community order. By contrast, the starting point for category 3 is a band A fine, with a sentencing range of conditional discharge to a band B fine.

Both for the s. 2(1) and s. 2(2) offence, the court must consider imposing a banning order (see **E21.3**). If no banning order is made, the court must give reasons.

B11.212 **Meaning of Terms** For the meaning of 'designated sporting event', see **B11.206**.

Sporting Events (Control of Alcohol etc.) Act 1985, s. 9

(2) 'Designated sports ground' means any place—
(a) used (wholly or partly) for sporting events where accommodation is provided for spectators, and
(b) for the time being designated, or of a class designated, by order made by the Secretary of State;

and an order under this subsection may include provision for determining for the purposes of this Act the outer limit of any designated sports ground.

...

(4) The period of a designated sporting event is the period beginning two hours before the start of the event or (if earlier) two hours before the time at which it is advertised to start and ending one hour after the end of the event, but—
(a) where an event advertised to start at a particular time on a particular day is postponed to a later day, the period includes the period in the day on which it is advertised to take place beginning two hours before and ending one hour after that time, and
(b) where an event advertised to start at a particular time on a particular day does not take place, the period is the period referred to in paragraph (a) above.

The articles to which s. 2 applies are defined in s. 2(3):

This section applies to any article capable of causing injury to a person struck by it, being—
(a) a bottle, can or other portable container (including such an article when crushed or broken) which—
(i) is for holding any drink, and
(ii) is of a kind which, when empty, is normally discarded or returned to, or left to be recovered by, the supplier, or
(b) part of an article falling within paragraph (a) above;

but does not apply to anything that is for holding any medicinal product (within the meaning of the Medicines Act 1968).

Possession of Flares, Fireworks, etc. at Sports Grounds

B11.213 **Sporting Events (Control of Alcohol etc.) Act 1985, s. 2A**

(1) A person is guilty of an offence if he has an article or substance to which this section applies in his possession—
(a) at any time during the period of a designated sporting event when he is in any area of a designated sports ground from which the event may be directly viewed, or
(b) *while entering or trying to enter* a designated sports ground at any time during the period of a designated sporting event at the ground.

(2) It is a defence for the accused to prove that he had possession with lawful authority.
(3) This section applies to any article or substance whose main purpose is the emission of a flare for purposes of illuminating or signalling (as opposed to igniting or heating) or the emission of smoke or a visible gas; and in particular it applies to distress flares, fog signals, and pellets and capsules intended to be used as fumigators or for testing pipes, but not to matches, cigarette lighters or heaters.
(4) This section also applies to any article which is a firework.

For the meaning of 'designated sporting event', see **B11.206**; for the meaning of 'designated sports ground', see **B11.212**.

Sentence and Procedure Offences under the Sporting Events (Control of Alcohol etc.) Act 1985, s. 2A are, by s. 8, triable summarily only, and punishable: **B11.214**

(a) in the case of an offence under s. 1A(2), a fine not exceeding level 4 on the standard scale;
(b) in the case of an offence under s. 1A(3), a fine not exceeding level 3 on the standard scale or imprisonment for a terms not exceeding three months, or both;
(c) in the case of an offence under s. 1A(4), a fine not exceeding level 2 on the standard scale.

NUISANCE OR DISTURBANCE ON NHS PREMISES

The CJIA 2008, s. 119, introduced the offence of causing nuisance or disturbance on NHS premises. The offence applies to both English and Welsh NHS premises (s. 119(4)). **B11.215**

Criminal Justice and Immigration Act 2008, s. 119

(1) A person commits an offence if—
  (a) the person causes, without reasonable excuse and while on NHS premises, a nuisance or disturbance to an NHS staff member who is working there or is otherwise there in connection with work,
  (b) the person refuses, without reasonable excuse, to leave the NHS premises when asked to do so by a constable or an NHS staff member, and
  (c) the person is not on the NHS premises for the purpose of obtaining medical advice, treatment or care for himself or herself.

Sentence

This is a summary only offence which attracts a maximum penalty of a fine not exceeding level 3 (CJIA 2008, s. 119(2)). **B11.216**

Defences

A person will not commit the offence if that person has a reasonable excuse for causing the nuisance or disturbance or refusing to leave the premises. Behaviour consequential to the receipt of upsetting news or bereavement may, for example, constitute a reasonable excuse. A reasonable excuse for not leaving the premises may, for example, include a situation where a dependant is on the premises concerned and the person causing a nuisance or disturbance has a responsibility to remain on the premises with this dependant. **B11.217**

Meaning of 'for the purpose of obtaining medical advice, treatment, etc'

A person ceases to be on the premises for the purpose of obtaining medical advice, treatment or care for himself or herself in two circumstances. First, once the person has received the advice, etc. (CJIA 2008, s. 119(3)(a)) and secondly, if the person has received the advice, etc. during the last eight hours (s. 119(3)(b)). **B11.218**

Powers of Removal

B11.219 The CJIA 2008, s.120, gives police officers and other authorised officers the power to use reasonable force if necessary to remove a person from NHS premises who they reasonably suspect is committing an offence under s. 119 or who has committed such an offence. However, an authorised officer cannot remove such a person if the officer has reason to believe that the person is in need of medical advice, etc. or that removal would endanger the person's mental or physical health (s. 120(4)). An 'authorised officer' is a duly authorised NHS staff member (s. 120(5)).

Section B12 Offences Relating to Weapons

FIRMS OFFENCES GENERALLY

B12.1 The Firearms Acts 1968 to 1997 control the possession etc. of firearms by dividing such weapons into a number of different categories, namely (i) firearms, (ii) firearms within s. 1 of the FA 1968 (certificate needed: see **B12.36**), (iii) prohibited weapons, (iv) shot guns and (v) air weapons. Section 8 of the F(A)A 1988 takes de-activated weapons out of a category into which they would otherwise have fallen (see **B12.20**), but there can be circumstances in which a de-activated weapon constitutes an 'imitation firearm'. Care needs to be taken in respect of any 'imitation firearm' because some offences expressly make reference to imitation firearms (see **B12.26**), while the reach of other offences extends to imitation firearms by operation of the FA 1982, ss. 1 and 2 (see **B12.30**). Many of the offences control ammunition (see **B12.24**) as well as firearms. It is important to distinguish between ammunition to which s.1 of the FA 1968 applies (certificate needed) and other ammunition that is not subject to s. 1; certain ammunition will be 'prohibited ammunition' (see **B12.60**).

Notwithstanding amendments that have been made to the firearms legislation by the PCA 2017 (notably Part 6, and see Circular 006/2017, *Firearms Controls*), aspects of the legislation remain unhappily drafted (notably, but not exclusively, in relation to 'air weapons') and much legislation has evolved piecemeal due, in part, to developments in the design and use of a number of devices. For example, devices that are popularly described as 'air guns' are not confined to the break-barrel piston-action type, but include carbon-dioxide bulb systems, or gas-cartridge-pellet systems. A number of air/gas powered guns have been designed to resemble traditional firearms (realistic imitation firearms). Such firearms are subject to legal controls (see **B12.32**). Note that the definition of a 'firearm' excludes an 'airsoft gun' (FA 1968, s. 57A): see **B12.8**.

A number of EU Directives currently apply in relation to firearms (e.g. Council Directive 91/477/EEC [1991] OJ L256/51, as amended by Directive (EU) 2017/853 [2017] OJ L137/22, but note prospective amendments under SI 2019 No. 742, reg. 58). Not all definitions in EU instruments mirror those found in UK firearms legislation.

Practitioners should be aware that in the event that the UK leaves the EU on 'IP completion day' and not on 'exit day' (European Union (Withdrawal Agreement) Act 2020, s. 39) a number of provisions of the FA 1968, the F(A)A 1988, the Firearms Acts (Amendment) Regulations 1992 (SI 1992 No. 2823), the Firearms (Amendment) Act 1988 (Amendment) Regulations 2011 (SI 2011 No. 2175) and Regulation (EU) 2015/2403 ([2015] OJ L333/62) may be the subject of legislative amendment (see the Law Enforcement and Security (Amendment) (EU Exit) Regulations 2019 (SI 2019 No. 742)).

Mode of Trial and Punishment

B12.2 Section 51(1) to (3) of the FA 1968 provide that the mode of trial, maximum punishments and powers of convicting courts with respect to offences created by that Act shall be as set out in sch. 6 to that Act, which is reproduced at **B12.6**.

Time-limits: Summary Trial

B12.3

Firearms Act 1968, s. 51

(4) Notwithstanding section 127(1) of the Magistrates' Courts Act 1980 . . . [Scotland] summary proceedings for an offence under this Act, other than an offence under section 22(3) or an offence relating specifically to air weapons, may be instituted at any time within four years after the commission of the offence:
Provided that no such proceedings shall be instituted in England after the expiration of six months after the commission of the offence unless they are instituted by, or by the direction of, the Director of Public Prosecutions.

Powers of Seizure and Forfeiture

B12.4 Sections 46 to 49 of the FA 1968 provide for powers of search, the demand by a constable for production of certificates, and police powers in relation to arms traffic (note pending amendments to s. 48 on 'IP completion day': SI 2019 No. 742).

Powers of forfeiture exercisable by a convicting court may be found in two places. Part II of sch. 6 to the FA 1968 (see **B12.7**) provides certain specific powers. Section 52 provides generally for forfeiture and disposal of firearms and for cancellation of certificates. Section 50(3) of the VCRA 2006 provides for ss. 46, 51(4), 52 and 58 of the FA 1968 to apply as if ss. 28, 29 and 35 of the 2006 Act were contained in the FA 1968.

The following powers also apply:

(a) Education Act 1996, s. 550AA (power of members of staff to search school pupils for weapons: the section now appears under the heading 'Powers to search pupils', as amended by the Apprenticeships, Skills, Children and Learning Act 2009, s. 242(1)). Note that s. 550AA now applies only to Wales whereas (more extensive) powers that are applicable in England exist under ss. 550ZA to 550ZD (Apprenticeships, Skills, Children and Learning Act 2009, s. 242, and the Education Act 2011, s. 2).
(b) Further and Higher Education Act 1992, s. 85B (power to search further education students for weapons). This section now applies only to Wales (for England, see ss. 85AA to 85AD, inserted by the Apprenticeships, Skills, Children and Learning Act 2009, s. 244; for Wales, see s. 245).
(c) CJA 1988, s. 139B (police power to search schools etc. for weapons).

In the absence of legitimate grounds for piercing the corporate veil, firearms or other property lawfully owned by a registered company or other corporation cannot be subject to a forfeiture order merely because an individual connected to that corporation has been convicted of an offence in relation to it (*Hyde* [2014] EWCA Crim 713).

Firearms Act 1968, s. 52

(1) Where a person—
 (a) is convicted of an offence under this Act (other than an offence under section 22(3) or an offence relating specifically to air weapons) or is convicted of a crime for which he is sentenced to imprisonment, or detention in a young offender institution . . . [Scotland] . . . or is subject to a detention and training order; or
 (b) has been ordered into a recognizance to keep the peace or to be of good behaviour, a condition of which is that he shall not possess, use or carry a firearm; or
 (c) is subject to a community order containing a requirement that he shall not possess, use or carry a firearm; or
 (d) [applies to Scotland only]
 the court by or before which he is convicted, or by which the order is made, may make such order as to the forfeiture or disposal of any firearm or ammunition found in his possession as the court thinks fit and may cancel any firearm certificate or shot gun certificate held by him.
(1A) In subsection (1)(c) 'community order' means—
 (a) a community order within the meaning of Part 12 of the Criminal Justice Act 2003, or a youth rehabilitation order within the meaning of Part 1 of the Criminal Justice and Immigration Act 2008, made in England and Wales, or
 (b) . . . [Scotland].
(2) Where the court cancels a certificate under this section—
 (a) the court shall cause notice to be sent to the chief officer of police by whom the certificate was granted; and
 (b) the chief officer of police shall by notice in writing require the holder of the certificate to surrender it; and
 (c) it is an offence for the holder to fail to surrender the certificate within 21 days from the date of the notice given him by the chief officer of police.
(3) A constable may seize and detain any firearm or ammunition which may be the subject of an order for forfeiture under this section.
(4) A court of summary jurisdiction or, in Scotland, the sheriff may, on the application of the chief officer of police, order any firearm or ammunition seized and detained by a constable under this Act to be destroyed or otherwise disposed of.
(5) In this section references to ammunition include references to a primer to which section 35 of the Violent Crime Reduction Act 2006 applies and to an empty cartridge case incorporating such a primer.

Appeals against Conviction for a Firearms Offence

As to the power of the Court of Appeal to substitute a firearms offence pursuant to the Criminal Appeal Act 1968, s. 3A, see *Lawrence* [2013] EWCA Crim 1054, [2014] 1 WLR 106. **B12.5**

Punishments under the Firearms Act 1968

Firearms Act 1968, sch. 6 **B12.6**

PART I TABLE OF PUNISHMENT

Section of this Act creating offence	General nature of offence	Mode of prosecution	Punishment	Additional provisions
Section 1(1)	Possessing etc. firearm or ammunition without certificate.	(a) Summary (b) On indictment	6 months or [an unlimited fine]; or both. (i) where the offence is committed in an aggravated form within the meaning of section 4(4) of this Act, 7 years, or a fine; or both. (ii) in any other case, 5 years or a fine; or both.	[Scotland only.]

Section of this Act creating offence	General nature of offence	Mode of prosecution	Punishment	Additional provisions
Section 1(2)	Non-compliance with condition of firearm certificate	Summary	6 months or [an unlimited fine]; or both.	
Section 2(1)	Possessing, etc. shot gun without shot gun certificate	(a) Summary (b) On indictment	6 months or [an unlimited fine]; or both. 5 years or a fine; or both.	[Scotland only.]
Section 2(2)	Non-compliance with condition of shot gun certificate.	Summary	6 months or [an unlimited fine]; or both.	[Scotland only.]
Section 3(1)	Trading in firearms without being registered as firearms dealer.	Summary	6 months or [an unlimited fine]; or both.	
Section 3(2)	Selling firearm to person without a certificate.	(a) Summary (b) On indictment	6 months or [an unlimited fine]; or both. 5 years or a fine; or both.	
Section 3(3)	Repairing, testing etc. firearm for person without a certificate.	(a) Summary (b) On indictment	6 months or [an unlimited fine]; or both. 5 years of a fine; or both.	
Section 3(5)	Falsifying certificate, etc. with view to acquisition of firearm.	(a) Summary (b) On indictment	6 months or [an unlimited fine]; or both. 5 years or a fine; or both.	
Section 3(6)	Pawnbroker taking firearm in pawn.	Summary	3 months or a fine of level 3 on the standard scale; or both.	
Section 4(1), (3)	Shortening a shot gun; conversion of firearms.	(a) Summary (b) On indictment	6 months or [an unlimited fine]; or both. 7 years or a fine; or both.	
Section 5(1)(a), (ab), (aba), (ac), (ad), (ae), (af) or (c)	Possessing prohibited weapons or ammunition.	On indictment	10 years or a fine, or both.	
Section 5(1)(b)	Possessing prohibited weapons designed for discharge of noxious liquid etc.	(a) Summary (b) On indictment	6 months or [an unlimited fine]; or both. 10 years or a fine; or both.	
Section 5(1A)(a)	Possessing firearm disguised as other object.	On indictment	10 years or a fine; or both.	
Section 5(1A)(b), (c), (d), (e), (f) or (g)	Possessing other prohibited weapons.	(a) Summary (b) On indictment	6 months or [an unlimited fine]; or both. 10 years or a fine; or both.	
Section 5(2A)	Manufacturing or distributing, or possessing for distribution, prohibited weapons or ammunition	On indictment	Imprisonment for life	
Section 5(5)	Non-compliance with condition of Defence Council authority.	Summary	6 months or [an unlimited fine]; or both.	
Section 5(6)	Non-compliance with requirement to surrender authority to possess, etc. prohibited weapon or ammunition.	Summary	A fine of level 3 on the standard scale.	

Section of this Act creating offence	General nature of offence	Mode of prosecution	Punishment	Additional provisions
Section 6(3)	Contravention of order under s. 6 (or corresponding Northern Irish order) restricting removal of arms.	Summary	3 months or, for each firearm or parcel of ammunition in respect of which the offence is committed, a fine of level 3 on the standard scale; or both.	Para. 2 of Part II of this Schedule applies.
Section 7(2)	Making false statement in order to obtain police permit.	Summary	6 months or [an unlimited fine]; or both.	
Section 9(3)	Making false statement in order to obtain permit for auction of firearms etc.	Summary	6 months or [an unlimited fine]; or both.	
Section 13(2)	Making false statement in order to obtain permit for removal of signalling apparatus.	Summary	6 months or [an unlimited fine]; or both.	
Section 16	Possession of firearm with intent to endanger life or injure property.	On indictment	Life imprisonment or a fine; or both.	
Section 16A	Possession of firearm or imitation firearm with intent to cause fear of violence.	On indictment	10 years or a fine; or both.	
Section 17(1)	Use of firearm or imitation firearm to resist arrest.	On indictment	Life imprisonment or a fine; or both.	Paras. 3 to 5 of Part II of this Schedule apply.
Section 17(2)	Possessing firearm or imitation firearm while committing an offence in schedule 1 or, in Scotland, an offence specified in Schedule 2.	On indictment	Life imprisonment or a fine; or both.	Paras. 3 and 6 of Part II of this Schedule apply.
Section 18(1)	Carrying firearm or imitation firearm with intent to commit indictable offence (or, in Scotland, an offence specified in Schedule 2) or to resist arrest.	On indictment	Life imprisonment or a fine; or both.	
Section 19	Carrying firearm or imitation firearm in public place.	(a) Summary except if the firearm is a firearm specified in section 5(1)(a), (ab), (aba), (ac), (ad), (ae) or (af) or section 5(1A)(a) of this Act.	6 months or [an unlimited fine]; or both.	
		(b) On indictment (but not if the firearm is an air weapon).	(i) if the weapon is an imitation firearm, 12 months or a fine; or both; (ii) in any other case, 7 years or a fine; or both.	

Section of this Act creating offence	General nature of offence	Mode of prosecution	Punishment	Additional provisions
Section 20(1)	Trespassing with firearm or imitation firearm in a building	(a) Summary except if the firearm is a firearm specified in section 5(1)(a), (ab), (aba), (ac), (ad), (ae) or (af) or section 5(1A)(a) of this Act. (b) On indictment (but not in the case of an imitation firearm or if the firearm is an air weapon).	6 months or [an unlimited fine]; or both. 7 years or a fine; or both.	
Section 20(2)	Trespassing with firearm or imitation firearm on land.	Summary	3 months or a fine of level 4 on the standard scale; or both.	
Section 21(4)	Contravention of provisions denying firearms to ex-prisoners and the like.	(a) Summary (b) On indictment	6 months or [an unlimited fine]; or both. 5 years or a fine; or both.	
Section 21(5)	Supplying firearms to person denied them under section 21.	(a) Summary (b) On indictment	6 months or [an unlimited fine]; or both. 5 years or a fine; or both.	
Section 21A	Person making improper use of air weapon.	Summary	A fine of level 3 on the standard scale.	Paras. 7 and 8 of Part II of this Schedule apply
Section 22(1)	Person under 18 acquiring firearm.	Summary	(i) Where the offence is committed in relation to a person aged 17 and in relation to a firearm other than an air weapon or ammunition other than ammunition for an air weapon, 3 months or [an unlimited fine]; or both; (ii) in any other case, 6 months or [an unlimited fine]; or both.	
Section 22(1A)	Person under 18 using certified firearm for unauthorised purpose.	Summary	3 months or [an unlimited fine] or both.	
Section 22(2)	Person under 14 having firearm in his possession without lawful authority.	Summary	6 months or [an unlimited fine]; or both.	

Section of this Act creating offence	General nature of offence	Mode of prosecution	Punishment	Additional provisions
Section 22(3)	Person under 15 having with him a shot gun without adult supervision.	Summary	A fine of level 3 on the standard scale.	Para. 8 of Part II of this Schedule applies.
Section 22(4)	Person under 18 having with him an air weapon or ammunition therefore.	Summary	A fine of level 3 on the standard scale.	Paras. 7 and 8 of Part II of this Schedule apply.
Section 23(1)	Person supervising a person under 18 and allowing him to make improper use of air weapon.	Summary	A fine of level 3 on the standard scale.	Paras. 7 and 8 of Part II of this Schedule apply.
Section 24(1)	Selling or letting on hire a firearm to person	Summary	(i) Where the offence is committed in relation to a person aged 17 and in relation to a firearm other than an air weapon or ammunition other than ammunition for an air weapon, 3 months or [an unlimited fine]; or both; (ii) in any other case, 6 months or [an unlimited fine]; or both.	
Section 24(2)	Supplying firearm or ammunition (being of a kind to which section 1 of this Act applies) to person under 18.	Summary	6 months or [an unlimited fine]; or both.	
Section 24(3)	Making gift of shot gun to person under 15.	Summary	A fine of level 3 on the standard scale.	Para. 9 of Part II of this Schedule applies.
Section 24(4)	Supplying air weapon to person under 14.	Summary	A fine of level 3 on the standard scale.	Paras. 7 and 8 of Part II of this Schedule apply.
Section 24ZA(1)	Failing to prevent minors from having air weapons	Summary	A fine of level 3 on the standard scale.	Paras. 7 and 8 of Part II of this Schedule apply.
Section 24A(1) or (2)	Acquisition by a minor of an imitation firearm and supplying him.	Summary	In England and Wales, 6 months or [an unlimited fine], or both. [Further provision re Scotland.]	
Section 25	Supplying firearm to person drunk or insane.	Summary	3 months or a fine of level 3 on the standard scale; or both.	

Section of this Act creating offence	General nature of offence	Mode of prosecution	Punishment	Additional provisions
Section 28A(7)	Making false statement in order to procure grant or renewal of a firearm or shot gun certificate.	Summary	6 months or [an unlimited fine]; or both.	
Section 29(3)	Making false statement in order to procure variation of a firearm certificate.	Summary	6 months or [an unlimited fine]; or both.	
Section 30D(3)	Failing to surrender certificate on revocation.	Summary	A fine of level 3 on the standard scale.	
Section 32B(5)	Failure to surrender expired European firearms pass.	Summary	A fine of level 3 on the standard scale.	
Section 32C(6)	Failure to produce European firearms pass or Article 7 authority for variation or cancellation etc.; failure to notify loss or theft of firearm identified in pass or to produce pass for endorsement.	Summary	3 months or [an unlimited fine]; or both.	
Section 38(8)	Failure to surrender certificate of registration or register of transactions on removal of firearms dealer's name from register.	Summary	A fine of level 3 on the standard scale.	
Section 39(1)	Making false statement in order to secure registration or entry in register of a place of business.	Summary	6 months or [an unlimited fine]; or both.	
Section 39(2)	Registered firearms dealer having place of business not entered in the register.	Summary	6 months or [an unlimited fine]; or both.	
Section 39(3)	Non-compliance with condition of registration.	Summary	6 months or [an unlimited fine]; or both.	
Section 40(5)	Non-compliance by firearms dealer with provisions as to register of transactions; making false entry in register.	Summary	6 months or [an unlimited fine]; or both.	
Section 42A	Failure to report transaction authorised by visitor's shot gun permit.	Summary	3 months or [an unlimited fine]; or both.	
Section 46	Obstructing constable or civilian officer in exercise of search powers.	Summary	6 months or [an unlimited fine]; or both.	

Section of this Act creating offence	General nature of offence	Mode of prosecution	Punishment	Additional provisions
Section 47(2)	Failure to hand over firearm or ammunition on demand by constable.	Summary	3 months, or a fine of level 4 on the standard scale; or both.	
Section 48(3)	Failure to comply with requirement of a constable that a person shall declare his name and address.	Summary	A fine of level 3 on the standard scale.	
Section 48A(4)	Failure to produce firearms pass issued in another Member State.	Summary	A fine of level 3 on the standard scale.	
Section 49(3)	Failure to give constable facilities for examination of firearms in transit, or to produce papers.	Summary	3 months or, for each firearm or parcel of ammunition in respect of which the offence is committed, a fine of level 3 on the standard scale; or both.	Para. 2 of Part II of this schedule applies.
Section 52(2)(c)	Failure to surrender firearm or shot gun certificate cancelled by court on conviction.	Summary	A fine of level 3 on the standard scale.	

Part II B12.7

1. [Applies to Scotland only.]
2. In the case of an offence against section 6(3) or 49(3) of this Act, the court before which the offender is convicted may, if the offender is the owner of the firearms or ammunition, make such order as to the forfeiture of the firearms or ammunition as the court thinks fit.

3.—(1) Where in England or Wales a person who has attained the age of seventeen is charged before a magistrates' court with an offence triable either way listed in schedule 1 to the Magistrates' Courts Act 1980 ('the listed offence') and is also charged before that court with an offence under section 17(1) or (2) of this Act, the following provisions of this paragraph shall apply.

(2) Subject to the following subparagraph the court shall proceed as if the listed offence were triable only on indictment and sections 18 to 23 of the said Act of 1980 (procedure for determining mode of trial of offences triable either way) shall not apply in relation to that offence.

(3) [Omitted except for rare cases where committal still applies.]

4. Where a person commits an offence under section 17(1) of this Act in respect of the lawful arrest or detention of himself for any other offence committed by him, he shall be liable to the penalty provided by Part I of this schedule in addition to any penalty to which he may be sentenced for the other offence.
5. If on the trial of a person for an offence under section 17(1) of this Act the jury are not satisfied that he is guilty of that offence but are satisfied that he is guilty of an offence under section 17(2), the jury may find him guilty of the offence under section 17(2) and he shall then be punishable accordingly.
6. The punishment to which a person is liable for an offence under section 17(2) of this Act shall be in addition to any punishment to which he may be liable for the offence first referred to in section 17(2).
7. The court by which a person is convicted of an offence under section 21A, 22(4), 23(1), 24(4) or 24ZA(1) of this Act may make such order as it thinks fit as to the forfeiture or disposal of the air weapon or ammunition in respect of which the offence was committed.
8. The court by which a person is convicted of an offence under section 21A, 22(3) or (4), 23(1), 24(4) or 24ZA(1) may make such order as it thinks fit as to the forfeiture or disposal of any firearm or ammunition found in his possession.
9. The court by which a person is convicted of an offence under section 24(3) of this Act may make such order is it thinks fit as to the forfeiture or disposal of the shot gun or ammunition in respect of which the offence was committed.

GENERAL DEFINITIONS

Meaning of 'Firearm'

B12.8 **Firearms Act 1968, s. 57**

(1) In this Act, the expression 'firearm' means—
 (a) a lethal barrelled weapon (see subsection (1B));
 (b) a prohibited weapon;
 (c) a relevant component part in relation to a lethal barrelled weapon or a prohibited weapon (see subsection (1D);
 (d) an accessory to a lethal barrelled weapon or a prohibited weapon where the accessory is designed or adapted to diminish the noise or flash caused by firing the weapon.

The definition was revised by the PCA 2017, s. 125, with effect from 2 May 2017, and appears to apply regardless of the date of the alleged offence.

Note that an 'airsoft gun' is not to be regarded as a 'firearm' for the purposes of the FA 1968 (s. 57A): see **B12.10**.

The meaning of 'prohibited weapon' is considered at **B12.60** ***et seq.***

'Lethal Barrelled Weapon': Elements

B12.9 **Lethal Barrelled Weapon** From 2 May 2017 the expression 'lethal barrelled weapon' (FA 1968, s. 57(1)(a)) is defined by the FA 1968, s. 57(1B):

> 'lethal barrelled weapon' means a barrelled weapon of any description from which a shot, bullet or other missile, with kinetic energy of more than one joule at the muzzle of the weapon, can be discharged.

Note that the permitted muzzle kinetic energy levels are higher in respect of an 'airsoft gun' (defined by s. 57A) and these must not be exceeded in order for such a gun to be excluded from the definition of a 'firearm' (see **B12.10**).

The permitted kinetic energy levels replace the common-law test for determining lethality of a barrelled weapon laid down in *Moore v Gooderham* [1960] 3 All ER 575 and *Thorpe* (1987) 85 Cr App R 107. It is submitted that save for the task of determining whether the relevant statutory permitted 'kinetic energy' level has been reached or exceeded (or would be if the weapon was in good working order), a more detailed analysis of the lethality of the weapon in question will rarely, if ever, be required.

B12.10 **BB Guns and Air-soft Guns** From 2 May 2017 the lethality of any 'lethal barrelled weapon' is determined in accordance with the FA 1968, s. 57(1B). This includes, it is submitted, BB guns and most air weapons.

An exception (see s. 57(1C)) relates to an 'airsoft gun', as defined by s. 57A and subject to the 'permitted kinetic energy' levels stated in s. 57A(4). Such guns are used in certain sports such as 'skirmishing' (see the Explanatory Notes to the PCA 2017, para. 143).

Section 57A(2) provides that:

> (2) An 'airsoft gun' is a barrelled weapon of any description which—
> (a) is designed to discharge only a small plastic missile (whether or not it is also capable of discharging any other kind of missile), and
> (b) is not capable of discharging a missile (of any kind) with kinetic energy at the muzzle of the weapon that exceeds the permitted level.

By s. 57A(3), a '"small plastic missile" is one that (a) is made wholly or partly from plastics, (b) is spherical, and (c) does not exceed 8 millimetres in diameter'. The permitted kinetic energy levels are '(a) in the case of a weapon which is capable of discharging two or more missiles successively without repeated pressure on the trigger, 1.3 joules; (b) in any other case, 2.5 joules' (s. 57A(4)).

Despite the use of the word 'airsoft' in s. 57A, and what is said in the Explanatory Notes to the PCA 2017 (para. 933), the section does not specify (surprisingly perhaps) that such a gun is one that must be powered by air, or be constructed of low density metal, and must not be rifled.

Shot, Bullet, or Missile can be Discharged The Home Office states that in the 'absence of a decision by a court', the Secretary of State takes the view that (among other things) 'captive-bolt stunning devices (where the bolt remains attached to the barrel) used in the slaughter of animals, operated by blank cartridges or pneumatically', should not be regarded as firearms within the definition of the Act (see *Guide on Firearms Licensing Law* (April 2016), para. 2.57). The argument may be that the words 'can be discharged' in the FA 1968, s. 57(1B), mean not merely that the missile is capable of passing down the barrel but that it is capable of being emitted clear of the muzzle. There is, however, no clear judicial decision to support so wide a proposition. **B12.11**

It is submitted that the words 'can be discharged' must be applied in the context of the permitted muzzle kinetic energy levels specified in the FA 1968. In *Rogers* [2011] EWCA Crim 1459, the Court of Appeal said that the difference between a 9mm *bullet* and a 9.3mm *barrel* may be a loss of pressure from the propelling gas and 'basically, the missile just rattles down the barrel and often comes out with a very low velocity' (at [16]). The determinative issue, however, may be whether the missile's kinetic energy at the muzzle exceeds 1 joule.

There is no justification for including within the definition of 'firearm' an item which could discharge a missile only in combination with other tools extraneous to that item. Thus, an old and damaged starting pistol with a partially drilled barrel could not be regarded as a 'prohibited weapon' (see **B12.60**), and thus a 'firearm' within s. 57, merely because it could be made to discharge a pellet with the aid of a vice or clamp, a mallet and metal punch (*Bewley* [2012] EWCA Crim 1457, [2013] 1 All ER 1). *Bewley* was applied in *Williamson* [2012] EWCA Crim 2114. See also *Heddell* [2016] EWCA Crim 443. *Freeman* [1970] 2 All ER 413 and *Cafferata v Wilson* [1936] 3 All ER 149 were disapproved in *Bewley* (in which *Kelly v MacKinnon* 1983 SLT 9 was cited and discussed).

For a discussion of the circumstances in which an item, or its parts, constitute 'component parts' within the definition of 'firearm' in s. 57, see **B12.15**.

Role of the Judge and Jury The question of whether a device is a 'lethal barrelled weapon' is a question of fact (noting the revised statutory definition of a 'firearm' in the FA 1968, s. 57(1)) (consider, e.g., *Singh* [1989] Crim LR 724). **B12.12**

Cases that predate the coming into force of the revised definition (2 May 2017), which were illustrative of the issue of *lethality*, are unlikely to be of assistance (it is submitted).

Meaning of 'Weapon' in the FA 1968, s. 57 The word 'weapon' is not defined by the FA 1968, and the PCA 2017 made no provision that clarifies whether the word 'weapon' adds anything to the definition of a 'firearm' for the purposes of the Firearms Acts (by contrast, the Canadian Criminal Code, s. 2, does provide a definition of 'weapon'; but see *Dunn* 2013 ONCA 539 (Ontario)). Unlike the Prevention of Crime Act 1953 (which controls the use of 'any article made or adapted for use for causing injury to a person, [etc.]'), the items brought under the control of the Firearms Acts encompass a wide range of uses and purposes in respect of persons, animals and property. The problem is illustrated, but not resolved, by *Formosa* [1991] 2 QB 1 (which held that *Titus* [1971] Crim LR 279 was correctly decided — ammonia in a water pistol was not within the FA 1968, s. 5(1)(b)). In *Formosa*, a Fairy Liquid washing-up bottle containing 400 millilitres of hydrochloric acid was held not to be a 'prohibited weapon' within the meaning of the FA 1968, s. 5(1)(b), because the bottle was not *altered* by being filled with the acid and, therefore, it was not a weapon 'designed or adapted' for the discharge of any noxious liquid within the meaning of the section. In the words of Lloyd LJ, a contrary construction 'would mean that a householder who filled a milk bottle with acid in order to destroy a wasps' nest would be in possession of a weapon adapted for the discharge **B12.13**

of a noxious liquid and would therefore be guilty of the offence of possessing a prohibited weapon; until, of course, he had used the acid for the purpose in question when the milk bottle would revert to its pristine innocence. That could not be right.' In his commentary to *Formosa* at [1990] Crim LR 868, Professor John Smith QC said: 'The answer surely is that the articles are not "weapons" . . . It would be hazardous to attempt an off-the-cuff definition of "weapon" but perhaps it requires something designed or adapted for use against the person of another.' Professor Smith might have gone on to include weapons for use against animals. On that analysis, neither a signalling parachute flare nor a 'firework' that emits a potentially lethal projectile would fall within s. 57 (when used for the purpose for which they were designed) and, if so, cases such as *Singh* [1989] Crim LR 724 (see **B12.12**) should be considered in that light. In *McKirdy* [1999] HCJ 5, the Scottish High Court did have regard to the purpose or function with which the object had been constructed (a 90mm length of bamboo cane reinforced along its length with copper wire from which a .22 shot could be fired applying an external force). The Court held that the use of the ordinary word 'weapon' was appropriate on the facts of that case. However, some provisions of the firearms legislation describe as 'firearms' apparatuses that are clearly not designed to be used as weapons (e.g., 'signalling apparatus' for ships and aircraft (FA 1968, s. 13), and starting pistols (F(A)A 1997, s. 5)). In certain cases the purpose for which the item was designed and used, and its objective characteristics, may be relevant matters (consider, albeit in the context of determining the relevant tariff on goods imported, *Airsoft Armoury Ltd v HMRC* [2012] UKFTT 145 (TC)).

B12.14 **Prohibited Weapon as Firearm (Whether Lethal Barrelled or Not)** The effect of the FA 1968, s. 57(1)(a), is that any prohibited weapon is a 'firearm' whether it is a 'lethal barrelled weapon' or not. In *W* [2007] EWCA Crim 3485 the Court of Appeal held that an electronic stun gun, resembling a torch, which is a 'prohibited weapon' within the meaning of s. 5(1)(b) (see **B12.61**), must necessarily be a firearm within the meaning of s. 57(1) of the Act, even though it may not be a 'lethal barrelled weapon' or capable of firing a missile. This wider meaning is clear from s. 57(1). All prohibited weapons are firearms but not all firearms are prohibited weapons. The Court added that what D actually possessed was merely a non-lethal self-defence weapon, but if convicted on the charge of possessing a disguised firearm contrary to s. 5(1A)(a), D would be subject to the minimum sentences applicable to firearms offences. As to whether or not the word 'weapon' has been used by the legislature to distinguish a toy gun from a device that is subject to the Firearms Acts, consider *Campbell v Hadley* (1876) 40 JP 756 and *Bryson v Gamage* [1907] 2 KB 630.

Component Parts

B12.15 The expression 'component part' is defined by the FA 1968, s. 57(1D):

> (1D) For the purposes of subsection (1)(c), each of the following items is a relevant component part in relation to a lethal barrelled weapon or a prohibited weapon—
> (a) a barrel, chamber or cylinder,
> (b) a frame, body or receiver,
> (c) a breech block, bolt or other mechanism for containing the pressure of discharge at the rear of a chamber,
>
> but only where the item is capable of being used as a part of a lethal barrelled weapon or a prohibited weapon.

Section 57(1D) should prevent legal arguments of the kind discussed in *Secretary of State for the Home Department, ex parte Impower* [1999] EWHC 309 (Admin) and *Ashton* [2007] EWCA Crim 234.

By the FA 1968, s. 57B, the Secretary of State may (by regulations made by statutory instrument) amend s. 57(1D) with respect to the meaning of a relevant 'component part' in relation to a lethal barrelled weapon or a prohibited weapon (subject to incidental, supplementary, or consequential, transitional, transitory, or saving provisions).

One effect of the final words of s. 57(1D) ('but only where the item is capable of being used as a part of a lethal barrelled weapon or a prohibited weapon') is that *Bewley* [2012] EWCA Crim 1457, [2013] 1 All ER 1 is overruled insofar as it held that if the weapon in question was not a lethal barrelled weapon from which any shot etc. can be discharged, then neither the item nor any part of it constitutes a 'component part of such a lethal weapon' (see s. 57(1)(b) as originally worded, and see the commentary in the 2017 edition of this work at B12.23).

Accessory Designed or Adapted to Diminish Noise or Flash Sound moderators (also known as 'silencers' or 'sound suppressors') are used legitimately for shooting game, deer or vermin, and may facilitate more effective pest control. They may reduce hearing damage to the shooter, or reduce noise nuisance (see the Home Office's *Guide on Firearms Licensing Law* (April 2016, tinyurl.com/yc25b3p6), para. 13.77). **B12.16**

There is a distinction between an 'accessory' and a 'component part' of a firearm (*Broome v Walter* [1989] Crim LR 725). Where something is an integral part of the firearm, then even though it may increase the lethal qualities of the firearm, it does not require a separate reference in a certificate or a separate certificate (*Broome v Walter*, in which *Watson v Herman* [1952] 2 All ER 70 is cited). Normally 'an accessory' is something readily detachable from an article that is capable of its ordinary use with or without the accessory (see also *Hedges* [1998] 1 Cr App R (S) 35).

Whether a sound moderator is an accessory to a firearm within the meaning of the FA 1968, s. 57(1) (see **B12.8**), is a question of fact (*Buckfield* [1998] EWCA Crim 1322). The question is to be answered by considering (a) whether the device can be used with D's firearm, and (b) whether D has the device for that purpose. The Court said:

> Where the silencer has been manufactured for use on the particular firearm in the defendant's possession, no further evidence will be required to establish that the silencer is an accessory to that weapon and should be shown on a firearm certificate. Where the silencer, as here, was manufactured for a weapon other than that in the defendant's possession, then the prosecution, to obtain a conviction under section 1(1)(a) of the Act, will have to prove that the device can be used with the defendant's firearm and that the defendant has the device for that purpose. The fact that the silencer may have been designed for quite a different weapon, such as a shotgun, does not prevent it being an accessory to a firearm if it can be used as such.

Professor Sir John Smith QC criticised the reasoning in *Buckfield* ([1998] Crim LR 673), stating (at p. 674), 'the question of fact is not whether the silencer "can be used", but whether it was "made or adapted", for use with the firearm. It was not. The section says nothing about the purpose of the possessor of the firearm or accessory.' It remains moot whether the possessor's purpose may be material in a case where a component or an accessory that could be used with a 'firearm' requiring, e.g., a firearm certificate (s. 1) was in fact intended to have legitimate use with a 'firearm' not requiring such a certificate (consider *Yong* [2015] EWCA Crim 852, [2015] 2 Cr App R 15 (228)).

Shot Gun

'Shot gun' has the meaning assigned to it by the FA 1968, s. 1(3)(a) (see s. 57(4): and see **B12.37**). **B12.17**

Air Weapon etc. and Gas Cartridge System

Some barrelled air/gas weapons are capable of being firearms within the meaning of the FA 1968, s. 57(1) (see **B12.12**), and a number of offences apply to such weapons, e.g., offences under the FA 1968, ss. 16, 16A, 17(1), 17(2), 18(1) and 19. Note, however, the definition of an 'airsoft gun' (FA 1968, s. 57A), which is exempted from the FA 1968. It is important to distinguish carefully between a CO_2 bulb system and gas cartridges that contain a projectile (see **B12.71**). **B12.18**

Imitation Firearm

See **B12.26**. **B12.19**

De-activated Weapons

Any firearm (including a prohibited weapon) which is de-activated in accordance with the FA 1968, s. 8, ceases to be a firearm. But the article can constitute an 'imitation firearm' in some circumstances, see **B12.26**. **B12.20**

Firearms (Amendment) Act 1988, s. 8

For the purposes of the principal Act and this Act it shall be presumed, unless the contrary is shown, that a firearm has been rendered incapable of discharging any shot, bullet or other missile, and has consequently ceased to be a firearm within the meaning of those Acts, if—

(a) it bears a mark which has been approved by the Secretary of State for denoting that fact and which has been made either by one of the two companies mentioned in section 58(1) of the principal Act or by such other person as may be approved by the Secretary of State for the purposes of this section; and

(b) that company or person has certified in writing that work has been carried out on the firearm in a manner approved by the Secretary of State for rendering it incapable of discharging any shot, bullet or other missile.

The companies mentioned in s. 58(1) are the Society of the Mystery of Gunmakers of the City of London (presumably a reference to the 'Worshipful Company of Gunmakers') and the Birmingham Proof House.

As to whether a 'component part' of a de-activated weapon falls within the definition of 'firearm' within the meaning of the FA 1968, s. 57(1), see **B12.15**.

B12.21 **Standards of De-activation: Regulation (EU) 2015/2403** Note that the following commentary is subject to amendments made to Regulation (EU) 2015/2403 by SI 2019 No. 742, reg. 58, that come into force on 'IP completion day'. With effect from 8 April 2016, Commission Implementing Regulation (EU) 2015/2403 ([2015] OJ L333/62) (as amended by Regulation (EU) 2018/337 ([2018] OJ L65/1) with effect from 28 June 2018), applies directly to the UK. Regulation (EU) 2015/2403 (entitled 'Establishing common guidelines on deactivation standards and techniques for ensuring that deactivated firearms are rendered irreversibly inoperable') applies from 28 June 2018 to firearms of all categories listed in part II of annex I to Directive 91/477/EEC (as amended by Directive (EU) 2017/853) (Article 1.1). Regulation (EU) 2015/2403 does not apply to firearms de-activated prior to 8 April 2016 'unless those firearms are transferred to another Member State or placed on the market' (Article 1.2).

The Regulation provides (among other things) that (i) the owner of a de-activated firearm shall retain the de-activation certificate at all times. If the de-activated firearm is placed on the market, it shall be accompanied by the de-activation certificate (Article 3.5); (ii) de-activated firearms shall be marked with a common unique marking in accordance with the template set out in annex II to the Regulations (as substituted by Regulation (EU) 2018/337) to indicate that they have been de-activated in accordance with the technical specifications set out in annex I (as substituted by Regulation (EU) 2018/337) (Article 5); (iii) Member States may introduce additional measures to de-activate firearms in their territory going beyond the technical specifications set out in annex I to the 2015 Regulations (Article 6.1); and (iv) de-activated firearms may be transferred to another Member State only if they bear the common unique marking and are accompanied by a de-activation certificate in accordance with the Regulation (Article 7.1).

B12.22 **Offence to Sell or Gift a 'defectively deactivated weapon'** The F(A)A 1988, s. 8A, makes it an offence for a person 'who owns or claims to own a defectively deactivated weapon (a) to make the weapon available for sale or as a gift to another person, or (b) to sell it or give it (as a gift) to another person' (s. 8A(1)). The word 'sale' includes 'exchange or barter' (s. 8A(9)). The offence is triable either way with statutory penalties specified in s. 8A(11).

By s. 8A(4), a weapon is 'defectively deactivated' if:

(a) it was at any time a firearm,

(b) it has been rendered incapable of discharging any shot, bullet or other missile (and, accordingly, has either ceased to be a firearm or is a firearm only by virtue of the Firearms Act 1982), but

(c) it has not been rendered so incapable in a way that meets the technical specifications for the deactivation of the weapon that apply at the time when the weapon is made available for sale or as a gift or (as the case may be) when it is sold or given as a gift.

Technical specifications that apply for the purposes of s. 8A may be published by the Secretary of State from time to time (s. 8A(5) to (7)).

Excepted from the above offences is any weapon 'made available for sale or as a gift' or 'sold or given' to a person who is outside the EU (or to persons all of whom are outside the EU) in circumstances where the consequence of the sale or gift is to transfer the weapon to a place outside the EU (s. 8A(2) and (3)).

No offence is committed under s. 8A in respect of a weapon sold or gifted etc. by or on behalf of one museum to another museum, provided that the weapon was 'rendered incapable' (i.e. de-activated) before 8 April 2016, and that each museum holds a 'museums firearms licence' (s. 8A(8)).

Notification of Possession or Transfer of a Deactivated Weapon The Firearms Regulations 2019 (SI 2019 No. 1420) came into force on 12 December 2019, but subject to a transitional provision, namely reg. 4. The regulations create two criminal offences (regs. 2 and 3: summary only) in respect of a person's failure to notify the 'appropriate national authority' (the Secretary of State in England and Wales and Scotland, or the Department of Justice in Northern Ireland: reg. 1(3)) that the person possesses a deactivated firearm or (as the case may be) has transferred a deactivated firearm. **B12.23**

For the purposes of the regulations, 'deactivated firearm' means a firearm that has been deactivated in accordance with the technical specifications set out in the document published by the Secretary of State under the F(A)A 1988, s. 8A(5); 'firearm' has the meaning given by the FA 1968, s. 57(1); and 'transfer' includes sell, give, let on hire for a period of more than 14 days or lend for a period of more than 14 days (reg. 1(3)).

Under reg. 2, a person commits an offence if that person transfers a deactivated firearm to another person, and the former does not give notice of the transfer to the Secretary of State. The notice must be given (i) before the deactivated firearm is transferred, or (ii) as soon as reasonably practicable after the transfer (reg. 2(2)(a)). The notice must describe the deactivated firearm and include (if known) the make, calibre and serial number (reg. 2(2)(b)); it must state the name and address of the person giving notice, and state the person to whom the deactivated firearm has been (or will be) transferred (reg. 2(2)(c)). The notice must be sent by registered post, by recorded delivery or by email to a postal or an electronic address published by the Secretary of State (reg. 2(2)(d), (3)).

Under reg. 3, a person will commit an offence if that person is in possession of a deactivated firearm and does not give notice of the deactivated firearm to the Secretary of State (reg. 3(1)(a), (b)). Notice must be given (i) on or before the day on which the person first possesses the deactivated firearm, or (ii) as soon as reasonably practicable after that date (reg. 3(3)(a)). Note that reg. 3 does not have effect until 14 March 2021 in respect of deactivated firearms that came into the person's possession before 14 September 2018 (reg. 4). The notice must describe the deactivated firearm and include (if known) the make, calibre and serial number (reg. 3(3)(b)) and it must state the person's name and address (reg. 3(3)(c)). The notice must be sent by registered post, by recorded delivery or by email to a postal or an electronic address published by the Secretary of State (reg. 3(3)(d), (4)). No offence is committed under reg. 3 if (i) a deactivated firearm was transferred to the person and the transferor gave notice of the transfer in accordance with reg. 2 (see reg. 3(1)(c)), or (ii) the person was in possession of the deactivated firearm for a period of 14 days or less (reg. 3(2)). In proceedings for an offence under reg. 3, it is a defence for the person to show a reasonable belief that the transferor had given, or would give, notice of the transfer in accordance with reg. 2 (reg. 3(5)).

Ammunition

Amendments are made to the FA 1968, ss. 5 and 5A, and the F(A)A 1997, s. 9, in respect of ammunition that expands on impact (PCA 2017, s. 129): see **B12.60**, **B12.61**, **B12.81**. **B12.24**

The FA 1968, s. 57(2), provides a general definition of 'ammunition'.

Firearms Act 1968, s. 57

(2) In this Act, the expression 'ammunition' means ammunition for any firearm and includes grenades, bombs and other like missiles, whether capable of use with a firearm or not, and also includes prohibited ammunition.

Section 58(3) provides that control over ammunition is in addition to, and not in derogation of, any enactment relating to the keeping and sale of explosives.

It is submitted that the Home Office's *Guide on Firearms Licensing Law* (April 2016, tinyurl.com/yc25b3p6), at para. 2.12, states correctly that:

> ...the definition of ammunition does not include ingredients and components of ammunition; it is only assembled ammunition that is controlled under the Act, not component parts. Empty cartridge cases, for example, are not 'ammunition'. There are two exceptions to this. The first is missiles for ammunition prohibited under section 5 of the 1968 Act, for example, expanding or armour-piercing bullets. Such missiles are themselves defined as 'ammunition' and are subject to control accordingly [see s. 5(1A)(g) at **B12.61**]...The second is primers — section 35 of the Violent Crime Reduction Act 2006 introduced controls on the purchase and sale of a cap type primer designed for use in metallic ammunition.

Cap-type Primers

B12.25 Section 35 of the VCRA 2006 creates summary offences in connection with cap-type primers designed for use in metallic ammunition for a firearm. By s. 35(2), it is an offence for a person to sell to another either (a) a primer to which s. 35 applies, or (b) an empty cartridge case incorporating such a primer, unless that other person falls within s. 35(3). The eight categories of persons falling within s. 35(3) include (a) a registered firearms dealer; (b) a person who sells by way of any trade or business either primers or empty cartridge cases incorporating primers, or both; (c) the holder of a certificate authorising possession of a firearm of a relevant kind; (d) the holder of a certificate authorising possession of ammunition of a relevant kind.

Section 35(4) of the VCRA 2006 makes it an offence for a person to buy or to attempt to buy (a) a primer to which s. 35 applies, or (b) an empty cartridge case incorporating such a primer, unless the person falls within s. 35(5). Although slightly different in phrasing, s. 35(5) covers the same persons as are covered by s. 35(3). Section 35 binds persons in the service of Her Majesty but such a person is expressly exempted from its restrictions if authorised as specified under s. 35(6). By s. 50(4) 'a person is in the service of Her Majesty if he is deemed to be in such service (or to be in the naval, military or air service of Her Majesty) for the purposes of and under section 54 of the 1968 Act (Crown application)'.

OFFENCES RELATING TO IMITATION FIREARMS

Introduction

B12.26 It is important to distinguish between (a) the general definition of an 'imitation firearm' within the meaning of the FA 1968, s. 57(4) (see **B12.27** *et seq.*), (b) those imitation firearms that have the appearance of being firearms which are subject to the FA 1968, s. 1, and which are readily convertible into such firearms (see **B12.30**) and (c) 'realistic imitation firearms' within the meaning of the VCRA 2006, s. 38 (see **B12.32**).

Offences Applying to Imitation Firearms by virtue of the Wording of the Section

B12.27 Some offences, *by their definition*, apply to 'imitation firearms', see, e.g., the FA 1968, s. 17(1) (use of a firearm to resist arrest). In such cases, the expression 'imitation firearm' has the following definition, according to s. 57(4).

Firearms Act 1968, s. 57

(4) ... 'imitation firearm' means any thing which has the appearance of being a firearm (other than such a weapon as is mentioned in section 5(1)(b) of this Act) whether or not it is capable of discharging any shot, bullet or other missile.

Weapons mentioned in s. 5(1)(b) constitute one category of prohibited weapons, i.e. a weapon designed or adapted for the discharge of any noxious liquid, gas or other thing (see **B12.61**).

'Appearance of Being a Firearm' Whether an item is an 'imitation firearm' is a matter for the tribunal of fact to decide, taking an objective view (*K v DPP* [2006] EWHC 2183 (Admin)), and taking into account the views of witnesses who saw the thing (citing *Morris and King* (1984) 79 Cr App R 104). The Divisional Court appears to have accepted as being correct the submission that once the tribunal of fact had found the thing to be an imitation firearm, its character cannot change depending on the knowledge and perception of the person against whom it is used. In *Morris and King*, D was in possession of two metal pipes bound together, giving the appearance of being a double-barrelled shot gun that could constitute an imitation firearm. In *Williams* [2006] EWCA Crim 1650, D told the victim that he had a gun; the relevant question was whether the thing (a bottle in a plastic bag) had the appearance of a firearm at the relevant time. **B12.28**

Device Must Be a 'Thing' that is Distinct from the Holder of It In *Bentham* [2005] UKHL 18, [2005] 2 All ER 65, the House of Lords held that, for a person to be in possession of an imitation firearm (FA 1968, s. 17(2); see **B12.104**), the 'thing' must be separate or distinct from himself. Therefore, the conviction for possession of an imitation firearm, where D put his hand inside a zipped-up jacket forcing the material out so as to give the impression that he had a gun, was quashed. **B12.29**

Readily Convertible Imitation Firearms: Firearms Act 1982

The FA 1982 applies to any article which has the appearance of being a firearm to which the FA 1968, s. 1, applies (see **B12.37**) and is readily convertible into such a firearm (FA 1982, s. 1(1)). In *Bewley* [2012] EWCA Crim 1457, [2013] 1 All ER 1, the Court of Appeal proceeded on the basis that, for the purposes of the FA 1982, the expression 'imitation firearm' has the meaning that appears in s. 57(4) of the 1968 Act. This is understandable given that under s. 1(3) (and (4)) of the 1982 Act (see below) the FA 1968 'shall apply in relation to an imitation firearm to which [the 1982 Act] applies as it applies to [a FA 1968, s. 1, firearm]'. However, it is arguable that it is unlikely that this is what Parliament intended, and that the expression has a discrete meaning given by s. 1(1) of the 1982 Act for the purposes of that Act. Section 57(4) excludes a s. 5(1)(b) weapon (i.e. one that is designed or adapted to discharge a noxious thing etc.). If s. 57(4) applies to the 1982 Act, the result would be that a gun that is designed to discharge gas, that looks like a s. 1 FA 1968 firearm, but which is readily convertible into a firearm, falls outside the 1982 Act. It will be noted that, whereas s. 57(4) of the FA 1968 does not limit the thing's appearance to a s. 1 firearm, s. 1(1) of the FA 1982 does do so. **B12.30**

The expression 'imitation firearm', for the purposes of the 1982 Act, applies to all offences which are concerned with a firearm to which the FA 1968, s. 1, applies (FA 1982, s. 1(2)), except ss. 4(3) and (4), 16 to 20 and 47 of the FA 1968 (FA 1982, s. 2(2)(a) and (b) and (3)). Air weapons are included whether or not they are specially dangerous (FA 1982, s. 1(4)(a)). The definition does not apply to component parts and accessories (s. 1(4)(b)).

In *Bewley*, the Court held that no conclusion can be reached as to whether an imitation firearm is or was readily convertible without proper consideration of the FA 1982, s. 1(6), and, if it was raised, the defence in s. 1(5). For a decision in which *Bewley* was considered but distinguished, see *Heddell* [2016] EWCA Crim 443.

Firearms Act 1982, ss. 1 and 2

1.—(1) This Act applies to an imitation firearm if—
(a) it has the appearance of being a firearm to which section 1 of the 1968 Act (firearms requiring a firearm certificate) applies; and
(b) it is so constructed or adapted as to be readily convertible into a firearm to which that section applies.
(2) Subject to section 2(2) of this Act and the following provisions of this section, the 1968 Act shall apply in relation to an imitation firearm to which this Act applies as it applies in relation to a firearm to which section 1 of that Act applies.
(3) Subject to the modifications in subsection (4) below, any expression given a meaning for the purposes of the 1968 Act has the same meaning in this Act.
(4) For the purposes of this section and the 1968 Act, as it applies by virtue of this section—
(a) the definition of air weapon in section 1(3)(b) of that Act (air weapons excepted from requirement of firearm certificate) shall have effect without the exclusion of any type declared by rules made by the Secretary of State under section 53 of that Act to be specially dangerous; and
(b) the definition of firearm in section 57(1) of that Act shall have effect without paragraphs (b) and (c) of that subsection (component parts and accessories).

...

(6) For the purposes of this section an imitation firearm shall be regarded as readily convertible into a firearm to which section 1 of the 1968 Act applies if—
(a) it can be so converted without any special skill on the part of the person converting it in the construction or adaptation of firearms of any description; and
(b) the work involved in converting it does not require equipment or tools other than such as are in common use by persons carrying out works of construction and maintenance in their own homes.

...

2.—(2) The following provisions of the 1968 Act do not apply by virtue of this Act to an imitation firearm to which this Act applies, that is to say—
(a) section 4(3) and (4) ...; and
(b) the provisions of that Act which relate to, or to the enforcement of control over, the manner in which a firearm is used or the circumstances in which it is carried;

but without prejudice, in the case of the provisions mentioned in paragraph (b) above, to the application to such an imitation firearm of such of those provisions as apply to imitation firearms apart from this Act.
(3) The provisions referred to in subsection (2)(b) are sections 16 to 20 and section 47.

If the FA 1982 does apply, a special defence is introduced by s. 1(5):

> In any proceedings brought by virtue of this section for an offence under the 1968 Act involving an imitation firearm to which this Act applies, it shall be a defence for the accused to show that he did not know and had no reason to suspect that the imitation firearm was so constructed or adapted as to be readily convertible into a firearm to which section 1 of that Act applies.

In *Williams* [2012] EWCA Crim 2162, [2013] 2 All ER 787, the Court of Appeal held that D shoulders the legal burden of proving the special defence introduced by the FA 1982, s. 1(5), which, in the judgment of the Court, was justified and proportionate, given that the defence was made available as an exception or modification to the strict liability approach adopted in respect of the FA 1968, ss. 1 and 5. See also the commentary to *Williams* at [2013] Crim LR 984 and **F3.35**. Concern has been expressed that the language of s. 1(6) is outdated and should be revised to reflect tools and equipment commonly available on the modern market: see *Firearms Control*, 3rd Report (December 2010), HC 447-1, House of Commons, at pp. 49–50; and see the Home Office's *Guide on Firearms Licensing Law* (April 2016).

Offences Concerning 'Realistic Imitation Firearms'

Definition of a 'realistic imitation firearm' B12.31

Violent Crime Reduction Act 2006, s. 38

(1) In sections 36 and 37 'realistic imitation firearm' means an imitation firearm which—
  (a) has an appearance that is so realistic as to make it indistinguishable, for all practical purposes, from a real firearm; and
  (b) is neither a de-activated firearm nor itself an antique.

(2) For the purposes of this section, an imitation firearm is not (except by virtue of subsection (3)(b)) to be regarded as distinguishable from a real firearm for any practical purpose if it could be so distinguished only—
  (a) by an expert;
  (b) on a close examination; or
  (c) as a result of an attempt to load or to fire it.

(3) In determining for the purposes of this section whether an imitation firearm is distinguishable from a real firearm—
  (a) the matters that must be taken into account include any differences between the size, shape and principal colour of the imitation firearm and the size, shape and colour in which the real firearm is manufactured; and
  (b) the imitation is to be regarded as distinguishable if its size, shape or principal colour is unrealistic for a real firearm.

The VCRA 2006 introduced restrictions, and created offences as well as defences (rather than exceptions) in relation to 'realistic imitation firearms' (defined by s. 38). In essence, these are imitations that are visually indistinguishable from 'real firearms' (defined by s. 38(7)), typically a 'modern firearm' (i.e. other than one the appearance of which would tend to identify it as having a design and mechanism of a sort first dating from before the year 1870: s. 38(8)). The VCRA 2006 does not define the term 'imitation firearm', but the Explanatory Notes to that Act state (para. 241) that, for the purposes of s. 38, the relevant definition is the one set out in the FA 1968, s. 57(4). Many realistic imitation firearms are air-powered BB guns (single shot, semi-automatic, and fully automatic fire), which are used in airsoft sports including 'skirmishing'. Such imitations take many forms, including rifles, pistols and submachine guns. An imitation firearm is to be regarded as '*unrealistic* for a real firearm' by virtue of its size and/or colour specified in the Violent Crime Reduction Act 2006 (Realistic Imitation Firearms) Regulations 2007 (SI 2007 No. 2606) (see **B12.33**). Nevertheless, an unrealistic imitation firearm may fall within s. 57(4) and both realistic and unrealistic imitations that discharge missiles may, depending on their specifications, be 'lethal barrelled' (see **B12.9**) or even a 'prohibited weapon' (see **B12.61**; and see the Home Office's *Guide on Firearms Licensing Law* (April 2016), at paras. 2.30 to 2.39). B12.32

Offences and Defences A person commits a summary offence contrary to s. 36(1) of the VCRA 2006 by (a) manufacturing a realistic imitation firearm; or (b) modifying an imitation firearm so that it becomes a realistic imitation firearm; or (c) selling a realistic imitation firearm; or (d) bringing a realistic imitation firearm into Great Britain or causing one to be brought into Great Britain. It is submitted that the 3D printing of a 'realistic imitation firearm' would be caught by s. 36(1)(a). B12.33

Specific 'defences' (rather than exemptions) to charges under s. 36 are set out in s. 37, namely, that it is for D to show that D's conduct was for the purpose only of making the imitation firearm in question available for one or more of the purposes specified in s. 37 (notably, for the purposes of a museum or gallery, theatrical performances, the production of films, the production of television programmes, certain historical re-enactments, and functions of persons in HM services). Further purposes have been added by the Violent Crime Reduction Act 2006 (Realistic Imitation Firearms) Regulations 2007, regs. 3 and 4 (whether as a defence to proceedings under s. 36 or under sch. 2, para. 4 to that instrument), namely, (a) the organisation and holding of 'permitted activities' (i.e. 'the acting out of military or law enforcement scenarios for the purposes of recreation': reg. 2) for which public liability insurance is held in relation to liabilities to third parties arising from or in connection with the organisation and holding of those activities; and (b) the purposes of display at a permitted event. These defences are intended to give some protection to those who hold airsoft 'skirmishing' activities, or fairs at which airsoft imitations are on display: see the Home Office's *Guide on Firearms Licensing Law* (April 2016), at paras. 2.33 to 2.35. The defences available under s. 37(1) and (3) of the VCRA 2006 impose an evidential burden on D (see s. 37(4)).

Offences: Not Conforming to Specifications for Realistic Imitation Firearms

B12.34 Under the VCRA 2006, s. 39(1), the Secretary of State may by regulations make provision requiring imitation firearms to conform to specifications which are (a) set out in regulations; or (b) approved by such persons and in such manner as may be so set out. Although s. 39 is silent on the point, the Explanatory Notes to the Act assert (at para. 246) that the definition of 'imitation firearm' for the purpose of s. 39 is the same as that for s. 38.

The Violent Crime Reduction Act 2006 (Realistic Imitation Firearms) Regulations 2007 make provision specifying sizes and colours which are to be regarded as *unrealistic* for a real firearm. The size of an imitation firearm is to be regarded as unrealistic for a real firearm only if the imitation firearm has dimensions that are less than a height of 38 millimetres and a length of 70 millimetres (reg. 6). The colour is to be regarded as unrealistic for a real firearm only if it is bright red, bright orange, bright yellow, bright green, bright pink, bright purple or bright blue (reg. 7). The Violent Crime Reduction Act 2006 (Specification for Imitation Firearms) Regulations 2011 (SI 2011 No. 1754) set out specifications for 'blank-firing imitation firearms' (regs. 3 and 4) and 'blank firing imitation revolvers' (regs. 5 and 6).

By virtue of s. 39(2), a person commits a summary offence if:

(a) he manufactures an imitation firearm which does not conform to the specifications required of it by regulations under that section;
(b) he modifies an imitation firearm so that it ceases to conform to the specifications so required of it;
(c) he modifies a firearm to create an imitation firearm that does not conform to the specifications so required of it; or
(d) he brings an imitation firearm which does not conform to the specifications so required of it into Great Britain or causes such an imitation firearm to be brought into Great Britain'.

Regulation 7 of SI 2011 No. 1754 provides that the offence in s. 39(2)(d) of the 2006 Act does not apply where the purpose involved was to make the imitation firearm available for one of the purposes set out in s. 37(2) (museum or gallery, theatre, film or TV production, re-enactment or HM services).

Supplying Imitation Firearms to Persons under 18

B12.35 See B12.127.

POSSESSING ETC. FIREARM OR AMMUNITION WITHOUT FIREARM CERTIFICATE

The Offence: Possessing, Purchasing or Acquiring a s. 1 Firearm

B12.36 **Firearms Act 1968, s. 1**

(1) Subject to any exemption under this Act, it is an offence for a person—
 (a) to have in his possession, or to purchase or acquire, a firearm to which this section applies without holding a firearm certificate in force at the time, or otherwise than as authorised by such a certificate;

(b) to have in his possession, or to purchase or acquire, any ammunition to which this section applies without holding a firearm certificate in force at the time, or otherwise than as authorised by such a certificate, or in quantities in excess of those so authorised.

It is also an offence for a person to fail to comply with a condition subject to which that person holds a firearm certificate (s. 1(2)). For rules relating to procedure and sentence, see **B12.3** and **B12.4**.

A 'firearm certificate' is defined by the FA 1968, s. 57(4), to mean 'a certificate granted by a chief officer of police under the [1968 Act] in respect of any firearm or ammunition to which section 1 of this Act applies and includes a certificate granted in Northern Ireland under section 1 of the Firearms Act 1920 or under an enactment of the Parliament of Northern Ireland amending or substituted for that section' (see generally **B12.42**).

Note that by s. 1 of the FA 1982, that Act applies to the FA 1968, s. 1, thus extending it to imitation firearms, as defined in the FA 1982 (see **B12.27**).

Firearms to which s. 1 Applies B12.37

Firearms Act 1968, s. 1

(3) This section applies to every firearm except—
   (a) a shot gun within the meaning of this Act, that is to say a smooth-bore gun (not being an air gun) which—
      (i) has a barrel not less than 24 inches in length and does not have any barrel with a bore exceeding 2 inches in diameter;
      (ii) either has no magazine or has a non-detachable magazine incapable of holding more than two cartridges; and
      (iii) is not a revolver gun; and
   (b) an air weapon (that is to say, an air rifle, air gun or air pistol which does not fall within section 5(1) and which is not of a type declared by rules made by the Secretary of State under section 53 of this Act to be specially dangerous).

(3A) A gun which has been adapted to have such a magazine as is mentioned in subsection (3)(a)(ii) above shall not be regarded as falling within that provision unless the magazine bears a mark approved by the Secretary of State for denoting that fact and that mark has been made, and the adaptation has been certified in writing as having been carried out in a manner approved by him, either by one of the two companies mentioned in section 58(1) of this Act or by such other person as may be approved by him for that purpose.

The 'two companies' referred to in s. 58(1) are the proof houses identified at **B12.20**.

The length of the barrel of a firearm shall be measured from the muzzle to the point at which the charge is exploded on firing (s. 57(6)(a)). 'Revolver', in relation to a smoothbore gun, means a gun containing a series of chambers, which revolve when the gun is fired (s. 57(2B)).

For exemptions relating to air weapons (i.e. s. 1(3)(b)), see **B12.38**.

Exemptions: Shot Guns, and Air Weapons that are Not Specially Dangerous

Section 1 of the FA 1968 applies to all firearms except shot guns and certain air weapons (the meaning of which is considered at **B12.17** and **B12.37**). Sawn-off shot guns are firearms to which s. 1 applies. From 2 May 2017 an 'airsoft gun' as defined by the FA 1968, s. 57A, is exempt from the 1968 Act. **B12.38**

Section 1(3)(b) exempts 'air weapons' (air rifle, air gun or air pistol) from the certification requirements of s. 1 except in three cases:

(a) The air weapon has been declared by the Secretary of State to be 'specially dangerous' because its kinetic energy exceeds limits prescribed by the Firearms (Dangerous Air Weapons) Rules 1969 (SI 1969 No. 47, as amended by SI 1993 No. 1490, r. 2). Thus, air pistols that develop kinetic energy of more than 6 ft/lb, and other air guns/rifles that develop kinetic energy of more than 12 ft/lb, are declared to be 'specially dangerous' (r. 2(1)(a)). It is submitted that, although a 'specially dangerous' weapon is likely to be 'lethal barrelled' (within the meaning of s. 57(1)), the element of lethality must also be established. Note that an air weapon is not 'specially dangerous' if it falls only within r. 2(1)(a) but is designed for use only when submerged in water (r. 2(2), disapplying r. 3). The effect of r. 2(2) is to exclude an air-powered underwater harpoon (unless it comes within r. 2(1)(b)).

(b) The air weapon is 'specially dangerous' because it is disguised as another object (SI 1969 No. 47, r. 2(1)(b)): and note s. 5(1A)(a) (see **B12.61**).

(c) The air weapon is a 'prohibited weapon' (i.e. it falls within s. 5(1): see **B12.61**). Any 'air rifle, air gun or air pistol which uses, or is designed or adapted for use with, a self-contained gas cartridge system' is a 'prohibited weapon' (s. 5(1)(af) (see **B12.71**). Note that a 'prohibited weapon' is a firearm (whether lethal barrelled or not) within the meaning of s. 57(1).

The exemption in s. 1(3)(b) was strictly construed in *Thorpe* [1987] 2 All ER 108 ('air' did not include 'carbon dioxide') but the FA(A)A 1997, s. 48, provides that references to 'an air rifle, airgun or air pistol' in s. 1(3)(b), and in the Firearms (Dangerous Air Weapons) Rules 1969, include such weapons that are powered by 'carbon dioxide'. It would therefore seem that weapons powered by gases other than carbon dioxide or air would not be exempt from s. 1.

Given that the expression 'firearm' in s. 57(1) includes the components of, and accessories to, lethal barrelled weapons, it follows that the components of, and accessories to, shot guns (other than those with a shortened barrel) and air weapons (other than those declared to be specially dangerous) are also not included in the phrase 'firearms to which s. 1 of the FA 1968 applies'.

Note that by virtue of the F(A)A 1988, s. 7(2), the conversion of a weapon into a shot gun or air weapon does not affect its classification as a firearm to which s. 1 applies.

Firearms (Amendment) Act 1988, s. 7

(2) Any weapon which—
 (a) has at any time since the coming into force of section 2 above been a weapon to which section 1 of the principal Act applies; or
 (b) would at any previous time have been such a weapon if those sections had then been in force,

shall if it has, or at any time has had, a rifled barrel less than 24 inches in length, be treated as a weapon to which section 1 of the principal Act applies notwithstanding anything done for the purpose of converting it into a shot gun or an air weapon.

(3) For the purposes of subsection (2) above there shall be disregarded the shortening of a barrel by a registered firearms dealer for the sole purpose of replacing part of it so as to produce a barrel not less than 24 inches in length.

B12.39 **Ammunition to which the Firearms Act 1968, s. 1, Applies** Section 1 applies to all ammunition except that excluded by s. 1(4).

Firearms Act 1968, s. 1

(4) This section applies to any ammunition for a firearm, except the following articles, namely—
 (a) cartridges containing five or more shot, none of which exceeds 0.36 inch in diameter;
 (b) ammunition for an airgun, air rifle or air pistol; and
 (c) blank cartridges not more than one inch in diameter measures immediately in front of the rim or cannelure of the base of the cartridge.

Primed cartridges (ones without gunpowder) are not excluded under s. 1(4)(c) because such a cartridge is capable of producing an explosive effect and it is therefore ammunition (*Stubbings* [1990] Crim LR 811, and see *Burfitt v A & E Kille* [1939] 2 KB 743).

B12.40 **Aggravated Offence: Shortened Shot Guns or Converted Firearms** The aggravated form of the offence (shortened shot guns and converted firearms) is to be found in the FA 1968, s. 4(4):

Firearms Act 1968, s. 4

(4) A person who commits an offence under section 1 of this Act by having in his possession, or purchasing or acquiring, a shot gun which has been shortened contrary to subsection (1) [of section 4] or a firearm which has been converted as mentioned in subsection (3) [of section 4] (whether by a registered firearms dealer or not), without holding a firearm certificate authorising him to have it in his possession, or to purchase or acquire it, shall be treated for the purposes of provisions of this Act relating to the punishment of offences as committing that offence in an aggravated form.

For the offence, contrary to s. 4(1), of shortening the barrel of a shot gun to a length less than 24 inches, see **B12.128**.

Indictment (for Offence under the Firearms Act 1968, s. 1(1)(a))

Statement of Offence **B12.41**

Possessing a firearm without holding a current firearm certificate contrary to section 1(1)(a) of the Firearms Act 1968.

Particulars of Offence

A on or about the .... day of........ was in possession of [or: purchased (or acquired)] a firearm to which section 1 of the Firearms Act 1968 applies, namely a ..., without holding a firearm certificate in force at that time.

As to procedure and sentence, see the FA 1968, ss. 51 and 52, at **B12.3** and **B12.4**, and sch. 6 at **B12.6**, and the cases listed at **B12.137**. As to those firearms and ammunition to which the FA 1968, s. 1, applies, see **B12.37** and **B12.38**.

Firearm Certificates: General Matters

A firearm certificate is a public document. **B12.42**

Firearm certificates are issued in accordance with the provisions of the Firearms Acts and in accordance with the Firearms Rules 1998 (SI 1998 No. 1941, as amended by SI 2017 No. 1281, SI 2018 No. 1042 (in force 16 October 2018) and SI 2019 No. 963 (in force 10 June 2019)): but see *Leatherdale v Surrey Police Headquarters* [1999] EWHC Admin 631.

The Firearms Rules are amended by the Firearms (Amendment) (No. 2) Rules 2019 (SI 2019 No. 1419), in force from 12 December 2019. Rules 3 and 5 are amended so that where the holder of the certificate is under the age of 18, arrangements must be in place for ensuring that either (i) the holder's parent or guardian or (ii) a person aged 18 or over who is authorised under the principal Act to have possession of firearms and ammunition (r. 3), or a shotgun (r. 5), must assume responsibility for the secure storage of the firearms and ammunition, or the shotgun, to which the certificate relates (and to do so in accordance with r. 3(4)(iv)(a) or r. 5(4)(iv)(a) as appropriate).

By the FA 1968, s. 27, a firearm certificate shall be granted where the chief officer of police is satisfied, (a) that the applicant is fit to be entrusted with a firearm to which s. 1 of the FA 1968 applies and is not a person prohibited by that Act from possessing such a firearm; (b) that the applicant has a good reason for having in his possession, or for purchasing or acquiring, the firearm or ammunition in respect of which the application is made; and (c) that in all the circumstances the applicant can be permitted to have the firearm or ammunition in his possession without danger to the public safety or to the peace. A chief constable must consider an application to grant, renew, or revoke a firearm or shotgun certificate with particular care, and the Crown Court must give careful and detailed consideration to any appeals arising from those decisions. Adherence to the rules of natural justice is an essential prerequisite to the lawfulness of any such decision. The extent of the procedural requirements that are necessary for fairness to be achieved will depend upon the nature of the decision and the context in which it is considered. The nature of the decision taken by the Crown Court may well engage the requirements of the ECHR, Article 6(1) (*R (Mason) v Winchester Crown Court* [2018] EWHC 1182 (Admin), [2019] 1 Cr App R 4 (43)).

In that case, a Practice Note was handed down by the Divisional Court in respect of appeals under the FA 1968, s. 44, against the revocation of a shotgun certificate pursuant to s. 30C of the 1968 Act.

Conditions may be imposed by the grant of a certificate on the use of a firearm. Certain conditions are statutorily imposed, for example, that any rifle or muzzle-loading pistol that is not a prohibited weapon (see **B12.60** ***et seq.***) may be used only for target shooting (F(A)A 1997, s. 44(1)). See the Home Office's *Guide on Firearms Licensing Law* (April 2016).

Failure to comply with a particular condition of the certificate may have the effect of depriving the holder of that certificate of a statutory exemption that would otherwise be available (e.g., humane killing of animals) or even deprive the holder of legal authority to possess the weapon: see, e.g., *Shahabi-Shack* [2014] EWCA Crim 2842, [2015] 1 WLR 2602 at [13]:

> ... in order to come within the exemption provided by [the F(A)A 1997, s. 3] the possession of the firearm must be in accordance with the firearms certificate and the conditions imposed by that certificate. There is, we think, an important distinction to be drawn between conditions that relate to the nature and functioning of the firearm itself and to other conditions relating, for example, to the use or secure storage of the firearm. It is not the breach of every condition upon the certificate that will render a firearm a prohibited weapon.

In *Paul* [1999] Crim LR 79, the Court of Appeal rejected the possibility of allowing the jury to approach the words in a firearm certificate as those of the ordinary English language (as in *Brutus v Cozens* [1973] AC 854):

> If [a firearm certificate] is to fulfil the clear statutory objective of providing a certain and effective system of control of particular firearms it is obvious and a matter of common sense that it should have a certain and consistent meaning. That can only be achieved by trial judges determining the meaning as a matter of law, leaving it to the jury in each case to determine ... whether the physical attributes of the firearm in question bring it within that meaning.

In *Paul* the trial judge correctly drew on the definition of 'slaughtering instrument' in s. 57(4) when defining 'humane killer' (as those words appeared in the certificate) as meaning 'a firearm specially designed or adapted for instantaneous slaughter of animals'; it would be for the jury to decide whether they covered the revolver in question, a Ruger .357. What matters is not the intention of the possessor/transferor or transferee but the physical characteristics of the weapon.

As to possession authorised in accordance with a European firearms pass or other documents for European purposes, see the FA 1968, ss. 32A to 32C.

Meaning of 'Acquire'

B12.43 The FA 1968, s. 57(4), provides that 'acquire' means 'hire, accept as a gift or borrow': the word 'acquisition' is to be construed accordingly.

Possession Generally

B12.44 Whether a person is in possession of a firearm is a question of fact (*Hall v Cotton* 1987] QB 504).

It is submitted that the *actus reus* of the offence under the FA 1968, s. 1(1), is that the firearm is physically in the custody or under the control of D (consider *DPP v Brooks* [1974] AC 862; *Warner v Metropolitan Police Commissioner* [1969] 2 AC 256). In *Uddin* [2005] EWCA Crim 2653, the Court of Appeal held that D was not in possession of the firearm (contrary to the FA 1968, s. 16; see **B12.93**) because, although he appeared to have intended to purchase the firearm, he never had his hands on the bag or the firearm within it. In different circumstances, D might have been considered to have acquired control of the firearm had the purchase gone through, even though he did not yet physically possess it. In *T* [2011] EWCA Crim 1646 the Court of Appeal held that, on the agreed facts of the case, the judge had been correct to hold that the momentary handling of a firearm by D, followed by his immediate rejection of it, did not constitute possession of it within the meaning of the FA 1968, s. 5(1). Possession is not confined to 'physical possession' (*North* [2001] EWCA Crim 544). The ability to demand that the property in question be removed (or the ability to remove it oneself) is no more than evidence of knowledge and acquiescence: it is not to be equated with actual control (consider *Kousar* [2009] EWCA Crim 139, [2009] 2 Cr App R 5 (88), and see *Case* [2015] EWCA Crim 2080 and *Jenkins v DPP* [2020] EWHC 1307 (Admin), in which *Kousar* was not cited). Custody and control of a firearm can 'reside' in different people. In *Sullivan v Earl of Caithness* [1976] QB 966, the Divisional Court held that an owner of firearms is in possession of them even if they are kept in another's custody. In *Woodage v Moss* [1974] 1 All ER 584, D was held to be in possession of a firearm when he was handed it by an unknown person to deliver it to a dealer as a surrendered weapon. Similarly, a person does not have to be present in the place where the firearm is kept in order to be in possession of it (*Hall v Cotton*).

It is important to note the distinction in the FA 1968 between being in 'possession' of a firearm and 'having a firearm with him'. This is a consistent distinction, so that where the conduct element of the offence is merely the fact of possession, that fact can be proved in the sense indicated in *Sullivan v Earl of Caithness* and it does not require the Crown to go further and to show that D had the firearm with him at the time of his committing or being arrested for the offence in question (*North*). The distinction is reinforced (it is submitted) by the observations of the Court of Appeal in *Veira* [2013] EWCA Crim 1823 at [15].

Possession and *Mens Rea*

The offences contrary to the FA 1968, ss. 1, 3, 5 and 19 (see **B12.36**, **B12.75** and **B12.110**), are strict liability offences (*Deyemi* [2007] EWCA Crim 2060, [2008] 1 Cr App R 25 (345) and *Warner v Metropolitan Police Commissioner* [1969] 2 AC 256: see **B19.28**). The offences should not be described as ones of 'absolute' liability (*Gregory* [2011] EWCA Crim 1712; see the commentary to *Deyemi* [2008] Crim LR 327, and consider *Zahid* [2010] EWCA Crim 2158, noting *Williams* [2012] EWCA Crim 2162, [2013] 2 All ER 787 and *Tinarwo* [2014] EWCA Crim 1409). **B12.45**

No *mens rea* is required except insofar as it is necessary to establish that D was in possession of the article (or, had it 'with him', as the case may be: see *Howells* [1977] QB 614 and *Jenkins v DPP* [2020] EWHC 1307 (Admin)). There is no distinction between cases where D believes that the contents of a container (e.g., a bag) were something innocent as opposed to not knowing what the contents were (*Zahid*). Thus, for the purpose of s. 1, D need know only that he is in possession of something which is, in fact, a firearm (or ammunition: see *Amos* [1999] EWCA Crim J0629; *Pommell* [1995] 2 Cr App R 607). D need not know that the thing in question was a firearm (*Hussain* [1981] 2 All ER 287, followed in *Vann* [1996] Crim LR 52). In *Vann*, D had a loaded weapon with her because 'she had the gun with her ... physically in her possession, and ... was aware that she had it, even if she was ignorant of the fact that it was a gun'. In *Harrison* [1996] 1 Cr App R 138, a case concerned with s. 19, the Court of Appeal held that, if a person claims to have been mistaken as to whether the item possessed was a loaded shot gun or loaded air weapon, the argument will not avail, provided the person knowingly had possession of the item. D was held to have been in possession of the contents of a rucksack (ammunition) notwithstanding that he had no idea of its contents, and was indeed mistaken as to whom it belonged, or as to its nature and quality (*Price v DPP* [1996] CLY 1469, following *Bradish* [1990] 1 QB 981, *Waller* [1991] Crim LR 381, *Steele* [1993] Crim LR 298, and *Harrison*: see also *Cremin* [2007] EWCA Crim 666).

In *Deyemi* [2007] EWCA Crim 2060, [2008] 1 Cr App R 25 (345), the Court of Appeal applied *Bradish* (see **B12.75**) and explained *Warner Metropolitan Police Commissioner*, and *Vann*. The case concerned the FA 1968, s. 5(1)(b) (see **B12.61**). The Court remarked that it would appear that Parliament had intended to impose a draconian prohibition on the possession of firearms for the obvious social purpose of controlling dangerous weapons. Insofar as the decision in *Vann* seeks to suggest that D may have a defence if ignorant of the nature of the object, that went too far (per Latham LJ, at [24]):

> It is based on the slender foundation of the obiter exposition of the effect of Warner ... by Lord Lane CJ in McNamara [(1988) 87 Cr App R 246] ... which itself was based upon one short passage in Lord Pearce's speech. As Auld J said in Bradish ... the Court's approach to 'possession' under the 1968 Act, has been to take the more restrictive view of Lord Morris and Lord Guest, and has rejected the 'half-way house' of which the 'nature' concept clearly forms part. In any event, that concept produces real logical difficulties, as its context in Lord Pearce's speech demonstrates. Sweets seem to us to be of a different nature from heroin; but according to Lord Pearce believing that the heroin tablets were sweets would not provide a defence.

B12.46 In *Amos* [1999] EWCA Crim J0629, it was held to be no defence for D to say that he had forgotten about his possession of an item or that he erroneously believed that it had been destroyed or disposed of, even if the original acquisition had been lawful under a firearm certificate.

EXEMPTIONS AND DEFENCES FOR THE PURPOSES OF THE FIREARMS ACT 1968, s. 1

B12.47 The FA 1968, s. 1(1), indicates that the offence is 'subject to any exemption under this Act'. Exemptions include the following.

(a) A holder of a police permit from the chief officer of police is exempted (FA 1968, s. 7(1); and see the Firearms Rules 1998, as amended).

(b) A registered firearms dealer (or his servant) may have in his possession, or purchase or acquire a firearm or ammunition in the ordinary course of that business without a certificate (FA 1968, s. 8(1)). The term 'firearms dealer' is defined by s. 57(4). The definition has been widened to include selling or transferring air weapons (VCRA 2006, s. 31(3)). Registration as a firearms dealer is governed by the FA 1968, ss. 33 to 39, and the Firearms Rules 1998, r. 10 and sch. 5.

(c) An auctioneer, carrier or warehouseman, or a servant of such a person, may have a firearm or ammunition in his possession in the ordinary course of business without a certificate (FA 1968, s. 9(1)).

(d) A licensed slaughterer (note SI 2015 No. 1782) may have in his possession, without a certificate, a slaughtering instrument (*Paul* [1999] Crim LR 79) or ammunition in any slaughterhouse or knacker's yard in which that person is employed (FA 1968, s. 10). Note the European Weapons Directive (Council Directive No. 91/477/EEC ([1991] OJ L256/51), as amended by Directive 2008/51/EC ([2008] OJ L179/5) and Directive (EU) 2017/853), see **B12.80**.

(e) There are a number of exemptions related to rifle or pistol clubs, sports, athletics and other approved activities (FA 1968, s. 11, and F(A)A 1988, s. 15). Approval is granted by the Secretary of State (s. 15). As to the European Weapons Directive, see **B12.80**.

(f) A person taking part in a theatrical performance or rehearsal or the production of a film may have a firearm in his possession without a certificate, but only during and for the purpose of the performance, rehearsal or production (FA 1968, s. 12).

(g) A person (i) may have in his possession a firearm, signalling apparatus or ammunition on board a ship or aircraft or at an aerodrome, provided it is equipment for same; or (ii) the person may remove signalling apparatus or ammunition, if it is aircraft equipment, from one aircraft to another at an aerodrome or into or from storage and keep such equipment in storage at an aerodrome; or (iii) with a permit from a constable, the person may remove a firearm, signalling apparatus or ammunition to or from a ship or aircraft at an aerodrome to or from a place specified in the permit (FA 1968, s. 13).

(h) The Proof Houses (see **B12.20**) and persons carrying firearms to or from such places (FA 1968, s. 58(1)).
(i) The FA 1968, s. 11A, authorises a person to possess a firearm or ammunition (without holding a firearm certificate) belonging to another person who holds a certificate, under instructions from and for the use of that other person, for sporting purposes only (s.11(1)). The conditions of s. 11A must be met and (in the case of a rifle) the borrower must be aged 17 years or over (FA 1968, s. 11A). Where a rifle is borrowed in the circumstances set out in s. 11A(1), the borrower may, without holding a firearm certificate, purchase or acquire ammunition on the premises, and have the ammunition in his possession on those premises for the period for which the firearm is borrowed (s. 11A(6)). However, the ammunition must be for use with the firearm, and the lender's firearm certificate must authorise the latter to have in his possession 'during that period ammunition of a quantity not less than that purchased or acquired by, and in the possession of, the borrower', and the borrower's possession and use of the ammunition must comply with any conditions set out in the firearm certificate (s. 11A(6)). Section 16 of the F(A)A 1988 was thus repealed (from 2 May 2017) by the PCA 2017, s. 130(2).
(j) A person who holds a visitor's permit granted by a chief officer of police under s. 17(2) to (9) of the F(A)A 1988, may have in his possession, without a certificate, a firearm or ammunition to which the FA 1968, s. 1, and the Firearms Rules 1998 apply. A visitor's shot gun permit does not authorise the purchase or acquisition of any shot gun with a magazine, except where s. 17(1A)(a) to (d) apply (s. 17(1A)). No visitor's permit will be issued unless the visitor produces a European firearms pass (see **B12.42**) and satisfies other criteria (s. 17(3A)). For summary offences relating to visitor permits, see the FA 1968, s. 17(1).
(k) Firearms acquired for export (see **B12.132** ***et seq.***) may be exempted. This exemption is primarily concerned with the acquisition of firearms for export, but must also cover their possession for that purpose.
(l) The holder of a museums firearms licence (F(A)A 1988, s. 19 and sch.).

Antique Firearms

Under the FA 1968, s. 58(2), an 'antique firearm' that is sold, transferred, purchased, acquired or possessed as a 'curiosity or ornament' is exempted from the firearms legislation save in relation to s. 21 and sch. 3 (possession of firearms by persons previously convicted of crime). **B12.48**

Antique Firearms: Legal Position until the PCA 2017, s. 126, is in Force Until such time as the amendments made to the FA 1968, s. 58, by the PCA 2017, s. 126, come into force, whether a firearm is an antique firearm is a question of fact and degree (*Richards v Curwen* [1977] 3 All ER 426; *Bennett v Brown* (1980) 71 Cr App R 109), and therefore a matter for a jury (*Burke* (1978) 67 Cr App R 220). It is not sufficient for D honestly and reasonably to believe that the firearm is an antique firearm; it must actually be so (*Howells* [1977] QB 614). **B12.49**

Antique Firearms: Legal Position after the PCA 2017, s. 126, is in Force From a day to be appointed, the expression 'antique firearm' is defined by the FA 1968, s. 58(2A), and its related provisions (s. 58(2B) to (2H)). The PCA 2017 does not affect the operation of the FA 1968, s. 58(2), by which an antique firearm is exempted from the 1968 Act if it is sold, transferred, purchased, acquired or possessed, as a curiosity or ornament. **B12.50**

A firearm will be 'antique' where either (i) it is chambered (either the original chamber or an identical replacement) (s. 58(2B)), and the chamber is 'designed for use with a cartridge of a description specified in regulations made by statutory instrument . . . (whether or not it is also capable of being used with other cartridges)', or (ii) the 'firearm's propulsion system is of a description specified in regulations made by statutory instrument' (s. 58(2C)). A further condition must be met if either 'a number of years specified [in regulations] has elapsed since the date on which the firearm was manufactured' (s. 58(2D)(a)), or 'the firearm was manufactured before a date specified in the regulations' (s. 58(2D)(b)).

The PCA 2017, s. 126(3), amends s. 58(2) so that an 'antique firearm' is not excluded from the provisions of the FA 1968 if it was used in the commission of an offence under the FA 1968, s. 19 (carrying a firearm in a public place) or s. 20 (trespassing with a firearm). Section 58(2) is unaltered in respect of an offence committed under s. 21 (possession of a firearm by a person previously convicted of crime).

Persons in the Service of the Crown

B12.51 Section 54 of the FA 1968 sets out the circumstances in which offences under the Firearms Acts are disapplied in respect of persons in the service of the Crown (see also *Heritage v Claxon* (1941) 85 SJ 323; *Tarttelin v Bowen* [1947] 2 All ER 837). The ABCPA 2014, s. 112, amended s. 54 so as to widen the exemptions that apply in relation to members and employees of the British Transport Police.

The PCA 2017, s. 38(6) (SI 2017 No. 1139, in force 15 December 2017), inserted s. 38(9A) into the Police Reform Act 2002 so that the chief officer of police of a police force must ensure that no person designated by the chief officer under the Police Reform Act 2002, s. 38 (civilian staff), is authorised to use a firearm, within the meaning given by the FA 1968, s. 57(1), in carrying out functions for the purposes of the designation. However, the Police Reform Act 2002, s. 38(9A), does not apply in respect of the use of a 'CS spray' (produced by the use of 2-chlorobenzalmalononitrile) or a 'PAVA spray' (produced by the use of pelargonic acid vanillylamide), or the use of a weapon of a description or for a purpose specified in regulations made by the Secretary of State.

From 15 December 2017 the PCA 2017, s. 39, brought special constables, community support volunteers and policing support volunteers within the scope of the FA 1968, s. 54(3)(ba); and, similarly, a community support volunteer or a policing support volunteer designated under the Police Reform Act 2002, s. 38 (as it applies by virtue of the Railways and Transport Safety Act 2003, s. 28) by the Chief Constable of the British Transport Police Force (FA 1968, s. 54(3)(g)).

OFFENCES RELATING TO SHOT GUNS

Possessing etc. Shot Gun without Shot Gun Certificate

B12.52 **Firearms Act 1968, s. 2**

(1) Subject to any exemption under this Act, it is an offence for a person to have in his possession, or to purchase or acquire, a shot gun without holding a certificate under this Act authorising him to possess shot guns.

As to procedure and sentence, see **B12.3** and **B12.4**. The meaning of 'shot gun' is considered at **B12.17**. This section does not extend to imitation firearms, see **B12.26**.

The term 'shot gun certificate' is defined by the FA 1968, s. 57(4), as 'a certificate granted by a chief officer of police … authorising a person to possess shot guns'. Such certificates are issued by chief officers of police under the FA 1968, s. 26B, the related provisions in Part II, and the Firearms Rules 1998 (as amended by SI 2017 No. 1281, SI 2019 No. 963, and SI 2019 No. 1419). Note that by the FA 1968, s. 28, and subject to s. 28(1A), a shot gun certificate shall be granted or renewed by the chief officer of police if the officer is satisfied that the applicant can be permitted to possess a shot gun without danger to the public safety or to the peace. But no such certificate shall be granted or renewed if the chief officer has reason to believe that the applicant is prohibited by the FA 1968 from possessing a shot gun; or the officer is satisfied that the applicant does not have a good reason for possessing, purchasing or acquiring a shot gun. Supplemental provisions relating to firearm certificates exist under the FA 1968, s. 28A, and (with effect from 17 April 2018) s. 28B (inserted by the PCA 2017, s. 131).

For the meaning of 'acquire', see **B12.43**. For the meaning of 'possession', see **B12.44**.

The exemptions applicable in the case of firearms from liability under the FA 1968, s. 1, also apply to this offence. In addition, holders of certificates granted in Northern Ireland are exempt (FA 1968, s. 15).

For the aggravated offence under the FA 1968, ss. 1 and 4, in respect of possessing a shortened shot gun, see **B12.40**.

Failure to Comply with Condition of Shot Gun Certificate

Firearms Act 1968, s. 2 **B12.53**

(2) It is an offence for a person to fail to comply with a condition subject to which a shot gun certificate is held by him.

This is a summary offence. For procedure and sentence, see **B12.3** and **B12.4**. The meaning of 'shot gun certificate' is considered at **B12.52**. For the meaning of 'shot gun', see **B12.17**.

SPECIFIC OFFENCES RELATING TO AIR WEAPONS

In relation to air weapons, the law in England and Wales differs from that in Scotland (see the Air Weapons and Licensing (Scotland) Act 2015). In Scotland, certain air weapons require an 'air weapon certificate'. However, in prescribed circumstances, a court in England and Wales may cancel an 'air weapon certificate' granted to a person under s. 5 of the 2015 Act (see the FA 1968, s. 52, together with art. 3 of the Air Weapons and Licensing (Scotland) Act 2015 (Consequential Provisions) Order 2017 (SI 2017 No. 452)). **B12.54**

Prohibition on Sale or Transfer of Air Weapons except by Registered Dealers

It is an offence if a person by way of trade or business (other than a registered firearms dealer) 'sells or transfers an air weapon, exposes such a weapon for sale or transfer or has such a weapon in his possession for sale or transfer' (FA 1968, s. 3(1)(c)). A 'firearms dealer' includes a person who sells or transfers air weapons (s. 57(4)). For the meaning of 'air weapon', see **B12.18** and **B12.38**. **B12.55**

Sales of Air Weapons by way of Trade or Business to Be Face to Face

Section 32 of the VCRA 2006 makes it an offence for a person to transfer possession of an air weapon, by way of trade or business, to an individual in Great Britain (who is not registered as a firearms dealer) other than when the buyer and seller are in the presence of each other. **B12.56**

Violent Crime Reduction Act 2006, s. 32

(1) This section applies where a person sells an air weapon by way of trade or business to an individual in Great Britain who is not registered as a firearms dealer.
(2) A person is guilty of an offence if, for the purposes of the sale, he transfers possession of the air weapon to the buyer otherwise than at a time when both—
 (a) the buyer, and
 (b) either the seller or a representative of his,
 are present in person.
(3) The reference in subsection (2) to a representative of the seller is a reference to—
 (a) a person who is employed by the seller in his business as a registered firearms dealer;
 (b) a registered firearms dealer who has been authorised by the seller to act on his behalf in relation to the sale; or
 (c) a person who is employed by a person falling within paragraph (b) in his business as a registered firearms dealer.

This is a summary offence. The maximum penalty is imprisonment for six months and/or an unlimited fine.

Age Limits on Purchasing and Selling Air Weapons

B12.57 By the FA 1968, s. 22(1), 'It is an offence for a person under the age of eighteen to purchase or hire any firearm or ammunition'. Note that an air weapon, which is 'lethal barrelled', is, by definition, a firearm within the meaning of s. 57 (see **B12.8**). Section 24(1) provides that '(1) It is an offence to sell or let on hire any firearm or ammunition to a person under the age of eighteen'. See also **B12.115**.

Air Weapons Safety

B12.58 A person (of any age) who fires an air weapon beyond premises commits an offence (whether supervised or not) unless the person has the consent of the occupier of any premises fired into or across (FA 1968, s. 21A).

Firearms Act 1968, s. 21A

(1) A person commits an offence if—
  (a) he has with him an air weapon on any premises; and
  (b) he uses it for firing a missile beyond those premises.

(2) In proceedings against a person for an offence under this section it shall be a defence for him to show that the only premises into or across which the missile was fired were premises the occupier of which had consented to the firing of the missile (whether specifically or by way of a general consent).

It is an offence for a person in possession of an air weapon to fail to take reasonable precautions to prevent any person under the age of 18 from having the weapon with him (FA 1968, s. 24ZA). A statutory defence exists by virtue of s. 24ZA(3).

'Premises' is defined by the FA 1968, s. 57(4), to include any land.

Person under 18 Having an Air Weapon and Ammunition

B12.59 Subject to the FA 1968, s. 23, it is an offence for a person under the age of 18 to have with him an air weapon, or ammunition for such a weapon (s. 22(4)).

Where a person is a member of a rifle club or miniature rifle club (for the time being approved by the Secretary of State for the purposes of the F(A)A 1988, s. 23 or s. 15), s. 23(2) of the FA 1968 provides that no offence is committed under s. 22(4) where a person has with him an air weapon or ammunition at a time when engaged as (a) a member, (b) in connection with target shooting, or (c) the person is using the weapon or ammunition at a shooting gallery, and where the only firearms used are either air weapons or miniature rifles not exceeding 0.23 inch calibre (s. 23(2)).

The offence contrary to s. 22(4) is summary only, punishable with a fine of level 3 on the standard scale, and an order of forfeiture or disposal of the air weapon or ammunition in respect of which the offence was committed (sch. 6).

POSSESSING OR DISTRIBUTING PROHIBITED WEAPONS OR AMMUNITION

Meaning of 'Prohibited Weapon' and 'Prohibited Ammunition'

B12.60 Section 5(2) of the FA 1968 defines 'prohibited weapon' and 'prohibited ammunition' (the words in square brackets will come into force on a day to be appointed: see the Offensive Weapons Act 2019, s. 54(4)):

> The weapons and ammunition specified in subsections (1) and (1A) of this section (including, [in the case of weapons, any devices falling within subsection (1)(ba) of this section and,] in the case

of ammunition, any missiles falling within subsection (1A)(g) of this section) are referred to in this Act as 'prohibited weapons' and 'prohibited ammunition' respectively.

It is important to ensure that the ammunition in question is 'prohibited ammunition' (*Buddington* [2015] EWCA Crim 1127).

Offence in Respect of Prohibited Weapons and/or Ammunition

Firearms Act 1968, s. 5 **B12.61**

(1) A person commits an offence if, without the authority, he has in his possession, or purchases, or acquires—
- (a) any firearm which is so designed or adapted that two or more missiles can be successively discharged without repeated pressure on the trigger;
- (ab) any self-loading or pump-action rifled gun other than one which is chambered for 0.22 rim-fire cartridges;
- (aba) any firearm which either has a barrel less than 30 centimetres in length or is less than 60 centimetres in length overall, other than an air weapon, a muzzle-loading gun or a firearm designed as signalling apparatus;
- (ac) any self-loading or pump-action smooth-bore gun which is not an air weapon or chambered for 0.22 rim-fire cartridges and either has a barrel less than 24 inches in length or is less than 40 inches in length overall;
- (ad) any smooth-bore revolver gun other than one which is chambered for 9 mm rim-fire cartridges or a muzzle-loading gun;
- (ae) any rocket launcher, or any mortar, for projecting a stabilised missile, other than a launcher or mortar designed for line-throwing or pyrotechnic purposes or as signalling apparatus;
- (af) any air rifle, air gun or air pistol which uses, or is designed or adapted for use with, a self-contained gas cartridge system;
- [(ag) any rifle with a chamber from which empty cartridge cases are extracted using—
  - (i) energy from propellant gas, or
  - (ii) energy imparted to a spring or other energy storage device by propellant gas, other than a rifle which is chambered for .22 rim-fire cartridges;]
- (b) any weapon of whatever description designed or adapted for the discharge of any noxious liquid, gas or other thing;
- [(ba) any device (commonly known as a bump stock) which is designed or adapted so that—
  - (i) it is capable of forming part of or being added to a selfloading lethal barrelled weapon (as defined in section 57(1B) and (2A)), and
  - (ii) if it forms part of or is added to such a weapon, it increases the rate of fire of the weapon by using the recoil from the weapon to generate repeated pressure on the trigger; and]
- (c) any cartridge with a bullet designed to explode on or immediately before impact, any ammunition containing or designed or adapted to contain any such noxious thing as is mentioned in paragraph (b) above and, if capable of being used with a firearm of any description, any grenade, bomb (or other like missile), or rocket or shell designed to explode as aforesaid.

(1A) Subject to section 5A of this Act [see **B12.80**], a person commits an offence if, without authority, he has in his possession, or purchases or acquires—
- (a) any firearm which is disguised as another object;
- (b) any rocket or ammunition not falling within paragraph (c) of subsection (1) of this section which consists in or incorporates a missile designed to explode on or immediately before impact and is for military use;
- (c) any launcher or other projecting apparatus not falling within paragraph (ae) of that subsection which is designed to be used with any rocket or ammunition falling within paragraph (b) above or with ammunition which would fall within that paragraph but for its being ammunition falling within paragraph (c) of that subsection;
- (d) any ammunition for military use which consists in or incorporates a missile designed so that a substance contained in the missile will ignite on or immediately before impact;
- (e) any ammunition for military use which consists in or incorporates a missile designed, on account of its having a jacket and hard-core, to penetrate armour plating, armour screening or body armour;

(f) any ammunition which is designed to be used with a pistol and incorporates a missile designed or adapted to expand on impact;
(g) anything which is designed to be projected as a missile from any weapon and is designed to be, or has been, incorporated in—
(i) any ammunition falling within any of the preceding paragraphs; or
(ii) any ammunition which would fall within any of those paragraphs but for its being specified in subsection (1) of this section.

(2) [See **B12.60**].
(2A) A person commits an offence if without authority—
(a) he manufactures any weapon [, device] or ammunition specified in subsection (1) of this section,
(b) he sells or transfers any prohibited weapon or prohibited ammunition,
(c) he has in his possession for sale or transfer any prohibited weapon or prohibited ammunition, or
(d) he purchases or acquires for sale or transfer any prohibited weapon or prohibited ammunition
(3) In this section 'authority' means an authority given in writing by—
(a) the Secretary of State (in or as regards England and Wales), or
(b) the Scottish Ministers (in or as regards Scotland).

...

(7) For the purposes of this section and section 5A of this Act—

...

(c) references to a missile's expanding on impact include references to its deforming in any predictable manner on or immediately after impact.

Note that the words in square brackets above (see s. 5(1)) are inserted by the Offensive Weapons Act 2019, s. 54, and will come into force on the appointed day save to the extent that the prohibitions on the purchase, acquisition, manufacture, sale, transfer, or purchase or acquisition of a weapon there mentioned, came into force on Royal Assent. The wording of s. 5(1A)(f) was revised by the PCA 2017, s. 129(2). The effect is to prohibit the possession, purchase or acquisition of expanding ammunition when used with a 'pistol', but to permit those actions (subject to the provisions of the firearms legislation) when used with a rifle (see **B12.81**).

Expressions in the Firearms Act 1968, s. 5

B12.62 **Prohibited Weapon** A person is in possession of a prohibited weapon even when it is in parts (*Pannell* (1982) 76 Cr App R 53, where D had possession of all the parts). A weapon may be a prohibited weapon even if one essential component is missing, such as the trigger (*Clarke* [1986] 1 All ER 846, and see *Brown* (1992) *The Times*, 27 March 1992, where it was held that a stun gun which did not work because of some unknown fault, and was not proved ever to have worked, was a prohibited weapon).

B12.63 **Firearm** A 'firearm', for the purposes of the FA 1968, s. 5(1)(a), is defined by s. 57(1) so as to include the component parts of a firearm (*Clarke* [1986] 1 All ER 846). In *Rogers* [2011] EWCA Crim 1459, the Court of Appeal held (allowing D's appeal against conviction under s. 5(1)(aba)) that it was impossible to describe the components in question as components of a firearm. It is submitted that, although the result is correct, the direct route was to hold that the article did not constitute a '*lethal* barrelled weapon' within the meaning of s. 57 (see **B12.9**). In any event, see now the FA 1968, s. 57(1D) (see **B12.15**).

B12.64 **Rocket or Ammunition for Military Use** By the FA 1968, s. 5(7)(a), 'any rocket or ammunition which is designed to be capable of being used with a military weapon shall be taken to be for military use'.

B12.65 **Meaning of Missiles Igniting on Impact** By the FA 1968, s. 5(7)(b), 'references to a missile designed so that a substance contained in the missile will ignite on or immediately before impact include references to any missile containing a substance that ignites on exposure to air'.

B12.66 **Meaning of Expanding Missiles** The FA 1968, s. 5(1A)(f) and 5(7)(c), apply to expanding ammunition that is popularly referred to as 'dum-dum bullets' (*Zahid* [2010] EWCA Crim 2158).

The F(A)A 1997, s. 9, amended the FA 1968, s. 5(1A)(f), to read that '*any* ammunition which incorporated a missile designed or adapted to expand on impact' (emphasis added) was prohibited. The wording of s. 5(1A)(f) was revised by the PCA 2017, s. 129(2), with effect from 2 May 2017. The effect is to prohibit the possession, purchase or acquisition of expanding ammunition when used with a 'pistol', but to permit those actions (subject to the provisions of the firearms legislation, and noting s. 5A(3): see **B12.80**) when used with a rifle. Section 129(4) of the PCA 2017 is a 'tidying up' provision that omits s. 9 of the 1997 Act. A consequential amendment was made by s. 129(3), so that the FA 1968, s. 5A(8)(a), reads 'references to expanding ammunition are references to any ammunition which *is designed to be used with a pistol and* incorporates a missile which is designed to expand on impact' (emphasis added): and see *Williamson* [2018] EWCA Crim 1576 where the ammunition in question was not hollow point 9 mm ammunition as first thought but jacketed soft point ammunition contrary to s. 5(1A)(f).

Section 5A(8)(b) remains unamended and provides that references to the missile for any such ammunition 'are references to anything which, in relation to any such ammunition, falls within section 5(1A)(g)'.

The Home Office's *Guide on Firearms Licensing Law* (April 2016), at para. 3.21, continues to provide important information about this type of ammunition (emphasis added):

> [Section 5(1A)(f)] refers to ammunition incorporating a projectile that is designed or adapted to expand in a controlled manner. It is the kind of ammunition used in deerstalking and vermin control because it is more likely than non-expanding ammunition to ensure a quick and humane kill. Semi-jacketed soft point and hollow point are typical forms of expanding ammunition, but care must be taken to distinguish between match target hollow point ammunition, which has a tiny hole at the front for manufacturing purposes, and true hollow point. Match hollow point rounds which are not designed to expand upon impact ... are not prohibited. Flat-nosed bullets, which are designed to prevent a magazine explosion caused by a pointed bullet resting on the primer of the cartridge ahead of it when the ammunition is used in a tubular magazine are also not prohibited. All bullets will distort on impact, *but only those which were designed or adapted to do so in a predictable manner fit this category.*

The italicised words are important because they reflect the thinking behind the wording of s. 5(7)(c) (see **B12.66**; see also **B12.81**).

Measuring Barrel Length and Overall Length The FA 1968, s. 5(8), provides that, for the purposes of s. 5(1)(aba) and (ac), 'any detachable, folding, retractable or other movable butt-stock shall be disregarded in measuring the length of any firearm'. Section 57(6)(a) provides that 'the length of the barrel of a firearm is measured from the muzzle to the point at which the charge is exploded on firing'. **B12.67**

Meaning of Muzzle-loading Gun The FA 1968, s. 5(9), provides that any reference in s. 5 to a muzzle-loading gun 'is a reference to a gun which is designed to be loaded at the muzzle end of the barrel or chamber with a loose charge and a separate ball (or other missile)'. **B12.68**

Meaning of Self-loading and Pump-action The FA 1968, s. 57(2A), provides that 'self-loading' and 'pump-action' in relation to any weapon 'mean respectively that it is designed or adapted (otherwise than as mentioned in section 5(1)(a)) so that it is automatically reloaded or that it is so designed or adapted that it is reloaded by the manual operation of the fore-end or forestock of the weapon'. **B12.69**

Meaning of Revolver Gun The FA 1968, s. 57(2B), provides that a 'revolver', in relation to a smooth-bore gun, 'means a gun containing a series of chambers which revolve when the gun is fired'. **B12.70**

Air Weapons with Self-contained Gas Cartridges For the meaning of 'air weapons', see **B12.38**. The legislation does not define the expression 'self-contained gas cartridge system', but the measure is directed against gas cartridges that contain a projectile (consider, e.g., the Brocock Air Cartridge System or the Tandem Air Cartridge system). Home Office Circular 01/2004 makes it clear that 'weapons that use a CO_2 bulb system are not affected because CO_2 bulbs do not contain a projectile and are not therefore self-contained'. **B12.71**

For the reasons given below, if, on 30 April 2004, a person had in his possession an air rifle, air gun or air pistol of the kind described in the FA 1968, s. 5(1)(af), then (a) s. 5(1) shall not prevent the person's continued possession of the air rifle, air gun or air pistol; (b) s. 1 shall apply; and (c) a chief officer of police may not refuse to grant or renew, and may not revoke or partially revoke, a firearm certificate on the ground that the person does not have a good reason for having the air rifle, air gun or air pistol in his possession (ASBA 2003, s. 39(4)). But these provisions do not apply to possession in the circumstances described in the FA 1968, s. 8, which is concerned with authorised dealing (ASBA 2003, s. 39(5)).

The explanation for the situation described above is that by virtue of the ASBA 2003, s. 39(3) — which inserted s. 5(1)(af) into the FA 1968 — it became an offence from 30 April 2004 (see SI 2003 No. 3300) for a person to possess, without the authority of the Secretary of State, 'any air rifle, air gun or air pistol which uses, or is designed or adapted for use with a self-contained gas cartridge system'. In respect of a person who possessed such a weapon before that date, the combined effect of the ASBA 2003, s. 39(4)(a) and (b), is that continued possession of such a weapon is not prohibited by the FA 1968, s. 5(1), but that s. 1 does apply (i.e. firearm certificate required: see **B12.36**). Accordingly, a person who had been in possession of a prohibited air weapon up to the commencement date, and who did not obtain a s. 1 certificate, would be guilty of an offence under s. 1 but not of an offence under s. 5 (*Goldsborough* [2015] EWCA Crim 1278, [2015] 1 WLR 4921).

Specific Issues Associated with Particular Prohibited Weapons

B12.72 **Firearms Act 1968, s. 5(1)(a)** Authorisation of prohibited weapons is a matter for the Secretary of State (*Leatherdale v Surrey Police Headquarters* [1999] EWHC Admin 631).

Note that s. 5(1)(a) does not apply to ammunition (*McLean* [2010] EWCA Crim 2398 at [28]). For useful examples of the types of weapons that fall within s. 5(1) and (1A), see the Home Office's *Guide on Firearms Licensing Law* (April 2016), ch. 3. For exemptions to the obligation to have the authority of the Secretary of State with respect to any of the activities mentioned in s. 5(1A), see **B12.80**.

A weapon satisfies s. 5(1)(a) if it is capable of burst fire, making it a weapon from which 'two or more missiles can be successively discharged'. This will be the case even if a weapon has been adapted and only experts would be able to make it operate as an automatic weapon. It was held in *Law* [1999] EWCA Crim J0201, that s. 5(1)(a) does not import either explicitly or implicitly any intention on the part of the designer or the adaptor. The vital words are 'can be successfully discharged'. *Law* has been criticised for going further than necessary because, on the facts, the weapon was originally constructed to be capable of fully automatic or semi-automatic fire, and this remained the position in the hands of a person with sufficient knowledge given that the modifications to the weapon were not wholly successful ([1999] Crim LR 837): but see *Rhodes* [2015] EWCA Crim 155, [2015] 2 Cr App R 16 (235), discussed at **B12.73**). For the meaning of 'firearm', see **B12.8**.

B12.73 **Firearms Act 1968, s. 5(1)(b)** A 'Lightning Strike' (a hand-held device from which electricity is emitted) is a prohibited weapon within s. 5(1)(b), because electricity is a noxious thing by reason of the stunning effect that it has on its victims, and is discharged from the device (*Flack v Baldry* [1988] 1 All ER 673 and see *W* [2007] EWCA Crim 3485). An empty bottle is not a weapon, and filling it with hydrochloric acid does not make it a prohibited weapon; merely to fill a bottle is not to 'adapt' it within the meaning of s. 5(1)(b) (*Formosa* [1991] 2 QB 1: see **B12.13**). The Court approved *Titus* [1971] Crim LR 279, where it was held that a water pistol is not a prohibited weapon even when used to discharge a noxious liquid. On the facts of *Ray* [2011] 6 Arch Rev 4 (HHJ Bevan QC, Luton Crown Court), a smoke grenade was held not to be a prohibited weapon under s. 5(1)(b). In *Rhodes* [2015] EWCA Crim 155, [2015] 2 Cr App R 16 (235) the Court of Appeal, citing *Law* [1999] EWCA Crim J0201 (see **B12.72**) and *Turek v Regional Court in Gliwice* [2011] EWHC 1556 (Admin), appears to have rejected the argument that the mere fact that a weapon which had not been designed for the purpose of discharging noxious gases but was *capable* of doing so was not sufficient to bring it within the meaning of weapon in s. 5(1)(b). Confusingly (perhaps), the Court said (at [19]): 'Whatever might be lawful in other countries, sale of a pistol which has the design capability and must have the deliberate design capability of discharging gas cartridges is not.' Clearly, there is a difference between 'design capability' and a '*deliberate* design capability'. The latter would undoubtedly be sufficient (it is submitted) to bring the item within s. 5(1)(b). Practitioners should note that the offence under s. 5(1)(b) is triable either way (see **B12.6**).

Firearms Act 1968, s. 5(1A)(a) The item must appear to be something that it is not, e.g., firearms that appear to be cameras or umbrellas, pepper or CS gas sprays that appear to be pens, or stun guns that resemble torches (*W* [2007] EWCA Crim 3485). It was held by the Appeal Court, High Court of Justiciary, in *Lord Advocate's Reference No. 1 of 2020* [2020] HCJAC 25, that whether a firearm is 'disguised as another object' (in this case a stun gun that also functioned as a torch) requires 'a straightforward objective assessment of whether the item is presented in such a way as to conceal that amongst its functions is that of a firearm'. This is 'critically a question of fact for the jury to determine on all the facts of the case'. The normal meanings of the word 'disguise' are to be adopted, and the matter 'must be determined from the perspective of the ordinary person in the street' (per Lady Dorrian, the Lord Justice Clerk (at [23]–[24])). Thus, the question is not whether the item was a multi-function device. **B12.74**

Strict Liability for s. 5 Offence

The offence under the FA 1968, s. 5, is one of strict liability (*Deyemi* [2007] EWCA Crim 2060, [2008] 1 Cr App R 25 (345); *Bradish* [1990] 1 QB 981, following *Howells* [1977] QB 614 and *Hussain* [1981] 2 All ER 287 (see **B12.45**), and distinguishing *Warner v Metropolitan Police Commissioner* [1969] 2 AC 256 insofar as it dealt with the 'container' cases). It is not appropriate to describe the offence as one of 'absolute' liability (*Gregory* [2011] EWCA Crim 1712). See also *Zahid* [2010] EWCA Crim 2158 and *Tinarwo* [2014] EWCA Crim 1409. **B12.75**

All that the prosecution need prove is that D knowingly had in his possession an article which was in fact a prohibited weapon. The fact of possession must be proved (see **B12.44**, especially *T* [2011] EWCA Crim 1646). It was submitted in *Bradish* that the weapon of which D was in possession was a spray canister containing CS gas and, therefore, he was not in possession of the contents of the container if he could show that he neither knew, nor could reasonably have been expected to know, that it was a prohibited weapon. The Court rejected this submission and that the facts did not disclose a 'container' case. The item was a prohibited weapon because of the combination of the canister itself and its contents. The 'container' was an essential part of the weapon.

In *Law* [1999] EWCA Crim J0201 the Court of Appeal held that the FA 1968, s. 5(1)(a), 'does not import either explicitly or implicitly any intention on the part of the designer or the adaptor'. The vital words are 'can be successfully discharged'. (Note that the transcript wrongly refers to 's. 5(1A)'; the case concerns s. 5(1)(a).)

On a day to be appointed, the PCA 2017, s.126, will amend the FA 1968 so that s. 5 will not apply (subject to an exception) to a person in possession of a device that ceases to be an 'antique firearm' by virtue of the FA 1968, s. 58(2A) to (2H), and the coming into force of regulations made under s. 58(2B). An application by the person for a certificate (or a renewed certificate) under ss.1 or 2 in respect of possession of the firearm may not be refused on the ground that the person does not have a good reason for having it in his possession (PCA 2017, s.126(6) and (7)).The exception concerns the person who carries on a business as a firearms dealer and the firearm is in his possession for the purpose of the business (s. 126(4) and (5), from a day to be appointed).

As to procedure and sentence, see ss. 51, 52 and sch. 6 at **B12.3**, **B12.4** and **B12.6** and also **B12.129**.

A Prohibited Weapon Keeps that Description even if Converted

B12.76 The F(A)A 1988 introduced an important change into the law as regards the conversion of weapons. Consequently, care needs to be taken in reading cases on the unamended version of s. 5 of the FA 1968, insofar as they are concerned with the conversion of weapons.

Firearms (Amendment) Act 1988, s. 7(1)

(1) Any weapon which—
(a) has at any time (whether before or after the passing of the Firearms (Amendment) Act 1997) been a weapon of a kind described in section 5(1) or (1A) of the principal Act (including any amendments to section 5(1) made under section 1(4) of this Act;
(b) is not a self-loading or pump-action smooth-bore gun which has at any such time been such a weapon by reason only of having had a barrel of less than 24 inches in length,
shall be treated as a prohibited weapon notwithstanding anything done for the purpose of converting it into a weapon of a different kind.

As to the de-activation of firearms, see **B12.20**.

Imitation Firearms and the Firearms Act 1968, s. 5

B12.77 It is submitted that possession (etc.) of an imitation 'prohibited weapon' would be an offence contrary to the FA 1968, s. 1 (certificate needed), if the weapon falls within the FA 1982, s. 1 (i.e. is readily convertible into a firearm: see **B12.30**). See also the Home Office's *Guide on Firearms Licensing Law* (April 2016), at para. 2.23.

AUTHORITY TO HANDLE PROHIBITED WEAPONS

Authority of the Defence Council as performed by the Secretary of State

B12.78 The Secretary of State may grant an authority (which must be in writing) permitting possession of a prohibited weapon or ammunition. The authority so granted must be subject to whatever conditions the Secretary of State sees fit to impose to secure that the prohibited weapon or ammunition does not endanger public safety or the peace (FA 1968, s. 5(1) and (2)). It is an offence to fail to comply with a condition of an authority (s. 5(5)). An authority may be revoked at any time by notice (s. 5(6)). As to procedure and sentence, see **B12.3** and **B12.4**.

Authority of the Secretary of State for Theatrical Performances

B12.79 The Secretary of State may, under the FA 1968, s. 12(2):

(a) authorise a person in charge of a theatrical performance or rehearsal or the production of a cinematograph film to have possession of a prohibited weapon if it is required for the purpose of the performance, rehearsal or production; and
(b) authorise, under s. 5, such other person as the person in charge of the performance etc. may select to have possession of it while taking part in the performance etc.

Exemptions to the Prohibitions Imposed by s. 5(1A)

B12.80 Section 5(1A) of the FA 1968 (see **B12.61**) is subject to s. 5A, which aims to ensure compliance with the European Weapons Directive (Council Directive No. 91/477/EEC; since amended by Directive 2008/51/EC and Directive (EU) 2017/853). It creates several exemptions to the obligation to have authority with regard to activities mentioned in s. 5(1A) in connection with any of the prohibited weapons or ammunition therein specified. Section 57(4A) makes provision to permit the use of a firearm or ammunition for specified purposes (e.g., sporting purposes, the shooting of vermin, competitions and estate management). Further exemptions apply in respect of persons who keep or exhibit the item in question as part of a collection (s. 5A(1)), or where a person's possession, purchase or acquisition of the weapon, ammunition or missile in question is exclusively in connection with the carrying on of activities in respect of which that person is recognised, for the purposes of the law of another Member State relating to firearms, as a collector of firearms or a body concerned in the cultural or historical aspects of weapons (s. 5A(3)). Note that s. 5A(3) is prospectively repealed by reg. 59(2) of SI 2019 No. 742.

Expanding Ammunition Exemptions

See also **B12.66**. Expanding ammunition when used in pistols is 'prohibited ammunition' by virtue of the FA 1968, s. 5(1A)(f) (as amended) (*Williamson* [2018] EWCA Crim 1576) but a number of exemptions from the requirement to have the authority of the Secretary of State apply to such ammunition for the purposes, and in the situations, specified in s. 5A(3). **B12.81**

Four categories of exemptions under s. 5A specifically relate to expanding ammunition:

(a) persons authorised by a firearm certificate or a visitor's firearm permit to possess, purchase or acquire, or to sell or transfer, expanding ammunition, or the missile for such ammunition, in order lawfully to shoot deer, to shoot vermin or (in the course of estate management activities) other wildlife, to kill animals humanely, or to shoot in order to protect other animals or humans (s. 5A(4)(a), (b)). Note that 'estate management activities' (referred to in s. 5A(4)(b)) relate to estates in Great Britain (*Lacey v Metropolitan Police Commissioner* [2000] Crim LR 853);
(b) persons who are entitled under the FA 1968, s. 10, to have a slaughtering instrument in their possession provided the expanding ammunition, or the missile for any such ammunition, in their possession is designed to be capable of being used with a slaughtering instrument (s. 5A(5));
(c) persons who sell or transfer expanding ammunition or the missile for such ammunition to persons who hold a certificate by virtue of the FA 1968, s. 5A(4) (s. 5A(6));
(d) persons who carry on the business of a firearms dealer, and who may deal in expanding ammunition or the missile for any such ammunition in the ordinary course of that business (s. 5A(7)).

A further exemption currently exists under s. 5A(3) in respect of the possession, purchase, or acquisition of ammunition or missiles, if exclusively in connection with the carrying on of activities by a person recognised by the law of another Member State as a collector of firearms or a body concerned in the cultural or historical aspects of weapons. However, note that this provision is prospectively repealed by reg. 59(2) of SI 2019 No. 742 on 'IP completion day'.

EXEMPTIONS: HANDLING PROHIBITED SMALL FIREARMS

Exemptions to the prohibition imposed by the FA 1968, s. 5(1)(aba) (see **B12.61**), are granted by the F(A)A 1997 and the Firearms (Amendment) (No. 2) Act 1997 in the situations set out below. Note that from 14 July 2014, the reference to s. 5(1)(aba) includes a reference to the FA 1968, s. 5(2A) (ABCPA 2014, s. 108(9), inserting s. 1(7A) into the F(A)A 1997). Failure to comply with a firearm certificate issued under the FA 1968, s. 1, may have the effect of rendering possession of a 'prohibited weapon' unlawful (*Shahabi-Shack* [2014] EWCA Crim 2842, [2015] 1 WLR 2602: see **B12.42**). **B12.82**

Slaughtering Instruments: s. 5(1)(aba) Exemption A person may have in his possession, purchase or acquire, or sell or transfer 'a slaughtering instrument if he is authorised by a firearm certificate to have the instrument in his possession, or to purchase or acquire it' (F(A)A 1997, s. 2(a)). A person may have in his possession 'a slaughtering instrument if he is entitled, under section 10 of the 1968 Act, to have it in his possession without a firearm certificate' (s. 2(b)). **B12.83**

Firearms Used for the Humane Killing of Animals: s. 5(1)(aba) Exemption A person may have in his possession, purchase or acquire, or sell or transfer 'a firearm if he is authorised by a firearm certificate to have the firearm in his possession, or to purchase or acquire it, subject to a condition that it is only for use in connection with the humane killing of animals' (F(A)A 1997, s. 3). **B12.84**

B12.85 **Shot Pistols Used for Shooting Vermin: s. 5(1)(aba) Exemption** A person may have in his possession, purchase or acquire, or sell or transfer 'a shot pistol if he is authorised by a firearm certificate to have the shot pistol in his possession, or to purchase or acquire it, subject to a condition that it is only for use in connection with the shooting of vermin' (F(A)A 1997, s. 4(1)). 'Shot pistol' means a smooth-bored gun which is chambered for .410 cartridges or 9mm rim-fire cartridges (s. 4(2)).

B12.86 **Races at Athletic Meetings: s. 5(1)(aba) Exemption** A person may 'have a firearm in his possession at an athletic meeting for the purpose of starting races at that meeting' (F(A)A 1997, s. 5(1)). A person may have in his possession, purchase or acquire, or sell or transfer 'a firearm if he is authorised by a firearm certificate to have the firearm in his possession, or to purchase or acquire it, subject to a condition that it is only for use in connection with starting races at athletic meetings' (F(A)A 1997, s. 5).

B12.87 **Trophies of War: s. 5(1)(aba) Exemption** A person may have in his possession 'a firearm which was acquired as a trophy of war before 1st January 1946 if he is authorised by a firearm certificate to have it in his possession' (F(A)A 1997, s. 6). A 'trophy of war' is not defined in the Firearms Acts but the Home Office's *Guide on Firearms Licensing Law* (April 2016), at para. 13.62, states that it is 'generally held to refer to firearms either carried on active service or captured from the enemy'.

B12.88 **Firearms of Historic Interest: s. 5(1)(aba) Exemption** The exemption provided by the F(A)A 1997, s. 7(4), is discrete from the 'antique firearm' exemption provided by s. 58(2) of the 1968 Act: see the Home Office's *Guide on Firearms Licensing Law* (April 2016), ch. 9.

(a) A person may have in his possession, purchase or acquire, or sell or transfer, a firearm which was (i) manufactured before 1 January 1919; and (ii) is of a specified description 'if he is authorised by a firearm certificate to have the firearm in his possession, or to purchase or acquire it, subject to a condition that he does so only for the purpose of its being kept or exhibited as part of a collection' (s. 7(1)). The Secretary of State may specify descriptions of firearms for the purposes of s. 7(1) if it appears to him that firearms of that description were manufactured before 1 January 1919 and ammunition for firearms of that type is not readily available (s. 7(2)). The Firearms (Amendment) Act 1997 (Firearms of Historic Interest) Order 1997 (SI 1997 No. 1537) has been made in exercise of that power.

(b) A person may have in his possession, or may purchase or acquire, or sell or transfer 'a firearm which is of particular rarity, aesthetic quality or technical interest, or is of historical importance, if he is authorised by a firearm certificate to have the firearm in his possession subject to a condition requiring it to be kept and used only at a designated place' (s. 7(3)). Places will be designated by the Secretary of State (s. 7(3)).

B12.89 **Weapons and Ammunition Used for Treating Animals: s. 5(1)(aba), (b), (c) Exemptions** This special exception applies to offences contrary to s. 5(1)(aba), (b) and (c) (see **B12.61**). A person may have in his possession, purchase or acquire, or sell or transfer 'any firearm, weapon or ammunition designed or adapted for the purpose of tranquillising or otherwise treating any animal, if he is authorised by a firearm certificate to possess, or to purchase or acquire, the firearm, weapon or ammunition subject to a condition restricting its use in connection with the treatment of animals' (F(A)A 1997, s. 8). Note that from 14 July 2014, the reference to s. 5(1)(aba), (b) and (c), includes a reference to the FA 1968, s. 5(2A) (ABCPA 2014, s. 108(9), inserting s. 1(7B) into the F(A)A 1997).

POSSESSION OF FIREARM WITH INTENT TO ENDANGER LIFE

B12.90 **Firearms Act 1968, s. 16**

It is an offence for a person to have in his possession any firearm or ammunition with intent by means thereof to endanger life or to enable another person by means thereof to endanger life whether any injury has been caused or not.

As to procedure and sentence, see ss. 51, 52 and sch. 6; **B12.3**, **B12.4** and **B12.6**, and the cases listed at **B12.137**. Note that this is an offence in the list of offences where convictions and/or allegations may be disclosed under the Domestic Violence Disclosure Scheme: see the *Domestic Violence Disclosure Scheme (DVDS) Guidance* (Home Office, December 2016).

Indictment

Statement of Offence **B12.91**

Having a firearm [ammunition] in possession with intent to endanger life, contrary to section 16 of the Firearms Act 1968.

Particulars of Offence

A on or about the... day of... at... had in his possession a firearm [ammunition], namely..., with intent by means thereof [with intent to enable another person by means thereof] to endanger life.

Note that the section applies to any 'firearm' (as defined by s. 57(1): see **B12.8**) or 'ammunition' (s. 57(2): see **B12.23**). Section 16 does not require the firearm or the ammunition to be prohibited (*Salih* [2007] EWCA Crim 2750, [2008] 2 All ER 319).

D must be 'in possession' of the firearm or ammunition: see **B12.44**.

No Extension to Imitation Firearms

Section 16 does not extend to imitation firearms, because there is no express reference to such firearms, and because the FA 1982, s. 2(2) and (3), make clear that that Act does not extend to s. 16. **B12.92**

Intent to Endanger Life

The FA 1968, s. 16, deals with two situations. The first is where D intends, by means of the firearm/ammunition, to endanger life; typically, D will have physical custody and control of the item in question. The second situation is where D intends to *enable another person* by means of a firearm/ammunition to endanger life, e.g., where D makes a firearm available to P and, by means thereof, to endanger life. The intent in each case is an intention to endanger life — not to kill. Note that in *Smith* [2014] EWCA Crim 2163, [2015] 1 WLR 937 the Court of Appeal held that s. 16 creates one offence, albeit that it is capable of being satisfied in two different situations. Accordingly, a *Brown* direction (see **D18.44**) is not required. **B12.93**

As the Court of Appeal pointed out in *Jones* [1997] QB 798, both limbs of s. 16 are concerned with possession by D of firearms or ammunition — not with their supply. It is the state of mind of D or the possessor that must be considered.

D must have intended to behave in such a way as will in fact, to D's knowledge, endanger life (*Brown* [1995] Crim LR 328 and *Anderson* [2006] EWCA Crim 833, disapproving the dictum in *East* [1990] Crim LR 413). A specific intent to endanger life has to be established (*Bathh* (28 May 1999 unreported)). The person whose life it is intended to endanger need not be in the UK (*El-Hakkoui* [1975] 2 All ER 146) and the intent need not be an immediate or unconditional one, although it is necessary that D has possession of a firearm or ammunition with a view to using it, if and when the occasion arises (*Bentham* [1973] QB 357 and *Jones* [1997] QB 798; and see *Spence* [2009] EWCA Crim 2736).

An intention to endanger life is not defined by the physical capabilities of any bullet at the time when the trigger comes to be pulled, so the intention could be present where the bullet or cartridge was a misfire. If D knew that the ammunition could not work, that may be relevant to intention (*Anderson*). The life that D intends to endanger must be someone else's and not D's own (*Norton* [1977] Crim LR 478).

Where the charge relates to the second limb of s. 16, i.e. possessing a firearm or ammunition with intent *to enable another* to endanger life, it is submitted that the prosecution must prove **B12.94** more than the mere fact of supply of a firearm to another. In *Jones* [1997] QB 798, the Court of Appeal said (emphasis added):

> The key to the problem is to identify the meaning of [the words 'to enable another person'] in the context in which they appear — in particular to determine the shade of meaning that the verb 'to enable' carries. *It plainly means something more than 'to give the opportunity', because to equate it with such an intent would indeed be to make the second limb offence almost one of strict liability and would certainly encompass the example of a man who negligently determines to hand a loaded firearm to an insufficiently responsible person — conduct which one cannot sensibly contemplate as running with the first limb in a section creating offences for which life imprisonment is provided*… [It] is not necessary to prove an immediate or unconditional intent that life shall be endangered — it is sufficient if the intent is that the firearm shall be used in a manner which endangers life as and when occasion requires. However, with that qualification it seems to us that *an intention on the part of the possessor that life shall be endangered is a requirement of the second as of the first limb. Whether on the facts of the particular case that intention has been proved is a question for the jury to determine, drawing such inferences as they properly may from the evidence… [T]here may be all the difference between possessing a gun with intent to supply it to a known poacher and possessing it with intent to supply it to a person known to have convictions for violent robberies.* Our conclusion… recognises the fallacy of placing all the emphasis or too much emphasis on the words 'to enable' rather than having regard to the whole phrase 'with intent to enable another to endanger life'. The essence of the offence is the intent to enable life to be endangered. *That is a specific intent and accordingly, if in the circumstances of the case the judge considers it necessary to elaborate upon a simple direction as to intent, he will need to have regard to the guidance to be derived from Nedrick, Hancock and Maloney.*

For a further illustration of the application of s. 16, see *Gander* [1997] EWCA Crim J0616 and *Thompson* [2013] EWCA Crim 57.

Virtual Certainty and Intention

B12.95 The reference in *Jones* [1997] QB 798 to the cases of *Moloney* [1985] AC 905, *Nedrick* [1986] 3 All ER 1, and *Hancock* [1986] AC 455 (and see now *Woollin* [1999] AC 82) means that the court may be required to grapple with the vexed problem of defining 'intention' in the context of consequences that are 'virtually certain' (sometimes termed 'oblique intention'). In *Smith and Hogan's Criminal Law* (15th edn, 2018), at p. 96 it is said that it 'is arguable that intention, in law, should extend to results known or believed by the actor to be conditions of the achievement of his purpose but should go no further'.

Notwithstanding the observations of the Court of Appeal in *Jones*, it is submitted that there are strong reasons why a direction along the lines set out in *Woollin* is best avoided if possible, not least because such a direction will very rarely be needed, and the 'virtual certainty' concept is not easily understood by lawyers or juries (consider, e.g., the issues canvassed in *R (Charles) v CCRC* [2017] EWHC 1219 (Admin), [2017] 2 Cr App R 14 (175)). The trial judge must make it clear to the jury that intent, for the purpose of s. 16, is not to be equated with indifference, negligence, or recklessness and must not leave the jury with the impression that D's appreciation that endangerment to life was a virtual certainty is to be equated with intention. Note the words of Lord Scarman, in *Hancock* (see **A2.5**). It is submitted that D's awareness that the consequences of the actions were 'virtually certain' may indicate whether D had the requisite intent or not, but it is not by itself the answer to the question (consider *Harte* [2006] NICC 2 at [20]) and *Royle* [2013] EWCA Crim 1461, [2014] 1 Cr App R (S) 49 (296)).

Intention to Endanger Life for an Unlawful Purpose

B12.96 Although there is nothing about an intention to endanger life unlawfully in the FA 1968, s. 16, the Court of Appeal held in *Georgiades* [1989] 1 WLR 759, that s. 16 did not exclude a defence in rare cases of an intention to endanger life *lawfully* (e.g., in self-defence). In *Stubbs* [2007] EWCA Crim 1714, the Court of Appeal held that for the issue of self-defence to be left to the jury there had to be evidence of fear of imminent attack. In *Salih* [2007] EWCA Crim 2750, [2008] 2 All ER 319, Hooper LJ said (at [16]–[18]):

> In our view, and in accordance with *Stubbs*..., the effectiveness of legislation designed to prevent the carrying of firearms or offensive weapons... would be 'seriously impaired' if anyone who reasonably feared that he might at some time be unlawfully attacked was allowed to carry such a weapon (see the commentary of Professor J C Smith QC in [1989] Crim LR 452). If at the moment at which the defendant is alleged to be in possession of a firearm (or offensive weapon...) he is anticipating an imminent attack and carrying the weapon for his own defence against a specific danger then that may be different... *Georgiades* establishes that if the defendant was acting in self defence at the moment when he is alleged to be in possession of a firearm, then he would not be guilty. However if the possession with intent to endanger life is alleged to have occurred at some time before that moment and at a time when he was not in immediate fear of attack, then, in accordance with *Stubbs*..., *Georgiades* will not apply.

It is submitted that it would rarely, if ever, be a defence to a charge under the FA 1968, s. 16, that D possessed the firearm to effect a citizen's arrest (consider, albeit in the context of s. 17, *List* [2011] EWCA Crim 2821).

POSSESSION OF FIREARM OR IMITATION FIREARM WITH INTENT TO CAUSE FEAR OF VIOLENCE

Firearms Act 1968, s. 16A **B12.97**

> It is an offence for a person to have in his possession any firearm or imitation firearm with intent—
> (a) by means thereof to cause, or
> (b) to enable another person by means thereof to cause,
> any person to believe that unlawful violence will be used against him or another person.

As to procedure and sentence, see **B12.3** and **B12.4**. Note that this is an offence in the list of offences where convictions and/or allegations may be disclosed under the Domestic Violence Disclosure Scheme: see the *Domestic Violence Disclosure Scheme (DVDS) Guidance* (Home Office, December 2016).

Indictment

Statement of Offence **B12.98**

> Having a firearm [an imitation firearm] in possession with intent to cause a person to believe that unlawful violence will be used against him or another, contrary to section 16A of the Firearms Act 1968.

Particulars of Offence

> A on or about the... day of... had in his possession a firearm [an imitation firearm], namely..., with intent by means thereof to cause V, to believe that unlawful violence would be used against him or another.

Elements

The unlawfulness of the threatened force is an essential element of the offence (*Elezaj* [2017] EWCA Crim 1713). For the meaning of 'firearm', see **B12.8**; for the meaning of 'imitation firearm', see **B12.26**. The concept of 'possession' is considered at **B12.44**. For the meaning of 'unlawful violence', see **B11.41**. **B12.99**

In *K v DPP* [2006] EWHC 2183 (Admin), the Divisional Court held that it was not fatal to a conviction under s. 16A that V was aware that the thing was an imitation firearm (but that fact might be relevant to sentence). D's purpose or intention was to make V fear unlawful violence. In *Stanulis v HM Advocate* [2014] HCJAC 133, the High Court of Justiciary (citing *Kelt*) could see no logic in the proposition that the intent to which s. 16A referred was confined to an essentially latent intention to commit some future act, which once realised by presenting the weapon (or imitation weapon), the temporal scope of s. 16A ended.

It is not appropriate to attempt to draw parallels with the provisions of the Prevention of Crime Act 1953 (see **B12.144**): 'the plain language of section 16A embraces the situation where an offender forms an intention to cause fear of violence at or immediately before his actions which are designed to cause such fear' (*Goluchowski* [2006] EWCA Crim 1972 at [18]).

USE OF FIREARM TO RESIST ARREST

B12.100 **Firearms Act 1968, s. 17**

(1) It is an offence for a person to make or attempt to make any use whatsoever of a firearm or imitation firearm with intent to resist or prevent the lawful arrest or detention of himself or another person.

As to sentence, see ss. 51 and 52 and sch. 6; **B12.3**, **B12.4** and **B12.6**, and the cases listed at **B12.137**.

Indictment

B12.101 *Statement of Offence*

Using firearm [imitation firearm] with intent to resist [or: prevent] arrest, contrary to section 17(1) of the Firearms Act 1968.

Particulars of Offence

A on or about the ... day of ... at ... used a firearm [an imitation firearm], namely ... with intent to resist his lawful arrest or detention [or: to prevent the lawful arrest or detention of X].

Alternative Verdicts

B12.102 **Firearms Act 1968, sch. 6, part II, para. 5**

If on the trial of a person for an offence under section 17(1) of this Act the jury are not satisfied that he is guilty of that offence but are satisfied that he is guilty of an offence under section 17(2), the jury may find him guilty of the offence under section 17(2) and he shall then be punishable accordingly.

As to the offence under s. 17(2), see **B12.104** to **B12.106**.

Firearms and Imitation Firearms

B12.103 By virtue of the FA 1968, s. 17(4), a restricted definition of 'firearm', as provided by s. 57(1) applies (see **B12.8**), except that component parts of and accessories to such firearms are not part of the definition for the purposes of the s. 17 offence (i.e. the definition in s. 57(1), except for paras. (b) and (c)).

Section 17 expressly refers to 'imitation firearm', and therefore it is the definition in s. 57(4), as applied by s. 17(4), that is relevant (see **B12.5**). The FA 1982 is not relevant to this offence.

POSSESSING FIREARM WHILE COMMITTING AN OFFENCE IN THE FIREARMS ACT 1968, sch. 1

B12.104 **Firearms Act 1968, s. 17**

(2) If a person, at the time of his committing or being arrested for an offence specified in schedule 1 to this Act, has in his possession a firearm or imitation firearm, he shall be guilty of an offence under this subsection unless he shows that he had it in his possession for a lawful object.

As to procedure and sentence, see ss. 51, 52 and sch. 6, **B12.3**, **B12.4** and **B12.6** and the cases listed at **B12.137**. See also **B12.101** and **B12.102**.

Elements

As to the (restricted) meaning of 'firearm' and 'imitation firearm' in the FA 1968, s. 17, generally, see **B12.103**. **B12.105**

An offence under s. 17(1) is committed where D has possession of the firearm or an imitation firearm. D need not 'have it with him' (see **B12.108**). There is a consistent use of the expressions 'possession' (see **B12.44**) and 'have with him' (see **B12.109**) in the FA 1968. Therefore, the same meaning of possession was applied in *North* [2001] EWCA Crim 544, as is applied to the offence contrary to the FA 1968, s. 1 (see **B12.36**). Having a firearm in order to carry out a citizen's arrest would not be lawful and therefore such a purpose would not constitute a 'lawful object' within the meaning of s. 17(2) (*List* [2011] EWCA Crim 2821).

Offences Specified in the Firearms Act 1968, sch. 1

The offences specified in sch. 1 are: **B12.106**

offences under the Criminal Damage Act 1971, s. 1 (damage to property);
offences under the OAPA 1861, ss. 20 to 22 (inflicting bodily injury, garrotting, criminal use of stupefying drugs), 30 (laying explosive to building), 32 (endangering railway passengers by tampering with track), 38 (assault with intent to commit offence or resist arrest) and 47 (assault);
offences under the Child Abduction Act 1984, Part I (abduction of children);
theft, robbery, burglary, blackmail and any offence under the Theft Act 1968, s. 12(1);
offences under the Police Act 1996, s. 90, Police and Fire Reform (Scotland) Act 2012 (assaulting or impeding police);
offences under the CJA 1991, s. 90(1) (assaulting prisoner custody officer);
offences under the CJPO 1994, s. 13(1) (assaulting secure training centre custody officer);
offences under the SOA 2003, ss. 1 (rape), 2 (assault by penetration), 4 (causing a person to engage in sexual activity involving penetration without consent), 5 (rape of a child under 13), 6 (assault by penetration of a child under 13), 8 (causing or inciting a child under 13 to engage in sexual activity involving penetration), 30 (sexual activity involving penetration with a person with a mental disorder impeding choice) and 31 (causing or inciting a person with a mental disorder impeding choice to engage in sexual activity involving penetration);
offences under the CJCA 2015, sch. 10, para. 14 or 24 (assaulting secure college custody officer);
aiding or abetting the commission of any such offence;
attempting to commit any such offence.

In *Nelson* [2001] QB 55, the Court of Appeal confirmed that the statute is clear that a specified offence need not have been committed, but D must have been lawfully arrested for one. However, in *Rutkahskas* [2014] EWCA Crim 425, a conviction under the FA 1968, s. 17, was quashed where D, having been charged with possessing a firearm at the time of committing a robbery, was acquitted of the robbery.

OFFENCES INVOLVING CARRYING OF FIREARMS

Carrying Firearm or Imitation Firearm with Intent to Commit an Indictable *Offence or to Resist Arrest*

Firearms Act 1968, s. 18 **B12.107**

(1) It is an offence for a person to have with him a firearm or imitation firearm with intent to commit an indictable offence, or to resist arrest or prevent the arrest of another, in either case while he has a firearm or imitation firearm with him.
(2) In proceedings for an offence under this section proof that the accused had a firearm or imitation firearm with him and intended to commit an offence, or to resist or prevent arrest, is evidence that he intended to have it with him while doing so.

As to procedure and sentence, see ss. 51, 52, sch. 6, **B12.3**, **B12.4** and **B12.6**, and the cases listed at **B12.137**.

Elements of the Offence

B12.108 There are three elements to this offence (*Stoddart* [1998] 2 Cr App R 25):

(a) that D had with him a firearm or imitation firearm;
(b) that D intended to have it with him; and
(c) that at the same time D had the intention to commit an indictable offence or to resist or prevent arrest.

The Court observed that (b) and (c) are distinct rather than composite elements of the offence. However, proving (b) and (c) is made easier by s. 18(2) (see **B12.107**).

The Court of Appeal in *Houghton* [1982] Crim LR 112, held that it is necessary to establish the intent only at the moment to which the charge relates, which in this case was when the imitation firearm was pulled out of a holster by D. The intent may be formed at the same time as D begins to have the gun with him. It need not be formed at any earlier stage. It is not necessary to show an intention to use the firearm in the furtherance of the indictable offence (*Stoddart*; applied in *Larkin* [2003] EWCA Crim 2739). The intent must be free from duress (*Fisher* [2004] EWCA Crim 3539).

The general definition of 'firearm' in the FA 1968, s. 57(1), applies, see **B12.8**. Since there is an express reference to 'imitation firearm', the definition in s. 57(4) applies, and the FA 1982 has no application, see **B12.27** and **B12.30**.

B12.109 **Have with Him** It was said in *Kelt* [1977] 3 All ER 1099 (per Scarman LJ) that 'the classic case of having a gun with you is if you are carrying it. But, even if you are not carrying it, you may yet have it with you, if it is immediately available to you. But if all that can be shown is possession in the sense that it is in your house or in a shed or somewhere where you have ultimate control, that is not enough.' For the contrasting meaning of 'possession', see **B12.44**; and consider *North* [2001] EWCA Crim 544. In *Pawlicki* [1992] 3 All ER 902, the Court of Appeal explained *Kelt* on the basis that the Court had attempted to highlight the importance of propinquity as a necessary ingredient distinguishing this offence from those relating to possession. Whilst rejecting the possibility of a statutory definition, the Court, adopting a purposive approach, relied upon a concept of 'ready accessibility' and decided that the defendants in an auction room had firearms with them which were in a car some 50 yards away. In *Bradish* [2004] EWCA Crim 1340, the defendants had made no arrangements that would have enabled them quickly to acquire the gun (kept in premises several miles away) in the course of a robbery if they had needed it for their purposes. On a common-sense basis, they did not have the gun with them (and consider *Henderson* [2016] EWCA Crim 965, [2016] 4 WLR 172).

Carrying Firearm in Public Place

B12.110 **Firearms Act 1968, s. 19**

> A person commits an offence if, without lawful authority or reasonable excuse (the proof whereof lies on him), he has with him in a public place—
> (a) a loaded shot gun,
> (b) an air weapon (whether loaded or not),
> (c) any other firearm (whether loaded or not) together with ammunition suitable for use in that firearm, or
> (d) an imitation firearm.

As to procedure and sentence, see ss. 51, 52, sch. 6, **B12.3**, **B12.4** and **B12.6** and the cases listed at **B12.137**. The offence is triable only summarily where the firearm is an air weapon. A s. 19 offence may be committed whether the air weapon is lethal barrelled or not (*Street v DPP* [2004]

EWHC 86 (Admin)). From a day to be appointed, the effect of the PCA 2017, s. 126(3), is that s. 19 of the FA 1968 will apply where an 'antique firearm' is involved.

By s. 57(4), a 'public place' includes 'any highway and any other premises or place to which at the material time the public have or are permitted to have access whether on payment or otherwise' (*Anderson v Miller* (1976) 64 Cr App R 178, where it was held that the space behind a shop counter is a public place).

For the meaning of 'imitation firearm' see **B12.27**. For the definition of 'shot gun' see **B12.17**.

The term 'loaded' has an extended meaning in the circumstances set out in s. 57(6) but note that the offence is committed for the purposes of s. 19(b) or (c) whether the weapon/firearm is loaded or not.

Firearms Act 1968, s. 57

(6) For purposes of this Act—

...

(b) a shot gun or an air weapon shall be deemed to be loaded if there is ammunition in the chamber or barrel or in any magazine or other device which is in such a position that the ammunition can be fed into the chamber or barrel by the manual or automatic operation of some part of the gun or weapon.

The offence under s. 19 is one of strict liability (see **B12.45**).

In *Jones* [1995] QB 235, the Court of Appeal held, following the Divisional Court in *Ross v Collins* [1982] Crim LR 368, that possession of a firearm or ammunition certificate was not in itself lawful authority to have a firearm and ammunition in a public place, and see *Cleaver* (6 October 1967 unreported) albeit decided under the FA 1967, s. 2 (the forerunner to s. 19 of the FA 1968).

Reasonable Excuse Whereas an honest, mistaken belief in facts, which if true would provide a lawful authority, is capable of being a reasonable excuse, there can be no reasonable excuse where the belief is in something which could not be lawful authority even if true, such as D's belief that a certificate was valid when it was, in fact, invalid (see also *Taylor v Mucklow* (1973) 117 SJ 792). **B12.111**

Reasonable excuse is unlikely to include a plea that D was unaware of the nature of the item that he had with him, or that the firearm was in a container and D did not know its contents nor had a reasonable opportunity to inspect, but the point was left undecided in *Vann*. However, in *Densu* [1998] 1 Cr App R 400 — a case that was decided in the context of the Prevention of Crime Act 1953, s. 1(1) — the Court of Appeal said that as a matter of principle:

> ... it cannot be possible for a defendant to argue, once found to have with him an offensive weapon, that he did not know it was an offensive weapon. The [Prevention of Crime Act 1953] is an Act aimed at eradicating the carrying of dangerous weapons in public. The whole purpose of the Act is to provide strict liability in respect of objects regarded as dangerous. To allow lack of knowledge to be raised as a reasonable excuse defence would defeat the purpose of imposing strict liability in respect of the possession of such a weapon.

It is unlikely (it is submitted) that the courts would apply a contrary principle where a 'reasonable excuse' defence is raised under the Firearms Acts.

Whether the imposition of the burden on D is compliant with the ECHR, Article 6, remains to be determined (see **F3.18**). Arguments against the reverse burden include the fact that the offence is triable either way and, on indictment, carries a high maximum penalty. On the other hand, the definitional elements of the offence must be proved by the prosecution and the offence deals with a serious problem.

PROHIBITION ON POSSESSION OR ACQUISITION OF FIREARMS BY CONVICTED PERSONS

B12.112 Section 21 of the FA 1968 imposes restrictions on the possession and acquisition of firearms by convicted persons. By s. 21(4), it is an offence for a person to contravene any of the provisions of s. 21(1) to (3A), which (in summary) provide that a person who has been sentenced to custody for life or to preventive detention, or to imprisonment, or to corrective training, youth custody or detention in a young offender institution (or Scottish equivalent) for three years or more, must not at any time have a firearm or ammunition in his possession (s. 21(1)).

A person who has been sentenced to imprisonment, youth custody, detention in a young offender institution (or Scottish equivalent), a secure training order, or a detention and training order for three months or more, but less than three years, must not at any time before the expiration of the period of five years from the date of his release have a firearm or ammunition in his possession (s. 21(2)). (For the meaning of 'date of release', see s. 21(2A).) It was held in *Fordham* [1970] 1 QB 77 that s. 21(2) has no application to suspended sentences: the word 'release' means release from actual custody.

Under s. 21(2C), a person who has been sentenced to imprisonment for a term of three months or more whose sentence is suspended must not have a firearm or ammunition in his possession at any time during the period of five years beginning with the second day after the date on which the sentence is passed.

A person who is subject to a recognizance to keep the peace or be of good behaviour with a condition relating to the possession of firearms (or the Scottish equivalent), a community order or a youth rehabilitation order must not, at any time during which the person is so subject, have a firearm or ammunition in his possession (s. 21(3)).

B12.113 As to procedure and sentence, see ss. 51, 52 and sch. 6 (see **B12.3**, **B12.4** and **B12.6**, and the cases listed at **B12.137**). If a person is prohibited in Northern Ireland from having a firearm or ammunition in his possession, he is also so prohibited in Great Britain (s. 21(3A)).

A person may apply to the Crown Court for the removal of such prohibitions (FA 1968, s. 21(6); *Gordon v Northampton Crown Court* (20 December 1999 unreported)). For the procedure, see s. 21(7) and sch. 3.

Section 21 does not extend to imitation firearms, because there is no express reference to such firearms and because the FA 1982 only extends to firearms to which the FA 1968, s. 1, applies, whereas this section applies to firearms generally.

Firearms Act 1968, s. 21

(5) It is an offence for a person to sell or transfer a firearm or ammunition to, or to repair, test or prove a firearm or ammunition for, a person whom he knows or has reasonable ground for believing to be prohibited by this section from having a firearm or ammunition in his possession.

The offence carries the same range of sentence as the offence contrary to s. 21(4) above (see sch. 6 at **B12.6**) and is triable either way.

PROHIBITION ON POSSESSION OR ACQUISITION OF FIREARMS BY PERSONS UNDER SPECIFIED AGES

B12.114 A series of summary offences created by the FA 1968, ss. 22 to 24, deals with the acquiring, having in possession, use, sale or letting to, supply to and making a gift to a young person of a variety of firearms. The requisite age of the young person is not the same in each case. As to procedure and sentence, see ss. 51, 52 and sch. 6 at **B12.3**, **B12.4** and **B12.6**, and the cases listed at **B12.137**. The following relevant definitions have been given above: 'firearm' (**B12.8**); 'shot gun' (**B12.17**); 'air weapon' (**B12.18**); 'ammunition' (**B12.23**); firearm to which the FA 1968, s. 1, applies (**B12.37**); ammunition to which the FA 1968, s. 1, applies (**B12.39**).

Person under 18 Acquiring Firearm or Imitation Firearm

Section 22(1) of the FA 1968 provides: '(1) It is an offence for a person under the age of eighteen to purchase or hire any firearm or ammunition'. See also **B12.57** in relation to air weapons. **B12.115**

Persons under 18 Possessing Firearm

A person under 18 may, as the holder of a certificate, have a firearm in his possession, but it is an offence to use that firearm for a purpose not authorised by the European Weapons Directive (FA 1968, s. 22(1A); see also **B12.80**). Note that this provision is prospectively repealed by reg. 59(3), SI 2019 No. 742, on 'IP completion day'. **B12.116**

Person under 14 Having Firearm in his Possession without Lawful Authority

It is an offence, contrary to the FA 1968, s. 22(2), for a person under the age of 14 to have in his possession any firearm or ammunition to which s. 1 of the 1968 Act or s. 15 of the F(A)A 1988 applies, except in circumstances where under s. 11(1), (3) or (4) of the 1968 Act, or s. 15 of the F(A)A 1988, the person is entitled to have possession of it without holding a firearm certificate. Since this offence refers to firearms to which s. 1 of the FA 1968 applies, the FA 1982 applies and so this section extends to imitation firearms within that Act, see **B12.30**. **B12.117**

Person under 15 Having with Him a Shot Gun without Adult Supervision

It is an offence, contrary to the FA 1968, s. 22(3), for a person under the age of 15 to have with him an assembled shot gun except while under the supervision of a person of or over the age of 21, or while the shot gun is so covered with a securely fastened gun cover that it cannot be fired. This section does not extend to imitation firearms because there is no express reference to such firearms and the FA 1982 does not apply. The offence consists in a person 'having with him' such a weapon, see **B12.109**. **B12.118**

Person under 18 Having with Him an Air Weapon or Ammunition

It is an offence, contrary to the FA 1968, s. 22(4), and subject to s. 23, for a person under the age of 18 to have with him an air weapon or ammunition for an air weapon. This section does not extend to imitation firearms, because there is no express reference to such firearms and the FA 1982 does not apply. As with the previous offence, this offence is concerned with a person having such a weapon with him (see **B12.109**). Section 23 provides certain defences. **B12.119**

Person under 18 Having with Him an Air Weapon or Ammunition and who is Acting under Supervision

By virtue of the FA 1968, s. 23(1), no offence is committed under s. 22(4) while the person is under the supervision of a person of or over the age of 21 but, where the person has with him an air weapon on any premises in circumstances where the person would be prohibited from having it with him but for s. 23, it is an offence for the *supervisor* to allow the person to use it for firing any missile beyond those premises. However, 'it shall be a defence for him to show that the only premises into or across which the missile was fired were premises the occupier of which had consented to the firing of the missile (whether specifically or by way of a general consent)' (s. 23(1A)). **B12.120**

Person aged 14 or over Having with Him an Air Weapon or Ammunition and who is Acting with the Consent of the Occupier of Private Premises

B12.121 It is not an offence under the FA 1968, s. 22(4), for a person of or over the age of 14 to have with him an air weapon or ammunition on private premises with the consent of the occupier (s. 23(3), as inserted by the ASBA 2003, s. 38(3)(b)). But, in those circumstances, it is an offence for the person to use the air weapon for firing any missile beyond those premises (see the FA 1968, s. 21A, at **B12.58**).

Selling or Letting on Hire to Person under 18

B12.122 Section 24(1) of the FA 1968 provides: 'It is an offence to sell or let on hire any firearm or ammunition to a person under the age of eighteen'. Section 24(1) does not extend to imitation firearms, because there is no express reference to such firearms and the FA 1982 does not apply. It is a defence, according to s. 24(5), to prove that the person charged with the offence believed the other person to be of or over the age mentioned in that provision and had reasonable grounds for that belief.

Supplying Certain Firearms or Ammunition to Person under 14

B12.123 It is an offence, contrary to the FA 1968, s. 24(2):

(a) to make a gift of or lend any firearm or ammunition to which s. 1 applies to a person under the age of 14; or
(b) to part with the possession of any such firearm or ammunition to a person under that age, except in circumstances where that person is entitled under s. 11(1), (3) or (4), or under the F(A)A 1988, s. 15, to have possession thereof without holding a firearm certificate.

Since this offence refers to firearms to which s. 1 of the FA 1968, applies, the FA 1982 applies and so this section extends to imitation firearms within the 1982 Act (see **B12.30**). As with the previous offence it is a defence to make a reasonable mistake as to age (see the defence under the FA 1968, s. 24(5)). It is also a defence if possession is permitted under s. 11(1), (3) or (4); or under the F(A)A 1988, s. 15 (sports, athletics and other approved activities; rifle and pistol clubs).

Making Gift of Shot Gun to Person under 15

B12.124 It is an offence, contrary to the FA 1968, s. 24(3), to make a gift of a shot gun or ammunition for a shot gun to a person under the age of 15. This section does not extend to imitation firearms because there is no express reference to such firearms and the FA 1982 does not apply. As with the offence contrary to the FA 1968, s. 24(1), it is a defence to make a reasonable mistake as to age (see the defence under s. 24(5)).

Supplying Air Weapon to Person under 18

B12.125 It is an offence, contrary to the FA 1968, s. 24(4):

(a) to make a gift of an air weapon or ammunition for an air weapon to a person under the age of 18; or
(b) to part with the possession of an air weapon or ammunition for an air weapon to a person under the age of 18 except where by virtue of s. 23 (see above) the person is not prohibited from having it with him.

There are the following defences to this offence:

(i) *As with the offence contrary* to the FA 1968, s. 24(1), it is a defence to make a reasonable mistake as to age; see the defence under s. 24(5).
(ii) A person may be entitled to have the weapon or ammunition with him under s. 23, see the offence under s. 22(4).

Failing to Prevent Minors from Having Air Weapons

For the FA 1968, s. 24ZA, see **B12.58**. **B12.126**

Supplying Imitation Firearms to Persons under 18

Section 24A of the FA 1968, inserted by the VCRA 2006, s. 40, makes it an offence for a person under the age of 18 to purchase an imitation firearm. **B12.127**

It is also an offence for a person to sell an imitation firearm to a person under the age of 18 (s. 24A(2)). It is a defence to show that the person charged with the offence (a) believed the other person to be aged 18 or over; and (b) had reasonable ground for that belief (s. 24A(3)). A person shall be taken to have shown the matters specified in s. 24A(3) if (i) sufficient evidence of those matters is adduced to raise an issue with respect to them; and (ii) the contrary is not proved beyond a reasonable doubt. For the definition of 'imitation firearm', see **B12.26**.

SHORTENING AND CONVERSION OF FIREARMS

Offence

Four offences are considered here. **B12.128**

(a) Section 4(1) of the FA 1968 makes it an offence to shorten the barrel of a shot gun to a length less than 24 inches. For the aggravated offence under s. 1 of possessing, purchasing or acquiring a shot gun which has been shortened contrary to s. 4(1) and see **B12.40**.
(b) Section 4(3) makes it an offence for a person other than a registered firearms dealer to convert into a firearm anything which, though having the appearance of being a firearm, is so constructed as to be incapable of discharging any missile through its barrel. (Note that this offence does not extend to imitation firearms that come within the FA 1982, ss. 1 and 2: see **B12.30**.)
(c) Section 6(1) of the F(A)A 1988 makes it an offence to shorten to a length of less than 24 inches the barrel of any smooth-bore gun to which the FA 1968, s. 1, applies, other than one which has a barrel with a bore exceeding two inches in diameter.
(d) The FA 1968, s. 4A, makes it an offence for a person 'other than a registered firearms dealer' to have in his possession or under his control an article '(a) . . . that is capable of being used (whether by itself or with other articles) to convert an imitation firearm into a firearm, and (b) the person intends to use the article (whether by itself or with other articles) to convert an imitation firearm into a firearm'.

By virtue of the FA 1968, s. 4(2), a registered firearms dealer does not commit the offence contrary to s. 4(1) if the barrel is shortened for the sole purpose of replacing a defective part of the barrel so as to produce a barrel not less than 24 inches in length. The F(A)A 1988, s. 6(2), provides the same defence to the offence under s. 6(1).

Procedure and Sentence

The length to which the barrel may be shortened is crucial for the first two offences, and this is to be measured, by virtue of s. 57(6)(a), from the muzzle to the point at which the charge is exploded on firing. **B12.129**

The first three offences summarised above are triable either way. The range of sentence for all three offences is the same, i.e. D is liable, on summary conviction, to a term of imprisonment not exceeding six months, or a fine not exceeding the prescribed sum, or both, and, on conviction on indictment, to a term of imprisonment not exceeding five years or a fine or both.

An offence committed under the FA 1968, s. 4A, is triable either way, and is punishable in England and Wales on summary conviction to imprisonment for a term not exceeding

12 months (or, in relation to offences committed before s. 154(1) of the CJA 2003 comes into force, six months) or to a fine, or to both; and on indictment to imprisonment for a term not exceeding five years or to a fine, or to both (s. 4A(2)).

As to the courts' power to order forfeiture or disposal of firearms and ammunition, see the FA 1968, ss. 51, 52 and sch. 6, at **B12.3**, **B12.4** and **B12.6**.

There is no offence-specific guideline but the Sentencing Council's *General Guideline: Overarching Principles* (see Supplement, **SG2-1**) is used for all offenders sentenced on or after 1 October 2019.

Definitions

B12.130 As to the meaning of: 'shot gun', see **B12.17**; 'smooth-bore gun to which section 1 of the Firearms Act 1968 applies', see **B12.37**; 'registered firearms dealer', see **B12.47**; 'firearm' see **B12.8**.

TRANSFER OF FIREARMS AND AMMUNITION TO BE IN PERSON

B12.131 The F(A)A 1997 introduced measures concerned with the transfer etc. of firearms and ammunition. In all cases it is an offence to breach the provisions provided for in ss. 32 to 35 of that Act. For transfers relating to air weapons, see **B12.55**.

The punishment and mode of trial of the offences depends upon whether the weaponry is a firearm or ammunition to which the FA 1968, s. 1, applies (F(A)A 1997, s. 36(a)) or a shotgun (s. 36(b)).

The offences to which these sentence and mode of trial provisions apply are set out in the detailed provisions of ss. 32 to 35 of the F(A)A 1997. It is an offence for a transferor, or a transferee, of weapons or ammunition which are specified in s. 32(1) to fail to comply with s. 32(2) (s. 32(3)).

A failure by a party to a transaction to which s. 33 applies (transfer of a firearm, including let or hire for more than 72 hours) to give the notice required by that section is an offence (s. 33(4)). The notice must be given within seven days of the transfer and must contain a description of the firearm in question (giving its identification number if any) and state the nature of the transaction and the name and address of the other party. Any such notice must be sent by registered post, recorded delivery or 'permitted electronic means' (s. 33(3), (3A)).

A failure, without reasonable excuse, to give the seven-day notice required by s. 34 in connection with the de-activation, destruction or loss of firearms is an offence (s. 34(4)). For the purposes of ss. 34 and 35, a firearm is de-activated 'if it would, by virtue of section 8 of the 1988 Act be presumed to be rendered incapable of discharging any shot, bullet or other missile' (s. 34(5)). (For s. 8 of the 1988 Act, see **B12.20**.) The s. 34(4) offence extends to ammunition which has been lost (whether by theft or otherwise) (s. 34(2)).

Section 35 creates two offences relating to the notification of events taking place outside Great Britain involving firearms which, broadly, mirror the offences under ss. 33 and 34.

BUSINESS, EXPORT AND OTHER TRANSACTIONS INVOLVING FIREARMS AND AMMUNITION

Scope of Offences

B12.132 There are various firearms offences concerned with business and other transactions. These can be considered in four separate groups reflecting the varying modes of trial and penalties.

Either-way offences:

(a) selling firearms to person without a certificate (FA 1968, s. 3(2));
(b) repairing, testing etc. firearms for person without a certificate (FA 1968, s. 3(3));
(c) falsifying a certificate etc. with a view to the acquisition of a firearm (FA 1968, s. 3(5));
(d) transfer of firearms not made in person (F(A)A 1997, s. 32);
(e) supplying firearms to person denied them under the FA 1968, s. 21(5) (this offence is dealt with at **B12.113**);
(f) trading in firearms without being registered as a firearms dealer (FA 1968, s. 3(1)).

Summary offences with maximum penalty three months' imprisonment and/or unlimited fine:

(a) failure to report transaction authorised by visitor's shot gun permit (FA 1968, s. 42A(3));
(b) failure by person who resides in Great Britain to report purchase or acquisition of firearms in other EU Member States (F(A)A 1988, s. 18A(6)). Note that s.18A is prospectively omitted by reg. 61(5) of SI 2019 No. 742 from 'IP completion day';
(c) failure of firearms dealer to include particulars of agreement as required by the European Weapons Directive and the F(A)A 1988, s. 18(1A) (s. 18(6)). Note that s. 18(1A) and (6) are prospectively omitted by SI 2019 No. 742 (reg. 61(4)(a), (c)) from 'IP completion day'.

Summary offences with maximum penalty six months' imprisonment and/or unlimited fine:

(a) failure of registered firearms dealer to notify police of export transaction (F(A)A 1988, s. 18(5));
(b) transfer of shot guns (F(A)A 1997, ss. 32(3), 33(4), 35(4), 36);
(c) restriction on sale of ammunition for smooth-bore guns (F(A)A 1988, s. 5(2)).

The offence contrary to the F(A)A 1988, s. 18(5), is designed to ensure that a registered firearms dealer who sells a firearm or shot gun to a person entitled to purchase the same under s. 18(1) without a certificate, sends a notice of the transaction within 48 hours to the chief officer of police. The required details of such a notice are laid down by s. 18(3). Under s. 5(2) it is an offence to sell certain ammunition to a person who is not a registered firearms dealer and is not permitted by a certificate or otherwise to have the gun for which certain ammunition is required. The ammunition covered is that to which the FA 1968, s. 1, does not apply and which can be used in a shot gun or smooth-bore gun to which that section applies.

Summary offences with maximum penalty six months' imprisonment and/or level 3 fine:

(a) pawnbroker taking firearm in pawn (FA 1968, s. 3(6));
(b) supplying firearm to person drunk or insane (FA 1968, s. 25);
(c) contravention of order prohibiting movement of arms and ammunition (FA 1968, s. 6(1), (3)).

The offence contrary to the FA 1968, s. 6(3), is supported by the power of the police, under s. 49, to search for and seize any firearms or ammunition which they have reason to believe are being removed in contravention of such an order. A person having custody or control of the firearms or ammunition must allow the police reasonable facilities to examine and inspect such articles and any documentation. Failure to comply with this power is a summary offence punishable in the same way as the offence contrary to s. 6(3).

Either-way Offences

Firearms Act 1968, s. 3 **B12.133**

(1) A person commits an offence if, by way of trade or business, he—
  (a) manufactures, sells, transfers, repairs, tests or proves any firearm or ammunition to which section 1 of this Act applies, or a shot gun; or
  (b) exposes for sale or transfer, or has in his possession for sale, transfer, test or proof any such firearm or ammunition, or a shot gun, or
  (c) sells or transfers an air weapon, exposes such a weapon for sale or transfer or has such a weapon in his possession for sale or transfer,

without being registered under this Act as a firearms dealer.

(2) It is an offence for a person to sell or transfer to any other person in the United Kingdom, other than a registered firearms dealer, any firearm or ammunition to which section 1 of this Act applies, or a shot gun, unless that other produces a firearm certificate authorising him to purchase or acquire it, or as the case may be, his shot gun certificate, or shows that he is by virtue of this Act entitled to purchase or acquire it without holding a certificate.

(3) It is an offence for a person to undertake the repair, test or proof of a firearm or ammunition to which section 1 of this Act applies, or of a shot gun, for any other person in the United Kingdom other than a registered firearms dealer as such, unless that other produces or causes to be produced a firearm certificate authorising him to have possession of the firearm or ammunition or, as the case may be, his shot gun certificate, or shows that he is by virtue of this Act entitled to have possession of it without holding a certificate.

...

(5) A person commits an offence if, with a view to purchasing or acquiring, or procuring the repair, test or proof of, any firearm or ammunition to which section 1 of this Act applies, or a shot gun, he produces a false certificate or a certificate in which any false entry has been made or personates a person to whom a certificate has been granted or knowingly or recklessly makes a statement false in any material particular.

As to procedure and sentence, see ss. 51, 52 and sch. 6 at **B12.3**, **B12.4** and **B12.6**, and the cases listed at **B12.137**.

The FA 1982, on readily convertible imitation firearms, applies to these offences (see **B12.30**).

For the meaning of: 'firearm or ammunition to which the FA 1968, s. 1, applies', see **B12.37**; 'shot gun', see **B12.17**; 'firearm certificate', see **B12.42**; 'shot gun certificate', see **B12.52**; 'registered firearms dealer', see **B12.52**. 'Transfer' is defined by the FA 1968, s. 57(4), as including let on hire, give, lend and part with possession, and 'transferee' and 'transferor' are construed accordingly.

B12.134 The offence in s. 3(2) is one of strict liability (*Paul* [1999] Crim LR 79). This must be true (it is submitted) of the similar offences. The test is an objective one: 'whether the firearm in question corresponds with the description relied on in a certificate produced by the transferee'. The intentions of the transferee as to use are irrelevant (*Paul*).

In the offence contrary to s. 3(5), the offence requires consideration of what is a 'false certificate', a 'false entry' or a 'false statement'. The consideration of the analogous phrases in the Forgery and Counterfeiting Act 1981 (see **B6.28** to **B6.32**) may be of assistance in ascertaining the meaning of these terms.

With respect to s. 3(1), relevant exemptions include exemption where D is authorised to deal with firearms, for persons in the service of the Crown, for proof houses, and where the firearm is an antique firearm sold or purchased as a curiosity or ornament, although all the exemptions in ss. 7 to 13, 15, 54 and 58(1) and (2) of the FA 1968, and ss. 15, 15B, 16A to 19 of the F(A)A 1988 apply (s. 16 of the F(A)A 1988 having been repealed; see **B12.47**(i)); and see generally **B12.47** to **B12.51**.

By s. 9(2) of the FA 1968 it is not an offence for an auctioneer to sell by auction, expose for sale by auction or have in his possession for sale by auction, a firearm or ammunition when the auctioneer is not a registered firearms dealer, provided the auctioneer has a permit from the chief officer of police and complies with the terms of that permit. It is a summary offence for a person knowingly or recklessly to make a statement false in any material particular for the purpose of procuring for himself or another the grant of such a permit (s. 9(3)).

The same exemptions apply to offences under the FA 1968, s. 3(2) and (3). In addition, by virtue of s. 8(2), it is not an offence under s. 3(2) for a person '(a) to part with possession of any firearm or ammunition, otherwise than in pursuance of a contract of sale or hire or by way of gift or loan, to a person who shows that he is by virtue of this Act entitled to have possession of the firearm or ammunition without holding a certificate, or (b) to return to another person a shot gun which he has lawfully undertaken to repair, test or prove for the other'. By virtue of s. 9(4) it is not an offence under s. 3(2) for a carrier or warehouseman, or a servant, to deliver any firearm or ammunition in the ordinary course of business or employment as such.

Failure to Comply with Instructions by Police Officers

Section 47(1) of the FA 1968 enables a constable to require a person whom the constable has reasonable cause to suspect (i) of having a firearm with him in a public place, or (ii) to be committing, or about to commit, elsewhere than in a public place, an offence contrary to ss. 18(1), (2) and 20 (see s. 47(6)), to hand over the firearm or any ammunition for examination by the constable. **B12.135**

It is an offence, contrary to the FA 1968, s. 47(2), for a person having a firearm or ammunition with him to fail to hand it over when required to do so by a constable acting under s. 47(1). Section 47 also provides a power of search of person and vehicle (s. 47(3) and (4)).

It is also an offence, contrary to s. 48(3), for a person to refuse to declare to a constable that person's name and address or to fail to give that person's true name and address when required to do so by a constable acting under s. 48. This enables a constable to require the production of a relevant certificate when the constable believes a person to be in possession of a firearm to which s. 1 applies, or a shot gun.

As to procedure and sentence, see ss. 51, 52 and sch. 6 at **B12.3**, **B12.4** and **B12.6**, and the cases listed at **B12.137**.

Miscellaneous Offences Relating to Permits, Certificates and Authorisations

A number of offences relate to the obtaining and use of permits, certificates and authorisations under the Firearms Acts 1968 to 1992. Reference has already been made to some of these offences under specific offences in the preceding parts of this section. In addition, the following summary offences have been created: **B12.136**

(a) To knowingly or recklessly make a statement which is false in any material particular in order to procure the grant or renewal of a firearm or shot gun certificate (FA 1968, s. 28A(7)). It is punishable with a term of imprisonment not exceeding six months and/or an unlimited fine.
(b) To knowingly or recklessly make a statement which is false in any material particular in order to procure the variation of a firearm certificate (s. 29(3)). It is punishable with a term of imprisonment not exceeding six months and/or an unlimited fine.
(c) To fail to surrender a certificate on revocation (s. 30D(3)). It is punishable with a fine not exceeding level 3 on the standard scale.
(d) On removal of a firearms dealer's name from the register, to fail to surrender a certificate of registration or register of transactions (s. 38(8)). It is punishable with a fine not exceeding level 3 on the standard scale.
(e) To knowingly or recklessly make a statement which is false in any material particular in order to secure firearms dealer registration or entry in the register of a place of business (s. 39(1)). It is punishable with a term of imprisonment not exceeding six months and/or an unlimited fine.
(f) For a registered firearms dealer to have a place of business not entered on the register (s. 39(2)). It is punishable with a term of imprisonment not exceeding six months and/or an unlimited fine.
(g) Not to comply with a condition of firearms dealer registration (s. 39(3)). It is punishable with a term of imprisonment not exceeding six months and/or an unlimited fine.
(h) For a firearms dealer not to comply with provisions as to the register of transactions and to make a false entry in the register (s. 40(5)). These offences are punishable with a term of imprisonment not exceeding six months and/or an unlimited fine.

(i) To fail to surrender a firearm or shot gun certificate cancelled by a court on conviction (s. 52(2)(c)). It is punishable with a fine not exceeding level 3 on the standard scale.
(j) To fail to comply with a notice from a chief officer of police who has revoked a certificate requiring the holder of the certificate to surrender forthwith the certificate and any firearms and ammunition which are in the holder's possession by virtue of the certificate (F(A)A 1988, s. 12(2)). The offence is punishable with imprisonment for a term not exceeding three months, or a fine not exceeding level 4 on the standard scale, or both.

Further summary offences (under the FA 1968, ss. 32B(5), 32C(6), 42A(3) and 48(4)) have been created to ensure compliance with the European Weapons Directive. Note the prospective amendments to ss. 32B, 32C, 42A, 48, 57, and sch. 6, part 1 (prosecution and punishment of offences) concerning entries relating to ss. 32B(5), 32C(6) and 48(4) by reg. 59 of SI 2019 No. 742, from 'IP completion day'.

SENTENCING FOR FIREARMS OFFENCES

B12.137 There is no offence-specific guideline for firearms offences but the Sentencing Council published a draft guideline for consultation during 2019 and anticipates issuing a definitive guideline during 2020. In the meantime, the *General Guideline: Overarching Principles* (see Supplement, **SG2-1**) is used for all offenders sentenced on or after 1 October 2019.

Several Court of Appeal decisions provide guidance on the appropriate sentencing bracket for the most serious firearms offences. *Avis* [1998] 1 Cr App R 420 (see **B12.138**) continues to be cited as to the principles to be applied, although for certain offences the sentence lengths have been overtaken by the requirement for minimum sentences. Section 51A of the FA 1968 provides for minimum custodial sentences to be imposed for certain firearms offences, unless (s. 51A(2)) the court is of the opinion that there are exceptional circumstances relating to the offence or to D which justify not doing so. The relevant offences are those under s. 5(1)(a), (ab), (aba), (ac), (ad), (ae), (af) or (c), (1A) or (2A) of the FA 1968. For a detailed discussion and cases on 'exceptional circumstances' to refrain from imposing the minimum term, see **E5.9**.

B12.138 The Court of Appeal in *Avis* [1998] 1 Cr App R 420 set guideline sentencing levels for a number of offences (endorsed and updated in *Wilkinson* [2009] EWCA Crim 1925, [2010] 1 Cr App R (S) 100 (628)). Lord Bingham CJ said that, given the clear public need to discourage unlawful possession and use of firearms (both real and imitation) and Parliament's intention expressed by the continuing increase in maximum penalties, the courts should treat offences under the FA 1968 as serious. Save for minor infringements which might be and were properly dealt with summarily, offences committed under ss. 1(1), 2(1), 3, 4, 5(1A), 16, 16A, 17(1) and (2), 18(1), 19 and 21(4) would generally merit custodial sentences, even on a plea of guilty and where D had no previous record. On breaches of ss. 4, 5, 16, 16A, 17(1) and (2), 18(1), 19 or 21, the custodial term was likely to be considerable, and where the four questions suggested by the court (set out below) yielded answers adverse to D, terms at or approaching the maximum might in a contested case be appropriate. An indeterminate sentence should, however, be imposed only where the established criteria for imposing such a sentence were met.

His lordship said that the appropriate level of sentence for firearms offences would, as for any other offence, depend on all the particular facts relevant to the offence and D, and it would be wrong for the Court of Appeal to prescribe unduly restrictive sentencing guidelines. However, it would usually be appropriate for the sentencing court to ask itself four questions:

(a) What sort of weapon was involved? Genuine weapons were more dangerous than imitation firearms, loaded firearms more dangerous than unloaded, unloaded for which ammunition was available more dangerous than where none was available. Possession of a firearm which had no lawful use, such as a sawn-off shot gun, would be viewed even more seriously than possession of a firearm capable of unlawful use.

(b) What, if any, use had been made of the firearm? The court had to take account of all the circumstances surrounding any use made of the firearm; the more prolonged and premeditated and violent, the more serious the offence was likely to be.
(c) With what intention, if any, did D possess or use the firearm? Generally, the more serious offences under the Act were those requiring proof of a specific criminal intent to endanger life, cause fear of violence, resist arrest, or commit an indictable offence. The more serious the act intended, the more serious the offence.
(d) What was D's record? The seriousness of any firearm offence was inevitably increased if D had an established record of committing firearms offences or crimes of violence.

An additional two questions were referred to by the Court in *Sheen* [2011] EWCA Crim 2461, [2012] 2 Cr App R (S) 3 (7), namely:

(e) Where was the firearm (or were the firearms) discharged, and who and how many were exposed to danger by its or their use?
(f) Was any injury or damage caused by the discharge of the firearm or firearms, and if so, how serious was it?

The Court of Appeal in *Wilkinson* endorsed the guidance given in *Avis*, with Lord Judge CJ emphasising (at [2]):

> Guns kill and maim, terrorise and intimidate. That is why criminals want them: that is why they use them: and that is why they organise their importation and manufacture, supply and distribution. Sentencing courts must address the fact that too many lethal weapons are too readily available: too many are carried: too many are used, always with devastating effect on individual victims and with insidious corrosive impact on the wellbeing of the local community.

The Court went on to note that *Avis* did not address large-scale importation and/or manufacture, sale and distribution of guns, saying that such offences were no less criminally reprehensible than the importation of drugs or possession of drugs with intent to supply. It was difficult to anticipate many such cases where an imminent risk to life was not an inevitable consequence of the offence. If so, the availability of a life sentence should not be dependent on proof of the specific intent required by s. 16 of the Act. However, where the statutory intent involving danger to life had been established, and it was clear that the firearms had subsequently been used with homicidal intent by others, the sentence on the importer or supplier should always reflect those dreadful consequences. The fact that the importer or supplier did not pull the trigger did not resolve the issue of dangerousness. In such cases, indeterminate sentences inevitably arose for consideration.

Importation or Distribution In *Harwozinski* [2019] EWCA Crim 1195 D was part of a series of conspiracies to convert blank-firing handguns, manufacture ammunition and to import both from the Czech Republic to the UK to enable others to endanger life, as indeed, they had done given that one of the weapons had been used in an attempted murder. D was dangerous and life sentences with a minimum of nine years and eight months were considered appropriate by the Court of Appeal. **B12.139**

A-G's Ref (No. 128 of 2015) [2016] EWCA Crim 54, [2016] 2 Cr App R (S) 12 (72) concerned a sophisticated criminal enterprise involving the distribution of firearms and ammunition to multiple criminal groups across the country. The Court of Appeal held that if life sentences are not passed in such cases, courts must impose long determinate sentences which reflect the hierarchy of the supply enterprise, the role played in individual transactions and any previous convictions in relation to guns. For the leader of the enterprise the starting point should be around 25 years; longer if there were previous convictions for firearms offences. Those under the leader should receive sentences reflecting the sentence for the leader, depending on the role they played. Those in other criminal groups who purchase guns, presumptively to 'kill and maim, terrorise and intimidate', should receive sentences of around 15 years, even without relevant prior convictions. Bearing in mind the mandatory minimum sentence of five years' imprisonment for possession of a gun, those assisting the transactions should receive sentences of at least eight years before plea discount. These observations were considered in *Dixon-Nash* [2019] EWCA Crim 1173, which involved the storage and transfer of a much smaller quantity of weapons, this time for a single criminal group. The family operation was rewarded with sentences after trial of 20 years for the leader, 14 years for his mother, who had acted as his 'key facilitator', and eight years' detention for his younger sister, aged 16 at the time of the offending.

B12.140 **Firearms in Use, or for Intended Use** In *Ray* [2019] EWCA Crim 2112 a sentence of 12 years' imprisonment imposed on D following his conviction for conspiring to possess a firearm with intent to endanger life was upheld. A sentence of ten years' imprisonment was appropriate in *Sugulle* [2013] EWCA Crim 170, [2013] 2 Cr App R (S) 61 (389) where D pleaded guilty to possession of a loaded revolver with intent to endanger life. The judge had considered the questions posed in *Avis* [1998] 1 Cr App R 420, and found that the gun was genuine, loaded, deadly, had no lawful purpose, and was in the possession of a man connected with gang-related activity. Another case of possession of a firearm with intent to endanger life is *Kumar* [2012] EWCA Crim 503, [2012] 2 Cr App R (S) 84 (487), where the Court of Appeal said that the appropriate sentence was five years and nine months on a guilty plea where D had acquired a gun after hearing threats that a gang was about to attack him, and had fired a shot from his house in the direction of the gang during the attack. See also *Adigun* [2013] EWCA Crim 171, [2013] 2 Cr App R (S) 58 (374). Possession of an imitation firearm with intent to resist arrest merited immediate custody in *Alcock* [2018] EWCA Crim 2940, in which D was resistant during arrest and produced what appeared to be a Browning pistol, leading police to flee. He was sentenced after a late plea to a 15-month suspended sentence. The Court of Appeal found that to be unduly lenient and substituted a sentence of three years' imprisonment. Possession of a firearm with intent to cause fear of violence merited a sentence of two years' imprisonment on conviction in *Carey* [2000] 1 Cr App R (S) 179, where D threatened police officers with an air pistol. In *Marsh* [2012] EWCA Crim 1217, [2013] 1 Cr App R (S) 18 (99), a sentence of nine months was appropriate following a guilty plea where D, a man of 36 with no relevant previous convictions, pointed an imitation firearm at some youths who had come to his home to complain about the offender's son. In *Moffat* [2014] EWCA Crim 332, [2014] 2 Cr App R (S) 37 (307) the Court Martial Appeal Court reduced a sentence of three years to one of 14 months in the case of a Leading Seaman who had confronted a Lieutenant Commander while in possession of an assault rifle but, when requested to hand over the weapon, had done so immediately. D, who was convicted after a trial, was found to have been suffering from an adjustment disorder which had impaired his judgement.

B12.141 **Simple Possession** In *Gourley* [1999] 2 Cr App R (S) 148, a sentence of four years' imprisonment for possessing a sawn-off shot gun without a certificate was reduced on appeal to three years. Although D had pleaded guilty, the offence was aggravated because live ammunition had been found along with the gun, the barrel had been shortened, and D had a previous conviction for violence. In *Hudson* [1998] 1 Cr App R (S) 124, the gun was of the same type but, in addition, was loaded and ready for use. The correct sentence, according to the Court of Appeal, was four years on a guilty plea. The Court of Appeal in *Higgins* [1998] 1 Cr App R (S) 333, confirmed that a distinction should be maintained when sentencing for possession of firearms other than shortened shot guns, but that sentences should nonetheless reflect public concerns about firearms generally. Fifteen months' imprisonment was appropriate in that case, where D was found to have a semi-automatic pistol and 55 rounds of ammunition at his home. It was accepted that D, who pleaded guilty, had taken the pistol from a nephew who had threatened to harm himself, but D had retained the weapon for six months, even after the nephew's death.

B12.142 **Consecutive or Concurrent Sentences** In *A-G's Ref (No. 57 of 2009) (Ralphs)* [2009] EWCA Crim 2555, [2010] 2 Cr App R (S) 30 (190) the Court of Appeal drew attention to the limited range of sentencing which is available when D is in possession of multiple prohibited firearms and is convicted of offences which carry a minimum sentence of five years' imprisonment (in the absence of exceptional circumstances), but a maximum sentence of only ten years, noting that where guilty pleas are entered, there is little room for case-specific flexibility. The Court was asked by the A-G to impose consecutive sentences amounting in total to double figures in order to mark the gravity of the offending. The Court refused, saying that in reality it was being asked to circumvent the statutory maximum sentence on the basis that it believes it to be too low and to disapply well-understood sentencing principles of which Parliament must be deemed to have been aware when the statutory maximum and minimum sentences were fixed. 'Tempting as it is to do so, that is a step too far' (at [29]). The problem, said the Court, must be addressed by legislation.

The principle in *Ralphs* was expressed with reference to a case in which all the relevant firearms and ammunition were found in the same place and had been received by D at the same time, and has not been followed in cases where firearms had been acquired at different times or stored in different locations (see, e.g., *Gribben* [2014] EWCA Crim 115, [2014] 2 Cr App R (S) 28 (229) and *Ullah* [2017] EWCA Crim 584. The question was revisited in *Asif* [2018] EWCA Crim 2297, [2019] 1 Cr App R (S) 26 (173), a case involving a single weapons cache found in a car. The Court concluded that where the principle in *Ralphs* applies, concurrent sentences should be imposed which in aggregate do not exceed the maximum of ten years' imprisonment, less such credit as may be appropriate in accordance with the sentencing guideline for any guilty pleas. The Court reiterated the need for Parliament to consider the issue (at [28]).

For the offence under the FA 1968, s. 19 (carrying a firearm in a public place: see **B12.110**), when tried summarily, see the *Magistrates' Court Sentencing Guidelines* (see Supplement, **SG10-98**).

Minimum Sentences For a full discussion, and cases on 'exceptional circumstances' for refraining from imposing minimum sentences, see **E.9**. **B12.143**

POSSESSION OF OFFENSIVE WEAPON

Prevention of Crime Act 1953, s. 1 **B12.144**

(1) Any person who without lawful authority or reasonable excuse, the proof whereof shall lie on him, has with him in any public place any offensive weapon shall be guilty of an offence.

Procedure

This offence is triable either way (Prevention of Crime Act 1953, s. 1(1)). Practitioners should be mindful of proposed amendments to the Prevention of Crime Act 1953 in the Sentencing Act 2020. **B12.145**

As to the compatibility with the ECHR, Article 8, of the CJPO 1994, s. 60, in respect of stop and search powers (without suspicion) for offensive weapons, see *R (Roberts) v Metropolitan Police Commissioner* [2015] UKSC 79, [2016] 1 WLR 210 and **D1.12**.

Indictment

Statement of Offence **B12.146**

Having an offensive weapon in a public place contrary to section 1 of the Prevention of Crime Act 1953.

Particulars of Offence

A on the ... day of ... had with him in a public place, namely ... an offensive weapon, namely ... without lawful authority or reasonable excuse.

'Time' and 'place' are material elements of the instant offence which must be accurately stated in the particulars of the offence (*Allamby* [1974] 3 All ER 126).

Where the weapon may be offensive under two of the categories of offensive weapons, the indictment need not contain two counts (*Flynn* (1985) 82 Cr App R 319).

Sentencing Guidelines

B12.147 The maximum penalty is: on conviction on indictment, imprisonment for a term not exceeding four years or a fine or both; on summary conviction, a term of imprisonment not exceeding six months and/or an unlimited fine (Prevention of Crime Act 1953, s. 1(1)). The Sentencing Council definitive guideline, *Bladed Articles and Offensive Weapons* (see Supplement, **SG14-1**), applies in relation to offenders sentenced on or after 1 June 2018, irrespective of the date of the offence. There are separate guidelines for offenders aged 18 and over, and for children and young people.

By virtue of the Prevention of Crime Act 1953, s. 1(2A) to (2G), where a person aged 16 or over is convicted of an offence under s. 1(1) and has at least one 'relevant conviction' the court must impose a prescribed minimum custodial sentence unless the court is of the opinion that there are particular circumstances which relate to the offence, the previous offence, or to the offender and which would make it unjust to do so in all the circumstances. The minimum sentence in the case of an offender aged 16 or 17 when convicted is a detention and training order for four months, and the minimum sentence in the case of an offender aged 18 or over when convicted is imprisonment or detention in a young offender institution for six months (see **E5.19**).

Meaning of 'Offensive Weapon'

B12.148 **Prevention of Crime Act 1953, s. 1**

(4) In this section ... 'offensive weapon' means any article made or adapted for use for causing injury to the person, or intended by the person having it with him for such use by him or by some other person.

There are three possible categories of offensive weapon (*Simpson* [1983] 1 WLR 1494):

(a) an article made for use for causing injury to the person, commonly known as a weapon that is offensive *per se*;
(b) an article adapted for use for causing injury to the person (e.g., a bottle that is broken to inflict injury);
(c) an article which the person carrying it intends to use for the purpose of causing injury to the person.

Frequently there is little or no distinction between the first two categories, but they must be distinguished from the third category, which requires proof that D intended to injure another person.

If the definition of an 'offensive weapon' requires elucidation (see the Prevention of Crime Act 1953, s.1(4)), a judge might fashion a direction using the words of s. 1(4) to make it clear that if the jury did not find that the article was made for causing injury to the person, then they had to consider whether the article which was being carried was intended to be used for causing injury to another person. The test is not 'is [the weapon] capable of causing injury?' (*Samuels* [2016] EWCA Crim 1876, citing *Simpson* [1983] 1 WLR 1494).

It is for the tribunal of fact to determine whether a weapon is offensive *per se*, i.e. that it is an article made for use for causing injury to the person (see, in particular, the decision of the Court of Appeal in *Williamson* (1978) 67 Cr App R 35, applied in *Dhindsa* [2005] EWCA Crim 1198, where it was for the jury to decide whether an item was a ring or a knuckle-duster); and see *Chen v DPP* (4 March 1997 unreported, Administrative Court), where a Kobutan martial arts bar was not, on the facts, offensive *per se*.

If an article has an innocent purpose, it will not be an offensive weapon *per se*. Thus, in *Petrie* [1961] 1 All ER 466, it was held that an ordinary razor is not an offensive weapon *per se* and, in *Humphreys* [1977] Crim LR 225, an ordinary penknife was held not to be an offensive weapon *per se*.

Items with a Dual Purpose For a consideration of the approach to be taken in cases where an item has the appearance of being an offensive weapon, but it may have another purpose (e.g., as a fashion accessory) such that it might be open to the tribunal of fact to find that the item was not an offensive weapon, see *DPP v Christof* [2015] EWHC 4096 (Admin), [2016] 2 Cr App R 6 (56), which concerned whether a belt buckle was a knuckleduster and in which *Simpson* [1983] 1 WLR 1494 and *DPP v Hynde* [1998] 1 WLR 1222 were applied; and see *Vasili* [2011] EWCA Crim 615, [2011] 2 Cr App R 5 (56) at **B12.152** and consider *Woods v Heywood* 1988 SCCR 434; see also *Lord Advocate's Reference No. 1 of 2020* [2020] HCJAC 25 (albeit in the context of a firearm 'disguised as another object' for the purposes of FA 1968, s. 5(1A)(a); **B12.74**). **B12.149**

Where there is doubt whether an article is an offensive weapon *per se*, the tribunal of fact must be directed to the statutory definition that must be applied in accordance with the statutory criteria (*Williamson* (1977) 67 Cr App R 35; *Simpson* [1983] 1 WLR 1494; *Humphries* (7 April 1987 unreported)).

Weapons Offensive *per se*

Where the article is an offensive weapon *per se*, the prosecution must prove that D had possession of the offensive weapon but need not prove a specific intent to injure (*Davis v Alexander* (1970) 54 Cr App R 398). The following are examples of weapons offensive *per se*. **B12.150**

Petrol Bombs A petrol bomb is an offensive weapon *per se* (*Akhtar* [2015] EWCA Crim 176, [2015] 2 Cr App R 7 (81)). **B12.151**

Knives A flick-knife is an offensive weapon *per se* (*Lawrence* (1971) 57 Cr App R 64; *Allamby* [1974] 3 All ER 126; *Gibson v Wales* [1983] 1 All ER 869). See also the Restriction of Offensive Weapons Act 1959, s. 1, at **B12.200**. Not all knives are offensive weapons *per se* (*Simpson*). Not all sheath knives are offensive weapons (*Simpson*) and consider *Coull v Guild* 1985 SLT 184. **B12.152**

An object which has all the characteristics of a flick-knife does not cease to be a flick-knife because it also has the secondary characteristic of being a lighter (*Vasili* [2011] EWCA Crim 615, [2011] 2 Cr App R 5 (56)).

In *Patterson v PC 108D PK* (1984) *The Times*, 21 June 1984, it was held that a lock knife is not an offensive weapon *per se*.

In a decision on the Aviation Security Act 1982, s. 4(2)(c), it was held that a butterfly knife is necessarily an article for use for causing injury to the person and judicial notice can be taken of that fact (see also *Garry v CPS* [2019] EWHC 636 (Admin), [2019] 1 WLR 3630, and *DPP v Hynde* [1998] 1 All ER 649, where the Court of Appeal referred to both the definition in the CJA 1988 and the decision in *Simpson*; and *DPP v Patterson* [2004] EWHC 2744 (Admin), which also concerned a butterfly knife).

Batons In *Houghton v Chief Constable of Greater Manchester* (1986) 84 Cr App R 319, it was held that a truncheon is an offensive weapon *per se*, in part because it does not possess *per se* any innocent quality. **B12.153**

'Shurikens' It is submitted that a 'shuriken' (Chinese throwing star) is offensive *per se* (*McGlennan v Clark* 1993 SLT 1069). **B12.154**

Rice Flails The conclusion by magistrates that a rice flail was an offensive weapon *per se* could not successfully be challenged on the facts adduced in *Copus v DPP* [1989] Crim LR 577. **B12.155**

Sword Sticks It was held in *Butler* [1988] Crim LR 695 that a sword stick is a weapon, offensive *per se*: see also *Davis v Alexander* to the same effect. **B12.156**

Statutory Classification of Articles Offensive *per se* Note that a list of offensive weapons appears in SI 1988 No. 2019 (as amended by SI 2002 No. 1668) for the purposes of the offence contrary to the CJA 1988, s. 141 (manufacture, sale or hire of offensive weapons; see **B12.201**). **B12.157**

In Scotland, the High Court of Justiciary has held that where it was clearly stated in a statutory instrument that an article was to be regarded as an offensive weapon, it could be regarded as an offensive weapon *per se* for the purposes of the Prevention of Crime Act 1953 (*McGlennan v Clark* 1993 SLT 1069).

Weapons Adapted to Cause Injury

B12.158 Whether an article is adapted to cause injury is a question of fact to be answered by the jury or magistrates (*Williamson* (1977) 67 Cr App R 35) and see *Warne v DPP* (3 June 1997 unreported), where the Divisional Court also made clear that the fact that the item was later used for a violent purpose was not necessarily determinative of the issue whether it had been adapted to cause injury. Thus, on the facts in *Warne*, a pick-axe handle, which had lost its head, had not been adapted for use for causing injury to the person.

Examples of items adjudged to have been adapted to cause injury include (a) a bottle which is deliberately broken so that the jagged end can be used to injure (*Simpson* [1983] 1 WLR 1494), (b) a potato with a razor blade inserted into it (*Williamson*), (c) half a pool cue (*Sills* [2006] EWHC 3383 (Admin)) and (d) a pair of sand gloves made for use as a weapon (*R* [2007] EWCA Crim 3312, [2008] 1 Cr App R 26 (357)).

If a jury wish some kind of experiment to be conducted in relation to the article in question, then whatever happens thereafter must take place in open court (*Higgins* (1989) *The Times*, 16 February 1989).

Weapons Intended to be Used to Cause Injury

B12.159 The prosecution must prove the element of specific intention (*Petrie* [1961] 1 All ER 466). The use to which the weapon is put might assist in determining what the intention of the possessor was (*Harrison v Thornton* (1966) 68 Cr App R 28; *Dayle* [1973] 3 All ER 1151; *Ohlson v Hylton* [1975] 2 All ER 490).

The charge should specify the time and place that D formed the intention to cause injury. It was said in *Allamby* [1974] 3 All ER 126 that it is not sufficient that D had the necessary intention at some earlier stage. However, this is inconsistent (it is submitted) with *Humphreys* [1977] Crim LR 225 where the Court drew a distinction (in effect) between an intention to injure that is formed ad hoc rather than an intention held while the weapon was being carried. Again, in *Tucker* [2016] EWCA Crim 593, Treacy LJ remarked (consistently with *Allamby*, albeit not cited) that there is an important distinction between an article (not offensive *per se*) that is introduced into a public place by a person with an intent to injure, and an article (already possessed lawfully and for good reason) that is used offensively to cause injury. Each case depends on its facts.

An intention to use the object or article as a weapon if the occasion were to arise may be sufficient. Recklessness as to how it might be used is not sufficient (*Byrne* [2003] EWCA Crim 3253, following *Patterson v Block* (12 September 1984 unreported)). The jury must be given carefully crafted directions regarding the meaning of 'intention' (see **A2.4**).

It is not settled whether 'injury to the person' includes self-inflicted injury but a proposition that it does do so was not challenged in the Divisional Court in *Bryan v Mott* (1975) 62 Cr App R 71. Although D's intention to commit suicide was not unlawful, he had no reasonable excuse for having the article in a public place for that purpose. On the other hand, a judge of the Crown Court ruled that an element in the offence was injury to a person other than the possessor of the weapon (*Fleming* [1989] Crim LR 71).

An intention to frighten or to intimidate is not an intention to cause injury unless D's intention was to cause injury by shock (*Rapier* (1979) 70 Cr App R 17, following *Edmonds* [1963] 2 QB 142, and explaining *Woodward v Koessler* [1958] 3 All ER 557). The trial judge must give careful directions in cases where it is appropriate to make the distinction (see also *Snooks* [1997] Crim LR 230). *Edmonds* was also followed in *Ali* [2012] EWCA Crim 934.

Distinction between 'Having it with Him' and 'Use' The offence contrary to s. 1(1) of the 1953 Act is concerned with the carrying of any offensive weapon and not with its use (a distinction drawn by Professor Sir John Smith, see *Smith, Hogan and Ormerod's Criminal Law* (15th edn, 2018), at p. 750 and see also p. 748, and by the courts (see, e.g., *Dayle* (1972) 58 Cr App R 100)). See also *C v DPP* [2001] EWHC Admin 1093, [2002] Crim LR 322. Thus, in *Jura* [1954] 1 QB 503, a conviction for an offence under the Prevention of Crime Act 1953, s. 1, was quashed where D had possession of an air rifle at a shooting gallery, which he used to fire at a woman companion. Although the use of the rifle was unlawful, his carrying of it (for which he had a reasonable excuse) was not. *Jura* was followed in *Dayle* [1974] 1 WLR 181, where the Court of Appeal held that it was open to a jury to find that there was no possession of an offensive weapon when an inoffensive article (a car jack) lawfully carried was offensively used (see also *Bryan v Mott* (1975) 62 Cr App R 71 at p. 73). **B12.160**

The use of an article as a weapon can (it is submitted) be dealt with by charging appropriate offences against the person. In *Veasey* [1999] Crim LR 158, the Court of Appeal confirmed that in cases where the real issue is the use of an offensive weapon, a charge of assault is 'quite adequate'. Again, in *Szewczyk* [2019] EWCA Crim 1811, [2020] 1 WLR 492, the Court of Appeal remarked that on a careful reading of *Ohlson v Hylton* 'it was clearly the intention of the Divisional Court, as with the Court of Criminal Appeal in *Jura* [1954] 1 QB 503, to apply a reading of the statute with a view to simple, straightforward charging; with a view to clarity — a clarity separating the charging of an offensive weapon being carried apart from assault, and the assault itself' (per Irwin LJ, at [19]).

In *Ohlson v Hylton* [1975] 2 All ER 490, a workman was held not to be guilty of the offence where he took a hammer from his work bag and struck a fellow traveller at an Underground station. The hammer was properly in his possession. Lord Widgery CJ said at pp. 728–9: **B12.161**

> ... I would hold that an offence under section 1 is not committed where a person arms himself with a weapon for *instant* attack on his victim. It seems to me that the section is concerned only with a man who, possessed of a weapon, forms the necessary intent before an occasion to use actual violence has arisen. In other words, it is not the actual use of the weapon with which the section is concerned, but the carrying of a weapon with intent to use it if occasion arises ...
>
> I accept that it is unnecessary for the prosecution to prove that the relevant intent was formed from the moment when the defendant set out on his expedition. An innocent carrying of say, a hammer can be converted into an unlawful carrying when the defendant forms the guilty intent, provided, in my view, that the intent is formed before the actual occasion to use violence has arisen.

Ohlson v Hylton was applied in *Humphreys* [1977] Crim LR 225, where the Court of Appeal held that no offence was committed where a person had a penknife on him, and then used it in desperation: it had not been carried in a public place with the necessary intent. In *Bates v Bulman* [1979] 1 WLR 1190, the Divisional Court held that D, who acquired an unopened clasp knife with the immediate intention of using it as an offensive weapon, did not commit the instant offence, because 'the purport of the [1953] Act ... is to cover the situation where an accused person ... has with him and is carrying an offensive weapon intending that it shall be used, if necessary, for offensive purposes' (per Stocker J). Stocker J also said that it:

> ... would be a rather academic and over-analytical approach [to make] a distinction between an innocent weapon subsequently used with the intention of an assault and which is being carried innocently ..., and a similar article which is acquired either by borrowing from somebody else or fortuitously by being picked up in the street.

The Court declined to follow *Harrison v Thornton* (1966) 68 Cr App R 28, where a stone that had been picked up by D during a fight was held to be an offensive weapon (and see also **B12.108**).

'Has with Him' and Knowledge

B12.162 **'Has with Him' and Possession Contrasted** It was held in *McCalla* (1988) 87 Cr App R 372, that to have something with one necessarily requires closer contact than mere possession: 'Every case of "having" is one of "possessing," but it does not necessarily follow that every case of "possessing" is one of "having" within the meaning of the relevant statutory provisions' (per May LJ at p. 378). See **B12.109** (albeit in the context of firearms). The Court of Appeal remarked in *Henderson* [2016] EWCA Crim 965, [2016] 4 WLR 172 (applying *Kelt* [1977] 1 WLR 1365 and *Pawlicki* [1992] 1 WLR 827) that the authorities indicate that in determining whether a person has a weapon 'with him', relevant considerations include the following: (i) possession of a weapon is a wider concept than having it 'with him'; (ii) having a weapon 'with him' is a wider concept than carrying it; (iii) the propinquity between the person and the weapon; (iv) whether the weapon is immediately available to the person; (v) the accessibility of the weapon; (vi) the context of any criminal enterprise embarked upon; and (vii) the purpose of the applicable statute.

B12.163 **Knowledge: General Principle** As a general principle, a person has something with him or it is in his possession if he *knows* that he has with him, or is in possession of, the object in question (*Cugullere* [1961] 1 WLR 858, at p. 860). A judge erred in his charge to the jury when he used words that might have made the jury think that a mere belief that a knife was somewhere in D's van would be sufficient (*Daubney* (2000) 164 JP 519). Similarly, in *Jolie* [2003] EWCA Crim 1543, [2004] 1 Cr App R 3 (44) (a case decided under the CJA 1988, s. 139), the Court of Appeal ruled that relevant to the element of possession was proof that D was either aware of the presence of the knife in the vehicle (when making the journey in the course of which D was stopped) or that D was responsible for putting the knife in the place where it was later found.

B12.164 **Lack of Knowledge that the Thing was a Weapon** In *Densu* [1998] 1 Cr App R 400, counsel, upon being shown by the Registrar of the Court of Appeal two unreported decisions of that Court (namely, *Vann* [1996] Crim LR 52 and *Matrix* [1997] Crim LR 901) abandoned the argument that the trial judge erred in ruling that the phrase 'has with him' was satisfied 'if the prosecution proved that the appellant merely knew that he had the baton with him but did not know that it was a weapon'. The Court of Appeal makes no comment on the abandonment of the argument but it is arguable that the point remains open. The cases referred to above are not ones concerned with the Prevention of Crime Act 1953. *Vann* [1996] Crim LR 52 is concerned with a 'have with him' offence, contrary to the FA 1968, s. 19 (and which followed *Hussain* [1981] 1 WLR 416, a possession offence under the FA 1968, s. 1: see **B12.110** and **B12.45**). *Matrix* [1997] Crim LR 901 is concerned with a possession offence contrary to the Protection of Children Act 1978. In both cases, the drugs decision of *Warner v Metropolitan Police Commissioner* [1969] 2 AC 256 (see **B19.28**), is relevant (it is submitted).

B12.165 **Forgetfulness** A person who forgets that the offensive weapon in the person's possession, nevertheless has it with him (*R (Bayliss) v DPP* [2003] EWHC 245 (Admin), reviewing, among other decisions, *McCalla* (1988) 87 Cr App R 372, *Russell* (1985) 81 Cr App R 315, and *Cugullere* [1961] 2 All ER 343: and see *Nicholson* [2006] EWCA Crim 1518, [2006] 1 WLR 2857). However, forgetfulness may be relevant to the issue of whether D had good reason for being in possession of the article (see **B12.170**).

B12.166 **Joint Possession** In *Edmonds* [1963] 2 QB 142, the Court of Appeal held (at pp. 149–50) that, in the case of persons alleged to have acted together to use an article to injure another, the appropriate direction is:

> ... consider the nature of each article and the case of each man individually and separately, and have regard to the circumstances as a whole and the time of day. Are you sure that each man intended to use the article he carried to injure someone? Alternatively, are you satisfied that he was party to a common purpose, with one or more of the others, of using one or more of the articles for inflicting injury upon someone? And, when you consider this alternative, you must first be sure that he knew that one or both of the others had the article which each of them was shown to be carrying.

Meaning of 'Public Place'

Prevention of Crime Act 1953, s. 1 **B12.167**

(4) In this section 'public place' includes any highway and any other premises or place to which at the material time the public have or are permitted to have access, whether on payment or otherwise...

Whether somewhere is a 'public place' is a question of fact; but whether it is capable of being such a place is a question of law (*Hanrahan* [2004] EWCA Crim 2943). In *Knox v Anderton* (1982) 76 Cr App R 156 the Divisional Court concluded that the upper landing of a block of flats, which could be reached without hindrance, was a 'public place', as there were no barriers or notices restricting access. By contrast, in *Williams v DPP* (1992) 95 Cr App R 415, the landing of a block of flats, to which access could be gained only by way of key, security code, tenants' intercom or caretaker, was not a 'public place' for the purposes of the CJA 1967, s. 91 (being drunk and disorderly, see **B11.198**), because only those admitted by or with the implied consent of the occupiers of the block of flats had access. See also **B11.54**.

B Part B Offences

Lawful Authority or Reasonable Excuse: the Burden of Proof

It is important to note that '[the] Act of 1953 is meant to deal with a person who goes out with an offensive weapon, it may be a cosh or a knife, without any reasonable excuse' (per Lord Goddard CJ in *Jura* [1954] 1 QB 503 at p. 506). **B12.168**

The Prevention of Crime Act 1953, s. 1(1) (see **B12.144**), lays the burden of proving either lawful authority or reasonable excuse upon D, but only when the possession of an offensive weapon has been established (*Petrie* [1961] 1 All ER 466). If the weapon is either made or adapted to be offensive, the prosecution must prove no more than simple possession of the article, whereas with the third category of offensive weapons (see **B12.148**) the prosecution must prove the requisite intent before the burden passes to D to prove either lawful authority or reasonable excuse.

The standard of proof required to establish a lawful authority or reasonable excuse is on a balance of probability and not beyond a reasonable doubt (*Brown* (1971) 55 Cr App R 478). See generally **F3.9** and **F3.53**. As to whether the imposition of the legal burden on D is open to challenge in the light of the human rights cases, consider *L v DPP* [2001] EWHC Admin 882, [2003] QB 137 (see **B12.182**) where it was held that in the context of the CJA 1988, s. 139(4), the reverse onus was permitted under the ECHR, Article 6(2).

Lawful Authority

The Divisional Court said in *Bryan v Mott* (1975) 62 Cr App R 71 at p. 73: **B12.169**

> The reference to lawful authority in the section is a reference to those people who from time to time carry an offensive weapon as a matter of duty — the soldier and his rifle and the police officer with his truncheon.

Private security guards do not have explicit lawful authority to carry, for example, a truncheon. They have neither a statutory power, nor a duty, to do so (*Bryan v Mott*). Any contractual duty would be irrelevant (*Spanner* [1973] Crim LR 704). Such a person may have a reasonable excuse (*Malnik v DPP* [1989] Crim LR 451) (see **B12.170**).

Reasonable Excuse

The issue of reasonable excuse should be determined only after a finding that the item is offensive *per se* or that D had an intention to cause injury at the material time (*Sundas* [2011] EWCA Crim 985). **B12.170**

In *Densu* [1998] 1 Cr App R 400, the Court of Appeal held that 'the cases where the defence of reasonable excuse will be available are restricted' and that the defence arises only once it is proved that D is in possession of an offensive weapon (e.g., an offensive weapon *per se* such as a truncheon). In *Densu* the Court of Appeal referred to an example provided by May LJ in *McCalla* (1988) 87 Cr App R 372, that might amount to a reasonable excuse:

> ... if someone driving along a road where earlier there had been a demonstration were to see and pick up a police truncheon which had obviously been dropped there and were to put it into the boot of his car, intending to take it to the nearest police station, and then were to be stopped within a few minutes, he would have a reasonable excuse for having the truncheon with him in the boot of the car.

It was said in *Garry v CPS* [2019] EWHC 636 (Admin), [2019] 1 WLR 3630, that whether the defence of reasonable excuse is made out depends on the facts of the case, in which regard the fact-finding tribunal enjoys a wide discretion. An innocent purpose for having an offensive weapon in a public place does not equate to a reasonable excuse. The court is entitled to consider necessity or immediate temporal connection between possession of the weapon and the purpose for which it was carried (at [16]). Proof that the weapon was for use at work is not dispositive of reasonable excuse. In many instances, when D proves use of the item for work, reasonableness of that use would not arise. That said, conclusive proof of a habit of using the weapon for work might prompt review of whether that use was reasonable (at [17]). One question for fact-finders is whether D's assertion that the weapon was used for work is credible.

In *Southwell v Chadwick* (1986) 85 Cr App R 235, the Court of Appeal accepted that, even if a machete knife in its scabbard and a catapult for use for killing grey squirrels were offensive *per se* (though they were not on the facts of that case), D had a reasonable excuse, namely to obtain food for his wild birds which he kept under licence.

In *DPP v Patterson* [2004] EWHC 2744 (Admin), the Divisional Court held that the magistrates were entitled to come to the conclusion that the excuse advanced by P, that he required the butterfly knife (offensive *per se*) to cut open feed for a horse and cut open bales of straw or hay, was capable of being a reasonable excuse on the facts of that case. The Court rejected the submission on behalf of the DPP that *Densu* is authority for the proposition that any factor relied on by D, which by its nature does not necessarily involve the possibility of the need for self-defence, is incapable of being a reasonable excuse for possession of a weapon offensive *per se*. There is nothing to suggest that the words 'reasonable excuse' should be fettered in that way. It was remarked in *N v DPP* [2011] EWHC 1807 (Admin) that there is no authority for the proposition that reasonable excuse should be determined subjectively: 'When a defendant claims that he had a reasonable excuse for possession of an offensive weapon because he believed he was at risk of imminent attack, it is for him to prove both the belief and the reasonableness of the belief on a balance of probabilities', per Supperstone J at [32]). Note **B12.183**, and the commentary to *Clancy* at [2012] Crim LR 548. However, when paras. 31 and 32 of the judgment in *N v DPP* are read together, it is clear (it is submitted) that the Court meant no more than that a reasonable excuse cannot be determined solely subjectively but that regard must be had to all the circumstances of the case (*Clancy* [2012] EWCA Crim 8, [2012] 2 Cr App R 7 (71) at [18]).

B12.171 **Self-defence** In *Evans and Hughes* [1972] 3 All ER 412, Lord Widgery CJ made the following statement of principle: '... it may be a reasonable excuse for the carrying of an offensive weapon that the carrier is in anticipation of imminent attack and is carrying it for his own personal defence'. Accordingly, the carrying of a weapon as a general precaution is insufficient to establish a reasonable excuse (*Evans v Hughes*, following *Evans v Wright* [1964] Crim LR 466 and *Grieve v Macleod* [1967] Crim LR 424), and this view has been confirmed by the Court of Appeal in *Densu* [1998] 1 Cr App R 400 (see also *Peacock* [1973] Crim LR 639; *Bradley v Moss* [1974] Crim LR 430; *Bryan v Mott* (1975) 62 Cr App R 71). In *N v DPP* [2011] EWHC 1807 (Admin), the Divisional Court rejected the submission that *Evans v Hughes* provides explicit guidance as to what lapse in time would be permissible when assessing whether D was in anticipation of imminent attack. The correct approach had been stated by Keene LJ in *McAuley* [2009] EWCA Crim 2130, [2010] 1 Cr App R 11 (148) at [13], namely: 'The reference in *Evans v Hughes* to "imminent attack" does not write those words into the statute and it remains for a jury to determine how imminent, how soon, how likely and how serious the anticipated attack has to be to constitute a good reason for possession of the bladed article'.

Ordinarily, one cannot legitimately arm oneself with an offensive weapon with which to repel unlawful violence when one has deliberately and knowingly brought about the situation in which such violence was liable to be inflicted (*Malnik v DPP* [1989] Crim LR 451, per Bingham LJ). Bingham LJ added that the position was quite different in the case of those to whom society has entrusted the responsibility for enforcing the law, and indeed there is a difference in the case of those such as security guards who are handling valuable property in the course of their ordinary occupation and have reason to fear attack.

Theatrical Occasions and Fancy Dress Where a weapon offensive *per se* was carried merely as theatrical property as part and parcel of fancy dress worn by a person going to or from a fancy dress party, the Court of Appeal accepted that the innocent motive could amount to a reasonable excuse (*Houghton v Chief Constable of Greater Manchester* (1987) 84 Cr App R 319). D (a former police officer) was dressed in a police uniform and carrying a truncheon. **B12.172**

Forgetfulness as 'Reasonable Excuse' Whereas the Prevention of Crime Act 1953, s. 1, employs the expression 'reasonable excuse', the CJA 1988, s. 139(4), provides a defence of 'good reason' (see **B12.182**). In *Jolie* [2003] EWCA Crim 1543, [2004] 1 Cr App R 3 (44), the Court of Appeal did not regard the distinction to be 'significant' (at [18]); and see *Clancy* [2012] EWCA Crim 8, [2012] 1 WLR 2536 (at [15]). Indeed, the same judicial decisions tend to be cited and discussed in respect of each expression. However, Professor Sir John Smith pointed out ([1998] Crim LR 347) that the defence in the CJA 1988 was intended to be a narrower one than that of reasonable excuse in the Prevention of Crime Act 1953 (see **B12.168**; and the discussion in *Smith v Shanks* [2014] HCJAC 25, 2014 SLT 626). **B12.173**

The issue of forgetfulness may have relevance in respect of two matters. First, as to whether or not D had the article 'with him' in a public place and, secondly, as to whether or not D's forgetfulness constitutes (or is capable of constituting) a defence of 'reasonable excuse' or 'good reason' (as the case may be). Different considerations apply to each matter. As to the former, see **B12.162** to **B12.165**. With respect to the latter, it is submitted that the relevant principles were correctly summarised by the Court of Appeal in *Tsap* [2008] EWCA Crim 2679 (at [21]):

(a) Mere forgetfulness that D has an offensive weapon with him cannot of itself provide a 'reasonable excuse' (or 'good reason') for having it (*Manning* [1998] Crim LR 198 (at [8]–[9]); *Hargreaves* [1999] EWCA Crim J0730).
(b) But, forgetfulness may be relevant as part of a wider set of circumstances relied upon as providing a 'reasonable excuse' (or 'good reason') (*McCalla* (1988) 87 Cr App R 372, at p. 379; *Glidewell* (1999) 163 JP 557).
(c) Each case depends on its own circumstances as to whether forgetfulness may afford D a defence (consider *Gregson* (1992) 96 Cr App R 240).
(d) Where matters go beyond mere forgetfulness, the issue of whether the defence is made out would normally (or almost invariably, *Ivey* [2000] EWCA Crim J0815) be left to the jury to decide.
(e) Cases may arise where a defence is based on more than mere forgetfulness, but the judge would be entitled to direct the jury that the evidence does not support a finding of 'reasonable excuse' (or 'good reason'). However, consider *Asmeron* [2013] EWCA Crim 435, [2013] 1 WLR 3457, and noting *Wang* [2005] UKHL 9, [2005] 2 Cr App R 8 (136).

Factors causing forgetfulness such as an illness or the taking of medication would be relevant (*Tsap* [2008] EWCA Crim 2679).

In *Hilton v Canterbury Crown Court* [2009] EWHC 2867 (Admin), D was entitled to have his defence considered and ruled upon, namely, that he had taken a knife from a friend in order to prevent something potentially dangerous occurring, that he had no realistic or reasonable opportunity to get rid of the knife, and thereafter had forgotten that he had the knife with him.

In *Glidewell* (1999) 163 JP 557 (a case decided under the PCA 1953) the fact that D did not introduce the weapons into his car; that the weapons had been in the car for a relatively short period of time, and that D was very busy on the night in question, all bore on the question of forgetfulness, and were matters for the jury to consider.

In *Ivey* [2000] EWCA Crim J0815, where forgetfulness was relevant to the reasonable excuse that D had put the knife in his pocket as part of moving his possessions from one house to another (the knife having been bought as an ornament) and he had had his possessions in his car for two weeks and had forgotten about the knife. See also *Lorimer* [2003] EWCA Crim 721.

In *Chahal v DPP* [2010] EWHC 439 (Admin), [2010] 2 Cr App R 5 (33), D's conviction for being in possession of a bladed article (a knife) in a public place was quashed because the magistrates erroneously regarded the 'casual' nature of D's work (at his uncle's factory) to be a relevant consideration. D claimed that he had forgotten about the knife after leaving the factory.

If D has what might be a good reason for possession of the item (e.g., a knife used regularly at work in a restaurant), that matter should be considered by the tribunal of fact, and if D had forgotten possessing the item, that is a factor in deciding whether D did have 'good reason' for possessing it (*Bird* [2004] EWCA Crim 964).

THREATENING WITH WEAPON IN PUBLIC

B12.174 **Prevention of Crime Act 1953, s. 1A**

(1) A person is guilty of an offence if that person—
  (a) has an offensive weapon with him or her in a public place,
  (b) unlawfully and intentionally threatens another person with the weapon, and
  (c) does so in such a way that there is an immediate risk of serious physical harm to that other person.

(2) For the purposes of this section physical harm is serious if it amounts to grievous bodily harm for the purposes of the Offences against the Person Act 1861.

Procedure and Sentence

B12.175 The offence under the Prevention of Crime Act 1953, s. 1A, is triable either way. On conviction on indictment, the maximum penalty is four years' imprisonment, a fine or both; on summary conviction, the maximum penalty is six months' imprisonment and/or an unlimited fine (s. 1A(4)). The Sentencing Council definitive guideline, *Bladed Articles and Offensive Weapons* (see Supplement, **SG14-1**), applies in relation to offenders sentenced on or after 1 June 2018, irrespective of the date of the offence. There are separate guidelines for offenders aged 18 and over, and for children and young people.

Where a person aged 16 or over is convicted of an offence under s. 1A, the court must impose a minimum custodial sentence (with or without a fine) unless the court is of the opinion that there are particular circumstances which relate to the offence or to the offender and which would make it unjust to do so in all the circumstances (s. 1A(5)). The minimum sentence in the case of an offender aged 16 or 17 when convicted is a detention and training order for four months, and the minimum sentence in the case of an offender aged 18 or over when convicted is imprisonment or detention in a young offender institution for six months (see **E5.17**).

Simple possession of an offensive weapon (under s. 1 of the 1953 Act) is an alternative verdict to a charge under s. 1A (s. 1A(10)).

Elements

Physical harm is 'serious' for the purposes of s. 1A if it amounts to grievous bodily harm for the purposes of the Offences against the Person Act 1861 (s. 1A(2)). For the meaning of grievous bodily harm, see **B2.67**. The terms 'offensive weapon' and 'public place' have the same meaning as in s. 1 (see **B12.148** *et seq*. and **B12.161**). **B12.176**

HAVING ARTICLE WITH BLADE OR POINT IN A PUBLIC PLACE

It is an offence triable either way, contrary to the CJA 1988, s. 139(1), for a person to have with him in a public place an article to which the section applies. **B12.177**

Criminal Justice Act 1988, s. 139

(1) Subject to subsections (4) and (5) below, any person who has an article to which this section applies with him in a public place shall be guilty of an offence.
(2) Subject to subsection (3) below, this section applies to any article which has a blade or is sharply pointed except a folding pocket knife.
(3) This section applies to a folding pocket knife if the cutting edge of its blade exceeds 3 inches.
(4) It shall be a defence for a person charged with an offence under this section to prove that he had good reason or lawful authority for having the article with him in a public place.
(5) Without prejudice to the generality of subsection (4) above, it shall be a defence for a person charged with an offence under this section to prove that he had the article with him—
   (a) for use at work;
   (b) for religious reasons; or
   (c) as part of any national costume.

...

(7) In this section 'public place' includes any place to which at the material time the public have or are permitted access, whether on payment or otherwise.

It was held by the Court of Appeal in *D* [2019] EWCA Crim 45, [2019] 1 Cr App R 33 (482) that, for the purposes of CJA 1988, s. 139, a pocketknife is not an apt description of a cut-throat razor.

Procedure and Sentence

The offence is punishable, on summary conviction, with a term of imprisonment not exceeding six months and/or an unlimited fine and, on conviction on indictment, a term of imprisonment not exceeding four years or a fine or both (CJA 1988, s. 139(6)). By virtue of s. 139(6A) to (6G), special provisions apply in respect of repeat offences committed after that date. See **B12.147** for comparable provisions and see **E5.19**. The Sentencing Council definitive guideline *Bladed Articles and Offensive Weapons* (see Supplement, **SG14-1**), applies in relation to offenders sentenced on or after 1 June 2018, irrespective of the date of the offence. There are separate guidelines for offenders aged 18 and over, and for children and young people. **B12.178**

Articles and 'Has with Him'

Section 139 covers any article which has a blade or is sharply pointed except 'a folding pocket knife'. A folding pocket knife is covered if the cutting edge of its blade exceeds three inches. **B12.179**

It was held in *Szewczyk* [2019] EWCA Crim 1811, [2020] 1 WLR 492, that the relevant article under s. 139 of the 1988 Act is not required to be either inherently offensive *per se,* nor carried with any offensive intent. For the *actus reus* of the offence to be made out, the article must simply conform to the description in the section (at [12]). The context of this provision and the Prevention of Crime Act 1953 differs (at [19]). The *actus reus* of the offence under s. 139 of the 1988 Act is established if D had a 'bladed article' with him in a public place, albeit for a short time.

If a knife is secured in the open position by a locking device, it is not 'a folding pocket knife' because it is not immediately foldable at all times by virtue of the folding process (*Harris v DPP* (1992) 96 Cr App R 235, and see *Fehmi v DPP* (1992) 96 Cr App R 235). *Harris* was followed in *Deegan* [1998] 2 Cr App R 121, where a challenge to the established meaning on the basis of what ministers said in *Hansard* was rejected because their statements lacked clarity. The Divisional Court held in *Sharma v DPP* [2018] EWHC 3330 (Admin) that the interpretation that has been given to the expression 'folding pocketknife' in the case law (citing *Harris v DPP* (1992) 96 Cr App R 235 and *Deegan* [1998] 2 Cr App R 121) is clear and straightforward and turns on whether the blade of the knife was immediately foldable at all times simply by applying pressure to the blade.

Determining whether an article falls within the CJA 1988, s. 139, is a matter of law for the judge to decide (*Davis* [1998] Crim LR 564). There is no room for applying the decision in *Brutus v Cozens* [1973] AC 854, because the 'issue was not the simple etymological meaning of the word "blade" '. The test is not whether the article is capable of causing injury, because the offence is limited to articles which 'happen to have something that could be described as a blade'. A common-sense test is to be applied, namely, that the article must be 'within the same broad category as a knife or a sharply pointed instrument'. Thus a screwdriver does not fall within s. 139, but cf. *Manning* [1998] Crim LR 198. The item need not be sharp but it must have a blade; therefore a blunt butter knife came within s. 139 (*Brooker v DPP* [2005] EWHC 1132 (Admin)). In *Docherty* [2014] EWCA Crim 1969, it was held that the trial judge had been wrong to direct the jury that they did not have to be sure of the nature of the knife in question. Its nature was important because, if it was a folding pocket knife, no offence was committed unless the cutting edge of the blade was more than three inches in length.

For the meaning of 'has with him', see **B12.162**.

Public Place

B12.180 'Public place' includes any place to which, at the material time, the public have or are permitted access, whether on payment or otherwise (s. 139(7)). In *Roberts* [2003] EWCA Crim 2753, [2004] 1 WLR 181, the Court of Appeal held that it did not include land adjacent to that to which the public had access. Unimpeded access to a place does not necessarily make it a public place; it must be determined whether public access was implied or tolerated (*Harriott v DPP* [2005] EWHC 965 (Admin)).

Defences

B12.181 Two defences are created by the CJA 1988, s. 139(4) and (5).

B12.182 **Good Reason or Lawful Authority (s. 139(4))** It is a defence for D to prove that there was good reason or lawful authority for having the article with him in a public place. D must prove the good reason on a balance of probabilities so that merely providing an uncontradicted explanation is not necessarily sufficient (*Godwin v DPP* (1993) 96 Cr App R 244). Having considered the effect of *Lambert* [2001] UKHL 37, [2002] 2 AC 545 (see **F3.9**), the Divisional Court in *L v DPP* [2001] EWHC Admin 882, [2003] QB 137 held that the reverse onus provision in s. 139 did not breach the ECHR, Article 6, as the prosecution have to prove that D knows that the relevant article was in his possession. Further, there is a strong public interest in bladed articles not being carried in public without good reason and, taking into account Parliament's decision, this requirement was not an improper infringement of rights. *L v DPP* was applied in *Matthews* [2003] EWCA Crim 813, [2004] QB 690.

The 'good reason' must relate to both D having the bladed article and having it with him in a public place (consider *Mohammed v Chief Constable of South Yorkshire Police* [2002] EWHC

406 (Admin) where the Divisional Court followed the approach in *Brutus v Cozens* [1973] AC 854 (see **B12.179**): and see *Deegan* [1998] 2 Cr App R 121).

In *Emmanuel* [1998] Crim LR 347, the Court of Appeal held that 'good reason' includes self-defence.

It was said in *Bown* [2003] EWCA Crim 1989, [2004] 1 Cr App R 13 (151), that it is for the judge to determine whether the explanation is capable of amounting to a good reason and, if it is so capable, it is for the jury to determine whether it did so amount. It was held that in some cases, a judge may be justified in ruling that certain facts are incapable of constituting a good reason, but should be slow to do so. The Court of Appeal remarked that the words in s. 139(4) are ordinary words of the English language. **B12.183**

In *Clancy* [2012] EWCA Crim 8, [2012] 2 Cr App R 7 (71), the Court of Appeal held (with regard, in particular, to *Manning* [1998] Crim LR 198, and *Jolie* [2003] EWCA Crim 1543, [2004] 1 Cr App R 3 (44)) that the expression 'good reason' is not one that calls for judicial explanation and thus it would be wrong for judges to hedge that expression 'with rules of law designed to limit its scope or meaning' (per Moore-Bick LJ). However, in *Asmeron* [2013] EWCA Crim 435, [2013] 1 WLR 3457, the Court of Appeal opined (at [22]) that *Clancy* was decided *per incuriam* in this respect because it is contrary to *Wang* [2005] UKHL 9, [2005] 1 All ER 782.

> The fact that a defence might be considered hopeless on the merits is not a good reason for a judge to withdraw it from the jury. The court can only rule that the explanation advanced by a defendant is incapable in law of amounting to a good reason or a reasonable excuse if it can properly be said, on the true construction of the Act, that it would be inconsistent with the essential nature and purpose of the offence for the defendant's explanation to be capable of amounting to a defence.

A fear of attack can constitute a 'good reason' within the meaning of s. 139(4): state of mind is not wholly irrelevant.

In *Giles* [2003] EWCA Crim 1287, it was held not to be sufficient that, in the case of a blade satisfying s. 139, D thought that he might use part of it, say the corkscrew. Self-harm appears not to be a 'good reason' (*Bown*). In *McAuley* [2009] EWCA Crim 2130, [2010] 1 Cr App R 11 (148), it was held that it could amount to a 'good reason' under s. 139(4) if D was carrying the knife for his own protection and could show on the balance of probabilities that he was in fear of an imminent attack. The Court of Appeal added (at [15]) that it remains for a jury to determine 'how imminent, how soon, how likely and how serious' the anticipated attack has to be to constitute a good reason for possession of the bladed article. It advised that 'it would normally be wise in such cases for a judge not to rule before hearing the evidence, because that evidence may turn out to be to some extent different from and certainly more detailed than that suggested in the documents' (such as the Defence Statement).

Forgetfulness In *R (Bayliss) v DPP* [2003] EWHC 245 (Admin), the Divisional Court accepted that there may be circumstances where forgetfulness is relevant to the defence of good reason (see **B12.173**), but it is not relevant to having the weapon with him (as to which see **B12.162**). **B12.184**

Religious Reasons, Work, National Costume (s. 139(5)) It is a defence for D to prove that he had the article with him for use at work, or for religious reasons, or as part of any national costume. Whether an article was for use for work (and therefore the other purposes also) is a matter to be determined in accordance with the approach in *Brutus v Cozens* [1973] AC 854 (see **B12.179**), as the statute uses words of the ordinary English language. It is a matter for the jury to determine having been so directed by the judge (*Manning* [1998] Crim LR 198). **B12.185**

In *Wang* [2005] UKHL 9, [2005] 1 All ER 782, D carried a bag which contained a curved martial arts sword, in its sheath. D claimed that he was a Buddhist and that he practised Shaolin, and that the knife was of a kind in which a Shaolin follower must become expert. The House of Lords held that had the trial judge directed the jury in the ordinary way, it seemed very likely that they would have convicted. However, the nature and extent of D's religious motivation had been the subject of evidence and his claim that he did not want to leave the weapon at home, with no one looking after it, was pre-eminently a matter for the jury.

ARTICLES AND OFFENSIVE WEAPONS ON SCHOOL [EDUCATION] PREMISES

Having Article with Blade or Point on School [Education] Premises

B12.186 It is an offence triable either way, contrary to the CJA 1988, s. 139A(1), for a person to have an article to which s. 139 applies (see **B12.177**) with him on school or further education premises. The words in square brackets are inserted by the Offensive Weapons Act 2019, s. 45, with effect from a day to be appointed. Section 45 will also substitute a revised subsection (6) and insert subsection (6A): neither provision is reproduced here.

Criminal Justice Act 1988, s. 139A

(1) Any person who has an article to which section 139 of this Act applies with him on school premises [or further education premises] shall be guilty of an offence.

(2) Any person who has an offensive weapon within the meaning of section 1 of the Prevention of Crime Act 1953 with him on school premises [or further education premises] shall be guilty of an offence.

(3) It shall be a defence for a person charged with an offence under subsection (1) or (2) above to prove that he had good reason or lawful authority for having the article or weapon with him on the premises in question.

(4) Without prejudice to the generality of subsection (3) above, it shall be a defence for a person charged with an offence under subsection (1) or (2) above to prove that he had the article or weapon in question with him—

(a) for use at work;
(b) for educational purposes,
(c) for religious reasons; or
(d) as part of any national costume.

...

(6) In this section and section 139B, 'school premises' means land used for the purposes of a school excluding any land occupied solely as a dwelling by a person employed at the school; and 'school' has the meaning given by section 4 of the Education Act 1996.

B12.187 **Procedure and Sentence** The offence is triable either way. It is punishable, on summary conviction, with a term of imprisonment not exceeding six months and/or an unlimited fine and, on conviction on indictment, a term of imprisonment not exceeding four years or a fine or both (CJA 1988, s. 139A(5)). By virtue of s. 139A(5A) to (5G), inserted by the CJCA 2015, s. 28, and having effect from 17 July 2015 (SI 2015 No. 778), special provisions apply in respect of repeat offences committed after that date. See **B12.147** for comparable provision and see **E5.19**. The Sentencing Council definitive guideline, *Bladed Articles and Offensive Weapons* (see Supplement, **SG14-1**), applies in relation to offenders sentenced on or after 1 June 2018, irrespective of the date of the offence. There are separate guidelines for offenders aged 18 and over, and for children and young people.

B12.188 **Elements** 'Has with him' will be understood in the same way as under the Prevention of Crime Act 1953 (see **B12.162**).

The Education Act 1996, s. 4(1), defines 'school'.

B12.189 It is a defence for D to prove that there was good reason or lawful authority for having the *article with him on the premises in question* (s. 139A(3)); as to lawful authority, see **B12.169** and **B12.170**. It is also a defence for D to prove that he had the article with him for use at work, for educational purposes, for religious reasons, or as part of any national costume (s. 139A(4)).

The imposition of a legal burden upon D is open to challenge in the light of the human rights cases on the 'reverse burden' (see **F3.18** but note **B12.181** to **B12.184**).

Power of Search and Seizure Under the CJA 1988, s. 139B, a constable has a power of entry to school premises (or, if s. 45(1) and (8) of the Offensive Weapons Act 2019 come into force, 'further education premises') to search the premises and any person on them for any article to which s. 139 applies or for any offensive weapon within the meaning of the Prevention of Crime Act 1953, s. 1, if the constable has reasonable grounds for suspecting that an offence under the CJA 1988, s. 139A or s. 139AA, is being or has been committed. If the constable finds any article which it is reasonable to suspect may be such an article, the constable may seize and retain it. Reasonable force may be used, if necessary. **B12.190**

For powers of search and seizure at schools, see **B12.4**.

Having Offensive Weapon on School Premises

It is an offence triable either way, contrary to the CJA 1988, s. 139A(2), for a person to have an offensive weapon as defined in the Prevention of Crime Act 1953 (see **B12.148** to **B12.161**) with him on school premises (or, if s. 45(1) and (4) of the Offensive Weapons Act 2019 come into force, 'further education premises'). 'Has with him' will be understood in the same way as under the Prevention of Crime Act 1953 (see **B12.162**). As to the meaning of 'school premises' and 'school' (and, if s. 45(1) and (7) of the Offensive Weapons Act 2019 come into force, 'further education premises'), see **B12.186**. It is punishable, on summary conviction, with a term of imprisonment not exceeding six months and/or an unlimited fine and, on conviction on indictment, to a term of imprisonment not exceeding four years or a fine or both (CJA 1988, s. 139A(5)(b)). The same defences as for the offence contrary to s. 139A(1) apply to this offence see **B12.186**). For the power of entry and search see **B12.190**. **B12.191**

THREATENING WITH ARTICLE WITH BLADE OR POINT OR OFFENSIVE WEAPON

Criminal Justice Act 1988, s. 139AA **B12.192**

(1) A person is guilty of an offence if that person—
- (a) has an article to which this section applies with him or her in a public place or on school premises,
- (b) unlawfully and intentionally threatens another person [('A')] with the article, and
- (c) does so in such a way that there is an immediate risk of serious physical harm to that other person. [does so in such a way that a reasonable person ('B') who was exposed to the same threat as A would think that there was an immediate risk of physical harm to B]

The Offensive Weapons Act 2019, s. 50(4), will amend subsection (1)(b) and replace subsection (1)(c) from a day to be appointed. The new text is shown in square brackets.

Procedure and Sentence

The offence under the CJA 1988, s. 139AA, is triable either way. On conviction on indictment, the maximum penalty is four years' imprisonment and/or a fine; on summary conviction, the maximum penalty is six months' imprisonment and/or an unlimited fine (s. 139AA(6)). The Sentencing Council definitive guideline, *Bladed Articles and Offensive Weapons* (see Supplement, **SG14-1**), applies in relation to offenders sentenced on or after 1 June 2018, irrespective of the date of the offence. There are separate guidelines for offenders aged 18 and over, and for children and young people. **B12.193**

Where a person aged 16 or over is convicted of an offence under s. 139AA, the court must impose a minimum custodial sentence (with or without a fine) unless the court is of the opinion that there are particular circumstances which relate to the offence or to the offender and which would make it unjust to do so in all the circumstances (s. 139AA(7)). The minimum sentence in the case of an offender aged 16 or 17 when convicted is a detention and training order for four months, and the minimum sentence in the case of an offender aged 18 or over when convicted is imprisonment or detention in a young offender institution for six months (see **E5.18**).

Possession of an article with a blade or point or of an offensive weapon (under s. 139 or 139A) is an alternative verdict to a charge under s. 139AA (s. 139AA(12)).

Elements

B12.194 In relation to a 'public place', the CJA 1988, s. 139AA, applies to an article to which s. 139 applies (s. 139AA(2); 'public place' has the same meaning as in s. 139: see **B12.177**). In relation to 'school premises', s. 139AA applies to (a) an article to which s. 139 applies; or (b) an 'offensive weapon' within the meaning of s. 1 of the Prevention of Crime Act 1953 (s. 139AA(3)). 'School premises' has the same meaning as in s. 139A (s. 139AA(5): see **B12.186**. Note that on a day to be appointed, s. 139AA(5) will be substituted by the Offensive Weapons Act 2019, s. 51(1), (4)(b)).

Physical harm is 'serious' for the purposes of s. 139AA if it amounts to grievous bodily harm for the purposes of the OAPA 1861 (s. 139AA(4)). For the meaning of 'grievous bodily harm', see **B2.67**. The term 'offensive weapon' has the same meaning as in the Prevention of Crime Act 1953, s. 1 (see **B12.148** ***et seq.***).

On a day to be appointed, the Offensive Weapons Act 2019, s. 51(2), will insert subsection (1A) into the CJA 1988, s. 139AA, making it an offence if a person:

> (1A) (a) has an article to which this section applies with them on further education premises,
> (b) unlawfully and intentionally threatens another person ('A') with the article, and
> (c) does so in such a way that a reasonable person ('B') who was exposed to the same threat as A would think that there was an immediate risk of physical harm to B.

The Offensive Weapons Act 2019, s. 51(3), will insert subsection (3A) into the CJA 1988, s. 139AA, to provide that:

> (3A) In relation to further education premises this section applies to each of these—
> (a) an article to which section 139 applies;
> (b) an offensive weapon within the meaning of section 1 of the Prevention of Crime Act 1953.

Section 139AA(5) will be amended to define the expression 'further education premises'.

OFFENCE OF THREATENING WITH OFFENSIVE WEAPON OR CORROSIVE SUBSTANCE IN A PRIVATE PLACE

B12.195 From a day to be appointed, it will be an offence contrary to the Offensive Weapons Act 2019, s. 52, for a person, while in a private place, to unlawfully and intentionally threaten another person with an 'article' or 'substance' to which the section applies (namely: (a) an offensive weapon within the meaning of the Prevention of Crime Act 1953, s. 1; (b) an article to which the CJA 1988, s. 139 (offence of having article with blade or point in public place), applies; or (c) a corrosive substance) and there is an immediate risk of serious physical harm to the other person (Offensive Weapons Act 2019, s. 52(2)).

'Private place' is defined by the Offensive Weapons Act 2019, s. 52(3) and (4). By s. 52(5), physical harm is 'serious' if it amounts to grievous bodily harm for the purposes of the OAPA 1861.

Sentence

B12.196 *By the Offensive Weapons Act 2019*, s. 52(6), a person guilty of an offence contrary to s. 52(1) is liable, on summary conviction, to imprisonment for a term not exceeding six months (or 12 months if committed after, and in the event that, s. 154(1) of the CJA 2003 comes into force), or to a fine or to both; or, on conviction on indictment, to imprisonment for a term not exceeding four years, to a fine or to both.

KNIVES OR OFFENSIVE WEAPONS IN PRISON

Under the Prison Act 1952, s. 40CA, a person who, without authorisation (defined by s. 40CA(5)), is in possession of any article inside a prison that has a blade, or is sharply pointed, or any other offensive weapon (as defined in the PACE 1984, s. 1(9), and the Prison Act 1952, s. 40CA(2)), is guilty of an offence (s. 40CA(1)). It is a defence for D to have reasonably believed in having authorisation to be in possession of the article, or that in all the circumstances, there was an overriding public interest which justified D being in possession of the article (s. 40CA(3)). The offence is triable either way. On conviction on indictment, the maximum penalty is four years' imprisonment and/or a fine; on summary conviction, the maximum penalty is six months' imprisonment and/or an unlimited fine (s. 40CA(4)). The Sentencing Council definitive guideline, *Bladed Articles and Offensive Weapons* (see Supplement, **SG14-1**), applies in relation to offenders sentenced on or after 1 June 2018, irrespective of the date of the offence. There are separate guidelines for offenders aged 18 and over, and for children and young people. By virtue of the guideline, the sentence categorisation for having a knife in prison will automatically be 1A, with a starting point for sentence of 18 months' imprisonment and a range to four years. **B12.197**

The circumstances of three pre-guideline cases illustrate the principles involved. In *Isham* [2016] EWCA Crim 831, renewed application for leave to appeal against a sentence of immediate custody of 12 months was refused. D, who was very heavily convicted, including with one previous conviction for possessing a knife in a public place, had barricaded himself into his cell and threatened officers who tried to enter it. D was found to be cutting himself with a razor blade, and an officer was cut on the hand. There was no evidence of brandishing of the blade. The Court of Appeal concluded that D had threatened the officers, and possession of any blade or knife in prison was a matter of serious concern given the closed environment and the potential for violence. In *Alderson* [2017] EWCA Crim 1050, [2017] 2 Cr App R (S) 53 (434), a sentence of 28 months' imprisonment, following early guilty pleas to a s. 40CA offence and one of assault by beating, was upheld on appeal. D, who had five previous convictions for 20 offences including 12 offences of battery, had removed a plastic table knife from the dining area on the wing and taken it into her cell. Later she approached another inmate and slashed at her neck with the plastic knife. Given the material the item was made with, the assault did not break the skin and caused only reddening. Those authorities were reviewed in *Skelton* [2017] EWCA Crim 2071, [2018] 1 Cr App R (S) 46 (351), where it was said that in a case where an improvised weapon was brandished to prison staff to reinforce a demand to be taken from the wing for the prisoner's own protection, a sentence of 21 months after trial was not manifestly excessive. The Court of Appeal indicated that deterrence is particularly vital within the prison context (at [19]):

> Possession of an offensive weapon threatens not only the individual concerned but those who are necessarily in close proximity to him. Tensions can be extremely high and other prisoners can contribute. The danger to prison officers who are to an extent confined within the prison with their charges is particularly acute if one of those charges obtains possession of a potentially lethal weapon. The danger does not just come from the person with the weapon, the vulnerability of prison officers is also from other prisoners who may take advantage of the situation.

POSSESSION OF CROSSBOW BY PERSON UNDER 18

It is a summary offence, contrary to the Crossbows Act 1987, s. 3, for a person under the age of 18 to have with him: (a) a crossbow which is capable of discharging a missile; or (b) parts of a crossbow which together (and without any other parts) can be assembled to form a crossbow **B12.198** capable of discharging a missile, unless the person is under the supervision of a person who is 21 years of age or older. The offence does not apply to crossbows with a draw weight of less than 1.4 kilograms (s. 5). A person guilty of the offence is liable to a fine not exceeding level 3 on the standard scale. The court may also make such order as it thinks fit as to the forfeiture or disposal of any crossbow or part of a crossbow in respect of which the offence was committed (s. 6). For other offences under the 1987 Act, see **B12.199** and **B12.207**.

For offences by trespassers on premises carrying weapons, see **B13.83** and **B13.84**.

Note that if ss. 31 and 70(1) of the Offensive Weapons Act 2019 come into force, the 1987 Act may be enforced by the local weights and measures authority within its area.

MANUFACTURE, SALE, HIRE AND PURCHASE OF WEAPONS

B12.199 There are four summary offences concerned with the manufacture etc. of various types of weapons generally:

(a) manufacture, sale or hire etc. of dangerous weapons, contrary to the Restriction of Offensive Weapons Act 1959, s. 1(1): **B12.200**;
(b) manufacture, sale and hire of offensive weapons, contrary to the CJA 1988, s. 141(1): **B12.201**;
(c) sale and letting on hire of a crossbow to a person under 18, contrary to the Crossbows Act 1987, s. 1: **B12.207**;
(d) purchase and hiring of a crossbow by a person under 18, contrary to the Crossbows Act 1987, s. 2: **B12.207**.

In addition to these offences, there are certain offences of a similar nature which relate only to knives (see **B12.208** ***et seq.***).

Note that the Policing and Crime Act 2009, s. 102 (not yet in force), inserts new ss. 141ZB to 141ZD into the CJA 1988, which prohibit the importation of offensive weapons subject to specified exceptions. Section 141(4) of the CJA 1988, which currently prohibits such importation, and related provisions will be repealed (see the Policing and Crime Act 2009, sch. 8, part 10).

Manufacture, Sale or Hire etc. of Dangerous Weapons

B12.200 **Restriction of Offensive Weapons Act 1959, s. 1**

(1) Any person who manufactures, sells or hires or offers for sale or hire or exposes or has in his possession for the purposes of sale or hire, or lends or gives to any other person—
  (a) any knife which has a blade which opens automatically by hand pressure applied to a button, spring or other device in or attached to the handle of the knife, sometimes known as a 'flick-knife' or 'flick gun'; or
  (b) any knife which has a blade which is released from the handle or sheath thereof by the force of gravity or the application of centrifugal force and which, when released, is locked in place by means of a button, spring, lever, or other device, sometimes known as a 'gravity knife',

shall be guilty of an offence and shall be liable on summary conviction to imprisonment for a term not exceeding six months or to [an unlimited fine] or to both such imprisonment and fine.

On a day to be appointed, the Offensive Weapons Act 2019, s. 43(1), will amend s. 1(a) of the 1959 Act to read:

(a) any knife which has a blade which opens automatically—
  (i) from the closed position to the fully opened position, or
  (ii) from a partially opened position to the fully opened position, by manual pressure applied to a button, spring or other device in or attached to the knife, and which is sometimes known as a 'flick knife' or 'flick gun'; or

On a day to be appointed, the Offensive Weapons Act 2019, s. 44, will insert three new subsections into the Restriction of Offensive Weapons Act 1959, s. 1:

(1A) Any person who possesses any knife of a kind described in subsection (1) is guilty of an offence.
(1B) A person guilty of an offence under subsection (1A) is liable—
 (a) on summary conviction in England and Wales, to imprisonment for a term not exceeding 51 weeks, to a fine or to both;
 (b) [Scotland.]
(1C) In relation to an offence committed before the coming into force of section 281(5) of the Criminal Justice Act 2003, subsection (1B)(a) has effect as if the reference to 51 weeks were to 6 months.

On a day to be appointed, the Offensive Weapons Act 2019, s. 44, will insert subsections (3) to (8) into the Restriction of Offensive Weapons Act 1959, s. 1, to provide further defences:

(3) It is a defence for a person charged in respect of any conduct of that person relating to a knife of a kind described in subsection (1)—
 (a) with an offence under subsection (1), or
 (b) with an offence under section 50(2) or (3) of the Customs and Excise Management Act 1979,
 to show that the conduct was only for the purposes of making the knife available to a museum or gallery to which this subsection applies.
(4) It is a defence for a person charged with an offence under subsection (1A) to show that they possessed the knife only in their capacity as the operator of, or as a person acting on behalf of, a museum or gallery.
(5) If the operator of, or a person acting on behalf of, a museum or gallery to which this subsection applies is charged with hiring or lending a knife of a kind described in subsection (1), it is a defence for them to show that they had reasonable grounds for believing that the person to whom they lent or hired it would use it only for cultural, artistic or educational purposes.
(6) Subsection (3) or (5) applies to a museum or gallery only if it does not distribute profits.
(7) In this section 'museum or gallery' includes any institution which has as its purpose, or one of its purposes, the preservation, display and interpretation of material of historical, artistic or scientific interest and gives the public access to it.
(8) A person is to be taken to have shown a matter mentioned in subsection (3), (4) or (5) if—
 (a) sufficient evidence of the matter is adduced to raise an issue with respect to it, and
 (b) the contrary is not proved beyond reasonable doubt.

In addition, the Restriction of Offensive Weapons Act 1959, s. 1(2), prohibits the importation of any such knife described in s. 1(1).

Manufacture, Sale and Hire of Offensive Weapons

Criminal Justice Act 1988, s. 141 **B12.201**

(1) Any person who manufactures, sells or hires or offers for sale or hire, exposes or has in his possession for the purpose of sale or hire, or lends or gives to any other person, a weapon to which this section applies shall be guilty of an offence ...

Subsection (4) also prohibits the importation of a weapon to which this section applies.

By virtue of the CJA 1988, s. 141(1), a person guilty of the offence is liable to imprisonment for a term not exceeding six months and/or an unlimited fine.

Possession of Certain Weapons in Private On a day to be appointed, the Offensive Weapons Act 2019, s. 46, will amend the CJA 1988, s. 141, by inserting subsections (1A) to (1F), making it an offence for a person to possess a weapon to which s. 141 applies in private (i.e., for England and Wales, other than in a public place, or school premises, or further education premises, or a prison: see s. 141(1C)). **B12.202**

Several defences are provided so that it will be a defence to show that the weapon in question is one of historical importance (new s. 141(7A)); or that the person possessed the weapon in question only in the capacity as the operator of, or as a person acting on behalf of, a museum or gallery (new s. 141(8A), or that the person possessed the weapon in question for educational purposes only (new s. 141(11ZA)), or that the person possessed the weapon in question only for one or more of the purposes specified in s. 141(11B) (new s. 141(11AA)).

B12.203 **Sentence** A person who possesses a weapon to which the CJA 1988, s. 141, applies, is liable on summary conviction in England and Wales to imprisonment for a term not exceeding six months (or 51 weeks if committed after, and in the event that, s. 281(5) of the CJA 2003 comes into force), or to a fine, or to both (CJA 1988, s. 141(1A)(a) and (1B), inserted by the Offensive Weapons Act 2019, s. 46(2), with effect from a day to be appointed).

B12.204 **Weapons** The weapons to which s. 141 applies are those listed in the schedule to the Criminal Justice Act 1988 (Offensive Weapons) Order 1988 (SI 1988 No. 2019), which was made under s. 141(2). This makes the following items offensive weapons for the purpose of the instant offence, other than weapons which are antiques.

Criminal Justice Act 1988 (Offensive Weapons) Order 1988 (SI 1988 No. 2019), sch.

1. ...
   (a) a knuckleduster, that is, a band of metal or other hard material worn on one or more fingers, and designed to cause injury, and any weapon incorporating a knuckleduster;
   (b) a swordstick, that is, a hollow walking-stick or cane containing a blade which may be used as a sword;
   (c) the weapon sometimes known as a 'handclaw', being a band of metal or other hard material from which a number of sharp spikes protrude, and worn around the hand;
   (d) the weapon sometimes known as a 'belt buckle knife', being a buckle which incorporates or conceals a knife;
   (e) the weapon sometimes known as a 'push dagger', being a knife the handle of which fits within a clenched fist and the blade of which protrudes from between two fingers;
   (f) the weapon sometimes known as a 'hollow kubotan', being a cylindrical container containing a number of sharp spikes;
   (g) the weapon sometimes known as a 'footclaw', being a bar of metal or other hard material from which a number of sharp spikes protrude, and worn strapped to the foot;
   (h) the weapon sometimes known as a 'shuriken', 'shaken' or 'death star', being a hard non-flexible plate having three or more sharp radiating points and designed to be thrown;
   (i) the weapon sometimes known as a 'balisong' or 'butterfly knife', being a blade enclosed by its handle, which is designed to split down the middle, without the operation of a spring or other mechanical means, to reveal the blade;
   (j) the weapon sometimes known as a 'telescopic truncheon', being a truncheon which extends automatically by hand pressure applied to a button, spring or other device in or attached to its handle;
   (k) the weapon sometimes known as a 'blowpipe' or 'blow gun' being a hollow tube out of which hard pellets or darts are shot by the use of breath;
   (l) the weapon sometimes known as a 'kusari gama', being a length of rope, cord, wire or chain fastened at one end to a sickle;
   (m) the weapon sometimes known as a 'kyoketsu shoge', being a length of rope, cord, wire or chain fastened at one end to a hooked knife;
   (n) the weapon sometimes known as a 'manrikigusari' or 'kusari', being a length of rope, cord, wire or chain fastened at each end to a hard weight or hand grip;
   (o) a disguised knife, that is any knife which has a concealed blade or concealed sharp point and is designed to appear to be an everyday object of a kind commonly carried on the person or in a handbag, briefcase, or other hand luggage (such as a comb, brush, writing instrument, cigarette lighter, key, lipstick or telephone);
   (p) a stealth knife, that is a knife or spike, which has a blade, or sharp point, made from a material that is not readily detectable by apparatus used for detecting metal and which is not designed for domestic use or for use in the processing, preparation or consumption of food or as a toy;
   (q) a straight, side-handled or friction-lock truncheon (sometimes known as a baton);
   (r) a sword with a curved blade of 50 centimetres or over in length; and for the purposes of this sub-paragraph, the length of the blade shall be the straight line distance from the top of the handle to the tip of the blade;

(s) the weapon sometimes known as a 'zombie knife', 'zombie killer knife' or 'zombie slayer knife', being a blade with—
 (i) a cutting edge;
 (ii) a serrated edge; and
 (iii) images or words (whether on the blade or handle) that suggest that it is to be used for the purpose of violence.

[(t) the weapon sometimes known as a 'cyclone knife' or 'spiral knife' being a weapon with—
 (i) a handle,
 (ii) a blade with two or more cutting edges, each of which forms a helix, and
 (iii) a sharp point at the end of the blade.]

When the Offensive Weapons Act 2019, s. 47(3), comes into force, para. 1(t) will be inserted into the schedule to the 1988 Order. As for para. 1(s) in relation to England and Wales, see SI 2016 No. 803.

By virtue of art. 2, a weapon is an antique for the purposes of the schedule if it was manufactured more than 100 years before the date of any offence alleged to have been committed in respect of the weapon (i.e. an offence contrary to the CJA 1988, s. 141(1) or, the Customs and Excise Management Act 1979, s. 50(2) or (3) (improper importation)). B12.205

It is a defence to show that D is:

(a) carrying out functions on behalf of the Crown or a visiting force (CJA 1988, s. 141(5) to (7)); or
(b) making a weapon available to a museum or gallery (s. 141(8), (10) and (11)); or
(c) a person acting on behalf of a museum or gallery loaning or hiring a weapon for proper purposes (s. 141(9));
(d) making the weapon available for theatre, film or television purposes (s. 141(11A) to (11C); SI 2008 No. 791).

Curved Blades: Defences B12.206

Criminal Justice Act 1988 (Offensive Weapons) Order 1988 (SI 1988 No. 2019), paras. 3 to 6

3. It shall be a defence for a person charged—
 (a) with an offence under section 141(1) [or (1A)] of the Criminal Justice Act 1988; or
 (b) with an offence under section 50(2) or (3) of the Customs and Excise Management Act 1979,

 in respect of any conduct of his relating to a weapon to which section 141 of the Criminal Justice Act 1988 applies by virtue of paragraph 1(r) to show that the weapon in question was made before 1954 or was made at any other time according to traditional methods of making swords by hand.

4. [(1)] It shall be a defence for a person charged—
 (a) with an offence under section 141(1) [or (1A)] of the Criminal Justice Act 1988; or
 (b) with an offence under section 50(2) or (3) of the Customs and Excise Management Act 1979,

 in respect of any conduct of his relating to a weapon to which section 141 of the Criminal Justice Act 1988 applies by virtue of paragraph 1(r) to show that his conduct was for the purpose only of making the weapon available for the purposes of the organisation and holding of a permitted activity for which public liability insurance is held in relation to liabilities to third parties arising from or in connection with the organisation and holding of such an activity.

 [(2) It is a defence for a person charged with an offence under section 141(1A) of the Criminal Justice Act 1988 in respect of any conduct of that person relating to a weapon to which section 141 of that Act applies by virtue of paragraph 1(r) to show that the person's conduct was for the purpose only of participating in a permitted activity of a kind mentioned in sub-paragraph (1).]

5. For the purposes of paragraph 4—

 'historical re-enactment' means any presentation or other event held for the purpose of re-enacting an event from the past or of illustrating conduct from a particular time or period in the past;

'insurance' means a contract of insurance or other arrangement made for the purpose of indemnifying a person or persons named in the contract or under the arrangement;
'permitted activity' means an historical re-enactment or a sporting activity;
'sporting activity' means the practising of a sport which requires the use of a weapon described in paragraph 1(r);
'third parties' includes participants in, and spectators of, a permitted activity and members of the public.

5A. [(1)] It shall be a defence for a person charged—
(a) with an offence under section 141(1) [or (1A)] of the Criminal Justice Act 1988; or
(b) with an offence under section 50(2) or (3) of the Customs and Excise Management Act 1979,

in respect of any conduct of his relating to a weapon to which section 141 of the Criminal Justice Act 1988 applies by virtue of paragraph 1(r) to show that his conduct was for the purpose only of making the weapon available for the purposes of use in religious ceremonies [for religious reasons].

[(2) It is a defence for a person charged with an offence under section 141(1A) of the Criminal Justice Act 1988 in respect of a weapon to which section 141 of the Criminal Justice Act 1988 applies by virtue of paragraph 1(r) to show that the person possessed the weapon for religious reasons only.

5B. (1) Sub-paragraph (2) applies to—
(a) a person charged with an offence under section 141(1) or (1A) of the Criminal Justice Act 1988 in respect of any conduct of the person relating to a curved sword, and
(b) a person charged with an offence under section 50(2) or (3) of the Customs and Excise Management Act 1979 in respect of any conduct of the person relating to a curved sword.

(2) It is a defence for the person to show that the person's conduct was for the purpose only of making the sword available for presentation by a Sikh to another person at a religious ceremony or other ceremonial event.

(3) It is a defence for a person charged with an offence under section 141(1) of the Criminal Justice Act 1988 of giving a curved sword to another person to show that the person's conduct consisted of the presentation of the sword by a Sikh to another person at a religious ceremony or other ceremonial event.

(4) It is a defence for a person charged with an offence under section 141(1A) of the Criminal Justice Act 1988 of possession of a curved sword in private to show that—
(a) the person was a Sikh at the time the offence is alleged to have been committed and possessed the sword for the purpose only of presenting it to another person at a religious ceremony or other ceremonial event, or
(b) the sword was presented to the person by a Sikh at a religious ceremony or other ceremonial event.

(5) In this paragraph—
'curved sword' means a weapon to which section 141 of the Criminal Justice Act 1988 applies by virtue of paragraph 1(r);
'Sikh' means a follower of the Sikh religion.]

6. For the purposes of paragraphs 3, 4 and 5A, a person shall be taken to have shown a matter specified in those paragraphs if—
(a) sufficient evidence of that matter is adduced to raise an issue with respect to it; and
(b) the contrary is not proved beyond a reasonable doubt.

Words in square brackets relate to amendments made by the Offensive Weapons Act 2019, s. 47, when in force.

B12.207 **Crossbows** It is an offence to sell or to let on hire a crossbow or a part of a crossbow to a person under the age of 18 (Crossbows Act 1987, s. 1). It is a defence that D believed the person to be 18 years of age or older and had reasonable ground for the belief. The maximum penalty is imprisonment for a term not exceeding six months and/or an unlimited fine.

A person under the age of 18 who buys or hires a crossbow or part of a crossbow is guilty of an offence (s. 2), and liable to a fine not exceeding level 3 on the standard scale. The crossbow or the relevant part may be forfeited or disposed of (s. 6(1) and (3)).

MANUFACTURE, MARKETING, SALE, HIRE AND PURCHASE OF KNIVES

The Offensive Weapons Act 1996, s. 6, created an offence relating to the sale of knives to persons under a specified age. The Knives Act 1997 has created two either-way offences (unlawful marketing of knives and publications in connection with the marketing of knives). All these offences are in addition to the summary offences mentioned at **B12.199**. **B12.208**

Sale of Knives and Certain Articles with Blade or Point to Persons under 18

Criminal Justice Act 1988, s. 141A **B12.209**

(1) ... any person who sells to a person under the age of 18 years an article to which this section applies shall be guilty of an offence and liable on summary conviction to imprisonment for a term not exceeding six months, or [an unlimited fine], or both.

By the CJA 1988, s. 141A(2), the offence applies to any knife, knife blade or razor blade, any axe, and any other article which has a blade or which is sharply pointed and which is made or adapted for use for causing injury to the person.

A grapefruit knife is a knife within the meaning of the CJA 1988, s. 141A, as amended by the Offensive Weapons Act 1996 (*R (Royal Borough of Windsor and Maidenhead) v East Berkshire Justices* [2010] EWHC 3020 (Admin), [2011] 1 Cr App R 21 (270)).

Section 141A does not apply to (a) any article described in the Restriction of Offensive Weapons Act 1959, s. 1 (see **B12.200**), (b) an order made under the CJA 1988, s. 141(2) (see **B12.201**), or (c) any order made under s. 141A itself (s. 141A(3)). As for the latter, see SI 1996 No. 3064, namely:

(a) a folding knife if the cutting edge of its blade does not exceed 7.62 centimetres (3 inches);
(b) razor blades permanently enclosed in a cartridge or housing where less than 2 millimetres of any blade is exposed beyond the place which intersects the highest point of the surfaces preceding and following such blades (Criminal Justice Act 1988 (Offensive Weapons) (Exemptions) Order 1996 (SI 1996 No. 3064), art. 2).

As to articles made or adapted to cause injury under the Prevention of Crime Act 1953, see **B12.158** and **B12.159**. It is a defence for a person charged with the offence to prove that all reasonable precautions were taken and due diligence exercised to avoid the commission of the offence (s. 141A(4)); the imposition of a legal burden upon D is arguably open to challenge in the light of the human rights jurisprudence regarding 'reverse burdens' (see **F3.18**). However, in *Croydon London Borough Council v Pinch A Pound (UK) Ltd* [2010] EWHC 3283 (Admin), [2011] 1 WLR 1189 the Divisional Court held that the statutory defence requires proof of two elements: the taking of all reasonable precautions and the exercise of all due diligence: the defence made available by the Act is couched in ordinary language.

Limitations on Defence to Offence under s. 141A: England and Wales

The Offensive Weapons Act 2019, s. 35(3), inserts a new s. 141B into the CJA 1988 from a day to be appointed: **B12.210**

[(1) This section applies if—
(a) a person ('the seller') is charged with an offence under section 141A (sale of bladed articles to persons under 18), and
(b) the seller was not in the presence of the person ('the buyer') to whom the article to which the charge relates was sold at the time of the sale.

(2) For the purposes of subsection (1)(b) the seller was not in the presence of the buyer at the time of the sale if—
 (a) where the seller is an individual, the seller or a person acting on the seller's behalf was not in the presence of the buyer at that time;
 (b) where the seller is not an individual, a person acting on the seller's behalf was not in the presence of the buyer at that time.
(3) The seller is not to be regarded as having proved that they took all reasonable precautions and exercised all due diligence to avoid the commission of the offence unless, as a minimum, they prove that the following conditions are met.
(4) Condition A is that, at the time the offence is alleged to have been committed—
 (a) the seller operated a system for checking that persons who bought articles to which section 141A applied by the same or a similar method of purchase to that used by the buyer were not under the age of 18, and
 (b) that system was likely to prevent persons under the age of 18 from buying such articles by that method.
(5) Condition B is that when the package containing the article was dispatched by the seller, it was clearly marked to indicate—
 (a) that it contained an article with a blade or which was sharply pointed (as the case may be), and
 (b) that, when finally delivered, it should only be delivered into the hands of a person aged 18 or over.
(6) Condition C is that the seller took all reasonable precautions and exercised all due diligence to ensure that, when finally delivered, the package would be delivered into the hands of a person aged 18 or over.
(7) Condition D is that the seller did not deliver the package, or arrange for its delivery, to a locker.
(8) Where the article to which section 141A applied was dispatched by the seller to a place from which it was to be collected by the buyer or a person acting on behalf of the buyer, references in subsections (5) and (6) to the final delivery of the article are to be read as its supply to the buyer or a person acting on behalf of the buyer from that place.
(9) In subsection (7) 'locker' means a lockable container to which the package was delivered with a view to its collection by the buyer, or a person acting on behalf of the buyer, in accordance with arrangements made between the seller and the buyer.]

Unlawful Marketing of Knives

B12.211 Knives Act 1997, s. 1

(1) A person is guilty of an offence if he markets a knife in a way which—
 (a) indicates, or suggests, that it is suitable for combat; or
 (b) is otherwise likely to stimulate or encourage violent behaviour involving the use of the knife as a weapon.

The offence is triable either way (s. 1(5)). The maximum penalty is: on conviction on indictment, imprisonment for a term not exceeding two years or a fine, or both; on summary conviction, imprisonment for a term not exceeding six months and/or an unlimited fine (s. 1(5)).

Elements

B12.212 'Knife' means an instrument which has a blade or is sharply pointed (s. 10). (Note that it is this definition that is relevant for the purposes of the CAJA 2009, Part 3, ch. 1 (anonymity investigations into offences of murder or manslaughter: see **D1.210**).) A person markets a knife if the person sells or hires it, offers, or exposes, it for sale or hire or has it in his possession for the purpose of sale or hire (s. 1(4)). A knife is suitable for combat if it is suitable for use as a weapon for inflicting injury on a person or causing a person to fear injury (s. 10). 'Violent behaviour' means an unlawful act inflicting injury on a person or causing a person to fear injury (s. 10).

An indication or suggestion that a knife is suitable for combat may, in particular, be given or made by a name or description which is applied to the knife, which is on the knife or any packaging in which it is contained or which is included in any advertisement which, expressly or by implication, relates to the knife (s. 1(3)).

Defences

Knives Act 1997, ss. 3 and 4 B12.213

3.—(1) It is a defence for a person charged with an offence under section 1 to prove that—
(a) the knife was marketed—
(i) for use by the armed forces of any country;
(ii) as an antique or curio; or
(iii) as falling within such other category (if any) as may be prescribed;
(b) it was reasonable for the knife to be marketed in that way; and
(c) there were no reasonable grounds for suspecting that a person into whose possession the knife might come in consequence of the way in which it was marketed would use it for an unlawful purpose.

...

4.—(1) It is a defence for a person charged with an offence under section 1 to prove that he did not know or suspect, and had no reasonable grounds for suspecting, that the way in which the knife was marketed—
(a) amounted to an indication or suggestion that the knife was suitable for combat; or
(b) was likely to stimulate or encourage violent behaviour involving the use of the knife as a weapon.

(2) It is a defence for a person charged with an offence under section 2 to prove that he did not know or suspect, and had no reasonable grounds for suspecting, that the way in which the knife was marketed—
(a) amounted to an indication or suggestion that the knife was suitable for combat; or
(b) was likely to stimulate or encourage violent behaviour involving the use of the knife as a weapon.

(3) It is a defence for a person charged with an offence under section 1 or 2 to prove that he took all reasonable precautions and exercised all due diligence to avoid committing the offence.

The imposition of a legal burden upon D is open to challenge in the light of the human rights cases on the 'reverse burden' (see **F3.18**).

Publications Relating to Knives

Knives Act 1997, s. 2 B12.214

(1) A person is guilty of an offence if he publishes any written, pictorial or other material in connection with the marketing of any knife and that material—
(a) indicates or suggests that the knife is suitable for combat; or
(b) is otherwise likely to stimulate or encourage violent behaviour involving the use of the knife as a weapon.

The maximum penalty is: on conviction on indictment, imprisonment for a term not exceeding two years and/or a fine; on summary conviction, imprisonment for a term not exceeding six months and/or an unlimited fine.

For definition of the terms used in s. 2, see **B12.212**.

Specific defences are provided by s. 4(2) and (3) (see **B12.213**).

DELIVERY OF BLADED PRODUCTS AND ARTICLES

Definitions of 'bladed product' and 'bladed article'

For the purposes of the Offensive Weapons Act 2019, ss. 38 to 40 (in force on a day to be appointed), a 'bladed product' means an 'article which (a) is or has a blade, and (b) is capable of causing a serious injury to a person which involves cutting that person's skin', but it does not include (in relation to England and Wales) an article described in the Restriction of Offensive Weapons Act 1959, s. 1 (see **B12.200**), or in an order made by the Secretary of State under the CJA 1988, s. 141A(3)(c) (Offensive Weapons Act 2019, s. 41(1) and (2)). B12.215

For the purposes of the Offensive Weapons Act 2019, s. 42, a 'bladed article' means 'an article to which section 141A of the Criminal Justice Act 1988 applies (as that section has effect in relation to England and Wales)' (Offensive Weapons Act 2019, s. 42(11)(a)).

Delivering a Bladed Product to Residential Premises or Locker

B12.216 A seller commits an offence (summary only) if, for the purposes of supplying a bladed product to the buyer (and the parties were not in each other's presence at the time of the sale), the seller delivers the product, or arranges for its delivery to 'residential premises (Offensive Weapons Act 2019, s. 38(2), (1), (4)). For the meaning of 'residential premises', see s. 38(5) and (6), the wording of which is identical to s. 3(5) and (6) (corrosive products; see **B12.228**).

The seller commits an offence (summary only) if, in like circumstances, the seller delivers (or arranges for delivery of) a bladed product 'to a locker' (s. 38(3), (1), (4)). For the meaning of 'locker', see s. 38(7), the wording of which is identical to s. 3(7) (corrosive products; see **B12.228**).

B12.217 **Sentence** A person guilty of an offence under the Offensive Weapons Act 2019, s. 38, is liable on summary conviction in England and Wales to imprisonment for a term not exceeding six months (or 51 weeks if committed after, and in the event that, the CJA 2003, s. 281(5), comes into force), or to a fine, or to both (Offensive Weapons Act 2019, s. 38(8)(a), (9)).

B12.218 **Defences** Various defences to a charge brought under s. 38(2) or (3) are afforded by s. 40:

(1) It is a defence to prove that all reasonable precautions were taken and all due diligence exercised to avoid the commission of the offence (s. 40(1)).
(2) It is a defence to prove that the bladed product was designed or manufactured for the buyer in accordance with specifications provided by the buyer (s. 40(4)).
(3) It is a defence to prove (s. 40(5)) that:
  (a) the bladed product was adapted for the buyer before its delivery in accordance with specifications provided by the buyer, and
  (b) the adaptations were made to enable or facilitate the use of the product by the buyer or its use for a particular purpose.
(4) It is a defence to prove that the accused reasonably believed that the buyer bought the bladed product for use for relevant sporting purposes or for the purposes of historical re-enactment (s. 40(6)).
(5) It is a defence for a seller charged with an offence under s. 38(2), of delivering a bladed product to residential premises, to prove that (see s. 40(2)):
  (a) at the time the offence is alleged to have been committed, the seller had procedures in place which were likely to ensure that any bladed product delivered by the seller to residential premises would be delivered into the hands of a person aged 18 or over, and
  (b) the seller took all reasonable precautions and exercised all due diligence to ensure that the product to which the charge relates would be delivered into the hands of a person aged 18 or over.
(6) It is a defence for a seller, charged with an offence under s. 38(2) of arranging for the delivery of a bladed product to residential premises, to prove that (see s. 40(3)):
  (a) the arrangement required the person with whom it was made to have procedures in place which were likely to ensure that any bladed products delivered to residential premises pursuant to the arrangement would be delivered into the hands of a person aged 18 or over, and
  (b) the seller took all reasonable precautions and exercised all due diligence to ensure that the product to which the charge relates would be delivered into the hands of a person aged 18 or over.
(7) The appropriate national authority may by regulations provide for other defences to the offence under s. 38 (s. 40(13)).

Delivering a Bladed Article to Persons under the Age of 18

From a day to be appointed, where the sale of a bladed product does not take place in the presence of the buyer, the body corporate (typically a courier company that has arranged with a seller, who is within the UK, to deliver 'bladed products' to a buyer) commits an offence contrary to the Offensive Weapons Act 2019, s. 39(6), if — with the requisite knowledge — the body corporate does not deliver it 'into the hands of a person aged 18 or over'. **B12.219**

It is submitted that the effect of s. 39(2) is that the buyer or the seller may be an 'individual' or 'not an individual' but, in either case, it includes a person acting on the buyer's or seller's behalf.

It is a defence for a person charged (in relation to England and Wales and Northern Ireland) to prove that all reasonable precautions were taken and all due diligence exercised to avoid the commission of the offence (s. 40(7)).

Sentence A person guilty of an offence contrary to s. 39(6) is liable on summary conviction in England and Wales to a fine (s. 39(7)). **B12.220**

MINDING A 'DANGEROUS WEAPON'

Section 28 of the VCRA 2006 creates an offence of using a person to mind a 'dangerous weapon', being a weapon intended to be made available for an unlawful purpose. By s. 28(3), 'dangerous weapon' means (a) a firearm other than an air weapon or a component part of, or accessory to, an air weapon; or (b) a weapon to which the CJA 1988, s. 141, applies (see **B12.201**). The penalties are set out in s. 29; the minimum sentence provisions in s. 29 are considered at **E5.14**. **B12.221**

Violent Crime Reduction Act 2006, ss. 28 and 29

28.—(1) A person is guilty of an offence if—
- (a) he uses another to look after, hide or transport a dangerous weapon for him; and
- (b) he does so under arrangements or in circumstances that facilitate, or are intended to facilitate, the weapon's being available to him for an unlawful purpose.

(2) For the purposes of this section the cases in which a dangerous weapon is to be regarded as available to a person for an unlawful purpose include any case where—
- (a) the weapon is available for him to take possession of it at a time and place; and
- (b) his possession of the weapon at that time and place would constitute, or be likely to involve or to lead to, the commission by him of an offence.

(3) In this section 'dangerous weapon' means—
- (a) a firearm other than an air weapon or a component part of, or accessory to, an air weapon; or
- (b) a weapon to which section 141 or 141A of the Criminal Justice Act 1988 applies (specified offensive weapons, knives and bladed weapons).

(4) [Scotland.]

29.—(1) This section applies where a person ('the offender') is guilty of an offence under section 28.

(2) Where the dangerous weapon in respect of which the offence was committed is a weapon to which section 141 or 141A of the Criminal Justice Act 1988 (specified offensive weapons, knives and bladed weapons) applies, the offender shall be liable, on conviction on indictment, to imprisonment for a term not exceeding 4 years or to a fine, or to both.

(3) Where—
- (a) at the time of the offence, the offender was aged 16 or over, and
- (b) the dangerous weapon in respect of which the offence was committed was a firearm mentioned in section 5(1)(a)–(af) or (c) or section 5(1A)(a) of the 1968 Act (firearms possession of which attracts a minimum sentence),

the offender shall be liable, on conviction on indictment, to imprisonment for a term not exceeding 10 years or to a fine, or to both.

(4) On a conviction in England and Wales, where—
- (a) subsection (3) applies, and
- (b) the offender is aged 18 or over at the time of conviction,

the court must impose (with or without a fine) a term of imprisonment of not less than 5 years, unless it is of the opinion that there are exceptional circumstances relating to the offence or to the offender which justify its not doing so.

(5) In relation to times before the commencement of paragraph 180 of schedule 7 to the Criminal Justice and Court Services Act 2000, the reference in subsection (4) to a sentence of imprisonment, in relation to an offender aged under 21 at the time of conviction, is to be read as a reference to a sentence of detention in a young offender institution.

(6) On a conviction in England and Wales, where—

(a) subsection (3) applies, and

(b) the offender is aged under 18 at the time of conviction,

the court must impose (with or without a fine) a term of detention under section 91 of the Powers of Criminal Courts (Sentencing) Act 2000 of not less than 3 years, unless it is of the opinion that there are exceptional circumstances relating to the offence or to the offender which justify its not doing so.

OFFENCES RELATING TO LASERS

B12.222 The Laser Misuse (Vehicles) Act 2018 creates new offences of shining or directing a laser beam towards a 'vehicle' or 'air traffic facility' and for connected purposes. The Act (insofar as it is in force) came into force at different times: s. 1 (England, Wales and Scotland; 10 July 2018, s. 4(3)); s. 2 (10 July 2018, s. 4(5)); s. 3 (interpretation) and s. 4 (extent, commencement) (10 May 2018, s. 4(2)).

By s. 3 of the Act, a 'vehicle' means any vehicle 'used for travel by land, water or air'; an 'aircraft' means 'any vehicle used for travel by air'; a 'vessel' has the meaning given by s. 255(1) of the Merchant Shipping Act 1995; and a 'laser beam' means 'a beam of coherent light produced by a device of any kind'. By s. 2(6) of the Act, an 'air traffic facility' means 'any building, structure, vehicle or other place from which air traffic services are provided', and 'air traffic services' has the meaning given by s. 98(1) of the Transport Act 2000. See also **B10.235**.

Vehicles

B12.223 A person commits an offence if a person shines or directs a laser beam towards a vehicle which is moving or ready to move, and the laser beam dazzles or distracts, or is likely to dazzle or distract, 'a person with control of the vehicle' (s. 1(1)). The reference to 'a person with control of the vehicle' is, in relation to an aircraft, a reference to any person on the aircraft who is engaged in controlling it, or in monitoring the controlling of it (s. 1(7)); and, in relation to a vessel, hovercraft or submarine, is a reference to the master, the pilot or any person engaged in navigating the vessel, hovercraft or submarine (s. 1(8)). A mechanically propelled vehicle, which is not moving or ready to move, but whose engine or motor is running, is to be treated for the purposes of s.1(1) as ready to move (s. 1(6)).

Air Traffic Services

B12.224 By s. 2 of the Act, an offence is committed if a person (a) shines or directs a laser beam towards an air traffic facility, or towards a person providing air traffic services, and (b) the laser beam dazzles or distracts, or is likely to dazzle or distract, a person providing air traffic services.

Defences

B12.225 Two statutory defences exist under s. 1(2) (vehicles) or under s. 2(2) (air traffic services): (a) that the person had a reasonable excuse for shining or directing the laser beam towards the vehicle, or (b) that the person, (i) did not intend to shine or direct the laser beam towards the vehicle, and *(ii) exercised* all due diligence and took all reasonable precautions to avoid doing so. A person will be taken to have shown a fact mentioned in s. 1(2) (or s. 2(2), as the case may be) if (a) sufficient evidence is adduced to raise an issue with respect to it, and (b) the contrary is not proved beyond reasonable doubt (s. 1(3); s. 2(3)).

Sentence

An offence under s. 1 or s. 2 is punishable on summary conviction, in England and Wales, to imprisonment for a term not exceeding six months (or 12 months upon the coming into force of the SA 2020, sch. 22, para. 24(2), formerly the CJA 2003, s. 154(1)) (Laser Misuse (Vehicles) Act 2018, s. 1(4), (5) or (as the case may be) s. 2(4), (5)). There is no offence-specific guideline for firearms offences but the Sentencing Council's *General Guideline: Overarching Principles* (see Supplement, SG2-1) is used for all offenders sentenced on or after 1 October 2019. **B12.226**

CORROSIVE PRODUCTS AND SUBSTANCES

The Offensive Weapons Act 2019, with effect from a day or days to be appointed, creates a number of offences in respect of the sale and delivery of 'corrosive products' and 'corrosive substances'. **B12.227**

Definition of a 'corrosive product'

A 'corrosive product' is either a *substance* listed in the first column of sch. 1 to the Offensive Weapons Act 2019, or it is a *product* that contains an aforementioned substance in a concentration higher than the limit set out for that substance (s. 1(11)), but it does not include a substance or product which is contained in a battery (s. 1(15)). The Secretary of State (in relation to England and Wales or Northern Ireland) may by regulations (and subject to consultation) add, modify, or remove, a substance or concentration specified in sch. 1 (s. 1(12) to (14)). **B12.228**

Name of substance and Chemical Abstracts Registry number (CAS RN)	Concentration limit (weight in weight)
Ammonium hydroxide (CAS RN 1336-21-6)	10% w/w
Formic acid (CAS RN 64-18-6)	10% w/w
Hydrochloric acid (CAS RN 7647-01-0)	10% w/w
Hydrofluoric acid (CAS RN 7664-39-3)	0% w/w
Nitric acid (CAS RN 7697-37-2)	3% w/w
Phosphoric acid (CAS RN 7664-38-2)	70% w/w
Sodium hydroxide (CAS RN 1310-73-2)	12% w/w
Sodium hypochlorite (CAS RN 7681-52-9)	10% w/w
Sulfuric acid (CAS RN 7664-93-9)	15% w/w

Sale of 'corrosive products' to a Person under the Age of 18

The Offensive Weapons Act 2019, s. 1, with effect from a day to be appointed, makes it an offence (summary only) for a person to sell a 'corrosive product' to a person under the age of 18. **B12.229**

It is a defence (in relation to England and Wales or Northern Ireland), subject to s. 2, for D to prove that all reasonable precautions were taken and all due diligence exercised to avoid the commission of the offence (s. 1(2)).

Where, at the time of the sale by an individual or (if the seller is not an individual) by the person acting on the seller's behalf (s. 2(2)) and the product was not sold in the presence of the buyer (i.e. a 'remote sale'), s. 2 provides that the seller is 'not to be regarded as having proved that they took all reasonable precautions and exercised all due diligence to avoid the commission of the [s. 1] offence' *unless as a minimum* the seller proves that the following conditions are met (see s. 2(2), (6) to (9)).

(1) Condition A (s. 2(6)) is that, at the time the offence is alleged to have been committed:
  (a) the seller operated a system for checking that persons who bought corrosive products by the same or a similar method of purchase to that used by the buyer were not under the age of 18, and
  (b) that system was likely to prevent persons under the age of 18 from buying corrosive products by that method.
(2) Condition B (s. 2(7)) is that when the package containing the corrosive product was dispatched by the seller, it was clearly marked to indicate:
  (a) that it contained a corrosive product, and
  (b) that, when finally delivered, it should only be delivered into the hands of a person aged 18 or over.
(3) Condition C (s. 2(8)) is that the seller took all reasonable precautions and exercised all due diligence to ensure that, when finally delivered, the package would be delivered into the hands of a person aged 18 or over.
(4) Condition D (s. 2(9)) is that the seller did not deliver the package, or arrange for its delivery, to a locker.

Where the 'final delivery' (condition B or C) is to a place from which the corrosive product is to be collected by the buyer (or a person acting on the buyer's behalf), conditions B and C are to be read as a supply to the buyer (or to the person acting on the buyer's behalf) from that place (s. 2(10)).

B12.230 **Sentence** A person guilty of an offence under the Offensive Weapons Act 2019, s. 1(1), is liable on summary conviction in England and Wales to imprisonment for a term not exceeding six months (or 51 weeks if committed after, and in the event that, the CJA 2003, s. 281(5), comes into force), or to a fine or to both (Offensive Weapons Act 2019, s. 1(7)(a), (8)).

Delivery of Corrosive Products to Residential Premises or Locker

B12.231 For the definition of 'corrosive product' see **B12.228**.

Where a person sells a 'corrosive product' to the buyer, at the time when the buyer and the seller (or, if the seller is not an individual, the person acting on the seller's behalf) were not in the presence of each other, the seller commits an offence (summary only) contrary to s. 3(2) of the Offensive Weapons Act 2019 if, 'for the purposes of supplying the corrosive product to the buyer, the seller delivers the product, or arranges for its delivery, to residential premises'. 'Residential premises' means 'premises used solely for residential purposes' (s. 3(5)), but the circumstances where premises are not residential premises 'include, in particular, where a person carries on a business from the premises' (s. 3(6)).

An offence (summary only) is committed contrary to s. 3(3) if that seller delivers the product, or arranges for its delivery, to a 'locker', i.e. 'a lockable container to which the corrosive product is delivered with a view to its collection by the buyer, or a person acting on behalf of the buyer, in accordance with arrangements made between the seller and the buyer' (s. 3(7)).

It is a defence to an offence charged under s. 3(2) or (3) for D to prove that all reasonable precautions were taken and all due diligence exercised to avoid the commission of the offence in question (s. 3(8), in relation to England and Wales and Northern Ireland).

B12.232 **Sentence** A person guilty of an offence under the Offensive Weapons Act 2019, s. 3, is liable on summary conviction in England and Wales to imprisonment for a term not exceeding six months (or 51 weeks if committed after, and in the event that, the CJA 2003, s. 281(5), comes into force), or to a fine, or to both (Offensive Weapons Act 2019, s. 3(11)(a), (12)).

Delivery (on Behalf of a Seller Overseas) of a Corrosive Product to Persons under 18 Years of Age

A body corporate (Offensive Weapons Act 2019, s. 4(1)(c)) commits an offence (summary only: contrary to s. 4(4)) if, when it delivers a 'corrosive product', it does not deliver the product 'into the hands of a person aged 18 or over', in circumstances where the seller (outside the UK: s. 4(1)(b)) sold a corrosive product to the buyer at a time when neither the seller nor the buyer was in each other's presence, and (prior to the sale) the seller had entered into an arrangement with the body corporate by which the latter agreed to deliver corrosive products (aware that it covered the delivery of such products). The seller and the buyer may be an 'individual' or 'not an individual' and, in either case, includes a person acting on the seller's or buyer's behalf (s. 4(2)). **B12.233**

For the definition of 'corrosive product', see **B12.228**.

A person *other than an individual* 'is outside the United Kingdom at any time if the person does not carry on a business of selling articles of any kind from premises in any part of the United Kingdom at that time' (s. 4(3)).

It is a defence to a charge under s. 4(4), for the body corporate to prove that all reasonable precautions were taken and all due diligence exercised to avoid the commission of the offence (s. 4(5)).

Sentence A person guilty of an offence under the Offensive Weapons Act 2019, s. 4, is liable on summary conviction in England and Wales to a fine (s. 4(10)(a)). **B12.234**

Offence of Having a 'Corrosive Substance' in a Public Place

A person commits an offence ('either way') contrary to the Offensive Weapons Act 2019, s. 6(1), if the person has a corrosive substance with him in a public place. **B12.235**

It is a defence for a person charged in England and Wales or Northern Ireland to prove 'that they had good reason or lawful authority for having the corrosive substance with them in a public place' (s. 6(2)). It is a defence without prejudice to the generality of s. 6(2) for a person 'to prove that they had the corrosive substance with them for use at work' (s. 6(3)).

For cases in relation to the issue of 'good reason' see **B12.182** (albeit in the context of the CJA 1988, s. 139); see also *Garry v CPS* [2019] EWHC 636 (Admin), [2019] 1 WLR 3630 (albeit in the context of the Prevention of Crime Act 1953, s. 1(1)) with regard to items or products used for work (see **B12.170**). For commentary in relation to the expression 'have with them', see **B12.162** and **B12.179**.

It is submitted that the issue that is likely to require prompt determination is whether the defences under s. 6(2) and (3) impose only an evidential burden on D.

Definitions The Offensive Weapons Act 2019, s. 6(9), includes the following definitions: **B12.236**

'corrosive substance' means a substance which is capable of burning human skin by corrosion;
'public place', in relation to England and Wales or Northern Ireland, includes any place to which, at the time in question, the public have or are permitted access, whether on payment or otherwise.

The definition of 'corrosive substance' is considerably wider than the expression 'corrosive product' (as the latter is defined by s. 1(11)).

Sentence A person guilty of an offence under the Offensive Weapons Act 2019, s. 6, is liable on summary conviction to imprisonment for a term not exceeding six months and/or a fine; and on conviction on indictment, to imprisonment for up to four years. The offence is subject to a mandatory minimum term of six months' imprisonment for an offender aged **B12.237**

16 or over with a qualifying conviction unless it would be unjust, in all the circumstances, to impose it (see s. 8(2)).

CAUSING EXPLOSION LIKELY TO ENDANGER LIFE OR PROPERTY

B12.238 **Explosive Substances Act 1883, s. 2**

> A person who in the United Kingdom or (being a citizen of the United Kingdom and Colonies) in the Republic of Ireland unlawfully and maliciously causes by any explosive substance an explosion of a nature likely to endanger life or to cause serious injury to property shall, whether any injury to person or property has actually been caused or not, be guilty of an offence . . .

Note that this is an offence in the list of offences where convictions and/or allegations may be disclosed under the Domestic Violence Disclosure Scheme: see the *Domestic Violence Disclosure Scheme (DVDS) Guidance* (Home Office, December 2016).

Indictment

B12.239 *Statement of Offence*

Causing an explosion contrary to section 2 of the Explosive Substances Act 1883.

Particulars of Offence

A on or about the . . . day of . . . maliciously caused by an explosive substance an explosion of a nature likely to endanger life or to cause serious injury to property, namely the explosion at . . . Town Hall on the . . . day of . . .

Procedure

B12.240 The offence is triable on indictment only (Explosive Substances Act 1883, s. 2) and is a class 2A offence.

Proceedings for a crime under this Act shall not be instituted except by or with the consent of the A-G (s. 7(1)); remands in custody or bail are expressly excluded from the operation of s. 7(1) by the Prosecution of Offences Act 1985, s. 25(2) (see *Whale* [1991] Crim LR 692, in which the proceedings for the offence contrary to s. 4 were held not to be effectively instituted until the committal proceedings). Further, in *Elliott* (1984) 81 Cr App R 115 at p. 121, the Court of Appeal concluded that the Explosive Substances Act 1883, s. 7, 'should be interpreted as meaning that instituting proceedings relates to the time when a person comes to court to answer the charge' so the relevant time is 'when he attends at the magistrates' court to answer the charge'; it held that any other interpretation would 'overlook and ignore' the provisions of the Prosecution of Offences Act 1985, s. 6.

Sentence

B12.241 The maximum penalty is imprisonment for life (Explosive Substances Act 1883, s. 2). Where the offence is committed in the context of terrorism, the Sentencing Council definitive guideline, *Terrorism Offences* (see Supplement, **SG32-4**), applies in respect of offenders aged 18 and over sentenced on or after 27 April 2018, irrespective of the date of the offence. In other circumstances the Sentencing Council's *General Guideline: Overarching Principles* (see Supplement, **SG2-1**) is used for all offenders sentenced on or after 1 October 2019.

In *Larsen* [2014] EWCA Crim 1514, [2014] 2 Cr App R (S) 81 (635) D pleaded guilty to one offence under s. 2 and one offence under s. 3 of the 1883 Act as well as two counts of arson. He had embarked on a sustained campaign of terror in the locality, setting two fires and causing an explosion with a device containing ball bearings. D, aged 46, had no previous convictions, there was no political motivation, and nobody had actually been injured. Sentences of 18 years' imprisonment concurrent for the two explosives offences were 'severe', but upheld by the Court of Appeal.

Powers of forfeiture and disposal of matter are provided by the Explosives Act 1875, ss. 89 and 96; these apply to this offence (1883 Act, s. 8(1)). See also **B12.249**.

Explosive Substance and Explosion

'Explosive substance' is 'deemed to include any materials for making any explosive substance; also any apparatus, machine, implement or materials used, or intended to be used, or adapted for causing, or aiding in causing, any explosion in or with any explosive substance; also any part of any such apparatus, machine or implement' (Explosive Substances Act 1883, s. 9(1)). Explosive substances have included a shot gun (*Downey* [1971] NI 224), a firearm (*Fegan* [1972] NI 80, (1971) 78 Cr App R 189), part of a vessel filled with an explosive substance (*Charles* (1892) 17 Cox CC 499) and electronic timers (*Berry (No. 3)* [1995] 1 WLR 7; and see *G* [2009] UKHL 13, [2010] 1 AC 43, where it was remarked (at [55]) that s. 9 would apply, for instance, to a timer), as well as the more obvious substances, such as dynamite or gunpowder (*Hallam* [1957] 1 QB 569), plaster gelatine and detonators (*Stewart* (1959) 44 Cr App R 29), and a stick of gelignite, a length of fuse and a detonator (*McCarthy* [1964] 1 All ER 95). The petrol in a petrol bomb combines with the air to create an explosive substance, so the petrol, bottle and wick are materials for making that explosive substance (*Bouch* [1983] QB 246; *Howard* [1993] Crim LR 213). **B12.242**

'Explosive' The Court of Appeal decided in *Wheatley* [1979] 1 All ER 954 that the definition of 'explosive' in the Explosives Act 1875, s. 3, applies to the 1883 Act. **B12.243**

Explosives Act 1875, s. 3

> The term 'explosive' in this Act — (1) Means gunpowder, nitro-glycerine, dynamite, guncotton, blasting powders, fulminate of mercury or of other metals, coloured fires and every other substance, whether similar to those above mentioned or not, used or manufactured with a view to producing a practical effect by explosion or a pyrotechnic effect; and (2) includes fog-signals, fireworks, fuses, rockets, percussion caps, detonators, cartridges, ammunition of all description, and every adaptation or preparation of an explosive as above defined.

In *Wheatley*, fire-dampened sodium chlorate mixture, used in a pipe bomb, was an explosive substance, even if it had only a pyrotechnic effect. In *Bouch*, the Court of Appeal held that 'pyrotechnic effect' has a broad meaning and is not limited to, e.g., fireworks. A flare is a pyrotechnic device. There does not have to be an explosion. A fireball produced by a petrol bomb has a pyrotechnic effect.

'Explosion' The meaning of 'explosion' was considered by the Court of Appeal in *Bouch* [1983] QB 246, where the definition used in the 1886 edition of the *Encyclopaedia Britannica* was approved: **B12.244**

> 'explosion' may for our purpose be defined as the sudden or extremely rapid conversion of a solid or liquid body of small bulk into gas or vapour, occupying very many times the volume of the original substance, and, in addition, highly expanded by the heat generated during the transformation. This sudden or very rapid expansion of volume is attained by an exhibition of force, more or less violent according to the constitution of the original substance and the circumstances of explosion. Any substance capable of undergoing such a change upon the application of heat, or other disturbing cause, is called 'explosive'.

The inevitable concomitant of a successful petrol bomb is an explosion because it produces a fireball, though it does not always have a blast effect. A petrol bomb will produce a blast effect where it does not ignite immediately upon impact but ignites after a pause. See also *Elliott* (1984) 81 Cr App R 115 adopting this approach.

'Who in the United Kingdom'

In *Ellis* (1991) 95 Cr App R 52, Swinton Thomas J held, on a motion to quash two counts in an indictment, that 'the words "who in the United Kingdom" do not govern the person but govern the acts'. In reaching this conclusion the judge had pointed out that 'to construe section **B12.245**

3 ... so as to limit the offence to a person who is physically present in the United Kingdom when he causes explosions runs not only wholly contrary to common sense but wholly contrary to the whole tenor of the law as it has developed over the last century and particularly over the last two decades'.

Mens Rea

B12.246 The *mens rea is* that the act must be done 'maliciously' (see **B2.69** and **A2.12**). It is often said that there is no need for foresight by D of (a) endangerment of life or (b) serious injury to property. The jury assesses the likelihood of either objectively. Without asserting that this proposition is incorrect, or overstated, consider *G* [2003] UKHL 50, [2004] 1 AC 1034 and *Cunningham* [1957] 2 QB 396.

Punishment of Accessories

B12.247 See **B12.261**.

Power of Search etc.

B12.248 Section 8(1) of the Explosive Substances Act 1883 extends certain powers in the Explosives Act 1875 to this offence. The powers are: to search for explosives (s. 73); to seize and detain explosives liable to forfeiture (s. 74); and to inspect wharves, carriages, boats etc. with explosives in transit (s. 75).

ATTEMPT TO CAUSE EXPLOSION OR MAKING OR KEEPING EXPLOSIVE WITH INTENT TO ENDANGER LIFE OR PROPERTY

B12.249 **Explosive Substances Act 1883, s. 3**

(1) A person who in the United Kingdom or a dependency or (being a citizen of the United Kingdom and Colonies) elsewhere unlawfully and maliciously—
  (a) does any act with intent to cause, or conspires to cause, by an explosive substance an explosion of a nature likely to endanger life, or cause serious injury to property, whether in the United Kingdom or elsewhere
  (b) makes or has in his possession or under his control an explosive substance with intent by means thereof to endanger life, or cause serious injury to property, whether in the United Kingdom or elsewhere, or to enable any other person so to do,

shall, whether any explosion does or does not take place, and whether any injury to person or property is actually caused or not, be guilty of an offence ...

Procedure

B12.250 The offence is triable on indictment only (Explosive Substances Act 1883, s. 3(1)) and is a class 2A offence. As to the need for the A-G's consent, see **B12.240**.

Sentence

B12.251 The maximum penalty is imprisonment for life (Explosive Substances Act 1883, s. 3(1)). Where the offence is committed in the context of terrorism, the Sentencing Council definitive guideline, *Terrorism Offences* (see Supplement, **SG32-4**), applies in respect of offenders aged 18 and over sentenced on or after 27 April 2018, irrespective of the date of the offence. In other circumstances the Sentencing Council's *General Guideline: Overarching Principles* (see Supplement, **SG2-1**) is used for all offenders sentenced on or after 1 October 2019. The explosive substance is forfeited. The related provisions of the Explosives Act 1875 (ss. 89 and 96) apply (s. 8(1)).

In *Martin* [1999] 1 Cr App R (S) 477, the Court of Appeal issued guidelines for the sentencing of this offence. Lord Bingham CJ said that the appropriate sentence would depend upon a number of factors, including the nature, size and likely effect of the explosive device, the nature and extent of any death, injury or damage caused, together with the role and motivation of the individual offenders. These guidelines informed the 15-year extended sentence (ten years' imprisonment, plus five years' extended licence) in *Hines-Randle* [2014] EWCA Crim 2364, which was itself referred to in *Pepper* [2019] EWCA Crim 2088 in which D was found at home with three petrol bombs designed, he said, for blowing up police. He was found to be dangerous, and his sentence of nine years' imprisonment with an extension of four years' licence was upheld.

Elements

As to the significance of 'in the United Kingdom', see **B12.245**; 'dependency' means the Channel Islands, the Isle of Man and any colony, other than a colony for whose external relations a country other than the UK is responsible (Explosive Substances Act 1883, s. 3(2)). *Abedin* [2004] EWCA Crim 2232 confirms that a jury is bound to acquit if it thinks that D's intention was to cause an explosion to endanger life or damage property abroad and not in the UK. **B12.252**

For the meaning of 'explosive substance' and 'explosive', see **B12.242** ***et seq***. For the meaning of 'making explosives', see **B12.255**.

'Maliciously'

The *mens rea* is that the act, whatever it might be, must be done 'maliciously' (see **B2.69** and **A2.12**). It would appear not to be possible to possess a substance maliciously if it is not known what the substance is. Thus the approach in the cases decided on the Explosive Substances Act 1883, s. 4, by the Court of Criminal Appeal in *Hallam* [1957] 1 QB 569 and *Stewart* (1959) 44 Cr App R 29 (see **B12.258**), may be applicable to this offence also, rather than the rules relating to possession developed in relation to controlled drugs (see **B19.27**). **B12.253**

Punishment of Accessories and Powers of Search

See **B12.261** for punishment of accessories. See **B12.248** for powers of search. **B12.254**

MAKING OR POSSESSION OF EXPLOSIVE UNDER SUSPICIOUS CIRCUMSTANCES

Explosive Substances Act 1883, s. 4 **B12.255**

(1) Any person who makes or knowingly has in his possession or under his control any explosive substance, under such circumstances as to give rise to a reasonable suspicion that he is not making it or does not have it in his possession or under his control for a lawful object, shall, unless he can show that he made it or had it in his possession or under his control for a lawful object, be guilty of an offence ...

Procedure

The offence is triable on indictment only (Explosive Substances Act 1883, s. 4(1)) and is a class 2A offence. As to the need for the A-G's consent, see **B12.229**. Note *McVitie* [1960] 2 QB 483 regarding particulars of the offence. **B12.256**

Sentence

On conviction on indictment, the maximum penalty is life imprisonment, and the explosive substance must be forfeited (Explosive Substances Act 1883, s. 4(1)). Where the offence was committed prior to 13 April 2014, the maximum sentence is 14 years' imprisonment. Where the offence is committed in the context of terrorism, the Sentencing Council definitive guideline, *Terrorism Offences* (see Supplement, **SG32-4**), applies in respect of offenders aged 18 and over sentenced on or after 27 April 2018, irrespective of the date of the offence. **B12.257**

In other circumstances the Sentencing Council's *General Guideline: Overarching Principles* (see Supplement, **SG2-1**) is used for all offenders sentenced on or after 1 October 2019.

A sentence of 42 months was upheld in *Lloyd* [2001] EWCA Crim 600, [2001] 2 Cr App R (S) 111 (493), where D, who had 14 previous convictions for weapons-related offences, pleaded guilty to making four explosive devices, but not intending to use them to cause harm. In *Riding* [2009] EWCA Crim 892, [2010] 1 Cr App R (S) 7 (37) it was held that a sentence of imprisonment was necessary for a 21-year-old man of good character who made a pipe bomb from instructions found on the internet, and kept it at his home. The sentence was reduced from 12 months to eight months. Four years' imprisonment was upheld in *Kasprzak* [2013] EWCA Crim 1531, [2014] 1 Cr App R (S) 20 (115), where D admitted eight offences of possessing an explosive substance after large quantities of chemicals and formulae for making explosives were found at his home. The sentence was ordered to run concurrently to a 20-year sentence for attempted murder, kidnapping and possession of an offensive weapon.

Possession, Control or Making and *Mens Rea*

B12.258 D must know that the substance is in his possession or control (*Berry (No. 3)* [1994] 2 All ER 913, at p. 918h). Note the extended meaning of 'explosive substance' in the Explosive Substances Act 1883, s. 9 (see **B12.231**). In *Hallam* [1957] 1 QB 569, the Court of Criminal Appeal decided the meaning of the section was clear and that 'the person must not only knowingly have in his possession the substance but must know that it is an explosive substance', but does not have to have 'any particular chemical knowledge'. The Court of Criminal Appeal followed this decision in *Stewart* (1959) 44 Cr App R 29. The word 'knowingly' prefaces 'possession' and 'control' and not 'making', but, nevertheless, 'all three categories of person must be shown to have known that the substance was an explosive substance' (*Berry (No. 3)*, at p. 918g). It was said in *Berry* that 'no person who makes a substance can be unaware that he had done so' although this must be read as being subject to the general defences (see **A3**).

The Court of Appeal in *Hallam* also said that 'if evidence is given that the person had the substance in his possession, and some evidence of circumstances which give rise to a reasonable suspicion that he had not got it for a lawful purpose is given, the jury are then entitled to infer that he knew it was an explosive substance'. However, there is nothing in this approach which should be interpreted as suggesting that the burden of proof is not on the prosecution to prove *mens rea*, and that is particularly so where the substance is not so obviously an explosive substance, e.g., a timer as opposed to gunpowder or gelignite. The jury must be sure that the maker intended the timer to be used to cause explosions (*Berry (No. 3)*, at p. 919).

Reasonable Suspicion

B12.259 'Reasonable suspicion' is an objective requirement, which must be proved by the prosecution (*Fegan* [1972] NI 80, (1971) 78 Cr App R 189). In *G* [2009] UKHL 13, [2010] 1 AC 43, their lordships made the point (at [56]) that whether the circumstances in which D was in possession or control of the article in question give rise to a reasonable suspicion depends (in part) on the nature of the article (e.g. a timer, petrol, or fertiliser) and the purpose for which that article might legitimately be applied by D. For example, many people have good reason for having petrol, but not 'semtex'.

Lawful Object

B12.260 In *Fegan* [1972] NI 80, (1971) 78 Cr App R 189, the Court of Criminal Appeal, Northern Ireland, held that 'the expression "lawful object" cannot be defined exhaustively or with precision'. The Court decided that possession and purpose must not be confused, so, 'possession of a firearm for the purpose of protecting the possessor, his wife or family from acts of violence may be possession for a lawful object'. That purpose 'cannot be founded on a mere fancy, or some aggressive motive' and the 'threatened danger must be reasonably and genuinely anticipated, must appear reasonably imminent, and must be of a nature which could not reasonably be met by more pacific means' (*Fegan*). The Court of Appeal in *A-G's Ref (No. 2 of 1983)* [1984] QB 456 agreed with this approach. The House of Lords appears to have adopted the same approach in *Berry* [1985] AC 246. The Court in *Fegan* held that a person cannot possess an item for a lawful object if the person also has it for an unlawful object. The Court of Appeal in *Campbell* [2004] EWCA Crim 2309, refused to grant leave to appeal against conviction where the trial judge had ruled that D never had a lawful reason for possession of the explosive substances, even if it was the case that they were made by him when he was young in order to put into hollow trees and down rabbit holes and had simply been retained as part of the detritus of childhood. It is necessary for people not to store explosive items without good reasons and D was irresponsible in doing what he had done. In *Riding* [2009] EWCA Crim 892, [2010] 1 Cr App R (S) 7 (37), the Court of Appeal rejected D's submission that 'lawful object' means the absence of criminal purpose rather than a positive object which is lawful. The Court held that 'lawful object' means the latter and not the former and that the conclusion is consistent with cases such *Fegan* and *A-G's Ref (No. 2 of 1983)*. In *Copeland* [2020] UKSC 8, [2020] 2 WLR 681 (and see the commentary to this case [2020] Crim LR 645), the Supreme Court held that the Court of Appeal in *Riding* had 'rightly held' that 'lawful object' in limb (2) of s. 4(1) does not mean 'the absence of criminal purpose', but rather requires D to identify 'a positive object which is lawful' (*Riding*, at [12]). It opined (at [31]) that the result in *Riding* was 'correct on the facts of the case'. There was no need for D to use an explosive substance to satisfy his curiosity whether he could successfully construct a pipe bomb: instead of filling it with gunpowder, he could have used an inert substance such as sand. It was not part of his case that he had made the pipe bomb in order to see if he could make it explode. Accordingly, the Court's statement in *Riding* that '[m]ere curiosity simply could not be a lawful object in the making of a lethal pipe bomb' had to be read in that context. However, the word 'object' is to be given its natural meaning (at [36]) and (in the opinion of the majority in *Copeland*) there is nothing unlawful about experimentation and self-education as objects, in themselves, so they are capable of being 'lawful objects' within the meaning of s. 4(1) of the 1883 Act (at [37]), and s. 4(1) has general application (at [40], per Lord Sales (with whom Lord Reed and Lord Carnwath agreed)):

> It can apply in the case of a teacher in the chemistry department of a school or university, or a person in a commercial research laboratory, who makes explosive substances or has them in his possession. If a charge were brought against such a person under section 4(1) and the prosecution was able to surmount the relatively low hurdle in limb (1) of the provision, the accused would be entitled to defend himself under limb (2) by proving that his object in making or keeping the substances was experimentation, education or research. It is apt to describe each of those as an 'object', as a matter of ordinary use of language.

The burden of proof of this defence lies upon D (*Berry (No. 3)* [1994] 2 All ER 913 at pp. 920 *et seq.* and *Fegan*) and it must be proved on a balance of probabilities (*Fegan*).

Punishment of Accessories

B12.261

Explosive Substances Act 1883, s. 5

> Any person who within or (being a subject of Her Majesty) without Her Majesty's dominions by the supply of or solicitation for money, the providing of premises, the supply of materials, or in any manner whatsoever, procures, counsels, aids, abets, or is accessory to, the commission of any crime under this Act, shall be guilty of [an offence], and shall be liable to be tried and punished for that crime, as if he had been guilty as a principal.

Notwithstanding s. 5, the commission of an offence contrary to s. 4 may be aided and abetted (*McCarthy* [1964] 1 All ER 95). For a general consideration of participation in crime, see **A4**, and, in particular, **A4.24**.

Powers of Search

See **B12.248** for powers of search. **B12.262**

CAUSING BODILY INJURY BY GUNPOWDER

B12.263 **Offences Against the Person Act 1861, s. 28**

> Whosoever shall unlawfully and maliciously, by the explosion of gunpowder or other explosive substance, burn, maim, disfigure, disable, or do any grievous bodily harm to any person, shall be guilty of [an offence].

Procedure and Sentence

B12.264 The offence is triable on indictment (OAPA 1861, s. 28) and is a class 2A offence.

The maximum penalty is imprisonment for life (s. 28). Where the offence is committed in the context of terrorism, the Sentencing Council definitive guideline, *Terrorism Offences* (see Supplement, SG32-4), applies in respect of offenders aged 18 and over sentenced on or after 27 April 2018, irrespective of the date of the offence. In other circumstances the Sentencing Council's *General Guideline: Overarching Principles* (see Supplement, SG2-1) is used for all offenders sentenced on or after 1 October 2019.

Elements

B12.265 In *Howard* [1993] Crim LR 213, the Court of Appeal decided that a petrol bomb is an explosive substance. The definition of 'explosive substance' under the Explosive Substances Act 1883 (see **B12.231**) was used by the trial judge and noted by the Court of Appeal. It clearly is of assistance, but may not be determinative of the concept as it appears in the OAPA 1861. It is submitted that the term should mean the same in both pieces of legislation. The Court of Appeal wondered if the trial judge should not have asked the jury to determine whether the petrol bomb was an explosive substance. This can be correct only if the jury were being asked to determine whether the facts about a petrol bomb satisfied the definition of explosive substance given to them by the judge.

It is to be assumed that the words 'burn, maim, disfigure, disable, or do any grievous bodily harm' will carry their ordinary meaning, unless a decision suggests otherwise. Indeed this was the approach of the Court of Appeal in interpreting the meaning of 'disable' in *James* (1979) 70 Cr App R 215. 'Maim' has a technical legal meaning which is injury of any part of a man's body which may make him less able to defend himself (12 *Halsbury's Statutes*, at p. 109), so there was no proof of an intent to maim or disable in *Sullivan* (1841) Car & M 209, where the blow was aimed at V's head, but it would have been otherwise had it been aimed at V's arm to prevent use of it. 'Disfigure' means to do an external injury which may detract from the personal appearance (12 *Halsbury's Statutes*, at p. 109). 'Disable' covers both permanent and temporary disablement (*James*, a decision on s. 29, and not applying *Boyce* (1824) 1 Mood CC 29). As to 'grievous bodily harm', see **B2.54**.

Mens Rea

B12.266 The *mens rea* is 'maliciously', which, it is submitted, refers both to the consequence as well as the explosion. As to the meaning of 'maliciously', see **B2.69** and **A2.12**.

CAUSING GUNPOWDER TO EXPLODE, SENDING AN EXPLOSIVE SUBSTANCE OR THROWING CORROSIVE FLUID WITH INTENT

B12.267 **Offences Against the Person Act 1861, s. 29**

> Whosoever shall unlawfully and maliciously cause any gunpowder or other explosive substance to explode, or send or deliver or to cause to be taken or received by any person any explosive substance or any other dangerous or noxious thing, or put or lay at any place, or cast or throw at or upon or otherwise apply to any person, any corrosive fluid or any destructive or explosive substance, with intent in any of the cases aforesaid to burn, maim, disfigure, or disable any person, or to do some grievous bodily harm to any person, shall, whether any bodily injury be effected or not, be guilty of [an offence].

Procedure and Sentence

This offence is triable on indictment (OAPA 1861, s. 29). As to the classification of the offence for the purpose of listing, see (in the context of an allegation of terrorism) CrimPD XIII, para. B and Annex 4 (see Supplement, **CPD.XIII.B** and **CPD.XIII.x4**). **B12.268**

On conviction on indictment, the maximum penalty is life imprisonment. Where the offence is committed in the context of terrorism, the Sentencing Council definitive guideline, *Terrorism Offences* (see Supplement, **SG32-4**), applies in respect of offenders aged 18 and over sentenced on or after 27 April 2018, irrespective of the date of the offence. In other circumstances the Sentencing Council's *General Guideline: Overarching Principles* (see Supplement, **SG2-1**) is used for all offenders sentenced on or after 1 October 2019.

Acid Attacks Note that the use of acid is specified as an aggravating factor in the Sentencing Council definitive guideline, *Assault* (see Supplement, **SG12-1**). In *Isaac* [2016] EWCA Crim 1907, sentences of ten and six years' detention were imposed on two young offenders, respectively, who had been convicted under the OAPA 1861, s. 29 (see also *Riley* [2017] EWCA Crim 243). In *Ardic* [2019] EWCA Crim 1836, [2020] 1 Cr App R (S) 59 (457), two offenders involved in an attack in which V was sprayed in the face with a corrosive substance, were found guilty of s. 29 offences and sentenced to custodial terms of 14 and 14½ years, extended in each case by three years. A third offender, who had brought the substance to the scene, had sprayed members of the public indiscriminately during the course of the attack and had been involved in earlier disorder, was sentenced to 17 years with a similar extension period. The trial judge had been right to use the factors within the s. 18 guideline to assess culpability and harm. However, in view of the length of the custodial element of the sentences there was no need for these admittedly dangerous offenders to receive extended sentences. Determinate sentences of 12, 14 and 16 years' imprisonment were substituted. In *Midmore* [2017] EWCA Crim 533, [2017] 2 Cr App R 8 (73), D1 and D2 were sentenced to 15 years' (with an extension period of five years) and nine years' imprisonment respectively for causing grievous bodily harm with intent (OAPA 1861, s. 18) by throwing sulphuric acid at the victim's face. D2 had pleaded guilty to the charge. **B12.269**

Elements

For the meaning of 'explosive substance' see **B12.231** and for 'burn, maim, disfigure, or disable', see **B12.265**. For 'grievous bodily harm', see **B2.54**. **B12.270**

In *Crawford* (1845) 2 Car & Kir 129, the Court for Crown Cases Reserved upheld a conviction on the basis that boiling water was 'destructive matter'. For the meaning of noxious thing, see **B2.91**.

Mens Rea

The *mens rea* of the offence consists of 'maliciously' doing one of the prohibited acts and with intent to produce one of the prohibited consequences. As to the meaning of 'maliciously', see **B2.69** and **A2.12**. As to 'intention', see **A2.4**. **B12.271**

PLACING GUNPOWDER NEAR A BUILDING ETC. WITH INTENT TO DO BODILY INJURY TO ANY PERSON

Offences Against the Person Act 1861, s. 30 **B12.272**

> Whosoever shall unlawfully and maliciously place or throw in, into, upon, against, or near any building, ship or vessel any gunpowder or other explosive substance, with intent to do any bodily injury to any person, shall, whether or not any explosion take place, and whether or not any bodily injury be effected, be guilty of [an offence].

Procedure and Sentence

The offence is triable on indictment (OAPA 1861, s. 30) and is a class 2A offence. **B12.273**

The maximum penalty is 14 years' imprisonment. Where the offence is committed in the context of terrorism, the Sentencing Council definitive guideline, *Terrorism Offences* (see Supplement, SG32-4), applies in respect of offenders aged 18 and over sentenced on or after 27 April 2018, irrespective of the date of the offence. In other circumstances the Sentencing Council's *General Guideline: Overarching Principles* (see Supplement, SG2-1) is used for all offenders sentenced on or after 1 October 2019.

Elements

B12.274 For the meaning of 'explosive substance', see **B12.242**. Although the substance need not explode, it must be capable of exploding, so to throw a bottle containing only gunpowder and an unlit fuse would not constitute the offence, because the act would merely be that of throwing a bottle (*Shephard* (1868) 19 LT 19 at p. 20).

Mens Rea

B12.275 The placing or throwing must be done 'maliciously' (as to which see **B2.69** and **A2.12**), and it must be done with intent to do bodily injury (as to 'intent', see **A2.4**). It is to be noted that the phrase is bodily injury and not grievous bodily harm. It appears to be a wider term in the sense that it need not be serious, but it may be more limited if it applies only to physical injury.

MAKING OR HAVING GUNPOWDER ETC. WITH INTENT TO COMMIT OR ENABLE ANY PERSON TO COMMIT A FELONY

B12.276 **Offences Against the Person Act 1861, s. 64**

> Whosoever shall knowingly have in his possession, or make or manufacture, any gunpowder, explosive substance, or any dangerous or noxious thing, or any machine, engine, instrument, or thing, with intent by means thereof to commit, or for the purpose of enabling any other person to commit, any of the felonies in this Act mentioned shall be guilty of an [offence].

Procedure and Sentence

B12.277 The offence is triable on indictment and is a class 2A offence.

The maximum penalty is two years' imprisonment. Where the offence is committed in the context of terrorism, the Sentencing Council definitive guideline, *Terrorism Offences* (see Supplement, SG32-4), applies in respect of offenders aged 18 and over sentenced on or after 27 April 2018, irrespective of the date of the offence. In other circumstances the Sentencing Council's *General Guideline: Overarching Principles* (see Supplement, **SG2-1**) is used for all offenders sentenced on or after 1 October 2019.

Elements

B12.278 For the meaning of 'possession', see, by analogy, the drug possession cases at **B19.27**, but note that the possession in this offence must be 'knowingly', see **B12.279**.

For the meaning of 'explosive substance', see **B12.242**. For the meaning of 'noxious thing', see **B2.91**.

Mens Rea

B12.279 The *mens rea* requires that there be an act (possession, making or manufacturing) which is done 'knowingly'. As to the meaning of 'knowingly', see **A2.14**. There must also be an intent to commit a felony within the OAPA 1861. As to the meaning of 'intent', see **A2.4**. The reference to 'felonies' is to any offence within the 1861 Act for D (not previously convicted) may be tried on indictment otherwise than at D's own instance (CLA 1967, s. 10 and sch. 2, para. 8).

FIREWORKS OFFENCES

There are a number of offences concerned with fireworks, including the throwing, casting, or the firing of any firework in or into any highway, street, thoroughfare or public place under the Explosives Act 1875, s. 80. On summary conviction for the s. 80 offence, the maximum penalty is an unlimited fine. Under the Penalties for Disorderly Behaviour (Amount of Penalty) Order 2002 (SI 2002 No. 1837), as amended, the s. 80 offence is a penalty offence and the amount payable is £90. The Fireworks Act 2003, s. 11(1), provides that any person who contravenes a prohibition imposed by fireworks regulations is guilty of an offence: see the Fireworks Regulations 2004 (SI 2004 No. 1836, as amended). Any person guilty of such an offence is liable, on summary conviction, to imprisonment for a term not exceeding six months and/or an unlimited fine (Fireworks Act 2003, s. 11(3)). The defence of due diligence, in the Consumer Protection Act 1987, s. 39, applies to this offence (Fireworks Act 2003, s. 11(7)). The offence under s. 11 is also a fixed penalty offence and attracts a penalty of £80 for persons aged 16 or over and £40 for persons under 16. Certain provisions of the Explosives Regulations 2014 (SI 2014 No. 1638) apply to 'fireworks' (defined by reg. 2). Breaches of the 2014 Regulations are offences contrary to the Health and Safety at Work Act 1974, s. 33. The Sentencing Council's *General Guideline: Overarching Principles* (see Supplement, **SG2-1**) is used for all offenders sentenced on or after 1 October 2019. **B12.280**

Possession of Pyrotechnic Articles at Musical Events

The PCA 2017, s. 134(1), makes it a summary only offence for a person to have a 'pyrotechnic article' in his possession at any time when the person is (a) at a place where a 'qualifying musical event' is being held, or (b) at any other place that is being used by 'a person responsible for the organisation of a qualifying musical event for the purpose of (i) regulating entry to, or departure from, the event, or (ii) providing sleeping or other facilities for those attending the event'. The offence thus applies to a person who carries out the forbidden action at any of the places specified in s. 134(1). By s. 134(2), the offence does *not* apply to a person who is responsible for organising the event, or to a person who has the article in his possession with the consent of the organiser of the event. **B12.281**

A 'pyrotechnic article' means an article that 'contains explosive substances, or an explosive mixture of substances, designed to produce heat, light, sound, gas or smoke, or a combination of such effects, through self-sustained exothermic chemical reactions, other than (a) a match, or (b) an article specified, or of a description specified, in regulations made by statutory instrument by the Secretary of State' (s. 134(4)).

A 'qualifying musical event' is one 'at which one or more live musical performances take place and which is specified, or of a description specified, in regulations made by statutory instrument by the Secretary of State' (s. 134(5), and see SI 2017 No. 306).

Penalties in Respect of an Offence under the Policing and Crime Act 2017, s. 134 By the PCA 2017, s. 134(3), a person guilty of an offence under s. 134(1) is liable on summary conviction to imprisonment for a term not exceeding 51 weeks (or, in relation to offences committed before the CJA 2003, s. 281(5), comes into force, three months), or to a fine not exceeding level 3 on the standard scale, or both. **B12.282**

Section B13 Offences Affecting Enjoyment of Premises

UNLAWFUL EVICTION AND HARASSMENT OF OCCUPIER

Definition

B13.1 The Protection from Eviction Act 1977, s. 1, creates three offences which may be considered together. The first offence, contrary to s. 1(2), is concerned with unlawful eviction (the statute using the words 'deprives'); the other two offences, contrary to s. 1(3) and (3A), are concerned with harassment of a residential occupier. The main differences between the two harassment offences is that the one contrary to s. 1(3) can be committed by any person and it is necessary to prove intention, whereas the offence contrary to s. 1(3A) can be committed only by the landlord or agent and no intention need be proved. Section 1(3) does not create two offences (*Schon v Camden London Borough Council* (1986) 84 LGR 830, per Glidewell LJ).

Protection from Eviction Act 1977, s. 1

(2) If any person unlawfully deprives the residential occupier of any premises of his occupation of the premises or any part thereof, or attempts to do so, he is guilty of an offence unless he proves that he believed, and had reasonable cause to believe, that the residential occupier had ceased to reside in the premises.

(3) If any person with intent to cause the residential occupier of any premises—

(a) to give up the occupation of the premises or any part thereof; or

(b) to refrain from exercising any right or pursuing any remedy in respect of the premises or part thereof;

does acts likely to interfere with the peace or comfort of the residential occupier or members of his household, or persistently withdraws or withholds services reasonably required for the occupation of the premises as a residence, he shall be guilty of an offence.

(3A) Subject to subsection (3B) below the landlord of a residential occupier or an agent of the landlord shall be guilty of an offence if—

(a) he does acts likely to interfere with the peace or comfort of the residential occupier or members of his household, or

(b) he persistently withdraws or withholds services reasonably required for the occupation of the premises in question as a residence,

and (in either case) he knows, or has reasonable cause to believe, that that conduct is likely to cause the residential occupier to give up the occupation of the whole or part of the premises or to refrain from exercising any right or pursuing any remedy in respect of the whole or part of the premises.

Procedure

The Protection from Eviction Act 1977, s. 6, provides that proceedings may be instituted by councils of districts and London boroughs, the Common Council of the City of London, councils of Welsh counties and county boroughs and the Council of the Scilly Isles. **B13.2**

The offence is triable either way. When tried on indictment it is normally a class 3 offence, but see CrimPD XIII, para. B (see Supplement, **CPD.XIII.B**) for the additional factors that the court considers on allocation.

Indictment

First Count **B13.3**

Statement of Offence

Unlawful eviction contrary to section 1(2) of the Protection from Eviction Act 1977.

Particulars of Offence

A on the... day of... unlawfully deprived V, the residential occupier, of his occupation of premises, namely..., by changing the locks of the said premises during the absence of V and the members of his household.

Second Count

Statement of Offence

Unlawful harassment contrary to section 1(3) of the Protection from Eviction Act 1977.

Particulars of Offence

A between the... day of... and the... day of... did acts likely to interfere with the peace and comfort of [or: withdrew (or withheld) services reasonably required for occupation, namely..., from] V, the residential occupier of premises at..., namely..., with intent to cause V to give up his occupation of the said premises [or: to refrain from exercising the right to...] [or: to refrain from pursuing a remedy of...], without reasonable cause to believe that he had ceased to reside in the premises.

Although strictly speaking in an indictment for the offence contrary to s. 1(3) there need be no reference to a 'persistent' withdrawing or withholding of services, as a matter of practice it is desirable that it should be included (*Abrol* [1972] Crim LR 318). It would not appear that s. 1(3) is a possible alternative offence to s. 1(2), although Glidewell LJ, giving the judgment of the Divisional Court in *Costelloe v Camden London Borough Council* [1986] Crim LR 249, stated that charging the two offences in the alternative would not be objectionable.

Sentence

The maximum penalty is: on summary conviction, imprisonment for a term not exceeding six months or a fine not exceeding the prescribed sum; on conviction on indictment, two years' imprisonment and/or a fine (Protection from Eviction Act 1977, s. 1(4)). **B13.4**

In *Khan* [2001] EWCA Crim 912, [2001] 2 Cr App R (S) 129 (553), a sentence of 15 months' imprisonment was upheld on conviction after a trial where D and four associates kicked down the door to V's flat when she was out, caused wanton damage to her possessions and made threats of violence against her. See also *Pittard* (1994) 15 Cr App R (S) 108.

Persons who can Commit Offence

The offences contrary to the Protection from Eviction Act 1977, s. 1(2) and (3), may be committed by 'any person', whereas the offence contrary to s. 1(3A) may be committed only by 'the landlord of a residential occupier or an agent of the landlord'. It may be that if the eviction is 'unlawful' within s. 1(2) only by virtue of the provisions of s. 3(1), the offence can be committed only by a landlord or agent (see **B13.11**). **B13.5**

Liability of Corporate Officers

B13.6 The Protection from Eviction Act 1977, s. 1(6), makes provision for the liability of officers of a body corporate which is guilty of one of the two offences:

Protection from Eviction Act 1977, s. 1

(6) Where an offence under this section committed by a body corporate is proved to have been committed with the consent or connivance of, or to be attributable to any neglect on the part of, any director, manager or secretary or other similar officer of the body corporate or any person who was purporting to act in any such capacity, he as well as the body corporate shall be guilty of that offence and shall be liable to be proceeded against and punished accordingly.

Meaning of 'Residential Occupier'

B13.7 **Protection from Eviction Act 1977, s. 1**

(1) In this section 'residential occupier', in relation to any premises, means a person occupying the premises as a residence, whether under a contract or by virtue of any enactment or rule of law giving him the right to remain in occupation or restricting the right of any other person to recover possession of the premises.

Provided an occupier has a right to remain in occupation, or the right of any other person to recover possession of the premises is restricted, the occupier is a 'residential occupier'. It has to be ascertained whether a given occupier has sufficient residential protection to qualify under this statute. In *Blankley* [1979] Crim LR 166, a Crown Court judge held, considering the earlier offence contrary to the Rent Act 1965, s. 30, that there was no case to answer since the occupier was not a tenant but merely a contractual licensee. With respect, this decision cannot be correct, since the Protection from Eviction Act 1977 is not concerned with whether the occupier is a tenant, but whether the occupation, granted by whatever means, satisfies the statutory requirements. Those requirements may be satisfied under a contractual licence. Lord Widgery CJ, giving the judgment of the Divisional Court, accepted in *Thurrock Urban District Council v Shina* (1972) 70 LGR 301 that a licensee could be a residential occupier, whilst recognising that a licence may more easily be terminated than a tenancy. This case is also a decision on the Rent Act 1965, s. 30. Of course, once a licence is ended, the person is usually no longer a residential occupier and falls outside the protection provided by these offences (*Portsmouth City Council, ex parte Knight* (1983) 82 LGR 184; *Surrey Heath Borough Council, ex parte Li* (1984) 16 HLR 79). In *R (N) v Lewisham London Borough Council* [2014] UKSC 62, [2015] AC 1259, the Supreme Court held that where a local authority provides accommodation under a temporary licence, pursuant to the duty in s. 188(1) of the Housing Act 1996, the Protection from Eviction Act 1977 does not apply.

The wider approach being advocated also follows from the decision of the Divisional Court in *Norton v Knowles* [1969] 1 QB 572 (a decision on the Rent Act 1965, s. 30) that a person living in a caravan which was not attached to the land was a residential occupier. Although the caravan was connected to the drains, water pipes and electricity supply and had a telephone, it does not appear that these factors were necessarily essential to the decision. What was essential was the relationship between the landlord and the caravan dweller.

Belief that Person Not Residential Occupier

B13.8 In relation to the harassment offence contrary to the Protection from Eviction Act 1977, s. 1(3), the Court of Appeal in *Phekoo* [1981] 3 All ER 84 held, on the basis that conviction for the offence is conviction for a truly criminal offence and attaches serious social stigma to D, that, where the issue is raised that D reasonably believed that the person who was harassed was not a residential occupier, it is for the Crown to prove that that belief was not honest. Although this decision directly applies only to the offence contrary to s. 1(3), there appears to be no good reason why it does not also apply to the offence contrary to s. 1(2) and (3A) (*Qureshi* [2011] EWCA Crim 676, [2012] 1 WLR 694). Whether it is still good law that there must be a reasonable basis for the belief, or whether the belief has only to be an honest one, is a question which is open. See the discussion of 'mistake' at **A3.2** to **A3.11**. For reasons of compliance with the ECHR, Article 6(2), it may be that the burden will be confirmed as lying on the prosecution (see *A-G's Ref (No. 1 of 2004)* [2004] EWCA Crim 1025, [2004] 4 All ER 457 and **F3.18** ***et seq.***).

Meaning of 'Premises'

Lord Widgery CJ, giving the judgment of the Divisional Court in *Thurrock Urban District Council v Shina* (1972) 70 LGR 301, decided that the word 'premises' in the Rent Act 1965, s. 30, the precursor to the Protection from Eviction Act 1977, should be given its normal wide meaning. He had no doubt that a single room, together with shared use of a bathroom and kitchen, did fall within the meaning of 'premises'. 'Premises' may include a caravan, together with the land upon which it stands (*Norton v Knowles* [1969] 1 QB 572). **B13.9**

Meaning of 'Occupying Premises as a Residence'

'Occupying premises as a residence' has the same meaning as it had in the Rent Act 1977 (*Schon v Camden London Borough Council* (1986) 84 LGR 830). Thus, a person may occupy premises as the person's residence although physically absent from them, provided that the absence is not, and is not intended to be, permanent, and either the person's spouse or some other member of the family is physically in occupation or, at the very least, the person's furniture and belongings remain in the premises. An occupier may be a resident of more than one residence (*Hampstead Way Investments Ltd v Lewis-Weare* [1985] 1 WLR 164). **B13.10**

Elements Specific to s. 1(2)

Unlawfully Depriving Occupier The Protection from Eviction Act 1977, s. 3(1), makes it unlawful for the owner to enforce against the occupier, otherwise than by court proceedings, the owner's right to recover possession of the premises where those premises have been let as a dwelling under a tenancy (which is not a statutorily protected tenancy or an excluded tenancy) and the tenancy has come to an end but the occupier continues to reside in the premises. In *Patel v Pirabakaran* [2006] EWCA Civ 685, [2006] 1 WLR 3112, a case under s. 2 of the 1977 Act on the meaning of 'let as a dwelling', Wilson LJ said (at [34]): 'the phrase "let as a dwelling" in s. 2 of the Act of 1977 means "let wholly or partly as a dwelling" and so applies to premises which are let for mixed residential and business purposes'. 'Dwelling' suggests a greater degree of settled occupation than 'residence', and could be equated with a person's home (*R (N) v Lewisham London Borough Council* [2014] UKSC 62, [2015] AC 1259). **B13.11**

The Court of Appeal in *Yuthiwattana* (1984) 80 Cr App R 55 was satisfied that s. 1(2) is concerned with eviction, and so an unlawful deprivation must have the character of an eviction although it need not be of a permanent character. Kerr LJ, giving the judgment of the court, said (at p. 63): 'cases which are more properly described as "locking out" or not admitting an occupier on one or even more isolated occasions, so that in effect he continues to be allowed to occupy the premises but is then unable to enter, seem to us to fall appropriately under subsection (3)(a) or (b), which deal with acts of harassment'.

Consequently the conviction under a count charging the offence contrary to s. 1(2) had to be quashed because the occupier was excluded for only one night. This decision was followed by the Divisional Court in *Costelloe v Camden London Borough Council* [1986] Crim LR 249, where Glidewell LJ held that there is an offence under s. 1(2) where the landlord intends to exclude the occupier permanently and the occupier thinks he or she has been excluded permanently, even if the landlord then has a change of heart and the occupier is later admitted. What matters is whether the exclusion appears to be permanent. Woolf J put the point slightly differently saying:

> The proper test is: What was the nature of the exclusion? Was it, whether it be short or long, an exclusion designed to evict the tenant from the premises? If it was, then it falls within section 1(2). If on the other hand all that occurred was the deprivation of the occupation of the premises for a short period of time and that was the object of the exercise, then it would not fall within section 1(2).

If the occupier decides to vacate the premises following a degree of pressure or intimidation from the landlord this will probably not amount to unlawful deprivation (*Salva v Singh-Potiwal* [2019] UKUT 307 (LC)) but it could amount to harassment.

B13.12 **Belief that Occupier had Ceased to Reside in Premises** No offence is committed if D believes, on reasonable grounds, that a residential occupier has ceased to reside in the premises. D bears the burden of proof. D's state of mind is a matter for the jury to determine. Thus the trial judge erred in *Davidson-Acres* [1980] Crim LR 50, when he himself decided questions as to the time and existence of D's belief.

Elements Specific to s. 1(3)

B13.13 **Harassment with Intent** It is essential under this offence to establish the necessary intent. If it is not present, it may be that an offence contrary to the Protection from Eviction Act 1977, s. 1(3A), has been committed. It has been held that the meaning of the word 'intent' must be approached in the same way as in the law of murder (*AMK (Property Management) Ltd* [1985] Crim LR 600). On the other hand, the House of Lords in *Burke* [1991] AC 135 held that 'intention' in this context means with the purpose or motive of causing the occupier to give up occupation of the premises. This would appear to be a more limited understanding of the word 'intent' than usually applies in criminal law, and might not, therefore, be followed in a case to which the usual understanding actually applied on the facts. See generally **A2.4**. The intention must be either to cause the occupier to give up the premises (s. 1(3)(a)), or to refrain from exercising any right or pursuing any remedy in respect of the premises (s. 1(3)(b)).

B13.14 With regard to s. 1(3)(a), the Court of Appeal allowed the appeals in part in *AMK* (*Property Management*) *Ltd* [1985] Crim LR 600 because the trial judge had not made clear to the jury that the consequences of the building work designed to refurbish a block of flats were not simply to be equated with an intention to evict. An intention to evict must be established and, whilst the works could have been carried out without an intention to evict, the company's acts were reasonable and not of the kind covered by s. 1(3)(a). Ormrod LJ, giving the judgment of the Court of Appeal in *McCall v Abelesz* [1976] QB 585 (a decision on the Rent Act 1965, s. 30), held that it is not sufficient to establish that D was completely indifferent as to cutting off the gas supply to the occupier, nor would it be sufficient for D simply to allow things to happen which might have the effect of causing the occupier to leave, since these could not be equated with an intent to cause the occupier to give up the occupation of the premises. If D realised that there was a real likelihood that these activities would result in the occupier leaving, the general approach to the meaning of 'intent' might result in a decision that D did intend to cause the occupier to give up occupation of the premises. Applying the orthodox interpretation of intent, the requirement should be that D at least foresaw the occupier leaving as a virtually certain result of D's conduct (as to the general approach to 'intent', see **A2.4**). The unlawful deprivation need relate only to part of the premises for the offence to be established.

B13.15 With regard to s. 1(3)(b), the Divisional Court in *Schon v Camden London Borough Council* (1986) 84 LGR 830 held that 'an intention to persuade [the occupier] to leave for a limited period of time in order to enable work to be done and thereafter to allow her to return, was not an intent to cause her to give up her occupation of the premises. Notwithstanding that, it would be an intent which fell within the second intention within s. 1(3) because it would be an intention to cause her to refrain from exercising her right to live in the premises and to be physically present in the premises.' Since the charge was specifically worded to refer to s. 1(3)(b), the necessary intent was not established and the appeal against conviction was allowed.

B13.16 ***Belief that Person Harassed Not Residential Occupier*** The decision of the Court of Appeal on this matter in *Phekoo* [1981] 3 All ER 84 applies to this offence, and is considered at **B13.8**.

Acts Likely to Interfere with Peace or Comfort The Protection from Eviction Act 1977 uses the phrase 'does acts', which requires that there be conduct on the part of the accused, but that phrase does not require that there be more than one act (*Polycarpou* (1978) 9 HLR 129). Consequently, removing the sole source of heat of a tenant would satisfy this requirement of the offence. **B13.17**

It may be that the Court of Appeal in *McCall v Abelesz* [1976] 1 QB 585 had in mind the need to establish personal conduct, as distinct from merely taking advantage of the consequences of the acts of others with the accused actually doing nothing. In *Ahmad* (1987) 84 Cr App R 64, the Court of Appeal held that the phrase 'does acts' does not impose a responsibility to rectify damage which D has already caused by an act done innocently. Thus, a later failure to take steps to rectify what D has caused, even if with the requisite intent, is not the doing of an act or acts for the purposes of s. 1(3). Clearly an act and not an omission is required, and the doctrine established by the House of Lords in *Miller* [1983] 2 AC 161 (see **A1.20**) does not apply. In *Yuthiwattana* (1984) 80 Cr App R 55, in addition to *the failure* to provide a front door key, which would not of itself have sufficed, there was proof of other sufficient acts which included entering the occupier's room without permission, removing his record player and records, and shouting at him.

Kerr LJ, delivering the judgment of the Court of Appeal in *Yuthiwattana* (1984) 80 Cr App R 55, and explaining the *obiter dictum* of Ormrod LJ in *McCall v Abelesz* [1976] 1 QB 585, held that it is not necessary that the acts in question should constitute a breach of the civil law, but simply that D's act be one calculated to interfere with the occupier's peace and comfort which was intended to cause the occupier to give up occupation of the premises. *Yuthiwattana* was approved by the House of Lords in *Burke* [1991] AC 135.

The relevant acts must be ones 'likely to' interfere with peace or comfort. It should be noted that until the amendment introduced by the Housing Act 1988, s. 29(1), this phrase read 'calculated to', which caused uncertainty. The phrase 'likely to' is a matter of objective analysis, not of realisation or calculation on the part of D.

Persistently Withdrawing or Withholding Services The word 'persistently' requires the withholding of services to be deliberate and continuous (*Abrol* [1972] Crim LR 318). The Divisional Court in *Westminster City Council v Peart* (1968) 66 LGR 561, a decision on the Rent Act 1965, s. 30, held that 'persistently' in the identically worded precursor of the present provision, refers to the withholding of as well as the withdrawing of services. Withdrawal of a service on one day was not sufficient to satisfy the element of persistency. Lord Parker CJ, giving the judgment of the court, left open the question of whether failing to pay for a gas or electricity supply, as a result of which a gas or electricity company disconnects the service, can properly be described as the landlord withholding a service. Clearly, where D permanently cuts off the electricity supply, there is a persistent withholding. **B13.18**

Elements Specific to s. 1(3A)

Landlord Harassing Residential Occupier The points made in relation to the offence contrary to s. 1(3) regarding the meaning of 'does acts likely to interfere with the peace or comfort of the residential occupier or members of his household' and 'persistently withdraws or withholds services reasonably required for the occupation of the premises in question as a residence', apply in full to the s. 1(3A) offence. However, the offence contrary to s. 1(3A) differs in that it can be committed only by a landlord (or agent) and it is not necessary to establish intention, although knowledge or belief must be established. In *Qureshi* [2011] EWCA Crim 676, [2012] 1 WLR 694 the issue for the Court of Appeal was whether D may be guilty of an offence under s. 1(3A) on the footing that D is vicariously liable for the act of another or others. The Court held that on its true construction s. 1(3A) requires the actual participation of D and that there is no room for vicarious liability. **B13.19**

B13.20 Meaning of 'Landlord'

Protection from Eviction Act 1977, s. 1

(3C) In subsection (3A) above 'landlord', in relation to a residential occupier of any premises, means the person who, but for—
(a) the residential occupier's right to remain in occupation of the premises, or
(b) a restriction on the person's right to recover possession of the premises,
would be entitled to occupation of the premises and any superior landlord under whom that person derives title.

If it is necessary to discover the identity of the landlord, a notice may be served on the landlord's agent or other person under s. 7 of the Act, requiring the disclosure of the landlord's full name and address. If such is not forthcoming, the person on whom the notice is served is guilty of a summary offence and liable to a fine not exceeding level 4 on the standard scale.

B13.21 **Knowledge or Belief** The landlord, though not requiring an intention, must know or have reasonable cause to believe that the residential occupier is likely to be caused to give up occupation of the premises (*R (McGowan) v Brent Justices* [2001] EWHC Admin 814).

Specific Defences

B13.22 The Protection from Eviction Act 1977, s. 1(2), provides that a person is not guilty of the eviction offence if 'he proves that he believed, and had reasonable cause to believe, that the residential occupier had ceased to reside in the premises'. D must prove the belief and its reasonable foundation on a balance of probabilities (*Desai* (1992) *The Times*, 3 February 1992).

Protection from Eviction Act 1977, s. 1

(3B) A person shall not be guilty of an offence under subsection (3A) above if he proves that he had reasonable grounds for doing the acts or withdrawing or withholding the services in question.

When the legal burden is on D, the standard required is proof on a balance of probabilities (see **F3.6** and **F3.53**). A trial judge is not obliged to leave this defence to the jury if it would be 'tenuous and specious' to do so (*Allen* [2013] EWCA Crim 676 at [14]).

Related Offences

B13.23 The offences contrary to the CLA 1977, Part I (see **B13.24** to **B13.37**), may be relevant. In particular, even if a person's activity does not fall within the Protection from Eviction Act 1977 offence because, for example, the 'victim' is not a residential occupier, the offence contrary to the CLA 1977, s. 6, using or threatening violence to secure entry, may nevertheless cover the relevant activity.

USE OR THREAT OF VIOLENCE FOR PURPOSE OF SECURING ENTRY TO PREMISES

Definition

B13.24 It is a summary offence, by virtue of the CLA 1977, s. 6(1), for any person, without lawful authority, to use or threaten violence 'for the purpose of securing entry into any premises for himself or for any other person', provided that:

(a) there is someone present on those premises at the time who is opposed to the entry which the violence is intended to secure; and
(b) the person using or threatening the violence knows that that is the case.

Procedure and Sentence

The CLA 1977, s. 12(8), provides that 'no rule of law ousting the jurisdiction of magistrates' courts to try offences where a dispute of title to property is involved shall preclude magistrates' courts from trying offences under this part of this Act'. By virtue of s. 6(5), a person found guilty of this offence is liable to imprisonment for a term not exceeding six months or a fine not exceeding level 5 on the standard scale, or both. **B13.25**

Elements

Some of the elements of this offence are further defined by the CLA 1977: **B13.26**

(a) *Uses or threatens violence*: according to s. 6(4)(a), it is immaterial whether the violence in question is directed against the person or against property.
(b) *Entry*: according to s. 6(4)(b), it is immaterial whether the entry which the violence is intended to secure is for the purpose of acquiring possession of the premises in question or for any other purpose. As to the meaning of entry in the analogous offence of burglary, see **B4.86**.
(c) *Premises*: according to s. 12, this means any building, any part of a building under separate occupation, any land ancillary to a building, the site comprising any building or buildings together with any land ancillary thereto. By s. 12(2) the references to a building apply to any structure other than a moveable one, and to any moveable structure, vehicle or vessel designed or adapted for residential purposes; and further that (i) part of a building is under separate occupation if anyone is in occupation or entitled to occupation of that part as distinct from the whole, and (ii) land is ancillary to a building if it is adjacent to it and used (or intended for use) in connection with the occupation of that building or any part of it.
(d) *Lawful authority* is considered in s. 6(2), which provides that the fact that a person has any interest in or right to possession or occupation of any premises shall not constitute lawful authority for the use or threat of violence by that person or anyone else for the purpose of securing entry into those premises.

Specific Defence

No offence is committed if the person is a displaced residential occupier or a protected intending occupier of the premises in question or is acting on behalf of such an occupier. If D adduces sufficient evidence of being, or of acting on behalf of, such an occupier D is presumed to be, or to be acting on behalf of, such an occupier unless the contrary is proved by the prosecution (CLA 1977, s. 6(1A)). When the legal burden is on D, the standard required is proof on a balance of probabilities (see **F3.6** and **F3.53**). **B13.27**

Displaced Residential Occupier Section 6(7) of the CLA 1977 makes clear that it is s. 12 which determines when a person is to be regarded as a 'displaced residential occupier' of any premises or of any access to any premises, which involves also considering the meaning of 'trespasser' (the meaning of 'premises' has been considered at **B13.26**). **B13.28**

Section 12(3) defines 'displaced residential occupier' by providing that any person who was occupying any premises as a residence immediately before being excluded from occupation by anyone who entered those premises, or any access to those premises, as a trespasser, is a displaced residential occupier of the premises for the purposes of this part of the Act, so long as that person continues to be excluded from occupation of the premises by the original trespasser or any subsequent trespasser. Such a person is also regarded, by s. 12(5), as a displaced residential occupier of any access to those premises.

Section 12(4) provides that a person who was occupying the premises in question as a trespasser immediately before being excluded from occupation, is not a displaced residential occupier of the premises. Section 12(6) provides an extended meaning of 'trespasser' so that anyone who enters or is on or in occupation of any premises by virtue of (a) any title derived from a trespasser, or (b) any licence or consent given by a trespasser or by a person deriving title from a trespasser, is treated as a trespasser for present purposes alone, and phrases involving a reference to a trespasser will be construed accordingly. Further s. 12(7) provides that anyone who is on any premises as a trespasser does not cease to be a trespasser by virtue of being allowed time to leave the premises, nor does anyone cease to be a displaced residential occupier of any premises by virtue of any such allowance of time to a trespasser.

In relation to any premises, 'access' means any part of any site or building within which those premises are situated which constitutes an ordinary means of access to those premises (whether or not that is its sole or primary use) (s. 12(1)(b)).

B13.29 **Protected Intending Occupier** Section 6(7) of the CLA 1977 also indicates that s. 12A has effect for determining when any person is to be regarded as a protected intending occupier of any premises (or any access to those premises: s. 12A(11)).

Criminal Law Act 1977, s. 12A

(1) For the purposes of this Part of this Act [part II] an individual is a protected intending occupier of any premises at any time if at that time he falls within subsection (2), (4) or (6) below.
(2) An individual is a protected intending occupier of any premises if—
 (a) he has in those premises a freehold interest or a leasehold interest with not less than two years still to run;
 (b) he requires the premises for his own occupation as a residence;
 (c) he is excluded from occupation of the premises by a person who entered them, or any access to them, as a trespasser; and
 (d) he or a person acting on his behalf holds a written statement—
  (i) which specifies his interest in the premises;
  (ii) which states that he requires the premises for occupation as a residence for himself; and
  (iii) with respect to which the requirements in subsection (3) below are fulfilled.
(3) The requirements referred to in subsection (2)(d)(iii) above are—
 (a) that the statement is signed by the person whose interest is specified in it in the presence of a justice of the peace or commissioner for oaths; and
 (b) that the justice of the peace or commissioner for oaths has subscribed his name as a witness to the signature.
(4) An individual is also a protected intending occupier of any premises if—
 (a) he has a tenancy of those premises (other than a tenancy falling within subsection (2)(a) above or (6)(a) below) or a licence to occupy those premises granted by a person with a freehold interest or a leasehold interest with not less than two years still to run in the premises;
 (b) he requires the premises for his own occupation as a residence;
 (c) he is excluded from occupation of the premises by a person who entered them, or any access to them, as a trespasser; and
 (d) he or a person acting on his behalf holds a written statement—
  (i) which states that he has been granted a tenancy of those premises or a licence to occupy those premises;
  (ii) which specifies the interest in the premises of the person who granted that tenancy or licence to occupy ('the landlord');
  (iii) which states that he requires the premises for occupation as a residence for himself; and
  (iv) with respect to which the requirements in subsection (5) below are fulfilled.
(5) The requirements referred to in subsection (4)(d)(iv) above are—
 (a) that the statement is signed by the landlord and by the tenant or licensee in the presence of a justice of the peace or commissioner for oaths;
 (b) that the justice of the peace or commissioner for oaths has subscribed his name as a witness to the signatures.

(6) An individual is also a protected intending occupier of any premises if—
(a) he has a tenancy of those premises (other than a tenancy falling within subsection (2)(a) or (4)(a) above) or a licence to occupy those premises granted by an authority to which this subsection applies;
(b) he requires the premises for his own occupation as a residence;
(c) he is excluded from occupation of the premises by a person who entered the premises, or any access to them, as a trespasser; and
(d) there has been issued to him by or on behalf of the authority referred to in paragraph (a) above a certificate stating that—
(i) he has been granted a tenancy of those premises or a licence to occupy those premises as a residence by the authority; and
(ii) the authority which granted that tenancy or licence to occupy is one to which this subsection applies, being of a description specified in the certificate.

(7) Subsection (6) above applies to the following authorities—
(a) any body mentioned in section 14 of the Rent Act 1977 (landlord's interest belonging to local authority etc.);
(b) the Regulator of Social Housing;
(ba) a non-profit registered provider of social housing;
(bb) a profit-making registered provider of social housing, but only in relation to premises which are social housing within the meaning of Part 2 of the Housing and Regeneration Act 2008;
(c) [repealed]; and
(d) a registered social landlord within the meaning of the Housing Act 1985...

(7A) Subsection (6) also applies to the Secretary of State if the tenancy or licence is granted by him under Part III of the Housing Associations Act 1985.

A freehold owner of former matrimonial premises is not a 'protected intending occupier' within the meaning of s. 12A, each of the provisions of which must be read conjunctively (*Wakolo v DPP* [2012] EWHC 611 (Admin)).

If a person makes a statement for the purposes of s. 12A(2)(d) or (4) which the person knows to be false in a material particular (see **B6.12** for meaning), or recklessly makes such a statement which is false in a material particular, the person commits an offence (s. 12A(8)) and is liable on summary conviction to imprisonment for a term not exceeding six months and/or an unlimited fine (s. 12A(10)). **B13.30**

OFFENCE OF SQUATTING IN A RESIDENTIAL BUILDING

Definition

Legal Aid, Sentencing and Punishment of Offenders Act 2012, s. 144 **B13.31**

(1) A person commits an offence if—
(a) the person is in a residential building as a trespasser having entered it as a trespasser,
(b) the person knows or ought to know that he or she is a trespasser, and
(c) the person is living in the building or intends to live there for any period.

(2) The offence is not committed by a person holding over after the end of a lease or licence (even if the person leaves and re-enters the building).

Procedure and Sentence

The offence is triable summarily. The maximum penalty is imprisonment for a term not exceeding six months or an unlimited fine or both (LASPO 2012, s. 144(5) and (6)). **B13.32**

Elements

By virtue of the LASPO 2012, s. 144(7), it is irrelevant whether a person entered the building as a trespasser before or after the commencement of the section. **B13.33**

The term 'building' includes any structure or part of a structure (including a temporary or moveable structure) and a building is 'residential' if it is designed or adapted, before the time of entry, for use as a place to live (s. 144(3)).

The fact that a person derives title from a trespasser, or has the permission of a trespasser, does not prevent the person from being a trespasser (s. 144(4)).

For a review of the s. 144 offence in the context of a civil claim for adverse possession by the squatter, see *R (Best) v Chief Land Registrar* [2015] EWCA Civ 17, [2016] QB 23.

ADVERSE OCCUPATION OF RESIDENTIAL PREMISES

Definition

B13.34 **Criminal Law Act 1977, s. 7**

(1) ...any person who is on any premises as a trespasser after having entered as such is guilty of an offence if he fails to leave those premises on being required to do so by or on behalf of—
(a) a displaced residential occupier of the premises; or
(b) an individual who is a protected intending occupier of the premises.

Procedure and Sentence

B13.35 The offence is triable summarily (CLA 1977, s. 7(5)). Where the offence relates to a protected intending occupier, a document purporting to be a certificate under the CLA 1977, s. 12A(6)(d) (see **B13.29**), is to be received in evidence and, unless the contrary is proved, is deemed to have been issued by or on behalf of the authority stated in the certificate (s. 12A(9)(b)).

The maximum penalty is imprisonment for a term not exceeding six months or an unlimited fine or both (s. 7(5)).

Elements

B13.36 Premises includes a reference to any access to them, whether or not such access itself constitutes premises within the meaning of the CLA 1977, Part II (s. 7(4)).

For the meaning of 'displaced residential occupier' and 'protected intending occupier', see **B13.28** and **B13.29**.

Specific Defences

B13.37 Section 7(3) provides that it is a defence for D to prove that:

(a) 'he believed that the person requiring him to leave the premises was not a displaced residential occupier or protected intending occupier of the premises or a person acting on behalf of a displaced residential occupier or protected intending occupier' (CLA 1977, s. 7(2));
(b) the premises in question are or form part of premises used mainly for non-residential purposes, and that D was not on any part of the premises used wholly or mainly for residential purposes.

When the legal burden is on D, the standard required is proof on a balance of probabilities (see **F3.6** and **F3.53**). For a summary of the case law relating to 'reverse burden' challenges under the HRA 1998, see **F3.18** ***et seq.*** Where D was requested to leave the premises by a person claiming to be or to act on behalf of a protected intending occupier of the premises, it is a defence for D to prove that, although asked to do so by D at the time D was requested to leave, that person failed at that time to produce to D a s. 12A statement or certificate (s. 12A(9)(a)) (see **B13.29** and *Forest Justices, ex parte Hartman* [1991] Crim LR 641).

TRESPASSING DURING THE CURRENCY OF AN INTERIM POSSESSION ORDER

Definition

Criminal Justice and Public Order Act 1994, s. 76 **B13.38**

(2) . . . a person who is present on premises as a trespasser at any time during the currency of the order commits an offence.

. . .

(4) A person who was in occupation of the premises at the time of service of the order but leaves them commits an offence if he re-enters the premises as a trespasser or attempts to do so after the expiry of the order but within the period of one year beginning with the day on which it was served.

Procedure and Sentence

The offences are triable summarily only. **B13.39**

The maximum penalty is a term of imprisonment not exceeding six months or an unlimited fine or both (CJPO 1994, s. 76(5)).

Elements

References to 'the order' are to be construed as referring to an interim possession order which has been made in respect of any premises and served in accordance with rules of court (CJPO 1994, s. 76(1)); references to 'the premises' are to the premises covered by the order (s. 76(1)). For the meaning of 'premises', which has the same meaning as in the CLA 1977, Part II, see **B13.26**. An interim possession order means an interim possession order (so entitled) made under rules of court for the bringing of summary proceedings for possession of premises which are occupied by trespassers (CJPO 1994, s. 75(4)). **B13.40**

A person who is in occupation of the premises at the time of service of the order is to be treated for the purposes of s. 76 as being present as a trespasser (s. 76(6)).

Specific Defence

Section 76(3) of the CJPO 1994 provides a specific defence to a charge under s. 76(2). No offence is committed by a person by leaving the premises within 24 hours of the time of service of the order and not returning, or if a copy of the order was not fixed to the premises in accordance with rules of court. When the legal burden is on D, the standard required is proof on a balance of probabilities (see **F3.6** and **F3.53**). For a summary of the case law relating to 'reverse burden' challenges under the HRA 1998, see **F3.18** ***et seq.*** **B13.41**

INTERIM POSSESSION ORDERS: FALSE OR MISLEADING STATEMENTS

Definition

Criminal Justice and Public Order Act 1994, s. 75 **B13.42**

(1) A person commits an offence if, for the purpose of obtaining an interim possession order, he—
  (a) makes a statement which he knows to be false or misleading in a material particular; or
  (b) recklessly makes a statement which is false or misleading in a material particular.

(2) A person commits an offence if, for the purpose of resisting the making of an interim possession order, he—
  (a) makes a statement which he knows to be false or misleading in a material particular, or
  (b) recklessly makes a statement which is false or misleading in a material particular.

Procedure and Sentence

B13.43 This offence is triable either way (CJPO 1994, s. 75(3)).

The maximum penalty is, on indictment, imprisonment for a term not exceeding two years or a fine or both, and, summarily, imprisonment for a term not exceeding six months or an unlimited fine or both (s. 75(3)).

Elements

B13.44 'Statement' in relation to an interim possession order, means any statement, in writing or oral and whether as to fact or belief, made in or for the purposes of the proceedings (CJPO 1994, s. 75(4)). For the meaning of 'interim possession order', see **B13.40**; for the meaning of 'premises', see **B13.26**.

AGGRAVATED TRESPASS

Definition

B13.45 **Criminal Justice and Public Order Act 1994, s. 68**

(1) A person commits the offence of aggravated trespass if he trespasses on land and, in relation to any lawful activity which persons are engaging in or are about to engage in on that or adjoining land, does there anything which is intended by him to have the effect—
(a) of intimidating those persons or any of them so as to deter them or any of them from engaging in that activity,
(b) of obstructing that activity, or
(c) of disrupting that activity.

Procedure and Sentence

B13.46 The offence is triable summarily (CJPO 1994, s. 68(3)). A charge is not void for duplicity where it states that the accused intended to 'deter, disrupt or obstruct' a hunt because these elements overlap. Therefore, there is no need for each element to be the subject of a separate charge (*Nelder v CPS* (1998) *The Times*, 11 June 1998).

The maximum penalty is imprisonment for a term not exceeding three months or a fine not exceeding level 4 on the standard scale or both (s. 68(3)).

Elements

B13.47 There are three elements to the offence: trespass on land; an intention to have one of three effects stated in subsections (a), (b) and (c) (despite the lack of the word 'or' after (a), Rafferty J in *Tilly v DPP* [2001] EWHC Admin 821 confirmed that this is the correct interpretation, but see the critical commentary at [2002] Crim LR 128); and an act done towards that end (*Winder v DPP* (1996) 160 JP 713; *Barnard v DPP* (1999) *The Times*, 9 November 1999). The act must be a 'distinct and overt act' apart from trespass, which calls for careful consideration in the context of the facts of a given case (*Peppersharp v DPP* [2012] EWHC 474 (Admin), (2012) 176 JP 257, approving *Barnard v DPP*). In *Bauer v DPP* [2013] EWHC 634 (Admin), [2013] 1 WLR 3617, the Divisional Court held that when UK Uncut protestors forced their way into a department store and, once inside, began to erect tents, beat drums and sound other loud instruments, and even play volleyball, there had been acts distinct from the initial trespass so as to justify convictions under s. 68(1). Whether the activity is lawful is defined by the CJPO 1994, s. 68(2).

Criminal Justice and Public Order Act 1994, s. 68

(2) Activity on any occasion on the part of a person or persons on land is 'lawful' for the purpose of this section if he or they may engage in the activity on the land on that occasion without committing an offence or trespassing on the land.

This requires that the activity or task be lawful. It does not require that the way it is to be done must be lawful. Clearing land and felling trees was the activity in question in *Hibberd v DPP* (27 November 1996 unreported); it was held to be a lawful activity, even though the means used may have been in breach of the Health and Safety at Work etc. Act 1974.

The Supreme Court in *Richardson v DPP* [2014] UKSC 8, [2014] 2 WLR 288 held that the intention of s. 68 is plainly to add the sanction of the criminal law to a trespass where, in addition to D invading the property of someone else where D is not entitled to be, D there disrupts an activity which the occupant is entitled to pursue. Not every incidental or collateral criminal offence can properly be said to affect the lawfulness of the activity, nor to render it criminal. It will do so only when the criminal offence is integral to the core activity carried on. It will not do so when there is some incidental or collateral offence, which is remote from the activity. If, however, a criminal offence integral to the core activity is raised, it may involve the court investigating extraneous facts or the conduct of third parties.

There is an 'activity' only where someone is present on the land who could be intimidated or not allowed to get on with what that person is entitled to (*Tilly v DPP* [2001] EWHC Admin 821). By the CJPO 1994, s. 68(5), 'land' does not include those highways and roads excluded for the purposes of s. 61(9) (see **B13.53**). Further, the word 'land' in the CJPO 1994, ss. 68 and 69, includes buildings. In *DPP v Chivers* [2010] EWHC 1814 (Admin), [2011] 1 All ER 367, the Administrative Court held that, in its unamended form, s. 68 did not include buildings within the definition of 'land' because of the inclusion of the phrase 'in the open air' (which was removed by the ASBA 2003); the purpose and effect of the amendment was quite plainly to negative the exclusion of buildings.

Where the charge is under s. 68(1)(c), an intention to disrupt must be proved, but actual disruption need not be established (*Winder v DPP* (1996) 160 JP 713). Further, the Divisional Court was satisfied that the decision of the magistrate that the requisite intention was present was justified, as the trespassers ran towards a hunt, that being an act that was not merely preparatory to actual disruption, although that running was not itself intended to disrupt the hunt. As to the possible application of the defence of property as an answer to the charge, see *DPP v Bayer* [2003] EWHC 2567 (Admin), [2004] 1 WLR 2856. **B13.48**

In *Ayliffe v DPP* [2005] EWHC 684 (Admin), [2006] QB 227, the Divisional Court was concerned with whether the offence was committed where protesters trespassed on sites and interfered with activity there that was in preparation for action in the Gulf and Iraq and held that following the Court of Appeal's decision in *Jones* [2004] EWCA Crim 1981, [2005] QB 259, and in the absence of express provision to the contrary, the term 'offence' in a domestic statute was ordinarily treated as referring to an offence committed in the domestic sphere against a common law or statutory rule. Since the 1994 Act did not define the word 'offence', that term, as used in s. 68(2), was to be understood as referring to an offence under domestic criminal law and not to the crime of aggression in international law. The crime of aggression in international law had not been assimilated into domestic law. The House of Lords, considering appeals affecting the accused in *Ayliffe* among others, supported that view (*Jones* [2006] UKHL 16, [2007] 1 AC 136).

Power to Remove Persons

Under the CJPO 1994, s. 69(1), the senior police officer present at the scene has the power to direct a person or persons to leave land if the officer reasonably believes: **B13.49**

(a) that a person is committing, has committed or intends to commit the offence of aggravated trespass on land; or
(b) that two or more persons are trespassing on land and are present there with the common purpose of intimidating persons so as to deter them from engaging in a lawful activity or of obstructing or disrupting a lawful activity.

If a person knowing that a direction under s. 69(1) has been given which applies to that person fails to leave the land as soon as practicable or, having left, again enters the land as a trespasser within the period of three months beginning with the day on which the direction was given, the person commits an offence and is liable on summary conviction to imprisonment for a term not exceeding three months or a fine not exceeding level 4 on the standard scale or both (s. 69(3)). If the police officer giving the direction does not communicate it, any constable at the scene may communicate it (s. 69(2)).

It is a defence for D to show (i) that D was not trespassing on land, or (ii) that D had a reasonable excuse for failing to leave the land as soon as practicable or, as the case may be, for again entering the land as a trespasser (s. 69(4)). When the legal burden is on D, the standard required is proof on a balance of probabilities (see **F3.6** and **F3.53**).

FAILURE TO LEAVE OR RE-ENTRY TO LAND AFTER POLICE DIRECTION TO LEAVE

Definition

B13.50 **Criminal Justice and Public Order Act 1994, s. 61**

(4) If a person knowing that a direction under subsection (1) above has been given which applies to him—
 (a) fails to leave the land as soon as reasonably practicable, or
 (b) having left again enters the land as a trespasser within the period of three months beginning with the day on which the direction was given,
he commits an offence...

Procedure and Sentence

B13.51 The offence is triable summarily.

The maximum penalty is imprisonment for a term not exceeding three months or a fine not exceeding level 4 on the standard scale or both (CJPO 1994, s. 61(4)).

Elements

B13.52 **Criminal Justice and Public Order Act 1994, s. 61**

(1) If the senior police officer present at the scene reasonably believes that two or more persons are trespassing on land and are present there with the common purpose of residing there for any period, that reasonable steps have been taken by or on behalf of the occupier to ask them to leave and—
 (a) that any of those persons has caused damage to the land or to property on the land or used threatening, abusive or insulting words or behaviour towards the occupier, a member of his family or an employee or agent of his, or
 (b) that those persons have between them six or more vehicles on the land, he may direct those persons, or any of them, to leave the land and to remove any vehicles or other property they have with them on the land.

In *R (Fuller) v Chief Constable of Dorset Police* [2001] EWHC Admin 1057, [2003] QB 480, the Administrative Court decided that s. 61 did not breach the ECHR, Article 6, because, although the police procedure applied without recourse to a court, it did not prevent a challenge through the courts to the power of arrest or prosecution or to the decision of the landowner (the local authority). Nor was s. 61 in breach of Article 8; whilst a measure that prevents travellers or gypsies from residing in their vehicles on land may breach Article 8, it does not necessarily do so, following *South Buckinghamshire District Council v Porter* [2001] EWCA Civ 1549, [2002]

1 All ER 425, as it may be justifiable under Article 8(2)) or, for similar reasons as applied to Article 8 under Article 1 of Protocol 1. Even more clearly, there was no breach of Article 3 (as to Article 8 rights and trespassers, see also *Kay v Lambeth London Borough Council* [2006] UKHL 10, [2006] 2 AC 465).

The offence is committed only where a direction to leave has been given. The Court in *Fuller* decided that it followed from construing s. 61 narrowly that, as a direction could be given to leave at some time in the future, the offence could not be committed before the time permitted in the direction had expired. Further, if the trespassers had not had an opportunity to comply with the landowner's request to leave, a direction under s. 61 was not lawful or valid.

Where the senior police officer reasonably believes that the person was not originally a trespasser on the land, a direction may still be made if the person has become a trespasser and the senior police officer reasonably believes that the conditions in s. 61(1) are satisfied after the person became a trespasser (s. 61(2)).

Definitions Section 61(9) of the CJPO 1994 defines certain terms used in the section. **B13.53**

(a) 'Land' does not include:
   (i) buildings other than agricultural buildings (within the meaning of the Local Government Finance Act 1988, sch. 5, paras. 3 to 8) or scheduled monuments (within the meaning of the Ancient Monuments and Archaeological Areas Act 1979);
   (ii) land forming part of a highway unless it is a footpath, bridleway or byway open to all traffic within the meaning of the Wildlife and Countryside Act 1981, Part III, is a restricted byway within the meaning of the Countryside and Rights of Way Act 2000, Part II or is a cycle track under the Highways Act 1980 or the Cycle Tracks Act 1984.
(b) 'Occupier' means the person entitled to possession of the land by virtue of an estate or interest held by him.
(c) Subject to the extension of its meaning with regard to common land (see below), 'trespass' means trespass as against the occupier of the land.
(d) In relation to damage to property on land, 'property' has the meaning in the Criminal Damage Act 1971, s. 10(1) (see **B8.7**), and 'damage' includes the deposit of any substance capable of polluting the land.
(e) 'Vehicle' includes:
   (i) any vehicle, whether or not it is in a fit state for use on roads, and includes any chassis or body, with or without wheels, appearing to have formed part of such a vehicle, and any load carried by, and anything attached to, such a vehicle; and
   (ii) a caravan as defined in the Caravan Sites and Control of Development Act 1960, s. 29(1).
(f) A person may be regarded as having a purpose of residing in a place notwithstanding that he has a home elsewhere.

Where the persons are on common land (i.e. land registered as common land in a register of common land kept under the Commons Act 2006, Part 1, and land which is subject to rights of common as defined in that Act), the references to trespassing or trespassers are references to acts and persons doing acts which constitute either a trespass as against the occupier or an infringement of the commoners' rights; references to 'the occupier' include the commoners or any of them or, in the case of common land to which the public has access, the local authority as well as any commoner (CJPO 1994, s. 61(7)). Persons are not trespassers as against any commoner or the local authority if they are permitted to be there by the other occupier (s. 61(8)(b)). The person must know of the direction and, it would appear, that it applies to that person (s. 61(4)). If the police officer giving the direction does not communicate it to the persons to be removed, any constable may do so (s. 61(3)).

Specific Defence

B13.54 It is a defence for D to show that D was not trespassing on the land, or had a reasonable excuse for failing to leave the land as soon as reasonably practicable or, as the case may be, for again entering the land as a trespasser (CJPO 1994, s. 61(6)). When the legal burden is on D, the standard required is proof on a balance of probabilities (see **F3.6** and **F3.53**).

Powers of Seizure

B13.55 A constable may seize and remove vehicles after a direction under the CJPO 1994, s. 61, has been given, provided the criteria in s. 62 are satisfied.

TRESPASSER'S FAILURE TO LEAVE LAND ON POLICE DIRECTION AFTER OCCUPIER'S REQUEST

Definition

B13.56 **Criminal Justice and Public Order Act 1994, s. 62B**

(1) A person commits an offence if he knows that a direction under section 62A(1) has been given which applies to him and—
(a) he fails to leave the relevant land as soon as reasonably practicable, or
(b) he enters any land in the area of the relevant local authority as a trespasser before the end of the relevant period with the intention of residing there.

The CJPO 1994, ss. 62A to 62E, create complementary offences and provide powers to remove trespassers where an alternative site is available.

Procedure and Sentence

B13.57 The offence is triable summarily.

The maximum penalty is imprisonment for a term not exceeding three months, a fine not exceeding level 4 on the standard scale, or both (CJPO 1994, s. 62B(3)).

Elements

B13.58 The power of the police to require someone to leave is provided by the CJPO 1994, s. 62A.

Criminal Justice and Public Order Act 1994, s. 62A

(1) If the senior police officer present at a scene reasonably believes that the conditions in subsection (2) are satisfied in relation to a person and land, he may direct the person—
(a) to leave the land:
(b) to remove any vehicle and other property he has with him on the land.
(2) The conditions are—
(a) that the person and one or more others ('the trespassers') are trespassing on the land;
(b) that the trespassers have between them at least one vehicle on the land;
(c) that the trespassers are present on the land with the common purpose of residing there for any period;
(d) if it appears to the officer that the person has one or more caravans in his possession or under his control on the land, that there is a suitable pitch on a relevant caravan site for that caravan or for each of those caravans;
(e) that the occupier of the land or a person acting on his behalf has asked the police to remove the trespassers from the land.
(3) A direction under subsection (1) may be communicated to the person to whom it applies by any constable at the scene.

(4) Subsection (5) applies if—
 (a) a police officer proposes to give a direction under subsection (1) in relation to a person and land, and
 (b) it appears to him that the person has one or more caravans in his possession or under his control on the land.
(5) The officer must consult every local authority within whose area the land is situated as to whether there is a suitable pitch for the caravan or each of the caravans on a relevant caravan site which is situated in the local authority's area.

Definitions The following terms are defined by the CJPO 1994, s. 62A(6). 'Caravan' and 'caravan site' have the same meaning as in the Caravan Sites and Control of Development Act 1960, Part 1. 'Relevant caravan site' means a caravan site which is (a) situated in the area of a local authority within whose area the land is situated; and (b) managed by a relevant site manager. 'Relevant site manager' means (a) a local authority within whose area the land is situated; (b) a registered social landlord (which definition may be amended by the Secretary of State: s. 62A(7) and (8)). 'Registered social landlord' means a body registered as a social landlord under the Housing Act 1996, ch. 1. **B13.59**

The 'relevant period' in s. 62B(1) is the period of three months starting with the day on which the direction is given (s. 62B(2)).

'Land' does not include buildings other than (a) agricultural buildings within the meaning of the Local Government Finance Act 1988, sch. 5, paras. 3 to 8, or (b) scheduled monuments within the meaning of the Ancient Monuments and Archaeological Areas Act 1979 (s. 62E(2)). 'Local authority' means (a) in Greater London, a London borough or the Common Council of the City of London, (b) in England outside Greater London, a county council, a district council or the Council of the Isles of Scilly, (c) in Wales, a county council or a county borough council (s. 62E(3)). 'Occupier', 'trespass', 'trespassing' and 'trespasser' have the meanings given by s. 61 in relation to England and Wales (see **B13.53**) (s. 62E(4)). 'The relevant land' means the land in respect of which a direction under s. 62A(1) is given (s. 62E(5)). 'The relevant local authority' means (a) if the relevant land is situated in the area of more than one local authority (but is not in the Isles of Scilly), the district council or county borough council within whose area the relevant land is situated, (b) if the relevant land is situated in the Isles of Scilly, the Council of the Isles of Scilly, (c) in any other case, the local authority within whose area the relevant land is situated (s. 62E(6)). 'Vehicle' has the meaning given by s. 61 (see **B13.53**) (s. 62E(7)). A person may be regarded as having a purpose of residing in a place even if that person has a home elsewhere (s. 62E(8)).

Common Land Modifications The CJPO 1994, ss. 62A to 62C, have effect in relation to common land with the modifications in s. 62D (s. 62D(1)). In that context, references to trespassing and trespassers have effect as if they were reference to acts, and persons doing acts, which constitute (a) a trespass as against the occupier, or (b) an infringement of the commoners' rights (s. 62D(2)). References to the occupier (a) in the case of land to which the public has access, include the local authority and any commoner, (b) in any other case, include the commoners or any of them (s. 62D(3)). Section 62D(1) does not (a) require action by more than one occupier, or (b) constitute persons trespassers as against any commoner or other local authority if they are permitted to be there by the other occupier (s. 62D(4)). 'Common land', 'commoner' and 'the local authority' have the meanings given by s. 61 (see **B13.53**). **B13.60**

Defences

Criminal Justice and Public Order Act 1994, s. 62B **B13.61**

(5) In proceedings for an offence under this section it is a defence for the accused to show—
 (a) that he was not trespassing on the land in respect of which he is alleged to have committed the offence, or

(b) that he had a reasonable excuse—
(i) for failing to leave the relevant land as soon as reasonably practicable, or
(ii) for entering land in the area of the relevant local authority as a trespasser with the intention of residing there, or
(c) that, at the time the direction was given, he was under the age of 18 years and was residing with his parent or guardian.

When the legal burden is on D, the standard required is proof on a balance of probabilities (see F3.6 and F3.53).

Power of Seizure

B13.62 A constable may seize and remove vehicles after a direction under the CJPO 1994, s. 62A(1), has been given, provided the criteria in s. 62C are satisfied.

FAILURE TO LEAVE AN EXCLUSION ZONE AFTER BEING ORDERED TO DO SO

Definition

B13.63 **Serious Organised Crime and Police Act 2005, s. 112**

(5) Any person who knowingly contravenes a direction given to him under this section is guilty of an offence...

Procedure and Sentence

B13.64 The offence is triable summarily.

The maximum penalty is imprisonment for a term not exceeding six months or a fine not exceeding level 4 on the standard scale or both (SOCPA 2005, s. 112(5)).

Elements

B13.65 **Serious Organised Crime and Police Act 2005, s. 112**

(1) A constable may direct a person to leave a place if he believes, on reasonable grounds, that the person is in the place at a time when he would be prohibited from entering it by virtue of—
(a) an order to which subsection (2) applies, or
(b) a condition to which subsection (3) applies.
(2) This subsection applies to an order which—
(a) was made, by virtue of any enactment, following the person's conviction of an offence, and
(b) prohibits the person from entering the place or from doing so during a period specified in the order.
(3) This subsection applies to a condition which—
(a) was imposed, by virtue of any enactment, as a condition of the person's release from a prison in which he was serving a sentence of imprisonment following his conviction of an offence, and
(b) prohibits the person from entering the place or from doing so during a period specified in the condition.
(4) A direction under this section may be given orally.

'Sentence of imprisonment' and 'prison' are to be construed in accordance with the Criminal Justice and Court Services Act 2000, s. 62(5) (s. 112(8)(a)). The reference to a release from prison includes a reference to a temporary release (s. 112(8)(b)). 'Place' includes an area (s. 112(9)).

Section 112 applies whether or not the order or condition in s. 112(1) was made or imposed before or after the commencement of s. 112 (s. 112(10)).

FAILURE TO LEAVE LAND OR RE-ENTRY TO LAND: RAVES

Definition

Criminal Justice and Public Order Act 1994, s. 63 **B13.66**

(6) If a person knowing that a direction has been given which applies to him—
 (a) fails to leave the land as soon as reasonably practicable, or
 (b) having left again enters the land within the period of 7 days beginning with the day on which the direction was given,

he commits an offence...

Procedure and Sentence

The offence is triable summarily. **B13.67**

The maximum penalty is imprisonment for a term not exceeding three months or a fine not exceeding level 4 on the standard scale or both (CJPO 1994, s. 63(6)). Where a person has been convicted of this offence and the court is satisfied that sound equipment which has been seized from the person under s. 64(4), or which was in the person's possession or control at the relevant time, has been used at the gathering, it may make an order for forfeiture in respect of that property in compliance with the provisions of s. 66 (s. 66(1)).

Elements

Section 63 of the CJPO 1994 applies only to gatherings of the kind specified in the s. 63(1); in the marginal note to s. 63, and in common parlance, such gatherings are called raves. The offence is committed only where a direction to leave has been given. **B13.68**

Criminal Justice and Public Order Act 1994, s. 63

(1) This section applies to a gathering on land in the open air of 20 or more persons (whether or not trespassers) at which amplified music is played during the night (with or without intermissions) and is such as, by reason of its loudness and duration and the time at which it is played, is likely to cause serious distress to the inhabitants of the locality; and for this purpose—
 (a) such a gathering continues during intermissions in the music and, where the gathering extends over several days, throughout the period during which the amplified music is played at night (with or without intermissions); and
 (b) 'music' includes sounds wholly or predominantly characterised by the emission of a succession of repetitive beats.

(1A) This section also applies to a gathering if—
 (a) it is a gathering of 20 or more persons who are trespassing on the land; and
 (b) it would be a gathering of a kind mentioned in subsection (1) above if it took place on land in the open air.

(2) If, as respects any land, a police officer of at least the rank of superintendent reasonably believes that—
 (a) two or more persons are making preparations for the holding there of a gathering to which this section applies,
 (b) ten or more persons are waiting for such a gathering to begin there, or
 (c) ten or more persons are attending such a gathering which is in progress, he may give a direction that those persons and any other persons who come to prepare or wait for or to attend the gathering are to leave the land and remove any vehicles or other property they have with them on the land.

The terms 'trespasser' and 'vehicle' have the same meaning as in s. 61 of the 1994 Act (see **B13.53**). 'Land in the open air' includes a place partly open to the air (s. 63(10)). See also *DPP v Chivers* [2010] EWHC 1814 (Admin), [2011] 1 WLR 2324.

The person must know of the direction and, it would appear, that it applies to the person (s. 63(6)). If the police officer giving the direction does not communicate it to the persons to be removed, any constable at the scene may do so (s. 63(3)). Persons shall be treated as having had a direction communicated to them if reasonable steps have been taken to bring it to their attention (s. 63(4)).

Exempt Persons and Gatherings

B13.69 Directions do not apply to 'exempt persons' (CJPO 1994, s. 63(5)). An 'exempt person', in relation to land (or any gathering on land), means 'the occupier, any member of his family and any employee or agent of his and any person whose home is situated on the land' (s. 63(10)). As to the meaning of 'occupier', see **B13.53**.

Directions do not apply, in England and Wales, to a gathering licensed by an entertainment licence (s. 63(9)(a)).

Specific Defence

B13.70 It is a defence to a charge under the CJPO 1994, s. 63(6), for D to show that there was had a reasonable excuse for failing to leave the land as soon as reasonably practicable or, as the case may be, for again entering the land (s. 63(7)). When the legal burden is on D, the standard required is proof on a balance of probabilities (see **F3.6** and **F3.53**).

The offence does not apply to a gathering in relation to a licensable activity within the meaning of the Licensing Act 2003, s. 1(1)(c) (provision of certain forms of entertainment) which is carried on under and in accordance with an authorisation within the meaning of s. 136 of that Act (s. 63(9)).

Further Offence

B13.71 A person commits an offence, contrary to the CJPO 1994, s. 63(7A), if (a) the person knows that a direction under s. 63(2) has been given which applies to that person, and (b) makes preparations for or attends a gathering to which s. 63 applies within the period of 24 hours starting when the direction was given. A person guilty of this offence is liable, on summary conviction, to imprisonment for a term not exceeding three months or a fine not exceeding level 4 on the standard scale, or both (s. 63(7B)).

Police Powers

B13.72 Sections 63 to 65 and 67 of the CJPO 1994 provide certain additional police powers for the purpose of controlling or prohibiting gatherings of the kind specified in s. 63(1) (see B13.68).

(a) A constable authorised to enter land for any purpose in accordance with s. 64(1) and (2) by a police officer of at least the rank of superintendent may enter the land without a warrant (s. 64(3)).
(b) A constable may seize and remove vehicles or sound equipment (as defined in s. 64(6)) after a s. 63 direction provided the criteria in s. 64(4) and (5) are satisfied. Any vehicles so seized and removed may be retained in accordance with regulations made by the Secretary of State (s. 67(1)). Any sound equipment so seized and removed may be retained until the conclusion of proceedings against the person from whom it was seized for an offence under s. 63 (s. 67(2)). Any authority is entitled to recover from a person from whom a vehicle has been seized such charges as may be prescribed in respect of the removal, retention, disposal and destruction of the vehicle by the authority (s. 67(4)).
(c) A constable in uniform has power, at a place within five miles of the boundary of the site of the rave, to stop a person, except an exempt person, whom the constable reasonably believes to be on the way to a rave and direct the person not to proceed in the direction of the rave (s. 65(1), (2) and (3)). It is a summary offence for a person, knowing that such a direction

has been given, to fail to comply with that direction, and such a person is liable on conviction to a fine not exceeding level 3 on the standard scale (s. 65(4)).

UNAUTHORISED CAMPERS: FAILURE TO LEAVE OR RETURNING TO THE LAND

Definition

Criminal Justice and Public Order Act 1994, s. 77 **B13.73**

(3) If a person knowing that a direction under subsection (1) has been given which applied to him—
  (a) fails, as soon as practicable, to leave the land or remove from the land any vehicle or other property which is the subject of the direction, or
  (b) having removed any such vehicle or property again enters the land with a vehicle within the period of three months beginning with the day on which the direction was given,
  he commits an offence . . .

Procedure and Sentence

The offence is triable summarily only. **B13.74**

The maximum penalty is a fine not exceeding level 3 on the standard scale (CJPO 1994, s. 77(3)).

Direction

Criminal Justice and Public Order Act 1994, s. 77 **B13.75**

(1) If it appears to a local authority that persons are for the time being residing in a vehicle or vehicles within that authority's area—
  (a) on any land forming part of a highway;
  (b) on any other unoccupied land; or
  (c) on any occupied land without the consent of the occupier,
  the authority may give a direction that those persons and any others with them are to leave the land and remove the vehicle or vehicles and any other property they have with them on the land.

Notice of a direction must be served on the persons to whom the direction applies, but it is sufficient for the direction to specify the land and (except where it applies to only one person) to be addressed to all occupants of the vehicles on the land, without naming them (s. 77(2)). Where it is impracticable to serve a direction on a person named in it, it is treated as duly served if a copy is fixed in a prominent place to the vehicle concerned; and where the direction is directed to unnamed occupants of vehicles, it is treated as duly served on those occupants if it is fixed in a prominent place to every vehicle on the land in question at the time when service is thus effected (s. 79(2)). The local authority must take such steps as are reasonably practicable to ensure that a copy of the direction is displayed on the land in question (otherwise than by being fixed to a vehicle) in a manner designed to ensure that it is likely to be seen by any person camping on the land (s. 79(3)). Notice of a direction is to be given by the local authority to the owner of the land and to any occupier of that land unless, after reasonable inquiries, it is unable to ascertain their names and addresses (s. 79(4)).

A direction operates to require persons who re-enter the land within the period of three months with vehicles or other property to leave and remove the vehicles or other property as it operates in relation to the persons and vehicles or other property on the land when the direction was given (s. 77(4)).

Definitions

Section 77(6) of the CJPO 1994 provides definitions for certain terms used in the section. **B13.76**
A person may be regarded as residing on any land notwithstanding that the person has a home

elsewhere. 'Land' means land in the open air. 'Vehicle' and 'occupier' are defined in the same terms as in s. 61 (see **B13.53**).

Specific Defence

B13.77 It is a defence for D to show that the failure to leave or to remove the vehicle or other property as soon as practicable, or the re-entry with a vehicle, was due to illness, mechanical breakdown or other immediate emergency (CJPO 1994, s. 77(5)). When the legal burden is on D, the standard required is proof on a balance of probabilities (see **F3.6** and **F3.53**).

Magistrates' Removal Order

B13.78 On a complaint made by a local authority, a magistrates' court, if satisfied that persons and vehicles in which they are residing are present on land within that authority's area in contravention of such a direction, may make an order requiring the removal of any vehicle or other property and any person residing in it (CJPO 1994, s. 78(1)). Such an order may authorise the local authority to take such steps as are reasonably necessary to ensure that the order is complied with and, in particular, may authorise the authority, by its officers and servants, to enter upon the land specified in the order, and to take, in relation to any vehicle or property to be removed in pursuance of the order, such steps for securing entry and rendering it suitable for removal as may be specified in the order (s. 78(2)). The local authority must give to the owner and occupier at least 24 hours' notice of its intention to enter any occupied land unless after reasonable inquiries it is unable to ascertain their names and addresses (s. 78(3)). A person who wilfully obstructs any person in the exercise of any power conferred by an order under s. 78 commits an offence and is liable, on summary conviction, to a fine not exceeding level 3 on the standard scale (s. 78(4)). Where a complaint is made, a summons issued by the court requiring the person(s) to whom it is directed to appear before it to answer to the complaint may be directed either to the occupant of a particular vehicle on the land in question or to all occupants of vehicles on the land in question, without naming them (s. 78(5)). There is no power to issue a warrant for arrest upon failure to appear (s. 78(6)). The owner and occupier of the land are entitled to appear and be heard at any proceedings (s. 79(4)).

TRESPASS ON A PROTECTED SITE

Definition

B13.79 Serious Organised Crime and Police Act 2005, s. 128

(1) A person commits an offence if he enters, or is on, any protected site in England and Wales or Northern Ireland as a trespasser.

Procedure and Sentence

B13.80 The offence is triable summarily only.

The maximum penalty is imprisonment for a term not exceeding six months or an unlimited fine or both (SOCPA 2005, s. 128(5)). No proceedings for the offence may be instituted against any person in England and Wales except by or with the consent of the A-G (s. 128(6)(a)).

Elements

B13.81 A 'protected site' means a nuclear site or a designated site (SOCPA 2005, s. 128(1A)). 'Nuclear site' means (a) so much of any premises in respect of which a nuclear site licence (within the meaning of the Nuclear Installations Act 1965) is for the time being in force as lies within the outer perimeter of the protection provided for those premises; and (b) so much of any other premises of which premises falling within paragraph (a) form a part as lies within that outer perimeter (s. 128(1B)). For this purpose (a) the outer perimeter of the protection provided for any premises is the line of the outermost fences, walls or other obstacles provided or relied on for protecting those premises from intruders; and (b) that line shall be determined on the assumption that every gate, door or other barrier across a way through a fence, wall or other obstacle is closed (s. 128(1C)). A 'designated site' means a site (a) specified or described (in any way) in an order made by the Secretary of State, and (b) designated for the purposes of s. 128 by the order (SOCPA 2005, s. 128(2)). The land that the Secretary of State may designate must be comprised in Crown land, or comprised in land belonging to Her Majesty in her private capacity or to the immediate heir to the Throne in his private capacity, or it must appear to the Secretary of State that it is appropriate to designate the site in the interests of national security (s. 128(3)). 'Site' means the whole or part of any building or buildings, or any land, or both (s. 128(8)(a)). 'Crown land' means land in which there is a Crown interest or a Duchy interest (s. 128(8)(b)). 'Crown interest' means an interest belonging to Her Majesty in right of the Crown and 'Duchy interest' means an interest belonging to Her Majesty in right of the Duchy of Lancaster or belonging to the Duchy of Cornwall (s. 128(9)). Sites have been designated by the Serious Organised Crime and Police Act 2005 (Designated Sites) Order 2005 (SI 2005 No. 3447) and the Serious Organised Crime and Police Act 2005 (Designated Sites under Section 128) Order 2007 (SI 2007 No. 930), as amended by SI 2012 Nos. 1769 and 2709, SI 2013 No. 1562, SI 2014 Nos. 411 and 2263, SI 2018 No. 4 and SI 2020 No. 15; the former designates 15 sites of military significance and the latter designates 14 sites associated with the government, the security services and the Royal family.

A person who is on any protected site as a trespasser does not cease to be a trespasser by virtue of being allowed time to leave the site (s. 128(7)).

A person cannot claim not to be a trespasser by virtue of the rights of the public in relation to access to land under the Countryside and Rights of Way Act 2000, s. 2(1), since that provision does not apply in respect of land in respect of which a designation order is in force (s. 131(1)).

Defence

Serious Organised Crime and Police Act 2005, s. 128 **B13.82**

(4) It is a defence for a person charged with an offence under this section to prove that he did not know, and had no reasonable cause to suspect, that the site in relation to which the offence is alleged to have been committed was a protected site.

When the legal burden is on D, the standard required is proof on a balance of probabilities (see **F3.6** and **F3.53**).

OTHER OFFENCES BY TRESPASSERS

Trespassing with Firearm in a Building or on Land

Firearms Act 1968, s. 20 **B13.83**

(1) A person commits an offence if, while he has a firearm or imitation firearm with him, he enters or is in any building or part of a building as a trespasser and without reasonable excuse (the proof whereof lies on him).
(2) A person commits an offence if, while he has a firearm or imitation firearm with him, he enters or is on any land as a trespasser and without reasonable excuse (the proof whereof lies on him).

The mode of trial for trespassing with firearm in a building is either way, although if the weapon is an air weapon or an imitation firearm, the offence is triable summarily only. The mode of trial for trespassing with a firearm on any land is summary only. As to the extension of the usual time-limit within which summary proceedings must be instituted, see **B12.3**.

The offence of trespassing with a firearm in a building is punishable, on summary conviction, with a term of imprisonment not exceeding six months and/or an unlimited fine; and, on conviction on indictment, with a term of imprisonment not exceeding five years and/or a fine. Where the s. 2(1) offence is committed 'in respect of a firearm or ammunition' specified in the FA 1968, s. 5(1)(a), (aba), (ac), (ad), (ae), (af), (c) or (1A)(a), the mandatory sentence provisions in s. 51A apply by virtue of s. 51A(1A) (see **E5.9**).

The offence of trespassing with a firearm on any land is punishable, on summary conviction, with a term of imprisonment not exceeding three months or a fine not exceeding level 4 on the standard scale or both. As to the courts' power to order forfeiture or disposal of firearms and ammunition, see **B12.4**.

The meaning of 'firearm' is considered at **B12.8**. Imitation firearms (see **B12.26**) fall within this section. The Firearms Act 1968, s. 20(3), defines 'land' as including land covered by water.

Trespassing with Weapon of Offence

B13.84 It is a summary offence, contrary to the CLA 1977, s. 8(1), for a person who is on any premises as a trespasser, after having entered as such, without lawful authority or reasonable excuse to have with him on the premises any weapon of offence. As to disputes as to title to property on summary trial, see **B13.25**.

By virtue of s. 8(3), a person guilty of this offence is liable to imprisonment for a term not exceeding three months or an unlimited fine or both.

The meanings of the words 'premises' and 'trespasser' have been considered at **B13.26** and **B13.28**. The phrase, 'weapon of offence' is defined by s. 8(2) as meaning any article made or adapted for causing injury to or incapacitating a person, or intended by the person having it with him for such use. The same definition of 'weapon of offence' is used in the offence of aggravated burglary contrary to the Theft Act 1968, s. 10. For further discussion of this subject, see **B4.101**.

Trespassing on Premises of Foreign Missions, etc.

B13.85 It is a summary offence, contrary to the CLA 1977, s. 9(1), for a person to enter or be on any premises to which s. 9 applies as a trespasser. As to disputes as to title to property on summary trial, see **B13.25**.

By virtue of s. 9(6), proceedings for this offence may not be instituted against any person except by or with the consent of the A-G.

By virtue of s. 9(5), a person guilty of this offence is liable to imprisonment for a term not exceeding six months or an unlimited fine or both.

The phrase 'enters as a trespasser' is partly defined by the 1977 Act, since meanings are given for 'entry' and 'trespasser' (see **B13.26** and **B13.28** respectively). Similar terms also appear in the offence of burglary (see **B4.86** and **B4.87**).

B13.86 The premises to which s. 9 applies are listed in s. 9(2):

Criminal Law Act 1977, s. 9

(2) This section applies to any premises which are or form part of—

(a) the premises of a diplomatic mission within the meaning of the definition in Article 1(i) of the Vienna Convention on Diplomatic Relations signed in 1961 as that Article has effect in the United Kingdom by virtue of section 2 of and Schedule 1 to the Diplomatic Privileges Act 1964;

(aa) the premises of a closed diplomatic mission;

(b) consular premises within the meaning of the definition in paragraph 1(j) of Article 1 of the Vienna Convention on Consular Relations signed in 1963 as that Article has effect in the United Kingdom by virtue of section 1 of and Schedule 1 to the Consular Relations Act 1968;

(bb) the premises of a closed consular post;
(c) any other premises in respect of which any organisation or body is entitled to inviolability by or under any enactment; and
(d) any premises which are the private residence of a diplomatic agent (within the meaning of Article 1(e) of the Convention mentioned in paragraph (a) above) or of any other person who is entitled to inviolability of residence by or under any enactment.

(2A) In subsection (2) above—
'the premises of a closed diplomatic mission' means premises which fall within Article 45 of the Convention mentioned in subsection (2)(a) above (as that Article has effect in the United Kingdom by virtue of the section and Schedule mentioned in that paragraph); and
'the premises of a closed consular post' means premises which fall within Article 27 of the Convention mentioned in subsection (2)(b) above (as that Article has effect in the United Kingdom by virtue of the section and Schedule mentioned in that paragraph).

Insofar as the general meaning of 'premises' is relevant, see **B13.26**. Section 9(4) creates an important evidential provision in relation to establishing whether given premises are covered by s. 9 or not, since in any proceedings for this offence 'a certificate issued by or under the authority of the Secretary of State stating that any premises were or formed part of premises of any description mentioned in paragraphs (a) to (d) of subsection (2) above at the time of the alleged offence shall be conclusive evidence that the premises were or formed part of premises of that description at that time'.

By virtue of s. 9(3), it is a defence for D to prove that D believed that the premises in question were not premises to which s. 9 applies. When the legal burden is on D, the standard required is proof on a balance of probabilities (see **F3.6** and **F3.53**).

Obstruction of Court Officers Executing Process against Unauthorised Occupiers

It is a summary offence, contrary to the CLA 1977, s. 10(1), and without prejudice to the Sheriffs Act 1887, s. 8(2), if a person resists or intentionally obstructs any person who is in fact an officer of a court engaged in executing any process issued by the High Court or any county court for the purpose of enforcing any judgment or order for the recovery of any premises or for the delivery of possession of any premises. As to disputes as to title to property on summary trial, see **B13.25**. **B13.87**

By virtue of s. 6(5), a person guilty of this offence is liable to imprisonment for a term not exceeding six months or an unlimited fine or both.

A similar phrase to 'resists or intentionally obstructs' appears in the offence involving the obstruction of a constable contrary to the Police Act 1996, s. 89(2) (see **B2.48**).

'Officer of a court' according to s. 10(6) means any sheriff, under sheriff, deputy sheriff, bailiff or officer of a sheriff, and officer of the county court.

The offence does not apply unless the judgment or order in question was given or made in proceedings brought under any provisions of rules of court applicable only in circumstances where the person claiming possession of any premises alleges that the premises in question are occupied solely by a person or persons (not being a tenant or tenants holding over after the termination of the tenancy) who entered into or remained in occupation of the premises without the licence or consent of the person claiming possession or any predecessor in title.

'Premises' in this section has a slightly wider meaning than in the other offences in Part II of the CLA 1977. Section 12 states that 'premises' means any building, any part of a building under separate occupation, any land ancillary to a building, the site comprising any building or buildings together with any land ancillary thereto, and (for the purposes only of ss. 10 and 11) any other place. The references to a building apply also to any structure other than a moveable one, and to any moveable structure, vehicle or vessel designed or adapted for residential purposes; and: **B13.88**

(a) part of a building is under separate occupation if anyone is in occupation or entitled to occupation of that part as distinct from the whole; and
(b) land is ancillary to a building if it is adjacent to it and used (or intended for use) in connection with the occupation of that building or any part of it.

By virtue of s. 10(3), it is a defence for D to prove that D believed that the person D was resisting or obstructing was not an officer of a court. When the legal burden is on D, the standard required is proof on a balance of probabilities (see **F3.6** and **F3.53**).

There is a related offence under s. 10(A1) of resisting or intentionally obstructing any person who is an enforcement officer, or is acting under the authority of an enforcement officer and is engaged in executing a writ issued from the High Court.

Trespassing on Licensed or Authorised Aerodromes

B13.89 It is an offence, contrary to the Civil Aviation Act 1982, s. 39, for a person to trespass on any land forming part of an aerodrome licensed in pursuit of an Air Navigation Order or authorised by a certificate under the Aerodromes Regulations. The maximum punishment is, on summary conviction, a fine not exceeding level 3 on the standard scale (s. 39(1)). No one may be convicted unless it is proved that, at the material time, notices warning trespassers of their liability under s. 39 were posted so as to be readily seen and read by members of the public, in such positions on or near the boundary of the aerodrome as appear to the court to be proper (s. 39(2)).

Trespassing on a Railway

B13.90 It is an offence, contrary to the British Transport Commission Act 1949, s. 55(1), to trespass on any railway lines, sidings, embankments, tunnels, cuttings or similar railway works. Under the Penalties for Disorderly Behaviour (Amount of Penalty) Order 2002 (SI 2002 No. 1837), as amended, this offence is a penalty offence and the amount payable is £60.

Poaching Offences

B13.91 There are five poaching offences, the primary focus of which is the protection of game rights, but which involve trespass to land (see the Game Act 1831, s. 30, the Night Poaching Act 1828, s. 1 and the Deer Act 1991, s. 1). Further, it is an offence to take or destroy fish from water which is private property or in which there is a private right of fishery (Theft Act 1968, sch. 1, para. 2(1)).

Section B14 Offences Against the Administration of Justice

PERJURY IN A JUDICIAL PROCEEDING

Perjury Act 1911, s. 1 **B14.1**

(1) If any person lawfully sworn as a witness or as an interpreter in a judicial proceeding wilfully makes a statement material in that proceeding, which he knows to be false or does not believe to be true, he shall be guilty of perjury, and shall, on conviction thereof on indictment, be liable to imprisonment for a term not exceeding seven years, or to a fine or to both imprisonment and fine.

(2) The expression 'judicial proceeding' includes a proceeding before any court, tribunal, or person having by law power to hear, receive, and examine evidence on oath.

(3) Where a statement made for the purposes of a judicial proceeding is not made before the tribunal itself, but is made on oath before a person authorised by law to administer an oath to the person who makes the statement, and to record or authenticate the statement, it shall, for the purposes of this section, be treated as having been made in a judicial proceeding.

(4) A statement made by a person lawfully sworn in England for the purposes of a judicial proceeding:
  (a) in another part of His Majesty's dominions; or
  (b) in a British tribunal lawfully constituted in any place by sea or land outside His Majesty's dominions; or
  (c) in a tribunal of any foreign state,

shall, for the purposes of this section, be treated as a statement made in a judicial proceeding in England.

(5) Where, for the purposes of a judicial proceeding in England, a person is lawfully sworn under the authority of an Act of Parliament:
  (a) in any other part of His Majesty's dominions; or
  (b) before a British tribunal or a British officer in a foreign country, or within the jurisdiction of the Admiralty of England;

a statement made by such person so sworn as aforesaid (unless the Act of Parliament under which it was made otherwise specifically provides) shall be treated for the purposes of this section as having been made in the judicial proceeding in England for the purposes whereof it was made.

(6) The question whether a statement on which perjury is assigned was material is a question of law to be determined by the court of trial.

This offence applies to intermediaries appointed under the YJCEA 1999, s. 29, as it applies to interpreters (s. 29(7)). This includes intermediaries who assist in the examination of a witness otherwise than in the course of judicial proceedings: the examination shall be taken to be part of the judicial proceeding in which that witness's evidence is given. **B14.2**

Procedure

Perjury in a judicial proceeding is triable only on indictment. It is normally a class 3 offence, but see CrimPD XIII, para. B (see Supplement, **CPD.XIII.B**), for the additional factors that the court considers on allocation. **B14.3**

Perjury Act 1911, s. 8

Where an offence against this Act or any offence punishable as perjury or as subornation of perjury under any other Act of Parliament is committed in any place either on sea or land outside the United Kingdom, the offender may be proceeded against, indicted, tried, and punished... in England.

It is not altogether clear whether this provision was intended to extend the ambit of the Act in any way, or whether it was, as the marginal note ('venue') suggests, intended merely to provide for the trial of any extra-territorial offences created under the preceding sections. On balance, the latter interpretation is to be preferred. The extra-territorial scope of s. 1, for example, is precisely governed by subsections (4) and (5), and these provisions would not have been necessary if s. 8 had any wider meaning. As to territorial jurisdiction generally, see **A8**.

Indictment

B14.4 *Statement of Offence*

Perjury contrary to section 1(1) of the Perjury Act 1911.

Particulars of Offence

A on the... day of..., having been lawfully sworn as a witness in a judicial proceeding, namely the trial of a criminal cause at the Central Criminal Court entitled The Queen v B.C., wilfully made a statement material in that proceeding which he knew to be false, namely that the accused B.C. had been in the City of Leicester on the... day of...

Perjury Act 1911, s. 12

(1) In an indictment—
   (a) for making any false statement or false representation punishable under this Act; or
   (b) for unlawfully, wilfully, falsely, fraudulently, deceitfully, maliciously, or corruptly taking, making, signing, or subscribing any oath, affirmation, solemn declaration, statutory declaration, affidavit, deposition, notice, certificate, or other writing,

   it is sufficient to set forth the substance of the offence charged, and before which court or person (if any) the offence was committed without setting forth the proceedings or any part of the proceedings in the course of which the offence was committed, and without setting forth the authority of any court or person before whom the offence was committed.

(2) In an indictment for aiding, abetting, counselling, suborning, or procuring any other person to commit any offence hereinbefore in this section mentioned, or for conspiring with any other person, or with attempting to suborn or procure any other person, to commit any such offence, it is sufficient—
   (a) where such offence has been committed, to allege that offence, and then to allege that the defendant procured the commission of the offence; and
   (b) where such offence has not been committed, to set forth the substance of the offence charged against the defendant without setting forth any matter or thing which it is unnecessary to aver in the case of an indictment for a false statement or false representation punishable under this Act.

Sentence

B14.5 The maximum penalty for perjury is seven years (Perjury Act 1911, s. 1). There is no definitive sentencing guideline for this offence.

A custodial sentence is almost always necessary since, as Roskill LJ said in *Davies* (1974) 59 Cr App R 311 at p. 313:

> It is often said there is too much perjury committed in courts, and it is regrettably true as everyone sitting in court knows. But it is one thing to suspect that perjury has been committed and another thing to prove it. Perjury is not always easy to prove. Perjurers are not easily brought to justice. *When they are they must be punished.*

In *Archer* [2002] EWCA Crim 1996, [2003] 1 Cr App R (S) 86 (446), a sentence of four years was upheld in respect of D who was convicted of two counts of perjury and two counts of perverting the course of justice, in respect of civil proceedings for libel which he had brought against a newspaper. The Court of Appeal held that there was no inherent difference in seriousness between perjury in civil as against criminal proceedings. Other factors were more relevant, including the number of offences committed, the timescale over which they had taken place, whether the lies were planned and persisted in, whether D had implicated others, and whether the perjury had affected the outcome of the original proceedings.

In *Hall* (1982) 4 Cr App R (S) 153 Talbot J (at p. 155) said that 'it is almost inconceivable that a sentence of less than three months would be given for a deliberate perjury in the face of the court', since 'such false evidence strikes at the whole basis of the administration of the law'. In that case a three-month sentence was upheld on a 62-year-old woman who had given false alibi evidence at a magistrates' court in respect of a man charged with assault occasioning actual bodily harm. A sentence of six months' imprisonment was upheld in *Healey* (1990) 12 Cr App R (S) 297, in respect of perjury committed in the course of a means inquiry in a magistrates' court. D appeared in court for failure to pay a fine of £200. He then gave evidence on oath that he was employed, and that the fine could be recovered by an attachment of earnings order. This evidence was untrue. In *Wittekind* [2010] EWCA Crim 646 the Court of Appeal said that a sentence of three years was too long for perjury committed in the course of an appeal in an Army disciplinary matter. No original serious offence was involved and, as a result of the custodial penalty, D would be discharged from the Army. The sentence was reduced to two years. By contrast, a sentence of four years' imprisonment for perjury was upheld in *Cunningham* [2007] EWCA Crim 524, [2007] 2 Cr App R (S) 61 (376), where D, a man with a previous conviction for an offence against justice, committed perjury in proceedings relating to a serious crime. **B14.6**

Meaning of 'Statements in Judicial Proceedings'

The effect of the Perjury Act 1911, s. 1 (2) and (3), is that perjury need not take the form of false evidence in court. A false affidavit sworn in connection with a judicial proceeding may amount to perjury, as may false evidence given on oath before a tribunal. **B14.7**

The position is slightly different in the case of false written evidence tendered in criminal proceedings under the CJA 1967, s. 9. Wilful falsity in such cases attracts a maximum penalty of two years and/or a fine, as opposed to the seven year maximum for perjury itself, but in all other respects the principles contained within the Perjury Act 1911 are applicable. The relevant offences are dealt with at **B14.20**.

The CJA 1988, s. 32, enables a person outside the UK to give evidence at a criminal trial in England or Wales through a live television link. As with evidence to which the Perjury Act 1911, s. 1(5), applies, any such evidence is treated for the purposes of the Perjury Act 1911, s. 1, as given in the trial concerned (CJA 1988, s. 32(3)).

By the European Communities Act 1972, s. 11(1)(a), all relevant provisions of the Perjury Act 1911 are applicable to statements made on oath before the CJEU, or any court attached thereto, whether or not the person responsible is a British citizen. See also the Evidence (European Court) Order 1976 (SI 1976 No. 428).

Meaning of 'Lawfully Sworn'

Evidence Act 1851, s. 16 **B14.8**

> Every court, judge, justice, officer, commissioner, arbitrator, or other person, now or hereafter having by law or by consent of parties authority to hear, receive, and examine evidence, is hereby empowered to administer an oath to all such witnesses as are legally called before them respectively.

A conviction for perjury is impossible if D was incompetent to testify in the proceedings in which the perjury is alleged to have been committed (*Clegg* (1868) 19 LT 47).

It is possible for a witness or interpreter to make a solemn affirmation in place of the oath, whether or not the taking of an oath would be contrary to that person's religious beliefs, and the Perjury Act 1911, s. 15(2), provides that references therein to 'oaths' and 'swearing' embrace affirmations. The affirming witness is thus equally subject to the Perjury Act 1911.

Perjury Act 1911, s. 15

(1) For the purposes of this Act, the forms and ceremonies used in administering an oath are immaterial, if the court or person before whom the oath is taken has power to administer an oath for the purpose of verifying the statement in question, and if the oath has been administered in a form and with ceremonies which the person taking the oath has accepted without objection, or has declared to be binding on him.

As to oaths and affirmations generally, see **F4.31** to **F4.36**.

Wilfulness

B14.9 It might seem at first sight that the requirement of wilfulness in the Perjury Act 1911, s. 1, is otiose, since the offence can be committed only by someone who does not believe the testimony to be true; but conduct is wilful only if it is deliberate or intentional (*Senior* [1899] 1 QB 283), and it must therefore be proved that any alleged perjury was not the result of a misunderstanding or a slip of the tongue, whereby D might perhaps have said something D did not mean (*Millward* [1985] QB 519). As to wilfulness generally, see **A2.13**.

Materiality

B14.10 'Material' means important or significant: something which matters. See *Mallett* [1978] 3 All ER 10, in which the Court of Appeal so construed the phrase 'false in a material particular', in a prosecution under the Theft Act 1968, s. 17(1), and *Lancaster* [2010] EWCA Crim 370, [2010] 3 All ER 402 at **B6.12**. Under the Perjury Act 1911, s. 1(6), the question of what is material is one of law (i.e. for the judge to decide). D must know of the falsity of the statement (or not believe in its truth) but need not know or believe it to be material (*Millward* [1985] QB 519).

The truth or falsity of D's statement need not be crucial to the outcome of the case. It would suffice, for example, if D's lies prevented the other side from pursuing a certain line of questioning which might have been material to an issue of credibility (*Millward* [1985] QB 519; and see also *Baker* [1895] 1 QB 797). A statement may also be material even though it ought strictly to have been excluded by the court or judge before whom it was made (*Gibbon* (1862) Le & Ca 109; cf. *Philpotts* (1851) 2 Den CC 302).

Clear examples of immaterial statements are hard to find amongst the reported cases. It was held in *Tate* (1871) 12 Cox CC 7 that it was not perjury for D to swear at X's trial for assault that he had seen X's wife commit adultery, because that would have been irrelevant to the question whether X had indeed committed the assault; but this decision has been doubted (*Hewitt* (1913) 9 Cr App R 192) and it has since been held that evidence is material if it may affect the likely penalty in criminal proceedings, even if it is immaterial to the question of liability (*Wheeler* [1917] 1 KB 283). A rare reported example of lies that were held to be immaterial is *Sweet-Escott* (1971) 55 Cr App R 316, where in committal proceedings D had denied having any previous convictions. He did have some; but these dated from over 20 years before, and it was held that they could not have made any difference to the outcome of the proceedings.

Truth or Falsity of the Statement

B14.11 On a literal interpretation of the Perjury Act 1911, s. 1, it would seem that D could be convicted of perjury as a result of a statement which D did not believe to be true, but which was in fact true after all. Prosecutions are hardly likely to be brought in respect of manifestly true statements, but if this literal interpretation is correct, it would ease the prosecution's task in cases where D's state of mind is easier to prove than the truth or falsity of the evidence. If, for example, D had testified that a certain incident occurred on 5 July, and the prosecution can prove that D could not possibly have known whether it occurred or not, this should suffice as proof of perjury, even if there is no evidence as to whether it did or did not occur (*Rider* (1986) 83 Cr App R 207).

This was indeed the position at common law (*Allen v Westley* (1629) Het 97) and although the Court of Appeal appears to have assumed in *Millward* [1985] QB 519 that proof of falsity is required under the Perjury Act 1911, this was unconsidered and strictly *obiter*. Most commentators support the literal interpretation, which also found some favour with the Court of Appeal in *Rider*, although the point was ultimately left open in that case.

It may at first seem rather difficult to reconcile the 'literal' interpretation of the Perjury Act 1911, s. 1, with s. 13, which effectively requires corroboration of any allegation of falsity before a conviction for perjury can be obtained, but the wording of s. 13 is not in fact inconsistent with that interpretation, as the Court of Appeal noted in *Rider*. As to s. 13, see **B14.16**.

False Statements of Opinion

An expression of opinion, not genuinely held by the witness making it, may amount to perjury (*Schlesinger* (1847) 10 QB 670). **B14.12**

Perjury Based on Inconsistent Statements

Where D has on separate occasions made two or more inconsistent statements on oath, and must have been guilty of deliberate perjury on at least one of those occasions, a conviction will not be possible unless the prosecution can prove which of the statements was perjured. **B14.13**

Prosecution for Perjury where Accused's Evidence Secured his Acquittal in Previous Trial

Where D has been acquitted of a criminal charge after giving sworn evidence of D's own innocence, further evidence may then come to light which tends to prove, not just that D lied, but that D must have been wrongly acquitted. If D is then tried for perjury, the prosecution may properly adduce evidence which is flatly inconsistent with the acquittal at the earlier trial. **B14.14**

The House of Lords in *DPP v Humphrys* [1977] AC 1 held that issue estoppel has no place in criminal proceedings, and the related doctrine laid down in *Sambasivam v Public Prosecutor* [1950] AC 458, under which it was said that the prosecution must accept D's innocence of any alleged crimes of which D has previously been acquitted, was rejected by the House in *Z* [2000] 2 AC 483. D's previous acquittal is accordingly no obstacle to a prosecution for perjury.

On the other hand, it may be oppressive and unfair for D to be prosecuted for perjury after being acquitted on the original charge, unless significant new prosecution evidence has become available to contradict D's original evidence. If the prosecution are merely hoping that a different jury might believe their original witnesses, the prosecution should be stayed as an abuse of process. This was recognised, both in *Humphrys* and in *Z*.

As to the effect of previous verdicts in criminal cases generally, see **F12**.

Proof of Previous Judicial Proceeding

If the fact of the proceeding at which the perjury is alleged to have taken place is not admitted, this may be proved by production of the record of the trial or, in the case of trials on indictment, in accordance with the Perjury Act 1911, s. 14. **B14.15**

Perjury Act 1911, s. 14

On a prosecution—

(a) for perjury alleged to have been committed on the trial of an indictment...; or

(b) for procuring or suborning the commission of perjury on any such trial,

> the fact of the former trial shall be sufficiently proved by the production of a certificate containing the substance and effect (omitting the formal parts) of the indictment and trial purporting to be signed by the clerk of the court, or other person having the custody of the records of the court where the indictment was tried, or by the deputy of that clerk or other person, without proof of the signature or official character of the clerk or person appearing to have signed the certificate.

D's allegedly perjured statements, if not admitted, may be proved by the testimony of persons who were present at the trial. One such witness would suffice, since s. 13 (see **B14.16**) applies only to evidence of falsity. Alternatively, the shorthand writer's record may be admissible under the CJA 2003, s. 117.

Requirement of Corroboration as to Falsity

B14.16 Perjury Act 1911, s. 13

> A person shall not be liable to be convicted of any offence against this Act, or of any offence declared by any other Act to be perjury or subornation of perjury, or to be punishable as perjury or subornation of perjury, solely upon the evidence of one witness as to the falsity of any statement alleged to be false.

This provision does not lay down any corroboration requirement as to the fact that D made the alleged statement, or as to D's knowledge or belief at the time (*O'Connor* [1980] Crim LR 43). If it is not being alleged that the statement was false (e.g., where it is alleged that neither D nor anyone else could have known whether it was true or not), then s. 13 has no application.

Where s. 13 does apply, its interpretation is troublesome. It does not expressly refer to 'corroboration' at all, and it was accordingly argued in *Hamid* (1979) 69 Cr App R 324 that, provided the prosecution case does not depend on a single witness as to falsity, the technicalities of the law relating to corroboration do not apply; but the Court of Appeal disagreed. It follows that a jury will need to be directed as to what other evidence might be capable of providing that corroboration, and the absence of any such direction will amount to a material irregularity. See also *Rider* (1986) 83 Cr App R 207, *Carroll* [1993] Crim LR 613 and *Cooper* [2010] EWCA Crim 979, [2010] 2 Cr App R 13 (92).

Although a single witness to falsity must be corroborated, this corroboration may take the form of documentary evidence, and may originate from D himself, as in *Threlfall* (1914) 10 Cr App R 112, where D had written a letter, parts of which appeared to be self-incriminating.

Where D is alleged to have confessed prior to the trial, the evidence of two witnesses to the confession has been held to be sufficient for the purposes of s. 13. It is not necessary that they should have witnessed confessions on separate occasions (*Peach* [1990] 2 All ER 966).

If the corroboration requirements in s. 13 cannot be satisfied, the protection it provides cannot be sidestepped by charging the same alleged act of perjury as perverting the course of justice (*Tsang Ping-Nam v the Queen* [1981] 1 WLR 1462 at p. 1466). In that case, however, there was no evidence that the initial statements given by D to the police (which differed from his testimony) were false. Had the evidence enabled him to be charged with perverting the course of justice on the basis of his original statements, s. 13 would not then have applied.

Aiding and Abetting etc.

B14.17 Perjury Act 1911, s. 7

> (1) Every person who aids, abets, counsels, procures, or suborns another person to commit an offence against this Act shall be liable to be proceeded against, indicted, tried and punished as if he were a principal offender.
>
> (2) Every person who incites another person to commit an offence against this Act shall be guilty of an offence, and, on conviction thereof on indictment, shall be liable to imprisonment, or to a fine, or to both such imprisonment and fine.

'Suborning' is merely another term, in this context, for procuring, and s. 7(1) thus adds nothing of significance to the general law of secondary participation in crime, as governed by the Accessories and Abettors Act 1861 (see generally A4.1 ***et seq.***).

The offence of incitement in s. 7(2) remains unaffected by the new law on aiding and encouraging crime because s. 7(2) is not one of the provisions listed in the SCA 2007, sch. 6, part 1 (see **A5.1**). The maximum term of imprisonment for an offence under s. 7(2) is limited by the PCC(S)A 2000, s. 77, to two years' imprisonment.

The Perjury Act 1911, s. 13 (see **B14.16**), applies to offences under this provision. All complicity offences are triable either way except complicity in an offence under the Perjury Act 1911, s. 1 (perjury in judicial proceedings).

OFFENCES AKIN TO PERJURY

False Testimony of Unsworn Child Witnesses in Criminal Proceedings

The Perjury Act 1911, s. 16(2), provides that nothing in that Act applies to the unsworn evidence of children (see **F4.21**) but under the YJCEA 1999, s. 57, children or other persons who wilfully give false evidence in criminal proceedings when testifying unsworn (by virtue of s. 56 of that Act: see **F4.27**), and who would be guilty of perjury if testifying on oath, will be guilty of a summary offence. The penalty for children (aged under 14) is a fine not exceeding £250; others may face a fine not exceeding £1,000 and/or imprisonment for a term not exceeding six months (YJCEA 1999, s. 57(2) and (3)). **B14.18**

False Unsworn Evidence under the Evidence (Proceedings in Other Jurisdictions) Act 1975

Perjury Act 1911, s. 1A **B14.19**

> If any person, in giving any testimony (either orally or in writing) otherwise than on oath, where required to do so by an order under section 2 of the Evidence (Proceedings in Other Jurisdictions) Act 1975, makes a statement:
> (a) which he knows to be false in a material particular, or
> (b) which is false in a material particular and which he does not believe to be true,
> he shall be guilty of [an offence] and shall be liable on conviction on indictment to imprisonment for a term not exceeding two years or a fine or both.

This section serves a function similar to that served in respect of sworn evidence by the Perjury Act 1911, s. 1(4) (see **B14.1**). In contrast to the uncertainty concerning the need for proof of actual falsity in prosecutions under s. 1, it is clear in this case that such proof is indeed required. As to the meaning of the phrase 'false in a material particular', see the discussion at **B14.10**.

Section 13 applies (see **B14.16**); and offences under this provision are triable either way (MCA 1980, s. 17 and sch. 1, para. 14).

False Written Statements Tendered in Criminal Proceedings

Criminal Justice Act 1967, s. 89 **B14.20**

> (1) If any person in a written statement tendered in evidence in criminal proceedings by virtue of section 9 of this Act, wilfully makes a statement material in those proceedings which he knows to be false or does not believe to be true, he shall be liable on conviction on indictment to *imprisonment* for a term not exceeding two years or a fine or both.
> (2) The Perjury Act 1911 shall have effect as if this section were contained in that Act.

The only obvious distinction between this offence and perjury itself lies in the maximum penalties, which stand at two years compared with the maximum of seven under the Perjury Act 1911, s. 1. Although there is no specific provision, it would seem that this offence is triable either way, since s. 89(2) assimilates s. 89 into the Perjury Act 1911 and, by virtue of the MCA 1980, s. 17 and sch. 1, para. 14, all offences under the Perjury Act 1911, except those under ss. 1,

3 and 4, are so triable. (Sections 3 and 4 of the Perjury Act 1911 expressly made offences under those sections triable either way.)

Section 13 of the Perjury Act 1911 is applicable to this offence: see **B14.16**.

As to the making of false statements in documents relating to civil proceedings, see the Civil Procedure Rules, r. 32.14(1), and **B14.49**.

False Statements Made on Oath outside Judicial Proceedings

B14.21 Perjury Act 1911, s. 2

If any person:

(1) being required or authorised by law to make any statement on oath for any purpose, and being lawfully sworn (otherwise than in a judicial proceeding) wilfully makes a statement which is material for that purpose and which he knows to be false or does not believe to be true; or

(2) wilfully uses any false affidavit for the purposes of the Bills of Sale Act 1878, as amended by any subsequent enactment,

he shall be guilty of [an offence], and, on conviction thereof on indictment, shall be liable to imprisonment for a term not exceeding seven years or to a fine or to both such imprisonment and fine.

The offence created by s. 2 is of limited application. Affidavits sworn in connection with judicial proceedings must be dealt with under the Perjury Act 1911, s. 1(3). As to statutory declarations, see s. 5, discussed in **B14.25**.

Section 13 applies (see **B14.16**), and offences under this provision are triable either way (MCA 1980, sch. 1, para. 14).

False Statements with Reference to Marriage

B14.22 Perjury Act 1911, s. 3

(1) If any person:

(a) for the purpose of procuring a marriage, or a certificate or licence for marriage, knowingly and wilfully makes a false oath, or makes or signs a false declaration, notice or certificate required under any Act of Parliament for the time being in force relating to marriage; or

(b) knowingly and wilfully makes, or knowingly and wilfully causes to be made, for the purpose of being inserted in any register of marriage, a false statement as to any particular required by law to be known and registered relating to any marriage; or

(c) forbids the issue of any certificate or licence for marriage by falsely representing himself to be a person whose consent to the marriage is required by law knowing such representation to be false; or

(d) with respect to a declaration made under section 16(1A) or 27B(2) of the Marriage Act 1949:

(i) enters a caveat under subsection (2) of the said section 16, or

(ii) makes a statement mentioned in subsection (4) of the said section 27B, which he knows to be false in a material particular,

he shall be guilty of [an offence,] and, on conviction thereof on indictment, shall be liable to imprisonment for a term not exceeding seven years or to a fine or to both imprisonment and fine and on summary conviction thereof shall be liable to [an unlimited fine].

(2) No prosecution for knowingly and wilfully making a false declaration for the purpose of procuring any marriage out of the district in which the parties or one of them dwell shall take place after the expiration of eighteen months from the solemnization of the marriage to which the declaration refers.

An offence under s. 3 can be committed only where D acts for the purpose of procuring a marriage or licence etc. but whether or not D succeeds in this purpose is irrelevant. A false statement cannot give rise to liability under s. 3(1)(a) or (b), unless it concerns something which must by law be stated correctly (*Frickey* [1956] Crim LR 421).

See also the Civil Partnership Act 2004, s. 80 (false statements etc. with reference to civil partnerships).

The Perjury Act 1911, s. 13 (see **B14.16**) applies both to s. 3 and to s. 80 of the 2004 Act (by virtue of s. 80(4)).

False Statements about Births and Deaths

Perjury Act 1911, s. 4 **B14.23**

(1) If any person:
  (a) wilfully makes any false answer to any question put to him by any registrar of births or deaths relating to the particulars required to be registered concerning any birth or death, or, wilfully gives to any such registrar any false information concerning any birth or death or the cause of any death; or
  (b) wilfully makes any false certificate or declaration under or for the purposes of any Act relating to the registration of births or deaths, or, knowing any such certificate or declaration to be false, uses the same as true or gives or sends the same as true to any person; or
  (c) wilfully makes, gives or uses any false statement or declaration as to a child born alive as having been still-born, or as to the body of a deceased person or still-born child in any coffin, or falsely pretends that any child born alive was still-born; or
  (d) makes any false statement with intent to have the same inserted in any register of births or deaths:

he shall be guilty of [an offence] and shall be liable:
  (i) on conviction thereof on indictment, to imprisonment for a term not exceeding seven years, or to a fine instead of the said punishments; and
  (ii) on summary conviction thereof, to [an unlimited fine].

(2) A prosecution on indictment for an offence against this section shall not be commenced more than three years after the commission of the offence.

As to the particulars requiring registration in relation to births or deaths, see the Births and Deaths Registration Act 1953, s. 39, and orders made thereunder. In contrast to the position under the Perjury Act 1911, s. 3, the wilful provision of any false information concerning a birth or death may involve liability, whether or not its provision was a strict legal requirement. **B14.24**

False statements as to the paternity of a child are obvious examples of the s. 4 offence, but cases of artificial insemination by donor (AID) can give rise to problems. The Family Law Reform Act 1987, s. 27, provides that, where a married couple agree to such a scheme, the child 'shall be treated as the child of the parties to the marriage', and this probably means that the husband can lawfully be registered as the father; but some doubts have been expressed as to this, especially since s. 27(3) precludes the inheritance of titles of honour by such children.

Section 13 of the Perjury Act 1911, applies: see **B14.16**.

False Statutory Declarations etc.

Perjury Act 1911, s. 5 **B14.25**

(1) If any person knowingly and wilfully makes (otherwise than on oath) a statement false in a material particular, and the statement is made:
  (a) in a statutory declaration; or
  (b) in an abstract, account, balance sheet, book, certificate, declaration, entry, estimate, inventory, notice, report, return, or other document which he is authorised or required to make, attest, or verify, by any public general Act of Parliament for the time being in force; or
  (c) in any oral declaration or oral answer which he is required to make by, under, or in pursuance of any public general Act of Parliament for the time being in force,

he shall be guilty of [an offence] and shall be liable on conviction thereof on indictment to imprisonment for any term not exceeding two years, or to a fine or to both such imprisonment and fine.

Perjury Act 1911, s. 15

(2) . . . The expression 'statutory declaration' means a declaration made by virtue of the Statutory Declarations Act 1835, or of any Act, order in council, rule or regulation applying or extending the provisions thereof;

As to the meaning of the phrase 'knowingly and wilfully' in this context, see *Sood* [1998] 2 Cr App R 355. The principal limitation on the scope of s. 5(b) and (c) is the need to prove that A was statutorily authorised or required to make the declaration etc. which is alleged to be false. It would not appear to suffice that the declaration was made in connection with, or for the purpose of procuring, some benefit which is the subject of legislative control; but false statements in such circumstances are frequently penalised under other legislation. See, e.g., the CJA 1925, s. 36, which creates an offence of making a statement which one knows to be untrue for the purpose of procuring a passport.

Section 13 applies to offences under s. 5 (see **B14.16**), and offences under s. 5 are triable either way (MCA 1980, s. 17 and sch. 1, para. 14).

False Declarations etc. to Obtain Registration for Carrying on a Vocation

B14.26 **Perjury Act 1911, s. 6**

(1) If any person:

(a) procures or attempts to procure himself to be registered on any register or roll kept under or in pursuance of any public general Act of Parliament for the time being in force of persons qualified by law to practise any vocation or calling; or

(b) procures or attempts to procure a certificate of the registration of any person on any such register or roll as aforesaid,

by wilfully making or producing or causing to be made or produced either verbally or in writing, any declaration, certificate, or representation which he knows to be false or fraudulent, he shall be guilty of [an offence] and shall be liable on conviction thereof on indictment to imprisonment for any term not exceeding 12 months, or to a fine, or to both such imprisonment and fine.

D should be charged with 'procuring' only where D's purpose under s. 6 (a) or (b) has succeeded. Where D fails in this, the charge should be one of attempting to procure, and this would be construed in accordance with the CAA 1981, s. 3: see generally **A5.72** ***et seq***.

Section 13 applies (see **B14.16**); and offences under s. 6 are triable either way (MCA 1980, s. 17 and sch. 1, para. 14).

Offences under the Land Registration Act 2002

B14.27 **Land Registration Act 2002, ss. 123 and 124**

123.—(1) A person commits an offence if in the course of proceedings relating to registration under this Act he suppresses information with the intention of—

(a) concealing a person's right or claim, or

(b) substantiating a false claim.

(2) A person guilty of an offence under this section is liable—

(a) on conviction on indictment, to imprisonment for a term not exceeding two years or to a fine;

(b) on summary conviction, to imprisonment for a term not exceeding six months or to [an unlimited fine], or to both.

124.—(1) A person commits an offence if he dishonestly induces another—

(a) to change the register of title or cautions register, or

(b) to authorise the making of such a change.

(2) A person commits an offence if he intentionally or recklessly makes an unauthorised change in the register of title or cautions register.

(3) A person guilty of an offence under this section is liable—

(a) on conviction on indictment, to imprisonment for a term not exceeding 2 years or to a fine;
(b) on summary conviction, to imprisonment for a term not exceeding six months or to [an unlimited fine], or to both.

(4) In this section, references to changing the register of title include changing a document referred to in it.

As to restrictions on the privilege against self-incrimination, see the Land Registration Act 2002, s. 125.

Relationship of Perjury Act 1911 to Other Enactments

Perjury Act 1911, s. 16 **B14.28**

(1) Where the making of a false statement is not only an offence under this Act, but also by virtue of some other Act is a corrupt practice or subjects the offender to any forfeiture or disqualification or to any penalty other than imprisonment, or fine, the liability of the offender under this Act shall be in addition to and not in substitution for his liability under such other Act.

(2) Nothing in this Act shall apply to a statement made without oath by a child under the provisions of the Prevention of Cruelty to Children Act 1904 and the Children Act 1908.

(3) Where the making of a false statement is by any other Act, whether passed before or after the commencement of this Act, made punishable on summary conviction, proceedings may be taken either under such other Act or under this Act:
Provided that where such an offence is by any Act passed before the commencement of this Act, as originally enacted, made punishable only on summary conviction, it shall remain only so punishable.

The provisions referred to in s. 16(2) have long been repealed. As to the position where a child gives false unsworn evidence in criminal proceedings, see **B14.18**.

PERVERTING THE COURSE OF JUSTICE

Definition

B14.29

It is an offence at common law to do an act tending and intended to pervert the course of public justice (including criminal investigations and proceedings before tribunals).

Procedure

This offence is triable only on indictment. It is normally a class 3 offence, but see CrimPD XIII, para. B (see Supplement, **CPD.XIII.B**) for the additional factors that the court considers on allocation. **B14.30**

Indictment

Statement of Offence **B14.31**

Perverting the course of justice.

Particulars of Offence

A on or about the . . . day of . . . did an act tending to pervert the course of justice, namely falsifying a number of documents, namely . . ., intended to be used as evidence in the prosecution of one X on indictment number . . . preferred against the said X according to law in the Central Criminal Court, intending that the course of justice should thereby be perverted.

Sentence

The maximum penalty is life imprisonment and/or a fine. There is no offence-specific guideline but the Sentencing Council's *General Guideline: Overarching Principles* (see Supplement, **SG2-1**) is used for all offenders sentenced on or after 1 October 2019. **B14.32**

Sentencing authorities were reviewed in *Abdulwahab* [2018] EWCA Crim 1399, [2018] 2 Cr App R (S) 46 (383), in which the Court of Appeal set out seriousness factors (at [14]):

> First, conduct which tends and is intended to pervert the course of justice strikes at the heart of the administration of justice and almost invariably calls for a custodial sentence. Deterrence is an important aim of sentencing in such cases, although, as was pointed out in *Radcliffe* [2016] EWCA Crim 2,7 [2016] 1 Cr App R (S) 65 (488), the necessary deterrence may sometimes be achieved by the imposition of an immediate custodial sentence without necessarily requiring a sentence of great length. Secondly, the appropriate sentence of course depends on the particular circumstances of the specific case. The circumstances vary across a very wide range. Therefore, only limited assistance can be derived from considering previous decisions in other cases.
>
> Thirdly, in assessing the seriousness of a particular offence, relevant factors include the seriousness of the underlying offence, the nature of the deceptive conduct, the period of time over which it was continued, whether it cast suspicion upon or led to the arrest of an innocent person, and the success or otherwise of the attempt to pervert the course of justice. In addition, of course, the offender's previous character and any personal mitigation must be taken into account.

In *Abdulwahab* D was involved in a serious case and deliberately persisted in what may have been a spontaneous lie made up during a police interview, and which was designed to help a friend. The lie ultimately had few adverse effects save his own imprisonment. He should have been sentenced to 15 months' imprisonment before credit for plea. The Court was referred to the Sentencing Council definitive guideline, *Imposition of Community and Custodial Sentences* (see Supplement, **SG9-1**), indicating that a prison sentence should not be suspended where appropriate punishment can only be achieved by immediate custody. The Court held that not only was that the case for this defendant, it will also be so in most cases of attempting to pervert the course of public justice.

The remaining cases set out below reflect the wide range of circumstances in which this offence may be committed and give illustrations of sentences. Some examples of witness intimidation may be prosecuted as perverting the course of justice, but there is an overlap with the statutory offence considered at **B14.50**.

B14.33 **Seeking to Avoid Prosecution** In *Griffin* [2019] EWCA Crim 563, [2019] 2 Cr App R (S) 32 (237) D sought to avoid prosecution for four driving offences by paying to be included in an elaborate scheme of identity fraud, enabling D to give false details as to the driver of his vehicles at relevant times. The sentencing judge started at three years bearing in mind the sophistication of the scheme, but the Court of Appeal felt a reduction was necessary bearing in mind D himself was not the mastermind. The starting point should have been two years, so with reduction for plea the resulting sentence should have been 16 months' immediate imprisonment. In *Snow* [2008] EWCA Crim 580, [2008] 2 Cr App R (S) 87 (497) D pleaded guilty to two counts of perverting the course of justice where he had twice given false details when stopped by the police for motoring matters. As a result of one deception, D's brother was convicted in his absence by a magistrates' court. Consecutive sentences of nine months on each count were upheld on appeal. Sentences of four months were appropriate for both offenders following guilty pleas in *Henderson* [2011] EWCA Crim 1152, [2012] 1 Cr App R (S) 18 (95), where a lorry driver asked a friend to 'take' his penalty points for speeding so that he could avoid disqualification; the friend did so, but the deception later came to light. In *Ratcliffe* [2016] EWCA Crim 27, [2016] 1 Cr App R (S) 65 (488) an enforcement camera had detected D's vehicle driving through a red light. D set about a persistent deception that the registration plates had been stolen, but admitted what had happened at a second plea and case management hearing. The Court of Appeal said that a sentence starting point of 19 months was very severe, but not manifestly excessive.

B14.34 **Concealing Evidence or Creating False Evidence** In *Matthews* [2009] EWCA Crim 1450, [2010] 1 Cr App R (S) 59 (373) a sentence of three years was upheld on the owner of a scrap metal company who attempted to conceal the cause of a fatal accident by arranging for the removal of evidence and telling employees to give a false account of what had happened.

In *Jones* [2008] EWCA Crim 348, [2008] 2 Cr App R (S) 75 (420), one of the worst cases, 12 years' imprisonment was upheld on D who attempted to intimidate a female witness in a murder case involving five defendants. The woman was subject to threats, and was promised a substantial sum of money if she would retract her evidence. The Court of Appeal said that the case was of 'utmost seriousness', and that D had set about derailing the trial for what had been a professional killing. There was no guilty plea and no mitigation. In *Asan* [2019] EWCA Crim 896 D intimidated the victim and her family over a two-year period. When investigated, D had used some relatively sophisticated techniques to convince police that hackers were planting incriminating evidence, including sending himself email material purporting to come from the alleged hackers and sending delayed texts at a time when he was distant from the handset to create an alibi. After pleading guilty, D was sentenced to a 12-month suspended sentence on the three indictments he faced, including six months' suspended imprisonment for the perverting counts. The Court of Appeal found all elements of the sentence to be unduly lenient and substituted a total of three years' imprisonment on the original matters and 18 months consecutive for the perverting counts. A sentence of three years' imprisonment was upheld in *Livesley* [2012] EWCA Crim 1100, [2013] 1 Cr App R (S) 27 (138), where D had submitted false references to the court in advance of being sentenced for a benefit fraud, with the effect that his sentence was suspended. *Livesley* was considered in *A-G's Ref (No. 123 of 2015) (Javed)* [2016] EWCA Crim 28, [2016] 1 Cr App R (S) 64 (479). D had submitted false references in mitigation, to the effect that he was a 'changed man'. The Court of Appeal said that where false references had been given, immediate custodial sentences of some length should be expected.

False Allegations of Crime Sentences in such cases may vary greatly depending on the consequences of the false allegations. If not charged as perverting the course of justice such conduct may be charged as stalking, which is covered by the *Intimidatory Offences* guideline (see Supplement, **SG27-1**, and sentencing cases at **B2.199** and **B2.207**). **B14.35**

In *Beale* [2019] EWCA Crim 665, [2019] 2 Cr App R 19 (194) a sentence of ten years' imprisonment after a trial was not considered manifestly excessive for D who made repeated false allegations of rape against multiple victims, and perjured herself while giving evidence in the trials that followed. One falsely accused man was convicted of rape and served nearly three years in prison, another was on bail for two years before the case was dropped, and a third fled the country to avoid prosecution for an offence he knew he had not committed. She was convicted of three counts of perjury and four counts of perverting the course of justice. The Court of Appeal commented that the harm to the victims was incalculable and that the sentence, though stern, was not excessive. By contrast, in *Day* [2009] EWCA Crim 2445, [2010] 2 Cr App R (S) 12 (73), D made a single false complaint of rape and the man who had been accused was detained for ten hours before release. The Court said that a false accusation of rape was not just a wrong against the man concerned but was also an attack on the criminal justice system, diverting scarce and expensive police resources. Although D had been 'far from well' when she made the complaint, the sentence of two years after a trial in this case was entirely appropriate and could have been longer.

In *Weiner* [2011] EWCA Crim 1249, [2012] 1 Cr App R (S) 6 (24) a sentence of ten years' imprisonment after a trial was appropriate for D who had planted indecent photographs of children on V's computer and then made an anonymous call to the police accusing V of possessing child pornography. V had been arrested, suffered unwelcome publicity, had been dismissed from his employment and forced to move house before the truth was uncovered. The Court of Appeal said that the degree of culpability and planning was worse than in many other false allegations of crime. In *Afford* [2013] EWCA Crim 633, [2014] 1 Cr App R (S) 2 (4) D told the police that he had been attacked by four Asian men, one of whom had slashed his face and said 'no white person should walk here'. D later admitted that he had made up the story, and had cut his own face. The Court of Appeal reduced a sentence of 12 months to one of eight months, commenting that the case was at the lower end of the scale, but the aggravating feature had been the risk of heightened racial tension in the area.

B14.36 **Helping an Offender** In *Sidhu* [2019] EWCA Crim 1034, [2019] 2 Cr App R (S) 34 (247) the Court of Appeal offered guidance on sentencing where D assists an offender to evade justice by disposing of a weapon or by helping the offender to leave the scene or flee the country. Following a fatal stabbing committed by one TA (see **B2.83**), KF and RS were each charged with perverting the course of justice: RS because he took, and apparently successfully disposed of, the knife used by TA; and KF because, having seen what TA had just done, he drove him away from the scene, enabling him to flee the country soon after. Each was sentenced to a term of two and a half years' imprisonment, expressed to include an element of deterrence. On appeal, RS's sentence was reduced to 22 months on the basis that his knowledge, role and culpability had not been as great as KF, but in all other respects the sentences were upheld, the Court of Appeal noting that a sentence reflecting, to some degree, a deterrent element as a warning to others may simply reflect the need to reduce crime. See also **B14.53**.

B14.37 **Bribery** Cases charged as bribery, such as *Patel* [2012] EWCA Crim 1243, [2013] 1 Cr App R (S) 48 (269) (see **B15.13**), may also be relevant. In that case D, a court clerk, had solicited bribes from motoring offenders due to appear before the magistrates' court. The appropriate starting point after trial would have been six years' imprisonment, reduced to four years for his plea. See also *Barnard* [2019] EWCA Crim 1206 at **B14.53**. Note that bribery offences are included in the Sentencing Council definitive guideline, *Fraud, Bribery and Money Laundering Offences* (see Supplement, **SG26-7**).

Substantive Offences, Conspiracy and Attempt

B14.38 Indictments tended to allege attempts or conspiracies to pervert the course of justice, because it was thought that actual perversion of the course of justice would often be difficult to prove. Indeed, this form of indictment was used even in some cases where the course of justice had been wholly frustrated (*Britton* [1973] RTR 502). It is now recognised, however, that an act which is intended to have this effect, and is capable of succeeding, may constitute the substantive offence, and should be charged accordingly. The Criminal Attempts Act 1981 does not generally have any application in such cases (unless perhaps D has failed to perform the act he intended) and references to 'attempts' to pervert the course of justice are accordingly misleading (*Rowell* [1978] 1 All ER 665; *Machin* [1980] 3 All ER 151; *Williams* (1991) 92 Cr App R 158). On the other hand, the common law principles governing jurisdiction over conspiracy or attempt abroad to commit offences in England and Wales (see **A5.62** and **A5.82**) apply equally to acts abroad that are intended to pervert the course of justice in England and Wales (*USA v Dempsey* [2018] EWHC 1724 (Admin), [2018] 4 WLR 110).

Where there appears to have been a conspiracy, there may sometimes be certain advantages in charging the statutory offence under the CLA 1977, s. 1; but see CrimPD II, para. 10A.3 (see Supplement, **CPD.10A**), on the use of conspiracy charges.

Acts which May Amount to Perverting the Course of Justice

B14.39 There is no closed list of acts which may give rise to an offence of perverting the course of justice and neither authority nor principle supports confining such acts to those giving rise to some other independent criminal wrongdoing (*Kenny* [2013] EWCA Crim 1, [2013] QB 896 at [35]: see also **B14.47**). Nor need the offence be concerned with a particular trial or investigation. Acts tending and intended to obstruct, divert or disrupt criminal proceedings or police investigations generally may suffice (*USA v Dempsey* [2018] EWHC 1724 (Admin), [2018] 4 WLR 110). However, some acts that do amount to this offence may (depending on the circumstances) more appropriately be charged as contempt of court, offences under the CLA 1967, s. 4 or s. 5, witness intimidation, perjury, subornation of perjury or wasting police time. In *Kenny* the Court of Appeal warned that any expansion of the offence should take place only incrementally and with caution, reflecting both principles of common law reasoning and the requirements of the ECHR, Article 7.

Perverting the course of justice requires some positive act; mere failure to point out an error, as where the wrong person is prosecuted, cannot suffice (*Headley* [1995] Crim LR 737), nor is the offence committed by a motorist who fails to report an accident until any alcohol in his body has been eliminated (*Clark* [2003] EWCA Crim 99, [2003] 2 Cr App R 23 (363)). In *Sookoo* [2002] EWCA Crim 800, the Court of Appeal warned that charges of perverting the course of justice should not without good reason be added to cases in which a suspect has merely told lies when questioned. In many cases such charges 'only serve to complicate the sentencing process'. See to similar effect *Hamshaw* [2003] EWCA Crim 2435.

Deliberately Assisting a Person to Evade Arrest *Thomas* [1979] QB 326 is an example of such a case. In contrast to the offence under the CLA 1967, s. 4 (see **B14.58**), it does not matter whether the offence was 'a relevant offence', and it is not strictly necessary to prove the guilt of the person assisted. Cf. *Spinks* [1982] 1 All ER 587. **B14.40**

Destroying, Falsifying or Concealing Potential Evidence This form of the offence can occur whether or not legal proceedings have already been instigated (*Vreones* [1891] 1 QB 360; *Murray* [1982] 2 All ER 225; *Firetto* [1991] Crim LR 208; *Rafique* [1993] 4 All ER 1; *Kiffin* [1994] Crim LR 449). It was said in *Selvage* [1982] QB 372 that, if proceedings have not been instigated at that time, an investigation must have been in progress; but this would fail to deal with measures designed to prevent an offence ever being discovered, and cannot be reconciled with *Vreones* or *T* [2011] EWCA Crim 729. In *Selvage*, D attempted to falsify details on X's driving licence, so as to obscure the fact he had endorsements; but this was with a view to protecting him if he should ever commit, and be charged with, a future road traffic offence. Insofar as the dicta in that case seem to refer to evidence in actual but undiscovered crimes or potential civil disputes, it is submitted that they are *obiter* and wrong. See also *Sharpe* [1938] 1 All ER 48 and *Sinha* [1995] Crim LR 68. An offence of perverting the course of justice may be committed by falsifying or procuring false evidence, even where D's motive was to procure what D believed would be a true and fair verdict; although this is ultimately a matter for the consideration of the jury (*A-G's Ref (No. 1 of 2002)* [2002] EWCA Crim 2392, [2003] Crim LR 410). **B14.41**

Interfering with Jurors or Witnesses Successful prosecutions have been brought in cases involving interfering with jurors (*Mickleburgh* [1995] 1 Cr App R 297) or interfering with potential witnesses, so as to prevent or dissuade them from testifying (*Kellett* [1976] QB 372; *Panayiotou* [1973] 3 All ER 112) or so as to persuade them to change their evidence. There must be an intent to influence the course or outcome of the case in some way (*Lalani* [1999] 1 Cr App R 481). If D knowingly sought to prevent true evidence being given, or to procure false evidence, then D's guilt is clear, even if no bribe, threat, undue pressure or other unlawful means were used (*Toney* [1993] 2 All ER 409). Problems may, however, arise where D claims that the object was to prevent a witness giving false evidence. In *T* [2008] EWCA Crim 183, the Court of Appeal approved (at [28]) this dictum from *Kellett*: **B14.42**

> We would not consider that the offence of attempting to pervert the course of justice would necessarily be committed by a person who tried to persuade a false witness, or even a witness he believed to be false, to speak the truth or to refrain from giving false evidence... [but] we think that however proper the end, the means must not be improper. Even if the intention of the meddler with a witness is to prevent perjury and injustice, he commits the offence if he meddles by unlawful means.

What is improper is generally a question of fact, but a jury should be directed that any threat, or any use of force, amounts to perversion of the course of justice, even where the threat is to take legal action for defamation or to exercise some other legal right, as long as the prosecution can prove necessary intent to influence the witness's evidence (*Toney*). One kind of threat should, however, be distinguished from the rest: a mere warning to a witness that false evidence may lead to prosecution for perjury should be insufficient to constitute an offence of perverting the course of justice. The new offences of witness or jury intimidation, which are created by the CJPO 1994, s. 51, operate in addition to, rather than in derogation of, the common law: see **B14.50**.

B14.43 **Offer or Agreement by Potential Witness** An offer or agreement by a potential witness to withhold (or, presumably, to change) evidence in return for payment etc. may amount to perverting the course of justice (*Bassi* [1985] Crim LR 671). *Bassi* has been criticised as being inconsistent with *Murray* [1982] 2 All ER 225, where it was said that the offence would only be complete where a person has done something which might, without further action on the person's part, lead to potential injustice; but it could be argued that the course of justice is jeopardised as soon as any such offer or agreement is made, even if the witness could eventually decide to tell the truth after all, and if *Bassi* is inconsistent with *Murray*, it is to be preferred. See also the CLA 1967, s. 5(1), discussed at **B14.69** to **B14.73**.

B14.44 **Confessing to Another's Crime or Serving Another's Sentence** Confessing or pleading to another person's crime in order to shield that person may amount to an offence (*Devito* [1975] Crim LR 175), as may completing an unpaid work requirement that has been imposed on another person by a court (*DPP v SK* [2016] EWHC 837 (Admin)).

B14.45 **Abuse of Police Discretion** Where D knowingly acts outside the limits of proper discretion, so as to shield or excuse another person (e.g., a friend) from criminal charges, this may amount to perverting the course of justice (*Coxhead* [1986] RTR 411). It is for the jury to decide whether D had any discretion to act in this way, and, if not, whether D might mistakenly have believed that to be the case (*Coxhead*). See also *Ward* [1995] Crim LR 398. As to the offence of corruptly exercising police powers, contrary to the CJCA 2015, s. 26, see **B15.32**.

B14.46 **False Allegations** Making false allegations against another person, intending that the person should be prosecuted or knowing that this is a possibility may be an offence (*Rowell* [1978] 1 All ER 665). Where false stories merely waste police time, a charge under the CLA 1967, s. 5(2), may be more appropriate (see **B14.82**) but even where no alleged offender is named, there may be a risk that an innocent person could be arrested and/or prosecuted, and this may accordingly amount to perverting the course of justice (*Cotter* [2002] EWCA Crim 1033, [2003] QB 951). It makes no difference if, unknown to D, the subject of these allegations has died, because the vice of the offence lies in the intent (*Brown* [2004] EWCA Crim 744). Where it can be proved that D acted with intent to pervert the course of justice (e.g., by falsely reporting a crime), it is not necessary to prove whether D intended to pervert the course of criminal or civil justice (*Iaquaniello* [2005] EWCA Crim 2029).

B14.47 **Breach of Restraint Orders** In *Kenny* [2013] EWCA Crim 1, [2013] QB 896 the Court of Appeal noted that where D deliberately defies a restraint order under the POCA 2002, condign punishment for contempt will almost invariably be available and will ordinarily provide a sufficient punishment and deterrent, but held that, where such defiance involves determined and sophisticated criminal conduct carefully orchestrated and designed to frustrate the intended effect of the restraint order, D cannot complain if the Crown instead pursue a charge of perverting the course of justice.

Compensation of Victims and Settlement of Disputes

B14.48 No offence is committed where one person merely offers to settle a civil dispute with another by offering (or asking for) payment, or where a third party offers such a settlement on behalf of one or other litigant (*Panayiotou* [1973] 3 All ER 112 at p. 1038).

The position becomes more complicated and uncertain where the offer is made to the victim of a crime, who is a potential prosecution witness; but the CLA 1967, s. 5(1) (see **B14.69**), appears to recognise that the victim would commit no offence merely by accepting an offer of 'reasonable compensation for loss or injury' in return for not disclosing the crime, and it may be inferred that the offeror would equally commit no offence. An agreement to accept more than such compensation (i.e. a bribe) would appear to be an offence under s. 5(1) and the offeror would be a party to this, whether or not the offeror is also guilty of perverting the course of justice (*Ali* [1993] Crim LR 396). And see, with regard to advertisements offering rewards for the return of stolen goods, the Theft Act 1968, s. 23.

OFFENCES AKIN TO PERVERSION OF THE COURSE OF JUSTICE

Certain other kinds of conduct might be regarded as amounting to the perversion of public justice, but are more commonly charged under other heads. Thus, by the Civil Procedure Rules, r. 32.14(1): **B14.49**

> Proceedings for contempt of court may be brought against a person if he makes, or causes to be made, a false statement in a document verified by a statement of truth without an honest belief in its truth.

Sanctions, including sentences of imprisonment, may accordingly be imposed in contempt proceedings if a person makes a false statement in a document verified by a statement of truth, where the statement has, or if persisted in would be likely to have, interfered with the course of justice, and that person does not have an honest belief in the truth of the statement and knew of its likelihood to interfere with the course of justice (*AXA Insurance UK plc v Rossiter* [2013] EWHC 3805 (QB); *Aziz v Ali* [2014] EWHC 4003 (QB)).

In addition to those offences dealt with at **B14.48** *et seq*., note that concealing or transferring the proceeds of criminal conduct for the purpose of avoiding prosecution may be punishable under the POCA 2002, s. 327, and 'tipping off' another person as to a proposed money laundering investigation may be punishable under s. 333 of that Act (see **B21** for the offences).

Intimidation of, or Retaliation against, Witnesses, Jurors and Others

The intimidation of witnesses, jurors or other persons involved in legal proceedings or investigations may be punishable at common law, not only as tending to the perversion of the course of justice (see **B14.42**), but also as contempt of court. Whether a judge should refer the matter to the CPS for possible prosecution or proceed to determine the matter under the judge's contempt jurisdiction is a matter for the judge's discretion (*AS* [2008] EWCA Crim 138). Retaliation against former witnesses etc. is also punishable as contempt (see **B14.102**). Indeed, any improper interference with or approach to a witness or juror (present, past or future), whether based on intimidation, bribery or persuasion, will almost invariably be punishable under one or other of those heads. See, e.g., *Mickleburgh* [1995] 1 Cr App R 297 and *A-G v Judd* [1995] COD 15 at **B14.102**. **B14.50**

Acts of intimidation or retaliation may, alternatively, be dealt with under the CJPO 1994, s. 51, or (where the victim is a witness or potential witness in a civil case) under the CJPA 2001, ss. 39 to 41 (*Sahin* [2009] EWCA Crim 2616). **B14.51**

Criminal Justice and Public Order Act 1994, s. 51

(1) A person commits an offence if—
  (a) he does an act which intimidates, and is intended to intimidate, another person ('the victim'),
  (b) he does the act knowing or believing that the victim is assisting in the investigation of an offence or is a witness or potential witness or a juror or potential juror in proceedings for an offence, and
  (c) he does it intending thereby to cause the investigation or the course of justice to be obstructed, perverted or interfered with.

(2) A person commits an offence if—
(a) he does an act which harms, and is intended to harm, another person or, intending to cause another person to fear harm, he threatens to do an act which would harm that other person,
(b) he does or threatens to do the act knowing or believing that the person harmed or threatened to be harmed ('the victim'), or some other person, has assisted in an investigation into an offence or has given evidence or particular evidence in proceedings for an offence, or has acted as a juror or concurred in a particular verdict in proceedings for an offence, and
(c) he does or threatens to do it because of that knowledge or belief.

(3) For the purposes of subsections (1) and (2) it is immaterial that the act is or would be done, or that the threat is made—
(a) otherwise than in the presence of the victim, or
(b) to a person other than the victim.

(4) The harm that may be done or threatened may be financial as well as physical (whether to the person or a person's property) and similarly as respects an intimidatory act which consists of threats.

(5) The intention required by subsection (1)(c) and the motive required by subsection (2)(c) above need not be the only or the predominating intention or motive with which the act is done or, in the case of subsection (2), threatened.

(6) A person guilty of an offence under this section shall be liable—
(a) on conviction on indictment, to imprisonment for a term not exceeding five years or a fine or both;
(b) on summary conviction, to imprisonment for a term not exceeding six months or [an unlimited fine] or both.

(7) If, in proceedings against a person for an offence under subsection (1) above, it is proved that he did an act falling within paragraph (a) with the knowledge or belief required by paragraph (b), he shall be presumed, unless the contrary is proved, to have done the act with the intention required by paragraph (c) of that subsection.

(8) If, in proceedings against a person for an offence under subsection (2) above, it is proved that within the relevant period—
(a) he did an act which harmed, and was intended to harm, another person, or
(b) intending to cause another person fear of harm, he threatened to do an act which would harm that other person,

and that he did the act, or (as the case may be) threatened to do the act with the knowledge or belief required by paragraph (b), he shall be presumed, unless the contrary is proved, to have done the act or (as the case may be) threatened to do the act with the motive required by paragraph (c) of that subsection.

(9) In this section—
'investigation into an offence' means such an investigation by the police or other person charged with the duty of investigating offences or charging offenders;
'offence' includes an alleged or suspected offence;
'potential', in relation to a juror, means a person who has been summoned for jury service at the court at which proceedings for the offence are pending;
'relevant prosecutor', 'requisition', 'single justice procedure notice' and 'written charge' have the same meaning as in section 29 of the Criminal Justice Act 2003; and
'the relevant period'—and
(a) in relation to a witness or juror in any proceedings for an offence, means the period beginning with the institution of the proceedings and ending with the first anniversary of the conclusion of the trial or, if there is an appeal or a reference under section 9 or 11 of the Criminal Appeal Act 1995, of the conclusion of the appeal;
(b) in relation to a person who has or is believed by the accused to have, assisted in an investigation into an offence, but was not also a witness in proceedings for an offence, means the period of one year beginning with any act of his, or any act believed by the accused to be an act of his, assisting in the investigation; and
(c) in relation to a person who both has or is believed by the accused to have, assisted in the investigation into an offence and was a witness in proceedings for the offence, means the period beginning with any act of his, or any act believed by the accused to be an act of his, assisting in the investigation and ending with the anniversary mentioned in paragraph (a) above.

Section 51(10) amplifies the definition of relevant period. Although, as s. 51(4) makes clear, the 'other person' in question does not have to be put in fear of physical violence, a full offence under s. 51 cannot be committed if that person refuses to be deterred or intimidated (*ZN* [2013] EWCA Crim 989, [2013] 4 All ER 331, not following *Patrascu* [2004] EWCA Crim 2417, [2004] 4 All ER 1006 on that point), nor can it be committed on the basis of a mistaken belief that an investigation is in progress (*Singh* [1999] Crim LR 681). A criminal attempt may, however, be committed in either case (see **A5.60**).

Relationship with Common-law Offence Apart from being triable either way, the offence created by s. 51(1) appears to offer few advantages over the common-law offence of perverting the course of justice (which is preserved under s. 51(11)). The latter would indeed be committed even if bribery or persuasion were used in place of intimidation. As to the burden of proof, the Court of Appeal in *A-G's Ref (No. 1 of 2004)* [2004] EWCA Crim 1025, [2004] 4 All ER 457 had 'no hesitation in concluding' that for this offence the legal burden of proof imposed on a defendant by s. 51(7) is both justified and proportional under the ECHR, Article 6. **B14.52**

In contrast, the offence created by s. 51(2) covers conduct that would not ordinarily amount to perverting the course of justice, and carries heavier penalties than those available for contempt of court (as to which, see **B14.99**). Committal for contempt may not, in any case, be a wholly satisfactory method of dealing with conduct of this type, especially where it occurs after the original trial has ended.

Sentence The maximum penalties are five years' imprisonment and unlimited fine on indictment, six months' imprisonment and unlimited fine when tried summarily. There is no offence-specific guideline but the Sentencing Council's *General Guideline: Overarching Principles* (see Supplement, **SG2-1**) is used for all offenders sentenced on or after 1 October 2019. **B14.53**

Where the offence occurs in relation to domestic violence proceedings the definitive sentencing guideline, *Domestic Abuse*, may be applicable (see Supplement, **SG6-1**). That guideline refers to controlling behaviours and coercive behaviours, both of which may be seen in the context of interference with witnesses in such cases.

In *Barnard* [2019] EWCA Crim 1206, the Court of Appeal reviewed earlier authorities, including *Smith* [2011] EWCA Crim 972, [2011] 2 Cr App R (S) 118 (676) which had concluded that the factors which bore on sentencing for this offence included whether the intimidation was isolated or part of a campaign, the content of any threat, whether the intimidation was accompanied by violence, the circumstances in which any threat was uttered, whether any encounter with a witness was premeditated or by chance and the impact on V. Overall a key factor was the public policy of ensuring the integrity of the justice system by imposing sentences which had a general deterrent effect. The Court in *Barnard* upheld a starting point of 16 months' imprisonment consecutive to a sentence for an offence under the OAPA 1861, s. 20, where D had made efforts to contact the witness, with full knowledge that D had been responsible for a serious assault that had caused significant injury and would face prison if the mattered was pursued, and D chose in the circumstances to offer the witness a bribe. By contrast in *Burrows* [2017] EWCA Crim 278 the sentence was reduced to 12 months, as D's meeting with the witness had not been planned. In *Williams* [1997] 2 Cr App R (S) 221 D, after having been convicted of false imprisonment and unlawful wounding, wrote to the victim of those offences from prison, threatening her with violence. For this offence under s. 51(2), to which D pleaded guilty, a further sentence of two years' imprisonment, *consecutive* to the three-year term being served, was upheld by the Court of Appeal. Harrison J noted that the offence under s. 51(2) carried a maximum of five years, as compared with two years for contempt of court, and said that such intimidation must be viewed extremely seriously.

Intimidation etc. of Witnesses in Civil Proceedings The CJPA 2001 makes similar provision (in ss. 39 to 41) to protect witnesses and potential witnesses in civil cases. Section 39 corresponds to the CJPO 1994, s. 51(1); the CJPA 2001, s. 40 corresponds to s. 51(2) of the 1994 Act. **B14.54**

Personating a Juror

B14.55 It is an offence at common law, punishable with a fine and imprisonment at large, to impersonate someone summoned for jury service, so as to sit in that person's place. The motive is irrelevant (*Clark* (1918) 82 JP 295).

Disposing of a Body with Intent to Prevent an Inquest

B14.56 The concealment, disposal or destruction of a corpse is a common-law offence, punishable with a fine and imprisonment at large, if done to prevent the holding of a lawful inquest as to the death (*Stephenson* (1884) 13 QBD 331). There is a separate common-law offence of preventing the decent and lawful burial of a body. This may be committed by anyone who unlawfully conceals or destroys a body whether to conceal an unlawful killing (as in *Hunter* [1974] QB 95) or for other reasons. In *Skidmore* [2008] EWCA Crim 1464 the offence was committed where a funeral director forgot to put an infant's body in the coffin for burial and attempted to conceal this blunder by placing it in the coffin of another deceased, which was in due course cremated.

B14.57 **Sentence** There is no offence-specific guideline but the Sentencing Council's *General Guideline: Overarching Principles* (see Supplement, **SG2-1**) is used for all offenders sentenced on or after 1 October 2019. In *Godward* [1998] 1 Cr App R (S) 385 D pleaded guilty to obstructing the coroner by concealing a body. The police found the decomposed body of a man in D's flat. D had failed to disclose the whereabouts of the body, despite being twice asked by the police to assist them in tracing him. Lord Bingham CJ, in the Court of Appeal, said that the most important factor was the intention of the perpetrator. If the purpose was to obstruct the course of justice and to make it difficult to bring home a charge against D or another person, the offence would merit punishment towards the top of the appropriate bracket. If such intention was lacking, a lesser sentence was appropriate. On the present facts, a prison sentence of four years was reduced to three years. See also *Blakemore* [1997] 2 Cr App R (S) 255.

As to sentencing for the offence of preventing a decent and lawful burial, Ouseley J commented in *Whiteley* [2001] 2 Cr App R (S) 25 (119) that this was a serious matter, capable of interfering with the administration of justice and causing grief for the bereaved. It deprived the deceased of a proper burial and sometimes raised anxieties in the minds of relatives as to whether the person had been dead when the attempts at concealment had been made. On the facts, where D had not been in any way responsible for the death but had assisted in removing the body of a man who was a drug addict from the flat where he had died to conceal it in a ditch, a sentence of 30 months was reduced to 18 months, with a further three months consecutive for failing to answer bail upheld. See also *Parry* (1986) 8 Cr App R (S) 476.

ASSISTING OFFENDERS

Definition

B14.58 **Criminal Law Act 1967, s. 4**

(1) Where a person has committed a relevant offence, any other person who, knowing or believing him to be guilty of the offence or of some other relevant offence, does without lawful authority or reasonable excuse any act with intent to impede his apprehension or prosecution shall be guilty of an offence.

(1A) In this section and section 5 below, 'relevant offence' means—
(a) an offence for which the sentence is fixed by law,
(b) an offence for which a person of 18 years or over (not previously convicted) may be sentenced to imprisonment for a term of five years (or might be so sentenced but for the restrictions imposed by section 33 of the Magistrates' Courts Acts 1980).

At common law, a person knowingly rendering assistance to someone who had committed a felony became an accessory after the fact, and thus guilty of that felony. This provision created a specific offence to replace that principle.

Procedure

Criminal Law Act 1967, s. 4 B14.59

(4) No proceedings shall be instituted for an offence under subsection (1)... except by or with the consent of the Director of Public Prosecutions.

Indictment

Statement of Offence B14.60

Assisting an offender contrary to section 4(1) of the Criminal Law Act 1967.

Particulars of Offence

A on the... day of..., X having committed a relevant offence, namely robbery, knowing or believing that X had committed the said offence or some other relevant offence, without lawful authority or reasonable excuse harboured X in his house, with intent to impede the apprehension or prosecution of X.

It must be proved that X did indeed commit the specified offence or some other offence for which X might have been convicted on an indictment alleging the specified offence (*Morgan* [1972] 1 QB 436). *Morgan* appears to have been overlooked in *Saunders* [2011] EWCA Crim 1571.

Alternative Verdicts

Criminal Law Act 1967, s. 4 B14.61

(2) If on the trial of an indictment for a relevant offence the jury are satisfied that the offence charged (or some other offence of which the accused might on that charge be found guilty) was committed, but find the accused not guilty of it, they may find him guilty of any offence under subsection (1)... of which they are satisfied that he is guilty in relation to the offence charged (or that other offence).

If D is not initially charged with a s. 4 offence, but with a substantive relevant offence, and the possibility of an alternative verdict under subsection (2) manifests itself in the course of the trial, D should be given sufficient opportunity to meet such a possibility. The issue should not be raised after the court has finished hearing evidence (*Cross* [1971] 3 All ER 641; *Vincent* (1972) 56 Cr App R 281).

Sentence

Where the principal offence is subject to a sentence fixed by law the maximum penalty is ten years, a fine, or both, on indictment (CLA 1967, s. 4(3)(a)); and six months and/or an unlimited fine summarily. Where the principal offence is subject to a sentence of 14 years, the maximum penalty is seven years and/or a fine on indictment (s. 4(3)(b)); and six months and/or an unlimited fine summarily. Where the principal offence is subject to a sentence of ten years, the maximum penalty is five years and/or a fine on indictment (s. 4(3)(c)); and six months and/or an unlimited fine summarily. In other cases: the maximum penalty is three years and/or a fine on indictment (s. 4(3)(d)); and six months and/or an unlimited fine summarily. There is no offence-specific guideline but the Sentencing Council's *General Guideline: Overarching Principles* (see Supplement, **SG2-1**) is used for all offenders sentenced on or after 1 October 2019. B14.62

A useful 'non-guideline' case which is nevertheless much cited is *A-G's Ref (No. 16 of 2009) (Yates)* [2009] EWCA Crim 2439, [2010] 2 Cr App R (S) 11 (64). Although the Court of Appeal said that it did not intend to lay down general guidelines, it set out some helpful principles that have come to inform many of the later cases. It was said that when assessing sentence for an offence of assisting an offender, the first issue is likely to be the nature and extent of the criminality of the offender for whom assistance was provided (the criminality involved the murder of a young boy). The second issue is the nature and extent of the assistance provided (in this case D had done all he could do, including washing down the offender in petrol to remove traces of evidence). The third issue is the extent to which the efforts to assist the offender damaged the interests of justice (here the administration of justice was slowed but ultimately not thwarted). Six years' detention in a young offender institution, imposed on a 19-year-old following conviction after a trial, was upheld in principle although reduced to five years for reasons of totality.

In *Knight* [2018] EWCA Crim 1755 D knew that police were looking for his friend in connection with a firearm. He helped him dispose of a bag and in due course pleaded guilty on the basis that he did not know its contents. In fact, the bag contained a loaded gun. The Court of Appeal found that the underlying criminality was grave. As to the second and third issues identified in *Yates*, the assistance given was not pre-planned, it was short-lived and it was largely ineffective, although D was on licence at the time. The appropriate sentence after trial should have been a term of 30 months. In *Solomons* [2019] EWCA Crim 807, a sentence of 16 months' imprisonment was appropriate for D who pleaded guilty to two counts of assisting an offender. When D became aware of an investigation into the offender's movements prior to committing offences of criminal damage and grievous bodily harm with intent, he had concealed a CCTV unit and had put tape over the number plates on the offender's van. D's intent was to impede the offender's arrest and prosecution, but those behaviours had been short-lived and ineffective. The sentencing judge had erred in imputing pre-knowledge to D of the substantive offences, a conclusion that could not properly be inferred from D's plea or the circumstances of the substantive offending. A three-year starting point was reduced to two years, which was further reduced for the guilty pleas to 16 months' imprisonment. In *Khatab* [2008] EWCA Crim 541, [2008] 2 Cr App R (S) 94 (530) a sentence of four years' imprisonment for assisting an offender by disposing of a weapon used to commit a murder was reduced on appeal to three years. In *Worthington-Hale* [2010] EWCA Crim 1664, [2011] 1 Cr App R (S) 64 (401) the appropriate sentence was 30 months' imprisonment for harbouring an offender who had committed a series of violent robberies and was himself later sentenced to nine years in prison.

The question of suspension was raised in *Begum* [2019] EWCA Crim 323, in which D, a qualified accountant, drove with the offender to Dover with the intention that they leave the country. The offender was subsequently convicted of murder. D was of good character and felt misguided loyalty to the offender, with whom she was in a relationship. No challenge was made to the length of the 15-month sentence of imprisonment, which the sentencing judge had said was already substantially reduced because of the mitigation, including the fact that the offence would almost certainly end D's professional career. It was argued the sentence should have been suspended. The Court acknowledged powerful personal mitigation and prospects of rehabilitation but concluded that an immediate sentence was necessary in such a case to mark the gravity of the offending.

Omissions

B14.63 This offence is not capable of taking the form of an omission. Shielding another person by silence etc. is rarely a crime, but see the CLA 1967, s. 5, and **B14.69**.

Requirement that Relevant Offence has been Committed

B14.64 An offence under the CLA 1967, s. 4, can be committed only where a relevant offence has previously been committed by the person assisted, and proof of that person's guilt is accordingly an essential element in proof of this offence (see **B14.60**).

It is not necessary for the person allegedly assisted by D to be convicted before D can be convicted of assisting (*Donald* (1986) 83 Cr App R 49), nor is that person's conviction conclusive proof of the person's guilt at D's subsequent trial for assisting; but the prior conviction of the person assisted *will* raise a presumption of guilt, and this will simplify the task of the prosecution at D's trial. It would be for the defence to prove, on balance of probabilities, that the conviction of the person assisted was wrong. See the PACE 1984, s. 74, and **F12.7**.

An acquittal is not proof of innocence, however. If, for example, D1 is accused of assisting D2 by impeding D2's apprehension or prosecution, D1 may be convicted on evidence that is not admissible against D2 or may plead guilty to assisting D2, only for D2 to be acquitted by the court or jury. In neither case will D2's acquittal necessarily undermine the safety of D1's conviction (*Zaman* [2010] EWCA Crim 209, [2010] 1 WLR 1304; *Saunders* [2011] EWCA Crim 1571). But if the court trying D1 has any reasonable doubts as to the guilt of D2, D1 must be acquitted. Cf. *Shannon* [1975] AC 717 (conviction of single conspirator).

Many of the problems arising from use of s. 4 can be avoided by charging D instead with perverting the course of justice: see **B14.29** to **B14.48**. In some cases there may be an overlap between s. 4 and the money laundering offences in the POCA 2002, Part 7 (see **B21**).

Knowledge of or Belief in the Guilt of the Person Assisted

By analogy with decisions concerning the offence of handling stolen goods (where knowledge or belief is similarly a *mens rea* element), it is clear that D must either know or positively believe in the guilt of the person assisted. Mere suspicion, however strong and well founded, would not suffice. On the other hand, the CLA 1967, s. 4(1), expressly provides that D may be guilty even if mistaken about what offence the person assisted has committed; and the language used is wide enough to embrace cases where D knew that the person assisted must have committed a serious offence, but had no idea what offence it may have been (*Morgan* [1972] 1 QB 436). **B14.65**

Intent to Impede Apprehension or Prosecution

The intent to impede the apprehension etc. of the person assisted is an ulterior intent. It is not necessary that the person assisted should have benefited from D's actions; indeed, they may be wholly unsuccessful and lead unwittingly to the person's immediate arrest. **B14.66**

Lawful Authority or Reasonable Excuse

The legal burden of proving absence of lawful authority etc. appears to rest on the prosecution (*Brindley* [1971] 2 QB 300). But the prosecution need not do so unless there is evidence before the court sufficient to raise the issue. See generally **F3.6** *et seq*. It is difficult to imagine what might amount to lawful authority or reasonable excuse in any normal circumstances. **B14.67**

No Offence of Attempting to Assist

There can be no offence of attempting to commit an offence under the CLA 1967, s. 4 (CAA 1981, s. 1(4)). **B14.68**

CONCEALING OFFENCES

Definition

Criminal Law Act 1967, s. 5 **B14.69**

(1) Where a person has committed a relevant offence, any other person who, knowing or believing that the offence or some other relevant offence has been committed, and that he has information which might be of material assistance in securing the prosecution or conviction of an offender for it, accepts or agrees to accept for not disclosing that information any consideration other than the making good of loss or injury caused by the offence, or the making of reasonable compensation for that loss or injury, shall be liable on conviction on indictment to imprisonment for not more than two years...

(5) The compounding of an offence other than treason shall not be an offence otherwise than under this section.

The term 'relevant offence' is defined by s. 4(1A) (see **B14.58**).

Procedure

B14.70 No proceedings shall be instituted for an offence under the CLA 1967, s. 5, except by or with the consent of the DPP (s. 5(3)).

Concealing a relevant offence is triable either way where the underlying offence is so triable (MCA 1980, s. 17 and sch. 1, para. 26). As in the case of assisting offenders, contrary to the CLA 1967, s. 4, an anomalous position arises with respect to the purely summary offence of taking a conveyance without authority (see **B14.59**).

Indictment

B14.71

Statement of Offence

Concealing a relevant offence contrary to section 5(1) of the Criminal Law Act 1967.

Particulars of Offence

A on the . . . day of . . ., X having committed a relevant offence, namely robbery, knowing or believing that the said or some other relevant offence had been committed and that he had information which might be of material assistance in securing the prosecution or conviction of X for it, accepted (or agreed to accept) consideration, namely a payment of £1,000, which was neither a making good of loss or injury caused by the said offence nor the making of reasonable compensation therefor, for not disclosing the said information.

Sentence

B14.72 The maximum penalty on indictment is two years (s. 5(1)). Summarily, the maximum penalty is six months and/or an unlimited fine. There is no offence-specific guideline but the Sentencing Council's *General Guideline: Overarching Principles* (see Supplement, **SG2-1**) is used for all offenders sentenced on or after 1 October 2019. As to sentencing, see the cases considered in respect of assisting offenders in **B14.62**.

Elements

B14.73 The common-law offences of misprision of felony and compounding a felony were both abolished by the CLA 1967. Misprision of treason remains an offence and there are now statutory offences of non-disclosure in relation to certain terrorist offences (see **B10.146** ***et seq.***) and money laundering (see **B21.30**). With these exceptions, the non-disclosure of offences cannot ordinarily be punishable. Compounding an offence other than treason cannot now be an offence other than under the CLA 1967, s. 5(1) (s. 5(5)).

The striking of a bargain, in which a promise of silence or non-disclosure is exchanged for consideration going beyond reasonable compensation to the victim, is another matter, and is punishable under s. 5(1). It is the agreement which constitutes the gist of the offence. It does not matter whether D subsequently keeps or breaks that agreement.

As with the CLA 1967, s. 4 (see **B14.58** to **B14.68**), the prosecution must prove that the other person did indeed commit a relevant offence (see **B14.64**); and where this might be difficult to prove there may similarly be advantages in charging D with perverting the course of justice. Demanding payment for silence may also amount to blackmail (see **B5.47**).

As with assisting offenders there can be no offence of attempting to commit an offence under this section (Criminal Attempts Act 1981, s. 1(4)).

OTHER OFFENCES RELATING TO OFFENDERS

Escape

B14.74 It is a common-law offence, punishable on indictment by a fine and imprisonment at large, to escape from legal custody. The escape may be from police custody following arrest (*Timmis*

[1976] Crim LR 129) or from custody or imprisonment etc. following remand or conviction (*Moss* (1985) 82 Cr App R 116).

In a case of alleged escape, the prosecution must prove that D was in custody; that D knew this (or was reckless as to whether this was the case or not); that the custody was lawful; and that D intentionally escaped from it (*Dhillon* [2005] EWCA Crim 2996, [2006] 1 WLR 1535; see also *Dillon v The Queen* [1982] AC 484). But it is irrelevant whether D was guilty of the crime for which D was arrested or imprisoned (*Waters* (1873) 12 Cox CC 390).

A partial definition of 'legal custody' is provided by s. 13(2) of the Prison Act 1952:

Prison Act 1952, s. 13

(2) A prisoner shall be deemed to be in legal custody while he is confined in, or is being taken to or from, any prison and while he is working, or is for any other reason, outside the prison in the custody or under the control of an officer of the prison and while he is being taken to any place to which he is required or authorised by or under this Act or the CJA 1982 to be taken, or is kept in custody in pursuance of any such requirement or authorisation.

The references to 'prison' apply equally to remand centres and young offender institutions (Prison Act 1952, s. 43(5)). The reference to 'an officer of the prison' is to be construed as a reference to a prisoner custody officer performing custodial duties at the prison (CJA 1991, s. 87(6)).

D is not lawfully confined if D has been erroneously kept in prison after the proper release date (*O'Connor* [2010] EWCA Crim 2842). D may be in lawful custody even though not physically restrained or guarded (e.g., where D is left unguarded in court). The question of whether D was in custody at the relevant time is primarily a question of fact, to be decided on a case-by-case basis (*Rumble* [2003] EWCA Crim 770). **B14.75**

It was held in *H v DPP* [2003] EWHC 878 (Admin), [2003] Crim LR 560 that a child was guilty of the offence of common-law escape by making off when briefly left unsupervised after being remanded into local authority accommodation. Such an order may be considered custodial, even if it does not specify secure accommodation. As to remands to local authority accommodation, see further **D7.133**.

In *Purchase* [2007] EWCA Crim 1740, [2008] 1 Cr App R (S) 58 (338) the Court of Appeal suggested that 'escape' cases fell into two categories. The first category included cases where a prisoner escaped under some personal pressure to do so, where sentences would be measured in months. The instant case involved a prisoner who absconded from an open prison and was at large for a fortnight. During that time he got into further trouble. A sentence of nine months' imprisonment, consecutive to the existing sentence, was upheld. See also *Banks-Nash* [2006] EWCA Crim 1211, [2007] 1 Cr App R (S) 18 (87), where 12 months was reduced to nine months, and *Golding* [2007] EWCA Crim 118, [2007] 2 Cr App R (S) 49 (309), where ten months was upheld, in each case consecutive to the existing sentence. The second category included cases where a criminal is aided in escape by confederates inside or outside prison, where sentences would be measured in years. An example is *Coughtrey* [1997] 2 Cr App R (S) 269, where four years' imprisonment was appropriate in the case of a man serving life imprisonment for murder who escaped from prison after burning through a perimeter fence with cutting equipment and scaling the outer wall by means of a ladder. He was at large for a week.

Breach of Prison

This offence is similar to escape, but must involve some breaking, cutting, or forcing in the course of the escape. It need not involve escape from an actual prison (forcing open a police station window would suffice) and need not involve any deliberate damage (*Haswell* (1821) Russ & Ry 458, where accidental dislodging of loose bricks while scaling the prison wall was held to suffice). **B14.76**

The case of *Coughtrey* [1997] 2 Cr App R (S) 269 provides sentencing guidelines for this offence. D was serving a life sentence for murder and escaped after two years by burning through the perimeter fence with cutting equipment and then scaling the outer wall. He gave himself up a week later. A sentence of seven years' imprisonment for prison breach was reduced on appeal to four years. McCowan LJ in the Court of Appeal noted that breaking prison is a very serious offence for which a substantial sentence of imprisonment is always to be expected because of the fear and apprehension it generates, the disruption to prison life, the violence and disorder that it may lead to, and the need to deter the culprit and others. Factors to be taken into account in fixing the length of the sentence will include (i) the nature and circumstances of the original offence, (ii) D's conduct while in prison, (iii) the methods employed in effecting escape and, in particular, whether any violence was used and whether there was extensive planning and outside assistance, (iv) whether D surrendered and how soon, and (v) a plea of guilty. If the original sentence is a determinate one, the sentence for prison breach should almost always be ordered to run consecutively. If the original sentence is a life sentence, the sentence for prison breach should usually be the same as if D had been serving a determinate sentence, but it will have to be served concurrently.

Remaining Unlawfully at Large after Recall and Remaining at Large after Temporary Release

B14.77 Under the Prisoners (Return to Custody) Act 1995, s. 1(1), a person who has been temporarily released in pursuance of rules made under the Prison Act 1952, s. 47(5), will be guilty of an offence if:

(a) without reasonable excuse he remains unlawfully at large at any time after the expiry of the period for which he was temporarily released; or
(b) knowing or believing an order recalling him to have been made, and while unlawfully at large by virtue of such an order, he fails, without reasonable excuse, to take all necessary steps for complying as soon as reasonably practicable with that order.

The offence does not apply to persons temporarily released from secure training centres (s. 1(2)). The CJCA 2015, s. 13 (in force from 13 April 2015), amended the 1995 Act so as to make the offence triable either way. It now has a maximum penalty of two years' imprisonment and/or a fine on indictment; six months and/or an unlimited fine summarily. This is in line with analogous offences of absconding or failing to return, but applies only where the period of temporary release expired before the amendments came into force; it was previously a summary only offence with a six months' maximum sentence.

The CJCA 2015, s. 12 (in force from 13 April 2015), inserted provisions into the Crime (Sentences) Act 1997 and the CJA 2003, by which persons recalled to prison under s. 32 of the Crime (Sentences) Act 1997 or ss. 254 or 255 of the CJA 2003 will commit offences if they fail, without reasonable excuse, to take all necessary steps to return to prison as soon as possible once notified of the recall orally or in writing.

The Crime (Sentences) Act 1997, s. 32ZA, and the CJA 2003, s. 255ZA, apply in relation to a person recalled to prison before or after commencement (CJCA 2015, s. 12(3)). Each offence is triable either way and is punishable on indictment by up to two years' imprisonment and/or a fine.

Assisting Escape and Harbouring Escapees

B14.78 Prison Act 1952, s. 39

(1) A person who—
(a) assists a prisoner in escaping or attempting to escape from a prison, or
(b) intending to facilitate the escape of a prisoner—
(i) *brings, throws or otherwise conveys anything into a prison,*
(ii) causes another person to bring, throw or otherwise convey anything into a prison, or

(iii) gives anything to a prisoner or leaves anything in any place (whether inside or outside a prison),

is guilty of an offence.

(2) A person guilty of an offence under this section is liable on conviction on indictment to imprisonment for a term not exceeding ten years.

Criminal Justice Act 1961, s. 22 B14.79

(2) If any person knowingly harbours a person who has escaped from a prison or other institution to which . . . section 39 [of this Act] applies, or who, having been sentenced in any part of the United Kingdom or in any of the Channel Islands or the Isle of Man to imprisonment or detention, is otherwise unlawfully at large, or who gives to any such person any assistance with intent to prevent, hinder or interfere with his being taken into custody, he shall be liable—

(a) on summary conviction, to imprisonment for a term not exceeding six months, or to [an unlimited fine] or to both;

(b) on conviction on indictment, to imprisonment for a term not exceeding ten years, or to a fine, or to both.

(2A) The reference in subsection (2) to a person who has been sentenced as mentioned there includes—

(a) a person on whom a custodial sentence within the meaning of the Armed Forces Act 2006 has been passed (anywhere) in respect of a service offence within the meaning of that Act;

(b) a person in respect of whom an order under section 214 of that Act (detention for commission of offence during currency of order) has been made.

These offences can each apply where the escape is from a prison, remand centre or young offender institution; but a s. 39 offence cannot be committed in respect of a person who escapes from custody whilst in transit to or from prison, or from court etc. (*Nicoll v Catron* (1985) 81 Cr App R 339; *Moss* (1985) 82 Cr App R 116) nor can a s. 22 offence be committed unless the person in question has already been sentenced to imprisonment or detention and is 'unlawfully at large'. It was suggested in both *Nicoll* and *Moss* that common-law offences could be committed by assisting a remand prisoner to escape from a court, etc. No specific common-law offence was identified in *Moss*, and *Nicoll* contains only a reference to perverting the course of justice; but there is also a common-law offence of forcible rescue from lawful custody (see 2 Hawk PC, ch. 21).

Sentence There is no offence-specific guideline but the Sentencing Council's *General Guideline: Overarching Principles* (see Supplement, **SG2-1**) is used for all offenders sentenced on or after 1 October 2019. The most serious reported sentencing case is *Bowman* [1997] 1 Cr App R (S) 282, where a sentence of seven years' imprisonment was upheld in respect of a conspiracy to assist prisoners to escape by smuggling a pistol into Durham Prison. The pistol was found after a search by prison officers. In *Walker* (1990) 12 Cr App R (S) 65, a sentence of nine months' imprisonment was upheld on D who pleaded guilty to aiding a prisoner to escape from an open prison by meeting him outside the prison and giving him a lift in his car. In *Williams* (1992) 13 Cr App R (S) 236, the appropriate sentence was said to be 15 months where D had changed places with a prisoner in an open prison for one night to allow the prisoner to spend a night at home. Twelve months' imprisonment was reduced to nine months in *Taylor* (1994) 15 Cr App R (S) 893 where D pleaded guilty to harbouring an escaped prisoner, his brother. B14.80

Mental Health Act 1983, s. 128 B14.81

(1) Where any person induces or knowingly assists another person who is liable to be detained in a hospital within the meaning of Part II of this Act or is subject to guardianship under this Act or is a community patient to absent himself without leave he shall be guilty of an offence.

(2) Where any person induces or knowingly assists another person who is in legal custody by virtue of section 137 [of this Act] to escape from such custody he shall be guilty of an offence.

(3) Where any person knowingly harbours a patient who is absent without leave or is otherwise at large and liable to be retaken under this Act or gives him any assistance with intent to prevent, hinder or interfere with his being taken into custody or returned to the hospital or other place where he ought to be he shall be guilty of an offence.

(4) Any person guilty of an offence under this section shall be liable—

(a) on summary conviction, to imprisonment for a term not exceeding six months or to [an unlimited fine], or to both;

(b) on conviction on indictment, to imprisonment for a term not exceeding two years or to a fine of any amount, or to both.

Wasting Police Time

B14.82 **Criminal Law Act 1967, s. 5**

(2) Where a person causes any wasteful employment of the police by knowingly making to any person a false report tending to show that an offence has been committed, or to give rise to apprehension for the safety of any persons or property, or tending to show that he has information material to any police inquiry, he shall be liable on summary conviction to imprisonment for not more than six months or to a fine of not more than level 4 on the standard scale or to both.

No proceedings for this offence may be instituted except by or with the consent of the DPP (CLA 1967, s. 5(3)). Under the Penalties for Disorderly Behaviour (Amount of Penalty) Order 2002 (SI 2002 No. 1837), the offence under s. 5(2) is a penalty offence and the amount payable is £90.

As to the relationship between the s. 5(2) offence and the more serious offence of perverting the course of justice, see *Cotter* [2002] EWCA Crim 1033, [2003] QB 951.

As to false (hoax) fire alarms, see the Fire and Rescue Services Act 2004, s. 49, discussed at **B11.97**.

CONTEMPT OF COURT IN RESPECT OF CRIMINAL PROCEEDINGS

B14.83 The following paragraphs deal with contempt of court, insofar as it affects criminal proceedings. Brief reference is made to the jurisdiction of the civil courts in respect of criminal contempt, and to civil contempt by breach of a restraint order. As to false statements in documents verified by statements of truth for the purpose of civil proceedings, see **B14.49**.

Nature of Contempt

B14.84 Criminal contempt of court can take a number of different forms. At common law, it has been defined as behaviour 'involving an interference with the due administration of justice, either in a particular case or more generally as a continuing process' (*A-G v Leveller Magazine Ltd* [1979] AC 440, per Lord Diplock at p. 449). It is not possible to provide an exhaustive list of the ways in which such contempt can be committed, although a substantial number of typical examples are given at **B14.102** to **B14.119**. As Donaldson MR said in *A-G v Newspaper Publishing plc* [1988] Ch 333 at p. 368:

> The law of contempt is based on the broadest of principles, namely that the courts cannot and will not permit interference with the due administration of justice. Its application is universal. The fact that it is applied in novel circumstances... is not a case of widening its application. It is merely a new example of its application.

Broadly based though it is, criminal contempt can nevertheless be categorised according to whether it is committed 'in the face of the court' or committed indirectly (i.e. a 'constructive' contempt, such as the publication of a book or article prejudicing a forthcoming trial in a way which may influence potential jurors or witnesses). Only the superior courts have jurisdiction to punish for constructive contempt (*Lefroy* (1873) LR 8 QB 134), whereas any court of record (including county courts and coroners' courts) may punish contempt in the face of the court.

(As to the position of magistrates' courts, see **B14.89**.) It does not follow that constructive contempt of an inferior court must go unpunished; jurisdiction to commit for such contempt may be exercised by the Divisional Court of the Queen's Bench Division (see **B14.96**).

Civil contempt typically involves disobedience to a court order (or an undertaking in lieu of an order). Breach of a restraint order made under the POCA 2002, s. 41, is no different in this respect from breach of a civil injunction and is thus properly classified as a civil contempt (*Director of the SFO v O'Brien* [2014] UKSC 23, [2014] 2 All ER 798). But either kind of contempt is subject to sanctions that include imprisonment (see **B14.99**) and the appropriate standard of proof is that of beyond reasonable doubt, even in cases of civil contempt to which civil rules of evidence apply (see, e.g., *Re Bramblevale Ltd* [1970] Ch 128). The ECHR, Article 6(2) and (3), are likewise equally applicable (*OB v Director of the SFO* [2012] EWCA Crim 901, [2012] 3 All ER 1017 at [21]) and this means that all contempt proceedings are criminal proceedings for the purposes of the LASPO 2012, s. 14 (see the Criminal Legal Aid (General) Regulations 2013 (SI 2013 No. 9), reg. 9(v) and *Devon County Council v Kirk* [2016] EWCA Civ 1221, [2017] 4 WLR 36 at [52]). **B14.85**

In cases of civil contempt it is usually left to any party aggrieved to instigate proceedings, and such party retains the right to waive the contempt. In contrast, cases of criminal contempt are generally prosecuted by the A-G or by the court acting of its own motion (*Home Office v Harman* [1983] 1 AC 280 per Lord Scarman at p. 310). This distinction is now reflected in the structure of CrimPR Part 48, in which different procedures are prescribed for contempt in the face of the court, on the one hand, and disobedience to court orders etc. on the other (see **B14.92** and Supplement, **R48.1** *et seq.*). Moreover, in cases of alleged civil contempt there is no power to remand an alleged contemnor in custody pending the hearing of his case.

Parties to Contempt

In *Balogh v St Albans Crown Court* [1975] QB 73, Lord Denning MR held that criminal contempt of court is governed by the ordinary principles of criminal liability. If this is correct, it follows that complicity in the offence, as a secondary party, would require *mens rea*, even where liability of the principal offender is strict under the Contempt of Court Act 1981 (see **B14.121** to **B14.128**). Where a corporation publishes material amounting to contempt, the corporation itself is the obvious principal offender, but a newspaper (or television etc.) editor would usually be regarded as a joint principal, because of that person's special responsibility for the content of the publication, and, where *mens rea* is required, an editor's *mens rea* could arguably be imputed to the company under the identification principle. **B14.86**

The dictum of Lord Goddard CJ in *Evening Standard Co. Ltd* [1954] 1 QB 578, that the liability of the editor and company is vicarious, is contrary to principle and has generally been doubted. Employees (e.g., reporters) are not publishers, but might be liable as secondary parties if they act with *mens rea*. See *Griffiths, ex parte A-G* [1957] 2 QB 192.

Courts and Tribunals Protected by the Law of Contempt

One must distinguish between the protection of the law of contempt, which is afforded to all courts and tribunals exercising the judicial power of the State, and the jurisdiction to punish for contempt, which is possessed at common law only by courts of record, and to differing extent according to whether the court is superior or inferior. (As to the position of magistrates' courts, see **B14.89**; as to the Crown Court, see **B14.91**.) **B14.87**

Tribunals which exercise administrative, rather than judicial, functions are not protected. It is not enough that they act judicially in discharging such functions (*A-G v British Broadcasting Corporation* [1981] AC 303; *General Medical Council v British Broadcasting Corporation* [1998] 3 All ER 426). Magistrates thus lose the protection of the law of contempt when sitting as licensing justices, this being an administrative function (*A-G v British Broadcasting Corporation* at p. 348).

Mode of Trial and Open Justice

B14.88 Cases of alleged contempt are tried by procedures which are peculiar to that offence. Contempt may be dealt with summarily (see **B14.89** *et seq.*) or by an application for committal made to the Divisional Court of the Queen's Bench Division (see **B14.96** *et seq.*). In *DPP v Channel Four Television Co. Ltd* [1993] 2 All ER 517, it was stated that 'sensitive' contempt cases, involving such issues as the duty of a journalist to disclose the source of information, should invariably be determined by the Divisional Court.

Proceedings for committal for contempt of court, including contempt in the face of the court, must ordinarily be conducted in accordance with the principles of open justice, irrespective of the court in which they are heard or of the proceedings in which they arise. Where, exceptionally, derogations from that principle are required, they must be no more than strictly necessary to achieve their purpose. See *Practice Direction: Committal for Contempt of Court — Open Court* [2015] 1 WLR 2195 and the associated Practice Guidance issued on 24 June 2015.

Jurisdiction and Procedure: Magistrates' Courts

B14.89 Magistrates' courts are not courts of record, but have jurisdiction to deal with contempt where that power is given by statute. In addition to the power to imprison fine defaulters, the MCA 1980, s. 63(3), empowers magistrates to deal with defaults in respect of other orders. This power is exercisable either of the court's own motion or by order on complaint (Contempt of Court Act 1981, s. 17). The maximum fine is £50 per day or £5,000; the maximum period of custody is two months. Some forms of contempt in the face of the court may be dealt with summarily under the MCA 1980, s. 97(4), or under the Contempt of Court Act 1981, s. 12. Under the CPIA 1996, s. 18, a court can also punish as contempt the use of disclosed prosecution material in contravention of s. 17 of that Act.

Magistrates' Courts Act 1980, s. 97

(4) If any person attending or brought before a magistrates' court refuses without just excuse to be sworn or give evidence, or to produce any document or thing, the court may commit him to custody until the expiration of such period not exceeding one month as may be specified in the warrant or until he sooner gives evidence or produces the document or thing or impose on him a fine not exceeding £2,500, or both.

Contempt of Court Act 1981, s. 12

(1) A magistrates' court has jurisdiction under this section to deal with any person who—
  (a) wilfully insults the justice or justices, any witness before or officer of the court or any solicitor or counsel having business in the court, during his or their sitting or attendance in court or in going to or returning from the court; or
  (b) wilfully interrupts the proceedings of the court or otherwise misbehaves in court.

(2) In any such case the court may order any officer of the court, or any constable, to take the offender into custody and detain him until the rising of the court; and the court may, if it thinks fit, commit the offender to custody for a specified period not exceeding one month or impose on him a fine not exceeding £2,500, or both.

(2A) A fine imposed under subsection (2) above shall be deemed, for the purposes of any enactment, to be a sum adjudged to be paid by a conviction.

(3) [Repealed.]

(4) A magistrates' court may at any time revoke an order of committal made under subsection (2) and, if the offender is in custody, order his discharge.

(5) Section 135 of the Powers of Criminal Courts (Sentencing) Act 2000 (limit on fines in respect of young persons) and the following provisions of the Magistrates' Courts Act 1980 apply in relation to an order under this section as they apply in relation to a sentence on conviction or finding of guilty of an offence, and those provisions of the Magistrates' Courts Act 1980 are sections 75 to 91 (enforcement); section 108 (appeal to Crown Court); section 136 (overnight detention in default of payment); and section 142(1) (power to rectify mistakes).

B14.90 The principles to be applied in exercising this jurisdiction are contained in CrimPR Part 48 (see Supplement, **R48.1** *et seq.* and also **B14.92** *et seq.*).

Section 12(1)(a) is not applicable where D has uttered threats rather than insults (*Havant Justices, ex parte Palmer* (1985) 149 JP 609, although uttering threats might involve 'misbehaviour' in court under s. 12(1)(b)). Magistrates have no jurisdiction over constructive contempt. This may, however, be dealt with by a Divisional Court under the Civil Procedure Rules, Part 81 (see **B14.96**).

Section 12(5) enables an appeal to be brought under the MCA 1980, s. 108, against conviction or sentence. In appropriate cases, the alleged contemnor may seek judicial review, or apply to the court to state a case for the High Court in accordance with the MCA 1980, s. 111 (*Haw v City of Westminster Magistrates' Court* [2007] EWHC 2960 (Admin), [2008] QB 888).

Jurisdiction and Procedure: the Crown Court

B14.91 By the Senior Courts Act 1981, s. 45(4), the Crown Court has, in relation to contempt and the enforcement of its orders, 'the like powers, rights, privileges and authority as the High Court'. This includes the power summarily to punish: disruptive, insulting or intimidating conduct in the courtroom or in its vicinity; disobedience to a witness summons (Criminal Procedure (Attendance of Witnesses) Act 1965, s. 3) or jury summons (Juries Act 1974, s. 20); misconduct under the Contempt of Court Act 1981, s. 9 (see **B14.114** and **B14.113**); failure to comply with its orders (such as investigation or restraint orders); and unauthorised use of disclosed prosecution material in contravention of the CPIA 1996, s. 17. As to failure to surrender to bail (which is not strictly speaking punishable as contempt), see D7.97.

Other forms of contempt (notably contempt involving publications prejudicial to current or forthcoming criminal trials) must be referred to a Queen's Bench Divisional Court in accordance with the Civil Procedure Rules, Part 81 (see **B14.96** ***et seq.***).

Criminal Procedure Rules, Part 48

B14.92 CrimPR Part 48 (see Supplement, **R48.1** *et seq.*), deals with procedures to be followed in a wide range of contempt cases before magistrates' courts, the Crown Court or the Court of Appeal. Part 48 does not deal with procedures in cases brought by order of committal before the Divisional Court, which are dealt with in the Civil Procedure Rules 1998, Part 81 (see **B14.97**).

Part 48 is divided into three sections. The first contains general rules (including rules governing the discharge or suspension of orders of imprisonment for contempt) and the second deals with procedures to be followed in cases involving allegations of obstruction, disruption or other forms of criminal contempt committed in the face of the court. The third section deals with procedures in cases where a party or some other person complains of disobedience to a court order, unauthorised use of disclosed prosecution material or other conduct akin to a civil contempt of court.

Where applicable, the rules supersede common-law principles and practice directions as to procedure in contempt cases, but are intended to reflect and codify previous good practice. This includes the principle that, wherever possible, a formal hearing must be held, even in cases involving contempt in the face of the court.

B14.93 **Rules Governing Proceedings for Contempt in the Face of the Court** Case law preceding the enlargement of CrimPR Part 48 emphasised the need to avoid unfairness to alleged contemnors. It was held that although a judge of the Crown Court has jurisdiction to deal immediately and summarily with contempt committed in the face of the court, that 'truly summary' procedure should be exercised only where 'the ends of justice really require such drastic means'. This is because 'it appears to be rough justice; it is contrary to natural justice; and it can only be justified if nothing else will do' (*Balogh v St Albans Crown Court* [1975] QB 73 per Stephenson LJ at p. 90). See also *AS* [2008] EWCA Crim 138.

An example of contempt that may call for immediate summary action is conduct which deliberately disrupts the trial, whether committed inside the courtroom or outside it. In *Morris v Crown Office* [1970] 2 QB 114, Welsh language campaigners who physically disrupted a sitting of the High Court were summarily committed to prison for three months. Less serious disruptions may also merit summary punishment, but there may be times when it would be wiser for the judge to rise, leaving those wishing to behave badly to do so in the absence of the judge (*Lewis* (1999) *The Times*, 4 November 1999).

The intimidation of witnesses or jurors during the course of a trial, or other forms of interference with them, has also been held to warrant an immediate judicial response. In *Goult* (1982) 76 Cr App R 140, D was summarily committed to prison by a Crown Court judge for intimidating jurors, both in and out of court. Lord Lane CJ said (at p. 144):

> There is every reason . . . for the judge to take the sort of steps which the judge took here . . . not only for the question of the dignity of the court, but also for the reassurance of other jurors who would be awaiting their call to duty in the court.

B14.94 CrimPR Part 48 preserves (in r. 48.5(3): see Supplement, **R48.5**) the discretion to deal immediately with an apparent contempt or postpone consideration of it until later, but r. 48.5(2) requires certain steps to be taken by a court, wherever possible, before it proceeds to conduct a hearing of any kind, including providing D with access to legal advice and the opportunity to reflect, explain or apologise. These steps reflect guidance previously given in cases such as *Moran* (1985) 81 Cr App R 51, *Hill* [1986] Crim LR 457 and *Wilkinson v S* [2003] EWCA Civ 95, [2003] 2 All ER 184.

A court (including, where the Contempt of Court Act 1981, s. 12, applies, a magistrates' court) may order D's detention in custody pending determination of the alleged contempt. By s. 12(2) and CrimPR 48.6, a magistrates' court may order such temporary detention only until the court rises, and must determine the case that same day, but the Crown Court or Court of Appeal are not so restricted and may detain D pending a review the next business day. Having reviewed the case, the court may then conduct a hearing or inquiry into the alleged contempt or postpone that inquiry and deal with it at some later date, in which case D must be released pending the hearing and must be served with a written statement of the allegations and details of the hearing date etc. in accordance with r. 48.7. The hearing itself (whether postponed or not) must be conducted in accordance with r. 48.8.

B14.95 **Proceedings for Contempt by Disobedience to a Court Order** CrimPR Part 48 deals separately with cases where it is alleged that a person has disobeyed an investigation or restraint order of the Crown Court; has improperly used prosecution material disclosed under the CPIA 1996, s. 17; or is guilty of any other conduct that can be dealt with by the Crown Court or Court of Appeal as a civil contempt. Such cases are governed by rr. 48.9 to 48.17 (see Supplement, **R48.9** ***et seq.***). Because proceedings for civil contempt of court are themselves civil proceedings, rr. 48.11 to 48.15 address the procedural requirements of the Civil Evidence Act 1995 in respect of hearsay evidence, any cross-examination of the maker of a hearsay statement, and any challenge to the credibility and consistency of the maker of such a statement.

As to circumstances in which it may be appropriate to adjourn proceedings for contempt by breach of a restraint order pending the outcome of a related criminal case, see *Payton* [2006] EWCA Crim 1226 and *AA* [2010] EWCA Crim 2805.

Jurisdiction and Procedure: the Divisional Court of the Queen's Bench Division

B14.96 The Divisional Court inherently possesses all the powers of a superior court and may act of its own motion in respect of any contempt committed against it; but its more important *jurisdiction in connection* with criminal cases is in committal proceedings instituted by the A-G or Solicitor-General for alleged interference with the due administration of justice (notably in respect of publications that are alleged to create a risk of prejudice to current or forthcoming trials).

Such proceedings are governed not by CrimPR Part 48 but by the Civil Procedure Rules, Part 81. Part 81, *inter alia*, supplants RSC Ord. 52, which was latterly set out in sch. 1 to the 1998 Rules, but only a few of the provisions of Part 81 apply to contempt in criminal cases.

Committal proceedings to which Part 81 applies are deemed to be civil proceedings for the purposes of rules of evidence and procedure, except that the criminal standard of proof applies along with the ECHR, Article 6 (*Daltel Europe Ltd v Makki* [2006] EWCA Civ 94, [2006] 1 WLR 2704). But they are criminal proceedings for the purposes of the LASPO 2012, s. 14 (see **B14.85**).

Civil Procedure Rules 1998 (SI 1998 No. 3132), rr. 81.12, 81.13 and 81.14 **B14.97**

81.12.—(1) This section regulates committal applications in relation to interference with the due administration of justice in connection with proceedings—

. . .

(e) which are criminal proceedings,

except where the contempt is committed in the face of the court or consists of disobedience to an order of the court or a breach of an undertaking to the court.

. . .

(3) A committal application under this section may not be made without the permission of the court.

81.13.—(1) Where contempt of court is committed in connection with any proceedings—

. . .

(e) which are criminal proceedings, the application for permission may be made only to a Divisional Court of the Queen's Bench Division.

81.14.—(1) The application for permission to make a committal application must be made by a Part 8 claim form which must include or be accompanied by—

(a) a detailed statement of the applicant's grounds for bringing the committal application; and

(b) an affidavit setting out the facts and exhibiting all documents relied upon.

(2) The claim form and the documents referred to in paragraph (1) must be served personally on the respondent unless the court otherwise directs.

(3) Within 14 days of service on the respondent of the claim form, the respondent—

(a) must file and serve an acknowledgment of service; and

(b) may file and serve evidence.

(4) The court will consider the application for permission at an oral hearing, unless it considers that such a hearing is not appropriate.

(5) If the respondent intends to appear at the permission hearing referred to in paragraph (4), the respondent must give 7 days' notice in writing of such intention to the court and any other party and at the same time provide a written summary of the submissions which the respondent proposes to make.

(6) Where permission to proceed is given, the court may give such directions as it thinks fit, and may—

(a) transfer the proceedings to another court; or

(b) direct that the application be listed for hearing before a single judge or a Divisional Court.

Permission will be granted only where the court is satisfied that the application discloses a reasonable basis for seeking committal, and where it is in the public interest to bring such proceedings. That may depend on whether the contempt appears sufficiently serious (*A-G v Pritchard* [2020] EWHC 607 (QB)).

The words of exception in the Civil Procedure Rules, r. 81.12(1)(e) were considered in *A-G v Yaxley-Lennon* [2019] EWHC 1791 (QB) at [93] *et seq*. Although they appear to dispense with the need for permission to be obtained in cases where committal is sought for breach of a reporting restriction order, the Divisional Court said that the removal of that important safeguard cannot have been intended.

Jurisdiction and Procedure: The Court of Appeal and the Supreme Court

The Court of Appeal and Supreme Court each possess the same inherent jurisdiction over contempt of court as the Crown Court and High Court. Contempt in the face of the Court of Appeal and contempt by disobedience to its orders must be dealt with according to the rules contained in CrimPR Part 48 (see **B14.92**). Other contempts may be dealt with by **B14.98** application for committal under the Civil Procedure Rules 1998, Part 81 (see **B14.97**). Such an application may be made to the Court of Appeal itself. As to contested contempt proceedings before the Supreme Court, see UKSC Practice Direction 1, paras. 1.2.11 and 1.3.4.

Penalties for Contempt

B14.99 Penalties for contempt of court are now governed by s. 14 of the Act.

Contempt of Court Act 1981, s. 14

(1) In any case where a court has power to commit a person to prison for contempt of court and (apart from this provision) no limitation applies to the period of committal, the committal shall (without prejudice to the power of the court to order his earlier discharge) be for a fixed term, and that term shall not on any occasion exceed two years in the case of committal by a superior court, or one month in the case of committal by an inferior court.

(2) In any case where an inferior court has power to fine a person for contempt of court and (apart from this provision) no limit applies to the amount of the fine, the fine shall not on any occasion exceed £2,500.

(2A) In the exercise of jurisdiction to commit for contempt of court or any kindred offence the court shall not deal with the offender by making an order under section 60 of the Powers of Criminal Courts (Sentencing) Act 2000 (an attendance centre order) if it appears to the court, after considering any available evidence, that he is under 17 years of age.

(2A) A fine imposed under subsection (2) above shall be deemed, for the purposes of any enactment, to be a sum adjudged to be paid by a conviction.

(3) [Repealed.]

(4) Each of the superior courts shall have the like power to make a hospital order or guardianship order under section 37 of the Mental Health Act 1983 or an interim hospital order under section 38 of that Act in the case of a person suffering from mental disorder within the meaning of that Act who could otherwise be committed to prison for contempt of court as the Crown Court has under that section in the case of a person convicted of an offence.

(4A) Each of the superior courts shall have the like power to make an order under section 35 of the said Act of 1983 (remand for report on accused's mental condition) where there is reason to suspect that a person who could be committed to prison for contempt of court is suffering from mental disorder within the meaning of that Act as the Crown Court has under that section in the case of an accused person within the meaning of the section.

(4A) For the purposes of the preceding provisions of this section the county court shall be treated as a superior court and not as an inferior court.

(4B) The preceding provisions of this section do not apply to the family court, but—
   (a) this is without prejudice to the operation of section 31E(1)(a) of the Matrimonial and Family Proceedings Act 1984 (family court has High Court's powers) in relation to the powers of the High Court that are limited or conferred by those provisions of this section, and
   (b) section 31E(1)(b) of that Act (family court has county court's powers) does not apply in relation to the powers of the county court that are limited or conferred by those provisions of this section.

(By oversight there are now *two* subsections numbered (2A) and *two* numbered (4A).)

As to the maximum penalties which may be imposed by magistrates' courts, see **B14.89**.

Section 14(1) applies to both civil and criminal contempt of court (*OB v Director of the SFO* [2012] EWCA Crim 901, [2012] 3 All ER 1017).

There is no power to detain in custody for contempt an offender who is under the age of 18 (*Byas* (1995) 16 Cr App R (S) 869). For offenders aged between 18 and 20 inclusive detention may be ordered where appropriate under the PCC(S)A 2000, s. 108 (see further **E15.5**). A committal to prison of a person aged 21 or over, or a committal under s. 108, is not a 'custodial sentence', as defined in the PCC(S)A 2000, s. 76. A committal cannot be suspended (*Morris v Crown Office* [1970] 2 QB 114). Courts dealing with persons found guilty of criminal contempt have no power to make a community order (*Palmer* [1992] 3 All ER 289).

Contempts Amounting to Other Offences Where the same conduct can amount both to contempt of court and to a more specific statutory offence (as is the case with deliberate non-attendance by a person summoned as a witness), the courts must have some regard to the maximum penalty in respect of the statutory offence when considering a possible penalty for contempt, but they are not bound by any such maximum if there are aggravating features (*Montgomery* [1995] 2 Cr App R 23). **B14.100**

Imprisonment without Legal Representation The PCC(S)A 2000, s. 83(1), which restricts the imprisonment of legally unrepresented persons (see **D20.78**), does not apply in cases of committal for contempt (*Newbury Justices, ex parte Pont* (1984) 78 Cr App R 255); but where CrimPR 48.5 (see Supplement, **R48.5**) applies, D must at least be allowed an opportunity to take advice before any hearing, unless D's behaviour makes this impracticable. **B14.101**

Forms of Contempt: Intimidation of or Interference with or Retaliation against Witnesses or Jurors

An attempt to interfere with jurors or witnesses, whether by way of intimidation, bribery or persuasion, may be punished as contempt at common law. This principle extends not only to litigants and members of the public but also to court officials and jury bailiffs, who should avoid any discussion of cases with jurors (*Mickleburgh* [1995] 1 Cr App R 297). In practice, such cases will ordinarily require police investigation, and may then more appropriately be dealt with under the CJPO 1994, s. 51 (see **B14.51**), or as conduct tending to pervert the course of justice. **B14.102**

Intimidation or harassment of former witnesses or jurors, or retaliation against them, is an equally serious matter (*A-G v Judd* [1995] COD 15). Although the original trial may be over, it is essential that former witnesses or jurors are protected, so that they will not be afraid to do their duty (*A-G v Butterworth* [1963] 1 QB 696).

In *Connolly v Dale* [1996] QB 120, a police inspector was found to be in contempt for obstructing attempts by an accused person's inquiry agent to obtain alibi evidence on behalf of his client, and for threatening him with prosecution under what is now the Police Act 1996, s. 89(2). This was despite the fact that the officer had acted in good faith, for the purpose, as he saw it, of preventing the contamination of identification evidence.

Sentence There is no offence-specific guideline but the Sentencing Council's *General Guideline: Overarching Principles* (see Supplement, **SG2-1**) is used for all offenders sentenced on or after 1 October 2019. **B14.103**

In *Wedlock* [1996] 1 Cr App R (S) 391 D had been on trial in the Crown Court for theft. After the principal prosecution witness had finished giving her evidence in chief the case was adjourned overnight. That evening D drove past the witness, threw something at her, and made an abusive remark. The Court of Appeal upheld the sentence of six months' imprisonment for the contempt. Six months' imprisonment was upheld in *Bryan* [1998] 2 Cr App R (S) 109, where D, the brother of a man on trial for murder, mouthed threatening words from the public gallery at a witness giving evidence in the case. See also *Stredder* [1997] 1 Cr App R (S) 209, where 12 months' imprisonment was upheld in a case where D, who was about to stand trial for theft, approached the sole prosecution witness in the court building, referred to damage which had been done to the witness's car, and said 'that was just a warning'.

Comparable sentences have been upheld by the Court of Appeal in respect of attempts to influence jurors. In *Curtis* [2012] EWCA Crim 945, [2013] 1 Cr App R (S) 28 (147) the offenders had followed three jurors on to a bus and sat close to them while one of the offenders held a loud conversation on her mobile phone making comments about the course of the trial. Sentences of five months and three months were upheld. In *Sparks* (1995) 16 Cr App R (S) 480, the offenders had sat in the public gallery in the Crown Court and, for their own amusement, made threatening gestures towards a juror. The jury had to be discharged as a result. Nine months' imprisonment was reduced to six months on appeal. In *Mitchell-Crinkley* [1998] 1 Cr App R (S) 368, D attended the trial of a friend and recognised one of the jurors. D telephoned the juror and told him that a previous jury in the case had failed to agree. Imprisonment for 12 months was upheld. See also **B14.50** ***et seq.***

Forms of Contempt: Disruption of Proceedings and Misbehaviour in Court

B14.104 A deliberate disruption of proceedings in court, whether staged by persons involved in those proceedings, or by demonstrators etc. may be punished as contempt, and in most cases will be dealt with by the court acting of its own motion. See *Morris v Crown Office* [1970] 2 QB 114. The same is true of misconduct, such as wolf-whistling at female jurors or witnesses (*Powell* (1993) 98 Cr App R 224), and of assaults on court officials whilst they are engaged in the administration of justice (*Re de Court* (1997) *The Times*, 27 November 1997). Whether noisy protests from the public gallery following conviction or sentence are so serious as to amount to contempt is a matter which the trial court or judge is usually best placed to decide, but in many cases the best way of dealing with it may be for the judge to rise, and let the disturbance subside (*Lewis* (1999) *The Times*, 4 November 1999). Outbursts in court may, however, be contempts, even in the absence of an intent to disrupt the proceedings (*Huggins* [2007] EWCA Crim 732, [2007] 2 Cr App R 8 (107)).

B14.105 **Sentence** There is no offence-specific guideline but the Sentencing Council's *General Guideline: Overarching Principles* (see Supplement, **SG2-1**) is used for all offenders sentenced on or after 1 October 2019. In *Phelps* [2009] EWCA Crim 2308, [2010] 2 Cr App R (S) 1 (1), D attacked two dock officers during the course of the sentencing hearing, punching and spitting. An alarm button was pressed and when further officers attended D continued to lash out with his fists. The judge dealt with the contempt immediately, imposing the maximum sentence of two years for contempt, consecutive to the other sentences. The Court of Appeal said that it had not been wrong for the judge to deal with the contempt summarily. There was no dispute as to what had happened, and the court had to act decisively. The conventional wisdom, however, was that in most cases a cooling-off period to allow D to calm down and apologise was appropriate. The sentence for the contempt was reduced to 21 months. In *Khan* [2018] EWCA Crim 2641 one defendant greeted a 'somewhat heated' exchange between the trial judge and a co-defendant's counsel with a slow hand clap. On the following court day he apologised, and the judge thereafter purported to sentence him to seven days' imprisonment for contempt. In that case the judge had not made clear at any stage that he considered the appellant to be in contempt of court and why, and that the proceedings were intended to be a contempt hearing, and nor did he provide the explanations required by CrimPR 48.5(2) and 48.6(3) (see Supplement, **R48.5** and **R48.6**). The Court of Appeal observed that it was not entirely clear at whom or what the behaviour was directed, given the events going on in the court at the time, but in any event, D's counsel had not been asked to address the question of sentence at all. The sentence was quashed in its entirety.

In *Walker* [2016] EWCA Crim 1851 the Court of Appeal considered the appropriate penalty following two findings of contempt of court constituted by D's outbursts during his sentencing hearing for an unrelated driving matter. The Court considered other authorities on committals for contempt and concluded that two periods of three months, to be served consecutive to each other as well as consecutive to the separate driving offence penalty, was excessive. In *McDaniel* (1990) 12 Cr App R (S) 44, D was aged 31 and had minor previous convictions. He attended the trial of his brother at the Crown Court where he and others had been warned about noisy conversations during the proceedings. When his brother was convicted and sentenced there was a general commotion during which D called the judge 'a dog'. A sentence of three months' imprisonment for addressing such personal abuse to the judge was reduced on appeal to 14 days.

Forms of Contempt: Committed by Witnesses, Jurors or Defendants

A juror who fails to attend court when duly summoned commits a summary offence under the Juries Act 1974, s. 20(1), but may alternatively be punished 'as if it were criminal contempt ... in the face of the court' (s. 20(2)). Jurors may likewise be punished for contempt if they refuse or fail to discharge their obligations in accordance with the jury oath (*Schot* [1997] 2 Cr App R 383) or conduct improper communications or research in defiance of the warnings given to them. See *A-G v Fraill* [2011] EWCA Crim 1629 (Admin), [2011] 2 Cr App R 21 (271). Note, however, that, since the Juries Act 1974, ss. 20A to 20C (see **B14.133** ***et seq.***), were brought into force on 13 April 2015, misconduct of the kind considered in *A-G v Fraill* may instead be dealt with as an indictable offence. **B14.106**

A witness who refuses to be sworn, or refuses to produce documents or answer questions properly put, will be in contempt. In *Wicks* (31 January 1995 unreported), the Court of Appeal emphasised that witnesses who have been threatened are not thereby excused from giving evidence. As to the liability of witnesses who fail to obey witness summonses, see **D15.93**. As to the position of journalists who wish to protect their sources of information, special provision is made by the Contempt of Court Act 1981, s. 10 (see **B14.115**).

As to contempt by a convicted defendant who refuses to appear in court for sentencing, see *Santiago* [2005] EWCA Crim 556, [2005] 2 Cr App R 24 (366) and *Collins* [2016] EWCA Crim 682 at **B14.107**. As to defendants who disrupt the trial or attempt to manipulate the jury, see *Baker* [2008] EWCA Crim 334.

Sentence There is no offence-specific guideline but the Sentencing Council's *General Guideline: Overarching Principles* (see Supplement, **SG2-1**) is used for all offenders sentenced on or after 1 October 2019. Guidance on sentencing for contempt where a witness refuses to give evidence has been provided by the Court of Appeal in *Montgomery* [1995] 2 Cr App R 23 and in *Robinson* [2006] EWCA Crim 613, [2006] 2 Cr App R (S) 88 (587). In the former case a sentence of 12 months' imprisonment for failure to attend court and persistent refusal to testify or explain the refusal was reduced to three months. In the latter case, where a defence witness gave evidence in chief but refused to answer any question in cross-examination, a sentence of four months' imprisonment was upheld on appeal. It emerges from these decisions that, in the absence of wholly exceptional circumstances, an immediate custodial sentence is appropriate for a refusal to testify, but that the sentence will often be shorter than that imposed in a case of interference with a witness or juror. The principal matters affecting sentence are the gravity of the offence being tried, the extent to which the failure to testify affected the course of the trial, whether the refusal was aggravated by defiance or impertinence to the judge, and the antecedents and personal circumstances of the contemnor. The contemnor should normally be sentenced at the end of the trial, or at least at the end of the prosecution case, to allow time to reconsider. See also *Cole* [1997] 1 Cr App R (S) 228. **B14.107**

In *Solicitor-General v Stoddart* [2017] EWHC 1361 (QB) a juror admitted that he had conducted internet research into the background of a defendant during a burglary trial, causing the conviction to be quashed. He received a four-month prison sentence suspended for 12 months. The Divisional Court did not doubt that an immediate custodial sentence is virtually inevitable for contempt of court but a suspension was considered acceptable given a two-year delay in the case. In the earlier case of *A-G v Dallas* [2012] EWHC 156 (Admin), [2012] 1 WLR 991 the feature of delay was absent. D, a juror, conducted online research into the accused's past, in defiance of the judge's instructions regarding misuse of the internet, and disclosed her findings to her fellow jurors, resulting in the discharge of the jury. She was sentenced to six months' imprisonment.

In *Collins* [2016] EWCA Crim 682, D, who deceived his doctor into certifying that he was too ill to stand trial with his co-defendants, and subsequently failed to attend his individual trial, was sentenced to six months' imprisonment for contempt. In *Chapman* [2012] EWCA Crim

1011, [2013] 1 Cr App R (S) 22 (117), 56 days' imprisonment was upheld in respect of a juror who absented herself from a trial to go on holiday.

Forms of Contempt: Contempt by Advocates

B14.108 An advocate who deliberately fails to attend a hearing with intent to hinder or delay the course of justice would be guilty of contempt (*Weston v Central Criminal Court Courts Administrator* [1977] QB 32); see also *West* [2014] EWCA Crim 1480, [2014] 2 Cr App R 28 (467), a case concerning the behaviour of a barrister of 'breathtaking arrogance', where Sir Brian Leveson P indicated (at 50) 'that not every failure to co-operate or refusal to attend court is a contempt; that is very different, however, from saying that failure to co-operate or refusal to attend court could never be a contempt: it clearly can be'. It could also be a contempt to persist in adducing inadmissible evidence, or in a forbidden line of questioning, or generally to disobey or disregard orders of the court or to treat the court with gross disrespect. It is not, however, contempt to do whatever is ethically and professionally appropriate to provide a client with zealous representation, even if this brings the advocate into conflict with the court for such is the advocate's duty. Failure to submit a defence statement complying with the CPIA 1996, ss. 5(5) and 6A, cannot be punished as a contempt of court on the part of either the defendant or the advocate (*Rochford* [2010] EWCA Crim 1928, [2011] 1 WLR 534).

The Legal Services Act 2007 created offences under ss. 14, 16 and 17 (carrying on a reserved activity when not entitled, employing someone to do so and pretending to be so entitled) and 181 (pretending to be a barrister). Each offence is an either-way offence punishable with imprisonment for two years on conviction on indictment and/or a fine, and with six months' imprisonment and/or an unlimited fine on summary conviction.

Forms of Contempt: Conduct or Publication Scandalising the Court

B14.109 Prior to the implementation of the CCA 2013, s. 33, the publication of scurrilous criticism or abuse that tended to discredit a court or judge (or the judicial system as a whole) could potentially be punished as a criminal contempt of court (*Gray* [1900] 2 QB 36). This law was rarely invoked in modern times, and s. 33 abolished it with effect from 25 June 2013.

Forms of Contempt: Publication Prejudicial to the Administration of Justice

B14.110 This is one of the most important and complex varieties of contempt. Prejudice may be caused, *inter alia*, by revealing matters which might be inadmissible in evidence, and which may influence jurors etc. (as in *Clarke, ex parte Crippen* (1910) 103 LT 636 and *Parke* [1903] 2 KB 432); by sensational and misleading coverage of a trial (see the comments of McCowan LJ in *Taylor* (1993) 98 Cr App R 361); by commenting on the merits of the case or prejudging it (*Hutchison, ex parte McMahon* [1936] 2 All ER 1514); by the vilification of a suspect under arrest (*A-G v MGN Ltd* [2011] EWHC 2074 (Admin), [2012] 1 WLR 2408) or by publicly disclosing sensitive material that was subject to a court order restricting such disclosure, even where the order was addressed to another (*A-G v Newspaper Publishing plc* [1997] 3 All ER 159). It may even involve harassment and intimidation of defendants, such as may affect their ability to participate in the trial (*A-G v Yaxley-Lennon* [2019] EWHC 1791 (QB)). The first question for the court in such cases is whether the publication created a substantial risk that the course of justice would be substantially impeded or prejudiced. The court must assess that risk by looking forward from the time of publication. It is no defence that by chance no jurors saw the offending material and no prejudice was caused (*A-G v Associated Newspapers Ltd* [2011] EWHC 418 (Admin), [2011] 1 WLR 2097). Members of the public who prejudge cases by posting comments on social media sites such as Twitter and Facebook may incur liability on the same basis as media organisations. As Sir Brian Leveson P warned in *Ex parte British Broadcasting Corporation*; *R v F* [2016] EWCA Crim 12, [2016] 2 Cr App R 13 (157) (at [43]):

> ... anyone posting a comment on a publicly available website which creates a substantial risk of causing serious prejudice faces the potential prospect of proceedings for contempt of court and we anticipate that the authorities will be alert to inform the Attorney General should such circumstances arise. This does not just apply to the appellant or any other media organisations: it applies to individuals who run the risk of causing real difficulty to the smooth progress of a fair trial.

Newspapers and other publishers may also commit contempt where they make payments to witnesses on terms which may encourage perjured evidence, or seek to pressurise litigants into abandoning their actions (*A-G v Hislop* [1991] 1 QB 514). Publication of material by one person, when another person has already been served with an injunction prohibiting disclosure of that material pending trial of the issue of its confidentiality, may be a criminal contempt by the publisher because it destroys the subject-matter of the dispute (*A-G v Times Newspapers Ltd* [1992] 1 AC 191; *A-G v Punch Ltd* [2002] UKHL 50, [2003] 1 AC 1046). It is not necessary that the publisher in such a case should intend to cause the harm that the third party injunction was ultimately designed to prevent. It is not for editors or broadcasters to decide (for example) whether publication of material which a third party has been ordered not to disclose would or would not harm the national interest. An honest belief on their part that no such harm would be caused is accordingly no defence (*A-G v Punch Ltd*).

Publication of material capable of prejudicing or impeding forthcoming legal proceedings does not necessarily amount to contempt. If the proceedings in question are not 'active' within the meaning of the Contempt of Court Act 1981 (see **B14.121**) or if there is no substantial risk of serious prejudice at the time of publication, then publication amounts to contempt only if there is proof of an intent to interfere with the course of justice in those proceedings. Recklessness or negligence will not suffice (*A-G v News Group Newspapers plc* [1989] QB 110; *A-G v Newspaper Publishing plc*). Where there is a substantial risk of serious prejudice to active proceedings, liability may be strict, but subject to certain defences (see generally **B14.121** to **B14.130**). **B14.111**

According to the Divisional Court in *A-G v News Group Newspapers plc*, publications which deliberately set out to prejudice possible future legal proceedings, and which do in fact create a real risk of such prejudice, may constitute contempt, even where those proceedings were not even imminent at the time of publication (e.g., where nothing had yet been done to instigate them). The case involved a highly prejudicial campaign run by the *Sun* newspaper with a view to ensuring that a doctor accused of raping a child would in due course be prosecuted. Watkins LJ acknowledged that this decision represented an extension of the law, but argued that the common law was 'a living body of law capable of adaption and expansion to meet fresh needs'. Doubts have subsequently been expressed as to the correctness of this view, which could be seen as a threat to investigative journalism. In *A-G v Sport Newspapers Ltd* [1991] 1 WLR 1194, a differently constituted Divisional Court held that material published by the *Sport* concerning a suspect in a murder inquiry did not amount to intentional interference in the course of justice, but Hodgson J went on to state (*obiter*) that *News Group Newspapers* was wrongly decided, and it seems that Bingham LJ would have been prepared to follow it only on the basis that he considered it wrong to depart from such a recent precedent.

Sentence There is no offence-specific guideline but the Sentencing Council's *General Guideline: Overarching Principles* (see Supplement, **SG2-1**) is used for all offenders sentenced on or after 1 October 2019. In *A-G v Malone* [2019] EWHC 3726 (QB) the A-G applied for D's committal to prison for contempt of court for breaching an injunction protecting the identity of one of James Bulger's killers. A television actress who had posted a photo on social media purporting to be of one of the killers of James Bulger, in breach of a worldwide injunction protecting his identity, was sentenced to eight months' imprisonment, suspended for two **B14.112**

B

Part B Offences

years. The threshold for a custodial sentence had undoubtedly been passed by her actions, but her personal mitigation led the Court to suspend the committal order. In *A-G v Paterson* [2019] EWHC 1914 (QB) D admitted recording a court hearing without permission and was committed to prison for 21 days, suspended for 12 months. The Court was referred to two earlier cases, *Cullinane* [2007] EWCA Crim 2682 and *A-G v Scarth* [2013] EWHC 194 (Admin), in which, in the former case, a sentence of four months' imprisonment was held to be excessive and on appeal a sentence was substituted which resulted in D's immediate release, while in the latter case, a sentence of 28 days was imposed, suspended for a period of 12 months.

In *A-G v News Group Newspapers Ltd* (1984) 6 Cr App R (S) 418 the Divisional Court dealt with a case where a newspaper had published, during the course of a trial, a picture of one of two defendants on trial for causing injury to their baby, with the wholly misleading headline: 'Baby was blinded by dad'. The contempt was not intentional and the newspaper apologised. There was a clear and grave risk to the trial, even if it was not, in fact, interrupted. The paper was fined £5,000, with Stephen Brown LJ underlining (at p. 420) the strict duty of care placed upon those who publish news items relating to trials to ensure that they do not run the risk of interfering with the course of justice.

Forms of Contempt: Misuse of Recording Devices in Court

B14.113 **Contempt of Court Act 1981, s. 9**

(1) Subject to subsection (4) below, it is a contempt of court—
   (a) to use in court, or bring into court for use, any tape recorder or other instrument for recording sound, except with the leave of the court;
   (b) to publish a recording of legal proceedings made by means of any such instrument, or any recording derived directly or indirectly from it, by playing it in the hearing of the public or any section of the public, or to dispose of it or any recording so derived, with a view to such publication;
   (c) to use any such recording in contravention of any conditions of leave granted under paragraph (a).

(2) Leave under paragraph (a) of subsection (1) may be granted or refused at the discretion of the court, and if granted may be granted subject to such conditions as the court thinks proper with respect to the use of any recording made pursuant to the leave; and where leave has been granted the court may at the like discretion withdraw or amend it either generally or in relation to any particular part of the proceedings.

(3) Without prejudice to any other power to deal with an act of contempt under paragraph (a) of subsection (1), the court may order the instrument, or any recording made with it, or both, to be forfeited; and any object so forfeited shall (unless the court otherwise determines on application by a person appearing to be the owner) be sold or otherwise disposed of in such manner as the court may direct.

(4) This section does not apply to the making or use of sound recordings for purposes of official transcripts of proceedings.

See *A-G v Pritchard* [2020] EWHC 607 (QB), in which it was no defence that D, a solicitor's clerk, made the illicit recordings only because he struggled to keep an accurate handwritten note of the proceedings.

Section 9 does not apply to the recording and broadcasting of certain proceedings in the Court of Appeal that are made in accordance with the Court of Appeal (Recording and Broadcasting) Order 2013 (SI 2013 No. 2786) or of sentencing remarks broadcast in accordance with the Crown Court (Recording and Broadcasting) Order 2020 (SI 2020 No. 637). In other cases, CrimPD I, paras. 6A.1 to 6A.6, *Unofficial Sound Recording of Proceedings* (see Supplement, **CPD.6A**) provide guidance on the exercise of the discretion to grant, withhold or withdraw leave to use equipment for recording sound or to impose conditions as to the use of any recording. (As to the power to order forfeiture of unauthorised recordings, see CrimPR 6.10 (see Supplement, **R6.10**).)

Forms of Contempt: Photography, Sketching, Tweeting and Mobile Telephones

B14.114 The taking of photographs or video in court is a summary offence under the CJA 1925, s. 41, as is the publication of such images. In some circumstances the prohibition extends to sketches of the proceedings. The maximum penalty (a level 3 fine) may however be considered inadequate as a punishment for serious offences, involving (e.g.) the deliberate flouting of the court's authority and the disruption or potential disruption of the proceedings. It may therefore be more fitting for such misconduct to be punished with imprisonment as contempt of court (*Solicitor-General v Cox* [2016] EWHC 1241 (QB), [2016] 2 Cr App R 15 (193); *Smith* [2016] EWCA Crim 1562; *A-G v Yaxley-Lennon* [2019] EWHC 1791 (QB)). It is an offence under s. 41(1) to:

(a) take or attempt to take in any court any photograph, or with a view to publication make or attempt to make in any court any portrait or sketch of any person, being a judge of the court or a juror or a witness in or a party to any proceedings before the court, whether civil or criminal; or
(b) publish any photograph, portrait or sketch taken or made in contravention of the foregoing provisions of this section or any reproduction thereof.

'Judge' includes a registrar, magistrate, justice and coroner (s. 41(2)(a)). Photography includes video; and the police are not exempt from the prohibition (*Loveridge* [2001] EWCA Crim 973, [2001] 2 Cr App R 29 (591)). Photography in the precincts of the court building is also covered (s. 41(2)(c)). The publication of sketches drawn from memory once outside the court is not prohibited; and s. 41 does not apply to the recording and broadcasting of certain proceedings in the Court of Appeal that are made in accordance with the Court of Appeal (Recording and Broadcasting) Order 2013 (SI 2013 No. 2786).

Mobile telephones must ordinarily be turned off in court, but a mobile phone (in silent mode) or small computer may be used by representatives of the media or legal commentators for the fair reporting of cases. Members of the public who wish to use such equipment must seek prior approval (CrimPD I, para. 6C: see Supplement, **CPD.6C** and **D3.140**). CrimPD I, para. 6D, provides for note-taking in court and states (at para. 6D.1) that the taking of notes 'on paper or by silent electronic means' is permitted as long as it does not interfere with the proper administration of justice.

Forms of Contempt: Refusal to Disclose Sources of Published Information

A journalist or other person who refuses to disclose the source of information that the journalist has published may be in contempt of court, but regard must be had to the Contempt of Court Act 1981, s. 10, which provides: **B14.115**

> No court may require a person to disclose, nor is any person guilty of contempt of court for refusing to disclose, the source of information contained in a publication for which he is responsible, unless it be established to the satisfaction of the court that disclosure is necessary in the interests of justice or national security or for the prevention of disorder or crime.

In order to satisfy the court of the necessity of disclosure, proof is required, on balance of probabilities; it is not enough merely to assert the need (*Secretary of State for Defence v Guardian Newspapers Ltd* [1985] AC 339). Nor is convenience the same thing as necessity; but necessity is a relative concept, and may be something less than absolute indispensability (*Re an Inquiry under the Company Securities (Insider Dealing) Act 1985* [1988] AC 660). 'Prevention of crime' includes the general control of crime and not just the prevention of specific acts (*Re an Inquiry under the Company Securities (Insider Dealing) Act 1985*). See generally **F9.23**.

Forms of Contempt: Breaches of Reporting Restrictions on Cases Heard in Public

Deliberate or reckless breach of reporting restrictions imposed under the Contempt of Court Act 1981, s. 4 (see **D3.125**) can also amount to contempt, even if it involves material that has already been in the public domain, and even if D lacked actual knowledge of the order (*A-G v Yaxley-Lennon* [2019] EWHC 1791 (QB) at [51] *et seq.*; *Horsham Justices, ex parte Farquharson* [1982] QB 762). CrimPD I, paras. 6B.1 to 6B.7, *Restrictions on Reporting Proceedings*, provide specific guidance on the exercise of this power (see Supplement, **CPD.6B**). For further guidance **B14.116** see *Reporting Restrictions in the Criminal Courts* (4th edn, revised May 2016), available at tinyurl.com/yak6uyma.

As to reporting restrictions generally, see **D3.125** ***et seq.***; for reporting restrictions when a case is sent to the Crown Court, see the CDA 1998, s. 52B, at **D10.51**.

See also *A-G v Harkins* [2013] EWHC 1455 (Admin), in which the A-G brought proceedings for contempt, not under s. 4, but under Part 81 of the Civil Procedure Rules in respect of the publication of photographs on Facebook, supposedly showing the notorious child murderers Thompson and Venables as adults, in breach of an injunction issued 'to the world' by the High Court.

Forms of Contempt: Publication of Matter Exempted from Disclosure in Court

B14.117 **Contempt of Court Act 1981, s. 11**

In any case where a court (having power to do so) allows a name or other matter to be withheld from the public in proceedings before the court, the court may give such directions prohibiting the publication of that name or matter in connection with the proceedings as appear to the court to be necessary for the purpose for which it was so withheld.

CrimPD I, paras. 6B.1 to 6B.7, *Restrictions on Reporting Proceedings*, provide specific guidance on the exercise of this power (see Supplement, **CPD.6B**). Breach of an order made under s. 11 could (as with breaches of orders under the Contempt of Court Act 1981, s. 4), constitute a statutory contempt. As to the principles of 'open justice', see **D3.122** ***et seq***.

The power to make such an order must not be used merely 'for the benefit of the comfort and feelings of defendants' as by safeguarding them from unwanted publicity or molestation (*Evesham Justices, ex parte McDonagh* [1988] QB 553). It is properly employed to safeguard the identity of children and young persons, complainants in rape cases, witnesses who might later be exposed to violence or blackmail, or revelation of whose identity might prejudice national security.

It may be necessary for a court to sit in camera when hearing evidence in support of an application under the Contempt of Court Act 1981, s. 11 (*Tower Bridge Magistrates' Court, ex parte Osbourne* (1989) 88 Cr App R 28).

Forms of Contempt: Publications Relating to Proceedings in Camera

B14.118 **Administration of Justice Act 1960, s. 12**

(1) The publication of information relating to proceedings before any court sitting in private shall not of itself be contempt of court except in the following cases, that is to say—
   (a) where the proceedings—
      (i) relate to the exercise of the inherent jurisdiction of the High Court with respect to minors;
      (ii) are brought under the Children Act 1989 or the Adoption and Children Act 2002; or
      (iii) otherwise relate wholly or mainly to the maintenance or upbringing of a minor;
   (b) where the proceedings are brought under the Mental Capacity Act 2005, or under any provision of the Mental Health Act 1983 authorising an application or reference to be made to the First-tier Tribunal, the Mental Health Review Tribunal for Wales or to the county court;
   (c) where the court sits in private for reasons of national security during that part of the proceedings about which the information in question is published;
   (d) where the information relates to a secret process, discovery or invention which is in issue in the proceedings;
   (e) where the court (having power to do so) expressly prohibits the publication of all information relating to the proceedings or of information of the description which is published.

(2) Without prejudice to the foregoing subsection, the publication of the text or a summary of the whole or part of an order made by a court sitting in private shall not of itself be

contempt of court except where the court (having power to do so) expressly prohibits the publication.

(3) In this section references to a court include references to a judge and to a tribunal and to any person exercising the functions of a court, a judge or a tribunal; and references to a court sitting in private include references to a court sitting in camera or in chambers.

(4) Nothing in this section shall be construed as implying that any publication is punishable as contempt of court which would not be so punishable apart from this section (and in particular where the publication is not so punishable by reason of being authorised by rules of court).

(5) Subsection (1) is subject to Part 2 of the Children, Schools and Families Act 2010 (family proceedings), and nothing in subsection (2) applies in relation to a contempt of court under section 11 of that Act (restriction on publication of information relating to family proceedings).

Section 12(5) was inserted by the Children, Schools and Families Act 2010, sch. 3, para. 4, and is not yet in force.

In *P v Liverpool Daily Post and Echo Newspapers plc* [1991] 2 AC 370, the House of Lords held that nothing in s. 12(1) prohibits publication of the fact that a court or tribunal is to sit etc., nor does it prohibit the naming of a person involved (but see **B14.117**).

Attempted Contempt

Criminal contempt can take the form either of conduct which is intended to interfere with the course of justice, or of conduct which tends to have that effect. It is not therefore essential that any real harm is done. If the intent is proved, the measures adopted may be hopelessly ineffective (*Castro, Skipworth's and the Defendant's Case* (1873) LR 9 QB 230), and if the tendency is proved, there may sometimes be an element of strict liability, although this is now largely confined to certain publications (see **B14.123**). **B14.119**

This leaves little scope for offences of attempted contempt, but one could have a case in which a person fails, not only to interfere with the proceedings, but to perform the act by which the person intends so to do. An example of such a case is *Balogh v St Albans Crown Court* [1975] QB 73, where Balogh intended to disrupt a trial by pumping laughing-gas into the court-room, but was arrested before he could do so. Doubts were expressed by Stephenson LJ about the very existence of any crime of attempted contempt, but Balogh had not in any case got beyond the stage of mere preparation, and the doubts were left unresolved. It is submitted that there are no compelling reasons for denying the existence of that offence (see the judgment of Lord Denning MR), but the problem will seldom arise in practice.

Mens Rea

It has been recognised that *mens rea* in criminal contempt cases is something of a minefield, owing to the piecemeal development of the common-law offence, and the lack of codification (see the observations of Lord Donaldson MR in *A-G v Newspaper Publishing plc* [1988] Ch 333 at p. 373). **B14.120**

At common law, some forms of contempt carried strict liability. Thus, in *Odhams Press Ltd, ex parte A-G* [1957] 1 QB 73, Odhams Press was held to be guilty of contempt for publishing an article which tended to prejudice the course of justice in a forthcoming trial, even though it was not informed that the trial was forthcoming, and was not even proved to have been reckless as to the possibility. This rule seems to have been confined in practice to publication cases (*A-G v English* [1983] 1 AC 116 per Lord Diplock at p. 141), and insofar as interference with the course of justice in 'particular proceedings' is concerned, it is now expressly so confined by ss. 1 and 2 of the Contempt of Court Act 1981, which indeed limit its application more tightly still (see **B14.121**).

This leaves two further issues to be considered. First, whether strict liability can still apply in any areas not covered by the Contempt of Court Act 1981; and secondly, whether anything less than a specific intent may suffice where strict liability is excluded under the Act. These issues are considered at **B14.129** and **B14.130** respectively.

Strict Liability: Contempt of Court Act 1981

B14.121 Contempt of Court Act 1981, ss. 1 and 2 and sch. 1

The strict liability rule

1. In this Act 'the strict liability rule' means the rule of law whereby conduct may be treated as a contempt of court as tending to interfere with the course of justice in particular legal proceedings regardless of intent to do so.

Limitation of scope of strict liability

2.—(1) The strict liability rule applies only in relation to publications, and for this purpose 'publication' includes any speech, writing, programme included in a programme service or other communication in whatever form, which is addressed to the public at large or any section of the public.
(2) The strict liability rule applies only to a publication which creates a substantial risk that the course of justice in the proceedings in question will be seriously impeded or prejudiced.
(3) The strict liability rule applies to a publication only if the proceedings in question are active within the meaning of this section at the time of the publication.
(4) Schedule 1 applies for determining the times at which proceedings are to be treated as active within the meaning of this section.
(5) In this section 'programme service' has the same meaning as in the Broadcasting Act 1990.

SCHEDULE 1

TIMES WHEN PROCEEDINGS ARE ACTIVE FOR PURPOSES OF SECTION 2

Preliminary

1. In this Schedule 'criminal proceedings' means proceedings against a person in respect of an offence, not being appellate proceedings or proceedings commenced by motion for committal or attachment in England and Wales or Northern Ireland; and 'appellate proceedings' means proceedings on appeal from or for the review of the decision of a court in any proceedings.

1ZA. [Scotland.]

1A. In paragraph 1 the reference to an offence includes a service offence within the meaning of the Armed Forces Act 2006.

2. Criminal, appellate and other proceedings are active within the meaning of section 2 at the times respectively prescribed by the following paragraphs of this Schedule; and in relation to proceedings in which more than one of the steps described in any of those paragraphs is taken, the reference in that paragraph is a reference to the first of those steps.

Criminal proceedings

3. Subject to the following provisions of this Schedule, criminal proceedings are active from the relevant initial step specified in paragraph 4 until concluded as described in paragraph 5.

4. The initial steps of criminal proceedings are:—
(a) arrest without warrant;
(b) the issue, or in Scotland the grant, of a warrant for arrest;
(c) the issue of a summons to appear; [or in Scotland the grant of a warrant to cite;]
(d) the service of an indictment or other document specifying the charge;
(e) except in Scotland, oral charge.
(f) [Scotland].

4A. Where as a result of an order under section 54 of the Criminal Procedure and Investigations Act 1996 (acquittal tainted by an administration of justice offence) proceedings are brought against a person for an offence of which he has previously been acquitted, the initial step of the proceedings is a certification under subsection (2) of that section; and paragraph 4 has effect *subject to this.*

5. Criminal proceedings are concluded—
(a) by acquittal or, as the case may be, by sentence;
(b) by any other verdict, finding, order or decision which puts an end to the proceedings;

(c) by discontinuance or by operation of law.
(d) [Scotland].

6. The reference in paragraph 5(a) to sentence includes any order or decision consequent on conviction or finding of guilt which disposes of the case, either absolutely or subject to future events, and a deferment of sentence under section 1 of the Powers of Criminal Courts (Sentencing) Act 2000, section 202 of the Criminal Procedure (Scotland) Act 1995 or Article 14 of the Treatment of Offenders (Northern Ireland) Order 1976.
7. Proceedings are discontinued within the meaning of paragraph 5(c)—
   (a) in England and Wales or Northern Ireland, if the charge or summons is withdrawn or a *nolle prosequi* entered;
   (aa) in England and Wales, if they are discontinued by virtue of section 23 of the Prosecution of Offences Act 1985;
   (ab) in England and Wales, if they are discontinued by virtue of paragraph 11 of Schedule 17 to the Crime and Courts Act 2013 (deferred prosecution agreements);
   (b) [Scotland];
   (c) in the case of proceedings in England and Wales or Northern Ireland commenced by arrest without warrant, if the person arrested is released, otherwise than on bail, without having been charged.
   (d) [Scotland].
8. [Repealed.]
9. Criminal proceedings in England and Wales or Northern Ireland cease to be active if an order is made for the charge to lie on the file, but become active again if leave is later given for the proceedings to continue.

9A. Where proceedings in England and Wales have been discontinued by virtue of section 23 of the Prosecution of Offences Act 1985, but notice is given by the accused under subsection (7) of that section to the effect that he wants the proceedings to continue, they become active again with the giving of that notice.

10. Without prejudice to paragraph 5(b) above, criminal proceedings against a person cease to be active—
   (a) if the accused is found to be under a disability such as to render him unfit to be tried or unfit to plead or, in Scotland, is found to be insane in bar of trial; or
   (b) if a hospital order is made in his case under section 51(5) of the Mental Health Act 1983 or Article 57(5) of the Mental Health (Northern Ireland) Order 1986 or, in Scotland, where an assessment order or a treatment order ceases to have effect by virtue of sections 52H or 52R respectively of the Criminal Procedure (Scotland) Act 1995,

   but become active again if they are later resumed.
11. Criminal proceedings against a person which become active on the issue or the grant of a warrant for his arrest cease to be active at the end of the period of 12 months beginning with the date of the warrant unless he has been arrested within that period, but become active again if he is subsequently arrested.

Other proceedings at first instance

12. Proceedings other than criminal proceedings and appellate proceedings are active from the time when arrangements for the hearing are made or, if no such arrangements are previously made, from the time the hearing begins, until the proceedings are disposed of or discontinued or withdrawn; and for the purposes of this paragraph any motion or application made in or for the purposes of any proceedings, and any pre-trial review in the county court, is to be treated as a distinct proceeding.
13. In England and Wales or Northern Ireland arrangements for the hearing of proceedings to which paragraph 12 applies are made within the meaning of that paragraph—
   (a) in the case of proceedings in the High Court for which provision is made by rules of court for setting down for trial, when the case is set down;
   (b) in the case of any proceedings, when a date for the trial or hearing is fixed.
14. [Scotland].

Appellate proceedings

15. Appellate proceedings are active from the time when they are commenced—
   (a) by application for leave to appeal or apply for review, or by notice of such an application;
   (b) by notice of appeal or of application for review;
   (c) by other originating process,

   until disposed of or abandoned, discontinued or withdrawn.

16. Where, in appellate proceedings relating to criminal proceedings, the court—
   (a) remits the case to the court below; or
   (b) orders a new trial or a *venire de novo*, or in Scotland grants authority to bring a new prosecution, any further or new proceedings which result shall be treated as active from the conclusion of the appellate proceedings.

B14.122 Prior to the enactment of these provisions, it had been held that the prejudging of court proceedings was necessarily contempt (see, e.g., *A-G v Times Newspapers Ltd* [1974] AC 273), and this is still true of publications which create a real risk of prejudicing a fair trial and which are intended to influence jurors, to dissuade one of the parties from contesting the case, or otherwise to interfere with the proceedings (*A-G v Hislop* [1991] 1 QB 514); but in the absence of proof of such intent, it would have to be proved that the prejudgment or other comment created a substantial risk of serious prejudice etc. in respect of active proceedings (as defined in sch. 1). Strict liability will then apply, subject to qualifications and defences contained or preserved within the Contempt of Court Act 1981, ss. 3 to 5 (see **B14.125** ***et seq.***).

B14.123 **Substantial Risk of Prejudice** The question whether a publication creates a substantial risk of serious prejudice etc. is ultimately one of fact (*Re Lonrho plc* [1990] 2 AC 154, per Lord Bridge at p. 208; *A-G v Times Newspapers Ltd* [2012] EWHC 3195 (Admin)). The creation of such a risk must accordingly be proved beyond reasonable doubt (*A-G v Unger* [1998] 1 Cr App R 308). 'Substantial' in this context does not mean 'weighty', but rather 'not insubstantial' or 'not minimal' (*A-G v News Group Newspapers Ltd* [1987] QB 1). Account may be taken of the likely effect of the publication on the parties, witnesses or court. Whilst it may sometimes be material, in assessing the risk of prejudice to any proceedings, that D has already confessed or has intimated an intention to plead guilty, it would be most dangerous for publishers to rely on such considerations, because pleas may be changed and confessions retracted or excluded from evidence (*A-G v Unger*). Still less should a publisher assume that the weight of evidence against D would place the outcome of any contested trial beyond doubt (*A-G v Unger*). The courts do however recognise that the proximity of the publication to any future trial may be an important consideration. The longer the interval between publication and trial, the less likely it is that any serious prejudice will be caused, especially if the publication contains nothing that could amount to inadmissible evidence (*A-G v News Group Newspapers Ltd*; *A-G v Independent Television News Ltd* [1995] 2 All ER 370; *A-G v Times Newspapers Ltd* [2012] EWHC 3195 (Admin); *A-G v Unger*). In contrast, the risk of prejudicing the court (and especially a jury) may be heightened by close contemporaneity and/or proximity to the trial, the vulnerability of D, the high profile of the case, the inclusion of material that is being withheld from evidence and/or any inaccuracy in the reporting (*A-G v Unger*; *A-G v Condé Nast Publications Ltd* [2015] EWHC 3322 (Admin)). The vilification of a suspect under arrest readily falls within the protective ambit of s. 2(2) as a potential impediment to the course of justice. In *A-G v MGN Ltd* [2011] EWHC 2074 (Admin), [2012] 1 WLR 2408, Lord Judge CJ said (at [31]):

> At the simplest level publication of such material may deter or discourage witnesses from coming forward and providing information helpful to the suspect, which may . . . help immediately to clear him of suspicion or enable his defence to be fully developed at trial. This may arise, for example, because witnesses may be reluctant to be associated with or perceived to be a supporter of the suspect, or, again, because they may begin to doubt whether information apparently favourable to the suspect could possibly be correct. Adverse publicity may impede the course of justice in a variety of different ways, but in the context we are now considering, it is not an answer that on the evidence actually available, the combination of the directions of the judge and the integrity of the jury would ensure a fair trial. The problem is that the evidence at trial may be incomplete just because its existence may never be known, or indeed may only come to light after conviction.

B14.124 In considering the test under s. 2(2) the question is in many cases whether the publication would have given rise to a seriously arguable ground of appeal if the trial had been allowed to continue and had proceeded to conviction (*A-G v Birmingham Post and Mail* [1999] 4 All ER 49 at 371; *A-G v Associated Newspapers Ltd* [2012] EWHC 2029 (Admin) at [11]), but it is not always the test to apply, and if seriously prejudicial material is published (even if only briefly and online) when proceedings are active, an investigation establishing that no juror actually saw or read it may not be a defence. The Divisional Court stated in *A-G v Yaxley-Lennon* [2019] EWHC 1791 (QB) at [72] that the notion of impeding the course of justice is a distinct one that engages very broad considerations, to do with the administration of justice and the public interest. As was pointed out in *A-G v Associated Newspapers Ltd* [2011] EWHC 418 (Admin), [2011] 2 Cr App R 9 (97) at [27], the assessment of risk at the time of publication is prospective, and 'in answering the statutory question whether a substantial risk was thereby created it is necessary to look at all the circumstances of the publication, including the time during which it was available for access and at what times of day it remained available'.

Where several prejudicial media accounts have been published, the conduct of each publisher must be looked at separately: the cumulative effect of the various publications cannot be lumped together. But if several newspapers etc. each publish prejudicial material, they cannot escape by contending that the damage has already been done by the others. It is sufficient that the latest publication has afforded an additional or further risk of prejudice or exacerbated and increased that risk (*A-G v Independent Television News* [1995] 2 All ER 370 at p. 381; *A-G v MGN Ltd* [1997] 1 All ER 456 at p. 460; *A-G v Associated Newspapers Ltd*).

In *A-G v Associated Newspapers Ltd* [2012] EWHC 2029 (Admin) an avalanche of material highlighting the depravity of the recently convicted serial child murderer, Levi Bellfield, appeared in the defendant's newspapers while the jury were still considering a further charge against him. This included material that had been ruled inadmissible at the trial. The jury was at once discharged and the publications were later found to have created substantial risk of prejudice within the scope of s. 2(2) even though the jury already knew many terrible things about Bellfield's character and had already convicted him of kidnapping and child murder. It is not, however, necessary that any application is made to abort the trial or discharge the jury (*A-G v Condé Nast Publications Ltd* [2015] EWHC 3322 (Admin)).

Applied this way, s. 2(2) applies the right kind of balance for the purposes of the ECHR, Article 10 (*A-G v MGN Ltd* [2011] EWHC 2074 (Admin), [2012] 1 WLR 2408 at [32]; *A-G v Associated Newspapers Ltd* at [11]).

Innocent Publication or Distribution

Contempt of Court Act 1981, s. 3 **B14.125**

(1) A person is not guilty of contempt of court under the strict liability rule as the publisher of any matter to which that rule applies if at the time of publication (having taken all reasonable care) he does not know and has no reason to suspect that relevant proceedings are active.
(2) A person is not guilty of contempt of court under the strict liability rule as the distributor of a publication containing any such matter if at the time of distribution (having taken all reasonable care) he does not know that it contains such matter and has no reason to suspect that it is likely to do so.
(3) The burden of proof of any fact tending to establish a defence afforded by this section to any person lies upon that person.

This section falls short of providing a general 'no fault' defence. In particular it does not protect publishers who are aware of the proceedings, but blamelessly unaware of the prejudicial effect of the publication (*Evening Standard Co. Ltd* [1954] 1 QB 578). Where proceedings are active in respect of a criminal case that arouses public interest, media organisations may be well advised to screen or disable public comments on any reports of that case (*Ex parte British Broadcasting Corporation; R v F* [2016] EWCA Crim 12; [2016] 2 Cr App R 13 (157) at [44]).

Fair and Accurate Reports of Proceedings

A person is not guilty of contempt of court under the strict liability rule in respect of a fair and accurate report of legal proceedings held in public, published contemporaneously and in good faith (Contempt of Court Act 1981, s. 4(1)). As to the limitations on that defence and the power to order postponement of a report, see **D3.125** and **B14.118**. **B14.126**

Discussion of Public Affairs

B14.127 **Contempt of Court Act 1981, s. 5**

A publication made as or as part of a discussion in good faith of public affairs or other matters of general public interest is not to be treated as a contempt of court under the strict liability rule if the risk of impediment or prejudice to particular legal proceedings is merely incidental to the discussion.

Whereas the Contempt of Court Act 1981, s. 3, creates defences to charges of contempt, s. 5 follows ss. 2 and 4(1) in restricting the scope of the strict liability rule itself, and the burden of proof does not lie on the alleged contemnor. If the publication is part of a wider discussion, the publisher is guilty of contempt under the strict liability rule only if it is proved that there is a substantial risk of prejudice to active proceedings (s. 2) and that this is not merely incidental to the wider discussion. See generally *A-G v English* [1983] 1 AC 116. But where an article went into the greatest detail about what purported to be the facts of an incident, it could not be described as 'merely incidental' to the wider discussion and s. 5 did not then apply (*A-G v Times Newspapers Ltd* (1983) *The Times*, 11 February 1983).

If, in the course of a wider discussion, the publisher intends to influence the outcome of proceedings, then (even apart from the good faith issue) the publisher may be guilty of contempt independently of the Act (see s. 6(c) at **B14.128**).

Contempt of Court Act 1981: General Provisions

B14.128 **Contempt of Court Act 1981, ss. 6 and 7**

6. Nothing in the foregoing provisions of this Act—
   (a) prejudices any defence available at common law to a charge of contempt of court under the strict liability rule;
   (b) implies that any publication is punishable as contempt of court under that rule which would not be so punishable apart from those provisions;
   (c) restricts liability for contempt of court in respect of conduct intended to impede or prejudice the administration of justice.
7. Proceedings for a contempt of court under the strict liability rule (other than Scottish proceedings) shall not be instituted except by or with the consent of the A-G or on the motion of a court having jurisdiction to deal with it.

Strict Liability: Where the Act Does Not Apply

B14.129 It is possible (but, it is submitted, unlikely) that strict liability may apply in certain circumstances not covered by the Contempt of Court Act 1981. This is because the Act only defines the scope of the strict liability rule insofar as it applies to conduct tending to interfere with particular proceedings. In *A-G v Newspaper Publishing plc* [1988] Ch 333, Sir John Donaldson MR suggested that examples of possible strict liability outside the scope of the Contempt of Court Act 1981 could include retaliation against a person who has given evidence in previous proceedings (which could themselves no longer be affected) and marrying a ward of court without the court's consent. The better view, however, would seem to be that such contempts do not carry strict liability. A person who punishes another for giving evidence or serving on a jury must at the very least be reckless as to the implications of the conduct on the due administration of justice, and this recklessness is the more probable basis of the person's liability. As for the wardship example (or other cases of interference with a court order), there is clear authority to the effect that recklessness as to the existence of the order is the minimum *mens rea* that will suffice (*Re F (A Minor) (Publication of Information)* [1977] Fam 58).

Cases in which Intent is Required by the Contempt of Court Act 1981

B14.130 Where the Contempt of Court Act 1981 expressly rules out any question of strict liability (e.g., in respect of publications tending to prejudice proceedings which may be forthcoming but which are not active), it is clear that a specific intent must be present. In *A-G v Newspaper Publishing plc* [1988] Ch 333, Lloyd LJ said:

> In cases covered by the Act to which the strict liability rule does not apply, there is no room for a state of mind which falls short of intention. There is no middle way.
>
> I would therefore hold that the *mens rea* required in the present case is an intent to interfere with the course of justice. As in other branches of the criminal law, that intent may exist, even though there is no desire to interfere with the course of justice. Nor need it be the sole intent. It may be inferred, even though there is no overt proof. The more obvious the interference with the course of justice, the more readily will the requisite intent be inferred.

See to the same effect *A-G v Newspaper Publishing plc* [1997] 3 All ER 159 per Lord Bingham CJ at p. 169.

Appeals

Appeals in contempt cases are usually governed by the Administration of Justice Act 1960, s. 13. An appeal against a finding of criminal contempt lies as of right. Leave is not required (*Hourigan* [2003] EWCA Crim 2306). **B14.131**

Administration of Justice Act 1960, s. 13

(1) Subject to the provisions of this section, an appeal shall lie under this section from any order or decision of a court in the exercise of jurisdiction to punish for contempt of court (including criminal contempt); and in relation to any such order or decision the provisions of this section shall have effect in substitution for any other enactment relating to appeals in civil or criminal proceedings.

(2) An appeal under this section shall lie in any case at the instance of the defendant and, in the case of an application for committal or attachment, at the instance of the applicant; and the appeal shall lie—
  - (a) from an order or decision of any inferior court not referred to in the next following paragraph, to the High Court;
  - (b) from an order or decision of the county court or any other inferior court from which appeals generally lie to the Court of Appeal, and from an order or decision (other than a decision on an appeal under this section) of a single judge of the High Court, or of any court having the powers of the High Court or of a judge of that court, to the Court of Appeal;
  - (bb) from an order or decision of the Crown Court to the Court of Appeal;
  - (c) from a decision of a single judge of the High Court on an appeal under this section, from an order or decision of a divisional court or the Court of Appeal (including a decision of either of those courts on an appeal under this section), and from an order or decision of the... Courts-Martial Appeal Court, to the Supreme Court.

(3) The court to which an appeal is brought under this section may reverse or vary the order or decision of the court below and make such other order as may be just; and without prejudice to the inherent powers of any court referred to in subsection (2) of this section, provision may be made by rules of court for authorising the release on bail of an appellant under this section.

(4) Subsections (2) to (4) of section 1 and section 2 of this Act shall apply to an appeal to the Supreme Court under this section as they apply to an appeal to the Supreme Court under the said section 1, except that so much of the said subsection (2) as restricts the grant of leave to appeal shall apply only where the decision of the court below is a decision on appeal to that court under this section.

(5) In this section 'court' includes any tribunal or person having power to punish for contempt; and references in this section to an order or decision of a court in the exercise of jurisdiction to punish for contempt of court include references—
  - (a) to an order or decision of the High Court, the Crown Court or the county court under any enactment enabling that court to deal with an offence as if it were contempt of court;
  - (b) to an order or decision of the county court, or of any court having the powers of the county court, under section 14, 92 or 118 of the County Courts Act 1984;
  - (c) to an order or decision of a magistrates' court under subsection (3) of section 63 of the Magistrates' Courts Act 1980,

(d) to an order or decision (except one made in Scotland or Northern Ireland) of the Court Martial, the Summary Appeal Court or the Service Civilian Court under section 309 of the Armed Forces Act 2006,

but do not include references to orders under section 5 of the Debtors Act 1869, or under any provision of the Magistrates' Courts Act 1980, or the County Courts Act 1984, except those referred to in paragraphs (b) and (c) of this subsection and except section 38 and 142 of the last mentioned Act so far as those sections confer jurisdiction in respect of contempt of court.

(6) This section does not apply to a conviction or sentence in respect of which an appeal lies under Part I of the Criminal Appeal Act 1968, or to a decision of the Criminal Division of the Court of Appeal under that Part of that Act.

B14.132 Section 13(1) and (2)(bb) give the Court of Appeal jurisdiction to hear an appeal against a refusal of bail by the Crown Court pending the determination of contempt proceedings against D (*Seramuga* [2005] EWCA Crim 370, [2005] 2 All ER 160).

Section 13(2) was considered by the Court of Appeal in *A-G v Hislop* [1991] 1 QB 514. It was held that the words 'application for committal or attachment' refer to the original application, rather than to the appeal itself: in other words, it gives a right of appeal to an unsuccessful applicant for a committal or attachment order. It does not matter if the applicant is actually seeking to have the alleged contemnor fined rather than committed to prison (this in any case being a matter for the court), nor if the alleged contemnor is a corporation which could not be committed or attached.

Appeals from the Crown Court were originally heard by the Civil Division of the Court of Appeal, but are now, more appropriately, heard by the Criminal Division (Senior Courts Act 1981, s. 53(2)(b)). Applying normal principles of statutory interpretation, the reference to the Court of Appeal in s. 13(2)(c) would be a reference to the civil division of that court (Senior Courts Act 1981, sch. 4, para. 3) but that would have the quite unintended effect of precluding any contempt appeal from the criminal division to the Supreme Court, and in *OB v Director of the SFO* [2012] EWCA Crim 901, [2012] 3 All ER 1017 the Court of Appeal held that this error should be judicially rectified in accordance with principles established in *Inco Europe v First Choice Distribution* [2000] 2 All ER 109. As to appeals from magistrates' courts, see *Haw v City of Westminster Magistrates' Court* [2007] EWHC 2960 (Admin), [2008] QB 888 (see **B14.90**).

RESEARCH AND OTHER PROHIBITED CONDUCT BY JURORS

B14.133 Some improper conduct by jurors formerly punishable only as contempt of court in accordance with the principles explained in *A-G v Fraill* [2011] EWCA Crim 1629 (Admin), [2011] 2 Cr App R 21 (271) (see **B14.106**) may now amount to an offence under the Juries Act 1974, ss. 20A to 20C. These provisions apply to jurors who improperly conduct and/or share their own research into the cases they are required to try (e.g., by conducting online searches), or who otherwise demonstrate an intent to try the case otherwise than on the basis of the evidence presented in court.

Such offences are triable only on indictment and punishable by imprisonment for a term not exceeding two years and/or a fine (ss. 20A(8), 20B(3) and 20C(6)). Proceedings may in each case be instituted only by or with the consent of the A-G (ss. 20A(9), 20B(4) and 20C(7)).

The power to deal with such misconduct as contempt remains, and circumstances might perhaps arise in which it would still be appropriate for it to be dealt with in that way (see **B14.93**), but in most cases prosecution for one or more of the new statutory offences will be more appropriate, by analogy with the principle set out in *Rimmington* [2005] UKHL 63, [2006] 1 AC 459 (see **B11.81**). As to the possibilities, see CrimPD VI, para. 26M.27 (see Supplement, **CPD.26M**).

Research by Jurors

Juries Act 1974, s. 20A B14.134

(1) It is an offence for a member of a jury that tries an issue in a case before a court to research the case during the trial period, subject to the exceptions in subsections (6) and (7).
(2) A person researches a case if (and only if) the person—
 (a) intentionally seeks information, and
 (b) when doing so, knows or ought reasonably to know that the information is or may be relevant to the case.
(3) The ways in which a person may seek information include—
 (a) asking a question,
 (b) searching an electronic database, including by means of the internet,
 (c) visiting or inspecting a place or object,
 (d) conducting an experiment, and
 (e) asking another person to seek the information.
(4) Information relevant to the case includes information about—
 (a) a person involved in events relevant to the case,
 (b) the judge dealing with the issue,
 (c) any other person involved in the trial, whether as a lawyer, a witness or otherwise,
 (d) the law relating to the case,
 (e) the law of evidence, and
 (f) court procedure.
(5) 'The trial period', in relation to a member of a jury that tries an issue, is the period—
 (a) beginning when the person is sworn to try the issue, and
 (b) ending when the judge discharges the jury or, if earlier, when the judge discharges the person.
(6) It is not an offence under this section for a person to seek information if the person needs the information for a reason which is not connected with the case.
(7) It is not an offence under this section for a person—
 (a) to attend proceedings before the court on the issue;
 (b) to seek information from the judge dealing with the issue;
 (c) to do anything which the judge dealing with the issue directs or authorises the person to do;
 (d) to seek information from another member of the jury, unless the person knows or ought reasonably to know that the other member of the jury contravened this section in the process of obtaining the information;
 (e) to do anything else which is reasonably necessary in order for the jury to try the issue.

Sharing Research with Other Jurors

Juries Act 1974, s. 20B B14.135

(1) It is an offence for a member of a jury that tries an issue in a case before a court intentionally to disclose information to another member of the jury during the trial period if—
 (a) the member contravened section 20A in the process of obtaining the information, and
 (b) the information has not been provided by the court.
(2) Information has been provided by the court if (and only if) it has been provided as part of—
 (a) evidence presented in the proceedings on the issue, or
 (b) other information provided to the jury or a juror during the trial period by, or with the permission of, the judge dealing with the issue.

...

(5) In this section, 'the trial period' has the same meaning as in section 20A.

Jurors Engaging in other Prohibited Conduct

Juries Act 1974, s. 20C B14.136

(1) It is an offence for a member of a jury that tries an issue in a case before a court intentionally to engage in prohibited conduct during the trial period, subject to the exceptions in subsections (4) and (5).
(2) 'Prohibited conduct' means conduct from which it may reasonably be concluded that the person intends to try the issue otherwise than on the basis of the evidence presented in the proceedings on the issue.

(3) An offence under this section is committed whether or not the person knows that the conduct is prohibited conduct.
(4) It is not an offence under this section for a member of the jury to research the case (as defined in section 20A(2) to (4)).
(5) It is not an offence under this section for a member of the jury to disclose information to another member of the jury.

...

(8) In this section, 'the trial period' has the same meaning as in section 20A.

Section 20C is a sweeping-up provision and, although it is potentially very broad, the 'prohibited conduct' to which it applies must (by s. 20C(4) and (5)) be something other than improper research or disclosure already proscribed under ss. 20A(2) to (4) or 20B. The different offences do not overlap. Should jurors be found for example to have used a ouija board to assist their deliberations (as in *Young* [1995] QB 324 (see **D19.29**)) that would appear to constitute a bizarre form of 'research' within s. 20A, but if they tossed a coin as a way of resolving a lack of agreement as to the verdict, that would clearly fall within s. 20C.

DISCLOSURES RELATING TO JURY DELIBERATIONS

B14.137 Under the Contempt of Court Act 1981, s. 8, it was a contempt of court to obtain, disclose or solicit any particulars of statements made, opinions expressed, arguments advanced or votes cast by members of a jury in the course of their deliberations in any legal proceedings. See further the 2015 edition of this work at B14.109.

The CJCA 2015, s. 74, repealed this provision, insofar as it applies to England and Wales, with effect from 13 April 2015, and replaced it with four provisions which it inserted into the Juries Act 1974, namely ss. 20D to 20G of that Act. Section 20D essentially restates the s. 8 prohibition.

Juries Act 1974, s. 20D

(1) It is an offence for a person intentionally—
    (a) to disclose information about statements made, opinions expressed, arguments advanced or votes cast by members of a jury in the course of their deliberations in proceedings before a court, or
    (b) to solicit or obtain such information,

subject to the exceptions in sections 20E to 20G.

Sections 20E to 20G limit the scope of the s. 20D offence through a series of exceptions, which are designed to ensure that the offence does not prohibit disclosures properly made or solicited for the purposes of enabling the jury to arrive at their verdict or in connection with the delivery of that verdict, nor preclude the proper reporting or investigation of alleged juror offences or irregularities. The structure and wording of ss. 20E to 20G suggest that they are not defences in respect of which D might bear any legal or evidential burden of proof, but operate as limitations on the ambit of the s. 20D offence itself. A Law Commission proposal that would have permitted academic research into jury deliberations has not been enacted.

As with ss. 20A to 20C, an offence under s. 20D is triable only on indictment and punishable by imprisonment for a term not exceeding two years and/or a fine (s. 20D(2)). Proceedings may likewise be instituted only by or with the consent of the A-G (s. 20D(3)).

BREACH OF NON-MOLESTATION OR RESTRAINING ORDERS

B14.138 The DVCVA 2004, s. 1, inserted s. 42A into the Family Law Act 1996. This makes breach of a non-molestation order (defined in s. 42 of the 1996 Act) a criminal offence, save where a power of arrest under the Family Law Act 1996, s. 47, remains attached to a non-molestation order made before that date (Domestic Violence, Crime and Victims Act (Commencement No. 9 and Transitional Provisions) Order 2007 (SI 2007 No. 1845), art. 3). It remains possible for breach of a non-molestation order to be dealt with as a civil contempt of court, but s. 42A(3) and (4) prevent D being punished twice for the same breach.

Family Law Act 1996, s. 42A

(1) A person who without reasonable excuse does anything that he is prohibited from doing by a non-molestation order is guilty of an offence.
(2) In the case of a non-molestation order made by virtue of section 45(1), a person can be guilty of an offence under this section only in respect of conduct engaged in at a time when he was aware of the existence of the order.
(3) Where a person is convicted of an offence under this section in respect of any conduct, that conduct is not punishable as a contempt of court.
(4) A person cannot be convicted of an offence under this section in respect of any conduct which has been punished as a contempt of court.
(5) A person guilty of an offence under this section is liable—
 (a) on conviction on indictment, to imprisonment for a term not exceeding five years, or a fine, or both;
 (b) on summary conviction, to imprisonment for a term not exceeding [6] months, or [an unlimited fine], or both.
(6) A reference in any enactment to proceedings under this Part, or to an order under this Part, does not include a reference to proceedings for an offence under this section or to an order made in such proceedings.
'Enactment' includes an enactment contained in subordinate legislation within the meaning of the Interpretation Act 1978.

Sentence

The Sentencing Council definitive guideline, *Breach Offences* (see Supplement, **SG15-6**), applies to all offenders aged 18 and over sentenced on or after 1 October 2018, irrespective of the date of the offence. That guideline supersedes the definitive guideline, *Breach of a Protective Order*, with effect from that date. **B14.139**

Section B15 Bribery and Misconduct in Public Office

THE BRIBERY ACT 2010 AND THE OLD LAW

B15.1 The Bribery Act 2010 was brought into force on 1 July 2011. Section 17 and sch. 2 abolished the common-law offences of bribery and embracery, and repealed the Public Bodies Corrupt Practices Act 1889 and the Prevention of Corruption Acts 1889 to 1916 (as to which see the 2015 edition of this work at B15.30 *et seq.*), but not the Honours (Prevention of Abuses) Act 1925 or the common-law offence of misconduct in public office. New offences were created by the Bribery Act 2010, ss. 1, 2, 6 and 7, subject to transitional provisions set out in s. 19(5) and (6).

Bribery Act 2010, s. 19

(5) This Act does not affect any liability, investigation, legal proceeding or penalty for or in respect of—
 (a) a common law offence mentioned in subsection (1) of section 17 which is committed wholly or partly before the coming into force of that subsection in relation to such an offence, or
 (b) an offence under the Public Bodies Corrupt Practices Act 1889 or the Prevention of Corruption Act 1906 committed wholly or partly before the coming into force of the repeal of the Act by schedule 2 to this Act.

(6) For the purposes of subsection (5) an offence is partly committed before a particular time if any act or omission which forms part of the offence takes place before that time.

The new offences have no retrospective effect and thus apply only to things done on or after the appointed date. But some overlap between the old and new law remains possible. If, for example, P offered a bribe to R (a public official) before the commencement date, but R agreed to receive it only on or after that date, R may then be charged with the new offence of 'being bribed' (Bribery Act 2010, s. 2, see **B15.11** *et seq.*); whereas P would have to be charged under the old law with offering that bribe, and R might also face charges under the old law if there is evidence that R 'corruptly solicited' the bribe before commencement contrary to the Public Bodies Corrupt Practices Act 1889, s. 1. If, however, the promised bribe was eventually given and received after commencement, there should be no difficulty in prosecuting both parties under the new law, without any need to resort to transitional provisions.

OFFENCES UNDER THE BRIBERY ACT 2010

The Structure of the Act

B15.2 The Bribery Act 2010 came into force on 1 July 2011. As to commencement, repeals and transitional provisions, see **B15.1**. The main or 'general' offences under the Act can be divided into the bribery of another person (contrary to s. 1) and being bribed (contrary to s. 2). These are separate and distinct offences because one can (for example) offer or request a bribe without the prior knowledge or agreement of the person who is intended to receive or provide it. The two general offences are supplemented by s. 6, which creates a discrete offence of bribing a foreign public official, and by s. 7, under which a commercial organisation may incur criminal liability if a person who performs services for it (such as an agent or employee) commits bribery on its behalf and it cannot prove that it had adopted appropriate procedures to prevent such conduct.

The general offences apply equally to bribery in the public sector and to bribery in connection with a business, trade or profession, thus largely eliminating problematic distinctions that affected the old law. The Act bases the new concept of bribery on the offer, promise or provision (or request, agreement to receive or acceptance) of a financial or other advantage for the purpose of inducing or rewarding the 'improper performance of a relevant function or activity'. It applies to individuals in the public service of the Crown as it applies to other individuals (s. 16), although there is a specific defence in s. 13 in respect of conduct that is necessary for the proper exercise of any function of one of the intelligence services, or for the proper exercise of any function of the armed forces when engaged on active service.

Meaning of Terms

Sections 3 and 4 of the Bribery Act 2010 define 'relevant function or activity' and 'improper **B15.3**
performance' for the purposes of ss. 1 and 2, and are themselves supplemented by s. 5, which further defines the 'expectation test' used in those provisions. Between them, these provisions adopt and apply 'threshold' and 'wrongfulness' tests developed by the Law Commission, on whose 2008 Report, *Reforming Bribery* (Law Com. No. 313) the Act is closely based. They are designed to ensure that personal or family arrangements and matters of private morality are kept outside the ambit of the offence, and to distinguish improper bribery on the one hand from legitimate rewards or inducements, on the other.

Bribery Act 2010, ss. 3, 4 and 5 **B15.4**

3.—(1) For the purposes of this Act a function or activity is a relevant function or activity if—
  (a) it falls within subsection (2), and
  (b) meets one or more of conditions A to C.
(2) The following functions and activities fall within this subsection—
  (a) any function of a public nature,
  (b) any activity connected with a business,
  (c) any activity performed in the course of a person's employment,
  (d) any activity performed by or on behalf of a body of persons (whether corporate or unincorporate).
(3) Condition A is that a person performing the function or activity is expected to perform it in good faith.
(4) Condition B is that a person performing the function or activity is expected to perform it impartially.
(5) Condition C is that a person performing the function or activity is in a position of trust by virtue of performing it.
(6) A function or activity is a relevant function or activity even if it—
  (a) has no connection with the United Kingdom, and
  (b) is performed in a country or territory outside the United Kingdom.
(7) In this section 'business' includes trade or profession.

4.—(1) For the purposes of this Act a relevant function or activity—
  (a) is performed improperly if it is performed in breach of a relevant expectation, and
  (b) is to be treated as being performed improperly if there is a failure to perform the function or activity and that failure is itself a breach of a relevant expectation.
(2) In subsection (1) 'relevant expectation'—
  (a) in relation to a function or activity which meets condition A or B, means the expectation mentioned in the condition concerned, and
  (b) in relation to a function or activity which meets condition C, means any expectation as to the manner in which, or the reasons for which, the function or activity will be performed that arises from the position of trust mentioned in that condition.
(3) Anything that a person does (or omits to do) arising from or in connection with that person's past performance of a relevant function or activity is to be treated for the purposes of this Act as being done (or omitted) by that person in the performance of that function or activity.

5.—(1) For the purposes of sections 3 and 4, the test of what is expected is a test of what a reasonable person in the United Kingdom would expect in relation to the performance of the type of function or activity concerned.

(2) In deciding what such a person would expect in relation to the performance of a function or activity where the performance is not subject to the law of any part of the United Kingdom, any local custom or practice is to be disregarded unless it is permitted or required by the written law applicable to the country or territory concerned.

(3) In subsection (2) 'written law' means law contained in—

(a) any written constitution, or provision made by or under legislation, applicable to the country or territory concerned, or

(b) any judicial decision which is so applicable and is evidenced in published written sources.

B15.5 The offer, request, provision or receipt of a financial or other advantage may thus fall beyond the scope of the new offences for a number of reasons. One possibility is that the offer, etc., is not intended to influence or reward the conduct of any public, business-related, employment or corporate function or activity, or any function or activity carried on by an unincorporated body of persons. But even if it is intended to influence or reward the performance of some such function or activity, the new general offences cannot be engaged unless at least one of the conditions in s. 3(3), (4) or (5) is also satisfied. There must in other words be an expectation (as defined in s. 5) that the functions in question will be carried out in good faith (condition A), or impartially (condition B), or the person performing it must be in a position of trust (condition C). In the absence of any such expectation, there can be no 'improper' performance of the relevant function or activity, as defined in s. 4. If, however, those tests are satisfied, it does not matter whether the function or activity in question was, or was intended to be, performed within the UK.

The Act does not attempt to define a 'financial or other advantage' (an expression also used in s. 6). If any issue arises as to whether something amounts to such an advantage for the purpose of the Act, it must be determined as a matter of common sense by the court or jury.

Commission Payments and Corporate Hospitality

B15.6 The Law Commission and the government each took the view that the provision or acceptance of 'corporate hospitality' in the business world does not ordinarily involve anything capable of amounting to a bribe. Although such hospitality may involve the provision and acceptance of 'financial or other advantages', there will ordinarily be no breach of any relevant expectation about the way that the recipients will behave. This is also the stated view of the DPP and the Director of the SFO, who issued joint guidance in March 2011 on prosecutorial decision-making under the Bribery Act 2010. There may, however, be circumstances in which the sheer scale of the hospitality is such as to suggest the opposite, and in other cases the offer or acceptance of 'hospitality' (e.g., to or by a judge or some other person acting in a position of trust or impartiality) would clearly be improper.

Similarly, an agent or broker who acts for a buyer of goods or services, but seeks or receives a commission payment from the supplier, will not ordinarily be regarded as acting improperly, but the prospect of earning such commission does create a potential conflict of interest and a prosecution for bribery might be possible if it can be proved that the purpose was to induce the agent to ignore the client's best interests in order to maximise the agent's own earnings.

GENERAL OFFENCES: BRIBING ANOTHER PERSON

Definition

B15.7 Bribery Act 2010, s. 1

(1) A person ('P') is guilty of an offence if either of the following cases applies.

(2) Case 1 is where—

(a) P offers, promises or gives a financial or other advantage to another person, and

(b) P intends the advantage—
  (i) to induce a person to perform improperly a relevant function or activity, or
  (ii) to reward a person for the improper performance of such a function or activity.

(3) Case 2 is where—
  (a) P offers, promises or gives a financial or other advantage to another person, and
  (b) P knows or believes that the acceptance of the advantage would itself constitute the improper performance of a relevant function or activity.

(4) In case 1 it does not matter whether the person to whom the advantage is offered, promised or given is the same person as the person who is to perform, or has performed, the function or activity concerned.

(5) In cases 1 and 2 it does not matter whether the advantage is offered, promised or given by P directly or through a third party.

Procedure

An offence under the Bribery Act 2010, s. 1, is triable either way. When tried on indictment it is normally a class 2C or 3 offence (depending on the complexity of the offence), but see CrimPD XIII, para. B (see Supplement, **CPD.XIII.B**), for the additional factors that the court considers on allocation. No prosecution may be instituted in England and Wales except by or with the consent of the DPP or the Director of the SFO (Bribery Act 2010, s. 10(1)). The relevant Director must exercise this function in person, unless incapacitated or out of the country, in which case the Director may give written authorisation to another person to exercise (but not sub-delegate) that function (s. 10(4) and (5)). **B15.8**

Some cases potentially falling within s. 1 may alternatively be prosecuted as offences under s. 6 (bribery of a foreign official: see **B15.15**). As to the potential application of the Fraud Act 2006, s. 13, see *Kensington International Ltd v Republic of Congo* [2007] EWCA Civ 1128, [2008] 1 WLR 1144 and **F10.8**.

Sentence

The maximum penalty for an offence under s. 1 is ten years' imprisonment and/or a fine. On summary conviction the maximum penalty is six months' imprisonment, and/or an unlimited fine (Bribery Act 2010, s. 11). **B15.9**

The definitive sentencing guideline, *Fraud, Bribery and Money Laundering Offences* (see Supplement, **SG26-7**) is applicable. The guideline applies to individual offenders aged 18 and over, and organisations. It applies to all offenders sentenced on or after 1 October 2014 regardless of the date of the offence. There is a separate part of the guideline applicable to corporate offenders.

Elements

The Bribery Act 2010, s. 1, appears to create a single umbrella offence that can be committed in either of two main ways (case 1 or case 2). In either case it is a conduct crime. P's offer, gift or promise need not be accepted by the person to whom it is offered and in a 'case 1' scenario it need not, even if accepted, result in the improper performance of any relevant function or activity. P must, however, intend such a result. If P offers a financial or other advantage to R, who undertakes no relevant function or activity, on the understanding that R will then seek to approach and influence a third party (S) who does, the criminality of P's conduct under s. 1 will depend on whether P *intends that S would be induced* to act improperly within the meaning of s. 4. If P does not intend to corrupt S, it is irrelevant whether P views the payment to R as a bribe or whether R accepts or receives it on that basis. **B15.10**

P may have a defence under s. 13 if it can be proved (on a balance of probabilities) that P's conduct was necessary for the proper exercise of any function of one of the intelligence services, or for the proper exercise of any function of the armed forces when engaged on active service.

By s. 13(6), this defence extends to secondary participation and inchoate offences, but it is excluded in cases that also infringe s. 6 (bribery of a foreign official: see **B15.15**).

As to jurisdiction over cases with a foreign element, see s. 12(1) to (4) at **B15.24**. As to the liability of senior officers of corporations (or persons purporting to act as such) for offences committed by the corporation with their consent or connivance, see s. 14 at **B15.25**.

GENERAL OFFENCES: BEING BRIBED

Definition

B15.11 **Bribery Act 2010, s. 2**

(1) A person ('R') is guilty of an offence if any of the following cases applies.
(2) Case 3 is where R requests, agrees to receive or accepts a financial or other advantage intending that, in consequence, a relevant function or activity should be performed improperly (whether by R or another person).
(3) Case 4 is where—
  (a) R requests, agrees to receive or accepts a financial or other advantage, and
  (b) the request, agreement or acceptance itself constitutes the improper performance by R of a relevant function or activity.
(4) Case 5 is where R requests, agrees to receive or accepts a financial or other advantage as a reward for the improper performance (whether by R or another person) of a relevant function or activity.
(5) Case 6 is where, in anticipation of or in consequence of R requesting, agreeing to receive or accepting a financial or other advantage, a relevant function or activity is performed improperly—
  (a) by R, or
  (b) by another person at R's request or with R's assent or acquiescence.
(6) In cases 3 to 6 it does not matter—
  (a) whether R requests, agrees to receive or accepts (or is to request, agree to receive or accept) the advantage directly or through a third party,
  (b) whether the advantage is (or is to be) for the benefit of R or another person.
(7) In cases 4 to 6 it does not matter whether R knows or believes that the performance of the function or activity is improper.
(8) In case 6, where a person other than R is performing the function or activity, it also does not matter whether that person knows or believes that the performance of the function or activity is improper.

Procedure

B15.12 An offence under the Bribery Act 2010, s. 2, is triable either way. When tried on indictment it is normally a class 2C or 3 offence (depending on the complexity of the offence), but see CrimPD XIII, para. B (see Supplement, **CPD.XIII.B**), for the additional factors that the court considers on allocation. No prosecution may be instituted in England and Wales except by or with the consent of the DPP or the Director of the SFO (Bribery Act 2010, s. 10(1)). For s. 10(4) and (5), see **B15.8**. As to the potential application of the Fraud Act 2006, s. 13, see *Kensington International Ltd v Republic of Congo* [2007] EWCA Civ 1128, [2008] 1 WLR 1144 and **F10.8**.

Sentence

B15.13 The maximum penalty for an offence under s. 2 is ten years' imprisonment and/or a fine. On summary conviction the maximum penalty is six months' imprisonment, and/or an unlimited fine (Bribery Act 2010, s. 11).

The definitive sentencing guideline, *Fraud, Bribery and Money Laundering Offences* (see Supplement, **SG26-7**) is applicable. The guideline applies to individual offenders aged 18 and over, and organisations. It applies to all offenders sentenced on or after 1 October 2014 regardless of the date of the offence. There is a separate part of the guideline applicable to corporate offenders.

Elements

Section 2 of the Bribery Act 2010 creates a single umbrella offence that can be committed in a number of different ways, the principal forms of which are labelled as cases 3, 4, 5 and 6. These will ordinarily be conduct crimes. This is true even of some offences falling within case 6, which reflects the Law Commission's view that, 'improper conduct may come before the advantage is conferred, and the other way around' (Law Com. No. 313 at para. 3.197). A case 6 offence may, however, take the form of a result crime if what is alleged is that a relevant function or activity was performed improperly by a third person at R's request etc., in consequence of R requesting, agreeing to receive or accepting a financial or other advantage. **B15.14**

In a case 4 scenario, R must be a person who performs (or is to perform) the relevant function or activity, as defined in s. 3, but in each of the other scenarios falling within s. 2 R need not be that person. There must, however, be a link between the advantage received or requested etc. by R and the improper performance (actual or intended) of a relevant function or activity by R or by some other person. In a case 3 scenario, R must intend that R or someone else will improperly perform a relevant function activity as a consequence of the advantage R has received, requested or agreed to receive; and in a case 5 scenario R must request, agree to receive or accept a reward for some such improper performance.

Mens rea is addressed in s. 2(7). R can commit an offence falling within cases 4, 5 or 6 without being aware of the wrongfulness of what is being done or proposed, but such awareness clearly *is* required in cases falling only within case 3.

P has a defence under s. 13 if it can be proved (on a balance of probabilities) that P's conduct was necessary for the proper exercise of any function of one of the intelligence services, or for the proper exercise of any function of the armed forces when engaged on active service. This defence also extends to secondary participation and inchoate offences (s. 13(6)).

As to jurisdiction over cases with a foreign element, see s. 12(1) to (4) at **B15.24**. As to the liability of senior officers of corporations (or persons purporting to act as such) for offences committed by the corporation with their consent or connivance, see s. 14 at **B15.25**.

BRIBERY OF FOREIGN PUBLIC OFFICIALS

Definition

Bribery Act 2010, s. 6 **B15.15**

(1) A person ('P') who bribes a foreign public official ('F') is guilty of an offence if P's intention is to influence F in F's capacity as a foreign public official.
(2) P must also intend to obtain or retain—
   (a) business, or
   (b) an advantage in the conduct of business.
(3) P bribes F if, and only if—
   (a) directly or through a third party, P offers, promises or gives any financial or other advantage—
      (i) to F, or
      (ii) to another person at F's request or with F's assent or acquiescence, and
   (b) F is neither permitted nor required by the written law applicable to F to be influenced in F's capacity as a foreign public official by the offer, promise or gift.
(4) References in this section to influencing F in F's capacity as a foreign public official mean influencing F in the performance of F's functions as such an official, which includes—
   (a) any omission to exercise those functions, and
   (b) any use of F's position as such an official, even if not within F's authority.
(5) 'Foreign public official' means an individual who—
   (a) holds a legislative, administrative or judicial position of any kind, whether appointed or elected, of a country or territory outside the United Kingdom (or any subdivision of such a country or territory),

(b) exercises a public function—
(i) for or on behalf of a country or territory outside the United Kingdom (or any subdivision of such a country or territory), or
(ii) for any public agency or public enterprise of that country or territory (or subdivision), or
(c) is an official or agent of a public international organisation.
(6) 'Public international organisation' means an organisation whose members are any of the following—
(a) countries or territories,
(b) governments of countries or territories,
(c) other public international organisations,
(d) a mixture of any of the above.
(7) For the purposes of subsection (3)(b), the written law applicable to F is—
(a) where the performance of the functions of F which P intends to influence would be subject to the law of any part of the United Kingdom, the law of that part of the United Kingdom,
(b) where paragraph (a) does not apply and F is an official or agent of a public international organisation, the applicable written rules of that organisation,
(c) where paragraphs (a) and (b) do not apply, the law of the country or territory in relation to which F is a foreign public official so far as that law is contained in—
(i) any written constitution, or provision made by or under legislation, applicable to the country or territory concerned, or
(ii) any judicial decision which is so applicable and is evidenced in published written sources.
(8) For the purposes of this section, a trade or profession is a business.

Procedure

B15.16 An offence under the Bribery Act 2010, s. 6, is triable either way. When tried on indictment it is normally a class 2C or 3 offence (depending on the complexity of the offence), but see CrimPD XIII, para. B (see Supplement, **CPD.XIII.B**), for the additional factors that the court considers on allocation. No prosecution may be instituted in England and Wales except by or with the consent of the DPP or the Director of the SFO (s. 10(1)). For s. 10(4) and (5), see **B15.8**. As to the potential application of the Fraud Act 2006, s. 13, see *Kensington International Ltd v Republic of Congo* [2007] EWCA Civ 1128, [2008] 1 WLR 1144 and **F10.8**.

Sentence

B15.17 The maximum penalty for an offence under s. 6 is ten years' imprisonment and/or a fine. On summary conviction the maximum penalty is six months' imprisonment, and/or an unlimited fine (Bribery Act 2010, s. 11).

The definitive sentencing guideline, *Fraud, Bribery and Money Laundering Offences* (see Supplement, **SG26-7**) is applicable. The guideline applies to individual offenders aged 18 and over, and organisations. It applies to all offenders sentenced on or after 1 October 2014 regardless of the date of the offence. There is a separate part of the guideline applicable to corporate offenders.

Elements

B15.18 The bribery of a public official (as defined in the Bribery Act 2010, s. 6(5)) may in some circumstances fall equally within the ambit of the general offence of bribery created by s. 1 (see **B15.7**) and the receipt of a bribe by such an official (which is not dealt with in s. 6) may sometimes fall within the ambit of s. 2 (see **B15.11**). The discrete offence created by s. 6, which shares the same territorial and extra-territorial ambit as the general offences, was included in order to ensure that the UK would comply with its obligations under the OECD Convention on Combating Bribery of Foreign Public Officials in International Business Transactions, and many of its terms are accordingly based on the terms of that Convention. The s. 6 offence can be developed and interpreted in light of those obligations and in line with international developments in the interpretation of the Convention without forcing the courts to develop or interpret the general offences in the same way.

The s. 6 offence has a narrower focus than the general offence created by s. 1, but will in some circumstances be easier to prove. P must act with the intent specified in s. 6(2) and must intend to influence the conduct of the official (F) in the performance of F's functions, but it need not be proved that P intended to induce or reward any 'improper performance' of those functions. No reference need be made to ss. 3, 4 or 5 of the Act. An attempt to influence F (directly or indirectly) through the offer or gift of a financial or other advantage will be lawful only where F is 'permitted or required by the written law applicable to F to be influenced in his capacity as a foreign public official by the offer, promise or gift'.

The advice of the Law Commission (at para. 5.76) was that a person who is anxious to avoid any infringement of this provision can almost always rely on one simple rule of thumb: 'Do not intentionally give advantages to foreign public officials, to gain or retain business, without a legal justification.' In some countries, however, 'facilitation payments' are routinely expected if officials are to perform the very functions that might legitimately be expected of them. In such circumstances, a prosecution for bribery brought under s. 1 might result in acquittal on the basis that no 'improper performance' by F was being encouraged, but a prosecution brought under s. 6 might well succeed, on the basis that the payment was nevertheless intended to influence F. This indeed is the firm view of the DPP and the Director of the SFO, although the guidance issued by the Directors is that in some such cases (e.g., those involving small payments or payments made under duress) the public interest may not always favour prosecution. **B15.19**

As to jurisdiction over bribery cases with a foreign element, see s. 12(1) to (4) at **B15.24**. As to the liability of senior officers of corporations (or persons purporting to act as such) for offences committed by the corporation with their consent or connivance, see s. 14 at **B15.25**.

FAILURE OF COMMERCIAL ORGANISATIONS TO PREVENT BRIBERY

Definition

Bribery Act 2010, ss. 7 and 8 **B15.20**

7.—(1) A relevant commercial organisation ('C') is guilty of an offence under this section if a person ('A') associated with C bribes another person intending—
(a) to obtain or retain business for C, or
(b) to obtain or retain an advantage in the conduct of business for C.
(2) But it is a defence for C to prove that C had in place adequate procedures designed to prevent persons associated with C from undertaking such conduct.
(3) For the purposes of this section, A bribes another person if, and only if, A—
(a) is, or would be, guilty of an offence under section 1 or 6 (whether or not A has been prosecuted for such an offence), or
(b) would be guilty of such an offence if section 12(2)(c) and (4) were omitted.
(4) See section 8 for the meaning of a person associated with C and see section 9 for a duty on the Secretary of State to publish guidance.
(5) In this section—
'partnership' means—
(a) a partnership within the Partnership Act 1890, or
(b) a limited partnership registered under the Limited Partnerships Act 1907, or a firm or entity of a similar character formed under the law of a country or territory outside the United Kingdom,
'relevant commercial organisation' means—
(a) a body which is incorporated under the law of any part of the United Kingdom and which carries on a business (whether there or elsewhere),
(b) any other body corporate (wherever incorporated) which carries on a business, or part of a business, in any part of the United Kingdom,
(c) a partnership which is formed under the law of any part of the United Kingdom and which carries on a business (whether there or elsewhere), or

(d) any other partnership (wherever formed) which carries on a business, or part of a business, in any part of the United Kingdom,

and, for the purposes of this section, a trade or profession is a business.

8.—(1) For the purposes of section 7, a person ('A') is associated with C if (disregarding any bribe under consideration) A is a person who performs services for or on behalf of C.

(2) The capacity in which A performs services for or on behalf of C does not matter.

(3) Accordingly A may (for example) be C's employee, agent or subsidiary.

(4) Whether or not A is a person who performs services for or on behalf of C is to be determined by reference to all the relevant circumstances and not merely by reference to the nature of the relationship between A and C.

(5) But if A is an employee of C, it is to be presumed unless the contrary is shown that A is a person who performs services for or on behalf of C.

Procedure

B15.21 An offence under the Bribery Act 2010, s. 7, is triable only on indictment (s. 11(3)). No prosecution may be instituted in England and Wales except by or with the consent of the DPP or the Director of the SFO (s. 10(1)). For s. 10(4) and (5), see **B15.8**.

An offence is committed under s. 7 irrespective of whether the acts or omissions which form part of the offence take place in the UK or elsewhere. Where no such acts or omissions take place in the UK, proceedings for the offence may be taken at any place in the UK (s. 12(5) and (6)).

Special rules apply to the prosecution of a partnership (as defined in s. 7(5)). Proceedings for an offence under s. 7 must be brought in the name of the partnership (not in that of any of the partners) and for the purposes of such proceedings the CJA 1925, s. 33, the MCA 1980, sch. 3, and CrimPR Part 4 (service of documents: see Supplement, **R4.1** *et seq.*) apply as if the partnership were a body corporate (Bribery Act 2010, s. 15).

Sentence

B15.22 A relevant commercial organisation convicted of an offence under s. 7 is liable to a fine (Bribery Act 2010, s. 11(3)). A fine imposed on a partnership is to be paid out of partnership assets (s. 15(3)).

The definitive sentencing guideline, *Fraud, Bribery and Money Laundering Offences* (see Supplement, **SG26-8**) is applicable. It applies to all offenders sentenced on or after 1 October 2014 regardless of the date of the offence. The guidance is to be found in the part of the guideline applicable to corporate offenders.

Elements

B15.23 The offence created by the Bribery Act 2010, s. 7 is not an offence of negligence, but an offence of strict liability, subject to a due diligence (or 'adequate procedures') defence contained in s. 7(2) that must be proved by C on a balance of probabilities. If no such defence is offered, C may be convicted without any evidence of fault on its part.

The prosecution must, however, prove that the associated person (A) is guilty of bribery committed on C's behalf, contrary to s. 1 or s. 6, or that A would have been so guilty but for the fact that the acts were committed abroad and A has no 'close connection with the United Kingdom' as defined in s. 12 (see **B15.24**).

In accordance with the Bribery Act 2010, s. 9, the Secretary of State has published guidance on procedures that relevant commercial organisations should put in place to prevent bribery by persons associated with them — the so-called 'six principles' (see tinyurl.com/ps7tbw8). These are not intended to be prescriptive and lack the force of law, but evidence of compliance with the six principles will inevitably assist a company or organisation that faces, or might otherwise face, a charge under s. 7. The six principles can be summarised as:

1. top-level commitment — senior management should provide leadership and demonstrate commitment to the prevention of bribery;
2. proportionality — greater efforts to prevent bribery may be expected of larger organisations and those exposed to potentially corrupt overseas markets, and/or high-risk transactions etc.;
3. risk assessment — research may be needed to assess the risks relating to markets and clients etc. with whom business is transacted;
4. due diligence — this is linked to risk assessment and may be linked to due diligence procedures familiar in other contexts;
5. communication (including training) — relevant employees etc. should be made aware of the law and receive training proportionate to the risks involved;
6. monitoring and review — this may involve internal and/or external review mechanisms that are proportionate to the organisation and the risks to which it is exposed.

TERRITORIAL AND EXTRA-TERRITORIAL APPLICATION

Bribery Act 2010, s. 12 **B15.24**

(1) An offence is committed under section 1, 2 or 6 in England and Wales, Scotland or Northern Ireland if any act or omission which forms part of the offence takes place in that part of the United Kingdom.
(2) Subsection (3) applies if—
  (a) no act or omission which forms part of an offence under section 1, 2 or 6 takes place in the United Kingdom,
  (b) a person's acts or omissions done or made outside the United Kingdom would form part of such an offence if done or made in the United Kingdom, and
  (c) that person has a close connection with the United Kingdom.
(3) In such a case—
  (a) the acts or omissions form part of the offence referred to in subsection (2)(a), and
  (b) proceedings for the offence may be taken at any place in the United Kingdom.
(4) For the purposes of subsection (2)(c) a person has a close connection with the United Kingdom if, and only if, the person was one of the following at the time the acts or omissions concerned were done or made—
  (a) a British citizen,
  (b) a British overseas territories citizen,
  (c) a British National (Overseas),
  (d) a British Overseas citizen,
  (e) a person who under the British Nationality Act 1981 was a British subject,
  (f) a British protected person within the meaning of that Act,
  (g) an individual ordinarily resident in the United Kingdom,
  (h) a body incorporated under the law of any part of the United Kingdom,
  (i) a Scottish partnership.
(5) An offence is committed under section 7 irrespective of whether the acts or omissions which form part of the offence take place in the United Kingdom or elsewhere.
(6) Where no act or omission which forms part of an offence under section 7 takes place in the United Kingdom, proceedings for the offence may be taken at any place in the United Kingdom.

Although s. 12(2) ensures that ss. 1, 2 or 6 may apply to things done abroad by persons (such as British citizens) who have a close UK connection, this ceases to be the case (as far as English law is concerned) if the only relevant acts or omissions take place in other parts of the UK. English jurisdiction may, however, be asserted (by virtue of s. 12(1)) if relevant acts or omissions take place both in England and Wales and elsewhere.

The offence under s. 7 has been described as one of 'universal jurisdiction', but this cannot be so because it can be committed only by a 'relevant commercial organisation' with close links to the UK (s. 7(5)). Moreover, s. 12(6) implies that if no act or omission occurs in England and Wales, English law still has no application to things done elsewhere in the UK.

LIABILITY OF SENIOR OFFICERS OF CORPORATIONS

B15.25 **Bribery Act 2010, s. 14**

(1) This section applies if an offence under section 1, 2 or 6 is committed by a body corporate or a Scottish partnership.
(2) If the offence is proved to have been committed with the consent or connivance of—
(a) a senior officer of the body corporate or Scottish partnership, or
(b) a person purporting to act in such a capacity,
the senior officer or person (as well as the body corporate or partnership) is guilty of the offence and liable to be proceeded against and punished accordingly.
(3) But subsection (2) does not apply, in the case of an offence which is committed under section 1, 2 or 6 by virtue of section 12(2) to (4), to a senior officer or person purporting to act in such a capacity unless the senior officer or person has a close connection with the United Kingdom (within the meaning given by section 12(4)).
(4) In this section—
'director', in relation to a body corporate whose affairs are managed by its members, means a member of the body corporate,
'senior officer' means—
(a) in relation to a body corporate, a director, manager, secretary or other similar officer of the body corporate, and
(b) in relation to a Scottish partnership, a partner in the partnership.

MISCONDUCT IN PUBLIC OFFICE

B15.26 The ingredients of the common-law offence of misconduct in public office were identified in *A-G's Ref (No. 3 of 2003)* [2004] EWCA Crim 868, [2005] 1 QB 73 and restated by the Court of Appeal in *Chapman* [2015] EWCA Crim 539, [2015] QB 883 in the following terms: the offence is committed where '(i) a public officer acting as such, (ii) wilfully neglects to perform his duty and/or wilfully misconducts himself, (iii) to such a degree as to amount to an abuse of the public's trust in the office holder, and (iv) does so without reasonable excuse or justification' (at [17]). A detailed analysis can be found in Law Commission Consultation Paper No. 229, *Reforming Misconduct in Public Office*, paras. 2.3 *et seq*.

A Public Officer, Acting as Such

B15.27 The principal offender must (whether remunerated or not) be a public office holder acting as such. Others may be guilty only as secondary parties. The concept of 'public office' was examined in *Belton* [2010] EWCA Crim 2857, [2011] QB 934. Magistrates, judges, registrars, council officials, ministers, civil servants and police officers are all public officers, as are prison staff (*King* [2013] EWCA Crim 1599, [2014] 1 Cr App R (S) 73 (462)) and prison nursing officers, including those employed by private companies operating prisons. As Leveson LJ explained in *Cosford* [2013] EWCA Crim 466, [2014] QB 81:

> Whether the prison is run directly by the state or indirectly through a private company paid by the state to perform this function does not alter the public nature of the duties of those undertaking the work: the responsibilities to the public are identical.

Police community support officers (*Bunyan* [2013] EWCA Crim 1885, [2014] 1 Cr App R (S) 65 (428)) and some police civilian employees may also be regarded as holding public office. In *DL* [2011] EWCA Crim 1259, [2011] 2 Cr App R 14 (159), a civilian employee in an Investigative Support Unit was convicted of conspiracy to commit the offence by passing confidential police information to a private investigator and to a member of the criminal fraternity. In *Ball* (7 October 2015 unreported) a former bishop of the Church of England was jailed for historic misconduct involving the sexual abuse of young clergymen under his authority. NHS paramedics or ambulance staff cannot in this context be regarded as holding public office. As Sir Brian Leveson P observed in *Mitchell* [2014] EWCA Crim 318, [2014] 2 Cr App R 2 (17) (at [17]), the public may have an interest in the duty owed by the NHS trust that employs them, but 'to focus on the overarching duty of the Trust would be to mean that every... employee of the Trust is a public officer; for an education authority, it would mean that every teacher... is a public officer. This is not correct.'

It is not enough that D is guilty of misconduct while holding office. In *Johnson v Westminster Magistrates' Court* [2019] EWHC 1709 (Admin), [2019] 2 Cr App R 30 (344) Rafferty LJ said (at [33]):

> The offence will be made out only if the manner in which the specific powers or duties of the office are discharged brings the misconduct within its ambit. Consequently at the time of the alleged misconduct the individual must be acting as, not simply whilst, a public official.

This clarifies that the alleged misconduct does not have to have occurred while D was discharging a power or duty, but the prosecution must be able to establish a nexus between D's conduct and the powers or duties of D's office. The practical consequence is that the prosecution must be able to identify the power or duty that D was purporting to exercise. This power or duty must be recognised by law as arising from D's public office. If there is a dispute about whether the function or duty in question arises from D's public office, this will be a matter for the judge to rule upon.

The Nature of the Misconduct

The offence may take a wide range of forms (for examples, see the cases cited at **B15.27** and **B15.29**) and may involve either a positive act, or an omission to act in circumstances where action is required (a notable example of an offence of omission is provided by *Dytham* [1979] QB 722 in which a police officer was convicted of misconduct through ignoring a serious and violent offence that was being committed in front of his eyes; see also **A1.19**). **B15.28**

Another case involving police misconduct is *A-G's Ref (No. 1 of 2007)* [2007] EWCA Crim 760, [2007] 2 Cr App R (S) 86 (544) in which a police officer was convicted for misusing the Police National Computer in order to supply confidential information to a known criminal. The latter case might now more appropriately be prosecuted as a corrupt exercise of police power, contrary to the CJCA 2015, s. 26 (see **B15.32**), but a case such as *Dytham* could not be, unless the inaction in question can be attributed to self-interest or an intent to benefit some other person.

A different kind of example is provided by *Bowden* [1996] 4 All ER 505 in which a local authority manager was convicted of the offence for improperly arranging for his men to carry out work at his girlfriend's house.

The Gravity of the Misconduct

Not every improper act or omission in public office will suffice to constitute the offence. The misconduct must be such as to harm the public interest and be deserving of condemnation and punishment. The unauthorised disclosure of confidential information to the media may raise particularly difficult questions concerning this public interest, and require very careful directions to a jury. In *Chapman* [2015] EWCA Crim 539, [2015] QB 883, Lord Thomas CJ said (at [33]–[34]): **B15.29**

> Those employed by the state in public office will generally be in breach of the duty owed by them to their employers or commanding officers by providing unauthorised information to the press. However, information is sometimes provided by such persons in breach of that duty where the provider of that information may benefit the public interest rather than harm it. The provision of the information may well in such a case be an abuse of trust by the office holder to his employer or commanding officer, even if the disclosure of the information may be in the public interest. It may therefore result in disciplinary action and dismissal of the officer holder. That is because the abuse of the trust reposed in the office holder by the employer/commanding officer in such a case is viewed through the prism of the relationship between the office holder and his employer or commanding

officer. That is not the prism through which a jury should approach the issue of the abuse of the public's trust in an office holder…

There are, we consider, two ways that the jury might be assisted in determining whether the misconduct is so serious. The first is to refer the jury to the need for them to reach a judgment that the misconduct is worthy of condemnation and punishment. The second is to refer them to the requirement that the misconduct must be judged by them as having the effect of harming the public interest.

See, to similar effect, *France* [2016] EWCA Crim 1588, [2017] 1 Cr App R 19 (296) and *Norman* [2016] EWCA Crim 1564, [2017] 1 Cr App R 8 (75). In the latter case, the Court of Appeal had no doubt that D, a prison officer, was properly convicted of misconduct through taking payments from journalists over several years in return for stories about prisoners and internal prison affairs. His conduct was clearly 'capable of damaging the efficient and effective running of the prison and undermining public confidence in its management' (at [46]).

Mens Rea

B15.30 Wilful misconduct involves 'deliberately doing something which is wrong, knowing it to be wrong or with reckless indifference as to whether it is wrong or not' (*A-G's Ref (No. 3 of 2003)* [2004] EWCA Crim 868, [2005] 1 QB 73 at [28]). For D to be convicted of misconduct in a public office, D must also know of the facts and circumstances which would lead a right-thinking member of the public to conclude that the misconduct is sufficiently serious as to satisfy the threshold test considered in **B15.29**. However, it is not necessary for the prosecution to prove that D reached that conclusion. It is sufficient to prove that D had the means of knowledge available to make the necessary assessment of the seriousness of the misconduct; the assessment is then for the jury (*Chapman* [2015] EWCA Crim 539, [2015] QB 883 at [48]).

When misconduct in a public office is alleged to have been committed in circumstances which involve the acquisition of property by theft or fraud, and in particular when the holder of a public office is alleged to have made improper claims for public funds in circumstances which are said to be criminal, it must be proved that D acted dishonestly. The question whether D was acting dishonestly or not is pre-eminently one for the jury after a correct direction from the judge (*W(M)* [2010] EWCA Crim 372, [2010] QB 787).

Sentence

B15.31 Misconduct in public office is triable only on indictment and is normally a class 3 offence, but see CrimPD XIII, para. B (see Supplement, **CPD.XIII.B**) for the additional factors that the court considers on allocation. The penalty is imprisonment and/or a fine, at the discretion of the court. There is no offence-specific guideline but the Sentencing Council's *General Guideline: Overarching Principles* (see Supplement, **SG2-1**), is used for all offenders sentenced on or after 1 October 2019.

The Court of Appeal addressed the principles to be applied in cases involving police officers in *A-G's Ref (No. 30 of 2010)* [2010] EWCA Crim 2261, [2011] 1 Cr App R (S) 106 (624) as follows (at [64]):

First, punishment and deterrence are always important elements in these cases: not only must police officers be deterred from misconduct, but also the public must see that condign punishment will be visited on police officers who betray the trust reposed in them and do not live up to the high standards of the police service. Secondly, an incentive… inevitably increases the seriousness of the offence. Third, misconduct, which encourages or permits criminals to behave in the belief that they will be kept informed of areas to avoid in connection with their criminal activities, or of those who might be informing on the police also increases its gravity. That is reflected in the observation of the learned judge who commented that [a criminal associate of the officer] had boasted that it was 'like having his own police station at the end of a phone'. Fourth, any misconduct that impacts on police operations moves the offence into a different category of gravity.

In that case a sentence of six years' imprisonment was imposed on an officer who was convicted of supplying intelligence information on multiple occasions to a drug dealer to enable him to escape detection.

In two more recent cases police officers received prison sentences for unauthorised access to computer records. In *Mungur* [2018] EWCA Crim 1062, [2018] 2 Cr App R (S) 33 (300) a police officer set up an undercover business accessing data about road traffic collisions to sell to solicitors, making unauthorised access to the police computer system over 20,000 times in six years and earning over £350,000 in the process. The scam had come to light when individuals who had reported accidents complained of unauthorised disclosure of personal information. The Court of Appeal said that such conduct seriously undermined public faith in the police force and the starting point after trial in such a case should be no less than six years. In *Harris* [2018] EWCA Crim 2002, [2019] 1 Cr App R (S) 18 (128) an appropriate sentence after trial of 32 months' imprisonment was upheld for a Sexual Offences Liaison Officer who accessed the Facebook account of the victim of a sexual offence using a password she had given him in connection with the case. He then copied historic images of her in school uniform to his private email account. He admitted the images were for his sexual gratification and that he had also accessed private data relating to other victims. The Court held that where the confidence of highly vulnerable people was at stake, deterrent sentences were to be expected and the sentence was well within the proper range.

In relation to prison officers, the smuggling of drugs and contraband may be prosecuted as misconduct in a public office. Where, in addition, prison security is or might be compromised, the sentences are likely to be severe. In *Bennett* [2019] EWCA Crim 762 a deterrent sentence was called for where a prison officer had brought Class B drugs into prison, engaged in sexual conduct with prisoners and passed on information concerning prison security measures. A sentence of six years' imprisonment on a plea was upheld. In *McCarthy* [2015] EWCA Crim 1117, [2015] 2 Cr App R (S) 47 (355) D pleaded guilty to assisting an offender and misconduct in public office when, in the context of her employment as a probation officer, she entered into a sexual relationship with an offender she was supervising, provided him with a mobile phone and lied to the police about the nature of the relationship. A sentence of 12 months' imprisonment on a guilty plea was upheld.

As to other officials, in *Shoyeju* [2014] EWCA Crim 486 a sentence of seven years' imprisonment on a senior officer working at the UK Border Agency's Asylum Screening Unit (following a late guilty plea) was not considered excessive and the limited guidance in *John-Ayo* [2008] EWCA Crim 1651, [2009] 1 Cr App R (S) 71 (416), where D received a nine-year prison sentence after trial, was approved. See also *Patel* [2012] EWCA Crim 1243, [2013] 1 Cr App R (S) 48 (269) (at **B15.13**) in which D, a court clerk, had solicited bribes from motoring offenders due to appear before the magistrates' court. The appropriate starting point after trial would have been six years' imprisonment, reduced to four years for his plea. By contrast, in *Kadiri* [2017] EWCA Crim 2667, [2019] 1 Cr App R (S) 25 (169) a suspended sentence was appropriate in the case of a former HMRC employee who had pleaded guilty to searching for the name and address of her husband's new partner.

CORRUPT OR IMPROPER EXERCISE OF POLICE POWERS AND PRIVILEGES

Definition

Criminal Justice and Courts Act 2015, s. 26 **B15.32**

(1) A police constable listed in subsection (3) commits an offence if he or she—
  (a) exercises the powers and privileges of a constable improperly, and
  (b) knows or ought to know that the exercise is improper.
(2) [See **B15.33**.]
(3) [See **B15.34**.]
(4) For the purposes of this section, a police constable exercises the powers and privileges of a constable improperly if—
  (a) he or she exercises a power or privilege of a constable for the purpose of achieving—
    (i) a benefit for himself or herself, or
    (ii) a benefit or a detriment for another person, and

(b) a reasonable person would not expect the power or privilege to be exercised for the purpose of achieving that benefit or detriment.

(5) For the purposes of this section, a police constable is to be treated as exercising the powers and privileges of a constable improperly in the cases described in subsections (6) and (7).

(6) The first case is where—

(a) the police constable fails to exercise a power or privilege of a constable,

(b) the purpose of the failure is to achieve a benefit or detriment described in subsection (4)(a), and

(c) a reasonable person would not expect a constable to fail to exercise the power or privilege for the purpose of achieving that benefit or detriment.

(7) The second case is where—

(a) the police constable threatens to exercise, or not to exercise, a power or privilege of a constable,

(b) the threat is made for the purpose of achieving a benefit or detriment described in subsection (4)(a), and

(c) a reasonable person would not expect a constable to threaten to exercise, or not to exercise, the power or privilege for the purpose of achieving that benefit or detriment.

(8) An offence is committed under this section if the act or omission in question takes place in the United Kingdom or in United Kingdom waters.

(9) In this section—

'benefit' and 'detriment' mean any benefit or detriment, whether or not in money or other property and whether temporary or permanent;

'United Kingdom waters' means the sea and other waters within the seaward limits of the United Kingdom's territorial sea.

(10) References in this section to exercising, or not exercising, the powers and privileges of a constable include performing, or not performing, the duties of a constable.

Procedure and Sentence

B15.33 An offence under the CJCA 2015, s. 26, is triable only on indictment and punishable by imprisonment for 14 years and/or a fine (s. 26(2)). By s. 26(11), nothing in s. 26 affects what constitutes the common-law offence of misconduct in public office, but as in other contexts in which specific statutory offences have been created alongside more general common-law ones, good practice may require that conduct clearly amounting to the statutory offence is charged accordingly, and the prosecution may thus be required to justify any decision to charge the common-law offence instead, as for example is the case with prosecutions for common-law conspiracy to defraud. See *Rimmington* [2005] UKHL 63, [2006] 1 AC 459 (at **B11.81**) and the A-G's Guidelines on conspiracy to defraud (see **appendix 2**). There is no offence-specific guideline but the Sentencing Council's *General Guideline: Overarching Principles* (see Supplement, **SG2-1**), is used for all offenders sentenced on or after 1 October 2019.

Elements

B15.34 By the CJCA 2015, s. 26(3), a constable may be a regular or special constable in any English or Welsh force or in the British Transport Police Force, a constable in the Civil Nuclear Constabulary or the Ministry of Defence Police or a National Crime Agency officer designated as having the powers and privileges of a constable, but the definition does not extend to PCSOs. Corrupt or improper conduct by a PCSO or civilian police employee may, however, still be punishable as misconduct in public office (see **B15.26**). Even in the case of a constable, some forms of misconduct fall outside the ambit of the s. 26 offence. In a case such as *Dytham* [1979] QB 722 (see **B15.28**), for example, D's failure to act would certainly appear to satisfy the requirements of s. 26(6)(a), but not s. 26(6)(b), unless keeping oneself out of harm's way and finishing work on time are construed as 'benefits' within the meaning of s. 26(4) and (9). A prosecution for the common-law offence might be considered more appropriate on such facts.

ABUSES IN RESPECT OF HONOURS

Under the Honours (Prevention of Abuses) Act 1925, s. 1, a person who accepts, obtains, gives or offers gifts or other valuable consideration, or who agrees to do so, as an inducement or reward for procuring, assisting or endeavouring to procure the grant of a dignity or title of honour to any person, is liable on conviction on indictment to imprisonment for a term not exceeding two years, and/or to a fine, or on summary conviction to three months' imprisonment and/or a fine not exceeding £5,000. This provision remains unaffected by the Bribery Act 2010. **B15.35**

Section B16 Revenue, Customs and Social Security Offences

INTRODUCTION

B16.1 Because the Inland Revenue and Customs and Excise were once separate government departments, legislation creating offences against the public revenue is contained in different Acts of Parliament. The Commissioners for Revenue and Customs Act 2005 created the department called HMRC, which exercises the functions previously exercised by those two departments.

PROSECUTIONS, PENALTIES AND MONEY SETTLEMENTS

B16.2 Frauds committed against the public revenue often involve Theft Act offences, such as false accounting (see **B6.3**), Fraud Act offences (see **B5.4**) or offences under the Perjury Act 1911, s. 5(1)(b) (see **B14.25**). They may instead be prosecuted as offences under revenue and customs legislation or as the common-law offence of cheating the public revenue. In some cases, tax frauds are not prosecuted because HMRC is willing in those cases to impose financial penalties and to accept a money settlement, once full disclosure has been made. In such a case, HMRC may decide to offer to a person suspected of tax fraud a Contractual Disclosure Facility, under which HMRC agrees not to carry out a criminal investigation if the person suspected admits fraud. See also, in relation to customs offences, the Customs and Excise Management Act 1979, s. 152 (see **B16.21**). In addition, civil remedies in tort may be available to the Commissioners (*Revenue and Customs Commissioners v Total Network SL* [2008] UKHL 19, [2008] 1 AC 1174; see **B16.9**).

CHEATING THE PUBLIC REVENUE

B16.3 The common-law offence of cheating the public revenue is triable only on indictment and punishable by a fine and/or imprisonment at large. It is a Group A offence for jurisdiction purposes under the CJA 1993, Part I (see **A8.10**).

In *Steed* [2011] EWCA Crim 75, Moses LJ stated (at [11]): 'Cheating consists of any form of fraudulent conduct, whether by making positive false representations,... or by concealing or omitting to disclose liability or income with the result that money is diverted from the Revenue and the Revenue is deprived of money to which it is entitled'. The offence may therefore be committed by dishonestly making false statements with intent to deceive or prejudice HMRC or the Department for Work and Pensions (*Hudson* [1956] 2 QB 252) or by dishonestly failing to declare a tax or national insurance liability. In *Mavji* [1987] 2 All ER 758, Michael Davies J said (at p. 1392): 'This appellant... had a statutory duty to make VAT returns and pay over to the Crown the VAT due. He dishonestly failed to do either. Accordingly, he was guilty of cheating... the public revenue. No further act or omission is required.' See also *Redford* (1988) 89 Cr App R 1.

Prosecutions for cheating the public revenue are generally reserved for the most serious and unusual offences. In *Dosanjh* [2013] EWCA Crim 2366, [2014] 1 WLR 1780, the Court of Appeal decided that Parliament had deliberately left this common-law offence untouched by statutory changes. It therefore remains appropriate to charge cheating the public revenue for the most serious revenue frauds for which statutory offences do not adequately reflect the criminality involved.

Following the decision of the Supreme Court in *Ivey v Genting Casinos (UK) Ltd* [2017] UKSC 67, [2018] AC 391, the question whether conduct is honest or dishonest is determined by the jury applying the standards of ordinary decent people. There is no requirement that the D must appreciate that what D has done is dishonest by those standards. See *Barton* [2020] EWCA Crim 575, especially at [84] and [105].

For charging and the appropriate preparation of the indictment where a course of conduct is alleged to amount to cheating the public revenue, see *Lunn* [2017] EWCA Crim 34, [2017] 2 Cr App R 5 (42). Where the judge has directed the jury that it is possible to convict on the basis of a single incident of cheating the public revenue, it is not permissible to sentence on the basis that the offence involved a course of conduct (*Khan* [2017] EWCA Crim 703).

Indictment

Statement of Offence B16.4

Cheating Her Majesty the Queen and Her Majesty's Revenue and Customs, contrary to common law.

Particulars of Offence

A, on the.... day of..., with intent to defraud and to the prejudice of Her Majesty the Queen and Her Majesty's Revenue and Customs of public revenue, cheated Her Majesty the Queen and Her Majesty's Revenue and Customs of public revenue, namely income tax, by delivering and/or causing to be delivered to an Inspector of Taxes a tax return for the year 20.. /20 .. showing income for the year to 5 April 20.. in respect of himself which was false, misleading and deceptive in that it omitted to declare all the income which he received during the said period.

Particulars of omitted income are –...

See *Allen* [2001] UKHL 45, [2002] 1 AC 509 at [5]–[7].

Sentencing

The definitive sentencing guideline, *Fraud, Bribery and Money Laundering Offences* (see Supplement, **SG26-4** and **B16.54**) includes guidance on sentencing for revenue fraud, including cheating the public revenue. The guideline applies to individual offenders aged 18 and over. Table 3 in the revenue fraud part of the guideline gives starting points and ranges of sentence for offending involving £2 million or more. For applications of the guideline in cases of cheating the public revenue, see *Chada* [2016] EWCA Crim 1955; *Lunn* [2017] EWCA Crim 34, [2017] 2 Cr App R 5 (42) at [88]–[102] and *Whitson-Dew* [2019] EWCA Crim 2131, [2020] 1 Cr App R (S) 56 (438). A separate part of the guideline gives starting points and ranges of sentence for corporate offenders. B16.5

FRAUDULENT EVASION OF INCOME TAX

Taxes Management Act 1970, s. 106A B16.6

(1) A person commits an offence if that person is knowingly concerned in the fraudulent evasion of income tax by that or any other person.

(2) A person guilty of an offence under this section is liable—

 (a) on summary conviction, to imprisonment for a term not exceeding [six] months or [an unlimited fine], or both;

(b) on conviction on indictment, to imprisonment for a term not exceeding seven years or a fine, or both.

In many respects, this offence mirrors the common-law offence of cheating, but only in respect of income tax evasion. The prosecution must prove knowledge, not just recklessness (*Godir* [2018] EWCA Crim 2294 at [15]–[17]). The words 'knowingly concerned' and 'fraudulent evasion' appear in the Customs and Excise Management Act 1979, s. 170(2) (see **B16.39**), and reference should be made to the case law under that section (see **B16.44** ***et seq.***).

Any dishonest attempt to evade or conceal one's income tax liabilities would appear to amount to an offence under s. 144; as would conduct that is intended to facilitate fraudulent evasion by another taxpayer. Those who dishonestly provide a taxpayer with false invoices or other documentation may be 'knowingly concerned' in the act of evasion. Paying a taxpayer a specially reduced fee in cash might also suffice, but only if the person making this payment knows that this is facilitating the dishonest non-disclosure of the payment by the taxpayer. See D Ormerod, 'Fraudulent Evasion of Income Tax' [2002] Crim LR 3.

The definitive sentencing guideline, *Fraud, Bribery and Money Laundering Offences* (see Supplement, **SG26-4**) includes guidance on sentencing for revenue fraud, including fraudulent evasion of income tax. Table 2 in the revenue fraud part of the guideline sets out the applicable starting points and ranges. See **B16.54** for a discussion of sentencing in revenue fraud cases.

In *Carr* [2016] EWCA Crim 2259, a case involving the fraudulent evasion of £400,000 income tax and VAT, the Court of Appeal assessed D's culpability as being on the cusp between categories A and B. The Court took three years' imprisonment as a starting point, which it reduced to two years because of D's guilty pleas. In *Tuck* [2018] EWCA Crim 2529 D pleaded guilty at trial to a charge of fraudulent evasion of at least £115,000 income tax. In the absence of category A high culpability features, the Court of Appeal took a starting point of two years and nine months' imprisonment, which it then reduced to one year and eight months' imprisonment to take account of strong personal mitigation and the late guilty plea.

FALSIFICATION ETC. OF DOCUMENTS CALLED FOR INSPECTION

B16.7 Falsification of documents with a view to deceiving tax inspectors may be charged as offences under various general provisions (e.g., false accounting, cheating or fraudulent evasion of income tax), but s. 20BB deals specifically with such behaviour.

Taxes Management Act 1970, s. 20BB

(1) Subject to subsections (2) and (3) below, a person shall be guilty of an offence if he intentionally falsifies, conceals, destroys or otherwise disposes of, or causes or permits the falsification, concealment, destruction or disposal of, a document which he has been required by an order under section 20BA above to deliver, or to deliver or to make available for inspection.

(2) A person does not commit an offence under subsection (1) above if he acts—
 (a) with the written permission of the tribunal, or an officer of the Board, or
 (b) after the document has been delivered.

(3) A person does not commit an offence under subsection (1) above if he acts after the end of the period of two years beginning with the date on which the order is made, unless before the end of that period an officer of Revenue and Customs has notified the person in writing that the order has not been complied with to the officer's satisfaction.

(4) [Repealed.]

(5) A person guilty of an offence under subsection (1) above shall be liable—
 (a) on summary conviction, to [an unlimited fine];
 (b) on conviction on indictment, to imprisonment for a term not exceeding two years or to a fine or to both.

For the similar offence under the Customs and Excise Management Act 1979, s. 168, see **B16.53**.

VAT FRAUDS

Section 72 of the Value Added Tax Act 1994 creates offences in relation to VAT. Sub-sections (2), (5) and (10) are set out as amended by the Taxation (Cross-border Trade) Act 2018, s. 43 and sch. 8, para. 63 (see **B16.11**), once those changes have been brought into force. **B16.8**

Value Added Tax Act 1994, s. 72

(1) If any person is knowingly concerned in, or in the taking of steps with a view to, the fraudulent evasion of VAT by him or any other person, he shall be liable—
- (a) on summary conviction, to a penalty of £20,000 or of three times the amount of the VAT, whichever is the greater, or to imprisonment for a term not exceeding 6 months or to both; or
- (b) on conviction on indictment, to a penalty of any amount or to imprisonment for a term not exceeding 7 years or to both.

(2) Any reference in subsection (1) above or subsection (8) below to the evasion of VAT includes a reference to the obtaining of—
- (a) the payment of a VAT credit; or
- (b) a refund under section 35 or 36 of this Act or section 22 of the [Value Added Tax Act 1983]; or
- (c) [repealed]
- (d) a repayment under section 39;

and any reference in those subsections to the amount of the VAT shall be construed—
- (i) in relation to VAT itself or a VAT credit, as a reference to the aggregate of the amount (if any) falsely claimed by way of credit for input tax and the amount (if any) by which output was falsely understated, and
- (ii) in relation to a refund or repayment falling within paragraph (b) or (d) above, as a reference to the amount falsely claimed by way of refund or repayment.

(3) If any person—
- (a) with intent to deceive produces, furnishes or sends for the purposes of this Act or otherwise makes use for those purposes of any document which is false in a material particular; or
- (b) in furnishing any information for the purposes of this Act makes any statement which he knows to be false in a material particular or recklessly makes a statement which is false in a material particular,

he shall be liable—
- (i) on summary conviction, to a penalty of £20,000 or, where subsection (4) or (5) below applies, to the alternative penalty specified in that subsection if it is greater, or to imprisonment for a term not exceeding 6 months or to both; or
- (ii) on conviction on indictment, to a penalty of any amount or to imprisonment for a term not exceeding 7 years or to both.

(4) In any case where—
- (a) the document referred to in subsection (3)(a) above is a return required under this Act, or
- (b) the information referred to in subsection (3)(b) above is contained in or otherwise relevant to such a return,

the alternative penalty referred to in subsection (3)(i) above is a penalty equal to three times the aggregate of the amount (if any) falsely claimed by way of credit for input tax and the amount (if any) by which output tax was falsely understated.

(5) In any case where—
- (a) the document referred to in subsection (3)(a) above is a claim for a refund under section 35 or 36 of this Act or section 22 of the [Value Added Tax Act 1983] or for a repayment under section 39, or
- (b) the information referred to in subsection (3)(b) above is contained in or otherwise relevant to such a claim,

the alternative penalty referred to in subsection (3)(i) above is a penalty equal to three times the amount falsely claimed.

(6) The reference in subsection (3)(a) above to furnishing, sending or otherwise making use of a document which is false in a material particular, with intent to deceive, includes a reference to furnishing, sending or otherwise making use of such a document, with intent to secure that a machine will respond to the document as if it were a true document.

(7) Any reference in subsection (3)(a) or subsection (6) above to producing, furnishing or sending a document includes a reference to causing a document to be produced, furnished or sent.

(8) Where a person's conduct during any specified period must have involved the commission by him of one or more offences under the preceding provisions of this section, then, whether or not the particulars of that offence or those offences are known, he shall, by virtue of this subsection, be guilty of an offence and liable—

(a) on summary conviction, to a penalty of £20,000 or, if greater, three times the amount of any VAT that was or was intended to be evaded by his conduct, or to imprisonment for a term not exceeding 6 months or to both; or

(b) on conviction on indictment to a penalty of any amount or to imprisonment for a term not exceeding 7 years or to both.

(9) [Repealed.]

(10) If any person acquires possession of or deals with any goods, or accepts the supply of any services, having reason to believe that VAT on the supply of the goods or services or on the importation of the goods has been or will be evaded, he shall be liable on summary conviction to a penalty of £20,000 or three times the amount of the VAT, whichever is the greater.

(11) If any person supplies or is supplied with goods or services in contravention of paragraph 4(2) of Schedule 11, he shall be liable on summary conviction to a penalty of £20,000.

(12) Subject to subsection (13) below, sections 145 to 155 of the [Customs and Excise Management Act 1979] (proceedings for offences, mitigation of penalties and certain other matters) shall apply in relation to offences under this Act (which include any act or omission in respect of which a penalty is imposed) and penalties imposed under this Act as they apply in relation to offences and penalties under the customs and excise Acts as defined in that Act; and accordingly in section 154(2) as it applies by virtue of this subsection the reference to duty shall be construed as a reference to VAT.

(13) In subsection (12) above the references to penalties do not include references to penalties under sections 60 to 70.

B16.9 Section 72 creates an offence of considerable width (*Revenue and Customs Commissioners v Total Network SL* [2008] UKHL 19, [2008] 1 AC 1174 at [136]). The words 'knowingly concerned' and 'fraudulent evasion' appear also in the Customs and Excise Management Act 1979, s. 170; for the case law on these phrases, see **B16.44** ***et seq.*** The Court of Appeal held in *McCarthy* [1981] STC 298 that a dishonest omission to register for VAT may constitute an offence of taking steps to evade that tax under what is now s. 72(1).

In *Hashash* [2006] EWCA Crim 2518 the Court of Appeal upheld convictions under s. 72 for participating in a 'carousel' fraud, whereby payment of VAT was avoided by a series of sales passing between different EU Member States. Liability to VAT is determined by the objective appearance of the transaction, regardless of any fraudulent intention.

HMRC may also recover the VAT evaded by a 'carousel' fraud as damages in the tort of conspiracy (*Revenue and Customs Commissioners v Total Network SL* [2008] UKHL 19, [2008] 1 AC 1174; *Revenue and Customs Commissioners v Sunico A/S* [2013] EWHC 941 (Ch)).

Section 72(8) enables a charge to be brought on the basis of a general deficiency. As to the circumstances in which this should be resorted to, see *Rasool* [1997] 4 All ER 439. As to the wording of indictments generally, see *Ike* [1996] Crim LR 515.

For the Customs and Excise Management Act 1979, ss. 145 to 154 (referred to in s. 72(12)), see **B16.14** to **B16.17**.

The definitive sentencing guideline, *Fraud, Bribery and Money Laundering Offences* (see Supplement, **SG26-4**), includes guidance on sentencing for revenue fraud, including fraudulent evasion of VAT and the making of a false statement for VAT purposes. Table 2 in the revenue fraud part of the guideline sets out the applicable starting points and ranges (see *Carr* [2016] EWCA Crim 2259 at [20]–[29] (**B16.6**) and **B16.54**). In *Mayet* [2015] EWCA Crim 456 D pleaded guilty to making fraudulent claims for credits and refunds of VAT totalling £35,000 over a period of four years. A sentence of 16 months' imprisonment was upheld.

In relation to suspending sentence of imprisonment for fraudulent evasion of VAT, see *Hashim* [2018] EWCA Crim 1695 at [7] (at **B16.57**).

Where fraudulent evasion of VAT is coupled with other offences, and concurrent sentences are passed, the court must consider the overall criminality (*Perks* [2016] EWCA Crim 1491 at [12]–[13]).

For sentencing in VAT cases charged as cheating the public revenue, see **B16.5**.

CORPORATE OFFENCES OF FAILURE TO PREVENT FACILITATION OF TAX EVASION

Part 3 of the Criminal Finances Act 2017 creates corporate offences, punishable by a fine, of failing to prevent facilitation of tax evasion offences by other persons. The offence under s. 45 consists of a failure to prevent facilitation of a UK tax offence. The offence under s. 46 consists of a failure to prevent facilitation of a foreign tax evasion offence. A company or partnership commits an offence if its employee or agent, when acting as such, or a person performing services on its behalf, commits a 'tax evasion facilitation offence' (as defined in ss. 45(5) and 46(6)). But it is a defence under ss. 45(2) and 46(3) for the company or partnership to prove that it had reasonable prevention procedures in place or that it was not reasonable to have any prevention procedures in place. These provisions came into force on 30 September 2017 (s. 58, and the Criminal Finances Act 2017 (Commencement No. 1) Regulations (SI 2017 No. 739), reg. 3). For a discussion of Part 3 see K Laird, 'The Criminal Finances Act 2017—an introduction' [2017] Crim LR 915 at pp. 930–939. **B16.10**

B

Part B Offences

Pursuant to s. 47 and the Facilitation of Tax Evasion Offences (Guidance About Prevention) Regulations (SI 2017 No. 876) the Chancellor of the Exchequer has published guidance about the procedures which companies and partnerships might put in place. This document, '*Tackling tax evasion: Government guidance for the corporate offence of failure to prevent the criminal facilitation of tax evasion*', is available at tinyurl.com/y83wjs9w.

Criminal Finances Act 2017, ss. 44 to 46 and 48

44.—(1) This section defines expressions used in this Part.

(2) 'Relevant body' means a body corporate or partnership (wherever incorporated or formed).

(3) 'Partnership' means—

(a) a partnership within the meaning of the Partnership Act 1890 or

(b) a limited partnership registered under the Limited Partnerships Act 1907,

or a firm or entity of a similar character formed under the law of a foreign country.

(4) A person (P) acts in the capacity of a person associated with a relevant body (B) if P is—

(a) an employee of B who is acting in the capacity of an employee,

(b) an agent of B (other than an employee) who is acting in the capacity of an agent, or

(c) any other person who performs services for or on behalf of B who is acting in the capacity of a person performing such services.

(5) For the purposes of subsection (4)(c) the question whether or not P is a person who provides services for or on behalf of B is to be determined by reference to all the relevant circumstances and not merely by reference to the nature of the relationship between P and B.

45.—(1) A relevant body (B) is guilty of an offence if a person commits a UK tax evasion facilitation offence when acting in the capacity of a person associated with B.

(2) It is a defence for B to prove that, when the UK tax evasion facilitation offence was committed—

(a) B had in place such prevention procedures as it was reasonable in all the circumstances to expect B to have in place, or

(b) it was not reasonable in all the circumstances to expect B to have any prevention procedures in place.

(3) In subsection (2) 'prevention procedures' means procedures designed to prevent persons acting in the capacity of a person associated with B from committing UK tax evasion facilitation offences.

(4) In this Part 'UK tax evasion offence' means—
(a) an offence of cheating the public revenue, or
(b) an offence under the law of any part of the United Kingdom consisting of being knowingly concerned in, or in taking steps with a view to, the fraudulent evasion of a tax.
(5) In this Part 'UK tax evasion facilitation offence' means an offence under the law of any part of the United Kingdom consisting of—
(a) being knowingly concerned in, or in taking steps with a view to, the fraudulent evasion of a tax by another person,
(b) aiding, abetting, counselling or procuring the commission of a UK tax evasion offence, or
(c) being involved art and part in the commission of an offence consisting of being knowingly concerned in, or in taking steps with a view to, the fraudulent evasion of a tax.
(6) Conduct carried out with a view to the fraudulent evasion of tax by another person is not to be regarded as a UK tax evasion facilitation offence by virtue of subsection (5)(a) unless the other person has committed a UK tax evasion offence facilitated by that conduct.
(7) For the purposes of this section 'tax' means a tax imposed under the law of any part of the United Kingdom, including national insurance contributions under—
(a) Part 1 of the Social Security Contributions and Benefits Act 1992, or
(b) Part 1 of the Social Security Contributions and Benefits (Northern Ireland) Act 1992.
(8) A relevant body guilty of an offence under this section is liable—
(a) on conviction on indictment, to a fine;
(b) on summary conviction in England and Wales, to a fine;
(c) [applies to Scotland and Northern Ireland only].

46.—(1) A relevant body (B) is guilty of an offence if at any time—
(a) a person commits a foreign tax evasion facilitation offence when acting in the capacity of a person associated with B, and
(b) any of the conditions in subsection (2) is satisfied.
(2) The conditions are—
(a) that B is a body incorporated, or a partnership formed, under the law of any part of the United Kingdom;
(b) that B carries on business or part of a business in the United Kingdom;
(c) that any conduct constituting part of the foreign tax evasion facilitation offence takes place in the United Kingdom;
and in paragraph (b) 'business' includes an undertaking.
(3) It is a defence for B to prove that, when the foreign tax evasion facilitation offence was committed—
(a) B had in place such prevention procedures as it was reasonable in all the circumstances to expect B to have in place, or
(b) it was not reasonable in all the circumstances to expect B to have any prevention procedures in place.
(4) In subsection (3) 'prevention procedures' means procedures designed to prevent persons acting in the capacity of a person associated with B from committing foreign tax evasion facilitation offences under the law of the foreign country concerned.
(5) In this Part 'foreign tax evasion offence' means conduct which—
(a) amounts to an offence under the law of a foreign country,
(b) relates to a breach of a duty relating to a tax imposed under the law of that country, and
(c) would be regarded by the courts of any part of the United Kingdom as amounting to being knowingly concerned in, or in taking steps with a view to, the fraudulent evasion of that tax.
(6) In this Part 'foreign tax evasion facilitation offence' means conduct which—
(a) amounts to an offence under the law of a foreign country,
(b) relates to the commission by another person of a foreign tax evasion offence under that law, and
(c) would, if the foreign tax evasion offence were a UK tax evasion offence, amount to a UK tax evasion facilitation offence (see section 45(5) and (6)).
(7) A relevant body guilty of an offence under this section is liable—
(a) on conviction on indictment, to a fine;
(b) on summary conviction in England and Wales, to a fine;
(c) [applies to Scotland and Northern Ireland only]

. . .

48.—(1) It is immaterial for the purposes of section 45 or 46 (except to the extent provided by section 46(2)) whether—
(a) any relevant conduct of a relevant body, or
(b) any conduct which constitutes part of a relevant UK tax evasion facilitation offence or foreign tax evasion facilitation offence, or
(c) any conduct which constitutes part of a relevant UK tax evasion offence or foreign tax evasion offence,
takes place in the United Kingdom or elsewhere.
(2) Proceedings for an offence under section 45 or 46 may be taken in any place in the United Kingdom.
(3) and (4) [Apply to Scotland only].

In addition to the definitions in ss. 44 to 46, 'conduct' includes acts and omissions, 'foreign country' means a country or territory outside the UK and 'tax' includes duty and any other form of taxation, however described (s. 52(1)).

The words 'art and part' in s. 45(5)(c) refer to accessory liability under Scots law.

By s. 49(2) no proceedings can be commenced in England and Wales except by or with the personal consent of the DPP or the Director of the SFO. If the Director concerned is unavailable and there is another person designated by the Director authorised to exercise that function when the Director is unavailable, that person may exercise the function, but must do so personally (s. 49(4) and (5)).

Section 50 contains supplementary provisions in respect of proceedings against and offences by partnerships.

CUSTOMS AND EXCISE: INTRODUCTION

The following paragraphs deal with the most important offences under the Customs and Excise Management Act 1979 and the Commissioners for Revenue and Customs Act 2005. Many such offences involve defrauding Her Majesty of duty payable on goods. It is therefore important to check not only the terms of the section creating the offence, but also the regulations setting out the circumstances in which a liability to duty arises. This affects not only the question whether the offence charged has been committed (*Chambers* [2008] EWCA Crim 2467; *Khan* [2009] EWCA Crim 588), but also the question whether the offender personally owed duty on goods for the purposes of confiscation proceedings (*Mackle* [2014] UKSC 5, [2014] AC 678; *CPS v Doran* [2015] EWCA Crim 384 and *Parker* [2018] EWCA Crim 1057; for further detail, see **E19.27**). **B16.11**

Following the withdrawal of the UK from the EU, the Taxation (Cross-border Trade) Act 2018, when brought into force, will regulate customs duty by reference to the importation of goods into the UK.

Time of Importation, Exportation, etc.

Most of the important offences involve breach of import or export control. The time at which import or export takes place is identified by s. 5 of the Customs and Excise Management Act 1979, as amended by the Taxation (Cross-border Trade) Act 2018, s. 29 and sch. 7, para. 6 (see **B16.11**). **B16.12**

Customs and Excise Management Act 1979, s. 5

(1) The provisions of this section shall have effect for the purposes of the customs and excise Acts.
(2) Subject to subsections (2A) and (6) below, the time of importation of any goods shall be deemed to be—
(a) where the goods are brought by sea, the time when the ship carrying them comes within the limits of a port;

(b) where the goods are brought by air, the time when the aircraft carrying them lands in the United Kingdom or the time when the goods are unloaded in the United Kingdom, whichever is the earlier;

(c) where the goods are brought by land, the time when the goods enter the United Kingdom.

(2A) If there is a relevant international arrangement with a country or territory outside the United Kingdom, the Commissioners may by regulations provide for the time of importation of any goods to be a time—

(a) which is earlier than the times set out in paragraph (a), (b) or (c) of subsection (2), and

(b) which is specified by reference to movement in or out of an area in the country or territory.

(2B) 'Relevant international arrangement' means an arrangement between Her Majesty's government in the United Kingdom and the government of the country or territory which includes provision in relation to the time at which goods are to be regarded as imported into the United Kingdom.

(3) [Repealed.]

(4) Subject to subsections (5), (5A) and (7) below, the time of exportation of any goods from the United Kingdom shall be deemed to be—

(a) where the goods are exported by sea or air, the time when the goods are shipped for exportation;

(b) where the goods are exported by land, the time when they are cleared by the proper officer at the last customs and excise station on their way to the boundary.

(5) In the case of goods of a class or description with respect to the exportation of which any prohibition or restriction is for the time being in force under or by virtue of any enactment which are exported by sea or air, the time of exportation shall be deemed to be the time when the exporting ship or aircraft departs from the last port or customs and excise airport at which it is cleared before departing for a destination outside the United Kingdom.

(5A) If there is a relevant international arrangement with a country or territory outside the United Kingdom, the Commissioners may by regulations provide for the time of exportation of any goods to be a time—

(a) which is earlier than the times set out in paragraph (a) or (b) of subsection (4), and

(b) which is specified by reference to movement in or out of an area in the country or territory.

(5B) 'Relevant international arrangement' means an arrangement between Her Majesty's government in the United Kingdom and the government of the country or territory which includes provision in relation to the time at which goods are to be regarded as exported from the United Kingdom.

(6) Goods imported by means of a pipe-line shall be treated as imported at the time when they are brought within the limits of a port or otherwise when they enter the United Kingdom.

(7) Goods exported by means of a pipe-line shall be treated as exported at the time when they are charged into that pipe-line for exportation.

(8) A ship shall be deemed to have arrived at or departed from a port at the time when the ship comes within or, as the case may be, leaves the limits of that port.

Procedural Provisions

B16.13 A number of specific procedural provisions apply to proceedings for any offence under the 1979 and 2005 Acts. It will be convenient to consider these before turning to the offences themselves.

Institution of Proceedings

B16.14 With limited exceptions, prosecutions under the Acts may be commenced by the Commissioners and in the name of an officer of the Customs and Excise Service.

Customs and Excise Management Act 1979, s. 145

(1) Subject to the following provisions of this section, no proceedings for an offence under the customs and excise Acts or for condemnation under Schedule 3 to this Act shall be instituted except—

(a) by or with the consent of the Director of Public Prosecutions, or

(b) by order of, or with the consent of, the Commissioners for Her Majesty's Revenue and Customs.

(2) Subject to the following provisions of this section, any proceedings under the customs and excise Acts instituted by order of the Commissioners in a magistrates court . . . shall be commenced in the name of an officer of Revenue and Customs.

(3) [Applies to Scotland only.]
(4) [Repealed.]
(5) Nothing in the foregoing provisions of this section, shall prevent the institution of proceedings for an offence under the customs and excise Acts by order and in any case in which he thinks it proper that proceedings should be so instituted.
(6) Notwithstanding anything in the foregoing provisions of this section, where any person has been detained for any offence for which he is liable to be detained under the customs and excise Acts, any court before which he is brought may proceed to deal with the case although the proceedings have not been instituted in accordance with this section.

This provision applies also to conspiracy to commit an offence under the Acts (*Whitehead* [1982] QB 1272). Where defendants had been arrested for being knowingly concerned in the fraudulent evasion of a prohibition of the importation of a controlled drug, contrary to the Customs and Excise Management Act 1979, s. 170 (see **B16.39**), their subsequent trial and conviction on a charge of conspiracy without an order of the Commissioners under s. 145(1) was not a nullity because s.145(6) allowed the court to deal with the case and not just the offence for which they had been arrested (*Keyes* [2000] 2 Cr App R 181).

Time-limits

Section 146A provides the following time-limits for instituting proceedings, which override the general limitation provisions of the MCA 1980, s. 127. **B16.15**

Customs and Excise Management Act 1979, s. 146A

(1) Except as otherwise provided in the customs and excise Acts, and notwithstanding anything in any other enactment, the following provisions shall apply in relation to proceedings for an offence under those Acts.
(2) Proceedings for an indictable offence shall not be commenced after the end of the period of 20 years beginning with the day on which the offence was committed.
(3) Proceedings for a summary offence shall not be commenced after the end of the period of three years beginning with that day but, subject to that, may be commenced at any time within six months from that date on which sufficient evidence to warrant the proceedings came to the knowledge of the prosecuting authority.
(4) For the purposes of subsection (3) above, a certificate of the prosecuting authority as to the date on which such evidence as is there mentioned came to that authority's knowledge shall be conclusive evidence of that fact.
(5) [Applies to Scotland only.]
(6) [Applies to Northern Ireland only.]
(7) In this section 'prosecuting authority', (a) in England and Wales means the DPP.

Knowledge of the prosecuting authority (formerly the Director of Revenue and Customs Prosecutions and now the DPP) does not include knowledge of Revenue and Customs staff (*Director of Revenue and Customs Prosecutions v NE Plastics Ltd* [2008] EWHC 3560 (Admin), [2009] 2 Cr App R 21 (358)).

Place of Trial

Customs and Excise Management Act 1979, s. 148 **B16.16**

(1) Proceedings for an offence under the customs and excise Acts may be commenced—
  (a) in any court having jurisdiction in the place where the person charged with the offence resides or is found; or
  (b) *if any* thing was detained or seized in connection with the offence, in any court having jurisdiction in the place where that thing was so detained or seized or was found or condemned as forfeited; or
  (c) in any court having jurisdiction anywhere in that part of the United Kingdom, namely—
    (i) England and Wales,
    (ii) Scotland, or
    (iii) Northern Ireland,

  in which the place where the offence was committed is situated.

(2) Where any such offence was committed at some place outside the area of any commission of the peace, the place of the commission of the offence shall, for the purposes of the jurisdiction of any court, be deemed to be any place in the United Kingdom where the offender is found or to which he is first brought after the commission of the offence.
(3) The jurisdiction under subsection (2) above shall be in addition to and not in derogation of any jurisdiction or power of any court under any other enactment.

Evidential Provisions

B16.17 The following provisions relate to the burden of proof as to certain documents and frequently recurring facts.

Customs and Excise Management Act 1979, s. 154

(1) An averment in any process in proceedings under the customs and excise Acts—
  (a) that those proceedings were instituted by the order of the Commissioners; or
  (b) that any person is or was a Commissioner, officer or constable, or a member of Her Majesty's armed forces or coastguard; or
  (c) that any person is or was appointed or authorised by the Commissioners to discharge, or was engaged by the orders or with the concurrence of the Commissioners in the discharge of, any duty; or
  (d) that the Commissioners have or have not been satisfied as to any matter as to which they are required by any provision of those Acts to be satisfied; or
  (e) that any ship is a British ship; or
  (f) that any goods thrown overboard, staved or destroyed were so dealt with in order to prevent or avoid the seizure of those goods,

shall, until the contrary is proved, be sufficient evidence of the matter in question.
(2) Where in any proceedings relating to customs or excise any question arises as to the place from which any goods have been brought or as to whether or not—
  (a) any duty has been paid or secured in respect of any goods; or
  (b) any goods or other things whatsoever are of the description or nature alleged in the information, writ or other process; or
  (c) any goods have been lawfully imported or lawfully unloaded from any ship, aircraft or railway vehicle; or
  (d) any goods have been lawfully loaded into any ship, aircraft or railway vehicle or lawfully exported or were lawfully water-borne; or
  (e) any goods were lawfully brought to any place for the purpose of being loaded into any ship, aircraft or railway vehicle or exported; or
  (f) any goods are or were subject to any prohibition of or restriction on their importation or exportation,

then where those proceedings are brought by or against the Commissioners, a law officer of the Crown or an officer, or against any other person in respect of anything purporting to have been done in pursuance of any power or duty conferred or imposed on him by or under the custom and excise Acts, the burden of proof shall be upon the other party to the proceedings.

The words 'ship, aircraft or railway vehicle' are substituted for the words 'ship or aircraft' by the Taxation (Cross-border Trade) Act 2018, s. 29 and sch. 7, para. 106 (see **B16.11**).

The reverse burden of proof in s. 154(2) is compatible with the ECHR, Article 6(2) (*Euro Wines (C&C) Ltd v Revenue and Customs Commissioners* [2018] EWCA Civ 46, [2018] 1 WLR 3248).

B16.18 **Commissioners for Revenue and Customs Act 2005, ss. 24 and 25A**

24.—(1) A document that purports to have been issued or signed by or with the authority of the Commissioners—
  (a) shall be treated as having been so issued or signed unless the contrary is proved, and
  (b) shall be admissible in any legal proceedings.
(2) A document that purports to have been issued by the Commissioners and which certifies any of the matters specified in subsection (3) shall (in addition to the matters provided for by subsection (1)(a) and (b)) be treated as accurate unless the contrary is proved.
(3) The matters mentioned in subsection (2) are—
  (a) that a specified person was appointed as a commissioner on a specified date,

(b) that a specified person was appointed as an officer of Revenue and Customs on a specified date,
(c) that at a specified time or for a specified purpose (or both) a function was delegated to a specified Commissioner,
(d) that at a specified time or for a specified purpose (or both) a function was delegated to a specified committee, and
(e) that at a specified time or for a specified purpose (or both) a function was delegated to another specified person.

(4) A photographic or other copy of a document acquired by the Commissioners shall, if certified by them to be an accurate copy, be admissible in any legal proceedings to the same extent as the document itself.

(5) Section 2 of the Documentary Evidence Act 1868 (proof of documents) shall apply to a Revenue and Customs document as it applies in relation to the documents mentioned in that section.

(6) In the application of that section to a Revenue and Customs document the Schedule to that Act shall be treated as if—
(a) the first column contained a reference to the Commissioners, and
(b) the second column contained a reference to a Commissioner or a person acting on his authority.

(7) In this section—
(a) 'Revenue and Customs document' means a document issued by or on behalf of the Commissioners, and
(b) a reference to the Commissioners includes a reference to the Commissioners of Inland Revenue and to the Commissioners of Customs and Excise.

25A.—(1) A certificate of an officer of Revenue and Customs that, to the best of that officer's knowledge and belief, a relevant sum has not been paid is sufficient evidence that the sum mentioned in the certificate is unpaid.

(2) In subsection (1) 'relevant sum' means a sum payable to the Commissioners under or by virtue of an enactment or under a contract settlement (within the meaning of section 25).

(3) Any document purporting to be such a certificate shall be treated as if it were such a certificate until the contrary is proved.

(4) Subsection (1) has effect subject to any provision treating the certificate as conclusive evidence.

General Provisions in Relation to Liability and Penalties

Section 149 makes provision for maximum terms of imprisonment in magistrates' courts. **B16.19**

Customs and Excise Management Act 1979, s. 149

(1) Where, in any proceedings for an offence under the customs and excise Acts, a magistrates' court in England or Wales or a court of summary jurisdiction in Scotland, in addition to ordering the person convicted to pay a penalty for the offence—
(a) orders him to be imprisoned for a term in respect of the same offence; and
(b) further (whether at the same time or subsequently) orders him to be imprisoned for a term in respect of non-payment of that penalty or default of a sufficient distress to satisfy the amount of that penalty,

the aggregate of the terms for which he is so ordered to be imprisoned shall not exceed 15 months.

(1A) In subsection (1)(b) as it applies to a magistrates' court in England and Wales the reference to default of sufficient distress to satisfy the amount of the penalty is a reference to want of sufficient goods to satisfy the amount, within the meaning given by section 79(4) of the Magistrates' Courts Act 1980.

(2) [Repealed.]

(3) [Applies to Northern Ireland only.]

By the MCA 1980, s. 79(4), references to want of sufficient goods to satisfy a sum of money are references to circumstances where a warrant of control has been issued for the sum to be recovered from a person, but it appears from the return to the warrant that the person's money and goods are insufficient to pay the amount outstanding.

B16.20 Section 150 contains a provision (s.150(1)) dealing with joint liability. Section 150(2) gives courts power to mitigate any pecuniary penalty. Section 150(3) provides that giving security for the payment of duty does not amount to a defence in proceedings under the customs and excise Acts.

Customs and Excise Management Act 1979, s. 150

(1) Where liability for any offence under the customs and excise Acts is incurred by two or more persons jointly, those persons shall each be liable for the full amount of any pecuniary penalty and may be proceeded against jointly or severally as [the] prosecuting authority (within the meaning of section 146A) may see fit.

(2) In any proceedings for an offence under the customs and excise Acts instituted in England, Wales or Northern Ireland, any court by whom the matter is considered may mitigate any pecuniary penalty as they see fit.

(3) In any proceedings for an offence or for the condemnation of any thing as being forfeited under the customs and excise Acts, the fact that security has been given by bond or otherwise for the payment of any duty or for compliance with any condition in respect of the non-payment of which or non-compliance with which the proceedings are instituted shall not be a defence.

...

B16.21 Section 152 gives the Commissioners power to mitigate penalties.

Customs and Excise Management Act 1979, s. 152

The Commissioners may, as they see fit—

(a) compound an offence (whether or not proceedings have been instituted in respect of it) and compound proceedings or for the condemnation of any thing as being forfeited under the customs and excise Acts; or

(b) restore, subject to such conditions (if any) as they think proper, any thing forfeited or seized under those Acts; or

(c) and (d) [repealed];

but paragraph (a) above shall not apply to proceedings on indictment in Scotland.

A person affected by a decision to refuse to restore an item forfeited or seized may ask the Commissioners to review that decision under the Finance Act 1994, s. 14, and, if still dissatisfied after that review, has a limited right of appeal to the First-tier Tribunal (Tax Chamber) under s. 16 (*Behzad Fuels (UK) Ltd v Revenue and Customs Commissioners* [2019] EWCA Civ 319, [2019] 4 WLR 104).

B16.22 Section 171 contains a number of further provisions as to offences and penalties. These relate to convictions of a person for more than one offence (s.171(1)), the meaning of 'prescribed sum' in relation to penalties (s.171(2)), the determination of the value of goods (s.171(3)), liability of officers of a company or other body corporate when an offence has been committed by the body corporate (s.171(4) and (4A)) and a default provision where the relevant time for ascertaining duty payable cannot be ascertained (s.171(5)). Section 171(5) is set out as amended by the Taxation (Cross-border Trade) Act 2018, s. 29 and sch. 7, para. 115 (see **B16.11**).

Customs and Excise Management Act 1979, s. 171

(1) Where—

(a) by any provision of any enactment relating to an assigned matter a punishment is prescribed for any offence thereunder or for any contravention of or failure to comply with any regulation, direction, condition or requirement made, given or imposed thereunder; and

(b) any person is convicted in the same proceedings of more than one such offence, contravention or failure,

that person shall be liable to that punishment for each such offence, contravention or failure of which he is so convicted.

(2) In this Act the 'prescribed sum', in relation to the penalty provided for an offence, means—

(a) if the offence was committed in England, Wales or Northern Ireland, the prescribed sum *within the meaning* of section 32 of the Magistrates' Courts Act 1980 (£1,000 or other sum substituted by order under section 143(1) of that Act);

(b) [Applies to Scotland only]
and in subsection (1)(a) above, the reference to a provision by which a punishment is prescribed includes a reference to a provision which makes a person liable to a penalty of the prescribed sum within the meaning of this subsection.

(3) Where a penalty for an offence under any enactment relating to an assigned matter is required to be fixed by reference to the value of any goods, that value shall be taken as the price which those goods might reasonably be expected to have fetched, after payment of any duty or tax chargeable thereon, if they had been sold in the open market at or about the date of the commission of the offence for which the penalty is imposed.

(4) Where an offence under any enactment relating to an assigned matter which has been committed by a body corporate is proved to have been committed with the consent or connivance of, or to be attributable to any neglect on the part of, any director, manager, secretary or other similar officer of the body corporate or any person purporting to act in any such capacity, he as well as the body corporate shall be guilty of that offence and shall be liable to be proceeded against and punished accordingly.
In this subsection 'director', in relation to any body corporate established by or under any enactment for the purpose of carrying on under national ownership any industry or part of an industry or undertaking, being a body corporate whose affairs are managed by the members thereof, means a member of that body corporate.

(4A) Subsection (4) shall not apply to an offence which relates to a matter listed in Schedule 1 to the Commissioners for Revenue and Customs Act 2005 (former Inland Revenue matters).

(5) Where in any proceedings for an offence under the customs and excise Acts any question arises as to the duty or the rate thereof chargeable on any imported goods, and it is not possible to ascertain the time at which a liability to import duty is incurred or the relevant excise duty point, that duty or rate shall be determined as if the time when the proceedings were commenced was the time at which the liability to import duty was incurred or, as the case may be, as if the time when the proceedings were commenced was the relevant excise duty point.

Appeals from Decisions of Magistrates' Courts

Unusually (see **D29**), the Customs and Excise Management Act 1979, s. 147(3), permits the prosecutor to appeal to the Crown Court against a decision of a magistrates' court in proceedings for an offence under the customs and excise Acts. **B16.23**

Customs and Excise Management Act 1979, s. 147

(3) In the case of proceedings in England and Wales, without prejudice to any right to require the statement of a case for the opinion of the High Court, the prosecutor may appeal to the Crown Court against any decision of a magistrates' court in proceedings for an offence under the customs and excise Acts.

The prosecutor may therefore appeal to the Crown Court against a sentence passed by the magistrates' court (*Customs and Excise Commissioners v Brunt* (1999) 163 JP 161). See also *Customs and Excise Commissioners, ex parte Wagstaff* [1998] Crim LR 287.

OFFENCES IN CONNECTION WITH COMMISSIONERS AND OFFICERS

Section 33 of the Commissioners for Revenue and Customs Act 2005 confers a power of arrest on an authorised officer of the Revenue and Customs if the officer reasonably suspects that a person has committed, is committing or is about to commit an offence under any of ss. 30 to 32. **B16.24**

Unlawful Assumption of Character of Commissioner or Officer

Commissioners for Revenue and Customs Act 2005, s. 30 **B16.25**

(1) A person commits an offence if he pretends to be a Commissioner or an officer of Revenue and Customs with a view to obtaining—
(a) admission to premises,

(b) information, or
(c) any other benefit.

This is a summary offence with a maximum penalty of six months' imprisonment and/or an unlimited fine.

Obstruction of and Assaults upon Officers etc.

B16.26 **Commissioners for Revenue and Customs Act 2005, ss. 31 and 32**

31.—(1) A person commits an offence if without reasonable excuse he obstructs—
(a) an officer of Revenue and Customs,
(b) a person acting on behalf of the Commissioners or an officer of Revenue and Customs, or
(c) a person assisting an officer of Revenue and Customs.

32.—(1) A person commits an offence if he assaults an officer of Revenue and Customs.

Section 31 creates a summary offence with a maximum penalty of six months' imprisonment and/or a fine at level 3 on the standard scale. The general principles concerning obstruction of a police officer (see **B2.48** to **B2.53**) apply. Thus a person who gives false information to officers of the Revenue and Customs, so making it harder for officers to perform their duty, is guilty of obstruction (*George* [1981] Crim LR 185).

For the powers of Customs officers to seize and detain goods liable to forfeiture, see the Customs and Excise Management Act 1979, s. 139. Customs officers also have power to detain goods pending determination of their duty status (*R (Eastenders Cash & Carry plc) v Revenue and Customs Commissioners* [2014] UKSC 34, [2015] AC 1101).

Section 32 creates a summary offence with a maximum penalty of six months' imprisonment and/or an unlimited fine.

IMPROPER IMPORTATION AND EXPORTATION OF GOODS

Improper Importation of Goods

B16.27 **Customs and Excise Management Act 1979, s. 50**

(1) Subsection (2) below applies to goods of the following descriptions, that is to say—
(a) goods chargeable with a duty which has not been paid; and
(b) goods the importation, landing or unloading of which is for the time being prohibited or restricted by or under any enactment.

(2) If any person with intent to defraud Her Majesty of any such duty or to evade any such prohibition or restriction as is mentioned in subsection (1) above—
(a) unships or lands in any port or unloads from any aircraft in the United Kingdom or from any vehicle which has entered the United Kingdom any goods to which this subsection applies, or assists or is otherwise concerned in such unshipping, landing or unloading; or
(b) removes from their place of importation or from any approved wharf, examination station, temporary storage facility, any place specified by an officer of Revenue and Customs under Part 1 of the Taxation (Cross-border Trade) Act 2018 as a place where the goods are required to be kept or customs and excise station any goods to which this subsection applies or assists or is otherwise concerned in such removal,

he shall be guilty of an offence under this subsection and may be arrested.

(3) If any person imports or is concerned in importing any goods contrary to any prohibition or restriction for the time being in force under or by virtue of any enactment with respect to those goods, whether or not the goods are unloaded, and does so with intent to evade the prohibition or restriction, he shall be guilty of an offence under this subsection and may be arrested.

Section 50(2) is set out as amended by the Taxation (Cross-border Trade) Act 2018, s. 29 and sch. 7, para. 44(1) and (2) (see **B16.11**).

Procedure, Evidence and Penalties This offence is triable either way. When tried on indictment it is a class 3 offence; CrimPD XIII, para. B (see Supplement, **CPD.XIII.B**). As to the power of arrest, see *Smith* [1973] QB 924. **B16.28**

As to evidence issues in the case of illegal importation, see **F1.18**.

Penalties are provided by the Customs and Excise Management Act 1979, s. 50(4): on indictment, a penalty of any amount, or imprisonment for a term not exceeding seven years or both; on summary conviction, a penalty of £20,000 or of three times the value of the goods, whichever is the greater, or imprisonment for a term not exceeding six months, or both. Enhanced penalties are provided for by s. 50(5) to (5AA), (5C) and sch. 1, in the following types of cases.

(i) Where the goods in respect of which the offence is committed are drugs, the importation of which is prohibited by the Misuse of Drugs Act 1971, s. 3 (see **B16.31**). If the drug is a Class A or Class B or temporary class drug (as to the meaning of which, see **B19.7**), on summary conviction the penalty is six months and/or a penalty not exceeding £20,000, or three times the value of the goods, whichever is the greater; on indictment there is a penalty of unlimited amount and, in the case of a Class A drug, life imprisonment, or, in the case of a Class B drug, 14 years' imprisonment. If the drug is a Class C drug (see **B19.7**), the penalty is on summary conviction three months and/or a penalty of £500, or three times the value of the goods, whichever is the greater. On indictment there is a penalty of unlimited amount and 14 years' imprisonment.
(ii) Where the importation is of any weapon or ammunition of a kind mentioned in the Firearms Act 1968, s. 5(1)(a), (ab), (aba), (ac), (ad), (ae), (af), (ag), (ba) or (c) or (1A)(a) (see **B12.61**), the maximum penalty on indictment is enhanced to life imprisonment.
(iii) Where the importation is of a counterfeit of a currency note or of a protected coin without the Treasury's consent (Forgery and Counterfeiting Act 1981, s. 20: see **B6.98**), the maximum penalty on indictment is enhanced to ten years' imprisonment.
(iv) Where the offence is in connection with nuclear material, the maximum penalty on indictment is 14 years' imprisonment.

Where the offence is committed in connection with the prohibition contained in the Import of Seal Skins Regulations 1996 (SI 1996 No. 2686), reg. 2, the maximum penalty is reduced to two years' imprisonment on indictment and a fine not exceeding £20,000 or three months' imprisonment, or both, on summary conviction (s. 50(5B)).

The definitive sentencing guideline, *Fraud, Bribery and Money Laundering Offences* (see Supplement, **SG26-4**) includes guidance on sentencing for revenue fraud, including for improper importation of goods. Table 2 in the revenue fraud part of the guideline sets out the applicable starting points and ranges. See **B16.54** for a discussion of sentencing in revenue fraud cases. In *Dobson* [2017] EWCA Crim 2435, [2018] 1 Cr App R (S) 37 (260) the Court of Appeal considered that nine months' imprisonment, before deduction for a guilty plea, was the appropriate sentence for the improper importation of an indecent item.

Elements As to prohibition or restriction, see *Superheater Co. Ltd v Commissioners of Customs and Excise* [1969] 2 All ER 469. **B16.29**

Goods which are unloaded at an airport and held in a customs area pending trans-shipment to a foreign destination are regarded as having been imported into the UK (*Smith* [1973] QB 924).

Duplication of Offences Section 50(7) of the Customs and Excise Management Act 1979 prevents duplication of offences and possible double jeopardy. **B16.30**

Customs and Excise Management Act 1979, s. 50

(7) In any case where a person would, apart from this subsection, be guilty of—
(a) an offence under this section in connection with the importation of goods contrary to a prohibition or restriction; and

(b) a corresponding offence under the enactment or other instrument imposing the prohibition or restriction, being an offence for which a fine or other penalty is expressly provided by that enactment or other instrument,

he shall not be guilty of the offence mentioned in paragraph (a) of this subsection.

Prohibition on Importation and Exportation of Controlled Drugs

B16.31 Section 3 of the MDA 1971 (see **B19.69**) creates a prohibition on the importation or exportation of a controlled drug (see **B19.7**), but does not expressly create an offence. Consequently, evasion of this prohibition should be charged as an offence of fraudulent evasion of duty (under the Customs and Excise Management Act 1979, s. 170; see **B16.39**) or as improper importation or exportation of goods (under ss. 50 and 68; see **B16.27** and **B16.34**). It is also possible, where appropriate, to charge a conspiracy to evade the prohibition imposed by the MDA 1971, s. 3.

Where a licence to import or export a controlled drug has been granted by the Secretary of State, the MDA 1971, s. 18(2) (see **B19.119**), makes it an offence to contravene any conditions imposed by the licence.

For sentencing guidelines relating to controlled drugs, including importation, see **B19.145** *et seq.*

Misdescription of Imported Goods

B16.32 **Customs and Excise Management Act 1979, s. 50**

(6) If any person—

(a) imports or causes to be imported any goods concealed in a container holding goods of a different description; or

(b) directly or indirectly imports, or causes to be imported, any chargeable goods found, whether before or after being released to a Customs procedure, not to correspond with any information provided under Part 1 of the Taxation (Cross-border Trade) Act 2018,

he shall be liable on summary conviction to a penalty of three times the value of the goods or level 3 on the standard scale, whichever is the greater.

Section 50(6)(b) is set out as substituted by the Taxation (Cross-border Trade) Act 2018, s. 29 and sch. 7, para. 44(1) and (3) (see **B16.11**).

This offence appears to be a strict liability offence. It meets the criteria for strict liability and in particular it emphasises the need to take care in the furnishing of information, packaging of imports, etc. (*Gammon (Hong Kong) Ltd v A-G of Hong Kong* [1985] AC 1; and see generally **A2.20**).

Improper Unloading of Goods Loaded etc. for Exportation

B16.33 **Customs and Excise Management Act 1979, s. 67**

(1) If any goods which have been loaded or retained on board any vehicle for exportation are not exported to and discharged at a place outside the United Kingdom but are unloaded in the United Kingdom, then, unless—

(a) the unloading was authorised by the proper officer; and

(b) except where the officer otherwise permits, any duty chargeable and unpaid on the goods is paid and any drawback or allowance paid in respect thereof is repaid,

the vehicle operator and any person concerned in the unshipping, relanding, landing, unloading or carrying of the goods from the vehicle without such authority, payment or repayment shall each be guilty of an offence under this section.

(2) The Commissioners may impose such conditions as they see fit with respect to any goods loaded or retained as mentioned in subsection (1) above which are permitted to be unloaded in the United Kingdom.

(3) If any person contravenes or fails to comply with, or is concerned in any contravention of or failure to comply with, any condition imposed under subsection (2) above he shall be guilty of an offence under this section.

(4) Where any goods loaded or retained as mentioned in subsection (1) above are—

(a) goods in an excise warehouse or goods which have been declared for a storage procedure;

(b) transit goods;

(c) other goods chargeable with a duty which has not been paid or goods which have been declared for an authorised use procedure or temporary admission procedure; or
(d) drawback goods,
then if any container in which the goods are held is without the authority of the proper officer opened, or any mark, letter or device on any such container or on any lot of the goods is without that authority cancelled, obliterated or altered, every person concerned in the opening, cancellation, obliteration or alteration shall be guilty of an offence under this section.

Section 67 is set out as amended by the Taxation (Cross-border Trade) Act 2018, s. 29 and sch. 7, para. 69 (see **B16.11**). 'Vehicle' is defined in sch. 7, para. 4(2)(l), as including a ship, aircraft or railway vehicle. The words 'the vehicle operator' are defined in sch. 7, para. 4(2)(m), as (a) in the case of a ship, the master of the ship; (b) in the case of an aircraft, the commander of the aircraft; (c) in the case of a railway vehicle, the person designated as train manager by the person operating the international service on which the railway vehicle is engaged; and (d) in the case of any other vehicle, the person in charge of the vehicle.

The offence is triable only summarily. The penalty is forfeiture of goods and a penalty of three times the value of the goods or level 3 on the standard scale, whichever is the greater (s. 67(5)).

Offences in Relation to Exportation of Prohibited or Restricted Goods

Customs and Excise Management Act 1979, s. 68 **B16.34**

(1) If any goods are—
(a) exported or shipped as stores; or
(b) brought to any place in the United Kingdom for the purpose of being exported or shipped as stores,
and the exportation or shipment is or would be contrary to any prohibition or restriction for the time being in force with respect to those goods under or by virtue of any enactment, the goods shall be liable to forfeiture and the exporter or intending exporter of the goods and any agent of his concerned in the exportation or shipment or intended exportation or shipment shall each be liable on summary conviction to a penalty of three times the value of the goods or level three on the standard scale, whichever is the greater.
(2) Any person knowingly concerned in the exportation or shipment as stores, or in the attempted exportation or shipment as stores, of any goods with intent to evade any such prohibition or restriction as is mentioned in subsection (1) above shall be guilty of an offence under this subsection and may be arrested

...

(5) If by virtue of any such restriction as is mentioned in subsection (1) above any goods may be exported only when consigned to a particular place or person and any goods so consigned are delivered to some other place or person, the vehicle in which they were exported shall be liable to forfeiture unless it is proved to the satisfaction of the Commissioners that both the owner of the vehicle and the vehicle operator—
(a) took all reasonable steps to secure that the goods were delivered to the particular place to which or person to whom they were consigned; and
(b) did not connive at or, except under duress, consent to the delivery of the goods to that other place or person.
(6) In any case where a person would, apart from this subsection be guilty of—
(a) an offence under subsection (1) or (2) above; and
(b) a corresponding offence under the enactment or instrument imposing the prohibition or restriction in question, being an offence for which a fine or other penalty is expressly provided by that enactment or other instrument,
he shall not be guilty of the offence mentioned in paragraph (a) of this subsection.

Section 68(5) is set out as amended by the Taxation (Cross-border Trade) Act 2018, s. 29 and sch. 7, para. 70 (see **B16.11**). For the meaning of 'vehicle' and 'vehicle operator' see **B16.33**.

Procedure and Penalties The offence is triable either way. When tried on indictment it is a class 3 offence; CrimPD XIII, para. B (see Supplement, **CPD.XIII.B**). As to the power of arrest, see *Smith* [1973] QB 924. **B16.35**

The Customs and Excise Management Act 1979, s. 68(3), (4) and (4A) and sch. 1, prescribe penalties. On summary conviction there may be imposed a penalty of £20,000 or of three times the value of the goods whichever is the greater, or imprisonment for a term not exceeding six months or both. On conviction on indictment there may be imposed a penalty of any amount, or imprisonment for a term not exceeding seven years, or both. Enhanced penalties, as under s. 50 (see **B16.28**), apply to dealing respectively with drugs, firearms and counterfeit notes and currency.

The penalties are also modified where a person is convicted of an offence contrary to s. 68(2) by virtue of the application of reg. 6 of the Controlled Drugs (Drug Precursors) (Community External Trade) Regulations 2008 (SI 2008 No. 296), as amended by the Law Enforcement and Security (Amendment) (EU Exit) Regulations 2019 (SI 2019 No. 742) (see **B19.138**). These regulations enable authorities to license operations involving substances useful for the manufacture of controlled drugs. In such a case, for an offence under s. 68(2), the maximum penalty on indictment is two years' imprisonment and, on summary conviction, is three months' imprisonment and/or a £5,000 fine.

Provision for forfeiture is made, subject to defences, by s. 68(5) above.

B16.36 **Elements** Under other legislation relating to national defence, it was held that a person may be convicted of an offence of unlawful exportation even though that person intends to bring the goods back to the UK (*Berner* (1953) 37 Cr App R 113).

A person can be concerned with the exportation of goods even if the acts which that person performs take place at a time other than that which constitutes exportation (see **B16.44** and **B16.45**). A person can be so concerned, for example, at a time prior to the departure of an aircraft (*Garrett v Arthur Churchill (Glass) Ltd* [1970] 1 QB 92).

The prosecution must show both that the export of the goods was prohibited (e.g., by the Export Control Order 2008 (SI 2008 No. 3231)), and that D knew that the goods fell into a prohibited category (*Daghir* [1994] Crim LR 945). The Customs and Excise Management Act 1979, s. 68(2), is cast in terms of evasion. This does not require an element of fraud or dishonesty, but is, rather, given its ordinary English meaning, i.e. 'to get around or avoid' (*Hurford-Jones* (1977) 65 Cr App R 263; see also *Bajwa* [2011] EWCA Crim 1093, [2012] 1 All ER 348 at [90] (see **B16.44**)).

In *Garrett v Arthur Churchill (Glass) Ltd* [1970] 1 QB 92, it was held that a person who hands over goods belonging to another, knowing that the other proposes to export them unlawfully, is knowingly concerned in the unlawful importation. The duty to hand over goods to their owner yields to the public interest in preventing such exportation.

Under art. 26 of the Export Control Order 2008, an export which would otherwise be forbidden may be licensed by the Secretary of State. Such a licence will not bar a prosecution under s. 68(2) where a shipment is in fact to a destination other than that specified in the licence. Even if it cannot be proved that a licence was obtained by misrepresentation, a prosecution may still be brought if the actor seeks to evade the prohibition by specifying a sham consignee (*Redfern* [1993] Crim LR 43).

IMPORTING OR EXPORTING A PSYCHOACTIVE SUBSTANCE

B16.37 **Psychoactive Substances Act 2016, s. 8**

(1) A person commits an offence if—
 (a) the person intentionally imports a substance,
 (b) the substance is a psychoactive substance,
 (c) the person knows or suspects, or ought to know or suspect, that the substance is a psychoactive substance, and

(d) the person—
(i) intends to consume the psychoactive substance for its psychoactive effects, or
(ii) knows, or is reckless as to whether, the psychoactive substance is likely to be consumed by some other person for its psychoactive effects.

(2) A person commits an offence if—
(a) the person intentionally exports a substance,
(b) the substance is a psychoactive substance,
(c) the person knows or suspects, or ought to know or suspect, that the substance is a psychoactive substance, and
(d) the person—
(i) intends to consume the psychoactive substance for its psychoactive effects, or
(ii) knows, or is reckless as to whether, the psychoactive substance is likely to be consumed by some other person for its psychoactive effects.

(3) In a case where a person imports or exports a controlled drug suspecting it to be a psychoactive substance, the person is to be treated for the purposes of this section as if the person had imported or exported a psychoactive substance suspecting it to be such a substance.
In this subsection 'controlled drug' has the same meaning as in the Misuse of Drugs Act 1971.

(4) Section 5 of the Customs and Excise Management Act 1979 (time of importation, exportation, etc.) applies for the purposes of this section as it applies for the purposes of that Act.

For the meaning of 'psychoactive substance', see s. 2 at **B19.123**. For the meaning of 'controlled drug' in the Misuse of Drugs Act 1971, see **B19.7** ***et seq.*** For s. 5 of the Customs and Excise Management Act 1979, see **B16.12**.

Section 11(3)(e) provides for exceptions to the offences. These exceptions are healthcare-related activities and approved scientific research listed and defined in sch. 2 to the Act.

Sentence

By the Psychoactive Substances Act 2016, s. 10(1), the maximum penalty on conviction on indictment is seven years' imprisonment or a fine or both; on summary conviction, the maximum penalty is six months, an unlimited fine or both. **B16.38**

FRAUDULENT EVASION OF DUTY ('SMUGGLING')

Customs and Excise Management Act 1979, s. 170 **B16.39**

(1) Without prejudice to any other provision of the Customs and Excise Acts 1979, if any person—
(a) knowingly acquires possession of any of the following goods, that is to say—
(i) goods which have been unlawfully removed from a warehouse or Queens warehouse;
(ii) goods which are chargeable with a duty which has not been paid;
(iii) goods with respect to the importation or exportation of which any prohibition or restriction is for the time being in force under or by virtue of any enactment; or
(b) is in any way knowingly concerned in carrying, removing, depositing, harbouring, keeping or concealing or in any manner dealing with any such goods,
and does so with intent to defraud Her Majesty of any duty payable on the goods or to evade any such prohibition or restriction with respect to the goods he shall be guilty of an offence under this section and may be arrested.

(2) Without prejudice to any other provision of the Customs and Excise Acts 1979, if any person is, in relation to any goods, in any way knowingly concerned in any fraudulent evasion or attempt at evasion—
(a) of any duty chargeable on the goods;
(b) of any prohibition or restriction for the time being in force with respect to the goods under or by virtue of any enactment; or
(c) of any provision of the Customs and Excise Acts 1979 or Part 1 of the Taxation (Cross-border Trade) Act 2018 applicable to the goods,
he shall be guilty of an offence under this section and may be arrested

Section 170(2)(c) is set out as amended by the Taxation (Cross-border Trade) Act 2018, s. 29 and sch. 7, para. 114 (see **B16.11**).

This offence relates to the smuggling of 'goods', defined in s. 1 as including stores and containers. For the offence of 'people smuggling' under the Immigration Act 1971, s. 25, see **B22.42**.

Procedure

B16.40 The offence is triable either way. When tried on indictment it is a class 3 offence; CrimPD XIII, para. B (see Supplement, **CPD.XIII.B**). The Customs and Excise Management Act 1979, s. 170(5), operates to prevent duplication of proceedings and possible double jeopardy problems.

Indictment (for Offences under s. 170(1)(b))

B16.41 *Statement of Offence*

Being knowingly concerned in concealing goods with intent to avoid prohibition on importation contrary to section 170(1)(b) of the Customs and Excise Management Act 1979.

Particulars of Offence

A on the ... day of ... was knowingly concerned in concealing goods, that is to say a quantity of a controlled drug, namely...valued at £..., with intent to evade the prohibition on importation of the said goods then in force pursuant to section 3 of the Misuse of Drugs Act 1971.

As to the Misuse of Drugs Act 1971, s. 3, see **B16.31** and **B19.69**.

Sentencing

B16.42 The maximum penalty on summary conviction is a penalty of £20,000 or of three times the value of the goods, whichever is the greater, and/or to imprisonment for a term not exceeding six months. The maximum penalty on indictment is a penalty of any amount and/or imprisonment for a term not exceeding seven years (Customs and Excise Management Act 1979, s. 170(3)).

In cases involving drugs, firearms and counterfeiting, penalties may be enhanced (s. 170(4) and (4A) and sch. 1). The enhancement is identical to that provided for in the case of s. 50 of the Act (see **B16.28**). For sentencing guidelines in drugs cases, see **B19.145 *et seq.*** In cases involving seal skins the maximum penalty is two years' imprisonment (s. 170(4B)).

The definitive sentencing guideline, *Fraud, Bribery and Money Laundering Offences* (see Supplement, **SG26-4**), includes guidance on sentencing for revenue fraud, including fraudulent evasion of excise duty. Table 2 in the revenue fraud part of the guideline sets out the applicable starting points and ranges. See **B16.54** for a discussion of sentencing in revenue fraud cases.

Scope of Offence

B16.43 These are wide prohibitions. Section 170 covers importing, exporting, those concerned in actual import and export, and even persons who cannot be proved to be implicated in an actual import or export; it is hard to think of anything in s. 170(2) which does not in fact come within s. 170(1) (*Neal* [1984] 3 All ER 156 at 160c–d). But a person could knowingly come into possession of unlawfully imported goods contrary to s. 170(1)(a)(iii) without being concerned in their importation contrary to s. 170(2)(b).

Actus Reus

B16.44 Evasion involves avoiding doing something which a person is under an obligation to do. A person evades an obligation by deliberately organising his or her affairs so as to be able to avoid doing what that person knows must be done (*Bajwa* [2011] EWCA Crim 1093, [2012] 1 All ER 348 at [90]–[93]). The words 'fraudulent evasion' in s. 170(2) do not require proof of acts of deceit practised on a customs officer (*A-G's Ref (No. 1 of 1981)* [1982] QB 848). When goods are smuggled into the UK by boat with the intention of avoiding the payment of duty, evasion takes place when the vessel enters the limits of the port (*Bajwa* at [94]).

In *Latif* [1996] 1 All ER 353 the House of Lords decided that s. 170(2) creates one offence which can be committed in one of two different ways, namely by evasion or an attempt at evasion (at pp. 365j–366a). Lord Steyn stated (at p. 362h) that it is inherent in the concept of an evasion that an importation has taken place. If no importation has taken place, no evasion has taken place. But if no importation has taken place, there may still be an attempted evasion, even if D's acts took place abroad.

The offence in s. 170(2) could relate to a single incident or a series of incidents forming an activity, any of which could be charged in a single count (*Martin* [1998] 2 Cr App R 385). Neither s. 170(1) nor (2) is restricted to those who form part of an original smuggling team (*Neal* [1984] 3 All ER 156). Therefore a person may be liable for acts done abroad prior to the actual smuggling, for participation in the act of entry itself, and for acts subsequent to entry relating, for example, to collection of the goods (*Jakeman* (1983) 76 Cr App R 223 at 228; *Sissen* [2001] 1 WLR 902 at [41]–[42]). Section 170B (see **B16.51**) creates a separate offence of being knowingly concerned in the taking of steps with a view to the fraudulent evasion of excise duty.

Evasion of the relevant prohibition is a continuing process; thus a person who, even after goods have been innocently imported by a carrier, falsely declares that his or her possessions contain no prohibited material, commits the offence (*Coughlan* (12 May 1997 unreported); *Bell* [2011] EWCA Crim 6 at [10]). However, a person cannot be guilty of fraudulent evasion if customs officers discover the planned importation of prohibited goods in advance and themselves arrange for the goods to be brought into the UK (*Latif* [1996] 1 All ER 353; see **A1.32**). But in those circumstances a person who planned to smuggle the goods could be guilty of an attempt at evasion (*Latif* at p. 364d–h) or conspiracy. In *Caippara* (1987) 87 Cr App R 316 the Court of Appeal held that a person may be guilty if proved willing to participate in a chain of activities which would result in drugs being imported into the UK, notwithstanding that customs officers substituted a harmless substance for them before delivery to the recipient. **B16.45**

The same principles as to when the substantive offence under s. 170 begins and ends appear in cases of conspiracy to evade a prohibition, etc. There can, it is said, be no abstract limit to the time when or place at which the crime is committed, provided always that the goods, the subject-matter of the charge, are goods which are the subject of a prohibition on importation and the acquisition is done knowingly and with intent to evade that prohibition or restriction (*Ardalan* [1972] 2 All ER 257 at p. 261c). Acts done after importation can be done in furtherance of a conspiracy since the conspiracy is not to import but to evade a restriction (*Borro* [1973] Crim LR 513).

It follows from *Quayle* [2005] EWCA Crim 1415, [2005] 1 All ER 988, especially at [54]–[56], and *Altham* [2006] EWCA Crim 7, [2006] 1 WLR 3287 (see **B19.38**) that no defence of necessity at common law in the interests of pain relief, whether for the person importing or others, can be raised to an unauthorised importation of a prohibited drug. **B16.46**

The fact of importation, where relevant, must be proved. It is then incumbent on D to prove factors in justification mentioned in s. 154 of the Act (see **B16.17**), such as that the goods were made here or that duty has been paid (*Watts* (1979) 70 Cr App R 187; *Mizel v Warren* [1973] 2 All ER 1149).

Mens Rea

Under s. 170(1), it must be shown that D knowingly acquired possession of certain goods or performed certain acts with intent to defraud Her Majesty or with intent to evade a relevant prohibition or restriction. In relation to knowingly harbouring goods, it is usually enough to show that goods which were subject to duty were found in D's possession (see also **F1.18**). This will establish a prima facie case of knowingly harbouring, subject to the accused's ability to rebut this by evidence casting doubt upon D's knowledge. Once the Crown has adduced a case of **B16.47** knowing possession, D must prove that the goods were in fact customed; see s. 154 (at **B16.17**) and *Cohen* [1951] 1 KB 505.

A person who presents goods for an assessment of duty does not act fraudulently by not disclosing the person's assessment of their worth, or by failing to alert a customs officer that the officer's valuation is wrong. In the absence of a false statement or concealment, the payment of duty demanded by a customs officer discharges the person's liability (*Customs and Excise Commissioners v Tan* [1977] AC 650).

B16.48 Under s. 170(2), the prosecution must prove fraudulent conduct in the sense of dishonest conduct deliberately intended to evade the prohibition or restriction with respect to, or the duty chargeable on, goods (*A-G's Ref (No. 1 of 1981)* [1982] QB 848). The prosecution must prove knowledge on D's part of the relevant circumstances, e.g., in a case of smuggling by sea, that the vessel had in fact entered territorial waters. Mere knowledge by the accused that at the relevant time there was a risk of entering territorial waters is not enough (*Panayi (No. 2)* [1989] 1 WLR 187).

D may have formed a guilty intent outside the UK. If the intent is formed abroad and acts constituting the offence are done there, liability will be complete. Subsequent repentance will not found a defence (*Jakeman* (1983) 76 Cr App R 223).

If a person engaged in the importation of goods believes that those goods are not subject to a restriction or prohibition, that person cannot be convicted (*Taaffe* [1984] AC 539). D is to be judged on the facts as D believed them to be. But if D believes the goods being imported are narcotics, whereas the substance is snuff, D may be convicted of attempting to evade a prohibition or restriction (*Shivpuri* [1987] AC 1).

It need not be proved that D was aware of the exact nature of the articles to which a restriction applies. Thus D who imports drugs believing them to be pornography will be liable for the offence (*Ellis* (1986) 84 Cr App R 235; *Hennessey* (1978) 68 Cr App R 419).

In respect of the importation of indecent material, it is enough if the person knows the material to be indecent; the precise nature of the indecency portrayed need not be known to the accused (*Forbes* [2001] UKHL 40, [2002] 2 AC 512). A person who knows the nature of the material imported and who believes it to be obscene will be liable for the offence even though no jury trying a case under the Obscene Publications Act 1959 has determined the article to be so: knowledge and belief suffice for guilt (*Dunne* (1998) 162 JP 399).

B16.49 Particular problems concern drugs where importation and exportation offences vary in severity according to whether the drug is a Class A, B, or C drug. Lord Bridge stated in *Shivpuri* [1987] AC 1 that the legislative history of the Misuse of Drugs Act 1971 makes clear that, while possession of class A, B, or C drugs are distinct offences, the offence of being concerned in importation requires proof only that D was aware of being engaged in evading restrictions on the importation of a prohibited article. Accordingly in *Siracusa* (1989) 90 Cr App R 340 it was held that the prosecution must prove that D knew that the goods in question were prohibited goods, but need not prove that D knew (precisely) what they were.

On a charge of conspiracy to supply controlled drugs, the prosecution must prove that D either (i) knew that the agreement related to the particular drug mentioned in the indictment, or (ii) knew that it related to a drug of the same class, without having any knowledge or belief as to it involving any particular drug, or (iii) believed that it related to another particular drug of the same class, or of a class attracting a greater penalty, or (iv) believed that it related to a drug of a class attracting a greater maximum penalty, without having any belief as to any particular drug, or (v) did not care at all what particular drug was involved. D would escape liability only where D mistakenly believed that the conspiracy related to a controlled drug of a class attracting a lesser maximum penalty (*Hanif* [2012] EWCA Crim 1968 at [14], following *Ayala* [2003] EWCA Crim 2047).

Offences under other provisions, e.g., regulations relating to the importation of animal products intended for human consumption, carry strict liability (see *Matudi* [2003] EWCA Crim 697 and **A2.20**).

Duplication of Offences As with s. 50(7) (see **B16.30**), s. 170(5) prevents duplication of offences and possible double jeopardy. **B16.50**

Customs and Excise Management Act 1979, s. 170

(5) In any case where a person would, apart from this subsection, be guilty of—
(a) an offence under this section in connection with a prohibition or restriction; and
(b) a corresponding offence under the enactment or other instrument imposing the prohibition or restriction, being an offence for which a fine or other penalty is expressly provided by that enactment or other instrument,
he shall not be guilty of the offence mentioned in paragraph (a) of this subsection.

Taking Preparatory Steps for Evasion of Excise Duty B16.51

Customs and Excise Management Act 1979, s. 170B

(1) If any person is knowingly concerned in the taking of any steps with a view to the fraudulent evasion, whether by himself or another, of any duty of excise on any goods, he shall be liable—
(a) on summary conviction, to a penalty of £20,000 or of three times the amount of the duty, whichever is the greater, or to imprisonment for a term not exceeding six months or to both; and
(b) on conviction on indictment, to a penalty of any amount or to imprisonment for a term not exceeding seven years or to both.
(2) Where any person is guilty of an offence under this section, the goods in respect of which the offence was committed shall be liable to forfeiture.

Untrue Declarations

Customs and Excise Management Act 1979, s. 167 **B16.52**

(1) If any person either knowingly or recklessly—
(a) makes or signs, or causes to be made or signed, or delivers or causes to be delivered to the Commissioners or an officer, any declaration, notice, certificate or other document whatsoever; or
(b) makes any statement in answer to any question put to him by an officer which he is required by or under any enactment to answer,
being a document or statement produced or made for any purpose or any assigned matter, which is untrue in any material particular, he shall be guilty of an offence under this subsection and may be arrested; and any goods in relation to which the document or statement was made shall be liable to forfeiture.
(2) Without prejudice to subsection (4) below, a person who commits an offence under subsection (1) above shall be liable—
(a) on summary conviction, to a penalty of £20,000, or to imprisonment for a term not exceeding six months, or to both; or
(b) on conviction on indictment, to a penalty of any amount, or to imprisonment for a term not exceeding two years, or to both.
(3) If any person—
(a) makes or signs, or causes to be made or signed, or delivers or causes to be delivered to the Commissioners or an officer, any declaration, notice, certificate or other document whatsoever; or
(b) makes any statement in answer to any question put to him by an officer which he is required by or under any enactment to answer,
being a document or statement produced or made for any purpose of any assigned matter, which is untrue in any material particular, then, without prejudice to subsection (4) below, he shall be liable on summary conviction to a penalty of level 4 on the standard scale.

In *Cross* [1987] Crim LR 43, it was held that the construction of documents is for the judge and not the jury (see also *Pioneer Shipping Ltd v BTP Tioxide Ltd (The Nema)* [1982] AC 724 at p. 736).

As to recklessness in this context, see *G* [2003] UKHL 50, [2004] 1 AC 1034 and **A2.8** *et seq.* generally. The offence under s. 167(3) would seem to be an offence of strict liability (*Patel v Comptroller of Customs* [1966] AC 356).

Counterfeiting Documents

B16.53 **Customs and Excise Management Act 1979, s. 168**

(1) If any person—
(a) counterfeits or falsifies any document which is required by or under any enactment relating to an assigned matter or which is used in the transaction of any business relating to an assigned matter; or
(b) knowingly accepts, receives or uses any such document so counterfeited or falsified; or
(c) alters any such document after it is officially issued; or
(d) counterfeits any seal, signature, initials or other mark of, or used by, any officer for the verification of such a document or for the security of goods or for any other purpose relating to an assigned matter,
he shall be guilty of an offence under this section and may be arrested.

Offences under s. 168(1) are triable either way. Under s. 168(2) the maximum on indictment is a penalty of any amount and/or imprisonment for a term not exceeding two years. On summary conviction, it is a penalty of £20,000 and/or imprisonment for a term not exceeding six months. See also **B16.7** for the similar offence under the Taxes Management Act 1970, s. 20BB.

In *Patel v Comptroller of Customs* [1966] AC 356, it was held that falsification and counterfeiting require *mens rea*. It may be helpful to refer to the law on these subjects under the Forgery and Counterfeiting Act 1981. See generally **B6.26** to **B6.29** and **B6.65**.

SENTENCING GUIDELINES FOR REVENUE FRAUD

B16.54 The definitive sentencing guideline, *Fraud, Bribery and Money Laundering Offences* (see Supplement, **SG26-4**), sets out guidance for sentencing for a range of revenue fraud offences. The guideline applies to offenders aged 18 and over and organisations sentenced on or after 1 October 2014, regardless of the date of the offence. The court is required to determine the offender's level of culpability (high, medium or lesser) and the harm, in monetary terms, calculated by reference to the amount obtained or intended to be obtained by the offending.

In respect of individuals, Table 2 in the revenue fraud part of the guideline sets out starting points and ranges of sentences for offences under the Value Added Tax Act 1994, s. 72, the Taxes Management Act 1970, s. 106A, and the Customs and Excise Management Act 1979, ss. 50 and 170, involving harm of up to £2 million. Table 3 sets out starting points and ranges of sentences for cheating the public revenue. The court then must consider any additional factors which increase or reduce the seriousness of the offence or which provide personal mitigation.

Under the revenue fraud part of the *Fraud, Bribery and Money Laundering Offences* guideline (see Supplement, **SG26-4**), all factors in the case are to be weighed to determine whether D's culpability is high, medium or lesser. Under this guideline the concept of a leading role, demonstrating high culpability, only applies where the offending is part of a group activity (*Carr* [2016] EWCA Crim 2259 at [22]–[25]). But the sophisticated nature of the offence, significant planning and fraudulent activity conducted over a sustained period of time are listed factors that may demonstrate high culpability by an individual acting alone.

B16.55 **Corporate Offenders** In respect of corporate offenders, the penalty will be a fine. A separate table sets out starting points and ranges for cheating the public revenue, offences under the Value Added Tax Act 1994, s. 72, and offences under the Customs and Excise Management

Act 1979, s. 170. The starting point and range are calculated by identifying the corporation's culpability (high, medium or lesser) and multiplying the harm figure, usually the actual or intended gross gain, by a percentage representing that culpability. The court then must consider whether there are further factors which indicate an adjustment to the level of fine (see further **A6.22**).

Drug Smuggling Sentencing in drug importation cases is covered by the definitive sentencing guideline, *Drug Offences* (see Supplement, **SG23-1** and **B19.149** to **B19.150**, **B19.156** and **B19.161**). Sentences for conspiracy to smuggle quantities of cocaine significantly in excess of the weights set out in the categories of harm in that guideline were considered in *Leitz* [2016] EWCA Crim 849 at [29]–[42]. In *Wright* [2017] EWCA Crim 126 a term of 24 years' imprisonment was held to be the appropriate starting point for a pilot who had flown large quantities of cocaine from Germany to the UK on eight occasions within three months. In *Jhurry* [2018] EWCA Crim 2799, [2019] Cr App R (S) 40 (274) (see **B19.149**) the Court of Appeal upheld a sentence taking a starting point of 25 years' imprisonment for a leading role by a baggage handler at Heathrow Airport in a conspiracy to import large quantities of high purity cocaine, reduced to 16 years for admissions in interview and an early plea of guilty. In *Birks* [2017] EWCA Crim 810 a sentence of 20 years' imprisonment for smuggling 12 kilograms of diamorphine was upheld. **B16.56**

Many smuggling cases involve group activity rather than an individual acting alone. Under the *Drug Offences* guideline, D's level of culpability is determined by whether D played a leading, significant or lesser role in the criminal activity. In *Nunez Lopez* [2015] EWCA Crim 1451 D was the driver of a lorry intercepted at Dover docks and containing 50 kilograms of cocaine. A sentence of 14 years' imprisonment on a guilty plea to a charge of fraudulent evasion of the prohibition on importation of cocaine was reduced to ten years as there was no evidence that D had played a leading role. In *Sperlinga* [2015] EWCA Crim 1842 a driver's role was also regarded as significant rather than leading, but was aggravated by the fact that he had committed the offence for substantial reward and had been involved in the concealment of the drugs. A sentence of 15 years' imprisonment was reduced to 12 years.

Lapse of time since apprehension, where this does not arise from D's conduct, is one of the factors reflecting personal mitigation listed in the *Fraud, Bribery and Money Laundering Offences* guideline, (see *Whitson-Dew* [2019] EWCA Crim 2131, [2020] 1 Cr App R (S) 56 (438)). This factor does not appear in the *Drug Offences* guideline. But these are expressed to be non-exhaustive lists and this factor was applied in *Khan* [2017] EWCA Crim 48 when reducing a sentence for conspiracy to smuggle cocaine from eight years to six and a half years.

Suspended Sentences In *Hashim* [2018] EWCA Crim 1695, a fraudulent evasion of VAT case of high culpability under the revenue fraud part of the *Fraud, Bribery and Money Laundering* sentencing guideline, Bean LJ observed (at [7]) that where there had been fraudulent activity over a sustained period of time, resulting in a far from negligible loss to HMRC, it was not generally right to suspend a sentence of imprisonment. In *Tuck* [2018] EWCA Crim 2529 (see **B16.6**) at [16]–[18] the length of the sentence for fraudulent evasion of income tax was substantially reduced because of D's good character and continuing health issues, but not suspended. **B16.57**

In *A-G v Peck* [2020] EWCA Crim 147 the Court of Appeal observed (at [51]) that, where a person imports and deals with Class A drugs over a long period of time, an immediate prison sentence of some length is almost always the outcome, even if that person is of positive good character with every expectation of good behaviour in the future. In that case the Court quashed as unduly lenient a suspended sentence of two years and substituted two years and nine months' immediate imprisonment. But in *Randhawa* [2017] EWCA Crim 1518 a sentence of 18 months' imprisonment for fraudulent evasion of duty on fuel was suspended for two years because D had been subjected to intimidation.

SOCIAL SECURITY OFFENCES

B16.58 The dishonest obtaining and/or retention of benefits may well involve the commission of offences under the Fraud Act 2006 (see **B5.4** ***et seq.***) or false accounting (see **B6.3**), but the Social Security Administration Act 1992, s. 111A, creates further offences carrying comparable penalties, while s. 112 creates a range of summary offences.

Dishonest Representations for Obtaining Benefit, etc.

B16.59 **Social Security Administration Act 1992, s. 111A**

(1) If a person dishonestly—
(a) makes a false statement or representation; or
(b) produces or furnishes, or causes or allows to be produced or furnished, any document or information which is false in a material particular,
with a view to obtaining any benefit or other payment or advantage under the relevant social security legislation (whether for himself or for some other person), he shall be guilty of an offence.

(1A) A person shall be guilty of an offence if—
(a) there has been a change of circumstances affecting any entitlement of his to any benefit or other payment or advantage under any provision of the relevant social security legislation;
(b) the change is not a change that is excluded by regulations from the changes that are required to be notified;
(c) he knows that the change affects an entitlement of his to such a benefit or other payment or advantage; and
(d) he dishonestly fails to give a prompt notification of that change in the prescribed manner to the prescribed person.

(1B) A person shall be guilty of an offence if—
(a) there has been a change of circumstances affecting any entitlement of another person to any benefit or other payment or advantage under any provision of the relevant social security legislation;
(b) the change is not a change that is excluded by regulations from the changes that are required to be notified;
(c) he knows that the change affects an entitlement of that other person to such a benefit or other payment or advantage; and
(d) he dishonestly causes or allows that other person to fail to give a prompt notification of that change in the prescribed manner to the prescribed person.

(1C) This subsection applies where—
(a) there has been a change of circumstances affecting any entitlement of a person ('the claimant') to any benefit or other payment or advantage under any provision of the relevant social security legislation;
(b) the benefit, payment or advantage is one in respect of which there is another person ('the recipient') who for the time being has a right to receive payments to which the claimant has, or (but for the arrangements under which they are payable to the recipient) would have, an entitlement; and
(c) the change is not a change that is excluded by regulations from the changes that are required to be notified.

(1D) In a case where subsection (1C) above applies, the recipient is guilty of an offence if—
(a) he knows that the change affects an entitlement of the claimant to a benefit or other payment or advantage under a provision of the relevant social security legislation;
(b) the entitlement is one in respect of which he has a right to receive payments to which the claimant has, or (but for the arrangements under which they are payable to the recipient) would have, an entitlement; and
(c) he dishonestly fails to give a prompt notification of that change in the prescribed manner *to the prescribed person.*

(1E) In a case where that subsection applies, a person other than the recipient is guilty of an offence if—
 (a) he knows that the change affects an entitlement of the claimant to a benefit or other payment or advantage under a provision of the relevant social security legislation;
 (b) the entitlement is one in respect of which the recipient has a right to receive payments to which the claimant has, or (but for the arrangements under which they are payable to the recipient) would have, an entitlement; and
 (c) he dishonestly causes or allows the recipient to fail to give a prompt notification of that change in the prescribed manner to the prescribed person.

(1F) In any case where subsection (1C) above applies but the right of the recipient is confined to a right, by reason of his being a person to whom the claimant is required to make payments in respect of a dwelling, to receive payments of housing benefit—
 (a) a person shall not be guilty of an offence under subsection (1D) or (1E) above unless the change is one relating to one or both of the following—
  (i) the claimant's occupation of that dwelling;
  (ii) the claimant's liability to make payments in respect of that dwelling; but
 (b) subsections (1D)(a) and (1E)(a) above shall each have effect as if after 'knows' there were inserted 'or could reasonably be expected to know'.

(1G) For the purposes of subsections (1A) to (1E) above a notification of a change is prompt if, and only if, it is given as soon as reasonably practicable after the change occurs.

(2) [Repealed.]

Elements 'Dishonestly' in the Social Security Administration Act 1992, s. 111A, has its normal meaning in criminal offences (*Department for Work and Pensions v Courts* [2006] EWHC 1156 (Admin) at [3]). See now *Ivey v Genting Casinos (UK) Ltd* [2017] UKSC 67, [2018] AC 391; *Barton* [2020] EWCA Crim 575, especially at [84] and [105] and **B4.54** ***et seq***. In *Boaden* [2019] EWCA Crim 2284, the Court of Appeal decided that the jury needed no help in the judge's summing-up in that case on the meaning of the word 'dishonestly' (at [51]). **B16.60**

'Benefit' is defined in s. 191 as meaning benefit under the Social Security Contributions and Benefits Act 1992 and includes universal credit, state pension under Part 1 of the Pensions Act 2014, a jobseeker's allowance, state pension credit, an employment and support allowance, personal independence payment and bereavement support payment under the Pensions Act 2014, s. 30.

The prosecution must prove that D knew that the change of circumstances had to be notified (*Zorlu* [2009] EWCA Crim 589) and that any change which a person failed to report would (and not merely could or might) have affected an entitlement to benefit etc. (*King v Kerrier District Council* [2006] EWHC 500 (Admin); *Coventry City Council v Vassell* [2011] EWHC 1542 (Admin) at [32]–[35]; *Webster* [2013] EWCA Crim 1714 at [41]). A change of circumstances will not affect entitlement unless, upon computation, the entitlement to benefit would be altered by the change (*Croydon London Borough Council v Shanahan* [2010] EWCA Crim 98 at [18]); see also *Mote* [2007] EWCA Crim 313 at [81]–[94]. Thus in *Passmore* [2007] EWCA Crim 2053, [2008] 1 Cr App R 12 (165) it was held that D committed no offence by failing to disclose that he had formed a company from which he had received no income.

Where the change of circumstances relied upon by the prosecution is that D started to live together with someone as partners or as man and wife, the judge does not need to define 'living together' to the jury (*State* [2018] EWCA Crim 394).

Where the prosecution rely on the word 'allows' in s. 111A(1B), they must prove that D failed to take some action that could appropriately have been taken that would have resulted in the other person discharging the obligation to report (*Tilley* [2009] EWCA Crim 1426, [2010] 1 WLR 605).

The word 'prompt' in s. 111A is an ordinary word to be given its natural meaning. The question whether 'prompt notification' has been given is one of fact (*Coventry City Council v Vassell*

[2011] EWHC 1542 (Admin) at [37]–[39]). The burden is on the prosecution to allege and prove that notification was not prompt (*Taffs v Chelmsford Crown Court* [2014] EWHC 889 (Admin) at [28]).

False Representations for Obtaining Benefit, etc.

B16.61 Section 112 complements s. 111A with a range of purely summary offences. These largely mirror the offences created by s. 111A and require similar knowledge of relevant matters, but do not require proof of dishonesty.

Social Security Administration Act 1992, s. 112

(1) If a person for the purpose of obtaining any benefit or other payment under the [relevant social security legislation] whether for himself or some other person, or for any other purpose connected with that legislation—
  (a) makes a statement or representation which he knows to be false; or
  (b) produces or furnishes, or knowingly causes or knowingly allows to be produced or furnished, any document or information which he knows to be false in a material particular,
he shall be guilty of an offence.

(1A) A person shall be guilty of an offence if—
  (a) there has been a change of circumstances affecting any entitlement of his to any benefit or other payment or advantage under any provision of the relevant social security legislation;
  (b) the change is not a change that is excluded by regulations from the changes that are required to be notified;
  (c) he knows that the change affects an entitlement of his to such a benefit or other payment or advantage; and
  (d) he fails to give a prompt notification of that change in the prescribed manner to the prescribed person.

(1B) A person is guilty of an offence under this section if—
  (a) there has been a change of circumstances affecting any entitlement of another person to any benefit or other payment or advantage under any provision of the relevant social security legislation;
  (b) the change is not a change that is excluded by regulations from the changes that are required to be notified;
  (c) he knows that the change affects an entitlement of that other person to such a benefit or other payment or advantage; and
  (d) he causes or allows that other person to fail to give a prompt notification of that change in the prescribed manner to the prescribed person.

(1C) In a case where subsection (1C) of section 111A above applies, the recipient is guilty of an offence if—
  (a) he knows that the change affects an entitlement of the claimant to a benefit or other payment or advantage under a provision of the relevant social security legislation;
  (b) the entitlement is one in respect of which he has a right to receive payments to which the claimant has, or (but for the arrangements under which they are payable to the recipient) would have, an entitlement; and
  (c) he fails to give a prompt notification of that change in the prescribed manner to the prescribed person.

(1D) In a case where that subsection applies, a person other than the recipient is guilty of an offence if—
  (a) he knows that the change affects an entitlement of the claimant to a benefit or other payment or advantage under a provision of the relevant social security legislation;
  (b) the entitlement is one in respect of which the recipient has a right to receive payments to which the claimant has, or (but for the arrangements under which they are payable to the recipient) would have, an entitlement; and
  (c) he causes or allows the recipient to fail to give a prompt notification of that change in the prescribed manner to the prescribed person.

(1E) Subsection (1F) of section 111A above applies in relation to subsections (1C) and (1D) above as it applies in relation to subsections (1D) and (1E) of that section.

(1F) For the purposes of subsections (1A) to (1D) above a notification of a change is prompt if, and only if, it is given as soon as reasonably practicable after the change occurs.

Elements While the offences under the Social Security Administration Act 1992, s. 112, do not require proof of dishonesty, s. 112(1A)(d) is to be read as requiring the prosecution to prove a mental element of knowingly failing to notify (*Coventry City Council v Vassell* [2011] EWHC 1542 (Admin) at [50]–[70]). Moreover, any 'change of circumstance' must be proved to have affected an entitlement (see **B16.60**). As to the meaning of 'allows' and 'prompt', see also **B16.60**. **B16.62**

Related Offences The fraudulent evasion of an obligation to make social security contributions is dealt with under the Social Security Administration Act 1992, s. 114. Any person 'knowingly concerned in the fraudulent evasion of any contributions which he or any other person is liable to pay' may be sentenced on indictment to imprisonment for up to seven years; or on summary conviction to an unlimited fine. For the words 'knowingly concerned' and 'fraudulent evasion', see **B16.44** and **B16.47**. **B16.63**

Procedure

The DPP has published (on www.cps.gov.uk) guidelines for the prosecution of benefit fraud cases. In addition, procedural provisions relating to the prosecution of offences under the Social Security Administration Act 1992 are contained in s. 116. **B16.64**

Social Security Administration Act 1992, s. 116

(1) Any person authorised by the Secretary of State in that behalf may conduct any proceedings under any provision of this Act other than section 114 or under any provision of the Jobseekers Act 1995 before a magistrates' court although not a barrister or solicitor.

(2) Notwithstanding anything in any Act—

(a) proceedings for an offence under this Act (other than proceedings to which paragraph (b) applies) or for an offence under the Jobseekers Act 1995 may be begun at any time within the period of 3 months from the date on which evidence, sufficient in the opinion of the Secretary of State to justify a prosecution for the offence, comes to his knowledge or within a period of 12 months from the commission of the offence, whichever period last expires; and

(b) proceedings brought by the appropriate authority for an offence under this Act relating to housing benefit or council tax benefit may be begun at any time within the period of 3 months from the date on which evidence, sufficient in the opinion of the appropriate authority to justify a prosecution for the offence, comes to the authority's knowledge or within a period of 12 months from the commission of the offence, whichever period last expires.

(2A) Subsection 2 above shall not be taken to impose any restriction on the time when proceedings may be begun for an offence under section 111A above.

(3) For the purposes of subsection (2) above—

(a) a certificate purporting to be signed by or on behalf of the Secretary of State as to the date on which such evidence as is mentioned in paragraph (a) of that subsection came to his knowledge shall be conclusive evidence of that date; and

(b) a certificate of the appropriate authority as to the date on which such evidence as is mentioned in paragraph (b) of that subsection came to the authority's knowledge shall be conclusive evidence of that date.

For the running of time within which a prosecution must be brought under s. 116(2), see *Eyeson v Milton Keynes Council* [2005] EWHC 1160 (Admin) and *Smith v North Somerset Council* [2007] EWHC 1767 (Admin). A certificate under s. 116(3) is conclusive unless it is inaccurate on its face or fraudulent (*Azam v Epping Forest District Council* [2009] EWHC 3177 (Admin), but it must comply strictly with the statutory requirements (*R (Chesterfield Poultry Ltd) v Sheffield Magistrates' Court* [2019] EWHC 2953 (Admin), [2020] 1 Cr App R 26 (419) at [23]–[26]). The Secretary of State may delegate the power to issue a certificate under s. 116

to a lawyer or prosecutor (*Mohammed v Department for Work and Pensions* [2012] EWHC 4220 (Admin)).

A heavy burden has to be discharged to stay prosecutions on the ground of abuse of process (*Department of Work and Pensions v Courts* [2006] EWHC 1156 (Admin)).

B16.65 **Sentence** The maximum sentence for an offence under the Social Security Administration Act 1992, s. 111A, is (i) on indictment, seven years' imprisonment and/or, a fine and (ii) on summary conviction, six months' imprisonment and/or an unlimited fine. The maximum sentence for the offences under s. 112 is three months' imprisonment and/or an unlimited fine.

The definitive sentencing guideline, *Fraud, Bribery and Money Laundering Offences* (see Supplement, **SG26-4**), sets out guidance for sentencing for benefit fraud offences under s. 111A. The court is required to determine D's level of culpability and the harm, in monetary terms. Table 1 in the benefit fraud part of the guideline sets out starting points and ranges of sentences. Table 2 sets out starting points and ranges for sentences for offences under s. 112. The guideline applies to offenders aged 18 and over who are sentenced on or after 1 October 2014, regardless of the date of the offence.

B16.66 In *Pettigrew* [2012] EWCA Crim 1998 D, who had a serious record for dishonesty, pleaded guilty to offences of fraud, obtaining by deception and failing to notify a change of circumstances. The Court of Appeal observed (at [13]) that it was not particularly helpful to attempt slavishly to bring the combination of offences into particular categories in the previous guideline and that a broader view, with assistance from that guideline, needed to be taken. In *Turner* [2010] EWCA Crim 2897, [2011] 2 Cr App R (S) 18 (102) the Court of Appeal upheld a judge's departure from that guideline in a case of repeated false declarations by D who had substantial means.

In *Hedman* [2017] EWCA Crim 830 concurrent sentences of 15 months' imprisonment were imposed following conviction at trial for five offences which involved dishonestly obtaining £30,000 over a period of five years without notifying changes of circumstances. In *Johnson* [2015] EWCA Crim 626, D, aged 64, had obtained £33,000 in benefits during a period of over ten years. She pleaded guilty at a late stage to five counts under s. 111A of the Social Security Administration Act 1992. A sentence of seven months' immediate imprisonment was upheld.

B16.67 **Suspended Sentences** In considering whether to suspend a sentence of imprisonment for offences under s. 111A the court should consider the definitive sentencing guideline, *Imposition of Community and Custodial Sentences* (see Supplement, **SG9-1**); and where D is facing a first custodial sentence the court should give specific reasons if no pre-sentence report has been obtained (*Mehmet* [2019] EWCA Crim 1303 at [10] and [14]). In *Bonner* [2013] EWCA Crim 1534, *Taylor* [2013] EWCA Crim 1668 and *Brindley* [2014] EWCA Crim 1104, each decided under the previous guideline, immediate custodial sentences were, on the facts, upheld. By contrast, in *Vincent* [2017] EWCA Crim 333 the sentence of imprisonment was suspended in view of D's position as a carer and previous good character. In *Mehmet* (at [15]–[16]) the Court of Appeal, having received a pre-appeal report, suspended the sentence.

When a court suspends a sentence of imprisonment for an offence under s. 112, requirements may be imposed for a duration longer than the three-month maximum term of imprisonment. In *Hale* [2013] EWCA Crim 2491 the Court of Appeal upheld a four-month night-time home curfew requirement.

Section B17 Offences Involving Misuse of Computers

UNAUTHORISED ACCESS OFFENCE ('HACKING')

Computer Misuse Act 1990, s. 1 **B17.1**

(1) A person is guilty of an offence if—
- (a) he causes a computer to perform any function with intent to secure access to any program or data held in any computer;
- (b) the access he intends to secure is unauthorised; and
- (c) he knows at the time when he causes the computer to perform the function that that is the case.

(2) The intent a person has to have to commit an offence under this section need not be directed at—
- (a) any particular program or data;
- (b) a program or data of any particular kind; or
- (c) a program or data held in any particular computer.

Procedure and Sentence

B17.2 The maximum penalty on indictment is imprisonment for a term not exceeding two years or a fine, or both (s. 1(3)(c)). On summary conviction, the maximum sentence is imprisonment for a term not exceeding six months or an unlimited fine, or both (s. 1(3)(a)). For cases giving some guidance on sentencing for offences under the Computer Misuse Act 1990, see **B17.15**.

Actus Reus

B17.3 The *actus reus* of the offence requires the accused to 'cause a computer to perform any function'. This is meant to exclude mere physical contact with a computer and the scrutiny of data without any interaction with a computer (thus the reading of confidential computer output, the reading of data displayed on the screen, or 'computer eavesdropping', are not covered). On the other hand there is no requirement that D should succeed in obtaining access to the program or data, or be successful in subverting computer security measures in place. A remote hacker would, thus, 'cause a computer to perform any function' if the hacker accessed it remotely and the computer responded, for example, by activating a computer security device or by offering a log-on menu. The substantive offence is thus drafted in such a way as to include conduct which might usually be thought to fall within the scope of the law of attempt. Secondary liability may arise where, for example, a person supplies a hacker with helpful information, such as a confidential computer password. The operator of a computer hacker 'bulletin board' might, therefore, come within the reach of the offence. The words 'any computer' in s. 1(1)(a) entail that the offence is not restricted to a case where D uses one computer to gain unauthorised access to the target computer. Instead, an offence may be committed when a person causes a computer to perform a function that grants the person unauthorised access to any program or data held within that same computer (*A-G's Ref (No. 1 of 1991)* [1993] QB 94). For a review of the s. 1 offence, see

Bow Street Metropolitan Stipendiary Magistrate, ex parte Government of the USA [2000] 1 Cr App R 61 per Lord Hobhouse at p. 72.

B17.4 The access to the program or data which D intends to secure must be 'unauthorised' access (s. 1(1)(b)). In *DPP v Bignell* [1998] 1 Cr App R 1, the Divisional Court held that the s. 1 offence was not committed where police officers, for private purposes, instructed a computer operator to extract details of two cars from a police computer. This was because the officers were entitled to access the computer, albeit only for legitimate police purposes. Astill J commented that the Act was designed to criminalise 'breaking into computer systems', and noted that misuse of the data once obtained was not covered by the Act but might constitute an offence under the Data Protection Act 1984, s. 5(2)(b) (which was then in force), and this clearly influenced the Divisional Court in holding that the conduct lay outside the 1990 Act. The decision in *Bignell* is open to criticism on the ground that, on an ordinary construction of language, authorising a person's access for one (legitimate) purpose ought not to be regarded as authorising the person's access for another (non-legitimate) purpose (see, by analogy, the burglary case of *Jones* [1976] 3 All ER 54 at **B4.88**). The authority of *Bignell* is undermined by the decision of the House of Lords in *Bow Street Metropolitan Stipendiary Magistrate, ex parte Government of the USA* [2000] 1 Cr App R 61. In that case one Allison, an employee of American Express, was authorised to access certain client accounts to check matters relating to credit. It was alleged that she in fact obtained access to other accounts and passed on confidential details to accomplices who were able to forge credit cards and obtain large sums of money. The issue was whether Allison could be extradited from England to the USA and the House of Lords, reversing the decision of the Divisional Court, held that she could. Lord Hobhouse had no difficulty in finding that the alleged conduct of Allison fell within the provisions of s. 1. His lordship held the Divisional Court in *Bignell* to have wrongly interpreted the concept of 'entitlement to control' in s. 17(5) of the 1990 Act as though it related to control of the computer. In fact, it concerned the ability to authorise certain individuals to access specific data on the computer. His lordship pointed out that the Divisional Court had fallen into error in asking itself whether D had authority to access data of that general kind, a mistake also made by the same court in the instant case. The correct question (applying the wording of s. 1 and s. 17(5)(a)) was whether the officers had authority to access the *actual data* involved. Even so, Lord Hobhouse thought that the outcome in *Bignell* was 'probably right'. It was distinguishable from the instant case because the police officers in *Bignell* had instructed the (innocent) computer operator to access the data. The access had been made by that person, and he had not exceeded his authority in doing so. It seems that in the circumstances there had been no 'unauthorised access', and hence an essential element of the *actus reus* was missing.

Mens Rea

B17.5 There are two limbs to the *mens rea* of the offence. The first limb is the 'intent to secure access to any program or data held in any computer'. The word 'any' makes it clear that the intent need not relate to the computer which the accused is at that time operating. The Computer Misuse Act 1990, s. 1(2), explains that D's intent need not be directed at any particular program or data, so as to include the hacker who accesses a computer without any clear idea of what will be found there. Recklessness is insufficient; still less would careless or inattentive accessing of the computer suffice for liability. The second limb is that D must know at the time of causing the computer to perform the function that the access which D intends to secure is unauthorised. The prosecution must prove both limbs.

No Public Interest Defence

B17.6 In *Coltman* [2018] EWCA Crim 2059, [2019] 2 Cr App R (S) 35 (432) D, a NHS employee, used the computer of a colleague to access a file to which he had no authorised access. The material from that file was later passed by D to a newspaper. D was charged with the offence under the Computer Misuse Act 1990, s. 1. In his defence statement D said that he had disclosed the material because it was in the public interest to do so. The Court of Appeal considered an interlocutory appeal on the issue of whether the 1990 Act should be read so as to allow for a potential 'public interest' defence. The Court held that nothing in the ECHR, Article 10, required a public interest defence to be read into s. 1 of the Act (see also **A7.56**). See, by contrast, the offence under the Data Protection Act 2018, s. 170 (at **B17.23**) where such a defence is clearly available.

Definitions

Computer Misuse Act 1990, s. 17 **B17.7**

(1) The following provisions of this section apply for the interpretation of this Act.
(2) A person secures access to any program or data held in a computer if by causing a computer to perform any function he—
    (a) alters or erases the program or data;
    (b) copies or moves it to any storage medium other than that in which it is held or to a different location in the storage medium in which it is held;
    (c) uses it; or
    (d) has it output from the computer in which it is held (whether by having it displayed or in any other manner);

    and references to access to a program or data (and to an intent to secure such access) shall be read accordingly.
(3) For the purposes of subsection (2)(c) above a person uses a program if the function he causes the computer to perform—
    (a) causes the program to be executed; or
    (b) is itself a function of the program.
(4) For the purposes of subsection (2)(d) above—
    (a) program is output if the instructions of which it consists are output; and
    (b) the form in which any such instructions or any other data is output (and in particular whether or not it represents a form in which, in the case of instructions, they are capable of being executed or, in the case of data, it is capable of being processed by a computer) is immaterial.
(5) Access of any kind by any person to any program or data held in a computer is unauthorised if—
    (a) he is not himself entitled to control access of the kind in question to the program or data; and
    (b) he does not have consent to access by him of the kind in question to the program or data from any person who is so entitled,

    but this subsection is subject to section 10.
(6) References to any program or data held in a computer include references to any program or data held in any removable storage medium which is for the time being in the computer; and a computer is to be regarded as containing any program or data held in any such medium.
(7) [Repealed.]
(8) An act done in relation to a computer is unauthorised if the person doing the act (or causing it to be done)
    (a) is not himself a person who has responsibility for the computer and is entitled to determine whether the act may be done; and
    (b) does not have consent to the act from any such person.

    In this subsection 'act' includes a series of acts.

The terms 'computer', 'data' and 'program' are not defined in the Computer Misuse Act 1990 and should, therefore, be given their ordinary meaning by the courts. Section 10 of the Act deals with access to computer material for law enforcement purposes.

UNAUTHORISED ACCESS OFFENCE WITH INTENT TO COMMIT FURTHER OFFENCES

Computer Misuse Act 1990, s. 2 **B17.8**

(1) A person is guilty of an offence under this section if he commits an offence under section 1 above ('the unauthorised access offence') with intent—
    (a) to commit an offence to which this section applies; or
    (b) to facilitate the commission of such an offence (whether by himself or by any other person);

and the offence he intends to commit or facilitate is referred to below in this section as the further offence.

(2) This section applies to offences—
(a) for which the sentence is fixed by law; or
(b) for which a person of 21 years of age or over (not previously convicted) may be sentenced to imprisonment for a term of five years (or, in England and Wales, might be so sentenced but for the restrictions imposed by section 33 of the Magistrates' Courts Act 1980).

(3) It is immaterial for the purposes of this section whether the further offence is to be committed on the same occasion as the unauthorised access offence or on any future occasion.

(4) A person may be guilty of an offence under this section even though the facts are such that the commission of the further offence is impossible.

Procedure and Sentence

B17.9 Section 2 of the Computer Misuse Act 1990 creates an offence triable either way. The maximum penalty on indictment is five years' imprisonment or a fine, or both (s. 2(5)(c)). The maximum penalty summarily is six months' imprisonment or an unlimited fine, or both (s. 2(5)(a)). For cases giving some guidance on sentencing for offences under the Computer Misuse Act 1990, see **B17.15**.

Elements

B17.10 The offence under s. 2 of the Computer Misuse Act 1990 is committing the unauthorised access offence under s. 1 (see **B17.1**) with intent to commit or facilitate the commission of a more serious 'further' offence. It is not necessary to prove that the intended further offence has actually been committed.

A person will be guilty of an offence under s. 2 in a range of situations. Obtaining the unauthorised access may, for example, be done with the intention of committing theft, such as by diverting funds, which are in the course of an electronic funds transfer, to D's own bank account, or to the bank account of an accomplice. It would also cover the case where D gained unauthorised access to sensitive information held on computer with a view to blackmailing the person to whom that information related.

Section 2(2) explains what qualifies as a further offence for the purposes of the s. 2 offence. Section 2(3) makes clear that D may intend to commit the further offence on the same occasion as the unauthorised access offence (as in the theft example just given) or on a future occasion (as in the blackmail example). Section 2(4) makes it possible to convict a person who intended to commit the further offence even if, on the facts, that would be impossible (e.g., where the intended blackmail victim was, unknown to the accused, dead). This rule is analogous to that in the Criminal Attempts Act 1981, s. 1(2), as applied in *Shivpuri* [1987] AC 1. See **A5.84**.

UNAUTHORISED ACTS WITH INTENT TO IMPAIR OPERATION OF COMPUTER ETC.

B17.11 **Computer Misuse Act 1990, s. 3**

(1) A person is guilty of an offence if—
(a) he does any unauthorised act in relation to a computer;
(b) at the time when he does the act he knows that it is unauthorised; and
(c) either subsection (2) or subsection (3) below applies.

(2) This subsection applies if the person intends by doing the act—
(a) to impair the operation of any computer;
(b) to prevent or hinder access to any program or data held in any computer;
(c) to impair the operation of any such program or the reliability of any such data.

(3) This subsection applies if the person is reckless as to whether the act will do any of the things mentioned in paragraphs (a) to (c) of subsection (2) above.

(4) The intention referred to in subsection (2) above, or the recklessness referred to in sub- section (3) above, need not relate to—
(a) any particular computer;
(b) any particular program or data; or
(c) a program or data of any particular kind.
(5) In this section—
(a) a reference to doing an act includes a reference to causing an act to be done;
(b) 'act' includes a series of acts;
(c) a reference to impairing, preventing or hindering something includes a reference to doing so temporarily.

Section 3 is an offence triable either way. The maximum penalty on indictment is imprisonment for a term not exceeding ten years or a fine, or both (s. 3(6)(c)). The maximum penalty summarily is imprisonment for a term not exceeding six months or an unlimited fine, or both (s. 3(6)(a)). **B17.12**

The effect of s. 3 is that a person commits an offence by performing any unauthorised act in relation to a computer, knowing it to be unauthorised, if the person intends by doing the act to do one of the things set out in s. 3(2), or is reckless as to whether by doing the act one of the things set out in s. 3(2) will be done.

When read in the context of the Computer Misuse Act 1990, s. 17 (see **B17.7**), it is clear that a wide range of different forms of conduct are included by s. 3. It covers all cases involving deliberate or reckless impairment of a computer's operation, preventing or hindering access to computer material by a legitimate user or impairing the operation or reliability of computer-held material. One form of the s. 3 offence would be the sending of a virus or malware to V's computer. D must know that the act was unauthorised.

In *DPP v Lennon* [2006] EWHC 1202 (Admin) the Divisional Court held that an offence under the substituted s. 3 was committed where a former employee of a company, acting on a grudge, impaired the operation of the company's computer by using a program to generate and send five million emails to the company. The Court rejected a defence argument under s. 17(8)(b) that the owner of a computer set up to receive emails must be taken to have consented to the sending of emails. It was held that such implied consent was not without limits and the owner could not be taken to consent to multiple emails being sent for the purpose of swamping the computer system. The Divisional Court was considering s. 17(8)(b) before its amendment in 2006 but its reasoning remains helpful to understanding the offence.

In *Zezev v Governor of HM Prison Brixton* [2002] EWHC 589 (Admin), [2002] 2 Cr App R 33 (515), it was held that an offence was committed under the substituted s. 3 where the accused placed on the files of another person's computer a bogus email which purported to come from a person who had not sent it. It does not have to be proved that D had any specific target computer, program or data in mind.

UNAUTHORISED ACTS CAUSING, OR CREATING RISK OF, SERIOUS DAMAGE

Computer Misuse Act 1990, s. 3ZA **B17.13**

(1) A person is guilty of an offence if—
(a) the person does any unauthorised act in relation to a computer;
(b) at the time of doing the act the person knows that it is unauthorised;
(c) the act causes, or creates a significant risk of, serious damage of a material kind; and
(d) the person intends by doing the act to cause serious damage of a material kind or is reckless as to whether such damage is caused.
(2) Damage is of a 'material kind' for the purposes of this section if it is—
(a) damage to human welfare in any place;
(b) damage to the environment of any place;

(c) damage to the economy of any country; or
(d) damage to the national security of any country.

(3) For the purposes of subsection (2)(a) an act causes damage to human welfare only if it causes—
(a) loss to human life;
(b) human illness or injury;
(c) disruption of a supply of money, food, water, energy or fuel;
(d) disruption of a system of communication;
(e) disruption of facilities for transport, or
(f) disruption of services relating to health

(4) It is immaterial for the purposes of subsection (2) whether or not an act causing damage—
(a) does so directly;
(b) is the only or main cause of the damage.

(5) In this section—
(a) a reference to doing an act includes a reference to causing an act to be done;
(b) 'act' includes a series of acts;
(c) a reference to a country includes a reference to a territory, and to any place in, or part or region of, a country or territory.

The SCA 2015, s. 41(2), inserted s. 3ZA with effect from 3 May 2015 (SI 2015 No. 820). This appears to be an aggravated form of the s. 3 offence. Section 3ZA is an offence triable only on indictment, punishable with imprisonment for a term not exceeding 14 years or a fine, or both. The sentencing powers of the court are greater if the offence is committed as a result of an act causing or creating a significant risk of (i) serious damage to human welfare of the kind mentioned in s. 3ZA(3)(a); or (ii) serious damage to national security, in which case the offence is punishable with imprisonment for life or a fine, or both (s. 3ZA(6) and (7)). The damage may occur, or be intended or risked to occur, in any country for the s. 3ZA offence to be established (s. 3ZA(2)).

Section 3ZA is designed to ensure that UK law is fully compliant with Directive 2013/40/EU on attacks against information systems ([2013] OJ L218/8). According to the explanatory notes issued alongside the SCA 2015, s. 3ZA is designed to cater for computer misuse where the damage is to, for example, critical national infrastructure and where the maximum penalty of ten years under s. 3 may be inadequate.

MAKING, SUPPLYING OR OBTAINING ARTICLES FOR USE IN OFFENCES UNDER s. 1 OR 3

B17.14 **Computer Misuse Act 1990, s. 3A**

(1) A person is guilty of an offence if he makes, adapts, supplies or offers to supply any article intending it to be used to commit, or to assist in the commission of, an offence under section 1, 3 or 3ZA.

(2) A person is guilty of an offence if he supplies or offers to supply any article believing that it is likely to be used to commit, or to assist in the commission of, an offence under section 1, 3 or 3ZA.

(3) A person is guilty of an offence if he obtains any article —
(a) intending to use it to commit, or to assist in the commission of, an offence under section 1, 3 or 3ZA, or
(b) with a view to its being supplied for use to commit, or to assist in the commission of, an offence under section 1, 3 or 3ZA.

(4) In this section 'article' includes any program or data held in electronic form.

Section 3A creates three offences triable either way, each punishable, on conviction on indictment, with imprisonment for a term not exceeding two years and/or a fine and, on summary conviction, with six months and/or an unlimited fine (s. 3A(5)). The SCA 2015, ss. 41(3) and 42, amended s. 3A with effect from 3 May 2015 (SI 2015 No. 820).

It is clear that the reason for the creation of this offence is to criminalise the market in electronic 'hacker tools' used for breaking into, or compromising, computer systems. The three offences under s. 3A are divisible into offences of 'making' (s. 3A(1)), 'supplying' (s. 3A(1) and (2)), and 'obtaining' (s. 3A(3)) such tools.

According to guidance notes published with the Police and Justice Act 2006, if D is charged with an offence under s. 3A(2) in relation to a quantity of articles, the prosecution would need to prove their case in relation to any particular one or more of those articles, but it would not be enough to prove that D believed that a certain proportion of the articles was likely to be used in connection with an offence under s. 1, 3 or 3ZA. In the offence under s. 3A(2) the relevant *mens rea* is 'belief' — by analogy with the offence of handling stolen goods it is submitted that mere suspicion would not be enough (see **B4.180**).

SENTENCING FOR OFFENCES UNDER THE COMPUTER MISUSE ACT 1990

There are no sentencing guidelines for offences under the Computer Misuse Act 1990. A number of earlier cases were considered in *Mangham* [2012] EWCA Crim 973, [2013] 1 Cr App R (S) 11 (62), where D pleaded guilty to offences under ss. 1 and 3. He had hacked into Facebook's computer and accessed and downloaded source code, which compromised confidential corporate information but not personal data. Facebook investigated and remedied the damage, which cost $200,000. A sentence of four months' imprisonment was appropriate. Cranston J said (at [19]) that aggravating features in computer misuse cases would be (i) whether the offence was planned or persistent, (ii) nature of the damage caused to the system and to the wider public interest, (iii) motive (including revenge) and extent of gain by the offender and (iv) whether the information had been passed on to others. The value of the intellectual property involved may also be relevant to sentencing. Among the mitigating factors D's psychological profile would be important. **B17.15**

In *Martin* [2013] EWCA Crim 1420, [2014] 1 Cr App R (S) 63 (414) the Court of Appeal dealt with a 21-year-old offender with a record of dishonesty offences, who pleaded guilty to five offences under s. 3 of the Act, one offence under s. 2, one offence under s. 1, and two offences under s. 3A. The total sentence of two years' imprisonment was upheld, together with a deprivation order under the PCC(S)A 2000, s. 143, in relation to various IT equipment. D had launched denial of service attacks on two university websites. Some two weeks of labour were expended to repair the damage he had done. Three days later he launched a similar attack on a police force website. Other illegal activity admitted involved the obtaining of bank account and other personal details on a named individual, requiring that individual to cancel his bank cards and change his passwords. A list of further potential targets was found at his home address. Leveson LJ said that the offences fell into the highest level of culpability, being carefully planned and targeted. The prevalence of computer crime, and its potential to cause enormous damage, cannot be understated. His lordship said that *Mangham* [2012] EWCA Crim 973, [2013] 1 Cr App R (S) 11 (62) should not be considered a benchmark for such cases, which are now likely to attract considerably longer sentences. For offending on the scale of *Martin*, sentences will be measured in years rather than months.

In *Mudd* [2017] EWCA Crim 1395, [2018] 1 Cr App R (S) 7 (33) D, who was aged between 16 and 18 over the course of the offending, admitted offences under ss. 1 and 3 of the Act and a further offence of concealing criminal property. He had devised a distributed denial of service program (DDoS) which he used himself and also sold to others. In total, 1.7 million DDoS attacks were launched at over half a million individual IP addresses or domain names. D received around £250,000 total payment for the program supplied. The judge considered pre-sentence, psychological and psychiatric reports, which agreed that D was autistic. Given the scale of the offending, and despite personal mitigation, the judge imposed a sentence of detention in a young offender institution for two years. The Court of Appeal upheld the custodial sentence but reduced it to 21 months. In *Needham* [2019] EWCA Crim 1541, the Court of Appeal upheld a total sentence of two years where D, aged 36, was convicted of offences under ss. 1 and 2 of the Act. The ex-employee, motivated by revenge, accessed his former firm's computers and deleted client accounts from its servers. Suspicion initially fell upon another employee; the financial loss was £500,000 and nine people lost their jobs as a result. The Court said that the judge had properly considered all relevant matters including D's mental health problems.

In *R (Pensions Regulator) v Workchain Ltd* [2019] EWCA Crim 1422 D was a corporate recruitment agency which provided temporary workers for business clients. The corporation was required to enrol eligible workers into a pension scheme, but steps were taken by company officers posing as workers to access online accounts to opt out of the scheme. The Pensions Regulator prosecuted the matter under the Computer Misuse Act 1990, s. 1. Suspended sentences and community orders were imposed on the company officers, who all pleaded guilty. The Court of Appeal reduced a fine of £200,000 imposed on the company itself to one of £100,000 to properly reflect the guilty pleas, and commented that loss of confidence in the integrity of the workplace pension scheme and the associated IT systems was likely to be a crucial head of harm, rather than just the financial gain to the company or the loss to the employees affected.

In some serious cases involving misuse of information held on police computers, offenders have been prosecuted for misconduct in public office (see **B15.26**) rather than for an offence under the 1990 Act. See, for example, *Kassim* [2005] EWCA Crim 1020, [2006] 1 Cr App R (S) 4 (12); *O'Leary* [2007] EWCA Crim 186, [2007] 2 Cr App R (S) 51 (317); *Lewis* [2010] EWCA Crim 496, [2010] 2 Cr App R (S) 104 (666) and *Wilkie* [2012] EWCA Crim 247, [2012] 2 Cr App R (S) 68 (393).

JURISDICTIONAL PROVISIONS

B17.16 Liability for offences under the Computer Misuse Act 1990, under ss. 1, 3 or 3ZA, requires proof of at least one 'significant link' with the 'home country concerned' which for the purposes of English law means England and Wales. By ss. 4 and 5, this link is satisfied where D was in England and Wales when the act in question was committed. Alternatively, it is satisfied where the targeted computer was situated in England and Wales. For territorial jurisdiction generally, see **A8.2**.

In contrast, s. 4(3) enables a s. 2 offence to be committed entirely abroad, provided that the 'further offence' would itself fall within English jurisdiction. If that offence is itself an extra-territorial offence, there need be no connection with England and Wales at all.

Section 4(4), read in conjunction with s. 8(1), applies s. 2 to cases in which the 'further offence' is an offence only under a foreign system of law, but would have qualified as a further offence within the meaning of s. 2(2) if committed within England and Wales. This applies only where the underlying s. 1 offence *does* have a significant link with England and Wales. For example, it would cover a case in which a defendant in England gains unauthorised access to a computer in France, with a view to committing a crime under French law that would have been punishable with imprisonment for five years or more if committed by an adult in England and Wales.

B17.17 **Computer Misuse Act 1990, ss. 4 and 5**

4.—(1) Except as provided below in this section, it is immaterial for the purposes of any offence under section 1, 3 or 3ZA above—

(a) whether any act or other event proof of which is required for conviction of the offence occurred in [England and Wales]; or

(b) whether the accused was in [England and Wales] at the time of any such act or event.

(2) Subject to subsection (3) below, in the case of such an offence at least one significant link with domestic jurisdiction must exist in the circumstances of the case for the offence to be committed.

(3) There is no need for any such link to exist for the commission of an offence under section 1 above to be established in proof of an allegation to that effect in proceedings for an offence under section 2 above.

(4) Subject to section 8 below, where—
(a) any such link does in fact exist in the case of an offence under section 1 above; and
(b) commission of that offence is alleged in proceedings for an offence under section 2 above;
section 2 above shall apply as if anything the accused intended to do or facilitate in any place outside [England and Wales] which would be an offence to which section 2 applies if it took place in [England and Wales] were the offence in question.
(4A) It is immaterial for the purposes of an offence under section 3A whether the accused was in the home country concerned at the time of any act or other event proof of which is required for conviction of the offence if there is a significant link with domestic jurisdiction in relation to the offence.
5.—(1) The following provisions of this section apply for the interpretation of section 4 above.
(1A) In relation to an offence under section 1, 3, 3ZA or 3A, where the accused was in a country outside the United Kingdom at the time of the act constituting the offence there is a significant link with domestic jurisdiction if—
(a) the accused was United Kingdom national at the time; and
(b) the act constituted an offence under the law of the country in which it occurred.
(1B) In subsection (1A)—
'country' includes territory;
'United Kingdom national' means an individual who is—
(a) a British citizen, a British overseas territories citizen, a British National (Overseas) or a British Overseas citizen;
(b) a person who under the British Nationality Act 1981 is a British subject; or
(c) a British protected person within the meaning of that Act.
(2) In relation to an offence under section 1, either of the following is a significant link with domestic jurisdiction—
(a) that the accused was in [England and Wales] at the time when he did the act which caused the computer to perform the function; or
(b) that any computer containing any program or data to which the accused by doing that act secured or intended to secure unauthorised access, or enabled or intended to enable unauthorised access to be secured, was in [England and Wales] at that time.
(3) In relation to an offence under section 3, either of the following is a significant link with domestic jurisdiction—
(a) that the accused was in [England and Wales] at the time when he did the unauthorised act (or caused it to be done); or
(b) that the unauthorised act was done in relation to a computer in [England and Wales].
(3A) In relation to an offence under section 3ZA, any of the following is also a significant link with domestic jurisdiction—
(a) that the accused was in the home country concerned at the time when he did the unauthorised act (or caused it to be done);
(b) that the unauthorised act was done in relation to a computer in the home country concerned;
(c) that the unauthorised act caused, or created a significant risk of, serious damage of a material kind (within the meaning of that section) in the home country concerned.

Sections 4 and 5 were amended by the SCA 2015, s. 43, with effect from 3 May 2015 (SI 2015 No. 820), by the insertion of ss. 4(4A) and 5(1A), (1B) and (3A). According to the explanatory notes issued alongside the SCA 2015, the effect of s. 5(1A) and (1B) is to permit prosecution of a UK national for any offence under the 1990 Act even where the conduct concerned has *no* other significant link to the UK, provided also that the offence was an offence in the country *where it took place*.

JURISDICTION OVER CONSPIRACY AND ATTEMPT

Section 6 of the Computer Misuse Act 1990 makes special provision for jurisdiction over inchoate offences of computer misuse, as does the CAA 1981, s. 1(1A) and (1B); but in practice, s. 1(1A) and (1B) are of no conceivable use to prosecutors, for the same reason that s. 1A of that Act is of no use: see **A5.82**. **B17.18**

Computer Misuse Act 1990, s. 6

(1) On a charge of conspiracy to commit an offence under this Act, the following questions are immaterial to the accused's guilt—
(a) the question where any person became a party to the conspiracy; and
(b) the question whether any act, omission or other event occurred in the home country concerned.
(2) On a charge of attempting to commit an offence under this Act the following questions are immaterial to the accused's guilt—
(a) the question where the attempt was made; and
(b) the question whether it had an effect in the home country concerned.

EVIDENCE OF FOREIGN LAW

B17.19 **Computer Misuse Act 1990, s. 8**

(1) A person is guilty of an offence triable by virtue of section 4(4) above only if what he intended to do or facilitate would involve the commission of an offence under the law in force where the whole or any part of it was intended to take place.
(2) [Repealed.]
(3) A person is guilty of an offence triable by virtue of section 1(1A) of the Criminal Attempts Act 1981 only if what he had in view would involve the commission of an offence under the law in force where the whole or any part of it was intended to take place.
(4) Conduct punishable under the law in force in any place is an offence under that law for the purposes of this section, however it is described in that law.
(5) Subject to subsection (7) below, a condition specified in [subsection (1) or (3)] above shall be taken to be satisfied unless not later than rules of court may provide the defence serve on the prosecution a notice—
(a) stating that, on the facts as alleged with respect to the relevant conduct, the condition is not in their opinion satisfied;
(b) showing their grounds for that opinion; and
(c) requiring the prosecution to show that it is satisfied.
(6) In subsection (5) above 'the relevant conduct' means—
(a) where the condition in subsection (1) above is in question, what the accused intended to do or facilitate;
(b) [Repealed.]
(c) where the condition in subsection (3) above is in question, what the accused had in view.
(7) The court, if it thinks fit, may permit the defence to require the prosecution to show that the condition is satisfied without the prior service of a notice under subsection (5) above.
(8) [Scotland.]
(9) In the Crown Court the question whether the condition is satisfied shall be decided by the judge alone.

OFFENCES UNDER THE DATA PROTECTION ACT 2018

B17.20 The Data Protection Act 1998 was largely repealed and replaced by the Data Protection Act 2018, which received Royal Assent on 23 May 2018. The 2018 Act sets new standards for protecting data in accordance with the General Data Protection Regulation (Regulation (EU) 2016/679 [2016] OJ L119/1, or 'GDPR'). The GDPR has been effective since 25 May 2018.

The 2018 Act generally updates pre-existing offences under the 1998 Act, introduces new data protection offences and contributes to the codification of the modern data protection regime. Definition of terms, scope and exemptions are set out at ss. 1 to 28. Principles of data protection and rights of the data subject are set out at ss. 34 to 42 and ss. 43 to 48 respectively. The obligations placed on data controllers and processors are set out at ss. 55 to 71. Controls on the *transfer of data to a third country or international* organisation, including by law enforcement authorities, are set out at ss. 72 to 78. Provisions concerning national security certificates and the reporting of infringements on the rights of data subjects are set out at ss. 79 to 81. The statutory authority and functions of the Information Commissioner ('ICO') are set out at ss. 114 to 141.

Following the departure of the UK from the EU, at the end of the transition period (31 December 2020) the GDPR is to be incorporated into UK domestic law under the European Union (Withdrawal) Act 2018 and the Data Protection, Privacy and Electronic Communications (Amendments) (EU Exit) Regulations (SI 2019 No. 419). The GDPR will become the UKGDPR.

Procedure

Proceedings for any criminal offence under the Act may be brought only by the ICO, or with the consent of the DPP (s. 197). Proceedings may be brought under the Act against a director, manager, secretary or similar officer, as well as the body corporate, where it is proved that breaches of the Act have occurred with the consent, connivance, or negligence of that person (s. 198). Certain offences under the Act are triable only summarily (s. 196(1)) while others are triable either way (s. 196(2)). **B17.21**

Data Processing Offences

The 2018 Act creates three new offences of potentially wide application: the knowing or reckless obtaining or disclosure of personal data without the consent of the controller (s. 170); the knowing or reckless re-identification of information that was previously de-identified (s. 171); and the alteration or concealment of information that should have been provided in response to a data subject access request, and in a way that prevents all or part of its disclosure (s. 173). **B17.22**

The s. 170 and s. 171 offences are triable either way (s. 196(2)). The s. 173 offence is summary only (s. 196(1)). Proceedings for an offence under s. 173 may be brought within six months of the day on which the prosecutor first knew of evidence that was sufficient to bring the proceedings. Proceedings are barred after the end of the period of three years from the date the offence was committed (s. 197(3) and (4)).

Other indictable offences under the 2018 Act are to be found in s. 132 (prohibiting the current or former ICO, or a member of the ICO's staff, from knowingly or recklessly disclosing confidential information without lawful authority), s. 144 (intentionally or recklessly making a false statement in response to an information notice), s. 148 (destroying or falsifying information and documents which are the subject of an information notice) and s. 184 (prohibiting employers from requiring that employees or contractors provide records obtained via subject access requests as a pre-condition of their employment or contract).

Relevant summary offences are to be found in s. 119 (obstructing an inspection by the ICO of personal data, where such inspection is necessary to discharge an international obligation, or failing without reasonable excuse to give any assistance that may be required with such an inspection) and sch. 15, para. 15 (obstructing the execution of a warrant).

All of the above data protection offences are recordable (s. 199).

Unlawful Obtaining etc. of Personal Data

Data Protection Act 2018, s. 170 **B17.23**

(1) It is an offence for a person knowingly or recklessly—
  (a) to obtain or disclose personal data without the consent of the controller,
  (b) to procure the disclosure of personal data to another person without the consent of the controller, or
  (c) *after obtaining* personal data, to retain it without the consent of the person who was the controller in relation to the personal data when it was obtained.

(2) It is a defence for a person charged with an offence under subsection (1) to prove that the obtaining, disclosing, procuring or retaining—
  (a) was necessary for the purposes of preventing or detecting crime,
  (b) was required or authorised by an enactment, by a rule of law or by the order of a court or tribunal, or
  (c) in the particular circumstances, was justified as being in the public interest.

(3) It is also a defence for a person charged with an offence under subsection (1) to prove that—
(a) the person acted in the reasonable belief that the person had a legal right to do the obtaining, disclosing, procuring or retaining,
(b) the person acted in the reasonable belief that the person would have had the consent of the controller if the controller had known about the obtaining, disclosing, procuring or retaining and the circumstances of it, or
(c) the person acted—
(i) for the special purposes,
(ii) with a view to the publication by a person of any journalistic, academic, artistic or literary material, and
(iii) in the reasonable belief that in the particular circumstances the obtaining, disclosing, procuring or retaining was justified as being in the public interest.
(4) It is an offence for a person to sell personal data if the person obtained the data in circumstances in which an offence under subsection (1) was committed.
(5) It is an offence for a person to offer to sell personal data if the person—
(a) has obtained the data in circumstances in which an offence under subsection (1) was committed, or
(b) subsequently obtains the data in such circumstances.
(6) For the purposes of subsection (5), an advertisement indicating that personal data is or may be for sale is an offer to sell the data.
(7) In this section—
(a) references to the consent of a controller do not include the consent of a person who is a controller by virtue of Article 28(10) of the GDPR or section 59(8) or 105(3) of this Act (processor to be treated as controller in certain circumstances);
(b) where there is more than one controller, such references are references to the consent of one or more of them.

The s. 170 offence may be established even if the data in question was originally lawfully obtained. For example, employees who are granted access to the lawfully obtained data of their employer's clients may commit the s. 170 offence by recklessly or knowingly disclosing that data without the consent of the data controllers. In *Shepherd v Information Commissioner* [2019] EWCA Crim 2 the Court of Appeal commented (*obiter*) that the defences set out in s. 170(2) clearly imposed a legal burden of proof upon the defence. The Court expressed no view on whether the provision is compatible with the defendant's ECHR, Article 6, rights.

The s. 170 offence builds on s. 55 of the 1998 Act. There have been no reported authorities that assist in understanding how the higher courts approach the sentencing exercise in respect of s. 170. It can, however, be assumed that sentencing authorities concerning the s. 55 offence are of assistance. In *Rooney* [2006] EWCA Crim 1841, D was convicted of two counts of unlawfully obtaining, and one count of unlawfully disclosing, personal data in breach of s. 55 of the 1998 Act. The offender had used her employment by Staffordshire Police to access private information about one police officer for personal reasons. She was found guilty and fined £700.

Sentence

B17.24 The enforcement of the Act is set out at ss. 142 to 181. Offences under the Act are punishable by way of a penalty notice issued by the ICO (s. 155). The penalty is an unlimited fine (s.196(1) and (2)). There is as yet no authoritative guidance on the appropriate level of fines for those convicted of offences under the Act. The court may order the forfeiture and destruction of material that was obtained as a result of offences, or used in connection with their commission (s. 196(4)). Any individual other than D having an interest in that data or material has the right to demonstrate to the court why it should not order forfeiture or destruction (s. 196(5)).

Section B18 Offences Involving Writing, Speech or Publication

PUBLISHING, OR HAVING FOR PUBLICATION FOR GAIN, AN OBSCENE ARTICLE

Definition

Obscene Publications Act 1959, s. 2 **B18.1**

(1) Subject as hereinafter provided, any person who, whether for gain or not, publishes an obscene article or who has an obscene article for publication for gain (whether gain to himself or gain to another) shall be liable . . .

Procedure

Offences under the Obscene Publications Act 1959, s. 2(1), are triable either way. When tried on indictment they are normally class 3 offences, but see CrimPD XIII, para. B (see Supplement, **CPD.XIII.B**), for the additional factors that the court considers on allocation. A prosecution must not be commenced more than two years after the commission of the offence (s. 2(3)). The CPS issued revised guidance in January 2019 (see tinyurl.com/y6mbm7lo) in relation to obscene publications including guidance on the provisions of the Obscene Publications Act 1959 Act generally, 'and in particular on how prosecutors should approach the question of obscenity' (see especially the revised guidance under the heading 'Evidential considerations'). **B18.2**

Where the article in question is a moving picture film of width 16mm or more, and the publication in question is by an exhibition of a film as defined in the Licensing Act 2003, then proceedings may not be instituted except by, or with the consent of, the DPP (Obscene Publications Act 1959, s. 2(3A)).

The Obscene Publications Act 1959, s. 2(4), provides that 'A person publishing an article shall not be proceeded against for an offence at common law consisting of the publication of any matter contained or embodied in the article where it is of the essence of the offence that the matter is obscene'. Subsection (4A) makes similar provision in respect of a film exhibition as defined in the Cinemas Act 1985. The rationale for these provisions was to prevent evasion by the prosecution of the defences available under the 1959 Act by charging the common-law offence of publishing an obscene libel, which has been abolished. Section 2(4) never did technically apply to the common-law offence of conspiracy to corrupt public morals since such a conspiracy does not consist of publication within s. 2(4) but rather the *agreement* to corrupt public morals by publishing (*Shaw v DPP* [1962] AC 220). The law officers, however, gave undertakings to Parliament in 1964 (*Parliamentary Debates (Hansard), House of Commons*, 3 June 1964, col. 1212) that conspiracy to corrupt public morals would not be used so as to circumvent the defences available under s. 4 of the 1959 Act. On the other hand, there is a separate offence at common law of outraging public decency (see **B3.350**), and conspiracy to do so, and this, it was held in *Gibson* [1990] 2 QB 619, is not barred by s. 2(4), even though in that case the offence involved the publication of an article (a human foetus earring) which was, in a loose sense, obscene. The article was not likely to deprave or corrupt and was therefore not obscene within the meaning of the 1959 Act and thus was **B18.3** not covered by s. 2(4). The Court of Appeal therefore upheld the convictions for outraging public decency.

For conspiracy to outrage public decency and conspiracy to corrupt public morals, see **A5.43**.

Indictment (for Offence of Having for Gain)

B18.4 *Statement of Offence*

Having an obscene article for publication for gain, contrary to section 2(1) of the Obscene Publications Act 1959.

Particulars of Offence

A on or about the... day of... had an obscene article, namely... for publication for gain to himself or another.

Sentence

B18.5 The maximum penalty is five years' imprisonment and/or a fine on indictment; six months' imprisonment and/or an unlimited fine summarily (Obscene Publications Act 1959, s. 2(1)). There is no offence-specific guideline but the Sentencing Council's *General Guideline: Overarching Principles* (see Supplement, **SG2-1**) is used for all offenders sentenced on or after 1 October 2019.

A number of Court of Appeal decisions deal with sentencing for offences in relation to obscene publications. In *Holloway* (1982) 4 Cr App R (S) 128, where D had been selling pornographic books, films and tapes on a commercial scale, Lawton LJ indicated that fines for such offending were simply added to the costs for future consumers and did little to deter the trade. Immediate custodial sentences should be imposed on those involved in any capacity in commercial exploitation of obscene material, with fines reserved for those whose involvement was inadvertent or non-commercial.

B18.6 A case towards the top end of the scale is *Snowden* [2009] EWCA Crim 1200, [2010] 1 Cr App R (S) 39 (233), where 30 months' imprisonment following a guilty plea was upheld. D was found to be in possession of some 55 DVDs categorised as obscene within the terms of the 1959 Act. Several involved scenes of sexual activity with animals. The offender admitted copying and distributing the DVDs to paying customers.

Custodial sentences of six months were approved in *Doorgashurn* (1988) 10 Cr App R (S) 195 and *Knight* (1990) 12 Cr App R (S) 319 where, in both cases, shopkeepers kept obscene books and video tapes for sale as part of their general trade. A fine of £2,000 was also imposed in the latter case. In *Knight*, Wright J regarded it as a significant aggravating factor that children's comics were for sale in the shop and that children could and sometimes did see the obscene material which was on display. Three months' imprisonment was appropriate in *Pace* [1998] 1 Cr App R (S) 121 where D worked as a 'front man' in a shop selling pornographic videos, and was convicted in respect of possession of one tape. The Court of Appeal indicated the continuing relevance of the guidelines in *Holloway*.

Meaning of 'Obscenity'

B18.7 **Obscene Publications Act 1959, s. 1**

(1) For the purposes of this Act an article shall be deemed to be obscene if its effect or (where the article comprises two or more distinct items) the effect of any one of its items is, if taken as a whole, such as to tend to deprave and corrupt persons who are likely, having regard to all relevant circumstances, to read, see or hear the matter contained or embodied in it.

Although this does not purport to be an exhaustive definition of obscenity, it is the only definition which counts for the purposes of the Act and the judge must not leave the jury with the impression that it is sufficient if the article is obscene in the ordinary sense of being 'filthy', 'loathsome' or 'lewd' (*Anderson* [1972] 1 QB 304). It is the tendency to deprave and corrupt which is important. This can refer merely to the effect on the mind in terms of stimulating fantasies and it is not necessary that physical or overt sexual activity should result (*DPP v Whyte*

[1972] AC 849). Indeed obscenity is not necessarily concerned with sexual depravity but has included in the past material advocating drug taking or violence (*John Calder (Publications) Ltd v Powell* [1965] 1 QB 509; *Calder and Boyars Ltd* [1969] 1 QB 151).

The persons likely to be depraved or corrupted need not be wholly innocent to begin with: the further corruption of the less innocent is also included. Nor is it necessary that all those likely to read, see or hear the article should be corrupted. It is sufficient that the article should tend to deprave or corrupt a significant proportion of them. This may be much less than 50 per cent but must not be numerically negligible (*DPP v Whyte* [1972] AC 849). However, where publication has been only to one person, the tendency to deprave and corrupt (or to further deprave and corrupt) that one person is sufficient (*GS* [2012] EWCA Crim 398, [2012] 1 WLR 3368).

It is the effect of the publication by D that counts (that is, the effect on persons likely to read, see or hear the article as a result of *that* publication) rather than the effect of publication by anyone else, 'unless it could reasonably have been expected that the publication by the other person would follow from publication by the person charged' (Obscene Publications Act 1959, s. 2(6)). **B18.8**

The fact that there are other materials in circulation which are as obscene as, or which are not materially different from, the articles in question is not of itself relevant nor does it render the articles in question acceptable. The jury should apply the standards of 'ordinary, decent right-minded people' to the actual articles before them (*Elliott* [1996] 1 Cr App R 432).

Admittedly shocking, disgusting and outrageous material may not be obscene if instead of tending to encourage, it would have precisely the opposite effect (per Salmon LJ in *Calder and Boyars Ltd* [1969] 1 QB 151 at p. 169) — a limitation on the meaning of obscenity approved by the Court of Appeal in *Anderson* [1972] 1 QB 304 as the 'aversion argument'.

See further on the meaning of obscenity the CPS revised guidance (2019) on obscene publications, and in particular the revised guidance under 'Evidential considerations' which includes an indication of conduct which 'will not likely fall to be prosecuted under the Act' provided that it meets four considerations relating to consent, lack of serious harm, not otherwise inextricably linked with other criminality, and likely audience not under 18 or otherwise vulnerable.

Meaning of 'Article'

The term 'article' is defined in the Obscene Publications Act 1959, s. 1(2), as 'any description of article containing or embodying matter to be read or looked at or both, any sound record, and any film or other record of a picture or pictures'. A video cassette is within s. 1(2) (*A-G's Ref (No. 5 of 1980)* [1981] 3 All ER 816). **B18.9**

Articles which are not themselves to be read or looked at or listened to are still treated as within s. 1(2) if they are 'intended to be used... for the reproduction or manufacture therefrom of articles containing or embodying matter to be read, looked at or listened to' (Obscene Publications Act 1964, s. 2(1), which thus now makes it clear that, for example, a photographic negative would be an article within the Obscene Publications Act 1959, s. 1(2), even if it was not itself to be looked at but merely used for producing prints). See also *Fellows* [1997] 1 Cr App R 244 (images held on computer disk in digitised form).

An 'article' may be regarded as a single item (e.g., a novel as in *Penguin Books* [1961] Crim LR 176), in which case, in assessing whether it has a tendency to deprave and corrupt, the jury should look at the effect of the article as a whole rather than at the effect in isolation of specific passages within it. However, an article may comprise a number of items (as in the case of the magazine in *Anderson* [1972] 1 QB 304); each item must then be judged individually and it is sufficient if the effect of any one of the items, taken as a whole, is to tend to deprave and corrupt. In *Anderson* [1972] 1 QB 304, Lord Widgery CJ said (at p. 312):

> A novelist who writes a complete novel and who cannot cut out particular passages without destroying the theme of the novel is entitled to have his work judged as a whole, but a magazine publisher

who has a far wider discretion as to what he will and will not insert by way of items is to be judged under the 1959 Act on what we call the item to item basis.

In *Goring* [1999] Crim LR 670, one film was treated as containing a number of distinct items, and whether a particular film is to be judged as a whole or on an item by item basis is a question of law for the judge.

Role of Expert Evidence

B18.10 Expert evidence is not admissible on the question whether an article is obscene since that is a matter for the jury. However, where the subject-matter of an article is beyond the experience of the ordinary person, such as the characteristics and effects of cocaine and the methods of ingesting it, expert evidence is admissible to inform the jury about that subject-matter. It then remains a matter entirely for the jury, armed with this information, whether an article advocating the taking of cocaine has a tendency to deprave or corrupt (*Skirving* [1985] QB 819). In contrast, where an article is concerned with sexual activity, the jury need no special information to assess that activity before proceeding to the question of whether the article itself is obscene.

Where the persons likely to be depraved or corrupted are members of a special class, such as primary schoolchildren, there may be a special rule allowing expert evidence on the likely effect of unusual material on them if a jury cannot be expected to understand the likely impact of the material without assistance (*DPP v A & BC Chewing Gum Ltd* [1968] 1 QB 159). However, it still remains, even in this 'highly exceptional' (*Anderson* [1972] 1 QB 304 at p. 313) type of case, for the jury to decide whether the factual effect should be classified as depraving or corrupting, and expert evidence would not be admissible on that issue.

As to expert evidence generally, see **F11**, especially **F11.16**.

Meaning of 'Publication'

B18.11 **Obscene Publications Act 1959, s. 1**

(3) For the purposes of this Act a person publishes an article who—
  (a) distributes, circulates, sells, lets on hire, gives, or lends it, or who offers it for sale or for letting for hire; or
  (b) in the case of an article containing or embodying matter to be looked at or a record, shows, plays or projects it, or, where the matter is data stored electronically, transmits that data.

(4) For the purposes of this Act a person also publishes an article to the extent that any matter recorded on it is included by him in a programme included in a programme service.

(5) Where the inclusion of any matter in a programme so included would, if that matter were recorded matter, constitute the publication of an obscene article for the purposes of this Act by virtue of subsection (4) above, this Act shall have effect in relation to the inclusion of that matter in that programme as if it were recorded matter.

(6) In this section 'programme' and 'programme service' have the same meaning as in the Broadcasting Act 1990.

In *Taylor* [1995] 1 Cr App R 131, the Court of Appeal held that a photographic developer, who develops a film sent by customers depicting obscene acts and who makes prints as requested and sends the prints back to those customers, publishes the prints by way of selling or distributing them. Even if there was only one customer to whom the print was sold, that would still be a publication, as is now confirmed in *GS* [2012] EWCA Crim 398, [2012] 2 Cr App R 14 (154), where it was explicitly decided that there can be publication to a single recipient (in this case not of photographic prints but of data—obscene paedophile comments—via internet relay chat).

The concluding words of s. 1(3)(b) relating to the transmission of electronically stored data were added by the CJPO 1994, sch. 9, para. 3, and were applied in *Waddon* [2000] All ER (D) 502 to the transmission of obscene images to a web site in the USA and then back again to a subscriber in the UK, which constituted publication within the jurisdiction. It seems from *Perrin* [2002]

EWCA Crim 747 that it is immaterial where the major steps to set up a web site are taken; it is the availability of the web pages within the jurisdiction that constitutes evidence of publication within s. 1(3)(b). See also *Sheppard* [2010] EWCA Crim 65, [2010] 2 All ER 850 and **A8.5**. In *GS* the publication was not the chat logs themselves but the logs were evidence of the 'comments that the defendant had typed and transmitted to the other party to the chat' so it seems that the act which transmits the data can be simultaneous with the act which stores the data electronically rather than the data having to be stored previously and then subsequently transmitted.

Having an Obscene Article for Publication for Gain

This form of the offence was added by the Obscene Publications Act 1964, s. 1(1), to deal with limitations on the publication form of the offence, notably that displaying an obscene article in a shop window does not amount to offering it for sale (*Mella v Monahan* [1961] Crim LR 175) and that supplying to a supposedly non-corruptible person (e.g., a police officer) may not be a publication tending to deprave or corrupt anyone (*Clayton* [1963] 1 QB 163). **B18.12**

By s. 1(2) of the 1964 Act 'a person shall be deemed to have an article for publication for gain if with a view to such publication he has the article in his ownership, possession or control'. Thus a person having obscene articles for sale in sex shops (cf. *O'Sullivan* [1995] 1 Cr App R 455) 'has' them '*for* publication for gain' even though the person may not yet have technically offered them for sale and actually published them in that sense. Since the provision deals with prospective publication rather than actual publication, s. 1(3)(b) of the 1964 Act provides that:

> . . . the question whether the article is obscene shall be determined by reference to such publication for gain of the article as in the circumstances it may reasonably be inferred he had in contemplation and to any further publication that could reasonably be expected to follow from it, but not to any other publication.

In a case such as *O'Sullivan*, the original prospective publication which it may reasonably be inferred D had in contemplation would be the sale in a sex shop, and the further publication that may reasonably be expected to follow from it (note the absence here of any reference to reasonably inferring *D's contemplation*) might (or might not, depending on the circumstances) include such matters as further circulation, lending, selling or showing the article by the original purchaser from the sex shop. The jury then must consider the tendency to deprave and corrupt as a result of those prospective publications. The Court of Appeal in *O'Sullivan* thought that the complexity of the direction to the jury necessitated by this provision and its relationship with the provisions of the Obscene Publications Act 1959 was such that the judge would be best advised to follow the order of the statutory provisions without attempting to improve upon them or to redefine the wording of the Acts. If a judge had any doubts about the proposed direction, the judge ought to commit it to writing and invite comment from counsel before they made their final speeches.

Things (such as negatives) from which obscene articles are to be made for publication but which things are not themselves to be published are deemed by s. 2(2) of the 1964 Act to be had for publication.

Defence of Having No Reasonable Cause to Suspect

Under the Obscene Publications Act 1959, s. 2(5), it is a defence for D to prove that 'he had not examined the article in respect of which he is charged' and that he 'had no reasonable cause to suspect that it was such that his publication of it would make him liable to be convicted of an offence under this section'. **B18.13**

This defence applies where the form of the alleged offence is publishing. Where the alleged offence is having for publication for gain, the Obscene Publications Act 1964, s. 1(3)(a), provides a similar defence except that it refers to 'no reasonable cause to suspect that it was such that his having it would make him liable'.

Defence of Public Good

B18.14 **Obscene Publications Act 1959, s. 4**

(1) Subject to subsection (1A) of this section a person shall not be convicted of an offence against section 2 of this Act... if it is proved that publication of the article in question is justified as being for the public good on the ground that it is in the interests of science, literature, art or learning, or of other objects of general concern.

Under s. 4(1A) the defence of public good does not apply to moving picture films or soundtracks but in relation to such articles there is instead a defence of public good 'on the ground that it is in the interests of drama, opera, ballet or any other art, or of literature or learning'. Section 4(2) declares 'that the opinion of experts as to the literary, artistic, scientific or other merits of an article may be admitted in any proceedings under this Act either to establish or to negative the said ground'. The issue of public good arises only if the article is first shown to be obscene and the expert evidence authorised by s. 4(2) is only admissible in relation to whether the article is in the interests of science, literature, art etc. and not in relation to whether the article is obscene in the first place. This should be pointed out to the jury (*A-G's Ref (No. 3 of 1977)* [1978] 3 All ER 1166). In *DPP v Jordan* [1978] AC 699, Lord Wilberforce said (at p. 719):

> The judgment to be reached under section 4(1) and the evidence to be given under section 4(2) must be in order to show that publication should be permitted in spite of obscenity—not to negative obscenity.

B18.15 The jury need some explanation of their task under s. 4, and should not be left, as was said in *Calder and Boyars Ltd* [1969] 1 QB 151 at p. 172, 'to sink or swim in its dark waters'. The Court of Appeal went on to say that the jury should consider:

> ...on the one hand, the number of readers they believe would tend to be depraved and corrupted by the book, the strength of the tendency to deprave and corrupt and the nature of the depravity or corruption. On the other hand they should assess the strength of the literary, sociological or ethical merit which they consider the book to possess. They should then weigh up all these factors and decide whether on balance the publication is proved to be justified as being for the public good.

It is for the jury to decide the issue of public good, the evidence of the experts going merely to the literary merits etc. which the jury then have to balance against the admitted obscenity of the article (*Penguin Books* [1961] Crim LR 176).

The phrase 'other objects of general concern' in s. 4(1) refers to objects falling within the same area as those specifically mentioned there, namely science, literature, art or learning, and thus expert evidence that obscene material is psychologically beneficial to persons with certain sexual tendencies in that it would relieve their sexual tensions and might divert them from antisocial activities is inadmissible (*DPP v Jordan* [1977] AC 699). On the other hand, the ethical merits of a book do come within 'other merits' in s. 4(2) and expert evidence on that issue is admissible (*Penguin Books*).

The word 'learning' in s. 4(1) is a noun and means the product of scholarship, rather than being a verb encompassing teaching. Expert evidence that obscene articles have merit for the purposes of sex education, or value in teaching or providing information about sexual matters, is not admissible because such matters are not in the interests of 'learning' as that word is used in s. 4(1) (*A-G's Ref (No. 3 of 1977)* [1978] 3 All ER 1166).

Search, Seizure and Forfeiture

B18.16 Section 3 of the Obscene Publications Act 1959 empowers a justice of the peace to issue a warrant for the search and seizure of obscene articles kept for publication for gain. A warrant which authorised a search for 'any other material of a sexually explicit nature' is on the face of it bad since such articles are not necessarily obscene (*Darbo v DPP* [1991] Crim LR 56).

The CJA 1967, s. 25, requires that the information must be laid by, or on behalf of, the DPP, or by a constable. The articles must then be brought before a justice of the peace who may issue a summons to the occupier of the premises from where the articles were seized to show cause why the articles should not be forfeited. See *Olympia Press Ltd v Hollis* [1973] 1 All ER 108 and RTH Stone, 'Obscene Publications: the problems persist' [1986] Crim LR 139 for discussion of the procedure. The defence of public good under s. 4(1) applies to the procedure under s. 3. So also does s. 2(2) of the Obscene Publications Act 1964 deeming negatives etc. to be had or kept for publication even though not themselves to be published. By virtue of the Prosecution of Offences Act 1985, s. 3(2)(d), it is the duty of the DPP to take over the conduct of any proceedings commenced by summons under the Obscene Publications Act 1959, s. 3. Section 3 (and, no doubt, the offence of having for publication for gain) applies equally to articles kept for publication abroad as it does to articles kept for publication in England and Wales (*Gold Star Publications Ltd v DPP* [1981] 2 All ER 257).

OBSCENE PERFORMANCES OF PLAYS

The obscene *performance* of a play, being unlike the written script of the play a transient thing, cannot amount to an article within the Obscene Publications Act 1959. Nor, it seems, does the performance of an obscene play amount to the publication of its script. However, the Theatres Act 1968, s. 2(2), makes it an offence 'if an obscene performance of a play is given, whether in public or private'. The offence is committed by 'anyone who (whether for gain or not) presented or directed' the performance and the penalties are the same as under the Obscene Publications Act 1959 (see **B18.1**), which is also echoed in the definition of obscenity (Theatres Act 1968, s. 2(1); cf. **B18.7**), in the time-limit of two years for prosecution (s. 2(3); cf. **B18.2**), the exclusion of proceedings at common law in respect of the performance of a play (s. 2(4)) and the defence of public good (s. 3, cf. **B18.14**). Section 7 of the Theatres Act 1968 contains a number of exceptions to the offence under s. 2 including the performance of a play given on a domestic occasion in a private dwelling, and s. 18 contains interpretation provisions explaining, *inter alia*, what is a play and who is, and who is not, to be treated as a presenter or director. **B18.17**

INDECENT DISPLAYS

Definition

Indecent Displays (Control) Act 1981, s. 1 **B18.18**

(1) If any indecent matter is publicly displayed the person making the display and any person causing or permitting the display to be made shall be guilty of an offence.

Procedure

Offences under the Indecent Displays (Control) Act 1981, s. 1(1), are, by s. 4(1) of the Act, triable either way. When tried on indictment they are normally class 3 offences, but see CrimPD XIII, para. B (see Supplement, **CPD.XIII.B**), for the additional factors that the court considers on allocation. **B18.19**

Sentence

The maximum penalty is two years and/or a fine on indictment; an unlimited fine summarily (Indecent Displays (Control) Act 1981, s. 4(1)). **B18.20**

Meaning of 'Indecent'

It seems clear that something can be indecent for the purposes of the Indecent Displays (Control) Act 1981 without being obscene for the purposes of the Obscene Publications Act 1959 (*Stanley* [1965] 2 QB 327, decided under the Post Office Act 1953, s. 11 — posting obscene or indecent matter). There is no defence of public good to a charge under the Indecent Displays (Control) Act 1981, s. 1(1). Section 1(5) provides that, in determining whether any displayed matter is indecent, '(a) there shall be disregarded any part of that matter which is not exposed to view'. **B18.21**

This underlines the fact that the offence is only concerned with that which is publicly displayed, so this is one occasion where one can judge a book (or magazine or any other article) by its cover. On the other hand, in assessing indecency, 'account may be taken of the effect of juxtaposing one thing with another' (s. 1(5)(b)).

Meaning of 'Matter'

B18.22 'Matter' includes 'anything capable of being displayed, except that it does not include an actual human body or any part thereof' (Indecent Displays (Control) Act 1981, s. 1(5)). By s. 1(2), 'Any matter which is displayed in or so as to be visible from any public place shall, for the purposes of this section, be deemed to be publicly displayed'.

Meaning of 'Public Place'

B18.23

Indecent Displays (Control) Act 1981, s. 1

(3) In subsection (2) above, 'public place', in relation to the display of any matter, means any place to which the public have or are permitted to have access (whether on payment or otherwise) while that matter is displayed except—
- (a) a place to which the public are permitted to have access only on payment which is or includes payment for that display; or
- (b) a shop or any part of a shop to which the public can only gain access by passing beyond an adequate warning notice;

but the exclusions contained in paragraphs (a) and (b) above shall only apply where persons under the age of 18 years are not permitted to enter while the display in question is continuing.

Section 1(6) sets out minimum requirements with which an adequate warning notice must comply.

Exclusions

B18.24 Section 1(4) of the Indecent Displays (Control) Act 1981 contains a number of exclusions for matter:

- (a) included in a television broadcasting service or other television programme service (as defined in the Broadcasting Act 1990), or
- (b) displayed in an art gallery or museum and only visible from within the gallery or museum, or
- (c) displayed by or with the authority of, and visible only from within a building occupied by, the Crown or a local authority, or
- (d) included in a performance of a play (as defined in the Theatres Act 1968) or a film exhibition (as defined in the Cinemas Act 1985).

OTHER OFFENCES

Sending Indecent etc. Articles through Post

B18.25

Postal Services Act 2000, s. 85

(3) A person commits an offence if he sends by post a postal packet which encloses—
- (a) any indecent or obscene print, painting, photograph, lithograph, engraving, cinematograph film or other record of a picture or pictures, book, card or written communication, or
- (b) any other indecent or obscene article (whether or not of a similar kind to those mentioned in paragraph (a)).

(4) A person commits an offence if he sends by post a postal packet which has on the packet, or on the cover of the packet, any words, marks or designs which are of an indecent or obscene character.

This offence is triable either way. The maximum penalty is 12 months and/or a fine on indictment; an unlimited fine summarily.

Whether something is 'obscene' under this section does not depend on the person or persons to whom the packet is addressed, but is to be determined using an objective test, regardless of the addressees (*Kosmos Publications Ltd v DPP* [1975] Crim LR 345; see also *Stanley* [1965] 2 QB 327; *Stamford* [1972] 2 QB 391; *Kirk* [2006] EWCA Crim 725).

Unsolicited Publications

Unsolicited Goods and Services Act 1971, s. 4 **B18.26**

(1) A person shall be guilty of an offence if he sends or causes to be sent to another person any book, magazine or leaflet (or advertising material for any such publication) which he knows or ought reasonably to know is unsolicited and which describes or illustrates human sexual techniques.
(2) A person found guilty of an offence under this section shall be liable on summary conviction to [an unlimited fine].
(3) A prosecution for an offence under this section shall not in England and Wales be instituted except by, or with the consent of, the DPP.

The sending of advertising material may be an offence even if that material does not itself describe or illustrate human sexual techniques (*DPP v Beate Uhse Ltd* [1974] QB 158).

Improper Use of Public Electronic Communications Network

Communications Act 2003, s. 127 **B18.27**

(1) A person is guilty of an offence if he—
 (a) sends by means of a public electronic communications network a message or other matter that is grossly offensive or of an indecent, obscene or menacing character; or
 (b) causes any such message or matter to be so sent.
(2) A person is guilty of an offence if, for the purpose of causing annoyance, inconvenience or needless anxiety to another, he—
 (a) sends by means of a public electronic communications network, a message that he knows to be false,
 (b) causes such a message to be sent; or
 (c) persistently makes use of a public electronic communications network.
(3) A person guilty of an offence under this section shall be liable, on summary conviction, to imprisonment for a term not exceeding six months or to [an unlimited fine], or to both.
(4) Subsections (1) and (2) do not apply to anything done in the course of providing a programme service (within the meaning of the Broadcasting Act 1990).

The CJCA 2015, s. 51, added s. 127(5) to (7), which extend the time-limits for taking proceedings under s. 127.

The term 'public electronic communications network' is defined in the 2003 Act, Part 2, ch. 1. **B18.28**
Messages (or 'tweets') on Twitter which are communicated and are accessible via the internet are covered (*Chambers v DPP* [2012] EWHC 2157 (Admin), [2013] 1 All ER 149). Programme services (excluded by s. 127(4)) are covered by the Obscene Publications Act 1959 (see **B18.11**). As to the meaning of *grossly* offensive under s. 127(1), see *DPP v Collins* [2006] UKHL 40, [2006] 4 All ER 602, where it was held by the House of Lords, contrary to the findings of the magistrates, that telephone messages sent to an MP about immigration and asylum issues (referring to 'Wogs', 'Pakis', 'Black bastards' and 'Niggers') were grossly offensive, irrespective of the actual reaction of the particular recipients. The offence is complete as soon as the message is sent (even if to an inanimate object, the answering machine in this case; see also *R (Chabloz) v CPS* [2019] EWHC 3094 (Admin), [2020] 1 Cr App R 17 (290) where the upload of a video to YouTube by D with the intention that people might view it was sufficient). The test for being grossly offensive was said in *DPP v Collins* to be (at [10]) whether the message is 'couched in terms liable to cause gross offence to those to whom it relates' (not necessarily the recipients). Although intention or awareness of the grossly offensive nature of the message was required, Lord Bingham said (at [12]) that:

> . . . a culpable state of mind will ordinarily be found where a message is couched in terms showing an intention to insult those to whom the message relates or giving rise to the inference that a risk of doing so must have been recognised by the sender.

Lord Carswell concluded (at [22]) that:

> ... the messages would be regarded as grossly offensive by reasonable persons in general, judged by the standards of an open and just multiracial society. The terms used were opprobrious and insulting, and not accidentally so. I am satisfied that reasonable citizens, not only members of the ethnic minorities referred to by the terms, would find them grossly offensive.

Lord Brown of Eaton-under-Heywood recognised (at [26]–[27]) that a conversation in these terms between two racists, neither of whom were offended, would be caught since the speakers would certainly know that the grossly offensive terms used were insulting to those to whom they applied and the section was intended to protect the integrity of the public communication system. The possible implications for certain types of telephone chat lines, given that the section also refers to messages of an obscene or indecent character, were expressly left open for another day.

In *Chambers v DPP* the meaning of 'menacing character' was considered. A 'tweet' intended to be a joke (and treated as such by all who read it), about blowing up an airport if it did not reopen by the time D was intending to travel the following week, was not of such character since it did not 'create fear or apprehension in those to whom it is communicated, or who may reasonably [be] expected to see it'. Quite apart from the absence of this *actus reus* requirement, on the facts, the mental element of this variation of the offence would further require (consistently with *DPP v Collins*) proof that D intended that the message should be of a menacing character or that D was aware of or recognised the risk at the time of sending the message 'that it may create fear or apprehension in any reasonable member of the public who reads or sees it'.

Chambers v DPP led to the DPP issuing guidelines as to the approach to be taken to the prosecution of communications sent on social media. The guidance was updated on the CPS web site on 21 August 2018 and includes a section on 'revenge pornography' (see **B18.31**).

In *Karsten v Wood Green Crown Court* [2014] EWHC 2900 (Admin), the meaning of menaces discussed in *Chambers* was applied in allowing an appeal against conviction (based on the only communication in which D was found to have been involved). The words used 'were nasty and anti-Semitic' but not 'menacing in the sense demanded by *Chambers v DPP*' (Cranston J at [19]). The words used seem to have fallen between two stools as being offensive, but not grossly offensive and not (in isolation) menacing. As Laws LJ put it (at [21]):

> The Crown Court found that the words were not grossly offensive; they were certainly offensive: a nasty, malicious anti-Semitic comment of which the appellant should be thoroughly ashamed, but they were not menacing. The courts need to be very careful not to criminalise speech which, however contemptible, is no more than offensive. It is not the task of the criminal law to censor offensive utterances.

B18.29 Under the Penalties for Disorderly Behaviour (Amount of Penalty) Order 2002 (SI 2002 No. 1837), an offence under s. 127 is a fixed penalty offence and the amount payable is £90.

The revised *Magistrates' Court Sentencing Guidelines* (see Supplement, **SG10-61**) apply in respect of the sentencing of offenders aged 18 and older who are sentenced on or after 24 April 2017 in relation to s. 127(1) and (2) of the Communications Act 2003.

Indecent or Offensive or Threatening Letters etc.

B18.30 **Malicious Communications Act 1988, s. 1**

(1) Any person who sends to another person—
  (a) a letter, electronic communication or article of any description which conveys—
    (i) a message which is indecent or grossly offensive;
    (ii) a threat; or
    (iii) information which is false and known or believed to be false by the sender; or
  (b) any article or electronic communication which is, in whole or part, of an indecent or grossly offensive nature,

is guilty of an offence if his purpose, or one of his purposes, in sending it is that it should, so far as falling within paragraph (a) or (b) above, cause distress or anxiety to the recipient or to any other person to whom he intends that it or its contents or nature should be communicated.

(2) A person is not guilty of an offence by virtue of subsection (1)(a)(ii) above if he shows—
(a) that the threat was used to reinforce a demand made by him on reasonable grounds; and
(b) that he believed, and had reasonable grounds for believing, that the use of the threat was a proper means of reinforcing the demand.

(2A) In this section 'electronic communication' includes—
(a) any oral or other communication by means of an electronic communications network; and
(b) any communication (however sent) that is in electronic form.

(3) In this section references to sending include references to delivering or transmitting and to causing to be sent, delivered or transmitted or delivered and 'sender' shall be construed accordingly.

By virtue of amendments made to s. 1 by the CJCA 2015, s. 32, the offence is triable either way. The maximum penalty is two years' imprisonment and/or a fine on indictment; six months and/or an unlimited fine on summary conviction (s. 1(4) to (6)). There is no offence-specific guideline but the Sentencing Council's *General Guideline: Overarching Principles* (see Supplement, **SG2-1**) is used for all offenders sentenced on or after 1 October 2019.

The terms of s. 1 were considered in *Connolly v DPP* [2007] EWHC 237 (Admin), [2008] 1 WLR 276. 'Indecent or grossly offensive' were said to be ordinary English words and thus it was impossible to say that the court below was not entitled to conclude that 'shocking and disturbing' close-up photographs of aborted foetuses and of an abortion were grossly offensive. They were intended to cause distress and anxiety to those who received them and the fact that there was also a political or educational motive behind D's actions was of no avail. Furthermore, to the extent that D was exercising her rights under the ECHR, Articles 9 and 10, to freedom of speech or religion in sending the material, the restriction on those rights effected by the criminal prosecution was justified under Articles 9(2) and 10(2) as being necessary for the protection of the rights of others, namely the rights of the employees of the three pharmacies who were in receipt of the photographs.

Disclosing Private Sexual Photographs and Films with Intent to Cause Distress

Definition **B18.31**

Criminal Justice and Courts Act 2015, s. 33

(1) It is an offence for a person to disclose a private sexual photograph or film if the disclosure is made—
(a) without the consent of an individual who appears in the photograph or film, and
(b) with the intention of causing that individual distress.

(2) But it is not an offence under this section for the person to disclose the photograph or film to the individual mentioned in subsection (1)(a) and (b).

(3) It is a defence for a person charged with an offence under this section to prove that he or she reasonably believed that the disclosure was necessary for the purposes of preventing, detecting or investigating crime.

(4) It is a defence for a person charged with an offence under this section to show that—
(a) the disclosure was made in the course of, or with a view to, the publication of journalistic material, and
(b) he or she reasonably believed that, in the particular circumstances, the publication of the journalistic material was, or would be, in the public interest.

(5) It is a defence for a person charged with an offence under this section to show that—
(a) he or she reasonably believed that the photograph or film had previously been disclosed for reward, whether by the individual mentioned in subsection (1)(a) and (b) or another person, and
(b) he or she had no reason to believe that the previous disclosure for reward was made without the consent of the individual mentioned in subsection (1)(a) and (b).

(6) A person is taken to have shown the matters mentioned in subsection (4) or (5) if—
(a) sufficient evidence of the matters is adduced to raise an issue with respect to it, and
(b) the contrary is not proved beyond reasonable doubt.
(7) For the purposes of subsections (1) to (5)—
(a) 'consent' to a disclosure includes general consent covering the disclosure, as well as consent to the particular disclosure, and
(b) 'publication' of journalistic material means disclosure to the public at large or to a section of the public.
(8) A person charged with an offence under this section is not to be taken to have disclosed a photograph or film with the intention of causing distress merely because that was a natural and probable consequence of the disclosure.

B18.32 **Procedure and Sentence** The offence is triable either way. The maximum penalty is two years' imprisonment and/or a fine on indictment; six months and/or an unlimited fine on summary conviction (s. 33(9), (11) and (12)). The Sentencing Council definitive guideline, *Intimidatory Offences* (see Supplement, **SG27-1**), applies in respect of offenders aged 18 and over, sentenced on or after 1 October 2018, irrespective of the date of the offence. When the offence is committed in a domestic context the Sentencing Council definitive guideline, *Domestic Abuse* (see Supplement, **SG6-1**), also applies. Special provision is made by sch. 8 for persons providing information society services.

In *Bostan* [2018] EWCA Crim 494, [2018] 2 Cr App R (S) 15 (112), D pleaded guilty to sending a topless image of his girlfriend to her mother, although he did not disseminate it further. A sentence of four months' imprisonment was reduced to three months on appeal.

B18.33 **Elements** The new offence was said to be enacted to deal with what has come to be known as 'revenge pornography', which refers to the publication, typically via the internet, of intimate images of former sexual partners without their consent. Although the updated CPS guidelines (21 August 2018) on prosecuting cases involving communications sent via social media indicate a number of possible existing offences which may be relevant to such conduct, depending on the exact circumstances, it was considered that the growing nature of the problem demanded a specifically targeted offence.

There is no requirement that the photograph or film should be in itself indecent or grossly offensive, but it must be a 'private sexual' photograph or film; 'private' and 'sexual' are defined in s. 35(2) and (3).

Criminal Justice and Courts Act 2015, s. 35

(2) A photograph or film is 'private' if it shows something that is not of a kind ordinarily seen in public.
(3) A photograph or film is 'sexual' if—
(a) it shows all or part of an individual's exposed genitals or pubic area,
(b) it shows something that a reasonable person would consider to be sexual because of its nature, or
(c) its content, taken as a whole, is such that a reasonable person would consider it to be sexual.

Section 35(4) and (5) provide for altered or combined images and effectively only bring those within the offence where it is the original image of the individual which is private and sexual as opposed to the way it has been altered or combined.

The gist of the offence is that the disclosure is done without the consent of an individual appearing in the photograph or film and with intent to cause distress to that individual. The meaning of disclosure is dealt with in s. 34(2): a person 'discloses' something to a person 'if, by any means, he or she gives or shows it to the person or makes it available to the person'. By s. 34(3), there may be disclosure whether or not done for reward and whether or not previously disclosed to the person. But it is not an offence to disclose to the person who appears in the photograph or film to whom it is intended to cause distress (s. 33(2)). However, this would not exclude liability where it is disclosed to someone appearing in the photograph or film with intent to cause distress to somebody else who appears in it.

Defences A number of defences are provided, including proving a reasonable belief 'that the disclosure was necessary for the purposes of preventing, detecting or investigating crime' (s. 33(3)), a defence relating to the publication of journalistic material in the public interest (s. 33(4)), and where there is a reasonable belief that the photograph or film had previously been disclosed for reward and no reason to believe that the previous disclosure for reward was made without the consent of the individual who appears in the photograph or film and to whom the current disclosure is intended to cause distress (s. 33(5)). In relation to the defences under s. 33(4) and (5), D has only an evidential burden (see s. 33(6) and contrast s. 33(3)). **B18.34**

Special Provision on Intent Section 33(8) provides that a person 'is not to be taken to have disclosed a photograph or film with the intention of causing distress merely because that was a natural and probable consequence of the disclosure'. This may at first sight seem unnecessary in the light of the CJA 1967, s. 8 (see **A2.34**), but s. 8 is concerned with intention or foresight of 'a result' whereas the new offence governed by s. 33(8) does not require any actual distress to have resulted but merely requires an intention to cause distress. **B18.35**

Publications Harmful to Children and Young Persons

Children and Young Persons (Harmful Publications) Act 1955, s. 2 **B18.36**

(1) A person who prints, publishes, sells or lets on hire a work to which this Act applies, or has any such work in his possession for the purpose of selling it or letting it on hire, shall be guilty of an offence and liable, on summary conviction, to imprisonment for a term not exceeding four months or to a fine not exceeding level 3 on the standard scale or to both.
Provided that, in any proceedings taken under this subsection against a person in respect of selling or letting on hire a work or of having it in his possession for the purpose of selling it or letting it on hire, it shall be a defence for him to prove that he had not examined the contents of the work and had no reasonable cause to suspect that it was one to which this Act applies.

(2) A prosecution for an offence under this section shall not, in England and Wales, be instituted except by, or with the consent of, the Attorney-General.

By s. 1, the works to which the Act applies are:

> ... any book, magazine or other like work which is of a kind likely to fall into the hands of children or young persons and consists wholly or mainly of stories told in pictures (with or without the addition of written matter) being stories portraying—
> (a) the commission of crimes; or
> (b) acts of violence or cruelty; or
> (c) incidents of a repulsive or horrible nature;
> in such a way that the work as a whole would tend to corrupt a child or young person into whose hands it might fall.

Section 3 provides powers of entry, search, seizure and, on conviction, forfeiture.

Indecent Photographs of Children

The offences under the Protection of Children Act 1978 dealing with indecent photographs of children are dealt with at **B3.320** ***et seq.*** **B18.37**

Video Recordings Act 1984 Offences

The Video Recordings Act 1984, repealed and revived by the Video Recordings Act 2010, established a system for the classification by the British Board of Film Classification of video works embodied in recordings supplied to the public through video rental and other outlets. This includes the classification of video works constituting video games, although since 2012 the classification of video games is undertaken by the Video Standards Council's Game Rating Authority. Sections 9 to 14 of the 1984 Act create various offences, all originally summary and punishable only by fines, relating to the supply, or possession for supply, of video recordings containing video works which have not been classified or with a false indication as to their classification etc. However, the CJPO 1994, s. 88, made the two most serious offences (under ss. 9 **B18.38** and 10 of the 1984 Act) indictable and punishable by a maximum of two years' imprisonment or six months on summary conviction. The other offences under the 1984 Act remain summary but the offences under ss. 11, 12 and 14 of the Act have been made imprisonable with a maximum sentence of six months.

The Video Recordings Act 2010 remedied a technical defect that had been discovered in the Video Recordings Act 1984, namely failure to notify the European Commission in accordance with applicable EU law (the Technical Standards Directive, Directive 83/189/EEC ([1983] OJ L109/8)). This meant that provisions relating to video classification and distribution were unenforceable within the UK, and when the defect came to light all current prosecutions were discontinued. The status of previous convictions under the 2010 Act was considered in *Interfact v Liverpool City Council* [2010] EWCA Crim 1486, [2011] QB 744 where, despite the defect in the legislation, they were found to be safe.

The legislation was the subject of a challenge to its legitimacy in *Dryzner* [2014] EWCA Crim 2438, a case arising out of the supply of videos for children imported from Poland which, although not having classification certificates, were in fact quite innocent in terms of their content. The Court of Appeal confirmed that the system set up by the Act did not amount to an unlawful interference with trade within the EU, contrary to Article 34 of the Treaty on the Functioning of the European Union. The legislation was permitted under Article 36 which qualified Article 34, *inter alia*, on grounds of public morality and the system of regulation requiring classification of videos, including the innocuous ones supplied by the appellants, was not unreasonable or disproportionate. Similarly, a challenge on human rights grounds on the basis of interference with freedom of expression under the ECHR, Article 10, was rejected since Article 10(2) qualified that right where a provision was justified on various grounds including for the protection of health or morals.

B18.39 In brief, the offences under the revised 1984 Act are as follows.

(a) supplying a video recording of an unclassified work (s. 9);
(b) possessing a video recording of an unclassified work for the purposes of supply (s. 10);
(c) supplying a video recording of a classified work to a person who has not attained the age specified in the classification certificate (s. 11);
(d) supplying a video recording with a restricted classification from a place other than a licensed sex shop (s. 12) (*Interfact Ltd v Liverpool City Council* [2005] EWHC 995 (Admin), [2005] 1 WLR 3118: it is the place of delivery rather than each despatch which counts, and mail order catalogues constitute 'offers' to supply illegally);
(e) supplying a video recording which does not comply with the requirements as to labelling (s. 13);
(f) supplying a video recording containing a false indication as to classification (s. 14).

Certain video works are exempted from the provisions of the 1984 Act. The meaning of an exempted work is set out in s. 2 of the Act. Broadly, a work is exempted if it is designed to inform, educate, instruct or is concerned with sport, religion or music. However, there always were restrictions on these exemptions which were further tightened as a result of amendments to s. 2 made by the Video Recordings Act 1984 (Exempted Video Works) Regulations 2014 (SI 2014 No. 2097). The changes were designed to ensure that anything that would attract an age rating of 12 or above will no longer be exempt (whereas previously it was possible in some cases for at least some material to be included in an exempt work which might otherwise have led to a 15 or 18 classification). Section 3 of the 1984 Act provides for the meaning of exempted supply, which includes a supply which is neither for reward nor in the course or furtherance of a business.

Possession of Extreme Pornographic Images

B18.40 This offence, created under the CJIA 2008, s. 63, is dealt with at **B3.344**.

Section B19 Offences Related to Drugs

AN OVERVIEW OF UK DRUG LEGISLATION

With the enactment of the Psychoactive Substances Act 2016 (PSA 2016; in force 26 May 2016), the UK now has three principal legislative schemes for regulating the production and distribution of drug substances and drug products for human consumption (namely, the MDA 1971, the Human Medicines Regulations 2012, and the PSA 2016). **B19.1**

Practitioners should be aware that in the event that the UK leaves the EU on 'IP Completion Day' (currently 31 December 2020), a number of existing UK/EU measures may be the subject of amendment, including the Controlled Drugs (Drug Precursors) (Intra-Community Trade) Regulations 2008 (see **B19.113, B19.138**), the Controlled Drugs (Drug Precursors) (Community External Trade) Regulations 2008 (see **B19.113, B19.139**), Regulation (EC) 273/2004 (see **B19.138**), Council Regulation (EC) 111/2005 (see **B19.139**), Delegated Regulation (EU) 2015/1011, Commission Implementing Regulation (EU) 2015/1013 and the PSA 2016 (see **B19.122**). Regulation (EC) No. 1920/2006 and Regulation (EU) 2017/2101 may be revoked (see the Law Enforcement and Security (Amendment) (EU Exit) Regulations 2019 (SI 2019 No. 742); and note the Human Medicines (Amendment etc.) (EU Exit) Regulations 2019 (SI 2019 No. 775) and the Medicines for Human Use (Clinical Trials) (Amendment) (EU Exit) Regulations 2019 (SI 2019 No. 744).

Controlled Drugs The principal statutory measure is the Misuse of Drugs Act 1971 (MDA 1971) by which drugs that are specified (according to their relative harm) in Classes A, B and C, in sch. 2 to the 1971 Act, are controlled. The restrictions and prohibitions imposed by the MDA 1971 are subject to the exceptions and exemptions set out in secondary legislation (notably in the Misuse of Drugs Regulations 2001 (SI 2001 No. 3998)). The MDA 1971 and its forerunners reflect the UK's commitment to comply with the three main United Nations Conventions (in respect of which the UK was a signatory) that aim to promote the global implementation of measures to restrict the use of specified substances to medical, therapeutic and research purposes. The three UN Conventions are the Single Convention on Narcotic Drugs 1961 (as amended by the 1972 Protocol), the Convention on Psychotropic Substances 1971, and the United Nations Convention Against Illicit Traffic in Narcotic Drugs and Psychotropic Substances 1988. Each **B19.2**

Convention has been amended. At its 63rd regular session (held in Vienna from 2 to 6 March 2020) the UN Commission on Narcotic Drugs placed 12 substances and one precursor under international control. To sch. I to the Single Convention on Narcotic Drugs of 1961 (as amended by the 1972 Protocol) are added *crotonylfentanyl* and *valerylfentanyl*. To sch. I to the Convention on Psychotropic Substances of 1971 is added DOC (*2,5-Dimethoxy-4-chloroamphetamine*); to sch. II are added AB-FUBINACA, 5F-AMB-PINACA (5F-AMB, 5F-MMB-PINACA), 5F-MDMB-PICA (5F-MDMB-2201), 4F-MDMB-BINACA, 4-CMC (*4-chloromethcathinone, clephedrone*), *N-ethylhexedrone*, and *alpha-PHP*; and to sch. IV are added *Flualprazolam* and *Etizolam*. With the support of the European Union (Council Decision (EU) 2020/286) *methyl alpha-phenylacetoacetate* (MAPA) (including its optical isomers) is added to Table I of the Convention against Illicit Traffic in Narcotic Drugs and Psychotropic Substances of 1988. There are a number of EU initiatives and measures that have similar objectives to those of the three main UN Conventions (e.g., the EU Drugs Strategy (2013–20) ([2012] OJ C402/1), the EU Action Plan on Drugs 2017–2020 ([2017] OJ C215/21) and the 'EU4Monitoring Drugs Project' 2019–2021 (tinyurl.com/y7323uvk)).

B19.3 **Medicinal Products** Many drug products and drug substances that fall within the definition of a 'medicinal product' are subject to the Human Medicines Regulations 2012 (SI 2012 No. 1916, as amended; see SI 2019 No. 199). The expression 'medicinal product' has the meaning given by reg. 2 of the 2012 Regulations (sch. 34, para. 31), which mirrors (almost exactly) the definition as it appears in Directive 2001/83/EC on the Community code relating to medicinal products for human use ([2001] OJ L311/67), art. 1(2). As to the latter, see Joined Cases C-358/13 and C-181/13 *D and G v Germany* (CJEU, 10 July 2014), in which the CJEU held that art. 1(2)(b) must be interpreted as not covering substances which produce effects that merely modify physiological functions but which are not such as to have any beneficial effects, either immediately or in the long term, on human health, and which are consumed solely to induce a state of intoxication and are, as such, harmful to human health (at [50]). In *Chapman* [2017] EWCA Crim 1743, [2018] 1 Cr App R 9 (122) the Court of Appeal held, in the context of the PSA 2016, and applying EU law, that canisters containing nitrous oxide manufactured for use unconnected with medicinal purposes were not 'medicinal products' within the meaning of the Human Medicines Regulations 2012. The regulatory regime of the 2012 Regulations contemplates that a substance may be a 'medicinal product' for one purpose (and thus subject to control under the 2012 Regulations) but not another (at [31]). See also *A guide to what is a medicinal product* (Medicines and Healthcare Products Regulatory Agency, March 2020, tinyurl.com/y8j7tu6t).

B19.4 **Non-exempted Psychoactive Substances (NEPS)** The PSA 2016 applies to all NEPS (i.e. drug substances which, when consumed, are capable of producing a psychoactive effect in a person). Both 'controlled drugs' and 'medicinal products' are exempted from the PSA 2016 (s. 3 and sch. 1) and are not 'psychoactive substances' for the purposes of that Act. The expressions 'legal highs', 'new psychoactive substances' or 'novel psychoactive substances' are best avoided. The latter two expressions (often styled in literature as 'NPS') tend to refer to those drugs that are not included in the schedules to the three UN Conventions mentioned at **B19.2** (and see Directive (EU) 2017/2103). In the context of UK drug laws, the acronym 'NPS' is misleading because many such substances have been controlled by the MDA 1971 for years.

B19.5 **Expert Drug Analysis** Given the existence of (i) the three above-mentioned drug-control statutory regimes, (ii) the use of generic definitions by which certain drugs are controlled under the MDA 1971, and (iii) the creation of criminal offences in respect of NEPS under the PSA 2016, it is essential that drug substances are correctly identified, and (in the case of the PSA 2016) that 'psychoactive effect' is properly established (consider the situation that arose in *Browne* [2018] EWCA Crim 2768, and see *Prosser* [2019] EWCA Crim 836). Drug identification of familiar controlled drugs (e.g., cocaine and MDMA) should cause few difficulties, but the correct identification of other drugs (to the standard of proof required in respect of criminal offences) may be a complex and time-consuming process. As for the role of experts, see *Chapman* [2017] EWCA Crim 1743, [2018] 1 Cr App R 9 (122), and consider *Pabon* [2018] EWCA Crim 420.

Spice Care should be taken in cases where reference is made to so-called 'spice', which is not a term formally recognised in science or in law, but is a colloquialism that usually refers to synthetic cannabinoid receptor agonist compounds (or products containing them) mixed with herbal material. There are many such compounds and it should not be assumed that all synthetic cannabinoids have the same effect on the body. It is important to note that three 'generations' of synthetic cannabinoids have been added (as controlled drugs) by way of generic definitions to the MDA 1971, sch. 2: see SI 2009 No. 3209 (first generation, in force 23 December 2009); SI 2013 No. 239 (second generation, in force February 2013), and SI 2016 No. 1109 (third generation, in force 14 December 2016, but note SI 2019 No.132). Consider also the report on 'Third Generation' synthetic cannabinoids, published by the Advisory Council on the Misuse of Drugs (November 2014). Other synthetic cannabinoids, which are not captured by the three generic definitions, might be caught by the PSA 2016, but this may depend on whether the substance in question is 'capable of producing a psychoactive effect in a person who consumes it' (PSA 2016, s. 2). The expression 'spice' has been in existence for some time: accordingly care must be taken to determine whether or not the synthetic cannabinoid in question was a 'controlled drug' at the material time. **B19.6**

CONTROLLED DRUGS

Meaning of 'Controlled Drug' and 'Temporary Class Drugs' **B19.7**

Misuse of Drugs Act 1971, s. 2

(1) In this Act—
  (a) the expression 'controlled drug' means any substance or product for the time being specified—
    (i) in Part I, II or III of Schedule 2, or
    (ii) in a temporary class drug order as a drug subject to temporary control (but this is subject to section 2A(6));
  (b) the expressions 'Class A drug', 'Class B drug' and 'Class C drug' mean any of the substances and products for the time being specified respectively in Part I, Part II and Part III of that Schedule; and
  (c) the expression 'temporary class drug' means any substance or product which is for the time being a controlled drug by virtue of a temporary class drug order;

and the provisions of Part IV of that Schedule shall have effect with respect to the meanings of expressions used in that Schedule.

Although not expressly stated in the MDA 1971, the drugs specified in sch. 2 to the Act are those that have a narcotic or psychoactive effect, or which have some medicinal indication. Thus, poisons (which do not have the aforementioned properties) tend not to be controlled under the MDA (consider, for example, the recommendation of the Advisory Council on the Misuse of Drugs (18 February 2019) not to include *2,4-dinitrophenol* within the schedule).

Temporary Class Drugs

Section 2 of the MDA 1971 was amended by the PRSRA 2011, s. 151 and sch. 17, para. 2, with the effect that substances and products that are the subject of a Temporary Class Drug Order ('TCDO') are 'controlled drugs' (see s. 2(1)(a)(ii) at **B19.7**). The relevant penalties are those that apply to Class B drugs (s. 25(2B)). **B19.8**

A 'temporary class drug' ceases to be a 'controlled drug' a year (or less, as specified in the order) after the order came into force (s. 2A(6)). Occasionally, a TCDO is renewed in respect of a given drug or drugs. Drugs previously the subject of a TCDO are often added to the MDA 1971, sch. 2 (and thus become controlled under the MDA by that route).

The following TCDOs have been made: SI 2016 No. 1126, SI 2016 No. 650, SI 2015 No. 1929, SI 2015 No. 1396, SI 2015 No. 1027, SI 2013 No. 1294 and SI 2012 No. 980. There are currently no TCDOs in force and, given the enactment of the PSA 2016, it is uncertain whether any further TCDOs will be made. Note that, by letter dated 18 October 2019, the Advisory Council on the Misuse of Drugs advised the Secretary of State for the Home

Department that, given the usefulness of TCDOs 'in dealing rapidly with highly dangerous compounds', the mechanism for making such orders should be retained 'at the present time'.

As for offences under the MDA 1971 that apply to temporary class drugs, as well as exemptions or exceptions (if any) that apply to such drugs under the MDA 1971, s. 7A, see the 2017 edition of this work.

'Substances and Products' Specified as Controlled Drugs in Class A, B or C

B19.9 Schedule 2 is frequently amended and the commencement provisions of amending legislation must not be overlooked.

Note that the wording of the MDA 1971, sch. 2, part 2, para. 1(ca) (Class B drugs), was substituted from 15 November 2019, by SI 2019 No.1323. From the same day, the Misuse of Drugs and Misuse of Drugs (Designation) (Amendment) (England, Wales and Scotland) Regulations 2019 (SI 2019 No. 1362) amended the Misuse of Drugs Regulations 2001 (SI 2001 No. 3998), sch. 1, para. 1(ld), as well as the Misuse of Drugs (Designation) (England, Wales and Scotland) Order 2015 (SI 2015 No. 704), sch. 1, para. 1(sa), by (in each case) substituting wording similar to revised para.1(ca).

The purpose of the amendments is to 'remove compounds which were not intended for control whilst retaining those which are known to be, or likely to be, misused, and where the misuse is having, or is capable of having, harmful effects' (see the Explanatory Memorandum to SI 2019 No. 1323), and see the Impact Assessment (HO0341) which stated (among other matters) that the original wording 'had an unintended consequence on the research community' and that, for example, the Advisory Council on the Misuse of Drugs had advised that some 40,000–90,000 compounds were captured by this wide definition which were not synthetic cannabinoids by their pharmacological action and therefore were not intended to be controlled under the 1971 Act and associated legislation.

The principal purpose of having the three classes of controlled drugs is to identify the maximum statutory penalty for a given class (*Free* [2013] EWCA Crim 589), but a secondary purpose (it is submitted) is that each class says something about the relative harm of drugs associated with that class.

Drugs are increasingly added to the list of controlled drugs by way of generic definitions. Practitioners should not assume that such definitions are free of ambiguity and should seek expert advice in appropriate cases (see **B19.6** in relation to so-called 'spice').

For an interpretation of the words 'any compound (not being a compound for the time being specified in [sch. 2] structurally derived from [the specified drug substance] by modification in any of the following ways' (as those words appear in various places in sch. 2 to the MDA 1971) consider, but with care, *Thomas v The Queen* [2019] SC (Bermuda) 15 App (19 February 2019).

Misuse of Drugs Act 1971, sch. 2

CONTROLLED DRUGS

PART I CLASS A DRUGS

1. The following substances and products, namely:—
   (a) Acetorphine.
   Alfentanil.
   Allylprodine.
   Alphacetylmethadol.
   Alphameprodine.
   Alphamethadol.
   Alphaprodine.
   Anileridine.
   Benzethidine.
   Benzylmorphine (3-benzylmorphine).
   Betacetylmethadol.
   Betameprodine.
   Betamethadol.
   Betaprodine.
   Bezitramide.
   Bufotenine.
   Carfentanil.
   Clonitazene.
   Coca leaf.
   Cocaine.
   Desomorphine.
   Dextromoramide.
   Diamorphine.
   Diampromide.

Diethylthiambutene.
Difenoxin (1-(3-cyano-3, 3-diphenylpropyl)-4-phenyl-piperidine-4-carboxylic acid).
Dihydrocodeinone *O*-carboxymethyloxime.
Dihydroetorphine.
Dihydromorphine.
Dimenoxadole.
Dimepheptanol.
Dimethylthiambutene.
Dioxaphetyl butyrate.
Diphenoxylate.
Dipipanone.
Drotebanol (3,4-dimethoxy-17-met hylmorphinan-6b, 14-diol).
Ecgonine, and any derivative of ecgonine which is convertible to ecgonine or to cocaine.
Ethylmethylthiambutene.
Eticyclidine.
Etonitazene.
Etorphine.
Etoxeridine.
Etryptamine.
Fentanyl.
Fungus (of any kind) which contains psilocin or an ester of psilocin.
Furethidine.
Hydrocodone.
Hydromorphinol.
Hydromorphone.
Hydroxypethidine.
Isomethadone.
Ketobemidone.
Levomethorphan.
Levomoramide.
Levophenacylmorphan.
Levorphanol.
Lofentanil.
Lysergamide.
Lysergide and other *N*-alkyl derivatives of lysergamide.
Mescaline.
Metazocine.
Methadone.
Methadyl acetate.
Methylamphetamine
Methyldesorphine.
Methyldihydromorphine (6-methyldihydromorphine).
Metopon.
Morpheridine.
Morphine.
Morphine methoromide, morphine *N*-oxide and other pentavalent nitrogen morphine derivatives.
Myrophine.
Nicomorphine (3,6-dinicotinoyl- morphine).
Noracymethadol.
Norlevorphanol.
Normethadone.
Normorphine.
Norpipanone.
Opium, whether raw, prepared or medicinal.
Oxycodone.
Oxymorphone.
Pethidine.
Phenadoxone.
Phenampromide.
Phenazocine.
Phencyclidine.
Phenomorphan.
Phenoperidine.
Piminodine.
Piritramide.
Poppy-straw and concentrate of poppy-straw.
Proheptazine.
Properidine (1-methyl-4-phenyl-piperidine-4-carboxylic acid isopropyl ester).
Psilocin.
Racemethorphan.
Racemoramide.
Racemorphan.
Remifentanil.
Rolicyclidine.
Sufentanil.
Tapentadol.
Tenocylidine.
Thebacon.
Thebaine.
Tilidate.
Trimeperidine.
(6aR,9R)-4-acetyl-N,N-diethyl-7-methyl-4,6,6a,7,8,9-hexahydroindolo [4,3-fg] quinoline-9-carboxamide (ALD-52).
4-Bromo-2,5-dimethoxy-a-m ethylphenethylamine.
4-Cyano-2-dimethylamino-4,4 -diphenylbutane.
4-Cyano-1-methyl-4-phenyl-piperidine.
1-Cyclohexyl-4-(1,2-diphenylethyl) piperazine (MT-45).
3,4-dichloro-N- [[1-(dimethylamino) cyclohexyl]methyl]benzamide (AH-7921).
3,4-dichloro-N-[2-(dimethylamino) cyclohexyl]-N-methylbenza-mide (U-47,700).
(6aR,9R)-N,N-diethyl-7-allyl-4,6,6a,7, 8,9-hexahydroindolo [4,3-fg] quinoline-9-carboxamide (AL-LAD).

(6aR,9R)-N,N-diethyl-7-ethyl-4,6,6a,7,8,9-hexahydroindolo[4,3-fg]quinoline-9-carboxamide (ETH-LAD).
(6aR,9R)-N,N-diethyl-7-propyl-4,6,6a,7,8,9-hexahydroindolo[4,3-fg]quinoline-9-carboxamide (PRO-LAD).
N,N-Diethyltryptamine.
2,4-dimethylazetidinyl{(6aR,9R)-7-methyl-4,6,6a,7,8,9-hexahydroindolo[4,3-fg]quinolin-9-yl}methanone (LSZ).
N,N-Dimethyltryptamine.
2,5-Dimethoxy-a,4-dimethylphenethylamine.
N-Hydroxy-tenamphetamine
1-Methyl-4-phenylpiperidine-4-carboxylic acid.
2-Methyl-3-morpholino-1,1- diphenylpropanecarboxylic acid.
4-Methyl-aminorex
4-Methyl-5-(4-methylphenyl)-4,5-dihydrooxazol-2-amine (4,4'-DMAR).
4-Phenylpiperidine-4-carboxylic acid ethyl ester.

(b) any compound (not being a compound for the time being specified in subparagraph (a) above) structurally derived from tryptamine or from a ring-hydroxy tryptamine by modification in any of the following ways, that is to say—
(i) by substitution at the nitrogen atom of the sidechain to any extent with alkyl or alkenyl substituents, or by inclusion of the nitrogen atom of the side chain (and no other atoms of the side chain) in a cyclic structure;
(ii) by substitution at the carbon atom adjacent to the nitrogen atom of the side chain with alkyl or alkenyl substituents;
(iii) by substitution in the 6-membered ring to any extent with alkyl, alkoxy, haloalkyl, thioalkyl, alkylenedioxy, or halide substituents;
(iv) by substitution at the 2-position of the tryptamine ring system with an alkyl substituent;
(ba) the following phenethylamine derivatives, namely:
Allyl(a-methyl-3,4-methylenedioxyphenethyl)amine
2-Amino-1-(2,5-dimethoxy-4-methylphenyl)ethanol
2-Amino-1-(3,4-dimethoxyphenyl)ethanol
Benzyl(a-methyl-3,4-methylenedioxyphenethyl)amine
4-Bromo-b,2,5-trimethoxyphenethylamine
N-(4-sec-Butylthio-2,5-dimethoxyphenethyl)hydroxylamine
Cyclopropylmethyl(a-methyl-3,4-methylenedioxyphenethyl)amine
2-(4,7-Dimethoxy-2,3-dihydro-1H-indan-5-yl)ethylamine
2-(4,7-Dimethoxy-2,3-dihydro-1H-indan-5-yl)-1-methylethylamine
2-(2,5-Dimethoxy-4-methylphenyl)cyclopropylamine
2-(1,4-Dimethoxy-2-naphthyl)ethylamine
2-(1,4-Dimethoxy-2-naphthyl)-1-methylethylamine
N-(2,5-Dimethoxy-4-propylthiophenethyl)hydroxylamine
2-(1,4-Dimethoxy-5, 6, 7,8-tetrahydro-2-naphthyl)ethylamine
2-(1,4-Dimethoxy-5,6,7,8-tetrahydro-2-naphthy1)-1-methylethylamine
a,a-Dimethyl-3,4-methylenedioxyphenethylamine
a,a-Dimethyl-3,4-methylenedioxyphenethyl(methyl)amine
Dimethyl(a-methyl-3,4-methylenedioxyphenethyl)amine
N-(4-Ethylthio-2,5-dimethoxyphenethyl)hydroxylamine
4-Iodo-2,5-dimethoxy-a-methylphenethyl(dimethyl)amine
2-(1,4-Methano-5,8-dimethoxy-1,2,3,4-tetrahydro-6-naphthyl)ethylamine
2-(1,4-Methano-5,8-dimethoxy-1,2,3,4-tetrahydro-6-naphthyl)1-methylethylamine
2-(5-Methoxy-2,2-dimethyl-2,3-dihydrobenzo[b]furan-6-yl)-1-methylethylamine
2-Methoxyethyl(a-methyl-3,4-methylenedioxyphenethyl)amine
2-(5-Methoxy-2-methyl-2,3-dihydrobenzo[b]furan-6-yl)-1-methylethylamine
b-Methoxy-3,4-methylenedioxyphenethylamine
1-(3,4-Methylenedioxybenzyl)butyl(ethyl)amine
1-(3,4-Methylenedioxybenzyl)butyl(methyl)amine
*2-(a-Methyl-3,4-methylenedioxy*phenethylamino)ethanol
a-Methyl-3,4-methylenedioxyphenethyl(prop-2-ynyl)amine
N-Methyl-N-(a-methyl-3,4-methylenedioxyphenethyl)hydroxylamine
O-Methyl-N-(a-methyl-3,4methylenedioxyphenethyl)hydroxylamine

a-Methyl-4-(methylthio)phenethylamine
b,3,4,5-Tetramethoxyphenethylamine
b,2,5-Trimethoxy-4-methylphenethylamine.

(c) any compound (not being methoxyphenamine or a compound for the time being specified in subparagraph (a) above) structurally derived from phenethylamine, an *N*-alkylphenethylamine, a-methylphenethylamine, an *N*-alkyl-a-methylphenethylamine, a-ethylphenethylamine, or an *N*-alkyl-a-ethylphenethylamine by substitution in the ring to any extent with alkyl, alkoxy, alkylenedioxy or halide substituents, whether or not further substituted in the ring by one or more other univalent substituents.

(d) any compound (not being a compound for the time being specified in subparagraph (a) above) structurally derived from fentanyl by modification in any of the following ways, that is to say,
   (i) by replacement of the phenyl portion of the phenethyl group by any heteromonocycle whether or not further substituted in the heterocycle;
   (ii) by substitution in the phenethyl group with alkyl, alkenyl, alkoxy, hydoxy, halogeno, haloalkyl, amino or nitro groups;
   (iii) by substitution in the piperidine ring with alkyl or alkenyl groups;
   (iv) by substitution in the aniline ring with alkyl, alkoxy, alkylenedioxy, halogeno or haloalkyl groups;
   (v) by substitution at the 4-position of the piperidine ring with any alkoxycarbonyl or alkoxyalkyl or acyloxy group;
   (vi) by replacement of the *N*-propionyl group by another acyl group;

(e) any compound (not being a compound for the time being specified in subparagraph (a) above) structurally derived from pethidine by modification in any of the following ways, that is to say,
   (i) by replacement of the 1-methyl group by an acyl, alkyl whether or not unsaturated, benzyl or phenethyl group, whether or not further substituted;
   (ii) by substitution in the piperidine ring with alkyl or alkenyl groups or with a propano bridge, whether or not further substituted;
   (iii) by substitution in the 4-phenyl ring with alkyl, alkoxy, aryloxy, halogeno or haloalkyl groups;
   (iv) by replacement of the 4-ethoxycarbonyl by any other alkoxycarbonyl or any alkoxyalkyl or acyloxy group;
   (v) by formation of an *N*-oxide or of a quaternary base.

(f) any compound (not being benzyl(α-methyl-3,4-methylenedioxyphenethyl)amine) structurally derived from mescaline, 4-bromo-2,5-dimethoxy-α-methylphenethylamine, 2,5-dimethoxy-α,4-dimethylphenethylamine, *N*-hydroxytenamphetamine, or a compound specified in sub-paragraph (ba) or (c) above, by substitution at the nitrogen atom of the amino group with a benzyl substituent, whether or not substituted in the phenyl ring of the benzyl group to any extent.

2. Any stereoisomeric form of a substance for the time being specified in paragraph 1 above not being dextromethorphan or dextrorphan.
3. Any ester or ether of a substance for the time being specified in paragraph 1 or 2 above not being a substance for the time being specified in Part II of this Schedule.
4. Any salt of a substance for the time being specified in any of paragraphs 1 to 3 above.
5. Any preparation or other product containing a substance or product for the time being specified in any of paragraphs 1 to 4 above.
6. Any preparation designed for administration by injection which includes a substance or product for the time being specified in any of paragraphs 1 to 3 of Part II of this Schedule.

Part II Class B Drugs

1. The following substances and products, *namely:—*
   (a) Acetyldihydrocodeine.
   Amphetamine.
   N-Benzyl-ethylphenidate
   Cannabinol.
   Cannabinol derivatives.
   Cannabis and cannabis resin.
   Codeine.
   Dihydrocodeine.
   Ethylmorphine (3-ethylmorphine).
   Ethylnaphthidate.
   Ethylphenidate
   Glutethimide.
   Isopropylphenidate (IPP or IPPD)
   Ketamine.
   Lefetamine.
   Lisdexamphetamine.
   Mecloqualone.
   Methaqualone.

Methcathinone.
Methylmorphenate
Methylnaphthidate (HDMP-28)
Methylphenidate.
a-Methylphenethylthydroxylamine
Methylphenobarbitone.
N-methyl-1-(thiophen-2-yl) propan-2-amine (methiopropamine or MPA)
Nicodine.
Nicodicodine (6-nicotinoyldihydrocodeine).
Norcodeine.
Pentazocine.
Phenmetrazine.
Pholcodine.
Propiram.
Propylphenidate
Zipeprol.
3,4-Dichloroethylphenidate
3,4-Dichloromethylphenidate (3,4-DCMP)
2-((Dimethylamino)methyl)-1-(3-hydroxyphenyl) cyclohexanol.
4-Fluoroethylphenidate
4-Fluoromethylphenidate
4-Methylmethylphenidate

(aa) Any compound (not being bupropion, cathinone, diethylpropion, pyrovalerone or a compound for the time being specified in sub-paragraph (a) above) structurally derived from 2–amino–1–phenyl–1–propanone by modification in any of the following ways, that is to say,
(i) by substitution in the phenyl ring to any extent with alkyl, alkoxy, alkylenedioxy, haloalkyl or halide substituents, whether or not further substituted in the phenyl ring by one or more other univalent substituents;
(ii) by substitution at the 3–position with an alkyl substituent;
(iii) by substitution at the nitrogen atom with alkyl or dialkyl groups, or by inclusion of the nitrogen atom in a cyclic structure.
(ab) Any compound structurally derived from 2–aminopropan–1–one by substitution at the 1-position with any monocyclic, or fused polycyclic ring system (not being a phenyl ring or alkylenedioxyphenyl ring system), whether or not the compound is further modified in any of the following ways, that is to say,
(i) by substitution in the ring system to any extent with alkyl, alkoxy, haloalkyl or halide substituents, whether or not further substituted in the ring system by one or more other univalent substituents;
(ii) by substitution at the 3–position with an alkyl substituent;
(iii) by substitution at the 2 amino nitrogen atom with alkyl or dialkyl groups, or by inclusion of the 2 amino nitrogen atom in a cyclic structure.
(ac) Any compound (not being pipradrol) structurally derived from piperidine, pyrrolidine, azepane, morpholine or pyridine by substitution at a ring carbon atom with a diphenyl-methyl group, whether or not the compound is further modified in any of the following ways, that is to say,
(i) by substitution in any of the phenyl rings to any extent with alkyl, alkoxy, haloalkyl or halide groups;
(ii) by substitution at the methyl carbon atom with an alkyl, hydroxyalkyl or hydroxy group;
(iii) by substitution at the ring nitrogen atom with an alkyl, alkenyl, haloalkyl or hydroxyalkyl group.
(b) Any 5,5 disubstituted barbituric acid.
(c) [2,3–Dihydro–5–methyl–3–(4–morpholinylmethyl)pyrrolo[1, 2, 3–de]–1,4–benzoxazin–6–yl]–1–naphthalenylmethanone.
3-Dimethylheptyl-11-hydroxyhexahydrocannabinol
[9–Hydroxy–6–methyl–3–[5–phenylpentan–2–yl] oxy–5, 6, 6a, 7, 8, 9, 10, 10a–octahydrophenanthridin–1–yl] acetate.
9-(Hydroxymethyl)–6, 6–dimethyl–3–(2–methyloctan–2–yl)–6a, 7, 10, 10a–tetrahydrobenzo[c]chromen–1–ol.
Nabilone
Any compound structurally derived from 3–(1–naphthoyl)indole, 3-(2-naphthoyl) indole, 1H-indol–3-yl–(1–naphthyl)methane or 1H-indol-3-yl-(2-naphthyl) methane by substitution at the nitrogen atom of the indole ring by alkyl, haloalkyl, alkenyl, cyanoalkyl, hydroxyalkyl, cycloalkylmethyl, cycloalkylethyl, (N-methylpiperidin-2-yl)methyl or 2–(4–morpholinyl)ethyl, whether or not further substituted in the indole ring to any extent and whether or not substituted in the naphthyl ring to any extent.

Any compound structurally derived from 3–(1–naphthoyl)pyrrole or 3-(2-naphthoyl) pyrrole by substitution at the nitrogen atom of the pyrrole ring by alkyl, haloalkyl, alkenyl, cyanoalkyl, hydroxyalkyl, cycloalkylmethyl, cycloalkylethyl, (N-methylpiperidin-2-yl) methyl or 2–(4–morpholinyl)ethyl, whether or not further substituted in the pyrrole ring to any extent and whether or not substituted in the naphthyl ring to any extent.

Any compound structurally derived from 1–(1–naphthylmethylene)indene or 1-(2-naphthylmethylene) indene by substitution at the 3–position of the indene ring by alkyl, haloalkyl, alkenyl, cyanoalkyl, hydroxyalkyl, cycloalkylmethyl, cycloalkylethyl, (N-methylpiperidin-2-yl)methyl or 2–(4–morpholinyl)ethyl, whether or not further substituted in the indene ring to any extent and whether or not substituted in the naphthyl ring to any extent.

Any compound structurally derived from 3–phenylacetylindole by substitution at the nitrogen atom of the indole ring by alkyl, haloalkyl, alkenyl, cyanoalkyl, hydroxyalkyl, cycloalkylmethyl, cycloalkylethyl, (N-methylpiperidin-2-yl)methyl or 2–(4–morpholinyl)ethyl, whether or not further substituted in the indole ring to any extent and whether or not substituted in the phenyl ring to any extent.

Any compound structurally derived from 2–(3–hydroxycyclohexyl)phenol by substitution at the 5–position of the phenolic ring by alkyl, alkenyl, cycloalkylmethyl, cycloalkylethyl or 2–(4–morpholinyl)ethyl, whether or not further substituted in the cyclohexyl ring to any extent.

Any compound structurally derived from 3-benzoylindole by substitution at the nitrogen atom of the indole ring by alkyl, haloalkyl, alkenyl, cyanoalkyl, hydroxyalkyl, cycloalkylmethyl, cycloalkylethyl, (N-methylpiperidin-2-yl)methyl or 2–(4–morpholinyl) ethyl, whether or not further substituted in the indole ring to any extent and whether or not substituted in the phenyl ring to any extent.

Any compound structurally derived from 3-(1-adamantoyl)indole or 3-(2-adamantoyl) indole by substitution at the nitrogen atom of the indole ring by alkyl, haloalkyl, alkenyl, cyanoalkyl, hydroxyalkyl, cycloalkylmethyl, cycloalkylethyl, (N-methylpiperidin-2-yl) methyl or 2–(4–morpholinyl)ethyl, whether or not further substituted in the indole ring to any extent and whether or not substituted in the adamantyl ring to any extent.

Any compound structurally derived from 3-(2,2,3,3-tetramethylcyclopropylcarbonyl) indole by substitution at the nitrogen atom of the indole ring by alkyl, haloalkyl, alkenyl, cyanoalkyl, hydroxyalkyl, cycloalkylmethyl, cycloalkylethyl, (N-methylpiperidin-2-yl) methyl or 2–(4–morpholinyl)ethyl, whether or not further substituted in the indole ring to any extent.

(ca) any compound (not being a compound for the time being specified in subparagraph (c) above) structurally related to 1-pentyl-3-(1-naphthoyl)indole (JWH-018), in that the four sub-structures, that is to say the indole ring, the pentyl substituent, the methanone linking group and the naphthyl ring, are linked together in a similar manner, whether or not any of the sub-structures have been modified, and whether or not substituted in any of the linked sub-structures with a benzyl or phenyl group and whether or not such compound is further substituted to any extent with alkyl, alkenyl, alkoxy, halide, haloalkyl or cyano substituents and, where any of the sub-structures have been modified, the modifications of the sub-structures are limited to any of the following, that is to say—

(i) replacement of the indole ring with indane, indene, indazole, pyrrole, pyrazole, imidazole, benzimidazole, pyrrolo[2,3-b]pyridine, pyrrolo[3,2-c]pyridine or pyrazolo[3,4-b] pyridine;

(ii) replacement of the pentyl substituent with alkyl, alkenyl, benzyl, cycloalkylmethyl, cycloalkylethyl, (N-methylpiperidin-2-yl)methyl, 2-(4-morpholinyl)ethyl or (tetrahydropyran-4-yl)methyl;

(iii) replacement of the methanone linking group with an ethanone, carboxamide, carboxylate, methylene bridge or methine group;

(iv) replacement of the 1-naphthyl ring with 2-naphthyl, phenyl, benzyl, adamantyl, cycloalkyl, cycloalkylmethyl, cycloalkylethyl, bicyclo[2.2.1]heptanyl, 1,2,3,4-tetrahydronaphthyl, quinolinyl, isoquinolinyl, 1-amino-1-oxopropan-2-yl, 1-hydroxy-1-oxopropan-2-yl, piperidinyl, morpholinyl, pyrrolidinyl, tetrahydropyranyl or piperazinyl.

(d) 1-Phenylcyclohexylamine or any compound (not being ketamine, tiletamine or a compound for the time being specified in paragraph 1(a) of Part 1 of this Schedule) structurally derived from 1-phenylcyclohexylamine or 2-amino-2-phenylcyclohexanone by modification in any of the following ways, that is to say,

(i) by substitution at the nitrogen atom to any extent by alkyl, alkenyl or hydroxyalkyl groups, or replacement of the amino group with a 1-piperidyl, 1-pyrrolidyl or 1-azepyl group, whether or not the nitrogen containing ring is further substituted by one or more alkyl groups;

(ii) by substitution in the phenyl ring to any extent by amino, alkyl, hydroxy, alkoxy or halide substituents, whether or not further substituted in the phenyl ring to any extent;

(iii) by substitution in the cyclohexyl or cyclohexanone ring by one or more alkyl substituents;

(iv) by replacement of the phenyl ring with a thienyl ring.

(e) Any compound (not being a compound for the time being specified in paragraph 1(ba) of Part 1 of this Schedule) structurally derived from 1-benzofuran, 2,3-dihydro-1-benzofuran, 1H-indole, indoline, 1H-indene, or indane by substitution in the 6-membered ring with a 2-ethylamino substituent whether or not further substituted in the ring system to any extent with alkyl, alkoxy, halide or haloalkyl substituents and whether or not substituted in the ethylamino side-chain with one or more alkyl substituents

2. Any stereoisomeric form of a substance for the time being specified in paragraph 1 of this Part of this Schedule.

2A. Any ester or ether of cannabinol or of a cannabinol derivative or of a substance for the time being specified in paragraph 1(ac), (c), (ca) or (d) of this Part of this Schedule.

3. Any salt of a substance for the time being specified in paragraph 1, 2 or 2A of this Part of this Schedule.

4. Any preparation or other product containing a substance or product for the time being specified in any of paragraphs 1 to 3 of this Part of this Schedule, not being a preparation falling within paragraph 6 of Part I of this Schedule.

Part III Class C Drugs

1. The following substances, namely:—

(a) Alprazolam.

Adinazolam (1-(8-Chloro-6-phenyl-4H-[1,2,4]triazolo[4,3-a][1,4]benzodiazepin-1-yl)-N,N-dimethylmethanamine)

Amineptine

Aminorex.

Benzphetamine.

Bromazepam.

Bromazolam (8-bromo-1-methyl-6-phenyl-4H-[1,2,4]triazolo[4,3-a][1,4]benzodiazepine).

7-bromo-5-(2-chlorophenyl)-1,3-dihydro-2H-1,4-benzodiazepin-2-one

Brotizolam.

Buprenorphine.

Camazepam.

Cathine.

Cathinone.

4'-Chlorodiazepam (7-Chloro-5-(4-chlorophenyl)-1-methyl-1,3-dihydro-2H-1,4-benzodiazepin-2-one).

Chlordiazepoxide.

Chlorphentermine.

Clobazam.

Clonazepam.

Clonazolam (6-(2-Chlorophenyl)-1-methyl-8-nitro-4H-[1,2,4]triazolo[4,3-a][1,4]benzodiazepine).

Clorazepic acid.

Clotiazepam.

Cloxazolam.

Delorazepam.

Deschloroetizolam (2-Ethyl-9-methyl-4-phenyl-6H-thieno[3,2-f][1,2,4]triazolo[4,3-a][1,4]diazepine)

Dextropropoxyphene.

Diazepam.

Diclazepam (7-Chloro-5-(2-chlorophenyl)-1-methyl-1,3-dihydro-2H-1,4-benzodiazepin-2-one)

Diethylpropion.

Estazolam.

Ethchlorvynol.

Ethinamate.

Ethyl loflazepate.

Etizolam

Fencamfamin.

Fenethylline.

Fenproporex.

Flubromazepam (7-Bromo-5-(2-fluorophenyl)-1,3-dihydro-2H-1,4-benzodiazepin-2-one).
Flubromazolam (8-Bromo-6-(2-fluorophenyl)-1-methyl-4H-[1,2,4]triazolo[4,3-a][1,4]benzodiazepine).
Fludiazepam.
Flunitrazepam.
Flurazepam.
Fonazepam (5-(2-Fluorophenyl)-7-nitro-1,3-dihydro-2H-1,4-benzodiazepin-2-one)
Gamma–butyrolactone
Halazepam.
Haloxazolam.
4-Hydroxy-n-butyric acid.
3-Hydroxyphenazepam (7-Bromo-5-(2-chlorophenyl)-3-hydroxy-1,3-dihydro-2H-1,4-benzodiazepin-2-one).
Ketazolam.
Khat
Loprazolam.
Lorazepam.
Lormetazepam.
Mazindol.
Meclonazepam (5-(2-Chlorophenyl)-3-methyl-7-nitro-1,3-dihydro-2H-1,4-benzodiazepin-2-one).
Medazepam.
Mefenorex.
Mephentermine.
Meprobamate.
Mesocarb.
Methyprylone.
Metizolam (4-(2-Chlorophenyl)-2-ethyl-6H-thieno[3,2-f][1,2,4]triazolo[4,3-a][1,4] diazepine).
Midazolam.
Nifoxipam (5-(2-Fluorophenyl)-3-hydroxy-7-nitro-1,3-dihydro-2H-1,4-benzodiazepin-2-one).
Nimetazepam.
Nitrazepam.
Nitrazolam (1-Methyl-8-nitro-6-phenyl-4H-[1,2,4]triazolo[4,3-a][1,4]benzodiazepine).
Nordazepam.
Oxazepam.
Oxazolam.
Pemoline.
Phendimetrazine.
Phentermine.
Pinazepam.
Prazepam.
Pyrazolam (8-Bromo-1-methyl-6-(2-pyridinyl)-4H-[1,2,4]triazolo[4,3-a][1,4]benzodiazepine).
Pyrovalerone.
Temazepam.
Tetrazepam.
Tramadol.
Triazolam.
N-Ethylamphetamine.
Zaleplon.
Zolpidem.
Zopiclone.

(b) 5α–Androstane–3,17–diol.
Androst-4-ene-3,17-diol.
1–Androstenediol.
1–Androstenedione
4–Androstene-3, 17-dione.
5–Androstenedione.
5–Androstene-3, 17-diol.
Atamestane.
Bolandiol.
Bolasterone.
Bolazine.
Boldenone.
Boldione.
Bolenol.
Bolmantalate.
1,4–Butanediol.
Calusterone.
4-Chloromethandienone.
Clostebol.
Danazol.
Desoxymethyltestosterone.
Dienedione (estra-4, 9-diene-3,17-dione).
Drostanolone.
Enestebol.
Epitiostanol.
Ethyloestrenol.
Fluoxymesterone.
Formebolone.
Furazabol.
Gabapentin (1-(aminomethyl) cyclohexaneacetic acid)
Gestrinone.
3–Hydroxy–5–androstan–17–one.
Mebolazine.
Mepitiostane.
Mesabolone.
Mestanolone.
Mesterolone.
Methandienone.
Methandriol.
Methenolone.
Methyltestosterone.
Metribolone.

Mibolerone.
Nandrolone.
19–Norandrostenedione.
19-Nor-4-Androstene-3, 17-dione.
19-Nor-5-Androstene-3, 17-diol.
19–Norandrosterone.
Norboletone.
Norclostebol.
Norethandrolone.
19–Noretiocholanolone.
Oripavine.
Ovandrotone.
Oxabolone.
Oxandrolone.
Oxymesterone.
Oxymetholone.
Pipradrol.
Prasterone.
Pregabalin ((S)-3-(aminomethyl)-5-methylhexanoic acid)
Propetandrol.
Prostanozol.
Quinbolone.
Roxibolone.
Silandrone.
Stanolone.
Stanozolol.
Stenbolone.
Testosterone.
Tetrahydrogestrinone.
Thiomesterone.
Trenbolone.

(c) any compound (not being Trilostane or a compound for the time being specified in sub-paragraph (b) above) structurally derived from 17-hydroxyandrostan-3-one or from 17-hydroxyestran-3-one by modification in any of the following ways, that is to say,
  (i) by further substitution at position 17 by a methyl or ethyl group;
  (ii) by substitution to any extent at one or more of positions 1, 2, 4, 6, 7, 9, 11 or 16, but at no other position;
  (iii) by unsaturation in the carbocyclic ring system to any extent, provided that there are no more than two ethylenic bonds in any one carbocyclic ring;
  (iv) by fusion of ring A with a heterocyclic system;
(ca) 1–benzylpiperazine or any compound structurally derived from 1–benzylpiperazine or 1–phenylpiperazine by modification in any of the following ways—
  (i) by substitution at the second nitrogen atom of the piperazine ring with alkyl, benzyl, haloalkyl or phenyl groups;
  (ii) by substitution in the aromatic ring to any extent with alkyl, alkoxy, alkylenedioxy, halide or haloalkyl groups.
(d) any substance which is an ester or ether (or, where more than one hydroxyl function is available, both an ester and an ether) of a substance specified in sub-paragraph (b) or described in sub-paragraph (c) above;
(e) Chorionic Gonadotrophin (HCG).
Non-human chorionic gonadotrophin.
Somatrem.
Zeranol.
Clenbuterol.
Somatotropin.
Somatropin.
Zilpatero

2. Any stereoisomeric form of a substance for the time being specified in paragraph 1 of this Part of this Schedule not being phenylpropanolamine.
3. Any salt of a substance for the time being specified in paragraph 1 or 2 of this Part of this Schedule.
4. Any preparation or other product containing a substance for the time being specified in any of paragraphs 1 to 3 of this Part of this Schedule.

Part IV Meaning of Certain Expressions Used in this Schedule

For the purposes of this Schedule the following expressions (which are not among those defined in section 37(1) of this Act) have the meanings hereby assigned to them respectively, that is to say—

'cannabinol derivatives' means the following substances, except where contained in cannabis or cannabis resin, namely tetrahydro derivatives of cannabinol and 3-alkyl homologues of cannabinol or of its tetrahydro derivatives;

'coca leaf' means the leaf of any plant of the genus *Erythroxylon* from whose leaves cocaine can be extracted either directly or by chemical transformation;

'concentrate of poppy-straw' means the material produced when poppy-straw has entered into a process for the concentration of its alkaloids;

'khat' means the leaves, stems or shoots of the plant of the species *Catha edulis*;

'medicinal opium' means raw opium which has undergone the process necessary to adapt it for medicinal use in accordance with the requirements of the British Pharmacopoeia, whether it is in the form of powder or is granulated or is in any other form, and whether it is or is not mixed with neutral substances;

'opium poppy' means the plant of the species *Papaver somniferum* L;

'poppy straw' means all parts, except the seeds, of the opium poppy after mowing;

'raw opium' includes powdered or granulated opium but does not include medicinal opium.

The inclusion of the concept of 'mowing' in the definition of 'poppy straw' in the MDA 1971, sch. 2, part IV, limits the extent of what is 'poppy straw' so that, on the facts in *Marwaha v UK Border Revenue Agency* [2017] EWHC 2321 (Admin), [2018] 1 WLR 758, [2018] 1 Cr App R 8 (105), poppy heads (with or without stalks) that had been harvested with care, were not mown. The Court applied a purposive approach to the legislation, and held that there was nothing to justify adopting a wider definition of 'mowing', such as to criminalise decorative uses for the dried poppy heads.

Provisions relating to Khat Khat, defined as 'the leaves, stems or shoots of the plant of the species *Catha edulis*', is classified as a Class C drug. It is a plant in which cathinone and cathine naturally subsist (Class C drugs when isolated from the plant). Khat is covered by the Misuse of Drugs (Designation) (England, Wales and Scotland) Order 2015 (SI 2015 No. 704), sch. 1, para. 1, the effect of which is to disapply s. 7(3) of the MDA 1971. It is also included in para. 1(a) of sch. 1 to the Misuse of Drugs Regulations 2001 (which specifies controlled drugs subject to the requirements of regs. 14, 15, 16, 18, 19, 20, 23, 26 and 27); the practical effect is to prohibit a doctor, dentist, veterinary practitioner, veterinary surgeon, pharmacist (or a person lawfully conducting a retail pharmacy business) possessing or applying khat for medicinal purposes. The CJPA 2001, s. 1(1), includes the possession of khat (and any preparation or other product containing khat) as an offence in respect of which a penalty notice may be given, and see the Police and Criminal Evidence Act 1984 (Codes of Practice) (Revision of Code E) Order 2016 (SI 2016 No. 35), para. 1. **B19.10**

For a sentencing example in relation to the importation of a large quantity of khat, see *Sidlauskas* [2014] EWCA Crim 2338, and note *Hamer* [2010] EWCA Crim 2053, [2011] 1 WLR 528.

Unnecessary to Distinguish between Drugs in Usual Form and Stereoisomeric Forms, Salts or Esters The MDA 1971, sch. 2, lists drugs in their basic and stereoisomeric forms, as well as their esters or salts. The Court of Appeal in *Greensmith* [1983] 3 All ER 444 held that the word 'cocaine' as used in para. 1 of sch. 2, part I (Class A drugs) is a generic word which includes within its ambit both the direct extracts of the coca leaf, the natural form, and whatever results from a chemical transformation listed in paras. 2 to 5. Having regard to *DPP v Goodchild* [1978] 2 All ER 161 (see **B19.12**) it is submitted that it would have been preferable had coca-leaf (which is separately specified as a controlled drug in sch. 2) not been described by the Court as 'cocaine'. *Greensmith* was applied in *A-G for the Cayman Islands v Roberts* [2002] UKPC 18, [2002] 1 WLR 1842. **B19.11**

The Court of Appeal held in *Watts* [1984] 2 All ER 380 that 'amphetamine' in sch. 2, part II, para. 1 (Class B drugs), includes generically all of its stereoisomers, pure dexamphetamine, pure levoamphetamine, or a racemic mixture of dexamphetamine and levoamphetamine.

Material Occurring Naturally Controlled drugs are defined by their chemical name (e.g., 'diamorphine' (heroin)). But 'any controlled drug described in [the MDA 1971, sch. 2] by its scientific name was not established by proof of possession of naturally occurring material of which the described drug was one of the constituents unseparated from the others ... and that was so whether or not the naturally occurring material was also included as another item in the list of controlled drugs' (*DPP v Goodchild* [1978] 2 All ER 161, per Lord Diplock, at p. 583). In the case of the latter **B19.12**

possibility, the offence would allude to the naturally occurring material, and not its constituent elements. Thus, cannabis, and fungus that contains psilocin, are described as such in sch. 2.

B19.13 **'Preparations' and 'Products' which Contain a Controlled Drug are Controlled** The word 'preparation' is not a technical word but 'a word to be addressed in its ordinary English meaning' (*Thomson* [2003] EWCA Crim 3477). The majority of appellate decisions that have considered the meaning of 'preparation' concern psilocybin mushrooms (now specifically controlled in the MDA 1971, sch. 2, part 1, para. 1(a)). In *Hodder v DPP* [1990] Crim LR 261, the Divisional Court held that to 'prepare' means 'to make ready or fit; to bring into a suitable state; to subject to a process of bringing it to a required state'. Freezing is not an act of preparation but of preservation. In order to prepare something it is not necessary to undertake a chemical or technical process (see *Stevens* [1981] Crim LR 568 and *Martin* [2006] EWCA Crim 109 in relation to naturally occurring material). A 'preparation' requires the substance to be altered by human action to put it into a condition in which it can be used for human consumption (*Stevens*; *Cunliffe* [1986] Crim LR 547, and consider *Heywood v Macrae* 1987 SCCR 627). Although *obiter*, it was remarked by the Divisional Court in *Jama v Senior Public Prosecutor, Germany* [2013] EWHC 3276 (Admin), [2014] 1 WLR 1843 at [38], that *Hodder v DPP* 'does not sit comfortably' with the observations of Lord Diplock in *DPP v Goodchild* [1978] 2 All ER 161. It did not seem to the Court that bundles of khat plants (as described in a European Arrest Warrant) could properly be regarded as a 'preparation or other product' containing cathinone, within the meaning of the MDA 1971, sch. 2, part III, para. 4, so as to bring the importation, exportation and supply of the plants themselves within the scope of the offences in ss. 3(1) and 4(1). The warrant did not suggest that anything had been done to the khat beyond picking it and bundling it up in parcels. In the opinion of the Court, it remained the natural plant, not a 'product' within the meaning of the statute (per Richards LJ at [38]). Note that khat is now a Class C controlled drug (SI 2014 No. 1352).

B19.14 In *Walker* [1987] Crim LR 565, the Court of Appeal declined to express any view as to whether merely picking psilocybin mushrooms is an act of preparation. Whether or to what extent the word 'product' includes packaged substances is not clear, but in *Hodder v DPP*, the Court of Appeal held that psilocybin mushrooms as 'picked, packaged and frozen' came within the meaning of the word 'product' or within the phrase 'or other product' as used in sch. 2, para. 5. Note that in *Greensmith* [1983] 3 All ER 444, the Court of Appeal remarked that any kind of matter comes within 'substance' whereas 'product' envisages the result of some kind of process. Difficulties have arisen in connection with *echinopsis peruviana* (cacti) in which mescaline subsists. In at least three cases concerning this plant material, proceedings for an offence under the MDA 1971 have been stayed (*Mardle* (14 December 2004 unreported), *Francis* (20 April 2005 unreported) and *Sette* (13 March 2006 unreported)). In *Sette*, the learned recorder stayed the case on the basis that the law was uncertain, and that HMRC had levied VAT on some vendors of this species of cactus. None of these first decision rulings has been the subject of detailed analysis by a higher court (but see *H* [2012] EWCA Crim 525, which raised similar issues with the same result). In any future cases involving this species of cactus, expert assistance might be required to specify the steps that need to be taken in order to put the plant into a usable condition. In *Aziz* [2012] EWCA Crim 1063, the Court of Appeal held (at [4]):

> ... that making an infusion out of the B-Caapi and the Chacruna amounted to producing by making a preparation. It did in any ordinary language and it did in law. It is not a question of altering the chemical make up of DMT. It is a question of putting it into a form in which it can be consumed, which is in any ordinary language preparation.

See also the commentary on *Aziz* at [2012] Crim LR 801. The Court of Appeal's reasoning would appear to be that, because the MDA 1971 controls 'preparations' that contain a controlled drug, a person can 'produce' a preparation (contrary to s. 4): consider *Williams* [2011] EWCA Crim 232 (see **B19.67**). If this means that every 'preparation' involved an act of 'production' then *Aziz* goes significantly further (it is submitted) than decisions such as *Hodder v DPP* and *Stevens*.

Meaning of 'Cannabis' and 'Cannabis Resin'

Misuse of Drugs Act 1971, s. 37 B19.15

'cannabis' (except in the expression 'cannabis resin') means any plant of the genus Cannabis or any part of any such plant (by whatever name designated) except that it does not include cannabis resin or any of the following products after separation from the rest of the plant, namely—
(a) mature stalk of any such plant,
(b) fibre produced from mature stalk of any such plant, and
(c) seed of any such plant,

'cannabis resin' means the separated resin, whether crude or purified, obtained from any plant of the genus *Cannabis*.

Note that 'cannabis' is not defined as a plant in which tetrahydrocannabinol (THC) subsists (either above a certain threshold or at all). In *Thomas* [1981] Crim LR 496, the Court of Appeal held that the substance was cannabis resin, even though on microscopic examination it was shown to contain elements of the natural form from which the resin had not been extracted. There was sufficient separated material, and *DPP v Goodchild* [1978] 2 All ER 161 did not lead to the conclusion that the wrong charge had been laid. In *Hill* (1993) 96 Cr App R 456, the Court of Appeal held that where the charge specifies the supply of 'cannabis resin' it is not enough to prove that D supplied either 'cannabis' or 'cannabis resin'. The Court distinguished *Best* (1979) 70 Cr App R 21 (see **B19.25**) where the charge particularised the drug as either cannabis or cannabis resin.

Proof of Substance as Controlled Drug

B19.16 Expert evidence (such as an analyst's certificate) is not required in all cases, but the prosecution must establish the identity of the drug referred to in the charge with sufficient certainty (*Hill* (1993) 96 Cr App R 456; see also *Gwilliam v DPP* [2010] EWHC 3312 (Admin), a case concerning herbal cannabis). This is particularly important for the reasons set out at **B19.5**. It should be noted that different penalties attach to each of the three statutory drug control regimes mentioned at **B19.2** to **B19.4**.

Note *R (Wright v CPS)* [2015] EWHC 628 (Admin) as to the importance of adhering to CrimPD V, paras. 19A.4 to 19A.6 (see Supplement, **CPD.19A**), with regard to expert evidence (see also *Chapman* [2017] EWCA Crim 1743, [2018] 1 Cr App R 9 (122)) and note the caution expressed in the introductory comments in **B19.120**. As the Administrative Court in *Wright* pointed out, the evidence, if relied on, must be capable of satisfying the criminal standard of proof. Although there are drug testing devices approved by the Home Office to identify a limited range of drugs for 'evidential purposes', it is submitted that the admissibility of the results of such devices is ultimately a matter for the courts: see Home Office Circular 013/2014 'The testing of substances suspected to be drugs controlled under the Misuse of Drugs Act 1971' and Home Office Circular 005/2017.

It was held in *Chatwood* [1980] 1 All ER 467 (in the context of the MDA 1971) that the admissions of D as to knowledge of the substance may constitute sufficient evidence to identify what it is. The Court of Appeal approved the statement of the law made by Lord Widgery CJ in *Bird v Adams* [1972] Crim LR 174:

> If a man admits possession of a substance which he says is a dangerous drug, if he admits it in circumstances like the present where he also admits that he has been peddling the drug, it is of course possible that the item in question was not a specified drug at all but the admission in those circumstances is not an admission of some fact about which the admitter knows nothing. This is the kind of case in which the appellant had certainly sufficient knowledge of the circumstances of his conduct to make his admission at least prima facie evidence of its truth and that was all that was required at the stage of the proceedings at which the submission to the justices was made.

The statements of the accused in *Chatwood* were sufficient to provide prima facie evidence of the nature of the substance in their possession. However, for the reasons given in this paragraph and at **B19.5**, the *Chatwood* approach needs to be applied with extreme care. D's opinion as to the nature of the substance possessed must be such that the opinion is reliable. As to admissions by D generally, see **F18**. See also *Bagshaw* [1995] Crim LR 433. For a useful discussion of this problem and the aforementioned cases, see *DPP v Buckley* [2007] IEHC 150 (a decision of the High Court of Ireland).

If evidence is disputed that a drug is the one alleged then it is important that this issue is raised in a timely fashion and challenged appropriately (consider *Griffiths* [2016] All ER (D) 192 (Feb)).

Regulations that Permit Actions with Respect to 'Controlled Drugs'

B19.17 The Misuse of Drugs Regulations 2001 contain provisions which make lawful certain acts which would otherwise be unlawful under the MDA 1971. They have been heavily amended (notably by SI 2018 No. 1055 to permit the wider use of 'cannabis-based product for medicinal use in humans', and for certain research purposes; see **B19.121**).

Note that by SI 2018 No. 682, the definition of 'prison' in regulation 2(1) has the same meaning as in the Investigatory Powers Act 2016, s. 49(3).

For reasons of space, this work no longer reproduces the 2001 Regulations, but they are available (as amended) via online law databases. The regulations must not be ignored.

A large number of controlled drugs are specified in schs. 1 to 5 to the 2001 Regulations. By reg. 3, 'Schedules 1 to 5 shall have effect for the purpose of specifying the controlled drugs to which certain provisions of these Regulations apply'. In other words, the intensity of legal control varies in respect of drugs falling within a given schedule. Drug substances and drug products listed in sch.1 to the 2001 Regulations are the most tightly controlled.

B19.18 **Power to Make Regulations** Section 7(1) of the MDA 1971 empowers the Secretary of State to make regulations to except from the MDA 1971, s. 5(1) (and ss. 3(1)(a) or (b) and 4(1)(a)) specified controlled drugs (and to make such other provision as he thinks fit) to make lawful an activity which, under ss. 4(1), 5(1), and 6(1), would otherwise be unlawful (and criminal under each section): see the Misuse of Drugs Regulations 2001. The Secretary of State is required to exercise this power to ensure that it is not unlawful under s. 5(1) for a doctor, dentist, veterinary practitioner, veterinary surgeon, pharmacist or person lawfully conducting a retail pharmacy business to have a controlled drug in his possession for the purpose of acting in such a capacity; similar provision is made with regard to the offence in s. 4(1) (s. 7(3)). However, that power is subject to s. 7(4), whereby the production, supply and possession of a drug may be made wholly unlawful, or unlawful except for research or other special purposes, or whereby the activities of practitioners, pharmacists and persons lawfully conducting retail pharmacy businesses may be made unlawful except where they act under a licence or other authority from the Secretary of State (see the Misuse of Drugs (Designation) (England, Wales and Scotland) Order 2015 (SI 2015 No. 704). Although cannabis is designated in para. 1(a) of the schedule to the 2015 Order (i.e., as a drug to which s. 7(4) applies) SI 2013 No. 624 excludes the cannabis-based medicine known as 'Sativex' from that designation, and see the Misuse of Drugs Regulations 2001, sch. 4, part I, para. 5, and note the position in relation to 'cannabis-based product for medicinal use in humans' pursuant to SI 2018 No. 1055. Similarly, in relation to a liquid formulation known as 'Epidyolex' that is placed in sch. 5 to the 2001 Regulations, see SI 2020 No. 559. Note also the Misuse of Drugs (Coronavirus) (Amendments Relating to the Supply of Controlled Drugs During a Pandemic etc.) Regulations 2020 (SI 2020 No. 468) that amend the 2001 Regulations to grant certain permissions in a pandemic situation.

B19.19 **Permitted Activities under the 2001 Regulations** Prescribed actions by persons specified in the regulations (e.g., constables, carriers, drug analysts, medical practitioners) are exempted from the general prohibitions or restrictions imposed by the MDA 1971 in respect of drugs that fall within a given schedule. For example, s. 3(1) (which prohibits the importation and exportation of controlled drugs) 'shall not have effect in relation to the drugs specified in Schedule 5' (reg. 4(1)). Section 5(1) (which prohibits the possession of controlled drugs) shall not have effect in relation to a fungus (of any kind) which contains psilocin or an ester of psilocin in the circumstances specified in reg. 4A.

Regulation 6A makes provision for the lawful supply of articles for administering or preparing controlled drugs. Regulation 12 permits the cultivation of cannabis plants when authorised by a licence of the Secretary of State. Regulations 15 to 17 provide for exemptions in relation to prescriptions.

Other regulations deal with requirements as to the marking of bottles and other containers, keeping of registers and records, furnishing of information and destruction of controlled drugs. Words and phrases are defined by reg. 2. In *Beneficent Spiritist Center Uniao Do Vegetal v Secretary of State for the Home Department* [2017] EWHC 1963 (Admin), the Divisional Court refused the claimant's renewed application for judicial review of a decision of the Secretary of State to refuse the claimant's application for a licence to import, possess and supply hoasca tea (ayahuasca) made from a plant material containing dimethyltryptamine (a Class A drug) for the purposes of consumption by its congregation. It was held (among other reasons) that the Secretary of State must justify the interference with the ECHR, Article 9, rights of the members of the claimant's congregation, but in approaching this matter the Secretary of State is entitled to a broad margin of appreciation (at [16]). In any event, there can be no presumption in favour of granting a licence under the provisions of the Misuse of Drugs Act 1971 and the regulations made thereunder.

The MDA 1971, s. 30, provides that a licence or other authority issued by the Secretary of State may be general or specific, and it may be issued on such terms and subject to such conditions (including, in the case of a licence, the payment of a prescribed fee) as the Secretary of State thinks proper, and may be modified or revoked at any time. **B19.20**

In *Dunbar* [1981] 1 All ER 188, the Court of Appeal had to consider the meaning of reg. 10(2) of the Misuse of Drugs Regulations 1973 (SI 1973 No. 797, revoked by SI 1985 No. 2066, which was itself revoked by SI 2001 No. 3998) in determining whether or not a doctor was unlawfully in possession of drugs. This case states a principle which is probably applicable to licences and authorisations generally. It was held that, for the purposes of reg. 10(2), it is not necessary for the doctor to have patients, since self-administration may well be appropriate. What matters is whether the doctor was acting bona fide in the capacity of a medical practitioner. This is a matter for the jury to decide (see also *Abraham* [2002] EWCA Crim 2870). In *Dunbar*, the jury had not been given the opportunity to consider whether D wanted the drugs for self-treatment or to commit suicide, and his conviction of unlawful possession was quashed. The mere fact that a person holds a licence, or authorisation, will not afford a defence where the possession of the drug is clearly outside the terms or conditions of the licence or authorisation, or is for an improper purpose. The issue must be left to the tribunal of fact to determine (*Abraham*).

Burden of Proof Relating to Exceptions under Regulations The leading case is *Hunt* [1987] AC 352. A statute may place a burden of proof on the accused by implication, although it does not do so expressly (as to the significance of *Hunt* on issues of burden of proof generally, see **F3.16**). Lord Griffiths said that the MDA 1971, s. 7(1), gives the Secretary of State power to make two kinds of exceptions: **B19.21**

(a) exceptions under s. 7(1)(a), whereby the power is given to provide that it is not an offence to possess certain drugs;

(b) exceptions under s. 7(1)(b), where the power is given to clothe certain persons with immunity from what would otherwise be unlawful acts, which is achieved by the remainder of the regulations.

Lord Griffiths said (at pp. 376–7):

> These latter regulations provide special defences to what would otherwise be unlawful acts and would, I accept, place a burden upon defendants to bring themselves within the exceptions if it were necessary to do so. I say 'if it were necessary to do so' because of the extreme improbability that an exempted person would be charged with an offence.

Hunt was decided with reference to the Misuse of Drugs Regulations 1973 (replaced by the 1985 and the 2001 Regulations). Their lordships held that as reg. 4 of the 1973 Regulations defined the essential ingredient of an offence, the prosecution must prove possession of the drug alleged beyond reasonable doubt. In *Hunt*, preparations of morphine containing not more than 0.2 per cent of morphine were exempted from the offence under s. 5(2), and the prosecution adduced no evidence of the composition of the preparation in question. It was held that the prosecution had failed to prove their case, and that D was entitled to an acquittal.

It follows that the incidence of proof may vary, depending upon which regulation is engaged. Where D shoulders a burden of proving a particular fact or matter, regard should be had to the decision of the House of Lords in *Lambert* [2001] UKHL 37, [2002] 2 AC 545 (see **B19.108** and **F3.18**; and consider *Keogh* [2007] EWCA Crim 528, [2007] 3 All ER 789 and *MK* [2018] EWCA Crim 667, [2019] QB 86).

OFFENCES UNDER THE MISUSE OF DRUGS ACT 1971

B19.22 It is submitted that, in the light of *Joseph* [2017] EWCA Crim 36, [2017] 1 Cr App R 33 (486) and *L* [2013] EWCA Crim 991, [2014] 1 All ER 113 (see **B22.17**), the fact that D was a trafficked child and that his criminal activities were integral to the circumstances in which he was a victim is relevant when deciding whether to prosecute on the basis of the public interest test (and to an 'abuse of process' argument). This consideration applies in relation to any offence under the MDA 1971 (consider *JXP* [2019] EWCA Crim 1280, and *V* [2015] EWCA Crim 1469). As to the circumstances in which a court may treat as mitigation (when sentencing for a drug trafficking offence) the fact that D is a victim of human trafficking, consider *Sidlauskas* [2014] EWCA Crim 2338 and see **A3**. As for the exploitation of children and other vulnerable persons in the context of the commission of drug trafficking offences, see *Mohammed* [2019] EWCA Crim 1881.

Possession of 'Controlled Drugs'

B19.23 **Misuse of Drugs Act 1971, s. 5**

(1) Subject to any regulations under section 7 of this Act for the time being in force, it shall not be lawful for a person to have a controlled drug in his possession.
(2) Subject to section 28 of this Act and to subsection (4) below, it is an offence for a person to have a controlled drug in his possession in contravention of subsection (1) above.
(2A) Subsections (1) and (2) do not apply in relation to a temporary class drug.

'Contravention' includes a failure to comply (s. 37(1)).

Note that the simple possession of cannabis and khat are 'penalty offences' for the purposes of the CJPA 2001 (see **D2.41**).

Given that the maximum sentence for the purposes of ss. 4(2) and (3)(a) to (c) and 5(2) and (3) depends upon the class of drug involved (see **B19.145**), it is arguable that the House of Lords' decision in *Courtie* [1984] AC 463 establishes that these provisions create more than one offence where the facts of a given case involve controlled drugs falling into different classes. However, the point is not free of difficulty having regard to s. 28(3)(a) and cases such as *Leeson* [2000] 1 Cr App R 233 (note also *Karpavicius v The Queen* [2002] UKPC 59, [2003] 1 WLR 169, in which *Courtie* was cited, albeit in the context of s. 6(2A) of the New Zealand Misuse of Drugs Act 1975). See also *Ellis* (1986) 84 Cr App R 235. Notwithstanding that it is unnecessary for the Crown to prove that D knew of the precise type and class of drug that D actually handled (see, e.g., *Bett* [1999] 1 All ER 600), it is submitted that it is best practice to charge by way of separate counts, on a single indictment, those controlled drugs that attract different maximum penalties (and see **B19.25**).

Procedure

B19.24 For powers of entry, search and seizure under the MDA 1971, see **B19.111**.

Offences under the MDA 1971, s. 5(2), are (by s. 25 of and sch. 4 to the Act) triable either way. When tried on indictment they are normally class 3 offences, but see CrimPD XIII, para. B (see Supplement, **CPD.XIII.B**), for the additional factors that the court considers on allocation.

Summary trial may be instituted by an information laid 12, rather than the usual six, months from the date of commission of the offence (MDA 1971, s. 25(4)).

For the liability of corporate officers, see **B19.40**.

Indictment

Statement of Offence **B19.25**

Possession of controlled drug contrary to section 5(2) of the Misuse of Drugs Act 1971.

Particulars of Offence

A on the ... day of ... unlawfully had in his possession a controlled drug of Class [A, B, or C] namely ... contrary to section 5(1) of the Misuse of Drugs Act 1971.

Where a count specifies more than one drug in the same class, the count does not offend the rules against duplicity (*Best* (1979) 70 Cr App R 21). But if the count specifies a particular controlled drug then the existence of that substance must be established (*Muir v Smith* [1978] Crim LR 293). Where a charge specifies a quantity of drugs, it is sufficient to prove that the accused acted in relation to part of that quantity and no question of a 'partial verdict' arises (*Peevey* (1973) 57 Cr App R 554).

It is not necessary to distinguish between a controlled drug and its stereoisomeric form, or a salt or ester in a count (see **B19.11**).

Sentencing Guidelines

See **B19.145** to **B19.165**. **B19.26**

Meaning of 'Possession'

Lord Hope in the House of Lords in *Lambert* [2001] UKHL 37, [2002] 2 AC 545, stated that 'there are two elements to possession. There is the physical element, and there is the mental element.' The approach of Lord Hope is reflected in the other judgments delivered in that case. It confirms the approach taken by the Court of Appeal in *McNamara* (1988) 87 Cr App R 246 (see **B19.29**), and is settled law (consider also *DPP v Brooks* [1974] AC 862 at **B19.33**). **B19.27**

Custody or Control 'The physical element involves proof that the thing is in the custody of the defendant or subject to his control', per Lord Hope in *Lambert* [2001] UKHL 37, [2002] 2 AC 545 (see also Lord Scarman in *Boyesen* [1982] AC 768). This is enlarged by the MDA 1971, s. 37(3): 'For the purposes of this Act the things which a person has in his possession shall be taken to include any thing subject to his control which is in the custody of another'. The ability to demand that the property in question be removed (or the ability to remove it oneself) is no more than evidence of knowledge and acquiescence: it is not to be equated with control (*Kousar* [2009] EWCA Crim 139, [2009] 2 Cr App R 5 (88), a case decided in the context of the Trade Marks Act 1994 but which, it is submitted, has relevance here: but note *Case* [2015] EWCA Crim 2080, in which *Kousar* was considered). **B19.28**

The description of possession given by Lord Wilberforce in *Warner v Metropolitan Police Commissioner* [1969] 2 AC 256, at pp. 310–11, remains relevant:

> The question, to which an answer is required, and in the end a jury must answer it, is whether in the circumstances the accused should be held to have possession of the substance, rather than mere control. In order to decide between these two, the jury should, in my opinion, be invited to consider all the circumstances — to use again the words of *Pollock and Wright* — the 'Modes or events' — by which the custody commences and the legal incident in which it is held. By these I mean relating them to typical situations, that they must consider the manner and circumstances in which the substance, or something which contains it, has been received, what knowledge or means of knowledge or guilty knowledge as to the presence of the substance, or as to the nature of what has been received, he had at the time of receipt or thereafter up to the moment when he is found with it; his legal relation to the substance or package (including his right of access to it). On such matters as these (not exhaustively stated) they must make the decision whether, in addition to physical control, he has, or ought to have imputed to him the intention to possess, or knowledge that he does possess, what is in fact a prohibited substance. If he has this intention or knowledge, it is not additionally necessary that he should know the nature of the substance.

For an interesting discussion of *Warner v Metropolitan Police Commissioner*, see *Tan Kiam Peng v Public Prosecutor* [2007] SGCA 38 (a decision of the Singapore Court of Appeal). The aspect of knowledge as a component of possession is dealt with at **B19.29**.

If a person orders a controlled drug, directing that it be sent by post to his or her address, the person is in possession of that drug from the time it arrives through the letter box (*Peaston* (1978) 69 Cr App R 203). A person smoking cannabis resin has that drug in his possession at the time of the smoking (*Chief Constable of Cheshire Constabulary v Hunt* (1983) 147 JP 567).

B19.29 **Knowledge of Possession** A person must be aware of being in possession of something which is, in fact, a controlled drug (regardless of whether the person knows it is a controlled drug or not): see *Warner v Metropolitan Police Commissioner* [1969] 2 AC 256, *Boyesen* [1982] AC 768 (at pp. 773–4), *McNamara* (1988) 87 Cr App R 246, and *Lambert* [2001] UKHL 37, [2002] 2 AC 545, where, for example, Lord Clyde states, 'The second element involves that the defendant knows that the thing in question is under his control. He need not know what its nature is, but so long as he knows that the thing, whatever it is, is under his control, it is in his possession' (and see *HKSAR v Hung Chan Wa* [2005] HKCA 231 at [36]–[37]). As to whether the prosecution need prove a conscious decision on the part of D to be in possession, consider *T* [2011] EWCA Crim 1646 (albeit in the context of the Firearms Act 1968). Ignorance of, or mistake as to, the quality of, the substance in question does not prevent D being in possession of it, provided that the substance turns out to be a controlled drug. Thus, D was in possession of the amphetamine tablets in a bottle in her holdall, even if she was mistaken as to their quality, in *Lockyer v Gibb* [1967] 2 QB 243 (consider also *Irving* [1970] Crim LR 642). In *Searle v Randolph* [1972] Crim LR 779, D knew that he had cigarettes; he simply made a mistake about the quality of the tobacco, and so was in possession of a controlled drug since one of the cigarettes contained cannabis. D's lack of knowledge of the quality of the thing might be a defence under the MDA 1971, s. 28 (see **B19.104**). It is important to keep this often-neglected provision in mind (see *Choudhury* [2008] EWCA Crim 3179 at **B19.105**).

A person does not possess something of which that person is completely unaware. If a drug is slipped secretly into someone's pocket, the person is not in possession of it (*Warner v Metropolitan Police Commissioner* and *McNamara*). D was not in possession in *Marriott* [1971] 1 All ER 595, where the cannabis resin on the knife could only be detected by a forensic scientist and D had no knowledge of any substance. A person remains in possession of something even if having forgotten about it (*Martindale* [1986] 3 All ER 25, following *Buswell* [1972] 1 All ER 75; cf. *Russell* (1984) 81 Cr App R 315).

B19.30 **Joint Possession** The expression 'joint possession' is liable to mislead. It is submitted that two situations need to be carefully contrasted. The first is where two or more persons are in possession of a controlled drug because each exercises control over the substance. A mere ability to control is not enough (see *Kousar* [2009] EWCA Crim 139, [2009] 2 Cr App R 5 (88) at **B19.28**, but note *Case* [2015] EWCA Crim 2080). Mere knowledge of the presence of a drug in the hands of a confederate is not enough: joint possession must be established (*Searle* [1971] Crim LR 592). Lord Widgery CJ, giving the judgment of the court, said: 'The sort of direction to which the deputy recorder should have opened the jury's mind was to ask them to consider whether these drugs formed a common pool from which all had the right to draw'. See also *Wright* (1975) 119 SJ 825, and consider *Montague* [2013] EWCA Crim 1781 (albeit in the context of firearms). In *Strong* (1989) *The Times*, 26 January 1990, the prosecution put the case on the basis that there was joint possession, that is, that each of the co-accused had control of one or more of the packages of cannabis. The Court of Appeal followed *Searle*, and said that what was being looked for was whether each person had the right to say what should be done with the cannabis. Mere presence in the same vehicle as the drugs, and knowing they were there, was not sufficient (and see *Irala-Prevost* [1965] Crim LR 606). In *Abbas* [2012] EWCA Crim 2517, [2013] 1 Cr App R 18 (255) it was said by the Court of Appeal (albeit in the context, presumably, of the FA 1968, s. 18) that, where knowledge and proof of joint possession depends upon the drawing of an inference, it is incumbent on a judge in summing up to identify the evidence of primary fact upon the basis of which, if it is accepted, a jury might infer knowledge and thus possession. However, it is submitted that directions will often be context-specific (and see *Sefaah* [2014] EWCA Crim 597).

The second situation is where D aids and abets another to be in possession of a controlled drug. In this situation, there must be some evidence of assistance, or encouragement, or some element of control: consider *Bland* [1988] Crim LR 41, *Conway* [1994] Crim LR 826, *McNamara* [1998] Crim LR 278, *Arshad* [2002] EWCA Crim 1549, *Jacobs* [2002] EWCA Crim 610, and *Bailey* [2004] EWCA Crim 2169. It should be noted that, on the question of knowledge, the prosecution are required to prove a stricter intent in the case of an aider or an abettor, namely that D knew that the principal was in possession of a controlled drug. It is not necessary that the prosecution prove the type of drug in question (*Patel* [1970] Crim LR 274, contrast *Fernandez* [1970] Crim LR 277).

Cases Involving Small Quantities of Controlled Drug

There are two points. First, the quantity of drug might be so slight as to amount, in reality, to nothing. Secondly, the fact that the quantity of drug is miniscule might be evidence of D's lack of knowledge of the existence of the thing. **B19.31**

Whether a Drug is Visible or Measurable Lord Widgery CJ, giving the majority judgment of the Divisional Court in *Bocking v Roberts* [1974] QB 307, said (at pp. 309–10): **B19.32**

> ... it is quite clear that the prosecution have to prove that there was some of the drug in the possession of the defendant to justify the charge, and the distinction which has to be drawn in cases of this kind is whether the quantity of the drug was enough to justify the conclusion that he was possessed of a quantity of the drug or whether, on the other hand, the traces were so slight that they really indicated no more than that at some previous time he had been in possession of the drug. It seems to me that that is the distinction that has to be drawn, although its application to individual cases is by no means easy.

This test was approved by the House of Lords in *Boyesen* [1982] AC 768. Lord Scarman said 'if it is visible, tangible, and measurable, it is certainly something'. It is submitted that the test may need to be applied mindful of the fact that modern scientific techniques may be capable of measuring minuscule amounts of a drug. See also *Worsell* [1970] 2 All ER 1183, *Graham* [1970] 2 All ER 1181, *Searle v Randolph* [1972] Crim LR 779, and see the discussion in *Williams v The Queen* [1978] HCA 49 at [18]. The House of Lords rejected a 'usability' test requiring that there be an amount of a drug sufficient to be used (or misused) for there to be something present. *Carver* [1978] QB 472 was overruled.

Minute Amount as Evidence of Lack of Knowledge Lord Scarman, in *Boyesen*, drew attention to the statement of Lord Diplock delivering the opinion of the Privy Council in *DPP v Brooks* [1974] AC 862, where he said: 'In the ordinary use of the word "possession", one has in one's possession whatever is, to one's own knowledge, physically in one's custody or under one's physical control'. Lord Scarman added, 'If the quantity in custody or control is so minute, the question arises: was it so minute that it cannot be proved that the accused knew he had it?' A good illustration, said Lord Scarman, is the New Zealand case of *Police v Emirali* [1976] 1 NZLR 286. Small quantities of drug were found in a vacuum cleaner which others had used, as well as a burned deposit on a metal clip of the type used for smoking marijuana cigarettes. The amount of the drug on the clip was only just measurable. On such facts D might properly argue against having been in possession of the substance at all; and see the approach taken by Stinson J in *Colyer* [1974] Crim LR 243. **B19.33**

Drugs in Containers

Two leading cases are *McNamara* (1988) 87 Cr App R 270, and *Lambert* [2001] UKHL 37, [2002] 2 AC 545. In *Lambert*, Lord Clyde said (at [126]): **B19.34**

> ... if the defendant is in possession of the container and knows that there is something in it, he will be taken to be in possession of the contents of the container.... Where the drug is in a container, it is sufficient for the prosecution to prove that the defendant had control of the container, that he knew of its existence and that there was something in it, and that the something was in fact the controlled drug which the prosecution alleges it to be. The prosecution does not require to prove that the accused knew that the thing was a controlled drug.

If D had no right to open the container and ascertain its contents, it is arguable that D was not in possession of the contents (*Warner v Metropolitan Police Commissioner* [1969] 2 AC 256, per Lord Morris at pp. 287 and 296, Lord Pearce at p. 306 and Lord Wilberforce at p. 312; *McNamara*; *Wright* (1975) 62 Cr App R 169. But consider, albeit in the context of firearms, *Deyemi* [2007] EWCA Crim 2060, [2008] 1 Cr App R 25 (345) at **B12.45**).

Subject to s. 28 of the MDA 1971, a mistake as to the nature of the contents will not avail the accused (cf. some of the statements of the House of Lords in *Warner v Metropolitan Police Commissioner* [1969] 2 AC 256, per Lord Reid at p. 281, Lord Morris at pp. 285, 290 and 296, Lord Guest at p. 302, Lord Pearce at p. 305 and Lord Wilberforce at p. 311).

Evidence Establishing Earlier Possession

B19.35 The existence of drug traces, or a minute quantity of a controlled drug, might be evidence that the accused had been in possession of a measurable/usable quantity of the substance (*Worsell* [1970] 2 All ER 1183; *Graham* [1970] 2 All ER 1181; consider *Hambleton v Callinan* [1968] 2 QB 427 concerning traces of a drug in a urine sample; and see *Olah v Court of Justice Miskolc (Hungary)* (27 April 2016 unreported, QBD) and *Spitans v Riga Regional Court* [2012] EWHC 472 (Admin)). However, it is important that care is taken in bringing charges on this basis. In *Pragliola* [1977] Crim LR 612, the Court of Appeal held that the charge of unlawful possession was oppressive and not justifiable where D was charged solely on the basis that a pipe, which contained a drug trace, was returned to him.

Mens Rea

B19.36 In *Lewis* (1988) 87 Cr App R 270, the Court of Appeal remarked that 'it is clear that if a defendant is proved to have knowledge of this control of prohibited articles, it is generally immaterial that he is in ignorance or under a mistake as to their extent or qualities'. This is the basic rule, but it is essential to read *Lewis* (and *Warner v Metropolitan Police Commissioner* [1969] 2 AC 256) with s. 28 of the MDA 1971 in mind (see *Lambert* [2001] UKHL 37, [2002] 2 AC 545 at **B19.108**, and note the commentary to *Lewis* by Professor Sir John Smith QC [1988] Crim LR 517. See also *Tan Kiam Peng v Public Prosecutor* [2007] SGCA 38).

Defence under s. 5(4)

B19.37 The MDA 1971, s. 5(4), provides a defence to simple possession (s. 5(2)) but the existence of that defence does not preclude any other defences being raised.

Misuse of Drugs Act 1971, s. 5

(4) In any proceedings for an offence under subsection (2) above in which it is proved that the accused had a controlled drug in his possession, it shall be a defence for him to prove—

(a) that, knowing or suspecting it to be a controlled drug, he took possession of it for the purpose of preventing another from committing or continuing to commit an offence in connection with that drug and that as soon as possible after taking possession of it he took all such steps as were reasonably open to him to destroy the drug or to deliver it into the custody of a person lawfully entitled to take custody of it; or

(b) that, knowing or suspecting it to be a controlled drug, he took possession of it for the purpose of delivering it into the custody of a person lawfully entitled to take custody of it and that as soon as possible after taking possession of it he took all such steps as were reasonably open to him to deliver it into the custody of such a person.

...

(6) Nothing in subsection (4) above shall prejudice any defence which it is open to a person charged with an offence under this section to raise apart from that subsection.

The defence under s. 5(4) proceeds on the assumption that the person knew or suspected that the thing which was in his possession was a controlled drug (*Lambert* [2001] UKHL 37, [2002] 2 AC 545 (at [56], [65] per Lord Hope and at [123] per Lord Clyde).

Where D buried drugs (e.g., cannabis) it was not sufficient to satisfy the defence in s. 5(4)(a) that the forces of nature might or would destroy the drugs eventually: rather it was for D to show that all such steps as were reasonably open were taken to destroy them and the acts of destruction must be D's (*Murphy* [2002] EWCA Crim 1587, [2003] 1 WLR 422). The Court of Appeal in *Dempsey* (1985) 82 Cr App R 291 made clear that the defence in s. 5(4)(b) is available only if D's purpose is to act in accordance with that subsection.

The decision in *Lambert* [2001] UKHL 37, [2002] 2 AC 545 (see **B19.108** and **F3.18**) means that the imposition of the persuasive burden in s. 5(4) is open to challenge (and consider *Keogh* [2007] EWCA Crim 528, [2007] 3 All ER 789).

Unavailable Defences

Necessity *Quayle* [2005] EWCA Crim 1415, [2006] 1 All ER 988 and *Altham* [2006] EWCA Crim 7, [2006] 1 WLR 3287 decide that necessity is not a defence to any of the offences under the MDA 1971 in circumstances where someone has possession of, is cultivating or is supplying cannabis in order to relieve pain. See also *Cotton* [2008] EWCA Crim 1279. In *Quayle*, the Court of Appeal pointed out that cannabis, cannabis resin and most cannabinoids are designated as drugs which may be used only for medical or scientific research (and they are drugs to which s. 7(4) of the MDA 1971 applies). Mance LJ said (at [54]): **B19.38**

> The effect of that designation is that, whatever benefits might be perceived or suggested for any individual patients, if these particular drugs were available for medical prescription and use (other than research), such individual benefits were and are in the legislator's view outweighed by disbenefits of strength sufficient in the national interest to require a general prohibition.

For further consideration of necessity, see **A3.47** to **A3.49**. For a decision of the ECtHR in relation to the medicinal use of cannabis, see *AM v Hungary* (2017) 65 EHRR SE2.

ECHR, Article 8 The ECHR, Article 8, is not engaged because a right to private life does not include a right to the possession of (or to cultivate) cannabis (*Morgan* [2002] EWCA Crim 721, and see (in the context of the ECHR, Article 9) *Taylor* [2001] EWCA Crim 2263, [2002] 1 Cr App R 37 (519) at **B19.62**). **B19.39**

Liability of Corporate Officers

Misuse of Drugs Act 1971, s. 21 **B19.40**

> Where any offence under this Act or Part II of the Criminal Justice (International Cooperation) Act 1990 committed by a body corporate is proved to have been committed with the consent or connivance of, or to be attributable to any neglect on the part of, any director, manager, secretary or other similar officer of the body corporate, or any person purporting to act in such capacity, he as well as the body corporate shall be guilty of that offence and liable to be proceeded against accordingly.

As to corporate liability generally, see **A6**.

SUPPLYING OR OFFERING TO SUPPLY ETC. CONTROLLED DRUG

Misuse of Drugs Act 1971, s. 4 **B19.41**

> (1) Subject to any regulations under section 7 of this Act, or any provision made in a temporary class drug order by virtue of section 7A, for the time being in force, it shall not be lawful for a person—
> (a) to produce a controlled drug; or
> (b) to supply or offer to supply a controlled drug to another.
> (2) ...
> (3) Subject to section 28 of this Act, it is an offence for a person—
> (a) to supply or offer to supply, a controlled drug to another in contravention of subsection 1 above; or
> (b) to be concerned in the supplying of such a drug to another in contravention of that subsection; or

(c) to be concerned in the making to another in contravention of that subsection of an offer to supply such a drug.

Given that s. 4(3) attracts different maximum penalties, depending on the class of drug involved, the indictment may need to be drafted with the effect of the decision of the House of Lords in *Courtie* [1984] AC 463 in mind (see **B19.23**). The Court of Appeal held in *Coker* [2019] EWCA Crim 420, [2019] 4 WLR 41 that s. 4(3) gives rise to 'three separate and distinct offences' (at [25]). See further **B19.49** and [2019] Crim LR 542.

Note that a 'controlled drug' includes substances or products subject to a 'temporary class drug order' (see s. 2(1)(a)(ii) at **B19.7**).

A number of elements are common to each of these offences (save for offers to supply), namely, (a) that there must be a 'controlled drug'; (b) that the activity with regard to that drug must involve a 'supply' in some form; and (c) that the activity must be in contravention of s. 4(1). The question of what substances are 'controlled drugs' is dealt with at **B19.7** ***et seq.*** It is important to keep in mind the potential reach of the offences of 'encouraging or assisting' an offence, created under the SCA 2007, part 2 (see also *S* [2011] EWCA Crim 2872, [2012] 2 All ER 793).

Procedure

B19.42 Offences under the MDA 1971, s. 4(3), are (by s. 25 of and sch. 4 to the Act) triable either way. When tried on indictment they are normally class 3 offences, but see CrimPD XIII, para. B (see Supplement, **CPD.XIII.B**), for the additional factors that the court considers on allocation. There may be circumstances when it is appropriate to charge, by way of a single count, conspiracy to produce and to supply a controlled drug (*Lewis* [2014] EWCA Crim 122).

Summary trial may be instituted by an information laid 12, rather than the usual six, months from the date of commission of the offence (MDA 1971, s. 25(4)).

For the liability of corporate officers, see **B19.40**.

Sentencing

B19.43 See **B19.145** to **B19.165**. The Drugs Act 2005 inserted s. 4A into the MDA 1971, which specifies for sentencing purposes an aggravating feature of supply of a controlled drug. If the offender convicted of an offence under s. 4(3) is aged 18 or over and the offence was committed on or in the vicinity of school premises, or the offence involved commission by the offender of a courier who at the relevant time was under 18, the sentencing court must treat such fact as an aggravating feature of the offence and must state in open court that the offence is so aggravated. It is submitted that s. 4A adds little to pre-existing sentencing principles that apply in cases of drug trafficking.

A minimum custodial sentence of seven years applies for the third Class A drug trafficking offence (see **E5.1**).

An offence under s. 4(3) is a drug trafficking offence within the meaning of the POCA 2002, sch. 2 (see **E19.18**).

A forfeiture order (see **E18.7**) or a confiscation order (see **E19**) may be imposed.

Meaning of 'Supply'

B19.44 The words 'supply' and 'supplying' mean the same whenever those words appear in the MDA 1971, as well as for the purposes of the regulations and orders made under the Act (see **B19.17**): see *Maginnis* [1987] AC 303. By s. 37(1) of the 1971 Act, 'supplying' includes distributing (consider *Moore* [1979] Crim LR 789 in which *King* [1978] Crim LR 288 was not followed). It is submitted that nothing said by the Court of Appeal in *Martin* [2014] EWCA

Crim 1940, [2015] 1 WLR 588 at [16] or in *Porja* [2017] EWCA Crim 17, [2017] 2 Cr App R 4 (34) (which concerned a charge under s. 4(3)(b): see **B19.49**) should be taken as modifying the speeches of their lordships in *Maginnis*.

There is a 'supply' where D purchases drugs on behalf of a third party, and then transfers the drug to that party (or where a drug is distributed within a small social group) (*Buckley* (1979) 69 Cr App R 371; *Denslow* [1998] Crim LR 566).

In *Maginnis*, Lord Keith, in a speech with which three other members of the House of Lords concurred, held that the word 'supply' is to be ascertained 'by reference to the ordinary natural meaning of the word together with any assistance which may be afforded by the context' (see also *Holmes v Chief Constable Merseyside Police* [1976] Crim LR 125). Lord Keith said (*Maginnis* at p. 309):

> The word 'supply', in its ordinary natural meaning, conveys the idea of furnishing or providing to another something which is wanted or required in order to meet the wants or requirements of that other. It connotes more than the mere transfer of physical control of some chattel or object from one person to another. No one would ordinarily say that to hand over something to a mere custodier was to supply him with it. The additional concept is that of enabling the recipient to apply the thing handed over to purposes for which he desires or has a duty to apply it. In my opinion it is not a necessary element in the conception of supply that the provision should be made out of the personal resources of the person who does the supplying. Thus if an employee draws from his employer's store materials or equipment which he requires for purposes of his work, it involves no straining of language to say that the storekeeper supplies him with those materials or that equipment, notwithstanding that they do not form part of the storekeeper's own resources and that he is merely the custodier of them. I think the same is true if it is the owner of the business who is drawing from his own storekeeper tools or materials which form part of his own resources. The storekeeper can be said to be supplying him with what he needs. If a trafficker in controlled drugs sets up a store of these in the custody of a friend whom he thinks unlikely to attract the suspicions of the police, and later draws on the store for the purposes of his trade, or for his own use, the custodier is in my opinion rightly to be regarded as supplying him with drugs.

The *Maginnis* approach provides little difficulty in a typical case where a person transfers both the custody and control of a controlled drug to another (*Mills* [1963] 1 QB 522).

Maginnis also deals with cases where D1 transfers drugs to D2 for 'safekeeping'. In *Maginnis*, **B19.45**
the House of Lords reconciled the cases of *Dempsey* (1985) 82 Cr App R 291 and *Delgado* [1984] 1 All ER 449, by holding that 'supply' involves more than a mere transfer of physical control of the item from one person to another but includes a further concept, namely, that of 'enabling the recipient to apply the thing handed over to purposes for which he desires or has a duty to apply it'. The result appears to be that if A gives drugs to B for safekeeping, A has not supplied B with them for the purposes of s. 4. But, were B to return the drugs to A (or where B intends to do so), B would be guilty of supplying the drugs to A (or possessing them with that intention) (*Panton* [2001] EWCA Crim 611, following *Maginnis*, where D, acting as a custodian of drugs, intended to return them to the depositor — D had therefore committed an offence contrary to s. 5(3)). In *Pentecost* [1998] EWCA Crim 865, the Court of Appeal held that the trial judge had not erred when he directed the jury that 'supply does not require a physical handing over as such by the custodian. It would be sufficient if, with the intention that the trafficker retakes the drugs, the custodian did something to enable the trafficker to achieve that object.' *Maginnis* [1987] AC 303 was considered in *Watson* [2014] EWCA Crim 196, where the Court of Appeal agreed with the single judge that questions of joint possession were irrelevant and that, on the facts of that case, the key elements of unlawful possession and intent to supply were established.

It is important not to confuse purpose, or intention, with motive (which is irrelevant) (*X* [1994] Crim LR 827, where D was a registered police informer; his motive of causing a drugs dealer to be caught did not affect whether there was a supply).

In *Harris* [1968] 2 All ER 49, it was held that injecting another with a drug in the recipient's possession is not 'supplying' that drug to the recipient, particularly since physical control was not transferred to the recipient. This case must be read with care (having regard to the fact that it pre-dates the MDA 1971).

Extra-territorial Effect

B19.46 In *Hussain (Shabbir)* [2010] EWCA Crim 970, [2011] QB 1 the Court of Appeal held (applying *Seymour v The Queen* [2007] UKPC 59, [2008] 1 AC 713) that the prohibition imposed by the MDA 1971 on supplying a controlled drug proscribes only the supply in the UK. D routinely transferred Class C drugs to a courier within the UK who would then deliver them to a customer abroad. The transfer to the courier did not amount to supply (*Maginnis* [1987] AC 303 applied). The fact that a custodian might act for profit did not turn the custodian into a supplier under the Act. The essence of supply was that the transfer had to be for the benefit of the transferee. Furthermore, the supply had to be within the jurisdiction. See also *Johnston* (2 March 1974 unreported), albeit decided in the context of rules relating to jurisdiction.

When Supply etc. is Lawful

B19.47 Conduct otherwise proscribed by the MDA 1971, s. 4(1), may be licensed or authorised by the Misuse of Drugs Regulations 2001 (see generally, **B19.17**). Various regulations provide exceptions and exemptions (e.g., for medical personnel, pharmacists and midwives, and for research activities).

Section 4(1)(b) and (3)(a): Offering to Supply

B19.48 An offer may be by words or conduct. If it is by words, it must be ascertained whether an offer to supply a controlled drug was made. Whether D had a controlled drug in his possession or had access to controlled drugs or whether the substance in his possession was a controlled drug at all is immaterial. The position might be different where the offer is made by conduct (*Mitchell* [1992] Crim LR 723; *Haggard v Mason* [1976] 1 All ER 337). Whether D intends to carry the offer into effect is irrelevant; the offence is complete upon the making of an offer to supply (*Goodard* [1992] Crim LR 588, see also *Gill* (1993) 97 Cr App R 215, *Showers* [1995] Crim LR 400, and *Haslock* [2001] EWCA Crim 1321). The offence is committed whether or not the offer is genuine. Once made, an offer cannot be withdrawn (*Prior* [2004] EWCA Crim 1147). It is not helpful to refer to principles of contract law in determining whether there is an offer (*Dhillon* [2000] Crim LR 760, and see *Prior*).

Section 4(3)(b): Being Concerned in Supply to Another

B19.49 The three ingredients of this offence were set out by the Court of Appeal in *Hughes* (1985) 81 Cr App R 344, at p. 348 (and reiterated in *Coker* [2019] EWCA Crim 420, [2019] 4 WLR 41):

(a) the supply of a drug to another in contravention of s. 4(1) of the MDA 1971;
(b) participation by D in an enterprise involving such supply; and
(c) D's knowledge of the nature of the enterprise, i.e. that it involved the supply of a drug.

In *Coker*, the Court added (at [29]) that the above elements are 'subject to such tailoring as is required for the individual facts'.

It was held in *Martin* [2014] EWCA Crim 1940, [2015] 1 WLR 588 that, for the purposes of s. 4(3)(b), it was not necessary for the prosecution to prove a past or completed supply. Lord Thomas CJ remarked (at [16]):

> The word 'supply' is a broad term. It does not by any stretch of the imagination result in a confinement to the expressions 'actual delivery' or 'past supply'. It refers to the entire process of supply.

The decision in *Martin* was applied in *Porja* [2017] EWCA Crim 17, [2017] 2 Cr App R 4 (34) (*Hughes* (1985) 81 Cr App R 344 and *Akinsete* [2012] EWCA Crim 2377 considered).

Martin and *Porja* bring the construction of s. 4(3)(b) closer to that decided by the High Court of Justiciary in Scotland (*Atkinson v HM Advocate* [2010] HCJAC 77; *Kerr v HM Advocate* 1986 SCCR 81) and, similarly, as decided by the courts of Jersey (*A-G v Antunes* [2003] JLR 144) and Guernsey (*Law Officers of the Crown v Bishop* (30 May 2013 unreported, Royal Court of Guernsey)). It was held in *Kerr* (at p. 87) that s. 4(3)(b) was 'purposely enacted in the widest terms and was intended to cover a great variety of activities both at the centre and also on the fringes of dealing in controlled drugs. It would, for example, in appropriate circumstances include the activities of financiers, couriers and other go-betweens, lookouts, advertisers, agents and many links in the chain of distribution' (see also *HM Advocate v Grant* [2007] HCJAC 71).

Section 4(3)(c): Concerned in the Making of an Offer to Supply

Noting the decisions of *Coker* and *Hughes* (see **B19.49**), it is submitted that the elements of an offence under s. 4(3)(c) are: (1) that D made an offer to supply a controlled drug to another in contravention of s. 4(1); (2) that D participated in an enterprise involving such offer to supply; and (3) that D knew the nature of the enterprise, namely that it involved such offering to supply. **B19.50**

Section 4: General Issues

'Concerned in' It is the duty of the judge to assist the jury as to the meaning of the phrase 'concerned in' (*Hughes* (1985) 81 Cr App R 344). **B19.51**

A person may be concerned by being involved at a distance in making an offer to supply a controlled drug (*Blake* (1978) 68 Cr App R 1).

'Enterprise' and 'participate' In *Baker* [2009] EWCA Crim 535 (not cited in *Martin* [2014] EWCA Crim 1940, [2015] 1 WLR 588; *Abi-Khalil* [2017] EWCA Crim 17, [2017] 2 Cr App R 4 (34) or *Coker* [2019] EWCA Crim 420, [2019] 4 WLR 41) Lord Judge CJ remarked (at [18]), 'We would caution against the danger of treating language used in the course of a judgment, which involves the interpretation of a criminal statute, as if it were the statute, or as if it replaced or amended the statute, at any rate, certainly where the statute is plain enough in its language and uses ordinary English to describe the offence'. The Court observed that neither the word 'enterprise' nor the word 'participate', as used by Robert Goff LJ in *Hughes*, appear in s. 4(3)(b). Accordingly, 'if a person introduces someone who wants to obtain heroin to someone who he knows is willing and able to supply it, and together they obtain heroin for which the person introduced to the vendor pays, on the basis that in due course the introducer will pay for his share, it is open to a jury to conclude that the introducer is concerned in the supplying of the heroin to the other person'. As to whether rules relating to accessorial liability have any application for the purposes of s. 4(3)(b) or (c), consider the Scots law cases of *Barclay v HM Advocate* [2020] HCJAC 8, and *HM Advocate v Hamil* 1998 SCCR 164. **B19.52**

Relationship between s. 4(3)(a), (b) and (c) Although the Court of Appeal in *Coker* described the wording of s. 4(3) as 'authoritatively explained in *Hughes* and *Martin* (endorsed in *Abi-Khalil*', aspects of the subsection may continue to be problematic. The Court held in (*Coker* at [25]) that s. 4(3) gives rise to 'three separate and distinct offences' and thus there is no room for an 'either/or' direction encompassing being concerned in the supplying of a controlled drug (s. 4(3)(b)) and the separate offence (under s. 4(3)(c)) of being concerned in the making of an *offer to supply* (at [32]). The Court expressed 'no view' on s. 4(3)(a) (supply or offer to supply a controlled drug). It added that nothing in the judgment deals with the situation where the indictment contains separate counts, one under s. 4(3)(b) and another under s. 4(3)(c) (at [35]). It is submitted that even if the offences are separate, the extent to which they are truly 'distinct' may require judicial clarification (noting that, in *Martin*, the Court held that the word 'supply' refers to 'the entire process of supply' (see **B19.49**). In a case where D has advertised, offered to supply, and supplied a controlled drug to another, how is the prosecution to proceed under s. 4(3)? It is submitted that many problems will be avoided if, as the Court in *Coker* stated, the **B19.53**

elements of the relevant offence are 'subject to such tailoring as is required for the individual facts' (see **B19.49**, and the case commentary to *Coker* at [2019] Crim LR 542).

B19.54 **'Another'** For the purposes of ss. 4 and 5(3), the 'another' cannot be someone charged in the same count, but it can be someone charged in other counts in the same indictment (*Smith* (14 February 1983 unreported), *Ferrera* (1984 unreported), *Adepoju* [1988] Crim LR 378, *Connelly* (1991) 156 JP 406, *Reeves* [2001] EWCA Crim 91, *Porja* [2017] EWCA Crim 17, [2017] 2 Cr App R 4 (34), and note *Gingell* (1999) 163 JP 648, which makes the same point in the context of a charge of handling stolen goods; see **B4.174**). For cases of conspiracy to supply to 'another' where that other is a co-conspirator, see *Drew* [2000] 1 Cr App R 91 and *Jackson* (1999) *The Times*, 13 May 1999; in neither judgment was the effect of *Adepoju* discussed. It is not clear whether the law in England and Wales mirrors that in Scotland, namely, that a single count, charged under s. 4(3)(a) or (b), may embrace more than one act of supply etc. (*HM Advocate v Grant* [2007] HCJAC 71).

Defence under s. 28

B19.55 The defence under the MDA 1971, s. 28, is discussed at **B19.104**. Note that s. 28 does not apply to *an offer* to supply a controlled drug (*Mitchell* [1992] Crim LR 723). This is because the offence is rooted in the making of the offer, and not in the quality of the substance offered (which, if it existed at all, might be innocuous).

POSSESSION OF CONTROLLED DRUG WITH INTENT TO SUPPLY

B19.56 **Misuse of Drugs Act 1971, s. 5**

(3) Subject to section 28 of this Act, it is an offence for a person to have a controlled drug in his possession, whether lawfully or not, with intent to supply it to another in contravention of section 4(1) of this Act.

As to whether the effect of the House of Lords' decision in *Courtie* [1984] AC 463 is that there is more than one offence under s. 5(3), see **B19.23**.

For the meaning of 'controlled drug', see **B19.7** *et seq.*; as to the meaning of 'possession', see **B19.27** *et seq.*

For circumstances in which possession may be lawful by virtue of the Misuse of Drugs Regulations 2001, see **B19.17**.

Procedure

B19.57 Offences under the MDA 1971, s. 5(3), are (by s. 25 of and sch. 4 to the Act) triable either way. When tried on indictment they are normally class 3 offences, but see CrimPD XIII, para. B (see Supplement, **CPD.XIII.B**) for the additional factors that the court considers on allocation.

Summary trial may be instituted by an information laid 12, rather than the usual six, months from the date of commission of the offence (MDA 1971, s. 25(4)).

For the liability of corporate officers, see **B19.40**.

Indictment

B19.58 The form of indictment provided at **B19.25** may be adapted by addition of the specific intent to the particulars of the offence.

Alternative Verdicts

B19.59 In *Blackford* (1989) 89 Cr App R 239, the Court of Appeal, exercising its general power under the CLA 1967, substituted a conviction of possession under the MDA 1971, s. 5(2), for that under s. 5(3) (but note *Yeardley* [2000] 2 WLR 366). In *Johnson* [2013] EWCA Crim 2001, the Court of Appeal, when quashing a conviction for an offence under the MDA 1971, s. 5(3), held that it did not suggest, any more than did the Court in *Hodson* [2009] EWCA Crim 1590, that every time that a jury is considering a count under s. 5(3) it will be necessary to leave simple possession in the alternative. It depends on the circumstances and the assessment of the trial judge as to what is fair. In the instant case, the jury should, at the least, have received assistance as to the evidence that was capable of establishing an intention to supply.

Sentence

See **B19.145** to **B19.165**. This is a drug trafficking offence within the meaning of the POCA 2002, sch. 2 (see **E19.18**). A minimum custodial sentence of seven years applies for the third Class A drug trafficking offence (see **E5.1**). A forfeiture order (see **E18.7**) or a confiscation order (see **E19**) may be imposed. **B19.60**

Intent to Supply

The expression 'supply', used in both ss. 4(3) and 5(3) of the MDA 1971, means the same in both contexts (*Maginnis* [1987] AC 303). For the meaning of 'supply', see **B19.44**. **B19.61**

For the purposes of s. 5(3), the prosecution need only establish that D had the controlled drug in his possession with the intention of supplying it to another. A mistake as to the drug in question is (subject to the MDA 1971, s. 28) irrelevant (*Leeson* [2000] 1 Cr App R 233).

'Intent to supply' means an intent on the part of the possessor of the drugs to supply, and not an intention that the drug should be supplied by another person (*Greenfield* (1983) 78 Cr App R 179).

To come within s. 5(3), the intention to supply must be an intention to supply the thing of which D is in possession (*Wright* [2011] EWCA Crim 1180, [2011] 2 Cr App R 15 (168)). It is submitted that *Wright* was decided on its special facts, namely, that there was no suggestion that D intended to supply the immature and unusable cannabis plants that were in his possession. *Wright* was doubted and distinguished in *McAtarsney* [2013] NICA 59.

As to proving an intent to supply, and the admissibility of evidence of large amounts of money, an extravagant lifestyle or drug equipment, see **F1.17**.

In *Downes* [1984] Crim LR 552, the Court of Appeal decided that where two people were in joint possession (for the meaning of this phrase, see **B19.30**) they were not both involved in a joint venture to supply unless both had an intention to supply. Mere knowledge on the part of one that the other intended to supply is not sufficient. It is submitted that this holds true if the case is put on the basis that each person was a principal offender. However, the s. 5(3) offence may be committed by way of secondary participation (Accessories and Abettors Act 1861, s. 8); it remains to be seen to what extent prosecutions are brought under the SCA 2007, part 2.

For the purposes of ss. 4 and 5(3), the 'another' cannot be someone charged in the same count, but it can be someone charged in other counts in the same indictment (see **B19.49**).

Defences

The defence under s. 28 is dealt with at **B19.104**. **B19.62**

In *Taylor* [2001] EWCA Crim 2263, [2002] 1 Cr App R 37 (519), D, a Rastafarian, argued that, as the prosecution had conceded that his possession with intent to supply cannabis was purely for religious purposes (see also **B11.146**), convicting him would be a breach of the ECHR, Article 9. The Court of Appeal held that there was no breach of Article 9 (or Article 8). Article 9(2) was satisfied as there was a pressing social need to combat the public health and public safety dangers arising from drugs such as cannabis. This was evidenced, in part, by the Single

Convention on Narcotic Drugs 1971; and see *Andrews* [2004] EWCA Crim 947 (a case under the Customs and Excise Management Act 1979, s. 170).

PRODUCTION OF CONTROLLED DRUG

B19.63 **Misuse of Drugs Act 1971, s. 4**

(2) Subject to section 28 of this Act, it is an offence for a person—
- (a) to produce a controlled drug in contravention of subsection (1) [of section 4]; or
- (b) to be concerned in the production of such a drug in contravention of that subsection by another.

For the meaning of 'controlled drug', see **B19.7** ***et seq.*** As to the circumstances in which production may be lawful pursuant to the Misuse of Drugs Regulations 2001, see **B19.17**.

Each of paras. (a) and (b) creates separate offences. As to whether the effect of the House of Lords' decision in *Courtie* [1984] AC 463 is that there is more than one offence under s. 4(2), see **B19.23**.

Procedure

B19.64 Offences under the MDA 1971, s. 4(2), are (by s. 25 of and sch. 4 to the Act) triable either way. When tried on indictment they are normally class 3 offences, but see CrimPD XIII, para. B (see Supplement, **CPD.XIII.B**), for the additional factors that the court considers on allocation.

Summary trial may be instituted by an information laid 12, rather than the usual six, months from the date of commission of the offence (MDA 1971, s. 25(4)).

For the liability of corporate officers, see **B19.40**.

There may be circumstances when it is appropriate to charge, by way of a single count, conspiracy to produce and to supply a controlled drug (*Lewis* [2014] EWCA Crim 122).

Sentence

B19.65 See **B19.145** to **B19.165**. This is a drug trafficking offence within the meaning of the POCA 2002, sch. 2 (see **E19.18**). A minimum custodial sentence of seven years applies for the third Class A drug trafficking offence (see **E5.1**). A forfeiture order (see **E18.7**) or a confiscation order (see **E19**) may be imposed for a drug trafficking offence.

Meaning of 'Produce', 'Concerned in Production'

B19.66 **Misuse of Drugs Act 1971, s. 37**

(1) ... 'produce', where the reference is to producing a controlled drug, means producing it by manufacture, cultivation or any other method, and 'production' has a corresponding meaning; ...

The Court of Appeal in *Russell* (1992) 94 Cr App R 351 held that the conversion of one form of Class A drug into another form of the same genus may be production and thus the conversion of the salt cocaine hydrochloride to free base cocaine (i.e. from a substance described in the MDA 1971, sch. 2, para. 4, to a substance described in sch. 2, para. 5) was an act of production. This was because it was 'the production of a substance (not by manufacture or cultivation but by "other means" [referring to the definition in s. 37(1), but, strictly, "any other method"]) with physical and chemical features different from the cocaine hydrochloride from which it springs, albeit sharing the same generic term, cocaine'.

Stripping a cannabis plant, which had been cut and harvested, is producing a controlled drug because the action, by 'other method', produces a part of the plant which is a controlled drug

(*Harris* [1996] 1 Cr App R 369). On the issue of whether a 'preparation' involves an act of 'production', see *Aziz* [2012] EWCA Crim 1063 (discussed at **B19.14**).

Being 'concerned in the production' (s. 4(2)(b)) does not require proof that the accused played an identifiable role in the production of the drug in question (*Nguyen* [2010] EWCA Crim 2658). However, in *Dunn* [2008] EWCA Crim 2308, the Court of Appeal proceeded on the basis that, for the purposes of s. 4(2), it must be shown that D participated in the enterprise and had knowledge of the nature of the enterprise. D had submitted that the words of Robert Goff LJ in *Hughes* (1985) 81 Cr App R 344 at p. 348, in relation to the supply limb of s. 4, could be transferred to the 'production limb'. Robert Goff LJ stated (in the context of s. 4(3)(b) and (c)): **B19.67**

> It appears to us that, for an offence to be shown to have been committed by a defendant contrary to subsection (b) or subsection (c), as the case may be, the prosecution has to prove (1) the supply of a drug to another, or as the case may be the making of an offer to supply a drug to another, in contravention of section 4(1) of the Act; (2) participation by the defendant in an enterprise involving such supply or, as the case may be, such offer to supply; and (3) knowledge by the defendant of the nature of the enterprise, i.e. that it involved supply of a drug or, as the case may be, offering to supply a drug.

But, in *Baker* [2009] EWCA Crim 535, the Court of Appeal remarked that neither the word 'enterprise' nor the word 'participate' appear in s. 4. Contrast the foregoing with *Farr* [1982] Crim LR 745.

In *Williams* [2011] EWCA Crim 232, the Court of Appeal held as a correct statement of the law that the addition of adulterants or bulking agents can amount to the production of a controlled drug. Presumably, users of heroin who mix the drug with water and cannabis users who mix the drug with tobacco (and those who bake a cannabis cake?) will have to rely on the discretion of prosecutors not to charge inappropriately.

In cases where it is alleged that D conspired to produce a controlled drug, it was held in *Kenning* [2008] EWCA Crim 1534, [2009] QB 221 that an agreement to aid and abet an offence cannot constitute a statutory conspiracy under the Criminal Law Act 1977, s. 1(1), but contrast *Dang* [2014] EWCA Crim 348, [2014] 1 WLR 3797 and see further **A5.52**. There could be no conviction for aiding, abetting and counselling or procuring an offence unless the *actus reus* of the substantive offence was shown to have occurred. Even if the aiders and abettors do all that they agree to do, their course of conduct will not 'necessarily amount' to the commission of an offence as required by s. 1(1).

Defence under s. 28

As to the defence under the MDA 1971, s. 28, see **B19.104**. **B19.68**

PROHIBITION ON IMPORTATION AND EXPORTATION OF CONTROLLED DRUGS

Misuse of Drugs Act 1971, s. 3 **B19.69**

(1) Subject to subsection (2) below—
 (a) the importation of a controlled drug: and
 (b) the exportation of a controlled drug,
 are hereby prohibited.
(2) Subsection (1) above does not apply—
 (a) to the importation or exportation of a controlled drug which is for the time being excepted from paragraph (a) or, as the case may be, paragraph (b) of subsection (1) above by regulations under section 7 of this Act or by provision made in a temporary class drug order by virtue of section 7A; or

(b) to the importation or exportation of a controlled drug under and in accordance with the terms of a licence issued by the Secretary of State and in compliance with any conditions attached thereto.

Section 3, which is of considerable importance, imposes a prohibition, but it does not create an offence. It is generally enforced by offences charged under the Customs and Excise Management Act 1979, namely, improper importation or exportation of goods, or the fraudulent evasion of a prohibition on importation or exportation of goods or, where appropriate, conspiracy to evade the prohibition contained in the section. As to these offences, see **B16.27** ***et seq.*** For the relationship between s. 3 offences and offences under the Customs and Excise Acts, see *Whitehead* [1982] QB 1272; and note *Marron* [2011] EWCA Crim 792.

The meaning of the term 'controlled drug' and the circumstances in which exemptions may be permitted by regulation are discussed in **B19.7** and **B19.17**.

CULTIVATING PLANT OF THE GENUS CANNABIS

B19.70 **Misuse of Drugs Act 1971, s. 6**

(1) Subject to any regulations under section 7 of this Act for the time being in force, it shall not be lawful for a person to cultivate any plant of the genus Cannabis.
(2) Subject to section 28 of this Act, it is an offence to cultivate any such plant in contravention of subsection (1) above.

Procedure

B19.71 Offences under the MDA 1971, s. 6, are (by s. 25 of and sch. 4 to the Act) triable either way. When tried on indictment they are normally class 3 offences, but see CrimPD XIII, para. B (see Supplement, **CPD.XIII.B**), for the additional factors that the court considers on allocation.

Summary trial may be instituted by an information laid 12, rather than the usual six, months from the date of commission of the offence (MDA 1971, s. 25(4)).

For the liability of corporate officers, see **B19.40**.

In the light of *Joseph* [2017] EWCA Crim 36, [2017] 1 Cr App R 33 (486) and *L* [2013] EWCA Crim 991, [2014] 1 All ER 113 (see **B22.17** and **B19.22**), the fact that D was a trafficked child and that his criminal activities were integral to the circumstances in which he was a victim is relevant when deciding whether to prosecute on the basis of the public interest test (and to an 'abuse of process' argument). Note that the s. 6 offence is not listed as a 'lifestyle offence' in the POCA 2002, sch. 2. In practice, conduct that could be charged under the MDA 1971, s. 6, is often charged as the 'production' of a controlled drug under s. 4 of the Act.

Sentence

B19.72 See **B19.145** to **B19.165**.

Meaning of 'Genus Cannabis'

B19.73 The definition of 'cannabis' provided in the MDA 1971, s. 37(1) (see **B19.15**), has limited (if any) application in the context of s. 6 of the Act. This is because the *actus reus* of the offence is explicitly the cultivation of the plant of the genus cannabis (and note the opening words to s. 37(1), 'except insofar as the context otherwise requires').

Meaning of 'Cultivate'

B19.74 This term is not defined in the Act. In *Tudhope v Robertson* 1980 JC 62, the High Court of Justiciary (Appeal) held that the Sheriff had taken too narrow and restricted view of the verb 'to cultivate' in relation to cannabis plants in a pot. *Quaere*, whether it would be sufficient that a person who did not introduce a plant of the genus *Cannabis* passively permitted it to thrive in a place over which that person has control without tending it, or whether some active steps must be taken to keep the plant alive or to cause it to grow. It may be more appropriate to charge possession in the former case. Note also *Kenning* [2008] EWCA Crim 1534, [2009] QB 221 (see **B19.67**).

Mens Rea

The prosecution are not required to prove that D knew that the plant cultivated was in fact cannabis (*Champ* (1981) 73 Cr App R 367), but note that D may have a defence under the MDA 1971, s. 28 (see **B19.104**). **B19.75**

When Cultivation May be Lawful

The Misuse of Drugs Regulations 2001 contain various exemptions from this prohibition. See, in particular, reg. 12, by virtue of which a person licensed by the Secretary of State may cultivate a plant of the genus *Cannabis* in accordance with the terms of the licence and in compliance with any conditions attached to it. **B19.76**

OFFENCES RELATING TO OPIUM

Misuse of Drugs Act 1971, s. 9 **B19.77**

Subject to section 28 of this Act, it is an offence for a person—

(a) to smoke or otherwise use prepared opium; or
(b) to frequent a place used for the purpose of opium smoking; or
(c) to have in his possession
  (i) any pipes or other utensils made or adapted for use in connection with the smoking of opium, being pipes or utensils which have been used by him or with his knowledge and permission in that connection or which he intends to use or permit others to use in that connection; or
  (ii) any utensils which have been used by him or with his knowledge and permission in connection with the preparation of opium for smoking.

Section 9 creates three discrete offences, rather than three methods of committing the same offence, in paras. (a), (b), and (c). Section 9(a) creates the only offence under the MDA 1971 where the actual *use* of a specified controlled drug is a criminal offence.

Procedure

Offences under the MDA 1971, s. 9, are (by s. 25 of and sch. 4 to the Act) triable either way. When tried on indictment they are normally class 3 offences, but see CrimPD XIII, para. B (see Supplement, **CPD.XIII.B**), for the additional factors that the court considers on allocation. **B19.78**

Summary trial may be instituted by an information laid 12, rather than the usual six, months from the date of commission of the offence (MDA 1971, s. 25(4)).

For the liability of corporate officers, see **B19.40**.

Sentence

See **B19.145** to **B19.165**. There is no offence-specific guideline but the Sentencing Council's *General Guideline: Overarching Principles* (see Supplement, **SG2-1**) is used for all offenders sentenced on or after 1 October 2019. **B19.79**

Elements and Defence

B19.80 By the MDA 1971, s. 37(1), 'prepared opium' means opium prepared for smoking and includes dross and any other residues remaining after opium has been smoked.

For the meaning of 'possession' in relation to the offence of the unlawful possession of a controlled drug, see **B19.27**.

The defence under s. 28 of the Act also applies to these offences (see **B19.104**).

PROHIBITION ON SUPPLY ETC. OF ARTICLES FOR ADMINISTERING OR PREPARING CONTROLLED DRUGS

B19.81 **Misuse of Drugs Act 1971, s. 9A**

(1) A person who supplies or offers to supply any article which may be used or adapted to be used (whether by itself or in combination with another article or other articles) in the administration by any person of a controlled drug to himself or another, believing that the article (or the article as adapted) is to be so used in circumstances where the administration is unlawful, is guilty of an offence.
(2) It is not an offence under subsection (1) above to supply or offer to supply a hypodermic syringe, or any part of one.
(3) A person who supplies or offers to supply any article which may be used to prepare a controlled drug for administration by any person to himself or another believing that the article is to be so used in circumstances where the administration is unlawful is guilty of an offence.
(4) [See **B19.85**]
(5) In this section, references to administration by any person of a controlled drug to himself include a reference to his administering it to himself with the assistance of another.

Note that a 'controlled drug' includes substances or products subject to a 'temporary class drug order' (see **B19.7** ***et seq.***).

Given that the penalty does not vary with the controlled drug in question, there are only two offences, one under s. 9A(1), and the other under s. 9A(3).

Procedure

B19.82 Offences under the MDA 1971, s. 9A, are (by s. 25 of and sch. 4 to the Act) triable only summarily. Summary trial may be instituted by an information laid 12, rather than the usual six, months from the date of commission of the offence (MDA 1971, s. 25(4)).

For the liability of corporate officers, see **B19.40**.

Sentence

B19.83 See **B19.145** to **B19.165**.

Elements

B19.84 Section 9A creates two offences. The focus of s. 9A(1) is on articles that may be used (or adapted) for the *administration* of a controlled drug by a person, whereas the focus of s. 9A(3) is on articles that may be used to *prepare* a controlled drug for such administration. The offences have rarely been preferred. Note that the *mens rea* requirement is strict: D must believe that the article '*is* to be... used' (not 'may be used') in circumstances where the administration is unlawful (a point central to the ruling of HH Judge Neil Clark, in *Abbas* (23 February 2015 unreported, Leeds Crown Court).

Section 9A is subject to the Misuse of Drugs Regulations 2001, reg. 6A (see **B19.81**).

As to the meaning of 'controlled drug', see **B19.7**.

It is not clear whether the definition given in *Maginnis* [1987] AC 303 of 'supply' applies to this offence (see **B19.44**).

Defences

To fall within the MDA 1971, s. 9A, the articles must be for the unlawful administration of a controlled drug. **B19.85**

Misuse of Drugs Act 1971, s. 9A

(4) For the purposes of this section, any administration of a controlled drug is unlawful except—
- (a) the administration by any person of a controlled drug to another in circumstances where the administration of the drug is not unlawful under section 4(1) of this Act,
- (b) the administration by any person of a controlled drug, other than a temporary class drug, to himself in circumstances where having the controlled drug in his possession is not unlawful under section 5(1) of this Act, or
- (c) the administration by any person of a temporary class drug to himself in circumstances where having the drug in his possession is to be treated as excepted possession for the purposes of this Act (see section 7A(2)(c)).

Notwithstanding s. 9A(1) and (3), certain persons may supply or offer to supply certain articles as laid down in the Misuse of Drugs Regulations 2001, reg. 6A.

OCCUPIERS AND THOSE CONCERNED IN MANAGEMENT OF PREMISES KNOWINGLY PERMITTING OR SUFFERING DRUG-RELATED ACTIVITIES

Misuse of Drugs Act 1971, s. 8 **B19.86**

A person commits an offence if, being the occupier or concerned in the management of any premises, he knowingly permits or suffers any of the following activities to take place on those premises, that is to say—
- (a) producing or attempting to produce a controlled drug in contravention of section 4(1) of this Act;
- (b) supplying or attempting to supply a controlled drug to another in contravention of section 4(1) of this Act, or offering to supply a controlled drug to another in contravention of section 4(1);
- (c) preparing opium for smoking;
- (d) smoking cannabis, cannabis resin or prepared opium.

Mitting J said in *Micek v District Court in Bruntal, Czech Republic* [2014] EWHC 621 (Admin) (at [7]) that:

> ... the offence is committed ... if the individual concerned, subject to satisfaction of all of the other elements of the offence including *mens rea*, is in a position to control what goes on in the relevant premises. He can do so as an occupier, merely by a licence or even by unlawful occupation of the premises, he can also do so as the owner of the premises or as someone having the right to manage them or control over them.

It is submitted that, for the purpose of s. 8(a) and (b), although it would be appropriate to charge by way of discrete counts those controlled drugs that attract different maximum penalties, it is not necessary for the Crown to prove with regard to a given count that D knew the particular identity and class of drug that was in fact being handled (*Bett* [1999] 1 All ER 600).

As to the meaning of 'controlled drug', see **B19.7** ***et seq.***; for 'producing', see **B19.66**; for 'supplying', see **B19.44**.

There is no definition of 'premises' in the MDA 1971, although it appears in other legislation where it is provided with a wide definition, e.g., under the Protection from Eviction Act 1977 (see **B13.9**).

It is a necessary ingredient of the offence under s. 8 that the requisite activity had actually taken place before a conviction can be sustained (see **B19.95**). For the purposes of s. 8(b), it is necessary for the supply actually to take place *on* the premises as s. 8 does not say 'from the premises' (*McGee* [2012] EWCA Crim 613, applying *Auguste* [2003] EWCA Crim 3929, [2004] 4 All ER 373). It is respectfully submitted that the decision in *McGee* is plainly correct. The opening words of s. 8 speak in terms of activities that 'take place on [the] premises'.

McGee was distinguished by the Court of Appeal in *McNaught* [2018] EWCA Crim 1588, where the phrasing of the indictment included the words 'supply' or 'attempting to supply' or 'offering to supply' rather than just 'supply'. The Court held that this allowed for a conviction on the basis that the offer of supply was completed from (on) the premises and that the handover took place elsewhere. It is conceivable that when s. 8(b) was enacted, Parliament envisaged that a typical 'offer to supply' would be an offer to supply or to share a cigarette containing cannabis rather than permitting premises to be used to facilitate commercial supplies of various controlled drugs. However, the decision in *McNaught* lends support (it is submitted) to the commentary in R Fortson, *Misuse of Drugs and Drug Trafficking Offences* (6th edn, 2012), ch. 7-008, that where the occupier etc. knowingly permits or suffers an offer to supply drugs to be made from, for example, a computer operated on premises, then the conduct falls within the MDA 1971, s. 8(b). As to whether an admission made by D would constitute sufficient evidence to prove that a prohibited activity took place on premises, consider *Chatwood* (1979) 70 Cr App R 39, and see *Abbott* (16 July 1982 unreported).

Procedure

B19.87 Offences under the MDA 1971, s. 9, are (by s. 25 of and sch. 4 to the Act) triable either way. When tried on indictment they are normally class 3 offences, but see CrimPD XIII, para. B (see Supplement, **CPD.XIII.B**), for the additional factors that the court considers on allocation.

Summary trial may be instituted by an information laid 12, rather than the usual six, months from the date of commission of the offence (MDA 1971, s. 25(4)).

For the liability of corporate officers, see **B19.40**.

Indictment

B19.88 *Statement of Offence*

Being the occupier [or: concerned in the management] of premises knowingly permitting or suffering [production] of a controlled drug, contrary to section 8 of the Misuse of Drugs Act 1971.

Particulars of Offence

A on or about the ... day of ..., being the occupier [or: being concerned in the management] of certain premises situated at and known as ..., knowingly permitted or suffered on the said premises the [production] of a controlled drug of Class B, namely ..., such [production] being contrary to section [4(1)] of the Misuse of Drugs Act 1971.

Sentence

B19.89 See **B19.145** to **B19.165**. There is no offence-specific guideline but the Sentencing Council's *General Guideline: Overarching Principles* (see Supplement, **SG2-1**) is used for all offenders sentenced on or after 1 October 2019.

Meaning of 'Occupier'

B19.90 Section 8 of the MDA 1971 is aimed at the occupiers or the managers of premises because it is they who may exercise immediate supervision over the activities carried on within them. It was held in

Tao [1977] QB 141 that the term 'occupier' should be given a common-sense interpretation. What should be avoided is an overly narrow or legalistic definition of that term. For the purposes of s. 8, D is in occupation of premises, whatever D's legal status, if the prosecution can show that D exercised control, or had the authority of another, to exclude persons from premises or to prohibit any of the activities referred to in s. 8. Accordingly, D does not have to be a tenant, or to have an estate in land, in order to be an 'occupier' for the purposes of s. 8. The Court of Appeal disapproved the reasoning in *Mogford* (1970) 63 Cr App R 168, where the trial judge (Neild J) had ruled that an 'occupier' was a person in 'legal possession of the premises and had control over them'. The Court pointed out that a person can be in legal possession of premises without being a tenant or having any estate in land (see *Errington v Errington* [1952] 1 KB 290 and contrast *Heslop v Burns* [1974] 3 All ER 406).

In *Tao*, the Court dismissed an undergraduate's appeal against conviction for an offence under s. 8, in circumstances where he had an exclusive contractual licence in respect of a college room, which gave him not merely a right to use the room but also sufficient exclusivity of possession to ensure that he was an occupier. Although he may not have been able to exclude college staff from entering his room, he could exclude cannabis smokers or, for that matter, any smoker. He was in a position to exercise control over the activities that took place there. The word 'occupies' is primarily a question of fact: consider *Brooks v Wassell* (8 November 1979 unreported).

Two further cases usefully illustrate the meaning of 'occupier' for the purposes of s. 8. In *Read v DPP* [1997] EWHC J0620, the Divisional Court dismissed an appeal by way of case stated against D's conviction of being the occupier of premises in which he knowingly permitted or suffered the smoking of cannabis to take place contrary to s. 8(d). D contended that he was not the occupier of the premises because the tenancy of the council house was in the name of his girlfriend with whom he had been cohabiting for some nine years. The Court held that D was clearly an occupier and his claim to the contrary was unrealistic. In *Coid* [1998] Crim LR 199, D was charged under s. 8. D was the boyfriend of Miss M: he cohabited with her at the premises although she was the tenant. When she was away, D would look after the premises. Drugs paraphernalia were found in the premises. When interviewed, D gave the address as being his. D's defence was in part that he was not an occupier for the purposes of the MDA 1971. The Court of Appeal held that Miss M's tenancy did not preclude D from being an occupier, which was a question of fact for the jury, and the judge gave a proper direction. **B19.91**

Meaning of 'Concerned in the Management of Premises'

To be a manager, D must run, organise and plan the use of the premises (*Josephs* (1977) 65 Cr App R 253), and so must be involved in more than menial or routine duties (*Abbott v Smith* [1965] 2 QB 662). A person satisfies the requirement of a manager even if the person has no lawful right or title to the premises (see *Josephs*). **B19.92**

'Knowingly Permits or Suffers'

The Court of Appeal in *Thomas* (1976) 63 Cr App R 65 held that 'knowingly' adds nothing to the words 'permits or suffers'. The word was probably included in the MDA 1971, s. 8, to put beyond doubt that proof of knowledge is required. This explains why the offence is not made subject to s. 28. Note that in *Sweet v Parsley* [1970] AC 132, the House of Lords decided that the word 'permits' in the forerunner to s. 8, imported *mens rea*. Wilful blindness as to forbidden activity taking place on premises may be sufficient, but mere suspicion is not (*Thomas*). For the purposes of s. 8(a) and (b), even where the particular drug is specified, it is not necessary for the Crown to prove more than knowledge of the production or supply of a controlled drug (*Bett* [1999] 1 All ER 600). D need not know the identity of the drug or its class. **B19.93**

In *Brock* [2001] 1 WLR 1159, a drop-in centre operated a policy that protected the confidentiality of clients in that no information was to be passed on without the express permission of the individual unless there was an element of danger, safety or personal harm involved. Whilst relevant, such policies are not determinative of the matter. It was for that reason that the trial judge directed the jury that 'the law does not permit you to write or operate a private policy so as to exempt you from the law's requirements'. The Court of Appeal held that: 'A belief by a defendant that he has taken reasonable steps does not afford any defence... It is not for the defendant to judge his own conduct', per Rose LJ. The Court added that: 'What the prosecution must prove to establish the offence of permitting under section 8(b) is (i) knowledge, actual or by closing eyes to the obvious, that heroin dealing is taking place; and (ii) unwillingness to prevent it, which can be inferred from failure to take reasonable steps readily available to prevent it'.

B19.94 In *Souter* [1971] 2 All ER 1151 (decided under s. 5 of the Dangerous Drugs Act 1965), Edmund Davies LJ said: 'The best indication of such unwillingness [to prevent the prohibited activity] is proof of failure to take reasonable steps readily available to prevent [it]. Conversely, all steps taken by the accused to prevent it have a direct bearing on the charge and should be brought to the attention of the jury.'

It is submitted that a further factor for the court to consider is whether D allowed the activity to go on 'not caring whether an offence was committed or not'. In *Souter*, Edmund Davies LJ adopted the test of 'permitting' as expressed by Lord Parker CJ in *Gray's Haulage v Arnold* [1966] 1 WLR 534. In the latter case, Lord Parker CJ stated (at p. 536) (albeit in the context of the RTA 1960, s. 73):

> It is of the very essence of the offence of permitting someone to do something that there should be knowledge. The case that is always referred to in this connection is *James & Son Ltd. v. Smee* [[1955] 1 QB 89] where in giving judgment I pointed out that knowledge is really of two kinds, actual knowledge, and knowledge which arises either from shutting one's eyes to the obvious, or, what is very much the same thing but put in another way, failing to do something or doing something not caring whether contravention takes place or not.

Mere acquiescence in what is taking place on premises is unlikely to amount to permitting that activity (*Bradbury* [1996] Crim LR 808).

The Divisional Court stated in *Taylor v Chief Constable of Kent* [1981] 1 WLR 606 that an occupier who permits another to cultivate cannabis plants permits or suffers their production (i.e. there is an overlap between the offences contrary to the MDA 1971, ss. 4 and 6: see **B19.63** and **B19.70**), and so commits an offence contrary to s. 8.

B19.95 In *Auguste* [2003] EWCA Crim 3929, [2004] 4 All ER 373 the Court of Appeal considered s. 8(d), and held that Parliament was seeking to deal with the situation where a person might discover, by reason of the smell of smoked cannabis, that this activity was taking place. Accordingly, the requisite activity had to be taking place for the offence to be committed.

ASSISTING IN OR INDUCING COMMISSION OUTSIDE UK OF OFFENCE PUNISHABLE UNDER CORRESPONDING LAW

B19.96 **Misuse of Drugs Act 1971, s. 20**

> A person commits an offence if in the United Kingdom he assists in or induces the commission in any place outside the United Kingdom of an offence punishable under the provisions of a corresponding law in force in that place.

Procedure

B19.97 The offence under the MDA 1971, s. 20, is (by s. 25 of and sch. 4 to the Act) triable either way. When tried on indictment it is normally a class 3 offence, but see CrimPD XIII, para. B (see Supplement, **CPD.XIII.B**), for the additional factors that the court considers on allocation. It is a 'listed offence' for the purposes of the SCA 2007, sch. 3 (encouraging or assisting a person to commit an inchoate offence: see **A5.31**).

Summary trial may be instituted by an information laid 12, rather than the usual six, months from the date of commission of the offence (MDA 1971, s. 25(4)).

For the liability of corporate officers, see **B19.40**.

Sentence

See **B19.145** to **B19.165**. There is no offence-specific guideline but the Sentencing Council's *General Guideline: Overarching Principles* (see Supplement, **SG2-1**) is used for all offenders sentenced on or after 1 October 2019. This is a drug trafficking offence within the meaning of the POCA 2002, sch. 2 (see **E19.18**). A minimum custodial sentence of seven years applies for the third Class A drug trafficking offence (see **E5.1**). A forfeiture order (see **E18.7**) or a confiscation order (see **E19**) may be imposed for a drug trafficking offence. **B19.98**

Meaning of 'Assisting'

Assisting is not to be narrowly construed but must be construed as an ordinary English word (*Vickers* [1975] 1 WLR 811; *Evans* (1977) 64 Cr App R 237; *Panayi* (1987) 86 Cr App R 261). In *Vickers* D was guilty when, as he had agreed, he took speaker cabinets to Italy, knowing that cannabis would then be loaded into them and shipped to the USA. In *Evans* D had assisted in the UK in the importation of cannabis into Canada from Brussels by the making of arrangements to provide for a human carrier and by carrying out those arrangements. **B19.99**

Commission of Offence outside UK

The offence outside the UK must have been committed (*Panayi* (1987) 86 Cr App R 261). It is only if such an offence is committed that there is something which can be assisted, so the convictions of the accused in *Panayi* were quashed when they had been arrested in British territorial waters having sailed from Spain in a yacht with a quantity of cannabis destined for Holland. If an offence is committed and D did an act of assistance, the offence under s. 20 of the MDA 1971 is committed even if it is not possible to identify the principal offender and the final act of importation was effected by an innocent third party (*Ahmed* [1990] Crim LR 648). **B19.100**

Meaning of 'Corresponding Law'

Misuse of Drugs Act 1971, s. 36 **B19.101**

(1) In this Act the expression 'corresponding law' means a law stated in a certificate purporting to be issued by or on behalf of the government of a country outside the United Kingdom to be a law providing for the control and regulation in that country of the production, supply, use, export and import of drugs and other substances in accordance with the provisions of the Single Convention on Narcotic Drugs signed at New York on 30 March 1961 or a law providing for the control and regulation in that country of the production, supply, use, export and import of dangerous or otherwise harmful drugs in pursuance of any treaty, convention or other agreement or arrangement to which the government of that country and Her Majesty's Government in the United Kingdom are for the time being parties.

(2) A statement in any such certificate as aforesaid to the effect that any facts constitute an offence against the law mentioned in the certificate shall be evidence, and in Scotland sufficient evidence, of the matters stated.

Mens Rea

The offence is not one of strict liability (*Vickers* [1975] 1 WLR 811). It is required that (a) D intended to assist, i.e. must know what he or she is doing and the purpose with which it is done (*Vickers*, at p. 818), and (b) D was aware that the person assisted was involved in drug smuggling (*Ahmed* [1990] Crim LR 648). It is not necessary to establish that D intended that the goods be imported into a particular country (*Ahmed*). **B19.102**

INCITEMENT

B19.103 **Misuse of Drugs Act 1971, s. 19**

It is an offence for a person . . . to incite another to commit an offence under any other provision of this Act.

The offence of incitement is triable and punishable in the same way as the substantive offence incited (MDA 1971, s. 25(3) and sch. 4). For examples, see *Marlow* [1997] EWCA Crim 1833 and *Jones* [2010] EWCA Crim 925, [2010] 2 Cr App R 10 (69). It is a 'listed offence' for the purposes of the SCA 2007, sch. 3 (encouraging or assisting a person to commit an inchoate offence: see **A5.31**).

DEFENCE UNDER THE MISUSE OF DRUGS ACT 1971, s. 28

B19.104 **Misuse of Drugs Act 1971, s. 28**

(1) This section applies to offences under any of the following provisions of this Act, that is to say section 4(2) and (3), section 5(2) and (3), section 6(2) and section 9.

(2) Subject to subsection (3) below, in any proceedings for an offence to which this section applies it shall be a defence for the accused to prove that he neither knew of nor suspected nor had reason to suspect the existence of some fact alleged by the prosecution which it is necessary for the prosecution to prove if he is to be convicted of the offence charged.

(3) Where in any proceedings for an offence to which this section applies it is necessary, if the accused is to be convicted of the offence charged, for the prosecution to prove that some substance or product involved in the alleged offence was the controlled drug which the prosecution alleges it to have been, and it is proved that the substance or product in question was that controlled drug, the accused—

(a) shall not be acquitted of the offence charged by reason only of proving that he neither knew nor suspected nor had reason to suspect that the substance or product in question was the particular controlled drug alleged; but

(b) shall be acquitted thereof—

(i) if he proves that he neither believed nor suspected nor had reason to suspect that the substance or product in question was a controlled drug; or

(ii) if he proves that he believed the substance or product in question to be a controlled drug, or a controlled drug of a description, such that, if it had in fact been that controlled drug or a controlled drug of that description, he would not at the material time have been committing any offence to which this section applies.

(4) Nothing in this section shall prejudice any defence which it is open to a person charged with an offence to which this section applies to raise apart from this section.

Note that the s. 28 defence cannot be 'read down', in reliance on the ECHR, Article 9, in order to provide for a religious exemption from the offence of possessing a Class A drug (*Aziz* [2012] EWCA Crim 1063, following *Taylor* [2001] EWCA Crim 2263, [2002] 1 Cr App R 37 (519)).

Relationship between s. 28(2) and (3)

B19.105 If D asserts 'that he did not know that the bag or other container which he was carrying contained a controlled drug and believed it contained a different type of article such as a video film, this defence arises under section 28(2) and not under section 28(3)' (per Lord Hutton in *Lambert* [2001] UKHL 37, [2002] 2 AC 545 at [181], applying *Salmon v HM Advocate* 1999 JC 67). The cases of *Lambert* and *Salmon* are essential reading as they lucidly explain the operation of s. 28 — a section which is often misunderstood: see *Barr* [2005] EWCA Crim 1764 (where *Lambert* was followed), and note *Carrera* [2002] EWCA Crim 2527, where the Court of Appeal said that 'following *Lambert* there may well be further debate as to the extent of the burden on the prosecution given the wording of s 28(2) and (3), but it is not necessary or appropriate to conduct that debate in order to resolve this appeal'. See also *Choudhury* [2008] EWCA Crim 3179 and consider *Aiton v HM Advocate* 2010 SLT 447.

B19.106 It is possible to read s. 28(2) and (3) in a highly restrictive way by focusing on the phrase 'which it is necessary for the prosecution to prove'. The point is best demonstrated by an example. If D is charged with possessing cocaine, with intent to supply it to another, contrary to s. 5(3), the prosecution must prove that D was in possession of a controlled drug of some description which turned out to be cocaine. But, on one interpretation, it would not be necessary for the prosecution to prove that D knew, believed, or suspected that the drug was cocaine, and it would be no defence for D to have thought the drug was amphetamine, and therefore (so the argument might run) D cannot make use of s. 28. However, if this construction of s. 28 is correct, it would mean that D would have no defence under s. 5(3) if D thought the substance was table salt. It is submitted that this is not a proper construction of s. 28. The offences under s. 6 (cultivating cannabis) and s. 9 (opium smoking) are 'subject to' s. 28. In each case, the controlled drug is specified in the section, but s. 28 is not confined to those two offences. The starting point is s. 28(2) which is qualified by s. 28(3). Thus, for the purposes of s. 5(3) it is necessary to prove that D was in possession of a substance that was a controlled drug of some description. As the High Court of Justiciary said in *Salmon*, 'subsection (3) turns out to be simply a particular example of the wider class of situations covered by subsection (2), viz. situations where the accused proves "that he neither knew nor suspected nor had reason to suspect the existence of some fact alleged by the prosecution which it is necessary for the prosecution to prove if he is to be convicted of the offence charged" '.

However, in *Leeson* [2000] 1 Cr App R 233 — a case that was decided prior to the decision of the House of Lords in *Lambert* and, in which *Salmon* was not cited — the Court of Appeal appears to have favoured a narrow interpretation of s. 28. D testified that he had stolen a bag out of a motor vehicle initially anticipating that the bag contained a quantity of 'smart clothes': he later noticed that the bag contained cannabis resin, scales and substances that he thought were amphetamine but which were in fact cocaine. The Court rejected D's submission that his error afforded him a defence under s. 28 on the grounds, (a) that proof that he 'neither knew of, nor suspected nor had reason to suspect' that a substance was cocaine, was not a lack of knowledge of the existence of a fact, alleged by the prosecution, which it was necessary for the prosecution to prove if he were to be convicted of the offence charged; (b) that the particulars of a count on an indictment that identified a substance as a particular controlled drug were not matters that the prosecution had to prove in order to obtain a conviction under s. 5(3); and (c) that s. 28(3)(b)(ii) did not afford D a defence because this was not a case where it was necessary for the prosecution to prove that some substance or product involved in the alleged offence was the controlled drug which the prosecution alleged it to have been. The Court held that 'under [s. 28(3)(a)] the accused is not to be acquitted by reason only of proving that he neither knew nor suspected nor had reason to suspect that the substance or product in question was the particular controlled drug alleged' because D admitted that he thought the substance was amphetamine and therefore he had no defence under s. 28 anyway.

B19.107 It is respectfully submitted that *Leeson* is best regarded as having been superseded by the decision of the House of Lords in *Lambert* in which the reasoning of the High Court of Justiciary in *Salmon* was discussed with approval (and see the commentary to *Leeson* at [2000] Crim LR 196). In *Salmon*, the Lord Justice General said (at pp. 72 to 73):

> The first part of subsec (3) shows that the subsection concerns the situation where it is necessary for the prosecution to prove that 'some *substance or product* involved in the alleged offence was the controlled drug which the prosecution alleges it to have been, and it is proved that the *substance or product* in question was that controlled drug' (emphasis added).
>
> It is significant that Parliament uses the words 'substance or product' rather than some more general word such as 'article'. In the clauses which I have quoted the words 'substance or product' can refer only to a substance or product which is actually a controlled drug — so it must be, say, the powder or tablets in question. That meaning must be carried through to the remainder of the subsection. Therefore in subsec (3)(b)(i), for instance, Parliament is saying that an accused is to be acquitted if he proves that he

neither believed nor suspected nor had reason to suspect that the *powder or tablets* in question were a controlled drug. It follows that the subsection is intended to deal with the limited situation where the Crown have proved that the accused person possessed or was concerned in supplying, say, tablets ('the substance or product'), which are proved to be Ecstasy tablets, but he says that he was mistaken about the nature or quality of the tablets.

A person in that position may say one of three things about the tablets. First, he may say that he did not know that they were Ecstasy tablets and had always thought that they were heroin. Even if the jury accept his evidence on this point, it does not constitute a defence, however, since he is not to be acquitted of possessing ecstasy tablets by proving that he did not know that the substance or product in question was the particular controlled drug alleged rather than another controlled drug (sec 28(3)(a)). Secondly, the accused may prove that he thought that the tablets in the bottle were aspirin and that he neither suspected nor had reason to suspect that they were a controlled drug. In that situation he is to be acquitted (sec 28(3)(b)(i)). Thirdly, there are situations where people are authorised to possess or supply particular drugs ... If a doctor were found to have Ecstasy tablets in his possession, it would be a defence for him to prove that he believed that the tablets were heroin tablets which he had in his possession for the purpose of acting in his capacity as a doctor (sec 28(3)(b)(ii)).

That being the scope of subsec (3), it is not apt to apply to the kind of case envisaged in *McNamara* where an accused says that he thought that the contents of a box on his motorcycle were pornographic or pirate videos rather than cannabis resin. In such a case the accused is not claiming that he did not know that the organic matter ('the substance or product in question') was a controlled drug. Rather, he is saying that he did not think that the cannabis resin was there at all: he thought that the box contained videos. It follows that, if the only possible basis for the motorcyclist's defence were sec 28(3), he would have no defence.

Incidence and Standard of Proof

B19.108 In *Lambert* [2001] UKHL 37, [2002] 2 AC 545, the House of Lords decided that the placing of a legal burden on the defence was contrary to the ECHR, Article 6. It did not issue a declaration of incompatibility, but, using the HRA 1998, s. 3, their lordships interpreted the MDA 1971, s. 28, so as to avoid incompatibility. The effect of *Lambert* seems to be that s. 28 imposes only an evidential burden upon D (but see further **F3.18**). *Lambert* was applied in *Lang* [2002] EWCA Crim 298; note also *Choudhury* [2008] EWCA Crim 3179; *R v CPS* (10 July 2008, unreported); *Carrera* [2002] EWCA Crim 2527; the judgment of the Appeal Court of the High Court of Justiciary in *Henvey v HM Advocate* [2005] HCJAC 10, and consider *Keogh* [2007] EWCA Crim 528, [2007] 3 All ER 789.

In *M* [2007] EWCA Crim 3228, the Court of Appeal purported to follow *Lambert* but, in doing so, it uncharacteristically fell into serious error (at [11]). The Court said that the trial judge's direction to the jury 'must explain the difference between an evidential burden and a legal burden of proof in terms that a jury can understand. It must then also explain that the evidential burden can be discharged on a balance of probabilities, but the legal burden on the Crown has to be discharged to a criminal burden of making the jury sure.' For a further illustration of the care that needs to be taken to ensure that the jury are correctly directed in relation to the incidence and standard of proof in the context of the MDA 1971, s. 28, see *Clarke* [2016] EWCA Crim 2228.

It is submitted that, following *Lambert*, a defence that is pursued under s. 28 ought to be dealt with in a manner akin to many other defences to a criminal charge such as self-defence (see, e.g., *DPP v Bailey* [1995] 1 Cr App R 257). In short, the question whether there is evidence sufficient to raise the issue under s. 28 for the jury's consideration is one for the trial judge to answer by applying common sense to the evidence in the case. Hopeless defences which have no factual basis of support do not have to be left to the jury.

B19.109 It is submitted that the correct approach was that stated by the High Court of Justiciary in *Henvey v HM Advocate* [2005] HCJAC 10:

(a) It must be emphasised that for the discharge of the burden there has to be evidence. As Lord Slynn of Hadley observed in *Lambert* (at [17]): 'It is not enough that the defendant in seeking to establish the evidential burden should merely mouth the words of the section'. Lord Hope stated (at [90]):

> But an evidential burden is not to be thought of as a burden which is illusory. What the accused must do is put evidence before the court which, if believed, could be taken by a reasonable jury to support his defence... It is what the common law requires of a defendant who wishes to invoke one of the common law defences such as provocation or duress.

(b) The evidence would have to cover each of the elements in the relevant subsection of s. 28. Thus, in the case of s. 28(2), the evidence would have to be to the effect that D neither knew of nor suspected nor had reason to suspect the existence of the fact alleged by the prosecution which it was necessary for the prosecution to prove if D was to be convicted of the offence charged.

(c) As was pointed out by the Lord Justice General in *Salmon v HM Advocate* 1999 JC 67 at p. 75, s. 28(2) does not require that D must necessarily have given evidence:

> Doubtless, that would often be the simplest mode of proof, but the necessary evidence might come, for example, from a 'mixed' statement or from witnesses speaking to what the accused was told was in the container or to the accused's apparent astonishment when the contents of the container were revealed and found to be a controlled drug.

(d) It is important to bear in mind that the question of whether the evidential burden has been discharged is a question of whether there is sufficient evidence for the purposes of the relevant subsection, for which it must be assumed that the evidence relied on is believed. Hence, as we have noted, Lord Hope spoke of the need for D to put evidence before the court 'which, if believed, could be taken by a reasonable jury to support his defence'. That is a matter for the trial judge, who would direct the jury accordingly.

(e) If that is the case, the Crown must meet that defence and satisfy the jury beyond reasonable doubt that it should be rejected. If the jury believe evidence that D neither knew of nor suspected nor had reason to suspect the existence of the relevant fact, D must be acquitted. Even if they are not prepared to go so far as to believe that evidence, but are left in reasonable doubt about that matter, D must also be acquitted. Thus, as Lord Clyde stated in *Lambert* (at [158]) in regard to a s. 5 case:

> If the jury are satisfied beyond reasonable doubt that the accused possessed the substance or product in question but are not satisfied beyond reasonable doubt that he knew that it was a controlled drug (or suspected or had reason to suspect that it was) then again they should acquit him. They can only convict if they are satisfied beyond reasonable doubt that the prosecution has proved possession of the controlled drug and, if the issue is raised, that the lines of defence set out in section 28 are without foundation.

(f) Where there is no issue as to whether D did not know or suspect or have reason to suspect the relevant fact, there is no need for the jury to be given directions in regard to s. 28. Thus, in a s. 4(3)(b) case where no such issue is raised on the evidence, D's conviction will depend on whether the tribunal of fact is satisfied that D was aware of being concerned in the supplying of something, and is further satisfied that that thing was in fact a controlled drug. If, on the other hand, there is evidence which, if believed, could support a defence under s. 28, the jury must be directed to acquit D if (a) they accept that evidence, or (b) they are left in reasonable doubt about that matter.

Self-induced intoxication is not a relevant consideration in the exercise of the statutory defence under s. 28(3)(b) (*Young* [1984] 2 All ER 164). **B19.110**

Section 28 does not apply to conspiracies to commit an MDA offence as they are not statutory offences created under the 1971 Act (*McGowan* [1990] Crim LR 399).

ENFORCEMENT PROVISIONS

Powers of Entry, Search and Seizure

B19.111 Misuse of Drugs Act 1971, s. 23

(1) A constable or other person authorised in that behalf by a general or special order of the Secretary of State (or in Northern Ireland either of the Secretary of State or the Ministry of Home Affairs for Northern Ireland) shall, for the purposes of the execution of this Act, have power to enter the premises of a person carrying on business as a producer or supplier of any controlled drugs and to demand the production of, and to inspect, any books or documents relating to dealings in any such drugs and to inspect any stocks of any such drugs.

(2) If a constable has reasonable grounds to suspect that any person is in possession of a controlled drug in contravention of this Act or of any regulations or orders made thereunder, the constable may—

(a) search that person, and detain him for the purpose of searching him;

(b) search any vehicle or vessel in which the constable suspects that the drug may be found, and for that purpose require the person in control of the vehicle or vessel to stop it;

(c) seize and detain, for the purposes of proceedings under this Act, anything found in the course of the search which appears to the constable to be evidence of an offence under this Act.

In this subsection 'vessel' includes a hovercraft within the meaning of the Hovercraft Act 1968; and nothing in this subsection shall prejudice any power of search or any power to seize or detain property which is exercisable by a constable apart from this subsection.

(3) If a justice of the peace (or in Scotland a justice of the peace, a magistrate or a sheriff) is satisfied by information on oath that there is reasonable ground for suspecting—

(a) that any controlled drugs are, in contravention of this Act or of any regulations or orders made thereunder, in the possession of a person on any premises; or

(b) that a document directly or indirectly relating to, or connected with, a transaction or dealing which was, or an intended transaction or dealing which would if carried out be, an offence under this Act, or in the case of a transaction or dealing carried out or intended to be carried out in a place outside the United Kingdom, an offence against the provisions of a corresponding law in force in that place, is in the possession of a person on any premises,

he may grant a warrant authorising any constable at any time or times within one month from the date of the warrant, to enter, if need be by force, the premises named in the warrant, and to search the premises and any persons found therein and, if there is reasonable ground for suspecting that an offence under this Act has been committed in relation to any controlled drugs found on the premises or in the possession of any such persons, or that a document so found is such a document as is mentioned in paragraph (b) above, to seize and detain those drugs or that document, as the case may be.

(3A) The powers conferred by subsection (1) above shall be exercisable also for the purposes of the execution of Part II of the Criminal Justice (International Co-operation) Act 1990 . . . [NI] . . . and subsection (3) above (excluding paragraph (a)) shall apply also to offences under section 12 or 13 of that Act of 1990, taking references in those provisions to controlled drugs as references to scheduled substances within the meaning of that Part.

B19.112 Note also s. 20 of the Health Act 2006 (power to enter and inspect 'relevant premises' for controlled drugs), the Controlled Drugs (Supervision of Management and Use) Regulations 2013 (SI 2013 No. 373), and the Controlled Drugs (Supervision of Management and Use) (Amendment) Regulations (SI 2020 No. 189), the effect of which is to amend, and to keep in force, the 2013 Regulations. See also the Controlled Drugs (Supervision of Management and Use) (Wales) Regulations 2008 (SI 2008 No. 3239), but note the prospective amendments made by the Retained EU Law (Miscellaneous Amendments) (Wales) (EU Exit) Regulations (SI 2019 No. 1281), reg. 7(5), in force on IP completion day and not on 'exit day' as specified in the European Union (Withdrawal Agreement) Act 2020. As to what amounts to 'reasonable grounds to suspect', see *O'Hara v Chief Constable of the RUC* [1997] AC 286 at p. 298 and *Coalter v HM Advocate* [2013] HCJAC 115, and consider *McKenzie v Procurator Fiscal* [2014]

HCJAC 132. In *McAughey v HM Advocate* [2013] HCJAC 163, the High Court of Justiciary (Appeal) remarked (citing *O'Hara* (among other cases) that the test relates to what was in the mind of the arresting officer when the power was exercised, and that the test is part subjective and part objective (at [10]–[14]). Where there is an application for the details of the information laid in support of a warrant to be disclosed, see *Metropolitan Police Commissioner v Bangs* [2014] EWHC 546 (Admin).

As to whether a police officer is acting in the execution of his duty notwithstanding the absence of evidence from the police officer of having had personal knowledge of the detail of the search warrant, see *Sykes v CPS* [2013] EWHC 3600 (Admin).

In *R (Daly) v Metropolitan Police Commissioner* [2018] EWHC 438 (Admin), [2018] 2 Cr App R 19 (274) the Divisional Court held that, for the purposes of the MDA 1971, s. 23(3), following the granting of a warrant, a subsequently established material mistake of fact cannot invalidate a warrant otherwise properly obtained. Provided that the police have not misled the court; have made full and frank disclosure, highlighting to the judge any material which is potentially adverse to the application in any material way; and have taken reasonable steps along the lines identified in the Code of Practice, the warrant is intended to provide protection in the absence of proof of malice. **B19.113**

In exercising any of the powers pursuant to s. 23, it is essential that constables comply with the PACE 1984, s. 2(2): (*Garjo* [2011] EWCA Crim 1169, citing *Bristol* [2007] EWCA Crim 3214, and see *Michaels v Highbury Corner Magistrates' Court* [2009] EWHC 2928 (Admin)). A pat-down search, as was conducted in *James v DPP* [2012] EWHC 1317 (Admin), is not 'a forcible search' (contrary to PACE Code A, para. 3.2), nor is the placing of a hand on the body of the individual, except perhaps in sensitive parts, the application of force or 'a forcible search'. If a suspect is to be kept in lawful custody for any period of time after the police search has been completed, the police must exercise another power to do so (such as arrest) (*Young v Procurator Fiscal* [2012] HCJAC 104).

Subject to any legislative amendments made as a consequence of the UK withdrawing from the EU, note that the powers conferred by s. 23(1) are also exercisable for the purposes of Articles 6 and 7 of Council Regulation (EC) No. 111/2005 ([2005] OJ L22/1) (as amended by Regulation (EU) No. 1259/2013 ([2013] OJ L330/30) and Regulation (EU) 2016/1443 ([2016] OJ L235/6)): see reg. 10 of the Controlled Drugs (Drug Precursors) (Community External Trade) Regulations 2008 (SI 2008 No. 296). Note also SI 2008 No. 295 with regard to intra-community trade (noting Regulation (EC) No. 273/2004 ([2004] OJ L47/1) as amended by Regulation (EU) 2016/1443).

The requirements set out in regs. 6 and 7 of SI 2008 No. 296, and s. 23(3) of the MDA 1971 (but excluding para. (a)), also apply to an offence preferred under reg. 6, 7 or 8. For these purposes, references made in s. 23 to 'controlled drugs' are to be taken as references to 'scheduled substances' within the meaning of Council Regulation (EC) No. 111/2005 (see reg. 2): see SI 2008 No. 296, reg. 10.

Offences of Obstruction, Concealment etc.

The powers of enforcement are supported by offences created by the MDA 1971, s. 23(4). **B19.114**

Misuse of Drugs Act 1971, s. 23

(4) A person commits an offence if he—
- (a) intentionally obstructs a person in the exercise of his powers under this section; or
- (b) conceals from a person acting in the exercise of his powers under subsection (1) above any such books, documents, stocks or drugs as are mentioned in that subsection; or
- (c) without reasonable excuse (proof of which shall lie on him) fails to produce any such books or documents as are so mentioned where their production is demanded by a person in the exercise of his powers under that subsection.

These offences are triable either way (MDA 1971, s. 25 and sch. 4).

As to sentence, see **B19.145** to **B19.165**.

In *Forde* (1985) 81 Cr App R 19, the Court of Appeal held that a person committed an offence under s. 23(4)(a) only if, on the facts of that case, D knew that he was being detained for the purposes of a search under s. 23(2)(a) and if the obstruction was intentional, that is to say the act viewed objectively, through the eyes of a bystander, did obstruct the constable's detention or search, and viewed subjectively, that is to say through the eyes of D himself, was intended so to obstruct. Note the case of *Bristol* [2007] EWCA Crim 3214, which concerned a charge under s. 23(4)(a) where there was no evidence that the police constable had taken reasonable steps to bring to D's attention the constable's name and name of the police station, and, until the constable had done so, the search could not be commenced; *Osman v DPP* (1999) 163 JP 725 was cited. *Bristol* was followed in *B v DPP* [2008] EWHC 1655 (Admin), and applied in *R (Michaels) v Highbury Corner Magistrates' Court* [2009] EWHC 2928 (Admin). These cases must be considered in conjunction with the PACE 1984, s. 2(2) and (3), which provide that a constable must not commence a search until reasonable steps have been taken to bring to the attention of the appropriate person (among other things) the constable's name and the name of the police station. A failure by the constable to identify name and station renders the subsequent search unlawful: 'It means that the officers were not then acting in the execution of their duty and no offence was committed under section 23(4)' (*R (Michaels) v Highbury Corner Magistrates' Court* at [9]; and see *Garjo* [2011] EWCA Crim 1169).

For consideration of the similar phrasing in the offence of the wilful obstruction of a police officer in the execution of his duty contrary to the Police Act 1996, s. 89(2), see **B2.48** to **B2.53** and *DPP v Meaden* [2003] EWHC 3005 (Admin), [2004] 1 WLR 945 in which s. 89(2) and the MDA 1971, s. 23, are discussed.

Note s. 21 of the Health Act 2006 (offences in connection with power to enter and inspect 'relevant premises' under s. 20 of that Act).

Drug-cutting Agents

B19.115 From 3 May 2015, part 4 of the SCA 2015 makes provision for the seizure of any substance on premises where an officer has reasonable grounds to suspect that it is intended for use as a 'drug-cutting agent', and for its forfeiture. The expression 'drug-cutting agent' is defined (somewhat narrowly) as a substance added to a controlled drug in connection with the unlawful supply or exportation of the drug (s. 65). A justice of the peace may issue a warrant (with or without notice: s. 52(5)) authorising a police or customs officer to enter premises ('all premises' or 'specified premises': s. 52(3)), and to search them for substances that appear to be intended for use as 'drug-cutting agents' (s. 52(1)).

The circumstances in which a 'drug-cutting agent' may be seized (without a warrant) by an officer lawfully on premises, are specified in s. 56. A container holding a substance seized under s. 55 or 56 may also be seized (s. 58).

Substances seized may initially be retained for the period specified in s. 59, with continued retention ordered by a magistrates' court in accordance with s. 60.

For powers of forfeiture, disposal, or return of seized substances, see ss. 61 and 63.

An appeal against a decision made under s. 61 exists pursuant to s. 62. The person to whom a substance belongs (which had been seized and retained) may make an application for compensation to a magistrates' court under s. 64 if no forfeiture order is made in respect of that substance.

OTHER OFFENCES RELATED TO MISUSE OF DRUGS

Contravention of Directions, Notices or Regulations Relating to Controlled Drugs

Directions It is an offence, contrary to the MDA 1971, s. 11(2), to contravene any directions given under s. 11(1) (as amended). The offence is punishable, on summary conviction, with imprisonment for a term not exceeding six months and/or an unlimited fine, and, on conviction on indictment, with imprisonment for a term not exceeding two years or a fine or both. **B19.116**

It is an offence, contrary to the MDA 1971, s. 12(6), to contravene a direction given under s. 12(2). When tried on indictment, the penalties are the same regardless of the class of drug involved. For the penalties available on conviction, see sch. 4 to the 1971 Act (set out at **B19.146**).

It is an offence, contrary to s. 13(3) of the MDA 1971, to contravene a direction given under s. 13(1) (as amended) or (2) of that Act. When an offence under s. 13(3) is tried on indictment, the penalties are the same regardless of the class of drug involved. For the penalties available on conviction, see sch. 4 (set out at **B19.146**). Note that s. 13 applies to a provision made in a TCDO.

It is an offence, contrary to s. 17(3), if a person 'without reasonable excuse (proof of which shall lie on him) fails to comply with any requirement to which he is subject' (e.g., a doctor) by virtue of s. 17(1) (power to obtain information from doctors etc., in certain circumstances, such as a particular drug-related social problem). For maximum penalties, see **B19.146**.

False Information It is an offence, contrary to s. 17(4), if a person, in purported compliance with a requirement imposed under s. 17(1), 'gives any information which he knows to be false in a material particular or recklessly gives any information which is so false'. It is an offence, contrary to s. 18(3), if a person, 'in purported compliance with any obligation to give information to which he is subject under or by virtue of regulations made under [the 1971 Act], gives any information which he knows to be false in a material particular or recklessly gives any information which is so false'. It is an offence, contrary to s. 18(4), if a person: **B19.117**

> for the purpose of obtaining, whether for himself or another, the issue or renewal of a licence or other authority under [the 1971 Act or any regulations made under it],...
> (a) makes any statement or gives any information which he knows to be false in a material particular or recklessly gives any information which is so false; or
> (b) produces or otherwise makes use of any book, record or other document which to his knowledge contains any statement or information which he knows to be false in a material particular.

For maximum penalties, see **B19.146**.

Contravention of Regulations It is an offence, contrary to the MDA 1971, s. 18(1), for a person to contravene any regulations made under the 1971 Act other than regulations relating to addicts. For maximum penalties, see **B19.146**. The significance of this offence, in particular, is that it means any breach of the Misuse of Drugs (Safe Custody) Regulations 1973 (SI 1973 No. 798, as amended) is an offence. **B19.118**

Contravening Licence Terms It is an offence, contrary to the MDA 1971, s. 18(2), for a person to contravene a condition or other term of a licence issued under s. 3 of the 1971 Act or of a licence or other authority under regulations made under the 1971 Act, not being a licence issued under regulations relating to addicts. For maximum penalties, see **B19.146**. **B19.119**

Prison Act 1952 Offences It is an offence, contrary to the Prison Act 1952, s. 40B(1), for a person to, without authorisation, (a) bring, throw or otherwise convey a List A article into or out of a prison, (b) cause another person to bring, throw or otherwise convey a List A article into or out of a prison, (c) leave a List A article in any place (whether inside or outside a prison) intending it to **B19.120**

come into the possession of a prisoner, or (d) knowing a person to be a prisoner, give a List A article to that person. For List A articles, see the Prison Act 1952, s. 40(2). By s. 40A(2)(a), a 'controlled drug' (as defined by the MDA 1971) is included in List A.

'Authorisation' means authorisation (a) in relation to all prisons (or prisons specified in the authorisation), by prison rules or by the Secretary of State; or (b) in relation to a particular prison, by the Secretary of State or by the governor or director of the prison (s. 40B(2)).

The offence is not one of strict liability but requires proof of *mens rea* (*Johnson* [2017] EWCA Crim 189, [2017] 2 Cr App R 6 (60); *M (D)* [2009] EWCA Crim 2615, [2010] 2 Cr App R 33 (383)).

By s. 40B(6), the offence is punishable on conviction on indictment to imprisonment for a term not exceeding ten years or to a fine (or both). For sentencing examples, see *O'Grady* [2020] EWCA Crim 414; *Smith (Rachel)* [2019] EWCA Crim 1077; *Hibbert* [2018] EWCA Crim 2047; *Hamilton* [2016] EWCA Crim 78, [2016] 2 Cr App R (S) 2 (7).

In *Johnson*, D pleaded guilty in a magistrates' court to an offence, charged under s. 40C(2)(a), of bringing, throwing or otherwise conveying a List C article into a prison intending it to come into the possession of a prisoner. The article was described by the Court of Appeal as '"spice" a synthetic cannabis "legal high"'. That offence (summary only) was not the subject of appeal before the Court of Appeal. It is submitted that this aspect of the case needs to be approached with considerable care. A List C article is any article or substance prescribed for the purposes of s. 40A(6) by prison rules. In the case of any prison, List C articles are those prescribed by r. 70A. In respect of any young offender institution, List C articles are those prescribed by r. 74A of the Young Offender Institution Rules 2000 (SI 2000 No. 3371). At the time of writing, no synthetic cannabinoids were listed in List C.

Practitioners should note the Prison and Young Offender Institution (Amendment) (No. 2) Rules 2018 (SI 2018 No. 960) and be aware of the limits of their application (drug testing of prisoners and inmates). The 2018 Rules amend the Prison Rules 1999 (SI 1999 No. 728) and the Young Offender Institution Rules 2000. Their effect is to substitute the definition of 'specified drug' in r. 2(1) of the 1999 and 2000 Rules with a revised definition and a new sch. 2. Various psychoactive substances, prescription-only medicines and pharmacy medicines are included.

CANNABIS-BASED PRODUCTS FOR MEDICINAL USE

B19.121 The Misuse of Drugs (Amendments) (Cannabis and Licence Fees) (England, Wales and Scotland) Regulations 2018 (SI 2018 No. 1055) came into force on 1 November 2018. They make a number of amendments to the Misuse of Drugs Regulations 2001 (SI 2001 No. 3998), the Misuse of Drugs (Designation) (England, Wales and Scotland) Order 2015 (SI 2015 No. 704) and the Misuse of Drugs (Licence Fees) Regulations 2010 (SI 2010 No. 2497). Their combined effect is to permit the wider use of 'cannabis-based medicinal products for human medicinal use' ('CBMP') and for certain research purposes.

A CBMP is defined by reg. 2(1) of the 2001 Regulations (inserted by the 2018 Regulations, reg. 3) as:

> ... a preparation or other product, other than one to which paragraph 5 of part 1 of Schedule 4 applies, which—
> (a) is or contains cannabis, cannabis resin, cannabinol or a cannabinol derivative (not being dronabinol or its stereoisomers);
> (b) is produced for medicinal use in humans; and—
> (c) is—
> (i) a medicinal product, or
> (ii) a substance or preparation for use as an ingredient of, or in the production of an ingredient of, a medicinal product;

All three elements of the definition ((a) to (c)) must be satisfied. A 'medicinal product' has the same meaning as in the Human Medicines Regulations 2012 (SI 2012 No. 1916).

'Cannabis', 'cannabis resin', 'cannabinol' and 'cannabinol derivatives' are Class B drugs (MDA 1971, sch. 2: see **B19.9**). 'Cannabis' and 'cannabis resin' are defined by s. 37 (see **B19.15**). The expression 'cannabinol derivatives' is defined by sch. 2, part IV (see **B19.9**).

'Cannabis' (not being the substance specified in sch. 4, part 1, para. 5 to the 2001 Regulations, i.e. a product known as '*Sativex*'), 'cannabis resin', 'cannabinol' and 'cannabinol derivatives (other than dronabinol or its stereoisomers)' are listed in sch. 1 to the 2001 Regulations and in sch. 1 to the 2015 Order (whereby the production, supply and possession of one of those substances is unlawful except for research or other special purposes; see **B19.18**).

The 2001 Regulations are amended so that a CBMP is not included within sch. 1 to the Regulations (2018 Regulations, reg. 6) but falls within sch. 2 (reg. 7). However, certain *forms* of a CBMP that are specified by paras. 2 to 5 of sch. 1 to the 2001 Regulations (e.g., an ester, a salt, or any preparation or other product containing a CBMP) must be one that is produced for medicinal use in humans (reg. 5A, inserted by the 2018 Regulations, reg. 7).

A CBMP is exempted from the 2015 Order (see the 2018 Regulations, reg. 9, amending sch. 1, part 1, para. 1(a); and inserting para. 10 (definition of a CBMP, and exempting esters, salts, preparations etc., produced for medicinal use in humans)).

Dronabinol has appeared in sch. 2 to the 2001 Regulations since the schedule was made (but is not defined therein). Dronabinol is *synthetically* produced *(–)-trans-Δ⁹-tetrahydrocannabinol* (THC). THC is also a (natural) cannabinoid of cannabis (and may be derived from it). The synthetic and natural cannabinoids are chemically identical and have the same International Non-proprietary Name (INN), namely, 'dronabinol'. In order to ensure that the position of dronabinol remains unaffected, and that references in the legislation to 'dronabinol' are to *synthetic* THC, reg. 3 of the 2018 Regulations inserts into reg. 2(1) of the 2001 Regulations a description of what is *not* dronabinol, namely, one that 'does not include any substance which (a) has the international non-proprietary name dronabinol (recommended by the World Health Organization); and (b) is derived from cannabis, cannabis resin or their constituents', and that 'stereoisomers of dronabinol are to be construed accordingly'.

Save for administration to animals for research purposes, a person must not order or supply a CBMP by way of or for the purpose of its administration, unless: (i) the supply is a 'special medicinal product' for use in accordance with a prescription or direction of a 'specialist medical practitioner'; or (ii) the product is an 'investigational medicinal product' without a 'marketing authorisation', for use in a 'clinical trial'; or (iii) it is a 'medicinal product' with a 'marketing authorisation' (2001 Regulations, reg. 16A(1), (2), inserted by the 2018 Regulations, reg 4). The expressions 'investigational medicinal product', 'marketing authorisation', and 'special medicinal product' have the same meanings as in the Human Medicines Regulations 2012 (reg. 16A(5)). A 'specialist medical practitioner' means a doctor included in the register of specialist medical practitioners kept under s. 34D of the Medical Act 1983 (the Specialist Register) (reg. 16A(6)).

A person must not self-administer a CBMP by the smoking of the product (other than for research purposes in accordance with reg. 13) (2001 Regulations, reg. 16A(3), inserted by the 2018 Regulations, reg. 4).

It is an offence to contravene any regulations made under the MDA 1971 other than regulations made in pursuance of s. 10(2)(h) or (i) of that Act. Note that import restrictions (administratively imposed) were changed on 2 March 2020 to help ensure that people with prescriptions for cannabis-based products for medicinal use do not have their treatment delayed or interrupted (see tinyurl.com/ydaq97ws).

PSYCHOACTIVE SUBSTANCES ACT 2016

Overview

B19.122 The PSA 2016 received Royal Assent on 28 January 2016. Sections 59, 61, 62 and 63 (and any power to make regulations under the Act) came into force on that date. The remaining provisions (and the ones of particular relevance to criminal law practitioners) came into force on 26 May 2016 (SI 2016 No. 553).

Save in respect of 'exempted activities', the PSA 2016 imposes a 'blanket' prohibition on acts of producing (s. 12(1)(a)), supplying (s. 12(1)(b)), offering to supply (s. 12(1)(c)), importing or exporting (s. 12(1)(d) and (e)) a non-exempted 'psychoactive substance' (defined by s. 2(1)) that is 'likely to be consumed by individuals for its psychoactive effect'. Exempted activities currently include 'Healthcare related activities' and 'Research' (s. 11 and sch. 2); and note the definition of a 'relevant ethics review body' as amended by the Higher Education and Research Act 2017, sch. 12, para. 29, with effect from 1 April 2018 to include 'United Kingdom Research and Innovation' (SI 2018 No. 241). The PSA 2016, s. 2(2), defines 'psychoactive effect' (see **B19.123**).

It is also a 'prohibited activity' to assist or to encourage the carrying on of any of the aforementioned activities (s. 12(1)(f)). The 'prohibited activities' stated in s. 12 are directly relevant to the exercise of the civil powers created under the PSA 2016, but s. 12 is also indicative of the purpose of the Act.

The statutory regime (in respect of which there is power to make regulations) is enforced by criminal offences created under the Act as well as by civil powers that are exercisable by specified 'senior officers' (defined by s. 13(7)), 'local authorities' (defined by s. 59(1)), and by the courts (notably magistrates' courts).

The PSA 2016 does not consolidate or codify other statutory regimes (notably the MDA 1971, TCDOs, or the Human Medicines Regulations 2012).

Each 'prohibited activity' referred to in s. 12(1) is the subject of a corresponding substantive criminal offence (ss. 4, 5(1) and (2), 7 and 8) that carries a maximum of seven years' imprisonment on indictment or, on summary conviction, six months or a fine, or both (s. 10(1)). The offences are criminal lifestyle offences for the purposes of the POCA 2002, part 2. For the purposes of sentencing, an offence under s. 5 (supply, offering to supply) is aggravated if the matters set out in s. 6 of the Act are established (i.e. the offence was committed in the vicinity of a school, the offender used a courier under the age of 18 years or the offence was committed in a custodial institution).

The Act does not create a specific general offence of simple possession of a psychoactive substance, but it is an offence to possess a psychoactive substance in a 'custodial institution' for consumption for its psychoactive effect (s. 9). That offence carries a maximum of two years' imprisonment on indictment, or six months or a fine on summary conviction or both (s.10(2)).

Sentencers may be assisted by guidelines published by the Sentencing Council on *Drug offences involving newer and less common drugs*, a document which does not have the status of a full guideline but which may nevertheless be taken into account in relevant cases.

The s. 9 offence is not a criminal lifestyle offence for the purposes of the POCA 2002.

Four other significant offences are created under the PSA 2016, namely:

(i) failing to comply with a prohibition/premises order (s. 26);
(ii) failing to comply with an access notice (s. 27);
(iii) obstructing a 'relevant enforcement officer' in the performance of any of the officer's functions under ss. 36 to 45 (s. 48(1));

(iv) failing without reasonable excuse to comply with a requirement made or a direction given by a 'relevant enforcement officer' in the exercise of any power conferred by ss. 37 to 45, or preventing any other person from complying with any such requirement or direction (s. 48(2)).

Practitioners would be well advised to obtain expert forensic opinion in cases where the identification of a drug substance, and/or whether it has psychoactive effect, is in issue. However, the observations made by the Court of Appeal in *Chapman* [2017] EWCA Crim 1743, [2018] 1 Cr App R 9 (122) (at [41]–[42]) are instructive in respect of experts who seek to address issues under the PSA 2016, namely, that they should limit their statements and reports to proper expert evidence (rather than argument which might have been deployed in Parliament by a legislator seeking to defeat the passage of legislation) and must comply with the provisions of the CrimPR (especially Part 19: see Supplement, **R19.1** *et seq.*) and the CrimPD (especially CrimPD V, 19A to 19C: see Supplement, **CPD.19A** *et seq.*).

Where proceedings for a 'prohibition order' are commenced in the youth court, those proceedings may remain there (if appropriate), notwithstanding that the subject of the proceedings has reached the age of 18 (Magistrates' Courts (Psychoactive Substances Act 2016) (Transfer of Proceedings) Rules 2016 (SI 2016 No. 546)).

For a detailed discussion of the offences, and other provisions of the 2016 Act, see R Fortson, 'The Psychoactive Substances Act 2016' [2016] Crim LR 301; the Explanatory Notes to the Act; Circular 004/2016: *Psychoactive Substances Act 2016*; the 'Psychoactive Substances Act 2016: Forensic Strategy' published by HM Government (tinyurl.com/yxvutdg2); and R Fortson, 'The Psychoactive Substances Act 2016: the "Medicinal Product" Exemption and Proving Psychoactivity' [2018] Crim LR 229.

For sentencing, see **B19.130**.

Meaning of 'Psychoactive Substance'

Psychoactive Substances Act 2016, ss. 2 and 3 and sch. 1 **B19.123**

2.—(1) In this Act 'psychoactive substance' means any substance which—
(a) is capable of producing a psychoactive effect in a person who consumes it, and
(b) is not an exempted substance (see section 3).

(2) For the purposes of this Act a substance produces a psychoactive effect in a person if, by stimulating or depressing the person's central nervous system, it affects the person's mental functioning or emotional state; and references to a substance's psychoactive effects are to be read accordingly.

(3) For the purposes of this Act a person consumes a substance if the person causes or allows the substance, or fumes given off by the substance, to enter the person's body in any way.

3.—(1) In this Act 'exempted substance' means a substance listed in Schedule 1.

(2) The Secretary of State may by regulations amend Schedule 1 in order to—
(a) add or vary any description of substance;
(b) remove any description of substance added under paragraph (a).

(3) to (5) [Procedure relating to making of regulations.]

Schedule 1

Exempted Substances

Controlled drugs

1 Controlled drugs (within the meaning of the Misuse of Drugs Act 1971).

Medicinal products

2 Medicinal products.
In this paragraph 'medicinal product' has the same meaning as in the Human Medicines Regulations 2012 (SI 2012/1916) (see regulation 2 of those Regulations).

Alcohol

3 Alcohol or alcoholic products.
In this paragraph—
'alcohol' means ethyl alcohol, and
'alcoholic product' means any product which—

(a) contains alcohol, and
(b) does not contain any psychoactive substance.

Nicotine and tobacco products

4 Nicotine.
5 Tobacco products.
In this paragraph 'tobacco product' means—
(a) anything which is a tobacco product within the meaning of the Tobacco Products Duty Act 1979 (see section 1 of that Act), and
(b) any other product which—
(i) contains nicotine, and
(ii) does not contain any psychoactive substance.

Caffeine

6 Caffeine or caffeine products.
In this paragraph 'caffeine product' means any product which—
(a) contains caffeine, and
(b) does not contain any psychoactive substance.

Food

7 Any substance which—
(a) is ordinarily consumed as food, and
(b) does not contain a prohibited ingredient.
In this paragraph—
'food' includes drink;
'prohibited ingredient', in relation to a substance, means any psychoactive substance—
(a) which is not naturally occurring in the substance, and
(b) the use of which in or on food is not authorised by an EU instrument.

It was held in *Rochester* [2018] EWCA Crim 1936, [2019] 1 WLR 1257 (a case concerning nitrous oxide, popularly known as 'laughing gas') that the natural meaning of the words 'produces a psychoactive effect in a person . . . by stimulating or depressing the person's central nervous system' in the PSA 2016, s. 2, encompassed the production of both a direct and an indirect effect. The statute was not concerned with a fine-grained question of biological analysis. Indirect effect was sufficient. A report of, and commentary to, this case appears at [2018] Crim LR 1002.

Meaning of 'medicinal product'

B19.124 It was held in *Chapman* [2017] EWCA Crim 1743, [2018] 1 Cr App R 9 (122) that canisters of nitrous oxide ('laughing gas') did not constitute an 'exempted substance' (for the purposes of the PSA 2016) as a 'medicinal product' within the meaning of the Human Medicines Regulations 2012, reg. 2. The 2012 Regulations contemplate that a substance may be a 'medicinal product' for one purpose (and thus subject to control under the 2012 Regulations) but not another (at [31]). In the circumstances of the conjoined appeals, the nitrous oxide in question was not a medicinal product. Lord Burnett CJ stated (at [32]):

> The gas no doubt modifies the physiological functions of those who inhale it, but it brings neither short term nor long-term beneficial effects to human health in these circumstances. The canisters in question were in fact manufactured for use unconnected with medical purposes, widely available and distributed for use in catering, which in itself is a strong indicator that they were not medicinal products. Furthermore, the purpose for which it was intended to supply the canisters was purely recreational with nothing whatsoever to do with health. This last feature coupled with the fact that the gas was intended to be used in circumstances which were not beneficial to health, indeed import some risk to health, was sufficient to take it outside the definition of medicinal product whatever label may have been on the boxes in which the canisters were originally packed.

Producing a Psychoactive Substance

B19.125 **Psychoactive Substances Act 2016, s. 4**

(1) A person commits an offence if—
(a) the person intentionally produces a psychoactive substance,
(b) the person knows or suspects that the substance is a psychoactive substance, and

(c) the person—
(i) intends to consume the psychoactive substance for its psychoactive effects, or
(ii) knows, or is reckless as to whether, the psychoactive substance is likely to be consumed by some other person for its psychoactive effects.
(2) This section is subject to section 11 (exceptions to offences).

The word 'producing' is partially defined by s. 59(2)(a) to mean producing the substance 'by manufacture, cultivation or any other method'. The Explanatory Notes state at para. 51 that D must intend to produce a psychoactive substance rather than any other substance. On this construction, the accidental production of a psychoactive substance is not caught by s. 4.

Supplying, or Offering to Supply, a Psychoactive Substance

Psychoactive Substances Act 2016, s. 5 **B19.126**

(1) A person commits an offence if—
(a) the person intentionally supplies a substance to another person,
(b) the substance is a psychoactive substance,
(c) the person knows or suspects, or ought to know or suspect, that the substance is a psychoactive substance, and
(d) the person knows, or is reckless as to whether, the psychoactive substance is likely to be consumed by the person to whom it is supplied, or by some other person, for its psychoactive effects.
(2) A person ('P') commits an offence if—
(a) P offers to supply a psychoactive substance to another person ('R'), and
(b) P knows or is reckless as to whether R, or some other person, would, if P supplied a substance to R in accordance with the offer, be likely to consume the substance for its psychoactive effects.
(3) For the purposes of subsection (2)(b), the reference to a substance's psychoactive effects includes a reference to the psychoactive effects which the substance would have if it were the substance which P had offered to supply to R.
(4) This section is subject to section 11 (exceptions to offences).

A partial definition of 'supplying' is given by s. 59(2)(b), namely that 'any reference to supplying a substance includes a reference to distributing it'. It seems likely that the word 'supply', as it appears in the PSA 2016 and in the MDA 1971, will be construed similarly (consider *Maginnis* [1987] AC 303, discussed at **B19.45**).

Section 5(2) (offering to supply) seems likely to be construed in terms similar to the offence of offering to supply a 'controlled drug' to another under the MDA 1971, s. 4 (see **B19.41**). Thus, the offence is in the making of the offer. By s. 5(3) of the PSA 2016, reference to a substance's 'psychoactive effects' includes a reference to the psychoactive effects which the substance would have 'if it were the substance which D had offered to supply to another'.

Possession of Psychoactive Substance with Intent to Supply

Psychoactive Substances Act 2016, s. 7 **B19.127**

(1) A person commits an offence if—
(a) the person is in possession of a psychoactive substance,
(b) the person knows or suspects that the substance is a psychoactive substance, and
(c) the person intends to supply the psychoactive substance to another person for its consumption, whether by any person to whom it is supplied or by some other person, for its psychoactive effects.
(2) This section is subject to section 11 (exceptions to offences).

A person must be in 'possession' of the substance (i.e. in its legal, technical, sense). By s. 59(3), possession includes items which are subject to that person's control but are in the custody of another person.

Importing or Exporting a Psychoactive Substance

B19.128 See **B16.37** for the offences of importing or exporting a psychoactive substance under the PSA 2016, s. 8.

Possession of a Psychoactive Substance in a Custodial Institution

B19.129 **Psychoactive Substances Act 2016, s. 9**

(1) A person commits an offence if—
  (a) the person is in possession of a psychoactive substance in a custodial institution,
  (b) the person knows or suspects that the substance is a psychoactive substance, and
  (c) the person intends to consume the psychoactive substance for its psychoactive effects.
(2) In this section 'custodial institution' has the same meaning as in section 6.
(3) This section is subject to section 11 (exceptions to offences).

Note that it is not sufficient that D is merely in possession of a psychoactive substance while in a 'custodial institution' (as defined by s. 6). It must be proved (among other things) that D intended to consume the psychoactive substance for its psychoactive effects (s. 9(1)(c)). No offence is committed if that act pertained to an 'exempted activity' (as defined in s. 11). Note that the s. 9 offence is not expressed as being limited to persons detained in a custodial institution.

Sentencing

B19.130 In *Waka* [2018] EWCA Crim 125, [2018 1 Cr App R (S) 54 (419) the Court of Appeal remarked that the Sentencing Council definitive guideline, *Drug Offences* (see Supplement, **SG23-1**), does not cover offences under the PSA 2016. It is not therefore a guideline which is 'relevant' within the narrow meaning of that word in the CAJA 2009, s. 125(1), or one which the court has a statutory obligation to follow. Nevertheless, this guideline is undoubtedly relevant in the broader sense of the word when sentencing for a similar offence (per Warby J at [15]):

> Until there are guidelines that apply to offences under the 2016 Act, we do consider that in a case such as the present a court should ordinarily have regard to the statutory guidelines for drug offences, and seek to sentence in a way that reflects the sentence that would apply to the drug and factual situation in the guideline which, on the information before the court, represent the closest approximation to the ones before the court.

For helpful sentencing guidance in relation to nitrous oxide, see *Miah* [2019] EWCA Crim 1478; *Halpin* [2019] EWCA Crim 892, in which *Waka* and *Grigas* [2017] EWCA Crim 1819 were cited.

SUPPLY OF INTOXICATING SUBSTANCE

B19.131 The Intoxicating Substances (Supply) Act 1985 was repealed by the PSA 2016, s. 60, and sch. 5, para. 1, with effect from 26 May 2016 (SI 2016 No. 553). See the 2016 edition of this work for details of the repealed provision.

MANUFACTURE AND SUPPLY OF SCHEDULED SUBSTANCES

B19.132 **Criminal Justice (International Co-Operation) Act 1990, s. 12**

(1) It is an offence for a person—
  (a) to manufacture a scheduled substance; or
  (b) to supply such a substance to another person,
knowing or suspecting that the substance is to be used in or for the unlawful production of a controlled drug.

A person does not commit an offence under s. 12(1) by manufacturing or, as the case may be, supplying the scheduled substance with the express consent of a constable (s. 12(1A)).

Procedure

No proceedings may be instituted in England and Wales except by or with the consent of the DPP or the Commissioners of Customs and Excise (Criminal Justice (International Co-operation) Act 1990, s. 21(2)(a)). The offence is triable either way (s. 12(2)). When tried on indictment it is a class 4 offence. **B19.133**

As to the position where the offence is committed on a British ship, see ss. 18 and 24. Section 21 of the MDA 1971 (liability of corporate officers — see **B19.40**) applies to this offence.

Sentence

The maximum penalty on conviction on indictment is imprisonment for a term not exceeding 14 years or a fine or both; on summary conviction, the maximum penalty is imprisonment for a term not exceeding six months or an unlimited fine (Criminal Justice (International Co-operation) Act 1990, s. 12(2)). This is a drug trafficking offence within the meaning of the POCA 2002, sch. 2 (see **E19.18**). A minimum custodial sentence of seven years applies for the third Class A drug trafficking offence (see **E5.1**). A confiscation order (see **E19**) or forfeiture order (see **E18.7**) may be imposed for a drug trafficking offence. Note that this is a 'serious offence' for the purposes of the SCA 2007, part 1 (serious crime prevention orders: see **D25.58**). Sentencers may be assisted by guidelines published by the Sentencing Council on *Drug offences involving newer and less common drugs*, a document which does not have the status of a full guideline but which may nevertheless be taken into account in relevant cases. **B19.134**

Scheduled Substance

A 'scheduled substance' for the purposes of the Criminal Justice (International Co-operation) Act 1990 is a substance specified in sch. 2 to that Act. Schedule 2 may be amended by Her Majesty by Order in Council. The substances are (in Table I) n-acetylanthranilic acid, ephedrine, ergometrine, ergotamine, isosafrole, lysergic acid, 3,4-methylene-dioxyphenyl-2-propanone, norephedrine, 1-phenyl-2-propanone, piperonal, pseudoephedrine, safrole and, (in Table II) acetic anhydride, acetone, anthranilic acid, ethyl ether, hydrochloric acid, methyl ethyl ketone (also referred to as 2-butanone or M.E.K.), phenylacetic acid, piperidine, potassium permanganate, sulphuric acid, and toluene. Also included are the salts of the substances listed in the Table (except hydrochloric acid and sulphuric acid) 'whenever the existence of such salts is possible'. **B19.135**

Note that the EU has legislated in respected of certain precursor chemicals: see Regulation (EC) No. 273/2004 (as amended by Regulations (EC) No. 219/2009, (EU) No. 1258/2013, (EU) 2016/1443 and (EU) 2018/729; see also (EC) No. 111/2005 (as amended) laying down rules for the monitoring of trade between the EU and third countries in drug precursors).

Unlawful Production of a Controlled Drug

The phrase 'controlled drug' has the same meaning as in the MDA 1971 (Criminal Justice (International Co-operation) Act 1990, s. 12(3)). For that definition, see **B19.7**. 'Unlawful production of a controlled drug' means production of such a drug which is unlawful by virtue of the MDA 1971, s. 4(1)(a) (Criminal Justice (International Co-operation) Act 1990, s. 12(3)). See **B19.63** ***et seq.*** **B19.136**

Supply

Supply is not defined in the Criminal Justice (International Co-operation) Act 1990, but it is presumed that it has the same meaning as in the MDA 1971 (see **B19.44**), as is explicitly the case in the regulations made under the Criminal Justice (International Co-operation) Act 1990, s. 13 (see **B19.138**). **B19.137**

CONTROLLED DRUGS (DRUGS PRECURSORS) REGULATIONS

Controlling the Production and Supply of Certain Scheduled Substances

B19.138 **Intra-community Trade** Note the commentary at **B19.1** regarding the future relationship between the UK and the EU. The relevant regulations are the Controlled Drugs (Drugs Precursors) (Intra-Community Trade) Regulations 2008 (SI 2008 No. 295). They should be read together with the 'Community Regulation', defined by reg. 2 of the 2008 Regulations as Regulation (EC) No. 273/2004 (the latter has been amended: see the Report on the Delegation of Power under (EC) No. 273/2004, COM(2018)159 final).

By reg. 6(1) of the 2008 Regulations, the obligations that are imposed by Regulation (EC) No. 273/2004, on 'operators' (as defined by Regulation (EC) No. 273/2004) by Article 5 (documentation), Article 7 (labelling) and Article 8 (notification of the competent authorities) shall be treated as if they are requirements imposed on them by regulations made under s. 13(1) of the 1990 Act, and as if references in those articles to 'scheduled substances' are references to scheduled substances within the meaning of part 2 of that Act. Where a person is convicted of an offence contrary to s. 13(5) of the 1990 Act, by virtue of reg. 6(1), s. 13(5)(a) of the 1990 Act shall have effect as if for the words '6 months' there are substituted the words '3 months'.

By reg. 7(1), an 'operator' who fails to comply with any of the requirements imposed by Article 3 of Regulation (EC) No. 273/2004 (requirements for placing on the market of scheduled substances) is guilty of an offence and liable (a) on summary conviction, to imprisonment for a term not exceeding three months and/or an unlimited fine; (b) on conviction on indictment, to imprisonment for a term not exceeding two years or a fine or both.

It is an offence, under the Criminal Justice (International Co-operation) Act 1990, s. 13, for a person to fail to comply with any requirement imposed by regulations made under that Act or, in purported compliance with any such requirement, to furnish information which he knows to be false in a material particular or recklessly to furnish information which is false in a material particular. The offence is triable either way and it is punishable on indictment with a maximum term of two years' imprisonment, and/or a fine. The maximum penalty, on summary conviction, is six months' imprisonment and/or an unlimited fine (s. 13(5)).

B19.139 **Community External Trade** Note the commentary at **B19.1**. The relevant regulations are the Controlled Drugs (Drugs Precursors) (External Trade) Regulations 2008 (SI 2008 No. 296). By reg. 5(2), the obligations imposed under Articles 3 to 5, 8 and 9 of Regulation (EC) No. 111/2005 shall be treated as if they are requirements imposed by regulations made under s. 13(1) of the 1990 Act (see **B19.138**), and as if references in those articles to scheduled substances are references to scheduled substances within the meaning of part 2 of that Act. Where a person is convicted of an offence contrary to s. 13(5) of the 1990 Act as a result of the application of reg. 5(2), s. 13(5)(a) of the 1990 Act (penalty on summary conviction) shall have effect as if for the words '6 months' there is substituted '3 months'.

SHIPS USED FOR ILLICIT TRAFFIC

B19.140 For offences in relation to controlled drugs on a British ship, see the Criminal Justice (International Co-operation) Act 1990, s. 19. Proceedings must be instituted by or with the consent of the DPP (s. 21(2)(a)). For jurisdiction, see s. 21(1).

Sentences for the offence vary according to the class of drug involved. As to whether the effect of the House of Lords' decision in *Courtie* [1984] AC 463 is that there is more than one offence, see **B19.23**. The offences are all triable either way (s. 19(4)). When tried on indictment they are class 4 offences.

Section 21 of the MDA 1971 (liability of corporate officers — see **B19.40**) applies to this offence.

Sentence

Where a class A drug is involved, the maximum penalty on indictment is imprisonment for life and/or a fine; on summary conviction, the maximum penalty is imprisonment for a term not exceeding six months and/or an unlimited fine (Criminal Justice (International Co-operation) Act 1990, s. 19(4)(a)). A minimum custodial sentence of seven years applies for the third Class A drug trafficking offence (see **E5.1**). **B19.141**

Where a Class B drug, or a temporary class drug, is involved, the maximum penalty on indictment is imprisonment for a term not exceeding 14 years and/or a fine; on summary conviction, the maximum penalty is imprisonment for a term not exceeding six months and/or an unlimited fine (s. 19(4)(b)).

Where a Class C drug is involved, the maximum penalty on indictment is imprisonment for a term not exceeding 14 years and/or a fine; on summary conviction, the maximum penalty is imprisonment for a term not exceeding three months and/or an unlimited fine (s. 19(4)(c)).

There is no offence-specific guideline but the Sentencing Council's *General Guideline: Overarching Principles* (see Supplement, **SG2-1**) is used for all offenders sentenced on or after 1 October 2019.

It is clearly established that where drugs have been intercepted on the high seas and those drugs were destined for a country other than England or Wales, the maximum available sentence for such offences in that other country is not a relevant sentencing consideration (*Maguire* [1997] 1 Cr App R (S) 130; *Wagenaar* [1997] 1 Cr App R (S) 178). For a further sentencing example (albeit in Scotland) see *Ekkebus v HM Advocate* [2002] ScotHC 77.

These are drug trafficking offences within the meaning of the POCA 2002, sch. 2 (see **E19.18**), so a forfeiture order (see **E18.7**) or a confiscation order (see **E19**) may be imposed.

Elements

The Criminal Justice (International Co-operation) Act 1990, s. 19(2), applies to a British ship, a ship registered in a State other than the UK which is a party to the Vienna Convention (a Convention State), and a ship not registered in any country or territory (s. 19(1)). Ship includes any vessel used in navigation; British ship means a ship registered in the UK or a colony (s. 24(1)). **B19.142**

'Controlled drug', and the classes of controlled drugs, have the same meaning as in the MDA 1971, see **B19.7** ***et seq.*** (s. 19(5)).

Since the defence in the MDA 1971, s. 28, applies, the meaning of possession in that Act should apply to the present offence. See **B19.27** ***et seq.***

As to the MDA 1971, s. 3(1), see **B19.69**. A certificate purporting to be issued by or on behalf of the government of any State to the effect that the importation or export of a controlled drug is prohibited by the law of that State shall be evidence of the matters stated (s. 19(3)).

It was made clear in *Dean* [1998] 2 Cr App R 171 that it is for the prosecution to prove, to the criminal standard of proof, that the ship in question is one to which s. 19 applies. The Court of Appeal said that it is 'sensible' to decide that issue at the outset of the trial rather than at the end of the prosecution case. On the facts of that particular case, the judge found that the ship was not registered anywhere and thus s. 19 was engaged.

B19.143 Enforcement powers, conferred by the 1990 Act, appear in sch. 3 to that Act. Section 20(1) of the Act provides that: 'The powers conferred on an enforcement officer by schedule 3 to this Act shall be exercisable in relation to any ship to which section 18 or 19 above applies for the purpose of detecting and the taking of appropriate action in respect of the offences mentioned in those sections'. Paragraph 2(1) of sch. 3 provides that: 'An enforcement officer may stop the ship, board it and, if he thinks it necessary in the exercise of his functions, require it to be taken to a port in the United Kingdom and detain it there'. Paragraph 4 provides that: 'If an enforcement officer has reasonable grounds to suspect that an offence mentioned in section 18 or 19 of this Act has been committed on a ship to which that section applies, he may (a) arrest without warrant any one whom he has reasonable grounds for suspecting to be guilty of the offence; and (b) seize and detain anything found on the ship which appears to him to be evidence of the offence'. In *Hoekstra v HM Advocate* [2002] ScotHC 343, the Appeal Court of the High Court of Justiciary held that before an enforcement officer could act under para. 4, the officer had to have pre-existing knowledge of reasonable grounds to suspect that an offence, mentioned in s. 18 or 19, had been committed. The wording of s. 19(2) meant that the aforementioned pre-existing knowledge (of reasonable grounds to suspect) extended to the issue of whether the ship concerned was one to which s. 19 applied. The Court had regard to a principle applied in *Leckie v Miln* 1982 SLT 177, that law enforcement officers cannot be treated as acting under and in terms of legal powers of which they are, at the time in question, ignorant and heedless. For requests made by UK customs officials to another State, to board a vessel that is flying an ensign of that State, see *Bolden* [1998] 2 Cr App R 171.

Defence

B19.144 The defence in the MDA 1971, s. 28, applies (Criminal Justice (International Co-operation) Act 1990, s. 19(5)). See **B19.104** for full details of the s. 28 defence.

SENTENCING GUIDELINES FOR OFFENCES UNDER THE MISUSE OF DRUGS ACT 1971

Maximum and Minimum Sentences

B19.145 Section 25 of the 1971 Act provides for maximum punishments to be set out in sch. 4 (see **B19.146**).

The Act distinguishes between three different types of drugs:

(a) Class A drugs (especially heroin, morphine, cocaine, LSD, opium and Ecstasy);
(b) Class B drugs (especially cannabis, cannabis resin, amphetamine and codeine); and
(c) Class C drugs (especially anabolic steroids, benzphetamine and pemoline).

A minimum custodial sentence of seven years must be imposed by the court where D, aged 18 or over, is convicted of a Class A drug trafficking offence committed after 1 October 1997, has been convicted of two other Class A drug trafficking offences, and there are no particular circumstances relating to any of the offences, or D, such that the imposition of a custodial sentence of at least seven years would be unjust in all the circumstances (PCC(S)A 2000, s. 110). For a detailed discussion of this topic, see **E5.1**.

Forfeiture and Confiscation

B19.146 For the court's powers of forfeiture under the MDA 1971, s. 27, see **E18.7**. For powers of confiscation, see **E19**.

Misuse of Drugs Act, sch. 4

Section 25

Schedule 4 Protection and Punishment of Offences

Section Creating Offence	General Nature of Offence	Mode of Prosecution	Punishment			
			Class A drug involved	Class B drug involved	Class C drug involved	General
Section 4(2)	Production, or being concerned in the production, of a controlled drug	(a) Summary	6 months or [an unlimited fine], or both	6 months or [an unlimited fine], or both	3 months or £2,500, or both	
		(b) On indictment	Life or a fine, or both	14 years or a fine, or both	14 years or a fine, or both	
Section 4(3)	Supplying or offering to supply a controlled drug or being concerned in the doing of either activity by another	(a) Summary	6 months or [an unlimited fine], or both	6 months or [an unlimited fine], or both	3 months or £2,500 or both	
		(b) On indictment	Life or a fine, or both	14 years or a fine, or both	14 years or a fine, or both	
Section 5(2)	Having possession of a controlled drug	(a) Summary	6 months or [an unlimited fine], or both	3 months or £2,500 or both	3 months or £1,000 or both	
		(b) On indictment	7 years or a fine, or both	5 years or a fine, or both	2 years or a fine, or both	
Section 5(3)	Having possession of a controlled drug with intent to supply it to another	(a) Summary	6 months [an unlimited fine], or both	6 months [an unlimited fine], or both	3 months or £2,500 or both	
		(b) On indictment	Life or a fine, or both	14 years or a fine, or both	14 years or a fine, or both	
Section 6(2)	Cultivation of cannabis plant	(a) Summary	—	—	—	6 months or [an unlimited fine], or both
		(b) On indictment	—	—	—	14 years or a fine, or both

Section Creating Offence	General Nature of Offence	Mode of Prosecution	Punishment			
			Class A drug involved	Class B drug involved	Class C drug involved	General
Section 8	Being the occupier, or concerned in the management, of premises and permitting or suffering certain activities to take place there	(a) Summary	6 months or [an unlimited fine], or both	6 months or [an unlimited fine], or both	3 months or £2,500 or both	
		(b) On indictment	14 years or a fine, or both	14 years or a fine, or both	14 years or a fine, or both	
Section 9	Offences relating to opium	(a) Summary	—	—	—	6 months or [an unlimited fine], or both
		(b) On indictment	—	—	—	14 years or a fine, or both
Section 11(2)	Contravention of direction relating to safe custody of controlled drugs	(a) Summary	—	—	—	6 months or [an unlimited fine], or both
		(b) On indictment	—	—	—	2 years or a fine, or both
Section 12(6)	Contravention of direction prohibiting practitioner etc. from possessing, supply etc. of controlled drugs	(a) Summary	6 months or [an unlimited fine], or both	6 months or [an unlimited fine], or both	3 months or £2,500 or both	
		(b) On indictment	14 years or a fine, or both	14 years or a fine, or both	14 years or a fine, or both	
Section 13(3)	Contravention of direction prohibiting practitioner etc. from prescribing, supplying etc. controlled drugs	(a) Summary	6 months or [an unlimited fine], or both	6 months or [an unlimited fine], or both	3 months or £2,500 or both	
		(b) On indictment	14 years or a fine, or both	14 years or a fine, or both	14 years or a fine, or both	
			—	—	—	2 years or a fine, or both
Section 17(3)	Failure to comply with notice requiring information relating to prescribing, supplying etc. of drugs	Summary	—	—	—	level 3 on the standard scale
Section 17(4)	Giving false information in purported compliance with notice requiring information relating to prescribing, supply etc. of drugs	(a) Summary	—	—	—	6 months or [an unlimited fine], or both
		(b) On indictment	—	—	—	2 years or a fine, or both

Section 18(1)	Contravention of regulations (other than regulations relating to addicts)	(a) Summary	—	—	—	6 months or prescribed sum, or both
Section 18(2)	Contravention of terms of licence or other authority (other than licence issued under regulations relating to addicts)	(a) Summary	—	—	—	6 months or [an unlimited fine], or both
		(b) On indictment	—	—	—	2 years or a fine, or both
Section 18(3)	Giving false information in purported compliance with obligation to give information imposed under or by virtue of regulations	(a) Summary	—	—	—	6 months or [an unlimited fine], or both
		(b) On indictment	—	—	—	2 years or a fine, or both
Section 18(4)	Giving false information, or producing documents etc. containing false statement etc. for purposes of obtaining issue or renewal of a licence or other authority	(a) Summary	—	—	—	6 months or [an unlimited fine], or both
		(b) On indictment	—	—	—	2 years or a fine, or both
Section 20	Assisting in or inducing commission outside United Kingdom of an offence punishable under a corresponding law	(a) Summary	—	—	—	6 months or [an unlimited fine], or both
		(b) On indictment	—	—	—	14 years or a fine, or both
Section 23(4)	Obstructing exercise of powers of search etc or concealing books, drugs, etc	(a) Summary	—	—	—	6 months or [an unlimited fine], or both
		(b) On indictment	—	—	—	2 years or a fine, or both

B19.147 The definitive sentencing guideline, *Drug Offences* (see Supplement, **SG23-1**), applies to all offenders aged 18 and over who are sentenced on or after 27 February 2012, irrespective of the date of the offence. The guideline covers (a) fraudulent evasion of a prohibition by bringing into or taking out of the UK a controlled drug, (b) supplying or offering to supply a controlled drug, (c) production of a controlled drug, (d) permitting premises to be used, and (e) possession of a controlled drug. The guideline supersedes a mass of case law issued under earlier authority. It was said by the Court of Appeal in *Dyer* [2013] EWCA Crim 2114, [2014] 2 Cr App R (S) 11 (61), in the context of street-dealing in Class A drugs, that the old case law had been superseded by the guideline and should no longer be relied upon.

Guideline Structure and Approach

B19.148 The definitive sentencing guideline, *Drug Offences* (see Supplement, **SG23-1**), requires the sentencer at Step One to determine the offence category by reference to the category of drug, the offender's culpability, and to the harm caused.

The guideline sets out, for each of the forms of offence covered, three levels of culpability at Step One: 'leading role', 'significant role' and 'lesser role'. A non-exhaustive list of characteristics which may demonstrate the particular offender's role is provided. The guideline then sets out, for each of the forms of offence covered, a three-fold or four-fold classification of 'category of harm' based upon indicative quantity of the drug concerned (upon which the sentencing starting point in each category is based). The various quantities listed in the guidelines are indicative only, and they are not thresholds (*Henry* [2013] EWCA Crim 1415, [2014] 1 Cr App R (S) 55 (347)).

In assessing harm, quantity is determined by the weight of the product. In *Kerley* [2015] EWCA Crim 1193, [2015] 2 Cr App R (S) 69 (475) the offenders fell to be sentenced for their involvement in a conspiracy to supply amphetamine. The drugs had been seized while stored 'wet', with a greater weight than if stored and sold 'dry'. The Court of Appeal said that normally dealers caught in possession of drugs should be sentenced on the basis of the weight of the drugs they had at the relevant time (the 'wet' weight in this case) and that evidence would have to be adduced before a different approach could be taken. The Court of Appeal in *Nnamani* [2015] EWCA Crim 596, [2015] 2 Cr App R (S) 23 (219) said that with matters of weight the guidelines had to be applied 'with realism', so that, where D had been found in possession of nearly 700 grams of cocaine of high purity and nearly 600 grams of a cutting agent for use with Class A drugs, the judge had been right to add the two amounts together to determine the weight for sentencing purposes. In principle, the purity of the drug concerned is not taken into account at Step One, but is dealt with at Step Two. However, as explained in *Kelly* [2014] EWCA Crim 1141, [2014] 2 Cr App R (S) 70 (549), a case involving conspiracy to supply Class A drugs, there can be circumstances where both quantity and purity of the drug is important in determining D's role. It was an 'obvious inference' that offenders who dealt with high-purity drugs were closer to the centre of operations than those who dealt with drugs which had been diluted for street use.

Having determined the applicable category under Step One, the sentencer should use the corresponding starting point to reach a sentence within the category range indicated in the guideline. The starting point applies to all offenders, irrespective of plea or previous convictions. The court should then consider further adjustment within the category range for aggravating or mitigating features, as set out in a non-exhaustive list.

The Court of Appeal in *Healey* [2012] EWCA Crim 1005, [2013] 1 Cr App R (S) 33 (176) provided a valuable detailed exposition on the proper approach of the courts to the guideline. Hughes LJ said that the sentencer's job was to read the guidelines for what they were, and it was not open to a judge to prefer and apply appellate guidance which pre-dated the guidelines. His lordship also said (at [9]–[10]):

> The format which is adopted by the Sentencing Council in producing its guidelines is to present the broad categories of offence frequently encountered pictorially in boxes. That is perhaps convenient,

> especially since it is necessary to condense the presentation as much as possible and to avoid discursive narrative on so wide a range of offending. It may be that the pictorial boxes which are part of the presentation may lead a superficial reader to think that adjacent boxes are mutually exclusive, one of the other. They are not. There is an inevitable overlap between the scenarios which are described in adjacent boxes. In real life, offending is found on a sliding scale of gravity with few hard lines. The guidelines set out to describe such sliding scales and graduations. In these guidelines, as in almost all such, there is a recognition that the two principal factors which affect sentencing for crime can broadly be collected together as, first, the harm the offence does, and secondly, the culpability of the offender...Quantity, which is a broad appreciation of harm, may well colour participation, which is a broad appreciation of culpability, and vice versa. What we have just said about sliding scales applies equally to both elements, both to culpability and to harm. In neither case do the boxes have hard edges.

The guidelines apply to cases of conspiracy. This was confirmed by the Court of Appeal in *Khan* [2013] EWCA Crim 800, [2014] 1 Cr App R (S) 10 (42), a case of conspiracy to supply Class A drugs. Treacy LJ said that in such a case a judge was entitled to consider the aggregate quantity of the drug (or drugs) involved. The role of the offender within the conspiracy would be very important, and an individual offender's limited part in the conspiracy had to be balanced against the seriousness of the offending as a whole. Where there is a conspiracy, and the amount of the drugs well exceeds the indicative amounts in the guideline, a judge is entitled to exceed the ceiling in the relevant category but the guideline should remain a valuable touchstone for sentence (*Cuni* [2018] EWCA Crim 600, [2018] 2 Cr App R (S) 18 (151)). A judge is entitled to use the relevant guideline for supply of drugs where D has been convicted of encouraging or assisting in that supply, contrary to s. 45 of the SCA 2007 (*Woodford* [2013] EWCA Crim 1098, [2014] 1 Cr App R (S) 32 (195)) or assisting contrary to s. 46 of that Act (*Hall* [2013] EWCA Crim 2499, [2014] 2 Cr App R (S) 20 (136)).

In *Waka* [2018] EWCA Crim 125, [2018] 1 Cr App R (S) 54 (419) the Court of Appeal considered an appeal against sentence for possession of cannabis and other psychoactive substances. The Court gave judicial guidance that, where a given chemical did not appear in the guideline, the correct approach would be to look to the guideline to establish the 'closest approximation'. Here the substance in question was a synthetic cannabinoid, and so the approximation required reference to the guideline for cannabis and Class B substances.

The prevalence of drug-related offending in a particular area should not normally be taken into account as an aggravating feature in sentencing (*Bondzie* [2016] EWCA Crim 552, [2016] 2 Cr App R (S) 28 (261)) unless there is sound and objective evidence to justify that course. See further **E1.22**.

Class A Drug Offences

Importation A minimum custodial sentence of seven years applies for the third Class A drug trafficking offence (see **E5.1**). **B19.149**

The guideline indicates that for an offender playing a 'leading role' in this offence, involving a Class A drug, and depending on the category of harm, the starting points are 14 years (category 1), 11 years (category 2), or eight years, six months (category 3). For an offender playing a 'significant role', the starting points are ten years, eight years, or six years. For an offender playing a 'lesser role', the starting points are eight years, six years, or four years, six months. In *Talebi* [2012] EWCA Crim 3040, [2013] 2 Cr App R (S) 49 (339), a case involving importation of 3.92 kilograms of opium, the Court of Appeal noted that the categories of harm in the guideline were based on indicative quantities of the drug concerned. While heroin and cocaine were listed there was no reference to opium. The Court concluded that for these purposes 1 kilogram of heroin should be regarded as equivalent to 8 kilograms of opium. The instant case was a category 2 importation with a starting point of 11 years. Applying 25 per cent discount for the guilty plea, the proper sentence was eight years' imprisonment. In *A-G's Refs (Nos. 15, 16 and 17 of 2012) (Lewis)* [2012] EWCA Crim 1414, [2013] 1 Cr App R (S) 52 (289), in the case of two offenders (D1 and D2) convicted of 'a massive importation' of 100 kilograms of diamorphine and 6 kilograms of cocaine, the Court of Appeal increased sentences totalling 13 years to 20 years for D1 and sentences totalling nine years to 13 years for D2, saying that D1 had played a 'leading/significant' role and D2 a 'significant' role in the offence. In *Haxihaj* [2016] EWCA Crim 83, [2016] 1 Cr App R (S) 72 (532), where D had played a leading role in a conspiracy to supply 70 kilograms of heroin at 44–53 per cent purity in two separate conspiracies, the appropriate starting points were 25 years and 30 years before substantial reductions for assistance provided to the prosecution and for pleas of guilty. In *Sanghera* [2016] EWCA Crim 94, [2016] 2 Cr App R (S) 15 (135) a starting point of 30 years for D who was playing a leading role but was not the mastermind in a relatively sophisticated operation to import and distribute 40 kilograms of cocaine, was reduced to 27 years before adjustment for plea. The Court of Appeal observed that although the quantity of drugs involved was eight times the indicative quantity for category 1, a starting point of 30 years should be reserved for 'massive' importations. *Sanghera* was applied in *Cuni* [2018] EWCA Crim 600, [2018] 2 Cr App R (S) 18 (151), which dealt with a long-running and sophisticated operation to distribute very large quantities of cocaine of about 90 per cent purity. Consignments which originated in South America were smuggled into the UK through France or Belgium via the Channel Tunnel, having been concealed in luxury cars. On one date alone, some 30 kilograms of cocaine, with a wholesale value of £1 million and a street value of £3.6 million, were intercepted and seized. The Court of Appeal said that this was a big conspiracy, but not 'really huge'. The judge should have taken a starting point of 28 years, and following reduction for plea the sentence should have been 19 years. Sentences on other appellants were upheld or, in one case, slightly reduced.

In *Jhurry* [2018] EWCA Crim 2799, [2019] 1 Cr App R (S) 40 (274) the Court of Appeal endorsed a submission that the sentence range for a leading role in a conspiracy to import Class A drugs, where the quantity substantially exceeds 100 kilograms, involves a starting point between 20 to 30 years' custody before discount for mitigating circumstances and plea of guilty. It went on to deal with the suggestion that additional credit for a very early indication of a guilty plea, and in particular, the *first* plea amongst a number of conspirators, could extend beyond one-third. The Court noted that the Sentencing Council's guideline, *Reduction in Sentence for a Guilty Plea* (see Supplement, SG5-1), expressly states, definitively, that the maximum level of reduction in sentence for a guilty plea is one-third. In the view of the Court, that would preclude any future submissions on this point. The judge had, however, been right to mark the significance of D being the first to enter a guilty plea not by additional credit, but by recognising that fact as clear evidence of D's remorse, a significant mitigating factor.

B19.150 **Drug Couriers and 'mules'** In *Attuh-Benson* [2004] EWCA Crim 3032, [2005] 2 Cr App R (S) 11 (52), the Court of Appeal stated that it was not appropriate at that time to reconsider the policy of passing long deterrent custodial sentences on drug couriers, who were not infrequently women with dependent children who came from under-developed countries and who would suffer considerable hardship in prison. The Court did say, however, that there was sufficient flexibility to allow judges to assess D's role, extent of culpability, attitude to the offence and personal circumstances. In *Robinson* [2004] EWCA Crim 360, [2004] 2 Cr App R (S) 72 (392), the Court of Appeal observed that, in some cases involving importation of drugs where a defence of duress has been run without success, it may still be necessary for the sentencer to hold a *Newton* hearing to determine whether there had been a degree of coercion short of duress (see also *Quinn* [2009] EWCA Crim 1097, [2010] 1 Cr App R (S) 34 (209)). The Sentencing Council has signalled a change of sentencing policy with respect to this particular group of drug offenders, with lower sentences now appropriate in some cases. It is significant, however, that the Council's press release which accompanied the guideline stressed that: 'A drug mule should not be confused with other types of offender sentenced for importation offences— if the court decides that he or she has a more significant role in importing drugs, then a longer sentence [sh]ould be passed'. In *Jaramillo* [2012] EWCA Crim 2101, [2013] 1 Cr App R (S) 110 (569), a case decided after the guideline came into effect, the four offenders pleaded guilty to importation of cocaine. They travelled as two couples, the first pair carrying 42.81 kilograms worth £7.2 million and the second pair carrying 33.89 kilograms, worth £5.29 million. It was accepted that the offenders were not organisers or managers. Sentences of ten years' detention in a young offender institution and 11 years' imprisonment respectively, were reduced to seven years and eight years. The offenders were, for the purposes of the guidelines, performing a lesser role, but importations of 5 kilograms or more fell within the scope of category 1. This was much more than 5 kilograms and the operation was on the most serious and commercial scale. Even so, the offenders had limited roles as couriers, but did not properly fall within the category of 'mules'. The original sentences did not recognise sufficiently the gap in culpability between those who managed and organised and those towards the lower end of the hierarchy.

Supply A minimum custodial sentence of seven years applies for the third Class A drug trafficking offence (see **E5.1**). **B19.151**

The guideline indicates that for an offender playing a 'leading role' in the offence, involving a Class A drug and depending on the category of harm, the starting point is 14 years (category 1); 11 years (category 2); eight years, six months (category 3); or five years, six months (category 4). For an offender playing a 'significant role', the starting point is ten years; eight years; four years, six months; or three years, six months. For an offender playing a 'lesser role', the starting point is seven years, five years, three years or 18 months. Sometimes an offence can straddle two categories, as in *Bakewell* [2015] EWCA Crim 1807, [2016] 1 Cr App R (S) 34 (201), where a guilty plea was tendered on the basis that the 13.61 grams of cocaine was principally for D's own use but he would have supplied some of his friends on a forthcoming weekend trip. The judge erred in placing the case within category 3, significant role. Lesser role was more appropriate. Three years and nine months' imprisonment was reduced to three years on appeal. The Court of Appeal in *Bondzie* [2016] EWCA Crim 552, [2016] 2 Cr App R (S) 28 (261) said, in relation to the sentencing of an offender for drugs supply in an area of the country where there was said to be a serious problem in relation to drugs, that the *Drug Offences* guideline (see Supplement, **SG23-1**) already took the collective social harm of offending into account. A judge should be very hesitant to increase sentence for reasons of local prevalence of offending, and should not do so without evidence provided to the court by a responsible body or senior police officer, such as to satisfy the judge that the local circumstances really were exceptional. See further **E1.22**.

In *Dyer* [2013] EWCA Crim 2114, [2014] 2 Cr App R (S) 11 (61) the offenders were eight people arrested as part of a single police operation. They appealed against sentences imposed following their guilty pleas to various offences of street dealing in Class A drugs. All had sold drugs to test purchase police officers. They appealed on the basis that the judge had misapplied the guideline. Leveson LJ said that for cases involving street dealing of drugs the harm caused was not quantified by the quantity of drugs. The particular guideline on supply, offering to supply, and possession with intent to supply operates slightly differently from the norm. A street dealer who was funding his own habit was 'motivated by financial advantage' and therefore played a *significant role* for the purpose of assessing his culpability under the guideline. The characteristic of 'some awareness and understanding of scale of operation' that pointed in other cases to D playing a significant role was less relevant to street dealing. It is important to note that any case of 'selling direct to users' drops straight into category 3. The fact that the sale was to a test purchase officer was not a reason to reduce the category since the identity of the person to whom the drugs were sold was a matter of chance. That leads (assuming Class A drugs) to a starting point of four years, six months and a category range of three years, six months to seven years. Drug purity becomes relevant at Step Two in the guideline, together with all relevant aggravating and mitigating factors (including but not limited to those listed). Then, of course, there should be an appropriate reduction for plea. The Court adjusted sentences in this case to terms ranging from three to five and a half years. Leveson LJ also said that the pre-guideline authorities on supply of drugs had been overtaken by the guideline, so reliance on *Afonso* [2004] EWCA Crim 2342, [2005] 1 Cr App R (S) 99 (560) was no longer appropriate. In *Leigh* [2015] EWCA Crim 1045, [2015] 2 Cr App R (S) 42 (332) D, who pleaded guilty to possession of cocaine with intent to supply, had been stopped by police and found to have nearly 15 grams of cocaine secreted in a plastic vessel in his anus. The basis of plea was that he was transporting the drugs across town for drug dealers. The Court of Appeal said that the offence clearly involved 'street dealing', even though no street deal would take place in the course of that particular journey. The offence fell into category 3, lesser role and the sentence of 26 months' imprisonment was upheld. In *Williams* [2014] EWCA Crim 765, [2014] 2 Cr App R (S) 58 (464) D pleaded guilty to possession of heroin with intent to supply, on the basis that he was storing the drugs at home for his supplier. There was 54 grams of heroin, capable of being divided into 288 deals. The judge took a starting point of three years, and reduced it by one third to reflect the plea. The Court of Appeal said that the judge had been entitled to place the offence into category 3 (indicative quantity 150 grams) even though D was not 'selling direct to users', since to have placed it in category 4 (indicative quantity 5 grams) would have understated his involvement.

Cases frequently have a combination of culpability elements from adjacent role categories. In *Osmani* [2018] EWCA Crim 2824 D pleaded guilty on the basis that he was a courier of a quantity of drugs and sought to be sentenced in a lesser role. The Court of Appeal noted that the amount he couriered was so large that he must have had some idea of the scale of the operation he was involved in and it was proper, in principle, to sentence him on the basis of a significant role even if only one of the five relevant characteristics indicative of 'significant role' was present. It would be fair, however, to sentence at the lower end of the relevant category.

The Court of Appeal in *Ajayi* [2017] EWCA Crim 1011, [2018] 4 WLR 42 gave guidance on the operation of the guideline in relation to the form of supply known as 'cuckooing', where retail drug dealers from metropolitan centres travel to a smaller provincial community to sell drugs, setting themselves up in local premises. Often they latch on to a local dealer and take over the operation. Large supplies will not be maintained in the provincial centre but will be the subject of re-supply from the metropolitan base. The practice of cuckooing is often achieved by exploiting local drug users and the exploitation of people to act as couriers or minders of drugs or money. Persons organising from the metropolitan base fall within a leading role, and a person operating as a local manager may also do so. Those involved who do not fall within a leading role will ordinarily fall into a significant role. Weight should be given to evidence of pressure, intimidation or reward. The offending may carry the hallmarks of professional crime above and beyond that of street dealing. Treacy LJ, giving the judgment of the Court, said that the judge should focus carefully on the evidence and the terms of the guideline to ensure appropriate categorisation, and the guidance was not intended to encourage a departure from the guideline.

In *Doforo* [2018] EWCA Crim 1506 the Court of Appeal considered aggravating features in a case of drug supply and said that D's previous conviction for Class A drug dealing was a very serious aggravating feature, noting that professional criminals who persist in dealing with Class A drugs, having previously been convicted and punished with a substantial term of imprisonment, would require appreciably longer terms of imprisonment when convicted again. It was necessary to deter such criminals and others like them who set about making the risk benefit calculation before engaging in this very deliberate and financially driven kind of offending. The rewards are very high—and so also must be the risks.

An argument that knowingly supplying cocaine to a police officer was an aggravating factor was, on the facts, rejected in *Wade* [2018] EWCA Crim 2429, [2019] 1 Cr App R (S) 31 (207). D was a long-standing friend of the officer, the supply was social supply, and there was no element of corruption.

As to a potential mitigating feature, the Court of Appeal in *Bird* [2013] EWCA Crim 1765, [2014] 1 Cr App R (S) 77 (478) said that while those who deal in drugs must understand that they take the risk that the drug they are selling could turn out to be Class A rather than (as they believed) Class B, a genuine misunderstanding by D as to the class of the drug is a factor in deciding where in the relevant Class A sentencing range the offence falls.

Supply to Serving Prisoner The guideline states that 'supply, other than by a person in position of responsibility, to a prisoner for gain without coercion' is indicative of a 'significant role'. In *Sanchez-Canadas* [2012] EWCA Crim 2204, [2013] 1 Cr App R (S) 114 (588) the Court of Appeal upheld a sentence of 45 months on D who attempted to supply 10.75 grams of heroin and 23 grams of cannabis into a prison by sending them concealed in a pair of trainers. The Court said that this was a category 4 significant role case, and a starting point of five years after a trial could not be faulted. The Court observed that it would be wrong to increase the harm category in a case such as this because of the enhanced value of drugs within a prison setting, but that most cases of drug supply into a prison would fall within 'significant role'. They will ordinarily demand a prison sentence even where there is no commercial motive and where the supplier has come under some moral pressure. By contrast, *Shahadat* [2017] EWCA Crim 822, [2017] 2 Cr App R (S) 32 (282) was a case of supply of Class A drugs by one prisoner to another, and the Court of Appeal said that category 3 (rather than 4) was appropriate because this was a form of 'street dealing', even though it had occurred within the prison walls. In *Hamilton* [2016] EWCA Crim 78, [2016] 2 Cr App R (S) 2 (7) the Court of Appeal said that it was legitimate to have regard to the drugs guideline when sentencing for smuggling drugs into prison under the Prison Act 1952, s. 40B. D, a single mother of two children, had been placed under emotional pressure to smuggle 6.88 grams of cocaine to an inmate during a prison visit. It was a category 4 lesser role case, aggravated by the supply to a prisoner. The appropriate starting point was 27 months, reduced to 18 months to reflect her guilty plea. In *Dickinson* [2017] EWCA Crim 2067, where D was caught trying to deliver 415 milligrams of crack cocaine and 14 tablets of Class C drugs, the Court of Appeal agreed with the approach in *Hamilton* and, despite strong personal mitigation, upheld an immediate prison sentence of six months. **B19.152**

This was further reinforced in *Severn* [2018] EWCA Crim 1441, [2018] 2 Cr App R (S) 48 (393), in which the sentencer identified the appropriate sentence after trial as 30 months, reduced to a sentence of 20 months' imprisonment after discount for plea, but not suspended. D was a woman with a small child, who was pregnant and who had supplied £280 worth of heroin to her partner only because she feared he would be in danger from other prisoners as a result of incurring debts to them. Upholding the sentence, the Court of Appeal said it was necessary to impose immediate custody even in such a case, otherwise there would be even greater pressure on the weak and vulnerable to contribute to prison disorder by taking drugs into prison.

Production A minimum custodial sentence of seven years applies for the third Class A drug trafficking offence (see **E5.1**). **B19.153**

The guideline indicates that for an offender playing a 'leading role' in the offence, involving a Class A drug and depending on the category of harm, the starting point is 14 years (category 1); 11 years (category 2); eight years, six months (category 3); or five years, six months (category 4). For an offender playing a 'significant role', the starting point is ten years; eight years; four years, six months; or three years, six months. For an offender playing a 'lesser role', the starting point is seven years, five years, three years or 18 months.

Permitting Use of Premises A minimum custodial sentence of seven years applies for the third Class A drug trafficking offence (see **E5.1**). **B19.154**

The guideline indicates that for category 1 (higher culpability and greater harm) the starting point is two years, six months; for offence category 2 (lower culpability and greater harm, or higher culpability and lesser harm) the starting point is 36 weeks; and for offence category 3 (lower culpability and lesser harm) the starting point is a medium level community order.

Possession The guideline indicates that for possession of a Class A controlled drug the starting point is a Band C fine within a category range of a Band A fine to 51 weeks' custody. In the pre-guideline case of *Roberts* [1997] 2 Cr App R (S) 187, a prisoner serving a four-year sentence for possession of heroin with intent to supply was found to be in possession of a small quantity of **B19.155**

heroin when searched by prison officers. The Court of Appeal stated that possession of drugs by a prisoner was more serious than possession of drugs outside prison, and upheld a consecutive sentence of 15 months' imprisonment. Possession of drugs in prison is an aggravating factor in the guideline.

Class B Drug Offences

B19.156 **Importation** The guideline indicates that for an offender playing a 'leading role' in this offence, involving a Class B drug, and depending on the category of harm, the starting points are eight years (category 1), six years (category 2), or four years (category 3). For an offender playing a 'significant role', the starting points are five years, six months; four years; or two years. For an offender playing a 'lesser role', the starting points are four years, two years, or one year.

In *A-G's Refs (Nos. 15, 16 and 17 of 2012) (Lewis)* [2012] EWCA Crim 1414, [2013] 1 Cr App R (S) 52 (289), D pleaded guilty to importation of 120 packages (240 kilograms) of methylethcathinone (street value around £3 million), 4 kilograms of cannabis resin (street value around £11,000) and 971 grams of moist (591 grams dry) amphetamine sulphate (street value around £9,000). The Court of Appeal found that this had been a highly professional commercial operation, and D played a very significant role in the chain of supply. There was little mitigation save for previous good character and a guilty plea. The Court said that the overall sentence should have been at least eight years before credit for plea, and the sentence of 42 months was increased to six years.

B19.157 **Supply** The guideline indicates that for an offender playing a 'leading role' in the offence, and depending on the category of harm, the starting point is eight years (category 1), six years (category 2), four years (category 3) and 18 months (category 4). For an offender playing a 'significant role', the starting point is five years, six months; four years; one year; and a high level community order. For an offender playing a 'lesser role', the starting point is three years, one year, a high level community order, or a low level community order. The Court of Appeal in *Brown* [2013] EWCA Crim 1726, [2014] 1 Cr App R (S) 84 (518), a case involving conspiracy to supply MDPV, said that, when determining the category of harm in the guideline, MDPV was to be treated as commensurate with amphetamine, and the potential for causing harm was the same for the same quantity of each drug. *Quick* [2017] EWCA Crim 66, [2017] 1 Cr App R (S) 54 (419) is a useful decision on sentencing for possession with intent to supply, where D was selling directly to users. The police found 256 grams of amphetamine sulphate at D's home, together with a large number of plastic bags. D said that the drugs were for his own use, but he was convicted after a trial. He had no previous convictions, and had recently become unemployed, which had led to him suffering from depression. The pre-sentence report recommended a suspended sentence. The Court of Appeal said that the judge had rightly characterised the offence as category 3 significant role, leading to a starting point of 12 months. The immediate sentence of nine months was upheld, although the Court said that a suspended sentence could have been imposed, and it would have been helpful if the judge had used the stepped approach in the guideline to explain why he had not done so. For considerations weighing for and against suspension of a custodial sentence, see the Sentencing Council definitive guideline, *Imposition of Community and Custodial Sentences* (see Supplement, **SG9-1**), and **E6.3**.

Supply of drugs to a serving prisoner is an important aggravating feature. In *Lea* [2017] EWCA Crim 1789 D was caught trying to convey two packages containing cannabis and a mobile phone. Despite strong personal mitigation and an early plea of guilty the Court of Appeal said that 12 months' imprisonment was appropriate, and the offence was too serious for the term to be suspended. In *Reynolds* [2017] 1 Cr App R (S) 42, [2017] 1 Cr App R (S) 42 (338) the Court of Appeal considered a number of earlier authorities and accepted that the default position for those convicted of taking contraband items into prison was an immediate custodial sentence, because such items contributed to disorder and criminality within prisons. D admitted conveying cannabis, contrary to the Prison Act 1953, s. 40B, and SIM cards, contrary to s. 40C, to her boyfriend in prison. Taking into account a psychiatric report and various matters of personal mitigation, the Court of Appeal suspended the original sentence of four months.

Production The guideline indicates that for an offender playing a 'leading role' in the offence, and depending on the category of harm, the starting points are eight years (category 1), six years (category 2), four years (category 3) and one year (category 4). For an offender playing a 'significant role', the starting points are five years, six months; four years; one year; and a high level community order. For an offender playing a 'lesser role', the starting points are three years, one year, a high level community order, and a Band C fine. **B19.158**

In *Dang* [2014] EWCA Crim 348, [2014] 1 WLR 3797 nine offenders were convicted of conspiracy to produce cannabis, in that they supplied hydroponic and other equipment to others to grow cannabis and also conspired to produce cannabis for themselves. This was done on an 'industrial scale', with evidence relating to some 56 cannabis production farms. Sentences ranging from four to 15 years were imposed, the judge noting that all the offenders came within category 1 and that 'skunk' cannabis, by virtue of its higher THC content, required a higher starting point, closer to that appropriate for Class A. All sentences were upheld by the Court of Appeal. In *Wiseman* [2013] EWCA Crim 2492, [2014] 2 Cr App R (S) 23 (162) six and a half years' imprisonment following a guilty plea was upheld in respect of an offender in a leading role in a cannabis cultivation operation capable of producing 120 kilograms per year. The Court of Appeal noted that, by contrast with the guideline for importation and supply, in the production guideline the description of cases which may fall into category 1 or category 2 did not give any indicative weight or quantity of plants. This was entirely understandable, since with importation or supply the specific charge would normally relate to an identified quantity of the drug whereas with production the issue was the amount the operation was 'capable of producing'. In the leading case of *Healey* [2012] EWCA Crim 1005, [2013] 1 Cr App R (S) 33 (176) the Court of Appeal dealt with a number of unrelated cases involving individual offenders growing relatively small numbers of cannabis plants in a loft or cellar, having invested in equipment for watering and lighting the plants which were intended for repeated cropping. Such offenders, displaying a 'determined approach to cultivation' play, according to the Court, a 'significant role', rather than a 'lesser role'. The offender Brearley, dealt with in *Healey*, was aged 45. He had a specially constructed room at the back of his garage, containing the usual equipment for the intensive cultivation of cannabis. At the time of arrest he had six plants but their potential yield was very high, as much as one and a third kilograms. He had spent £600 on the equipment. The offence was aggravated by involving other people to assist him crop the plants. In addition he had bypassed the electricity meter. He claimed that the product was all for his own use, and that was accepted by the judge. The Court said that the proper sentence based on a significant role, category 3, would have been 12 months after a trial, eight months on a plea of guilty. In *Bamford* [2012] EWCA Crim 820, [2013] 1 Cr App R (S) 4 (26), a rather similar case decided under the guideline but before the decision in *Healey*, six months' imprisonment was reduced on appeal to nine weeks on the basis of D's 'lesser role'. In *Descombre* [2013] EWCA Crim 72, [2013] 2 Cr App R (S) 51 (345) D had established a 'cannabis factory' in an outbuilding which had produced three crops of cannabis. There were 60 mature plants with a potential yield of about 5 kilograms. The Court approved the judge's finding that D performed a leading role in a commercial operation and upheld a sentence of 40 months' imprisonment following a plea of guilty. In *Soloman* [2015] EWCA Crim 64, [2015] 1 Cr App R (S) 57 (401) D admitted possession of 18 immature cannabis plants, together with equipment for cultivation. The judge found that the method of cultivation would have provided a higher yield than the figure suggested in the guideline, and that recovered text messages showed that the operation was closer to a commercial than a domestic one, thereby taking the case into category 3 rather than 4. The Court of Appeal upheld the sentence of nine months' imprisonment following a guilty plea. The Court of Appeal in *Wicks* [2013] EWCA Crim 1414, [2014] 1 Cr App R (S) 57 (355) said that the judge had been entitled to take into account information in a community impact statement about the significant risk of associated offending, including violent crime, in an area where cannabis factories were in operation.

B19.159 **Permitting Use of Premises** The guideline indicates that for a Class B controlled drug the starting point for category 1 is one year within a category range of 26 weeks to 18 months, for category 2 the starting point is a high level community order within a category range of low level community order to 26 weeks and for category 3 the starting point is a Band C fine within a category range of a Band A fine to a low level community order.

B19.160 **Possession** The guideline indicates that for possession of a Class B controlled drug the starting point is a Band B fine within a category range of a discharge to 26 weeks' custody.

Class C Drug Offences

B19.161 **Importation** The guideline indicates that for an offender playing a 'leading role' in this offence, involving a Class C drug, and depending on the category of harm, the starting points are five years (category 1); three years, six months (category 2); or 18 months (category 3). For an offender playing a 'significant role', the starting points are three years, 18 months, or 26 weeks. For an offender playing a 'lesser role', the starting points are 18 months, 26 weeks, or a high level community order. In *Pearce* [2015] EWCA Crim 1291, [2015] 2 Cr App R (S) 70 (480), D imported and sold steroids to the value of £58,000, making £20,000 profit. He acted as a 'sole trader', and there was no hierarchy of supply. The Court of Appeal said that his role lay somewhere between significant and leading, and reduced a sentence of 30 months' imprisonment to one of 20 months.

B19.162 **Supply** The guideline indicates that for an offender playing a 'leading role' in the offence, and depending on the category of harm, the starting point is five years (category 1); three years, six months (category 2); 18 months (category 3); and 26 weeks (category 4). For an offender playing a 'significant role', the starting point is three years, 18 months, 26 weeks, and a high level community order. For an offender playing a 'lesser role', the starting point is 18 months, 26 weeks, a high level community order, or a low level community order.

Sentences of 21 months and three years were appropriate on pleas of guilty for two offenders involved in the commercial supply of steroids in the pre-guideline case of *Higgins* [2010] EWCA Crim 2599, [2011] 2 Cr App R (S) 2 (3). In *Dalessandro* [2008] EWCA Crim 1501, [2009] 1 Cr App R (S) 29 (154) sentences totalling two years' imprisonment would have been appropriate for an offender who pleaded guilty to possession of various Class C drugs, including anabolic steroids and GHB, with intent to supply them to competitive bodybuilders. The sentences were in fact reduced to 18 months for reasons of delay in prosecuting the case. In *Dix* [2010] EWCA Crim 1498, [2011] 1 Cr App R (S) 45 (305) a sentence of 21 months was upheld where D had pleaded guilty to supplying ketamine on a regular basis to his friends for a profit. He was not a user of the drug. His involvement occurred over a substantial period of time and involved a substantial quantity of the drug, significantly more than that found in *Johnson* [2009] EWCA Crim 2745, [2010] 2 Cr App R (S) 24 (154), where 18 months' imprisonment was reduced to 12 months in the case of an offender convicted after a trial of possession of ketamine with intent to supply. Containers of the drug were found at his home in sufficient quantity to make 2,600 deals with a retail price of about £11,000.

B19.163 **Production** The guideline indicates that for an offender playing a 'leading role' in the offence, and depending on the category of harm, the starting points are five years (category 1); three years, six months (category 2); 18 months (category 3); and 26 weeks (category 4). For an offender playing a 'significant role', the starting points are three years, 18 months, 26 weeks, and a high level community order. For an offender playing a 'lesser role', the starting points are 18 months, 26 weeks, a high level community order and a Band C fine.

Permitting Use of Premises The guideline indicates that for a Class C controlled drug the starting point for category 1 is 12 weeks within a category range of high level community order to 26 weeks (although when tried summarily the maximum penalty is 12 weeks), for category 2 the starting point is a low level community order within a category range of a Band C fine to a high level community order, and for category 3 the starting point is a Band A fine within a category range of a discharge to a Band C fine. **B19.164**

Possession The guideline indicates that for possession of a Class C controlled drug the starting point is a Band A fine within a category range of a discharge to a medium level community order. **B19.165**

Section B20 Offences Relating to Dangerous Dogs and Animal Welfare

OFFENCES UNDER THE DANGEROUS DOGS ACT 1991

Control and Possession of Dogs Bred for Fighting

B20.1 The Dangerous Dogs Act 1991, s. 1, controls the possession, disposal and breeding of pit bull terriers. It also applies to the Japanese tosa, dogo Argentino and fila Braziliero. In *Knightsbridge Crown Court, ex parte Dunne* [1994] 4 All ER 491, it was held that s. 1 applies to dogs possessing a substantial number of breed characteristics, even if some other characteristics are missing. Some pit bull/Staffordshire crosses may therefore fall within s. 1. As to the burden of proof, s. 5(5) provides:

> If in any proceedings it is alleged by the prosecution that a dog is one to which section 1 . . . applies it shall be presumed that it is such a dog unless the contrary is shown by the accused by such evidence as the court considers sufficient; and the accused shall not be permitted to adduce such evidence unless he has given the prosecution notice of his intention to do so not later than the 14th day before that on which the evidence is to be adduced.

Section 5(5) applies only to criminal proceedings and not where a destruction order is sought without a prosecution (*Walton Street Magistrates' Court, ex parte Crothers* (1996) 160 JP 427, but in *Henderson v Metropolitan Police Commissioner* [2018] EWHC 666 (Admin), [2018] 1 WLR 5029, it was held that in a civil case only the owner of the dog, or a person with a relationship to the dog such that its destruction would be an interference with their right to family or private life under the ECHR, Article 8, may contend that it is not a dog to which s. 1 applies). In *Bates v UK* (1996) Appln 26280/95, 16 January, the European Human Rights Commission considered the burden imposed by s. 5(5) to be compatible with the presumption of innocence under the ECHR, Article 6(2), but this is difficult to reconcile with *Lambert* [2001] UKHL 37, [2002] 2 AC 545. It may yet be necessary for s. 5 to be reinterpreted as imposing only an evidential burden on the defence (see **F3.18**).

B20.2 **Offences and Exemptions** Under s. 1(3) of the Act, it is an offence to possess or have custody of any dog to which s. 1 applies (except under a power of seizure or a destruction order), but, by s. 1(5) and the Dangerous Dogs Exemption Schemes (England and Wales) Order 2015 (SI 2015 No. 138), this does not apply in cases where the dog in question is covered by a certificate of exemption and the conditions of that exemption (neutering, microchipping, insurance etc.) are observed or (under an interim exemption scheme) where a chief officer of police has released the dog into the possession of a person seeking such exemption. Details of the exemption and interim exemption schemes can be found in the 2015 Order, and further guidance was provided by the Divisional Court in *Webb v Chief Constable of Avon and Somerset* [2017] EWHC 3311 (Admin), [2018] 1 WLR 5001. Defra maintains an 'Index of Exempted Dogs' for this purpose.

Section 1(2) of the 1991 Act creates further offences:

Dangerous Dogs Act 1991, s. 1

(2) No person shall—
  (a) breed, or breed from, a dog to which this section applies;
  (b) sell or exchange such a dog or offer, advertise or expose such a dog for sale or exchange;
  (c) make or offer to make a gift of such a dog or advertise or expose such a dog as a gift;

(d) allow such a dog of which he is the owner or of which he is for the time being in charge to be in a public place without being muzzled and kept on a lead; or
(e) abandon such a dog of which he is the owner or, being the owner or for the time being in charge of such a dog, allow it to stray.

Penalties and Defences in Relation to Offences under s. 1

Dangerous Dogs Act 1991, s. 1 **B20.3**

(7) Any person who contravenes this section is guilty of an offence and liable on summary conviction to imprisonment for a term not exceeding six months or [an unlimited fine] or both except that a person who publishes an advertisement in contravention of subsection 2(b) or (c)—
(a) shall not on being convicted be liable to imprisonment if he shows that he published the advertisement to the order of someone else and did not himself devise it; and
(b) shall not be convicted if, in addition, he shows that he did not know and had no reasonable cause to suspect that it related to a dog to which this section applies.

Voluntary intoxication is no defence to a charge under s. 1(7) (*DPP v Kellett* [1994] Crim LR 916). Indeed it seems clear from s. 1(7)(b) that the offence is one of strict liability, as are those created by s. 3 (see **B20.5**). The revised definitive sentencing guideline on *Dangerous Dog Offences* (see Supplement, **SG21-1**) applies to all offenders aged 18 and over sentenced on or after 1 July 2016. The guidelines apply, *inter alia*, to the offences under s. 1(2) and (3). As to disqualification and destruction orders, see **B20.11**.

Definitions The term 'advertisement' is defined in the Dangerous Dogs Act 1991, s. 10(2), as including any means of bringing a matter to the attention of the public; 'public place' is defined in s. 10(2) as meaning any street, road or other place to which the public have or are permitted access, whether for payment or otherwise (*Cummings v DPP* (1999) *The Times*, 26 March 1999), and includes the common parts of a building containing two or more separate dwellings. A pit bull terrier sitting in a car parked in a public place is itself in a public place and must be muzzled in accordance with s. 1(2)(d) (*Bates v DPP* (1993) 157 JP 1004). Muzzling remains necessary even if the dog is ill and would be distressed by muzzling; no defence of necessity applies in such circumstances (*Cichon v DPP* [1994] Crim LR 918). However, a private path or driveway is not a public place merely because visitors or postmen may use it when calling on the owner (*Fellowes v DPP* (1993) 157 JP 936) The same may be true even of a shared driveway, if this is private property (*Bogdal* [2008] EWCA Crim 1; and see also *C* [2007] EWCA Crim 1757). **B20.4**

Dangerous Dogs Act 1991, ss. 6 and 7

6. Where a dog is owned by a person who is less than sixteen years old any reference to its owner in section 1(2)(d) or (e) or 3 above shall include a reference to the head of the household, if any, of which that person is a member or, in Scotland, to the person who has his actual care and control.

7.—(1) In this Act—
(a) references to a dog being muzzled are to its being securely fitted with a muzzle sufficient to prevent it biting any person; and
(b) references to its being kept on a lead are to its being securely held on a lead by a person who is not less than sixteen years old.

Failing to Keep Dogs under Proper Control

The offences of failing to keep a dog under proper control were significantly amended by the ABCPA 2014, with effect from 13 May 2014. The principal amendment involved the repeal of s. 3(3) and with it the need for any offence to take place in a public place or in a place where the dog is not permitted to be. Special provision is, however, made for 'householder' cases involving trespassers or supposed trespassers within a dwelling. **B20.5**

Dangerous Dogs Act 1991, s. 3

(1) If a dog is dangerously out of control in any place in England or Wales (whether or not a public place)—
(a) the owner; and

B

Part B Offences

(b) if different, the person for the time being in charge of the dog,

is guilty of an offence, or, if the dog while so out of control injures any person or assistance dog, an aggravated offence, under this subsection.

(1A) A person ('D') is not guilty of an offence under subsection (1) in a case which is a householder case.

(1B) For the purposes of subsection (1A) 'a householder case' is a case where—

(a) the dog is dangerously out of control while in or partly in a building, or part of a building, that is a dwelling or is forces accommodation (or is both), and

(b) at that time—

(i) the person in relation to whom the dog is dangerously out of control ('V') is in, or is entering, the building or part as a trespasser, or

(ii) D (if present at that time) believed V to be in, or entering, the building or part as a trespasser.

Section 76(8B) to (8F) of the Criminal Justice and Immigration Act 2008 (use of force at place of residence [see **A3.58**]) apply for the purposes of this subsection as they apply for the purposes of subsection (8A) of that section (and for those purposes the reference in section 76(8D) to subsection (8A)(d) is to be read as if it were a reference to paragraph (b)(ii) of this subsection).

(2) In proceedings for an offence under subsection (1) above against a person who is the owner of a dog but was not at the material time in charge of it, it shall be a defence for the accused to prove that the dog was at the material time in the charge of a person whom he reasonably believed to be a fit and proper person to be in charge of it.

B20.6 Sentence

Dangerous Dogs Act 1991, s. 3

(4) A person guilty of an offence under subsection (1) above other than an aggravated offence is liable on summary conviction to imprisonment for a term not exceeding six months or [an unlimited fine] or both; and a person guilty of an aggravated offence under that subsection is liable—

(a) on summary conviction, to imprisonment for a term not exceeding six months or [an unlimited fine] or both;

(b) on conviction on indictment, to imprisonment for a term not exceeding the relevant maximum specified in subsection (4A) or a fine or both.

(4A) For the purposes of subsection (4)(b), the relevant maximum is—

(a) 14 years if a person dies as a result of being injured;

(b) 5 years in any other case where a person is injured;

(c) 3 years in any case where an assistance dog is injured (whether or not it dies).

The revised definitive sentencing guideline on *Dangerous Dog Offences* (see Supplement, **SG21-1**) applies to all offenders aged 18 and over sentenced on or after 1 July 2016. The guidelines apply, *inter alia*, to the offences under s. 3(1) which attract the different maximum penalties set out in s. 3(4) and (4A). In *Leonard* [2020] EWCA Crim 135 three dogs escaped from a garden and bit two victims, requiring one, a child, to have surgery to his arm. The case was properly categorised in the medium category with a starting point of 18 months' imprisonment. In view of the character of the dogs, D's responsible efforts to manage them securely, and his plea and genuine remorse, the sentence of ten months' imprisonment should have been suspended.

For destruction and disqualification orders following conviction see **B20.11**.

B20.7 Alternative Verdict When D is charged on indictment with an aggravated offence it is not open to a jury to convict D of a simple (non-aggravated) offence because, by s. 3(4), such an offence is summary only and is not specified for the purposes of the CLA 1967, s. 6(3) (*Williams* [2011] EWCA Crim 1716).

B20.8 *Actus Reus* Save where s. 3(1A) applies ('householder cases') and provided that the offence is alleged to have occurred after 1 October 2014 (see **B20.5**), it no longer matters whether a dog is out of control on the owner's property or elsewhere. An aggravated offence may now be committed where, for example, D's dog bites a visitor inside D's house, a postman walking up D's front path, or somebody stealing strawberries in D's garden. See, e.g., *Blake v CPS* [2017] EWHC 1608 (Admin).

The question whether someone other than the owner is 'in charge' of the dog is one of fact and degree and should ordinarily be left to the jury (*Rawlings* [1994] Crim LR 433). More than one person may be in charge of a dog at any given time (*L v CPS* [2010] EWHC 341 (Admin)). As to the scope of the defence under s. 3(2), see *Huddart* [1999] Crim LR 568.

The offences created by s. 3(1) may be committed by both the owner (subject to the s. 3(2) defence) *and* the person in charge of the dog. The owner is not exempt from liability just because someone else is in charge of the dog at the time.

Under s. 3, the type of dog is irrelevant; it is enough to show that it was dangerously out of control. Section 10(3) provides:

> . . . a dog shall be regarded as dangerously out of control on any occasion on which there are grounds for reasonable apprehension that it will injure any person or assistance dog, whether or not it actually does so, but references to a dog injuring a person or there being grounds for reasonable apprehension that it will do so do not include references to any case in which the dog is being used for a lawful purpose by a constable or a person in the service of the Crown.

It is submitted that references to dogs injuring persons must, in this context, be confined to bites, etc., directly inflicted by dogs and should not include traffic injuries indirectly caused by dogs running loose on a road, but the point has yet to be decided in the courts.

A dog may be dangerously out of control even when on a lead, if its handler cannot properly control or restrain it (*Gedminintaite* [2008] EWCA Crim 814). By s. 10(3) liability can arise only where the dog behaves in such a way that there are 'reasonable grounds for apprehension that it will injure any person or assistance dog', but in *Rafiq v DPP* (1997) 161 JP 412 it was held that, even if a dog bites without warning, 'this is itself capable of being conduct giving grounds for reasonable apprehension of injury'. Anyone witnessing it is likely to fear it will cause further harm.

Even where it seems likely that a dog may injure someone, the words 'dangerously out of control' must be given their natural meaning. If, for example, X teases Y's dog in a cruel and stupid way, it may be apparent to any onlooker that X is likely to be bitten, but it does not follow that the dog is out of control.

Where the dog is owned by a person under the age of 16, s. 6 (see **B20.4**) applies.

Strict Liability It is clear that s. 3 imposes strict liability. It was enacted for reasons of public safety, and would become very much harder to enforce if some fault element, such as negligence, had to be proved against the owner or handler of a dog which becomes dangerously out of control. It therefore places the onus squarely upon dog owners, etc., to ensure their dogs are kept under control (*Bezzina* [1994] 3 All ER 964). But, although this provision creates an offence of 'situational liability' and does not specify how or why the dog may have come to be thus out of control, the Court of Appeal in *Robinson-Pierre* [2013] EWCA Crim 2396, [2014] 1 WLR 2368 rejected an argument that Parliament intended liability to be absolute, 'in the sense that criminal liability may follow notwithstanding the absence of any act or omission of the defendant contributing to the prohibited state of affairs'. The offence instead requires 'proof of an act or omission by the defendant (with or without fault) that to some more than minimal degree caused or permitted the prohibited state of affairs to come about' (per Pitchford LJ at [42]). It follows that D cannot properly be convicted if the dog in question was allowed to get out of control as a result of third-party acts or omissions that D did not cause and had no power to control or prevent. **B20.9**

Seizure

The Dangerous Dogs Act 1991, s. 5(1), provides for the seizure of dogs to which s. 1 of the Act applies or dogs that appear to be dangerously out of control in a public place. Section 5(2) deals with warrants for the seizure of dogs on private premises. Guidance as to enforcement is provided by Defra (see *Dangerous dogs law: Guidance for enforcers* at tinyurl.com/yc7p58se). **B20.10**

Destruction and Disqualification following Conviction

B20.11 **Dangerous Dogs Act 1991, ss. 4 and 4A**

4.—(1) Where a person is convicted of an offence under section 1 or 3(1) above or of an offence under an order made under section 2 above the court—

(a) may order the destruction of any dog in respect of which the offence was committed and, subject to subsection (1A) below, shall do so in the case of an offence under section 1 or an aggravated offence under section 3(1) above; and

(b) may order the offender to be disqualified, for such period as the court thinks fit, for having custody of a dog.

(1A) Nothing in subsection (1)(a) above shall require the court to order the destruction of a dog if the court is satisfied—

(a) that the dog would not constitute a danger to public safety; and

(b) where the dog was born before 30th November 1991 and is subject to the prohibition in section 1(3) above, that there is a good reason why the dog has not been exempted from that prohibition.

(1B) For the purposes of subsection (1A)(a), when deciding whether a dog would constitute a danger to public safety, the court—

(a) must consider—

(i) the temperament of the dog and its past behaviour, and

(ii) whether the owner of the dog, or the person for the time being in charge of it, is a fit and proper person to be in charge of the dog, and

(b) may consider any other relevant circumstances.

(2) Where a court makes an order under subsection (1)(a) above for the destruction of a dog owned by a person other than the offender, the owner may appeal to the Crown Court against the order.

(3) A dog shall not be destroyed pursuant to an order under subsection (1)(a) above—

(a) until the end of the period for giving notice of appeal against the conviction, or against the order; and

(b) if notice of appeal is given within that period, until the appeal is determined or withdrawn,

unless the offender and, in a case to which subsection (2) above applies, the owner of the dog give notice to the court that made the order that there is to be no appeal.

(4) Where a court makes an order under subsection (1)(a) above it may—

(a) appoint a person to undertake the destruction of the dog and require any person having custody of it to deliver it up for that purpose; and

(b) order the offender to pay such sum as the court may determine to be the reasonable expenses of destroying the dog and of keeping it pending its destruction.

(5) Any sum ordered to be paid under subsection (4)(b) above shall be treated for the purposes of enforcement as if it were a fine imposed on conviction.

4A.—(1) Where—

(a) a person is convicted of an offence under section 1 above or an aggravated offence under section 3(1) above;

(b) the court does not order the destruction of the dog under section 4(1)(a) above; and

(c) in the case of an offence under section 1 above, the dog is subject to the prohibition in section 1(3) above,

the court shall order that, unless the dog is exempted from that prohibition within the requisite period, the dog shall be destroyed.

(2) Where an order is made under subsection (1) above in respect of a dog, and the dog is not exempted from the prohibition in section 1(3) above within the requisite period, the court may extend that period.

(3) Subject to subsection (2) above, the requisite period for the purposes of such an order is the period of two months beginning with the date of the order.

(4) Where a person is convicted of an offence under section 3(1) above, the court may order that, unless the owner of the dog keeps it under proper control, the dog shall be destroyed.

(5) An order under subsection (4) above—

(a) may specify the measures to be taken for keeping the dog under proper control, whether by muzzling, keeping on a lead, excluding it from specified places or otherwise; and

(b) if it appears to the court that the dog is a male and would be less dangerous if neutered, may require it to be neutered.

(6) Subsections (2) to (4) of section 4 above shall apply in relation to an order under subsection (1) or (4) above as they apply in relation to an order under subsection (1)(a) of that section.

Any person who has custody of a dog in contravention of s. 4(1)(b), or who fails to comply with a requirement imposed under s. 4(4)(a) commits a summary offence and is liable to an unlimited fine (s. 4(8)).

Destruction orders are imposed not by way of punishment, but for reasons of public safety. Non-compliance with a contingent destruction order is not an offence, but as the Divisional Court explained in *Chief Constable of Merseyside Police v Doyle* [2019] EWHC 2180 (Admin), at [25], the MCA 1980, s. 63, gives magistrates' courts power to suspend, rescind or vary such orders, and:

> In cases where there has been a failure of proper control, at least if it is more than trivial, accidental or momentary, and if there has not been any material change of circumstances since the time of the making of the contingent destruction order, then the ordinary position will be that the contingent destruction order should be implemented and the dog destroyed.

As to the making of destruction orders or contingent destruction orders following seizure under s. 5, where there are no criminal proceedings (whether because the owner cannot be found or for any other reason) or where returning the dog to its owner would result in the owner breaching the prohibition under s. 1, see s. 4B of the Act and *Dodsworth v Chief Constable of Yorkshire* [2019] EWHC 330 (Admin). In the later case of *R (Golding) v Crown Court at Maidstone* [2019] EWHC 2029 (Admin), [2019] 1 WLR 5939 it was pointed out that the civil regime is in some respects less flexible than the one governing orders following conviction.

The revised sentencing guideline on *Dangerous Dog Offences* (see Supplement, **SG21-1**), which applies to all offenders aged 18 and over sentenced on or after 1 July 2016, contains guidance in relation to the making of a destruction order, a contingent destruction order or an order disqualifying a person from having custody of a dog. **B20.12**

The considerations listed in s. 4(1B) were in practice taken into account even before that provision was inserted by the ABCPA 2014. In *Flack* [2008] EWCA Crim 204, [2008] 2 Cr App R (S) 70 (395) (a case involving an aggravated offence under s. 3(1)), it was held that a 'suspended destruction order' was appropriate in a case where D was a conscientious dog owner of good character, and where the dog had not previously been aggressive. D was ordered to comply with conditions relating to the muzzling of the dog, that the dog wear a special collar and be kept on a lead at all times in public. *Flack* was applied in *Baballa* [2010] EWCA Crim 1950, [2011] 1 Cr App R (S) 50 (329), where destruction might otherwise have followed for an offence under s. 1(3). However, the default assumption to be made in respect of any pit bull, or other dog to which s. 1 applies, is that it represents a danger to public safety and should accordingly be destroyed (s. 4(1)(a)). This assumption applies unless the court is affirmatively satisfied that (subject to compliance with the terms of a conditional order) the dog would not constitute a danger to public safety. The burden of proving this would be on the defence.

In cases involving convictions under s. 3, Collins J in *Kelleher v DPP* [2012] EWHC 2978 (Admin) noted the distinction between aggravated and non-aggravated offences and the burden of proof governing destruction orders in each case. He said (at [11], [12] and [15]):

> It is clear that s. 4A(4) applies both to aggravated and non-aggravated offences. The power to make a destruction order applies in both cases . . . in the case of an aggravated offence the burden is on the defendant to show that the dog is not a danger to public safety, otherwise a destruction order is mandatory. It is, as it were, the other way around in the case of a non-aggravated offence: the court will not make a destruction order unless, on the material, the court takes the view that a destruction order is necessary.
>
> The test, which . . . should be applied in either case, essentially relates to whether the dog is a danger to the public. If it is, whichever way round . . . the burden lies for showing it, then the destruction

> order is appropriate. What the court must do in the case of a non-aggravated offence is to decide whether, on the basis that the dog is a danger to the public, a destruction order should follow. However, s. 4A enables the court, instead of making an immediate destruction order, to make what is described as a 'contingent destruction order', that is to say a destruction order unless the dog is kept under proper control by whatever measures are considered to be appropriate ...
>
> The court is only required to make a destruction order in the case of a pit bull or an aggravated offence [under s. 3].

An immediate destruction was warranted in *Fitzgerald* [2017] EWCA Crim 514 where D's dog had been trained to be aggressive and had bitten a paramedic who tried to assist D; and in *Blake v CPS* [2017] EWHC 1608 (Admin) following an attack on a child, even though the dog had never shown signs of such behaviour before, and even though the attack had occurred on the owner's own property. Such an order was also considered appropriate in *R (Killeen) v Birmingham Crown Court* [2018] EWHC 174 (Admin), where a large and aggressive dog had bitten a dog warden, terrorised the family living next door to it, and appeared quite beyond the control of its owner. The risk of another potentially serious incident was in each of these three cases obvious if destruction was not ordered. By contrast, in *Jones-Wharton* [2019] EWCA Crim 2188 the Court of Appeal quashed a destruction order made in respect of 'Chico', a Staffordshire terrier, following its involvement in an aggravated s. 3(1) offence, but imposed a conditional order under s. 4A with terms designed to ensure that the public would not be endangered by the decision to spare the dog's life, including requirements for the dog to be kept securely in the property, to be taken out in public only by a responsible person over 16 and only if the dog was muzzled and held on a double lead. Other terms included a requirement for training with a registered dog trainer (for both owner and dog), and for third party liability insurance to be in place for the life of the dog.

B20.13 The only conditions that may be imposed when making a contingent destruction order in relation to a pit bull or any other dog falling within s. 1 are those that may be imposed under the Dangerous Dogs Exemption Schemes (England and Wales) Order 2015, art. 4 (*R (Sandhu) v Isleworth Crown Court* [2012] EWHC 1658 (Admin)), although the granting of any certificate of exemption will also be dependent in all cases on satisfaction of requirements listed in art. 10 of that Order. Breach of any of the terms of exemption (e.g., by failing to maintain the requisite liability insurance) means the dog ceases to be exempted, and the owner etc. may thus be prosecuted for an offence (or further offence) under s. 1, but this does not revive any destruction order that pre-dated the grant of a certificate of exemption, nor is there any other provision in the Act or the Scheme authorising the automatic destruction of a dog which ceases to be exempted (*R (Ali) v Chief Constable of Merseyside* [2014] EWHC 4772 (Admin)).

In cases other than those involving s. 1 dogs, the conditions attached to contingent destruction orders may be more flexible. See, e.g., *Devon* [2011] EWCA Crim 1073 (order made conditional on rehousing with suitable owners) and *Jones-Wharton* [2019] EWCA Crim 2188 (in which a long list of conditions was imposed on appeal—see the judgment at [18]).

In deciding whether to make a disqualification order and whether to order the destruction of any dog, a court may have regard to any voluntary undertaking offered by D as to D's future conduct (*Haynes* [2003] EWCA Crim 3247, [2004] 2 Cr App R (S) 9 (36); see also *Singh* [2013] EWCA Crim 2416).

In *Holland* [2002] EWCA Crim 1585, [2003] 1 Cr App R (S) 60 (288) (a case involving an aggravated offence under s. 3(3)(a) in which the grandchild of D's neighbour was attacked by D's bull terrier in the neighbour's own garden), it was held that a disqualification order was appropriate in addition to the destruction of the dog, and that such an order could not solely limit D from keeping dangerous dogs but would necessarily ban her from keeping any dog at all. It was open to her to apply to have the disqualification lifted after one year, but the success of such an application might turn on the breed she intended to keep, the security of her property and who her neighbours were at that time.

As to the competence of expert witnesses in cases concerning dangerousness and destruction orders, see *Rogers* [2016] EWCA Crim 801, [2016] 2 Cr App R (S) 36 (370).

Addressing Alleged Breaches of a Contingent Destruction Order

The question of how alleged breaches of a contingent destruction order should be addressed was considered in detail in *Chief Constable of Merseyside Police v Doyle* [2019] EWHC 2180 (Admin). It was argued that the statute provided no mechanism for resolving factual disputes and there could therefore be no effective mechanism for enforcement. The argument was given short shrift. The Divisional Court held that magistrates had ample power to deal with any such allegation, which should proceed by way of complaint in the civil jurisdiction of the magistrates' court. The magistrates will determine to the civil standard whether there was non-compliance and if so whether the contingent destruction order should be implemented by the making of any necessary orders under s. 4(4)(a) and (b) of the 1991 Act or whether it should be varied, suspended or revoked. The magistrates would consider the circumstances at the time when implementation is sought, an exercise which will involve determination of the facts relating to the non-compliance, including the reasons for, and the duration and the nature of, any failure of proper control. It would also be likely to involve consideration of the facts as specified in s. 4(1A)(a) and thus s. 4(1B) of the 1991 Act in the circumstances as they exist at that time. The Court noted that the circumstances at this point may be significantly different from those which existed at the time of the making of the original contingent destruction order, and at a time when the age and physical condition of the dog may have been significantly different. Where there has been a failure of proper control, at least if it is more than trivial, accidental or momentary, and if there has not been any material change of circumstances since the time of the making of the contingent destruction order, then the ordinary position will be that the contingent destruction order should be implemented and the dog destroyed. Prior to any destruction occurring, however, there remains a right of appeal under s. 4(2) of the 1991 Act, just as there was in relation to the original order. **B20.14**

OTHER OFFENCES RELATING TO DANGEROUS OR FEROCIOUS DOGS

The Dangerous Dogs Act 1991 does not reduce the powers of courts under the Dogs Act 1871, s. 2. Orders requiring the destruction or proper control of dangerous dogs may still be made under that provision, whether or not any person has been injured, and may require a dog to be muzzled and/or castrated (Dangerous Dogs Act 1991, s. 3(5) and (6)). Under the Dangerous Dogs Act 1989, s. 1(3), it is an offence, punishable on summary conviction by a fine not exceeding level 3 on the standard scale, not to comply with a control or destruction order; and where under that Act an owner has been disqualified from having custody of a dog, contravention of that order is punishable by an unlimited fine (Dangerous Dogs Act 1989, s. 1(6)). **B20.15**

By the Town Police Clauses Act 1847, s. 28, it remains an offence punishable by a maximum of 14 days' imprisonment for any person 'in any street, to the obstruction, annoyance, or danger of residents or passengers', to suffer to be at large any unmuzzled ferocious dog, or set on or urge any dog or other animal to attack, worry, or put in fear any person or animal.

Control of Guard Dogs

Guard Dogs Act 1975, s. 1 **B20.16**

(1) A person shall not use or permit the use of a guard dog at any premises unless a person ('the handler') who is capable of controlling the dog is present on the premises and the dog is under the control of the handler at all times while it is being so used except while it is secured so that it is not at liberty to go freely about the premises.

(2) The handler of a guard dog shall keep the dog under his control at all times while it is being used as a guard dog at any premises except—
   (a) while another handler has control over the dog; or
   (b) while the dog is secured so that it is not at liberty to go freely about the premises.

(3) A person shall not use or permit the use of a guard dog at any premises unless a notice containing a warning that a guard dog is present is clearly exhibited at each entrance to the premises.

Under the Guard Dogs Act 1975, s. 5, non-compliance with s. 1 is an offence punishable on summary conviction by an unlimited fine.

Before any liability can be imposed under the Guard Dogs Act 1975, it must be proved or admitted that the dog was being used 'to protect — (a) premises; or (b) property kept on the premises; or (c) a person guarding the premises or such property' (s. 7). It is not enough that a large dog (even one kept on commercial premises) may have developed a 'guard dog's instinct' (*Kelly v DPP* [2008] EWHC 597 (Admin)).

OFFENCES UNDER THE ANIMAL WELFARE ACT 2006

B20.17 The principal provisions of the Animal Welfare Act 2006 came into force in England on 6 April 2007 and in Wales on 28 March 2007. A number of other provisions relating to animals and animal welfare remain in force, including substantial parts of the Performing Animals (Regulation) Act 1925, the Pet Animals Act 1951, the Animal Boarding Establishments Act 1963, the Riding Establishments Acts 1964 and 1970, the Breeding of Dogs Acts 1973 and 1991 and the Sale of Dogs (Welfare) Act 1999.

The Animal Welfare Act 2006 does not apply to any invertebrate creature (see s. 1(1) and (5)), nor to any foetus or embryo (s. 1(2)), but regulations made under the Act may amend its scope in either respect in accordance with s. 1(3) and (4).

The protection of the Act extends only to 'protected animals'. A protected animal is defined in s. 2 as one of a kind commonly domesticated in the British Isles or one which is under the control of man (whether on a permanent or temporary basis) or not living in a wild state. Feral cats and stray dogs fall within this definition, as do pets, farm animals, animals kept in zoos or wildlife parks, and animals which may recently have escaped from human control, but which are not yet 'living wild'. Wild animals such as foxes or badgers are not ordinarily protected under the Act, but any that have been captured or rescued are protected for as long as they remain in care or captivity. As to the prohibition of certain cruel or potentially cruel methods of taking or killing wild animals, see the Wildlife and Countryside Act 1981, s. 11. Captive wild birds may be protected both under the 2006 Act and under s. 8 of the 1981 Act (*R (RSPCA) v Shinton* [2003] EWHC 1696 (Admin)).

B20.18 Some offences under the 2006 Act can be committed only by a person who is 'responsible for an animal'. An animal for which some person is responsible (such as a pet rat) must necessarily be a protected animal, even if other animals of the same species, living wild, would not be.

By s. 3, a person may be responsible for an animal either on a permanent or temporary basis. Persons running boarding kennels or veterinary practices clearly have temporary responsibility for animals in their care, but responsibility may also extend to a person who agrees to feed, clean and water a neighbour's animals for a few days. A person who owns an animal shall always be regarded as responsible for it, but references to being responsible for an animal include being in charge of it; and by s. 3(4) 'a person shall be treated as responsible for any animal for which a person under the age of 16 years of whom he has actual care and control is responsible'. For an illustration of the kind of case in which this rule may be important, see *R (RSPCA) v C* [2006] EWHC 1069 (Admin) and **B20.28**.

B20.19 By ss. 58 and 59, nothing in the Act applies to anything lawfully done under the Animals (Scientific Procedures) Act 1986 or to anything which occurs in the normal course of fishing.

As to application to the Crown, see s. 60; as to the liability of directors, managers and officers for offences committed by bodies corporate, see s. 57.

The only offences examined in this work are those created by ss. 4, 7, 8 and 9. Other offences include those concerned with the docking of dogs' tails and other prohibited procedures involving protected animals (ss. 5 and 6, together with associated regulations), the unlawful transfer of animals by way of sale or prize to children under the age of 16 (s. 11), and the unlicensed commission of specified activities for which a licence under the Act is required (s. 13).

Regulations made under s. 12 of the 2006 Act and applicable to Wales differ from those applicable to England. For example, electronic dog or cat training collars that may be used to administer shocks are banned in Wales (Animal Welfare (Electronic Collars) (Wales) Regulations 2010 (SI 2010 No. 943, W 97)) but in England a partial ban proposed by DEFRA will continue to allow the use of 'safety fence' collars that are triggered when the animal attempts to stray (*Electronic Collar Manufacturers Association v Secretary of State for Environment, Food and Rural Affairs* [2019] EWHC 2813 (Admin)).

Search Warrants, Seizures and Prosecutions

The Animal Welfare Act 2006, s. 52, sets out conditions for the granting of search warrants under the Act. Section 18 enables constables or authorised inspectors to take necessary measures in relation to animals found in distress (which may involve taking possession of the animals or even destroying them). The importance of the principle of legality in the exercise of those powers was stressed by the Divisional Court in *R (RSPCA) v Colchester Magistrates' Court* [2015] EWHC 1418 (Admin), in which evidence of offences exposed only by the misuse of such powers was held to have been correctly excluded under the PACE 1984, s. 78. The Animal Welfare Act 2006, s. 30, permits prosecutions to be brought by local authorities. No specific provision is made for prosecutions to be brought by the RSPCA, but it retains (and exercises) its common-law power to prosecute, and in *Lamont-Perkins v RSPCA* [2012] EWHC 1002 (Admin) it was held that any prosecutor, including the RSPCA, may in appropriate cases invoke the provisions of s. 31. **B20.20**

Animal Welfare Act 2006, s. 31

(1) Notwithstanding anything in section 127(1) of the Magistrates' Courts Act 1980, a magistrates' court may try an information relating to an offence under this Act if the information is laid—
  (a) before the end of the period of three years beginning with the date of the commission of the offence, and
  (b) before the end of the period of six months beginning with the date on which evidence which the prosecutor thinks is sufficient to justify the proceedings comes to his knowledge.

(2) For the purposes of subsection (1)(b)—
  (a) a certificate signed by or on behalf of the prosecutor and stating the date on which such evidence came to his knowledge shall be conclusive evidence of that fact, and
  (b) a certificate stating that matter and purporting to be so signed shall be treated as so signed unless the contrary is proved.

Section 31 (and identical provisions in related regulations, such as the Welfare of Animals at the Time of Killing (England) Regulations 2015 (SI 2015 No. 1782), reg. 41) have been considered by appellate courts on several occasions, notably in *Woodward* [2017] EWHC 1008 (Admin), in which much of the earlier case law was reviewed. The following propositions can be derived from this and subsequent case law:

1. A certificate does not have to be issued before proceedings are commenced (*RSPCA v King* [2010] EWHC 637 (Admin); *Letherbarrow v Warwickshire County Council* [2014] EWHC 4820 (Admin)). It can be issued at any time, at least until the close of the prosecution case.

2. A prosecutor can avail himself of a s. 31 certificate only if that certificate fully complies with the statutory requirements. An unsigned file copy of a missing certificate does not so comply, even if accompanied by a signed letter stating that such a certificate was indeed issued (*RSPCA v King*).
3. The issue of a defective certificate does not, however, preclude the subsequent issue of a valid certificate subject to that new certificate complying with the statutory requirements and not being patently incorrect, fraudulent or an abuse of the court (*Woodward*).
4. The relevant date for the purposes of s. 31(1)(b) is that on which the individual within the CPS or other relevant organisation who is responsible for making the decision to prosecute (see *Letherbarrow* and *Woodward*) concludes that there is evidence sufficient to justify bringing the proceedings. It is not the date on which the relevant evidence was placed on that person's desk or inbox, but nor is it necessarily the date on which the prosecutor concludes that it is in the public interest to prosecute (*Chesterfield Poultry Ltd v Sheffield Magistrates' Court* [2019] EWHC 2953 (Admin), [2020] 1 Cr App R 26 (419)). In *Riley v CPS* [2016] EWHC 2531 (Admin), [2017] 1 WLR 505, a CPS prosecutor could rely on a s. 31 certificate, even though the Food Standards Agency became aware of the facts giving rise to the charge several months before notifying the CPS. The Agency was not the prosecutor and the statutory requirements did not apply to it.
5. If there is no certificate (or none that is valid) the court must instead determine (on the basis of available evidence) whether the prosecution was brought within the relevant time-limits (*Azam v Epping Forest District Council* [2009] EWHC 3177 (Admin)).
6. In the absence of fraud, a certificate in proper form which contains no error on its face is not merely conclusive evidence of the date when particular pieces of evidence came to the prosecutor's knowledge. It is conclusive evidence of the relevant date from which the six-month period begins to run, and is not open to challenge by reference to extraneous evidence showing that it is wrong or even plainly wrong. To hold otherwise would depart from a clear and consistent line of authority which rests on sound principles. The presumptively conclusive nature of a s. 31 certificate would otherwise be undermined (*Downes v RSPCA* [2017] EWHC 3622 (Admin), [2018] 2 Cr App R 3 (25); *Chesterfield Poultry Ltd v Sheffield Magistrates' Court*).

Seizure of animals under s. 18(5) of the Act does not in itself amount to commencement of proceedings for these purposes (*RSPCA v Webb* [2015] EWHC 3802 (Admin)).

Penalties and Orders

B20.21 Offences under the Animal Welfare Act 2006 are triable only summarily. The maximum penalty in respect of offences under ss. 4, 5, 6(1) and (2), 7, 8, 9 and 34(9) is imprisonment for a term not exceeding six months and/or a fine. The maximum penalty for any other offence is six months and/or a fine not exceeding level 4 on the standard scale (s. 32). The *Magistrates' Court Sentencing Guidelines* on animal cruelty apply (see Supplement, **SG10-57**).

On conviction, D may be deprived of the animal in question (s. 33), and may be disqualified from owning, keeping or participating in the keeping of animals (s. 34(2)), disqualified from dealing in animals (s. 34(3)) and/or disqualified from transporting or arranging for the transport of animals (s. 34(4)), but such an order cannot prevent D from living at an address where animals are kept by other members of the same household (*Patterson v RSPCA* [2013] EWHC 4531 (Admin)). As to what may amount to 'keeping' an animal, see *R (Arthur) v RSPCA* [2005] EWHC 2616 (Admin). Disqualification may be ordered in respect of animals generally or in respect of animals of one or more kinds (s. 34(5)) and may be made for such period as the court thinks fit (s. 34(1) and see *Ward* [2010] EWHC 347 (Admin)). Disqualification will ordinarily extend to each of the relevant activities specified in the subsection under which the order is made (*R (RSPCA) v Guildford Crown Court* [2012] EWHC 3392 (Admin)), so a court that disqualifies D from *keeping* animals would be unlikely to permit D to *participate in the keeping* of animals (unless perhaps the HRA 1998, s. 3, requires such an interpretation of s. 34). Breach of a disqualification order is an offence under s. 34(9).

The interaction between possible orders was considered in *Barker v RSPCA* [2018] EWHC 880 (Admin), [2018] 2 Cr App R (S) 13 (92), in which D kept an ill dog and several flea-ridden puppies crated for extended periods. An order made by the magistrates' court under s. 34 to disqualify D from keeping any animals for seven years was varied by the Crown Court on appeal simply to exclude the keeping of a pet terrapin about which there were no concerns. Upholding both the general disqualification and the specific exclusion, the High Court examined (at [48]–[50]) the criteria for imposing three types of disqualification order: (a) an order covering all animals; (b) a disqualification limited to animals of a particular type, such as horses; or (c) an 'exclusory order' relating to all animals *save* for a particular type to which harm was unlikely. The key point was that disqualification orders are designed to be protective of animals, rather than punitive to defendants.

Section 34 does not address the problem that arose in *R (RSPCA) v Chester Crown Court* [2006] EWHC 1273 (Admin), in which the Divisional Court reluctantly concluded that a disqualification under the Protection of Animals Act 1911, s. 1, could not impose a limit on the number of animals that could be kept. Sedley J suggested in that case that, 'Parliament [may] want to consider whether [that] kind of order . . . should not be authorised by future animal protection legislation', but no such provision has been made.

As to the seizure of animals in connection with a disqualification order, see ss. 35 and 36. As to the making of orders for the destruction of animals, see ss. 37 and 38. As to the forfeiture of equipment used in connection with offences, see s. 40. As to the cancellation of licences or the disqualification of a person from holding a licence, see s. 42.

Unnecessary Suffering

Animal Welfare Act 2006, s. 4 **B20.22**

(1) A person commits an offence if—
  (a) an act of his, or a failure of his to act, causes an animal to suffer,
  (b) he knew, or ought reasonably to have known, that the act, or failure to act, would have that effect or be likely to do so,
  (c) the animal is a protected animal, and
  (d) the suffering is unnecessary.
(2) A person commits an offence if—
  (a) he is responsible for an animal,
  (b) an act, or failure to act, of another person causes the animal to suffer,
  (c) he permitted that to happen or failed to take such steps (whether by way of supervising the other person or otherwise) as were reasonable in all the circumstances to prevent that happening, and
  (d) the suffering is unnecessary.
(3) The considerations to which it is relevant to have regard when determining for the purposes of this section whether suffering is unnecessary include—
  (a) whether the suffering could reasonably have been avoided or reduced;
  (b) whether the conduct which caused the suffering was in compliance with any relevant enactment or any relevant provisions of a licence or code of practice issued under an enactment;
  (c) whether the conduct which caused the suffering was for a legitimate purpose, such as—
    (i) the purpose of benefiting the animal, or
    (ii) the purpose of protecting a person, property or another animal;
  (d) whether the suffering was proportionate to the purpose of the conduct concerned;
  (e) whether the conduct concerned was in all the circumstances that of a reasonably competent and humane person.
(3A) In determining for the purposes of subsection (1) whether suffering is unnecessary in a case where it was caused by conduct for a purpose mentioned in subsection (3)(c)(ii), the fact that the conduct was for that purpose is to be disregarded if—
  (a) the animal was under the control of a relevant officer at the time of the conduct,

(b) it was being used by that officer at that time, in the course of the officer's duties, in a way that was reasonable in all the circumstances, and
(c) that officer is not the defendant.

(3B) In subsection (3A) 'relevant officer' means—
(a) a constable;
(b) a person (other than a constable) who has the powers of a constable or is otherwise employed for police purposes or is engaged to provide services for police purposes;
(c) a prisoner custody officer within the meaning of Part 4 of the Criminal Justice Act 1991.

(3C) The Secretary of State may by regulations amend subsection (3B). Only a person in the public service of the Crown may be specified in subsection (3B) by virtue of regulations under this subsection.

(4) Nothing in this section applies to the destruction of an animal in an appropriate and humane manner.

B20.23 The offences created by s. 4(1) and (2) extend to omissions as well as to positive acts, and to mental suffering as well as physical (see s. 62(1)); but on general principles an omission can be seen as 'causing' suffering only in cases where the person in question was under a duty to prevent it. Thus, if D ignores the suffering of an injured dog found lying in the road, this will not ordinarily amount to any offence; but if D was responsible for the dog's injury (or has care of the dog), the position may be different. D may then be under a duty to mitigate the animal's suffering. See generally **A1.14** ***et seq.***

In serious cases, other charges, carrying heavier penalties, may sometimes be appropriate, as in *Mills* [2017] EWCA Crim 1077, where D was properly indicted for criminal damage and firearms offences after shooting several pet cats in a residential area.

The *mens rea* required for an offence under s. 4 was considered in *R (Gray) v Aylesbury Crown Court* [2013] EWHC 500 (Admin), [2013] 3 All ER 346 and in *Riley v CPS* [2016] EWHC 2531 (Admin), [2017] 1 WLR 505. It must be proved that D knew, or ought reasonably to have known, both that D's conduct would cause an animal to suffer and that the suffering was unnecessary. No offence is committed where D acts in the honest and reasonable, albeit mistaken, belief that such actions are necessary for or beneficial to the animal's welfare, nor is any offence committed where D could not have been aware of the incident that gave rise to the suffering. But ignorance of an animal's illness or condition may not invariably be a defence, because a person having care of an animal must ensure that it is inspected sufficiently regularly for conditions that would cause suffering to be brought to veterinary attention (*Patterson v RSPCA* [2013] EWHC 4531 (Admin)).

Section 4(3) requires allowance to be made for a number of possible factors when determining whether any suffering was 'unnecessary'. Police horses used for riot control may, for example, be exposed to a risk of injury from flying stones or even petrol bombs, but their exposure to such risks may be considered necessary. Section 4(3A) (as inserted by the Animal Welfare (Service Animals) Act 2019, with effect from 8 June 2019) curtails the ability of those charged with causing unnecessary suffering to police dogs, police horses etc. to argue that they were protecting themselves or their property, etc. No such defence can now succeed if the service animal in question was being properly used in accordance with that provision.

Administration of Poisons

B20.24 **Animal Welfare Act 2006, s. 7**

(1) A person commits an offence if, without lawful authority or reasonable excuse, he—
(a) administers any poisonous or injurious drug or substance to a protected animal, knowing it to be poisonous or injurious, or
(b) causes any poisonous or injurious drug or substance to be taken by a protected animal, knowing it to be poisonous or injurious.

(2) A person commits an offence if—
(a) he is responsible for an animal,
(b) without lawful authority or reasonable excuse, another person administers a poisonous or injurious drug or substance to the animal or causes the animal to take such a drug or substance, and

(c) he permitted that to happen or, knowing the drug or substance to be poisonous or injurious, he failed to take such steps (whether by way of supervising the other person or otherwise) as were reasonable in all the circumstances to prevent that happening.
(3) In this section, references to a poisonous or injurious drug or substance include a drug or substance which, by virtue of the quantity or manner in which it is administered or taken, has the effect of a poisonous or injurious drug or substance.

This provision, which replaces the offence of wilful poisoning formerly contained in the Protection of Animals Act 1911, s. 1(1)(d), is not intended to cover cases of accidental poisoning. According to the accompanying notes for guidance, the term 'administer' should be understood as indicating a deliberate action.

Animal Fights and Related Activities

Animal Welfare Act 2006, s. 8 **B20.25**

(1) A person commits an offence if he—
  (a) causes an animal fight to take place, or attempts to do so;
  (b) knowingly receives money for admission to an animal fight;
  (c) knowingly publicises a proposed animal fight;
  (d) provides information about an animal fight to another with the intention of enabling or encouraging attendance at the fight;
  (e) makes or accepts a bet on the outcome of an animal fight or on the likelihood of anything occurring or not occurring in the course of an animal fight;
  (f) takes part in an animal fight;
  (g) has in his possession anything designed or adapted for use in connection with an animal fight with the intention of its being so used;
  (h) keeps or trains an animal for use for in connection with an animal fight;
  (i) keeps any premises for use for an animal fight.
(2) A person commits an offence if, without lawful authority or reasonable excuse, he is present at an animal fight.
(3) A person commits an offence if, without lawful authority or reasonable excuse, he—
  (a) knowingly supplies a video recording of an animal fight,
  (b) knowingly publishes a video recording of an animal fight,
  (c) knowingly shows a video recording of an animal fight to another, or
  (d) possesses a video recording of an animal fight, knowing it to be such a recording, with the intention of supplying it.
(4) Subsection (3) does not apply if the video recording is of an animal fight that took place—
  (a) outside Great Britain, or
  (b) before the commencement date.
(5) Subsection (3) does not apply—
  (a) in the case of paragraph (a), to the supply of a video recording for inclusion in a programme service;
  (b) in the case of paragraph (b) or (c), to the publication or showing of a video recording by means of its inclusion in a programme service;
  (c) in the case of paragraph (d), by virtue of intention to supply for inclusion in a programme service.

Note that s. 8(3) to (5) have not yet been brought into force.

This provision targets a wide range of activities connected with animal fights — defined as 'an occasion on which a protected animal is placed with an animal, or with a human, for the purpose of fighting, wrestling or baiting' (s. 8(7)). A wild animal, such as a badger, which has been captured for the purpose of being baited by dogs, will itself be a protected animal whilst in captivity. **B20.26**

If a fight or intended fight is to fall within the meaning of s. 8, it cannot be the by-product of a chance meeting but rather must be a contrived or artificial creation specifically for the purpose of a fight. This may involve measures being taken to prevent one or more of the animals from escaping but this may not be necessary (e.g., where a pair of fighting dogs are placed together). Animal fights often involve money but this is not a necessary ingredient of the offence (*RSPCA v McCormick* [2016] EWHC 928 (Admin), [2016] 1 WLR 2641).

Section 8 does not proscribe the use of an animal (such as a terrier or ferret) for legitimate pest control or the video-recording of an animal being used for such a purpose. Where, however, pest control is combined with sport or betting (e.g., betting on the number of rats killed by a terrier) it would appear to fall within the scope of s. 8.

The offence under s. 8(1)(h) extends not only to those who actually keep or train the animals, but to those who use agents or trainers to do so on their behalf (*Wright v Reading Crown Court* [2017] EWHC 2643 (Admin)). If one or more of the animals is a dog to which the Dangerous Dogs Act 1991, s. 1, applies, the persons involved may also be guilty of offences under that Act (see **B20.1** *et seq.*).

The Welfare Offence

B20.27 **Animal Welfare Act 2006, s. 9**

(1) A person commits an offence if he does not take such steps as are reasonable in all the circumstances to ensure that the needs of an animal for which he is responsible are met to the extent required by good practice.
(2) For the purposes of this Act, an animal's needs shall be taken to include—
 (a) its need for a suitable environment,
 (b) its need for a suitable diet,
 (c) its need to be able to exhibit normal behaviour patterns,
 (d) any need it has to be housed with, or apart from, other animals, and
 (e) its need to be protected from pain, suffering, injury and disease.
(3) The circumstances to which it is relevant to have regard when applying subsection (1) include, in particular—
 (a) any lawful purpose for which the animal is kept, and
 (b) any lawful activity undertaken in relation to the animal.
(4) Nothing in this section applies to the destruction of an animal in an appropriate and humane manner.

B20.28 The current regulations applicable to farmed animals in England (Welfare of Farmed Animals (England) Regulations 2007 (SI 2007 No. 2078)) cover the welfare of all farmed animals (as defined in reg. 3), including those kept on common land. Other codes of practice deal with the welfare of cats, dogs, donkeys, rabbits, privately kept non-human primates and game birds reared for sporting purposes. The Welsh Assembly publishes codes of practice for Wales that may differ in some respects from those applicable to England.

Section 9(1) sets a purely objective standard of care which a person responsible for an animal is required to provide (*R (Gray) v Aylesbury Crown Court* [2013] EWHC 500 (Admin), [2013] 3 All ER 346). There is some potential overlap between s. 9 and s. 4 of the Act (see **B20.22**). Where, for example, an animal that requires human care is abandoned, or deprived of essential veterinary care, an offence will ordinarily be committed under s. 9; if, as is likely, this leads to suffering (cold, hunger, distress, etc.) there may be a further offence under s. 4. There should however be no conviction and certainly no penalty imposed under s. 9 where the facts relied upon for that conviction are essentially the same as those that gave rise to a conviction under s. 4; but that may not be the case where (as in *Gray*) the s. 9 conviction relates to different incidents and/or different or additional animals.

Although the test under s. 9 is an objective one, it may be necessary for a court to consider, not just whether the animal(s) in question received a reasonable standard of care, but whether D acted reasonably in the circumstances. In *R (RSPCA) v C* [2006] EWHC 1069 (Admin), in which a girl aged 15 was charged under the Protection of Animals Act 1911, s. 1, with causing unnecessary suffering to her cat by 'unreasonably' failing to secure essential veterinary treatment for it, it was held that account must be taken of her youth and of the fact that she had been told by her father (who pleaded guilty) that no such treatment was required. Newman J said (at [15]):

> The issue which the justices had to decide was whether or not this ... girl had acted reasonably or unreasonably in acceding to the opinion her father had expressed ... That involved considering whether it

was reasonable for her to go along with her father's view of the position, having regard to her age and position in the household, whether it was for her to take any other action, as she could have done, and whether it was reasonable or unreasonable for her to fail to take that other action.

Cases decided under the 1911 Act cannot necessarily be relied upon when construing provisions of the 2006 Act (a point strongly emphasised in *R (Gray) v Aylesbury Crown Court*), but the reasoning in *R (RSPCA) v C* appears wholly consistent with the wording of s. 9 itself so may still be considered good law.

It remains to be seen how strictly the concept of 'good practice' will be interpreted and enforced outside the highly regulated farming context; but arguably any dog or cat owner who fails to keep the animal fully vaccinated against common diseases now risks prosecution under s. 9, because 'good practice' surely requires regular vaccination. **B20.29**

Section 10 of the Act enables inspectors (as defined in s. 51) to issue 'improvement notices' where they are of the opinion that s. 9 requirements are not being met. Such notices must give the responsible person time in which to rectify the problem specified in the notice; but this does not preclude the instigation of proceedings without notice for clear breaches of welfare principles.

Section B21 Offences Relating to Money Laundering and the Proceeds of Criminal Conduct

INTRODUCTION

B21.1 Part 7 of the POCA 2002 creates a series of 'money laundering' offences (ss. 327 to 329) which (subject to the transitional arrangements explained below) have supplanted offences previously contained in the CJA 1988, ss. 93A to 93C, and the Drug Trafficking Act 1994, ss. 49 to 51. Sections 330 to 332 of the 2002 Act create offences of failure to disclose cases of suspected money laundering. The non-disclosure offences (which supplant the Drug Trafficking Act 1994, s. 52) are capable of commission only by persons in the 'regulated sector', comprising industries identified as exposed to the greatest risk of money laundering as defined in sch. 9 to the Act (as amended). The current offences differ from s. 52 of the 1994 Act in that they extend to matters concerning the proceeds of all types of criminal conduct, and not just to those concerning the proceeds of drug trafficking. Finally, s. 333A creates an offence of 'tipping off' another person as to the fact that a report of suspected money laundering has been made, where this tip-off is likely to prejudice any subsequent investigation. This provision supplants s. 93D(2) of the 1988 Act and s. 53(2) of the 1994 Act. As to the origins, scope and purpose of Part 7 generally, see parts 5 to 8 of Brooke LJ's judgment in *Bowman v Fels* [2005] EWCA Civ 226, [2005] 4 All ER 609.

In Part 8 of the 2002 Act, s. 342 (see **B21.34**) creates an offence involving conduct likely to obstruct or prejudice a money laundering, civil recovery, 'detained cash' or confiscation investigation. This goes well beyond the offences previously contained in s. 93D(1) of the 1988 Act and s. 53(1) of the 1994 Act.

B21.2 Parts 7 and 8 of the Act were brought into force on 24 February 2003 (Proceeds of Crime Act 2002 (Commencement No. 4, Transitional Provisions and Savings) Order 2003 (SI 2003 No. 120)), but subject to art. 3 of that Order. This provides that the current provisions do *not* apply where the conduct allegedly constituting an offence under those provisions began before 24 February 2003 and ended on or after that date. The old law continues to apply in such circumstances. See *Montila* [2003] EWCA Crim 3082, [2005] 1 All ER 113, *Saik* [2006] UKHL 18, [2007] 1 AC 18 (see **A5.58**) and *Khanani* [2009] EWCA Crim 276.

As to the power of the FCA (the successor in this respect to the FSA) to bring prosecutions for offences under the POCA 2002, see *Rollins* [2010] UKSC 39, [2010] 4 All ER 880.

Criminal liability may also be incurred by 'relevant persons' in the regulated sector for failure to comply with requirements imposed on them by the Money Laundering, Terrorist Financing and Transfer of Funds (Information on the Payer) Regulations 2017 (SI 2017 No. 692, as amended by SI 2019 No. 1511), or the Money Laundering Regulations 2007 (SI 2007 No. 2157). The 2007 Regulations remain applicable to any alleged breaches that began before *26 June 2017. As to offences under the 2017 Regulations, see* **B21.35**.

MONEY LAUNDERING AND CRIMINAL PROPERTY

Money Laundering

The term 'money laundering', although widely used in the POCA 2002, is potentially misleading. By s. 340(11), 'money laundering' is defined as an act which constitutes an offence under ss. 327, 328 or 329, an inchoate version of such an offence, secondary participation in such an offence or (by s. 340(11)(d)) an act which would constitute any of the above if it were done in the UK. As to the interpretation of para. (d) in respect of things done abroad, see *Rogers* [2014] EWCA Crim 1680, [2015] 1 WLR 1017 and **A8.5**. The offences under ss. 327 to 329 do not, however, use the terms 'money' or 'laundering' to define their scope. They are concerned instead with 'criminal property', as defined in s. 340(2) to (10). **B21.3**

Criminal Property

Proceeds of Crime Act 2002, s. 340 **B21.4**

(2) Criminal conduct is conduct which—
 (a) constitutes an offence in any part of the United Kingdom, or
 (b) would constitute an offence in any part of the United Kingdom if it occurred there.
(3) Property is criminal property if—
 (a) it constitutes a person's benefit from criminal conduct or it represents such a benefit (in whole or part and whether directly or indirectly), and
 (b) the alleged offender knows or suspects that it constitutes or represents such a benefit.
(4) It is immaterial—
 (a) who carried out the conduct;
 (b) who benefited from it;
 (c) whether the conduct occurred before or after the passing of this Act.
(5) A person benefits from conduct if he obtains property as a result of or in connection with the conduct.
(6) If a person obtains a pecuniary advantage as a result of or in connection with conduct, he is to be taken to obtain as a result of or in connection with the conduct a sum of money equal to the value of the pecuniary advantage.
(7) References to property or a pecuniary advantage obtained in connection with conduct include references to property or a pecuniary advantage obtained in both that connection and some other.
(8) If a person benefits from conduct his benefit is the property obtained as a result of or in connection with the conduct.
(9) Property is all property wherever situated and includes—
 (a) money;
 (b) all forms of property, real or personal, heritable or moveable;
 (c) things in action and other intangible or incorporeal property.
(10) The following rules apply in relation to property—
 (a) property is obtained by a person if he obtains an interest in it;
 (b) references to an interest, in relation to land in England and Wales or Northern Ireland, are to any legal estate or equitable interest or power;
 (c) references to an interest, in relation to land in Scotland, are to any estate, interest, servitude or other heritable right in or over land, including a heritable security;
 (d) references to an interest, in relation to property other than land, include references to a right (including a right to possession).

Section 340 has been considered by the Court of Appeal on several occasions, and by the Supreme Court in *GH* [2015] UKSC 24, [2015] 1 WLR 2126. Its importance is that property that does not fall within the terms of s. 340 cannot be 'criminal property' for the purpose of any of the offences in Part 7 of the Act.

Facts, Knowledge and Suspicion The definition of criminal property in the POCA 2002, s. 340(3), includes both *actus reus* and *mens rea* elements. Criminal property must represent, in whole or in part, a person's benefit from *actual* criminal conduct as defined in s. 340(2). This **B21.5**

must be criminal conduct other than the alleged money laundering itself (see further **B21.7**). In addition D must know or suspect this fact. It was suggested in *Ogden* [2016] EWCA Crim 6, [2016] 1 Cr App R 29 (447) that, 'Illegal drugs by their nature always represent criminal property' but (with respect), as well as there being circumstances in which their possession is lawful, there may be cases in which D does not even suspect they are drugs at all. The proceeds of crime may indeed be 'criminal property' as far as D1 is concerned, but not as far as D2 is concerned, depending on what each knows or suspects.

As to 'suspicion', the interpretation adopted by the Court of Appeal in *Da Silva* [2006] EWCA Crim 1654, [2007] 4 All ER 900, in the context of the CJA 1988, s. 93A, may be considered applicable to offences under the POCA 2002. Longmore LJ said in that case:

> The defendant must think that there is a possibility, which is more than fanciful, that the relevant facts exist. A vague feeling of unease would not suffice. But the statute does not require the suspicion to be 'clear' or 'firmly grounded and targeted on specific facts', or based upon 'reasonable grounds'.

Unfounded suspicion can never give rise to criminal liability under Part 7 of the Act (*GH* [2015] UKSC 24, [2015] 1 WLR 2126) but, if D positively believes that he or she is dealing with criminal property, D's actions may give rise to liability for an inchoate offence, such as attempting to commit a money laundering offence, even if the belief proves to have been mistaken (*Pace* [2014] EWCA Crim 186, [2014] 1 WLR 2687 and see **A5.80** and **A5.84**).

B21.6 **Proving the Criminal Derivation of Property** In *Anwoir* [2008] EWCA Crim 1354, [2008] 2 Cr App R 36 (532) the Court of Appeal identified two ways in which the Crown may prove that property derives from crime, namely: (a) by showing that it derives from criminal conduct of a specific kind; or (b) by proving that the circumstances in which it was handled create an irresistible inference that it can only have been derived from crime. *Anwoir* has been followed in a number of subsequent cases, including *F* [2008] EWCA Crim 1868, *Anwar* [2013] EWCA Crim 1865 and *Otegbola* [2017] EWCA Crim 1147, and is consistent with earlier authority, such as *Craig* [2007] EWCA Crim 2913 and *K* [2007] EWCA Crim 491, [2007] 1 WLR 2262. In the latter case, the Court held that it was open to a jury to infer that a large sum concealed in the assets of a business represented criminal property, even though 'the prosecution could not identify the provenance of the money'. This inference was possible because of the elaborate false documentation that had been created in an attempt to disguise its existence and origins. Nobody needs to launder clean money, and one of the purposes of the 2002 Act was to avoid the problems that used to arise where it was clear that property had criminal origins, but unclear whether it derived from drug trafficking or other criminal activity (cf. *El Kurd* [2001] Crim LR 234).

As the Privy Council noted in *DPP (Mauritius) v Bolah* [2011] UKPC 44, [2012] 1 WLR 1737, there is some tension between the *Anwoir* line of authority and *NW* [2008] EWCA Crim 2, [2009] 1 WLR 965, which appears to suggest that the general class or type of crime involved must at least be identified, by analogy with the position in civil proceedings under Part 5 of the Act (as to which, see **D8.19**). Laws LJ said in *NW*:

> We do not consider that Parliament can have intended a state of affairs in which... no particulars whatever need to be given or proved of a cardinal element in the case, namely the criminal conduct relied on.

But *NW* was carefully considered in *Anwoir* where Latham LJ suggested that the problem in the earlier case was that the prosecution had no evidence as to the derivation of D's assets other than the fact that he had no other identifiable means of support. That is very different from a case where D has clearly been taking active measures to falsify or conceal the source of wealth. See also *Kuchhadia* [2015] EWCA Crim 1252, [2015] 2 Cr App R 32 (447), in which Macur LJ said (at [21]):

> There is no reason why the prosecution could not rely on alternative or several allegations of different criminal conduct provided that they can prove at least one to the criminal standard to the satisfaction of the jury.

Where the prosecution allege that property is or may be the proceeds of a particular predicate offence, or the issue arises during the course of the trial, the trial judge should direct the jury as to at least the essential elements of that offence (*Gabriel* [2006] EWCA Crim 229, [2007] 2 Cr App R 11 (139); *Yip* [2010] EWCA Crim 1381). Where the issue of a particular predicate offence is raised only by the jury during their deliberations, no such direction is needed (*Solanki* [2020] EWCA Crim 47). In such circumstances, the Court of Appeal has indicated that the preferable course of action is to instruct the jury that the offence 'had never been part of the prosecution, had never been subject to any evidence and the jury should simply not speculate on that matter any further' (*Anwar* [2013] EWCA Crim 1865 at [40]).

Property Must Already be Criminal Property when Laundered As the Supreme Court explained in *GH* [2015] UKSC 24, [2015] 1 WLR 2126: **B21.7**

> It is a prerequisite of the offences created by ss. 327, 328 and 329 that the property alleged to be criminal property should have that quality or status at the time of the alleged offence. It is that pre-existing quality which makes it an offence for a person to deal with the property, or to arrange for it to be dealt with, in any of the prohibited ways.

Thus, in the context of an offence of transferring criminal property contrary to s. 327(1) of the Act, the property concealed, disguised, converted or transferred must be criminal property at the time it is concealed, disguised, converted or transferred (*Loizou* [2005] EWCA Crim 1579, [2005] 2 Cr App R 37 (618)).

In *GH* D set up bank accounts. His accomplice, B, deceived victims into making payments into those accounts for 'insurance cover' that was never provided. B was given control of the accounts. This was held to be a money-laundering arrangement, contrary to s. 328(1). It did not matter that no relevant criminal property yet existed when B and D first entered into this arrangement, as long as it related to property which was criminal property at the time when the arrangement began to operate on it. The sums credited to the accounts were indeed criminal property because they were obtained through fraud perpetrated on the victims. Lord Toulson said:

> A thief is not guilty of acquiring criminal property by his act of stealing it from its lawful owner, but that does not prevent him from being guilty thereafter of an offence under one or other, or both, of those sections by possessing, using, concealing, transferring it and so on.

In *Haque* [2019] EWCA Crim 1028, [2020] 1 Cr App R 12 (218), D had been charged with acquiring criminal property contrary to s. 329(1)(a) having received funds which were of legitimate origin but which had been transferred into a joint account by virtue of fraud. The Court of Appeal, applying *GH*, accepted the funds were not criminal property at the time they had been acquired and noted that D should have been charged under s. 328 or s. 329(1)(b) or (c) to capture D's conduct after the funds had been acquired, at which point they became criminal property.

In *Gabriel* [2006] EWCA Crim 229, [2007] 2 Cr App R 11 (139), the Court of Appeal rejected arguments that profits made from legitimate trading would, if not declared to the Revenue (or, in the case of benefit claimants, to the Department for Work and Pensions) thereby become criminal property. Gage LJ said (at [21] and [22]):

> We recognise that the failure to declare profits for the purposes of income tax may give rise to an offence, but that does not make the legitimate trading in goods an offence of itself.

Gage LJ nevertheless accepted that in some circumstances a false declaration or a failure to disclose a change in circumstances may give rise to the obtaining of a pecuniary advantage, within the meaning of s. 340(6); and in *K* [2007] EWCA Crim 491, [2007] 1 WLR 2262 the Court of Appeal accordingly held that, where D had fraudulently under-declared the takings of his business so as to evade income tax and VAT, he thereby obtained a pecuniary advantage as a result of cheating the public revenue (see **B16.3**). Dyson LJ said (at [21]):

> Suppose that over a two year period D fraudulently under-declares the takings of his business by £250,000 per annum with the result that he deprives the Revenue of £100,000 in income tax and £25,000 in VAT

> in each of the two years. In each year, D has obtained a pecuniary advantage of £125,000 as a result of his cheating the Revenue. That is a 'benefit' within the meaning of s 340(3)(a) of POCA. The undeclared takings of £500,000 '*represent*' that benefit '*in part*' within the meaning of s 340(3)(a) in the sense that the undeclared takings of £500,000 should have borne tax and a sum representing or equivalent to part of that figure should have been paid in tax.

See to similar effect *William* [2013] EWCA Crim 1262.

B21.8 **Criminal Property and Foreign Law** The concept of 'criminal property' may still in some circumstances include property derived from activities abroad that are lawful under local law. As originally drafted, the POCA 2002 made no concessions to local law, but amendments to the principal money laundering offences came into force on 15 May 2006 (ss. 327(2A), 328(3) and 329(2A)). These effectively exempt the proceeds of most, but not all, 'locally lawful' activities from the operation of the Act. By virtue of the Proceeds of Crime Act 2002 (Money Laundering: Exceptions to Overseas Conduct Defence) Order 2006 (SI 2006 No. 1070), they do not, however, exempt the proceeds of conduct which would have constituted an offence punishable by imprisonment for a maximum term in excess of 12 months in any part of the UK if it occurred there, other than the proceeds of conduct that would have amounted to an offence under the Gaming Act 1968 (now repealed), an offence under the Lotteries and Amusements Act 1976 (now repealed) or an offence under ss. 23 or 25 of the Financial Services and Markets Act 2000.

AUTHORISED DISCLOSURE AND APPROPRIATE CONSENT

B21.9 A person is not guilty of a money laundering offence if the person makes an 'authorised disclosure' and acts with the 'appropriate consent'. These terms are defined in ss. 338 and 335, respectively; and see also the guidance issued by the NCA, available at tinyurl.com/y472r28v.

Proceeds of Crime Act 2002, s. 338

(1) For the purposes of this Part a disclosure is authorised if—
  (a) it is a disclosure to a constable, a customs officer or a nominated officer by the alleged offender that property is criminal property, and
  (b) [repealed]
  (c) the first, second or third condition set out below is satisfied.
(2) The first condition is that the disclosure is made before the alleged offender does the prohibited act.
(2A) The second condition is that—
  (a) the disclosure is made while the alleged offender is doing the prohibited act,
  (b) he began to do the act at a time when, because he did not then know or suspect that the property constituted or represented a person's benefit from criminal conduct, the act was not a prohibited act, and
  (c) the disclosure is made on his own initiative and as soon as is practicable after he first knows or suspects that the property constitutes or represents a person's benefit from criminal conduct.
(3) The third condition is that—
  (a) the disclosure is made after the alleged offender does the prohibited act,
  (b) he has a reasonable excuse for his failure to make the disclosure before he did the act, and
  (c) the disclosure is made on his own initiative and as soon as it is practicable for him to make it.
(4) An authorised disclosure is not to be taken to breach any restriction on the disclosure of information (however imposed).
(5) A disclosure to a nominated officer is a disclosure which—
  (a) is made to a person nominated by the alleged offender's employer to receive authorised disclosures, and
  (b) is made in the course of the alleged offender's employment.
(6) References to the prohibited act are to an act mentioned in section 327(1), 328(1) or 329(1) (as the case may be).

References to a constable include a person authorised for these purposes by the NCA (s. 340(13)).

Proceeds of Crime Act 2002, s. 335 B21.10

(1) The appropriate consent is—
  (a) the consent of a nominated officer to do a prohibited act if an authorised disclosure is made to the nominated officer;
  (b) the consent of a constable to do a prohibited act if an authorised disclosure is made to a constable;
  (c) the consent of a customs officer to do a prohibited act if an authorised disclosure is made to a customs officer.
(2) A person must be treated as having the appropriate consent if—
  (a) he makes an authorised disclosure to a constable or a customs officer, and
  (b) the condition in subsection (3) or the condition in subsection (4) is satisfied.
(3) The condition is that before the end of the notice period he does not receive notice from a constable or customs officer that consent to the doing of the act is refused.
(4) The condition is that—
  (a) before the end of the notice period he receives notice from a constable or customs officer that consent to the doing of the act is refused, and
  (b) the moratorium period has expired.
(5) The notice period is the period of seven working days starting with the first working day after the person makes the disclosure.
(6) The moratorium period is the period of 31 days starting with the day on which the person receives notice that consent to the doing of the act is refused.
(6A) Subsection (6) is subject to—
  (a) section 336A, which enables the moratorium period to be extended by court order in accordance with that section, and
  (b) section 336C, which provides for an automatic extension of the moratorium period in certain cases (period extended if it would otherwise end before determination of application or appeal proceedings etc)
(7) A working day is a day other than a Saturday, a Sunday, Christmas Day, Good Friday or a day which is a bank holiday under the Banking and Financial Dealings Act 1971 in the part of the United Kingdom in which the person is when he makes the disclosure.
(8) References to a prohibited act are to an act mentioned in section 327(1), 328(1) or 329(1) (as the case may be).
(9) A nominated officer is a person nominated to receive disclosures under section 338.

Section 336 details conditions under which a nominated officer may give appropriate consent.

The Criminal Finances Act 2017, s. 10 (which came into force on 31 October 2017), amended the provisions of the POCA 2002 relating to authorised disclosure and appropriate consent by inserting ss. 335(6A), 336(8A) and 336A to 336D. These provisions enable a court to order an extension of the moratorium period (as defined in s. 335(6)) beyond the usual 31-day maximum. By s. 336A, the court can grant an extension for up to 31 further days where it is satisfied that the investigation is being conducted diligently and expeditiously; further time is required for it; and the extension sought is reasonable. Applications for such extensions must be made before the original moratorium period has expired and can be made only by a senior officer (as defined in s. 336D).

Section 336A is complemented by s. 336C, by which the initial moratorium period is automatically extended by up to 31 days, if it would otherwise end before the determination or disposal by the court of an application under s. 336A, or of an appeal against a decision relating to such an application. In addition, where the court initially refuses an application for an extension, s. 336C(7) extends the moratorium period (if it would otherwise expire) by up to five working days beginning with the day on which the court refuses the application, to give time for an appeal to be brought.

Extensions to the moratorium period under ss. 336A and 336C are limited to a maximum of 186 days in total.

By s. 336B the court is empowered to exclude 'interested persons' (as defined by s. 336D) or their representatives from proceedings under s. 336A and (where certain conditions are met) to withhold specified information from them. The court must be satisfied before ordering the withholding of such information that there are reasonable grounds to believe that its disclosure might lead to interference with or harm to evidence or witnesses, hinder or interfere with the gathering of information or the recovery of property, or put national security at risk.

B21.11 In *Bowman v Fels* [2005] EWCA Civ 226, [2005] 4 All ER 609 the Court of Appeal held (at [95]) that 'the issue or pursuit of ordinary legal proceedings with a view to obtaining the court's adjudication upon the parties' rights and duties is not to be regarded as an arrangement or a prohibited act within ss. 327–9'. It follows that lawyers conducting litigation are not required to make disclosure to the NCA and obtain NCA consent merely because of a suspicion that the proceedings might in some way facilitate the acquisition, retention, use or control of criminal property by one or more of the parties.

Where disclosure is required, as Laddie J explained in *Squirrell Ltd v National Westminster Bank plc* [2005] EWHC 664 (Ch), [2006] 2 All ER 784 at [17], the constable (or NCA officer) or customs officer may simply give consent (s. 335(1)). Alternatively, consent may be assumed if the party has made an authorised disclosure and has not received, within seven working days, notice that consent is refused (s. 335(3)). If notice of refusal is given, the applicable moratorium period must expire before that party can safely deal with the property in question (s. 335(4)).

OFFENCES UNDER THE PROCEEDS OF CRIME ACT 2002

Offences of Concealment, etc.

B21.12 **Proceeds of Crime Act 2002, s. 327**

(1) A person commits an offence if he—
- (a) conceals criminal property;
- (b) disguises criminal property;
- (c) converts criminal property;
- (d) transfers criminal property;
- (e) removes criminal property from England and Wales or from Scotland or from Northern Ireland.

(2) But a person does not commit such an offence if—
- (a) he makes an authorised disclosure under section 338 and (if the disclosure is made before he does the act mentioned in subsection (1)) he has the appropriate consent;
- (b) he intended to make such a disclosure but had a reasonable excuse for not doing so;
- (c) the act he does is done in carrying out a function he has relating to the enforcement of any provision of this Act or of any other enactment relating to criminal conduct or benefit from criminal conduct.

(2A) Nor does a person commit an offence under subsection (1) if—
- (a) he knows, or believes on reasonable grounds, that the relevant criminal conduct occurred in a particular country or territory outside the United Kingdom, and
- (b) the relevant criminal conduct—
  - (i) was not, at the time it occurred, unlawful under the criminal law then applying in that country or territory, and
  - (ii) is not of a description prescribed by an order made by the Secretary of State.

(2B) In subsection (2A) 'the relevant criminal conduct' is the criminal conduct by reference to which the property concerned is criminal property.

(2C) A deposit-taking body that does an act mentioned in paragraph (c) or (d) of subsection (1) does not commit an offence under that subsection if—
- (a) it does the act in operating an account maintained with it, and
- (b) the value of the criminal property concerned is less than the threshold amount determined under section 339A for the act.

(3) Concealing or disguising criminal property includes concealing or disguising its nature, source, location, disposition, movement or ownership or any rights with respect to it.

B21.13 **Indictment**

Statement of Offence

Concealing criminal property, contrary to section 327(1)(e) of the Proceeds of Crime Act 2002.

Particulars of Offence

D on or about the... day of... concealed in his home criminal property, namely... knowing or suspecting it to represent in whole or in part the proceeds of drug trafficking committed by E.

The explanatory notes to the Act suggest that s. 327 'creates one of three principal money laundering offences', but the structure of the section suggests that it creates not one but five separate offences (one in each of s. 327(1)(a) to (e)) and the Act contains no clear indication to the contrary. This contrasts with other statutes, such as the Public Order Act 1986, which specifically states in s. 7(2) that ss. 1 to 5 of that Act each create only one offence. An indictment that merely alleges 'money laundering, contrary to s. 327' would thus appear to be duplicitous. See generally **D11.45** ***et seq.***

Procedure and Sentence (Offences under ss. 327, 328 and 329) These offences are each triable either way (s. 334). When tried on indictment they are class 2C or 3 offences (CrimPD XIII, para. B: see Supplement, **CPD.XIII.B**). The maximum penalty is 14 years' imprisonment and/or a fine following conviction on indictment; six months and/or an unlimited fine on summary conviction. Where criminal property has been laundered or disposed of in various ways over a period of time, it may be legitimate for the prosecution to allege a general deficiency as in comparable cases of handling or theft. See CrimPR 10.2(2) (see Supplement, **R10.2**), and *Martin* [2012] EWCA Crim 902. **B21.14**

As to the potential application of the Fraud Act 2006, s. 13, see *JSC BTA Bank v Ablyazov* [2009] EWCA Civ 1124, [2010] 1 WLR 976 and **F10.8**.

The definitive sentencing guideline, *Fraud, Bribery and Money Laundering Offences* (see Supplement, **SG26-6**) covers offences under ss. 327 to 329. The guideline applies to all individual offenders aged 18 and over and to organisations sentenced on or after 1 October 2014 regardless of the date of the offence. A separate part of the guideline applies to corporate offenders.

In *Olarinoye* [2015] EWCA Crim 1503, D was convicted after trial on two counts of acquiring criminal property contrary to s. 329. He had 'played a part in a classic money laundering enterprise of some sophistication'. The sums involved totalled just over £46,000 of which £7,900 went into D's own accounts. The frauds behind the money laundering involved the use of forged documents, stolen cheques and identity theft. The victims were individuals, small businesses and a charity, the Dogs Trust. Having considered the guideline, the Court of Appeal upheld sentences totalling two years' imprisonment and rejected submissions that a suspended sentence was appropriate.

An important post-guideline authority is *Ogden* [2016] EWCA Crim 6, [2016] 1 Cr App R 29 (447), where the offenders were convicted of converting criminal property contrary to s. 327 in the context of drug dealing. It was noted by the Court of Appeal that the money laundering sentencing guidelines were markedly lower than the drugs guidelines and that, on the particular facts, the sentencing judge had passed sentences which were weighted too heavily towards the latter. Attention was drawn to the passage in the money laundering guideline which states that '[t]o complete the assessment of harm, the court should take into account the level of harm associated with the underlying offence to determine whether it warrants upward adjustment of the starting point within the range, or in appropriate cases, outside the range'. To the same effect is *Campbell* [2017] EWCA Crim 213, [2017] 1 Cr App R (S) 57 (440). Further, in *Fulton* [2017] EWCA Crim 308, [2017] 2 Cr App R (S) 11 (63), the Court of Appeal dealt with a sophisticated money laundering operation relating to an underlying European VAT fraud. Between March and November 2011 transactions involving £30 million had taken place, involving a tax loss to the Revenue of about £17.5 million. The Court said that the criminality of the money laundering must in the first instance be judged by the nature and total scale of that activity, and it was the whole amount involved, not just that part which comprised the criminal property (the 'dirty money'), which impacted on the financial system. Sentences of seven years and four and a half years were upheld. A different kind of case is *Scott* [2015] EWCA Crim 937, [2015] 2 Cr App R (S) 48 (361), where D, a man of 51 with a significant criminal record, was convicted for his part in a cash-in-transit robbery, in which over £25,000 in cash was stolen. Dye was released on the **B21.15** stolen notes, staining them. After serving his sentence D retrieved some of the cash from a hiding place and, acting with others, laundered the cash by purchasing low-value train tickets from ticket machines, keeping the change as clean money. He pleaded guilty to money laundering on the second day of trial, and was sentenced to three years' imprisonment, based upon culpability A and harm category 5 in the money laundering guideline. The Court of Appeal upheld the sentence, agreeing with the judge that D was the prime mover in the offence, had a poor record and was on licence at the time of the offence, and observing that it was hard to imagine a worse case of 'not learning the lessons of the earlier sentence'.

In *Sula* [2017] EWCA Crim 27, the Court of Appeal provided guidance on sentencing under the money laundering sentencing guidelines where the amount of money bordered categories. On the facts, the sum of £500,000 bordered on both category 4 and category 3. The Court concluded that the judge erred in fixing upon 30 months. A straight-line graph between the starting points for sums of £300,000 and £1 million indicates that for a sum of £500,000 a starting point of around 24 months is appropriate.

B21.16 **Elements** The scope of the offences created by s. 327 is potentially very broad. Dishonesty is not required, and although 'criminal property' is defined in the POCA 2002, s. 330, as representing a benefit of criminal conduct, the 'conversion' of such property may fall within the ambit of s. 327 whether or not any such benefit accrues from that conversion (*Ogden* [2016] EWCA Crim 6, [2016] 1 Cr App R 29 (447) at [51]). The same goes for the other offences under s. 327 (concealing, disguising or removing criminal property). On a literal reading of s. 327, a thief who conceals, disguises or sells property that has just been stolen may thereby commit offences under that section, as may someone who suspects (correctly) that the property that person converts or exports represents the benefit of another person's crime (s. 340(3)(b)). In *Fazal* [2009] EWCA Crim 1697, [2010] 1 WLR 694, D allowed his bank account to be used by a friend to launder money, and it was held that he was guilty of converting criminal property (contrary to s. 327(1)(c)) whenever such monies were deposited in, retained in, or withdrawn from the account. Where property is purchased for 'adequate consideration', s. 329(2) provides a defence to a charge of unlawful acquisition, use or possession under s. 329(1) (see **B21.22**) but this defence cannot apply if the charge is converting, transferring or removing the property under s. 327.

Section 327(2) creates defences to charges under s. 327(1). D does not bear any legal or persuasive burden in respect of those defences, but must presumably bear an evidential burden. The prosecution therefore need not address any such issues unless these are raised by admissible evidence.

Money Laundering Arrangements

B21.17 **Proceeds of Crime Act 2002, s. 328**

(1) A person commits an offence if he enters into or becomes concerned in an arrangement which he knows or suspects facilitates (by whatever means) the acquisition, retention, use or control of criminal property by or on behalf of another person.

(2) But a person does not commit such an offence if—
  (a) he makes an authorised disclosure under section 338 and (if the disclosure is made before he does the act mentioned in subsection (1)) he has the appropriate consent;
  (b) he intended to make such a disclosure but had a reasonable excuse for not doing so;
  (c) the act he does is done in carrying out a function he has relating to the enforcement of any provision of this Act or of any other enactment relating to criminal conduct or benefit from criminal conduct.

(3) Nor does a person commit an offence under subsection (1) if—
  (a) he knows, or believes on reasonable grounds, that the relevant criminal conduct occurred in a particular country or territory outside the United Kingdom, and
  (b) the relevant criminal conduct—
    (i) was not, at the time it occurred, unlawful under the criminal law then applying in that country or territory, and
    (ii) is not of a description prescribed by an order made by the Secretary of State.

(4) In subsection (3) 'the relevant criminal conduct' is the criminal conduct by reference to which the property concerned is criminal property.
(5) A deposit-taking body that does an act mentioned in subsection (1) does not commit an offence under that subsection if—
 (a) it does the act in operating an account maintained with it, and
 (b) the arrangement facilitates the acquisition, retention, use or control of criminal property of a value that is less than the threshold amount determined under section 339A for the act.

Indictment, etc. **B21.18**

Statement of Offence

Entering into or becoming concerned in a money laundering arrangement, contrary to section 328(1) of the Proceeds of Crime Act 2002.

Particulars of Offence

D on or about the day of...entered into or became concerned in an arrangement, namely the opening by E of an account at...under a false name, knowing or suspecting that this arrangement facilitated the retention, use or control of criminal property by E or by other persons unknown.

In contrast to ss. 327 and 329, s. 328 appears to create a single offence, which may be committed in various ways. It is analogous in this respect to the offence of handling stolen goods (see **B4.159**). As to procedure and sentence, see **B21.14**.

Elements Section 328 requires a definite arrangement which D knows or suspects facilitates (and not just 'will or may facilitate') the acquisition of criminal property by or on behalf of another person, who must already be identified or at least identifiable (*Dare v CPS* [2012] EWHC 2074 (Admin)). It potentially affects not only deliberate or dishonest offenders, but also banks, accountants and legal advisers, etc., who become suspicious as to the legality of the means by which their clients have acquired any of the funds or other property they are asked to deal with or manage. As Laddie J explained in *Squirrell Ltd v National Westminster Bank plc* [2005] EWHC 664 (Ch), [2006] 2 All ER 784 at [16]: **B21.19**

> The purpose of s. 328(1) is not to turn innocent third parties...into criminals. It is to put them under pressure to provide information to the relevant authorities to enable the latter to obtain information about possible criminal activity and to increase their prospects of being able to freeze the proceeds of crime...A party caught by s. 328(1) can avoid liability if he brings himself within the statutory defence created by s. 328(2)...

In *Squirrell*, Laddie J's view was that 'Even if [the client's account] does *not* contain funds which are, in fact, criminal property and no offence has been committed [by the client] s. 328(1) bites if [the bank] has a relevant suspicion'. But this interpretation was clearly wrong in light of the decision of the House of Lords in *Montila* [2003] EWCA Crim 3082, [2005] 1 All ER 113 (not referred to in *Squirrell*), which the Supreme Court in *GH* [2015] UKSC 24, [2015] 1 WLR 2126 (see **B21.7**) confirmed to be equally applicable to offences under the POCA 2002. Unfounded suspicion alone cannot give rise to any offence under s. 328. The property in question must actually be criminal property within the meaning of s. 340, if not when the initial arrangement is made then when it is put into operation. **B21.20**

In *Bowman v Fels* [2005] EWCA Civ 226, [2005] 4 All ER 609, the Court of Appeal rejected arguments that, if a lawyer acting for a client in legal proceedings discovers or suspects anything in the proceedings that may facilitate the acquisition, retention, use or control (usually by the lawyer's own client or the client's opponent) of criminal property, the lawyer must immediately notify the relevant authority (now the NCA) of this belief in order to avoid being guilty of a s. 328 offence. Brooke LJ said (at [83]):

> [Section 328] is...not intended to cover or affect the ordinary conduct of litigation by legal professionals. That includes any step taken by them in litigation from the issue of proceedings and the securing of injunctive relief or a freezing order up to its final disposal by judgment. We do not

consider that either the European or the United Kingdom legislator can have envisaged that any of these ordinary activities could fall within the concept of 'becoming concerned in an arrangement which . . . facilitates the acquisition, retention, use or control of criminal property'.

B21.21 The wording of s. 328(2) does not suggest that D bears any legal or persuasive burden in respect of the defences it creates, but D must bear an evidential burden. The prosecution therefore need not address any such issues unless these have been raised by admissible evidence.

Offences of Acquisition, Use or Possession

B21.22 **Proceeds of Crime Act 2002, s. 329**

(1) A person commits an offence if he—
(a) acquires criminal property;
(b) uses criminal property;
(c) has possession of criminal property.
(2) But a person does not commit such an offence if—
(a) he makes an authorised disclosure under section 338 and (if the disclosure is made before he does the act mentioned in subsection (1)) he has the appropriate consent;
(b) he intended to make such a disclosure but had a reasonable excuse for not doing so;
(c) he acquired or used or had possession of the property for adequate consideration;
(d) the act he does is done in carrying out a function he has relating to the enforcement of any provision of this Act or of any other enactment relating to criminal conduct or benefit from criminal conduct.
(2A) Nor does a person commit an offence under subsection (1) if—
(a) he knows, or believes on reasonable grounds, that the relevant criminal conduct occurred in a particular country or territory outside the United Kingdom, and
(b) the relevant criminal conduct—
(i) was not, at the time it occurred, unlawful under the criminal law then applying in that country or territory, and
(ii) is not of a description prescribed by an order made by the Secretary of State.
(2B) In subsection (2A) 'the relevant criminal conduct' is the criminal conduct by reference to which the property concerned is criminal property.
(2C) A deposit-taking body that does an act mentioned in subsection (1) does not commit an offence under that subsection if—
(a) it does the act in operating an account maintained with it, and
(b) the arrangement facilitates the acquisition, retention, use or control of criminal property of a value that is less than the threshold amount determined under section 339A for the act.
(3) For the purposes of this section—
(a) a person acquires property for inadequate consideration if the value of the consideration is significantly less than the value of the property;
(b) a person uses or has possession of property for inadequate consideration if the value of the consideration is significantly less than the value of the use or possession;
(c) the provision by a person of goods or services which he knows or suspects may help another to carry out criminal conduct is not consideration.

B21.23 **Indictment, etc.**

Statement of Offence

Acquiring criminal property, contrary to section 329(1)(a) of the Proceeds of Crime Act 2002.

Particulars of Offence

D on or about the day of . . . acquired criminal property, namely . . . knowing or suspecting it to represent in whole or in part the proceeds of drug trafficking committed by E.

There may be room for argument as to whether s. 329(1)(a) to (c) each create a distinct offence, or whether they represent three different ways of committing a single offence created by s. 329(1). See the discussion of s. 327 at **B21.13**. The form of indictment shown above should be acceptable in either case. As to procedure and sentence, see **B21.14**.

Elements Section 329 does not distinguish between criminal property that represents the benefit of some other person's crime and that which represents the benefits of a crime which D has just committed. A thief who uses or retains possession of property that has just been stolen (this being criminal property as defined in s. 340) must therefore be guilty of an offence under s. 329(1)(b) or (c), the maximum penalty for which is twice that for basic theft. It does not follow that such a charge would be appropriate. It might indeed be considered perverse. The structure of the money laundering offences appears to rely on the assumption that they will be applied sensibly and that prosecutors will not attempt to exploit the more bizarre or extreme possibilities that they create. On the other hand, it is apparent that charges are now being laid under s. 329 in some cases where D might previously have faced more charges of theft or handling (see, e.g., *Hogan v DPP* [2007] EWHC 978 (Admin), [2007] 1 WLR 2944 and *Wilkinson v DPP* [2006] EWHC 3012 (Admin)). **B21.24**

Dishonesty is not required under s. 329, nor need D know or believe that the property in question is criminal property. Mere suspicion will suffice (see s. 340(3)(b)).

Defences are provided under s. 329(2) to (2C). D bears no legal or persuasive burden in respect of those defences, but does bear an evidential burden (*Hogan v DPP*). The prosecution therefore need not address any such issues unless these have been raised by D. Where property is purchased for 'adequate consideration', s. 329(2)(c) provides a defence to someone who is charged with unlawful acquisition, use or possession under s. 329(1), but this cannot apply if the person is charged instead with an offence under s. 327. **B21.25**

In *Gabriel* [2006] EWCA Crim 229, [2007] 2 Cr App R 11 (139), Gage LJ offered this advice to prosecutors in cases involving s. 329 (at [29]):

> There can be no doubt that the money laundering provisions of the Proceeds of Crime Act 2002 are draconian. The scope of section 329 is wide. It requires proof of no more *mens rea* than suspicion. The danger is that juries will be tempted to think that it is for the defence to prove innocence rather than the prosecution to prove guilt. In *R v Loizou* [2005] EWCA 1579, the prosecution had set out the factors upon which it relied and from which it submitted the jury could draw proper inferences. In our judgment it is a sensible practice for the prosecution, as was done in *Loizou*, either by giving particulars, or at least in opening, to set out the facts upon which it relies and the inferences which it will invite the jury to draw as proof that the property was criminal property. In doing so it may very well be that the prosecution will be able to limit the scope of the criminal conduct alleged.

Sentence A sentence of 12 months' imprisonment for the offence under s. 329 was upheld in *Valentine* [2011] EWCA Crim 1463, [2012] 1 Cr App R (S) 42 (246). D was married to a man who was eventually sentenced to life imprisonment for offences including robbery and conspiracy to murder. The man headed a criminal gang, and the profits made from criminal activity funded a lavish lifestyle for the couple, including expensive cars and jewellery and many foreign trips. **B21.26**

Money Laundering, Stolen Goods and Wrongful Credits

There are overlaps between the money laundering offences and several existing offences, including those of assisting offenders, concealing offences and perverting the course of justice. The most important overlaps, however, appear to be with handling stolen goods (Theft Act 1968, s. 22; see **B4.159** *et seq.*) and dishonestly retaining a wrongful credit (Theft Act 1968, s. 24A: see **B4.184** *et seq.*). **B21.27**

The term, 'stolen goods', as defined in s. 24 of the Theft Act 1968, includes money and other property which directly or indirectly represents (or has previously represented) the proceeds of theft, blackmail, a s. 15 deception offence, or fraud (within the meaning of the Fraud Act 2006) in the hands of the original thief, etc., or in the hands of a dishonest handler of stolen goods. Such property may be criminally 'handled' in a number of ways, but D must be proved to have been dishonest and to have 'known or believed' that the property in question was stolen goods. Mere suspicion is never enough (see **B4.179**). If the goods were allegedly stolen abroad, outside English jurisdiction, it will be necessary to prove the content of the relevant foreign law (*Ofori* (1994) 99 Cr App R 223). D cannot ordinarily be convicted of handling the proceeds of D's own crime, unless D is proved to have done so for the benefit of another. Finally, in cases involving cheques, money transfers or the proceeds of bank accounts, care must be taken to avoid the problems identified (or created) by the House of Lords in *Preddy* [1996] AC 815 (see **B4.187**).

B21.28 A money laundering offence may be easier to establish than any Theft Act offence. By the POCA 2002, s. 340(3), the property in question may represent the proceeds of any crime under UK law, and it suffices that D merely suspects this (*Pace* [2014] EWCA Crim 186, [2014] 1 WLR 2867). In *Hickey* [2007] EWCA Crim 542, D pleaded guilty to an offence under s. 327(1)(c) (see **B21.12**) on the basis that he had suspected that a vehicle he delivered to a buyer had been stolen. It is not clear whether a charge of handling could ever have been proved on the facts of that case, but it was accepted that there was no reason to suppose that he had been aware that the theft of the vehicle had been connected to a domestic burglary. The courts have made statements discouraging the use of money laundering charges in cases that might more accurately be described as ones of handling (*Wilkinson v DPP* [2006] EWHC 3012 (Admin); *GH* [2015] UKSC 24, [2015] 1 WLR 2126 at [49]) but the choice of charge where there is an overlap is ultimately that of the prosecutor (see *Roberts* [2014] EWCA Crim 1475 and the commentary at [2015] Crim LR 458).

The exact crime from which the property is derived need not be established, nor need anyone have been convicted in respect of it. D may even be guilty of 'money laundering', by using, possessing or retaining the proceeds of D's own (previous) criminal conduct (cf. *Rose* [2008] EWCA Crim 239, [2008] 2 Cr App R 15 (202)); but amendments made to the 2002 Act by the SOCPA 2005, s. 102, now ensure that D will not ordinarily be guilty of any of the principal money laundering offences where D knows, or believes on reasonable grounds, that the relevant 'criminal' conduct occurred (or is occurring) in a country or territory outside the UK, and is not (or was not at that time) criminal under the applicable local law. This defence will not apply if the relevant conduct is of a type described by an order made by the Secretary of State.

Where D's bank or building society account contains the proceeds of thefts or frauds, a money laundering charge may similarly be an easier charge to prove than a charge under the Theft Act 1968, s. 24A. It would again avoid the need for proof of D's dishonesty or knowledge as to the provenance of the funds.

Jurisdiction

B21.29 None of the money laundering offences in the POCA 2002 are listed as Group A offences for jurisdictional purposes under the CJA 1993, Part I (see **A8.10**) but, as long as the money laundering offence takes place in England and Wales, it does not matter if the property concerned is the product of criminal conduct committed elsewhere in the world. As to 'cross-frontier' offences, see also *Rogers* [2014] EWCA Crim 1680, [2015] 1 WLR 1017 and the analysis of that case at **A8.5**.

Failure to Disclose Possible Money Laundering

B21.30 Sections 330, 331 and 332 create offences of failure to disclose possible money laundering activities (as defined in s. 340(11)). Actual knowledge or suspicion is not essential under ss. 330 or 331. It suffices in either case that D has 'reasonable grounds' for suspicion. Section 330 deals with failures by persons working in the 'regulated sector' (financial services etc.) as defined in sch. 9 to the Act.

Proceeds of Crime Act 2002, s. 330

(1) A person commits an offence if the conditions in subsections (2) to (4) are satisfied.
(2) The first condition is that he—
(a) knows or suspects, or
(b) has reasonable grounds for knowing or suspecting,
that another person is engaged in money laundering.
(3) The second condition is that the information or other matter—
(a) on which his knowledge or suspicion is based, or
(b) which gives reasonable grounds for such knowledge or suspicion,
came to him in the course of a business in the regulated sector.
(3A) The third condition is—
(a) that he can identify the other person mentioned in subsection (2) or the whereabouts of any of the laundered property, or
(b) that he believes, or it is reasonable to expect him to believe, that the information or other matter mentioned in subsection (3) will or may assist in identifying that other person or the whereabouts of any of the laundered property.
(4) The fourth condition is that he does not make the required disclosure to—
(a) a nominated officer, or
(b) a person authorised for the purposes of this Part by the Director General of the National Crime Agency,
as soon as is practicable after the information or other matter mentioned in subsection (3) comes to him.
(5) The required disclosure is a disclosure of—
(a) the identity of the other person mentioned in subsection (2), if he knows it,
(b) the whereabouts of the laundered property, so far as he knows it, and
(c) the information or other matter mentioned in subsection (3).
(5A) The laundered property is the property forming the subject-matter of the money laundering that he knows or suspects, or has reasonable grounds for knowing or suspecting, that other person to be engaged in.
(6) But he does not commit an offence under this section if—
(a) he has a reasonable excuse for not making the required disclosure,
(b) he is a professional legal adviser or relevant professional adviser and—
(i) if he knows either of the things mentioned in subsection (5)(a) and (b), he knows the thing because of information or other matter that came to him in privileged circumstances, or
(ii) the information or other matter mentioned in subsection (3) came to him in privileged circumstances, or
(c) subsection (7) or (7B) applies to him.
(7) This subsection applies to a person if—
(a) he does not know or suspect that another person is engaged in money laundering, and
(b) he has not been provided by his employer with such training as is specified by the Secretary of State by order for the purposes of this section.
(7A) Nor does a person commit an offence under this section if—
(a) he knows, or believes on reasonable grounds, that the money laundering is occurring in a particular country or territory outside the United Kingdom, and
(b) the money laundering—
(i) is not unlawful under the criminal law applying in that country or territory, and
(ii) is not of a description prescribed in an order made by the Secretary of State.
(7B) This subsection applies to a person if—
(a) he is employed by, or is in partnership with, a professional legal adviser or a relevant professional adviser to provide the adviser with assistance or support,
(b) the information or other matter mentioned in subsection (3) comes to the person in connection with the provision of such assistance or support, and
(c) the information or other matter came to the adviser in privileged circumstances.
(8) In deciding whether a person committed an offence under this section the court must consider whether he followed any relevant guidance which was at the time concerned—
(a) issued by a supervisory authority or any other appropriate body,
(b) approved by the Treasury, and

(c) published in a manner it approved as appropriate in its opinion to bring the guidance to the attention of persons likely to be affected by it.

(9) A disclosure to a nominated officer is a disclosure which—
(a) is made to a person nominated by the alleged offender's employer to receive disclosures under this section, and
(b) is made in the course of the alleged offender's employment.

(9A) But a disclosure which satisfies paragraphs (a) and (b) of subsection (9) is not to be taken as a disclosure to a nominated officer if the person making the disclosure—
(a) is a professional legal adviser or relevant professional adviser,
(b) makes it for the purpose of obtaining advice about making a disclosure under this section, and
(c) does not intend it to be a disclosure under this section.

(10) Information or other matter comes to a professional legal adviser or relevant professional adviser in privileged circumstances if it is communicated or given to him—
(a) by (or by a representative of) a client of his in connection with the giving by the adviser of legal advice to the client,
(b) by (or by a representative of) a person seeking legal advice from the adviser, or
(c) by a person in connection with legal proceedings or contemplated legal proceedings.

(11) But subsection (10) does not apply to information or other matter which is communicated or given with the intention of furthering a criminal purpose.

(12) Schedule 9 has effect for the purpose of determining what is—
(a) a business in the regulated sector;
(b) a supervisory authority.

(13) An appropriate body is any body which regulates or is representative of any trade, profession, business or employment carried on by the alleged offender.

(14) A relevant professional adviser is an accountant, auditor or tax adviser who is a member of a professional body which is established for accountants, auditors or tax advisers (as the case may be) and which makes provision for—
(a) testing the competence of those seeking admission to membership of such a body as a condition for such admission; and
(b) imposing and maintaining professional and ethical standards for its members, as well as imposing sanctions for non-compliance with those standards.

B21.31 The guidance referred to in s. 330(8) includes that issued by the Joint Money Laundering Steering Group, available at www.jmlsg.org.uk, and (for those in the legal sector) by the Legal Sector Affinity Group (available at tinyurl.com/ycbr6v9w).

Section 330 differs from the other provisions in Part 7 in that it refers not to 'criminal property', but to 'the laundered property', which is defined in s. 330(5A). This is a narrower concept than 'criminal property' in that property may be criminal property whether it has been laundered or not. Read in isolation, s. 330(5A) might at first sight appear capable of referring to unfounded suspicions of money laundering. This seems indeed to have been the view of the High Court of Justiciary in *Ahmad v HM Advocate* [2009] HCJAC 60; but if this was the intended meaning, it is remarkable that D could not then escape conviction by proving that no money laundering was in fact taking place, whereas D *could* escape conviction by proving (under s. 330(7A)) that D believed it was occurring abroad, in circumstances where it would then have been legal (*Montila* [2003] EWCA Crim 3082, [2005] 1 All ER 113).

Section 331 creates a broadly similar offence, applicable to nominated officers in the regulated sector, who have themselves received information as to suspected money laundering in consequence of disclosures made to them under s. 330.

Section 332 deals with failures by nominated officers to whom disclosures have been made under s. 337 (protected disclosures) or s. 338 (authorised disclosures).

B21.32 **Penalties and Procedure for Offences under ss. 330 to 332** Offences under ss. 330 to 332 are *triable either way (s. 334)*. When tried on indictment they are normally a class 3 offence, but see CrimPD XIII, para. B (see Supplement, **CPD.XIII.B**), for the additional factors that the court considers on allocation. The maximum penalty is five years' imprisonment and/or a fine following conviction on indictment; six months and/or an unlimited fine on summary conviction. There is no offence-specific guideline but the Sentencing Council's *General Guideline: Overarching Principles* (see Supplement, **SG2-1**) is used for all offenders sentenced on or after 1 October 2019.

In *Swan* [2011] EWCA Crim 2275, [2012] 1 Cr App R (S) 90 (542) a sentence of nine months' imprisonment was appropriate where the offenders, who ran a safe deposit company, failed to disclose circumstances giving rise to reasonable grounds to suspect that money laundering was taking place. The Court of Appeal noted that the maximum penalty for the offence was five years, and that sentences towards the top of the range would be reserved for those involved in regulated businesses who knew that money laundering was going on. In the instant case, if the Court had been dealing with an isolated instance a lower sentence would have been proper, but there had been guilty pleas to seven counts of assisting undercover police officers in laundering money without being reported and advising how identity might be concealed.

In *Griffiths* [2006] EWCA Crim 2155, [2007] 1 Cr App R (S) 95 (581), D, a solicitor, was convicted of failing to make a required disclosure under s. 330. D had carried out a conveyance on a house in circumstances where there were reasonable grounds to suspect that others were engaged in money laundering. Sentence was reduced from 15 months' imprisonment to six months. See also *Duff* [2002] EWCA Crim 2117, [2003] 1 Cr App R (S) 88 (466).

Tipping-off

The POCA 2002, s. 333(1), created an offence of making a disclosure likely to prejudice a money laundering investigation which is being undertaken or may in the future be undertaken by law enforcement authorities. This was replaced by the Terrorism Act 2000 and the Proceeds of Crime Act 2002 (Amendment) Regulations 2007 (SI 2007 No. 3398), reg. 3 and sch. 2, with five new sections (ss. 333A to 333E) in accordance with Directive 2005/60/EC on the prevention of the use of the financial system for the purpose of money laundering and terrorist financing ([2005] OJ L309/15) (Third Money Laundering Directive). Section 333A provides a direct replacement for s. 333, whereas ss. 333B to 333D give effect to certain exceptions specified in Article 28 of the Directive. Section 333E provides definitions. **B21.33**

Proceeds of Crime Act 2002, s. 333A

(1) A person commits an offence if—
  (a) the person discloses any matter within subsection (2);
  (b) the disclosure is likely to prejudice any investigation that might be conducted following the disclosure referred to in that subsection; and
  (c) the information on which the disclosure is based came to the person in the course of a business in the regulated sector.

(2) The matters are that the person or another person has made a disclosure under this Part—
  (a) to a constable,
  (b) to an officer of Revenue and Customs,
  (c) to a nominated officer, or
  (d) to a National Crime Agency officer authorised for the purposes of this Part by the Director General of that Agency,

of information that came to that person in the course of a business in the regulated sector.

(3) A person commits an offence if—
  (a) the person discloses that an investigation into allegations that an offence under this Part has been committed is being contemplated or is being carried out;
  (b) the disclosure is likely to prejudice that investigation; and
  (c) the information on which the disclosure is based came to the person in the course of a business in the regulated sector.

(4) A person guilty of an offence under this section is liable—
  (a) on summary conviction to imprisonment for a term not exceeding three months, or to [an unlimited fine], or to both;
  (b) on conviction on indictment to imprisonment for a term not exceeding two years, or to a fine, or to both.

(5) This section is subject to—
(a) section 333B (disclosures within an undertaking or group etc),
(b) section 333C (other permitted disclosures between institutions etc), and
(c) section 333D (other permitted disclosures etc).

Prejudicing Investigations

B21.34 Part 8 of the Act deals with criminal and civil investigations into suspected money laundering activities.

Proceeds of Crime Act 2002, s. 342

(1) This section applies if a person knows or suspects that an appropriate officer... is acting (or proposing to act) in connection with a confiscation investigation, a civil recovery investigation, a detained cash investigation, a detained property investigation, a frozen funds investigation, an exploitation proceeds investigation or a money laundering investigation which is being or is about to be conducted.
(2) The person commits an offence if—
(a) he makes a disclosure which is likely to prejudice the investigation, or
(b) he falsifies, conceals, destroys or otherwise disposes of, or causes or permits the falsification, concealment, destruction or disposal of, documents which are relevant to the investigation.
(3) A person does not commit an offence under subsection (2)(a) if—
(a) he does not know or suspect that the disclosure is likely to prejudice the investigation,
(b) the disclosure is made in the exercise of a function under this Act or any other enactment relating to criminal conduct or benefit from criminal conduct or in compliance with a requirement imposed under or by virtue of this Act,
(ba) the disclosure is of a matter within section 333A(2) or (3)(a) (money laundering: tipping off) and the information on which the disclosure is based came to the person in the course of a business in the regulated sector, or
(bb) the disclosure is made in the exercise of a function under Part 7 of the Coroners and Justice Act 2009 (criminal memoirs etc) or in compliance with a requirement imposed under or by virtue of that Act, or
(c) he is a professional legal adviser and the disclosure falls within subsection (4).
(4) A disclosure falls within this subsection if it is a disclosure—
(a) to (or to a representative of) a client of the professional legal adviser in connection with the giving by the adviser of legal advice to the client, or
(b) to any person in connection with legal proceedings or contemplated legal proceedings.
(5) But a disclosure does not fall within subsection (4) if it is made with the intention of furthering a criminal purpose.
(6) A person does not commit an offence under subsection (2)(b) if—
(a) he does not know or suspect that the documents are relevant to the investigation, or
(b) he does not intend to conceal any facts disclosed by the documents from any appropriate officer... carrying out the investigation.

This provision must be read in conjunction with the POCA 2002, s. 341, which defines the various investigations listed in s. 342(1).

It is clear that s. 342(2)(a) and (b) each create a separate offence. Penalties and procedure for either offence are the same as for offences under ss. 330 to 332 (see **B21.32**).

See also the SCA 2007, s. 69 (improper 'further disclosure' by D of protected information which has been directly or indirectly disclosed to D by a public authority).

OFFENCES UNDER MONEY LAUNDERING REGULATIONS

B21.35 The *Money Laundering, Terrorist Financing and Transfer of Funds (Information on the Payer) Regulations 2017* replaced the Money Laundering Regulations 2007 on 26 June 2017 with provisions that implement the EU Fourth Money Laundering Directive (Directive (EU)

2015/849 [2015] OJ L141/73) and enable the UK to enforce the EU Funds Transfer Regulation (Regulation (EU) 2015/847 [2015] OJ L141/1). The 2017 Regulations were amended by the Money Laundering and Terrorist Financing (Amendment) Regulations 2019 (SI 2019 No. 1511), which transposed the EU Fifth Money Laundering Directive (Directive (EU) 2018/843 [2018] OJ L 156/43) into UK law. The detailed content of the Regulations falls well beyond the scope of this work, but brief reference will be made to the offences created by Part 9, ch. 3, of the Regulations. It should be noted that these offences do not apply to regulatory infringements that began before 26 June 2017. The 2007 Regulations will continue to apply in such cases. For offences flowing from breaches of new regulatory requirements inserted by SI 2019 No. 1511, the infringement must have commenced on or after 10 January 2020.

The principal offence-creating provisions under the 2017 Regulations are contained in regs. 86 to 88, which are supplemented by provisions dealing with: the power to institute criminal proceedings (reg. 89); jurisdiction and territorial extent (reg. 90); proceedings against partnerships or unincorporated associations (reg. 91); and the liability of the officers of corporations, partnerships or unincorporated associations (reg. 92).

The various offences created by regs. 86 to 98 are each punishable on summary conviction by up to three months' imprisonment and/or a fine, and on indictment by up to two years' imprisonment and/or a fine.

By reg. 86(1), if D breaches any 'relevant requirement' imposed, D may be guilty of an offence. 'Relevant requirements' for this purpose are listed in sch. 6 to the Regulations (as amended). No *mens rea* is specified, but by reg. 86(2):

> (2) In deciding whether a person has committed an offence under paragraph (1), the court must decide whether that person followed—
> (a) any guidelines issued by the European Supervisory Authorities in accordance with Article 17, 18.4 and 48.10 of the fourth money laundering directive or Article 25 of the funds transfer regulation; and
> (b) any relevant guidance which was at the time—
> (i) issued by the FCA; or
> (ii) issued by any other supervisory authority or appropriate body and approved by the Treasury.

Regulation 86(3) meanwhile provides that D cannot be guilty of this offence if D took all reasonable steps and exercised all due diligence to avoid committing it.

By reg. 87, D may be guilty of an offence if D knows or suspects that an appropriate officer is acting (or proposing to act) in connection with an investigation into a potential contravention of a relevant requirement which is being or is about to be conducted; and either (a) makes a disclosure which is likely to prejudice the investigation; or (b) falsifies, conceals, destroys or otherwise disposes of, or causes or permits the falsification, concealment, destruction or disposal of, documents which are relevant to the investigation.

Regulation 87(3) to (8) identify a range of circumstances in which a disclosure otherwise falling within (a) will be considered innocent or lawful, including disclosure by a professional legal adviser in the course of advising a client or in connection with actual or contemplated legal proceedings (but not with the intention of furthering any criminal purpose).

By reg. 88(1) it is an offence for D knowingly or recklessly to provide false or misleading information in purported compliance with a requirement under the Regulations; and by reg. 88(3) it is an offence to disclose information in contravention of a relevant (sch. 6) requirement, although D has a defence to the reg. 88(3) offence if it can be proved D acted under a reasonable belief that the disclosure was lawful, or that the information had already been made available to the public.

Section B22 Modern Slavery, Trafficking and Immigration Offences

SLAVERY, SERVITUDE AND FORCED OR COMPULSORY LABOUR

B22.1 The CAJA 2009, s. 71 (as to which, see the 2015 edition of this work at B2.198 *et seq.*) was enacted in order to ensure compliance with the ECHR, Article 4, by which (1) 'No one shall be held in slavery or servitude' and (2) 'No one shall be required to perform forced or compulsory labour'. Under Article 4(3), the term 'forced or compulsory labour' excludes:

(a) any work required to be done in the ordinary course of detention imposed according to the provisions of Article 5 of this Convention or during conditional release from such detention;
(b) any service of a military character or, in case of conscientious objectors in countries where they are recognised, service exacted instead of compulsory military service;
(c) any service exacted in case of an emergency or calamity threatening the life or well-being of the community; and
(d) any work or service which forms part of normal civic obligations.

It also sought to ensure compliance with the UK's obligations under the International Labour Organisation Conventions on Forced Labour, which require the illegal exaction of forced or compulsory labour to be punishable as a criminal offence. Section 71 is supplanted by s. 1 of the Modern Slavery Act 2015. In *Rooney* [2019] EWCA Crim 681, the Court of Appeal highlighted (at [55]) that in enacting s. 1(3), (4) and (5) of the 2015 Act, Parliament made it explicit that a jury should consider all the circumstances of the case when deciding whether all the ingredients of an offence had been proved. Section 5 of the 2015 Act increased maximum sentences to life, supplemented by the power to make slavery and trafficking reparation, prevention and risk orders (as to which, see **E11**, **E21** and **D25** respectively).

Definition

B22.2 **Modern Slavery Act 2015, s. 1**

(1) A person commits an offence if—
(a) the person holds another person in slavery or servitude and the circumstances are such that the person knows or ought to know that the other person is held in slavery or servitude, or
(b) the person requires another person to perform forced or compulsory labour and the circumstances are such that the person knows or ought to know that the other person is being *required to perform forced or compulsory labour.*

(2) In subsection (1) the references to holding a person in slavery or servitude or requiring a person to perform forced or compulsory labour are to be construed in accordance with Article 4 of the Human Rights Convention.

(3) In determining whether a person is being held in slavery or servitude or required to perform forced or compulsory labour regard may be had to all the circumstances.
(4) For example, regard may be had—
  (a) to any of the person's personal circumstances (such as the person being a child, the person's family relationships, and any mental or physical illness) which may make the person more vulnerable than other persons;
  (b) to any work or services provided by the person, including work or services provided in circumstances which constitute exploitation within section 3(3) to (6).
(5) The consent of a person (whether an adult or a child) to any of the acts alleged to constitute holding the person in slavery or servitude, or requiring the person to perform forced or compulsory labour, does not preclude a determination that the person is being held in slavery or servitude, or required to perform forced or compulsory labour.

Procedure and Sentence

Offences under s. 1 are triable either way. The maximum penalty on conviction on indictment is life imprisonment or a fine or both; six months or an unlimited fine or both on summary conviction (s. 5(1) and (4)). Subsections 5(1)(a) and (b) create separate offences. The Court of Appeal provided guidance for sentencing under the old law in *A-G's Ref (Nos. 2, 3, 4 and 5 of 2013) (Connors)* [2013] EWCA Crim 234, [2013] 2 Cr App R (S) 71 (451). Lord Judge CJ said that, where the circumstances of the offences were broadly similar, slavery was the gravest offence, followed by servitude and then by enforced or compulsory labour, but it was wrong to suggest that a sentence for enforced or compulsory labour would always be lower than for servitude etc. Relevant considerations were the nature and degree of the deception or coercion involved in persuading the worker to join the organisation, the nature and degree of subsequent exploitation after arrival, conditions of work, level and methods of control over the workers, level and extent of vulnerability of and harm (including psychological and financial) to V, and the nature and extent of the organisation and D's role within it. These offences involved deliberate degrading of human beings. It was difficult for victims to report their plight to the authorities. When offenders were brought to justice substantial sentences were required. Offenders in this case were sentenced on conviction after a trial to terms ranging from six and a half years to four years and three years. The Court regarded the sentences as lenient but not so lenient as to require adjustment. A degree of assistance in sentencing could also be derived from *A-G's Ref (Nos. 37, 38 and 65 of 2010)* [2010] EWCA Crim 2880, [2011] 2 Cr App R (S) 31 (186) (see **B22.13**) and *A-G's Ref (Nos. 146 and 147 of 2015) (Edet)* [2016] EWCA Crim 347, a case concerned with servitude. **B22.3**

In *Rooney* [2019] EWCA Crim 681 the Court of Appeal stated that *Joyce* [2017] EWCA Crim 337 did not necessarily mark an upward trend in sentencing for every case for forced or compulsory labour, because each case depended on its own facts. What is important is the circumstances of the offending and the harm caused by it (at [72]). Sentencing in *Rooney* for the forced or compulsory labour count alone ranged from four years three months (on a plea of guilty) to ten years six months for different individuals and their relative roles in the conspiracy. The features of offending that made it necessary (at [71]) to impose lengthy sentences included the duration of the conspiracy, the number of workers, the physical conditions in which they were accommodated, the physical demands of the work they were required to undertake, and derisory pay (see also **B22.8**).

Interpretation

In interpreting the s. 1 offence, the courts must continue to have regard both to the ECHR, Article 4, and to relevant case law concerning it. It was held in *Siliadin v France* (2006) 43 EHRR 16 (287) that the Convention is a 'living instrument' and the terms used in Article 4 are themselves to be construed in accordance with their use in other treaties, such as the 1927 Slavery Convention, by which 'slavery is the status or condition of a person over whom any or **B22.4** all of the powers attaching to the right of ownership are exercised' (at [122]). Servitude includes an obligation to provide one's services that is imposed by the use of coercion, and is to be linked with the definition of slavery (at [124]).

Forced or compulsory labour is 'all work or service which is exacted from any person under the menace of any penalty and for which the person has not offered himself voluntarily' (*Siliadin v France* at [116]). The Court of Appeal reflected in *K* [2011] EWCA Crim 1691, [2013] QB 82 that in descending order of gravity, slavery is at the top of hierarchy, servitude in the middle and forced or compulsory labour at the bottom. The Court concluded (at [42]):

> Where 'forced or compulsory labour' is concerned, the menace of a penalty can be exerted in various ways. It can be direct; it can also be indirect. Constraint can be mental or physical. It can be imposed by force of circumstances. Where it is alleged that one person has been compulsorily employed by another, the level of pay he or she has received, if any, may have evidential importance. It may point to coercion; it may bear on an employee's ability to escape from his or her employer's control. On its own, however, a derisory level of wages is not tantamount to coercion.

In terms of defining exploitation, a focus on the economics of the relationship in *K* diluted the test the jury had to apply to one appropriate in an employment law context. The alleged failure of D to remunerate V at, or anywhere near, the level of national minimum wage was not determinative of guilt (at [44]).

In *Rooney* [2019] EWCA Crim 681, the Court emphasised that all circumstances must be considered, with 'low pay being a relevant factor but not in itself sufficient to amount to forced compulsory labour' (at [56]). The Court stated that there would be circumstances of exploitation which would not amount to the offence of forced compulsory labour, such as where an employer merely pays very low wages or flouts health and safety requirements.

Forced or compulsory labour as set out in *Van der Mussele v Belgium* (1984) 6 EHRR 163 is derived from ILO Convention No. 29 and is cited as 'all work or service which is exacted from any person under the menace of any penalty and for which the said person has not offered himself voluntarily'. In *Rantsev v Cyprus and Russia* (2010) 51 EHRR 1 (1), the ECtHR considered that: 'For forced or compulsory labour to arise … there must be some physical or mental constraint, as well as some overriding of the person's will'.

In *Tibet Mentes v Turkey* (2018) 67 EHRR 13 (434), the ECtHR considered circumstances of workers in airport shops who had voluntarily agreed to conditions of work involving continuous 24 hour shifts. There was no mental or physical coercion to work overtime. The ECtHR found (at [67]) that forced or compulsory labour refers to physical or mental constraint. 'Compulsory' could not refer to just any form of legal compulsion or obligation. In *Tibet Mentes* the mere possibility of being dismissed for refusal did not amount to the 'menace of penalty' for there to be an Article 4 breach. In *CN v France* (2012) Appln. 67724/09, 11 October 2012, it was recognised (at [77]) that the 'penalty' could take subtler forms, or a psychological nature, such as threats to denounce victims to the police or immigration authorities when their employment status was illegal.

No issue arose of breach of Article 4 in cases where an employee was not paid for work done, but work was performed voluntarily and entitlement to payment was not disputed (*Sokur v Ukraine* (2005) Appln. 29439/02, 26 April 2005). In *Chowdhury v Greece* (2017) Appln. 21884/15, 30 March 2017, the circumstances of irregular migrants working in the strawberry picking industry in difficult physical conditions and without wages, under the supervision of armed guards, constituted forced labour.

Persons accused of keeping others (usually vulnerable women, children or immigrants) in servitude as 'domestic slaves' may thereby commit offences such as false imprisonment or assault (*Pearson-Gaballonie* [2007] EWCA Crim 3504).

HUMAN TRAFFICKING

The Modern Slavery Act 2015, ss. 2 and 3, set out the human trafficking offence and replace the two trafficking offences under the SOA 2003 and the Asylum and Immigration (Treatment of Claimants, etc.) Act 2004. The consolidated offence relates to trafficking for all forms of exploitation. This 'human trafficking' offence extends to arranging or facilitating travel within the jurisdiction (as where victims are shipped from one house or locality to another), international travel and even travel within the borders of another country, subject to restrictions (under s. 2(7)) on the extra-territorial liability of those who are not UK nationals. The trafficking must be carried out with a view to exploitation of the persons 'trafficked', which (by s. 3) may include unlawful organ removal or sexual exploitation, as well as slavery, servitude or compulsory labour. **B22.5**

Other provisions in the Act include trafficking and preventative orders for the protection of victims of such trafficking (such as slavery and trafficking risk orders, see **D25.79**; slavery and trafficking prevention orders, see **E21.40**) and specific provision for compensating victims of human trafficking (slavery and trafficking reparation orders, see **E16.17**).

Definitions

Section 2 defines human trafficking and s. 3 explains the meaning of exploitation. **B22.6**

Modern Slavery Act 2015, ss. 2 and 3

2.—(1) A person commits an offence if the person arranges or facilitates the travel of another person ('V') with a view to V being exploited.

(2) It is irrelevant whether V consents to the travel (whether V is an adult or a child).

(3) A person may in particular arrange or facilitate V's travel by recruiting V, transporting or transferring V, harbouring or receiving V, or transferring or exchanging control over V.

(4) A person arranges or facilitates V's travel with a view to V being exploited only if—
- (a) the person intends to exploit V (in any part of the world) during or after the travel, or
- (b) the person knows or ought to know that another person is likely to exploit V (in any part of the world) during or after the travel.

(5) 'Travel' means—
- (a) arriving in, or entering, any country,
- (b) departing from any country,
- (c) travelling within any country.

(6) A person who is a UK national commits an offence under this section regardless of—
- (a) where the arranging or facilitating takes place, or
- (b) where the travel takes place.

(7) A person who is not a UK national commits an offence under this section if—
- (a) any part of the arranging or facilitating takes place in the United Kingdom, or
- (b) the travel consists of arrival in or entry into, departure from, or travel within, the United Kingdom.

3.—(1) For the purposes of section 2 a person is exploited only if one or more of the following subsections apply in relation to the person.

Slavery, servitude and forced or compulsory labour

(2) The person is the victim of behaviour—
- (a) which involves the commission of an offence under section 1, or
- (b) which would involve the commission of an offence under that section if it took place in England and Wales.

Sexual exploitation

(3) Something is done to or in respect of the person—
- (a) which involves the commission of an offence under—
  - (i) section 1(1)(a) of the Protection of Children Act 1978 (indecent photographs of children), or
  - (ii) Part 1 of the Sexual Offences Act 2003 (sexual offences), as it has effect in England and Wales, or
- (b) which would involve the commission of such an offence if it were done in England and Wales.

Removal of organs etc

(4) The person is encouraged, required or expected to do anything—
  (a) which involves the commission, by him or her or another person, of an offence under section 32 or 33 of the Human Tissue Act 2004 (prohibition of commercial dealings in organs and restrictions on use of live donors) as it has effect in England and Wales, or
  (b) which would involve the commission of such an offence, by him or her or another person, if it were done in England and Wales.

Securing services etc by force, threats or deception

(5) The person is subjected to force, threats or deception designed to induce him or her—
  (a) to provide services of any kind,
  (b) to provide another person with benefits of any kind, or
  (c) to enable another person to acquire benefits of any kind.

Securing services etc from children and vulnerable persons

(6) Another person uses or attempts to use the person for a purpose within paragraph (a), (b) or (c) of subsection (5), having chosen him or her for that purpose on the grounds that—
  (a) he or she is a child, is mentally or physically ill or disabled, or has a family relationship with a particular person, and
  (b) an adult, or a person without the illness, disability, or family relationship, would be likely to refuse to be used for that purpose.

Procedure and Jurisdiction

B22.7 An offence under the Modern Slavery Act 2015, s. 2, is triable either way. The human trafficking offence may be committed by a UK national anywhere in the world. For non-UK nationals, it may be committed where any part of the arranging, facilitation or travel takes place in the UK.

Sentence

B22.8 The maximum penalty on conviction on indictment is life imprisonment; on summary conviction, the maximum is six months and/or an unlimited fine (s. 5).

In *Zielinski* [2017] EWCA Crim 758, the Court of Appeal considered a sentence for counts of arranging or facilitating the travel of another for exploitation (s. 2) and conspiring with others to require another to perform forced or compulsory labour (s. 1). The sentence was increased to seven years. Over nine months D had tricked Polish nationals into travelling to the UK on the promise of well-paid work. Individuals were subject to threats and violence, identity cards were never returned. Living conditions in the UK were appalling and only a small percentage of earnings was handed over. The Court considered *A-G's Ref (Nos. 2, 3, 4 and 5 of 2013) (Connors)* [2013] EWCA Crim 324, [2013] 2 Cr App R (S) 71 (451) and *A-G's Ref (Nos. 37, 38 and 65 of 2010)* [2010] EWCA Crim 2880, [2011] 2 Cr App R (S) 31 (186), highlighting that all cases depend on their own particular facts. Of note was that a maximum of life applied under the Modern Slavery Act 2015, rather than 14 years (though in sentencing for a conspiracy spanning matters under legislation both pre and post the Modern Slavery Act 2015, it would be necessary to bear in mind if a significant part of the offending took place when a 14-year maximum sentence applied (*MC* [2019] EWCA Crim 1026 at [56])). The sentencing judge in *Zielinksi* had been correct in setting out the significant factors as to gravity of offending as being the level of organisation and planning, the deception in persuading the victims to travel to the UK, the duration and persistence of conspiracy, the poor accommodation provided, the methods used to control the victims, the level of vulnerability of the victims, the level of harm caused by offending and the offending being for financial gain. In *Egeresi* [2019] EWCA Crim 675 sentences were reduced to five years and four years' imprisonment for offences under the Modern Slavery Act 2015, s. 2. Economic exploitation went further than confiscation of wages, and included third party loans and overdrafts and the control of bank accounts. Factors taken into account included the significant degree of planning, deception in terms of the false promise of work and significant financial gain.

In *Iyamu* [2018] EWCA Crim 2166, [2019] 1 Cr App R (S) 19 (132) D was convicted after a trial of five offences contrary to the Modern Slavery Act 2015, s. 2, of arranging or facilitating the travel of five young women from Nigeria across north Africa and through Europe. They had been made to travel in life-threatening conditions and were forced into sexual exploitation as prostitutes. The concurrent sentences of 13 years' imprisonment imposed after trial were found to be unduly lenient. The Court of Appeal imposed sentences of 17 years' imprisonment in their place. In *Mohammed (Zakaria)* [2019] EWCA Crim 1881, an overall sentence of 12 years was appropriate in relation to a 21-year-old drug dealer who exploited children in county lines activity (seven years for five counts of human trafficking contrary to the Modern Slavery Act 2015, s. 2, and consecutive five years for conspiracy to supply). The children exploited were aged 14 and 15 and taken from Birmingham to Lincoln where they lived in poor accommodation, dealing cocaine and heroin. The Court of Appeal indicated it was not for the Court to set a sentencing guideline, but did provide relevant sentencing considerations (at [37]):

(a) Where the person whose travel was arranged with a view to exploitation was a child, the offence inevitably would be more serious than a case where the person was an adult.
(b) Where the exploitation involved the commission of serious criminal offences, the exploitation offence would be especially grave.
(c) The number of children whose travel was facilitated or arranged would be of importance.
(d) The offence would be aggravated if the same child was the subject of travel with a view to exploitation more than once.

Section 2 is an offence listed under the CJA 2003, schs. 15 and 15B, so dangerousness provisions may apply. There are powers to confiscate the assets of offenders under the POCA 2002 (see **E19**) and to make slavery and trafficking reparation orders under the Modern Slavery Act 2015, s. 8 (see **E16.17**).

Elements

The Modern Slavery Act 2015, s. 2, clarifies that V's consent to the travel (whether an adult or child) is irrelevant. A person may, in particular, arrange or facilitate V's travel by recruiting V, transporting or transferring V, harbouring or deceiving V or transferring or exchanging control of V. The language is intended to reflect the definitions of trafficking set out in the Convention on Action against Trafficking and the associated Palermo Protocol (explanatory notes to the Modern Slavery Act 2015, para. 26). **B22.9**

Internal trafficking, namely travel within the UK, is caught by the ambit of s. 2. The legislation and explanatory notes do not state what the minimum amount of travel could be. In *Ali (Yasir)* [2015] EWCA Crim 1279, [2015] 2 Cr App R 33 (457), the Court of Appeal considered (at [80]) that 'the fact that [travel] may be short does not affect whether or not the offence is committed ... It is self-evident that walking, for instance, between adjacent rooms, or other journeys involving truly minimal distances ... may well be outside the ambit of this provision because there is a clear geographical element to this offence ... It would lead to absurdity to try to stipulate, for instance, a minimum number of miles, or that the journey must be planned with a clear destination, before the provision is engaged.'

The *mens rea* of the offence is set out in s. 2(4). This is satisfied if the arranging or facilitating is done with the view to V being exploited, if either D intends to exploit V or knows or ought to know that any other person is likely to do so.

The definition of 'exploitation' in s. 3 is consistent with the combination of trafficking offences under the Asylum and Immigration (Treatment of Claimants, etc.) Act 2004, s. 4 (see **B22.11**), and the SOA 2003, s. 59A (see **B3.268**). The case law prior to the 2015 Act is still relevant when considering the definition of exploitation (see **B22.15**).

The impact of s. 3(2)b, (3)b and (4)b is to ensure that equivalent conduct committed outside England and Wales also comes within the definition of the Act, even though for jurisdictional reasons it would not amount to an offence in English law (explanatory notes, para. 32).

The type of exploitation covered in s. 3(5) includes where a person is subject to force, threats or deception designed to induce that person to provide a service of any kind, or providing a person with benefits. It includes matters such as forcing a person to engage in activities like begging and shop theft, but is not limited to criminal offences.

Associated Offence

B22.10 Under the Modern Slavery Act 2015, s. 4, a person commits an offence if the person commits any offence with the intention of committing an offence under s. 2 (including aiding, abetting, counselling or procuring such an offence). The explanatory notes (para. 36) state that this separate offence under s. 4 was intended to capture preparatory criminal conduct which amounted to a lesser offence, e.g., theft of a vehicle with the intention of using that vehicle to traffic individuals, and in order to attract the higher penalties in s. 5.

This offence is triable either way. The maximum penalty on conviction on indictment is ten years' imprisonment; on summary conviction, it is six months' imprisonment and/or an unlimited fine. However, where the offence under s. 4 is committed by kidnapping or false imprisonment, the maximum penalty is life imprisonment.

Asylum and Immigration (Treatment of Claimants, etc.) Act 2004, s. 4

B22.11 With effect from 31 July 2015, the Asylum and Immigration (Treatment of Claimants, etc.) Act 2004, s. 4, was repealed and replaced by the offence under the Modern Slavery Act 2015, s. 5 (see **B22.1** and SI 2015 No. 1476). For offences that pre-date 31 July 2015, s. 4 is applicable in relation to trafficking (the relevant amended s. 4 in force at the time should be used). The CAJA 2009, s. 71, is applicable to offences pre-dating 31 July 2015 in relation to slavery/servitude and forced labour (see the 2015 edition of this work and **B22.1**).

Asylum and Immigration (Treatment of Claimants, etc.) Act 2004, s. 4

(1A) A person ('A') commits an offence if A intentionally arranges or facilitates—
- (a) the arrival in, or entry into, the United Kingdom or another country of another person ('B'),
- (b) the travel of B within the United Kingdom or another country, or
- (c) the departure of B from the United Kingdom or another country,

with a view to the exploitation of B.

(1B) For the purposes of subsection (1A)(a) and (c) A's arranging or facilitating is with a view to the exploitation of B if (and only if)—
- (a) A intends to exploit B, after B's arrival, entry or (as the case may be) departure but in any part of the world, or
- (b) A believes that another person is likely to exploit B, after B's arrival, entry or (as the case may be) departure but in any part of the world.

(1C) For the purposes of subsection (1A)(b) A's arranging or facilitating is with a view to the exploitation of B if (and only if)—
- (a) A intends to exploit B, during or after the journey and in any part of the world, or
- (b) A believes that another person is likely to exploit B, during or after the journey and in any part of the world.

...

(4) For the purposes of this section a person is exploited if (and only if)—
- (a) he is the victim of behaviour that contravenes Article 4 of the Human Rights Convention (slavery and forced labour),
- (b) he is encouraged, required or expected to do anything—
  - (i) as a result of which he or another person would commit an offence under section 32 or 33 of the Human Tissue Act 2004 as it has effect in the law of England and Wales, or

(ii) which, were it done in England and Wales, would constitute an offence within subparagraph (i),

(c) he is subjected to force, threats or deception designed to induce him—
(i) to provide services of any kind,
(ii) to provide another person with benefits of any kind, or
(iii) to enable another person to acquire benefits of any kind, or

(d) a person uses or attempts to use him for any purpose within sub-paragraph (i), (ii) or (iii) of paragraph (c), having chosen him for that purpose on the grounds that—
(i) he is mentally or physically ill or disabled, he is young or he has a family relationship with a person, and
(ii) a person without the illness, disability, youth or family relationship would be likely to refuse to be used for that purpose.

(4A) A person who is a UK national commits an offence under this section regardless of—
(a) where the arranging or facilitating takes place, or
(b) which country is the country of arrival, entry, travel or (as the case may be) departure.

(4B) A person who is not a UK national commits an offence under this section if—
(a) any part of the arranging or facilitating takes place in the United Kingdom, or
(b) the United Kingdom is the country of arrival, entry, travel or (as the case may be) departure.

Section 4 was in force from 26 April 2013 to 30 July 2015.

Procedure and Jurisdiction An offence under s. 4 is triable either way. An immigration officer has a power of arrest in respect of this offence (Asylum and Immigration (Treatment of Claimants, etc.) Act 2004, s. 14(2)(p)). **B22.12**

Extended jurisdiction provisions apply by virtue of s. 4.

Sentence The maximum penalty on conviction on indictment is 14 years' imprisonment and/or a fine. On summary conviction, the maximum is six months and/or an unlimited fine (ss. 4(5) and 5(11)). **B22.13**

In *A-G's Ref (Nos. 37, 38 and 65 of 2010)* [2010] EWCA Crim 2880, [2011] 2 Cr App R (S) 31 (186) the Court of Appeal gave guidance on relevant factors when sentencing for s. 4 (at [17]):

> (1) the nature and degree of deception or coercion exercised upon the incoming worker; (2) the nature and degree of exploitation exercised upon the worker on arrival in the workplace; (3) the level and methods of control exercised; (4) the level of vulnerability of the incoming worker; (5) the degree of harm suffered by the worker; (6) the level of organisation and planning behind the scheme, the gain sought or achieved, and the offender's role within the organisation; (7) the number of those exploited; and (8) previous convictions for similar offences.

The Court indicated that the fact that V was a family member might constitute some mitigation, but the fact that V was a stranger would not be considered an aggravating feature (at [26]). The case concerned a conspiracy to traffic persons for the purpose of exploitation. General deterrence was appropriate when assessing the sentence. The starting point would have been six years, and sentences of four years' imprisonment were imposed allowing for double jeopardy.

In *A-G's Ref (Nos. 2, 3, 4 and 5 of 2013) (Connors)* [2013] EWCA Crim 324, [2013] 2 Cr App R (S) 71 (451) the Court of Appeal considered sentences relating to the CAJA 2009, s. 71, in relation to a count of conspiracy to require a person to perform forced or compulsory labour. There was pre-existing vulnerability of the victims, who were forced to work long hours for minimal wages and were subjected to threats and violence. The Court stated that 'sentences must make clear that ... every vulnerable victim of exploitation will be protected by the criminal law' and that 'substantial sentences are required, ... realistically addressing the criminality of the defendants' (at [10]). Sentences varying between six years and two years, three months imposed by the trial judge were not adjusted.

In *A-G's Ref (No. 35 of 2016) (Rafiq)* [2016] EWCA Crim 1368 the Court of Appeal upheld a sentence of 27 months' imprisonment for conspiring to arrange or facilitate travel contrary to s. 4(1). The Court considered that D was an 'end user', an employer who willingly colluded in

B

Part B Offences

employing five Hungarian nationals for wages of £10 per week, and (at [21]) that he did so 'for his own financial benefit in alleviating pressure on his ailing business. By the time the victims had been deceived and trafficked to this country, they were in a vulnerable position.' The Court refused to give general guidance in sentencing these cases, indicating (at [26]) that they were fact-sensitive and further that the provisions of the 2015 Act replaced s. 4.

In *Naseem* [2019] EWCA Crim 2279 the Court of Appeal noted that there was no definitive sentencing guideline in relation to s. 4 offences. In this case, a family targeted vulnerable victims, deceiving them into entering the UK and going on to use them as cheap labour. The exploitation continued over several years and was purely for their financial advantage; a good deal of planning and organisation was involved. Minimal pay was given and victims were told they owed substantial debts to the family and had to involve themselves in criminality in obtaining benefits. Victims were kept in good conditions and not subject to violence, but were encouraged to incur debt. Sentences of six and a half years were imposed for the head of the enterprise, and three and a half years and 18-month sentences sustained for other members of the family.

B22.14 **Elements** Section 4 was considered in *K* [2018] EWCA Crim 1432 in the context of teenage drug couriers used in 'county lines' drug operations. The Court of Appeal considered (at [44]) that a purposive approach was to be adopted in determining the intent of Parliament for s. 4. In particular, the design of s. 4 was to protect the vulnerable from trafficking and to comply with the State's duty under various international instruments. The words 'arranging' or 'facilitating' within the statute were necessarily broad, and it was not sensible to lay down precise definitions of these terms (at [46]). The Court identified the correct approach to the wording of s. 4(4)d, 'having chosen him for that purpose on the grounds that ... he is young'. It concluded that while a courier's youth had to be one of the reasons for the choice of that courier, it did not need to be the sole or main reason (at [55]). In addition, the word 'chosen' was to be given a natural and broad meaning, and was not simply limited to the words 'initially recruited'. Importantly, the Court highlighted that there was no need to prove a lack of consent on the part of a young courier or any element of coercion (at [60]), for the intention of the Act was to protect the young and vulnerable from their own decision-making.

B22.15 **Exploitation** As originally enacted, 'exploitation' was defined as (a) behaviour contravening the ECHR, Article 4 (slavery and forced labour); (b) encouraging, requiring or expecting V to do anything which would amount to an offence under the Human Organ Transplant Act 1989; (c) subjecting V to force, threats or deception to induce V to provide services or benefits of any kind or to enable someone else to acquire benefits; or (d) requesting or inducing V to undertake an activity because V is mentally or physically ill or disabled, young or has a family relationship, when another person without those characteristics is likely to refuse or resist. This definition was amended by the Borders, Citizenship and Immigration Act 2009, s. 54, which modified the original definition of exploitation. Specifically, the original requirement in s. 4(4)(d) of the 2004 Act for an individual to have *been requested or induced to undertake an activity* was replaced by a provision that omits altogether the requirement for a request or inducement to undertake an activity.

In *SK* [2011] EWCA Crim 1691, [2013] QB 82, D's conviction pursuant to s. 4(1) was quashed because the trial judge had failed properly to direct the jury on the effect of the ECHR, Article 4. The Court of Appeal analysed the case law of the Strasbourg Court in *Siliadin v France* (2005) 43 EHRR 16 (287) and *Rantsev v Cyprus and Russia* (2010) 51 EHRR 1 (1), and found assistance in what has been described as the hierarchy of the denial of personal autonomy to which Article 4 and thus s. 4 of the 2004 Act relate. The International Labour Organisation has developed a list of indicators of forced labour that was endorsed by the Supreme Court in *Hounga v Allen* [2014] UKSC 47, [2014] 1 WLR 2889. Where two or more of the indicators are present, the situation qualifies, according to the ILO, as forced labour. The indicators include: (a) threats or actual physical harm to the worker; (b) restriction of movement and confinement to the workplace or to a limited area; (c) debt bondage, where the worker works to pay off a debt or loan, and is not paid for working though the employer may provide food and accommodation; (d) withholding of wages or excessive wage reduction; (e) retention of passport and identity documents; (f) threat of denunciation to the authorities.

Trafficking into the UK for Sexual Exploitation

For this offence and related offences under the Sexual Offences Act 2003, see **B3.267** *et seq.* **B22.16**

CONSIDERATIONS PRIOR TO PROSECUTION OF VICTIMS OF TRAFFICKING OR SLAVERY

A victim of human trafficking is defined in Article 4 of the Council of Europe Convention on Action against Trafficking in Human Beings, 2005 and Article 2 of Directive 2011/36/EU on preventing and combating trafficking in human beings and protecting its victims ([2011] OJ L101/1) (the Trafficking Directive). **B22.17**

Abuse of Process for Cases Prior to the Modern Slavery Act 2015

The jurisdiction to stay an indictment as an abuse of process where D is a victim of human trafficking was considered by the Court of Appeal in *LM* [2010] EWCA Crim 2327, [2011] 1 Cr App R 12 (135) and *L* [2013] EWCA Crim 991, [2014] 1 All ER 113. In *LM* it was outlined that the protection principles behind such an abuse of process submission are provided for in the non-punishment provisions in Article 26 of the Convention and Article 8 of the Trafficking Directive. The Court of Appeal in *DS* [2020] EWCA Crim 285 considered that the lacuna existing prior to the Modern Slavery Act 2015 coming into force was one filled by the abuse of process doctrine. Hughes LJ, when ruling on the application of Article 26, held in *LM* (at [10]]) that prosecutors are required to conduct a three-stage exercise of judgement: (1) is there reason to believe that the person has been trafficked? If so, then (2) if there is clear evidence of a credible common-law defence the case will be discontinued in the ordinary way on evidential grounds, but, importantly, (3) even where there is not, but the offence may have been committed as a result of compulsion arising from the trafficking, prosecutors should consider whether the public interest lies in proceeding to prosecute or not. In *LM* the Court held that the word 'compelled' was not limited to the circumstances in which the English common-law defences of duress and necessity apply. In respect of (3), where D is a child (under 18 years old), the prosecutors should treat as a primary consideration whether it would be in the best interests of the child to prosecute (*L* at [20]–[21]). **B22.18**

Lord Judge CJ further held in *L* (at [17]):

> In the context of an abuse of process argument on behalf of an alleged victim of trafficking, the court will reach its own decision on the basis of the material advanced in support of and against the continuation of the prosecution. Where a court considers issues relevant to age, trafficking and exploitation, the prosecution will be stayed if the court disagrees with the decision to prosecute. The fears that the exercise of the jurisdiction to stay will be inadequate are groundless.

Lord Judge CJ had earlier stated (at [16]):

> In any case, where it is necessary to do so, whether issues of trafficking or other questions arise, the court reviews the decision to prosecute through the exercise of its jurisdiction to stay. The court protects the rights of a victim of trafficking by overseeing the decision of the prosecutor and refusing to countenance any prosecution which fails to acknowledge and address the victim's subservient situation, and the international obligations to which the United Kingdom is a party. The role of the court replicates its role in relation to *agent provocateurs*. It stands between the prosecution and the victim of trafficking where the crimes are committed as an aspect of the victim's exploitation (see *R v Loosely A-G's Ref (No. 3 of 2000)* [[2001] EWCA Crim 1214, [2001] 2 Cr App R 26 (472)] ...).

Abuse of Process for Cases Following the Modern Slavery Act 2015

B22.19 In *DS* [2020] EWCA Crim 285, the Court of Appeal considered that the jurisdiction to stay proceedings as an abuse of process was an important, but limited power of a criminal court. The Court noted that for cases prior to the Modern Slavery Act 2015 there was a lacuna, which the courts filled by the abuse of process doctrine. However, for cases following enactment of s. 45, the responsibility for deciding the facts relevant to the status of an individual as a victim of trafficking is 'unquestionably that of the jury'. The Court concluded (at [40]):

> Cases to which the MSA 2015 applied should proceed on the basis they will be stayed only if an abuse of process as conventionally defined is found. This involves two categories of abuse, as is well known. The first is that a fair trial is not possible and the second is that it would be wrong to try the defendant because of some misconduct by the state in bringing about the prosecution.

The Court made the fundamental observation (at [39(ii)]):

> The Convention and the Directive are not directly applicable in domestic law. It is for Parliament and the executive to decide how to give effect to the international obligations of the United Kingdom, and where it does so by legislation the function of the court is to apply that legislation. The Directive required Member States of the European Union to put in place arrangements that reflect its requirements. We have not identified any clear gap between the provisions of the 2015 Act and those obligations, and in our judgment the CPS Guidance means that the CPS is 'entitled' not to prosecute for the purposes of Article 8 of the Directive.

In considering Article 4, the Court of Appeal concluded that the positive obligation on the State to protect victims of trafficking was to 'endeavour to provide for the physical safety of victims of trafficking while in their territories and to establish comprehensive policies and programmes to prevent and combat trafficking' (*Rantsev v Cyprus and Russia* (2010) 51 EHRR 1 (1)). It was not expressed in terms of non-prosecution. *DS* concerned forced or compulsory labour, namely the lowest level of gravity of oppression, below 'slavery' and 'servitude'. There was no basis for deriving a positive obligation not to prosecute victims of forced or compulsory labour. If any such obligation did exist it would be heavily qualified. There was no basis for concluding that the qualifications found in the common law of duress, in s. 45 of the Modern Slavery Act 2015, and the CPS Guidance were inadequate so that there was a violation of any such positive obligation under Article 4 of the ECHR that might exist.

The Supreme Court in *MS (Pakistan) v Secretary of State for the Home Department* [2020] UKSC 9, [2020] 1 WLR 1373 (at [34]) considered that there is a positive obligation under Article 4 to take operational measures to protect an individual where the authorities were aware or ought to have been aware of the circumstances giving rise to a credible suspicion that an identified individual had been or was at real and immediate risk of being trafficked or exploited.

National Referral Mechanism

B22.20 The Secretary of State provides for a formal identification of a victim of trafficking, known as the National Referral Mechanism. Suspected victims are referred by first responders (which include police, immigration authorities, local authorities and certain NGOs) to the Single Competent Authority for a decision to be made on whether the individual is a victim of modern slavery. The identification of an individual as a victim of trafficking is a two-stage process. The first part is the 'reasonable grounds decision', acting as an initial filter, the Single Competent Authority deciding whether it was 'reasonable to believe' that the person was a victim of trafficking on the information available. The standard of proof is that the Single Competent Authority 'suspects but cannot prove' that a person was a potential victim. The second stage involves a further inquiry and leads to a 'conclusive grounds decision' as to whether the person is in fact a victim, and the standard of proof applied at this stage is the balance of probabilities (*R (MN) v Secretary of State for the Home Department* [2018] EWHC 3268 (QB)). Further details on methods of referral into the National Referral Mechanism are set out in the Home Office's *Statutory Guidance for England and Wales for the Modern Slavery Act 2015* (March 2020, tinyurl.com/y6v5guu7). The

CPS is not a first responder. If a prosecutor comes to the conclusion that a suspect should be referred to the Single Competent Authority for a National Referral Mechanism decision this must be done through the police. The Single Competent Authority aims to make reasonable grounds decisions within five working days of receiving a referral. In *R (DS) v Secretary of State for the Home Department* [2019] EWHC 3046 (Admin), the policy that referral for reconsideration of a negative decision could only be made by a first responder was considered to be unlawful, by not permitting reconsideration requests from parties other than a first responder. That entailed an abdication of the State's responsibility to perform the identification duty in cases where a negative decision had to be reconsidered in the light of relevant new material. The National Referral Mechanism correctly included a discretionary power to reopen negative decisions which had to be exercised in accordance with the duty to identify victims, or it would dilute the protection afforded by way of the Council of Europe Convention on Action against Trafficking in Human Beings and the ECHR, Article 4. In *L* the Court held (at [28]) that, when considering the weight to be placed on such decisions:

> Whether the concluded decision of the competent authority is favourable or adverse to the individual it will have been made by an authority vested with the responsibility for investigating these issues, and although the court is not bound by the decision, unless there is evidence to contradict it, or significant evidence that was not considered, it is likely that the criminal courts will abide by it.

The Court of Appeal reinforced the decision of *L* in *GS* [2018] EWCA Crim 1824, [2019] 1 Cr App R 7 (84) by considering that decisions by the First-tier Tribunal and the Competent Authority as to whether an individual is a victim of trafficking do not bind prosecutors or the court, but would be 'respected (subject to submissions as to their basis or limitations) unless there is a good reason not to follow them' (at [76]). See also *O* [2019] EWCA Crim 1389 at [18] where the Court emphasised that the decision of a First-tier Tribunal judge would likely be followed where there was no evidence to contradict it. In *JXP* [2019] EWCA Crim 1280, the Court noted (at [54]) that 'the Competent Authority is a specialist authority with particular expertise and knowledge in this area of trafficking'. The Court accepted the conclusion of the Competent Authority, notwithstanding finding that an important aspect of D's account was in their view deserving of a more rigorous analysis than appeared in the Minute. The CPS guidance (see **B22.22**) sets out that a conclusive grounds decision by the Single Competent Authority is to be taken into account in deciding whether D is a victim of trafficking and whether the offending has a very close nexus with the exploitation. No case before the Court of Appeal has yet determined if the decision of the Single Competent Authority is admissible before a jury.

It is important that D understands that even after receiving a negative conclusive grounds decision, it is still possible to mount a defence under the Modern Slavery Act 2015, s. 45, before a jury (*S* [2020] EWCA Crim 765, at [36]–[39]). The Court of Appeal reflected that the nuances of the word 'conclusive' may be lost even on well-educated lay people fluent in English, let alone a foreign national not fluent in the language.

In *MS (Pakistan) v Secretary of State for the Home Department* [2020] UKSC 9, [2020] 1 WLR 1373, the Supreme Court held (at [11]) that immigration tribunals are in no way bound by the decision of the National Referral Mechanism.

B22.21 Where D has not come forward as a victim of trafficking until after conviction and sentence, the Court of Appeal has still quashed the conviction as unsafe on the premise that had the evidence been made known to the prosecution at the material time, no prosecution would have been brought (*O* [2011] EWCA Crim 2226; *LZ* [2012] EWCA Crim 1867). *GB* [2020] EWCA Crim 2 concerned an appeal where a guilty plea had been entered. The Court considered (at [36]) that if a 'guilty plea is entered without due consideration of the relevant principles concerning the criminal liability of victims of trafficking, the plea is not regarded as an impediment to the court's consideration of appeals'. See also *S* [2014] EWCA Crim 2919, where the Court of Appeal accepted the decision of the First-tier Tribunal that an appellant's life in the UK was 'entirely consistent with the manner in which such vulnerable people are trafficked into this country and then held captive and forced into domestic servitude'. In *GS* a conviction for drug importation was sought to be appealed more than nine years after the conviction in 2007. The Court considered that this was a 'change in law' case, given there had been a material change in law and practice concerning the rights of victims of trafficking since 2007, one example being the stark difference in the guidance published by the CPS. A 'substantial injustice' would be required in terms of granting 'exceptional' leave. And here (distinct from *Ordu* [2017] EWCA Crim 4, [2017] 1 Cr App R 21 (319)) a 'substantial injustice' was shown, because of the risk the conviction presented to D's immigration status. Unlike *GS*, in *O* [2019] EWCA Crim 1389 the Court of Appeal concluded that a conviction relating to July 2008 and an appeal nine years afterwards did not amount to a 'change in law' case. The Court considered that 'substantial injustice' did exist where, because of the conviction, D suffered continued detrimental impact in obtaining employment, making applications for citizenship and the ability to accompany her children on school trips. In *GB* [2020] EWCA Crim 2 the Court concluded that substantial injustice was demonstrated where D was at continuing risk of being re-trafficked and the conviction had potential implications for future Home Office decisions on her status (at [37]–[38]).

Guidance

B22.22 The CPS has published detailed guidance on 'Human Trafficking, Smuggling and Slavery' (30 April 2020, tinyurl.com/y8fejjox) which considers the prosecutorial discretion concerning accused potential victims of trafficking and provides examples of offences most frequently committed by victims of trafficking in its section on 'Indicators of trafficking'. These offences are wide reaching and include benefit fraud, drug production and identity offences. The CPS guidance sets out that 'prosecutors should have regard to the duty of the prosecutor to make proper enquiries in criminal prosecutions involving individuals who may be victims of trafficking or slavery'. The guidance outlines that inquiries should be made by advising the law enforcement agency which investigated the original offence that it must investigate D's trafficking and slavery situation; and advising that D is referred through the National Referral Mechanism for victim identification (see **B22.20**). The assessment process to be adopted by prosecutors in applying the Full Code Test includes the following questions:

1. Is there a reason to believe that the person is a victim of trafficking or slavery?
2. Is there clear evidence of a credible common law of duress?
3. Is there clear evidence of a statutory defence under s. 45 of the MSA 2015?
4. Is it in the public interest to prosecute? (Even where there is no clear evidence of duress or s. 45 defence, or it is an offence under schedule 4 this must still be considered.)

The guidance highlights that where a decision has already been taken to charge and prosecute a suspect, but further credible evidence comes to light, e.g. in mitigation or a pre-sentence report, then prosecutors should seek an adjournment and ensure that the suspect is referred through the National Referral Mechanism and the steps in the assessment process are carried out. See *N* [2019] EWCA Crim 984 where the Court of Appeal considered that there was sufficient information that D was a victim of trafficking. The defence advocate should have raised an issue; it would also have been open to the judge to raise the issue and the prosecutor should have asked for an adjournment.

All law enforcement officers are able to refer potential victims of slavery/trafficking to the National Referral Mechanism. Such steps must be taken regardless of whether there has been any indication of a guilty plea. An adult must consent to being referred; no consent is required in relation to a child.

B22.23 An updated practice note has been published by the Law Society on 'Victims of modern slavery' (*30 April 2020, tinyurl.com/rqrpzrx*). This contains guidance on referral mechanisms into the National Referral Mechanism and issues of client confidentiality.

STATUTORY DEFENCE UNDER THE MODERN SLAVERY ACT, s. 45

The Modern Slavery Act 2015, s. 45, provides a statutory defence for slavery or trafficking victims who commit an offence. **B22.24**

Modern Slavery Act 2015, s. 45

(1) A person is not guilty of an offence if—
   (a) the person is aged 18 or over when the person does the act which constitutes the offence,
   (b) the person does that act because the person is compelled to do it,
   (c) the compulsion is attributable to slavery or to relevant exploitation, and
   (d) a reasonable person in the same situation as the person and having the person's relevant characteristics would have no realistic alternative to doing that act.

(2) A person may be compelled to do something by another person or by the person's circumstances.

(3) Compulsion is attributable to slavery or to relevant exploitation only if—
   (a) it is, or is part of, conduct which constitutes an offence under section 1 or conduct which constitutes relevant exploitation, or
   (b) it is a direct consequence of a person being, or having been, a victim of slavery or a victim of relevant exploitation.

(4) A person is not guilty of an offence if—
   (a) the person is under the age of 18 when the person does the act which constitutes the offence,
   (b) the person does that act as a direct consequence of the person being, or having been, a victim of slavery or a victim of relevant exploitation, and
   (c) a reasonable person in the same situation as the person and having the person's relevant characteristics would do that act.

(5) For the purposes of this section—
   'relevant characteristics' means age, sex and any physical or mental illness or disability;
   'relevant exploitation' is exploitation (within the meaning of section 3) that is attributable to the exploited person being, or having been, a victim of human trafficking.

(6) In this section references to an act include an omission.

(7) Subsections (1) and (4) do not apply to an offence listed in Schedule 4.

(8) The Secretary of State may by regulations amend Schedule 4.

For the s. 45 defence to apply, the first requirement is that the person has done 'the act which constitutes the offence'. If the defence is raised on the evidence, it is for the prosecution to prove that it does not apply. In *MK* [2018] EWCA Crim 667, [2019] QB 86 the Court of Appeal stated (at [45]):

> [Section 45] does not implicitly require the defendant to bear the legal or persuasive burden of proof of any element of the defence. The burden on a defendant is evidential. It is for the defendant to raise evidence of each of those elements and for the prosecution to disprove one or more of them to the criminal standard in the usual way.

See also the discussion at **A3.54** and the *Crown Court Compendium* (July 2020), ch. 18-6, as to the application of the Modern Slavery Act 2015, s. 45. For victims of trafficking or slavery the CPS guidance on 'Human Trafficking, Smuggling and Slavery' (see **B22.22**) outlines considerations that should be taken into account. Victims of trafficking may include UK nationals and non-UK nationals. In relation to county lines offending, consider CPS typology (see **B22.30**).

The 'relevant characteristics' identified in s. 45(5) mirror the common-law position in relation to duress and *Bowen* [1996] 2 Cr App R 157. However an issue may arise as to whether a 'reasonable person in the same situation' as D should be assessed in the context of D's experience of slavery or having been a victim of human trafficking. See the *Crown Court Compendium* (July 2020), ch. 18-6, for sample directions. PTPH forms now ask defence advocates to specifically highlight if it is alleged that D is a victim of modern slavery. This is critical to ensure that consideration is given to the public interest test at an early stage, and if a defence under the Modern Slavery Act 2015, s. 45, is relied upon.

B22.25 Schedule 4 to the Act specifies a long list of offences to which the statutory defence under s. 45 does not apply. This includes, but is not limited to, murder, manslaughter, kidnap, false imprisonment and perverting the course of justice. In relation to the OAPA 1861, the defence does not apply to various offences including ss. 16, 18 and 20 (e.g., on an indictment containing one count of actual bodily harm and one of s. 20 grievous bodily harm, the defence under s. 45 would apply to the former but not the latter). Most firearms offences, most sexual offences under the SOA 2003, robbery and burglary with intent to inflict grievous bodily harm, arson and death by dangerous driving are also excluded from the application of s. 45.

The Modern Slavery Act 2015 offences under ss. 1 and 2 (slavery/servitude and forced labour, and human trafficking) are not excluded. In relation to immigration offences, the s. 45 defence cannot apply to the Immigration Act 1971, s. 25 (assisting unlawful immigration to a Member State). Where s. 45 does not apply, other options available include the EU Trafficking Directive, representations as to whether the prosecution is in the public interest, and abuse of process.

'Compulsion' or 'compelled'

B22.26 These terms are set out in the non-punishment provisions of the Trafficking Directive, Article 8, and the Convention on Action against Trafficking in Human Beings 2005, Article 26. The Explanatory Report to the Trafficking Convention interprets 'compelled' as 'the requirement that victims have been compelled to be involved in unlawful activities shall be understood as comprising, at a minimum, victims that have been subject to any of the illicit means referred to in Article 4 (the trafficking definition), when such involvement results from compulsion'. The Modern Slavery Act 2015, s. 45(2), provides that a person can be compelled to commit an offence either by another person or by that person's own circumstances (explanatory notes, para. 220).

In *Joseph* [2017] EWCA Crim 36, [2017] 1 Cr App R 33 (486), the Court of Appeal considered that s. 45 was enacted by Parliament without providing for retrospective protection and as a result the law of duress does not need to be developed in line with s. 45 (at [28]). The Court stated that the decision of the competent authority as to whether a person had been trafficked for the purposes of exploitation was not binding on the court (at [20(viii)]).

B22.27 The trafficking *acquis* distinguishes between child and adult victims of trafficking. The definition of trafficking and the application of the non-punishment provisions set out in the Convention on Action against Trafficking in Human Beings are markedly different in key respects. A child need only show, *inter alia*, that he or she was recruited, moved, transferred or harboured for the purpose of exploitation in order to establish the fact of being a trafficked child. A child does not need to establish that any of these elements (including exploitation) was achieved through, *inter alia*, force or coercion. A child will be a trafficked child if the criminality is bound up in the trafficking experience (*L* [2013] EWCA Crim 991, [2014] 1 All ER 113).

In *Joseph* [2017] EWCA Crim 36, [2017] 1 Cr App R 33 (486), when determining whether there is a nexus between the crime committed by the child defendant and the trafficking, the Court of Appeal held that a child does not need to establish that he or she was compelled to commit the criminal offence (at [22] and [35]). In *MK* [2018] EWCA Crim 667, [2019] QB 86, the Court stated (at [24]):

> Whereas in the case of an adult the defence requires that a reasonable person in the same situation with the same relevant characteristics would have 'no realistic alternative' to doing the criminal act, in the case of a child it simply requires that a reasonable person in the same situation and with the child's relevant characteristics would do what the child did.

Age Dispute Issues

B22.28 Where any issue as to D's age arises, it must be addressed at the first court appearance. Alternatively, issues should be raised at the PTPH and appropriate adaptations made to ensure potential problems are not overlooked (*L* [2013] EWCA Crim 991, [2013] 2 Cr App R 23

(247) at [25], [31] and [32]). The Children and Young Persons Act 1933, s. 99(1), directs the court to make 'due inquiry' as to D's age (and see E7.2).

Due inquiry includes such evidence as may be forthcoming at the hearing of the case. Effective participation by a child in relation to the 'due inquiry' is essential and likely to require adjournments. See also the Merton guidelines as summarised in *MVN v Greenwich London Borough Council* [2015] EWHC 1942 (Admin). Note that in *R (ZM) v Croydon London Borough Council* [2016] UT 559, in a judicial review capacity the Upper Tribunal concluded that age cannot be accurately assessed from dental X-rays and maturity.

If at the end of a 'due inquiry' D's age remains in doubt, then D must be treated as a child (see Article 10(3) of the Council of Europe Convention on Action Against Trafficking in Human Beings, *L* at [25], and the Modern Slavery Act 2015, s. 51).

Even if a court determines that an individual should be considered as an adult defendant, it does not prevent the fact that the individual is under 18 from being raised at trial in the context of a s. 45 defence.

Nexus

In *GS* [2018] EWCA Crim 1824, [2019] 1 Cr App R 7 (84) the Court of Appeal summarised the principles that apply following *LM, L* and *Joseph* [2017] EWCA Crim 36, [2017] 1 Cr App R 33 (486) in relation to the discretion to prosecute victims of trafficking. The Court confirmed (at [76]) that neither 'Article 26 of ECAT nor Article 8 of the Directive confers a blanket immunity from prosecution on victims of trafficking'. Further, that the UK's international obligations require 'careful and fact sensitive exercise by prosecutors of their discretion as to whether it was in the public interest to prosecute a victim of trafficking'. In exercising that discretion, the Court considered there was no closed list of factors bearing on the prosecutor's discretion to proceed and that: **B22.29**

> Factors obviously impacting on the discretion to prosecute go to the nexus between the crime committed by the Defendant and the trafficking. If there is no reasonable nexus between the offence and the trafficking then, generally, there is no reason why (on trafficking grounds) the prosecution should not proceed. If there is a nexus, in some cases the level of compulsion will be such that it will not be in the public interest for the prosecution to proceed. In other cases, it will be necessary to consider whether the compulsion was continuing and what, if any, reasonable alternatives were available for the VOT. There will be cases where a decision to prosecute will be justified but due allowance can be made for mitigating factors at the sentencing stage.

An assessment that a person is a victim of trafficking does not necessarily extinguish culpability. In *EK* [2018] EWCA Crim 2961 it was accepted that D had been a victim of trafficking at the material time of her convictions. The convictions concerned conspiracy to control prostitution for gain, possessing false identity documents and removing criminal property. Yet in this instance the Court of Appeal concluded that her position as a victim of trafficking did not extinguish her culpability or so diminish it as to cast doubt on the decision to prosecute. In *O* [2019] EWCA Crim 1389, D had been subjected to sexual exploitation prior to entry into the UK and was then coerced into commission of criminal offences involving fraudulent cashing of travellers cheques and use of a false identity card. The Court considered (at [37]) that the offences took place in the 'context of a life of sexual exploitation and repeated trafficking', and concluded that 'they are both integral to, and consequent upon, the trafficking and exploitation so as to extinguish culpability'. In evaluating such trafficking, this could include events which took place within the UK. The *Crown Court Compendium* (July 2020), ch. 18-6, highlights that the judge, as well as the defence and prosecution, must be alert to the possibility that D is a victim of modern slavery or trafficking. Even if not expressly raised by D, it may become apparent from the evidence. See also *N* [2019] EWCA Crim 984, where a conviction was quashed by the Court of Appeal, noting that there was sufficient information before the Court that D was a victim of trafficking when he pleaded guilty. The Court considered this should have been apparent to the defence advocate or could have been raised by the judge as an issue, and the prosecution should have followed the guidance and asked for an adjournment in order to make proper inquiries, for referral into the National Referral Mechanism to take place. If that had been done, D would likely have been successful in the s. 45 defence. In *GB* [2020] EWCA Crim 2, the Court considered there to be a clear nexus between the use of a false passport and D's experience as a victim of trafficking. She was a victim of sexual exploitation and was attempting to travel to Canada from Italy in order to escape from her traffickers when she passed through the jurisdiction. She was six months pregnant at the time and highly vulnerable. The Court considered it unrealistic to expect D to extricate herself from the person helping her to escape, or that she would be familiar with the immigration rules and her ability to claim asylum in the UK. The Court found that D was under a compulsion in the 'broad sense', which meant that her culpability was extinguished as a matter of reality and that it was not in the public interest for her to be prosecuted [at (40)].

County Lines Offending

B22.30 In *K* [2018] EWCA Crim 143 the Court of Appeal highlighted (at [1]) the 'worrying development' of the use of county lines, identifying that:

> To avoid detection and promote the supply of drugs, drugs dealers run 'county drug lines' using couriers, often teenagers to take drugs from a large city to towns some distance away. The use of county drug lines is a very worrying development and is a method of supplying drugs that is becoming increasingly prevalent.

For further guidance see CPS, *County Lines Typology* (June 2018, tinyurl.com/y5hxn69l). This details the approach to be taken in criminal investigations, prosecutions and safeguarding of vulnerable persons subjected to county lines offending. In addition the CPS guidance on 'Human Trafficking, Smuggling and Slavery' (see **B22.22**) considers county lines offending and sets out that 'where there may be consideration of charge and prosecution of vulnerable children or adults, prosecutors should consider applying the statutory defence or CPS policy on the non-prosecution of suspects who may be victims of trafficking'. Best practice guidance has been issued by the Ministry of Justice for YOTs and frontline practitioners (1 October 2019, tinyurl.com/ybvvqlx5). It provides the template for referral pathways when responding and safeguarding children involved in county lines. The guidance stresses that a collaborative multi-agency approach is paramount. Child criminal exploitation is defined as occurring where 'an individual or group takes advantage of power to coerce, control, manipulate or deceive a child or young person under the age of 18. The victim may have been criminally exploited even if the activity appears consensual.' Indicators of county lines exploitation referenced by the MOJ Guidance includes:

(a) persistently going missing from school or home or care;
(b) children travelling to locations they have no obvious connection with;
(c) unexplained acquisition of money, clothes or mobile phones;
(d) relationships with controlling or older individuals and groups;
(e) suspicion of physical assault or unexplained injuries;
(f) carrying weapons;
(g) gang association or isolation from peers.

Anonymity Orders

B22.31 Consideration should be given in cases concerning victims of trafficking and modern slavery to anonymity orders. On the particular facts of *L and N* [2017] EWCA Crim 2129, the Court of Appeal granted anonymity orders in each case on the basis of risk of reprisals to the applicants and their families for having given an account of their trafficking (at [33] and [52]). However, the Court emphasised that anonymity orders could only be justified where strictly necessary (at [13]) and declined to give general guidance on them (at [15]). An anonymity order was again provided under the Contempt of Court Act 1981, s. 11, where in *S* [2020] EWCA Crim 765, an individual was recognised as a victim of trafficking and had named the two men who compelled him to look after cannabis plants, opening him up to the risk of reprisals. In *O* [2019] EWCA Crim 1389, the Court granted an anonymity order to an applicant whose ECHR, Article 3, rights had been engaged. The Court took into account information the applicant had provided about her trafficking, the violence and repercussions she had faced and the potential risks to her and her children. In addition, if D is charged on the same indictment with an individual possibly responsible for D's trafficking or relevant exploitation, practitioners should consider the possibility of severance as well.

ENTRY WITHOUT LEAVE

Immigration Act 1971, s. 24 B22.32

(1) A person who is not a British citizen shall be guilty of an offence punishable on summary conviction with [an unlimited fine] or with imprisonment for not more than six months, or with both, in any of the following cases—
 (a) if contrary to this Act he knowingly enters the United Kingdom in breach of a deportation order or without leave;
 (b) if, having only a limited leave to enter or remain in the United Kingdom, he knowingly either—
  (i) remains beyond the time limited by the leave; or
  (ii) fails to observe a condition of the leave;
 (c) if, having lawfully entered the United Kingdom without leave by virtue of section 8(1) above, he remains without leave beyond the time allowed by section 8(1);
 (d) if, without reasonable excuse, he fails to comply with any requirement imposed on him under Schedule 2 to this Act to report to a medical officer of health, or to attend, or submit to a test or examination, as required by such an officer;
 ...
 (f) if he disembarks in the United Kingdom from a ship or aircraft after being placed on board under Schedule 2 or 3 to this Act with a view to his removal from the United Kingdom;
 (g) if he embarks in contravention of a restriction imposed by or under an Order in Council under section 3(7) of this Act;
 (h) if the person is on immigration bail within the meaning of Schedule 10 to the Immigration Act 2016 and, without reasonable excuse, the person breaches a bail condition within the meaning of that Schedule.

Procedure

An immigration officer may arrest without warrant any person who has committed or attempted to commit any offence under the Immigration Act 1971, s. 24 (except s. 24(1)(d)), or whom the officer has reasonable grounds for suspecting of committing or attempting to commit such an offence (s. 28A(1) and (2)). B22.33

An offence under the Immigration Act 1971, s. 24, is a summary only offence (s. 24(1)). An extended time-limit for prosecution applies to offences under s. 24(1)(a) and (c) (ss. 24(3) and 28).

Extended time limits for prosecution apply (s. 28(1A)) of six months from the date of committing the breach of an immigration bail condition or within three months of first having been arrested for that breach (if this is later).

Sentence

The maximum sentence for illegal entry and any other offence under the Immigration Act 1971, s. 24, is six months' imprisonment and/or an unlimited fine (s. 24(1)). B22.34

Elements

A person who is a British citizen cannot commit this offence. The offence of illegal entry requires actual entry. It is committed only if no leave at all was granted. The offence requires proof that D B22.35

knowingly entered the UK without leave of an immigration officer or in breach of a deportation order. The offence is committed on the day of entry only and is not a continuing offence.

The burden of proof for the offence is normally on the prosecution. However, an exception is made in cases brought within six months of the date of entry. In those cases the burden is on D to show, on the balance of probabilities, that D entered the UK legally (Immigration Act 1971, s. 24(4)(b)). It is arguable that this reversal of the legal burden of proof is contrary to the presumption of innocence contained in the ECHR, Article 6(2), particularly since leave to enter may be granted orally (Immigration (Leave to Enter and Remain) Order 2000 (SI 2000 No. 1161), art. 8(3)) and so might be difficult to prove. On the presumption of innocence and Article 6(2), see further **F3.18**.

The offence of overstaying under s. 24(1)(b) is committed at any time when the immigrant knows that leave has expired but remains in the UK, but can be charged only once for any period of overstay (s. 24(1A)). Overstaying requires proof of limited leave, the expiry date of this leave and proof of knowledge of remaining beyond the date of expiry of leave. If, before the original grant of leave expired, D had made an application to the Secretary of State for an extension of leave, before the original grant of leave expired, the original period of leave is deemed to have been extended by virtue of the Immigration Act 1971, s. 3C, until the application is finally determined. Final determination of an application encompasses any subsequent appeal against a refusal to extend leave.

OBTAINING LEAVE BY DECEPTION

B22.36 **Immigration Act 1971, s. 24A**

(1) A person who is not a British citizen is guilty of an offence if, by means which include deception by him:—
  (a) he obtains or seeks to obtain leave to enter or remain in the United Kingdom; or
  (b) he secures or seeks to secure the avoidance, postponement or revocation of enforcement action against him.

(2) 'Enforcement action', in relation to a person, means—
  (a) the giving of directions for his removal from the United Kingdom ('directions') under Schedule 2 to this Act or section 10 of the Immigration and Asylum Act 1999;
  (b) the making of a deportation order against him under section 5 of this Act; or
  (c) his removal from the United Kingdom in consequence of directions or a deportation order.

Procedure

B22.37 An immigration officer may arrest without warrant any person who has committed or attempted to commit any offence under the Immigration Act 1971, s. 24A, or whom the officer has reasonable grounds for suspecting of committing or attempting to commit such an offence (s. 28A(1) and (2)). The offence of deception can be committed in a control zone in France or Belgium, and powers of arrest are exercisable by police there (Nationality, Immigration and Asylum Act 2002 (Juxtaposed Controls) Order 2003 (SI 2003 No. 2818), arts. 11 to 13).

The deception offence under s. 24A is triable either way (s. 24A(3)).

Indictment

B22.38 *Statement of Offence*

Obtaining leave to enter or remain in the United Kingdom by deception contrary to section 24A(1) and (3) of the Immigration Act 1971.

Particulars of Offence

A on the … day of …/on a day between the … day of … and the … day of … not being a British citizen, obtained/sought to obtain leave to enter or remain in the United Kingdom/the avoidance, postponement or revocation of enforcement against him by means of deception namely [*specify deception*].

Sentence

The maximum penalty for the deception offence when tried summarily is six months' imprisonment and/or an unlimited fine; on conviction on indictment the maximum is two years' imprisonment and/or a fine (s. 24A(3)). **B22.39**

If D is convicted or pleads guilty before a magistrates' court in respect of the s. 24A offence, it is likely that D will be committed to the Crown Court for sentence. For all but the most minor offences, an immediate custodial sentence can be expected.

The Court of Appeal held in *Heng Pit Ding* [2010] EWCA Crim 1979, [2011] 1 Cr App R (S) 91 (546) that the 1971 Act did not draw a distinction between the use of deception to obtain entry and the use of deception to remain in the UK and therefore there was no distinction for sentencing purposes. The Court held that the mischief in both types of cases was that the conduct undermined the system of border control. The Court reaffirmed the sentencing guidance in *Ali (Nasir)* [2001] EWCA Crim 2874, [2002] 2 Cr App R (S) 32 (115), which endorsed what Rose LJ stated in *Daljit Singh* [1999] 1 Cr App R (S) 490:

> ... although a plea of guilt will always attract an appropriate discount, previous good character and personal circumstances of mitigation are of very limited value in cases of this kind, which should generally be sentenced on a deterrent basis ... Extensive or sophisticated alteration of a passport will always be an aggravating feature.
>
> ... cases involving the use of false passports will almost always merit a significant period of custody ... this will usually be within the range of six to nine months, even on a guilty plea of a person of good character.

Where the purpose of the entry is to claim asylum, different considerations apply. In *R (K) v Croydon Crown Court* [2005] EWHC 478 (Admin), [2005] 2 Cr App R (S) 96 (578), a four-month detention and training order imposed by a youth court on a 17-year-old asylum seeker who used deception on entry was quashed as wrong in principle, and a conditional discharge substituted. The Divisional Court emphasised the role and the power of the agent in that case.

In *Kishientine* [2004] EWCA Crim 3352, [2005] 2 Cr App R (S) 28 (156), it was considered that the apparent strength of an asylum claim should not be taken into account by the court where that claim had not yet been determined by the Secretary of State. Nor should it treat D's imminent removal as justifying a lower sentence than would otherwise have been given (*A-G's Ref (Nos. 1 and 6 of 2008)* [2008] EWCA Crim 677, [2008] 2 Cr App R (S) 99 (557)).

Bashir [2019] EWCA Crim 1229 concerned the fraudulent sale to individuals who wished to enter or remain in the UK of a 'confirmation of acceptance to study' at two colleges at which no education was to be offered. The Court of Appeal found that the fraudulent activity may not have extended over a long period of time but the attempts made were determined, involved relatively large sums of money and were a significant abuse of the points-based system of the Immigration Rules. Sentences were uplifted to eight years, three years and 11 months and four years respectively.

Elements

A person who is a British citizen cannot commit this offence. **B22.40**

The deception offence can be committed by seeking to enter as well as by actually entering, and also embraces action taken to remain in the UK and to prevent or defer removal. It has been used against failed asylum seekers who have sought asylum again under a different identity (*Nagmadeen* [2003] EWCA Crim 2004). The deception must be material (but it does not have to be the sole means of obtaining entry, etc.) and must be by D personally.

There are also offences relating to false registration cards and immigration stamps under ss. 26A and 26B of the 1971 Act.

Defences

B22.41 The statutory defence under the Immigration and Asylum Act 1999, s. 31 (see **B22.73**), applies to this offence as well as the Modern Slavery Act 2012, s. 45 (see **B22.24**).

FACILITATING UNLAWFUL IMMIGRATION

B22.42 **Immigration Act 1971, s. 25**

(1) A person commits an offence if he—
- (a) does an act which facilitates the commission of a breach or attempted breach of immigration law by an individual who is not a citizen of the European Union,
- (b) knows or has reasonable cause for believing that the act facilitates the commission of a breach or attempted breach of immigration law by the individual, and
- (c) knows or has reasonable cause for believing that the individual is not a citizen of the European Union.

Section 25(1)(a) and (c) will be amended by the Immigration, Nationality and Asylum (EU Exit) Regulations 2019 (SI 2019 No. 745), reg. 4, from a date to be appointed. The words 'not a citizen of the European Union' will be amended to read 'neither a citizen of the European Union, nor a national of the United Kingdom'.

Procedure and Jurisdiction

B22.43 An immigration officer may arrest without warrant a person who has committed or is attempting to commit this offence, or whom the officer has reasonable grounds for suspecting of committing or attempting to commit the offence (Immigration Act 1971, s. 28A(3)).

The offence is triable either way (s. 25(6)). The offence under s. 25(1) of assisting unlawful immigration applies to things done whether inside or outside the UK (s. 25(4)). The definition of a Member State under s. 25(7) includes any Member State of the EU (s. 25(2)) or Iceland and Norway, which are treated as Member States for this purpose by virtue of art. 2 of the Immigration (Assisting Unlawful Immigration) (Section 25 List of Schengen Acquis States) Order 2004 (SI 2004 No. 2877). Following amendments to be made on a date to be appointed under the Immigration, Nationality and Asylum (EU Exit) Regulations 2019, the definition of a national of the UK will include a British citizen, a person who is a British subject by virtue of Part 4 of the British Nationality Act 1981 with a right of abode in the UK and a person who is a British overseas territories citizen by virtue of a connection with Gibraltar.

Indictment

B22.44 *Statement of Offence*

Assisting unlawful immigration to the United Kingdom contrary to section 25 of the Immigration Act 1971.

Particulars of Offence

A on the ... day of .../on a day between the ... day of ... and the ... day of ... did an act which facilitated the commission of a breach of immigration law by [*specify name*], who is not a citizen of the European Union, knowing or having reasonable cause to believe that the act facilitated the commission of a breach of immigration law by him, and that he is not a citizen of the European Union.

Sentence

B22.45 The maximum sentence is 14 years' imprisonment and/or a fine on conviction on indictment; six months' imprisonment and/or an unlimited fine on summary conviction (Immigration Act 1971, s. 25(6)).

Le and Stark [1999] 1 Cr App R (S) 422 provides an important guideline judgment in relation to the previous s. 25(1)(a) offence of 'assisting illegal entry' into the UK. At that stage, the maximum sentence was one of seven years, and not 14. Lord Bingham CJ stated (at p. 425): 'The offence is one which calls very often for deterrent sentences and as the statistics make plain, the problem of illegal entry is on the increase.' The Court of Appeal indicated that the appropriate penalty for all but the most minor offences would be one of immediate custody. The offence would be aggravated where (a) the offence had been repeated, (b) it was committed for financial gain, (c) the illegal entry was facilitated for strangers as opposed to a spouse or a close family member, (d) in cases of conspiracy, the offence had been committed over a period, (e) there had been a high degree of planning, organisation and sophistication, (f) D had played a prominent role or (g) the offence was committed in relation to a large number of illegal entrants. *Le and Stark* was considered and applied in *Oliviera* [2012] EWCA Crim 2279, [2013] 2 Cr App R (S) 4 (18) in the context of sham marriages, the Court noting that the statutory maximum at the time of *Le and Stark* had since increased from seven years' imprisonment to 14 years. In *Rotsias* [2013] EWCA Crim 2470, the Court referred to the 'net effect' of *A-G's Ref (Nos. 37, 38 and 65 of 2010)* [2010] EWCA Crim 2880, [2011] 2 Cr App R (S) 31 (186), namely that offences under s. 25 of the 1971 Act will routinely attract sentences of between three and eight years. Further, that where an individual sentence will stand in this range will depend on the features of aggravation identified by Lord Bingham in *Le and Stark*. In respect of sham marriages, see *Olusanya* [2012] EWCA Crim 900, [2013] 1 Cr App R (S) 32 (170), where the Court upheld sentences of 32 months' imprisonment for the first accused and 16 months for the second.

In *A-G's Ref (Nos. 49 and 50 of 2015) (Bakht)* [2015] EWCA Crim 1402, [2016] 1 Cr App R **B22.46** (S) 4 (14), a case focusing on visa applications supported by false documents relating to educational studies, it was recognised that the exploitation of others, the 'acute human misery visited on a number of young who were dedicated to educational advancement' (at [29]), was relevant, leading to an increase in sentences to eight and five years' imprisonment respectively. In *Patel (Dilipkumar)* [2014] EWCA Crim 265 (advice on falsifying applications) a sentence of four years' imprisonment for a man of good character on a guilty plea was upheld. Sentences totalling ten years for facilitating illegal entry, living on the earnings of prostitution, kidnapping and incitement to rape, for men involved in arranging the illegal entry of women who were then required to work as prostitutes, were increased to a total of 23 years in *A-G's Ref (No. 6 of 2004) (Plakici)* [2004] EWCA Crim 1275, [2005] 1 Cr App R (S) 19 (83). The Court of Appeal upheld a sentence of nine years' imprisonment for a conspiracy to facilitate a breach of immigration law, which involved an operation that ran for three months and was sophisticated, planned and organised (*Wolanski* [2013] EWCA Crim 1020). In *A-G's Ref (No. 28 of 2014)* [2014] EWCA Crim 1723 the Court increased a sentence of four years and six months to eight years in respect of a five-year conspiracy, the acts in furtherance of which involved providing security guards (who were either in the UK unlawfully or had no right to work) to construction companies. With the exception of 'illegal entry' the factors in *Le and Stark* were present together with the additional factor of exploitation (in terms of hours and poor wages) of those who were employed. As the case did not involve illegal entry, the gravamen of the offence was not equated with fraud. The offending was 'damaging to immigration controls but also to the UK's economic interests' (at [25]). See also *Ali (Nogib)* [2018] EWCA Crim 405 concerning offenders with roles in smuggling people, including fugitives out of the UK to the EU. Those with a central role should have received eight-year sentences and those acting as 'taxi drivers' for the trips, two and a half years. In *Bazegurore* [2020] EWCA Crim 375, the Court of Appeal upheld sentences of nine years for a conspiracy to facilitate the breach of immigration law, after a lorry containing 11 illegal immigrants was stopped. Two months after that incident, the appellants were apprehended in Belgium for similar offences, and faced separate proceedings. The Court considered (at [16]) that in general a court will sentence on the basis of the facts 'before it', and that it was neither unjust nor disproportionate to require those engaged in international criminality to bear the risk of sanctions in multiple jurisdictions of potentially variable severity (at [19]).

B22.47 At the other end of the scale, a sentence of ten months' imprisonment was imposed on appeal where D had brought her husband to the UK using a false passport (*Nenartoniene* [2009] EWCA Crim 2659) and a sentence of nine months was imposed on appeal for D who had brought his widowed sister-in-law to the UK using his wife's passport (*Darays* [2009] EWCA Crim 2654). For an offence not considered particularly sophisticated, nor carried out for financial gain, the Court considered a ten-month sentence on appeal appropriate (*Walid* [2016] EWCA Crim 1120). In *Seferi* [2012] EWCA Crim 1404, [2013] 1 Cr App R (S) 63 (350), the Court of Appeal rejected the submission of disparity with the co-defendant who received a suspended sentence, and upheld a 12-month custodial sentence in a case where an illegal entrant was found in the boot of D's car. In *Roman* [2017] EWCA Crim 6, [2017] 1 Cr App R (S) 43 (343), the Court considered the appropriate level of discount to be one third for an individual who pleaded guilty at the preliminary hearing, but who later absconded, for otherwise the effect would be to penalise her for her Bail Act offences. In *Bani* [2020] EWCA Crim 233, the Court reduced the sentence to five years, in a case involving the use of a dinghy to cross the Channel. There was considered to be planning, organisation and sophistication in the offence. The Court found the offence not to be for financial gain, but to share the costs with other Iranian nationals who wanted to make the same trip.

A person convicted of an offence under s. 25 will also be subject to the forfeiture provisions in s. 25C. An offence under s. 25 is designated a 'lifestyle offence' under the POCA 2002 (see **E19.17**). It follows that the imposition of a serious crime prevention order is applicable (see **D25.58**).

Elements

B22.48 The offence applies only where the person (or persons) 'assisted' is not a citizen of a Member State of the EU or a citizen of Iceland or Norway. The *actus reus* is an act which 'facilitates' a breach of 'immigration law'. 'Immigration law' is defined in s. 25(2) as a law that has effect in a Member State which regulates entitlement to (a) enter the State, (b) transit across the State, or (c) be in the State. The offence thus covers acts facilitating illegal entry or stay in other Member States. The immigration laws of Member States are to be conclusively proved by a certificate from the government concerned (s. 25(3)) (*Bina (Arya)* [2014] EWCA Crim 1444, [2014] 2 Cr App R 30 (496)). It also includes acts assisting non-EU citizens who entered the UK lawfully to remain unlawfully.

In *Kapoor* [2012] EWCA Crim 435, [2012] 2 Cr App R 11 (125) the Court of Appeal held that for the purposes of s. 25(2) an immigration law is a law that determines whether a person is lawfully or unlawfully either entering the UK, or in transit or being in the UK. Thus if a person, with the necessary knowledge or reasonable cause to believe, facilitates the unlawful entry or unlawful presence in the UK of a person who is not a citizen of the EU, the offence is committed. The Court held that the Asylum and Immigration (Treatment of Claimants, etc.) Act 2004, s. 2 (as to which see **B22.60**), was not an 'immigration law' for the purposes of s. 25(2). In *Bina (Arya)* [2014] EWCA Crim 1444, [2014] 2 Cr App R 30 (496), the Court of Appeal considered (at [30]) that there was nothing in s. 25 requiring that an EU national who had been aided must not be an asylum seeker. The fact that there may have been a parallel offence under s. 25A was not an answer to the charge.

B22.49 The particulars to the offence should set out which immigration law is alleged to have been breached. An indictment charging an offence of assisting unlawful immigration that did not set out the particular immigration law alleged to have been breached had not rendered a conviction unsafe where there had been no request to provide further particulars and D had conceded that he had carried out acts that had facilitated breaches in immigration laws (*Dhall* [2013] EWCA Crim 1610). The offence can be facilitated whether or not the breach is committed (e.g. finding a sham bride for a proposed sham marriage, but no completion of the marriage ceremony (*Ali (Nazakat)* [2015] EWCA Crim 43, [2015] 1 Cr App R 32 (494)). There is no need for a judge to direct a jury on the meaning of 'facilitates' (*Ali (Nazakat)*). Although no offence under s. 24A needs to have been committed for the completion of the s. 25 offence, an element of the *actus reus* is complicit dishonesty on the part of the person whose entry or stay is facilitated (e.g., the visa applicant knew that the documents that had been provided by D and on which the applicant relied in making the visa application were false); proof of dishonesty on the part of D is not sufficient (*Kaile* [2009] EWCA Crim 2868). In *Javaherifard* [2005] EWCA Crim 3231, the Court of Appeal held, following *Singh and Meeuwsen* [1972] 1 All ER 122, that it is possible to facilitate entry by acts close to but following actual entry (e.g. by making arrangements to get illegal entrants away quickly from the port of disembarkation).

Acts done abroad before 30 January 2008 (before s. 25(4) was amended) by persons who are not British nationals cannot constitute an offence under s. 25 (*Rechack* [2006] EWCA Crim 2975).

The *mens rea* of the offence under s. 25 is actual knowledge or having reasonable cause to believe, i.e. being negligent as to circumstances which would have put the reasonable person on notice of matters in s. 25(1)(b) and (c) (see **A2.17**). The *mens rea* for conspiracy counts is nothing short of knowledge or intention and is not equated to the *mens rea* for the substantive offence under the Immigration Act 1971, s. 25(1). This was confirmed by the Court of Appeal in *Ali (Arie)* [2019] EWCA Crim 2448, [2020] 1 Cr App R 21 (371). The Court highlighted (at [22]) that for conspiracy counts, where people to be smuggled have already been identified as a group and the defendants are aware of who they are, the indictment for conspiracy should be formulated so that *mens rea* is 'knowledge of the facts or circumstances'. If however, the people to be smuggled are not yet identified, the indictment should be drafted on the basis of intention. The conviction was upheld. D's defence at trial was that he was not present and not involved, rather than any issue about 'reasonable cause to believe'. **B22.50**

D cannot rely on the protection of Article 31 of the Convention Relating to the Status of Refugees (the 'Refugee Convention') (see **B22.86**) in relation to facilitating the entry into the UK of another (*Sternaj v DPP* [2011] EWHC 1094 (Admin)). In *Sternaj* the Divisional Court remarked that in the case where the accused were registered asylum seekers who facilitated the entry of the son of one of the accused using another child's passport, the prosecution might question whether it was in the public interest to prosecute. Nor can D rely upon the statutory defence under the Modern Slavery Act 2015, s. 45.

The defence of duress of circumstances has been used at first instance when those smuggled in were refugees and smuggling was the only way to secure their safety from a threat or serious injury (*Martin* [1989] 1 All ER 652; *Pommell (Fitzroy Derek)* [1995] 2 Cr App R 601; *Abdul-Hussein* [1999] Crim LR 570; *Cairns* [1999] 2 Cr App R 137).

OTHER OFFENCES RELATING TO ASSISTING ENTRY

Helping Asylum Seeker to Enter the UK

Immigration Act 1971, s. 25A **B22.51**

(1) A person commits an offence if—
  (a) he knowingly and for gain facilitates the arrival or attempted arrival in, or the entry or attempted entry into, the United Kingdom of an individual, and
  (b) he knows or has reasonable cause to believe that the individual is an asylum-seeker.

Procedure and Jurisdiction An immigration officer may arrest without warrant a person who has committed or is attempting to commit this offence, or whom the officer has reasonable grounds for suspecting of committing or attempting to commit the offence (Immigration Act 1971, s. 28A(3)). **B22.52**

The offence is triable either way (ss. 25A(4) and 25(6)). The offence applies to things done inside or outside the UK (ss. 25A(4) and 25(4)).

B22.53 **Indictment**

Statement of Offence

Helping an asylum-seeker to enter the United Kingdom contrary to section 25A of the Immigration Act 1971.

Particulars of Offence

A on the ... day of .../on a day between the ... day of ... and the ... day of ... knowingly and for gain facilitated the arrival in the United Kingdom of [*specify name*], a person whom he knew or had reasonable cause for believing to be an asylum-seeker.

B22.54 **Sentence** The maximum sentence is 14 years' imprisonment and/or a fine on indictment; six months' imprisonment and/or an unlimited fine summarily (Immigration Act 1971, ss. 25A(4) and 25(6)). Reported sentences range from six months' imprisonment for smuggling a husband (*Ozdemir* [1996] 2 Cr App Rep (S) 64) to 30 months for bringing in a brother on another brother's passport (*Toor* [2003] EWCA Crim 185, [2003] 2 Cr App Rep (S) 57 (349)). In *Bina (Arya)* [2014] EWCA Crim 1444, [2014] 2 Cr App R 30 (496), the Court of Appeal upheld a sentence of nine years that had been imposed for various offences, including one count under s. 25A. The Court considered (at [40]) that 'to facilitate the entry of asylum seekers is to obtain gain from the acutely vulnerable'.

The offence is designated a 'lifestyle offence' for the purposes of the POCA 2002 (see **E19.17**). It follows that the imposition of a serious crime prevention order is applicable (see **D25.58**).

B22.55 **Elements** Section 25A of the Immigration Act 1971 reproduces the offence which was previously set out in the Immigration Act 1971, s. 25(1)(b). Since the right to claim asylum is protected by the Universal Declaration on Human Rights, the act of assisting asylum seekers to arrive in the UK and claim asylum cannot therefore be unlawful *per se*, and the gravamen of this offence is profiteering. Thus financial gain is an essential element of the offence. Section 25A does not apply to anything done by persons acting on behalf of an organisation that aims to assist asylum seekers and does not charge for its services (s. 25A(3)). D must know or 'have reasonable cause to believe' that the individual D is assisting is an 'asylum-seeker'. 'Asylum seeker' is defined in s. 25A(2) as someone who 'intends' to claim that to remove that person from the UK would be a breach of the UK's obligations under (a) the Refugee Convention or (b) the ECHR. This presumably means that D could be guilty of this offence even though D did not make a claim under the Refugee Convention or the ECHR, provided it can be established that D intended to make such a claim. Section 25A applies in the case of an asylum seeker who arrives in or enters the UK without any breach of immigration law being committed by the person gaining entry (*Sternaj v DPP* [2011] EWHC 1094 (Admin)).

Assisting Entry to the UK in Breach of Deportation or Exclusion Order

B22.56 **Immigration Act 1971, s. 25B**

(1) A person commits an offence if he—
  (a) does an act which facilitates a breach or attempted breach of a deportation order in force against an individual who is a citizen of the European Union, and
  (b) knows or has reasonable cause for believing that the act facilitates a breach or attempted breach of the deportation order.

(2) Subsection (3) applies where the Secretary of State has made an order excluding an individual from the United Kingdom on the grounds of public policy, public security or public health, other than a temporary exclusion order.

(3) A person commits an offence if he—
  (a) does an act which assists the individual to arrive in, enter or remain, or attempt to arrive in, enter or remain in the United Kingdom,
  (b) knows or has reasonable cause for believing that the act assists the individual to arrive in, enter or remain, or attempt to arrive in, enter or remain in the United Kingdom, and
  (c) knows or has reasonable cause for believing that the Secretary of State has made an order excluding the individual from the United Kingdom on the grounds of public policy, public security or public health.

Procedure and Jurisdiction An immigration officer may arrest without warrant a person who has committed or is attempting to commit this offence, or whom the officer has reasonable grounds for suspecting of committing or attempting to commit the offence (Immigration Act 1971, s. 28A(3)). **B22.57**

The offence is triable either way (ss. 25A(4) and 25(6)). The offence also applies to things done inside or outside the UK (ss. 25B(4) and 25(4), as amended).

Sentence The maximum sentence is 14 years' imprisonment and/or a fine on indictment; six months' imprisonment and/or an unlimited fine summarily (Immigration Act 1971, ss. 25B(4) and 25(6)). There are no guideline judgments issued for this offence. **B22.58**

The forfeiture provisions discussed at **B22.47** also apply to this offence (s. 25C(1)). The offence is designated a 'lifestyle offence' for the purposes of the POCA 2002 (see **E19.17**). It follows that the imposition of a serious crime prevention order is applicable (see **D25.58**).

Elements An offence under the Immigration Act 1971 s. 25B, applies only where the person being assisted is a citizen of the EU. It therefore complements the offence at s. 25, which applies only where the person assisted is not an EU citizen. It is a defence that D did not know or have reasonable cause to believe that the person being assisted was the subject of a deportation or exclusion order. **B22.59**

FAILURE TO PRODUCE IMMIGRATION DOCUMENTS, ETC.

Definition

Asylum and Immigration (Treatment of Claimants, etc.) Act 2004, s. 2 **B22.60**

(1) A person commits an offence if at a leave or asylum interview he does not have with him an immigration document which—
  (a) is in force, and
  (b) satisfactorily establishes his identity and nationality or citizenship.
(2) A person commits an offence if at a leave or asylum interview he does not have with him, in respect of any dependent child with whom he claims to be travelling or living, an immigration document which—
  (a) is in force, and
  (b) satisfactorily establishes the child's identity and nationality or citizenship.
(3) But a person does not commit an offence under subsection (1) or (2) if—
  (a) the interview referred to in that subsection takes place after the person has entered the United Kingdom, and
  (b) within the period of three days beginning with the date of the interview the person provides to an immigration officer or to the Secretary of State a document of the kind referred to in that subsection.
(4) It is a defence for a person charged with an offence under subsection (1)—
  (a) to prove that he is an EEA national,
  (b) to prove that he is a member of the family of an EEA national and that he is exercising a right under the EU Treaties in respect of entry to or residence in the United Kingdom,
  (c) to prove that he has a reasonable excuse for not being in possession of a document of the kind specified in subsection (1),
  (d) to produce a false immigration document and to prove that he used that document as an immigration document for all purposes in connection with his journey to the United Kingdom, or
  (e) to prove that he travelled to the United Kingdom without, at any stage since he set out on *the journey*, having possession of an immigration document.
(5) It is a defence for a person charged with an offence under subsection (2) in respect of a child—
  (a) to prove that the child is an EEA national,
  (b) to prove that the child is a member of the family of an EEA national and that the child is exercising a right under the EU Treaties in respect of entry to or residence in the United Kingdom,
  (c) to prove that the person has a reasonable excuse for not being in possession of a document of the kind specified in subsection (2),
  (d) to produce a false immigration document and to prove that it was used as an immigration document for all purposes in connection with the child's journey to the United Kingdom, or

(e) to prove that he travelled to the United Kingdom with the child without, at any stage since he set out on the journey, having possession of an immigration document in respect of the child.

(6) Where the charge for an offence under subsection (1) or (2) relates to an interview which takes place after the defendant has entered the United Kingdom—
(a) subsections (4)(c) and (5)(c) shall not apply, but
(b) it is a defence for the defendant to prove that he has a reasonable excuse for not providing a document in accordance with subsection (3).

(7) For the purposes of subsections (4) to (6)—
(a) the fact that a document was deliberately destroyed or disposed of is not a reasonable excuse for not being in possession of it or for not providing it in accordance with subsection (3), unless it is shown that the destruction or disposal was—
(i) for a reasonable cause, or
(ii) beyond the control of the person charged with the offence, and
(b) in paragraph (a)(i) 'reasonable cause' does not include the purpose of—
(i) delaying the handling or resolution of a claim or application or the taking of a decision,
(ii) increasing the chances of success of a claim or application, or
(iii) complying with instructions or advice given by a person who offers advice about, or facilitates, immigration into the United Kingdom, unless in the circumstances of the case it is unreasonable to expect non-compliance with the instructions or advice.

(8) A person shall be presumed for the purposes of this section not to have a document with him if he fails to produce it to an immigration officer or official of the Secretary of State on request.

Under the Immigration, Nationality and Asylum (EU Exit) Regulations 2019 (SI 2019 No. 745), reg. 14, the words 'EU Treaties' in s. 2(4)(b) and (5)(b) will be replaced with 'retained EU law' from a date to be appointed.

Procedure

B22.61 A power of arrest is granted to an immigration officer who reasonably suspects that a person has committed an offence under the Asylum and Immigration (Treatment of Claimants, etc.) Act 2004, s. 2 (s. 2(10)).

The offence is triable either way.

Sentence

B22.62 The maximum penalty on conviction on indictment is two years' imprisonment and/or a fine. On summary conviction, the maximum is six months and/or an unlimited fine. In normal circumstances, a custodial sentence is inevitable (*Bei Bei Wang* [2005] EWCA Crim 293, [2005] 2 Cr App R (S) 13 (492), in which a ten-month sentence in a young offender institution on an 18-year-old offender was reduced to two months, and a recommendation for deportation quashed). However, in *MJ* (20 July 2007 unreported), the Court of Appeal held that a custodial sentence was generally inappropriate for an unaccompanied minor committing the offence. Appeals allowed in *Weng and Wang* [2005] EWCA Crim 2248, [2006] 1 Cr App R (S) 97 (582) resulted in sentences of three months, and in *Lu Zhu Ai* [2005] EWCA Crim 936, [2006] 1 Cr App R (S) 5 (18), a reduced sentence of five months. In *Jeyarasa* [2014] EWCA Crim 2545, [2015] 1 Cr App R (S) 39 (290), D stated that an agent had provided him with travel documents to show French authorities, which were taken back before arrival in the UK. Although the Court of Appeal considered it relevant that D's asylum claim failed, this did not mean that the guidance in *Lu Zhu Ai* should be disregarded. The sentence was reduced to six months.

Elements

B22.63 The essence of the offence is that D has destroyed a document en route since carriers are required to ensure that their passengers have appropriate documentation prior to embarking on their journey. This destruction would be with a view to concealing evidence of identity, age or nationality in order to increase the chances of being allowed to remain in the UK.

If D is travelling with a dependent child, it is also an offence not to have such documentation in respect of the child.

Defence

D has the legal burden of proving, on a balance of probabilities, a defence under the Asylum and Immigration (Treatment of Claimants, etc.) Act 2004, s. 2(4) (*Embaye* [2005] EWCA Crim 2865). It is a defence for the D (a) to prove that D, or the child for whom D is responsible, is an EEA national, (b) to prove that D or the child is a family member of an EEA national exercising a Treaty right, (c) to prove that D has a reasonable excuse for not being in possession of a 'document of the kind' needed at the interview to prove identity, (d) to produce a false document and to prove it was used for all purposes in connection with the journey to the UK, or (e) to prove that at no stage of the journey to the UK did D have a passport or similar document. The term 'reasonable excuse' is not defined under the Act. However, the spirit of the Refugee Convention has been incorporated within the reasonable excuse provision and is equivalent to the 'good cause' demanded in the defence under the Immigration and Asylum Act 1999, s. 31 (see **B22.86**). The Court of Appeal has indicated that sentencing judges should be alert to the need to hold *Newton* hearings in order to differentiate between those who had never possessed a passport or had only possessed one for a very short time and those who had destroyed it and were advancing false mitigation (*Bei Bei Wang* [2005] EWCA Crim 293, [2005] 2 Cr App R (S) 13 (492)). See also *Safari* [2005] EWCA Crim 830, [2006] 1 Cr App R (S) 1 (1), where the Court of Appeal considered that a *Newton* hearing was required before a sentencing judge could reach the decision that the offenders gave their documents to an agent to conceal their identities and details of their movements. **B22.64**

In *Thet v DPP* [2006] EWHC 2701 (Admin), [2007] 2 All ER 425 Lord Phillips CJ held that the Asylum and Immigration (Treatment of Claimants, etc.) Act 2004, s. 2(3), (4)(c) and (6), referred to valid documents only. Someone who has been unable to obtain a valid passport in his or her home country has a reasonable excuse for not producing it, and does not have to prove additionally a reasonable excuse for disposal of a false immigration document used to enter the UK. In *Mohammed and Osman* [2007] EWCA Crim 2332, [2008] 1 WLR 1130, the Court of Appeal accepted this interpretation of s. 2(4)(c) and (6)(b), but held that the fact that a claimant never had a genuine travel document did not provide a defence under s. 2(4)(e). This judgment results in the phrase 'immigration document' having different meanings in different subsections, which is unsatisfactory. A conviction for entering the UK without a passport was quashed where a judge had wrongly withdrawn the defence of reasonable excuse under s. 2(4)(c) before the trial had begun; there was evidence to support the defence and it would not have been perverse of the jury to conclude that the defence was made out on the evidence before them (*Asmeron* [2013] EWCA Crim 435, [2013] 1 WLR 3457).

The imposition of a legal burden of proof on D when seeking to rely on the statutory defence is not incompatible with the presumption of innocence contained in the ECHR, Article 6(2) (see *Embaye* [2005] EWCA Crim 2865 and **F3.18** ***et seq.***), even if the defence may not fully comply with Article 31 of the Refugee Convention where D is a bona fide asylum claimant. For Article 31, see **B22.86**.

FAILURE TO COMPLY WITH REQUIREMENT TO PROVIDE INFORMATION REQUIRED TO OBTAIN TRAVEL DOCUMENT

Under the Asylum and Immigration (Treatment of Claimants, etc.) Act 2004, s. 35(1), the Secretary of State may require a person to take specified action if the Secretary of State thinks that the action will, or may, enable a travel document to be obtained to facilitate the person's deportation or removal. Under s. 35(3) a person commits an offence by failing without reasonable excuse to comply with a requirement of the Secretary of State under s. 35(1). In *Secretary* **B22.65** *of State for the Home Department v JM (Zimbabwe)* [2017] EWCA Civ 1669, [2018] 1 WLR 2329 the Court of Appeal (Civil Division) considered the correct construction of s. 35 and concluded that the Secretary of State could not lawfully require a foreign national who was unlawfully in the UK to tell officials in the person's home country that the person agreed to return voluntarily when that was not the case.

Procedure

B22.66 A power of arrest is granted to an immigration officer who reasonably suspects that a person has committed an offence under the Asylum and Immigration (Treatment of Claimants, etc.) Act 2004, s. 35(3) (s. 35(5)).

The offence is triable either way.

Sentence

B22.67 The maximum penalty on conviction on indictment is two years' imprisonment and/or a fine. On summary conviction, the maximum is six months and/or an unlimited fine (s. 35(4)).

Elements

B22.68 Fear of persecution in the home country was held not to constitute a reasonable excuse for non-compliance with a requirement to attend for interview by officials of that country's embassy in *Tabnak* [2007] EWCA Crim 380, [2007] 1 WLR 1317, where the Court of Appeal considered that reasonable excuse should relate to ability, not willingness to comply. The Court accepted in *Amirthanathan* [2003] EWHC 1107 (Admin) that 'once an appeal is lodged it is inappropriate to require a person to give an interview to the authorities of the destination country to facilitate the obtaining of a travel document, since the interview might lead to information being provided which might put the claimant or his family at risk'. Home Office guidance on the Asylum and Immigration (Treatment of Claimants, etc.) Act 2004, s. 35(3), indicates that travel difficulties and health emergencies might constitute reasonable excuses. The burden of proof is an evidential one for D. Once the defence of reasonable excuse is raised by D it will be for the prosecution to disprove it to the criminal standard.

FALSE DOCUMENT AND IDENTITY OFFENCES

Forgery and Counterfeiting Offences

B22.69 The Forgery and Counterfeiting Act 1981 creates the following offences which may be relevant in an immigration context: s. 1 — forgery (see **B6.36**); s. 2 — copying a false instrument (see **B6.41**); s. 3 — using a false instrument (see **B6.46**); s. 4 — using a copy of a false instrument (see **B6.46**); s. 5 — offences relating to stamps, share certificates etc. (see **B6.51**).

Accused Required to Provide Nationality in Court

B22.70 Section 86(A) of the Courts Act 2003 and CrimPR 3.16(5) (see Supplement, **R3.16**) introduce a requirement that D provide details, including name, date of birth and nationality, in criminal proceedings. If without reasonable excuse D fails when required to do so, or provides false or incomplete details, an offence is committed. The information given in response is not admissible in any other criminal proceedings against D, other than under s. 86A. A maximum penalty of six months' imprisonment and/or a fine applies (s. 86A(5)). This section came into force on 13 November 2017 (PCA 2017, s. 162).

Offences under the Identity Documents Act 2010

B22.71 The Identity Documents Act 2010 repeals and re-enacts offence-creating provisions and definitions previously found in the Identity Cards Act 2006, ss. 25 and 26. By s. 13(1) of the 2010

Act, 'the repeal and re-enactment ... does not affect the continuity of the law'; and by s. 13(3), '[a]ny reference (express or implied) in any enactment, instrument or document to a provision of this Act is to be read as including, in relation to times, circumstances or purposes in relation to which any corresponding provision repealed by this Act had effect, a reference to that corresponding provision' — so far as the context permits.

Identity Documents Act 2010, ss. 4 to 9

4.—(1) It is an offence for a person ('P') with an improper intention to have in P's possession or under P's control—

(a) an identity document that is false and that P knows or believes to be false,

(b) an identity document that was improperly obtained and that P knows or believes to have been improperly obtained, or

(c) an identity document that relates to someone else.

(2) Each of the following is an improper intention—

(a) the intention of using the document for establishing personal information about P;

(b) the intention of allowing or inducing another to use it for establishing, ascertaining or verifying personal information about P or anyone else.

(3) In subsection (2)(b) the reference to P or anyone else does not include, in the case of a document within subsection (1)(c), the individual to whom it relates.

...

5.—(1) It is an offence for a person ('P') with the prohibited intention to make or to have in P's possession or under P's control—

(a) any apparatus which, to P's knowledge, is or has been specially designed or adapted for the making of false identity documents, or

(b) any article or material which, to P's knowledge, is or has been specially designed or adapted to be used in the making of such documents.

(2) The prohibited intention is the intention—

(a) that P or another will make a false identity document, and

(b) that the document will be used by somebody for establishing, ascertaining or verifying personal information about a person.

...

6.—(1) It is an offence for a person ('P'), without reasonable excuse, to have in P's possession or under P's control—

(a) an identity document that is false,

(b) an identity document that was improperly obtained,

(c) an identity document that relates to someone else,

(d) any apparatus which, to P's knowledge, is or has been specially designed or adapted for the making of false identity documents, or

(e) any article or material which, to P's knowledge, is or has been specially designed or adapted to be used in the making of such documents.

...

7.—(1) For the purposes of sections 4 to 6 'identity document' means any document that is or purports to be—

(a) an immigration document,

(b) a United Kingdom passport (within the meaning of the Immigration Act 1971),

(c) a passport issued by or on behalf of the authorities of a country or territory outside the United Kingdom or by or on behalf of an international organisation,

(d) a document that can be used (in some or all circumstances) instead of a passport,

(e) a licence to drive a motor vehicle granted under Part 3 of the Road Traffic 1988 or under Part 2 of the Road Traffic (Northern Ireland) Order 1981, or

(f) a driving licence issued by or on behalf of the authorities of a country or territory outside the United Kingdom.

(2) In subsection (1)(a) 'immigration document' means—

(a) a document used for confirming the right of a person under the EU Treaties in respect of entry or residence in the United Kingdom,

(b) a document that is given in exercise of immigration functions and records information about leave granted to a person to enter or to remain in the United Kingdom, or

(c) a registration card (within the meaning of section 26A of the Immigration Act 1971).

...

8.—(1) For the purposes of sections 4 and 5 'personal information', in relation to an individual ('A'), means—
(a) A's full name,
(b) other names by which A is or has previously been known,
(c) A's gender,
(d) A's date and place of birth,
(e) external characteristics of A that are capable of being used for identifying A,
(f) the address of A's principal place of residence in the United Kingdom,
(g) the address of every other place in the United Kingdom or elsewhere where A has a place of residence,
(h) where in the United Kingdom and elsewhere A has previously been resident,
(i) the times at which A was resident at different places in the United Kingdom or elsewhere,
(j) A's current residential status,
(k) residential statuses previously held by A, and
(l) information about numbers allocated to A for identification purposes and about the documents (including stamps or labels) to which they relate.

(2) In subsection (1) 'residential status' means—
(a) A's nationality,
(b) A's entitlement to remain in the United Kingdom, and
(c) if that entitlement derives from a grant of leave to enter or remain in the United Kingdom, the terms and conditions of that leave.

9.—(1) 'Apparatus' includes any equipment, machinery or device and any wire or cable, together with any software used with it.

(2) In relation to England and Wales and Northern Ireland, an identity document is 'false' only if it is false within the meaning of Part 1 of the Forgery and Counterfeiting Act 1981 (see section 9(1)).

(3) An identity document was 'improperly obtained' if—
(a) false information was provided in, or in connection with, the application for its issue to the person who issued it, or
(b) false information was provided in, or in connection with, an application for its modification to a person entitled to modify it.

(4) In subsection (3)—
(a) 'false' information includes information containing any inaccuracy or omission that results in a tendency to mislead,
(b) 'information' includes documents (including stamps and labels) and records, and
(c) the 'issue' of a document includes its renewal, replacement or re-issue (with or without modifications).

(5) References to the making of a false identity document include the modification of an identity document so that it becomes false.

(6) This section applies for the purposes of sections 4 to 6.

B22.72 **Procedure and Jurisdiction** Offences under the Identity Documents Act 2010, ss. 4 and 5, are triable only on indictment (ss. 4(4) and 5(3)) and are normally class 3 offences, but see CrimPD XIII, para. B (see Supplement, **CPD.XIII.B**), for the additional factors that the court considers on allocation. Offences under s. 6 are triable either way (s. 6(2)). All are Group A offences for jurisdiction purposes under the CJA 1993, Part I (see **A8.10**).

B22.73 **Defence for Refugees and Victims of Trafficking** Refugees who satisfy certain conditions under the Immigration and Asylum Act 1999, s. 31, may have a defence to charges brought under the Identity Documents Act 2010. See further *Mateta* [2013] EWCA Crim 1372, [2014] 1 All ER 152 and **B22.86**. Victims of trafficking and modern day slavery may have a statutory defence under the Modern Slavery Act 2015, s. 45 (see **B22.27**). See also *K* [2017] EWCA Crim 486 and *M* [2016] EWCA Crim 1326.

B22.74 **Alternative Verdicts** Based on the usual principles of law governing alternative verdicts (CLA *1967, s. 6(3)*: see **D19.41 *et seq.***), it is submitted that on an indictment for an offence under the Identity Documents Act 2010, s. 4 or 5, the jury may return a verdict of guilty of an offence under s. 6. It may, nevertheless, be prudent to add alternative counts.

Sentence The maximum sentence for an offence under the Identity Documents Act 2010, s. 4 or 5, is ten years or a fine (or both) (ss. 4(4) and 5(3)). The maximum sentence for an offence under s. 6 when tried on indictment is two years; on summary conviction, it is six months or an unlimited fine or both. B22.75

An immediate custodial sentence would ordinarily be imposed for possession of false documents (contrary to the Identity Documents Act 2010) in an immigration context because such offences are inimical to proper immigration control (*Carneiro* [2007] EWCA Crim 2170, [2008] 1 Cr App R (S) 95 (571)). In *Ovieriakhi* [2009] EWCA Crim 452, [2009] 2 Cr App R (S) 91 (607) the Court of Appeal, in reviewing past authorities, considered there to be a scale ranging from the use or possession of false passports for the purpose of evading controls on entry into the UK to the use of a document other than a passport by a person lawfully present in order to obtain employment or a bank account. In *Acheampong* [2015] EWCA Crim 1894 the Court endorsed the sentencing guidance in *Ovieriakhi* and substituted a sentence of eight months for one of 12 months. The Court noted that the passport used was not false, was not used to gain entry into the UK but instead to gain work, was lent to D by her sister and was used by D to secure work in an attempt to support her child, and, further, that D had never been lawfully entitled to be in the UK or to work in the UK. In *Mehmeti* [2019] EWCA Crim 751, the Court reduced a sentence to six months, as a false identity document was not used for immigration purposes. In *Aderemi* [2018] EWCA Crim 1502, the Court imposed a sentence of six months, given that the only misuse of false identity documents was to obtain work. Earlier guidance in *Kolawole* [2004] EWCA Crim 3047, [2005] 2 Cr App R (S) 14 (71) (12 to 18 months for a person of good character on a guilty plea) was said to apply to the former category, which is to be distinguished from cases where a false passport is used to gain work or open a bank account whether the individual is lawfully present in the UK or not. Unlawful presence in the UK has now been held to be an aggravating factor for sentencing purposes. See *Lasgaa* [2014] EWCA Crim 1822, a case involving an offence contrary to the Identity Documents Act 2010, s. 4, where the Court of Appeal departed from *Omowanle* [2009] EWCA Crim 2286. Six months 'has now become a standard sentence for somebody using a false document to obtain employment contrary to immigration controls, in circumstances where they plead at the first opportunity and have a good character' (*Osei* [2009] EWCA Crim 2287). Where the effect of the deception had been long-term and very advantageous to D, the sentence of 12 months was deemed appropriate (*Boateng* [2013] EWCA Crim 2306).

In *Cheema* [2002] EWCA Crim 325, [2002] 2 Cr App R (S) 79 (356), the Court of Appeal considered a sentence of three years appropriate under the previous legislation of the Forgery and Counterfeiting Act 1981 for having custody or control of 12 false passports, intending that they would be used as genuine passports. In *Kuosmanen* [2004] EWCA Crim 1861, [2005] 1 Cr App R (S) 71 (354), when sentencing in relation to the possession of 250 counterfeit passports with intent, a sentence of five years' imprisonment was upheld.

Elements Although the Identity Documents Act 2010 replaces two lengthy sections in the 2006 Act with six shorter ones, no obvious change is made to the form or structure of the three offences involved. Section 4 effectively restates the offence previously found in s. 25(1) and (2); s. 5 similarly restates the offence previously found in s. 25(3) and (4), and s. 6 is identical in every respect to the old s. 25(5). The s. 25(5) offence was considered by the Court of Appeal in *Unah* [2011] EWCA Crim 1837, [2012] 1 All ER 122, in which it was held that whether D's ignorance of a document's falsity would amount to a 'reasonable excuse' for possessing it must be a question of fact. The same must accordingly be true of the offence under s. 6. B22.76

One possible caveat arises from the definition of 'improper intention' in s. 4(2). In contrast to the concept of 'requisite intent' it replaces, and in contrast to that of 'prohibited intent' in

s. 5(2), it might be possible to construe that definition as non-exhaustive. In other words, there may perhaps be some (as yet unidentified) forms of 'improper intention' beyond those listed in s. 5(2)(a) and (b). The fact that in this respect the wording of the new provision differs from the one it replaced might suggest this. On the other hand, such an intention could easily have been made more obvious by use of the word 'includes'.

The s. 6 offence corresponds to that in the Forgery and Counterfeiting Act 1981, s. 5(4) (see **B6.51** *et seq.*). 'Possession or control' in the former provision broadly corresponds to 'custody or control' in the latter (see **B6.56**) and the concept of 'lawful excuse' must have the same meaning in each case. As to this, see **B6.57**.

B22.77 **Defence** The Supreme Court in *SXH* [2017] UKSC 30, [2017] 1 WLR 1401 held that, in deciding whether to institute criminal proceedings, the CPS are required to apply a two-stage test. They must first consider whether there is enough evidence to provide a realistic prospect of conviction and, if that is satisfied, decide whether the prosecution would be in the public interest. D, an asylum applicant, was prosecuted under the Identity Cards Act 2006, s. 25(1). During the course of the proceedings D was recognised as a refugee and thereafter the CPS offered no evidence. D brought proceedings against the CPS, the Home Office and the police for damages on various grounds including a breach of her rights under the ECHR, Article 8. The Supreme Court unanimously dismissed the appeal, having held (at [34]) that it was difficult to envisage circumstances in which the initiation of a prosecution against a person reasonably suspected of committing a criminal offence could itself be a breach of that person's human rights. It does not matter that prosecution is not obligatory in the UK; whether it is in the public interest to prosecute is not the same as whether a prosecution would breach an individual's Article 8 rights. Article 8 is therefore not applicable to the decision to prosecute. The CPS could be criticised regarding the length of time taken to conclude that D's s. 31 defence would succeed. Even if the original decision to prosecute was an error of judgement by the CPS this would not have breached Article 8. Lord Kerr (at [41]–[46]) raised the possibility that the continuation of the decision to prosecute beyond the time that it should have been recognised that D had an answerable defence under s. 31 constituted an interference with D's freedom of liberty under the ECHR, Article 5, and with Article 8 rights.

ILLEGAL WORKING

Employing Illegal Worker

B22.78 **Immigration, Asylum and Nationality Act 2006, s. 21**

(1) A person commits an offence if he employs another ('the employee') knowing that the employee is disqualified from employment by reason of the employee's immigration status.

(1A) A person commits an offence if the person—

(a) employs another person ('the employee') who is disqualified from employment by reason of the employee's immigration status, and

(b) has reasonable cause to believe that the employee is disqualified from employment by reason of the employee's immigration status.

(1B) For the purposes of subsections (1) and (1A) a person is disqualified from employment by reason of the person's immigration status if the person is an adult subject to immigration control and—

(a) the person has not been granted leave to enter or remain in the United Kingdom, or

(b) the person's leave to enter or remain in the United Kingdom—

(i) is invalid,

(ii) has ceased to have effect (whether by reason of curtailment, revocation, cancellation, passage of time or otherwise), or

(iii) is subject to a condition preventing the person from accepting the employment.

The provisions of the 2006 Act apply only in respect of employment commenced on or after 29 February 2008 (SI 2008 No. 310, art. 2(1)(b)).

Procedure The offences are triable either way (Immigration, Asylum and Nationality Act 2006, s. 21(2)). A body corporate can commit the offences, and provision is made in s. 22 for a body (whether corporate or not) to be treated as knowing, or having reasonable cause to believe, a fact if a person within that body with responsibility for an aspect of the employment knows the fact or has such reasonable cause to believe. **B22.79**

Sentence The maximum penalty on conviction on indictment is five years' imprisonment and/or a fine. On summary conviction, the maximum is six months and/or an unlimited fine. **B22.80**

Elements The criminal offence applies not only to individual employers but also companies and partnerships (Immigration, Asylum and Nationality Act 2006, s. 22). The offence can be committed by an employer who either knows or has reasonable cause to believe that a person is working without leave. **B22.81**

Illegal Working

Immigration Act 1971, s. 24B **B22.82**

(1) A person ('P') who is subject to immigration control commits an offence if—
  (a) P works at a time when P is disqualified from working by reason of P's immigration status, and
  (b) at that time P knows or has reasonable cause to believe that P is disqualified from working by reason of P's immigration status.
(2) For the purposes of subsection (1) a person is disqualified from working by reason of the person's immigration status if—
  (a) the person has not been granted leave to enter or remain in the United Kingdom, or
  (b) the person's leave to enter or remain in the United Kingdom—
    (i) is invalid,
    (ii) has ceased to have effect (whether by reason of curtailment, revocation, cancellation, passage of time or otherwise), or
    (iii) is subject to a condition preventing the person from doing work of that kind.

...

(8) The reference in subsection (1) to a person who is subject to immigration control is to a person who under this Act requires leave to enter or remain in the United Kingdom.
(9) Where a person is on immigration bail within the meaning of Part 1 of Schedule 10 to the Immigration Act 2016—
  (a) the person is to be treated for the purposes of subsection (2) as if the person had been granted leave to enter the United Kingdom, but
  (b) any condition as to the person's work in the United Kingdom to which the person's immigration bail is subject is to be treated for those purposes as a condition of leave.

Procedure The offence is summary only (Immigration Act 1971, s. 24B(3)). **B22.83**

Sentence The maximum penalty is six months' imprisonment and/or an unlimited fine (s. 24B(3)(a) and (4)). A person convicted of the offence may also have earnings seized under the POCA 2002 (s. 24B(5)). **B22.84**

Elements The offence is committed where a person works without having been granted leave to enter or remain in the UK, or the person's leave to enter or remain in the UK is invalid, has ceased to have effect or the person is subject to a condition preventing the person from undertaking work of that kind. Section 24B(10) defines 'working' widely so as to include working 'under or for the purposes of a contract for services', 'under a contract personally to do work' or for 'a purpose related to a contract to sell goods'. The term 'contract' means a contract whether express or implied and, if express, whether oral or in writing (s. 24B(13)). **B22.85**

STATUTORY DEFENCE UNDER THE IMMIGRATION AND ASYLUM ACT 1999, s. 31

Article 31 of the Convention Relating to the Status of Refugees

B22.86 Section 31 of the Immigration and Asylum Act 1999 sets out defences, based on Article 31 of the Refugee Convention, to an offence under the Immigration Act 1971, s. 24A (entry etc. by deception), and certain other offences, including offences under the Forgery and Counterfeiting Act 1981, Part 1 (see **B6.26**), and the Identity Documents Act 2010, ss. 4 and 6 (see **B22.71**). The statutory defence in s. 31 was introduced following the decision of the Divisional Court in *Uxbridge Magistrates' Court, ex parte Adimi* [1999] 4 All ER 520, which held that the government's obligations under Article 31 of the Refugee Convention required that criminal sanctions were not imposed on refugees who entered the UK illegally provided that they made themselves known to the relevant authorities without delay. A 'refugee' is as defined in Article 1A of the Refugee Convention. The statutory defence in s. 31 is significantly narrower in its scope than the protection afforded by Article 31(1) of the Refugee Convention according to *Adimi*. It applies to those who have claimed refugee status, but whose cases have not yet been dealt with, if the prosecution cannot disprove beyond a reasonable doubt that they are refugees (*Makuwa* [2006] EWCA Crim 175, [2006] 1 WLR 2755). In *Asfaw* [2008] UKHL 31, [2008] 1 AC 1061 the House of Lords held that since s. 31 was intended to give effect to Article 31 of the Refugee Convention, the defence provided by it should not be read as limited to offences attributable to a refugee's illegal entry into or presence in the UK, but rather as providing immunity (if conditions contained therein are fulfilled) from the imposition of criminal penalties for offences attributable to the attempt of a refugee to leave this country in the continuing course of a flight from persecution, even after a short stopover in transit. In *Mateta* [2013] EWCA Crim 1372, [2014] 1 All ER 152 the Court of Appeal summarised the main elements of the s. 31 defence as follows (at [21]):

i) The defendant must provide sufficient evidence in support of his claim to refugee status to raise the issue and thereafter the burden falls on the prosecution to prove to the criminal standard that he is not a refugee (section 31 Immigration and Asylum Act 1999 and *Mukuwa* [[2006] EWCA Crim 175, [2006] 1 WLR 2755 at] [26]) unless an application by the defendant for asylum has been refused by the Secretary of State, when the legal burden rests on him to establish on a balance of probabilities that he is a refugee (s. 31(7) of the [1999 Act] and *Sadighpour* [[2012] EWCA Crim 2669, [2013] 1 Cr App R 20 (269) at] [38]–[40]);

ii) If the Crown fails to disprove that the defendant was a refugee (or if the defendant proves on a balance of probabilities he is a refugee following the Secretary of State's refusal of his application for asylum), it then falls to a defendant to prove on the balance of probabilities that
   a) that he did not stop in any country in transit to the United Kingdom for more than a short stopover (which, on the facts, was explicable, see (iv) below) or, alternatively, that he could not reasonably have expected to be given protection under the Refugee Convention in countries outside the United Kingdom in which he stopped; and, if so:
   b) he, presented himself to the authorities in the UK 'without delay', unless (again, depending on the facts) it was explicable that he did not present himself to the authorities in the United Kingdom during a short stopover in this country when travelling through to the nation where he intended to claim asylum;
   c) he had good cause for his illegal entry or presence in the UK; and
   d) *he made a claim for asylum* as soon as was reasonably practicable after his arrival in the UK, unless (once again, depending on the facts) it was explicable that he did not present himself to the authorities in the United Kingdom during a short stopover in this

country when travelling through to the nation where he intended to claim asylum. (s. 31(1) [of the 1999 Act]; *Sadighpour* [18] and [38]–[40]; *Jaddi* [[2012] EWCA Crim 2565 at] [16] and [30]).

iii) The requirement that the claim for asylum must be made as soon as was reasonably practicable does not necessarily mean at the earliest possible moment (*Asfaw* [[2008] UKHL 31, [2008] 1 AC 1061 at] [16]; *R v M (A)* [[2010] EWCA Crim 2400, [2011] 1 Cr App R 35 (432) at] [9]).

iv) It follows that the fact that a refugee stopped in a third country in transit is not necessarily fatal and may be explicable: the refugee has some choice as to where he might properly claim asylum. The main touchstones by which exclusion from protection should be judged are the length of the stay in the intermediate country, the reasons for delaying there and whether or not the refugee sought or found protection de jure or de facto from the persecution from which he or she was seeking to escape [(*Asfaw* [26]; *R v M (A)* [9])].

v) The requirement that the refugee demonstrates 'good cause' for his illegal entry or presence in the United Kingdom will be satisfied by him showing he was reasonably travelling on false papers (*Ex p Adimi* [[2001] QB 667] at 679H).

The Court went on to consider the obligation to provide advice on the parameters of the s. 31 defence (at [24]): **B22.87**

i) There is an obligation on those representing defendants charged with an offence of possession of an identity document with improper intention to advise them of the existence of a possible section 31 defence if the circumstances and instructions generate the possibility of mounting this defence, and they should explain its parameters (*R v M (A)* [10]).

ii) The advisers should properly note the instructions and the advice given (*R v M (A)* [56]).

iii) If an accused's representatives failed to advise him about the availability of this defence, on an appeal to the Court of Appeal … the court will assess whether the defence would 'quite probably' have succeeded (*R v M (A)* [13]).

iv) It is appropriate for the Court of Appeal to assess the prospects of an asylum defence succeeding by reference to the findings of the First-tier Tribunal (Immigration and Asylum Chamber), if available (*Sadighpour* [35]).

For further application of *Mateta* see *M* [2016] EWCA Crim 1326. In *Zaredar* [2016] EWCA Crim 877, the Court of Appeal observed that the Law Society should be appraised of the judgment and encouraged, as a matter of professional training and conduct, to draw the issue of failures to provide legal advice on s. 31 to the attention of its members.

The role of an agent is an important consideration in any immigration offence or the application of the s. 31 statutory defence. In *K* [2005] EWHC 478 (Admin), [2005] 2 Cr App R (S) 96 (578), in a judicial review of the decision of the Crown Court to uphold a sentence of four months' detention and training for an offence under the Immigration Act 1971, s. 24A, the Divisional Court held, in granting the application, that it could only interfere with the sentence of the Crown Court in circumstances where there had been an excess of jurisdiction or the sentence was wrong in law. In this case, however, the important feature of the role of the agent, while it had been mentioned before the Crown Court, had not been supported by authority and the issue was not properly brought home to the court. Two cases had stated that some asylum seekers were so much under the influence of their agent that they could not be criticised for accepting implicitly what they were told by him (*R (Q) v Secretary of State for the Home Department* [2003] EWCA Civ 364, [2004] QB 36; *R (S)* [2003] EWHC 1941 (Admin), [2004] HLR 16). Furthermore, the powerful influence of the agent was underpinned by acknowledgement within the control of immigration screening procedures of the particular care that needed to be taken when interviewing and screening minors and the need for a responsible adult to be present, which did not happen in this case. The absence of a responsible adult made it all the more important to take into account the influence that the agent must have had on K. If the influence of the agent had been properly brought home to the Crown Court, it would not have been possible to say that custody was the only appropriate means of dealing with K. To ignore that fact amounted to an error of law. Therefore, the Crown Court did err as a matter of law in upholding the sentence of detention and a conditional discharge was substituted for the sentence of detention.

In practice, the information received on waiver of legal professional privilege will be crucial. In *Ghorbani* [2015] EWCA Crim 275 D had chosen to plead guilty in circumstances where the statutory defence had been drawn to her attention by her legal advisers. The appeal was dismissed notwithstanding that the statutory defence would 'quite probably have succeeded'. In *Malak* [2018] EWCA Crim 1693, a guilty plea was rendered equivocal in relation to a Syrian national who had explained at the airport his true position (which was accepted by the sentencing judge) of having fled Syria to travel to the UK to claim asylum. There was no improper intention on his part and D had not been advised of the availability of the s. 31 defence. Following release from custody, D was recognised as a refugee.

In *Mulugeta* [2015] EWCA Crim 6, where D had pleaded guilty to an offence under the Immigration Act 1971, s. 24A(1), the Court of Appeal emphasised the need to be able to satisfy all the elements of the defence as outlined in *Mateta*. Though the Crown conceded that D's legal advisers had 'inadequately considered, if at all' the statutory defence, the Court held that there was no nexus between D's claim to refugee status and his deception and that the defence would not have been available to him.

B22.88 The statutory defence under s. 31 does not apply to the offence of illegal entry, and did not apply to the statutory predecessor of s. 24A. A conviction for deception under s. 24A was quashed in *R (Badur) v Birmingham Crown Court* [2006] EWHC 539 (Admin), on the basis that it should have been charged under the statutory predecessor of s. 24A, and D would have been able to avail himself of the broader defence which relied directly on the Refugee Convention, Article 31, instead of being limited to the statutory defence under s. 31 of the 1999 Act. See also *Kamalanathan* [2010] EWCA Crim 1335 and *Sadeghi* [2014] EWCA Crim 2933.

The defence under s. 31 does not apply to the offence of facilitating the entry into the UK of another (*Sternaj v DPP* [2011] EWHC 1094 (Admin)). In *Mirahessari* [2016] EWCA Crim 1733, the defence under s. 31 did not apply where the applicants' criminality went substantially further than trying to enter the UK with either false documents or no documents. The applicants were trying to enter the UK in a dangerous manner which obstructed railway traffic through the Channel Tunnel. In *Ordu* [2017] EWCA Crim 4, [2017] 1 Cr App R 21 (319), the Court of Appeal refused an extension of time for a refugee to apply for permission against his conviction for possession of identity documents with intent. Although the law had changed after his conviction in such a way that had it applied at the time of trial he would have had a defence, D had been released from prison, his licence had expired and the conviction was spent. The Court held that no substantial injustice would occur if the application was dismissed.

DEPORTATION AND DEPRIVATION OF CITIZENSHIP

Automatic Deportation

B22.89 The UK Borders Act 2007 provides for automatic deportation provisions which are contained in ss. 32 to 39. One example is sentences that are over 12 months' immediate custody. Under the Immigration, Nationality and Asylum (EU Exit) Regulations 2019 (SI 2019 No. 745), reg. 17(2), the words 'or an Irish citizen' will be added to the definition of 'foreign criminal' in s. 32(1)(a) from a date to be appointed. See **E20.1**.

Recommendation for Deportation

A recommendation for deportation is a power still available to the courts following the UK Borders Act 2007, but would apply only to cases involving a short custodial sentence of under 12 months' duration or where a non-custodial penalty has been imposed upon the offender (see **E20.1**). **B22.90**

Deprivation of Citizenship

The grounds upon which a British Citizen (or any other British national) may be deprived of citizenship under the British Nationality Act 1981 are as follows. First, where the Secretary of State is satisfied that doing so is 'conducive to the public good' (s. 40(2)) and the person would not be left stateless as a result (s. 40(4)). Second, where the Secretary of State is satisfied, regardless of whether or not it will render that person stateless, that a naturalised citizen has behaved in a manner seriously prejudicial to the vital interests of the UK and the Secretary of State has reasonable grounds to believe that the person is able, under the law of the country or territory outside the UK, to become a national of such a country or territory. Third, where the Secretary of State is satisfied that registration or naturalisation has been obtained by fraud, false representation or concealment of material facts. **B22.91**

Under s. 40(4A), the Secretary of State is not prevented from making an order under s. 40(2) to deprive a person of a citizenship status if: that person has become a citizen by naturalisation; the Secretary of State is satisfied that the deprivation is conducive to the public good because the person, while having that citizenship status, has behaved in a manner which is seriously prejudicial to the vital interests of the UK etc.; and the Secretary of State has reasonable grounds for believing that the person is able, under the law of a country or territory outside the UK, to become a national of such a country or territory.

Section C1 Definitions and Basic Principles in Road Traffic Cases

DEFINITIONS

Accident

The word 'accident' has been given a number of different meanings depending upon the context in which it is used. In *Chief Constable of West Midlands Police v Billingham* [1979] 2 All ER 182, the Divisional Court expressed a preference for an 'ordinary man' test, stating that the definition of the word by the Court of Appeal in *Morris* [1972] 1 All ER 384 as 'some unintended occurrence which has an adverse physical result' should be understood in relation to the facts of that case. Nonetheless, the Court did state (per Bridge LJ) that the word 'accident' was 'capable of applying to an untoward occurrence which has adverse physical results' even if one event in the chain was deliberate. The main doubt at one time was whether an accident could result from one or more intentional or deliberate acts. **C1.1**

In *Chief Constable of Staffordshire v Lees* [1981] RTR 506, the argument that a 'deliberate act' does not constitute an 'accident' for the purposes of the Road Traffic Acts was rejected. In that case the defendant deliberately drove his car at a locked gate. The Divisional Court held that an 'accident' could be said to have occurred within the meaning of the RTA 1972, s. 8(2), when arising through a deliberate and intended act, provided that any ordinary person would say that there had been an accident owing to the presence of a motor vehicle on a road. Bingham J stated (at p. 510):

> It would be an insult to common sense if a collision involving a motor car arising from some careless and inadvertent act entitled a constable to exercise his powers under the [Road Traffic] Act but a similar result caused by a deliberate antisocial act did not. Previous cases have made it clear that one should look at the ordinary meaning of the word 'accident'.

In *Morris* [1972] 1 All ER 384, Lord Widgery CJ acknowledged the possibility of a *de minimis* argument where the physical consequences were so trivial that an ordinary person would not regard the occurrence as an accident. In *Currie* [2007] EWCA Crim 926, [2007] 2 Cr App R 18 (246), the Court of Appeal held that the term must be given a common-sense meaning and that an accident is not restricted to untoward or unintended consequences having an adverse physical effect, confirming that some physical impact is not an essential element.

Stapylton [2012] EWCA Crim 728, [2013] 1 Cr App R (S) 12 (68), applying *Mayor v Oxford* (1980) 2 Cr App R (S) 280, confirmed that any accident resulting from driving where the vehicle has run off the road and collided with some stationary object was clearly an accident which occurred 'owing to the presence of a motor vehicle on a road', even though the collision happened off the road.

Driver and Driving

The definition of 'driver' is set out in the RTA 1988, s. 192 (see C1.31). It includes, except in cases of causing death by dangerous driving, a person who is steering, as well as any other person engaged in driving. As respects establishing the identity of the driver of a vehicle concerned in an offence, there is no general presumption that the owner of a vehicle is the **C1.2** driver of it at a particular time, notwithstanding the various statutory provisions that establish owner liability in certain specific circumstances; the question of the driver's identity is one of fact on which the tribunal must be sure (*Clarke v DPP* (1992) 156 JP 605; *Powell v DPP* [1992] RTR 270; *Browning* (1991) 94 Cr App R 109, concerning car identification). Evidence of ownership is merely one strand in the evidential rope which may go to establish the identity of the driver. All the evidence relating to the issue, including circumstantial evidence, can properly be considered together (*McCombie v Liverpool City Magistrates' Court* [2011] EWHC 758 (Admin)).

In *Evans v Walkden* [1956] 3 All ER 64, occupying the front passenger seat and supervising the driver, thereby being in a position to assume control if necessary, was held not to be equivalent to being in control, with the result that the supervisor was not a 'driver'. *Langman v Valentine* [1952] 2 All ER 803 was distinguished because there the degree of control exercised throughout by the supervisor was considerably greater.

The act of driving is a physical one which can only be performed by a natural person, and the words 'drive' and 'driver' should be construed accordingly. Consequently, the Divisional Court declined to make the respondent, a limited company, vicariously liable for an offence under the RTRA 1984, s. 8(1) (*Richmond London Borough Council v Pinn and Wheeler Ltd* [1989] RTR 354). See **C1.5** for examples of 'driving'.

C1.3 In *MacDonagh* [1974] QB 448 (a five-judge Court of Appeal), the essence of driving was said to be the use of 'the driver's controls for the purpose of directing the movement of the vehicle'. The defendant, who was disqualified from driving, having been asked by a police officer to move the car, explained that it had been pushed with both feet remaining on the road and one hand on the steering wheel. The jury were directed that this could properly be described as driving. Allowing the appeal, Lord Widgery CJ stated (at p. 451):

> There are an infinite number of ways in which a person may control the movement of a motor vehicle, apart from the orthodox one of sitting in the driving seat and using the engine for propulsion. He may be coasting down a hill with the gears in neutral and the engine switched off; he may be steering a vehicle which is being towed by another. As has already been pointed out, he may be sitting in the driving seat while others push, or half sitting in the driving seat but keeping one foot on the road in order to induce the car to move. Finally, as in the present case, he may be standing in the road and himself pushing the car with or without using the steering wheel to direct it. Although the word 'drive' must be given a wide meaning, the courts must be alert to see that the net is not thrown so widely that it includes activities which cannot be said to be driving a motor vehicle in any ordinary use of that word in the English language.

Controlling the movement and direction of a motor cycle by pushing and steering with the ignition and lights on constituted 'driving', as long as the defendant was wearing motor cyclist's clothing and a crash helmet (*McKoen v Ellis* [1987] RTR 26).

In *Selby v DPP* [1994] RTR 157n, Taylor LJ stated (at p. 162) that 'riding' is carried out 'if a person is being carried on a motor cycle as it moves on its wheels, whether propelled by the engine or by his feet or by gravity', which would seem to be equally applicable as the test for 'driving' a motor cycle (*Gunnell v DPP* [1994] RTR 151).

C1.4 Once the act of driving has commenced, ascertained by applying the *MacDonagh* test, it continues until it terminates, and a person may still be 'driving' although the vehicle is stationary (*Pinner v Everett* [1969] 3 All ER 257; *Skelton* [1995] Crim LR 635). In *Edkins v Knowles* [1973] QB 748, it was emphasised that the reason for stopping is relevant, as it may be part of the journey, e.g., traffic lights or a junction, or may mark a break in the journey, in which case the length of break and whether the driver leaves the vehicle become important. The issue is one of fact and degree, just as it is at the end of a journey, when various activities connected with driving must be completed before the driving is terminated, e.g., switching off the ignition and securing the vehicle. The court must consider the period of time and the circumstances to decide whether the person still in the driving seat was 'driving' (*Planton v DPP* [2001] EWHC Admin 450, [2002] RTR 9 (107)).

Examples of Driving *MacDonagh* [1974] QB 448 was followed in *McQuaid v Anderton* [1981] 1 WLR 154, in which the appellant, who was disqualified, was steering a towed vehicle which had an operational braking system. The Divisional Court held that the method of propulsion was irrelevant and dismissed his appeal. **C1.5**

A person steering a vehicle from the passenger seat, over an appreciable period of time, was driving, as was the person sitting in the driver's seat (*Tyler v Whatmore* [1976] RTR 83), but a momentary seizure of the steering wheel causing the vehicle to leave the road, whilst borderline, could not properly be described as 'driving' (*Jones v Pratt* [1983] RTR 54). In neither case did the court consider the interpretation provisions and any possible definition of 'steersman'. *Jones v Pratt* was followed in *DPP v Hastings* [1993] RTR 205, where there was a similar momentary seizure of the wheel. Although the seizure in *Hastings* was intended to cause danger, there was no finding that the driver relinquished control and the seizure was regarded as 'an act of interfering with the driving of the car rather than an act of driving in itself'.

In *Burgoyne v Phillips* [1983] RTR 49, releasing the handbrake and sitting in the car with the steering locked and the engine off whilst the vehicle moved by reason of gravity was held to be driving, although the defendant had left the keys to the car elsewhere. In *Leach v DPP* [1993] RTR 161, however, sitting in the driving seat of a stationary motor vehicle with hands on the steering wheel and the engine off was held not to be, *per se*, driving within the meaning of the RTA 1988, s. 163(1), so as to make it an offence to fail to stop for a constable. Where the engine is on but forward propulsion is being prevented because the handbrake remains applied so that the vehicle's wheels merely spin then, applying *MacDonagh*, this amounts to driving (*DPP v Alderton* [2003] EWHC 2917 (Admin), [2004] RTR 23 (367)). However, in *Whelehan v DPP* [1995] RTR 177, quite apart from admitting having driven to the location where the defendant was found by a constable, the Divisional Court concluded that being discovered in the driving seat of a stationary motor vehicle on a road at 1.20 a.m. with the keys in the ignition switch afforded sufficient evidence from which to infer that the defendant had driven to that location. **C1.6**

Kneeling on the driving seat, releasing the handbrake and attempting to re-apply the handbrake was material upon which justices might find a defendant was driving (*Rowan v Chief Constable of Merseyside* (1985) *The Times*, 10 December 1985).

Mechanical Defect

Where a driver is deprived of control of a motor vehicle as a result of a mechanical defect of which the driver has no knowledge, real or constructive, then such a defect is a defence to a charge of careless driving and a charge of contravening the regulations relating to pedestrian crossings and there seems little or no reason why its principles should not be of wider application. **C1.7**

This defence of mechanical or latent defect stems from *Kay v Butterworth* (1945) 61 TLR 452, *Simpson v Peat* [1952] 2 QB 24, *Hill v Baxter* [1958] 1 QB 227, and the general proposition that in cases not involving fault the law should seek to avoid the imposition of any criminal sanction.

In *Spurge* [1961] 2 QB 205, the appellant had recently purchased a car with a tendency to move to the right when the brakes were applied, and had been convicted of dangerous driving (as it existed before the RTA 1988, s. 2, was enacted). His appeal was dismissed and Salmon J stressed that successful reliance on the defence would be rare and that it did not apply where the defect was known, or would have been discovered by the exercise of reasonable prudence. He stated (at p. 212) that: 'The essence of the defence is that the danger has been created by a sudden total loss of control in no way due to any fault on the part of the driver'. It is for the defence to raise the issue, but the onus of disproving it remains with the prosecution.

C1.8 In *Burns v Bidder* [1967] 2 QB 227, the Divisional Court allowed an appeal against a pedestrian crossing offence as the convicting magistrate failed to consider the defence of mechanical defect at all, wrongly believing the offence to be absolute. James J stated (at pp. 240–1):

> The cases of the driver suddenly stung by a swarm of bees or suffering a sudden epileptic form of disabling attack, or a vehicle being propelled forward by reason of another vehicle hitting it from behind, are illustrations of where no offence may be shown, because control over the vehicle is taken completely out of the hands of the driver, and his failure to accord precedence on that account would be no offence.
>
> Likewise in my view a sudden removal of control over the vehicle occasioned by a latent defect of which the driver did not know and could not reasonably be expected to know would render the resulting failure to accord precedence no offence, provided he is in no way at fault himself.

Where the possibility exists of mechanical defect being raised in response to a charge, it is desirable to have in place procedures ensuring that the vehicle concerned will not be scrapped until all inquiries, including those on behalf of a defendant, have been completed (see, e.g., *Beckford* [1996] 1 Cr App R 96).

Motor Vehicle and Mechanically Propelled Vehicle

C1.9 The term 'motor vehicle' is defined in the RTA 1988, s. 185 (see **C1.31**), as a mechanically propelled vehicle intended or adapted for use on roads. A mechanically propelled vehicle does not need to be intended or adapted for such use; whether a vehicle is mechanically propelled remains a question of fact. Section 185 is expressly subject to the Chronically Sick and Disabled Persons Act 1970, s. 20, so an invalid carriage used in accordance with the conditions prescribed by that section will not be a 'motor vehicle' for the purpose of certain offences, e.g., the RTA 1988, s. 5 (*Croitoru v DPP* [2016] EWHC 1645 (Admin), [2017] 1 WLR 1130).

A vehicle which has more than one source of power does not cease to be 'mechanically propelled', even though it is propelled by means other than an engine at the relevant time (*Floyd v Bush* [1953] 1 All ER 265). This extends to a vehicle which is being towed, even though that vehicle may be in such a poor condition that it could not be propelled under its own power, and even though it was at the same time a 'trailer', a 'vehicle' drawn by a 'motor vehicle' (*Cobb v Whorton* [1971] RTR 392).

A suitably adapted vehicle, even though originally constructed for use on the roads, may, as a question of fact, cease to be a 'motor vehicle' within the meaning of s. 185, as in *Lawrence v Howlett* [1952] 2 All ER 74, where the auxiliary engine had been removed from a moped making it into a 'pedal cycle'. Normally, however, only when it is clear that a vehicle will not become mobile again can it be said that it ceases to be a 'motor vehicle', and in each case that is a question of fact for the court.

C1.10 In *Burns v Currell* [1963] 2 QB 433, Lord Parker CJ, adopting a 'reasonable person' test as to the use of the vehicle, stated (at p. 440):

> ...in the ordinary case... there will be little difficulty in saying whether a particular vehicle is a motor vehicle or not. But to define exactly the meaning of the words 'intended or adapted' is by no means easy. I think that the expression 'intended'... does not mean 'intended by the user of the vehicle either at the moment of the alleged offence or for the future'.

This case was followed in *Chief Constable of Avon and Somerset Constabulary v F (A Juvenile)* [1987] RTR 378, where Glidewell LJ said (at pp. 382–3):

> I emphasise that that test is what would be the view of the reasonable man as to the general user of this particular vehicle; not what was the particular user to which this particular defendant put it... if a reasonable man were to say 'Yes, this vehicle might well be used on the road', then, applying the test, the vehicle is intended or adapted for such use. If that be the case, it is nothing to the point if the individual defendant says: 'I normally use it for scrambling and I am only pushing it along the road on this occasion because I have no other means of getting it home', or something of that sort.

The test was also applied in *DPP v Saddington* [2001] RTR 15 (227), in relation to a motorised scooter, the 'Go-ped', to conclude that, although the vehicle was incapable of being registered as such and fell foul of the construction and use regulations, it was a 'motor vehicle' for the purposes of the RTA 1988, s. 185(1). This conclusion was reached because a reasonable person would say that one of the scooter's uses would be general use on the roads. See, in relation to a Segway, *Coates v CPS* [2011] EWHC 2032 (Admin), (2011) 175 JP 401.

For a motor vehicle to change its character from that intended by the manufacturer, a very substantial or dramatic alteration would be required for it to cease to be a motor vehicle; the addition of something that may make the vehicle unusable on a road might suffice, but the absence of registration plates, reflectors, lights or the speedometer would be insufficient (*DPP v Ryan* [1992] RTR 13). **C1.11**

In *Maddox v Storer* [1963] 1 QB 451, the Divisional Court stated that it was necessary to look to the context in which the word 'adapted' was used, and when used alone it was held to have the adjectival meaning of 'being fit and apt for the purpose'. If used disjunctively, as an alternative to 'constructed', its meaning was 'being altered so as to make it fit'.

In *Millard v Turvey* [1968] 2 QB 390, a chassis without a cab, doors, roof, windscreen or seats for the accommodation of passengers was held to be a motor vehicle, albeit under construction, but was not a 'motor tractor'. In *Tahsin* [1970] RTR 88, it was held that a moped did not cease to be a 'motor vehicle' merely because its engine would not work. A moped, however, does not become a motor cycle merely because one pedal is missing (*G (A Minor) v Jarrett* [1981] RTR 186). For a vehicle to change in such a manner requires an alteration in its design or construction.

Owner

See the RTA 1988, s. 192, at **C1.31**. **C1.12**

In relation to a vehicle which is subject to a hiring or hire-purchase agreement, 'owner' includes the person in possession of the vehicle under that agreement. Even if the person lawfully in possession of the vehicle under a hiring agreement parts with it to a third party, who may then drive the vehicle without documents, insurance etc., unless the agreement provides for instant termination of the hire, so that property in the vehicle immediately reverts to the person who has legal title to the vehicle, the third party would not commit an offence under the Theft Act 1968, s. 12, although both that third person and the person in possession of the vehicle under the hiring agreement may be guilty of other offences relating to the absence of insurance, etc.

Road or Other Public Place

Road The word 'road' is defined by the RTA 1988, s. 192 (see **C1.31**). It includes any highway and any other road to which the public has access, including bridges over which a road passes. The *Concise Oxford Dictionary* defines 'road' as 'a line of communication between places for use of pedestrians, riders, and vehicles'. The RTA 1988, s. 34(1)(b), includes footpaths and bridleways as being within the definition of a road. **C1.13**

In *Clarke v Kato* [1998] 4 All ER 417, at p. 422, the House of Lords confirmed that whether a place which is not a highway is a 'road' within the meaning of the RTA 1988, s. 192, is a question of fact to be determined after consideration of its physical character and the function it exists to serve. Lord Clyde gave the following guidance:

> One obvious feature of a road as commonly understood is that its physical limits are defined or at least definable. It should always be possible to ascertain the sides of a road or to have them ascertained. Its location should be identifiable as a route or way. It will often have a prepared surface and have been manufactured or constructed. But it may simply have developed by the repeated passage of traffic over the same area of land. It may be continuous, like a circular route, or it may come to a termination, as in the case of a cul-de-sac. A road may run on a single line without diversion or it may have branches.
>
> . . . it is also necessary to consider the function of the place in order to see if it qualifies as a road. Essentially a road serves as a means of access. It leads from one place to another and constitutes a

Part C Road Traffic Offences

route whereby travellers may move conveniently between the places to which and from which it leads. It is thus a defined or at least a definable way intended to enable those who pass over it to reach a destination. Its precise extent will require to be a matter of detailed decision as matter of fact in the particular circumstances. Lines may require to be drawn to determine the point at which the road ends and the destination has been reached. Where there is a door or a gate the problem may be readily resolved. Where there is no physical point which can be readily identified, then by an exercise of reasonable judgment an imaginary line will have to be drawn to mark the point where it should be held that the road has ended. Whether or not a particular area is or is not a road eventually comes to be a matter of fact.

Accordingly, a place that can reasonably be described as a car park does not, save in exceptional circumstances, qualify as a road, and in the event of a carriageway being found to exist within its bounds which does so qualify, the remaining area will retain its integrity as a car park. Trafalgar Square is a road (*Sadiku v DPP* [2000] RTR 155). In *Barrett v DPP* [2009] EWHC 423 (Admin), [2010] RTR 2 (8), a route between points marked on a plan which was a roadway with defined edges, road marking and signs was confirmed to be a road.

C1.14 In *Price v DPP* [1990] RTR 413, where the defendant drove across a pavement (part of which was maintained at public expense and part of which was privately owned) thereby causing a pedestrian to jump out of the way, it was held that the justices were fully entitled to conclude that the pavement as a whole constituted a road and the defendant was, therefore, properly convicted of driving without reasonable consideration for another road user.

In *Hawkins v Phillips* [1980] RTR 197, a filter lane or slip road was held to be part of the main carriageway for the purposes of the RTRA 1967. 'Highway' is defined as a 'public road, main route by land or water'. In *Lang v Hindhaugh* [1986] RTR 271, a footpath which was not designed for motor vehicles or passable by motor cars was held to be a highway.

In *Worth v Brooks* [1959] Crim LR 855, the grass verge by the side of a carriageway was held to form part of the highway which itself constituted a road. In *Avery v CPS* [2011] EWHC 2388 (Admin), [2012] RTR 8 (87), where the physical boundary of the road was in issue, it being asserted that the wheels of the vehicle driven by the defendant remained on a private driveway, the Divisional Court held that any material encroachment on the air-space vertically above the road was sufficient to justify a conclusion that the vehicle concerned was on the road, because the legislation seeks to protect the public from the effects of drunken driving in a place where they might be expected to pass and repass in safety. In *Dunmill v DPP* [2004] EWHC 1700 (Admin), (2004) *The Times*, 15 July 2004, a grass area within a camp site, which may have been a public place, was held not to be a road.

In *Holliday v Henry* [1974] RTR 101, an ingenious attempt to avoid a vehicle being 'on' a road by placing a roller skate under each wheel was rejected by the Divisional Court, which stated that it was perfectly clear that the vehicle was 'on' the road.

C1.15 The question of whether a particular road is one to which the public has access is one of fact and degree (*Waterfield* [1964] 1 QB 164). In any case where use by the public may not be readily apparent, *Hallett v DPP* [2011] EWHC 488 (Admin) emphasises the need for the prosecution to adduce evidence of such use.

The primary intended use of a place, irrespective of whether it is publicly or privately owned, does not appear to be of relevance (*Price v DPP* [1990] RTR 413). A road which is not maintainable and manageable at public expense does not preclude it from being 'a road open to the public' as that expression refers to a road to which the public has access (*DPP v Cargo Handling Ltd* [1992] RTR 318).

C1.16 **Other Public Place** It is a truism to state that a public place is one to which the public has access. It is not, however, definitive. Whether such access is sufficient for a finding that the place is a 'public place' for the purposes of the Road Traffic Acts is a question of fact and degree to be arrived at after consideration of the evidence (*Planton v DPP* [2001] EWHC Admin 450, [2002] RTR 9 (107)). Justices are entitled to use their 'local knowledge' in arriving at their conclusion on this point, but it is good practice to inform the prosecution and defence so that they can comment (*Bowman v DPP* [1991] RTR 263).

In *DPP v Vivier* [1991] RTR 205, a case under the RTA 1988, s. 5(1)(a), the Divisional Court gave wide consideration to the meaning of 'public place'. The defendant had been driving a car in a caravan park which covered 80 acres and contained between three and four miles of road. The number of people present in the caravan park, whether admitted as caravanners, campers, or their guests, varied between 800 and 3,500, depending on the time of year. The Divisional Court referred to *Montgomery v Loney* [1959] NILR 171, in which the distinction was drawn between members of the general public and persons who belong to a special class of members of the public and who have 'some reason personal to them for their admittance', such as postmen, meter readers and employees going to work along a factory road, concluding that 'the decision whether a place was a place to which the public had access...was a matter of fact and degree but whether the material for consideration sufficed to support one view or the other was a matter of law'.

Whether a place is a public place can be identified by looking at the people who use it and their reasons for doing so. In *DPP v Vivier*, Simon Brown J separated such persons into two categories: those who seek entry for the purposes of the occupier, including guests, postmen or meter readers going to a private house, recognised as a special class of people distinct from members of the general public, and those who seek entry for their own purposes and yet are screened in the sense of having to satisfy certain conditions for admission. In the latter case, the court needs to ask whether 'those admitted pass through the screening process for a reason, or on account of some characteristic, personal to themselves', or whether in truth they are 'merely members of the public who are being admitted as such and processed simply so as to make them subject to payment and whatever other conditions the landowner chooses to impose'. **C1.17**

In *DPP v Coulman* [1993] RTR 230, the Divisional Court concluded that, after disembarking at Dover Eastern Docks into the Freight Immigration Lanes, the respondent continued to be present there as a member of the public, rather than in any other special capacity, with the consequence that the Lanes constituted a public place for the purposes of the RTA 1988, s. 5. In *Havell v DPP* (1994) 158 JP 680, however, use of a car park (which was readily accessible from the road, without restricted access and not marked as being private) as a member of a bona fide club whose membership was not of such a size 'that it was indistinguishable from the public at large in the locality' did not constitute use as a member of the general public; therefore the defendant's appeal against a conviction for being 'in charge' of a motor vehicle on a road or other public place whilst unfit through drink or drugs was allowed. A company car park for the use of staff, customers and other visitors is not a public place unless there is proof of actual use of that car park by members of the public (*Spence* [1999] RTR 353). A car park adjoining a main road and used by members of the public generally is a public place (*May v DPP* [2005] EWHC 1280 (Admin)). In *Filmer v DPP* [2006] EWHC 3450 (Admin), [2007] RTR 28 (330), Fulford J indicated that 'the critical distinction is between private land to which the public have access at the time in question, on the one hand, and private land which is closed to the public at the material time or is only open to particular people, on the other'. These cases were further discussed in *Richardson v DPP* [2019] EWHC 428 (Admin), [2019] 4 WLR 46, in which it was confirmed that the presence or absence of any barrier is not determinative and there ought to be some evidence why any member of the general public should go to the place rather than only those having pre-ordained business there. In *Cowan v DPP* [2013] EWHC 192 (Admin), (2013) 177 JP 474, an internal roadway within Kingston Hill University campus was held not to be a public place; students, having a right to occupy their rooms and use the facilities on the campus, were doing so not as members of the public but by virtue of being students, and their visitors were accessing the site not as ordinary members of the public but for the purposes of those occupiers of the site.

Vehicle

The word 'vehicle' does not appear to have been given any statutory meaning, and may therefore include things as diverse as a bicycle or a poultry shed on wheels (*Garner v Burr* [1951] **C1.18**

1 KB 31). The *Concise Oxford English Dictionary* defines 'vehicle' as a 'carriage or conveyance of any kind used on land'.

BASIC PRINCIPLES

Aiding, Abetting, Counselling, Procuring

C1.19 For the meaning of these terms, see generally the Accessories and Abettors Act 1861, s. 8; the MCA 1980, s. 44(1); and **A4.1** *et seq*. See also *Martin* [2010] EWCA Crim 1450, [2011] RTR 4 (46) for guidance on jury directions that could be used in respect of a qualified supervising driver who is charged with aiding and abetting resulting from failing to act to intervene when accompanying a learner driver.

By the MCA 1980, s. 44, a person convicted of aiding, abetting, counselling or procuring a summary offence is guilty of the like offence, and if the substantive offence carries endorsement the defendant's licence must be endorsed and the defendant may be disqualified.

Where disqualification is mandatory for the principal offence (e.g., driving with excess alcohol in the breath), a person convicted of aiding and abetting etc. is liable to discretionary disqualification by virtue of the RTOA 1988, s. 34(5) (see **C7.8**), and the person's licence must be endorsed with ten penalty points (RTOA 1988, s. 28(1)(b)).

Attempts

C1.20 As to attempts generally, see **A5.72** *et seq*.

By virtue of the CAA 1981, s. 1(4) (see **A5.72**), it is not possible to attempt the commission of an offence which is purely summary, unless such an offence is created by statute (e.g., the RTA 1988, s. 5(1)(a), attempting to drive a motor vehicle on a road after consuming so much alcohol that the proportion of it in the breath etc. exceeds the prescribed limit). In *Mason v DPP* [2009] EWHC 2198 (Admin), [2010] RTR 11 (120), the Divisional Court suggested that embarking on the full offence of driving would occur when turning on the engine, but not when merely opening the vehicle's door. The CAA 1981, s. 3, enacts similar provisions in relation to statutory attempts as are contained in s. 1(2), (3) and (4) of the Act.

Automatism and Insanity

C1.21 As to insanity generally, see **A3.23** to **A3.33**. As to automatism generally, see **A3.12**.

Questions of fitness to plead and insanity are determined under the Criminal Procedure (Insanity) Act 1964 (see **D12.2** *et seq*.). In indictable offences, where these issues are raised, the magistrates' court is obliged to commit to the Crown Court in pursuance of that statute.

In the magistrates' court questions relating to automatism usually arise in the form of defences of involuntary behaviour on the part of the driver. (See also mechanical defect at **C1.7**, and duress or necessity at **A3.35** to **A3.49**.)

C1.22 In *Hill v Baxter* [1958] 1 QB 277, Lord Goddard CJ, having quoted a famous dictum of Humphreys J in *Kay v Butterworth* (1945) 61 TLR 452, went on to say (at p. 283):

> I agree that there may be cases where the circumstances are such that the accused could not really be said to be driving at all. Suppose he had a stroke or an epileptic fit, both instances of what may properly be called acts of God; he might well be in the driver's seat even with his hands on the wheel, but in such a state of unconsciousness that he could not be said to be driving. A blow from a stone or an attack by a swarm of bees I think introduces some conception akin to *novus actus interveniens*.

In such circumstances, the defendant is not 'driving' but has been rendered incapable of physical control of the vehicle. This is not automatism of the type considered in *Bailey* [1983] 2 All ER 503 and *Hardie* [1985] 3 All ER 848, but nonetheless arises without fault and should not therefore be the subject of any criminal sanction. There must, however, be 'a total destruction of voluntary control'; impaired or reduced control is not enough (*A-G's Ref (No. 2 of 1992)* [1994] QB 91, as endorsed in *Coley* [2013] EWCA Crim 223). The prosecution must establish the manner of the defendant's driving and then the defendant must adduce evidence of being totally unable to control the car (*C* [2007] EWCA Crim 1862). The lack of control must arise from causes which do not bring the defendant within the M'Naghten rules. Thus driving with 'a reduced or imperfect awareness', which is brought on by the repetitive stimuli experienced on a long journey and which reduces a driver's capacity to avoid collisions, cannot, as a matter of law, found a defence of automatism. Similarly, in *Watmore v Jenkins* [1962] 2 QB 572, Winn J pointed out that a finding by the justices that the defendant 'continued to perform the functions of driving, after a fashion' for five miles on a road which was not straight, was inconsistent with a finding of automatism 'extending throughout the whole of the distance… to which it related'.

Causing

A number of offences in the Road Traffic Acts may be committed by causing or permitting the use of, as well as using, a vehicle in a prohibited manner. Each of these gives rise to a separate offence. **C1.23**

'Causing' demands a positive act on the part of the defendant (*Price v Cromack* [1975] 2 All ER 113). It also requires prior knowledge. In *Milstead v Sexton* [1964] Crim LR 474, the defendant was convicted of causing a car to be used on a road where that car was being towed and the defendant was driving the towing vehicle. In *Ross Hillman Ltd v Bond* [1974] QB 435, the defendant was a limited company which owned a number of vehicles and employed a number of drivers, all of whom had been warned against driving their vehicles while overloaded. One of the employees drove a vehicle while it was overloaded. Allowing the defendant's appeal, May J stated (at p. 446):

> Unassisted by any authority I would as a matter of ordinary English construe both the word 'causes' and the word 'permits' in section 40(5)(b) of the Act of 1972 as requiring prior knowledge of the facts constituting the unlawful user… if, as I think and as is supported by authority, actual user of a vehicle in contravention of the regulations is an absolute offence, and if, as I also think, a master 'uses' the vehicle which his servant is driving on that master's business, then I think that the mischief against which the regulations are directed, that of having unsafe vehicles on the roads is adequately dealt with. Having regard to the ordinary meaning of 'causes' I do not find it surprising that, whereas on given facts a master charged with using will be convicted, on the same facts a master charged with causing that use will be acquitted.

In *Mounsey v Campbell* [1983] RTR 36, the defendant caused an obstruction by parking a van immediately in front of another motor vehicle so that vehicle was unable to move. The defence had argued that it was only when the defendant refused to move the van that the vehicle became an obstruction, and therefore the proper charge should have been one of 'permitting'. This argument was described as 'nebulous' by the Divisional Court, which found that the initial act of parking and subsequent refusal to move the vehicle could both constitute 'causing'. **C1.24**

A company which shut its eyes to the failure of its employee to fill in tachograph records could not be said to have 'caused' that failure. Such wilful ignorance may amount to 'permitting' but falls short of the 'positive mandate or… other sufficient act required for the offence' (*Redhead Freight Ltd v Shulman* [1989] RTR 1).

Permitting

In *Vehicle Inspectorate v Nuttall* [1999] 3 All ER 833, the House of Lords drew a distinction between positive acts where a person 'allows' or 'authorises' the use of the vehicle by another and omissions which amount to 'failure to take reasonable steps to prevent' such use. When the second, wider meaning applies to the context of the offence charged, it is not an offence of strict liability and, therefore, requires proof of nothing less than wilfulness or recklessness. This may **C1.25** be demonstrated by adducing actual evidence or by raising a rebuttable presumption. For example, in respect of regulatory tachograph requirements, if the employer fails to take reasonable steps to prevent employee drivers from contravening the statutory provisions, it raises a rebuttable presumption that the necessary mental element has been established (per Lord Steyn at p. 637C). The evidence adduced must, however, be capable of supporting such a presumption (*Yorkshire Traction Co. Ltd v Vehicle Inspectorate* [2001] EWHC Admin 190, [2001] RTR 34 (518)).

For 'permission' involving a positive act, proof of prior knowledge remains necessary (*Ross Hillman Ltd v Bond* [1974] QB 435). This connotes express or implied permission or acquiescence as much as direct participation.

'Knowledge' includes actual and constructive knowledge, such as 'the state of mind of a man who shuts his eyes to the obvious or allows his servant to do something in the circumstances where a contravention is likely, not caring whether a contravention takes place or not' (*James & Son Ltd v Smee* [1955] 1 QB 78, per Parker J at p. 91). Where justices had found that an employer did not know and had no reasonable cause to suspect that one of this vehicles had a defective braking system, it was not open to them to convict of an offence of permitting the vehicle's use, notwithstanding that the defendant would have had no answer to a charge of 'using' the vehicle in a defective condition (*Robinson v DPP* [1991] RTR 315).

C1.26 Negligence not amounting to recklessness did not justify an inference that a managing director, someone who might be said to be 'the "brains" of the company rather than its hands', was wilfully shutting an eye to the obvious, and therefore that a company was guilty of permitting the use of a vehicle on a road with defective brakes (*Hill & Sons (Botley and Denmead) Ltd v Hampshire Chief Constable* [1972] RTR 29).

That decision closely follows *Magna Plant Ltd v Mitchell* [1966] Crim LR 394, in which Lord Parker CJ said:

> A company was not criminally liable in the absence of knowledge of the facts constituting the offence for the failure of a servant to whom it had delegated a task. The servant was not in the position of the brains of the company and his knowledge could not be imputed to a director…

However, an employer's failure to operate an adequate, or any, system of checking tachograph charts was regarded as sufficiently reckless 'shutting of the eyes' so as to amount to implied knowledge in *Vehicle Inspectorate v Shane Raymond Nuttall t/a Redline Coaches* (1997) 161 JP 701. The test is one of fact and degree. For corporate liability, see **A6**.

C1.27 In cases of no insurance, permitting has a stricter interpretation. Where an owner allows the use of a vehicle, believing that use to be insured, such a belief is no defence to a charge of permitting the uninsured use of the vehicle (*Lyons v May* [1948] 2 All ER 1062; *Baugh v Crago* [1975] RTR 453). In exceptional circumstances a conditional permission to use a vehicle only with insurance does not constitute an offence (*Sheldon Deliveries Ltd v Willis* [1972] RTR 217; *Newbury v Davis* [1974] RTR 367), but such a defence must be regarded with extreme caution before it is capable of application (*DPP v Fisher* [1991] RTR 93, where it was held that the permission must be given direct to the would-be driver).

Using

C1.28 'Using' has a restricted meaning when found in the same section as 'causing' and 'permitting'. In such cases it is only the driver (or the driver's employer, when the driver is driving on that employer's business) who can be said to be 'using' the vehicle (*Mickleborough v BRS (Contracts) Ltd* [1977] RTR 389; *Jones v DPP* [1999] RTR 1; *Interlink Express Parcels Ltd v Night Truckers Ltd* [2000] RTR 324, where the vehicles were owned by another party). 'User' must involve an element of controlling, managing or operating the vehicle by the person concerned (*Hatton v Hall* [1997] RTR 212). For a non-driver of the vehicle, this element could exist as a result of a joint venture to use it for a particular purpose or where the passenger procures the making of the journey (*O'Mahoney v Joliffe* [1999] RTR 245); whether it does is a question of fact and degree.

These propositions extend to cases where the word 'use' is found, either alone, or in conjunction with another word such as 'keeps' (*James & Son Ltd v Smee* [1955] 1 QB 78; *Richardson v Baker* [1976] RTR 56). Use, however, by a person other than a servant, even a business partner, does not constitute use by the owner, albeit that the vehicle is being driven at the owner's request and with that person's full knowledge (*Crawford v Haughton* [1972] 1 All ER 535; *Garrett v Hooper* [1973] RTR 1). That sort of use may, of course, amount to 'permitting' or even 'causing'. However, *Hallett Silberman v Cheshire County Council* [1993] RTR 32 shows that a vehicle which exceeds its permitted weight may be being used by the owner even if its driver is self-employed and provides the tractor unit. The decision rests heavily on the degree of control exercised by the defendants, who supplied the trailer and chose the route; as such their position was analogous to that of an employer. By contrast, in *DPP v Seawheel Ltd* (1994) 158 JP 444, mere ownership of a part of the assembly on which a load was carried and which was secured to the trailer was insufficient to establish use; the tractor and trailer unit were owned by a person who had contracted to transport the load and there was no finding that the defendants were in possession of any of the relevant parts. It was suggested *obiter*, however, that a wider meaning should be given to 'use' when applied to a trailer rather than when applied to a lorry. However, where 'use' appears in a provision in conjunction with 'drive or cause or permit to be driven', 'use' will be construed more broadly so as to cover the owner of a vehicle used for the owner's purposes or on the owner's behalf and being driven by someone other than an employee (*Richmond upon Thames London Borough Council v Morton* [2000] RTR 79). **C1.29**

Vehicles left unattended on a road can still be regarded as being used, as 'use' has been held to mean 'having the use of' for these purposes (*Eden v Mitchell* [1975] RTR 425). Accordingly, the mere fact of having two defective tyres did not preclude the vehicle's use and the owner's intention in respect of using the vehicle was held to be irrelevant. Similarly, in *Elliott v Grey* [1960] 1 QB 367, despite having an engine that did not work, no battery and no petrol, the vehicle in question was being 'used' without insurance, as it could be moved, albeit not driven. The distinction drawn in *Hewer v Cutler* [1974] RTR 155, that immobile vehicles whose wheels would not rotate were outside the definition of 'use', was found to be unjustified by Mitchell J in *Pumbien v Vines* [1996] RTR 37. In that case the vehicle's tyres were deflated, the handbrake was on, the rear brakes were seized and the gearbox contained no oil because there was a leak in the transmission pipe. It was held that, provided the vehicle was a 'motor vehicle' within the definition of the RTA 1988, s. 185 (see generally **C1.31**), and was on a road, the owner had the use of it on a road, whether at the material time it could move on its wheels or not. This decision has also apparently removed the requirement of an 'element of controlling, managing or operating the vehicle as a vehicle' (*Nichol v Leach* [1972] RTR 476), in the sense of the vehicle being capable of movement 'as a vehicle'. Consequently, for the purposes of the RTA 1988, ss. 47 and 143, 'use' should be accorded the same meaning and mobility of the vehicle is irrelevant. **C1.30**

INTERPRETATION PROVISIONS OF ROAD TRAFFIC ACT 1988

Road Traffic Act 1988, ss. 185, 186, 189, 192 **C1.31**

185.—(1) In this Act—

'heavy locomotive' means a mechanically propelled vehicle which is not constructed itself to carry a load other than any of the excepted articles and the weight of which unladen exceeds 11690 kilograms,

'heavy motor car' means a mechanically propelled vehicle, not being a motor car, which is constructed itself to carry a load or passengers and the weight of which unladen exceeds 2540 kilograms,

'invalid carriage' means a mechanically propelled vehicle the weight of which unladen does not exceed 254 kilograms and which is specially designed and constructed, and not merely adapted, for the use of a person suffering from some physical defect or disability and is used solely by such a person,

'light locomotive' means a mechanically propelled vehicle which is not constructed itself to carry a load other than any of the excepted articles and the weight of which unladen does not exceed 11690 kilograms but does exceed 7370 kilograms,

'motor car' means a mechanically propelled vehicle, not being a motor cycle or an invalid carriage, which is constructed itself to carry a load or passengers and the weight of which unladen—

(a) if it is constructed solely for the carriage of passengers and their effects, is adapted to carry not more than seven passengers exclusive of the driver and is fitted with tyres of such type as may be specified in regulations made by the Secretary of State, does not exceed 3050 kilograms,

(b) if it is constructed or adapted for use for the conveyance of goods or burden of any description, does not exceed 3050 kilograms, or 3500 kilograms if the vehicle carries a container or containers for holding for the purposes of its propulsion any fuel which is wholly gaseous at 17.5 degrees Celsius under a pressure of 1.013 bar or plant and material for producing such fuel,

(c) does not exceed 2540 kilograms in a case not falling within subparagraph (a) or (b) above,

'motor cycle' means a mechanically propelled vehicle, not being an invalid carriage, with less than four wheels and the weight of which unladen does not exceed 410 kilograms,

'motor tractor' means a mechanically propelled vehicle which is not constructed itself to carry a load, other than the excepted articles, and the weight of which unladen does not exceed 7370 kilograms,

'motor vehicle' means, subject to section 20 of the Chronically Sick and Disabled Persons Act 1970 (which makes special provision about invalid carriages, within the meaning of that Act), a mechanically propelled vehicle intended or adapted for use on roads, and 'trailer' means a vehicle drawn by a motor vehicle.

(2) In subsection (1) above 'excepted articles' means any of the following: water, fuel, accumulators and other equipment used for the purpose of propulsion, loose tools and loose equipment.

186.—(1) For the purposes of section 185 of this Act, a side car attached to a motor vehicle, if it complies with such conditions as may be specified in regulations made by the Secretary of State, is to be regarded as forming part of the vehicle to which it is attached and as not being a trailer.

(2) For the purposes of section 185 of this Act, in a case where a motor vehicle is so constructed that a trailer may by partial super-imposition be attached to the vehicle in such a manner as to cause a substantial part of the weight of the trailer to be borne by the vehicle, that vehicle is to be deemed to be a vehicle itself constructed to carry a load.

(3) For the purposes of section 185 of this Act, in the case of a motor vehicle fitted with a crane, dynamo, welding plant or other special appliance or apparatus which is a permanent or essentially permanent fixture, the appliance or apparatus is not to be deemed to constitute a load or goods or burden of any description, but is to be deemed to form part of the vehicle.

(4)–(6) [Regulations.]

189.—(1) For the purposes of the Road Traffic Acts—

(a) a mechanically propelled vehicle being an implement for cutting grass which is controlled by a pedestrian and is not capable of being used or adapted for any other purpose,

(b) any other mechanically propelled vehicle controlled by a pedestrian which may be specified by regulations made by the Secretary of State for the purposes of this section and section 140 of the Road Traffic Regulation Act 1984, and

(c) an electrically assisted pedal cycle of such a class as may be prescribed by regulations so made, is to be treated as not being a motor vehicle.

(2) In subsection (1) above 'controlled by a pedestrian' means that the vehicle either—

(a) is constructed or adapted for use only under such control, or

(b) is constructed or adapted for use either under such control or under the control of a person carried on it, but is not for the time being in use under, or proceeding under, the control of a person carried on it.

192.—(1) In this Act—

. . .

'bridleway' means a way over which the public have the following, but no other, rights of way: a right of way on foot and a right of way on horseback or leading a horse, with or without a right to drive animals of any description along the way,

'carriage of goods' includes the haulage of goods,

'cycle' means a bicycle, a tricycle, or a cycle having four or more wheels, not being in any case a motor vehicle,

'driver', where a separate person acts as a steersman of a motor vehicle, includes (except for the purposes of section 1 of this Act) that person as well as any other person engaged in the driving of the vehicle, and 'drive' is to be interpreted accordingly,

'footpath', in relation to England and Wales, means a way over which the public have a right of way on foot only,

'goods' includes goods or burden of any description,

'goods vehicle' means a motor vehicle constructed or adapted for use for the carriage of goods, or a trailer so constructed or adapted,

'highway authority', in England and Wales, means—

(a) in relation to a road for which he is the highway authority within the meaning of the Highways Act 1980, the Secretary of State, and

(b) in relation to any other road, the council of the county, metropolitan district or London borough, or the Common Council of the City of London, as the case may be;

'international road haulage permit' means a licence, permit, authorisation or other document issued in pursuance of an EU instrument relating to the carriage of goods by road between member States or an international agreement to which the United Kingdom is a party and which relates to the international carriage of goods by road,

'owner', in relation to a vehicle which is the subject of a hiring agreement or hire-purchase agreement, means the person in possession of the vehicle under that agreement,

'prescribed' (except in section 5A) means prescribed by regulations made by the Secretary of State,

'road'—

(a) in relation to England and Wales, means any highway and any other road to which the public has access, and includes bridges over which a road passes, and

(b) [Applies only to Scotland.];

'the Road Traffic Acts' means the Road Traffic Offenders Act 1988, the Road Traffic (Consequential Provisions) Act 1988 (so far as it reproduces the effect of provisions repealed by that Act) and this Act,

'statutory', in relation to any prohibition, restriction, requirement or provision, means contained in, or having effect under, any enactment (including any enactment contained in this Act),

'the Traffic Acts' means the Road Traffic Acts and the Road Traffic Regulation Act 1984,

'traffic sign' has the meaning given by section 64(1) of the Road Traffic Regulation Act 1984,

'tramcar' includes any carriage used on any road by virtue of an order under the Light Railways Act 1896, and

'trolley vehicle' means a mechanically propelled vehicle adapted for use on roads without rails under power transmitted to it from some external source (whether or not there is in addition a source of power on board the vehicle).

(1A) In this Act—

(a) any reference to a county shall be construed in relation to Wales as including a reference to a county borough; and

(b) section 17(4) and (5) of the Local Government (Wales) Act 1994 (references to counties and districts to be construed generally in relation to Wales as references to counties and county boroughs) shall not apply.

(2) [Applies only to Scotland.]

(3) References in this Act to a class of vehicles are to be interpreted as references to a class defined or described by reference to any characteristics of the vehicles or to any other circumstances whatsoever and accordingly as authorising the use of 'category' to indicate a class of vehicles, however defined or described.

Section C2 Procedure and Evidence in Road Traffic Cases

PROCEDURE

Notice of Intended Prosecution

C2.1 **Road Traffic Offenders Act 1988, ss. 1 and 2**

1.—(1) Subject to section 2 of this Act, a person shall not be convicted of an offence to which this section applies unless—

(a) he was warned at the time the offence was committed that the question of prosecuting him for some one or other of the offences to which this section applies would be taken into consideration, or

(b) within 14 days of the commission of the offence a summons (or, in Scotland, a complaint) for the offence was served on him, or

(c) within 14 days of the commission of the offence a notice of the intended prosecution specifying the nature of the alleged offence and the time and place where it is alleged to have been committed, was—

(i) in the case of an offence under section 28 or 29 of the Road Traffic Act 1988 (cycling offences), served on him,

(ii) in the case of any other offence, served on him or on the person, if any, registered as the keeper of the vehicle at the time of the commission of the offence.

(1A) A notice required by this section to be served on any person may be served on that person—

(a) by delivering it to him;

(b) by addressing it to him and leaving it at his last known address;

(c) by sending it by registered post, recorded delivery service or first class post addressed to him at his last known address.

(2) A notice shall be deemed for the purposes of subsection (1)(c) above to have been served on a person if it was sent by registered post or recorded delivery service addressed to him at his last known address, notwithstanding that the notice was returned as undelivered or was for any other reason not received by him.

(3) The requirement of subsection (1) above shall in every case be deemed to have been complied with unless and until the contrary is proved.

(4) Schedule 1 to this Act shows the offences to which this section applies.

2.—(1) The requirement of section 1(1) of this Act does not apply in relation to an offence if, at the time of the offence or immediately after it, an accident occurs owing to the presence on a road of the vehicle in respect of which the offence was committed.

(2) [Exception for fixed penalty notices.]

(3) Failure to comply with the requirement of section 1(1) of this Act is not a bar to the conviction of the accused in a case where the court is satisfied—

(a) that neither the name and address of the accused nor the name and address of the registered keeper, if any, could with reasonable diligence have been ascertained in time for a summons or, as the case may be, a complaint to be served or for a notice to be served or sent in compliance with the requirement, or

(b) that the accused by his own conduct contributed to the failure.

(4) Failure to comply with the requirement of section 1(1) of this Act in relation to an offence is not a bar to the conviction of a person of that offence by virtue of the provisions of—

(a) section 24 of this Act, or

(b) any of the enactments mentioned in section 24(6);

but a person is not to be convicted of an offence by virtue of any of those provisions if section 1 applies to the offence with which he was charged and the requirement of section 1(1) was not satisfied in relation to the offence charged.

The oral warning referred to in s. 1(1)(a) must have been understood by the defendant. The test was set out in *Gibson v Dalton* [1980] RTR 410, by Donaldson LJ (at pp. 413–14): C2.2

> The obligation on the prosecutor is to warn the accused, not merely to address a warning to him or to give a warning. The mischief to which this section is directed is clear. It is that motorists are entitled to have it brought to their attention at a relatively early stage that there is likely to be a prosecution in order that they may recall and, it may be, record the facts as they occurred at the time.... But a warning which does not get through to the accused person is of no value at all, and prima facie, therefore, the words might be expected to mean that the warning must get through....
>
> If, viewing the matter objectively, one would expect that the words addressed to the accused person would have been heard and understood by him, then prima facie he was warned within the meaning of the statute. But it is only a prima facie case. It is open to the defendant to prove, if he can, that he did not understand or hear or appreciate the warning and therefore that he was not warned.

The warning must have been given 'at the time' the offence was committed, which is a matter of fact and degree judged on what was reasonable (*Okike* [1978] RTR 489). In *Stacey* [1982] RTR 20, the Court of Appeal held that this issue was to be decided by the judge and added that whether the chain of circumstances was unbroken and whether all that took place was connected with the incident were relevant factors.

The warning must relate to one or other of the offences to which s. 1 applies as set out in sch. 1 to the Act. These include: dangerous driving (see **C3.39**); careless, and inconsiderate, driving (see **C6.1**); leaving a vehicle in a dangerous position (see **C6.16**); failing to comply with traffic directions (see **C6.22**) and traffic signs (see **C6.25**); and speeding (see **C6.58**). It need not specify the particular offence or offences but rather their nature. Alternative verdicts may be entered in accordance with the provisions of the Criminal Law Act 1967, s. 6(3), or the RTOA 1988, s. 24 (see **C2.8**), if the requirements of s. 1(1) have been complied with in relation to the original offence charged.

If the warning was not given at the time then a summons must be served within 14 days. The MCA 1980, s. 47, offers a saving provision where service by post has not been proved, enabling a second summons to be issued on the same information. In other cases a notice of intended prosecution must be served within 14 days on the driver or registered keeper of the vehicle. Service is deemed under s. 1(2) if sent by registered post or recorded delivery service, as long as it was sent so as to be delivered, in the ordinary course of post, within the 14 days (*Groome v Driscoll* [1969] 3 All ER 1638). Such deeming of service is unavailable where the notice of intended prosecution was actually delivered after the end of the 14-day period, despite having been posted in accordance with the rebuttable presumption in CrimPR 4.11 (see Supplement, **R4.11**), so that it would be delivered within that time-limit (*Gidden v Chief Constable of Humberside* [2009] EWHC 2924 (Admin), [2010] 2 All ER 75, where the cause was a postal strike). C2.3

Section 1(3) places the burden of proving failure to comply with the section on the defence on a balance of probabilities. Unless and until the defendant has given evidence of not having received the notice, the warning that must be given is deemed to have been given under s. 1(3) (*Hall v CPS* [2013] EWHC 2544 (Admin)). Because the question of service is a highly technical point, where the evidence is lacking on this issue it falls within the discretion of the court to grant an adjournment to allow the parties the chance to deal with the matter properly and fully (*R (Taylor) v Southampton Magistrates' Court* [2008] EWHC 3006 (Admin), (2009) 173 JP 17).

The requirement in s. 1 does not apply if there has been an accident of which the defendant was aware or which the defendant has deliberately ignored, but if the incident was so trivial that the driver was unaware of it a notice of intended prosecution is necessary (*Bentley v Dickinson* [1983] RTR 356). For these purposes, 'accident' should be given a common-sense meaning and not be restricted to untoward or unintended consequences having an adverse physical effect (*Currie* [2007] EWCA Crim 926, [2007] 2 Cr App R 18 (246)). The principle applied in *Bentley v Dickinson*, however, does not extend to cases where the driver's injuries are so severe that the driver has no recollection of the accident (*DPP v Pidhajeckyj* [1991] RTR 136). There must be a sufficient causal link C2.4

between the offence and the accident before the warning can be dispensed with (*Myers* [2007] EWCA Crim 599, [2007] 2 Cr App R 19 (258)).

Section 2(3) contains a saving where the prosecution have acted with reasonable diligence or where the accused's own conduct has contributed to a failure to comply with s. 1. In *Pledge* [2019] EWCA Crim 912, [2019] 4 WLR 110, relying on information found on the Police National Computer, which derived from the DVLA, was found to be reasonable diligence. Where the court is satisfied that s. 2(3)(a) applies, that is the end of the requirement to serve a summons within 14 days; it does not set a second period of 14 days running once the name and address have been ascertained (*R* [2012] EWCA Crim 2887). In the Crown Court, determining this issue is a matter for the judge rather than the jury (*Currie*).

Time-limits

C2.5 The MCA 1980, s. 127, lays down a general time-limit of six months for the laying of an information for a summary offence, subject to any enactment which expressly permits a longer period. *Brown v DPP* [2019] EWHC 798 (Admin), [2019] RTR 34 (449) explains when the six-month period expires for the purpose of 'issuing' under the CJA 2003, s. 29.

The RTOA 1988, s. 6, provides for an extended time-limit in relation to certain offences specified in sch. 1 to the Act. These include: driving while disqualified (see **C6.40**); insurance offences (see **C6.46** and **C6.50**); false statements (see **C4.20**) and certain offences relating to driving licences. In those cases proceedings may be commenced within a period of six months from the date on which sufficient evidence came to the prosecutor's knowledge; that date is conclusively proved by a signed certificate (*Haringey Magistrates' Court, ex parte Amvrosiou* (13 June 1996 unreported, QBD), which raised the possibility that fraud or inaccuracy on the face of the certificate might have an effect on conclusiveness). No proceedings are to be brought more than three years after the offence.

A traffic examiner employed by the vehicle inspectorate to investigate traffic offences, but not authorised to decide whether to prosecute, is not a prosecutor for the purposes of the 1988 Act (*Swan v Vehicle Inspectorate* [1997] RTR 187).

Duty to Produce Licence to Court

C2.6 **Road Traffic Offenders Act 1988, s. 7**

(1) A person who is prosecuted for an offence involving obligatory or discretionary disqualification and who is the holder of a licence must—
  (a) cause it to be delivered to the proper officer of the court not later than the day before the date appointed for the hearing, or
  (b) post it, at such a time that in the ordinary course of post it would be delivered not later than that day, in a letter duly addressed to the clerk and either registered or sent by the recorded delivery service, or
  (c) have it with him at the hearing

'Licence' includes a Community licence (RTOA 1988, s. 91A(1)).

Where the procedure for trial by a single justice on the papers applies (see **D22.33**), s. 7(1) does not apply and special provision is made by s. 7(1A) to (1C) (introduced by the CJCA 2015, sch. 11, para. 9) for the delivery of the licence to a designated officer.

Notification as to Disabilities

C2.7 **Road Traffic Offenders Act 1988, s. 22**

(1) If in any proceedings for an offence committed in respect of a motor vehicle it appears to the court that the accused may be suffering from any relevant disability or prospective disability (within the meaning of Part III of the Road Traffic Act 1988) the court must notify the Secretary of State.

'Relevant disability' means the disabilities set out in the Motor Vehicles (Driving Licences) Regulations 1999 (SI 1999 No. 2864), Part VI. There must be some evidence of such a disability before the court may notify the Secretary of State.

Alternative Verdicts

C2.8

Road Traffic Offenders Act 1988, s. 24

(A1) Where—
(a) a person charged with manslaughter in connection with the driving of a mechanically propelled vehicle by him is found not guilty of that offence, but
(b) the allegations in the indictment amount to or include an allegation of any of the relevant offences, he may be convicted of that offence.

(A2) For the purposes of subsection (A1) above the following are the relevant offences—
(a) an offence under section 1 of the Road Traffic Act 1988 (causing death by dangerous driving),
(aa) an offence under section 1A of that Act (causing serious injury by dangerous driving),
(b) an offence under section 2 of that Act (dangerous driving),
(ba) an offence under section 3ZC of that Act (causing death by driving: disqualified drivers),
(bb) an offence under section 3ZD of that Act (causing serious injury by driving: disqualified drivers),
(c) an offence under section 3A of that Act (causing death by careless driving when under the influence of drink or drugs), and
(d) an offence under section 35 of the Offences against the Person Act 1861 (furious driving).

(1) Where—
(a) a person charged with an offence under a provision of the Road Traffic Act 1988 specified in the first column of the table below (where the general nature of the offences is also indicated) is found not guilty of that offence, but
(b) the allegations in the indictment or information (or in Scotland complaint) amount to or include an allegation of an offence under one or more of the provisions specified in the corresponding entry in the second column,

he may be convicted of that offence or of one or more of those offences.

Offence charged	Alternative
Section 1 (causing death by dangerous driving)	Section 2 (dangerous driving) Section 2B (causing death by careless, or inconsiderate, driving) Section 3 (careless, and inconsiderate, driving)
Section 1A (causing serious injury by dangerous driving)	Section 2 (dangerous driving) Section 3 (careless and inconsiderate driving)
Section 2 (dangerous driving)	Section 3 (careless, and inconsiderate, driving)
Section 2B (causing death by careless, or inconsiderate, driving)	Section 3 (careless, and inconsiderate, driving)
Section 3ZC (causing death by driving: disqualified drivers)	Section 103(1)(b) (driving while disqualified)
Section 3ZD (causing serious injury by driving: disqualified drivers)	Section 103(1)(b) (driving while disqualified)
Section 3A (causing death by careless driving when under influence of drink or drugs)	Section 2B (causing death by careless, or inconsiderate, driving) Section 3 (careless and inconsiderate driving) Section 4(1) (driving when unfit to drive through drink or drugs) Section 5(1)(a) (driving with excess alcohol in breath, blood or urine) Section 7(6) (failing to provide specimen) Section 7A(6) (failing to give permission for laboratory test)
Section 4(1) (driving or attempting to drive when unfit to drive through drink or drugs)	Section 4(2) (being in charge of a vehicle when unfit to drive through drink or drugs)
Section 5(1)(a) (driving or attempting to drive with excess alcohol in breath, blood or urine)	Section 5(1)(b) (being in charge of a vehicle with excess alcohol in breath, blood or urine)
Section 5A(1)(a) and (2) (driving or attempting to drive with concentration of specified controlled drug above specified limit)	Section 5A(1)(b) and (2) (being in charge of a vehicle with concentration of specified controlled drug above specified limit)
Section 28 (dangerous cycling)	Section 29 (careless, and inconsiderate, cycling)

(2) Where the offence with which a person is charged is an offence under section 3A of the Road Traffic Act 1988, subsection (1) above shall not authorise his conviction of any offence of attempting to drive.
(3) Where a person is charged with having committed an offence under section 4(1), 5(1)(a) or 5A(1)(a) and (2) of the Road Traffic Act 1988 by driving a vehicle, he may be convicted of having committed an offence under the provision in question by attempting to drive.
(4) Where by virtue of this section a person is convicted before the Crown Court of an offence triable only summarily, the court shall have the same powers and duties as a magistrates' court would have had on convicting him of that offence.
(5) [Applies only to Scotland.]
(6) This section has effect without prejudice to section 6(3) of the Criminal Law Act 1967 (alternative verdicts on trial on indictment)... and section 23 of this Act.

C2.9 Where the charge is one under the RTA 1988, s. 4(1) (see **C5.58**), s. 5(1)(a) (see **C5.33**) or s. 5A(1)(a) and (2) (see **C5.54**), it is open to the magistrates to convict of 'being in charge' or, on a charge relating to driving, of attempting to drive (s. 24(3)). However, s. 24(2) states that where the offence charged is that under the RTA 1988, s. 3A, no alternative verdict involving attempting to drive is authorised. If the conviction is in the Crown Court and the offence is one that is triable only summarily, for example where the conviction is under s. 3 of the 1988 Act (careless driving) as an alternative to a count alleging causing death by dangerous driving under s. 1, the powers of the Crown Court will be the same as those of the magistrates (s. 24(4)).

The six-month time-limit imposed by the MCA 1980, s. 127, does not apply (*Coventry Justices, ex parte Sayers* [1979] RTR 22).

C2.10 In *Jeavons* [1990] RTR 263, a case of reckless driving, the prosecution alleged that the accused and another were racing, although this was denied in interview. The co-accused pleaded guilty and the appellant did not give evidence. The judge did not leave an alternative verdict of careless driving to the jury. His decision was upheld on the basis that it is for the judge to exclude irrelevant charges and allegations as well as to ensure that the indictment covers offences which the facts might disclose. In the instant case, if the prosecution's case of 'racing' was rejected by the jury there was, in the circumstances, no ground for an allegation of careless driving. However, where there is a live issue as to the quality of a defendant's driving, the alternative verdict of careless driving should be left to the jury (*Cambray* [2006] EWCA Crim 1708, [2007] RTR 10 (128)). In *Griffiths* [1998] Crim LR 348, the Court of Appeal held that, in the absence of a verdict of not guilty on the count of dangerous driving, there was no power under s. 24(1) for the jury to return a verdict of guilty of careless driving. For these purposes, a finding of no case to answer is equivalent to a finding of not guilty, thus making available the alternative verdict (*DPP v Smith* [2002] EWHC 1151 (Admin), [2002] Crim LR 970). Where the defendant has already been acquitted of the 'lesser' charge (by the prosecution offering no evidence or otherwise), the alternative verdict is not available on the trial of the 'greater' charge and that should be made clear to the arbiters of fact (*DPP v Khan* [1997] RTR 82). For a full discussion of alternative verdicts and the relevant procedure, see **D19.41** ***et seq.***

Information as to Date of Birth and Sex

C2.11 The RTOA 1988, s. 25, imposes requirements on magistrates' courts convicting a person of an offence involving obligatory or discretionary disqualification, or any offence prescribed by regulations under the RTA 1988, s. 105, to ascertain the defendant's date of birth, if unknown, through ordering its provision in writing. A person, having provided a date of birth, may be required by written notice from the Secretary of State left at, delivered or sent to the person's latest known address, to provide verification of that date of birth or to give a statement in writing specifying the person's different name at the time of birth (s. 25(5)). When dealing with a written guilty plea, if the defendant's sex is unknown, the court must order it to be provided in writing. Knowingly failing to comply with any s. 25 requirement is punishable by a fine up to level 3.

Duty to Provide Information

Road Traffic Act 1988, s. 172 C2.12

(1) This section applies—
 (a) to any offence under the preceding provisions of this Act except—
  (i) an offence under Part V, or
  (ii) an offence under section 13, 16, 51(2), 61(4), 67(9), 68(4), 96 or 120, and to an offence under section 178 of this Act,
 (b) to any offence under sections 25, 26 and 27 of the Road Traffic Offenders Act 1988,
 (c) to any offence against any other enactment relating to the use of vehicles on roads, and
 (d) to manslaughter, or in Scotland culpable homicide, by the driver of a motor vehicle.

(2) Where the driver of a vehicle is alleged to be guilty of an offence to which this section applies—
 (a) the person keeping the vehicle shall give such information as to the identity of the driver as he may be required to give by or on behalf of a chief officer of police, and
 (b) any other person shall if required as stated above give any information which it is in his power to give and may lead to identification of the driver.

(3) Subject to the following provisions, a person who fails to comply with a requirement under subsection (2) above shall be guilty of an offence.

(4) A person shall not be guilty of an offence by virtue of paragraph (a) of subsection (2) above if he shows that he did not know and could not with reasonable diligence have ascertained who the driver of the vehicle was.

(5) Where a body corporate is guilty of an offence under this section and the offence is proved to have been committed with the consent or connivance of, or to be attributable to neglect on the part of, a director, manager, secretary or other similar officer of the body corporate, or a person who was purporting to act in any such capacity, he, as well as the body corporate, is guilty of that offence and liable to be proceeded against and punished accordingly.

(6) Where the alleged offender is a body corporate, . . . or the proceedings are brought against him by virtue of subsection (5) above or subsection (11) below, subsection (4) above shall not apply unless, in addition to the matters there mentioned, the alleged offender shows that no record was kept of the persons who drove the vehicle and that the failure to keep a record was reasonable.

(7) A requirement under subsection (2) may be made by written notice served by post; and where it is so made—
 (a) it shall have effect as a requirement to give the information within the period of 28 days beginning with the day on which the notice is served, and
 (b) the person on whom the notice is served shall not be guilty of an offence under this section if he shows either that he gave the information as soon as reasonably practicable after the end of that period or that it has not been reasonably practicable for him to give it.

(8) Where the person on whom a notice under subsection (7) above is to be served is a body corporate, the notice is duly served if it is served on the secretary or clerk of that body.

(9) For the purposes of section 7 of the Interpretation Act 1978 as it applies for the purposes of this section the proper address of any person in relation to the service on him of a notice under subsection (7) above is—
 (a) in the case of the secretary or clerk of a body corporate, that of the registered or principal office of that body or (if the body corporate is the registered keeper of the vehicle concerned) the registered address, and
 (b) in any other case, his last known address at the time of service.

(10) In this section—
 'registered address', in relation to the registered keeper of a vehicle, means the address recorded in the record kept under the Vehicle Excise and Registration Act 1994 with respect to that vehicle as being that person's address, and
 'registered keeper', in relation to a vehicle, means the person in whose name the vehicle is registered under that Act;
 and references to the driver of a vehicle include references to the rider of a cycle.

Foster v DPP [2013] EWHC 2039 (Admin), (2014) 178 JP 15 highlights the necessity of a charge for non-compliance specifying a date for the offence as one *after* the period of 28 days following service of the notice requiring information to be given (s. 172(7)(a)) has passed. C2.13

The justices must be satisfied that the document requiring information as to the identity of the driver was sent on behalf of a chief officer of police (although, by virtue of the Infrastructure Act 2015, s. 22(2), a requirement may also be sent on behalf of the Chief Constable of the British Transport Police Force), but there is no need for that document to be signed, provided the document's authenticity can clearly be established by the prosecution (*Arnold v DPP* [1999] RTR 99). If the justices conclude that the defendant did not receive the notice, it follows that they must regard the notice as not having been sent (*Krishevsky v DPP* [2014] EWHC 1755 (Admin), (2014) 178 JP 369). The justices need to be aware whether it is alleged that the defendant was the keeper of the vehicle or 'any other person', although, for the purpose of submissions on duplicity, s. 172 creates only one offence (*Mohindra v DPP* [2004] EWHC 490 (Admin), [2005] RTR 7 (95)). Where there are joint registered keepers with a common last known address, a single notice, attaching only one form on which to reply, constitutes making a lawful requirement for the purposes of s. 172 (*Lynes v DPP* [2012] EWHC 1300 (Admin), [2013] RTR 13 (199)). Section 172 does not create a duty, as such, on a registered keeper to make sure the keeper (or someone else) is available at the registered address to receive relevant communications; however, a failure to be available for this purpose is a factor making it difficult, if not impossible, for a registered keeper to discharge the burden of proving a defence under s. 172(7)(b) (*R (Purnell) v Snaresbrook Crown Court* [2009] EWHC 934 (Admin), [2011] RTR 35 (452) and *Whiteside v DPP* [2011] EWHC 3471 (Admin), (2012) 176 JP 103, where it was suggested a registered keeper may need to consider establishing some system to handle correspondence sent during extended absences). *Whiteside v DPP* also confirmed that the offence does not require proof of *mens rea*, being within the exception articulated in *Sweet v Parsley* [1970] AC 132 (see **A2.23**) by Lord Reid because the offence was 'not criminal in any real sense but was an act which in the public interest was prohibited under penalty', and that service by post in accordance with CrimPR 4.4(2)(a) (see Supplement, **R4.4**) is effective even if the defendant has not personally received the notice but accepts that it was delivered to the defendant's address.

The obligation to provide information is mandatory. Where a written response is required, giving the information sought orally will not suffice to fulfil the obligation because the scheme of the section is designed to produce a document that can be accepted as evidence against the driver (*DPP v Broomfield* [2002] EWHC 1962 (Admin), [2003] RTR 5 (108)). However, responding in writing, albeit not on the official form, but providing all the information required and signing the letter, can suffice to bring the defendant within the defence in s. 172(4) (*Jones v DPP* [2004] EWHC 236 (Admin), [2004] RTR 20 (331)). Leaving the completed form in a post tray at work is insufficient to comply with the obligation to return it (*Phiri v DPP* [2017] EWHC 2546 (Admin), distinguishing the position of using the post office directly or a private posting company, which may be accepted as compliance). A response by the driver to an earlier request sent to a different person as the registered keeper does not provide a defence to failing to respond to a subsequent notice sent directly to the defendant in the capacity of the driver (*Duff v DPP* [2009] EWHC 675 (Admin)). Because of the relationship with the RTOA 1988, s. 12, where the form is not signed then, even where it contains the information required, its return will not fulfil the s. 172 requirements (*Mawdesley v Chief Constable of Cheshire Constabulary* [2003] EWHC 1586 (Admin), [2004] 1 All ER 58; *Francis v DPP* [2004] EWHC 591 (Admin), (2004) 168 JP 492). Attempting to limit the use to which the provision of the required information can be put will not prevent it being used for the purpose envisaged by the RTOA 1988, s. 12 (see **C2.18**: *R (Hatton) v Chief Constable of Devon and Cornwall Constabulary* [2008] EWHC 209 (Admin)). If the keeper of the vehicle pleads ignorance as to who was the driver, the onus is on the keeper to show that the identity of the driver was unknown, and could not with reasonable diligence have been ascertained. For the purposes of the defence in s. 172(4), the relevant date at which knowledge of who was driving needs to be assessed is the time at which the request is made, rather than the earlier time of when the driving occurred (*Atkinson v DPP* [2011] EWHC 706 (Admin), (2012) 176 JP 57). Where the defendant claims not to have been the driver but knew that only one other person had access to the vehicle, it is a clear inference that that other person was the driver at the time in question and the defendant is obliged to say so (*R (Flegg) v Southampton and New Forest Justices* [2006] EWHC 396 (Admin), (2006) 170 JP 373). In those circumstances, the defence in s. 172(4) is unavailable. The extent to which the keeper has been open with the police and provided information about who else may have been driving is relevant to the defence (*Lord Howard of Lympne v DPP* [2018] EWHC 100 (Admin), [2019] RTR 4 (33)). When the justices reject a defence under s. 172(4), they must exercise care to ensure that they provide readily understandable reasons for doing so (*Weightman v DPP* [2007] EWHC 634 (Admin), [2007] RTR 45 (565)). In the case of any person other than the keeper, the onus is on the prosecution to establish that the person had information which may have led to the identification of the driver and which it was in that person's power to give.

Where the defendant admits to having been the driver concerned in the alleged offence, the statement provided under s. 172 can still be used by the prosecution to prove that fact, because to do so does not violate the right to a fair trial conferred by the ECHR, Article 6, and the privilege against self-incrimination implicit in that general right because s. 172 is not a disproportionate measure (*Brown v Stott* [2003] 1 AC 681, which was applied by the Divisional Court in *DPP v Wilson* [2001] EWHC Admin 198, [2002] RTR 6 (37) and *Hayes v DPP* [2004] EWHC 277 (QB)). This domestic approach was endorsed by the ECtHR in *O'Halloran and Francis v UK* (2008) 46 EHRR 21 (397), in which it was confirmed (at [57]) that people 'who choose to keep and drive motor cars can be taken to have accepted certain responsibilities and obligation as part of the regulatory regime relating to motor vehicles, and in the legal framework of the United Kingdom, these responsibilities include the obligation, in the event of suspected commission of road traffic offences, to inform the authorities of the identity of the driver on that occasion'. In doing so, the Court focused on the nature and degree of compulsion used to obtain the evidence, the existence of any relevant safeguards in the procedure, and the use to which any material so obtained is put. When balancing these issues the Court concluded that the essence of the right to remain silent and the privilege against self-incrimination had not been destroyed. C2.14

It is not hearsay evidence to refer to records relating to the making of the requirement and note the absence of any reply (*DPP v Leigh* [2010] EWHC 345 (Admin)); the record is not being used for the purpose of establishing any fact or opinion because what counts is what it does not say.

Contravention of s. 172 constitutes an offence for which the defendant can be disqualified or face an endorsement of six penalty points on the driving record. It also attracts a fine up to level 3 on the standard scale. A fixed penalty of £200 is available in respect of this offence. The *Magistrates' Court Sentencing Guidelines* (see Supplement, **SG10-106**) give fine band C as the starting point. C2.15

EVIDENCE

Admissibility of Highway Code

The RTA 1988, s. 38(8), defines 'the Highway Code' as the Code comprising directions for the guidance of persons using roads issued under the RTA 1930, s. 45, and subsequently revised. C2.16

Section 38(7) provides that a failure to observe a provision of the Code shall not of itself render a person liable to criminal proceedings, but any such failure may be relied upon by any party to civil or criminal proceedings as tending to establish or negative any liability in question in those proceedings. In appropriate cases, the provisions of the Code can be used as guidance when a judge sums up to the jury, e.g., on what might constitute dangerous driving (*Taylor* [2004] EWCA Crim 213). The subsection does not provide for the admissibility of evidence of due observance of the Code. But a defendant may rely on the failure of any other person to observe a relevant provision of the Code (*Baker v E. Longhurst & Sons Ltd* [1933] 2 KB 461; *Croston v Vaughan* [1938] 1 KB 540).

Evidence by Certificate as to Driver, Owner or User

The RTOA 1988, s. 11, makes provision for evidence relating to the driver, user or owner to be adduced through a certificate in the prescribed form signed by a constable or a traffic warden C2.17

(Functions of Traffic Wardens Order 1970 (SI 1970 No. 1958)). The certificate confirms that the person specified therein stated that on a particular occasion the mechanically propelled vehicle referred to was driven or used by, or belonged to, that person, or a firm in which the person was a partner, or a corporation of which the person was a director, officer or employee at the time of the statement. The certificate is admissible as evidence of who drove or used the vehicle, or to whom it belonged on that occasion. Its admissibility is dependent on a copy being served in the prescribed manner not less than seven days before the hearing or trial and the absence of any counter-notice from the defendant served on the prosecution not later than three days before the hearing or trial requiring the person who signed the certificate to attend. The form of the certificate and rules for service are prescribed by the Evidence by Certificate Rules 1961 (SI 1961 No. 248).

Section 11 provides an exception to the 'hearsay' rule. The offences to which the section applies are those set out in sch. 1 to the RTOA 1988 and 'any offence against any other enactment relating to the use of vehicles on roads'. These include the majority of the offences under the RTA 1988 and the RTOA 1988. Section 11 also applies to 'any offence against any other enactment relating to the use of vehicles on roads'.

Proof of Identity of Driver in Summary Proceedings

C2.18 **Road Traffic Offenders Act 1988, s. 12**

(1) Where on the summary trial in England and Wales of an information for an offence to which this subsection applies—

(a) it is proved to the satisfaction of the court, on oath or in manner prescribed by Criminal Procedure Rules, that a requirement under section 172(2) of the Road Traffic Act 1988 to give information as to the identity of the driver of a particular vehicle on the particular occasion to which the information relates has been served on the accused by post, and

(b) a statement in writing is produced to the court purporting to be signed by the accused that the accused was the driver of that vehicle on that occasion,

the court may accept that statement as evidence that the accused was the driver of that vehicle on that occasion.

As to proving service, see CrimPR 4.12 (see Supplement, **R4.12**). The offences to which the section applies are those set out in sch. 1 to the RTOA 1988 and 'any offence against any other enactment relating to the use of vehicles on roads'.

C2.19 In cases where identity becomes an issue and there is no s. 12 statement, the justices will be permitted to assess the sufficiency of the evidence from other sources (*Creed v Scott* [1976] RTR 488), such as relevant information about the registered keeper given to the police when questioned, which, when checked, corresponds to details held on the Police National Computer (*DPP v Bayliff* [2003] EWHC 539 (Admin)). Indeed, where there has been no prior notice that identity is an issue, relying on evidence by way of a dock identification may be permissible (*Karia v DPP* [2002] EWHC 2175 (Admin), (2002) 166 JP 753).

Admissibility of Records of Secretary of State

C2.20 The RTOA 1988, s. 13, enables statements reflecting the content of a part of the records maintained by the Secretary of State in connection with any functions exercisable by virtue of the RTA 1988, Part III, or a part of any other records maintained by the Secretary of State with respect to vehicles, to be admissible in proceedings as evidence of any fact stated therein to the same extent as oral evidence would be admissible. The document containing the statement must be authenticated by a person duly authorised by the Secretary of State. Upon conviction of a summary offence under the Traffic Acts or the Road Traffic (Driver Licensing and Information Systems) Act 1989, s. 13 permits the court, in the absence of the defendant, to take account of any previous conviction or order specified in the document as if the defendant had appeared and admitted it (s. 13(3A)). Similarly, in respect of other offences involving obligatory or discretionary disqualification, where the document refers to a previous conviction for such an offence or any order made on conviction and is proved to have been served on the defendant not less than seven days before its production in court, in the absence of the defendant, the court may take it into account on the same basis (s. 13(4)).

The records to be maintained and which are admissible (s. 13(5)) are set out in the Vehicle and Driving Licences Records (Evidence) Regulations 1970 (SI 1970 No. 1997). They usually take the form of a computer printout from the DVLA at Swansea, appropriately endorsed for use in accordance with the general rules for adducing evidence at trial or producing information for sentencing purposes set out in CrimPR Part 24 (see Supplement, **R24.1** *et seq.*).

Admissibility of Evidence from Prescribed Devices

Road Traffic Offenders Act 1988, s. 20 **C2.21**

(1) Evidence (which in Scotland shall be sufficient evidence) of a fact relevant to proceedings for an offence to which this section applies may be given by the production of—
  (a) a record produced by a prescribed device, and
  (b) (in the same or another document) a certificate as to the circumstances in which the record was produced signed by a constable or by a person authorised by or on behalf of the chief officer of police for the police area in which the offence is alleged to have been committed;

but subject to the following provisions of this section.

...

(6) In proceedings for an offence to which this section applies, evidence (which in Scotland shall be sufficient evidence)—
  (a) of a measurement made by a device, or of the circumstances in which it was made, or
  (b) that a device was of a type approved for the purposes of this section, or that any conditions subject to which an approval was given were satisfied,

may be given by the production of a document which is signed as mentioned in subsection (1) above and which, as the case may be, gives particulars of the measurement or of the circumstances in which it was made, or states that the device was of such a type or that, to the best of the knowledge and belief of the person making the statement, all such conditions were satisfied.

(7) For the purposes of this section a document purporting to be a record of the kind mentioned in subsection (1) above, or to be a certificate or other document signed as mentioned in that subsection or in subsection (6) above, shall be deemed to be such a record, or to be so signed, unless the contrary is proved.

(8) Nothing in subsection (1) or (6) above makes a document admissible as evidence in proceedings for an offence unless a copy of it has, not less than seven days before the hearing or trial, been served on the person charged with the offence; and nothing in those subsections makes a document admissible as evidence of anything other than the matters shown on a record produced by a prescribed device if that person, not less than three days before the hearing or trial or within such further time as the court may in special circumstances allow, serves a notice on the prosecutor requiring attendance at the hearing or trial of the person who signed the document.

As to the requirement for corroboration of the opinion evidence of a witness concerning speed in such cases, and the use of measurements as corroboration, see the RTRA 1984, s. 89; *Nicholas v Penny* [1950] 2 KB 466; and *Swain v Gillet* [1974] RTR 446. **C2.22**

Section 20(2) provides that s. 20 applies to offences under the RTRA 1984, ss. 16, 17(4), 88(7) and 89(1) (speeding offences: see **C6.58**), offences under that Act in respect of bus lanes or routes for use by buses only, and offences under the RTA 1988, s. 36(1) (failure to comply with automatic traffic light signal: see **C6.25**), offences under the Vehicle Excise and Registration Act 1994, s. 29(1) (using or keeping an unlicensed vehicle on a public road), and offences under the HGV Road User Levy Act 2013, s. 11(1) (using or keeping heavy goods vehicle if levy not paid). Section 20 also applies to offences of driving a vehicle on the hard shoulder of a motorway and failing to comply with an indication given by a light signal not to enter, or proceed in, a traffic lane (SI 2017 No. 294). Section 20 is just one of the means of proving the offence; other methods of proof remain available (*R (Seroka) v Redhill Magistrates' Court* [2012] EWHC 3827 (Admin)).

In the case of any offence to which s. 20 applies, the prosecution will be able to rely on evidence produced by automatic devices of a specified and approved type, without the need for corroboration. For these purposes, a photograph is accepted as a record produced by the device, even though it is not produced directly because of the need for developing the negative before it becomes readable, after which printing is the most convenient medium for use (*Griffiths v DPP* [2007] EWHC 619 (Admin), [2007] RTR 44 (547)). The evidence must be accompanied by the appropriate certificate signed by a constable or other authorised person, and, where there is such a certificate, s. 20(7) imposes the burden on the defence of disproving that the document is a record. Where that evidence and certificate are served not less than seven days before the hearing or trial and there is no counter-notice from the defendant in accordance with s. 20(8), they may be tendered in evidence without the necessity of anyone being called to prove them (*DPP v Thornley* [2006] EWHC 312 (Admin), (2006) 170 JP 385). Any document served under s. 20(8) must be capable of being used for the purpose intended; if it is only a poor quality copy, that does not constitute 'service' and the document itself is rendered inadmissible under the subsection. However, in any case where s. 20(8) does not apply, the evidence from the prescribed device can be adduced in the conventional way. The approach to take to a disclosure application under the CPIA 1996, s. 8 (see **D9.27**), in respect of a device relied on for a speeding offence was considered in *R (DPP) v Caernarfon Crown Court* [2019] EWHC 767 (Admin), applying *R (DPP) v Manchester and Salford Magistrates' Court* [2017] EWHC 3719 (Admin), [2019] 1 WLR 2617.

C2.23 Prescribed devices include those facilitating radar measurement of speed (Road Traffic Offenders (Prescribed Devices) Order 1992 (SI 1992 No. 1209)); photographic imaging to calculate speed (Road Traffic Offenders (Prescribed Devices) Order 1999 (SI 1999 No. 162)); and measurement of odometer pulses between two points (Road Traffic Offenders (Prescribed Devices) Order 2008 (SI 2008 No. 1332)). In addition, there are bus lane cameras (Road Traffic Offenders (Additional Offences and Prescribed Devices) Order 1997 (SI 1997 No. 384)), a generic device relating to vehicle movements on motorways (Road Traffic Offenders (Prescribed Devices) Order 2019 (SI 2019 No. 920)) and traffic light cameras (Road Traffic Offenders (Prescribed Devices) (No. 2) Order 1992 (SI 1992 No. 2843), and see *Robbie the Pict v CPS* [2009] EWHC 1176 (Admin)). *Brotherston v DPP* [2012] EWHC 136 (Admin), (2012) 176 JP 153 confirms that the RTOA 1988, s. 20, enables technological advances to be accommodated without the need for amending primary legislation. There is nothing in the provisions to suggest that Parliament intended that the description of the device in the statutory instrument needed to be more specific than the generic description in the original form of s. 20; the 'description' of the device does not need to identify the particular brand of the product.

Connell v CPS [2011] EWHC 158 (Admin), (2011) 175 JP 151 confirms that the RTOA 1988, s. 20, constitutes a self-contained code, offering a particular method of adducing evidence before the court. Accordingly, an officer providing oral evidence of the officer's opinion of a vehicle's speed, supported by a reading from a prescribed but non-approved device, can lawfully found a conviction for speeding (see **C6.61**). In *Barber v DPP* [2006] EWHC 3137 (Admin), [2007] RTR 25 (300), the constable's explanation about why 'Timeout' appeared on stills produced by the device in question was accepted and this did not render the stills inadmissible. A device remains an approved device even if one of the pre-operative tests is not performed (*R (Bray) v Bristol Crown Court* [2009] EWHC 3018 (Admin)). See also *Iaciofano v DPP* [2010] EWHC 2357 (Admin), [2011] RTR 15 (205), in respect of the Police Pilot Provida device. Unlike in Scotland, there is no requirement to prove that the device had been tested for accuracy before it can provide corroborating evidence (*Clarke v CPS* [2013] EWHC 366 (Admin), (2014) 178 JP 7).

Section C3 Offences Relating to Driving Triable on Indictment

MANSLAUGHTER

Manslaughter is considered here only in relation to so-called 'motor' or 'vehicular' manslaughter. As to manslaughter generally, see **B1.34** to **B1.51**. **C3.1**

Indictment

For the form of indictment for manslaughter, see **B1.38**. **C3.2**

Elements

In general see **B1.63** ***et seq.*** **C3.3**

The RTA 1988, s. 38, is applicable; see **C2.16**.

Defences

Automatism, mechanical defect and duress. See **C1.21**, **C1.7** and **A3.35** to **A3.52**. See also *Riddell* [2017] EWCA Crim 413, [2017] 2 Cr App R 3 (22) on self-defence and *Renouf* [1986] 2 All ER 449 at **C3.42**. **C3.4**

Punishment

See generally **B1.51**. **C3.5**

Life imprisonment and/or a fine. See *Pimm* [1994] RTR 391.

By the RTOA 1988, s. 34 and sch. 2, part II, disqualification for at least two years and endorsement are obligatory, unless the court finds 'special reasons'. Manslaughter by the use of a motor vehicle carries between three and 11 penalty points for the purposes of the RTOA 1988, s. 35. The offence also carries mandatory retesting by way of an extended driving test (see **C7.32**). Forfeiture of a motor vehicle used in connection with the crime may be ordered (see **E18.1**).

Sentence

The definitive sentencing guideline, *Manslaughter* (see Supplement, **SG25-1**), must generally be followed where the offender is aged 18 or over. Accordingly, earlier cases may no longer provide assistance for the sentencing exercise, confirming the approach indicated by the Court of Appeal in *Brown* [2005] EWCA Crim 2868, [2006] 1 Cr App R (S) 124 (727). The principle that the sentencing judge must bear in mind that the offence is more serious than causing death by dangerous driving still applies, because the risk of death is higher, so will generally merit a proportionately greater sentence than for the statutory offence (*A-G's Ref (No. 14 of 2001)* [2001] EWCA Crim 1235, [2002] 1 Cr App R (S) 25 (106)). The guideline differentiates **C3.6** between gross negligence manslaughter, where the sentencing range is between one and 18 years' custody, and unlawful act manslaughter, where the range is between one and 24 years' custody. In respect of both types of manslaughter, those ranges are subdivided into four categories depending on the level of culpability, with starting points in each such range generally at around the mid-point. Factors increasing the seriousness of the offence, or reducing it or reflecting personal mitigation, are also set out to follow in making appropriate adjustments.

CAUSING DEATH BY DANGEROUS DRIVING

C3.7 **Road Traffic Act 1988, s. 1**

> A person who causes the death of another person by driving a mechanically propelled vehicle dangerously on a road or other public place is guilty of an offence.

This offence is triable only on indictment.

Indictment

C3.8 *Statement of Offence*

> Causing death by dangerous driving, contrary to section 1 of the Road Traffic Act 1988.

Particulars of Offence

> D, on the…day of…, drove a mechanically propelled vehicle dangerously on a road [or public place], namely…, and thereby caused the death of V.

In *Roberts* [2013] EWCA Crim 785, [2013] RTR 32 (436), the Court of Appeal commented that, because in sentencing terms it is generally considered more serious, charging causing death by dangerous driving (when supported by the evidence) was preferable to opting to charge aggravated vehicle taking instead.

Elements

C3.9 The RTA 1988, s. 38, and the RTOA 1988, s. 11, are applicable; see **C2.16** and **C2.17**. For the meaning of 'public place', see **C1.16**.

For the purposes of the RTA 1988, s. 1, the definition of 'driver' does not include a separate person acting as a steersman. One of the tests for dangerous driving must be satisfied, producing a causal link to the death.

C3.10 **Tests for Dangerous Driving** Section 2A sets out to define what constitutes dangerous driving.

Road Traffic Act 1988, s. 2A

> (1) For the purposes of sections 1, 1A and 2 above a person is to be regarded as driving dangerously if (and, subject to subsection (2) below, only if)—
> (a) the way he drives falls far below what would be expected of a competent and careful driver, and
> (b) it would be obvious to a competent and careful driver that driving in that way would be dangerous.
>
> (2) A person is also to be regarded as driving dangerously for the purposes of sections 1 and 2 above if it would be obvious to a competent and careful driver that driving the vehicle in its current state would be dangerous.
>
> (3) In subsections (1) and (2) above 'dangerous' refers to danger either of injury to any person or of serious damage to property; and in determining for the purposes of those subsections what would be expected of, or obvious to, a competent and careful driver in a particular case, regard shall be had not only to the circumstances of which he could be expected to be aware but also to any circumstances shown to have been within the knowledge of the accused.
>
> (4) In determining for the purposes of subsection (2) above the state of a vehicle, regard may be had to anything attached to or carried on or in it and to the manner in which it is attached or carried.

C3.11 Section 2A relies on an objective test. Danger refers to the danger of injury to a person or serious damage to property. *Mens rea* plays no part in the offence (*Loukes* [1996] 1 Cr App R 444 at p. 450):

> Proof of guilt depends on an objective standard of driving, namely, what would have been obvious to a competent and careful driver. The accused driver's state of mind is relevant only if and to the extent that it attributes additional knowledge to the notional competent and careful driver... It should be noted too that the threshold of proof is high. It must be shown that the defect was 'obvious' to a 'competent and careful driver'. It is not enough to show in the case of such a driver that, say, if he had examined the vehicle by going underneath it, he would have seen the defect.

The standard of driving must fall 'far below' that expected of a 'competent and careful' driver and it must be obvious to a 'competent and careful' driver that the manner of driving is dangerous. The prosecution must demonstrate both elements before s. 2A(1) is satisfied (*Brooks* [2001] EWCA Crim 1944). Care needs to be taken by the prosecution not to seek to adduce inadmissible evidence about the defendant's past bad driving (*McKenzie* [2008] EWCA Crim 758, [2008] RTR 22 (277)). When directing a jury, the judge must avoid watering down the requirement for the driving to fall 'far below' the standard expected so that it confuses the test with that for careless driving (*Jeshani* [2005] EWCA Crim 146). The introduction of the concept of a careful driver as an objective observer places the question of what constitutes dangerous driving within the province of the tribunal of fact. Speed alone is not sufficient to found a conviction for dangerous driving (*DPP v Milton* [2006] EWHC 242 (Admin), [2006] RTR 21 (264)). When determining what was expected of the competent and careful driver in the situation in which the defendant was driving, taking into account the driving skills of the particular defendant is inconsistent with the objective test set out in the RTA 1988, s. 2A(3) (*Bannister* [2009] EWCA Crim 1571, [2010] 2 All ER 841). Accordingly, the special skill (or indeed lack of skill) of a driver is an irrelevant circumstance in considering whether the driving is dangerous. The provisions of the Highway Code, whilst certainly not conclusive, may still merit careful consideration as guidance as to the standards to be attributed to a careful and competent driver (*Taylor* [2004] EWCA Crim 213).

The CPS guidance on charging practice in relation to traffic offences gives the following examples of driving that may support an allegation of dangerous driving: **C3.12**

(a) racing or competitive driving;
(b) failing to have a proper and safe regard for vulnerable road users such as cyclists, motorcyclists, horse riders, the elderly and pedestrians or when in the vicinity of a pedestrian crossing, hospital, school or residential home;
(c) speed which is highly inappropriate for the prevailing road or traffic conditions;
(d) aggressive driving, such as sudden lane changes, cutting into a line of vehicles or driving much too close to the vehicle in front;
(e) disregard of traffic lights and other road signs, which, on an objective analysis, would appear to be deliberate;
(f) disregard of warnings from fellow passengers;
(g) overtaking that could not have been carried out safely;
(h) driving when knowingly suffering from a medical or physical condition that significantly and dangerously impairs the offender's driving skills such as having an arm or leg in plaster, or impaired eyesight;
(i) driving when knowingly deprived of adequate sleep or rest;
(j) driving a vehicle knowing it has a dangerous defect or is poorly maintained or is dangerously loaded;
(k) using a hand-held mobile phone or other hand-held electronic equipment when the driver was avoidably and dangerously distracted by that use;
(l) driving while avoidably and dangerously distracted such as while reading a newspaper/map, talking to and looking at a passenger, selecting and lighting a cigarette or by adjusting the controls of electronic equipment such a radio, hands-free mobile phone or satellite navigation equipment;
(m) a brief but obvious danger arising from a seriously dangerous manoeuvre. This covers situations where a driver has made a mistake or an error of judgement that was so substantial that it caused the driving to be dangerous even for only a short time.

In *A-G's Ref (No. 17 of 2009)* [2009] EWCA Crim 1003, [2010] 1 Cr App R (S) 12 (62), the Court of Appeal confirmed that there is never any excuse for texting or using a hand-held mobile phone while driving. Filming events or taking photographs while driving, either with a camera or the camera function on a mobile phone, may be evidence of dangerous driving, according to the Divisional Court (*DPP v Barreto* [2019] EWHC 2044 (Admin), [2020] RTR 2 (15)). In addition, by reference to the guidance in *Cooksley* [2003] EWCA Crim 996, [2003] 3 All ER 40, further factors might be callous behaviour at the time, e.g., throwing a victim off the vehicle or failing to stop, or causing death (and presumably, where applicable, serious injury) in the course of an escape or an attempt to avoid detection. These are indicative only and not conclusive as to the type of behaviour which might constitute dangerous driving.

C3.13 Dangerous State of Driver The fact that a driver was adversely affected by alcohol is a circumstance relevant to the issue of dangerous driving, but it is not in itself determinative to prove the offence (*Webster* [2006] EWCA Crim 415, [2006] 2 Cr App R 6 (103)). In *Woodward* [1995] 3 All ER 79, the Court of Appeal distinguished the line of cases which had developed in relation to reckless driving and reaffirmed the earlier principle from *McBride* [1962] 2 QB 167 (a five-judge Court of Appeal), where Ashworth J stated (at p. 172):

> ... if a driver is adversely affected by drink, this fact is a circumstance relevant to the issue whether he was driving dangerously. Evidence to this effect is of probative value and is admissible in law. In the application of this principle two further points should be noticed. In the first place, the mere fact that the driver has had drink is not of itself relevant: in order to render evidence as to the drink taken by the driver admissible, such evidence must tend to show that the amount of drink taken was such as would adversely affect a driver or, alternatively, that the driver was in fact adversely affected. Secondly, there remains in the court an overriding discretion to exclude such evidence if in the opinion of the court its prejudicial effect outweighs its probative value.

The provisions of the RTOA 1988, s. 15 (see **C5.41**), are applicable only to the alcohol-related offences specified therein. Accordingly, where only a single specimen has been taken from which to assess the level of the defendant's alcohol consumption, such evidence is still admissible on the issue of whether the defendant drove dangerously (*Ash* [1999] RTR 347). There is no requirement to prove whether the defendant was above or below the prescribed limit, as that is not an element of the offence (*Mari* [2009] EWCA Crim 2677, [2010] RTR 17 (192)); evidence of the amount of alcohol consumed and said to affect the defendant's ability to drive suffices.

A similar approach is likely to be adopted in relation to a driver adversely affected by drugs contrary to the RTA 1988, s. 5A (see **C5.54**).

In *Marison* [1997] RTR 457, driving in a dangerously defective state owing to diabetes was considered no different to driving in a dangerously defective state owing to alcohol, constituting circumstances of which the defendant could be expected to be aware and of which the defendant had knowledge, within the meaning of the RTA 1988, s. 2A(3).

C3.14 Dangerous State of Vehicle The offence may also be committed if the state of a vehicle, including any attachment or load and the way in which it is attached or carried, would make driving it dangerous in the eyes of a 'competent and careful' driver. In relation to the dangerous state of the vehicle being 'obvious', no special definition is required when directing the jury; however it would not be a misdirection to indicate that it can arise from an inspection which is something between a fleeting glance and a long look (*Marsh* [2002] EWCA Crim 137). It could be argued that some loads and vehicles (e.g., certain tractor units and their attachments) are inherently dangerous. However, where the vehicle benefits from specific authorisation from the Secretary of State for use on public roads, there must usually be evidence that the vehicle has been manoeuvred in such a way as to create a danger beyond that otherwise inherent in its use on a road, because 'current state' implies something different from the vehicle's original or manufactured state (*Marchant* [2003] EWCA Crim 2099, [2004] 1 All ER 1187).

Where the mere act of taking an inherently dangerous vehicle on the road amounts to dangerous driving, it potentially falls within the RTA 1988, s. 2A(2) and also s. 2A(1)(a) and (b). To that extent s. 2A(2) is superfluous, but it underlines the point that driving a vehicle in a dangerous condition may well constitute an offence under s. 1, 1A or 2 (depending on the consequences of the dangerous driving) as well as under the construction and use regulations (see also *Spurge* [1961] 2 QB 205 and *Robert Millar Contractors Ltd* [1970] 2 QB 54). The danger presented by the current state of the vehicle must, however, be capable of being seen or realised at first glance, in the sense of being 'evident to' the competent and careful driver, before it can be regarded as 'obvious'; it should not be discoverable only by taking some additional steps to ascertain the vehicle's defective state (*Strong* [1995] Crim LR 428). Moreover, where the driver is an employee driving the employer's vehicle, it will be important to consider the instructions given to the driver about checking the vehicle's condition. Unless those instructions appear inadequate, the driver cannot be expected to do more than comply with them (*Roberts* [1997] RTR 462); such compliance satisfies the 'competent and careful driver' test.

Causal Link to Fatality The prosecution need to establish that death resulted from the accused's dangerous driving. In *Jenkins* [2012] EWCA Crim 2909, [2013] RTR 21 (288), which involved parking a vehicle so as to restrict visibility for other road users, the Court of Appeal stressed that the offence relates to causing death *by* driving and not causing death *while* driving, clarifying that the driving is not required to be coterminous with the impact resulting in the death. It should be noted that danger to the person is not qualified by any adjective and therefore, as long as it is not *de minimis*, any danger to any person, even though slight, if obvious to the 'competent and careful' driver, would suffice. In *Hennigan* [1971] 3 All ER 133, a case of causing death by reckless driving under the RTA 1960, the recklessness consisted mainly of the speed at which the defendant was driving; the driver of the other car, which contained the two persons who were killed, may well have been substantially to blame for the accident. The Court of Appeal held that there was nothing in the legislation which required the manner of the accused's driving to be a substantial or major cause of the accident, as long as it was 'a cause and something more than *de minimis*'. An acceptable direction to the jury is that they do not have to be sure that the defendant's driving 'was the principal, or a substantial, cause of the death, as long as [they] are sure that it was a cause and that there was something more than a slight or a trifling link' (*Kimsey* [1996] Crim LR 35). In *Girdler* [2009] EWCA Crim 2666, [2010] RTR 28 (307), the Court of Appeal offered guidance about the most appropriate way to direct the jury where the accused alleges that a second collision is the immediate cause of death and so constitutes a *novus actus interveniens*, breaking the chain of causation. If the jury are sure that the accused drove dangerously and also sure that the dangerous driving was more than a slight or trifling link to the death(s), the jury could also be told that the accused 'will have caused the death(s) only if you are sure that it could sensibly have been anticipated that a fatal collision might occur in the circumstances in which the second collision did occur'. It was made clear in *A* [2020] EWCA Crim 407 that a jury would not need to be sure that the particular circumstances of the collision or 'the exact form' of the subsequent act were reasonably foreseeable. All that had to be sensibly anticipated in that case was that another vehicle might leave the carriageway and collide with the respondent's car which was parked on the hard shoulder of the motorway. C3.15

Defences

Automatism, mechanical defect and duress. See **C1.21**, **C1.7** and **A3.35** to **A3.52**. See also *Riddell* [2017] EWCA Crim 413, [2017] 2 Cr App R 3 (22) on self-defence and *Renouf* [1986] 2 All ER 449 at **C3.42**. No offence is committed under s. 1 where the driving was in a public place other than a road in the course of an authorised motoring event (RTA 1988, s. 13A). C3.16

Alternative Verdicts

The RTOA 1988, s. 24, provides alternative verdicts of dangerous driving and careless, and inconsiderate, driving under the RTA 1988, ss. 2 and 3 (see **C2.8**). See also *Fairbanks* [1986] 1 WLR 1202 (discussed at **D19.60**) and *Jeavons* [1990] RTR 263. An alternative verdict of causing death by careless or inconsiderate driving under the RTA 1988, s. 2B, is also available (see **C3.27**). Section 24 operates without prejudice to the CLA 1967, s. 6(3). Accordingly, no separate count for such an offence is required. Indeed, as careless driving has not been specified under the CJA 1988, s. 40, a separate count for that offence would be invalid, thereby rendering ineffective a guilty plea entered in respect of it (*Davis* (19 April 1996 unreported)). By the C3.17

RTOA 1988, s. 2, a failure to warn a suspect of an intended prosecution or to serve such a warning notice does not act as a bar to conviction of the alternative offences.

Punishment

C3.18 The maximum sentence is 14 years' imprisonment and/or a fine. In the absence of 'special reasons', disqualification for not less than two years and endorsement are obligatory (RTOA 1988, s. 34(4) and sch. 2). The offence carries between three and 11 penalty points and mandatory retesting by way of an extended driving test (see **C7.32**). Forfeiture of the motor vehicle used for the purpose of the crime may be ordered (see **E18.1**).

Sentence

C3.19 The sentencing guideline, *Causing Death by Driving* (see Supplement, **SG22-1**), must generally be followed where the offender is aged 18 or over. The guideline creates three levels of seriousness drawn principally by reference to the standard of the offender's driving. Determinants of seriousness include the offender's awareness of the risk associated with the driving involved, the effect of alcohol or drug consumption, driving at an inappropriate speed, other instances of serious culpable behaviour and where the victim was a vulnerable road user. Examples are provided to enable the offending behaviour to be categorised. For the most serious level 1 offences, involving a deliberate decision to drive very badly and an apparent disregard for the great danger to others resulting, the sentencing range is from seven to 14 years' imprisonment, with a starting point of eight years. For level 2 offences, which create a substantial risk of danger, the sentencing range is four to seven years' imprisonment, with a starting point of five years. For level 3 offences, which create a significant risk of danger, the sentencing range is two to five years' imprisonment, with a starting point of three years. Because of the consequences flowing therefrom, it is important to select the correct level (*Carswell* [2009] EWCA Crim 1848; *A-G's Ref (No. 150 of 2015)* [2016] EWCA Crim 459, [2016] 2 Cr App R (S) 16 (147)) and to indicate clearly what it is when pronouncing sentence (*Farmer* [2010] EWCA Crim 2851), although some overlap exists and the levels are not 'impermeable' (*Salam* [2012] EWCA Crim 2264). Within a level, care is required to place the offending at the appropriate point, because there is considerable disparity between, e.g., the top and bottom of a sentencing range (*Allen* [2017] EWCA Crim 458). In *Amin* [2015] EWCA Crim 1074, the Court of Appeal stressed that 'the examples provided in the guideline are no more than examples'. Because each case turns on its own facts, in *Maciulevictus* [2015] EWCA Crim 1270 it was similarly noted that caution needs to be exercised when referring to previous decisions, especially references from the A-G, which are focused on leniency of sentences. The guideline is to be interpreted flexibly, in a nuanced way sensitive to the facts of the case (*Paul* [2013] EWCA Crim 2034, [2014] 2 Cr App R (S) 7 (38)). The list of circumstances set out is not exhaustive, meaning that not all cases will fit precisely into a given level (*Torkington* [2013] EWCA Crim 2183). In *Collins* [2018] EWCA Crim 113, the Court of Appeal stressed that a sentencing judge, being engaged in an overall, evaluative assessment, rather than a technical exercise, must consider the relevant driving in the round, taking account of the factors identified in the guideline and any other relevant circumstances to determine an appropriate starting point. The guideline also lists the additional aggravating and mitigating factors to be taken into account in adjusting the sentence from the starting point applicable for each level of offence. Where more than one death occurs, it was confirmed in *Brown (Robert Anthony)* [2018] EWCA Crim 1775, [2019] 1 Cr App R (S) 10 (72) that this is reflected in the sentence as an aggravating factor rather than being justification for imposing consecutive, as opposed to concurrent, sentences. The Court of Appeal emphasised, endorsing the approach in *Noble* [2002] EWCA Crim 1713, [2003] 1 Cr App R (S) 65 (312), that concurrent sentences were appropriate because there had been a single episode of dangerous driving. The same principle applies if the aggravating factor is an offence of causing serious injury by dangerous driving (see **C3.33**) arising out of the same episode of driving (*Morrison* [2018] EWCA Crim 981, [2018] 2 Cr App R (S) 31 (284)). Guidance was offered in *Soare* [2018] EWCA Crim 465, [2018] 2 Cr App R (S) 3 (15) that the starting point where two deaths are caused might be increased by 50 per cent, emphasising that this was not an automatic increase, and commenting (at [19]) that 'it is impossible to adequately reflect by term of imprisonment the value of the lives lost'. In *Dudan* [2019] EWCA Crim 2414, which was a reference by the A-G and involved driving causing three fatalities, the Court of Appeal regarded 12 years' imprisonment as the appropriate starting point following trial and, because this was two years higher than the sentencing judge's starting point, considered that such a difference crossed the threshold for being regarded as unduly lenient, resulting in the final sentence being increased from six years and eight months to eight years' imprisonment. Street racing is regarded very seriously (*Mannan* [2016] EWCA Crim 1082, [2016] 2 Cr App R (S) 37 (396)), as is never having passed a driving test (*Collins*). Mobile telephone use during the period shortly preceding the offence is likely to be regarded as an aggravating factor (*Arora* [2014] EWCA Crim 104; *Gard* [2017] EWCA Crim 21, [2017] 1 Cr App R (S) 45 (358)). In *Cody* [2014] EWCA Crim 1819, the deceased being a policeman courageously discharging his public duty was a significant aggravating factor. Where the offender is of good character and has an impeccable driving record, a bigger discount than would be the case through slavishly following the guideline can be justified (*Bolam* [2009] EWCA Crim 2462).

CAUSING DEATH BY CARELESS DRIVING WHEN UNDER THE INFLUENCE OF DRINK OR DRUGS

Road Traffic Act 1988, s. 3A **C3.20**

(1) If a person causes the death of another person by driving a mechanically propelled vehicle on a road or other public place without due care and attention, or without reasonable consideration for other persons using the road or place, and—
  (a) he is, at the time when he is driving, unfit to drive through drink or drugs, or
  (b) he has consumed so much alcohol that the proportion of it in his breath, blood or urine at that time exceeds the prescribed limit, or
  (ba) he has in his body a specified controlled drug and the proportion of it in his blood or urine at that time exceeds the specified limit for that drug, or
  (c) he is, within 18 hours after that time, required to provide a specimen in pursuance of section 7 of this Act, but without reasonable excuse fails to provide it, or
  (d) he is required by a constable to give his permission for a laboratory test of a specimen of blood taken from him under section 7A of this Act, but without reasonable excuse fails to do so,

  he is guilty of an offence.
(2) For the purposes of this section a person shall be taken to be unfit to drive at any time when his ability to drive properly is impaired.
(3) Subsection (1)(b), (ba), (c) and (d) above shall not apply in relation to a person driving a mechanically propelled vehicle other than a motor vehicle.

This offence is triable only on indictment.

Indictment

Statement of Offence **C3.21**

Causing death by careless driving when under the influence of drink or drugs, contrary to s. 3A(1) of the Road Traffic Act 1988.

Particulars of Offence

D, on the... day of..., caused the death of V by driving a motor [or mechanically propelled] vehicle on a road [or public place], namely..., without due care and attention [or reasonable consideration for other persons using the road [or place]] and after having consumed so much alcohol that the proportion of it in his breath [or blood or urine] at the time exceeded the prescribed limit [or when unfit to drive through drink or drugs etc.].

Elements

For the meaning of 'careless' and 'without reasonable consideration', see **C6.3** and **C6.6**. For the meaning of 'public place', see **C1.16**. **C3.22**

The RTA 1988, s. 38, and the RTOA 1988, s. 11, are applicable; see **C2.16** and **C2.17**.

The offence can be committed in ten separate ways. The prosecution need to establish either that the accused was driving without due care and attention or without reasonable consideration for other persons using the road, that the death of another person was caused by the manner of that driving and that at the time the accused came within one of the five paragraphs in s. 3A(1). The prosecution would therefore have to prove careless driving, the requisite causal link and the related 'drink driving' or 'drug driving' offence in exactly the same way as if both offences had been charged (see **C6.1** *et seq.* and **C5.9**, **C5.33**, **C5.54** and **C5.58**). The offence does not require any causal connection between the alcohol or drugs and the death (*Shepherd* [1994] 2 All ER 242).

In applying the appropriate test to determine whether a defendant has driven without due care and attention, the jury are entitled to look at all the circumstances of the case, including evidence that the defendant had been affected by alcohol or had taken such an amount of alcohol as would be likely to affect a driver (*Millington* [1996] RTR 80). Thus, the principle stated in *McBride* [1962] 2 QB 167 (see **C3.13**) in relation to causing death by dangerous driving applies equally to the offence in s. 3A(1). See also *Coe* [2009] EWCA Crim 1452, [2010] 3 All ER 83, especially relating to the RTA 1988, s. 3A(1)(c).

Evidence of impairment would normally be provided by a doctor who examines the accused, but evidence may also be provided by non-expert witnesses. It may take the form of a description of the actions of the accused, including the manner of driving, as long as the witness does not express an opinion as to the condition of the accused. In relation to any drug not legitimately available in the UK, the jury need to consider in the round whether its presence in the body makes the accused unfit (*Beach* [2013] EWCA Crim 1783).

If the offence relates to s. 3A(1)(c), the request to provide a specimen must be made within 18 hours, presumably from the time of driving rather than the time of death.

Section 3A(1)(b), (ba), (c) and (d) apply only where the driving is of a 'motor vehicle', but the offence under s. 3A(1)(a) may be committed whilst driving any 'mechanically propelled vehicle'.

Defences

C3.23 Duress and mechanical defect. See **A3.35** to **A3.52** and **C1.7**. Automatism may be a defence (see **C1.21**), but in practice will be very difficult to establish given the nature of this offence and the possibility of interpreting such a situation as arising from self-induced intoxication. See also **C5.51**.

Alternative Verdicts

C3.24 The RTOA 1988, s. 24 (see **C2.8**), provides alternative verdicts under the RTA 1988, ss. 3, 4(1), 5(1)(a), 7(6) and 7A(6), but not under the RTA 1988, s. 5A(1)(a) and (2). An alternative verdict under the RTA 1988, s. 2B, is also available (see **C3.27**). It would therefore seem that, if someone is accused of an offence based on s. 3A(1)(c), the accused could theoretically be convicted, for example, of driving whilst unfit even though the indictment contains an allegation of refusing to provide a specimen.

Punishment

C3.25 The maximum sentence is 14 years' imprisonment and/or a fine (CJA 2003, s. 285). In the absence of 'special reasons', disqualification for not less than two years and endorsement are obligatory. The offence carries between three and 11 penalty points. Retesting by way of an extended driving test is mandatory (see **C7.32**). Forfeiture of the motor vehicle used for the purpose of the crime may be ordered (see **E18.1**).

Sentence

C3.26 The sentencing guideline, *Causing Death by Driving* (see Supplement, **SG22-1**), must generally be followed where the offender is aged 18 or over. The guideline creates three bands of seriousness depending on the amount by which the offender exceeded the prescribed or, as the case may be, specified limit or the manner of the failure to provide the specimen required. In *Roberts* [2018] EWCA Crim 2965, [2019] 1 Cr App R (S) 49 (417), the approach to these three levels was described as 'somewhat outdated'. In respect of each of those bands, the sentencing range and starting point are fixed by reference to whether the careless or inconsiderate driving arose from momentary inattention with no aggravating factors or was not far short of dangerousness, or whether it fell somewhere in-between (see, e.g., *Nwokedi* [2010] EWCA Crim 132). The lowest starting point is 18 months' imprisonment, where the sentencing range is from 26 weeks to four years, and the highest is eight years' imprisonment, where the sentencing range is seven to 14 years. In *Wood* [2019] EWCA Crim 2078, where the defendant was found to have driven while just over four times above the specified limit in respect of cannabis, and the driving was within the speed limit but still viewed as being close to dangerous in all the circumstances, a sentence of five years and three months' imprisonment was upheld. The guideline also lists the additional aggravating and mitigating factors to be taken into account in adjusting the sentence from the starting point applicable for each category of offence. In *Williams* [2014] EWCA Crim 147, it was suggested that a compassionate act of shepherding the accused from the scene should be distinguished from the aggravating factor of fleeing after the offence. The sentencing judge should remember that the consumption of alcohol and carelessness, e.g., arising from speeding, are constituent elements of the offence and not of themselves aggravating factors (*Smith* [2011] EWCA Crim 2844). In *Thorogood* [2010] EWCA Crim 2123, the Court of Appeal confirmed the appropriateness of a sentencing court taking into account the age of the offender as personal mitigation, warranting a further reduction in the starting point before applying any discount arising from a guilty plea. In *Wilson* [2019] EWCA Crim 1141, the difficulty of how to reflect any contribution of the deceased to the death was acknowledged, but it was made clear that it must be factored in so as to be fair. *Blakely* [2015] EWCA Crim 704, in which a sentence of ten years' imprisonment was upheld, offers an example of a case of very bad driving justifying a starting point close to the maximum sentence. From *Perera* [2017] EWCA Crim 2238 and *Bond* [2017] EWCA Crim 2329, it appears that the possibility of a sentence of imprisonment being suspended is remote.

CAUSING DEATH BY CARELESS, OR INCONSIDERATE, DRIVING

Road Traffic Act 1988, s. 2B **C3.27**

> A person who causes the death of another person by driving a mechanically propelled vehicle on a road or other public place without due care and attention, or without reasonable consideration for other persons using the road or place, is guilty of an offence.

This offence is triable either way.

Indictment

Statement of Offence **C3.28**

> Causing death by careless [or inconsiderate] driving, contrary to s. 2B of the Road Traffic Act 1988.

Particulars of Offence

> D, on the... day of..., drove a mechanically propelled vehicle on a road [or public place], namely..., without due care and attention [or reasonable consideration for other persons using the road [or place]], and thereby caused the death of V.

Elements

The offence will require proof of an underlying offence under the RTA 1988, s. 3 (see **C6.1** ***et seq.***), together with a causal link to a fatality (see **C3.15**). **C3.29**

The RTA 1988, s. 38, and the RTOA 1988, ss. 1, 11 and 12(1), are applicable; see **C2.1**, **C2.16**, **C2.17** and **C2.18**.

Where tachograph evidence relating to the driving just prior to the fatal collision is used, the directions to the jury should put it into context as forming part of the background and explain its relevance (e.g., as demonstrating that the defendant slowed down) (*Greenhalgh* [2014] EWCA Crim 2084). Although there is no rule of law which requires a magistrates' court to adjourn any trial involving a fatal road traffic accident until the inquest has been concluded, as a matter of practice it is desirable to do so (*Smith v DPP* [2000] RTR 36). However, a s. 2B offence should not be treated as 'unlawful killing' for the purposes of the conclusion of an inquest (*R (Wilkinson) v HM Coroner for the Greater Manchester District* [2012] EWHC 2755 (Admin), (2012) 176 JP 665).

Alternative Verdicts

C3.30 The RTOA 1988, s. 24, provides an alternative verdict under the RTA 1988, s. 3 (see **C2.8**). As for other offences, where the defendant has already been acquitted of the s. 3 charge (by the prosecution offering no evidence), the alternative verdict is no longer available and that should be made clear to the arbiters of fact (*DPP v Khan* [1997] RTR 82).

Punishment

C3.31 On indictment, the maximum sentence is five years' imprisonment and/or a fine; on summary trial, it is six months' imprisonment and/or an unlimited fine. Disqualification is obligatory. The offence carries obligatory endorsement with between three and 11 penalty points.

Sentence

C3.32 The sentencing guideline, *Causing Death by Driving* (see Supplement, **SG22-1**), must generally be followed where the offender is aged 18 or over. For the least serious offences arising from momentary inattention with no aggravating factors, a community order is indicated. For the most serious offences where the driving falls not far short of dangerous driving, the starting point is 15 months' imprisonment, with the sentencing range being 36 weeks to three years. For all other cases of careless or inconsiderate driving, the starting point is 36 weeks' imprisonment, with the sentencing range being a community order (high) to two years' imprisonment. The guideline also lists the additional aggravating and mitigating factors to be taken into account in adjusting the sentence from the starting point applicable for each band of offence. Where there are multiple aggravating factors, moving above the top starting point in the category range can be permissible (*Adeyemi* [2016] EWCA Crim 2201). *Landon* [2011] EWCA Crim 1755, [2012] 1 Cr App R (S) 71 (402), in which a sentence of 20 months' youth detention was upheld, provides an example of the difficulties encountered in cases in the highest category of culpability involving a young driver. For a significant lapse of concentration for 14 seconds, a sentence of 12 months' imprisonment was justified (*Forster* [2012] EWCA Crim 2142), whereas a single misjudgment could be regarded as momentary inattention where a custodial sentence may not even be warranted (*Campbell* [2009] EWCA Crim 2459, [2010] 2 Cr App R (S) 28 (175)). See also *Fleury* [2013] EWCA Crim 2273, [2014] 2 Cr App R (S) 14 (109) relating to a foreign driver's forgetfulness. Careless driving of a large vehicle is regarded as more serious because of the greater likelihood of causing injury (*Evans* [2019] EWCA Crim 2358). Driving deliberately over an object in the road, which could have been avoided and turned out to be a person, was categorised as brief inattention, but the offender's failure to contact the police thereafter and being evasive when spoken to were regarded as serious aggravating factors (*Wild* [2015] EWCA Crim 1202). Not using an available onboard camera covering what was otherwise a blind spot on an articulated lorry was an aggravating factor (*Magee* [2017] EWCA Crim 972, [2017] 2 Cr App R (S) 40 (354)). *Wilkinson* [2019] EWCA Crim 702 contains a detailed analysis of why an immediate custodial sentence for the middle category is likely to follow. The statutory minimum disqualification period may be all that is justified in respect of one short instance of inattention (*Hall* [2010] EWCA Crim 2135), although there is no reason in principle or fact where the offending is outside the bottom category not to consider increasing the disqualification period (*Bagshawe* [2013] EWCA Crim 127, [2013] 2 Cr App R (S) 62 (393)). See also *Scott* [2018] EWCA Crim 521. Ordering retesting is not mandatory, but the sentencer should consider whether the defendant, when resuming driving, will be competent for the safety of other road users (*Coe* [2015] EWCA Crim 169) and, if ordering an extended retest, must explain why, otherwise the order will be susceptible to appeal (*Sanmuhalingam* [2019] EWCA Crim 1286). It is highly likely that there will be a reduction in the offender's culpability where the fatal collision was largely the responsibility of the deceased (*Arshad* [2011] EWCA Crim 2092, [2012] 1 Cr App R (S) 86 (511)).

CAUSING SERIOUS INJURY BY DANGEROUS DRIVING

Road Traffic Act 1988, s. 1A **C3.33**

(1) A person who causes serious injury to another person by driving a mechanically propelled vehicle dangerously on a road or other public place is guilty of an offence.

(2) In this section 'serious injury' means—

(a) in England and Wales, physical harm which amounts to grievous bodily harm for the purposes of the Offences Against the Person Act 1861...

This offence is triable either way. It applies to driving occurring on or after 3 December 2012.

Elements

C3.34 For the meaning of 'dangerous' and 'dangerous driving', see **C3.10** ***et seq***. For the meaning of 'public place', see **C1.16**. For 'grievous bodily harm', see **B2.60**.

The RTA 1988, s. 38, and the RTOA 1988, ss. 11 and 12(1), are applicable; see **C2.16**, **C2.17** and **C2.18**.

Defences

C3.35 Automatism, mechanical defect and duress. See **C1.21**, **C1.7** and **A3.35** ***et seq***. No offence is committed under the RTA 1988, s. 1A, where the driving took place in a public place other than a road in the course of an authorised motoring event (s. 13A).

Alternative Verdicts

C3.36 The RTOA 1988, s. 24, provides an alternative verdict under the RTA 1988, ss. 2 (dangerous driving) and 3 (careless, and inconsiderate, driving); see **C2.8**. *DPP v Khan* [1997] RTR 82 (see **C3.30**) must also be borne in mind.

Punishment

C3.37 The maximum sentence on indictment is five years' imprisonment and/or a fine; on summary trial, it is six months' imprisonment and/or an unlimited fine. Disqualification is obligatory. The offence carries obligatory endorsement with between three and 11 penalty points. Retesting by way of an extended driving test is mandatory (see **C7.32**). Forfeiture of the vehicle used may also be ordered (see **E18.1**).

Sentence

C3.38 In *Jenkins* [2015] EWCA Crim 105, [2015] 1 Cr App R (S) 70 (491), Treacy LJ heavily criticised the maximum penalty of five years' imprisonment, commenting that it afforded insufficient headroom to sentencers when dealing with bad cases by comparison to the maximum sentence of 14 years where a fatality occurs. *Dewdney* [2014] EWCA Crim 1722, [2015] 1 Cr App R (S) 5 (36) confirms that, in the absence of a specific sentencing guideline for this offence, reference should be made to the sentencing guideline, *Causing Death by Driving* (see Supplement, **SG22-1**), with appropriate modifications. This was repeated in *Shaw* [2018] EWCA Crim 2932 and *Burton* [2019] EWCA Crim 2396. Sentencers might wish to identify a broader band of conduct and not just proceed on the basis of the very worst imaginable case. Having regard to the maximum sentence, care is needed not to choose an unwarranted high starting point (*Leatham* [2016] EWCA Crim 2150; *Mirza* [2019] EWCA Crim 1322). However, the approach should not be too mechanistic (*Rimmer* [2015] EWCA Crim 490, where the appropriateness of the final sentence reached was emphasised). *McAll* [2017] EWCA Crim *2024, [2018] 1 Cr App R (S) 32 (232)* involved a police emergency responder with a good driving record, which was weighty mitigation, in a case where the harm was high, leading to six months' suspended imprisonment and no reason to go above the mandatory two-year disqualification. Account may be taken of all injuries caused by the defendant's driving and not only those serious ones relating directly to the offence charged (*Aziz* [2016] EWCA Crim 1945, [2017] 1 Cr App R (S) 28 (199)). In *Leahy* [2018] EWCA Crim 2858, leg injuries, even though involving surgery, were said to be at the lower end of injuries regarded as serious. Where consumption of alcohol is involved, reference can also be made to the guidelines in respect of an offence under the RTA 1988, s. 3A, again with appropriate modifications to reflect the different consequences (*Vincer* [2014] EWCA Crim 2743, [2015] 2 Cr App R (S) 51 (353)). In *Iqbal* [2014] EWCA Crim 2353, having regard to the totality principle, sentences of 40 months' imprisonment concurrent following guilty pleas on three counts were upheld, even though none individually warranted a starting point of the maximum sentence. *Sandulache* [2015] EWCA Crim 1502 offers an example of the Court of Appeal concluding that it was inappropriate to take a starting point of the maximum sentence of five years' imprisonment. The case concerned 'a very bad piece of driving, involving as it did the deliberate and unjustified taking of a risk', which was in contravention of road markings and created an obvious danger to other road users. As such, it equated to level 1. However, the offender had no previous convictions at all, held a valid licence, was insured, did not fail to stop at the scene or take any other steps to evade detection and was not under the influence of alcohol or drugs. Although there was high culpability, it did not warrant starting at the maximum sentence available. In *Hanson* [2019] EWCA Crim 2298, an appeal against a three-year sentence for imprisonment was dismissed. The ground put forward was that the sentence was manifestly excessive as the case involved 'no bad driving' but 'speed only'. This was rejected in its entirety and a loss of time order of 14 days made. The appeal against the length of disqualification of six years and six months could not be interfered with; the trial judge was in the best position to know the relevant facts and any reduction would be 'tinkering'. See *Ellis* [2014] EWCA Crim 593, [2014] 2 Cr App R (S) 50 (410) and *Ali* [2017] EWCA Crim 571 in relation to disqualification for the offence.

DANGEROUS DRIVING

C3.39 Road Traffic Act 1988, s. 2

> A person who drives a mechanically propelled vehicle dangerously on a road or other public place is guilty of an offence.

This offence is triable either way. In the absence of an election by the defendant, CrimPD II, para. 9A.1 (see Supplement, **CPD.9A**), requires courts to follow the *Allocation* sentencing guideline (see Supplement, **SG1-1**) which requires that cases should generally be tried summarily unless the magistrates' court's sentencing powers are insufficient or for reasons of unusual legal, procedural or factual complexity.

Indictment

C3.40 *Statement of Offence*

> Dangerous driving, contrary to section 2 of the Road Traffic Act 1988.

Particulars of Offence

> D, on the ... day of ..., drove a mechanically propelled vehicle dangerously on a road [or public place], namely ...

Elements

C3.41 For the meaning of 'dangerous' and 'dangerous driving', see **C3.10** ***et seq***. For the meaning of 'public place', see **C1.16**.

The RTA 1988, s. 38, and the RTOA 1988, ss. 1, 11 and 12(1), are applicable; see **C2.1**, **C2.16**, **C2.17** and **C2.18**.

In *Vaid* [2015] EWCA Crim 298, [2015] Crim LR 532, DNA was found on the driver's airbag, which had been deployed in a collision, and was used to disprove the defendant's claim that he had only been a passenger in the vehicle. See also *Bech* [2018] EWCA Crim 448. Where the evidence permits, charging aggravated vehicle-taking as well as dangerous driving does not result in double jeopardy nor in itself does it amount to an abuse of process (*Harding* [1995] Crim LR 733). However, where the defendant has previously been convicted of another offence arising out of the same incident, e.g., an excess alcohol offence, then pursuing a separate charge of dangerous driving subsequently is wrong; the prosecution must choose their course of action from the outset or no later than before the conclusion of the first set of proceedings (*Phipps* [2005] EWCA Crim 33).

Defences

C3.42 Automatism, mechanical defect and duress. See **C1.21**, **C1.7** and **A3.35** to **A3.52**. No offence is committed under this section where the driving took place in a public place other than a road in the course of an authorised motoring event (RTA 1988, s. 13A).

Although likely to be rare, self-defence is in principle available where the particular facts of the case so permit (*Riddell* [2017] EWCA Crim 413, [2017] 2 Cr App R 3 (22)). There must be force used through driving dangerously (or, it seems, carelessly) in response to actual or perceived force or threat of force. Although creating an apparent anomaly, fleeing from such threatened or actual force by driving away does not give rise to the defence because the defendant would not in fact be using force to meet force. This decision reflects and develops earlier decisions such as *Renouf* [1986] 2 All ER 449 and *Morris* [2013] EWCA Crim 436, [2014] 1 WLR 16, in which using only such force as was reasonable to assist in the lawful arrest of the offenders in accordance with the CLA 1967, s. 3(1) (see **A3.55**), was recognised, on the particular facts of such cases, as capable of excusing or providing a defence to a charge of dangerous driving, and so, by extension, to offences of causing death by dangerous driving, causing serious injury by dangerous driving or manslaughter.

Alternative Verdicts

C3.43 The RTOA 1988, s. 24, provides an alternative verdict under the RTA 1988, s. 3 (see **C2.8**). *DPP v Khan* [1997] RTR 82 (see **C3.30**) must also be borne in mind.

Punishment

C3.44 The maximum sentence on indictment is two years' imprisonment and/or a fine; on summary trial, it is six months' imprisonment and/or an unlimited fine. Disqualification is obligatory. The offence carries obligatory endorsement with between three and 11 penalty points. Retesting by way of an extended driving test is mandatory (see **C7.32**). Forfeiture of the vehicle used may also be ordered (see **E18.1**).

Sentence

C3.45 When conducting a sentencing exercise, it is a point of principle that proper regard must be taken of the maximum sentence of two years' imprisonment and the extent of the culpability of the offender (*Pettit* [2010] EWCA Crim 2107; *Raynham* [2011] EWCA Crim 1032; *Gaskin* [2013] EWCA Crim 244). When selecting the appropriate starting point, sentencers must be realistic about just how bad the driving was (*Wilson* [2013] EWCA Crim 1745, [2014] 1 Cr App R (S) 79 (490)). A very bad example of dangerous driving may justify a starting point at two years (*Ellis* [2016] EWCA Crim 1398, [2017] 1 Cr App R (S) 4 (15); *Mahmood* [2017] EWCA Crim 1449, where the car had deliberately been used as a weapon), but care must also be taken to leave some headroom for the most serious offences (*Freeman* [2016] EWCA Crim 1818). Sentencers should be hesitant about increasing a sentence because of local prevalence of this type of offending and, if it is to be raised by the prosecution, this should be done expressly and by reference to relevant material, or, if believed to be an issue by the court, submissions on the point should be invited, with reasons given when sentencing about the extent to which it has been a factor (*Khalid* [2017] EWCA Crim 592).

In *Shoaib* [2012] EWCA Crim 2742, which involved prolonged high-speed driving where it was lucky no damage or injury was inflicted, the sentence of 22 months' imprisonment was upheld. In *Templeton* [1996] 1 Cr App R (S) 380, the offender drove for nearly four minutes at speeds of up to 70 mph in a built-up area, travelling about three miles and crossing seven red lights. Nine months' imprisonment and disqualification for two years was upheld. In *Kahar* [2018] EWCA Crim 2522, a persistent course of driving at excessive speeds through residential areas, including driving head-on towards oncoming traffic, aggravated by not holding a licence or being insured, was regarded as so dangerous that, despite the appellant being aged just 19, 12 months' detention was upheld and suspension of that sentence could not be justified. An appeal against a sentence of 18 months' imprisonment was dismissed in *Imtiaz* [2019] EWCA Crim 2077. The appeal was on the basis that the sentence was manifestly excessive and wrong in principle as the appellant was told that he would receive one third credit for his guilty plea, and his time spent on recall was counted despite his being told it would not be. It was held that the three driving offences merited a sentence of 20 months' imprisonment after trial, and therefore a sentence of 12 months, to account for the guilty plea, was not inappropriate. The appellant had no right to any credit for time spent on recall as there was nothing exceptional about his case. In *Joseph* [2001] EWCA Crim 1195, [2002] 1 Cr App R (S) 20 (74), dangerous driving resulting in personal injury to a traffic warden attracted a deterrent sentence of ten months' imprisonment and disqualification for two years. Even where the defendant is young and the period of driving involved is short, a short custodial sentence can still be warranted (*Barnes* [2011] EWCA Crim 2127). The seriousness of the offence may well preclude the court from suspending the sentence (*Sweeney* [2018] EWCA Crim 1410). In *Kennion* [1997] RTR 421, the Court of Appeal commented that 'where otherwise perfectly respectable people of impeccable character lose control when sitting behind the wheel of a motor car because they imagine in some way that they have been provoked', i.e. road rage, they 'can expect immediate custodial sentences', a sentiment reiterated in *William* [2016] EWCA Crim 362, [2016] 2 Cr App R (S) 3 (12). *Harvey* [2016] EWCA Crim 1701 endorsed the approach of *Howells* [2002] EWCA Crim 1608, [2003] 1 Cr App R (S) 61 (292), in which it was suggested that a sentence of between six and 12 months' imprisonment is appropriate for a road rage case where no collision or injury results, alcohol plays no part, but there is evidence of intent to cause fear through furious driving in a temper. Even in such cases, general principles about the appropriate period of disqualification apply (see **C7.36**) and should not be so long as to impair the prospects of rehabilitation (*Warke* [2014] EWCA Crim 2354; *Sinclair* [2014] EWCA Crim 2599). Other principles identified in *Islam* [2019] EWCA Crim 1494 included the length required to prevent harm to the public and the punitive element in disqualification from driving. The former would be particularly relevant to cases involving young accused, who could be expected to grow out of their tendency to drive dangerously; the accused in *Islam*, aged 27, could be expected to be beyond that stage. However, the Court of Appeal recognised that it remained the position that there was no formula by which a court could measure the right length of a disqualification: it was a judicial decision which should produce a result tailored to the offender and the offence. In *Kargbo* [2019] EWCA Crim 2226, a ten-year period of disqualification was deemed to be manifestly excessive, even for someone with a history of this sort of offending, and it was substituted for a period of five years. Where the defendant had never passed a driving test, disqualifying for six years was merited and so upheld (*Wilson* [2019] EWCA Crim 2410). In *Henry* [2018] EWCA Crim 2794, which involved alcohol consumption and very high speeds for a significant period, the fact that the appellant had no history of driving offences had been factored into the length of custodial sentence, but was not apparently reflected in the disqualification imposed, which was accordingly reduced to three years. *McCafferty* [2011] EWCA Crim 509 and *Tombs* [2019] EWCA Crim 1100 provide examples of cases in which the minimum period of disqualification was appropriate. When sentencing for offences of dangerous driving and driving while disqualified committed on the same occasion, the latter offence should not attract a consecutive sentence but rather be regarded as aggravating the dangerous driving offence (*Cosby* [2020] EWCA Crim 69).

C3.46 In *Fitzpatrick* [2003] EWCA Crim 1399, the trial judge was criticised for wrongly taking into account that the driving had resulted in a fatality where this was not the offender's fault or even part of the prosecution case against the defendant.

Reference can also usefully be made to the *Magistrates' Court Sentencing Guidelines* (see Supplement, **SG10-64**); where the offence is being dealt with summarily, the guideline must generally be followed.

CAUSING DEATH BY DRIVING: UNLICENSED OR UNINSURED DRIVERS

C3.47

Road Traffic Act 1988, s. 3ZB

A person is guilty of an offence under this section if he causes the death of another person by driving a motor vehicle on a road and, at the time when he is driving, the circumstances are such that he is committing an offence under—

(a) section 87(1) of this Act (driving otherwise than in accordance with a licence), or
(c) section 143 of this Act (using motor vehicle while uninsured or unsecured against third party risks).

This offence is triable either way.

Section 3ZB was amended by the CJCA 2015, sch. 6, para. 1, so as to remove the offence of causing death by driving where at the time of driving the defendant is also committing an offence of driving while disqualified under s. 103(1)(b) (see **C3.51**).

Elements

The offence requires proof of one of the underlying offences under the RTA 1988 (see **C6.37** and **C6.46**), together with a causal link to a fatality (see generally **C3.15**). In *Hughes* [2013] UKSC 56, [2013] 1 WLR 2461, the Supreme Court clarified that the key words in s. 3ZB are 'causes... death... by driving' and, because this is a penal statute, it falls to be construed with a degree of strictness in favour of the accused. There must be something more than 'but for' causation. Section 3ZB 'requires at least some act or omission in the control of the car, which involves some element of fault, whether amounting to careless/inconsiderate driving or not, and which contributes in some more than minimal way to the death. It is not necessary that such act or omission be the principal cause of the death' (at [36]). In terms of directions to the jury, 'it is not necessary for the Crown to prove careless or inconsiderate driving, but... there must be something open to proper criticism in the driving of the defendant, beyond the mere presence of the vehicle on the road, and which contributed in some more than minimal way to the death' (at [33]). See, as an example of *Hughes* being applied, *Uthayakmar* [2014] EWCA Crim 123. In *Wilson* [2018] EWCA Crim 1184, [2019] RTR 24 (267) it was emphasised that the causal link in question is between the driving and the death rather than the driving and the collision. D had been driving at 10 mph above the speed limit when he hit a pedestrian. Expert evidence showed that this significantly and materially increased the likelihood of death, even though a collision may have been unavoidable. D was therefore liable on the basis that his driving had contributed in some more than minimal way to death. **C3.48**

The RTOA 1988, ss. 11 and 12(1), are applicable; see **C2.17** and **C2.18**.

Punishment

The maximum sentence on indictment is two years' imprisonment and/or a fine; on summary trial, it is six months' imprisonment and/or an unlimited fine. Disqualification is obligatory. The offence carries obligatory endorsement with between three and 11 penalty points. **C3.49**

Sentence

The sentencing guideline, *Causing Death by Driving* (see Supplement, **SG22-1**), must generally be followed where the offender is aged 18 or over. The guideline sets out the starting points and sentencing ranges for the various ways in which the offence can be committed and lists the additional aggravating and mitigating factors to be taken into account in adjusting the sentence from the starting point applicable for each band of offence. **C3.50**

CAUSING DEATH BY DRIVING: DISQUALIFIED DRIVERS

Road Traffic Act 1988, s. 3ZC **C3.51**

A person is guilty of an offence under this section if he or she
(a) causes the death of another person by driving a motor vehicle on a road. and
(b) at that time, is committing an offence under section 103(1)(b) of this Act (driving while disqualified).

This offence is triable only on indictment. It applies only in respect of offences committed on or after 13 April 2015.

Elements

The offence requires proof of the underlying offence under the RTA 1988, s. 103(1)(b) (see **C6.40**), together with a causal link to a fatality (see generally **C3.15**). See also **C3.48**. **C3.52**

The RTOA 1988, ss. 11 and 12(1), are applicable; see **C2.17** and **C2.18**.

Alternative Verdicts

C3.53 The RTOA 1988, s. 24, provides an alternative verdict under the RTA 1988, s. 103(1)(b) (see **C6.40**).

Punishment

C3.54 The maximum sentence is ten years' imprisonment and/or a fine. Disqualification is obligatory. The offence carries obligatory endorsement with between three and 11 penalty points. Forfeiture of the vehicle used may also be ordered (see **E18.1**).

CAUSING SERIOUS INJURY BY DRIVING: DISQUALIFIED DRIVERS

C3.55 **Road Traffic Act 1988, s. 3ZD**

(1) A person is guilty of an offence under this section if he or she
 (a) causes serious injury to another person by driving a motor vehicle on a road, and
 (b) at that time, is committing an offence under section 103(1)(b) of this Act (driving while disqualified).

This offence is triable either way. It applies only in respect of offences committed on or after 13 April 2015.

Elements

C3.56 The offence requires proof of the underlying offence under the RTA 1988, s. 103(1)(b) (see **C6.40**), together with a causal link to the injury. By s. 3ZD(2), 'serious injury' is defined as 'physical harm which amounts to grievous bodily harm' within the meaning of the OAPA 1861 (see **B2.60**). See also **C3.48**.

The RTOA 1988, ss. 11 and 12(1), are applicable; see **C2.17** and **C2.18**.

Alternative Verdicts

C3.57 The RTOA 1988, s. 24, provides an alternative verdict under the RTA 1988, s. 103(1)(b) (see **C6.40**).

Punishment

C3.58 The maximum sentence on conviction on indictment is four years' imprisonment and/or a fine. On summary conviction, the maximum sentence is six months' imprisonment and/or an unlimited fine. Disqualification is obligatory. The offence carries obligatory endorsement with between three and 11 penalty points. Forfeiture of the vehicle used may also be ordered (see **E18.1**).

WANTON OR FURIOUS DRIVING

C3.59 **Offences Against the Person Act 1861, s. 35**

Whosoever, having the charge of any carriage or vehicle, shall by wanton or furious driving or racing, or other wilful misconduct, or by wilful neglect, do or cause to be done any bodily harm to any person whatsoever, shall be guilty of an offence…

This offence is triable only on indictment.

Indictment

C3.60 *Statement of Offence*

Causing bodily harm, contrary to section 35 of the Offences Against the Person Act 1861.

Particulars of Offence

D, on the…day of…, having the charge of a taxi cab [or carriage etc.], by wanton [or furious] driving [or racing etc.] caused bodily harm to V.

Elements

The RTA 1988, s. 38, is applicable if the offence is committed on a 'road'. See **C1.13** and **C2.16**. **C3.61**

The offence can be committed whether or not the conduct takes place on a road (*Cooke* [1971] Crim LR 44; *Knight* [2004] EWCA Crim 2998). It also covers any kind of vehicle or carriage, including bicycles (*Parker* (1895) 59 JP 793).

The definition of 'driving' in this context is generally thought to be the older definition, which would include bicycles and even box carts, although such 'vehicles' or 'carriages' would often be propelled manually or by means of pedals and could rarely be said to be 'driven' in the modern sense of that term. 'Wanton' has no technical meaning, and may be construed in the light of its ordinary dictionary definition of irresponsible, capricious, unrestrained or random. In *Knight*, the Court of Appeal accepted as correct the trial judge's direction on the meaning of 'wanton' as effectively recklessness, involving the defendant in 'driving in such a manner as to create an obvious and serious risk of causing physical harm to some other person who might happen to be using the road, or doing substantial damage to property' and 'that in driving in that manner [the defendant] did so without having given any thought to the possibility of there being any such risk, or having recognised that there was some risk involved, had nonetheless gone on to take it'.

Alternative Verdicts

Assault occasioning actual bodily harm, contrary to the OAPA 1861, s. 47. Common assault, contrary to the CJA 1988, s. 39, but only if specifically included as a separate count on the indictment (*Mearns* [1991] QB 82). **C3.62**

Punishment

The offence carries two years' imprisonment and/or a fine. In *Ghasanfer* [2018] EWCA Crim 1083, [2018] RTR 30 (452), a sentence of ten months' imprisonment suspended for two years was substituted for the original sentence of 15 months' immediate imprisonment to reflect that the offence does not require proof of deliberate conduct. Where the offence is committed in respect of a mechanically propelled vehicle, endorsement is obligatory, it carries between three and nine penalty points and disqualification is discretionary (Road Safety Act 2006, s. 28). The offence is not otherwise endorsable but disqualification may be ordered under the PCC(S)A 2000, s. 147 (see **E21.14**), if an assault is involved and the accused was driving a motor vehicle. Forfeiture of the vehicle used for the purposes of the crime may be ordered (see **E18.1**). **C3.63**

CAUSING DANGER TO ROAD-USERS

Road Traffic Act 1988, s. 22A **C3.64**

(1) A person is guilty of an offence if he intentionally and without lawful authority or reasonable cause—
  (a) causes anything to be on or over a road, or
  (b) interferes with a motor vehicle, trailer or cycle, or
  (c) interferes (directly or indirectly) with traffic equipment,
  in such circumstances that it would be obvious to a reasonable person that to do so would be dangerous.

(2) In subsection (1) above 'dangerous' refers to danger either of injury to any person while on or near a road, or of serious damage to property on or near a road; and in determining for the purposes of that subsection what would be obvious to a reasonable person in a particular case, regard shall be had not only to the circumstances of which he could be expected to be aware but also to any circumstances shown to have been within the knowledge of the accused.

(3) In subsection (1) above 'traffic equipment' means—
  (a) anything lawfully placed on or near a road by a highway authority;
  (b) a traffic sign lawfully placed on or near a road by a person other than a highway authority;
  (c) any fence, barrier or light lawfully placed on or near a road—
    (i) in pursuance of section 174 of the Highways Act 1980, or section 65 of the New Roads and Street Works Act 1991 (which provide for guarding, lighting and signing in streets where works are undertaken), or

(ii) by a constable or a person acting under the instructions (whether general or specific) of a chief officer of police.

(4) For the purposes of subsection (3) above anything placed on or near a road shall unless the contrary is proved be deemed to have been lawfully placed there.

(5) In this section 'road' does not include a footpath or bridleway.

This offence is triable either way. In *Curtis* [2009] EWCA Crim 1225, [2010] 1 Cr App R (S) 31 (193), it was suggested that, because of the prejudice involved, an offence under s. 22A(1) should not have been dealt with at the trial of offences under the Protection from Harassment Act 1997, s. 4(1).

Indictment

C3.65

Statement of Offence

Causing danger to road users, contrary to section 22A(1) of the Road Traffic Act 1988.

Particulars of Offence

D, on the... day of..., intentionally and without lawful authority or reasonable cause interfered with a motor vehicle [or trailer, cycle or traffic equipment], namely..., [or caused... to be on [or over] a road, namely...,] in such circumstances that to do so was dangerous.

Elements

C3.66 The prosecution must establish that the accused intentionally performed the act. As to the burden of proof in relation to a defence of acting with lawful authority or reasonable cause, see **F3.11** ***et seq.***

The danger which arises must be of serious damage to property or of injury to any person while on or near a road. The test is an objective one but the danger must exist and must be obvious to a reasonable person. In other words there has to be a serious likelihood that injury or serious damage may be the result of the actions of the accused. In *DPP v D* [2006] EWHC 314 (Admin), [2006] RTR 38 (461), where a large road sign had been placed by the defendant and another on the carriageway without authorisation, the Divisional Court held that the proper test is not what would be obvious to a reasonable and prudent driver but rather whether a reasonable bystander, whether a motorist or not and being fully aware that not all drivers do drive carefully and well, would consider the act in question to represent an obvious danger. It is not necessary for injury or damage to result and it seems that any injury, however slight and as long as it could be termed an injury, would qualify. The extent of the potential damage or injury must, of course, have relevance to any sentence.

In *Meeking* [2012] EWCA Crim 641, [2012] 1 WLR 3349, a case of unlawful act manslaughter in which the act involved endangering road users contrary to the RTA 1988, s. 22A(1)(b), the Court of Appeal clarified that s. 22A(1)(b) is not confined to acts done to the vehicle before it is driven, but also covers interference creating a danger while the vehicle is in the process of being driven. Further, the conduct can take place within the vehicle rather than only external to it, such as dropping objects on to it. It is, however, a misdirection for the judge to refer to interference with the driver of the vehicle as opposed to interference with the vehicle itself (*Maxwell* [2014] EWCA Crim 417, [2014] RTR 27 (411)).

Punishment

C3.67 The maximum sentence on indictment is seven years' imprisonment and/or a fine; on summary trial, it is six months' imprisonment and/or an unlimited fine. The offence is not endorsable.

Section C4 Offences Relating to Documents Triable on Indictment

FORGERY, ALTERATION ETC. OF DOCUMENTS ETC.

Goods Vehicles (Licensing of Operators) Act 1995, s. 38 **C4.1**

(1) A person is guilty of an offence if, with intent to deceive, he—
 (a) forges, alters or uses a document or other thing to which this section applies;
 (b) lends to, or allows to be used by, any other person a document or other thing to which this section applies; or
 (c) makes or has in his possession any document or other thing so closely resembling a document or other thing to which this section applies as to be calculated to deceive.

(2) This section applies to the following documents and other things, namely—
 (a) any operator's licence;
 (b) any document, plate, mark or other thing by which, in pursuance of regulations, a vehicle is to be identified as being authorised to be used, or as being used, under an operator's licence;
 (c) any document evidencing the authorisation of any person for the purposes of sections 40 and 41;
 (d) any certificate of qualification under section 49; and
 (e) any certificate or diploma such as is mentioned in paragraph 13(1) or (1A) of Schedule 3.

Indictment

Statement of Offence **C4.2**

Forgery [or Use etc.] of a document [or licence etc.] with intent to deceive, contrary to section 38(1) of the Goods Vehicles (Licensing of Operators) Act 1995.

Particulars of Offence

D, on the... day of..., with intent to deceive, forged [or used etc.] a document [or licence etc.], namely...

Statement of Offence

Making [or Possessing] a document [or licence etc.] with intent to deceive, contrary to section 38(1) of the Goods Vehicles (Licensing of Operators) Act 1995.

Particulars of Offence

D, on the... day of..., with intent to deceive, made [or had in his possession] a document [or thing] so closely resembling an operator's licence [or document etc.] as to be calculated to deceive.

This offence is triable either way.

Elements

The RTOA 1988, s. 6 (see **C2.5**), applies by virtue of the Goods Vehicles (Licensing of Operators) Act 1995, s. 51. **C4.3**

As to forgery, see s. 38(4) of the 1995 Act and, generally, **B6.36** *et seq*. The term 'operator's licence' is defined in s. 2(1) of the 1995 Act and the vehicles authorised to be used under such a licence are set out in s. 5(1). Power to seize documents or articles is contained in s. 41. See also *Vehicle Operator Services Agency v FM Conway Ltd* [2012] EWHC 2930 (Admin), [2013] RTR 17 (242).

Punishment

C4.4 The offence under s. 38 is punishable on summary conviction by an unlimited fine, or on indictment by a term of imprisonment not exceeding two years and/or a fine (s. 38(3)).

Sentence

C4.5 See *Raven* (1988) 10 Cr App R (S) 354 and C4.9.

FALSE RECORDS OR ENTRIES RELATING TO DRIVERS' HOURS

C4.6 **Transport Act 1968, s. 99**

(5) Any person who makes, or causes to be made, any entry in a book, register or document kept or carried for the purposes of regulations under section 98 [of this Act] which he knows to be false or, with intent to deceive, alters or causes to be altered any such record or entry shall be liable—
  (a) on summary conviction, to [an unlimited fine];
  (b) on conviction on indictment, to imprisonment for a term not exceeding two years.

Indictment

C4.7 *Statement of Offence*

Making [or Causing] a false record [or entry] [to be made], contrary to section 99(5) of the Transport Act 1968.

Particulars of Offence

D, on the...day of..., made [or caused to be made] an entry in a book [or register etc.] kept [or carried] for the purposes of regulations under section 98 of the Transport Act 1968, namely..., which he knew to be false.

This offence is triable either way.

Elements

C4.8 This offence has a narrower application following the introduction by the Passenger and Goods Vehicles (Recording Equipment) Regulations 2005 (SI 2005 No. 1904) of separate provisions relating to digital tachographs. Regulations made under s. 98 are the Drivers' Hours (Goods Vehicles) (Keeping of Records) Regulations 1987 (SI 1987 No. 1421) which provide for the making of entries in the driver's record book according to the instructions contained therein. These regulations apply to certain work-related journeys and impose obligations upon employers, where relevant, as well as drivers. In any proceedings under s. 99(5), it is necessary for the prosecution to establish that the record or book etc. is being 'carried for the purpose' of the relevant regulation, and as certain vehicles are exempt, a thorough examination of the various provisions is essential. In *JF Alford Transport Ltd* [1997] 2 Cr App R 326, the Court of Appeal held that knowledge of and passive acquiescence in a principal's offence under s. 99(5) is insufficient to amount to aiding and abetting its commission, but indicated that such knowledge and an ability to control the action of an offender coupled with a deliberate decision to refrain from doing so might suffice.

Sentence

C4.9 In *Raven* (1988) 10 Cr App R (S) 354, the offender was involved in the running of a haulage business, a number of whose vehicles had their tachograph wiring interfered with. He had entered into an agreement with another man to operate using that man's operator's licence and discs. Two drivers said that they were instructed by the appellant, from time to time, to drive with the tachograph switched off. The appellant had previous relevant convictions. The sentence of nine months' imprisonment following guilty pleas to six counts was upheld. In *Potter* [1999] 2 Cr App R (S) 448, the Court of Appeal substituted three months' imprisonment for the nine months imposed and concluded that where the offender is not in a managerial position and had not therefore corrupted others, a lower sentence may be justified. However, in *Saunders* [2001] EWCA Crim 93, [2001] 2 Cr App R (S) 63 (301), eight months' imprisonment was upheld in spite of the offenders not occupying managerial positions because of the number of offences and the lengthy period over which they were committed. The Court of Appeal approved the judge's sentencing remarks, which stressed the importance of safety provisions, the unfairness of competition to 'fair traders', the level of sophistication shown, the public danger which must have arisen, and the fraudulent nature of the offenders' activities.

FORGERY, ALTERATION ETC. OF LICENCES, MARKS, TRADE PLATES ETC.

Vehicle Excise and Registration Act 1994, s. 44 **C4.10**

(1) A person is guilty of an offence if he forges, fraudulently alters, fraudulently uses, fraudulently lends or fraudulently allows to be used by another person anything to which subsection (2) applies.

(2) This subsection applies to—
- (a) to (c) [repealed],
- (d) a registration mark,
- (e) a registration document, and
- (f) a trade plate (including a replacement trade plate).

Indictment

Statement of Offence **C4.11**

Forgery [or Fraudulent use etc.] of a registration document, contrary to section 44(1) of the Vehicle Excise and Registration Act 1994.

Particulars of Offence

D, on the... day of..., forged [or fraudulently used etc.] a registration document, namely...

Procedure and Evidence

The admissibility of records maintained by the Secretary of State is governed by the Vehicle Excise and Registration Act 1994, s. 52. **C4.12**

Elements

For the purposes of the Vehicle Excise and Registration Act 1994, s. 44, 'fraudulently' means dishonestly deceiving a police officer or other person responsible for a public duty. The approach to dishonesty set out in *Ivey v Genting Casinos (UK) Ltd* [2017] UKSC 67, [2018] AC 391 and confirmed in *Barton* [2020] EWCA Crim 575 (see also **B4.55**) is applicable. There is no requirement to prove an intention to cause any economic loss (*Terry* [1984] AC 374). In *Johnson* [1995] RTR 15, it was held that an offence under the Vehicles (Excise) Act 1971, s. 26 (which s. 44 of the 1994 Act replaced), relating to fraudulent use of a vehicle licence (which was formerly covered under s. 44) could be committed only where there was evidence that the vehicle was being or had been used on a public road while displaying the offending licence. **C4.13**

Forgery does not necessarily connote an intention to defraud but may be taken to include an intention to deceive for the purposes of the Vehicle Excise and Registration Act 1994 (*Clifford v Bloom* [1977] RTR 351; *Clayton* (1980) 72 Cr App R 135).

In *Macrae* (1995) 159 JP 359, the offence was said to involve the defendant having the intent that the defendant or another should use the item to induce a third party to accept it as genuine and by reason of so accepting it to do or not to do some act to that third party's or another's prejudice as a result of such acceptance as genuine in connection with the performance of any duty, i.e. akin to the ulterior intent found in the Forgery and Counterfeiting Act 1981 (see **B6.36** ***et seq***).

Punishment

C4.14 On indictment, the maximum sentence for an offence under the Vehicle Excise and Registration Act 1994, s. 44, is two years' imprisonment and/or a fine; on summary conviction, an unlimited fine. See *Weston* [2011] EWCA Crim 2334 and *Gallucci* [2014] EWCA Crim 766.

FORGERY OF DOCUMENTS ETC.: ROAD TRAFFIC ACT 1988, s. 173

C4.15 Road Traffic Act 1988, s. 173

(1) A person who, with intent to deceive—
- (a) forges, alters or uses a document or other thing to which this section applies, or
- (b) lends to, or allows to be used by, any other person a document or other thing to which this section applies, or
- (c) makes or has in his possession any document or other thing so closely resembling a document or other thing to which this section applies as to be calculated to deceive,

is guilty of an offence.

(2) This section applies to the following documents and other things—
- (a) any licence under any Part of this Act
- (b) any test certificate, goods vehicle test certificate, plating certificate, certificate of conformity or Minister's approval certificate (within the meaning of Part II of this Act),
- (c) any certificate required as a condition of any exception prescribed under section 14 of this Act,
- (cc) any seal required by regulations made under section 41 of this Act with respect to speed limiters,
- (d) any plate containing particulars required to be marked on a vehicle by regulations under section 41 of this Act or containing other particulars required to be marked on a goods vehicle by sections 54 to 58 of this Act or regulations under those sections,
- (dd) any document evidencing the appointment of an examiner under section 66A of this Act,
- (e) any records required to be kept by virtue of section 74 of this Act,
- (f) any document which, in pursuance of section 89(3) of this Act, is issued as evidence of the result of a test of competence to drive,
- (ff) any document evidencing the successful completion of a driver training course provided in accordance with regulations under section 99ZA of this Act,
- (g) any certificate under section 133A or any badge or certificate prescribed by regulations made by virtue of section 135 of this Act,
- (h) any certificate of insurance under Part VI of this Act,
- (j) any document produced as evidence of insurance in pursuance of Regulation 6 of the Motor Vehicles (Compulsory Insurance) (No. 2) Regulations 1973 (SI 1973 No. 2143),
- (k) any document issued under regulations made by the Secretary of State in pursuance of his power under section 165(2)(a) of this Act to prescribe evidence which may be produced in lieu of a certificate of insurance,
- (l) any international road haulage permit, and

(m) a certificate of the kind referred to in section 34B(1) of the Road Traffic Offenders Act 1988.

(3) In the application of this section to England and Wales 'forges' means makes a false document or other thing in order that it may be used as genuine.

When s. 37(8) of the Road Safety Act 2006 is brought into force, a new s. 173(2)(n) will be inserted so as to include 'any document produced as evidence of the passing of an appropriate driving test' (as defined in the RTOA 1988, s. 36) within s. 173. When para. 27 of sch. 6 to that Act is implemented, s. 173(2)(g) will be replaced with three paragraphs expanding the documents already mentioned to include reference to a document evidencing the passing of an examination to give driving instruction or the completion of training for such instructors. **C4.16**

Indictment

The form provided in **C4.2** may be adapted for use in relation to offences under this section. **C4.17**

Elements

'Use' extends to use by an employer, see **C1.28**. **C4.18**

Particular words must be read 'against the mischief which that particular section seeks to avoid or prevent'; the production of a driving licence unconnected with any driving on the road is not 'using' it for the purposes of the RTA 1988, s. 173 (*Howe* [1982] RTR 45).

A document which has been completed by someone other than the proper person does not cease to be a document to which the section applies for the purposes of 'using' (*Pilditch* [1981] RTR 303).

A forged document which is not specified within s. 173 but which closely resembles a document there specified is not 'used', but may fall within s. 173(1)(c) (*Holloway v Brown* [1978] RTR 537).

Where an 'intent to deceive' has been established, it is not necessary for the prosecution to prove that the defendant knew the documents were false; if that was the case, the statute would include the word 'knowingly'. Such an intent may be shown by evidence that 'they were irregular documents either by way of irregular acquisition or by the irregular disposing of them' (*Greenberg* [1942] 2 All ER 344, per Birkett J at p. 347). The Court of Criminal Appeal in *Greenberg* also stated that it is unnecessary to allege or prove an intent to deceive any particular person. Knowledge that the documents are false may, however, be relevant to the issue of whether the defendant had an 'intent to deceive'.

In *Cleghorn* [1938] 3 All ER 398, a certificate of insurance which had been cancelled was held to be properly described as one resembling a certificate of insurance. Similarly, in *Aworinde* [1996] RTR 66, bogus blank insurance certificates were held to be documents so closely resembling certificates as to be calculated to deceive.

'Calculated to deceive' means 'likely to deceive' (*Davison* [1972] 3 All ER 1121; *Turner v Shearer* [1972] 1 All ER 397).

Punishment

On conviction on indictment, the maximum sentence is two years' imprisonment and/or a fine; on summary conviction, an unlimited fine. **C4.19**

FALSE STATEMENTS ETC.: ROAD TRAFFIC ACT 1988, s. 174

C4.20 Road Traffic Act 1988, s. 174

(1) A person who knowingly makes a false statement for the purpose—
(a) of obtaining the grant of a licence under any Part of this Act to himself or any other person, or
(b) of preventing the grant of any such licence, or
(c) of procuring the imposition of a condition or limitation in relation to any such licence, or
(ca) of obtaining a document evidencing the successful completion of a driver training course provided in accordance with regulations under section 99ZA of this Act, or
(d) of securing the entry or retention of the name of any person in the register of approved instructors maintained under Part V of this Act, or
(dd) of obtaining the grant to any person of a certificate under section 133A of this Act, or
(e) of obtaining the grant of an international road haulage permit to himself or any other person,
is guilty of an offence.
(2) A person who, in supplying information or producing documents for the purposes either of sections 53 to 60 and 63 of this Act or of regulations made under sections 49 to 51, 61, 62 and 66(3) of this Act—
(a) makes a statement which he knows to be false in a material particular or recklessly makes a statement which is false in a material particular, or
(b) produces, provides, sends or otherwise makes use of a document which he knows to be false in a material particular or recklessly produces, provides, sends or otherwise makes use of a document which is false in a material particular,
is guilty of an offence.
(3) A person who—
(a) knowingly produces false evidence for the purposes of regulations under section 66(1) of this Act, or
(b) knowingly makes a false statement in a declaration required to be made by the regulations,
is guilty of an offence.
(4) A person who—
(a) wilfully makes a false entry in any record required to be made or kept by regulations under section 74 of this Act, or
(b) with intent to deceive, makes use of any such entry which he knows to be false,
is guilty of an offence.
(5) A person who makes a false statement or withholds any material information for the purpose of obtaining the issue—
(a) of a certificate of insurance under Part VI of this Act, or
(b) of any document issued under regulations made by the Secretary of State in pursuance of his power under section 165(2)(a) of this Act to prescribe evidence which may be produced in lieu of a certificate of insurance,
is guilty of an offence.

When para. 28 of sch. 6 to the Road Safety Act 2006 is brought into force, a new s. 174(1)(da) will be inserted, referring to a document evidencing the passing of an examination to give driving instruction or the completion of training for such instructors.

Elements

C4.21 There is no requirement that the making of the false statement results in any gain or advantage accruing to the defendant (*Jones v Meatyard* [1939] 1 All ER 140) or, presumably, to a third person.

The offence in s. 174(5) of making a false statement for the purpose of obtaining the issue of an insurance certificate is one of strict liability. However, in *Cummerson* [1968] 2 QB 534, it was indicated that the other offence created by the provision of withholding material information for that purpose may well require proof that the act was done consciously. In *Power v Provincial*

Insurance plc [1998] RTR 60, the Court of Appeal decided that a motorist correctly regarded his conviction for driving whilst unfit as being 'spent' by reference to the rehabilitation period applying to the fine imposed and not the period of effectiveness of the endorsement on the driving licence relating to a period of disqualification. This meant that he had been entitled to answer negatively the question whether he had been convicted of an offence for which an order of endorsement had been made, which in turn meant that he had not made a false statement under s. 174(5).

Punishment

On conviction on indictment, the maximum sentence is two years' imprisonment and/or a fine; on summary conviction, six months' imprisonment and/or an unlimited fine. C4.22

Section C5 Drink-Driving and Drug-Driving Offences

PRELIMINARY TESTING

C5.1 **Road Traffic Act 1988, ss. 6, 6A, 6B, 6C, 6D and 6E**

6.—(1) If any of subsections (2) to (5) applies a constable may require a person to co-operate with any one or more preliminary tests administered to the person by that constable or another constable.

(2) This subsection applies if a constable reasonably suspects that the person—
- (a) is driving, is attempting to drive or is in charge of a motor vehicle on a road or other public place, and
- (b) has alcohol or a drug in his body or is under the influence of a drug.

(3) This subsection applies if a constable reasonably suspects that the person—
- (a) has been driving, attempting to drive or in charge of a motor vehicle on a road or other public place while having alcohol or a drug in his body or while unfit to drive because of a drug, and
- (b) still has alcohol or a drug in his body or is still under the influence of a drug.

(4) This subsection applies if a constable reasonably suspects that the person—
- (a) is or has been driving, attempting to drive or in charge of a motor vehicle on a road or other public place, and
- (b) has committed a traffic offence while the vehicle was in motion.

(5) This subsection applies if—
- (a) an accident occurs owing to the presence of a motor vehicle on a road or other public place, and
- (b) a constable reasonably believes that the person was driving, attempting to drive or in charge of the vehicle at the time of the accident.

(6) A person commits an offence if without reasonable excuse he fails to co-operate with a preliminary test in pursuance of a requirement imposed under this section.

(7) A constable may administer a preliminary test by virtue of any of subsections (2) to (4) only if he is in uniform.

(8) In this section—
- (a) a reference to a preliminary test is to any of the tests described in sections 6A to 6C, and
- (b) 'traffic offence' means an offence under—
  - (i) a provision of Part II of the Public Passenger Vehicles Act 1981,
  - (ii) a provision of the Road Traffic Regulation Act 1984,
  - (iii) a provision of the Road Traffic Offenders Act 1988 other than a provision of Part III, or
  - (iv) a provision of this Act other than a provision of Part V.

6A.—(1) A preliminary breath test is a procedure whereby the person to whom the test is administered provides a specimen of breath to be used for the purpose of obtaining, by means of a device of a type approved by the Secretary of State, an indication whether the proportion of alcohol in the person's breath or blood is likely to exceed the prescribed limit.

(2) A preliminary breath test administered in reliance on section 6(2) to (4) may be administered only at or near the place where the requirement to co-operate with the test is imposed.

(3) A preliminary breath test administered in reliance on section 6(5) may be administered—
- (a) at or near the place where the requirement to co-operate with the test is imposed, or
- (b) if the constable who imposes the requirement thinks it expedient, at a police station specified by him.

6B.—(1) A preliminary impairment test is a procedure whereby the constable administering the test—
(a) observes the person to whom the test is administered in his performance of tasks specified by the constable, and
(b) makes such other observations of the person's physical state as the constable thinks expedient.
(2) and (3) [Secretary of State's power to issue code of practice and contents of such a code.]
(4) A preliminary impairment test may be administered—
(a) at or near the place where the requirement to co-operate with the test is imposed, or
(b) if the constable who imposes the requirement thinks it expedient, at a police station specified by him.
(5) A constable administering a preliminary impairment test shall have regard to the code of practice under this section.
(6) A constable may administer a preliminary impairment test only if he is approved for that purpose by the chief officer of the police force to which he belongs.
(7) A code of practice under this section may include provision about—
(a) the giving of approval under subsection (6), and
(b) in particular, the kind of training that a constable should have undergone, or the kind of qualification that a constable should possess, before being approved under that subsection.
6C.—(1) A preliminary drug test is a procedure by which a specimen of sweat or saliva is—
(a) obtained, and
(b) used for the purpose of obtaining, by means of a device of a type approved by the Secretary of State, an indication whether the person to whom the test is administered has a drug in his body and if so–
(i) whether it is a specified controlled drug;
(ii) if it is, whether the proportion of it in the person's blood or urine is likely to exceed the specified limit for that drug.
(2) A preliminary drug test may be administered—
(a) at or near the place where the requirement to co-operate with the test is imposed, or
(b) if the constable who imposes the requirement thinks it expedient, at a police station specified by him.
(3) Up to three preliminary drug tests may be administered.
6D.—(1) A constable may arrest a person without warrant if as a result of a preliminary breath test or preliminary drug test the constable reasonably suspects that—
(a) the proportion of alcohol in the person's breath or blood exceeds the prescribed limit, or
(b) the person has a specified controlled drug in his body and the proportion of it in the person's blood or urine exceeds the specified limit for that drug.
(1A) The fact that specimens of breath have been provided under section 7 of this Act by the person concerned does not prevent subsection (1) above having effect if the constable who imposed on him the requirement to provide the specimens has reasonable cause to believe that the device used to analyse the specimens has not produced a reliable indication of the proportion of alcohol in the breath of the person.
(2) A constable may arrest a person without warrant if—
(a) the person fails to co-operate with a preliminary test in pursuance of a requirement imposed under section 6, and
(b) the constable reasonably suspects that the person has alcohol or a drug in his body or is under the influence of a drug.
(2A) A person arrested under this section may, instead of being taken to a police station, be detained at or near the place where the preliminary test was, or would have been, administered, with a view to imposing on him there a requirement under section 7 of this Act.
(3) A person may not be arrested under this section while at a hospital as a patient.
6E.—(1) A constable may enter any place (using reasonable force if necessary) for the purpose of—
(a) imposing a requirement by virtue of section 6(5) following an accident in a case where the constable reasonably suspects that the accident involved injury of any person, or
(b) arresting a person under section 6D following an accident in a case where the constable reasonably suspects that the accident involved injury of any person.

(2) This section—
  (a) does not extend to Scotland, and
  (b) is without prejudice to any rule of law or enactment about the right of a constable in Scotland to enter any place.

Making the Requirement

C5.2 **Circumstances in which Requirement can be Imposed** A preliminary test may be required only when one of the situations specified in s. 6(2) to (5) is satisfied. Hospital patients are accorded added protection (see the RTA 1988, s. 9, and **C5.23**). If reliance is placed on 'reasonable belief' following an accident, a higher standard than 'reasonable suspicion' can still be expected (see, e.g., *Johnson v Whitehouse* [1984] RTR 38), although 'belief' does not equate to 'knowledge' (*Bunyard v Hayes* [1985] RTR 348).

The power of the police to stop a vehicle is contained in the RTA 1988, s. 163. There is nothing to prevent random stopping, but the law requires one of the conditions in s. 6(2) to (5) to be complied with before a preliminary test is administered. In *Chief Constable of Gwent v Dash* [1986] RTR 41, police were stopping vehicles at random in order to apprehend drivers who might be suspected of having excess alcohol in their bodies. Macpherson J, giving the judgment of the Divisional Court, said (at p. 46, emphasis added):

> ... there is no restriction upon the stopping of motorists by a policeman *in the execution of his duty* and the subsequent requirement for a breath test should the policeman then and there genuinely suspect the ingestion of alcohol. It may be said by some to be bad luck that such a situation arises but it is not unlawful provided the officer is in uniform and acts without oppression, or caprice, or some false pretence or proved 'malpractice'.

The Court did, however, distinguish cases where persons are arrested in their own house in a situation similar to that in *Morris v Beardmore* [1981] AC 446. See *DPP v Godwin* [1991] RTR 303 and **C5.46**.

C5.3 The necessary suspicion may result from information supplied by others and may arise after a motorist has ceased to drive, so long as it relates to the period when the person was actually driving (s. 6(3) and (5) and see also *Moss v Jenkins* [1975] RTR 25 and *Blake v Pope* [1986] 3 All ER 185). Evidence of what the officer has been told is admissible if it goes to the officer's state of mind at the time of requiring the specimen of breath. Whilst the absence of a ground under which to administer a preliminary test may invalidate an arrest under s. 6D, it should not invalidate the subsequent procedure unless the court exercises its discretion to exclude evidence under the PACE 1984, s. 78 (*Griffiths v Willett* [1979] RTR 195), or as a result of human rights violations. In *DPP v Wilson* [1991] RTR 284, it was held that the power to exclude evidence could arise from *Fox* [1986] AC 281 or *Chief Constable of Gwent v Dash* [1986] RTR 41, and co-existed with a wide discretion under s. 78, but there is no duty on the police to warn a driver of a potential offence and failure to do so may not be oppressive.

If the device used is itself specified in the schedule to the approval order, no further identification or specification is required from the prosecution (*Breckon v DPP* [2007] EWHC 2013 (Admin), [2008] RTR 8 (96)). If the device used to administer a roadside breath test is of a type that could be used to obtain an evidential specimen (see **C5.9**), the justices must exercise care to ensure that they understand which type of test was being conducted and the consequences flowing therefrom. If the police evidence is that the device was not operating so as to give an accurate evidential reading and that goes unchallenged, or is preferred, the test is a s. 6 preliminary test (*DPP v Karamouzis* [2006] EWHC 2634 (Admin)). Where the test is a preliminary one, the prosecution are not obliged to disclose to the defence the results in figures from that roadside test (*Smith v DPP* [2007] EWHC 100 (Admin), [2007] 4 All ER 1135; *Breckon v DPP*); the test remains indicative only as to whether the constable should arrest the suspect with a view to securing an evidential specimen thereafter.

Where consumption of alcohol is suspected, the constable is likely to continue to require a roadside breath test. Where, however, the suspect appears unfit, the constable may, if previously given approval by the force's chief officer in accordance with s. 6B(6), administer an impairment test in accordance with the code of practice issued by the Secretary of State, which is designed to ascertain whether the perceived unfitness to drive is due to drink or drugs. Alternatively, a decision to administer a preliminary drug test by means of an approved device and to take a specimen of sweat or saliva might be taken. As s. 6(1) refers to 'any one or more preliminary tests', it is clear that they are not mutually exclusive and the constable could require co-operation with each of the tests in turn, if only to eliminate any suspicions as to both alcohol and drugs. C5.4

As regards requiring a preliminary breath test, failing to follow the manufacturer's instructions about allowing a 20-minute gap to elapse after the consumption of alcohol before commencing the test will render the roadside procedure unlawful so that no offence under s. 6(6) will be committed, but that does not of itself affect the lawfulness of the subsequent Intoximeter procedure (*DPP v Kay* [1999] RTR 109).

Other Conditions for Requirement The constable making a requirement by virtue of any of s. 6(2) to (4) must be 'in uniform', i.e. the officer should be easily identifiable as a constable. The absence of a helmet (*Wallwork v Giles* [1970] RTR 117) or the wearing of a raincoat (*Taylor v Baldwin* [1976] RTR 265) did not affect the conclusion that the constable was still in uniform. Justices are also able to rely on their knowledge of how the local constabulary operates (*Cooper v Rowlands* [1971] RTR 291, in relation to a motor patrol officer; *Richards v West* [1980] RTR 215, in relation to special constables) and, in the absence of evidence to the contrary, they are entitled to infer or assume from the surrounding circumstances that a constable is in uniform (*Gage v Jones* [1983] RTR 508). C5.5

Under s. 6A(2), a preliminary breath test in a situation not involving an accident must be administered at or near the place where the requirement is made but, in relation to a person required to undertake a preliminary breath test as a result of an accident or a preliminary impairment or drug test, it may be administered either at or near the place where the requirement is made (usually the roadside) or at a police station (see, e.g., *Moore* [1994] RTR 360).

The requirement must be made using words of sufficient clarity, although there is no set formula for any particular words to be uttered. In relation to the old s. 6 offence, using 'I wish to give you a breath test' (*Clarke* [1969] 2 QB 91) or 'I intend to give you a breath test' (*O'Boyle* [1973] RTR 445) sufficed. Adapting such wording to cover the impairment or drug test, adding whatever further explanation is appropriate, should be adequate. As long as the constable speaks the words in the reasonable belief that they would be, and were being, heard and understood, it is not necessary to prove they were actually both heard and understood (*Nicholls* [1972] 2 All ER 186). There is no need to produce physically a breath test device, provided that an opportunity to comply with the requirement is given (*DPP v Swan* [2004] EWHC 2432 (QB)).

Failure to Co-operate with a Preliminary Test

Section 6(6) creates a single offence of failing, without a reasonable excuse, to co-operate with a preliminary test when required to do so. The RTOA 1988, ss. 11 and 12(1), apply; see **C2.17** and **C2.18**. For the meaning of the terms 'accident', 'driving', 'motor vehicle', 'road or other public place', and 'attempting to drive', see **C1.1, C1.2, C1.9, C1.13** and **C1.20**. For the meaning of 'in charge', see **C5.36**. The term 'fail' includes a refusal (RTA 1988, s. 11). Whether there is a failure is a question of fact and degree. If a person does not take advantage of the opportunity to take the test provided by the constable, there will in principle be a failure (*Ferguson* [1970] RTR 395). C5.6

C5.7 **Reasonable Excuse** Once the defence have raised a 'reasonable excuse', it is for the prosecution to negative it (*Rowland v Thorpe* [1970] 3 All ER 195). A claim by the defendant that none of the pre-conditions for making the requirement existed does not constitute a reasonable excuse (*Downey* [1970] RTR 257). In *Chief Constable of Avon and Somerset Constabulary v Singh* [1988] RTR 107, it was held that a failure to provide a roadside breath test merely because the accused claimed that he had not been driving at the time did not constitute a reasonable excuse. His understanding of what was being required of him was held to be irrelevant, because he was putting forward a false story as to the driving of the vehicle. The Divisional Court did accept that, in certain circumstances, a failure to understand the nature of the obligation might constitute a reasonable excuse, but added that before something could amount to an excuse 'it has to be causative in this sense, that it was the reason why the thing was not done'. This reasoning appears equally valid in relation to impairment and drug preliminary tests. A medical condition, such as a chest complaint, may constitute a reasonable excuse for failing to co-operate, or where the person required to provide a specimen is 'physically or mentally unable to provide it or its provision would entail a substantial risk to health' (*Lennard* [1973] 2 All ER 831). See also **C5.26** and **C5.29**.

C5.8 **Punishment** The penalty is a fine up to level 3 on the standard scale. The *Magistrates' Court Sentencing Guidelines* (see Supplement, **SG10-106**) give fine band B as the starting point. Disqualification is discretionary but, in the absence of 'special reasons', endorsement with four penalty points is obligatory.

EVIDENTIAL SPECIMENS

C5.9 **Road Traffic Act 1988, ss. 7 and 7A**

7.—(1) In the course of an investigation into whether a person has committed an offence under section 3A, 4 or 5 of this Act a constable may, subject to the following provisions of this section and section 9 of this Act, require him—

(a) to provide two specimens of breath for analysis by means of a device of a type approved by the Secretary of State, or

(b) to provide a specimen of blood or urine for a laboratory test.

(1A) In the course of an investigation into whether a person has committed an offence under section 5A of this Act a constable may, subject to subsections (3) to (7) of this section and section 9 of this Act, require the person to provide a specimen of blood or urine for a laboratory test.

(2) A constable may make a requirement under this section to provide specimens of breath only if—

(a) the requirement is made at a police station or a hospital,

(b) the requirement is imposed in circumstances where section 6(5) of this Act applies, or

(c) the constable is in uniform.

(2A) and (2B) [Repealed.]

(2C) Where a constable has imposed a requirement on the person concerned to co-operate with a relevant breath test at any place, he is entitled to remain at or near that place in order to impose on him there a requirement under this section.

(2CA) For the purposes of subsection (2C) 'a relevant breath test' is a procedure involving the provision by the person concerned of a specimen of breath to be used for the purpose of obtaining an indication whether the proportion of alcohol in his breath or blood is likely to exceed the prescribed limit.

(2D) If a requirement under subsection (1)(a) above has been made at a place other than at a police station, such a requirement may subsequently be made at a police station if (but only if)—

(a) a device or a reliable device of the type mentioned in subsection (1)(a) above was not available at that place or it was for any other reason not practicable to use such a device there, or

(b) the constable who made the previous requirement has reasonable cause to believe that the device used there has not produced a reliable indication of the proportion of alcohol in the breath of the person concerned.

(3) A requirement under this section to provide a specimen of blood or urine can only be made at a police station or at a hospital; and it cannot be made at a police station unless—

(a) the constable making the requirement has reasonable cause to believe that for medical reasons a specimen of breath cannot be provided or should not be required, or

(b) specimens of breath have not been provided elsewhere and at the time the requirement is made a device or a reliable device of the type mentioned in subsection (1)(a) above is not available at the police station or it is then for any other reason not practicable to use such a device there,

(bb) a device of the type mentioned in subsection (1)(a) above has been used (at the police station or elsewhere) but the constable who required the specimens of breath has reasonable cause to believe that the device has not produced a reliable indication of the proportion of alcohol in the breath of the person concerned,

(bc) as a result of the administration of a preliminary drug test, the constable making the requirement has reasonable cause to believe that the person required to provide a specimen of blood or urine has a drug in his body, or

(c) the suspected offence is one under section 3A, 4 or 5A of this Act and the constable making the requirement has been advised by a medical practitioner or a registered health care professional that the condition of the person required to provide the specimen might be due to some drug;

but may then be made notwithstanding that the person required to provide the specimen has already provided or been required to provide two specimens of breath.

(4) If the provision of a specimen other than a specimen of breath may be required in pursuance of this section the question whether it is to be a specimen of blood or a specimen of urine and, in the case of a specimen of blood, the question who is to be asked to take it shall be decided (subject to subsection (4A)) by the constable making the requirement.

(4A) Where a constable decides for the purposes of subsection (4) to require the provision of a specimen of blood, there shall be no requirement to provide such a specimen if—

(a) the medical practitioner who is asked to take the specimen is of the opinion that, for medical reasons, it cannot or should not be taken; or

(b) the registered health care professional who is asked to take it is of that opinion and there is no contrary opinion from a medical practitioner;

and, where by virtue of this subsection there can be no requirement to provide a specimen of blood, the constable may require a specimen of urine instead.

(5) A specimen of urine shall be provided within one hour of the requirement for its provision being made and after the provision of a previous specimen of urine.

(5A) A constable may arrest a person without warrant if—

(a) the person fails to provide a specimen of breath when required to do so in pursuance of this section, and

(b) the constable reasonably suspects that the person has alcohol in his body.

(6) A person who, without reasonable excuse, fails to provide a specimen when required to do so in pursuance of this section is guilty of an offence.

(7) A constable must, on requiring any person to provide a specimen in pursuance of this section, warn him that a failure to provide it may render him liable to prosecution.

7A.—(1) A constable may make a request to a medical or health care practitioner for him to take a specimen of blood from a person ('the person concerned') irrespective of whether that person consents if—

(a) that person is a person from whom the constable would (in the absence of any incapacity of that person and of any objection under section 9) be entitled under section 7 to require the provision of a specimen of blood for a laboratory test;

(b) it appears to that constable that that person has been involved in an accident that constitutes or is comprised in the matter that is under investigation or the circumstances of that matter;

(c) it appears to that constable that that person is or may be incapable (whether or not he has purported to do so) of giving a valid consent to the taking of a specimen of blood; and

(d) it appears to that constable that that person's incapacity is attributable to medical reasons.

(2) A request under this section—

(a) shall not be made to a medical or health care practitioner who for the time being has any responsibility (apart from the request) for the clinical care of the person concerned; and

(b) shall not be made to a practitioner other than a police medical or health care practitioner unless—
(i) it is not reasonably practicable for the request to be made to a police medical or health care practitioner; or
(ii) it is not reasonably practicable for such a practitioner (assuming him to be willing to do so) to take the specimen.

(3) It shall be lawful for a medical or health care practitioner to whom a request is made under this section, if he thinks fit—
(a) to take a specimen of blood from the person concerned irrespective of whether that person consents; and
(b) to provide the sample to a constable.

(4) If a specimen is taken in pursuance of a request under this section, the specimen shall not be subjected to a laboratory test unless the person from whom it was taken—
(a) has been informed that it was taken; and
(b) has been required by a constable to give his permission for a laboratory test of the specimen; and
(c) has given his permission.

(5) A constable must, on requiring a person to give his permission for the purposes of this section for a laboratory test of a specimen, warn that person that a failure to give the permission may render him liable to prosecution.

(6) A person who, without reasonable excuse, fails to give his permission for a laboratory test of a specimen of blood taken from him under this section is guilty of an offence.

(7) In this section—
'medical or health care practitioner' means a medical practitioner or a registered health care professional;
'police medical or health care practitioner' means a medical practitioner, or a registered health care professional, who is engaged under any agreement to provide medical or health care services for purposes connected with the activities of a police force.

Initial Procedural Requirements

C5.10 The requirement to provide specimens must arise 'in the course of an investigation', which does not imply any greater formality than is normally involved in the plain and ordinary meaning of the word 'investigation' (*Graham v Albert* [1985] RTR 352). As with a preliminary test (see C5.2), the 'requirement' does not have to be in any formalised language, provided it amounts to a requirement and is made at a permitted location. A requirement made otherwise than by strictly following the guidance contained in a standard form covering the police station testing process is not automatically unlawful (*DPP v Coulter* [2005] EWHC 1533 (Admin)). The requirement can, where a portable evidential breath test device is available, be made at the roadside (although requiring a preliminary test under the RTA 1988, ss. 6 and 6A (see **C5.1**), remains an option available to the constable). The requirement can be made at a police station or, when appropriate, at a hospital (see **C5.23**). Having made the requirement at such a place, the RTA 1988, s. 7, is silent as to the actual taking of the specimen, which implies that it can be done elsewhere (*Pascoe v Nicholson* [1981] 2 All ER 769; *Russell v Devine* [2003] UKHL 24, [2003] 1 WLR 1187), when taken by a medical practitioner. Any challenge to the qualifications of the person who took the blood sample must be raised in a timely fashion and not left as a last-minute defence ambush in closing (*Whitfield v DPP* [2006] EWHC 1414 (Admin)). When the requirement is made at a hospital, there is no obligation to explain why a breath specimen cannot be required (*Jones v DPP* [2004] EWHC 236 (Admin), [2004] RTR 20 (331)).

In *Brown v Gallacher* [2003] RTR 17 (239), the Scottish High Court of Justiciary dismissed an argument that the answers given and specimens provided under this statutory procedure should be disregarded because they infringe the privilege against self-incrimination protected by the ECHR, Article 6.

Where there is some doubt as to who was driving the motor vehicle at the relevant time, a constable may require all the persons suspected of driving to provide a specimen (*Pearson v*

Metropolitan Police Commissioner [1988] RTR 276). Indeed, the defendant need not have been driving the motor vehicle on a road or other public place provided the requirement for a specimen is made in the course of an investigation and is made in good faith (*Hawes v DPP* [1993] RTR 116).

At a police station, where there has been a positive result from administering a preliminary drug test, the constable will move directly to requiring a specimen of blood or urine under s. 7(3)(bc), but where consumption of alcohol is suspected, the constable will first consider whether the person should be required to provide two specimens of breath. Unless one of the situations set out in s. 7(3) arises, the constable will proceed to make that requirement, which involves giving the statutory warning necessary under s. 7(7) (see **C5.21**). If the person provides two specimens of breath as required, the lower reading will dictate whether no further action is taken (see **C5.12**) or a charge under the RTA 1988, s. 5(1), will be pursued (see **C5.33**). If the person fails to provide the specimens as required, the constable may proceed to require an alternative specimen of blood or urine (see **C5.14** ***et seq.***) or a charge under the RTA 1988, s. 7(6), may be pursued (see **C5.25**). In order to make what is being said understood, the constable may repeat any requirement as many times as is felt appropriate. **C5.11**

Breath Specimens

Road Traffic Act 1988, s. 8 **C5.12**

(1) ...of any two specimens of breath provided by any person in pursuance of section 7 of this Act that with the lower proportion of alcohol in the breath shall be used and the other shall be disregarded.

If the lower of the two specimens of breath provided is 39 microgrammes in 100 millilitres or less, proceedings under the RTA 1988, s. 5(1), are not usually instituted.

If the device were thought to be unreliable, s. 7(3) provides the grounds for requiring blood or urine (see **C5.15**). For more detailed information about how the option of providing a replacement specimen has been dealt with when it was available, see previous editions of this work.

It is not unfair or improper for the police to insist on a specimen being provided before legal advice is obtained, except possibly where the police refuse to allow a suspect access to a solicitor who is ready and immediately available; even then there would be powerful arguments why the discretion to exclude evidence under the PACE 1984, s. 78, should not be exercised (*Chalupa v CPS* [2009] EWHC 3082 (Admin), (2010) 174 JP 111). **C5.13**

Medical Reason

The question of what constitutes a 'medical reason' by virtue of which a specimen of breath cannot be provided or should not be required for the purposes of the RTA 1988, s. 7(3)(a) (see **C5.9**), is a question for the constable. What is important is the state of knowledge of the constable and his or her reasonable state of belief, bearing in mind that the constable is a lay person. Unlike under s. 7(4), there is no obligation for the constable to take medical advice before reaching a conclusion (*Steadman v DPP* [2002] EWHC 810 (Admin), [2003] RTR 2 (10)). As long as the constable has 'reasonable cause to believe' that a specimen of breath cannot be provided or should not be required for medical reasons then that is sufficient, whether or not the medical reason advanced appears, 'in the cold light of day', to be an unsatisfactory one for declining to provide a specimen of breath (*Davies v DPP* [1989] RTR 391, per Neill LJ). **C5.14**

Where the defendant uses best endeavours to provide a specimen, and in the absence of any other reason for not complying, incapacity due to being upset, shaken, intoxicated and distressed can amount to a medical reason (*Webb v DPP* [1992] RTR 299, applying *Davies v*

DPP). Intoxication alone may constitute such a medical reason (*Young v DPP* [1992] RTR 328). The taking of medication is also capable of amounting to a medical reason (*Wade v DPP* [1996] RTR 177). If a medical opinion is given to the constable, it will properly inform the reasonableness of the officer's conclusion on this issue, however wrong that opinion may be (*Andrews v DPP* [1992] RTR 1). If the conclusion is that there was no medical reason for the defendant's failure to provide, the officer may proceed to charge a s. 7(6) offence (*Longstaff v DPP* [2008] EWHC 303 (Admin), [2008] RTR 17 (212)).

In relation to tendering advice in accordance with the RTA 1988, s. 7(3)(c), that the condition of the person might be due to some drug, the doctor is not limited to the findings from the examination the doctor conducts at the police station, but is entitled to take into account all relevant information, including what the doctor has been told by police officers (*Angel v Chief Constable of South Yorkshire* [2010] EWHC 883 (Admin)).

If a medical reason is advanced as to why a specimen of blood, which a constable has decided to be appropriate, cannot or should not be taken, the validity of the reason can be determined under s. 7(4A) only by a medical practitioner (*Townson v DPP* [2006] EWHC 2007 (Admin)).

Reliability of Device

C5.15 Two situations may arise. The constable may already know that the device at the police station is not working properly or may discover it is malfunctioning during the procedure (RTA 1988, s. 7(3)(b)) and move directly to consideration of whether to advance the investigation by requiring a blood or urine sample. In this context, the question of reliability is subjective and depends upon the officer's reasonable belief (*Thompson v Thynne* [1986] RTR 293). That reasonable belief can be formed as a result of information provided to the officer by another (*Kelsey v DPP* [2008] EWHC 127 (Admin)). Alternatively, breath specimens may have been provided as a result of which the investigating officer is presented objectively with reasonable cause to believe in the unreliability of the analysis produced (RTA 1988, s. 7(3)(bb)). This might occur where the difference between the two readings is considerable (e.g., above 20 per cent: *DPP v Smith* [2000] RTR 341; above 15 per cent: *Stewart v DPP* [2003] EWHC 1323 (Admin), [2003] RTR 35 (529)) or where the reading that is produced is wholly inconsistent with the defendant's admitted alcohol consumption and perceived physical state (although this course of action was not taken in the circumstances considered in *DPP v Spurrier* [2000] RTR 60). This might also arise where the officer has attempted two cycles of specimens with the device with the second specimen each time being recorded as 'ambient failure' (*Hussain v DPP* [2008] EWHC 901 (Admin), [2008] RTR 30 (382)). An 'ambient failure' message during an earlier attempt does not make the device unreliable in respect of a subsequent test if the court can be satisfied the device was functioning reliably and, in reaching such a conclusion, one factor that can be taken into account is the reading produced by the roadside test (*Kang v DPP* [2016] EWHC 3014 (Admin), [2017] 4 WLR 3). However, where the officer is told that the defendant burped during the process, that information does not render the analysis produced by the device unreliable (*McNeil v DPP* [2008] EWHC 1254 (Admin), [2008] RTR 27 (359), explaining the consequences of *Zafar v DPP* [2004] EWHC 2468 (Admin), [2005] RTR 18 (220): see **C5.34**).

Where the device is regarded as unreliable, the printout can be adduced in evidence to support the belief of the investigating officer without the need to comply with prior service in accordance with the RTOA 1988, s. 16 (see **C5.37**). Where no valid specimens for the purposes of the RTA 1988, s. 11(3), have been provided, the officer is entitled to require provision of two further specimens of breath (*Hussain*), and in other circumstances the officer may choose first to invite (but not require) provision of further specimens of breath or proceed directly to

A specimen of urine provided after the one-hour period referred to in the RTA 1988, s. 7(5), is still admissible to prove an offence under s. 5(1) (*DPP v Baldwin* [2000] RTR 314). The significance of the one-hour limit is that, once it passes, the investigating officer can charge a s. 7(6) offence but, should the officer choose to exercise the discretion available, the officer can await provision of the specimen of urine required.

In *Ryder v CPS* [2011] EWHC 4003 (Admin), (2012) 176 JP 558, where the defendant had been catheterised at the time of consenting to provide a sample of urine, the Court of Appeal concluded that the 'providing' occurred when the catheter bag was emptied and not at the time the urine left the defendant. Consequently, the fact that there was evidence of a continuous flow of urine from the defendant's body into the catheter bag did not mean that there had only been a single specimen provided (unlike the conclusion on different facts in *Prosser v Dickeson* [1982] RTR 96, where the investigating officer had inappropriately interfered in the process of providing samples); the earlier emptying and discarding of the contents of the catheter bag amounting to provision of a previous specimen, as required by the RTA 1988, s. 7(5). This conclusion is consistent with the guidance offered by May LJ in *Nugent v Ridley* [1987] RTR 412 that the specimen to be analysed must be 'a fresh specimen and properly reflects the bodily condition of the person from whom it is taken'.

Warning

The warning in the RTA 1988, s. 7(7), is mandatory and must be understood by the person required to provide the specimen. However, it is mandatory only when a requirement is actually made and is not needed if the constable *invites* a suspect to provide further samples (*Edmond v DPP* [2006] EWHC 463 (Admin), [2006] RTR 18 (229)). If the suspect does not understand the warning, it is invalid; the subsequent procedure is then ineffectual and a defence becomes available to a charge under s. 7(6) (*Simpson v Spalding* [1987] RTR 221; *Chief Constable of Avon and Somerset Constabulary v Singh* [1988] RTR 107). A court is permitted to draw the inference, if the evidence supports it, that someone being asked to do something in a police station by a police officer with the assistance of an accredited interpreter of the relevant language has been asked the correct question, understands it and also the consequences of not responding (*Bielecki v DPP* [2011] EWHC 2245 (Admin), (2011) 175 JP 369). A finding that the defendant understood the request for a specimen being made and the penal warning attached thereto is not affected by the fact that the defendant was being detained under the Mental Health Act 1983, s. 136 (*Francis v DPP* [1997] RTR 113). At a hospital (see **C5.23**), the warning must still be given by a constable and cannot lawfully be given by a doctor (*Beatrice v DPP* [2004] EWHC 2416 (QB)). However, self-induced intoxication rendering a person incapable of understanding what was being said does not provide such a defence or a reasonable excuse for failing to provide as required (*DPP v Beech* [1992] RTR 239). **C5.21**

A failure to give the warning in s. 7(7) or to comply with any of the appropriate statutory procedures will render evidence of the specimen inadmissible under the RTOA 1988, s. 15(2), even if there is no prejudice to the defendant (*Murray v DPP* [1993] RTR 209). There is no automatic requirement for the prosecution to retain CCTV footage of the custody suite in order to show that the warning was given (*Morris v DPP* [2008] EWHC 2788 (Admin), (2009) 173 JP 41). If the defence wish to take issue about the alleged failure to warn, this should occur openly and during the course of the evidence rather than only in closing submissions (*R (Parker) v Crown Court at Bradford* [2006] EWHC 3213 (Admin), [2007] RTR 30 (369); *Malcolm v DPP* [2007] EWHC 363 (Admin), [2007] 3 All ER 578, where the late timing of the submission provided special circumstances justifying the court, even after retiring to consider its verdict, giving permission for further prosecution evidence to be adduced; *Cox v DPP* [2009] EWHC 3595 (Admin), [2010] RTR 18 (199)).

Detention of Persons Affected by Alcohol or a Drug

C5.22 By virtue of the RTA 1988, s. 10, following a requirement for a specimen of breath, blood or urine, a person may be detained at a police station until it appears to a constable that, if the person were driving or attempting to drive, an offence under s. 4, 5 or 5A of the Act would not be committed. If the specimen was provided otherwise than at the police station, the constable may arrest the person and take the suspect to a police station for detention on the same basis, unless the suspect is at a hospital as a patient and such action would be prejudicial to that patient's proper care and treatment. If, however, it appears to the constable that there is no likelihood of the suspect driving or attempting to drive with impaired ability or while above the prescribed limit for alcohol or any of the specified limits for controlled drugs then the suspect may not be detained under s. 10. If a question arises in relation to detention as to whether or not a person's ability to drive is, or might be, impaired through drugs, the constable must consult a medical practitioner and act on the advice given in response.

Protection for Hospital Patients

C5.23 Road Traffic Act 1988, s. 9

(1) While a person is at a hospital as a patient he shall not be required to co-operate with a preliminary test or to provide a specimen under section 7 of this Act unless the medical practitioner in immediate charge of his case has been notified of the proposal to make the requirement; and—
(a) if the requirement is then made, it shall be for co-operation with a test administered, or for the provision of a specimen, at the hospital, but
(b) if the medical practitioner objects on the ground specified in subsection (2) below, the requirement shall not be made.

(1A) While a person is at a hospital as a patient, no specimen of blood shall be taken from him under section 7A of this Act and he shall not be required to give his permission for a laboratory test of a specimen taken under that section unless the medical practitioner in immediate charge of his case—
(a) has been notified of the proposal to take the specimen or to make the requirement; and
(b) has not objected on the ground specified in subsection (2).

(2) The ground on which the medical practitioner may object is—
(a) in a case falling within subsection (1), that the requirement or the provision of the specimen or (if one is required) the warning required by section 7(7) of this Act would be prejudicial to the proper care and treatment of the patient; and
(b) in a case falling within subsection (1A), that the taking of the specimen, the requirement or the warning required by section 7A(5) of this Act would be so prejudicial.

For the RTA 1988, s. 7A, see **C5.9**.

C5.24 A person is at a hospital when the person is within the hospital's curtilage and is there for treatment, even as an out-patient. Once the treatment has been completed, the person is no longer a patient within the meaning of s. 9 (*A-G's Ref (No. 1 of 1976)* [1977] 3 All ER 557). The doctor who is directly responsible for the patient is the medical practitioner in immediate charge of the patient's case. Common-sense evidential conclusions when identifying that medical practitioner are permissible (*Cherpion v DPP* [2013] EWHC 615 (Admin)). The medical practitioner must be notified of the proposal to take blood and must not raise any objection; formal consent is not mandatory (*Bryan* [2008] EWCA Crim 1568, [2009] RTR 4 (29)).

In *Burton upon Trent Justices, ex parte Woolley* [1995] RTR 139, the Divisional Court decided that there is no obligation for the constable to inform a driver who is a patient at a hospital why a specimen of breath cannot be taken but, at some stage during the process at the hospital, the constable must ask the driver whether there is any reason why a specimen of blood should not be taken. Thereafter, the details of the procedure laid down in *DPP v Warren* [1993] AC 319 and *DPP v Jackson* [1999] 1 AC 406 (see **C5.17** ***et seq.***) should be followed. Where a constable has information supplied by, or presumably about, a person under investigation which relates to a possible medical reason for being unable to provide a specimen, the officer is required to relay that specific information to the doctor dealing with the patient (*Butler v DPP* [2001] RTR 28 (430)). A requirement lawfully made under s. 9 remains valid after the patient's discharge from hospital; it must therefore be complied with unless it is abundantly plain that, following discharge, the investigating officer is setting in train the s. 7 procedure (*Webber v DPP* [1998] RTR 111).

Failure to Provide an Evidential Specimen

The RTOA 1988, ss. 11 and 12(1), apply; see **C2.17** and **C2.18**. 'Fail' includes a refusal (RTA 1988, s. 11). Whether there is a refusal is a matter of fact for the justices to decide (*Smyth v DPP* [1996] RTR 59; *Plackett v DPP* [2008] EWHC 1335 (Admin), (2008) 172 JP 455). Where a motorist initially declined to provide the required specimens of breath but within some five seconds indicated a wish to reverse that position, the only possible conclusion was that there had not been a refusal. Clear words of denial, such as saying 'No, no, no', even before the investigating officer chooses between a specimen of blood or urine, will probably amount to a refusal (*Burke v DPP* [1999] RTR 387). If the defendant's conduct shows a lack of willingness to provide the specimen required, or the defendant imposes unacceptable terms for the specimen to be provided, then a failure may well be made out (*DPP v Swan* [2004] EWHC 2432 (QB), where the Court commented that *Mackey* [1977] RTR 146 should not be understood as imposing a threshold of outrageousness in behaviour before it can constitute a failure to provide). **C5.25**

In *DPP v Darwen* [2007] EWHC 337 (Admin) and *Rweikiza v DPP* [2008] EWHC 386 (Admin), the importance of the conjunctive 'and' in s. 11(3) was stressed, making it clear that the specimen provided must both be sufficient (e.g., in volume) and provided in such a way as to enable the analysis of it to be satisfactorily achieved. If either of these criteria is not satisfied, there will be a failure to provide the required specimen. The offence crystallises at the point of failing to provide, meaning there is no requirement to consider the alternative specimen procedure (*DPP v Camp* [2017] EWHC 3119 (Admin)).

In *DPP v Butterworth* [1995] 1 AC 381, the House of Lords confirmed that the RTA 1988, s. 7(6), creates only one offence. Accordingly, a charge stating that 'having been required to provide a specimen of breath/blood/urine for analysis, [the defendant] failed without reasonable excuse to do so' was found not to be duplicitous (*Worsley v DPP* [1995] Crim LR 572, where the prosecution then adduced evidence of failure to provide only one type of specimen), even though the information looks capable of relating to three separate demands for three separate specimens. Amending the charge to substitute the correct type of specimen required for the type mistakenly included is permissible, although this should usually occur prior to the date fixed for trial (*Williams v DPP* [2009] EWHC 2354 (Admin)). The essence of the offence is that the police are investigating whether the person committed any of the offences in ss. 3A, 4 and 5 of the 1988 Act and so there is no need to identify in the charge a specific offence to which the mind of the investigating officer was directed.

Although s. 7(6) creates a single offence, two charges can be brought against the same defendant where two separate failures are alleged (*Chichester Justices, ex parte DPP* [1994] RTR 175). Moreover, the subsequent provision of a different specimen below the prescribed limit as a consequence of a separate request may not cure the initial failure to provide without a reasonable excuse (*Lorimer v Russell* 1996 SLT 501).

Reasonable Excuse It is a defence to a charge under the RTA 1988, s. 7(6), to have had a reasonable excuse for the failure to provide the specimen required. Although there is no statutory requirement to advance a medical reason at the time of attempting but failing to provide the specimen, if the defendant omits to mention a condition of which the defendant is aware, this is unlikely to be accepted by the justices subsequently as a reasonable excuse (*Piggott v DPP* [2008] EWHC 305 (Admin), [2008] RTR 16 (199)). However, where there is a refusal or deliberate failure to provide the specimen required, it cannot subsequently be justified by **C5.26**

reference to a medical condition which was not alluded to at the time (*DPP v Furby* [2000] RTR 181; *DPP v Lonsdale* [2001] EWHC Admin 95, [2001] RTR 29 (444); *R (Martiner) v DPP* [2004] EWHC 2484 (Admin)). There must be an attempt to provide which is unsuccessful because of a physical or mental disability before reasonable excuse can be raised as a defence.

Once a defence of reasonable excuse is raised, it is for the prosecution to negative it. If the justices' decision suggests they have misapplied these respective burdens, the resulting conviction will be liable to be quashed (*McKeon v DPP* [2007] EWHC 3216 (Admin), [2008] RTR 14 (165)). What constitutes a 'reasonable excuse' must always remain a matter of fact for the court. But in *Lennard* [1973] 2 All ER 831, Lawton LJ said (at p. 487):

> In our judgment no excuse can be adjudged a reasonable one unless the person from whom the specimen is required is physically or mentally unable to provide it or the provision of the specimen would entail a substantial risk to his health.

C5.27 Normally, expert medical evidence of the physical or mental incapacity to provide the specimen is required to support the defence and demonstrate the existence of the necessary causative link between the incapacity and the failure to provide (*DPP v Crofton* [1994] RTR 279; *DPP v Brodzky* [1997] RTR 425n; *DPP v Grundy* [2006] EWHC 1157 (Admin)). To be admissible, evidence supporting the defence must be indicated appropriately and in a timely fashion (*Writtle v DPP* [2009] EWHC 236 (Admin), [2009] RTR 28 (367), deploring defence ambushes). Where a substantial risk to health is advanced, alternative approaches to the provision of the specimen should be considered before assessing the reasonableness of the excuse (*DPP v Mukandiwa* [2005] EWHC 2977 (Admin), [2006] RTR 24 (304), where a potentially dangerous trance state triggered by the sight of blood could have been avoided by looking away and did not relate directly to the taking of the blood specimen required).

C5.28 Post-accident stress cannot, without evidence showing mental or physical disability, constitute a reasonable excuse for failing to provide a specimen (*DPP v Eddowes* [1991] RTR 35). In *De Freitas v DPP* [1993] RTR 98, a phobia of catching AIDS, established by medical evidence, amounted to a reasonable excuse. If a medical reason is claimed as a reason for not providing a specimen of blood, a medical practitioner's opinion that such a reason is not a medical one is conclusive.

Where a medical reason is advanced as a reasonable excuse, the justices should still give proper weight to the other evidence relating to the defendant's failure to provide, e.g., where the defendant, after having satisfactorily provided a roadside test and the first specimen of breath required, put the device's tube to the defendant's mouth and yet no breath was registered (*DPP v Radford* [1995] RTR 86). Only if the justices' decision in this respect is perverse will there be grounds to interfere on appeal.

Even without medical evidence justices are entitled, if they have the test in *Lennard* well in mind, to find that shock combined with inebriation which renders a defendant physically incapable may amount to a reasonable excuse (*DPP v Pearman* [1992] RTR 407; *DPP v Crofton* [1994] RTR 279). However, in *DPP v Camp* [2017] EWHC 3119 (Admin), the Divisional Court rejected self-induced intoxication as capable of amounting to a reasonable excuse because to allow it would be contrary to Parliament's intention. Justices should be wary of using their own knowledge of a medical condition which is not supported by or is beyond the evidence before them (*DPP v Curtis* [1993] RTR 72).

C5.29 **Non-medical Reasons** Omitting to warn the defendant that there is a time-limit for completing the breathalyser process, after which the Intoximeter stops functioning, will not amount to a reasonable excuse (*DPP v Coyle* [1996] RTR 287). Indeed, *Cosgrove v DPP* [1997] RTR 153 confirmed that the investigating officer is not obliged to permit the driver the test's full three minutes in which to provide the required specimens. This was reaffirmed in *Watson v DPP* [2006] EWHC 3429 (Admin), where the defendant's insistence on being permitted to go to the lavatory between provision of the first and second breath specimens was not accepted as a reasonable excuse.

Failure to provide a specimen because the defendant was waiting for the arrival of, or telephone advice from, a solicitor did not amount to a reasonable excuse (*DPP v Skinner* [1990] RTR 231 and *DPP v Varley* (1999) 163 JP 443, following *DPP v Billington* [1988] 1 All ER 435). The decision in *Smith v Hand* [1986] RTR 265 was explained as applying only to cases where the defendant has been told positively that waiting for the defendant's solicitor is allowed, although *Billington* clearly makes the distinction between imposing a condition and merely making a request in relation to the provision of legal advice. This principle does not violate the ECHR, Article 6(3) (*Campbell v CPS* [2002] EWHC 1314 (Admin), (2002) 166 JP 742; *Kennedy v CPS* [2002] EWHC 2297 (Admin), (2003) 167 JP 267; *Myles v DPP* [2004] EWHC 594 (Admin), [2004] 2 All ER 902). A very short delay before carrying out the test may be accommodated to permit a suspect to consult a solicitor, but thereafter the balance lies in favour of conducting the test promptly (*Gearing v DPP* [2008] EWHC 1695 (Admin), [2009] RTR 7 (72); *Chalupa v CPS* [2009] EWHC 3082 (Admin), (2010) 174 JP 111, suggesting the solicitor must be immediately available). In *Dickinson v DPP* [1989] Crim LR 741, legal advice given to the defendant by a solicitor who accompanied the defendant to the police station to the effect that the defendant should refuse a specimen was held not to constitute a reasonable excuse. Where the defendant makes provision of the specimen required conditional on having sight of a law book, that does not amount to a reasonable excuse (*DPP v Noe* [2000] RTR 351). Neither is insisting upon reading the PACE 1984 codes of practice before providing a specimen of breath a 'reasonable excuse' for failing to provide it (*DPP v Cornell* [1990] RTR 254).

In *DPP v Rous* [1992] RTR 246, it was held that the procedure as to the provision of specimens does not constitute an interview and therefore there is no discretion under the PACE 1984, s. 78, to exclude evidence relating to the procedure. Indeed, para. 11.1A of PACE Code C specifically states that procedures under s. 7 do not constitute interviewing. In *DPP v Whalley* [1991] RTR 161, a finding that the notice given to detained persons misled the accused to think he had a right to consult the codes before further procedures were undertaken was not enough to constitute a reasonable excuse for failing to provide a specimen. **C5.30**

Punishment Where the offender was driving or attempting to drive, the penalty is six months' imprisonment and/or an unlimited fine. Disqualification and endorsement are, in the absence of 'special reasons', obligatory. The offence carries between three and 11 penalty points. **C5.31**

In any other case, the penalty is three months' imprisonment and/or a fine up to level 4 on the standard scale. Disqualification is discretionary, but endorsement with ten penalty points, in the absence of 'special reasons', is obligatory.

Forfeiture of the vehicle may be ordered under either situation (see **E18.1**).

Sentence In *Waltham Forest Justices, ex parte Barton* [1990] RTR 49, the Divisional Court indicated that, where a defendant is charged with failing to provide a specimen at the police station, the charge itself should indicate that 'the specimen was required to ascertain the ability of the defendant at the time he was driving or attempting to drive'. The decision in *DPP v Butterworth* [1995] 1 AC 381, however, makes it clear that there is no need to specify in the charge whether the allegation is that the defendant was only 'in charge' or driving or attempting to drive. Lord Slynn stated (at p. 394) that 'the question whether the person was driving or in charge of the motor vehicle is not part of the inquiry into whether there has been a refusal for the purposes of section 7(6). That question only becomes relevant after conviction and goes to the appropriate penalty.' Accordingly, the charge itself does not need to indicate whether the defendant faces a mandatory or discretionary disqualification, although the prosecution might be asked informally on what basis the case is being put. **C5.32**

Where the prosecution case is put on the 'in charge' basis, sentence can be passed only on the basis that the defendant was 'in charge' and not driving (*George v DPP* [1989] RTR 217). Consequently, if there is no evidence adduced that the defendant was driving, the court must sentence only on the 'in charge' basis (*Cawley v DPP* [2001] EWHC Admin 83).

The *Magistrates' Court Sentencing Guidelines* (see Supplement, **SG10-92** and **SG10-93**) must generally be followed.

DRIVING, OR BEING IN CHARGE, WITH ALCOHOL CONCENTRATION ABOVE PRESCRIBED LIMIT

C5.33 **Road Traffic Act 1988, s. 5**

(1) If a person—
  (a) drives or attempts to drive a motor vehicle on a road or other public place, or
  (b) is in charge of a motor vehicle on a road or other public place,
  after consuming so much alcohol that the proportion of it in his breath, blood or urine exceeds the prescribed limit he is guilty of an offence.

(2) It is a defence for a person charged with an offence under subsection (1)(b) above to prove that at the time he is alleged to have committed the offence the circumstances were such that there was no likelihood of his driving the vehicle whilst the proportion of alcohol in his breath, blood or urine remained likely to exceed the prescribed limit.

(3) The court may, in determining whether there was such a likelihood as is mentioned in subsection (2) above, disregard any injury to him and any damage to the vehicle.

Elements

C5.34 The RTOA 1988, ss. 11 and 12(1), apply; see **C2.17** and **C2.18**. For the meaning of the terms 'driving', 'road or other public place' and 'attempting', see **C1.2** and **C1.5**, **C1.13** and **C1.16**, and **C1.20**. Where the only evidence of 'driving' is in a confession that is inadmissible as a result of non-compliance with the PACE 1984, it cannot be relied upon to found a conviction under the RTA 1988, s. 5(1)(a) (*Charles v DPP* [2009] EWHC 3521 (Admin), [2010] RTR 34 (402)). An intoxicated driver who is intending to drive but who is prevented from doing so before getting into the vehicle has not committed the *actus reus* of attempting to drive (*Mason v DPP* [2009] EWHC 2198 (Admin), [2010] RTR 11 (120)). The RTA 1988, s. 11, sets out the 'prescribed limit'. If the lower reading in breath is 39 microgrammes in 100 millilitres or less, proceedings are not usually instituted. In *DPP v Johnson* [1995] 4 All ER 53, the Divisional Court held that the meaning of 'consuming' was sufficiently wide to cover ingestion otherwise than by mouth and the important element of the offence was the concentration of alcohol in the driver's body at the relevant time. In *Zafar v DPP* [2004] EWHC 2468 (Admin), [2005] RTR 18 (220), it was confirmed that 'breath' in this context is not confined to deep lung air and should be given its dictionary definition ('air exhaled from any thing').

C5.35 Section 5 creates nine separate offences of driving, or attempting to drive or being in charge of a motor vehicle, each with an alcohol concentration above the prescribed limit in relation to breath, blood or urine (*Bolton Justices, ex parte Khan* [1999] Crim LR 912). The charge must state which specimen is to be relied upon by the prosecution. Referring to more than one type of specimen renders the charge bad for duplicity. However, a late amendment to the charge to refer to the correct specimen is likely to be permitted as it should not prejudice the defendant, who knows that driving with excess alcohol in the defendant's body is what is being alleged (*Fenwick v Valentine* 1994 SLT 485).

As regards secondary participation in an offence under s. 5, a supervising driver who was aware that the learner driver had drunk so much that the alcohol level in his body must have exceeded the prescribed limit was held to have been properly convicted of aiding and abetting the offence, even though the driver had not been required to provide a specimen (*Carter v Richardson* [1974] RTR 314, where this was a proper inference to draw from the behaviour of the defendant when the police arrived, because the defendant had lied about who was the driver). Lacing the drinks of a person who then drives may involve procuring an offence under s. 5; the defendant must be proved to have known that the person whose drink was laced was going to drive and that the ordinary result of lacing the drinks would be to raise the driver's alcohol level above the prescribed limit (*A-G's Ref (No. 1 of 1975)* [1975] QB 773). Alternatively, as McCullough J stated in *Blakely v DPP* [1991] RTR 405 (at p. 415):

> It must, at the least, be shown that the accused contemplated that his act would or might bring about or assist the commission of the principal offence.

In Charge It was confirmed in *Drake v DPP* [1994] RTR 411 that a person can be in charge of a motor vehicle when the vehicle is immobile. In *Leach v Evans* [1952] 2 All ER 264, a motorist emerging from a public house considerably under the influence of alcohol told a police officer that he was looking for his van, walked towards it and was then arrested within three yards of it. Lord Goddard CJ posed the question: if the motorist was not in charge of the van, who was? This principle was followed in *Haines v Roberts* [1953] 1 All ER 344, where Lord Goddard CJ said (at p. 311): **C5.36**

> It may be that, if a man goes to a public house and leaves his car outside or in the car park and, getting drunk, asks a friend to look after the car for him or to take it home, he has put it in charge of somebody else; but if he has not put it in charge of somebody else he is in charge until he does. His car is out on the road or in the car park — it matters not which — and he is in charge.

In *DPP v Watkins* [1989] QB 821, it was held that a person was in charge of a vehicle if the person acted in a manner which showed that the person had assumed control or intended to assume control of the vehicle preparatory to driving it. Thereafter the burden of proving the statutory defence in the RTA 1988, s. 5(2), shifts to the defendant (see **C5.51**). Amongst factors which merited consideration were:

(a) whether and where the defendant was in the vehicle or how far the defendant was from it;
(b) what the defendant was doing at the relevant time;
(c) whether the defendant was in possession of a key that fitted the ignition;
(d) whether there was evidence of an intention to take or assert control of the car by driving or otherwise;
(e) whether any other person was in, at or near the vehicle and, if so, the like particulars in respect of that person.

Where the defendant was the owner of the car in which the defendant was found sitting holding the ignition keys, in the absence of any suggestion of another person being in charge, it is an inescapable conclusion that the defendant was in charge (*CPS v Bate* [2004] EWHC 2811 (Admin)).

Evidence as to Specimens

Road Traffic Offenders Act 1988, s. 16 **C5.37**

(1) Evidence of the proportion of alcohol or a drug in a specimen of breath, blood or urine may, subject to subsections (3) and (4) below and to section 15(5) and (5A) of this Act, be given by the production of a document or documents purporting to be whichever of the following is appropriate, that is to say—
  (a) a statement automatically produced by the device by which the proportion of alcohol in a specimen of breath was measured and a certificate signed by a constable (which may but need not be contained in the same document as the statement) that the statement relates to a specimen provided by the accused at the date and time shown in the statement, and
  (b) a certificate signed by an authorised analyst as to the proportion of alcohol or any drug found in a specimen of blood or urine identified in the certificate.

(2) Subject to subsections (3) and (4) below, evidence that a specimen of blood was taken from the accused with his consent by a medical practitioner or a registered health care professional may be given by the production of a document purporting to certify that fact and to be signed by a medical practitioner or a registered health care professional.

(3) Subject to subsection (4) below—

(a) a document purporting to be such a statement or such a certificate (or both such a statement and such a certificate) as is mentioned in subsection (1)(a) above is admissible in evidence on behalf of the prosecution in pursuance of this section only if a copy of it either has been handed to the accused when the document was produced or has been served on him not later than seven days before the hearing, and

(b) any other document is so admissible only if a copy of it has been served on the accused not later than seven days before the hearing.

(4) A document purporting to be a certificate (or so much of a document as purports to be a certificate) is not so admissible if the accused, not later than three days before the hearing or within such further time as the court may in special circumstances allow, has served notice on the prosecutor requiring the attendance at the hearing of the person by whom the document purports to be signed.

(5) [Applies only to Scotland.]

(6) A copy of a certificate required by this section to be served on the accused or a notice required by this section to be served on the prosecutor may be served personally or sent by registered post or recorded delivery service.

C5.38 **Printouts** In *Garner v DPP* [1990] RTR 208 (following *Castle v Cross* [1984] 1 All ER 87), the Court of Appeal held that the admissibility of the 'statement automatically produced by the device' (commonly called 'the printout') did not just arise through the RTOA 1988, s. 16(1). The statement is in itself an admissible document and represents real evidence as long as it is properly produced. The purpose and effect of s. 16 is to enable the printout together with an appropriate certificate to be tendered at the hearing and to 'be capable of establishing the facts stated in it without the necessity of anybody being called' (per Stocker LJ at p. 184). In short, s. 16(1)(a) is permissive. It does not stipulate the only manner in which evidence of analysis can be given. It provides one method for proving the proportion of alcohol in a breath specimen (*Thom v DPP* [1994] RTR 11; *R (Leong) v DPP* [2006] EWHC 1575 (Admin); *R (CPS) v Sedgemoor Justices* [2007] EWHC 1803 (Admin)). Other routes of admissibility are available, including the hearsay provisions of the CJA 2003, s. 116 (*Brett v DPP* [2009] EWHC 440 (Admin), [2009] 1 WLR 2530: see **C5.40**).

The printout and the operator's certificate may be separate or contained in the same document. Section 16(4) relates to the operator's, medical practitioner's and analyst's certificates, and not to the printout (*Temple v Botha* [1985] Crim LR 517). On a plea of guilty, there is no need to produce the original printout from the device. If there is a genuine change of plea, reasonable adjournments must be given to the prosecution if there is a problem about production of the printout (*Tower Bridge Magistrates' Court, ex parte DPP* [1989] RTR 118).

C5.39 A failure to produce the printout in evidence in a case where the officer does not give evidence of the reading, the officer's familiarity with the device, its working or calibration means that the prosecution have failed to establish a case against the defendant (*Hasler v DPP* [1989] RTR 148). Evidence of the breath alcohol reading, in the absence of the printout, is not, in itself, sufficient to found a conviction (*Owen v Chesters* [1985] RTR 191). The prosecution should establish that the device is working correctly by evidence relating to the calibration. An officer giving such evidence has to be trained in the use and manner of performance of the device so as to understand the calibration process and to recognise that, unless the result of the process lies within accepted limits, the device may be unreliable (*Denneny v Harding* [1986] RTR 350). Even where the operator's knowledge of the device has been shown in cross-examination to be less than perfect, provided there is nothing to show the decision was irrational, it is still open to the court to conclude that the operator has been adequately trained so as to be qualified to conduct the procedure and that the device has functioned reliably (*Haggis v DPP* [2003] EWHC 2481 (Admin), [2004] 2 All ER 382). The operator is entitled to give oral evidence, without production of the printout being a pre-condition, so as to support a conviction, provided that the evidence demonstrates the actual reading on which the charge is founded and demonstrates that the device was working properly and reliably, i.e. by the operator looking at the figures on the device's display (*Thom v DPP* [1994] RTR 11; *Greenaway v DPP* [1994] RTR 17). There is also a discretion to permit the prosecution to remedy an oversight to adduce such evidence during their case by calling appropriate evidence later on, especially where the interests of justice outweigh any prejudice to the defendant (*Cook v DPP* [2001] Crim LR 321; *Leeson v DPP* [2000] RTR 385). The exact procedures of various approved devices differ, so that reliance on the steps in respect of the wrong one, perhaps as a result of references in authorities, will not assist (*Mercer v DPP* [2003] EWHC 225 (Admin), (2003) 167 JP 441, which drew the distinction between the Lion Intoxilyser 6000 and the old Lion Intoximeter 3000).

A printout timed according to Greenwich Mean Time is admissible even though British Summer Time was operating at the time the defendant provided the specimen (*Parker v DPP* [1993] RTR 283). Indeed, in *DPP v McKeown* [1997] 1 All ER 737, a printout recording a wholly inaccurate time due to a malfunctioning clock was still held admissible because that malfunction did not affect the way in which the computer processed, stored or retrieved the information used to generate the statement in evidence. This reasoning has been applied to typographical errors on the face of printouts which clearly do not affect the proper functioning of the device (*Reid v DPP* [1999] RTR 357; *DPP v Barber* (1999) 163 JP 457).

Service of Certificate The certificate under the RTOA 1988, s. 16(2), is termed an HORT/5. Section 16(3) imposes a duty to serve the analyst's certificate, which cannot be waived if this method of admissibility is relied upon (*Tobi v Nicholas* [1988] RTR 343). However, where only the lack of a signature on the certificate is an issue, and not service itself, strict proof of service can be waived (*Louis v DPP* [1998] RTR 354). The obligation imposed is treated as being to offer a copy of the printout to the defendant, so that a refusal to accept it in order to argue that it has not been 'handed' as required will not render the contents of the printout inadmissible (*McCormack v DPP* [2002] EWHC 173 (Admin), [2002] RTR 20 (355)). If the defendant wishes to challenge the lack of service of any of the certificates, this must be done before the contents are put in evidence (*Banks* [1972] 1 All ER 1041), although the challenge does not have to be made immediately and may be permitted if made a few minutes later, so that the defendant first has time to consider the implications of the issue (*R (Wooldridge) v DPP* [2003] EWHC 1663 (Admin)), but attempting to do so only in closing is too late (*Jeffreys v DPP* [2006] EWHC 1377 (Admin)). **C5.40**

Section 16(6) provides for service of various notices, and s. 16(4) for the service of a counter-notice. Oral notice will not suffice and, if there is any issue as to whether a document complies with these provisions, the justices will have to determine as a matter of fact whether it constitutes a notice (*R (Stavrinou) v Horseferry Road Justices* [2006] EWHC 566 (Admin); *R (DPP) v Chorley Magistrates' Court* [2006] EWHC 1795 (Admin)). This procedure provides an alternative method of service to that contained in the CJA 1967, s. 9 (*DPP v Stephens* [2006] EWHC 1860 (Admin), where it was pointed out that the methods specified in s. 16(6) are exhaustively listed). In *Brett v DPP* [2009] EWHC 440 (Admin), [2009] 1 WLR 2530, upon service of a s. 16(4) counter-notice, if the analyst is unavailable to attend in person, the CJA 2003, s. 116 (see **F17.7**), may enable the evidence to be admitted as hearsay, although, in the event of the trial being adjourned, the position on whether attendance can be achieved must be reviewed. If the prosecution seek an adjournment arising from their failure to warn the officer to attend following receipt of a s. 16(4) counter-notice, the court should be wary about acceding to that application (*R (Decani) v City of London Magistrates' Court* [2017] EWHC 3422 (Admin)). If there is any issue factually as to whether the offer of supplying one part of the sample was made to the accused, that is an issue for trial, making an application for disclosure of the sample pursuant to the CPIA 1996, s. 8, inappropriate (*Beattie v CPS* [2018] EWHC 787 (Admin)), because non-compliance with the procedure under s. 15 would render inadmissible the evidence of the analysis on which the prosecution wished to rely.

Where evidence is adduced from someone who is not an authorised analyst, the s. 16 mechanism is not applicable and the usual process for admitting expert evidence must be followed (*R (CPS) v Sedgemoor Justices* [2007] EWHC 1803 (Admin)).

Admissibility of Specimens

C5.41

Road Traffic Offenders Act 1988, s. 15

(1) This section and section 16 of this Act apply in respect of proceedings for an offence under any of sections 3A to 5A of the Road Traffic Act 1988 (driving offences connected with drink or drugs); and expressions used in this section and section 16 of this Act have the same meaning as in sections 3A to 10 of that Act.

(2) Evidence of the proportion of alcohol or any drug in a specimen of breath, blood or urine provided by or taken from the accused shall, in all cases (including cases where the specimen was not provided or taken in connection with the alleged offence), be taken into account and—

(a) it is to be assumed, subject to subsection (3) below, that the proportion of alcohol in the accused's breath, blood or urine at the time of the alleged offence was not less than in the specimen;

(b) it is to be assumed, subject to subsection (3A) below, that the proportion of a drug in the accused's blood or urine at the time of the alleged offence was not less than in the specimen.

(3) The assumption in subsection (2)(a) above shall not be made if the accused proves—

(a) that he consumed alcohol before he provided the specimen or had it taken from him and—

(i) in relation to an offence under section 3A, after the time of the alleged offence, and

(ii) otherwise, after he had ceased to drive, attempt to drive or be in charge of a vehicle on a road or other public place, and

(b) that had he not done so the proportion of alcohol in his breath, blood or urine would not have exceeded the prescribed limit and, if it is alleged that he was unfit to drive through drink, would not have been such as to impair his ability to drive properly.

(3A) The assumption in subsection (2)(b) above shall not be made if the accused proves—

(a) that he took the drug before he provided the specimen or had the specimen taken from him and—

(i) in relation to an offence under section 3A, after the time of the alleged offence, and

(ii) otherwise, after he had ceased to drive, attempt to drive or be in charge of a vehicle on a road or other public place, and

(b) that had he not done so the proportion of the drug in his blood or urine—

(i) in the case of a specified controlled drug, would not have exceeded the specified limit for that drug, and

(ii) if it is alleged that he was unfit to drive through drugs, would not have been such as to impair his ability to drive properly.

(4) A specimen of blood shall be disregarded unless—

(a) it was taken from the accused with his consent by a medical practitioner or a registered health care professional; or

(b) it was taken from the accused by a medical practitioner or a registered health care professional under section 7A of the Road Traffic Act 1988 and the accused subsequently gave his permission for a laboratory test of the specimen.

(5) Where, at the time a specimen of blood or urine was provided by the accused, he asked to be provided with such a specimen, evidence of the proportion of alcohol or any drug found in the specimen is not admissible on behalf of the prosecution unless—

(a) the specimen in which the alcohol or drug was found is one of two parts into which the specimen provided by the accused was divided at the time it was provided, and

(b) the other part was supplied to the accused.

(5A) Where a specimen of blood was taken from the accused under section 7A of the Road Traffic Act 1988, evidence of the proportion of alcohol or any drug found in the specimen is not admissible on behalf of the prosecution unless—

(a) the specimen in which the alcohol or drug was found is one of two parts into which the specimen taken from the accused was divided at the time it was taken; and

(b) any request to be supplied with the other part which was made by the accused at the time when he gave his permission for a laboratory test of the specimen was complied with.

Section 15 does not apply to offences contrary to the RTA 1988, s. 3A(1)(c) and (d) (*Coe* [2009] EWCA Crim 1452, [2010] 3 All ER 83).

Incomplete breath specimens, even if they purport to give a reading, are inadmissible against the defendant (*R (Willicott) v DPP* [2001] EWHC Admin 415, (2002) 166 JP 385). Under the RTA 1988, s. 7(1)(a), a constable may require provision of two specimens of breath. Accordingly, only the first two specimens actually provided are admissible (*Howard v Hallett* [1984] RTR 353). In this case, the first Intoximeter procedure resulted in only one specimen being provided because of the constable's error, so the full procedure was recommenced resulting in the provision of three specimens in total. The Divisional Court rejected the prosecution's attempt to ignore the first procedure entirely and so rely on the lower of the second and third specimens provided. It ruled that the third specimen was the one to be disregarded as being outside the s. 7 statutory procedure and that the lower of the first two readings was the specimen on which the prosecution were obliged to found their case. On the basis that s. 7(1)(b) enables a constable to require a specimen of blood, only the first specimen of blood or urine taken ought to be admissible. **C5.42**

Where blood has been taken on two occasions and then divided, the resulting analysis is inadmissible (*Dear v DPP* [1988] RTR 148). In *DPP v Elstob* [1992] RTR 45, it was held that the phrase 'divided at the time' in the RTOA 1988, s. 15(5)(a), meant that the taking and division of the specimen had to be closely linked in time and performed as part of the same event, even though it is inevitable that some time will pass between the two acts. It is important to maintain the integrity of what occurs, and therefore it is desirable (albeit not strictly necessary for compliance with the statute) for the defendant to be present. Incorrect labelling by a police doctor of the part specimen handed to the defendant, in pursuance of s. 15(5)(b), is not fatal to the admissibility of evidence relating to the proportion of alcohol or drug found in the specimen, unless it is supplied in such a way as to deter or prevent the defendant from having it analysed (*Butler v DPP* [1990] RTR 377). In order to comply with s. 15(5)(b), the defendant's part does not need to be handed physically to the defendant but can be supplied by being made available, e.g., through provision to a friend in such a way that the defendant must have known what had become of it (*R (O'Connell) v DPP* [2006] EWHC 1419 (Admin)). There is no obligation to give the defendant a choice as to which of the two parts of the sample to take (*R (Lidington) v DPP* [2006] EWHC 1984 (Admin)). If there is any issue factually as to whether the offer of supplying one part of the sample was made to the accused, that is an issue for trial, making an application for disclosure of the sample pursuant to the CPIA 1996, s. 8, inappropriate (*Beattie v CPS* [2018] EWHC 787 (Admin)), because non-compliance with the procedure under s. 15 would render inadmissible the evidence of the analysis on which the prosecution wished to rely. In *Afolayan v CPS* [2012] EWHC 1322 (Admin), although Form MG DD/A had not been properly completed, the Divisional Court concluded that the justices had evidence from the police and from what the analyst said about the specimen the analyst had received entitling them to prefer that evidence to the defendant's evidence that the blood sample taken from the defendant had not been sealed, as required, in the defendant's presence. **C5.43**

Where the laboratory analysing the sample subdivides it for the purpose of analysis, it is lawful to use the average result and not necessary to use only the lowest result (*DPP v Welsh* (1997) 161 JP 57). In *Bolton Magistrates' Court, ex parte Scally* [1991] 1 QB 537, where the reliability of the blood analysis was impugned because the sample had been taken using a cleaning swab impregnated with alcohol, the Divisional Court quashed the conviction. Similarly, in *Gregory v DPP* [2002] EWHC 385 (Admin), (2002) 166 JP 400, opinion evidence explaining possible discrepancies in the analysis in a borderline case, which resulted from contact with the fluoride preservative in the container into which the blood was transferred after being divided, should not have been disregarded at trial, with the consequence that the conviction was quashed. However, in *Carter v DPP* [2006] EWHC 3328 (Admin), [2007] RTR 22 (257), following *R (Dhaliwal) v DPP* [2006] EWHC 1149 (Admin), the Divisional Court concluded that, unless there is something suggesting otherwise, justices are entitled to presume that the procedures laid down for the preparation of analysts' kits have been carried out correctly. Any failure to notify the defendant of the procedure set out in s. 15(5) will harm the prosecution's case irreparably (*Anderton v Lythgoe* [1985] 1 WLR 222); the same consequence is likely in respect of the procedure in s. 15(5A). Where a point is taken on this procedure, it must be taken before evidence of the analysis is adduced (*Hudson v Hornby* [1973] RTR 4).

C5.44 **Challenging the Specimen Evidence** In *Twigg* [2019] EWCA Crim 1553, [2020] RTR 10 (103), after reviewing the authorities relating to whether there was a rule of automatic application that non-compliance with the requirements of the RTA 1988 meant the evidence of the analysis of the specimen was inadmissible (e.g. by reference to *Murray v DPP* [1993] RTR 209), the Court of Appeal concluded that no such rule exists. Instead, the issue of non-compliance must be viewed in the context of the overall consideration of fairness under the PACE 1984, s. 78. In that case, where the defendant had lied to the medical practitioner about whether he had taken drugs, a breach of s. 7(3)(c) did not require the judge to exclude the specimen as evidence. The PACE 1984, s. 78, can also be used to make a general challenge to the admissibility of the printout from the Intoximeter (e.g., relating to the compensatory element where the device detects a substance believed to be acetone, reducing the alcohol reading accordingly: *Ashton v DPP* [1998] RTR 45). However, challenging the reliability of the device so as to render the evidence produced inadmissible is notoriously difficult. The justices should assume the device to have been in good working order until the contrary is proved (*Anderton v Waring* [1986] RTR 74). They can infer from the device being of a type approved by the Secretary of State that it contains the original and approved software (*Skinner v DPP* [2004] EWHC 2914 (Admin), [2005] RTR 17 (202)). Firm case management of challenges to the evidence of a specimen was suggested, and guidance given, in *R (Hassani) v West London Magistrates' Court* [2017] EWHC 1270 (Admin), (2017) 181 JP 253.

In *Tower Bridge Magistrates' Court, ex parte DPP* [1989] RTR 118, the Divisional Court quashed a witness summons issued by the magistrates' court for a police officer to produce the service record and machine log in respect of the device used, castigating the defence for engaging on a fishing expedition. Disclosure to establish that an approved device has been altered in such a way as to take it out of type approval should be ordered only after production of some material justifying the application, not on the basis of mere assertion from the defendant that there had been an unapproved modification (*DPP v Wood* [2006] EWHC 32 (Admin), (2006) 170 JP 177). Any suggestion that the device was working unreliably must be related to the particular facts of the case before the justices rather than generally (*DPP v Brown* [2001] EWHC Admin 931, [2002] RTR 23 (395)). There should be evidence raising a realistic possibility that the device malfunctioned and a general assertion alleging failure to comply with the manufacturer's recommendations does not amount to such evidence (*Scheiner v DPP* [2006] EWHC 1516 (Admin)). Whether a modification made to a device which is ordinarily an approved device takes it out of type approval involves a broad common-sense consideration of whether the build and function of the device still has the character, essence and identity of the device with type approval (*R (Coxon) v Manchester City Magistrates' Court* [2010] EWHC 712 (Admin)). Tests by experts pointing to the unreliability of the device in relation to an aspect of its functions that is wholly irrelevant to the reliability of the evidence adduced in the defendant's case will not deprive the device of its type approval by the Secretary of State (*DPP v Memery* [2002] EWHC 1720 (Admin), [2003] RTR 18 (249)). In *DPP v Walsall Magistrates' Court* [2019] EWHC 3317 (Admin), disclosure orders made under the CPIA 1996, s. 8(2), in respect of the service histories of Lion Intoxilyser 6000UK devices were quashed on the basis that, following the approach in *R (DPP) v Manchester and Salford Magistrates' Court* [2017] EWHC 3719 (Admin), [2019] 1 WLR 2617, they should have not have been made, further emphasising the need for evidence to be adduced in support of such an application explaining the use to which the material sought would be put (*R (DPP) v Caernarfon Crown Court* [2019] EWHC 767 (Admin)).

C5.45 There is no obligation on the prosecution to disclose to the defence the evidence of the proportion of alcohol found in a roadside breath test where it is not being put in evidence and relied upon in accordance with s. 15(2). Applications under the CPIA 1996, s. 8(2), for such disclosure, with a view to seeing if those readings provided the foundation for a challenge to the evidential specimen on which the prosecutions were based, were rejected in *Murphy v DPP* [2006] EWHC 1753 (Admin) and *Smith v DPP* [2007] EWHC 100 (Admin), [2007] 4 All ER 1135.

Evidence of the amount of alcohol allegedly taken prior to providing the specimen relied on by the prosecution may be used to challenge the reliability of the evidence relating to the specimen (*Cracknell v Willis* [1988] AC 450). However, this will often depend on the evidence of the defendant alone and, in the absence of the right to provide a sample of blood or urine, the defendant is unlikely to prevail. For example, in *Lafferty v DPP* [1995] Crim LR 429, the defendant adduced evidence as to the amount of alcohol consumed supported by expert evidence indicating that, on such a level of consumption, the Intoximeter reading should not have been as high as it was; if the defendant's evidence to that effect was accepted, it followed that the device was unreliable. The Divisional Court decided that the justices had properly admitted evidence of the results of the roadside breath test, as this went to the veracity of the defendant when attacking the reliability of the device, which attack the prosecution was entitled to rebut by any relevant evidence. It is not strictly necessary to adduce expert evidence establishing the reading which should have been produced on the basis of what the defendant claims to have consumed (*DPP v Spurrier* [2000] RTR 60) but, except in exceptional circumstances, to do so is always likely to make the defendant's evidence more credible.

In summary, for evidence of a specimen required under the RTA 1988, s. 7(1), to be admissible under the RTOA 1988, s. 15(2), all the procedural requirements of the RTA 1988, ss. 7 and 8, including the mandatory warning under s. 7(7), must be fully complied with, even where no prejudice results from a breach of those requirements (*Murray v DPP* [1993] RTR 209). A blood sample provided voluntarily by the defendant before being suspected of an offence is also admissible under s. 15(2) (*DPP v Carless* [2005] EWHC 3234 (Admin)).

Excluding Improperly Obtained Specimens

Since the decision in *Fox* [1986] AC 281, a lawful arrest is not an essential prerequisite for lawfully requiring a specimen under the RTA 1988, s. 7. Indeed, subject to general principles about the admissibility of evidence illegally or unlawfully obtained (see **F2.1** *et seq.*), it is arguable that no irregularity in the preliminary testing procedure under ss. 6 to 6E can have any effect on the subsequent procedure under s. 7 (*DPP v Wilson* [2009] EWHC 1988 (Admin), [2009] RTR 29 (375); *R (CPS) v Wolverhampton Magistrates' Court* [2009] EWHC 3467 (Admin)). Similarly, because time is of the essence and the police are not required to delay the breath test procedure in order for the defendant to obtain legal advice (see **C5.29**), the PACE 1984, s. 58 (right of access to solicitor: see **D1.55**), will not usually be breached, and it follows that s. 78 of that Act cannot be invoked to justify exclusion of the evidence of the test (*Chalupa v CPS* [2009] EWHC 3082 (Admin), (2010) 174 JP 111). *Miller v DPP* [2018] EWHC 262 (Admin), [2018] RTR 19 (278), provides an example where failure to have an appropriate adult present at the police station when conducting the drink-drive procedure where the suspect was known to have learning difficulties and autism constituted a breach of PACE Code C and led to the evidence obtained being excluded. **C5.46**

The decision in *Fox* did, however, recognise a discretion to exclude otherwise admissible evidence obtained by some trick, deception or other impropriety as envisaged in *Sang* [1980] AC 402. In *Matto v Wolverhampton Crown Court* [1987] RTR 337, officers followed the appellant on to private property, continued to administer a breath test to him and then arrested him after their implied licence to remain had been terminated. The Crown Court was of the opinion that, in order to exercise the discretion under the PACE 1984, s. 78, it must find that the police officers were knowingly acting in excess of their powers, and therefore acting in bad faith, and that evidence had been obtained other than voluntarily. In allowing the appeal, Woolf LJ stated that the approach of the Crown Court was wrong (at p. 347):

> ... it was at least open to the Crown Court, if the matter had been properly left before them, for them to have come to a conclusion that what happened at the house was still affecting the fairness of what happened in the police station and, because it affected the fairness of what happened at the police station, that would in turn give rise to an argument as to the admissibility of the evidence under section 78 of the Police and Criminal Evidence Act 1984.

C5.47 In *Thomas* [1991] RTR 292, Tudor-Evans J stated (at p. 294):

> ... in principle and upon authority, it is open to a defendant to argue that the procedures at the police station were so tainted by the previous conduct of the police at the roadside that there was a discretion to exclude the evidence of what happened at the police station.

It is not normally permissible, however, to raise this type of issue before the Divisional Court if it was not raised initially before the justices themselves (*Braham v DPP* [1996] RTR 30).

The Statutory Assumption

C5.48 The assumption in the RTOA 1988, s. 15(2) (see **C5.41**), relates to the proportion of alcohol or drug in the defendant's specimen at the time of the offence. It applies only to trials and is not the sole basis, whether guilt is established by plea or otherwise, on which to sentence (*Goldsmith v DPP* [2009] EWHC 3010 (Admin), [2010] RTR 20 (219)). The assumption is not rebuttable (*Beauchamp-Thompson v DPP* [1988] RTR 54; *Millard v DPP* [1990] RTR 201) and a court is not competent to receive expert evidence aimed at undermining the assumption (*Griffiths v DPP* [2002] EWHC 792 (Admin), (2002) 166 JP 629). The assumption has been found not to be incompatible with the presumption of innocence in the ECHR, Article 6(2) (*Parker v DPP* [2001] RTR 16 (240); *Drummond* [2002] EWCA Crim 527, [2002] 2 Cr App R 25 (352)).

The assumption provides the 'floor' in relation to the amount of alcohol in the defendant's breath or alcohol or drug in the defendant's blood or urine at the relevant time. Accordingly, the prosecution are entitled to produce evidence by way of back-calculation to show that, at the time of driving, attempting to drive or being in charge, the proportion was even higher than the specimen shows and was therefore in excess of the applicable prescribed or specified limit. In *Gumbley v Cunningham* [1988] QB 170, the appellant driver was involved in a fatal accident at 11.15 p.m. Four hours and 20 minutes later, the appellant provided a specimen of blood analysed at 59 milligrammes per 100 millilitres. The prosecution adduced evidence to demonstrate that persons of the height, age, weight and physical condition of the appellant would, at the time of driving, have had alcohol in their body in the range of 120 to 130 milligrammes in blood. In upholding the conviction in the Divisional Court, Mann J said (at p. 181):

> Evidence which is material to the question of what was the proportion of alcohol at the moment of driving must be admissible. The provisions of [the RTOA 1988, s. 15(2) and (3)] do not preclude evidence other than that revealed by a specimen to show a greater level of alcohol although, subject to the 'hip-flask' defence, the specimen will always provide a 'not less' or base figure. If that figure is above the prescribed limit, other evidence is unnecessary to establish the offence.
>
> Our conclusion means that those who drive whilst above the prescribed limits cannot necessarily escape punishment because of the lapse of time. However, our conclusion also means that in cases where a sample provided a substantial period of time after driving has ceased shows a level below the prescribed limit justices may find themselves confronted with evidence of a complicated and scientific nature.... We think it needs to be said, therefore, that in our view the prosecution should not seek to rely on evidence of back-calculation save where that evidence is easily understood and clearly persuasive of the presence of excess alcohol at the time when a defendant was driving. Moreover, justices must be very careful especially where there is conflicting evidence not to convict unless, upon the scientific and other evidence which they find it safe to rely on, they are sure an excess of alcohol was in the defendant's body when he was actually driving as charged.

Where the analyses of two specimens of blood or urine differ, it is for the justices to evaluate all the evidence before them. If in any reasonable doubt, they should choose that most favourable to the defendant (*Froggatt v Allcock* [1975] RTR 372n).

Defences

C5.49 **The Statutory 'Hip-flask' Defence** Section 15(3) of the RTOA 1988 (see **C5.41**) affords a defence to a charge under the RTA 1988, s. 5, where the defendant claims that the fact that there is alcohol in the defendant's body above the prescribed limit is attributable to consumption after the event to an extent that, but for that later consumption of alcohol, evidence from the specimen would not have resulted in an offence being made out. Once the statutory assumption (see **C5.48**) has to be made, the onus shifts to the defendant to raise the 'hip-flask' defence (*Patterson v Charlton* [1986] RTR 18). The defendant must prove, on the balance of probabilities, not only that the reading was wrong but also that at the relevant time the defendant's alcohol level was below the prescribed limit (*DPP v Tooze* [2007] EWHC 2186 (Admin)). In *Drummond* [2002] EWCA Crim 527, [2002] 2 Cr App R 25 (352), the Court of Appeal decided not to 'read down' s. 15(3) under the HRA 1998, s. 3, so that it imposes only an evidential burden (see, e.g., *Lambert* [2001] UKHL 37, [2002] 2 AC 545 at **F3.18**) and ruled that the persuasive burden imposed does not interfere with the presumption of innocence in the ECHR, Article 6(2), because it is no greater an interference than is necessary. This approach was confirmed as remaining correct post-*Sheldrake* (see **C5.51**) in *DPP v Ellery* [2005] EWHC 2513 (Admin).

The defence also extends to offences under the RTA 1988, ss. 3A and 4 (see **C3.20** and **C5.58**). **C5.50**
In the case of an offence under s. 3A, evidence of post-accident consumption of alcohol is admissible even if the defendant drove after the accident because s. 3A looks at the state of intoxication at the time the cause of death arose. In *Dawson v Lunn* [1986] RTR 234, Robert Goff LJ said (at p. 238):

> ...there are circumstances in which, as a matter of common sense, laymen can reach a perfectly sensible conclusion unaided by scientific evidence. We need only to take the simple case of somebody who satisfies the justices on the evidence that he had drunk only a small amount before driving, and that after ceasing to drive he had drunk a substantial quantity of alcohol. The justices can then conclude as laymen, reliably and confidently... that the defendant has satisfied them, on the balance of probabilities, that he has consumed alcohol after ceasing to drive and that had he not done so the proportion of alcohol in his breath, or blood, or urine would not have exceeded the prescribed limit. But there must be cases where the justices cannot sensibly draw that conclusion themselves unaided by expert evidence.

He went on to adopt the passage in *Pugsley v Hunter* [1973] 2 All ER 10 (a case on 'special reasons'), where Lord Widgery CJ observed that 'unless the case really is an obvious one... the only way in which a defendant can discharge the onus is by calling medical evidence'. The Court of Appeal also discouraged reliance upon extracts from scientific journals. Except perhaps in the clearest of cases, the defendant must therefore call scientific evidence (*DPP v Singh* [1988] RTR 209). Where there is no expert evidence, the justices should avoid drawing their own conclusions about the probable effect of the claimed consumption of alcohol (*Lonergan v DPP* [2002] EWHC 1263 (Admin), [2003] RTR 12 (188)) and must be careful when assessing the credibility of the defendant (*DPP v Dukolli* [2009] EWHC 3097 (Admin)). Where the justices have the benefit of expert evidence, despite apparent discrepancies, they may be entitled to find that the defendant has discharged the onus placed upon the defendant (*DPP v Lowden* [1993] RTR 349).

If expert evidence is to be called, it should be disclosed to the prosecution to avoid unnecessary adjournments (*DPP v O'Connor* [1992] RTR 66).

Other Defences Section 5(2) of the RTA 1988 provides a defence to an allegation of 'in **C5.51**
charge' of the vehicle, based on the likelihood of the defendant driving while still above the prescribed limit. In *Sheldrake v DPP* [2004] UKHL 43, [2005] 1 AC 264, the House of Lords determined that there was no need to 'read down' this reverse onus of proof as an evidential burden only (as the majority of the Divisional Court had, relying on the presumption of innocence in the ECHR, Article 6(2)) and that this was a provision properly imposing a legal burden on the defendant, which was justified as pursuing a legitimate objective that was neither unreasonable or arbitrary. See **F3.18** for a full discussion of the 'reverse burden'.

It is not sufficient for the defendant to prove a lack of intention to drive. The question is whether the defendant has shown that there is no likelihood of driving while still over the prescribed limit (*CPS v Thompson* [2007] EWHC 1841 (Admin), [2008] RTR 5 (70)); 'likelihood' means real risk (*Sheldrake v DPP* [2003] EWHC 273 (Admin), [2004] QB 487). In *Drake v DPP* [1994] RTR 411, the Divisional Court held that the presence of a wheel clamp on a motor vehicle could not be disregarded when considering the likelihood of the defendant driving. Medical or other expert evidence will almost inevitably be required to establish the probable alcohol level at the time at which the defendant will next drive (*DPP v Frost* [1989] RTR 11), unless the length of time involved makes that conclusion obvious. As to duress, see **A3.35** to **A3.52**.

Since *Loake v CPS* [2017] EWHC 2855 (Admin), [2018] QB 998, which confirmed that the defence of insanity is of general application, *DPP v H* [1997] 1 WLR 1406, which suggested that insanity could not be raised as a defence to a s. 5 charge because there is no *mens rea* element to which it can relate, is not to be followed.

Punishment

C5.52 For offences of driving or attempting to drive, the penalty is six months' imprisonment and/or an unlimited fine. Disqualification and endorsement are obligatory unless there are 'special reasons', and the offence carries between three and 11 penalty points. An order for forfeiture may be made under either offence (see E18.1).

The offence of being 'in charge' is punishable by imprisonment for up to three months and/or a fine up to level 4 on the standard scale. Disqualification is discretionary; endorsement with ten penalty points is obligatory.

Sentence

C5.53 The *Magistrates' Court Sentencing Guidelines* (see Supplement, **SG10-79** and **SG10-80**) must generally be followed; the guidelines set out the starting points and sentencing ranges by reference to the amount above the prescribed limit found in the specimen and provide examples of aggravating and mitigating factors. In particular, they indicate that, as a starting point, a custodial sentence might properly be considered for readings of 120 microgrammes in 100 millilitres of breath (equating to 276 milligrammes in 100 millilitres of blood or 367 milligrammes in 100 millilitres of urine). In *Nokes* [1978] RTR 101, it was accepted that there is no rule that a first offence should not attract a custodial sentence if the facts show it to be appropriate.

DRIVING, OR BEING IN CHARGE, WITH CONTROLLED DRUG ABOVE SPECIFIED LIMIT

C5.54 **Road Traffic Act 1988, s. 5A**

(1) This section applies where a person ('D')—
  (a) drives or attempts to drive a motor vehicle on a road or other public place, or
  (b) is in charge of a motor vehicle on a road or other public place,
  and there is in D's body a specified controlled drug.
(2) D is guilty of an offence if the proportion of the drug in D's blood or urine exceeds the specified limit for that drug.
(3) It is a defence for a person ('D') charged with an offence under this section to show that—
  (a) the specified controlled drug had been prescribed or supplied to D for medical or dental purposes,
  (b) D took the drug in accordance with any directions given by the person by whom the drug was prescribed or supplied, and with any accompanying instructions (so far as consistent with any such directions) given by the manufacturer or distributor of the drug, and
  (c) D's possession of the drug immediately before taking it was not unlawful under section 5(1) of the Misuse of Drugs Act 1971 (restriction of possession of controlled drugs) because of an exemption in regulations made under section 7 of that Act (authorisation of activities otherwise unlawful under foregoing provisions).
(4) The defence in subsection (3) is not available if D's actions were—

(a) contrary to any advice, given by the person by whom the drug was prescribed or supplied, about the amount of time that should elapse between taking the drug and driving a motor vehicle, or
(b) contrary to any accompanying instructions about that matter (so far as consistent with any such advice) given by the manufacturer or distributor of the drug.

(5) If evidence is adduced that is sufficient to raise an issue with respect to the defence in subsection (3), the court must assume that the defence is satisfied unless the prosecution proves beyond reasonable doubt that it is not.
(6) It is a defence for a person ('D') charged with an offence by virtue of subsection (1)(b) to prove that at the time D is alleged to have committed the offence the circumstances were such that there was no likelihood of D driving the vehicle whilst the proportion of the specified controlled drug in D's blood or urine remained likely to exceed the specified limit for that drug.
(7) The court may, in determining whether there was such a likelihood, disregard any injury to D and any damage to the vehicle.

This is an offence expressly dealing with drug-driving, inserted by the CCA 2013, s. 56. It can be regarded as a development of the 'unfit' offence in the RTA 1988, s. 4, although there is no requirement to prove impairment (see **C5.61**). It is broadly similar to the alcohol-related offence in the RTA 1988, s. 5.

Elements

The RTOA 1988, ss. 11 and 12(1) apply; see **C2.17** and **C2.18**. For the meaning of the terms 'driving', 'road or other public place' and 'attempting', see **C1.2** and **C1.5**, **C1.13** and **C1.16** and **C1.20**. **C5.55**

Because of the similarities with the offences in the RTA 1988, s. 5, see also generally **C5.34** to **C5.36**. The RTOA 1988, ss. 15 and 16, apply, see generally **C5.37** to **C5.47**. On the approach to take to the statutory assumption in respect of the proportion of a specified controlled drug in a person's body, see generally **C5.48**.

The Drug Driving (Specified Limits) (England and Wales) Regulations 2014 (SI 2014 No. 2868), specify 17 controlled drugs and their corresponding specified limits, each of which is expressed in microgrammes per litre of blood. For example, the limits for amphetamine, cocaine, diazepam, methadone, morphine and temazepam are 250, 10, 550, 500, 80 and 1,000 respectively. No limits have yet been set in relation to urine.

Defences

Section 5A(3) and (4) provide a defence for a defendant who shows that the drug in question was prescribed or supplied for medical or dental purposes, was used in accordance with appropriate instructions or directions and was not possessed by the defendant contrary to the MDA 1971. The defendant bears the evidential burden of raising the defence and thereafter the prosecution must disprove it beyond reasonable doubt (s. 5A(5)). **C5.56**

The RTA 1988, s. 5A(6), provides a defence in respect of an allegation that the defendant was 'in charge' of the vehicle similar to that contained in s. 5(2) (see **C5.51**). In determining the likelihood, the court is permitted to disregard any injury to the defendant or damage to the vehicle (s. 5A(7)).

Punishment

For offences of driving or attempting to drive, the penalty is six months' imprisonment and/or an unlimited fine. Disqualification and endorsement are obligatory unless there are 'special reasons', and the offence carries between three and 11 penalty points. Forfeiture of the vehicle may be ordered (see **E18.1**). **C5.57**

The offence of being 'in charge' carries three months' imprisonment and/or a fine up to level 4 on the standard scale. Disqualification is discretionary; endorsement with ten penalty points is obligatory.

The *Magistrates' Court Sentencing Guidelines*, which must generally be followed, are likely to be supplemented to explain how to assess the offence seriousness by reference to the different levels of controlled drug found in the defendant's body, as well as by reference to the nature of the offending activity, and provide examples of aggravating and mitigating factors. As a temporary measure, the Sentencing Council has published guidance, which sentencers are not obliged to follow in the same manner as a definitive sentencing guideline, but which helpfully summarises how to assess the seriousness of the offence and offers appropriate starting points, as well as setting out the other aggravating and mitigating factors that might be relevant. In *Hussain* [2018] EWCA Crim 2361, [2019] RTR 19 (228), derivatives of both cocaine and cannabis were found in the defendant's blood. Evidence of a second drug is one of the factors mentioned in the guidance as increasing the seriousness of the offence. It was further noted that the defendant's vehicle contained a passenger who had been exposed to risk and the defendant was at the time subject to a suspended custodial sentence. The guidance suggests a disqualification range of 29 to 36 months 'where there is evidence of one or more factors that increase seriousness and one or more aggravating factors' and the defendant's disqualification for 30 months was upheld. In a case at the lower end of culpability, involving one aggravating factor (presence of a passenger) and two mitigating factors (the short distance driven and no relevant convictions) a disqualification period of 26 months was reduced to one of 14 months (*Ewbank* [2019] EWCA Crim 1732).

DRIVING, OR BEING IN CHARGE, WHEN UNDER THE INFLUENCE OF DRINK OR DRUGS

C5.58 **Road Traffic Act 1988, s. 4**

(1) A person who, when driving or attempting to drive a mechanically propelled vehicle on a road or other public place, is unfit to drive through drink or drugs is guilty of an offence.
(2) Without prejudice to subsection (1) above, a person who, when in charge of a mechanically propelled vehicle which is on a road or other public place, is unfit to drive through drink or drugs is guilty of an offence.
(3) For the purposes of subsection (2) above, a person shall be deemed not to have been in charge of a mechanically propelled vehicle if he proves that at the material time the circumstances were such that there was no likelihood of his driving it so long as he remained unfit to drive through drink or drugs.
(4) The court may, in determining whether there was such a likelihood as is mentioned in subsection (3) above, disregard any injury to him and any damage to the vehicle.
(5) For the purposes of this section, a person shall be taken to be unfit to drive if his ability to drive properly is for the time being impaired.

Elements

C5.59 The RTOA 1988, ss. 11 and 12(1), apply; see **C2.17** and **C2.18**. The RTA 1988, s. 11, defines 'drugs' as including any intoxicant other than alcohol. For the meaning of the terms 'driving', 'motor vehicle', 'road or other public place' and 'attempting', see **C1.2** and **C1.5**, **C1.9**, **C1.13** and **C1.16** and **C1.20**. For 'in charge', see **C5.36**.

Section 4 creates three separate offences. The prosecution must establish that the defendant was driving or attempting to drive, or was in charge of a motor vehicle on a road or public place, and that at the time the defendant's ability to drive properly was impaired through drink or drugs. The charge may read 'drink or drugs' without either being duplicitous or bad for uncertainty.

Drugs

C5.60 Medicines are drugs for the purposes of the RTA 1988, s. 4, and include, e.g., insulin and toluene (*Armstrong v Clark* [1957] 2 QB 391; *Bradford v Wilson* (1983) 78 Cr App R 77). In *Watmore v Jenkins* [1962] 2 QB 572, the defendant had been overtaken by a hypoglycaemic episode and coma through a fall in the level of cortisone and a consequent increase in the level of insulin, brought about by a combination of injected insulin and an improvement in liver function following recovery from an attack of jaundice. In those unusual circumstances, the Divisional Court upheld an acquittal of driving whilst unfit through drugs as the justices were entitled to 'entertain a reasonable doubt whether the injected insulin was more than a predisposing or historical cause' of the defendant's state.

In *Ealing Magistrates' Court, ex parte Woodman* [1994] RTR 181, the conviction of a diabetic suffering a hypoglycaemic attack was quashed because there was no evidence entitling the stipendiary magistrate to conclude that the presence of insulin in the applicant's blood was the real effective cause of the attack. The Divisional Court decided that it would only be appropriate to rely on s. 4 in such cases where there is evidence of a clear overdose of insulin having been taken by the defendant.

Evidence of Impairment

This may be provided by the opinion evidence of an expert witness, normally a doctor, who has examined the defendant, even if the defendant has refused to be examined, and the doctor's testimony should be treated as that of any 'independent expert witness giving evidence to assist the court', whether the doctor is a police surgeon or anyone else (*Lanfear* [1968] 2 QB 77). Opinion evidence of the defendant's state or of the amount the defendant has drunk may be given even by a lay witness, but the opinion of such a lay witness as to whether the defendant was fit to drive is not admissible. Nor could a lay witness give evidence as to the amount of alcohol in the defendant's blood. As to opinion evidence by lay witnesses generally, see **F11.2**. **C5.61**

The prosecution are not obliged to adduce opinion evidence of an expert witness in order to establish the defendant's impairment to drive, provided that the totality of the evidence actually adduced suffices to satisfy the justices of this element (*Leetham v DPP* [1999] RTR 29). Such evidence may include the manner of the driving, the defendant's apparent physical state and any admission made relating to the consumption of drugs and, presumably, alcohol. Observations of a defendant's performance in a preliminary impairment test under the RTA 1988, s. 6B, should also be capable of being adduced as relevant evidence on this point.

The prosecution may adduce evidence of the amount of alcohol or a drug in a specimen properly provided by the defendant under the RTA 1988, s. 7. Such evidence is admissible by virtue of the RTOA 1988, ss. 15 and 16 (see **C5.41** and **C5.37**).

Defences

The RTA 1988, s. 4(3), provides a defence to an allegation that the defendant was 'in charge' of the vehicle similar to that contained in s. 5(2) (see **C5.51**). The defence imposes a permissible legal burden, rather than just an evidential burden, on the defendant (*Sheldrake v DPP* [2004] UKHL 43, [2005] 1 AC 264: see **C5.51**). **C5.62**

The defence may also adduce evidence of post-incident consumption to rebut the assumption that the defendant was unfit at the time of the alleged offence (see the RTOA 1988, s. 15(3), and **C5.49**). Evidence of post-incident drug use may provide a defence in comparable circumstances.

Punishment

For offences of driving or attempting to drive when unfit, the penalty is a maximum of six months' imprisonment and/or an unlimited fine. Endorsement and disqualification for one year are obligatory unless there are 'special reasons'. The offence carries between three and 11 penalty points. Forfeiture of the vehicle may be ordered (see **E18.1**). **C5.63**

The offence of being 'in charge' carries three months' imprisonment and/or a fine up to level 4 on the standard scale. Disqualification is discretionary but endorsement with ten penalty points is obligatory.

The *Magistrates' Court Sentencing Guidelines* (see Supplement, **SG10-143** and **SG10-144**) must generally be followed; the guidelines explain how to assess the category applicable to the offence by reference to culpability and harm and provide examples of aggravating and mitigating factors.

INTERPRETATION OF THE ROAD TRAFFIC ACT 1988, ss. 3A TO 10

C5.64 **Road Traffic Act 1988, s. 11**

(1) The following provisions apply for the interpretation of sections 3A to 10 of this Act.

(2) In those sections—

'controlled drug' has the meaning given by section 2 of the Misuse of Drugs Act 1971,

'drug' includes any intoxicant other than alcohol,

'fail' includes refuse,

'hospital' means an institution which provides medical or surgical treatment for in-patients or out-patients,

'the prescribed limit' means, as the case may require—

(a) 35 microgrammes of alcohol in 100 millilitres of breath,

(b) 80 milligrammes of alcohol in 100 millilitres of blood, or

(c) 107 milligrammes of alcohol in 100 millilitres of urine,

or such other proportion as may be prescribed by regulations made by the Secretary of State,

'registered health care professional' means a person (other than a medical practitioner) who is—

(a) a registered nurse; or

(b) a registered member of a health care profession which is designated for the purposes of this paragraph by an order made by the Secretary of State.

'specified', in relation to a controlled drug, has the meaning given by section 5A(8).

(2ZA) [Relates to power to make regulations under subsection (2).]

(2A) A health care profession is any profession mentioned in section 60(2) of the Health Act 1999 other than the profession of practising medicine and the profession of nursing.

(2B) [Procedure for making orders under subsection (2).]

(3) A person does not co-operate with a preliminary test or provide a specimen of breath for analysis unless his co-operation or the specimen—

(a) is sufficient to enable the test or the analysis to be carried out, and

(b) is provided in such a way as to enable the objective of the test or analysis to be satisfactorily achieved.

(4) A person provides a specimen of blood if and only if—

(a) he consents to the taking of such a specimen from him; and

(b) the specimen is taken from him either by a medical practitioner or by a registered health care professional.

Section C6 Summary Traffic Offences

CARELESS AND INCONSIDERATE DRIVING

Road Traffic Act 1988, s. 3 **C6.1**

> If a person drives a mechanically propelled vehicle on a road or other public place without due care and attention, or without reasonable consideration for other persons using the road or place, he is guilty of an offence.

Elements

C6.2 The RTOA 1988, ss. 1, 11 and 12(1), apply; see **C2.1**, **C2.17** and **C2.18**.

For the meaning of the terms 'drive', 'mechanically propelled vehicle' and 'road or other public place' see **C1.2** and **C1.5**, **C1.9** and **C1.13**, and **C1.16**. Section 3 creates two separate offences, commonly called 'careless driving' and 'driving without reasonable consideration'.

The term 'other persons using the road' includes persons who are pedestrians or passengers in vehicles, including that driven by the defendant, as well as other motorists (*Pawley v Wharldall* [1966] 1 QB 373).

Careless Driving

C6.3 Under the RTA 1988, s. 3ZA(2) and (3), the single test for driving without due care and attention is 'if (and only if)' the way the person drives 'falls below what would be expected of a competent and careful driver'. In addition to this objective standard, the court can consider any particular matters known at the time to the driver because, in determining what would be expected of a careful and competent driver, 'regard shall be had not only to the circumstances of which he could have been expected to be aware but also to any circumstances shown to have been within the knowledge of the accused'.

Previous case law, e.g., *Simpson v Peat* [1952] 2 QB 24, *DPP v Cox* (1993) 157 JP 1044 and the *obiter* comments of Lord Diplock in *Lawrence* [1982] AC 510, has effectively been codified. In *Jones v CPS* [2019] EWHC 2826 (Admin), [2020] 1 WLR 99, the approach taken by *Webster* [2006] EWCA Crim 415, [2006] 2 Cr App R 6 (103) to the construction of the statutory test for dangerous driving (see **C3.13**) was adapted so as to apply to careless driving (at [34]):

> It is not sufficient merely to rely on the condition of the driver in order to prove the offence of careless driving or of causing death by careless driving. The condition of the driver is relevant and admissible. But it does not determine whether the way in which the defendant drove was careless.

C6.4 Departure from the standard of driving required by the Highway Code, whilst not in itself an offence, may well establish liability under the RTA 1988, s. 3, but adherence to the Highway

Code may, equally, negative such a liability. For the admissibility of the provisions of the Highway Code, see the RTA 1988, s. 38, and **C2.16**. Each case must be objectively decided on its own facts in the surrounding circumstances. Only if the court considers that the driver has or must have failed to exercise the degree of care and attention which the reasonable, prudent and competent driver would have exercised, should a conviction result. It follows that a particular manner of driving may be careless in one situation but not in another.

On occasions, e.g., where a driver veers off in the course of overtaking and collides with an oncoming vehicle, the only inference that can be drawn is that the defendant drove carelessly. To draw another inference, such as mechanical defect, without any evidence to support that inference means that the justices have misdirected themselves (*DPP v Tipton* (1992) 156 JP 172). Crossing a road's dividing line is prima facie evidence of carelessness, necessitating an explanation which is acceptable on the facts (*Mundi v Warwickshire Police* [2001] EWHC Admin 448).

In *DPP v Parker* [1989] RTR 413, the defendant, who had been driving in a line of traffic which came to a halt, ran into the back of the car in front which then ran into another car in front. The defendant was not driving fast immediately before the collision and, because of rain, road conditions were wet and slippery. The Divisional Court held that while such driving might in other circumstances be sufficient to constitute an offence, whether it was sufficient in this case had been a question of fact. There was insufficient material to justify a finding that the justices' decision on the facts was perverse, and the prosecution's appeal accordingly failed.

C6.5 The CPS guidance on charging practice in traffic offences gives the following examples of driving which may amount to driving without due care and attention:

(a) overtaking on the inside;
(b) driving inappropriately close to another vehicle;
(c) inadvertently driving through a red light;
(d) emerging from a side road into the path of another vehicle;
(e) tuning a car radio;
(f) using a hand-held mobile phone or other hand-held electronic equipment where the driver was avoidably distracted by that use; and
(g) selecting and lighting a cigarette or similar where the driver was avoidably distracted by that use.

These are indicative only and not conclusive as to the type of behaviour which might constitute careless driving. The Divisional Court in *DPP v Barreto* [2019] EWHC 2044 (Admin), [2020] 1 Cr App R 6 (142) confirmed that filming events or taking photographs while driving, either with a camera or the camera function on a mobile phone, or making any other use of a phone while driving, may be cogent evidence of careless driving (at [51]).

Driving without Reasonable Consideration

C6.6 By virtue of the RTA 1988, s. 3ZA(4), this offence is made out *only* if other road users are inconvenienced by the driving of the defendant. Evidence of such inconvenience may be provided either by the direct testimony of another road user, or by inference to be drawn from evidence of the reactions or behaviour of other road users. *DPP v Waller* [2018] EWHC 3303 (Admin) clarified that the question whether the defendant's driving inconvenienced another road user falls to be determined on the whole of the evidence, so even if the complainant's evidence was that there had been no inconvenience that is not determinative on that issue.

The CPS guidance on charging practice in traffic offences gives the following examples of conduct appropriate for a charge of driving without reasonable consideration:

(a) flashing of lights to force other drivers in front to give way;
(b) *misuse of any* lane (including cycling lanes) to avoid queuing or gain some other advantage over other drivers;
(c) unnecessarily remaining in an overtaking lane;

(d) unnecessarily slow driving or braking without good cause;
(e) driving with undipped headlights that dazzle oncoming drivers, cyclists or pedestrians;
(f) driving through a puddle causing pedestrians to be splashed; and
(g) driving a bus in such a way as to alarm passengers.

Defences

Mechanical defect, automatism and duress of circumstances (*Backshall* [1998] 1 WLR 1506); see **C1.7**, **C1.21** and **A3.47**. In principle, self-defence may be available (see *Riddell* [2017] EWCA Crim 413, [2017] 2 Cr App R 3 (22) at **C3.42**). No offence is committed under s. 3 where the driving took place in a public place other than a road in the course of an authorised motoring event (RTA 1988, s. 13A). **C6.7**

Alternative Verdicts

See the RTOA 1988, s. 24, set out at **C2.8**. **C6.8**

On a trial on indictment for an offence under the RTA 1988, s. 1, 1A, 2, 2B or 3A, the jury may find the defendant guilty of an offence under s. 3 (unless the defendant has already been acquitted of it: *DPP v Khan* [1997] RTR 82), and the Crown Court has the same sentencing powers as a magistrates' court when that occurs. Where the prosecution have not accepted a guilty plea to careless driving and the defendant has been found not guilty of dangerous driving, without an alternative verdict having been entered, the previous guilty plea is a nullity and the court cannot proceed to sentence in respect of it (*McGregor-Read* [1999] Crim LR 860). The requirement for a notice under s. 1(1) of the RTOA 1988 is waived by s. 2(4) of that Act as long as the original requirement for a warning notice, if any, has been complied with.

It is not open to the prosecution to accept a plea of guilty to a charge of careless driving which has been committed for trial under the CJA 1988, s. 41, and offer no evidence on the indictable offence of reckless (now dangerous) driving (*Foote* [1993] RTR 171). Offences committed for trial under s. 41 can be dealt with only following a conviction for an indictable offence arising out of circumstances which are the same as or connected with the summary offence.

If a defendant is acquitted, by magistrates, of an offence under s. 2, the court may direct or allow a charge for an offence under s. 3 to be preferred (RTOA 1988, s. 24(3)). This power extends to the Crown Court on an appeal against conviction for dangerous driving (*Killington v Butcher* [1979] Crim LR 458; Senior Courts Act 1981, s. 79(3)). The requirement for a notice of intended prosecution is waived by the RTOA 1988, s. 2(6), as long as the original requirement for a warning notice, if any, has been complied with.

In *Coventry Justices, ex parte Sayers* [1979] RTR 22, the Divisional Court held that the six-month time limit did not apply to a charge preferred under s. 24(3).

Powers to Stop, Seize and Remove Vehicles

Police Reform Act 2002, s. 59 **C6.9**

(1) Where a constable in uniform has reasonable grounds for believing that a motor vehicle is being used on any occasion in a manner which—
  (a) contravenes section 3 or 34 of the Road Traffic Act 1988 (careless and inconsiderate driving and prohibition of off-road driving), and
  (b) is causing, or is likely to cause, alarm, distress or annoyance to members of the public, he shall have the powers set out in subsection (3).
(2) A constable in uniform shall also have the powers set out in subsection (3) where he has reasonable grounds for believing that a motor vehicle has been used on any occasion in a manner falling within subsection (1).
(3) Those powers are—
  (a) power, if the motor vehicle is moving, to order the person driving it to stop the vehicle;
  (b) power to seize and remove the motor vehicle;

(c) power, for the purposes of exercising a power falling within paragraph (a) or (b), to enter any premises on which he has reasonable grounds for believing the motor vehicle to be;
(d) power to use reasonable force, if necessary, in the exercise of any power conferred by any of paragraphs (a) to (c).

(4) A constable shall not seize a motor vehicle in the exercise of the powers conferred on him by this section unless—
(a) he has warned the person appearing to him to be the person whose use falls within subsection (1) that he will seize it, if that use continues or is repeated; and
(b) it appears to him that the use has continued or been repeated after the warning.

(5) Subsection (4) does not require a warning to be given by a constable on any occasion on which he would otherwise have the power to seize a motor vehicle under this section if—
(a) the circumstances make it impracticable for him to give the warning;
(b) the constable has already on that occasion given a warning under that subsection in respect of any use of that motor vehicle or of another motor vehicle by that person or any other person;
(c) the constable has reasonable grounds for believing that such a warning has been given on that occasion otherwise than by him; or
(d) the constable has reasonable grounds for believing that the person whose use of that motor vehicle on that occasion would justify the seizure is a person to whom a warning under that subsection has been given (whether or not by that constable or in respect the same vehicle or the same or a similar use) on a previous occasion in the previous twelve months.

(6) A person who fails to comply with an order under subsection (3)(a) is guilty of an offence and shall be liable, on summary conviction, to a fine not exceeding level 3 on the standard scale.
(7) Subsection (3)(c) does not authorise entry into a private dwelling house.
(8) The powers conferred on a constable by this section shall be exercisable only at a time when regulations under section 60 are in force.
(9) In this section—
'driving' has the same meaning as in the Road Traffic Act 1988;
'motor vehicle' means any mechanically propelled vehicle, whether or not it is intended or adapted for use on roads; and
'private dwelling house' does not include any garage or other structure occupied with the dwelling house, or any land appurtenant to the dwelling house.

C6.10 The Police (Retention and Disposal of Motor Vehicles) Regulations 2002 (SI 2002 No. 3049) were made under s. 60.

The Secretary of State is empowered to appoint 'stopping officers' for specified purposes in relation to commercial vehicles (Road Vehicles (Powers to Stop) Regulations 2011 (SI 2011 No. 996)).

Punishment

C6.11 The offence carries an unlimited fine. Disqualification is discretionary but endorsement, in the absence of 'special reasons', with between three and nine penalty points is obligatory. In appropriate cases, the court may disqualify the defendant until a driving test is passed under the RTOA 1988, s. 36 (see *Miller* (1994) 15 Cr App R (S) 505 at **C7.34**). Because the offence does not carry obligatory disqualification, it is not permitted to disqualify until an extended driving test is passed (*Kruger* [2012] EWCA Crim 2166, [2013] 1 Cr App R (S) 17 (608)). A fixed penalty of £100 is available for this offence (Fixed Penalty Offences Order 2013 (SI 2013 No. 1565)).

Sentence

C6.12 The *Magistrates' Court Sentencing Guidelines* (see Supplement, **SG10-60**) must generally be followed; the guidelines explain how to assess the category applicable to the offence by reference to culpability and harm and provide examples of aggravating and mitigating factors. The starting points are fines of differing bands. When a maximum fine of £5,000 applied, the guidelines indicated that this should be reserved only for the worst instances of careless driving where the defendant also has the means to pay (*Holman* [2010] EWCA Crim 107, [2010] RTR 23 (257) and *Christie* [2012] EWCA Crim 35, [2012] 2 Cr App R (S) 46 (273), where the fine was reduced to £3,000 in respect of a defendant, recently returned from America, pulling out from a car park into a main road causing an approaching vehicle to take evasive action and driving the wrong way down the road for 185 metres before being involved in a head-on collision). An argument that it was wrong in principle to disqualify two police officers, who had driven separate vehicles on a motorway at speeds exceeding 90 mph when there was no operational need to do so, because it would deprive the public of the services they provided, was rejected in *Perkins* [2012] EWCA Crim 218 (although, having regard to all the circumstances of the case, the eight-month discretionary disqualifications were quashed). In *Mitchell* [2017] EWCA Crim 456, having been convicted of careless driving as an alternative to a count of causing serious injury by dangerous driving (see **C3.33** ***et seq.***), a five-year disqualification, described as more appropriate to dangerous driving, was replaced by one of two years.

As to compensation orders, see **E16**, particularly **E16.1**.

MOTOR RACING ON HIGHWAYS

Road Traffic Act 1988, s. 12 **C6.13**

(1) A person who promotes or takes part in a race or trial of speed between motor vehicles on a public way is guilty of an offence.

Elements

The RTOA 1988, ss. 11 and 12(1), apply; see **C2.17** and **C2.18**. **C6.14**

The Deregulation Act 2015, s. 73, has made s. 12(1) subject to ss. 12A to 12F, which enable highway authorities to make motor race orders. Such orders (see, e.g., SI 2017 No. 390) permit designated bodies to hold races or trials of speed on public ways.

Punishment

The offence carries a fine of up to level 4 on the standard scale. Unless 'special reasons' are established, there is a minimum disqualification from driving for a period of 12 months. Persons who 'promote' or 'take part' must be disqualified even though they are not drivers. The offence is endorsable with between three and 11 penalty points. **C6.15**

LEAVING VEHICLE IN DANGEROUS POSITION

Road Traffic Act 1988, s. 22 **C6.16**

If a person in charge of a vehicle causes or permits the vehicle or a trailer drawn by it to remain at rest on a road in such a position or in such condition or in such circumstances as to involve a danger of injury to other persons using the road, he is guilty of an offence.

Elements

For the meaning of the terms 'causing', 'permitting' and 'using', see **C1.23**, **C1.25** and **C1.28**. The RTOA 1988, ss. 1, 11 and 12(1), apply; see **C2.1**, **C2.17** and **C2.18**. **C6.17**

Section 22 applies to any vehicle, not just a motor vehicle. The offence may be established either where the vehicle itself involves a danger of injury (e.g., if it is on fire or parked on a hill without brakes and secured only by stones or bricks placed under the wheels), or where, because of its position on the road, it creates a danger. For example, parking a car or other vehicle on the corner of a busy intersection, obstructing the view of other motorists emerging from a side road, involves a danger of injury, because motorists would be forced to emerge 'blind' and, however cautiously this was done, the likelihood of a collision and consequent injury would remain.

Punishment

C6.18 A fine up to level 3 on the standard scale applies. If the offence is committed in respect of a motor vehicle, disqualification is discretionary and endorsement with three penalty points is obligatory. A fixed penalty of £100 is available for this offence.

RESTRICTION OF CARRIAGE OF PERSONS ON MOTOR CYCLES

C6.19 **Road Traffic Act 1988, s. 23**

(1) Not more than one person in addition to the driver may be carried on a motor bicycle.
(2) No person in addition to the driver may be carried on a motor bicycle otherwise than sitting astride the motor cycle and on a proper seat securely fixed to the motor cycle behind the driver's seat.
(3) If a person is carried on a motor cycle in contravention of this section, the driver of the motor cycle is guilty of an offence.

Elements

C6.20 The RTOA 1988, ss. 11 and 12(1), apply; see C2.17 and C2.18.

Punishment

C6.21 The offence carries a fine up to level 3. Disqualification is discretionary and endorsement with three penalty points obligatory. A fixed penalty of £100 is available for this offence.

NEGLECT OR REFUSAL TO COMPLY WITH TRAFFIC DIRECTIONS GIVEN BY CONSTABLE

C6.22 **Road Traffic Act 1988, s. 35**

(1) Where a constable or traffic officer is for the time being engaged in the regulation of traffic in a road, a person driving or propelling a vehicle who neglects or refuses—
  (a) to stop the vehicle, or
  (b) to make it proceed in, or keep to, a particular line of traffic,
  when directed to do so by the constable in the execution of his duty or the traffic officer (as the case may be) is guilty of an offence.
(2) Where—
  (a) a traffic survey of any description is being carried out on or in the vicinity of a road, and
  (b) a constable or traffic officer gives to a person driving or propelling a vehicle a direction—
    (i) to stop the vehicle,
    (ii) to make it proceed in, or keep to, a particular line of traffic, or
    (iii) to proceed to a particular point on or near the road on which the vehicle is being driven or propelled,
  being a direction given for the purposes of the survey (but not a direction requiring any person to provide any information for the purposes of a traffic survey),
  the person is guilty of an offence if he neglects or refuses to comply with the direction.
(3) The power to give such a direction as is referred to in subsection (2) above for the purposes of a traffic survey shall be so exercised as not to cause any unreasonable delay to a person who indicates that he is unwilling to provide any information for the purposes of the survey.

Elements

C6.23 The RTOA 1988, ss. 1, 11 and 12(1), apply; see C2.1, C2.17 and C2.18.

This section extends to any vehicle as long as it is being driven or propelled. The reference to a constable includes a traffic warden if the warden is engaged in accordance with s. 35 in the regulation of traffic in the road.

There are two offences created. For an offence under s. 35(2), the constable must be giving a direction for the purposes of a traffic survey. Under s. 35(1), the constable must be acting in the execution of the constable's duty, which in this case means a duty to protect life and property arising from the dangers created by unregulated traffic (*Hoffman v Thomas* [1974] 2 All ER 233; *Johnson v Phillips* [1976] 3 All ER 682). It is arguable, therefore, that for s. 35 to operate, the constable must have been engaged upon traffic duties and not exercising powers either under the PACE 1984 or the RTA 1988, s. 163.

Punishment

The offence carries a fine up to level 3. If the offence is committed in respect of a motor vehicle, disqualification is discretionary, but endorsement with three penalty points is obligatory. The *Magistrates' Court Sentencing Guidelines* (see Supplement, **SG10-108**) give fine band A as the starting point. A fixed penalty of £100 is available for this offence. **C6.24**

FAILURE TO COMPLY WITH INDICATION GIVEN BY TRAFFIC SIGN

Road Traffic Act 1988, s. 36 **C6.25**

(1) Where a traffic sign, being a sign—
  (a) of the prescribed size, colour and type, or
  (b) of another character authorised by the relevant authority under the provisions in that behalf of the Road Traffic Regulation Act 1984,
  has been lawfully placed on or near a road, a person driving or propelling a vehicle who fails to comply with the indication given by the sign is guilty of an offence.
(2) A traffic sign shall not be treated for the purposes of this section as having been lawfully placed unless either—
  (a) the indication given by the sign is an indication of a statutory prohibition, restriction or requirement, or
  (b) it is expressly provided by or under any provision of the Traffic Acts that this section shall apply to the sign or to signs of a type of which the sign is one;
  and, where the indication mentioned in paragraph (a) of this subsection is of the general nature only of the prohibition, restriction or requirement to which the sign relates, a person shall not be convicted of failure to comply with the indication unless he has failed to comply with the prohibition, restriction or requirement to which the sign relates.

Elements

The RTOA 1988, ss. 1, 11, 12(1) and 20, apply; see **C2.1**, **C2.17**, **C2.18** and **C2.21**. **C6.26**

Traffic signs are prescribed by regulations made under the RTRA 1984, s. 64. If a sign indicates a statutory prohibition, restriction or requirement, or if it is expressly provided under any provision of the Traffic Acts that the section applies to the sign, a failure to comply with it is an offence.

The main regulatory instrument is the Traffic Signs Regulations and General Directions 2016 (SI 2016 No. 362), which provides a comprehensive statutory framework. Failure to comply with any traffic sign may constitute an offence but only failure by a person driving a motor vehicle to comply with a sign of a kind specified within the regulations carries endorsement and disqualification. The signs so specified include 'Stop' and 'Give Way' signs at junctions (sch. 9, part 8, para. 2), traffic lights (sch. 14, part 4, para. 2) and matrix signs and lights signals for the control of moving traffic on motorways and dual carriageway roads (sch. 15, part 4, para. 7(2)).

Signs for use only in temporary situations are included in sch. 14.

To prove contravention of a 'Stop' sign, it is necessary to show either that the vehicle did not stop before crossing the line or, if the line is unclear, before entering the major road, or that the vehicle when proceeding past the line or entering the major road, if that line is not clearly visible, did so in a manner likely to cause danger to the driver of another vehicle on the major road or so as to cause that driver to change speed or course so as to avoid an accident (sch. 9, part 7).

C6.27 For contravention of a red light, it is necessary to prove that the vehicle proceeded beyond the stop line. Schedule 14, part 1, para. 5, contains a waiver of the prohibition conveyed by the red light for vehicles used for the purposes listed in para. 5(6), including ambulance, fire brigade or police purposes, and substitutes instead a requirement that the vehicle will not proceed beyond the stop line in such a manner or at such a time as to be likely to endanger any person or to cause the driver of another vehicle to change its speed or course in order to avoid an accident. As to when a vehicle is properly classified as a vehicle used for ambulance purposes, see *DPP v Issler* [2014] EWHC 669 (Admin), [2014] 1 WLR 3686, discussed at **C6.34**. In *Craggy v Chief Constable of Cleveland Police* [2009] EWCA Civ 1128, albeit in a civil context, expecting the driver of an emergency vehicle to drive in such a manner that the driver could stop in the event of another emergency vehicle emerging from the junction was held to impose an unreasonably high burden well beyond what can be expected of a reasonable and prudent driver.

The prohibition contained by 'double white lines' operates not only to prevent the vehicle crossing those lines, but also to forbid vehicles stopping on any length of road along which the marking has been placed. Schedule 9, part 7, para. 9 does, however, contain certain exemptions for vehicles which have to cross the line for the purposes of obtaining access or to pass a stationary vehicle, to enable passengers to board and alight, and so forth. Stopping within double white lines to pick up a taxi fare is not an offence (*McKenzie v DPP* [1997] RTR 175).

Where there was a failure to place a white arrow before solid double white lines in the centre of the road the lines were not a sign 'lawfully placed' for the purposes of the regulations and directions then in force and failure to comply with the double white lines was, therefore, not an offence contrary to s. 36 of the RTA 1988 (*O'Halloran v DPP* [1990] RTR 62).

Punishment

C6.28 The offence carries a fine up to level 3. If committed in respect of a motor vehicle by a failure to comply with a specified sign (see **C6.26**), disqualification is discretionary, but endorsement with three penalty points is obligatory. The *Magistrates' Court Sentencing Guidelines* (see Supplement, **SG10-108**) give fine band A as the starting point. A fixed penalty of £100 is available for this offence.

USING VEHICLE IN DANGEROUS CONDITION

C6.29

Road Traffic Act 1988, s. 40A

(1) A person is guilty of an offence if he uses, or causes or permits another to use, a motor vehicle or trailer on a road when—
(a) the condition of the motor vehicle or trailer, or of its accessories or equipment, or
(b) the purpose for which it is used, or
(c) the number of passengers carried by it, or the manner in which they are carried, or
(d) the weight, position or distribution of its load, or the manner in which it is secured,
is such that the use of the motor vehicle or trailer involves a danger of injury to any person.

Elements

C6.30 The RTOA 1988, ss. 11 and 12(1), apply; see **C2.17** and **C2.18**. For the meaning of the terms 'using', 'causing' and 'permitting' see **C1.28**, **C1.23**, and **C1.25**. The RTOA 1988, ss. 14 and

17, make provision about the admissibility of authenticated records as evidence of matters stated therein and of evidence relating to weights and dates of manufacture being presumed to be accurately marked on vehicles.

Section 40A puts into statute the more important construction and use requirements and widens the scope of their operation. For example, if the circumstances applying in *Young and CF Abraham (Transport) Ltd v CPS* [1992] RTR 194 (see **C6.35**) were to be repeated, s. 40A(d) would apply. Where a passenger is carried in the rear of a van and there are no seats or restraints of any kind there, the speed at which the van is driven will be a material consideration in relation to whether the manner of carriage is such as to involve a danger of injury under s. 40A(c) (*Akelis v Normand* 1997 SLT 136). Section 40A(c) involves considering objectively whether there was a danger inherent in the circumstances in which the vehicle was being driven at the material time (*Gray v DPP* [1999] RTR 339). Accordingly, when assessing that danger, justices can take into account the locality of the offence and the prevailing traffic conditions but must disregard any consequences, such as a serious accident, of the driving involved (*DPP v Potts* [2000] RTR 1). In *R (Vehicle and Operator Services Agency) v Henderson* [2004] EWHC 3118 (Admin), where the wheel nuts on a 32-tonne lorry were so loose that they could be removed by hand, the Divisional Court held that s. 40A is an offence of strict liability in that it is unnecessary for the prosecution to prove any state of mind on the part of the person using the motor vehicle in that condition. The magistrates must ask, as a matter of fact, whether D used the vehicle when its condition involved a danger of injury to any person. The danger may be to the driver, or any other road-user, and the statute does not require that the danger be imminent, merely that it exists. In this case the wheel was a danger before it became an imminent danger because its condition could deteriorate rapidly and unpredictably.

Punishment

The offence is endorsable with three penalty points; disqualification is discretionary. In respect of a second offence committed within three years of a previous s. 40A offence, in the absence of 'special reasons', disqualification for six months is obligatory, although for other offences it will remain discretionary only (Road Safety Act 2006, s. 25(1)). However, the RTOA 1988, s. 48(1), forbids the court from disqualifying or ordering any penalty points to be ordered if the defendant proves that the defendant did not know, and had no reasonable cause to suspect, that the use of the vehicle involved a danger of injury to any person. Where the offence is committed in respect of a goods vehicle or a vehicle adapted to carry more than eight passengers, the level of fine which may be imposed is unlimited; in other cases, a fine up to level 4 may be imposed. The *Magistrates' Court Sentencing Guidelines* (see Supplement, **SG10-107**) must generally be followed; they apply to the various offences covered and explain the appropriate starting points for fine bands, differentiating between drivers, driver-owners and owner-companies. A fixed penalty of £100 is available for this offence. **C6.31**

CONTRAVENTION OF CONSTRUCTION AND USE REGULATIONS

Road Traffic Act 1988, s. 41A **C6.32**

(1) A person who—
  (a) contravenes or fails to comply with a construction and use requirement as to brakes, steering-gear or tyres, or
  (b) uses on a road a motor vehicle or trailer which does not comply with such a requirement, or causes or permits a motor vehicle or trailer to be so used, is guilty of an offence.

Section 41B makes contravention of a requirement in relation to the weight of a goods vehicle or a passenger vehicle adapted to carry more than eight passengers an offence. It is a defence if the vehicle is proceeding to or from the nearest available weighbridge, which means the nearest one factually, irrespective of the driver's knowledge of its existence (*Vehicle and Operator Services Agency v F & S Gibbs Transport Services Ltd* [2006] EWHC 1109 (Admin), [2007] RTR 17 (193)). In addition a 5 per cent excess may be excluded in certain circumstances. It is not essential for a certificate as to the accuracy of the weighbridge to be produced provided there is other evidence from which its accuracy can be ascertained (*Kelly Communications Ltd v DPP* [2002] EWHC 2752 (Admin), (2003) 167 JP 73).

When the Road Safety Act 2006, s. 18, is brought into force, a new offence under the RTA 1988, s. 41C, will be created prohibiting vehicles being fitted with, or a person using a vehicle carrying, 'speed assessment equipment detection devices', which are devices 'the purpose, or one of the purposes, of which is to detect, or interfere with the operation of, equipment used to assess the speed of motor vehicles'.

Section 42 makes contravention of the other construction and use requirements an offence and extends this to cover 'using', 'causing' or 'permitting'.

Mobile Telephones, etc.

C6.33 The RTA 1988, s. 41D, deals specifically with a contravention or failure to comply with a requirement about not driving a motor vehicle in a position which does not give proper control or a full view of the road or traffic ahead or not driving, or supervising the driving, of a motor vehicle while using a hand-held mobile telephone or other hand-held interactive communication device. The offence extends to 'causing' or 'permitting' (see **C1.23** and **C1.25**). The principal reason for carving out such a specific offence was to make endorsement with penalty points obligatory and disqualification discretionary, thereby raising its seriousness closer to the alternative of charging driving without due care and attention.

Elements

C6.34 The RTOA 1988, ss. 11 and 12(1), apply to the RTA 1988, ss. 41A, 41B, 41D and 42 (and, in due course, will apply to the RTA 1988, s. 41C); see **C2.17** and **C2.18**. For the meaning of the terms 'using', 'causing' and 'permitting', see **C1.28**, **C1.23**, and **C1.25**. The relevant requirements are those contained in the Road Vehicles (Construction and Use) Regulations 1986 (SI 1986 No. 1078).

In order to show that a vehicle does not fall within any of the definitions contained either in the regulations or the Act, the burden of proof is on the defendant (*Wakeman v Catlow* [1977] RTR 174). To qualify as a motor vehicle used for ambulance purposes, the vehicle used 'must at the very least be capable of conveying sick, injured or disabled persons and do so with such frequency that this core activity may fairly and properly be designated as its primary use' (*DPP v Issler* [2014] EWHC 669 (Admin), [2014] 1 WLR 3686).

C6.35 Regulations 13 to 18 and sch. 3 deal with brakes. Even if a trailer is not required to have brakes under reg. 18, any brakes fitted must be maintained in efficient working order (*DPP v Young* [1991] RTR 56). Regulation 27 deals with tyres.

Regulation 100 deals with vehicles which are in a dangerous condition and loads which cause a danger. See the RTA 1988, s. 42(2), for a statutory defence to a summons alleging a failure to comply with a requirement relating to any description of weight applicable to a goods vehicle. In *Young and CF Abraham (Transport) Ltd v CPS* [1992] RTR 194, a trailer loaded with an excavator collided with a footbridge because the excavator arms and bucket had not been lowered. The driver and the company were prosecuted for using a trailer for an unsuitable purpose 'as to cause or be likely to cause danger or nuisance to any person . . . on a road'. The Divisional Court decided that the risk came from the incorrect loading rather than the use of the trailer and that, in such circumstances, the offence was not made out.

In respect of an offence under the RTA 1988, s. 41D, reg. 110 imposes a range of restrictions involving driving-related activities that cannot be undertaken whilst the person is using a hand-held mobile telephone or a prescribed hand-held device. In *DPP v Barreto* [2019] EWHC 2044 (Admin), [2020] 1 Cr App R 6 (142), which related to D filming the scene of a collision using the camera function on a mobile telephone while driving, it was held that this did not contravene reg. 110 and constitute the offence under the RTA 1988, s. 41D, because the 'using' to which that prohibition refers is confined to using the interactive communication function of the device. Regulation 110(5) contains specific exceptions for calls to the emergency services, where it is a response to a genuine emergency and if it would be unsafe or impracticable to cease the driving-related activity before making the call, and reg. 110(5A) adds a further exemption when using the device to perform a remote parking manoeuvre in compliance with the conditions specified in relation thereto.

Punishment

A breach of s. 41A is endorsable with three penalty points; disqualification is discretionary. However, the RTOA 1988, s. 48(2), forbids the court to disqualify or order any penalty points if the defence prove the defendant did not know, and had no reasonable cause to suspect, that the facts of the case were such that the offence would be committed. Where an offence is committed in respect of a goods vehicle or a vehicle adapted to carry more than eight passengers, the level of fine which may be imposed is unlimited; in other cases, a fine up to level 4. A fixed penalty of £200 is available. **C6.36**

Breaches of s. 41B or 42 are not endorsable. Section 41B carries an unlimited fine and graduated fixed penalties (see **C7.3**) are applicable to various offences thereunder, up to a maximum of £300. Section 42 carries a fine up to level 4 if committed in respect of a goods vehicle or a vehicle adapted to carry more than eight passengers; in other cases, a fine of up to level 3.

The s. 41D(b) offence of using a hand-held mobile telephone or other device is endorsable with six penalty points and a fixed penalty of £200 is available. The other s. 41D offences are endorsable with three penalty points and a fixed penalty of £100 is available. In all cases disqualification is discretionary. Where an offence is committed in respect of a goods vehicle or a vehicle adapted to carry more than eight passengers, a fine up to level 4 may be imposed; in other cases, a fine up to level 3.

Breach of s. 41C (not yet in force) will be subject to the same penalty as a speeding offence, i.e. it is endorsable with between three and six penalty points or three points when a fixed penalty is imposed. It will carry a fine up to level 4 if committed on a special road (such as a motorway); in other cases, a fine up to level 3.

The *Magistrates' Court Sentencing Guidelines* (see Supplement, **SG10-107** and **SG10-108**) must generally be followed; they apply to the various offences covered and explain the appropriate starting points for fine bands, differentiating between drivers, driver-owners and owner-companies.

DRIVING OTHERWISE THAN IN ACCORDANCE WITH A LICENCE

Road Traffic Act 1988, s. 87 **C6.37**

(1) It is an offence for a person to drive on a road a motor vehicle of any class otherwise than in accordance with a licence authorising him to drive a motor vehicle of that class.
(2) It is an offence for a person to cause or permit another person to drive on a road a motor vehicle of any class otherwise than in accordance with a licence authorising that other person to drive a motor vehicle of that class.

This offence encompasses driving without 'L' plates or (an alternative applicable only within Wales) 'D' plates, without supervision, driving under age and driving without a licence.

Elements

The RTOA 1988, ss. 11 and 12(1), apply; see **C2.17** and **C2.18**. For the meaning of 'cause' and 'permit', see **C1.23** and **C1.25**. **C6.38**

Section 88 of the RTA 1988 creates certain exceptions. The approach to proof is the same as for the offence of no insurance (see **C6.47**).

Drivers with licences issued by foreign countries are subject to the Motor Vehicles (International Circulation) Order 1975 (SI 1975 No. 1208). If a person resident abroad and temporarily resident in Great Britain holds a Convention driving permit, a foreign driving permit or a British Forces (BFG) driving licence, it shall be lawful for that person to drive during a period of 12 months from the person's last entry into the UK (unless the person is under the minimum age or disqualified by court order). A Community licence holder normally resident in Great Britain is not obliged to exchange the licence issued by that other country for one issued under the RTA 1988 so as to obtain continuing authorisation to drive (s. 99A of the Act), the only requirement being to deliver the Community licence within 12 months to the Secretary of State and provide certain information (s. 99B of the Act).

Punishment

C6.39 The offence carries a fine up to level 3. If the offender's driving would not have been in accordance with a licence that could have been granted, then, in the absence of 'special reasons', disqualification is discretionary and endorsement with between three and six penalty points is obligatory. A fixed penalty of £100 is available.

An offence of causing or permitting a person to drive without an appropriate licence contrary to s. 87(2) is punishable only by a fine up to level 3 on the standard scale. The *Magistrates' Court Sentencing Guidelines* (see Supplement, **SG10-106**) give fine band A as the starting point and note that if no licence has ever been held that is an aggravating factor.

DRIVING WHILE DISQUALIFIED

C6.40 Road Traffic Act 1988, s. 103

(1) A person is guilty of an offence if, while disqualified for holding or obtaining a licence, he—
  (a) obtains a licence, or
  (b) drives a motor vehicle on a road.
(2) A licence obtained by a person who is disqualified is of no effect (or, where the disqualification relates only to vehicles of a particular class, is of no effect in relation to vehicles of that class).
(3) [Repealed.]
(4) Subsection (1) above does not apply in relation to disqualification by virtue of section 101 of this Act.
(5) Subsection (1)(b) above does not apply in relation to disqualification by virtue of section 102 of this Act.
(6) In the application of subsection (1) above to a person whose disqualification is limited to the driving of motor vehicles of a particular class by virtue of—
  (a) section 102, 117 or 117A of this Act, or
  (b) subsection (9) of section 36 of the Road Traffic Offenders Act 1988 (disqualification until test is passed),

the references to disqualification for holding or obtaining a licence and driving motor vehicles are references to disqualification for holding or obtaining a licence to drive and driving motor vehicles of that class.

Elements

C6.41 In the absence of duress, the RTA 1988, s. 103(1)(b), creates an offence of strict liability. It is usual to produce either the register of the magistrates' court where the defendant was disqualified, or a properly certified extract. A conviction may be proved under the PACE 1984, s. 73, by the production of a certificate signed by the clerk of the court. (As to the proof of convictions generally, see **F12.1** *et seq.*) Other authorised methods of proving the conviction are equally admissible, but it is not necessary to prove that the defendant knew of the disqualification (*Taylor v Kenyon* [1952] 2 All ER 726). The disqualification may be one imposed in the Republic of Ireland in respect of which notification has been given in accordance with the

Agreement on the Mutual Recognition of Driving Disqualifications (CJCA 2015, s. 31 and sch. 7; SI 2017 No. 189).

In *Derwentside Justices, ex parte Heaviside* [1996] RTR 384, the Divisional Court held that strict proof linking the defendant to the person named in the certificate of conviction is required. In doing so, it identified three methods by which this requirement could be satisfied: an admission under the CJA 1967, s. 10; comparison of fingerprints; or evidence from a person who was present in court when the disqualification was imposed. The fear that this list was exhaustive was allayed by subsequent decisions of the Divisional Court (*Derwentside Justices, ex parte Swift* [1997] RTR 89; *DPP v Mansfield* [1997] RTR 96; *DPP v Mooney* [1997] RTR 434). Consequently, whilst strict proof is necessary (and failure by the prosecution to adduce any such evidence cannot be cured by information provided by the clerk to the court from computerised court records (*R (Kingsnorth) v DPP* [2003] EWHC 768 (Admin)), the prosecution can rely on any admissible evidence from which it could properly be concluded that the defendant and the individual named in the certificate are one and the same person, and the issue is one for the court to determine on the basis of the evidence placed before it. For example, admissions in an interview with the police provide sufficient evidence (*Moran v CPS* (2000) 164 JP 562). Where the defendant has an unusual name, proof that it is identical to that of a person previously disqualified raises a prima facie case that the defendant is that disqualified person (*Olakunori v DPP* [1998] COD 443), especially if the person has also lied about the person's identity. Even where the personal details of the defendant are not uncommon, a match with those recorded on the certificate of conviction establishes a prima facie case which, in the absence of any contradictory evidence, will be sufficient for the court to convict (*Pattison v DPP* [2005] EWHC 2938 (Admin), [2006] 2 All ER 317).

In *Thames Magistrates' Court, ex parte Levy* (1997) *The Times*, 17 July 1997, it was confirmed that the offence of driving while disqualified can be committed during a period of disqualification which is not suspended pending an appeal (see the RTOA 1988, s. 39, and **C7.40**), even where the conviction which led to the disqualification is subsequently quashed (see also *RD* [2019] EWCA Crim 1545). Similarly, the offence can be committed in the period between disqualification following conviction and the swearing of a statutory declaration under the MCA 1980, s. 14, as the earlier proceedings become void from the time of the declaration and not *ab initio* (*Singh v DPP* [1999] RTR 424). **C6.42**

Where a person has been disqualified until a test is passed, under the RTOA 1988, s. 36, failure to comply with the conditions of a provisional driving licence is an offence under s. 103(1)(b). This would seem to be the case whether or not the defendant has actually obtained such a licence (*Scott v Jelf* [1974] RTR 256). The defendant bears the burden of showing that a provisional licence is held and that the defendant was complying with the conditions attached to it at the time of the driving in question (*DPP v Baker* [2004] EWHC 2502 (Admin), (2004) 168 JP 617). For the purposes of s. 103, such disqualifications persist regardless of whether elements of the original sentence would enable the offence in respect of which disqualification was imposed to be regarded as spent (*Re Hamill* [2001] EWHC Admin 762).

If a defendant drives on a 'road', his mistaken belief that it was not a road is incapable of amounting to a defence (*Miller* [1975] 2 All ER 974).

Aiding and abetting the offence of driving while disqualified requires knowledge of the disqualification; this may be actual or constructive, in the sense that the defendant failed to make inquiries which a reasonable person should have made, or deliberately ignored the possibility of the driver being disqualified (*Pope v Minton* [1954] Crim LR 711; *Bateman v Evans* [1964] Crim LR 601).

Defences

Duress or necessity may provide a defence in the proper circumstances. See **A3.35** to **A3.52**. **C6.43**

Indictment

C6.44 The CJA 1988 made the offence summary only, but provides in s. 40 (see **D11.17**) for certain circumstances where it may be included in an indictment and that thereafter it 'shall be tried in the same manner as if it were an indictable offence'. Consequently, the offence is no longer an 'indictable offence' within the meaning of the CAA 1981 (see **A5.72**), and the offence of attempting to drive while disqualified has ceased to exist.

Punishment

C6.45 The maximum sentence is six months' imprisonment and/or an unlimited fine. Disqualification is discretionary but endorsement is obligatory. The offence carries six penalty points. Forfeiture of the vehicle used may also be ordered (see **E18.1**). The *Magistrates' Court Sentencing Guidelines* (see Supplement, **SG10-72**) must generally be followed; the guidelines explain how to assess the category applicable to the offence by reference to culpability and harm and provide examples of aggravating and mitigating factors. The sentencing ranges overlap, but only the most serious category states a custodial sentence as being the starting point. See *Pegrum* (1986) 8 Cr App R (S) 27 for a case in which the maximum term of imprisonment (then one year) was upheld. There is nothing wrong in principle in imposing a consecutive sentence to that imposed for another offence arising out of the same incident, e.g., aggravated vehicle-taking (*Forbes* [2005] EWCA Crim 2069).

USING ETC. MOTOR VEHICLE WITHOUT INSURANCE

C6.46 **Road Traffic Act 1988, s. 143**

(1) Subject to the provisions of this Part of this Act—
  (a) a person must not use a motor vehicle on a road or other public place unless there is in force in relation to the use of the vehicle by that person such a policy of insurance as complies with the requirements of this Part of this Act, and
  (b) a person must not cause or permit any other person to use a motor vehicle on a road or other public place unless there is in force in relation to the use of the vehicle by that other person such a policy of insurance as complies with the requirements of this Part of this Act.
(2) If a person acts in contravention of subsection (1) above he is guilty of an offence.
(3) A person charged with using a motor vehicle in contravention of this section shall not be convicted if he proves—
  (a) that the vehicle did not belong to him and was not in his possession under a contract of hiring or of loan,
  (b) that he was using the vehicle in the course of his employment, and
  (c) that he neither knew nor had reason to believe that there was not in force in relation to the vehicle such a policy of insurance as is mentioned in subsection (1) above.
(4) This Part of this Act does not apply to invalid carriages.

Elements

C6.47 The RTOA 1988, ss. 6, 11, and 12(1), apply; see **C2.5**, **C2.17** and **C2.18**. For the meaning of the terms 'use', 'cause' and 'permit', see **C1.28**, **C1.23** and **C1.25**.

The burden of proof rests on the defendant, who is therefore required to produce evidence of a valid insurance policy (*DPP v Kavaz* [1999] RTR 40), whether or not there has been any requirement to produce this under the pro forma HORT/1 or otherwise (*DPP v Hay* [2005] EWHC 1395 (Admin), [2006] RTR 3 (32)). Once a certificate is produced, the burden shifts back to the prosecution where the allegation is that the use of the vehicle extends beyond the terms of the policy, e.g., it is being used for business purposes when the policy is limited to social and domestic purposes (*DPP v Whittaker* [2015] EWHC 1850 (Admin), [2016] 1 WLR 1035).

For the owner of a vehicle to be convicted of using without insurance when it was being driven by someone else, it has to be proved that the defendant owned the vehicle and that the driver at the time was employed by the owner and was, at the material time, acting in the course of the driver's employment (*Jones v DPP* [1999] RTR 1).

The section imposes strict liability irrespective of knowledge, even if the charge is for 'causing' or 'permitting' (*Lyons v May* [1948] 2 All ER 1062; *Tapsell v Maslen* [1967] Crim LR 53). However, if the person who allows the use of a vehicle does so on the express condition that the user insures it, that person is not 'permitting' the uninsured use of the vehicle within the meaning of s. 143 (*Newbury v Davis* [1974] RTR 367). That case, however, appears to be confined to its own facts. In *DPP v Fisher* [1992] RTR 93, the Divisional Court declined to follow *Newbury* where the driver of the vehicle was not in communication directly with the owner even though the owner only authorised the use of the vehicle by a suitably insured person. Conditional authorisation amounts to permission.

Section 144 of the RTA 1988 contains certain exceptions. The requirements of a policy of insurance are set out in the RTA 1988, s. 145.

By s. 161, 'policy of insurance' includes a covering note. By s. 147(1), a policy of insurance is of no effect under s. 143 until delivered to the party by whom the policy is effected. The burden is on the defendant to prove the facts necessary to establish the statutory defence for employees in s. 143(3).

A policy of insurance obtained by misrepresentation or non-disclosure of material facts is not a 'policy of insurance' for the purposes of the RTA 1930, s. 36(4) (*Guardian Assurance Co. Ltd v Sutherland* [1939] 2 All ER 246, per Branson J). A voidable policy does, however, satisfy the requirements of s. 143 until it is avoided (*Durrant v MacLaren* [1956] 2 Lloyd's Rep 70; *Adams v Dunne* [1978] RTR 281). **C6.48**

Payment of petrol money on a regular 'school run' which went beyond the bounds of mere social kindness may bring the vehicle (if it is adapted to carry more than eight passengers) within the meaning of the term 'public service vehicle' (*DPP v Sikondar* [1993] RTR 90). This may in turn vitiate a policy of insurance so as to bring the driver within the ambit of s. 143.

Punishment

Disqualification is discretionary, but endorsement with between six and eight penalty points is obligatory. The level of fine which may be imposed is unlimited. A fixed penalty of £300 is available (Fixed Penalty Offences Order 2003 (SI 2003 No. 1253)). The *Magistrates' Court Sentencing Guidelines* (see Supplement, **SG10-114**) must generally be followed; the guidelines indicate starting points to be considered by reference to culpability and harm and provide examples of aggravating and mitigating factors. *Cox* [2018] EWCA Crim 1871 provides an example of a significant reduction from 12 months to two months for a category 1 offence. **C6.49**

KEEPING VEHICLE NOT MEETING INSURANCE REQUIREMENTS

The RTA 1988, s. 144A, concerns the offence of keeping a vehicle which does not meet the insurance requirements (as defined therein). The offence is designed to ensure so far as possible that all relevant vehicles are covered by appropriate minimum levels of insurance. Various exceptions to the requirement are established under s. 144B and in the Motor Vehicles (Insurance Requirements) Regulations 2011 (SI 2011 No. 20), which also deal with disclosure of information by the Motor Insurers' Information Centre and the availability of a fixed penalty. The offence is not endorsable. **C6.50**

FAILING TO STOP AND FAILING TO REPORT ACCIDENT

C6.51 **Road Traffic Act 1988, s. 170**

(1) This section applies in a case where, owing to the presence of a mechanically propelled vehicle on a road or other public place, an accident occurs by which—
(a) personal injury is caused to a person other than the driver of that mechanically propelled vehicle, or
(b) damage is caused—
(i) to a vehicle other than that mechanically propelled vehicle or a trailer drawn by that mechanically propelled vehicle, or
(ii) to an animal other than an animal in or on that mechanically propelled vehicle or a trailer drawn by that mechanically propelled vehicle, or
(iii) to any other property constructed on, fixed to, growing in or otherwise forming part of the land on which the road or place in question is situated or land adjacent to such land.

(2) The driver of the mechanically propelled vehicle must stop and, if required to do so by any person having reasonable grounds for so requiring, give his name and address and also the name and address of the owner and the identification marks of the vehicle.

(3) If for any reason the driver of the mechanically propelled vehicle does not give his name and address under subsection (2) above, he must report the accident.

(4) A person who fails to comply with subsection (2) or (3) above is guilty of an offence.

(5) If, in a case where this section applies by virtue of subsection (1)(a) above, the driver of a motor vehicle does not at the time of the accident produce such a certificate of insurance or other evidence, as is mentioned in section 165(2)(a) of this Act—
(a) to a constable, or
(b) to some person who, having reasonable grounds for so doing, has required him to produce it, the driver must report the accident and produce such a certificate or other evidence.
This subsection does not apply to the driver of an invalid carriage.

(6) To comply with a duty under this section to report an accident or to produce such a certificate of insurance or other evidence, as is mentioned in section 165(2)(a) of this Act, the driver—
(a) must do so at a police station or to a constable, and
(b) must do so as soon as is reasonably practicable and, in any case, within 24 hours of the occurrence of the accident.

(7) A person who fails to comply with a duty under subsection (5) above is guilty of an offence, but he shall not be convicted by reason only of a failure to produce a certificate or other evidence if, within seven days after the occurrence of the accident, the certificate or other evidence is produced at a police station that was specified by him at the time when the accident was reported.

(8) In this section 'animal' means horse, cattle, ass, mule, sheep, pig, goat or dog.

Elements

C6.52 For the meaning of the terms 'accident', 'driver' and 'vehicle', see **C1.1**, **C1.2** and **C1.18**.

The RTOA 1988, ss. 11 and 12(1), apply; see **C2.17** and **C2.18**.

Section 170(2) creates one offence which may be committed in a number of different ways. Section 170(3) creates a separate offence, as does s. 170(7) (*DPP v Bennett* [1993] RTR 175). In *R (Parker) v Crown Court at Bradford* [2006] EWHC 3213 (Admin), [2007] RTR 30 (369), an attempt to challenge the insertion in s. 170(1) of 'or other public place' by the Motor Vehicles (Compulsory Insurance) Regulations 2000 (SI 2000 No. 726) (since revoked) was unsuccessful.

The object of s. 170 is to identify the parties involved for the purposes of both civil and criminal proceedings. To that end, it is a question of fact whether providing the name and address of a third party satisfies the requirements of the section (*DPP v McCarthy* [1999] RTR 323); in that case, the driver provided his name and the address of his solicitors, which was found to be sufficient. It is not necessary for the motor vehicle to be directly involved with the accident, but the prosecution must establish causation because of the presence of the defendant's motor vehicle on the road (*Quelch v Phipps* [1955] 2 QB 107). Nor is it necessary for the driver to be physically present in the vehicle at the time of the accident (provided being outside the vehicle does not terminate the act of 'driving': see **C1.2** and **C1.5**) (*Cawthorn v DPP* [2000] RTR 45).

In *Harding v Price* [1948] 1 KB 695, it was established that where a driver is unaware of an accident, the driver cannot be aware of a duty to stop or report and is entitled to be acquitted. When it is sought to establish this, the onus of proof rests on the defendant (see also *Hampson v Powell* [1970] 1 All ER 929).

Following such an accident as is mentioned in s. 170(1), the driver is obliged to remain at the scene for a reasonable time so that the driver's obligations under s. 170(2) can be fulfilled (*Lee v Knapp* [1967] 2 QB 442; *Ward v Rawson* [1978] RTR 498). The obligation does not extend to searching out persons who might be entitled to the information required under s. 170(2) (*Mutton v Bates* [1984] RTR 256).

Whether the vehicle is stopped at the appropriate point is a question of fact; where a driver chose to drive on for 80 yards before stopping and returning to the scene of the accident, the Divisional Court was not prepared to interfere with a decision finding that this constituted a failure to stop as required, because it could not be said to be one which no court, properly directing itself upon the law, could rationally have arrived at (*McDermott v DPP* [1997] RTR 474). Under s. 170(2), a driver is required to stop immediately so that witnesses might make themselves known and any person wishing to request the driver's particulars might do so (*Hallinan v DPP* [1998] Crim LR 754). The requirement to stop imposed by the RTA 1988, s. 170, arises almost immediately the relevant event takes place and so the offence is complete as soon as the failure to do so occurs. Consequently, in *Attwater* [2010] EWCA Crim 2399, [2011] RTR 12 (173), it was confirmed that, once that moment has passed, the driver in question is no longer committing an offence and the use of force envisaged by the CJA 1967, s. 3 (to prevent an offence being committed), cannot be relied upon as a defence. C6.53

Partial compliance with the requirements will not suffice, but if a driver has stopped and has not been required to provide any or all of the details mentioned in s. 170(2), the driver will fulfil the obligation, subject, however, to a duty to report the accident in the manner prescribed by s. 170(6) if there has been no provision of the driver's name and address. The obligation to report an accident under s. 170(3) therefore exists whenever the driver's name and address have not been provided.

In *DPP v Drury* [1989] RTR 165, it was held that a driver who is not aware of an accident but who subsequently becomes aware of it, must report the accident to a police station personally if becoming aware within 24 hours of the accident occurring. Reporting an accident by telephone is insufficient, and the obligation appears to be one that must, in the absence of physical impossibility, be performed personally (*Wisdom v Macdonald* [1983] RTR 186). The obligations under s. 170 are not negated by police attendance at the scene of the accident and the defendant being conveyed to hospital (*DPP v Hay* [2005] EWHC 1395 (Admin), [2006] RTR 3 (32)).

In an accident involving more than one other person or vehicle, the driver may be required to provide details to a number of people, and failure to provide those details to anyone who has reasonable grounds for requiring them is an offence. If, however, the driver has furnished particulars, including name and address, to at least one person and has satisfied all other requests made, then it is suggested the driver is not obliged to report the accident in the manner prescribed by s. 170(6), unless personal injury has been caused to someone other than the driver. C6.54

Where personal injury is caused to anyone other than the driver of the vehicle, the driver must produce the driver's insurance certificate (or such other documentation as would satisfy s. 165(2)(a) of the Act) at the time of the accident either to a constable or any other person who has reasonable grounds for requesting its production. If the driver does not produce insurance (or such other documentation as would satisfy s. 165(2)(a) of the Act), either because the driver was not able to or was not so required, the accident must be reported in the manner prescribed by s. 170(6).

Punishment

An offence under s. 170(4) is punishable with up to six months' imprisonment and/or an unlimited fine. Disqualification is discretionary but endorsement, with between five and ten penalty points, C6.55

is obligatory. Forfeiture of the vehicle concerned may also be ordered (see **E18.1**). The *Magistrates' Court Sentencing Guidelines* (see Supplement, **SG10-95**) must generally be followed.

PEDESTRIAN CROSSING REGULATIONS

C6.56 The RTRA 1984, s. 25, enables the Secretary of State to make regulations in respect of vehicles and pedestrians at and in the vicinity of crossings. The current regulations are in the Traffic Signs Regulations and General Directions 2016 (SI 2016 No. 362, as amended by SI 2017 No. 1086). There is a saving at reg. 14(5) for Pelican crossings complying with the requirements of the revoked 1997 Regulations (SI 1997 No. 2400). Contravention of the regulations is an offence punishable by a fine up to level 3 on the standard scale. Disqualification when a motor vehicle is involved is discretionary, but endorsement with three penalty points is obligatory. The regulations apply to all vehicles. The *Magistrates' Court Sentencing Guidelines* (see Supplement, **SG10-108**) give fine band A as the starting point.

FAILING TO STOP AT SCHOOL CROSSING

C6.57 The RTRA 1984, s. 28, creates specific offences of failing to comply with a stop sign exhibited by a uniformed school crossing patrol and causing a vehicle to be put in motion so long as the sign continues to be exhibited. The sign is prescribed by the Traffic Signs Regulations and General Directions 2016 (SI 2016 No. 362) (see, in particular, reg. 3(2) and sch. 14, part 2). The driver of a motor vehicle must stop unless the sign has been removed by the time the vehicle arrives at the crossing (*Franklin v Langdown* [1971] 3 All ER 662). A fine up to level 3 on the standard scale may be imposed. Disqualification when a motor vehicle is involved is discretionary, but endorsement with three penalty points is obligatory.

SPEEDING

C6.58 **Road Traffic Regulation Act 1984, s. 89**

(1) A person who drives a motor vehicle on a road at a speed exceeding a limit imposed by or under any enactment to which this section applies shall be guilty of an offence.
(2) A person prosecuted for such an offence shall not be liable to be convicted solely on the evidence of one witness to the effect that, in the opinion of the witness, the person prosecuted was driving the vehicle at a speed exceeding a specified limit.
(3) The enactments to which this section applies are—
  (a) any enactment contained in this Act except section 17(2);
  (b) section 2 of the Parks Regulation (Amendment) Act 1926; and
  (c) any enactment not contained in this Act, but passed after 1 September 1960, whether before or after the passing of this Act.
(4) If a person who employs other persons to drive motor vehicles on roads publishes or issues any timetable or schedule, or gives any directions, under which any journey, or any stage or part of any journey, is to be completed within some specified time, and it is not practicable in the circumstances of the case for that journey (or that stage or part of it) to be completed in the specified time without the commission of such an offence as is mentioned in subsection (1) above, the publication or issue of the timetable or schedule, or the giving of the directions, may be produced as prima facie evidence that the employer procured or (as the case may be) incited the persons employed by him to drive the vehicle to commit such an offence.

Elements

C6.59 The section applies only to 'motor vehicles', see **C1.9**. The RTOA 1988, ss. 1, 11 and 12(1) apply; see **C2.1**, **C2.17** and **C2.18**.

Depending on the context and circumstances, driving at grossly excessive speed might constitute dangerous driving (see **C3.11**).

Section 87 of the 1984 Act exempts motor vehicles being used for fire service, police or ambulance purposes (the latter extending to a vehicle responding to an emergency at the request of an NHS ambulance service), if observance of the speed limit would be likely to hinder the purpose for which they are being used. Where a vehicle is not constructed, adapted or used for the purpose of conveying sick, injured or disabled persons, it may not be an ambulance benefiting from this exemption (*Ashton v CPS* [2005] EWHC 2729 (Admin); *Lord-Castle v DPP* [2009] EWHC 87 (Admin); *DPP v Issler* [2014] EWHC 609 (Admin), [2014] 1 WLR 3686 and see **C6.34**). When the Road Safety Act 2006, s. 19, is brought into force, it will substitute a new s. 87, which will enable the coverage to include additional purposes whilst limiting the exemption to drivers who have satisfactorily completed an appropriate course of training.

Incorrectly sited speed restriction signs will not invalidate the speed limit imposed by a relevant enactment (*Wawrzynczyk v Chief Constable of Staffordshire Constabulary* (2000) *The Times*, 16 March 2000), provided no doubt that they sufficiently advise drivers of that speed limit in the location of the alleged offence and do not mislead. At the geographical point where the motorist exceeds the speed limit, the requisite signs must be capable of conveying the reduced limit to the motorist in sufficient time to enable the reduction from a previously lawful speed to within the new limit, which will not be the case if the signs are obscured by overgrown hedgerows (*Coombes v DPP* [2006] EWHC 3263 (Admin), [2007] RTR 31 (383)).

The specific defence available in respect of inadequate signage applies only where the road is not a restricted one by reason of the system of street lighting (*Humber v DPP* [2008] EWHC 2932 (Admin)). The requirement for the prosecution to adduce evidence demonstrating compliance with the Traffic Signs Regulations and General Directions 2002 (now revoked and replaced by the 2016 measure (SI 2016 No. 362, as amended by SI 2017 No. 1086)) was confirmed in *DPP v Butler* [2010] EWHC 669 (Admin), where a terminal speed limit sign located within 50 metres of a street lamp was not illuminated, as required, in darkness. However, in order to secure a conviction, there is no requirement that all the signage in the whole area to which a limit applies is compliant, provided that there is adequate compliant signage providing guidance as to the speed limit to be observed in the road leading up to the point of enforcement (*Peake v DPP* [2010] EWHC 286 (Admin), [2011] RTR 3 (33)). Where there is more than *de minimis* non-compliance with the statutory obligations relating to signage, the court needs to engage in a balancing exercise, weighing the public interest in setting and enforcing speed limits and the protections afforded to motorists and assessing whether adequate guidance has been given about the speed limit to be observed at the point on the road where the offence occurs (*Jones v DPP* [2011] EWHC 50 (Admin), [2012] RTR 3 (19)). **C6.60**

If it is alleged that the road in question is a restricted road by reason of the street lighting being no more than 200 yards apart and the defendant puts the prosecution to strict proof, such proof must be provided (*Martin v Harrow Crown Court* [2007] EWHC 3193 (Admin)). A traffic authority for a road can make an order that a road that is not a restricted road by reason of the positioning of street lighting shall become a restricted road for the purpose of imposing a 30 mph speed limit (see, e.g., *DPP v Evans* [2004] EWHC 2785 (Admin), (2004) 169 JP 237). In *DPP v Wells* [2007] EWHC 3259 (Admin), [2008] RTR 23 (288), it was held that charging such an offence under s. 89 is permissible even where the offence could alternatively be charged under s. 14 (temporary prohibition or restriction).

Evidence from an approved device is admissible to prove speeding offences under s. 89 (see the RTOA 1988, s. 20 at **C2.21**). Where there is evidence providing reasonable doubt in contradiction to the evidence from an approved device, this may lead to acquittal. In *DPP v Marrable* [2020] EWHC 566 (Admin), the DPP appealed by way of case stated against an acquittal by magistrates for D's speeding charge. The DPP submitted that the magistrates were wrong to have relied upon GPS evidence that indicated D had been travelling at between 53 and 54 mph as opposed to prosecution evidence, from an approved 'Trucam' device, that he had travelled at 72 mph where there was a 50 mph limit. It was held that the GPS evidence was enough to provide a reasonable doubt that D had travelled above the speed limit.

C6.61 Section 89(2) provides a statutory requirement of corroboration. Opinion evidence as to speed is admissible but, because of the danger of inaccuracy inherent in such evidence, it was felt necessary to require corroboration. See generally *Nicholas v Penny* [1950] 2 KB 466 and *Swain v Gillet* [1974] RTR 446. The reading of a police car's speedometer is capable of supplying the necessary corroboration, even if there is no evidence of testing, though the weight of such evidence is open to question (*Swain v Gillet*). It would satisfy the statutory requirement to have the opinion evidence of two or more witnesses, provided that their observations occurred at the same time (*Brighty v Pearson* [1938] 4 All ER 127).

Factual evidence, however, does not require corroboration, and evidence of the speed recorded on the speedometer of a police car, driven at an even distance behind the appellant's car, was held to be sufficient to sustain a conviction (*Nicholas v Penny* [1950] 2 KB 466). The speedometer does not need to be tested, and in the absence of evidence to the contrary can be presumed, as can radar guns, radar speed meters and other mechanical instruments, to be in order at the material time (*Castle v Cross* [1984] 1 All ER 87; *Burton v Gilbert* [1984] RTR 162).

The expert evidence of a 'Collision Investigator', which entails the reconstruction of events from various tests, skid marks and damage, is considered to be based on more than mere opinion where the investigator describes the facts on which the opinion is based (*Crossland v DPP* [1988] 3 All ER 712).

Punishment

C6.62 A fine up to level 3 may be imposed. Disqualification is discretionary. Endorsement, with three penalty points when a fixed penalty is imposed and with between three and six penalty points in any other case, is obligatory. When the Road Safety Act 2006, s. 17, is brought into force, the range of penalty points applicable will increase to between two and six points; the 2006 Act also provides for a range of penalty points when a fixed penalty is imposed (see C7.3). Special reasons may be capable of being advanced, e.g., when driving too quickly to deal with an emergency situation (see C7.58). The *Magistrates' Court Sentencing Guidelines* (see Supplement, **SG10-133**) must generally be followed; the guidelines indicate starting points to be considered by reference to the speed recorded relative to the limit in question and provide examples of aggravating and mitigating factors.

Section C7 Sentencing

GENERAL PRINCIPLES

Fines and Imprisonment

The RTOA 1988, s. 33, provides that the maximum punishments for offences against the Traffic Acts should be those set out in sch. 2, part I, col. 4 (see **C8.1**). References therein to years or months are references to terms of imprisonment. **C7.1**

Forfeiture of Motor Vehicle

Section 143 of the PCC(S)A 2000 (see **E18.1** *et seq.*) makes it possible, in some circumstances, for a court to order the forfeiture of a motor vehicle where it has been used in committing or facilitating the commission of an offence. **C7.2**

Fixed Penalties

Part III of the RTOA 1988 contains provisions relating to fixed penalties. The 'fixed penalty offences' are listed in the RTOA 1988, sch. 3 (see **C8.3**), and include many of the less serious offences which are most commonly committed. A 'fixed penalty notice' is 'a notice offering the opportunity of the discharge of any liability to conviction for the offence to which the notice relates by payment of a fixed penalty' which 'must give such particulars of the circumstances alleged to constitute the offence to which it relates as are necessary for giving reasonable information about the alleged offence' (RTOA 1988, s. 52(1) and (2)). The amount of fixed penalty is specified by the Fixed Penalty Order 2000 (SI 2000 No. 2792), made under the RTOA 1988, s. 53. Graduated fixed penalties are available in relation to offences in respect of drivers' hours (and related recording equipment) for goods and passenger vehicles, certain roadworthiness defects, and overloading; the amounts payable are determined by reference to the nature of the offence, its severity, where it has taken place and whether the offender appears to have committed other prescribed offences during a prescribed period. **C7.3**

A fixed penalty notice may be given to a person where a constable in uniform or a vehicle examiner has reason to believe that a fixed penalty offence is being, or has been, committed by that person (RTOA 1988, s. 54). If the offence in question is endorsable, however, a fixed penalty notice can be given only if the person's driving record shows that the person will not be liable, once the penalty points for the instant offence are added, to disqualification under the RTOA 1988, s. 35 (see **C7.24**) and the licence is surrendered to be dealt with in accordance with the provisions of Part III. Where the constable or vehicle examiner cannot access the driving record to check that the person will not be liable to disqualification or where no licence can be produced at the time, the constable or examiner may give the person a notice to produce the licence at a police station, within seven days if the notice is given by a constable or within 14 days if given by an examiner. If, upon inspection, a fixed penalty is similarly available, a fixed penalty notice must be given at that time. A similar procedure exists for drivers who do not have a GB licence but whose driving records enable endorsement of a fixed penalty offence (see **C7.50**).

C7.4 A suspended enforcement period follows the giving of a fixed penalty notice, during which no proceedings may be brought against the recipient in respect of the offence (RTOA 1988, s. 78(2)). The period must be at least 21 days and is usually 28 days. If the fixed penalty is paid before the end of the suspended enforcement period that ends matters except, in the case of an endorsable offence, where the endorsement is entered on the person's driving record and any licence surrendered is returned (s. 57(3)). Instead of paying the fixed penalty, the recipient may give notice requesting a hearing in respect of the offence, in which case it will subsequently be tried summarily (s. 55(2)). If the recipient takes no action before the end of the suspended enforcement period, an amount of one and a half times the amount of the fixed penalty may be registered under s. 71 for enforcement against that person as a fine (s. 55(3)). For an endorsable offence, upon notice of the registration as a fine, endorsement is entered on the person's driving record and any surrendered licence duly returned.

A fixed penalty notice may be affixed to a stationary vehicle by a constable or vehicle examiner who has reason to believe that an offence which does not carry obligatory endorsement is being, or has on that occasion been, committed (s. 62). A similar suspended enforcement period follows and, if the fixed penalty is paid within that period, that ends the matter (s. 78(2)) or, if notice is given requesting a hearing, stating therein that the person was the driver at the time of the alleged offence, the case will subsequently be tried summarily (s. 63(3)). If no payment is made or hearing requested, a notice may be served on the person appearing to be the owner of the vehicle concerned (s. 63(2)). If there is no response to that notice within the time permitted by it, an amount of one and a half times the amount of the fixed penalty may be registered under s. 71 for enforcement against the person so served as a fine (s. 64(2)). Alternatively, the person served may request a hearing on that person's behalf or on behalf of some other person who was the driver at the relevant time (s. 63(6)). Unless it is proved that the vehicle in question was in the possession of some other person without the consent of the person served with the s. 63 notice, the person so served is conclusively presumed to have been the driver of the vehicle at the time of the alleged offence (s. 64(5) and (6)).

Financial Penalty Deposits

C7.5 Under the RTOA 1988, Part 3A, consisting of ss. 90A to 90F, in an appropriate case, where a person believed to have committed an applicable offence fails to provide 'an address in the United Kingdom at which the constable or vehicle examiner considers it is likely that it would be possible to find the person whenever necessary to do so in connection with the proceedings, fixed penalty notice or conditional offer', a requirement for a financial penalty deposit can be made (s. 90A(4)). The requirement is to make payment of 'the appropriate amount' immediately or within 'the relevant period' which varies according to the situation. The Road Safety (Financial Penalty Deposit) Order 2009 (SI 2009 No. 491) specifies that the requirement can be made in respect of the person in charge of the vehicle for any offence listed being committed, or which has been committed, on a road or other public place. The appropriate amount is set out in the Road Safety (Financial Penalty Deposit) (Appropriate Amount) Order 2009 (SI 2009 No. 492, as amended), and is generally fixed by reference to the size of the applicable fixed penalty or graduated fixed penalty but, for offences likely to be tried by a court, is set at £500. Where more than one offence is involved on a single occasion, the maximum aggregate amount that can be required is £1,500.

The amount so paid is then used to pay any uncontested fixed penalty notice. If the person chooses to contest the commission of the offence and is unsuccessful, the payment made is off-set against all, or part, of the fine imposed. If the offender is successful, or the matter does not come to court within the time permitted for a prosecution to be commenced or 12 months, whichever is shorter, the amount is refunded with interest, calculated by reference to the Bank of England base rate at the beginning of the day on which the financial penalty deposit was made (Road Safety (Financial Penalty Deposit) (Interest) Order 2009 (SI 2009 No. 498)).

Prohibition on Driving Under the RTOA 1988, s. 90D, where a person on whom a financial penalty deposit requirement is imposed does not make an immediate payment of the amount required, the constable or vehicle examiner is entitled, but not obliged, to give notice in writing to the person prohibiting the driving of the vehicle of which the person was in charge at the time of the offence. In doing so, a direction in writing may also be given to the person concerned that the vehicle in question must be removed to another specified place. The prohibition on driving will continue until the deposit is paid, a fixed penalty arising from the offence is paid, the person is convicted or acquitted of the offence, the person is told there will be no prosecution for the offence, or the prosecution period expires. Detailed provisions relating to these powers, also covering other instances where driving is prohibited in accordance with the Road Safety Act 2006, sch. 4, are contained in the Road Safety (Immobilisation, Removal and Disposal of Vehicles) Regulations 2009 (SI 2009 No. 493). **C7.6**

Production of Licence

Road Traffic Offenders Act 1988, s. 27 **C7.7**

(1) Where a person who is the holder of a licence is convicted of an offence involving obligatory or discretionary disqualification, and a court proposes to make an order disqualifying him or an order under section 44 of this Act, the court must, unless it has already received them, require the licence to be produced to it.

(2) [Repealed.]

(3) If the holder of the licence has not caused it to be delivered, or posted it, in accordance with section 7 of this Act and does not produce it as required under this section or section 301 of the Criminal Justice Act 2003, section 146 or 147 of the Powers of Criminal Courts (Sentencing) Act 2000,... then, unless he satisfies the court that he has applied for a new licence and has not received it—
   (a) he is guilty of an offence, and
   (b) the licence shall be suspended from the time when its production was required until it is produced to the court and shall, while suspended, be of no effect.

(4) Subsection (3) above does not apply where the holder of the licence—
   (a) has caused a current receipt for the licence issued under section 56 of this Act to be delivered to the proper officer of the court not later than the day before the date appointed for the hearing, or
   (b) has posted such a receipt, at such time that in the ordinary course of post it would be delivered not later than that day, in a letter duly addressed to the proper officer and either registered or sent by the recorded delivery service, or
   (c) surrenders such a receipt to the court at the hearing, and produces the licence to the court immediately on its return.

(4A) Subsection (3) above does not apply where section 7(1B) applies in relation to the proceedings and the holder of the licence—
   (a) has caused a current receipt for the licence issued under section 56 to be delivered to the designated officer specified in the single justice procedure notice within the period described in section 7(1B)(a),
   (b) has posted it to that officer within that period in such manner as is described in section 7(1B)(b), or
   (c) surrenders such a receipt to the court at the hearing described in section 7(1B)(c),

   and produces the licence to the court immediately on its return.

'Licence' includes a Community licence (RTOA 1988, s. 91A(1)).

When a request is made to a convicted person to produce that person's driving licence, a failure to produce it is, unless an application has been made for a new licence which has not yet been received or s. 27(4) applies, an offence punishable by a fine up to level 3 on the standard scale. The licence is also suspended until it is produced, and if the offender drives during that suspension, an offence under the RTA 1988, s. 87(1) (see **C6.37**) is committed.

OBLIGATORY AND DISCRETIONARY DISQUALIFICATION

Obligatory Disqualification

C7.8 **Road Traffic Offenders Act 1988, s. 34**

(1) Where a person is convicted of an offence involving obligatory disqualification, the court must order him to be disqualified for such period not less than 12 months as the court thinks fit unless the court for special reasons thinks fit to order him to be disqualified for a shorter period or not to order him to be disqualified.

(1A) Where a person is convicted of an offence under section 12A of the Theft Act 1968 (aggravated vehicle-taking), the fact that he did not drive the vehicle in question at any particular time or at all shall not be regarded as a special reason for the purposes of subsection (1) above.

(2) Where a person is convicted of an offence involving discretionary disqualification, and either—
(a) the penalty points to be taken into account on that occasion number fewer than 12, or
(b) the offence is not one involving obligatory endorsement, the court may order him to be disqualified for such period as the court thinks fit.

(3) Where a person convicted of an offence under any of the following provisions of the Road Traffic Act 1988, that is—
(aa) section 3A (causing death by careless driving when under the influence of drink or drugs),
(a) section 4(1) (driving or attempting to drive while unfit),
(b) section 5(1)(a) (driving or attempting to drive with excess alcohol),
(ba) section 5A(1)(a) and (2) (driving or attempting to drive with concentration of specified controlled drug above specified limit),
(c) section 7(6) (failing to provide a specimen) where that is an offence involving obligatory disqualification,
(d) section 7A(b) (failing to allow a specimen to be subjected to laboratory test) where that is an offence involving obligatory disqualification; has within the 10 years immediately preceding the commission of the offence been convicted of any such offence, subsection (1) above shall apply in relation to him as if the reference to 12 months were a reference to three years.

(4) Subject to subsection (3) above, subsection (1) above shall apply as if the reference to 12 months were a reference to two years—
(a) in relation to a person convicted of—
(i) manslaughter, . . . or
(ii) an offence under section 1 of the Road Traffic Act 1988 (causing death by dangerous driving), or
(iia) an offence under section 1A of that Act (causing serious injury by dangerous driving), or
(iib) an offence under section 3ZC of that Act (causing death by driving: disqualified drivers), or
(iic) an offence under section 3ZD of that Act (causing serious injury by driving: disqualified drivers), or
(iii) an offence under section 3A of that Act (causing death by careless driving while under the influence of drink or drugs), and
(b) in relation to a person on whom more than one disqualification for a fixed period of 56 days or more has been imposed within the three years immediately preceding the commission of the offence.

(4A) For the purposes of subsection (4)(b) above there shall be disregarded any disqualification imposed under section 26 of this Act or section 147 of the Powers of Criminal Courts (Sentencing) Act 2000 or section 248 of the Criminal Procedure (Scotland) Act 1995 (offences committed by using vehicles) and any disqualification imposed in respect of an offence of stealing a motor vehicle, an offence under section 12 or 25 of the Theft Act 1968, an offence under section 178 of the Road Traffic Act 1988, or an attempt to commit such an offence.

(4AA) For the purposes of subsection (4)(b), a disqualification is to be disregarded if the period of disqualification would have been less than 56 days but for an extension period added pursuant to—
(a) section 35A or 35C,
(b) section 248D of the Criminal Procedure (Scotland) Act 1995,
(c) section 147A of the Powers of Criminal Courts (Sentencing) Act 2000.

(4B) Where a person convicted of an offence under section 40A of the Road Traffic Act 1988 (using vehicle in dangerous condition etc.) has within the three years immediately preceding the commission of the offence been convicted of any such offence, subsection (1) above shall apply in relation to him as if the reference to twelve months were a reference to six months.

(5) The preceding provisions of this section shall apply in relation to a conviction of an offence committed by aiding, abetting, counselling or procuring, or inciting to the commission of, an offence involving obligatory disqualification as if the offence were an offence involving discretionary disqualification.

(6) This section is subject to section 48 of this Act.

The reference in s. 34(5) to incitement has effect as a reference to (or to conduct amounting to) encouraging or assisting the offences under Part 2 of the SCA 2007 (see SI 2008 No. 2504).

Where a person is convicted of an offence involving obligatory disqualification, the court must order that person to be disqualified for a minimum period of 12 months in the absence of special reasons (see **C7.53**). Where the offence is one of manslaughter by the driver of a motor vehicle or is an offence under the RTA 1988, s. 1, 1A, 3ZC, 3ZD or 3A, the minimum period of disqualification is two years; the minimum period is also two years where the offender has had two or more periods of disqualification of 56 days or more within the period of three years preceding the commission of the offence. A second or subsequent conviction for an offence relating to 'drink driving' or 'drug driving' (i.e. under s. 3A, 4(1), 5(1)(a), 5A(1)(a) and (2), 7(6) or 7A(6)) carries a minimum period of disqualification of three years, if it is committed within ten years of another such conviction. See also **C7.36**. **C7.9**

In *Learmont v DPP* [1994] RTR 286, the Divisional Court ruled that the justices, when sentencing the appellant for the instant offence of dangerous driving, had been wrong to conclude that an 18-month disqualification and a concurrent disqualification arising from the four notional penalty points imposed for that offence were two disqualifications of 56 days or more within the relevant three-year period; they were imposed for a single offence, thereby rendering the increased minimum period for disqualification inapplicable.

A person convicted of aiding and abetting etc. an offence mentioned in the RTOA 1988, s. 34(3), must be disqualified for three years if the person is subsequently convicted of an offence mentioned in s. 34(3) (*Makeham v Donaldson* [1981] RTR 511).

If the court disqualifies for any of the substantive offences under the RTOA 1988, s. 34, it does not order endorsement with any penalty points relating to that offence; the driving record is endorsed with particulars of the offence. The points relating to that offence are disregarded for the purposes of s. 35 (*Martin v DPP* [2000] RTR 188). **C7.10**

Discretionary Disqualification

Where a disqualification is discretionary, courts may not consider, except in the more serious cases, that disqualification is appropriate, particularly where it is a first offence. It 'should generally be restricted to cases involving bad driving, persistent motoring offences or the use of vehicles for the purposes of crime' (per Morland J in *Callister* [1993] RTR 70). In that case, theft of a vehicle by sale while it was subject to a credit agreement did not fall into any of those categories. Each case must be taken on its own merits, bearing in mind that certain types of offence will be viewed with greater seriousness. Offences of using a vehicle without insurance and failing to stop after an accident or to report an accident are always viewed seriously and often attract disqualification, even as a first offence. Also viewed seriously is driving while disqualified. **C7.11**

The penalty points to be taken into account are set out in the RTOA 1988, s. 29 (see **C7.19**), and include any attributable to the offence or offences for which the defendant is before the court and any points previously endorsed, unless the defendant has been disqualified under s. 35 since their imposition. The effect of s. 29 is that, where an offender has 12 or more points to be taken into account, the court may not disqualify for the substantive offence unless the offence is one which carries discretionary disqualification without obligatory endorsement; in such circumstances, it would seem that Parliament intended the penalty points procedure to take priority.

C7.12 In any case where a magistrates' court is considering imposing a period of disqualification and the person to be disqualified is not present in court, the court must, unless the single justice notice procedure applies (see **D22.33**) and the accused has indicated a wish to make representations, adjourn in order to warn the defendant that it has disqualification in mind (MCA 1980, s. 11(4) and (5A)). If the defendant fails to attend, the court may disqualify in the defendant's absence or, more usually, issue a warrant under the MCA 1980, s. 13, to compel the defendant's attendance. Before a court imposes disqualification in a case where it is discretionary, either the defendant or the defendant's representative should be warned and then given the opportunity to address the court (*Ireland* (1988) 10 Cr App R (S) 474; *Money* (1988) 10 Cr App R (S) 237).

Meaning of 'Offence Involving Obligatory Disqualification' and 'Offence Involving Discretionary Disqualification'

C7.13 **Road Traffic Offenders Act 1988, s. 97**

(1) For the purposes of this Act, an offence involves obligatory disqualification if it is an offence under a provision of the Traffic Acts specified in column 1 of Part I of Schedule 2 to this Act or an offence specified in column 1 of Part II of that Schedule and either—
  (a) the word 'obligatory' (without qualification) appears in column 5 (in the case of Part I) or column 2 (in the case of Part II) against the offence, or
  (b) that word appears there qualified by conditions or circumstances relating to the offence which are satisfied or obtain.

(2) For the purposes of this Act, an offence involves discretionary disqualification if it is an offence under a provision of the Traffic Acts specified in column 1 of Part I of Schedule 2 to this Act or an offence specified in column 1 of Part II of that Schedule and either—
  (a) the word 'discretionary' (without qualification) appears in column 5 (in the case of Part I) or column 2 (in the case of Part II) against the offence, or
  (b) that word appears there qualified by conditions or circumstances relating to the offence which are satisfied or obtain.

Reduced Disqualification following Course

C7.14 Sections 34A to 34C of the RTOA 1988 set up a procedure for driver retraining for offenders convicted of drink-driving offences under the RTA 1988, s. 3A, 4, 5 or 7, where the court has disqualified for not less than 12 months under the RTOA 1988, s. 34, and provide an incentive to drivers to attend such courses by reducing the period of disqualification for those who do.

C7.15 For an order to be made, the period of disqualification must be at least 12 months and the 'reduced period' of disqualification cannot be less than three months or more than a quarter of the entire period of disqualification. An order cannot be made if the offender has completed an approved course under the RTOA 1988, s. 30A or s. 34A, for a specified offence within the previous three years (see **C7.22**) or in respect of an offender still within the probationary period for newly qualified drivers (see **C7.44**). The offender must be aged at least 17. Before making a s. 34A order, the court must be satisfied that a place is available, that the offender agrees to the order and that it is explained to the offender that the fees for the course must be paid in advance and how much those fees are. This provision has certain disadvantages for the impecunious offender, particularly if that offender has relied on driving for previous employment.

Section 34B deals with certificates in relation to completion of the course. The order reducing the period of disqualification does not come into effect until the certificate has been received by the proper officer of the supervising court. If the certificate is received by the court before the end of the 'reduced period', the order reducing the period of disqualification comes into effect on the day that the certificate is received. The organiser of the retraining course may refuse to give a certificate for the reasons specified in s. 34B(4). If a certificate is not given to the offender in accordance with s. 34B, an application may be made to the supervising court which, if successful, has the effect of a certificate duly received by the court. Section 41A of the RTOA 1988 enables the court to suspend a disqualification pending determination of such an application.

Section 34BA makes provision for approval of courses and s. 34C deals with the powers of the Secretary of State or the National Assembly for Wales to give guidance to course organisers and other supplementary matters. See the Rehabilitation Courses (Relevant Drink Offences) Regulations 2012 (SI 2012 No. 2939, as amended by SI 2015 No. 366) or, as the case may be, the Rehabilitation Courses (Relevant Drink Offences) (Wales) Regulations 2013 (SI 2013 No. 372), for further details.

PENALTY POINTS

Road Traffic Offenders Act 1988, s. 28 C7.16

(1) Where a person is convicted of an offence involving obligatory endorsement, then, subject to the following provisions of this section, the number of penalty points to be attributed to the offence is—
   (a) the number shown in relation to the offence in the last column of Part I or Part II of Schedule 2 to this Act, or
   (b) where a range of numbers is shown, a number within that range.

(2) Where a person is convicted of an offence committed by aiding, abetting, counselling or procuring, or inciting to the commission of, an offence involving obligatory disqualification, then, subject to the following provisions of this section, the number of penalty points to be attributed to the offence is 10.

(3) For the purposes of sections 57A(6) and 77A(8) of this Act, the number of penalty points to be attributed to an offence is—
   (a) where both a range of numbers and a number followed by the words '(fixed penalty)' is shown in the last column of part 1 of Schedule 2 to this Act in relation to the offence, that number,
   (b) where a range of numbers followed by the words 'or appropriate penalty points (fixed penalty)' is shown there in relation to the offence, the appropriate number of penalty points for the offence, and
   (c) where only a range of numbers is shown there in relation to the offence, the lowest number in the range.

(3A) For the purposes of subsection (3)(b) above the appropriate number of penalty points for an offence is such number of penalty points as the Secretary of State may by order made by statutory instrument prescribe.

(3B) An order made under subsection (3A) above in relation to an offence may make provision for the appropriate number of penalty points for the offence to be different depending on the circumstances, including (in particular)—
   (a) the nature of the contravention or failure constituting the offence,
   (b) how serious it is,
   (c) the area, or sort of place, where it takes place, and
   (d) whether the offender appears to have committed an offence or offences of a description in the order during a period so specified.

(4) Where a person is convicted (whether on the same occasion or not) of two or more offences committed on the same occasion and involving obligatory endorsement, the total number of penalty points to be attributed to them is the number or highest number that would be attributed on a conviction of one of them (so that if the convictions are on different occasions the number of penalty points to be attributed to the offences on the later occasion or occasions shall be restricted accordingly).

(5) In a case where (apart from this subsection) subsection (4) above would apply to two or more offences, the court may if it thinks fit determine that that subsection shall not apply to the offences (or, where three or more offences are concerned, to any one or more of them).

(6) Where a court makes such a determination it shall state its reasons in open court and, if it is a magistrates' court . . . shall cause them to be entered in the register . . . of its proceedings.
(7) to (9) [Powers of Secretary of State to alter penalty points and matters consequent.]

The reference in s. 28(2) to incitement has effect as a reference to (or to conduct amounting to) encouraging or assisting the offences under Part 2 of the SCA 2007 (SI 2008 No. 2504).

C7.17 Aiding and abetting etc. an offence involving obligatory disqualification, such as driving with excess alcohol, carries ten penalty points but does not entail mandatory disqualification. In offences not involving obligatory disqualification, secondary participation entails the same punishment as for the principal.

If an attempted offence is summary only, then it must be statutory (e.g., attempting to drive while unfit through drink or drugs), and the penalty is set out in the RTOA 1988, sch. 2, part I, col. 7 (see **C8.1**). If it is triable either way then, by virtue of the CAA 1981, s. 4(1)(b), the same liability to penalties exists as for the complete offence.

By virtue of the RTOA 1988, s. 28, the court may, following a determination under s. 28(5), order the endorsement of the driving record with penalty points in relation to more than one offence committed on the same occasion. Points would then be aggregated for the purposes of the RTOA 1988, s. 35 (disqualification for repeated offences: see C7.24) and the Road Traffic (New Drivers) Act 1995 (surrender of licences: see C7.44).

The effect of s. 28 is to give the court a discretion to impose penalty points in respect of two or more offences committed on the same occasion and thereby aggregate the penalty points imposed in order to disqualify under the 'penalty points' system (s. 28(5)). Reasons must be given in open court and magistrates must enter the reasons in the court register (see *Ishmail* [2018] EWCA Crim 1411 and *Sage* [2019] EWCA Crim 934, [2019] 2 Cr App R (S) 50 (407) for the consequences of not having s. 28(4) drawn to the sentencer's attention). The power can be used where none of the offences is so serious as to merit disqualification in its own right but the totality of the offending merits disqualification, possibly because of the number of offences or because the offences are of different types.

C7.18 In *Johnson v Finbow* [1983] 1 WLR 879, the appellant was charged with offences of failing to stop after an accident and failing to report the accident to the police. The Divisional Court accepted that there was an argument that the offences were not committed on the 'same occasion', but Robert Goff LJ, giving the judgment of the court, went on to say (at pp. 882–3):

> . . . looking at the matter more broadly (and, for my part, I think more sensibly), it can be said that the lapse of time, although significant, is not sufficiently great to be able to say, as a matter of common sense, that those offences were committed on different occasions. It is true that they were committed at different moments of time; indeed, they might even have been committed on different days. On the other hand, they certainly arose out of the same accident. And when one sees how closely they are connected with the accident, and how very similar, in fact, the two offences are in their nature, then I think the proper conclusion is that when arising out of the same accident these two offences are committed on the same occasion.

In *Johnston v Over* (1984) 6 Cr App R (S) 420, the defendant had parked two vehicles outside his home. He was charged with two offences of 'using' a vehicle without insurance. The Divisional Court stated that whether an offence was 'committed on the same or on different occasions' depended upon the facts of each case, and that in this case, as a matter of common sense, both offences were committed on the same occasion.

Offences which are committed on separate occasions have the number or highest number of penalty points awarded separately, and, if committed within three years of each other, those points are added up for the purposes of the RTOA 1988, s. 35.

Points to be Taken into Account on Conviction

Road Traffic Offenders Act 1988, s. 29 C7.19

(1) Where a person is convicted of an offence involving obligatory endorsement, the penalty points to be taken into account on that occasion are (subject to subsection (2) below)—
   (a) any that are to be attributed to the offence or offences of which he is convicted, disregarding any offence in respect of which an order under section 34 of this Act is made, and
   (b) any that were on a previous occasion ordered to be endorsed on his driving record, unless the offender has since that occasion and before the conviction been disqualified under section 35 of this Act.

(2) If any of the offences was committed more than three years before another, the penalty points in respect of that offence shall not be added to those in respect of the other.

The effect of s. 29 is that penalty points remain on the driving record; it is not 'wiped clean' by a disqualification under the RTOA 1988, s. 34. If a disqualification is imposed under s. 34, no points in respect of that offence can be taken into account on that occasion because they must be disregarded, although points in respect of other offences being dealt with remain relevant. Thus if a defendant is convicted of two offences committed on the same occasion, one of which carries mandatory disqualification, points on the other offence will be taken into account for the purposes of s. 35 (see **C7.24**). Where there is a disqualification under s. 34, the driving record is not endorsed with penalty points (*Campbell* [2009] EWCA Crim 2459, [2010] 2 Cr App R (S) 28 (175); *Burrows* [2017] EWCA Crim 278). C7.20

Even if the offender is disqualified for an offence before the court, the relevant number of penalty points (denoted in the RTOA 1988, sch. 2, part I, col. 7) must still be 'taken into account' for the purposes of s. 35.

A previous disqualification under the penalty points system has the effect of wiping the driving record clean. Points ordered since the disqualification must be taken into account even if they are imposed in respect of an offence committed before the disqualification, unless, of course, the offence was committed more than three years before another.

For the purposes of s. 29, the date of conviction means the date on which sentence is imposed (*Brentwood Justices, ex parte Richardson* (1992) 95 Cr App R 187).

Modification where Fixed Penalty Points also in Question

Road Traffic Offenders Act 1988, s. 30 C7.21

(1) Sections 28 and 29 of this Act shall have effect subject to this section in any case where—
   (a) a person is convicted of an offence involving obligatory endorsement, and
   (b) the court is satisfied that his driving record has been or is liable to be endorsed under section 57A or 77A of this Act in respect of an offence (referred to in this section as the 'connected offence') committed on the same occasion as the offence of which he is convicted.

(2) The number of penalty points to be attributed to the offence of which he is convicted is—
   (a) the number of penalty points to be attributed to that offence under section 28 of this Act apart from this section, less
   (b) the number of penalty points required to be endorsed on his driving record under section 57A or 77A of this Act in respect of the connected offence (except so far as they have already been deducted by virtue of this paragraph).

The offences to which the procedure applies are set out in the RTOA 1988, sch. 3 (see **C8.3**). Where the 'fixed penalty' procedure (see **C7.3**) has been, or is being, used in respect of an offence which arose on the 'same occasion' as the offence for which the defendant's driving record is to be endorsed, the number of penalty points to be imposed in respect of that offence is the highest number of points attributable under the RTOA 1988, s. 28, less the number of points already endorsed under the fixed penalty procedure.

Reduced Penalty Points for Attendance on Courses When the Road Safety Act 2006, s. 34, is brought into force, it will introduce a new range of courses designed, when successfully completed, to remove from the offender's driving record three penalty points (or fewer where, for the instant C7.22

offence, the court endorsed fewer). This is intended to offer an element of retraining for repeat offenders and enable such offenders to benefit from the incentive of reducing the risk of being disqualified on reaching 12 or more penalty points under the RTOA 1988, s. 35 (see **C7.24**).

Sections 30A to 30D will be inserted into the RTOA 1988. The offences to be covered are (a) careless, and inconsiderate, driving; (b) failing to comply with traffic signs; and (c) speeding. The opportunity to attend a course will not be available to anyone who has completed a course under s. 30A or 34A (see **C7.14**) in the previous three years or a person who commits the offence during the probationary period for newly qualified drivers (see **C7.44**). These courses will be quite distinct from the Driver Improvement Scheme and Speed Awareness Courses operated by the police without court involvement.

Previously Endorsed Particulars

C7.23 **Road Traffic Offenders Act 1988, s. 31**

(1) Where a person is convicted of an offence involving obligatory or discretionary disqualification—
  (a) any existing endorsement on his driving record is prima facie evidence of the matters endorsed, and
  (b) the court may, in determining what order to make in pursuance of the conviction, take those matters into consideration.

(2) [Applies only to Scotland.]

This is one of a number of ways by which previous convictions may be proved. In addition, an extract from the Criminal Records Office may be produced by the prosecution and is admissible if agreed by the defendant. On a number of occasions the only evidence relating to the defendant's driving record will be contained in a computer printout from the DVLA, which may be admitted under the RTOA 1988, s. 13 (see **C2.20**). In other circumstances previous convictions may be proved under the PACE 1984, ss. 73 to 75 (see generally, **F12.1** *et seq.*).

PENALTY POINTS DISQUALIFICATION

C7.24 **Road Traffic Offenders Act 1988, s. 35**

(1) Where—
  (a) a person is convicted of an offence to which this subsection applies, and
  (b) the penalty points to be taken into account on that occasion number 12 or more,

  the court must order him to be disqualified for not less than the minimum period unless the court is satisfied, having regard to all the circumstances, that there are grounds for mitigating the normal consequences of the conviction and thinks fit to order him to be disqualified for a shorter period or not to order him to be disqualified.

(1A) Subsection (1) above applies to—
  (a) an offence involving discretionary disqualification and obligatory endorsement, and
  (b) an offence involving obligatory disqualification in respect of which no order is made under section 34 of this Act.

(2) The minimum period referred to in subsection (1) above is—
  (a) six months if no previous disqualification imposed on the offender is to be taken into account, and
  (b) one year if one, and two years if more than one, such disqualification is to be taken into account;

  and a previous disqualification imposed on an offender is to be taken into account if it was for a fixed period of 56 days or more and was imposed within the three years immediately preceding the commission of the latest offence in respect of which penalty points are taken into account under section 29 of this Act.

(3) Where an offender is convicted on the same occasion of more than one offence to which subsection (1) above applies—
  (a) not more than one disqualification shall be imposed on him under subsection (1) above,
  (b) in determining the period of the disqualification the court must take into account all the offences, and
  (c) for the purposes of any appeal any disqualification imposed under subsection (1) above shall be treated as an order made on the conviction of each of the offences.

(4) No account is to be taken under subsection (1) above of any of the following circumstances—
  (a) any circumstances that are alleged to make the offence or any of the offences not a serious one,
  (b) hardship, other than exceptional hardship, or

(c) any circumstances which, within the three years immediately preceding the conviction, have been taken into account under that subsection in ordering the offender to be disqualified for a shorter period or not ordering him to be disqualified.

(5) References in this section to disqualification do not include a disqualification imposed under section 26 of this Act or section 147 of the Powers of Criminal Courts (Sentencing) Act 2000 . . . or a disqualification imposed in respect of an offence of stealing a motor vehicle, an offence under section 12 or 25 of the Theft Act 1968, an offence under section 178 of the Road Traffic Act 1988, or an attempt to commit such an offence.

(5A) The preceding provisions of this section shall apply in relation to a conviction of an offence committed by aiding, abetting, counselling, procuring, or inciting to the commission of, an offence involving obligatory disqualification as if the offence were an offence involving discretionary disqualification.

(6) [Applies only to Scotland.]

(7) This section is subject to section 48 of this Act.

The reference in s. 35(5A) to incitement has effect as a reference to (or to conduct amounting to) encouraging or assisting the offences under Part 2 of the SCA 2007 (SI 2008 No. 2504).

The purpose of the procedure, colloquially termed 'totting up', is to punish repeated offences which in themselves are not sufficiently grave to warrant disqualification, but which taken together indicate repeated offences of bad driving or disregard for the law. When considering the proper sentence for an offence carrying discretionary disqualification, the court should first consider whether that is warranted. In doing so, it will have regard to the defendant's full relevant driving record. If it considers that a mandatory period of disqualification under the RTOA 1988, s. 35, would be the best disposal, the court can exercise its discretion not to disqualify under s. 34, and to impose an appropriate number of penalty points to bring the defendant within s. 35 (*Jones v DPP* [2001] RTR 8 (80)). As such, ss. 34 and 35 are complementary rather than mutually exclusive. **C7.25**

Once points have been imposed they are added to any other points imposed in respect of offences committed within three years of the latest offence or offences (points to be taken into consideration). If the total is 12 or more, the court is obliged to disqualify under the RTOA 1988, s. 35. This disqualification is mandatory unless the court finds mitigating circumstances. It is in addition to, but not consecutive to, any disqualification which the court may order for the offences before it on that day.

Even if the court disqualifies for a substantive offence, it is obliged to take into account other offences which were committed and to take into account and attribute points in accordance with the RTOA 1988, ss. 28 and 29, with a view to disqualification under s. 35. Points are not endorsed under s. 44 (see **C7.46**) if there is a penalty points disqualification. **C7.26**

The effect of a disqualification under the penalty points procedure is to wipe the driving record clean. If the defendant is subsequently convicted of an offence, previously endorsed points are not taken into consideration, but the fact of a penalty points disqualification is relevant to any future points disqualification.

Period of Disqualification under the Road Traffic Offenders Act 1988, s. 35 The disqualification must be for a minimum period, unless there are grounds for mitigating the normal consequences and the court thinks fit to order a shorter period or no disqualification at all. See also **C7.36**. **C7.27**

If the offender has no previous disqualification of 56 days or more imposed within three years of the commission of the latest offence for which penalty points are to be taken into account, the period is six months. If there is one such disqualification in the three years, the period is a minimum of one year. If there are two or more such disqualifications imposed within three years of the commission of the latest offence, the minimum period is two years. Disqualifications under the RTOA 1988, s. 26, and the PCC(S)A 2000, s. 147, are not to be taken into account.

Mitigating Circumstances Mitigating circumstances may be circumstances which relate to the offender or the offence, and may include the offender's record and good works. **C7.28**

The RTOA 1988, s. 35(4), specifically excludes circumstances which are alleged to make the offence not serious, hardship, other than exceptional hardship, and any 'mitigating circumstances' which have been advanced as such during the three years preceding the conviction for the latest offence. For those reasons the RTOA 1988, s. 47, requires grounds for mitigating the normal consequences of the conviction to be stated in open court, and entered in the court register if the case is heard by a magistrates' court.

It is for the offender to establish that grounds being advanced are different from any previously put before the court (*Sandbach Justices, ex parte Pescud* (1983) 5 Cr App R (S) 177). In practice, most of the mitigating circumstances advanced relate to 'exceptional hardship'. In *Owen v Jones* (1987) 9 Cr App R (S) 34, the Divisional Court expressed the view that in the vast majority of cases justices would need to have evidence to satisfy themselves of the existence of exceptional hardship, but that on occasions they might rely upon their own knowledge. In that case a police officer had acquired a total of 13 points and, if disqualified, would have, by the usual practice of the Chief Constable, been forced to resign, thereby losing both employment and somewhere to live. This practice was known to the bench, who did not require the defendant to provide evidence, as they found that the facts amounted to exceptional hardship.

C7.29 'Exceptional hardship' is often advanced in relation to the offender's employment. In those circumstances the court might consider whether a licence to drive is necessary for the offender either to go to work or because the person's occupation is, or entails, driving. Such matters as hours and pattern of work, together with the distances to be travelled in order to reach the place of work and the availability of public transport, are relevant, as are details of the person's age and health and any other means of transport available. If loss of the licence may mean loss of employment or reduced wages, the court may consider any unusual hardship that may result to the family of the defendant and any unusual hardship that may be occasioned to them if the defendant were to be disqualified. The fact that the defendant runs a business, with employees dependent upon that business and the defendant's ability to drive, may be considered, but the court should be careful to inquire as to other means of transport or available methods of effecting the person's necessary business.

The court must have regard to all the circumstances. This has been held to include, in the case of a young offender with a bad record who was disqualified for two years under the penalty points procedure, the counter-productive nature of long periods of disqualification. In *Thomas* [1983] 3 All ER 756, upon reducing the disqualification from two years to one, Lord Lane CJ said (at p. 1491):

> ...with persons like the present appellant, who seem to be incapable of leaving motor vehicles alone, to impose a period of disqualification which will extend for a substantial period after their release from prison may well, and in many cases certainly will, invite the offender to commit further offences in relation to motor vehicles. In other words a long period of disqualification may well be counter-productive and so contrary to the public interest. So well established has this sentencing policy become in recent years that it is not necessary to refer to a line of cases.

Given the breadth of the discretion under s. 35(1), it can be exercised in cases where the unreasonable length of time between the offence resulting in a penalty points disqualification and the imposition of that sentence violates the ECHR, Article 6; in such a case, an appropriate remedy may be the reduction of the usual period of disqualification, or even imposing no disqualification at all (*Miller v DPP* [2004] EWHC 595 (Admin), [2005] RTR 3 (44), applying *A-G's Ref (No. 2 of 2001)* [2001] EWCA Crim 1568, [2001] 1 WLR 1869).

DISQUALIFICATION GENERALLY

Interim Disqualification

C7.30 **Road Traffic Offenders Act 1988, s. 26**

(1) Where a magistrates' court—

(a) commits an offender to the Crown Court under section 6 of the Powers of Criminal Courts (Sentencing) Act 2000 or any enactment mentioned in subsection (4) of that section, or

(b) remits an offender to another magistrates' court under section 10 of that Act, to be dealt with for an offence involving obligatory or discretionary disqualification, it may order him to be disqualified until he has been dealt with in respect of the offence.

(2) Where a court in England and Wales—

(a) defers passing sentence on an offender under section 1 of that Act in respect of an offence involving obligatory or discretionary disqualification, or

(b) adjourns after convicting an offender of such an offence but before dealing with him for the offence,

it may order the offender to be disqualified until he has been dealt with in respect of the offence.

(3) [Applies only to Scotland.]

(4) Subject to subsection (5) below, an order under this section shall cease to have effect at the end of the period of six months beginning with the day on which it is made, if it has not ceased to have effect before that time.

(5) [Applies only to Scotland.]

(6) Where a court orders a person to be disqualified under this section ('the first order'), no court shall make a further order under this section in respect of the same offence or any offence in respect of which an order could have been made under this section at the time the first order was made.

(7) to (9) [Production of licences and consequences of failure to produce.]

(10) to (11) [Duty to send notice of order to Secretary of State and contents of notice.]

(12) Where on any occasion a court deals with an offender—

(a) for an offence in respect of which an order was made under this section, or

(b) for two or more offences in respect of any of which such an order was made,

any period of disqualification which is on that occasion imposed under section 34 or 35 of this Act shall be treated as reduced by any period during which he was disqualified by reason only of an order made under this section in respect of any of those offences.

(13) Any reference in this or any other Act (including any Act passed after this Act) to the length of a period of disqualification shall, unless the context otherwise requires, be construed as a reference to its length before any reduction under this section.

Section 26 enables magistrates, when committing an offender to the Crown Court under the PCC(S)A 2000, s. 6 (see **D23.55**), remitting an offender to another court, deferring sentence or adjourning, to disqualify the offender from driving until the case has been finally dealt with. Any period of disqualification finally imposed by the court, without regard to the period of interim disqualification, is reduced accordingly by the administrative authorities (*Edwards v Wheelan* 1999 SLT 917). Such an order is termed a 'first order' and only one such order may be made under s. 26. In *Needham* [2016] EWCA Crim 455, [2016] 1 WLR 4449, because of the effects of the RTOA 1988, ss. 35A and 35B, it was suggested that it might be inappropriate to impose interim disqualifications on offenders remanded in custody. However, to avoid injustice, it is open to the court when determining the period of the disqualification under the RTOA 1988, s. 34, to take any remand time into account (*Maughan* [2020] EWCA Crim 170). The order may only be made for a maximum of six months inclusive of the day on which the order is made (see, e.g., *Mascerenas* [2018] EWCA Crim 1467). The defendant's licence must be produced, which the court must retain. Failure to do so is an offence unless the licence has been posted in accordance with s. 7 of the Act (see **C2.6**), a new licence has been applied for but not received, or the defendant tenders a valid receipt under s. 56 of the Act and immediately produces the licence to the court on its return. **C7.31**

Disqualification Pending Passing of Driving Test

Road Traffic Offenders Act 1988, s. 36 **C7.32**

(1) Where this subsection applies to a person the court must order him to be disqualified until he passes the appropriate driving test.

(2) Subsection (1) above applies to a person who is disqualified under section 34 of this Act on conviction of—

(a) manslaughter . . . by the driver of a motor vehicle, or

(b) an offence under section 1 (causing death by dangerous driving), section 1A (causing serious injury by dangerous driving) or section 2 (dangerous driving) of the Road Traffic Act 1988.

(3) Subsection (1) above also applies—
   (a) to a person who is disqualified under section 34 or 35 of this Act in such circumstances or for such period as the Secretary of State may by order prescribe, or
   (b) to such other persons convicted of such offences involving obligatory endorsement as may be so prescribed.

(4) Where a person to whom subsection (1) above does not apply is convicted of an offence involving obligatory endorsement, the court may order him to be disqualified until he passes the appropriate driving test (whether or not he has previously passed any test).

(5) In this section—
   'appropriate driving test' means—
   (a) an extended driving test, where a person is convicted of an offence involving obligatory disqualification or is disqualified under section 35 of this Act,
   (b) a test of competence to drive, other than an extended driving test, in any other case,
   'extended driving test' means a test of competence to drive prescribed for the purposes of this section, and
   'test of competence to drive' means a test prescribed by virtue of section 89(3) of the Road Traffic Act 1988.

(6) In determining whether to make an order under subsection (4) above, the court shall have regard to the safety of road users.

(7) Where a person is disqualified until he passes the extended driving test—
   (a) any earlier order under this section shall cease to have effect, and
   (b) a court shall not make a further order under this section while he is so disqualified.

(8) Subject to subsection (9) below, a disqualification by virtue of an order under this section shall be deemed to have expired on production to the Secretary of State of evidence, in such form as may be prescribed by regulations under section 105 of the RTA 1988, that the person disqualified has passed the test in question since the order was made.

(9) A disqualification shall be deemed to have expired only in relation to vehicles of such classes as may be prescribed in relation to the test passed by regulations under that section.

(10) [Repealed.]

C7.33 The effect of s. 36 is to make disqualification until a test is passed mandatory for those offenders convicted of offences specified in s. 36(2). The obligation to disqualify under s. 36 also extends to such persons disqualified under ss. 34 and 35 as may be prescribed and to such other persons convicted of offences involving obligatory endorsement as may be prescribed. Where an offender is already subject to an order to take an extended driving test, by virtue of the RTOA 1988, s. 36(7)(b), a sentencing court cannot impose a further order to take such a test (*Abdullahi* [2010] EWCA Crim 1886; *Weafer* [2019] EWCA Crim 1072).

The matters to be tested during an 'extended driving test' are broadly similar to those prescribed for the 'ordinary' driving test, but its minimum length is 60 minutes, considerably longer than the normal test of competence to drive (Motor Vehicles (Driving Licences) Regulations 1999 (SI 1999 No. 2864), reg. 41). Under the RTOA 1988, s. 36(5), when imposing a discretionary disqualification, e.g., for careless driving (*Owen* [2012] EWCA Crim 170), driving while disqualified (*Watson* [2013] EWCA Crim 2316) or assault occasioning actual bodily harm (*Large* [2011] EWCA Crim 2970), the sentencing court cannot disqualify until an extended driving test is passed; that option is confined to cases where the offence involves obligatory disqualification or the defendant is being disqualified for accumulating penalty points under the RTOA 1988, s. 35, but the court is permitted to order an ordinary test to be retaken. If the sentencing court omits to order disqualification until an extended test is passed when such an order is required, this cannot be rectified on appeal owing to the CAA 1981, s. 11(3) (*Mohammed* [2019] EWCA Crim 1582). When the Road Safety Act 2006, s. 37, is brought into force, the definition of 'appropriate driving test' will be modified so that it will enable the Secretary of State to prescribe by regulations the circumstances in which the test to be passed must be an extended one. This is clearly intended to broaden the circumstances in which the more stringent post-disqualification test will be applicable before the driver fully returns to the roads.

The power to order a person to take a driving test where the person has been convicted of an offence involving obligatory endorsement which has not been prescribed under s. 36(3)(b) may be exercised only after the court has had regard to the safety of road users in accordance with s. 36(6). The insertion of s. 36(6) seems to indicate that such a regard is paramount in deciding whether to exercise the discretion to disqualify. This implies that all courts should consider using s. 36 when it is not mandatory to order a retest. Nonetheless, on the previous authorities an order was to be made only on evidence that the ability of the defendant to drive is in some way in question. It should not be used as an additional punishment but only where because of 'age or infirmity or the circumstances of the offence a person may not be a competent driver' (*Buckley* (1988) 10 Cr App R (S) 477). There is no principle that it is inappropriate to disqualify someone who was merely a passenger (*Beech* [2016] EWCA Crim 1746, [2016] 4 WLR 182). **C7.34**

In *Miller* (1994) 15 Cr App R (S) 505, the Court of Appeal upheld the sentencing judge's order that the offender be disqualified until passing a driving test on the ground that it was clear the offender's driving was grossly incompetent. A plea of guilty to careless driving had been entered on an indictment alleging dangerous driving. The offender had never passed a driving test and had numerous previous convictions, including ten for driving while disqualified. In *Bannister* [1991] RTR 1, where the offender was imprisoned for three months and disqualified for two years and thereafter until a test was passed, the Court of Appeal took the view that competence to drive included proper regard for other road users as well as control of the vehicle.

If an offender is disqualified under the RTOA 1988, s. 36, a provisional driving licence must be obtained before driving and its conditions of use must be complied with, or else the offender may run the risk of being convicted under the RTA 1988, s. 103 (*Hunter v Coombs* [1962] 1 All ER 904; *DPP v Barker* [2004] EWHC 2502 (Admin), (2004) 168 JP 617).

Offender Escaping Consequences of Endorsable Offence by Deception

Where a sentencing court was deceived by a defendant being dealt with for an offence involving obligatory endorsement about any circumstance that may have had a bearing on whether to disqualify the defendant or the length of disqualification to impose, the RTOA 1988, s. 49, enables the court subsequently dealing with the defendant on conviction for an offence arising from that deception, after taking into account any order made by the original sentencing court, to exercise the same powers and duties regarding an order for disqualification as were available to the original court, i.e. to resentence for the original endorsable offence. **C7.35**

Length of Disqualification

A period of disqualification is forward-looking and designed to be preventative rather than backward-looking and punitive (*Hussain* [2009] EWCA Crim 2582; *Bell* [2013] EWCA Crim 2549). The main purpose of disqualification is to protect the public from the risk posed by an offender driving, meaning that a low risk may not warrant a lengthy period of disqualification, although there is, or may be, an element of punishment (*Barker* [2017] EWCA Crim 257). **C7.36**

For offences committed on or after 13 April 2015 (see SI 2015 No. 819), the RTOA 1988, s. 35A (as amended by the CJCA 2015, s. 30(1)), provides that a defendant who is sentenced to a custodial sentence as well as a disqualification under the RTOA 1988, s. 34 or 35, must be disqualified for 'the appropriate extension period', as set out in s. 35A(4), in addition to the period being imposed in respect of s. 34 or 35. The overall period of disqualification will effectively be increased by the period actually spent in custody. In cases where the court proposes to impose a period of disqualification as well as imposing, for a separate offence, immediate custody (or where the defendant is already a serving prisoner), s. 35B requires the court to consider the diminished effect of disqualification as a distinct penalty. In *Needham* [2016] EWCA Crim 455, [2016] 1 WLR 4449, the Court of Appeal (at [31]) provided a checklist for applying these sections:

- Step 1—does the court intend to impose a 'discretionary' disqualification under s. 34 or 35 for any offence?
  YES—go to Step 2.
- Step 2—does the court intend to impose a custodial term for that **same** offence?
  YES—s. 35A applies and the court must impose an extension period (see s. 35A(4)(h) for that **same** offence and consider Step 3).
  NO—s. 35A does not apply at all—go on to consider s. 35B and Step 4.
- Step 3—does the court intend to impose a custodial term for **another** offence (which is longer or consecutive) or is the defendant already serving a custodial sentence?
  YES—then consider what increase ('uplift') in the period of 'discretionary disqualification' is required to comply with s. 35B(2) and (3). In accordance with s. 35B(4), ignore any custodial term imposed for an offence involving disqualification under s. 35A.

  Discretionary period + extension period + uplift = total period of disqualification

  NO—no need to consider s. 35B at all.

  Discretionary period + extension period = total disqualification period
- Step 4—does the court intend to impose a custodial term for **another** offence or is the defendant already serving a custodial sentence?
  YES—then consider what increase ('uplift') in the period of 'discretionary disqualification' is required to comply with s. 35B(2) and (3).

  Discretionary period + uplift = total period of disqualification

These sections must be strictly adhered to and the sentence expressed accurately by reference to each component period (*Watson* [2016] EWCA Crim 2119). In *Bogart* [2020] EWCA Crim 831, it was recognised that this is a complicated exercise where judges need the assistance of counsel so that the constituent parts of the sentence are properly announced in open court, rather than falling to be corrected administratively or involving wasting court time on appeal. Where the length of disqualification cannot be increased in accordance with the CAA 1981, s. 11(3), the make-up of the disqualification period may need to be recast on appeal (*Jolly* [2016] EWCA Crim 2193). Where any term of imprisonment on appeal is reduced, it follows that the extension period or uplift should be reconsidered (*Saunders* [2016] EWCA Crim 1855; *Quibell* [2016] EWCA Crim 2195). An example of the effect of imposing a consecutive custodial sentence for another offence is *Bealing* [2017] EWCA Crim 1262. Imposing a disqualification for life inevitably incorporates any applicable extension period (*Lusher* [2016] EWCA Crim 2055). These principles apply in the same manner to extended disqualification periods imposed pursuant to the PCC(S)A 2000, ss. 147A and 147B (*Vasey* [2017] EWCA Crim 434).

C7.37 In arriving at the length of disqualification which is appropriate, the court should not have regard to the application of the RTOA 1988, s. 42 (see **C7.42**), and the power of the court to remove a disqualification, but merely to the length of time that is appropriate for the offence before it (*Bannister* [1991] RTR 1). The disqualification runs from the date of sentence rather than being capable of being made to run consecutively to a period of disqualification previously imposed (*Hellyer* [2015] EWCA Crim 1410). Disqualifications take effect immediately and cannot be postponed (*Holmes* [2018] EWCA Crim 131).

In general, when considering the length of disqualification courts should attempt to avoid long periods because lengthy disqualifications tend to be counterproductive and often hamper the offender in the job market, sometimes leading to further crime, in particular driving while disqualified. Care needs to be taken not to over-sentence in a case where there is no apparent appreciable risk to the public (*Dadson* [2013] EWCA Crim 1887). Where no reason is given, or found, relating to protecting the public or as punishment relating to a disqualification longer than the mandatory minimum period, that longer disqualification is susceptible to reduction on appeal (*Desouza* [2020] EWCA Crim 804). However, the court must also consider its duty to protect the public, and a lengthy period of disqualification to enable the defendant to mature may be justified (*Gibbons* (1987) 9 Cr App R (S) 21). An appellate court faced with an appeal that the disqualification period is manifestly excessive must consider the period in the context of the sentence imposed and ancillary orders as a whole (*Evans* [2019] EWCA Crim 2358). Where the defendant is a professional driver holding a foreign licence, whose livelihood will only be minimally affected because the disqualification will not adversely change the ability to continue driving in mainland Europe, the principle of protecting the public while not unduly impacting on employment prospects can be met with what might otherwise be regarded as a longer period of disqualification than would be appropriate in a purely domestic context (*Sertvytis* [2017] EWCA Crim 2246).

Disqualification for life may be imposed (*Tunde-Olarinde* [1967] 2 All ER 491), but such a disqualification is inappropriate and wrong in principle in the absence of either psychiatric evidence or evidence of many previous convictions which indicates that the defendant would be a danger to the public for an indefinite period if subsequently allowed to drive (per Morland J in *King* (1992) 13 Cr App R (S) 668). In *King*, although the appellant had used his car as a weapon, he had no previous convictions which related to dangerous or careless driving. The Court of Appeal reduced the period of disqualification from life to five years on the basis that the judge had failed to give weight to the rehabilitative principle set out in *Russell* [1993] RTR 249n. Similarly, in *Rivano* (1994) 158 JP 288, the Court of Appeal decided that there were no very exceptional circumstances requiring disqualification for life or leading to the conclusion that, at the age of only 30, the appellant would be a danger to the public indefinitely. In *Buckley* (1994) 15 Cr App R (S) 695, however, the fact that the appellant had such an appalling driving record, including six convictions for reckless driving, demonstrated an astonishing readiness to imperil the public and clearly satisfied the second limb in *King*; in those circumstances disqualification for life was justified. **C7.38**

When considering the period for which to disqualify a defendant whose licence has already been revoked because of a relevant disability, it is wrong in principle for the court to disqualify indefinitely (*Harrison* [2004] EWCA Crim 1527). The period of disqualification should reflect the offence and the offender's driving record and concerns about public safety arising from that disability are more appropriately dealt with through DVLA procedures for restoring the licence once the disability is no longer a factor.

Where the length of sentence alone is being challenged on appeal (which is preferable to instituting proceedings for judicial review), the appropriate test to apply is whether the sentence is 'truly astonishing' (*Tucker v DPP* [1992] 4 All ER 901; *Ealing Justices, ex parte Scrafield* [1994] RTR 195). In cases involving additional factors, the 'harsh and oppressive' test might be more appropriate. **C7.39**

Appeal against and Suspension of Disqualification

Under the RTOA 1988, s. 38(1), a person disqualified by an order of a magistrates' court under s. 34 or 35 may appeal against the order in the same manner as against a conviction. Section 39(1) provides that any court which makes an order disqualifying a person may, if it thinks fit, suspend the disqualification pending an appeal against the order. **C7.40**

Effect of Order of Disqualification

Upon being disqualified by court order, under the RTOA 1988, s. 37, the defendant's licence is generally treated as being revoked from the beginning of the disqualification. Revocation does not operate for short disqualifications of less than 56 days for endorsable offences or on interim disqualification under the RTOA 1988, s. 26 (see **C7.30**). If disqualified under the RTOA 1988, s. 36, until a retest is passed (see **C7.32**), and if not otherwise disqualified, a provisional licence can be obtained at the end of the fixed period of disqualification. **C7.41**

Removal of Disqualification

The RTOA 1988, s. 42, enables a person to apply to the court by which the person was disqualified to remove that disqualification. This option is not available for a disqualification imposed under the RTOA 1988, s. 36(1) (requiring a retest: see **C7.32**). An application can be made only after a certain period of the disqualification has been served: two years if the disqualification was for less than four years; otherwise half of the period of disqualification, **C7.42** subject to never having to wait longer than five years. The court is able to reconsider the length of disqualification and may take into account the person's conduct since the disqualification was imposed. If an application is refused, a further application may not be made until at least three months have elapsed.

C7.43 By the RTOA 1988, s. 43, any period of suspension shall be disregarded in determining the expiration of a period of disqualification. Thus, if a defendant is disqualified for three years and during that period the disqualification is suspended for three months, then the expiry of the disqualification is three years and three months after the date of disqualification.

CrimPR 29.2 (see Supplement, **R29.2**) sets out the requirements for an application under s. 42. There is no power to award the applicant costs but even if successful the applicant may be ordered to pay the costs of the application. There appears to be nothing to prevent the court from fixing the hearing date at any stage as long as the application is actually heard after the expiry of the 'relevant time'.

Probationary Period for Newly Qualified Drivers

C7.44 The Road Traffic (New Drivers) Act 1995, s. 1, establishes a probationary period of two years commencing from the day on which a person becomes a qualified driver, during which time a driver is more at risk of having the driving licence withdrawn through disqualification than following its completion.

A person becomes a 'qualified driver' on the first occasion of passing a UK driving test or a driving test conducted in any EEA State, the Isle of Man, any of the Channel Islands or Gibraltar (s. 1(2)). By virtue of s. 7, the period may be terminated early if the person is disqualified until a driving test is passed under the RTOA 1988, s. 36 (see **C7.32**), or if the person has already had to surrender the licence under the terms of the 1995 Act and has since been granted a full driving licence after retaking and passing a driving test.

During the probationary period, if the driver commits an offence or offences involving obligatory endorsement where the penalty points to be taken into account under the RTOA 1988, s. 29 (see **C7.19**), are six or more, the sentencing court or fixed penalty clerk must send a notice, together with the driver's licence, to the Secretary of State (s. 2), who must then serve a notice on the driver revoking the licence (s. 3). (Schedule 1 to the 1995 Act makes similar provisions for the surrender and revocation of test certificates and provisional driving licences, where the driver has not yet applied for a full driving licence.) There is no discretion involved although 'special reasons' (see **C7.53**) may, if appropriate, be raised against endorsement to prevent such an eventuality. In *Benson* [2012] EWCA Crim 2993, having indicated that the defendant's careless driving did not merit disqualification, but warranted a 'significant number' of points, without consideration of the effect of the 1995 Act, the sentencer imposed six penalty points. Revocation of the licence was only discovered some years later when the appellant sought to change the address shown on the licence. The situation was remedied by granting leave to appeal out of time and then substituting five penalty points instead.

C7.45 Where a licence is revoked the holder has to retake and pass an 'ordinary' driving test for each class of vehicle affected by the revocation before being able to drive unsupervised and being eligible to apply once again for a full driving licence (s. 4). After passing the retest, however, no probationary period attaches, otherwise persistent offenders could find themselves in a vicious circle of retesting.

By s. 5, if the driver appeals against the conviction or penalty points that led to the person's licence being revoked under s. 3 and the Secretary of State receives due notification, the licence will be temporarily restored to the driver pending determination of the appeal. If the appeal is successful, a new full licence will be granted and, if appropriate, the probationary period will continue to run. If the appeal fails to reduce the relevant penalty points below six, the temporary licence will be treated as revoked. These provisions are supplemented by the New Drivers (Appeals Procedure) Regulations 1997 (SI 1997 No. 1098).

Any penalty points which lead to the revocation of a licence remain effective for the normal three-year period from the date of commission of the offence (RTOA 1988, s. 29(2): see **C7.19**).

Revocation of the driving licence does not 'wipe clean' the person's driving record for the purposes of disqualification for repeated offences under s. 35 (see **C7.24**). A short discretionary disqualification under s. 34(2), would, however, lead to there being no penalty points to be taken into account. If the sentencer declines to impose a discretionary disqualification, there should be some consideration of the effect on the defendant of awarding six or more penalty points, where the range for the offence permits a lower number (*Edmunds* [2000] 2 Cr App R (S) 62). The sentencing court should bear in mind the intention of the 1995 Act to require newly qualified drivers whose driving is poor to face retesting.

ENDORSEMENT

Road Traffic Offenders Act 1988, ss. 44 and 44A **C7.46**

44.—(1) Where a person is convicted of an offence involving obligatory endorsement, the court must order there to be endorsed on his driving record particulars of the conviction and also—
- (a) if the court orders him to be disqualified, particulars of the disqualification, or
- (b) if the court does not order him to be disqualified—
  - (i) particulars of the offence, including the date when it was committed, and
  - (ii) the penalty points to be attributed to the offence.

(2) Where the court does not order the person convicted to be disqualified, it need not make an order under subsection (1) above if for special reasons it thinks fit not to do so.

(3) [Applies only to Scotland.]

(4) This section is subject to section 48 of this Act.

44A.—(1) Where the court orders the endorsement of a person's driving record with any particulars or penalty points it must send notice of the order to the Secretary of State.

(2) On receiving the notice, the Secretary of State must endorse those particulars or penalty points on the person's driving record.

(3) A notice sent by the court to the Secretary of State in pursuance of this section must be sent in such manner and to such address and contain such particulars as the Secretary of State may require.

In all cases involving obligatory or discretionary disqualification, the court, in the absence of 'special reasons' (see **C7.53**) or the operation of the RTOA 1988, s. 48, or the Mental Health Act 1983, s. 37 (see **E22.2**), is obliged to order particulars of the offence to be endorsed on the offender's driving record: see **C7.50**). Each offence is denoted by a particular code, and the DVLA is notified. Where the offender is not disqualified, penalty points must also be endorsed (RTOA 1988, s. 44). Where the offender is disqualified, penalty points in respect of that offence must not additionally be endorsed (*Usaceva* [2015] EWCA Crim 166, [2016] 1 All ER 741) nor should points be endorsed in respect of another offence committed on the same occasion (*Fisher* [2019] EWCA Crim 1066; *Thomas* [2020] EWCA Crim 513, which also relates to summary offences committed to the Crown Court under the PCC(S)A 2000). **C7.47**

The number of points applicable to an offence is set out in the RTOA 1988, sch. 2, part I, col. 7. Certain offences carry a variable number of points (see **C8.1**). In cases involving variable penalty points, the court should allow mitigation before arriving at any decision as to the number of points that should be imposed.

The points to be endorsed should reflect the seriousness of the offence. Therefore, an offence of driving without due care and attention consisting of momentary inattention might be suitably endorsed with three or four penalty points, whereas an offence consisting of prolonged, blatantly bad driving should carry a higher number of points to reflect the greater degree of culpability.

If there are a number of offences committed on the 'same occasion' then, subject to the RTOA 1988, s. 28 (see **C7.16**), the points to be endorsed are those relating to the offence which carries the highest number. Thus, if a defendant is convicted of careless driving and a construction and use offence, the highest number of penalty points relates to the careless driving. If the penalty points are the same for both offences, then it is normal practice to endorse the more serious offence with the points. Where penalty points for a fixed penalty have already been endorsed, **C7.48** the maximum number of points available to the court in respect of an offence committed on the same occasion must be reduced accordingly (see C7.21; *Green v O'Donnell* 1997 SCCR 315). If a period of disqualification is obligatory or imposed under the court's discretionary powers, no penalty points in respect of other offences committed on the 'same occasion' are endorsed (*Martin v DPP* [2000] RTR 188 and *Ahmed v McLeod* [2000] RTR 201n, respectively).

It is not unusual for a defendant to face a number of charges relating to different occasions. In those circumstances the court must establish the total number of points for each occasion, and is then obliged to aggregate those points for the purposes of the penalty points procedure.

The fact that an endorsement to which s. 45(7) applies remains effective beyond the time after which the conviction to which it attaches may be spent under the Rehabilitation of Offenders Act 1974 (see E24) does not constitute a violation of the right to private life in the ECHR, Article 8(1) (*R (Pearson) v DVLA* [2002] EWHC 2482 (Admin), [2003] RTR 20 (292)).

Meaning of 'Offence Involving Obligatory Endorsement'

C7.49 **Road Traffic Offenders Act 1988, s. 96**

For the purposes of this Act, an offence involves obligatory endorsement if it is an offence under a provision of the Traffic Acts specified in column 1 of Part I of Schedule 2 to this Act or an offence specified in column 1 of Part II of that Schedule and either—

(a) the word 'obligatory' (without qualification) appears in column 6 (in the case of Part I) or column 3 (in the case of Part II) against the offence, or
(b) that word appears there qualified by conditions relating to the offence which are satisfied.

For the RTOA 1988, sch. 2, see **C8.1**.

System of Endorsement

C7.50 **Driving Record** With effect from 8 June 2015 (see SI 2015 No. 560), driving licence counterparts in Great Britain (and Community counterparts) were abolished under the Road Safety Act 2006, s. 10 and sch. 3. Endorsements, penalty points and disqualifications are entered solely on to an individual's electronic driving record maintained by the DVLA. These records are 'designed to be endorsed with particulars relating to offences committed by the person under the Traffic Acts' (RTA 1988, s. 97A). This uniform, centralised system of offending records enables those who need to do so to access the database of records in order to ascertain whether the person with whom they are dealing is liable to disqualification under the RTOA 1988, s. 35.

C7.51 A driver who holds a GB driving licence is still required to produce it, but is no longer required to produce the counterpart. This obligation applies whether production is to the court or on being given a fixed penalty notice. In the case of a person who does not hold a GB driving licence, the RTOA 1988, s. 57A, enables a fixed penalty clerk, upon payment of the fixed penalty before the end of the suspended enforcement period, to send relevant particulars to be entered on the person's driving record.

Combination of Disqualification and Endorsement with Orders for Discharge

C7.52 The RTOA 1988, s. 46, makes provision as to the combination of orders for disqualification and endorsement with the provisions in the PCC(S)A 2000, s. 14, which have the effect of treating a conviction in respect of which a discharge is imposed as if it were not a conviction at all (see **E12.6**). Section 46(1) provides that the PCC(S)A 2000, s. 14(3), does not operate to prevent the court from endorsing an offender's driving record or disqualifying the person from driving. Section 46(2) provides that the PCC(S)A 2000, s. 14(1), does not operate to prevent a court from taking into account previous orders of disqualification or endorsement imposed on an occasion when the offender was discharged.

SPECIAL REASONS

General

A finding of 'special reasons' allows the court a discretion as to whether or not it: C7.53

(a) disqualifies under the RTOA 1988, s. 34(1); or
(b) endorses under the RTOA 1988, s. 44.

A 'special reason' was defined in *Whittal v Kirby* [1947] KB 194 as being special to the facts of the offence and not the offender. In doing so the Divisional Court adopted the definition in *Crossan* [1939] NI 106 (at pp. 112–13):

> A 'special reason' within the exception is one which is special to the facts of the particular case, that is, special to the facts which constitute the offence. It is, in other words, a mitigating or extenuating circumstance, not amounting in law to a defence to the charge, yet directly connected with the commission of the offence, and one which the court ought properly to take into consideration when imposing punishment. A circumstance peculiar to the offender as distinguished from the offence is not a 'special reason' within the exception.

Although *Wickins* (1958) 42 Cr App R 236 broadly confirmed these requirements, in *Jarvis v DPP* (2001) 165 JP 15, in respect of cases where excess alcohol offending is in issue, preference was expressed for the analysis of the position contained in *Jackson* [1970] 1 QB 647. Where a defendant's medical condition is found not to amount to a defence to a charge of failing to provide a specimen, it does not automatically mean that the same medical condition cannot constitute 'special reasons' (*Woolfe v DPP* [2006] EWHC 1497 (Admin), [2007] RTR 16 (187)).

As unreasonable delay in the determination of the charge does not relate to the facts of the offence so such delay cannot constitute a special reason (*Miller v DPP* [2004] EWHC 595 (Admin), [2005] RTR 3 (44)).

The onus of establishing that there are 'special reasons' lies with the defence on a balance of probabilities. Where there has been a trial resulting in a conviction and the defendant then advances special reasons, justices should readily accede to an application that a defendant be recalled when the earlier evidence has not fully dealt with the relevant facts (*DPP v Kinnersley* [1993] RTR 105). In most cases (save for obvious ones), the justices might expect to hear expert evidence, particularly where the defence seek to establish that drinks were laced, although where corroboration does not exist or is unavailable for some good reason it is still open to the court to find special reasons where the defendant's evidence is believed (*Watson v Adam* 1996 SLT 459). Notice of the defence's intention to produce evidence of such special reasons should be given to the prosecution so that unnecessary adjournments are avoided. Failure to notify the prosecution could reflect on the bona fides of the defendant (*DPP v O'Connor* [1992] RTR 66; see also *Pugsley v Hunter* [1973] 2 All ER 10). The defendant's failure to give an appropriate explanation or account at the time of arrest or commission of the offence does not, as a matter of law, exclude the possibility of a finding that special reasons exist, but it would usually form an important factor for the court in considering all the relevant circumstances of a case (*DPP v Kinnersley*). C7.54

'Special reasons' may be advanced on appeal to the Crown Court as part of an appeal against sentence, or, if an appeal against conviction includes an appeal against sentence, where the Crown Court have upheld the conviction. The appeal is by way of rehearing of the evidence relevant to the issue of whether or not there are special reasons and, if so, as to how the discretion is to be exercised. Where special reasons have not been found an appeal by way of case stated is a more convenient procedure than an application for judicial review (*DPP v O'Connor*).

Exercise of Power is Discretionary In *St. Albans Crown Court, ex parte O'Donovan* [2000] 1 Cr App R (S) 344, the Divisional Court noted that, whilst it did not rule out the possibility, following a finding of 'special reasons', of imposing a period of disqualification greater than the C7.55

mandatory minimum, there would have to be compelling reasons to do so. In *Ex parte Donovan*, the defendant was nearly three times above the prescribed limit but had only driven a very short distance and had not posed any appreciable risk of danger to anyone. A disqualification of 12 months was substituted for the original 20 months.

Even where 'special reasons' have been established, there is no obligation to exercise the discretion and the court may still disqualify and endorse as it considers appropriate. In cases involving obligatory disqualification, the court may find 'special reasons' and not disqualify but still endorse. In cases where disqualification is discretionary, the court may find 'special reasons' and still endorse. In *Agnew v DPP* [1991] RTR 147, a case of careless driving, the Divisional Court found that the conditions were satisfied but refused to exercise its discretion. The applicant was a police officer on a training exercise who had gone through a red light, failing to follow instructions in treating the light in the same way as a 'give way' sign. Morland J quoted Lord Widgery CJ in *Taylor v Rajan* [1974] QB 424, that 'justices should only exercise the discretion in favour of the driver in clear and compelling circumstances'. He then went on to say (at p. 150):

> There are two competing considerations: the need for realistic police driver training in actual road conditions and the safety of lawful users of the highway, motorists and pedestrians. The second must always be paramount.

C7.56 Whether or not to exercise the discretion 'is peculiarly a question for [the justices], seeing and hearing the witnesses and making their assessment of the answers which are given to them, to determine whether in the circumstances it is a case in which they, in the exercise of that discretion, feel justified in imposing penalties other than disqualification' (per Beldam J in *Donahue v DPP* [1993] RTR 156). In *DPP v Bristow* [1998] RTR 100, the Divisional Court held that the key question justices should ask themselves when assessing if special reasons exist and whether their discretion should be exercised is what a sober, reasonable and responsible friend of the defendant, who was present at the time but who was a non-driver and thus unable to help, would have advised in the circumstances: drive or not drive. Unless the justices thought it was a real possibility rather than just an off-chance that such a friend would have advised the defendant to drive, they should not find special reasons and exercise their discretion.

Endorsement under s. 44 includes endorsement with penalty points. If the court does exercise the discretion not to endorse with particulars of the conviction, there is no power to endorse penalty points separately. Nor is there any power to endorse either without penalty points or with a lesser number than the amount set out in sch. 2 to the Act.

As shown in the examples that follow, the question of what constitutes 'special reasons' depends upon the facts of any particular case within the overall test as expressed in *Whittal v Kirby* [1947] KB 194 (see **C7.53**). As long as the justices or Crown Court have properly directed themselves in accordance with that test, the appellate courts will not interfere with their finding. Many of the cases relate to drink-related offences where the defendant may be anxious to avoid a mandatory disqualification. The courts have consistently sought to limit the application of 'special reasons' to cases which are plainly meritorious.

C7.57 **'Laced' Drinks** 'Laced' drinks as a special reason received a comprehensive review in *DPP v O'Connor* [1992] RTR 66. The Divisional Court held that the defence must show:

(a) that the defendant's drink or drinks had been laced;
(b) that the defendant did not know or suspect that the drink had been laced;
(c) that, if the defendant had not taken the laced drink, the defendant's level of alcohol would not have exceeded the prescribed limit.

Evidence needs to be examined with some care and expert evidence, which justices should normally expect to receive, is usually highly relevant as it goes to both credibility and whether the driver's admitted, voluntary consumption of alcohol would have taken the driver above the prescribed limit (per Woolf LJ at p. 79). In appropriate cases, public funding should be made available to enable a defendant to adduce expert evidence to support a plea of special reasons in 'laced drinks' cases (*Gravesham Magistrates' Court, ex parte Baker* [1998] RTR 451).

The need for a two-stage process was stressed, and Woolf LJ stated (at p. 81E):

> ... in cases where there is erratic driving, or there is a substantial amount of alcohol in the defendant's bloodstream, justices will want to consider carefully whether, even if special reasons are established, this is a case where the defendant should have appreciated that he was not in a condition in which he should have driven.

An inability to distinguish between the relative alcoholic strengths of different drinks will not suffice (*Beauchamp-Thompson v DPP* [1988] RTR 54), otherwise it could give rise to a licence to 'lace' one's own drinks. Assuming, without inquiry, that a drink contains no alcohol will not constitute special reasons (*Robinson v DPP* [2003] EWHC 2718 (Admin), (2004) 168 JP 522, where the Divisional Court suggested *obiter* that even after inquiry and being told that the drink did not contain alcohol, readings that are very high should still not result in the justices exercising their discretion in favour of the defendant). The difficulties presented when advancing special reasons were highlighted in *R (Knifton) v DPP* [2011] EWHC 3850 (Admin), where the Divisional Court decided that the justices, following careful scrutiny of the evidence given, had been entitled to conclude that the defendant had known, or at very least suspected, that the drinks consumed had been laced.

Handling Emergencies In principle, driving in an emergency is recognised as being capable of amounting to special reasons. When raised, it is the justices' task to decide whether the facts amount to, and were, special reasons and then to decide what effect, if any, this has on the sentence to be imposed (*DPP v Upchurch* [1994] RTR 366; *DPP v Knight* [1994] RTR 374). In doing so, the court can divide the driving into separate chapters to ascertain whether there was any interruption after which a fresh explanation would be required as to why the defendant had chosen to drive again (*DPP v Goddard* [1998] RTR 463). C7.58

In *Aichroth v Cottee* [1954] 2 All ER 856, Lord Goddard CJ stated (at p. 1127) that the 'mere fact that there is a sudden emergency will not be enough if it is shown that there are other reasonable methods of meeting it'. In *DPP v Cox* [1996] RTR 123, the defendant was a key-holder at a golf club and was contacted in the night when the burglar alarm was activated. Despite the short distance involved and having consumed a considerable amount of alcohol, the defendant drove to the club premises without considering alternative methods of responding to the alarm. The Divisional Court confirmed that the issue of whether an emergency exists must be viewed objectively and held that the justices were justified in concluding that this was an emergency within the guidelines of *Aichroth v Cottee*. When considering if special reasons not to disqualify exist and deciding objectively whether a reasonable or sober person would have advised the defendant to drive in the perceived urgent situation in which the defendant was placed, it is appropriate to take into account the amount of alcohol consumed and the fact that the danger to road users would have been obvious (*DPP v Heathcote* [2011] EWHC 2536 (Admin), (2011) 175 JP 530). Where it was apparent to the defendant that the onset of a diabetic hypoglycaemic attack was occurring, special reasons may be available on a charge of speeding if, and only if, the decision to exceed the speed limit was a reasonable means by which to bring the vehicle to a halt at the nearest convenient moment (*Warring-Davies v CPS Bradford* [2009] EWHC 1172 (Admin), [2009] RTR 35 (431)).

A private crisis, such as being blackmailed by a threat of crying rape, can justify a finding of special reasons as long as the justices guard against being taken in by hard luck stories and approach the issue in the proper objective fashion (*DPP v Enston* [1996] RTR 324). Provided justices have considered all the relevant facts, have reached a conclusion on those facts that could not be said to be perverse and have directed themselves properly on the law, the Divisional Court should be very slow to overturn the decision of the justices, even if it does not agree with the conclusions of the justices as to the facts (*Chapman v O'Hagan* [1949] 2 All ER 690). See also *Ashton v CPS* [2005] EWHC 2729 (Admin), which involved a defendant being en route to collect a liveried ambulance to answer a call-out. C7.59

In *DPP v Whittle* [1996] RTR 154, however, the Divisional Court overturned a finding of special reasons on grounds of a medical emergency, reaffirming the objective approach required, because the reasonable man would not have regarded the situation as one in which no other course of action was possible. The defendant's spouse had been driving and complained of dizziness and blurred vision, so the defendant had taken over the driving, but was also driving fellow passengers home when stopped by the police. In passing, Simon Brown LJ wondered whether a genuine medical emergency might more properly fall within the complete defence of duress of circumstances (see **A3.50**) rather than being raised only as a special reason. In cases involving the risk of death or serious injury, such a course would certainly be advisable.

C7.60 **Relevance of Distance Driven** In *Chatters v Burke* [1986] 3 All ER 168, following an accident the defendant drove the motor vehicle a very short distance from a field onto the side of the highway, where the defendant stopped, got out, and waited for the arrival of the police. Charges of driving with excess alcohol and no insurance were preferred. The finding of 'special reasons' was upheld and seven matters which ought to be taken into account in such cases were listed (at p. 1327):

> First of all they should consider how far the vehicle was in fact driven; secondly, in what manner it was driven; thirdly, what was the state of the vehicle; fourthly, whether it was the intention of the driver to drive any further; fifthly, the prevailing conditions with regard to the road and the traffic upon it; sixthly, whether there was any possibility of danger by contact with other road users; and finally, what was the reason for the vehicle being driven at all.

C7.61 In *DPP v Humphries* [2000] RTR 52, the Divisional Court recognised the importance of this guidance whilst adding that the presence or absence of any factor would not automatically produce a particular conclusion. In this case, an argument in favour of finding 'special reasons' founded on the short distance actually driven was rejected because the intention of the defendant had been to drive much further had he not been apprehended. In contrast, in *DPP v Heritage* [2002] EWHC 2139 (Admin), (2002) 166 JP 772, where the vehicle had been moved to a parking place and was then involved in a collision, having regard to the very short distance driven and all the surrounding circumstances, the justices were entitled to conclude that special reasons existed on a conviction for no insurance.

In *DPP v Corcoran* [1991] RTR 329, the respondent, having parked in the street due to being late for the theatre, drove some 40 yards to a car park from which a colleague was to collect the car on the following day. The car was travelling without lights, albeit slowly, and there were pedestrians in the vicinity but no other vehicles were visible and no danger was caused to other road users. The lack of danger by contact with other road users and the distance travelled were central to the decision to uphold the justices' finding of special reasons. But other factors, such as the availability of alternative courses of action to that of driving, can lead to the opposite conclusion (*R (DPP) v Oram* [2005] EWHC 964 (Admin)).

In *Daniels v DPP* [1992] RTR 140, the appellant, in the course of attempting to start a motor cycle, travelled 35 yards and was then arrested on suspicion of theft. As the defendant claimed that the subsequent refusal to provide the required specimen was attributable to having been distracted by the charge of theft (which was not being pursued), on those particular facts the Divisional Court accepted that this could be found to amount to 'special reasons'.

C7.62 **No Insurance** In cases concerning no insurance, a mistaken, albeit honest, belief that there was insurance has been held to be insufficient to amount to 'special reasons' in the absence of reasonable grounds for the belief (*Knowler v Rennison* [1947] KB 488; *DPP v Robson* [2001] EWHC Admin 496), particularly where responsibility for withdrawal of insurance cover rested on the defendant (*R (Smith) v DPP* [2003] EWHC 1080 (Admin)). Where a defendant made inquiry as to whether there was insurance cover and was assured that there was, this may amount to reasonable grounds, and special reasons (*Marshall v McLeod* 1998 SCCR 317). The mere fact that a vehicle is parked and unlikely to be driven while uninsured will not amount to 'special reasons' (*Heywood v O'Connor* 1994 SLT 254). In *DPP v Powell* [1993] RTR 266, the defendant's view that there was no requirement for insurance to road test a motorised children's bike, which the defendant regarded as being a toy, was held to come within the test set out in *Whittal v Kirby* [1947] KB 194 (see **C7.53**). See also *DPP v Murray* [2001] EWHC Admin 848, which concerned a Go-Ped.

Other Reasons It can be 'special reasons' where the investigating officer incorrectly informs the defendant that failure to provide the required specimen will not necessarily lead to a period of disqualification (*Bobin v DPP* [1999] RTR 375). **C7.63**

Although fear of AIDS is potentially a defence to a charge of refusing to provide a specimen if it is medically established as a phobia (see *De Freitas v DPP* [1993] RTR 98 at **C5.28**), it was also held, in *DPP v Kinnersley* [1993] RTR 105, to be capable of being a 'special reason' for not disqualifying after a refusal to give a breath specimen.

Stating Grounds for Not Disqualifying or Endorsing or Shortening Period of Disqualification

Road Traffic Offenders Act 1988, s. 47 **C7.64**

(1) In any case where a court exercises its power under section 34, 35 or 44 of this Act not to order any disqualification or endorsement or to order disqualification for a shorter period than would otherwise be required, it must state the grounds for doing so in open court and, if it is a magistrates' court..., must cause them to be entered in the register... of its proceedings.

Any court must state, in open court, the grounds on which it has found 'special reasons' or 'mitigating circumstances', but despite the use of the word 'must', the Divisional Court in *Barnes v Gevaux* [1981] RTR 236 held that this requirement was discretionary in cases where the power to disqualify is discretionary.

INTERPRETATION PROVISIONS

Road Traffic Offenders Act 1988, s. 98 **C7.65**

(1) In this Act—
'disqualified' means disqualified for holding or obtaining a licence and 'disqualification' is to be construed accordingly,
'drive' has the same meaning as in the Road Traffic Act 1988,
'licence' means a licence to drive a motor vehicle granted under Part III of that Act,
'provisional licence' means a licence granted by virtue of section 97(2) of that Act,
'the provisions connected with the licensing of drivers' means sections 7, 8, 22, 25 to 29, 31, 34 to 48, 91ZA, 91A, 96 and 97 of this Act,
'road'—
(a) in relation to England and Wales, means any highway and any other road to which the public has access, and includes bridges over which a road passes, and
(b) [Applies only to Scotland.],
'the Road Traffic Acts' means the Road Traffic Act 1988, the Road Traffic (Consequential Provisions) Act 1988 (so far as it reproduces the effect of provisions repealed by that Act) and this Act, and
'the Traffic Acts' means the Road Traffic Acts and the Road Traffic Regulation Act 1984, and
'Community licence', 'EEA State' and 'Northern Ireland licence' have the same meanings as in Part III of the Road Traffic Act 1988.

(2) Sections 185 and 186 of the Road Traffic Act 1988 (meaning of 'motor vehicle' and other expressions relating to vehicles) apply for the purposes of this Act as they apply for the purposes of that Act.

(3) In the Schedules to this Act—
'RTRA' is used as an abbreviation for the Road Traffic Regulation Act 1984, and
'RTA' is used as an abbreviation for the Road Traffic Act 1988 or, if followed by '1989', the Road Traffic (Driver Licensing and Information Systems) Act 1989.

(4) Subject to any express exception, references in this Act to any Part of this Act include a reference to any Schedule to this Act so far as relating to that Part.

Section C8 Schedules 2 and 3 to the Road Traffic Offenders Act 1988

C8.1

Road Traffic Offenders Act 1988, sch. 2

SCHEDULE 2
PROSECUTION AND PUNISHMENT OF OFFENCES
PART I
OFFENCES UNDER THE TRAFFIC ACTS

(1) Provision creating offence	(2) General nature of offence	(3) Mode of prosecution	(4) Punishment	(5) Disqualification	(6) Endorsement	(7) Penalty points
Offences under the Road Traffic Regulation Act 1984						
RTRA section 5	Contravention of traffic regulation order.	Summarily.	Level 3 on the standard scale.			
RTRA section 8	Contravention of order regulating traffic in Greater London.	Summarily.	Level 3 on the standard scale.			
RTRA section 11	Contravention of experimental traffic order.	Summarily.	Level 3 on the standard scale.			
RTRA section 13	Contravention of experimental traffic scheme in Greater London.	Summarily.	Level 3 on the standard scale.			
RTRA section 16(1)	Contravention of temporary prohibition or restriction.	Summarily.	Level 3 on the standard scale.	Discretionary if committed in respect of a speed restriction.	Obligatory if committed in respect of a speed restriction.	3–6 or 3 (fixed penalty).
RTRA section 16C(1)	Contravention of prohibition or restriction relating to relevant event.	Summarily.	Level 3 on the standard scale.			
RTRA section 17(4)	Use of special road contrary to scheme or regulations.	Summarily.	Level 4 on the standard scale.	Discretionary if committed in respect of a motor vehicle otherwise than by unlawfully stopping or allowing the vehicle to remain at rest on a part of a special road on which vehicles are in certain circumstances permitted to remain at rest.	Obligatory if committed as mentioned in the entry in column 5.	3–6 or 3 (fixed penalty) if committed in respect of a speed restriction, 3 in any other case.
RTRA section 18(3)	One-way traffic on trunk road.	Summarily.	Level 3 on the standard scale.			

(1) Provision creating offence	(2) General nature of offence	(3) Mode of prosecution	(4) Punishment	(5) Disqualification	(6) Endorsement	(7) Penalty points
RTRA section 20(5)	Contravention of prohibition or restriction for roads of certain classes.	Summarily.	Level 3 on the standard scale.			
RTRA section 25(5)	Contravention of pedestrian crossing regulations.	Summarily.	Level 3 on the standard scale.	Discretionary if committed in respect of a motor vehicle.	Obligatory if committed in respect of a motor vehicle.	3
RTRA section 28(3)	Not stopping at school crossing.	Summarily.	Level 3 on the standard scale.	Discretionary if committed in respect of a motor vehicle.	Obligatory if committed in respect of a motor vehicle.	3
RTRA section 29(3)	Contravention of order relating to street playground.	Summarily.	Level 3 on the standard scale.	Discretionary if committed in respect of a motor vehicle.	Obligatory if committed in respect of a motor vehicle.	2
RTRA section 35A(1)	Contravention of order as to use of parking place.	Summarily.	(a) Level 3 on the standard scale in the case of an offence committed by a person in a street parking place reserved for disabled persons' vehicles or in an off-street parking place reserved for such vehicles, where that person would not have been guilty of that offence if the motor vehicle in respect of which it was committed had been a disabled person's vehicle. (b) Level 2 on the standard scale in any other case.			
RTRA section 35A(2)	Misuse of apparatus for collecting charges or of parking device or connected apparatus.	Summarily.	Level 3 on the standard scale.			
RTRA section 35A(5)	Plying for hire in parking place.	Summarily.	Level 2 on the standard scale.			
RTRA section 43(5)	Unauthorised disclosure of information in respect of licensed parking place.	Summarily.	Level 3 on the standard scale.			
RTRA section 43(10)	Failure to comply with term or conditions of licence to operate parking place.	Summarily.	Level 3 on the standard scale.			
RTRA section 43(12)	Operation of public offstreet parking place without licence.	Summarily.	[An unlimited fine.]			

(1) Provision creating offence	(2) General nature of offence	(3) Mode of prosecution	(4) Punishment	(5) Disqualification	(6) Endorsement	(7) Penalty points
RTRA section 47(1)	Contraventions relating to designated parking places.	Summarily.	(a) Level 3 on the standard scale in the case of an offence committed by a person in a street parking place reserved for disabled persons' vehicles where that person would not have been guilty of the offence if the motor vehicle in respect of which it was committed had been a disabled person's vehicle. (b) Level 2 in any other case.			
RTRA section 47(3)	Tampering with parking meter.	Summarily.	Level 3 on the standard scale.			
RTRA section 52(1)	Misuse of parking device.	Summarily.	Level 2 on the standard scale.			
RTRA section 53(5)	Contravention of certain provisions of designation orders.	Summarily.	Level 3 on the standard scale.			
RTRA section 53(6)	Other contraventions of designation orders.	Summarily.	Level 2 on the standard scale.			
RTRA section 61(5)	Unauthorised use of loading area.	Summarily.	Level 3 on the standard scale.			
RTRA section 88(7)	Contravention of minimum speed limit.	Summarily.	Level 3 on the standard scale.			
RTRA section 89(1)	Exceeding speed limit.	Summarily.	Level 3 on the standard scale.	Discretionary.	Obligatory.	3–6 or 3 (fixed penalty).
RTRA section 104(5)	Interference with notice as to immobilisation device.	Summarily.	Level 2 on the standard scale.			
RTRA section 104(6)	Interference with immobilisation device.	Summarily.	Level 3 on the standard scale.			
RTRA section 105(5)	Misuse of disabled person's badge (immobilisation devices).	Summarily.	Level 3 on the standard scale.			
RTRA section 105(6A)	Misuse of recognised badge (immobilisation devices).	Summarily.	Level 3 on the standard scale.			
RTRA section 108(2) (or that subsection as modified by section *109(2)* and (3))	Non-compliance with notice (excess charge).	Summarily.	Level 3 on the standard scale.			

(1) Provision creating offence	(2) General nature of offence	(3) Mode of prosecution	(4) Punishment	(5) Disqualification	(6) Endorsement	(7) Penalty points
RTRA section 108(3) (or that subsection as modified by section 109(2) and (3))	False response to notice (excess charge).	Summarily.	[An unlimited fine.]			
RTRA section 112(4)	Failure to give information as to identity of driver.	Summarily.	Level 3 on the standard scale.			
RTRA section 115(1)	Mishandling or faking parking documents.	(a) Summarily. (b) On indictment.	(a) [An unlimited fine.] (b) 2 years.			
RTRA section 115(2)	False statement for procuring authorisation.	Summarily.	Level 4 on the standard scale.			
RTRA section 116(1)	Non-delivery of suspect document or article.	Summarily.	Level 3 on the standard scale.			
RTRA section 117(1)	Wrongful use of disabled person's badge.	Summarily.	Level 3 on the standard scale.			
RTRA section 117(1A)	Wrongful use of recognised badge.	Summarily.	Level 3 on the standard scale.			
RTRA section 129(3)	Failure to give evidence at inquiry.	Summarily.	Level 3 on the standard scale.			
Offences under the Road Traffic Act 1988						
RTA section 1	Causing death by dangerous driving	On indictment.	14 years.	Obligatory.	Obligatory.	3–11
RTA section 1A	Causing serious injury by dangerous driving	(a) Summarily. (b) On indictment.	(a) [6 months] or [an unlimited fine] or both. (b) 5 years or a fine or both.	Obligatory	Obligatory.	3–11
RTA section 2	Dangerous driving.	(a) Summarily. (b) On indictment.	(a) 6 months or [an unlimited fine] or both. (b) 2 years or a fine or both.	Obligatory.	Obligatory.	3–11
RTA section 2B	Causing death by careless, or inconsiderate, driving.	(a) Summarily. (b) On indictment.	(a) [6 months] or [an unlimited fine] or both. (b) 5 years or a fine or both.	Obligatory.	Obligatory.	3–11
RTA section 3	Careless, and inconsiderate, driving.	Summarily.	[An unlimited fine.]	Discretionary.	Obligatory.	3–9
RTA section 3ZB	Causing death by driving: unlicensed or uninsured drivers.	(a) Summarily. (b) On indictment.	(a) [6 months] or [an unlimited fine] or both. (b) 2 years or a fine or both.	Obligatory.	Obligatory.	3–11

(1) Provision creating offence	(2) General nature of offence	(3) Mode of prosecution	(4) Punishment	(5) Disqualification	(6) Endorsement	(7) Penalty points
RTA section 3ZC	Causing death by driving: disqualified drivers	On indictment	10 years or a fine or both	Obligatory.	Obligatory.	3–11
RTA section 3ZD	Causing serious injury by driving: disqualified drivers	(a) Summarily. (b) On indictment.	(a) On conviction in England and Wales: [6] months or a fine or both. [Applies only to Scotland.] (b) 4 years or a fine or both	Obligatory.	Obligatory.	3–11
RTA section 3A	Causing death by careless driving when under influence of drink or drugs.	On indictment.	14 years or a fine or both.	Obligatory.	Obligatory.	3–11
RTA section 4(1)	Driving or attempting to drive when unfit to drive through drink or drugs.	Summarily.	6 months or [an unlimited fine] or both.	Obligatory.	Obligatory.	3–11
RTA section 4(2)	Being in charge of a mechanically propelled vehicle when unfit to drive through drink or drugs	Summarily.	3 months or level 4 on the standard scale or both.	Discretionary.	Obligatory.	10
RTA section 5(1)(a)	Driving or attempting to drive with excess alcohol in breath, blood or urine.	Summarily.	6 months or [an unlimited fine] or both.	Obligatory.	Obligatory.	3–11
RTA section 5(1)(b)	Being in charge of a motor vehicle with excess alcohol in breath, blood or urine.	Summarily.	3 months or level 4 on the standard scale or both.	Discretionary.	Obligatory.	10
RTA section 5A(1)(a) and (2)	Driving or attempting to drive with concentration of specified controlled drug above specified limit.	Summarily.	On conviction in England and Wales: [6 months] or [an unlimited fine] or both. [Applies only to Scotland.]	Obligatory.	Obligatory.	3–11
RTA section 5A(1)(b) and (2)	Being in charge of a motor vehicle with concentration of specified controlled drug above specified limit.	Summarily.	On conviction in England and Wales: [6 months] or level 4 on the standard scale or both. [Applies only to Scotland.]	Discretionary.	Obligatory.	10
RTA section 6	Failing to co-operate with a preliminary test.	Summarily.	Level 3 on the standard scale.	Discretionary.	Obligatory.	4
RTA section 7	Failing to provide specimen for analysis or laboratory test.	Summarily.	(a) Where the specimen was required to ascertain ability to drive or proportion of alcohol or proportion of a specified controlled drug at the time offender was driving or attempting to drive, 6 months or [an unlimited fine] or both. (b) In any other case, 3 months or level 4 on the standard scale or both.	(a) Obligatory in case mentioned in column 4(a). (b) Discretionary in any other case.	Obligatory.	(a) 3–11 in case mentioned in column 4(a). (b) 10 in any other case.

(1) Provision creating offence	(2) General nature of offence	(3) Mode of prosecution	(4) Punishment	(5) Disqualification	(6) Endorsement	(7) Penalty points
RTA section 7A	Failing to allow specimen to be subjected to laboratory test.	Summarily.	(a) Where the test would be for ascertaining ability to drive or proportion of alcohol or proportion of a specified controlled drug at the time offender was driving or attempting to drive, 6 months or [an unlimited fine] or both. (b) In any other case, 3 months or level 4 on the standard scale or both.	(a) Obligatory in the case mentioned in column 4(a). (b) Discretionary in any other case.	Obligatory.	(a) 3–11, in case mentioned in column 4(a). (b) 10 in any other case.
RTA section 12	Motor racing and speed trials on public ways.	Summarily.	Level 4 on the standard scale.	Obligatory.	Obligatory.	3–11
RTA section 13	Other unauthorised or irregular competitions or trials on public ways.	Summarily.	Level 3 on the standard scale.			
RTA section 14	Driving or riding in a motor vehicle in contravention of regulations requiring wearing of seat belts.	Summarily.	Level 2 on the standard scale.			
RTA section 15(2)	Driving motor vehicle with child in front not wearing seat belt or with child in a rear-facing child restraint in front seat with an active air bag.	Summarily.	Level 2 on the standard scale.			
RTA section 15(4)	Driving motor vehicle with child in rear not wearing seat belt.	Summarily.	Level 2 on the standard scale.			
RTA section 15A(3) or (4)	Selling etc. in certain circumstances equipment as conducive to the safety of children in motor vehicles.	Summarily.	Level 3 on the standard scale.			
RTA section 15B	Failure to notify bus passengers of the requirement to wear seat belt.	Summarily.	Level 4 on the standard scale.			
RTA section 16	Driving or riding motor cycles in contravention of regulations requiring wearing of protective headgear.	Summarily.	Level 2 on the standard scale.			
RTA section 17	Selling, etc., helmet not of the prescribed type as helmet for affording protection for motor cyclists.	Summarily.	Level 3 on the standard scale.			

(1) Provision creating offence	(2) General nature of offence	(3) Mode of prosecution	(4) Punishment	(5) Disqualification	(6) Endorsement	(7) Penalty points
RTA section 18(3)	Contravention of regulations with respect to use of headworn appliances on motor cycles.	Summarily.	Level 2 on the standard scale.			
RTA section 18(4)	Selling, etc., appliance not of prescribed type as approved for use on motor cycles.	Summarily.	Level 3 on the standard scale.			
RTA section 19	Prohibition of parking of heavy commercial vehicles on verges, etc.	Summarily.	Level 3 on the standard scale.			
RTA section 21	Driving or parking on cycle track.	Summarily.	Level 3 on the standard scale.			
RTA section 22	Leaving vehicles in dangerous positions.	Summarily.	Level 3 on the standard scale.	Discretionary if committed in respect of a motor vehicle.	Obligatory if committed in respect of a motor vehicle.	3
RTA section 22A	Causing danger to road users.	(a) Summarily. (b) On indictment.	(a) 6 months or [an unlimited fine] or both. (b) 7 years or a fine or both.			
RTA section 23	Carrying passenger on motor-cycle contrary to section 23.	Summarily.	Level 3 on the standard scale.	Discretionary.	Obligatory.	3
RTA section 24	Carrying passenger on bicycle contrary to section 24.	Summarily.	Level 1 on the standard scale.			
RTA section 25	Tampering with motor vehicles.	Summarily.	Level 3 on the standard scale.			
RTA section 26	Holding or getting on to vehicle, etc., in order to be towed or carried.	Summarily.	Level 1 on the standard scale.			
RTA section 27	Dogs on designated roads without being held on lead.	Summarily.	Level 1 on the standard scale.			
RTA section 28	Dangerous cycling.	Summarily.	Level 4 on the standard scale.			
RTA section 29	Careless, and inconsiderate, cycling.	Summarily.	Level 3 on the standard scale.			
RTA section 30	Cycling when unfit through drink or drugs.	Summarily.	Level 3 on the standard scale.			
RTA section 31	Unauthorised or irregular cycle racing or trials of speed on public ways.	Summarily.	Level 1 on the standard scale.			
RTA section 32	Contravening prohibition on persons under 14 driving electrically assisted pedal cycles.	Summarily.	Level 2 on the standard scale.			
RTA section 33	Unauthorised motor vehicle trial on footpaths or bridleways.	Summarily.	Level 3 on the standard scale.			
RTA section 34	Driving mechanically propelled vehicles elsewhere than on roads.	Summarily.	Level 3 on the standard scale.			

(1) Provision creating offence	(2) General nature of offence	(3) Mode of prosecution	(4) Punishment	(5) Disqualification	(6) Endorsement	(7) Penalty points
RTA section 35	Failing to comply with traffic directions.	Summarily.	Level 3 on the standard scale.	Discretionary, if committed in respect of a motor vehicle by failure to comply with a direction of a constable or traffic officer.	Obligatory if committed as described in column 5.	3
RTA section 36	Failing to comply with traffic signs.	Summarily.	Level 3 on the standard scale.	Discretionary, if committed in respect of a motor vehicle by failure to comply with an indication given by a sign specified for the purposes of this paragraph in regulations under RTA section 36.	Obligatory if committed as described in column 5.	
RTA section 37	Pedestrian failing to stop when directed.	Summarily.	Level 3 on the standard scale.			
RTA section 40A	Using vehicle in dangerous condition etc.	Summarily.	(a) [An unlimited fine] if committed in respect of a goods vehicle or a vehicle adapted to carry more than eight passengers. (b) Level 4 on the standard scale in any other case.	(a) Obligatory if committed within three years of a previous conviction of the offender under section 40A. (b) Discretionary in any other case.	Obligatory.	3
RTA section 41A	Breach of requirement as to brakes, steering-gear or tyres.	Summarily.	(a) [An unlimited fine] if committed in respect of a goods vehicle or a vehicle adapted to carry more than eight passengers. (b) Level 4 on the standard scale in any other case.	Discretionary.	Obligatory.	3
RTA section 41B	Breach of requirement as to weight: goods and passenger vehicles.	Summarily.	[An unlimited fine.]			
RTA section 41D	Breach of requirements as to control of vehicle, mobile telephones etc.	Summarily.	(a) Level 4 on the standard scale if committed in respect of a goods vehicle or a vehicle adapted to carry more than eight passengers. (b) Level 3 on the standard scale in any other case.	Discretionary.	Obligatory.	(a) 3, in the case of an offence under section 41D(a). (b) 6, in the case of an offence under section 41D(b).

(1) Provision creating offence	(2) General nature of offence	(3) Mode of prosecution	(4) Punishment	(5) Disqualification	(6) Endorsement	(7) Penalty points
RTA section 42	Breach of other construction and use requirements.	Summarily.	(a) Level 4 on the standard scale if committed in respect of a goods vehicle or a vehicle adapted to carry more than eight passengers. (b) Level 3 on the standard scale in any other case.			
RTA section 47	Using, etc., vehicle without required test certificate being in force.	Summarily.	(a) Level 4 on the standard scale in the case of a vehicle adapted to carry more than eight passengers. (b) Level 3 on the standard scale in any other case.			
Regulations under RTA section 49 made by virtue of section 51(2)	Contravention of requirement of regulations (which is declared by regulations to be an offence) that driver of goods vehicle being tested be present throughout tests or drive, etc., vehicle as and when directed.	Summarily.	Level 3 on the standard scale.			
RTA section 53(1)	Using, etc., goods vehicle without required plating certificate being in force.	Summarily.	Level 3 on the standard scale.			
RTA section 53(2)	Using, etc., goods vehicle without required goods vehicle test certificate being in force.	Summarily.	Level 4 on the standard scale.			
RTA section 53(3)	Using, etc., goods vehicle where Secretary of State is required by regulations under section 49 to be notified of an alteration to the vehicle or its equipment but has not been notified.	Summarily.	Level 3 on the standard scale.			
Regulations under RTA section 61 made by virtue of subsection (4)	Contravention of requirement of regulations (which is declared by regulations to be an offence) that driver of goods vehicle being tested after notifiable alteration be present throughout test and drive, etc., vehicle as and when directed.	Summarily.	Level 3 on the standard scale.			
RTA section 63(1)	Using, etc., goods vehicle without required certificate being in force showing that it complies with type approval requirements applicable to it.	Summarily.	Level 4 on the standard scale.			

(1) Provision creating offence	(2) General nature of offence	(3) Mode of prosecution	(4) Punishment	(5) Disqualification	(6) Endorsement	(7) Penalty points
RTA section 63(2)	Using, etc., certain goods vehicles for drawing trailer when plating certificate does not specify maximum laden weight for vehicle and trailer.	Summarily.	Level 3 on the standard scale.			
RTA section 63(3)	Using, etc., goods vehicle where Secretary of State is required to be notified under section 59 of alteration to it or its equipment but has not been notified.	Summarily.	Level 3 on the standard scale.			
RTA section 64	Using goods vehicle with unauthorised weights as well as authorised weights marked on it.	Summarily.	Level 3 on the standard scale.			
RTA section 65	Supplying vehicle or vehicle part without required certificate being in force showing that it complies with type approval requirements applicable to it.	Summarily.	[An unlimited fine.]			
RTA section 65A	Light passenger vehicles and motor cycles not to be sold without EC certificate of conformity.	Summarily.	[An unlimited fine.]			
RTA section 66C(1)	Impersonating a stopping officer etc. with intent to deceive	Summarily.	[An unlimited fine.]			
RTA section 66C(2)	Resisting or wilfully obstructing a stopping officer	Summarily.	One month or level 3 on the standard scale or both.			
RTA section 67	Obstructing testing of vehicle by examiner on road or failing to comply with requirements of RTA section 67 or Schedule 2.	Summarily.	Level 3 on the standard scale.			
RTA section 68	Obstructing inspection, etc., of vehicle by examiner or failing to comply with requirement to take vehicle for inspection.	Summarily.	Level 3 on the standard scale.			
RTA section 71	Driving, etc., vehicle in contravention of prohibition on driving it as being unfit for service, or refusing, neglecting or otherwise failing to comply with direction to remove a vehicle found overloaded.	Summarily.	[An unlimited fine.]			
RTA section 74	Contravention of regulations requiring goods vehicle operator to inspect, and keep records of inspection of, goods vehicles.	Summarily.	Level 3 on the standard scale.			

(1) Provision creating offence	(2) General nature of offence	(3) Mode of prosecution	(4) Punishment	(5) Disqualification	(6) Endorsement	(7) Penalty points
RTA section 75	Selling, etc., unroadworthy vehicle or trailer or altering vehicle or trailer so as to make it unroadworthy.	Summarily.	[An unlimited fine.]			
RTA section 76(1)	Fitting of defective or unsuitable vehicle parts.	Summarily.	[An unlimited fine.]			
RTA section 76(3)	Supplying defective or unsuitable vehicle parts.	Summarily.	Level 4 on the standard scale.			
RTA section 76(8)	Obstructing examiner testing vehicles to ascertain whether defective or unsuitable part has been fitted, etc.	Summarily.	Level 3 on the standard scale.			
RTA section 77	Obstructing examiner testing condition of used vehicle at sale rooms, etc.	Summarily.	Level 3 on the standard scale.			
RTA section 78	Failing to comply with requirement about weighing motor vehicle or obstructing authorised person.	Summarily.	[An unlimited fine.]			
RTA section 81	Selling, etc., pedal cycle in contravention of regulations as to brakes, bells, etc.	Summarily.	Level 3 on the standard scale.			
RTA section 83	Selling, etc., wrongly made tail lamps or reflectors.	Summarily.	[An unlimited fine.]			
RTA section 87(1)	Driving otherwise than in accordance with a licence.	Summarily.	Level 3 on the standard scale.	Discretionary in a case where the offender's driving would not have been in accordance with any licence that could have been granted to him.	Obligatory in the case mentioned in column 5.	3–6
RTA section 87(2)	Causing or permitting a person to drive otherwise than in accordance with a licence.	Summarily.	Level 3 on the standard scale.			
RTA section 92(7C)	Failure to deliver licence revoked by virtue of section 92(7A) to Secretary of State.	Summarily.	Level 3 on the standard scale.			
RTA section 92(10)	Driving after making false declaration as to physical fitness.	Summarily.	Level 4 on the standard scale.	Discretionary.	Obligatory.	3–6
RTA section 93(3)	Failure to deliver revoked licence to Secretary of State.	Summarily.	Level 3 on the standard scale.			
RTA section 94(3) and that subsection as applied by RTA section 99D or 109C	Failure to notify Secretary of State of onset of, or deterioration in, relevant or prospective disability.	Summarily.	Level 3 on the standard scale.			

(1) Provision creating offence	(2) General nature of offence	(3) Mode of prosecution	(4) Punishment	(5) Disqualification	(6) Endorsement	(7) Penalty points
RTA section 94(3A) and that subsection as applied by RTA section 99D(b) or 109C(c)	Driving after such a failure.	Summarily.	Level 3 on the standard scale.	Discretionary.	Obligatory.	3–6
RTA section 94A	Driving after refusal of licence under section 92(3), revocation under section 93 or service of a notice under section 99C or 109B.	Summarily.	6 months or [an unlimited fine] or both.	Discretionary.	Obligatory.	3–6
RTA section 96	Driving with uncorrected defective eyesight, or refusing to submit to test of eyesight.	Summarily.	Level 3 on the standard scale.	Discretionary.	Obligatory.	3
RTA section 99(5)	Driving licence holder failing to surrender licence.	Summarily.	Level 3 on the standard scale.			
RTA section 99B(11)	Driving after failing to comply with a requirement under section 99B(7) or (10).	Summarily.	Level 3 on the standard scale.			
RTA section 99C(4)	Failure to deliver Community licence to Secretary of State when required by notice under section 99C.	Summarily.	Level 3 on the standard scale.			
RTA section 103(1)(a)	Obtaining driving licence while disqualified.	Summarily.	Level 3 on the standard scale.			
RTA section 103(1)(b)	Driving while disqualified.	(a) Summarily, in England and Wales. (b) [Scotland] (c) [Scotland]	(a) 6 months or [an unlimited fine] or both. (b) [Scotland] (c) [Scotland]	Discretionary.	Obligatory.	6
RTA section 109B(4)	Failing to deliver Northern Ireland licence to Secretary of State when required by notice under section 109B.	Summarily.	Level 3 on the standard scale.			
RTA section 114	Failing to comply with conditions of LGV, PCV licence or LGV Community licence, or causing or permitting person under 21 to drive LGV or PCV in contravention of such conditions.	Summarily.	Level 3 on the standard scale.			
RTA section 115A(4)	Failure to deliver LGV or PCV Community licence when required by notice under section 115A.	Summarily.	Level 3 on the standard scale.			
RTA section 118	Failing to surrender revoked or suspended LGV or PCV licence.	Summarily.	Level 3 on the standard scale.			

(1) Provision creating offence	(2) General nature of offence	(3) Mode of prosecution	(4) Punishment	(5) Disqualification	(6) Endorsement	(7) Penalty points
Regulations made by virtue of RTA section 120(5)	Contravention of provision of regulations (which is declared by regulations to be an offence) about LGV or PCV drivers; licences or LGV or PCV Community licence.	Summarily.	Level 3 on the standard scale.			
RTA section 123(4)	Giving of paid driving instruction by unregistered and unlicensed person or their employers.	Summarily.	Level 4 on the standard scale.			
RTA section 123(6)	Giving of paid instruction without there being exhibited on the motor car a certificate of registration or a licence under RTA Part V.	Summarily.	Level 3 on the standard scale.			
RTA section 125(2B)	Failure, on application to be registered in respect of driving instruction, to notify Registrar of relevant or prospective disability.	Summarily.	Level 3 on the standard scale.			
RTA section 133C(4)	Failure by registered or licensed driving instructor to notify Registrar of onset of, or deterioration in, relevant or prospective disability.	Summarily.	Level 3 on the standard scale.			
RTA section 133D	Giving of paid driving instruction by persons required to hold emergency control certificates or their employers without emergency control certificate or in unauthorised motor car.	Summarily.	Level 3 on the standard scale.			
RTA section 135	Unregistered instructor using title or displaying badge, etc., prescribed for registered instructor, or employer using such title, etc., in relation to his unregistered instructor or issuing misleading advertisement, etc.	Summarily.	Level 4 on the standard scale.			
RTA section 136	Failure of instructor to surrender to Registrar certificate or licence.	Summarily.	Level 3 on the standard scale.			
RTA section 137	Failing to produce certificate of registration or licence as driving instructor.	Summarily.	Level 3 on the standard scale.			
RTA section 143	Using motor vehicle while uninsured.	Summarily.	[An unlimited fine.]	Discretionary.	Obligatory.	6–8
RTA section 144A	Keeping vehicle which does not meet insurance requirements.	Summarily.	Level 3 on the standard scale.			

(1) Provision creating offence	(2) General nature of offence	(3) Mode of prosecution	(4) Punishment	(5) Disqualification	(6) Endorsement	(7) Penalty points
RTA section 147	Failing to surrender certificate of insurance to insurer on cancellation or to make statutory declaration of loss or destruction.	Summarily.	Level 3 on the standard scale.			
RTA section 154	Failing to give information, or wilfully making a false statement, as to insurance when claim made.	Summarily.	Level 4 on the standard scale.			
Regulations under RTA section 160 made by virtue of paragraph 2(1) of schedule 2A	Contravention of provisions of regulations (which is declared by regulations to be an offence) prohibiting removal of or interference with immobilisation notice.	Summarily.	Level 2 on the standard scale.			
Regulations under RTA section 160 made by virtue of paragraph 2(2) of schedule 2A	Contravention of provisions of regulations (which is declared by regulations to be an offence) prohibiting removal or attempted removal of immobilisation device.	Summarily.	Level 3 on the standard scale.			
Regulations under RTA section 160 made by virtue of paragraph 2(3) of schedule 2A	Contravention of provisions of regulations (which is declared by regulations to be an offence) about display of disabled person's badge.	Summarily.	Level 3 on the standard scale.			
RTA section 163	Failing to stop mechanically propelled vehicle or cycle when required.	Summarily.	(a) [An unlimited fine] if committed by a person driving a mechanically propelled vehicle. (b) Level 3 on the standard scale if committed by a person riding a cycle.			
RTA section 164	Failing to produce driving licence or to state date of birth, or failing to provide the Secretary of State with evidence of date of birth, etc.	Summarily.	Level 3 on the standard scale.			
RTA section 165	Failing to give certain names and addresses or to produce certain documents.	Summarily.	Level 3 on the standard scale.			

(1) Provision creating offence	(2) General nature of offence	(3) Mode of prosecution	(4) Punishment	(5) Disqualification	(6) Endorsement	(7) Penalty points
RTA section 168	Refusing to give, or giving false, name and address in case of reckless, careless or inconsiderate driving or cycling.	Summarily.	Level 3 on the standard scale.			
RTA section 169	Pedestrian failing to give constable his name and address after failing to stop when directed by constable controlling traffic.	Summarily.	Level 1 on the standard scale.			
RTA section 170(4)	Failing to stop after accident and give particulars or report accident.	Summarily.	6 months or [an unlimited fine] or both.	Discretionary.	Obligatory.	5–10
RTA section 170(7)	Failure by driver, in case of accident involving injury to another, to produce evidence of insurance or to report accident.	Summarily.	Level 3 on the standard scale.			
RTA section 171	Failure by owner of motor vehicle to give police information for verifying compliance with requirement of compulsory insurance.	Summarily.	Level 4 on the standard scale.			
RTA section 172	Failure of person keeping vehicle and others to give police information as to identity of driver, etc., in the case of certain offences.	Summarily.	Level 3 on the standard scale.	Discretionary if committed otherwise than by virtue of subsection (5) or (11).	Obligatory if committed otherwise than by virtue of subsection (5) or (11).	6
RTA section 173	Forgery, etc., of licences, certificates of insurance and other documents and things.	(a) Summarily. (b) On indictment.	(a) [An unlimited fine.] (b) 2 years.			
RTA section 174	Making certain false statements, etc., and withholding certain material information.	(a) Summarily. (b) On indictment.	(a) 6 months or [an unlimited fine] or both. (b) 2 years or a fine or both.			
RTA section 175	Issuing false documents.	Summarily.	Level 4 on the standard scale.			
RTA section 177	Impersonation of, or of person employed by, authorised examiner.	Summarily.	Level 3 on the standard scale.			
RTA section 178	[Scotland.]					
RTA section 180	Failing to attend, give evidence or produce documents to, inquiry held by Secretary of State, etc.	Summarily.	Level 3 on the standard scale.			
RTA section 181	Obstructing inspection of vehicles after accident.	Summarily.	Level 3 on the standard scale.			

(1) Provision creating offence	(2) General nature of offence	(3) Mode of prosecution	(4) Punishment	(5) Disqualification	(6) Endorsement	(7) Penalty points
RTA schedule 1 paragraph 6	Applying warranty to equipment, protective helmet, appliance or information in defending proceedings under RTA section 15A, 17 or 18(4) where no warranty given, or applying false warranty.	Summarily.	Level 3 on the standard scale.			
Offences under this Act						
Section 25 of this Act.	Failing to give information as to date of birth or sex to court or to provide Secretary of State with evidence of date of birth, etc.	Summarily.	Level 3 on the standard scale.			
Section 26 of this Act.	Failing to produce driving licence to court making order for interim disqualification.	Summarily.	Level 3 on the standard scale.			
Section 27 of this Act.	Failing to produce licence to court for endorsement on conviction of offence involving obligatory endorsement or on committal for sentence, etc., for offence involving obligatory or discretionary disqualification when no interim disqualification ordered.	Summarily.	Level 3 on the standard scale.			
Section 62 of this Act.	Removing fixed penalty notice fixed to vehicle.	Summarily.	Level 2 on the standard scale.			
Section 67 of this Act.	False statement in response to notice to owner.	Summarily.	[An unlimited fine.]			
Section 90D(6) of this Act.	Driving, etc., vehicle in contravention of prohibition for failure to pay financial penalty deposit, etc.	Summarily.	[An unlimited fine.]			

C8.2

Part II
Other Offences

(1) Offence	(2) Disqualification	(3) Endorsement	(4) Penalty points
Manslaughter or, in Scotland, culpable homicide by the driver of a motor vehicle.	Obligatory.	Obligatory.	3–11
An offence under section 35 of the Offences against the Persons Act 1861 (furious driving).	Discretionary.	Obligatory if committed in respect of a mechanically propelled vehicle.	3–9
An offence under section 12A of the Theft Act 1968 (aggravated vehicle-taking).	Obligatory	Obligatory	3–11
Stealing or attempting to steal a motor vehicle.	Discretionary.		
An offence or attempt to commit an offence in respect of a motor vehicle under section 12 of the Theft Act 1968 (taking conveyance without consent of owner etc. or, knowing it has been so taken, driving it or allowing oneself to be carried in it).	Discretionary.		
An offence under section 25 of the Theft Act 1968 (going equipped for stealing, etc.) committed with reference to the theft or taking of motor vehicles.	Discretionary.		

C8.3

Road Traffic Offenders Act 1988, sch. 3

Schedule 3
Fixed Penalty Offences

(1) Provision creating offence	(2) General nature of offence
Offence under the Highways Act 1835	
Section 72 of the Highways Act 1835	Cycling/driving on the footway.
Offences under the Transport Act 1968	
Section 96(11) of the Transport Act 1968	Contravention of any requirement of domestic drivers' hours code.
Section 96(11A) of that Act	Contravention of any requirement of applicable Community rules as to periods of driving, etc.
Section 97(1) of that Act	Using vehicle in contravention of requirements relating to installation, use or repair of recording equipment in accordance with EU Tachographs Regulation.
Section 97ZA(1) and (2) of that Act	Using vehicle in contravention of requirements relating to installation, use or repair or recording equipment in accordance with the AETR.
Section 98(4) of that Act	Contravention of regulations made under section 98 or any requirement as to books, records or documents of applicable Community rules.
Section 99(4) of that Act	Failing to comply with requirements relating to inspection or records or obstructing an officer, but only insofar as the offences relates to:— (i) failing to comply with any requirement under section 99(1)(a); or (ii) obstructing an officer in exercise of powers under 99(2)(a) or 99(3).

(1) Provision creating offence	(2) General nature of offence
Section 99ZD(1) of that Act	Failing to comply with requirements relating to inspection of recording equipment or records (whether electronic or hard copy) made by or stored on recording equipment except where that offence is committed by:— (i) failing to sign a hard copy of downloaded data when required to do so under section 99ZC (1); or (ii) obstructing an officer in exercise of powers under section 99ZF.
Section 99C of that Act	Failure to comply with prohibition or direction in relation to driving vehicle.
Offence under the Road Traffic (Foreign Vehicles) Act 1972	
Section 3(1) of the Road Traffic (Foreign Vehicles) Act 1972.	Driving, etc., foreign goods vehicle or foreign public service vehicle in contravention of prohibition etc.
Offence under the Greater London Council (General Powers) Act 1974	
Section 15 of the Greater London Council (General Powers) Act 1974.	Parking vehicles on footways, verges, etc.
Offence under the Highways Act 1980	
Section 137 of the Highways Act 1980.	Obstructing a highway, but only where the offence is committed in respect of a vehicle.
Offences under the Public Passenger Vehicles Act 1981	
Section 12(5) of the Public Passenger Vehicles Act 1981.	Using public service vehicle on road except under PSV operators' licence.
Offences under the Road Traffic Regulation Act 1984	
RTRA section 5(1)	Using a vehicle in contravention of a traffic regulation order outside Greater London.
RTRA section 8(1)	Breach of traffic regulation order in Greater London.
RTRA section 11	Breach of experimental traffic order.
RTRA section 13	Breach of experimental traffic scheme regulations in Greater London.
RTRA section 16(1)	Using a vehicle in contravention of temporary prohibition or restriction of traffic in case of execution of works, etc.
RTRA section 17(4)	Wrongful use of special road.
RTRA section 18(3)	Using a vehicle in contravention of provision for oneway traffic on trunk road.
RTRA section 20(5)	Driving a vehicle in contravention of order prohibiting or restricting driving vehicles on certain classes of roads.
RTRA section 25(5)	Breach of pedestrian crossing regulations, except an offence in respect of a moving motor vehicle other than a contravention of regulations 23, 24, 25 and 26 of the Zebra, Pelican and Puffin Pedestrian Crossings Regulations and General Directions 1997.
RTRA section 29(3)	Using a vehicle in contravention of a street playground order.
RTRA section 35A(1)	Breach of an order regulating the use, etc., of a parking place provided by a local authority, but only where the offence is committed in relation to a parking place provided on a road.

(1) Provision creating offence	(2) General nature of offence
RTRA section 47(1)	Breach of a provision of a parking place designation order and other offences committed in relation to a parking place designated by such an order, except any offence of failing to pay an excess charge within the meaning of section 46.
RTRA section 53(5)	Using vehicle in contravention of any provision of a parking place designation order having effect by virtue of section 53(1)(a) (inclusion of certain traffic regulation provisions).
RTRA section 53(6)	Breach of a provision of a parking place designation order having effect by virtue of section 53(1)(b) (use of any part of a road for parking without charge).
RTRA section 88(7)	Driving a motor vehicle in contravention of an order imposing a minimum speed limit under section 88(1)(b).
RTRA section 89(1)	Speeding offences under RTRA and other Acts.
Offences under the Road Transport (International Passenger Services) Regulations 1984 (SI 1984/748)	
Regulation 19(1) of the Road Transport (International Passenger Services) Regulations 1984.	Using vehicle for Community regulated carriage of passengers by road otherwise than in accordance with authorisation or certificate, etc.
Regulation 19(2) of those Regulations	Using vehicle for ASOR regulated or Community regulated carriage of passengers by road without having correctly completed passenger waybill or without carrying top copy of waybill on vehicle throughout journey.
Offences under the Road Traffic Act 1988	
RTA section 3	Driving mechanically propelled vehicle on a road or other public place without due care and attention, or without reasonable consideration.
RTA section 14	Breach of regulations requiring wearing of seat belts.
RTA section 15(2)	Breach of restriction on carrying children in the front of vehicles.
RTA section 15(4)	Breach of restriction on carrying children in the rear of vehicles.
RTA section 16	Breach of regulations relating to protective headgear for motor cycle drivers and passengers.
RTA section 18(3)	Breach of regulations relating to head-worn appliances (eye protectors) for use on motor cycles.
RTA section 19	Parking a heavy commercial vehicle on verge or footway.
RTA section 22	Leaving vehicle in dangerous position.
RTA section 23	Unlawful carrying of passengers on motor cycles.
RTA section 24	Carrying more than one person on a pedal cycle.
RTA section 34	Driving mechanically propelled vehicle elsewhere than on a road.
RTA section 35	Failure to comply with traffic directions.
RTA section 36	Failure to comply with traffic signs.

(1) Provision creating offence	(2) General nature of offence
RTA section 40A	Using vehicle in dangerous condition, etc.
RTA section 41A	Breach of requirement as to brakes, steering-gear or tyres.
RTA section 41B	Breach of requirement as to weight: goods and passenger vehicles.
RTA section 41D	Breach of requirements as to control of vehicle, mobile telephone etc.
RTA section 42	Breach of other construction and use requirements.
RTA section 47	Using, etc., vehicle without required test certificate being in force.
RTA section 71(1)	Driving, etc., vehicle in contravention of prohibition on driving it as being unfit for service or overloaded, or failing to comply with direction to remove a vehicle found overloaded.
RTA section 87(1)	Driving vehicle otherwise than in accordance with requisite licence.
RTA section 143	Using motor vehicle while uninsured.
RTA section 163	Failure to stop vehicle on being so required.
RTA section 172	Failure of person keeping vehicle and others to give the police information as to identity of driver, etc., in the case of certain offences.
Offence under this Act	
Section 90D(6)	Driving, etc., vehicle in contravention of prohibition on driving, or failing to comply with direction to remove vehicle on failure to make a financial penalty deposit payment.
Offences under the Goods Vehicles (Community Authorisations) Regulations 1992 (SI 1992/3077)	
Regulation 3 of the Goods Vehicles (Community Authorisations) Regulations 1992.	Using goods vehicle without Community authorisation.
Regulation 7 of those Regulations	Using vehicle under Community authorisation in contravention of conditions governing authorisation.
Offences under the Vehicle Excise and Registration Act 1994	
Section 34 of that Act.	Using trade licence for unauthorised purposes or in unauthorised circumstances, etc.
Section 42 of that Act.	Driving or keeping a vehicle without required registration mark.
Section 43 of that Act.	Driving or keeping a vehicle with registration mark obscured, etc.
Section 43C of that Act.	Using an incorrectly registered vehicle.
Section 59 of that Act.	Failure to fix prescribed registration mark to a vehicle in accordance with regulations made under section 23(4)(a) of that Act.
Offence under the Goods Vehicles (Licensing of Operators) Act 1995	
Section 2(5) of the Goods Vehicles (Licensing of Operators) Act 1995.	Using goods vehicle on road for carriage of goods except under operator's licence.

(1) Provision creating offence	(2) General nature of offence
Offences under the Public Service Vehicles (Community Licences) Regulations 1999 (SI 1999/1322)	
Regulation 3 of the Public Service Vehicles (Community Licences) Regulations 1999.	Using public service vehicle on road without Community licence.
Regulation 7 of those Regulations	Using public service vehicle under Community licence in contravention of conditions governing use of licence.
Offences under the Road Transport (Passenger Vehicles Cabotage) Regulations 1999 (SI 1999/3413)	
Regulation 3 of the Road Transport (Passenger Vehicles Cabotage) Regulations 1999.	Using vehicle on road for UK cabotage operations without Community licence.
Regulation 4 of those Regulations	Using vehicle on road for UK cabotage operation without control document.
Regulation 7(1) of those Regulations	Driver failing to produce Community licence on request when vehicle required to have licence on board.
Regulation 7(3) of those Regulations	Driver failing to produce control document on request when vehicle required to have control document on board.
Offence under the Vehicle Drivers (Certificates of Professional Competence) Regulations 2007 (SI 2007/605)	
Regulation 11(7) of the Vehicle Drivers (Certificates of Professional Competence) Regulations 2007.	Driver of relevant vehicle failing to produce on request evidence or document required to be carried under regulation 11(1), (3) or (5).
Offence under the Goods Vehicles (Community Licences) Regulations 2011 (SI 2011/2633)	
Regulation 4 of the Goods Vehicles (Community Licences) Regulations 2011.	Using a vehicle in Great Britain in contravention of the requirement to possess a Community licence.
Offence under the HGV Road User Levy Act 2013	
Section 11 of the HGV Road User Levy Act 2013.	Using or keeping heavy goods vehicle if HGV road user levy not paid.
Offences under the Haulage Permits and Trailer Registration Act 2018	
Section 8(1) of the Haulage Permits and Trailer Registration Act 2018	Operator using a goods vehicle in breach of regulations under section 1(1) of that Act without reasonable excuse.
Section 8(2) of that Act	Driver of a goods vehicle breaching a requirement under section 6(2)(a) of that Act to produce a permit without reasonable excuse.
Section 8(3) of that Act	Wilfully obstructing an examiner exercising powers under section 6 of that Act.
Section 8(4)(a) of that Act	Breaching a prohibition under section 7 of that Act without reasonable excuse.
Offences under the Trailer Registration Regulations 2018 (SI 2018/1203)	
Regulation 5 of the Trailer Registration Regulations 2018	Keeping or using a trailer that has not been registered under those Regulations on a journey to or through a foreign country that is a contracting party to the 1968 Vienna Convention on Road Traffic ('the 1968 Convention').
Regulation 19(1)(a) of those Regulations	Using a registered trailer with an expired registration document on a journey to or through a foreign country that is a contracting party to the 1968 Convention.

(1) Provision creating offence	(2) General nature of offence
Regulation 19(1)(f) of those Regulations	Failing to produce a trailer registration document when required to do so.
Regulation 19(1)(g) of those Regulations	Failing to fix a registration plate on a registered trailer in accordance with those Regulations.
Regulation 19(1)(h) of those Regulations	Displaying a trailer registration mark on a trailer that is not assigned to that trailer.
Regulation 20 of those Regulations	Keeping or using an incorrectly registered trailer on a road.
Regulation 21 of those Regulations	Keeping or using a registered trailer on a road with a registration mark that is obscured.
Regulation 22(a) of those Regulations	Wilfully obstructing a person carrying out an inspection of a trailer under those Regulations.

Section D1 Powers of Investigation

POLICE POWERS IN THE INVESTIGATION OF CRIME

Police powers of investigation, including arrest, detention, interrogation, entry and search of premises, personal search and the taking of samples and various procedures for identification are largely governed by the PACE 1984 and/or the associated PACE Codes of Practice. These powers are dealt with in this section, but see **F2** for the admission (and exclusion) of evidence obtained in breach of the PACE 1984 or the PACE Codes, **F18** for the admission of confession evidence and **F19** for the treatment of identification evidence at trial. **D1.1**

There are eight PACE Codes of Practice, A to H, issued by the Secretary of State under the authority of the PACE 1984, ss. 66 and 67. Codes A to D and G are set out in **appendix 1**. The current versions of the codes are as follows:

- Code A — in force from 19 March 2015 (SI 2015 No. 418).
- Code B — in force from 27 October 2013 (SI 2013 No. 2685).
- Code C — in force from 21 August 2019 (SI 2019 No. 1157).
- Code D — in force from 23 February 2017 (SI 2017 No. 103).
- Code E — in force from 31 July 2018 (SI 2018 No. 829).
- Code F — in force from 31 July 2018 (SI 2018 No. 829).
- Code G — in force from 12 November 2012 (SI 2012 No. 1798).
- Code H — in force from 21 August 2019 (SI 2019 No. 1157).

Code A does not apply to stop and search powers under the TA 2000, which are governed by separate codes of practice given effect by the Terrorism Act 2000 (Codes of Practice for the Exercise of Stop and Search Powers) Order 2012 (SI 2012 No. 1794) (see **B10.25**). However, it does apply to powers under the Terrorism Prevention and Investigations Measures Act 2011 to search persons without them being arrested. Code B includes powers to enter and search premises for the purposes of serving, monitoring and enforcing TPIM notices.

A failure by a police officer or other person required to have regard to provisions of the codes does not, of itself, render that officer liable to criminal or civil proceedings (PACE 1984, s. 67(10)). However, to the extent that they are relevant, the codes are admissible in evidence in criminal or civil proceedings (PACE 1984, s. 67(11)). See further **F18.8** (in relation to exclusion of confession evidence under the PACE 1984, s. 76) and **F2.7** (in relation to the exclusion of any prosecution evidence under the PACE 1984, s. 78).

Investigations in Connection with Terrorism

D1.2 Where persons are detained for examination under the TA 2000, s. 53 and sch. 7, their treatment is governed by the TA 2000, sch. 8, part 1. Similarly, where persons are detained for examination under the C-TBSA 2019, s. 22 and sch. 3, part 1, their treatment is governed by sch. 3, parts 2 and 3. Persons detained for examination under both the TA 2000, s. 53 and sch. 7, and the C-TBSA 2019, s. 22 and sch. 3, part 1, are not treated as being in police detention for the purpose of the PACE 1984, and the PACE Codes do not apply to them. The detention of persons arrested under the TA 2000, s. 41 (on suspicion of being a terrorist), is governed by sch. 8 to that Act rather than by the PACE 1984. They are not treated as being arrested for an offence, but whilst they are detained at a police station they are deemed to be in police detention for the purposes of the PACE 1984 (PACE 1984, s. 118(2)). PACE Code H applies to their detention whilst they have not been charged, and if they are detained for post-charge questioning under the C-TA 2008, s. 22. Subject to the latter, Code C will apply if they are charged with an offence or if they are being questioned about any offence after charge without a s. 22 authorisation having been given. Note that there is a separate code of practice for video recording with sound of interviews of persons detained under the TA 2000, s. 42 or sch. 7, and of persons detained for post-charge questioning (see the Terrorism Act 2000 (Video Recording with Sound of Interviews and Associated Code of Practice) Order 2012 (SI 2012 No. 1792), and the Counter-Terrorism Act 2008 (Code of Practice for the Video Recording with Sound of Post-Charge Questioning) Order 2012 (SI 2012 No. 1793)). PACE Code D does apply to persons arrested under the TA 2000, s. 41, except for those provisions relating to photographs, fingerprints, skin impressions, body samples and impressions of people. PACE Codes E and F also do not apply to such persons. See generally **B10.14** ***et seq***.

Investigations by Non-police Officers

D1.3 The PACE 1984 is applied (with modifications) to investigations conducted and persons detained by Revenue and Customs officers by the PACE 1984, s. 114(2), and the Police and Criminal Evidence Act 1984 (Application to Revenue and Customs) Order 2015 (SI 2015 No. 1783). The PACE 1984 is also applied (with modifications) to investigations conducted by immigration officers and designated customs officers under the Borders, Citizenship and Immigration Act 2009, Part 1, by s. 23 of that Act and the Police and Criminal Evidence Act 1984 (Application to immigration officers and designated customs officers in England and Wales) Order 2013 (SI 2013 No. 1542). The PACE 1984 is applied to investigations conducted under the Armed Forces Act 2006 and to persons under arrest under that Act by the PACE 1984, s. 113(1), and the Police and Criminal Evidence Act 1984 (Armed Forces) Order 2009 (SI 2009 No. 1922).

The Director General of the NCA has the power to designate a member of Agency staff as a person having the powers of a constable, Revenue and Customs officer and/or immigration officer (CCA 2013, s. 10 and sch. 5). Where a person is designated as having powers of a constable, that person has all the powers and privileges of a constable (sch. 5, para. 11). The PACE 1984 applies to them and the exercise of their powers by virtue of the Crime and Courts Act 2013 (Application and Modification of Certain Enactments) Order 2014 (SI 2014 No. 1704), art. 3, which applies in respect of the NCA by virtue of the CCA 2013, sch. 8, part 4. For this purpose, the PACE 1984 is subject to the modifications set out in sch. 1 to the Order, the most important of which are:

(a) references to 'police officer' and 'officer' are normally to be treated as references to a 'designated person' under the CCA 2013;
(b) where authorisation is required for a search under the PACE 1984, s. 18, reference to an inspector is replaced by reference to a grade 3 officer;
(c) references to 'police station' (e.g., in relation to fingerprinting, volunteers and fingerprints and samples) are to be treated as references to a 'National Crime Agency office';
(d) 'National Crime Agency office' means a place for the time being occupied by the NCA.

Persons other than police officers who are charged with the duty of investigating offences or charging offenders are required in the discharge of that duty to have regard to any relevant provision of the codes (PACE 1984, s. 67(9)). Whether a person is charged with such a duty is a question of fact in each case. It has been held to include officers of the SFO (*Director of the SFO, ex parte Saunders* [1988] Crim LR 837; *Gill* [2003] EWCA Crim 2256, [2003] 4 All ER 681); trading standards officers (*Dudley MBC v Debenhams* (1994) 159 JP 18; *Tiplady* (1995) 159 JP 548); store detectives (*Bayliss* (1993) 98 Cr App R 235); investigators employed by the Federation Against Copyright Theft (*Joy v Federation Against Copyright Theft Ltd* [1993] Crim LR 588; *Halawa v Federation Against Copyright Theft* [1995] 1 Cr App R 21); and commercial investigators when interviewing an employee (*Twaites* (1990) 92 Cr App R 106). However, it was decided in *Seelig and Spens* [1992] 4 All ER 429 that inspectors from the Department of Trade and Industry (now the Department for Business, Energy and Industrial Strategy) appointed under the Companies Acts, were not persons charged with such a duty. A similar conclusion was drawn in respect of local tax inspectors in *Doncaster* [2008] EWCA Crim 5, and of a line manager investigating possible fraud by an employee in *Welcher* [2007] EWCA Crim 480, [2007] 2 Cr App R (S) 83 (519). In both *Taylor (Martin)* [2000] EWCA Crim 2922 and *Harper* [2019] EWCA Crim 343, [2019] 4 WLR 39 it was held that a prison officer was not a person charged with the duty of investigating offences, but on the facts in *Devani* [2007] EWCA Crim 1926, [2008] 1 Cr App R 4 (65) the contrary conclusion was drawn.

The PACE Codes apply to Revenue and Customs officers where they are conducting 'relevant investigations' (Police and Criminal Evidence Act 1984 (Application to Revenue and Customs) Order 2015, art. 3(1) and sch. 1). However, they do not apply to the civil investigation of tax fraud procedure (see HM Revenue and Customs Code of Practice 9 (June 2014, tinyurl.com/ydgygdnd)). The PACE Codes do not apply to an investigation under the Armed Forces Act 2006, but dedicated codes have been issued under the PACE 1984, s. 113(3). For the detention and treatment of a person arrested on a European Arrest Warrant, see **D1.38**.

Certain police powers can be exercised by civilian staff designated by a chief constable as a community support officer or policing support officer, or by a volunteer designated as a community support volunteer or policing support volunteer (Police Reform Act 2002, Part 4, as amended by the PCA 2017, Part 3, ch. 1, brought fully into force on 15 December 2017 by the Policing and Crime Act 2017 (Commencement No. 5 and Transitional Provisions) Regulations 2017 (SI 2017 No. 1139)). Chief constables may determine which police powers are to be conferred on such officers or volunteers and may confer any police power other than an excluded power or duty listed in sch. 3B, part 1. A designated officer or volunteer must have regard to any relevant provision of the PACE Codes in the exercise or performance of the officer's powers and duties (PACE 1984, s. 67(9A)).

The PACE 1984, s. 114B, empowers the Secretary of State to make regulations applying any provisions of the Act which relate to the investigation of offences by police officers to the investigation of labour market offences conducted by labour abuse prevention officers.

REASONABLE SUSPICION

A number of police powers are premised upon the constable having reasonable grounds for suspicion. For example, stop and search under the PACE 1984, Part I, requires a constable to have 'reasonable grounds for suspecting that he will find stolen or prohibited articles' etc. and some, but not all, powers of arrest under s. 24 depend on the officer having reasonable grounds for suspicion. This reflects the ECHR, Article 5(1)(c), which permits a person to be deprived of liberty 'on reasonable suspicion of having committed an offence or when it is reasonably considered necessary to prevent his committing an offence or fleeing after having done so'. It should be contrasted with the expression 'reasonable grounds for believing', found in the PACE 1984, s. 24(4) (the necessity for arrest), s. 37(2) (detention without charge) and s. 38(1) (bail **D1.4** following charge), which implies a more stringent test. Reasonable suspicion relates to the existence of facts and not to the state of the law. An officer who reasonably but mistakenly proceeds on a particular view of the law, and thus exercises his or her power of arrest, does not have reasonable suspicion (*Todd v DPP* [1996] Crim LR 344). However, in the absence of a specific statutory requirement to such effect, the precise legal power under which the constable acts does not have to have been identified (*R (Rutherford) v Independent Police Complaints Commission* [2010] EWHC 2881 (Admin)).

Reasonable suspicion is not defined in the PACE 1984. It is explained in relation to stop and search powers in PACE Code A, paras. 2.2 to 2.6B, and requires both a genuine suspicion on the part of the officer concerned and an objective basis for that suspicion (para. 2.2). In relation to arrest, Code G provides that there 'must be some reasonable, objective grounds for the suspicion, based on known facts and information' (para. 2.3A). Note for Guidance 2 states that facts and information should not be confined to those which tend to indicate guilt, but should include facts and information that tend to dispel suspicion, and Note for Guidance 2A provides examples in respect of self-defence and the use of force by school staff.

It has been held that reasonable suspicion requires both that the constable carrying out the arrest actually suspects (a subjective test) and that a reasonable person in possession of the same facts as the constable would also suspect (an objective test). In addition the arrest must be *Wednesbury* reasonable (*Castorina v Chief Constable of Surrey* (1988) 138 NLJ 180; *Salmon v Chief Constable of the Police Service of Northern Ireland* [2013] NIQB 10; *Parker v Chief Constable of Essex Police* [2018] EWCA Civ 2788, [2019] 1 WLR 2238; *Smith v Chief Constable of the Police Service for Northern Ireland* [2019] NIQB 39). The test for whether an officer has reasonable grounds for suspicion for the purposes of stop and search under the PACE 1984, Part I, is the same in all material respects (*Howarth v Metropolitan Police Commissioner* [2011] EWHC 2818 (Admin)). Whether the constable had reasonable suspicion must be determined according to what the constable knew and perceived at the time; reasonableness is to be evaluated without reference to hindsight (*Redmond-Bate v DPP* (1999) 163 JP 789). Information required to form a reasonable suspicion is of a lower standard than that required to establish a prima facie case. Prima facie proof must be based on admissible evidence whereas reasonable suspicion may take into account matters which are not admissible in evidence or matters which, while admissible, could not form part of a prima facie case (*Hussien v Chong Fook Kam* [1970] AC 942). Whilst it is not necessary to have identified the specific suspicious offence (*Coudrat v Commissioners of Her Majesty's Revenue and Customs* [2005] EWCA Civ 616), the constable must reasonably suspect the existence of facts amounting to an offence of a kind in mind (*Chapman v DPP* (1988) 89 Cr App R 190).

D1.5 In forming a reasonable suspicion a constable may rely on hearsay, provided that it is reasonable and that the constable believes it (*Clarke v Chief Constable of North Wales Police* [2000] All ER (D) 477). Thus a constable may arrest a person as a result of radio information, or even an anonymous telephone call, provided that the person arrested corresponds to the description in the message (*King v Gardner* (1979) 71 Cr App R 13; *DPP v Wilson* [1991] RTR 284); the constable may act on the word of an informant, although such a source should be treated with considerable reserve (*James v Chief Constable of South Wales* [1991] 6 CL 80). The constable may rely on an entry in the police national computer, unless in the light of all the circumstances some further inquiry is called for before suspicion can properly crystallise (*Hough v Chief Constable of Staffordshire Police* [2001] EWCA Civ 39); or on a briefing from another police officer (*Alford v Chief Constable of Cambridgeshire* [2009] EWCA Civ 100) or investigator such as an officer from the SFO (*R (Rawlinson) v Central Criminal Court* [2012] EWHC 2254 (Admin), [2013] 1 WLR 1634). The arresting officer is not under a duty to check information supplied, and an arrest will be lawful even if the information was incorrect (*R (Tchenguiz) v Director of the SFO [2012] EWHC 2254 (Admin), [2013]* 1 WLR 1634; *R (Chatwani) v NCA* [2015] EWHC 1283 (Admin)). The mere fact that an arresting officer has been instructed by a superior to effect an arrest is not sufficient (*O'Hara v Chief Constable of the Royal Ulster Constabulary* [1997]

AC 286; *Olden* [2007] EWCA Crim 726). A belief that a superior officer probably did have information justifying an arrest which was not conveyed to the arresting officer does not suffice (*Metropolitan Police Commissioner v Raissi* [2008] EWCA Civ 1237, [2009] QB 564).

Evidence of particular opportunity may give rise to reasonable suspicion. Where police, having taken all reasonable steps to discover the perpetrator of an offence, are left with the suspicion that one of a number of persons must have been the culprit, this may be sufficient to arrest those persons (*Cummings v Chief Constable of Northumbria Police* [2003] EWCA Civ 1844; *Parker v Chief Constable of Essex Police* [2018] EWCA Civ 2788, [2019] 1 WLR 2238). The police may be justified in making such arrests even though there is a possibility that another or other persons may have committed the offence. The matter is one of degree (*Al Fayed v Metropolitan Police Commissioner* [2004] EWCA Civ 1579). Similar principles also apply to search of groups of people under the PACE 1984, Part I (*Howarth v Metropolitan Police Commissioner* [2011] EWHC 2818 (Admin), followed in *Tuthill v York Magistrates' Court* [2011] EWHC 3760 (Admin); and see Code A, paras. 2.6 and 2.6A). A constable who has reasonable grounds to suspect that an offence has been committed is not obliged to discount all possible defences or seek complete proof before carrying out an arrest (*Ward v Chief Constable of Avon and Somerset Constabulary* (1986) *The Times*, 26 June 1986; *McCarrick v Oxford* [1983] RTR 117; but see Code G, Note for Guidance 2).

Use of arrest is permissible in order to interview and/or seek further evidence from a suspect, **D1.6**
or as a means of exercising control over a suspect with a view to securing a confession or other information where it is necessary to bring matters to a head speedily, to preserve evidence or to prevent the further commission of crime (*Al Fayed v Metropolitan Police Commissioner*). Furthermore, an arrest is lawful if carried out for an ulterior purpose, e.g., to install a listening device in the arrested person's house for the purpose of investigating another offence, provided that there are reasonable grounds for suspicion in relation to the offence for which the person was arrested (*Chalkley* [1998] QB 848). However, these cases must now be considered in the context of the requirement that an arrest must be necessary (see **D1.25**). The police must not mislead the suspect as to the true nature of the investigation, e.g., by failing to tell a suspect arrested for burglary that the victim has died (*Kirk* [1999] 4 All ER 698, and see **D1.17**).

THE USE OF FORCE

The PACE 1984, s. 117, provides that where any provision of the Act confers a power on a constable **D1.7**
and does not provide that the power may be exercised only with the consent of a person other than a police officer, the officer may use reasonable force, if necessary, in the exercise of the power. This would include force used in connection with a stop and search under the PACE 1984, Part I, entry and search of premises under s. 17, arrest under s. 24, detention of a person at a police station under the PACE 1984, Part IV, search of a person under s. 54, intimate search of a detained person under s. 55, finger-printing without consent under s. 61 and the taking of a non-intimate sample without consent under s. 63. It would not include the use of force in connection with the conduct of a visual identification procedure governed by PACE Code D, or the taking of an intimate sample under s. 62, since these require consent. A civilian designated under the Police Reform Act 2002, s. 38, may, in exercising those powers, use reasonable force in the same circumstances as a constable (Police Reform Act 2002, s. 38(8), and Code C, para. 1.14). In addition, the CLA 1967, s. 3, empowers any person to use such force as is reasonable in the circumstances in the prevention of crime, or in effecting or assisting in the lawful arrest of an offender or suspected offender or of persons unlawfully at large (see **A3.55** *et seq.*).

In determining what force is reasonable, the court may take into account all the circumstances including the nature and degree of the force used, the gravity of the offence for which arrest is to be made, the harm that would flow from the use of force against the suspect, and the possibility of effecting the arrest or preventing the harm by other means. The fact that the force used results in serious injury does not necessarily make it unreasonable (*Roberts v Chief Constable of Kent* [2008] EWCA Civ 1588; *McDonnell v Metropolitan Police Commissioner* [2015] EWCA Civ 573); and *McCarthy v Chief Constable of Merseyside* [2016] EWCA Civ 1257; but contrast *Minio-Paluello v Metropolitan Police Commissioner* [2011] EWHC 3411 (QB), in which it was held that the degree of force used was neither reasonable nor proportionate. The use of excessive force will not render the arrest unlawful (*Simpson v Chief Constable of South Yorkshire Police* (1991) *The Times*, 7 March 1991).

D1.8 **Use of Handcuffs** Handcuffs should be used only where they are reasonably necessary to prevent an escape or to prevent a violent breach of the peace by a prisoner (*Lockley* (1864) 4 F & F 155). The same rule applies to the handcuffing of prisoners in court (*Cambridge Justices, ex parte Peacock* (1992) 156 JP 895; *Horden* [2009] EWCA Crim 388, [2009] 2 Cr App R 24 (406)). It would seem that, where handcuffs are unjustifiably resorted to, their use will constitute a trespass even though the arrest itself is lawful (*Taylor* (1895) 59 JP 393; *Bibby v Chief Constable of Essex* (2000) 164 JP 297).

POWERS TO STOP AND SEARCH

D1.9 Police powers to stop and search people and vehicles are conferred by the PACE 1984, and a range of other legislation. See PACE Code A, annex A (see **appendix 1**), for a summary of the main stop and search powers. The PACE 1984, ss. 2 and 3, impose a number of obligations on officers conducting a stop and search irrespective of the legislative authority for it. Code A applies to all police powers of stop and search other than those conducted under the Aviation Security Act 1982, s. 27(2), and the PACE 1984, s. 6(1), and similar powers under the TA 2000 (see Code A, para. 1.03, and **B10.25**). Community support officers designated under the Police Reform Act 2002, Part 4, do not have powers of stop and search under the PACE 1984, but do have such powers under some other legislation (see Code A, annex C, for a summary of such powers).

Stop and Search Powers Requiring Reasonable Suspicion

D1.10 The main stop and search power requiring reasonable suspicion is that under the PACE 1984, Part I. For reasonable suspicion see **D1.4** and PACE Code A, paras. 2.2 to 2.6B (see **appendix 1**).

Police and Criminal Evidence Act 1984, s. 1

(1) A constable may exercise any power conferred by this section—
  (a) in any place to which at the time when he proposes to exercise the power the public or any section of the public has access, on payment or otherwise, as of right or by virtue of express or implied permission; or
  (b) in any other place to which people have ready access at the time when he proposes to exercise the power but which is not a dwelling.

(2) Subject to subsection (3) to (5) below, a constable—
  (a) may search—
    (i) any person or vehicle;
    (ii) anything which is in or on a vehicle,
    for stolen or prohibited articles, any article to which subsection (8A) below applies[, any substance to which subsection (8AA) below applies] or any firework to which subsection (8B) below applies; and
  (b) may detain a person or vehicle for the purpose of such a search.

(3) This section does not give a constable power to search a person or vehicle or anything in or on a vehicle unless he has reasonable grounds for suspecting that he will find stolen or prohibited articles or, any article to which subsection (8A) below applies[, any substance to which subsection (8AA) below applies] or any firework to which subsection (8B) below applies.

(4) If a person is in a garden or yard occupied with and used for the purposes of a dwelling or on other land so occupied and used, a constable may not search him in the exercise of the power conferred by this section unless the constable has reasonable grounds for believing—
  (a) that he does not reside in the dwelling; and
  (b) that he is not in the place in question with the express or implied permission of a person who resides in the dwelling.

(5) If a vehicle is in a garden or yard occupied with and used for the purposes of a dwelling or on other land so occupied and used, a constable may not search the vehicle or anything in or on it in the exercise of the power conferred by this section unless he has reasonable grounds for believing—
  (a) that the person in charge of the vehicle does not reside in the dwelling; and
  (b) that the vehicle is not in the place in question with the express or implied permission of a person who resides in the dwelling.
(6) If in the course of such a search a constable discovers an article which he has reasonable grounds for suspecting to be a stolen or prohibited article, an article to which subsection (8A) below applies[, any substance to which subsection (8AA) below applies] or a firework to which subsection (8B) below applies, he may seize it.
(7) An article is prohibited for the purposes of this Part of this Act if it is—
  (a) an offensive weapon; or
  (b) an article—
    (i) made or adapted for use in the course of or in connection with an offence to which this sub-paragraph applies; or
    (ii) intended by the person having it with him for such use by him or by some other person.
(8) The offences to which subsection (7)(b)(i) above applies are—
  (a) burglary;
  (b) theft;
  (c) offences under section 12 of the Theft Act 1968 (taking motor vehicle or other conveyance without authority);
  (d) fraud (contrary to section 1 of the Fraud Act 2006); and
  (e) offences under section 1 of the Criminal Damage Act 1971 (destroying or damaging property).
(8A) This subsection applies to any article in relation to which a person has committed, or is committing or is going to commit an offence under section 139 or section 139AA of the Criminal Justice Act 1988.
[(8AA) This subsection applies to any substance in relation to which a person has committed, or is committing or is going to commit an offence under section 6 of the Offensive Weapons Act 2019 (offence of having a corrosive substance in a public place).]
[(8AB) In this section references to such a substance include an article which contains such a substance.]
(8B) This subsection applies to any firework which a person possesses in contravention of a prohibition imposed by fireworks regulations.
(8C) In this section—
  (a) 'firework' shall be construed in accordance with the definition of 'fireworks' in section 1(1) of the Fireworks Act 2003; and
  (b) 'fireworks regulations' has the same meaning as in that Act.
(9) In this Part of this Act 'offensive weapon' means any article—
  (a) made or adapted for use for causing injury to persons; or
  (b) intended by the person having it with him for such use by him or by some other person.

The power is available only in public places, but this is given a particular meaning by s. 1(1)(a) and (b), (4) and (5).

The words in square brackets have been inserted by the Offensive Weapons Act 2019, s. 10, and will come into force on a date to be appointed.

Stop and Search Powers Not Requiring Reasonable Suspicion

Stop and search powers that do not require reasonable suspicion include those under the CJPO 1994, ss. 60 and 60AA, and the CJA 1988, s. 139B, although under the latter power the constable must have reasonable grounds to believe that an offence under s. 139A (having a bladed or pointed article or offensive weapon on school premises) or s. 139AA (threatening with article with blade or point or offensive weapon) has been or is being committed. For stop and search powers under the TA 2000 that do not require reasonable suspicion, see **B10.25**. **D1.11**

D1.12 Section 60 of the CJPO 1994 gives the police the power to stop and search where an officer of the rank of inspector or above has given the appropriate authorisation under s. 60(1). Authorisation may be granted if the officer reasonably believes:

(a) that incidents involving serious violence may take place in any locality in the constable's police area, and that it is expedient to give an authorisation under this section to prevent their occurrence (s. 60(1)(a));
(b) that an incident involving serious violence has occurred in the constable's police area, a dangerous instrument or offensive weapon used in the incident is being carried by a person in that area, and it is expedient to give an authorisation to find the instrument or weapon (s. 60(1)(aa)); or
(c) that persons are carrying dangerous instruments or offensive weapons in any locality in the constable's police area without good reason (s. 60(1)(b)).

Authorisation may be granted for up to 24 hours, although this may be extended by an officer of the rank of superintendent or above by a further 24 hours (CJPO 1994, s. 60(1) and (3)). It must be given in writing specifying the grounds on which it is given, and the locality in which and the period during which the powers are exercisable (s. 60(9)). An authorisation given under s. 60(1)(aa) need not be in writing if that is not practicable, but must be recorded in writing as soon as is practicable (s. 60(9ZA)).

Where an authorisation is in force any constable in uniform may stop any pedestrian and search the pedestrian or anything carried by the pedestrian for offensive weapons or dangerous instruments, or may stop any vehicle and search the vehicle, the driver and any passenger for a like purpose (s. 60(4)). Section 60(5) provides that this power may be exercised whether or not the constable has any grounds for suspecting that the person or vehicle is carrying such weapons or instruments. However, under Code A, para. 2.14A, the selection of persons and vehicles to be stopped and, if appropriate, searched should reflect an objective assessment of the nature of the incident or weapon in question and the individuals and vehicles thought likely to be associated with that incident or those weapons. It was held in *R (Roberts) v Metropolitan Police Commissioner* [2015] UKSC 79, [2016] 1 WLR 210 that, while engaging the ECHR, Article 8, exercise of the power of stop and search under s. 60 did not breach Article 8 rights.

A person, or driver of a vehicle, stopped or searched under s. 60 is entitled to a written statement that he or she was so stopped or searched if this is applied for within 12 months (s. 60(10) and (10A)). In addition, the information and recording requirements of the PACE 1984, ss. 2 and 3, apply (see **D1.13**).

The CJPO 1994, s. 60AA, provides for a power to require the removal of any item which a constable reasonably believes a person is wearing wholly or mainly for the purpose of concealing identity, and power to seize an item which a person intends to wear for such a purpose. The power is exercisable where an authorisation under s. 60 is in place, but a separate authorisation may be given under s. 60AA(3) and (4).

Conduct of Stop and Search Powers

D1.13 The consent of the person concerned is not a sufficient authority for a search. PACE Code A, para. 1.5, provides that a search must not be conducted in the absence of a relevant power. The various statutory powers contain different provisions regarding the conduct of a stop and search. Most enable both persons and vehicles to be searched, although some are confined to one or the other. Some are exercisable anywhere whereas others can only be carried out in a public place or in specific premises or areas such as schools or ports. Some require the officer to be in uniform, but others do not. For a summary, see Code A, annex A (**appendix 1**). The requirement, under the PACE 1984, s. 2(b)(i), and Code A, para. 3.9, that an officer who is not in uniform provide documentary evidence of being a constable before carrying out a search is mandatory (*Bristol* [2007] EWCA Crim 3214; *B v DPP* [2008] EWHC 1655 (Admin)).

Code A sets out minimum requirements that must be observed when powers to stop and search to which Code A applies are exercised. Reasonable force may be used, although co-operation should be sought even if the person initially objects to the search (PACE 1984, s. 117; Code A, para. 3.2; *James v DPP* [2012] EWHC 1317 (Admin); see also **D1.7**). A person may be detained for the purpose of carrying out a search although the period for which the person is detained must be reasonable and be kept to a minimum (PACE 1984, s. 1(2)(b); Code A, para. 3.3). It was held in *R (Gillan) v Metropolitan Police Commissioner* [2006] UKHL 12, [2006] 2 AC 307, that, provided it is properly conducted, a short period of detention (in that case 20 minutes) for the purposes of stop and search does not engage the ECHR, Article 5 (but see **B10.25**). The search must be conducted at or near the place where the person or vehicle was stopped (Code A, para. 3.4), although a place is 'near' if it is within a reasonable travelling distance (Code A, Note for Guidance 6). If a search requires the removal of more than outer clothing this cannot normally be done in public (PACE 1984, s. 2(9)(a); Code A, para. 3.5). Before a search of a person or an attended vehicle is conducted the officer must take reasonable steps to give the person the information set out in the PACE 1984, s. 2, and Code A, paras. 3.8 to 3.11 (*Bristol* [2007] EWCA Crim 3214). It was held in *R (Michaels) v Highbury Corner Magistrates' Court* [2009] EWHC 2928 (Admin) that this applies even if the officer conducting the search and the person who is the subject of the search are well known to each other. Recording requirements are set out in the PACE 1984, s. 3, and Code A, section 4.

POWERS OF ARREST: GENERAL PROVISIONS

Powers of Arrest

Police powers of arrest without a warrant in relation to criminal offences are principally governed by the PACE 1984, s. 24. Most other statutory powers of arrest were repealed by the SOCPA 2005, s. 111 and sch. 7, although a number of pre-PACE statutory powers are preserved by the PACE 1984, sch. 2, and there are extensive cross-border powers of arrest under the CJPO 1994 (see **D1.31** ***et seq.***). Civilian powers of arrest are governed by the PACE 1984, s. 24A. The other remaining power of arrest without a warrant is the common-law power of arrest for breach of the peace (see **D1.33**). Arrest under a warrant is governed by a number of statutory provisions (see **D1.35** ***et seq.***). **D1.14**

Legal Characteristics of Arrest

'Arrest' is not defined by the PACE 1984, or other legislation, and there is some inconsistency in the case law. One approach is that a person is arrested if, as a result of what is said or done, the person is under compulsion and is not free to go (*Alderson v Booth* [1969] 2 QB 216; *Inwood* (1973) 57 Cr App R 529; *Spicer v Holt* [1977] AC 987). Arrest is an ordinary English word, and whether or not a person has been arrested depends not on the legality of the arrest but on whether the person has been deprived of liberty to go where he or she pleases (*Lewis v Chief Constable of the South Wales Constabulary* [1991] 1 All ER 206). A second approach is that context and purpose are relevant. In *Austin v Metropolitan Police Commissioner* [2009] UKHL 5, [2009] 1 AC 564 the House of Lords distinguished between a deprivation of liberty and a restriction of movement. Whether a situation amounts to a deprivation of liberty as opposed to a restriction of movement is a matter of degree and intensity and is highly fact-sensitive. A whole range of factors has to be considered including the individual's specific situation, the context in which the restriction occurs and the purpose of the confinement or restriction (see also *Shields v Chief Constable of Merseyside Police* [2010] EWCA Civ 1281; *Austin v UK* (2012) 55 EHRR 14 (359); *Walker v Metropolitan Police Commissioner* [2014] EWCA Civ 897, [2015] 1 Cr App R 22 (283)). The decisions in *Austin* and *Walker* were followed in *R (Jalloh (formerly Jollah) v Secretary of State for the Home Department* [2020] UKSC 4, [2020] 2 WLR 418 where it was held that there may be imprisonment at common law without there being a deprivation **D1.15** of liberty under the ECHR, Article 5. In *Iqbal* [2011] EWCA Crim 273, [2011] 1 WLR 1541 it was held that a person who was handcuffed by a police officer and told that he would be arrested later by other officers was not under arrest (although he was unlawfully detained). Under the *Lewis* approach these circumstances would clearly have amounted to an arrest, albeit an unlawful arrest because D was not told that he was under arrest as required by the PACE 1984, s. 28(1). Taking hold of a person's arm for the purpose of simply drawing attention to what is being said, without an intention to detain or arrest, is neither an arrest nor an actionable trespass to the person unless it goes beyond what is acceptable by the ordinary standards of everyday life (*Mepstead v DPP* (1996) 160 JP 475; *Pegram v DPP* [2019] EWHC 2673 (Admin)); and the same is true where an officer takes a drunk person by the arm to steady him for his own safety (*McMillan v CPS* [2008] EWHC 1457 (Admin)). However, if an officer takes hold of a person's arm to detain that person while the officer decides whether to arrest, this does amount to a trespass (*Wood v DPP* [2008] EWHC 1056 (Admin); *Elkington v DPP* [2012] EWHC 3398 (Admin)); and detaining a person by confinement in a restricted space, without any intention of arrest, amounts to unlawful imprisonment (*Walker v Metropolitan Police Commissioner* [2014] EWCA Civ 897, [2015] 1 WLR 312; and see **B2.45** ***et seq.***).

D1.16 There is no necessary assumption that an arrest will be followed by a charge (*Holgate-Mohammed v Duke* [1984] AC 437). Although the power to arrest must be exercised for a proper purpose, it was affirmed in *Chalkley* [1998] QB 848 that the fact that an arrest is motivated by a desire to investigate another, more serious, offence does not render it invalid provided there are valid grounds for the arrest. An arrest for an offence will, however, be unlawful, even though made on the basis of reasonable suspicion, where the officer knows at the time of arrest that there is no possibility of a charge being made. Conversely, it is clear that, even though a complainant withdraws the complaint, a constable may still arrest a suspect where hoping by so doing to obtain a confession (*Plange v Chief Constable of South Humberside Police* (1992) *The Times*, 23 March 1992). If the lawfulness of an arrest carried out by an officer at the request of another is challenged, it is for the police to prove that the officer who asked for the arrest to be made acted in good faith in making the request (*Copeland v Metropolitan Police Commissioner* [2014] EWCA Civ 1014, [2015] 3 All ER 391; but see **D1.5**). The burden of proof of lawful arrest is on the police; if an arrest is lawful, the burden of proving excessive force is on the complainant (*Durrant v Chief Constable of Avon and Somerset Constabulary* [2014] EWHC 2922 (QB)). Reasonable force may be used to effect an arrest (PACE 1984, s. 117; CLA 1967, s. 3; and see **D1.7**).

Communication of Fact of and Grounds for Arrest

D1.17 Where a person is arrested (whether or not for an offence), otherwise than by being informed of being under arrest, the arrest is unlawful unless the person is informed of being under arrest as soon as is practicable after the arrest (PACE 1984, s. 28(1)). If the arrest is by a constable, this applies even if the fact of arrest is obvious (s. 28(2)). Further, an arrest is unlawful unless the arrested person is informed of the ground for the arrest at the time of the arrest, or as soon as is practicable after the arrest (s. 28(3)). If the arrest is by a constable, this applies even if the grounds for arrest are obvious (s. 28(4)). The person must also be informed why arrest was believed to be necessary (for the purposes of s. 24(4)), although failure to do so will not render the arrest unlawful (Code G, para. 2.2).

The test for whether the words used were sufficient is whether, having regard to all the circumstances of the case, the person arrested was told, in simple, non-technical language that the person could understand, the essential legal and factual grounds for the arrest (*Taylor v Chief Constable of Thames Valley Police* [2004] EWCA Civ 858, [2004] 1 WLR 3155; *Adler v CPS* [2013] EWHC 1968 (Admin)). According to PACE Code C, Note for Guidance 10B, and Code G, Note for Guidance 3, where a person is arrested for an offence that person must be informed of the nature of the suspected offence, and when and where it was allegedly committed.

D1.18 The information need not be given by the arresting officer but may be given by a colleague (*Nicholas v Parsonage* [1987] RTR 199; *Dhesi v Chief Constable of West Midlands Police* (2000) *The Times*, 9 May 2000). Where no reasons are given at the time of arrest because it is impracticable to inform the suspect, acts done at the time of arrest do not become retrospectively invalid because of a later failure to inform the suspect (*DPP v Hawkins* [1988] 3 All ER 673; *Lewis v Chief Constable of the South Wales Constabulary* [1991] 1 All ER 206). The words used will suffice even though they are apt to describe more than one offence, provided that they aptly describe the offence for which the arrest is made (*Abbassy v Metropolitan Police Commissioner* [1990] 1 All ER 193; *Clarke v Chief Constable of North Wales Police* [2000] All ER (D) 477). It was held in *Walker v Metropolitan Police Commissioner* [2014] EWCA Civ 897, [2015] 1 WLR 312 that, on the facts, informing a person that he or she was arrested for 'public order' was sufficient. An arresting officer may not, however, lead a person to think that the officer is arresting him or her for one offence when in truth the officer wishes to arrest the person for another (*Christie v Leachinsky* [1947] AC 573; *Abbassy v Metropolitan Police Commissioner*; *Waters v Bigmore* [1981] RTR 356).

In addition to the information required under s. 28, a person who is arrested, or who is further arrested (e.g., under the PACE 1984, s. 31), must be cautioned at the time of arrest or as soon as is practicable afterwards unless it is impracticable to do so because of the person's condition or behaviour at the time or the person has already been cautioned immediately before arrest (e.g., where initially questioned regarding a suspected offence without being arrested) (Code C, para. 10.4, and Code G, para. 3.4). The terms of the caution are set out in Code C, para. 10.5 (see **appendix 1**). Failure to administer a caution does not render the arrest unlawful, although it may provide grounds for exclusion of evidence under the PACE 1984, s. 76 or 78 (*Miller* [2007] EWCA Crim 1891).

The nature and circumstances of the offence leading to the arrest, the reason(s) why the arrest was necessary, the giving of the caution, and anything said by the arrested person at the time of arrest must be recorded by the arresting officer in the officer's pocket book (or other method used for recording information) (Code G, para. 4.1). This record must be made at the time of the arrest unless impracticable, in which case it must be completed as soon as possible thereafter (Code G, para 4.2). If the arrested person is subsequently detained at a police station, the information given by the arresting officer as to the circumstances and reason(s) for the arrest must be recorded in, or attached to, the custody record (Code G, para. 4.3).

Resisting Arrest

D1.19 A person has an unqualified right at common law to resist an unlawful arrest (*Christie v Leachinsky* [1947] AC 573), but must not use excessive force in doing so (*Wilson* [1955] 1 All ER 744; *Long* (1836) 7 C & P 314). Whilst excessive force in resisting arrest may amount to an offence, the person using excessive force would not be guilty of assaulting a constable in the execution of his duty (*Kenlin v Gardiner* [1967] 2 QB 510). These principles extend to a person resisting or assaulting an officer who goes to the assistance of another officer who is carrying out an unlawful arrest (*Cumberbatch v CPS* [2009] EWHC 3353 (Admin)), unless the assisting officer had an independent lawful justification for intervention (*Dixon v CPS* [2018] EWHC 3154 (Admin), [2018] 4 WLR 160). An officer who genuinely and reasonably believes that he or she is authorised by a court order to arrest a person and that the person is in breach of the order acts in the execution of his or her duty even if the power conferred by the order is erroneous (*Ahmed v CPS* [2017] EWHC 1272 (Admin)). The defence of self-defence is, in principle, available in respect of obstruction or assault on a police officer in the execution of his duty even where an arrest is lawful (*Oraki v DPP* [2018] EWHC 115 (Admin), [2018] QB 1086; *Wheeldon v CPS* [2018] EWHC 249 (Admin)).

It would seem that avoiding arrest, or even questioning short of arrest, by running away when approached by police can amount to wilful obstruction of the police in the execution of their duty, contrary to the Police Act 1996, s. 89(2) (*Sekfali v DPP* [2006] EWHC 894 (Admin)).

However, there is some difficulty in reconciling this with the established principle that a person does not commit wilful obstruction or any other offence (except where statute provides otherwise) by refusing to give the police his or her name and address or to answer police questions (*Rice v Connolly* [1966] 2 QB 414); and with the decision in *Iqbal* [2011] EWCA Crim 273, [2011] 1 WLR 1541, in which it was held that a person did not commit an offence by refusing to wait to be arrested (see also **B2.51** *et seq.*).

Action following Arrest

D1.20 Where a person is arrested at any place other than a police station, or is taken into custody by a constable following an arrest made by a civilian, the constable is normally obliged to take the person to a designated police station as soon as is practicable thereafter (PACE 1984, s. 30(1), (1A), (1B) and (2)). In exceptional circumstances the person may be taken to a non-designated station (s. 30(3) to (6)). The constable may delay taking the arrested person to a police station or releasing on bail under s. 30A if the person's presence at a place other than a police station is necessary in order to carry out such investigations as it is reasonable to carry out immediately (s. 30(10) and (10A)), but the reasons must be recorded (s. 30(11)). This might include taking the suspect from one place to another to check an alibi (*Dallison v Caffery* [1965] 1 QB 348), search of the arrested person under s. 32(2)(a) (see **D1.96**), or entry and search of premises under s. 32(2)(b) or s. 18(1) and (5) (see **D1.171**). A constable who is satisfied that there are no grounds for keeping the arrested person under arrest or releasing on bail under s. 30A must release the person (s. 30(7) and (7A)), and the facts must be recorded (s. 30(8) and (9)).

D1.21 Notwithstanding the above, an arrested person may, instead of being taken to a police station, be released either without bail or on bail, to attend at a police station on a future date (s. 30A(1) to (3)). The release may only be on bail if the officer is satisfied that this is necessary and proportionate in all the circumstances, and it is authorised by an officer of the rank of inspector or above (PACE 1984, s. 30A(1A), inserted by the PCA 2017, s. 52(4)). If the person is released on bail, conditions may be imposed for the purpose of securing surrender, preventing further offences, preventing interference with witnesses or obstruction of the administration of justice, or for the person's own protection (s. 30A(3B)). An application to vary conditions may be made to the police and, thereafter, to a magistrates' court (ss. 30CA and 30CB).

A person released on bail in these circumstances must be given a notice informing the person of the offence to which the arrest relates, of the grounds of arrest, that the person is required to attend a police station and of any conditions imposed, and opportunities for seeking a variation of those conditions. The notice must also specify the police station which the person is required to attend and the time required for attendance. The person may be required to attend a different police station from that originally notified (s. 30B(1) to (6)). These provisions do not apply to a person released without bail under s. 30A. A release on bail is limited to 28 days commencing on the day after the day on which the person was arrested for the offence in relation to which bail is granted (PACE 1984, s. 30B(8), inserted by the PCA 2017, s. 62(8)).

A person released under s. 30A (with or without bail) may be re-arrested without warrant if, since the release, new evidence has come to light or an examination or analysis of existing evidence has been made which could not reasonably have been made before the release (s. 30C(4), as amended by the PCA 2017, s. 65(2)). Any person released on bail under s. 30A who fails to attend at a police station as required and any person whom a constable has reasonable grounds for suspecting has broken any conditions imposed may be arrested without warrant; but the police have no power to arrest for an anticipated breach of conditions or failure to surrender. The person must then be taken to a police station (which may be the specified police station or any other police station) as soon as practicable after an arrest. Although breach of conditions, and failure to attend a police station, do not constitute offences, an arrest under these provisions counts as an arrest for an offence for the purposes of the PACE 1984, ss. 30 and 31 (s. 30D).

The PACE 1984 makes no provision regarding arrest of a person released without bail under s. 30A other than in the circumstances provided for by s. 30(c)(4).

ARREST WITHOUT WARRANT

Police powers of arrest without warrant are largely governed by the PACE 1984, s. 24 (but see **D1.30** *et seq.*), and civilian powers of arrest by s. 24A. Under s. 24 a police officer may arrest for any offence, but civilian powers of arrest are confined to indictable offences (see **D1.69**). In both cases the power is subject to a test of necessity. Section 24 is supplemented by PACE Code of Practice G (see **D1.1**). Other powers of arrest without warrant, cross-border powers of arrest, and arrest for breach of the peace, are also dealt with in this section. **D1.22**

Powers of arrest are generally discretionary; if the conditions are satisfied the officer (or civilian) may arrest, but is not required to. However, where a person has been arrested for an offence and is at a police station in consequence of that arrest, and it appears to the police that, if released, the person would be liable to arrest for some other offence, the person must be arrested for that other offence (PACE 1984, s. 31).

Police Powers of Arrest

Police and Criminal Evidence Act 1984, s. 24 **D1.23**

(1) A constable may arrest without a warrant—
  (a) anyone who is about to commit an offence;
  (b) anyone who is in the act of committing an offence;
  (c) anyone whom he has reasonable grounds for suspecting to be about to commit an offence;
  (d) anyone whom he has reasonable grounds for suspecting to be committing an offence.
(2) If a constable has reasonable grounds for suspecting that an offence has been committed, he may arrest without a warrant anyone whom he has reasonable grounds to suspect of being guilty of it.
(3) If an offence has been committed, a constable may arrest without a warrant—
  (a) anyone who is guilty of the offence;
  (b) anyone whom he has reasonable grounds for suspecting to be guilty of it.
(4) But the power of summary arrest conferred by subsection (1), (2) or (3) is exercisable only if the constable has reasonable grounds for believing that for any of the reasons mentioned in subsection (5) it is necessary to arrest the person in question.
(5) The reasons are—
  (a) to enable the name of the person in question to be ascertained (in the case where the constable does not know, and cannot readily ascertain, the person's name, or has reasonable grounds for doubting whether a name given by the person as his name is his real name);
  (b) correspondingly as regards the person's address;
  (c) to prevent the person in question—
    (i) causing physical injury to himself or any other person;
    (ii) suffering physical injury;
    (iii) causing loss of or damage to property;
    (iv) committing an offence against public decency (subject to subsection (6)); or
    (v) causing an unlawful obstruction of the highway;
  (d) to protect a child or other vulnerable person from the person in question;
  (e) to allow the prompt and effective investigation of the offence or of the conduct of the person in question;
  (f) to prevent any prosecution for the offence from being hindered by the disappearance of the person in question.
(6) Subsection (5)(c)(iv) applies only where members of the public going about their normal business cannot reasonably be expected to avoid the person in question.

Reasonable Suspicion Arrest under the PACE 1984, s. 24(1)(c) and (d), (2) and (3)(b), requires the officer to have reasonable grounds for suspicion (see **D1.4**). However, the PACE 1984, s. 24(1)(a) and (b), and (3)(a), permit arrest without reasonable suspicion. Thus, provided it can be established that the relevant condition is satisfied (e.g., that the person was in the act of **D1.24**

committing an offence), the arrest will be lawful even if it cannot be established that the officer had reasonable grounds for suspicion. The scope for justifying an arrest by reference to the powers that do not require reasonable suspicion was emphasised in *Shields v Chief Constable of Merseyside Police* [2010] EWCA Civ 1281, although the Court of Appeal did not consider whether these powers comply with the reasonable suspicion requirement of the ECHR, Article 5(1)(c) (see **D1.4**).

D1.25 **Necessity** In addition to the conditions set out in the PACE 1984, s. 24(1) to (3), the officer must have reasonable grounds for believing that arrest is necessary for any of the reasons set out in s. 24(5) (s. 24(4)). 'Necessary' cannot be regarded as a synonym for 'desirable' or 'convenient' (*R (TL) v Chief Constable of Surrey Police* [2017] EWHC 129 (Admin), [2017] 1 Cr App R 29 (431); *Metropolitan Police Commissioner v MR* [2019] EWHC 888 (QB)). The necessity test involves a similar mixed subjective/objective test to that required for reasonable grounds for suspicion (*Graham v West (Chief Constable of West Mercia)* [2011] EWHC 4 (QB); *Parker v Chief Constable of Essex Police* [2018] EWCA Civ 2788, [2019] 1 WLR 2238). The objective element requires the officer to have 'solid grounds' for believing that arrest is necessary, for example, that the suspect would hide or destroy evidence; a theoretical possibility is not sufficient (*Hanningfield v Chief Constable of Essex* [2013] EWHC 243 (QB), [2013] 1 WLR 3632, cited with approval in *B v Chief Constable of the Police Service of Northern Ireland* [2015] EWHC 3691 (Admin)). PACE Code G notes that arrest 'represents an obvious and significant interference' with the right to liberty (para. 1.2), and the decision to arrest must be fully justified and the officer must consider whether the necessary objectives can be met by other, less intrusive, means (para. 1.3). The officer does not have to be satisfied that there is no viable alternative to arrest; concluding that arrest is the practical and sensible option is sufficient. However, the officer must make some evaluation of the feasibility of achieving the object of the arrest by some alternative means, such as by inviting the suspect to attend for interview (*Re Alexander* [2009] NIQB 20). Voluntary attendance at a police station may be, but is not necessarily, a viable alternative to arrest (*Hayes v Chief Constable of Merseyside Police* [2011] EWCA Civ 911, [2012] 1 WLR 517).

An officer who does not consider alternatives short of arrest is open to challenge (*Richardson v Chief Constable of West Midlands Police* [2011] EWHC 773 (QB), [2011] 2 Cr App R 1 (1)), but 'the challenge, if it comes, is not one which requires the officer's decision to be subjected to a full-blown public law reasons challenge. It is one which requires it to be shown that on the information known to the officer there were reasonable grounds for believing arrest to be necessary, for an identified section 24(5) reason' (*Hayes v Chief Constable of Merseyside Police*, followed in *Fitzpatrick, Wilkey and Thomas, Body and White (a firm) v Metropolitan Police Commissioner* [2012] EWHC 12 (Admin) and *Metropolitan Police Commissioner v MR* [2019] EWHC 888 (QB)). See also Code G, para. 2.6, and Note for Guidance 2C.

D1.26 Code G, para. 1.3, provides that it is essential that the power of arrest is exercised in a 'non-discriminatory and proportionate manner' and it is submitted that, in considering whether arrest is necessary, the officer must take into account the nature and seriousness of the suspected offence (and see Code G, para. 2.8). Further, in considering whether the police have sufficiently considered alternatives to arrest, it would seem to follow from *Hanningfield* that account should be taken of whether an arrest was carried out in the context of a planned operation, or was a response to immediate and urgent events.

D1.27 Code G, para. 2.9, provides some explanation of the various necessity conditions. In relation to s. 24(5)(a) and (b) it states that an address is satisfactory for the purposes of serving a summons, or requisition and charge, if the person will be at the address for a sufficiently long period to facilitate service, or if some other person at the address given will accept service on the person's behalf. Where the suspect gives his or her name and/or address, the officer must have reasonable grounds for doubting the name or address given for arrest to be necessary (Code G, para. 2.9(b)). A constable cannot be said to doubt it simply because in the past other persons suspected of a like offence have not given correct particulars (*G v DPP* [1989] Crim LR 150).

In certain circumstances, loss of or damage to property, for the purposes of s. 24(5)(c)(iii), could include the offender's own property, such as where a violent husband, having assaulted his wife, is believed likely to damage the matrimonial home or objects in it. The condition under s. 24(5)(c)(iv) applies only where members of the public going about their normal business cannot reasonably be expected to avoid the person in question (s. 24(6)). In relation to s. 24(5)(c)(v) it is irrelevant that the police have previously permitted an act of obstruction to take place there (*Arrowsmith v Jenkins* [1963] 2 QB 561).

Section 24(5)(e) permits arrest in order to allow the prompt and effective investigation of the offence or of the conduct of the person in question. It is difficult to see how an arrest could be justified by reference to a need to investigate the conduct of the person unless that involves investigation of the offence of which the person is suspected. Code G, para. 2.9(e), gives examples of the circumstances in which this condition may be satisfied, including where there is a need to enter and search property, search the person, or take fingerprints, photographs, etc. However, many such investigative acts may be carried out with the consent of the person concerned so they may not, in themselves, justify an arrest of a person willing to co-operate. Furthermore, in the case of an intention to enter and search property, if the circumstances permit, the police should proceed by way of an application for a search warrant under the PACE 1984, s. 8, rather than an arrest followed by a search under s. 18 (*R (TL) v Chief Constable of Surrey Police* [2017] EWHC 129 (Admin), [2017] 1 Cr App R 29 (431)). It was held in *B v Chief Constable of the Police Service of Northern Ireland* [2015] EWHC 3691 (Admin) that the fact that an officer may wish to place a person on conditional bail following interview did not, in itself, render an arrest necessary. However, in *R (TL) v Chief Constable of Surrey Police* the Divisional Court stated that this was confined to the facts, and that an arrest could be necessary for this purpose where, for example, there are grounds to believe that bail conditions are required to protect a witness from intimidation. Where a person attends at a police station voluntarily, arrest is justified only if new information coming to light after the arrangements were made indicates that voluntary attendance is no longer a practical alternative. The possibility that a volunteer may leave during the interview is not a valid reason for arresting the volunteer before the interview commences (Code G, Note for Guidance 2G; cf. *Hayes v Chief Constable of Merseyside Police* [2011] EWCA Civ 911, [2012] 1 WLR 517). **D1.28**

In relation to s. 24(5)(f), Code G, para. 2.9, states that the condition may be satisfied if there are reasonable grounds for believing that the person will fail to attend court if not arrested, or if the grant of bail under the PACE 1984, s. 30A, would not be enough to deter the person from trying to evade prosecution. Given the reasonable belief requirement in s. 24(4), there must be some objective basis for the belief. Mere suspicion that the person may not turn up in court should not be sufficient.

Civilian Powers of Arrest

Police and Criminal Evidence Act 1984, s. 24A **D1.29**

(1) A person other than a constable may arrest without a warrant—
 (a) anyone who is in the act of committing an indictable offence;
 (b) anyone whom he has reasonable grounds for suspecting to be committing an indictable offence.
(2) Where an indictable offence has been committed, a person other than a constable may arrest without a warrant—
 (a) anyone who is guilty of the offence;
 (b) anyone whom he has reasonable grounds for suspecting to be guilty of it.
(3) But the power of summary arrest conferred by subsection (1) or (2) is exercisable only if—
 (a) the person making the arrest has reasonable grounds for believing that for any of the reasons mentioned in subsection (4) it is necessary to arrest the person in question; and
 (b) it appears to the person making the arrest that it is not reasonably practicable for a constable to make it instead.
(4) The reasons are to prevent the person in question—
 (a) causing physical injury to himself or any other person;
 (b) suffering physical injury;

(c) causing loss of or damage to property; or
(d) making off before a constable can assume responsibility for him.

(5) This section does not apply in relation to an offence under Part 3 or 3A of the Public Order Act 1986.

Section 24A provides for a more restricted scheme of powers of arrest for persons other than constables. These powers apply only to indictable offences (s. 24A(1) and (2)), which includes offences triable either way as well as indictable-only offences (see **D1.69**). Unlike a constable, a civilian cannot arrest for an anticipated offence. If a civilian arrests a person under s. 24A(2) for an offence the civilian believes has been committed, the arrest will be unlawful if it cannot be established that an indictable offence was in fact committed (*Self* [1992] 3 All ER 476, decided under the former version of s. 24, but the same principles apply). However, where an arrest is carried out under s. 24A(1)(b), there is no requirement that an indictable offence has actually been committed (*Sowande v CPS* [2017] EWHC 1234 (Admin)). A civilian making an arrest must have reasonable grounds for believing that, for any of the reasons mentioned in s. 24A(4), it is necessary to arrest the person and it must appear that it is not practicable for a constable to make the arrest instead (s. 24A(3)). The necessity conditions under s. 24A(4) are more limited than those that apply to constables under s. 24(5).

Other Powers of Arrest

D1.30 The PACE 1984, s. 26 and sch. 2, preserve certain powers of arrest enacted prior to the PACE 1984.

Police and Criminal Evidence Act 1984, sch. 2

PRESERVED POWERS OF ARREST	
1952 c. 52	Section 49 of the Prison Act 1952.
1952 c. 67	Section 13 of the Visiting Forces Act 1952.
1969 c. 54	Section 32 of the Children and Young Persons Act 1969.
1971 c. 77	Section 24(2) of the Immigration Act 1971 and paragraphs 17, 24 and 33 of Schedule 2 and paragraph 7 of Schedule 3 to that Act.
1976 c. 63	Section 7 of the Bail Act 1976.
1983 c. 20	Sections 18, 35(10), 36(8), 38(7), 136(1) and 138 of the Mental Health Act 1983.
1984 c. 47	Section 5(5) of the Repatriation of Prisoners Act 1984.

A constable has a power to arrest a person released on bail in criminal proceedings where (a) there are reasonable grounds to believe the person is not likely to surrender to custody or is likely to break any bail conditions, (b) there are reasonable grounds to suspect that the person has broken the bail conditions, or (c) where that person was released on bail with a surety or sureties, a surety notifies the constable in writing that the bailed person is unlikely to surrender to custody and that for that reason the surety wishes to be relieved of his or her obligations as a surety (BA 1976, s. 7(3)). A Customs and Excise officer has a similar power to arrest a suspect who the officer has reasonable grounds for believing is not likely to surrender to custody where the person has been released on bail in respect of possession of controlled drugs, drug trafficking or money laundering (CJA 1988, s. 151). For powers of arrest in respect of a person granted bail before being taken to a police station, see **D1.21**, and in respect of a person granted bail under the PACE 1984, Part IV, see **D1.197**.

Many statutory powers of arrest enacted before and after the PACE 1984 were repealed by the SOCPA 2005, s. 111 and sch. 7. However, the police still have various statutory powers of arrest other than those granted by the PACE 1984, s. 24, or preserved by sch. 2. For example, they may arrest a person for the purpose of taking fingerprints or samples (PACE 1984, s. 63A(4) and sch. 2A, para. 17), and may arrest a person who is reasonably suspected to be a terrorist (see **B10.14** *et seq.*). The police also have powers to remove a person to a place of safety under the Mental Health Act 1983, s. 136(1) (see **D1.63**). For powers of arrest in respect of service offences, see the Armed Forces Act 2006, Part 3, ch. 1.

Cross-border Powers of Arrest

The CJPO 1994, Part X (ss. 136 to 140), makes extensive provision for cross-border powers of arrest within the UK. Section 136 concerns the cross-border execution of warrants. A warrant issued in one part of the UK in the name of an innocent person (as in the context of personation by the true offender) remains valid until annulled. Where police arrest the person named in the warrant, they will not be liable for wrongful arrest or false imprisonment provided that they acted without malice (*McGrath v Chief Constable of the Royal Ulster Constabulary* [2001] UKHL 39, [2001] 2 AC 731). **D1.31**

By s. 137, constables from one part of the UK who have reasonable grounds for suspecting that an offence has been committed or attempted in their jurisdiction may arrest a suspected person in another part of the UK. An arrest can be carried out under this provision where the conditions which would enable the officers to arrest lawfully in their own jurisdiction are satisfied. Following arrest, the arrested person must be taken to a police station in accordance with s. 137(7). By s. 137A similar powers are granted to constables to arrest a person in their own jurisdiction where they have reasonable grounds for suspecting that the person has committed a specified offence in another part of the UK. 'Specified offence' is defined in s. 137B. Constables of a police force in England and Wales or Northern Ireland must have reasonable grounds for believing that arrest is necessary to allow the prompt and effective investigation of the offence, or to prevent any prosecution for the offence from being hindered by the disappearance of the person (s. 137A(1)). Constables of a police force in Scotland must be satisfied that it would not be in the interests of justice to delay the arrest to enable a warrant to be obtained under s. 136 or to enable a power of arrest under s. 137 to be exercised. A person arrested under s. 137A may only be detained to enable an arrest warrant under s. 136 to be obtained, or to enable the person to be re-arrested under s. 137 (s. 137C). For the maximum periods for which a person arrested under s. 137A may be detained, see s. 137C(2) to (7).

The Finance Act 2007, s. 87, as amended by the PCA 2017, s. 118, provides that all of the cross-border powers of arrest are exercisable by Revenue and Customs officers in relation to any of the functions of HMRC or Revenue and Customs officers. This means that the powers are available in relation to both tax and customs matters. Designated customs officials and NCA officers who are designated with the powers of Revenue and Customs officers are also able to exercise cross-border powers of arrest.

Reasonable force may be used in effecting an arrest under the CJPO 1994, s. 137 or s. 137A (s. 137(8)(a), and s. 137A(6)(d)). Generally, the powers of a constable ancillary to arrest are those that apply in the jurisdiction in which the suspected offence was committed (see s. 137(8) and 138(2), and s. 137A(6) and (7) respectively). The rights of persons arrested under these provisions are governed by s. 137(8)(c) and s. 137D respectively. Powers of search available in respect of an arrest under ss. 136, 137 and 137A are governed by s. 139 (as amended by the PCA 2017, sch. 17, para. 4). **D1.32**

The scheme further provides for reciprocal powers of arrest. Where a police constable in England or Wales would have powers to arrest, a constable from Scotland or Northern Ireland who is in England or Wales has the same powers of arrest (s. 140(1)). Reciprocal powers apply in favour of a constable from England or Wales in Scotland or Northern Ireland (s. 140(3), (4) and (5)). The scheme is premised upon the arresting officer having the same powers and coming under the same obligations as if the officer were a local constable operating under local law.

Arrest for Breach of the Peace

Any person, whether constable or civilian, has a common-law power of arrest where (a) a breach of the peace is committed in the person's presence, (b) the person effecting the arrest reasonably believes that such a breach will be committed in the immediate future by the person arrested, or (c) a breach of the peace has been committed or the person effecting the arrest reasonably **D1.33** believes that a breach of the peace has occurred and that a further breach is threatened. In order to comply with the ECHR, Article 5(1)(c), an arrest must be for the purpose of bringing the person before a competent legal authority, but an arrest is lawful notwithstanding that the person is released before it was practical to bring the person before a court (*R (Hicks) v Metropolitan Police Commissioner* [2017] UKSC 9, [2017] AC 256, which was approved on appeal to the ECtHR in *Eiseman-Renyard v UK* (2019) Appln 57884/17, 5 March 2019). A breach of the peace occurs 'whenever harm is actually done or is likely to be done to a person or in his presence to his property, or a person is in fear of being so harmed through an assault, affray, riot, unlawful assembly or other disturbance' (*Howell* [1982] QB 416, at p. 427). For guidance on immediacy in relation to conduct in a domestic setting, see *Wragg v DPP* [2005] EWHC 1389 (Admin) and *Demetriou v DPP* [2012] EWHC 2443 (Admin).

Reasonable belief is an objective requirement in the sense that the court must determine whether the belief was reasonable having regard to the circumstances as perceived by the person carrying out the arrest at the time (*Redmond-Bate v DPP* (1999) 163 JP 789). Where a reasonable apprehension of an imminent breach of the peace exists, the preventive action taken must be reasonable, necessary and proportionate. For action short of arrest, see *R (Laporte) v Chief Constable of Gloucestershire* [2006] UKHL 55, [2007] 2 AC 105; *Austin v Metropolitan Police Commissioner* [2009] UKHL 5, [2009] 1 AC 564, and *R (McClure and Moos) v Metropolitan Police Commissioner* [2012] EWCA Civ 12. The power to arrest for an apprehended breach of the peace caused by apparently lawful conduct is exceptional (*Foulkes v Chief Constable of Merseyside Police* [1998] 3 All ER 705; *Bibby v Chief Constable of Essex Police* (2000) 164 JP 297). For powers of entry to deal with a breach of the peace, see **D1.174**.

D1.34 A person arrested for breach of the peace may be held in custody at a police station, but the officer concerned must have an honest belief, based upon objective and reasonable grounds, that detention is necessary in order to prevent a breach of the peace. If this condition is not satisfied, and no other grounds for detention exist, the person must be released (*Chief Constable of Cleveland Police v McGrogan* [2002] EWCA Civ 86). Breach of the peace is not an offence under domestic law, although it may be treated as criminal for the purposes of the ECHR (*Steel v UK* (1999) 28 EHRR 603) and, therefore, detention of a person arrested for breach of the peace is not governed by the PACE 1984, s. 37. It was held in *Williamson v Chief Constable of West Midlands Police* [2003] EWCA Civ 337, [2004] 1 WLR 14 (followed in *Hicks*) that PACE Code C did not apply to a person detained at a police station following arrest for breach of the peace because such a person was not arrested for an offence and therefore was not in police detention. However, whilst some powers and obligations under the PACE 1984 apply only in respect of persons in police detention (see **D1.40**), the right to consult a solicitor (see **D1.55**) and the right to notification (see **D1.52**) apply to persons 'arrested and held in custody'. Furthermore, Code C, para. 1.10, states that the code (other than the detention review provisions in s. 15) applies to people in custody at police stations 'whether or not they have been arrested', and it would be a strange result if a person arrested for breach of the peace had less protection than a person who is in custody without having been arrested.

ARREST UNDER WARRANT

Warrants Issued by Magistrates' Courts

D1.35 The most important of the statutes which authorise arrest under warrant for a criminal offence is the MCA 1980. Section 1 empowers a justice to issue a warrant on the basis of a written information substantiated on oath that a person has, or is suspected of having, committed an offence. Such a warrant may or may not be endorsed for bail. If endorsed for bail, the warrant will (if relevant) specify the amounts in which any sureties are to be bound. If bail is to be granted with sureties, the police must release the offender if the sureties approved by the officer enter into recognizances in accordance with the endorsement. The person bailed is then obliged to appear before a magistrates' court at the time and place named in the recognizance (s. 117).

The power of a magistrates' court to issue a warrant for the arrest of any person who has attained the age of 18 years is limited by s. 1(4). The offence concerned must be indictable, or punishable with imprisonment, or the person's address must be not sufficiently established for a summons to be served. A warrant to arrest any person for non-appearance before a magistrates' court must not be issued unless the offence to which the warrant relates is also punishable with imprisonment or where the court, having convicted the defendant, proposes to impose a disqualification. In the case of private prosecutions for certain offences, listed in s. 1(4D), a warrant must not be issued without consent of the DPP (s. 1(4A)).

Power is given under the MCA 1980, s. 13, to issue a warrant for the arrest of a person who has failed to appear to answer a summons. Power to issue a warrant for arrest in respect of a person who has been granted bail and who fails to surrender to custody or who, having surrendered to custody, then goes absent before the court is ready to deal with the case, is governed by the BA 1976, s. 7.

Warrants Issued by the Crown Court

Section 80(2) of the Senior Courts Act 1981 provides that, where an indictment has been signed but the person charged has not been sent for trial, the Crown Court may issue a summons requiring that person to appear before it or may issue an arrest warrant. A similar power applies where a person charged with or convicted of an offence has entered into a recognizance to appear at the Crown Court and fails to do so. A warrant for arrest may be endorsed for bail, in which case the officer in charge of the police station to which D is taken has the same powers and duties as in the parallel case where the warrant is issued by magistrates (s. 81). **D1.36**

Procedural Requirements Governing Arrest Warrants For the procedural requirements governing arrest warrants, see CrimPR 13.2 (terms of warrants for arrest), 13.4 (information to be included in a warrant), 13.5 (execution of a warrant) and 13.7 (warrant issued when the court office is closed). **D1.37**

Extradition Cases

For powers of arrest in extradition cases, see **D31.4** and **D31.7**. **D1.38**

A person arrested under the extradition provisions may be held in custody at a police station until produced before the appropriate court, but is not treated as being in police detention for the purposes of the PACE 1984, s. 118(2) (see **D1.40**). The person's treatment whilst at a police station is governed by codes of practice issued under the Extradition Act 2003, s. 173 (see the Extradition Act 2003 (Police Powers: Codes of Practice) Order 2003 (SI 2003 No. 3336)).

Execution of Warrants

The principal provision dealing with the execution of warrants is the MCA 1980, s. 125. This is supplemented by ss. 125A and 125B, which extend powers of execution to civilian enforcement officers and other approved persons and bodies. Section 125 provides that a warrant of arrest issued by a justice of the peace remains in force until it is executed or ceases to have effect in accordance with rules of court, and that it may be executed anywhere in England and Wales by any person to whom it is directed or by any constable acting within his or her police area. The effect of this, taken together with the Police Act 1996, s. 30, is to enable such a warrant to be executed by a constable anywhere in England and Wales and adjacent UK waters. Furthermore, any constable may execute the warrant in his or her own police area even though it is addressed to a constable in another police area. Police have a discretion as to when to execute a warrant, but the discretion must be exercised reasonably. The term 'immediately' in such a warrant refers to taking the person before the court and not to when the arrest may be made. In certain circumstances, it may be reasonable for police to investigate a criminal matter before executing a **D1.39** default warrant of which they are aware (*Henderson v Chief Constable of Cleveland Police* [2001] EWCA Civ 335, [2001] 1 WLR 1103).

A warrant to which s. 125A(1) or s. 125D applies may be executed by any person entitled to execute it even though it is not in the person's possession at the time (s. 125D(1) and (2)). It must be shown to the person arrested, if demanded, as soon as practicable (s. 125D(4)). These provisions do not, however, apply to a search warrant or other warrant which must be in the constable's possession at the time (*Purdy* [1975] QB 288, and see **D1.169**).

A constable who arrests a person under warrant must inform the person of the reason for the arrest and that the constable is acting under warrant (PACE 1984, s. 28).

DETENTION AND TREATMENT OF SUSPECTS

Applicability of PACE and Codes of Practice

D1.40 **General** The detention and treatments of suspects is regulated by the PACE 1984, parts IV and V, and PACE Code C. The PACE 1984 distinguishes between persons in police detention and others who may be held in custody at a police station. A person is in police detention if the person has been taken to a police station after being arrested for an offence or under the TA 2000, s. 41, or has been arrested at a police station after attending voluntarily or accompanying a constable to it, and is detained there or detained elsewhere in the charge of a constable (PACE 1984, s. 118(2)). Similarly, a person is in police detention if in the custody of a designated civilian detention, investigating or escort officer by virtue of the Police Reform Act 2002, sch. 4, paras. 22, 34(1) or 35(3) (PACE 1984, s. 118(2A)). A person who is at court after being charged is not in police detention (s. 118(2)); neither is a person who attends a police station to answer to live link bail in accordance with a direction under the CDA 1998, s. 57C (PACE 1984, s. 46ZA(2)), unless an exception in s. 46ZA(3) applies (see **D2.46**).

Many of the police powers in the PACE 1984 relate only to persons in police detention. However, certain rights such as the right of intimation (under s. 56) and the right to legal advice (under s. 58), apply to persons arrested and held in custody at a police station or other premises, and apply irrespective of whether the person was arrested for an offence.

D1.41 Code C applies to persons in custody at a police station whether or not they have been arrested (subject to the exceptions in Code C, para. 1.12), and to persons removed to a police station as a place of safety under the Mental Health Act 1983, ss. 135 and 136 (see **D1.63**). However, section 15 of Code C (concerning reviews of detention) applies only to persons in police detention. Whilst a person arrested under the TA 2000, s. 41, and taken to a police station is in police detention, Code H rather than Code C applies unless and until the person is charged with an offence (Code H, para. 1.2, and see **D1.2**), and many aspects of detention are governed by the TA 2000, sch. 8. For the application of Code C to a person detained following arrest for breach of the peace, see **D1.34**.

D1.42 **Persons Remanded to Police Custody** Where a magistrates' court has power to remand a person in custody, it may commit the person to detention at a police station (MCA 1980, s. 128(7)). A person so committed is treated as being in police detention for the purposes of the PACE 1984, s. 39 (duty of the custody officer to ensure that detainees are treated in accordance with PACE and the Codes), and the detention is subject to review under the PACE 1984, s. 40 (MCA 1980, s. 128(8)(c) and (d)). The person is not to be kept in police detention unless it is necessary for the purpose of inquiring into other offences, and must be taken back before the magistrates' court that committed him or her as soon as that need ceases (s. 128(8)(a) and (b)). A magistrates' court has a similar power, under the CJA 1988, s. 152(1) and (1A), to commit a person brought before the court in respect of certain drugs offences to the custody of a constable for up to 192 hours, but the legislation is silent on the applicability of the PACE 1984. In any event Code C applies (other than section 15) if, as a result, the person is held in custody in a police station.

Volunteers A person who, for the purpose of assisting with an investigation, attends voluntarily at a police station or at any other place where a constable is present, or who accompanies a constable to a police station or such other place without having been arrested, is entitled to leave at will unless arrested. This could include victims and witnesses as well as suspects. If the constable decides that the person is to be prevented from leaving at will, the constable is to inform the suspect at once that the suspect is under arrest and (presumably only if at a police station) bring the suspect before the custody officer (PACE 1984, s. 29; Code C, para. 3.21). If the suspect is not placed under arrest but is cautioned (see **D1.83**), the officer administering the caution must immediately inform the suspect that he or she is not under arrest, and is free to leave if so wished, and that free and independent legal advice may be obtained (Code C, para. 3.21). The officer must also inform the person of the grounds and reasons for suspecting him or her of the offence(s) concerned. If the relevant location is any place or premises for which the interviewer requires the person's informed consent to remain, reference to being free to leave means that the person may withdraw consent and require the officer to leave (Code C, para. 3.22). **D1.43**

Many of the provisions of the PACE 1984 and Code C do not apply to a volunteer even when at a police station since the volunteer is neither in police detention nor held in custody. However, a volunteer is entitled to legal advice at any time, and to communicate with anyone outside a police station, and must be treated with no less consideration than a person who is in custody (Code C, Note for Guidance 1A). For the rights, entitlements and safeguards that apply to a volunteer interviewed by the police, see Code C, paras. 3.21 and 3.21A.

The Custody Officer

Where a person has been arrested, that person must normally be taken to a police station (subject to the power to release under the PACE 1984, ss. 30(7) and 30A (s. 30(1): see **D1.20** ***et seq.***). The person may be taken to any police station, unless it is anticipated that detention of more than six hours will be necessary, in which case the person should be taken to a police station designated under s. 35 (s. 30(3) to (6)). One or more custody officers must be appointed for each designated police station (s. 36(1)). A custody officer must be of at least the rank of sergeant (s. 36(3)). If a custody officer is not readily available, or if a person is taken to a non-designated police station, another officer may perform the role although that officer must normally not be involved in the investigation of an offence for which the person is in detention (s. 36(4) to (7)). **D1.44**

A person who has been arrested for an offence can only be kept in police detention in accordance with the PACE 1984, Part IV (s. 34(1)). Such a person may be detained at a police station only on the authority of the custody officer (s. 37(1)), and may not be released except on the custody officer's authority (s. 34(2) and (3)). Generally, it is the responsibility of the custody officer to ensure that a person in police detention is treated in accordance with the PACE 1984 and the Codes of Practice, although responsibility is temporarily transferred to any officer to whom custody of the person is transferred in accordance with the Codes of Practice (s. 39(1) to (3)).

Custody Records

A custody record must be opened as soon as is practicable in respect of each person who is *brought to a police station* under arrest, or who is arrested at a police station after having attended voluntarily, or who attends a police station in accordance with bail granted under the PACE 1984, s. 30A (Code C, para. 2.1: see **D1.20**). A custody record does not have to be opened in respect of a volunteer who is not arrested. The custody officer is responsible for recording in the custody record all matters that are required by the PACE 1984 or the Codes of Practice to be recorded (s. 39(1)(b) and Code C, para. 2.3). If the detained person is transferred to another police station, the custody record or a copy of it must accompany the person, and must show the time of and reason for the transfer (Code C, para. 2.3). It is **D1.45**

Part D Procedure

not clear whether a new custody record should be opened where a person is further detained on surrendering to custody following a release on police bail or whether the original custody record should be continued. However, time in police detention before the release on bail will normally count for the purpose of calculating the maximum periods of detention (see D1.67).

D1.46 Both the PACE 1984 and the Codes of Practice provide for the many matters that must be recorded in the custody record. The former requirement to record everything that a person has with him or her when detained is now at the discretion of the custody officer (PACE 1984, s. 54, as amended by the CJA 2003, s. 8). If a record is made, it does not have to be in the custody record (s. 54(2A)), although Home Office Circular 60/2003, para. 5.5, states that the detained person should be asked to check any record that is made, and sign it as correct. For details of what must be recorded when a healthcare professional is called in to examine a detained person, see Code C, paras. 9.15 and 9.16.

A solicitor or appropriate adult must be permitted to inspect the 'whole of the detainee's custody record' as soon as practicable after arrival at a police station, and at any time during the period of detention (Code C, para. 2.4). A detained person, lawyer or appropriate adult must be permitted, on giving reasonable notice, to inspect the custody record after the person has left police detention (Code C, para. 2.5), and is entitled to receive a copy of the custody record for up to 12 months after release (Code C, para. 2.4A).

The Decision to Detain

D1.47 **The Initial Decision** Where a person is arrested for an offence, whether without a warrant or under a warrant not endorsed for bail, the custody officer at the station where the person is detained must determine whether there is sufficient evidence to charge the suspect with the offence for which the suspect is arrested (PACE 1984, s. 37(1)). It has been held that in making the determination the custody officer is not required to inquire into the lawfulness of the arrest (*DPP v L* [1999] Crim LR 752; *Al Fayed v Metropolitan Police Commissioner* [2004] EWCA Civ 1579). However, Code C, para. 3.4(b), now provides that documents essential for the purpose of challenging the lawfulness of arrest or detention must be disclosed to the suspect at the time that the custody officer determines whether detention is necessary, and Note for Guidance 3ZA requires the investigating officer to bring to the officer's attention any documents which appear to undermine the need to keep the suspect in custody. Arguably, therefore, the custody officer should at least take a view on the legality of the arrest on the basis of any such documents that are brought to the custody officer's attention.

The test for determining whether there is sufficient evidence to charge is not statutorily defined. The DPP has issued statutory guidance for the purposes of s. 37(7) (see **D2.2**), but this is not binding in respect of a decision under s. 37(1) (*R (G) v Chief Constable of West Yorkshire Police* [2008] EWCA Civ 28, [2008] 1 WLR 550). It seems likely that the test is sufficient evidence to give a realistic prospect of conviction (see Code C, para. 16.1). However, the *Director's Guidance on Charging* creates an anomaly since, where a person had been detained following a determination that there is not sufficient evidence to charge under s. 37(1), it provides that in some circumstances the test for determining whether there is sufficient evidence to charge for the purposes of s. 37(7) is the lower threshold test (see **D2.4**).

The custody officer must make the determination as soon as is practicable after the arrested person arrives at the station or, if the arrest occurs there, as soon as possible after the arrest (s. 37(10)). The custody officer may detain the person at the police station for so long as is necessary to discharge this function (s. 37(1)). If the custody officer determines that there is not sufficient evidence to charge, the arrested person is to be dealt with in accordance with the PACE 1984, s. 37(2) (see **D1.49**). If the custody officer determines that there is sufficient evidence to charge, the arrested person must be dealt with in accordance with s. 37(7) (see *R (G) v Chief Constable of West Yorkshire Police* and **D2.2** and **D2.7**).

A person who attends a police station to answer to bail granted under s. 30A, or returns to a police station to answer to bail otherwise granted by police under the PACE 1984, Part IV, or is arrested under s. 30D (having failed to answer to bail granted under s. 30A) or s. 46A (having failed to answer to bail otherwise granted under Part IV), is to be treated as arrested for the offence for which bail was granted (s. 34(7)). A person arrested under the RTA 1988, s. 6D, or the Transport and Works Act 1992, s. 30(2) (arrest under the breath-test procedure), is also to be treated as having been arrested for an offence (PACE 1984, s. 34(6)). **D1.48**

A custody officer who becomes aware at any time that the grounds for detaining a suspect in police custody have ceased to apply and who is not aware of any other grounds which would justify continued detention must release the suspect immediately (s. 34(2)), such release normally being without bail (s. 34(5)). The custody officer must not, however, release a suspect who appears to have been unlawfully at large when arrested (s. 34(4)). Further, if the offence for which the person was arrested is one in respect of which a sample for the purpose of drug-testing may be taken (see **D1.120**), release may be delayed for up to 24 hours from the relevant time (see **D1.68**) for the purpose of enabling a sample to be taken (s. 37(8A) and (8B)).

Insufficient Evidence to Charge If the custody officer determines that there is not sufficient evidence to charge an arrested person, the custody officer must release the person with or without bail unless there are reasonable grounds for believing that detention of the suspect without charge is necessary to secure or preserve evidence relating to an offence for which the suspect is under arrest or to obtain evidence by questioning (PACE 1984, s. 37(2)). If the custody officer does have such a belief, he or she may authorise the person to be kept in police detention (s. 37(3)), and must make a written record of the grounds for detention as soon as is practicable (s. 37(4); Code C, para. 3.4), normally in the presence of the person (s. 37(5) and (6)). **D1.49**

The requirement that the officer believes that detention is necessary creates, in principle, a stringent test. That was certainly the view of the then Secretary of State when he explained the provision to Parliament during passage of the original Bill, indicating that it meant more than simply desirable or convenient. It was held in *Al Fayed v Metropolitan Police Commissioner* [2004] EWCA Civ 1579, that whilst the question of reasonable belief that detention is necessary involves an objective element, it is to be determined by reference to whether the custody officer acted reasonably in deciding that detention was necessary. However, it is submitted that if, viewed objectively, detention was not necessary, the officer could not have acted reasonably in so believing.

The Procedural Requirements Where the custody officer authorises detention, the procedural requirements are largely governed by PACE Code C. The officer must inform the detained person of the right to legal advice (**D1.55**) and *the right to* have someone informed of the arrest (**D1.52**), and ask the person whether he or she wishes to exercise those rights (Code C, paras. 3.1 and 3.5). The officer must also inform the person of the right to consult the Codes of Practice, the right to interpretation and translation (if applicable), and the right to be informed about the offence (para. 3.1); and must make available to the suspect or the suspect's solicitor documents and materials necessary to challenge the lawfulness of the arrest and detention (para. 3.4(b) and Note for Guidance 3ZA). In addition, the custody officer must give the person a written notice containing the information set out in para. 3.2. A risk assessment must be carried out, and any necessary steps taken (paras. 3.6 to 3.10). **D1.50**

If the detained person is a child or young person (which, for these purposes, includes those under 18 years: see Code C, paras. 1.5 and 1.5A), the custody officer, or other custody staff, must ascertain the person responsible for the child or young person's welfare and inform that person of the arrest and detention (Code C, para. 3.13, and see **D1.63**). If the child or young person is known to be the subject of a court order under which a person or organisation is responsible for supervision or monitoring, the custody officer must also inform that person or organisation (para. 3.14). Where the detained person is a child or young person or mentally disordered or otherwise mentally vulnerable, the officer must inform the appropriate adult and ask that adult to come to the police station (para. 3.15; and see *Miller v DPP* [2018] EWHC 262 (Admin)). If the detained person is deaf or there is doubt about the person's hearing or speaking ability, or ability to speak or understand English, and the custody officer cannot establish effective communication, the custody officer must call in an interpreter (para. 3.12: see **D1.91**). If the person is blind or seriously visually handicapped or is unable to read, the custody officer should ensure that the person's solicitor, relative, the appropriate adult or some other person likely to take an interest is available to help in checking any documentation. Where Code C requires written consent or signification then the person who is assisting may be asked to sign instead if the detained person so wishes (para. 3.20). In each case, a person who appears to come within the category of persons requiring special treatment must be treated as such. Code C, para. 1.13C, states:

> if there is doubt as to whether the person should be treated, or continue to be treated, as being male or female in the case of:
> (i) a search or other procedure to which this Code applies which may only be carried out or observed by a person of the same sex as the detainee; or
> (ii) any other procedure which requires action to be taken or information to be given that depends on whether the person is to be treated as being male or female; then the gender of the detainee and other parties concerned should be established and recorded in line with Annex L [para. 4] of this Code.

D1.51 A detained person who is a foreign national must be informed of the right to communicate with his or her High Commission, embassy or consulate (Code C, para. 3.3 and section 7). If the person is a citizen of a foreign country with which a bilateral consular convention or agreement is in force, the appropriate High Commission, embassy or consulate must be informed, unless the person is a refugee or is seeking political asylum, in which case UK Visas and Immigration must be informed, and UKVI will determine whether notification is to be given (paras. 7.2 and 7.4). These obligations and rights apply in addition to the right to notification of arrest under the PACE 1984, s. 56. There is no provision for delay even where delay in notification of arrest (see **D1.53**) or delay in access to legal advice (see **D1.61**) is authorised. It was held in *R (Centre for Advice on Individual Rights in Europe) v Secretary of State for the Home Department* [2018] EWCA Civ 2837, [2019] 1 WLR 3002 that routinely asking foreign national detainees about their nationality was merely asking for information and did not amount to unlawful systematic verification as prohibited by the Citizens' Rights Directive 2004/38/EC ([2004] OJ L158/77), Article 14(2).

Notification of Arrest

D1.52 **The Right to Notification** A person who has been arrested (whether or not for an offence) and who is being held in custody at a police station or other premises has a right, at the person's request, to have one friend, or relative or other person who is known to him or her or who is likely to take an interest in his or her welfare, told of the arrest and the place of detention. This is to be done as soon as is practicable (PACE 1984, s. 56(1)). The custody officer must inform the suspect of this right (Code C, para. 3.1(i)), and ask whether the suspect wishes to exercise it (para. 3.5(a)(iii)).

The person chosen by the detainee is to be informed of the detainee's whereabouts at public expense and, if the detainee requests, on each occasion that the detainee is taken to another police station (s. 56(8) and Code C, para. 5.3). If that person cannot be contacted, the detainee may choose up to two alternatives. If they too cannot be contacted, the custody officer or the person in charge of the investigation has discretion to allow further attempts until the information has been conveyed (para. 5.1). If the detainee does not know of anyone to contact for advice, the custody officer should bear in mind local voluntary bodies who may be able to help (Code C, Note for Guidance 5C).

Delaying Notification Where a person is detained for an indictable offence (see **D1.69**), an officer of the rank of inspector or above may authorise delay in giving notification of the detention for up to 36 hours from the relevant time (PACE 1984, s. 56(2) and (3)). For the meaning of 'relevant time', see **D1.68**. Authorisation may be given either orally or in writing, but if done orally the authorisation is to be confirmed in writing as soon as practicable (s. 56(4)). The officer may authorise delay only if there are reasonable grounds for believing that any of the conditions in s. 56(5) or (5A) is satisfied. These are the same conditions that apply to a decision to delay access to a lawyer under s. 58 (see **D1.61**). If delay is authorised, the detained person must be told the reason for it, and that reason must be noted on the custody record (s. 56(6)). **D1.53**

Other Similar Rights A detainee may receive visits at the custody officer's discretion (Code C, para. 5.4), and Code C Note for Guidance 5B indicates that visits should be allowed where possible. **D1.54**

A detainee is entitled to writing materials and to speak on the telephone for a reasonable time to one person, although this may be delayed or denied if the person is detained in respect of an indictable offence (see **D1.69**) and an officer of the rank of inspector or above considers that sending a letter or making a telephone call may result in any of the consequences set out in Code C, annex B, paras. 1 and 2 (Code C, para. 5.6). Any delay or denial of the above rights should be proportionate and should last for no longer than is necessary (para. 5.7A). The detainee must be told that what he or she says in any communication, other than one to the detainee's solicitor, may be read or listened to and may be given in evidence (para. 5.7).

If a friend or relative of a detainee, or a person with an interest in a detainee's welfare, asks where the detainee is then this information must be given provided that the detainee agrees and delay in notification under the PACE 1984, s. 56, has not been authorised (Code C, para. 5.5 and annex B).

Right of Access to Solicitor

The Right to Consult a Solicitor A person who is arrested (whether or not for an offence) and held in custody at a police station or other premises has a right, at his or her request, to consult a solicitor privately at any time (PACE 1984, s. 58; Code C, para. 6.1). 'Held in custody' has been given a more restricted meaning than simply 'in custody' and describes the situation where a custody officer has made a decision that the person should be detained (*Kerawalla* [1991] Crim LR 451). However, in *Ambrose v Harris* [2011] UKSC 43, [2011] 1 WLR 2435 the Supreme Court held that the ECHR, Article 6(1) and (3)(c), require that a person who suffers a significant curtailment of freedom of action is entitled to legal assistance. Thus the right to legal assistance may apply prior to the decision to detain a person at a police station, and even before the person has been formally arrested. The right applies to all persons held in custody including those who are children or young persons, or mentally disordered or vulnerable. An appropriate adult has an independent right to legal advice even if the child or young person or vulnerable adult does not want one, although a child or young person cannot be forced to see a solicitor if he or she does not wish to do so (Code C, paras. 3.19 and 6.5A). While the statutory right does not apply in respect of a prisoner on remand in custody at a magistrates' court, there is a common-law right to consult a solicitor as soon as is reasonably practicable and police cannot refuse access to a prisoner in custody simply because the request falls outside customary hours (*Chief Constable of South Wales, ex parte Merrick* [1994] 2 All ER 560). **D1.55**

A person must be told of the right to free legal advice when brought to a police station under arrest, or when arrested having initially attended voluntarily (Code C, paras. 3.1 and 6.1); immediately before the beginning or recommencement of any interview at a police station or other authorised place of detention (para. 11.2); before a review of detention is conducted or before a decision is made whether to extend the period of detention (para. 15.4); after charge or being informed that the person may be prosecuted, where a police officer wishes to bring to the person's attention any statement or the content of any interview, or where the person is re-interviewed (paras. 16.4 and 16.5); before being asked to provide an intimate sample (Code D, para. 6.3); before an intimate drug search is conducted under the PACE 1984, s. 55(1)(b) (Code C, annex A, para. 2B), or an x-ray or ultrasound scan is taken under s. 55A(1) (Code C, annex K, para. 3); before the person is (exceptionally) interviewed after charge (Code C, para. 16.5); and before an identification parade or group or video identification is conducted (Code D, para. 3.17). Where appropriate, information should be provided regarding the availability of the duty solicitor (*Vernon* [1988] Crim LR 445, distinguished in *Beeres v CPS* [2014] EWHC 283 (Admin), [2014] 2 Cr App R 8 (101)). (See also **D1.43** as to the position of volunteers attending police stations.)

D1.56 If, on being informed or reminded of the right to legal advice, the person declines to speak to a solicitor, the officer must tell the person that the right to legal advice includes the right to speak to a solicitor on the telephone, and ask whether the person wishes to do so. If the person still declines legal advice, the officer must ask why, and record any answer. Once it is clear that the person does not wish to speak to a solicitor at all, the officer must cease to ask the person for reasons for the decision (Code C, para. 6.5). No attempt should be made to dissuade a suspect from obtaining legal advice (para. 6.4). It was held in *McGowan v B* [2011] UKSC 54, [2011] 1 WLR 3121 that for waiver of the right to legal assistance to be valid it is normally sufficient that the person is told of the right, understands what the right is, and that the waiver is made freely and voluntarily. The prosecution are not required to establish that a suspect understood all of the implications of the decision (*Saunders* [2012] EWCA Crim 1380, [2012] 2 Cr App R 26 (321)). However, suspects 'who are of low intelligence or are vulnerable for other reasons or who are under the influence of drugs or alcohol may need to be given more than the standard formulae if their right to fair trial is not to be compromised' (*McGowan v B* at [47]). See also *Jude v HM Advocate* [2011] UKSC 55. Wrongful denial of access to a solicitor may lead to the exclusion of evidence (see **F2.7** and **F18.33**). A suspect cannot be refused access to a solicitor simply because the police fear that the solicitor will advise the suspect not to answer questions (Code C, annex B, para. 4; *Alladice* (1988) 87 Cr App R 380).

The word 'solicitor' is not defined in the PACE 1984, but Code C defines it for the purposes of the Code to include a solicitor holding a practising certificate, or an accredited or probationary representative included on the register maintained by the Legal Aid Agency (Code C, para. 6.12, and see Code D, para. 2.6, Code E, para. 1.5, and Code F, para. 1.5). By implication, 'solicitor' does not include a representative (who is neither accredited nor probationary) of a solicitor acting privately, although arguably a solicitor acting privately can send such a representative to advise at the police station if the client consents.

D1.57 By Code C, para. 6.12A, an accredited or probationary representative may be denied access to a police station if an officer of the rank of inspector or above considers that to grant access will hinder the investigation. Hindering of the investigation does not include giving proper legal advice. Code C, para. 6.13, provides that the officer should take into account whether the credentials of an accredited or probationary representative have been satisfactorily established, whether the person is of suitable character to give advice, and any other matters in any written letter or authorisation provided by the solicitor concerned. A person with a criminal record, save for a minor offence, is unlikely to be suitable. Responsibility for assessing these matters rests with the investigating officer, who may have regard to but is not fettered by general statements of force policy. The primary question is whether allowing a particular individual access to advise the detainee may prejudice the investigation (*R (Thompson) v Chief Constable of the Northumberland Constabulary* [2001] EWCA Civ 321, [2001] 1 WLR 1342). As the Divisional Court said in *Chief Constable of Avon and Somerset, ex parte Robinson* [1989] 2 All ER 15, where a person is ostensibly capable of giving advice, he or she cannot be excluded simply because the police believe that the person will give poor advice.

There is no similar provision for a solicitor (as opposed to a representative) to be excluded from a police station. However, a solicitor (including a representative) may be required to leave an interview if an officer of the rank of superintendent or above considers that by his or her misconduct the solicitor has prevented the proper putting of questions to the client (Code C, paras. 6.9 to 6.11). A solicitor is not guilty of misconduct for seeking to challenge an improper question or the manner in which it is put or for advising the client not to reply to particular questions or if the solicitor wishes to give the client further legal advice. Code C, Note for Guidance 6D, suggests that misconduct could include answering questions on the client's behalf or providing written replies for the client to quote. However, this would not include the situation where a solicitor drafts a statement to be handed, or read out, to the police in interview (see, e.g., *Knight* [2003] EWCA Crim 1977, [2004] 1 WLR 340).

Section 58(1) of the PACE 1984 grants a right to consult 'privately' with a solicitor. Code C, Note for Guidance 6J, describes this as 'fundamental', and states that facilities to enable private consultation with a solicitor, whether in person or on the telephone, should normally be provided. The consultation should be both unsupervised and unobserved by police officers (*R (L)* [2010] EWCA Crim 924, [2011] 1 WLR 359). The House of Lords determined that the power to conduct surveillance under the RIPA 2000, Part II, overrides s. 58(1) (*McE v Prison Service of Northern Ireland* [2009] UKHL 15, [2009] 1 AC 908), but that authorisation under the provisions governing directed surveillance (as opposed to intrusive surveillance) is not proportionate, and infringes the ECHR, Article 8(2). The Regulation of Investigatory Powers (Extension of Authorisation Provisions: Legal Consultation) Order 2010 (SI 2010 No. 461) provides that directed surveillance to be carried out on premises used for the purpose of legal consultations (which include police stations) must be treated as intrusive surveillance. The Regulation of Investigatory Powers (Covert Human Intelligence Sources: Matters Subject to Legal Privilege) Order 2010 (SI 2010 No. 123) makes similar provision regarding the authorisation of the use of covert human intelligence sources whose activities involve obtaining access to matters subject to legal privilege. For further limitations on the right to consult in terrorist investigations, see **B10.18**. **D1.58**

Action When a Request is Made Where a person makes a request to consult a solicitor the person must, subject to the power to delay (see **D1.61**), be permitted to consult a solicitor as soon as practicable and the custody officer must act without delay to secure the provision of advice (PACE 1984, s. 58(4), and Code C, para. 6.5). It was held in *Gearing v DPP* [2008] EWHC 1695 (Admin), [2009] RTR 7 (72) that a delay of 22 minutes between the request for legal advice and action by the police to contact a solicitor amounted to a breach of s. 58(4). Code C, Note for Guidance 6B, sets out the arrangements for obtaining legal advice. These arrangements give rise to considerable practical difficulties. In particular, given the lack of private telephone facilities in many police stations, securing advice under the CDS Direct scheme may lead to a breach of the right to consult a solicitor privately (see **D1.58**). A solicitor may advise more than one client in an investigation, and any question of a conflict of interest is for the solicitor to determine in accordance with any professional code of conduct (Code C, Note for Guidance 6G, and see *R (McDonagh) v Chief Constable of Leicestershire Constabulary* [2013] EWHC 4690 (Admin)). **D1.59**

Although s. 58 does not expressly give a right to have a solicitor present in a police interview, s. 58(1) states that the person has a right to consult a solicitor 'at any time', and Code C, para. 6.8, provides that a detainee who has been permitted to consult a solicitor must, on request, be allowed to have the solicitor present during interview unless the exceptions in para. 6.6 apply. **D1.60**

Subject to the power to delay access to a solicitor under s. 58(8) to (11), once a person has asked to consult a solicitor the person must not be interviewed or continue to be interviewed until that consultation has taken place unless any of the conditions in Code C, para. 6.6(b) to (d), is satisfied. Note that if an interview is conducted in the absence of legal advice under para. 6.6(b) (but not para. 6.6(c) or (d)), inferences under the CJPO 1994, ss. 34, 36 or 37 (see **F20**), cannot be drawn and the modified caution under Code C, annex C, para. 2, must be given. Notwithstanding these provisions, in the absence of compelling reasons, interviewing a person who has requested legal advice before it has been received, or the use of evidence so obtained, is likely to amount to a breach of the right to fair trial under the ECHR, Article 6 (*Cadder v HM Advocate* [2010] UKSC 43, [2010] 1 WLR 2601). The statutory drink/driving procedure under the RTA 1988 (or the Transport and Works Act 1992, s. 31) is not an interview and is therefore not subject to delay pending legal advice (Code C, para. 11.1A). Thus failure to permit access to a solicitor before the procedure is carried out does not afford the suspect a reasonable excuse for failure to provide a specimen (*DPP v Billington* [1988] 1 All ER 435; see also *Kennedy v CPS* [2002] EWHC 2297 (Admin); *Cowper v DPP* [2009] EWHC 2165 (Admin); *Chalupa v CPS* [2009] EWHC 3082 (Admin)).

D1.61 **Delaying Access to a Solicitor** Delaying access to a solicitor is permitted only where the person is detained in respect of an indictable offence (see **D1.69**), has not been charged, and delay is authorised by an officer of the rank of superintendent or above (PACE 1984, s. 58(6), and Code C, annex B). The officer may authorise delay only if there are reasonable grounds for believing that exercising the right:

(a) will lead to interference with or harm to evidence connected with an indictable offence or interference with or physical injury to other people (s. 58(8)(a));
(b) will lead to the alerting of other people suspected of having committed such an offence but not yet arrested for it (s. 58(8)(b));
(c) will hinder the recovery of any property obtained as a result of such an offence (s. 58(8)(c)); or
(d) where the person detained for the indictable offence has benefited from criminal conduct (within the meaning of the POCA 2002, Part 2), it will hinder the recovery of the value of the property constituting the benefit (s. 58A).

Where these conditions are satisfied, access to a solicitor may be delayed only for as long as the grounds exist, and in any case no longer than 36 hours from the relevant time (s. 58(5); Code C, annex B, para. 6). For the meaning of 'relevant time' see **D1.68**. If the police seek a warrant of further detention (see **D1.72**), the suspect must be allowed access to a solicitor in reasonable time before the hearing even if this is within the 36-hour period (Code C, annex B, para. 7).

D1.62 These provisions create a stringent test for delaying access to a solicitor and, given that the authorising officer must have 'reasonable grounds' for the 'belief' that access 'will' lead to one or more of the consequences, there should be some objective basis for that belief. In *Samuel* [1988] QB 615, the Court of Appeal held that (a) the police officer must believe that one of the statutory grounds for exclusion applies, and (b) that belief must be reasonable. The police officer must believe that the consequence will very probably happen. It will rarely happen that a police officer will be entitled to believe that a solicitor will knowingly pass on information in breach of the statute, and any grounds put forward would have to be specific to the solicitor concerned. Solicitors are also unlikely to be unwitting dupes, and suspicion that the suspect will try to use the solicitor thus must be specific to that solicitor, e.g., where he or she is known or suspected to be a member of a criminal gang. This is reinforced by Code C, annex B, Note for Guidance B3. However, in *Re McNamee and McDonnell LLP's application for judicial review* [2014] NICA 13, the Northern Ireland Court of Appeal suggested a less stringent test: a real risk that the nominated solicitor would pass on information, rather than a belief that the solicitor very probably would do so. See also *Alladice* (1988) 87 Cr App R 380, *Davison* [1988] Crim LR 442 and *James* [2008] EWCA Crim 1869.

If a decision is made to delay access to a particular solicitor the suspect must be allowed to choose another solicitor (Code C, annex B, para. 3). If delay is authorised, the detained person must be told the reason for it, and the reason must be noted on the custody record (annex B, para. 13). Once the grounds for delay cease to exist the suspect must be asked, as soon as is practicable, whether he or she wants to exercise the right to a solicitor and the custody record must be noted accordingly (annex B, para. 6).

In the absence of compelling reasons, delaying access to a solicitor under these provisions is likely to amount to a breach of the right to a fair trial under the ECHR, Article 6 (*Cadder v HM Advocate* [2010] UKSC 43, [2010] 1 WLR 2601). In *Ibrahim v UK* [2016] ECHR 750, [2017] Crim LR 877 the Grand Chamber of the ECtHR found that an absence of 'compelling reasons' in respect of the fourth applicant meant that the onus was 'on the Government to demonstrate convincingly why, exceptionally and in the specific circumstances of the case, the overall fairness of the trial was not irretrievably prejudiced by the restriction on access to legal advice'. However in *Abdurahman* [2019] EWCA Crim 2239, [2020] 1 Cr App R 27 (439) the Court of Appeal expressed doubt as to whether a 'strong presumption of irretrievable prejudice' should apply in such a case and considered this to be a significant extension of existing Strasbourg case law. The Court declined to form a final view of the issue.

In respect of the other three applicants in *Ibrahim v UK* the Grand Chamber of the ECtHR found that in the context of the London bombings of 21 July 2005 there were compelling reasons to conduct 'safety' interviews in respect of those applicants in the absence of their lawyers. Therefore, the decision to delay access under the TA 2000, sch. 8, para. 8 (which is in similar terms to the PACE 1984, s. 58(8)), did not breach the right to a lawyer under the ECHR, Article 6(3)(c) (see also **A7.44** and **B10.18**). Note that inferences under the CJPO 1994, ss. 34, 36 or 37 (see **F20**), are not permitted where the person was at an authorised place of detention and had not been allowed an opportunity to consult a solicitor prior to being questioned (CJPO 1994, ss. 34(2A), 36(4A) and 37(3A), and see **D1.85**).

Children and Young People and Mentally Disordered or Vulnerable Persons

For the initial action to be taken in respect of children and mentally disordered persons, and those with other forms of vulnerability, see **D1.50**. **D1.63**

In the case of young people, anyone who appears to be under the age of 18 years is a 'juvenile' for the purposes of Part IV of the PACE 1984 (PACE 1984, s. 37(15), and see Code C, para. 1.5). The PCA 2017, s. 73, substituted the age of 18 years for 17 years for a number of other purposes under the PACE 1984: conditions attached to bail following arrest, for the person's own welfare or in his or her own interests (s. 30A(3B)(d)) (see **D1.21**); testing for the presence of class A drugs (s. 63B(5A) and (10)) (see **D1.122**); and for the purposes of the meaning of 'appropriate consent' (s. 65(1)) (see **D1.105** (fingerprints), **D1.107** (footwear impressions), **D1.110** (intimate samples), and **D1.112** (non-intimate samples)). The Children Act 2004, s. 11, requires the police to take into account the need to safeguard and promote the welfare of children in discharging their functions, but does not impose additional obligations (*R (C) v Metropolitan Police Commissioner* [2011] EWHC 2317 (Admin), [2012] 1 All ER 953; and see **D2.52**).

With regard to mental disorder or vulnerability, if an officer has any reason to suspect that a person of any age may be vulnerable, in the absence of clear evidence to dispel that suspicion, the person must be treated as such for the purposes of the Codes of Practice (Code C, para. 1.4). Code C, para. 1.4, sets out the actions that a custody officer (in the case of a detained person) or an officer investigating the case (in the case of a person who has not been arrested or detained) must take to establish whether such a reason may exist. It has been held that suspicion may be dispelled following examination by a forensic medical officer (*Beattie* [2018] NICA 1)). The meaning of the term 'vulnerable' is set out in Code C, para. 1.13(d), and Note for Guidance 1G.

It is imperative that a mentally disordered or otherwise mentally vulnerable person detained under the Mental Health Act 1983, s. 136, be assessed as soon as possible (Code C, para. 3.16). The Mental Health Act 1983, ss. 135 and 136, provide that: (a) before deciding to remove a person to, or to keep a person at, a place of safety, a constable must, if practicable, consult a registered medical practitioner, registered nurse, approved mental health practitioner, or a person of a description specified in regulations made by the Secretary of State; (b) a child cannot be detained in a police cell as a place of safety; and (c) the maximum period that a person can be detained at a police station is reduced from 72 hours to 24 hours, which may be extended by 12 hours where authorised by the responsible medical practitioner. The detention of adults at a police station as a place of safety is further regulated by the Mental Health Act 1983 (Places of Safety) Regulations 2017 (SI 2017 No. 1036) (issued under the Mental Health Act 1983, s. 136A(2)). These regulations provide that a police station may only be used as a place of safety in respect of an adult where the relevant decision-maker is satisfied that: (a) the behaviour of the person poses an imminent risk of serious injury or death to him or herself or another; (b) because of that risk, no place of safety other than a police station can reasonably be expected to detain the person; and (c) the requirement in reg. 4(1)(b) (so far as reasonably practicable, a healthcare professional is present and available to the detained person throughout the period of detention at the police station) will be met. Detention in such circumstances must be authorised by an officer of the rank of inspector or above (reg. 2). See also Department of Health/Home Office Guidance for the implementation of changes to police powers and places of safety provisions in the Mental Health Act 1983 (October 2017, tinyurl.com/ya42fd25).

D1.64 **Appropriate Adult** 'Appropriate adult', in the case of a young suspect, is defined as a parent or guardian or, if the child or young person is in the care of a local authority or voluntary organisation, a person representing that authority or organisation, a social worker of a local authority, or (failing these) some other responsible person who is not a police officer, employed by the police, under the direction or control of a chief police officer, or a person who provides services under contractual arrangements (but without being employed by the chief police officer) to assist that force in relation to the discharge of its chief officer's functions (Code C, para. 1.7(a)). See also the PACE 1984, s. 63B(10) (testing for the presence of class A drugs), the CDA 1998, s. 66ZA(7) (youth cautions), and the CJA 2003, s. 161(8) (pre-sentence drug testing), all of which were amended by the PCA 2017, s. 79. An estranged parent whom an arrested child or young person does not wish to attend and to whom the child or young person specifically objects should not act as an appropriate adult (Code C, Note for Guidance 1B; *DPP v Blake* [1989] 1 WLR 432). Similarly, an illiterate parent with a low IQ who cannot appreciate the gravity of the situation in which his or her child is placed should not act as an appropriate adult (*Morse* [1991] Crim LR 195). Where the child or young person is in care, the relevant social worker or representative should be prepared to attend as soon as practicable (*DPP v Blake*).

'Appropriate adult' in the case of a person who is mentally disordered or vulnerable is defined as a relative, guardian or other person responsible for care or custody of the person, someone who has experience of dealing with such persons (but who is not a police officer or police employee) or, failing these, some other responsible adult aged 18 years or older who is not a police officer or police employee (Code C, para. 1.7(b)). Code C, Note for Guidance 1D, states that it may be more satisfactory for the appropriate adult to be someone who is experienced or trained in the care of mentally disordered or vulnerable people, although the suspect's wishes should be respected where practicable.

D1.65 A solicitor attending a police station on a suspect's behalf should not act as an appropriate adult (Code C, Note for Guidance 1F; *Lewis* [1996] Crim LR 260). A person should not be the appropriate adult if the person (a) is suspected of involvement in the suspected offence, (b) is the victim or a witness, (c) is involved in the investigation, or (d) has received admissions from the suspect before acting as the appropriate adult (Code C, Note for Guidance 1B). A social worker or a member of a youth offending team should also refrain from acting as an appropriate adult if the suspect has made admissions to him or her (Code C, Note for Guidance 1C).

D1.66 **Role of the Appropriate Adult** The role of the appropriate adult is to safeguard the rights, entitlements and welfare of children and vulnerable persons. Among other things, appropriate adults are expected to (a) support, advise and assist detainees when they are given or asked to provide information or participate in any procedure; (b) observe whether the police are acting properly and fairly, and to inform an officer of the rank of inspector or above if they consider that they are not; (c) assist detainees to communicate with the police while respecting their right to say nothing unless they want to; and (d) help them to understand their rights and ensure that those rights are protected and respected (Code C, para. 1.7A). Code C, para. 11.17, describes a similar role for appropriate adults during police interviews. If the appropriate adult or the detainee asks for legal advice, the provisions of Code C, section 6, apply (para. 3.19, and see **D1.55**). The presence of an appropriate adult during a consultation between suspect and lawyer which would otherwise attract legal advice privilege does not destroy that privilege (*A Local Authority v B* [2008] EWHC 1017 (Fam)).

Generally, a child or young person or mentally disordered or vulnerable person must not be interviewed by the police or asked to provide a written statement in the absence of an appropriate adult, unless delay would be likely to lead to interference with or harm to evidence connected with an offence, interference with or physical harm to other people or serious loss of or damage to property, to alerting other suspects not yet arrested, or to hindering the recovery of property obtained in consequence of commission of the offence. If an interview at a police station is necessary for one or more of these reasons, it must be authorised by an officer of the rank of superintendent or above (Code C, paras 11.1, 11.15 and 11.18 to 11.20). Further, the appropriate adult has specific roles in respect of legal advice (para. 6.5A) and intimate and strip searches (Code C, annex A, paras 5 and 11(c)). In the case of identification and other evidential procedures that require 'appropriate consent', the PACE 1984, s. 65(1), provides that, in the case of a person who has attained the age of 14 years but is under 18 years, consent is required from the young person and his or her parent or guardian, but that, in the case of a person under 14 years, only the consent of the parent or guardian is required. Note that if the appropriate adult is not a parent or guardian, he or she cannot give consent.

Detention Time-limits

The normal maximum period of detention without charge is 24 hours from the relevant time (PACE 1984, s. 41(1)). For the meaning of 'relevant time' see **D1.68**. Subject to the powers to extend detention without charge, if at the expiry of that time the person has not been charged, he or she must be released, either on bail or without bail (s. 41(7)). The period of detention without charge may be extended in respect of a person under arrest for an indictable offence; for up to a total of 36 hours from the relevant time by an officer of the rank of superintendent or above (see **D1.69**); and for up to a total of 96 hours from the relevant time by a magistrates' court (see **D1.72**). Where a detention time-limit has expired and the person is released without charge, he or she may not be re-arrested without warrant for the offence for which the person was previously arrested (subject to the power to arrest for failure to answer to police bail under s. 46A) unless, since the release, new evidence has come to light or an examination or analysis of existing evidence has been made which could not reasonably have been made before (ss. 41(9), 42(11) and 43(19), as amended by the PCA 2017, s. 65). **D1.67**

For the purpose of calculating maximum periods of detention, time normally runs continuously from the relevant time. However, where a detainee is removed to hospital for medical treatment, time spent at the hospital or travelling to or from hospital does not count, except for any time spent questioning the person for the purpose of obtaining evidence in respect of an offence (s. 41(6)). Note that a person in police detention at a hospital must not be questioned without the agreement of a responsible doctor (Code C, para. 14.2). If a person is questioned in these circumstances, the person is entitled to consult a solicitor (see **D1.55**).

The Relevant Time Normally, the relevant time is the time an arrested person arrives at the first police station, or 24 hours after arrest, whichever is the earlier (PACE 1984, s. 41(2)(a)). However, this basic definition is modified in the circumstances set out in s. 41(2)(b) to (6). Where a person released on police bail under the PACE 1984, Part IV, is detained when attending at the police station to surrender to custody, or is arrested under s. 46A for failure to **D1.68**

surrender to custody, the relevant time is that which applies to the original detention; however, any time during which the person was on bail is not included (PACE 1984, s. 47(6)).

If a person is arrested other than under s. 46A, e.g., because there is new evidence justifying a further arrest (see **D1.67**), the relevant time will be that relating to the subsequent arrest (s. 47(7)).

Note that the relevant time is not necessarily the same time as that for determining the timing of reviews of detention, which may be some time later (see **D1.76**).

Detention for More than 24 Hours, up to 36 Hours

D1.69 A person can be detained without charge beyond 24 hours only if three conditions are met (PACE 1984, s. 42(1)). These are:

(a) that a police officer of the rank of superintendent or above who is responsible for the police station at which the person is detained has reasonable grounds for believing that such detention is necessary to secure or preserve evidence relating to an offence for which the person is under arrest or to obtain such evidence by questioning him;
(b) that the offence for which the person is under arrest is an indictable offence;
(c) that the investigation is being conducted diligently and expeditiously.

As to (a), the requirement for reasonable grounds for belief that detention is necessary is the same as under the PACE 1984, s. 37(2) (see **D1.49**). As to (b), an indictable offence is one that is triable only on indictment or is triable either-way. Low-value shoplifting (as defined by the MCA 1980, s. 22A(3): see **D6.27**) is an indictable offence for the purposes of the PACE 1984 (ABCPA 2014, s. 176(6)). Documents and materials essential to challenging the lawfulness of a detainee's arrest and detention must be made available to the detainee or his or her solicitor (Code C, paras. 3.4(b) and 15.0).

If the above conditions are met, the officer may authorise detention for up to 36 hours from the relevant time (see **D1.68**). If detention is authorised for less than 36 hours, further detention up to the maximum 36 hours may be authorised provided that the above conditions still apply (PACE 1984, s. 42(2)). No authorisation under s. 42(1) may be made more than 24 hours after the relevant time. Thus retrospective authorisation is not permitted. Further, by s. 42(4), the decision to authorise detention beyond 24 hours cannot be made before the second review of detention under s. 40 (see **D1.76**). Authorisation may be granted by an officer using live link, provided that the conditions for using live link are satisfied (s. 45ZA, inserted by the PCA 2017, s. 74(2)). 'Live link' is defined in s. 45ZA(8). Note that Code C, Note for Guidance 15F, has not been revised to take account of the live link provision.

D1.70 If it is proposed to transfer a person to police detention in another police area, in determining whether to authorise detention without charge beyond 24 hours, the officer must have regard to the distance and the time the journey would take (s. 42(3)). Presumably, if the time involved is likely to take detention beyond the 36 hours permitted, the review officer will have either to refuse the transfer or a warrant of further detention will have to be sought (see **D1.72**).

A person whose extended detention has been ordered under the foregoing procedure must be released from detention either with or without bail at the expiration of 36 hours unless either the person has been charged with an offence or a warrant of further detention has been granted by a magistrates' court (s. 42(10)). A person who has been released may not be re-arrested for the same offence unless new evidence justifying such a course has come to light (s. 42(11) and see **D1.67**).

D1.71 Before deciding whether to authorise detention under s. 42(1) or (2), the officer must give the detained person, or solicitor if available at the time that the decision is to be made (and appropriate adult, if relevant (Code C, para. 15.3)), an opportunity to make representations about the decision (s. 42(6)). If the detainee is likely to be asleep at the time the decision is made it should, if the legal obligations and time constraints permit, be brought forward, but if the detainee is asleep he or she need not be woken (Code C, Note for Guidance 15C). Representations may be given orally or in writing (s. 42(7)). It has been held that the requirement under s. 42(6) is mandatory, so that a purported authorisation without providing such an opportunity was invalid (*In the matter of an application for a warrant of further detention* [1988] Crim LR 296, although this is a magistrates' court decision). The officer may decline to hear oral representations from the suspect if the officer considers that the detainee's condition or behaviour is such as to render him or her unfit to do so (s. 42(8)).

If an officer authorises detention beyond 24 hours, and the detainee has not at that time taken advantage of the right to have someone informed of the arrest or the right to consult a solicitor, the officer must (a) inform the detainee of his or her rights, (b) decide whether the detainee should be permitted to exercise them, (c) record the decision in the custody record, and (d) if the officer decides to refuse to allow the detainee to exercise either of the rights, must also record the grounds for the decision in the detainee's custody record (s. 42(9)).

Detention for More than 36 Hours

Warrant of Further Detention Detention without charge beyond 36 hours from the relevant time (see **D1.68**) is permitted only where a magistrates' court issues a warrant of further detention (PACE 1984, s. 43(1)). A magistrates' court is defined for this purpose as a court consisting of two or more justices sitting otherwise than in open court (PACE 1984, s. 45(1)). A warrant hearing may be conducted by means of live link provided that the conditions set out in s. 45ZA(1) and (2) are satisfied, and the court so directs. 'Live link' is defined in s. 45ZB(4). **D1.72**

The application must be made on oath by a constable and supported by an information (s. 43(1) and (14)). In order to issue a warrant the court must be satisfied that there are reasonable grounds for believing that further detention is justified (s. 43(1)), which must be determined in accordance with the criteria set out in s. 43(4). The hearing is *inter partes*. The detainee must be given a copy of the information and be brought before the court for the hearing (s. 43(2)). Prior to the hearing, documents and materials that are essential to challenging the lawfulness of the detainee's arrest and detention must be made available to the detainee or his or her solicitor (Code C, paras. 3.4(b) and 15.0(b)). The detainee is entitled to be legally represented at the hearing. If the detainee is not so represented but wishes to be, the court must adjourn the hearing to enable representation. The detainee may be held in detention during the adjournment (s. 41(3)). No limit is placed on the time for which an adjournment may be granted.

An application for a warrant of further detention must, as a general rule, be made before the expiry of 36 hours from the relevant time (s. 43(4)(a): but see also **D1.68**). For this purpose, the time of the application is the time that the constable makes the application on oath and gives evidence (*Sedgefield Justices, ex parte Milne* (5 November 1987 unreported)). This period may be extended where it is not practicable for the magistrates' court to which the application will be made to sit before the expiry of the period but where it will sit within six hours following the 36-hour period (s. 43(4)(c)). If the application cannot be heard before the expiry of the 36-hour period, the custody officer is to note in the detainee's custody record the fact that the detainee was detained for the extra period and the reason why (s. 43(6)). If the application is made outside the 36-hour period and the magistrates' court considers that it would have been reasonable for the police to have made the application before the expiry of the period, it must dismiss the application (s. 43(7), and see *Slough Justices, ex parte Stirling* (1987) 151 JP 603). **D1.73**

If the court is not satisfied that there are reasonable grounds for believing that further detention is justified, it must dismiss the application or adjourn the hearing of it to a time not later than 36 hours from the relevant time (s. 43(8)). The person may be kept in police detention during any period of adjournment (s. 43(9)). If, therefore, the court sits at a time close to the 36-hour limit, it may well not be possible for the police to obtain an adjournment in order to strengthen their case. Furthermore, where an application for a warrant of further detention has been refused, no further application may be made under s. 43 unless fresh evidence has come to light since the refusal (s. 43(17)). This, of course, assumes that the hearing took place before the expiry of the 36-hour period and that it is possible for the detainee still to be in lawful custody. If the application for a warrant is refused, the police must either charge or release the detainee, either on bail or without bail (s. 43(15)). However, if the refusal was made before the expiry of the 24-hour limit (**D1.67**) or any extension granted under s. 42 (see **D1.69**), the detainee need not be released before the expiry of that period (provided that the conditions for detention without charge continue to be satisfied) (s. 43(16)).

If the court is satisfied that there are reasonable grounds for believing that further detention is justified, it may issue a warrant of further detention for a maximum period of 36 hours (s. 43(12)). Within that limit, where it is intended to transfer a detainee to another police area, the court must have regard to the distance and time involved in a journey (s. 43(13)). The warrant must state the time at which it is issued and the period for which it is granted (s. 43(10)). At the expiry of a warrant of further detention the detainee must, unless the warrant is extended under the PACE 1984, s. 44, be charged or released, either on bail or without bail. If released on bail, the detainee may not be re-arrested without a warrant for the offence for which he or she was previously arrested unless new evidence justifying a further arrest has come to light since the release (s. 43(19), and see **D1.67**).

D1.74 **Extension of Warrant of Further Detention** A magistrates' court may, on an application on oath and supported by an information, extend a warrant of further detention issued under the PACE 1984, s. 43, provided it is satisfied that there are reasonable grounds for believing that the further detention is justified (s. 44(1)). Such extension may be made for any period which the court thinks fit, having regard to the evidence before it, but it may not be for longer than 36 hours, and the total period for which the person is to be held in detention may not exceed 96 hours from the relevant time (see **D1.68**). There is no formal limit to the number of occasions on which such a further extension may be granted, but the total period of 96 hours cannot be exceeded (s. 44(1) to (4)). An application for an extension of a warrant of further detention may be conducted by means of live link provided that the conditions set out in s. 45ZA(1) and (2) are satisfied, and the court so directs. 'Live link' is defined in s. 45ZB(4).

The court must be furnished with the same particulars as are required in the original application, and the detainee has the same rights of representation (s. 44(6)). The police are under the same obligation to provide documents and materials that are essential to challenging the lawfulness of the arrest and detention as for the original warrant application (see **D1.72**). If the extension is refused, the detainee must either be released (with or without bail) or charged save that, if the application for extension is made before the expiry of the period specified in the warrant itself, the detainee may be held until the expiry of that period (provided that the conditions for detention without charge continue to be satisfied) (s. 44(7) to (8)).

Reviews of Detention

D1.75 The PACE 1984, s. 40, requires that the detention of persons in police detention (see **D1.40**) be periodically reviewed in order to determine whether continued detention is justified (see also Code C, section 15). The review requirement applies both to persons who have not been charged and those who have been charged, but does not apply to a person who is at court after being charged since such a person is not in police detention (PACE 1984, s. 118(2)). The statutory review requirement does not apply to volunteers (see **D1.43**), to persons who have been *taken to a police station as a place of safety* under the Mental Health Act 1983, nor to persons who have been arrested other than for an offence (e.g., under a fine default warrant or for fingerprints to be taken under the PACE 1984, s. 63A(4) and sch. 2A, para. 17). However, the detention of persons who are held in custody but who are not in police detention as defined by the PACE 1984, s. 118(2), should still be reviewed periodically, as a matter of good practice, in order to check the power under which they are held, the conditions of their detention, and that appropriate action is being taken in respect of them (Code C, Note for Guidance 15B). The statutory review requirements do apply to persons who are deemed to be arrested for an offence (see **D1.40**) and to persons who have been remanded to a police station under the MCA 1980, s. 128(7) (see **D1.42**). They also apply to persons detained at a police station in respect of whom a warrant of further detention has been issued or extended by a magistrates' court (see **D1.72**).

In the case of persons who have been arrested and charged, reviews of detention must be conducted by the custody officer. For persons who have not been charged, they must be conducted by an officer of at least the rank of inspector who has not been directly involved in the investigation (PACE 1984, s. 40(1)). In either case the officer concerned is referred to as a 'review officer' (s. 40(2)).

Timing of Reviews The first review must be conducted no later than six hours after detention was first authorised under the PACE 1984, s. 37 (which may be later than the 'relevant time': see **D1.68**) (PACE 1984, s. 40(3)(a)). The second and subsequent reviews must be carried out no later than nine hours after the previous review (s. 40(3)(b) and (c)). A review may be postponed if it is impracticable to carry it out by the latest time specified (s. 40(4)(a)). The statute gives two examples. The first is where the review officer is satisfied that a review would interrupt questioning then in progress and would prejudice the investigation. The second is where no review officer is readily available at that time (s. 40(4)(b)). However, these are not exhaustive. If a detainee is asleep when a review is conducted he or she need not be woken up, but if the detainee is likely to be asleep when a review is due to be conducted, the review officer should consider bringing the review forward (Code C, Note for Guidance 15C). A postponed review must be carried out as soon as is practicable (s. 40(5)), and the review officer is required to record the reasons for any postponement in the custody record (s. 40(7); Code C, para. 15.3). The timing of subsequent reviews is not affected, so that they must be carried out no later than nine hours after the latest time at which the review should have been conducted (s. 40(6)). However, if a review is brought forward, the next review must be conducted no later than nine hours after the time that the review was in fact conducted. **D1.76**

Failure to carry out a timely review of a person's detention in custody before charge renders previously lawful detention unlawful and amounts to the tort of false imprisonment (*Roberts v Chief Constable of the Cheshire Constabulary* [1999] 2 All ER 326).

Criteria for Reviews In the case of a person not yet charged at the time of the review, the review officer must determine whether there is sufficient evidence to charge and, if not, whether detention is necessary for the reasons set out in the PACE 1984, s. 37(2) (s. 40(8) and (8A) and see **D1.49**). If a person is held because he or she was not in a fit state to be dealt with, the review officer must determine whether the person is now in a fit state (s. 40(9)). **D1.77**

If a person has already been charged at the time of review, the review officer must consider whether to order release on bail, applying the same principles as those which the custody officer is obliged to employ under s. 38(1) to (6B) (s. 40(10) and (10A) and see **D2.49**).

If directions relating to a person in police detention given by a higher-ranking officer are at variance with an actual or proposed decision or action of the review officer, the matter must be immediately referred to an officer of the rank of superintendent or above who is in charge of the station (s. 40(11)).

Procedural Requirements Reviews of detention under the PACE 1984, s. 40(1)(b) (i.e. reviews conducted prior to charge, other than those involving consideration of whether detention is to continue beyond 24 hours (see **D1.69**)), may be conducted in person, by telephone (s. 40A(1)) or by video-conferencing facilities (s. 40A(2) and the Police and Criminal Evidence Act 1984 (Remote Reviews of Detention) Regulations 2014 (SI 2014 No. 3279)). It is for the **D1.78**

officer conducting the review to determine which of these forms of communication is to be used, and in making this decision the officer should take into account the factors set out in Code C, para. 15.3C. See Code C, paras. 15.9 to 15.11, for further explanation.

Before determining whether to authorise continued detention the review officer must decide, in consultation with the investigating officer, what documents and materials which are essential for challenging the lawfulness of the arrest and detention must be made available to the detainee (Code C, paras. 3.4(b) and 15.0(a)). The review officer must also give either the detained person (unless asleep), or any solicitor representing the detained person who is available at the time of the review, an opportunity to make representations about the detention (PACE 1984, ss. 40(12), 40A(3) and (4) and 45A(6) and (7)). Code C, para. 15.3, however, provides that this opportunity is to be given to the detainee 'and' to his or her solicitor and, where relevant, to the appropriate adult. The review officer also has discretion to allow other persons having an interest in the person's welfare to make representations (para. 15.3A). Before conducting a review, the review officer must ensure that the detained person is reminded of the entitlement to free legal advice (para. 15.4). The detainee or solicitor may make representations either orally or in writing, but the review officer need not hear oral representations from a detainee whom the officer considers unfit to make such representations by reason of his or her condition or behaviour (PACE 1984, s. 40(13) and (14); Code C, para. 15.3B).

D1.79 A note must be made in the custody record of the fact that the detainee was reminded of the right to legal advice, details of a review conducted by telephone and the outcome of the review (Code C, paras. 15.12 to 15.16); if continued detention is authorised, any comment made by the detainee or his or her solicitor must also be recorded (para. 15.3). Any written representations made must be retained (para. 15.15).

INTERROGATION OF SUSPECTS

D1.80 The interrogation of suspects is governed partly by common law, partly by the PACE 1984, but primarily by PACE Code C (see **appendix** 1). Code C contains rules regulating the treatment of persons who are being questioned, and the questioning itself, principally in sections 10, 11 and 12. For the application of Code C to the police and to others, see **D1.1** and **D1.3**. Recording of interviews is governed by Code E (audio-recording) and Code F (visual recording with sound). Code C, section 12, lays down certain rules governing the physical conditions of, and the treatment of detainees in, interviews conducted at police stations.

Interviews Generally

D1.81 **Definition of Interview** 'Interview' is widely defined by Code C, para. 11.1A, in purposive terms. An interview is the 'questioning of a person regarding their involvement or suspected involvement in a criminal offence or offences which, under para. 10.1, must be carried out under caution'. By para. 10.1, a person whom there are grounds to suspect of an offence 'must be cautioned before any questions about an offence, or further questions if the answers provide the grounds for suspicion, are put to them if either the suspect's answers or their silence, (i.e. failure or refusal to answer or answer satisfactorily) may be given in evidence to a court in a prosecution'. However, it further provides that a caution is not necessary if questions are for other purposes, such as:

(a) solely to establish identify or ownership of a vehicle;
(b) to obtain information in accordance with a statutory requirement, e.g., under the RTA 1988, s. 165 (note that the statutory drink-driving procedure is not an interview: *DPP v D (a Juvenile)* (1992) 94 Cr App R 185);
(c) in furtherance of the proper and effective conduct of a search (although if questioning goes further, e.g., to establish whether drugs found were intended to be supplied to another, a caution will be necessary: *Langiert* [1991] Crim LR 777; *Khan* [1993] Crim LR 54; *Raphaie* [1996] Crim LR 812); or

(d) to seek verification of a written record of comments made by the person outside an interview.

It follows that questioning of a person in circumstances where a caution does not have to be administered does not amount to an interview for the purposes of Code C. Conversely, questioning of a person about an offence of which there are grounds to suspect him or her will amount to an interview even if the person has not been arrested and no decision to arrest has been made. The reference to 'an offence' means that a caution must be given if the person is questioned about an offence other than that for which he or she has been arrested if there are grounds to suspect the person of it. See further **D1.43** concerning safeguards applying to interviews of volunteers, and **D1.83** regarding cautioning.

Where an Interview May be Conducted The general rules for the conduct of interviews are contained in Code C, section 11. Following a decision to arrest a suspect, he must normally be interviewed only at a police station or other authorised place of detention (Code C, para. 11.1). The reference to 'a decision to arrest' means that if a police officer has decided to arrest a person, the arrest should not be delayed in order to question the suspect before doing so. The requirement that an interview be conducted at a police station is subject to exception where delay would be likely to: **D1.82**

(a) lead to interference with or harm to evidence connected with an offence, interference with or physical harm to other persons, or serious loss of, or damage to, property; or
(b) lead to the alerting of other persons suspected of having committed an offence but not yet arrested for it; or
(c) hinder the recovery of property obtained in consequence of the commission of an offence (para. 11.1).

Interviewing in any of these circumstances must cease once the relevant risk has been averted or the necessary questions have been put to avert the risk (Code C, para. 11.1).

The PACE 1984, s. 39, as amended by the PCA 2017, s. 75, makes provision enabling persons in police detention to be interviewed by an officer who is not at the police station, using live link. 'Live link' is defined for this purpose by s. 39(3E). Section 39(3A) enables a custody officer, 'in accordance with any code of practice issued under this Act', to transfer or permit the transfer of the detained person to a police officer for the purpose of a live link interview conducted by another officer. See further Code C, paras. 12.9A and 12.9B. The officer who is not at the police station has the same duty as the officer to whom custody of the person has been entrusted to ensure that the person is treated in accordance with the provisions of the PACE 1984 and the Codes of Practice (s. 39(3B); Code C, para. 3.21A).

Cautions and Special Warnings It follows from Code C, para. 10.1 (see **D1.81**), that a caution must be administered at the commencement of an interview as defined in Code C, para. 11.1A, whether or not it is conducted at a police station. The suspect must also be reminded that he or she is under caution at the recommencement of an interview after any break, and if there is any doubt, the caution should be given again in full (para. 10.8). The caution must also be given on arrest (para. 10.4, and see **D1.18**). **D1.83**

The normal caution is set out in Code C, para. 10.5, as follows:

> You do not have to say anything. But it may harm your defence if you do not mention when questioned something which you later rely on in Court. Anything you do say may be given in evidence.

Minor deviation from these words is permissible provided that the sense of the caution is preserved (para. 10.7). Where an interpreter is used, the fact that the caution is not perfectly translated will not render it invalid provided that the essential features are adequately conveyed to the suspect (*Koc* [2008] EWCA Crim 77). If it appears that the suspect does not understand the caution, the person giving it should explain it in his or her own words (Code C, Note for Guidance 10D).

If a suspect is (exceptionally) interviewed after charge (see **D1.93**), or interviewed in circumstances where the suspect has requested a solicitor but has not been permitted to consult with one (see **D1.55** *et seq.*), the terms of the caution are those set out in Code C, annex C, para. 2 as follows: 'You do not have to say anything, but anything you do say may be given in evidence'. The reason for the different caution is that in such circumstances inferences cannot be drawn under the CJPO 1994, ss. 34, 36 or 37. Although Code C does not require a caution to be given if a statement is taken after charge, it should be given (*Pall* (1992) 156 JP 424).

D1.84 Whilst Code C, para. 10.1, requires a caution to be given to a person 'whom there are grounds to suspect' of an offence, Note for Guidance 10A explains this phrase by stating that there must be 'some reasonable, objective grounds for the suspicion, based on known facts or information'. This accords with the decision in *James* [1996] Crim LR 650, and this qualification of the expression was not disputed in *Shillibier* [2006] EWCA Crim 793. If correct, however, it means that insofar as the caution has a protective purpose, it does not apply to the questioning of a person in respect of whom there is some suspicion not amounting to a reasonable suspicion, even though what the person says may subsequently be used in evidence against him or her. Whether there are sufficient grounds for a caution to be administered is an objective question, and does not simply depend on how the police officer regarded the matter (*Williams* [2012] EWCA Crim 264). In *Ibrahim v UK* [2016] ECHR 750 the police deliberately decided not to caution the fourth applicant when, on being interviewed as a witness, he started to incriminate himself, and the UK government accepted that he should have been cautioned at this point. This can be contrasted with the position in *Shepherd* [2019] EWCA Crim 1062, [2019] 2 Cr App R 26 (282) where it was found that there was no obligation to caution when the police officers were unaware of the existence of a byelaw which could have given rise to a reasonable suspicion. For examples of interpretation of the cautioning requirement by the courts, see *Senior* [2004] EWCA Crim 454, [2004] 3 All ER 9, in which it was held that a caution should have been given, and *Perpont* [2004] EWCA Crim 2562; *Ridehalgh v DPP* [2005] EWHC 1100 (Admin), [2005] RTR 26 (353) and *Sneyd v DPP* [2006] EWHC 560 (Admin), in which the decision went the other way. Failure to administer a caution in circumstances where it is required is a significant and substantial breach of Code C, although it will not necessarily result in exclusion of evidence of the interview (compare *Armas-Rodriguez* [2005] EWCA Crim 1981 and *Devani* [2007] EWCA Crim 1926, [2008] 1 Cr App R 4 (65) with *Miller* [2007] EWCA Crim 1891). Similarly, giving the wrong caution will not necessarily lead to exclusion (*Ibrahim* [2008] EWCA Crim 880, [2009] 1 WLR 578; but see *Charles v DPP* [2009] EWHC 3521 (Admin), [2010] RTR 34 (402)).

Whenever a person is interviewed he or she, and solicitor if represented, must be given, before the interview, sufficient information to make it possible to understand the nature of the suspected offence and why the person is suspected of committing it (Code C, para. 11.1A). In *Kirk* [1999] 4 All ER 698, D was arrested for theft and was not told that V had died; believing himself to be facing a charge of theft only, he made admissions. It was held that these should have been excluded. See also *Charles v DPP*. The disclosure obligation in Code C, para. 11.1A, has been extended to reflect the requirements of EU Directive 2012/13/EU, Article 6 (see **A9.26**), but does not require the disclosure of details at a time which might prejudice the investigation. The decision on what should be disclosed rests with the investigating officer, who must make a record of what was disclosed and when it was disclosed.

D1.85 In addition to the caution, where a suspect is interviewed at a police station or other authorised place of detention following arrest and:

(a) is asked to account for any object, mark or substance, or mark on such objects found on his or her person, in or on his or her clothing or footwear, otherwise in his or her possession, or in the place where the arrest took place; or
(b) to account for his or her presence at the place where the arrest took place,

a special warning must be given in the terms set out in Code C, para. 10.11. Inferences cannot be drawn if the warning is not given (CJPO 1994, ss. 36(4) and 37(3)). The requirement to give a special warning does not apply where the person who has requested a solicitor is interviewed without having been given an opportunity to consult the solicitor, since inferences from refusal or failure to account cannot be drawn as a result of the CJPO 1994, ss. 36(4A) and 37(3A) (Code C, para. 10.10).

Information about Legal Advice Prior to the commencement or recommencement of an interview at a police station or other authorised place of detention, the interviewing officer must, unless access to a solicitor has been delayed or one of the exceptions applies, remind the suspect of the entitlement to free legal advice and that the interview can be delayed for legal advice to be obtained (Code C, para. 11.2, and see **D1.55** *et seq*.). Violations of a suspect's entitlement to legal advice may lead to the exclusion of evidence (see **F2.7** and **F18.34**). **D1.86**

Significant Statement or Silence At the beginning of an interview carried out at a police station or other authorised place of detention, the interviewing officer must, after cautioning the suspect, put to the suspect any significant statement or silence which occurred in the presence and hearing of a police officer or other police staff (and which has not been put in the course of a previous interview) (Code C, para. 11.4). A significant statement is one which appears to be capable of being used in evidence, and in particular a direct admission of guilt. It does not include what a suspect is alleged to have said as part of the conduct constituting the offence (*DPP v Lawrence* [2007] EWHC 2154 (Admin), [2008] 1 Cr App R 10 (147)). A significant silence is a failure or refusal to answer a question, or answer satisfactorily when under caution which might, allowing for the restrictions on drawing inferences from silence, give rise to an adverse inference under the CJPO 1994 (para. 11.4A). **D1.87**

Conduct of the Interview No police officer or other interviewer may try to obtain answers to questions or to elicit a statement by the use of oppression, nor indicate, except in answer to a direct question, what action the police will take if the suspect answers or refuses to answer questions or make a statement. If the suspect asks the officer directly what action will be taken in any of those events, the officer may inform the suspect of the proposed action, which could be, e.g., keeping the person in detention if further action is to be taken. The proposed action must, however, be proper and warranted (Code C, para. 11.5). Thus it was improper for the police to tell a church organist accused of theft from choirboys that the police would interview all of the choirboys if he did not confess (*Howden-Simpson* [1991] Crim LR 49). The police should not seek a confession by offering a caution (*R (U) v Metropolitan Police Commissioner* [2002] EWHC 2486 (Admin), [2003] 1 WLR 897, overturned but not in this respect by *R (R) v Durham Constabulary* [2005] UKHL 21, [2005] 1 WLR 1184; and see Ministry of Justice guidance, *Simple Cautions for Adult Offenders* (see **D2.24**), paras. 42 and 59). **D1.88**

Apart from this, the PACE 1984 and Code C provide little, if any, guidance on the proper conduct of interviews, although the case law provides some indication of what is acceptable. It has been held to be legitimate for police officers to pursue their interrogation of a suspect with a view to eliciting admissions even where the suspect denies involvement in the offence or declines to answer specific questions (*Holgate-Mohammed v Duke* [1984] AC 437). In *Mason* [1988] 3 All ER 481, it was held that a confession should be excluded where the police falsely informed D that incriminating fingerprints had been found, although the fact that his solicitor was also deceived may have been an important factor. In *Maclean* [1993] Crim LR 687, it was noted that not every trick will result in exclusion of evidence, but in *Imran and Hussain* [1997] Crim LR 754, the Court of Appeal stated that there was a positive duty on the police not to actively mislead a suspect.

The asking of hypothetical questions is permissible, although it may need to be approached with care (*Stringer* [2008] EWCA Crim 1222). Police questioning which is carried on after repeated denials or refusals may become oppressive (*Paris* (1993) 97 Cr App R 99). Hectoring and bullying throughout an interview has been held to be oppressive (*Beales* [1991] Crim LR 118), whereas questioning that was rude and discourteous, with raised voices and some bad language, was not (*Emmerson* (1991) 92 Cr App R 284). See further **F2.29** and **F18.34** ***et seq.*** on exclusion of evidence.

D1.89 **When Interviews Should Cease** The interview of a person who has not been charged or informed that he or she may be prosecuted must cease when the officer in charge of the investigation is satisfied that all the questions the officer considers relevant to obtaining accurate and reliable information about the offence have been put to the suspect, the officer has taken account of other available evidence, and the officer (or the custody officer in the case of a detained suspect) reasonably believes there is sufficient evidence to provide a realistic prospect of conviction (Code C, para. 11.6). This, of course, is subject to the limits imposed by the PACE 1984 on the maximum periods of detention without charge (see **D1.67**), and the provisions regarding breaks in interviews and rest periods in Code C, section 12 (for application of the provision regarding rest periods, see *Beeres v CPS* [2014] EWHC 283 (Admin), [2014] 2 Cr App R 8 (101)). The fact that the conditions in para. 11.6 are satisfied does not preclude officers in Revenue cases or acting under the confiscation provisions of the POCA 2002 from inviting a suspect to complete a formal question-and-answer record after the interview is completed. (Code C, para. 11.6 refers to the confiscation provisions of the CJA 1988 or the Drug Trafficking Act 1994, but presumably this is an error.)

Code C, para. 11.6, gives the police a large degree of latitude in determining when interviewing should cease since it appears to permit the police to continue questioning beyond the point when they are satisfied that there is sufficient evidence to charge if, e.g., the officer believes that further questions could or should be put to the suspect. However, there is some inconsistency within Code C and thus uncertainty about the effect of para. 11.6. It provides that in the case of a detained suspect (presumably, as opposed to a volunteer) it is for the custody officer and not the investigating officer to determine whether there is sufficient evidence to charge. On the other hand, para. 16.1 states that when the officer in charge of the investigation believes that there is sufficient evidence to provide a realistic prospect of conviction, the suspect must be taken to the custody officer without delay. It may be that this is intended to reflect the fact that the custody officer has formal responsibility for making the decision as to whether there is sufficient evidence to charge. However, para. 16.1 implies that when the officer in charge of the investigation is so satisfied, the suspect must be taken to the custody officer even though the investigating officer still may have further questions to put to the suspect. In any event, under the PACE 1984, s. 37(7), once the custody officer determines that there is sufficient evidence to charge the person the custody officer must proceed under that subsection, which would normally preclude further interviewing. 'Sufficient evidence to charge' is not defined, but the *Director's Guidance on Charging* provides that the custody officer must normally apply the full code test (see **D2.4**).

Where a person is detained in respect of more than one offence, Code C, para. 16.1, provides that it is permissible to delay informing the custody officer until the conditions are satisfied in respect of each of the offences. This, however, conflicts with the mandatory provisions of s. 37(7).

Recording of Interviews

D1.90 Interviews of suspects, whether or not conducted at a police station, must normally be contemporaneously recorded (Code C, para. 11.7). Further, any comment that might be relevant to the suspected offence made by a suspect outside the context of an interview, including unsolicited comments, must be recorded and, where practicable, the suspect must be given the opportunity to verify the record (para. 11.13). This includes relevant comments made by way of a reply to the issuing of a fixed penalty notice (*R (Karia) v Hampshire Constabulary* [2015] EWHC 4083 (Admin)). Failure to comply with the recording requirements has led to exclusion of evidence of what was allegedly said (see, e.g., *Canale* [1990] 2 All ER 187;

Keenan [1990] 2 QB 54), but this is not always so (see, e.g., *Waters* [1989] Crim LR 62; *Dures* [1997] 2 Cr App R 247).

Interviews conducted under caution (see **D1.81**), whether or not at a police station, must normally be recorded using an authorised recording device (Code E, para. 2.1). For regulations governing the use of an authorised recording device, see Code E, section 3. For the circumstances in which an interview may be conducted in writing, see Code E, para. 2.3. For the provisions governing the audio-recording of interviews generally, see Code E. Visual recording of police interviews is not mandatory in any police force area, but where such facilities are available and a police officer chooses to use them, regard must be had to Code F.

Special Categories of Persons

A child or young person or a mentally disordered or vulnerable person (see **D1.63**) must not be interviewed or asked to provide or sign a written statement in the absence of the appropriate adult unless the conditions for conducting an interview away from a police station under Code C, para 11.1, are satisfied (see **D1.82**), or the interview is authorised by an officer of the rank of superintendent or above under Code C, para. 11.18 (Code C, para. 11.15, and annex E). A child or young person should be interviewed at his or her place of education only in exceptional circumstances and then only if the principal or principal's nominee agrees. Efforts should be made to notify parents and the appropriate adult. In cases of necessity, and provided that the school was not the victim of the alleged offence, the principal may act as the appropriate adult (Code C, para. 11.16). The appropriate adult is to be reminded of his or her functions as adviser and observer as well as that of facilitating communication with the person being interviewed (para. 11.17). As to the special rules applying where a child who is to be interviewed is a ward of court, see CrimPD V, paras. 17A.1 to 17A.8 (see Supplement, **CPD.17A**); and see *Re A Ward of Court* [2017] EWHC 1022 (Fam), [2017] Fam 369 in which it was held that judicial consent is not required before a police interview of a ward of court. **D1.91**

A person whom the custody officer has determined requires an interpreter (Code C, paras. 3.5(c)(ii) and 3.12, and see **D1.50**) must not be interviewed without an interpreter unless authorised by an officer of the rank of superintendent or above, being satisfied that delaying the interview will lead to the consequences in Code C, para. 11.1(a) to (c), and that the interview would not significantly harm the person's physical or mental state (para. 11.18). Normally, the interpreter must be physically present, but Code C, paras. 13.1ZA and 13.12, make provision for interpretation to be provided by live link if the custody officer or interviewer are satisfied that this would not adversely affect or otherwise undermine or limit the suspect's ability to communicate confidently and effectively. If live link is used, the modifications to various procedures as set out in Code C, annex N, part 2, apply. Where a suspect cannot read and an interview is recorded in writing, the record must be read over to the suspect who must be asked to verify it (Code C, para. 11.11).

Intoxicated Persons

Code C, para. 11.18, precludes the interviewing of any person who is unable to appreciate the significance of questions and their answers, or to understand what is happening because of the effects of drink, drugs or any illness, ailment or condition, unless it is authorised by an officer of the rank of superintendent (such authorisation being subject to the same conditions as for a person who requires an interpreter). **D1.92**

Effect of Charge

Generally, a person who has been charged with, or informed that he or she may be prosecuted for, an offence cannot be interviewed or otherwise asked questions about that offence (Code C, para. 16.5). Different provisions apply where the offence is a terrorism offence within the **D1.93** meaning of the C-TA 2008, s. 27 (as amended on 12 April 2019 by the C-tBSA 2019, s. 23(1) and sch. 4, paras. 40 and 42; see **B10.14 *et seq.***). In *Charles v DPP* [2009] EWHC 3521 (Admin), [2010] RTR 34 (402), interviewing a person about an offence of driving whilst under the influence of alcohol in circumstances where he had already been informed that he would be charged with the offence of being in charge of a motor vehicle whilst under the influence was held to be a breach of para. 16.5. There are two exceptions to the prohibition on interviewing after charge. First, the person may be questioned if an officer wishes to bring to the person's notice any written statement made by another person or the content of an interview with another person. In such a case, the officer must hand to the accused a true copy of any such statement or interview record, but must not do or say anything to invite any reply or comment, except to caution the accused (Code C, para. 16.4). A police officer may read the statement or record to an illiterate person. If the person is a child or young person or is mentally disordered or mentally vulnerable, the copy or interview record must be given or shown to the appropriate adult (para. 16.4A).

The second exception is where an interview is necessary for the purpose of preventing or minimising harm or loss to some other person or to the public, to clear up an ambiguity in a previous answer or statement, or where it is in the interests of justice that the person should be presented with and should have an opportunity to comment on information concerning the offence which has come to light since the person was charged or informed that he or she may be prosecuted (para. 16.5).

In either case, the person must first be cautioned in the terms set out in paras. 16.4(a) or 16.5(a). Inferences under the CJPO 1994 cannot be drawn in such circumstances (see Code C, annex C, para. 1(b)). The person must also be reminded of the right to legal advice.

Serious Fraud and other Serious Crime

D1.94 Different rules apply in relation to investigation of certain serious or complex frauds. While the police are obliged to follow the normal procedure when questioning suspects, including the administration of a caution, the Director of the SFO has power under the CJA 1987, s. 2, to require a person under investigation or any other person whom the Director has reason to believe has relevant information to produce documents and to provide an explanation of them. This includes the right to re-interview witnesses even following the delivery of a case statement by the defence (*Turner* (1993) *The Times*, 2 July 1993). The Director is not obliged to provide the interviewee with advance information on the subject-matter of the interview but may do so should it be deemed helpful and not likely to prejudice the investigation (*SFO, ex parte Maxwell* (1992) *The Independent*, 7 October 1992). The court has no power to direct liquidators of an insolvent company not to comply with a notice served by the SFO requesting production of transcripts of examinations under the Insolvency Act 1986, s. 236. It is for the judge at the criminal trial to determine whether to admit such a transcript at the criminal trial. In *R (KBR Inc.) v Director of the SFO* [2018] EWHC 2368 (Admin), [2019] 2 WLR 267, which is subject to appeal to the Supreme Court, it was held that the power to require the production of material under the CJA 1987, s. 2(3), had extraterritorial effect if the relevant foreign company had a 'sufficient connection' to the UK jurisdiction. A person who without reasonable excuse fails to comply with a requirement under s. 2 commits an offence punishable on summary conviction with up to six months' imprisonment and/or a fine not exceeding level 5. Note, however, that compulsion to attend for interview or to provide information where the person is at risk of criminal prosecution in respect of those matters may amount to an interference with rights under the ECHR, Article 6; but this depends upon the nature of the regulatory regime and the information sought (*O'Halloran v UK* [2008] 46 EHRR 21 (397)).

It would seem that the fact that a person who is required to answer questions in the course of an inquiry by the SFO is the spouse of a party charged with fraud is not a reasonable excuse for declining to answer questions (*Director of the SFO, ex parte Johnson* [1993] COD 58). This seemingly follows from the consideration that such inquiries are administrative, and must represent something of a triumph of form over function.

For restrictions on the use in evidence of information obtained by virtue of the CJA 1987, s. 2, see s. 2(8) and (8AA), and see further **F10.45** and **F20.1**. **D1.95**

For powers of search under the CJA 1987, s. 2, see the review of the procedure and authorities in *R (Energy Financing Team Ltd) v Bow Street Magistrates' Court* [2005] EWHC 1626 (Admin), [2006] 4 All ER 285.

Similar powers to those under CJA 1987, s. 2, are available to the DPP under the SOCPA 2005, Part 2, in respect of certain offences. See further **D1.205** ***et seq.***

For the obligation to answer questions or to provide information under a serious crime prevention order granted under the SCA 2007, Part 1, see **D25.58**.

SEARCH OF THE PERSON

Search on Arrest

A constable who arrests a person elsewhere than at a police station may search that person if the constable has reason to believe that the person may present a danger to him or herself or others (PACE 1984, s. 32(1)), and may seize and retain anything found if there are reasonable grounds for believing that the person might use it to cause physical injury to him or herself or others (s. 32(8)). The constable may also search the person for anything which that person might use to escape from lawful custody or which might be evidence in relation to an offence, provided that there is reasonable cause to believe that the arrested person has such material on his or her person (s. 32(2) and (5)). The officer may seize and retain anything, other than an item subject to legal privilege, if there are reasonable grounds for believing that the person may use it to assist with escape from lawful custody or that it is evidence of an offence or has been obtained in consequence of the commission of an offence (s. 32(9)). 'Reasonable grounds' implies a mixed subjective/objective test (see **D1.4**). Seizure of car keys under s. 32 from a person arrested on suspicion of burglary and who had been placed in a police car was held in *Churchill* [1989] Crim LR 226 to be unlawful since the keys were not evidence of any crime, although they could have been seized under the officer's general duty to preserve property. **D1.96**

Search under s. 32(2) is authorised only to the extent that it is reasonably required for the purpose of discovering any such thing or evidence (s. 32(3)). The reference to 'an' offence means that the power is not limited to search for or seizure of an item which may be evidence relating to the offence for which the person has been arrested. Unlike the power to search premises under s. 32(2)(b), the offence for which the person has been arrested does not have to be an indictable offence. Where the search takes place in public, the constable may only require the arrested person to remove an outer coat, jacket or gloves, but is authorised to search a person's mouth (s. 32(4)). Hats, turbans and other forms of head-wear are not mentioned in s. 32(4) and thus it would seem that a person cannot be required to remove them in public. However, note the power of a constable in uniform, in an area where an authorisation under the CJPO 1994, s. 60, is in force (see **D1.12**), to require a person to remove any item which the constable reasonably believes is being worn wholly or mainly for the purpose of concealing identity (s. 60AA). Note also that the power to photograph an arrested person without consent under the PACE 1984, s. 64A(1), is supplemented by a power to require the person to remove any item worn on or over the whole or part of the face or head (s. 64A(2): see **D1.118**).

Search at the Police Station

With the exception of searches following arrest under the TA 2000, s. 41 (for which see **B10.24**), searches by a constable of persons in police detention (see **D1.40**), including intimate searches, **D1.97** can take place only under the authority of the PACE 1984 (s. 53(1)). A person who attends at a police station to answer to 'live link bail' (see **D2.46**) is not in police detention, but see **D1.98** regarding search and seizure powers.

The custody officer at a police station is obliged to ascertain everything which a person has with him or her when brought to the station after having been arrested (PACE 1984, s. 54(1); Code C, para. 4.1; and see *Davies v Chief Constable of Merseyside Police* [2015] EWCA Civ 114, [2015] 1 WLR 2865, in which it was held that Code C, section 4, applies to the exercise of all powers under s. 54). In order to do so, the person may be searched if the custody officer considers it necessary in order to ascertain what property the person has, but only to the extent that the custody officer considers it necessary for that purpose (s. 54(6); para. 4.1). The custody officer must also ascertain what property the suspect may have acquired for an unlawful or harmful purpose while in custody, and is responsible for the safe-keeping of property taken from the detainee and kept at the police station (Code C, para. 4.1). For recording requirements, see **D1.45**.

The custody officer may seize and retain anything in the possession of the detainee, save for clothes and personal effects. These may be seized only if the custody officer believes that the person from whom they are seized may use them to cause physical injury to him or herself or another, to damage property, to interfere with evidence, to escape, or if the custody officer has reasonable grounds for believing that they may be evidence relating to an offence (PACE 1984, s. 54(3), (4), (6B) and (6C); Code C, para. 4.2). In respect of most of these criteria, the custody officer need only have a subjective belief that seizure is necessary, but in respect of articles of supposed evidentiary value, the belief must be based on reasonable grounds. Paragraphs 4.2 and 4.3 of Code C expressly state that a detained person may retain clothing and personal effects other than cash and other items of value, at his or her own risk, unless the custody officer considers that the detainee might use them in the manner noted above or they are needed as evidence.

A person from whom an article is seized is to be told the reason for the seizure unless the person is either violent or likely to become so, is incapable of understanding what is said, or is in urgent need of medical attention (PACE 1984, s. 54(5); Code C, paras. 1.8 and 4.2).

D1.98 Under the PACE 1984, s. 54A, searches and examinations may be authorised by an officer of the rank of inspector or above for the purpose of ascertaining whether a detained person has any mark (such as a tattoo) that would tend to identify him or her as a person involved in the commission of an offence (s. 54A(1)(a)), or so as to facilitate the ascertainment of the person's identity (s. 54A(1)(b)). See also Code D, paras. 5.1 to 5.11. By s. 54A(2), authorisation may be given under s. 54A(1)(a) only if appropriate consent (see the PACE 1984, s. 65(1)) has been withheld or it is not practicable to obtain it (for examples, see Code D, Note for Guidance 5D). Authorisation may be given under s. 54A(1)(b) only if the person has refused to identify him or herself or the officer has reasonable grounds for suspecting that the person is not who he or she claims to be (s. 54A(3)). An identifying mark found on such a search or examination may be photographed (s. 54A(5)). The PACE 1984, ss. 54B and 54C, permit a police constable to search a person attending a police station to answer to live link bail (see **D2.46**), and to seize and retain anything that may jeopardise the maintenance of order, or the safety of any person, in the police station, or which may be evidence of, or relating to, an offence. An intimate search cannot be carried out under s. 54A (s. 54A(8)) or s. 54B (s. 54B(5)), and if the search or examination requires the removal of more than outer clothing it must be treated as a strip search and conducted in accordance with Code C, annex A, para. 11.

Strip Searches

D1.99 A strip search is a search that is not an intimate search, but which involves the removal of more than outer clothing (Code C, annex A, para. 9). A strip search should not be routinely conducted, and should be carried out only if it is considered necessary to remove an article which the detained person would not be allowed to keep and the officer reasonably considers that the detainee might have concealed such an article (Code C, annex A, para. 10). It was held in *Davies v Chief Constable of Merseyside Police* [2015] EWCA Civ 114, [2015] 1 WLR 2865 that annex A applies to all powers under the PACE 1984, s. 54, including the removal of clothing which it is believed may be used by a person to injure him or herself. The conduct of strip searches is governed by Code C, annex A, para. 11; in particular, they may be carried out only by a constable of the same sex as the person being searched (annex A, para. 11(a)). Code C, para. 1.13C and Annex L, specify the approach to be adopted in establishing gender for the purposes of searching (see also **D1.50**).

Intimate Searches, X-rays and Ultrasound Scans

Intimate Searches A person who has been arrested and is in police detention (see **D1.40**) may, under certain circumstances, be subjected to an intimate search, i.e. a search consisting of a physical examination of the bodily orifices other than the mouth (PACE 1984, ss. 54 and 65(1)). An intimate search cannot be authorised for the purpose of securing evidence relating to an offence, nor must it be conducted whilst carrying out a search or examination under s. 54A. 'Bodily orifice' is not defined but would include ears, nose, anus and vagina. Physical insertion into a bodily orifice amounts to an intimate search, as does any application of force to an orifice or its immediate surroundings, such as the removal of something within an orifice. Code C, annex A, para. 11(e), implies that touching an orifice in these circumstances would also amount to an intimate search. **D1.100**

An intimate search can be conducted only if an officer of the rank of inspector or above authorises it. Such officer must have reasonable grounds for believing that the detained person has concealed an article which could be used to cause physical injury to him or herself or others, and which the person might so use while in police detention or in the custody of a court (s. 55(1)(a)). Authorisation may also be granted if the officer has reasonable grounds for believing that such a person may have concealed on him or her a Class A drug and is in possession of it with the appropriate criminal intent (i.e. either to supply it to another or to export it with intent to evade a prohibition or restriction: s. 55(17)) (s. 55(1)(b)). In either case the officer must have reasonable grounds for believing that the article in question cannot be found unless the detainee is intimately searched (s. 55(2)). The reasons why an intimate search is considered necessary must be explained to the person before the search takes place (Code C, annex A, para. 2A). Intimate searches are not limited to circumstances where a person has been arrested for an indictable or recordable offence, although searches conducted under s. 55(1)(b) will, by definition, relate to such offences.

Authorisation may be given either orally, subject to confirmation in writing, or in writing (PACE 1984, s. 55(3)). Consent of the person to be searched is not required for a search under s. 55(1)(a), and reasonable force can be used in order to carry it out (PACE 1984, s. 117). Appropriate consent (see s. 65(1) for definition) in writing is required for a search under s. 55(1)(b). In the latter case the person to be searched must be told of the authorisation and the reasons for it (s. 55(3B)). If consent to a search under s. 55(1)(b) (but not a search under s. 55(1)(a)) is refused without good cause, proper inferences may be drawn (s. 55(13A)), but where consent has been refused force may not be used.

The general rule is that an intimate search should be carried out by a suitably qualified person, i.e. a registered medical practitioner or a registered nurse (s. 55(17)). Searches under s. 55(1)(b) must always be so carried out (s. 55(4) and (5)). Searches under s. 55(1)(a) must normally be carried out by a suitably qualified person, but may be conducted by a constable where an officer of the rank of inspector or above considers that this would not be practicable (s. 55(5) and (6)); such a search may be carried out by a civilian detention officer (Police Reform Act 2002, sch. 4, para. 28). A search under s. 55(1)(a) by anyone other than a suitably qualified person should **D1.101** be considered only as a last resort (Code C, annex A, para. 3A) — an example might be where a suspect is believed to have concealed a poisonous drug in his anus. No intimate search of an arrested child or young person or a mentally vulnerable person may be carried out unless the appropriate adult of the same sex is present or the suspect requests the presence of a particular adult of the opposite sex who is readily available. In the case of a child or young person, the search may take place in the absence of the appropriate adult only if the child or young person approves this in the adult's presence (Code C, annex A, para. 5). A constable may not carry out an intimate search of a person of the opposite sex, but this restriction does not apply to a search carried out by a medically qualified person; a minimum of two people other than the detainee must be present (Code C, annex A, para. 6). The person to be searched, if not legally represented, must be reminded of the entitlement to free legal advice (Code C, para. 6.5, and annex A, para. 2B).

Intimate searches may be carried out only at a police station, a hospital, surgery or other medical premises, although an intimate search under s. 55(1)(b) may not be carried out at a police station (PACE 1984, s. 55(8) and (9); Code C, annex A, para. 4). 'Medical premises' is not defined but presumably could, e.g., include a workplace health centre. As soon as possible after completion of an intimate search, the parts of the body searched and the reason for the search (and in the case of a search under s. 55(1)(b), the fact of and grounds for the authorisation and the fact that appropriate consent was given) must be recorded in the custody record (s. 55(10) and (11)).

D1.102 A person from whom anything is seized is to be told the reason why, unless the person is incapable of understanding or is violent or likely to become so (s. 55(13)). Articles found in an intimate search may be seized and retained by the police for the same reasons as justify seizure and retention in the case of a non-intimate search (s. 55(12), and see **D1.97**).

D1.103 **X-rays and Ultrasound Scans** By the PACE 1984, s. 55A(1), an X-ray or ultrasound scan may be taken if authorised by an officer of at least the rank of inspector, who has reasonable grounds for believing that a person who has been arrested and is in police detention (see **D1.40**) may have swallowed a Class A drug and was in possession of it with the appropriate criminal intent (see s. 55A(1) and **D1.100**) before the arrest. The officer granting the authorisation must inform the person concerned of the authorisation and of the reasons for it (s. 55A(3)). Neither an X-ray nor an ultrasound scan may be taken without appropriate consent (see s. 65(1) for definition) (s. 55A(2)). The procedures may be carried out by the same categories of person, and at the same places, as for an intimate search under s. 55(1)(b) (s. 55A(4)), and similar recording requirements apply (s. 55A(5)). Inferences may be drawn against a person who refuses consent (s. 55A(9)), but force may not be used.

BIOMETRIC IMPRESSIONS AND SAMPLES

D1.104 The police have wide powers to take, use and retain biometric samples and impressions, and also footwear impressions, both with and without consent, although intimate samples cannot be taken without consent in any circumstances. Generally there is a distinction between powers that may be exercised in respect of a person who is in police detention (see **D1.40**) and those that apply where a person is not in police detention, although in respect of the latter there are powers to require a person to attend a police station for the purpose of taking fingerprints or samples, with a power of arrest in default (PACE 1984, s. 63A(4) and sch. 2A). The statutory provisions are supplemented by Code D, sections 4 and 6.

Fingerprints and Footwear Impressions

D1.105 **Fingerprints** The taking of fingerprints in connection with a criminal investigation is governed by the PACE 1984, s. 61, and by PACE Code D, Part 4(A) (see **appendix 1**).

Police and Criminal Evidence Act 1984, s. 61

(1) Except as provided by this section no person's fingerprints may be taken without the appropriate consent.

(2) Consent to the taking of a person's fingerprints must be in writing if it is given at a time when he is at a police station.

(3) The fingerprints of a person detained at a police station may be taken without the appropriate consent if—
   (a) he is detained in consequence of his arrest for a recordable offence; and
   (b) he has not had his fingerprints taken in the course of the investigation of the offence by the police.

(3A) Where a person mentioned in paragraph (a) of subsection (3) or (4) has already had his fingerprints taken in the course of the investigation of the offence by the police, that fact shall be disregarded for the purposes of that subsection if—
   (a) the fingerprints taken on the previous occasion do not constitute a complete set of his fingerprints; or
   (b) some or all of the fingerprints taken on the previous occasion are not of sufficient quality to allow satisfactory analysis, comparison or matching (whether in the case in question or generally).

(4) The fingerprints of a person detained at a police station may be taken without the appropriate consent if—
   (a) he has been charged with a recordable offence or informed that he will be reported for such an offence; and
   (b) he has not had his fingerprints taken in the course of the investigation of the offence by the police.

(4A) The fingerprints of a person who has answered to bail at a court or police station may be taken without the appropriate consent at the court or station if—
   (a) the court, or
   (b) an officer of at least the rank of inspector,
authorises them to be taken.

(4B) A court or officer may only give an authorisation under subsection (4A) if—
   (a) the person who has answered to bail has answered to it for a person whose fingerprints were taken on a previous occasion and there are reasonable grounds for believing that he is not the same person; or
   (b) the person who has answered to bail claims to be a different person from a person whose fingerprints were taken on a previous occasion.

(5) An officer may give an authorisation under subsection (4A) above orally or in writing but, if he gives it orally, he shall confirm it in writing as soon as is practicable.

(5A) The fingerprints of a person may be taken without the appropriate consent if (before or after the coming into force of this subsection) he has been arrested for a recordable offence and released and—
   (a) in the case of a person who is on bail, he has not had his fingerprints taken in the course of the investigation of the offence by the police; or
   (b) in any case, he has had his fingerprints taken in the course of that investigation but
      (i) subsection (3A)(a) or (b) above applies, or
      (ii) subsection (5C) below applies.

(5B) The fingerprints of a person not detained at a police station may be taken without the appropriate consent if (before or after the coming into force of this subsection) he has been charged with a recordable offence or informed that he will be reported for such an offence and—
   (a) he has not had his fingerprints taken in the course of the investigation of the offence by the police; or
   (b) he has had his fingerprints taken in the course of that investigation but
      (i) subsection (3A)(a) or (b) above applies, or
      (ii) subsection 5C below applies.

(5C) This subsection applies where—
   (a) the investigation was discontinued but subsequently resumed, and
   (b) before the resumption of the investigation the fingerprints were destroyed pursuant to section 63D(3) below.

(6) Subject to this section, the fingerprints of a person may be taken without the appropriate consent if (before or after the coming into force of this subsection)—

(a) he has been convicted of a recordable offence, or
(b) he has been given a caution in respect of a recordable offence which, at the time of the caution, he has admitted, and

either of the conditions mentioned in subsection (6ZA) below is met.

(6ZA) The conditions referred to in subsection (6) above are—
(a) the person has not had his fingerprints taken since he was convicted or cautioned;
(b) he has had his fingerprints taken since then but subsection (3A)(a) or (b) above applies.

(6ZB) Fingerprints may only be taken as specified in subsection (6) above with the authorisation of an officer of at least the rank of inspector.

(6ZC) An officer may only give an authorisation under subsection (6ZB) above if the officer is satisfied that taking the fingerprints is necessary to assist in the prevention or detection of crime.

(6A) A constable may take a person's fingerprints without the appropriate consent if—
(a) the constable reasonably suspects that the person is committing or attempting to commit an offence, or has committed or attempted to commit an offence; and
(b) either of the two conditions mentioned in subsection (6B) is met.

(6B) The conditions are that—
(a) the name of the person is unknown to, and cannot be readily ascertained by, the constable;
(b) the constable has reasonable grounds for doubting whether a name furnished by the person as his name is his real name.

(6C) The taking of fingerprints by virtue of subsection (6A) does not count for any of the purposes of this Act as taking them in the course of the investigation of an offence by the police.

(6D) Subject to this section, the fingerprints of a person may be taken without the appropriate consent if—
(a) under the law in force in a country or territory outside England and Wales the person has been convicted of an offence under that law (whether before or after the coming into force of this subsection and whether or not he has been punished for it);
(b) the act constituting the offence would constitute a qualifying offence if done in England and Wales (whether or not it constituted such an offence when the person was convicted); and
(c) either of the conditions mentioned in subsection (6E) below is met.

(6E) The conditions referred to in subsection (6D)(c) above are—
(a) the person has not had his fingerprints taken on a previous occasion under subsection (6D) above;
(b) he has had his fingerprints taken on a previous occasion under that subsection but subsection (3A)(a) or (b) above applies.

(6F) Fingerprints may only be taken as specified in subsection (6D) above with the authorisation of an officer of at least the rank of inspector.

(6G) An officer may only give an authorisation under subsection (6F) above if the officer is satisfied that taking the fingerprints is necessary to assist in the prevention or detection of crime.

(7) Where a person's fingerprints are taken without the appropriate consent by virtue of any power conferred by this section—
(a) before the fingerprints are taken, the person shall be informed of—
(i) the reason for taking the fingerprints;
(ii) the power by virtue of which they are taken; and
(iii) in a case where the authorisation of the court or an officer is required for the exercise of the power, the fact that the authorisation has been given; and
(b) those matters shall be recorded as soon as practicable after the fingerprints are taken.

(7A) If a person's fingerprints are taken at a police station, or by virtue of subsection (4A), (6A) at a place other than a police station, whether with or without the appropriate consent—
(a) before the fingerprints are taken, an officer (or, where by virtue of subsection (4A), (6A) the fingerprints are taken at a place other than a police station, the constable taking the fingerprints) shall inform him that they may be the subject of a speculative search; and
(b) the fact that the person has been informed of this possibility shall be recorded as soon as is practicable after the fingerprints have been taken.

(8) If he is detained at a police station when the fingerprints are taken, the matters referred to in subsection (7)(a)(i) to (iii) above and, in the case falling within subsection (7A) above, the fact referred to in paragraph (b) of that subsection shall be recorded on his custody record.

(8B) Any power under this section to take the fingerprints of a person without the appropriate consent, if not otherwise specified to be exercisable by a constable, shall be exercisable by a constable.

(9) Nothing in this section—
   (a) affects any power conferred by paragraph 18(2) of Schedule 2 to the Immigration Act 1971; or
   (b) applies to a person arrested or detained under the terrorism provisions or detained under Part 1 of Schedule 3 to the Counter-Terrorism and Border Security Act 2019.
(10) Nothing in this section applies to a person arrested under an extradition arrest power.

'Fingerprints' means any record, produced by any method, of the skin pattern and other physical characteristics or features of a person's fingers or palms (s. 65(1)). 'Appropriate consent' means: (a) in relation to a person who has attained the age of 17 years, the consent of that person; (b) in relation to a person who has not attained that age but has attained the age of 14 years, the consent of that person and his or her parent or guardian; and (c) in relation to a person who has not attained the age of 14 years, the consent of his or her parent or guardian (s. 65(1)). A 17-year-old is treated as an adult for these purposes (but see **D1.63**). If the person is at a police station, consent must be in writing (Code D, para. 4.2). 'Recordable offence' means an offence specified by the Secretary of State in regulations issued under the PACE 1984, s. 27(4), and includes all imprisonable offences and certain non-imprisonable offences (and see Code D, Note for Guidance 4A). The reference to a person 'detained at a police station' is assumed to be a reference to a person in 'police detention' (see **D1.40**). **D1.106**

The power under s. 61(6A) to (6C) to take the fingerprints of a person who has not been arrested is not confined to circumstances where the person is suspected of a recordable offence. Furthermore, since the absence of an arrest is not a precondition, the power could be used to take the fingerprints of a person who has been arrested for a non-recordable offence provided that one of the conditions in s. 61(6B) is satisfied (and see Code D, Note for Guidance 4C). Although fingerprints taken under s. 61(6A) are not regarded as being taken in the course of the investigation of an offence (s. 61(6C)), they can be used for the purpose of a speculative search (s. 63A(1ZA)).

Footwear Impressions The taking of footwear impressions in connection with a criminal investigation is governed by the PACE 1984, s. 61A, and Code D, Part 4(C). 'Footwear' is not defined in the PACE 1984, nor in Code D. **D1.107**

Police and Criminal Evidence Act 1984, s. 61A

(1) Except as provided by this section, no impression of a person's footwear may be taken without the appropriate consent.
(2) Consent to the taking of an impression of a person's footwear must be in writing if it is given at a time when he is at a police station.
(3) Where a person is detained at a police station, an impression of his footwear may be taken without the appropriate consent if—
   (a) he is detained in consequence of his arrest for a recordable offence, or has been charged with a recordable offence, or informed that he will be reported for a recordable offence; and
   (b) he has not had an impression taken of his footwear in the course of the investigation of the offence by the police.
(4) Where a person mentioned in paragraph (a) of subsection (3) above has already had an impression taken of his footwear in the course of the investigation of the offence by the police, that fact shall be disregarded for the purposes of that subsection if the impression of his footwear taken previously is—
   (a) incomplete; or
   (b) is not of sufficient quality to allow satisfactory analysis, comparison or matching (whether in the case in question or generally).
(5) If an impression of a person's footwear is taken at a police station, whether with or without the appropriate consent—
   (a) before it is taken, an officer shall inform him that it may be the subject of a speculative search; and
   (b) the fact that the person has been informed of this possibility shall be recorded as soon as is practicable after the impression has been taken, and if he is detained at a police station, the record shall be made on his custody record.

(6) In a case where, by virtue of subsection (3) above, an impression of a person's footwear is taken without the appropriate consent—
(a) he shall be told the reason before it is taken; and
(b) the reason shall be recorded on his custody record as soon as is practicable after the impression is taken.
(7) The power to take an impression of the footwear of a person detained at a police station without the appropriate consent shall be exercisable by any constable.
(8) Nothing in this section applies to any person—
(a) arrested or detained under the terrorism provisions or detained under Part 1 of Schedule 3 to the Counter-Terrorism and Border Security Act 2019
(b) arrested under an extradition arrest power.

For the meanings of 'appropriate consent', 'recordable offence' and 'detained at a police station', see **D1.106**.

Body Samples and Dental or Skin Impressions

D1.108 The taking of body samples, skin impressions (including footprints) and dental impressions in connection with a criminal investigation is governed by the PACE 1984, ss. 62 and 63, and by Code D, section 6 (see **appendix** 1). The powers differ as between intimate and non-intimate samples.

D1.109 **Intimate Samples** Intimate samples are defined as blood, semen or tissue fluid; urine; pubic hair; dental impressions; and swabs taken from the genitals or pubic hair or from orifices other than the mouth (s. 65(1)). Hair samples (other than pubic hair) are non-intimate, even if plucked with roots for DNA testing, provided that no more are plucked than the person taking the sample reasonably considers to be necessary for a sufficient sample (s. 63A(2)). Section 62 does not apply to the taking of urine and blood samples for the purposes of the RTA 1988, ss. 4 to 11, or the Transport and Works Act 1992, ss. 26 to 38 (see **C5.1** ***et seq.***).

D1.110 **Police and Criminal Evidence Act 1984, s. 62**

(1) Subject to section 63B below an intimate sample may be taken from a person in police detention only—
(a) if a police officer of at least the rank of inspector authorises it to be taken; and
(b) if the appropriate consent is given.
(1A) An intimate sample may be taken from a person who is not in police detention but from whom, in the course of the investigation of an offence, two or more non-intimate samples suitable for the same means of analysis have been taken which have proved insufficient—
(a) if a police officer of at least the rank of inspector authorises it to be taken; and
(b) if the appropriate consent is given.
(2) An officer may only give an authorisation under subsection (1) or (1A) above if he has reasonable grounds—
(a) for suspecting the involvement of the person from whom the sample is to be taken in a recordable offence; and
(b) for believing that the sample will tend to confirm or disprove his involvement.
(2A) An intimate sample may be taken from a person where—
(a) two or more non-intimate samples suitable for the same means of analysis have been taken from the person under section 63(3E) below (persons convicted of offences outside England and Wales etc) but have proved insufficient;
(b) a police officer of at least the rank of inspector authorises it to be taken; and
(c) the appropriate consent is given.
(2B) An officer may only give an authorisation under subsection (2A) above if the officer is satisfied that taking the sample is necessary to assist in the prevention or detection of crime.
(3) An officer may give an authorisation under subsection (1) or (1A) or (2A) above orally or in writing but, if he gives it orally, he shall confirm it in writing as soon as is practicable.
(4) The appropriate consent must be given in writing.
(5) Before an intimate sample is taken from a person, an officer shall inform him of the following—
(a) the reason for taking the sample;
(b) the fact that authorisation has been given and the provision of this section under which it has been given; and

(c) if the sample was taken at a police station, the fact that the sample may be the subject of a speculative search.

(6) The reason referred to in subsection (5)(a) above must include, except in a case where the sample is taken under subsection (2A) above, a statement of the nature of the offence in which it is suspected that the person has been involved.

(7) After an intimate sample has been taken from a person, the following shall be recorded as soon as practicable—
(a) the matters referred to in subsection (5)(a) and (b) above;
(b) if the sample was taken at a police station, the fact that the person has been informed as specified in subsection (5)(c) above; and
(c) the fact that the appropriate consent was given.

(8) If an intimate sample is taken from a person detained at a police station, the matters required to be recorded by subsection (7) above shall be recorded in his custody record.

(9) In the case of an intimate sample which is a dental impression, the sample may be taken from a person only by a registered dentist.

(9A) In the case of any other form of intimate sample, except in the case of a sample of urine, the sample may be taken from a person only by—
(a) a registered medical practitioner; or
(b) a registered health care professional.

(10) Where the appropriate consent to the taking of an intimate sample from a person was refused without good cause, in any proceedings against that person for an offence—
(a) the court, in determining—
(i) whether to commit that person for trial; or
(ii) whether there is a case to answer; and
(aa) a judge, in deciding whether to grant an application made by the accused under paragraph 2 of Schedule 3 to the Crime and Disorder Act 1998 (applications for dismissal); and
(b) the court or jury, in determining whether that person is guilty of the offence charged, may draw such inferences from the refusal as appear proper.

(11) Nothing in this section applies to the taking of a specimen for the purposes of any of the provisions of sections 4 to 11 of the Road Traffic Act 1988 or of sections 26 to 38 of the Transport and Works Act 1992.

(12) Nothing in this section applies to a person arrested or detained under the terrorism provisions; and subsection (1A) shall not apply where the non-intimate samples mentioned in that subsection were taken under paragraph 10 of Schedule 8 to the Terrorism Act 2000.

(13) Nothing in this section applies to a person detained under Part 1 of Schedule 3 to the Counter-Terrorism and Border Security Act 2019; and subsection (1A) does not apply where the non-intimate samples mentioned in that subsection were taken under Part 2 of that Schedule.

For the meanings of 'appropriate consent' and 'recordable offence', see **D1.106**, and for 'police detention' see **D1.40**. In addition to the information that must be given under s. 62(5), the person must also be warned of the consequences of refusal under s. 62(10) (Code D, para 6.3(b)).

Non-intimate Samples Non-intimate samples are defined as a sample of hair other than pubic hair; a sample taken from a nail or from under a nail; a swab taken from any part of a person's body other than a part from which a swab taken would be an intimate sample; saliva; or a skin impression (s. 65(1)). Unlike intimate samples, non-intimate samples may be taken without consent in a wide range of circumstances. **D1.111**

Police and Criminal Evidence Act 1984, s. 63 **D1.112**

(1) Except as provided by this section, a non-intimate sample may not be taken from a person without the appropriate consent.

(2) Consent to the taking of a non-intimate sample must be given in writing.

(2A) A non-intimate sample may be taken from a person without the appropriate consent if two conditions are satisfied.

(2B) The first is that the person is in police detention in consequence of his arrest for a recordable offence.

(2C) The second is that—
(a) he has not had a non-intimate sample of the same type and from the same part of the body taken in the course of the investigation of the offence by the police, or
(b) he has had such a sample taken but it proved insufficient.

(3) A non-intimate sample may be taken from a person without the appropriate consent if—
(a) he is being held in custody by the police on the authority of a court; and
(b) an officer of at least the rank of inspector authorises it to be taken without the appropriate consent.

(3ZA) A non-intimate sample may be taken from a person without the appropriate consent if (before or after the coming into force of this subsection) he has been arrested for a recordable offence and released and—
(a) in the case of a person who is on bail, he has not had a non-intimate sample of the same type and from the same part of the body taken from him in the course of the investigation of the offence by the police; or
(b) in any case, he has had a non-intimate sample taken from him in the course of that investigation but—
(i) it was not suitable for the same means of analysis, or
(ii) it proved insufficient, or
(iii) subsection (3AA) below applies.

(3A) A non-intimate sample may be taken from a person (whether or not he is in police detention or held in custody by the police on the authority of a court) without the appropriate consent if he has been charged with a recordable offence or informed that he will be reported for such an offence and—
(a) he has not had a non-intimate sample taken from him in the course of the investigation of the offence by the police; or
(b) he has had a non-intimate sample taken from him in the course of that investigation but—
(i) it was not suitable for the same means of analysis, or
(ii) it proved insufficient,
(iii) subsection (3AA) below applies or
(c) he has had a non-intimate sample taken from him in the course of that investigation and—
(i) the sample has been destroyed pursuant to section 64ZA below or any other enactment, and
(ii) it is disputed, in relation to any proceedings relating to the offence, whether a DNA profile relevant to the proceedings is derived from the sample.

(3AA) This subsection applies where the investigation was discontinued but subsequently resumed, and before the resumption of the investigation—
(a) any DNA profile derived from the sample was destroyed pursuant to section 63D(3) below, and
(b) the sample itself was destroyed pursuant to section 63R(4), (5) or (12) below.

(3B) Subject to this section, a non-intimate sample may be taken from a person without the appropriate consent if (before or after the coming into force of this subsection)—
(a) he has been convicted of a recordable offence, or
(b) he has been given a caution in respect of a recordable offence which, at the time of the caution, he has admitted, and

either of the conditions mentioned in subsection (3BA) below is met.

(3BA) The conditions referred to in subsection (3B) above are—
(a) a non-intimate sample has not been taken from the person since he was convicted or cautioned;
(b) such a sample has been taken from him since then but—
(i) it was not suitable for the same means of analysis, or
(ii) it proved insufficient.

(3BB) A non-intimate sample may only be taken as specified in subsection (3B) above with the authorisation of an officer of at least the rank of inspector.

(3BC) An officer may only give an authorisation under subsection (3BB) above if the officer is satisfied that taking the sample is necessary to assist in the prevention or detection of crime.

(3C) A non-intimate sample may also be taken from a person without the appropriate consent if he is a person to whom section 2 of the Criminal Evidence (Amendment) Act 1997 applies (persons detained following acquittal on grounds of insanity or finding of unfitness to plead).

(3D) [Not in force.]

(3E) Subject to this section, a non-intimate sample may be taken without the appropriate consent from a person if—
(a) under the law in force in a country or territory outside England and Wales the person has been convicted of an offence under that law (whether before or after the coming into force of this subsection and whether or not he has been punished for it);

(b) the act constituting the offence would constitute a qualifying offence if done in England and Wales (whether or not it constituted such an offence when the person was convicted); and
(c) either of the conditions mentioned in subsection (3F) below is met.

(3F) The conditions referred to in subsection (3E)(c) above are—
(a) the person has not had a non-intimate sample taken from him on a previous occasion under subsection (3E) above;
(b) he has had such a sample taken from him on a previous occasion under that subsection but—
(i) the sample was not suitable for the same means of analysis, or
(ii) it proved insufficient.

(3G) A non-intimate sample may only be taken as specified in subsection (3E) above with the authorisation of an officer of at least the rank of inspector.

(3H) An officer may only give an authorisation under subsection (3G) above if the officer is satisfied that taking the sample is necessary to assist in the prevention or detection of crime.

(4) An officer may only give an authorisation under subsection (3) above if he has reasonable grounds—
(a) for suspecting the involvement of the person from whom the sample is to be taken in a recordable offence; and
(b) for believing that the sample will tend to confirm or disprove his involvement.

(5) An officer may give an authorisation under subsection (3) above orally or in writing but, if he gives it orally, he shall confirm it in writing as soon as is practicable.

(5A) An officer shall not give an authorisation under subsection (3) above for the taking from any person of a non-intimate sample consisting of a skin impression if–
(a) a skin impression of the same part of the body has already been taken from that person in the course of the investigation of the offence; and
(b) the impression previously taken is not one that has proved insufficient.

(6) Where a non-intimate sample is taken from a person without the appropriate consent by virtue of any power conferred by this section—
(a) before the sample is taken, an officer shall inform him of—
(i) the reason for taking the sample;
(ii) the power by virtue of which it is taken; and
(iii) in a case where the authorisation of an officer is required for the exercise of the power, the fact that the authorisation has been given; and
(b) those matters shall be recorded as soon as practicable after the sample is taken.

(7) The reason referred to in subsection (6)(a)(i) above must include, except in a case where the non-intimate sample is taken under subsection (3B) or (3E) above, a statement of the nature of the offence in which it is suspected that the person has been involved.

...

(8B) If a non-intimate sample is taken from a person at a police station, whether with or without the appropriate consent—
(a) before the sample is taken, an officer shall inform him that it may be the subject of a speculative search; and
(b) the fact that the person has been informed of this possibility shall be recorded as soon as practicable after the sample has been taken.

(9) If a non-intimate sample is taken from a person detained at a police station, the matters required to be recorded by subsection (6) or (8B) above shall be recorded in his custody record.

(9ZA) The power to take a non-intimate sample from a person without the appropriate consent shall be exercisable by any constable.

(9A) Subsection (3B) above shall not apply to
(a) any person convicted before 10th April 1995 unless he is a person to whom section 1 of the Criminal Evidence (Amendment) Act 1997 applies (persons imprisoned or detained by virtue of pre-existing conviction for sexual offence etc.); or
(b) a person given a caution before 10th April 1995.

(10) Nothing in this section applies to a person arrested or detained under the terrorism provisions or detained under Part 1 of Schedule 3 to the Counter-Terrorism and Border Security Act 2019.

(11) Nothing in this section applies to a person arrested under an extradition arrest power.

For the meanings of 'appropriate consent' and 'recordable offence', see **D1.106**, and for 'police detention' see **D1.40**. A 'qualifying offence' for the purpose of s. 63(3E) is defined in s. 65A, and includes certain violent, sexual or terrorist offences, or inchoate versions thereof. For skin impressions consisting of ear-prints see *Kempster* [2008] EWCA Crim 975, [2008] 2 Cr App R 19 (256), and **F19.37**.

Speculative Searches

D1.113 Under the PACE 1984, s. 63A, fingerprints, impressions of footwear, samples or the information derived from samples may be used for the purpose of speculative searches as prescribed in that section.

Police and Criminal Evidence Act 1984, s. 63A

(1) Where a person has been arrested on suspicion of being involved in a recordable offence or has been charged with such an offence or has been informed that he will be reported for such an offence, fingerprints, impressions of footwear or samples or the information derived from samples taken under any power conferred by this Part of this Act from the person may be checked against—

(a) other fingerprints, impressions of footwear or samples to which the person seeking to check has access and which are held by or on behalf of any one or more relevant law-enforcement authorities or which are held in connection with or as a result of an investigation of an offence;

(b) information derived from other samples if the information is contained in records to which the person seeking to check has access and which are held as mentioned in paragraph (a) above.

(1ZA) Fingerprints taken by virtue of section 61(6A) above may be checked against other fingerprints to which the person seeking to check has access and which are held by or on behalf of any one or more relevant law-enforcement authorities or which are held in connection with or as a result of an investigation of an offence.

(1A) In subsection (1) and (1ZA) above 'relevant law-enforcement authority' means–

(a) a police force;

(b) the National Crime Agency;

(d) a public authority (not falling within paragraphs (a) to (c)) with functions in any part of the British Islands which consist of or include the investigation of crimes or the charging of offenders;

(e) any person with functions in any country or territory outside the United Kingdom which–

(i) correspond to those of a police force; or

(ii) otherwise consist of or include the investigation of conduct contrary to the law of that country or territory, or the apprehension of persons guilty of such conduct;

(f) any person with functions under any international agreement which consist of or include the investigation of conduct which is–

(i) unlawful under the law of one or more places,

(ii) prohibited by such an agreement, or

(iii) contrary to international law, or the apprehension of persons guilty of such conduct.

(1B) The reference in subsection (1A) above to a police force is a reference to any of the following–...

(1C) Where–

(a) fingerprints, impressions of footwear or samples have been taken from any person in connection with the investigation of an offence but otherwise than in circumstances to which subsection (1) above applies, and

(b) that person has given his consent in writing to the use in a speculative search of the fingerprints, of the impressions of footwear or of the samples and of information derived from them, the fingerprints or impressions of footwear or, as the case may be, those samples and that information may be checked against any of the fingerprints, impressions of footwear, samples or information mentioned in paragraph (a) or (b) of that subsection.

(1D) A consent given for the purposes of subsection (1C) above shall not be capable of being withdrawn.

(1E) Where fingerprints or samples have been taken from any person under section 61(6) or 63(3B) above (persons convicted etc), the fingerprints or samples, or information derived from the samples, may be checked against any of the fingerprints, samples or information mentioned in subsection (1)(a) or (b) above.

(1F) Where fingerprints or samples have been taken from any person under section 61(6D), 62(2A) or 63(3E) above (offences outside England and Wales etc), the fingerprints or samples, or information derived from the samples, may be checked against any of the fingerprints, samples or information mentioned in subsection (1)(a) or (b) above.

...

For the meaning of 'recordable offence', see **D1.106**.

Powers to Require Attendance at Police Station

The PACE 1984, s. 63A(4) and sch. 2A, contain powers to require attendance at a police station for the purpose of taking fingerprints and samples. **D1.114**

Police and Criminal Evidence Act 1984, sch. 2A **D1.115**

PART I

FINGERPRINTING

Persons arrested and released

1.—(1) A constable may require a person to attend a police station for the purpose of taking his fingerprints under section 61(5A).

(2) The power under sub-paragraph (1) above may not be exercised in a case falling within section 61(5A)(b)(i) (fingerprints taken on previous occasion insufficient etc.) after the end of the period of six months beginning with the day on which the appropriate officer was informed that section 61(3A)(a) or (b) applied.

(3) In sub-paragraph (2) above 'appropriate officer' means the officer investigating the offence for which the person was arrested.

(4) The power under sub-paragraph (1) above may not be exercised in a case falling within section 61(5A)(b)(ii) (fingerprints destroyed where investigation interrupted) after the end of the period of six months beginning with the day on which the investigation was resumed.

Persons charged etc

2.—(1) A constable may require a person to attend a police station for the purpose of taking his fingerprints under section 61(5B).

(2) The power under sub-paragraph (1) above may not be exercised after the end of the period of six months beginning with—

(a) in a case falling within section 61(5B)(a) (fingerprints not taken previously), the day on which the person was charged or informed that he would be reported, or

(b) in a case falling within section 61(5B)(b)(i) (fingerprints taken on previous occasion insufficient etc.), the day on which the appropriate officer was informed that section 61(3A)(a) or (b) applied, or

(c) in a case falling within section 61(5B)(b)(ii) (fingerprints destroyed where investigation interrupted), the day on which the investigation was resumed.

(3) In sub-paragraph (2)(b) above 'appropriate officer' means the officer investigating the offence for which the person was charged or informed that he would be reported.

Persons convicted etc. of an offence in England and Wales

3.—(1) A constable may require a person to attend a police station for the purpose of taking his fingerprints under section 61(6).

(2) Where the condition in section 61(6ZA)(a) is satisfied (fingerprints not taken previously), the power under sub-paragraph (1) above may not be exercised after the end of the period of two years beginning with—

(a) the day on which the person was convicted or cautioned or

(b) if later, the day on which this schedule comes into force.

(3) Where the condition in section 61(6ZA)(b) is satisfied (fingerprints taken on previous occasion insufficient etc.), the power under sub-paragraph (1) above may not be exercised after the end of the period of two years beginning with—

(a) the day on which an appropriate officer was informed that section 61(3A)(a) or (b) applied, or

(b) if later, the day on which this Schedule comes into force.

(4) In sub-paragraph (3)(a) above 'appropriate officer' means an officer of the police force which investigated the offence in question.

(5) Sub-paragraphs (2) and (3) above do not apply where the offence is a qualifying offence (whether or not it was such an offence at the time of the conviction or caution).

4. [Repealed.]

Persons convicted etc. of an offence outside England and Wales

5. A constable may require a person to attend a police station for the purpose of taking his fingerprints under section 61(6D).

Multiple attendance

6.—(1) Where a person's fingerprints have been taken under section 61 on two occasions in relation to any offence, he may not under this schedule be required to attend a police station to have his fingerprints taken under that section in relation to that offence on a subsequent occasion without the authorisation of an officer of at least the rank of inspector.

(2) Where an authorisation is given under sub-paragraph (1) above—

(a) the fact of the authorisation, and

(b) the reasons for giving it,

shall be recorded as soon as practicable after it has been given.

PART 2

INTIMATE SAMPLES

Persons suspected to be involved in an offence

7. A constable may require a person to attend a police station for the purpose of taking an intimate sample from him under section 62(1A) if, in the course of the investigation of an offence, two or more non-intimate samples suitable for the same means of analysis have been taken from him but have proved insufficient.

Persons convicted etc. of an offence outside England and Wales

8. A constable may require a person to attend a police station for the purpose of taking a sample from him under section 62(2A) if two or more non-intimate samples suitable for the same means of analysis have been taken from him under section 63(3E) but have proved insufficient.

PART 3

NON-INTIMATE SAMPLES

Persons arrested and released

9.—(1) A constable may require a person to attend a police station for the purpose of taking a non-intimate sample from him under section 63(3ZA).

(2) The power under sub-paragraph (1) above may not be exercised in a case falling within section 63(3ZA)(b)(i) or (ii) (sample taken on a previous occasion not suitable etc.) after the end of the period of six months beginning with the day on which the appropriate officer was informed of the matters specified in section 63(3ZA)(b)(i) or (ii).

(3) In sub-paragraph (2) above, 'appropriate officer' means the officer investigating the offence for which the person was arrested.

(4) The power under sub-paragraph (1) above may not be exercised in a case falling within section 63(3ZA)(b)(iii) (sample, and any DNA profile, destroyed where investigation interrupted) after the end of the period of six months beginning with the day on which the investigation was resumed.

Persons charged etc.

10.—(1) A constable may require a person to attend a police station for the purpose of taking a non-intimate sample from him under section 63(3A).

(2) The power under sub-paragraph (1) above may not be exercised in a case falling within section 63(3A)(a) (sample not taken previously) after the end of the period of six months beginning with the day on which he was charged or informed that he would be reported.

(3) The power under sub-paragraph (1) above may not be exercised in a case falling within section 63(3A)(b)(i) or (ii) (sample taken on a previous occasion not suitable etc.) after the end of the period of six months beginning with the day on which the appropriate officer was informed of the matters specified in section 63(3A)(b)(i) or (ii).

(4) In sub-paragraph (3) above 'appropriate officer' means the officer investigating the offence for which the person was charged or informed that he would be reported.

(5) The power under sub-paragraph (1) above may not be exercised in a case falling within section 63(3A)(b)(iii) (sample, and any DNA profile, destroyed where investigation interrupted) after the end of the period of six months beginning with the day on which the investigation was resumed.

Persons convicted etc. of an offence in England and Wales

11.—(1) A constable may require a person to attend a police station for the purpose of taking a non-intimate sample from him under section 63(3B).

(2) Where the condition in section 63(3BA)(a) is satisfied (sample not taken previously), the power under sub-paragraph (1) above may not be exercised after the end of the period of two years beginning with—

(a) the day on which the person was convicted or cautioned, or

(b) if later, the day on which this schedule comes into force.

(3) Where the condition in section 63(3BA)(b) is satisfied (sample taken on a previous occasion not suitable etc.), the power under sub-paragraph (1) above may not be exercised after the end of the period of two years beginning with—
   (a) the day on which an appropriate officer was informed of the matters specified in section 63(3BA)(b)(i) or (ii), or
   (b) if later, the day on which this schedule comes into force.
(4) In sub-paragraph (3)(a) above 'appropriate officer' means an officer of the police force which investigated the offence in question.
(5) Sub-paragraphs (2) and (3) above do not apply where—
   (a) the offence is a qualifying offence (whether or not it was such an offence at the time of the conviction or caution), or
   (b) he was convicted before 10th April 1995 and is a person to whom section 1 of the Criminal Evidence (Amendment) Act 1997 applies.

12. [Repealed.]

Persons convicted etc. of an offence outside England and Wales

13. A constable may require a person to attend a police station for the purpose of taking a non-intimate sample from him under section 63(3E).

Multiple exercise of power

14.—(1) Where a non-intimate sample has been taken from a person under section 63 on two occasions in relation to any offence, he may not under this schedule be required to attend a police station to have another such sample taken from him under that section in relation to that offence on a subsequent occasion without the authorisation of an officer of at least the rank of inspector.
(2) Where an authorisation is given under sub-paragraph (1) above—
   (a) the fact of the authorisation, and
   (b) the reasons for giving it, shall be recorded as soon as practicable after it has been given.

Part 4

General and Supplementary

Requirement to have power to take fingerprints or sample

15. A power conferred by this schedule to require a person to attend a police station for the purposes of taking fingerprints or a sample under any provision of this Act may be exercised only in a case where the fingerprints or sample may be taken from the person under that provision (and, in particular, if any necessary authorisation for taking the fingerprints or sample under that provision has been obtained).

Date and time of attendance

16.—(1) A requirement under this schedule—
   (a) shall give the person a period of at least seven days within which he must attend the police station; and
   (b) may direct him so to attend at a specified time of day or between specified times of day.
(2) In specifying a period or time or times of day for the purposes of sub-paragraph (1) above, the constable shall consider whether the fingerprints or sample could reasonably be taken at a time when the person is for any other reason required to attend the police station.
(3) A requirement under this schedule may specify a period shorter than seven days if—
   (a) there is an urgent need for the fingerprints or sample for the purposes of the investigation of an offence; and
   (b) the shorter period is authorised by an officer of at least the rank of inspector.
(4) Where an authorisation is given under sub-paragraph (3)(b) above—
   (a) the fact of the authorisation, and
   (b) the reasons for giving it, shall be recorded as soon as practicable after it has been given.
(5) If the constable giving a requirement under this Schedule and the person to whom it is given so agree, it may be varied so as to specify any period within which, or date or time at which, the person must attend; but a variation shall not have effect unless confirmed by the constable in writing.

Enforcement

17. A constable may arrest without warrant a person who has failed to comply with a requirement under this schedule.

D1.116 Where a person is required under sch. 2A to attend a police station for the purpose of having fingerprints or samples taken, the person must be given be given at least seven days' notice unless there is an urgent need for them to be taken for the purposes of an investigation (Code D, annex G). A non-intimate sample may be taken under s. 63(3B) only if it is authorised by an officer of at least the rank of inspector, and a requirement to attend in order to provide such a sample under sch. 2A, para. 11, is unlawful if the demand was made before authorisation was given (*R (R) v A Chief Constable* [2013] EWHC 2864 (Admin), [2014] 1 Cr App R 16 (222)). A person arrested under sch. 2A, para. 17, and taken to a police station is not in police detention (see **D1.40**). Paragraph 17 permits a constable to arrest a person for failing to attend a police station for the purpose of taking an intimate sample under sch. 2A, paras. 7 or 8, despite the fact that such a sample can only be taken with appropriate consent (see **D1.106**); although refusal to consent could result in inferences under s. 62(10).

Retention or Destruction of Biometric Data

D1.117 Provisions governing the retention and destruction of fingerprints, footwear impressions, and samples, and information derived from samples, are set out in the PACE 1984, ss. 63D to 63U, as amended by the PCA 2017, s. 70. See further the National Police Chiefs' Council's *Record Deletion Guidance* (tinyurl.com/kxy7w5b). For the rules governing orders for the retention of fingerprints and other biometric data, see CrimPR 47.42 to 47.45 (see Supplement, **R47.42** ***et seq.***). For the use in evidence of biometric data, see **F19.27** ***et seq.***

POWERS TO PHOTOGRAPH SUSPECTS

D1.118 Powers to take, retain and use photographs are governed by the PACE 1984, s. 64A(1), which provides that a person detained at a police station (see **D1.106**) may be photographed with the appropriate consent (see **D1.106**), or without such consent if it is withheld or it is not practicable to obtain it. Section 64A(1A) gives power to the police to photograph a person other than at a police station where that person has been: (a) arrested by a constable; (b) taken into custody by a constable after being arrested by a person other than a constable; (c) made the subject of a requirement to wait with a community support officer under the Police Reform Act 2002, sch. 4, para. 2(3) or (3B); (d) been given a direction by a constable under the ABCPA 2014, s. 35 (directions excluding a person from an area); or (e) been given a notice under various provisions set out in s. 64A(1B)(d) to (g) which relate to penalty notices and fixed penalty offences. Again, the power may be exercised with appropriate consent or without it if it is withheld or it is not practicable to obtain it (s. 64A(1A)). References to taking a photograph include references to using any process by means of which a visual image may be produced, and include a moving image (s. 64A(6) and (6A)). The powers to take photographs of persons detained in a police station or elsewhere are also governed by Code D, paras. 5.12 to 5.18, and powers to photograph persons at a police station but who are not detained (i.e. those who are voluntarily at a police station) are set out in paras. 5.19 to 5.24. Taking and retaining photographs of persons who have not been arrested may amount to a breach of the ECHR, Article 8 (*Mengesha v Metropolitan Police Commissioner* [2013] EWHC 1695 (Admin)).

D1.119 The particular relevance of the statutory power to take photographs is that the police may use force in order to take them. In addition to their general powers to use force under the PACE 1984, s. 117 (see **D1.7**), s. 64A(2) provides that for the purpose of taking a photograph the police may require the removal of any item or substance worn on or over the whole or any part of the head or face of the person, and may remove the item or substance if the requirement is not complied with. Force may not be used in connection with taking the photograph of a person who is voluntarily at a police station (Code D, para. 5.21).

A photograph taken under s. 64A may be used by, or disclosed to, any person for any purpose related to the prevention or detection of crime, the investigation of an offence, or the conduct of a prosecution, or to the enforcement of any sentence (s. 64A(4)(a)). After being so used or disclosed, the photograph may be retained but may not be used or disclosed except for a purpose so related (s. 64A(4)(b)). In *R (RMC and FJ) v Metropolitan Police Commissioner* [2012] EWHC 1681 (Admin), [2012] 1 WLR 3007, the Divisional Court concluded that the law and guidance then in force (the National Policing Improvement Agency Code of Practice and Guidance on the Management of Police Information; see now College of Policing Authorised Professional Practice, *Information Management*) failed to strike a fair balance between competing public and private interests or meet the requirements of proportionality, and was objectionable for the same reasons as those that led to the judgment of the ECtHR in *S v United Kingdom* (2009) 48 EHRR 50 (1169). In particular, no adequate distinction was drawn between those convicted and those who were not charged or not convicted.

The search or examination of a suspect with a view to finding and, if necessary, photographing, any distinguishing marks or injuries is governed by the PACE 1984, s. 54A, and Code D, paras. 5.1 to 5.11 (see **D1.98**).

DRUG TESTING FOR CLASS A DRUGS

The power to test for Class A drugs is governed by the PACE 1984, s. 63B, supplemented by s. 63C, and by Code C, section 17. **D1.120**

Where a person is in police detention (see **D1.40**), a sample of urine or a non-intimate sample may be taken for the purpose of ascertaining whether the person has any specified Class A drug in his or her body provided that the person has been brought before a custody officer (s. 63B(5D)) and the following conditions are satisfied:

(a) either the arrest condition or the charge condition is met;
(b) both the age condition and the request condition are met; and
(c) the notification condition is met in relation to the arrest condition, the charge condition or the age condition (as relevant) (s. 63B(1)(a) to (c)).

Arrest and Charge Conditions

The 'arrest condition' is satisfied if the suspect has been arrested for, but not charged with, a trigger offence or any offence where an inspector or above, having reasonable grounds for suspecting that the misuse by that person of any specified Class A drug caused or contributed to the offence, authorises a sample to be taken (PACE 1984, s. 63B(1A)). The 'charge condition' is satisfied if the suspect has been charged with a trigger offence or any offence where an inspector or above, having reasonable grounds for suspecting that the misuse by that person of any specified Class A drug caused or contributed to the offence, authorises a sample to be taken (s. 63B(2)). If a sample is taken on the basis that the arrest condition was satisfied, no further sample can be taken under s. 63B during the same continuous period of detention unless the suspect remains in police detention in respect of another offence in respect of which the arrest condition is satisfied (s. 63B(5B) and (5C); Code C, para. 17.9). A 'specified' Class A drug has the same meaning as in the Criminal Justice and Court Services Act 2000, Part III. The term 'trigger offence' is defined in sch. 6 of the 2000 Act, and the offences are conveniently set out in Code C, Note for Guidance 17E (see **appendix 1**). **D1.121**

Age and Request Conditions

Where the arrest condition is met, the 'age condition' is that the person has attained the age of 18; where the charge condition is met, the 'age condition' is that the person has attained the **D1.122** age of 14 (PACE 1984, s. 63B(3)). The 'request condition' is simply that a police officer has requested the suspect to give the sample (s. 63B(4)). Before requesting a sample the suspect must be warned that failure without good cause to provide the sample requested renders the suspect liable to prosecution (s. 63B(5); Code C, Note for Guidance 17A). The suspect must also be told the purpose of taking the sample, that authorisation has been given (where required), and of the right to have someone informed of the arrest, to obtain legal advice and to consult the Codes of Practice (Code C, para. 17.6). Where the suspect is a child or young person, the making of the request, the warning that refusal may amount to an offence, and the taking of a sample must be in the presence of an appropriate adult (s. 63B(5A); Code C, para. 17.7).

Notification Condition

D1.123 The 'notification condition' is that the relevant chief officer has been notified by the Secretary of State that appropriate arrangements have been made for the police area as a whole, or for the particular police station in which the suspect is in police detention (PACE 1984, s. 63B(4A)). All police forces are permitted to introduce drug-testing, although not all forces have done so.

The authorisation and grounds for suspicion (where authorisation is required), the warning as to the consequences of refusal, and the time at which the sample is given, must be recorded in the custody record (s. 63C(3) and (4); Code C, para. 17.2).

Failure without good cause to provide a sample is an offence punishable, on summary conviction, with up to three months' imprisonment and/or a fine not exceeding level 4 (ss. 63B(8) and 63C(1)). If the suspect does refuse to provide a sample, the police cannot use force to obtain one (Code C, para. 17.14).

Detention for the Purposes of Drug-testing

D1.124 Where a person has been arrested for a relevant offence (see **D1.121**), he or she may be detained for up to 24 hours from the relevant time (see **D1.68**) in order for a sample to be taken even though the custody officer would otherwise have decided that the suspect should be released on bail under the PACE 1984, s. 37(2) (bail without charge), s. 37(7)(a)(i) (release without charge and on bail with a view to the CPS making the charge decision), or s. 37(7)(b) (release without charge and on bail but not for that purpose) (s. 37(8A) and (8B); Code C, para. 17.10). Where the arrest condition (but not the charge condition) is satisfied in respect of one offence (offence 1) and the suspect's release would be required before a sample could be taken but for continued detention in respect of an offence that does not satisfy the arrest condition (offence 2), the suspect may have a sample taken while in continued detention provided that it is taken within 24 hours of the suspect's arrest for offence 1 (s. 63B(5C); Code C, para. 17.10). Thus, if a person is charged with an offence that did satisfy the arrest condition, and a sample could not be taken before charging, but the person continues to be detained in respect of an offence that does not satisfy the arrest condition, a sample may be taken during that period of further detention, provided that it is taken within 24 hours of the arrest for the first offence. Where a sample may be taken from a person under s. 63B, but the person is charged before a sample is taken and the custody officer would otherwise release the person on bail under s. 38, the custody officer may authorise detention for up to six hours from the time of charge in order for a sample to be taken (s. 38(1)(a)(iiia) and (2); Code C, para. 17.10).

Consequences of a Positive Drug Test

D1.125 Where a suspect aged 18 years or older has tested positive for a specified Class A drug under the PACE 1984, s. 63B, the police may, before the suspect is released, impose a requirement that the suspect attend an initial assessment of his or her drug misuse and remain for the duration of the assessment. Where the suspect is tested prior to charge, the requirement can be imposed even if the suspect is not subsequently charged with an offence. Failure to attend or to remain at the assessment is an offence carrying imprisonment up to three months and/or a fine not exceeding level 4 (Drugs Act 2005, s. 12(3) and (4); Code C, para. 17.17). When such a requirement is imposed the suspect must be told of the time and place for the assessment and be warned that failure without good cause to attend and to remain renders the suspect liable for prosecution (Code C, para. 17.18). The suspect must also be given a written notice containing this information (para. 17.19) and the process must be entered in the custody record (para. 17.20). There are also provisions (in police stations where the chief officer has been notified by the Secretary of State that follow-up assessment arrangements are available) to require a person who is required to attend an initial assessment also to attend a follow-up assessment, and there are similar provisions regarding enforcement (Drugs Act 2005, ss. 10 to 12, and Code C, paras. 17.17 to 17.20).

A sample taken under s. 63B may be disclosed only for the purposes set out in s. 63B(7). Although it must be retained until the person's first appearance at court (Code C, para. 17.16(b)), it cannot be used for the purpose of prosecuting for an offence, other than those offences mentioned in s. 63B(7). The purposes are: **D1.126**

(a) for the purpose of informing a decision as to bail, whether by the police or by a court (s. 63B(7)(a));
(b) for the purpose of informing a decision about the imposition of a conditional caution (s. 63B(7)(aa));
(c) for the purpose of informing any decision about the supervision of the person in police detention, in custody or on bail (s. 63B(7)(b));
(d) following conviction, for the purpose of informing any decision about sentence, and any decision about supervision or release (s. 63B(7)(c));
(e) for the purpose of a drugs assessment which the suspect is required to attend by the police by virtue of the Drugs Act 2005, s. 9(2) (initial assessment) or s. 10(2) (follow-up assessment) (s. 63B(7)(ca));
(f) for the purposes of a prosecution under the Drugs Act 2005, s. 12(3) (for failure to attend or remain at an initial assessment), or s. 24(3) (for failure to attend or remain at a follow-up assessment) (s. 63B(7)(cb));
(g) for the purpose of ensuring that appropriate advice and treatment is made available to the person concerned (s. 63B(7)(d)).

VISUAL IDENTIFICATION AND RECOGNITION PROCEDURES

Visual identification and recognition procedures are governed by PACE Code D (see **D1.1**). Code D distinguishes between identification of a suspect by an eye-witness (part 3(A)), recognition by controlled showing of films, photographs and images (part 3(B)), and recognition by uncontrolled viewing of films, photographs and images (part 3(C)), and sets out different procedures to be followed in respect of each section. The most recent revision of Code D, which introduced the distinction between parts 3(B) and 3(C), takes account of the decisions in a number of cases, including *Lariba* [2015] EWCA Crim 478 and *Deakin* [2012] EWCA Crim 2637. For the evidential implications of failure by the police to comply with relevant identification procedures, see **F19.4**. It has been held that Code D was not designed to apply to situations in which the police seek to connect a suspect with events that occurred many years previously, when the suspect's appearance was markedly different (*Folan* [2003] EWCA Crim 908). Code D makes no reference to identification procedures after charge, although it was implied in *Joseph* [1994] Crim LR 48 that this is permissible. **D1.127**

Which Part Applies?

D1.128 The procedures in Code D, part 3(A) (identification of a suspect by an eye-witness), apply when an eye-witness has seen a person committing a crime or in any other circumstances which tend to prove or disprove the involvement of the person seen in the crime (Code D, para. 3.0). This part of the code sets out the procedures to be followed to test the ability of that eye-witness to identify a person suspected of involvement in the offence as the person seen on the previous occasion. The procedures in Code D, part 3(B) (recognition by controlled showing of films, photographs and images), are for the purpose of testing whether a person recognises anyone in an image, but must not be used in respect of eye-witnesses (Code D, para. 3.34). The procedures in Code D, part 3(C) (recognition by uncontrolled viewing of films, photographs and images), are for the purpose of identifying and tracing suspects, and may involve both eye-witnesses and/or others who, by definition, are not known to the police. Note for Guidance 3AA states that the eye-witness identification procedures in part 3(A) should not be used to test whether a witness can recognise a person as someone known but, rather confusingly, states that in such cases the procedures in part 3(B) or (C) should be used. However, as noted above, the part 3(B) procedure cannot be used in respect of eye-witnesses (although an eye-witness could be shown visual images by virtue of para. 3.3 and annex E). It is clear that part 3(A) applies where an eye-witness known to the police may be able to identify the person seen committing a crime, and that under part 3(C) images may be seen by an eye-witness who recognises a person in the image, and who may then contact the police as a result. What is not so clear is which part applies where an eye-witness known to the police may, or thinks that he or she may, recognise the person seen committing the offence.

D1.129 The case law on the distinction between identification and recognition (and thus on the question of whether an identification procedure should be conducted) has not always been consistent, although all were decided in the context of previous versions of Code D. If a witness clearly knows the person suspected of committing a crime and is able to name that person, an identification procedure would not be mandatory (*H v DPP* [2003] EWHC 133 (Admin)). However, if the recognition is less certain, and particularly if the suspect disputes the purported recognition, the courts have held that an identification procedure should be held. See, e.g., *Fergus* [1992] Crim LR 363, where the witness had only seen the suspect once before and had been told his name by a third party (see also *Byrne* [2004] EWCA Crim 979; and cf. *France* [2012] UKPC 28). Further, it has been held that an identification procedure should have been held, even though the witness named the suspect, where the latter disputed the purported recognition (*Conway* (1990) 91 Cr App R 143; *Harris* [2003] EWCA Crim 174).

Identification of a Suspect by an Eye-witness under Code D, part 3(A)

D1.130 In all potential identification cases, Code D, para. 3.1, requires a record to be made of the description of the 'suspect' (meaning the person allegedly seen at the scene of the crime etc.) as first given by the witness. This description must, where practicable, be disclosed to the 'suspect' (in this case, meaning the person who is suspected of committing the offence) or the suspect's solicitor before any identification procedures are undertaken. The procedure to be followed depends upon whether or not there is a 'known' suspect. References to a suspect being 'known' mean there is sufficient information known to the police to establish that there are reasonable grounds to suspect a particular person of involvement in the offence (Code D, para. 3.1A(a)). In *Preddie* [2011] EWCA Crim 312 a street identification of suspects who had already been arrested on the basis that they fitted the description given by the witness was held to be a breach of Code D.

D1.131 **Procedures where the Suspect is Not Known** Where a suspect's identity is not known, Code D, paras. 3.2 and 3.3, allow witnesses to be taken to a particular neighbourhood or place to see whether they can identify the person they saw in relation to the alleged crime. Paragraph 3.2 states that while the rules governing formal identification procedures do not apply directly, the principles should as far as practicable be followed, and provides examples of the appropriate procedures.

The showing of photographs must be carried out in accordance with Code D, annex E (Code D, para. 3.3). Only one eye-witness at a time may be shown photographs, and must be shown at least 12 photographs at a time which should, as far as possible, all be of a similar type. The eye-witness must be told that a photograph of the person seen may not be among them, and must not be prompted or guided in any way. If an eye-witness makes a positive identification from photographs then, unless the person identified can be eliminated from the inquiry, no further witnesses may be shown photographs; instead, a video identification or parade etc. should be arranged unless there is no dispute about the suspect's identification. Similarly, if the use of other visual images points to a known suspect who can be asked to participate in an identification procedure, the likeness must not then be shown to other witnesses (annex E, paras. 6 and 8).

Procedures where the Suspect is Known Where a suspect is 'known' (see **D1.130**), the procedure to be followed depends upon whether the suspect is 'available'. A suspect is 'available' if he or she is immediately available or will be within a reasonably short time and is willing to take an effective part in a video identification, identification parade or group identification which it is practicable to arrange (Code D, para. 3.1A(b)). A suspect may be available even if not under arrest provided he or she is likely to be arrested, or will otherwise be available (e.g., by agreeing to attend a video identification voluntarily) in the near future. If a suspect who is 'known' refuses the identification procedure which is proposed by the police, the suspect (or solicitor or appropriate adult) may make representations as to why another procedure should be used. The identification officer (see **D1.136**) 'shall, if appropriate,' arrange for the suspect to be offered a suitable and practicable alternative. The words 'if appropriate' indicate that the police need not give in to objections that appear to be merely obstructive, misguided or petulant. If for any reason the identification officer decides that it is not suitable and practicable to offer an alternative procedure, the reasons for that decision must be recorded (para. 3.15). If the consent of the suspect cannot be obtained he or she may, in effect, be treated as not being available. **D1.132**

If a suspect is known but not available, the identification officer may make arrangements for a video identification or a group identification if this is practicable (para. 3.21). If not practicable, the identification officer may make arrangements for a confrontation by the witness (para. 3.23). Force may not be used in order to facilitate an identification procedure where the suspect attempts to hide his face (*Jones* (1999) *The Times*, 26 March 1999, and see Code D, annex D, para. 3) but, where there are reasonable grounds to suspect that, if forewarned, the suspect would take steps to avoid being identified, para. 3.20 permits the identification officer to arrange for images to be obtained for use in a video identification procedure before the usual information and notice is given to the suspect under paras. 3.17 and 3.18. **D1.133**

If a suspect is known and available, Code D, para. 3.4, provides that a video identification, identification parade or group identification 'may' be used (para. 3.4). However, this should be read subject to para 3.12, which sets out the circumstances in which such a procedure must be held, as follows:

(a) where an eye-witness has identified or purported to have identified a suspect, or there is a witness who expresses an ability to identify the suspect, or where there is a reasonable chance of the witness being able to do so; and
(b) the eye-witness has not been given an opportunity to identify the suspect in a video or group identification or identification parade; and
(c) the suspect disputes being the person the witness claims to have seen.

If these conditions are satisfied, an identification procedure must be held unless it is not practicable or it would serve no useful purpose in proving or disproving whether the suspect was involved in committing the offence.

It was held in *Bates v CPS* [2015] EWHC 2346 (Admin) that a police officer who, on stopping a driver for a suspected offence, took down the personal details provided by that person and subsequently reported them, was not an eye-witness for the purpose of para. 3.12(a).

An identification procedure may also be held if the officer in charge of the investigation considers that this would be useful (para. 3.13).

The term 'suspect' in para. 3.12 is, unfortunately, used to convey two different meanings: in (a) above it refers to the person that the witness says was seen committing the crime etc.; in (c) above it refers to the person who is now under arrest or is otherwise suspected of having committed the offence, and who is asked to participate in the identification procedure.

D1.134 Whether a witness expresses an ability to identify the suspect or there is a reasonable chance of the witness being able to do so is, of course, a matter of fact, but it is suggested that the police should err on the side of caution.

> If an eyewitness of a criminal incident makes plain to the police that he cannot identify the culprit, it will very probably be futile to invite that witness to attend an identification [procedure]. If an eyewitness may be able to identify clothing worn by a culprit, but not the culprit himself, it will probably be futile to mount an identification [procedure] rather than simply inviting the witness to identify the clothing. If a case is one of pure recognition of someone well known to the eyewitness, it may again be futile to hold an identification [procedure]. But save in cases such as these, or other exceptional circumstances, the effect of [Code D] is clear: if (a) the police have sufficient information to justify the arrest of a particular person for suspected involvement in an offence, and (b) an eyewitness has identified or may be able to identify that person, and (c) the suspect disputes his identification as a person involved in the commission of that offence, an identification [procedure] must be held. … (*Forbes* [2001] 1 AC 473 at p. 486, per Lord Bingham)

Code D was revised after the decision in *Forbes* [2001] 1 AC 473 so that an identification procedure does not have to be held if it would serve no useful purpose. However, it was held in *Callie* [2009] EWCA Crim 283 that this does not permit the police to carry out a proportionality exercise. The question is whether an identification procedure might produce relevant evidence. Thus, for example, the fact that one witness has made a positive identification does not mean that inviting other witnesses to view an identification procedure would serve no useful purpose (*Gojra* [2010] EWCA Crim 1939).

Whether the suspect disputes being the person the witness claims to have seen should normally be straightforward. It would include circumstances where the suspect admits being at the scene but denies being involved in the offence (*Hope* [1994] Crim LR 118; *K* [2003] EWHC 351 (QB)). However, it does not include circumstances where the suspect merely disagrees with his or her level of involvement in an alleged offence.

D1.135 Given the availability of the video identification procedure, cases where an identification procedure is not practicable should be relatively rare. A procedure may be impracticable if the suspect has distinctive features that cannot be appropriately disguised, although it is permissible for the police to modify video images, or to use other means of modifying the appearance of the suspect and/or the comparators used in the identification procedure, provided care is taken (*Martin* [2002] EWCA Crim 251; *Pecco* [2010] EWCA Crim 972; and see Code D, annex A, paras. 2A to 2C). The police must make their decision regarding practicability on reasonable grounds (*Britton* [1989] Crim LR 144).

The question of whether an identification procedure would serve a useful purpose has arisen in cases where there has previously been a positive identification, and also where the circumstances are on the cusp of recognition. In *Popat (No. 2)* [2000] Crim LR 54, decided under a former version of Code D, it was held that an identification parade was not necessary where there had been a 'full and satisfactory informal identification of the suspect by the witness' (although note that the circumstances where an 'informal' identification can be conducted are limited to where the suspect is not 'known': see **D1.130**). In *Harris* [2003] EWCA Crim 174 it was held that a formal identification procedure would have served a useful purpose where a purported recognition, based upon the accused having attended the same school as the witnesses two years previously, was disputed by the accused.

Types and Conduct of Identification Procedures

Identification Officer and Investigating Officers The arrangements for, and conduct of, identification procedures under Code D are the responsibility of the 'identification officer', an officer not below the rank of inspector who is not otherwise involved with the investigation (Code D, para. 3.11). However, Code D permits substantial delegation of this officer's duties (and those of the custody officer: see **D1.44**) to other officers or to civilian police employees (para. 2.21). Certain duties may also be performed by the custody officer, in respect of the 'notice to suspect' requirements under paras. 3.17 to 3.19, where the identification procedure is to be carried out at a later date, and an inspector is not available to act as identification officer. No officer or other person involved in the investigation may take part in the formal identification procedures, except as specifically provided by Code D, or act as the identification officer (para. 3.11). In particular, an officer involved in the investigation must not take witnesses to the identification procedure (*Gall* (1990) 90 Cr App R 64; *Ryan* [1992] Crim LR 187), although it appears that the officer is permitted to take the suspect to the procedure (*Jones* [1992] Crim LR 365, and see **D1.139**). **D1.136**

Choice of Identification Procedure Code D provides for four possible procedures by which a known suspect may be placed before witnesses in order to establish if they can identify the suspect. Priority is given to video identification, but an identification parade may be offered if a video identification is not practicable or if a parade is both practicable and more suitable than a video identification. The identification officer and the officer in charge of the investigation must consult with each other to determine which procedure is to be offered (para. 3.14). A group identification may be offered initially only if the officer in charge of the investigation considers it is more suitable than either a video identification or an identification parade and the identification officer considers it is practicable to arrange (para. 3.16). Confrontation remains the last resort, to be used only if all other options (including covertly recorded video, etc.) are impracticable (para. 3.23). Whichever procedure is adopted, it must be carried out in accordance with the appropriate annex to Code D. **D1.137**

Video Identification Code D, annex A, sets out the procedures to be followed in a video identification. A video identification must ordinarily be conducted with the suspect's consent, but may in certain circumstances be conducted covertly (Code D, paras. 3.21 and 3.22, and Note for Guidance 3D). Annex A, paras. 2A to 2C, set out the procedures to be followed if the suspect has unusual physical features, and paras. 7 to 9 deal with the opportunities to be given to the suspect or the suspect's solicitor to be involved in the procedure. **D1.138**

Identification Parades Code D, annex B, sets out the procedures to be followed in holding an identification parade, and includes a requirement that a video recording normally be made of a parade (para. 23). Annex B, para. 10, sets out the procedure to be followed if the suspect has unusual physical features, and paras. 1, 3, 6, 8 and 13 deal with the opportunities to be given to the suspect or the suspect's solicitor to be involved in the procedure. **D1.139**

Regrettably, some deficiencies revealed in past cases have not been addressed by the revisions to Code D. Annex B lays down strict rules to prevent contact between witnesses, or between witnesses *and investigating officers*, during a parade or immediately before it (see paras. 14 to 16) but still says nothing about the propriety of such contact once the witnesses in question have viewed the parade. See *Willoughby* [1999] 2 Cr App R 82 and **F19.4**.

Group Identification Code D, annex C, sets out the procedures to be followed in holding a group identification. It seeks to ensure that, as far as possible, such procedures follow the same principles as identification parades so that the conditions are fair to the suspect in the way they test the witness's ability to make an identification. The conditions under which group **D1.140**

D

Part D Procedure

identifications take place cannot be controlled to the same degree as video identification or parades but, under para. 6, the identification officer must reasonably expect that over the period the witness observes the group the witness will be able to see, from time to time, a number of others (in addition to the suspect) whose appearance is broadly similar. In *Jamel* [1993] Crim LR 52, a group identification was arranged on the basis that a parade was impracticable. D was of mixed race, and the identification was held in a street where one might have expected a variety of individuals of various races to pass by. In the event, nobody of mixed race but D appeared, and he was identified by the witness. The Court of Appeal declined to find fault with this procedure, but indicated that a different view would have been taken had the identification procedure been held in an overwhelmingly white neighbourhood.

A group identification must ordinarily be conducted with the suspect's consent, but may in certain circumstances be conducted covertly (Code D, paras. 3.21 and 3.22, and Note for Guidance 3D). It may be held in either a public place or a secure environment (such as a prison or police station) and the suspect may be part of either a moving or a stationary group. Annex C makes provision for each type of case. An identification carried out in accordance with annex C remains a group identification notwithstanding that at the time of being seen by the witness the suspect was alone rather than in a group (para. 10).

Paragraphs 3, 11, 13, and 27 deal with the opportunities to be given to the suspect or the suspect's solicitor to be involved in the procedure.

D1.141 **Confrontation** Confrontation of a suspect by a witness is governed by Code D, annex D. Force may not be used even if the suspect attempts to hide his or her face (see para. 3, and **D1.132**). A confrontation must normally not take place in the absence of the suspect's legal adviser etc. (para. 4). Confrontation is in some respects little better than dock identification, and the courts will almost certainly exclude such evidence if the limited safeguards required under annex D have been breached (see, e.g., *Powell v DPP* [1992] RTR 270; *Samms* [1991] Crim LR 197). Judicial mistrust of confrontation can most clearly be seen in *Joseph* [1994] Crim LR 48, where the police had done their best to arrange for a parade, group identification or video identification, but without success. The prosecution sought to proceed on the basis of other evidence, but D demanded a confrontation before the trial, in the misguided hope that the witnesses would not identify him. He was in fact identified by two witnesses, and the trial judge admitted that evidence on the basis that D had asked for the confrontation. However, the Court of Appeal considered that the weakness of this evidence required its exclusion under the PACE 1984, s. 78.

D1.142 **Qualified Identification** In some cases, a witness may qualify the identification of the suspect by indicating that he or she 'cannot be quite certain', or is only '90 per cent sure'. An accused should not be convicted on qualified identification evidence alone (*George* [2002] EWCA Crim 1923), but it may still have some probative value when adduced in support of other more positive evidence. Although Code D states in a number of places (e.g., annex A, para. 13) that care must be taken not to direct the witness's attention to any particular image or person, it remains largely silent on the subject of a qualified identification. It would clearly be improper for the police to encourage a witness to be more positive once the initial video identification or parade process has been concluded (e.g., by telling the witness that he or she has 'got the right one'). As Lord Bingham CJ observed in *Willoughby* [1999] 2 Cr App R 82:

> There ... would be the utmost ground for concern if there were any question of the police nudging, prompting or encouraging any witness ... to make a more positive identification of a suspect. ... It would seem to us important that a witness should not be told whether an identification is right or wrong until after the witness has made any further statement that the witness may wish.

Controlled Recognition Procedures under Code D, part 3(B)

D1.143 Part 3(B) of Code D applies when, for the purposes of obtaining evidence of recognition, a person (including a police officer) who is not an eye-witness views a film, photograph or other visual medium and is asked whether he or she recognises anyone who is shown in the material as someone who is known to him or her (para. 3.34). The procedure is to be distinguished from the showing of photographs or other visual images to an eye-witness where a suspect is not known (see **D1.131**). The procedures to be adopted under Code D, part 3(B), aimed at safeguarding against mistaken recognition and the possibility of collusion, are set out in Code D, para. 3.35. The recording requirements are set out in Code D, paras. 3.36 and 3.37. The revised procedures largely deal with the concerns expressed in cases such as *Smith* [2008] EWCA Crim 1342, [2009] 1 Cr App R 36 (521); *McGrath* [2009] EWCA Crim 1758 and *Moss* [2011] EWCA Crim 252.

Uncontrolled Recognition Procedures under Code D, part 3(C)

Code D, part 3(C), applies when, for the purpose of identifying and tracing suspects, films, photographs of incidents or other images are shown to the public (which may include police officers and police staff) through national or local media, or social media, or are circulated through local or national communications systems, and the viewing is not formally controlled and supervised as set out in part 3(B). A copy of the visual media that are released must be kept (para. 3.39). The officer responsible for circulating or making available the visual media must make arrangements to ensure that where a person indicates in response to a viewing that he or she may have information relating to the identity and whereabouts of anyone seen in the viewing, the person is asked to give details of the circumstances, and that a record is made of the circumstances and the conditions under which the viewing took place, as soon as is practicable (para. 3.41). **D1.144**

A person who comes forward as a result of viewing the visual media released may be an eye-witness; that is, he or she saw a person committing a crime or in any other circumstances which tend to prove or disprove the involvement of that person in a crime (Code D, para. 3.0). If, subsequently, an identification procedure is conducted in relation to a known suspect (see **D1.132**), the suspect or the suspect's solicitor must be allowed to view the visual media released prior to the conduct of an identification procedure, provided this is practical and would not unreasonably delay the investigation (para. 3.39). Each eye-witness involved in such an identification procedure must be asked, after taking part, whether he or she has seen any film, photograph or image relating to the offence or any description of the suspect which has been broadcast or published, and the reply recorded. If so, the eye-witness must be asked to give details of the circumstances, and a record must be made (para. 3.41). **D1.145**

VOICE IDENTIFICATION

There is no PACE code on voice identification, and it is mentioned only briefly in Code D. Paragraph 1.2 states that nothing in Code D precludes the use of aural identification procedures, and annex B, para. 18, states that a witness may ask any member of an identification parade to speak. In such a case, the witness should first be asked if he or she can make a purely visual identification, and must be reminded that participants will have been chosen on the basis of their appearance only. Members of the parade may then be asked to comply with the request of the witness to hear them speak. Code D makes no direct provision for cases in which the attempted identification is to be made on the basis of voice alone. This is unfortunate, because there is clear evidence that the risks of mistaken identification are very great. See, e.g., *Roberts* [2000] Crim LR 183 and *Chenia* [2002] EWCA Crim 2345, [2003] 2 Cr App R 6 (83). **D1.146**

One possible approach is to adapt the usual Code D procedures, so as to hold what is in effect a 'voice identification parade'. In *Hersey* [1998] Crim LR 281, the Court of Appeal upheld a conviction based largely on evidence derived from such a parade, although it was acknowledged that voice identification shares many of the dangers of visual identification, and should be subject at trial to analogous warnings derived or adapted from the *Turnbull* guidelines. See further **F19.24**. Home Office Circular 57/2003, *Advice on the use of voice identification parades*, states that the police should not attempt to conduct 'live' voice identification procedures, but should use a procedure involving recorded voices of both the suspect and the comparators. In *Flynn* [2008] EWCA Crim 970, [2008] 2 Cr App R 20 (266), the Court of Appeal set out a critical assessment of the problems associated with voice identification, stating that it was more likely to be reliable when carried out by experts using acoustic and spectrographic, and sophisticated auditory, techniques, than by lay persons. For a detailed examination of the issues, see D Ormerod, 'Sounds Familiar? — Voice Identification Evidence' [2001] Crim LR 595 and 'Sounding out Expert Voice Identification' [2002] Crim LR 771, and J Robson, 'A Fair Hearing? The Use of Voice Identification Parades in Criminal Investigations in England and Wales' [2017] Crim LR 36.

ENTRY AND SEARCH UNDER WARRANT

D1.147 Powers of entry and search of premises, both under a warrant and without a warrant, are governed by a number of statutes, although the main general power of search under warrant is governed by the PACE 1984, Part II. The PACE 1984, ss. 15 (safeguards) and 16 (execution of warrants), apply to warrants issued to a constable under any enactment. For examples of other powers of search under warrant, see PACE Code B, Note for Guidance 2A (see **appendix 1**). CrimPR 47.24 to 47.30 (see Supplement, **R47.24** ***et seq.***) include provisions governing applications for and the content of warrants. Search of premises and seizure is also governed by Code B which applies to search of p\remises for the purposes and under the powers set out in Code B, para. 2.3. For the powers of designated civilian investigating officers to apply for a warrant under the PACE 1984, s. 8, and the application of other provisions governing search and seizure to such civilians, see the Police Reform Act 2002, sch. 4, part 2. For the powers to search for and seize the proceeds of crime, see **D8**. For disclosure by courts of information or documents from records or case materials, see CrimPR 5.7 (see Supplement, **R5.7**).

All statutory powers of search enacted before the PACE 1984 ceased to have effect in relation to the authorisation of searches for items subject to legal professional privilege, excluded material and special procedure material consisting of documents or other records (PACE 1984, s. 9(2)). The TA 2000 makes separate provision for the search of premises in respect of terrorism (**B10.23**). For powers of entry and search in relation to serious fraud, see the CJA 1987, s. 2, and CrimPR 47.29; those powers were comprehensively reviewed in *R (Energy Financing Team Ltd) v Bow Street Magistrates' Court* [2005] EWHC 1626 (Admin), [2006] 4 All ER 285. For powers of entry and search under the SOCPA 2005, Part 2, see **D1.208**. The SCA 2015, Part 4, governs 'search and seizure' warrants authorising a police or customs officer to enter premises and search them for substances that appear to be intended for use as drug-cutting agents. For powers relating to search warrants and production orders relating to a European investigation order, see the Criminal Justice (European Investigation Order) Regulations 2017 (SI 2017 No. 730), Part 3, and CrimPR Parts 47 and 49 (see Supplement, **R47.1** ***et seq.*** and **R49.1** ***et seq.***).

Items Subject to Legal Privilege

D1.148 The term 'items subject to legal privilege' is defined in the PACE 1984, s. 10(1). It includes lawyer-client communications made in connection with the giving of legal advice to the client, and also: (a) communications between either of these or a representative and another person if it was in connection with or in contemplation of and for the purpose of legal proceedings; and (b) items enclosed with or referred to in any of these communications when such items are in the possession of a person entitled to possession of them (see **F10.33** ***et seq.***). If such items are in the possession of a person not so entitled it would appear that the protection afforded by the PACE 1984 is lost. Material in the hands of a solicitor which is not subject to legal privilege is special procedure material (*Norwich Crown Court, ex parte Chethams* [1991] COD 271). However, in accordance with the common-law rule governing privilege, if any items are held with the intention of furthering a criminal purpose they are not to be regarded as items subject to legal privilege (s. 10(2): see further **F10.36** *et seq.*).

Excluded Material

D1.149 'Excluded material' means the following material if it is 'held in confidence' (PACE 1984, s. 11(1)):

(a) personal records acquired or created in a trade, business, profession or other occupation or for the purpose of any office, paid or unpaid;
(b) human tissue or tissue fluid taken for purposes of diagnosis or medical treatment;
(c) journalistic material consisting of documents or records.

Material of types (a) and (b) is 'held in confidence' if there is an express or implied undertaking to that effect, or a statutory requirement to restrict disclosure or maintain secrecy (s. 11(2)). Material of type (c) is 'held in confidence' if it is held subject to such an undertaking, restriction or obligation and has been so held since it was first acquired or created for the purpose of journalism (s. 11(3)). It cannot acquire the status of excluded material at a later time in order to avoid a search and seizure.

'Personal records' means records concerning an individual (living or dead) who can be identified from them, and relating to that person's physical or mental health, spiritual counselling, or counselling for personal welfare by a voluntary organisation, or a person with responsibility for so doing, either by virtue of office or occupation or on authority from a court to supervise that person (e.g., probation officers, members of the clergy) (s. 12). Hospital records of patients' admissions and discharges are excluded material because they relate to the physical or mental health of persons who could be identified from them (*Cardiff Crown Court, ex parte Kellam* (1993) *The Times*, 3 May 1993).

'Journalistic material' means material acquired or created for the purposes of journalism, but only if it is in the possession of a person who acquired it or created it for that purpose. That person will be deemed to have acquired it for that purpose if it was given to him or her with the intention that it be used for that purpose (s. 13).

D

Part D Procedure

Special Procedure Material

D1.150 'Special procedure material' means (PACE 1984, s. 14(1) and (2)):

(a) material, other than items subject to legal privilege and excluded material, acquired or created in a trade, business, profession or occupation, or for the purpose of any office paid or unpaid, where it is held in confidence subject to an express or implied undertaking to that effect or a statutory requirement to restrict disclosure or maintain secrecy; and
(b) 'journalistic material' other than that already falling within the meaning of excluded material.

Material acquired by an employee in the course of employment, or by a company from an associated company, is special procedure material only if it was so immediately before it was acquired (s. 14(3)); it cannot later be redesignated as confidential. Material created by an employee in the course of employment, or by a company on behalf of an associated company, is special procedure material only if it would have been had the employer or associated company created it (s. 14(4) and (5)). For guidance on applications for 'special procedure' search warrants see *R (S) v Chief Constable of British Transport Police* [2013] EWHC 2189 (Admin), [2014] 1 WLR 1647.

Warrant Issued by a Justice of the Peace

D1.151 On application by a constable, a justice of the peace may issue a warrant to a constable to enter and search premises if the justice has reasonable grounds for believing: (a) that an indictable offence (see **D1.69**) has been committed; (b) that there is material on the premises (defined at **D1.156**) which is likely to be of substantial value (whether by itself or together with other material) to the investigation of the offence (defined at **D.157**); (c) that the material is likely to be relevant evidence (defined at **D.157**) and (d) that it not consist of or include items subject to legal privilege, excluded material or special procedure material (s. 8(1); see *Bates v Chief Constable of Avon and Somerset Constabulary* [2009] EWHC 942 (Admin); *Power-Hynes v Norwich Magistrates' Court* [2009] EWHC 1512 (Admin) and *R (Sharer) v City of London Magistrates' Court* [2016] EWHC 1412 (Admin)). See further CrimPR 47.26 to 47.28 (see Supplement, **R47.26**).

Although warrants under s. 8 relate to premises rather than persons, an 'all premises warrant' may be issued in respect of all premises occupied or controlled by the person named in the application (see **D1.153**). 'Premises' is defined for all purposes in the PACE 1984 as including any place and, in particular, includes:

(a) any vehicle, vessel, aircraft or hovercraft;
(b) any offshore installation within the meaning of the Mineral Workings (Offshore Installations) Act 1971, s. 1;
(c) any renewable energy installation within the meaning of the Energy Act 2004, Part 2, ch. 2;
(d) any tent or movable structure (PACE 1984, s. 23).

D1.152 Section 23 does not refer to premises that consist of a number of dwellings. However, s. 32(7), in respect of search on arrest, limits the power to search in respect of such premises to the dwelling in which the person was arrested or in which the person was immediately before arrest, and any parts of the premises which the occupier of any such dwelling uses in common with other occupiers of dwellings comprised in the premises. There are similar provisions in s. 17(2)(b). It is submitted that the same principles should apply to entry and search under other powers. There is no statutory test to determine whether rooms in premises that are individually occupied constitute separate dwellings. On the facts in *Thomas v DPP* [2009] EWHC 3906 (Admin) it was held that, where homeless persons were granted a licence to occupy a bedroom in a house containing three bedrooms, with use of communal parts, each bedroom comprised a separate dwelling.

D1.153 **All Premises and Specific Premises Warrants** Warrants fall into one of two categories. The first is a 'specific premises warrant' which permits search of one or more sets of premises specified in the application (PACE 1984, s. 8(1A)(a)). The second is an 'all premises warrant' which permits search of any premises occupied or controlled by a person specified in the application, including such sets of premises as are so specified (s. 8(1A)(b)). In addition to the conditions in s. 8(1) (see **D1.151**), before granting an 'all premises warrant' a justice of the peace must be satisfied that, because of the particulars of the indictable offence specified in s. 8(1)(a), there are reasonable grounds for believing that it is necessary to search premises occupied or controlled by the person in question which are not specified in the application in order to find material of substantial value to the investigation and that it is not reasonably practicable to specify in the application all the premises that the person controls which might need to be searched (s. 8(1B)). Where an all premises warrant is issued, premises that are not specified in the warrant must not be entered or searched without the prior written authority of an officer of the rank of inspector who is not involved in the investigation (s. 16(3A)).

Either form of warrant may authorise multiple entries and searches of the premises if a justice of the peace is satisfied that it is necessary so to authorise in order to achieve the purpose for which the warrant is issued (s. 8(1C)). A warrant authorising multiple entries may authorise an unlimited number of entries or limit them to a maximum (s. 8(1D)), but any entry or search must be made within three months from the date of issue of the warrant (s. 16(3)). After the first entry and search under such a warrant, subsequent entries or searches may be conducted only with the prior written authority of an officer of the rank of inspector who is not involved in the investigation (s. 16(3B)).

Conditions for Issuing a Warrant A warrant under s. 8(1) cannot be issued unless at least one of the conditions in s. 8(3) is satisfied: **D1.154**

(a) that it is not practicable to communicate with any person entitled to grant entry to the premises; or
(b) if it is, that it is not practicable to communicate with any person entitled to grant access to the evidence; or
(c) that entry to the premises will not be granted unless a warrant is produced; or
(d) that the purpose of a search may be frustrated or seriously prejudiced unless a constable arriving at the premises can secure immediate entry to them.

It is not a condition precedent to the issue of a magistrates' court warrant that other methods have been tried and failed or would be bound to fail, nor that no other statutory procedure for securing the material exists (*Billericay Justices, ex parte Frank Harris (Coaches) Ltd* [1991] Crim LR 472). Where there are grounds for seeking search warrants, the police are entitled to choose when to apply for them and when, within the time permitted by law, to execute them (*Chief Constable of Warwickshire Constabulary, ex parte Fitzpatrick*). However, the warrant is invalid if the police do not identify the s. 8(3) condition(s) that they rely upon (*Redknapp v Commissioner of the City of London Police* [2008] EWHC 1177 (Admin), [2008] 1 All ER 229).

A constable may obtain access to excluded material or special procedure material for the purposes of a criminal investigation by making an application under the PACE 1984, sch. 1 (see **D1.161**). However, a magistrate is not barred from issuing a search warrant under s. 8(1) because there may be special procedure or excluded material on the premises; the issue of a warrant is barred only if the material falls into these categories and is or forms part of the subject-matter of such an application (*Ex parte Fitzpatrick* [1999] 1 All ER 65). The position is otherwise if the warrant is not sufficiently specific so that such material is likely to be included (*Power-Hynes v Norwich Magistrates' Court* [2009] EWHC 1512 (Admin)).

Powers on Executing a Warrant A constable may seize and retain anything for which a search has been authorised under a warrant issued under the PACE 1984, s. 8 (s. 8(2)). This does not extend to seizing a car parked in a car park where there was insufficient evidence that the car park was part of the premises within the scope of the warrant (*Wood v North Avon Magistrates' Court* [2009] EWHC 3614 (Admin)). See further **D1.178** ***et seq***. **D1.155**

Unless the statute explicitly so provides, a warrant to enter and search premises does not confer a power to search persons found therein (*Hepburn v Chief Constable of Thames Valley* [2002] EWCA Civ 1841; *DPP v Meaden* [2003] EWHC 3005 (Admin), [2004] 1 WLR 945). However, it is permissible to take reasonable and necessary steps to detain persons found therein in the course of execution of the warrant (*Connor v Chief Constable of Merseyside* [2006] EWCA Civ 1549).

Access to Excluded or Special Procedure Material

The PACE 1984, s. 9(1), enables access to be obtained to excluded material and special procedure material for the purposes of a criminal investigation if the procedures set out in sch. 1 to the Act are followed. Schedule 1 applies not only to police investigations but also to investigations of indictable offences by the Department for Business, Energy and Industrial Strategy (BEIS). A BEIS investigator may apply for an order or warrant to obtain special procedure material in connection with a BEIS investigation (PACE 1984, s. 114A, and the Police and Criminal Evidence Act (Department of Trade and Industry Investigations) Order 2002 (SI 2002 No. 2326)). Special procedure material in the hands of a court can be made the subject of a production order, pursuant to the Crime (International Co-operation) Act 2003, s. 13, notwithstanding the absence of express provision in that section (*R (Secretary of State for the Home Department) v Southwark Crown Court* [2013] EWHC 4366 (Admin), [2014] 1 WLR 2529). **D1.156**

D1.157 **Access Conditions** There are two sets of access conditions in the PACE 1984, sch. 1, one of which must be satisfied for a production order to be made.

The first set of access conditions (sch. 1, para. 2) is fulfilled if:

(a) There are reasonable grounds for believing:
   (i) that an indictable offence has been committed (see **D1.69**);
   (ii) that there is material which consists of special procedure material or includes special procedure material and does not include excluded material on premises specified in the application or on premises occupied or controlled by a person specified in the application (including all such premises on which there are reasonable grounds for believing that there is such material as it is reasonably practicable so to specify);
   (iii) that the material is likely to be of substantial value to the investigation. It was held in *R (BBC) v Newcastle Crown Court* [2019] EWHC 2756 (Admin), [2020] 1 Cr App R 16 (274) that the term 'criminal investigation' in the PACE 1984 had the same definition as that under the CPIA 1996, s. 22(1), namely 'an investigation conducted by police officers with a view to it being ascertained — (a) whether a person should be charged with an offence, or (b) whether a person charged with an offence is guilty of it' (see **D9.6** ***et seq.***). Therefore, an application made for a production order while an accused was standing trial was still made for the purpose of a 'criminal investigation';
   (iv) that the material is likely to be relevant evidence. It was held in *R (BBC) v Newcastle Crown Court* that the phrase 'relevant evidence' was defined in the PACE 1984, s. 8(4), as 'anything that would be admissible in evidence at a trial for the offence'. The Divisional Court cited with approval the House of Lords' decision in *Derby Magistrates' Court, ex parte B* [1996] AC 487 which held that in order for the information sought to constitute 'material evidence' it must be 'immediately admissible *per se* and without more'. The Court found that the test of likelihood does not require the judge to assess the likelihood that the material *may* become admissible if certain events occur at trial. Therefore, if the material sought is not likely to be 'immediately admissible', it ceases to be 'relevant evidence'. This is why material is not relevant evidence simply because it could be used as a basis for cross-examination (*Norwich Crown Court, ex parte Chethams* [1991] COD 271).

(b) Other methods of obtaining the special procedure material have failed or have not been tried because it appeared they would be bound to fail. Thus if, e.g., a motion under the Bankers' Books Evidence Act 1879 (see **F8.35**) would be possible, it must be shown that such a motion was brought and failed or that the material could not have been secured by such a motion (*Crown Court at Lewes, ex parte Hill* (1991) 93 Cr App R 60). An application cannot however be impugned simply because some further and remote step to uncover evidence might possibly have been taken. What matters is the belief of the constable at the time the application is made. There must be cogent grounds for the belief; a bare assertion will not do (*R (Ashbolt) v Leeds Crown Court* [2020] EWHC 1588 (Admin); *R (Newcastle United Football Club) v Revenue and Customs Commissioners* [2017] EWHC 2402 (Admin), [2017] 4 WLR 187; *R (S) v Chief Constable of the British Transport Police* [2013] EWHC 2189 (Admin), [2014] 1 WLR 1647).

(c) It is in the public interest to produce or allow access to the material, having regard (i) to the benefit likely to accrue to the investigation if the material is obtained; and (ii) to the circumstances under which the person in possession of the material holds it.

The second set of access conditions (sch. 1, para. 3) requires that there are reasonable grounds for believing that there is material which consists of or includes excluded or special procedure material:

(a) on such premises specified in the application; or

(b) on premises occupied or controlled by a person specified in the application (including such premises on which there are reasonable grounds for believing that there is such material as it is reasonably practicable so to specify), in respect of which the issue of a warrant under an enactment other than sch. 1 would have been appropriate and available but for the repeal by s. 9(2) of all the provisions allowing warrants to be issued to search for this type of material.

Procedure The procedure is set out in the PACE 1984, sch. 1, and CrimPR 47.4 to 47.10 (see Supplement, R47.4 *et seq.*). An application must be made to a circuit judge (extended to a district judge (magistrates' court) if and when the Courts Act 2003, sch. 4, para. 6, is brought into force). Before an order to produce or a search warrant is applied for, careful consideration must be given to what material it is hoped a search might reveal, and the application must also make it clear that the material sought relates to the crime under investigation (*Central Criminal Court, ex parte AJD Holdings* [1992] Crim LR 669). It is not sufficient for the information laid in support of the application merely to recite the statutory conditions, without any statement of the facts or matters on which the application is based (*R (S) v Chief Constable of the British Transport Police* [2013] EWHC 2189 (Admin), [2014] 1 WLR 1647). An order to produce special procedure material may be made even though some of the material is not of that description. This avoids making separate but necessarily sequential applications (*Preston Crown Court, ex parte McGrath* [1993] COD 103). A mobile telephone may properly be made the subject of a warrant under s. 9 and sch. 1, even where legally privileged material may be found on it, provided that the wording of the warrant clearly excludes any such material from that which may be sought or seized (*R (A) v Central Criminal Court* [2017] EWHC 70 (Admin), [2017] 1 WLR 3567). **D1.158**

Notice of an application to make an order must be served on the person in possession of the material (sch. 1, para. 8), and all information on which the applicant intends to rely must be made available (*R (British Sky Broadcasting Ltd) v Central Criminal Court* [2011] EWHC 3451 (Admin), [2012] QB 785). That person must not conceal, destroy, alter or dispose of the material without leave of a judge or written permission of a constable until the application is dismissed or abandoned, or the person has complied with the order (para. 11). Failure to comply with an order is to be treated as a contempt of court (para. 15).

Bodies such as banks in respect of which such applications are made often let them go by default. It is thus particularly important that the judge be given adequate material to enable a reliable judgement to be formed. This will include details of the charges, the dates covered by them, whether previous steps to secure the evidence have been tried and failed, and what the nature of the material is.

A suspect has no statutory right to be heard on an application for access, but the judge has discretion to hear the suspect where this appears likely to be helpful (*Crown Court at Lewes, ex parte Hill* (1991) 93 Cr App R 60).

The Order If satisfied that one or other of the access conditions is fulfilled, the judge may make an order requiring the person in possession of the material to produce it to a constable to be taken away, or to give a constable access to it, within a specified period, normally seven days (PACE 1984, sch. 1, paras. 1 and 4). Once such an order has been made it cannot be rescinded; the only recourse is judicial review (*Liverpool Crown Court, ex parte Wimpey plc* [1991] Crim LR 635). **D1.159**

The approach which a judge should take towards applications is set out in *Crown Court at Lewes, ex parte Hill* (1991) 93 Cr App R 60 and *R (Bright) v Central Criminal Court* [2001] 1 WLR 662. The Divisional Court in *Ex parte Hill* stated that the Act provides a careful balance between the public interest in the effective investigation and prosecution of crime and the interests of citizens in protecting their personal and property rights. The circuit judge is entrusted with the primary duty of giving effect to that scheme and must exercise his or her powers with great care and caution. The circuit judge must be shown such material as is necessary to enable him or her to be satisfied before making the order, and should be told anything which, to the knowledge of the applicant, might weigh against making such an order (*Leeds Crown Court, ex parte Hill* [1991] COD 197; *Acton Crown Court, ex parte Layton* [1993] Crim LR 458; *R (Virdee) v NCA* [2018] EWHC 1119 (Admin), [2018] 1 WLR 5073). The circuit judge should not allow the police to engage in a fishing expedition. Any order made must be specific as to the material sought. For an application of these principles, when production orders were quashed, see *R (British Sky Broadcasting Ltd) v Chelmsford Crown Court* [2012] EWHC 1295 (Admin), [2012] 2 Cr App R 33 (454). In cases involving national security the judge must at least be presented with a properly drafted, careful summary. In particularly sensitive cases the judge may wish to adapt the procedure which applies to applications for public interest immunity to deal with the matter (*R (Bright) v Central Criminal Court*).

Even if the access conditions are made out, the judge has discretion to refuse to grant the order. Such an exercise of discretion would no doubt be rare. Discretion, however, enables the judge to weigh fundamental principles and, for example, may in a proper case lead to the conclusion that there would be disproportion between what might be gained to the investigation as against the stifling of public debate (*R (Bright) v Central Criminal Court* per Judge LJ, explaining *Northamptonshire Magistrates' Court, ex parte DPP* (1991) 93 Cr App R 396).

D1.160 There has been some disagreement as to whether a judge may be inhibited from making an order for production by reason of the fact that the person to whom it is addressed may incriminate him or herself (*R (Bright) v Central Criminal Court* [2001] 1 WLR 662). In *Malik v Manchester Crown Court* [2008] EWHC 1362 (Admin), [2008] 4 All ER 403 the Divisional Court suggested that, in view of the uncertain state of the law, judges should treat the privilege against self-incrimination as an important factor to be taken into account when exercising their discretion in respect of pre-existing documents. However, having reviewed the authorities, the Court in *R (River East Supplies Ltd) v Nottingham Crown Court* [2017] EWHC 1942 (Admin), 2 Cr App R 27 (384) expressed doubt that this was correct: 'the privilege, on the best view of existing and binding authority, as well as in accordance with principle and policy, does not apply to "independent" documents. On that basis, no question of the exercise of judicial discretion would arise' (at [102]).

Where the material consists of information stored in any electronic form, the order is to produce material in a form in which it can be taken away and in which it is visible and legible or from which it can be produced in a visible and legible form. An order to give access is to be understood in the same sense (sch. 1, para. 5).

Where an order to produce requires the presentation or production of emails, which require the recipient of the order to modify or interfere with a telecommunications system (an offence under the IPA 2016, s. 3), the order takes precedence over the prohibition in the 2016 Act (see *R (NTL Group Ltd) v Ipswich Crown Court* [2002] EWHC 1585 (Admin), [2003] QB 131; IPA 2016, s. 6, and **B9.91**).

Search Warrant Issued by Judge

D1.161 A judge may issue a warrant authorising a constable to enter and search premises if one or other of two conditions is satisfied (PACE 1984, sch. 1, para. 12).

The first condition is that the judge is satisfied that either set of access conditions (see **D1.157**) is fulfilled and that any of the following are also fulfilled (sch. 1, para. 14):

(a) that it is not practicable to communicate with a person entitled to grant entry to the premises;
(b) if it is, that it is not practicable to communicate with a person entitled to grant access to the material;
(c) that there is a statutory restriction on disclosure or obligation of secrecy and disclosure contained in any enactment, and disclosure would be in breach of the statute unless a warrant is issued; or
(d) that service of notice of an application for an order would seriously prejudice the investigation (see *R (Ashbolt) v Leeds Crown Court* [2020] EWHC 1588 (Admin)).

The term 'practicable' bears a wider meaning than feasible or physically possible. The court may consider not only the available means of communication, but also all the circumstances, including the nature of the inquiries and the persons against whom they are directed. The usual procedure where a solicitor's office is to be searched would be by order to produce, but a search warrant may be proper where the firm is under investigation (*Leeds Crown Court, ex parte Switalski* [1991] Crim LR 559; *Maidstone Crown Court, ex parte Waitt* [1988] Crim LR 384; *Central Criminal Court, ex parte Hutchinson* [1996] COD 14). However, a search warrant was quashed in *R (Faisaltex Ltd) v Preston Crown Court* [2008] EWHC 2832 (Admin), [2009] 1 WLR 1687 where there was no evidence that proceeding by way of a production order might seriously prejudice the investigation: 'A solicitor was not to be regarded as somehow tainted and unreliable because, e.g., he acted for someone charged with or convicted of a criminal offence'. Similarly, in *R (Hart) v Crown Court at Blackfriars* [2017] EWHC 3091 (Admin), the Divisional Court quashed a production order because, while HMRC had not misled the judge on the applicable law or underlying facts, it had failed to disclose sufficient information in relation to its contention that service of notice of an application for an order would seriously prejudice the investigation.

The second condition is that the second set of access conditions (see **D1.157**) is fulfilled and that there has been a failure to comply with an order under sch. 1, para. 4 (**D1.159**).

The approach which a judge must take towards an application for a search warrant is set out in *Crown Court at Lewes, ex parte Hill* (1991) 93 Cr App R 60 (see **D1.159**). **D1.162**

The judge may not issue an 'all premises warrant' (**D1.153**) unless satisfied that there are reasonable grounds for believing that it is necessary to search premises occupied or controlled by the person in question which are not specified in the application, as well as those which are, in order to find the material in question, and that it is not reasonably practicable to specify all the premises occupied or controlled by the person which might need to be searched (sch. 1, para. 12A).

In searching premises, a constable is entitled to impose reasonable obligations on persons found therein in order to make the search effective. The constable may, thus, require persons found in the premises to go to or remain in a particular part of the premises while the search is carried out (*DPP v Meaden* [2003] EWHC 3005 (Admin), [2004] 1 WLR 945), and see **D1.155**).

A constable may seize and retain anything for which such a search has been authorised (sch. 1, para. 13). See further **D1.178** ***et seq.***

Procedural Requirements and Safeguards Courts have consistently held that the issue of a search warrant is a very severe interference with individual liberty, is a step which should be taken only after mature consideration of the facts, and that the officer making the application is under a duty of full disclosure of relevant matters (*R (Chatwani) v NCA* [2015] EWHC 1283 (Admin), in which the Divisional Court criticised the NCA for failing 'to have any regard to the fundamentals of the statutory scheme'). The necessary foundation for the issue of a warrant should be on the face of the information unless there are good reasons for not including it, and both the applicant and the court must be able to identify the basis for the grant of the warrant. However, information may be withheld from the applicant if it is not in the public interest to disclose it, even if what falls to be disclosed cannot, without more, support the various conclusions necessary for a warrant to be issued (*Haralambous v St Albans Crown Court* [2018] UKSC 1, [2018] AC 236). If information additional to that in the information is provided to the court, both the applicant and the court must keep a written record of it (*R (Austen) v Chief Constable of Wiltshire* [2011] EWHC 3385 (Admin)). Whilst the PACE 1984 does not require a court to give reasons why the conditions for issue of a warrant are satisfied, in most cases, and particularly where the information is given or supplemented orally, the court should ensure that reasons for its decision are given and recorded (*R (Glenn & Co. (Essex) Ltd) v HM Commissioners for Revenue and Customs* [2011] EWHC 2998 (Admin), [2012] 1 Cr App R 22 (291)). However, the absence of reasons will not necessarily be fatal if a sufficient basis for the issue of the warrant may be discerned (*R (Newcastle United Football Club Ltd) v Revenue and Customs Commissioners* [2017] EWHC 2402 (Admin), [2017] 4 WLR 187). **D1.163**

All entries on and searches of premises under a warrant issued *under any enactment* are unlawful unless they comply with ss. 15 and 16 of the PACE 1984, although see *R (Glenn & Co. (Essex) Ltd) v HM Commissioners for Revenue and Customs*, in which a failure to supply a copy of a warrant to the occupier did not, on the facts, render the search unlawful. Code B, para 1.3A, provides a reminder that the Equality Act 2010 makes it unlawful for police officers to discriminate against, harass or victimise any person on the grounds of the 'protected characteristics' of age, disability, gender reassignment, race, religion or belief, sex and sexual orientation, marriage and civil partnership, pregnancy and maternity when using their powers.

D1.164 **The Application** Procedure on an application for a warrant, and the conduct of the hearing, is governed by the PACE 1984, s. 15, and CrimPR 47.25, 47.26 and 47.28 (see Supplement, **R47.25** ***et seq.***), supplemented by Code B. A constable who applies for a warrant must state the ground on which the application is made; the enactment under which the warrant would be issued; and, if the application is for a warrant authorising entry and search on more than one occasion, the ground on which such a warrant is applied for, and whether the constable seeks a warrant authorising an unlimited number of entries or (if not) the maximum number of entries desired (PACE 1984, s. 15(2)(i) to (iii)). In *R (Lees) v Solihull Magistrates' Court* [2013] EWHC 3779 (Admin) warrants were declared unlawful because they were too vague and general, and failed properly to identify the items to which they related (see also *R (Cheema) v Nottingham and Newark Magistrates' Court* [2013] EWHC 3790 (Admin)).

PACE Code B, requires, *inter alia*, that before making an application the officer must take reasonable steps to check the accuracy of the information, that it is recent, and that it has not been provided maliciously or irresponsibly (and see *R (G) v Metropolitan Police Commissioner* [2011] EWHC 3331 (Admin)). It also prohibits any application being made on the basis of information provided anonymously unless corroboration has been sought (Code B, para. 3.1). The officer must make reasonable inquiries to ascertain information about the premises to be searched, the likely occupier and the articles concerned (Code B, paras. 3.2 and 3.3). A failure to carry out basic steps to verify the connection between the premises and the offence under investigation may amount to a breach of the ECHR, Article 8 (*Keegan v UK* (2007) 44 EHRR 33 (716)). If there is reason to believe that a search might have an adverse effect on community relations, the local police/community liaison officer must be consulted, unless the search is needed urgently in which case he or she must be consulted as soon as practicable after the search (Code B, para. 3.5). Furthermore, a constable must not, when applying for a warrant, state that the purposes of the search will be frustrated or prejudiced unless immediate access is granted where the constable does not believe this to be so. In particular no such statement can properly be made where the subject of the search has already demonstrated that he or she is prepared to co-operate in producing material. Police acting in conjunction with another agency must form their own opinion whether it is necessary to apply for a warrant (*Reading Justices, ex parte South West Meat Ltd* [1992] Crim LR 672).

D1.165 No application for a search warrant or production order under the PACE 1984, sch. 1, may be made without the prior written authority of an officer of at least the rank of inspector, except in the case of urgency when an application to a justice of the peace may be authorised by the senior officer on duty (Code B, para. 3.4(a)). In the case of an application for a production order under the TA 2000, sch. 5, authorisation must be given by an officer of at least the rank of superintendent (Code B, para. 3.4(b)).

D1.166 An application for a warrant covering one or more sets of premises specified in the application must specify each set of premises which it is desired to enter and search (s. 15(2A)(a)). Under s. 15(2A)(b), an application for an all premises warrant (see **D1.153**) must specify (i) as many *sets of premises which it is* desired to enter and search as it is reasonably practicable to specify; (ii) the person who is in occupation or control of those premises and any other premises which it is desired to enter and search; (iii) why it is necessary to search more premises than those specified in sub-para. (i); and (iv) why it is not reasonably practicable to specify all the premises which it is desired to enter and search (see also CrimPR 47.28(5) to (7), and Code B, para. 3.6). A constable who wishes to search only a part of premises divided into separate dwellings and the common parts of those premises must make this clear in the information when applying for the warrant (*South Western Magistrates' Court, ex parte Cofie* [1996] 1 WLR 885). The application must be made *ex parte* and supported by an information in writing (s. 15(3)). The constable must answer on oath any questions put by the justice of the peace or the judge at a hearing of an application (s. 15(4)).

If an application is refused, no further application may be made unless supported by additional grounds (Code B, para. 3.8).

The application must disclose anything known or reported to the applicant that might reasonably be considered capable of undermining any of the grounds of the application (CrimPR 47.26(3)), and bare compliance with the statutory requirements regarding the information to be disclosed on an application for a warrant may not be sufficient. The test adopted in *R (Rawlinson) v Central Criminal Court* [2012] EWHC 2254 (Admin), [2013] 1 WLR 1634 was whether the errors or non-disclosure in the application would in fact have made a difference to the decision to issue a warrant (and not whether they *might* have made a difference). This was followed in *R (Golfrate Property Management Ltd) v Southwark Crown Court* [2014] EWHC 840 (Admin), [2014] 2 Cr App R 12 (145), in which the lack of 'full and frank' disclosure resulted in the warrants being set aside, and in *Zinga* [2012] EWCA Crim 2357, in which failure to disclose the intended prosecutor did not vitiate the warrant. However, this approach was doubted in *R (Mills) v Sussex Police* [2014] EWHC 2523 (Admin), [2015] 1 WLR 2199, where it was held that the preferred test 'is whether the information that it is alleged should have been given to the magistrate might reasonably have led him to refuse to issue the warrant'. See also *Vuciterni v Brent Magistrates' Court* [2012] EWHC 2140 (Admin), in which warrants were quashed where there was a failure to disclose doubts about whether the activities being investigated were unlawful. While a material mistake of fact leading to unfairness can be available as a ground of judicial review in some circumstances (*R (DPP) v Sunderland Magistrates' Court* [2018] EWHC 229 (Admin), [2018] 1 WLR 2195), it cannot invalidate a warrant otherwise properly obtained (*R (Daly) v Metropolitan Police Commissioner* [2018] EWHC 438 (Admin), [2018] 1 WLR 2221). **D1.167**

Note that a court may consider a request for disclosure of information laid in support of an application for a warrant after the warrant has been executed, and for any additional information relied upon by the court when granting the warrant. See further CrimPR 5.7 (see Supplement, **R5.7**). However, this is subject to a power to refuse disclosure on the grounds of public interest immunity (see *R (Terra Services Ltd) v NCA* [2019] EWHC 3165 (Admin); *Competition Markets Authority v Concordia International RX (UK) Ltd* [2018] EWCA Civ 1881, [2019] 1 All ER 699; *R (Haralambous) v St Albans Crown Court* [2018] UKSC 1, [2018] AC 236; *Metropolitan Police Commissioner v Bangs* [2014] EWHC 546 (Admin) and **D9.49**). The court is entitled to adopt a closed material procedure in judicial review proceedings concerning the legality of a search warrant issued ex parte under the PACE 1984, ss. 8 and 15(3) (*Haralambous*). However, it would be a 'rare case' where the appointment of a special advocate could be justified (*R (Terra Services Ltd) v NCA* [2020] EWHC 130 (Admin), [2020] 1 WLR 1149 at [24]).

The Warrant The general requirements governing warrants are contained in the PACE 1984, s. 15(5) to (7), and CrimPR 47.27 (see Supplement, **R47.27**); but note that legislation governing specific warrants may include particular requirements. A warrant can authorise entry on only one occasion unless it specifies that it authorises multiple entries (PACE 1984, s. 15(5)). If it authorises multiple entries, it must also specify whether the number of entries authorised is unlimited or limited to a specified maximum (s. 15(5A)). It must specify the name of the person applying for it (the name of the police unit is not sufficient: *R (G) v Metropolitan Police Commissioner* [2011] EWHC 3331 (Admin)), the date of issue, the Act under which it is issued, the premises to be searched, and, so far as is practicable, the identity of the articles or persons sought (s. 15(6), and see *R (Anand) v Revenue and Customs Commissioners* [2012] EWHC 2989 (Admin); *Van der Pijl* **D1.168**

v Kingston Crown Court [2012] EWHC 3745 (Admin), [2013] 1 WLR 2706; *R (Hoque) v City of London Magistrates' Court* [2013] EWHC 725 (Admin) and *Re O'Neill's Application for Judicial Review* [2017] NIQB 37). As to specifying the articles sought, see *R (Hicks) v Metropolitan Police Commissioner* [2012] EWHC 1947 (Admin) and *R (Sweeney) v Westminster Magistrates' Court* [2014] EWHC 2068 (Admin). For the purposes of the PACE 1984, s. 8(1), 'material' has a broad meaning, and is capable of covering a computer or hard disk even though the information contained therein might include irrelevant material (*R (Faisaltex Ltd) v Preston Crown Court* [2008] EWHC 2832 (Admin), [2009] 1 WLR 1687; *Cabot Global Ltd v Barkingside Magistrates' Court* [2015] EWHC 1458 (Admin), [2015] 2 Cr App R 26 (355)).

Each set of premises to be searched must be specified or, in the case of an all premises warrant, the person who is in occupation or control of the premises to be searched together with any premises under the person's occupation or control which can be specified and are to be searched (s. 15(6)(a)(iv)). Two copies must be made of a specific premises warrant which specifies only one set of premises and does not authorise multiple entries; and as many copies as are reasonably required may be made of any other kind of warrant (s. 15(7)). A warrant may be issued which is directed at all premises occupied or controlled by a specified person and, at the same time, one which specifies some of those premises (CrimPR 47.25(6)(c) (see Supplement, **R47.25**); and see *Redknapp v Commissioner of the City of London Police* [2008] EWHC 1177 (Admin), [2008] 1 All ER 229).

D1.169 **Execution of the Warrant** Entry and search under a warrant must be at a reasonable hour unless it appears to the constable executing it that its purpose may otherwise be frustrated (PACE 1984, s. 16(5)). It must be carried out within three months from the date of its issue (s. 16(3)). A warrant authorising entry and search 'on one occasion' does not require the police to complete the search in one calendar day (*R (Sher) v Chief Constable of Greater Manchester Police* [2010] EWHC 1859 (Admin), [2011] 2 All ER 364). A warrant may be executed by any constable and may authorise persons to accompany the constable (s. 16(2)). A person so authorised has the same powers as the accompanied constable in respect of the execution of the warrant and the seizure of anything to which it relates (s. 16(2A)). Such a person may, however, exercise those powers only when in the company of and under the supervision of a constable (s. 16(2B); *Reading Justices, ex parte South West Meat Ltd* [1992] Crim LR 672). Civilians designated as investigating officers under the Police Reform Act 2002 have certain powers to execute warrants (see sch. 4 to that Act).

Where the occupier of premises is present, the constable must identify him or herself and, if not in uniform, produce his or her identity (warrant) card, produce the search warrant and supply a copy to the occupier, including any schedule (PACE 1984, s. 16(5); *R (Glenn & Co. (Essex) Ltd) v HM Commissioners for Revenue and Customs* [2011] EWHC 2998 (Admin), [2012] 1 Cr App R 22 (291); *R (Global Cash & Carry Ltd) v Birmingham Magistrates' Court* [2013] EWHC 528 (Admin)). If the occupier is not present, the constable must do these things in relation to the person who appears to be in charge of the premises (s. 16(6)). If there is no person present who appears to be in charge, a copy of the warrant must be left in a prominent place on the premises (s. 16(7)). The police practice of completing the address by hand as the warrant is executed amounts to a breach of s. 16(5) (*R (Bhatti) v Croydon Magistrates' Court* [2009] EWHC 3004 (Admin)).

D1.170 The search may be conducted only to the extent required for the purpose for which it was issued (s. 16(8)), but provided a warrant is executed for the purpose for which it had been obtained, it is irrelevant that execution was timed to produce some collateral advantage (*R (Pearce) v Metropolitan Police Commissioner* [2013] EWCA Civ 866). As to what may be seized by a constable lawfully in premises, see **D1.178**. An executed warrant must be endorsed with information about whether the articles or persons sought were found, and whether any other articles were seized. Unless the warrant is a specific premises warrant specifying one set of premises only, the constable must endorse separately in respect of each set of premises entered and searched (s. 16(9)). The warrant must be returned to the appropriate officer in the magistrates' court or other court that issued it when it has been executed or, in the case of a specific premises warrant which has not been executed, an all premises warrant or any warrant authorising multiple entries, upon the expiry of three months or sooner (s. 16(10) and (10A)). Returned warrants are to be retained by those persons for 12 months (s. 16(11)). This is so that the occupier of the premises to which the warrant related may exercise the right under s. 16(12) to inspect the warrant.

ENTRY AND SEARCH WITHOUT WARRANT

A search of premises is always permissible with the consent of a person entitled to grant entry, although consent should be obtained in writing (Code B, section 5). Police constables have powers of entry and search without a warrant under the PACE 1984, ss. 17, 18 and 32, and also under a variety of other statutes (see Code B, Note for Guidance 2B, for examples: see **appendix 1**). The police also have common-law powers of entry in respect of breach of the peace (**D1.33**). Designated civilian investigating officers also have certain powers of entry and search without a warrant (Police Reform Act 2002, s. 38(9) and sch. 4). Code B applies to searches under the PACE 1984, ss. 17, 18 and 32, and to most other searches by police for the purposes of investigation of an alleged offence, whether with or without consent (Code B, para. 2.3). **D1.171**

Entry for the Purposes of Arrest etc.

The PACE 1984, s. 17(1), empowers a constable to enter and search any premises (for definition, see **D1.151**): **D1.172**

(a) to execute a warrant of arrest issued in connection with or arising out of criminal proceedings, or a warrant of commitment issued under the MCA 1980, s. 76 (s. 17(1)(a));
(b) to arrest a person for an indictable offence (s. 17(1)(b), and see **D1.69** for the meaning of indictable offence);
(c) to arrest a person for an offence under the Public Order Act 1936, s. 1 (prohibition of uniforms in connection with political objects) or the Public Order Act 1986, s. 4 (fear or provocation of violence); the RTA 1988, s. 4 (driving etc. when under the influence of drink or drugs) or s. 163 (failure to stop when required to do so by a constable in uniform); the Transport and Works Act 1992, s. 27 (offences involving drink or drugs); for an offence to which the Animal Health Act 1981, s. 61, applies; or an offence under the Animal Welfare Act 2006, ss. 4, 5, 6(1) and (2), 7 and 8(1) and (2) (s. 17(1)(c) and (caa));
(d) provided the constable is in uniform, to arrest a person for an offence under any enactment contained in the CLA 1977, ss. 6 to 8 or 10 (offences relating to entering and remaining on property), or the CJPO 1994, s. 76 (failure to comply with an interim possession order), or the LASPO 2012, s. 144 (squatting in residential building) (s. 17(1)(c) and (3));
(e) to arrest a child or young person who has been remanded to local authority or youth detention accommodation under the CYPA 1969, s. 32(1A) (s. 17(1)(ca));
(f) to arrest a person under the PACE 1984, s. 30D(1) or (2A) (arrest where a person granted bail under s. 30A fails to attend the police station or where a constable has reasonable grounds for suspecting that the person has broken bail conditions); the PACE 1984, s. 46A(1) or (1A) (arrest where a person granted bail under the PACE 1984, Part IV, fails to attend the police station or where a constable has reasonable grounds for suspecting that the person has broken bail conditions); the BA 1976, s. 5B(7) (arrest where a person fails to surrender to custody in accordance with a court order); the BA 1976, s. 7(3) (arrest where a person is not likely to surrender to custody, etc.); and the LASPO 2012, s. 97(1) (arrest where a child is suspected of breaking conditions of remand) (s. 17(1)(cab), as inserted by the PCA 2017, s. 72);
(g) to recapture a person who is, or who is deemed to be, unlawfully at large while liable to be detained in a prison, remand centre, young offender institution, or secure training centre, or in pursuance of the PCC(S)A 2000, s. 92 (dealing with children and young persons

guilty of grave crimes), or to recapture a person who is unlawfully at large and whom the constable is pursuing (s. 17(1)(cb) and (d));

(h) to save life or limb or prevent serious damage to property (s. 17(1)(e)), which includes saving someone from self-harm (*Baker v CPS* [2009] EWHC 299 (Admin)).

D1.173 When entering premises to search for a person (except for the purpose of saving life or preventing property damage), the constable must have reasonable grounds for believing that the person sought is on the premises (s. 17(2)(a)). A constable may enter any dwelling in which there are reasonable grounds for believing the person may be, and, where the premises consist of two or more dwellings, the constable may enter any parts of the premises used in common by the occupiers (s. 17(2)(b)). For entry under s. 17(1)(e), the officer must apprehend that some serious or dangerous incident has occurred, or is likely to occur; it is not enough that the officer is merely concerned for the welfare of someone in the premises (*Syed v DPP* [2010] EWHC 81 (Admin), [2010] 1 Cr App R 34 (480)).

If a constable has power to arrest a person under an extradition arrest power, the constable may enter and search any premises for the purposes of exercising the power of arrest if there are reasonable grounds for believing that the person is on the premises (Extradition Act 2003, s. 161(2)). In this case, the relevant Code of Practice is the Extradition Act Code B (see **D1.38**).

Force may be used to enter premises where it is necessary to do so. Where the occupier of the premises is present and can be spoken to, forcible entry will not be justified unless the constable explains by what right and for what purpose he or she seeks to enter (*Lineham v DPP* [2000] Crim LR 861). That reason must be lawful: a wish to talk to a suspect cannot, for example, be elided into a wish to arrest a suspect. There is an exception to the duty above where the circumstances are such as to make it impossible, impracticable or unnecessary to give such an explanation to the occupier (*O'Loughlin v Chief Constable of Essex* [1998] 1 WLR 374).

Any search made must be restricted to that which is reasonably required to achieve the object of the search (s. 17(4)).

D1.174 Other than the power of entry to deal with or prevent a breach of the peace, all common-law powers of a constable to enter premises without a warrant were abolished by the PACE 1984, s. 17(5). A constable does not have the power to enter premises to carry out an investigation as to whether a further breach of the peace would occur (*Friswell v Chief Constable of Essex Police* [2004] EWHC 3009 (QB)). The power of a constable under s. 17(1)(d) to enter and search premises to recapture a person who is unlawfully at large and whom the constable is pursuing extends to entry to retake a mental patient unlawfully at large provided that such a patient is liable to be retaken and returned to a hospital and provided that the pursuit of such person is almost contemporaneous with the entry to the premises, a term which is somewhat wider than 'hot pursuit'. Where the element of contemporaneity cannot be satisfied, but the situation is one of real emergency, the police could enter the premises under their common-law powers relating to breach of the peace which were specifically preserved by s. 17(6) (*D'Souza v DPP* (1993) 96 Cr App R 278).

Entry and Search on Arrest

D1.175 Where a person is arrested for an indictable offence (see **D1.69**), a constable may enter and search any premises (for definition, see **D1.151**) where the person was at the time of or immediately before the arrest, for evidence relating to the offence for which the person was arrested (PACE 1984, s. 32(2)(b)). Despite the wording of s. 32(1), the power is not confined to circumstances where a constable has reasonable grounds for believing that the arrested person may present a danger to him or herself or others (*Hanningfield v Chief Constable of Essex Police* [2013] EWHC 243 (QB), [2013] 1 WLR 3632). Where the premises consist of two or more dwellings, the power is confined to the dwelling where the arrest took place, or where the person arrested was immediately before arrest, and to common areas (s. 32(7)). The power extends to the search of vehicles and, in the case of ticket touting (see **B11.133**), extends to the search of any vehicle which the constable has reasonable grounds for believing was being used for any purpose connected with the offence. Unlike the power under the PACE 1984, s. 18, the power under s. 32 applies to premises irrespective of whether the person arrested owns, occupies or controls them. However, it does not extend to the search of premises belonging to the arrested person's friends and associates at which the person was not arrested even though it may be suspected that incriminating items are to be found there (*R (Hewitson) v Chief Constable of Dorset Police* [2003] EWHC 3296 (Admin)).

Entry and search is limited to premises that the person was in at the time of the arrest or 'immediately before' the arrest. In contrast to the power under s. 18, s. 32 is an immediate power and it is not permissible for the police to return to premises to search them several hours after the arrest (*Badham* [1987] Crim LR 202). In *Hewitson* it was indicated that a gap of two hours and ten minutes was too long. In such circumstances a power of search may, but will not necessarily, be available under s. 18.

The power of entry and search is available only if the constable has reasonable grounds for believing that there is evidence for which a search is permitted (s. 32(6)). Search is permitted only to the extent that is reasonably required for the purpose of discovering any such thing (s. 32(3)). Whether police entered for that purpose is a question of fact (*Beckford* (1991) 94 Cr App R 43).

Powers of seizure are governed by the PACE 1984, s. 19 (see **D1.178**).

Entry and Search after Arrest

Where a person has been arrested for an indictable offence (see **D1.69**), a constable may enter and search any premises (for definition, see **D1.151**) occupied or controlled by that person provided that the constable has reasonable grounds for suspecting that there is on the premises evidence (other than items subject to legal privilege) relating to that offence or to some other indictable offence which is connected with or similar to that offence (PACE 1984, s. 18(1)). The term 'occupied or controlled' is not defined in the PACE 1984. The premises must as a fact, or perhaps as a matter of mixed fact and law, be occupied or controlled by the person under arrest; reasonable suspicion that the person occupies or controls them is not enough (*Khan v Metropolitan Police Commissioner* [2008] EWCA Civ 723 and see Code B, para. 4.3). A short stay may be sufficient to amount to 'occupation', but it must be such as to support the belief that it will have caused or contributed to the evidence sought being on the premises (*R (AB and CD) v Huddersfield Magistrates' Court* [2014] EWHC 1089 (Admin), [2015] 1 WLR 4737). **D1.176**

It would be possible, provided the conditions are satisfied, for a search to be conducted under both s. 18 and s. 32. For example, where a person is arrested at the house of an acquaintance, that house could be searched under s. 32 and the person's own house searched under s. 18. It has been held that the safeguards governing search and seizure under the PACE 1984, Part II, should not be systematically circumvented by arrest motivated primarily by an intention to search under s. 18 or s. 32 (*R (TL) v Chief Constable of Surrey Police* [2017] EWHC 129 (Admin), [2017] 1 Cr App R 29 (431)). However, it was held in *R (Virdee) v NCA* [2018] EWHC 1119 (Admin), [2018] 1 WLR 5073 that where a search warrant could be obtained or post-arrest powers used, investigators have a choice as to which powers to use.

Generally, entry and search under s. 18 is permissible only if it is authorised in writing in advance by an officer of at least the rank of inspector (s. 18(4)). The officer must not give authorisation unless satisfied that the premises are occupied or controlled by the arrested person and that the necessary grounds exist (Code B, para. 4.3). Code B gives no guidance on what action the officer should take to be satisfied that the premises are occupied or controlled by the arrested person, but it is submitted that the same principles as apply prior to making an application for a search warrant should apply to authorisation under s. 18 (see **D1.164**). A constable can enter and search under s. 18 without such authorisation and before the person is taken to a police station or released on bail under s. 30A (see **D1.20**) if the presence of the person at a place other than a police station is necessary for the effective investigation of the offence (s. 18(5) and (5A)). In such a case, the constable must inform an officer of at least the rank of inspector as soon as practicable (s. 18(6)). An officer who authorises or is informed under s. 18(6) of such a search must make a written record of the grounds for the search and the nature of the evidence sought (s. 18(7)). If the person in occupation or control of the premises at the time of the search is in police detention at the time the record is to be made, it must be made a part of the custody record (s. 18(8)).

D1.177 While the authorisation requirements of s. 18 are mandatory, a failure to comply with them fully (as by not specifying precisely the grounds of the search and the property to be searched for) will not necessarily render the search unlawful. While the section is to be obeyed, the court will, in determining the consequences of any breach, have regard to whether the failure to record prejudiced the person arrested (*Krohn v DPP* [1997] COD 345). It is submitted that, as with entry to carry out an arrest, a constable must first demand entry (where this is practicable) before resorting to force (see **D1.172**).

The constable may seize and retain anything for which he or she may search (s. 18(2)). The scope of the search must be restricted to that which is reasonably required for the purpose of discovering such evidence (s. 18(3)).

Where a constable has entered premises in order to arrest under an extradition arrest power (**D1.38**), he or she may seize and retain anything on the premises that there are reasonable grounds for believing has been obtained in consequence of the commission of an offence, or is evidence in relation to an offence, and that it is necessary to seize it in order to prevent it being concealed, lost, damaged, altered or destroyed (Extradition Act 2003, s. 161(4)). In this case, the relevant code of practice is the Extradition Act Code B (see **D1.38**).

SEIZURE OF, ACCESS TO AND RETENTION OF MATERIALS

Powers of Seizure

D1.178 Where a constable executes a warrant under the PACE 1984, s. 8 or sch. 1, he or she has specific powers to seize and retain anything for which the search has been authorised (s. 8(2) and sch. 1, paras. 4 and 13). Similarly, where a search of premises is conducted under s. 18, or a search of the person under s. 32(1) or s. 32(2)(a) (but not of premises under s. 32(2)(b)), a constable has specific powers to seize and retain materials (ss. 18(2), and 32(8) and (9)). Other search powers may also contain provisions regarding what may be seized. In addition to specific powers of seizure and retention, a constable who is lawfully on any premises (see **D1.151** for definition) has power:

(a) to seize anything which is on the premises if the constable has reasonable grounds to believe that it has been obtained in consequence of the commission of an offence, or that it is evidence in relation to an offence, and that it is necessary to seize it in order to prevent it being concealed, lost, altered or destroyed (PACE 1984, s. 19(2) and (3));

(b) where the constable has similar reasonable grounds, to require that information which is stored in any electronic form and is accessible from the premises be produced in a form in which it can be taken away and which is in a visible and legible form or in a form (such as a disk) from which a visible and legible version can be produced (s. 19(4)) — this power is in addition to any power otherwise conferred (s. 19(5)), including common-law powers (*Cowan v Condon* [2000] 1 WLR 254).

The power under s. 19 is exercisable whether the constable is lawfully on premises by consent or as a result of a statutory or common-law power, and is not limited to indictable offences. No power of seizure conferred by any statute applies to items which the constable has reasonable grounds for believing to be subject to legal privilege (PACE 1984, s. 19(6)), but this must be interpreted by reference to the CJPA 2001, s. 50 (see **D1.180**).

The power under s. 19(2) and (3) to seize anything 'which is on the premises' includes the premises themselves if they are readily moveable, e.g., a car or caravan (*Cowan v Condon*). However, it does not extend to seizing things that are not on the premises, such as a car parked in a car park adjacent to the premises (*Wood v North Avon Magistrates' Court* [2009] EWHC 3614 (Admin)). A trivial excess of power in seizing an object not authorised by a warrant will not vitiate the legality of a search (*Inland Revenue Commissioners, ex parte Rossminster* [1980] AC 952; *A-G of Jamaica v Williams* [1998] AC 351; *Chesterfield Justices, ex parte Bramley* [2000] QB 576). Property that has been unlawfully seized cannot be re-seized at a police station to which it has been taken on the basis that the officer is then lawfully on those premises (*R (Cook) v SOCA* [2010] EWHC 2119 (Admin), [2011] 1 WLR 144). However, in such circumstances, if an application is made under the CJPA 2001, s. 59(5)(b), a judge may authorise retention under s. 59(6) (*R (El-Kurd) v Winchester Crown Court* [2011] EWHC 1853 (Admin); cf. *R (Chatwani) v NCA* [2015] EWHC 1283 (Admin)). **D1.179**

The power to require any information stored in electronic form and which is accessible from the premises to be produced in a form in which it can be taken away etc. is specifically extended to powers of seizure under any enactment contained in an Act passed before or after the PACE 1984, and under the PACE 1984, ss. 8 and 18 and sch. 1, para. 13 (s. 20).

Code B, para. 8.1, requires that records be kept of all searches of premises and specifies the information that must be recorded, which includes anything seized. A search register, containing all search records, must be kept at each sub-divisional (or equivalent) police station (Code B, para. 9.1).

For powers to seize and retain the proceeds of crime, see **D8**.

Powers to 'seize and sift'

The CJPA 2001, s. 50, enables a person who is lawfully on premises and to whom a power of seizure listed in the CJPA 2001, sch. 1, part 1 applies, to seize the whole or part of a suspect item so as to remove it from the premises for the purpose of determining whether it falls within the power. It is a condition of exercise of the power that the determination cannot be reasonably practicably determined on the premises (s. 50(1)). Where the seizable property cannot reasonably practicably be separated from something else in which it is comprised, both the article and that from which it cannot be separated may be seized (s. 50(2)). The factors to be considered in determining reasonable practicability are set out in s. 50(3) and include length of time, numbers of persons needed, damage to property from separation, the apparatus necessary and prejudice to the use of separated property. The powers of seizure referred to in the CJPA 2001, sch. 1, are remarkably comprehensive and include powers of seizure under the PACE 1984, parts II and III. They go beyond the normal range of police activities and include enforcement activities conducted by a wide range of other authorities. Note that Revenue and Customs officers have the same powers in respect of the provisions concerning legally privileged material as police officers (s. 67). **D1.180**

The CJPA 2001, s. 51, contains similar powers in respect of seizure from the person. The powers to which s. 51 apply are set out in the CJPA 2001, sch. 1, part 2 (s. 51(5)). For guidance on seizure, retention and return of property seized under ss. 50 and 51, see Code B, paras. 7.7 to 7.17 (see **appendix 1**).

Provision is made under s. 52 for giving notice of the exercise of the powers under ss. 50 and 51. It was held in *R (Dulai) v Chelmsford Magistrates' Court* [2012] EWHC 1055 (Admin), [2012] 2 Cr App R 19 (229) that non-compliance with s. 52 did not necessarily render a seizure under s. 50 unlawful. Examination and return of anything seized under ss. 50 and 51 is governed by s. 53. Essentially, the examination should be carried out as soon as possible, should be confined to the purpose of verification, and the property should be kept separate from other articles seized. While the use of in-house staff as 'independent' lawyers to determine questions of whether material may be covered by legal professional privilege would be unlawful, their use in a preliminary sift of documents is not (*R (McKenzie) v Director of the SFO* [2016] EWHC 102 (Admin), [2016] 1 WLR 1308). Note that seized property that may be subject to the obligation to return may include copies made of an electronic document that has been seized (*Business Energy Solutions Ltd v Preston Crown Court* [2018] EWHC 1534 (Admin), [2018] 1 WLR 4887).

D1.181 Specific provision is made in s. 54 for the return of articles seized under ss. 50 or 51 which attract legal privilege. The meaning of 'legal privilege' depends upon the statute in which the phrase is used. The definition in the PACE 1984, s. 10 (see **D1.148**), remains unaltered (CJPA 2001, s. 65). If at any time after seizure it appears to the person having possession of the seized property that it is an item subject to legal privilege or has such an item comprised in it, that person is under a duty to return the property as soon as reasonably practicable after the seizure. This is subject to exception where the legally privileged item is comprised within property for which the person had power to search and which the person is not required to return either under s. 54 or s. 55 (s. 55 concerns excluded and special procedure material). This is itself subject to the proviso that return is not required where separation is not reasonably practicable without prejudicing the use, for lawful purposes, of that part of the article (s. 54(1) and (2)). The power of retention under s. 56 does not authorise retention of anything that must be returned under s. 54 (s. 56(4), and see **D1.183**).

Access to and Retention of Seized Material

D1.182 In respect of seizures under any enactment, on the request of either the occupier of premises on which the material was seized or the person having custody or control of it immediately before seizure, the constable or accompanying person must provide a record of what was seized within a reasonable time of the request (PACE 1984, s. 21(1) and (2)). If requested by the person who had custody or control of the item immediately before it was seized, or by someone acting on the person's behalf, the officer in charge of the investigation must allow that person access to the item under the supervision of a constable (s. 21(3)). Similarly the officer must allow access for photographing or copying, or arrange for it to be photographed or copied and supply the photograph or copy to the person requesting it within a reasonable time (s. 21(4), (6) and (7)). A constable may also photograph or copy anything he or she has power to seize without such a request (s. 21(5)). The request does not need to be acceded to if there are reasonable grounds to believe that it would prejudice any investigation, or any criminal proceedings resulting therefrom, to do so (s. 21(8)).

D1.183 The common-law power of the police to preserve *exhibits* is well established (*Lushington, ex parte Otto* [1894] 1 QB 420). Anything seized or taken away by a constable or accompanying person under s. 19 or s. 20 may be retained as long as is necessary in all the circumstances (s. 22(1)). In particular, anything seized for the purposes of a criminal investigation may be retained for use as evidence at a trial, or forensic examination or further investigation, unless a photograph or copy would suffice, and where there are reasonable grounds for believing it has been obtained in consequence of the commission of an offence, anything may be retained in order to establish its lawful owner (s. 22(2) and (4)). In relation to the latter, the police may retain the material only for so long as that purpose continues (*Malone v Metropolitan Police Commissioner* [1980] QB 49; *Gough v Chief Constable of the West Midlands Police* [2004] EWCA Civ 206; *Settelen v Metropolitan Police Commissioner* [2004] EWHC 2171 (Ch)). However, the police have a short 'period of grace' during which they can retain the material to consider whether, for example, an application should be made to retain it under the POCA 2002 (*R (Iqbal) v Luton and*

South Bedfordshire Magistrates' Court [2011] EWHC 705 (Admin)). Where the thing seized is a residential caravan, the legality of its retention must be determined by whether it strikes a fair balance between the right to private life under the ECHR, Article 8, and the public interest, including the prevention of disorder or crime (*Chief Constable of Wiltshire Constabulary v McDonagh* [2008] EWHC 654 (QB)).

The police cannot retain items seized because they may be used to cause physical injury, or to damage property, or to interfere with evidence, or to assist in escape from lawful custody, when the person from whom they were seized is no longer in police detention or the custody of the court or has been released on bail (s. 22(3), and see *Chief Constable of Merseyside Police v Owens* [2012] EWHC 1515 (Admin)). However, they can retain material, even after the CPS has decided not to prosecute, for use in a private prosecution (*Scopelight Ltd v Chief Constable of Northumbria Police Force* [2009] EWCA Civ 1156, [2010] QB 438).

It follows from these provisions that the only permitted use of seized material is for the purpose of investigating and prosecuting crime, after which they must be returned to their true owner. Documents and information may be communicated to others for the purpose of investigation and prosecution, and may perhaps be disclosed to other public authorities. They may not be made available to private individuals for private purposes (*Marcel v Metropolitan Police Commissioner* [1992] Ch 225).

Section 22(5) declares that the provisions of s. 22 do not affect the power of a court to make an order in respect of property under the Police (Property) Act 1897, s. 1. The procedure for applications under the 1897 Act is governed by CrimPR 47.37 to 47.40 (see Supplement, **R47.37** *et seq.*). **D1.184**

In addition to the provisions in the PACE 1984, s. 22, retention of seized property is also governed by the CJPA 2001, s. 56. Section 56 concerns property seized by any constable who is lawfully on premises or by 'relevant persons' (as to which see s. 56(4A) and (5), referring, e.g., to warrants under the Companies Act 1985) accompanying a constable, and to property seized by a constable carrying out a lawful search of any person. Retention of such property is authorised if there are reasonable grounds for believing that it is property obtained in consequence of the commission of an offence and that its retention is necessary to prevent it being concealed, lost, damaged, altered or destroyed (s. 56(2) and see *R (Chief Constable of South Yorkshire) v Sheffield Crown Court* [2014] EWHC 81 (Admin)). The power also extends to property that is believed to be evidence in relation to any offence where its retention is required for the same purposes (s. 56(3)). Powers to obtain hard copies of information stored in electronic form are powers of seizure (s. 60). It follows that the powers of retention etc. apply to such material. **D1.185**

By the CJPA 2001, s. 59, any person with a relevant interest in property seized under the authority, or purported authority, of a relevant power of seizure (which may include a person from whom the property has been seized, or the police or other authority which has seized it) may apply to the appropriate judicial authority for the return of the whole or part of the seized property (s. 59(2)). The grounds for such an application are set out in s. 59(3) (and see CrimPR 47.38). There is no general rule preventing an application under s. 59 until every issue in a judicial review claim has been resolved (*R (HS) v South Cheshire Magistrates' Court* [2015] EWHC 3415 (Admin)). Where an application under s. 59 has been made, the relevant judicial authority may give such directions as it thinks fit as to the examination, retention, separation or return of the whole or part of the seized property (s. 59(5)). For relevant case law, see *R (El-Kurd) v Winchester Crown Court* [2011] EWHC 1853 (Admin); *R (Dulai) v Chelmsford Magistrates' Court* [2012] EWHC 1055 (Admin), [2013] 1 WLR 220; *AC, RC, BK, and GST v Nottingham and Newark Magistrates' Court* [2013] EWHC 3790 (Admin); *R (Panesar) v Central Criminal Court* [2014] EWCA Civ 1613, [2015] 1 WLR 2577; *R (Chaudhary) v Bristol Crown Court* [2014] EWHC 4096 (Admin); [2015] 1 Cr App R 18 (221); *R (Kouyoumjian) v Hammersmith Magistrates' Court* [2014] EWHC 4028 (Admin)). The court has a discretion under s. 59(6) to authorise the retention of property which has been unlawfully seized if it is satisfied that an investigating agency would either succeed in a notional application for a fresh search warrant under s. 59(7)(a) or that one of the orders identified in s. 59(7)(b) for the production of property would be granted (s. 56(6) and see *R (HMRC Commissioners) v Maidstone Crown Court* [2018] EWHC 2219 (Admin) and **D.154, D1.157, D1.161**). The investigating agency's conduct must be examined as a whole by the court in considering whether to authorise retention and is not limited to instances of bad faith (*R (Chatwani) v NCA* [2015] EWHC 1283 (Admin)). This consideration includes any breach of the duty of candour in judicial review proceedings (*R (Brook) v Preston Crown Court* [2018] EWHC 2024 (Admin)).

For the power to restrict disclosure to a person seeking the return of seized material under s. 59, see *Haralambous v St Albans Crown Court* [2018] UKSC 1, [2018] AC 236 (see **D1.163**), which was considered in *Competition Markets Authority v Concordia International RX (UK) Ltd* [2019] EWCA Civ 1881, [2019] 1 All ER 699.

POLICE BAIL WITHOUT CHARGE

Powers and Duties to Release with or without Bail

D1.186 The police have a variety of powers and duties under the PACE 1984 to release (with or without bail) persons arrested and taken to, or detained at, a police station in respect of an offence, but not charged. These have been significantly modified by amendments introduced by the PCA 2017, Part 4, ch. 1. For the power to grant bail to an arrested person without taking him or her to a police station, see **D1.20**. For the power to release (with or without bail) in circumstances where a custody officer is satisfied that there is sufficient evidence to charge, see **D2.2** ***et seq.*** The police do not have power to release on bail without charge a person arrested and detained under the TA 2000, s. 41 (*R (I) v City of Westminster Magistrates' Court* [2008] EWHC 2146 (Admin)).

D1.187 The PACE 1984, s. 34(2), provides that, where a custody officer becomes aware, in relation to a person in police detention (see **D1.40**), that grounds for detention have ceased to apply and the officer is not aware of any other grounds to justify detention, the immediate release from custody of the detained person must be ordered (unless it appears to the officer that the person was unlawfully at large when arrested: s. 34(4)). Such release must be without bail unless it appears to the custody officer that there is a need for further investigation of any matter in connection with which the person was detained at any time during the period of detention or that in respect of any such matter proceedings may be taken against the person (or, if achild or young person, that he or she may be given a youth caution), and the pre-conditions for bail are satisfied, in which case the release must be on bail (s. 34(5) and (5A)).

Where a person arrested either without warrant or under a warrant not endorsed for bail is taken before a custody officer under s. 37(1), and the officer determines that there is not sufficient evidence to charge, the person must be released without bail (unless the pre-conditions for bail are satisfied, in which case the release must be on bail), unless the officer has reasonable grounds for believing that detention is necessary for one or more of the specified grounds (s. 37(2) and (3), and see **D1.49**). If the officer determines that there is sufficient evidence to charge, the detainee must be dealt with in accordance with s. 37(7) (see **D2.2**).

D1.188 If the officer conducting a review of detention under s. 40 (see D1.75) concludes that detention can no longer be justified by reference to the conditions in s. 37, the officer must release the person without bail, unless the pre-conditions for bail are satisfied, in which case the release must be on bail (s. 40(8) and (8A)). Where a detained person has not been charged at the expiry of 24 hours after the relevant time, he or she must be released without bail (unless the pre-conditions for bail are satisfied, in which case the release must be on bail) unless further detention is authorised under s. 42 or 43 (s. 41(7)). A similar provision applies at the expiry of the 36-hour time-limit (s. 42(10)), or where an application for a warrant or extension of a warrant of further detention is refused (unless the 36 hours or the existing warrant have not expired (s. 43(15) and (16) and s. 44(7) and (8)), or where a warrant expires (s. 43(18)). There is no similar provision where an extended warrant expires, but it is submitted that the same principles must apply.

The 'pre-conditions for bail' are: **D1.189**

(a) that the custody officer is satisfied that releasing the person on bail is necessary and proportionate in all the circumstances (having regard, in particular, to any conditions of bail which would be imposed); and
(b) that an officer of the rank of inspector or above, having considered any representations made by the person or legal representative, authorises the release on bail (PACE 1984, s. 50A, as inserted by the PCA 2017, s. 59).

The PACE 1984 imposes no overall limit on the period for which bail can be granted, but this is subject to the limitations and provisions for extension introduced by the PCA 2017, Part 4, ch. 1 (see **D1.192** ***et seq.***) A person who is released without bail is commonly referred to as being released under investigation although this term does not feature in the PACE 1984. The National Police Chiefs' Council's *Operational guidance for pre-charge bail and released under investigation* (January 2019, tinyurl.com/y9retwnq) sets out the test for continued investigation in cases where a suspect has been released under investigation (RUI): 'The RUI process...must be capable of withstanding scrutiny, having due regard to proportionality and necessity in the circumstances' (p. 3). 'Investigations [in] which suspects are on RUI must be conducted expeditiously to ensure all parties are not subject to long delays' (p. 4). 'A supervisor should endorse the investigation log with an initial Expected Finish Date (EFD)' (p. 5). The guidance also outlines 'suggested good practice' that 'once a suspect has been released, investigations must have a documented supervisory review at least every 30 days (or every 10 days if high priority and safeguarding is an issue) until the investigation has been completed and a disposal actioned' (p. 5). Subsequent reviews will be conducted by an inspector at three months and superintendent at six months who must satisfy themselves that the RUI case is being 'managed expeditiously and further investigation is appropriate'. At each review 'the investigating officer must ensure the victim, suspect and their legal advisor...is provided with an update on the progress of the investigation' (p. 5). **D1.190**

Powers to Impose Conditions

A release on bail under the PACE 1984, Part IV (which includes all of the powers to grant bail mentioned in **D1.186** except for bail granted under s. 30A), is deemed to be a release on bail in accordance with the BA 1976, ss. 3, 3A, 5 and 5A, as those sections apply to bail granted by a constable. Conditions can be attached to bail granted under the PACE 1984, Part IV, except ss. 37(CA(2)(b) and 37A(2)(b) (PACE 1984, s. 47(1A), as amended by the PCA 2017, s. 62(3)). For the power to attach conditions to bail granted under s. 30A, see **D1.20**. Such conditions (including requiring a surety or security) can be imposed as appear necessary for the purpose of ensuring that the person surrenders to custody, does not commit an offence on bail, does not interfere with witnesses or otherwise obstruct the course of justice, and/or for his or her own protection (or where the person is under 18 years, for his or her own welfare or own interests) (PACE 1984, s. 47(1A), and BA 1976, ss. 3(6) and 3A(5)). Any condition may be imposed other than a condition that the person reside in a bail hostel, make him or herself available for the purposes of a court report, or attend an interview with a lawyer (BA 1976, s. 3A(2)). A surety can be required only for the purpose of securing surrender to custody (*R (Shea) v Winchester Crown Court* [2013] EWHC 1050 (Admin)). It has been held in relation to a court's power to impose bail conditions that in considering whether and what conditions to impose, the court must perceive a real and not merely fanciful risk of the relevant outcome (*Mansfield Justices, ex parte Sharkey* [1985] QB 613), and it is submitted that the same principle must apply to a decision by a police officer. **D1.191**

For the right of a person to apply for variation or removal of bail conditions, see **D2.47**.

The Period of Bail and Extensions

D1.192 **Initial Maximum Period** The initial maximum period for which bail can be granted is three months beginning with the person's bail date in an SFO case, or 28 days in an FCA case or any other case (s. 47ZB(1)). The bail start date is the day after the day on which the person was arrested, irrespective of the actual day on which the person is released on bail (PACE 1984, s. 47ZB(4)(a)). An 'FCA case' is a case in which the 'relevant offence' in relation to the person is being investigated by the FCA, and a senior officer confirms that this is the case. An 'SFO case' is a case in which the relevant offence in relation to the person is being investigated by the Director of the SFO, and a senior officer confirms that this is the case (s. 47ZB(4)(b) to (c)). The 'relevant offence' is the offence in respect of which the power to release the person on bail is exercised (s. 47ZA(8)). A 'senior officer' is an officer of the rank of at least superintendent (s. 47ZB(4)(d)). The bail period does not run, or is suspended, during the period that a person is released on bail under the PACE 1984, s. 37(7)(a) or s. 37C(2)(b), in order for a Crown prosecutor to make a charging decision (unless the prosecutor requests further information from the police in order to make the decision, in which case the period is treated as running during the time that the police are gathering the further information) (s. 47ZL). If a person who has been bailed is in hospital as an in-patient at any time on the day on which the applicable bail period would end, the running of the bail period is treated as having been suspended for any day on which the person is an in-patient (s. 47ZM(4) and (5)). Where the person had previously been released under the PACE 1984, s. 30A (street bail), in connection with the matter for which he or she is in police detention, the period spent on street bail counts towards the period of 28 days for the purposes of s. 47ZB(1)(b) (s. 47ZM(1) to (3)).

D1.193 **Extension of the Period of Bail** Extension of the period of bail beyond the initial maximum periods depends upon whether some or all of the following conditions are satisfied:

Condition A: the decision-maker has reasonable grounds for suspecting the person to be guilty of the relevant offence.

Condition B: the decision-maker has reasonable grounds for believing, in a case where the person is, or is to be, released on bail under the PACE 1984, s. 37(7)(c) or s. 37CA(2)(b), that further time is needed for making a decision as to whether to charge the person with the relevant offence; or otherwise, that further investigation is needed of any matter in connection with the relevant offence.

Condition C: that the decision-maker has reasonable grounds for believing, in a case where the person is, or is to be, released on bail under the PACE 1984, s. 37(7)(c) or s. 37CA(2)(b), that the decision as to whether to charge the person with the relevant offence is being made diligently and expeditiously; or otherwise, that the investigation is being conducted diligently and expeditiously.

Condition D: that the decision-maker has reasonable grounds for believing that the release on bail of the person is necessary and proportionate in all the circumstances (having regard, in particular, to any conditions of bail which are, or are to be, imposed (PACE 1984, s. 47ZC(2) to (5)).

D1.194 In an FCA case or any case other than an SFO case, or a case where an extension has been authorised under the PACE 1984, s. 47ZD, and designated as exceptionally complex, a senior officer may extend the period of bail to the end of the period of three months beginning with the person's bail date provided the officer is satisfied that conditions A to D are met. Before making a decision, the officer must arrange for the person or the person's legal representative to be informed that a determination is to be made, consider any representations made, and subsequently inform the person of the determination made (s. 47ZD). In an SFO case, or a case where an extension has been authorised under s. 47ZD and which has been designated by a qualifying prosecutor as being exceptionally complex, an appropriate decision-maker may extend the period of bail to the end of the period of six months beginning with the person's bail date, provided the decision-maker is satisfied that conditions A to D are met. A 'qualifying prosecutor' is a prosecutor of a description designated for this purpose by the Chief Executive of the FCA, the Director of the SFO or the DPP. An 'appropriate decision-maker' is a designated member of staff of the FCA (in an FCA case), a member of the SFO who is of the Senior Civil Service (in an SFO case), or a qualifying police officer (i.e. a police officer of the rank of commander or assistant chief constable or above). Before making a decision, the appropriate decision-maker must arrange for the person or the person's legal representative to be informed that a determination is to be made (and if a qualifying police officer, consult a qualifying prosecutor), consider any representations made, and subsequently inform the person of the determination (PACE 1984, s. 47ZE).

In (a) an SFO case, (b) a case where bail has been extended under the PACE 1984, s. 47ZD, or (c) a case where bail has been extended under s. 47ZE, an application may be made to a magistrates' court to extend the period of bail. In order to extend bail, the court must be satisfied that conditions B to D are met. If it is so satisfied, and it is likely that the decision or investigations referred to in condition B will be made or completed within six months beginning with the person's bail date in the case of (a) or (b), or nine months in the case of (c), then the court may extend the period of bail for such a period. If satisfied that conditions B to D are met, but it is unlikely that the decision will be made or investigations completed if a longer period of bail is not granted, the court may extend bail by nine months in the case of (a) or (b), or 12 months in the case of (c), beginning with the person's bail date (s. 47ZF). The PACE 1984, s. 47ZG, provides that a court can further extend the bail period if it is satisfied that conditions B to D are met. The maximum period of extension is three months from the end of the current applicable bail period if it is likely that the decision or investigations referred to in condition B will be made or completed within that period, or six months if it is not likely that the decision or investigations will be made or completed within the three-month period. Provided the relevant conditions continue to be satisfied, there is no limit on the number of extensions of bail that may be granted. **D1.195**

Applications to extend bail under the PACE 1984, ss. 47ZF and ss. 47ZG, are to be made before the applicable bail period expires, and are normally to be determined by a single justice of the peace on written evidence (s. 47ZI). However, an application is to be heard orally (but not in open court) if a single justice of the peace considers that the interests of justice require an oral hearing, or the effect of the application would be to extend the applicable bail period so that it ends after the end of the period of 12 months beginning with the person's start bail date and either that person, or the person making the application, requests an oral hearing (s. 47ZI(2) and (3)). Where an oral hearing is held, the justices may direct that the person to whom the application relates and the person's legal representative be excluded from any part of the hearing (s. 47ZI(5)). The applicant may apply to the court for it to authorise that specified information be withheld from the person to whom the application relates and the person's legal representative. The court can grant such an application if it is satisfied that there are reasonable grounds for believing that the specified information is sensitive information. Information is sensitive if its disclosure would have one or more of the following results: **D1.196**

(a) evidence connected with an indictable offence would be interfered with or harmed;
(b) a person would be interfered with or physically injured;
(c) a person suspected of having committed an indictable offence but not yet arrested for the offence would be alerted;
(d) the recovery of property obtained as a result of an indictable offence would be hindered (s. 47ZH).

An application under s. 47ZH is to be determined by a single justice of the peace on written evidence unless the justice determines that the interests of justice require an oral hearing (s. 47ZI(7)).

Enforcement

D1.197 A person who has been released under the PACE 1984, ss. 41(7), 42(10), 43(18) or 47(2), may be re-arrested if, since release, new evidence has come to light or an examination or analysis of existing evidence has been made which could not reasonably have been made before the release (ss. 41(9), 42(11), 43(19) and 47(2) respectively, as amended by the PCA 2017, s. 65). With the exception of arrest under s. 47(2), this applies irrespective of whether the release was on bail or without bail. It would seem that where a person has been released without bail, in the absence of new evidence, etc., the person cannot be re-arrested for the offence in relation to which he or she was originally arrested since otherwise the provisions on re-arrest would not be necessary.

A person released on conditional bail may be arrested by a constable having reasonable grounds for suspecting that the person has broken any of the conditions (s. 46A(1A)). A person granted bail to return to a police station (whether conditional or not) is under a duty to do so, and may be arrested if he or she fails to attend the police station at the appointed time (s. 46A(1)). The person must then be taken to the police station at which he or she was required to surrender as soon as practicable (s. 46A(1A)), and is treated as having been arrested for an offence for the purposes of ss. 30 (duty to take arrested person to a police station) and 31 (arrest for further offence) (s. 46A(2) and (3)). If the person had been released under s. 37(7)(a) and the Crown Prosecutor has not made a charge decision under the PACE 1984, s. 37B, the custody officer may either charge or release the person on bail again (s. 37C(2) and (3)). The duty to attend at the police station on the appointed date is subject to the power of a custody officer to give notice in writing to the person that attendance is not required (s. 47(4)). Unlike under the BA 1976, s. 7(3), there is no power of arrest in respect of an anticipated breach of conditions or failure to surrender. Breach of conditions is not an offence (subject to the following exception), but failure without reasonable cause to surrender to custody is an offence (BA 1976, s. 6, as applied by the PACE 1984, s. 47(1)). Where a person is released without charge and on bail under the PACE 1984, Part IV, and the release is subject to a travel restriction condition, breach of the condition is an offence (PCA 2017, ss. 68 and 69). 'Travel restriction condition' is defined in s. 68(2).

Where a person returns to the police station in accordance with bail (or fails to surrender and is arrested and taken to the police station), the custody officer may authorise further detention only if the grounds in s. 37(2) are satisfied (as a result of s. 34(7)). However, this does not apply where the person was released on bail under s. 37(7)(a), in which case the person may be kept in police detention to enable a charge decision to be made in accordance with ss. 37B or 37C (s. 37D(4)). Where a person returns to the police station in accordance with the grant of bail, including live link bail under s. 46ZA(4), or is arrested for failure to surrender to bail under s. 46A(1) or s. 46ZA(5), time spent in police detention before the release on bail (but not any time whilst on bail) counts for the purpose of calculating the maximum period of detention without charge (s. 47(6): see also **D1.67**). However, this is not the case if the person has been re-arrested on the grounds of new evidence, in which case the detention clock starts again.

INTERCEPTION OF COMMUNICATIONS AND SURVEILLANCE

D1.198 Interception of communications, the gathering and retention of communications data, and surveillance are principally regulated by the IPA 2016 and the RIPA 2000, although there are other relevant statutes including the Police Act 1997 and the Intelligence Services Act 1994. The interception of communications provisions of the RIPA 2000, Part I, have been repealed and replaced by parts 1 to 7 of the IPA 2016, but the provisions of the RIPA 2000 governing surveillance and covert human intelligence sources remain unaffected.

Interception of Communications

The interception of communications, and the gathering and retention of communications data, are regulated by the IPA 2016, parts 1 to 7. Interception of communications and obtaining communications data without lawful authority under the Act are offences (ss. 3 and 11) (see also **B9.84**). Lawful authority may be granted by warrant (part 2, chapter 1), but certain interceptions may be lawfully carried out without a warrant (ss. 6 and 44 to 52). Note in particular that interception of a communication that is sent by, or intended for, a person who has consented to the interception is lawful provided that it is authorised as directed surveillance (s. 44). The grounds for issuing a warrant are set out in s. 20. **D1.199**

Substantial restrictions apply to the use of intercepted material (see **F2.33** ***et seq.***)

Surveillance and Covert Human Intelligence Sources

Part II of the RIPA 2000 regulates the use of intrusive and directed surveillance, and covert human intelligence sources. Use of these methods without authorisation does not amount to an offence, and there is no similar limitation on evidence to that found in s. 17 (*Kelly* [2007] EWCA Crim 1715). They are defined in s. 26, and it is an essential feature of each that the activity be 'covert' (defined in s. 26(9)). Surveillance is intrusive if it is carried out in relation to anything taking place on any residential premises or private vehicle, and involves the presence of an individual on the premises or vehicle or is carried out by means of a surveillance device (s. 26(3)). A police van is not a private vehicle (*Plunkett* [2013] EWCA Crim 261, [2013] 1 WLR 3121). However, there are certain exceptions to this definition in s. 26(4) to (6). Surveillance is directed if it is undertaken for the purposes of a specific investigation or operation in such a manner as is likely to result in private information being obtained, and is otherwise than by way of an immediate response to events or circumstances the nature of which is that it would not be reasonably practicable for an authorisation to have been sought (s. 26(2)). In this way, surveillance by general CCTV cameras, or by an officer who in the course of a routine patrol decides to follow a suspicious looking person in the street, does not come within the definition, and therefore does not require authorisation under the Act. There is an overlap between the provisions governing the authorisation of intrusive surveillance under the RIPA 2000 and those in the Police Act 1997, Part III, and the Intelligence Services Act 1994, s. 5, governing entry on to or interference with property. A covert human intelligence source is defined in the RIPA 2000, s. 26(7) and (8), and could include both an informant and a police officer acting undercover. Children can act as covert human intelligence sources (*R (Just for Kids Law) v Secretary of State for the Home Department* [2019] EWHC 1772 (Admin), [2019] 2 Cr App R 31 (356)). Civilian staff or volunteers designated under the Police Reform Act 2002, s. 38 (see **D1.3**), cannot be authorised to establish contact in person with another person (RIPA 2000, s. 29(6A)), although they could be authorised to do so online, e.g. as part of an online child sexual abuse investigation. **D1.200**

Authorisation of intrusive surveillance must be by a senior authorising officer (of the rank of chief constable or equivalent) or by the Secretary of State (s. 32(1)). The grounds for authorisation are set out in s. 32(2) to (4). Authorisation of directed surveillance or the use of a covert human intelligence source must be by designated persons (of the rank of superintendent or equivalent) (ss. 28(1) and 29(1)). Authorisations granted by designated local authority officers do not take effect unless approved by a judicial authority (s. 32A). The grounds for authorisation are set out in s. 28(2) and (3), and s. 29(2) and (3) respectively. The person giving authorisation must believe that the operation is necessary (*Brett* [2005] EWCA Crim 983). In the absence of exceptional circumstances, the lawfulness of surveillance would normally be sufficiently demonstrated by the production of the surveillance commissioner's or authorising officer's signed approval and the defence would not normally be entitled to see the authorisation or the material on which it was based (*GS* [2005] EWCA Crim 887). For surveillance carried out on premises used for the purpose of legal consultations and the use of covert human intelligence sources whose activities involve obtaining access to matters subject to legal privilege, see **D1.58**. **D1.201**

The RIPA 2000 does not apply to surveillance which is not covert or not conducted by the police (or other regulated agency). Thus, for example, it does not govern the overt taking of photographs of potential demonstrators (which it was held in *R (Wood) v Metropolitan Police Commissioner* [2009] EWCA Civ 414, [2010] 1 WLR 123 may breach the ECHR, Article 8) or the overt use of automated facial recognition technology (*R (Bridges) v Chief Constable of South Wales Police* [2019] EWHC 2341 (Admin), [2020] 1 Cr App R 3 (52)). Evidence discovered by means of a camera erected by the accused's neighbours, the location of which was known to the accused, could be relied upon by the prosecution and would not be excluded under the PACE 1984, s. 78 (*Rosenberg* [2006] EWCA Crim 6).

INVESTIGATORY POWERS UNDER THE CRIME (OVERSEAS PRODUCTION ORDERS) ACT 2019

D1.202 The Crime (Overseas Production Orders) Act 2019 enables an 'appropriate officer' to apply to the Crown Court for an overseas production order ('OPO') requiring a person based overseas to produce or give access to 'electronic data' regardless as to where it is stored (ss. 1, 4, 5(4)(a), 6). A non-disclosure requirement may be included within the OPO (s. 8). A person must comply with the OPO within seven days of the date of service unless a judge orders otherwise (s. 5(4)(b), (5)). An application to vary or revoke an OPO can be made by an appropriate officer or any person affected by the order or by the Secretary of State (s. 7). See CrimPR 47.66 to 47.71 (see Supplement, **R47.66** *et seq.*).

An 'appropriate officer' is defined under s. 2(1) as:

(i) a constable; or
(ii) an officer of Revenue and Customs; or
(iii) a member of the SFO; or
(iv) an accredited financial investigator if the officer is exercising that function for the purpose of a confiscation or money laundering investigation within the meaning of Part 8 of the POCA 2002 (s. 2(2)); or
(v) a counter-terrorism financial investigator if the officer is exercising that function for the purpose of a terrorist investigation relating to terrorist property (s. 2(3)) or is a sch. 5A counter-terrorism financial investigator and is exercising that function for the purpose of a terrorist financing investigation (s. 2(4)); or
(vi) is a person appointed by the FCA under the FSMA 2000, s. 168(3) or (5), to conduct an investigation; or
(vii) is a person of a description specified in regulations made by the Secretary of State.

Definitions

D1.203 'Electronic data' is broadly defined as 'any data stored electronically' (s. 3(2)) regardless of where it is stored (s. 6(4)(a)) but does not include 'excepted electronic data' (s. 3(3)).

'Excepted electronic data' means electronic data that is (a) an item subject to legal privilege with the same meaning as the PACE 1984, s. 10 (s. 3(6)) (see **D1.148**), or (b) a personal record which is a confidential personal record.

The term 'personal record' is defined at s. 3(7) in essentially identical terms to the PACE 1984, s. 12 (see **D1.149**). A 'personal record' is 'confidential' if it was created in circumstances giving rise to an obligation of confidence and that obligation continues to be owed, or it is held subject to a restriction on disclosure or an obligation of secrecy contained in an enactment (whenever passed or made) (s. 3(8)). Therefore, an OPO cannot require the production of material that is protected by legal professional privilege or personal records that are a confidential personal record.

Requirements

A Crown Court judge must have reasonable grounds for believing that each of the requirements set out in s. 4(2) to (7) are met (s. 4(1)), namely that: D1.204

- s. 4(2): the person against whom an order is sought operates or is based in a country outside the UK which is a party to or participates in a 'designated international co-operation arrangement' (see further s. 4(8));
- s. 4(3): (a) that an indictable offence has been committed and proceedings have been instituted or the offence is being investigated or (b) the order is sought for the purpose of a terrorism investigation (as defined by the TA 2000, s. 32);
- s. 4(4): the person against whom the order is sought has possession or control of all or part of the electronic data;
- s. 4(5): all or part of the electronic data is likely to be of substantial value to the investigation or proceedings as mentioned in s. 4(3)(a) and (b);
- s. 4(6): all or part of the electronic data is likely to be relevant evidence in respect of the offence mentioned at s. 4(3)(a) (this subsection has no application to terrorism investigations under s. 4(3)(b)). 'Relevant evidence' is defined as anything that would be admissible in evidence in proceedings in relation to the offence (s. 4(11));
- s. 4(7): that it is in the public interest for the OPO to be made having regard to both the benefit likely to accrue, if the data is obtained, to the proceedings or investigation as mentioned in s. 4(3)(a) and (b) and the circumstances under which the person against whom the order is sought has possession or control of any of the data.

On 28 February 2020 the Overseas Production Orders and Requests for Interception (Designation of Agreement) Regulations 2020 (SI 2020 No. 38), reg. 2(a), designated the Agreement between the United Kingdom and the United States of America on Access to Electronic Data for the Purpose of Countering Serious Crime (7 October 2019) as a relevant treaty for the purposes of the Crime (Overseas Production Orders) Act 2019, s. 1(5)(b), which means that the Agreement is now a 'designated international co-operation arrangement'. These provisions will enable Overseas Production Orders to be made in respect of electronic data governed by US law.

INVESTIGATORY POWERS UNDER THE SERIOUS ORGANISED CRIME AND POLICE ACT 2005

Powers Relating to Disclosure and Production

Part 2 of the SOCPA 2005 confers powers on the DPP, referred to as 'the Investigating Authority', in relation to the giving of disclosure notices (s. 60(1) and (5)). These may be delegated to a Crown Prosecutor or to a Revenue and Customs Prosecutor (s. 60(2) and (3)). These powers apply to the offences specified in s. 61(1). D1.205

Serious Organised Crime and Police Act 2005, s. 61

(1) This Chapter applies to the following offences—
- (a) any offence listed in Schedule 2 to the Proceeds of Crime Act 2002 (lifestyle offences: England and Wales);
- (b) any offence listed in Schedule 4 to that Act (lifestyle offences: Scotland);
- (ba) any offence listed in Schedule 5 to that Act (lifestyle offences: Northern Ireland);
- (c) any offence under sections 15 to 18 of the Terrorism Act 2000 (offences relating to fund-raising, money laundering etc.);
- (d) any offence under section 170 of the Customs and Excise Management Act 1979 (fraudulent evasion of duty) or section 72 of the Value Added Tax Act 1994 (offences relating to VAT) which is a qualifying offence;

(e) any offence under section 17 of the Theft Act 1968 (false accounting), or section 17 of the Theft Act (Northern Ireland) 1969 (false accounting) or any offence at common law of cheating in relation to the public revenue, which is a qualifying offence;
(f) any offence under section 1 of the Criminal Attempts Act 1981, or Article 3 of the Criminal Attempts and Conspiracy (Northern Ireland) Order 1983 or in Scotland at common law, of attempting to commit any offence in paragraph (c) or any offence in paragraph (d) or (e) which is a qualifying offence;
(g) any offence under section 1 of the Criminal Law Act 1977, or Article 9 of the Criminal Attempts and Conspiracy (Northern Ireland) Order 1983 or in Scotland at common law, of conspiracy to commit any offence in paragraph (c) or any offence in paragraph (d) or (e) which is a qualifying offence;
(h) any offence under the Bribery Act 2010.
(i) any offence under section 45 or 46 of the Criminal Finances Act 2017 (failure to prevent the facilitation of UK tax evasion offences or foreign tax evasion offences).
(j) any offence under regulations under section 1 of the Sanctions and Anti-Money Laundering Act 2018 (sanctions regulations) which is specified by those regulations by virtue of section 17(8) of that Act

(2) For the purposes of subsection (1) an offence in paragraph (d) or (e) of that subsection is a qualifying offence if the Investigating Authority certifies that in his opinion—
(a) in the case of an offence in paragraph (d) or an offence of cheating the public revenue, the offence involved or would have involved a loss, or potential loss, to the public revenue of an amount not less than £5,000;
(b) in the case of an offence under section 17 of the Theft Act 1968 or section 17 of the Theft Act (Northern Ireland) 1969, the offence involved or would have involved a loss or gain, or potential loss or gain, of an amount not less than £5,000.

D1.206 **Disclosure, Production and Retention** The Investigating Authority may issue a disclosure notice where it appears: (a) that there are reasonable grounds for suspecting that an offence specified in the SOCPA 2005, s. 61, has been committed; (b) that any person has information, whether documentary or not, which relates to a matter relevant to the investigation of the offence; and (c) that there are reasonable grounds for believing that information which may be provided by that person in compliance with a disclosure notice is likely to be of substantial value (whether or not by itself) to that investigation (s. 62(1)). Note that the information sought need not be directly probative of an offence nor need it be admissible in evidence.

A disclosure notice, which must be in writing and signed or countersigned by the Investigating Authority, may require the person to answer questions, provide information or produce a document, or documents of any particular description, relevant to the offence (s. 62(3) to (5)).

An authorised person may take copies of or extracts from any documents produced and may require the person producing them to provide an explanation for any of them (s. 62(2)). Documents so produced may be retained for so long as the Investigating Authority considers it necessary to retain them (rather than copies) (s. 62(3)). The Investigating Authority may retain such documents if there are reasonable grounds for believing that any such documents may have to be produced for the purpose of legal proceedings and that they might otherwise be unavailable for such purposes (s. 62(3)). If a person required to produce documents does not do so, an authorised person may require the person to state, to the best of his or her knowledge and belief, where they are (s. 63(5)).

D1.207 **Privilege** Legal professional privilege is fully protected. A person may not be required to answer any privileged question, provide any privileged information, or produce any privileged document (SOCPA 2005, s. 64(1) to (4)), nor may the person be required to produce any excluded material (s. 64(5) and the PACE 1984, s. 11). Furthermore, a person may not be required to disclose any information or produce any document in respect of which he or she *owes an obligation of confidence by virtue* of carrying on any banking business unless the person to whom the obligation is owed consents to disclosure or production, or the requirement is made by or in accordance with a specific authorisation given by the Investigating Authority (s.

64(8) and (9)). It is thus apparent that, while legal professional privilege cannot be overridden by the Investigating Authority, banking secrecy may be so overridden.

Power to Enter, and to Seize Documents

Where a person has been required by a disclosure notice to produce documents but has not done so, or it is not practicable to give a disclosure notice requiring production, or the giving of such a notice might seriously prejudice the investigation into a relevant offence, a justice of the peace may issue a warrant at the instance of the Investigating Authority. Such an application must be made by way of information on oath (SOCPA 2005, s. 66(1) and (2)). The justice must be satisfied that the documents are on the premises specified. **D1.208**

The warrant authorises an appropriate person named in it, accompanied by such other persons as he or she deems necessary, to enter and search the specified premises using such reasonable force as is necessary, to take possession of documents appearing to be of a description specified in the information or to take any other steps which appear to be necessary for preserving or preventing interference with any such documents. Similar steps may be taken in respect of computer disks which appear to contain the information sought. Copies and extracts of documents may be taken. Any person in the premises may be required to provide an explanation of any such documents or information or to state where any such documents or information may be found and may be required to give the person executing the warrant such assistance as may reasonably be required for the taking of copies or extracts (s. 66(1) and (4)).

It would seem that the obligation to provide an explanation of documents or information must, consistent with the HRA 1998, not require the person directly to incriminate him or herself.

Provision is made to ensure that premises entered in the absence of the occupier are left secure (s. 66(6)).

As with documents or devices produced under notice, the Investigating Authority may retain the document or device for so long as the Authority considers it necessary to retain it rather than a copy in aid of the investigation (s. 66(7)). Retention of the document or device is also authorised where the Investigating Authority has reasonable grounds for believing that the document or device may have to be produced for the purposes of any legal proceedings and that it might otherwise be unavailable for those purposes (s. 66(8)). There is no 'reasonable cause to believe' requirement where retention is for the purposes of the investigation, but there is such a requirement where retention is in aid of the possible production of the document or device in legal proceedings. **D1.209**

The power to take possession of or make copies extends only to those items disclosure or production of which can be compelled under this statutory scheme (s. 66(9)).

Failure without reasonable cause to comply with any requirement imposed under ss. 62 or 63 is a summary offence punishable with imprisonment not exceeding six months and/or a fine not exceeding level 5 (ss. 67(1) and (4) and 175). Knowingly or recklessly making a false or misleading statement in a material particular is an either-way offence punishable on indictment with imprisonment for up to two years and/or an unlimited fine and punishable on summary conviction with six months and/or a fine not exceeding the statutory maximum (ss. 67(2) and (5) and 175). Wilful obstruction of any person in the exercise of any of the warrant powers conferred by s. 66 is a summary offence punishable in the same way as an offence under s. 67(1) (s. 67(3) and (4)).

ANONYMITY IN INVESTIGATIONS

The CAJA 2009, Part 3, ch. 1 (ss. 74 to 85), contains provisions for investigation anonymity orders, which are a response to the difficulties in persuading witnesses of serious gang-related crime to give evidence. **D1.210**

By s. 74, an 'investigation anonymity order' is an order in respect of a specified person which prohibits the disclosure of information which identifies the specified person as a person who is or was able and willing to assist a 'specified qualifying criminal investigation' or that might enable the specified person to be identified as such a person. The qualifying offences are murder and manslaughter, provided death is caused either by the victim being shot with a firearm or being injured with a knife. A criminal investigation is a qualifying criminal investigation if it is conducted wholly or in part with a view to ascertaining whether a person should be charged with a 'qualifying offence' or whether a person charged with a qualifying offence is guilty of it (s. 75).

Section 76(10) makes it an offence to disclose information in contravention of an investigation anonymity order. Section 76(3) to (9) set out circumstances in which the prohibition against disclosure would not be contravened.

D1.211 An order may be made on application by, *inter alia*, a police force, the Director General of the NCA or the DPP (s. 77). The order is made by a justice of the peace who must be satisfied that there are reasonable grounds for believing that the following conditions, set out in s. 78(3) to (8), are satisfied:

(a) a qualifying offence has been committed;
(b) the person likely to have committed the offence — the 'relevant person' — is a person aged at least 11 but under 30;
(c) that at the time the offence was committed the relevant person is likely to have been a member of a group which it is possible to identify from the criminal activities that its members appear to engage in and it appears that the majority of the persons in the group are aged at least 11 but under 30;
(d) the person who would be specified in the order has reasonable grounds for fearing intimidation or harm if identified as a person who is or was willing and able to assist the investigation;
(e) the person who would be specified in the order is able to provide information that would assist the criminal investigation and is more likely than not, as a consequence of the making of the order, to provide such information.

For the procedure governing applications for investigation anonymity orders, see CrimPR 47.45 to 47.49 (see Supplement, **R47.45** *et seq.*). For witness anonymity orders, see **D14.72**.

Section D2 The Decision to Prosecute and Diversion

THE DECISION TO PROSECUTE

The decision to prosecute is governed by the PACE 1984, ss. 37, 37A and 37B, the Code for Crown Prosecutors and the *Director's Guidance on Charging*. The Code for Crown Prosecutors was most recently revised in October 2018 (see **appendix 3**). The *Director's Guidance on Charging* was most recently revised in May 2013 (5th edn, tinyurl.com/y9ez44oq). The general scheme governing the decision to prosecute in police investigations is that the custody officer has responsibility for determining whether there is sufficient evidence to charge, but the decision to charge rests with either the custody officer or a Crown Prosecutor, depending on the nature of the charge and the likely plea. **D2.1**

Commencement of criminal proceedings by way of charge is dealt with in this section. For commencement by way of summons, or written charge and requisition, see **D5.2** ***et seq.***

Sufficient Evidence to Charge

If the custody officer determines that there is sufficient evidence to charge an arrested person with the offence for which he or she was arrested, the person must be (PACE 1984, s. 37(7), as amended by the PCA 2017, s. 54): **D2.2**

(a) released without charge and on bail (s. 37(7)(a)(i)), or kept in police detention (s. 37(7)(a)(ii)), for the purpose of enabling the DPP (in practice, normally a Crown Prosecutor) to make a decision under s. 37B (whether there is sufficient evidence to charge and, if so, whether the person should be charged and what the charge should be, or whether the person should be given a caution);
(b) released without charge and without bail unless the pre-conditions for bail are satisfied (see **D1.189**) (s. 37(7)(b));
(c) released without charge and on bail if those pre-conditions are satisfied but not for the purpose mentioned in s. 37(7)(a) (s. 37(7)(c)); or
(d) charged (s. 37(7)(d)).

This is subject to s. 41(7), which provides that at the expiry of a detention time-limit a person who has not been charged must be released either on bail or without bail (see **D1.67** ***et seq.***). The decision as to how a person is to be dealt with under s. 37(7) is that of the custody officer (s. 37(7A)), but in making the decision the custody officer must have regard to the *Director's Guidance on Charging* (s. 37A(3)). Once the custody officer has determined that there is sufficient evidence to charge, action under s. 37(7) is mandatory (*R (G) v Chief Constable of West Yorkshire Police* [2008] EWCA Civ 28, [2008] 1 WLR 550). For the test for determining when interviewing should cease and a person be brought before a custody officer, see **D1.89**.

Generally, where a person is released and the custody officer determines that either there is not sufficient evidence to charge, or there is sufficient evidence to charge but the person should not be charged or given a caution for an offence, the custody officer must give written notice that the person is not to be prosecuted. Such a notice does not prevent prosecution of the person if new evidence comes to light after the notice was given. This applies where a person is released under the PACE 1984, ss. 34(5), 37(2), 37(7)(b) or (c), 37CA(2), 41(7), 42(10), 43(15) or (18) and 44(7) (PACE 1984, ss. 34(5B) to (5E), 37(6A) to (6C), 37(8ZA), 37CA(5) to (7), **D2.3**

D

Part D Procedure

41(10) to (12), 42(12) to (14), 43(20) to (22) and 44(9) to (11) respectively, as inserted by the PCA 2017, ss. 66 and 67). Unlike the reference to 'new evidence' in relation to re-arrest (see **D1.197**), the reference to 'new evidence' in these provisions does not explicitly extend to an examination or analysis of existing evidence that could not reasonably have been made before the person's release.

D2.4 The test for whether there is sufficient evidence to charge is not statutorily defined. PACE Code C, paras. 11.6 and 16.1, imply that it means sufficient evidence to provide a realistic prospect of conviction (which is the test for the evidential stage of the 'full code test' — see **D2.11**). Under the *Director's Guidance on Charging* this is the test that must normally be applied both in determining whether there is sufficient evidence to charge and in determining whether to charge (para. 8). However, the *Guidance* provides that a lower, threshold test may be applied by custody officers in determining whether to refer a case to a Crown Prosecutor for a charge decision where the conditions for making a charge decision on the basis of the threshold test are met (paras. 8 and 11, and see **D2.14**); or, exceptionally, where the custody officer makes a charge decision in a case that should normally be referred to a prosecutor for a charge decision (see **D2.9**). The *Guidance* and the Code for Crown Prosecutors provide that a Crown Prosecutor can make a charge decision on the basis of the threshold test in certain circumstances (see **D2.14**).

Where the person is dealt with under s. 37(7)(a), an officer involved in the investigation must, as soon as practicable, send to the DPP (in practice a Crown Prosecutor) such information as is specified in the *Director's Guidance on Charging* (s. 37B(1) and *Guidance*, para. 26 and annex A). If the prosecutor determines that there is sufficient evidence to charge, the person may be charged having been detained for this purpose under s. 37(7)(a)(ii), or may be charged when answering to bail granted under s. 37(7)(a)(i). Alternatively, the person may be charged by means of a written charge and requisition (s. 37B(8)). If the prosecutor determines that there is not sufficient evidence to charge, or that there is sufficient evidence to charge but that the person should not be charged or given a caution, the custody officer must give the person written notice that he or she is not to be prosecuted (s. 37B(5)).

D2.5 It would seem that the purpose of s. 37(7)(b) and (c) is, despite the fact that the custody officer has determined that there is sufficient evidence to charge, to permit the person to be released without charge whilst further investigations are carried out. In respect of a release under s. 37(7)(c) (or under s. 37CA(2)(b)), the provisions regarding the maximum periods of bail, and extension of bail, set out at **D1.192** ***et seq.***, apply. Where a person is released without bail under s. 37(7)(b), it would seem that, in practice, if a decision is made to prosecute, this would have to be by way of a written charge and requisition unless there is new evidence justifying re-arrest (see **D1.197**) or the person is willing to attend the police station voluntarily for the purpose of charge.

Where a person is bailed without charge, the question arises whether, on surrendering to custody following release under s. 37(7)(c), the person can then be further detained without charge. On returning to the police station, the person is to be treated as arrested for the offence in connection with which bail was granted (s. 34(7)). If the test for determining whether there is sufficient evidence to charge is the same for s. 37(1) and (7) (or was so treated in a particular case), it is difficult to see how detention under s. 37(2) would be possible since the custody officer would have determined that there was sufficient evidence to charge in order to grant bail under s. 37(7)(c). Since under the current version of the *Director's Guidance on Charging* the test for determining whether there is sufficient evidence to charge is normally the 'full code test', it would seem that the meaning is the same.

The PACE 1984, s. 37(7)(b) and (c), permit the custody officer to release the person without charge even if there is sufficient evidence to charge, but in either case it would enable the person to be dealt with by way of an out-of-court disposal, such as by means of a caution, at some later date (see **D2.24**).

Where a person is arrested under the provisions of the CJA 2003, Part 10, which allow a person to be retried after being acquitted of a serious offence which is a qualifying offence under sch. 5, and further prosecution is not precluded by s. 75(3) (see **D12.40** ***et seq.***), the PACE 1984, s. 37, is modified and, in particular, an officer of at least the rank of superintendent (who has not directly been involved in the investigation) must determine whether the evidence available or known is sufficient for the case to be referred to a prosecutor to consider whether consent should be sought for an application in respect of that person under the CJA 2003, s. 76 (CJA 2003, s. 87). **D2.6**

If the police continue to detain a person without charge beyond the point at which the charge decision should have been made, that detention is likely to be unlawful. Further, it may be argued that inferences should not be drawn from any 'silence' (see **F20.42**) since the CJPO 1994, s. 34, does not permit inferences from 'silence' after charge.

Detention for More than One Offence Code C, para. 16.1, provides that, where a person is detained in respect of more than one offence, it is permissible to delay bringing the person before the custody officer with a view to a decision being made under s. 37(7) until the officer in charge of the investigation reasonably believes that there is sufficient evidence to provide a realistic prospect of conviction in respect of all the offences in respect of which the person is being detained. This may be *ultra vires* since s. 37(7) is in mandatory terms and does not cater for such circumstances, but the point does not appear to have been authoritatively determined. **D2.7**

Responsibility for Making the Charge Decision

Under the *Director's Guidance on Charging*, responsibility for making a charge decision may rest with either a Crown Prosecutor or a custody officer. A Crown Prosecutor must make a charge decision in respect of all indictable-only offences, and any either-way offence in respect of which, under the *Guidance*, a custody officer is not permitted to make a charge decision (see below). In cases where more than one charge may be appropriate, and at least one of them must be referred to a prosecutor for a charge decision, all matters must be referred to the prosecutor. The decision on charge may be made by a custody officer (under the PACE 1984, s. 37(7)(d)) in respect of any summary only offence (including criminal damage where the value of the loss or damage is less than £5,000) irrespective of likely plea. A custody officer may also make a charge decision in respect of an either-way offence where it is anticipated that the person charged will plead guilty and it is suitable for sentence in a magistrates' court provided it is not one of the following (*Director's Guidance on Charging*, para. 15): **D2.8**

- a case requiring the consent to prosecute of the DPP or a law officer (see **D2.16**);
- a case involving death;
- connected with terrorist activity or official secrets;
- classified as hate crime or domestic violence under CPS policies;
- an offence of violent disorder or affray;
- causing grievous bodily harm or wounding, or actual bodily harm;
- an offence under the SOA 2003 committed by or upon a person under 18 years; or
- an offence under the Licensing Act 2003.

The *Guidance* provides that a case may be considered suitable for sentence in a magistrates' court unless the loss or damage relating to the charge is more than £5,000 or would exceed that sum if more than one offence is charged (or taken into consideration); or the overall circumstances of the offence are so serious that the court may decide that a sentence of more than six months' imprisonment justifies sending the case to the Crown Court; or the offence has been committed whilst the suspect was subject to a Crown Court order then in force (para. 18).

A custody officer may also, provided it is authorised by an inspector, charge a person with an offence that under the *Guidance* should be referred to a Crown Prosecutor for a charge decision where the continued detention of the suspect after charge is justified and it is not possible to obtain a prosecutor's authority for the charge before the expiry of any relevant detention time-limit (see **D1.67** ***et seq.***). In making a charge decision, the custody officer may apply the **D2.9** threshold test (see **D2.14**) and the case must be referred to a prosecutor as soon as possible after charge and not later than the time proposed for the first appearance in a magistrates' court (*Director's Guidance on Charging*, para. 20).

The Tests for Deciding Whether to Charge

D2.10 **Full Code Test** In deciding whether to charge, a Crown Prosecutor or custody officer (where they are permitted to charge) must normally apply the 'full code test' set out in the Code for Crown Prosecutors (*Director's Guidance on Charging*, para. 8, and see **appendix 3**). The full code test has two stages: the evidential stage and the public interest stage.

D2.11 **Evidential Stage** The evidential stage requires prosecutors (or custody officers, as the case may be) to be satisfied that there is sufficient evidence to provide a realistic prospect of conviction in respect of each charge. They must consider what the defence case may be and how it is likely to affect the prosecution case. Prosecutors must also consider whether there is any material held by the police, or which may be obtained through reasonable lines of inquiry, which could affect the decision to charge. The Code for Crown Prosecutors describes it as an objective test (para. 4.7), meaning that a court properly directed and acting in accordance with the law is more likely than not to convict the defendant of the alleged offence. However, it was held in *R (FB) v DPP* [2009] EWHC 106 (Admin), [2009] 1 Cr App R 38 (580) that in deciding whether there is a realistic prospect of conviction, rather than take a statistical approach prosecutors should imagine themselves to be the fact finder and ask whether, on balance, the evidence was sufficient to merit a conviction taking into account what they knew about the defence case. See further the Code for Crown Prosecutors, paras. 4.6 to 4.8, at **appendix 3**, and the discussion of the evidential stage test in *Da Silva v UK* (2016) 63 EHRR 12 (589) at [265]–[276].

D2.12 **Public Interest Stage** The public interest stage of the test must be applied only after the prosecutor (or custody officer, as the case may be) has determined that the evidential stage is satisfied. If the prosecutor (or custody officer) has determined that there is sufficient evidence to give a realistic prospect of conviction, a prosecution should normally proceed unless there are public interest factors that outweigh those in favour of prosecution, or the prosecutor (or custody officer) is satisfied that the public interest may be properly served by offering the offender the opportunity to have the matter dealt with by an out-of-court disposal (Code for Crown Prosecutors, para. 4.9). The factors to be taken into account are set out in the Code for Crown Prosecutors, para. 4.14, and now require prosecutors to assess whether suspects have benefited from criminal conduct, when considering their culpability (para. 4.14(b)). Although not specifically mentioned in the Code for Crown Prosecutors, in cases where the trafficking of human beings is an obvious possibility the police should make suitable inquiries and the prosecutor should take it into account in deciding, especially, whether to prosecute or to continue a prosecution (*LM* [2010] EWCA Crim 2327, [2011] 1 Cr App R 12 (135); *N* [2012] EWCA Crim 189, [2013] QB 379; *L* [2013] EWCA Crim 991, [2014] 1 All ER 113 and *O* [2019] EWCA Crim 752); for a full discussion of the treatment of victims of trafficking or slavery, see **B22.1** ***et seq.*** As to factors relevant to determining whether it is in the public interest to prosecute complainants in rape or domestic violence cases who have apparently been pressurised or coerced into retracting their initial complaint, see *A (RJ)* [2012] EWCA Crim 434, [2012] 2 Cr App R 8 (80). Decisions to prosecute in such cases must always be referred to the DPP. The *Rape and Sexual Offences* guidance (April 2019, tinyurl.com/yxy6fxcj) stipulates that for such offences the public interest test is almost always met.

CPS guidance on dealing with suspects with mental health conditions (October 2019, tinyurl.com/sfqvhyx) requires investigators to draw the attention of the decision-maker to relevant material relating to the suspect's mental health, where it may be a live issue. In such cases, the decision-maker is required to consider the impact of the suspect's mental health at the evidential and public interest stages.

D2.13 **Selecting the Charges** Charges should be selected which reflect the seriousness and extent of the offending, give the court adequate powers to sentence and impose appropriate post-conviction orders, and enable the case to be presented in a clear and simple way (Code for Crown Prosecutors, para. 6.1). A prosecutor (or custody officer, as the case may be) should not proceed with more charges than are necessary just to encourage an accused to plead guilty to a few, nor proceed with a more serious charge just to encourage an accused to plead guilty to a less serious one (Code for Crown Prosecutors, para. 6.3). In making a charge decision, consideration should be given to alternatives to prosecution (Code for Crown Prosecutors, paras. 7.1 and 7.2, and see **D2.24**).

Threshold Test As an exception to the normal rule, Crown Prosecutors may charge on the basis of the threshold test in the circumstances set out in the Code for Crown Prosecutors, paras. 5.2 to 5.10. The test sets out five conditions, all of which must be met before the suspect can be charged. **D2.14**

(1) There must be 'reasonable grounds to suspect that the person to be charged has committed the offence' (paras. 5.3 to 5.4).
(2) The prosecutor must be satisfied that there are 'reasonable grounds to believe that the continuing investigation will provide further evidence, within a reasonable period of time, so that when all the evidence is considered together, including material which may point away from as well as towards a particular suspect, it is capable of establishing a realistic prospect of conviction in accordance with the Full Code Test' (para. 5.5). In reaching a decision regarding this condition, the prosecutor must consider the factors set out in para. 5.7.
(3) The seriousness or the circumstances of the case must justify the making of an immediate charging decision (para. 5.8).
(4) There must be continuing substantial grounds to object to bail (para. 5.9).
(5) The prosecutor must apply the public interest stage of the Full Code test based on the information available at the time (para. 5.10).

A decision to charge under the threshold test must be kept under review, and the full code test must be applied as soon as is reasonably practicable and in any event before the expiry of any applicable custody time-limit or extended custody time-limit (para. 5.11). A previous version of the threshold test was disapproved in *G v Chief Constable of West Yorkshire Police* [2006] EWHC 3485 (Admin) as a test for determining whether to charge. The revised version of the test still enables a person to be charged on the basis of a level of suspicion that is little different than that required for arrest, although there is a requirement that the prosecutor (and exceptionally a custody officer) has reasonable grounds for believing that continuing investigation will produce sufficient evidence within a reasonable period of time to establish a realistic prospect of conviction.

The Process of Charging

Responsibility for charging a person rests with the custody officer. Where the charge decision is made by a Crown Prosecutor, the decision must be notified to an officer involved in the investigation of the case (PACE 1984, s. 37B(4)). The person to be charged must, if still in police detention, be charged in accordance with the prosecutor's decision; if the person has been released on bail, he or she must be charged on return to a police station to answer bail or through the written charge and requisition procedure established by the CJA 2003, s. 29 (s. 37B(6) and (8)). On being charged the person must be cautioned in the terms set out in Code C, para. 16.2, unless the restrictions on drawing inferences apply (see **D1.83**), in which case the person must be cautioned in the terms set out in Code C, annex C, para. 2. The person must be given a written notice showing particulars of the offence(s) for which he or she is charged, including the name of the officer in the case (or warrant number in cases where Code C, para. 2.6A, or Code H, para. 2.8, apply), the police station and reference number for the case, and confirmation of the caution. As far as possible, the particulars of the charge must be stated in simple terms, but they must show the precise offence with which the person is charged (Code C, para. 16.3). Where the person charged does not understand the language used in the document, a translation must be provided as soon as is practicable, although such translation may be provided orally (Code C, para. 13.10B, and annex M). The custody officer must, when determining whether to detain or grant bail to the person following charge, consider what documents (if any) must be disclosed to the person on the grounds that they are essential to enable the lawfulness of the arrest or detention to be challenged (Code C, para. 16.7A). **D2.15**

Cases where Consent is Required

D2.16 **Offences Requiring Consent** The institution of criminal proceedings for certain offences, or for offences in certain circumstances, requires the consent of either the A-G or the DPP or, in some cases, some other person such as a relevant government minister.

In general, the A-G's consent is required where issues of public policy, national security or relations with other countries may affect the decision whether to prosecute. An example is the Suppression of Terrorism Act 1978, s. 4(4) (see **A8.24**), by which the A-G must sanction any proceedings in the UK for terrorist offences allegedly committed in a convention country. Other examples are offences of bribery under the Official Secrets Act 1911 (s. 8); offences of stirring up racial hatred etc. contrary to Part III of the POA 1986 (s. 27); contempt of court under the strict liability rule (Contempt of Court Act 1981, s. 8); juror's research and disclosure offences (Juries Act 1974, ss. 20A to 20D); war crimes (War Crimes Act 1991, s. 1); and offences contrary to the Explosive Substances Act 1883 (s. 7).

Offences for which consent of the DPP is required include: offences of theft or criminal damage where the property in question belongs to the accused's spouse (Theft Act 1968, s. 30(4)); offences of assisting offenders and wasting police time (Criminal Law Act 1967, ss. 4(4) and 5(3)); encouraging or assisting another's suicide (Suicide Act 1961, s. 2(4)); riot (POA 1986, s. 7(1)); offences under the Bribery Act 2010; and certain terrorism offences under the TA 2000 (TA 2000, s. 117). For the DPP's policy on prosecuting in cases of encouraging or assisting suicide, see **B1.141**.

It was held in *R (Uberoi) v City of Westminster Magistrates' Court* [2008] EWHC 3191 (Admin), [2009] 1 WLR 1905 that, despite the clear wording of the CJA 1993, s. 61(2), the Financial Services Authority has power to prosecute for insider dealing under Part V of that Act without obtaining consent. The Financial Services and Markets Act 2000, s. 402, empowered the Financial Services Authority to institute proceedings for such an offence and s. 401(2) enabled it to do so on its own authority. The principle would apply equally to the powers of the Financial Conduct Authority to institute proceedings: see **B7.21**.

CPS guidance, *Consents to Prosecute* (December 2018, tinyurl.com/y9d9zpdc), annex 1, contains a useful list of prosecutions requiring consent by the A-G or the DPP.

D2.17 **Form and Timing of Consent** The A-G's consent to a prosecution is normally signified in writing, although there would appear to be no bar to its being given orally (per Lord Widgery CJ in *Cain* [1976] QB 496 at p. 502C). The consent need not specify the precise form of charges to which approval is given. Thus, in *Cain*, the Court of Appeal held that the Crown Court had had jurisdiction to try D for possessing explosives under suspicious circumstances contrary to the Explosive Substances Act 1883, s. 4, even though the A-G's consent did not refer specifically to s. 4, but merely stated in general terms that the A-G consented to the prosecution of D 'for an offence or offences contrary to the provisions of the [1883 Act]'. Although it is theoretically open to an accused to challenge the validity of an apparent consent on the basis that the A-G did not genuinely consider the propriety or otherwise of a prosecution, the initial presumption in the case of a written consent is that it would not have been issued unless the A-G had 'applied himself to his duty, considered the relevant facts, and reached a conclusion upon them' (*Cain* at p. 502F).

By the Prosecution of Offences Act 1985, s. 1(7), the consent of the DPP to a prosecution may be given on the DPP's behalf by a Crown Prosecutor. Consent is deemed to have been given by the DPP if a Crown Prosecutor has determined that there is sufficient evidence to charge, identified the relevant offence, and notified the police of the decision (*Walker* [2016] EWCA Crim 751, [2016] 2 Cr App R 24 (325)).

Section 26 provides that a document duly signed and purporting to be a consent to prosecution shall be admissible as prima facie evidence that consent has in fact been given.

D2.18 Legislation requiring consent normally states that consent is required in order that proceedings be instituted. However, the Prosecution of Offences Act 1985, s. 25(2), provides that lack of consent does not prevent the arrest without warrant, or the issue or execution of a warrant for arrest, of a person for any offence, or the remand in custody or on bail, of any person. The CPS guidance, *Consents to Prosecute*, states that consent should be obtained or given: in the case of indictable-only offences, before the sending hearing; in the case of either-way offences, before the plea before venue procedure; and in the case of summary-only offences, before plea is taken. Where a prosecution is commenced by summons, consent should be sought or given before the information is laid; where commencement is by written charge and requisition, consent should be sought before they are issued. Where the voluntary bill procedure is used, consent must be obtained or given before the application for the bill is made. In the case of proceedings in magistrates' courts, failure to comply renders the proceedings a nullity. In Crown Court proceedings, however, the court may use its powers under the Courts Act 2003, s. 66, to reconvene as a magistrates' court and, provided consent has by then been given, can proceed from the point at which proceedings are instituted.

Time-limits

For time-limits relating to summary offences, see **D21.17** *et seq*. For abuse of process resulting from delay, see **D3.73** *et seq*. **D2.19**

Immunity from Prosecution

For immunity by reason of age see **A3.73**. For jurisdictional immunities see **A8.25**. **D2.20**

Judicial Review of Prosecution Decisions

Decision to Prosecute Generally, a decision to prosecute is not susceptible to judicial review since it may be challenged within the trial process itself, notably by an application to stay proceedings on the grounds of abuse of process. Arguments relating to abuse of process may and should be raised in the course of the criminal trial itself save in wholly exceptional circumstances (*R (Pepushi) v CPS* [2004] EWHC 798 (Admin), (2004) *The Times*, 21 May 2004). However, it is not for the trial judge to determine the proportionality of a decision to prosecute unless it amounted to an abuse of process (*James v DPP* [2015] EWHC 3296 (Admin), [2016] 1 WLR 2118, disapproving *Dehai v CPS* [2005] EWHC 2154 (Admin)). It thus appears that in the absence of dishonesty, *mala fides* or some exceptional circumstance, a decision to prosecute cannot normally be challenged by way of judicial review (*DPP, ex parte Kebilene* [2000] 2 AC 326). In *R (E) v DPP* [2011] EWHC 1465 (Admin), [2012] 1 Cr App R 6 (68) the Divisional Court was willing to quash a decision to prosecute a young girl for sexual offences on her infant sisters, although the facts were unusual. In a review by the CPS of a decision not to prosecute, it is not contrary to natural justice for a decision to be made without giving the accused an opportunity to make representations (*R (S) v CPS* [2015] EWHC 2868 (Admin), [2016] 1 WLR 804). It has been held that a decision to prosecute rather than caution is susceptible to judicial review, but there is a heavy burden on the applicant which may be insurmountable (*Chief Constable of Kent, ex parte L* (1991) 93 Cr App R 416). The courts are reluctant to intervene in such a decision unless breach of an authority's clear and settled policy is established (*Metropolitan Police Commissioner, ex parte Thompson* [1977] 1 WLR 1519; *R (Mondelly) v Metropolitan Police Commissioner* [2006] EWHC 2370 (Admin)). In *R (Robson) v CPS* [2016] EWHC 2191 (Admin), [2017] 1 Cr App R 5 (36) the decision to prosecute rather than to offer a conditional caution, in accordance with the prohibition on offering a conditional caution in a domestic violence case in the *Director's Guidance on Adult Conditional Cautions*, was quashed; the Divisional Court holding that the rule must be interpreted to permit exceptions. For abuse of process see **D3.66** *et seq*. **D2.21**

Decision Not to Prosecute A decision not to prosecute is susceptible to judicial review because no other remedy is available (*DPP, ex parte Manning* [2001] QB 330), but the cases show that the power to review such a decision will be exercised sparingly. Generally, the court will only intervene if the decision not to prosecute was arrived at as a result of some unlawful policy, or from a failure to act in accordance with the DPP's settled policy, or because the decision was perverse (i.e. it was a decision which no reasonable prosecutor could have made) (*DPP, ex parte C* [1995] 1 Cr App R 136, followed in *R (O'Brien) v DPP* [2013] EWHC 3741 (Admin)). Prosecutorial **D2.22**

decision-makers have a significant margin of discretion, however the margin allowed the decision-maker depends upon the circumstances of the case. Where the issues involve an assessment of disputed evidence or the public interest, the court will be slow to interfere. If the issue is essentially one of law, the court will more readily be prepared to find that the decision-maker's conclusion was wrong (*Campaign Against Anti-Semitism v DPP* [2019] EWHC 9 (Admin)). In *R (John-Baptiste) v DPP* [2019] EWHC 1130 (Admin), the fact that two experienced prosecutors came to different conclusions when considering whether the evidential test was satisfied demonstrated that there was nothing irrational or perverse in the decision ultimately taken: it confirmed that more than one view could be taken on the evidence.

In *Ex parte Manning* the Administrative Court was willing to intervene in respect of a decision, made without giving reasons, not to prosecute a person who had been identified in an inquest as being responsible for an unlawful killing. Relief has also been granted where a decision not to prosecute amounted to a breach of the victim's right to private life under the ECHR, Article 8 (*R (Waxman) v CPS* [2012] EWHC 133 (Admin)). See also *R (Dennis) v DPP* [2006] EWHC 3211 (Admin); *R (Da Silva) v DPP* [2006] EWHC 3204 (Admin); *R (FB) v DPP* [2009] EWHC 106 (Admin), [2009] 1 Cr App R 38 (580) and *NXB v CPS* [2015] EWHC 631 (QB). Note that under the Victims' Right to Review Scheme, victims have a right to request a review of a CPS decision not to prosecute or to terminate criminal proceedings (see *Victims' Right to Review Guidance* (July 2016, tinyurl.com/ydduf6g6)). Victims do not have a right to make representations, but are given a fair opportunity to do so, and to have them taken into account by the decision-maker, under para. 42 of the guidance (*R (FNM) v DPP* [2020] EWHC 870 (Admin)). When a review is requested, it is important that those requesting the review are able to understand the reviewing lawyer's decision and the reasons for conclusions made (*R (Torpey) v DPP* [2019] EWHC 1804 (Admin)). The policy of the CPS to refuse to review a decision to prosecute some, but not all, possible suspects is lawful (*R (AC) v DPP* [2018] EWCA Civ 2092, [2019] 1 Cr App R 12 (170)). The policy of the CPS which prevents the consideration of a request for a review prior to the termination of a case where no evidence is offered is also lawful (*R (Hayes) v CPS* [2018] EWHC 327 (Admin), [2018] 2 Cr App R 7 (76)).

A policy not to prosecute for certain classes of offence or in certain situations is, in principle, susceptible to judicial review (*Metropolitan Police Commissioner, ex parte Blackburn* [1968] 2 QB 118). Conversely, a refusal by the DPP to undertake not to prosecute an offence or a class of offences may not be reviewed. The executive may not suspend or dispense with the execution of the laws without Parliamentary consent. Exercise of the discretion not to prosecute must depend upon a consideration of the public interest in the light of offences already committed (*R (Pretty) v DPP* [2001] UKHL 61, [2002] 1 AC 800).

Note that the DPP has the power to take over a private prosecution by virtue of the Prosecution of Offences Act 1985, s. 6(1), and may continue the prosecution, or discontinue it if either the evidential sufficiency stage or public interest stage of the Full Code Test is not satisfied. The factors to be taken into account in making such decisions are set out in CPS Legal Guidance, *Private Prosecutions* (October 2019, tinyurl.com/yazntmd4), which was approved, in this respect, by the Supreme Court in *R (Gujra) v CPS* [2012] UKSC 52, [2013] 1 AC 484. See also the guidance published by the Private Prosecutors' Association, available at https://private-prosecutions.com.

Private prosecutors owe a duty of candour when applying *ex parte* for the issue of a summons in the magistrates' court (*R (Kay) v Leeds Magistrates' Court* [2018] EWHC 1233 (Admin), [2018] 2 Cr App R 27 (425)). When considering whether to issue a summons for a private prosecution after the CPS had discontinued a prosecution in respect of the same facts, magistrates should consider whether the allegation was of an offence known to law and, if so, whether the ingredients of the offence are prima facie present; whether a summons was time barred; whether the court had jurisdiction; whether the informant had the necessary authority to prosecute; and any other relevant facts. However, a private prosecutor is not bound by the full code test in the Code for Crown Prosecutors (*R (Charlson) v Guildford Magistrates' Court* [2006] EWHC 2318 (Admin), [2006] 3 All ER 163).

In the case of decisions made by the A-G, the superintendence of the A-G over the DPP is one stage removed from prosecutorial decisions made on a case-by-case basis. Successful challenges to such decisions will therefore be rarer still than those of the DPP (*R (Slade) v HM A-G of England and Wales* [2018] EWHC 3573 (Admin)).

Decision to Caution A decision to caution rather than to prosecute is susceptible to review at the instance of the victim. The giving of a conditional caution as an alternative to prosecution was successfully challenged by the victim in *R (Guest) v DPP* [2009] EWHC 594 (Admin), [2009] 2 Cr App R 26 (426) on the grounds that it was inappropriate for an offence of assault occasioning actual bodily harm and that the decision did not comply with the Conditional Cautioning Code of Practice. Further, a prosecution following the quashing of the conditional caution would not necessarily be stayed as an abuse of process. **D2.23**

The courts are reluctant to interfere with a decision to caution at the instance of the person cautioned, but a decision to caution may be challenged if it is made in breach of the statutory scheme (*R (Owusu-Yianoma) v Chief Constable of Leicestershire Constabulary* [2017] EWHC 576 (Admin)), or contrary to settled policy (e.g., the relevant Ministry of Justice guidance); such as where there was no clear and reliable admission (*R (Wyman) v Chief Constable of Hampshire Constabulary* [2006] EWHC 1904 (Admin)) or where there was insufficient evidence to give a realistic prospect of conviction, and the resulting caution was in breach of the recipient's rights under the ECHR, Article 8 (*R (Mohammed) v Chief Constable of West Midlands* [2010] EWHC 1228 (Admin)). In *Caetano v Metropolitan Police Commissioner* [2013] EWHC 375 (Admin) the Divisional Court was willing to quash a caution where it was not in the public interest. Reliance by the police on an out-of-date circular may, but will not necessarily, result in quashing of a caution (*R (Lee) v Chief Constable of Essex* [2012] EWHC 283 (Admin)).

In principle, the fact that a person has been cautioned for an offence does not prevent a subsequent private prosecution for the same offence (*Hayter v L* [1998] 1 WLR 854). However, a prosecution in such circumstances may be stayed as an abuse if the accused was assured during the process of administering the caution that he or she would not be prosecuted (*Jones v Whalley* [2006] UKHL 41, [2007] 1 AC 63). Current Ministry of Justice guidance, *Simple Cautions for Adult Offenders* (April 2015, tinyurl.com/y7btwew3), states that when a caution is administered, the offender should be informed in writing that it may not preclude a subsequent prosecution (at para. 90). In *R (Lowden) v Gateshead Magistrates' Court* [2016] EWHC 3536 (Admin), [2017] 2 Cr App R 1 (1), the claimant successfully challenged a district judge's refusal to issue a summons in circumstances where the police, in administering a caution, had not positively indicated that there would be no subsequent prosecution.

ALTERNATIVES TO PROSECUTION

There are two main alternatives to prosecution. The first is the system of cautions: simple cautions and conditional cautions for adults; and youth cautions and youth conditional cautions. There is also a non-statutory cautioning scheme for possession of small amounts of cannabis, set out in *ACPO Guidance on Cannabis Possession for Personal Use*. The second alternative is fixed penalty notices. See **D2.12** for the general factors to be taken into account by prosecutors in deciding whether to offer an out-of-court disposal rather than to prosecute. For deferred prosecution agreements under the CCA 2013, see **D12.106**. The CPS has issued guidance on *Cautioning and Diversion* (September 2019, tinyurl.com/sgva9ny) covering simple and conditional cautions, penalty notices for disorder and protection for spent cautions. **D2.24**

Simple Cautions (Adults)

Simple cautions for adults, unlike youth cautions and conditional cautions, are a non-statutory disposal and are available only in respect of persons who have attained the age of 18 years. They are governed by Ministry of Justice guidance, *Simple Cautions for Adult Offenders*. However, they are subject to statutory restrictions under the CJCA 2015, ss. 17 and 18. **D2.25**

See also the *Director's Guidance on Charging*, para. 9 (see **D2.1**). The decision-making process is set out in section two of *Simple Cautions for Adult Offenders*.

A caution may be given in respect of an indictable-only offence only in exceptional circumstances relating to the offender or the offence and with the consent of the DPP (CJCA 2015, s. 17(2)). If the offence is an either-way offence specified in the Criminal Justice and Courts Act 2015 (Simple Cautions) (Specification of Either-Way Offences) Order 2015 (SI 2015 No. 790), a caution may be given only in exceptional circumstances relating to the offender or the offence (s. 17(3)). Specified offences include most sexual offences, and many drugs offences involving Class A drugs. In the case of non-specified either-way offences and summary-only offences, where the person has been convicted of, or cautioned for, a similar offence in the two years prior to the admitted offence, a caution may be given only in exceptional circumstances relating to the offender, the offence admitted or the previous offence (s. 17(4)). It is for a police officer not below a rank specified in the Criminal Justice and Courts Act 2015 (Simple Cautions) (Specification of Police Ranks) Order 2015 (SI 2015 No. 830) to determine whether there are exceptional circumstances, or whether a previous offence is similar to the current offence; where s. 17(2) applies the specified rank is superintendent and where s. 17(3) applies it is inspector. That decision must be made in accordance with guidance issued by the Secretary of State (s. 17(5) and (6) and SI 2015 No. 830).

D2.26 **Criteria for a Simple Caution** In determining whether a simple caution is appropriate, the police or Crown Prosecutor must apply the Full Code Test, which includes both the evidential and public interest stages (see **D2.10** ***et seq.***) (*Simple Cautions for Adult Offenders*, para. 27). A simple caution cannot be given to a person who does not make a clear and reliable admission (para. 23, and see *R (Wyman) v Chief Constable of Hampshire Constabulary* [2006] EWHC 1904 (Admin), in which there was not a clear and reliable admission in respect of an offence under the SOA 2003, s. 3). If the admission is made outside the context of a formal interview, the method of obtaining and recording the admission must be compliant with the provisions of the PACE 1984 (para. 26). The admission of guilt must be made before the person can be invited to accept a caution, and the admission must not be induced by the offer of a caution (paras. 24 and 77, and *R (R) v Durham Constabulary* [2005] UKHL 21, [2005] 2 All ER 369). The requirement in *Simple Cautions for Adult Offenders*, para. 78, that the police must inform the offender of the evidence against him or her before administering a caution, does not extend to an obligation to disclose documents (*R (Manser) v Metropolitan Police Commissioner* [2015] EWHC 3642 (Admin)).

An overview of the factors to be taken into account in considering whether a simple caution is appropriate is set out in annex A of the guidance.

D2.27 **Consent of the Suspect** A simple caution cannot be imposed on a person who refuses to accept it, and the implications of accepting a caution must be explained to the person before he or she is invited to accept it (*Simple Cautions for Adult Offenders*, paras. 77 and 80). The person must be given the opportunity to consult a solicitor before a simple caution is administered (para. 78).

D2.28 **Procedure for Administering Simple Caution and its Consequences** A simple caution should be administered by a custody officer or a suitably trained person to whom authority to administer cautions has been delegated (*Simple Cautions for Adult Offenders*, para. 79). The officer must ensure that the offender understands that there is no obligation to make an immediate decision on whether to accept a simple caution, and can take legal advice on whether to accept it, and ensure that the offender understands the implications of the caution. The offender should be asked to sign a form setting out the implications of the caution (para. 82). Although a caution is not a criminal conviction, if it is imposed for a recordable offence it is entered on the Police National Computer and forms part of the offender's criminal record. Fingerprints and other identification data can be taken and retained, and in the case of a relevant sexual offence the person is placed on the sex offenders register for two years (see **E23.1** ***et seq.***). A simple caution may be taken into account by the Disclosure and Barring Service in making a decision about the suitability of persons to work with children and adults (para. 73). Note, however, that in

R (Gallagher) v Secretary of State for the Home Department [2019] UKSC 3, [2019] 2 WLR 509, the Supreme Court found that the scheme for disclosure of cautions, convictions and reprimands was incompatible with the ECHR, Article 8, in so far as it applied the 'multiple conviction rule' and in relation to the requirement to disclose warnings and reprimands. Under the Police Act 1997, ss. 113A(3) and (6)(b) and 113B(3) and (9)(b), the multiple conviction rule provides that where a person has more than one conviction of whatever nature, any conviction of whatever nature is a 'relevant matter' falling to be disclosed in a criminal record certificate. See also **D2.33** for the Supreme Court's ruling in relation to warnings and reprimands.

A caution may be cited in any subsequent court proceedings. However, simple cautions are covered by the Rehabilitation of Offenders Act 1974, so that they are immediately spent when administered (paras. 65 to 74, and see further **E24.1*et seq.***). A caution may be quashed if the person is not informed of the consequences of accepting a caution (*R (Stratton) v Chief Constable of Thames Valley Police* [2013] EWHC 1561 (Admin)). Normally, a person cannot be prosecuted for an offence in respect of which the person has been cautioned, although he or she may be prosecuted if new evidence comes to light suggesting that the offence committed is more serious than appeared at the time the decision to offer a caution was made. The fact that a simple caution has been administered may not preclude a private prosecution (paras. 74 and 90, and see **D2.23**).

Youth Cautions

Youth cautions for offenders aged 17 and under are governed by the CDA 1998, ss. 66ZA and 66ZB. **D2.29**
Guidance on youth cautions has been issued under s. 66ZA(5): see *Youth Cautions: Guidance for Police and Youth Offending Teams* (April 2013, tinyurl.com/y8otmpwk). A reprimand or warning imposed before the provisions came into effect is to be treated as a youth caution (LASPO 2012, s. 135(5)).

Criteria for a Youth Caution A constable may give a child or young person a youth caution if: **D2.30**

(a) the constable decides that there is sufficient evidence to charge the child or young person,
(b) the child or young person admits to the constable having committed the offence, and
(c) the constable does not consider that the child or young person should be prosecuted or given a youth conditional caution in respect of the offence (s. 66ZA(1)).

In making a decision, the constable should have regard to the guidance, *Youth Cautions: Guidance for Police and Youth Offending Teams*, and to the ACPO Youth Offender Case Disposal Gravity Factor Matrix (March 2013, tinyurl.com/y76lfub9).

With regard to (b) above, it was held in *R (M) v Leicestershire Constabulary* [2009] EWHC 3640 (Admin) that the admission must be a clear and reliable admission to all elements of the offence. This was in respect of a decision to administer a final warning, but the same principles should apply. For the relevance of age in determining whether the *mens rea* of certain crimes is satisfied, or the availability of certain defences, see **A3.74**.

There is no requirement that the child or young person (or parent or guardian) give consent before a youth caution is administered. It was held in *R (R) v Durham Constabulary* [2005] UKHL 21, [2005] 2 All ER 369, in relation to a final warning, that since a warning was not the determination of a criminal charge, the absence of a consent requirement was not a breach of the ECHR, Article 6 (confirmed by the ECtHR in *R v UK* (2007) 44 EHRR SE17 (228)).

Decision to Give a Youth Caution The guidance, *Youth Cautions: Guidance for Police and Youth Offending Teams*, sets out the factors to be taken into account in deciding whether it is appropriate to give a youth caution (paras. 4.3 to 4.24). There is no statutory prohibition on administering a youth caution to a child or young person who has previously been given a caution or youth conditional caution, or who has previously been convicted of an offence (see paras. 4.15 to 5.17 for relevant factors). It is for the police (rather than a Crown Prosecutor) to decide whether to administer a youth caution but presumably, as with a simple caution for an adult (see **D2.25**), a Crown Prosecutor may advise on, or authorise, the giving of a youth caution. **D2.31**

D2.32 **Process of Administering a Youth Caution** The constable administering a youth caution must explain to the child or young person (and to the appropriate adult if relevant) in ordinary language the effect of the caution and any relevant guidance published by the Secretary of State (s. 66ZA(3) and (4)). See further, *Youth Cautions: Guidance for Police and Youth Offending Teams*, section 9. A youth caution must be given in the presence of an appropriate adult as defined in s. 66ZA(7) (as amended by the PCA 2017, s. 79(2)) (s. 66ZA(2)).

D2.33 **Consequences of a Youth Caution** Where a youth caution has been administered, the constable must refer the child or young person to a youth offending team as soon as practicable (CDA 1998, s. 66ZB(1)). If the child or young person has not previously been so referred and has not previously been given a youth conditional caution, the youth offending team may assess the child or young person and may arrange participation in a rehabilitation programme (s. 66ZB(3)). Otherwise, the youth offending team must assess the child or young person, and arrange for participation in a rehabilitation programme unless they consider it inappropriate to do so (s. 66ZB(2)). For guidance on what should be included in a rehabilitation programme, the manner in which any failure to participate in such a programme is to be recorded, and the persons to be notified of such failure (published under s. 66ZB(4)), see *Youth Cautions: Guidance for Police and Youth Offending Teams.*

A youth caution does not count as a conviction, but the caution and any report on failure to participate in a rehabilitation programme may be cited in criminal proceedings in the same circumstances as a conviction may be cited (s. 66ZB(7)). Youth cautions are covered by the Rehabilitation of Offenders Act 1974, and are immediately spent when administered (see further **E24.1** ***et seq.***). If the offence is one that is covered by the SOA 2003, Part 2 (see **E23.1** ***et seq.***), the child or young person will be placed on the sex offenders register for a period of two and a half years.

In *R (Gallagher) v Secretary of State for the Home Department* [2019] UKSC 3, [2019] 2 WLR 509, the Supreme Court held that a scheme requiring disclosure of warnings and reprimands (which were replaced by youth cautions in 2013: see **D2.29**) was inconsistent with their purpose. See also **D2.28.**

D2.34 Where a person (a) has received two or more youth cautions and is convicted of an offence committed within two years beginning with the date of the last of those cautions, or (b) has received a youth conditional caution followed by a youth caution and is convicted of an offence committed within two years beginning with the date of the youth caution, the court must not impose a conditional discharge unless it is of the opinion that there are exceptional circumstances relating to the offence or the person that justify it doing so. If so justified, the fact that the court is of that opinion and the reasons for that opinion must be stated in open court (s. 66ZB(5) and (6)).

Where a child or young person is informed that he or she will be reported for a recordable offence, the usual rules regarding the taking of fingerprints and non-intimate samples apply. Where a child or young person is released, on bail or otherwise (e.g., for a decision to be taken about a youth caution), and a youth caution is subsequently administered for a recordable offence, fingerprints or a non-intimate sample may be taken without consent (see **D1.105** and **D1.112**).

Conditional Cautions

D2.35 Conditional cautions for those who have attained the age of 18 are governed by the CJA 2003, Part 3, and the *Code of Practice for Adult Conditional Cautions*, issued under the CJA 2003, s. 25 (introduced by the Criminal Justice Act 2003 (Conditional Cautions: Code of Practice) Order 2013 (SI 2013 No. 801)). In addition, regard should be had to the *Director's Guidance on Adult Conditional Cautions* (November 2019, tinyurl.com/yc4vglbu), issued by the DPP under the PACE 1984, s. 37A and the CPS guidance on *Restorative Justice* (September 2019, tinyurl.com/vrw7f6w) to be used alongside the Code of Practice for Adult Conditional Cautions. Youth conditional cautions for persons under the age of 18 are governed by the CDA 1998, ss. 66A to 66H, and the *Code of Practice for Youth Conditional Cautions* (introduced by the Crime and Disorder Act 1998 (Youth Conditional Cautions: Code of Practice) Order 2013 (SI 2013 No. 613)). In addition, regard should be had to the *Director's Guidance on Youth Conditional Cautions* (November 2019, tinyurl.com/y9nncxl5), issued by the DPP under the PACE 1984, s. 37A.

An assessment of the seriousness of the offence is the starting point for considering whether a conditional caution may be appropriate. In respect of adults, a conditional caution should not be imposed where the circumstances of an offence indicate that an immediate custodial sentence or high level community order is the appropriate sentence, unless specific provisions concerning foreign nationals apply, or the exceptional circumstances set out in the *Director's Guidance on Adult Conditional Cautions* are met. The seriousness of the offence and the range of penalties likely to be imposed must be considered, taking into account the *Magistrates' Court Sentencing Guidelines*. Specific either-way offences with a starting point at high level community order or period of imprisonment are set out in annex A. In respect of youths, the police decision-makers will apply the *ACPO Youth Offender Disposal Gravity Matrix*. A youth conditional caution for an indictable only offence will only be appropriate in the most exceptional circumstances; such a case must be referred to a prosecutor to determine whether the exceptional circumstances are met. In *R (Guest) v DPP* [2009] EWHC 594 (Admin), [2009] 2 Cr App R 26 (426), a conditional caution given to an adult was quashed where it was given for an offence which was too serious. **D2.36**

A conditional caution is defined as 'a caution which is given in respect of an offence committed by the offender and which has conditions attached to it' (CJA 2003, s. 22(2); CDA 1998, s. 66A(2)). The decision whether there is sufficient evidence to charge and that a conditional caution should be given may be made by either a Crown Prosecutor or a police officer. In deciding whether a conditional caution is a suitable disposal, account must be taken of the factors set out in the relevant guidance; but it has been held that the prohibition in the *Director's Guidance on Adult Conditional Cautions* on offering a conditional caution in respect of a domestic violence offence must be interpreted so as to permit exceptions (*R (Robson) v CPS* [2016] EWHC 2191 (Admin), [2017] 1 Cr App R 5 (36)). Where a youth conditional caution is given, the authorised person must refer the offender to a youth offending team as soon as practicable (CDA 1998, s. 66A(6A)).

Criteria for a Conditional Caution A conditional caution may be imposed if each of five requirements is satisfied (CJA 2003, s. 23 (adults); CDA 1998, s. 66B (youths)): **D2.37**

(a) The *authorised person* has evidence that the offender has committed an offence.
(b) The *relevant prosecutor or authorised person* decides there is sufficient evidence to charge and that a conditional caution should be given. In making this decision, the evidential and public interest stages of the full code test must be applied (see **D2.10** to **D2.12**).
(c) The offender admits the offence to the *authorised person*. Following authority on similar provisions relating to simple cautions, and reprimands and warnings, the admission must be clear and reliable, and must not be induced by the offer of a conditional caution (see **D2.26**).
(d) The *authorised person* explains the effects of the conditional caution to the offender and warns that failure to comply with any of the conditions renders the offender liable to be prosecuted for the original offence. If the offender is aged 16 or under, the explanation and warning must be given in the presence of an appropriate adult (CDA 1998, s. 66B(5)).
(e) The offender signs a document which contains details of the offence, an admission of having committed it, consent to the conditional caution, and the conditions that are attached to the caution.

An *authorised person* is a constable, a designated civilian investigating officer or a person authorised for this purpose by the relevant prosecutor (CJA 2003, s. 22(4); CDA 1998, s. 66A(7)). A *relevant prosecutor* means the A-G, Director of the SFO, DPP, Secretary of State or a person specified in an order made by the Secretary of State (CJA 2003, s. 27; CDA 1998, s. 66H(e)).

Conditions that May be Imposed A condition can be imposed provided it has the purpose of facilitating the rehabilitation of the offender, ensuring that the offender makes reparation for the offence or punishing the offender (CJA 2003, s. 22(3); CDA 1998, s. 66A(3)). A condition can include a requirement that the offender pay a financial penalty up to a prescribed maximum (Criminal Justice Act 2003 (Conditional Cautions: Financial Penalties) Order 2013 (SI 2013 No. 615)). The position is likewise for youth conditional cautions, although the maximum amounts of financial penalties are lower (Crime and Disorder Act 1998 (Youth Conditional Cautions: Financial Penalties) Order 2013 (SI 2013 No. 608)). See also Home **D2.38**

Office guidance, *Using Conditional Cautions with Sobriety Requirements* (November 2013, tinyurl.com/y99e5ky6).

The CJA 2003, s. 22(3D) to (3G), enable conditions to be attached to an adult conditional caution given to a relevant foreign offender that have the objective of bringing about the departure of the offender and/or ensuring that the offender does not return to the UK for a specified period of time. The term 'relevant foreign offender' is defined by s. 22(3G).

Conditions must be appropriate, proportionate and achievable (*Code of Practice for Adult Conditional Cautions*, para. 2.21; *Code of Practice for Youth Conditional Cautions*, para. 8.1). A relevant prosecutor or authorised person may, with consent of the offender, vary the conditions attached to a conditional caution by modifying or omitting any of the conditions or adding a condition (CJA 2003, s. 23B; CDA 1998, s. 66D).

D2.39 **Repeat Cautions** A previous conviction or caution does not preclude the use of a conditional caution or youth conditional caution, although a second caution should not normally be given for the same or a similar offence unless there are exceptional circumstances indicating that it may be appropriate (*Code of Practice for Adult Conditional Cautions*, paras. 2.11 and 2.13; *Code of Practice for Youth Conditional Cautions*, paras. 6.4 and 6.6).

D2.40 **Consequences of a Conditional Caution** Failure without reasonable cause to comply with any of the conditions imposed under a conditional caution renders the person liable to prosecution for the original offence (CJA 2003, s. 24(1); CDA 1998, s. 66E(1)), and the document that the person has signed (see **D2.37**) will be admissible in evidence (CJA 2003, s. 24(2); CDA 1998, s. 66E(2)). Although a conditional caution is not a criminal conviction, if it is imposed for a recordable offence it is entered on the Police National Computer and forms part of the offender's criminal record. Fingerprints and other identification data can be taken and retained and, in the case of a relevant sexual offence, the person is placed on the sex offenders register for two years (see **E23.1** ***et seq.***). Conditional cautions may be cited in any subsequent court proceedings. They are covered by the Rehabilitation of Offenders Act 1974, and are spent at the end of the 'relevant period for the caution', i.e. normally three months after the date on which they were given (see further **E24.1** ***et seq.***). A constable having reasonable grounds for believing that a person who is subject to a conditional caution has failed, without reasonable cause, to comply with any of its conditions, may arrest the person without warrant (CJA 2003, s. 24A(1)). Following arrest, the person may be charged with the offence for which the conditional caution was imposed, released without charge to enable a charge decision to be made, or released without charge and without bail (with or without any variation in the conditions attached to the caution) (s. 24A(2)). Where a person is so arrested, various provisions of the PACE 1984 apply with modifications (s. 24B). These provisions are applied to youth conditional cautions by the CDA 1998, s. 66E(4) and (5).

Fixed Penalty Notices

D2.41 **Fixed Penalty Notices under the CJPA 2001** The CJPA 2001, ss. 1 and 2, make provision for fixed penalty notices in respect of the list of offences set out in s. 1. They include being drunk in a highway, other public place or licensed premises (Licensing Act 1872, s. 12), disorderly behaviour while drunk in a public place (CJA 1967, s. 91), wasting police time or giving a false report (Criminal Law Act 1967, s. 5(2)), theft (Theft Act 1968, s. 1, but limited by guidance to retail thefts up to £100), destroying or damaging property (Criminal Damage Act 1971, s. 1(1), but limited by guidance to damage not exceeding £300), behaviour likely to cause harassment, alarm or distress (POA 1986, s. 5), and possession of cannabis or Khat and related offences (Misuse of Drugs Act 1971, s. 5(2)).

Penalty notices are defined in the CJPA 2001, s. 2(4), as notices that offer the opportunity, by paying a penalty, 'to discharge any liability to be convicted of the offence to which the notice relates'. Where a police officer has reason to believe that a person aged 18 or over has committed a penalty offence, the officer may give the person a penalty notice in respect of the offence

(s. 2(1)). Guidance provides that only one penalty notice should be issued to a person for retail theft, and a notice should not be issued for retail theft or criminal damage to a person who is a known substance misuser. Guidance on fixed penalty notices is provided by the Ministry of Justice: *Penalty notices for disorder (PNDs)* (June 2014, tinyurl.com/jkczv2y).

Section 3 sets out the requirements to be met for the notice to be valid. It must: **D2.42**

(a) state the alleged offence;
(b) give such particulars of the circumstances alleged to constitute the offence as are necessary to provide reasonable information about it;
(c) specify the suspended enforcement period (as to which see s. 5) and explain its effect;
(d) state the amount of the penalty;
(e) state where the penalty may be paid; and
(f) inform the recipient of the right to ask to be tried for the alleged offence and explain how that right may be exercised.

The amount of the penalty is fixed by the Penalties for Disorderly Behaviour (Amount of Penalty) Order 2002 (SI 2002 No. 1837), as amended, *inter alia*, by SI 2013 No. 1579; the fixed penalty payable is £90 or £60, depending on the nature of the offence. A penalty notice may include an education option if it arises from an offence in relation to which there is an approved educational course.

Section 4 sets out the effect of a penalty notice. Where the recipient of a notice asks to be tried for the alleged offence, proceedings may be brought. Such a request must be made by the recipient in the manner specified in the penalty notice and before the end of the period of suspended enforcement (defined in s. 5). If, by the end of the suspended enforcement period, the penalty has not been paid but the recipient has not made a request to be tried, a sum equal to one and a half times the amount of the penalty may be registered under s. 8 for enforcement as a fine. These provisions are modified in the case of a penalty notice with an education option (see the CJPA 2001, ss. 4(6) to (10) and 5(2)). **D2.43**

Proceedings for the offence to which a penalty notice relates may not be brought until the end of the period of 21 days beginning with the date on which the notice was given. If the penalty is paid before the end of this 'suspended enforcement period', no proceedings may be brought for the offence (s. 5). Section 5 does not apply if the person to whom the penalty notice was given has made a request to be tried. Where a fixed penalty notice has been imposed, prosecution for an offence arising from the same circumstances is permissible if evidence of a more serious offence than that for which the penalty was imposed comes to light (*Gore* [2009] EWCA Crim 1424, [2009] 1 WLR 2454). A penalty notice is not a conviction, and does not amount to an admission of guilt nor to proof that a crime has been committed (*Hamer* [2010] EWCA Crim 2053, [2011] 1 WLR 528: see also **F14.8**).

Fixed Penalty Notices under the ASBA 2003 The ASBA 2003, s. 43, makes provision for penalty notices in respect of offences listed in s. 44(1). **D2.44**

Where an authorised officer of a local authority has reason to believe that a person has committed an offence to which these provisions apply, the officer may give that person a notice offering the opportunity of discharging any liability to conviction for that offence by payment of a penalty (s. 43(1)). However, this does not apply if the authorised officer considers that the commission of the offence, in the case of damage to property, also involves the commission of an offence under the CDA 1998, s. 30 (racially or religiously aggravated criminal damage) or, in the case of any other relevant offence, was motivated (wholly or partly) by hostility towards a person based upon membership (or presumed membership) of a racial or religious group, or towards members of a racial or religious group based on their membership of that group (s. 43(2)).

Where a person is given a penalty notice in respect of an offence, no proceedings may be instituted for that offence (or any other offence to which the provisions apply arising out of the same circumstances) until 14 days after the date of the notice (s. 43(4)). The person cannot be convicted of that offence (or any other relevant offence arising out of the same circumstances) if the penalty specified in the notice is paid within 14 days. The penalty notice must 'give such particulars of the circumstances alleged to constitute the offence as are necessary for giving reasonable information of the offence' (s. 43(5)). Where payment is made by post, it is deemed to have been made at the time at which that letter would be delivered in the ordinary course of post (s. 43(8)).

Section 43B empowers the authorised officer of the local authority to require the person to give his or her name and address. Failure to give name and address (or giving a false or inaccurate address) is an offence under s. 43B(2), punishable with a fine on level 3 of the standard scale.

D2.45 **Other Fixed Penalty Notice Provisions** There are a number of statutory provisions for fixed penalty notices in environmental protection legislation. These include fixed penalties for:

- depositing waste and leaving litter (Environmental Protection Act 1990, ss. 33, 87 and 88);
- failure to provide specified receptacles for household or commercial waste (Environmental Protection Act 1990, s. 47ZA);
- failure to comply with a community protection notice under the ABCPA 2014, s. 48 (s. 52 of that Act);
- failure to comply with a consumption of alcohol prohibition order under s. 63, and failure to comply with a public spaces protection order under s. 67, of the ABCPA 2014 (s. 68 of that Act);
- exceeding permitted noise levels in a dwelling after service of a notice contrary to the Noise Act 1996, s. 4 (s. 8 of that Act);
- abandoning a vehicle contrary to the Refuse Disposal (Amenity) Act 1978, s. 2 (s. 2A of that Act);
- exposing two or more vehicles for sale on a road or repairing vehicles on a road for profit contrary to the Clean Neighbourhoods and Environment Act 2005, ss. 3 or 4 (s. 6 of that Act);
- failure to nominate a key-holder where an audible intruder alarm is installed on premises in an alarm notification area contrary to the Clean Neighbourhoods and Environment Act 2005, s. 71(4) (s. 73 of that Act).

For traffic offences in respect of which a fixed penalty notice can be imposed under the RTOA 1988, sch. 3, see **C8.3**.

BAIL FOLLOWING CHARGE

D2.46 Where a person arrested for an offence otherwise than under a warrant endorsed for bail is charged with an offence the custody officer must, subject to the CJPO 1994, s. 25 (see **D2.50**), release the person from detention either on bail or without bail, unless one or more of the conditions in the PACE 1984, s. 38, is satisfied (s. 38(1); see **D2.50**). This is subject to the power under s. 37(8A) and (8B) to detain the person for the purpose of a Class A drug test (see **D1.124**). A person charged with murder cannot be granted bail by a custody officer (s. 38(1)(c)). Where a person is granted bail under s. 38(1), the custody officer must appoint for the court appearance a date which is no later than the first sitting of the relevant magistrates' court after the date on which the person is charged, unless notified that the appearance cannot be accommodated until a later date, in which case the officer must appoint that later date (PACE 1984, s. 47(3A)). Alternatively, the custody officer may bail a person to attend a police station pursuant to a live link direction under the CDA 1998, s. 57C (PACE 1984, s. 47(3)(b)). Live link bail is now available in all local justice areas. For pre-trial hearings by television link, see **D5.38**; for bail from a court, see **D7**. For Home Office guidance on bail and refusal of bail by criminal courts and police officers, see tinyurl.com/tnxubaf.

Power to Impose Conditions

D2.47 A release on bail under s. 38(1) is deemed to be a release on bail granted in accordance with the BA 1976, ss. 3, 3A, 5 and 5A, as they apply to bail granted by a constable (PACE 1984,

s. 47(1)), and the 'normal powers to impose conditions of bail' (as defined in the BA 1976, s. 3(6)) apply (PACE 1984, s. 47(1A)). Such conditions (including requiring a surety or security) can be imposed as appear necessary for the purpose of ensuring that the person surrenders to custody, does not commit an offence on bail, does not interfere with witnesses or otherwise obstruct the course of justice and/or for his or her own protection (or where the person is under 18 years, for his or her own welfare or own interests) (PACE 1984, s. 47(1A); BA 1976, ss. 3(6) and 3A(5)). Any condition may be imposed other than a condition that the person reside in a bail hostel, be available for the purposes of a court report, or attend an interview with a lawyer (BA 1976, s. 3A(2)). A surety can be required only for the purpose of securing surrender to custody (*R (Shea) v Winchester Crown Court* [2013] EWHC 1050 (Admin)). It has been held in relation to a court's power to impose bail conditions that, in considering whether and what conditions to impose, the court must perceive a real and not merely fanciful risk of the relevant outcome (*Mansfield Justices, ex parte Sharkey* [1985] QB 613), and it is submitted that the same principle must apply to a decision by a police officer.

A person who has been made subject to bail conditions may apply to the same or another custody officer serving at the same station for the conditions to be varied, and in doing so the officer may impose conditions or more onerous conditions (BA 1976, s. 3A(4)). The person may, alternatively or in addition, apply to a magistrates' court for variation, and again the court may impose conditions or more onerous conditions (PACE 1984, s. 47(1D) and (1E)). The procedure for reconsideration by a magistrates' court of a bail decision by a police officer, including a decision as to the imposition of conditions, is set out in CrimPR 14.6 (see Supplement, **R14.6**). The application must be made in writing and served on the other party, the court officer and any surety. It must specify any decision that the applicant wants the court to make, each offence charged (or for which the person was arrested) and the decision and the reasons given for it. In considering variation or removal of conditions, a court can take into account a police officer's opinion that the person is a flight risk even though the source of the information giving rise to the officer's opinion has not been disclosed (*R (Ajaib) v Birmingham Magistrates' Court* [2009] EWHC 2127 (Admin)). There is no appeal against the decision of a magistrates' court, but the decision is susceptible to judicial review (*R (Carson) v Ealing Magistrates' Court* [2012] EWHC 1456 (Admin)).

Enforcement of Bail

Police bail granted under the PACE 1984, s. 38, is enforceable in the same way as bail granted **D2.48** by a court. Failure to surrender to custody at the appointed time without reasonable cause is an offence under the BA 1976, s. 6, and the person subject to bail may be arrested if the person fails to surrender or if a police officer has reasonable grounds for believing that the person is not likely to surrender to custody (s. 7). Breach of bail conditions is not an offence but a person released on bail subject to conditions may be arrested if a constable has reasonable grounds for believing that the person is likely to breach any of the conditions, or for suspecting that any of the conditions has been broken. Furthermore, if the person was released subject to a surety, the person on bail may be arrested if the surety notifies the police in writing that the person is unlikely to surrender to custody and that the surety wants to be relieved of the obligations as surety (s. 7(3)). The court at which the suspect is due to appear may extend bail by fixing a later time at which the suspect is to surrender, whether or not bail was granted subject to a surety (MCA 1980, s. 43(1)).

DETENTION FOLLOWING CHARGE

As noted in **D2.46**, where a person arrested for an offence otherwise than under a warrant **D2.49** endorsed for bail is charged with an offence, the custody officer must, subject to the CJPO

1994, s. 25, release the person from detention either on bail or without bail, unless one or more of the conditions in the PACE 1984, s. 38, is satisfied (s. 38(1)). The officer must determine what, if any, documents or materials should be made available to the detained person by virtue of Code C, para. 3.4(b) (documents and materials that are essential for challenging the lawfulness of the arrest and detention) (Code C, para. 16.7A). It was held in *Hutt v Metropolitan Police Commissioner* [2003] EWCA Civ 1911 that where the arrest leading to the detention was unlawful, bail could not be denied under s. 38(1). However, it is submitted that this would not be the case if the nature of the illegality was such that it could be, and was, 'cured' (e.g., where a failure to comply with the requirement under the PACE 1984, s. 28, to inform the arrested person of the grounds for arrest is 'cured' by the arrested person subsequently being given this information). It is an abuse of process for the investigating officer to oppose bail following charge where the officer had promised that, if the person voluntarily returned to the UK and surrendered to the police, bail would be granted (*R (Hauschildt) v Highbury Corner Magistrates' Court* [2007] EWHC 3494 (Admin)).

Where a person charged with an offence is kept in police detention or, in the case of a child, is detained by a local authority in accordance with the PACE 1984, s. 38(6) (see **D2.52**), the police must bring the person before a magistrates' court (s. 46(1)). A person may be treated as having been so brought if attending through a live link (see **D5.38**). If the person is to be brought before a magistrates' court in the local justice area in which the police station is situated, that must be done as soon as is practicable, and in any event no later than the first sitting after the person is charged with the offence (s. 46(2)). This will result in the accused person being brought before the court on the day of charging or on the next day, unless the next day is a Sunday, Christmas Day or Good Friday (s. 46(8)). If no magistrates' court for the area is due to sit in either period, the custody officer must inform the relevant court office that there is a charged and detained person who must be brought before the court (s. 46(3)). Arrangements must then be made for a magistrates' court to sit not later than the day after the day following the date of charge (s. 46(6)(a) and (7)(a)).

Grounds for Withholding Bail

D2.50 The restrictions on bail under the CJPO 1994, s. 25, mean that where a person is charged with certain specified offences, and that person already has a conviction (including a finding of not guilty by reason of insanity, a finding under the Criminal Procedure (Insanity) Act 1964, s. 4A(3) (unfitness to plead) that a person did the act or made the omission charged, or conviction for an offence for which the person was absolutely or conditionally discharged) for any of certain specified offences in any part of the UK (or a conviction for culpable homicide), bail may only be granted if the custody officer is satisfied that there are exceptional circumstances which justify the grant of bail. The offences concerned are set out in s. 25(2) (see **D7.10**).

Where the previous conviction was for manslaughter or culpable homicide, the restriction only applies if the person received a custodial sentence (CJPO 1994, s. 25(3)). No guidance is given in the Act as to the meaning of 'exceptional circumstances' nor as to the relationship between s. 25 and the PACE 1984, s. 38. It would seem that the custody officer would still have to be satisfied that one or more of the s. 38 conditions applies before withholding bail, but in practice, it is highly unlikely that a custody officer would grant bail in the circumstances covered by s. 25. It was held in *R (O) v Crown Court at Harrow* [2003] EWHC 868 (Admin), [2003] 1 WLR 2756, that s. 25 does not violate the ECHR, Article 5 (right to liberty and security), provided that it is not construed too narrowly.

D2.51 The grounds for withholding bail under the PACE 1984, s. 38(1), are as follows.

(a) The person's name or address cannot be ascertained, or the custody officer has reasonable grounds for doubting whether the name or address given by the suspect is real (s. 38(1)(a)(i)).

(b) The custody officer has reasonable grounds for believing that the person arrested will fail to appear in court to answer bail (s. 38(1)(a)(ii)).
(c) Where the person was arrested for an imprisonable offence, the custody officer has reasonable grounds for believing that the detention of the person is necessary to prevent him or her from committing an offence (s. 38(1)(a)(iii)). Note that it refers to a person *arrested* for as opposed to *charged* with an imprisonable offence. It is suggested that the wording follows from the general structure of the section, and that the ground should be relied upon to deny bail only where a person is charged with such an offence.
(d) In a case where a sample may be taken under the PACE 1984, s. 63B (testing for Class A drugs), the custody officer has reasonable grounds for believing that the detention of the person is necessary to enable the sample to be taken (s. 38(1)(a)(iiia)). In this case the person cannot be kept in police detention after the end of the period of six hours beginning when the person was charged with the offence (s. 38(2)).
(e) Where the person was arrested for a non-imprisonable offence, the custody officer has reasonable grounds for believing that detention is necessary to prevent him or her from causing physical injury to any other person or from causing loss of or damage to property (s. 38(1)(a)(iv)).
(f) The custody officer has reasonable grounds for believing that detention is necessary to prevent the person from interfering with the administration of justice or with the investigation of offences or of a particular offence (s. 38(1)(a)(v)).
(g) The custody officer has reasonable grounds for believing that detention is necessary for the person's own protection (s. 38(1)(a)(vi)).
(h) The person is charged with murder (s. 38(1)(c)).

By s. 38(7A), 'imprisonable offence' has the same meaning as in the BA 1976, sch. 1 (see **D7.151**). In considering the above grounds, other than (a) and (g), the custody officer must have regard to the nature and seriousness of the offence, and the probable penalty; the character, antecedents, associations and community ties of the detained person; the person's record in respect of previous grant of bail; the strength of the evidence; and any other relevant consideration (PACE 1984, s. 38(2A)).

Detention of Children after Charge

D2.52 The grounds for withholding bail under the PACE 1984, s. 38(1), apply to children in the same way as they apply to adults except that ground (d) applies only if the child has attained the minimum age (see **D1.122**), and that bail may also be withheld if the custody officer has reasonable grounds for believing that the child ought to be detained in the child's own interests (s. 38(1)(b)). For the definition of 'child', see **D1.63**.

Where a child is kept in police detention after charge under s. 38(1) (but not under some other power), the child must be dealt with in accordance with s. 38(6) to (7). Section 38(6) provides that the custody officer must arrange for the child to be transferred to local authority accommodation unless the officer certifies:

(a) that, by reason of such circumstances as are specified in the certificate, it is impracticable to do so; or
(b) in the case of an arrested juvenile who has attained the age of 12 years, that no secure accommodation is available and that keeping the juvenile in other local authority accommodation would not be adequate to protect the public from serious harm.

In October 2017 the Home Office published a *Concordat on Children in Custody* (available at tinyurl.com/ydbe6y5t), with the objective of supporting police forces and local authorities in England in complying with their statutory responsibilities with regard to children in custody, and to bring about a decrease in the number of children held overnight in police stations.

D2.53 With regard to practicability, Code C, Note for Guidance 16D, provides that neither the child's behaviour nor the nature of the offence with which the child is charged provides grounds for the custody officer to retain the child in police custody rather than to arrange a transfer to local authority accommodation; impracticability concerns transport and travel requirements. It also states that lack of secure local authority accommodation does not make it impracticable for the custody officer to transfer the child, noting that the availability of secure accommodation is only a factor in relation to a child aged 12 or over when the local authority accommodation would not be adequate to protect the public from serious harm.

Furthermore, Note for Guidance 16D provides that the obligation to transfer a child to local authority accommodation applies as much to a child charged during the daytime as to a child who is to be held overnight, subject to the requirement under s. 46(1) and (2) to bring a person charged and kept in police detention or detained in local authority accommodation under these provisions before a court as soon as is practicable. In *R (M) v Gateshead Metropolitan Borough Council* [2006] EWCA Civ 221, [2006] QB 650, the Court of Appeal held that local authorities should have a reasonable system in place to enable them to respond to such requests under s. 38(6), but that they were not under an absolute duty to provide secure accommodation. Where the request was made at 00.20 a.m., with a view to the child being produced in court at 10 a.m. the same day, it was wholly impracticable for the local authority to provide accommodation. The obligation under s. 38(6) does not arise where a child is not charged, for example, where the child is arrested under the BA 1976, s. 7, for breach of bail conditions (*R (BG) v Chief Constable of West Midlands Constabulary* [2014] EWHC 4374 (Admin)).

D2.54 The PACE 1984, s. 38(6)(b), provides that, in the case of children who have attained the age of 12 years, the custody officer can take into account the lack of secure accommodation where keeping the suspect in other local authority accommodation would not be adequate to protect the public from the risk of serious harm. It is understood that this subsection was intended to apply only to children of that age who were charged with violent or sexual offences. However, s. 38(6A) provides that 'any reference, in relation to an arrested juvenile charged with a violent or sexual offence, to protecting the public from serious harm from him shall be construed as a reference to protecting members of the public from death or serious personal injury, whether physical or psychological, occasioned by further such offences committed by him'. Therefore, the possibility of keeping a child in police custody after charge under s. 38(6) is not confined to those charged with a violent or sexual offence. The justification of 'protecting the public from serious harm' is defined only in respect of those charged with a violent or sexual offence. It is suggested, however, that this definition gives an indication of the gravity of the threat of harm to the public that would be required in order to keep a child charged with any other offence in police custody.

Note that although s. 38(6)(b) refers to the non-availability of secure accommodation, the police cannot insist that the local authority place the child in secure accommodation even if it is available. 'Secure accommodation' has a technical meaning, and a local authority cannot restrict the liberty of a child in its care otherwise than in approved secure accommodation. A child aged 12 or over but under the age of 18 who is detained following charge under the PACE 1984, s. 38(6), may not be placed in secure accommodation unless it appears that any accommodation other than that provided for the purpose of restricting liberty is inappropriate because the child is likely to abscond from other accommodation, or is likely to injure him or herself or other people if kept in other accommodation. A child aged 10 or 11 who is detained under s. 38(6) may not be placed in secure accommodation unless it appears that there is a history of absconding and the child is likely to abscond from any other description of accommodation, and is likely thereby to suffer significant harm, or it appears that if kept in any other description of accommodation the child is likely to injure him or herself or other persons. For England, see the Children

Act 1989, s. 25, and the Children (Secure Accommodation) Regulations 1991 (SI 1991 No. 1505), reg. 6, as amended by the Children (Secure Accommodation) (Amendment) (England) Regulations 2015 (SI 2015 No. 1883), reg. 2; for Wales, see the Social Services and Well-being (Wales) Act 2014, s. 119, and the Children (Secure Accommodation) (Wales) Regulations 2015 (SI 2015 No. 1988), reg. 15(1), as amended by the Children (Secure Accommodation) (Wales) (Amendment) Regulations 2016 (SI 2016 No. 312), reg. 2(8).

If a child is kept in police custody under s. 38(6)(a) or (b), the custody officer must certify the reasons, and this certificate must be produced to the court before which the child first appears (s. 38(7)). **D2.55**

Section D3 Courts, Parties and Abuse of Process

INTRODUCTION

D3.1 The criminal trial of an adult takes place either in the Crown Court or in a magistrates' court. The criminal trial of a child or young person usually takes place in a special form of magistrates' court, known as the youth court, but sometimes takes place in either the Crown Court or an ordinary magistrates' court. The first part of this section describes the status, structure, judges and main heads of jurisdiction of the Crown Court and ordinary magistrates' courts. Youth courts are described in **D24**.

THE CROWN COURT

Creation and Status

D3.2 The Crown Court was created by the Courts Act 1971, and replaced the former courts of assize and quarter sessions and a number of other criminal courts. The Crown Court derives its jurisdiction from the Senior Courts Act 1981. Its practice and procedure are prescribed, *inter alia*, by the CrimPR (see Supplement, **R1.1** *et seq*.).

The Crown Court is regarded as a *single* court. It follows that, although the Crown Court sits in many different locations and a case will normally be tried at a location near where the offence allegedly occurred, the trial may take place at any location of the Crown Court. The choice of location will depend on the nature of the offence charged (offences are divided into three classes, determining the level of judge who should preside), the convenience of the parties, the desirability of expediting the trial and any directions given by the presiding judge of the relevant circuit as to the locations to which the magistrates' courts in the area of the circuit should normally send cases for trial. See CrimPD XIII for detailed guidance on listing, especially Part E on allocation of business within the Crown Court (see Supplement, **CPD.XIII.E**).

In status, the Crown Court occupies a somewhat ambiguous position. Like the High Court, it is a Senior Court and a superior court of record (Senior Courts Act 1981, s. 45(1)), with the same powers in relation to, e.g., contempt and enforcement of its orders as are possessed by the High Court (s. 45(4)). Furthermore, when it exercises its jurisdiction in relation to trials on indictment, appeals from its decisions lie only to the Court of Appeal (Criminal Division), just as appeals from the High Court go to the Court of Appeal (Civil Division). On the other hand, decisions of the Crown Court which do not relate to trial on indictment (e.g., a decision taken in respect of an appeal from a magistrates' court) may be challenged in the High Court either by an appeal by way of case stated or by application for judicial review (see ss. 28(2) and 29(3) of the 1981 Act). Thus, for some purposes the Crown Court is treated as being on a par with the High Court, while for other purposes it is subject to the same supervisory jurisdiction that the High Court exercises in relation to magistrates' courts.

Structure

The many different locations in which the Crown Court sits are classified according to (a) geographical position and (b) status. As to (a), every location belongs to one of six 'circuits': (i) Midlands, (ii) North-Eastern, (iii) Northern, (iv) Wales, (v) Western, and (vi) South-Eastern. Each circuit is presided over by a High Court judge called the 'presiding judge', who has responsibility for taking certain decisions about the administration and distribution of work on the circuit. If considered desirable, a circuit may have both a senior presiding judge and one or more other presiding judges to assist. As to (b), locations are either first, second or third tier. At first-tier locations, High Court judges regularly sit; at third-tier locations, High Court judges do not normally sit. Each circuit contains locations of each of the three tiers. The most serious cases will normally be committed to either a first or second-tier location, so that there will be at least the possibility of the trial being conducted by a High Court judge. The presiding judge for the circuit has overall responsibility for listing at all courts on his or her circuit (see CrimPD XIII, which deals with listing in detail (see Supplement, **CPD.XIII.A**)). At each location of the Crown Court, there is a senior judge (known as the 'resident judge') who is responsible, *inter alia*, for the distribution of work amongst the judges allocated to that court and for providing a link between the judiciary and the court administration. **D3.3**

Judges

Senior Courts Act 1981, s. 8 **D3.4**

(1) The jurisdiction of the Crown Court shall be exercisable by—
   (a) any judge of the High Court; or
   (b) any circuit judge, recorder, qualifying judge advocate or District Judge (Magistrates' Courts); or
   (c) subject to and in accordance with the provisions of sections 74 and 75(2), a judge of the High Court, circuit judge, recorder or qualifying judge advocate sitting with not more than four justices of the peace,

and any such persons when exercising the jurisdiction of the Crown Court shall be judges of the Crown Court.

For ss. 74 and 75(2) (justices sitting in Crown Court), see **D3.9**. Section 8(1) must be read in conjunction with s. 24 (deputy circuit judges) — see **D3.8**.

There are thus three principal categories of Crown Court judge, namely High Court judges, circuit judges and recorders. All proceedings in the Crown Court must be heard before a single professional judge of the court except where there is provision for justices to sit with such a judge (s. 73(1)).

The Armed Forces Act 2011 amended s. 8(1)(b) to add any 'qualifying judge advocate' to the list of judges who can exercise the jurisdiction of the Crown Court; however, such judges will not have jurisdiction in relation to an appeal from a youth court (s. 8(1A)).

High Court Judges By virtue of the Senior Courts Act 1981, s. 10(2)(c), a person cannot be appointed as a judge of the High Court without satisfying the judicial-appointment eligibility condition on a seven-year basis or having been a circuit judge for at least two years. The process for appointing High Court judges is governed by the Constitutional Reform Act 2005, ss. 85 to 93. The Senior Courts Act 1981, s. 9(4), also enables the appointment of deputy High Court judges to facilitate the disposal of business in the High Court or the Crown Court (those appointed must be eligible for appointment as High Court judges). **D3.5**

CrimPD XIII, Part E, requires that certain categories of case must normally be tried by a High Court judge (see Supplement, **CPD.XIII.E**).

Circuit Judges The office of circuit judge was created by the Courts Act 1971. Circuit judges are appointed 'to serve in the Crown Court and county courts and to carry out such other judicial **D3.6**

functions as may be conferred on them under this or any other enactment' (Courts Act 1971, s. 16(1)). To be appointed as a circuit judge, the applicant must satisfy the judicial-appointment eligibility condition on a seven-year basis, or else be a recorder, or a person who has held (as a full-time appointment for at least three years) one of the offices listed in the Courts Act 1971, sch. 2, part 1A (s. 16(3)).

City and borough councils are able to appoint a judge as 'Honorary Recorder' (a title which is not to be confused with the part-time judges discussed at **D3.7**); Honorary Recorders have no additional judicial functions but are expected to engage in local civic affairs and events. If an Honorary Recorder is appointed, it is usually the Resident Judge.

D3.7 **Recorders** Recorders are appointed 'to act as part-time judges of the Crown Court and to carry out such other judicial functions as may be conferred on them under this or any other enactment' (Courts Act 1971, s. 21(1)). By s. 21(2), to be appointed as a recorder, the applicant must satisfy the judicial-appointment eligibility condition on a seven-year basis. The appointment must specify the term for which the recorder is appointed and the frequency and duration of the occasions during that term on which the recorder must be available to undertake his or her duties (s. 21(3)). The original term of appointment must be extended by the Lord Chancellor (with the agreement of the recorder) unless the Lord Chief Justice agrees that the Lord Chancellor should decline to extend the appointment because of the incapacity or misbehaviour of the recorder (s. 21(4A) to (4C)). When not sitting, the recorder may (and normally does) revert to private practice. The major difference between a circuit judge and a recorder is that the former is a full-time and the latter a part-time appointment.

D3.8 **Deputy Circuit Judges** The Courts Act 1971, s. 24, enables the Lord Chief Justice (with the concurrence of the Lord Chancellor) to appoint deputy circuit judges where it is expedient to do so as a temporary measure in order to facilitate the disposal of business in (*inter alia*) the Crown Court. A person may be appointed as a deputy circuit judge having previously held office as a judge of the Court of Appeal or of the High Court or as a circuit judge.

D3.9 **Justices** For the hearing of appeals from a magistrates' court, the Crown Court *must* normally include not less than two and not more than four justices, none of whom took part in the decision under appeal (Senior Courts Act 1981, s. 74(1); CrimPR 34.11(1)(a): see Supplement, **R34.11**). The exceptions are that the Crown Court may include only one justice of the peace if the presiding judge decides that the start of the appeal hearing would otherwise be delayed unreasonably, or else one or more of the justices who started hearing the appeal is absent (r. 34.11(2)(a)).

Rule 34.11(1)(b) provides that, where the appeal is from a youth court, each justice of the peace must be qualified to sit as a member of a youth court.

Role of the Justices in the Crown Court

D3.10 When the Crown Court comprises a judge sitting with a justice or justices, the decision of the court may be by a majority (Senior Courts Act 1981, s. 73(3)). It follows that the justices may out-vote the professional judge, although if an even-numbered court is equally divided the professional judge has a casting vote (s. 73(3)). The principle that the justices participate equally with the judge in the decisions of the court applies not only to the determination of the appeal, but also to interlocutory decisions (e.g., about the admissibility of evidence). Thus, in *Orpin* [1975] QB 283, Lord Widgery CJ said (at p. 287) that the justices should be given an opportunity of taking part in the decision as to whether disputed evidence was admissible or not. It is up to the judge whether to retire for the purpose, or whether to consult with the justices briefly and informally on the bench. However, his lordship went on to say that, in matters of law, 'the lay justices must take a ruling from the presiding judge in precisely the same way as the jury is required to take his ruling when the jury considers its verdict'.

The role of the justices was further considered in *Newby* (1984) 6 Cr App R (S) 148. Criticising the judge for announcing sentence immediately after defence counsel's plea in mitigation, and without any apparent consultation with the justices (although there had been consultation before coming into court and the passing of notes during counsel's speech), Caulfield J said (at p. 150):

> [W]here a ... judge is sitting with justices, the court consists of the presiding judge and the justices who sit with the judge, and of course on matters of fact the majority decision decides. So obviously there has to be consultation between the presiding judge and the justices who sit with him ...
>
> This court would like to emphasise that where a learned judge is sitting with magistrates, not only should he consult his fellow magistrates by law but he should make sure that the court appreciates that he has consulted. It is not necessary for the court to retire after each particular case. There is nothing wrong in notes being passed between members of the court. But when it comes to the point of sentence having to be given, it is far wiser for the court to show the public that the court is a composite court and that each member has a view which is expressed eventually through the president or chairman of the court.

It is submitted that his lordship's remarks are applicable not only to the passing of sentence but to all decisions (whether interlocutory or final) taken by a court which includes justices.

Modes of Address

According to CrimPD XII, paras. B.1 and B.2 (see Supplement, **CPD.XII.B**), circuit judges, recorders and deputy circuit judges should all be addressed when sitting in court as 'Your Honour', save that any circuit judge sitting at the Central Criminal Court (and any senior circuit judge who is the honorary recorder of the city in which he or she sits) should be addressed as 'My Lord' or 'My Lady'. **D3.11**

High Court judges sitting in the Crown Court should be addressed as 'My Lord' or 'My Lady', as they would in the High Court. In cause lists, forms and orders, the following descriptions are appropriate:

Circuit judges	His (or Her) Honour Judge A
Recorders	Mr (or Mrs) Recorder B
Deputy circuit judges	His (or Her) Honour CD, sitting as a deputy circuit judge.

Jurisdiction

The main function of the Crown Court is as a court of trial (known as 'trial on indictment', as the charges faced by the accused are set out in a document known as an indictment). However, the Crown Court also hears appeals, against conviction and/or sentence, from magistrates' courts, and also passes sentence in those cases which are committed to it for sentence by magistrates' courts. **D3.12**

Trial on Indictment

The Crown Court has exclusive jurisdiction over trials on indictment (Senior Courts Act 1981, s. 46(1), which provides that 'all proceedings on indictment shall be brought before the Crown Court'). This jurisdiction is not geographically restricted: 'The jurisdiction of the Crown Court ... shall include jurisdiction in proceedings on indictment for offences *wherever committed* ...' (s. 46(2), emphasis added). The effect of s. 46(2) is that, assuming the alleged offence is indictable and is an offence in respect of which the English criminal courts accept jurisdiction, the Crown Court will have jurisdiction to try the accused for it. **D3.13**

Appeals

A person convicted by a magistrates' court may, if he or she pleaded not guilty, appeal to the Crown Court against conviction and/or sentence; if the person pleaded guilty, he or she may appeal only against sentence (MCA 1980, s. 108, and see **D29.2** ***et seq.***). **D3.14**

Committal for Sentence

D3.15 Various statutory provisions enable magistrates' courts to commit an offender to the Crown Court to be sentenced. These are described fully at **D23.29** *et seq*.

Summary Offences

D3.16 In certain circumstances the Crown Court may have jurisdiction to deal with certain summary offences, pursuant to the CJA 1988, s. 40 (see **D11.17**). Moreover, by virtue of the Courts Act 2003, s. 66, a Crown Court judge (whether a High Court judge, circuit judge, or recorder) may exercise the powers of a district judge (magistrates' court). So, for example, it would be possible for a Crown Court judge in the Crown Court to deal with a summary offence that is linked with an indictable offence without the case having to go back to a magistrates' court: under s. 66, the judge would be able to deal with the summary offence as if he or she were a magistrate (following the procedure that would be adopted in the magistrates' court).

Bail

D3.17 As well as being able to grant bail during the course of a trial on indictment or other proceedings before it, the Crown Court has jurisdiction, *inter alia*, to grant bail to a person: (a) who has been sent to it in custody for trial or sentence; (b) who is appealing to it from a magistrates' court following the imposition of a custodial sentence by the justices; (c) who is appealing from it to the Court of Appeal and has been granted a certificate that the case is fit for appeal; or (d) who has been remanded in custody by a magistrates' court following an argued bail application (Senior Courts Act 1981, s. 81). Bail is covered in detail in **D7**.

Contempt etc.

D3.18 The Senior Courts Act 1981, s. 45(4), provides that 'the Crown Court shall, in relation to the attendance and examination of witnesses, any contempt of court, the enforcement of its orders and all other matters incidental to its jurisdiction, have the like powers, rights, privileges and authority as the High Court'. In particular, the Crown Court is able to deal summarily (i.e. without the empanelling of a jury) with any contempt committed in the face of the court (see generally **B14.83** *et seq*.). The generality of s. 45(4) is subject to the proviso that, for purposes of securing the attendance of witnesses, the Crown Court must use the powers given to it by the Criminal Procedure (Attendance of Witnesses) Act 1965, s. 8, and not proceed by way of subpoena.

MAGISTRATES' COURTS

D3.19 Magistrates' courts consist of justices of the peace. The great majority of justices are unpaid lay men or women; a minority are salaried district judges (magistrates' courts) who are legally qualified. The bulk of the criminal jurisdiction of magistrates' courts has to be exercised by a court consisting of at least two lay justices sitting in open court. However, district judges almost invariably sit alone. The law on justices and magistrates' courts is contained principally in: (a) the Courts Act 2003 (appointment, removal etc. of justices and organisation of magistrates' courts); (b) the MCA 1980 (jurisdiction and powers of the courts); and (c) the CrimPR (detailed practice and procedure).

The MCA 1980, s. 148(1), provides that 'the expression "magistrates' court" means any justice or justices of the peace acting under any enactment or by virtue of his or their commission or under the common law'. Thus, whenever a justice or justices sit for the purpose of exercising their jurisdiction as justices they constitute a magistrates' court. Where proceedings fall into a number of distinct stages (as when a magistrates' court, after convicting an offender and imposing a fine, subsequently takes steps to enforce payment of the fine), the court for the later stage need not be constituted by the same justices as constituted the court on the first occasion, so long as both magistrates' courts are acting in the same local justice area (s. 148(2)).

Justices of the Peace (Magistrates)

The titles 'justice' or 'justice of the peace' and 'magistrate' are interchangeable. Justices are appointed by the Lord Chancellor 'on behalf and in the name of Her Majesty' (Courts Act 2003, s. 10). The Lord Chancellor normally acts on the recommendation of local advisory committees. Lay justices are appointed for the whole of England and Wales but are assigned to one or more local justice areas by the Lord Chief Justice. Under s. 10(3), every lay justice is capable of acting in any local justice area. **D3.20**

Save in the special case of district judges (magistrates' courts) (see **D3.21**), justices are not required to possess any particular qualifications, whether legal or otherwise. There is, however, an obligation on new justices to complete a course of basic instruction in the duties which they will be carrying out.

Justices, other than district judges (magistrates' courts), are not paid a salary for their work. They are, however, entitled to a travelling and/or subsistence allowance, and to compensation for loss of earnings etc. (Courts Act 2003, s. 15).

District Judges (Magistrates' Courts)

Although the great majority of justices are lay, a minority are both paid and legally qualified. The latter (formerly known as stipendiary magistrates) are now properly described as district judges (magistrates' courts). Provisions regarding their appointment, removal, remuneration etc. are contained in the Courts Act 2003, ss. 22 to 26. **D3.21**

To be appointed as a district judge, the applicant must satisfy the judicial-appointment eligibility condition on a five-year basis (s. 22(1)); the same applies to deputy district judges (s. 24(1)). A district judge has jurisdiction to sit as a magistrate anywhere in England and Wales (s. 25(1)). District judges (and deputy district judges) sit alone in the magistrates' court.

According to CrimPD XIII, annex 1 (see Supplement, **CPD.XIII.x1**), district judges should generally be deployed to hear cases involving complex points of law, evidence, or procedure, as well as longer cases, but are also expected to take a share of the more routine work and, occasionally, to sit with lay justices.

Under the Courts Act 2003, s. 65, a district judge (magistrates' courts) is empowered to exercise some of the powers of a Crown Court judge: sch. 4 sets out a number of interlocutory matters falling within the jurisdiction of district judges before a case is ready to go before a Crown Court judge.

Structure of the Magistrates' Courts System

Magistrates' courts are organised on the basis of local justice areas (Courts Act 2003, s. 8), which are listed in the Local Justice Areas Order 2005 (SI 2005 No. 554), sch. 1, as amended. **D3.22**

Jurisdiction

Under the MCA 1980, s. 2(1), a magistrates' court has jurisdiction to try any summary offence and (subject to the mode of trial procedure) any offence which is triable either way, irrespective of where the offence was committed. If the accused is convicted of a summary offence, the court may sentence the accused to anything up to the maximum penalty provided for by the statute creating the offence. A magistrates' court may try an either-way offence allegedly committed by an adult if (a) the offence is not so serious that the court's powers of punishment in the event of conviction would be inadequate, and (b) the accused agrees (ss. 18 to 21); in the event of **D3.23** conviction, the court may impose a penalty of anything up to six months' imprisonment and/or an unlimited fine (s. 32(1)). Where a magistrates' court has convicted an adult of an either-way offence, it may commit the offender to the Crown Court for sentence if the court considers its powers of punishment to be inadequate (PCC(S)A 2000, s. 3).

A magistrates' court may send someone accused of an indictable offence (whether triable only on indictment or triable either way) for trial in the Crown Court no matter where the offence was allegedly committed.

A youth court is a form of magistrates' court and has jurisdiction to try children or young people for any offence (other than homicide and certain firearms offences), whether indictable or summary, although in certain circumstances the court may choose instead to send the child or young person to the Crown Court for trial (MCA 1980, s. 24).

D3.24 A magistrates' court may adjourn proceedings and remand the accused either on bail (except where the charge is murder) or in custody (ss. 10(1) and 128). There is also power to grant bail to: (a) an offender whose case has been adjourned for inquiries to be made prior to the passing of sentence (s. 10(3)); (b) a person, other than one charged with murder, who is being committed to the Crown Court for sentence (PCC(S)A 2000, s. 3); and (c) a person who is appealing to the Crown Court or the High Court against conviction or sentence by the magistrates (MCA 1980, s. 113).

Magistrates' courts are responsible for enforcing the payment of fines, both those fines imposed by a magistrates' court and those imposed by the Crown Court (Courts Act 2003, s. 97 and schs. 5 and 6; PCC(S)A 2000, s. 140; MCA 1980, ss. 75 to 91). Magistrates' courts also act as supervising courts for community orders and, if an offender is brought before the court for allegedly failing to comply with the requirements of the order, the court may impose a penalty for the breach of the community order, or (if the community order was imposed by a magistrates' court) resentence the offender for the original offence, or (if the original order was made by the Crown Court) commit the offender to the Crown Court to be dealt with (CJA 2003, sch. 8, part 2).

Constitution and Place of Sitting

D3.25 Unless an enactment specifically provides to the contrary, a magistrates' court may not try a charge summarily unless it is composed of at least two justices (MCA 1980, s. 121(1)). This applies whether the offence charged is summary or indictable. Similarly, a court holding a means inquiry under s. 82 of the 1980 Act in respect of a fine defaulter must comprise at least two justices (s. 121(2)). The maximum number of justices who may sit in a criminal case is three (Justices of the Peace Rules 2016 (SI 2016 No. 709), r. 4). In practice, the court almost always consists of two or three justices. If they include the chairman or one of the deputy chairmen elected by the justices for the local justice area at their annual meeting, then the chairman or deputy presides unless he or she asks one of the others to do so (Courts Act 2003, s. 18). A justice may preside before having been included on a list of approved court chairmen only if under the supervision of a justice who is on the list of approved court chairmen and has completed the prescribed chairman training course (r. 5(2)). In the absence of a justice entitled to preside, the justices present may appoint one of their number to preside in court to deal with any case if the justices present are satisfied as to the suitability of the magistrate proposed and (unless by reason of illness, circumstances unforeseen when the justices to sit were chosen, or other emergency no such justice is present) that magistrate has completed (or is undergoing) a chairman training course (r. 5(3) and (4)).

The justices composing the court before which any proceedings take place must remain present throughout the proceedings, save that (a) if one or more absent themselves but the court nonetheless is still validly constituted having regard to the nature of the proceedings and the provisions of the MCA 1980, s. 121, then the proceedings may continue before the remaining justices (s. *121(6)*), and (b) where the court has convicted an accused and adjourned before sentence, the court which passes sentence need not be composed of the same justices who formed the 'convicting' court (s. 121(7)).

Any decision of the bench may be arrived at by a majority. In the event of an even-numbered court being equally divided, the court must adjourn for rehearing before a differently constituted bench. D3.26

District judges (magistrates' courts) may, and normally do, sit alone in criminal proceedings (Courts Act 2003, s. 26).

Under the Courts Act 2003, s. 30(3), the Lord Chancellor may, with the concurrence of the Lord Chief Justice, give directions as to the distribution and transfer of the general business of magistrates' courts between the places where magistrates' courts sit. Such directions may, under s. 30(5), require a defendant to appear at a place in the local justice area in which the offence is alleged to have been committed, or in which the person charged with the offence resides, or in which the witnesses (or the majority of the witnesses) reside; or a place (not necessarily in the same local justice area) where other cases raising similar issues are being dealt with. Section 30(7) empowers the Lord Chancellor to give directions as to the days on which, and times at which, magistrates' courts may sit; subject to these directions, the business of magistrates' courts may be conducted on any day and at any time (s. 30(8)).

Powers of a Single Lay Justice

The CDA 1998, s. 49(1), provides that a number of powers of a magistrates' court may be exercised by a single justice of the peace. The list includes extending bail, or imposing or varying conditions of bail; dismissing a charge where no evidence is offered by the prosecution; making an order for the payment of defence costs out of central funds; requesting a pre-sentence report following a plea of guilty and, for that purpose, giving an indication of the seriousness of the offence; requesting a medical report and, for that purpose, remanding the accused in custody or on bail; remitting an offender to another court for sentence; extending, with the consent of the accused, a custody time-limit or an overall time-limit; giving, varying or revoking directions for the conduct of a trial (including directions as to the timetable for the proceedings, the attendance of the parties, the service of documents (including summaries of any legal arguments relied on by the parties), and the manner in which evidence is to be given); and giving, varying or revoking orders for separate or joint trials in the case of two or more accused or two or more charges. D3.27

The MCA 1980, s. 16A, enables a single justice to deal with non-imprisonable summary offences 'on the papers' unless the accused either objects to this procedure or else indicates an intention to plead not guilty.

Justices' Legal Advisers

The Courts and Tribunals (Judiciary and Functions of Staff) Act 2018, s. 3(1), states that: D3.28

> The Schedule [to the Act] provides for authorised court and tribunal staff—
> (a) to provide legal advice to judges of the family court and justices of the peace, and
> (b) to exercise judicial functions where procedure rules so provide.

One important effect of this Act is the abolition of the role (but not the functions) of the justices' clerk. Section 3 of the 2018 Act was brought into force from 6 April 2020 by the Courts and Tribunals (Judiciary and Functions of Staff) Act 2018 (Commencement) Regulations 2020 (SI 2020 No. 24).

By virtue of the 2018 Act, the Courts Act 2003, ss. 27 to 29, are replaced with new provisions. As amended, s. 28(1) of the 2003 Act provides that:

> The Lord Chief Justice may authorise a person—
> (a) to give advice to justices of the peace about matters of law (including procedure and practice) on questions arising in connection with the discharge of their functions, including questions arising when the person is not personally attending on them, and

(b) to bring to the attention of justices of the peace, at any time when the person thinks appropriate, any point of law (including procedure and practice) that is or may be involved in any question so arising.

Authorised persons giving legal advice must have such qualifications as are prescribed in regulations made by the Lord Chancellor (s. 28(3)). The qualifications required are set out in the Authorised Court Staff (Legal Advice Functions) Qualifications Regulations 2020 (SI 2020 No. 98). Those qualified to give legal advice to magistrates include barristers, solicitors and Fellows of the Chartered Institute of Legal Executives.

D3.29 The CrimPR use the phrase 'authorised court officer' in place of justices' clerk or assistant clerk. Under CrimPR 2.4(3) (see Supplement, **R2.4**), authorised court officers may not (amongst other things):

(a) authorise a person's committal to prison;
(b) authorise a person's arrest (except to secure that person's attendance at court in respect of an offence of which he or she has been accused or convicted in a case in which no objection is made by or on behalf of that person to the issue of the warrant);
(c) grant or withhold bail, save in the limited circumstances permitted by CrimPR 2.8;
(d) adjudicate on guilt, except for acquitting a defendant against whom the prosecutor offers no evidence, convicting a defendant who pleads guilty, or giving a prosecutor permission to withdraw a case;
(e) determine the admissibility of evidence;
(f) set ground rules for the conduct of questioning of vulnerable witnesses;
(g) make findings of fact for the purpose of sentence, defer or pass sentence, impose a penalty or commit a defendant to the Crown Court for sentence;
(h) make a costs orders unless the party or person ordered to pay costs agrees;
(i) grant a search warrant.

CrimPR 2.8 (see Supplement, **R2.8**) sets out a list of functions that may be exercised by an authorised court officer. Such a person may (amongst other things):

(a) fix, cancel or vary the date, time or place for a hearing, including a trial, or adjourn a hearing;
(b) adjourn, remit or transfer proceedings from one local justice area to another;
(c) determine an application to extend a time-limit set by a rule or by the court, unless the effect would be to affect the date of any hearing that has been fixed, including a trial, or significantly to affect the progress of the case in any other way;
(d) issue a summons at the request of a public prosecutor;
(e) give a prosecutor permission to withdraw a case;
(f) grant bail where the defendant already is on bail and the conditions, if any, to which that bail is subject will remain the same, or else the bail conditions will be varied or imposed with the agreement of both parties.

D3.30 An authorised court officer who is legally qualified may also exercise the functions listed in CrimPR 2.8(4) to (11). These paragraphs empower the court officer (amongst other things) to:

(a) conduct early administrative hearings (under the CDA 1998, s. 50);
(b) give, vary or revoke 'live link' directions;
(c) extend time-limits set by a rule or by the court;
(d) give, vary or revoke an order for separate or joint trials in respect of two or more defendants or two or more offences, if all parties agree;
(e) give, vary or revoke directions for the conduct of proceedings, including the timetable for the case, the attendance of the parties, the service of documents (including summaries of any legal arguments relied on by the parties), and the manner in which evidence is to be given;
(f) issue a summons;

(g) give a prosecutor permission to withdraw a charge;
(h) dismiss a prosecution where the prosecutor offers no evidence;
(i) amend a charge;
(j) send a defendant to the Crown Court for trial if the offence is triable only on indictment or a notice has been served under the CDA 1998, s. 51B or 51C (prosecutor's notice requiring sending for trial in a case of serious or complex fraud or a case in which a child is to be called as a witness);
(k) issue a warrant for a person's arrest to secure that the person attends court proceedings relating to an offence of which he or she has been accused or convicted in a case in which no objection is made by or on behalf of that person to the issue of the warrant;
(l) grant bail where the defendant is present, the prosecutor agrees to the grant of bail, and the conditions, if any, to which that bail will be subject will remain the same as before, or will be varied or imposed with the agreement of the parties;
(m) issue a witness summons;
(n) convict a defendant who has pleaded guilty;
(o) request a pre-sentence report where a defendant pleads guilty;
(p) direct the commissioning of a medical report;
(q) make or vary an order for a party to pay costs, if both parties agree; make or vary an order for another person to pay costs, if that person agrees; make an order for costs out of central funds;
(r) make a legal aid representation order on an appeal against a refusal of legal aid (but a court officer may not decline to make such an order).

DISQUALIFICATION OF JUDGES AND MAGISTRATES FROM HEARING PARTICULAR CASES

A magistrate may be disqualified from adjudicating in certain proceedings either by reason of the rule of natural justice that a member of a tribunal must not be biased, or by reason of a specific statutory provision. Where a justice sits when he or she ought not to have done, the decision of the court is liable to be quashed through the High Court issuing a quashing order upon an application for judicial review. However, the issue of such an order is discretionary, and so, if a party knew of an objection to a justice before the commencement of the proceedings but failed to ask the justice to withdraw, the order may be refused. **D3.31**

Judicial review is not available to challenge matters relating to trial on indictment (Senior Courts Act 1981, s. 29(3)), though any issue regarding bias on the part of the trial judge could be raised in any appeal to the Court of Appeal (Criminal Division) to show that the conviction was unsafe.

Actual or Apparent Bias

If a magistrate or judge has a direct interest in the outcome of the case, he or she will obviously be disqualified from hearing that case. In other cases where the question of possible bias is raised, the test to be applied is that laid down in *Porter v Magill* [2001] UKHL 67, [2002] 2 AC 357, where Lord Hope of Craighead (at [103]) said: **D3.32**

> The question is whether the fair-minded and informed observer, having considered the facts, would conclude that there was a real possibility that the tribunal was biased.

His lordship noted (at [88]) that there is a close relationship between the concepts of independence and impartiality. He quoted from the case of *Findlay v UK* (1997) 24 EHRR 221 at [73], where the ECtHR said:

> ... in order to establish whether a tribunal can be considered as 'independent', regard must be had *inter alia* to the manner of appointment of its members and their term of office, the existence of guarantees against outside pressures and the question whether the body presents an appearance of

> independence. As to the question of 'impartiality', there are two aspects to this requirement. First, the tribunal must be subjectively free from personal prejudice or bias. Secondly, it must also be impartial from an objective viewpoint, that is, it must offer sufficient guarantees to exclude any legitimate doubt in this respect. The concepts of independence and objective impartiality are closely linked…

Lord Hope commented that, in both cases, 'the concept requires not only that the tribunal must be truly independent and free from actual bias, proof of which is likely to be very difficult, but also that it must not appear in the objective sense to lack these essential qualities'.

D3.33 In *Helow v Secretary of State for the Home Department* [2008] UKHL 62, [2008] 1 WLR 2416, Lord Hope of Craighead (at [2]) observed that the fair-minded and informed observer 'is the sort of person who always reserves judgment on every point until she has seen and fully understood both sides of the argument. She is not unduly sensitive or suspicious… But she is not complacent either. She knows that fairness requires that a judge must be, and must be seen to be, unbiased.' Lord Mance (at [39]) said that the question of whether a tribunal is biased is one of law, to be answered in the light of the relevant facts, which may include a statement from the judge as to what the judge knew at the time. The court is not necessarily bound to accept any such statement at face value, but there can be no question of cross-examining the judge on it, and no attention will be paid to any statement by the judge as to the impact of any knowledge on his or her mind. In *Oldfield* [2011] EWCA Crim 2910, [2012] 1 Cr App R 17 (211), Jackson LJ reiterated (at [34]) that the fair-minded and informed observer is 'neither complacent nor unduly sensitive or suspicious. He or she has access to all facts known by the general public. He or she knows how things are usually done. He or she is aware that judges have years of relevant training and experience. He or she is aware of the terms of the judicial oath.'

The importance of avoiding the appearance of bias was emphasised in *S (K)* [2009] EWCA Crim 2377, [2010] 1 WLR 2511. The Court of Appeal had to consider a case where a judge had discharged the jury because jury-tampering had come to light and ruled (pursuant to the CJA 2003, s. 46) that a judge-only trial was appropriate. The defence argued that the judge could not continue to try the case because of bias. Lord Judge CJ (at [41]) said that the Court could not 'countenance, let alone permit the verdicts in a criminal trial to be returned by a jury which is actually or apparently biased. An identical principle must apply whenever the verdict is to be returned by a judge sitting on his own.' His lordship went on to say that: 'It is clear that the absence of judicial bias does not answer the separate question whether an informed objective bystander might legitimately conclude that such bias is a realistic possibility'. So far as the CJA 2003, s. 46, is concerned, his lordship said (at [42]) that 'it is inconceivable that the consequence of discharging a jury on the ground that it has been contaminated could result in a trial by judge alone which was inconsistent with the well-established principles relating to the necessary absence of bias or apparent bias in the tribunal'.

D3.34 The test for bias was also considered, in the context of a magistrates' court, in *R (B) v Wolverhampton Youth Court* [2009] EWHC 2706 (Admin), where the Divisional Court held that there was no automatic bar to a magistrate hearing a case on the basis that she taught at a school where D had formerly been a pupil; nor would it normally be a bar if a justice had previously dealt with someone from the same family (per Pill LJ at [11]). Similarly, in *R (Hewitt) v Denbighshire Magistrates' Court* [2015] EWHC 2956 (Admin), D, who was an anti-hunting campaigner, was charged with assaulting a terrierman. It was argued that the district judge hearing the case ought to have recused himself on the basis that he had once, as a solicitor, represented another terrierman charged with an offence under the Hunting Act 2004, and had on another occasion represented a member of the Countryside Alliance charged with throwing an egg at the deputy prime minister. There was no other evidence of his involvement in hunting or in the Countryside Alliance. The district judge declined to recuse himself during the trial, but did so at the sentencing stage 'as a matter of expediency' to avoid a further protracted hearing of allegations of apparent bias. Wyn Williams J upheld the conviction and held that the district judge ought not to have recused himself at all.

Bench's Knowledge of Accused's Record or Pending Matters

There is no blanket rule that the justices must be unaware that there are other charges outstanding against the accused in the same court or that there are offences for which the accused is awaiting sentence. Where a submission is made that such knowledge disqualifies the justices from acting, they have a discretion to order that the case be tried by a differently constituted bench, but if, having applied the correct test, they conclude that it is proper for them to continue with the case, the Divisional Court will not interfere with their decision (*Weston-super-Mare Justices, ex parte Shaw* [1987] QB 640). **D3.35**

Similar considerations apply where a justice knows from previous dealings with the accused that the accused is of bad character. The question is whether, having regard to the circumstances of the particular case, there is a real danger of bias on the part of the justice were he or she to sit. In *R (S) v Camberwell Green Youth Court* [2004] EWHC 1043 (QB), Moses J (at [40]) observed that 'the mere fact that a justice is aware of a previous conviction is not sufficient to disqualify that justice from trying the case of an accused of whose previous conviction the justice is aware'. This case involved a district judge (rather than lay justices), but it is submitted that the outcome would have been the same had the court comprised lay justices.

The fact that previous convictions may be admissible in the range of circumstances set out in the CJA 2003, ss. 101 to 106, makes it even less likely that knowledge of previous convictions will be sufficient to disqualify a magistrate from hearing a case. In *R (Robinson) v Sutton Coldfield Magistrates' Court* [2006] EWHC 307 (Admin), [2006] 4 All ER 1029, the Divisional Court considered the position of justices where an application is made to adduce bad character evidence pursuant to the CJA 2003, s. 101. Hallett LJ said (at [21]): **D3.36**

> Where an application is made to adduce bad character evidence before a magistrates' court, the justices will, of necessity, hear details of the conviction in order to rule on the application. If the application fails they will put the convictions out of mind when they hear the case. The fact that they know the details of the previous convictions does not disqualify them from discharging their role as fact finders in the trial.

Other Interlocutory Rulings by Justices

Unless there are special circumstances, the making of an interlocutory ruling on the admissibility of evidence does not deprive justices of the ability to continue the hearing of the trial. Justices should, therefore, not normally disqualify themselves from hearing a trial merely because they have ruled in favour of an *ex parte* application by the prosecution for non-disclosure of material on the ground of public interest immunity (*R (DPP) v Acton Youth Court* [2001] EWHC Admin 402, [2001] 1 WLR 1828, expressly approved by the House of Lords in *H* [2004] UKHL 3, [2004] 2 AC 134). **D3.37**

Specific Statutory Provision Disqualifying Justices from Hearing Particular Cases

A justice who is a member of a local authority as defined by the Courts Act 2003, s. 41(6) (e.g., a county council, district council, London borough council, parish or community council or police authority) may not be a member of the Crown Court or of a magistrates' court in any proceedings brought by or against (or by way of appeal from the decision of) the authority or any committee or officer of the authority (Courts Act 2003, s. 41). However, s. 41(5) states that 'no act is invalidated merely because of the disqualification under this section of the person by whom it is done'. **D3.38**

Disqualification of Judges of the Crown Court from Hearing Particular Cases

The rule that nobody may be a judge in his or her own cause applies to all courts. The position as far as Crown Court judges are concerned was considered in *Mulvihill* [1990] 1 WLR 438. D was charged with conspiracy to rob a number of banks and building societies, including **D3.39** the National Westminster Bank. The trial judge owned a number of shares in National Westminster Bank plc. Brooke J, giving the judgment of the Court of Appeal, said (at p. 444):

> The function of a Crown Court judge conducting a criminal trial on indictment with a jury is very different from that of a lay justice who is one of the primary decision makers in summary proceedings in a magistrates' court; and although [the trial judge] had to make direct decisions on the admissibility of evidence, . . . we do not consider that the hypothetical reasonable bystander would reasonably suspect that it was not possible for him to reach a fair decision because of the existence of his shareholding in one of the institutions whose branch office was robbed . . . a judge in a criminal trial is not, save possibly in some very exceptional circumstances, called upon to declare that he has some remote interest in premises which have become the scene of a crime.

So far as lay justices sitting in the Crown Court are concerned, CrimPR 34.11(a)(ii) (see Supplement, **R34.11**) provides that a lay justice may sit in the Crown Court on an appeal from a magistrates' court only if the lay justice did not take part in the decision under appeal. It follows that a justice is disqualified from sitting only if he or she sat on the bench which convicted or passed sentence on the accused. If a justice was involved in a hearing other than the trial (or sentencing hearing), such as a bail application or mode of trial hearing, the usual principles governing bias would apply.

PARTIES TO CRIMINAL PROCEEDINGS

D3.40 The usual parties to criminal proceedings are the prosecutor and the accused. In *Re Pinochet Ugarte* (2000) *The Times*, 16 February 2000, it was indicated that, while there were many bodies representing the interests of victims and other persons who might wish to take part in such proceedings, there would need to be overwhelming reasons why they should be allowed to intervene in cases other than those being heard by the Supreme Court, which concern pure points of law, and which might well merit different consideration.

Prosecutor

D3.41 The great majority of prosecutions are commenced either by the police and the CPS or by the officers of governmental or quasi-governmental organisations such as local authorities, the Environment Agency and the Department for Work and Pensions.

So far as 'private' prosecutions are concerned (in other words, those not brought by the police or by another public authority), these have to be brought by applying to a magistrates' court for the issue of a summons (historically known as 'laying an information'). In *R (Gladstone plc) v Manchester City Magistrates' Court* [2004] EWHC 2806 (Admin), [2005] 2 All ER 56, the Divisional Court held that, unless the application for a summons is required by statute to be made by any particular person, any person may make it where the offence is not an individual grievance, provided that the prosecution can establish a public interest and benefit as opposed to a purely private interest in criminal proceedings. However, in *Ewing v Davis* [2007] EWHC 1730 (Admin), [2007] 1 WLR 3223, Mitting J pointed out that, historically, there has never been a requirement that a private prosecutor has to show a public interest where the prosecution is brought under a public general Act. This power has not been fettered by modern statute. His lordship went on to hold that public interest in a private prosecution is established by the nature of the offence as defined in the statute that creates it, not by the circumstances leading up to it. His lordship concluded that *R (Gladstone plc) v Manchester City Magistrates' Court* should not be taken as an invitation to magistrates to examine the circumstances of alleged offences and their relation to the private prosecutor. The fact that a prosecution may be brought by a public authority does not prevent a private prosecution taking place. For example, a prosecution for causing unnecessary suffering to an animal, contrary to the Animal Welfare Act 2006, s. 4, could be brought by a local authority (pursuant to its powers under the Local Government Act 1972, s. 222) but this does not prevent a private prosecution being brought by, for example, the RSPCA (*Woodward* [2017] EWHC 1008 (Admin)). In *AB* [2017] EWCA Crim 534, [2017] 2 Cr App R 25 (347), the Court of Appeal held that a local authority has the power to prosecute only by virtue of s. 222 (it has no free-standing common law right to prosecute); moreover, a prosecution under s. 222 is permissible only if it is brought for the benefit of the inhabitants of the local authority's area as such (and not for a wider public benefit purpose).

It is important to note that private prosecutors are required to comply with the overriding objective in the same way as 'public' prosecutors are. As the Divisional Court pointed out in *R (Kay) v Leeds Magistrates' Court* [2018] EWHC 1233 (Admin), [2018] 4 WLR 91, at [23]:

> (1) Whilst the Code for Crown Prosecutors does not apply to private prosecutions, a private prosecutor is subject to the same obligations as a Minister for Justice as are the public prosecuting authorities — including the duty to ensure that all relevant material is made available both for the court and the defence.
>
> (2) Advocates and solicitors who have the conduct of private prosecutions must observe the highest standards of integrity, of regard for the public interest and duty to act as a Minister for Justice in preference to the interests of the client who has instructed them to bring the prosecution — owing a duty to the court to ensure that the proceeding is fair.

In *D Ltd v A* [2017] EWCA Crim 1172, the Court of Appeal made a similar point, citing with approval *Zinga* [2014] EWCA Crim 52, [2014] 1 Cr App R 27 (382), where Lord Thomas CJ had said (at [61]) that barristers and solicitors who have conduct of private prosecutions 'must observe the highest standards of integrity, of regard for the public interest and duty to act as a Minister for Justice . . . in preference to the interests of the client who has instructed them to bring the prosecution'.

Who Should Commence a Prosecution?

CrimPR 7.2 (see Supplement, **R7.2**) refers to a prosecution being started by 'a prosecutor'. **D3.42**
In *Rubin v DPP* [1990] 2 QB 80, Watkins LJ expressed the view that a prosecution should be brought in the name of an individual. This proposition was, however, doubted by Woolf LJ in *Ealing Justices, ex parte Dixon* [1990] 2 QB 91; even so, his lordship thought it preferable for an individual to start the prosecution, albeit that he was acting on behalf of a body corporate.

Commencement of Proceedings against Suspects Arrested by the Police

The procedure for charging a suspect at a police station is described at **D2**. It is a procedure **D3.43**
which, by its very nature, must take place at a police station. In a minority of cases, under the PACE 1984, s. 37(1), the responsibility for deciding whether or not a person should be charged rests with the custody officer on duty at the station where the suspect is being detained at the relevant time (see s. 37(7) especially). However, in most cases the custody officer must first consult with a Crown Prosecutor before charging the suspect, or release the suspect on bail under s. 37(7)(a), to enable a charging decision to be taken by the CPS. The CPS will then decide whether there is sufficient evidence to charge the person with an offence.

Moreover, under the Prosecution of Offences Act 1985, s. 3(2), it is the duty of the DPP to take over the conduct of all criminal proceedings instituted on behalf of a police force. Proceedings are instituted on behalf of a police force only where the police force has investigated and arrested the suspect and brought him or her before the custody officer. In *R (Hunt) v CCRC* [2001] QB 1108, the Divisional Court rejected the argument that an Inland Revenue prosecution should have been conducted by the CPS because the suspect had been charged by a custody officer at a police station. Similarly, in *Stafford Justices, ex parte Commissioners of Customs and Excise* [1991] 2 QB 339, where D was arrested by customs officers for alleged drug trafficking offences but was taken to a police station and formally charged by the custody officer, it was held by the Divisional Court that where a person such as a customs officer has investigated an offence and arrested a suspect, he or she does not, by taking that suspect to a police station to be charged by a custody officer, thereby surrender prosecution of the proceedings to the DPP. This reasoning was followed in *Croydon Justices, ex parte Holmberg* (1993) 157 JP 277, where it was held that the seeking of police assistance (in this case by a trading standards officer) does not of itself turn proceedings into police proceedings.

The Director of Public Prosecutions

D3.44 Insofar as the State plays a direct role in the prosecution system, it does so through the DPP and the law officers of the Crown (the A-G and Solicitor-General).

The office of DPP is governed by the Prosecution of Offences Act 1985. The DPP is a barrister or solicitor of at least ten years' standing, appointed by the A-G (Prosecution of Offences Act 1985, s. 2). The functions of the DPP are discharged under the superintendence of the A-G (s. 3(1)). The DPP's duties are listed in s. 3(2) and include (amongst other duties) the following:

(a) To take over the conduct of all criminal proceedings instituted by or on behalf of a police force, other than 'specified proceedings', namely those listed in the schedule to the Prosecution of Offences Act 1985 (Specified Proceedings) Order 1999 (SI 1999 No. 904), as amended. The list of specified offences includes various road traffic offences, offences under the POA 1986, s. 5, criminal damage where the value involved does not exceed £5,000 and theft where the offence constitutes low-value shoplifting (see **D6.27**). An offence ceases to be a specified offence if a summons or requisition has been issued in respect of it, unless (if the offence is a summary one) the accused is also served with the paperwork necessary to enable him or her to plead guilty by post under the MCA 1980, s. 12, or (if the offence is triable either way) the accused is served with the statement of facts, or prosecution witness statements, which will be placed before the court if the accused pleads guilty. Moreover, proceedings for an offence cease to be specified once a magistrates' court has begun to hear evidence in those proceedings. Proceedings which would otherwise be 'specified' for the purposes of s. 3 are not so specified if they were instituted by way of charge under the PACE 1984, s. 37(7)(d), if the accused was aged under 16 when proceedings were started, or if at any time a magistrates' court indicates that it is considering imposing a custodial sentence for the offence in question. The Prosecution of Offences Act 1985 (Specified Proceedings) (Amendment) Order 2018 (SI 2018 No. 198) clarifies that the DPP is not under a duty to take over conduct of criminal proceedings dealt with in accordance with the Single Justice Procedure established by the MCA 1980, s. 16A.

(b) To institute and conduct criminal proceedings in any case where it appears to the DPP appropriate to do so either on account of the importance or difficulty of the case or for any other reason.

(c) To take over the conduct of all binding-over proceedings instituted on behalf of a police force.

(d) To take over the conduct of any criminal proceedings instituted by the NCA.

(e) To have the conduct of extradition proceedings (see **D31**).

(f) To advise police forces, to the extent the DPP considers appropriate, on all matters relating to criminal offences.

(g) To appear for the prosecution when directed by the court to do so on:
   (i) appeals from the High Court to the Supreme Court in criminal cases;
   (ii) appeals from the Crown Court to the Court of Appeal (Criminal Division) and from thence to the Supreme Court; and
   (iii) appeals to the Crown Court against the exercise by a magistrates' court of its powers under s. 12 of the Contempt of Court Act 1981 to deal with offences of contempt of the court.

(h) To have the conduct of applications for orders under the ABCPA 2014 (criminal behaviour orders), and to apply for discharge or variation of such orders.

(i) To discharge the duties conferred under the POCA 2002, parts 5 and 8 (civil recovery of the proceeds of unlawful conduct, civil recovery investigations and disclosure orders in relation to confiscation investigations).

(j) To discharge such other functions as may from time to time be assigned to the DPP by the A-G.

D3.45 Where the DPP has the conduct of proceedings in consequence of the duties imposed under s. 3 of the 1985 Act, he or she may discontinue the proceedings or take any other step in relation to them, including the bringing of an appeal and the making of representations in respect of applications for bail (s. 15(3)).

Further duties imposed on the DPP by the 1985 Act include issuing a Code for the guidance of Crown Prosecutors in the performance of various aspects of their duties (s. 10). Another duty resting on the DPP is to give or refuse consent to a prosecution in those cases where statute provides that the prosecutor may not proceed without it (see **D2.16** for prosecutions requiring the DPP's consent).

The Crown Prosecution Service

Section 3(2)(a) of the Prosecution of Offences Act 1985 requires the DPP to 'take over the conduct of all criminal proceedings... instituted on behalf of a police force'. To enable the DPP to perform this task, the Act also provided for the creation of the CPS, of which the DPP is the head (s. 1(1)(a)). **D3.46**

The CPS is not instructed by the police—acting on behalf of the DPP it *takes over* prosecutions begun by the police, and therefore exercises an independent judgment in deciding any legal questions which arise.

CPS Involvement in the Charging Process The CPS is involved in deciding what charges (if any) should be preferred in all but the most minor cases. For discussion of the CPS involvement in the charging process, see **D2.1** ***et seq.*** **D3.47**

Crown Prosecutors For CPS administrative purposes, the country is divided into areas, with a Chief Crown Prosecutor for each area (Prosecution of Offences Act 1985, s. 1(4)). The DPP may designate any member of the CPS who is a barrister or solicitor to be a Crown Prosecutor (s. 1(3)). Crown Prosecutors have the same rights of audience as practising solicitors, which means essentially that they may appear for the Service in magistrates' courts but, unless they have been granted rights of audience in the higher courts, not in the Crown Court (see **D3.117** for rights of audience in general). Furthermore, without prejudice to any other functions as a member of the CPS, a Crown Prosecutor has 'all the powers of the Director as to the institution and conduct of proceedings but shall exercise those powers under the direction of the Director' (s. 1(6)). Where an enactment prevents any step being taken without the DPP's consent, or requires any step to be taken by or in relation to the DPP, the consent or step may be taken by or in relation to a Crown Prosecutor (s. 1(7)). Thus, the DPP may delegate to Crown Prosecutors the power to sanction a prosecution in cases where proceedings require consent. **D3.48**

In *Liverpool Crown Court, ex parte Bray* [1987] Crim LR 51, it was confirmed that the DPP's powers may be exercised by Crown Prosecutors acting within the general authority delegated to them and without express instructions from the DPP. Thus, the DPP's powers to take over the conduct of privately commenced prosecutions and to serve a notice discontinuing a prosecution are, in practice, exercised by Crown Prosecutors rather than the DPP personally. The risk of individual Crown Prosecutors coming to widely divergent decisions in similar factual situations is reduced to some extent by s. 10 of the Prosecution of Offences Act 1985, which requires the DPP to issue a Code for Crown Prosecutors giving guidance on the general principles to be applied by them in: (a) determining whether proceedings for an offence should be instituted or (if already instituted) continued; (b) determining what charge(s) should be preferred; and (c) considering what representations should be made to a magistrates' court about mode of trial (see **D2.10** and, for the full text of the Code, see **appendix 3**). **D3.49**

The Prosecution of Offences Act 1985 also empowers the DPP to appoint persons who are not members of the Service to institute or take over the conduct of such criminal proceedings as the DPP may assign to them (s. 5(1)). The appointed person must have a general qualification (within the meaning of the Courts and Legal Services Act 1990, s. 71). A person appointed under s. 5(1) has, in conducting the proceedings, all the powers of a Crown Prosecutor, **D3.50** but has to exercise those powers subject to any instructions given by a Crown Prosecutor (s. 5(2)). Section 5 places no fetter on the circumstances in which the DPP may exercise the power to assign cases to non-CPS personnel. In practice, the volume of CPS work in the magistrates' courts is such that some has to be delegated to agents under s. 5. An agent is, however, expected to obtain authority from a CPS lawyer before taking steps in relation to a case such as offering no evidence on a charge or accepting a bind-over (contrast the independence that prosecuting counsel in the Crown Court enjoys: see **D16.4**).

Section 7A of the Prosecution of Offences Act 1985 gives the DPP power to appoint staff who are not legally qualified. These staff are now known as 'associate prosecutors', and may represent the CPS on bail applications and on other pre-trial applications, such as requests for adjournments. They may conduct trials but only where the offence in question is a non-imprisonable summary offence. Section 7A of the 1985 Act also empowers associate prosecutors to represent the CPS in proceedings relating to 'preventative civil orders' (including criminal behaviour orders).

Review of CPS Decision Not to Prosecute

D3.51 Following *Killick* [2011] EWCA Crim 1608, [2012] 1 Cr App R 10 (121) and Directive 2012/29/EU establishing minimum standards on the rights, support and protection of victims of crime ([2012] OJ L315/57), a person who is alleged to have suffered harm directly caused by criminal conduct may seek a review of a decision not to prosecute the person(s) suspected to have committed the criminal conduct which caused the harm suffered by the complainant. Article 11.1 of the Directive states that:

> Member States shall ensure that victims, in accordance with their role in the relevant criminal justice system, have the right to a review of a decision not to prosecute. The procedural rules for such a review shall be determined by national law.

Guidance on the operation of the scheme is contained in the CPS *Victims' Right to Review Scheme* (issued in 2013 and revised in 2016). The right of review arises where (i) the CPS decide not to charge the suspect; (ii) proceedings against the suspect are discontinued (or withdrawn in a magistrates' court case), thereby ending those proceedings; (iii) no evidence is offered in those proceedings (with the result that the defendant is acquitted); or (iv) the charges are left to 'lie on the file', marked 'not to be proceeded with without the leave of the Crown Court or the Court of Appeal'.

Where no evidence has been offered, that decision cannot be reversed (since the accused stands acquitted of the offence and so cannot be re-prosecuted for it); however, as was pointed out in *Hayes v CPS* [2018] EWHC 327 (Admin), [2018] 1 WLR 4106 (at [51]), such a review could lead to 'an admission of error, coupled with an apology'.

The CPS *Victims' Right to Review Scheme* states that certain decisions fall outside the scope of the scheme. The list includes cases where:

- charges are brought in respect of some (but not all) allegations made or against some (but not all) possible suspects;
- a single charge or charges are terminated but another charge or related charges continue;
- proceedings against one (or more) defendants are terminated but related proceedings against other defendants continue;
- a single charge or charges are substantially altered but proceedings continue;
- some charges are left to lie on file.

The common factor in this set of exceptions is that someone has been charged with something. In *R (AC) v DPP* [2018] EWCA Civ 2092, [2019] 1 WLR 917, the Court of Appeal (Civil Division) upheld the decision of the Divisional Court that 'extending the VRR to cases where one suspect is not charged but another is would raise proportionality concerns and significantly undermine operational prosecutorial discretion with potentially serious resource implications' (see [31] and [35]). Article 11 does not preclude the CPS from identifying some situations where the scheme does not apply. This includes excluding from the scope of the scheme cases where conducting a review would not be proportionate.

A decision not to prosecute may also be challenged by way of judicial review (see **D2.22**). However, in *R (Monica) v DPP* [2018] EWHC 3508 (Admin), [2019] 1 Cr App R 28 (363), the Court noted (at [46]) four key principles:

(1) Particularly where a CPS review decision is exceptionally detailed, thorough, and in accordance with CPS policy, it cannot be considered perverse ...
(2) A significant margin of discretion is given to prosecutors ...
(3) Decision letters should be read in a broad and common sense way, without being subjected to excessive or overly punctilious textual analysis.
(4) It is not incumbent on decision-makers to refer specifically to all the available evidence. An overall evaluation of the strength of a case falls to be made on the evidence as a whole, applying prosecutorial experience and expert judgment.

The Attorney-General

The main functions of the A-G in respect of criminal proceedings are as follows: **D3.52**

(a) Appointment of the DPP, whose functions are discharged 'under the superintendence of the Attorney-General' (Prosecution of Offences Act 1985, ss. 2 and 3(1)).
(b) Instituting and conducting the prosecution of offences of exceptional gravity or complexity, especially those which impinge upon the security of the State and/or this country's relationships with other countries. The A-G may bring prosecutions for contempt of court. The A-G may also take over the conduct of a privately commenced prosecution (or direct the DPP to do so). Very occasionally, the A-G appears in court to represent the prosecution.
(c) Certain offences may only be prosecuted by or with the consent of the A-G (see **D2.16**).
(d) Issuing guidelines on aspects of prosecution practice.
(e) At any stage after the indictment against an accused has been signed and before the verdict, the A-G may enter a *nolle prosequi*, which terminates the prosecution.
(f) The A-G may invite the Court of Appeal to clarify a point of law where an accused has been acquitted (CJA 1972, s. 36; see **D28.1**).
(g) The A-G may refer a sentence to the Court of Appeal on the ground that it is unduly lenient (CJA 1988, s. 36; see **D28.3**).

By virtue of the Law Officers Act 1997, s. 1, the functions of the A-G may be discharged by the Solicitor-General.

The Serious Fraud Office

The SFO was set up by the CJA 1987. It is headed by a Director, who is appointed and superintended by the A-G (s. 1(2)). Its functions are to 'investigate any suspected offence which appears to [the Director] on reasonable grounds to involve serious or complex fraud', and to initiate and conduct (or take over and then conduct) any criminal proceedings relating to such fraud (s. 1(3) and (5)). Functions are also conferred under the POCA 2002, parts 5 and 8 (civil recovery of the proceeds of unlawful conduct, civil recovery investigations and disclosure orders in relation to confiscation investigations). The Director may designate any barrister or solicitor who is a member of the Office to have the same powers as the Director in relation to the institution and conduct of proceedings (s. 1(7) and (8)). The DPP's duties in relation to the initiation and/or conduct of proceedings where a case appears to be of difficulty or importance do not extend to serious frauds under investigation by the SFO (Prosecution of Offences Act 1985, s. 3(2)). **D3.53**

National Crime Agency

The NCA was created by the CCA 2013, s. 1. By virtue of s. 1(4) and (5), the NCA has a 'crime-reduction function' (securing that efficient and effective activities to combat organised crime and serious crime are carried out, whether by the NCA or by other law enforcement agencies) and a 'criminal intelligence function' (gathering, storing, processing, analysing, and disseminating information that is relevant to activities to combat crime, including organised or **D3.54** serious crime). The NCA discharges the crime-reduction function through (for example) investigating offences relating to organised or serious crime, and carrying out activities to combat organised and serious crime, including by instituting criminal proceedings (s. 1(7)), as well as by working with other enforcement agencies (s. 1(8)). The crime-reduction function does not include the function of the NCA itself prosecuting offences (s. 1(10)), and so any prosecutions instituted by the NCA are carried on by the CPS.

Government Departments and Statutory Bodies

D3.55 Several government departments regularly initiate and conduct criminal prosecutions, e.g., the Department for Business, Energy and Industrial Strategy for violations of the Companies Acts and the Department for Work and Pensions for fraudulent benefit claims.

Some non-governmental statutory bodies also have the power to institute criminal proceedings. For example, the Financial Conduct Authority has power to bring prosecutions for offences under the FSMA 2000 (see s. 401 of that Act and **B7.21**) and for certain other offences, such as offences under the CJA 1993, Part V (insider dealing) (see the FSMA 2000, s. 402). In *Rollins* [2010] UKSC 39, [2010] 1 WLR 1922, the issue was whether the Financial Services Authority (the predecessor to the FCA) had power to prosecute offences of money laundering contrary to the POCA 2002, ss. 327 and 328, or whether the FSA's powers to prosecute criminal offences were limited to the offences referred to in the FSMA 2000, ss. 401 and 402 (which do not include offences under the POCA 2002). The Supreme Court rejected the contention that ss. 401 and 402 create a complete regime of offences that the Financial Services Authority has the power to prosecute, holding that the Financial Services Authority was entitled to prosecute other offences (e.g., offences under the POCA 2002). In reaching this conclusion, which is presumably equally applicable to the FCA, Lord Dyson noted (at [15]) that the purpose of s. 401 is not to *confer* the power to prosecute, but to *limit* the persons who may prosecute for offences under that Act. His lordship also referred (at [10]) to *R (Hunt) v CCRC* [2001] QB 1108, where Lord Woolf CJ had said (at [20]) that, if an ordinary member of the public can bring proceedings for breaches of the criminal law, it would be surprising if the Inland Revenue (as HMRC was then known) were not in a similar position.

Prosecutions by Other Persons

D3.56 Section 6(1) of the Prosecution of Offences Act 1985 provides that: 'Nothing in this Part [of the Act] shall preclude any person from instituting any criminal proceedings to which the Director's duty to take over the conduct of proceedings does not apply'. Since the DPP is only required to take over prosecutions begun by the police, it follows that, save in those limited categories of cases where a statute other than the 1985 Act requires a prosecution to have the prior consent of either the DPP or the A-G, there is no restriction on the right of any individual to bring criminal proceedings. This applies whether the individual acts in a purely personal capacity or in the course of duties for a local authority, government department, business enterprise or other organisation.

It should be borne in mind that a private prosecution is initiated by making an application to a magistrates' court for the issue of a summons. This application (formerly known as laying an information) amounts to the commencement of proceedings and is therefore the 'conduct of litigation' under the Legal Services Act 2007, sch. 2, and a 'reserved legal activity' within the meaning of s. 12 of that Act. If proceedings are commenced on behalf of a private prosecutor by someone who is acting as an agent for the prosecutor, those proceedings will be void if the agent is not authorised to conduct litigation under the 2007 Act (*Media Protection Services Ltd v Crawford* [2012] EWHC 2373 (Admin), [2013] 1 WLR 1068). It should be noted, however, that CrimPR 46.1(2) (see Supplement, **R46.1**) permits a 'member, officer, or employee of a prosecutor' to apply for a summons on the prosecutor's behalf.

In *Zinga* [2014] EWCA Crim 52, [2014] 1 WLR 2228, it was held that a private prosecutor is entitled to initiate confiscation proceedings under the POCA 2002, s. 6.

In *Bow Street Metropolitan Stipendiary Magistrate, ex parte South Coast Shipping Co.* [1993] QB 645, the Divisional Court held that the fact that the public prosecuting authorities had instituted proceedings for a minor offence arising out of an incident did not preclude a private prosecution for a more serious offence, where there was evidence suggesting culpability. The case arose from the sinking of the Thames pleasure cruiser, the *Marchioness*, by the *Bowbelle*, a disaster in which 51 people died. The master of the *Bowbelle* had been charged under merchant shipping legislation, and was tried twice, the jury failing to reach a verdict on each occasion. A private prosecution for manslaughter was then instituted against the owners of the *Bowbelle* and others. The magistrate's decision to send them for trial was upheld by the Divisional Court. **D3.57**

In *Barry v Birmingham Magistrates' Court* [2009] EWHC 2571 (Admin), [2010] 1 Cr App R 13 (160), Cranston J said (at [13]) that 'there is no requirement for a person seeking to have a summons issued to approach the police first'. However, he observed that, 'in a particular case it may be a relevant circumstance whether or not the person seeking a summons has approached the police. The failure of the police to proceed in a particular case may demonstrate that it is hopeless.'

In *R (Holloway) v Bhui* [2019] EWHC 1731 (Admin), [2020] 1 Cr App R 8 (171), Males LJ observed (at [19]) that, in their role as 'ministers of justice', all prosecutors (including private prosecutors) have a 'duty to undertake an independent and objective analysis of the evidence before commencing proceedings to determine whether there is a realistic prospect of a conviction'. This analysis 'requires an assessment not only of what evidence exists, but also of whether it is reliable and credible, and whether there is other evidence which might affect the position'. His lordship went on to say (at [20]) that private prosecutors, because of their interest in the proceedings, 'may lack the objectivity required to undertake such an analysis'. It will therefore often be prudent 'to bring a proposed prosecution to the attention of the police or prosecution authorities and to take legal advice'. His lordship emphasised that this is not a legal precondition to bringing a private prosecution, and that a failure to do so is not in itself 'improper' (for the purpose of a wasted costs order under the POA 1985, s. 19; see **D33.34** ***et seq.***), but 'it may give rise to an inference that a private prosecutor was determined to go ahead regardless of the prospects of success or…may simply indicate that no proper analysis of evidential sufficiency has been carried out'.

A private prosecutor may wish to see evidence, such as witness statements, in the possession of the police or the CPS. In *Scopelight Ltd v Chief Constable of Northumbria* [2009] EWCA Civ 1156, [2010] QB 438, it was held that the PACE 1984, s. 22, does not preclude the police from retaining seized property where that property was required for the purpose of investigating or prosecuting an offence, even where the CPS had notified the parties of its decision not to prosecute those from whom the property had been seized. The police then have power to determine whether it is necessary in all the circumstances that the property seized should be retained for further examination or for use as evidence at a trial for an offence. Leveson LJ (at [53]) said: **D3.58**

> If a prosecution is not to be pursued by the CPS but some other public or private body wishes to pursue a private prosecution, the relevant circumstances include (but are not limited to): the identity and motive of the potential prosecutor; the gravity of the allegation along with the reasoning behind the negative decision of the CPS and thus the extent to which, in this case, the public have a legitimate interest in the criminal prosecution of this conduct; the police view of the significance of what has been retained; and any material fact concerning the proposed defendant. All this falls to be considered so that a balanced decision can be reached upon whether retention is necessary 'in all the circumstances'. Such a decision would be capable of challenge on traditional public law grounds.

However, the bringing of a private prosecution does not confer a right of access to statements, photographs or reports in the hands of the police or the CPS, even if the request is a legitimate one and even if they are essential to the success of the prosecution (*DPP, ex parte Hallas* (1987) 87 Cr App R 340). Nonetheless, once the matter has been sent for Crown Court trial, the prosecution is deemed to be on behalf of the Crown, and so disclosure may be ordered (*Pawsey* [1989] Crim LR 152).

On restraint of vexatious prosecutions, see **D3.65**.

DISCONTINUANCE OF AND JUDICIAL RESTRAINT ON CRIMINAL PROSECUTION

Discontinuance of Prosecutions Conducted by the DPP

D3.59 Where the DPP is conducting a prosecution (this includes CPS prosecutions), the DPP (or a Crown Prosecutor) may, at any time during the 'preliminary stages' of the proceedings, give notice to the court that he or she does not want the proceedings to continue (Prosecution of Offences Act 1985, s. 23(3)). 'Preliminary stage' does *not* include: (a) any stage of the proceedings after the court has begun to hear evidence for the prosecution at a summary trial of the offence; or (b) any stage of the proceedings after the accused has been sent for trial for the offence. However, the exclusion (by s. 23(2)) of cases that have been sent for trial to the Crown Court is negated to a large extent by s. 23A. This specifically provides for a notice of discontinuance to be served where a case has been sent to the Crown Court for trial under the CDA 1998, s. 51. The notice may be served on the Crown Court 'at any time before the indictment is preferred' (s. 23A(2)).

The effect of the DPP giving notice of discontinuance under s. 23 is that the proceedings are discontinued from the giving of the notice. However, they may be revived by the accused giving notice that he or she wishes them to continue (s. 23(3) and (7)). The apparent purpose of allowing the accused to insist on the case continuing is, first, that a full hearing may establish innocence and vindicate the accused in a way which the mere withdrawal of proceedings could not, and, secondly, if there is an acquittal following trial the accused may rely on the plea of autrefois acquit if further proceedings are commenced. This is significant because notice of discontinuance does not guarantee that the proceedings will not be revived should additional evidence later be discovered (s. 23(9) provides that discontinuance shall not prevent the subsequent institution of fresh proceedings in respect of the same offence).

D3.60 When giving notice to the court under s. 23(3), the DPP must give reasons for not wanting the proceedings to continue (s. 23(5)). The DPP must also inform the accused that notice has been given and that the accused has the right to require the proceedings to be continued, but the DPP is not obliged to indicate to the accused the reasons for desiring discontinuance (s. 23(6)). If the accused has been charged at the police station and the DPP wishes to discontinue before there has even been a court appearance, it is merely necessary to serve notice to that effect on the accused, and the accused does not then have the right to require the proceedings to continue (s. 23(4)).

Where proceedings are discontinued under s. 23A, the discontinuance takes effect from the giving of that notice (s. 23A(2)). The notice must give reasons for the decision to discontinue the proceedings (s. 23A(3)) but the DPP (or Crown Prosecutor) is not obliged to give the accused any indication of the reasons for not wanting the proceedings to continue (s. 23A(4)). Under s. 23A(5), the discontinuance of proceedings under s. 23A does not prevent the institution of fresh proceedings in respect of the same offence. However, unlike discontinuance under s. 23, there is no provision for the accused to insist that the proceedings continue.

The procedure to be followed under s. 23 or s. 23A is set out in CrimPR Part 12 (see Supplement, **R12.1** *et seq.*).

The decision to discontinue a prosecution may be challenged by way of judicial review if that decision is based on an irrational (and therefore) unlawful application of the provisions of the Code for Crown Prosecutors which govern the decision to prosecute (*R (FB) v DPP* [2009] EWHC 106 (Admin), [2009] 1 Cr App R 38 (580)).

Offering No Evidence

D3.61 Instead of discontinuing proceedings under the Prosecution of Offences Act 1985, s. 23 or 23A (see D3.59), the prosecution may simply offer no evidence at the trial. *Cooke v DPP* (1992) 95 Cr App R 233 makes it clear that the statutory power to discontinue a prosecution is additional to the common-law power to offer no evidence. Offering no evidence is appropriate where the prosecution wish to withdraw the case against the accused but it is too late to discontinue the proceedings under s. 23 or 23A.

It would appear that the court has no power to prevent the offering of no evidence (see Lord Lane CJ in *Canterbury and St Augustine Justices, ex parte Klisiak* [1982] QB 398 at p. 411C–D and *Horseferry Road Magistrates' Court, ex parte O'Regan* (1986) 150 JP 535). However, where an accused pleads guilty to one offence on the basis that the prosecution will offer no evidence on another offence, the court may require the prosecution to reconsider the matter if the guilty plea would not give the court the appropriate power to sentence the criminality alleged by the prosecution. CrimPD VII, para. B.2 (see Supplement, **CPD.VII.B**), says that a prosecution advocate who is considering whether to accept a plea to a lesser charge may invite the judge to approve the proposed course of action; if such an indication is sought, 'the advocate must abide by the decision of the judge'. Paragraph B.3 goes on to state that, if the prosecution advocate has not invited the judge to approve the acceptance of a lesser charge, it is open to the judge to express dissent with the course proposed and to 'invite the advocate to reconsider the matter with those instructing him or her'. Where the issue remains unresolved after that reconsideration, the judge can require that the DPP or the Director of the relevant prosecuting authority should be consulted (para. B.4).

If the prosecution offer no evidence, the accused stands acquitted (see the CJA 1967, s. 17, and the MCA 1980, s. 27, which apply to trial on indictment and summary trial of either-way offences respectively).

An alternative to offering no evidence in the Crown Court is to invite the court to order that the count in question should be left 'on the file'. Where that is done, the accused is not acquitted of the offence in question, but proceedings may be reinstated only with the leave of the Crown Court or the Court of Appeal.

Discontinuance by the DPP of Private Prosecutions

The Prosecution of Offences Act 1985, s. 6(2), gives the DPP discretion to take over the conduct of proceedings begun by somebody other than him or herself. The DPP might take over a private prosecution to ensure, in the public interest, that it is conducted efficiently. However, since the DPP also has power to discontinue proceedings of which the DPP has the conduct, it follows that the DPP can prevent the continuance of a privately commenced prosecution by taking over its conduct and then serving notice of discontinuance. **D3.62**

In *Raymond v A-G* [1982] QB 839 the Court of Appeal considered whether it was legitimate for the DPP to take over a prosecution with the sole purpose of offering no evidence. Sir Sebag Shaw said (at pp. 846H–847D):

> ...when the Director intervenes in a prosecution which has been privately instituted he may do so not exclusively for the purpose of pursuing it by carrying it on, but also with the object of aborting it; that is to say, he may 'conduct' the proceedings in whatever manner may appear expedient in the public interest. The Director will thus intervene in a private prosecution where the issues in the public interest are so grave that the expertise and the resources of the Director's office should be brought to bear in order to ensure that the proceedings are properly conducted from the point of view of the prosecution.
>
> On the other hand, there may be what appear to the Director substantial reasons in the public interest for not pursuing a prosecution privately commenced. What may emerge from those proceedings might have an adverse effect upon a pending prosecution involving far more serious issues. The Director, in such a case, is called upon to make a value judgment. Unless his decision is manifestly such that it could not be honestly and reasonably arrived at it cannot, in our opinion, be impugned.

The DPP has a published policy setting out the circumstances in which the CPS will take over a private prosecution. The section of the policy dealing with taking over private prosecutions in order to discontinue them states that:

> A private prosecution should be taken over and stopped if, upon review of the case papers, either the evidential sufficiency stage or the public interest stage of the Full Code Test is not met.

The Code goes on to give examples of factors which 'would be damaging to the interests of justice if the private prosecution was not discontinued'. These include cases where the prosecution would interfere with the investigation or prosecution of another offence; the prosecution is vexatious (within the meaning of the Senior Courts Act 1981, s. 42) or malicious; the prosecuting authorities have promised the defendant that he or she will not be prosecuted at all (a promise of immunity from prosecution); or the defendant has already (and appropriately) been given a simple caution or a conditional caution for the offence.

The lawfulness of the approach of the CPS to taking over private prosecutions in order to discontinue them was considered by the Supreme Court in *R (Gujra) v CPS* [2012] UKSC 52, [2013] 1 AC 484. It was held (by a 3:2 majority) that this policy did not frustrate the right, under the Prosecution of Offences Act 1985, s. 6(1), to bring a private prosecution. It was therefore lawful for the DPP to apply to private prosecutions the same tests (namely, evidential sufficiency and public interest) which apply to cases brought by the CPS.

D3.63 **Prosecution of Offences Act 1985, ss. 23 and 23A**

23.—(1) Where the Director of Public Prosecutions has the conduct of proceedings for an offence, this section applies in relation to the preliminary stages of those proceedings.

(2) In this section, 'preliminary stage' in relation to proceedings for an offence does not include—
(a) any stage of the proceedings after the court has begun to hear evidence for the prosecution at a summary trial of the offence; or
(b) any stage of the proceedings after the accused has been sent for trial for the offence.

(3) Where, at any time during the preliminary stages of the proceedings, the Director gives notice under this section to the designated officer for the court that he does not want the proceedings to continue, they shall be discontinued with effect from the giving of that notice but may be revived by notice given by the accused under subsection (7) below.

(4) Where, in the case of a person charged with an offence after being taken into custody without a warrant, the Director gives him notice, at a time when no magistrates' court has been informed of the charge, that the proceedings against him are discontinued, they shall be discontinued with effect from the giving of that notice.

(5) The Director shall, in any notice given under subsection (3) above, give reasons for not wanting the proceedings to continue.

(6) On giving any notice under subsection (3) above the Director shall inform the accused of the notice and of the accused's right to require the proceedings to be continued; but the Director shall not be obliged to give the accused any indication of his reasons for not wanting the proceedings to continue.

(7) Where the Director has given notice under subsection (3) above, the accused shall, if he wants the proceedings to continue, give notice to that effect to the designated officer for the court within the prescribed period; and where notice is so given the proceedings shall continue as if no notice had been given by the Director under subsection (3) above.

(8) Where the designated officer for the court has been so notified by the accused he shall inform the Director.

(9) The discontinuance of any proceedings by virtue of this section shall not prevent the institution of fresh proceedings in respect of the same offence.

[(10) Meaning of 'prescribed'.]

23A.—(1) This section applies where—
(a) the Director of Public Prosecutions, or a public authority (within the meaning of section 17 of this Act), has the conduct of proceedings for an offence; and
(b) the accused has been sent for trial for the offence.

(2) Where, at any time before the indictment is preferred, the Director or authority gives notice under this section to the Crown Court sitting at the place specified in the notice under section 51D(1) of the Crime and Disorder Act 1998 that he or it does not want the proceedings to continue, they shall be discontinued with effect from the giving of that notice.

(3) The Director or authority shall, in any notice given under subsection (2) above, give reasons for not wanting the proceedings to continue.

(4) On giving any notice under subsection (2) above the Director or authority shall inform the accused of the notice; but the Director or authority shall not be obliged to give the accused any indication of his reasons for not wanting the proceedings to continue.

(5) The discontinuance of any proceedings by virtue of this section shall not prevent the institution of fresh proceedings in respect of the same offence.

Nolle Prosequi by the Attorney-General

Either the prosecution or defence may apply informally to the A-G for entry of a *nolle prosequi* to halt criminal proceedings. The commonest reason for the power being exercised is that the accused is physically or mentally unfit to be produced in court and the incapacity is likely to be permanent, but there may be other exceptional situations in which a *nolle prosequi* is the best means of halting proceedings which the prosecution agree ought not to be continued. **D3.64**

The power of the A-G to enter a *nolle prosequi* is not shared by the DPP, but it may be viewed as complementing the latter's powers under the Prosecution of Offences Act 1985, ss. 23 and 23A.

Court Order Restricting the Commencement of a Prosecution

By s. 42(1)(c) of the Senior Courts Act 1981, the A-G may apply to the High Court for a 'criminal proceedings order'. Such an order prevents the person against whom it is made or applying for the issue of a summons or for a voluntary bill of indictment without leave of the High Court (s. 42(1A)). Before making the order, the High Court must, after giving the proposed subject the opportunity of making representations, be satisfied that the subject has 'habitually and persistently and without any reasonable ground...instituted vexatious prosecutions (whether against the same person or different persons)'. Where an order has been made, leave to apply for a summons or a voluntary bill may not be given unless the High Court is satisfied that (a) the institution of the prosecution would not be an abuse of the criminal process; and (b) the applicant has reasonable grounds for instituting it (s. 42(3A)). There is no appeal against refusal of leave (s. 42(4)). **D3.65**

An application for permission to apply for judicial review falls within the definition of 'civil proceedings' even if the decision under challenge relates to a criminal cause or matter, and so a person who has been declared a vexatious litigant and who is subject to a 'civil proceedings order' under s. 42(1A) of the 1981 Act, requires leave (under s. 42) to make the application (*Ewing v DPP* [2010] EWCA Civ 70).

ABUSE OF PROCESS: THE POWER TO STAY PROCEEDINGS

According to *County of London Quarter Sessions, ex parte Downes* [1954] 1 QB 1 at p. 6, once an indictment has been preferred, the accused must be tried unless: **D3.66**

(a) the indictment is defective (e.g., it contains counts that are improperly joined and so does not comply with CrimPR 3.29(4): see Supplement, **R3.29**);
(b) a 'plea in bar' applies (such as autrefois acquit);
(c) a '*nolle prosequi*' is entered by the A-G to stop the proceedings; or
(d) the indictment discloses no offence that the court has jurisdiction to try (e.g., the offence is based on a statutory provision that was not in force at the date the accused allegedly did the act complained of).

To this list must be added cases where it would amount to an abuse of process to continue with the prosecution. Where proceedings would amount to an abuse of process, the court may order that those proceedings be stayed. The usual effect of a stay is that the case against the accused is stopped permanently. Given the nature of the grounds upon which a case may properly be regarded as an abuse of process, it would only be in exceptional cases that there would be any basis for lifting a stay that has been imposed. An example of such a case, however, is *Gadd* [2014] EWHC 3307 (QB), where Globe J granted a voluntary bill of indictment to allow the accused to be prosecuted for offences which had been stayed by a magistrates' court in 1998 (the stay being subsequently upheld by the Divisional Court). His lordship decided that, in the circumstances prevailing at the time of the application for a voluntary bill (including, in particular, the fact that there were other allegations to be tried), the interests of justice no longer required that the proceedings be stayed. A voluntary bill was therefore granted. An application for leave to appeal against conviction was subsequently dismissed by the Court of Appeal (*Gadd* [2015] All ER (D) 141 (Nov)).

The Meaning of 'Abuse of Process'

D3.67 In *Beckford* [1996] 1 Cr App R 94, Neill LJ said (at p. 100) that the 'constitutional principle which underlies the jurisdiction to stay proceedings is that the courts have the power and the duty to protect the law by protecting its own purposes and functions'. His lordship quoted the words of Lord Devlin in *Connelly v DPP* [1964] AC 1254 at p. 1354, that the courts have 'an inescapable duty to secure fair treatment for those who come or are brought before them'. In *Maxwell* [2010] UKSC 48, [2011] 1 WLR 1837 (at [13]), cited in *Warren v A-G for Jersey* [2011] UKPC 10, [2012] 1 AC 22 (at [22]), Lord Dyson summarised the two categories of case in which the court has the power to stay proceedings for abuse of process:

> It is well established that the court has the power to stay proceedings in two categories of case, namely (i) where it will be impossible to give the accused a fair trial, and (ii) where it offends the court's sense of justice and propriety to be asked to try the accused in the particular circumstances of the case. In the first category of case, if the court concludes that an accused cannot receive a fair trial, it will stay the proceedings without more. No question of the balancing of competing interests arises. In the second category of case, the court is concerned to protect the integrity of the criminal justice system. Here a stay will be granted where the court concludes that in all the circumstances a trial will offend the court's sense of justice and propriety (per Lord Lowry in *R v Horseferry Road Magistrates' Court, ex p Bennett* [1994] 1 AC 42 (at 74G)), or will undermine public confidence in the criminal justice system and bring it into disrepute (per Lord Steyn in *Latif* [1996] 1 WLR 104 (at 112F)).

In *Crawley* [2014] EWCA Crim 1028, [2014] 2 Cr App R 16 (214), Sir Brian Leveson P summarised the scope of abuse of process thus (at [17]–[18]):

> [T]here are two categories of case in which the court has the power to stay proceedings for abuse of process. These are, first, where the court concludes that the accused can no longer receive a fair hearing; and, second, where it would otherwise be unfair to try the accused or, put another way, where a stay is necessary to protect the integrity of the criminal justice system. The first limb focuses on the trial process and where the court concludes that the accused would not receive a fair hearing it will stay the proceedings; no balancing exercise is required. The second limb concerns the integrity of the criminal justice system and applies where the Court considers that the accused should not be standing trial at all, irrespective of the potential fairness of the trial itself.
>
> ... [T]here is a strong public interest in the prosecution of crime and in ensuring that those charged with serious criminal offences are tried. Ordering a stay of proceedings, which in criminal law is effectively a permanent remedy, is thus a remedy of last resort.

His lordship observed (at [21]) that 'cases in which it may be unfair to try the accused (the second category of case) will include, but are not confined to, those cases where there has been bad faith, unlawfulness or executive misconduct'. In such a case, 'the court is concerned not to create the perception that it is condoning malpractice by law enforcement agencies or to convey the impression that it will adopt the approach that the end justifies the means: the touchstone is the integrity of the criminal justice system' (at [23]). In *Horseferry Road Magistrates' Court, ex parte Bennett* [1994] 1 AC 42, Lord Griffiths (at p. 61H) said that if the courts have a power to interfere with the prosecution in such cases:

> ... it must be because the judiciary accept a responsibility for the maintenance of the rule of law that embraces a willingness to oversee executive action and to refuse to countenance behaviour that threatens either basic human rights or the rule of law... I have no doubt that the judiciary should accept this responsibility in the field of criminal law.

D3.68 There are thus two main categories of abuse of process:

(a) cases where the court concludes that the accused cannot receive a fair trial;
(b) cases where the court concludes that it would be unfair for the accused to be tried.

The former focuses on the trial process; the latter is applicable where the accused should not be standing trial at all (irrespective of the fairness of the actual trial).

In *D Ltd v A* [2017] EWCA Crim 1172, David LJ noted (at [35]) that it is 'important to bear in mind that the two limbs to the exercise of this jurisdiction to stay are legally distinct and have to be considered separately: considerations that may be relevant to the first limb may not be relevant to the second limb and vice versa. Moreover, the second limb requires a balance of the competing interests, whereas the first limb does not.' The Court of Appeal (at [63]) accepted the argument that failures on the part of the prosecution are not of themselves ordinarily relevant to the first limb of abuse of process. The key issue is whether the consequences of those failures are such as to deprive the defendant of a fair trial. Thus, 'for the purposes of the limb one argument one has to assess the prejudicial effect of that conduct on the fairness of the trial' (at [66]).

In *DPP v Humphrys* [1977] AC 1, Lord Salmon (at p. 46) commented that a judge does not have 'any power to refuse to allow a prosecution to proceed merely because he considers that, as a matter of policy, it ought not to have been brought. It is only if the prosecution amounts to an abuse of the process of the court and is oppressive and vexatious that the judge has the power to intervene.'

In very rare cases, the court may intervene to prevent an abuse of process before a suspect has been formally charged. However, the court will order that a police investigation be discontinued, on the basis that there is no prospect of an eventual prosecution, only in the most exceptional cases. Where there were unquestionably reasonable grounds initially to suspect a person under investigation, the court should be very slow to second-guess the police in deciding at what point the suspect can be dismissed from the inquiry. To hold otherwise would involve an unwelcome blurring of the separate roles of court and prosecutor/investigator (*R (C) v Chief Constable of A* [2006] EWHC 2352 (Admin), per Underhill J at [32]). **D3.69**

One consequence of the fact that the test for abuse of process is much higher than the judge simply taking the view that the case should not have been brought is that it is not an abuse of process to prosecute someone where the evidence against that person is weak. It follows that a judge has no power to prevent the prosecution from presenting their evidence merely on the basis that the judge considers a conviction unlikely (*A-G's Ref (No. 2 of 2000)* [2001] 1 Cr App R 36 (503)), although the judge may, if he or she sees fit, stop the case at the close of the prosecution evidence.

Key Issues in Abuse of Process Cases

Two key questions run through many of the authorities: (1) To what extent is the accused prejudiced? (2) To what degree are the rule of law and the administration of justice undermined by the behaviour of the investigators or the prosecution? **D3.70**

As well as invoking the right to a fair trial under the ECHR, Article 6, those seeking to establish abuse of process may also rely on the overriding objective set out in CrimPR Part 1 (see Supplement, **R1.1** ***et seq.***), which requires everyone involved in any way in a criminal case to prepare and conduct the case in accordance with the overriding objective to deal with the case 'justly' (which term includes the requirement to deal with the defence fairly and to deal with the case efficiently and expeditiously: see **D4**).

There is no definitive list of complaints which are capable of amounting to abuse of process, but it is possible to derive some broad categories of abuse from the case law. For example: lengthy delay which causes prejudice to the accused; failure to honour an undertaking given to the accused; failing to secure evidence or destroying evidence; tactical manipulation or misuse of procedures in order to deprive the accused of some protection provided by the law, or taking unfair advantage of a technicality; entrapment; abuse of executive power.

Magistrates' Courts

Much of the case law on abuse of process comes from cases tried in the Crown Court. However, abuse of process can also be raised in a magistrates' court. In *Horseferry Road Magistrates' Court, ex* **D3.71** *parte Bennett* [1994] 1 AC 42, the House of Lords ruled that the jurisdiction exercised by magistrates to protect the court's process from abuse is confined strictly to matters directly affecting the fairness of the trial of the particular accused with whom they were dealing (such as delay or unfair manipulation of court procedures). It does not extend to a wider supervisory jurisdiction to uphold the rule of law. The rationale is that supervision of the use of executive power is a responsibility that is vested in the High Court. Where such an issue arises, the magistrates should adjourn the matter so that an application can be made to the Divisional Court, which is the proper forum for deciding the matter (per Lord Griffiths at p. 64). It follows that, where it is contended that a summary trial should not take place because it would be unfair to try the accused (as opposed to the question being whether the accused can have a fair trial), the issue of abuse of process should be dealt with by the High Court, not in the magistrates' court (*Nembhard v DPP* [2009] EWHC 194 (Admin); *R (Smith) v CPS* [2010] EWHC 3593 (Admin)). However, as the Divisional Court observed in *R (Kay) v Leeds Magistrates' Court* [2018] EWHC 1233 (Admin), [2018] 4 WLR 91, at [30], the 'wide category of cases over which the magistrates' court has jurisdiction includes investigation of the *bona fides* of the prosecution or of whether the prosecution has been instituted oppressively or unfairly — including, since a magistrate has jurisdiction to refuse to issue a summons that is vexatious, the jurisdiction to stay proceedings on such a summons at a later stage'; alternatively, the magistrates' court can adjourn the case to enable the matter to be considered by the Divisional Court.

In *R (Salubi) v Bow Street Magistrates' Court* [2002] EWHC 919 (Admin), [2002] 1 WLR 3073, it was held that the fact that magistrates are required, under the transfer procedure in the CDA 1998, s. 51(1), to send cases to Crown Court 'forthwith' does not necessarily preclude them from exercising their jurisdiction to stay the proceedings as an abuse of process in an appropriate case. However, it would be appropriate to do so only in rare cases where the defence establish bad faith or serious misconduct. The Divisional Court reiterated that a magistrates' court's power to stay criminal proceedings for abuse of process is strictly confined to matters directly affecting the fairness of a trial before it and that this power should be exercised sparingly. The Court said that where the point is complex or novel it should normally be left for resolution in the Crown Court or the High Court. It should be borne in mind that an abuse of process application may be made immediately after the case arrives at the Crown Court (per Auld LJ at [20]–[21]).

In *DPP v Gowing* [2013] EWHC 4614 (Admin), Beatson LJ emphasised (at [29]) that it is important that magistrates who are considering staying proceedings recognise 'the exceptional nature of the jurisdiction to stay proceedings'. This means that there must be 'a firm factual basis for staying' the proceedings. His lordship added (at [31]) that, where there are failures on the part of prosecutors, the power to stay proceedings 'should not be used to punish prosecutors where a fair trial remains possible'.

In *R (Barons Pub Co. Ltd) v Staines Magistrates' Court* [2013] EWHC 898 (Admin), Sir John Thomas P made it clear (at [36]) that a magistrates' court has 'no power of review of a prosecutorial decision other than through an abuse of process application'. He added that such an application 'in itself is an exceptional remedy'; moreover, it is only where an abuse of process application cannot be made that an application can be made to the High Court by way of judicial review of the decision to prosecute.

Burden and Standard of Proof

D3.72 The defence bear the burden of establishing abuse on the balance of probabilities (*Telford Justices, ex parte Badhan* [1991] 2 QB 78).

However, it should be noted that in *S (SP)* [2006] EWCA Crim 756, [2006] 2 Cr App R 23 (341), the Court of Appeal observed that the decision whether or not to grant a stay by reason of delay is an exercise in judicial assessment dependent on judgement, rather than on any conclusion as to fact based on evidence. It is, therefore, potentially misleading to use the language of burden and standard of proof, which is more apt to an evidence-based fact-finding process (per Rose LJ at [20]).

It may well be that this comment should be taken as applying to abuse of process applications generally (i.e. it is not limited to those where delay is an issue), since the balancing of competing interests is at the heart of all abuse claims. Nonetheless, it remains the case that there is, effectively, a presumption that the trial should go ahead unless there is a compelling reason for stopping the trial from taking place. For example, the Court of Appeal confirmed in *E* [2012] EWCA Crim 791 that, where delay is said to amount to abuse of process, 'the burden of proof or persuasion lies on the defendant' to show that a fair trial is no longer possible (per Rix LJ at [22]).

Delay

There is no general time-limit within which proceedings have to be commenced where the alleged offence is indictable. However, in the case of summary offences, there is a six-month time-limit by virtue of the MCA 1980, s. 127 (see **D21.17**). **D3.73**

Where delay is deliberate, it is likely to be held to amount to an abuse of process. For example, in *Brentford Justices, ex parte Wong* [1981] QB 445, proceedings (for careless driving) were commenced (just) within the six-month period permitted for summary offences by the MCA 1980, s. 127, but the summons was not served until three months later. The prosecutor accepted that the delay was because he had not then reached a firm decision on whether to take proceedings, and he was trying to keep his options open. The Divisional Court held that the case could properly be regarded as one where the proceedings should be stayed, since this was a deliberate attempt by the prosecutor to gain further time in which to reach a decision, thereby defeating the time-limit set by s. 127.

Inadvertent Delay Where deliberate delay in bringing the case to court cannot be shown, the defence may nonetheless apply for the proceedings to be stayed on the ground of abuse of process if (a) there has been inordinate or unconscionable delay due to the prosecution's inefficiency, and (b) prejudice to the defence from the delay is either proved or to be inferred (per Lloyd LJ in *Gateshead Justices, ex parte Smith* (1985) 149 JP 681). **D3.74**

In *Bow Street Stipendiary Magistrate, ex parte DPP* (1989) 91 Cr App R 283, the Divisional Court made it clear that, to amount to an abuse of process, delay has to produce 'genuine prejudice and unfairness' (per Watkins LJ at p. 296). In some cases, however, prejudice will be inferred from substantial delay, and the prosecution will then have to rebut that inference of prejudice (p. 297). Such an inference 'is more easily drawn when dealing with a single brief but confused event which must depend on the recollections of those involved' (p. 300). Similarly, in *Telford Justices, ex parte Badhan* [1991] 2 QB 78, the Divisional Court said (at p. 91) that, where the period of delay is long, it is legitimate for the court to infer prejudice without proof of specific prejudice.

Effect of Delay on Fairness of Trial In *A-G's Ref (No. 1 of 1990)* [1992] QB 630 (at pp. 643–4), Lord Lane CJ said that: **D3.75**

> Stays imposed on the grounds of delay or for any other reason should only be employed in exceptional circumstances... In principle, therefore, even where the delay can be said to be unjustifiable, the imposition of a permanent stay should be the exception rather than the rule. Still more rare should be cases where a stay can properly be imposed in the absence of any fault on the part of the complainant or prosecution. Delay due merely to the complexity of the case or contributed to by the actions of the defendant himself should never be the foundation for a stay... [N]o stay should be imposed unless the defendant shows on the balance of probabilities that owing to the delay he will suffer serious prejudice to the extent that no fair trial can be held: in other words, that the continuance of the prosecution amounts to a misuse of the process of the court. In assessing whether there is likely to be prejudice and if so whether it can properly be described as serious, the following matters should be borne in mind: first, the power of the judge at common law and under the PACE 1984 to regulate the admissibility of evidence; secondly, the trial process itself, which should ensure that all relevant factual issues arising from delay will be placed before the jury as part of the evidence for their consideration, together with the powers of the judge to give appropriate directions to the jury before they consider their verdict.

D3.76 The same approach was adopted by the House of Lords in *A-G's Ref (No. 2 of 2001)* [2003] UKHL 68, [2004] 2 AC 72. Two questions had been certified by the Court of Appeal: (1) whether criminal proceedings may be stayed on the ground that there had been a breach of the reasonable time requirement in the ECHR, Article 6(1), in circumstances where the accused cannot demonstrate any prejudice arising from the delay; and (2) when the relevant time period commences in the determination of whether, for the purposes of Article 6(1), a criminal charge has been heard within a reasonable time. The House of Lords ruled that criminal proceedings may be stayed on the ground that there had been a violation of the reasonable time requirement in the Article 6(1), only if '(a) there can no longer be a fair hearing, or (b) it would otherwise be unfair to try the defendant' (per Lord Bingham at [24]). It was said that it would be anomalous if breach of the reasonable time requirement were to have an effect that is more far-reaching than breach of the accused's other Article 6(1) rights. Lord Bingham said that the remedy for such a breach must be 'effective, just and proportionate'. It follows that a stay of the proceedings would not be an appropriate remedy 'if any lesser remedy will be just and proportionate in all the circumstances'. His lordship added that, if breach of the reasonable time requirement is established retrospectively (in other words, used as a ground for appeal against conviction), it would not be appropriate to quash any conviction unless the hearing was unfair or it was unfair to try the accused at all (at [24]).

D3.77 Regarding the second question, it was held that, for the purposes of the requirement under Article 6(1) that a criminal charge must be heard within a reasonable time, the relevant period commences at the earliest time at which a person was officially alerted to the likelihood of criminal proceedings against him or her (per Lord Bingham at [27]). This will normally be when the person is charged or served with a summons or written charge. In *Burns v HM Advocate* [2008] UKPC 63, [2009] 1 AC 720, it was held that the reasonable time requirement must be interpreted and applied in a way that will tend to achieve its purpose, which is to avoid undue uncertainty on the part of a person charged, and so the matter ought to be examined from the perspective of the individual concerned (per Lady Cosgrove at [53]).

So far as the ECtHR is concerned, 'the reasonableness of the length of proceedings must be assessed in the light of the circumstances of the case and with reference to the following criteria: the complexity of the case, the conduct of the applicants and the relevant authorities and what was at stake for the applicants' (*Bullen and Soneji v UK* [2009] ECHR 28).

D3.78 In *S (SP)* [2006] EWCA Crim 756, [2006] 2 Cr App R 23 (341), the Court of Appeal summarised the position as follows: (a) even where delay is unjustifiable, a permanent stay should be the exception rather than the rule; (b) where there is no fault on the part of the complainant or prosecution, it will be very rare for a stay to be granted; (c) no stay should be granted in the absence of serious prejudice to the accused, so that no fair trial can be held; (d) when assessing possible serious prejudice, the judge should bear in mind the power to regulate the admissibility of evidence, and that the trial process itself should ensure that all the relevant factual issues arising from delay will be placed before the jury for their consideration; (e) if the judge's assessment is that a fair trial is possible, a stay should not be granted (per Rose LJ at [21]).

In *Spiers v Ruddy* [2007] UKPC D2, [2008] 1 AC 873, the Privy Council reiterated that a stay of proceedings is a last resort. Lord Bingham of Cornhill CJ said (at [16]) that where there has (or may have been) such delay in the conduct of proceedings as to breach a party's right to trial within a reasonable time, but where the fairness of the trial has not been or will not be compromised, 'such delay does not give rise to a continuing breach which cannot be cured save by a discontinuation of proceedings. It gives rise to a breach which can be cured, even where it cannot be prevented, by expedition, reduction of sentence or compensation, provided always that the breach, where it occurs, is publicly acknowledged and addressed.'

The need for the accused to demonstrate that the delay has caused prejudice was emphasised in *Brants v DPP* [2011] EWHC 754 (Admin). Jackson LJ said (at [47]) that delay alone by the prosecution cannot warrant the staying of proceedings as an abuse of process: 'There is a public interest in prosecuting offences which transcends any consideration of punishing the prosecution for delay. If delay by the prosecution does not cause prejudice to the defence, then normally it would not be appropriate to stay proceedings for abuse of process.'

An example of a case where there was held to be a lack of prejudice (and hence no abuse of process) was *Central Criminal Court, ex parte Randle* [1991] 1 All ER 370. The accused appeared in court some 23 years after the alleged offences, and applied for the proceedings to be stayed on the ground of unreasonable delay. The Divisional Court noted that they had published a book in 1989, which had provided much of the material upon which the prosecution relied. In the light of its contents, the plea of failing memory could not be advanced, and so there was no prejudice to them. Where a case turns largely on documentary evidence, and it is possible for witnesses to refresh their memories from documents, delay is unlikely to cause prejudice to the accused. A further example is found in *LG* [2018] EWCA Crim 736, where a pedestrian was killed after being struck by a motorcycle ridden by D. The accident occurred in December 2010. A decision not to prosecute D was taken in June 2011. This decision was apparently not formally communicated to D. The daughter of the deceased sought a review of the decision not to prosecute D. In June 2014, the Independent Police Complaints Commission concluded that the original investigation had been carried out in accordance with proper police standards. The deceased's daughter challenged this conclusion, and it was reviewed in October 2014. A report from a new accident investigation was produced in June 2016. In May 2017, D was charged with causing death by careless driving. The Crown Court stayed the proceedings as an abuse of process. Following an appeal by the prosecution against that terminating ruling, the Court of Appeal reversed the stay and ordered the resumption of the proceedings in the Crown Court. Davis LJ said (at [29]) that the judge had conflated aspects of the requirements of the second limb relating to abuse of process (where it is not fair for the defendant to be tried at all) with aspects of the requirements of the first limb relating to abuse of process (where the accused can no longer have a fair trial), and had 'failed to assess whether there was significant prejudice, over and above the natural disappointed expectations of the [accused], such that a fair trial could no longer be had'. His lordship added (at [30]) that it is:

> ... an important element of the interests of justice that conduct which is adjudged by those entrusted with making the prosecutorial decision to be criminal with sufficient prospects of successful prosecution should ordinarily be the subject of criminal proceedings. The rights and interests of victims and their families are not simply to be subordinated to those of a defendant in any given case. Further, ... the public interest in prosecuting offences transcends any considerations of punishing the prosecution for delay — always, of course, we add, subject to the delay not having given rise to any significant prejudice to the defence which cannot be accommodated by the trial process.

So far as appeals against refusals of stays are concerned, *Ali v CPS* [2007] EWCA Crim 691 emphasises that the question for the Court of Appeal is not whether the judge was correct to refuse to stay the proceedings, but rather whether the effect of the delay is such as to lead the court to the conclusion that the verdict was unsafe.

Where the issue of delay is raised at the stage when the magistrates are contemplating the transfer **D3.79**
of the case to the Crown Court, it is submitted that the magistrates should refuse to transfer the case on the basis of delay only in cases where it is patent that a fair trial could not take place; in other cases, the magistrates should send the case to the Crown Court and allow a Crown Court judge to consider whether steps can be taken to enable the accused to have a fair trial (e.g., specific directions to the jury about the effect of the delay on the ability of the accused to conduct the defence).

Mitigating the Effects of Delay Where the defence argue that the proceedings amount to an **D3.80**
abuse of process because of delay in bringing the prosecution, an important consideration is whether a direction to the jury about the effect of the delay is a sufficient remedy for the accused. The *Crown Court Compendium* (July 2020), ch. 10-4, includes in an example direction the need

to 'bear in mind that the passage of time is likely to have affected the memory of each of the witnesses about exactly what happened all those years ago' and to 'be aware that the passage of time may have put D at a serious disadvantage. He may not be able to remember details now that could have helped him.' Significantly, the example direction concludes, 'You should take the long delay into account in D's favour each of these ways when you are deciding whether or not the prosecution have proved that D is guilty, so that you are sure of it'.

In *H* [1998] 2 Cr App R 161 at p. 168, the Court of Appeal said that a direction on delay 'should be given in any case where it is necessary for the purposes of being even-handed as between complainant and defendant'. In *M* [2000] 1 Cr App R 49, it was said that trial judges should tailor their directions to the circumstances of the particular case. The Court of Appeal added that, where the evidence was cogent, such a warning might not be necessary and its absence would not necessarily render a conviction unsafe, particularly when counsel's submissions at trial had not highlighted any specific risk of prejudice.

D3.81 **Sexual Offences and Delay** It is often the case that allegations involving sexual offences emerge a long time after the alleged abuse took place. Such cases have come to be regarded as a separate category so far as delay is concerned. The view generally taken by the courts is that the unfairness can be minimised by a direction to the jury to take proper account of the fact that the accused was handicapped in defending the case because of the length of time which has elapsed since the alleged offence was committed. Any residual prejudice is regarded as outweighed by the importance of prosecuting such serious offences. In *E* [2004] EWCA Crim 1441, [2004] 2 Cr App R 36 (621), the Court of Appeal said that juries should be trusted to make allowances not only for the lapse of time but also for the difficulties faced by an accused who could only deny the offence (per Keith J at [17]).

D3.82 In *MacKreth* [2009] EWCA Crim 1849, Rix LJ noted (at [39]) that, despite the matter being considered in a number of subsequent cases, the relevant principles regarding delay, including delay in cases involving alleged sexual offences, are still to be found in *A-G's Ref (No. 1 of 1990)* [1992] QB 630 (see **D3.75**). It follows that this case should be the first point of reference regarding delay. Nonetheless, in *F (TB)* [2011] EWCA Crim 726, [2011] 2 Cr App R 13 (145) (a case concerning a 62-year-old man who had been convicted of committing sexual offences against his step-daughter and daughter between 30 and 40 years earlier) Jackson LJ, having reviewed the relevant authorities, set out the following five propositions in relation to criminal prosecutions brought after a long delay (at [37]):

> (i) The court should stay proceedings on some or all counts of the indictment for abuse of process if, and only if, it is satisfied on balance of probabilities that by reason of delay a fair trial is not possible on those counts.
> (ii) It is now recognised that usually the proper time for the defence to make such an application and for the judge to rule upon it is at trial, after all the evidence has been called.
> (iii) In assessing what prejudice has been caused to the defendant on any particular count by reason of delay, the court should consider what evidence directly relevant to the defence case has been lost through the passage of time. Vague speculation that lost documents or deceased witnesses might have assisted the defendant is not helpful. The court should also consider what evidence has survived the passage of time. The court should then examine critically how important the missing evidence is in the context of the case as a whole.
> (iv) Having identified the prejudice caused to the defence by reason of the delay, it is then necessary to consider to what extent the judge can compensate for that prejudice by emphasising guidance given in standard directions or formulating special directions to the jury. Where important independent evidence has been lost over time, it may not be known which party that evidence would have supported. There may be cases in which no direction to the jury can dispel the resultant prejudice which one or other of the parties must suffer, but this depends on the facts of the case.
> (v) If the complainant's delay in coming forward is unjustified, that is relevant to the question whether it is fair to try the defendant so long after the events in issue. In determining whether the complainant's delay is unjustified, it must be firmly borne in mind that victims of sexual abuse are often unwilling to reveal or talk about their experiences for some time and for good reason.

In *F (S)* [2011] EWCA Crim 1844, [2012] QB 703, a five-judge court presided over by Lord Judge CJ repeated that, where a judge is considering an application to stay proceedings on the ground of prejudice resulting from delay in the institution of proceedings, the appropriate test is to be found in *A-G's Ref (No. 1 of 1990)*. Lord Judge emphasised (at [39]) that the decision whether the trial should be stayed because it would constitute an abuse of process is not to be elided with the separate and distinct question which may arise at the end of the prosecution case, namely whether (applying the principles in *Galbraith* [1981] 2 All ER 1060) there is a case to answer. A judge should not decide the question of whether there should be a stay by assessing whether a conviction would be unsafe. In most cases involving allegations of sexual offences which occurred a long time ago, the reasons for the delay in making the complaint, and whether and how the delay is explained or justified, will bear directly on the credibility of the complainant and so will be an essential part of the factual matrix on which the jury must make its decision. An abuse of process argument cannot succeed unless prejudice has been caused to the accused, and so the explanation for delay is relevant to an application to stay only if it bears on how readily the fact of prejudice to the accused may be shown. Unjustified delay is not, by itself, a sufficient reason for a stay (at [40]). Most importantly, Lord Judge CJ said (at [45]) that it is only in the exceptional cases where a fair trial is not possible that abuse of process applications are justified on the grounds of delay. His lordship said that the best safeguard against unfairness to either side in such cases is the trial process itself, and an evaluation by the jury of the evidence. **D3.83**

In *Halahan* [2014] EWCA Crim 2079, where the Court of Appeal upheld the decision to allow D to be prosecuted for indecent assault during the period June 1974 to June 1977, the Court cited with approval *RD* [2013] EWCA Crim 1592, where Treacy LJ had said (at [15]):

> In considering the question of prejudice to the defence, it seems to us that it is necessary to distinguish between mere speculation about what missing documents or witnesses might show, and missing evidence which represents a significant and demonstrable chance of amounting to decisive or strongly supportive evidence emerging on a specific issue in the case. The court will need to consider what evidence directly relevant to the appellant's case has been lost by reason of the passage of time. The court will then need to go on to consider the importance of the missing evidence in the context of the case as a whole and the issues before the jury. Having considered those matters, the court will have to identify what prejudice, if any, has been caused to the appellant by the delay and whether judicial directions would be sufficient to compensate for such prejudice as may have been caused or whether in truth a fair trial could not properly be afforded to a defendant.

An important question is *when* an abuse application should be made, if one is to be made. In *Smolinski* [2004] EWCA Crim 1270, [2004] 2 Cr App R 40 (661), Lord Woolf CJ had said (at [9]) that, if an abuse of process application is to be made, the best time for doing so is after any evidence has been called: the judge, having had an opportunity of seeing the witnesses, can then come to a conclusion as to whether the trial should proceed or whether the evidence is such that it would not be safe for a jury to convict. However, in *F (S)*, the Court of Appeal signalled a different approach. Lord Judge CJ said (at [45]): **D3.84**

> Where there are genuine grounds for an application to stay on the basis that a fair trial will be impossible because of incurable prejudice to the defendant caused by delay, that application is, by its nature, preliminary to rather than part of the trial process. The contention is that the trial should not take place at all. If it is to be made, notice should be given before the trial begins. In the end of course the time when it should be dealt with by argument and ruling is a matter for the trial judge. Although we can envisage cases in which, for example, the application is based on prejudice resulting from the absence of long-lost evidence... and where the evaluation of the significance of the absence of such evidence may best be undertaken at the close of the Crown's case, in general the question whether the trial should proceed at all should take place before evidence is called.

His lordship reasoned that, if the ruling is deferred, there is a significant danger that the submissions to the judge would conflate the principles applicable to a submission of no case to answer

D

Part D Procedure

with those applicable to abuse of process. There is also the point that, if the issue is not dealt with before the evidence is heard, the complainant will have been through the ordeal of giving evidence, which is unfair if the proceedings are then held to be an abuse of process. His lordship went on to say, though the Court did not propose to be prescriptive, 'unless there is a specific reason for deferment, an application to stay on abuse of process grounds is preliminary to the trial, and ought normally to be dealt with at the outset'.

Failing to Obtain, Losing or Destroying Evidence

D3.85 In *Dobson* [2001] EWCA Crim 1606, the Court of Appeal considered the position where police had failed to obtain CCTV footage relating to D's defence of alibi. Potter LJ said (at [34]) that, in determining whether there was an abuse of process, it was appropriate to consider:

(a) What was the duty of the police?
(b) Did the police fail in their duty by not obtaining or retaining the appropriate video footage?
(c) If so, was there serious prejudice which rendered a fair trial impossible in the light of such failure?
(d) Alternatively, did the police failure result from such bad behaviour, in the sense of bad faith or serious fault, as to render it unfair that the accused should be tried at all?

In the instant case, the police should have looked at the CCTV footage, and had failed in their duty to do so. However, the prejudice was not 'serious' because it was uncertain that the footage would have assisted the defence; moreover, D was in a position to understand the relevance of the footage and could have requested it and/or sought other evidence to support his alibi. There was no question of malice or intentional omission, as opposed to oversight, on behalf of the police. The judge was therefore right to conclude that a fair trial was possible and the conviction was upheld.

D3.86 In reaching that conclusion, the Court in *Dobson* adopted the approach which was taken in what is now to be regarded as the leading authority on such cases, *R (Ebrahim) v Feltham Magistrates' Court* [2001] EWHC Admin 130, [2001] 1 WLR 1293. Brooke LJ said (at [16]) that the starting point must be whether there was a duty on the investigator to obtain and/or retain the material in question. That question will be answered mainly through the provisions of the Code of Practice issued under Part II of the CPIA 1996 (see **D9**). If there was no duty to obtain or retain the evidence in question, there can be no grounds to stay the proceedings for failure to do so. If there was a duty, and that duty has been breached, there has to be either an element of bad faith, or at the very least some serious fault, on the part of the police or the prosecution authorities, for this ground of challenge to succeed (at [23]). Moreover, it has to be clear that the accused could not be fairly tried (at [24]).

Brooke LJ went on to say (at [25]):

> Two well-known principles are frequently invoked in this context when a court is invited to stay proceedings for abuse of process:
> (i) The ultimate objective of this discretionary power is to ensure that there should be a fair trial according to law, which involves fairness both to the defendant and the prosecution, because the fairness of a trial is not all one sided; it requires that those who are undoubtedly guilty should be convicted as well as that those about whose guilt there is any reasonable doubt should be acquitted.
> (ii) The trial process itself is equipped to deal with the bulk of the complaints on which applications for a stay are founded.

In many 'missing evidence' cases, the defence will be able to make use of the absence of that evidence, arguing that its absence should help to create a reasonable doubt in the minds of the jury or magistrates as to the guilt of the accused. Brooke LJ (at [27]) expressed the point thus:

> It must be remembered that it is a commonplace in criminal trials for a defendant to rely on 'holes' in the prosecution case, for example, a failure to take fingerprints or a failure to submit evidential material to forensic examination. If, in such a case, there is sufficient credible evidence, apart from the missing evidence, which, if believed, would justify a safe conviction, then a trial should proceed,

> leaving the defendant to seek to persuade the jury or justices not to convict because evidence which might otherwise have been available was not before the court through no fault of his. Often the absence of a video film or fingerprints or DNA material is likely to hamper the prosecution as much as the defence.

The relevance of the missing evidence has to be considered very carefully. In *D* [2013] EWCA Crim 1592, Treacy LJ (at [15]) said:

> In considering the question of prejudice to the defence, it seems to us that it is necessary to distinguish between mere speculation about what missing documents or witnesses might show, and missing evidence which represents a significant and demonstrable chance of amounting to decisive or strongly supportive evidence emerging on a specific issue in the case. The court will need to consider what evidence directly relevant to the appellant's case has been lost by reason of the passage of time. The court will then need to go on to consider the importance of the missing evidence in the context of the case as a whole and the issues before the jury. Having considered those matters, the court will have to identify what prejudice, if any, has been caused to the appellant by the delay and whether judicial directions would be sufficient to compensate for such prejudice as may have been caused or whether in truth a fair trial could not properly be afforded to a defendant.

Sometimes, evidence is 'missing' because it was not gathered in the first place. In *E* [2018] EWCA Crim 2426, for example, D argued that a prosecution amounted to an abuse of process because the police had failed to seize the mobile phone of one of two complainants who alleged that D had sexually assaulted them. Sir Brian Leveson P said (at [32]) that:

> ... the proper approach is to look at whether the trial will be fair generally. That requires a consideration of all the circumstances of the case: it is a fact sensitive decision. The circumstances primarily revolve around the issues in the case and the likelihood that information relevant to those issues and of assistance to the defence would have been revealed by the material, had it been seized and retained. It is not, of course, permissible to speculate but, in many cases, it may be possible to draw proper inferences about what is missing from the material that is available. In that regard, consideration must also be given to whether any potential unfairness to a defendant would be removed by the trial process which involves the strength of any other evidence and the material that the defence could utilise in a trial.

In *CB* [2020] EWCA Crim 790, Fulford LJ stressed (at [75]) that 'mobile telephones or other devices should not be obtained as a matter of routine by investigators from witnesses', adding (at [76]) that 'the electronic or digital nature of many modern records does not change or dilute the test for disclosure, which remains whether it might reasonably be considered capable of undermining the prosecution's case or assisting the case for the accused'.

The relevance of fault on the part of the prosecution should not be over-emphasised. In *Clay* [2014] EWHC 321 (Admin), D had been driving a lorry which collided with the rear of a car. The police had released the car and allowed the insurer to dispose of it. D argued that, because he had been deprived of the ability to examine the state of the car (in particular, whether the brake lights were working), the failure by the police to retain the vehicle resulted in the proceedings amounting to an abuse of process. Pitchford LJ (at [46]–[48]) considered the decision in *Ebrahim*, and concluded:

> With great respect to the court in *Ebrahim*, it seems to me that the question of whether the defendant can have a fair trial does not logically depend upon whether anyone was 'at fault' in causing the exigency that created the unfairness. If vital evidence has as a matter of fact been lost to the defendant whether occasioned by the fault of the police or not, the issue is whether that disadvantage can be accommodated at his trial so as to ensure that his trial is fair. There is in this respect no difference between an unfair trial occasioned by delay and an unfair trial occasioned by the loss of vital evidence.

Burton J added (at [75]) that the justices in the present case were entitled to conclude that 'injustice to the defendant could be avoided by judicious regulation of the trial'.

In *PR* [2019] EWCA Crim 1225, [2019] 2 Cr App R 22 (227), the Court of Appeal had to consider whether the trial judge was right to allow the case to proceed when evidence gathered by the police in 2002, relevant to D's defence, had been destroyed by water damage and was unavailable for the trial in 2018. Fulford LJ (at [65]) observed that:

> . . . there is no rule that if material has become unavailable, that of itself means the trial is unfair because, for instance, a relevant avenue of inquiry can no longer be explored with the benefit of the missing documents or records. It follows that there is no presumption that extraneous material must be available to enable the defendant to test the reliability of the oral testimony of one or more of the prosecution's witnesses. In some instances, this opportunity exists; in others it does not. It is to be regretted if relevant records become unavailable, but when this happens the effect may be to put the defendant closer to the position of many accused whose trial turns on a decision by the jury as to whether they are sure of the oral evidence of the prosecution witness or witnesses, absent other substantive information by which their testimony can be tested.

His lordship went on to say (at [66]) that:

> . . . the question of whether the defendant can receive a fair trial when relevant material has been accidentally destroyed will depend on the particular circumstances of the case, the focus being on the nature and extent of the prejudice to the defendant. A careful judicial direction, in many instances, will operate to ensure the integrity of the proceedings.

For a stay to be granted, the court must be satisfied that the trial process cannot remove the unfairness caused by the absence of the evidence in question. Fulford LJ observed (at [71]) that imposing a stay in situations of missing records:

> . . . will only occur when the trial process, including the judge's directions, is unable adequately to deal with the prejudice caused to the defence by the absence of the materials that have been lost.

In the instant case, there had been a 'substantial amount of material that could be used to test the reliability and credibility of the complainant' (at [72]). Moreover, the trial judge had given an 'impeccable' direction to the jury on the issue of the missing evidence, Fulford LJ noting (at [73]) that:

> The judge's directions to the jury should include the need for them to be aware that the lost material, as identified, may have put the defendant at a serious disadvantage, in that documents and other materials he would have wished to deploy had been destroyed. Critically, the jury should be directed to take this prejudice to the defendant into account when considering whether the prosecution had been able to prove, so that they are sure, that he or she is guilty.

D3.87 In *Allan* [2017] EWCA Crim 2396, Simon LJ observed (at [29]):

> The central question [for the trial judge] was whether there could be fair trial for both parties bearing in mind that the trial process is usually able to address the sort of problems that arises from this type of issue. The burden was on the defence to show, on the balance of probabilities, the applicant would suffer serious prejudice to such an extent that a trial would not be fair.

In that case, two women had been the victims of attempted rape and indecent assault. Thirteen years later D was arrested for an unrelated matter and found to match the DNA profile of the assailant. In the meantime, most of the paperwork and exhibits for the original investigation had been lost. New statements were taken from the victims, police officers and other witnesses. The Court held that if there was sufficiently credible evidence, apart from the missing evidence, on which a jury properly directed could convict, then the trial should proceed. Simon LJ (at [30]) said that the trial judge was:

> . . . plainly correct in her conclusion that the DNA analysis was a firm evidential basis for the prosecution case. The defence was able to put before the jury the agreed facts in relation to the missing evidence, 'the holes in the prosecution case' to use the phrase of Brooke LJ in *Ebrahim*. They were able to cross-examine as to why material was mislaid or was otherwise no longer available. They were able to address the jury on these matters, and there was nothing in the missing evidence which *might 'taint' the DNA evidence.*

In *Ali v CPS* [2007] EWCA Crim 691, the Court of Appeal emphasised that the mere fact that missing material might have assisted the defence will not necessarily lead to a stay. In considering whether or not to order a stay, the court will have regard to whether there is sufficiently credible evidence, apart from the missing evidence, leaving the defence to exploit the gaps left by the missing evidence. Moses LJ said (at [30]) that the 'rationale for refusing a stay is the existence of credible evidence, itself untainted by what has gone missing'.

The principles relevant to cases involving lost evidence were helpfully summarised by Gross LJ in *DPP v Fell* [2013] EWHC 562 (Admin) (at [15]), emphasising that a stay is to be granted only in exceptional cases:

> The party seeking a stay must make good to the civil standard that, owing to the missing evidence, he will suffer serious prejudice to the extent that no fair trial can be held and that, accordingly, the continuance of the prosecution would amount to a misuse of the process of the court.

His lordship added that the grant of the stay in a case where it is not suggested that there has been serious culpability or bad faith on the part of the prosecutor or investigator 'is, effectively, a measure of last resort. It caters for and only for those cases which cannot be accommodated with all their imperfections within the trial process.' It would, however, be 'a very different situation' if evidence had gone missing through serious culpability or bad faith.

The ability of the trial process to counteract potential unfairness is a very important consideration.

Failure to Disclose Evidence

Failure on the part of the prosecution to comply with the disclosure obligations created by the CPIA 1996, ss. 3 and 7A, may (in appropriate cases) amount to an abuse of process. However, in *DPP v Petrie* [2015] EWHC 48 (Admin), Gross LJ (at [39]) noted that, in some cases, 'a wholesale failure on the part of the prosecution to comply with its disclosure obligations may require the prosecution to offer no evidence, in accordance with the professional code for prosecutors and the guidance set out in the CPS/ACPO Disclosure Manual'. His lordship observed that the 'possibility of such an outcome serves to illuminate that only rarely will recourse to an abuse of process argument be necessary or appropriate'. Some of the relevant factors to be taken into account when deciding whether non-disclosure amounts to abuse of process were considered in *Salt* [2015] EWCA Crim 662, [2015] 1 WLR 4905; they included the gravity of the charges, the denial of justice to the complainants, the necessity for proper attention to be paid to disclosure, the nature and materiality of the failures, the conduct of the defence, the waste of court resources, the effect on the jury and the availability of sanctions other than halting proceedings. **D3.88**

Going Back on a Promise, Legitimate Expectation and Double Jeopardy

In *Croydon Justices, ex parte Dean* [1993] QB 769, Staughton LJ said (at p. 778) that 'the prosecution of a person who has received a promise, undertaking or representation from the police that he will not be prosecuted is *capable* of being an abuse of process' (emphasis added). In such circumstances, it is not necessary for the accused to show that there was bad faith on the part of the police. **D3.89**

An example of a prosecution change of mind amounting to an abuse of process is *Bloomfield* [1997] 1 Cr App R 135. D was charged with possession of a Class A controlled drug. At a preliminary hearing, prosecuting counsel indicated to the defence that the Crown wished to offer no evidence because it was accepted that D had been the victim of a set-up. Owing to the presence in court of certain people, it would have been embarrassing to the police and prosecution if no evidence had been offered that day, so counsel spoke to the judge in his room. An order was then made in open court to adjourn the case and relist it 'for mention'. The CPS subsequently arranged a conference with new prosecuting counsel and informed the defence that there had been a change of plan and that the Crown intended to continue the prosecution against D. It was held by the Court of Appeal that allowing the prosecution to go ahead amounted to an abuse of process since, whether or not there was prejudice to the accused, it would bring the administration of justice into disrepute if the Crown were permitted to revoke its original decision, particularly as it had been made in the presence of the judge (per Staughton LJ at p. 143).

D3.90 **Cautions** The administration of a caution may lead to a subsequent prosecution being held to be an abuse of process. In *Jones v Whalley* [2006] UKHL 41, [2007] 1 AC 63 (see **D2.23**), a private prosecution was held to be an abuse of process because D had previously been cautioned by the police for the offence in question, and the terms of the caution had said, expressly, that he would not have to go before a criminal court in connection with the matter. The House of Lords observed that allowing a private prosecution to proceed, despite an assurance that the offender would not have to go to court, would tend to undermine not only the non-statutory system of cautions, but also the statutory schemes for cautioning young offenders and adult offenders (per Lord Rodger of Earlsferry at [25]). Their lordships also noted that the abuse complained of was not abuse impairing the fairness of the trial (since evidence of D's admission to the offence, and of the caution administered by the police, could be excluded), but went to the fairness of trying D at all (per Lord Bingham at [13]). The same principles apply to young offenders.

D3.91 In *DPP v Alexander* [2010] EWHC 2266 (Admin), [2011] 1 WLR 653, the Divisional Court considered the effect of a caution in the context of the doctrine of autrefois (see **D12.20** *et seq.*). Stanley Burnton LJ said (at [6]):

> A caution is not a conviction for the purposes of those defences, notwithstanding that a caution will only be administered if the accused person admits his guilt. The principles of autrefois convict and autrefois acquit are applicable only where there has been a finding by a court of guilt or innocence. They have no application to an extra-judicial procedure, such as the administration of a simple caution

However, his lordship went on to say (at [9]) that, where criminal conduct has been the subject of an agreed caution, 'in the absence of good reason for it to be the subject of a subsequent prosecution, such a prosecution will generally constitute an abuse of the process of the court'. He added that examples of cases where a prosecution might be justified despite the earlier administration of caution include instances where information or evidence is obtained subsequent to the caution (e.g., details of injury to a victim significantly exceeding what had previously been known). In *R (Lowden) v Gateshead Magistrates' Court* [2016] EWHC 3536 (Admin), [2017] 2 Cr App R 1 (1), Blake J reiterated (at [54]) that the existence of a simple caution administered by the police or the CPS is not in itself a bar to a private prosecution being brought, but it may be an abuse of process for a private prosecution to be brought if an assurance was given in the course of administering the caution that there would be no prosecution.

D3.92 **Fixed Penalty Notices** The application of the doctrine of abuse to cases which have been dealt with by way of fixed penalty notices was considered in *Gore* [2009] EWCA Crim 1424, [2009] 1 WLR 2454, where the two accused had each received a fixed penalty notice for public disorder. The following day, the police reviewed the CCTV evidence of the incident and decided that the fixed penalty notices were inappropriate, arrested the two accused and charged them with inflicting grievous bodily harm. The Court of Appeal ruled that there had been no improper escalation of charge, nor any departure from any reasonable expectation that the accused would not be prosecuted, where more serious consequences of their conduct and evidence justifying prosecution for an offence of violence came to light after the issue of the notice (per Lord Judge CJ at [16]).

In *R (Gavigan) v Enfield Magistrates' Court* [2013] EWHC 2805 (Admin), the accused received fixed penalty notices but, rather than paying the fixed penalty, they indicated that they wished the matter to be dealt with by a court. The decision was then taken to prosecute them for the offence (rather than dealing with the matter as a contested fixed penalty notice). This had the consequence that, if convicted, the accused were liable to a custodial sentence. However, Mitting J said (at [15]) that there is 'simply no principle or policy reason that requires that a person, who has rejected the opportunity to pay a fixed penalty ... should not thereafter be prosecuted for any offence arising out of the same set of facts for those in respect of which the notice was issued'.

Prosecution Changes of Mind Giving an indication that the case will be dropped does not necessarily mean that it will be an abuse of process for the prosecution to have a change of mind. In *Mulla* [2003] EWCA Crim 1881, [2004] 1 Cr App R 6 (72), D was charged with causing death by dangerous driving. On the morning of the first day of the trial, the prosecution indicated that they would be willing to accept a plea of guilty to careless driving. The judge was dissatisfied with the decision and asked the prosecutor to reconsider. In the afternoon, after having reconsidered the matter, the prosecution indicated that they had decided to proceed with the original charge of causing death by dangerous driving. The Court of Appeal held that this did not amount to an abuse of process. This was not a case in which D's hopes were raised, later to be dashed, since he knew from the beginning of the proceedings in court that the judge did not approve of the course which the prosecution were proposing to take. The Court said that factors to be considered include what view is expressed by the judge when the prosecution gives its indication, the period of time over which the prosecution reconsider the matter before they change their mind, whether or not the accused's hopes have been inappropriately raised, and whether there has been, by reason of the change of course by the prosecution, any prejudice to the defence (per Rose LJ at [22]). **D3.93**

In *Abu Hamza* [2006] EWCA Crim 2918, [2007] QB 659, the Court of Appeal said that, where a person has been told he will not be prosecuted for an offence, 'it is not likely to constitute an abuse of process to proceed with a prosecution unless (i) there has been an unequivocal representation by those with the conduct of the investigation or prosecution of a case that the defendant will not be prosecuted and (ii) the defendant has acted on that representation to his detriment. Even then, if facts come to light which were not known when the representation was made, these may justify proceeding with the prosecution despite the representation' (per Lord Phillips CJ at [54]). His lordship added (at [51]) that 'it is usually in the public interest that those who are reasonably suspected of criminal conduct should be brought to trial. Only in rare circumstances will it be offensive to justice to give effect to this public interest.' Similarly, in *Killick* [2011] EWCA Crim 1608, [2012] 1 Cr App R 10 (121), Thomas LJ noted (at [43]) that there must be 'a clear unequivocal representation ... upon which the defendant relies to his detriment'. Even then, however, 'there can be circumstances where, even in that situation, it would not be an abuse of process to proceed'. **D3.94**

A key question is whether the accused has been treated unjustly. In *DPP v B* [2008] EWHC 201 (Admin), D originally faced a single charge of sexual assault. However, when he appeared before the Crown Court, the judge considered that the single count failed to reflect the criminality which was alleged against D, the complainant having alleged that she had been sexually abused by D over a period of years. The prosecution subsequently sought to bring 17 charges of sexual assault against D, to reflect the years over which the sexual abuse had occurred. The Divisional Court held that this did not amount to an abuse of process. Latham LJ pointed out (at [10]) that proceedings should be stayed for abuse of process only 'in very exceptional circumstances, where it can properly be said that the consequence would be injustice, or where the circumstances giving rise to the proceedings in respect of which the application is made offend one's sense of justice overall'. His lordship accepted (at [12]) that D was clearly at risk of a substantially greater sentence than he would have been under the original charge, but said that this was not unjust since D was not going to be exposed to any sentence other than the proper sentence that should be imposed for the offences which were established (whether through guilty pleas or following trial) against him. By contrast, *CPS v Mattu* [2009] EWCA Crim 1483 concerned a detailed 'basis of plea' which had been agreed upon and approved by the court. It was held that it would be an abuse of process to prosecute related matters where the case advanced by the prosecution was wholly inconsistent with that basis of plea. In the instant case, the basis of plea was comprehensive and carefully drafted, with the prosecution involved in agreeing its terms for submission to the court; the judge considered it to be a suitable basis for sentence and proceeded to sentence. The basis of plea had therefore achieved a status which precluded the prosecution from attempting to go behind it (per Pill LJ at [19]). However, his lordship observed (at [20]) **D3.95** that 'there will be cases, where, for example, fresh evidence emerges and circumstances change, in which it may be possible for the prosecution to circumvent a basis of plea they have agreed'.

D3.96 Another important aspect of abuse of process is whether the decision to prosecute is inconsistent with a *legitimate* expectation held by the accused. In *LM* [2010] EWCA Crim 2327, [2011] 1 Cr App R 12 (135), Hughes LJ said (at [15]) that:

> Criminal courts in England and Wales do not decide whether a person ought to be prosecuted or not. They decide whether an offence has been committed. They may, however, also have to decide whether a legal process to which a person is entitled, or to which he has a legitimate expectation, has been neglected to his disadvantage.

In *Antoine* [2014] EWCA Crim 1971, [2015] 1 Cr App R 8 (81), D pleaded guilty to charges of possession of a firearm, and possession of ammunition without a certificate. He was subsequently charged with possession of a prohibited firearm and possession of a firearm following a detention and training order. The question on appeal was whether the prosecution for the latter offences should have been stayed as an abuse of process, given that D had already been convicted and sentenced for lesser offences arising out of the same facts. Thirlwall J, giving the judgment of the Court of Appeal, said (at [31]) that this 'was not an escalation from minor charges to more serious charges', but rather was 'a move from misconceived charges to correct charges'. Her ladyship went on to say (at [33] and [34]):

> We have no hesitation in concluding that the judge was justified in finding that there were special circumstances here which required that the prosecution continue. The court's sense of justice and propriety was not offended nor was public confidence in the criminal justice system undermined. On the contrary, a stay would have brought the criminal justice system into disrepute.
>
> We have made it plain that we accept that serious mistakes were made but there was no bad faith and the mistakes were rectified within a very short time. The fact that the fault lay with the Crown Prosecution Service did not require the grant of a stay, given the circumstances of this case.

D3.97 In *Dowty* [2011] EWCA Crim 3138 and *Killick* [2011] EWCA Crim 1608, [2012] 1 Cr App R 10 (121), the Court of Appeal referred to what is now para. 10 of the Code for Crown Prosecutors (see **appendix 3**), which says that occasionally there may be reasons why the CPS will overturn a decision not to prosecute or when it will re-start a prosecution, particularly if the case is serious. The examples given include cases where a review of the original decision shows that it was wrong and, in order to maintain confidence in the criminal justice system, a prosecution should be brought despite the earlier decision, and cases which are stopped because of a lack of evidence but where more significant evidence is discovered later. It is submitted that a decision taken in accordance with the Code is unlikely to be overturned by the courts.

D3.98 It should be noted, however, that a 'prosecution which did not constitute an abuse of process at the date of conviction cannot acquire that characteristic, on the basis of new or amended prosecutorial guidance or policy subsequently issued' (*A (RJ)* [2012] EWCA Crim 434, [2012] 2 Cr App R 8 (80), per Lord Judge CJ at [86]).

D3.99 Given that a victim of an alleged offence has a right to ask the CPS to review a decision not to prosecute the alleged perpetrator, it is inevitable that some decisions not to prosecute a suspect will be reversed. In *R (S) v CPS* [2015] EWHC 2868 (Admin), [2016] 1 WLR 804, for example, D was charged with rape, following the review by the CPS of its earlier decision not to prosecute him. He sought judicial review of the decision to charge. It was argued that the CPS guidance on the review process was unlawful because it provides that a suspect is not to be made aware of a victim's request for a review, and so the suspect has no opportunity to make representations to the independent reviewing prosecutor. The Divisional Court rejected that submission. Sir Brian Leveson P said (at [17]):

> The principal policy reason for this provision in the Guidance is that the Guidance requires the independent prosecutor to take account only of information available at the time of the decision under review. That information will include any explanation put forward by the suspect/defendant in the course of the investigation prior to the decision under review. Natural justice does not

> require a decision maker who is assessing only pre-existing material and who is prohibited from taking into account new evidence or information from the party seeking the review to invite a response from a third party who may be affected by the result of the review. The Guidance is a lawful policy in its entirety.

His lordship went on to say (at [28]) that a decision to prosecute in such a case will almost invariably be upheld if it is challenged by way of judicial review, given the existence of other remedies:

> If it is alleged that the prosecution is an abuse of process, the trial judge will determine it. Deficiencies in the evidence can be exposed either at dismissal proceedings or at the close of the prosecution case. Suffice to say that I consider it difficult to conceive any circumstance in which the type of decision made in this case might be subject to successful judicial review.

Immunity from Prosecution The SOCPA 2005, s. 71, makes provision for immunity from prosecution. It provides that, if a specified prosecutor (i.e. the DPP, the Director of the SFO, the Financial Conduct Authority, the Prudential Regulation Authority (in the case of the investigations under the FSMA 2000), the Bank of England and the Secretary of State for Business, Energy and Industrial Strategy, or a prosecutor acting on their behalf) thinks that, for the purposes of the investigation or prosecution of any offence, it is appropriate to offer any person immunity from prosecution, he or she may give the person a written 'immunity notice' (s. 71(1)). A person who has been given such a notice cannot be prosecuted for an offence of a description specified in the notice unless he or she fails to comply with any of the conditions specified in the notice, in which case the notice ceases to have effect (s. 71(2) and (3)). Given the clear statutory wording, a court would have little option but to regard a prosecution brought in breach of s. 71 as an abuse of process. The issue of immunity notices is restricted to indictable and either-way offences (s. 71(1)). **D3.100**

Modern Slavery Act 2015, s. 45 In *DS* [2020] EWCA Crim 285, the Court of Appeal noted (at [18]) that, where an accused may have a defence under the Modern Slavery Act 2015, s. 45(4) (defence for victims of slavery or trafficking who commit an offence), a prosecutor should consider four questions when applying the Full Code Test in the Code for Crown Prosecutors (see **D2.10**). These are: **D3.101**

(1) whether there is a reason to believe that the person is a victim of trafficking or slavery;
(2) if so, whether there is 'clear evidence of a credible common law defence of duress';
(3) if so, the accused should not be charged or the prosecution should be discontinued; if not, whether there is clear evidence of a statutory defence under s. 45;
(4) if so, then the accused should not be charged or the prosecution should be discontinued; if not, whether it is in the public interest to prosecute.

Even where there is no clear evidence of duress or of a s. 45 defence (or where s. 45 does not apply, because the offence is excluded under sch. 4), the public interest must be considered, with the prosecutor taking into account all the circumstances of the case, 'including the seriousness of the offence and any direct or indirect compulsion arising from their trafficking situation'. See also **B22.19**.

Manipulation of Procedure

An example of something that may amount to manipulation of procedure is where a charge alleging a summary offence is replaced with one alleging an indictable offence, or vice versa. Paragraph 6.4 of the Code for Crown Prosecutors (see **appendix 3**) makes it clear that the charge should not be changed simply because of the decision made as to trial venue. In *Canterbury and St Augustine Justices, ex parte Klisiak* [1982] QB 398, it was said that the court should interfere with the prosecution's decision as to what offences to proceed upon only 'in the most obvious circumstances which disclose blatant injustice' (per Lord Lane CJ at p. 411). It has to be clear that the change in the charge is not a bona fide result of a reassessment of the appropriateness of the original charge. It is only appropriate to interfere where the court concludes that the prosecution were acting in bad faith, in the sense of deliberately **D3.102** manipulating the system to deprive an accused of his or her rights (*Sheffield Justices, ex parte DPP* [1993] Crim LR 136).

Another situation where allegations of manipulation can be made is where the accused is charged with a different offence at the time when the custody time-limit for the original offence is about to expire (or has expired), so that a new custody time-limit starts to run. In *R (Wardle) v Leeds Crown Court* [2001] UKHL 12, [2002] 1 AC 754, for example, a murder charge was replaced with a manslaughter charge when the custody time-limit was about to expire. Their lordships held that the bringing of a new charge would be an abuse of process if the bringing of that charge cannot be justified on the facts of the case by the prosecutor and the court is satisfied that it has been brought solely with a view to obtaining the substitution of a fresh custody time-limit (per Lord Hope of Craighead at [99]).

In *Wokingham Borough Council v Scott* [2019] EWCA Crim 205, [2020] 4 WLR 2, the Court of Appeal had to consider an abuse of process claim based on the fact that the prosecutor (a local authority) intended to seek a confiscation order under the POCA 2002, in which case, the prosecuting authority 'would have received 37½% of the fruits of the order', suggesting an inference that the authority was seeking to prosecute the defendants 'to claw back public money already expended on the case' (see [31]). Hallett LJ (at [63]) acknowledged that a confiscation order may act as a deterrent to offending but noted a potential conflict of interest arising from a financial interest in the outcome of the prosecution, saying that:

> . . .the prosecutor must be scrupulous in avoiding any perception of bias. The possibility of a [confiscation] order being made in the prosecutor's favour should play no part in the determination of the evidential and public interest test within the Code for Crown Prosecutors.

In the present case, however, there was also a question as to whether the possibility of a confiscation order was in fact necessary in order to deter further breaches of the relevant planning regulations. Hallett LJ (at [64]) observed that a deterrent effect appeared to have been achieved already through civil injunctive proceedings:

> On the facts of this case, given we have heard nothing to justify the decision to prosecute at least ten of the defendants after the injunctive relief was granted and [D] was made subject to a suspended sentence of imprisonment, it raises the distinct possibility that making of a POCA order in [the local authority's] favour was one of the grounds for the decision to prosecute them. If it was, it should not have been. As far as [D] is concerned, there may be a stronger argument that a POCA order generally was a legitimate consideration as a deterrent to continued breaches of planning controls, but we note that after the committal proceedings, any failure to comply with the enforcement notice could be met by a sentence of imprisonment. There were no further breaches and one must question what deterrent effect a POCA order might have.

In *R (Kombou) v Crown Court at Wood Green* [2020] EWHC 1529, the Adminisrative Court reiterated (at [84]) that a prosecuting authority must be 'scrupulous to ensure that a decision to prosecute is not motivated, and does not appear to be motivated, by the prospect of financial gain'. However, the Court added (at [85]) that:

> It is not. . . the case that a decision to prosecute will inevitably be open to successful challenge if it might eventually lead to a confiscation order from which the prosecuting authority will benefit. . . . There is a crucial distinction between investigators legitimately considering the possibility of confiscation proceedings, and the decision-maker being improperly motivated to decide in favour of prosecution by the prospect of financial gain to the authority.

It is submitted that one way of refuting a suggestion of bias or improper motives might be for the prosecuting authority to ensure that it documents carefully the basis upon which it was decided that there was sufficient evidence to give rise to a realistic prospect of conviction and that it was *in the public interest to prosecute.*

Abuse of process can also be used in cases which fall just outside the scope of the autrefois principle but where it would nonetheless be unfair to allow a further prosecution to take place. For example, in *Beedie* [1998] QB 356, D was charged with offences under health and safety legislation and, following his conviction, he was charged with manslaughter arising out of the same facts. The Court of Appeal ruled that it was an abuse of process to have sequential trials for offences on an ascending scale of gravity. In *J (JF)* [2013] EWCA Crim 569, [2014] QB 561, Sir John Thomas P said (at [29]) that, in any case where the narrow application of the autrefois principle would result in unfairness or injustice to an accused to the extent of amounting to oppression, 'the remedy lies in the power of the court to stay the proceedings'.

Entrapment

In *A-G's Ref (No. 3 of 2000) (Looseley)* [2001] UKHL 53, [2001] 1 WLR 2060, the House of Lords said that, although entrapment is not a substantive defence in English law, where an accused can show entrapment, the court may stay the proceedings as an abuse of the court's process or it may exclude evidence pursuant to the PACE 1984, s. 78. Of these two remedies, the grant of stay (rather than the exclusion of evidence at the trial) should normally be regarded as the appropriate response, since a prosecution founded on entrapment would be an abuse of the court's process. Police conduct which brings about state-created crime is unacceptable and improper, and to prosecute in such circumstances would be an affront to the public conscience. However, if the accused already had the intent to commit a crime of the same or a similar kind, and the police did no more than give the accused the opportunity to fulfil that existing intent, that is unobjectionable (per Lord Nicholls of Birkenhead at [19] and [21]). A useful guide is to consider whether the police did no more than present the accused with an unexceptional opportunity to commit a crime. The yardstick for the purposes of this test is, in general, whether the police conduct preceding the commission of the offence was no more than might have been expected from others in the circumstances ([23]). As Lord Hutton put it (at [101]), particular emphasis is placed on the need: **D3.103**

> ... to consider whether a person has been persuaded or pressurised by a law enforcement officer into committing a crime which he would not otherwise have committed, or whether the officer did not go beyond giving the person an opportunity to break the law, when he would have behaved in the same way if some other person had offered him the opportunity to commit a similar crime, and when he freely took advantage of the opportunity presented to him by the officer.

Ultimately, however, the overall consideration is always whether the conduct of the police or other law enforcement agency was so seriously improper as to bring the administration of justice into disrepute (Lord Nicholls at [25]). In applying this test, the court has regard to all the circumstances of the case, including those listed by Lord Nicholls at [26]–[28]: (a) the nature of the offence (the use of proactive techniques is more appropriate in some circumstances than others, depending on secrecy and difficulty of detection, and the manner in which the particular criminal activity is carried on); (b) the reason for the particular police operation (having reasonable grounds for suspicion is one way good faith may be established, but having grounds for suspicion of a particular individual was not always essential); (c) the nature and extent of police participation in the crime (the greater the inducement held out by the police, and the more forceful or persistent the police overtures, the more readily might a court conclude that the police overstepped the boundary). It is also clear from this case that there is no appreciable difference between the requirements of Article 6 (or the Strasbourg jurisprudence on Article 6, such as *Teixeira de Castro v Portugal* (1999) 28 EHRR 101: see **A7.37**) and English law.

In *M* [2011] EWCA Crim 648, Stanley Burnton LJ said (at [15]) that there 'may be a difficult line to draw between legitimate police conduct and improper entrapment. In general, however, conduct that is open to a finding of such entrapment as to render a prosecution improper involves some pressure or persuasion on the defendant to commit the crime. Providing the opportunity for the commission of the crime will not of itself lead to a finding of entrapment.' His lordship concluded (at [18]) that it is: **D3.104**

> ... an inherent aspect of any undercover police operation that the undercover police officer insinuates himself into the confidence of those involved in the criminal conduct at which the operation

is directed. For an officer who has so insinuated himself to offer an opportunity to a defendant to commit a criminal offence, in the absence of persuasion or pressure or the offer of a significant inducement, will not generally result in its being an abuse of the process to prosecute the person who takes that opportunity to commit an offence.

The principles to be applied where entrapment is alleged were set out *Moore* [2013] EWCA Crim 85. Rix LJ referred (at [52]) to Professor Ormerod's article, 'Recent Developments in Entrapment' [2006] Covert Policing Review 65, and noted that Professor Ormerod identifies five factors as of particular relevance: (i) reasonable suspicion of criminal activity as a legitimate trigger for the police operation (a control mechanism for testing the police's good faith); (ii) authorisation and supervision of the operation as a legitimate control mechanism (to ensure proper control of the operation); (iii) necessity and proportionality of the means employed to police particular types of offence; (iv) the concepts of 'unexceptional opportunity' and causation; and (v) authentication of the evidence (i.e. of the conversations and contacts).

Another example is *Palmer* [2014] EWCA Crim 1681, where the police set up a covert operation in which local criminals could incriminate themselves by selling stolen property to officers who posed as the operators of a dishonest pawnshop business. Arrests were made only once a large number of offenders had incriminated themselves over a period of several months. Hallett LJ said (at [79]):

> ... These were commercial premises open to the public; no-one was forced or badgered into entering them. The officers were instructed on how to behave, and reminded repeatedly of their obligations. Everything relevant was recorded and retained. The operation was constantly monitored and the officers properly supervised. The Surveillance Commissioner was satisfied there was nothing untoward in what they were doing. The operation may have lasted for over a year but that was to be expected given its scale and the fact that the officers had to build up trade and develop the confidence of those with stolen property to sell. The length of the operation overall was not excessive in all the circumstances.

The Court of Appeal therefore rejected the defence argument on entrapment, holding that there had been 'no affront to justice' (at [80]).

In *Syed* [2018] EWCA Crim 2809, the Court of Appeal rejected the argument that *Looseley* is incompatible with the jurisprudence of the ECtHR. Gross LJ (at [108]) observed that:

> ...the rationale is essentially the same, in both approaches. It involves a concern for the integrity of the criminal justice system. Ends do not necessarily justify means. Criminal proceedings amounting to an affront to the public conscience on account of the improper conduct of state agents may be stayed. Were it otherwise, the administration of justice would be brought into disrepute. In the context of entrapment, the Court must stand between the state and its citizens. Equally however, the Court understands the public interest in combating crime and bringing criminals to justice; it recognises the need for intrusive techniques including undercover operations to do so, especially in the context of serious crime. Therefore, the use of undercover techniques could not of themselves infringe the right to a fair trial. But the right to a fair trial must not be sacrificed on grounds of expediency. Accordingly, as a matter of striking the correct balance between these competing and profoundly important interests, there are limits as to what is acceptable by way of police, intelligence or security work and safeguards must be in place.

Moreover, 'working definitions of entrapment are essentially the same' in the approach taken in both domestic law and Strasbourg jurisprudence (at [109]).

Arguments relating to entrapment are generally confined to cases involving actions by the police or other 'official' investigators. However, in *TL* [2018] EWCA Crim 1821, [2018] 1 WLR 6037, it was argued that the actions of a 'paedophile hunter', U, amounted to entrapment and so justified a stay on the ground of abuse of process. Lord Burnett CJ noted (at [31]) that the principles explained in *Looseley* 'apply to the conduct of agents of the state. Involvement of agents of the state in unacceptable behaviour is at the heart of the reasoning.

It is the court's unwillingness to approbate seriously wrongful conduct by the state, by entertaining a prosecution, that is the foundation of this aspect of the abuse jurisdiction.' However, 'the conduct of a private citizen may in theory found a stay of proceedings as an abuse of process'. A prosecution needs evidence, and 'it is not inconceivable that, given sufficiently gross misconduct by a private citizen, it would be an abuse of the court's process (and a breach of article 6) for the state to seek to rely on the product of that misconduct' (at [32]). His lordship cited with approval the judgment of Goldring J in *Council for the Regulation of Health Care Professionals v General Medical Council* [2006] EWHC 2784 (Admin), [2007] 1 WLR 3094 (at [81]):

> [G]iven sufficiently gross misconduct by the non-state agent, it would be an abuse of the court's process (and a breach of Article 6) for the state to seek to rely on the resulting evidence. In other words, so serious would the conduct of the non-state agent have to be that reliance upon it in the court's proceedings would compromise the court's integrity.

Lord Burnett went on to say (at [35]) that a 'starting point in considering whether the conduct of a private citizen should result in a stay of proceedings is to ask whether the same, or similar, conduct by a police officer would do so'. On the facts of the instant case, if police officers 'had engaged in broadly similar conduct an application to stay the proceedings as an abuse of process should have failed' (at [37]). There was nothing in U's conduct that made it inappropriate for the prosecution to proceed (at [39]).

Abuse of Executive Power

In *Horseferry Road Magistrates' Court, ex parte Bennett* [1994] 1 AC 42, D had been brought back forcibly to the UK in disregard of extradition procedures that were available. This was held to amount to an abuse of process even though a fair trial was possible. The point was that D should not have been before the court in the first place. **D3.105**

Likewise, in *Mullen* [2000] QB 520, the security services and police had procured D's unlawful deportation from Zimbabwe. The Court of Appeal ruled that, even if no complaint can be made as to the fairness of the trial itself, unconscionable conduct on the part of the authorities in bringing the accused before the court *may* amount to an abuse of process. However, it is not invariably an abuse of process, since every case should be approached on its own facts. There may be cases where the 'seriousness of the crime is so great relative to the nature of the abuse of process that it would be a proper exercise of judicial discretion to permit a prosecution to proceed or to allow a conviction to stand notwithstanding an abuse of process in relation to the defendant's presence within the jurisdiction' (per Rose LJ at pp. 536–7).

This was the approach adopted by the House of Lords in *Latif* [1996] 1 All ER 353. D was convicted of being knowingly concerned in the importation into the UK of heroin which had been brought into the country by an undercover customs officer. The House of Lords held that whether the proceedings should have been stayed on the ground of abuse was a matter of discretion for the judge, who had to decide whether the matters said to constitute abuse of process amounted to what Lord Steyn described (at p. 112) as an 'affront to the public conscience'. His lordship added that this requires the judge to balance the public interest in ensuring that those who are charged with serious crimes should be tried against the competing public interest in not conveying the impression that the court will adopt the approach that the end justifies any means (p. 113). In the instant case, the judge had been entitled to conclude that the proceedings should not be stayed; for similar reasons, the judge had not erred in not exercising his discretion to exclude the core of the prosecution case.

In cases such as these, a stay will be granted where the court concludes that, in all the circumstances, a trial will 'offend the court's sense of justice and propriety' (per Lord Lowry in *Ex parte Bennett*, at p. 74G) or will 'undermine public confidence in the criminal justice system and bring it into disrepute' (per Lord Steyn in *Latif*, at p. 112F).

D3.106 In *Ahmed* [2011] EWCA Crim 184 (a case where D had allegedly been subject to torture outside the UK), Hughes LJ said (at [24]) that the jurisdiction to stay for abuse of process may be exercised 'where, by reason of gross executive misconduct manipulating the process of the court, the defendant has been deprived of the protection of the rule of law and it would as a result be unfair to put him on trial at all'. His lordship added that 'the jurisdiction does not exist to discipline the police or other executive arms of the State (although of course it will incidentally do so), but rather to protect the integrity of the processes of justice'. The Court of Appeal upheld the refusal of a stay on the basis that the judge had been right to hold that what is required is a connection between the alleged wrongdoing and the trial. In *Ahmed*, no evidence which was the product of torture or other ill-treatment was adduced at the trial, and the investigation did not amount, directly or indirectly, to employing the product of torture to make a case against D (at [39]).

Bringing Justice into Disrepute

D3.107 Closely related to abuse of executive power are cases where the investigators have behaved in a way that is wholly improper. In *Grant* [2005] EWCA Crim 1089, [2006] QB 60, for example, the police unlawfully recorded privileged conversations between D and his legal adviser. No useful evidence was gathered in this way, and so there was nothing to exclude under the PACE 1984, s. 78. The Court of Appeal said that such unlawful acts, amounting as they did to a deliberate violation of a suspect's right to legal professional privilege, were 'so great an affront to the integrity of the justice system, and therefore the rule of law, that the associated prosecution was thereby rendered abusive and ought not to be countenanced by the court' (per Laws LJ at [54]), despite the absence of any actual prejudice to the accused. (As to covert surveillance and the RIPA 2000, see *McE v Prison Service of Northern Ireland* [2009] UKHL 15, [2009] 1 AC 908 at **D1.58**.)

D3.108 However, in *Warren v A-G for Jersey* [2011] UKPC 10, [2012] 1 AC 22, the Privy Council said that the decision in *Grant* was wrong (per Lord Dyson, at [36]). This was because it was 'difficult to avoid the conclusion that in *Grant* the proceedings were stayed in order to express the court's disapproval of the police misconduct and to discipline the police', which is an impermissible use of the power to stay proceedings. Lord Dyson referred to an earlier decision of the Supreme Court, *Maxwell* [2010] UKSC 48, [2011] 1 WLR 1837 (a case involving serious misconduct by the police), where he had said (at [13]) that:

> It is well established that the court has the power to stay proceedings in two categories of case, namely (i) where it will be impossible to give the accused a fair trial, and (ii) where it offends the court's sense of justice and propriety to be asked to try the accused in the particular circumstances of the case. In the first category of case, if the court concludes that an accused cannot receive a fair trial, it will stay the proceedings without more. No question of the balancing of competing interests arises. In the second category of case, the court is concerned to protect the integrity of the criminal justice system ...

Warren involved illegal cross-border audio surveillance and so fell within the second category of case. The arguments for and against a stay were set out by Lord Dyson SJC at [46]–[50]. The case for a stay was 'of considerable weight': the misconduct was very serious (it involved misleading the Jersey Attorney-General and the Chief of Police, and the authorities of three foreign States) and, without the product of the unlawfulness, there would have been no trial. However, there were also factors which, taken cumulatively, 'weighed heavily against a stay': the offence was very serious; the ringleader 'was a professional drug dealer of the first order'; the 'unwise' advice of the Crown Advocate mitigated, to some extent, the gravity of the misconduct of the police; there had been no attempt to mislead the Jersey court; and there was 'real urgency' in the case and it was 'in these circumstances that the police cut corners and acted unlawfully'. Lord Kerr (at [83]) went on to summarise some of the principles which have emerged from recent case law on abuse of process:

> (i) [A stay in the second category of case] should be granted where necessary to protect the integrity of the criminal justice system.

(ii) A balancing of interests should be conducted in deciding whether a stay is required to fulfil this primary purpose... [W]here a stay is being considered in order to protect the integrity of the criminal justice system, 'the public interest in ensuring that those that are charged with grave crimes should be tried' will always weigh in the balance [per Lord Steyn in *Latif* [1996] 1 All ER 353 at p. 113A-B, who] mentioned that a possible counter-vailing factor was that the impression should not be created that the court is giving its sanction to an approach that the end justifies any means. With the emphasis that is given in this and other cases to statements that prosecutorial or police misbehaviour will never be condoned, this may not be as significant a consideration as heretofore...

(iii) The 'but for' factor (i.e. where it can be shown that the defendant would not have stood trial but for executive abuse of power) is merely one of various matters that will influence the outcome of the inquiry as to whether a stay should be granted. It is not necessarily determinative of that issue.

(iv) A stay should not be ordered for the purpose of punishing or disciplining prosecutorial or police misconduct. The focus should always be on whether the stay is required in order to safeguard the integrity of the criminal justice system.

The approach to be taken in such cases was summarised by the Court of Appeal in *Norman* [2016] EWCA Crim 1564, [2017] 1 Cr App R 8 (75) (at [23]):

> First it must be determined whether and in what respects the prosecutorial authorities have been guilty of misconduct. Secondly it must be determined whether such misconduct justifies staying the proceedings as an abuse. This second stage requires an evaluation which weighs in the balance the public interest in ensuring that those charged with crimes should be tried against the competing public interest in maintaining confidence in the criminal justice system and not giving the impression that the end will always be treated as justifying any means. How the discretion will be exercised will depend upon the particular circumstances of each case, including such factors as the seriousness of the violation of the accused's rights; whether the police have acted in bad faith or maliciously; whether the misconduct was committed in circumstances of urgency, emergency or necessity; the availability of a sanction against the person(s) responsible for the misconduct; and the seriousness of the offence with which the accused is charged. These are merely examples of factors which may be relevant. Each case is fact specific.

In *Tague v Governor of HM Prison, Full Sutton* [2015] EWHC 3576 (Admin), [2016] 1 Cr App R 15 (209), D had absconded during his trial in 2000 and fled to Spain. He was convicted in his absence and in 2013 he was extradited to England pursuant to a European Arrest Warrant. He alleged that his extradition from Spain had been tainted by abuse of process, in that the order for extradition had been conditional upon the UK acknowledging and agreeing that, once surrendered, he would be entitled to a re-trial. That was not possible and the SOCA (whose functions have since been taken over by the NCA) had been negligent in agreeing to such a condition. Rejecting an application for habeas corpus, the Divisional Court ruled that the SOCA's conduct could not be characterised as so serious that to require D to serve the sentence of imprisonment imposed upon him after a trial in which he took full part would constitute an affront to justice or undermine the confidence of the public in the justice system. Rather, it was clear that the public would consider the converse to be a more accurate description of the case. It should be noted that counsel for the NCA had conceded that the doctrine of abuse of process could be extended to events which took place after the trial. The Court proceeded on the basis of that concession, making it clear that it was not deciding that the doctrine of abuse could be so extended. Given that a key function of the doctrine of abuse of process is to protect the integrity of the criminal justice system, it is submitted that it is appropriate that this doctrine should apply post-conviction.

Private Prosecutions In *R (Dacre) v City of Westminster Magistrates' Court* [2008] EWHC 1667 (Admin), [2009] 1 WLR 2241, the Divisional Court considered abuse in the context of private prosecutions. Latham LJ (at [26]) said that in deciding whether 'it would offend the court's sense of justice for the prosecution to proceed... both motive and conduct can clearly be relevant. As far as motive is concerned, proceedings tainted by *mala fides* or spite or some other oblique motive may fall into this category.' However, he went on to note (at [27]) that it had **D3.109**

been held in *Bow Street Metropolitan Stipendiary Magistrate, ex parte South Coast Shipping Co. Ltd* [1993] QB 645, that the mere presence of an indirect or improper motive in launching a prosecution did not necessarily vitiate it, and the court would be slow to halt such a prosecution in the case of mixed motives unless the conduct was truly oppressive. Drawing an analogy with the principles relating to entrapment in relation to public prosecutions (set out in *A-G's Ref (No. 3 of 2000) (Looseley)* [2001] UKHL 53, [2001] 1 WLR 2060: see **D3.103**), his lordship went on to hold (at [31]) that there is 'no reason in principle why ... a private prosecution should not be considered an abuse of process if the crime which is the subject of the prosecution is one that has been encouraged by the private prosecutor or when in some other way the private prosecutor has essentially created the same mischief as that about which he or she complains'. In *D Ltd v A* [2017] EWCA Crim 1172, the Court reiterated (at [41]) that the 'legal principles relating to stay on the ground of abuse apply in precisely the same way to private prosecutions as they do to public prosecutions', adding (at [59) that it is 'well established that mixed motives do not of themselves necessarily vitiate the prosecution'.

D3.110 **Actions of Third Parties** In *Momodou* [2005] EWCA Crim 177, [2005] 1 WLR 3442, Judge LJ (at [54]) observed that 'notwithstanding that the prosecution or prosecuting authority may be blameless ... [t]he activities of third parties may constitute an abuse of process', although in most cases 'difficulties, even great difficulties, created for the defence are almost always capable of being addressed by the trial process itself', making it unnecessary to halt a prosecution as an abuse (see **D15.103** for further discussion of this case). Whether or not a fair trial is possible is, of course, a fact-specific question: in *Athwal* [2009] EWCA Crim 789, [2009] 1 WLR 2430, the Court of Appeal rejected an argument that refusal by the Legal Services Commission to fund particular inquiries had rendered the trial unfair; in *Crawley* [2014] EWCA Crim 1028, [2014] 2 Cr App R 16 (214), where a stay was overturned in a case where the accused had been unable to find representation because of a refusal by the self-employed Bar to accept the fees which were payable for such work, the Court of Appeal held that other remedies short of a stay could have been deployed.

Procedure for Making Abuse of Process Applications

D3.111 **Crown Court** CrimPR 3.28 (see Supplement, **R3.28**) applies where the accused wants the Crown Court to stay the case on the grounds that the proceedings are an abuse of the court, or are otherwise unfair. The accused must give written notice of the application to the prosecutor (and to any co-accused) and to the court as soon as practicable after becoming aware of the grounds for applying. The application should be dealt with at a pre-trial hearing, unless the grounds for the application do not arise until trial. The application must explain the grounds on which it is made; include or identify all supporting material; specify 'relevant events, dates and propositions of law'; and identify any witness the accused wants to call to give evidence in person. A party who wishes to make representations in opposition to the application must serve written representations on the court and the other parties within ten business days of the service of the application. According to CrimPD I, paras. 3C.3 and 3C.4 (see Supplement, **CPD.3C**), the advocate appearing for the applicant must serve a skeleton argument on the court and on the other parties at least five clear working days before the application is due to be heard, and the prosecution advocate must serve a responsive skeleton argument at least two clear working days before the hearing. The skeleton arguments must set out any propositions of law to be advanced, together with any authorities (identifying specific passages) that are relied on.

D3.112 **Magistrates' Courts** No specific procedure is laid down for raising abuse of process in a magistrates' court, but it is essential that the court hears from both the prosecution and the defence. In *Clerkenwell Stipendiary Magistrate, ex parte Bell* (1991) 159 JP 669, the magistrate heard evidence from a police officer explaining the reason for the delay but declined to hear evidence from the accused. The Divisional Court held that this was a breach of natural justice and quashed the decision to send the accused to the Crown Court for trial. Similarly, in *Crawley Justices, ex parte DPP* (1991) 155 JP 841, the Divisional Court quashed the decision of the justices to dismiss the case because of delay, since the bench had not heard the full facts before coming to their decision.

LEGAL REPRESENTATION AND RIGHTS OF AUDIENCE

Rights of Audience

Under the Legal Services Act 2007, s. 12(1)(a), the exercise of a right of audience is a 'reserved legal activity'. By virtue of s. 13, a person is permitted to carry out a reserved legal activity only if he or she is an 'authorised person' in relation to that activity; under s. 18, an 'authorised person' is someone who is 'authorised to carry on the relevant activity by a relevant approved regulator' (such as the Bar Standards Board or the Solicitors Regulation Authority). **D3.113**

Section 19 exempts certain persons from the requirement to be authorised to conduct particular reserved legal activities. For example, under sch. 3, para. 1(2), a person is exempt if he or she is not an authorised person but has a right of audience granted by the court 'in relation to those proceedings'. In *Southwark Crown Court, ex parte Tawfick* [1995] Crim LR 658, Glidewell LJ, construing a similar provision in earlier legislation, accepted the argument that the statute gave 'any court the power in its discretion to grant to any person a right of audience related to particular proceedings'.

CrimPR 46.2 (see Supplement, **R46.2**) requires a party who is not legally aided to give notice to the court and to each other party, within five business days, of the appointment or dismissal of a legal representative. CrimPR 46.3 (see Supplement, **R46.3**) sets out the procedure to be followed where a party who is legally aided wishes to select a different legal representative to the one named in the legal aid representation order.

The Prosecution in the Crown Court

At common law, the prosecution at a trial on indictment had to be legally represented. In *George Maxwell (Developments) Ltd* [1980] 2 All ER 99, the trial judge ruled that the case would fail for want of prosecution unless the complainant (who had brought a private prosecution) instructed solicitors and counsel (since, once the indictment was signed, the proceedings continued in the name of the Crown). However, in *Southwark Crown Court, ex parte Tawfick* [1995] Crim LR 658, it was said that the discretion which was then conferred on the court by the Courts and Legal Services Act 1990 (and which is now to be found in the Legal Services Act 2007, sch. 3) could be used to allow an unrepresented prosecutor to conduct a prosecution in the Crown Court. However, Glidewell LJ added that the discretion would be exercised only 'occasionally', and that it would be only in 'exceptional circumstances' that a Crown Court judge would allow the complainant to conduct the prosecution case. **D3.114**

The Accused in the Crown Court

The accused is entitled to decline legal representation and present the case in person. If the accused is represented during the initial stages of a trial on indictment and then wishes to dispense with the services of counsel, application to that effect must be made to the trial judge, who has a discretion to refuse to release counsel. It is, however, rare for the accused's application to be refused. In *Lyons* (1979) 68 Cr App R 104, Waller LJ said (at p. 108) that 'it may well be that in the vast majority of cases a judge, faced with an application to dispense with counsel ... would allow the application ... But at the end of the day it is a matter for the discretion of the learned judge.' **D3.115**

The court has a common-law power to prevent an unrepresented accused from cross-examining in an oppressive manner (*Brown* [1998] 2 Cr App R 364). Moreover, the YJCEA 1999, ss. 34 to 39, prohibits unrepresented defendants from cross-examining complainants and child witnesses in trials for certain specified offences, and the court has the power to prohibit cross-examination of witnesses by unrepresented defendants in any other case if satisfied that the quality of evidence given by the witness on cross-examination is likely to be diminished if the cross-examination is conducted or continued by the accused in person, and that a prohibition would not be contrary to the interests of justice. There are provisions for the appointment of representatives to conduct cross-examination on behalf of unrepresented defendants. The procedural aspects of the restriction on cross-examination by an accused acting in person are set out in CrimPR Part 23 (which applies both to the Crown Court and to the magistrates' courts: see Supplement, **R23.1** ***et seq.***).

D3.116 In *Ulcay* [2007] EWCA Crim 2379, [2008] 1 WLR 1209, D changed his instructions at the close of the prosecution case, and his legal representatives withdrew on the grounds of professional embarrassment. The judge refused an application from the new representatives for a two-week adjournment and the new representatives also withdrew. D remained unrepresented during the trial. The Court of Appeal had to decide whether his subsequent conviction was safe. Sir Igor Judge P gave guidance (at [28]) on what should be done by defence counsel where the accused changes instructions during the trial:

> It is for counsel to decide whether, consistent with his obligations to his client, and the court, and the rules of his profession, he is so professionally embarrassed that he cannot continue with the case. If so, again consistent with his duty to the court, but without contravening the legal privilege which underpins his professional relationship with his client, he should inform the court of his situation, providing such explanation as he can, to enable the judge to decide how to proceed. It is difficult to imagine cases in which it would be appropriate for the trial judge to direct counsel that he must continue with a case, or refuse him permission to withdraw on the grounds of professional embarrassment if, having heard counsel explain his position, counsel remains unpersuaded that he may properly continue to act, not least because counsel will almost certainly be better informed than the judge, in particular because there are likely to be considerations which he may be unable to reveal.

His lordship held (at [36]) that, in the circumstances, the judge was entitled to exercise his discretion to refuse the lengthy adjournment sought by counsel, since a lengthy adjournment would have necessitated the discharge of the jury, thereby causing prejudice to the co-accused and public inconvenience and cost (or else trying D separately from his co-accused, with the cost and inconvenience that would involve).

Rights of Audience in the Crown Court

D3.117 By virtue of the regulatory regime established by the Legal Services Act 2007 (see **D3.113**), rights of audience in the Crown Court are conferred upon barristers, and upon solicitors with rights of audience in the higher courts.

Magistrates' Courts

D3.118 In the magistrates' court, neither the prosecutor nor the accused need be legally represented. A private prosecutor, for example, may appear in person, as when the victim of an alleged assault takes out a summons against the assailant and then both argues the case and gives the principal evidence for the prosecution. In the case of police prosecutions, however, the Prosecution of Offences Act 1985, s. 3(2)(a), requires the DPP (through the CPS) to take over the conduct of the prosecution.

Representation in a magistrates' court may be either by counsel or by solicitor, since both have rights of audience. Legal Executives (regulated by the Chartered Institute of Legal Executives) also have a right of audience in magistrates' courts.

Arranging for Legal Representation for the Prosecution

D3.119 It is the responsibility of the CPS to arrange for the prosecution to be legally represented in cases where the DPP has the conduct of the proceedings. Crown Prosecutors commonly represent the

CPS at proceedings in magistrates' courts. For trials on indictment (and, in practice, for appeals to the Crown Court and committals for sentence), the CPS are obliged to brief an advocate with the right of audience in the Crown Court unless the case is conducted by a Crown Prosecutor with a right of audience in the higher courts. There is nothing to stop the CPS briefing an advocate for a specific case in a magistrates' court, although the usual practice is to employ a solicitor or barrister as agent (under the Prosecution of Offences Act 1985, s. 5) to handle the entire CPS list for a court session.

Major prosecuting authorities other than the CPS (such as the Department for Work and Pensions and local authorities) have legally qualified staff to prepare and present cases. Otherwise, a private prosecutor who wishes to be legally represented must instruct solicitors (who may, of course, brief counsel). Various enactments also permit certain types of prosecution in the magistrates' courts to be presented by officials who are not practising solicitors and may not even be lawyers, e.g., the Local Government Act 1972, s. 223, and the Social Security Administration Act 1992, s. 116 (note, however, that s. 116ZA restricts the power of local authorities to bring proceedings relating to housing benefit and council tax benefit offences following the creation of the Single Fraud Investigation Service).

Arranging for Legal Representation for the Accused

An accused secures legal representation by instructing solicitors. It is open to the accused to apply for public funding (through the Criminal Defence Service) to cover the costs. To be eligible for legal aid (whether in the Crown Court or in a magistrates' court), the accused must satisfy both a merits test (that public funding is in the 'interests of justice') and a means test (see **D32.1** *et seq*. for details). Some publicly funded representation is provided through a system of salaried public defenders, but the majority is provided through solicitors in private practice who carry out what is still generally referred to as 'legal aid' work. **D3.120**

There will be occasions when counsel withdraws from the case after the trial has started. In *Bain* [2020] UKPC 10, Lord Hamblen noted (at [40]) that there is no absolute right to legal representation. Where counsel seeks to withdraw during the course of a trial, the judge should consider:

> (i) persuading counsel to remain; (ii) explaining clearly to the defendant the difficulties he may face if he tries to proceed at trial on his own and without representation; (iii) affording, where appropriate, time for reflection or a cooling-off period; (iv) the prejudice that the defendant will suffer if counsel withdraws, and (v) whether there should be an adjournment to enable the defendant to try to obtain alternative representation.

The decision to allow a trial to continue with an unrepresented defendant 'is a matter of the trial judge's discretion, but it is a discretion which must be carefully exercised'. Relevant factors to be considered by the judge include:

> (i) whether the defendant is at fault and, if so, the degree of such fault; (ii) whether there is any suggestion of manipulation or abuse; (iii) whether the defendant wishes to represent himself and, if so, the extent to which that is a matter of free and informed choice; (iv) the history of the proceedings and the stage which the trial has reached; (v) the apparent abilities of the defendant; (vi) the seriousness of the charges and the complexity of the issues in the case and the extent to which skilled representation is likely to be needed; (vii) the availability of alternative representation; (viii) whether an adjournment will be required and, if so, the impact of any adjournment on the proper conduct of the case, including in relation to the availability of witnesses.

Use of a McKenzie Friend

In *Conaghan* [2017] EWCA Crim 597, [2017] 2 Cr App R 19 (240), the Court of Appeal said (at [16]) that the term 'McKenzie friend' is not appropriate in the Court of Appeal (Criminal Division), suggesting that terms such as 'applicant's friend' or 'applicant's helper' might be more appropriate. The Court went on to say that it would allow a non-qualified third party to address the Court only in exceptional circumstances, to be decided on a case-by-case basis. **D3.121**

OPEN JUSTICE

The General Rule that Proceedings Should be in Open Court

D3.122 It has long been established that criminal trials should take place in open court and be freely reported. The following principles may be derived from Lord Diplock's speech in *A-G v Leveller Magazine Ltd* [1979] AC 440 at p. 450:

(a) The normal rule is that criminal proceedings should be conducted publicly.
(b) Nonetheless, courts do have power to order that the public be excluded.
(c) The exercise of the power, in common with any other derogation from the principles of open justice, should be strictly confined to cases where the public's presence would 'frustrate or render impracticable the administration of justice'.

In *Sarker* [2018] EWCA Crim 1341, [2018] 1 WLR 6023, Lord Burnett CJ reiterated (at [29]) a principle that runs through the relevant case law, that 'the default position is the general principle that all proceedings in courts and tribunals are conducted in public. This is the principle of open justice. Media reports of legal proceedings are an extension of the concept of open justice.'

The importance of open justice is apparent (for example) in CrimPR 25.2 (see Supplement, **R25.2**), which provides that, in the case of Crown Court trials, the general rule is that the trial must be in public. However, this is subject to the court's power to impose a restriction on reporting what takes place at a public hearing, or public access to what otherwise would be a public hearing, or to withhold information from the public during a public hearing, or to order that a trial is to take place in private. There is corresponding provision for magistrates' court trials in CrimPR 24.2 (which provides that the general rule is that the hearing must be in public, but the court may exercise its power to impose reporting restrictions, withhold information from the public or order a hearing in private: see Supplement, **R24.2**). Indeed, the MCA 1980, s. 121(4), requires a magistrates' court to sit in open court when trying an accused or imposing a sentence of imprisonment.

It should also be noted that CrimPR 25.12 (Crown Court: see Supplement, **R25.12**) stipulates that, where the written statement of a witness (including an expert witness) is admitted into evidence, each relevant part of the statement must be read or summarised aloud, unless the court otherwise directs. In magistrates' courts a similar obligation arises under CrimPR 24.5 (see Supplement, **R24.5**) but it applies only where a member of the public (including any reporter) is present.

CrimPD I, para. 3N.17 (see Supplement, **CPD.3N**), makes the point that the principle of open justice applies equally where electronic means of communication are used to conduct a hearing. It follows that, where a participant attends a public hearing by live link or telephone, his or her participation must be (so far as possible) equally audible and, if applicable, equally visible to the public as if he or she were physically present.

In *Billington* [2017] EWCA Crim 618, [2017] 2 Cr App R (S) 22 (171), the Court of Appeal (at [32]) emphasised the importance of sentencing judges delivering their sentencing remarks in open court, in order to ensure 'that the public at large, which includes the press who might cover a sentencing exercise, are made fully aware of the reasons for the sentence passed'.

CrimPD I, para. 6E.2 (see Supplement, **CPD.6E**), refers to *R (O'Connor) v Aldershot Magistrates' Court* [2016] EWHC 2792 (Admin), [2017] 1 WLR 2833, where it was noted (at [29]) that the 'right to attend a public court hearing and to enter the court building . . . is not unqualified', and adds that the court 'has an inherent power to restrict public access to the courtroom where it is necessary to do so in the interests of justice, for example to prevent disorder'.

Paragraph 6E.3 states that during criminal proceedings in a Crown Court there are some specific parts of proceedings whereby it may be appropriate for a judge to restrict movement in the public gallery, citing *R (Ewing) v Isleworth Crown Court* [2019] EWHC 288 (Admin), [2019] 2 Cr

App R 9 (74), where Bean LJ had observed (at [23]) that there are 'sensitive moments, generally of brief duration, [when] it is necessary for the court to be still so that the process can take place without distraction and in a manner which preserves the dignity and solemnity of the proceedings'. Paragraph 6E.3 stipulates that access may be restricted to prevent comings and goings in the public gallery during:

(a) arraignment;
(b) empanelling and swearing in of the jury;
(c) oath taking or affirmation;
(d) return of verdict by a jury;
(e) passing of sentence by a judge.

In addition, para. 6E.4 notes that, in *Ewing*, the Court made clear that it would be unlawful to issue a blanket policy that restricted access during other parts of the proceedings. Accordingly:

> Unless the judge has specifically directed restrictions to access to the public gallery for good reason in a particular case, then at all other times, it is expected that the public can enter and leave the courtroom as they require, provided they do so quietly and without disrupting proceedings.

The reference to preventing people entering or leaving court during the passing of sentence should not be taken as restricting the importance of sentencing remarks being delivered in open court (as required in *Billington* [2017] EWCA Crim 618, [2017] 4 WLR 114, at [32]).

The Coronavirus Act 2020, s. 53 and sch. 23, have made temporary modifications to the CJA 2003, ss. 51 to 56 and sch. 3A, to give the court power to direct live link attendance by certain participants at 'eligible criminal proceedings'. For full details, see the Special Supplement, **D3.124A** ***et seq.***

Sitting in Private A decision to sit in private (sometimes described as sitting 'in camera' or 'in chambers') is not justified merely on the ground that, having regard to the nature of the witness's proposed evidence, he or she would find it embarrassing to testify publicly (*Malvern Justices, ex parte Evans* [1988] QB 540). Even when it is claimed that the safety of a witness or party will be endangered by an open hearing, the court should consider carefully whether he or she can be adequately protected by means less drastic than totally excluding the public. In *Reigate Justices, ex parte Argus Newspapers* (1983) 5 Cr App R (S) 181, the Divisional Court emphasised that it is only in exceptional circumstances that a court may depart from the rule that justice has to be administered in public. Hearing a matter in private is a course of last resort and the justices should have applied their minds to how else they might have dealt with the matter (e.g., an order under the Contempt of Court Act 1981, s. 11, protecting the identity of the accused). **D3.123**

In *Re Guardian News and Media Ltd* [2014] EWCA Crim 1861, [2015] 1 Cr App R 4 (36), there was an application for a trial to be held in private. Gross LJ said (at [10]):

> The Rule of Law is a priceless asset of our country and a foundation of our Constitution. One aspect of the Rule of Law — a hallmark and a safeguard — is open justice, which includes criminal trials being held in public and the publication of the names of defendants. Open justice is both a fundamental principle of the common law and a means of ensuring public confidence in our legal system; exceptions are rare and must be justified on the facts. Any such exceptions must be necessary and proportionate. No more than the minimum departure from open justice will be countenanced.

His lordship went on to say (at [16]) that 'considerations of national security will not *by themselves* justify a departure from the principle of open justice', adding (at [17]) that:

> ... open justice must, however, give way to the yet more fundamental principle that the paramount object of the Court is to *do* justice ... Accordingly, where there is a serious possibility that an insistence on open justice in the national security context would frustrate the administration of justice, for example, by deterring the Crown from prosecuting a case where it otherwise should do so, a departure from open justice may be justified.

His lordship also said (at [47]) that the court had grave concern as to the cumulative effects of holding a criminal trial in camera and also anonymising the accused, concluding that the court found it 'difficult to conceive of a situation where both departures from open justice will be justified'.

In *Yam v UK* [2020] ECHR 41, the ECtHR said that the ECHR, Article 6(1), does not prohibit courts from derogating from the requirement to hold hearings in public, 'where the special features of the case justify such a course of action' (at [53]). The ECtHR applies a test of 'strict necessity', and so the national court 'must make a specific finding that exclusion is necessary to protect a compelling governmental interest and must limit secrecy to the extent necessary to preserve that interest' (at [54]). The Court went on to note that, where national security is at issue, 'the very reasons for excluding the public may themselves be subject to confidentiality arrangements and respondent Governments may be reluctant to disclose details to this Court', and there will be cases where the Court is 'asked to assess whether the exclusion of the public and the press met the strict necessity test without itself having access to the material on which that assessment was made at the domestic level' (at [55]). The Court said that it was 'not well-equipped to challenge the national authorities' judgment that national security considerations arise', but added that 'measures affecting fundamental human rights must be subject to some form of adversarial proceedings before an independent body competent to review the reasons for the decision'. It follows that, in cases where the Court does not have sight of the material on which decisions restricting human rights are based (because of national security concerns), it will 'scrutinise the national decision-making procedure to ensure that it incorporated adequate safeguards to protect the interests of the person concerned' (at [56]). It will also be relevant, when determining whether a decision to hold criminal proceedings in private was compatible with the right to a public hearing, 'whether public interest considerations were balanced with the need for openness, whether all evidence was disclosed to the defence and whether the proceedings as a whole were fair' (at [57]).

D3.124 **Procedure** CrimPR 6.6 and 6.7 (see Supplement, **R6.6** and **R6.7**) set out the procedure for an application for an order that all or part of a trial be held in private. The application must be made not less than five business days before the trial is due to begin and the application must be served on the Crown Court and each other party. The appropriate officer of the Crown Court must then ensure that a copy of the notice is prominently displayed in the vicinity of the courtroom. The application must be determined at a hearing, which must be in private unless the court otherwise directs, after the accused has been arraigned but before the jury is sworn. A court must not hear a trial in private until the business day after it orders such a trial or the disposal of any appeal or review of the order, if later. It should be borne in mind that special rules govern public access to youth courts (see **D24.13**).

Freedom of the Media to Report Court Proceedings

D3.125 Section 4(1) of the Contempt of Court Act 1981 protects the freedom of the media to publish 'fair and accurate' reports of legal proceedings held in public, so long as they are published 'contemporaneously and in good faith'.

In *R (Guardian News and Media Ltd) v City of Westminster Magistrates' Court* [2012] EWCA Civ 420, [2013] QB 618, the Court of Appeal (Civil Division) had to consider whether a district judge had power to allow a newspaper to inspect and take copies of affidavits, witness statements and correspondence, which had been supplied to the judge for the purposes of extradition hearings but which had not been read out in open court (though they were referred to during the course of the hearings). Toulson LJ, with whose judgment the Master of the Rolls agreed, said (at [69]) that the courts have an inherent jurisdiction to determine how the principle of open justice should be applied. His lordship observed (at [76]) that the newspaper had 'a serious journalistic purpose in seeking access to the documents', and said that, unless 'some strong contrary argument can be made out, the courts should assist rather than impede such an exercise' (at [77]).

He observed (at [79]) that 'the purpose of the open justice principle... is to enable the public to understand and scrutinise the justice system of which the courts are the administrators'. His lordship added (at [83]) that 'the practice of receiving evidence without it being read in open court potentially has the side effect of making the proceedings less intelligible to the press and the public', and went on to say that the time has now come for the courts to acknowledge that in some cases public access to documents referred to in open court might be necessary. He said (at [85]):

> In a case where documents have been placed before a judge and referred to in the course of proceedings,... the default position should be that access should be permitted on the open justice principle; and where access is sought for a proper journalistic purpose, the case for allowing it will be particularly strong. However, there may be countervailing reasons... The court has to carry out a proportionality exercise which will be fact-specific. Central to the court's evaluation will be the purpose of the open justice principle, the potential value of the material in advancing that purpose and, conversely, any risk of harm which access to the documents may cause to the legitimate interests of others.

His lordship concluded (at [87]) that, since the newspaper had put forward good reasons for having access to the documents sought, and that there was no suggestion that this would give rise to any risk of harm to any other party, or that it would place any great burden on the court, the application should be allowed.

This case was cited in *Marine A* [2013] EWCA Crim 2367, [2014] 1 WLR 3326, where Lord Judge CJ, applying CrimPD I, para. 5B.9 (see Supplement, **CPD.5B**; the text was subject to minor amendment in April 2018), said (at [52]) that the court is bound to 'have regard to the rights of victims, parties, witnesses and any third parties whose rights may be engaged by the release to the public of material presented in court'. His lordship went on to consider the position of journalists, saying (at [56]) that:

> ...it is clear that those who inform public debate on matters of public interest as journalists (whether in the print, broadcasting or internet media) are accorded a special position, given the role of journalism in enabling proper and effective participation in a democratic society.

Lord Judge then considered the test to be applied where restrictions on publication of the identity of the accused are sought, saying (at [84]) that 'a defendant in a criminal trial must be named save in rare circumstances'. However, 'the Court has a power to withhold the name and address of a defendant in cases where circumstances justify that', although 'such cases would be rare. Any derogation from open justice, and any interference with the right to report a criminal trial, must be both necessary and proportionate' (at [85]). His lordship added (at [88]) that an order that an accused should not be identified 'will not be necessary, if some other measure is available to protect those rights of the individuals, and that other measure would be proportionate'.

At the conclusion of the trial to which *Re Guardian News and Media Ltd* [2014] EWCA Crim 1861, [2015] 1 Cr App R 4 (36) related, the media parties argued that there was no longer a significant risk that the administration of justice would be frustrated if the media were to publish reports of the trial and that there was therefore no longer a continuing justification for the restrictions on reporting the trial that were imposed by the Court of Appeal in that case. That challenge was dismissed in *Re Guardian News and Media Ltd* [2016] EWCA Crim 11, [2016] 1 WLR 1767. Lord Thomas CJ said (at [47]) that, when the DPP makes an application for part of the proceedings to be held in private, 'the court proceeds on the basis that the principle of open justice is fundamental to the rule of law and to democratic accountability'. His lordship referred to the decision of the House of Lords in *Scott v Scott* [1913] AC 417, and observed (at [49]) that it is:

> ...for the DPP, as the party seeking to curtail the principle of open justice, to make a very clear case. The stringency of the test was expressed by Viscount Haldane in *Scott v Scott* at p. 438 as requiring it to be shown that a hearing in camera was 'strictly necessary' and 'that by nothing short of the exclusion of the public can justice be done'...

Lord Thomas CJ went on (at [51]–[53]) to hold that:

> Where the reason for departing from the principle of open justice is based on reasons relating to national security, it is for the court and the court alone to determine if the stringent test has been met. It, and it alone, decides whether the evidence or material in question should be heard in public or not.
>
> In making that decision the court will pay the highest regard to what is stated by the Secretary of State in his or her Certificate. As Lord Hoffman made clear in *Secretary of State for the Home Department v Rehman* [2003] 1 AC 153 at [50]–[57], a court should not depart from the view of the Secretary of State on national security issues, provided there is an evidential basis for the decision of the Secretary of State. That is because under our constitution the identification and delineation of national security interests is for the Executive branch of the state. Although the circumstances will be very rare, the court is also free to depart from the views set out in the Certificate as to the weight to be attached to the national security interests. That is because it is always for the court to make the decision on whether those interests necessitate the departure from the principle of open justice.
>
> Thus when a prosecutor seeks a ruling from the court in relation to hearing evidence in camera, it is for the court to determine that application by deciding whether the evidence or material in issue should or should not be heard in camera. The test for the court is one of necessity…

His lordship also emphasised (at [63]) that the decision of the court to hear evidence in private, or to withhold information from the public and/or the press, is 'subject to continuous review during the trial in the light of any changes in circumstances and to review at the conclusion of the trial'.

D3.126 Under the Administration of Justice Act 1960, s. 12 (see **B14.118**), there is no automatic rule that the reporting of proceedings held in private amounts to contempt — just as when public proceedings were reported, it has to be shown that the reporting involved a substantial risk of prejudice to the administration of justice (per Lord Scarman in *A-G v Leveller Magazine Ltd* [1979] AC 440 at p. 472F–G).

D3.127 **Postponing Reporting of Proceedings** Section 4(2) of the Contempt of Court Act 1981 empowers the court, if it appears to be 'necessary for avoiding a substantial risk of prejudice to the administration of justice' in those proceedings, to 'order that the publication of any report of the proceedings, or any part of the proceedings, be postponed for such period as the court thinks necessary for that purpose'. In *Sarker* [2018] EWCA Crim 1341, [2018] 1 WLR 6023, Lord Burnett CJ noted (at [22]) that applications for orders under s. 4(2) must set out clearly '(i) *how* contemporaneous fair and accurate reports of the trial will cause a substantial risk of prejudice? and (ii) *why* a postponement order would avoid the identified risk of prejudice'.

D3.128 **Scope of Order** CrimPD I, para. 6B.3 (see Supplement, **CPD.6B**), makes it clear that, before exercising its discretion to impose reporting restrictions, the court must 'follow precisely the statutory provisions under which the order is to be made, paying particular regard to what has to be established, by whom and to what standard'. Paragraph 6B.4 sets out a number of general principles, for example: that the court must 'keep in mind the fact that every order is a departure from the general principle that proceedings shall be open and freely reported'; that the court 'must be satisfied that the purpose of the proposed order cannot be achieved by some lesser measure'; that the terms of the order must be 'proportionate' (so as to comply with the ECHR, Article 10); that the parties (and any interested party, including representatives of the media) must be given a chance to make representations; that the order must be in precise terms (if practicable, agreed with the advocates in the case), stating the power under which it is made, its precise scope and purpose, and when it will cease to have effect. Paragraph 6B.1 makes reference to a document entitled *Reporting Restrictions in the Criminal Courts* (revised May 2016, tinyurl.com/lluexdb), a practical guide to the statutory and common-law principles which should be applied (which has been adopted by the Judicial College, the Media Lawyers' Association, the Society of Editors and the News Media Association).

Examples of situations in which the power given to the courts by the Contempt of Court Act 1981, s. 4(2), may be of value include: (a) when an accused is to be tried successively on separate indictments (or several accused are to be tried separately for connected offences) and reports of the evidence given at the trial held first are likely to prejudice jurors for the later trials; and (b) when evidence and/or argument is put before the judge at a trial on indictment in the absence of the jury, the purpose of sending the jury out being to prevent their being prejudiced by, for example, evidence which the judge ultimately rules to be inadmissible.

In *Sarker* [2018] EWCA Crim 1341, [2018] 1 WLR 6023, Lord Burnett CJ emphasised the need for very careful judicial scrutiny of applications for reporting restrictions (at [23]–[28]). His lordship went on to summarise the approach that should be taken to applications under s. 4(2), saying (at [30]): **D3.129**

> i) The first question is whether reporting would give rise to a substantial risk of prejudice to the administration of justice in the relevant proceedings . . . If not, that will be the end of the matter.
> ii) If such a risk is perceived to exist, then the second question arises: would a section 4(2) order eliminate it? If not, there could be no necessity to impose such a ban. On the other hand, even if the judge is satisfied that an order would achieve the objective, he or she would still have to consider whether the risk could satisfactorily be overcome by some less restrictive means. If so, it could not be said to be 'necessary' to take the more drastic approach . . .
> iii) If the judge is satisfied that there is indeed no other way of eliminating the perceived risk of prejudice; it still does not necessarily follow that an order has to be made. The judge may still have to ask whether the *degree* of risk contemplated should be regarded as tolerable in the sense of being 'the lesser of two evils'. It is at this stage that value judgments may have to be made as to the priority between the competing public interests; fair trial and freedom of expression/open justice . . .

The word 'substantial' in this context means 'not insubstantial' or 'not minimal' (at [31]). The exceptional nature of reporting restrictions is emphasised when his lordship makes the point that, in most cases, 'no possible prejudice to the immediate trial could arise from the publication of contemporaneous reports of the trial itself (at least so much of the proceedings that take place in front of the jury)', given that (i) the jury will have heard the evidence or submissions that are the subject of the report; and (ii) the jury will have been directed by the judge to try the case on the evidence presented during the trial, not to carry out any research themselves, to ignore any media reports that they may see of the case they are trying. Moreover, the court must proceed on the basis that juries are committed to the right of the accused to receive a fair trial and that they will abide by the directions given by the judge, and that media reports of the trial will be 'responsible, fair and accurate' (at [32]).

As regards cases of sequential or connected trials, his lordship observed (at [34]) that, where a s. 4(2) order is made in the first trial to protect the second trial or retrial, 'the judge must still consider carefully the nature of the prejudice that is relied upon to justify the order'. If the subsequent trial will take place some months after the first, the court should bear in mind the 'fade factor', namely the effect of the lapse of time between publication and trial.

If any order is thought to be required, the key question is whether a less restrictive order might avoid the risk of prejudice that has been identified. Lord Burnett noted that it may be sufficient to limit the order to the postponement of the identification of certain persons involved in the first trial or to particular aspects of the evidence. Accordingly, 'consideration must be given to whether an order stopping short of a total postponement of reporting of the proceedings can be fashioned' (at [35]).

It follows that a 'blanket' postponement order under s. 4(2) should be regarded as a last resort; if there is an alternative way of avoiding a substantial risk of prejudice, that alternative should be preferred.

Finally, Lord Burnett said that it was not strictly accurate to say that the court ultimately had a discretion whether to make an order under s. 4(2); rather the court was required 'to make a value judgment about the competing rights and interests' (at [36]).

In *Ex parte MGN Ltd* [2011] EWCA Crim 100, [2011] 1 Cr App R 31 (387), an order under s. 4(2) had been made to protect witnesses in a murder trial. Lord Judge CJ said (at [22]) that the use of s. 4(2) 'for the purposes of alleviating the difficulties of giving evidence, even if evidence has to be given in more than one trial, is rarely appropriate'. If the conditions for an order under s. 4(2) are established in the case of a particular witness, so that the order is 'justified in accordance with principle, then the order should be made'. However, the protection of witnesses is 'more appropriately secured by statutory measures designed for the purpose', such as reporting restrictions, or special measures under the YJCEA 1999, ss. 23 to 30, 'designed to enable witnesses to give of their best'.

D3.130 In *R (Press Association) v Cambridge Crown Court* [2012] EWCA Crim 2434, [2013] 1 WLR 1979, Lord Judge CJ pointed out (at [13]) that s. 4(2) 'is aimed at the postponement of publication rather than a permanent ban'. It follows that an order prohibiting publication for an indefinite period, which amounts in effect to the imposition of a permanent ban, should not be made under s. 4(2). Indeed, in *Times Newspapers Ltd* [2007] EWCA Crim 1925, [2008] 1 WLR 234, the Court of Appeal held that s. 4(2), unlike s. 11 (see **D3.135**), is designed to enable the court to prevent the publication of a report of proceedings where such publication will prejudice the conduct of those proceedings, or specific pending proceedings. It permits only postponement, and the need for postponement cannot subsist beyond the end of the proceedings in question (per Lord Phillips CJ, at [12]).

The powers of the court to postpone publication under s. 4(2) are exhaustive, and so the court has no inherent power in addition to the terms of that provision (*Newtownabbey Magistrates' Court, ex parte Belfast Telegraph Newspapers Ltd* (1997) *The Times*, 27 August 1997).

D3.131 In *Clerkenwell Stipendiary Magistrate, ex parte The Telegraph plc* [1993] QB 462, the Divisional Court confirmed that the court has a discretion to hear representations from the press regarding the making of a s. 4(2) order. Although the power is discretionary, it would generally be right to exercise it by hearing from the press, who are best qualified to represent that public interest in publicity which the court has to take into account in performing the necessary balancing exercise (per Mann LJ at p. 471).

In *Ex parte British Broadcasting Corporation; R v F* [2016] EWCA Crim 12, [2016] 2 Cr App R 13 (157), the Court of Appeal had to deal for the first time with prejudicial comments posed by members of the public on social media linked to the websites or Facebook pages of various media organisations. Sir Brian Leveson P said (at [39]) that 'the comparative exercise is not whether a s. 4(2) order is necessary because otherwise there will be no protection ... but, rather, even if an order could be made under s. 4(2), whether the mechanism of proceeding by s. 45(4) of the Senior Courts Act 1981 renders it a disproportionate interference with the Article 10 ECHR rights of the press and the importance rightly attached to contemporaneous reporting of criminal proceedings which attract considerable entirely legitimate public interest'. The Court ordered the media organisations not to place any report of the trial in question on their respective Facebook pages and to disable the ability for users to post comments on their respective news websites on any report of the trial published by the media organisations on their own websites. In *Sarker* [2018] EWCA Crim 1341, [2018] 1 WLR 6023, Lord Burnett CJ noted (at [33]) that judges may fear that publication online of fair and accurate contemporaneous reports will give rise to a risk of prejudice arising from third parties making prejudicial comments upon the reports of proceedings (or providing links to prejudicial material).

His response was that the risk of prejudicial third-party commentary in user-generated content should not be exaggerated, since media organisations are able to disable any facility allowing comments to be made on website reports of jury trials and, perhaps more significantly, that this sort of 'parasitic damage' is not a risk of prejudice arising (directly) from fair and accurate reporting and so cannot justify the imposition of a reporting restriction order under s. 4(2).

Effect of the ECHR: the Balancing Exercise In *Re S (a Child) (Identification: restriction on publication)* [2004] UKHL 47, [2005] 1 AC 593, the House of Lords reiterated the substance of the decision about the interplay between the ECHR, Articles 8 (respect for private and family life) and 10 (freedom of expression), in *Campbell v MGN Ltd* [2004] UKHL 22, [2004] 2 AC 457: (a) neither article has precedence over the other; (b) where the values under the two articles are in conflict, an intense focus on the comparative importance of the specific rights being claimed in the individual case is necessary; (c) the justifications for interfering with or restricting each right must be taken into account; (d) the proportionality test must be applied to each (per Lord Steyn at [17]). His lordship went on to say (at [30]): **D3.132**

> A criminal trial is a public event. The principle of open justice puts, as has often been said, the judge and all who participate in the trial under intense scrutiny. The glare of contemporaneous publicity ensures that trials are properly conducted. It is a valuable check on the criminal process. Moreover, the public interest may be as much involved in the circumstances of a remarkable acquittal as in a surprising conviction. Informed public debate is necessary about all such matters. Full contemporaneous reporting of criminal trials in progress promotes public confidence in the administration of justice. It promotes the values of the rule of law.

On this basis, it was held that the press should not be restrained from publishing the identity of the accused in a murder trial in order to protect the privacy of the accused's child, who was not involved in the criminal proceedings.

In *Re Trinity Mirror plc* [2008] EWCA Crim 50, [2008] QB 770, a five-judge Court of Appeal (including the Presidents of the QBD and the Family Division) said that it is 'impossible to over-emphasise the importance to be attached to the ability of the media to report criminal trials ... this represents the embodiment of the principle of open justice in a free country. An important aspect of the public interest in the administration of criminal justice is that the identity of those convicted and sentenced for criminal offices should not be concealed' (Sir Igor Judge P at [32]). On this basis, the Court set aside an order protecting the identity of D's children, saying (at [33]) that: **D3.133**

> Everyone appreciates the risk that innocent children may suffer prejudice and damage when a parent is convicted of a serious offence ... However ... if the court were to uphold this ruling so as to protect the rights of the defendant's children under Article 8, it would be countenancing a substantial erosion of the principle of open justice, to the overwhelming disadvantage of public confidence in the criminal justice system, the free reporting of criminal trials and the proper identification of those convicted and sentenced in them. Such an order cannot begin to be contemplated unless the circumstances are indeed properly to be described as exceptional.

More recently, in *Blackman* [2017] EWCA Crim 326, the Court of Appeal refused an application by media organisations to disclose video recordings taken by a marine during the killing of a wounded insurgent in Afghanistan, holding that, on balance, the considerations against disclosure (sufficient information already in the public domain and the risk of endangerment of a number of people) outweighed the principles of open justice and the rights of the media under the ECHR, Article 10.

The Supreme Court, in *Khuja v Times Newspapers Ltd* [2017] UKSC 49, [2018] 1 Cr App R 1 (1), heard an appeal against the lifting of an order under s. 4(2). C had been named in the course of a trial as a suspect, but had never been charged with an offence. Lord Sumption, giving the judgment of the majority of the justices, said (at [29]) that, when considering the question whether the open justice principle may be satisfied without adversely affecting the claimant's

Convention rights by permitting proceedings in court to be reported but without disclosing the claimant's name, the test to be applied

> is whether the public interest served by publishing the facts extended to publishing the name. In practice, where the court is satisfied that there is a real public interest in publication, that interest has generally extended to publication of the name. This is because the anonymised reporting of issues of legitimate public concern are less likely to interest the public and therefore to provoke discussion.

His lordship went on (at [34]) to explain why the majority of justices had decided to allow C's identity to be revealed. C had not applied for the trial to be conducted so as to withhold his identity (had such an application been made, different considerations would have applied). His application was to prohibit the reporting, however fair or accurate, of matters which were discussed at a public trial; these were not matters in respect of which he could have had any reasonable expectation of privacy. Moreover, the impact on his family life of what was said about him at the trial was no different in kind from the impact of many disagreeable statements which may be made about individuals at a high profile criminal trial; the impact on his family life was also indirect and incidental, as he had not participated in any capacity at the trial, and nothing that was said at the trial related to his family. Furthermore, the order sought by C would not prevent the identification of a party to the criminal proceedings or even of a witness, making it more difficult to justify preventing publication of his identity. His lordship went on to say that:

> The policy which permits media reporting of judicial proceedings does not depend on the person adversely affected by the publicity being a participant in the proceedings. It depends on (i) the right of the public to be informed about a significant public act of the state, and (ii) the law's recognition that, within the limits imposed by the law of defamation, the way in which the story is presented is a matter of editorial judgment, in which the desire to increase the interest of the story by giving it a human face is a legitimate consideration. [The claimant's] identity is not a peripheral or irrelevant feature of this particular story.

Finally, Lord Sumption said (at [35]) that 'restrictions on the reporting of proceedings in open court are particularly difficult to justify. It may in some cases be easier to justify managing the trial in a way which avoids the identification of those with a sufficient claim to anonymity'. Applications for anonymity in the courtroom will generally raise various issues, including the fairness of the trial and the existence and extent of any legitimate public interest in the applicant's identity. His lordship concluded that 'if there is a solution to the problem of collateral damage to those not directly involved in criminal proceedings, that is where it is to be found'.

D3.134 **Contempt of Court Act 1981, s. 4**

(1) Subject to this section a person is not guilty of contempt of court under the strict liability rule in respect of a fair and accurate report of legal proceedings held in public, published contemporaneously and in good faith.

(2) In any such proceedings the court may, where it appears to be necessary for avoiding a substantial risk of prejudice to the administration of justice in those proceedings, or in any other proceedings pending or imminent, order that the publication of any report of the proceedings, or any part of the proceedings, be postponed for such period as the court thinks necessary for that purpose.

(2A) Where in proceedings for any offence which is an administration of justice offence for the purposes of section 54 of the Criminal Procedure and Investigations Act 1996 (acquittal tainted by an administration of justice offence) it appears to the court that there is a possibility that (by virtue of that section) proceedings may be taken against a person for an offence of which he has been acquitted, subsection (2) of this section shall apply as if those proceedings were pending or imminent.

(3) For the purposes of subsection (1) of this section ... a report of proceedings shall be treated as published contemporaneously—

(a) in the case of a report of which publication is postponed pursuant to an order under subsection (2) of this section, if published as soon as practicable after that order expires;

(b) in the case of a report of allocation or sending proceedings of which publication is permitted by virtue only of subsection (6) of section 52A of the Crime and Disorder Act 1998 ('the 1998 Act'), if published as soon as practicable after publication is so permitted;
(c) in the case of a report of an application of which publication is permitted by virtue only of sub-paragraph (5) or (7) of paragraph 3 of Schedule 3 to the 1998 Act, if published as soon as practicable after publication is so permitted.

The procedure to adopt where a person is alleged to be in breach of an order under s. 4 was considered in *Yaxley-Lennon* [2018] EWCA Crim 1856, [2018] 2 Cr App R 30 (475). Lord Burnett CJ (at [27]) noted that a judge may deal summarily with a contempt which amounts to an interference in the course of the proceedings. However, his lordship went on to say (at [28]) that, even in cases where a court considers it necessary to proceed summarily to deal with a contempt, it is 'often wise ... to adjourn the contempt hearing to a later date and sometimes before a different judge', in order to avoid any question of bias. Indeed, in most cases concerning an interference with the public course of justice, the judge will refer the matter to the A-G. His lordship then emphasised the need for procedural fairness in contempt proceedings, 'including the need to particularise the alleged contempt at the outset. An alleged contemnor must know what it is he has done which is said to amount to a contempt of court so that he can decide whether to accept responsibility or contest the allegation' (at [29]). The court should therefore follow the procedure set out in CrimPR Part 48 (see Supplement, **R48.1** *et seq.*). Although the Court of Appeal, in *West* [2014] EWCA Crim 1480, [2015] 1 WLR 109, had said that 'strict observance of the provisions is essential' (per Sir Brian Leveson P, at [34]), the Court in *Yaxley-Lennon* said that it was not the case that any and every breach of the rules invalidates a finding of contempt. Rather, the criminal courts should adopt the same procedure as the civil and family courts, applying *Nicholls v Nicholls* [1997] 1 WLR 314, where Lord Woolf MR had said (at p. 327) that, as long as the contemnor had received 'a fair trial and the order has been made on valid grounds', the existence of a defect in the process 'will not result in the order being set aside except in so far as the interests of justice require this to be done', and that the interests of justice 'will not require an order to be set aside where there is no prejudice caused as a result of errors in the application to commit or in the order to commit'.

Imposition of a Permanent Ban on Reporting Certain Matters

In addition to their power to postpone publication of court reports by virtue of an order under the Contempt of Court Act 1981, s. 4(2), the courts are empowered to impose a *permanent* ban on the reporting of certain matters. **D3.135**

Contempt of Court Act 1981, s. 11

In any case where a court (having power to do so) allows a name or other matter to be withheld from the public in proceedings before the court, the court may give such directions prohibiting the publication of that name or matter in connection with the proceedings as appear to the court to be necessary for the purpose for which it was so withheld.

The terms of s. 11 show that an order under it may be without limitation of time but may only be made where the court has legitimately exercised its common law power to receive evidence or other information without allowing it to be disclosed to the public (*Re Trinity Mirror plc* [2008] EWCA Crim 50, [2008] QB 770). It is therefore a pre-condition to the making of an order on the basis of s. 11 that the court, having the power to do so, has withheld the name or other matter from the public in the proceedings before it (*R (Press Association) v Cambridge Crown Court* [2012] EWCA Crim 2434, [2013] 1 WLR 1979, per Lord Judge CJ, at [14]). CrimPD I, paras. 6B.1 to 6B.7 (see Supplement, **CPD.6B**), apply to orders under s. 11 as well as to orders under s. 4(2).

In *Re Times Newspapers Ltd* [2008] EWCA Crim 2559, [2009] 1 WLR 1015, Latham LJ (at [12]) noted that an important aspect of open justice is that defendants' names should be made public. However, 'there is no doubt that a court may, in appropriate circumstances, order that the identity of a defendant can be protected from publicity by withholding his or her name'. The **D3.136** power to do so comes, not from the Contempt of Court Act 1981, s. 11, but from the common law, which enables an order for anonymity to be made if the court is satisfied that the administration of justice would otherwise be seriously affected (at [17]). Nonetheless, as Lord Hope of Craighead said in *A-G's Ref (No. 3 of 1999) (BBC's application to set aside or vary a reporting restriction order*) [2009] UKHL 34, [2010] 1 AC 145 (at [28]), even 'significant' interference with the rights of the accused under the ECHR, Article 8, may be 'proportionate when account is taken of the weight that must be given to the competing right to freedom of expression' under Article 10.

In *R (Yam) v Central Criminal Court* [2016] AC 771, C sought a variation of an order made under s. 11 so that the sensitive material could be deployed in an application to the ECtHR. The Supreme Court upheld the refusal to permit disclosure to the ECtHR of material heard in private before the ECtHR had decided what disclosure it required.

The ECtHR ruled in *Yam v UK* [2020] ECHR 41, at [81], that the fact that, 'despite an invitation by the applicant, no request for particular documents has been made by the Court will, in most cases, be fatal to [an] allegation of a failure to comply with Article 34 obligations'. The Court went on to say (at [82]):

> ...even where such a request has been made and refused, there will not necessarily be a failure to comply with Article 34 obligations if measures affecting fundamental human rights have been subject to some form of adversarial proceedings before an independent body competent to review the reasons for the decision and the relevant evidence.

In *Yam*, the decision to maintain the confidential nature of the in camera material in respect of the proceedings before the ECtHR had been reviewed by the domestic courts, whose judgments explained why the material should remain confidential and why they did not consider it appropriate to vary the order to allow disclosure to the ECtHR (see [82]).

D3.137 **Children and Young People** So far as children and young people appearing in an adult court are concerned, under the YJCEA 1999, s. 45, the onus is on the Crown Court or magistrates' court to make an order protecting the child or young person's anonymity (see **D24.75**). The opposite applies in the youth court, where reporting restrictions to protect the child or young person's identity apply automatically (see the CYPA 1933, s. 49, and **D24.14**).

D3.138 **Sexual Offences** Under the Sexual Offences (Amendment) Act 1992, the alleged victim in a case involving one of the sexual offences listed in s. 2 of the Act (including rape) is entitled to anonymity. Once an allegation of one of the offences in question has been made, nothing may be published which is likely to lead members of the public to identify the alleged victim (s. 1(1)). In reporting the proceedings at and prior to a trial for one of the offences covered by the 1992 Act, the media are obliged to omit anything likely to disclose the complainant's identity, even if that information was given in open court. Under s. 1(1), the restriction continues for the lifetime of the complainant. Under s. 3, the prohibition on publicity may be lifted by order of the court if either: (a) publicity is required by the accused so that witnesses will come forward and the conduct of the defence is likely to be seriously prejudiced if the direction is not given (s. 3(1)); or (b) the trial judge is satisfied that imposition of the prohibition imposes a substantial and unreasonable restriction on the reporting of the proceedings and it is in the public interest to relax the restriction (s. 3(2)).

D3.139 **'Reporting Directions'** The YJCEA 1999, s. 46, provides for a party to make an application for the court to give reporting directions in relation to a witness (other than the accused) who has attained the age of 18. The effect of the direction is that 'no matter relating to the witness shall during the witness's lifetime be included in any publication if it is likely to lead members of the public to identify him as being a witness in the proceedings' (s. 46(6)). The court may make such a direction in respect of an eligible witness if it determines that the direction is likely to improve the quality of the evidence of the witness, or his or her co-operation in the case preparation of any party to the proceedings (s. 46(2)). Eligibility for a direction arises where the quality of evidence or the witness's co-operation is likely to be diminished by reason of fear or distress on the part of the witness in connection with being identified by members of the public as a witness in the proceedings (s. 46(3)). Generally, the direction has effect for the lifetime of the witness (s. 46(6)).

Under the YJCEA 1999, s. 45A, the court may make a reporting direction in relation to a witness (other than the accused) who is under the age of 18 when the proceedings commence. The direction is that, during that person's lifetime, information must not be 'included in any publication if it is likely to lead members of the public to identify that person as being concerned in the proceedings' (s. 45A(2)). The grounds for making a direction under s. 45A are the same as those under s. 46 (s. 45A(2) and (3)).

For the purposes of ss. 45A and 46, the protected information includes the person's name and address, the identity of any school or other educational establishment the person attends, and the identity of any place of work; the restriction also applies to any still or moving picture of the person. In *ITN News v R* [2013] EWCA Crim 773, [2014] 1 WLR 199, the Court of Appeal noted (at [31]) that a still or moving picture of a witness may be prohibited if the 'eligibility' test is satisfied, even if the name and identity of that witness is otherwise known. The Court added that, even when a reporting restriction is appropriate, 'it should be no wider than necessary to avoid any diminution in the quality of the evidence to be given by the witness'.

Under CrimPR 6.2 (see Supplement, **R6.2**), where a court is (i) imposing a restriction on the reporting of what takes place at a public hearing or on public access to what otherwise would be a public hearing, (ii) is allowing the withholding of information from the public during a public hearing or (iii) is ordering that a trial should take place in private, the court must have regard to the importance of dealing with criminal cases in public and of allowing a public hearing to be reported to the public. CrimPR 6.4 (see Supplement, **R6.4**) sets out the procedure to be followed where such restrictions are sought, including any application for a 'reporting direction' (under the YJCEA 1999, s. 46). Under CrimPR 6.6 (see Supplement, **R6.6**), a party who is seeking an order that some or all of a trial should be heard in private must make a written application not less than five business days before the trial is due to begin, explaining the reasons for the application and, in particular, why no measures other than a private trial order would suffice.

The provisions in s. 46 do not apply to the accused (and the reporting restrictions in s. 45 expire when the accused attains the age of 18). An accused who has attained the age of 18 and who wishes to continue to benefit from anonymity may seek a permanent injunction restraining the press and all other persons from publishing his or her name or identity (as in, e.g., *A and B v Persons Unknown* [2016] EWHC 3295 (Ch), where such an order was granted because the claimants, who had (when they were children) been convicted of very serious crimes, would otherwise have been at risk of attack by vigilantes and other persons seeking revenge against them).

Live Text-based Communications from Court

CrimPD I, para. 6C, 'clarifies the use which may be made of live text-based communications, such as mobile email, social media (including Twitter) and internet enabled laptops in and from courts throughout England and Wales'. A member of the public who is in court and who wishes to use live text-based communications during court proceedings, must first apply for permission to activate and use a mobile phone, small laptop or similar piece of equipment which can, if permission is granted, be used solely to make live, text-based communications of the proceedings (para. 6C.7). The 'paramount question' for the judge, when deciding whether to give permission, is whether it may 'interfere with the proper administration of justice' (para. 6C.9). In the context of a criminal trial, the danger to the administration of justice is likely to be most acute where, for example, 'witnesses who are out of court may be informed of what has already happened in court and so coached or briefed before they then give evidence', or where information posted (e.g., on Twitter) 'about inadmissible evidence may influence members of a jury' (para. 6C.11). However, to enable the media to produce fair and accurate reports of **D3.140** the proceedings, a representative of the media or a legal commentator who wishes to use live, text-based communications from court may do so without making an application to the court (para. 6C.8). It may be necessary for the judge to limit live, text-based communications to representatives of the media for journalistic purposes, and to disallow their use by the wider public in court, if (for example) it is necessary to limit the number of mobile electronic devices in use at any given time (para. 6C.12). Permission to use live, text-based communications from court may be withdrawn by the court at any time (para. 6C.14).

Taking Notes in Court

D3.141 CrimPD I, para. 6D.1 (see Supplement, **CPD.6D**), clarifies that, so long as it does not interfere with the proper administration of justice, anyone who attends a court hearing 'may quietly take notes, on paper or by silent electronic means'. The permission of the court is not required. However, para. 6D.2 makes it clear that it is within the power of the court to prohibit note taking by one or more specified individuals 'if that is necessary and proportionate to prevent unlawful conduct' or if there is reason to believe that the individual(s) are in fact engaged in the transmission of live text-based communications from court without the permission required by para. 6C.7. Paragraph 6D.3 adds that the existence of reporting restrictions, without more, is not a sufficient reason to prohibit note taking (though it may need to be made clear to those taking notes that the reporting restrictions affect what may be communicated to others). This guidance adopts the approach taken in *Ewing v Newport Crown Court* [2016] EWHC 183 (Admin), [2016] 1 Cr App R 32 (516), where it was held (at [23]) that the 'default position' is that 'those who attend public court hearings should be free to make notes of what occurs'. However, the court may, for good reason, withdraw the liberty to make notes; the 'paramount question for the judge if considering withdrawing that liberty would be whether the note-taking in question would be likely to interfere with the proper administration of justice' (at [24]).

Appeals against Derogations from Open Justice

D3.142 **Criminal Justice Act 1988, s. 159**

(1) A person aggrieved may appeal to the Court of Appeal, if that court grants leave, against—
- (a) an order under section 4 or 11 of the Contempt of Court Act 1981 made in relation to a trial on indictment;
- (aa) an order made by the Crown Court under section 58(7) or (8) of the Criminal Procedure and Investigations Act 1996 in a case where the court has convicted a person on a trial on indictment;
- (b) any order restricting the access of the public to the whole or any part of a trial on indictment or to any proceedings ancillary to such a trial; and
- (c) any order restricting the publication of any report of the whole or any part of a trial on indictment or any such ancillary proceedings;

and the decision of the Court of Appeal shall be final.

...

(5) On the hearing of an appeal under this section the Court of Appeal shall have power—
- (a) to stay any proceedings in any other court until after the appeal is disposed of;
- (b) to confirm, reverse or vary the order complained of; and
- (c) to make such order as to costs as it thinks fit.

D3.143 Section 159 creates a specific right to appeal against orders of the Crown Court derogating from the principle of open justice. The procedure to be followed is set out in CrimPR Part 40 (see Supplement, **R40.1** ***et seq.***). In *Re A* [2006] EWCA Crim 4, [2006] 1 WLR 1361, the Court of Appeal confirmed that media representatives and the accused both fall within the description of persons who may be 'aggrieved' within s. 159(1). It should be noted that an appeal under s. 159 can be brought even after the reporting restriction order has been discharged (*Sarker* [2018] *EWCA Crim 1341, [2018]* 1 WLR 6023, at [2]).

Section 159(5) contemplates the trial on indictment being stayed while the appeal is determined. The power to stay the trial is necessary because quashing an order derogating from open justice after the relevant proceedings have been completed will often serve no practical purpose, since by that time any harm resulting from the order has already been done.

CrimPR 36.6(3) (see Supplement, **R36.6**) stipulates that, where the appellant wants to appeal against an order restricting public access to a trial, the court may decide both the application for permission to appeal and the appeal itself without a hearing but must, in any event, announce its decision on such an appeal at a hearing in public. The Court of Appeal therefore has a discretion to hold a hearing.

Magistrates' Court Cases Section 159 of the CJA 1988 does not extend to decisions of magistrates' courts or to decisions made by the Crown Court otherwise than in connection with trials on indictment (e.g., on an appeal from magistrates). In respect of such decisions, the remedy of an aggrieved person is to apply to the Divisional Court for judicial review. This has the disadvantage that, even if the remedy sought is granted, it may come too late to be of practical value. **D3.144**

Section D4 Criminal Procedure Rules and Case Management

THE RULES AND PRACTICE DIRECTION ARE THE LAW

D4.1 The Criminal Procedure Rules and the Criminal Practice Direction (which are referred to below as the 'CrimPR' and 'CrimPD') apply to all criminal proceedings in the magistrates' courts, Crown Court and Court of Appeal (Criminal Division). The Criminal Procedure Rules 2015 (SI 2015 No. 1490), which had effect from 5 October 2015, were fully revised by the Criminal Procedure Rules 2020 (SI 2020 No. 759), in force from 5 October 2020 (see Supplement, **R1.1** ***et seq.***).

The temporary changes to the CrimPR 2015 required by the Coronavirus Act 2020 were given effect by the Criminal Procedure (Amendment No. 2) (Coronavirus) Rules 2020 (SI 2020 No. 417), in force from 14 April 2020. Therefore full sets of the CrimPR 2015 show alternate versions of rr. 2, 3, 5, 14, 18, 24, 25, 28, 47 and 50. Those alternate versions are carried through into the CrimPR 2020 by r. 2.1(4) of the CrimPR 2020.

The CrimPR, being made by Statutory Instrument, and the CrimPD, being issued by the Lord Chief Justice, are binding law as CrimPD, para. 1A.3 (see Supplement, **CPD.1A**), now explains:

> The Criminal Procedure Rules and the Criminal Practice Directions are the law. Together they provide a code of current practice that is binding on the courts to which they are directed, and which promotes the consistent administration of justice. Participants must comply with the Rules and Practice Direction, and directions made by the court, and so it is the responsibility of the courts and those who participate in cases to be familiar with, and to ensure that these provisions are complied with.

The status of the CrimPD was explained by Sir Brian Leveson P in *Valiati v DPP* [2018] EWHC 2908 (Admin), [2019] 1 Cr App R 17 (216), at [12]:

> It is important to underline that the directions pass through the Criminal Procedure Rule Committee and are issued by the Lord Chief Justice pursuant to s. 74 of the Courts Act 2003 and Schedule 2 (Part 1) of the Constitutional Reform Act 2005. They represent the current practice and bind the courts to which they are directed. In that regard, they are identical to the practice directions for civil proceedings (s. 74 of the 2003 Act being in substantially the same terms as s. 5 of the Civil Procedure Act 1997) in respect of which Waller and Dyson LJJ said in Secretary of *State for Communities and Local Government v Bovale Ltd* [2009] EWCA Civ 171 at [28]:
>
>> 'The issue of a practice direction is the exercise of an inherent power, . . . and . . . it cannot be open to another judge of the court to which the practice direction is intended to apply to ignore that practice direction or to suggest in a judgment that a practice direction should no longer be followed in that court.'
>
> The value of the Criminal Procedure Rules and the Practice Directions is that they provide a code which govern the practice of all criminal litigation and go a long way to ensuring that justice is administered consistently throughout the country.

Much of the law set out in the CrimPD originates from authorities but it may well be a development of those principles and has a binding nature independent of them.

The inspiration for the rules came, in large part, from the *Review of the Criminal Courts of England and Wales* carried out by Auld LJ (the 'Auld report') in October 2001, and the first rules came into effect on 4 April 2005.

Sir Brian Leveson's *Review of Efficiency in Criminal Proceedings* was published in January 2015 and effect was given to many of the recommendations by amendments to the CrimPR and

CrimPD and a number of linked initiatives under the heading of Better Case Management. The specific mechanisms by which this is achieved are addressed in **D15**.

The case management provisions of the CrimPR and CrimPD are supported by the *Better Case Management Handbook* issued by the Senior Presiding Judge on 8 January 2018 and which has the status of guidance (see tinyurl.com/ydgab7z5).

Components of the Rules and Practice Direction

The CrimPR and CrimPD are divided into subject divisions, which follow the chronological progress of a criminal case. They are set out in full in the Supplement. Individual provisions are dealt with in the relevant sections of this work. Two parts of the CrimPR particularly give effect to the intention to enhance efficiency and support the Better Case Management process. Those are: **D4.2**

(a) Part 1: The Overriding Objective (see **D4.3**); and
(b) Part 3: Case Management (see **D4.7**).

THE OVERRIDING OBJECTIVE

Criminal Procedure Rules 2020, rr. 1.1 to 1.3 **D4.3**

1.1—(1) The overriding objective of this procedural code is that criminal cases be dealt with justly.
(2) Dealing with a criminal case justly includes—
(a) acquitting the innocent and convicting the guilty;
(b) dealing with the prosecution and the defence fairly;
(c) recognising the rights of a defendant, particularly those under Article 6 of the European Convention on Human Rights;
(d) respecting the interests of witnesses, victims and jurors and keeping them informed of the progress of the case;
(e) dealing with the case efficiently and expeditiously;
(f) ensuring that appropriate information is available to the court when bail and sentence are considered; and
(g) dealing with the case in ways that take into account—
(i) the gravity of the offence alleged,
(ii) the complexity of what is in issue,
(iii) the severity of the consequences for the defendant and others affected, and
(iv) the needs of other cases.

1.2—(1) Each participant, in the conduct of each case, must—
(a) prepare and conduct the case in accordance with the overriding objective;
(b) comply with these Rules, practice directions and directions made by the court; and
(c) at once inform the court and all parties of any significant failure (whether or not that participant is responsible for that failure) to take any procedural step required by these Rules, any practice direction or any direction of the court. A failure is significant if it might hinder the court in furthering the overriding objective.
(2) Anyone involved in any way with a criminal case is a participant in its conduct for the purposes of this rule.

1.3—(1) The court must further the overriding objective in particular when—
(a) exercising any power given to it by legislation (including these Rules);
(b) applying any practice direction; or
(c) interpreting any rule or practice direction.

The Balance of Rights and Duties

The elements included in the overriding objective stated in CrimPR 1.1(1) are expanded upon in r. 1.1(2). These recognise that all those who participate in proceedings have rights to be considered as well as obligations to undertake so as to ensure the efficient expedition of justice. **D4.4**

This approach was elaborated by the Court of Appeal in *Jisl* [2004] EWCA Crim 696 (at [114]):

> The starting point is simple. Justice must be done. The defendant is entitled to a fair trial: and, which is sometimes overlooked, the prosecution is equally entitled to a reasonable opportunity to present the evidence against the defendant. It is not however a concomitant of the entitlement to a fair trial that either or both sides are further entitled to take as much time as they like, or for that matter, as long as counsel and solicitors or the defendants themselves think appropriate. Resources are limited. The funding for courts and judges, for prosecuting and the vast majority of defence lawyers is dependent on public money, for which there are many competing demands. Time itself is a resource. Every day unnecessarily used, while the trial meanders sluggishly to its eventual conclusion, represents another day's stressful waiting for the remaining witnesses and the jurors in that particular trial, and no less important, continuing and increasing tension and worry for another defendant or defendants, some of whom are remanded in custody, and the witnesses in trials which are waiting their turn to be listed. It follows that the sensible use of time requires judicial management and control…

See also **D4.9**.

However, the rules have limitations. In *Hubner v District Court of Prostejov, Czech Republic* [2009] EWHC 2929 (Admin), the Divisional Court emphasised that the overriding objective could not affect the interpretation of substantive law or regulate 'the manner in which principles of law must be interpreted or construed' (per Elias LJ at [7]). Similarly, the CrimPR allow for case management but do not permit a judge to halt proceedings with which the judge disagrees (per Leveson LJ in *B (F)* [2010] EWCA Crim 1857, [2011] 1 WLR 844, at [26]).

The Balance of the Criteria

D4.5 In *Holmes v SGB Services* [2001] EWCA Civ 354, addressing the corresponding provisions of the Civil Procedure Rules, Buxton LJ said that the court had to balance all the criteria identified in CrimPR 1.1 without giving any one of them undue weight. However, this should not be interpreted as undermining the traditional status of the presumption of innocence. This was made clear by the Lord Chief Justice when he introduced the CrimPR, stating:

> The presumption of innocence and a robust adversarial process are essential features of English legal tradition and of the defendant's right to a fair trial. The overriding objective acknowledges those rights. It must not be read as detracting from a defendant's right to silence or from the confidentiality properly attaching to what passes between a lawyer and his client.

The requirement in r. 1.1(2)(b) of 'dealing with the prosecution and the defence fairly' should be read in the context of jurisprudence of the ECtHR, which emphasises the principle of equality of arms (see, e.g., *Kaufman v Belgium* (1986) 50 DR 98 at p. 115). However, this is not unqualified. In *Malcolm v DPP* [2007] EWHC 363 (Admin), [2007] 1 WLR 1230, the Divisional Court said that the requirement for the prosecution to prove their case in its entirety before closing the case 'had an anachronistic, and obsolete, ring', as the prosecution should be permitted to address points raised for the first time after that stage, which ought properly to have been raised in advance as part of the management of the case. In *Graham* [2019] EWCA Crim 2141 the decision of the trial judge to allow the prosecution to re-open their case to adduce further evidence after D's evidence-in-chief had been completed was upheld. CrimPR 25.9(2)(i) (see Supplement, **R25.9**) was not confined to rebuttal evidence.

There is a notable contrast between the formulae in r. 1.1(2)(c) and (d), which properly reflects the presumption of innocence. Whereas the rights of the defendant (particularly those under the ECHR, Article 6) have to be recognised (r. 1.1(2)(c)), there is a different formula, namely 'respecting the interests', in r. 1.1(2)(d), in relation to other parties in the case. It is therefore clear that proposition (c) takes precedence over proposition (d) where they come into conflict.

CrimPR 1.1(2)(e) is closely related to the provisions on case management, which are dealt with in **D4.7**; r. 1.1(2)(f) applies to agencies responsible for records of antecedents, and pre-sentence and medical reports, and underlines their duty to assist the court by ensuring that the relevant information is available at the crucial time when decisions as to bail and sentence are considered;

and r. 1.1(2)(g) imports the civil concept of proportionality into the overall objective, in accordance with the concern for resources identified by the Court of Appeal in *Jisl* [2004] EWCA Crim 696. It would be unrealistic to expect equivalent resources to be devoted to a case that ought to be tried in the magistrates' court and one that was indictable only. Again, the factors to be taken into account under this element of 'dealing justly' must be fleshed out by the approach of the courts to case management (see **D4.7**).

Duties Imposed on Participants

The remaining rules in Part 1 deal with the duty of the participants in the case to prepare and conduct the case in accordance with the overriding objective, and to comply with the rules and directions that the court makes. By CrimPR 1.2(2), 'Anyone involved in any way with a criminal case is a participant in its conduct for the purposes of this rule'. **D4.6**

This obligation was stressed by the Court of Appeal in *Phillips* [2007] EWCA Crim 1042, when Clarke J said (at [37]) 'not only must judges be robust in their case management decisions ... but the parties who are ordered to take steps must take them'.

The court itself is fixed with a duty to implement the overriding objective by CrimPR 1.3, through its case management functions.

CASE MANAGEMENT

CrimPR Part 3 operates together with CrimPD I (see Supplement, **CPD.1A**), which was re-cast as part of Better Case Management. **D4.7**

Rules 3.1 to 3.15 (see Supplement, **R3.1** ***et seq.***) apply to the management of all cases in the magistrates' courts and the Crown Court, including the Crown Court acting in its appellate capacity; rr. 3.19 to 3.34 apply to the preparation of Crown Court trials and rr. 3.16 to 3.18 to the magistrates' court. Rule 3.10 makes specific rules for the obtaining of medical reports by the court other than for sentencing purposes where, exceptionally, they are ordered by the court rather than obtained by the parties.

The Rationale

Rules 3.2(1) and (3) lay down that the court must further the overriding objective (see **D4.3**) by 'actively managing the case' and do so by giving any direction appropriate as early as possible. **D4.8**

This is not new. The need for active case management is a theme that the Court of Appeal has emphasised in a series of decisions and this was confirmed in the Leveson Review. In *Jisl* [2004] EWCA Crim 696, Judge LJ stated (at [116]–[118]):

> Active, hands on, case management, both pre-trial and throughout the trial itself, is now regarded as an essential part of the judge's duty. The profession must understand that this has become and will remain part of the normal trial process, and that cases must be prepared and conducted accordingly ...
>
> Once the issue has been identified, in a case of any substance at all, (and this particular case was undoubtedly a case of substance and difficulty) the judge should consider whether to direct a timetable to cover pre-trial steps, and eventually the conduct of the trial itself, not rigid, nor immutable, and fully recognising that during the trial at any rate the unexpected must be treated as normal, and making due allowance for it in the interests of justice. To enable the trial judge to manage the case in a way which is fair to every participant, pre-trial, the potential problems, as well as the possible areas for time saving, should be canvassed. In short, a sensible informed discussion about the future management of the case and the most convenient way to present the evidence, whether disputed or not, and where appropriate, with admissions by one or other or both sides, should enable the judge to make a fully informed analysis of the future

> timetable, and the proper conduct of the trial. The objective is not haste and rush, but greater efficiency and better use of limited resources by closer identification of and focus on critical rather than peripheral issues. When trial judges act in accordance with these principles, the directions they give, and where appropriate, the timetables they prescribe in the exercise of their case management responsibilities, will be supported in this Court. Criticism is more likely to be addressed to those who ignore them.

In *R (Hassani) v West London Magistrates' Court* [2017] EWHC 1270 (Admin), the Divisional Court emphasised that active case management was the duty of the criminal courts and that increased firmness and rigour was needed.

The Court's Role

D4.9 Rule 3.2(2) (see Supplement, **R3.2**) sets out a list of elements of active case management, based upon early identification of the issues, needs of witnesses, achieving certainty about what is to be done, by whom and when, and by the setting of a procedural timetable. There are obligations to monitor the progress of the case and compliance with directions, discourage delay, promote cooperation and avoid unnecessary hearings and, as to the evidence, to ensure that, whether disputed or not, it is presented in the shortest and clearest way. In turn r. 3.5 sets out the court's case management powers which include at r. 3.5(2)(h) the power to require that issues in the case should be identified in writing and to determine the order they are decided in. Rule 3.13 identifies powers to manage the trial or appeal itself, once again emphasising that the court must establish, with the assistance of the parties, what are the disputed issues and consider setting a timetable.

These provisions are consistent with authority from the Court of Appeal. For example:

(a) In *Bryant* [2005] EWCA Crim 2079, that it will support efforts by the trial judge to move a case forward at a reasonable speed, provided that the accused receives a fair trial.
(b) In *B* [2005] EWCA Crim 805, that the case management powers of the judge could be exercised to place limits on cross-examination and that the entitlement to a fair trial was not inconsistent with proper judicial control over the use of court time. See also *Heppenstall* [2007] EWCA Crim 2485.
(c) In *K* [2006] EWCA Crim 724, [2006] 2 All ER 552, that the case management powers in the CrimPR enable a judge to deal with issues preliminary to trial by way of written submissions, and to limit the length of those submissions (see **D9.26**).
(d) In *Boardman* [2015] EWCA Crim 175, [2015] 1 Cr App R 33 (504), that the judge's case management powers would justify the exclusion of late served prosecution evidence. As to the consequences of failures in disclosure, see also *Salt* [2015] EWCA Crim 662, [2015] 2 Cr App R 27 (376) at **D9.28**.

Where the ruling was made pre-trial then the CPIA 1996, s. 40(5), provides that 'no application may be made [for discharge or variation of such a ruling] unless there has been a material change in circumstances since the ruling was made or, if a previous application has been made, since the application (or last application) was made'. The same principle applies to rulings made during the trial (*Lashley* [2005] EWCA Crim 2016, at [20]).

Balancing Efficiency and Fairness

D4.10 Achieving effective case management must be tempered by the imperatives of justice, as outlined in CrimPR 1.1. This was emphasised by the Administrative Court in *S v DPP* [2006] EWHC 1207 (Admin), and illustrated by the approach in *R (Drinkwater) v Solihull Magistrates' Court* [2012] EWHC 765 (Admin), where it was stressed that the decision to proceed with a trial in D's absence was not to be made solely for reasons of expedition. Moreover, the court's power does not extend to the quashing of properly preferred indictments or otherwise using the overriding objective to challenge established legal principles (*B (F)* [2010] EWCA Crim 1857, [2011] 1 WLR 844, and see also *H (S)* [2010] EWCA Crim 1931, [2011] 1 Cr App R 14 (182)).

Case Management Directions The court may give any direction and take any step actively to manage a case unless that would be inconsistent with legislation including the CrimPR, and r. 3.5 identifies ways in which the court can act. D4.11

There are obligations on the court to give directions for the early conclusion of the case and to facilitate the attendance of witnesses and the participation of all including the defendant (r. 3.8). This includes extensive powers in rr. 3.8(6) and (7) to control the treatment and questioning of witnesses or defendants including setting ground rules or by r. 3.13 to require parties to identify witness requirements, points of law and to limit the examination of witnesses or the duration of any stage of the proceedings.

An increasingly important aspect of case management is the obligation on the court by r. 3.2(2)(h) and (3) and (4) to further the overriding objective by making use of technology by way of live links. The extent to which hearings can be conducted by video or audio was extended by amendments to relevant legislation made by the Coronavirus Act 2020 and consequent amendments to the CrimPR (see the Special Supplement, **D3.124F** and **D3.124G**).

CrimPR 3.19 to 3.34, supplemented by CrimPD I, paras. 3A.16 to 3A.28, encourage case management at pre-trial hearings in the Crown Court while CrimPR 3.16 to 3.18, supplemented by CrimPD I, paras. 3A.4 to 3A.15, regulate pre-trial hearings in the magistrates' court.

Protocols Relating to Complex Cases A protocol on the 'Control and Management of Heavy Fraud and Other Complex Criminal Cases' was issued by the Lord Chief Justice in March 2005. To make allowance for the changes brought about in Better Case Management a pilot case-management regime suitable for such cases was begun in October 2015 at four Crown Courts (Birmingham, Manchester, Kingston and Southwark). That has yet to result in any national guidance and, for the present, such cases are managed on an ad hoc basis, so far as possible within the principles of Better Case Management. D4.12

The Duties of the Parties

CrimPR 3.3 imposes on the parties a duty actively to assist the court in fulfilling the court's obligation actively to manage the case which therefore includes assisting the court in the early identification of the real issues. See also rr. 3.5(1)(h) and 3.11(a). Following the recommendations of the Leveson Review this was supplemented by a duty of direct engagement between identified representatives who have case ownership responsibilities. This is, in turn, supported by the obligation in r. 3.27 to notify the court of the identity of the intended defence trial advocate. D4.13

The obligation to assist the court in identifying the real issues is separate from the statutory provisions relating to disclosure (see **D9.29**).

CrimPD I, para. 1A.1, now explains:

> The presumption of innocence and an adversarial process are essential features of English and Welsh legal tradition and of the defendant's right to a fair trial. But it is no part of a fair trial that questions of guilt and innocence should be determined by procedural manoeuvres. On the contrary, fairness is best served when the issues between the parties are identified as early and as clearly as possible. As Lord Justice Auld noted, a criminal trial is not a game under which a guilty defendant should be provided with a sporting chance. It is a search for truth in accordance with the twin principles that the prosecution must prove its case and that a defendant is not obliged to inculpate himself, the object being to convict the guilty and acquit the innocent.

The reference to Auld LJ is to *Gleeson* [2003] EWCA Crim 3357, [2004] 1 Cr App R 29 (406) (at [36]). In *R (Hassani) v West London Magistrates' Court* [2017] EWHC 1270 (Admin), Irwin LJ said (at [9]–[10]):

> The criminal law is not a game to be played in the hope of a lucky outcome, a game to be played as long and in as involved a fashion as the paying client is able and prepared to afford. . . . Courts must

> consider the Criminal Procedure Rules, which are to be employed actively so as to preclude game playing and ensure that the courts only have to address real issues with some substance.

CrimPD I, para. 1A.2, now explains:

> Further, it is not just for a party to obstruct or delay the preparation of a case for trial in order to secure some perceived procedural advantage, or to take unfair advantage of a mistake by someone else. If courts allow that to happen it damages public confidence in criminal justice. The Rules and the Practice Directions, taken together, make it clear that courts must not allow it to happen.

The courts have shown themselves ready to act to identify the issues early and to deny the defence any advantage from failing to do so. See also *R (Lawson) v Stafford Magistrates' Court* [2007] EWHC 2490 (Admin); *Writtle v DPP* [2009] EWHC 236 (Admin), [2009] RTR 28 (369); *Penner* [2010] EWCA Crim 1155; *R (DPP) v Sunderland Magistrates* [2018] EWHC 229 (Admin), [2018] 2 Cr App R 20 (285).

However, the limits to the scope of a case management order which required disclosure of details of defence witnesses, and the implications for litigation privilege and legal professional privilege, were demonstrated in *R (Kelly) v Warley Magistrates' Court* [2007] EWHC 1836 (Admin), [2008] 1 WLR 2001, where the Divisional Court found that, although contemporary principles as to the proper conduct in litigation accorded greater weight to the dictates of good case management, they could not of themselves usurp a litigant's historic right not to disclose information until it was presented from the protection of litigation privilege or legal professional privilege. In *Randell v DPP* [2018] EWHC 1048 (Admin), it was held that a failure by D to engage by identifying issues on the Preparation for Effective Trial form could not be taken as an acceptance of the truth of V's statement nor consent to its being adduced as hearsay.

Case Progression Officers

D4.14 CrimPR 3.4 (see Supplement, **R3.4**) requires each of the parties, and the court, to appoint a case progression officer at the commencement of proceedings, and to inform the other participants of how to contact that person. The case progression officer is thereafter responsible for progressing the case, ensuring that party's compliance with court directions, and alerting other parties to anything which may interfere with the smooth progress of the case. CrimPD I, para. 3A.24, states: 'As far as possible, case progression should be managed without a hearing in the courtroom, using electronic communication in accordance with CrimPR 3.5(2)(d)'.

Practical Case Management

D4.15 CrimPR Part 3 is supplemented by CrimPD I, Part 3 (see Supplement **CPD.3A**), and the forms to be used for case management purposes, set out in CrimPD, annex D.

For cases that are contested and which are to proceed in the magistrates' court the parties are required to complete the Preparation for Effective Trial (PET) form. For cases that are to be sent to the Crown Court the Better Case Management (BCM) form is completed on sending, and the Plea and Trial Preparation Hearing (PTPH) form at that hearing at the Crown Court (paras. 3A.3, 3A.11). The respective forms are intended to promote engaged hearings properly to plan the further stages of the case, a standardised approach to case preparation, and to minimise the need for further hearings.

Issues of case management that are addressed in more detail elsewhere in this work include the following:

(a) the Better Case Management process, involving early guilty plea hearings and PTPH (see **D15.41**);
(b) the provisions relating to issues of disclosure (see **D9**);
(c) the provisions relating to preparatory hearings (see **D15.51**).

Failure to Comply with Rules, Directions and Time-limits

While the court has a power to extend a time-limit set by CrimPR Part 3 even after expiry (r. 3.15(1)(a)), an important aspect of the exercise of the court's case management powers is the consequences of any failure of the parties to comply with the rules or directions of the court, including time-limits. The proper approach to be adopted is that identified in *Musone* [2007] EWCA Crim 1237, [2007] 1 WLR 2467, where the Court of Appeal was concerned with whether the trial judge had correctly rejected the attempt by one accused to adduce evidence of the previous bad character of the other at a late stage — so late as to be in breach of the time-limit for service of a notice of an application to adduce such evidence (see also **F13.70**). **D4.16**

The Court observed that the trial judge was entitled to exclude such evidence where he concluded that D1 was deliberately manipulating the process so as to prevent D2 from dealing with the evidence properly. It would be rare for a judge to exclude evidence of substantial probative value just because the time-limits had not been complied with, but it would be proper to do so where such exclusion was the only means to ensure fairness.

The same approach was adopted in cases such as *R (Robinson) v Sutton Coldfield Magistrates' Court* [2006] EWHC 307 (Admin), [2006] 2 Cr App R 13 (208) and *Delay* [2006] EWCA Crim 1110, namely that the court should consider whether the other parties have been prejudiced by the late notice of the application, and the reasons for the delay, before deciding whether evidence should be excluded as a consequence of the breach of the rules.

Although these cases all relate to notice of a bad character application, the same approach has been taken in relation to the consequences of failures to comply with the rules in other areas (*R (Robinson) v Abergavenny Magistrates' Court* [2007] EWHC 2005 (Admin)). See also *Ensor* [2009] EWCA Crim 2519, [2010] 1 Cr App R 18 (255), where the failure of the defence to comply with the notice requirements for expert evidence resulted in the exclusion of that evidence.

The obligation on 'participants' does not just relate to their own compliance with the Rules. They are also expected to notify the court and all parties 'at once . . . of any significant failure' of compliance by others (r. 1.2(1)(c)). In *Boardman* [2015] EWCA Crim 175, [2015] 1 Cr App R 33 (504), Sir Brian Leveson P invoked the overriding objective, referred to *Jisl* [2004] EWCA Crim 696 and added, *obiter* (at [40]):

> . . . the fact that the defence solicitors did not alert the court to the problems of non-disclosure at a time when something could have been done about it (but left the complaint so late that the trial date could not be met) meant that the court was deprived of the opportunity of an earlier listing to resolve the issues [when they] could be resolved and maintain the trial date. It would be perfectly open to the judge to decide that the consequences of such a failure of duty on the part of the defence should be to reject a complaint of prejudice consequent upon the need for an adjournment. In each case, the impact of whatever breaches are established will be for the judge to assess, bearing in mind the particular circumstances of the case and the overriding objective.

In *R (Hassani) v West London Magistrates' Court* [2017] EWHC 1270 (Admin), the Divisional Court noted that CrimPR 1.2(1)(c) obliged the defence to notify the court of the late service of documentation by the prosecution in good time, rather than to raise the issue only at trial, and stated (at [12]):

> If the defence are going to suggest that some document or some piece of service is missing, they must do so early. If they do not, then it is open to the court to find that the point was raised late, and any direction then sought to produce a document or to apply for an adjournment may properly be refused.

That a late application or renewal may lead to refusal was confirmed by Lord Burnett CJ in *DPP v Walsall Magistrates' Court* [2019] EWHC 3317 (Admin) at [57]–[59].

Section D5 Starting a Prosecution and Preliminary Proceedings in Magistrates' Courts

INTRODUCTION

D5.1 This section describes the preliminary proceedings in the magistrates' court which precede either the summary trial of an accused or being sent to the Crown Court for trial.

PROCEDURE FOR STARTING A PROSECUTION AND SECURING PRESENCE OF ACCUSED

Introduction

D5.2 The first appearance of an accused before a magistrates' court may be secured in a number of different ways:

(a) The accused may be arrested and, after the police have sought advice from the CPS, charged by the police (the details of the offence(s) will appear on a charge sheet).
(b) The accused may be arrested and then granted police bail while the CPS decide whether there is sufficient evidence to justify a charge; the CPS may then start a prosecution by using the 'written charge and requisition' procedure established by the CJA 2003, s. 29 (where available).
(c) The accused may be arrested and then be granted police bail, subject to a requirement of returning to the police station on a specified date; during the intervening period the CPS decide whether there is sufficient evidence to justify a charge and, if so, when the accused returns to the police station, the police will charge the accused with the offence(s) specified by the CPS.
(d) The accused may be served with a written charge and requisition (under the CJA 2003, s. 29) without first having been arrested.
(e) An application may be made to a magistrates' court for the issue of a summons (or an arrest warrant) requiring the accused to attend before it (this process is sometimes referred to as 'laying an information'). A prosecutor who is not a 'relevant prosecutor' for these purposes (see **D5.4**) cannot use the written charge and requisition process but must instead apply for the issue of a summons by the magistrates' court.

Much of the relevant legislation (such as the MCA 1980) refers to trial of an 'information' by a magistrates' court. For these purposes, an 'information' is the application to the magistrates' court for a summons requiring the accused to attend the court to answer the allegation of having committed an offence. Moreover, the CJA 2003, s. 30(5), provides that references to an 'information' are to be construed as including a 'written charge', and references to a 'summons' are to be construed as including a 'requisition'.

D5.3 The powers and procedures for arresting an accused without warrant, questioning at a police station and then charging are dealt with in detail in **D1**, which also deals with the circumstances *in which the police may refuse to bail* a person who has been charged and the period within which that person must be brought before a magistrates' court. This section considers the other means of securing the presence of the accused before the court.

Written Charge and Requisition Procedure

The CJA 2003, s. 29, applies only to prosecutions brought by a 'relevant prosecutor'. By virtue of s. 29(5), s. 29 applies to prosecutions brought by the following (or by someone authorised to institute criminal proceedings on their behalf): D5.4

(a) a police force;
(b) the Director of the SFO;
(c) the DPP (and therefore the CPS);
(d) the Director General of the NCA;
(e) the A-G (not yet in force);
(f) a person specified by the Secretary of State in an order under the CJA 2003, s. 29(5)(h).

Those so designated as 'relevant prosecutors' include the Secretary of State for Work and Pensions, the Secretary of State for Health in England and Wales, the Secretary of State for Business, Energy and Industrial Strategy, the Driver and Vehicle Standards Agency, Transport for London, the Environment Agency, specified local authorities (including county and district councils, and London borough councils), the Natural Resources Body for Wales, railway operators (for the purpose of prosecuting a railway offence), certain tramway operators and the TV licensing authority.

Under s. 29(1), a prosecutor to whom these provisions apply may institute criminal proceedings against a person by issuing a 'written charge', which charges the person with an offence. Under s. 29(2), where the prosecutor issues a written charge, a 'requisition' must be issued at the same time; this requires the accused to appear before a magistrates' court to answer the written charge. The written charge and requisition must be served on the accused and a copy of both must be served on the court named in the requisition (s. 29(3)).

This method of commencing criminal proceedings is available only where the prosecutor is a 'relevant prosecutor' (i.e. a prosecuting body specified under the legislation).

Where a 'relevant prosecutor' issues a written charge, the relevant magistrates' court must be notified immediately. However, notification of the requirement to attend court is communicated to the accused by the prosecutor through service of the 'requisition' which accompanies the written charge (not by the magistrates' court, as is the case where a summons is issued). D5.5

Section 30(4) makes it clear that the written charge and requisition procedure does not affect the ability of a 'relevant prosecutor' to apply for the issue of an arrest warrant under the MCA 1980, s. 1 (see **D5.8**).

As the magistrates' court is not involved in the issuing of the written charge and requisition, there will be no possibility of the magistrates preventing a prosecution from being brought in this way. However, it is submitted that the decision to issue a written charge and requisition could be amenable to judicial review, and an application for the case to be dismissed as an abuse of process would also be available in appropriate cases.

In *Brown v DPP* [2019] EWHC 798 (Admin), [2019] 2 Cr App R 6 (48), the Divisional Court rejected the submission that the issuing of a written charge arises only when the written charge is posted to the accused. Irwin LJ (at [19]) noted that the 'issuing' of the written charge and its service are discrete steps. The Court also rejected the submission that the information contained in the written charge must be in the public domain, in the sense of being placed before a court or being served, before issue can be held to be complete. It follows that the written charge can be regarded as issued 'when the document comprising the written charge is completed, with all relevant details and in the form needed for service' (at [20]). Provided this is, in the case of a summary offence (to which the six-month time-limit in the MCA 1980, s. 127, applies), done within six months of the offence in question, the written charge will have been issued in time. His lordship went on to observe (at [22]) that, if there is 'an inordinate or unwarranted or unjustified but significant delay before such a written charge is served', that may amount to abuse of process. It would therefore 'be wise for prosecutors, as a matter of practice, to ensure in every case that both the issue and service ... are completed before six months from the relevant offences, so as to put paid to any suggestion of such unwarranted delay'.

In *DPP v McFarlane* [2019] EWHC 1895 (Admin), [2020] 1 Cr App R 4 (112), the Divisional Court reiterated (at [28]) that criminal proceedings are 'instituted' by the issue of a written charge pursuant to the CJA 2003, s. 29, regardless of whether a requisition (or a single justice procedure notice, see **D5.6**) is issued and regardless of whether the charge and requisition (or single justice procedure notice) are served on the accused. It was also held that the s. 29 procedure is available where the prosecution sought to add one or more new charges to existing proceedings for which the attendance of the accused has already been secured. This includes a requirement to issue a requisition, even if it serves no practical purposes (per Males LJ, at [18]). The effect of this part of the decision is now enshrined in CrimPR 7.3(3) (see Supplement, **R7.3**), which provides that a prosecutor who alleges an offence against an accused who is due to attend, or attends, court in response to another allegation, must set out the additional allegation in terms that comply with r. 7.3(1) (see **D5.14**) and, as soon as practicable, either serve the additional allegation on the court officer and the defendant, or present the additional allegation orally to the court, with a written statement of that allegation. In *McFarlane* it was held that failure to issue a requisition and/or failure to serve the documents is a procedural defect that does not render the institution of proceedings a nullity (at [24]). To the extent that such failure causes prejudice to an accused, 'the court's jurisdiction to stay proceedings as an abuse of process provides a sufficient remedy'. In the case under consideration, where D was already before the Court, there was no question of any prejudice at all. It is likely that the same principles would apply even though the requirement to serve a written charge and requisition in such a case is now contained in the CrimPR.

In *Young v DPP* [2020] EWHC 976 (Admin), the issue again arose whether proceedings for a summary offence had been commenced within the required six months. The Administrative Court confirmed that, whether or not the magistrates purport to act under the MCA 1980, s. 8A (pre-trial rulings), whether proceedings have been commenced in time is a matter that is appropriate to be dealt with by a preliminary ruling. The Court reiterated (at [35]) that:

> ... the only document the issue of which within six months of the offence is relevant to the question of jurisdiction is the written charge. If the written charge was issued within that six-month period, ... it is irrelevant to that question of jurisdiction when the SJPN was issued or whether it was issued and served at the same time as the written charge.

Single Justice Procedure Notice

D5.6 The CJA 2003, s. 29, as amended by the CJCA 2015, s. 46, provides that, where a 'relevant prosecutor' issues a written charge, either a 'requisition' or a 'single justice procedure notice' must be issued at the same time. A single justice procedure notice requires the recipient to serve on the magistrates' court specified in the notice a written notification stating whether the recipient desires to plead guilty or not guilty and, if the intended plea is guilty, whether the case should be dealt with in accordance with the single justice procedure set out in the MCA 1980, s. 16A (CJA 2003, s. 29(2B)). This procedure is limited to cases where the accused has attained the age of 18, is charged with a summary offence that does not carry imprisonment, intends to plead guilty and does not object to the matter being dealt with by a single justice without a hearing (and therefore without requiring the accused to attend court).

Applying for the Issue of a Summons

D5.7 **The Application ('Information')** The written charge and requisition procedure is not available in the case of private prosecutions (i.e. prosecutions where the prosecutor is not a 'relevant prosecutor', as defined by the CJA 2003, s. 29(5)); these must be commenced by making an application to the magistrates' court for the issue of a summons. Historically, this has been known as 'laying information', though this phrase does not appear in CrimPR Part 7. The CJA 2003, s. 30(4)(b), provides that nothing in s. 29 affects the power of a person who is not a relevant prosecutor to serve an information for the purpose of obtaining the issue of a summons, or a warrant, under the MCA 1980, s. 1.

Under CrimPR 7.2(1) (see Supplement, **R7.2**) a prosecutor who wants the court to issue a summons must either serve a written application on the court, or present an application orally to the court (but with a written record of the allegation(s) made by the prosecutor). By virtue of CrimPR 7.2(3), the application must set out the allegation(s) made by the applicant and, if there is a time limit for prosecution of the offence(s), demonstrate that the application is made in time.

Unless the prosecution is being brought by or on behalf of a 'public authority' (as defined by the Prosecution of Offences Act 1985, s. 17(6), which governs recovery of prosecution costs, and includes the police, the CPS, government departments, and local authorities), the application must also set out concisely the grounds for asserting that the accused has committed the alleged offence(s), and must disclose details of any previous such application by the same applicant in respect of any allegation now made, and of any current or previous proceedings brought by another prosecutor in respect of any of the allegations now made. The application must also include a statement that, to the best of the applicant's knowledge, information and belief, the allegations contained in the application are substantially true, the evidence on which the applicant relies will be available at the trial, and that the application discloses all the information that is material to what the court must decide (CrimPR 7.2(6)). Where the latter statement is made orally, it must (unless the court directs otherwise) be made on oath or affirmation (r. 7.2(7)).

CrimPR 7.2 refers to 'a prosecutor' applying for the issue of a summons. It is questionable whether an application for a summons may be served on behalf of an unincorporated association. It seems to follow from *Rubin v DPP* [1990] 2 QB 80 that an application for a summons should be served by a named, actual person and must disclose the identity of that person. However, in *Ealing Justices, ex parte Dixon* [1990] 2 QB 91, Woolf LJ said that he had reservations as to the reasoning which had underpinned the conclusion reached in *Rubin*, that a prosecution must be by an individual rather than a corporate person. Nonetheless, his lordship said (at p. 101) that he would 'regard it as preferable' for an individual to be named, albeit that the individual is acting on behalf of a body corporate. **D5.8**

In *Norwich Justices, ex parte Texas Homecare* [1991] Crim LR 555, the applications had been signed by the senior environmental health officer, who had no authority to do so under the relevant legislation. The applications were later amended to substitute the signature of the person who did have the necessary authority, but the amendment took place after the six-month deadline for commencing the prosecution had elapsed. The Divisional Court quashed the convictions, holding that where the person applying for a summons has no authority to do so, the application is a nullity, and this was not curable by amendment.

Service of the Application Service of written applications is governed by CrimPR Part 4 (see Supplement, **R4.1** *et seq.*). Rule 4.2(2) states that, where electronic service of a document is permitted by r. 4.6, 'the general rule is that the person serving it must use that method'. Otherwise, under r. 4.3(1)(e), a document may be served on the court 'by handing it to a court officer with authority to accept it at the relevant court office'; under r. 4.4, a document may be served by leaving the document at or sending it by first class post to the relevant court office, or via the Document Exchange (r. 4.5). Rule 4.11 states that, where a document is handed over, it is served that day; where it is sent by post or via the DX, the second business day after the day on which it was posted or left at the DX; where it is sent by email, it is served the same day if sent no later than 2.30 p.m. (otherwise, it is served the following day). In *Begum v Luton Borough Council* [2018] EWHC 1044 (Admin), [2018] 1 WLR 3792, an application for several summonses was left with a court security guard. The guard did not have authority to accept documents. The Divisional Court held that the recipient must have authority to receive the document on behalf of the court. It followed that the application was to be regarded as having been left at the court office (and so, under r. 4.11(2)(a), deemed to have been served the following business day), not served on a court officer (and deemed to have been served the same day). It should be noted that the CrimPR do not specify who has authority to receive documents: that is a matter for HM Courts and Tribunals Service. **D5.9**

D5.10 **The Summons**

The MCA 1980, s. 1(1), provides that:

> (1) On an information being laid before a justice of the peace that a person has, or is suspected of having, committed an offence, the justice may issue—
> (a) a summons directed to that person requiring him to appear before a magistrates' court to answer the information, or
> (b) a warrant to arrest that person and bring him before a magistrates' court.

A justices' clerk (or an assistant clerk who has been specifically authorised by the justices' clerk for that purpose) may issue a summons but not a warrant (Justices' Clerks Rules 2005 (SI 2005 No. 545), sch. 1, paras. 1 and 2).

D5.11 **Decision to Issue a Summons** The decision whether to issue a summons 'is a judicial function which must, therefore, be performed judicially' (per Lord Roskill in *Manchester Stipendiary Magistrate, ex parte Hill* [1983] 1 AC 328 at pp. 342F–343D). The exercise of this function was considered by the Divisional Court in *R (Kay) v Leeds Magistrates' Court* [2018] EWHC 1233 (Admin), [2018] 4 WLR 91. The Court referred (at [21]–[22]) to a line of authority starting with *West London Metropolitan Stipendiary Magistrate, ex parte Klahn* [1979] WLR 933 (per Lord Widgery CJ, at pp. 935F–936E), and summarised the relevant principles thus:

> (1) The magistrate must ascertain whether the allegation is an offence known to the law, and if so whether the essential ingredients of the offence are prima facie present; that the offence alleged is not time-barred; that the court has jurisdiction; and whether the informant has the necessary authority to prosecute.
> (2) If so, generally the magistrate ought to issue the summons, unless there are compelling reasons not to do so — most obviously that the application is vexatious (which may involve the presence of an improper ulterior purpose and/or long delay); or is an abuse of process; or is otherwise improper.
> (3) Hence the magistrate should consider the whole of the relevant circumstances to enable him to satisfy himself that it is a proper case to issue the summons and, even if there is evidence of the offence, should consider whether the application is vexatious, an abuse of process, or otherwise improper.
> (4) Whether the applicant has previously approached the police may be a relevant circumstance.
> (5) There is no obligation on the magistrate to make enquiries, but he may do so if he thinks it necessary.
> (6) A proposed defendant has no right to be heard, but the magistrate has a discretion to: (a) require the proposed defendant to be notified of the application; (b) hear the proposed defendant if he thinks it necessary for the purpose of making a decision.

The Court went on to discuss what was described as the 'duty of candour' when making such applications. Reference was made (at [24]) to *Grays Justices, ex parte Low* [1988] 3 All ER 834, where Nolan J said (at p. 837J) that 'the withholding of material information is in itself a critical factor in determining whether a summons should be set aside as an abuse of the process of the court'. The Court then pointed out (at [25]) that this duty has been described in a number of ways, including as a duty of 'full and frank disclosure'; a duty 'not to mislead the judge in any material way'; a duty to disclose 'any material which is potentially adverse to the application'. At [26], the Court quoted the words of Hughes LJ in *Re Stanford International Bank Ltd* [2010] EWCA Civ 137, [2011] Ch 33 (at [191]):

> In effect a prosecutor seeking an *ex parte* order must put on his defence hat and ask himself what, if he were representing the defendant or a third party with a relevant interest, he would be saying to the judge, and, having answered that question, that is what he must tell the judge.

If a summons is issued in a case where it should not have been, it is open to the defendant to apply to the magistrates' court to stay the proceedings as an abuse of process (see **D3.66** ***et seq.***).

In *R (Johnson) v Westminster Magistrates' Court* [2019] EWHC 1709 (Admin), [2019] 2 Cr App R 30 (344), the Court reiterated (at [7]) that, when determining whether to issue a summons, a magistrate 'must ascertain whether the allegation is of an offence known to law, and if so whether the essential ingredients of the offence are prima facie present'. Where it is argued that the magistrate erred in law by reaching a decision that no magistrate, properly directing him or herself as to the ingredients of the offence, could reasonably have reached, this is a public law challenge that is therefore amenable to judicial review (see [17]–[19]).

In *R (Charlson) v Guildford Magistrates' Court* [2006] EWHC 2318 (Admin), [2006] 1 WLR 3494, the Divisional Court considered the approach to be adopted by magistrates if they are considering whether to issue a summons for a private prosecution where the CPS had already brought and discontinued a prosecution arising out of the same events. Silber J said (at [19]) that, where justices are considering whether to accede to an application to issue a summons for a private prosecution where the CPS have already brought a prosecution which is still proceeding, they should, in the absence of special circumstances, be slow to issue a summons at the behest of a private prosecutor. **D5.12**

Delay in Issue of Summons The MCA 1980, s. 1, does not require that the issue of a summons must follow immediately upon the consideration of the application by the court (*Fairford Justices, ex parte Brewster* [1976] QB 600). It is open to the prosecutor to serve the application on the court and then suggest that a summons should not be issued immediately (e.g., because the accused is out of the country and service could not be effected for a considerable time). However, if the delay between the making of the application and the issue of the summons is so great as to be unreasonable and to cause prejudice, then the High Court has a discretion to intervene by way of judicial review (see **D29.25** ***et seq.***) and quash the summons (*Ex parte Brewster* at p. 604F–H). Moreover, an application for a summons should be served on the court with the intention of having the consequent summons served as soon as reasonably possible. Therefore, if the prosecutor has not in fact decided whether to proceed at the time of applying for the summons but is concerned merely that any possible prosecution should not be out of time, this conduct could amount to an abuse of the process of the court and the magistrates therefore had the power to stay the proceedings if the prosecutor then decided to proceed (*Brentford Justices, ex parte Wong* [1981] QB 445). **D5.13**

Content of the Written Charge or Application for a Summons

CrimPR 7.3(1) (see Supplement, **R7.3**) provides that an application for a summons (or for an arrest warrant) or a written charge must contain: **D5.14**

(a) a statement of the offence which describes the offence 'in ordinary language' and (if the offence is created by statute) identifies the legislation that creates it; and
(b) sufficient particulars of the conduct constituting the commission of the offence to make clear what the prosecutor alleges against the defendant (including the value of any damage or theft alleged where that value is known and where it affects the exercise of the court's powers, as will be the case with criminal damage where the value involved does not exceed £5,000, and shoplifting where the value involved does not exceed £200: see **D6.20** and **D6.27** respectively).

Where a number of incidents, taken together, amount to a course of conduct (having regard to the time, place or purpose of commission), those incidents may be included in the allegation (r. 7.3(2)). Moreover, a single document may contain more than one charge (r. 7.2(9)).

Under r. 7.4(3) (see Supplement, **R7.4**), a requisition or summons must contain a notice setting out when and where the accused must attend the court, and must specify each offence in respect of which it has been issued. Additionally, a summons must identify the issuing court, and a requisition must identify the person under whose authority it is issued.

Beyond the general statement in r. 7.3 that the offence that is alleged should be described in ordinary language and give sufficient particulars of the conduct alleged, there is little guidance on how it should be drafted. However, reference to a particular statutory provision may cure an apparent defect by making plain what might otherwise be ambiguous (*Karpinski v City of Westminster* [1993] Crim LR 606, followed in *DPP v Short* [2001] EWHC Admin 885).

Insufficient Particulars If insufficient particulars of the offence are given, an application for further particulars may be made at any time after the charge has been preferred (*Aylesbury Justices, ex parte Wisbey* [1965] 1 All ER 602 at p. 345). In *Nash v Birmingham Crown Court* [2005] EWHC 338 (Admin), it was held that if documents that are served fail to give sufficient information to the accused as to the nature of the charge that is alleged, that does not of itself render the proceedings a nullity or any resulting conviction unsafe, provided that the requisite information is given to the accused in good **D5.15**

time (so as to be able to answer the allegations that are being made). The accused is entitled to that information and its provision is capable of curing the defect in the summons or written charge (per Stanley Burnton J at [26]). In such a case it may well be appropriate for the prosecution to apply to amend the wording of the charge (under the MCA 1980, s. 123), with the defence being granted an adjournment if they may have been misled by the original error. In *R (Mohamed) v London Borough of Waltham Forest* [2020] EWHC 1083 (Admin), [2020] 1 WLR 2929, the Divisional Court reiterated (at [24]) that 'if insufficient information has been provided by a prosecutor to a magistrate to justify the issue of a summons, but a summons has in fact been issued, the subsequent criminal proceedings do not become a nullity'. This is because 'the subsequent provision of sufficient information may remedy the earlier deficiency of information so that the criminal proceedings are fair'. The Court added that 'if sufficient information could never be provided to the magistrate, the Court may quash the decision to issue a summons based on the insufficient information'.

Service of the Summons or Requisition

D5.16 A summons or requisition may be served on an individual by handing it to the individual (CrimPR 4.3(1)(a)) or by leaving it at, or sending it by first class post to, an address where it is reasonably believed that the individual will receive it (r. 4.4(1) and (2)(a)).

Service of a summons or requisition on a corporation may be effected by handing it to a person holding a senior position in that corporation (r. 4.3(1)(b)) or by leaving it at, or sending it by first class post to, its principal office in England and Wales or, if there is no readily identifiable principal office, any place in England and Wales where it carries on its activities or business (r. 4.4(1) and (2)(b)).

Issue of Warrant for Arrest

D5.17 The MCA 1980, s. 1(1)(b), provides that whenever a justice has power to issue a summons, it is possible alternatively to issue a warrant for the arrest of the person named in the application, provided that:

(a) the application is in writing (s. 1(3); CrimPR 7.2(2)); and
(b) where the person in respect of whom the warrant is to be issued has attained the age of 18, the offence to which the warrant relates is an indictable offence or is punishable with imprisonment or else the person's address is not sufficiently established for a summons, or a written charge and requisition, to be served on that person (s. 1(4); CrimPR 7.2(4)).

It is submitted that a magistrate should not issue a warrant if a summons or requisition, as the case may be, would appear to be an effective means of securing the accused's attendance before the court. Moreover, given that a police officer may arrest (without warrant) a person for any offence provided that the officer has reasonable grounds for believing that the arrest is necessary (for example) to allow the prompt and effective investigation of the offence or to prevent any prosecution for the offence from being hindered by the disappearance of the suspect (see the PACE 1984, s. 24, and **D1.14**), an application for an arrest warrant will generally be unnecessary, as the suspect can be arrested without one. It follows that the use of a warrant for arrest issued under s. 1 of the 1980 Act is the least common means of commencing proceedings.

Whenever magistrates issue an arrest warrant they have a discretion to 'back it for bail', i.e. they may direct that, having been arrested, the person arrested shall thereafter be bailed by the police to attend court on a named day (see s. 117 of the 1980 Act). The backing for bail may be unconditional or conditional on the accused providing sureties.

Under the MCA 1980, s. 1(4A), where a person who is not a relevant prosecutor authorised to issue requisitions applies for a summons in respect of a qualifying offence (i.e. an offence listed in s. 1(4C)) committed outside the UK, an arrest warrant can be issued only with the consent of the DPP.

D5.18 The MCA 1980, s. 1(6), specifically provides that, if the offence alleged is indictable (this term includes either-way offences), a warrant for arrest may be issued under s. 1 notwithstanding that a summons (or written charge and requisition) has already been issued. If the offence is summary and the process initially takes the form of a summons or a requisition, it would seem that there is no power to issue a warrant under s. 1, although circumstances may subsequently arise which justify a warrant under other provisions of the Act.

Effect of Defect in Process on Jurisdiction of Court

The jurisdiction of a magistrates' court to determine mode of trial for an either-way offence, to try such an offence summarily or to send it to the Crown Court to be tried on indictment is dependent, *inter alia*, on the accused appearing or being brought before the court (MCA 1980, ss. 2(3) to (4) and 18). However, there is no express requirement in those provisions that the accused's presence shall have been obtained by lawful means. Therefore, if the accused in fact appears before the court (e.g., in answer to a summons or requisition) or is brought before the court following arrest, the magistrates will have jurisdiction to deal with the case even if the process by which the attendance of the accused was secured was faulty, provided, of course, that any other preconditions of jurisdiction are satisfied (*Hughes* (1879) 4 QBD 614, approved by the House of Lords in *Manchester Stipendiary Magistrate, ex parte Hill* [1983] 1 AC 328 at pp. 344–5). **D5.19**

DISCLOSURE OF INITIAL DETAILS OF PROSECUTION CASE

CrimPR Part 8 (see Supplement, **R8.1** *et seq.*) applies in every case (r. 8.1(1)). Rule 8.2(1)(a) requires the prosecutor, as soon as practicable (and, in any event, no later than the beginning of the day of the first hearing), to provide to the court 'initial details' of the prosecution case. These initial details of the prosecution case do not have to be supplied automatically to the accused; rather, r. 8.2(2) provides that, if the accused requests the initial details, the prosecutor must serve them as soon as practicable (and, in any event, no later than the beginning of the day of the first hearing); if the accused does not request those details, the prosecutor must make them available to the accused at, or before, the beginning of the day of the first hearing (r. 8.2(3)). **D5.20**

What constitutes 'initial details' of the prosecution case is defined by r. 8.3. Where, immediately before the first hearing in the magistrates' court, the accused was in police custody for the offence charged, initial details comprise a 'summary of the circumstances of the offence', and the accused's criminal record (if any). If the accused is not in custody, initial details comprise: a summary of the circumstances of the offence; any account given by the accused in interview (set out either in the summary or in a separate document); any written witness statements (including exhibits) that the prosecutor has available at that stage and which the prosecutor considers to be material to plea, or to whether the case should be tried in a magistrates' court or the Crown Court, or to sentence; the accused's criminal record (if any); and any available statement of the effect of the offence on victims or their family (or on others).

It is submitted that the reference to a magistrates' court in Part 8 should be taken to include youth courts, and so these provisions apply equally to cases in the youth court where the accused is under the age of 18.

CrimPD I, para. 3A.4, states that the information supplied pursuant to CrimPR 8.3 must be sufficient to allow the accused and the court, at the first hearing, to take an informed view on plea and (where applicable) venue for trial. Paragraph 3A.12 makes the point that, if the accused is on bail and the prosecutor does not anticipate a guilty plea at the first hearing in a magistrates' court, the initial details of the prosecution case that are provided for that first hearing must be sufficient to assist the court to identify the real issues and to give appropriate directions for an effective trial (regardless of whether the trial is to be heard in the magistrates' court or the Crown Court). Moreover, by virtue of para. 3A.13, as well as the material required by CrimPR Part 8, the information required by the Preparation for Effective Trial form must be available to be submitted at the first hearing, and the parties must complete that form.

Failure to Comply

Part 8 contains no specific sanction if the prosecution fail to supply the required initial details. **D5.21**
However, it is submitted that it would be open to the magistrates' court to make a direction (under

CrimPR 3.5: see Supplement, **R3.5**) requiring the prosecution to comply. It should be noted that r. 3.5(6)(a) provides that, if a party fails to comply with direction given by the court, the court may (for example) adjourn the hearing (see **D5.22**). Failure on the part of the prosecution to comply with Part 8 is likely to result in an adjournment (and possibly a costs sanction under r. 3.5(6)(b)).

Moreover, CrimPR 8.4 applies where the prosecutor wants to introduce information contained in a document listed in r. 8.3 but has not served that document on the accused or made that information available. In such cases, the prosecutor will not be permitted to 'introduce that information unless the court first allows the defendant sufficient time to consider it'.

However, it would appear that the court cannot dismiss the charge(s) brought by the prosecution because of non-compliance with a request for initial details of the prosecution case (*King v Kucharz* (1989) 153 JP 336). In *R (AP, MD and JS)* [2001] EWHC Admin 215, the Divisional Court held that, even taking into account the coming into force of the HRA 1998, the court does not have jurisdiction to dismiss proceedings for abuse of process simply on the basis of the failure to supply the information now required by Part 8.

ADJOURNMENTS AND REMANDS ON BAIL AND IN CUSTODY

Power to Adjourn

D5.22 At any stage before the case is sent to the Crown Court for trial or before (or during) a summary trial, a magistrates' court may adjourn the proceedings (see the MCA 1980, ss. 10 and 18, and **D5.29**).

D5.23 A substantial body of case law on the approach to be taken to applications for adjournments (the effect of which was summarised in *Picton* [2006] EWHC 1108 (Admin)) had developed over the years. However, CrimPD VI, para. 24C.6 (see Supplement, **CPD.24C**), stipulates that the Practice Direction now codifies the relevant principles, that the Practice Direction supersedes those judgments, and that it is to the Practice Direction that magistrates' courts must refer in the first instance.

Paragraphs 24C.5 to 24C.26 address applications to adjourn on the day of the trial. Paragraph 24C.7 emphasises that the 'starting point is that the trial should proceed', and refers to *DPP v Petrie* [2015] EWHC 48 (Admin), where Gross LJ observed (at [19]) that, 'efficiency, expedition, the discouraging of delay and the avoidance of unnecessary hearings are adjuncts of dealing with cases justly and it may be said, in the summary jurisdiction, summarily. Adjournments . . . run contrary to these important objectives.' His lordship went on to say (at [20]):

> Although there are of course instances where the interests of justice require the grant of an adjournment, this should be a course of last rather than first resort — and after other alternatives have been considered . . . It is essential that parties to proceedings in the magistrates' court should proceed on the basis of a need to get matters right first time; any suggestion of a culture readily permitting an opportunity to correct failures of preparation should be firmly dispelled.

Paragraph 24C.8 adds that a magistrates' court 'may keep in mind that, if appropriate, the court's decision may be re-opened' (under the MCA 1980, s 142, which empowers a magistrates' court to set aside a conviction; see **D22.73**), and that 'avenues of appeal by way of rehearing or of review are open to the parties' (see **D29** on appeals from magistrates' courts).

Paragraph 24C.9 identifies a number of principles that are relevant to applications to adjourn trials:

(i) the court's duty to deal justly with the case, which includes doing justice between the parties;
(ii) the court 'must have regard to the need for expedition. Delay is generally inimical to the interests of justice and brings the criminal justice system into disrepute. Proceedings in a magistrates' court should be simple and speedy';
(iii) applications for adjournments 'should be rigorously scrutinised and the court must have a clear reason for adjourning. To do this, the court must review the history of the case' (this may of course be taken to militate against repeated adjournments);

(iv) where the prosecutor asks for an adjournment, the court must consider not only the interest of the accused in getting the matter dealt with without delay, 'but also the public interest in ensuring that criminal charges are adjudicated upon thoroughly, with the guilty convicted as well as the innocent acquitted'; with a more serious charge, 'the public interest that there be a trial will carry greater weight';
(v) where the accused asks for an adjournment, the court 'must consider whether he or she will be able to present the defence fully without an adjournment and, if not, the extent to which his or her ability to do so is compromised';
(vi) the court must consider the consequences of an adjournment and its impact on the ability of witnesses and of the accused accurately to recall events;
(vii) the 'impact of adjournment on other cases', since relisting one case 'almost inevitably delays or displaces the hearing of others', and so the 'length of the hearing and the extent of delay in other cases will need to be considered'.

The Practice Direction goes on to address the relevance of fault. Paragraph 24C.10 observes that a potential consequence of the starting point, that the trial should proceed without an adjournment, may be that the prosecutor is unable to prove the prosecution case, or that the accused is unable to explore an issue. However, that 'may be a just consequence of inadequate preparation. Even in the absence of fault on the part of either party it may not be in the interests of justice to adjourn, notwithstanding that an imperfect trial may be the result.' Paragraph 24C.11 makes the point that, if the adjournment is needed because of fault on the part of the applicant, that 'weighs against' granting the adjournment (depending on the 'gravity of the fault'). Paragraph 24C.12 says that a fault will be regarded as serious 'if the relevant act or omission has been repeated, especially where it has caused a previous adjournment, or where there is no reasonable explanation for that act or omission', adding that the 'more serious the default, the less willing the court will be to adjourn'. Another issue that may be relevant where a party has been at fault is whether the other party, if aware of the fault, drew 'attention to that fault promptly and explicitly'; if not, the court 'may look less favourably on any application by that other party for an adjournment, especially if that application might reasonably have been made before the trial date' (para. 24C.13).

Paragraph 24C.14 notes that the length of the adjournment that is sought is a relevant consideration: the 'shorter the necessary adjournment, the less objectionable it will be' (subject to the 'ability of the court to accommodate it without undue impact on other cases'). In any event, courts must 'make every effort to make the adjournment as short as possible, for example by using time vacated by another trial or by conducting the hearing at another court house'. Indeed, in some cases 'it may be possible to achieve a just outcome by a short adjournment to later on the same day'.

If the reason for the application to adjourn is that the applicant 'seeks more time in which to raise or explore an issue', an important consideration is whether that party has 'reasonable grounds' for the late identification of that issue; in the absence of such grounds, failure to ensure early identification of issues 'will constitute a fault' for these purposes (para. 24C.15).

The Practice Direction also addresses failure to serve evidence in time as a basis for seeking an adjournment. Paragraph 24C.21 notes that it should 'rarely be the case that an application to adjourn based on a failure to serve evidence is made on the day of trial. The court is entitled to expect that evidence will have been served in good time and in accordance with the directions of the court.' Paragraph 24C.22 requires the court to 'conduct a rigorous inquiry into the nature of the evidence', and to consider 'whether any of what is sought has been served, and if so when; the volume and the significance of what is sought; and the time likely to be needed for its consideration'. In particular, the court 'must satisfy itself that any material still sought is relevant and that the party seeking it has a right to it'. In some circumstances, 'a failure to serve evidence can be addressed by refusing to admit it instead of by adjourning the trial to allow it to be served'.

Paragraph 24C.24 goes on to state that, where the accused seeks an adjournment on the basis of a prosecution failure to disclose material that ought to have been disclosed under the CPIA 1996 (see **D9.13** ***et seq.***), the court 'should consider whether the matter can be resolved by the giving of disclosure immediately'; if not, the court should apply the principles that are applicable where a party is at fault. Paragraph 24C.26 notes that, if the accused has served a defence statement (see **D9.29** ***et seq.***) and asks for further disclosure, the court may hear an application under the CPIA 1996, s. 8 (see **D9.26** ***et seq.***), immediately, 'provided that there is sufficient time available for the application itself and then for the defence to consider any material disclosed in consequence of it'.

Applications for adjournments where the accused fails to attend are considered at **D22.17** ***et seq.***, and applications where a witness fails to appear are considered at **D22.27**.

D5.24 **Repeated Applications** Where an adjournment has been refused, the court can change its mind only if there is a good reason. A further application should therefore be made only if there has been a material change of circumstances. In *R (Watson) v Dartford Magistrates' Court* [2005] EWHC 905 (Admin), for example, the prosecution had (before the date fixed for trial) sought an adjournment due to the non-availability of two witnesses. The magistrates refused the application. On the date fixed for trial, the prosecution made a further application for an adjournment. This time, the application was successful. The Divisional Court held that the magistrates were wrong to allow the adjournment, since there had not been a change in circumstances since the first request to adjourn the trial. Similarly, in *R (F) v Knowsley Youth Court* [2006] EWHC 695 (Admin), an application for an adjournment was heard by a bench of lay justices on the morning of the day of the trial. The application was refused. In the afternoon, at the beginning of the trial (before a district judge), the prosecution made another application for an adjournment. The district judge, who was made aware that a similar application had been made to a different bench that morning, allowed the application. The defendants sought judicial review of the district judge's decision. It was held that the district judge should have refused the application. In the absence of a change of circumstances, he was not entitled to revisit the decision to refuse an adjournment.

Applications to Vacate Trial

D5.25 CrimPD VI, para. 24C.30 (see Supplement, **CPD.24C**), requires that applications to vacate trials should be made 'promptly and in writing, in advance of the date of trial'. Such applications will usually be dealt with 'outside the courtroom', and will be considered in accordance with the principles applicable to adjournments (see **D5.23**).

Paragraph 24C.31 emphasises that the parties must provide 'full and accurate information to the court to enable it to assess where the interests of justice lie'. An application to vacate should include:

(i) the reason for the application;
(ii) a chronology of the case, 'recording the dates of compliance with any directions and of communication between the parties';
(iii) an 'assessment of the interests of justice', including an indication of 'the likely effect should the court conclude that the trial should proceed on the date fixed';
(iv) any restrictions on the future availability of witnesses;
(v) any likely changes to the number of witnesses or the way in which the evidence will be presented, and any impact on the trial time estimate.

Paragraph 24C.32 stipulates that, on receipt of an application to vacate, each other party should serve their response on the court and on the applicant within two business days (unless the court otherwise directs). Any request for the matter to be determined at a hearing (rather than on the papers) should be served with the application (or response, as the case may be), together with the reasons for that request.

Reasons

D5.26 Reasons for granting, or refusing, an adjournment should be given, but they do not have to be elaborate, so long as the basis for the decision is clear (*Essen v DPP* [2005] EWHC 1077 (Admin), at [29])).

Challenging Decisions on Adjournments

It is possible to challenge the grant or refusal of an adjournment by way of judicial review (see **D29.25** ***et seq.***). However, the Divisional Court will be 'particularly slow' to interfere with a decision to refuse an adjournment, given the discretionary nature of that decision (per Clarke J in *R (CPS) v Uxbridge Magistrates* [2007] EWHC 205 (Admin), at [5]). **D5.27**

In *DPP v Petrie* [2015] EWHC 48 (Admin), Gross LJ said (at [21]) that the grant or refusal of an adjournment 'is a paradigm example of a discretionary case management decision where an appeal ought only to succeed on well-recognised but limited grounds (for example, error of principle, error of law or where the decision can properly be characterised as plainly wrong)'. An example of such a case is *Pari-Jones v CPS* [2018] EWHC 3482 (Admin), where the magistrates' court had refused an adjournment despite the fact that neither D nor her solicitor could attend court because of bad weather. Andrews J, remitting the case for retrial, said (at [12]) that it was 'self-evident that if the magistrates had taken into account all the relevant considerations and if they had balanced [D's] right to a fair trial with the lack of fault caused by the weather conditions, the fact that she had already attended court previously, and all the other relevant considerations, they could not have refused this adjournment'. A similar approach was taken in *R (Parashar) v Sunderland Magistrates' Court* [2019] EWHC 514 (Admin), where it was held that 'the decision to fix a date for a trial at which the prosecution expert could attend and the defence expert (whose report had been served in good time) could not was clearly wrong' (per Bean LJ, at [46]). His lordship noted that if the trial had proceeded on that basis, D's ability to present his defence 'would have been seriously compromised and the trial would inevitably have been unfair'. Simler J concurred, saying (at [49]):

> To insist on a trial date on which the prosecution expert was available but the defence expert was not was wrong and would have led to an unfair trial. There is a high public interest in summary trials taking place quickly and on the day set for trial, and in adjournments not being granted absent compelling reasons. But it is also necessary as a matter of fairness and in the interests of justice, where a defence request to vacate a trial date is made, to consider whether, if it is not granted, the defendant will be able fully to present his defence, and if he will not be able to do so, the degree to which the defence will be compromised.

Offering No Evidence where Adjournment Refused If the prosecution seek an adjournment but the magistrates refuse to adjourn and the prosecutor offers no evidence, with the effect that the charge is dismissed, the magistrates cannot subsequently hear the case. In *R (O) v Stratford Youth Court* [2004] EWHC 1553 (Admin), key prosecution witnesses failed to attend. The justices refused an adjournment; the prosecution thereupon offered no evidence and the justices dismissed the charge. The prosecutor then discovered that the complainant had by then arrived at court and made a request that the court be reconvened. The magistrates agreed to do so; they overturned their refusal to adjourn and rescinded their dismissal of the charge. It was held by the Divisional Court that, where the prosecution have offered no evidence and the court has dismissed the charge, it is not open to the justices to reopen the case. In such a case, the justices are *functus officio*, and any further hearing against the accused in relation to that matter will inevitably give rise to a successful plea of autrefois acquit on the accused's behalf (per Rose LJ at [8]). **D5.28**

Statutory Provisions on Power to Adjourn The power to adjourn is contained in the MCA 1980, ss. 10(1) and 18(4). **D5.29**

Magistrates' Courts Act 1980, ss. 10 and 18

10.—(1) A magistrates' court may at any time, whether before or after beginning to try an information, adjourn the trial, and may do so, notwithstanding anything in this Act, when composed of a single justice.

(2) The court may when adjourning either fix the time and place at which the trial is to be resumed, or, unless it remands the accused, leave the time and place to be determined later by the court.

...

(4) On adjourning the trial of an information the court may remand the accused and, where the accused has attained the age of 18 years, shall do so if the offence is triable either way and—
(a) on the occasion on which the accused first appeared, or was brought, before the court to answer to the information he was in custody or, having been released on bail, surrendered to the custody of the court; or
(b) the accused has been remanded at any time in the course of proceedings on the information;
and, where the court remands the accused, the time fixed for the resumption of the trial shall be that at which he is required to appear or be brought before the court in pursuance of the remand or would be required to be brought before the court but for section 128(3A) below.

18.—(1) Sections 19 to 23 below shall have effect where a person who has attained the age of 18 years appears or is brought before a magistrates' court on an information charging him with an offence triable either way and—
(a) he indicates under section 17A above that (if the offence were to proceed to trial) he would plead not guilty, or
(b) his representative indicates under section 17B above that (if the offence were to proceed to trial) he would plead not guilty.

...

(4) A magistrates' court proceeding under sections 19 to 23 below may adjourn the proceedings at any time, and on doing so on any occasion when the accused is present may remand the accused, and shall remand him if—
(a) on the occasion on which he first appeared, or was brought, before the court to answer to the information he was in custody or, having been released on bail, surrendered to the custody of the court; or
(b) he has been remanded at any time in the course of proceedings on the information;
and where the court remands the accused, the time fixed for the resumption of the proceedings shall be that at which he is required to appear or be brought before the court in pursuance of the remand or would be required to be brought before the court but for section 128(3A) below.

D5.30 **Remanding the Accused on Adjournments** The MCA 1980, s. 128(1), provides that, whenever a magistrates' court has power to remand a person, it may either remand in custody or remand on bail, in accordance with the BA 1976. Accordingly, the references in ss. 10 and 18 to 'remanding' an accused mean either a remand in custody (i.e. committing the accused to custody to be brought before the court at the end of the period of remand or at such earlier time as the court may require), or a remand on bail in accordance with the provisions of the BA 1976 (i.e. directing the accused to appear before the court at the end of the period of the remand or, if bail is made continuous, directing that the accused appear at every time to which the proceedings may be adjourned) (MCA 1980, s. 128(1) and (4)).

Section 18 governs adjournments until allocation (mode of trial) has been determined. Section 10 applies to appearances for summary offences up until conviction, and to appearances for either-way offences from after mode of trial has been determined in favour of summary trial to conviction. Sections 10(4) and 18(4) provide (in almost identical terms) that, on adjourning proceedings for an either-way offence, the court must remand the accused (on bail or in custody) unless the accused: (a) first appeared in answer to a summons or requisition (as opposed to being brought before the court in custody or appearing in answer to police bail); and (b) has not been remanded at an earlier hearing.

It follows that the magistrates may, at their discretion, adjourn without remanding the accused: (a) at all appearances for summary offences up to conviction; and (b) at appearances for either-way offences up to either a determination for trial on indictment or summary conviction, provided the accused initially appeared in answer to a summons or requisition and has not subsequently been remanded. In *R (Iqbal) v Canterbury Crown Court* [2020] EWHC 452 (Admin), Carr J (at [48]), having noted that the Court had been informed that defence solicitors currently advise their clients that, if they are released under investigation and then receive a postal requisition, they would not be remanded in custody if they comply (and have in the past complied) with their attendance requirements, unless there is a material change in circumstances, said that if this was indeed a practice, 'there is no proper or principled basis for it. The full history and background will be taken into account by a court ... but there can never be any guarantee of bail once a defendant is charged.' Nonetheless, it is submitted that, where a defendant appears in court in response to a written charge and requisition, the question of bail arises only if the magistrates' court chooses to remand the defendant rather than simply adjourning the case; in such a case, the question of remanding the accused is likely to arise only if there appears to be a good reason for considering a remand in custody.

Where a case is simply adjourned, there is no need to fix the date for the next hearing at the time of adjourning, whereas if there is a remand the adjournment date must be fixed forthwith and is the date to which the accused is remanded. An accused who is not remanded and who then fails to appear on the date to which the case is adjourned commits no offence, but it may be possible either for an arrest warrant to be issued or for the proceedings to be conducted in the absence of the accused. An accused who has been remanded on bail and who then fails without reasonable cause to surrender to custody commits an offence under the BA 1976.

Period of Remand in Custody

The maximum period for which a magistrates' court may remand an accused in custody is 'eight clear days' (MCA 1980, s. 128(6)). This is subject to the following exceptions: **D5.31**

(a) following summary conviction, there may be a remand in custody of up to three weeks (four weeks if the remand is not in custody) for inquiries, such as a pre-sentence report, to be made into the most suitable method of dealing with the accused (MCA 1980, s. 10(3));
(b) following the court being satisfied that the accused 'did the act or made the omission charged', there may be a remand in custody of up to three weeks (four weeks if on bail) for a medical examination and reports if the court considers that an inquiry should be made into the physical or mental condition of the accused before deciding how to proceed (PCC(S)A 2000, s. 11(1) and (2));
(c) where mode of trial is determined in favour of summary trial but the court is not constituted so as to proceed immediately to trial (e.g., because it consists of a single lay justice), there may be a remand in custody to a date on which the court will be properly constituted even if the remand is for a period exceeding eight clear days (MCA 1980, s. 128(6)(c));
(d) where s. 128A of the MCA 1980 applies, a second or subsequent remand in custody may be for up to 28 clear days; and
(e) an accused who is already being detained under a custodial sentence may be remanded in custody for up to 28 clear days or the anticipated release date, whichever is the shorter (MCA 1980, s. 131).

Further Remands A person who is brought before the court after an earlier remand may be remanded again (MCA 1980, s. 128(3)). Thus, there may be several remand hearings before the case is sent to the Crown Court or the commencement of summary trial. The only limitation on the number of remands is the general discretion of magistrates to refuse an adjournment if it would be against the interests of justice (e.g., because they consider that the party requesting the adjournment should have been ready to proceed on the present occasion). By s. 130, a court remanding an accused in custody may order that, for subsequent remands, the accused be brought up before a different magistrates' court nearer to the prison where the accused is to be confined while on remand. That alternate court then enjoys the same powers in relation to remand that the original court would otherwise have. **D5.32**

The MCA 1980, s. 128, is without prejudice to the provisions of s. 129. Under s. 129(1), in the absence of the accused the magistrates may remand the accused to a convenient date, and any restrictions on the period of the remand which would otherwise be imposed by s. 128(6) do not apply. Section 129(1) applies whether the remand is in custody or on bail, but is restricted to cases where non-attendance on the day originally fixed is due to 'illness or accident'. In *Hillman v Governor of Bronzefield Prison* (24 May 2013 unreported), it was held that the failure to produce an accused in court because of an error in the administrative process is capable of amounting to an 'accident' within the meaning of s. 129(1), thus enabling the magistrates to remand the

D

Part D Procedure

accused in custody in her absence. Moreover, by virtue of s. 129(3), where an accused has been remanded on bail, the court may grant bail in the absence of the accused simply by appointing a later time for appearance. Section 129(3) applies only to remands on bail but places no restrictions on the reasons for which the court may choose to exercise its powers under the subsection. Thus, bail may be granted under s. 129(3) where it becomes apparent during the remand period that the court will not have time to deal with the case on the day originally fixed, or where the accused fails to attend but some acceptable reason is advanced for the non-appearance (not necessarily sickness or accident). Where bail is granted in such a case, the court may also 'enlarge' the recognizances of any sureties (i.e. they will be under an obligation to secure the accused's attendance on the new hearing date).

Remands in Custody in the Absence of Accused

D5.33 To avoid the necessity for an accused to be brought before the court in custody when it is apparent that no effective progress in the case will be possible at the hearing to which the accused would otherwise be brought, a remand in custody may take place in the absence of the accused under the MCA 1980, s. 128(3A) to (3E). A remand in absence may take place only if the accused:

(a) has consented (at an earlier hearing) to not being present at future remands (s. 128(3A)(a));
(b) has a legal representative acting in the case, although the representative need not be present in court (s. 128(3B));
(c) has not been remanded in absence on more than two consecutive occasions prior to the present application for remand in absence (s. 128(3A)(b)); and
(d) has not withdrawn consent (s. 128(3A)(d)).

D5.34 To facilitate the giving of consent to remands in absence, it is provided in s. 128(1A) to (1C) that, where magistrates are proposing to remand in custody an accused who is present in court (s. 128(1A)(b)), they shall, assuming the accused is legally represented in court (s. 128(1A)(d)), explain the possibility of further remands being in absence and ask whether the accused consents to that procedure being adopted. It is a precondition of the accused being asked for consent to remands in absence that the legal representative is present in court (s. 128(1B)), whereas (assuming consent has been given) the remands in absence themselves can, and normally do, take place without the attendance of a lawyer, provided the accused still has a lawyer acting in the case. The restriction on the number of consecutive remands in absence to a maximum of three means that the accused cannot be remanded for more than approximately a month without being brought before the court. The accused could, on attending after three remands in absence, agree to the next three remands being in absence. If a case is listed for a formal remand in absence, but it appears to the magistrates that the conditions for such a remand are not in fact satisfied (e.g., because the accused has withdrawn consent or no longer has a legal representative), they must remand the accused for the shortest period possible that will enable the accused to be brought before them (s. 128(3C) to (3D)). It should be noted that, although remands in absence are pure formalities, the rule that remands in custody shall not exceed eight clear days must still be complied with, in the sense that the accused's case must be listed within each eight-day period so that the magistrates can formally remand to the next appropriate date.

Remands in absence are limited to cases where the court is adjourning under ss. 5, 10(1) or 18(4) of the 1980 Act (i.e. adjournments prior to or during summary trial or sending the case for Crown Court trial). If the adjournment is under s. 10(3) or the PCC(S)A 2000, s. 11 (see **D5.30**), the period of a custodial remand may extend to three weeks but there is no power to remand in absence.

Remands in Custody for up to 28 Days

D5.35 Under s. 128A of the MCA 1980, a magistrates' court may remand an accused in custody for a period exceeding eight clear days if (by virtue of s. 128A(2)):

(a) the accused has previously been remanded in custody for the same offence;
(b) the accused is now before the court; and

(c) the court (after allowing the parties to make representations) has fixed a date on which it expects that it will be possible for the next stage in the proceedings, other than a hearing relating to a further remand in custody or on bail, to take place.

This final requirement is that the next hearing should be an effective hearing. In the case of either-way offences, the next effective hearing after the accused becomes eligible for an extended remand will be the hearing to determine plea and allocation. The maximum period of a remand under s. 128A is 28 clear days or to the date of the next effective hearing, whichever is the shorter (s. 128A(2)(i) and (ii)). Section 128A does not apply on the occasion of a first remand in custody (s. 128A(2)(a)), although the accused may at that stage be invited to consent to the next three remands being in absence (see **D5.32**). The making of a remand under s. 128A does not affect the right of the accused to apply for bail during the period of that remand (s. 128A(3)). The preservation of the right to make a bail application even though there has been a 28-day remand in custody entitles the defence to put before the magistrates immediately any relevant change in circumstances that arises during the period of the remand.

Remand on Bail

Under the MCA 1980, s. 128(6)(a), the accused may be remanded for a period greater than eight clear days if the remand is on bail and both the accused and the prosecution agree to a longer period of remand. **D5.36**

Statutory Provisions on Duration of Remands **D5.37**

Magistrates' Courts Act 1980, ss. 128 to 131

128.—(1) Where a magistrates' court has power to remand any person, then, subject to section 4 of the Bail Act 1976 and to any other enactment modifying that power, the court may—
(a) remand him in custody, that is to say, commit him to custody to be brought before the court, subject to subsection (3A) below, at the end of the period of remand or at such earlier time as the court may require; or
(b) where it is trying an offence alleged to have been committed by that person or has convicted him of an offence, remand him on bail in accordance with the Bail Act 1976, that is to say, by directing him to appear as provided in subsection (4) below; or
[(c) relates to bail in non-criminal proceedings.]

(1A) Where—
(a) on adjourning a case under section 10(1), 17C, 18(4) or 24C above the court proposes to remand or further remand a person in custody; and
(b) he is before the court; and
(c) [repealed]; and
(d) he is legally represented in that court,

it shall be the duty of the court—
(i) to explain the effect of subsections (3A) and (3B) below to him in ordinary language; and
(ii) to inform him in ordinary language that, notwithstanding the procedure for a remand without his being brought before a court, he would be brought before a court for the hearing and determination of at least every fourth application for his remand, and of every application for his remand heard at a time when it appeared to the court that he had no solicitor acting for him in the case.

(1B) For the purposes of subsection (1A) above a person is to be treated as legally represented in a court if, but only if, he has the assistance of counsel or a solicitor to represent him in the proceedings in that court.

(1C) After explaining to an accused as provided by subsection (1A) above the court shall ask him whether he consents to hearing and determination of such applications in his absence.

(2) Where the court fixes the amount of a recognizance under subsection (1) above or section 8(3) of the Bail Act 1976 with a view to its being taken subsequently the court shall in the meantime commit the person so remanded to custody in accordance with paragraph (a) of the said subsection (1).

(3) Where a person is brought before the court after remand, the court may further remand him.

D

Part D Procedure

(3A) Subject to subsection (3B) below, where a person has been remanded in custody and the remand was not a remand under section 128A below for a period exceeding eight clear days, the court may further remand him (otherwise than in the exercise of the power conferred by that section) on an adjournment under section 10(1), 17C, 18(4) or 24C above without his being brought before it if it is satisfied—
(a) that he gave his consent, either in response to a question under subsection (1C) above or otherwise, to the hearing and determination in his absence of any application for his remand on an adjournment of the case under any of those provisions; and
(b) that he has not by virtue of this subsection been remanded without being brought before the court on more than two such applications immediately preceding the application which the court is hearing; and
(c) [repealed]; and
(d) that he has not withdrawn his consent...

(3B) The court may not exercise the power conferred by subsection (3A) above if it appears to the court, on an application for a further remand being made to it, that the person to whom the application relates has no solicitor acting for him in the case (whether present in court or not).

(3C) Where—
(a) a person has been remanded in custody on an adjournment of a case under section 10(1), 17C, 18(4) or 24C above; and
(b) an application is subsequently made for his further remand on such an adjournment; and
(c) he is not brought before the court which hears and determines the application; and
(d) that court is not satisfied as mentioned in subsection (3A) above, the court shall adjourn the case and remand him in custody for the period for which it stands adjourned.

(3D) An adjournment under subsection (3C) above shall be for the shortest period that appears to the court to make it possible for the accused to be brought before it.

(3E) Where—
(a) on an adjournment of a case under section 10(1), 17C, 18(4) or 24C above a person has been remanded in custody without being brought before the court; and
(b) it subsequently appears—
(i) to the court which remanded him in custody; or
(ii) to an alternate magistrates' court to which he is remanded under section 130 below,

that he ought not to have been remanded in custody in his absence, the court shall require him to be brought before it at the earliest time that appears to the court to be possible.

(4) Where a person is remanded on bail under subsection (1) above the court may... direct him to appear...—
(a) before that court at the end of the period of remand; or
(b) at every time and place to which during the course of the proceedings the hearing may be from time to time adjourned;

and, where it remands him on bail conditionally on his providing a surety when it is proceeding with a view to transfer for trial, may direct that the recognisance of the surety be conditioned to secure that the person so bailed appears—
(c) at every time and place to which during the course of the proceedings the hearing may be from time to time adjourned and also before the Crown Court in the event of the person so bailed being committed for trial there.

(5) Where a person is directed to appear or a recognisance is conditioned for a person's appearance in accordance with paragraph (b) or (c) of subsection (4) above, the fixing at any time of the time for him next to appear shall be deemed to be a remand; but nothing in this subsection or subsection (4) above shall deprive the court of power at any subsequent hearing to remand him afresh.

(6) Subject to the provisions of sections 128A and 129 below, a magistrates' court shall not remand a person for a period exceeding eight clear days, except that—
(a) if the court remands him on bail, it may remand him for a longer period if he and the other party consent;
(b) where the court adjourns a trial under section 10(3) or section 11 of the Powers of Criminal Courts (Sentencing) Act 2000, the court may remand him for the period of the adjournment;
(c) where a person is charged with an offence triable either way, then, if it falls to the court to try the case summarily but the court is not at the time so constituted, and sitting in such a place, as will enable it to proceed with the trial, the court may remand him until the next occasion on which it will be practicable for the court to be so constituted, and to sit in such a place, as aforesaid, notwithstanding that the remand is for a period exceeding eight clear days.

[(7) and (8) concern committing an accused to police detention for a period not exceeding three clear days where there is a need to question him about other offences — see **D1.42**.]

128A.—(1) [Power of Secretary of State to implement this section in specified areas or for specified proceedings.]

(2) A magistrates' court may remand the accused in custody for a period exceeding eight clear days if—

(a) it has previously remanded him in custody for the same offence; and

(b) he is before the court,

but only if, after affording the parties an opportunity to make representations, it has set a date on which it expects that it will be possible for the next stage in the proceedings, other than a hearing relating to a further remand in custody or on bail, to take place, and only—

(i) for a period ending not later than that date; or

(ii) for a period of 28 clear days,

whichever is the less.

(3) Nothing in this section affects the right of the accused to apply for bail during the period of remand.

[(4) Making of statutory instruments under the section.]

129.—(1) If a magistrates' court is satisfied that any person who has been remanded is unable by reason of illness or accident to appear or be brought before the court at the expiration of the period for which he was remanded, the court may, in his absence, remand him for a further time; and section 128(6) above shall not apply.

(2) Notwithstanding anything in section 128(1) above, the power of a court under subsection (1) above to remand a person on bail for a further time—

(a) where he was granted bail in criminal proceedings, includes power to enlarge the recognisance of any surety for him to a later time;

[(b) concerns bail in non-criminal proceedings.]

(3) Where a person remanded on bail is bound to appear before a magistrates' court at any time and the court has no power to remand him under subsection (1) above, the court may in his absence—

(a) where he was granted bail in criminal proceedings, appoint a later time as the time at which he is to appear and enlarge the recognisances of any sureties for him to that time;

[(b) concerns bail in non-criminal proceedings];

and the appointment of the time ... shall be deemed to be a further remand.

[(4) concerns enlargement of a surety's recognisance upon sending for trial.]

130.—(1) A magistrates' court adjourning a case under section 10(1), 17C, 18(4) or 24C above, and remanding the accused in custody, may, if he has attained the age of 17, order that he be brought up for any subsequent remands before an alternate magistrates' court nearer to the prison where he is to be confined while on remand.

[(2) to (5) and sch. 5 contain detailed provisions governing remands to alternate magistrates' courts.]

131.—(1) When a magistrates' court remands an accused person in custody and he is already detained under a custodial sentence, the period for which he is remanded may be up to 28 clear days.

(2) But the court shall inquire as to the expected date of his release from that detention; and if it appears that it will be before 28 clear days have expired, he shall not be remanded in custody for more than eight clear days or (if longer) a period ending with that date.

PRE-TRIAL HEARINGS BY TELEVISION LINK

The CDA 1998, ss. 57A, 57B, 57D and 57E, enable the court to direct that an accused who is in custody may appear at preliminary hearings, and at sentencing hearings, via a 'live link' from prison or from a police station. Under s. 57A(2), the accused is to be treated as present in court when attending via a live link (defined, by s. 57A(3), so as to require that that the accused be able to see and hear, and to be seen and heard by, the court during the hearing). CrimPR 3.2(4) (see Supplement, **R3.2**) strongly encourages the use of live links; moreover, CrimPD I, para. 3N.1 (see Supplement, **CPD.3N**), says that where it is 'lawful and in the interests of justice to do so, courts should exercise their statutory and other powers to conduct hearings by live link or telephone'. Paragraph 3N.4 emphasises that all participants must be able to hear and, in the **D5.38** case of a live link, see each other clearly, and notes that, if a hearing is open to the public, use of media such as Skype or Facetime, which are not generally considered secure from interception, may not be objectionable (as the information is in the public domain anyway). Paragraph 3N.8 states that, in principle, nothing prohibits the conduct of a pre-trial hearing by live link or telephone with each participant, including the member(s) of the court, in a different location (sometimes described as a 'virtual hearing'), so long as the hearing can be witnessed by the public (e.g. by public attendance at a venue from which the participants can all be seen and heard (if by live link), or heard (if by telephone)).

The Coronavirus Act 2020, s. 54 and sch. 24, have made temporary modifications to the CDA 1998, ss. 57A to 57B and sch. 3A, to give the court power to direct 'live link' attendance at 'preliminary hearings'. For full details, see the Special Supplement, **D15.40A** *et seq.*

Preliminary Hearings where Accused in Custody

D5.39 Under the CDA 1998, s. 57B, the Crown Court or a magistrates' court (for these purposes, this includes a single justice: s. 57B(7)) may direct that an accused who is likely to be held in custody during a preliminary hearing is to attend that hearing by way of live link (a 'live link direction'). Under s. 57B(4), if there is a hearing in relation to the making (or rescinding) of such a direction, the court may require or permit attendance via a live link. It follows that the accused does not have to be physically present in court for a live link direction to be given (and so the court may give such a direction in writing or immediately before the start of a hearing with the accused present via a live link). Under s. 57B(5), the court is required to give the parties the opportunity to make representations before giving (or rescinding) a live link direction. If a magistrates' court decides not to give a live link direction where it has power to do so, it must state its reasons in open court and record the reasons in the court register (s. 57B(6)).

Preliminary Hearings where Accused at Police Station

D5.40 The CDA 1998, s. 57C, empowers a magistrates' court (but not the Crown Court) to direct the accused to attend a preliminary hearing via a live link from a police station. By virtue of s. 57C(3) and (4), this provision applies both to an accused who is detained at the police station in connection with the offence in question, and to an accused who has been bailed to return to the police station for a live link appearance in connection with the offence, known as 'live link bail' (PACE 1984, s. 47(3), allows the police to grant bail subject to a duty to appear at a police station for the purpose of a live link hearing). The CDA 1998, s. 57C(10), makes it clear that an accused answering to 'live link bail' is to be treated as having surrendered to the custody of the court as from the time when it makes a live link direction in respect of that accused. Under s. 57C(6A), a live link direction may be given only if the court is satisfied that it is not contrary to the interests of justice to do so. However, the consent of the accused is not required.

Proceeding to Sentence

D5.41 Under the CDA 1998, s. 57D, where an accused attends a preliminary hearing over a live link (pursuant to s. 57B or 57C) and pleads guilty to the offence (or, if it is an either-way offence, indicates a guilty plea and so is deemed to have pleaded guilty under the 'plea before venue' procedure), and the court proposes to proceed immediately to sentencing, the accused may continue to attend through the live link provided the court is satisfied that it is not contrary to the interests of justice for this to take place (s. 57D(2)). Section 57D(3) provides that, where a preliminary hearing over a live link continues as a sentencing hearing, the offender can give oral evidence over the live link only if the court is satisfied that it is not contrary to the interests of justice.

OPTIONS WHEN THE ACCUSED FAILS TO APPEAR

D5.42 If an accused who has been bailed to appear at a magistrates' court fails to do so, the court may (assuming the provisions of the MCA 1980, s. 12 (pleading guilty by post) or 16A (trial by single justice on the papers in certain cases where the accused pleads guilty), are not applicable):

(a) issue an arrest warrant under the BA 1976, s. 7; or
(b) extend bail in accordance with the MCA 1980, s. 129(3); or
(c) proceed in the absence of the accused under the MCA 1980, s. 11(1) (see **D5.43**).

Trial in Absence of the Accused

If the accused fails to appear for the trial in the magistrates' court, the case may (if the accused is under 18) or must (if the accused has attained the age of 18 and it does not appear to the court to be contrary to the interests of justice to do so) proceed in the accused's absence (MCA 1980, s. 11(1); see also CrimPR 24.12(3): see Supplement, **R24.12**). However, where the prosecution commenced by issue of a summons or requisition, it must be proved to the satisfaction of the court that either the summons (or requisition, as the case may be) was served a reasonable time before the hearing or the accused appeared on a previous occasion to answer the charge (MCA 1980, s. 11(2)). Summary trial in the absence of the accused is considered in more detail at **D22.14**. **D5.43**

Bench Warrants

Should the court decide to adjourn the trial rather than proceeding in the absence of the accused, it may issue an arrest warrant under the MCA 1980, s. 13(1), provided that the offence to which the warrant relates is punishable with imprisonment, or the court, having convicted the accused, is proposing to impose a disqualification (s. 13(3) and (3A)). Where proceedings were initiated by the issue of a summons (or requisition), it must be proved to the satisfaction of the court that the summons (or requisition) was served on the accused a reasonable time before the trial (or adjourned trial, as the case may be), unless the current adjournment is a second or subsequent adjournment and the accused was present in court on the occasion of the last adjournment and was informed of the time for the adjourned hearing on that occasion (s. 13(2), (2A) and (2B)). **D5.44**

Although warrants under s. 13 are not expressly limited to prosecutions commenced by way of summons or requisition, reliance on that section in cases where the accused has been bailed to appear is unnecessary because non-attendance in answer to bail may be dealt with by issue of a warrant under the BA 1976, s. 7. If a prosecution for an indictable offence is commenced by way of summons (or by written charge and requisition) and the accused does not appear, a warrant cannot be issued under s. 13 of the 1980 Act unless and until it is determined to try the case summarily (as the power conferred by s. 13 is to issue a warrant when the *trial* is adjourned), but the prosecutor is entitled to apply for the issue of an arrest warrant under the MCA 1980, s. 1 (see s. 1(6), which provides that, where the offence charged is indictable, a warrant may be issued under s. 1 notwithstanding the previous issue of a summons or written charge and requisition).

If a warrant for arrest is issued the court may, at its discretion, 'back it for bail' (MCA 1980, s. 117); this means that the court directs that, once arrested, the person may thereafter be bailed by the police to attend court on a specified date. This may be appropriate where, for example, there is some suggestion that the accused has a good reason for non-attendance but there is no (or insufficient) evidence to support this suggestion (making it inappropriate simply to extend bail under the MCA 1980, s. 129(3)). The execution of such warrants is sometimes seen as a waste of police resources, and so magistrates' courts have been encouraged to use warning letters instead (see **D7.99**). **D5.45**

Full discussion of the options open to the court where an accused who is on bail fails to attend court may be found in **D7**.

Section D6 Classification of Offences and Determining Allocation (Mode of Trial)

INTRODUCTION

D6.1 Criminal trials in England and Wales are either trials on indictment in the Crown Court or summary trials in a magistrates' court. This section deals with (a) the classification of offences according to whether they: (i) must be tried on indictment, or (ii) may be tried either on indictment or summarily, or (iii) must be tried summarily; and (b) the procedure for determining the appropriate mode of trial in those cases where there is a choice.

CLASSIFICATION OF OFFENCES

Definition of the Classes of Offences

D6.2 There are, as regards mode of trial, three classes of offence — namely, (a) those triable only on indictment, (b) those triable only summarily, and (c) those triable either way: see the MCA 1980, ss. 17 to 25. These sections must be read in conjunction with sch. 1 to the Interpretation Act 1978.

Interpretation Act 1978, sch. 1

(a) 'indictable offence' means an offence which, if committed by an adult, is triable on indictment, whether it is exclusively so triable or triable either way;
(b) 'summary offence' means an offence which, if committed by an adult, is triable only summarily;
(c) 'offence triable either way' means an offence, other than an offence triable on indictment only by virtue of [s. 40] of the Criminal Justice Act 1988 which, if committed by an adult, is triable either on indictment or summarily;

and the terms 'indictable', 'summary' and 'triable either way', in their application to offences, are to be construed accordingly.

The Interpretation Act 1978 qualifies the above definitions with the rider that 'references . . . to the way or ways in which an offence is triable are to be construed without regard to the effect, if any, of section 22 of the Magistrates' Courts Act 1980 on the mode of trial in a particular case'. The broad effect of s. 22 of the MCA 1980 is that the offences under s. 1 of the Criminal Damage Act 1971 involving damage not exceeding the relevant sum (currently £5,000) must be dealt with as if they were triable only summarily (see **D6.20**).

D6.3 Where an Act contains the phrase 'indictable offence' without any further qualification, it must be understood to mean both those offences which, in the case of an adult, *must* be tried on indictment and those which (again in the case of an adult) carry the right to trial on indictment although they can be tried summarily with the agreement of the accused and of the magistrates. Summary offences, on the other hand, are entirely distinct from indictable offences and must always be tried summarily, unless s. 40 of the CJA 1988 applies. The reason for the Interpretation Act 1978 definitions referring each time to the possible mode of trial in the case of an adult is that special rules apply to the trial of children and young people, greatly restricting the use of trial on indictment (see s. 24 of the MCA 1980 and **D24**).

The CJA 1988, s. 40, enables certain specified summary offences to appear on an indictment if they are linked to an indictable offence for which the accused has been sent to the Crown Court for trial (see **D11.17**). Those offences include common assault; taking a motor vehicle without consent; driving whilst disqualified; and criminal damage where the value of the damage does not exceed £5,000 (and so the provisions of the MCA 1980, s. 22, apply: see **D6.20**). Moreover, under the CLA 1967, s. 6(3A), a jury can (by way of alternative verdict under s. 6(3)) convict an accused of a summary offence to which the CJA 1988, s. 40, applies, even if a count charging the offence is not included in the indictment (see **D19.42**).

Determining the Class of an Offence

An offence is triable either way if either : (a) it is listed in the MCA 1980, sch. 1 (see **D6.5**) (the MCA 1980, s. 17, provides that, without prejudice to any other enactment by virtue of which an offence is triable either way, the offences listed in sch. 1 shall be so triable); or (b) the enactment creating the offence (where the offence is a statutory one) specifies one penalty on summary conviction and a different (invariably greater) penalty on conviction on indictment. If the statute provides for a maximum penalty imposable on summary conviction but does not provide for a penalty on conviction on indictment, the offence is summary. If the statute provides only for a penalty on conviction on indictment, the offence is triable only on indictment (unless the offence is listed in the MCA 1980, sch. 1). Common-law offences (i.e. offences not created by statute) are all indictable offences and are triable only on indictment unless listed in the MCA 1980, sch. 1. **D6.4**

Attempts are covered by the CAA 1981, s. 4(1)(c), the rule being — as it is for allegations of aiding and abetting — that the offence is triable either way only if the substantive offence is so triable.

The CAA 1981, s. 1(4), provides that s. 1 (which creates the offence of attempting to commit an offence) applies to any offence which, if it were completed, would be triable in England and Wales as an indictable offence. Section 4(1)(c) provides that a person guilty under s. 1 of attempting to commit an either-way offence is liable, on summary conviction, to any penalty that could have been imposed on summary conviction of that offence.

Magistrates' Courts Act 1980, s. 17 and sch. 1 **D6.5**

17.—(1) The offences listed in Schedule 1 to this Act shall be triable either way.
(2) Subsection (1) above is without prejudice to any other enactment by virtue of which any offence is triable either way.

SCHEDULE 1

OFFENCES TRIABLE EITHER WAY BY VIRTUE OF SECTION 17

1. Offences at common law of public nuisance.
1A. An offence at common law of outraging public decency.
2. [Repealed.]
3. Offences consisting in contravention of section 13 of the Statutory Declarations Act 1835 (administration by a person of an oath etc. touching matters in which he has no jurisdiction).
4. Offences under section 36 of the Malicious Damage Act 1861 (obstructing engines or carriages on railways).
5. Offences under the following provisions of the Offences against the Person Act 1861—
   (a) section 16 (threats to kill);
   (b) section 20 (inflicting bodily injury, with or without a weapon);
   (c) section 26 (not providing apprentices or servants with food etc.);
   (d) section 27 (abandoning or exposing a child);
   (e) section 34 (doing or omitting to do anything so as to endanger railway passengers);

(f) section 36 (assaulting a clergyman at a place of worship etc.);
(g) section 38 (assault with intent to resist apprehension);
(h) section 47 (assault occasioning bodily harm);
(i) section 57 (bigamy);
(j) section 60 (concealing the birth of a child).

6. Offences under section 20 of the Telegraph Act 1868 (disclosing or intercepting messages).
7. Offences under section 13 of the Debtors Act 1869 (transactions intended to defraud creditors).
8. Offences under section 5 of the Public Stores Act 1875 (obliteration of marks with intent to conceal).
9. Offences under section 12 of the Corn Returns Act 1882 (false returns).
10. [Repealed.]
11. Offences under section 3 of the Submarine Telegraph Act 1885 (damaging submarine cables).
12. Offences under section 13 of the Stamp Duties Management Act 1891 (offences in relation to dies and stamps).
13. Offences under section 8(2) of the Cremation Act 1902 (making false representations etc. with a view to procuring the burning of any human remains).
14. All offences under the Perjury Act 1911 except offences under—
    (a) section 1 (perjury in judicial proceedings);
    (b) section 3 (false statements etc. with reference to marriage).
    (c) section 4 (false statements etc. as to births or deaths).
15. [Repealed.]
16. Offences under section 17 of the Deeds of Arrangement Act 1914 (trustee making preferential payments).
17. [Repealed.]
18. Offences under section 8(2) of the Census Act 1920 (disclosing census information).
19. Offences under section 36 of the Criminal Justice Act 1925 (forgery of passports etc.).
20. Offences under section 11 of the Agricultural Credits Act 1928 (frauds by farmers).

21 to 25. [Repealed.]

26. The following offences under the Criminal Law Act 1967—
    (a) offences under section 4(1) (assisting offenders); and
    (b) offences under section 5(1) (concealing arrestable offences and giving false information),
    where the offence to which they relate is triable either way.
27. [Repealed.]
28. All indictable offences under the Theft Act 1968 except—
    (a) robbery, aggravated burglary, blackmail and assault with intent to rob;
    (b) burglary comprising the commission of, or an intention to commit, an offence which is triable only on indictment;
    (c) burglary in a dwelling if any person in the dwelling was subjected to violence or the threat of violence.
29. Offences under the following provisions of the Criminal Damage Act 1971—
    section 1(1) (destroying or damaging property);
    section 1(1) and (3) (arson);
    section 2 (threats to destroy or damage property);
    section 3 (possessing anything with intent to destroy or damage property).
30. Offences in relation to stamps issued for the purpose of national insurance under the provisions of any enactments as applied to those stamps.

31 and 32. [Repealed.]

33. Aiding, abetting, counselling or procuring the commission of any offence listed in the preceding paragraphs of this Schedule except paragraph 26.

ALLOCATION: DETERMINATION OF MODE OF TRIAL

Introduction

D6.6 Sections 17A to 21 of the MCA 1980 set out the method of determining allocation (mode of trial) when an adult is charged with an either-way offence. The first stage ('plea before venue') ascertains the accused's intended plea (see **D6.7**); if the intended plea is (or is deemed to be) not guilty, the second stage is to determine whether the case will be tried in a magistrates' court or in the Crown Court (see **D6.8**).

Section 22 provides for a special procedure where the charge is one of criminal damage (see **D6.20**), and s. 23 allows for proceedings under ss. 19 to 22 to be carried out in the absence of the accused provided certain conditions are satisfied (see **D6.9**). Section 25 relates to changing the decision about mode of trial originally taken (see **D6.30**).

The relevant statutory provisions are set out at **D6.19**.

Plea before Venue

The initial procedure set out in the MCA 1980, s. 17A (see **D6.19**), applies whenever a person who has attained the age of 18 appears before a magistrates' court charged with an either-way offence (MCA 1980, s. 17A(1)). This procedure must be complied with before any evidence is called for purposes of a summary trial or the case is sent for Crown Court trial, and (subject to certain exceptions, considered at **D6.9**) should take place in the presence of the accused (s. 17A(2)). The steps in the standard procedure are as follows: **D6.7**

(a) The charge is written down (if that has not already been done) and read to the accused (s. 17A(3)).
(b) The court explains that the accused may indicate whether the plea would be guilty or not guilty if the offence were to proceed to trial. The court should explain that, if the accused indicates a plea of guilty, the proceedings will be treated as a summary trial at which a guilty plea has been tendered, and that the accused may be committed for sentence under the PCC(S)A 2000, s. 3, if the court is of the opinion that its powers of punishment are inadequate (see **D23.30**), or under s. 3A, if it appears to the court that the criteria for the imposition of a sentence under the CJA 2003, s. 226A (the 'dangerous offender' provisions), apply (s. 17A(4); see **D23.49**).
(c) The court asks the accused to indicate whether (if the offence were to proceed to trial) the plea would be guilty or not guilty (s. 17A(5)).
(d) If the accused indicates a guilty plea, the court proceeds as if the accused had pleaded guilty at summary trial (s. 17A(6)), and so moves on to the sentencing stage.
(e) If the accused indicates a not guilty plea, an allocation ('mode of trial') hearing must take place, pursuant to s. 18 (s. 17A(7)). If the accused fails to give an indication of intended plea, the court will regard this as an indication of an intention to plead not guilty and so will go on to determine allocation under s. 18 (s. 17A(8)).

Allocation

Where the accused has indicated an intention to plead not guilty to an either-way offence (or has failed to give an indication as to plea), the court must proceed to determine allocation (s. 18(1); see **D6.19**). The steps in this stage of the procedure are as follows: **D6.8**

(a) The court affords the prosecution and defence the opportunity to make representations about whether the offence is more suitable for summary trial or trial on indictment (s. 19(2)(b)). At that stage, the prosecution must also be given the opportunity of informing the magistrates of any previous convictions recorded against the accused (s. 19(2)(a)), since the existence of relevant previous convictions would affect the appropriate sentence.
(b) The court then must decide whether the offence appears to be more suitable for summary trial or for trial on indictment (s. 19(1)). Section 19(3) provides that the court, when deciding which mode of trial is more suitable, must consider:
    (i) whether the sentence which a magistrates' court would have power to impose for the offence would be adequate;
    (ii) any representations made by the prosecution or the accused; and
    (iii) allocation guidelines issued by the Sentencing Council under the CAJA 2009, s. 120 (see **D6.14**).

D

Part D Procedure

(c) If it appears to the court that summary trial is more appropriate, the court explains to the accused that:
   (i) such is the court's view, and that the accused can either consent to be tried summarily or elect to be tried on indictment in the Crown Court; and
   (ii) if the accused is tried summarily and convicted, the magistrates may commit the accused to the Crown Court for sentence if they are of the opinion that greater punishment should be inflicted than they have power to inflict (PCC(S)A 2000, s. 3; see **D23.30**) or if it appears to the court that the criteria for the imposition of a sentence under the CJA 2003, s. 226A (dangerous offenders), would be met (s. 20(1) and (2); see **D23.49**).
(d) At that point, the accused may request that the magistrates indicate whether, if the accused were to be tried summarily and were to plead guilty at that stage, the sentence would be custodial or non-custodial (s. 20(3)). The magistrates are not obliged to give such an indication (s. 20(4)). If the court does give an indication of sentence, it must ask the accused whether he or she wishes, on the basis of the indication, to reconsider the indication of plea which was given (s. 20(5)). If the accused does wish to do so, the court must ask for a fresh indication of intended plea, and so the 'plea before venue' stage is repeated (s. 20(6)).
(e) If the accused indicates an intention to plead guilty following an indication of sentence, this is regarded as a guilty plea (s. 20(7)), and the magistrates' court will proceed to sentence, if necessary adjourning for a pre-sentence report; in such a case, a custodial sentence will be available only if such a sentence was indicated by the court (s. 20A(1)). Where an indication of sentence is given and the accused does not choose to plead guilty on the basis of it, the sentence indication is not binding on the magistrates who later try the case summarily, or on the Crown Court if the accused elects trial on indictment (s. 20A(3)).
(f) If the court does not give an indication of sentence (either because the accused does not seek one or the court declines to give one), or if the accused seeks and receives an indication of sentence but does not then wish to reconsider the indication of plea, or if the accused goes through the plea before venue stage a second time but does not indicate an intention to plead guilty, then the accused is asked whether he or she consents to summary trial (s. 20(8) and (9)).
(g) Depending on the choice made by the accused, the court either proceeds to summary trial or sends the case to the Crown Court for trial under the CDA 1998, s. 51 (s. 20(9)).
(h) If, on the other hand, it appears to the court that trial on indictment is more appropriate, it tells the accused that this is so and proceeds to send the case to the Crown Court under the CDA 1998, s. 51 (s. 21).

It follows that summary trial of an either-way offence is possible only if the magistrates' court and the accused both agree to summary trial. If the magistrates decline jurisdiction, the case will be sent to the Crown Court for trial; likewise, if the magistrates accept jurisdiction but the accused elects trial on indictment, the case will be sent to the Crown Court for trial.

It should be noted that the procedure for determining allocation is modified in the case of low-value criminal damage and shoplifting (see **D6.20** and **D6.27** respectively).

Presence of the Accused

D6.9 The accused must generally be present at the 'plea before venue' hearing (MCA 1980, s. 17A(2)) and when allocation is determined (s. 18(2); see **D6.19**). However, by virtue of s. 17B, the 'plea before venue' hearing may take place in the absence of the accused if:

(a) the accused is represented by a legal representative; and
(b) the court considers that, by reason of the accused's disorderly conduct before the court, it is not practicable for proceedings under s. 17A to be conducted in the presence of the accused; and
(c) the court considers that it should proceed in the absence of the accused.

In such a case, the representative is asked to indicate whether the accused intends to plead guilty or not guilty (s. 17B(2)(b)); if the representative indicates a guilty plea, the court proceeds as if the accused had pleaded guilty (s. 17B(2)(c)). Otherwise, the court proceeds to determine allocation under s. 18 (s. 17B(2)(d) and (3)).

The allocation hearing can take place in the absence of the accused under either s. 18(3) or s. 23.

(a) Under s. 18(3), the court may determine allocation in the absence of the accused if it considers that, by reason of disorderly conduct before the court, it is not practicable for the proceedings to be conducted in the presence of the accused. Where there is a legal representative present in court, the representative speaks on behalf of the accused (s. 18(3)).
(b) Under s. 23, the court may determine allocation in the absence of an accused who is represented by a legal representative who signifies to the court that the accused consents to the mode of trial proceedings being conducted in the absence of the accused, and the court is satisfied that there is good reason for the proceedings being so conducted (s. 23(1)). The phrase 'good reason' is not defined; sickness is an obvious example, but it is submitted that 'good reason' extends beyond that. Assuming the court does proceed in the accused's absence and considers that the offence is more suitable for summary trial, consent to such a trial may be signified by the legal representative, in which event 'the court shall proceed to ... summary trial' (s. 23(4)(a)). Clearly, this does not require the magistrates to commence the trial forthwith, as they are entitled to adjourn under the general power given them by s. 10(1) if an immediate hearing is impracticable or undesirable (e.g., because of the accused's absence). If the court considers that trial on indictment is more appropriate, or if the legal representative does not signify that the accused consents to summary trial, then the court must proceed to send the case to the Crown Court for trial under the CDA 1998, s. 51 (s. 23(4)(b) and (5)).

It should be noted that the court may use a live television link in a case where the accused is held in custody and facilities are available there (CDA 1998, s. 57B: see **D5.38**).

CONDUCT OF PLEA BEFORE VENUE AND ALLOCATION HEARINGS

General

The 'plea before venue' hearing and the subsequent hearing to determine allocation may take place before a single justice (ss. 17E(1) and 18(5) respectively), but in practice it is almost invariably the case that a lay bench will consist of at least two justices. **D6.10**

The determination of plea and allocation need not necessarily take place on the first occasion when an accused charged with an either-way offence appears before magistrates. Section 17C empowers the court to adjourn proceedings under s. 17A or s. 17B (the 'plea before venue' hearing), and s. 18(4) allows the court to adjourn proceedings under ss. 19 to 23 (the allocation hearing). In either case, if the court does adjourn, it must remand the accused (either in custody or on bail) to the date fixed for the resumption of the proceedings, unless the accused first appeared in answer to a summons, or written charge and requisition, and has not subsequently been remanded, in which case the court has a discretion simply to adjourn (without remanding the accused).

It is submitted that magistrates are to be regarded as proceeding under ss. 17A to 23 from when an accused first appears charged with an either-way offence to when mode of trial is finally determined. Therefore, any adjournment during that period will be by virtue of s. 17C or s. 18(4).

Effect of Guilty Plea Indication at Plea before Venue Hearing

If sentence is not passed immediately (e.g., because the court requires a pre-sentence report), the case will have to be adjourned (see **D23.2**). In *Rafferty* [1999] 1 Cr App R 235, the Court **D6.11** of Appeal held that where a plea of guilty is entered at the 'plea before venue' hearing, this will not usually alter the position regarding bail. When a person who has been on bail enters a guilty plea at the 'plea before venue' hearing, the usual practice should be to continue the bail, even if it is anticipated that a custodial sentence will be imposed by the Crown Court, unless there is good reason for remanding in custody (per Thomas J at p. 237).

If the magistrates take the view that their sentencing powers are insufficient, they can commit the offender to the Crown Court for sentence, under the PCC(S)A 2000, s. 3 (see **D23.30**).

If sentence is to be passed in the magistrates' court, the procedure set out in **D23.6** *et seq*. will be followed.

By virtue of the Sentencing Council's definitive guideline, *Reduction in Sentence for a Guilty Plea* (see Supplement, **SG5-1**), where a guilty plea is indicated 'at the first stage of proceedings' a reduction of one-third should (unless any of the exceptions set out in guideline apply) be made. The first stage 'will normally be the first hearing at which a plea or indication of plea is sought and recorded by the court'. Where a guilty plea is indicated after the first stage of proceedings, the maximum level of reduction is reduced to one-quarter. It follows that, where the offence is triable either way, a guilty plea should be entered at the 'plea before venue' hearing in order to attract the maximum reduction in sentence.

Binding Effect of Indication of Sentence

D6.12 Where the court gives an indication of sentence under the MCA 1980, s. 20(4), and the accused then indicates a guilty plea (under s. 20(7)), s. 20A(1) stipulates that 'no court (whether a magistrates' court or not) may impose a custodial sentence for the offence unless such a sentence was indicated in the indication of sentence' given under s. 20(4). However, this is subject to the proviso contained in s. 20A(2), which refers to the PCC(S)A 2000, ss. 3A(4), 4(8) and 5(3).

The PCC(S)A 2000, s. 3A(2), requires a magistrates' court to commit an offender to the Crown Court for sentence where it appears to the magistrates' court that the criteria for the imposition of a sentence under the CJA 2003, s. 226A (extended sentences for dangerous offenders) would be met; it follows that an indication of a non-custodial sentence does not oust the power of the court to commit for sentence under s. 3A (see s. 3A(4)), or the power of the Crown Court to impose an extended sentence under s. 226A (see s. 5(3)).

Section 4(8) applies where the magistrates' court commits an offender to the Crown Court for sentence under s. 4(2) on the basis that the accused has indicated an intention to plead guilty to an either-way offence (and therefore is deemed to have pleaded guilty to it) and is also being sent to the Crown Court for trial in respect of one or more related offences. This power to commit for sentence is not ousted by an indication of sentence under the MCA 1980, s. 20(4). However, the ambit of this provision is limited by the PCC(S)A 2000, s. 5(3), which makes it clear that the powers of the Crown Court are freed from the restriction imposed by s. 20A(1) only where the offence committed for sentence under the PCC(S)A 2000, s. 4(2), is a specified offence (i.e. specified under the CJA 2003, s. 224) in respect of which the magistrates' court has stated (under s. 4(4)) that, in its opinion, it also had power to commit the offender for sentence under s. 3A(2).

Indication of Not Guilty Plea: Magistrates' Decision Whether to Accept Jurisdiction

D6.13 If the accused indicates a not guilty plea (or gives no indication, and so is deemed to be indicating a guilty plea), the court must consider whether to offer the accused the opportunity to consent to summary trial. Section 19(3) of the MCA 1980 sets out the matters to which the magistrates must have regard in considering whether summary trial or trial on indictment is more appropriate. The most important consideration for the magistrates (and for the parties, when making their representations) is whether the sentencing powers of the magistrates would be adequate to deal with the offence(s) in the event of the accused being convicted.

Where the accused is charged with more than one offence, the magistrates are required to look at the totality of the allegations, and not at each offence in isolation. Thus the magistrates can, and should, decline jurisdiction if they take the view that their sentencing powers are insufficient to deal with the totality of the offending, even if each offence taken by itself would not merit a harsher sentence than the magistrates could impose for that individual offence. The maximum penalty which magistrates can currently impose on summary conviction for an either-way offence is usually six months' imprisonment (an aggregate total of up to 12 months' imprisonment if the court is dealing with two or more either-way offences) and/or an unlimited fine.

Although the maximum sentence available in the magistrates' court is the most important factor when considering whether or not a case is suitable for summary trial, it is open to the magistrates to consider other factors. In *Horseferry Road Magistrates' Court, ex parte K* [1997] QB 23, for example, the Divisional Court accepted that a possible defence of insanity might make the case more suitable for trial on indictment.

Allocation Guideline The Sentencing Council's definitive guideline, *Allocation* (see Supplement, **SG1-1**), states that, in general, either-way offences should be tried summarily unless either: **D6.14**

- the outcome would clearly be a sentence in excess of the court's powers for the offence(s) concerned after taking into account personal mitigation and any potential reduction for a guilty plea; or
- for reasons of unusual legal, procedural or factual complexity, the case should be tried in the Crown Court. This exception may apply in cases where a very substantial fine is the likely sentence; other circumstances where this exception will apply are likely to be 'rare and case specific'.

The guideline goes on to say that, in cases with no factual or legal complications, the court should bear in mind its power to commit for sentence after a trial, and may retain jurisdiction notwithstanding that the likely sentence might exceed its powers. It is submitted that the practical effect is that, if the magistrates are uncertain of the adequacy of their sentencing powers, they should err on the side of offering the accused the option of summary trial.

The guideline also says that 'all parties should be asked by the court to make representations as to whether the case is suitable for summary trial'. The court should refer to the relevant definitive offence-specific guidelines (if any) to assess the likely sentence for the offence in the light of the facts alleged by the prosecution case, taking into account all aspects of the case (including those advanced by the defence, including any personal mitigation to which the defence wish to refer).

Where the court decides that the case is suitable to be dealt with in the magistrates' court, it must warn the accused that all sentencing options remain open and that, if the accused consents to summary trial and is convicted by the court or pleads guilty, the accused may be committed to the Crown Court for sentence.

Turning to the power to commit for sentence under the PCC(S)A 2000, s. 3 (see **D23.30**), **D6.15** the guideline notes that there is ordinarily no statutory restriction on committing an either-way offence for sentence following conviction. The general power of the magistrates' court to commit to the Crown Court for sentence after a finding that a case is suitable for summary trial and/or conviction continues to be available where the court is of the opinion 'that the offence or the combination of the offence and one or more offences associated with it was so serious that the Crown Court should, in the court's opinion, have the power to deal with the offender in any way it could deal with him if he had been convicted on indictment'. An important consequence of this approach is that the magistrates' court does not, in order to commit for sentence under s. 3, have to be in possession of new information making the offence appear more serious than it did when the court initially accepted jurisdiction at the allocation hearing.

The guideline adds that, when deciding whether to commit for sentence, the court should refer to any definitive guideline to arrive at the appropriate sentence, taking into account all the circumstances of the case (including personal mitigation and the appropriate guilty plea reduction). In borderline cases, the magistrates' court should consider obtaining a pre-sentence report before deciding whether to commit to the Crown Court for sentence.

Finally, the guideline says that where the offending is so serious that the court is of the opinion that the Crown Court should have the power to deal with the offender, the case should be committed to the Crown Court for sentence even if a community order may be the appropriate sentence (the guideline notes that this will allow the Crown Court to deal with any breach of a community order, if that is the sentence passed). It is submitted that this provision will be relevant only in exceptional cases, for example where the offence merits a custodial sentence in excess of the powers of the magistrates' court but where a community sentence might be appropriate in light of mitigation put forward by the offender.

D6.16 **Allocation Where There Are Co-accused** CrimPR 9.2(6)(a) (see Supplement, **R9.2**) provides that, where the court is dealing on the same occasion with two or more accused who are charged jointly with an offence that can be tried in the Crown Court, the court must explain that, if one of them is sent to the Crown Court for trial, the other(s) must also be sent for trial in the Crown Court for the offence that is jointly charged and for any other offence which the court decides is related to that offence. This is so even if the court has, by then, decided that the case against the other accused is suitable for summary trial. To prevent having to repeat the procedure where the case has been found suitable for summary trial in respect of one accused but a co-accused then elects Crown Court trial, r. 9.2(6)(b) states that the court may ask the accused questions to help it decide in what order to deal with them (this would include questions about intention to elect Crown Court trial). In any event, by virtue of r. 9.2(7), if the court is dealing on the same occasion with two or more accused who are jointly charged and it accepts jurisdiction in respect of one of them but another is then sent for Crown Court trial (this would be as a result of that accused electing Crown Court trial), the court must deal again with the accused in respect of whom it has accepted jurisdiction (sending that accused instead to the Crown Court for trial). This has the effect of reversing the decision of the House of Lords in *Brentwood Justices, ex parte Nicholls* [1992] 1 AC 1, where it had been held that a case remained suitable for summary trial even if a co-accused had elected Crown Court trial.

CrimPR 9.2 is a consequence of the effect of the CDA 1998, s. 51(5), which provides that, where one accused is sent to the Crown Court for trial and another adult appears before the court (on the same or a subsequent occasion) charged jointly with the first accused with an either-way offence that appears to the court to be related to an offence for which the first accused was sent for trial, the court must, where it is the same occasion, or may, where it is a subsequent occasion, send the other adult to the Crown Court for trial for that either-way offence. This is so even if that offence would otherwise be suitable for summary trial (see **D10.9**).

Prosecution Influence on the Allocation Decision

D6.17 The overall effect of the mode of trial provisions in the MCA 1980 is that summary trial may be vetoed either by the court or by the accused, but not by the prosecution. The most the prosecution can do is to make representations that trial on indictment would be more appropriate having regard to the gravity of the offence. However, where either (a) the case involves fraud of such seriousness or complexity that it is appropriate that the management of the case should without delay be taken over by the Crown Court, or (b) the accused is charged with an offence which involves an assault on, or injury or a threat of injury to, a person or is charged with certain other specified offences and a child will be called as a witness at the trial and, for the purpose of avoiding any prejudice to the welfare of the child, the case should be taken over and proceeded with without delay by the Crown Court, then the prosecutor can serve a notice, under the CDA 1998, s. 51B or s. 51C respectively (see **D10.34** ***et seq.***). The effect of such a notice is that the magistrates' court is required, by s. 51(2)(c), to send the case forthwith to the Crown Court for trial instead of conducting a plea before venue hearing under s. 17A (s. 17A(10)).

Accused's Decision Whether to Consent to Summary Trial

It is sometimes asserted that one advantage of summary trial is that there is a limit on the sentence which the magistrates' court can pass (six months' imprisonment for one 'either-way' offence, an aggregate of 12 months for two or more). However, this advantage is nullified by the power of the magistrates to commit the accused to be sentenced in the Crown Court under the PCC(S)A 2000, s. 3. **D6.18**

One potential advantage of trial on indictment is that submissions on the admissibility of evidence can be made in the absence of the jury, with the obvious benefit that the jury do not find out about any matters that are ruled inadmissible. However, under the Courts Act 2003, sch. 3, a bench of magistrates may give a pre-trial ruling on the admissibility of evidence and that ruling binds the bench that tries the case (see **D21.35**).

Another supposed advantage of trial on indictment is that the defence are entitled to receive copies of the written statements of the witnesses to be called by the prosecution as part of the process whereby the case is transferred to the Crown Court. However, as a matter of good practice, the prosecution also provide to the defence all the evidence upon which they propose to rely in a summary trial. Thus, an accused who is to be tried in the magistrates' court should be in the same position as one being tried in the Crown Court as regards obtaining copies of the prosecution witness statements.

One possible advantage of magistrates' court trial is that it is shorter and less formal than trial on indictment, and is therefore also cheaper (likely to be particularly relevant if the accused is not legally aided).

Statutory Provisions on Mode of Trial

Magistrates' Courts Act 1980, ss. 17A to 17C, 18 to 21 and 23 **D6.19**

17A.—(1) This section shall have effect where a person who has attained the age of 18 years appears or is brought before a magistrates' court on an information charging him with an offence triable either way.

(2) Everything that the court is required to do under the following provisions of this section must be done with the accused present in court.

(3) The court shall cause the charge to be written down, if this has not already been done, and to be read to the accused.

(4) The court shall then explain to the accused in ordinary language that he may indicate whether (if the offence were to proceed to trial) he would plead guilty or not guilty, and that if he indicates that he would plead guilty—
- (a) the court must proceed as mentioned in subsection (6) below; and
- (b) he may be committed for sentence to the Crown Court under section 3 of the Powers of Criminal Courts (Sentencing) Act 2000 if the court is of such opinion as is mentioned in subsection (2) of that section.

(5) The court shall then ask the accused whether (if the offence were to proceed to trial) he would plead guilty or not guilty.

(6) If the accused indicates that he would plead guilty the court shall proceed as if—
- (a) the proceedings constituted from the beginning the summary trial of the information; and
- (b) section 9(1) above was complied with and he pleaded guilty under it.

(7) If the accused indicates that he would plead not guilty section 18(1) below shall apply.

(8) If the accused in fact fails to indicate how he would plead, for the purposes of this section and section 18(1) below he shall be taken to indicate that he would plead not guilty.

(9) Subject to subsection (6) above, the following shall not for any purpose be taken to constitute the taking of a plea—
- (a) asking the accused under this section whether (if the offence were to proceed to trial) he would plead guilty or not guilty;
- (b) an indication by the accused under this section of how he would plead.

17B.—(1) This section shall have effect where—

(a) a person who has attained the age of 18 years appears or is brought before a magistrates' court on an information charging him with an offence triable either way,

(b) the accused is represented by a legal representative,

(c) the court considers that by reason of the accused's disorderly conduct before the court it is not practicable for proceedings under section 17A above to be conducted in his presence, and

(d) the court considers that it should proceed in the absence of the accused.

(2) In such a case—

(a) the court shall cause the charge to be written down, if this has not already been done, and to be read to the representative;

(b) the court shall ask the representative whether (if the offence were to proceed to trial) the accused would plead guilty or not guilty;

(c) if the representative indicates that the accused would plead guilty the court shall proceed as if the proceedings constituted from the beginning the summary trial of the information, and as if section 9(1) above was complied with and the accused pleaded guilty under it;

(d) if the representative indicates that the accused would plead not guilty section 18(1) below shall apply.

(3) If the representative in fact fails to indicate how the accused would plead, for the purposes of this section and section 18(1) below he shall be taken to indicate that the accused would plead not guilty.

(4) Subject to subsection (2)(c) above, the following shall not for any purpose be taken to constitute the taking of a plea—

(a) asking the representative under this section whether (if the offence were to proceed to trial) the accused would plead guilty or not guilty;

(b) an indication by the representative under this section of how the accused would plead.

17C. A magistrates' court proceeding under section 17A or 17B above may adjourn the proceedings at any time, and on doing so on any occasion when the accused is present may remand the accused, and shall remand him if—

(a) on the occasion on which he first appeared, or was brought, before the court to answer to the information he was in custody or, having been released on bail, surrendered to the custody of the court; or

(b) he has been remanded at any time in the course of proceedings on the information;

and where the court remands the accused, the time fixed for the resumption of proceedings shall be that at which he is required to appear or be brought before the court in pursuance of the remand or would be required to be brought before the court but for section 128(3A) below.

18.—(1) Sections 19 to 23 below shall have effect where a person who has attained the age of 18 years appears or is brought before a magistrates' court on an information charging him with an offence triable either way and—

(a) he indicates under section 17A above that (if the offence were to proceed to trial) he would plead not guilty, or

(b) his representative indicates under section 17B above that (if the offence were to proceed to trial) he would plead not guilty.

(2) Without prejudice to section 11(1) above [proceeding to summary trial of an information in the absence of the accused if he does not appear], everything that the court is required to do under sections 19 to 22 below must be done before any evidence is called and, subject to subsection (3) below and section 23 below, with the accused present in court.

(3) The court may proceed in the absence of the accused in accordance with such of the provisions of sections 19 to 22 below as are applicable in the circumstances if the court considers that by reason of his disorderly conduct before the court it is not practicable for the proceedings to be conducted in his presence; and subsections (3) to (5) of section 23 below, so far as applicable, shall have effect in relation to proceedings conducted in the absence of the accused by virtue of this subsection (references in those subsections to the person representing the accused being for this purpose read as references to the person, if any, representing him).

(4) A magistrates' court proceeding under sections 19 to 23 below may adjourn the proceedings at any time, and on doing so on any occasion when the accused is present may remand the accused, and shall remand him if—

(a) on the occasion on which he first appeared, or was brought, before the court to answer to the information he was in custody or, having been released on bail, surrendered to the custody of the court; or

(b) if he has been remanded at any time in the course of proceedings on the information;

and where the court remands the accused, the time fixed for the resumption of the proceedings shall be that at which he is required to appear or be brought before the court in pursuance of the remand or would be required to be brought before the court but for section 128(3A) below [accused being remanded in custody agreeing to future remands in custody taking place in accused's absence].

(5) The functions of a magistrates' court under sections 19 to 23 below may be discharged by a single justice, but the foregoing provision shall not be taken to authorise the summary trial of an information by a magistrates' court composed of less than two justices.

19.—(1) The court shall decide whether the offence appears to it more suitable for summary trial or for trial on indictment.

(2) Before making a decision under this section, the court—

(a) shall give the prosecution an opportunity to inform the court of the accused's previous convictions (if any); and

(b) shall give the prosecution and the accused an opportunity to make representations as to whether summary trial or trial on indictment would be more suitable.

(3) In making a decision under this section, the court shall consider—

(a) whether the sentence which a magistrates' court would have power to impose for the offence would be adequate; and

(b) any representations made by the prosecution or the accused under subsection (2)(b) above,

and shall have regard to any allocation guidelines (or revised allocation guidelines) issued as definitive guidelines under section 170 of the Criminal Justice Act 2003.

(4) Where—

(a) the accused is charged with two or more offences; and

(b) it appears to the court that the charges for the offences could be joined in the same indictment or that the offences arise out of the same or connected circumstances,

subsection (3)(a) above shall have effect as if references to the sentence which a magistrates' court would have power to impose for the offence were a reference to the maximum aggregate sentence which a magistrates' court would have power to impose for all of the offences taken together.

(5) In this section any reference to a previous conviction is a reference to—

(a) a previous conviction by a court in the United Kingdom;

(aa) a previous conviction by a court in another member State of a relevant offence under the law of that State; or

(b) a previous conviction of a service offence within the meaning of the Armed Forces Act 2006.

(5A) For the purposes of subsection (5)(aa) an offence is 'relevant' if the offence would constitute an offence under the law of any part of the United Kingdom if it were done in that part at the time when the allocation decision is made.

(6) If, in respect of the offence, the court receives a notice under section 51B or 51C of the Crime and Disorder Act 1998 (which relate to serious or complex fraud cases and to certain cases involving children respectively), the preceding provisions of this section and sections 20, 20A and 21 below shall not apply, and the court shall proceed in relation to the offence in accordance with section 51(1) of that Act.

20.—(1) If the court decides under section 19 above that the offence appears to it more suitable for summary trial, the following provisions of this section shall apply (unless they are excluded by section 23 below).

(2) The court shall explain to the accused in ordinary language—

(a) that it appears to the court more suitable for him to be tried summarily for the offence;

(b) that he can either consent to be so tried or, if he wishes, be tried on indictment;

(c) that if he is tried summarily and is convicted by the court, he may be committed for sentence to the Crown Court under section 3 or (if applicable) section 3A of the Powers of Criminal Courts (Sentencing) Act 2000 if the court is of such opinion as is mentioned in subsection (2) of the applicable section.

(3) The accused may then request an indication ('an indication of sentence') of whether a custodial sentence or non-custodial sentence would be more likely to be imposed if he were to be tried summarily for the offence and to plead guilty.

(4) If the accused requests an indication of sentence, the court may, but need not, give such an indication.

(5) If the accused requests and the court gives an indication of sentence, the court shall ask the accused whether he wishes, on the basis of the indication, to reconsider the indication of plea which was given, or is taken to have been given, under section 17A or 17B above.

(6) If the accused indicates that he wishes to reconsider the indication under section 17A or 17B above, the court shall ask the accused whether (if the offence were to proceed to trial) he would plead guilty or not guilty.

(7) If the accused indicates that he would plead guilty the court shall proceed as if—
- (a) the proceedings constituted from that time the summary trial of the information; and
- (b) section 9(1) above were complied with and he pleaded guilty under it.

(8) Subsection (9) below applies where—
- (a) the court does not give an indication of sentence (whether because the accused does not request one or because the court does not agree to give one);
- (b) the accused either—
  - (i) does not indicate, in accordance with subsection (5) above, that he wishes; or
  - (ii) indicates, in accordance with subsection (5) above, that he does not wish, to reconsider the indication of plea under section 17A or 17B above; or
- (c) the accused does not indicate, in accordance with subsection (6) above, that he would plead guilty.

(9) The court shall ask the accused whether he consents to be tried summarily or wishes to be tried on indictment and—
- (a) if he consents to be tried summarily, shall proceed to the summary trial of the information; and
- (b) if he does not so consent, shall proceed in relation to the offence in accordance with section 51(1) of the Crime and Disorder Act 1998.

20A.—(1) Where the case is dealt with in accordance with section 20(7) above, no court (whether a magistrates' court or not) may impose a custodial sentence for the offence unless such a sentence was indicated in the indication of sentence referred to in section 20 above.

(2) Subsection (1) above is subject to sections 3A(4), 4(8) and 5(3) of the Powers of Criminal Courts (Sentencing) Act 2000.

(3) Except as provided in subsection (1) above—
- (a) an indication of sentence shall not be binding on any court (whether a magistrates' court or not); and
- (b) no sentence may be challenged or be the subject of appeal in any court on the ground that it is not consistent with an indication of sentence.

21. If the court decides under section 19 above that the offence appears to it more suitable for trial on indictment, the court shall tell the accused that the court has decided that it is more suitable for him to be tried on indictment, and shall proceed in relation to the offence in accordance with section 51(1) of the Crime and Disorder Act 1998.

23.—(1) Where—
- (a) the accused is represented by counsel or a solicitor who in his absence signifies to the court the accused's consent to the proceedings for determining how he is to be tried for the offence being conducted in his absence; and
- (b) the court is satisfied that there is good reason for proceeding in the absence of the accused,

the following provisions of this section shall apply.

(2) Subject to the following provisions of this section, the court may proceed in the absence of the accused in accordance with such of the provisions of sections 19 to 22 above as are applicable in the circumstances.

(3) If, in a case where subsection (1) of section 22 above applies, it appears to the court as mentioned in subsection (4) of that section, subsections (5) and (6) of that section shall not apply and the court—
- (a) if the accused's consent to be tried summarily has been or is signified by the person representing him, shall proceed in accordance with subsection (2) of that section as if that subsection applied; or
- (b) if that consent has not been and is not so signified, shall proceed in accordance with subsection (3) of that section as if that subsection applied.

(4) If the court decides under section 19 above that the offence appears to it more suitable for summary trial then—
- (a) if the accused's consent to be tried summarily has been or is signified by the person representing him, section 20 above shall not apply, and the court shall proceed to the summary trial of the information; or

(b) if that consent has not been and is not so signified, section 20 above shall not apply and the court shall proceed in relation to the offence in accordance with section 51(1) of the Crime and Disorder Act 1998.

(5) If the court decides under section 19 above that the offence appears to it more suitable for trial on indictment, section 21 above shall not apply and the court shall proceed in relation to the offence in accordance with section 51(1) of the Crime and Disorder Act 1998.

[26. Powers ancillary to s. 23 to issue a summons or warrant for arrest in respect of the accused if either the court considers that he should be present while the mode of trial is determined or, having proceeded in his absence and adjourned without remanding him prior to committal or transfer proceedings, he does not appear for the resumption of the hearing.]

SPECIAL PROCEDURE FOR CRIMINAL DAMAGE CHARGES

Procedure on Criminal Damage Charges

If the accused is charged with a 'scheduled offence', the allocation procedure must be preceded by consideration of the value involved in the offence (s. 22(1); see **D6.26**). Depending on what that value is, the accused may be deprived of the right to elect trial on indictment, notwithstanding that the offence is otherwise triable either way. **D6.20**

Scheduled offences comprise: (a) offences of damaging or destroying property contrary to s. 1 of the Criminal Damage Act 1971, excluding those committed by fire; and (b) aiding, abetting, counselling or procuring such offences, or attempting or encouraging them (MCA 1980, sch. 2). Some offences under the Criminal Damage Act 1971 are *not* scheduled offences, including:

(a) those committed by damaging or destroying property by fire (these are expressly excluded from scheduled offences by the terms of the MCA 1980, sch. 2); and

(b) those committed with intent to endanger life or being reckless as to the endangering of life contrary to the Criminal Damage Act 1971, s. 1(2): although not expressly dealt with in sch. 2, these cannot be scheduled offences because they are not in the list of offences under the 1971 Act that are triable either way (see the MCA 1980, sch. 1, para. 29), and so they are triable only on indictment.

It should also be noted that conspiracy to commit criminal damage is not a scheduled offence (*Ward* [1997] 1 Cr App R (S) 442).

Value Involved If the accused is charged with an offence of criminal damage to which the provisions of the MCA 1980, s. 22, apply, then the court must give the accused the opportunity to indicate plea (pursuant to s. 17A). It must then consider, having regard to any representations made by the prosecution and defence, whether the 'value involved' in the offence exceeds the 'relevant sum', currently £5,000 (MCA 1980, s. 22(1)). If the property was allegedly destroyed or damaged beyond repair, the value involved is what it would probably have cost to purchase a replacement in the open market at the time of the offence; if the property was repairable, the value involved is the probable market cost of repairs or the probable market replacement cost, whichever is the less (sch. 2). In *Colchester Magistrates' Court, ex parte Abbott* [2001] EWHC Admin 136, the Divisional Court made it clear that the value on which the magistrates must focus is the value of the damage to the property itself; they should not concern themselves with any consequential losses which might have been sustained as a result of the damage. **D6.21**

If it appears to the magistrates that the value involved clearly does *not* exceed the relevant sum, they must proceed as if the offence charged were triable only summarily (s. 22(2)). Consequently, the allocation provisions of the 1980 Act do not apply and the accused has no right to elect trial on indictment.

If it appears to the court clear that the value involved exceeds the relevant sum, it is obliged to determine allocation in accordance with the usual procedure, just as for any other either-way offence (s. 22(3)).

Where, for any reason, it is not clear to the court whether the value involved does or does not exceed the relevant sum, it must explain to the accused that he or she may consent to summary trial and that, if consent is given, a summary trial will take place and (in the event of conviction) liability to imprisonment or a fine will be limited in accordance with the provisions of s. 33 of the 1980 Act (see **D6.26**). The accused is then asked for consent. Depending on the accused's response, the court either proceeds to summary trial or embarks on the ordinary procedure for determining mode of trial (s. 22(5) and (6)).

D6.22 The MCA 1980, s. 17D(1), provides that where the accused, at the plea before venue hearing, indicated a guilty plea to an offence to which s. 22 applies (and so is deemed to have pleaded guilty to it), the court must consider whether, having regard to any representations made by the accused or by the prosecutor, the value involved exceeds £5,000. If it appears clear to the court that the value involved does not exceed £5,000, or it is unclear whether the value involved exceeds £5,000, the court's sentencing powers are subject to the limits set out in the MCA 1980, s. 33, and there is no power to commit for sentence under the PCC(S)A 2000, s. 3 or s. 4. Section 33 provides that where the accused is convicted of an offence to which s. 22 applies (this includes conviction following a guilty plea under s. 17A(6) and conviction following summary trial of a criminal damage offence where either the court decided that the value involved clearly did not exceed £5,000 or, by virtue of s. 22(5), the accused consented to summary trial in a case where the court was in doubt as to the value involved), then the maximum penalty that may be imposed in the event of conviction is three months' imprisonment or a fine of £2,500, and the court has no power to commit for sentence under the PCC(S)A 2000, s. 3. If the accused is tried summarily in a case where the value involved clearly exceeded the relevant sum but summary trial was nevertheless offered and accepted, the penalties available are as for any either-way offence (currently six months' imprisonment and/or a fine); moreover, there may be a committal for sentence under the PCC(S)A 2000, s. 3.

D6.23 **Procedure for Determining the Value Involved** The court is required by the MCA 1980, s. 22(1), to have regard to the 'representations' of the parties when considering the value involved in a criminal damage offence. This does not entail an obligation to hear evidence. In *Canterbury and St Augustine Justices, ex parte Klisiak* [1982] QB 398 at p. 413D–E, Lord Lane CJ said that 'the word "representations" implies something less than evidence. It comprises submissions, coupled with assertions of fact and sometimes production of documents . . . The nearest analogy is, perhaps, the speech in mitigation after a finding or plea of guilty in a criminal trial.' However, the court has a discretion to hear evidence on the question of the value involved if it wishes to do so (*Ex parte Klisiak* at p. 413D–E).

In a case where there is real difficulty in arriving at an appropriate basis for calculating the value involved, the prosecution are entitled to say that they will not seek to prove that the accused caused any more damage than can be established with clarity. Acting on that assurance, the court may conclude that the value was clearly less than the relevant sum even though, in the absence of such an assurance and adopting an alternative method of calculation, the question would have remained doubtful and the accused could therefore have elected trial on indictment (*Salisbury Magistrates' Court, ex parte Mastin* (1986) 84 Cr App R 248).

Two or More Criminal Damage Charges

D6.24 If the accused is 'charged on the same occasion with two or more scheduled offences and it appears to the court that they constitute or form part of a series of two or more offences of the same or a similar character', then the relevant consideration is the *aggregate* value involved in the offences (MCA 1980, s. 22(11); see **D6.26**). In other words, the accused will retain the right to trial on indictment if the value of the offences added together exceeds the relevant sum (£5,000), even if the value of each offence taken individually was under the relevant sum.

The reference in s. 22(11) to a 'series of two or more offences of the same or similar character' connotes that the aggregate value is the relevant value where the offences could be joined together in the same indictment under CrimPR 3.29(4) (see Supplement, **R3.29**), which governs joinder of counts in an indictment (see **D11.63** ***et seq.***). Thus, s. 22(11) applies where the offences are founded on the same facts (effectively, amounting to a single incident) or constitute a series of offences that are linked by closeness in time and geographical location.

Section 22(11) applies where the accused is 'charged on the same occasion' with two or more scheduled offences. This phrase could be construed to mean either being charged at the police station (where that is the way in which proceedings were commenced) or appearing before a magistrates' court to answer charges. In *Harvey* [2020] EWCA Crim 354, [2020] 4 WLR 50, the Court of Appeal construed the phrase 'charged on the same occasion' to mean 'appearing at the magistrates' court to answer the charges' on the same occasion. It follows that an accused may be charged with offences on separate occasions at a police station but, if the first court appearance for those charges is at the same hearing, then the accused is charged on the same occasion with those offences and their value can be aggregated. **D6.25**

Statutory Provisions on Criminal Damage Mode of Trial

Magistrates' Courts Act 1980, ss. 17D, 22 and 33 and sch. 2 **D6.26**

17D.—(1) If—
(a) the offence is a scheduled offence (as defined in section 22(1) below);
(b) the court proceeds in relation to the offence in accordance with section 17A(6) or 17B(2)(c) above; and
(c) the court convicts the accused of the offence,
the court shall consider whether, having regard to any representations made by him or by the prosecutor, the value involved (as defined in section 22(10) below) appears to the court to exceed the relevant sum (as specified for the purposes of section 22 below).

(2) If it appears to the court clear that the value involved does not exceed the relevant sum, or it appears to the court for any reason not clear whether the value involved does or does not exceed the relevant sum—
(a) subject to subsection (4) below, the court shall not have power to impose on the accused in respect of the offence a sentence in excess of the limits mentioned in section 33(1)(a) below; and
(b) sections 3 and 4 of the Powers of Criminal Courts (Sentencing) Act 2000 shall not apply as regards that offence.

(3) Subsections (9) to (12) of section 22 below shall apply for the purposes of this section as they apply for the purposes of that section (reading the reference to subsection (1) in section 22(9) as a reference to subsection (1) of this section).

(4) Subsection (2)(a) above does not apply to an offence under section 12A of the Theft Act 1968 (aggravated vehicle-taking).

22.—(1) If the offence charged by the information is one of those mentioned in the first column of Schedule 2 to this Act (in this section referred to as 'scheduled offences') then the court shall, before proceeding in accordance with section 19 above, consider whether, having regard to any representations made by the prosecutor or the accused, the value involved (as defined in subsection (10) below) appears to exceed the relevant sum. For the purposes of this section the relevant sum is £5,000.

(2) If, where subsection (1) above applies, it appears to the court clear that, for the offence charged, the value involved does not exceed the relevant sum, the court shall proceed as if the offence were triable only summarily, and sections 19 to 21 above shall not apply.

(3) If, where subsection (1) above applies, it appears to the court clear that, for the offence charged, the value involved exceeds that relevant sum, the court shall thereupon proceed in accordance with section 19 above in the ordinary way without further regard to the provisions of this section.

(4) If, where subsection (1) above applies, it appears to the court for any reason not clear whether, for the offence charged, the value involved does or does not exceed the relevant sum, the provisions of subsections (5) and (6) below shall apply.

(5) The court shall cause the charge to be written down, if this has not already been done, and read to the accused, and shall explain to him in ordinary language—
  (a) that he can, if he wishes, consent to be tried summarily for the offence and that if he consents to be so tried, he will definitely be tried in that way; and
  (b) that if he is tried summarily and is convicted by the court, his liability to imprisonment or a fine will be limited as provided in section 33 below.

(6) After explaining to the accused as provided by subsection (5) above, the court shall ask him whether he consents to be tried summarily and—
  (a) if he so consents, shall proceed in accordance with subsection (2) above as if that subsection applied;
  (b) if he does not so consent, shall proceed in accordance with subsection (3) above as if that subsection applied.

[(7) Repealed.]

[(8) No appeal to the Crown Court against conviction for a scheduled offence on the ground that the decision as to the value involved was mistaken.]

[(9) Where a juvenile and an adult are jointly charged with a scheduled offence, the juvenile as well as the adult may make representations as to the value involved.]

[(10) 'The value involved' to be given the meaning set out in sch. 2, and 'material time', when used in sch. 2, means the time of the alleged offence.]

(11) Where—
  (a) the accused is charged on the same occasion with two or more scheduled offences and it appears to the court that they constitute or form part of a series of two or more offences of the same or a similar character; or
  (b) the offence charged consists in [intentionally encouraging or assisting a person] to commit two or more scheduled offences,

this section shall have effect as if any reference in it to the value involved were a reference to the aggregate of the values involved.

(12) Subsection (8) of section 12A of the Theft Act 1968 (which determines when a vehicle is recovered) shall apply for the purposes of paragraph 3 of Schedule 2 to this Act as it applies for the purposes of that section.

33.—(1) Where in pursuance of subsection (2) of section 22 above a magistrates' court proceeds to the summary trial of an information, then, if the accused is summarily convicted of the offence—
  (a) subject to subsection (3) below the court shall not have power to impose on him in respect of that offence imprisonment for more than 3 months or a fine greater than level 4 on the standard scale; and
  (b) Section 3 of the Powers of Criminal Courts (Sentencing) Act 2000 [committal for sentence if the magistrates' powers of punishment inadequate] shall not apply as regards that offence.

(2) In subsection (1) above 'fine' includes a pecuniary penalty but does not include a pecuniary forfeiture or pecuniary compensation.

(3) Paragraph (a) of subsection (1) above does not apply to an offence under section 12A of the Theft Act 1968 (aggravated vehicle-taking).

Schedule 2

Offences for which the Value Involved is Relevant to the Mode of Trial

[Column 1 shows the offences subject to the special procedure; column 2 defines the value involved, and column 3 indicates how the value involved is calculated.]

Offence	Value involved	How measured
1. Offences under section 1 of the Criminal Damage Act 1971 (destroying or damaging property), excluding any offence committed by destroying or damaging property by fire.	As regards property alleged to have been destroyed, its value. As regards property alleged to have been damaged, the value of the alleged damage.	What the property would probably have cost to buy in the open market at the material time. (a) If immediately after the material time the damage was capable of repair— (i) what would probably then have been the market price for the repair of the damage, or (ii) what the property alleged to have been damaged would probably have cost to buy in the open market at the material time, whichever is the less; or (b) if immediately after the material time the damage was beyond repair, what the said property would probably have cost to buy in the open market at the material time.
2. The following offences, namely (a) aiding, abetting, counselling or procuring the commission of any offence mentioned in paragraph 1 above; (b) attempting to commit any offence so mentioned; and (c) inciting another to commit any offence so mentioned.	The value indicated in paragraph 1 above for the offence alleged to have been aided, abetted, counselled or procured, or attempted or incited.	As for the corresponding entry in paragraph 1 above.
3. Offences under section 12A of the Theft Act 1968 (aggravated vehicle-taking) where no allegation is made under subsection (1)(b) other than of damage, whether to the vehicle or other property or both.	The total value of the damage alleged to have been caused.	(1) In the case of damage to any property other than the vehicle involved in the offence, as for the corresponding entry in paragraph 1 above, substituting a reference to the time of the accident concerned for any reference to the material time. (2) In the case of damage to the vehicle involved in the offence— (a) if immediately after the vehicle was recovered the damage was capable of repair— (i) what would probably then have been the market price for the repair of the damage, or (ii) what the vehicle would probably have cost to buy in the open market immediately before it was unlawfully taken, whichever is the less; or (b) if immediately after the vehicle was recovered the damage was beyond repair, what the vehicle would probably have cost to buy in the open market immediately before it was unlawfully taken.

SPECIAL PROVISION FOR LOW-VALUE SHOPLIFTING

D6.27 The MCA 1980, s. 22A (see **D6.28**), provides that 'low-value' shoplifting (defined as shoplifting where the value of the stolen goods does not exceed £200) is triable only summarily. However, s. 22A(2) goes on to provide that, where an accused who has attained the age of 18 is charged with low-value shoplifting, the court must, before the summary trial of the offence begins, give the accused the opportunity of electing Crown Court trial for the offence; if the accused elects to be so tried, the magistrates' court must send the case to the Crown Court for trial. Unlike the special procedure for criminal damage (under the MCA 1980, s. 22), in the case of low-value shoplifting the accused retains the right to elect Crown Court trial. CrimPR 9.7(4)(c) (see Supplement, **R9.7**) makes it clear that, where the offence is low-value shoplifting, the magistrates' court must offer the accused the opportunity to require trial in the Crown Court.

In *McDermott-Mullane* [2016] EWCA Crim 2239, [2017] 4 WLR 127, D was charged with low-value shoplifting, together with another summary offence and an either-way offence. She did not elect Crown Court trial in respect of the shoplifting, but was sent to the Crown Court for trial. At the Crown Court, the prosecution did not proceed with the either-way offence or the other summary offence. The only charge before the Crown Court, therefore, was the shoplifting. The court ruled that the indictment was a nullity because, unless the accused elects Crown Court trial, low-value shoplifting is not capable of forming the sole count of an indictment (at [27]); only the magistrates' court had power to deal with the offence of low-value shoplifting unless the accused elected Crown Court trial (at [31]).

Where the accused is 'charged on the same occasion' with two or more offences of low-value shoplifting, the value of the offences is aggregated, and s. 22A applies only if the total value does not exceed £200 (s. 22A(4)(b)). The phrase, 'charged on the same occasion', is to be construed in the same way as it is for the purposes of the special criminal damage provisions (see **D6.25**) (*Harvey* [2020] EWCA Crim 354, [2020] 4 WLR 50, at [20]).

In *Maxwell* [2017] EWCA Crim 1233, [2018] 1 Cr App R 5 (76), the Court of Appeal ruled that low-value shoplifting charges cannot be aggregated with shoplifting offences to which s. 22A does not apply (and so it is only the 'low-value' offences that can be aggregated). In this case, the three low-value offences came nowhere near £200 in total and so were (unless the accused elected Crown Court trial) triable only summarily. The Court also rejected the suggestion that the CDA 1998, s. 40 (see **D11.17**), applies to low-value shoplifting. The Secretary of State has power (under s. 40(4)) to specify additional offences by statutory instrument; however, low-value shoplifting has not been so specified.

Similarly, in *Burrows* [2019] EWCA Crim 889, D was sent for trial for going equipped for stealing (TA 1968, s. 25), having elected Crown Court trial for that offence. A related offence of theft was sent for trial under the CDA 1998, s. 51(3) (see **D10.7**). The theft charge was included in the indictment. However, the theft was an offence of low-value shoplifting and, because D had not elected Crown Court trial in respect of that offence, it remained a summary offence. The Court of Appeal noted (at [9]) that only summary offences that are listed in the CJA 1988, s. 40, can be joined to an indictment. Low-value shoplifting is not one of the offences listed in s. 40 and so, 'in the absence of an election by the accused it cannot be included as a count on the indictment'. It followed that the charge of theft should have been dealt with by the Crown Court in accordance with the procedure set out in the CDA 1998, sch. 3, para. 6 (see **D10.29**).

D6.28 **Magistrates' Courts Act 1980, s. 22A**

(1) Low-value shoplifting is triable only summarily.
(2) But where a person accused of low-value shoplifting is aged 18 or over, and appears or is brought before the court before the summary trial of the offence begins, the court must give the person the opportunity of electing to be tried by the Crown Court for the offence and, if the person elects to be so tried—
   (a) subsection (1) does not apply, and

(b) the court must proceed in relation to the offence in accordance with section 51(1) of the Crime and Disorder Act 1998.

(3) 'Low-value shoplifting' means an offence under section 1 of the Theft Act 1968 in circumstances where—
(a) the value of the stolen goods does not exceed £200,
(b) the goods were being offered for sale in a shop or any other premises, stall, vehicle or place from which there is carried on a trade or business, and
(c) at the time of the offence, the person accused of low-value shoplifting was, or was purporting to be, a customer or potential customer of the person offering the goods for sale.

(4) For the purposes of subsection (3)(a)—
(a) the value of the stolen goods is the price at which they were being offered for sale at the time of the offence, and
(b) where the accused is charged on the same occasion with two or more offences of low-value shoplifting, the reference to the value involved has effect as if it were a reference to the aggregate of the values involved.

(5) [Maximum sentence.]

(6) A person convicted of low-value shoplifting by a magistrates' court may not appeal to the Crown Court against the conviction on the ground that the convicting court was mistaken as to whether the offence was one of low-value shoplifting.

(7) For the purposes of this section, any reference to low-value shoplifting includes aiding, abetting, counselling or procuring the commission of low-value shoplifting.

FAILURE TO COMPLY WITH THE ALLOCATION PROCEDURE

Failure to comply with the statutory allocation procedure renders the proceedings a nullity. **D6.29**
In *Kent Justices, ex parte Machin* [1952] 2 QB 355, it was held that, because the jurisdiction of magistrates' courts to try either-way offences derives solely from statute, any failure to comply with the statutory procedure laid down for determining allocation renders any summary trial which follows that defective procedure *ultra vires* and therefore a nullity. In *Ashton* [2006] EWCA Crim 794, [2007] 1 WLR 181, it was held that, in the absence of a clear indication that Parliament intended jurisdiction automatically to be removed following a procedural failure, the decision of the court should be based on an assessment of the interests of justice, with particular focus on whether there was a real possibility that the prosecution or the defence may suffer prejudice. If that risk is present, the court should then decide whether it is just to permit the proceedings to continue. This meant that a number of authorities, including *Machin*, would have to be reconsidered (at [67]–[69]). However, in *R (Rahmdezfouli) v Wood Green Crown Court* [2013] EWHC 2998 (Admin), [2014] 1 WLR 1793, Mackay J said (at [16]):

> [T]he legislature in enacting s. 17A must have intended ... that where a magistrates' court declined or failed to follow the requirements of the section it was acting without jurisdiction every bit as much as if, for instance, it had purported to try a defendant on a charge of homicide.

The effect of this decision is that failure to comply with the allocation process as it is set out in the MCA 1980 is to be regarded as nullifying any proceedings which follow that defective procedure.

The same approach was taken in *Westminster City Council v Owadally* [2017] EWHC 1092 (Admin), [2017] 2 Cr App R 18 (223). At the plea before venue hearing, guilty pleas were indicated on behalf of the accused by their counsel. The Divisional Court held (at [45]) that, as in the Crown Court, an accused in a magistrates' court must enter a guilty plea personally. The requirements of s. 17A are to be treated as going to the jurisdiction of the court. It follows that, if a guilty plea is not entered by the accused personally, that plea (and any proceedings subsequent to that plea, such as committal for sentence) is to be regarded as a nullity.

VARIATION OF ORIGINAL DECISION AS TO ALLOCATION

Introduction

D6.30 Variation of the allocation decision is governed by the MCA 1980, s. 25 (see **D6.31**), which enables the prosecution to make an application to the magistrates (before the start of the summary trial) to reconsider their acceptance of summary jurisdiction.

By virtue of s. 25(2), where the accused has consented to summary trial (the magistrates having first accepted jurisdiction), the prosecution may apply to the court for the offence to be tried on indictment instead (s. 25(2)). This application must be made before the summary trial begins and must be dealt with by the court before any other application or issue in relation to the summary trial is dealt with (s. 25(2A)). Under s. 25(2B), the court may accede to the application 'only if it is satisfied that the sentence which a magistrates' court would have power to impose for the offence (or offences, where they constitute or form part of a series of two or more offences of the same or a similar character) would be inadequate'. If the court agrees to the prosecution application, the case is sent to the Crown Court for trial under the CDA 1998, s. 51.

D6.31 **Magistrates' Courts Act 1980, s. 25**

(1) Subsections (2) to (2D) below shall have effect where a person who has attained the age of 18 appears or is brought before a magistrates' court on an information charging him with an offence triable either way.

(2) Where the court is required under section 20(9) above to proceed to the summary trial of the information, the prosecution may apply to the court for the offence to be tried on indictment instead.

(2A) An application under subsection (2) above—

(a) must be made before the summary trial begins; and

(b) must be dealt with by the court before any other application or issue in relation to the summary trial is dealt with.

(2B) The court may grant an application under subsection (2) above but only if it is satisfied that the sentence which a magistrates' court would have power to impose for the offence would be inadequate.

(2C) Where—

(a) the accused is charged on the same occasion with two or more offences; and

(b) it appears to the court that they constitute or form part of a series of two or more offences of the same or a similar character,

subsection (2B) above shall have effect as if references to the sentence which a magistrates' court would have power to impose for the offence were a reference to the maximum aggregate sentence which a magistrates' court would have power to impose for all of the offences taken together.

(2D) Where the court grants an application under subsection (2) above, it shall proceed in relation to the offence in accordance with section 51(1) of the Crime and Disorder Act 1998.

WITHDRAWAL BY ACCUSED OF ORIGINAL CONSENT

General

D6.32 The approach a magistrates' court should adopt when an accused who has already chosen between summary trial and trial on indictment asks to withdraw the original consent to summary trial was considered by McCullough J in *Birmingham Justices, ex parte Hodgson* [1985] QB 1131. The following propositions emerge from his judgment:

(a) The magistrates have a discretion to permit the accused to withdraw consent to summary trial, notwithstanding that the provisions now contained in the MCA 1980, s. 20(9)(a), state that, if an accused consents to be tried summarily, the court *shall* proceed to summary trial. It would seem that the accused could, in theory, be allowed to reconsider consent to summary trial even after the trial on a not guilty plea has begun. However, it is submitted that, once a significant portion of the prosecution evidence has been given, a change of election should be allowed only in very exceptional circumstances, since otherwise the defence might be tempted to ask to withdraw consent to summary trial as a tactical ploy simply because the trial seems to be going badly.

(b) In exercising their discretion whether to accede to an application to withdraw consent, magistrates must have regard to the 'broad justice' of the situation (per Lord Widgery CJ in *Southampton Justices, ex parte Briggs* [1972] 1 All ER 573 at p. 280). They are entitled to take into account: (i) that the accused had the right to elect Crown Court trial fully explained; (ii) that the accused understood those rights; (iii) that the accused voluntarily consented to be tried summarily; and (iv) that there were no unusual, difficult or grave features in the case (*Lambeth Metropolitan Stipendiary Magistrate, ex parte Wright* [1974] Crim LR 444, as explained by McCullough J in *Ex parte Hodgson* [1985] QB 1131 at p. 1140A–C).

(c) Consent to summary trial given when unrepresented and intending to plead guilty through a misunderstanding of the law is invalid because, even if the accused understands the nature of the choice in the sense of knowing the difference between trial on indictment and summary trial, the accused does not truly appreciate the *significance* of the choice (*Ex parte Hodgson*, see especially p. 1146D–H).

(d) It is implicit in the judgment of McCullough J that the fact that the accused was unrepresented when consenting to summary trial is not sufficient by itself to compel the court to allow a withdrawal of consent, even if the accused is subsequently advised that trial on indictment would be preferable. Conversely, although having had legal advice before consenting would obviously be a very powerful argument against an application to withdraw consent, there is no reason to suppose that it must inevitably be decisive.

(e) Most important, where the material before the magistrates shows that the accused, when consenting to summary trial, did not properly understand the 'nature and significance' of the choice, the broad justice of the situation demands that the accused be allowed to withdraw consent (*Ex parte Hodgson* [1985] QB 1131 at pp. 1144–5).

(f) Where it is said that the accused did not understand the nature and significance of the choice, the court's view that the case is, in fact, more suitable for summary trial is *not* a factor which should tell against an application to withdraw consent (per McCullough J in *Ex parte Hodgson* [1985] QB 1131 at p. 1145A–B and *Ex parte Weekes* [1985] QB 1147 at p. 1152C–E).

Where the accused is arguing a lack of understanding of the consequences of the original consent to summary trial, it is for the accused to establish that fact, whether by giving evidence or by other means. Moreover, if the justices hearing the application are different from those who originally sat, they must receive evidence as to what occurred at the earlier hearing (*Forest Magistrates' Court, ex parte Spicer* (1989) 153 JP 81). The accused's consent to summary trial is likely, in practice, to be closely connected to the plea. If, having consented to summary trial, the accused pleads guilty but is then allowed to change the plea to not guilty, permission should be given to withdraw consent to summary trial, so that the allocation procedure can be repeated (*Bow Street Magistrates' Court, ex parte Welcombe* (1992) 156 JP 609). **D6.33**

Challenging Refusal of Magistrates to Allow Withdrawal of Consent

If an application by the accused to withdraw consent to summary trial is refused, the refusal may be challenged by means of an application for judicial review (see **D29.25** *et seq*.). It will, however, be necessary to show either that the magistrates took into account irrelevant factors or ignored relevant ones when deciding to hold the accused to the original decision, or that they acted so unreasonably that no bench properly directing itself could have reached their decision. **D6.34**

In *Highbury Corner Metropolitan Stipendiary Magistrate, ex parte Weekes* [1985] QB 1147, for example, D, who was aged 17, had not had the opportunity to consult a lawyer and did not properly understand what a Crown Court was. In those circumstances, it was plainly unreasonable for the magistrate to have rejected the defence application that the consent to summary trial be withdrawn.

ADJUSTMENT OF CHARGES TO DICTATE ALLOCATION

D6.35 It is possible for the prosecution to replace an existing charge with a new charge. Where the prosecution choose to replace an offence which is triable either way with an offence which is triable only summarily, the accused is thereby deprived of the possibility of trial by jury. In *Canterbury and St Augustine Justices, ex parte Klisiak* [1982] QB 398, it was held that the court can prevent the prosecution from doing this only 'in the most obvious circumstances which disclose blatant injustice' (per Lord Lane CJ at p. 411F). In *Sheffield Justices, ex parte DPP* [1993] Crim LR 136, the Divisional Court said that it would be appropriate to interfere with the prosecutor's decision to replace an either-way charge with a summary-only charge only if there was evidence that the prosecutor had done so in order to manipulate the system (in other words, acting in bad faith). However, in *DPP v Hammerton* [2009] EWHC 921 (Admin), [2010] QB 79, where D was charged with attempted theft (triable either way) but the prosecution subsequently sought to replace the charge with one of interfering with a motor vehicle (a summary offence), Davis J pointed out that the courts now have to take into account the CrimPR, and in particular the overriding objective and said (at [24] and [30]) that:

> ... the language of 'proper and appropriate' better conveys the correct approach in cases of this kind ... I doubt if it now needs be shown that bad faith as such needs be shown in all cases before an application to substitute a new charge can be disallowed ...
>
> ... in the vast majority of cases everyone concerned will be entirely content for a lesser charge to be substituted. But where a lesser charge is to be substituted, first, it must be proper and appropriate to the facts of the case; secondly, the application should be made promptly and not left until the last minute, at all events without any proper explanation; and, thirdly, an eye should also be kept on considerations of the good administration of justice and the wider picture.

For example, the impact on any co-accused might be relevant.

D6.36 It is also possible for a charge which is triable either way to be replaced with a charge that is triable only on indictment. However, in *Brooks* [1985] Crim LR 385, the Court of Appeal warned that it would be unjust and wrong for the prosecution to do this if the magistrates have already accepted jurisdiction in respect of the either-way offence, since the prosecution would be frustrating the decision reached by the justices. The principles were summarised by Neill LJ in *Redbridge Justices, ex parte Whitehouse* [1992] 94 Cr App R 332 (at p. 338):

> (3) ... If the prosecution ... seek to prefer new charges or to substitute charges or to offer no evidence on certain charges the justices should consider the matter on its merits. The fact that the prosecution wish to add or substitute new charges either to ensure that the case is tried summarily or to ensure that it is tried in the Crown Court is not a ground for refusing the issue of a summons or other process provided that on the facts disclosed the justices are satisfied that the course proposed by the prosecution is proper and appropriate in the light of the facts put before them. Thus clearly the justices should not agree to the addition of a charge which is triable only on indictment if the facts are incapable of supporting such a charge and the fresh charge can be seen to be a device designed to deprive the justices of their jurisdiction to try the case themselves. (4) If the justices have already decided to try a matter summarily and the case is then adjourned, any later application by the prosecution to add an additional charge which would have the effect of making summary trial no longer possible should be scrutinised with particular care. The prosecution cannot be allowed improperly to frustrate the earlier decision of the justices. However, I do not understand the decision in *Brooks* ... as meaning that once the justices have decided on summary trial there are no circumstances in which the prosecutor can properly seek to add a further charge which is triable only on indictment ... (5) If the justices acting within their jurisdiction exercise their discretion

> bona fide and bring their minds to bear on the question whether they ought to grant a further summons or not, this Court is very unlikely to interfere except in an exceptional case where the decision satisfies the strict test of being unreasonable in a *Wednesbury* sense.

It must also be borne in mind that the Code for Crown Prosecutors, para. 6.4 (see **appendix 3**), states that: 'Prosecutors should not change the charge simply because of the decision made by the court or the defendant about where the case will be heard'.

CHALLENGING A DECISION BY A MAGISTRATES' COURT TO ACCEPT JURISDICTION

It is difficult for the prosecution to mount a challenge against a decision in favour of summary trial, since it is essentially a matter within the magistrates' discretion. An application to quash a decision to accept jurisdiction will succeed only if the magistrates' decision was so obviously wrong that no reasonable magistrate could have arrived at it (*McLean, ex parte Metropolitan Police Commissioner* [1975] Crim LR 289). Nevertheless, in an appropriately clear-cut case, the Divisional Court will grant judicial review. In *Northampton Magistrates' Court, ex parte Commissioners of Customs and Excise* [1994] Crim LR 598, for example, D was charged with a VAT fraud which, on the prosecution case, had caused a loss of £193,000. The magistrates decided to try him summarily and the prosecution sought judicial review. The Divisional Court said that the correct approach was to ask whether the acceptance of jurisdiction was 'truly astonishing'. Here they must have concluded that it was, as they allowed the application and remitted the matter with a direction to the magistrates to reject jurisdiction. **D6.37**

SUMMARY OFFENCES IN THE CROWN COURT

It follows from the basic definition of a summary offence as one which is triable *only* summarily that the question of mode of trial for such an offence does not normally arise. However, the CJA 1988, s. 40, provides that where certain specified summary offences (including common assault, driving while disqualified, taking a motor vehicle without the owner's consent, and criminal damage where the value involved does not exceed £5,000) are disclosed by the evidence on the basis of which an accused has been sent for trial in respect of an indictable offence, and the summary offence is either founded on the same facts as the indictable offence or forms with it a series of offences of the same or similar character, then the prosecution may include a count for the summary offence on the indictment and, if the accused pleads not guilty, the charge will be tried by a jury (see **D11.17**). **D6.38**

The CDA 1998, s. 51(6), provides that, where the court sends an accused for trial in respect of an indictable-only or either-way offence, it must also send the accused to the Crown Court for trial for any summary offence which appears to the court to be related to the offence(s) which are sent for trial, provided that the summary offence is punishable with imprisonment or involves disqualification from driving. Unless the summary offence is one to which the CJA 1988, s. 40, applies and is added to the indictment, sch. 3, para. 6, governs the procedure in respect of the summary offence (see **D10.29**). If the accused is convicted on the indictment, the Crown Court must, assuming it agrees that the summary offence is related to the offence(s) sent for trial under s. 51, ask the accused to enter a plea to the summary offence. If a guilty plea is entered, the Crown Court may deal with the offender in respect of that offence in any way in which a magistrates' court could have done; if a not guilty plea is entered, the powers of the Crown Court cease in respect of the summary offence (save that the court may dismiss the charge if the prosecution inform the court that they would not desire to submit evidence in respect of it). It is submitted that (even though para. 6 is silent as to the possibility) it would also be open to a Crown Court judge to try the summary offence, sitting as a district judge (magistrates' courts) under the Courts Act 2003, s. 66 (see **D3.16**).

Section D7 Bail

INTRODUCTION

D7.1 Bail in criminal proceedings is governed by the Bail Act 1976 (BA 1976) (see s. 1(6) of the Act). 'Bail in criminal proceedings' is defined in s. 1(1) of the Act as: '(a) bail grantable in or in connection with proceedings for an offence to a person who is accused or convicted of the offence, or (b) bail grantable in connection with an offence to a person who is under arrest for the offence or for whose arrest for the offence a warrant (endorsed for bail) is being issued'. The procedural rules relating to bail are set out in CrimPR Part 14 (see Supplement, **R14.1** *et seq.*). This section is chiefly concerned with bail from magistrates' courts and the Crown Court. For bail in appeals to the Court of Appeal, see **D7.5** and **D27.14**.

The BA 1976 is set out at **D7.134** *et seq.*

COURTS' POWER TO GRANT BAIL

Bail by Magistrates' Courts

D7.2 A magistrates' court, when adjourning a case, may remand the accused (see the MCA 1980, ss. 10(1) and 18(4), at **D5.29**, for the jurisdiction to adjourn and remand at the preliminary stages of a case). Under the MCA 1980, s. 128(1), a remand by a magistrates' court may be in custody or on bail, in accordance with the BA 1976. For the time restrictions on remands in custody and the possibility of remands in the absence of the accused, see **D5.33**. Magistrates also have power to grant bail for the period of any remand for reports etc. after summary conviction (see the MCA 1980, s. 10(3), and also the PCC(S)A 2000, s. 11, for remands on bail for medical examination). Where a magistrates' court sends an accused to the Crown Court for trial under the CDA 1998, s. 51, the accused may be kept in custody or released on bail (see **D10**). Similarly, committals for sentence may be in custody or on bail. Where a magistrates' court has summarily convicted an accused and passed a custodial sentence, it may grant bail pending the determination of an appeal to the Crown Court or to the Divisional Court by way of case stated (MCA 1980, s. 113). The CAJA 2009, s. 115, provides that a person charged with murder may not be granted bail except by order of a Crown Court judge (see **D7.3**).

Bail by the Crown Court

Under the Senior Courts Act 1981, s. 81(1)(a) to (g), the Crown Court may grant bail to any person: D7.3

(a) who has been sent in custody for trial in the Crown Court;
(b) who has been given a custodial sentence following conviction in the magistrates' court (whether by guilty plea or a finding of guilty after trial) and who is appealing to the Crown Court against conviction and/or sentence;
(c) who is in the custody of the Crown Court pending disposal of the case (so whenever the Crown Court adjourns a trial or adjourns between conviction and sentence, it has a discretion to grant the accused bail for the period of the adjournment);
(d) and (e) whose case has been decided by the Crown Court but who has applied to the court to state a case for the Divisional Court's opinion or is seeking judicial review of the decision;
(f) to whom the Crown Court has granted a certificate that the case is fit for appeal to the Court of Appeal, whether against conviction or against sentence; and
(g) who has been remanded in custody by a magistrates' court on adjourning a case under the PCC(S)A 2000, s. 11, the CDA 1998, s. 52(5), or the MCA 1980, ss. 10, 17C, 18 or 24C, provided the magistrates' court has granted a certificate that, before refusing bail, it heard full argument.

All the above powers are subject to the CJPO 1994, s. 25 (see **D7.8**).

Bail Jurisdiction in Murder Cases The CAJA 2009, s. 115(1), provides that a person charged with murder may not be granted bail except by order of a Crown Court judge. A person who appears before a magistrates' court charged with murder must be committed (in custody) to the Crown Court (s. 115(4)). A Crown Court judge must then make a decision about bail as soon as reasonably practicable and, in any event, within the period of 48 hours (excluding weekends and public holidays) beginning with the day after the day on which the person appears before the magistrates' court (s. 115(3)). These provisions apply whether or not the accused is charged with any offences in addition to the murder charge (s. 115(6)). D7.4

Bail by Court of Appeal (Criminal Division)

The Court of Appeal has jurisdiction to grant bail to a person who has served notice of appeal or notice of application for leave to appeal against conviction and/or sentence in the Crown Court (Criminal Appeal Act 1968, s. 19). The Court of Appeal also has power to bail a person who is appealing from it to the Supreme Court (s. 36). These powers are again subject to the CJPO 1994, s. 25 (see **D7.8**). D7.5

Where the Court of Appeal quashes a conviction and orders a retrial, it has power to grant bail under the Criminal Appeal Act 1968, s. 8(2)(a). However, in *X* [2004] All ER (D) 400 (Feb), it was held that once a fresh indictment has been preferred in the Crown Court following the quashing of a conviction and the ordering of a retrial, the Court of Appeal no longer has jurisdiction in relation to bail. It follows that, once a fresh indictment has been preferred, jurisdiction in relation to bail belongs with the Crown Court.

PRINCIPLES GOVERNING BAIL

Presumption in Favour of Bail

Section 4(1) of the BA 1976, together with sch. 1 (see **D7.142**), creates a rebuttable presumption in favour of bail (sometimes referred to, somewhat inaccurately, as a 'right to bail'). It provides that: 'A person to whom this section applies shall be granted bail except as provided in Schedule 1 to this Act'. Subsections (2) to (4) of s. 4 then define the persons who benefit from the presumption in favour of bail. They are any person: D7.6

(a) who appears before the Crown Court or a magistrates' court in the course of or in connection with proceedings for an offence, or applies to a court for bail (or for a variation of the conditions of bail) in connection with those proceedings (s. 4(2));

(b) who has been convicted of an offence and whose case is adjourned for reports before sentencing (s. 4(4)); and
(c) who has been brought before the court under the CJA 2003, sch. 8, for alleged breach of a requirement of a community order (s. 4(3)).

Apart from cases where the accused has been convicted and the hearing has been adjourned for pre-sentence reports, s. 4(1) does *not* apply once a person has been convicted of an offence (as is made clear in the proviso to s. 4(2)). Therefore, an appellant seeking bail pending determination of an appeal against conviction and/or sentence cannot rely on the presumption in favour of bail. Neither can an offender who is committed to the Crown Court for sentence following conviction in a magistrates' court. In both those situations, there is power to grant bail, but its grant or refusal is entirely at the discretion of the court. It should also be noted that s. 4(1) does not apply to bail from the police station, although, once a detainee has been charged, the PACE 1984, s. 38(1), imposes on the custody officer a duty to grant bail unless its refusal can be justified on grounds similar to those which would justify a court refusing bail under the BA 1976 (see **D2.46** ***et seq.***). Whenever bail is granted in criminal proceedings (whether or not subject to the presumption in s. 4), the general provisions of the Act concerning bail apply (e.g., a person who fails without reasonable cause to surrender commits an offence under s. 6).

D7.7 **Bail Following Indication of Guilty Plea at 'Plea before Venue' Hearing** In *Rafferty* [1999] 1 Cr App R 235, the Court of Appeal dealt with the position where an accused enters a guilty plea at the 'plea before venue' procedure (see **D6.11** ***et seq.***), and is then committed for sentence to the Crown Court. Thomas J said (at p. 237) that, in most such cases, it would not be usual to alter the position as regards bail or custody. When a person who had been on bail pleads guilty at the plea before venue, the usual practice should be to continue bail, even if it is anticipated that a custodial sentence will be imposed by the Crown Court, unless there are good reasons for remanding the accused in custody. If the accused is in custody, then it would be unusual, if the reasons for the remand in custody remain unchanged, to alter the position.

Exceptions to the Presumption in Favour of Bail

D7.8 **No Bail for Homicide or Rape if Previous Conviction** Under the CJPO 1994, s. 25 (see **D7.10**), the court may not grant bail to an accused who is charged with (or has been convicted of) murder, attempted murder, manslaughter, rape or attempted rape, or certain other offences under the SOA 2003, if the accused has been convicted of any of these offences (or culpable homicide) in the past, unless it is of the opinion that there are exceptional circumstances which justify it. In a case where the previous conviction was for manslaughter, the restriction applies only if the accused received a custodial sentence for that offence. 'Conviction' is widely defined to include a finding that the defendant was not guilty by reason of insanity, or was found to have done the act or made the omission charged in a case where the defendant was unfit to plead. Previous convictions in other EU Member States are treated as being relevant previous convictions if the corresponding offences in the UK would be so treated.

It was suggested by the Law Commission in its paper *Bail and the Human Rights Act 1998* (Law Com No. 269) that the CJPO 1994, s. 25, is liable to be misunderstood and applied in a way which is incompatible with the ECHR, Article 5. The problem with s. 25 is that it appears to create a statutory presumption against the grant of bail in cases to which it applies. If so, it conflicts with the Convention's starting point of the presumption of liberty, and substitutes a presumption of custodial remand. The Commission suggested that the court should go through the usual process of balancing factors for and against the granting of bail. Because of the provisions of s. 25, however, it should give special weight to those counting against the grant of bail. Thus, the court would take all relevant circumstances into account, but might nonetheless deny bail because the case fell within s. 25, where it might not otherwise have done so.

D7.9 Section 25 was considered by the House of Lords in *R (O) v Harrow Crown Court* [2006] UKHL 42, [2007] 1 AC 249. The particular issue was the effect of s. 25 upon the right to bail of a defendant during the currency of the custody time-limit provided by the Prosecution of Offences Act 1985, s. 22, and upon the expiry of such a custody time-limit (see **D15.7** *et seq.* for detailed discussion of custody time-limits). The House of Lords held that, where an application for bail is made during the currency of the custody time-limit, s. 25 should be read as placing an evidential burden on the accused to 'point to or produce material which supports the existence of exceptional circumstances' (per Lord Carswell at [12]); if the accused fails to do so, bail should be denied. Lord Brown of Eaton-under-Heywood (at [35]) said that in the vast majority of cases, the court will be able to reach a clear view one way or the other whether the conditions for withholding bail, specified by the BA 1976, sch. 1, are satisfied. However, the court may occasionally be left unsure as to whether the defendant should be released on bail. This is the only situation in which the burden of proof assumes any relevance, and in such a case bail would have to be granted. That must be, said his lordship, the 'default position', and s. 25 should be read down to make that plain. Dealing with the relationship between s. 25 and the custody time-limit provisions, it was held that s. 25 operates to disapply the ordinary requirement under the Prosecution of Offences (Custody Time Limits) Regulations 1987, reg. 6(6), that bail should be granted automatically to anyone whose custody time-limit has expired. Their lordships held that, thus applied, s. 25 is compatible with the ECHR, Article 5(3).

In *O'Dowd v UK* (2012) 54 EHRR 8 (187), D complained that the CJPO 1994, s. 25, unfairly discriminates against those with previous convictions for certain offences. The ECtHR noted (at [81]) that D's previous convictions arose from an incident which was factually very similar to the alleged offences with which D was subsequently charged and so were 'comparable both in nature and degree of seriousness'. In those circumstances, D could not 'claim to be in an analogous position to a defendant charged with the same offence who does not have a previous similar offence' (at [82]). It followed that D's complaint was 'manifestly ill-founded'. Presumably, the answer would be different if the offences lacked that degree of similarity.

Criminal Justice and Public Order Act 1994, s. 25 **D7.10**

(1) A person who in any proceedings has been charged with or convicted of an offence to which this section applies in circumstances to which it applies shall be granted bail in those proceedings only if the court or, as the case may be, the constable considering the grant of bail is of the opinion that there are exceptional circumstances which justify it.

(2) This section applies, subject to subsection (3) below, to the following offences, that is to say—
- (a) murder;
- (b) attempted murder;
- (c) manslaughter;
- (d) rape under the law of Scotland;
- (e) an offence under section 1 of the Sexual Offences Act 1956 (rape);
- (f) an offence under section 1 of the Sexual Offences Act 2003 (rape);
- (g) an offence under section 2 of that Act (assault by penetration);
- (h) an offence under section 4 of that Act (causing a person to engage in sexual activity without consent), where the activity caused involved penetration within subsection (4)(a) to (d) of that section;
- (i) an offence under section 5 of that Act (rape of a child under 13);
- (j) an offence under section 6 of that Act (assault of a child under 13 by penetration);
- (k) an offence under section 8 of that Act (causing or inciting a child under 13 to engage in sexual activity), where an activity involving penetration within subsection (2)(a) to (d) of that section was caused;
- (l) an offence under section 30 of that Act (sexual activity with a person with a mental disorder impeding choice), where the touching involved penetration within subsection (3)(a) to (d) of that section;
- (m) an offence under section 31 of that Act (causing or inciting a person, with a mental disorder impeding choice, to engage in sexual activity), where an activity involving penetration within subsection (3)(a) to (d) of that section was caused;
- (ma) to (mh) [equivalent offences under the law of Northern Ireland]
- (n) an attempt to commit an offence within any of paragraphs (d) to (mh).

(3) This section applies in the circumstances described in subsection (3A) or (3B) only.

(3A) This section applies where—

(a) the person has been previously convicted by or before a court in any part of the United Kingdom of any offence within subsection (2) or of culpable homicide, and

(b) if that previous conviction is one of manslaughter or culpable homicide—

(i) the person was then a child or young person, and was sentenced to long-term detention under any of the relevant enactments, or

(ii) the person was not then a child or young person, and was sentenced to imprisonment or detention.

(3B) This section applies where—

(a) the person has been previously convicted by or before a court in another member State of any relevant foreign offence corresponding to an offence within subsection (2) or to culpable homicide, and

(b) if the previous conviction is of a relevant foreign offence corresponding to the offence of manslaughter or culpable homicide—

(i) the person was then a child or young person, and was sentenced to detention for a period in excess of 2 years, or

(ii) the person was not then a child or young person, and was sentenced to detention.

(4) This section applies whether or not an appeal is pending against conviction or sentence.

(5) In this section—

'conviction' includes—

(a) a finding that a person is not guilty by reason of insanity;

(b) a finding under section 4A(3) of the Criminal Procedure (Insanity) Act 1964 (cases of unfitness to plead) that a person did the act or made the omission charged against him; and

(c) a conviction of an offence for which an order is made discharging the offender absolutely or conditionally;

and 'convicted' shall be construed accordingly;

'the relevant enactments' means—

(a) as respects England and Wales, section 91 of the Powers of Criminal Courts (Sentencing) Act 2000;

(b) as respects Scotland, sections 205(1) to (3) and 208 of the Criminal Procedure (Scotland) Act 1995;

(c) as respects Northern Ireland, section 73(2) of the Children and Young Persons Act (Northern Ireland) 1968;

'relevant foreign offence', in relation to a member State other than the United Kingdom, means an offence under the law in force in that member State.

(5A) For the purposes of subsection (3B), a relevant foreign offence corresponds to another offence if the relevant foreign offence would have constituted that other offence if it had been done in any part of the United Kingdom at the time when the relevant foreign offence was committed.

D7.11 **Murder** Under the BA 1976, sch. 1, part I, para. 6ZA, an accused who is charged with murder may not be granted bail unless the court is of the opinion that there is no significant risk that the accused will, if released on bail, commit an offence that would, or would be likely to, cause physical or mental injury to any other person. Again, the presumption in favour of bail is effectively reversed.

REFUSING BAIL TO AN ACCUSED CHARGED WITH AN INDICTABLE OFFENCE

D7.12 Part I of sch. 1 to the 1976 Act sets out the circumstances in which an accused may be refused bail if charged with (or awaiting sentence for) at least one offence that is triable on indictment and punishable with imprisonment (part IA applies where the offences(s) are imprisonable summary offences, and part II applies when none of the offences are imprisonable; see D7.35 *et seq*).

An unconvicted accused charged with an offence which is imprisonable and triable on indictment need not be granted bail if one or more of the grounds for a remand in custody (listed in the BA 1976, sch. 1, part I, paras. 2 to 6A) is applicable. The first — and most commonly relied on — ground (para. 2) subdivides into three (see **D7.13**). As regards offenders convicted but remanded for reports, there is a further ground (para. 7) on which reliance may also be placed. The statutory grounds for refusing bail are as follows.

Risk of Absconding, Further Offences or Interference with Witnesses

Bail Act 1976, sch. 1, para. 2 **D7.13**

(1) The defendant need not be granted bail if the court is satisfied that there are substantial grounds for believing that the defendant, if released on bail (whether subject to conditions or not) would—
   (a) fail to surrender to custody, or
   (b) commit an offence while on bail, or
   (c) interfere with witnesses or otherwise obstruct the course of justice, whether in relation to himself or any other person.

Standard of Proof The opening words of para. 2(1) do *not* require the court to be satisfied that the consequences specified in subparagraphs (a) to (c) will in fact occur in the event of bail being granted, or even to be satisfied that they are more likely than not to occur. The court must merely be satisfied that there are 'substantial grounds for believing' that they would occur. Although the question posed by para. 2 is whether substantial grounds exist for believing that a future event will occur and to that extent is a question of fact, it is not a question which can be answered according to the usual rules of evidence. Thus in *Re Moles* [1981] Crim LR 170 it was held that a police officer explaining the objections to bail was entitled to recount what he had been told by a potential witness about the threats the latter had received, with a view to showing that the granting of bail would lead to further interference with witnesses. In *Mansfield Justices, ex parte Sharkey* [1985] QB 613, Lord Lane CJ referred to *Re Moles* and said (at p. 626A), 'there is no requirement for formal evidence to be given [at an application for bail] ... It was for example sufficient for the facts to be related to the justices at second hand by a police officer.' Current practice when presenting objections to bail in a magistrates' court is not even to have a police officer present, but for the CPS representative to argue that bail is inappropriate on the basis of information supplied by the police and included in the case file. **D7.14**

In *R (F) v Southampton Crown Court* [2009] EWHC 2206 (Admin), the judge had refused to grant bail because he was 'not sure' D would 'turn up or stay out of trouble'. On appeal, Collins J (at [3]) noted that the correct test under the BA 1976 'requires the judge to have substantial grounds for believing that the defendant before him would fail to surrender, commit offences on bail, or transgress one of the other provisions in schedule 1'. The judge had therefore applied the wrong test. As Collins J said (at [8]): 'It is not a question of him not being sure that the defendant would turn up or stay out of trouble'; rather, 'he was only entitled to refuse bail if there were substantial grounds for believing that he would breach [his bail], he would fail to turn up or would commit further offences'. The case was therefore remitted to the Crown Court for reconsideration applying the correct test. **D7.15**

The importance of applying the correct test was emphasised again in *R (Shehzad) v Newcastle Crown Court* [2012] EWHC 1453 (Admin). In that case, the Crown Court judge had said that D had 'every reason to fail to surrender, there is the possibility of further offences and there is a risk of interference with witnesses, principally of course the principal witness for the prosecution. In those circumstances I refuse his application for bail.' An application for judicial review was made on the basis that the judge's phraseology suggested that he had applied a lower threshold of satisfaction in relation to the various matters that can operate as a basis for refusing bail than the 'substantial grounds for believing' test. Foskett J (at [10] and [11]) said that the Crown Court judge was extremely experienced, applied the statutory test on an almost daily basis and was therefore 'very unlikely to have misapplied the usual approach to decisions of this nature'. However, it was right for D to have his case 'assessed by the correct statutory formulation', so the refusal of bail was quashed and the matter remitted to the Crown Court to be dealt with by another judge. A similar approach was taken in *Charles* [2012] EWHC 2581 (Admin), where the Divisional Court accepted (at [24]) D's submission that, when the bail ruling was read as a whole, it appeared that 'the learned judge failed to ask himself the right questions'.

D7.16 **No Real Prospect of a Custodial Sentence** Paragraph 1A of sch. 1 provides that para. 2 does not apply where the accused has attained the age of 18, and has not been convicted of an offence in those proceedings, and it appears to the court that there is no real prospect that the accused will be sentenced to a custodial sentence in the proceedings. In such a case, bail cannot be withheld on any of the grounds set out in para. 2.

D7.17 **Relevant Factors** Certain factors to which the court should have regard when taking a decision under para. 2 are listed in para. 9. These factors are:

(a) the nature and seriousness of the offence and the probable method of dealing with the offender for it (see **D7.18**);
(b) the character, antecedents, associations and community ties of the accused (see **D7.19** and **D7.20**);
(c) the accused's 'record' for having answered bail in the past (see **D7.21**);
(d) the strength of the evidence against the accused (see **D7.22**); and
(e) if the court is satisfied that there are substantial grounds for believing that the accused would commit an offence while on bail, the risk that the accused may engage in conduct likely to cause physical or mental injury to anyone else (see **D7.23**).

D7.18 *Nature and seriousness of offence (para. 9(a)).* The relevance of the offence alleged being serious is that the accused will know that, if convicted, a severe sentence is likely and it will therefore be tempting to abscond rather than run the risk of such a sentence. The gravity of the charge is not an automatic reason for refusing bail (although, by virtue of the CJPO 1994, s. 25, an accused must normally be refused bail where the charge is, e.g., homicide or rape and the accused has previously been convicted of such an offence (see **D7.8**)). Indeed, in *Hurnam v State of Mauritius* [2005] UKPC 49, [2006] 1 WLR 857, the Privy Council said that the seriousness of an offence cannot be treated as a conclusive reason for refusing bail to an unconvicted suspect. Lord Bingham said (at [15]):

> The seriousness of the offence and the severity of the penalty likely to be imposed on conviction may well ... provide grounds for refusing bail, but they do not do so of themselves, without more: they are factors relevant to the judgment whether, in all the circumstances, it is necessary to deprive the applicant of his liberty. Whether or not that is the conclusion reached, clear and explicit reasons should be given.

The statutory presumption in favour of bail continues to apply after conviction where there is an adjournment for the preparation of a pre-sentence report before sentence is passed. In *R (R) v Snaresbrook Crown Court* [2011] EWHC 3569 (Admin), the Divisional Court considered the refusal of bail because of the likelihood of a custodial sentence. Holman J said (at [24]) that, of itself, 'the mere fact that a person has been convicted and a custodial sentence is inevitable, is not sufficient to trigger the exception to bail. It still is necessary that the court is satisfied that there are substantial grounds for believing that one of the statutory exceptions [to the presumption in favour of bail] applies.' This point is reiterated at [31], where his lordship said that, 'even the inevitability of a custodial sentence is not itself an exception to the right to bail, unless it justifies a court being satisfied that there are substantial grounds for believing that the defendant would fail to surrender to custody'.

D7.19 *Character and antecedents (para. 9(b)).* This refers primarily to previous convictions. These may make a custodial sentence more likely (especially if the accused, if convicted of the present offence, will be in breach of a suspended sentence of imprisonment). Moreover, a person of previous good character is more likely to be trusted by the courts than one with a criminal record. Previous convictions under the BA 1976, s. 6, for failing to surrender to custody in answer to bail are especially relevant (see subparagraph (c)).

Associations and community ties (para. 9(b)). The word 'associations' is generally taken to refer to undesirable friends with criminal records. Examining the 'community ties' of the accused involves looking at how easy it would be to abscond and how much the accused has to lose by absconding. Relevant factors include the following: How long has the accused lived at the present address? Does the accused have a partner? Does the accused have dependent children? Is the accused in employment? If so, for how long? Does the accused have a mortgage or a protected tenancy? An accused of 'no fixed abode' or living in short-term accommodation is not automatically debarred from bail, but the ease of disappearing to another address is a factor to be considered. **D7.20**

Bail record (para. 9(c)). Considering the bail record of the accused requires the court to consider whether the accused has absconded in the past. Absconding in earlier proceedings is regarded as evidence of a risk that the accused may do so again. **D7.21**

Strength of the prosecution evidence (para. 9(d)). This is relevant to whether an accused would answer bail, in the sense that one who knows there is a good chance of being acquitted is less likely to abscond than one who anticipates almost certain conviction. It can be argued that there is no point in the accused absconding if an acquittal is likely anyway. Conversely, if the prosecution case is strong, so that conviction is likely, the accused may abscond rather than 'face the music' (especially if a custodial sentence is likely). It is also relevant that a remand in custody followed by acquittal creates a manifest, if sometimes unavoidable, injustice. In borderline cases, where the arguments against bail are strong but not overwhelming, the court may prefer to run the risk of the accused absconding etc. rather than run the risk of an acquittal after a long period in custody on remand. **D7.22**

Risk of injury to someone else (para. 9(e)). Where the court is satisfied that there are substantial grounds for believing that the accused would commit an offence while on bail, the court considers whether that offence is likely to cause physical or mental injury to any other person. **D7.23**

Paragraph 9 concludes with the words 'as well as to any others [i.e. considerations] which appear to be relevant', thus making it clear that the considerations mentioned in para. 9(a) to (e) are *not* exhaustive. Those 'others' might include the fact that the accused has previously committed offences while on bail, or the suggestion that potential prosecution witnesses have already received threats and/or are known to the accused, who could therefore locate them if at liberty. Also, it should be noted that the BA 1976, s. 4(9), stipulates that 'in taking any decisions required by Part I or II of Schedule 1 to this Act, the considerations to which the court is to have regard include, so far as relevant, any misuse of controlled drugs by the defendant'.

Other Grounds for Withholding Bail

Part I of sch. 1 to the BA 1976 (see **D7.151** *et seq.*) sets out other grounds for withholding bail: risk of injury to an 'associated person' (para. 2ZA); where the accused is already on bail for another offence (para. 2A); for the accused's own protection (para. 3); where the accused is already serving a custodial sentence for another offence (para. 4); where the court has insufficient information (para. 5); where the accused has absconded in the present proceedings (para. 6). Additionally, where the accused is charged with murder, para. 6ZA restricts the circumstances in which bail can be granted. **D7.24**

Domestic Violence: Risk to an 'Associated Person' By virtue of para. 2ZA, the accused need not be granted bail if the court is satisfied that there are substantial grounds for believing that, **D7.25**

if released on bail, the accused would commit an offence while on bail by engaging in conduct that would, or would be likely to, cause physical or mental injury to an associated person, or else cause such a person to fear such injury. For this purpose, an 'associated person' is a person who is associated with the accused within the meaning of the Family Law Act 1996, s. 62(3) (the definition includes people who are or have been married to each other, or who are or have been civil partners; cohabitants or former cohabitants; people who live or have lived in the same household, otherwise than as an employee, tenant, lodger or boarder; relatives; people who have or have had an intimate personal relationship with each other which is or was of significant duration; and in relation to any child, a parent or person who has or has had parental responsibility for the child).

D7.26 **Accused Already on Bail** Under para. 2A, the accused need not be granted bail if it appears to the court that the accused was on bail in respect of another offence on the date of the current offence. However, by virtue of para. 1A, para. 2A does not apply where the accused has attained the age of 18, and has not been convicted of an offence in the current proceedings, and it appears to the court that there is no real prospect that the accused will be sentenced to a custodial sentence in the proceedings.

D7.27 **Own Protection** Under para. 3, the accused need not be granted bail if the court is satisfied that remaining in custody would be for the accused's own protection. This will (for example) cover cases where the offence alleged has caused anger in the area where it was committed and there is a risk of members of the public exacting retribution on the person believed to be responsible. Where the accused is a child or young person, bail may be refused under para. 3 if the accused should be kept in custody 'for his own welfare'.

D7.28 **Already in Custody** Under para. 4, the accused need not be granted bail if already serving a custodial sentence. Paragraph 4 applies only if the accused is in custody pursuant to a *sentence*, not when in custody as a result of a remand in other proceedings that are currently outstanding. Where an accused is certain to be in custody for the foreseeable future, the court may find it more convenient to grant what may be regarded as technical bail; this avoids the restrictions on the periods for which remands in custody may be ordered and the consequent need to bring the accused back to court for further remand hearings.

D7.29 **Insufficient Time** Under para. 5, the accused need not be granted bail if the court is satisfied that, owing to lack of time since the commencement of the proceedings, it has not been practicable to obtain sufficient information for the purposes of taking the decision on bail. In such cases, the court might remand in custody (possibly for a shorter than usual period) to enable the necessary information to be discovered. Paragraph 5 might apply, for example, where the police are not satisfied that the accused has given them correct particulars and think the accused may have previous convictions under another name, or if time is needed to check an address, or if inquiries are still in hand which may reveal the offence to be more serious than originally supposed and/or that the accused has committed additional offences. It is submitted that para. 5 should be relied on sparingly, and should not be used to justify dilatoriness on the part of the police or the prosecution in marshalling their objections to bail.

A remand in custody under para. 5 does not amount to a decision to withhold bail for the purposes of para. 2 of part IIA, and so does not restrict further applications for bail (see **D7.70**).

D7.30 **Absconded in the Present Proceedings** Under para. 6, the accused need not be granted bail if arrested under the BA 1976, s. 7, having previously been released on bail in connection with the current proceedings (see **D7.147**). However, by virtue of para. 1A, para. 6 does not apply where the accused has attained the age of 18, and has not been convicted of an offence in the current proceedings, and it appears to the court that there is no real prospect that the accused will be sentenced to a custodial sentence in the proceedings.

Bail in Cases Involving Abuse of Drugs Paragraphs 6A to 6C of the BA 1976, sch. 1, part I, provide that an accused aged 18 or over may not be granted bail, unless the court is of the opinion that there is no significant risk of the accused committing an offence while on bail, where the three conditions set out in para. 6B apply, namely: **D7.31**

(1) there is drug test evidence (by way of a lawful test obtained under the PACE 1984, s. 63B, or the CJA 2003, s. 161) that there is a specified Class A drug in the person's body;
(2) either the accused is charged with an offence under the Misuse of Drugs Act 1971, s. 5(2) or (3), and the offence relates to a specified Class A drug, or the court is satisfied that there are substantial grounds for believing that the misuse of a specified Class A drug caused or contributed to the offence with which the accused is charged or that offence was motivated wholly or partly by intended misuse of a specified Class A drug; and
(3) the person does not agree to undergo an assessment (carried out by a suitably qualified person) of dependency upon or a propensity to misuse any specified Class A drugs, or has undergone such an assessment but does not agree to participate in any relevant follow-up which has been offered.

If an assessment or follow-up is proposed and agreed to, it will be a condition of bail that it is undertaken (BA 1976, s. 3(6D)).

The phrase 'may not' is a prohibitive one and makes it plain that the court should not grant bail unless satisfied that there was no significant risk of the accused committing offences while on bail. In essence, the presumption created by the BA 1976, s. 4, is reversed and it becomes necessary for the court to be persuaded that there is no significant risk of the accused committing an offence if released on bail (cf. *R (Wiggins) v Harrow Crown Court* [2005] EWHC 882 (Admin), per Collins J, at [24]).

Under sch. 1, para. 2(2), where the accused falls within these drugs provisions, para. 2 (refusal of bail where there are substantial grounds for believing that the accused will fail to surrender to custody etc.: see **D7.13**) does not apply unless the court is of the opinion that there is no significant risk of the accused committing an offence while on bail.

Convicted Offenders: Adjourning for Reports

Under the BA 1976, sch. 1, part I, para. 7, if the case of a convicted offender is adjourned for inquiries or reports, bail need not be granted if it appears to the court that it would be impracticable to complete the inquiries or make the report without the accused being kept in custody (e.g., because the accused would not voluntarily attend for purposes such as seeing a probation officer or being medically examined). It is submitted that, where a court needs a pre-sentence report before it will be in a position to decide the appropriate sentence, the normal practice should be to grant bail unless there are exceptional reasons for keeping the offender in custody. It should be borne in mind that a remand in custody might appear to be prejudging the question of whether the ultimate sentence should be custodial. **D7.32**

Children and Young People

The BA 1976, sch. 1 (see **D7.151** ***et seq.***), contains some additional provisions that are specific to cases where the accused is under the age of 18. Paragraph 9AA provides that, if the accused is under the age of 18 and it appears to the court that the accused was on bail (in respect of other proceedings) at the date of the current alleged offence, the court must (when deciding whether it is satisfied that there are substantial grounds for believing that the accused will, if released on bail, commit an offence) give 'particular weight' to the fact that the accused was on bail in respect of another alleged offence on the date of the current alleged offence. **D7.33**

Paragraph 9AB(3) applies where the accused is under the age of 18 and it appears to the court that, having been released on bail in connection with the proceedings for the present offence, the accused has failed to surrender to custody. In such a case, the court must (when deciding whether it is satisfied that there are substantial grounds for believing that the accused will, if released on bail, fail to surrender to custody) give 'particular weight' to certain matters: where the accused did not have reasonable cause for the failure to surrender to custody, the fact of the failure to surrender to custody; and where the accused did have reasonable cause for the failure to surrender to custody, the fact of the failure to surrender to custody as soon as reasonably practicable after the appointed time for surrender.

D7.34 **Criminal Damage** The BA 1976, s. 9A (see **D7.150**), provides that, where an accused under the age of 18 is charged with an offence to which the MCA 1980, s. 22, applies (i.e. criminal damage where the value involved does not exceed £5,000), and the trial of that offence has not begun, a magistrates' court (this includes a youth court) considering whether to withhold or grant bail must consider, having regard to any representations from the prosecution and the accused person, whether the value exceeds £5,000. If the value involved does not exceed £5,000, the BA 1976, sch. 1, part IA (see **D7.35**) will apply.

REFUSING BAIL TO AN ACCUSED CHARGED WITH SUMMARY AND NON-IMPRISONABLE OFFENCES

Imprisonable Summary Offences

D7.35 Under the BA 1976, sch. 1, part I, para. 1(2) (see **D7.151**), where the offence is a summary offence punishable with imprisonment, or an offence to which the MCA 1980, s. 22, applies (criminal damage where the value involved does not exceed £5,000), part I of sch. 1 does not apply. In such cases, the BA 1976, sch. 1, part IA, applies instead (see **D7.158** ***et seq.***). Under part IA, the exceptions to the presumption in favour of bail are as follows:

(a) where the accused has previously been granted bail and has failed to surrender to custody in those proceedings, and the court believes, in view of that failure, that the accused would, if released on bail, fail to surrender to custody (para. 2);
(b) where the accused was on bail on the date of the current alleged offence and the court is satisfied that there are substantial grounds for believing that, if released on bail, the accused would commit an offence while on bail (para. 3);
(c) where the court is satisfied that there are substantial grounds for believing that, if released on bail, the accused would commit an offence while on bail by engaging in conduct that would, or would be likely to, cause physical or mental injury to an associated person (as defined by the Family Law Act 1996, s. 62, see **D7.25**), or cause such a person to fear physical or mental injury, i.e. domestic violence (para. 4);
(d) where the court is satisfied that the accused should be kept in custody for the accused's own protection (or welfare, if a child or young person) (para. 5);
(e) where the accused is already serving a custodial sentence (para. 6);
(f) where the accused has been arrested under the BA 1976, s. 7, and the court is satisfied that there are substantial grounds for believing that, if released on bail, the accused would fail to surrender to custody, commit an offence while on bail or interfere with witnesses or otherwise obstruct the course of justice (whether in relation to the accused or any other person) (para. 7);
(g) where the court is satisfied that it has not been practicable to obtain sufficient information for the purpose of taking the decision on whether to grant bail for want of time since the institution of the proceedings (para. 8); and
(h) where part I, paras. 6A to 6C (see **D7.31**), would otherwise be applicable were the current offence an indictable one (para. 9).

D7.36 **No Real Prospect of a Custodial Sentence** The BA 1976, sch. 1, part IA, para. 1A, provides that para. 2 (failure to surrender to custody), para. 3 (committing offences while on bail) and para. 7 (accused arrested under s. 7) do not apply where the accused has attained the age of 18, and has not been convicted of an offence in the proceedings, and it appears to the court that there is 'no real prospect that the defendant will be sentenced to a custodial sentence in the proceedings'.

Non-imprisonable Offences

Part II of sch. 1 to the BA 1976 (see **D7.161** *et seq.*) sets out the reasons which permit the refusal of bail to an accused charged solely with one or more offences that are not punishable with imprisonment. The grounds for withholding bail in such cases are as follows: **D7.37**

(a) where the accused is under the age of 18 or has been convicted of an offence in those proceedings and (in either case), having been previously granted bail in criminal proceedings, has failed to surrender to custody and the court believes, in view of that failure, that the accused would fail to surrender to custody (para. 2);
(b) where the court is satisfied that the accused should be kept in custody for his or her own protection (or welfare, if a child or young person) (para. 3);
(c) where the accused is already serving a custodial sentence (para. 4);
(d) where the accused is under the age of 18 or has been convicted of an offence in those proceedings, and (in either case) has been arrested under the BA 1976, s. 7, and the court is satisfied that there are substantial grounds to believe that the accused would fail to surrender to custody, commit an offence on bail, or interfere with witnesses or otherwise obstruct the course of justice (para. 5);
(e) where the accused has been arrested under s. 7 and the court is satisfied that there are substantial grounds for believing that, if released on bail, the accused would commit an offence while on bail by engaging in conduct that would, or would be likely to, cause physical or mental injury to an associated person (as defined by the Family Law Act 1996, s. 62, see **D7.25**), or to cause such a person to fear such injury, i.e. domestic violence (para. 6).

It should be noted that the grounds of 'risk of absconding etc.' and 'insufficient time' for refusing bail to someone charged with imprisonable offences do *not* apply where the offences are non-imprisonable.

BAIL AND THE EUROPEAN CONVENTION ON HUMAN RIGHTS

Article 5 of the ECHR (see **A7.48**), which provides that 'everyone has the right to liberty', has clear relevance to bail. It lays down that no one shall be deprived of their liberty save in the six sets of circumstances specified in Article 5(1)(a) to (f). The list of exceptions is exhaustive, and has been described in Strasbourg as ensuring that no one is deprived of liberty in an 'arbitrary fashion' (*Engel v Netherlands* (1979–80) 1 EHRR 647). **D7.38**

The Law Commission (Law Com No. 269) considered the impact of the HRA 1998 on the law governing decisions taken by the police and the courts to grant or refuse bail in criminal proceedings. The Commission noted that Article 5 of the ECHR states that, although reasonable suspicion that the detained person has committed an offence can be sufficient to justify pre-trial detention for a short time, the national authorities must thereafter show additional grounds for detention. They summarised the five additional grounds recognised under the ECHR as follows, namely where the purpose of detention is to avoid a real risk of:

(1) failure to attend trial;
(2) interference with evidence or witnesses, or obstruction of the course of justice;
(3) commission of an offence while on bail;

(4) harm to the accused against which the accused would be inadequately protected; or
(5) a disturbance to public order.

The Law Commission concluded that there are no provisions in the BA 1976 which are incompatible with Convention rights. However, the Commission did produce a guide to assist decision-makers to apply the Act in a way that is compatible with the ECHR. This emphasises that an accused should be refused bail only where detention is necessary for a purpose which Strasbourg jurisprudence has recognised as legitimate, in the sense that detention may be compatible with the accused's right to release under Article 5(3). Thus, a domestic court exercising its powers in a way which is compatible with the Convention rights should refuse bail only where it can be justified under both the ECHR, as interpreted in Strasbourg jurisprudence, and domestic legislation. The guidance also points out that detention will be necessary only if the risk relied upon as the ground for withholding bail could not be adequately addressed by the imposition of appropriate bail conditions. Thus, the Commission concluded that conditional bail should be used in preference to a remand in custody where a bail condition could adequately address the risk that would otherwise justify detention. Furthermore, the court refusing bail should give reasons for finding that a remand in custody is necessary. Those reasons should be closely related to the individual circumstances pertaining to the accused, and be capable of supporting the conclusion of the court.

D7.39 In *R (Thompson) v Central Criminal Court* [2005] EWHC 2345 (Admin), Collins J (at [10]) said:

> The approach under the Bail Act is entirely consistent with the approach which the European Court has regarded as proper under Article 5, namely there must be a grant of bail unless there are good reasons to refuse. The approach therefore really is not should there be bail granted but should custody be opposed, that is, is it necessary for the defendant to be in custody. That is the approach that the court should take. Only if persuaded that it is necessary should a remand in custody take place. It would be necessary if the court decides that whatever conditions can be reasonably imposed in relation to bail there are nevertheless substantial grounds for believing that the defendant will either fail to surrender to custody, commit an offence, interfere with witnesses or otherwise obstruct justice.

In *R (Fergus) v Southampton Crown Court* [2008] EWHC 3273 (Admin), Silber J (at [20]) said that there was a 'high threshold' before bail can be withheld, namely that an accused should be remanded in custody only if that is 'necessary'.

Strasbourg Case Law

D7.40 Under Article 5, a person charged with an offence must be released pending trial unless there are 'relevant and sufficient' reasons to justify continued detention (*Wemhoff v Germany* (1979–80) 1 EHRR 55, at [12]). The case law of the ECtHR shows that this is interpreted in a way that is very similar to the UK's BA 1976. The grounds accepted by the ECtHR for withholding bail include:

(1) *The risk that the accused will fail to appear at the trial.* This has been defined as requiring 'a whole set of circumstances ... which give reason to suppose that the consequences and hazards of flight will seem to him to be a lesser evil than continued imprisonment' (*Stogmuller v Austria* (1979–80) 1 EHRR 155, at [15]). The court can take account of 'the character of the person involved, his morals, his home, his occupation, his assets, his family ties, and all kinds of links with the country in which he is being prosecuted' (*Neumeister v Austria* (1979–80) 1 EHRR 91, at [10]). The likely sentence is relevant but cannot of itself justify the refusal of bail (*Letellier v France* (1992) 14 EHRR 83, at [43]).

(2) *The risk that the accused will interfere with the course of justice* (e.g., interfering with witnesses, warning other suspects, destroying relevant evidence). There must be an identifiable risk and there must be plausible evidence in support (cf. *Clooth v Belgium* (1992) 14 EHRR 717).
(3) *Preventing the commission of further offences.* There must be good reason to believe that the accused will commit offences while on bail (cf. *Toth v Austria* (1992) 14 EHRR 551).
(4) *The preservation of public order.* Bail may be withheld where the nature of the alleged crime and the likely public reaction to it are such that the release of the accused may give rise to public disorder (*Letellier v France*, at [51]).

Article 5 of the Convention also allows the imposition of conditions on the grant of bail.

In *O'Dowd v UK* (2012) 54 EHRR 8 (187), the ECtHR observed (at [68]) that: **D7.41**

> Whether it is reasonable for an accused to remain in detention must be assessed in each case according to its special features. Continued detention can be justified in a given case only if there are specific indications of a genuine requirement of public interest which, notwithstanding the presumption of innocence, outweighs the rule of respect for individual liberty laid down in Article 5 of the Convention . . .

It follows, said the Court (at [69]), that it falls to the 'national judicial authorities to ensure that, in a given case, the pre-trial detention of an accused person does not exceed a reasonable time'. The Court went on to say (at [70]) that the 'persistence of reasonable suspicion that the person arrested has committed an offence is a condition *sine qua non* for the lawfulness of the continued detention, but after a certain lapse of time it no longer suffices'. At that point, there must not only be 'sufficient' grounds to justify the deprivation of liberty, but the 'national authorities' (i.e. the prosecution) must display 'special diligence' in the conduct of the proceedings. In assessing whether the 'special diligence' requirement has been met, regard must be had 'to periods of unjustified delay, to the overall complexity of the proceedings and to any steps taken by the authorities to speed up proceedings to ensure that the overall length of detention remains "reasonable" '.

The Court ruled (at [73]) that the 'due diligence' required by the Prosecution of Offences Act 1985, s. 22(3) (extension of custody time-limits: see **D7.43**), cannot be equated to the 'special diligence' required by Article 5(3). The Court went on to explain that:

> . . . unlike the approach of the domestic courts to compliance with the 1985 Act, in assessing compliance with Article 5(3), this Court will examine the proceedings as a whole and assess any particular periods of inactivity or delay by the authorities within the context of the overall period of pre-trial detention, with particular regard to any recognition by the authorities of the length of time already spent in detention and the need to take additional steps to bring about a more speedy trial.

The Court found no breach of Article 5(3) on the facts in *O'Dowd*. This was largely because D had contributed substantially to the overall length of his pre-trial detention (e.g., by dismissing his legal advisers shortly before hearings, which resulted in the hearings being postponed).

'Equality of Arms' in Context of Bail

It should be noted that the 'equality of arms' principle applies to bail applications (*Woukam Moudefo v France* (1991) 13 EHRR 549). This includes: **D7.42**

(a) the right to disclosure of prosecution evidence for purposes of making a bail application: *Lamy v Belgium* (1989) 11 EHRR 529, at [29] (the decision of the Divisional Court, *DPP, ex parte Lee* [1999] 2 Cr App R 304, largely accords with this);
(b) the requirement that the court should give reasons for the refusal of bail (*Tomasi v France* (1993) 15 EHRR 1, at [84]) and should permit renewed applications for bail at reasonable intervals (*Bezicheri v Italy* (1990) 12 EHRR 210, at [21]).

BAIL AND CUSTODY TIME-LIMITS

D7.43 Grafted on to the general system of a presumption in favour of bail which is lost if one or more of the exceptions described above applies are special rules applying where the prosecution fail to comply with the custody time-limits contained in the Prosecution of Offences (Custody Time Limits) Regulations 1987 (SI 1987 No. 299) (see **D15.7** ***et seq.***). For either-way offences, the maximum period of custody between the accused's first appearance and the start of summary trial, or the time when the court decides whether to send the accused to the Crown Court for trial, is 70 days (reg. 4(2)). However, if, before the expiry of 56 days following the day of the accused's first appearance, the court decides to proceed to summary trial, the maximum period of custody between the accused's first appearance and the start of the summary trial is 56 days (reg. 4(3)). For indictable-only offences, the maximum period of custody between the accused's first appearance and the time when the court decides to send the accused to the Crown Court for trial is 70 days (reg. 4(4)). For summary offences, the maximum period of custody beginning with the date of the accused's first appearance and ending with the date of the start of the summary trial is 56 days (reg. 4(4A)). Where a case is sent for trial in the Crown Court, the maximum period of custody between the time when the accused is sent for trial and the start of the trial is 182 days (reg. 5(6B)).

Under reg. 6(6), where the Crown Court is notified that the custody time-limit applicable to an accused in custody pending trial on indictment is about to expire, it must grant bail as from the expiry of the time-limit. By reg. 6(1) to (5), the prosecution must notify the Crown Court, at least five days before expiry of the time-limit, whether they intend to ask the Crown Court to impose conditions on the grant of bail. They must also arrange for the accused to be brought before the court within the two days preceding expiry. This is without prejudice to the prosecution's right to apply for an extension of the time-limit under the Prosecution of Offences Act 1985, s. 22(3).

The 1987 Regulations make no express provision as to the procedure to be adopted in a magistrates' court when a custody time-limit is about to expire. The fact that an accused who has not been granted bail must appear before the magistrates at regular intervals (because of the restrictions on the period for a remand in custody) perhaps makes it unnecessary to provide expressly for bringing the accused before the court in anticipation of the expiry of a custody time-limit.

D7.44 Regulation 8 modifies the BA 1976 in that, where a custody time-limit has expired, the words 'except as provided in Schedule 1 to this Act' are treated as omitted from s. 4(1) of the Act. The effect is to give the accused an absolute right to bail. Moreover, s. 3 of the 1976 Act (which deals with the conditions which may be imposed when granting bail, considered at **D7.45** ***et seq.***) is also modified so as to prevent a court, when bailing an accused entitled to bail by reason of the expiry of a custody time-limit, from imposing requirements of a surety or deposit of security or any other condition which has to be complied with *before* release on bail (although it can impose conditions such as residence, curfew or reporting to a police station which have to be complied with *after* release). Moreover, following the grant of bail, the accused may not be arrested without warrant (under s. 7 of the BA 1976) on the ground that a police officer believes the accused is unlikely to surrender to custody or has, or is likely, to break a condition of bail.

If the accused is granted bail because the custody time-limit has expired, the right to bail continues only until a plea has been entered. Thereafter, the court can withhold bail if any of the reasons for doing so under the BA 1976 apply (*Croydon Crown Court, ex parte Lewis* (1994) 158 JP 886).

These provisions apply to proceedings in the youth court even though the usual distinction between summary and indictable offences does not apply there (*Stratford Youth Court, ex parte S* [1998] 1 WLR 1758).

For a full discussion of custody time-limits, see **D15.7** ***et seq.***

CONDITIONS OF BAIL

The BA 1976, s. 3, governs the duties resting on a person granted bail in criminal proceedings and the various requirements which may be attached to a grant of bail. Where the court grants 'unconditional' bail, the accused has simply to surrender to custody (i.e. attend court) at the date and time specified (s. 3(1)). However, the court may impose a wide range of additional requirements by granting bail subject to specific conditions, known as 'conditional bail' (s. 3(6)). **D7.45**

CrimPR 14.16 (see Supplement, **R14.16**) applies where the court may impose a bail condition requirement with which the accused must comply while in another EU Member State (to be monitored and enforced by that Member State); r. 14.17 applies where another EU Member State requests the monitoring and enforcement of an accused's compliance with a supervision measure imposed by an authority in that other State.

Duty to Surrender to Custody

A person granted bail in criminal proceedings is under a duty to surrender to custody (BA 1976, s. 3(1)). 'Surrender to custody' is defined in s. 2(2) as surrendering into the custody of the court the accused has been bailed to attend. For discussion of what precisely is meant by surrendering to the custody of a court, see **D7.101**. The date fixed for surrender to custody may be varied to a later date (see the MCA 1980, ss. 43 and 129, for a magistrates' court's powers in this respect). Failure without reasonable cause to surrender to custody is an offence under the BA 1976, s. 6 (see **D7.110**). **D7.46**

By s. 3(2) of the 1976 Act, an accused granted bail in criminal proceedings may not be bailed on his or her own recognizance (in other words, an accused may not act as his or her own surety). The accused may, however, be required to provide other people to stand surety, under s. 3(4) (see **D7.55**), or may be required to give security for his or her surrender to custody, under s. 3(5) (see **D7.60**).

Conditions that May be Imposed by the Court

By virtue of the BA 1976, s. 3(6) (see **D7.136**), a person who is granted bail may be required by the court to comply with such requirements as appear to the court necessary to secure that the person: **D7.47**

(a) surrenders to custody;
(b) does not commit an offence on bail;
(c) does not interfere with witnesses or otherwise obstruct the course of justice;
(d) is available for the making of inquiries or a report to assist in sentencing (this condition may be imposed only it appears to be necessary to do so for the purpose of enabling inquiries or a report to be made: sch. 1, part I, para. 8(1A)); and
(e) attends an interview with a legal representative (this will nearly always be a solicitor).

Conditions may also be imposed for the protection of the accused (or, if a child or young person, for the accused's own welfare or interests).

The BA 1976, sch. 1, part I, para. 8(1), provides that no conditions may be imposed unless it appears to the court that it is 'necessary' to do so either (a) for the purpose of preventing the occurrence of any of the events mentioned in sch. 1, para. 2(1), or for the accused's own protection or, if a child or young person, for the accused's own welfare or interests. The events mentioned in sch. 1, part I, para. 2, are precisely the same as those mentioned in paras. (a) to (c) of s. 3(6): failure to surrender to custody, commission of further offences and interference with witnesses. There is thus an almost complete overlap between s. 3(6) and sch. 1, part I, para. 8. This was attributed by Lord Lane CJ in *Mansfield Justices, ex parte Sharkey* [1985] QB 613 to 'indifferent drafting' (at p. 625C). Counsel for the applicants argued that para. 8 impliedly restricted the imposition of requirements to cases where the court was satisfied that there were substantial grounds for believing that one of the adverse consequences would occur unless bail was made **D7.48** conditional. However, this argument was rejected by the Divisional Court. Having quoted s. 3(6) and para. 8, Lord Lane explained their effect in the context of a condition imposed to prevent further offences. His lordship said (at p. 625E):

> In the present circumstances the question the justices should ask themselves is a simple one: 'Is this condition *necessary* for the prevention of the commission of an offence when on bail?' They are not obliged to have substantial grounds. It is enough if they perceive a *real and not a fanciful risk* of the offence being committed. Thus, section 3(6) and paragraph 8 give the court a wide discretion to inquire whether the condition is necessary [emphasis added].

It followed that the justices were *not* obliged to have substantial grounds for believing that a repetition of the accused's conduct would occur. It was enough that they perceived a 'real risk' of that happening. Although set out in the context of determining the legality of conditions imposed to prevent offences while on bail, the Lord Chief Justice's reasoning is equally applicable to conditions designed to prevent the accused absconding or interfering with witnesses.

A similar approach was adopted in *R (CPS) v Chorley Justices* [2002] EWHC 2162 (Admin), where the Divisional Court noted that the only prerequisite for imposing conditions on bail is that, in the circumstances of the particular case, imposition of the condition is necessary to achieve the aims specified in that section (e.g., preventing the accused from absconding, or committing offences while on bail, or interfering with witnesses or otherwise obstructing the course of justice).

D7.49 The BA 1976 refers to some specific conditions (such as sureties and security) but it does not contain a definitive list of conditions that may be imposed. The court may impose *any* condition so long as it is necessary to prevent the accused from absconding, committing offences etc. Under CrimPR 14.5(4) (see Supplement, **R14.5**) a prosecutor who wants the court to impose a condition must specify the condition and explain what purpose it would serve.

Commonly imposed conditions include:

(a) a condition of residence, often expressed as a condition that the accused is to live and sleep at a specified address;
(b) a condition that the accused is to notify any changes of address to the police;
(c) a condition of reporting (whether daily, weekly or at other intervals) to a local police station;
(d) a curfew (i.e. the accused must be at a specified address between certain hours);
(e) a condition that the accused is not to enter a certain area or building or go within a specified distance of a certain address;
(f) a condition that the accused is not to contact (whether directly or indirectly) the victim of the alleged offence and/or any other probable prosecution witness; and
(g) a condition that the accused's passport must be surrendered to the police (sometimes with an additional restriction to prevent the accused from applying for travel documents).

Conditions (a), (b), (c) and (g) are particularly relevant to reducing the risk of absconding. A special form of residential condition is that the accused is to reside at a bail hostel or probation hostel. When imposing such a condition the court may, and normally will, impose an additional requirement that the accused must comply with the rules of the hostel (s. 3(6ZA)). In the case of a convicted offender being remanded for reports, a requirement of residence at a hostel may be imposed not simply to reduce the risk of absconding but, additionally or alternatively, to assess the offender's suitability for being dealt with by means of a community order. Conditions (d) and (e) are designed to prevent the commission of offences when on bail. A curfew may be appropriate where the offence with which the accused is charged was allegedly committed at night; a geographical restriction is useful if the offence was one of violence committed at a certain address (in effect, the accused is ordered to stay away from the address). Conditions (e) and (f) may be imposed to minimise the risk of interference with witnesses.

Under CrimPR 14.11 (see Supplement, **R14.11**) the accused must, as soon as practicable, notify the prosecutor of the address at which the accused will live and sleep if released on bail with a condition of residence. The prosecutor must help the court to assess the suitability of an address proposed as a condition of residence. **D7.50**

In *R (CPS) v Chorley Justices* [2002] EWHC 2162 (Admin), D was granted bail subject to a curfew condition. The magistrates' court ruled that there was no jurisdiction to impose an additional condition requested by the prosecution, that D should 'be required during the hours of the curfew to present himself at the door of his home if requested to do so by a police officer'. The CPS sought judicial review of this refusal. The Divisional Court held that there is power under s. 3(6) to impose such 'door-step' conditions, but it is a question of fact in each case whether such a condition is necessary.

Electronic Monitoring

Electronic monitoring (colloquially known as 'tagging') is available as a condition of bail under the BA 1976, s. 3(6ZAA). This condition is often combined with a curfew condition. **D7.51**

Adults Section 3AB of the 1976 Act governs the imposition of electronic monitoring requirements where the accused has attained the age of 18. Such a requirement may be imposed only if the court is satisfied that, without the electronic monitoring requirement, the accused would not be granted bail (s. 3AB(2)). **D7.52**

Children and Young People Section 3AA applies where the accused is under the age of 18. It stipulates that an electronic monitoring requirement cannot be imposed unless the accused is at least 12 years old. Moreover, the child or young person must have been charged with, or convicted of, either (a) a violent or sexual offence, or an offence punishable in the case of an adult with at least 14 years' imprisonment, or (b) one or more imprisonable offences which amount (or would amount if convicted of the present charge) to a recent history of repeatedly committing imprisonable offences while remanded on bail or subject to a custodial remand (s. 3AA(3)). Moreover, a youth offending team must have confirmed the suitability of the requirement for the accused (s. 3AA(5)). **D7.53**

Non-imprisonable Offences

In *Bournemouth Magistrates' Court, ex parte Cross* (1989) 89 Cr App R 90, the Divisional Court confirmed that conditions can be imposed on bail under the BA 1976, s. 3(6), where the offence in question is non-imprisonable. **D7.54**

Sureties

A person granted bail in criminal proceedings may be required, before release on bail, to provide one or more sureties to secure the person's surrender to custody (BA 1976, s. 3(4), see **D7.136**). Section 3(4) does not place any fetter on the discretion to demand a surety (cf. s. 3(6)). However, sch. 1, part I, para. 8, provides that no conditions shall be imposed under, *inter alia*, s. 3(4) unless they appear to the court necessary to prevent the occurrence of any of the events mentioned in sch. 1, part I, para. 2(1) (i.e. failure to surrender to custody, the commission of one or more offences while on bail, or interference with witnesses or obstruction of the course of justice). In *R (Shea) v Winchester Crown Court* [2013] EWHC 1050 (Admin), the Divisional Court ruled that there is no power (under the BA 1976 or otherwise) to require a surety to ensure no further offending: a surety can be sought only for the purpose of securing surrender to custody, and not for any other purpose. It follows that one or more sureties should be required only in cases where there appears to be a risk of absconding. **D7.55**

The position is different where the accused is under the age of 17 (see **D7.59**).

D7.56 **Who Can be a Surety?** The BA 1976, s. 8 (see **D7.148**), contains detailed provisions about the taking of sureties. In considering whether a proposed surety is suitable, regard may be had, *inter alia*, to the factors set out in s. 8(2).

(a) The financial resources of the proposed surety: could the surety pay the sum which is promised? In *Birmingham Crown Court, ex parte Rashid Ali* (1999) 163 JP 145, Kennedy LJ (at p. 147) said that 'it is irresponsible (and possibly a matter for consideration by a professional disciplinary body) for a qualified lawyer or legal executive to tender anyone as a surety unless he or she has reasonable grounds for believing that the surety will, if necessary, be able to meet his or her financial undertaking'.
(b) The character of the proposed surety and any previous convictions: is the surety a trustworthy person?
(c) The proximity (whether kinship, place of residence or otherwise) of the proposed surety to the accused: for example, is the proposed surety a friend, relative or employer? The most important consideration under this heading is the relationship of the proposed surety to the accused: will the surety have the ability to influence the accused so as to ensure attendance at court at the appointed time? Put another way, would the fact that the surety stands to lose money if the accused absconds operate on the mind of the accused so as to act as a deterrent against absconding?

D7.57 **Taking the Surety** The normal consequence for a surety if an accused fails to answer to bail is that the surety is ordered to forfeit the entire sum which was promised (the 'recognizance'). As the surety is promising to pay money rather than handing over any money at the outset, it is therefore important for the court to be assured that the surety has sufficient funds with which to honour the undertaking given to the court. A proposed surety who is present in court is asked how the sum promised would be paid if the accused were to abscond. It is also standard practice for the police to check whether the proposed surety has previous convictions; if so, and depending on their age and nature, objection may be made to that person acting as a surety. If no satisfactory surety is forthcoming at court, but the court is willing to grant bail subject to the provision of a satisfactory surety, the court simply fixes the amount in which the surety is to be bound and the accused remains in custody unless and until the court's requirement can be fulfilled (BA 1976, s. 8(3)). To facilitate early release where the sureties are not at court, they may enter into their recognizances outside court (s. 8(4)). Paragraphs (a) to (d) of s. 8(4), in conjunction with CrimPR 14.14(3)(b) (see Supplement, **R14.14**), list the persons who may accept a surety's recognizance: a justice of the peace; a justices' clerk; a police officer who is either of the rank of inspector or above or who is in charge of a police station; or the 'defendant's custodian' (i.e. the governor of the prison or remand centre where the accused is being held); or, if bail has been granted by the Crown Court, an officer of that court. The court granting bail may, however, specify the person (or class of person) before whom the surety is to be taken or require that the surety be taken in court (see the opening words of s. 8(4)). If a person asked to accept a surety outside court refuses to do so due to lack of satisfaction about the surety's suitability, the surety may apply either to the court which fixed the amount of the recognizance in which the surety was to be bound, or to any magistrates' court, for that court to take the recognizance; that court must, if satisfied of the surety's suitability, take the recognizance (s. 8(5)).

It is quite common to have two or more sureties. If the court will grant bail only subject to a recognizance of a certain amount and that amount is beyond the means of one of the proposed sureties, then one or more additional sureties will have to be found.

For discussion of the consequences for the surety if the accused absconds, see **D7.121**.

D7.58 **Making Sureties Continuous** Where bail is granted subject to a requirement for sureties, the surety's recognizance may be conditioned to secure that the accused 'appears at every time and place to which during the course of the proceedings the hearing may be from time to time adjourned' and also before the Crown Court in the event of the accused being sent there for trial (MCA 1980, s. 128(4)). Making the sureties continuous in this way is a useful device to avoid the sureties having to come to court for each remand hearing. If they have not been made continuous and are not at court, the accused, even if granted bail on precisely the same terms as previously, cannot be released until the undertakings have been renewed (e.g., by going to a local police station). Section 128(4)(c) even empowers magistrates to make the sureties' recognizances extend beyond the date when the case is sent to the Crown Court for trial (i.e. at a remand hearing they undertake to secure the accused's attendance before the Crown Court if the accused is sent there for trial). Where the accused's bail is conditional both on sureties and other conditions, there is no obligation to inform the sureties should the other conditions be relaxed or varied (*Wells Street Magistrates' Court, ex parte Albanese* [1982] QB 333).

In *Evans* [2011] EWCA Crim 2842, [2012] 1 WLR 1192, Hughes LJ (at [33]) said that, where a magistrates' court has sent the accused to Crown Court, bail and any recognizance will lapse on the first appearance in the Crown Court and cannot carry through to subsequent adjournments in the Crown Court. However, if the Crown Court renews bail, it does have the power to make the recognizance continuous for all future appearances. This, said his lordship:

> ... underlines the importance of attention being paid to the terms of a defendant's bail, particularly at the conclusion of the first hearing in the Crown Court. At that point conditions of bail should always be considered. Of course it is sufficient to do so briefly by simply reimposing conditions previously placed there by the magistrates, if that is appropriate and especially if there is no objection. But in both surety cases and non-surety cases an assessment of bail is required at the end of the first hearing in each Crown Court.

Parent Standing Surety for a Child or Young Person The general rule is that the obligations of a surety extend only to securing the accused's attendance at court, and so a surety is *not* responsible for preventing any other possible defaults of the accused while on bail (e.g., intimidation of witnesses or breach of a condition of bail). However, the BA 1976, s. 3(7), provides that, where the accused is under the age of 17, and a parent or guardian stands surety, the court may require the parent or guardian to secure that the accused complies with any condition of bail imposed by virtue of s. 3(6), (6ZAA), or (6A). A requirement under s. 3(7) can be imposed only with the consent of the parent or guardian, and the sum promised may not exceed £50. **D7.59**

Deposit of Security

Under the BA 1976, s. 3(2) (see **D7.136**), a person cannot stand as surety for him or herself. However, persons granted bail may be required to give 'security' for their surrender to custody, i.e. deposit with the court money or some other valuable item which will be liable to forfeiture in the event of non-attendance in answer to bail (BA 1976, s. 3(5)). As with sureties, security may be required as a condition of bail only if it is considered necessary to prevent absconding. Where security has been given in pursuance of s. 3(5) and the person bailed absconds, the court may, unless there appears to have been reasonable cause for the failure to surrender to custody, order forfeiture of the security (s. 5(7) to (9)). **D7.60**

In *R (Stevens) v Truro Magistrates' Court* [2001] EWHC Admin 558, [2002] 1 WLR 144, it was held that it is permissible for a third party to make available an asset to an accused for use as security, and that the court can accept such an asset. However, as it is the accused who gives the security, the arrangements the accused might make with those who assist with the provision of the requisite security are not a matter for the court. There is no obligation for the third party to be notified before the security is forfeited on the accused's non-attendance.

Other Statutory Bail Conditions

There are a number of other conditions which may be imposed on the grant of bail pursuant to various provisions of the BA 1976. **D7.61**

D7.62 **Drug Assessments** Section 3(6C) to (6E) of the BA 1976 (see **D7.136**) provide that where:

(a) the conditions set out in para. 6B of part I of sch. 1 are satisfied (namely, the accused is aged 18 or over, there is drug test evidence that there is a specified Class A drug in the accused's body, and either the offence is a drugs offence associated with a specified Class A drug or the court is satisfied that there are substantial grounds for believing that the misuse of a specified Class A drug caused or contributed to that offence or provided its motivation), and
(b) the accused has been offered an assessment of dependency upon or propensity to misuse any specified Class A drugs (or such an assessment has been carried out and follow-up has been offered), and
(c) the accused has agreed to undergo that assessment or participate in any follow-up,

then the court, if it grants bail, is required to impose as a condition that the accused must both undergo the relevant assessment and participate in any relevant follow-up that is proposed or, if a relevant assessment has been carried out, that the accused must participate in the relevant follow-up (s. 3(6D)).

D7.63 **Co-operation in the Making of Reports** One of the purposes for which the court may impose a requirement under the BA 1976, s. 3(6), is to ensure that the accused will be 'available for the purpose of enabling inquiries or a report to be made to assist the court in dealing with him for the offence' (s. 3(6)(d)). For obvious reasons, such a requirement will not generally be considered until the stage of an adjournment between conviction and sentence. However, there are two situations in which the court is obliged — not merely empowered — to make a requirement under s. 3(6)(d), and both can arise even before conviction. Those situations are:

(a) Where a magistrates' court is dealing with an imprisonable offence, it may adjourn the case under the PCC(S)A 2000, s. 11(1), for a medical examination, provided that the court is satisfied that the accused did the act or made the omission charged, and is of the opinion that an inquiry ought to be made into the physical or mental condition of the accused before the method of proceeding is determined. Although such an adjournment is conditional on the court being satisfied that the accused committed the *actus reus* of the offence, there is no need for a conviction to have been recorded. The purpose of ordering the examination is usually to discover whether the accused's mental condition is such that the accused might be dealt with by means such as a hospital order (whether with or without a prior conviction for the offence charged) or a community order with a condition for medical treatment. Under s. 11(3), where there is an adjournment under s. 11(1) and the magistrates remand the accused on bail, the court *shall* impose conditions under the BA 1976, s. 3(6). Those conditions must include requirements that the accused: (i) submits to examination by a duly qualified medical practitioner (or, if the inquiry is into the accused's mental condition and the court so directs, by two practitioners); and (ii) for the purpose of the examination, attends at such place as the court directs and complies with any directions given for that purpose.
(b) Where a court grants bail to an accused charged with murder, it must, unless satisfied that satisfactory reports on the accused's mental condition have already been obtained, impose as conditions of bail requirements that the accused must undergo examination by two medical practitioners (including a psychiatrist approved under the Mental Health Act 1983) and attend such place as directed for the purpose of the examination (BA 1976, s. 3(6A) and (6B)). The importance in such cases of obtaining full medical and, in particular, psychiatric reports on the accused while still on remand prior to trial is that the reports may lay the foundation for a defence of diminished responsibility or, alternatively, assist the prosecution in rebutting such a defence. In *Central Criminal Court, ex parte Porter* [1992] Crim LR 121, the Divisional Court said that if no such condition was imposed, then the decision to grant bail would be a nullity.

D7.64 **Taking Legal Advice** The court also has power to require an accused, as a condition of bail, to attend an interview with a legal adviser before the next appearance in court (BA 1976, s. 3(6)(e)).

The aim is to save the time of the court by ensuring that the accused receives legal advice, in advance of the hearing, to decide on how to respond to the charge. Clearly, if the accused indicates a wish not to be legally represented, such a condition should not be imposed. If the condition is attached, then the accused should be told of the consequences of failing to comply.

Applications to Vary the Conditions of Bail

Where bail has been granted subject to conditions, the accused may apply for the conditions to be varied (BA 1976, s. 3(8)(a)). The application should be made to the court which granted bail or, where the accused has been sent to the Crown Court for trial, or committed to the Crown Court for sentence, to the Crown Court. Furthermore, the prosecution may make a similar application either for existing conditions to be varied or, in a case where the court originally granted unconditional bail, for conditions to be imposed (s. 3(8)(b)). A party who intends to apply for a variation of bail conditions must give advance notice to the court and to the other party, explaining what is sought and why. CrimPR 14.7 applies to such applications (see **D7.67**). Under r. 14.7(2)(c), the application must be served not less than two business days before any hearing in the case at which the applicant wants the court to consider it, if such a hearing is already due. The court may determine an application to vary a condition without a hearing if the variation has been agreed by the parties (r. 14.7(7)(c)); if there is to be a hearing, it should take place no later than the fifth business day after the application was served (r. 14.7(6)(b)). **D7.65**

Breach of Bail Conditions

Breach of any condition which has been imposed may result in the accused being arrested without warrant under the BA 1976, s. 7(3), and bail being withdrawn. See **D7.102**. **D7.66**

PROCEDURE FOR BAIL APPLICATIONS IN MAGISTRATES' COURTS

Application Procedure

The Coronavirus Act 2020, s. 54 and sch. 24, have made temporary modifications to the CDA 1998, ss. 57A to 57B and sch. 3A, to give the court power to direct 'live link' attendance at 'preliminary hearings'. Under the CDA 1998, s. 57B(8) and sch. 3A, para. 3, specific prohibitions and limitations on the power to direct attendance by live link apply to disputed bail hearings. For full details, see the Special Supplement, **D5.40B**. **D7.67**

Guidance on the procedure to be followed for bail applications is contained in CrimPR Part 14 (see Supplement, **R14.1** *et seq.*). Rule 14.2(1)(a) states that a decision on bail cannot be made unless each party (and any surety directly affected by the decision) is present (in person or via live link) or has had an opportunity to make representations. However, where the accused is in custody, bail may be considered in the absence of an accused who has waived the right to attend, or who was present when bail was refused on a previous occasion and who has been in custody continuously since then (r. 14.2(1)(b)). Rule 14.2(2) states that a bail hearing may take place in public or in private.

Assuming the presumption in favour of bail applies by virtue of the BA 1976, s. 4(1), the onus is on the court to justify any refusal of bail in accordance with sch. 1 to the Act. This applies both when the accused first appears and at all subsequent appearances while remaining within the scope of s. 4(1) (sch. 1, part IIA, para. 1).

The question of bail is always a matter for the court. However, when adjourning the case of an unconvicted accused to whom s. 4(1) applies and who is entitled to make an argued bail application under sch. 1, part IIA (see **D7.70**), normal practice is to ask the prosecution if they have any objections to bail. The prosecution representative then summarises the objections (or, as the case may be, states that there are no objections). The CPS case file will contain information, **D7.68** supplied by the police, which sets out the objections to bail, if any, and the basis of those objections. The prosecution advocate usually has little alternative but to base the objections on this information unless a police officer connected with the case is present in court and able to provide additional information. The justices will normally be told of the accused's previous convictions (including any convictions for failure to surrender to custody) when the prosecution give their objections to bail. Following the prosecution objections, the defence representative (or the accused in person if unrepresented) may present the arguments for bail (whether conditional or unconditional). Even where the defence choose not to make a bail application, it is submitted that the prosecution should present at least cursory objections to bail so that the court will be able to base a refusal on one or more of the reasons contained in sch. 1.

The question of bail is normally dealt with on the basis of submissions from the prosecution and defence. Rule 14.5(2) requires the prosecutor to provide the court with all information in the prosecutor's possession that is relevant to the question of bail. Where the prosecution oppose bail, the prosecutor is required to specify each statutory exception to the presumption in favour of bail on which the prosecution rely, and each consideration the prosecution argue to be relevant (r. 14.5(3)).

There is no requirement for formal evidence to be given (*Re Moles* [1981] Crim LR 170; *Mansfield JJ, ex parte Sharkey* [1985] QB 613 at p. 626, per Lord Lane CJ). Either party may, however, adduce evidence in support of their respective arguments, e.g., a police officer to substantiate the objections to bail, or proposed sureties to further the application for bail. Such witnesses give their evidence on the *voir dire* form of oath, to answer truthfully all such questions as the court may ask.

The prosecution will not normally reply to the application for bail by the defence. However, the prosecutor does have a right to reply to the defence submissions if this is necessary to correct alleged misstatements of fact in what the defence have said (*Isleworth Crown Court, ex parte Commissioner of Customs and Excise* [1990] Crim LR 859).

Having heard the prosecution objections to bail, and the answer of the defence to those objections, the court announces its decision on the grant or withholding of bail.

D7.69 **Effect on Procedure of the Human Rights Act 1998** The compatibility of the procedure adopted in the case of contested bail hearings with the safeguards in the ECHR, Articles 5 and 6, was examined (in the context of a hearing involving an accused arrested for breach of a bail condition) in *R (DPP) v Havering Magistrates' Court* [2001] 1 WLR 805 (see **D7.106**). In that case the need for formal evidence and procedures was rejected in favour of proper account being taken of the quality of the material upon which the court is asked to adjudicate, with D being given a full and fair opportunity to comment on, and answer, that material (per Latham LJ, at [41]).

Right to Make Repeated Argued Bail Applications

D7.70 An accused who has been remanded in custody may make a fully argued application at the next hearing, regardless of whether that application repeats arguments that were placed before the previous bench (BA 1976, sch. 1, part IIA, para. 2; see **D7.163**). Unless the accused consents to being remanded while absent, the next hearing will take place within eight clear days (MCA 1980, s. 128(6)). (Section 128A of the MCA 1980, which permits remands in custody of up to 28 days, applies only if the accused has already been remanded in custody for the offence on at least one previous occasion.) Therefore, the wait between being refused bail on a first appearance and being able to argue again for bail on a second appearance is relatively short. However, should that second argued application fail, the BA 1976, sch. 1, part IIA, para. 3, is applicable. This provides that, at subsequent hearings, the court 'need not hear arguments as to fact or law which it has heard previously'. This is so even though at each hearing the court should nominally consider whether the accused ought to remain in custody (sch. 1, part IIA, para. 1). Paragraph 3 effectively entitles the magistrates to treat the finding of the previous bench (that there were grounds for refusing bail) as a form of *res iudicata*. They may therefore refuse to hear argument in favour of bail, and need consider the question only to the limited extent of satisfying themselves that the accused has exhausted the argued bail applications to which the accused is entitled as of right and that there has been no material change of circumstances since the last argued application to enable the matter to be reopened.

The Law Commission Paper, *Bail and the Human Rights Act 1998* (Law Com No. 269), contains guidance aiming to ensure that the provisions relating to a change in circumstances are applied in a way that is compatible with the ECHR. This guidance states (at paras. 12.23 and 13.33) that courts should be willing, at regular intervals of 28 days, to consider arguments that the passage of time constitutes, in the particular case before the court, a change in circumstances so as to require full argument. If the court finds that the passage of time does amount to a relevant changed circumstance, or that there are other circumstances which may be relevant to the need to detain the accused that have changed or come to notice since the last fully argued bail hearing, then a full bail application should follow in which all the arguments, old and new, could be put forward and taken into account.

Part IIA of sch. 1 to the BA 1976 was intended to give statutory effect to the decision of the Divisional Court in *Nottingham Justices, ex parte Davies* [1981] QB 38. That decision may therefore be regarded as a useful aid to the interpretation of part IIA. Donaldson LJ said (at pp. 43–4): **D7.71**

> ... I accept that the fact that a bench of the same or a different constitution has decided on a previous occasion or occasions that one or more of the schedule 1 exceptions applies and has accordingly remanded the accused in custody, does not absolve the bench on each subsequent occasion from considering whether the accused is entitled to bail, whether or not an application is made.
>
> However, this does not mean that the justices should ignore their own previous decision or a previous decision of their colleagues. Far from it. On those previous occasions, the court will have been under an obligation to grant bail unless it was satisfied that a schedule 1 exception was made out. If it was so satisfied, it will have recorded the exceptions which in its judgment were applicable. This ... is a finding by the court that schedule 1 circumstances then existed and it is to be treated like every other finding of the court. It is *res iudicata* or analogous thereto. It stands as a finding unless and until it is overturned on appeal. ... It follows that on the next occasion when bail is considered [by the magistrates] the court should treat, as an essential fact, that at the time when the matter of bail was last considered, schedule 1 circumstances did indeed exist. Strictly speaking, they can and should only investigate whether that situation has changed since then ...
>
> I would inject only one qualification to the general rule that justices can and should only investigate whether the situation has changed since the last remand in custody. The finding on that occasion that schedule 1 circumstances existed will have been based upon matters known to the court at that time. The court considering afresh the question of bail is both entitled and bound to take account not only of a change in circumstances which has occurred since that last occasion, but also of circumstances which, although they then existed, were not brought to the attention of the court. ... The question is a little wider than 'Has there been a change?' It is 'Are there any new considerations which were not before the court when the accused was last remanded in custody?'

Interpretation of Part IIA The BA 1976, sch. 1, part IIA, paras. 2 and 3 (see **D7.163**), oblige the court to consider any relevant arguments, whether of fact or of law, which were not before the court when bail was refused. This is so whether the argument arises out of a change in circumstances since the last unsuccessful application, or is an argument that could have been put on the previous occasion but, for whatever reason, was not. In *R (B) v Brent Youth Court* [2010] EWHC 1893 (Admin), there had been two bail applications to the magistrates' court and one at the Crown Court; the defence sought to make a further application to the magistrates on the basis, *inter alia*, of a new set of possible conditions. The magistrates ruled that the possibility of new conditions did not amount to a change of circumstances and that the revised conditions could have been put before the court on a previous occasion; accordingly, they refused to hear the application. This refusal was quashed by the Divisional Court. Wilkie J referred to part IIA and said (at [9]) that the: **D7.72**

> ... effect of this is that the court is obliged to entertain two bail applications regardless of whether the arguments put forward in the second are arguments which have been advanced previously. But

> if those arguments are sought to be put forward a third time the court is not obliged to entertain them, though it may do so. But this only applies to the extent that arguments put forward as to fact or law are arguments which the court has heard previously.

He went on to say that this is almost invariably referred to as the 'change of circumstance' condition but that this phrase 'does not accurately reflect the statutory provisions'. Thus, the key question is whether the argument (of fact or law) was one which was put before the court on an earlier occasion, not whether it could have been put to the court previously.

Paragraph 2 does not state, as it might have done, that the accused is entitled to two fully argued bail applications. It merely provides that, *at the first hearing* after the accused was refused bail, an application for bail may be supported with any argument of fact or law, regardless of whether it was previously advanced. Thus, on a literal interpretation of para. 2, if an accused chooses not to make a bail application on the occasion of the first appearance and is accordingly remanded in custody, a fully-argued application may be made at the next appearance but, if that application fails, no further argued application may be made unless it includes matters which have not previously been placed before the court. It follows that an accused seeking bail who wants two opportunities to do so in the magistrates' court should make applications on both the first and second remand appearances.

In *Calder Justices, ex parte Kennedy* (1992) 156 JP 716, the Divisional Court held that a decision under sch. 1, part I, para. 5 (that it has not been practicable to obtain sufficient information whether to grant bail) is not a decision not to grant bail, since the justices are merely saying that they are not in a position to decide the question of bail. It does not therefore count for the purposes of para. 2 of part IIA of sch. 1.

In *Dover and East Kent Justices, ex parte Dean* (1992) 156 JP 357, D made no bail application on his first appearance and consented to be remanded in his absence for three weeks under the MCA 1980, s. 128 (see **D5.37**). D appeared before the justices at the end of that period and wished to make a bail application, but the magistrates ruled that he was not entitled to make an application . The Divisional Court held that the occasions when he had been remanded in his absence were not 'hearings' for the purpose of para. 2, and so he had a right to make a bail application when he came before the justices at the end of the period of remand by consent.

Where the accused has exhausted the automatic entitlement of fully-argued applications but claims that a new consideration has arisen which was not placed before the court on the earlier occasions, para. 3 could be construed merely as obliging the court to hear the argument of fact or law not previously advanced, rather than obliging it to reopen the entire question of bail. It is submitted, however, that to consider only the new matter(s) in isolation from the other arguments for bail would be an artificial exercise, and that the identifying of a new consideration relevant to bail should entitle the accused to make a further full bail application in which both the fresh and the old arguments may be relied on.

It must also be borne in mind that para. 3 merely states that, at the third and subsequent remand hearings, the court 'need not' hear arguments which it has heard previously. It therefore does not debar the court from entertaining yet another fully-argued application, but gives it a discretion to hear a further bail application even in the absence of fresh information.

Care must be taken by the court in expressing the reason for the refusal of bail where para. 3 is applicable. Since in theory the court is obliged to consider bail each time an accused who is entitled to the benefit of the BA 1976, s. 4(1), appears before it in custody, it is unwise for the magistrates simply to say that they were not prepared to consider the matter of bail. It is more appropriate to say: 'As there is no new material before us relevant to the question of bail, bail will be refused'. This avoids giving the impression that they have simply refused to consider the question (per Ormrod LJ in *Slough Justices, ex parte Duncan* (1982) 75 Cr App R 384 at p. 389).

Extending Bail in the Absence of the Accused

The MCA 1980, s. 129(1), applies if the court is satisfied that, on the day to which the accused was remanded, he or she is unable to attend 'by reason of illness or accident'. It may then remand the accused again in his or her absence. Notwithstanding s. 128(6), a remand in custody under s. 129(1) may exceed eight clear days. Section 129(1) applies regardless of whether the remand is in custody or on bail. Thus, if an accused remanded in custody on an earlier occasion is ill in prison and will not be well enough to attend court for several weeks, the magistrates may extend the period of the remand until such time as a recovery is likely. **D7.73**

By contrast with s. 129(1), s. 129(3) applies only if the accused has been remanded on bail. The subsection permits the court to appoint, in the absence of the accused, a later time as the time at which the accused is to appear. The appointment of the new time is deemed to be a further remand (s. 129(3)). This power is useful when unforeseen developments mean that the case will not be able to proceed on the date to which it was originally adjourned. By agreement between the court and the parties, a new date can be fixed without the necessity for the accused appearing. The power is also useful when the accused fails to appear on the date to which the accused was bailed but an acceptable explanation for this non-appearance is put before the court. Instead of issuing an arrest warrant, the magistrates may simply adjourn and enlarge bail in the absence of the accused.

Whenever bail is extended under either s. 129(1) or (3), the recognizances of the sureties may be correspondingly 'enlarged' to secure the accused's appearance on the new date (s. 129(2)(a) and (3)(a)).

The powers conferred by the MCA 1980, s. 129, should be distinguished from the power under s. 128(3A) to remand an accused in custody on up to three consecutive occasions without being brought before the court if the accused has consented not to be produced (see **D5.33**).

STATING AND RECORDING DECISIONS ABOUT BAIL

Section 5 of the BA 1976 imposes a number of requirements about the giving and recording of decisions about bail and the reasons for those decisions. **D7.74**

Duty to Make a Record of the Decision

Where a court grants bail, or withholds bail from someone to whom the BA 1976, s. 4, applies, or appoints a different time or place for a person granted bail to surrender to custody, or varies any conditions of bail or imposes conditions in respect of bail, it must make a record of the decision. The accused is entitled to a copy of the record on request (BA 1976, s. 5(1)). **D7.75**

Reasons for Decisions relating to Bail

Where a magistrates' court or the Crown Court: (a) withholds bail from an accused prima facie entitled to bail under the BA 1976, s. 4, or (b) imposes conditions on the grant of bail to such a person, or varies conditions that have previously been imposed, it must give reasons for withholding bail or, as the case may be, imposing or varying conditions of bail (BA 1976, s. 5(3)). The purpose of the giving of reasons is to enable the accused to consider making an application for bail (or for the variation or removal of conditions of bail) to another court. A note of the reasons must be included in the record of the court's decision (s. 5(4)). The accused must be given a copy of the note (s. 5(4)), unless the decision was taken by the Crown Court and the accused is legally represented, in which case a copy need be provided only if the legal representative so requests (s. 5(5)). It should be noted that the obligation to give reasons under s. 5(4) arises only if the accused has the benefit of the presumption of bail conferred by s. 4. If, for example, bail pending appeal is refused to a person summarily convicted and given a custodial sentence, the court is not required by the BA 1976 to explain the refusal, since the case falls outside s. 4. **D7.76**

In *R (Rojas) v Snaresbrook Crown Court* [2011] EWHC 3569 (Admin), the Divisional Court considered the duty under s. 5(3) to give reasons for withholding bail. Holman J said (at [21]) that such reasons had to 'extend to a minimum reasonable level of adequacy, and had to identify the ground or grounds upon which the court was satisfied that bail should now be refused, and with a minimum level of adequacy identify the case specific reasons for being so satisfied'. In *R (Fergus) v Southampton Crown Court* [2008] EWHC 3273 (Admin), Silber J (at [21]) said that the reason for withholding bail 'must relate to the facts. Such a reason must be more than merely reciting that one of the statutory grounds has been made out. The underlying facts have to be put forward.' In other words, the factual basis for holding that one or more of the statutory grounds for withholding bail has been substantiated must be articulated clearly.

Reasons for Granting Bail

D7.77 Where a magistrates' court or the Crown Court grants bail to a person to whom the BA 1976, s. 4, applies after hearing representations from the prosecutor in favour of withholding bail, it must give reasons for its decision (s. 5(2A)), and those reasons must be included in the record of the court's decision, a copy of which must be given to the prosecutor if requested (s. 5(2B)).

Certificates of Full Argument

D7.78 Section 5(6A) to (6C) of the BA 1976 deal with certificates of full argument. Section 5(6A) applies where a magistrates' court adjourns a case under the PCC(S)A 2000, s. 11, or the CDA 1998, s. 52(5), or the MCA 1980, s. 10, 17C, 18 or 24C, and remands the accused in custody after hearing a fully-argued bail application (s. 5(6A)(a)). In such a case, the court must issue a certificate confirming that full argument was heard if either the court has not previously heard full argument on a bail application made by the accused in the proceedings in question, or it has previously heard such argument but is satisfied that there has been a change in circumstances or that new considerations have been placed before it (s. 5(6A)(b)). In a case where the court has heard a second or subsequent fully argued application on the basis of a change in circumstances or new considerations, the certificate must state what the change was (s. 5(6B)). The accused must be given a copy of the certificate (s. 5(6C)). The significance of the issue of a certificate of full argument is that the right to apply to the Crown Court for bail is dependent on it (Senior Courts Act 1981, s. 81(1)(g) and (1J)).

It should be noted that an adjournment during a summary trial (under the MCA 1980, s. 10) includes an adjournment for reports after conviction, so the obligation to issue a certificate may arise if the accused is remanded in custody at that stage. Moreover, the obligation to issue a certificate also applies where bail is refused on an adjournment under the PCC(S)A 2000, s. 11, for medical reports.

Informing Unrepresented Accused of Right to Apply to Crown Court

D7.79 Where a magistrates' court withholds bail and sends an unrepresented accused for trial to the Crown Court or issues a certificate under s. 5(6A), the accused must be informed of the right to apply to the Crown Court for bail (BA 1976, s. 5(6)).

OPTIONS OPEN TO AN ACCUSED REMANDED IN CUSTODY OR ON CONDITIONAL BAIL BY MAGISTRATES

D7.80 An accused who has been refused bail by a magistrates' court may apply for bail to the Crown Court. An appeal can also be made against a decision of a magistrates' court to impose conditions on bail.

Appeal to the Crown Court

D7.81 The right to apply to the Crown Court for bail is contained in the Senior Courts Act 1981, s. 81(1) (see **D27.17**). Section 81(1)(g) provides that the Crown Court may grant bail to any person who has been remanded in custody by a magistrates' court on adjourning a case under the PCC(S)A 2000, s. 11, or the CDA 1998, s. 52(5), or the MCA 1980, s. 10, 17C, 18 or 24C. However, s. 81(1J) provides that the Crown Court may grant bail under s. 81(1)(g) only if the magistrates' court which remanded the accused in custody has certified (under the BA 1976, s. 5(6A)) that it 'heard full argument on his application for bail before it refused the application'. The right to apply to the Crown Court is thus dependent on a fully-argued application having been made before the magistrates. Where a fully-argued bail application is refused by magistrates, the defence should therefore obtain a certificate of full argument from the court which may then be used to permit a further application to the Crown Court.

If the Crown Court confirms the refusal of bail, it may be possible (in exceptional cases) for the accused to seek judicial review of that decision (see **D7.89**).

An accused who has been sent for trial under the CDA 1998, s. 51 or 51A, may apply to the Crown Court for bail by virtue of s. 81(1)(a) of the 1981 Act, which empowers the Crown Court to grant bail to any person who has been sent in custody to appear before it. At this stage, there is no need to rely on a certificate of full argument.

Appeal against Imposition of Conditions

The CJA 2003, s. 16(1), enables an accused to appeal to the Crown Court against the imposition of certain bail conditions, namely those set out in s. 16(3), that the person concerned: **D7.82**

(a) resides away from a particular place or area,
(b) resides at a particular place other than a bail hostel,
(c) has to provide a surety or sureties, or security,
(d) remains indoors between certain hours,
(e) is to be subject to an electronic monitoring requirement under the BA 1976, s. 3(6ZAA), or
(f) makes no contact with another person.

The right of appeal under s. 16 can be exercised only if the accused has previously made an application to the magistrates (under the BA 1976, s. 3(8)(a): see **D7.136**) for the conditions to be varied or if the conditions were imposed following an application by the prosecution under the BA 1976, s. 3(8)(b) or s. 5B(1) (s. 16(4), (5) and (6)). Once the Crown Court has disposed of the appeal, no further appeal can be brought under s. 16 unless an application or further application under the BA 1976, s. 3(8)(a), is made to the magistrates' court after the appeal (s. 16(8)).

PROCEDURE FOR BAIL APPLICATIONS IN THE CROWN COURT

Notice of Appeal

CrimPR 14.8 (see Supplement, **R14.8**) applies when the accused wants to apply to the Crown Court for bail after bail has been withheld by a magistrates' court or to appeal to the Crown Court after a magistrates' court has refused an application by the accused (under the BA 1976, s. 3(8)(a)) to vary a condition of bail (r. 14.8(1)). Written notice of the intention to make the application must be given to the magistrates' court, the Crown Court and the prosecutor (and any surety affected or proposed) as soon as reasonably practicable after the decision of the magistrates' court (r. 14.8(2)). The notice must explain why bail should not be withheld, or why the condition of bail under appeal should be varied (as the case may be), should identify any further information or legal argument that has become available since the decision of the magistrates' court and, where it is an application for bail, should attach a copy of the certificate that the magistrates heard full argument as to bail (r. 14.8(3)). **D7.83**

If the prosecution oppose the application, they must notify the Crown Court and the accused at once, and must serve notice of the reasons for opposing the application (r. 14.8(5)).

Unless the Crown Court directs otherwise, the application or appeal should be heard no later than the business day after notice of the application or appeal was served (r. 14.8(6)).

The Hearing

D7.84 The application may be heard in public or in private (CrimPR 14.2(2): see Supplement, **R14.2**); however, such applications are often heard in private. The application will be heard by a circuit judge or recorder. The hearing follows the pattern of a bail application in the magistrates' court, with counsel for the prosecution summarising the objections to bail and counsel for the applicant responding to those objections.

If bail is granted to an accused who was refused it by magistrates at a remand hearing, the Crown Court may direct the accused to appear 'at a time and place which the magistrates' court could have directed' and the recognizance of any surety shall be conditioned accordingly (Senior Courts Act 1981, s. 81(1H)). Any sureties required by the Crown Court may enter into their recognizances before, *inter alia*, an officer of the Crown Court, a police officer who is either in charge of a police station or of the rank of inspector or above, or the governor of the prison where the accused is presently detained (BA 1976, s. 8(4); CrimPR 14.14(3)(b): see Supplement, **R14.14**).

D7.85 When considering whether a bail application should be heard in public, the Crown Court should apply the principles laid down in *R (Malik) v Central Criminal Court* [2006] EWHC 1539 (Admin), [2007] 1 WLR 2455. The court must start from the 'fundamental presumption in favour of open justice' (per Gray J at [40]). The court must therefore consider whether it is necessary, in the interests of justice, to depart from the ordinary rule of open justice. The judgment makes it clear that this is not an exercise of discretion (which implies a judicial choice between two or more equally proper courses), but of judgement as to whether a departure from the norm is justified (at [30]). It may, for example, be appropriate for the court to sit in private if the delay involved in arranging a public hearing would defeat the purpose of the application (at [31]). It may be in the interests of the accused for the bail application to be heard in private, e.g., (a) where the prosecution need to rehearse a damaging case against the accused; (b) where the prosecution intend to give detailed reasons for fearing that the accused will not surrender if given bail; (c) where the accused's previous convictions will be referred to; (d) where it will or may be necessary to reveal personal and confidential information about the accused or about prosecution witnesses or others; and (e) where the court may need to be told about information which has been provided to the prosecuting authorities by the accused or by someone else connected with the case (at [33]). Gray J added that it does not follow that bail applications must be listed and called on in open court and then adjourned to the judge's chambers only if a case is made for doing so. He said that there is nothing objectionable in listing bail applications on the provisional assumption that the interests of justice call for a closed hearing, so long as any application to sit in public is acceded to unless there is a sound reason for excluding the public. Such an application will ordinarily come from one or both of the parties, but it may also legitimately come from the media or some other third party (at [35]). Another point which emerges from Malik is that, where the accused has legal representation, there is no right to be produced from prison for the purposes of a bail application. Gray J pointed out that the increasing use of video links between the court and the prison where the accused is detained effectively removes any disadvantage to the accused by reason of not being physically present when the application for bail is heard (at [38]). It is submitted that it follows from this that where no video link is available, a request for an accused to be produced should be looked on more favourably by the court.

The Coronavirus Act 2020, s. 54 and sch. 24, have made temporary modifications to the CDA 1998, ss. 57A to 57B and sch. 3A, to give the court power to direct 'live link' attendance at 'preliminary hearings'. Under the CDA 1998, s. 57B(8) and sch. 3A, para. 3, specific prohibitions and limitations on the power to direct attendance by live link apply to disputed bail hearings. For full details, see the Special Supplement, **D5.40B**.

Repeated Bail Applications in the Crown Court

D7.86 Part IIA of sch. 1 to the BA 1976 (see **D7.70**) applies to bail applications in the Crown Court just as it applies to applications before the magistrates. Therefore, if one application for bail has already been made to the Crown Court, a further argued application may not be presented unless there are fresh arguments or considerations to put before the court.

Application for Bail during the Crown Court Proceedings

CrimPD III, para. 14G.2 (see Supplement, **CPD.14G**), makes the point that, once the trial has begun, the grant of bail during adjournments (such as lunch-time or overnight) is a matter for the discretion of the trial judge (or magistrates, as the case may be). Paragraph 14G.3 states that an accused who was on bail before the trial should not be refused bail during the trial unless, in the opinion of the court, there are 'positive reasons' to justify such refusal. Two examples are given: (a) a point has been reached where there is a real danger that the accused will abscond, either because the case is going badly for the defence, or for any other reason, or (b) there is a real danger that the accused may interfere with witnesses, jurors or a co-accused. Paragraph 14G.4 states that, where the accused has been found guilty, the question of bail should be decided in the light of the gravity of the offence, any friction between co-accused, and the likely sentence. **D7.87**

BAIL BY THE HIGH COURT

Statutory Bail Jurisdiction of the High Court

There are a number of instances where the High Court has a statutory jurisdiction to grant bail: **D7.88**

(1) Under the CJA 1967, s. 22(1), the High Court may entertain an application for bail (or to vary bail conditions) if the accused is appealing by way of case stated against conviction (or sentence, although such appeals are rarely appropriate) and the magistrates have withheld bail or granted only conditional bail (see **D29.23**).
(2) Under the CJA 1948, s. 37, the High Court may also grant bail where the applicant:
   (a) is appealing to the High Court by way of case stated from a decision of the Crown Court (s. 37(1)(b)(i)) — in practice, this will be where an accused appeals from the magistrates' court to the Crown Court and then seeks to appeal to the High Court from the decision of the Crown Court (see **D29.37**);
   (b) is appealing from the Crown Court to the High Court by way of judicial review, seeking an order quashing the decision of the Crown Court (s. 37(1)(b)(ii)) — again this will be the case where the accused is challenging a decision of the Crown Court in its appellate capacity (see **D29.25**); and
   (c) has been convicted or sentenced by a magistrates' court and is appealing to the High Court by way of judicial review, seeking an order quashing the decision of the magistrates (s. 37(1)(d)).

Challenging Refusal of Bail by the Crown Court by Way of Judicial Review

The Senior Courts Act 1981, s. 29(3), excludes judicial review of the Crown Court 'in matters relating to trial on indictment'. However, in *R (M) v Isleworth Crown Court* [2005] EWHC 363 (Admin), Maurice Kay LJ (at [7]) said that 'a decision as to *bail at an early stage of criminal proceedings* [emphasis added] does not relate to trial on indictment as that expression has been interpreted in cases such as *R v Manchester Crown Court, ex parte DPP* (1994) 98 Cr App R 461', in that such a decision does not arise in the issue between the Crown and the accused formulated by the indictment (the test propounded in that case by Lord Browne-Wilkinson). It followed that the Divisional Court had jurisdiction to review a bail decision by the Crown Court. Having ruled that judicial review was available in such cases, Maurice Kay LJ went on to say (at [11]–[12]): **D7.89**

> ... I am in no doubt that it is a jurisdiction which we should exercise very sparingly indeed. ... The test must be on *Wednesbury* principles, but robustly applied and with this court always keeping in mind that Parliament has understandably vested the decision in judges in the Crown Court who have everyday experience of, and feel for, bail applications. Of course if bail were to be

> refused on a basis such as 'I always refuse in this type of case', or some other unjudicial basis, then this court would and should interfere.

Put another way, nothing short of 'irrationality' entitles the High Court to interfere (*R (Galliano) v Crown Court at Manchester* [2005] EWHC 1125 (Admin), per Collins J, at [11]). As Collins J said in *R (on the application of Wiggins) v Harrow Crown Court* [2005] EWHC 882 (Admin) (at [35]):

> What this Court [i.e. the Divisional Court] has to do is to decide whether in all the circumstances the decision made by the Crown Court judge was one which fell within ... the 'bounds of reasonableness' ... What matters is that the Court has to be persuaded that the decision was not one which the judge below was entitled to reach. That will very rarely be the position ...

The point was reiterated by Hooper LJ in *R (N) v Leeds Crown Court* [2005] EWHC 3352 (Admin), where his lordship said (at [16]) that:

> On review [of a decision to withhold bail] the Divisional Court's role is narrow. It is not for this court to decide for itself the matter afresh. This court will not interfere unless in all the circumstances the decision made by the Crown Court Judge was one which fell outside the bounds of reasonableness. The court has to be persuaded that the decision was not one which the judge below was entitled to reach. This will very rarely be the position.

In *R (Iqbal) v Canterbury Crown Court* [2020] EWHC 452 (Admin), the Divisional Court again made the point that what is required in such cases 'is the robust application of *Wednesbury* principles' (at [38]).

It should be noted that s. 29(3) of the 1981 Act does prevent a challenge by way of judicial review to a decision by a trial judge *during* a Crown Court trial to revoke the bail of the accused (*R (Uddin) v Leeds Crown Court* [2013] EWHC 2752 (Admin), [2014] 1 WLR 1742). Similarly, *AF v Crown Court at Kingston* [2017] EWHC 2706 (Admin), [2018] 1 Cr App R 32 (521) concerned an application for judicial review of the refusal of bail to a defendant who had been convicted in the Crown Court and had then been remanded in custody prior to being sentenced. The Divisional Court ruled that, because the decision to withhold bail was clearly related to trial on indictment, it had no jurisdiction. Holroyde LJ (at [26]) said that 'there can in my judgment be no doubt that a decision refusing bail between the jury's verdict and sentence in the Crown Court is a matter relating to trial on indictment'; judicial review was therefore precluded by the SCA 1981, s. 29(3).

However, there may be cases where judicial review can be granted despite s. 29(3). In *R (DPP) v Aylesbury Crown Court* [2017] EWHC 2987 (Admin), [2018] 1 Cr App R 22 (325), the Divisional Court was invited to consider an application for judicial review of a decision on a costs order in the context of proceedings on indictment. The court held that judicial review was possible, despite s. 29(3), if 'there is a jurisdictional error of sufficient gravity to take the case out of the jurisdiction of the Crown Court' (per Sharp LJ, at [7]). It is submitted that the same principle could apply where the challenge relates to bail.

D7.90 In *R (Shergill) v Harrow Crown Court* [2005] EWHC 648 (Admin), the Divisional Court said that a claim for judicial review of the decision of a Crown Court judge to refuse bail should be put before a judge of the Administrative Court or, in the vacation, the vacation judge. The judge may indicate that there is absolutely no chance that the decision would be overturned and reject it out of hand. Otherwise, the matter should then be heard orally as soon as possible, normally within 48 hours (with notice being given to the Crown Court and the prosecution). Secondly, it is essential that reasons given by a Crown Court judge for refusing bail are recorded so that, if any application for judicial review is made, the Administrative Court has a record of the reasons for refusal. Further guidance on procedure was given in *R (Allwin) v Snaresbrook Crown Court* [2005] EWHC 742 (Admin), where it was said that it will not generally be appropriate to grant bail on an interim application on the papers. The Administrative Court judge should direct an oral hearing within a day or two to determine the issue. If, at that hearing, the court is minded to review the Crown Court's decision, permission will be granted, all procedural requirements will be abridged, and the matter will be remitted to the Crown Court to formally grant bail. Such hearings will normally be dealt with by a single judge.

Where the High Court does quash a refusal of bail, it will normally remit the matter to the court below for the question of bail to be reconsidered. It will be rare for the High Court to substitute its own decision. In *R (R) v Snaresbrook Crown Court* [2011] EWHC 3569 (Admin), Holman J said (at [29]): **D7.91**

> If this court considers ... that there has been significant procedural error, it should remit the substantive issue of bail for reconsideration by the judge, who is currently conducting this case in the Crown Court, unless this court can properly conclude that no reasonable judge, properly directing himself, could have withdrawn or could now withdraw bail (subject to any appropriate conditions or varied conditions). If I am satisfied that not only this judge, but no judge acting reasonably and lawfully, could fail to grant bail (subject to any appropriate conditions), then it is no more than a waste of time and expense to remit the matter to the Crown Court. If, however, there is still room for a discretionary decision to withdraw bail, then that is a decision which should be made by the Crown Court judge, but after hearing submissions on behalf of the claimant and possibly the prosecution.

PROSECUTION APPLICATIONS RELATING TO BAIL

Prosecution Right of Appeal against Decision to Grant Bail

The Bail (Amendment) Act 1993 (see **D7.165**) confers upon the prosecution the right to appeal (i) to the Crown Court against a decision by a magistrates' court to grant bail (s. 1(1)), and (ii) to appeal to the High Court when the Crown Court grants bail other than in the context of an appeal against the grant of bail by a magistrates' court under s. 1(1) (s. 1(1B) and (1C)). **D7.92**

Under s. 1(1) to (3), this right is limited to cases where:

(a) the accused is charged with, or convicted of, an offence which is (or would be in the case of an adult) punishable by imprisonment; and
(b) the prosecution is conducted by or on behalf of the DPP (this includes prosecutions conducted by the CPS), or by a prosecutor specified in the schedule to the Bail (Amendment) Act 1993 (Prescription of Prosecuting Authorities) Order 1994 (SI 1994 No. 1438), which includes the SFO; the Department of Business, Energy and Industrial Strategy; and the Department for Work and Pensions; and a universal service provider within the meaning of the Postal Services Act 2011; and
(c) before bail was granted, the prosecution made representations that bail should not be granted.

Procedure

The Bail (Amendment) Act 1993 (see **D7.165**) and CrimPR 14.9 (see Supplement, **R14.9**) lay down the procedural requirements with which the prosecution must comply in order to exercise its right. First, they must give oral notice of appeal at the conclusion of the proceedings in which bail was granted, and before the accused is released from custody (s. 1(4) of the 1993 Act). In *Isleworth Crown Court, ex parte Clarke* [1998] 1 Cr App R 257, this requirement was held to be satisfied where notice was given to the court officer about five minutes after the court rose but before the accused had been released from custody. The Divisional Court held that a delay of five minutes or so, especially where an accused had not yet been released from custody, did not bring the case into a category in which it could be said that oral notice was not given at the conclusion of the proceedings. Moreover, since notice can properly be given to the court officer, it is not necessary that the justices should themselves be in court. **D7.93**

Following the oral notice of appeal, the accused must be remanded in custody until the appeal is determined or otherwise disposed of (s. 1(6)). The oral notice given under s. 1(4) must be confirmed in writing, served on the court and the accused within two hours after the conclusion of the proceedings (s. 1(5)); otherwise the appeal is deemed to be disposed of (s. 1(7)) and the accused will be released on bail on the terms on which it was granted by the court when it granted bail.

In *R (Jeffrey) v Warwick Crown Court* [2002] EWHC 2469 (Admin), the prosecutor served the written notice of appeal three minutes late. The Divisional Court held that Parliament did not intend that the time-limit for serving notice of appeal should defeat an appeal if the prosecution had given itself ample time to serve the notice within the two-hour period, had used due diligence to serve the notice within that period, and the failure to do so was not the fault of the prosecution but was due to circumstances outside its control (per Hooper J at [11]). Furthermore, the Court said that the delay of three minutes had not caused D any prejudice, since he knew at the conclusion of the proceedings before the magistrates that the prosecution was exercising its right of appeal and he knew that he was being detained in custody as a result of the oral application for him to be remanded in custody until the appeal was disposed of (at [9]).

Jeffrey was followed in *R (Cardin) v Birmingham Crown Court* [2017] EWHC 2101 (Admin), [2018] 1 Cr App R 3 (50). D had been granted bail despite opposition from the prosecution; the prosecutor gave oral notice of an intention to appeal the granting of bail, and written notice of the intention to appeal the granting of bail was given to the court officer at the magistrates' court approximately an hour later. However, the written notice was not served on D because he had (in error) already been sent to the prison where he was to be held pending the disposal of the prosecution appeal against the grant of bail; attempts by the court to secure service of the notice on D at the prison were unsuccessful. The question to be decided was whether the Crown Court had jurisdiction to hear the appeal against the grant of bail to D, given that the notice of appeal had not been served on him. Andrews J (at [40]) described the question to be decided as 'whether s. 1(7) should be construed so as to deprive the appellate court of jurisdiction to reverse a decision by the magistrates to grant bail if the prosecution could not have served the defendant within the two hours, however hard it tried'. The Court ruled (at [46]) that:

> . . . it cannot have been Parliament's intention that the Crown should lose the opportunity to reverse a decision that was wrong in principle, with the result that a defendant who might abscond or commit further offences or interfere with prosecution witnesses was released on bail, if the reason why the notice of appeal was not served in time (or indeed at all) was outside the prosecution's control.

The Court (at [47]) based its conclusion in part on the use of the word 'fails' in s. 1(7):

> The word 'fails' in this context carries with it an implication of fault, and would not generally be used to describe the situation in which a person is unable to do something. One dictionary definition of 'fails' is 'to neglect to do something', and in our judgment that is the sense, rather than the wider sense of 'being unsuccessful in achieving one's goals', in which the word should be understood in this specific context.

The appeal must be heard (by the Crown Court or the High Court, as the case may be) within 48 hours, excluding weekends and public holidays (s. 1(8)). In *Middlesex Guildhall Crown Court, ex parte Okoli* [2001] 1 Cr App R 1 (1), the Divisional Court construed this as meaning that the appeal hearing must commence within two working days of the date of the decision to grant bail. The Court rejected the contention that the appeal had to commence literally within 48 hours of the moment upon which oral notice had been given.

D7.94 The appeal takes the form of a rehearing. The judge may remand the accused in custody or grant bail with or without conditions (s. 1(9)). The hearing may be in held in public or in private (CrimPR 14.2(2): see Supplement, **R14.2**). Under r. 14.2(1)(c), the accused is entitled to be present at the hearing of the appeal unless the court is satisfied that the accused has waived the right to attend or that it would be just to proceed in the absence of the accused. It is submitted that it will rarely be 'just' to proceed in the absence of an accused who wishes to be present. In *Allen v UK* (2010) 51 EHRR 22 (555), it was held that a refusal to allow the applicant to attend the hearing of the prosecution's appeal against bail being granted amounted to a breach of Article 5(4), mainly because the prosecution appeal against bail is regarded as a re-hearing of the application for bail; it followed that 'the applicant should have been afforded the same guarantees at the prosecution's appeal as at first instance'. It should be noted, however, that a person is to be treated as present in court when, by virtue of a live link direction, the person attends the hearing through a live link (see the CDA 1998, ss. 57A and 57B, at **D5.38**).

Although the MCA 1980, ss. 128, 128A and 129 (see **D5.31** ***et seq.***), do not directly bind the Crown Court, where the accused has not yet been sent to the Crown Court for trial, and the judge decides to remand the accused in custody, the judge must stipulate a date which is in accordance with the powers of the justices under those sections (*Re Szakal* [2000] 1 Cr App R 248, followed in *Remice v HMP Belmarsh* [2007] EWCA Crim 936, [2008] 1 Cr App R (S) 5 (23)).

Guidance on the Use of the Power of Prosecution Appeal Guidance issued by the CPS in their Legal Guidance Manual (www.cps.gov.uk/legal-guidance/bail) states that, in considering whether an appeal is appropriate, 'the key factor to consider is the level of risk posed to a victim, group of victims or the public at large'. **D7.95**

Prosecution Application for Reconsideration of Bail

Under the BA 1976, s. 5B, the prosecution can, in certain circumstances, apply for the grant of bail by a magistrates' court (or by a police officer) to be reconsidered (s. 5B(A1)). The power to make such an application is limited to indictable offences, including those that are triable either way (s. 5B(2)). Any application must be based on information which was not available to the court (or police officer) granting bail when the decision was taken (s. 5B(3)). **D7.96**

CrimPR 14.7 (see Supplement, **R14.7**) applies, *inter alia*, to an application by the prosecution to withdraw bail granted by a court, or to impose or vary a bail condition. The application must be in writing and must explain the reason for the application and identify the material information that has come to light since the most recent bail decision was made (r. 14.7(2)(a) and (3)(c)). The notice must be served on the accused and the court (and on any surety affected) not less than two business days before the hearing of the application (r. 14.7(2)(b) and (c)). Unless the court directs otherwise, an application to withdraw bail should be heard no later than the second business day after service of the notice, and an application to impose or vary a bail condition should be heard no later than the fifth business day after service of the notice (r. 14.7(6)). Where the application is for reconsideration of the grant of police bail, r. 14.6, which is in similar terms to r. 14.7, applies.

When an application is made by the prosecutor under the BA 1976, s. 5B, the court may vary the bail conditions, or impose conditions if the original grant of bail was unconditional, or withhold bail altogether (s. 5B(1)). In deciding what order to make, the court must act in accordance with the presumption in favour of bail contained in s. 4 and sch. 1 (s. 5B(4)). If the decision is to withhold bail and the accused is before the court, the accused will be remanded in custody. If not before the court, the accused must be ordered to surrender to custody (s. 5B(5)(b)) and is liable to arrest without warrant upon failure without reasonable cause to surrender to custody in accordance with the order (s. 5B(7)). A person who is arrested pursuant to s. 5B(7) must be taken before a magistrate within 24 hours (excluding Sundays), and the magistrate must remand the person in custody (s. 5B(8)).

Section 5B(8A) stipulates that, where the court refuses to withhold bail from the accused after hearing representations from the prosecutor in favour of withholding bail, the court must give reasons for refusing to withhold bail. Those reasons must be set out in the record of the court's decision, a copy of which must be given to the prosecutor if so requested (s. 5B(8C)).

FAILURE TO COMPLY WITH BAIL

Where an accused who has been granted bail in criminal proceedings fails to comply with the obligations imposed thereby, two main questions arise. The first is how the court should **D7.97** ensure that the accused will attend court for the remaining stages of the proceedings; the second is how the accused (and any sureties) will be dealt with in consequence of the breach of bail.

Powers of the Court when a Bailed Accused Fails to Appear

D7.98 When a person who is on bail fails to surrender to custody in answer to bail, the court has a number of options.

(1) The court may issue an arrest warrant (often called a 'bench warrant'), under the BA 1976, s. 7(1). This applies whatever court the accused was bailed to attend and regardless of whether bail was granted by the custody officer at the police station or by the court itself at an earlier hearing. The usual form of warrant simply orders that the accused be arrested and brought to court. However, at the court's discretion, the warrant may be 'backed for bail' (see **D7.99**), either with or without a requirement for sureties. Where the accused fails to appear, a bench warrant will normally be issued. It should be noted that the Justices' Clerks Rules 2005 (SI 2005 No. 545), sch. 1, para. 3, empowers a clerk to issue a warrant of arrest, whether or not endorsed for bail, for failure to surrender to court, where there is no objection on behalf of the accused.
(2) Instead of issuing a warrant, a magistrates' court may adjourn and extend the accused's bail under the MCA 1980, s. 129 (see **D7.73**). Similarly, the Crown Court, in appropriate cases, may simply order that the case be stood out of the list and take no further action in respect of the accused (who will remain under an obligation to attend whenever the case is next listed). Such a course of action is appropriate only where the court is satisfied that there is a good reason for the accused's non-attendance (e.g., a doctor's certificate has been sent to the court indicating that the accused is unfit to attend).
(3) It may be possible to proceed in the absence of the accused (though it should be borne in mind that if the offence is triable either way, a magistrates' court may try the case only with the consent of the accused, and that consent must be given at a hearing at which the accused is present unless the court is satisfied that there is a good reason for absence and the accused is represented by a lawyer who consents to summary trial on behalf of the accused: see **D6.9**).

D7.99 **Warrants Backed for Bail** Where the court decides to issue an arrest warrant, the warrant may be endorsed with a direction that the person named in it, having been arrested, shall then be released on bail (see the MCA 1980, s. 117, and the SCA 1981, s. 81(4), respectively, for the power of magistrates and the Crown Court). This is generally known as 'backing the warrant for bail'. Such warrants are, however, sometimes viewed as consuming a disproportionate amount of police time and effort in return for little or no advantage. A possible alternative to the issue of a warrant backed for bail where the accused fails to attend is to send a warning letter, directing the accused to attend on the date of the next hearing and warning of the consequences of non-attendance, namely that failure to attend the next hearing is likely to result in the court proceeding in the accused's absence or issuing a bench warrant that is not backed for bail.

D7.100 **Proof of Inability to Attend Court** CrimPD III, para. 14B.2 (see Supplement, **CPD.14B**), states that an accused who will be unable to attend court for medical reasons must supply the court with a certificate from a GP (or another appropriate medical practitioner, such as a hospital doctor) in advance of the hearing. Without a medical certificate, or if an unsatisfactory certificate is provided, the court is likely to consider that the accused has failed to surrender (para. 19B.3).

It should be noted that a medical certificate, in order to justify non-attendance at court, should *make it clear that the accused is unfit to* attend court. A certificate that the accused is unfit for work may not necessarily be accepted as evidence of unfitness to attend court (CrimPD I, para. 5C.4; see Supplement, **CPD.5C**).

Surrender to Custody

The power to issue a warrant under the BA 1976, s. 7(1), arises only if the accused fails to surrender to custody at the time appointed. In this context, 'surrendering to custody' merely connotes complying with whatever procedure is prescribed by the court for those answering to their bail: 'if a court provides a procedure which, by some form of direction, by notice or orally, instructs a person surrendering to bail to report to a particular office or to a particular official, when he complies with that direction he surrenders to his bail' (*DPP v Richards* [1988] QB 701, per Glidewell LJ at p. 711). Thus, if a court operates a system whereby persons on bail are required to report to an usher and are then allowed to wait in the court precincts until their case is called, a person who so reports has surrendered to custody. It follows that, if the accused subsequently goes away before the court is ready to deal with the case, the accused has not absconded within the meaning of s. 6, and so a warrant may *not* be issued under s. 7(1). However, this situation is covered by s. 7(2), which provides that, where a person who has been released on bail in criminal proceedings is absent from the court (without permission from the court) at any time after surrendering to custody but before the court is ready to begin or resume the hearing of the proceedings, the court may issue an arrest warrant. D7.101

In *Central Criminal Court, ex parte Guney* [1996] AC 616, the House of Lords held that, where an accused is formally arraigned in the Crown Court, the arraignment amounts to surrender to the custody of the court. The accused's further detention is therefore within the discretion and power of the judge and, unless the judge grants bail, the accused will remain in custody pending and during the trial. It also followed that the obligations of any surety are also extinguished at that point. In *Kent Crown Court, ex parte Jodka* (1997) 161 JP 638, the Divisional Court held that bail granted by magistrates ceases when the defendant surrenders to the custody of the Crown Court, whether or not the defendant is arraigned (i.e. enters a plea) at that hearing. It follows that the jurisdiction of the magistrates to grant bail does not extend beyond the first occasion on which a defendant surrenders to the Crown Court (*Choudhry v Birmingham Crown Court* [2007] EWHC 2764 (Admin), per Gibbs J at [33]).

In *Evans* [2011] EWCA Crim 2842, [2012] 1 WLR 1192, the Court of Appeal had to consider what amounts to surrender to custody in the Crown Court. Hughes LJ noted (at [15]) that 'what constitutes surrender has necessarily to vary to some extent according to the arrangements which are made for accepting surrender at any particular court'. His lordship (at [20]) summarised the practical effect of the decision of the House of Lords in *Guney* thus: 'once arraignment has taken place, however informal its particular circumstances may be, the court must review the question of bail and if a surety is involved direct a fresh taking of a recognizance... [W]henever else it may happen surrender is deemed to have taken place on arraignment.' His lordship went on to say (at [27]) that surrender is normally accomplished by way of entry into the dock. However, in the Crown Court, 'surrender may also be accomplished by the commencement of any hearing before the judge where the defendant is formally identified and whether he enters the dock or not'. Consequently, the Court rejected (at [28]) the suggestion that reporting to the usher amounts to surrender. The Court reasoned (at [29], [32] and [36]):

> ... in the absence of either stepping into the dock in a Crown Court or in such a court being formally identified for the purposes of hearing, the defendant has not put himself into anything which can properly be called 'custody'. Nor... has he overtly subjected himself to the directions of the court.
>
> ... once a defendant arrives at the Crown Court building he is in one sense not entirely at liberty to come and go as he wishes. That, however, does not... mean that he has thereby surrendered... [M]ere arrival at the Crown Court building does not constitute surrender and could not do so. The correct analysis seems to us to be not that he has surrendered but that he knows that he may be required at any moment to do so and in consequence he would be very unwise to wander away.
>
> ... in the absence of special arrangements either particular to the court or particular to the individual case, surrender to the Crown Court is accomplished when the defendant presents himself to

> the custody officers by entering the dock or where a hearing before the judge commences at which he is formally identified as present... [I]f there has been no previous surrender, as ordinarily there will have been, it is also accomplished by arraignment... [T]he position in the Magistrates' Court may be the same, but may easily differ...

Breach of Bail Conditions

D7.102 Under s. 7(3) of the BA 1976, where an accused has been bailed to attend a court, a police officer may arrest the accused without warrant prior to the surrender date if:

(a) the officer has reasonable grounds for believing that the accused is not likely to surrender to custody; or
(b) the officer has reasonable grounds for believing that the accused has broken, or is likely to break, any condition of bail; or
(c) a surety has given written notice to the police that the person bailed is unlikely to surrender to custody and for that reason the surety wishes to be relieved of any obligations.

Following arrest under s. 7(3), s. 7(4) stipulates that the person arrested must be brought before a magistrate as soon as practicable and, in any event, within 24 hours (excluding Sundays (s. 7(7)), and so a person arrested on a Saturday under s. 7(3) need not be brought before a magistrate until the following Monday). The wording of s. 7(4) makes it clear that the person arrested must be brought before a single justice (s. 7(4)(a)); the justice need not be sitting in a courtroom. Where, however, the accused is arrested under s. 7(3) within 24 hours of the time appointed for surrender to custody, the accused must be brought before the court at which surrender to custody should have taken place (s. 7(4)(b)).

In *Governor of Glen Parva Young Offender Institution, ex parte G* [1998] QB 877, D was arrested for breach of bail conditions. He was taken to the cells of a magistrates' court within 24 hours of arrest but was not brought before a magistrate until two hours after the expiry of the 24-hour time-limit. The Divisional Court held that the detention after 24 hours was unlawful, as s. 7(4) requires the defendant to be brought before a justice of the peace (not merely brought within the court precincts or to the court cells) within 24 hours of arrest. The importance of dealing with the accused within 24 hours was again emphasised in *R (Culley) v Crown Court sitting at Dorchester* [2007] EWHC 109 (Admin), where it was held that the time-limit under s. 7 is a strict one. It follows that the justice is required to complete the required investigation and decision-making in relation to the matter within the 24-hour period. If the justice fails to do so, the continued custody of the accused becomes unlawful from the moment the 24-hour period has expired. If the justice purports to remand the accused in custody after that time, the order is *ultra vires* and unlawful (per Forbes J at [20]).

D7.103 **Arrest Following Grant of Conditional Bail by the Crown Court** In *R (Ellison) v Teesside Magistrates' Court* [2001] EWHC Admin 11, the Divisional Court held that, where an accused has been sent for trial to the Crown Court, and is subsequently arrested for breach of a bail condition, the jurisdiction to deal with the accused under s. 7 of the BA 1976 must be exercised by a magistrate. Thus, the magistrate must deal with the matter; there is no power to commit the accused to the Crown Court to be dealt with. Lord Woolf CJ (at [9]) said that:

> The idea of remanding in custody to the Crown Court a defendant who breaches a condition of his bail so that the Crown Court can then deal with bail thereafter is misconceived. The appropriate course for the magistrates to take is to remand or commit the defendant to the Crown Court until his trial or further order. If the superior court wishes to grant bail, that can be done. Any order made by the superior court would then override the decision of the magistrates. But the making of an order to a fixed date (as was done in this case) was inappropriate.

It follows from this that, even after the accused has been sent to the Crown Court for trial, an alleged breach of a bail condition must be dealt with by a magistrate (since that is what is required under the BA 1976, s. 7(4)). If the magistrate finds that there has been no breach of a bail condition, the accused will remain on bail as before. If the magistrate finds that there has been a breach of bail, bail may be allowed to continue as before, or more stringent conditions may be imposed. If the magistrate finds that the accused has indeed breached a bail condition, and decides that the withholding of bail (as opposed to granting bail but on more onerous conditions) would be appropriate, the magistrate should revoke bail and remand the accused in custody until the date fixed for the trial or further order of the Crown Court. It is then open to the Crown Court to grant bail should the accused then apply for bail to the Crown Court.

Procedure where the Accused is Brought before the Court under s. 7 The question for a magistrate before whom a person is brought under the BA 1976, s. 7, is whether that person is likely to fail to surrender to custody, or else has broken or is likely to break any condition of bail (as the case may be). If of the opinion that any of those matters is established, the magistrate may remand the accused in custody (s. 7(5)). Alternatively, the magistrate may grant bail subject to different conditions. In most cases, where bail is granted under s. 7(5), more onerous conditions will be imposed. **D7.104**

The power to remand in custody under s. 7(5) is subject to the proviso contained in s. 7(5A). This applies where an accused who has attained the age of 18 was released on bail, and has not yet been convicted in the current proceedings. In such a case, a magistrate cannot withhold bail under s. 7 if it appears that there is 'no real prospect that the person will be sentenced to a custodial sentence in the proceedings'.

Where the magistrate is *not* of the opinion that the accused is likely to fail to surrender to custody or has broken, or is likely to break, a condition of bail, bail *must* be granted on the same conditions (if any) as were originally imposed.

Nature of a s. 7 Inquiry In *R (Hussain) v Derby Magistrates' Court* [2001] EWHC Admin 507, [2001] 1 WLR 2454, it was confirmed that there is no need for the court to hear evidence; instead it can base its decision on representations from the prosecution and the defence. Likewise, in *R (Thomas) v Greenwich Magistrates' Court* [2009] EWHC 1180 (Admin), Hickinbottom J ruled that, in considering whether the accused has broken any condition of bail, a justice is entitled to rely upon hearsay material, so long as the material is properly evaluated. **D7.105**

In *R (Vickers) v West London Magistrates' Court* [2003] EWHC 1809 (Admin), D was arrested and brought before the justices for failing to comply with the bail conditions. He sought to raise a defence of reasonable excuse; however, the justices ruled that no such defence exists under the BA 1976, s. 7. Gage J (at [16]–[18]) held that s. 7(5) requires a two-stage approach. First, the justice must determine whether there has been a breach of a bail condition (if there has been no breach of a condition, then the accused is entitled to be granted bail on precisely the same conditions as before); secondly, if there has been a breach, the justice is obliged to consider whether or not the bailed person should be granted bail again. In carrying out the first stage of that process, the justice must act fairly and give the accused a chance to answer the allegation of breach. That does not, however, include an inquiry as to whether the arrested person had any reasonable excuse for breaching bail (since s. 7 makes no mention of such a defence and, indeed, s. 7 does not create a criminal offence). The second stage (assuming that the justice is satisfied that there has been a breach) is the point at which the reasons for the breach of bail become relevant. At that stage, the justice must consider all the issues relating to 'reasonable excuse' when deciding whether or not to grant bail. The breach of bail will be a factor, but only one factor, as to whether the bailed person is granted bail again.

Human Rights Issues and the Summary Procedure under s. 7 In *R (DPP) v Havering Magistrates' Court* [2001] 1 WLR 805, the Divisional Court considered s. 7 in the context of the ECHR, Articles 5 and 6. It held that Article 6 (the right to a fair trial) has no direct relevance where magistrates are exercising their judgement whether to remand a person in custody following breach of bail conditions, since s. 7 does not create any criminal offence. However, the Court went on to hold that Article 5 is directly relevant. Latham LJ summarised (at [35]) the effect of Article 5 and the relevant Strasbourg case law thus: 'where a decision is taken to deprive **D7.106**

somebody of his liberty, that should only be done after he has been given a fair opportunity to answer the basis upon which such an order is sought'. His lordship went on to hold that the procedure adopted under s. 7 is entirely compatible with the requirements of Article 5. These proceedings are, by their nature, emergency proceedings to determine whether or not a person, who had not been considered to present risks which would have justified a remand in custody in the first instance, did subsequently present such risks. When exercising the power to detain, the magistrate is not entitled to order detention by reason simply of the finding of a breach. The fact of a breach is evidence of a relevant risk arising, but it is no more than one of the factors which the magistrate must consider in exercising discretion. The magistrate is required to come to an honest and rational opinion on the material presented, that material not being restricted to admissible evidence in the strict sense. In doing so, the magistrate must bear in mind the consequences for the person arrested, namely the risk of loss of liberty, in the context of the presumption of innocence. The procedural task of the magistrate is to ensure that the person arrested has a full and fair opportunity to comment on, and answer, the material before the court; if that material includes evidence from a witness who gives oral testimony, there must be an opportunity to cross-examine. Likewise, if the person arrested wishes to give oral evidence, the person is entitled to do so (*R (DPP) v Havering Magistrates' Court* at [38]–[41]).

D7.107 **No Power to Adjourn Proceedings under s. 7** In *R (DPP) v Havering Magistrates' Court* [2001] 1 WLR 805, the Divisional Court confirmed that there is no power for magistrates to adjourn the hearing once a person has been brought before them under s. 7 of the BA 1976. Parliament has to be taken to have determined that there should be a swift and relatively informal resolution of the issues raised, and so the court must do its best to come to a fair conclusion on the relevant day; if it cannot do so, it will not be of the opinion that the relevant matters have been made out which could justify detention (per Latham LJ at [44]).

D7.108 **No Separate Offence under s. 7** It should be emphasised that the BA 1976, s. 7, merely confers a power of arrest. It does not create a separate offence (per Hobhouse J in *Rowland* (14 February 1991 unreported, CA), cited by Dyson LJ in *Gangar* [2008] EWCA Crim 2987 at [12]).

D7.109 **Breach of Bail Conditions as Contempt of Court** Failure to comply with conditions of bail can also amount to contempt of court, but that fact is of limited practical relevance. In *Ashley* [2003] EWCA Crim 2571, [2004] 1 WLR 2057, D was convicted of contempt of court, arising out of breaches of bail conditions. He had been released on bail subject to conditions that required him to surrender his passport and not to leave the country. He broke both conditions but returned to face trial on the appointed day. The Court of Appeal held that the purpose of placing restrictions on an individual's movement under the BA 1976 is to ensure attendance at trial. If the conduct breaching bail is known about at the time, that bail could be revoked. Furthermore, even though s. 7 does not itself create any offence, there may be cases where breach of a bail condition gives rise to a further offence (e.g., where witnesses are intimidated). In the present case, although D had breached bail conditions by leaving the country, he did return for his trial. It followed that the judge did not have power to deal with him by way of contempt of court.

Offence of Failure to Surrender

D7.110 The BA 1976, s. 6, creates the offence of absconding. Under s. 6(1), a person who has been released on bail and who fails, without reasonable cause, to surrender to custody, is guilty of an offence. The burden of showing reasonable cause is on the accused (s. 6(3)). Moreover, a person who had reasonable cause for failing to surrender on the appointed day nevertheless commits an offence by failing to surrender as soon after the appointed time as is reasonably practicable (s. 6(2)). It follows that an accused who has a reasonable excuse for failing to attend court must surrender to custody as soon as reasonably practicable after that excuse ceases to apply (and commits an offence under s. 6 if not). The meaning of 'surrendering to custody' in s. 6(1) and (2) is considered at **D7.101**).

An offence under s. 6(1) or (2) is 'punishable either on summary conviction or as if it were a criminal contempt of court' (s. 6(5)). An offender summarily convicted of an offence under s. 6 is liable to imprisonment for up to three months and/or a fine of any amount (s. 6(7)). A magistrates' court which has convicted the offender of a s. 6 offence may commit the offender to the Crown Court for sentence if either it considers that the offence merits greater punishment than it has power to inflict, or it is sending the offender for trial to the Crown Court for another offence and it considers that the Crown Court should deal with the absconding as well (s. 6(6)). An offender who is committed to the Crown Court for sentence, or who is dealt with in the Crown Court as if guilty of a criminal contempt, is liable to imprisonment for up to 12 months and/or an unlimited fine (s. 6(7)). **D7.111**

In *Scott* [2007] EWCA Crim 2757 D arrived at court over half an hour late, because he had overslept. The defence argued that this was *de minimis*, and that no Bail Act offence should have been put to him. The Court of Appeal rejected this argument, holding that 'the mere fact that a defendant is only slightly late cannot afford him a defence' (per Toulson LJ at [14]). His lordship added (at [15]) that, even accepting, for the sake of argument, the possibility that there could be circumstances where an accused's late arrival at court was so truly marginal that it would be '*Wednesbury* unreasonable' to pursue it, that would be a rare case. His lordship explained this approach (at [16]–[17]): **D7.112**

> Even if a delay is small it can still cause inconvenience and waste of time. If a culture of lateness is tolerated the results can be cumulative and bad for the administration of justice. If the message given to this appellant had been that being half-an-hour late did not really matter, it would have been the wrong message to him and to other people ... It was submitted that it was disproportionate and draconian that it should now be on his record that he failed to surrender at the appointed time. Why so? It is a matter of fact he did fail to attend at the appointed time. It was submitted that this could have an unduly harsh effect in the future because another court might refuse him bail. If the message received by defendants is that a failure to answer to their bail on time may have an adverse effect on obtaining bail in future, we cannot see this as a cause for complaint.

Procedure for Prosecuting Offences under the Bail Act 1976, s. 6 The BA 1976, s. 6(5), provides that an offence under s. 6(1) or (2) is punishable either on summary conviction or as if it were a criminal contempt of court. However, in *Lubega* (1999) 163 JP 221, the Court of Appeal confirmed that s. 6(5) did not have the effect of converting an offence under the Act to a contempt of court. It followed that the judge was not entitled to deal with the matter in the same way as an ordinary contempt of court. **D7.113**

The procedure to be followed under the BA 1976, s. 6, is set out in CrimPD III, paras. 14C.1 to 14C.8 (see Supplement, **CPD.14C**). An accused who has absconded after being granted bail by a court should normally be brought, as soon as appropriate after arrest, before the court at which the proceedings in respect of which bail was granted are to be heard (para. 14C.3). There is no requirement to apply for a summons or to issue a written charge and requisition. It is regarded as more appropriate that the court itself should initiate the proceedings by its own motion, although the prosecutor may invite the court to take proceedings (para. 14C.4). Where the court initiates proceedings (with or without an invitation from the prosecutor), the prosecutor is expected to assist the court, for example by cross-examining the accused (para. 14C.7). In practice, many magistrates' courts informally ask absconders or their legal representative the reason for the non-appearance. If the explanation seems prima facie satisfactory, the bench indicates that no further action is necessary; otherwise the charge is put to the accused. Where a bench, on the occasion of an absconder's first appearance after absconding, indicates, albeit informally, that no charge need be preferred, that decision is binding on subsequent benches (*France v Dewsbury Magistrates' Court* (1988) 152 JP 301).

Where bail was granted by a magistrates' court on sending the accused to the Crown Court for trial or sentence, the trial for the Bail Act offence should take place in the Crown Court. The Crown Court judge will sit alone, without a jury (*Schiavo v Anderton* [1987] QB 20, at p. 34A). **D7.114**

CrimPD III, para. 14C.5, states that the court should not, without good reason, adjourn proceedings under s. 6 until the conclusion of the proceedings in respect of which bail was granted; rather, the court should deal with the bail matter 'as soon as is practicable' (taking into account when the proceedings in respect of which bail was granted are expected to conclude, the seriousness of the offence for which the defendant is already being prosecuted, the type of penalty that might be imposed for the Bail Act offence and the original offence, and any other relevant circumstances).

A certified copy of the record made under the BA 1976, s. 5(1), of the granting of bail is evidence of the time and place at which the accused should have surrendered. The court file will show whether the accused did in fact surrender. Thus, although it is in theory possible for the prosecution to call the evidence of absconding, the basic facts will usually be established from court documents. The prosecution's role is therefore essentially one of testing in cross-examination any reason put forward by the accused to explain the non-appearance.

D7.115 Failure to Answer Police Bail When the accused has absconded after being granted police bail, the decision whether to initiate proceedings under the BA 1976, s. 6, will be taken by the police and/or the CPS (CrimPD III, para. 14C.1: see Supplement, **CPD.14C**); the offence should be dealt with on the first appearance after arrest, unless an adjournment is necessary (para. 14C.2). The prosecutor will conduct the proceedings and, if the accused denies absconding, will call the evidence to prove the case (para. 14C.7). Failure to answer police bail is dealt with by commencement of proceedings in the usual way, using the written charge and requisition procedure, under s. 6(11). Section 6(10) disapplies the MCA 1980, s. 127 (which prevents summary proceedings from being instituted more than six months after the commission of an offence), in respect of offences under the BA 1976, s. 6: instead s. 6(12) to (14) provide that such an offence may not be tried unless proceedings are commenced either within six months of the commission of the offence, or within three months of the date when the defendant surrenders to custody, or is arrested in connection with the offence for which bail was granted, or appears in court in respect of that offence. This ensures that a defendant cannot escape prosecution under s. 6 merely by absconding for more than six months.

D7.116 Reasonable Excuse The offence under the BA 1976, s. 6, is made out only if the court finds that the accused did not have a 'reasonable cause' for failing to surrender to custody. It follows that it is imperative that the accused be given the opportunity to put forward an explanation for the non-attendance. In *Davis* (1986) 8 Cr App R (S) 64, it was said that the court should give the accused an opportunity to explain, and invite submissions from counsel; an unrepresented accused should be given the chance to apply for legal representation or, at the very least, be given the fullest possible opportunity of offering some excuse (if any) for the non-attendance. In *Boyle* [1993] Crim LR 40, Steyn LJ said that it is necessary to invite counsel to call evidence on the s. 6 charge; if counsel does not wish to call evidence, he or she should be invited to address the judge on the question of guilt or otherwise. The judge should then announce the finding and, if it be a finding of guilt, should give reasons at that stage. If there is a finding of guilt, the judge should then invite counsel to address the question of mitigation and only then should the judge impose a sentence.

Being mistaken about the day on which one should have appeared was held in *Laidlaw v Atkinson* (1986) *The Times*, 2 August 1986 not to amount to a reasonable cause.

A medical certificate will usually provide the accused with sufficient evidence to defend a charge of failure to surrender, but it should be noted that the court is not absolutely bound by a medical certificate and may require the medical practitioner who issued it to give evidence or the court may exercise its discretion to disregard a certificate it finds to be unsatisfactory (CrimPD I, para. 5C.3: see *Supplement*, ***CPD.5C***).

D7.117 Sentencing Council Guidelines Definitive guidelines for failure to surrender to bail are to be found in the Sentencing Council's guideline, *Breach Offences* (see Supplement, **SG15-1**).

Failure to surrender which represents a 'deliberate attempt to evade or delay justice' is the most serious category of culpability; the lowest category of culpability is where the reason for the failure to surrender is just short of amounting to reasonable cause. Failure to attend a Crown Court hearing resulting in substantial delay and/or interference with the administration of justice is the most serious category of harm; failure to attend a magistrates' court hearing with that result is the middle category of harm; cases where the non-attendance does not result in substantial delay and/or interference with the administration of justice are in the lowest category of harm. The aggravating features identified in the guideline include a history of breaches of court orders or police bail and distress caused to victims and/or witnesses. The mitigating factors specifically identified are: genuine misunderstanding of bail or its requirements, prompt voluntary surrender, and the accused being sole or primary carer for a dependent relative.

CrimPD III, para. 14C.9 (see Supplement, **CPD.14C**) says that the offence under s. 6 'stands apart from the proceedings in respect of which bail was granted. The seriousness of the offence can be reflected by an appropriate and generally separate penalty being imposed for the Bail Act offence.' CrimPD III, para. 14C.10, goes on to state that, where the appropriate penalty is a custodial sentence, consecutive sentences should be imposed unless there are circumstances that make this inappropriate. **D7.118**

Moreover, the Court of Appeal in *White* [2002] EWCA Crim 2952, [2003] 2 Cr App R (S) 29 (133) held that there is no principle of law that the sentence for failing to surrender to custody should be proportionate to the sentence for the substantive offence of which the accused stands convicted. Indeed, it pointed out that in *Neve* (1986) 8 Cr App R (S) 270, a sentence of six months' imprisonment for failing to surrender to custody was upheld, even though the accused had been acquitted of the substantive offence.

In *Hourigan* [2003] EWCA Crim 2306, the Court of Appeal made the point that it is inappropriate for a judge in the Crown Court to impose a sentence of less than five days' imprisonment for an offence under s. 6, having regard to the fact that the MCA 1980, s. 132, prohibits magistrates from imposing sentences of less than five days' imprisonment. **D7.119**

Relationship between the BA 1976, ss. 6 and 7

In *Evans* [2011] EWCA Crim 2842, [2012] 1 WLR 1192, D's advocate in the Crown Court went into the courtroom where the case was likely to be heard and told the usher that D was in the building. D later walked out of the building and did not return. When his case was called on, he was not there, and a bench warrant for his arrest was issued. He was subsequently dealt with for the offence of failing to surrender to bail, contrary to the BA 1976, s. 6(1). Hughes LJ (at [9]–[11]) noted that the Act distinguishes between two situations: first, where an accused is on bail but fails without reasonable excuse to surrender to custody (defined in s. 2(2) as 'surrendering himself into the custody of the court... at the time and place for the time being appointed for him to do so'); secondly, where an accused has surrendered to bail but then is absent from the court before the hearing either begins or resumes, as the case may be. The first situation constitutes an offence under s. 6(1); the second situation, however, does not, but the court may issue a warrant for the accused's arrest under s. 7(2). His lordship observed that the second situation would fall within the common-law offence of escape (*Rumble* [2003] EWCA Crim 770). **D7.120**

Consequences for Sureties when Accused Absconds

If an accused who has been granted bail subject to the provision of one or more sureties fails to surrender at the appointed time, there is a presumption that the court will order forfeiture of the recognizance(s) (i.e. order the sureties to pay the amounts which they had promised to pay). The court does, however, have a discretion, in exceptional circumstances, to order that the surety pay less than the full sum or even to order that none of the sum promised should in fact be forfeited. **D7.121**

The power to forfeit recognizances which relate to the accused appearing in a magistrates' court is contained in the MCA 1980, s. 120(1) and (1A). Section 120(1A)(a) provides that if the accused fails to appear in court, the court 'shall ... declare the recognizance to be forfeited'. The word 'shall' connotes a duty rather than mere power. However, having declared the automatic forfeiture of any recognizance entered into by a surety, the court is required to issue a summons to the surety to appear before it (unless, of course, already present) to explain why the sum should not be paid (s. 120(1A)(b)). If the surety fails to answer the summons, the court has the discretion to proceed in the surety's absence, provided it is satisfied that the summons has been correctly served (s. 120(1A)). The MCA 1980, s. 120(3), provides that the court may, instead of requiring the surety to pay the whole sum that was promised, require payment of only part of that sum or may remit the sum altogether.

There is no express provision for forfeiture of recognizances which relate to the accused appearing in the Crown Court. It is clear from case law, however, that the Crown Court is to be regarded as having the power to order the forfeiture of a recognizance.

Forfeiture of a recognizance given by a surety, whether in respect of appearance by the accused in a magistrates' court or the Crown Court, is dealt with by CrimPR 14.15 (see Supplement, **R14.15**), which requires the court to serve notice on the surety (and on the accused and the prosecution) of the hearing at which the court will consider forfeiture of the recognizance, and stipulates that forfeiture must not be ordered within five business days of the service of the notice.

Principles Governing Forfeiture of Surety

D7.122 The principles governing forfeiture of a surety's recognizance have been set out in a number of cases, including *Southampton Justices, ex parte Green* [1976] QB 11, *Horseferry Road Stipendiary Magistrate, ex parte Pearson* [1976] 2 All ER 264 and *Crown Court at Wood Green, ex parte Howe* [1992] 1 WLR 702. Before making an order, the court should consider both the surety's means and the extent of the surety's responsibility for the accused's non-appearance, including any steps taken to ensure that the accused would surrender. However, there is a strong presumption that the surety should forfeit the full amount that was promised. As it was put in *Ex parte Pearson* at p. 514C:

> ... the surety has seriously entered into a serious obligation and ought to pay the amount which he or she has promised unless there are circumstances in the case, either relating to ... means or ... culpability, which make it fair and just to pay a smaller sum.

The authorities were reviewed extensively by McCullough J in *Uxbridge Justices, ex parte Heward-Mills* [1983] 1 All ER 530. His lordship then summarised their effect thus (at p. 62A–B):

> ... the more important principles to be derived from the authorities [are] as follows. (1) When a defendant for whose attendance a person has stood surety fails to appear, the full recognisance should be forfeited, unless it appears fair and just that a lesser sum should be forfeited or none at all. (2) The burden of satisfying the court that the full sum should not be forfeited rests on the surety and is a heavy one. It is for him to lay before the court the evidence of want of culpability and of means on which he relies. (3) Where a surety is unrepresented the court should assist him by explaining these principles in ordinary language, and giving him the opportunity to call evidence and advance argument in relation to them.

D7.123 **Want of Means** In both *Southampton Justices, ex parte Green* [1976] QB 11 and *Uxbridge Justices, ex parte Heward-Mills* [1983] 1 All ER 530, the orders for forfeiture were quashed because the magistrates had failed properly to take into account the surety's want of means. Nevertheless, the cases emphasise that the burden is on the surety to show impecuniosity. If a surety wishes to put forward evidence on the matter, the court is under a duty to consider it even if, when being accepted as surety, the surety had claimed to have the necessary funds (*Ex parte Heward-Mills*, at p. 63). However, there is no obligation on the court to initiate the inquiry (*Ex parte Heward-Mills*, at p. 63). Moreover, it is submitted that if a proper inquiry was conducted into the surety's means at the time the undertaking was accepted, the surety should be relieved from that obligation on financial grounds only if something unforeseen has arisen between then and the consideration of forfeiture which prevents that obligation being met. Otherwise the surety benefits from having misled the court which accepted the undertaking.

In *Leicestershire Stipendiary Magistrate, ex parte Kaur* (2000) 164 JP 127, the appellant had stood surety in the sum of £150,000. To pay that sum she would have had to sell the matrimonial home. Rose LJ, having reviewed the authorities, summarised the guiding principles thus:

1. Justices have a wide discretion under s. 120 whether to remit in whole or in part;
2. In exercising that discretion, they must plainly have regard only to the surety's assets. The assets of other persons are not assets which can properly be called upon to satisfy a surety's liability;
3. Want of culpability by a surety in the accused's failure to appear is not in itself a reason for not forfeiting or for remitting a recognisance. But there may be circumstances ... where the amount forfeited may be reduced because a culpable surety has made very considerable efforts to carry out his or her undertaking;
4. Regard may properly be had to a surety's share in the equity of a matrimonial home when a recognisance is being entered into;
5. When enforcement of a recognisance is being considered under s. 120, the means of the surety at that time is one of the factors to be considered and, at that stage, the impact on both the surety and on others, if the matrimonial home has to be sold to satisfy the recognisance, is a relevant factor when deciding whether to remit a recognisance in whole or in part.

Culpability According to *Warwick Crown Court, ex parte Smalley* [1987] 1 WLR 237, there is no requirement of proof that any blame attached to the surety for the accused's failure to surrender. The Divisional Court rejected the suggestion that there had to be some fault on the part of the surety for the recognizance to be forfeited. The authorities on this point were reviewed in *Reading Crown Court, ex parte Bello* [1992] 3 All ER 353. Parker LJ (at p. 363C–D) summarised the position as follows: **D7.124**

> The failure of the accused to surrender when required triggers the power to forfeit but the court, before deciding what should be done, must enquire into the question of fault. If it is satisfied that the surety was blameless throughout it would then be proper to remit the whole of the amount of the recognisance and in exceptional circumstances this would ... be the only proper course.

In *Maidstone Crown Court, ex parte Lever* [1995] 2 All ER 35, the Court of Appeal signalled a robust approach to the question of culpability. One of two sureties discovered that D had not been home for two nights. That surety telephoned the other surety and the police. Attempts by the police to apprehend D were unsuccessful. The judge ordered the first surety to forfeit £35,000 (out of a recognizance of £40,000) and the other £16,000 (out of a recognizance of £19,000). The Court of Appeal upheld this decision. Butler-Sloss LJ said (at p. 930) that 'the presence or absence of culpability is a factor but the absence of culpability ... is not in itself a reason to reduce or set aside the obligations entered into by the surety to pay in the event of a failure to bring the defendant to court'. The reason for the adoption of a fairly strict approach to the forfeiture of recognizances was set out by Butler-Sloss LJ at p. 931, where her ladyship quotes from Lord Widgery CJ in *Southampton Justices, ex parte Corker* (1976) 120 SJ 214: **D7.125**

> The real pull of bail, the real effective force that it exerts, is that it may cause the offender to attend his trial rather than subject his nearest and dearest who has gone surety for him to undue pain and discomfort.

Nonetheless, it is clear that there may be circumstances where the amount forfeited might be reduced because the surety has made considerable efforts to carry out the responsibilities undertaken.

In *Choudhry v Birmingham Crown Court* [2007] EWHC 2764 (Admin), Gibbs J helpfully summarised (at [15]) the principles to be derived from *Ex parte Lever*: **D7.126**

(a) The purpose of a recognizance is to bring the defendant to court for trial.
(b) The forfeiture of recognizance is not a penalty imposed on the surety for misconduct.

(c) It is for the surety to establish to the satisfaction of the court that there are grounds upon which the court may remit from forfeiture part or, wholly exceptionally, the whole recognizance.
(d) The absence of culpability on the part of the surety is not of itself a reason to set aside or reduce the obligation entered into.
(e) Absence of culpability is a factor to be considered. The court may, in the exercise of a wide discretion, decide it would be fair and just to estreat some or all of the recognizance.

His lordship added (on the basis of *Uxbridge Justices, ex parte Heward-Mills* [1983] 1 All ER 530) that 'the burden of satisfying the court that the full sum should not be forfeited rests upon the surety and is a heavy one'.

In *Harrow Crown Court, ex parte Lingard* [1998] EWHC 233 (Admin), Dyson J (at [20]), with whom Lord Bingham CJ agreed, said that it was clear that in an exceptional case, where the surety is 'entirely blameless and the failure of the defendant to surrender to bail is wholly outside the control of, and unforeseeable by, the surety', the court may 'in the exercise of its discretion remit the whole or a substantial part of the amount of the recognizance'. In *Choudhry v Birmingham Crown Court*, however, Gibbs J (at [43]) emphasised that, although the court may so remit, there is no principle of law which requires it to do so. It is thus a matter entirely within the discretion of the court.

The position regarding forfeiture of recognizances is summarised in CrimPD III, para. 14F.5 (see Supplement, **CPD.14F**), which states that, even if a surety makes best efforts to ensure the attendance of the accused at court, the surety remains liable for the full amount, except at the discretion of the court. However, the court should take into account the presence or absence of culpability on the part of the surety (though this 'is not in itself a reason to reduce or set aside the obligations entered into by the surety'), and the means of a surety (particularly if those means have changed since the obligation was taken on). Moreover, the court should order forfeiture of 'no more than is necessary, in public policy, to maintain the integrity and confidence of the system of taking sureties'.

D7.127 In *Wells Street Magistrates' Court, ex parte Albanese* [1982] QB 333, the Divisional Court considered the position where the conditions of bail have been varied. Ralph Gibson J, giving the judgment of the court, declined to hold that a court, if it varies the conditions of bail in a case in which there is a surety, is under a duty to give notice of the change to the surety. However, an unnotified variation in bail conditions may be relevant to the question of forfeiture of the recognizance. In *Choudhry v Birmingham Crown Court*, Gibbs J (at [35]), ruled that it is both possible and lawful for a recognizance in Crown Court proceedings to be expressed as continuous until the conclusion of proceedings in the Crown Court. If an order is subsequently made varying the conditions of bail, unconnected with the sureties, this does not give rise to the need for sureties to be taken afresh. His lordship went on to say (at [36]) that if, at the commencement of the trial (when bail falls to be reconsidered), the accused is allowed to continue on bail (whether on the same or varied terms), that amounts to a fresh grant of bail. However, that does not necessarily mean that sureties must be taken again. Provided that the recognizances were in terms which made it clear that they continued to bind the surety until the end of the trial, they would remain in force so long as bail was granted in terms which required that they did so (at [37]).

Forfeiture of Security

D7.128 Where the accused (or somebody on behalf of the accused) has given security for the accused's surrender to custody in pursuance of a requirement imposed under the BA 1976, s. 3(5), and the court is satisfied that the accused has absconded, then the court may, unless satisfied that the accused had reasonable cause for the failure to surrender, order forfeiture of part or all of the security (s. 5(7) and (8)). Section 5(8A) to (8C) set out a procedure by which the accused may apply to have an order under s. 5(7) remitted on the grounds that there was in fact reasonable cause for not surrendering to custody. The principles to be applied in deciding whether or not to order forfeiture of a security are no doubt analogous to those which apply when forfeiture of a surety's recognizance is under consideration.

DETENTION WHEN BAIL IS REFUSED

Detention of Adults

Where a court refuses bail to an accused aged 21 or over, the accused is detained in a prison until the next hearing (MCA 1980, ss. 128(1) and 150(1)). An accused aged 18 to 20 inclusive who is remanded in custody must be committed to a remand centre if one is available (CJA 1948, s. 27(1)); otherwise the accused is committed to a prison. **D7.129**

Remands to Police Custody

A magistrates' court may, instead of remanding the accused in custody, commit the accused to detention at a police station for a period not exceeding three clear days (MCA 1980, s. 128(7)). This may be done only if it is necessary for the purposes of inquiries into offences other than the one(s) for which the accused is appearing before the court (s. 128(8)(a)). The accused must be brought back before the magistrates' court as soon as that need ceases (s. 128(8)(b)). While detained at the police station, the accused is entitled to the same protection as regards conditions of detention, and periodic review of the continuing need for detention, as would have been the case had the arrest taken place without warrant on suspicion of having committed an offence (s. 128(8)(c) and (d)). **D7.130**

Children and Young People Refused Bail

As regards a court's decision whether to grant bail to a child or young person (defined in the BA 1976, s. 2(2), as someone under the age of 18), the only special rules applying are that (a) bail can be refused if that is necessary for the accused's own welfare (sch. 1, para. 3), and (b) a parent or guardian may be asked to stand surety for the accused's compliance with any conditions of bail that may be imposed, as well as standing surety for the accused's appearance at court (s. 3(7)). However, where bail is *refused* in the case of a person aged under 18, the consequences are significantly different. **D7.131**

The LASPO 2012, ss. 91 to 107, set out the options open to the court where a child or young person is refused bail. Section 91 applies where a person under 18 is charged with, or convicted of, one or more offences: it provides that, if the child or young person is not released on bail, the court must remand the child or young person to local authority accommodation, in accordance with s. 92, or to youth detention accommodation, in accordance with s. 102.

Remands to Local Authority Accommodation

Under the LASPO 2012, s. 92, a remand to local authority accommodation is defined as a remand to accommodation provided by or on behalf of the local authority designated by the court; that authority must provide or arrange for the provision of accommodation for the accused. Section 93 enables the court to impose conditions when remanding to local authority accommodation: s. 93(1) provides that the accused can be required to comply with any conditions that could be imposed under the BA 1976, s. 3(6). Also, under s. 93(2), compliance with those conditions may be secured through the imposition of electronic monitoring, provided that the requirements set out in s. 94 are met. Those requirements are as follows: **D7.132**

(i) the accused must have attained the age of 12;
(ii) one or more of the offences must be imprisonable;
(iii) one or more of the offences must be a violent or sexual offence (as specified in the CJA 2003, sch. 15) or an offence punishable (in the case of an adult) with at least 14 years' imprisonment, or else the offence(s) must amount, or (assuming the accused is convicted) would amount, to a recent history of committing imprisonable offences while on bail or subject to a custodial remand;
(iv) the court must be satisfied that electronic monitoring is available; and
(v) a youth offending team must have informed the court that the imposition of an electronic monitoring condition would be suitable for that person.

Under s. 93(3), a court remanding a child or young person to local authority accommodation may also impose requirements on the designated authority to secure compliance with the conditions imposed on the accused; the court can also stipulate that the accused must not be placed with a named person. The court must first consult with the designated authority (s. 93(4)). Under s. 93(5), where a child or young person has been remanded to local authority accommodation, the court may, on the application of the designated authority, impose any conditions that could be imposed under s. 93(1) or (2) when a court is remanding a child or young person to local authority accommodation. Under s. 93(6), the local authority or the accused can apply for the variation or revocation of any of the conditions which have been imposed.

Under s. 97, a police officer may arrest a child or young person without warrant if the person has been remanded to local authority accommodation, conditions were imposed under s. 93, and the officer has reasonable grounds for suspecting that any of those conditions has been broken (s. 97(1)). A person arrested under s. 97(1) must be brought before a magistrate within 24 hours of arrest (excluding Sundays). Under s. 97(5), if the magistrate is of the opinion that the person has broken any condition imposed under s. 93, the person must be remanded under s. 91 (i.e. either to local authority accommodation or to youth detention accommodation). If the magistrate is not of that opinion, the child or young person must be remanded to the place of remand at the time of the arrest, subject to the same conditions as before.

Remands to Youth Detention Accommodation

D7.133 Remand to 'youth detention accommodation' means remand to a secure children's home, a secure training centre, a young offender institution, or detention accommodation for detention and training orders (s. 102). Remand to youth detention accommodation is possible only where either of two sets of conditions (set out in ss. 98 and 99) is satisfied (s. 91(4)).

The conditions in s. 98 are as follows:

(i) the accused must have attained the age of 12;
(ii) one or more of the offences must be a violent or sexual offence (as specified in the CJA 2003, sch. 15), or an offence punishable (in the case of an adult) with at least 14 years' imprisonment;
(iii) the court must be of the opinion, after considering all the options for remand, that only a remand to youth detention accommodation would be adequate to protect the public from death or serious personal injury (whether physical or psychological) occasioned by further offences committed by the accused, or to prevent the accused committing imprisonable offences;
(iv) either the accused is legally represented at court, or else one of the following applies: representation was provided but has been withdrawn because of the accused's conduct or because it appeared that the accused's financial resources were such that the accused was not eligible for such representation, or representation was refused because it appeared that the accused's financial resources were such that the accused was ineligible for such representation, or the accused has refused or failed to apply for representation.

The conditions in s. 99 are:

(i) the accused must have attained the age of 12;
(ii) there must be a real prospect that the accused (if convicted) will be sentenced to a custodial sentence;
(iii) one or more of the offences is imprisonable;
(iv) either the accused has a recent history of absconding while subject to a custodial remand and one or more of the present offences is alleged (or found) to have been committed while remanded to local authority accommodation or youth detention accommodation, or the offence(s) amount, or (if the accused is convicted) would amount, to a recent history of committing imprisonable offences while on bail or subject to a custodial remand.

Additional conditions (the necessity condition and the legal representation conditions) apply—they are the same as those set out at (iii) and (iv) under s. 98.

TEXT OF THE BAIL ACT 1976

Bail Act 1976 D7.134

Preliminary

Meaning of 'bail in criminal proceedings'

1.—(1) In this Act 'bail in criminal proceedings' means—
(a) bail grantable in or in connection with proceedings for an offence to a person who is accused or convicted of the offence, or
(b) bail grantable in connection with an offence to a person who is under arrest for the offence or for whose arrest for the offence a warrant (endorsed for bail) is being issued, or
(c) bail grantable in connection with extradition proceedings in respect of an offence.
(2) In this Act 'bail' means bail grantable under the law (including common law) for the time being in force.
(3) Except as provided by section 13(3) of this Act, this section does not apply to bail in or in connection with proceedings outside England and Wales.
. . .
(5) This section applies—
(a) whether the offence was committed in England or Wales or elsewhere, and
(b) whether it is an offence under the law of England and Wales, or of any other country or territory.
(6) Bail in criminal proceedings shall be granted (and in particular shall be granted unconditionally or conditionally), in accordance with this Act.

Other definitions

2.—(1) In this Act, unless the context otherwise requires, 'conviction' includes— D7.135
(a) a finding of guilt,
(b) a finding that a person is not guilty by reason of insanity,
(c) a finding under section 11(1) of the Powers of Criminal Courts (Sentencing) Act 2000 (remand for medical examination) that the person in question did the act or made the omission charged, and
(d) a conviction of an offence for which an order is made discharging the offender absolutely or conditionally, and 'convicted' shall be construed accordingly.
(2) In this Act, unless the context otherwise requires—
'bail hostel' means premises for the accommodation of persons remanded on bail,
'bail in non-extradition proceedings' means bail in criminal proceedings of the kind mentioned in section 1(1)(a),
'child' means a person under the age of fourteen,
'court' includes a judge of a court or a justice of the peace and, in the case of a specified court, includes a judge or (as the case may be) justice having powers to act in connection with proceedings before that court,
'Courts Martial Appeal rules' means rules made under section 49 of the Courts Martial Appeals Act 1968,
'custodial sentence' means a sentence or order mentioned in section 76(1) of the Powers of Criminal Courts (Sentencing) Act 2000 or any corresponding sentence or order imposed or made under any earlier enactment,
'extradition proceedings' means proceedings under the Extradition Act 2003,
'imprisonable offence' means an offence punishable in the case of an adult with imprisonment,
'offence' includes an alleged offence,
'probation hostel' means premises for the accommodation of persons who may be required to reside there by a community order under section 177 of the Criminal Justice Act 2003,
'prosecutor', in relation to extradition proceedings, means the person acting on behalf of the territory to which extradition is sought,
'sexual offence' means an offence specified in Part 2 of Schedule 15 to the Criminal Justice Act 2003,
'surrender to custody' means, in relation to a person released on bail, surrendering himself into the custody of the court or of the constable (according to the requirements of the grant of bail) at the time and place for the time being appointed for him to do so,
'vary', in relation to bail, means imposing further conditions after bail is granted, or varying or rescinding conditions,

'violent offence' means murder or an offence specified in Part 1 of Schedule 15 to the Criminal Justice Act 2003,

'young person' means a person who has attained the age of 14 and is under the age of 18.

(3) Where an enactment (whenever passed) which relates to bail in criminal proceedings refers to the person bailed appearing before a court it is to be construed unless the context otherwise requires as referring to his surrendering himself into the custody of the court.

(4) Any reference in this Act to any other enactment is a reference thereto as amended, and includes a reference thereto as extended or applied, by or under any other enactment, including this Act.

Incidents of bail in criminal proceedings

General provisions

D7.136 3.—(1) A person granted bail in criminal proceedings shall be under a duty to surrender to custody, and that duty is enforceable in accordance with section 6 of this Act.

(2) No recognizance for his surrender to custody shall be taken from him.

(3) Except as provided by this section—

(a) no security for his surrender to custody shall be taken from him,

(b) he shall not be required to provide a surety or sureties for his surrender to custody, and

(c) no other requirement shall be imposed on him as a condition of bail.

(4) He may be required, before release on bail, to provide a surety or sureties to secure his surrender to custody.

(5) He may be required, before release on bail, to give security for his surrender to custody. The security may be given by him or on his behalf.

(6) He may be required to comply, before release on bail or later, with such requirements as appear to the court to be necessary—

(a) to secure that he surrenders to custody,

(b) to secure that he does not commit an offence while on bail,

(c) to secure that he does not interfere with witnesses or otherwise obstruct the course of justice whether in relation to himself or any other person,

(ca) for his own protection or, if he is a child or young person, for his own welfare or in his own interests,

(d) to secure that he makes himself available for the purpose of enabling inquiries or a report to be made to assist the court in dealing with him for the offence,

(e) to secure that before the time appointed for him to surrender to custody, he attends an interview with an authorised advocate or authorised litigator, as defined by section 119(1) of the Courts and Legal Services Act 1990;

and, in any Act, 'the normal powers to impose conditions of bail' means the powers to impose conditions under paragraph (a), (b), (c) or (ca) above.

(6ZAA) The requirements which may be imposed under subsection (6) include electronic monitoring requirements.

The imposition of electronic monitoring requirements is subject to section 3AA (in the case of a child or young person granted bail in criminal proceedings of the kind mentioned in section 1(1)(a) or (b)), section 3AAA (in the case of a child or young person granted bail in connection with extradition proceedings), section 3AB (in the case of other persons) and section 3AC (in all cases).

(6ZAB) In this section and sections 3AA to 3AC 'electronic monitoring requirements' means requirements imposed for the purpose of securing the electronic monitoring of a person's compliance with any other requirement imposed on him as a condition of bail.

(6ZA) Where he is required under subsection (6) above to reside in a bail hostel or probation hostel, he may also be required to comply with the rules of the hostel.

(6A) In the case of a person accused of murder the court granting bail shall, unless it considers that satisfactory reports on his mental condition have already been obtained, impose as conditions of bail—

(a) a requirement that the accused shall undergo examination by two medical practitioners for the purpose of enabling such reports to be prepared; and

(b) a requirement that he shall for that purpose attend such an institution or place as the court directs and comply with any other directions which may be given to him for that purpose by either of those practitioners.

(6B) Of the medical practitioners referred to in subsection (6A) above at least one shall be a practitioner approved for the purposes of section 12 of the Mental Health Act 1983.

(6C) Subsection (6D) below applies where—

(a) the court has been notified by the Secretary of State that arrangements for conducting a relevant assessment or, as the case may be, providing relevant follow-up have been made

for the local justice area in which it appears to the court that the person referred to in subsection (6D) would reside if granted bail; and
(b) the notice has not been withdrawn.
(6D) In the case of a person ('P')—
(a) in relation to whom paragraphs (a) to (c) of paragraph 6B(1) of Part 1 of Schedule 1 to this Act apply (including where P is a person to whom the provisions of Part 1A of Schedule 1 apply);
(b) who, after analysis of the sample referred to in paragraph (b) of that paragraph, has been offered a relevant assessment or, if a relevant assessment has been carried out, has had relevant follow-up proposed to him; and
(c) who has agreed to undergo the relevant assessment or, as the case may be, to participate in the relevant follow-up,
the court, if it grants bail, shall impose as a condition of bail that P both undergo the relevant assessment and participate in any relevant follow-up proposed to him or, if a relevant assessment has been carried out, that P participate in the relevant follow-up.
(6E) In subsections (6C) and (6D) above—
(a) 'relevant assessment' means an assessment conducted by a suitably qualified person of whether P is dependent upon or has a propensity to misuse any specified Class A drugs;
(b) 'relevant follow-up' means, in a case where the person who conducted the relevant assessment believes P to have such a dependency or propensity, such further assessment, and such assistance or treatment (or both) in connection with the dependency or propensity, as the person who conducted the relevant assessment (or conducts any later assessment) considers to be appropriate in P's case, and in paragraph (a) above 'Class A drug' and 'misuse' have the same meaning as in the Misuse of Drugs Act 1971, and 'specified' (in relation to a Class A drug) has the same meaning as in Part 3 of the Criminal Justice and Court Services Act 2000.
(6F) In subsection (6E)(a) above, 'suitably qualified person' means a person who has such qualifications or experience as are from time to time specified by the Secretary of State for the purposes of this subsection.
(7) If a parent or guardian of a person under the age of seventeen consents to be surety for the person for the purposes of this subsection, the parent or guardian may be required to secure that the person complies with any requirement imposed on him by virtue of subsection (6), (6ZAA) or (6A) above but—
(a) no requirement shall be imposed on the parent or the guardian by virtue of this subsection where it appears that the person will attain the age of 17 before the time to be appointed for him to surrender to custody; and
(b) the parent or guardian shall not be required to secure compliance with any requirement to which his consent does not extend and shall not, in respect of those requirements to which his consent does extend, be bound in a sum greater than £50.
(8) Where a court has granted bail in criminal proceedings that court or, where that court has sent a person on bail to the Crown Court for trial or committed him on bail to the Crown Court to be sentenced or otherwise dealt with, that court or the Crown Court may on application—
(a) by or on behalf of the person to whom bail was granted, or
(b) by the prosecutor or a constable,
vary the conditions of bail or impose conditions in respect of bail which has been granted unconditionally.
(9) This section is subject to subsection (3) of section 11 of the Powers of Criminal Courts (Sentencing) Act 2000 (conditions of bail on remand for medical examination).
(10) This section is subject, in its application to bail granted by a constable, to section 3A of this Act.

3AA.—(1) A court may not impose electronic monitoring requirements on a child or young person released on bail in criminal proceedings of the kind mentioned in section 1(1)(a) or (b) unless each of the following conditions is met. **D7.137**
(2) The first condition is that the child or young person has attained the age of twelve years.
(3) The second condition is that—
(a) the child or young person is charged with or has been convicted of a violent or sexual offence, or an offence punishable in the case of an adult with imprisonment for a term of fourteen years or more; or
(b) he is charged with or has been convicted of one or more imprisonable offences which, together with any other imprisonable offences of which he has been convicted in any proceedings—
(i) amount, or

(ii) would, if he were convicted of the offences with which he is charged, amount, to a recent history of repeatedly committing imprisonable offences while remanded on bail or subject to a custodial remand.

(4) The third condition is that the court is satisfied that the necessary provision for dealing with the person concerned can be made under arrangements for the electronic monitoring of persons released on bail that are currently available in each local justice area which is a relevant area.

(5) The fourth condition is that a youth offending team has informed the court that in its opinion the imposition of electronic monitoring requirements will be suitable in the case of the child or young person.

(6) to (10) [Repealed.]

(11) The references in subsection (3)(b) to an imprisonable offence include a reference to an offence—

(a) of which the child or young person has been convicted outside England and Wales, and

(b) which is equivalent to an offence that is punishable with imprisonment in England and Wales.

(12) The reference in subsection (3)(b) to a child or young person being subject to a custodial remand is to the child or young person being—

(a) remanded to local authority accommodation or youth detention accommodation under section 91 of the Legal Aid, Sentencing and Punishment of Offenders Act 2012,

(b) remanded to local authority accommodation under section 23 of the Children and Young Persons Act 1969 or to prison under that section as modified by section 98 of the Crime and Disorder Act 1998 or under section 27 of the Criminal Justice Act 1948, or

(c) subject to a form of custodial detention in a country or territory outside England and Wales while awaiting trial or sentence in that country or territory or during a trial in that country or territory.

D7.138 3AAA.—(1) A court may not impose electronic monitoring requirements on a child or young person released on bail in connection with extradition proceedings unless each of the following conditions is met.

(2) The first condition is that the child or young person has attained the age of twelve years.

(3) The second condition is that—

(a) the conduct constituting the offence to which the extradition proceedings relate, or one or more of those offences, would, if committed in England and Wales, constitute a violent or sexual offence or an offence punishable in the case of an adult with imprisonment for a term of fourteen years or more, or

(b) the offence or offences to which the extradition proceedings relate, together with any other imprisonable offences of which the child or young person has been convicted in any proceedings—

(i) amount, or

(ii) would, if the child or young person were convicted of that offence or those offences, amount,

to a recent history of committing imprisonable offences while on bail or subject to a custodial remand.

(4) The third condition is that the court is satisfied that the necessary provision for dealing with the child or young person concerned can be made under arrangements for the electronic monitoring of persons released on bail that are currently available in each local justice area which is a relevant area.

(5) The fourth condition is that a youth offending team has informed the court that in its opinion the imposition of electronic monitoring requirements will be suitable in the case of the child or young person.

(6) The references in subsection (3)(b) to an imprisonable offence include a reference to an offence—

(a) of which the child or young person has been accused or convicted outside England and Wales, and

(b) which is equivalent to an offence that is punishable with imprisonment in England and Wales.

(7) The reference in subsection (3)(b) to a child or young person being subject to a custodial remand is to the child or young person being—

(a) remanded to local authority accommodation or youth detention accommodation under section 91 of the Legal Aid, Sentencing and Punishment of Offenders Act 2012,
(b) remanded to local authority accommodation under section 23 of the Children and Young Persons Act 1969 or to prison under that section as modified by section 98 of the Crime and Disorder Act 1998 or under section 27 of the Criminal Justice Act 1948, or
(c) subject to a form of custodial detention in a country or territory outside England and Wales while awaiting trial or sentence in that country or territory or during a trial in that country or territory.

3AB.—(1) A court may not impose electronic monitoring requirements on a person who has attained the age of eighteen unless each of the following conditions is met. **D7.139**
(2) The first condition is that the court is satisfied that without the electronic monitoring requirements the person would not be granted bail.
(3) The second condition is that the court is satisfied that the necessary provision for dealing with the person concerned can be made under arrangements for the electronic monitoring of persons released on bail that are currently available in each local justice area which is a relevant area.

3AC.—(1) Where a court imposes electronic monitoring requirements as a condition of bail, the requirements must include provision for making a person responsible for the monitoring. **D7.140**
(2) A person may not be made responsible for the electronic monitoring of a person on bail unless he is of a description specified in an order made by the Secretary of State.
(3) to (6) [Rule-making powers.]
(7) For the purposes of section 3AA, 3AAA or 3AB a local justice area is a relevant area in relation to a proposed electronic monitoring requirement if the court considers that it will not be practicable to secure the electronic monitoring in question unless electronic monitoring arrangements are available in that area.
(8) Nothing in sections 3, 3AA, 3AAA or 3AB is to be taken to require the Secretary of State to ensure that arrangements are made for the electronic monitoring of persons released on bail.

Conditions of bail in case of police bail

3A.—(1) Section 3 of this Act applies, in relation to bail granted by a custody officer under Part IV of the Police and Criminal Evidence Act 1984 in cases where the normal powers to impose conditions of bail are available to him, subject to the following modifications. **D7.141**
(2) Subsection (6) does not authorise the imposition of a requirement to reside in a bail hostel or any requirement under paragraph (d) or (e).
(3) Subsections (6ZAA), (6ZA), (6A) to (6F) shall be omitted.
(4) For subsection (8), substitute the following—
'(8) Where a custody officer has granted bail in criminal proceedings he or another custody officer serving at the same police station may, at the request of the person to whom it was granted, vary the conditions of bail; and in doing so he may impose conditions or more onerous conditions.'
(5) Where a constable grants bail to a person no conditions shall be imposed under subsections (4), (5), (6) or (7) of section 3 of this Act unless it appears to the constable that it is necessary to do so—
(a) for the purpose of preventing that person from failing to surrender to custody, or
(b) for the purpose of preventing that person from committing an offence while on bail, or
(c) for the purpose of preventing that person from interfering with witnesses or other-wise obstructing the course of justice, whether in relation to himself or any other person, or
(d) for that person's own protection or, if he is a child or young person, for his own welfare or in his own interests.
(6) Subsection (5) above also applies on any request to a custody officer under subsection (8) of section 3 of this Act to vary the conditions of bail.

Bail for accused persons and others

General right to bail of accused persons and others

4.—(1) A person to whom this section applies shall be granted bail except as provided in Schedule 1 to this Act. **D7.142**

(2) This section applies to a person who is accused of an offence when—
(a) he appears or is brought before a magistrates' court or the Crown Court in the course of or in connection with proceedings for the offence, or
(b) he applies to a court for bail or for a variation of the conditions of bail in connection with the proceedings.

This subsection does not apply as respects proceedings on or after a person's conviction of the offence.

(2A) This section also applies to a person whose extradition is sought in respect of an offence, when—
(a) he appears or is brought before a court in the course of or in connection with extradition proceedings in respect of the offence, or
(b) he applies to a court for bail or for a variation of the conditions of bail in connection with the proceedings.

(2B) But subsection (2A) above does not apply if the person is alleged to have been convicted of the offence.

(3) This section also applies to a person who, having been convicted of an offence, appears or is brought before a magistrates' court or the Crown Court to be dealt with under—
(za) Schedule 1 to the Powers of Criminal Courts (Sentencing) Act 2000 (referral orders: referral back to appropriate court),
(zb) Schedule 8 to that Act (breach of reparation order),
(a) Schedule 2 to the Criminal Justice and Immigration Act 2008 (breach, revocation or amendment of youth rehabilitation orders),
(b) Part 2 of Schedule 8 to the Criminal Justice Act 2003 (breach of requirement of community order), or
(c) the Schedule to the Street Offences Act 1959 (breach of orders under section 1(2A) of that Act).

(4) This section also applies to a person who has been convicted of an offence and whose case is adjourned by the court for the purpose of enabling inquiries or a report to be made to assist the court in dealing with him for the offence.

(5) Schedule 1 to this Act also has effect as respects conditions of bail for a person to whom this section applies.

(6) In Schedule 1 to this Act 'the defendant' means a person to whom this section applies and any reference to a defendant whose case is adjourned for inquiries or a report is a reference to a person to whom this section applies by virtue of subsection (4) above.

(7) This section is subject to section 41 of the Magistrates' Courts Act 1980 (restriction of bail by magistrates' court in cases of treason).

(8) This section is subject to section 25 of the Criminal Justice and Public Order Act 1994 (exclusion of bail in cases of homicide and rape).

(9) In taking any decisions required by Part I or II of Schedule 1 to this Act, the considerations to which the court is to have regard include, so far as relevant, any misuse of controlled drugs by the defendant ('controlled drugs' and 'misuse' having the same meanings as in the Misuse of Drugs Act 1971).

Supplementary

Supplementary provisions about decisions on bail

D7.143 5.—(1) Subject to subsection (2) below, where—
(a) a court or constable grants bail in criminal proceedings, or
(b) a court withholds bail in criminal proceedings from a person to whom section 4 of this Act applies, or
(c) a court, or officer of a court or constable appoints a different time or place for a person granted bail in criminal proceedings to surrender to custody, or
(d) a court or constable varies any conditions of bail or imposes conditions in respect of bail in criminal proceedings,

that court, officer or constable shall make a record of the decision in the prescribed manner and containing the prescribed particulars and, if requested to do so by the person in relation to whom the decision was taken, shall cause him to be given a copy of the record of the decision as soon as practicable after the record is made.

(2) Where bail in criminal proceedings is granted by endorsing a warrant of arrest for bail the constable who releases on bail the person arrested shall make the record required by subsection (1) above instead of the judge or justice who issued the warrant.

(2A) Where a magistrates' court or the Crown Court grants bail in criminal proceedings to a person to whom section 4 of this Act applies after hearing representations from the prosecutor in favour of withholding bail, then the court shall give reasons for granting bail.

(2B) A court which is by virtue of subsection (2A) above required to give reasons for its decision shall include a note of those reasons in the record of its decision and, if requested to do so by the prosecutor, shall cause the prosecutor to be given a copy of the record of the decision as soon as practicable after the record is made.

(3) Where a magistrates' court or the Crown Court—
(a) withholds bail in criminal proceedings, or
(b) imposes conditions in granting bail in criminal proceedings, or
(c) varies any conditions of bail or imposes conditions in respect of bail in criminal proceedings,
and does so in relation to a person to whom section 4 of this Act applies, then the court shall, with a view to enabling him to consider making an application in the matter to another court, give reasons for withholding bail or for imposing or varying the conditions.

(4) A court which is by virtue of subsection (3) above required to give reasons for its decision shall include a note of those reasons in the record of its decision and shall (except in a case where, by virtue of subsection (5) below, this need not be done) give a copy of that note to the person in relation to whom the decision was taken.

(5) The Crown Court need not give a copy of the note of the reasons for its decision to the person in relation to whom the decision was taken where that person is represented by counsel or a solicitor unless his counsel or solicitor requests the court to do so.

(6) Where a magistrates' court withholds bail in criminal proceedings from a person who is not represented by counsel or a solicitor, the court shall—
(a) if it is sending him for trial to the Crown Court, or if it issues a certificate under subsection (6A) below inform him that he may apply to the High Court or to the Crown Court to be granted bail;
(b) [Repealed].

(6A) Where in criminal proceedings—
(a) a magistrates' court remands a person in custody under section 52(5) of the Crime and Disorder Act 1998, section 11 of the Powers of Criminal Courts (Sentencing) Act 2000 or any of the following provisions of the Magistrates' Courts Act 1980—
(i) [Repealed.]
(ii) section 10 (adjournment of trial);
(iia) section 17C (intention as to plea: adjournment);
(iii) section 18 (initial procedure on information against adult for offence triable either way),
(iv) section 24C (intention as to plea by child or young person: adjournment),
after hearing full argument on an application for bail from him; and
(b) either—
(i) it has not previously heard such argument on an application for bail from him in those proceedings; or
(ii) it has previously heard full argument from him on such an application but it is satisfied that there has been a change in his circumstances or that new considerations have been placed before it,
it shall be the duty of the court to issue a certificate in the prescribed form that they heard full argument on his application for bail before they refused the application.

(6B) Where the court issues a certificate under subsection (6A) above in a case to which paragraph (b)(ii) of that subsection applies, it shall state in the certificate the nature of the change of circumstances or the new considerations which caused it to hear a further fully argued bail application.

(6C) Where a court issues a certificate under subsection (6A) above it shall cause the person to whom it refuses bail to be given a copy of the certificate.

(7) Where a person has given security in pursuance of section 3(5) above, and a court is satisfied that he failed to surrender to custody then, unless it appears that he had reasonable cause for his failure, the court may order the forfeiture of the security.

(8) If a court orders the forfeiture of a security under subsection (7) above, the court may declare that the forfeiture extends to such amount less than the full value of the security as it thinks fit to order.

(8A) to (9A) [Procedure for taking and forfeiting a security.]

(10) [Meaning of 'prescribed'.]
(11) This section is subject, in its application to bail granted by a constable, to section 5A of this Act.

Supplementary provisions in cases of police bail

D7.144 5A.—(1) Section 5 of this Act applies, in relation to bail granted by a custody officer under Part IV of the Police and Criminal Evidence Act 1984 in cases where the normal powers to impose conditions of bail are available to him, subject to the following modifications.
(1A) Subsections (2A) and (2B) shall be omitted.
(2) For subsection (3) substitute the following—
'(3) Where a custody officer, in relation to any person,—
(a) imposes conditions in granting bail in criminal proceedings, or
(b) varies any conditions of bail or imposes conditions in respect of bail, in criminal proceedings,
the custody officer shall, with a view to enabling that person to consider requesting him or another custody officer, or making an application to a magistrates' court, to vary the conditions, give reasons for imposing or varying the conditions.'
(3) For subsection (4) substitute the following—
'(4) A custody officer who is by virtue of subsection (3) above required to give reasons for his decision shall include a note of those reasons in the custody record and shall give a copy of that note to the person in relation to whom the decision was taken.'
(4) Subsections (5) and (6) shall be omitted.

Reconsideration of decisions granting bail

D7.145 5B.—(A1) This section applies in any of these cases—
(a) a magistrates' court has granted bail in criminal proceedings in connection with an offence to which this section applies or proceedings for such an offence;
(b) a constable has granted bail in criminal proceedings in connection with proceedings for such an offence;
(c) a magistrates' court or a constable has granted bail in connection with extradition proceedings.
(1) The court or the appropriate court in relation to the constable may, on application by the prosecutor for the decision to be reconsidered,—
(a) vary the conditions of bail,
(b) impose conditions in respect of bail which has been granted unconditionally, or
(c) withhold bail.
(2) The offences to which this section applies are offences triable on indictment and offences triable either way.
(3) No application for the reconsideration of a decision under this section shall be made unless it is based on information which was not available to the court or constable when the decision was taken.
(4) Whether or not the person to whom the application relates appears before it, the magistrates' court shall take the decision in accordance with section 4(1) (and Schedule 1) of this Act.
(5) Where the decision of the court on a reconsideration under this section is to withhold bail from the person to whom it was originally granted the court shall—
(a) if that person is before the court, remand him in custody, and
(b) if that person is not before the court, order him to surrender himself forthwith into the custody of the court.
(6) Where a person surrenders himself into the custody of the court in compliance with an order under subsection (5) above, the court shall remand him in custody.
(7) A person who has been ordered to surrender to custody under subsection (5) above may be arrested without warrant by a constable if he fails without reasonable cause to surrender to custody in accordance with the order.
(8) A person arrested in pursuance of subsection (7) above shall be brought as soon as practicable, and in any event within 24 hours after his arrest, before a justice of the peace for the local justice area in which he was arrested and the justice shall remand him in custody.
In reckoning for the purposes of this subsection any period of 24 hours, no account shall be taken of Christmas Day, Good Friday or any Sunday.

(8A) Where the court, on a reconsideration under this section, refuses to withhold bail from a relevant person after hearing representations from the prosecutor in favour of withholding bail, then the court shall give reasons for refusing to withhold bail.
(8B) In subsection (8A) above, 'relevant person' means a person to whom section 4(1) (and Schedule 1) of this Act is applicable in accordance with subsection (4) above.
(8C) A court which is by virtue of subsection (8A) above required to give reasons for its decision shall include a note of those reasons in any record of its decision and, if requested to do so by the prosecutor, shall cause the prosecutor to be given a copy of any such record as soon as practicable after the record is made.
(9) [Indicates what may be covered by the CrimPR.]

Offence of absconding by person released on bail

6.—(1) If a person who has been released on bail in criminal proceedings fails without reasonable cause to surrender to custody he shall be guilty of an offence. **D7.146**
(2) If a person who—
 (a) has been released on bail in criminal proceedings, and
 (b) having reasonable cause therefor, has failed to surrender to custody,
 fails to surrender to custody at the appointed place as soon after the appointed time as is reasonably practicable he shall be guilty of an offence.
(3) It shall be for the accused to prove that he had reasonable cause for his failure to surrender to custody.
(4) A failure to give to a person granted bail in criminal proceedings a copy of the record of the decision shall not constitute a reasonable cause for that person's failure to surrender to custody.
(5) An offence under subsection (1) or (2) above shall be punishable either on summary conviction or as if it were a criminal contempt of court.
(6) Where a magistrates' court convicts a person of an offence under subsection (1) or (2) above the court may, if it thinks—
 (a) that the circumstances of the offence are such that greater punishment should be inflicted for that offence than the court has power to inflict, or
 (b) in a case where it sends that person for trial to the Crown Court for another offence, that it would be appropriate for him to be dealt with for the offence under subsection (1) or (2) above by the court before which he is tried for the other offence, commit him in custody or on bail to the Crown Court for sentence.
(7) A person who is convicted summarily of an offence under subsection (1) or (2) above and is not committed to the Crown Court for sentence shall be liable to imprisonment for a term not exceeding three months or to a fine not exceeding level 5 on the standard scale or to both and a person who is so committed for sentence or is dealt with as for such a contempt shall be liable to imprisonment for a term not exceeding 12 months or to a fine or to both.
(8) In any proceedings for an offence under subsection (1) or (2) above a document purporting to be a copy of the part of the prescribed record which relates to the time and place appointed for the person specified in the record to surrender to custody and to be duly certified to be a true copy of that part of the record shall be evidence of the time and place appointed for that person to surrender to custody.
(9) For the purposes of subsection (8) above—
 (a) 'the prescribed record' means the record of the decision of the court, officer or constable made in pursuance of section 5(1) of this Act;
 (b) the copy of the prescribed record is duly certified if it is certified by the appropriate officer of the court or, as the case may be, by the constable who took the decision or a constable designated for the purpose by the officer in charge of the police station from which the person to whom the record relates was released;
 (c) 'the appropriate officer' of the court is—
  (i) in the case of a magistrates' court, the designated officer for the court;
  (ii) in the case of the Crown Court, such officer as may be designated for the purpose in accordance with arrangements made by the Lord Chancellor;
  (iii) in the case of the High Court, such officer as may be designated for the purpose in accordance with arrangements made by the Lord Chancellor;
  (iv) in the case of the Court of Appeal, the registrar of criminal appeals or such other officer as may be authorised by him to act for the purpose;
  (v) in the case of the Courts Martial Appeal Court, the registrar or such other officer as may be authorised by him to act for the purpose.

(10) Section 127 of the Magistrates' Courts Act 1980 shall not apply in relation to an offence under subsection (1) or (2) above.

(11) Where a person has been released on bail in criminal proceedings and that bail was granted by a constable, a magistrates' court shall not try that person for an offence under subsection (1) or (2) above in relation to that bail (the 'relevant offence') unless either or both of subsections (12) and (13) below applies.

(12) This subsection applies if an information is laid for the relevant offence within 6 months from the time of the commission of the relevant offence.

(13) This subsection applies if an information is laid for the relevant offence no later than 3 months from the time of the occurrence of the first of the events mentioned in subsection (14) below to occur after the commission of the relevant offence.

(14) Those events are—
  (a) the person surrenders to custody at the appointed place;
  (b) the person is arrested, or attends at a police station, in connection with the relevant offence or the offence for which he was granted bail;
  (c) the person appears or is brought before a court in connection with the relevant offence or the offence for which he was granted bail.

Liability to arrest for absconding or breaking conditions of bail

D7.147 7.—(1) If a person who has been released on bail in criminal proceedings and is under a duty to surrender into the custody of a court fails to surrender to custody at the time appointed for him to do so the court may issue a warrant for his arrest.

(1A) Subsection (1B) applies if—
  (a) a person has been released on bail in connection with extradition proceedings,
  (b) the person is under a duty to surrender into the custody of a constable, and
  (c) the person fails to surrender to custody at the time appointed for him to do so.

(1B) A magistrates' court may issue a warrant for the person's arrest.

(2) If a person who has been released on bail in criminal proceedings absents himself from the court at any time after he has surrendered into the custody of the court and before the court is ready to begin or to resume the hearing of the proceedings, the court may issue a warrant for his arrest; but no warrant shall be issued under this subsection where that person is absent in accordance with leave given to him by or on behalf of the court.

(3) A person who has been released on bail in criminal proceedings and is under a duty to surrender into the custody of a court may be arrested without warrant by a constable—
  (a) if the constable has reasonable grounds for believing that that person is not likely to surrender to custody;
  (b) if the constable has reasonable grounds for believing that that person is likely to break any of the conditions of his bail or has reasonable grounds for suspecting that that person has broken any of those conditions; or
  (c) in a case where that person was released on bail with one or more surety or sureties, if a surety notifies a constable in writing that that person is unlikely to surrender to custody and that for that reason the surety wishes to be relieved of his obligations as a surety.

(4) A person arrested in pursuance of subsection (3) above—
  (a) shall, except where he was arrested within 24 hours of the time appointed for him to surrender to custody, be brought as soon as practicable and in any event within 24 hours after his arrest before a justice of the peace; and
  (b) in the said excepted case shall be brought before the court at which he was to have surrendered to custody.

(4A) A person who has been released on bail in connection with extradition proceedings and is under a duty to surrender into the custody of a constable may be arrested without warrant by a constable on any of the grounds set out in paragraphs (a) to (c) of subsection (3).

(4B) A person arrested in pursuance of subsection (4A) above shall be brought as soon as practicable and in any event within 24 hours after his arrest before a justice of the peace for the petty sessions area in which he was arrested.

(5) A justice of the peace before whom a person is brought under subsection (4) above may, subject to subsections (5A) and (6) below, if of the opinion that that person—
  (a) is not likely to surrender to custody, or
  (b) has broken or is likely to break any condition of his bail,

remand him in custody or commit him to custody, as the case may require, or alternatively, grant him bail subject to the same or to different conditions, but if not of that opinion shall grant him bail subject to the same conditions (if any) as were originally imposed.

(5A) A justice of the peace may not remand a person in, or commit a person to, custody under subsection (5) if—
(a) the person has attained the age of eighteen,
(b) the person was released on bail in non-extradition proceedings,
(c) the person has not been convicted of an offence in those proceedings, and
(d) it appears to the justice of the peace that there is no real prospect that the person will be sentenced to a custodial sentence in the proceedings.

(6) Where a person brought before a justice under subsection (4) or (4B) is a child or young person and the justice does not grant him bail, subsection (5) above shall have effect subject to the provisions of section 91 of the Legal Aid, Sentencing and Punishment of Offenders Act 2012 (remands of children otherwise than on bail).

(7) In reckoning for the purposes of this subsection any period of 24 hours, no account shall be taken of Christmas Day, Good Friday or any Sunday.

(8) In the case of a person charged with murder or with murder and one or more other offences—
(a) subsections (4) and (5) have effect as if for 'justice of the peace' there were substituted 'judge of the Crown Court',
(b) subsection (6) has effect as if for 'justice' (in both places) there were substituted 'judge', and
(c) subsection (7) has effect, for the purposes of subsection (4), as if at the end there were added 'Saturday or bank holiday'.

Bail with sureties

8.—(1) This section applies where a person is granted bail in criminal proceedings on condition that he provides one or more surety or sureties for the purpose of securing that he surrenders to custody. **D7.148**

(2) In considering the suitability for that purpose of a proposed surety, regard may be had (amongst other things) to—
(a) the surety's financial resources;
(b) his character and any previous convictions of his; and
(c) his proximity (whether in point of kinship, place of residence or otherwise) to the person for whom he is to be surety.

(3) Where a court grants a person bail in criminal proceedings on such a condition but is unable to release him because no surety or no suitable surety is available, the court shall fix the amount in which the surety is to be found and subsections (4) and (5) below, or in a case where the proposed surety resides in Scotland subsection (6) below, shall apply for the purpose of enabling the recognizance of the surety to be entered into subsequently.

(4) Where this subsection applies the recognizance of the surety may be entered into before such of the following persons or descriptions of persons as the court may by order specify or, if it makes no such order, before any of the following persons, that is to say—
(a) where the decision is taken by a magistrates' court, before a justice of the peace, a justices' clerk or a police officer who either is of the rank of inspector or above or is in charge of a police station or, if Criminal Procedure Rules so provide, by a person of such other description as is specified in the rules;
(b) where the decision is taken by the Crown Court, before any of the persons specified in paragraph (a) above or, if Criminal Procedure Rules so provide, by a person of such other description as is specified in the rules;
(c) where the decision is taken by the High Court or the Court of Appeal, before any of the persons specified in paragraph (a) above or, if Criminal Procedure Rules so provide, by a person of such other description as is specified in the rules;
(d) where the decision is taken by the Court Martial Appeal Court, before any of the persons specified in paragraph (a) above or, if Court Martial Appeal Rules so provide, by a person of such other description as is specified in the rules;

and Civil Procedure Rules, Criminal Procedure Rules or Court Martial Appeal Rules may also prescribe the manner in which a recognizance which is to be entered into before such a person is to be entered into and the persons by whom and the manner in which the recognizance may be enforced.

(5) Where a surety seeks to enter into his recognizance before any person in accordance with subsection (4) above but that person declines to take his recognizance because he is not satisfied of the surety's suitability, the surety may apply to—
(a) the court which fixed the amount of the recognizance in which the surety was to be bound, or
(b) a magistrates' court.
(6) Where this subsection applies, the court, if satisfied of the suitability of the proposed surety, may direct that arrangements be made for the recognizance of the surety to be entered into in Scotland before any constable, within the meaning of the Police (Scotland) Act 1967, having charge at any police office or station in like manner as the recognizance would be entered into in England or Wales.
(7) Where, in pursuance of subsection (4) or (6) above, a recognizance is entered into otherwise than before the court that fixed the amount of the recognizance, the same consequences shall follow as if it had been entered into before that court.

Miscellaneous

Offence of agreeing to indemnify sureties in criminal proceedings

D7.149 9.—(1) If a person agrees with another to indemnify that other against any liability which that other may incur as a surety to secure the surrender to custody of a person accused or convicted of or under arrest for an offence, he and that other person shall be guilty of an offence.
(2) An offence under subsection (1) above is committed whether the agreement is made before or after the person to be indemnified becomes a surety and whether or not he becomes a surety and whether the agreement contemplates compensation in money or in money's worth.
(3) Where a magistrates' court convicts a person of an offence under subsection (1) above the court may, if it thinks—
(a) that the circumstances of the offence are such that greater punishment should be inflicted for that offence than the court has power to inflict, or
(b) in a case where it sends that person for trial to the Crown Court for another offence, that it would be appropriate for him to be dealt with for the offence under subsection (1) above by the court before which he is tried for the other offence,
commit him in custody or on bail to the Crown Court for sentence.
(4) A person guilty of an offence under subsection (1) above shall be liable—
(a) on summary conviction, to imprisonment for a term not exceeding 3 months or to a fine not exceeding the prescribed sum or to both; or
(b) on conviction on indictment or if sentenced by the Crown Court on committal for sentence under subsection (3) above, to imprisonment for a term not exceeding 12 months or to a fine or to both.
(5) No proceedings for an offence under subsection (1) above shall be instituted except by or with the consent of the Director of Public Prosecutions.

Bail decisions relating to persons aged under 18 who are accused of offences mentioned in schedule 2 to the Magistrates' Courts Act 1980

D7.150 9A.—(1) This section applies whenever—
(a) a magistrates' court is considering whether to withhold or grant bail in relation to a child or young person who is accused of a scheduled offence; and
(b) the trial of that offence has not begun.
(2) The court shall, before deciding whether to withhold or grant bail, consider whether, having regard to any representations made by the prosecutor or the accused child or young person, the value involved does not exceed the relevant sum for the purposes of section 22.
(3) The duty in subsection (2) does not apply in relation to an offence if—
(a) a determination under subsection (4) has already been made in relation to that offence; or
(b) the accused child or young person is, in relation to any other offence of which he is accused which is not a scheduled offence, a person to whom Part 1 of Schedule 1 to this Act applies.
(4) *If where the duty in subsection* (2) applies it appears to the court clear that, for the offence in question, the amount involved does not exceed the relevant sum, the court shall make a determination to that effect.

(5) In this section—
(a) 'relevant sum' has the same meaning as in section 22(1) of the Magistrates' Courts Act 1980 (certain either way offences to be tried summarily if value involved is less than the relevant sum);
(b) 'scheduled offence' means an offence mentioned in schedule 2 to that Act (offences for which the value involved is relevant to the mode of trial); and
(c) 'the value involved' is to be construed in accordance with section 22(10) to (12) of that Act.

[**10.** and **11.** Repealed.]
[**12.** Amendments, repeals and transitional provisions.]
[**13.** Short title, commencement, application and extent.]

Schedule 1

Persons Entitled to Bail: Supplementary Provisions

Part I

Defendants Accused or Convicted of Imprisonable Offences

Defendants to whom Part I applies

1.—(1) Subject to sub-paragraph (2) and paragraph 1A, the following provisions of this Part of this Schedule apply to the defendant if— **D7.151**
(a) the offence or one of the offences of which he is accused or convicted in the proceedings is punishable with imprisonment, or
(b) his extradition is sought in respect of an offence.
(2) But those provisions do not apply by virtue of sub-paragraph (1)(a) if the offence, or each of the offences punishable with imprisonment, is—
(a) a summary offence; or
(b) an offence mentioned in schedule 2 to the Magistrates' Courts Act 1980 (offences for which the value involved is relevant to the mode of trial) in relation to which—
(i) a determination has been made under section 22(2) of that Act (certain either way offences to be tried summarily if value involved is less than the relevant sum) that it is clear that the value does not exceed the relevant sum for the purposes of that section; or
(ii) a determination has been made under section 9A(4) of this Act to the same effect.

1A.—(1) The paragraphs of this Part of this Schedule mentioned in sub-paragraph (2) do not apply in relation to bail in non-extradition proceedings where—
(a) the defendant has attained the age of 18,
(b) the defendant has not been convicted of an offence in those proceedings, and
(c) it appears to the court that there is no real prospect that the defendant will be sentenced to a custodial sentence in the proceedings.
(2) The paragraphs are—
(a) paragraph 2 (refusal of bail where defendant may fail to surrender to custody, commit offences on bail or interfere with witnesses),
(b) paragraph 2A (refusal of bail where defendant appears to have committed indictable or either way offence while on bail), and
(c) paragraph 6 (refusal of bail where defendant has been arrested under section 7).

Exceptions to right to bail

2.—(1) The defendant need not be granted bail if the court is satisfied that there are substantial grounds for believing that the defendant, if released on bail (whether subject to conditions or not) would— **D7.152**
(a) fail to surrender to custody, or
(b) commit an offence while on bail, or
(c) interfere with witnesses or otherwise obstruct the course of justice, whether in relation to himself or any other person.
(2) Where the defendant falls within paragraph 6B, this paragraph does not apply unless—
(a) the court is of the opinion mentioned in paragraph 6A, or
(b) paragraph 6A does not apply by virtue of paragraph 6C.

2ZA.—(1) The defendant need not be granted bail if the court is satisfied that there are substantial grounds for believing that the defendant, if released on bail (whether subject to conditions or not), would commit an offence while on bail by engaging in conduct that would, or would be likely to, cause—
(a) physical or mental injury to an associated person; or
(b) an associated person to fear physical or mental injury.
(2) In sub-paragraph (1) 'associated person' means a person who is associated with the defendant within the meaning of section 62 of the Family Law Act 1996.
2A. The defendant need not be granted bail if—
(a) the offence is an indictable offence or an offence triable either way, and
(b) it appears to the court that the defendant was on bail in criminal proceedings on the date of the offence.
2B. The defendant need not be granted bail in connection with extradition proceedings if—
(a) the conduct constituting the offence would, if carried out by the defendant in England and Wales, constitute an indictable offence or an offence triable either way; and
(b) it appears to the court that the defendant was on bail on the date of the offence.
3. The defendant need not be granted bail if the court is satisfied that the defendant should be kept in custody for his own protection or, if he is a child or young person, for his own welfare.
4. The defendant need not be granted bail if he is in custody in pursuance of a sentence of a court or a sentence imposed by an officer under the Armed Forces Act 2006.
5. The defendant need not be granted bail where the court is satisfied that it has not been practicable to obtain sufficient information for the purpose of taking the decisions required by this Part of this Schedule for want of time since the institution of the proceedings against him.
6.—(1) The defendant need not be granted bail if, having previously been released on bail in, or in connection with, the proceedings, the defendant has been arrested in pursuance of section 7.
6ZA. If the defendant is charged with murder, the defendant may not be granted bail unless the court is of the opinion that there is no significant risk of the defendant committing, while on bail, an offence that would, or would be likely to, cause physical or mental injury to any person other than the defendant.

Exception applicable to drug users in certain areas

D7.153 6A. Subject to paragraph 6C below, a defendant who falls within paragraph 6B below may not be granted bail unless the court is of the opinion that there is no significant risk of his committing an offence while on bail (whether subject to conditions or not).
6B.—(1) A defendant falls within this paragraph if—
(a) he is aged 18 or over,
(b) a sample taken—
(i) under section 63B of the Police and Criminal Evidence Act 1984 (testing for presence of Class A drugs) in connection with the offence; or
(ii) under section 161 of the Criminal Justice Act 2003 (drug testing after conviction of an offence but before sentence),
has revealed the presence in his body of a specified Class A drug;
(c) either the offence is one under section 5(2) or (3) of the Misuse of Drugs Act 1971 and relates to a specified Class A drug, or the court is satisfied that there are substantial grounds for believing—
(i) that misuse by him of any specified Class A drug caused or contributed to the offence; or
(ii) (even if it did not) that the offence was motivated wholly or partly by his intended misuse of such a drug; and
(d) the condition set out in sub-paragraph (2) below is satisfied or (if the court is considering on a second or subsequent occasion whether or not to grant bail) has been, and continues to be, satisfied.
(2) The condition referred to is that after the taking and analysis of the sample—
(a) a relevant assessment has been offered to the defendant but he does not agree to undergo it; or
(b) he has undergone a relevant assessment, and relevant follow-up has been proposed to him, but he does not agree to participate in it.

(3) In this paragraph and paragraph 6C below—
(a) 'Class A drug' and 'misuse' have the same meaning as in the Misuse of Drugs Act 1971;
(b) 'relevant assessment' and 'relevant follow-up' have the meaning given by section 3(6E) of this Act;
(c) 'specified' (in relation to a Class A drug) has the same meaning as in Part 3 of the Criminal Justice and Court Services Act 2000.

6C. Paragraph 6A above does not apply unless—
(a) the court has been notified by the Secretary of State that arrangements for conducting a relevant assessment or, as the case may be, providing relevant follow-up have been made for the local justice area in which it appears to the court that the defendant would reside if granted bail; and
(b) the notice has not been withdrawn.

Exception applicable only to defendant whose case is adjourned for inquiries or a report

7. Where his case is adjourned for inquiries or a report, the defendant need not be granted bail **D7.154**
if it appears to the court that it would be impracticable to complete the inquiries or make the report without keeping the defendant in custody.

Restriction of conditions of bail

8.—(1) Subject to subparagraph (3) below, where the defendant is granted bail, no conditions **D7.155**
shall be imposed under subsections (4) to (6B) or (7) (except subsection (6)(d) or (e)) of section 3 of this Act unless it appears to the court that it is necessary to do so—
(a) for the purpose of preventing the occurrence of any of the events mentioned in paragraph 2(1) of this Part of this Schedule, or
(b) for the defendant's own protection or, if he is a child or young person, for his own welfare or in his own interests.

(1A) No condition shall be imposed under section 3(6)(d) of this Act unless it appears to be necessary to do so for the purpose of enabling inquiries or a report to be made.

(2) Subparagraphs (1) and (1A) above also apply on any application to the court to vary the conditions of bail or to impose conditions in respect of bail which has been granted unconditionally.

(3) The restriction imposed by subparagraph (1A) above shall not apply to the conditions required to be imposed under section 3(6A) of this Act or operate to override the direction in section 11(3) of the Powers of Criminal Courts (Sentencing) Act 2000 to a magistrates' court to impose conditions of bail under section 3(6)(d) of this Act of the description specified in the said section 11(3) in the circumstances so specified.

Decisions under paragraph 2

9. In taking the decisions required by paragraph 2(1), or in deciding whether it is satisfied as men- **D7.156**
tioned in paragraph 2ZA(1), or of the opinion mentioned in paragraph 6ZA or 6A of this Part of this Schedule, the court shall have regard to such of the following considerations as appear to it to be relevant, that is to say—
(a) the nature and seriousness of the offence or default (and the probable method of dealing with the defendant for it),
(b) the character, antecedents, associations and community ties of the defendant,
(c) the defendant's record as respects the fulfilment of his obligations under previous grants of bail in criminal proceedings,
(d) except in the case of a defendant whose case is adjourned for inquiries or a report, the strength of the evidence of his having committed the offence or having defaulted,
(e) if the court is satisfied that there are substantial grounds for believing that the defendant, if released on bail (whether subject to conditions or not), would commit an offence while on bail, the risk that the defendant may do so by engaging in conduct that would, or would be likely to, cause physical or mental injury to any person other than the defendant,

as well as to any others which appear to be relevant.

9AA.—(1) This paragraph applies if—
(a) the defendant is a child or young person, and
(b) it appears to the court that he was on bail in criminal proceedings on the date of the offence.

(2) In deciding for the purposes of paragraph 2(1) of this Part of this Schedule whether it is satisfied that there are substantial grounds for believing that the defendant, if released on bail (whether subject to conditions or not), would commit an offence while on bail, the court shall give particular weight to the fact that the defendant was on bail in criminal proceedings on the date of the offence.

9AB.—(1) Subject to sub-paragraph (2) below, this paragraph applies if—

(a) the defendant is a child or young person, and

(b) it appears to the court that, having been released on bail in or in connection with the proceedings for the offence, he failed to surrender to custody.

(2) Where it appears to the court that the defendant had reasonable cause for his failure to surrender to custody, this paragraph does not apply unless it also appears to the court that he failed to surrender to custody at the appointed place as soon as reasonably practicable after the appointed time.

(3) In deciding for the purposes of paragraph 2(1) of this Part of this Schedule whether it is satisfied that there are substantial grounds for believing that the defendant, if released on bail (whether subject to conditions or not), would fail to surrender to custody, the court shall give particular weight to—

(a) where the defendant did not have reasonable cause for his failure to surrender to custody, the fact that he failed to surrender to custody, or

(b) where he did have reasonable cause for his failure to surrender to custody, the fact that he failed to surrender to custody at the appointed place as soon as reasonably practicable after the appointed time.

(4) For the purposes of this paragraph, a failure to give to the defendant a copy of the record of the decision to grant him bail shall not constitute a reasonable cause for his failure to surrender to custody.

[Note: Paragraphs 9AA and 9AB are in force only in respect of offences which attract a life sentence: see SI 2006 No. 3217.]

Cases under section 128A of Magistrates' Courts Act 1980

D7.157 **9B.** Where the court is considering exercising the power conferred by section 128A of the Magistrates' Courts Act 1980 (power to remand in custody for more than 8 clear days), it shall have regard to the total length of time which the accused would spend in custody if it were to exercise the power.

Part IA

Defendants Accused or Convicted of Imprisonable Offences to which Part I Does Not Apply

Defendants to whom Part IA applies

D7.158 **1.** Subject to paragraph 1A, the following provisions of this Part apply to the defendant if—

(a) the offence or one of the offences of which he is accused or convicted is punishable with imprisonment, but

(b) Part 1 does not apply to him by virtue of paragraph 1(2) of that part.

1A.—(1) The paragraphs of this Part of this Schedule mentioned in sub-paragraph (2) do not apply in relation to bail in, or in connection with, proceedings where—

(a) the defendant has attained the age of 18,

(b) the defendant has not been convicted of an offence in those proceedings, and

(c) it appears to the court that there is no real prospect that the defendant will be sentenced to a custodial sentence in the proceedings.

(2) The paragraphs are—

(a) paragraph 2 (refusal of bail for failure to surrender to custody),

(b) paragraph 3 (refusal of bail where defendant would commit further offences on bail), and

(c) paragraph 7 (refusal of bail in certain circumstances when arrested under section 7).

Exceptions to right to bail

D7.159 **2.** The defendant need not be granted bail if—

(a) it appears to the court that, having been previously granted bail in criminal proceedings, he has failed to surrender to custody in accordance with his obligations under the grant of bail; and

(b) the court believes, in view of that failure, that the defendant, if released on bail (whether subject to conditions or not) would fail to surrender to custody.

3. The defendant need not be granted bail if—

(a) it appears to the court that the defendant was on bail in criminal proceedings on the date of the offence; and

(b) the court is satisfied that there are substantial grounds for believing that the defendant, if released on bail (whether subject to conditions or not) would commit an offence while on bail.

4.—(1) The defendant need not be granted bail if the court is satisfied that there are substantial grounds for believing that the defendant, if released on bail (whether subject to conditions or not), would commit an offence while on bail by engaging in conduct that would, or would be likely to, cause—
(a) physical or mental injury to an associated person; or
(b) an associated person to fear physical or mental injury.
(2) In sub-paragraph (1) 'associated person' means a person who is associated with the defendant within the meaning of section 62 of the Family Law Act 1996.
5. The defendant need not be granted bail if the court is satisfied that the defendant should be kept in custody for his own protection or, if he is a child or young person, for his own welfare.
6. The defendant need not be granted bail if he is in custody in pursuance of a sentence of a court or a sentence imposed by an officer under the Armed Forces Act 2006
7. The defendant need not be granted bail if—
(a) having been released on bail in or in connection with the proceedings for the offence, he has been arrested in pursuance of section 7 of this Act; and
(b) the court is satisfied that there are substantial grounds for believing that the defendant, if released on bail (whether subject to conditions or not) would fail to surrender to custody, commit an offence while on bail or interfere with witnesses or otherwise obstruct the course of justice (whether in relation to himself or any other person).
8. The defendant need not be granted bail where the court is satisfied that it has not been practicable to obtain sufficient information for the purpose of taking the decisions required by this Part of this Schedule for want of time since the institution of the proceedings against him.

Application of paragraphs 6A to 6C of Part 1

9. Paragraphs 6A to 6C of Part 1 (exception applicable to drug users in certain areas and related provisions) apply to a defendant to whom this Part applies as they apply to a defendant to whom that Part applies. **D7.160**

Part II

Defendants Accused or Convicted of Non-imprisonable Offences

Defendants to whom Part II applies

1. Where the offence or every offence of which the defendant is accused or convicted in the proceedings is one which is not punishable with imprisonment the following provisions of this Part of this Schedule apply. **D7.161**

Exceptions to right to bail

2. The defendant need not be granted bail if— **D7.162**
(za) the defendant—
(i) is a child or young person, or
(ii) has been convicted in the proceedings of an offence;
(a) it appears to the court that, having been previously granted bail in criminal proceedings, he has failed to surrender to custody in accordance with his obligations under the grant of bail; and
(b) the court believes, in view of that failure, that the defendant, if released on bail (whether subject to conditions or not) would fail to surrender to custody.
3. The defendant need not be granted bail if the court is satisfied that the defendant should be kept in custody for his own protection or, if he is a child or young person, for his own welfare.
4. The defendant need not be granted bail if he is in custody in pursuance of a sentence of a court or a sentence imposed by an officer under the Armed Forces Act 2006.
5. The defendant need not be granted bail if—
(za) the defendant—
(i) is a child or young person, or
(ii) has been convicted in the proceedings of an offence;
(a) having been released on bail in or in connection with the proceedings for the offence, he has been arrested in pursuance of section 7 of this Act; and
(b) the court is satisfied that there are substantial grounds for believing that the defendant, if released on bail (whether subject to conditions or not) would fail to surrender to custody, commit an offence on bail or interfere with witnesses or otherwise obstruct the course of justice (whether in relation to himself or any other person).

6.—(1) The defendant need not be granted bail if—
(a) having been released on bail in, or in connection with, the proceedings for the offence, the defendant has been arrested in pursuance of section 7, and
(b) the court is satisfied that there are substantial grounds for believing that the defendant, if released on bail (whether subject to conditions or not), would commit an offence while on bail by engaging in conduct that would, or would be likely to, cause—
(i) physical or mental injury to an associated person, or
(ii) an associated person to fear physical or mental injury.
(2) In sub-paragraph (1) 'associated person' means a person who is associated with the defendant within the meaning of section 62 of the Family Law Act 1996.

Part IIA

Decisions Where Bail Refused on Previous Hearing

D7.163 1. If the court decides not to grant the defendant bail, it is the court's duty to consider, at each subsequent hearing while the defendant is a person to whom section 4 above applies and remains in custody, whether he ought to be granted bail.
2. At the first hearing after that at which the court decided not to grant the defendant bail he may support an application for bail with any argument as to fact or law that he desires (whether or not he has advanced that argument previously).
3. At subsequent hearings the court need not hear arguments as to fact or law which it has heard previously.

Part III

[Interpretation]

D7.164 1. For the purposes of this Schedule the question whether an offence is one which is punishable with imprisonment shall be determined without regard to any enactment prohibiting or restricting the imprisonment of young offenders or first offenders.
2. References in this Schedule to previous grants of bail include—
(a) bail granted before the coming into force of this Act;
(b) as respects the reference in paragraph 2A of Part 1 of this Schedule (as substituted by paragraph 16 of Schedule 11 to the Legal Aid, Sentencing and Punishment of Offenders Act 2012), bail granted before the coming into force of that paragraph;
(c) as respects the references in paragraph 6 of Part 1 of this Schedule (as substituted by paragraph 17 of Schedule 11 to the Legal Aid, Sentencing and Punishment of Offenders Act 2012), bail granted before the coming into force of that paragraph;
(d) as respects the references in paragraph 9AA of Part 1 of this Schedule, bail granted before the coming into force of that paragraph;
(e) as respects the references in paragraph 9AB of Part 1 of this Schedule, bail granted before the coming into force of that paragraph;
(f) as respects the reference in paragraph 5 of Part 2 of this Schedule (as substituted by section 13(4) of the Criminal Justice Act 2003), bail granted before the coming into force of that paragraph;
(g) as respects the reference in paragraph 6 of Part 2 of this Schedule, bail granted before the coming into force of that paragraph.
3. References in this Schedule to a defendant's being kept in custody or being in custody include (where the defendant is a child or young person) references to his being kept or being in accommodation pursuant to a remand under section 91(3) or (4) of the Legal Aid, Sentencing and Punishment of Offenders Act 2012 (remands to local authority accommodation or youth detention accommodation).
4. In this Schedule—
'court', in the expression 'sentence of a court' includes a service court as defined in section 12(1) of the Visiting Forces Act 1952 and 'sentence', in that expression, shall be construed in accordance with that definition;
'default', in relation to the defendant, means the default for which he is to be dealt with under Part 2 of Schedule 8 to the Criminal Justice Act 2003 (breach of requirement of order).

TEXT OF THE BAIL (AMENDMENT) ACT 1993

Bail (Amendment) Act 1993, s. 1

D7.165

(1) Where a magistrates' court grants bail to a person who is charged with or convicted of an offence punishable by imprisonment, the prosecution may appeal to a judge of the Crown Court against the granting of bail.

(1A) Where a magistrates' court grants bail to a person in connection with extradition proceedings, the prosecution may appeal to the High Court against the granting of bail.

(1B) Where a judge of the Crown Court grants bail to a person who is charged with, or convicted of, an offence punishable by imprisonment, the prosecution may appeal to the High Court against the granting of bail.

(1C) An appeal under subsection (1B) may not be made where a judge of the Crown Court has granted bail on an appeal under subsection (1).

(2) Subsections (1) and (1B) above apply only where the prosecution is conducted—
  (a) by or on behalf of the Director of Public Prosecutions; or
  (b) by a person who falls within such class or description of person as may be prescribed for the purposes of this section by order made by the Secretary of State.

(3) An appeal under subsection (1), (1A) or (1B) may be made only if—
  (a) the prosecution made representations that bail should not be granted; and
  (b) the representations were made before it was granted.

(4) In the event of the prosecution wishing to exercise the right of appeal set out in subsection (1), (1A) or (1B) above, oral notice of appeal shall be given to the court which has granted bail at the conclusion of the proceedings in which bail has been granted and before the release from custody of the person concerned.

(5) Written notice of appeal shall thereafter be served on the court which has granted bail and the person concerned within two hours of the conclusion of such proceedings.

(6) Upon receipt from the prosecution of oral notice of appeal from its decision to grant bail the court which has granted bail shall remand in custody the person concerned, until the appeal is determined or otherwise disposed of.

(7) Where the prosecution fails, within the period of two hours mentioned in subsection (5) above, to serve one or both of the notices required by that subsection, the appeal shall be deemed to have been disposed of.

(8) The hearing of an appeal under subsection (1), (1A) or (1B) above against a decision of the court to grant bail shall be commenced within forty-eight hours, excluding weekends and any public holiday (that is to say, Christmas Day, Good Friday or a bank holiday), from the date on which oral notice of appeal is given.

(9) At the hearing of any appeal by the prosecution under this section, such appeal shall be by way of re-hearing, and the judge hearing any such appeal may remand the person concerned in custody or may grant bail subject to such conditions (if any) as he thinks fit.

(10) In relation to a person under the age of 18—
  (a) the references in subsections (1) and (1B) above to an offence punishable by imprisonment are to be read as references to an offence which would be so punishable in the case of an adult; and
  (b) the references in subsections (6) and (9) above to remand in custody are to be read subject to the provisions of Chapter 3 of Part 3 of the Legal Aid, Sentencing and Punishment of Offenders Act 2012 (remands of children otherwise than on bail).

(11) [Rule-making power.]

(12) In this section—
  'extradition proceedings' means proceedings under the Extradition Act 2003;
  'magistrates' court' and 'court' in relation to extradition proceedings means a District Judge (Magistrates' Courts) designated in accordance with section 67 or section 139 of the Extradition Act 2003;
  'prosecution' in relation to extradition proceedings means the person acting on behalf of the territory to which extradition is sought.

Section D8 Assets Recovery

INTRODUCTION

D8.1 The powers of investigating, preserving and recovering the proceeds of crime may be broadly divided into eight categories:

(a) civil freezing and recovery of criminal property in the High Court;
(b) taxation of criminal profits;
(c) seizure and summary forfeiture of cash, listed assets and bank balances;
(d) powers of investigation;
(e) criminal restraint orders;
(f) seizure of realisable property other than cash;
(g) post-conviction confiscation (see **E19**).

Accredited Financial Investigators

D8.2 The 'Accredited Financial Investigator' has a significant role to play in this field, being authorised, for example, to exercise powers of investigation. An accredited financial investigator is someone who has been trained and accredited under s. 3 of the POCA 2002. The authorities which may provide financial investigators, such as the Department for Works and Pensions, are identified in the Proceeds of Crime Act 2002 (References to Financial Investigators) (England and Wales) Order 2015 (SI 2015 No. 1583).

HIGH COURT: CIVIL RECOVERY ORDERS

D8.3 The POCA 2002, Part 5, contains provisions permitting the 'civil recovery' of property that is or represents property obtained through criminal conduct. Chapter 2 of Part 5 concerns civil recovery in the High Court. The burden of proof lies on the applicant 'enforcement authority', except where an unexplained wealth order has been obtained in respect of property and not complied with (see **D8.55**). An enforcement authority that is undertaking a 'civil recovery investigation' may apply for a number of investigative orders (see **D8.36**). For civil recovery pursuant to an overseas request see Part 5 of the Proceeds of Crime Act 2002 (External Requests and Orders) Order 2005 (SI 2005 No. 3181). For civil recovery in the magistrates' court see the POCA 2002, Part 5, chs. 3 (see **D8.12**), 3A (see **D8.27**) and 3B (see **D8.33**).

Overview

D8.4 Claims for civil recovery, brought by the 'enforcement authority', are governed by the Civil Recovery Practice Direction (July 2013). An enforcement authority may be the NCA (which replaced the Assets Recovery Agency and the SOCA), the DPP, the Director of the SFO, HMRC or the FCA. To start proceedings the enforcement authority must reasonably believe that the value of the property claimed is not less than £10,000, being the threshold sum (specified by the Secretary of State under s. 287). If the enforcement authority proves to the civil standard the existence of 'property obtained through unlawful conduct' ('recoverable property', as to which see **D8.6**) or property that represents such property, the court may make an order vesting the property in a 'trustee for civil recovery', who is a receiver with wide powers to realise the property. Proceedings may not be taken in respect of cash alone (s. 282(2)). An order may not be made if it would be incompatible with the ECHR (see s. 266 and *NCA v Azam* [2015] EWCA Civ 1234, [2016] 1 WLR 2560). The Limitation Act 1980, ss. 27A and 27B, fix the limitation period at 20 years from the date upon which the cause of action accrued (PACA 2009, s. 62). Under s. 282A, the court may make orders in defined circumstances in relation to property outside England and Wales, thereby reversing the Supreme Court decision to the contrary in *SOCA v Perry* [2012] UKSC 35, [2013] 1 AC 182.

Unlawful Conduct

In broad terms, 'unlawful conduct' (which must be proven to obtain an order for civil recovery) means crime wherever it is committed; more precisely, it is conduct that is unlawful under UK criminal law or, if it occurs in another country or territory, conduct contrary to the criminal law of that country which would be unlawful if it occurred in the UK (s. 241). From 31 January 2018, s. 241(2A) (introduced by the Criminal Finances Act 2017, s. 13) applies, so that 'unlawful conduct' also includes conduct occurring outside the UK which 'constitutes, or is connected with, the commission of a gross human rights abuse or violation' (defined in s. 241A) and which, if it occurred in the UK, would be an offence triable under the criminal law, regardless of whether it was an offence in the country where it occurred. **D8.5**

Recoverable Property

'Recoverable property' is property 'obtained through unlawful conduct' (POCA 2002, s. 304(1)), or property into which such property may be traced. Property is obtained by a person through unlawful conduct if it is obtained 'by or in return for the conduct', whether the conduct is that person's or another's (s. 242(1)). If such property is disposed of, it is recoverable in the hands of the recipient (s. 304(2)) unless the recipient obtained the property in good faith, for value and without notice (s. 308(1)). Property may be 'traced' into other property where the replacement property 'represents' the original property (s. 305(1)). Thus, if stolen goods are sold for cash, both the cash and the stolen goods are recoverable property. If recoverable property is 'mixed' with other property, the portion of the mixed property which is attributable to the recoverable property represents the recoverable property (s. 306). Any profit accruing on recoverable property is itself recoverable (s. 307). Property is not recoverable in certain situations specified in s. 308, for example where a restraint order applies to it. **D8.6**

Interim Orders

The POCA 2002, ss. 245A to 245G, authorise the High Court to make a 'property freezing order' in respect of property and, where necessary, also to appoint a receiver in respect of that property. In principle, a property freezing order prohibits 'any person to whose property the order applies from in any way dealing with the property' (s. 245A(2)). However, an order may be varied to 'exclude' permitted ways of dealing with the property from the general prohibition under s. 245C. The court may make an exclusion for the purpose of enabling a person to meet legal expenses in respect of the proceedings. The power to make such an exclusion should be exercised with a view to ensuring, so far as practicable, that there is no undue prejudice to the right to recover the property (s. 245C(8)), but subject to s. 245C(6), which requires the court to have regard to the desirability of the person being represented in the proceedings. If the person has other assets to pay for representation or there are specific indications that the person has such assets, the court should not grant the exclusion (see *SOCA v Azam* [2013] EWCA Civ 970, [2014] 1 All ER 206 and the Proceeds of Crime Act 2002 (Legal Expenses in Civil Recovery Proceedings) Regulations 2005 (SI 2005 No. 3382)). **D8.7**

Sections 246 to 247 and 250 to 255 authorise the High Court to make an interim receiving order in respect of property, the effect of which is to order the detention, custody, or preservation of property and the appointment of an interim receiver.

Applications for freezing orders and interim receiving orders may be made without notice. Such applications may be granted 'on the papers' and there is no requirement to give reasons (*Nuttall v NCA* [2016] EWHC 1911 (Admin), [2016] 4 WLR 134 (albeit concerning a disclosure order) disapproving of *NCA v Simkus* [2016] EWHC 255 (Admin), [2016] 1 WLR 3481).

Guidance

D8.8 The power to bring proceedings for civil recovery is not conditional upon there having been a successful criminal prosecution. A civil settlement would not be appropriate for those who committed serious crimes such as corruption of senior foreign government officials and they should not be viewed or treated in any different way to other criminals. It would be inconsistent with basic principles of justice for the criminality of corporations to be glossed over by a civil, as opposed to a criminal, sanction (*Innospec Ltd* [2010] Lloyd's Rep FC 462). See also *R (Director of the Assets Recovery Agency) v He* [2004] EWHC 3021 (Admin). The A-G and the Secretary of State issued guidance under the POCA 2002, s. 2A: *Asset Recovery Powers for Prosecutors* (November 2012, tinyurl.com/y8t97zm6). As to deferred prosecution agreements, see **D12.106**.

An acquittal is no bar to civil recovery proceedings in respect of the very same conduct. In *SOCA v Namli* [2013] EWHC 1200 (QB), Males J stated that 'an acquittal whether here or abroad is not conclusive of the defendant's innocence'. It was, however, evidence on which reliance could be placed, though it did not have the status of a formal presumption, and its weight was a matter to be determined, taking account of the circumstances. The weight of an acquittal could be affected by the reason for it: e.g., if it was prompted by procedural defects rather than an assessment of the merits, it might carry 'very little weight'. In *SOCA v Gale* [2011] UKSC 1, [2011] 2 All ER 1 the Supreme Court held that there is nothing in the 'confusing' jurisprudence of the European Court to support a conclusion that the criminal standard must apply to proof of criminal conduct in civil recovery proceedings — in that case, the appellant had been acquitted in Portuguese criminal proceedings. Thus, in serious criminal cases, legal advice should include the possibility that, even if acquitted, the defendant's assets (including property that may have been sold or given away) could be pursued through the High Court. Mortgage providers are advised to spell out in their application forms that a deliberate misstatement could lead to a civil recovery order (*SOCA v Pelekanos* [2009] EWHC 2307 (QB)). Although civil recovery proceedings are barred in respect of property which has been taken into account for the purposes of a confiscation order under s. 308(9), that will not preclude proceedings for civil recovery where the confiscation order is quashed on appeal (*Director of the Assets Recovery Agency v Singh* [2005] EWCA Civ 580, [2005] 1 WLR 3747). Moreover, the admission of evidence that has been ruled inadmissible in criminal proceedings on the basis that it was obtained unlawfully is not an abuse of process. The civil court applies different criteria for the exclusion of evidence under r. 32.1 of the Civil Procedure Rules 1998, and in accordance with the overriding objective. Where evidence has been excluded in criminal proceedings it is the circumstances that led to the exclusion, rather than the fact of the exclusion, that are relevant to admissibility in the civil proceedings (*Olden v SOCA* [2010] EWCA Civ 143).

TAXATION

D8.9 Under Part 6 of the POCA 2002, the NCA may take over the tax collection functions of HMRC in cases where the NCA has reasonable grounds to suspect that taxable income, gains or profits are the proceeds of crime. There is no statutory prohibition on the NCA (a) seeking recovery of property on the basis that it derives from criminal conduct, and (b) assessing an individual for the tax arising in respect of income received from that same criminal conduct.

MAGISTRATES' COURTS: SEIZURE, DETENTION AND FORFEITURE

Part 5 of the POCA 2002 contains three schemes for the summary forfeiture of property that is 'recoverable' or intended for use in unlawful conduct: cash ch. 3, see **D8.11**, 'listed assets' ch. 3A, see **D8.27** and money held in bank accounts ch. 3B, see **D8.33**. **D8.10**

Search and Seizure of Cash

Proceeds of Crime Act 2002, s. 289 **D8.11**

(1) If an officer of Revenue and Customs, a constable, an SFO officer or an accredited financial investigator is lawfully on any premises and has reasonable grounds for suspecting that there is on the premises cash—
(a) which is recoverable property or is intended by any person for use in unlawful conduct, and
(b) the amount of which is not less than the minimum amount,
he may search for the cash there.
(1A) to (1E) [Concern searches of vehicles.]
(2) If an officer of Revenue and Customs, a constable, an SFO officer or an accredited financial investigator has reasonable grounds for suspecting that a person (the suspect) is carrying cash—
(a) which is recoverable property or is intended by any person for use in unlawful conduct, and
(b) the amount of which is not less than the minimum amount,
he may exercise the following powers.
(3) The officer, constable, SFO officer or accredited financial investigator may, so far as he thinks it necessary or expedient, require the suspect—
(a) to permit a search of any article he has with him,
(b) to permit a search of his person.
(4) An officer, constable, SFO officer or accredited financial investigator may—
(a) in exercising powers by virtue of subsection (1D), detain the vehicle for so long as is necessary for their exercise,
(b) in exercising powers by virtue of subsection (3)(b), detain the suspect for so long as is necessary for their exercise.
(5) The powers conferred by this section—
(a) are exercisable only so far as reasonably required for the purpose of finding cash,
(b) are exercisable by an officer of Revenue and Customs only if he has reasonable grounds for suspecting that the unlawful conduct in question relates to an assigned matter (within the meaning of the Customs and Excise Management Act 1979),
(c) are exercisable by an SFO officer or accredited financial investigator only in relation to the following—
(i) premises ... (in the case of subsection (1)),
(ii) vehicles and suspects ... (in the case of subsections (1D) and (4)(a)),
(iii) suspects ... (in the case of subsections (2), (3) and (4)(b)).
(6) Cash means—
(a) notes and coins in any currency,
(b) postal orders,
(c) cheques of any kind, including travellers' cheques,
(d) bankers' drafts,
(e) bearer bonds and bearer shares,
found at any place in the United Kingdom.
(7) Cash also includes any kind of monetary instrument which is found at any place in the United Kingdom, if the instrument is specified by the Secretary of State by an order ...
(8) This section does not require a person to submit to an intimate search or strip search (within the meaning of section 164 of the Customs and Excise Management Act 1979).

General Chapter 3 of Part 5 of the POCA 2002 provides for powers of search, seizure and forfeiture of cash. 'Cash' includes postal orders, all forms of cheque, bankers' drafts, bearer bonds, gaming vouchers, fixed-value casino tokens and betting receipts (and any kind of monetary **D8.12**

instrument specified by the Secretary of State) 'found at any place in the United Kingdom' (s. 289(6) and (7)).

D8.13 **Searches** Searches are governed by the Cash Searches Code of Practice 2018. They may be conducted by constables, officers of Revenue and Customs, SFO officers and accredited financial investigators. Searches need prior approval from a magistrate or, if that is not practical, from a 'senior officer' (as defined by the POCA 2002, s. 290(4)) unless 'in the circumstances it is not practicable to obtain that approval' beforehand (s. 290). If a search is conducted without the authority of a magistrate, and no cash is seized or seized cash is released within 48 hours, a written report must be completed specifying the reasons for the search and why prior approval was not practicable (s. 290(6) and (7)).

To exercise the powers of search under the POCA 2002, s. 289, the officer must have reasonable grounds for suspecting (a) that cash which is recoverable property or which is intended by any person for use in unlawful conduct is on the premises or is being carried by a person, and (b) that the amount of cash is not less than £1,000 (Proceeds of Crime Act 2002 (Recovery of Cash in Summary Proceedings: Minimum Amount) Order 2006 (SI 2006 No. 1699)). Where individuals hold less than the minimum amount, but together hold £1,000 or more, the amounts may be aggregated if there are grounds for suspecting that they have a common source or destination (*Commissioners of Customs and Excise v Duffy* [2002] EWHC 425 (Admin), (2002) *The Times*, 4 April 2002).

The powers of search, as they are exercisable by a constable, extend to immigration officers in respect of a limited class of 'unlawful conduct' (Borders Act 2007, s. 24). In the case of officers of Revenue and Customs, searches are permitted only if the officer has reasonable grounds for suspecting that the unlawful conduct relates to an 'assigned matter' as defined by the Customs and Excise Management Act 1979 — essentially any matter in relation to which the Commissioners are 'for the time being required in pursuance of any enactment to perform any duties'. (The Criminal Finances Act 2017, s. 18, removed certain restrictions on the powers of officers of Revenue and Customs in connection with searches for and seizure of cash.)

There is power to search vehicles which are in a public place or other readily accessible place other than a dwelling where 'it appears to the officer … that the vehicle is under the control of a person (the suspect) who is in or in the vicinity of the vehicle' (POCA 2002, s. 289(1A) to (1E)).

Section 164A of the Customs and Excise Management Act 1979 permits HMRC to exercise certain investigative powers when searching for recoverable property or enforcing compliance with Regulation (EC) No. 1889/2005 on controls of cash entering or leaving the Community ([2005] OJ L309/9).

D8.14 The power to search premises requires the officer to be lawfully on those premises and is exercisable 'only so far as reasonably required for the purpose of finding cash'. Involuntary 'intimate' or 'strip searches' within the meaning of the Customs and Excise Management Act 1979, s. 164, are not permitted (POCA 2002, s. 289(8)), except, it appears, where the search is conducted at the border (Customs and Excise Management Act 1979, s. 164A).

D8.15 **Proceeds of Crime Act 2002, s. 294**

(1) An officer of Revenue and Customs, a constable, an SFO officer or an accredited financial investigator may seize any cash if he has reasonable grounds for suspecting that it is—
  (a) recoverable property, or
  (b) intended by any person for use in unlawful conduct.
(2) An officer of Revenue and Customs, a constable, an SFO officer or an accredited financial investigator may also seize cash part of which he has reasonable grounds for suspecting to be—
  (a) recoverable property, or
  (b) intended by any person for use in unlawful conduct,
  if it is not reasonably practicable to seize only that part.
(2A) to (2C) [Repealed.]
(3) This section does not authorise the seizure of an amount of cash if it or, as the case may be, the part to which his suspicion relates, is less than the minimum amount.

(4) This section does not authorise the seizure by an SFO officer or an accredited financial investigator of cash found in Scotland.

Seizure Constables (and, by reason of the Borders Act 2007, s. 24, immigration officers), officers of Revenue and Customs, SFO officers and accredited financial investigators may seize cash if they have reasonable grounds for suspecting that it is recoverable property or is intended by any person for use in unlawful conduct (POCA 2002, s. 294(1)). It would be an abuse of power to seize cheques whose production had been ordered pursuant to a criminal investigation when the real reason for seeking the production was to enable the cheques to be seized (*R (Merida Oil Traders Ltd) v Central Criminal Court* [2017] EWHC 747 (Admin), [2017] 1 WLR 3680). The whole of a cash amount may be seized if it is not reasonably practicable to sever it from a suspected amount (s. 294(2)). Cash seized under the PACE 1984 (see **D1.178**) may be re-seized under these provisions. Where the PACE powers expire (e.g., where criminal proceedings are abandoned), the authority is allowed a reasonable period of grace before re-seizure under s. 294 (*R (Iqbal) v Luton and South Bedfordshire Magistrates' Court* [2011] EWHC 705 (Admin)). The initial 48-hour limit on detention of cash (see **D8.17**) commences only on the re-seizure under s. 294 (*Chief Constable of Merseyside v Hickman* [2006] EWHC 451 (Admin)). **D8.16**

Detention in Anticipation of Proceedings

Once seized, cash may be detained for investigation, including to make use of the powers exercisable by the Crown Court in respect of a 'detained cash investigation', namely production orders (see **D8.41**) and search warrants (see **D8.44**). **D8.17**

The initial time-limit for detention is 48 hours, although this may be extended upon application by a magistrate for a period of six months. Weekends, Christmas Day, Good Friday and bank holidays are excluded from the 48-hour calculation (POCA 2002, s. 295(1A) and (1B)). Applications, which are made on Form A, are governed by the Magistrates' Courts (Detention and Forfeiture of Cash) Rules 2002 (SI 2002 No. 2998). There are two conditions under s. 295(5) and (6) for continued detention of cash: first, that there are reasonable grounds for suspecting that the cash is recoverable or intended to be used in unlawful conduct and, secondly, that either (a) continued detention is 'justified' while the derivation of the cash is further investigated (and use of the term 'justified' imports, it is submitted, an element of judgement as to the appropriateness of further detention, e.g., where the investigation has not been pursued with due expedition), or (b) consideration is being given to bringing 'in the United Kingdom or elsewhere' proceedings against 'any person' for an offence with which the cash is 'connected', or (c) such proceedings have commenced but have not concluded.

If the application for detention is successful, the court must give notice of the order and a copy of it to the person from whom the cash was seized and to any other person known to be affected by the order. The cash must be deposited in an interest-bearing account. Subsequent applications may seek orders for further detention up to a maximum of two years (s. 295). While the cash is detained pursuant to a court order the person from whom the cash was seized may apply for the return of any part of the cash. To succeed on the application the person must satisfy the court that the above conditions no longer apply (s. 297(3)). It is an abuse of process to seek a High Court declaration of ownership while proceedings continue (*Capper v Chaney and Metropolitan Police Commissioner* [2010] EWHC 1704 (Ch)). If the holding authority is satisfied that detention is no longer justified, it may, after notifying the court, release the cash in whole or in part (s. 297).

Forfeiture

Proceeds of Crime Act 2002, s. 298 **D8.18**

(1) While cash is detained under section 295, 297C or 297D, an application for the forfeiture of the whole or any part of it may be made—
  (a) to a magistrates' court by the Commissioners of Customs and Excise, an accredited financial investigator, a constable or an SFO officer,
  (b) [Scotland].

(2) The court or sheriff may order the forfeiture of the cash or any part of it if satisfied that the cash or part—
  (a) is recoverable property, or
  (b) is intended by any person for use in unlawful conduct.
(3) But in the case of recoverable property which belongs to joint tenants, one of whom is an excepted joint owner, the order may not apply to so much of it as the court thinks is attributable to the excepted joint owner's share.
(4) Where an application for the forfeiture of any cash is made under this section, the cash is to be detained (and may not be released under any power conferred by this chapter) until any proceedings in pursuance of the application (including any proceedings on appeal) are concluded.

D8.19 **The Power** Cash may be forfeited where the court is satisfied that it is 'recoverable property' or 'is intended by any person for use in unlawful conduct' (POCA 2002, s. 298(2)). The Court is only concerned with the nature of the cash (its origins or intended use) and the fact that the cash was seized unlawfully (e.g. because as a historic fact the seizing officer did not have the relevant state of mind) is irrelevant (*R (Campbell) v Bromley Magistrates Court* [2017] EWCA Civ 1161). Proceedings are in the nature of a civil complaint and, as such, are regulated by the MCA 1980, ss. 51 to 74. The standard of proof is 'the balance of probabilities' (s. 241(3)). A magistrates' court may order the forfeiture of all or part of any cash if satisfied that it is either recoverable property or was intended for use by any person in criminal conduct (s. 298). In *Ahmed v Revenue and Customs Commissioners* [2013] EWHC 2241 (Admin), the High Court reduced an order for forfeiture to avoid a disproportionate interference with the owner's property rights under the ECHR. Where a parallel prosecution is brought, it may be appropriate to detain the cash but not to commence a forfeiture application until the criminal proceedings are concluded. 'It is ... important that care is taken to ensure that the fair trial of a defendant is not prejudiced by anything arising in civil proceedings in the magistrates' court and steps should be taken accordingly. Liaison between police acting under Part 5 of the 2002 Act and the prosecuting authority is essential' (*Payton* [2006] EWCA Crim 1226 at [31]).

Applications for forfeiture are made on Form G and the procedure is governed by the Magistrates' Courts (Detention and Forfeiture of Cash) Rules 2002 (SI 2002 No. 2998). Magistrates assume effective service of documents unless the contrary is shown but may treat notice of the proceedings as ineffective if the respondent demonstrates that the notice was not received (2002 Rules, r. 9). The power to exclude evidence under the PACE 1984, s. 78, is not available in forfeiture proceedings (*Revenue and Customs Commissioners v Pisciotto* [2009] EWHC 1991 (Admin)). The admission of hearsay evidence is governed by the Magistrates' Courts (Hearsay Evidence in Civil Proceedings) Rules 1999 (SI 1999 No. 681).

D8.20 **Recoverable Property** The definition of recoverable property is the same as that in civil recovery proceedings (see **D8.6**). For consideration of the position in relation to the product or earnings of unlawful immigrant workers, see *R (Chief Constable of the Greater Manchester Police) v City of Salford Magistrates' Court* [2008] EWHC 1651 (Admin), [2009] 1 WLR 1023; *Xu* [2008] EWCA Crim 2372; *Nuro v Home Office* [2014] EWHC 462 (Admin) and *Paulet v UK* (2015) 61 EHRR 39 (994).

The meaning of 'unlawful conduct' is the same as that applicable to civil recovery (see **D8.5**). To establish that property is 'recoverable' there is no need to prove specific criminal conduct. It is sufficient to show that property was obtained through a specified kind of unlawful conduct or, where the POCA 2002, s. 242(2)(b), is relied on, the applicant must at least show that the cash was obtained through conduct of one of a number of kinds, each of which would have been unlawful (see also *Wiese v UK Border Agency* [2012] EWHC 2549 (Admin)). According to Moore-Bick LJ in *Szepietowski* (at [107]), the applicant:

> ... need not prove the commission of any specific criminal offence, in the sense of proving that a particular person committed a particular offence on a particular occasion. Nonetheless, I think it is necessary for her to prove that specific property was obtained by or in return for a criminal offence of an identifiable kind (robbery, theft, fraud or whatever) or, if she relies on section 242(2), by or in return for one or other of a number of offences of an identifiable kind.

A pleading that the respondent 'has committed immigration offences, acquisitive criminal offences, mortgage fraud and laundered the proceeds of these (and possible other offences) in addition to cheating the public revenue' may be 'sufficient indication of the alleged "kinds" of conduct to satisfy the requirements of the statute' (Carnwath LJ in *Olupitan* at [24]).

Where the criminal conduct relied on is 'money laundering', it appears to be sufficient, applying *Anwoir* [2008] EWCA Crim 1354, [2008] 2 Cr App R 36 (532), that the way in which the cash was handled gives rise to the irresistible inference that it can only be derived from crime. Thus, provided the cash can be inferred to have been obtained through money laundering it is not necessary to identify the underlying criminal conduct (this was the approach of the High Court in *NCA v Khan* [2017] EWHC 27 (QB)). The same logic cannot be applied to other types of criminal offending: it is insufficient to claim that property derives from unlawful conduct of an unspecified kind (see *Angus v UK Border Agency* [2011] EWHC 461 (Admin), followed in *Bapinder Sandhu v Chief Constable of the West Midlands Police* [2019] EWHC 3316 (Admin)) (but see **D8.22** for an explanation of how this line of authority is effectively circumvented).

In *Director of the Assets Recovery Agency v Green* [2005] EWHC 3168 (Admin), Sullivan J explained that, by contrast with civil recovery of tangible assets, greater latitude in inference was reasonable in cash forfeiture cases in the context of society's abandonment of cash as a lawful medium for large transactions:

> ... conduct consisting in the mere fact of having a very large sum of cash in the form of banknotes in one's possession in certain circumstances (eg at an airport) may well provide reasonable grounds for suspicion and demand an answer. By contrast, conduct consisting of the mere fact of being in possession of other types of property, expensive jewellery, houses, cars and so forth, or the mere fact of having a lavish lifestyle or of living beyond one's apparent means, do not, without anything more, provide reasonable grounds for suspicion demanding an explanation.

The evidence in support of an application may include evidence that the cash has been hidden and untruthful or inconsistent explanation(s) offered for its possession. Where the defendant has lied in the context of formal questioning as to the source or destination of cash, the court may be entitled to infer that it is related to unlawful conduct (*Muneka v Commissioners of Customs and Excise* [2005] EWHC 495 (Admin)). The background circumstances may be relevant: e.g., that the suspected person was travelling to a well-known centre for the supply of drugs. The cash itself may be contaminated with traces of drugs which are not explicable in terms of normal contamination of notes in circulation (*Pruijsen v Customs and Excise Commissioners* (18 October 1999 unreported)). Moreover, there may be specific evidence to associate the carrier of cash with illegal activity on a previous occasion. Previous convictions are admissible (*Ali v Best* (1997) 161 JP 393; *Isleworth Crown Court, ex parte Marland* (1998) 162 JP 251). In certain circumstances, the applicant may even rely upon a previous acquittal (*Customs and Excise Commissioners v Thorpe* (18 November 1996 unreported); *Commissioners of Customs and Excise v T* (1998) 162 JP 193). As to whether forfeiture following an acquittal is ECHR compliant, see *Scottish Ministers v Doig* [2009] CSIH 34, 2009 SLT 1106. **D8.21**

'Intended ... for use in unlawful conduct' This is the alternative basis for the forfeiture of cash. In *Begum v West Midlands Police* [2012] EWHC 2304 (Admin), [2013] 1 All ER 1261 D had been found with £7,000 cash that she had not declared in her application for state benefits. These circumstances did not establish her intention to 'use' the cash in unlawful conduct. Where the circumstances are such that the court may infer that cash was obtained through unlawful conduct, albeit of an unidentifiable kind, the court may order the cash to be forfeited on the basis that it was intended for use in unlawful conduct, as any 'use' of the cash would almost inevitably involve the commission of a criminal offence (money laundering). This was the effect of the decision in *Fletcher v Chief Constable of Leicestershire Constabulary* [2013] EWHC 3357 (Admin), where concealed cash was handed in by an innocent third party. The decision largely circumvents the restriction on the forfeiture of cash imposed by *Angus v UK Border Agency* [2011] EWHC 461 (Admin) (see **D8.20**). **D8.22**

D8.23 **Detention Pending Proceedings** Where an application for forfeiture is made, the cash is to be detained and may not be released until any proceedings in pursuance of the application (including any proceedings on appeal) are concluded (POCA 2002, s. 295(4)). In *R (Chief Constable of Lancashire Constabulary) v Burnley Magistrates' Court* [2003] EWHC 3308 (Admin), magistrates had refused an application to extend the initial 48-hour detention on the basis that the police did not have reasonable grounds to detain the cash. However, the magistrates omitted to order the release of the cash under s. 297(2). Before the 48 hours expired, the police applied for forfeiture. The Administrative Court held that, absent bad faith, it was not possible to characterise the Chief Constable's decision as an abuse without having considered carefully the proper ambit of the exercise of his duty to the public. The Chief Constable was at liberty to make the application he did. The statutory provision permitted it and the decision of the justices did not prevent it. There was no evidence that the Chief Constable's purpose was to detain rather than forfeit. Had the justices wished, they could have brought an end to the period of detention under s. 295(1). There is no statutory requirement that all available evidence should be in place before the forfeiture application is made.

Cash may also be detained under s. 297C or s. 297D where it is the subject of a forfeiture notice (see **D8.26**) or, if the notice lapses, for a further period of 48 hours.

D8.24 **Third Parties** Third parties who claim to own the cash may apply for it to be released in the course of detention or forfeiture proceedings 'or at any other time' (POCA 2002, s. 301). A victim of crime may apply in circumstances where it can be shown (a) that V was deprived of the cash, or of property that it represents, by unlawful conduct, (b) that it was not 'recoverable property' immediately before V was deprived of it, and (c) that the cash belongs to V. Other owners may apply for the release of the cash. Where the applicant is not the person from whom the cash was seized but appears to be the owner of the cash then, provided the person from whom the cash was seized does not object, the cash may be released if the court is satisfied that the conditions for detention are no longer met or the cash is not recoverable property (s. 301(4)). The cash may be released either to the applicant or to the person from whom it was seized. A third party who was not given notice of the forfeiture proceedings may be able to recover cash that has been forfeited by means of judicial review (*R (Galldorf Takarmanvgvarto es Kereskedelmi Zartkoroen Mokodo Reszvenytarsasag) v Folkestone Magistrates' Court* [2017] EWHC 2019 (Admin)).

D8.25 **Compensation and Costs** Where no forfeiture order is made, the person from whom the cash was seized or the person to whom it belongs may apply for compensation (POCA 2002, s. 302). An application is a complaint within the meaning of the MCA 1980, s. 127, and, accordingly, a six-month time-limit runs from the date when the money was returned (*Davis v Chief Constable of Leicestershire* [2012] EWHC 3388 (Admin)). A similar entitlement applies where the cash is not forfeited pursuant to a forfeiture notice. Compensation will normally be no more than the accrued interest but, if the court is satisfied that the person has suffered loss as a result of the detention and 'the circumstances are exceptional', it may order reasonable additional compensation. In exercising its power under the MCA 1980, s. 64(1), to make 'such order as to costs ... as it thinks just and reasonable' to a successful respondent, a magistrates' court should not start from the presumption that costs followed the event but from the presumption that no order should be made against a police or regulatory authority that has acted honestly, reasonably, properly and on grounds that reasonably appeared to be sound unless an order was justified by other factors relevant to the magistrates' discretion such as undue financial prejudice or the fact that the conduct of the public authority had been unreasonable or in some other way open to criticism (*R (Perinpanathan) v City of Westminster Magistrates' Court* [2010] EWCA Civ 40, [2010] 1 WLR 1508; *Bennett v Chief Constable of Merseyside Police* [2018] EWHC 3591 (Admin)). In *R (Stone) v Camberwell Green Magistrates' Court* [2010] EWHC 2333 (Admin), the Divisional Court declined to resolve whether, in a case where forfeiture proceedings were resolved by agreement, there is power to award costs, either under the MCA 1980, s. 64, or the Courts Act 1971, s. 52.

Any party aggrieved by the making or non-making of a forfeiture order may appeal to the Crown Court (POCA 2002, s. 299). The application must be made within 30 days of the forfeiture order and that deadline may not be extended (*R (Lamai) v West London Magistrates' Court* (6 July 2000 unreported)).

Forfeiture Notices A 'senior officer' who is satisfied that detained cash is recoverable property or is intended for use in unlawful conduct may serve a forfeiture notice which, if no objection is made, results in the forfeiture of the cash (POCA 2002, ss. 297A to 297G). The notice must specify, *inter alia*, the period for objecting which 'must be at least 30 days starting with the day after the notice is given' (s. 297B). The notice lapses if an objection is made within that period (s. 297C(4)) but the cash may be detained for a further 48 hours (s. 297D). A person aggrieved by forfeiture pursuant to a notice may apply to the magistrates' court to set aside the forfeiture within a period of 30 days (which may be extended in exceptional circumstances) of the end of the objection period (s. 297E). **D8.26**

Forfeiture of Listed Assets

Overview The Criminal Finances Act 2017, s. 15, inserted ch. 3A into Part 5 of the POCA 2002 with effect from 16 April 2018. This is a scheme for the summary forfeiture of listed assets (s. 303B(1): precious metals, precious stones, watches, artistic works, face-value vouchers and postage stamps). The scheme has similarities with that for the forfeiture of cash (see **D8.11**) and is governed by the Magistrates' Courts (Detention and Forfeiture of Listed Assets) Rules 2017 (SI 2017 No. 1297). The Secretary of State has issued a code of practice (Proceeds of Crime Act 2002 (Recovery of Listed Assets: Code of Practice) (England and Wales and Scotland) Regulations 2018 (SI 2018 No. 85)). Part 5A of the Proceeds of Crime Act 2002 (External Requests and Orders) Order 2005 (SI 2005 No. 3181) contains a similar scheme for the seizure, detention and forfeiture of listed assets, pursuant to a request from overseas. **D8.27**

Search and Seizure Relevant officers (an officer of Revenue and Customs, constable, SFO officer or accredited financial investigator) who are lawfully on any premises may search them where there are reasonable grounds to suspect that a 'seizable' listed asset is on the premises (POCA 2002, s. 303C). A listed asset is 'seizable' if its value is at least £1,000 and it is, in whole or in part, 'recoverable' or intended for use in criminal conduct. **D8.28**

The power of search extends, in defined circumstances, to searches of vehicles (s. 303C(2)) and searches of persons suspected of carrying listed assets (s. 303C(6)). There is no requirement, as there is in relation to searches for cash (see **D8.13**), for the searching officer to obtain 'prior approval'. Property may be seized if there are reasonable grounds to suspect that it is: (i) a listed asset, (ii) worth at least £1,000 (the value of multiple assets may be aggregated), and (iii) recoverable or intended by any person for use in unlawful conduct (s. 303J). Seized property must be 'safely stored' and may be subjected to tests to establish whether it is in fact a listed asset (s. 303M).

Detention Property that has been seized may be detained, provided the relevant reasonable grounds for suspicion remain, for an initial period of six hours and then, with the permission of a senior officer, for a further period not exceeding 42 hours (POCA 2002, s. 303K). Further detention may, upon application, be authorised by a magistrates' court for an initial period not exceeding six months. Upon further application, the court may order further detention but may not order the property to be detained beyond the end of the period of two years beginning with the date of the first order (s. 303L). Detention of an asset may be ordered if the court is satisfied that: (i) it is a listed asset, (ii) whose value is not less than £1,000 (the value of multiple assets may be aggregated and the court need only be satisfied as to the value of the asset or assets on the first application for detention), and (iii) one of two conditions listed in s. 303L is met: **D8.29**

Proceeds of Crime Act 2002, s. 303L

(8) Condition 1 is that there are reasonable grounds for suspecting that the property is recoverable property and that either—

(a) its continued detention is justified while its derivation is further investigated or consideration is given to bringing (in the United Kingdom or elsewhere) proceedings against any person for an offence with which the property is connected, or

(b) proceedings against any person for an offence with which the property is connected have been started and have not been concluded.

(9) Condition 2 is that there are reasonable grounds for suspecting that the property is intended to be used in unlawful conduct and that either—

(a) its continued detention is justified while its intended use is further investigated or consideration is given to bringing (in the United Kingdom or elsewhere) proceedings against any person for an offence with which the property is connected, or

(b) proceedings against any person for an offence with which the property is connected have been started and have not been concluded.

The court may, upon an application by the person from whom the property was seized, order the release of the property if the conditions for its ongoing detention are no longer met (s. 303N). Other persons who are not the person from whom the property was seized may apply for the release of the property (s. 303V). Persons who establish that they are a 'victim' (as defined) may obtain the release of property. An officer who is satisfied that the detention of property may no longer be justified may, after notifying the magistrates' court, release that property (s. 303N).

D8.30 **Forfeiture** While a listed asset is detained, the magistrates' court may, upon application, order the forfeiture of property if satisfied that the property is: (i) a listed asset and (ii) recoverable property or intended by any person for use in unlawful conduct. Where an asset is forfeitable only in part, the court may (where there is agreement) allow the owner of the part that is not forfeitable to retain the asset in return for a payment equal to the value of the part that is forfeitable. In doing so the court may provide for the vesting, creating or extinguishing of any interest in property (POCA 2002, s. 303Q). In default of agreement the matter must be transferred to the High Court if the value of the asset is £10,000 or more and the matter may be so transferred in any other case (s. 303R). Detailed provisions allow the magistrates court or High Court (as the case may be) to extinguish or sever interests in the part of an asset that is not forfeitable and for payment to be made to the holder of that interest (s. 303R).

D8.31 **Realisation** Property that is forfeited is to be realised by a relevant officer (POCA 2002, s. 303T) and the proceeds distributed in accordance with any orders of the court requiring payment (s. 303U): (i) to the holder of an interest which has been extinguished or severed; (ii) by way of legal expenses; (iii) to reimburse the reasonable costs of storing or insuring the property. The remainder is paid to the consolidated fund.

D8.32 **Compensation and Appeal** Where property is not forfeited, the court may order compensation where there is consequential loss and the circumstances are exceptional (POCA 2002, s. 303W).

Extensive appeal rights are available to persons aggrieved by the various types of order which the magistrates' court may make. Appeals, which must be made within 30 days of the impugned order, lie to the Crown Court (s. 303S(3)). It appears that an appeal against a decision of the High Court would be to the Court of Appeal (Civil Division). Detained property which is subject to an application for forfeiture remains detained until any appeal proceedings are concluded (s. 303O(9)).

Forfeiture of Money Held in Bank Accounts

D8.33 **Overview** The Criminal Finances Act 2017, s. 16, inserted ch. 3B into Part 5 of the POCA 2002 with effect from 31 January 2018. This is a scheme for the forfeiture of money held in bank and building society accounts upon the application of an 'enforcement officer' (an officer of Revenue and Customs, constable, SFO officer, accredited financial investigator or immigration officer). The scheme has similarities with that for the forfeiture of cash (see **D8.11**) and is governed by the Magistrates' Courts (Freezing and Forfeiture of Money in Bank and Building Society Accounts) Rules 2017 (SI 2017 No. 1297). Part 5B of the Proceeds of Crime Act 2002 (External Requests and Orders) Order 2005 contains a similar scheme for the freezing and forfeiture of bank balances, pursuant to a request from overseas.

Freezing Orders The magistrates' court may make an 'account freezing order', pursuant to the POCA 2002, s. 303Z3, for a period not exceeding two years where it is satisfied that there are reasonable grounds for suspecting that money held in an account is 'recoverable property' (which has the same meaning as in civil recovery proceedings, see **D8.6**) or intended by any person for use in unlawful conduct (s. 303Z3). Applications for such an order may be made without notice (s. 303Z1(4)) and may only be made in respect of money which is at least the minimum amount of £1,000 (s. 303Z2(1)). The applicant enforcement officer must be, or have been authorised by, a 'senior officer' (s. 303Z2(2)). The court may vary an order upon application by an enforcement officer or any affected person (s. 303Z4), including by way of making 'exclusions' to enable a person to meet reasonable living expenses or to carry on a trade, business, profession or occupation (s. 303Z5). The court may make an exclusion for the purpose of enabling a person to meet legal expenses in respect of the proceedings but the power should be exercised with a view to ensuring, so far as practicable, that there is not undue prejudice to the taking of any steps to forfeit the money (s. 303Z5(8)), but subject to the desirability that the person should be represented in proceedings under Part 5 (s. 303Z5(6), and see **D8.7** on the similar regime for exclusions in the High Court). Powers of investigation available in connection with a 'frozen funds investigation' include production orders and search warrants (see **D8.41** and **D8.44**). **D8.34**

Forfeiture Where an account freezing order is in force in respect of money the magistrates' court may, upon application, order its forfeiture if satisfied that the money or part of it is recoverable property, or is intended by any person for use in unlawful conduct. If the court makes, or declines to make, an order in respect of any or all of the money claimed, an aggrieved party may appeal to the Crown Court (s. 303Z16) and the lower court may order the continuation of the freezing order pending the appeal (s. 303Z15). Where an account freezing order is made but none of the money in the account is forfeited, the court may order compensation where there is consequential loss and the circumstances are exceptional (s. 303Z18). **D8.35**

Where an account freezing order is in force in respect of money and a senior officer is satisfied that the money is recoverable or intended by any person for use in criminal conduct, the officer may give an account forfeiture notice which complies with the requirements of s. 303Z9(4) and the Proceeds of Crime Act 2002 (Administrative Forfeiture Notices) (England and Wales and Northern Ireland) Regulations 2017 (SI 2017 No. 1223). If no objection is received within 30 days, the amount of money stated in the notice is forfeited and the bank must transfer the amount to a nominated account. An aggrieved person may apply within a period of 30 days (which may be extended in exceptional circumstances) to set aside the forfeiture (s. 303Z12).

POWERS OF INVESTIGATION

General

Part 8 of the POCA 2002 contains an armoury of judicial orders for the purposes of the investigation and pursuit of criminal property: **D8.36**

(a) production orders;
(b) search and seizure warrants;
(c) disclosure orders;
(d) customer information orders;
(e) account monitoring orders;
(f) unexplained wealth orders.

A similar arsenal of powers is available to assist investigations being conducted by an overseas authority (see the Proceeds of Crime Act 2002 (External Investigations) Order 2013 (SI 2013 No. 2605) and the Proceeds of Crime Act 2002 (External Investigations) Order 2014 (SI 2014 No. 1893). All of the orders may be made on *ex parte* application. On the importance of candour, see *R (Merida Oil*

Traders Ltd) v Central Criminal Court [2017] EWHC 747 (Admin), [2017] 1 WLR 3680. The general exercise of these functions is governed by two codes of practice which came into force on 31 January 2018: the Investigative Powers of Prosecutors Code of Practice and the Investigations Code of Practice. CrimPR Part 47 also applies (see Supplement, **R47.1** *et seq.*).

Where the statutory criteria are met for making a particular investigative order, the court must nevertheless decide whether to exercise its discretion (*Southwark Crown Court, ex parte Customs and Excise Commissioners* [1990] 1 QB 650). Where an order may lead to the discovery of material relevant to a criminal investigation (which might have been obtained pursuant to an investigative order under the PACE 1984) the court may still grant the order if the 'dominant purpose' of the application is to obtain evidence to support the investigation into criminal property (cf. *Southwark Crown Court, ex parte Bowles* [1998] AC 641).

The Codes are admissible in evidence and a court 'may take account of any failure to comply with [their] provisions in determining any question in the proceedings' (ss. 377(7) and 377A(8)). However, failure to comply with any provision of the Codes will not *of itself* render a person liable to criminal or civil proceedings.

D8.37 **Investigations** The conditions for the making of the various orders differ according to the type of investigation involved.

(a) A 'confiscation investigation' is 'an investigation into (a) whether a person has benefited from his criminal conduct, (b) the extent or whereabouts of his benefit from his criminal conduct, or (c) the amount available in respect of the person or the extent or whereabouts of realisable property available for satisfying a confiscation order made in respect of him' (POCA 2002, s. 341(1)): see **E19**.
(b) A 'civil recovery investigation' is an investigation into whether property is or has been recoverable property or associated property, who holds or has held property, what property a person holds or has held or the nature, extent or whereabouts of property (s. 341(2)). The scope of such an investigation was widened by s. 341A to include an investigation into 'other property' held by a person who appears to hold or to have held recoverable property or associated property. By s. 341(3), an investigation does not qualify as a civil recovery investigation if proceedings for a recovery order in respect of the property have started, if an interim receiving or administration order applies, if the property has been detained as cash or a 'listed asset' (see **D8.27**), or is subject to an account freezing order (see **D8.34**).
(c) A 'detained cash investigation' is an investigation for the purposes of cash forfeiture into the derivation of detained cash or into whether it is intended to be used in unlawful conduct (s. 341(3A)).
(d) A 'detained property investigation' is an investigation into the derivation of 'listed assets' detained pursuant to ch. 3A of Part 5 or into whether such property is intended to be used in unlawful conduct (s. 341(3B)).
(e) A 'frozen funds investigation' is an investigation into the derivation of monies frozen pursuant to ch. 3B of Part 5 or into whether such property is intended to be used in unlawful conduct (s. 341(3C)).
(f) A 'money laundering investigation' is an investigation into 'whether a person has committed a money laundering offence' (s. 341(4)).
(g) An 'exploitation proceeds investigation' is an investigation under Part 7 of the CAJA 2009 (criminal memoirs etc.) (s. 341(5)).

D8.38 **Jurisdiction of Courts** Only a High Court judge may make an order as part of a civil recovery investigation or exploitation proceeds investigation; orders that are part of any other form of investigation may be granted by a judge of the Crown Court (POCA 2002, s. 343) including a detained cash investigation, a detained property investigation and a frozen funds investigation. An unexplained wealth order (see **D8.55**) may be made only by the High Court. The fact that there are concurrent or overlapping investigations (e.g. a money laundering investigation and a frozen funds investigation) does not, of itself, affect the power of the court to make an order. For example, the fact that a bank account is subject to a frozen funds investigation does not prevent the court from making a disclosure order for the purposes of a concurrent money laundering investigation in relation to that account (*Re NCA* [2020] EWHC 268 (Admin)).

Mutual Assistance Detailed provision is made for the exercise of powers by the Director of the NCA, the DPP or the Director of the SFO in assisting an 'external investigation'. The provisions of the Proceeds of Crime Act 2002 (External Investigations) Order 2014 (SI 2014 No. 1893) are analogous to those concerning a 'confiscation investigation' in Part 8 of the POCA 2002. The provisions of the Proceeds of Crime Act 2002 (External Investigations) Order 2013 (SI 2013 No. 2605) are analogous to those concerning a 'civil recovery investigation'. The POCA 2002, s. 447(3), defines an external investigation as: **D8.39**

> ... an investigation by an overseas authority into—
> (a) whether property has been obtained as a result of or in connection with criminal conduct, ...
> (aa) the extent or whereabouts of property obtained as a result of or in connection with criminal conduct, or
> (b) whether a money laundering offence has been committed.

For general guidance on mutual assistance, see *Van der Pijl v Secretary of State for the Home Department* [2014] EWHC 281 (Admin), [2014] Lloyd's Rep FC 362; *R (Secretary of State for the Home Department) v Southwark Crown Court* [2013] EWHC 4366 (Admin), [2014] 1 WLR 2529 and *USA v Abacha* [2014] EWCA Civ 1291, [2015] 1 WLR 1917.

Prejudicing an Investigation

A person commits an offence if, knowing or suspecting that an investigation is being, or is about to be conducted, the person makes a disclosure that is likely to prejudice it (s. 342(2)(a)) or 'falsifies, conceals, destroys or otherwise disposes of' relevant documents or causes or permits another to do so (s. 342(2)(b)). See **B21.34** for details. **D8.40**

Production Orders

Proceeds of Crime Act 2002, ss. 345 and 346 **D8.41**

> **345.**—(1) A judge may, on an application made to him by an appropriate officer, make a production order if he is satisfied that each of the requirements for the making of the order is fulfilled.
> (2) The application for a production order must state that—
> (a) a person specified in the application is subject to a confiscation investigation, a civil recovery investigation, an exploitation proceeds investigation or a money laundering investigation, or
> (b) property specified in the application is subject to a civil recovery investigation, a detained cash investigation, a detained property investigation or a frozen funds investigation.
> (3) The application must also state that—
> (a) the order is sought for the purposes of the investigation;
> (b) the order is sought in relation to material, or material of a description, specified in the application;
> (c) a person specified in the application appears to be in possession or control of the material.
> (4) A production order is an order either—
> (a) requiring the person the application for the order specifies as appearing to be in possession or control of material to produce it to an appropriate officer for him to take away, or
> (b) requiring that person to give an appropriate officer access to the material, within the period stated in the order.
> (5) The period stated in a production order must be a period of seven days beginning with the day on which the order is made, unless it appears to the judge by whom the order is made that a longer or shorter period would be appropriate in the particular circumstances.
> **346.**—(1) These are the requirements for the making of a production order.
> (2) There must be reasonable grounds for suspecting that—
> (a) in the case of a confiscation investigation, the person the application for the order specifies as being subject to the investigation has benefited from his criminal conduct;
> (b) in the case of a civil recovery investigation—

D

Part D Procedure

(i) the person the application for the order specifies as being subject to the investigation holds recoverable property or associated property,
(ii) that person has, at any time, held property that was recoverable property or associated property at the time, or
(iii) the property the application for the order specifies as being subject to the investigation is recoverable property or associated property;

(ba) in the case of a detained cash investigation into the derivation of cash, the property the application for the order specifies as being subject to the investigation, or a part of it, is recoverable property;
(bb) in the case of a detained cash investigation into the intended use of cash, the property the application for the order specifies as being subject to the investigation, or a part of it, is intended by any person to be used in unlawful conduct;
(bc) in the case of a detained property investigation into the derivation of property, the property the application for the order specifies as being subject to the investigation, or a part of it, is recoverable property;
(bd) in the case of a detained property investigation into the intended use of property, the property the application for the order specifies as being subject to the investigation, or a part of it, is intended by any person to be used in unlawful conduct;
(be) in the case of a frozen funds investigation into the derivation of money held in an account in relation to which an account freezing order made under section 303Z3 has effect (a 'frozen account'), the property the application for the order specifies as being subject to the investigation, or a part of it, is recoverable property;
(bf) in the case of a frozen funds investigation into the intended use of money held in a frozen account, the property the application for the order specifies as being subject to the investigation, or a part of it, is intended by any person to be used in unlawful conduct;
(c) in the case of a money laundering investigation, the person the application for the order specifies as being subject to the investigation has committed a money laundering offence;
(d) in the case of an exploitation proceeds investigation, the person the application for the order specifies as being subject to the investigation is within subsection (2A).

(2A) A person is within this subsection if, for the purposes of Part 7 of the Coroners and Justice Act 2009 (criminal memoirs etc), exploitation proceeds have been obtained by the person from a relevant offence by reason of any benefit derived by the person.
This subsection is to be construed in accordance with that Part.

(3) There must be reasonable grounds for believing that the person the application specifies as appearing to be in possession or control of the material so specified is in possession or control of it.

(4) There must be reasonable grounds for believing that the material is likely to be of substantial value (whether or not by itself) to the investigation for the purposes of which the order is sought.

(5) There must be reasonable grounds for believing that it is in the public interest for the material to be produced or for access to it to be given, having regard to—
(a) the benefit likely to accrue to the investigation if the material is obtained;
(b) the circumstances under which the person the application specifies as appearing to be in possession or control of the material holds it.

D8.42 **Terms and Effect of the Order** A production order requires the person appearing to be in possession or control of specified material to produce it to the appropriate officer for removal or for inspection normally within seven days of the order; the period may be lengthened or shortened as 'appropriate in the particular circumstances' (POCA 2002, s. 345(4) and (5)). Orders may be made in relation to material in the possession or control of a government department (s. 350).

A judge can supplement a production order by making an order requiring entry to premises to allow the appropriate officer to obtain access to the material (s. 347). The material may be copied or retained for 'so long as it is necessary to retain it' in connection with the relevant investigation and, in particular, until any proceedings are concluded (s. 348(6) and (7)). Specific provisions apply to '*information contained* in a computer' (s. 349) so as to ensure the material is visible and legible.

An order does not require a person to produce or give access to privileged or excluded material (s. 348). 'Privileged material' is 'any material which the person would be entitled to refuse to produce on grounds of legal professional privilege in proceedings in the High Court' (s. 348(2)). Under s. 379 'excluded material' has the same meaning as in the PACE 1984, s. 11 (see **D1.149**). In broad terms it means material that is held in confidence and that falls into the following categories: (a) personal, occupational or business records, (b) human tissue or tissue fluid taken for medical diagnosis or treatment, or (c) journalistic documents or records.

Production orders and orders to grant entry 'have effect as if they were orders of the court' (s. 351(7)). In other words, breaches of the orders are punishable as contempt of court.

Requirements A judge may grant a production order if satisfied that each of the necessary requirements is fulfilled (ss. 345 and 346). The first requirement is that 'there must be reasonable grounds for suspecting' the particular state of affairs applicable to the type of investigation (POCA 2002, s. 346(2)(a) to (d); see **D8.41**). **D8.43**

The remaining three requirements are common to all the forms of investigation. There must be reasonable grounds for 'believing' (a) that the person specified in the application is in possession or control of the 'material' (s. 346(3)), (b) that the material 'is likely to be of substantial value (whether or not by itself) to the investigation' (s. 346(4)), and (c) that 'it is in the public interest for the material to be produced or for access to it to be given', having regard to the likely benefit if it is obtained and to the circumstances under which the specified person holds the material (s. 346(5)). As to the unlawful use by investigators of the production order regime to secure property in order to seize it with a view to its forfeiture, see **D8.16**. As to the required reasonable grounds for 'believing', see *Assets Recovery Agency (Ex parte) (Jamaica)* [2015] UKPC 1, [2015] Lloyd's Rep FC 203, where Lord Hughes explained (at [19]) that 'the test is concerned not with proof but the existence of grounds (reasons) for believing (thinking) something, and with the reasonableness of those grounds'. The application must specify the material and the person believed to be in possession or control of it (s. 345(3)).

Only an 'appropriate officer' may apply. The meaning of 'appropriate officer' varies according to the type of investigation (see s. 378): (a) in a confiscation investigation, it means an NCA officer, an accredited financial investigator, a constable, an SFO officer, an officer of Revenue and Customs or an immigration officer; (b) in a civil recovery investigation, it means an NCA officer, the director of the SFO, the DPP, an officer of Revenue and Customs or an FCA officer; (c) in a money laundering or detained cash investigation, it means a constable, an SFO officer, an accredited financial investigator, an officer of Revenue and Customs or an immigration officer; (d) in a detained property investigation or frozen funds investigation, it means a constable, an SFO officer, an accredited financial investigator or an officer of Revenue and Customs; (e) in an exploitation proceeds investigation, it means an NCA officer.

Search and Seizure Warrants

Proceeds of Crime Act 2002, ss. 352 and 353 **D8.44**

352.—(1) A judge may, on an application made to him by an appropriate officer, issue a search and seizure warrant if he is satisfied that either of the requirements for the issuing of the warrant is fulfilled.

(2) The application for a search and seizure warrant must state that—

(a) a person specified in the application is subject to a confiscation investigation, a civil recovery investigation, an exploitation proceeds investigation or a money laundering investigation, or

(b) property specified in the application is subject to a civil recovery investigation, a detained cash investigation, a detained property investigation or a frozen funds investigation.

(3) The application must also state—

(a) that the warrant is sought for the purposes of the investigation;

(b) that the warrant is sought in relation to the premises specified in the application;

(c) that the warrant is sought in relation to material specified in the application, or that there are reasonable grounds for believing that there is material falling within section 353(6), (7), (7A), (7B) or (8) on the premises.

(4) A search and seizure warrant is a warrant authorising an appropriate person—
(a) to enter and search the premises specified in the application for the warrant, and
(b) to seize and retain any material found there which is likely to be of substantial value (whether or not by itself) to the investigation for the purposes of which the application is made.
(5) An appropriate person is—
(a) [repealed];
(b) a Financial Conduct Authority officer, a National Crime Agency officer, an officer of Revenue and Customs or a member or of the staff of the relevant Director, if the warrant is sought for the purposes of a civil recovery investigation;
(c) a constable, an SFO officer, an accredited financial investigator or an officer of Revenue and Customs or an immigration officer, if the warrant is sought for the purposes of a detained cash investigation, a confiscation investigation or a money laundering investigation;
(ca) a constable, an SFO officer, an accredited financial investigator or an officer of Revenue and Customs, if the warrant is sought for the purposes of a detained property investigation;
(cb) a constable, an SFO officer, an accredited financial investigator or an officer of Revenue and Customs, if the warrant is sought for the purposes of a frozen funds investigation;
(d) a National Crime Agency officer, if the warrant is sought for the purposes of an exploitation proceeds investigation.
(5A) In this Part 'relevant Director'—
(a) in relation to England and Wales, means the Director of Public Prosecutions or the Director of the Serious Fraud Office; and
(b) [Northern Ireland.]
(6) The requirements for the issue of a search and seizure warrant are—
(a) that a production order made in relation to material has not been complied with and there are reasonable grounds for believing that the material is on the premises specified in the application for the warrant, or
(b) that section 353 is satisfied in relation to the warrant.
(7) The reference in paragraph (c), (ca) and (cb) of subsection (5) to an accredited financial investigator is a reference to an accredited financial investigator who falls within a description specified in an order made for the purposes of that paragraph by the Secretary of State under section 453.
(8) [Concerns the CrimPR.]
353.—(1) This section is satisfied in relation to a search and seizure warrant if—
(a) subsection (2) applies, and
(b) either the first or the second set of conditions is complied with.
(2) This subsection applies if there are reasonable grounds for suspecting that—
(a) in the case of a confiscation investigation, the person specified in the application for the warrant has benefited from his criminal conduct;
(b) in the case of a civil recovery investigation—
(i) the person specified in the application for the warrant holds recoverable property or associated property,
(ii) that person has, at any time, held property that was recoverable property or associated property at the time, or
(iii) the property specified in the application for the warrant is recoverable property or associated property;
(ba) in the case of a detained cash investigation into the derivation of cash, the property specified in the application for the warrant, or a part of it, is recoverable property;
(bb) in the case of a detained cash investigation into the intended use of cash, the property specified in the application for the warrant, or a part of it, is intended by any person to be used in unlawful conduct;
(bc) in the case of a detained property investigation into the derivation of property, the property specified in the application for the warrant, or a part of it, is recoverable property;
(bd) in the case of a detained property investigation into the intended use of property, the property specified in the application for the warrant, or a part of it, is intended by any person to be used in unlawful conduct;
(be) in the case of a frozen funds investigation into the derivation of money held in an account in relation to which an account freezing order made under section 303Z3 has effect (a 'frozen account'), the property specified in the application for the warrant, or a part of it, is recoverable property;

(bf) in the case of a frozen funds investigation into the intended use of money held in a frozen account, the property specified in the application for the warrant, or a part of it, is intended by any person to be used in unlawful conduct;
(c) in the case of a money laundering investigation, the person specified in the application for the warrant has committed a money laundering offence;
(d) in the case of an exploitation proceeds investigation, the person specified in the application for the warrant is specified in section 346(2A).

(3) The first set of conditions is that there are reasonable grounds for believing that—
(a) any material on the premises specified in the application for the warrant is likely to be of substantial value (whether or not by itself) to the investigation for the purposes of which the warrant is sought,
(b) it is in the public interest for the material to be obtained, having regard to the benefit likely to accrue to the investigation if the material is obtained, and
(c) it would not be appropriate to make a production order for any one or more of the reasons in subsection (4).

(4) The reasons are—
(a) that it is not practicable to communicate with any person against whom the production order could be made;
(b) that it is not practicable to communicate with any person who would be required to comply with an order to grant entry to the premises;
(c) that the investigation might be seriously prejudiced unless an appropriate person is able to secure immediate access to the material.

(5) The second set of conditions is that—
(a) there are reasonable grounds for believing that there is material on the premises specified in the application for the warrant and that the material falls within subsection (6), (7), (7A), (7B), (7C), (7D), (7E), (7F), (8) or (8A),
(b) there are reasonable grounds for believing that it is in the public interest for the material to be obtained, having regard to the benefit likely to accrue to the investigation if the material is obtained, and
(c) any one or more of the requirements in subsection (9) is met.

(6) In the case of a confiscation investigation, material falls within this subsection if it cannot be identified at the time of the application but it—
(a) relates to the person specified in the application, the question whether he has benefited from his criminal conduct or any question as to the extent or whereabouts of his benefit from his criminal conduct or of realisable property available for satisfying a confiscation order made in respect of him, and
(b) is likely to be of substantial value (whether or not by itself) to the investigation for the purposes of which the warrant is sought.

(7) In the case of a civil recovery investigation, material falls within this subsection if it cannot be identified at the time of the application but it—
(a) relates to the person or property specified in the application, or to any of the questions listed in subsection (7ZA), and
(b) is likely to be of substantial value (whether or not by itself) to the investigation for the purposes of which the warrant is sought.

(7ZA) Those questions are—
(a) where a person is specified in the application, any question as to—
(i) what property the person holds or has held,
(ii) whether the property is or has been recoverable property or associated property, or
(iii) the nature, extent or whereabouts of the property, and
(b) where property is specified in the application, any question as to—
(i) whether the property is or has been recoverable property or associated property,
(ii) who holds it or has held it,
(iii) whether a person who appears to hold or to have held it holds or has held other property,
(iv) whether the other property is or has been recoverable property or associated property, or
(v) the nature, extent or whereabouts of the specified property or the other property.

(7A) In the case of a detained cash investigation into the derivation of cash, material falls within this subsection if it cannot be identified at the time of the application but it—
(a) relates to the property specified in the application, the question whether the property, or a part of it, is recoverable property or any other question as to its derivation, and

D

Part D Procedure

(b) is likely to be of substantial value (whether or not by itself) to the investigation for the purposes of which the warrant is sought.

(7B) In the case of a detained cash investigation into the intended use of cash, material falls within this subsection if it cannot be identified at the time of the application but it—

(a) relates to the property specified in the application or the question whether the property, or a part of it, is intended by any person to be used in unlawful conduct, and

(b) is likely to be of substantial value (whether or not by itself) to the investigation for the purposes of which the warrant is sought.

(7C) In the case of a detained property investigation into the derivation of property, material falls within this subsection if it cannot be identified at the time of the application but it—

(a) relates to the property specified in the application, the question whether the property, or a part of it, is recoverable property or any other question as to its derivation, and

(b) is likely to be of substantial value (whether or not by itself) to the investigation for the purposes of which the warrant is sought.

(7D) In the case of a detained property investigation into the intended use of property, material falls within this subsection if it cannot be identified at the time of the application but it—

(a) relates to the property specified in the application or the question whether the property, or a part of it, is intended by any person to be used in unlawful conduct, and

(b) is likely to be of substantial value (whether or not by itself) to the investigation for the purposes of which the warrant is sought.

(7E) In the case of a frozen funds investigation into the derivation of money held in a frozen account, material falls within this subsection if it cannot be identified at the time of the application but it—

(a) relates to the property specified in the application, the question whether the property, or a part of it, is recoverable property or any other question as to its derivation, and

(b) is likely to be of substantial value (whether or not by itself) to the investigation for the purposes of which the warrant is sought.

(8) In the case of a money laundering investigation, material falls within this subsection if it cannot be identified at the time of the application but it—

(a) relates to the person specified in the application or the question whether he has committed a money laundering offence, and

(b) is likely to be of substantial value (whether or not by itself) to the investigation for the purposes of which the warrant is sought.

(8A) In the case of an exploitation proceeds investigation, material falls within this subsection if it cannot be identified at the time of the application but it—

(a) relates to the person specified in the application, the question whether exploitation proceeds have been obtained from a relevant offence in relation to that person, any question as to the extent or whereabouts of any benefit as a result of which exploitation proceeds are obtained or any question about the person's available amount, and

(b) is likely to be of substantial value (whether or not by itself) to the investigation for the purposes of which the warrant is sought.

This subsection is to be construed in accordance with Part 7 of the Coroners and Justice Act 2009 (criminal memoirs etc).

(9) The requirements are—

(a) that it is not practicable to communicate with any person entitled to grant entry to the premises;

(b) that entry to the premises will not be granted unless a warrant is produced;

(c) that the investigation might be seriously prejudiced unless an appropriate person arriving at the premises is able to secure immediate entry to them.

(10) An appropriate person is—

(a) [repealed];

(b) a Financial Conduct Authority officer, a National Crime Agency officer, an officer of Revenue and Customs, or a member or of the staff of the relevant Director, if the warrant is sought for the purposes of a civil recovery investigation;

(c) a constable, an SFO officer, an accredited financial investigator, an officer of Revenue and Customs or an immigration officer, if the warrant is sought for the purposes of a detained cash investigation, a confiscation investigation or a money laundering investigation;

(ca) a constable, an SFO officer, an accredited financial investigator or an officer of Revenue and Customs, if the warrant is sought for the purposes of a detained property investigation;

(cb) a constable, an SFO officer, an accredited financial investigator or an officer of Revenue and Customs, if the warrant is sought for the purposes of a frozen funds investigation;

(d) a National Crime Agency officer, if the warrant is sought for the purposes of an exploitation proceeds investigation.

(11) The reference in paragraph (c) of subsection (10) to an accredited financial investigator is a reference to an accredited financial investigator who falls within a description specified in an order made for the purposes of that paragraph by the Secretary of State under section 453.

The Powers A search and seizure warrant authorises an appropriate officer (see **D8.43**) to enter and search specified premises and to seize and retain any material 'which is likely to be of substantial value (whether or not by itself) to the investigation' (POCA 2002, s. 352(4)). Lord Thomas CJ emphasised in *R (Golfrate Property Management) v Southwark Crown Court* [2014] EWHC 840 (Admin), [2014] 2 Cr App R 12 (145) at [26], that resources should be made available to ensure that judges have sufficient time to scrutinise an application and give a reasoned decision (although, as to the requirement to give reasons for making a 'disclosure order', see *Nuttall v NCA* [2016] EWHC 1911 (Admin), [2016] 4 WLR 134). He continued (at [27]): 'At all events, a judge faced with such an application requires the presentation of a full and clear picture of what lies behind it and to be told of matters that might tell against it. The target of the application is entitled to expect such candour.' **D8.45**

Essentially, a warrant is available only (a) where a production order has not been complied with and there are reasonable grounds for believing that the material is on the specified premises (s. 352) or (b), (i) where it is in the public interest to obtain the material and the material is likely to be of substantial value to the investigation but it is not appropriate to make a production order, notwithstanding that the requirements can be made out, because it is not practicable to communicate with the interested parties or because the investigation might be seriously prejudiced unless immediate access is obtained (s. 353(3) and (4)); or (ii) where the material is likely to be of substantial value to the investigation but cannot be identified in advance and it is not practicable to communicate with the interested parties or because the investigation might be seriously prejudiced unless immediate access is obtained (s. 353(5)). A warrant does not confer the right to seize 'privileged' or 'excluded' material (s. 354). Where property has been seized pursuant to a technically defective warrant, the Crown Court may authorise the retention of the property under the CJPA 2001, s. 59, on the ground that, were it to be returned, it would immediately become appropriate to issue a fresh warrant (*R (El-Kurd) v Winchester Crown Court* [2011] EWHC 1853 (Admin)). See also *R (Panesar) v Central Criminal Court* [2014] EWCA Civ 1613, [2015] 1 WLR 2577 at **D1.185**.

The exercise of these powers is governed by the SCA 2015, sch. 2, and by the Investigations Code of Practice. The control of search warrant use under the PACE 1984 has been extended to searches under a POCA warrant in confiscation, money laundering, detained cash, detained property and frozen funds investigations (see the POCA 2002, s. 355, and the Proceeds of Crime Act 2002 (Application of Police and Criminal Evidence Act 1984) Order 2015 (SI 2015 No. 759)). The PACE 1984 provisions that apply are the safeguards in respect of search warrants (PACE 1984, s. 15), the execution of warrants (s. 16), access and copying (s. 21) and retention (s. 22). For details of these provisions, see **D1.164** ***et seq***. Certain modifications of the provisions are set out in the 2015 Order. Similar but more limited controls on the execution of a warrant granted by a High Court judge apply to civil recovery investigations (s. 356). **D8.46**

Section 22 of the Criminal Finances Act 2017 inserted s. 356A into the POCA 2002, which created a number of offences in relation to obstruction of the execution of search and seizure warrants.

Disclosure Orders

Proceeds of Crime Act 2002, ss. 357 and 358 **D8.47**

357.—(1) A judge may, on an application made to him by the relevant authority, make a disclosure order if he is satisfied that each of the requirements for the making of the order is fulfilled.

(2) No application for a disclosure order may be made in relation to a detained cash investigation a detained property investigation or a frozen funds investigation.

(3) The application for a disclosure order must state that—
(a) a person specified in the application is subject to a confiscation investigation which is being carried out by an appropriate officer and the order is sought for the purposes of the investigation, or
(b) a person specified in the application or property specified in the application is subject to a civil recovery investigation and the order is sought for the purposes of the investigation,
(ba) a person specified in the application is subject to a money laundering investigation which is being carried out by an appropriate officer and the order is sought for the purposes of the investigation, or
(c) a person specified in the application is subject to an exploitation proceeds investigation and the order is sought for the purposes of the investigation.
(4) A disclosure order is an order authorising an appropriate officer to give to any person the appropriate officer considers has relevant information notice in writing requiring him to do, with respect to any matter relevant to the investigation for the purposes of which the order is sought, any or all of the following—
(a) answer questions, either at a time specified in the notice or at once, at a place so specified;
(b) provide information specified in the notice, by a time and in a manner so specified;
(c) produce documents, or documents of a description, specified in the notice, either at or by a time so specified or at once, and in a manner so specified.
(5) Relevant information is information (whether or not contained in a document) which the appropriate officer concerned considers to be relevant to the investigation.
(6) A person is not bound to comply with a requirement imposed by a notice given under a disclosure order unless evidence of authority to give the notice is produced to him.
(7) In this Part 'relevant authority' means—
(a) in relation to a confiscation investigation, an appropriate officer; and
(b) in relation to a civil recovery investigation, a Financial Conduct Authority officer, a National Crime Agency officer, an officer of Revenue and Customs or the relevant Director; and
(ba) in relation to a money laundering investigation, an appropriate officer, and
(c) in relation to an exploitation proceeds investigation, National Crime Agency officer.

358.—(1) These are the requirements for the making of a disclosure order.
(2) There must be reasonable grounds for suspecting that—
(a) in the case of a confiscation investigation, the person specified in the application for the order has benefited from his criminal conduct;
(b) in the case of a civil recovery investigation—
(i) the person specified in the application for the order holds recoverable property or associated property,
(ii) that person has, at any time, held property that was recoverable property or associated property at the time, or
(iii) the property specified in the application for the order is recoverable property or associated property;
(ba) in the case of a money laundering investigation, the person specified in the application for the order has committed a money laundering offence;
(c) in the case of an exploitation proceeds investigation, the person specified in the application for the order is a person within section 346(2A).
(3) There must be reasonable grounds for believing that information which may be provided in compliance with a requirement imposed under the order is likely to be of substantial value (whether or not by itself) to the investigation for the purposes of which the order is sought.
(4) There must be reasonable grounds for believing that it is in the public interest for the information to be provided, having regard to the benefit likely to accrue to the investigation if the information is obtained.

As to the meaning of 'reasonable grounds for believing', see **D8.43**.

D8.48 **Effect of the Order** A disclosure order under the POCA 2002, s. 357, enables an appropriate officer (see **D8.43**) to give notice to any person considered to have relevant information requiring that person to respond in any or all of three ways: to answer questions at a specified time and place; to provide information at a time and in a manner specified in the notice; and/or to produce documents or documents of a description, specified in the notice, by a time and in a manner specified in the notice. 'Relevant information' is defined as information the appropriate officer considers to be relevant to an investigation (s. 357(6)).

An application may be made by the relevant authority (ss. 367(7) and 378). An order may now be granted in relation to a money laundering investigation (as a result of changes brought about by the Criminal Finances Act 2017, s. 7, in force from 31 January 2018) but not in relation to investigations into detained cash, detained property and frozen funds (see **D8.37**). Notice may be given to anyone that the appropriate officer considers has relevant information. A notice made under a disclosure order (see **D8.50**) may not be sent to persons who are not within the jurisdiction (*SOCA v Perry* [2012] UKSC 35, [2013] 1 AC 182).

The two conditions for the making of an order are essentially questions of fact, namely, whether there are reasonable grounds for believing that the material would likely be of substantial value and that it would be in the public interest that the material should be produced (*R (Malik) v Manchester Crown Court* [2008] EWHC 1362 (Admin), [2008] 4 All ER 403).

An order does not confer the right to require persons to answer privileged questions, provide privileged information, produce privileged documents or produce 'excluded material' (s. 361). (See **D8.42** for the meaning of these terms.) 'A lawyer' may be required to provide a client's name and address. The privilege against self-incrimination does not allow a person to refuse to produce 'independent' or pre-existing documents (*R (River East Supplies Ltd) v Crown Court at Nottingham* [2017] EWHC 1942 (Admin), [2017] 2 Cr App R 27 (384)).

For a discussion of the disclosure order regime, see *NCA v Simkus* [2016] EWHC 255 (Admin), [2016] 1 WLR 3481, referring to: the right of a person to apply to set aside an order (at [15]); the obligation on the claimant, unless the court's permission is obtained, to provide the 'target' of an order with a copy of the evidence relied upon once the investigation is 'overt' (at [50]–[52]); and the power to make an order not being limited to discovering the whereabouts of known property but it may also be used to identify property not yet known (at [53]–[64]).

Generally, a statement made in response to a requirement of a disclosure order may not be used in evidence against the maker in criminal proceedings (s. 360(1)). Its use is permissible, however, in confiscation proceedings, in a prosecution for having failed without reasonable excuse to comply with the disclosure order, or in a prosecution for perjury. Moreover, an order may not be resisted on the basis that disclosure would breach the privilege against self-incrimination because it may lead to prosecution for an offence under s. 328 (entering or being concerned in a money laundering arrangement: see **B21.17**); such an offence is a 'related' offence within the meaning of the Fraud Act 2006, s. 13, and no privilege applies (*JSC BTA Bank v Ablyazov* [2009] EWCA Civ 1124, [2010] 1 WLR 976). More widely, the statement is admissible in any prosecution when the person 'in giving evidence' makes an inconsistent statement (s. 360(2)). **D8.49**

It is a summary offence to fail to comply with a requirement of a disclosure order without reasonable excuse (s. 359(1)) and it is an offence triable either way if, in purported compliance, a person knowingly or recklessly makes a false or misleading statement (s. 359(3)).

Disclosure Notices under the SOCPA 2005 For the power of the DPP to issue 'disclosure notices', see **D1.205**. **D8.50**

Customer Information Orders

Proceeds of Crime Act 2002, ss. 363 to 365 **D8.51**

363.—(1) A judge may, on an application made to him by an appropriate officer, make a customer information order if he is satisfied that each of the requirements for the making of the order is fulfilled.

(1A) No application for a customer information order may be made in relation to a detained cash investigation, a detained property investigation or a frozen funds investigation.

(2) The application for a customer information order must state that—

(a) a person specified in the application is subject to a confiscation investigation, a civil recovery investigation, an exploitation proceeds investigation or a money laundering investigation.

(b) [omitted by the CCA 2013, sch. 19.]

(3) The application must also state that—
(a) the order is sought for the purposes of the investigation;
(b) the order is sought against the financial institution or financial institutions specified in the application.
(4) An application for a customer information order may specify—
(a) all financial institutions,
(b) a particular description, or particular descriptions, of financial institutions, or
(c) a particular financial institution or particular financial institutions.
(5) A customer information order is an order that a financial institution covered by the application for the order must, on being required to do so by notice in writing given by an appropriate officer, provide any such customer information as it has relating to the person specified in the application.
(6) A financial institution which is required to provide information under a customer information order must provide the information to an appropriate officer in such manner, and at or by such time, as an appropriate officer requires.
(7) If a financial institution on which a requirement is imposed by a notice given under a customer information order requires the production of evidence of authority to give the notice, it is not bound to comply with the requirement unless evidence of the authority has been produced to it.

364.—(1) 'Customer information', in relation to a person and a financial institution, is information whether the person holds, or has held, an account or accounts at the financial institution (whether solely or jointly with another) and (if so) information as to—
(a) the matters specified in subsection (2) if the person is an individual;
(b) the matters specified in subsection (3) if the person is a company or limited liability partnership or a similar body incorporated or otherwise established outside the United Kingdom.
(2) The matters referred to in subsection (1)(a) are—
(a) the account number or numbers;
(b) the person's full name;
(c) his date of birth;
(d) his most recent address and any previous addresses;
(e) the date or dates on which he began to hold the account or accounts and, if he has ceased to hold the account or any of the accounts, the date or dates on which he did so;
(f) such evidence of his identity as was obtained by the financial institution under or for the purposes of any legislation relating to money laundering;
(g) the full name, date of birth and most recent address, and any previous addresses, of any person who holds, or has held, an account at the financial institution jointly with him;
(h) the account number or numbers of any other account or accounts held at the financial institution to which he is a signatory and details of the person holding the other account or accounts.
(3) The matters referred to in subsection (1)(b) are—
(a) the account number or numbers;
(b) the person's full name;
(c) a description of any business which the person carries on;
(d) the country or territory in which it is incorporated or otherwise established and any number allocated to it under the Companies Act 2006 or corresponding legislation of any country or territory outside the United Kingdom;
(e) any number assigned to it for the purposes of value added tax in the United Kingdom;
(f) its registered office, and any previous registered offices, under the Companies Act 2006 (or corresponding earlier legislation) or anything similar under corresponding legislation of any country or territory outside the United Kingdom;
(g) its registered office, and any previous registered offices, under the Limited Liability Partnerships Act 2000 or anything similar under corresponding legislation of any country or territory outside Great Britain;
(h) the date or dates on which it began to hold the account or accounts and, if it has ceased to hold the account or any of the accounts, the date or dates on which it did so;
(i) such evidence of its identity as was obtained by the financial institution under or for the purposes of any legislation relating to money laundering;
(j) the full name, date of birth and most recent address and any previous addresses of any person who is a signatory to the account or any of the accounts.

(4) The Secretary of State may by order provide for information of a description specified in the order—
(a) to be customer information, or
(b) no longer to be customer information.
(5) Money laundering is an act which—
(a) constitutes an offence under section 327, 328 or 329 of this Act or section 18 of the Terrorism Act 2000, or
(aa) constitutes an offence under section 415(1A) of this Act; or
(b) would constitute an offence specified in paragraph (a) or (aa) if done in the United Kingdom.

365.—(1) These are the requirements for the making of a customer information order.
(2) In the case of a confiscation investigation, there must be reasonable grounds for suspecting that the person specified in the application for the order has benefited from his criminal conduct.
(3A) In the case of a civil recovery investigation, there must be reasonable grounds for suspecting that the person specified in the application—
(a) holds recoverable property or associated property, or
(b) has, at any time, held property that was recoverable property or associated property at the time.
(4) In the case of a money laundering investigation, there must be reasonable grounds for suspecting that the person specified in the application for the order has committed a money laundering offence.
(5) In the case of any investigation, there must be reasonable grounds for believing that customer information which may be provided in compliance with the order is likely to be of substantial value (whether or not by itself) to the investigation for the purposes of which the order is sought.
(6) In the case of any investigation, there must be reasonable grounds for believing that it is in the public interest for the customer information to be provided, having regard to the benefit likely to accrue to the investigation if the information is obtained.

Effect, Procedure and Requirements A customer information order requires a 'financial institution' on written notice to provide 'customer information' to an 'appropriate officer' (see **D8.43**) (POCA 2002, s. 363(5)). 'Customer information' can amount to the most detailed information about financial accounts and account holders (s. 364). **D8.52**

Procedure is governed by CrimPR Part 47 (see Supplement, **R47.1** *et seq.*). Separate rules apply in civil recovery investigations. The applicant must be an 'appropriate officer', whose office and rank are dependent on the type of investigation (see s. 378 at **D8.43**).

An order is not available to support a detained cash investigation, a detained property investigation, or a frozen funds investigation. There must be reasonable grounds for suspecting the particular state of affairs applicable to the type of investigation. In addition there must be 'reasonable grounds for believing' (see **D8.43**) that an order is in the 'public interest and the customer information is likely to be of 'substantial value to the investigation'.

In keeping with the provisions relating to disclosure orders, a statement made by a financial institution in response to a customer information order cannot be used against it in criminal proceedings other than in confiscation proceedings, in a prosecution under s. 366 for non-compliance with the order itself or in any prosecution where the financial institution makes an inconsistent statement (s. 367). An application to vary or discharge the order may be made by the original applicant for the order or by 'any person affected by the order' (s. 369).

A financial institution commits an offence if it fails to comply with an order without reasonable excuse (s. 366(1)) or if, in purported compliance, it knowingly or recklessly makes a false or misleading statement (s. 366(3)). The latter is triable either way.

Account Monitoring Orders

Proceeds of Crime Act 2002, ss. 370 and 371 **D8.53**

370.—(1) A judge may, on an application made to him by an appropriate officer, make an account monitoring order if he is satisfied that each of the requirements for the making of the order is fulfilled.
(1A) No application for an account monitoring order may be made in relation to a detained cash investigation, a detained property investigation or a frozen funds investigation.

(2) The application for an account monitoring order must state that—
(a) a person specified in the application is subject to a confiscation investigation, a civil recovery investigation, an exploitation proceeds investigation or a money laundering investigation.
(3) The application must also state that—
(a) the order is sought for the purposes of the investigation;
(b) the order is sought against the financial institution specified in the application in relation to account information of the description so specified.
(4) Account information is information relating to an account or accounts held at the financial institution specified in the application by the person so specified (whether solely or jointly with another).
(5) The application for an account monitoring order may specify information relating to—
(a) all accounts held by the person specified in the application for the order at the financial institution so specified,
(b) a particular description, or particular descriptions, of accounts so held, or
(c) a particular account, or particular accounts, so held.
(6) An account monitoring order is an order that the financial institution specified in the application for the order must, for the period stated in the order, provide account information of the description specified in the order to an appropriate officer in the manner, and at or by the time or times, stated in the order.
(7) The period stated in an account monitoring order must not exceed the period of 90 days beginning with the day on which the order is made.

371.—(1) These are the requirements for the making of an account monitoring order.
(2) In the case of a confiscation investigation, there must be reasonable grounds for suspecting that the person specified in the application for the order has benefited from his criminal conduct.
(3A) In the case of a civil recovery investigation, there must be reasonable grounds for suspecting that the person specified in the application holds recoverable property or associated property.
(4) In the case of a money laundering investigation, there must be reasonable grounds for suspecting that the person specified in the application for the order has committed a money laundering offence.
(5) In the case of any investigation, there must be reasonable grounds for believing that account information which may be provided in compliance with the order is likely to be of substantial value (whether or not by itself) to the investigation for the purposes of which the order is sought.
(6) In the case of any investigation, there must be reasonable grounds for believing that it is in the public interest for the account information to be provided, having regard to the benefit likely to accrue to the investigation if the information is obtained.

D8.54 **Effect, Procedure and Requirements** An account monitoring order requires a financial institution to provide an appropriate officer (see **D8.43**) with specified information 'relating to an account or accounts held' solely or jointly by a specified person ('account information') for the period stated in the order (POCA 2002, s. 370) which must not exceed 90 days from the date of the order. An order 'has effect in spite of any restriction on the disclosure of information (however imposed)' (s. 374); this appears to override any claim of confidentiality or data protection.

Procedure is governed by CrimPR Part 47 (see Supplement, **R47.1** *et seq.*). The requirements under s. 371 closely resemble those of the other orders. An order is not available to support a detained cash investigation, a detained property investigation, or a frozen funds investigation. There must be reasonable grounds for suspecting the particular state of affairs applicable to the type of investigation. In addition there must be 'reasonable grounds for believing' (see **D8.43**) that an order is in the 'public interest' and the customer information is likely to be of 'substantial value to the investigation'. There are restrictions similar to those relating to other orders on the use in criminal proceedings of a statement by a financial institution in response to an order (s. 372). An application to vary or discharge the order may be made by the original applicant for the order or by 'any person affected by the order' (s. 375).

Unexplained Wealth Orders

D8.55 The following provisions came into force on 31 January 2018.

Proceeds of Crime Act 2002, ss. 362A to 362D

362A.—(1) The High Court may, on an application made by an enforcement authority, make an unexplained wealth order in respect of any property if the court is satisfied that each of the requirements for the making of the order is fulfilled.

(2) An application for an order must—

(a) specify or describe the property in respect of which the order is sought, and

(b) specify the person whom the enforcement authority thinks holds the property ('the respondent') (and the person specified may include a person outside the United Kingdom).

(3) An unexplained wealth order is an order requiring the respondent to provide a statement—

(a) setting out the nature and extent of the respondent's interest in the property in respect of which the order is made,

(b) explaining how the respondent obtained the property (including, in particular, how any costs incurred in obtaining it were met),

(c) where the property is held by the trustees of a settlement, setting out such details of the settlement as may be specified in the order, and

(d) setting out such other information in connection with the property as may be so specified.

(4) The order must specify—

(a) the form and manner in which the statement is to be given,

(b) the person to whom it is to be given, and

(c) the place at which it is to be given or, if it is to be given in writing, the address to which it is to be sent.

(5) The order may, in connection with requiring the respondent to provide the statement mentioned in subsection (3), also require the respondent to produce documents of a kind specified or described in the order.

(6) The respondent must comply with the requirements imposed by an unexplained wealth order within whatever period the court may specify (and different periods may be specified in relation to different requirements).

(7) In this Chapter 'enforcement authority' means—

(a) the National Crime Agency,

(b) Her Majesty's Revenue and Customs,

(c) the Financial Conduct Authority,

(d) the Director of the Serious Fraud Office, or

(e) the Director of Public Prosecutions (in relation to England and Wales) or the Director of Public Prosecutions for Northern Ireland (in relation to Northern Ireland).

362B.—(1) These are the requirements for the making of an unexplained wealth order in respect of any property.

(2) The High Court must be satisfied that there is reasonable cause to believe that—

(a) the respondent holds the property, and

(b) the value of the property is greater than £50,000.

(3) The High Court must be satisfied that there are reasonable grounds for suspecting that the known sources of the respondent's lawfully obtained income would have been insufficient for the purposes of enabling the respondent to obtain the property.

(4) The High Court must be satisfied that—

(a) the respondent is a politically exposed person, or

(b) there are reasonable grounds for suspecting that—

(i) the respondent is, or has been, involved in serious crime (whether in a part of the United Kingdom or elsewhere), or

(ii) a person connected with the respondent is, or has been, so involved.

(5) It does not matter for the purposes of subsection (2)(a)—

(a) whether or not there are other persons who also hold the property;

(b) whether the property was obtained by the respondent before or after the coming into force of this section.

(6) For the purposes of subsection (3)—

(a) regard is to be had to any mortgage, charge or other kind of security that it is reasonable to assume was or may have been available to the respondent for the purposes of obtaining the property;

(b) it is to be assumed that the respondent obtained the property for a price equivalent to its market value;

(c) income is 'lawfully obtained' if it is obtained lawfully under the laws of the country from where the income arises;

(d) 'known' sources of the respondent's income are the sources of income (whether arising from employment, assets or otherwise) that are reasonably ascertainable from available information at the time of the making of the application for the order;

(e) where the property is an interest in other property comprised in a settlement, the reference to the respondent obtaining the property is to be taken as if it were a reference to the respondent obtaining direct ownership of such share in the settled property as relates to, or is fairly represented by, that interest.

(7) In subsection (4)(a), 'politically exposed person' means a person who is—

(a) an individual who is, or has been, entrusted with prominent public functions by an international organisation or by a State other than the United Kingdom or another EEA State,

(b) a family member of a person within paragraph (a),

(c) known to be a close associate of a person within that paragraph, or

(d) otherwise connected with a person within that paragraph.

(8) Article 3 of Directive 2015/849/EU of the European Parliament and of the Council of 20 May 2015 applies for the purposes of determining—

(a) whether a person has been entrusted with prominent public functions (see point (9) of that Article),

(b) whether a person is a family member (see point (10) of that Article), and

(c) whether a person is known to be a close associate of another (see point (11) of that Article).

(9) For the purposes of this section—

(a) a person is involved in serious crime in a part of the United Kingdom or elsewhere if the person would be so involved for the purposes of Part 1 of the Serious Crime Act 2007 (see in particular sections 2, 2A and 3 of that Act);

(b) section 1122 of the Corporation Tax Act 2010 ('connected' persons) applies in determining whether a person is connected with another.

(10) Where the property in respect of which the order is sought comprises more than one item of property, the reference in subsection (2)(b) to the value of the property is to the total value of those items.

362C.—(1) This section applies in a case where the respondent fails, without reasonable excuse, to comply with the requirements imposed by an unexplained wealth order in respect of any property before the end of the response period.

(2) The property is to be presumed to be recoverable property for the purposes of any proceedings taken in respect of the property under Part 5, unless the contrary is shown.

(3) The presumption in subsection (2) applies in relation to property—

(a) only so far as relating to the respondent's interest in the property, and

(b) only if the value of that interest is greater than the sum specified in section 362B(2)(b). It is for the court hearing the proceedings under Part 5 in relation to which reliance is placed on the presumption to determine the matters in this subsection.

(4) The 'response period' is whatever period the court specifies under section 362A(6) as the period within which the requirements imposed by the order are to be complied with (or the period ending the latest, if more than one is specified in respect of different requirements).

(5) For the purposes of subsection (1)—

(a) a respondent who purports to comply with the requirements imposed by an unexplained wealth order is not to be taken to have failed to comply with the order (see instead section 362D);

(b) where an unexplained wealth order imposes more than one requirement on the respondent, the respondent is to be taken to have failed to comply with the requirements imposed by the order unless each of the requirements is complied with or is purported to be complied with.

(6) Subsections (7) and (8) apply in determining the respondent's interest for the purposes of subsection (3) in a case where the respondent to the unexplained wealth order—

(a) is connected with another person who is, or has been, involved in serious crime (see subsection (4)(b)(ii) of section 362B), or

(b) is a politically exposed person of a kind mentioned in paragraph (b), (c) or (d) of subsection (7) of that section (family member, known close associates etc of individual entrusted with prominent public functions).

(7) In a case within subsection (6)(a), the respondent's interest is to be taken to include any interest in the property of the person involved in serious crime with whom the respondent is connected.

(8) In a case within subsection (6)(b), the respondent's interest is to be taken to include any interest in the property of the person mentioned in subsection (7)(a) of section 362B.

(9) Where an unexplained wealth order is made in respect of property comprising more than one item of property, the reference in subsection (3)(b) to the value of the respondent's interest in the property is to the total value of the respondent's interest in those items.

362D.—(1) This section applies in a case where, before the end of the response period (as defined by section 362C(4)), the respondent complies, or purports to comply, with the requirements imposed by an unexplained wealth order in respect of any property in relation to which the order is made.

(2) If an interim freezing order has effect in relation to the property (see section 362J), the enforcement authority must determine what enforcement or investigatory proceedings, if any, it considers ought to be taken in relation to the property.

(3) A determination under subsection (2) must be made within the period of 60 days starting with the day of compliance.

(4) If the determination under subsection (2) is that no further enforcement or investigatory proceedings ought to be taken in relation to the property, the enforcement authority must notify the High Court of that fact as soon as reasonably practicable (and in any event before the end of the 60 day period mentioned in subsection (3)).

(5) If there is no interim freezing order in effect in relation to the property, the enforcement authority may (at any time) determine what, if any, enforcement or investigatory proceedings it considers ought to be taken in relation to the property.

(6) A determination under this section to take no further enforcement or investigatory proceedings in relation to any property does not prevent such proceedings being taken subsequently (whether as a result of new information or otherwise, and whether or not by the same enforcement authority) in relation to the property.

(7) For the purposes of this section—
- (a) the respondent complies with the requirements imposed by an unexplained wealth order only if all of the requirements are complied with,
- (b) references to the day of compliance are to the day on which the requirements imposed by the order are complied with (or, if the requirements are complied with over more than one day, the last of those days), and
- (c) where an order requires the sending of information in writing to, or the production of documents at, an address specified in the order, compliance with the order (so far as relating to that requirement) occurs when the written information is received, or the documents are produced, at that address, and in paragraphs (a) to (c) references to compliance include purported compliance.

(8) In this section 'enforcement or investigatory proceedings' means any proceedings in relation to property taken under—
- (a) Part 2 or 4 (confiscation proceedings in England and Wales or Northern Ireland) (in relation to cases where the enforcement authority is also a prosecuting authority for the purposes of that Part),
- (b) Part 5 (civil recovery of the proceeds of unlawful conduct), or
- (c) this Chapter.

Effect, Procedure and Requirements The Criminal Finances Act 2017, s. 1, introduced, with effect from 31 January 2018, a new investigative measure known as an unexplained wealth order requiring a person holding property to 'explain' the person's interest in that property (POCA 2002, ss. 362A to 362I). An application for an order is normally made *ex parte*, in private and, as such, the normal rules on open justice do not apply (*NCA v Hussain* [2020] EWHC 432 (Admin)). An unexplained wealth order may be made in respect of property (provided it is worth more than £50,000) where there are reasonable grounds for suspecting that the known sources of lawful income of the person holding the property would have been insufficient for the purposes of enabling that person to obtain it. In conducting this exercise, care should be taken where the applicant seeks to place reliance on complex property transactions to establish a suspicion about the provenance of funds. As explained by Lang J in *NCA v Baker* [2020] EWHC 822 (Admin) at [97], drawing on the case law concerned with freezing orders, the use of complex offshore structures or trusts is not, without more, a ground for believing that they have been set up, or are being used, for wrongful purposes, such as money laundering. There are lawful reasons—privacy, security, tax **D8.56**

mitigation—why very wealthy people invest their capital in complex offshore corporate structures or trusts. An order under s. 362A is one which requires the holder of the property to make a statement containing the matters particularised in s. 362A(3). The privilege against self-incrimination does not provide a basis for refusing to respond to an order (*NCA v Hajiyeva* [2020] EWCA Civ 108 at [53]). An unexplained wealth order is only available where the property is held by a person who falls within s. 362B(4). A person falls within s. 352B(4) if the court is satisfied that the person is 'politically exposed' as that term is defined by s. 362B(7) (and see *NCA v Hajiyeva*, at [23]–[29]) or if there are reasonable grounds for suspecting that the person, or a person 'connected with' him or her, is involved in or has been involved in 'serious crime'.

By reason of s. 362C, a failure, without reasonable excuse, to comply with any requirement imposed by an unexplained wealth order in respect of any property has the effect of establishing a presumption that such property is recoverable property for the purposes of any Part 5 (civil forfeiture) proceedings that may be taken. In any such proceedings it would be open to a respondent to rebut that presumption. Moreover, the presumption only applies where there has been a demonstrable non-compliance (without reasonable excuse), which is to be distinguished from 'purported compliance'.

In cases of 'compliance or purported compliance' with the requirements of an unexplained wealth order, the presumption that the property is 'recoverable' does not apply. In such cases, it falls to the enforcement authority to decide, within a period of 60 days of the date of compliance, what if any enforcement or investigatory proceedings ought to be taken, namely, confiscation proceedings (POCA 2002, Part 2), civil proceedings for the recovery of property (Part 5) or investigatory proceedings (Part 8, ch. 2).

Where the High Court makes an unexplained wealth order it may at the same time make an interim freezing order (s. 362J) and appoint a receiver (s. 362N). An interim freezing order may be made where the court considers it 'necessary for the purposes of avoiding the risk of any recovery order that might subsequently be obtained being frustrated'. An interim freezing order gives the enforcement authority an opportunity to decide what if any further action to take, such as obtaining a restraint order (part 2) or a property freezing order or interim receiving order (part 5). Section 362K contains power to vary or discharge an interim freezing order and specifies the cases in which an order must be discharged. The court may (as with property freezing orders) make an interim freezing order subject to 'exclusions' to permit a person to meet expenses (s. 362L). Where property is believed to be located outside the UK, the enforcement authority or (where appointed) a receiver may (ss. 362S to 362T) send a request for assistance in the freezing or management of that property.

It is a criminal offence triable either way for a person with the relevant state of mind (knowledge or recklessness) to make a materially false or misleading statement in purported compliance with an unexplained wealth order (s. 362E). Where the order contains a penal notice, non-compliance is punishable as a contempt (*NCA v Hajiyeva* [2018] EWHC 2534 (Admin), [2018] 1 WLR 5887 at [94]).

RESTRAINT ORDERS

D8.57 **Proceeds of Crime Act 2002, ss. 40 and 41**

40.—(1) The Crown Court may exercise the powers conferred by section 41 if any of the following conditions is satisfied.

(2) The first condition is that—
 (a) a criminal investigation has been started in England and Wales with regard to an offence, and
 (b) there are reasonable grounds to suspect that the alleged offender has benefited from his criminal conduct.

(3) The second condition is that—
 (a) proceedings for an offence have been started in England and Wales and not concluded, and
 (b) there is reasonable cause to believe that the defendant has benefited from his criminal conduct.

(4) The third condition is that—
 (a) an application by the prosecutor has been made under section 19, 20, 27 or 28 and not concluded, or the court believes that such an application is to be made, and
 (b) there is reasonable cause to believe that the defendant has benefited from his criminal conduct.

(5) The fourth condition is that—
 (a) an application by the prosecutor has been made under section 21 and not concluded, or the court believes that such an application is to be made, and
 (b) there is reasonable cause to believe that the court will decide under that section that the amount found under the new calculation of the defendant's benefit exceeds the relevant amount (as defined in that section).

(6) The fifth condition is that—
 (a) an application by the prosecutor has been made under section 22 and not concluded, or the court believes that such an application is to be made, and
 (b) there is reasonable cause to believe that the court will decide under that section that the amount found under the new calculation of the available amount exceeds the relevant amount (as defined in that section).

(7) The second condition is not satisfied if the court believes that—
 (a) there has been undue delay in continuing the proceedings, or
 (b) the prosecutor does not intend to proceed.

(8) If an application mentioned in the third, fourth or fifth condition has been made the condition is not satisfied if the court believes that—
 (a) there has been undue delay in continuing the application, or
 (b) the prosecutor does not intend to proceed.

(9) If the first condition is satisfied—
 (a) references in this Part to the defendant are to the alleged offender;
 (b) references in this Part to the prosecutor are to the person the court believes is to have conduct of any proceedings for the offence;
 (c) section 77(9) has effect as if proceedings for the offence had been started against the defendant when the investigation was started.

41.—(1) If any condition set out in section 40 is satisfied the Crown Court may make an order (a restraint order) prohibiting any specified person from dealing with any realisable property held by him.

(2) A restraint order may provide that it applies—
 (a) to all realisable property held by the specified person whether or not the property is described in the order;
 (b) to realisable property transferred to the specified person after the order is made.

(2A) A restraint order must be made subject to an exception enabling relevant legal aid payments to be made (a legal aid exception).

(2B) A relevant legal aid payment is a payment that the specified person is obliged to make—
 (a) by regulations under section 23 or 24 of the Legal Aid, Sentencing and Punishment of Offenders Act 2012, and
 (b) in connection with services provided in relation to an offence which falls within subsection (5),

whether the obligation to make the payment arises before or after the restraint order is made.

(3) A restraint order may be made subject to other exceptions, and an exception may in particular—
 (a) make provision for reasonable living expenses and reasonable legal expenses;
 (b) make provision for the purpose of enabling any person to carry on any trade, business, profession or occupation.

(4) But where an exception to a restraint order is made under subsection (3), it must not make provision for any legal expenses which—
 (a) relate to an offence which falls within subsection (5), and
 (b) are incurred by the defendant or by a recipient of a tainted gift.

(5) These offences fall within this subsection—
 (a) the offence mentioned in section 40(2) or (3), if the first or second condition (as the case may be) is satisfied;
 (b) the offence (or any of the offences) concerned, if the third, fourth or fifth condition is satisfied.

(5A) A legal aid exception—
 (a) must be made subject to prescribed restrictions (if any) on—
  (i) the circumstances in which payments may be made in reliance on the exception, or
  (ii) the amount of the payments that may be made in reliance on the exception,

(b) must be made subject to other prescribed conditions (if any) and
(c) may be made subject to other condition·

(5B) Any other exception to a restraint order may be made subject to conditions.

(6) Subsection (7) applies if—
(a) a court makes a restraint order, and
(b) the applicant for the order applies to the court to proceed under subsection (7) (whether as part of the application for the restraint order or at any time afterwards).

(7) The court may make such order as it believes is appropriate for the purpose of ensuring that the restraint order is effective.

(7A) Subsections (7B) and (7C) apply where the Crown Court makes a restraint order (by virtue of the first condition in section 40) as a result of a criminal investigation having been started in England and Wales with regard to an offence.

(7B) The court—
(a) must include in the order a requirement for the applicant for the order to report to the court on the progress of the investigation at such times and in such manner as the order may specify (a 'reporting requirement'), and
(b) must discharge the order if proceedings for the offence are not started within a reasonable time (and this duty applies whether or not an application to discharge the order is made under section 42(3)).

(7C) The duty under subsection (7B)(a) does not apply if the court decides that, in the circumstances of the case, a reporting requirement should not be imposed, but the court—
(a) must give reasons for its decision, and
(b) may at any time vary the order so as to include a reporting requirement (and this power applies whether or not an application to vary the order is made under section 42(3)).

(7D) In considering whether to make an order under subsection (7), the court must, in particular, consider whether any restriction or prohibition on the defendant's travel outside the United Kingdom ought to be imposed for the purpose mentioned in that subsection.

(8) A restraint order does not affect property for the time being subject to a charge under any of these provisions—
(a) section 9 of the Drug Trafficking Offences Act 1986;
(b) section 78 of the Criminal Justice Act 1988;
(c) Article 14 of the Criminal Justice (Confiscation) (Northern Ireland) Order 1990 (SI 1990 No. 2588);
(d) section 27 of the Drug Trafficking Act 1994;
(e) Article 32 of the Proceeds of Crime (Northern Ireland) Order 1996 (SI 1996 No. 1299).

(9) Dealing with property includes removing it from England and Wales.

(10) In this section 'prescribed' means prescribed by regulations made by the Secretary of State.

The SCA 2015, s. 11, amended ss. 40 and 41. The test applied under s. 40 where a criminal investigation has started is no longer 'reasonable cause to believe' but 'reasonable grounds to suspect'.

Power to Make an Order

D8.58 Under earlier legislation, restraint orders could be granted only by the High Court. Under the POCA 2002, Part 2, the jurisdiction is transferred to the Crown Court. For a useful summary of the statutory scheme and procedure, see *Re Windsor* [2011] EWCA Crim 143, [2011] 1 WLR 1519.

A restraint order is a preventive measure imposed in support of any confiscation order that may be or has been made. The purpose of a confiscation order is to recover a sum of money not exceeding the value of property obtained by the defendant from criminal conduct. A restraint order operates to prohibit 'any specified person from dealing with any realisable property held by him' (s. 41(1)). Realisable property is 'any free property' held by the defendant or by the recipient of a 'tainted gift' (s. 83). The reference to 'tainted gifts' ensures that the value of property can be restrained and recovered even when it has been 'gifted' into the hands of another. Property is 'free' unless it is subject to a recovery or forfeiture order or a forfeiture notice (s. 82). Property is held by a person who has an 'interest' in it. This is not necessarily confined to the holding of a legal or equitable interest in the property. In the context of a VAT carousel fraud, all the conspirators may be treated as having obtained the proceeds of the conspiracy which may be the subject of a restraint order (*Ahmad* [2014] UKSC 36, [2015] AC 299).

Ancillary to a restraint order, the court 'may make such order as it believes is appropriate for the purpose of ensuring that the restraint order is effective' (s. 41(7)). Frequently, defendants are required to provide statements disclosing their finances (*Re O (Disclosure Order)* [1991] 2 QB 520) or to repatriate assets (*DPP v Scarlett* [2000] 1 WLR 515). In principle, such orders are available against third parties. The power has been used to permit a police officer to convert into sterling bitcoin that was subject to restraint (*Teresko* [2018] Crim LR 81). Property that has been seized by or produced to 'an appropriate officer' (see **D8.43**) under a statutory power may be detained as part of the restraint order (s. 41A). The s. 41(7) power has been used to permit the police to convert bitcoin into sterling (*Teresko* [2018] Crim LR 81).

Basis for Making an Order

The satisfaction of any one of five 'conditions' in the POCA 2002, s. 40, provides the basis for **D8.59** a restraint order. The first condition is that (a) 'a criminal investigation has been started with regard to an offence' (s. 40(2)(a)) and there 'are reasonable grounds to suspect that the alleged offender has benefited from his criminal conduct' (s. 40(2)(b), as amended by the SCA 2015, s. 11(1)). In this context, delay in making the application would not itself justify not making an order (*Ready Rentals Ltd (in liquidation) v Ahmed* [2016] EWHC 1996 (Ch)), although that factor might be relevant to the existence or otherwise of a risk of dissipation (see **D8.63**). The second and third conditions are that (b) 'proceedings have been started' and (c) there is an unconcluded application (or an application that the court believes is to be made) for reconsideration of confiscation or an application in respect of an absconded defendant and, in each of these two cases, that there 'is reasonable cause to believe' that the defendant has benefited from the criminal conduct.

The SCA 2015, s. 11(2), amended the POCA 2002, s. 41, so that where the court makes an order under the first condition it must (a) include in the order a requirement for the applicant to report on the progress of the investigation at such times and in such manner as the order may specify, and (b) discharge the order if proceedings for the offence are not started within a reasonable time. The duty to make a reporting requirement will not apply if the court decides that, in the circumstances of the case, one should not be imposed, but the court must then give reasons for its decision, and may at any time vary the order so as to include a reporting requirement. Transitional provisions require that restraint orders may not be made under (a) above where an offence which is the subject of an investigation was committed before 24 March 2003 (Proceeds of Crime Act 2002 (Transitional Provisions, Savings and Amendment) Order (SI 2003 No. 333), art. 5). However, the applicant does not need to establish that all the offences under investigation occurred after that date. All that is required to establish jurisdiction is that an offence that may, following conviction, give rise to a confiscation order under the POCA 2002 is under investigation at the time of the application (*RCPO v Hill* [2005] EWCA Crim 3271).

The fourth and fifth conditions are that an application to reconsider the amount of benefit or the available amount determined in previous confiscation proceedings is not concluded (or that the court believes such an application is to be made) and there is reasonable cause to believe that the new amount will exceed the original amount. The second to fourth conditions are not satisfied if the court believes that there has been undue delay in continuing the proceedings or application or that the prosecutor does not intend to proceed. Whether there has been 'undue delay' depends on an analysis of the complexity of the case, the extent of the delay and the reasons for it (*R* [2016] EWCA Crim 1938).

It appears that, for the purposes of the first two conditions, there need not necessarily be a con- **D8.60** nection between the current criminal investigation or proceedings and the 'criminal conduct' from which the person is believed to have benefited (*RCPO v Hill* [2005] EWCA Crim 3271). 'Criminal conduct' simply means any conduct that constitutes an offence in England and Wales or that would constitute an offence if it occurred here (s. 76). Accordingly, the conditions for a restraint order simply anticipate the twin components of a confiscation order — a conviction for an offence and a finding that the defendant has benefited from 'his criminal conduct'.

Exercise of the Power

D8.61 The POCA 2002, s. 69, provides a 'legislative steer'. The powers of the court and of receivers must be exercised:

(a) with a view to securing the availability of the value of the property to satisfy any confiscation order;
(b) in a case where no order has yet been made, with a view to ensuring that the property does not decrease in value;
(c) 'without taking account of any obligation of the defendant or the recipient of a tainted gift if the obligation conflicts with the object of satisfying any confiscation order'.

The three objectives are subject to rules that:

(i) a person other than the defendant or a recipient of a tainted gift should be allowed to retain or recover the value of any interest held by him;
(ii) in respect of realisable property held by the recipient of a tainted gift, the powers should be exercised with a view to realising no more than the value for the time being of that gift;
(iii) where no confiscation order has yet been made, and the defendant or a recipient of a tainted gift makes an application, the court should not order the sale of property which cannot be replaced

The underlying purpose of the legislation is to prevent the dissipation of realisable property, whether legitimately acquired or not.

D8.62 **Property to be Restrained** Any property in which, on a good arguable case, a defendant or suspect holds an interest is liable to be restrained (*Compton* [2002] EWCA Civ 1720). Likewise, property is liable to be restrained if there is a good arguable case that it is property which is held by a company in respect of which the corporate veil may be pierced (**E19.30**) or held by the recipient of a tainted gift (**E19.54**). Section 69(2)(c) of the POCA 2002 requires the courts to ignore any debt owed by the restrained person to an unsecured third-party creditor, so that the existence of such a debt would not empower the court to vary a restraint order unless there was no conflict with the object of satisfying any confiscation order that had been or might be made. The statutory provisions had changed significantly since the pre-2002 Act legislation (*Re X (Restraint Order: Variation)* [2004] EWHC 861 (Admin), [2005] QB 133, superseded by *SFO v Lexi Holdings plc (In Administration)* [2008] EWCA Crim 1443, [2009] QB 376). Where there are concurrent matrimonial proceedings, it may be possible to order the transfer of the innocent partner's share as ancillary relief in those proceedings thus taking that share out of the calculation of the amount available for restraint or confiscation (*Webber v CPS* [2006] EWHC 2893 (Fam), [2007] 1 WLR 1052; *Customs and Excise Commissioners v MCA* [2002] EWCA Civ 1039, [2003] Fam 55; *CPS v Grimes* [2003] 2 FLR 510; *Hedges* [2004] EWCA Crim 2133; *X v X* [2005] EWHC 296 (Fam), [2005] 2 FLR 487). This should not be regarded as 'open season to collusive agreements between dishonest former spouses'. 'As a matter of justice and public policy', the fact that family assets are derived from crime will be 'the decisive factor'; they should not be distributed to satisfy ancillary relief claims (*CPS v Richards* [2006] EWCA Civ 849, [2006] 2 FLR 1220).

The amount of property to be restrained should not exceed the amount of any confiscation order which has been or may be made, but the anticipated confiscation order may be large, particularly in a case of alleged or proven 'criminal lifestyle', in which case, because the statutory assumptions as to benefit would apply, an unlimited order may be justified (*K* [2005] EWCA Crim 619).

D8.63 **Risk of Dissipation** As a basic principle, 'if there is no [risk that property will be dissipated] ... or the risk is merely fanciful, the order ought not to be made since, *ex hypothesi*, it would not be necessary for the achievement of its only proper purpose' (*Re AJ and DJ* (9 December 1992 unreported) per Glidewell LJ). Since a restraint order amounts to an interference with the right to peaceful enjoyment of possessions under Article 1 of Protocol 1 to the ECHR, there can be no justification for an order unless such a risk exists (*Re B (Restraint Order)* [2008] EWCA Crim 1374, [2009] 1 Cr App R 14 (203)). Where dishonesty is alleged, there will usually be reason to fear that assets will be dissipated. Prosecutors should be alive to the possibility that there may be no risk in fact and, where no dissipation has occurred over a long period, they should explain why dissipation is now feared. Where the respondent has had ample opportunity to dissipate assets but has not done so and has disclosed the existence of other assets, the prosecutor and judge must provide a reasoned explanation for an order (*Re B*).

Candour Prosecutors proceeding *ex parte* have a duty to make full and frank disclosure but, as they act in the public interest, a failure of disclosure should not result in the sanction of discharging the order save where their behaviour was appalling (*Jennings v CPS* [2005] EWCA Civ 746, [2005] 4 All ER 391). If the court considers that the prosecution have failed to consider the risk or failed to put relevant material before the court, but that the public interest still requires an order, the court may disallow the prosecution costs (*Stanford International Bank v SFO* [2010] EWCA Civ 137, [2011] Ch 33; *Jennings v CPS*). **D8.64**

Restrictions on Restraint Orders

No distress may be levied against any restrained property, nor may there be forfeiture for breach of a tenancy agreement without leave of the Crown Court (POCA 2002, s. 58(2) and (3)). Where other court proceedings are pending in respect of restrained property, the other court has a discretion whether to stay those proceedings once it has given an opportunity for the applicant for the restraint order and any receiver to make representations (s. 58(6)). **D8.65**

External Requests and Orders

The principal legislation governing assistance to and from EU countries is the Criminal Justice and Data Protection (Protocol No. 36) Regulations 2014 (SI 2014 No. 3141). These provide for the 'mutual recognition' of restraint orders through the provision of a 'certificate'. Under reg. 6, if any of the property to which an application for a 'domestic restraint order' (i.e. an order under the POCA 2002, s. 41) relates is property in a Member State other than the UK, the prosecutor may ask the Crown Court to make a certificate. The Crown Court may make a certificate if it makes a domestic restraint order in relation to property in the other Member State and it is satisfied that there is a good arguable case that the property has been or is likely to be used for the purposes of an offence or is the proceeds of an offence. The 2014 Regulations set out the subsequent procedure. They also set out the steps to be taken on receipt of an overseas restraint order accompanied by a certificate. There is limited scope to challenge the domestic recognition of an overseas restraint order made under the 2014 Regulations (*A v DPP* [2016] EWCA Crim 1393, [2017] 1 WLR 713). Most challenges should be directed to the Member State whose restraint order has been 'recognised'. **D8.66**

A separate scheme of assistance permits the Crown Court to make a 'restraint order' prohibiting dealing with property which is the subject of an 'external request' made by any foreign jurisdiction (Proceeds of Crime Act 2002 (External Requests and Orders) Order 2005 (SI 2005 No. 3181) and s. 444). An external request 'is a request by an overseas authority to prohibit dealing with relevant property which is identified in the request' (s. 447(1)). Property is 'relevant property' if there are reasonable grounds to believe that it may be needed to satisfy an external order which has been or may be made (s. 447(7)). An external order is an order made by an overseas court in criminal proceedings for the recovery of specified property or a sum of money (s. 447(3)). Appeals are governed by the Proceeds of Crime Act 2002 (External Requests and Orders) Order 2005 (England and Wales) (Appeals under Part 2) Order 2012 (SI 2012 No. 138). **D8.67**

The 2005 Order was amended by the Proceeds of Crime Act 2002 (External Requests and Orders) (Amendment) Order 2013 (SI 2013 No. 2604) so that an enforcement authority (see **D8.4**) may obtain from the High Court a 'prohibition order'. A prohibition order caters for a case where the anticipated 'external order' may be civil in nature. A prohibition order operates to prevent any person to whose property the order applies from dealing with property in England and Wales or Northern Ireland subject to detailed exceptions. The enforcement authority may not apply for an order unless it believes that the aggregate value is not less than £10,000.

In March 2015, the Home Office published its 12th version of guidance for overseas authorities on *Requests for Mutual Legal Assistance in Criminal Matters* (tinyurl.com/yayx28dt).

Procedure

D8.68 The 'prosecutor' or an accredited financial investigator may apply for a restraint order (POCA 2002, s. 42(1) and (2)). As the Financial Services Authority had power to bring a prosecution for money laundering (see **D3.55**), it could apply for an order (*Rollins* [2010] UKSC 39, [2010] 4 All ER 880); this principle is likely to hold good for the Financial Conduct Authority.

Procedure is governed by CrimPR 33.51 to 33.55 (see Supplement, **R33.51** ***et seq.***). An application may be made without notice, although whether such an application is necessary should be carefully considered (*Malabu Oil and Gas Ltd v DPP* [2016] Lloyd's Rep FC 108). The application should be determined by the resident judge or a nominated judge (CrimPD XIII, para. G.9; see Supplement, **CPD.G9**) and in an appropriate case a judge of the High Court (*Director of the SFO v Lexi Holdings plc (in administration)* [2008] EWCA Crim 1443, [2009] QB 376).

Restraint proceedings have been held to be civil in nature (*Re S (Restraint Order: Release of Assets)* [2004] EWCA Crim 2374, [2005] 1 WLR 1338 at [53]), although the making of the relevant rules in the CrimPR is premised on restraint proceedings being a 'criminal cause or matter' (Courts Act 2003, s. 68). In any event, ss. 2 to 4 of the Civil Evidence Act 1995, which deal with hearsay evidence, apply. Indeed, hearsay evidence 'of whatever degree' is expressly admissible (s. 46(1)).

D8.69 The application must be made in writing and it must be supported by a witness statement, which must contain (CrimPR 33.51(3)):

(a) the grounds for the application;
(b) details of the realisable property and of the person holding that property;
(c) the grounds for, and full details of, any application for an ancillary order; and
(d) where the application is made by an accredited financial investigator, a statement that he has been authorised to make the application.

D8.70 The court may make exceptions to the order to allow for reasonable living or legal expenses or 'for the purpose of enabling any person to carry on any trade, business, profession or occupation' (POCA 2002, s. 41(3)). The order must not make provision for legal expenses attributable to the investigation or proceedings to which the restraint order relates (see s. 41(4), *Re S (Restraint Order: Release of Assets)* [2004] EWCA Crim 2374, [2005] 1 WLR 1338 and *CPS v Campbell* [2009] EWCA Crim 997, [2010] 1 WLR 650; this has been held to be compatible with the ECHR, see *AP v CPS* [2007] EWCA Crim 3128, [2008] 1 Cr App R 39 (497)). However, s. 41(2A) allows for monthly legal aid payments to be met (see also the Restraint Order (Legal Aid Exception and Relevant Legal Aid Payments) Regulations 2015 (SI 2015 No. 868)). As a general rule the defendant is entitled to enjoy the standard of life previously experienced and is entitled to meet continuing expenses as they arise, although this may not extend to keeping up an excessively 'Rolls Royce lifestyle' (*Re Peters* [1988] QB 871; *Re D* (28 October 1992 unreported)). As to the relevance of unrestrained assets in deciding whether to make an exception, see (in the civil recovery context) *SOCA v Azam* [2013] EWCA Civ 970, [2013] 1 WLR 3800. No variation of the order is necessary to enable solicitors instructed by the defendant to transfer funds from the defendant's client account to its office account in satisfaction of legal fees incurred prior to the making of the order (*Irwin Mitchell v RCPO* [2008] EWCA Crim 1741, [2009] 3 All ER 530).

D8.71 **Discharge** An application to discharge the order may be made by the original applicant or by 'any person affected by the order' (s. 42(3)). The order must be discharged on the conclusion of the proceedings unless the Court of Appeal orders a retrial and the order has remained in force (s. 42(6A), as inserted by the SCA 2015, s. 12) or, where the order was made for the purposes of an investigation, if proceedings are not started within a reasonable time (s. 42(7): see *S* [2019] EWCA Crim 1728, [2020] 1 Cr App R 13 (228), holding that there is no requirement for the prosecution to act 'as rapidly as possible' and it is unhelpful to place a gloss on the phrase 'reasonable time'). Note, however, that where a confiscation order is made the confiscation proceedings are not concluded until the confiscation order is satisfied or discharged (s. 85(5)).

Breach A breach of an order may be dealt with by the Crown Court by committal for contempt of court (*M* [2008] EWCA Crim 1901, [2009] 1 WLR 1179; Senior Courts Act 1981, s. 45(4)). Contempt in this context is civil and not criminal (*OB v Director of the SFO* [2012] EWCA Crim 67, [2012] 3 All ER 999). Accordingly, the principle of speciality does not prevent an extradited person from being dealt with for such a contempt (*Director of the SFO v O'Brien* [2014] UKSC 23, [2014] AC 1246). A deterrent element is appropriate in the sentence (*Adewunmi* [2008] EWCA Crim 71, [2008] 2 Cr App R (S) 52 (326)). A breach is capable, without more illegality beyond the contempt itself, of constituting the offence of perverting the course of justice (*Kenny* [2013] EWCA Crim 1, [2013] 3 All ER 85). However, the Court added that '[i]n cases of breach of restraint orders, nothing we have said should encourage prosecutors to charge perverting the course of justice where it is unnecessary to do so; ordinarily the sanction of contempt of court will suffice'. **D8.72**

Receivers

If necessary, the court may order that property be managed by a management receiver (POCA 2002, s. 48). The court may confer specific powers upon the receiver that include powers to take possession of the property, commence and conduct legal proceedings, enter into contracts, employ agents and to 'take any other steps the court thinks appropriate'. The receiver may realise so much of the property as is necessary to meet the receiver's own remuneration and expenses (s. 49(2)(d)) and may do so even if the assets were beneficially owned by a third party, with the defendant having only the bare legal title to them (*Heath Sinclair v Glatt* [2009] EWCA Civ 176, [2009] 4 All ER 724). **D8.73**

Where a restraint order is discharged on the basis that the legal conditions are not met, there can be no subsequent order that the receiver's costs and expenses, previously incurred, should be met from the restrained property — but there is power under the law of restitution to order the prosecutor to meet the receiver's costs and expenses (*Barnes v Eastenders Cash & Carry plc* [2013] UKSC 60, [2014] AC 1).

A court-appointed receiver is not an agent of either party but, in effect, an officer of the court (*Re Andrews* [1991] 3 WLR 1236). In cases of urgency, where it is feared that notice may result in dissipation of the property, the application to appoint a receiver may be made at the same time as an *ex parte* restraint application. The orders made must, however, be in the narrowest terms consistent with the need to act effectively, and ought not to include a general power of sale. In such circumstances, should it become necessary for the receiver to dispose of property, the receiver should return to court on notice for further directions (*Re P* [1999] 4 All ER 473). The Act itself prevents the court from providing the receiver with power to 'manage or otherwise deal with the property' or to realise any of it for payments to the receiver, without first giving 'persons holding interests in the property a reasonable opportunity to make representations' (s. 49(8)).

Persons who are or who may be affected by the receiver's actions, as well as the receiver, may apply for such directions as the court believes are appropriate (s. 62) or for variation or discharge of the order (s. 63). No distress may be levied against any realisable property, nor may there be forfeiture for breach of a tenancy agreement without leave of the Crown Court (s. 58(2) and (3)). Where other proceedings are pending in respect of the property, the other court has a discretion whether to stay those proceedings once it has given an opportunity for the applicant for the restraint order and any receiver to make representations (s. 58(6)).

Self-incrimination

D8.74 Under the High Court jurisdiction, the privilege against self-incrimination was maintained by the inclusion of a prohibition on the use of any statement of assets in a criminal prosecution (*Re O (Disclosure Order: Disclosure of Assets)* [1991] 1 All ER 330). Orders drawn under the new procedures in the Crown Court should contain a clear and specific statement to this effect. This will not prevent the use of such statements in subsequent confiscation proceedings.

Appeal

D8.75 There is no right of appeal against the making of a restraint order. A person affected by an order must first apply to vary or discharge the order (POCA 2002, s. 42(3)). Where a decision on the application is made, both the original applicant and any person affected by the order has a right of appeal to the Court of Appeal, and thereafter to the Supreme Court (POCA 2002, ss. 43 and 44). Property detained under a restraint order which is discharged may continue to be detained until 'there is no further possibility' of an appeal (s. 44A).

SEIZURE OF REALISABLE PROPERTY

D8.76 The POCA 2002, ss. 47A to 47S, grant powers to 'an appropriate officer' to search premises, people and vehicles and to seize realisable property other than cash or 'exempt property'.

'Exempt property' means (a) equipment, including vehicles, that is necessary for the defendant's personal use in employment, business or vocation and (b) household items and furniture necessary 'for satisfying the basic domestic needs of the defendant and the defendant's family' (s. 47C(4)). An 'appropriate officer' is an officer of Revenue and Customs, an immigration officer, a constable, an SFO officer or an accredited financial investigator.

The Secretary of State has issued a revised code of practice governing all the matters connected with these powers (Proceeds of Crime Act 2002 (Search, Seizure and Detention of Property: Code of Practice) Order 2018 (SI 2018 No. 82)) which came into force on 31 January 2018.

Power to Seize Property

D8.77 In order to seize property, the officer must first be satisfied that one of the seven statutory conditions is met (POCA 2002, s. 47B(1)). The first two conditions (s. 47B(2) and (3)) both require (a) that a criminal investigation into an indictable offence 'has been started' in England or Wales, (b) that a person has been arrested for the offence, but (c) that proceedings have not yet been started. The first condition additionally requires that, where a restraint order is not in force, there 'are reasonable grounds to suspect' that the person has benefited from conduct constituting the offence (s. 47B(2)(d), as amended by the SCA 2015, s. 13). There is no such requirement under the second condition where a restraint order is in force.

The third and fourth conditions apply where proceedings have been started but not concluded (s. 47B(4) and (5)). Again, they are distinguished by whether a restraint order is in force. Where no order is in force, the third condition requires 'reasonable cause' for believing that the defendant has benefited.

The fifth condition (s. 47B(6)) operates where the prosecutor has made or where the officer believes the prosecutor will make an application under s. 19 or s. 20 (reconsideration of the case or benefit where no confiscation order has been made) or under s. 27 or s. 28 (confiscation order against an absconding defendant). There must be a reasonable belief that the defendant has benefited from criminal conduct. The sixth and seventh conditions relate to applications under ss. 21 and 22 for reconsideration of the benefit or available amount (see **E19.49**) where a confiscation order has been made (s. 47B(7) and (8))). For either condition to be met, there must be a reasonable belief that the court will raise the benefit or available amount figures respectively.

The power of seizure itself is contained in s. 47C. It is exercisable only where the officer is satisfied that there are reasonable grounds for suspecting that (a) the property may otherwise be made unavailable for satisfying any confiscation order that has been or may be made against the defendant or (b) the value of the property may otherwise be diminished as a result of conduct by the defendant or any other person. **D8.78**

Use of the power to seize property requires 'appropriate approval' unless it is not practicable to obtain approval beforehand (s. 47C(6)(a)). This means approval by a justice of the peace or, if that is not practicable, a senior officer (s. 47G). As to the restrictions on the powers as they apply to an officer of Revenue and Customs and an immigration officer, see s. 47C(6A) and (6B) respectively.

Seized property may be detained initially for 48 hours (s. 47J). A magistrates' court may extend the period (s. 47M). Thereafter, detention may continue while an application to make or vary a restraint order is extant. The application must be made during the initial or extended period.

Ancillary Powers

Complementary powers to search people, premises and vehicles are to be found in the POCA 2002, ss. 47D to 47F. The exercise of these powers also requires 'appropriate approval' unless impracticable (see **D8.78**). **D8.79**

Relevant Statutory Extracts

Proceeds of Crime Act 2002, ss. 47A to 47F and 47J to 47N **D8.80**

47A.—(1) In sections 47B to 47S 'appropriate officer' means—
(a) an officer of Revenue and Customs,
(aa) an immigration officer,
(b) a constable, or
(c) an accredited financial investigator.
(2) In subsection (1)(c) the reference to an accredited financial investigator is a reference to an accredited financial investigator who falls within a description specified in an order made for the purposes of that provision by the Secretary of State under section 453.

47B.—(1) An appropriate officer may exercise the power conferred by section 47C if satisfied that any of the following conditions is met.
(2) The first condition is that—
(a) a criminal investigation has been started in England and Wales with regard to an indictable offence,
(b) a person has been arrested for the offence,
(c) proceedings for the offence have not yet been started against the person in England and Wales,
(d) there are reasonable grounds to suspect that the person has benefited from conduct constituting the offence, and
(e) a restraint order is not in force in respect of any realisable property.
(3) The second condition is that—
(a) a criminal investigation has been started in England and Wales with regard to an indictable offence,
(b) a person has been arrested for the offence,
(c) proceedings for the offence have not yet been started against the person in England and Wales, and
(d) a restraint order is in force in respect of any realisable property.
(4) The third condition is that—
(a) proceedings for an indictable offence have been started in England and Wales and have not been concluded,
(b) there is reasonable cause to believe that the defendant has benefited from conduct constituting the offence, and
(c) a restraint order is not in force in respect of any realisable property.
(5) The fourth condition is that—
(a) proceedings for an indictable offence have been started in England and Wales and have not been concluded, and
(b) a restraint order is in force in respect of any realisable property.

(6) The fifth condition is that—
(a) an application by the prosecutor has been made under section 19, 20, 27 or 28 and not concluded, or the officer believes that such an application is to be made, and
(b) there is reasonable cause to believe that the defendant has benefited from criminal conduct.
(7) The sixth condition is that—
(a) an application by the prosecutor has been made under section 21 and not concluded, or the officer believes that such an application is to be made, and
(b) there is reasonable cause to believe that the court will decide under that section that the amount found under the new calculation of the defendant's benefit exceeds the relevant amount (as defined in that section).
(8) The seventh condition is that—
(a) an application by the prosecutor has been made under section 22 and not concluded, or the officer believes that such an application is to be made, and
(b) there is reasonable cause to believe that the court will decide under that section that the amount found under the new calculation of the available amount exceeds the relevant amount (as defined in that section).
(9) The third or fourth condition is not met if the officer believes that—
(a) there has been undue delay in continuing the proceedings, or
(b) the prosecutor does not intend to proceed.
(10) If an application mentioned in the fifth, sixth or seventh condition has been made the condition is not met if the officer believes that—
(a) there has been undue delay in continuing the application, or
(b) the prosecutor does not intend to proceed.
(11) In relation to the first or second condition references in sections 47C to 47S to the defendant are to the person mentioned in that condition.
(12) In relation to the first or second condition section 77(9) has effect as if proceedings for the offence had been started against the defendant when the investigation was started.

47C.—(1) On being satisfied as mentioned in section 47B(1) an appropriate officer may seize any realisable property if the officer has reasonable grounds for suspecting that—
(a) the property may otherwise be made unavailable for satisfying any confiscation order that has been or may be made against the defendant, or
(b) the value of the property may otherwise be diminished as a result of conduct by the defendant or any other person.
(2) But the officer may not seize—
(a) cash, or
(b) exempt property.
(3) 'Cash' has the same meaning as in section 289.
(4) 'Exempt property' means—
(a) such tools, books, vehicles and other items of equipment as are necessary to the defendant for use personally in the defendant's employment, business or vocation;
(b) such clothing, bedding, furniture, household equipment, provisions or other things as are necessary for satisfying the basic domestic needs of the defendant and the defendant's family.
(5) In relation to realisable property which is free property held by the recipient of a tainted gift, references in subsection (4) to the defendant are to be read as references to the recipient of that gift. Section 47B(11) is subject to this subsection.
(6) The power conferred by this section—
(a) may be exercised only with the appropriate approval under section 47G unless, in the circumstances, it is not practicable to obtain that approval before exercising the power, and
(aa) where applicable, in accordance with subsection (6A) or (6B).
(6A) The power conferred by this section is exercisable by an officer of Revenue and Customs only if the officer has reasonable grounds for suspecting that conduct constituting the relevant offence relates to an assigned matter (within the meaning of the Customs and Excise Management Act 1979).
(6B) The power conferred by this section is exercisable by an immigration officer only if the officer has reasonable grounds for suspecting that conduct constituting the relevant offence—
(a) relates to the entitlement of one or more persons who are not nationals of the United Kingdom to enter, transit across, or be in, the United Kingdom (including conduct which relates to conditions or other controls on any such entitlement), or
(b) is undertaken for the purposes of, or otherwise in relation to, a relevant nationality enactment.
(7) 'Relevant offence' means—

(a) in a case where the officer is satisfied that the first, second, third or fourth condition in section 47B is met, the offence mentioned in that condition,
(b) in a case where the officer is satisfied that any of the other conditions in section 47B is met, the offence (or any of the offences) concerned.

(8) [Defines 'relevant nationality enactment'.]

47D.—(1) If an appropriate officer is lawfully on any premises the officer may search the premises for the purpose of finding any property which—
(a) the officer has reasonable grounds for suspecting may be found there, and
(b) if found there, the officer intends to seize under section 47C.

(2) The power conferred by this section may be exercised only with the appropriate approval under section 47G unless, in the circumstances, it is not practicable to obtain that approval before exercising the power.

(3) 'Premises' has the meaning given by section 23 of the Police and Criminal Evidence Act 1984.

47E.—(1) An appropriate officer may exercise the following powers if the officer has reasonable grounds for suspecting that a person is carrying property that may be seized under section 47C.

(2) The officer may, so far as the officer thinks it necessary or expedient for the purpose of seizing the property under that section, require the person—
(a) to permit a search of any article with the person,
(b) to permit a search of the person.

(3) An officer exercising a power under subsection (2) may detain the person for so long as is necessary for its exercise.

(4) A power conferred by this section may be exercised only with the appropriate approval under section 47G unless, in the circumstances, it is not practicable to obtain that approval before exercising the power.

(5) This section does not require a person to submit to an intimate search or strip search (within the meaning of section 164 of the Customs and Excise Management Act 1979).

47F.—(1) The powers specified in subsection (4) are exercisable if—
(a) an appropriate officer has reasonable grounds for suspecting that a vehicle contains property that may be seized under section 47C, and
(b) it appears to the officer that the vehicle is under the control of a person who is in or in the vicinity of the vehicle.

(2) The powers are exercisable only if the vehicle is—
(a) in any place to which, at the time of the proposed exercise of the powers, the public or any section of the public has access, on payment or otherwise, as of right or by virtue of express or implied permission, or
(b) in any other place to which at that time people have ready access but which is not a dwelling.

(3) But if the vehicle is in a garden or yard or other land occupied with and used for the purposes of a dwelling, the officer may exercise the powers under subsection (4) only if the officer has reasonable grounds for believing—
(a) that the person does not reside in the dwelling, and
(b) that the vehicle is not in the place in question with the express or implied permission of another who resides in the dwelling.

(4) The officer may, so far as the officer thinks it necessary or expedient for the purpose of seizing the property under section 47C, require the person to—
(a) permit entry to the vehicle,
(b) permit a search of the vehicle.

(5) An officer exercising a power under subsection (4) may detain the vehicle for so long as is necessary for its exercise.

(6) A power conferred by this section may be exercised only with the appropriate approval under section 47G unless, in the circumstances, it is not practicable to obtain that approval before exercising the power.

47J.—(1) This section applies if an appropriate officer seizes property under section 47C.

(2) The property may be detained initially for a period of 48 hours.

(3) The period of 48 hours is to be calculated in accordance with section 47H(7).

47K.—(1) This section applies if—
(a) property is detained under section 47J, and
(b) no restraint order is in force in respect of the property.

(2) If within the period mentioned in section 47J an application is made for a restraint order which includes provision under section 41A authorising detention of the property, the property may be detained until the application is determined or otherwise disposed of.

(3) If such an application is made within that period and the application is refused, the property may be detained until there is no further possibility of an appeal against—
(a) the decision to refuse the application, or
(b) any decision made on an appeal against that decision.
(4) In subsection (2) the reference to the period mentioned in section 47J includes that period as extended by any order under section 47M.
47L.—(1) This section applies if—
(a) property is detained under section 47J,
(b) a restraint order is in force in respect of the property, and
(c) the order does not include provision under section 41A authorising the detention of the property.
(2) If within the period mentioned in section 47J an application is made for the order to be varied so as to include provision under section 41A authorising detention of the property, the property may be detained until the application is determined or otherwise disposed of.
(3) If such an application is made within that period and the application is refused, the property may be detained until there is no further possibility of an appeal against—
(a) the decision to refuse the application, or
(b) any decision made on an appeal against that decision.
47M.—(1) This section applies if—
(a) property is detained under section 47J,
(b) no restraint order is in force in respect of the property, and
(c) no application has been made for a restraint order which includes provision under section 41A authorising detention of the property.
(2) A magistrates' court may by order extend the period for which the property or any part of it may be detained under section 47J if satisfied that—
(a) any of the conditions in section 47B is met (reading references in that section to the officer as references to the court),
(b) the property or part is realisable property other than exempt property (within the meaning of section 47C(4)), and
(c) there are reasonable grounds for suspecting that—
(i) the property may otherwise be made unavailable for satisfying any confiscation order that has been or may be made against the defendant, or
(ii) the value of the property may otherwise be diminished as a result of conduct by the defendant or any other person.
(3) An application for an order may be made by—
(a) the Commissioners for Her Majesty's Revenue and Customs,
(aa) an immigration officer,
(b) a constable,
(c) an accredited financial investigator, or
(d) the prosecutor.
(4) If the property was seized in reliance on the first or second condition in section 47B, 'the prosecutor' means a person who is to have conduct of any proceedings for the offence.
(5) An order under this section must provide for notice to be given to persons affected by it.
(6) In this section 'part' includes portion.
47N.—(1) An order under section 47M may be discharged or varied.
(2) An application for variation or discharge of the order may be made by—
(a) a person mentioned in section 47M(3), or
(b) any person affected by the order.
(3) On an application under this section the court must discharge the order if—
(a) the order was made on the ground that the first or second condition in section 47B was met but proceedings for the offence mentioned in that condition have not been started within a reasonable time,
(b) the order was made on the ground that the third or fourth condition in section 47B was met but proceedings for the offence mentioned in that condition have now been concluded,
(c) the order was made on the ground that the fifth, sixth or seventh condition in section 47B was met but the application mentioned in that condition has now been concluded or, as the case may be, has not been made within a reasonable time.
(4) *An order made under section 47M lapses if a restraint order is made in respect of the property to which it relates (but provision authorising detention of the property may have been included in the restraint order by virtue of section 41A).*

Section D9 Disclosure

INTRODUCTION

Types of Disclosure

Before a contested criminal trial, an obligation arises on both parties to disclose to each other certain information concerning the case. The obligation varies between the prosecution and the defence, and the stage of the proceedings. **D9.1**

In broad terms the prosecution must disclose to an accused:

(a) the case upon which it will rely at trial; and
(b) other material relating to the case which the prosecution does not intend to use, known as 'unused material'.

Unlike its more expansive use in civil proceedings, in criminal proceedings the term 'disclosure' is generally understood to relate to the service by the prosecution on the defence of unused material (as in (b) above), and disclosure by the defence of the essence of the case upon which they propose to rely at trial.

As will be apparent, the obligation on the defence to provide disclosure is significantly more limited than that which applies to the prosecution. The rationale underlying this difference is the unequal resources at the disposal of the State (prosecuting) on the one hand, and the individual (defendant), on the other.

Following the collapse of a number of recent trials owing to failings in disclosure, and the increasing challenges posed by the volume of digital material involved in fraud cases, the disclosure regime has come under increased public scrutiny in recent years and is a topic of contemporary debate. The twin concerns are that deficiencies in disclosure may undermine the fairness of a trial (for a defendant) and the security of a conviction on appeal (for a victim). These matters in turn raise the possibility of undermining the general public's confidence in the criminal justice system. It seems likely that changes in the disclosure regime will follow in the near term. However, there would seem to be little need to change the current statutory regime (discussed further below). Rather, changes are likely to focus on the operation of disclosure in practice at the level of the police and among prosecutors, improved training and execution, and the greater use of technology. The allocation and availability of resources is likely to remain a matter of political debate.

This section is concerned with the disclosure of unused material by the prosecution and the disclosure of the defence case. As for the extent to which the prosecution are required to disclose their case in a trial on indictment (that is to say their evidential case), see **D15.70** ***et seq.*** This section considers disclosure once criminal proceedings have commenced. For disclosure of material pre-charge, see **D1**.

The Statutory Regime and the Common Law

The statutory regime governing the disclosure of unused material by the prosecution and the disclosure of the defence case is set out in the CPIA 1996, Part I (ss. 1 to 21), and supplemented **D9.2** by the Code of Practice issued under the CPIA 1996, s. 23 ('CPIA Code'), CrimPR Part 15 (see Supplement, **R15.1** *et seq.*), and a variety of other sources (see **D9.5**).

Prior to the CPIA 1996, common-law rules developed concerning the disclosure of prosecution material. However, following a number of high-profile miscarriages of justice in which failures in disclosure played a part (notably *Ward* [1993] 1 WLR 619; see further **D9.50**), a statutory scheme was developed. The statute followed, broadly, the recommendations of the Royal Commission on Criminal Justice (the Runciman Commission, July 1993).

The circumstances in which the CPIA 1996 now applies are set out in s. 1 (see **D9.3**). In summary, the regime is compulsory in relation to cases sent to the Crown Court to be tried on indictment. The statutory duties begin with the arrival of the case (by whatever route) in the Crown Court (s. 1(2)) and end with the conclusion of the trial, whether by conviction, acquittal, or the discontinuation of proceedings (s. 7A(1)(b)). The regime may also apply to any summary trial, including those in the youth court (see **D9.37**).

The CPIA 1996 expressly provides that it displaces the common law in cases to which it applies save in respect of common-law rules governing whether disclosure is in the public interest (see s. 21 and **D9.49**). It should be noted, however, that the position at common law remains relevant and that circumstances may arise in which a prosecutor may be required to disclose material to the defence outside the scheme of the CPIA 1996 (e.g., in connection with a bail application at an early stage, or following the conclusion of proceedings). The right for a defendant to have adequate time and facilities to prepare the defence is also expressly protected by the ECHR, Article 6(3)(b). The essential consideration for a prosecutor is whether disclosure of any material to the defence is required in accordance with the interests of justice and fairness. As Lord Bingham observed in *H* [2004] UKHL 3, [2004] 2 AC 134 at [14], prosecution disclosure is a requirement of basic fairness (the CPIA 1996 notwithstanding):

> Fairness ordinarily requires that any material held by the prosecution which weakens its case or strengthens that of the defendant, if not relied on as part of its formal case against the defendant, should be disclosed to the defence. Bitter experience has shown that miscarriages of justice may occur where such material is withheld from disclosure. The golden rule is that full disclosure of such material should be made.

It is important to note that while the principle of fairness informs the duty of disclosure at all stages of proceedings, it does not follow that fairness requires the same level of disclosure at each stage. In respect of the position at common law prior to the engagement of the CPIA 1996, see **D9.14** and *DPP, ex parte Lee* [1999] 2 All ER 737. In relation to the position following a conviction, see **D9.24**, *Nunn* [2014] UKSC 37, [2015] AC 225 and *Gohil* [2018] EWCA Crim 140, [2018] WLR 3697.

The legislative regime under the CPIA 1996 envisages a staged approach to the disclosure of unused prosecution material and the defence case:

(a) A statutory duty (reinforced by the CPIA Code) obliges police officers investigating an offence to record and retain all information and material, gathered or generated, that may be relevant to the investigation (see **D9.10**).
(b) Material which is relevant to the investigation but is not expected to form part of the prosecution case should be provided by the police to the prosecutor for review (see **D9.12** to **D9.13**).
(c) The prosecution must apply the statutory test in the CPIA 1996, s. 3, to that material and must disclose any material meeting that test, usually together with a schedule of all the other material recorded and retained (see **D9.13** to **D9.28**: separate obligations apply as regards material which is intended to be used).
(d) The defence, in turn, have a duty to inform the prosecution of the case which they intend to present at trial (see **D9.29** to **D9.47**).

(e) The prosecution are, throughout proceedings, under a duty to disclose material which meets the statutory test for disclosure, which may prompt further disclosure (e.g., following the defence statement (see **D9.24**)).
(f) Following service of the defence statement and any further disclosure (or a failure to make further disclosure), an accused may make further applications for disclosure (see **D9.26**).

The CPIA 1996 provides for applications to be made to the court in circumstances where there is a dispute about whether the prosecution should disclose certain unused material (see **D9.26**); and there are sanctions laid down for a defendant who fails to provide details of the case on a timely basis and/or provides false or inconsistent information (see **D9.42**).

Criminal Procedure and Investigations Act 1996, s. 1 **D9.3**

(1) This Part applies where—
 (a) a person is charged with a summary offence in respect of which a court proceeds to summary trial and in respect of which he pleads not guilty,
 (b) a person who has attained the age of 18 is charged with an offence which is triable either way, in respect of which a court proceeds to summary trial and in respect of which he pleads not guilty, or
 (c) a person under the age of 18 is charged with an indictable offence in respect of which a court proceeds to summary trial and in respect of which he pleads not guilty.
(2) This Part also applies where—
 (a) to (c) [repealed];
 (cc) a person is charged with an offence for which he is sent for trial,
 (d) a count charging a person with a summary offence is included in an indictment under the authority of section 40 of the Criminal Justice Act 1988 (common assault etc.),
 (e) a bill of indictment charging a person with an indictable offence is preferred under the authority of section 2(2)(b) of the Administration of Justice (Miscellaneous Provisions) Act 1933 (bill preferred by direction of Court of Appeal, or by direction or with consent of a judge),
 (f) a bill of indictment charging a person with an indictable offence is preferred under section 22B(3)(a) of the Prosecution of Offences Act 1985, or
 (g) following the preferment of a bill of indictment charging a person with an indictable offence under the authority of section 2(2)(ba) of the Administration of Justice (Miscellaneous Provisions) Act 1933 (bill of indictment preferred with consent of Crown Court judge following approval of deferred prosecution agreement), the suspension of the proceedings against the person under paragraph 2(2) of Schedule 17 to the Crime and Courts Act 2013 is lifted under paragraph 2(3) of that Schedule.
(3) This Part applies in relation to alleged offences into which no criminal investigation has begun before the appointed day.
(4) For the purposes of this section a criminal investigation is an investigation which police officers or other persons have a duty to conduct with a view to it being ascertained—
 (a) whether a person should be charged with an offence, or
 (b) whether a person charged with an offence is guilty of it.

Commencement Dates The disclosure provisions of Part I of the CPIA 1996 apply to any alleged offence for which a criminal investigation began on or after 1 April 1997. **D9.4**

A number of major amendments were made to Part I by the CJA 2003 and are now in force. Certain provisions in the CJA 2003 have yet to be implemented, however, and care is needed in reading the detail of the legislation by reference to the time at which the investigation began. The main amendments yet to come into force are:

(a) defence disclosure to co-accused (CPIA 1996, s. 5(5A), (5B) and (5D), inserted by the CJA 2003, s. 33(1));
(b) updated disclosure by the defence (CPIA 1996, s. 6B, inserted by the CJA 2003, s. 33(3));
(c) notification of names of experts instructed by the defence (CPIA 1996, s. 6D, inserted by the CJA 2003, s. 35 — in practice this provision is concerned with a situation in which an expert report is not served: see CrimPR Part 19 (see Supplement, **R19.1** *et seq.*), and **D9.68** to **D9.69**).

D9.5 **Additional Sources** The CPIA 1996 is supplemented by a number of additional sources of guidance:

(a) The CPIA Code (March 2015) (see **D9.6**).
(b) CrimPR Part 15 (see Supplement, **R15.1** *et seq.*), and CrimPD IV, paras. 15A.1 and 15A.2 (see Supplement, **CPD.15A**).
(c) The Judicial Protocol on the Disclosure of Unused Material in Criminal Cases ('Judicial Disclosure Protocol') (December 2013) (see **appendix 4**).
(d) The Attorney-General's Guidelines on Disclosure for investigators, prosecutors and defence practitioners ('A-G's Guidelines') (December 2013) (see **appendix 4**).
(e) The CPS/Police Disclosure Manual ('CPS Disclosure Manual') (December 2018, tinyurl.com/y8krxa8q).
(f) The Code of Practice for Arranging and Conducting Interviews of Witnesses Notified by the Accused (see **D9.35**).
(g) The 2013 Protocol and Good Practice Model on Disclosure of Information in Cases of Alleged Child Abuse and Linked Criminal and Care Directions Hearings ('Child Abuse Disclosure Protocol') (October 2013, tinyurl.com/yc833avt) (though see *Re H (Children)* [2018] EWFC 61 for criticism of this protocol and proposals for improvement).

CrimPR Part 15 sets out the procedure to be followed on applications to the court for unused material and on public interest immunity applications, as well as the requirements for giving notice to the court about prosecution and defence disclosure. The notes to that section also contain a useful summary of the requirements of the CPIA 1996.

CrimPD IV, para. 15A.1, requires that all parties are familiar with their obligations, in particular under the CPIA 1996 and the CPIA Code, and must comply with the Judicial Disclosure Protocol and the A-G's Guidelines.

The full text of the Judicial Disclosure Protocol is to be found at **appendix 4**. It sets out the principles to be applied to, and the importance of, disclosure; the expectations of the court and its role in disclosure, in particular in relation to case management; and guidance on the consequences of any failure of the prosecution or defence to comply with their obligations. Its emphasis is on prosecution-led disclosure and a constructive approach on both sides, supported by robust judicial case management. It proposes that all requests by the defence for further disclosure should now be made on the s. 8 application form (see further **D9.26**), even if no hearing is sought in the first instance. There is extensive guidance in the protocol on material held by third parties.

The Child Abuse Disclosure Protocol represents best practice in child abuse cases and should be consulted in all cases of concurrent criminal and Family Court proceedings involving a child.

The A-G's Guidelines are also set out at **appendix 4**. For ease of reference they are structured in the same way as the Judicial Disclosure Protocol and the two documents are to be read together. In particular, the A-G's Guidelines emphasise the importance of prosecution-led disclosure and of applying the CPIA regime thoughtfully, tailored where appropriate to the type of investigation or prosecution in question. Among other matters the guidelines provide for the preparation of Disclosure Management Documents in large and complex Crown Court trials. The A-G's Supplementary Guidelines on Digitally Stored Material (2011) are included as an annex.

The CPS 'Guidelines on Communication Evidence' (updated 26 January 2018), while not concerned with disclosure specifically, are also worthy of note for their observations on the examination of mobile telephone evidence and its particular relevance to cases involving sexual offences.

THE INVESTIGATION STAGE

The responsibilities of investigators in relation to unused material are set out in a variety of sources, but chiefly the CPIA Code. This was revised and reissued in March 2015 to take account of changes recommended by the Magistrates' Court Disclosure Review, designed to enable police disclosure officers to adopt a streamlined procedure in magistrates' court cases. **D9.6**

The CPIA Code applies to all criminal investigations carried out by police officers (see the CPIA 1996, s. 22) and, under s. 26, persons other than police officers charged with the duty of conducting criminal investigations (see **D9.7**).

The CPIA Code, para. 2.1, takes its definition of a criminal investigation from the CPIA 1996, s. 22, and provides a number of examples:

> . . . a *criminal investigation* is an investigation conducted by police officers with a view to it being ascertained whether a person should be charged with an offence, or whether a person charged with an offence is guilty of it. This will include:
>
> — investigations into crimes that have been committed;
> — investigations whose purpose is to ascertain whether a crime has been committed, with a view to the possible institution of criminal proceedings; and
> — investigations which begin in the belief that a crime may be committed, for example when the police keep premises or individuals under observation for a period of time, with a view to the possible institution of criminal proceedings.

Criminal Procedure and Investigations Act 1996, ss. 22 and 26 **D9.7**

22.—(1) For the purposes of [Part II] a criminal investigation is an investigation conducted by police officers with a view to it being ascertained—
 (a) whether a person should be charged with an offence, or
 (b) whether a person charged with an offence is guilty of it.
(2) In [Part II] references to material are to material of all kinds, and in particular include references to—
 (a) information and
 (b) objects of all descriptions.
(3) In [Part II] references to recording information are to putting it in a durable or retrievable form (such as writing or tape).

26.—(1) A person other than a police officer who is charged with the duty of conducting an investigation with a view to it being ascertained—
 (a) whether a person should be charged with an offence, or
 (b) whether a person charged with an offence is guilty of it,
shall in discharging that duty have regard to any relevant provision of a code which would apply if the investigation were conducted by police officers.
(2) A failure—
 (a) by a police officer to comply with any provision of a code for the time being in operation by virtue of an order under section 25, or
 (b) by a person to comply with subsection (1),
shall not in itself render him liable to any criminal or civil proceedings.
(3) In all criminal and civil proceedings a code in operation at any time by virtue of an order under section 25 shall be admissible in evidence.
(4) If it appears to a court or tribunal conducting criminal or civil proceedings that—
 (a) any provision of a code in operation at any time by virtue of an order under section 25, or
 (b) any failure mentioned in subsection (2)(a) or (b),
is relevant to any question arising in the proceedings, the provision or failure shall be taken into account in deciding the question.

Responsibilities of Investigators and Disclosure Officers

The CPIA Code sets out the varying functions of individuals within a criminal investigation and their particular responsibilities as regards the disclosure process (albeit that different **D9.8** functions may be performed by the same individual). Among the definitions in the CPIA Code, certain key roles are notable, namely: an 'investigator' — any police officer involved in the conduct of a criminal investigation; a 'disclosure officer' — the police officer responsible for examining material retained by the police during the investigation and for revealing material to the prosecutor; and the 'officer in charge of an investigation' — the police officer responsible for directing a criminal investigation, including ensuring that proper procedures are in place for recording information, retaining records of information and other material in the investigation (para. 2.1). The CPIA Code emphasises the need to retain clear records of the identities of the persons performing these roles; that they are carried out by suitably experienced individuals, independent of the investigation; and that the investigative process is tailored to the circumstances of each case (paras. 3.3 to 3.7). Notably, the CPIA Code puts a police officer (the disclosure officer) at the centre of the disclosure process, as opposed to a qualified lawyer; a scheme that has not been without controversy. For a critical review of this regime by HM Inspectorate of Constabulary and HM Inspectorate of the CPS see 'Making it Fair: The Disclosure of Unused Material in Volume Crown Court Cases' (July 2017, tinyurl.com/y7ckf7br).

The CPIA Code provides for delegation under arrangements for joint investigations (para. 3.4) (though note *Khan* [2011] EWCA Crim 2240).

D9.9 The A-G's Guidelines also deal with the duties of investigators and disclosure officers in paras. 15 to 27 (see **appendix 4**). The key obligations are to retain and record relevant material, to review it, and to reveal it to the prosecutor.

Under the Guidelines, investigators and disclosure officers are required to be fair and objective and to work together with prosecutors on disclosure issues (para. 15). Investigators and disclosure officers must approach their duties in a 'thinking manner', not as a box-ticking exercise, and should be deployed on cases commensurate with their skills, training and experience (para. 16). Disclosure officers must draw to the attention of the prosecutor any material where there is doubt as to whether it is disclosable (para. 26). An investigator who believes that a person may have information which satisfies the statutory test for disclosure cannot decline to make inquiries of that person in order to avoid the need to disclose what that person might say (*Joof* [2012] EWCA Crim 1475). For a case considering the obligations on an investigator to pursue reasonable lines of inquiry and obtain and preserve evidence more generally see *E* [2018] EWCA Crim 2426. In larger cases there may be a number of disclosure officers, but there must always be a lead officer (para. 18). Disclosure officers must inspect, view or listen to all relevant material. In some cases, a detailed examination of all seized material may be required. In others, this would be virtually impossible and the Supplementary A-G's Guidelines (see **D9.10**), dealing with digitally stored material, may apply (A-G's Guidelines, para. 21) (see also *R* [2015] EWCA Crim 1941, [2016] 1 WLR 1872 and **D9.13**). Relevant material must be retained but, if it later becomes apparent that it is incapable of impact, retention is no longer required (para. 25). Disclosure officers must seek the advice of prosecutors when in doubt as to their responsibilities (para. 26). In relation to digital material, investigators and prosecutors are to be transparent with the defence and the courts about how the prosecution have approached complying with their disclosure obligations, and the defence will be expected to play their part in defining the real issues in the case (Supplementary A-G's Guidelines, para. 3).

In recent years there has been increasing emphasis on the need for the investigators and disclosure officers to perform their roles better. For a discussion in the context of the Court Martial, see *Mayende* [2015] EWCA Crim 1566. (See also 'Making It Fair' at **D9.8**.) Following the collapse of several cases owing to serious errors in the disclosure process, the Justice Select Committee has now conducted a review of disclosure procedures in general. The A-G and the DPP have also published reviews of the disclosure process. (See also 'A joint review of the disclosure process in the case of R v Allan' (Metropolitan Police/CPS, January 2018, tinyurl.com/yc5phkf5).)

Duty to Record and Retain Material

Under the CPIA Code, investigators must record, in a durable or retrievable form, all material which may be relevant to the investigation and which is not already recorded. This obligation to record includes negative information, e.g., the fact that a number of people present at a particular place and time saw nothing unusual (para. 4.1). **D9.10**

The investigator is also responsible for retaining all material obtained in a criminal investigation that may be relevant to the investigation (para. 5.1).

What amounts to material that is 'relevant to an investigation' is a widely drawn definition. The CPIA Code provides (para. 2.1) that material will fall within this category if it appears to an investigator or disclosure officer that it has merely some bearing on any offence under investigation or any person being investigated, or on the surrounding circumstances of the case. Thus, material is to be considered potentially relevant unless it is actually incapable of having any impact on the case.

'Material' includes material gathered in the course of the investigation (e.g., documents seized in the course of searching premises) and generated by the investigation (e.g., interview records) (para. 2.1).

The CPIA Code expressly identifies that the duty to retain material will include, for example, the following categories of material: crime reports, including crime report forms, relevant parts of incident report books and police officers' notebooks; final versions of witness statements; draft versions of witness statements where their content differs from the final version; interview records (written or taped); expert reports and schedules; any material casting doubt upon the reliability of a confession; and any material casting doubt on the reliability of a witness (para. 5.4). The CPIA Code also makes clear that the duty to retain material does not extend to items purely ancillary to the above categories which possess no independent significance, such as duplicates of documents (para. 5.6).

Material must be retained at least until criminal proceedings are concluded. In the event of a conviction, material must be retained until the convicted person is released from custody or discharged from hospital (where a custodial sentence or hospital order is imposed) and, in any event, for at least six months from the date of conviction (paras. 5.7 to 5.10).

Where an appeal against conviction is in progress, when the release or discharge occurs, or at the end of the six months, the material must be retained until the appeal is determined. A similar rule applies where an application is considered by the CCRC (para. 5.10).

Specific provision is made for the recording and retention of digital material under the Supplementary A-G's Guidelines. Digital material not imaged at the location of a search should be imaged when reasonably practicable (para. A17) and no more digital material may be seized than is justified (para. A20). It must be examined as soon as reasonably practicable and consideration must be given to allowing the person from whom it was seized, or anyone with an interest in it, to be present during the examination (para. A22). No digital material may be seized which an investigator has reasonable grounds to believe is subject to legal professional privilege, other than under the additional powers of seizure in the CJPA 2001 (para. A28). Guidance is also given in the A-G's Supplementary Guidelines as to retention of digital material (paras. A23 to A27), sifting (paras. A38 to A44), record keeping (paras. A45 to A48), scheduling (paras. A49 to A52) and third-party material (paras. A53).

In considering the potential relevance of material to an investigation, it is notable that the CPS Disclosure Manual states that reports, advices and other communications between the CPS and police will usually be of an administrative nature or derivative in that they contain professional opinion based on evidential material or material already subject to revelation and they will usually have no bearing on the case and will thus be irrelevant (ch. 4, p. 15). Clearly, however, all such material falls for consideration on its individual merits and in the particular circumstances. **D9.11**

Duty to Reveal Material to the Prosecutor

D9.12 The CPIA Code, para. 6, establishes a procedure whereby retained material which may be relevant to an investigation, but which the disclosure officer believes will not form part of the prosecution case, must be listed on a schedule. The obligation to prepare a schedule arises in all cases likely to be heard in the Crown Court and all cases in the magistrates' court where the accused is likely to plead not guilty.

In Crown Court cases, the disclosure officer must prepare a schedule on a form, known as the MG6C, which lists such retained material. In magistrates' court cases where the accused is likely to plead not guilty, a streamlined disclosure certificate (a template for which is in the annex to the CPIA Code), is prepared (para. 6.5). It is these schedules which the prosecutor will review when making decisions as to whether material is to be disclosed to the defence, applying the relevant statutory test.

Any 'sensitive material' should be listed in a separate schedule or, exceptionally, disclosed to the prosecutor separately. Sensitive material is defined as material which the investigator believes would give rise to a real risk of serious prejudice to an important public interest if it were to be disclosed (para. 2.1) (see further **D9.49**). Paragraph 6.15 provides examples of such material, ranging from material relating to national security to material given in confidence, and includes material relating to informants, undercover police officers, premises used for police surveillance, techniques used in the detection of crime, and material relating to child witnesses (e.g., material generated by a local authority social services department).

The A-G's Guidelines (see **appendix** 4) emphasise that descriptions by disclosure officers in non-sensitive schedules should be clear and accurate and must contain sufficient detail to enable the prosecutor to make an informed decision on disclosure (para. 23). Sensitive schedules must contain sufficient information to enable the prosecutor to decide whether the material should be viewed, bearing in mind its confidential nature (para. 24).

An investigator should draw the prosecutor's attention to any material which might satisfy the test for prosecution disclosure (see **D9.15**) and must give the prosecutor a copy of any material falling within certain categories in the CPIA Code, para. 7.3, including information provided by an accused which indicates an explanation for the offence and any material relating to the reliability of a confession or a prosecution witness.

The Court of Appeal has observed that 'corporate knowledge' operates in respect of information which falls to be disclosed; the prosecution duty to disclose is not rendered redundant if officers withhold information from counsel, or if officers withhold information from one another (*Grant* [2015] EWCA Crim 1815).

At the conclusion of the process, a disclosure officer must certify to the prosecutor that to the best of the officer's knowledge and belief the duties imposed under the code have been complied with (CPIA Code, para. 9.1).

PROSECUTION DISCLOSURE

Responsibilities of Prosecutor to Review Material

D9.13 It is the prosecutor's task to review the schedule(s) provided by the disclosure officer and to assess the need to make disclosure of the underlying material to the defence. That task is undertaken applying the statutory test for disclosure contained in the CPIA 1996, s. 3 (see **D9.15**). However, the duty on a prosecutor to review material and, where necessary, direct the disclosure of that material is a continuing one and the disclosure should be kept under review throughout *proceedings (see **D9.24**)*.

The A-G's Guidelines require prosecutors to do all that they can to facilitate proper disclosure. This includes probing actions taken by disclosure officers, reviewing schedules and, if necessary, taking action to correct or improve them (paras. 28 to 30). Prosecutors must consider any defence statement thoroughly, even if it points to other lines of inquiry. A prosecutor should advise the investigator if any such lines of inquiry should be pursued and challenge the lack of, or inadequate, defence statements in writing (paras. 31 to 33). (As to defence statements generally see **D9.29**.)

Prosecution advocates must ensure that all material which ought to be disclosed is disclosed to the defence, satisfy themselves that they are in possession of all relevant material and that they have been fully instructed as regards disclosure matters, and keep all disclosure decisions under review (paras. 35 to 37).

In *Olu* [2010] EWCA Crim 2975, [2011] 1 Cr App R 33 (404), the Court of Appeal (while upholding the conviction) observed that it is the task of the prosecutor to identify the issues in the case and for the disclosure officer to act under the prosecutor's guidance; the disclosure regime will not work in practice unless the disclosure officer is directed by the prosecutor as to what is likely to be most relevant and important so that the officer approaches the matter through the exercise of judgement, not simply as a schedule-completing exercise. The Court of Appeal has also emphasised the need for disclosure officers to receive proper training (*Malook* [2011] EWCA Crim 254, [2012] 1 WLR 633).

In *R* [2015] EWCA Crim 1941, [2016] 1 WLR 1872 the Court of Appeal considered the particular problems faced by the prosecution in long and complex fraud cases involving the seizure of large volumes of material, encompassing several terabytes of electronic data, where it was not possible to review all of the material seized. Having considered the law and existing guidance, the Court drew a number of conclusions from which five broad propositions may be identified which are of particular relevance to cases involving large quantities of digital material:

(a) The prosecution are, and must be, in the driving seat at the stage of primary disclosure.
(b) The prosecution must encourage dialogue and prompt engagement with the defence.
(c) The law is prescriptive of the result of disclosure, not the method by which the process should operate.
(d) The process should be subject to robust case management by the judge, utilising the full range of case management powers.
(e) Flexibility is critical.

Among other matters, the Court endorsed the practice of 'dip sampling' material and the use of search tools by the prosecution to satisfy the disclosure obligation in a practicable and effective manner where the quantity of material to be reviewed would be unmanageable otherwise (though it noted that disclosure of the methodology of such sampling or searching would be important).

Disclosure Post-charge but Prior to Statutory Obligation The scheme under the CPIA 1996 requires service of unused material at particular points (see **D9.23**), but, at common law and under the A-G's Guidelines, investigators and prosecutors must recognise that the interests of justice and fairness in the particular circumstances of any case may require disclosure of material after the commencement of proceedings but before the statutory duty arises (A-G's Guidelines, paras. 14 and 44). Likewise, the CPIA Code requires disclosure with the initial details of the case of material that might assist the defence with the early preparation of its case or at a bail hearing, irrespective of the anticipated plea (paras. 6.6 and 7.1). Examples of such material cited in the Code are relevant previous convictions of key prosecution witnesses and statements that have been withdrawn by witnesses. (As for the disclosure of previous convictions of witnesses generally see *HM Advocate v Murtagh* [2009] UKPC 36, [2011] 1 AC 731.) **D9.14**

In *DPP, ex parte Lee* [1999] 2 All ER 737, the Divisional Court considered whether the prosecution had a duty to disclose unused material in indictable-only offences prior to committal (prior to its abolition). The Court found that there might well be circumstances in which it would be helpful to the defence to know of unused material at an earlier stage. For example:

(a) the previous convictions of the alleged victim when they might be expected to help the defence in a bail application;
(b) material to help an application to stay proceedings as an abuse of process;
(c) material to help the accused prepare for trial, e.g., eye-witnesses whom the prosecution did not intend to use.

Kennedy LJ said that a responsible prosecutor should consider whether fairness required that some of this material might be disclosed. The question was: what immediate disclosure (if any) did justice and fairness require in the circumstances of the case? The Court found that the extent of the disclosure required at this stage was not the 'full blown' extent required under the CPIA 1996.

The Statutory Test: Initial Disclosure

D9.15 Though prosecution disclosure may be required in other circumstances (see **D9.14**), the main duty of the prosecution to make disclosure of material other than its case arises under the CPIA 1996, s. 3.

Section 3 requires a prosecutor to disclose previously undisclosed material to the accused if it 'might reasonably be considered capable of undermining the case for the prosecution against the accused, or of assisting the case for the accused'.

If there is no disclosable material, the accused must be given a written statement to that effect. The court officer must be informed by the prosecutor at the same time (CrimPR 15.2: see Supplement, **R15.2**).

Prosecution material is defined in s. 3(2) and includes material which the prosecutor possesses or has been allowed to inspect under the provisions of the CPIA Code.

In determining whether unused material should be revealed to the defence as part of the disclosure process, as noted above, the statutory test is whether it might reasonably be considered capable of:

(a) undermining the case for the prosecution against the accused; or
(b) assisting the case for the accused.

It is important to emphasise that the test is an objective one and is to be approached impartially. Something can be said to be undermined if it becomes more likely to fall (or fail) as a result. The prosecution case will be more likely to fail if material points to a defect, discrepancy or inconsistency in that case.

In *Barkshire* [2011] EWCA Crim 1885, the Court of Appeal stated that the statutory test extends to anything available to the prosecution which might undermine confidence in the accuracy of evidence called by the prosecution, or which might provide a measure of support for the defence at trial. In that case, the failure of the prosecution to make proper disclosure of material relating to the role and activities of an undercover officer, as well as other material supportive of the defence case, where the materials were pertinent to a potential submission of abuse of process by way of entrapment and had the capacity to support the defence of necessity and justification, had rendered the trial unfair and the convictions unsafe.

The prosecution case might also be undermined as a result of a particular defence which the accused may or may not run. Clearly it is not possible to say with certainty, at the stage of initial disclosure, precisely what course the defence will take. That will come into focus after the service of a defence statement, though it will only be known for sure at trial. However, it is submitted that the fact that material in the possession of the prosecution raises a new issue in the case which might reasonably be considered capable of assisting the defence is likely to meet the statutory test for its disclosure.

In *Whale* [2016] EWCA Crim 742, the Court of Appeal considered a renewed application for leave to appeal on whether the scope of s. 3 required the disclosure of materials (in that case emails) created and retained by D but no longer held by him, which would serve as an aide-memoire as regards the events which formed the subject of the trial. The Court refused leave. It was found to be unarguable that the CPIA 1996 regime applied to documentation created (or received) by an accused and that documents said to be required for memory refreshing fell within its scope. (See also *Hayes* [2015] EWCA Crim 1944.)

In *H* [2004] UKHL 3, [2004] 2 AC 134, the House of Lords made clear that s. 3 does not require disclosure of material which is either neutral in effect or which is adverse to the accused, whether because it strengthens the prosecution or weakens the defence. For examples of cases where material was rightly withheld because nothing in it served to exculpate the accused, see *Khan* [2007] EWCA Crim 2911 and *Yockney* [2012] EWCA Crim 2974.

The Court of Appeal has previously observed that there has been a wide range of serious misunderstandings as to the ambit of unused material to which the defence is entitled and as to the role to be played by the judge. The Judicial Disclosure Protocol states that 'it is ... essential that the trial process is not overburdened or diverted by erroneous and inappropriate disclosure of unused prosecution material' (para. 3). It continues by stating that the 'overarching principle is that unused prosecution material will fall to be disclosed if, and only if, it satisfies the test for disclosure applicable to the proceedings in question, subject to any overriding public interest considerations' (para. 4). Prosecution advocates are cautioned against seeking to abrogate their responsibilities under the CPIA 1996 by disclosing material which does not pass the test for disclosure (para. 37). **D9.16**

However, the Judicial Protocol also warns that failure to disclose material to the defence remains the biggest single cause of miscarriages of justice. Likewise the CCRC has recently re-stated its view that the non-disclosure of material, at or before trial, which could have been of assistance to the defence remains a major cause of miscarriages of justice. The Court of Appeal has been critical of prosecutors who have appeared to apply a modified form of s. 3, based on whether the disclosable material goes to an issue on which they believe that the Crown will ultimately prevail (see, e.g., *Gohil* [2018] EWCA Crim 140, [2018] 1 WLR 3697).

In *Rowe and Davis v UK* (2000) 30 EHRR 1 (see **D9.52**), the ECtHR emphasised that the right to a fair trial means that the prosecution authorities should disclose to the defence all material evidence in their possession for and against the accused. Considering the case, the House of Lords in *H* noted that this had been the domestic law under the A-G's 1981 Guidelines on Disclosure but had ceased to be so in 1996 with the enactment of the CPIA. In this limited sense the House of Lords appeared to contemplate a possibility that the legislation may be out of line with the Strasbourg jurisprudence, though the point was not developed. The matter has now received the consideration of the Court of Appeal in *Syed* [2018] EWCA Crim 2809, [2019] 1 Cr App R 21 (267) in the context of cases of entrapment. Gross LJ giving the judgment of the Court observed that, while there were inevitable terminological and other differences of detail, there was no material conceptual difference between the requirements of disclosure in English law and under the ECHR. The central concern was always fairness. There was no absolute entitlement to disclosure, under the CPIA or the ECHR, **D9.17**

The A-G's Guidelines (see **appendix** 4) set out some factors for a prosecutor to consider in deciding whether the s. 3 test is met for the purposes of initial disclosure in relation to any piece of material, including the following (paras. 6 to 8): **D9.18**

(a) the use that might be made of the material in cross-examination;
(b) its capacity to support submissions that could lead to the exclusion of evidence, a stay of proceedings or a finding that any public authority had acted incompatibly with the accused's rights under the ECHR;

(c) its capacity to suggest an explanation or partial explanation of the accused's actions;
(d) the capacity of the material to have a bearing on scientific or medical evidence in the case.

In addition, material relating to the accused's mental or physical health, intellectual capacity, or to any ill-treatment which the accused may have suffered in custody is said to be likely to fall within the test for disclosure (para. 8).

For large and complex cases in the Crown Court, the A-G's Guidelines require that careful thought is given by prosecutors to prosecution-led disclosure from the very earliest stage (para. 50), a point reinforced by the Court of Appeal in *R* [2015] EWCA Crim 1941, [2016] 1 WLR 1872. A clear investigation and prosecution policy must be devised and the approach to disclosure set out in a Disclosure Management Document, tailored to the individual case, which sets out the prosecution's approach to disclosure, dealing with such matters as digital, video and third-party material, and reasonable lines of inquiry, as well as their understanding of the defence case. Such a document should be served on the court and the defence at an early stage (para. 51).

D9.19 A prosecutor may disclose material to the defence either by providing a copy of the material or allowing inspection at a reasonable time and place (CPIA 1996, s. 3(3)). However, material must not be disclosed under s. 3 if a court has concluded that it is not in the public interest that it be disclosed (s. 3(6) and see **D9.49** to **D9.67**). Nor may material be disclosed if its disclosure is prohibited by the IPA 2016, s. 56 (CPIA 1996, s. 3(7)). As for the disclosure of previous convictions of witnesses (including victims) and the extent to which this constitutes a lawful interference with the ECHR, Article 8, rights of the person whose convictions are to be disclosed, see the Privy Council decision in *HM Advocate v Murtagh* [2009] UKPC 36, [2011] 1 AC 731.

D9.20

Criminal Procedure and Investigations Act 1996, s. 3

(1) The prosecutor must—
(a) disclose to the accused any prosecution material which has not previously been disclosed to the accused and which might reasonably be considered capable of undermining the case for the prosecution against the accused, or of assisting the case for the accused, or
(b) give to the accused a written statement that there is no material of a description mentioned in paragraph (a).
(2) For the purposes of this section prosecution material is material—
(a) which is in the prosecutor's possession, and came into his possession in connection with the case for the prosecution against the accused, or
(b) which, in pursuance of a code operative under Part II, he has inspected in connection with the case for the prosecution against the accused.
(3) Where material consists of information which has been recorded in any form the prosecutor discloses it for the purposes of this section—
(a) by securing that a copy is made of it and that the copy is given to the accused, or
(b) if in the prosecutor's opinion that is not practicable or not desirable, by allowing the accused to inspect it at a reasonable time and a reasonable place or by taking steps to secure that he is allowed to do so;

and a copy may be in such form as the prosecutor thinks fit and need not be in the same form as that in which the information has already been recorded.
(4) Where material consists of information which has not been recorded the prosecutor discloses it for the purposes of this section by securing that it is recorded in such form as he thinks fit and—
(a) by securing that a copy is made of it and that the copy is given to the accused, or
(b) if in the prosecutor's opinion that is not practicable or not desirable, by allowing the accused to inspect it at a reasonable time and a reasonable place or by taking steps to secure that he is allowed to do so.
(5) Where material does not consist of information the prosecutor discloses it for the purposes of this section by allowing the accused to inspect it at a reasonable time and a reasonable place or by taking steps to secure that he is allowed to do so.
(6) Material must not be disclosed under this section to the extent that the court, on an application by the prosecutor, concludes it is not in the public interest to disclose it and orders accordingly.

(7) Material must not be disclosed under this section to the extent that it is material the disclosure of which is prohibited by section 56 of the Investigatory Powers Act 2016.

(8) The prosecutor must act under this section during the period which, by virtue of section 12, is the relevant period for this section.

Service of Schedule

In addition to providing material under s. 3, under s. 4 of the CPIA 1996, where the prosecutor has been given a schedule of unused material by a police officer under the CPIA Code (see **D9.12**), that schedule must be served on the accused when the prosecutor makes disclosure of unused material under s. 3. **D9.21**

Criminal Procedure and Investigations Act 1996, s. 4

(1) This section applies where—
   (a) the prosecutor acts under section 3, and
   (b) before so doing he was given a document in pursuance of provision included, by virtue of section 24(3), in a code operative under Part II.

(2) In such a case the prosecutor must give the document to the accused at the same time as the prosecutor acts under section 3.

Summary Trials — Nature of Prosecution's Obligations

By virtue of s. 1(1), the CPIA 1996 partially incorporates summary proceedings into the statutory disclosure scheme (see **D9.2**). The prosecution's duty of disclosure applies whenever the accused pleads not guilty and the court proceeds to summary trial. The CPIA Code provides for a streamlined disclosure process in such cases, involving a simplified disclosure schedule (para. 6 and see also **D9.12** and **D9.14**). The Judicial Disclosure Protocol states that the principles relating to disclosure apply equally in the magistrates' courts. It follows that, whilst disclosure of unused material is undoubtedly essential in order to achieve justice, misconceived applications for disclosure, or inappropriate disclosure, must be avoided (see para. 30). Prosecutors are required to take into account information provided as to the defence case in the case management forms when conducting any review of material (para. 33). The A-G's Guidelines require prosecutors to be alert to the possibility that material may exist which should be disclosed to the defence prior to the CPIA requirements applying to the case (para. 44). **D9.22**

Time-limits for Disclosure

There are no statutory time-limits for disclosure of unused material in the Crown Court. Provision was made in the legislation for a time-limit to be laid down by statutory instrument but no such instrument has ever been made affecting Crown Court cases. That being the case, the default position is set out in the CPIA 1996, s. 13(1): disclosure must be made as soon as reasonably practicable after the happening of a particular event, such as service of the prosecution case. In magistrates' court cases, the CPIA Code stipulates that where a streamlined disclosure certificate is required (see **D9.12** and **D9.22**) it must be disclosed to the accused either at the hearing at which a not guilty plea is entered, or as soon as possible following a formal indication from the accused or the accused's representative that a not guilty plea will be entered at the hearing (para. 10.1). **D9.23**

The Judicial Disclosure Protocol requires that, if there is a preliminary hearing, the judge should seize the opportunity to impose an early timetable for disclosure and to identify any likely problems including as regards third-party material and material that will require an application to the Family Court (para. 9). The court should keep the timetable for prosecution and defence disclosure under review from the first hearing (para. 7). Large and complex cases will require robust case management by the judiciary, and the courts should be provided with an up-to-date timetable for disclosure whenever there are material changes as a result of difficulties that emerge (paras. 38 and 39).

Continuing Duty to Review

D9.24 Under the CPIA 1996, s. 7A, a prosecutor remains under a continuing duty to review questions of disclosure, applying a test in the same terms as s. 3 (see **D9.20**). If, at any time before the accused is acquitted or convicted, the prosecutor forms the opinion that there is material which might undermine the prosecution case, or be reasonably expected to assist the accused's defence, it must be disclosed to the accused as soon as reasonably practicable, provided that it is not prohibited under s. 7A(8) (public interest) or (9) (relating to the RIPA 2000). Where the court has ruled against disclosure on public interest grounds, it must keep under review the question whether it is still in the public interest not to disclose the material affected by its order.

In practice, the duty of continuing disclosure is most likely to crystallise either on service of the defence case statement or during the trial itself as the issues develop.

After service of the defence case statement (see **D9.29**), the CPIA Code requires, in effect, a repeat exercise of the process for initial disclosure. An investigator must again look at the material retained and draw the prosecutor's attention to any material which might reasonably be considered capable of undermining the prosecution case or of assisting the defence if it were to be disclosed (para. 8.3). If the investigator comes into possession of any new material after complying with these duties, it must be revealed to the prosecutor (para. 8.3). This may trigger a requirement for disclosure by the prosecution (see also the A-G's Guidelines, paras. 37 and 42). The disclosure officer must also certify compliance with the duties imposed by the CPIA Code after consideration of the defence statement and whenever a schedule of material is otherwise given or material is revealed to the prosecutor (para. 9.1).

The duty of continuing review may be triggered during the course of a trial where, for example, a prosecution witness gives evidence which is materially inconsistent with a statement made earlier to the police. If the defence are unaware of the statement, prosecuting counsel should disclose it so that it can be used by the defence in cross-examination to challenge the witness's evidence (*Clarke* (1931) 22 Cr App R 58).

The position so far as summary trial is concerned is dealt with at **D9.63**.

Following conviction there is no general duty on the State (through the police or CPS) to continue to investigate. The statutory duties of disclosure under the CPIA 1996 terminate with a conviction, acquittal or discontinuation of the proceedings (s. 7A(1)). However, between conviction and sentence, there is a common-law duty to disclose any material that is not known to the accused but which may be relevant to sentence, such as information which might assist in placing the accused's role in the correct context vis-à-vis other offenders (*Gohil* [2018] EWCA Crim 140, [2018] 1 WLR 3697; *R (Nunn) v Chief Constable of Suffolk Police* [2014] UKSC 37, [2015] AC 225; A-G's Guidelines, para. 71). In *Onuigbo (also known as Okoronkwo)* [2014] EWCA Crim 65, [2014] Lloyd's Rep FC 302, the Court of Appeal approved a statement in the CPS Disclosure Manual (para. 21.3) that the common law, A-G's Guidelines and the ECHR, Article 6, obliged a prosecutor to continue to review unused material, particularly following the receipt of any response to a confiscation statement.

Once proceedings are complete the prosecution are still under a duty at common law to consider disclosure of any material which might cast doubt on the safety of conviction and to make disclosure of such material unless there is a good reason not to. Pending an appeal, the prosecution are obliged to disclose any material not previously disclosed relevant to an identified ground of appeal. (See further *Gohil*, *Nunn* and A-G's Guidelines, para. 72.) As the Supreme Court observed in *Nunn*, ordinarily post-conviction disclosure will only arise in respect of material which has come into the prosecution's possession after trial (otherwise it should have been disclosed previously). In cases where a failure in disclosure comes to light, however, the common law requires that it be corrected to make available what should have been available at trial as well as material relevant to the grounds of appeal.

Criminal Procedure and Investigations Act 1996, s. 7A **D9.25**

(1) This section applies at all times—
 (a) after the prosecutor has complied with section 3 or purported to comply with it, and
 (b) before the accused is acquitted or convicted or the prosecutor decides not to proceed with the case concerned.
(2) The prosecutor must keep under review the question whether at any given time (and, in particular, following the giving of a defence statement) there is prosecution material which—
 (a) might reasonably be considered capable of undermining the case for the prosecution against the accused or of assisting the case for the accused, and
 (b) has not been disclosed to the accused.
(3) If at any time there is any such material as is mentioned in subsection (2) the prosecutor must disclose it to the accused as soon as is reasonably practicable (or within the period mentioned in subsection (5)(a), where that applies).
(4) In applying subsection (2) by reference to any given time the state of affairs at that time (including the case for the prosecution as it stands at that time) must be taken into account.
(5) Where the accused gives a defence statement under section 5, 6 or 6B—
 (a) if as a result of that statement the prosecutor is required by this section to make any disclosure, or further disclosure, he must do so during the period which, by virtue of section 12, is the relevant period for this section;
 (b) if the prosecutor considers that he is not so required, he must during that period give to the accused a written statement to that effect.
(6) For the purposes of this section prosecution material is material—
 (a) which is in the prosecutor's possession and came into his possession in connection with the case for the prosecution against the accused, or
 (b) which, in pursuance of a code operative under Part 2, he has inspected in connection with the case for the prosecution against the accused.
(7) Subsections (3) to (5) of section 3 (method by which prosecutor discloses) apply for the purposes of this section as they apply for the purposes of that.
(8) Material must not be disclosed under this section to the extent that the court, on an application by the prosecutor, concludes it is not in the public interest to disclose it and orders accordingly.
(9) Material must not be disclosed under this section to the extent that it is material the disclosure of which is prohibited by section 56 of the Investigatory Powers Act 2016.

Defence Applications for Disclosure from the Prosecution

If an accused has served a defence statement (see **D9.29**) and the prosecution have complied, purported to comply, or failed to comply, with the procedure for further disclosure (see **D9.24**), an accused may apply under the CPIA 1996, s. 8, for an order for disclosure of material which should have been disclosed under s. 7A, i.e. material which the prosecutor should have disclosed as material which might reasonably be considered capable of undermining the prosecution case or assisting the accused's case. Such an application may relate to material actually held or inspected by the prosecutor (s. 8(3)), as well as to any material which the prosecutor would be entitled to hold or inspect if requested (s. 8(4)). **D9.26**

In the Judicial Disclosure Protocol, para. 26 (see **appendix** 4), it is emphasised that the s. 8 procedure is not intended for blanket requests from the defence and that requests for specific disclosure of unused prosecution material which are not referable to any issue in the case identified by the defence case statement should be rejected (see also *DPP v Wood* [2006] EWHC 32 (Admin)).

The procedure for making an application under s. 8 is set out in CrimPR 15.5 (see Supplement, **R15.5**). In *K* [2006] EWCA Crim 724, [2006] 2 All ER 552, the Court of Appeal stated that the case management powers contained in the CrimPR permitted the judge to deal with issues of disclosure exclusively by reference to written submissions, and also to limit their length. The necessary public element of any hearing was sufficiently achieved if the accused, and any media present for the hearing, were supplied with copies of written submissions if they wished to see them.

D9.27 **Criminal Procedure and Investigations Act 1996, s. 8**

(1) This section applies where the accused has given a defence statement under section 5, 6 or 6B and the prosecutor has complied with section 7A(5) or has purported to comply with it or has failed to comply with it.
(2) If the accused has at any time reasonable cause to believe that there is prosecution material which is required by section 7A to be disclosed to him and has not been, he may apply to the court for an order requiring the prosecutor to disclose it to him.
(3) For the purposes of this section prosecution material is material—
  (a) which is in the prosecutor's possession and came into his possession in connection with the case for the prosecution against the accused,
  (b) which, in pursuance of a code operative under Part II, he has inspected in connection with the case for the prosecution against the accused, or
  (c) which falls within subsection (4).
(4) Material falls within this subsection if in pursuance of a code operative under Part II the prosecutor must, if he asks for the material, be given a copy of it or be allowed to inspect it in connection with the case for the prosecution against the accused.
(5) Material must not be disclosed under this section to the extent that the court, on an application by the prosecutor, concludes it is not in the public interest to disclose it and orders accordingly.
(6) Material must not be disclosed under this section to the extent that it is material the disclosure of which is prohibited by section 17 of the Regulation of Investigatory Powers Act 2000.

Consequences of Prosecution Non-disclosure

D9.28 A failure on the part of the prosecution to make proper disclosure may, in serious cases, provide a basis on which a defendant may apply to stay proceedings as an abuse of process, to exclude certain evidence, or appeal. In *R (L)* [2010] EWCA Crim 924, [2011] 1 WLR 359, the Court of Appeal upheld a decision of the trial judge to stay proceedings as an abuse where the CPS had wrongly declined to comply with a CPIA 1996, s. 8, order for disclosure, on the mistaken basis that to do so may amount to an offence (given that the order required the copying of indecent images). The test, however, sets a high bar. In *Salt* [2015] EWCA Crim 662, [2015] 2 Cr App R 27 (376) the Lord Chief Justice overturned the decision of a trial judge to stay proceedings as an abuse notwithstanding very serious failings in the disclosure of unused material. It was observed that the proper sanction as regards these failures could be a wasted costs order. The well-known principle in *A-G's Ref (No. 3 of 2000) (Looseley)* [2001] UKHL 53, [2001] 1 WLR 2060, that a stay for abuse was not to be used to sanction the prosecution or the police, was reiterated. The principles applicable in abuse applications concerning non-disclosure were also considered in *R* [2015] EWCA Crim 1941, [2016] 1 WLR 1872 and *E* [2018] EWCA Crim 2426. For the factors involved when an application for a stay is made generally, see **D3.66 *et seq***.

So far as concerns late disclosure leading to the exclusion of evidence and the collapse of a prosecution, see *Boardman* [2015] EWCA Crim 175. See also *Brants v DPP* [2011] EWHC 754 (Admin); *Prosecution Appeal: R v O* [2011] EWCA Crim 2854; *Salt* [2015] EWCA Crim 662, [2015] 1 WLR 4905; *Butler* [2015] EWCA Crim 854; *O'Meally* [2015] EWCA Crim 905 and *Kelly* [2015] EWCA Crim 817.

As to the approach to failures in disclosure undermining the safety of a conviction, see (among others) *Gohil* [2018] EWCA Crim 140, [2018] 1 WLR 3697; *Poole* [2017] EWCA Crim 208; *Wang Yam* [2017] EWCA Crim 1414; *Garland* [2016] EWCA Crim 1743, [2017] 4 WLR 117 and also, e.g., *Hadley* [2006] EWCA Crim 2544; *Alibhai* [2004] EWCA Crim 681; *Ward* [1993] 1 WLR 619 (though note that in *Ali* [2019] EWCA Crim 1527, at [42], the Court of Appeal described the test for disclosure set out in *Ward*—pre-CPIA 1996—as an 'over-correction') and *Smith* [2004] EWCA Crim 2212. It is not necessary to show, in a case of disclosure failure, that the undisclosed item might have shifted the balance or opened up a new line of defence. However, a conviction will not be considered unsafe if the undisclosed material can be said to be insignificant to any real issue in the trial.

For a consideration of circumstances in which non-disclosure may amount to a breach of the ECHR, Article 6, see the Scottish appeal of *Macklin v HM Advocate* [2015] UKSC 77, [2017] 1

All ER 32. See also *McInnes v HM Advocate* [2010] UKSC 7, 2010 SC (UKSC) 28, (mentioned in *Wang Yam* and *Garland*).

The courts have increasingly emphasised the importance of having regard to the overall objective of the CrimPR and the directions of trial judges in order to deal with criminal cases justly and to treat the prosecution and defence fairly when making decisions on appeal points relating to non-disclosure. The conduct of the defence, in drawing failings in disclosure to light, for example, is also likely to be considered material.

In the appellate cases, the courts have repeatedly emphasised the distinction to be drawn between whether, on the one hand, material ought to have been disclosed by the prosecution and, on the other, the consequences of that violation. It is only in cases where, in the light of a failure of disclosure, it can be considered that the conviction is unsafe that an appeal will succeed.

DEFENCE STATEMENTS

The Defence Statement

By the CPIA 1996, s. 5, once the case is sent to the Crown Court and the prosecution case is served, the accused must give a defence statement to the court and the prosecutor. The defence statement is a written statement setting out the basis on which the case will be defended. The areas that the statement must cover are set out in s. 6A of the CPIA 1996 and include: **D9.29**

- the nature of the accused's defence, including any particular defences upon which the accused intends to rely;
- the matters of fact on which the accused takes issue with the prosecution, with the reasons why;
- particulars of the matters of fact on which the accused intends to rely for the purposes of defence; and
- any points of law which the accused wishes to take, with any authorities relied upon.

It should be stressed that the duty of disclosure imposed on the defence is different to that which is meant by the prosecution 'duty of disclosure'. In respect of the defence, it is a duty to reveal the case which will be presented at trial (rather than, as in the case of the prosecution, to disclose unused material).

The degree of detail which is currently required by the CPIA 1996 results from a perception among some prosecutors and members of the judiciary that defence lawyers were providing defence statements that were couched in too general terms, so that the intended benefits of their introduction in terms of improved case management were not being realised. In *Bryant* [2005] EWCA Crim 2079, the Court of Appeal said that a defence statement consisting of a general denial of the counts in the indictment, accompanied by a statement that D took issue with any witness giving evidence contrary to his denial, was 'woefully inadequate'. However, notwithstanding *Bryant*, if the accused raises no positive case at all in a defence statement and simply requires the Crown to prove its case, there is no failure to comply with the CPIA 1996, s. 6A, as long as the defence statement makes clear that this is the accused's position (*Rochford* [2010] EWCA Crim 1928, [2011] 1 WLR 534, as explained in *Malcolm* [2011] EWCA Crim 2069). The distinction between the two cases rests on the difference between a positive but *unspecified* challenge to the evidence of a witness, as against an approach which ensures the Crown proves its case. **D9.30**

The Judicial Disclosure Protocol, para. 17 (see **appendix** 4), states: 'Judges expect a defence statement to contain a clear and detailed exposition of the issues of fact and law'. The Protocol requires judges to examine the defence statement with care to ensure that it complies with the formalities required by the CPIA 1996 (para. 19) and to investigate any failure by the defence to comply with its obligations (see para. 20).

In appropriate circumstances the principle that there must be equality of arms will mean that the prosecution must spell out the inferences that they will be asking the trier of fact to draw from the facts adduced in their evidence, given that the defence are obliged to set out their reasoning for disputing issues of fact in that evidence. It follows that the scope of the defence statement should be viewed in the context of what might reasonably be required of the defence at a stage when they may not be clear about the way in which the prosecution put their case.

Legal professional privilege and the accused's privilege against self-incrimination are unaffected by s. 6A. The accused is required to disclose what is going to happen at the trial, but is not required to disclose the confidential discussions with lawyers, nor is the accused obliged to self-incriminate if the accused does not want to. A lawyer cannot properly advise an accused not to file a defence statement or to omit from it something that is required to be there by s. 6A. For these propositions, see *Rochford and R (Kelly) v Warley Magistrates' Court* [2007] EWHC 1836 (Admin), [2008] 1 WLR 2001.

In January 2011, the Bar Standards Board published revised guidance for counsel on the preparation of defence statements. The guidance states that counsel ought not to accept any instructions to draft or settle a defence statement unless given the opportunity and adequate time to gain proper familiarity with the case and to comply with fundamental requirements which are set out in the guidance.

D9.31 As regards disclosure between co-accused, in *Cairns* [2002] EWCA Crim 2838, [2003] 1 WLR 796 the trial judge had declined to order disclosure of the defence statements of D's co-accused, ruling that disclosure of such statements under the CPIA 1996, s. 5(5), was only as between the accused and the Crown. The Court of Appeal overturned the decision, finding that the prosecutor's duty under s. 7 extended to disclosure of defence statements made by a co-accused. Failing that, the judge should have ordered disclosure under s. 8. If s. 33 of the CJA 2003 comes fully into effect, the matter will be governed by s. 5(5A), (5B) and (5D) of the CPIA 1996. In a multi-accused case, the court will be able to order each of the accused to give copies of his or her defence statement to the co-accused. The court may act of its own motion, or in response to an application by any party, specifying the period within which the statement must be served.

A further amendment to the defence duty of disclosure is envisaged in the CPIA 1996, s. 6B, which is inserted by the CJA 2003, s. 33(3), but it is not yet in force.

D9.32 The question of the authorship of the defence statement (or an updating statement, or a statement that no updating is necessary) is dealt with in s. 6E(1). It deems that, where an accused's solicitor purports to give such a statement on behalf of the accused, it is to be treated as given on behalf of the accused unless the contrary is proved. Of course, evidence can be adduced to show that it was not given with the accused's authority, but that may have adverse consequences where legal professional privilege is waived as a result (see **F10.40**).

At trial, the judge may direct that the jury receive a copy of any defence statement (whether initial or updated), edited to exclude any reference to inadmissible evidence. This can be done of the judge's own motion or on application, but only if it would help the jury to understand the case or resolve any issue in it (s. 6E(4) to (6)). A judge's conclusion that a defence statement should be shown to the jury to help it understand the case, exercising powers under s. 6E(5)(b), cannot be attacked on appeal unless it can be shown that the conclusion was unreasonable (*Sanghera* [2012] EWCA Crim 16, [2012] 2 Cr App R 17 (196)).

In *Attique* [2018] EWCA Crim 552, [2019] 1 WLR 66 it was a ground of appeal that lawyers acting for D had erroneously failed to include in the Defence Case Statement a fact which D had later raised at trial and which had then been the subject of an adverse inference direction. Dismissing the appeal on the facts, the Court of Appeal found as a matter of principle that it is not open to a defendant to omit from the defence statement matters about which the defendant has been inconsistent to avoid hostages to fortune and then to complain that a particular fact had been mentioned at an earlier stage. If, however, a matter of fact is omitted in error and instructions have been consistent throughout, prosecuting counsel should be informed and the defence statement amended.

Alibi

If the defence statement discloses an alibi, particulars of alibi must be given under the CPIA 1996, s. 6A(2). The names, addresses and dates of birth (or as much of this information as is known) of any alibi witnesses whom the accused intends to call must be contained within the defence statement. If the accused does not know any of these details, any information in the accused's possession that might assist in identifying or finding any such witness must be given. Changes in relation to alibi witnesses, or the later discovery of the information required by statute, must be dealt with by the procedure for updated disclosure when this is in force. Alibi evidence is defined in s. 6A(3) as 'evidence tending to show that by reason of the presence of the accused at a particular place or in a particular area at a particular time he was not, or was unlikely to have been, at the place where the offence is alleged to have been committed at the time of its alleged commission' (see **D17.15**). The statutory obligation to provide the details of the witness is triggered by the accused's belief that the witness is able to assist; it is not necessary that the witness can give evidence or is willing to do so (*Re Joseph Hill & Co, Solicitors* [2013] EWCA Crim 775, [2014] 1 WLR 786). **D9.33**

Notification of Details of Defence Witnesses

The defence are under a duty to notify the court and the prosecutor, separately from the defence statement, of any witnesses they intend to call at trial, other than the defendant and any alibi witnesses already notified (CPIA 1996, s. 6C). The defence must provide names, addresses, dates of birth or, if any such details are not known, other identifying information. Notice of intention to call a witness must be given within 14 days (in the case of summary proceedings) and 28 days (in the case of Crown Court proceedings) from the date when the prosecutor complies, or purports to comply, with the duty to disclose under s. 3 (Criminal Procedure and Investigations Act 1996 (Defence Disclosure Time Limits) Regulations 2011 (SI 2011 No. 209), reg. 2). There is provision for applications for extensions of this period (reg. 3) and for treatment of weekends and bank holidays (reg. 2(4)). Any change in the plans to call witnesses (including a decision not to call a previously notified witness or to call a witness not previously notified) must be dealt with by way of an amended notice to the court and the prosecutor. It seems clear from *R (Kelly) v Warley Magistrates' Court* [2007] EWHC 1836 (Admin), [2008] 1 WLR 2001 that these provisions override litigation privilege and legal professional privilege to the extent that such privileges are inconsistent with reasonable requirements for the proper working of the provisions (see **F10.16** ***et seq.***). **D9.34**

The Code of Practice for Arranging and Conducting Interviews of Witnesses Notified by the Accused, made under s. 21A of the CPIA 1996, contains guidance to police officers and other persons charged with the duty of investigating offences in relation to interviews of witnesses notified by the accused (either to support an alibi or otherwise). Any such person must have regard to the Code (s. 21A(3)). Any provision of the Code or any failure to have due regard to the Code can be taken into account by a civil or criminal court or tribunal where relevant to deciding any question (s. 21A(13)). The Code deals with such matters as the information to be provided to the witness and the accused before any interview may take place, the arrangements for the interview, attendance of solicitors on behalf of the accused and the interviewee, and recording of the interview. **D9.35**

In *Rochford* [2010] EWCA Crim 1928, [2011] 1 WLR 534, the case of *Penner* [2010] EWCA Crim 1155 was cited by the Court of Appeal as authority for the proposition that the combination of the provisions concerning notification of details of defence witnesses and the CrimPR have abolished, or at least are designed to abolish, trial by ambush.

The Law Society has issued a practice note setting out the obligations and ethical considerations that defence solicitors should consider when conducting a case involving defence witnesses, including dealing with defence witness notices.

D9.36 **Criminal Procedure and Investigations Act 1996, ss. 5, 6A, 6C and 6E**

5.—(1) Subject to subsections (2) to (4), this section applies where—
(a) [Part I] applies by virtue of section 1(2), and
(b) the prosecutor complies with section 3 or purports to comply with it.
(2) [Repealed.]
(3) [Repealed.]
(3A) Where [Part I] applies by virtue of section 1(2)(cc), this section does not apply unless—
(a) copies of the documents containing the evidence have been served on the accused under regulations made under para. 1 of Schedule 3 to the Crime and Disorder Act 1998; and
(b) a copy of the notice under subsection (7) of section 51 of that Act has been served on him under that subsection.
(4) Where [Part I] applies by virtue of section 1(2)(e), this section does not apply unless the prosecutor has served on the accused a copy of the indictment and a copy of the set of documents containing the evidence which is the basis of the charge.
(5) Where this section applies, the accused must give a defence statement to the court and the prosecutor.
(5A) [Not yet in force: see **D9.4**].
(5B) [Not yet in force: see **D9.4**].
(5C) A defence statement that has to be given to the court and the prosecutor (under subsection (5)) must be given during the period which, by virtue of section 12, is the relevant period for this section.
(5D) [Not yet in force: see **D9.4**].

6A.—(1) For the purposes of this Part a defence statement is a written statement—
(a) setting out the nature of the accused's defence, including any particular defences on which he intends to rely,
(b) indicating the matters of fact on which he takes issue with the prosecution,
(c) setting out, in the case of each such matter, why he takes issue with the prosecution,
(ca) setting out particulars of the matters of fact on which he intends to rely for the purposes of his defence, and
(d) indicating any point of law (including any point as to the admissibility of evidence or an abuse of process) which he wishes to take, and any authority on which he intends to rely for that purpose.
(2) A defence statement that discloses an alibi must give particulars of it, including—
(a) the name, address and date of birth of any witness the accused believes is able to give evidence in support of the alibi, or as many of those details as are known to the accused when the statement is given;
(b) any information in the accused's possession which might be of material assistance in identifying or finding any such witness in whose case any of the details mentioned in paragraph (a) are not known to the accused when the statement is given.
(3) For the purposes of this section evidence in support of an alibi is evidence tending to show that by reason of the presence of the accused at a particular place or in a particular area at a particular time he was not, or was unlikely to have been, at the place where the offence is alleged to have been committed at the time of its alleged commission.
(4) [Power to make regulations.]

6C.—(1) The accused must give to the court and the prosecutor a notice indicating whether he intends to call any persons (other than himself) as witnesses at his trial and, if so—
(a) giving the name, address and date of birth of each such proposed witness, or as many of those details as are known to the accused when the notice is given;
(b) providing any information in the accused's possession which might be of material assistance in identifying or finding any such proposed witness in whose case any of the details mentioned in paragraph (a) are not known to the accused when the notice is given.
(2) Details do not have to be given under this section to the extent that they have already been given under section 6A(2).
(3) The accused must give a notice under this section during the period which, by virtue of section 12, is the relevant period for this section.

(4) If, following the giving of a notice under this section, the accused—
(a) decides to call a person (other than himself) who is not included in the notice as a proposed witness, or decides not to call a person who is so included, or
(b) discovers any information which, under subsection (1), he would have had to include in the notice if he had been aware of it when giving the notice,
he must give an appropriately amended notice to the court and the prosecutor.

6E.—(1) Where an accused's solicitor purports to give on behalf of the accused—
(a) a defence statement under section 5, 6 or 6B, or
(b) a statement of the kind mentioned in section 6B(4),
the statement shall, unless the contrary is proved, be deemed to be given with the authority of the accused.

Defence Statements in Cases Tried Summarily

In cases tried summarily there is no obligation on the defence to provide a defence statement. **D9.37** However, once the prosecutor has complied (or purported to comply) with the duty to disclose unused material (see **D9.15**), the accused may give the prosecutor and the court a defence statement (CPIA 1996, s. 6). In the absence of a defence statement, the accused cannot make an application for specific disclosure under s. 8, and the court cannot make any orders for disclosure of unused prosecution material (see s. 8(1) and **D9.26**). As to the use of the s. 8 procedure in the magistrates' court in the context of breathalyser cases and the need for some evidential basis on which a s. 8 request must be premised, see *DPP v Manchester and Salford Magistrates' Court* [2017] EWHC 3719 (Admin) and *DPP v Walsall Magistrates' Court* [2019] EWHC 3317 (Admin).

Where the accused chooses to serve a defence statement this must be done within 14 days from the date on which the prosecutor complies or purports to comply with the initial duty of disclosure (Criminal Procedure and Investigations Act 1996 (Defence Disclosure Time Limits) Regulations 2011, reg. 2: see **D9.40**). The court has power to extend this time-limit on the application of the accused (reg. 3).

If the accused provides a defence statement, the requirements in s. 6A as to the contents of the statement apply. The voluntary regime applies to summary trial, whether it is of a summary or an either-way offence or even (in the case of a child or young person) of an indictable-only offence (s. 1(1)). The Magistrates' Courts Protocol makes the following points in respect of defence statements:

(1) Defence advocates must give consideration at an early stage to whether to serve such a statement.
(2) Defence statements must contain a clear and detailed exposition of the issues of fact and law in the case and courts should examine them with care to ensure that they comply with the formalities required by the CPIA.
(3) Where late service of a defence statement results in potential delay to the proceedings, any application to adjourn for further disclosure or to make an application under s. 8 must be scrutinised carefully by the court.
(4) Any case which raises difficult issues of disclosure should be referred to a district judge, where one is available.

Notwithstanding the absence of a requirement to serve a defence statement, the defence must identify the real issues in a case in accordance with the overriding objective in CrimPR 1.1 (see Supplement, **R1.1**) (*Robinson v Abergavenny Magistrates' Court* [2007] EWHC 2005 (Admin)).

Criminal Procedure and Investigations Act 1996, s. 6 **D9.38**

(1) This section applies where—
(a) [Part I] applies by virtue of section 1(1), and
(b) the prosecutor complies with section 3 or purports to comply with it.
(2) The accused—
(a) may give a defence statement to the prosecutor, and
(b) if he does so, must also give such a statement to the court.
...

(4) If the accused gives a defence statement under this section he must give it during the period which, by virtue of section 12, is the relevant period for this section.

Defence Admissions in Case Management Forms

D9.39 In *R (Firth) v Epping Justices* [2011] EWHC 388 (Admin), [2011] 4 All ER 326, judicial review was sought of the decision of a magistrates' court to rely in committal proceedings upon the defence statement in a case progression form, made through D's counsel, which admitted contact with the victim of an assault but on the basis of self-defence. The contention was that admitting the document offended the principle that an accused could not be required to self-incriminate. The Divisional Court refused the application, stating that it was repugnant to the new approach to criminal justice in the CrimPR whereby both sides disclosed the nature of their case. If the circumstances were such that an admission was tainted by unfairness, it could be excluded under the PACE 1984, s. 78. The effect of this decision has been modified to an extent by *Newell* [2012] EWCA Crim 650, [2012] 1 WLR 3142, where the Court of Appeal made clear that, while admissions by legal representatives in case progression forms are admissible in evidence, it will rarely be appropriate not to exercise discretion under s. 78 to exclude them, provided the case is conducted following the letter and the spirit of the CrimPR.

Defence Statements in Cases Tried in the Crown Court—Time-limits

D9.40 By the Criminal Procedure Investigations Act 1996 (Defence Disclosure Time Limits) Regulations 2011, reg. 2, the defence statement must be served within 28 days of the prosecution's compliance (or purported compliance) with the duty of initial disclosure. The defence may apply for an extension, but the application must be made before the deadline expires (reg. 3). The application must not be granted unless the court is satisfied that it would not be reasonable to require the accused to give a defence statement within 28 days. There is no limit to the number of applications that may be made (reg. 3). Time runs from the date of service of a statement by the prosecution under the CPIA 1996, s. 3(1)(h), not from service of the scheduled unused material; however, the right to further disclosure is not lost if there is a short delay in serving the defence statement (*DPP v Wood* [2006] EWHC 32 (Admin); *Murphy v DPP* [2006] EWHC 1753 (Admin)).

The Judicial Disclosure Protocol recognises that there may be some instances when there may be a well-founded defence application to extend the 28-day limit for serving a proper defence statement to enable an appropriate defence statement to be filed (para. 10). Extensions will not be granted lightly or as a matter of course. If an extension is sought, the application ought to be accompanied by an appropriate explanation (para. 12).

There is clearly a burden on defence representatives to embark on detailed preparation soon after receipt of the prosecution case. However, this responsibility cannot be discharged unless the prosecution make timely disclosure of unused material. As it is put in the Judicial Disclosure Protocol, para. 10, for effective case management 'the defence must have a proper opportunity to review the case papers and consider initial disclosure, with a view to preparing a properly completed defence statement'.

D9.41 **Criminal Procedure and Investigations Act 1996 (Defence Disclosure Time Limits) Regulations 2011 (SI 2011 No. 209), regs. 2 and 3**

2.—(1) The relevant period for sections 5 (compulsory disclosure), section 6 (voluntary disclosure) and section 6C (notification of intention to call defence witnesses) begins with the day on which the prosecutor complies, or purports to comply, with section 3 (initial duty of prosecutor to disclose).

(2) In a case where Part 1 applies by virtue of section 1(1) (application of Part 1 in respect of summary proceedings), the relevant period for section 6 and section 6C expires at the end of 14 days beginning with the first day of the relevant period.

(3) In a case where Part 1 applies by virtue of section 1(2) (application of Part 1 in respect of Crown Court proceedings), the relevant period for section 5 and section 6C expires at the end of 28 days beginning with the first day of the relevant period.

(4) Where the relevant period would expire on a Saturday, Sunday, Christmas Day, Good Friday or any day that under the Banking and Financial Dealings Act 1971 is a bank holiday in England and Wales, the relevant period is treated as expiring on the next day that is not one of those days.
(5) Paragraphs (2) and (3) are subject to regulation 3.

3.—(1) The court may by order extend (or further extend) the relevant period by so many days as it specifies.
(2) The court may only make such an order—
 (a) on an application by the accused; and
 (b) if it is satisfied that it would be unreasonable to require the accused to give a defence statement under section 5 or section 6, or give notice under section 6C, as the case may be, within the relevant period.
(3) Such an application must—
 (a) be made within the relevant period;
 (b) specify the grounds on which it is made; and
 (c) state the number of days by which the accused wishes the relevant period to be extended.
(4) There is no limit on the number of applications that may be made under paragraph (2)(a).

Sanctions for Failure in Providing Defence Materials

Section 11 of the CPIA 1996 lays down sanctions for failure in defence disclosure which apply if the accused: **D9.42**

(a) fails to give the initial defence statement required under s. 5 in respect of Crown Court cases;
(b) gives the initial defence statement after the 14-day period during which it must be served in the magistrates' court or after the 28-day period during which it must be served in the Crown Court (see **D9.40**);
(c) fails to provide an updated statement required under s. 6B(1) or a statement that no updating is necessary under s. 6B(4) (note, however, that s. 6B is not yet in force);
(d) supplies the documents in (c) outside the applicable time-limit;
(e) sets out inconsistent defences in the defence statement;
(f) puts forward a defence at trial that was not mentioned in the defence statement;
(g) relies on a matter that should have been mentioned in the defence statement to comply with s. 6A, but was not;
(h) gives evidence of alibi or call a witness to give evidence in support of alibi without having complied with the provisions relating to notification of alibi witnesses;
(i) calls a witness not included or adequately identified in the notice of defence witnesses.

The above list is a summary of s. 11(2) as amended by the CJA 2003, s. 39, and the CJIA 2008, s. 60(2).

In the event that any of the issues identified above applies, the court may comment upon the failure in question (s. 11(5)). Other parties (the prosecution and co-accused) may also comment upon any defect in disclosure, but in certain circumstances such comment requires the leave of the court. Those circumstances are where the defect that triggers the sanction is a failure to mention a point of law (including failure to mention a point about admissibility of evidence or abuse of process) or authority to be relied on, failure to give notice of or adequately identify a witness, or failure to give such notice in time (s. 11(6) and (7)). **D9.43**

If any of the above deficiencies applies, the court or jury may also draw such inferences as appear proper in deciding whether the accused is guilty of the offence concerned (s. 11(5)(b)). The accused may not, however, be convicted solely on the basis of such an inference (s. 11(10)). It seems that the wording of s. 11(5)(b) would preclude the use of an inference from defective disclosure to bolster the prosecution case against a submission of no case to answer, since the phrase 'whether the accused is guilty of the offence concerned' is not apt to describe the decision which the court has to make on such a submission. The context in which such an inference can be drawn is therefore narrower than that applicable to inferences from silence under the

CJPO 1994, s. 34 (see **F20.4**), which explicitly allows an inference to be drawn when the court determines whether there is a case to answer, reserving the wording replicated in s. 11(5)(b) of the 1996 Act to apply to the verdict.

If there is a failure of defence disclosure by breaching any of the requirements of the CPIA 1996, the only sanctions available to the court are those contained in s. 11. Therefore, the court cannot punish by way of contempt of court a failure to comply with its direction to amend (or provide) the defence statement (*Rochford* [2010] EWCA Crim 1928, [2011] 1 WLR 534); it cannot rule as inadmissible the evidence of alibi witnesses on the basis that no defence statement had been served providing details of them (*R (Tinnion) v Reading Crown Court* [2009] EWHC 2930 (Admin), [2010] RTR 24 (263)); and it cannot decline to allow the accused to put forward matters in cross-examination which go to a relevant issue because the material on which such cross-examination is based is produced at a very late stage with no advance notice (*T* [2012] EWCA Crim 2358). The appropriate sanction in all these instances is adverse comment and for the court or jury to be able to draw such inferences as may be proper. Where a failure to provide a defence statement results in additional expense for the prosecution, a wasted costs order may be appropriate (*SVS Solicitors* [2012] EWCA Crim 319).

D9.44 Section 6E(2) of the CPIA 1996 provides that where it appears to the judge at a pre-trial hearing (see **D15.39** ***et seq.***) that the accused has failed to serve a defence statement, or to update it when required to do so, or to serve notice of intention to call defence witnesses, so that there may be comment made or inferences drawn under s. 11(5), the judge must warn the accused of that possibility. Curiously, this provision is fully in force even though the provision relating to updated statements (s. 6B) is not yet in force.

In *Essa* [2009] EWCA Crim 43, the Court of Appeal rejected the argument that the CPIA 1996, s. 11(5), is incompatible with the right to a fair trial under the ECHR, Article 6. The Court said that the use of s. 11(5) is subject to judicial control. In particular the judge can interfere and stop the cross-examination if it is unfair, and, if unfair cross-examination has been embarked upon, it is open to the judge to tell the jury to disregard it. In those circumstances, s. 11(5) is compatible with the Convention.

D9.45 **Circumstances in which Comment may be Made** Section 11 makes further provision about the making of comments and drawing of inferences in two sets of circumstances:

(a) where the defect in question is that the accused put forward a defence different from that set out in the defence statement, the court must have regard to the extent of any difference, and whether there is any justification for it (s. 11(8));
(b) where the defect concerns failure to give notice of, or identify adequately, a defence witness, the court must have regard to whether there is any justification for the failure (s. 11(9));

In cases where there is apparent inconsistency between the defence statement and the case run by the defence at trial, the judge needs to decide whether the jury should be permitted to draw an inference from the inconsistency, in accordance with the CPIA 1996, s. 11(5)(b). In *Wheeler* (2000) 164 JP 565, D was charged with knowingly importing cocaine from Jamaica. He had been arrested at Gatwick when drugs were found in his possession. In interview and later in evidence at his trial, he gave an explanation concerning his possession of the drugs which was inconsistent with his defence statement. In cross-examination, he said that the statement was a mistake. The trial judge gave no specific direction to the jury about the inconsistency. On appeal, it was D's case, and was accepted by his solicitors, that the defence statement did not reflect his instructions, and had not been approved by him. The appeal was allowed on the basis that the judge ought to have given the jury a specific direction on how to approach that inconsistency, given the fact that D's credibility had been crucial to his case. The Court of Appeal said that it would have been wise for the judge to have accepted that the fault lay with the solicitors, given that the conduct of the defence at trial was in accordance with the version of events that he gave in interview. There will inevitably be a proportion of cases in which defence disclosure is defective, whether due to errors by defence lawyers, a failure by the accused to be organised enough to attend to give instructions, or a lack of focus on the importance of the issues involved. It is right to stress the need for caution in such circumstances.

There is a presumption that a defence statement is issued with the authority of the accused, subject to proof to the contrary (s. 6E(1): see **D9.32**). It is submitted, however, that the reasoning of the Court of Appeal in *Wheeler* is still a helpful guideline. In *Wheeler* it was also suggested that defence statements should be signed, to acknowledge their accuracy and avoid disputes. A related issue arose in *R (Sullivan) v Crown Court at Maidstone* [2002] EWHC 967 (Admin), [2002] 4 All ER 427, in which the High Court found that a local practice direction by the resident judge that all defence statements were to be signed by the accused was unlawful, on the ground that there was no power to make it. **D9.46**

Where the judge decides to allow the jury to draw an inference in a case where there is apparent inconsistency between the defence statement and the case run by the defence at trial, it is usually unhelpful for the judge to give at the same time a direction as to lies in accordance with *Lucas* [1981] QB 720; but if the factual context of the case is that the accused is entitled to the protection of a *Lucas* direction then that protection should be incorporated in the judge's direction to the jury concerning the inference (see *Hackett* [2011] EWCA Crim 380, [2011] 2 Cr App R 3 (35), the principles of which appear to apply to situations in which comment is permissible under the CPIA 1996, s. 11, discussed more fully at **F20.26**).

Criminal Procedure and Investigations Act 1996, s. 11 **D9.47**

(1) This section applies in the three cases set out in subsections (2), (3) and (4).
(2) The first case is where section 5 applies and the accused—
  (a) fails to give an initial defence statement,
  (b) gives an initial defence statement but does so after the end of the period which, by virtue of section 12, is the relevant period for section 5,
  (c) is required by section 6B to give either an updated defence statement or a statement of the kind mentioned in subsection (4) of that section but fails to do so,
  (d) gives an updated defence statement or a statement of the kind mentioned in section 6B(4) but does so after the end of the period which, by virtue of section 12, is the relevant period for section 6B,
  (e) sets out inconsistent defences in his defence statement, or
  (f) at his trial—
    (i) puts forward a defence which was not mentioned in his defence statement or is different from any defence set out in that statement,
    (ii) relies on a matter (or any particular of any matter of fact) which, in breach of the requirements imposed by or under section 6A, was not mentioned in his defence statement [words in brackets added by CJIA 2008, s. 60(2): for commencement date, see **D9.4**],
    (iii) adduces evidence in support of an alibi without having given particulars of the alibi in his defence statement, or
    (iv) calls a witness to give evidence in support of an alibi without having complied with section 6A(2)(a) or (b) as regards the witness in his defence statement.
(3) The second case is where section 6 applies, the accused gives an initial defence statement, and the accused—
  (a) gives the initial defence statement after the end of the period which, by virtue of section 12, is the relevant period for section 6, or
  (b) does any of the things mentioned in paras. (c) to (f) of subsection (2).
(4) The third case is where the accused—
  (a) gives a witness notice but does so after the end of the period which, by virtue of section 12, is the relevant period for section 6C, or
  (b) at his trial calls a witness (other than himself) not included, or not adequately identified, in a witness notice.
(5) Where this section applies—
  (a) the court or any other party may make such comment as appears appropriate;

(b) the court or jury may draw such inferences as appear proper in deciding whether the accused is guilty of the offence concerned.

(6) Where—

(a) this section applies by virtue of subsection (2)(f)(ii) (including that provision as it applies by virtue of subsection (3)(b)), and

(b) the matter which was not mentioned is a point of law (including any point as to the admissibility of evidence or an abuse of process) or an authority,

comment by another party under subsection (5)(a) may be made only with the leave of the court.

(7) Where this section applies by virtue of subsection (4), comment by another party under subsection (5)(a) may be made only with the leave of the court.

(8) Where the accused puts forward a defence which is different from any defence set out in his defence statement, in doing anything under subsection (5) or in deciding whether to do anything under it the court shall have regard —

(a) to the extent of the differences in the defences, and

(b) to whether there is any justification for it.

(9) Where the accused calls a witness whom he has failed to include, or to identify adequately, in a witness notice, in doing anything under subsection (5) or in deciding whether to do anything under it the court shall have regard to whether there is any justification for the failure.

(10) A person shall not be convicted of an offence solely on an inference drawn under sub-section (5).

(11) [not yet in force: see **D9.4**].

(12) In this section—

(a) 'initial defence statement' means a defence statement given under section 5 or 6;

(b) 'updated defence statement' means a defence statement given under section 6B;

(c) a reference simply to an accused's 'defence statement' is a reference—

(i) where he has given only an initial defence statement, to that statement;

(ii) where he has given both an initial and an updated defence statement, to the updated defence statement;

(iii) where he has given both an initial defence statement and a statement of the kind mentioned in section 6B(4), to the initial defence statement;

(d) a reference to evidence in support of an alibi shall be construed in accordance with section 6A(3);

(e) 'witness notice' means a notice given under section 6C.

ROLE OF THE COURT

D9.48 The Judicial Disclosure Protocol clearly states that the disclosure process is to be 'led by the prosecution so as to trigger comprehensive defence engagement, supported by robust judicial management' (para. 6). While recognising that failure to disclose material to the defence remains the biggest single cause of miscarriages of justice, the Protocol also states that it is essential that the trial process is not overburdened or diverted by erroneous and inappropriate disclosure or by misconceived applications. The burden of disclosure must not be allowed to render the prosecution of cases impracticable. Accordingly, the Protocol emphasises the need for all involved to understand the statutory requirements and to undertake their roles with rigour, in a timely manner (paras. 1 to 3). The overarching principle to be applied is 'that unused material will fall to be disclosed if, and only if, it satisfies the test for disclosure applicable to the proceedings in question, subject to any overriding public interest considerations' (para. 4).

The courts are to:

(a) set realistic timetables for prosecution and defence disclosure (paras. 7, 9, 10 and 16);

(b) grant extensions only in response to an appropriate explanation for the request (para. 12);

(c) not allow the prosecution to abdicate their responsibility for reviewing unused material by allowing the defence to inspect everything on the schedule of non-sensitive unused material (para. 13);

(d) examine defence case statements with care to ensure that they comply with the formalities, investigate any failures and, if appropriate, give a warning about the possibility of an adverse inference being drawn (paras. 19 to 21);

(e) cease making blanket orders for disclosure and instead reject requests which are not referable to an issue identified in the defence case statement and which satisfy the test for disclosure (para. 26);
(f) allow adequate time to deal with disclosure issues at the plea and case management hearing (paras. 28 to 29).

Particular issues affecting magistrates' courts are dealt with at paras. 30 to 37. As to the role and case management powers of the court at the stage of primary disclosure in particular, see *R* [2015] EWCA Crim 1941, [2016] 1 WLR 1872.

PUBLIC INTEREST IMMUNITY

Circumstances may arise in a case in which material held by the prosecution and tending to undermine the prosecution or assist the defence cannot be disclosed to the defence, fully or even at all, without the risk of prejudice to an important public interest. In such circumstances the courts may be justified in ordering that the material is withheld from disclosure, but they must only allow this to the minimum extent necessary to protect the public interest in question and must never imperil the overall fairness of the trial (*H* [2004] UKHL 3, [2004] 2 AC 134). Applications by the prosecution to the court to withhold material in these circumstances are known as public interest immunity applications. Although the 1996 Act generally disapplies the rules of common law in relation to the prosecution duty of disclosure (s. 21(1)), it expressly preserves 'the rules of common law as to whether disclosure is in the public interest' (s. 21(2)). The provisions of the CPIA 1996 which provide for disclosure to the accused allow relevant material to be withheld on public interest grounds only if the court so decides (ss. 3(6) and 8(5)). **D9.49**

For the circumstances in which public interest immunity may be claimed, see **F9**. This section deals with the procedure in respect of such claims.

Background

The law concerning public interest immunity (previously known as Crown privilege) developed in civil proceedings (*Duncan v Cammell Laird & Co. Ltd* [1942] AC 624; *Conway v Rimmer* [1968] AC 910). Until the mid-1990s there were few reported cases concerning public interest immunity in criminal proceedings because it was left largely to the judgment of the prosecution as to whether material should be withheld. Only exceptionally were courts called upon to make a ruling. That position changed with the case of *Ward* [1993] 2 All ER 577. D had been convicted of multiple murder and explosives offences. It later transpired, however, that the prosecution had failed to disclose material relevant to her alleged confessions and certain scientific evidence. In upholding her appeal, the Court of Appeal made it clear that the court, rather than the prosecution, had to be the final arbiter as to whether the prosecution were entitled to avoid disclosure on the basis of public interest immunity. It would be wrong to allow the prosecution to withhold material documents on public interest grounds without giving notice of that fact to the defence. The court could then, if necessary, be asked to rule on the legitimacy of the prosecution's asserted claim. If the prosecution were not prepared to have the issue of public interest immunity determined by a court, they would inevitably have to abandon the case. **D9.50**

The requirement set out in *Ward* to give notice to the defence of an application in every case seemed likely in some instances to lead to the material in question being compromised. Accordingly, some months after *Ward* was decided, the Court of Appeal laid down guidance as to the procedure to be followed in public interest immunity cases in the case of *Davis* [1993] 2 All ER 643. Lord Taylor CJ stated that: **D9.51**

(a) If the prosecution wish to rely on public interest immunity to justify non-disclosure then, in most cases, they must notify the defence that they are applying for a ruling by the court, and indicate to the defence at least the category of the material which they hold. The defence must then have the opportunity of making representations to the court.

(b) Where, however, the public interest would be injured if disclosure was made of the category of material, the prosecution should still notify the defence of the application, but need not specify the category of material. The defence would be able to address the court on the procedure to be adopted but the application itself would be *ex parte*. If the court on that application found that there should be an *inter partes* application it would so order. If not, it would rule on the *ex parte* application.

(c) In a highly exceptional case where even to reveal that an *ex parte* application was to be made would injure the public interest, the prosecution could apply to the court *ex parte* without notice. Again, if the court on hearing the application considered that notice should have been given to the defence, or even that the normal *inter partes* hearing should have been adopted, it would so order.

Lord Taylor emphasised the importance of the court keeping the situation under review.

CrimPR 15.3 (see Supplement, **R15.3**) in effect reproduces the procedure laid down in *Davis* (see **D9.58**).

Public Interest Immunity and Article 6

D9.52 The procedural fairness of public interest immunity has been examined in a number of decisions of the ECtHR.

In *Rowe and Davis v UK* (2000) 30 EHRR 1, the Court gave an important ruling concerning the approach to be adopted when public interest immunity issues arise for determination. The following points emerge from the Court's unanimous decision:

(a) The right to a fair trial means that the prosecution should disclose to the defence all material evidence in their possession for and against the accused.

(b) That duty of disclosure is not absolute, and 'in any criminal proceedings there may be competing interests, such as national security or the need to protect witnesses at risk of reprisals or keep secret police methods of investigation, which must be weighed against the rights of the accused'.

(c) Only such measures restricting the rights of the defence to disclosure as are strictly necessary are permissible under the ECHR, Article 6(1).

(d) Any difficulties caused to the defence by a limitation on their rights must be sufficiently counterbalanced by the procedure followed by the court.

(e) The task of the ECtHR is to ascertain whether the decision-making procedure applied in each case complies with the requirements of adversarial proceedings and equality of arms and incorporates adequate safeguards to protect the interest of the accused.

In *Rowe and Davis* it was necessary for the ECtHR to consider whether procedural failures at first instance could be remedied at a later stage. The judge at first instance had not considered material that had been withheld by the prosecution during the trial. On appeal the Court of Appeal had adopted an *ex parte* procedure to consider the material that had been withheld. The ECtHR found that this procedure did not remedy the unfairness of the judge at first instance in not considering the material. If he had considered the material, they found, he could have monitored the importance of the undisclosed evidence at a stage when it could have affected the course of the trial. Further, since the Court of Appeal hearing had been *ex parte*, they had been reliant upon prosecution counsel and transcripts of the trial for an understanding of the possible relevance of the undisclosed material. The ECtHR reached a similar conclusion in *Atlan v UK* (2002) 34 EHRR 33 (833), a case in which the prosecution had repeatedly denied the existence of undisclosed material and the judge had not been informed of the true position. See also *Dowsett v UK* (2004) 38 EHRR 41 (845).

D9.53 The case of *Jasper v UK* (2000) 30 EHRR 441 established that an *ex parte* procedure at first instance would not necessarily breach Article 6(1). The ECtHR held (by a majority of nine to eight) that there was no breach because, although the application for an order permitting non-disclosure had been heard on an *ex parte* basis, the defence were notified that the application had been made; the trial judge gave them as much information regarding the nature of the withheld evidence as possible without revealing what it was; and the defence were permitted to outline their case to the judge. The Court reached the same conclusion in *Fitt v UK* (2000) 30 EHRR 480, which was decided on the same day on similar grounds.

In *Botmeh* [2001] EWCA Crim 2226, [2002] 1 WLR 531, it was argued that an *ex parte* procedure could not be adopted by the Court of Appeal, but was confined to proceedings at first instance. The argument was rejected. There was nothing in the judgments *Rowe* and *Atlan* to suggest that *ex parte* examination of material by the Court of Appeal was of itself unfair.

In the light of these authorities, it appears that the procedures for handling public interest immunity applications in our domestic courts (set out at **D9.54** to **D9.65**) are compliant with Article 6 (see also para. 68 of the A-G's Guidelines which states that rigid adherence with the principles set out in *H* [2004] UKHL 3, [2004] 2 AC 134 is necessary to ensure compliance with Article 6). As for a case considering the proper approach to handling public interest immunity material and applications in the Court of Appeal, where that material was not considered or available at first instance, see *Clarke* [2017] EWCA Crim 37, [2017] 1 Cr App R 28 (421).

Approach of the Courts to Public Interest Immunity

In *H* [2004] UKHL 3, [2004] 2 AC 134, the House of Lords provided a template by which courts are to make public interest immunity decisions. Judges are to address a series of questions in sequential order: **D9.54**

(1) The court must first identify whether the material which the prosecution seeks to withhold is material that may weaken the prosecution case or strengthen that of the defence. If the material cannot be so described — because for instance it is neutral or damaging to the accused — then it should not be disclosed. If it can be so described, the golden rule is that disclosure should be made unless public interest immunity considerations prevent it.
(2) Next, in determining whether public interest immunity applies, the court is to apply the test of whether there is a real risk of serious prejudice to an important and identified public interest. If the material does not satisfy that test, it does not attract public interest immunity and must be disclosed.
(3) If the material does attract public interest immunity, the court must then consider whether the accused's interests can be protected without disclosure or whether disclosure can be ordered to an extent or in a way which will give adequate protection to the public interest in question and also afford adequate protection to the interests of the defence.
(4) In considering whether limited disclosure is possible, the court must give consideration to ordering the prosecution to make admissions, prepare summaries or extracts of evidence, or provide documents in an edited or anonymised form.
(5) If the court is minded to order limited disclosure of this kind, it must first ask whether it represents the minimum derogation necessary to protect the public interest in question. If not, then it must order more disclosure. If, however, the effect of limited disclosure may be to render the whole trial process unfair to the accused, fuller disclosure should be ordered even if this leads the prosecution to discontinue the proceedings.
(6) The issue of disclosure of the material should be reviewed as the trial unfolds, evidence is adduced and the defence advanced.

If material is capable of being disclosed in redacted or edited form or by way of summaries, it ought not to be necessary to place it before the court for a decision under (4) above. The A-G's Guidelines state that prosecutors should aim to disclose as much of the material as they properly can and should only seek a judicial ruling in truly borderline cases (para. 65). The

Judicial Disclosure Protocol also encourages redactions, e.g., by removing personal details from a statement (para. 55(c)).

Practice and Procedure of Investigators

D9.55 Material which might in due course be made the subject of a public interest immunity application must be recorded by investigators in a 'sensitive schedule'. As to the contents of the schedule, see **D9.12**. Detailed guidance as to the assessment of sensitivity and the preparation of the schedule is contained in the CPS Disclosure Manual, ch. 8. Investigators are to specify the reasons why the material is sensitive, the degree of sensitivity attaching to the material, the consequences of revealing it to the defence, the significance of the material to the issues in the trial, the involvement of third parties in bringing the material to the attention of the police, the implications for continuance of the prosecution if disclosure is ordered, and whether it is possible to disclose the material without compromising its sensitivity. In considering the material, prosecutors are to consider the possibility of prejudice to the public interest through direct harm or indirectly through incremental or cumulative harm.

Inclusion of material upon a 'sensitive' schedule is in no way conclusive of the question of whether its disclosure is in the public interest. That question is for determination by the court. The principle articulated in *Ward* [1993] 2 All ER 577 (see **D9.50**) is reflected in the terms of the 1996 Act: the court, rather than the prosecutor (let alone the investigator) is the arbiter as to whether disclosure can be avoided on the basis of public interest immunity. Further, it is clear that the categories of 'sensitive material' identified in the CPIA Code are wider than the types of material which the courts have been prepared to consider subject to public interest immunity. For example, the CPIA Code gives as an example of sensitive material, 'material given in confidence'; but the fact that material has been given in confidence is not sufficient of itself to ensure that it attracts public interest immunity so as to enable the prosecution to avoid disclosing it (see **F9.30**). Nonetheless public interest immunity applications are likely to be founded on material which is contained in the 'sensitive' schedule.

Preparation of Applications

D9.56 The procedure that the prosecutor must follow in making an application for a public interest ruling is set out in CrimPR 15.3 (see Supplement, **R15.3**). Detailed guidance is also contained in the CPS Disclosure Manual, ch. 13. The rules specify that applications must be in writing and must explain why it would not be in the public interest to disclose the material (r. 15.3(2)). The guidance emphasises that applications to the court will be rare and should be considered only if the other options of disclosing the material in a way that does not compromise the public interest in issue; or abandoning the case; or disclosing the material because it is in the overall public interest to do so, have been discounted or there is no agreement between the prosecutor, investigators or agencies, or the court's assistance is required to assess whether material should be disclosed. CrimPR 15.3(3)(a)(iii) reflects this point by requiring that the prosecutor must specify why no measure such as an admission of fact, or disclosure by summary, extract or edited copy would protect both the public interest and the defendant's right to a fair trial. Chapter 13 of the CPS Disclosure Manual contains practical details about arranging the application and making the accompanying written submission. The Judicial Disclosure Protocol also deals with the written submission. It discourages formulaic expressions and encourages the use of schedules in complex cases which set out the specific objection in relation to each item and leave a space for the decision (para. 55(d)).

CrimPR 15.3(2) makes provision for service of notices on the accused and interested parties where appropriate.

In *Menga* [1998] Crim LR 58, the Court of Appeal emphasised that prosecution counsel should ensure, so far as possible, sight of all material in respect of which public interest immunity is to be claimed before the trial commences so that the applications can be made at the most convenient time. For a case involving the accidental disclosure of material subject to public interest immunity in the context of an application for a warrant, see *R (Hafeez) v Southwark Crown Court* [2018] EWHC 954 (Admin).

Categories of Hearing

CrimPR 15.3(2)(b)(iii) and (4) (see Supplement, **R15.3**) in effect reproduces the procedure laid down in *Davis* [1993] 2 All ER 643 (see **D9.51**). In Type 1 applications, a notice of application is served on the accused by the prosecutor. Type 2 applications arise where the prosecutor has reason to believe that to reveal to the accused the nature of the material to which the application relates would have the effect of disclosing that which the prosecutor contends should not in the public interest be disclosed. In such cases, the prosecutor is not to serve a notice but instead must notify the accused that a Type 2 application has been made. Type 3 applications arise where the prosecutor has reason to believe that to reveal to the accused the fact of an application being made would have the effect of disclosing that which the prosecutor contends should not in the public interest be disclosed. In such cases, no notice is required. **D9.57**

The Judicial Disclosure Protocol stipulates that in Type 1 and 2 applications proper notice to the defence is necessary to allow them to make focused submissions to the court. The notice should be as specific as possible, though it is accepted that in some cases only the generic nature of the material can properly be identified (para. 55(b)). To this end, CrimPR 15.3(4) provides that, where the prosecutor serves only part of the application on the defendant, the prosecutor must mark the other part to show that it is only for the court; and in that other part must explain why it has been withheld from the defendant. The judge should always ask the prosecution to justify the form of notice given or the decision not to give a notice (Judicial Disclosure Protocol, para. 55(b)). If the judge takes the view that the defence should have had notice of the application, or of the nature of the material, or that the application should be made *inter partes*, then it is plain that the judge should direct accordingly, as Lord Taylor CJ observed in *Davis* (see **D9.51**).

In *Smith* [1998] 2 Cr App R 1, the Court of Appeal stressed that no *ex parte* application should be made in circumstances where there was nothing to be said which could not be said in the presence of defence counsel.

As to when a departure from open justice may be justified for *ex parte* hearings concerning material which does not meet the disclosure test, but nonetheless raises issues of public interest immunity, see *Ali* [2019] EWCA Crim 1527, [2020] 1 Cr App R 1 (1) at [50]. See also *Connor* [2019] EWCA Crim 96 for a case in which the submission that the prosecution had misused the *ex parte* procedure to address the judge on matters which did not relate to disclosure, in breach of the principle of open justice, was held to be totally without merit. Sensitive material had been placed before the judge to enable the judge to exercise case management powers in a manner which was intended to, and did ensure that the defendants had a fair trial.

Procedure in Court

Hearings are to take place in private unless the court otherwise directs and may take place, wholly or in part, in the defendant's absence (CrimPR 15.3(6): see Supplement, **R15.3**). Where the defendant is present, the court is to hear the prosecutor and any interested party first, then the defendant, in the presence of them all, and then once more the prosecutor and any interested party, but this time in the defendant's absence, unless it directs that other arrangements are to take place (r. 15.3(7)). The court is to determine the application only if satisfied that it has been able to take adequate account of such rights of confidentiality as apply to the material, and the defendant's right to a fair trial (r. 15.3(8)). **D9.58**

In *Jackson* [2000] Crim LR 377, the Court of Appeal stressed that it is imperative that in all cases the Crown is scrupulously accurate in the information provided in *ex parte* public interest immunity hearings. The judge must personally examine or view the evidence, so as to have the facts of what it contained in mind. Only then can the judge be in a position to balance the competing interests of public interest immunity and fairness to the party claiming disclosure (see also, on that point, *K (TD)* (1993) 97 Cr App R 342). In *Law* (1996) *The Times*, 15 August 1996, the Court of Appeal held that, in deciding whether to order the prosecution to disclose information, the judge was not restricted to considering only evidence admissible in a court of law. The judge was entitled to see additional material, even if it amounted to hearsay evidence.

In *Templar* [2003] EWCA Crim 3186, Latham LJ warned against frequent meetings between the judge and prosecuting counsel in chambers in order to consider public interest immunity issues, where D and his lawyers were absent. In the instant case there were some 36 such meetings in a period of five months. Although there was in fact no impropriety, he warned of the danger that prosecuting counsel and judge might come to use the procedure as a 'mutual support mechanism', with the result that repeated visits to chambers might blur their appreciation of the respective tasks which they faced.

In *G* [2004] EWCA Crim 1368, [2004] 1 WLR 2932, highly sensitive evidence was disclosed accidentally to the defence counsel and solicitor. The trial judge ordered them not to pass the information in question to anyone else, including their clients. It was held in the course of an interlocutory appeal that this order must be quashed as it would undermine the lawyer-client relationship.

D9.59 Public interest immunity applications must be recorded. The judge should give some short statement of reasons; this is often best done document by document as the hearing proceeds (Judicial Disclosure Protocol, para. 55(e)).

As to the procedure where the Court of Appeal reviews the conduct by the trial judge of a public interest immunity hearing, see **D27.32** and *McDonald* [2004] EWCA Crim 2614. See also *Clarke* [2017] EWCA Crim 37, [2017] 1 Cr App R 28 (421).

Use of Special Advocates and Confidentiality Rings

D9.60 In *Rowe and Davis* (2000) 30 EHRR 1 (see **D9.52**), it was argued on behalf of the applicants that the exclusion of the defence from the *ex parte* procedure conducted by the Court of Appeal should have been counterbalanced by the introduction of a special independent counsel who could argue the relevance of the undisclosed evidence, test the strength of the prosecution claim to public interest immunity, and safeguard against the risk of judicial error or bias. The court found a violation of the ECHR, Article 6, without the need to address this question but the issue arose again in *Edwards v UK* (2003) 15 BHRC 189. In that case, the tribunal of fact was the trial judge, who had to decide whether to exclude evidence because the accused had been entrapped. Material was produced to the trial judge in *ex parte* hearings. The defence was not aware of the material. The ECtHR found that the defence should have been given the opportunity to counter the evidence and show the judge that it was mistaken or unreliable. A procedure which denied the defence that opportunity on an issue which was so fundamental to a fair trial failed to comply 'with the requirements to provide adversarial proceedings and equality of arms' or to incorporate 'adequate safeguards to protect the interests of the accused'. During the course of the judgment, the role of special counsel was again canvassed, and mentioned with some approval by the court. Accordingly, in *H* [2004] UKHL 3, [2004] 2 AC 134, the House of Lords were invited to state that special counsel should be appointed wherever material which the prosecution seek to withhold is, or may be, relevant to a disputed issue of fact which the judge has to decide in order to rule on an application which will effectively determine the outcome of the proceedings. In particular, it was argued that such an appointment should be made whenever the defence rely on entrapment as a basis for staying the case as an abuse of process or excluding prosecution evidence. The House of Lords declined to hold that special counsel should always be appointed in such circumstances, saying that this would place the trial judge in a straitjacket. Lord Bingham did make it clear, however, that the appointment of special counsel may be a necessary step in appropriate cases to ensure that the contentions of the prosecution are tested and the interests of the accused protected. As to *H*, see further **D9.54**.

In *Chisholm* [2010] EWCA Crim 258 the Court of Appeal made some tentative observations about the use of special counsel in an appeal against conviction. The view was expressed that, in many cases, if the judge reads the closed material that will obviate the need for special counsel, but that it may be necessary in cases: (a) where the court wishes to ensure that it has all the material which it ought to have; (b) where special counsel would wish to present any argument on the basis of the material not known to the applicant; or (c) the court feels that questions arise which require special counsel in the interests of justice. (See also *McDonald* [2004] EWCA Crim 2614 and *Ebcin* [2005] EWCA Crim 2006.) As to the use of special counsel in relation to legal argument concerning a possible abuse of process, see *Austin* [2013] EWCA Crim 1028, [2014] 1 WLR 1045. For a recent case declining the use of special counsel see *Knaggs* [2018] EWCA Crim 1863.

An alternative means of ensuring that the interests of the defendant are protected in cases where material cannot be disclosed might be found in *R (Mohammed) v Secretary of State for Defence* [2012] EWHC 3454 (Admin), [2013] 2 All ER 897, a claim for judicial review. Moses LJ (sitting alone) held that there is no principle which prohibits a court considering whether to uphold or reject a claim for public interest immunity from ordering that, whilst the claim should not be upheld, nonetheless the documents or material should only be disclosed to those identified within a confidentiality ring on terms to be specified in an undertaking agreed by the parties. However, such an approach has since been doubted (by Ouseley LJ) in the context of judicial review (*AHK v Secretary of State for the Home Department* [2013] EWHC 1426 (Admin)).

Interventions of Third Parties

Section 16 of the CPIA 1996 provides for interventions by interested third parties when the court is considering the issue of public interest immunity. An example of such a third party intervention may be found in *R (B) v Crown Court at Stafford* [2006] EWHC 1645 (Admin), [2007] 1 WLR 1524, in which the issue was the disclosure to the defence of V's medical records. D had sought the records by way of service of a witness summons on the relevant health care authority, following which the Crown Court ordered that a full set of the records be produced by the authority at a public interest immunity hearing. The Divisional Court found that the Crown Court had acted unlawfully and that V had been entitled to service of the application and representation at the public interest immunity hearing, consistent with her ECHR, Article 8, rights. **D9.61**

Criminal Procedure and Investigations Act 1996, s. 16

Where—

(a) an application is made under section 3(6), 7A(8), 8(5), 14(2) or 15(4),
(b) a person claiming to have an interest in the material applies to be heard by the court, and
(c) he shows that he was involved (whether alone or with others and whether directly or indirectly) in the prosecutor's attention being brought to the material,

the court must not make an order under section 3(6), 7A(8), 8(5), 14(3) or 15(5) (as the case may be) unless the person applying under paragraph (b) has been given an opportunity to be heard.

The nature of the duty of prosecutors towards informants was considered in *R (WV) v CPS* [2011] EWHC 2480 (Admin). The Divisional Court quashed a decision of the CPS to disclose the identity of an informant (WV) to the defence without having put the issue before a judge to consider. The facts of the case involved a real and substantial risk that WV might be killed if his identity was revealed. The Court said it was of the highest importance to public confidence in the administration of justice that a decision to break an express or implied undertaking of confidence as to the identity of an informant or other provider of information, without informed consent from that individual, is made by a judge.

Categories of Public Interest Material

D9.62 For examples of circumstances in which the prosecution can successfully claim immunity from disclosure, see **F9.10** *et seq*., especially **F9.14**.

Review of Public Interest Immunity Decisions

D9.63 Once a court has made a decision to exclude material from consideration on public interest immunity grounds, the approach that is taken with regard to reviewing the decision differs as between cases tried summarily and cases tried on indictment under the CPIA 1996, ss. 14 and 15. In summary trials, under s. 14, it is necessary for the accused to apply for the decision to be reviewed, whereas in cases tried on indictment (s. 15) the court is under a duty to keep under review the question whether it is still not in the public interest to disclose the affected material. For an example of a case in the Crown Court where a judge ought to have reversed his original decision, see *Giles* [2011] EWCA Crim 2259. In that case the prosecution alleged that D1 and D2 were jointly engaged through companies in a missing trader fraud. The judge had made three public interest immunity rulings: two at a very early stage of the trial and one after the evidence-in-chief of D1. D2's defence was that he did not know the companies were engaged in fraud. The information that was withheld related to a separate investigation into D1 alone of money laundering involving another company of which D2 was company secretary. There was no suggestion that D2 was involved in wrongdoing in that other matter. The Court of Appeal, allowing D2's appeal, held that whilst the early rulings by the judge could not be criticised, the effect of maintaining them, especially after the conclusion of D1's evidence-in-chief, was to deny D2's counsel the possibility of putting allegations to D1 in cross-examination, and making a good deal of them in his closing speech. D2's case was by no means hopeless and a jury might have reached a different verdict.

D9.64 The difference in approach between cases tried summarily and those tried on indictment under the legislation originates from the dual role of the magistrates as triers of both fact and law; a matter which was considered in *South Worcester Justices, ex parte Lilley* [1995] 4 All ER 186. Shortly put, the issue is that when the magistrates in their role as triers of law conduct a review of documents for which immunity is claimed, it may appear to prejudice them in their role as triers of fact. The problem is compounded when the review is conducted *ex parte*, in the absence of the accused and the defence lawyer. As a result, a new bench may be needed to try the case after the original bench rules against disclosure. If that new bench were under a duty of continuous review, it would mean that it would be impossible ever to recruit a bench which was immune from the contamination which results from looking at the relevant material. Hence the onus is put on the accused to make the application (see also *Stipendiary Magistrate for Norfolk, ex parte Taylor* (1997) 161 JP 773; *R (DPP) v Acton Youth Court* [2001] EWHC Admin 402, [2001] 1 WLR 1828; *R (Ratra) v DPP* [2004] EWHC 87 (Admin)). The procedure for conducting a review is set out in CrimPR 15.6 (see Supplement, **R15.6**), and is similar to the procedure used in the initial application (see **D9.57**).

D9.65 **Criminal Procedure and Investigations Act 1996, ss. 14 and 15**

14.—(1) This section applies where [Part I] applies by virtue of section 1(1).

(2) At any time—
(a) after a court makes an order under section 3(6), 7A(8) or 8(5), and
(b) before the accused is acquitted or convicted or the prosecutor decides not to proceed with the case concerned,
the accused may apply to the court for a review of the question whether it is still not in the public interest to disclose material affected by its order.

(3) In such a case the court must review that question, and if it concludes that it is in the public interest to disclose material to any extent—
(a) it shall so order, and
(b) it shall take such steps as are reasonable to inform the prosecutor of its order.

(4) Where the prosecutor is informed of an order made under subsection (3) he must act accordingly having regard to the provisions of [Part I] (unless he decides not to proceed with the case concerned).

15.—(1) This section applies where [Part I] applies by virtue of section 1(2).

(2) This section applies at all times—

(a) after a court makes an order under section 3(6), 7A(8) or 8(5), and

(b) before the accused is acquitted or convicted or the prosecutor decides not to proceed with the case concerned.

(3) The court must keep under review the question whether at any given time it is still not in the public interest to disclose material affected by its order.

(4) The court must keep the question mentioned in subsection (3) under review without the need for an application; but the accused may apply to the court for a review of that question.

(5) If the court at any time concludes that it is in the public interest to disclose material to any extent—

(a) it shall so order, and

(b) it shall take such steps as are reasonable to inform the prosecutor of its order.

(6) Where the prosecutor is informed of an order made under subsection (5) he must act accordingly having regard to the provisions of [Part I] (unless he decides not to proceed with the case concerned).

Intercept Material

Section 56 of the IPA 2016 prevents the fact of interception of a subject's communications and the product of that interception being relied upon or referred to by any party to criminal proceedings. It is given further effect by ss. 3(7) and 7A(9) of the CPIA 1996 (repealed by the CJA 2003, sch. 37, part 3, para. 1). Schedule 3 to the IPA 2016 provides for the exceptions to the prohibition, including at para. 21, in order to allow disclosure to a prosecutor to enable that person to determine what is required in order to ensure that the prosecution is fair. This duty may require the prosecutor to make admissions of fact, discontinue part of the case, not rely on certain evidence, or put the case in a different way. It may also require disclosure to the judge so that the judge may sum up the case in a particular way, give appropriate directions to the jury or require admissions of fact from the prosecution. The A-G's Section 18 RIPA Prosecutors Intercept Guidelines (see **appendix 2**) give detailed guidance on the approach to be taken by prosecutors. At the time of publication this has not been updated to reflect the IPA 2016; however, given the similarities between the two legislative regimes it is submitted that the earlier guidelines and authorities remain relevant. **D9.66**

In *Khyam* [2008] EWCA Crim 1612, [2009] 1 Cr App R (S) 77 (455) the Court of Appeal considered the interrelation of ss. 17 and 18 of the RIPA 2000 (the predecessor provisions to the IPA 2016, s. 56). The Court found that the circumstances which might lead to a departure from the prohibition in s. 17 must be highly unusual and material. It is clear from *Austin* [2013] EWCA Crim 1028, [2014] 1 WLR 1045 that s. 17 does not prevent the prosecution relying on intercepts and recordings made in a country outside the UK and in accordance with the laws of the other country concerned.

Since the prohibition affects both prosecution and defence, arguments concerning the right in the ECHR, Article 6(1), to equality of arms are not likely to be available. The position is different, however, with regard to non-disclosure of evidence. In *Khyam*, it was noted that the regulation of intercept material falls outside the normal disclosure process in criminal trials. Nonetheless, the ECHR is applicable. In *Natunen v Finland* (2009) 49 EHRR 32 (810), telephone intercept material had been destroyed by the investigating authorities in compliance with domestic law with the consequence that D was deprived of material which could have justified his defence. The ECtHR held that Article 6(3)(b) guaranteed D 'adequate time and facilities for the preparation of his defence' and therefore implied that the substantive defence activity on his behalf may comprise everything which was 'necessary' to prepare the main trial. Failure to disclose material evidence to the defence, where that material contained particulars which could enable D to exonerate himself or have his sentence reduced, would constitute a refusal of facilities necessary for the preparation of the defence. Whilst D had been able to put **D9.67** questions during the trial concerning all his conversations with the other parties, his argument had been rejected for lack of supporting evidence. The significance of the destroyed records was therefore plain.

EXPERT EVIDENCE

Experts and Content of Report

D9.68 CrimPR Part 19 (see Supplement, **R19.1** *et seq.*) consolidates the rules on expert evidence. An expert has a duty to help the court to achieve the overriding objective by giving opinion which is objective and unbiased and within the expert's area or areas of expertise (CrimPR 19.2(1)). This duty overrides any obligation to the client or person paying for the expert's services (r. 19.2(2)). For consideration of the importance of a prosecutor ensuring an expert is properly qualified and prepared see *Pabon* [2018] EWCA Crim 420. Part 19 goes on to provide explicit rules about the form in which expert evidence should be introduced, including such information as the court may need to decide whether the expert's opinion is reliable, about service of the evidence, and about the use of the court's case management powers to define what is in dispute between the experts. A failure to make timely disclosure of an expert's report entitles the judge to refuse to allow the report to go to the jury (*Ensor* [2009] EWCA Crim 2519, [2010] 1 Cr App R 18 (255)). In *Asiedu* [2015] EWCA Crim 714, [2015] 2 Cr App R 8 (95) an appeal against conviction was dismissed where some addendums to an expert report were not disclosed, on the basis that the expert evidence had not influenced D's guilty plea.

D9.69 There is no obligation on the defence, either at common law or under the CPIA 1996, to reveal material which is not to be used at trial. (However, s. 6D, inserted by the CJA 2003, s. 35, but not yet brought into force, might seem to run counter to this principle.)

THIRD-PARTY PROVISION OF INFORMATION

D9.70 Sometimes the information which the accused needs for the defence will be in the hands of someone other than the prosecution — a 'third party' as far as the criminal case is concerned. In such cases, there may nonetheless be an obligation on the investigator to obtain the information. Alternatively, the third party may give up the information, voluntarily or under compulsion.

Obligations of Prosecutors

D9.71 Paragraph 3.5 of the CPIA Code of Practice requires investigators to pursue all reasonable lines of inquiry, whether these point towards or away from the suspect. The obligation to make disclosure under the CPIA 1996 and the A-G's Guidelines cannot be avoided by declining to make an inquiry which might produce disclosable material (see *Joof* [2012] EWCA Crim 1475 and **D9.9**); but see also *Boardman* [2015] EWCA Crim 175, [2015] 1 Cr App R 33 (504) at [28] for a statement to the effect that prosecutors are not required to investigate matters or obtain evidence which may help the defence, though no reference was made in *Boardman* to para. 3.5 of the CPIA Code or to *Joof*. For a case considering the obligation on the SFO to obtain material from a company which is the subject of a deferred prosecution agreement, where the information is requested by an individual defendant, see *R (AL) v SFO* [2018] EWHC 856 (Admin), [2018] 2 Cr App R 13 (170). Where such investigation reveals the existence of material held by a third party which may be relevant to the investigation but such material is not obtained, the third party must be informed of the investigation and invited to retain the material in case a request for disclosure is made. While speculative inquiries of third parties are not required, and there must be some reason to believe that they hold relevant material (CPIA Code, para. 3.6), the test of what are reasonable investigative steps in the circumstances is likely to start from the position of a persistent prosecutor who does not readily take 'no' for an answer (see *R (AL)*). The margin of discretion attributable to a prosecutor in pursing third party disclosure is confined by considerations of fairness at common law and under the ECHR, Article 6 (*R (AL)*). In *DPP v Wood* [2006] EWHC 32 (Admin), the Administrative Court stated that a simple failure on the part of the prosecution to identify and obtain third-party material would not justify a stay of proceedings. A stay could be justified only if the material had significance in relation to a real issue which was damaging to the prosecution or helpful to the defence and the prosecutor had failed to act in accordance with the permissible limits of the A-G's Guidelines (as to which, see **D9.72**). The Court also stated that there were circumstances where a third party's refusal to co-operate would require proceedings to be stayed even in the absence of any prosecutorial misconduct.

In relation to the obtaining of relevant material from outside the EU, the Court of Appeal in *Flook* [2009] EWCA Crim 682, [2010] 1 Cr App R 30 (434) noted that the power of the courts to obtain third party material is limited. It stated that there cannot be an absolute obligation on the Crown to disclose such material since it does not hold the material; the obligation is to take reasonable steps to obtain it. This reasoning is adopted in the Judicial Disclosure Protocol at paras. 51 to 53, and reiterated in the A-G's Guidelines at paras. 59 to 64.

The obligation on a prosecutor to seek the disclosure from third parties of material which if in the prosecutor's hands would be disclosable was explored at first instance in *George* (December 2009 unreported). In that case the Office of Fair Trading had entered into a leniency agreement with employees of Virgin Atlantic Airways whereby, in exchange for immunity from prosecution, they were to co-operate fully with its investigation, to the extent if necessary of waiving any claim to legal professional privilege. On an application by the accused under the CPIA 1996, s. 8, for disclosure by the OFT of material over which legal professional privilege was claimed, Owen J, having become satisfied that the material was highly relevant, held that the OFT ought reasonably to press for disclosure of the material, notwithstanding the claim to privilege, on the basis that, failing a satisfactory response, it might revoke the immunity. For deferred prosecution agreements, see **D12.106**.

Voluntary Production of Information

There are a number of instances where special procedures have evolved which will result in voluntary production of material. These procedures are increasingly of interest in the context of private prosecutions. **D9.72**

(a) *Material held by government departments and other Crown bodies.* The A-G's Guidelines, paras. 53 to 55, establish a procedure by which such material may be disclosed. The prosecution team are not to be regarded as being in constructive possession of such material but they must take reasonable steps to identify such material, including notifying the body of the nature of the prosecution case and of relevant issues. In turn government departments and other Crown bodies have a public law duty to co-operate with a criminal investigation, as well as duties of candour. Statutory prohibitions on disclosure of material usually allow an exception for disclosure for the purposes of criminal proceedings, but questions of legal professional privilege or public interest immunity may nevertheless arise which may affect the willingness of Crown bodies to disclose information in their possession.

(b) *Material held by other agencies.* The A-G's Guidelines, para. 56, provides that the prosecution should take steps to obtain material or information in the possession of a third party (e.g., a local authority, social services department, hospital, doctor or school) if it might reasonably be considered capable of undermining the prosecution case or assisting the defence (i.e. to fulfil the test for primary or secondary disclosure). Paragraph 57 deals with the situation where the police or prosecutors meet with a refusal by the third party to supply such material or information. Such refusal might be made, for instance, if the third party considers that it owes a duty of confidentiality to a person in respect of whom the material relates, or that person's Article 8 right to privacy is engaged, and this overrides its duty to co-operate with the criminal investigation. If, despite the reasons put forward for refusal by the third party, it still appears reasonable to seek its production, and the provisions of the relevant statutes are satisfied, the prosecutor or investigator should apply for a witness summons requiring the third party to produce the material to the court. But there should be consultation with the agency before disclosure is made since there may be public interest reasons justifying withholding disclosure.

(c) *Others.* Third parties which are not public authorities have no obligation at common law to co-operate with an investigation. They may also owe duties of confidentiality arising out of a professional relationship such as a banking relationship. In such circumstances the third party may feel obliged to insist that he produces material in response to an order of the court (see **D9.73**). For an example of voluntary disclosure of credit information, however, see *Bhatti* [2015] EWCA Crim 1305, [2016] 1 Cr App R 1 (1).

Compulsory Production Route

D9.73 At an early stage, investigators have powers, under the PACE 1984, s. 8 and sch. 1, to compel third parties to produce material for the purposes of a criminal investigation (see **D1.147** to **D1.170**). Once a person is charged, and a third party is not prepared to hand over relevant material, the course of action available to the prosecution or the accused is to seek a witness summons. The procedure is laid down by the Criminal Procedure (Attendance of Witnesses) Act 1965, s. 2(1) (for the text, see **D15.94**), as far as Crown Court trial is concerned. In magistrates' courts, it is governed by the MCA 1980, s. 97 (see **D21.32**). The procedure involves issuing a witness summons to compel the third party to attend with the document(s) to give evidence, and/or to produce the document(s) in advance. The person seeking the witness summons must satisfy the court that:

(a) the third party is likely to be able to give, or produce, evidence which is likely to be material in the proceedings; and
(b) it is in the interests of justice to issue a summons to secure the attendance of that person to give evidence or to produce the document or thing.

D9.74 Under amendments introduced by the CPIA 1996, s. 66, there is a procedure for advance production whereby a summons which is issued under s. 2 may require the directed person to produce any document or thing at a place stated in the summons and at a time stated for inspection by the person applying for the summons. If on inspection the applicant for the summons concludes that the document or thing is not required, the applicant can apply to the court for a direction that the summons is of no further effect (see the Criminal Procedure (Attendance of Witnesses) Act 1965, ss. 2A and 2B).

Under CrimPR Part 17 (see Supplement, **R17.1** *et seq.*) an application must be made by a party 'as soon as practicable after becoming aware of the grounds for doing so' (r. 17.3(1)). It may be made orally or in writing unless a document is required to be produced or confidential information is to be given in which case the application must be in writing and served on the proposed witness and, if the court so directs, a person to whom the evidence relates and another party (r. 17.5(3)). The application must identify the proposed witness and explain what evidence the witness can give or produce, why it is likely to be material, and why it would be in the interests of justice to issue a summons, warrant or order (r. 17.3(2)). At the hearing (or, if it is issued without notice, subsequently), the third party will have an opportunity to make representations including, for example, as to the evidence said to be held, its materiality, or any other considerations (including rights of confidentiality) as to the existence of the summons or its contents. For the availability of costs in relation to answering a witness summons see the Guide to Allowances under Part V of the Costs in Criminal Cases (General) Regulations 1986.

In relation to banking material, either the prosecution or the defence may apply to magistrates or to the Crown Court for an order to inspect or take copies. See the Bankers' Books Evidence Act 1879 at **F8.35**.

In *Brushett* [2001] Crim LR 471, the Court of Appeal considered a case where disclosure of reports held by social services departments was sought by the accused in a case of alleged sexual abuse of children. Their lordships characterised the principles governing disclosure by third parties as 'narrower' than those where the prosecution held such material. They indicated that disclosure should nevertheless be granted, for example, where there had been false accusations by the subject of the report in the past, or where there had been sexual activity with another adult. **D9.75**

In *Alibhai* [2004] EWCA Crim 681, Longmore LJ pointed out various unsatisfactory features of the procedure for disclosure of material held by third parties as follows:

(a) It is not possible to issue a witness summons to a person outside the jurisdiction.
(b) A witness summons to produce a 'document or thing' will not elicit information.
(c) The 'document or thing' must itself be likely to be material evidence, and a witness summons will not be issued for documents which will not themselves constitute evidence in the case but merely give rise to a line of inquiry which might result in evidence being obtained, still less for documents merely capable of use in cross-examination as to credit.
(d) There is no provision for the prosecution or defence, unless they so agree, to examine the documents before they are produced to the court as a result of the witness summons.

The Judicial Disclosure Protocol (see **appendix** 4) gives guidance as to the approach of the courts to requests for third-party material (paras. 44 to 50). It states that speculative inquiries without any proper basis in relation to third-party material (whether by the prosecution or the defence) must be discouraged, and that, in appropriate cases, the court will consider making an order for wasted costs where the application is clearly unmeritorious and misconceived. **D9.76**

The possibility that the civil courts may be used as a means to compel the disclosure of information for use in criminal proceedings arises as a result of the decision of the Divisional Court in *R (Mohamed) v Secretary of State for Foreign and Commonwealth Affairs (No. 1)* [2008] EWHC 2048 (Admin), [2009] 1 WLR 2579. In that case, the Court made a *Norwich Pharmacal* order requiring disclosure by the Foreign Secretary of material which it considered was essential to a fair trial in criminal proceedings in the USA for terrorist offences. The case raises the interesting possibility that applications may be made for *Norwich Pharmacal* orders in future in circumstances in which the arguably stricter requirements of the witness summons procedure would not allow for the disclosure of information by a third party. For another instance, see *R (Omar) v Secretary of State for Foreign and Commonwealth Affairs* [2011] EWCA Civ 1587 in which the Court of Appeal (Civil Division) held that the information sought from the Foreign Secretary could potentially assist the applicant in defending a charge in Ugandan proceedings which, if proven against him, could result in the death penalty.

Section D10 Sending Cases from the Magistrates' Court to the Crown Court

INTRODUCTION

D10.1 All adults accused in criminal cases make their first appearance in the magistrates' court. If the offence is triable only in the Crown Court, the accused must be sent to that court for trial. If it is triable either way, the accused will be sent to the Crown Court for trial only if the accused indicates, or is deemed to indicate, a not guilty plea at the 'plea before venue' hearing and the allocation ('mode of trial') hearing that follows results in a decision in favour of Crown Court trial; in either case, the case is sent for trial to the Crown Court under the CDA 1998, s. 51 (see **D6**).

There remains one other way of securing the Crown Court trial of an accused, namely the 'voluntary bill of indictment' (see **D10.65**).

The special rules relating to accused who are under the age of 18, in particular the CDA 1998, s. 51A, are considered in **D24**.

Need for a Formal Transfer to the Crown Court

D10.2 The necessity for a formal transfer of the case to the Crown Court for trial arises from the Administration of Justice (Miscellaneous Provisions) Act 1933, s. 2(2).

Administration of Justice Act (Miscellaneous Provisions) Act 1933, s. 2

(2) Subject as hereinafter provided no bill of indictment charging any person with an indictable offence shall be preferred unless either—
(a) the person charged has been sent for trial for the offence; or
(b) the bill is preferred by the direction of the Court of Criminal Appeal or by the direction or with the consent of a judge of the High Court...
(ba) the bill is preferred with the consent of a judge of the Crown Court following a declaration by the court under paragraph 8(1) of Schedule 17 to the Crime and Courts Act 2013 (court approval of deferred prosecution agreement); or
(c) the bill is preferred under section 22B(3)(a) of the Prosecution of Offences Act 1985:
Provided that—
(i) where the person charged has been sent for trial, the bill of indictment against him may include, either in substitution for or in addition to any count charging an offence specified in the notice under section 51D(1) of the Crime and Disorder Act 1998, any counts founded on material which, in pursuance of regulations made under paragraph 1 of Schedule 3 to that Act, was served on the person charged, being counts which may lawfully be joined in the same indictment...

D10.3 The phrase 'bill of indictment' in s. 2 means simply a draft indictment (which is the term now used in CrimPR Part 10: see Supplement, **R10.1** *et seq.*), prepared by or on behalf of the prosecution. It is 'preferred' by being sent to the Crown Court. It follows from s. 2 of the 1933 Act that a trial on indictment may not validly take place unless:

(a) the accused has been sent for trial under the CDA 1998, s. 51 or s. 51A;
(b) the Court of Appeal has directed the preferment of a bill of indictment (which occurs where the Court of Appeal quashes a conviction but then exercises its discretion, under the Criminal Appeal Act 1968, s. 7, to order that the successful appellant be retried); or

(c) the bill is preferred by the direction or with the consent of a High Court judge (a 'voluntary bill of indictment').

The effect of the proviso to s. 2(2) is that, provided the accused was validly sent for trial on a charge of an indictable offence, the indictment that is drafted may include counts for other indictable offences, in respect of which the accused was not sent for trial, provided that those offences are disclosed by the evidence on the basis of which the case was originally sent to the Crown Court and can properly be joined in the same indictment. See **D11** for detailed discussion of indictments.

Court of First Appearance

Whether the offence is triable either way or triable only on indictment, the accused's first appearance will be in a magistrates' court. The MCA 1980, s. 2(2), provides: **D10.4**

> A magistrates' court has jurisdiction under sections 51 and 51A of the Crime and Disorder Act 1998 in respect of any offence committed by a person who appears or is brought before the court.

SENDING CASES TO THE CROWN COURT UNDER THE CRIME AND DISORDER ACT 1998, s. 51

The CDA 1998, s. 51(1) (see **D10.44**), provides that, where an adult appears or is brought before a magistrates' court charged with an offence to which these provisions apply, the court must send the accused 'forthwith' to the Crown Court for trial for the offence. This is, however, subject to the magistrates' power (under s. 52(5)) to adjourn if necessary. **D10.5**

By virtue of s. 51(2)(a) and (b), these provisions apply where the offence is triable only on indictment, or where the offence is triable either way and the allocation hearing (sometimes known as the 'mode of trial' hearing) has resulted in a decision in favour of trial on indictment, either because the magistrates have declined jurisdiction or else the accused has elected Crown Court trial rather than summary trial (see **D6.6** *et seq.*). Under s. 51(2)(c), the magistrates must also send the accused forthwith to the Crown Court where notice has been given under s. 51B (serious fraud cases) or s. 51C (child witness cases) (see **D10.45** and **D10.46**).

Either-way Offences under s. 51

The CDA 1998, s. 50A(3) (see **D10.43**), sets out various steps which must be taken where the offence is triable either way (unless notice is given under s. 51B or 51C): **D10.6**

(a) 'plea before venue': the accused is asked to indicate an intention to plead guilty or not guilty;
(b) in the event of an indication of a not guilty plea (or no indication), the allocation (mode of trial) procedure: the prosecution and, if they wish, the defence make representations as to whether the case is suitable for summary trial and the court then decides whether to accept jurisdiction and offer summary trial to the accused;
(c) if the magistrates' court declines jurisdiction, or if the accused elects trial on indictment, the case is sent for trial to the Crown Court under s. 51.

The procedure for determining mode of trial for either-way offences is considered in detail at **D6.6** *et seq.*

Related Either-way and Summary Offences

The CDA 1998, s. 51(3) (see **D10.44**), goes on to provide that, where the court sends an adult for trial under s. 51(1), it must also send the accused to the Crown Court for trial for any either-way or summary offence with which the accused is charged and which appears to the court to be related to the offence being sent to the Crown Court under s. 51(1) (provided that, if the offence is a summary offence, it is punishable with imprisonment or disqualification from driving). Under s. 51E(c), an either-way offence is related to an indictable offence if the charge for **D10.7** the either-way offence could be joined in the same indictment as the charge for the indictable offence (by virtue of CrimPR 3.29(4) (see Supplement, **R3.29**), this will require consideration, *inter alia*, of whether the charges are founded on the same facts, or form (part of) a series of offences of the same or a similar character), and under s. 51E(d), a summary offence is related to an indictable offence if it arises out of circumstances that are the 'same as or connected with' those giving rise to the indictable offence.

In *Maxwell* [2017] EWCA Crim 1233, [2018] 1 Cr App R 5 (76), Treacy LJ observed (at [30]) that the test for summary offences 'appears to be narrower than that applicable to either-way offences' and that this 'would be consistent with an intention that only those summary offences which have a close link to more serious offences sent to the Crown Court should trouble that court'. His lordship noted (at [31]) that s. 51(3)(b) uses the phrase, 'appears to the court to be related to the offence', and said that this 'provides leeway to the justices. A determination that there is an apparent connection between the circumstances of the offences is something less than a determination that in fact they are connected.' His lordship contrasted this with the language of the CDA 1998, sch. 3, para. 6 (see **D10.29**), which deals with the power of the Crown Court to deal with a summary offence and 'places an obligation on the Crown Court to consider whether in fact the summary offence is related to an indictable offence for which he was sent for trial'.

In *Osman* [2017] EWCA Crim 2178, [2018] 1 Cr App R 23 (337), it had to be decided whether the summary offence of failure to surrender (BA 1976, s. 6) was 'related to' the indictable offences for which D had been sent for trial. The Court concluded (at [22]):

> It is clear to us that the Bail Act offence did not arise out of 'circumstances connected with those giving rise to the indictable offence'. There was obviously a connection between the Bail Act offence and the substantive offences in that it was for the substantive offences that he had been granted bail and failed to surrender. But the circumstances giving rise to the substantive offence had no connection with the circumstances out of which the Bail Act offence arose. If that were so, then every Bail Act offence would be 'related' to the substantive offence, with the consequence that there would always be a mandatory obligation under s. 51(3)(b) to send the linked Bail Act offence to the Crown Court for trial. That could not possibly be correct . . .

The test applicable to linked summary offences was considered again in *Merritt* [2019] EWCA Crim 1514. D was arrested for shoplifting; when at the police station, he racially abused police officers. He was charged with an either-way offence relating to that abuse and elected Crown Court trial. The offence of shoplifting fell within the MCA 1980, s. 22, as the value involved did not exceed £200, and so (because he did not elect Crown Court trial in respect of that offence) it had to be dealt with as a summary offence. It was therefore sent to the Crown Court under the CDA 1998, s. 51(3). The Court of Appeal adopted the same reasoning as in *Osman*, holding (at [18]) that, although there was a clear connection between the shoplifting and the racially aggravated harassment (D would not have abused the officers had he not been arrested for shoplifting), the 'circumstances' giving rise to the shoplifting had no connection with the circumstances of the racially aggravated harassment at the police station approximately four hours later. It followed that the summary offence did not arise out of circumstances that were the same as or connected with those giving rise to the either-way offences.

One of the consequences of the provisions contained in s. 51(3) is that, if the accused is charged with an indictable-only offence, there will not be any question as to mode of trial in respect of any related either-way offences with which the accused is charged (since any either-way offences will be sent for trial automatically alongside the indictable-only offence). If a summary offence is sent to the Crown Court under s. 51(3), it will be dealt with in accordance with the CDA 1998, sch. 3, para. 6 (see **D10.29**).

D10.8 If *an adult has already* been sent to the Crown Court for trial under s. 51(1) and then subsequently appears before a magistrates' court charged with an either-way or summary offence that appears to the court to be related to the offence sent for trial under s. 51(1), the court *may* send the accused to the Crown Court for trial for the either-way or summary offence (provided that, if the offence is a summary one, it is punishable with imprisonment or disqualification from driving) (s. 51(4)). Note that this is a discretionary power, not a mandatory duty. It follows from the discretionary nature of the power to send for trial under s. 51(4) that there will be a plea before venue and mode of trial hearing in respect of an either-way offence to which s. 51(4) applies.

Co-accused

CrimPR 9.2(6) and (7) (see Supplement, **R9.2**) make it clear that, where there are co-accused and one accused elects Crown Court trial, the magistrates' court must send any other accused charged with the same offence (or a related offence) to the Crown Court for trial, even if the offence(s) in question would otherwise be suitable for summary trial (see **D6.16**). **D10.9**

The CDA 1998, s. 51(5) (see **D10.44**), applies where the court sends an adult for trial (under s. 51(1) or (3)), and another adult appears before the court, either on the same or a subsequent occasion, charged jointly with the first adult with an either-way offence, and that offence appears to the court to be related to an offence for which the first adult was sent for trial under s. 51(1) or (3). The court must (where it is the same occasion), or may (where it is a subsequent occasion), send the other adult to the Crown Court for trial for the either-way offence. Where the court sends an adult for trial under s. 51(5), it must (by virtue of s. 51(6)) at the same time send D to the Crown Court for trial for any either-way or summary offence with which D is charged and which appears to the court to be related to the offence for which D is sent for trial (provided that, if it is a summary offence, it is punishable with imprisonment or disqualification from driving).

Co-accused under the Age of 18 Section 51(7) (see **D10.44**) covers the situation where an adult and a person under the age of 18 are jointly charged. It applies where the court sends an adult to the Crown Court for trial under s. 51(1), (3) or (5), and a child or young person appears before the court (on the same or a subsequent occasion) charged jointly with the adult with an indictable offence for which the adult is sent for trial under s. 51(1), (3) or (5), or charged with an indictable offence that appears to the court to be related to that offence. The court 'shall, if it considers it necessary in the interests of justice to do so, send the child or young person forthwith to the Crown Court for trial for the indictable offence'. Under s. 51(8), where the court sends a child or young person for trial under s. 51(7), it may at the same time send D to the Crown Court for trial for any indictable or summary offence with which D is charged and which appears to the court to be related to the offence for which D is sent for trial (again, if the offence is a summary one, it must be punishable with imprisonment or disqualification from driving). **D10.10**

Subsidiary Matters

Where a summary offence is sent to the Crown Court for trial under s. 51, the summary trial for that offence is regarded as having been adjourned by the magistrates' court without fixing the time and place for its resumption (s. 51(10)). **D10.11**

Under s. 51(13), the functions of a magistrates' court under s. 51 may be discharged by a single justice.

Section 51A contains equivalent provisions to s. 51 for cases where defendants who are under the age of 18 are to be sent to the Crown Court for trial (see **D24**).

Presence of the Accused

The CDA 1998, s. 51(1), applies where the accused is 'before a magistrates' court'. If the accused does not appear in court for the s. 51 hearing, the court may issue an arrest warrant (see the MCA 1980, s. 1(6), and the BA 1976, s. 7(1), which are applicable, respectively, where the accused fails to answer to a summons or requisition, or fails to answer to bail, whether that bail was granted by the police or by a magistrates' court; see **D5.17** and **D7.98**). **D10.12**

Reporting Restrictions

D10.13 Reporting restrictions in respect of allocation and sending proceedings are governed by the CDA 1998, s. 52A (see **D10.50**). The only details that may be published or broadcast are those permitted by s. 52A (s. 52A(1)). For reporting restrictions generally, see **D3.128**.

The purpose of the restrictions is to prevent potentially prejudicial reporting of the case prior to the conclusion of any trial. Therefore, s. 52A(6) makes it clear that the restrictions do not apply where the accused enters a plea of guilty at the 'plea before venue' hearing or after the conclusion of the accused's trial (or, where there is more than one defendant, the trial of the last to be tried).

D10.14 **Nature of Restrictions** The matters that may be reported are listed in the CDA 1998, s. 52A(7). They include the identity of the court and the name of the justice(s); the name, age, home address and occupation of the accused; the offence(s) with which the accused is or are charged; the names of counsel and solicitors engaged in the proceedings; arrangements regarding bail; and whether legal aid has been granted. Where notice has been given under s. 51B (serious fraud cases; see **D10.34**), the press may also report 'relevant business information' (defined in s. 52(9) to include the name and address of any business being carried on by the accused).

Contravention of the reporting restrictions is an offence under s. 52B, punishable, on summary conviction, by an unlimited fine. Proceedings may be brought only by, or with the consent of, the A-G.

D10.15 **Lifting the Restrictions** Under the CDA 1998, s. 52A(2), the magistrates can order that the restrictions do not apply to particular allocation or sending proceedings (in other words, they can lift the reporting restrictions). Where the accused (or any of the accused) objects to the lifting of the restrictions, the court may lift the restrictions only if it is satisfied, after hearing representations from (each of) the accused, that it is in the interests of justice to do so (s. 52A(3) and (4)).

It is submitted that it should be very rare for the court to lift reporting restrictions other than upon an application by the accused, since the restrictions exist for the protection of the accused.

In *Leeds Justices, ex parte Sykes* [1983] 1 All ER 460, it was held (construing earlier legislation) that, in the event of disagreement between the defendants, the burden was on the accused who wanted reporting to show that it was in the interests of justice for the normal restrictions to be lifted. Griffiths LJ said (at pp. 134H–135B) that 'the interests of justice incorporate as a paramount consideration that the defendants should have a fair trial' and that, because Parliament has laid down a general rule against reporting, 'a powerful case' has to made out to lift the reporting restrictions. His lordship suggested (at p. 137B) that an application for restrictions to be lifted on the ground that publicity might induce potential witnesses for the defendant making the application to come forward would 'merit really serious consideration by the justices'.

The court must give all the co-accused a chance to make representations. Failure to do so is a serious breach of procedure and is likely to result in the quashing of the order lifting the reporting restrictions (*Wirral District Magistrates' Court, ex parte Meikle* (1990) 154 JP 1035).

D10.16 **Contempt of Court Act 1981** The provisions dealing with cases where there are several accused and one of them wants to have the reporting restrictions lifted are necessary because, even if it were practicable to report only those parts of the proceedings relating to the accused who wants the restrictions lifted and omit everything relating to the others, the court has no power under the CDA 1998, s. 52A, to make an order to that effect. Construing earlier legislation, Griffiths LJ, in *Leeds Justices, ex parte Sykes* [1983] 1 All ER 460 (at p. 136A), said that, 'If the reporting restrictions are to be lifted, then they are to be lifted ... in their entirety. They cannot be lifted piecemeal.' The justices therefore cannot pick and choose which of the restrictions are lifted and which remain. However, it is submitted that they can achieve a similar result by first lifting reporting restrictions through an order under s. 52A and then making a further order under the Contempt of Court Act 1981, s. 4(2), postponing contemporaneous reporting of some of the evidence until after the trial on indictment (*Horsham Justices, ex parte Farquharson* [1982] QB 762).

In *Sarker* [2018] EWCA Crim 1341, [2019] 1 Cr App R 3 (27) Lord Burnett CJ said (at [22]) that 'the explanation for why the order [under s. 4(2)] is necessary needs to address, clearly (and ordinarily in writing): (i) how contemporaneous fair and accurate reports of the trial will cause a substantial risk of prejudice? and (ii) why a postponement order would avoid the identified risk of prejudice?' (see **D3.125** *et seq.*).

Effecting the Transfer: s. 51D

Under the CDA 1998, s. 51D(1) (see **D10.47**), the magistrates' court specifies, in a notice, the offence(s) for which the accused is being sent for trial and the location of the Crown Court where the trial is to take place. A copy of the notice is served on the accused and a copy is sent to the Crown Court (s. 51D(2)). The location of the Crown Court to which the accused is sent for trial is chosen by the magistrates' court having regard to the convenience of the defence, the prosecution and the witnesses; the desirability of expediting the trial (i.e. how soon a courtroom will become available); and any directions given by the Lord Chief Justice under the Senior Courts Act 1981, s. 75(1) (CrimPR 9.3(3): see Supplement, **R9.3**) (s. 51D(4)). **D10.17**

In *R (Bentham) v Governor of HM Prison Wandsworth* [2006] EWHC 121 (Admin), D argued that the notice failed to comply with the statutory requirements. The Divisional Court ruled that the decision of substance is that of magistrates to send the accused to the Crown Court for trial. Only thereafter, and by way of an administrative act, is the notice prepared. No particular form is prescribed, nor is there any provision dealing with the consequences of a defective notice. It follows, said the court, that defects in the notice do not invalidate (or render ineffective) an otherwise valid (or effective) sending.

The various documents that the magistrates' court must send to the Crown Court are listed in CrimPR 9.5 (see Supplement, **R9.5**).

Each magistrates' court is informed of the location to which it should normally send defendants for trial, and (in the absence of any representations to the contrary by any of the parties) it will automatically send the accused to that location. Nonetheless, in some cases either the prosecution or the defence may invite the magistrates to send the case to a different location of the Crown Court. This may be appropriate if, for example, the offence with which the defendant is charged has aroused such ill feeling locally that a fair trial at the nearest location of the Crown Court may not be possible. If the magistrates do not accede to a request to transfer the case to a particular location of the Crown Court, or if the location specified by the magistrates subsequently appears unsatisfactory to one of the parties, there are two other ways of moving the trial: **D10.18**

(a) the Senior Courts Act 1981, s. 76(2), empowers an officer of the Crown Court to alter the place of trial;
(b) if the transfer is not effected administratively, either party may make an application to the Crown Court, under s. 76(3) of the 1981 Act for the venue of the trial to be altered. Applications to vary the location of the trial under s. 76 are heard by a Crown Court judge, usually sitting in private.

Service of Evidence and Draft Indictment

Under the Crime and Disorder Act 1998 (Service of Prosecution Evidence) Regulations 2005 (SI 2005 No. 902), reg. 2, where a person is sent for trial under s. 51, copies of the documents containing the evidence on which the charge(s) are based must, within 70 days (50 days if the accused is in custody) from the date on which the accused was sent for trial, be served on the accused and on the Crown Court. Under reg. 3, the prosecutor may apply orally or in writing to **D10.19** the Crown Court for an extension (or further extension) of that period. Where the prosecutor wishes to make an oral application under reg. 3, written notice of the intention to do so must be given to the court and to the accused (reg. 4). Under reg. 5, any written application under reg. 3 must be sent to the court and to the accused, and must specify the grounds for the application. The accused may make written representations in response within three days of service of the application.

In *Fehily v Governor of Wandsworth Prison* [2002] EWHC 1295 (Admin), [2003] 1 Cr App R 10 (153), the Divisional Court held that failure by the prosecution to comply with the time-limit does not render the prosecution a nullity. Furthermore, the Crown Court has jurisdiction to extend time on an application by the prosecution even if the application is made after the expiry of the time-limit.

D10.20 Except where the indictment is generated electronically under CrimPR 10.3 (see Supplement, **R10.3**), the draft indictment must be served on the Crown Court within 20 business days of service on the accused of the copies of the documents containing the evidence on which the charge(s) are based (CrimPR 10.4(2)). The indictment may contain any count that is supported by the evidence contained in the papers served by the prosecution, either in addition to or in substitution for the charges upon which the defendant was sent to the Crown Court by the magistrates' court (Administration of Justice (Miscellaneous Provisions) Act 1933, s. 2(2)). Any such counts must, however, be capable of being joined in the same indictment in accordance with CrimPR 3.29(4) (see Supplement, **R3.29**), and so should be founded on the same facts or form (part of) a series of offences of the same or a similar character (see *Lombardi* [1989] 1 All ER 992 and **D11.14** ***et seq.***).

Bail

D10.21 Under the CDA 1998, s. 52(1) (see **D10.49**), the accused may be sent to the Crown Court in custody or on bail. It should be borne in mind that the presumption in favour of bail (under the BA 1976, s. 4) continues to operate, and so bail may be withheld only if one or more of the statutory grounds for withholding bail under sch. 1 to the 1976 Act are made out (see **D7.12** ***et seq.***).

Plea and Trial Preparation Hearings

D10.22 CrimPR 3.21(1)(b) (see Supplement, **R3.16**) requires the Crown Court to conduct a plea and trial preparation hearing (PTPH). Where a magistrates' court sends a case to the Crown Court for trial, the magistrates' court must set a date for a PTPH at the Crown Court (in accordance with CrimPR 9.7(5)(a): see Supplement, **R9.7**). Unless the accused has indicated an intention to plead guilty (in which case, the magistrates' court must make arrangements for the Crown Court to take the accused's plea as soon as possible (CrimPR 9.7(5)(a)(i)), the PTPH must be held within 28 days of sending (CrimPD I, para. 3A.11). An indictment should be lodged at least seven days in advance of the PTPH (para. 3A.16).

Applications for Dismissal

D10.23 Under the CDA 1998, sch. 3, para. 2(1) (see **D10.52**), the accused may (after the date when the accused is served with the documents containing the evidence on which the charge(s) are based, but before the date of the arraignment) apply orally or in writing to the Crown Court for the charge(s) to be dismissed. Where such an application is made, the judge must dismiss any charge (and quash any count relating to it in the indictment) if it appears that the evidence against the applicant would not be sufficient to ensure a proper conviction (para. 2(2)).

D10.24 **Procedure** The accused may make an oral application for dismissal only after giving written notice of intention to do so (CDA 1998, sch. 3, para. 2(3)).

The procedure for an application to dismiss a charge is contained in CrimPR 3.20 (see Supplement, **R3.20**). Rule 3.20(2)(a) requires the accused to apply in writing not more than 20 business days after service of the prosecution evidence (and before arraignment). Copies of the application must be served on the prosecution and on any co-accused (r. 3.20(2)(b)). The application must 'explain why the prosecution evidence would not be sufficient for the defendant to be properly convicted'; ask for a hearing, if the accused wants one (and, if so, explain why a hearing is needed); identify any witnesses whom the accused wants to call to testify; and identify any material that the accused thinks will be needed to determine the application (r. 3.20(2)(c)). If the prosecution wish to oppose the application, they must serve notice to that effect not more than ten business days after service of the accused's notice, explaining their grounds of opposition, explaining why a hearing is needed if the prosecution are seeking one and identifying any witnesses and relevant material (r. 3.20(3)). Under r. 3.20(4), the court may determine the application at a hearing (in public or in private) or without a hearing. The court may shorten or extend the limits imposed by r. 3.20 (r. 3.20(5)(a)). If the intention to make an application to dismiss is raised at the PTPH, the accused will not be arraigned, and a timetable will be set for service of the written application.

Where a charge is dismissed under the CDA 1998, sch. 3, para. 2, further proceedings in respect of that charge may be brought only by means of the preferment of a voluntary bill of indictment (para. 2(6)); see **D10.69** ***et seq.***). **D10.25**

Challenging the Decision to Dismiss a Charge The accused cannot challenge the decision of the Crown Court judge not to dismiss a charge under the CDA 1998, sch. 3, para. 2, by way of judicial review. In *R (Snelgrove) v Woolwich Crown Court* [2004] EWHC 2172 (Admin), [2005] 1 WLR 3223, the Divisional Court held that a decision under sch. 3 not to dismiss the charge is an order in a matter relating to trial on indictment for the purposes of the Senior Courts Act 1981, s. 29(3), and so judicial review is not available. The Court reasoned that, following the sending of a case to the Crown Court, that court has jurisdiction in the matter and in all decisions concerning the issue between the accused and the Crown, and so those decisions necessarily relate to the trial on indictment; moreover, a decision whether to dismiss the charge affects the conduct of the trial, in that it determines whether the trial proceeds (per Auld LJ at [43]). In *R (O) v Central Criminal Court* [2006] EWHC 256 (Admin), the Divisional Court reaffirmed that a judge's decision to refuse to dismiss a case under the CDA 1988, sch. 3, para. 2, was a matter relating to trial on indictment, and therefore not susceptible to judicial review. **D10.26**

In *Thompson* [2006] EWCA Crim 2849, [2007] 1 WLR 1123, it was held that the Crown's right of appeal under the CJA 2003, s. 58 (see **D16.73** ***et seq.***), does not extend to a judge's ruling pursuant to the CDA 1998, sch. 3, para. 2, since that procedure can only lead to the dismissal of a charge or the quashing of an indictment, rather than the acquittal of the defendant. It follows that the only remedy for the prosecution in the face of the dismissal of a charge is to seek the preferment of a voluntary bill of indictment under sch. 3, para. 2(6).

Test on Dismissal Applications In *R (Inland Revenue Commissioners) v Crown Court at Kingston* [2001] EWHC Admin 581, [2001] 4 All ER 721, it was held that, on an application to dismiss (under earlier legislation), the judge was required to take into account the whole of the evidence against the accused, and that it was not appropriate for the judge to view any evidence in isolation from its context and other evidence (per Stanley Burnton J at [16]). The judge is not bound to assume that a jury would make every possible inference capable of being drawn against the accused but, where the case depends on the inferences or conclusions to be drawn from the evidence, the judge must assess the inferences or conclusions that the prosecution propose to ask the jury to draw, and decide whether it appears that the jury could properly draw those inferences and come to those conclusions (at [16]). It is submitted that the same principles would necessarily apply to applications to dismiss under the CDA 1998, sch. 3, para. 2. The decision in *R (Snelgrove) v Woolwich Crown Court* [2004] EWHC 2172 (Admin), [2005] 1 WLR 3223 (see **D10.26**) means that the court in *R (Inland Revenue Commissioners) v Crown Court at Kingston* should not have entertained the application for judicial review of the decision of the Crown Court judge, but it is submitted that the Divisional Court's ruling about the test to be applied in such cases remains valid nonetheless. **D10.27**

D10.28 **Reporting Restrictions** Reporting restrictions in relation to applications for the dismissal of charges are governed by the CDA 1998, sch. 3, para. 3. The restrictions apply automatically but can be lifted, under para. 3(2), by the judge dealing with the application. Under para. 3(8), reporting must be limited to details such as the identity of the judge, the names, ages, home addresses and occupations of the accused and witnesses; the offence(s) with which the defendant(s) are charged; the names of counsel and solicitors engaged in the proceedings; arrangements as to bail; whether legal aid has been granted. Contravention of these restrictions is a summary offence under para. 3(10), punishable with an unlimited fine. Where there is more than one defendant, and one of them objects to the making of an order lifting the restrictions, the judge is required to lift them if, and only if, satisfied (after hearing representations from the defendants) that it is in the interests of justice to do so (para. 3(3)).

Power of Crown Court to Deal with Summary Offence

D10.29 The CDA 1998, sch. 3, para. 6 (see **D10.56**), sets out what happens when the accused has been sent for trial for a related summary offence. If (and only if) the accused is convicted on the indictment, the Crown Court judge has first to consider whether the summary offence is indeed related to the indictable offence(s) for which the accused was sent for trial. For these purposes, the summary offence is related to the indictable offence if it 'arises out of circumstances which are the same as or connected with those giving rise' to the indictable offence (para. 6(12)). If the judge is so satisfied, the accused is asked to enter a plea (para. 6(3)). If the accused pleads guilty, the Crown Court will pass sentence, but subject to the limitations on sentence applicable to a magistrates' court (para. 6(4)). If the accused pleads not guilty, para. 6(5) provides that the powers of the Crown Court cease in respect of the summary offence, save that the Crown Court may dismiss the charge if the prosecution indicate that they do not wish to proceed with the charge (para. 6(6)); if the prosecution do wish to proceed with the charge, they must do so in the magistrates' court.

Paragraph 6(8) makes it clear that the provisions of para. 6 do not apply where the summary offence in question is one to which the CJA 1988, s. 40, applies (see **D11.17**) and that offence has been added to the indictment.

The Courts Act 2003, s. 66, affects the power of the Crown Court to deal with summary-only offences in that it confers on Crown Court judges the 'powers of a justice of the peace who is a District Judge (Magistrates' Courts)'. It is submitted that the effect of this provision is that, if the Crown Court is left with a summary offence, the judge may, if the accused pleads not guilty, try the offence as if the judge were a magistrate instead of remitting the accused to the magistrates' court to be tried for the summary offence. It should be emphasised that this provision simply empowers the Crown Court judge to try the summary offence as a magistrate, and so there is no obligation to do so. If the judge chooses not to try the offence, the trial will (assuming the prosecution wish to proceed with it) take place in the magistrates' court (the proceedings in the magistrates' court for the summary offence being treated, by virtue of the CDA 1998, s. 51(10), as if the court had adjourned them under the MCA 1980, s.10, without fixing the time and place for their resumption, when the summary offence was sent to the Crown Court under s. 51).

If the Court of Appeal quashes a conviction for the indictable offence to which a summary offence is related, that court must also set aside the conviction for the summary offence and may direct that no further proceedings in relation to the offence are to be undertaken (para. 6(9)). If the Court of Appeal does not so direct, it is open to the prosecution to proceed against the accused in the magistrates' court in respect of that summary offence.

In *Wilson* [2019] EWCA Crim 2410, the Court of Appeal confirmed that it does not have jurisdiction to hear an appeal against conviction for a summary offence which has been sent to the Crown Court under the CDA 1998, s. 51, and for which a guilty plea has been entered following D's conviction for one or more offences on indictment. In the cases under consideration, fresh evidence showed that the convictions for the summary offences, albeit following guilty pleas, were unsafe. To quash the convictions, the Court of Appeal had to reconstitute itself as a Divisional Court.

Accused No Longer Facing an Offence Sent for Trial

The CDA 1998, sch. 3, para. 7 (see **D10.57**), deals with the procedure to be adopted where the accused has been sent for trial for an indictable offence but, as a result of amendment of the indictment or because of a successful application for one or more charges to be dismissed, the indictment no longer includes a 'main offence'. The term 'main offence' is defined in para. 7(9) as either (a) an offence for which the accused has been sent to the Crown Court for trial under s. 51(1), or (b) an offence for which the accused has been sent for trial under s. 51(5) (which applies where a co-accused is charged with a related either-way offence) or s. 51A(6) (which applies where there is a co-accused aged under 18, and an adult is charged with a related either-way offence), in respect of which the conditions for sending to the Crown Court for trial under the relevant subsection continue to be satisfied. **D10.30**

If the accused still faces an allegation of an either-way offence, the Crown Court must go through a mode of trial procedure, which preserves the accused's right to be tried summarily for an either-way offence only where the accused consents to this, and also preserves the court's discretion to rule that the case is too serious for summary trial. First, the accused is asked to indicate an intention to plead guilty or not guilty (para. 7(5)). If the accused indicates a guilty plea, the Crown Court proceeds to the sentencing stage for that offence (para. 7(6)). If the accused indicates a not guilty plea, the court decides whether the case is more suitable for summary trial or for trial on indictment (para. 7(7)).

Paragraph 8 enables the court to proceed under para. 7 ('plea before venue') in the absence of the accused where the accused is legally represented and the court considers that, because of disorderly conduct before the court, it is not practicable to conduct the proceedings in the presence of the accused. In such a case, the representative is asked to give the indication as to plea.

Before deciding whether the case is more suitable for summary trial or for trial on indictment, the court must give the prosecution an opportunity to inform the court of the accused's previous convictions (if any), and must give the prosecution and the accused an opportunity to make representations as to whether summary trial or trial on indictment would be more suitable (para. 9(2)). In reaching its decision, the court must consider whether the sentence that a magistrates' court would have power to impose for the offence(s) would be adequate, and must have regard to the allocation guidelines issued by the Sentencing Council under the CAJA 2009, s. 122 (para. 9(3)). Under para. 10, if the Crown Court considers that an offence is more suitable for summary trial, the accused is given the choice of trial on indictment or summary trial. If the Crown Court considers that the offence is more suitable for trial on indictment, the accused is informed that this is so (para. 11).

It should be noted that the special procedure for determining mode of trial for criminal damage where the value involved is less than £5,000 (see the MCA 1980, s. 22, at **D6.21**) is also applicable in this context (para. 14).

The allocation ('mode of trial') proceedings under para. 9 can be dealt with in the absence of the accused if the accused is legally represented, the legal representative signifies the accused's consent to the proceedings being conducted in his or her absence, and the court is satisfied that there is good reason for proceeding in the absence of the accused (para. 15(1)). If the court decides that the case is more suitable for summary trial and the legal representative indicates that the accused wishes to be tried summarily, the court will remit the accused for trial to the magistrates' court; otherwise, the trial will take place in the Crown Court (para. 15(3)). **D10.31**

In *Ashton* [2006] EWCA Crim 794, [2007] 1 WLR 181, the Court of Appeal held (at [55]) that a Crown Court judge exercising the power to sit as a district judge under the Courts Act 2003,

s. 66, may determine allocation and (assuming the accused pleads guilty or, following summary trial in front of the judge sitting as a district judge, is found guilty) commit the defendant for sentence and then (sitting as a Crown Court judge) sit as the sentencing court.

D10.32 **Procedural Irregularities** In *Haye* [2002] EWCA Crim 2476, D was charged with robbery. He was sent for trial at the Crown Court pursuant to the CDA 1998, s. 51. At the Crown Court, the prosecution dropped the charge of robbery (an indictable-only offence) and replaced it with a charge of theft (triable either way). D pleaded not guilty to the theft charge. When the matter came on for trial, D was re-arraigned on the theft charge and entered a guilty plea. He subsequently appealed against conviction on the ground that the procedure set out in the CDA 1998, sch. 3, para. 7, had not been followed prior to the arraignment on the theft charge. In particular, he complained that proper consideration had not been given to the question of whether he should be tried summarily or whether the Crown Court should continue to deal with the case. He argued that the proceedings that followed the plea of guilty were, therefore, a nullity. The Court of Appeal agreed, holding that any failure to comply with the statutory procedure in relation to the right of an accused to make representations and/or to exercise choice as to mode of trial would have the consequence that, if the matter proceeded to trial, the hearing would be regarded as *ultra vires* and liable to be quashed. In the present case, D had been deprived of an opportunity of seeking to persuade the judge that summary trial would be more suitable. It followed that the proceedings in relation to the indictment alleging theft were a nullity.

However, *Haye* was considered by the Court of Appeal in *Ashton* [2006] EWCA Crim 794, [2007] 1 WLR 181. The Court said that, in the light of the decision of the House of Lords in *Soneji* [2005] UKHL 49, [2006] 1 AC 340 and the earlier Court of Appeal decision in *Sekhon* [2002] EWCA Crim 2954, [2003] 1 WLR 1655, 'we are confident that if *Haye* was decided now the result would have been the other way' (per Fulford J at [69]). The Court reached this conclusion on the basis that, in the light of those two authorities and of the overriding objective in the CrimPR, and in the absence of a clear indication that Parliament intended jurisdiction automatically to be removed following a procedural failure, the decision of the court should be based on an assessment of the interests of justice and, in particular, on whether there is a real possibility that the prosecution or the defence might suffer prejudice. If there is a risk of prejudice, a court should go on to decide whether it is just to permit the proceedings to continue. In other words, procedural failings do not generally render the proceedings invalid, they merely give the court a discretion whether to proceed with the case (*Ashton* at [4] and [9]).

D10.33 The approach laid down by *Ashton* was followed in *Thwaites* [2006] EWCA Crim 3235, where D was sent for trial to the Crown Court charged with conspiracy to handle stolen goods. However, he was arraigned and tried on an indictment containing counts of burglary, but no indictable-only offence. During the course of the trial, it was discovered that the judge had failed to conduct the allocation procedure required by the CDA 1998, sch. 3, in respect of the either-way charges on the indictment. The trial judge ruled that, had the correct procedure been followed, the case would have been found as suitable only for trial on indictment, and so D had suffered no prejudice from the failure to conduct the mode of trial procedure. The Court of Appeal agreed, holding that earlier authorities such as *Haye* are no longer good law and that there was no unfairness or prejudice to D, who had received a fair trial.

The Court of Appeal revisited the consequences of failure to comply with para. 7 in *Gul* [2012] EWCA Crim 1761, [2013] 1 WLR 1136. D had been sent for trial in respect of an indictable-only offence but the indictment as eventually drafted contained only either-way offences. The Crown Court did not go through the procedure laid down in para. 7, but instead simply took D's plea. D pleaded not guilty but was convicted by a jury. The Court of Appeal rejected the argument that the trial was a nullity. Lord Judge CJ (at [23]–[24]) said:

> The entitlement of the defendant is to make submissions in support of summary trial if he wishes to do so, but the defendant does not enjoy an unfettered entitlement to summary trial. The ultimate decision must be made by the court. If however the defendant wishes to be tried summarily and the

> court has failed to give him the opportunity to ask for it, there is nothing in the procedure which prevents an application by him to that effect. ... If the decision is made by the Crown Court that the case is more suitable for summary trial, only then does the defendant have the right to elect trial by jury. He has no corresponding right to elect summary trial ... the complaint here is no more and no less than that the defendant, like the prosecution, was not invited to make representations about the mode of trial. Thereafter no application to do so was made. The omission of that procedural step did not vitiate the indictment or the process before the Crown Court ... What is more, any defect in the process, which meant that the defendant was not invited to make submissions about the possible suitability of summary trial was readily curable: the defendant could and should have made an appropriate application. In these circumstances, with a remedy available to the defendant, it is inconceivable that Parliament intended that the consequence of non-compliance would be to render subsequent proceedings in the Crown Court a nullity.

It is clear from this that the approach taken in *Thwaites* is to be preferred to that taken in *Haye*.

Notices in Serious or Complex Fraud Cases: s. 51B

Under the CDA 1998, s. 51B(1) (see **D10.45**), a notice may be given in respect of an indictable offence if the prosecution are of the opinion (a subjective test) that the evidence in the case (a) is sufficient for the person charged to be put on trial for the offence, and (b) reveals a case of fraud 'of such seriousness or complexity that it is appropriate that the management of the case should without delay be taken over by the Crown Court'. This provision applies only where the prosecution is being brought by a 'designated authority' (or under s. 51B(7), one of its officers). The designated authorities are the DPP (this includes the CPS), the Director of the SFO, and the Secretary of State (s. 51B(9)). Where a notice has been given to the magistrates' court under s. 51B, the case must be sent forthwith to the Crown Court for trial, under s. 51(1). Under s. 51B(6), the effect of the notice under s. 51B is that, apart from ancillary matters such as granting bail and legal aid, the functions of the magistrates' court cease in relation to the case. **D10.34**

In the unlikely event that the magistrates accept jurisdiction at a mode of trial hearing in such a case, any such notice must be given before any summary trial begins (s. 51B(5)). The effect of the notice is that, apart from ancillary matters such as granting bail and legal aid, the functions of the magistrates' court cease in relation to the case (s. 51B(6)). A decision to give a notice under s. 51B is not subject to appeal and cannot be questioned in any court (s. 51B(8)).

The notice, which must be given to the magistrates' court at which the accused appears (s. 51B(4)), must specify the proposed place of trial; in selecting that place, s. 51B(3) provides that the designated authority must have regard to the same matters as magistrates must take into account (under s. 51D(4)) when deciding where to send an accused for trial (see **D10.17**). Except where the indictment is generated electronically under CrimPR 10.3, the indictment must be preferred within 20 business days of the giving of notice (subject to the power of the Crown Court to extend that time limit) (CrimPR 10.4(2): see Supplement, **R10.4**).

In *Wrench* [1996] 1 Cr App R 340 (decided under earlier legislation), it was held that, if one of the charges is one to which the transfer provisions apply, then the procedure can also be used in respect of any other offences which can properly be joined on the same indictment. (This aspect of *Wrench* is not affected by the disapproval of that case in *T* [2001] 1 Cr App R 32 (446).) It is submitted that the same principle would apply to transfers under s. 51B. **D10.35**

Because the case is sent to the Crown Court under s. 51, the ability to apply to the Crown Court for the charges to be dismissed (under the CDA 1998, sch. 3, para. 2) applies equally where a notice is given under s. 51B.

Notices in Certain Cases Involving Children: s. 51C

Under the CDA 1998, s. 51C(1) (see **D10.46**), a notice may be given by the DPP (in practice, notice will usually be given by a Crown Prosecutor, since the DPP is able to delegate this function under s. 51C(5)) if of the opinion (a subjective test) that (a) the evidence in the case is **D10.36** sufficient for the person charged to be put on trial for the offence, (b) a child will be called as a witness at the trial and (c) in order to avoid any prejudice to the welfare of the child, the case 'should be taken over and proceeded with without delay by the Crown Court'. This provision applies only to the offences specified in s. 51C(3), which lists a number of specific sexual or violent offences but also includes any offence that involves an assault on, or injury or a threat of injury to, a person and any offence under the Modern Slavery Act 2015, s. 1. Where a notice has been given to a magistrates' court under s. 51C, the case must be sent forthwith to the Crown Court for trial, under s. 51(1). A decision to give a notice under s. 51C is not subject to appeal and cannot be questioned in any court (s. 51C(6)).

For the purposes of s. 51C, 'child' is defined in s. 51C(7) as a person who is under the age of 17 or any person of whom a video recording (as defined in the YJCEA 1999, s. 63(1)) was made when the person was under the age of 17 with a view to its admission as the person's evidence-in-chief in the trial.

D10.37 Under s. 51C(4), the effect of the notice under s. 51C is that, apart from ancillary matters such as granting bail and legal aid, the functions of the magistrates' court cease in relation to the case. Except where the indictment is generated electronically under CrimPR 10.3, the indictment must be preferred within 20 business days of the giving of notice (subject to the power of the Crown Court to extend that time limit) (CrimPR 10.4(2)).

Cases where notice has been served under s. 51C are sent for trial under s. 51, and so it is possible for the accused to apply to the Crown Court for the dismissal of the charge(s) under the CDA 1998, sch. 3, para. 2.

D10.38 **Accused under the Age of 18** In *Fareham Youth Court and Morey, ex parte CPS* (1999) 163 JP 812, it was held that where the youth court has determined that a child or young person should be tried summarily, the prosecution cannot reverse that decision by issue of a notice of transfer. In *T* [2001] 1 Cr App R 32 (446), Kay LJ (at [37]) said that, where the defendant is under the age of 18, the DPP should not transfer the case to the Crown Court unless satisfied that a magistrates' court would be likely to find that it ought to be possible to sentence the defendant under the PCC(S)A 2000, s. 91 (see **D24.27** ***et seq.***).

Depositions for Use in the Trial

D10.39 The CDA 1998, sch. 3, para. 4 (see **D10.54**), empowers a magistrate to issue a summons requiring a person to attend before a magistrate to have evidence taken in the form of a deposition. Under para. 4(1), before issuing the summons, the magistrate must be satisfied that the person is likely to be able to give material evidence (or to produce a relevant document or other exhibit) on behalf of the prosecution for an offence that has been sent to the Crown Court for trial, and that it is in the interests of justice to issue a summons to secure the attendance of the witness. Under CrimPR Part 17 (see Supplement, **R17.1** ***et seq.***), the procedure for obtaining a witness summons under para. 4 is the same as in the case of an application for a witness summons in the context of a summary trial or trial on indictment.

If the prosecutor makes the application on oath and the magistrate is satisfied that the summons would not result in the attendance of the witness, the magistrate may issue an arrest warrant instead of a summons (para. 4(3)). If a summons is issued and the witness fails to attend in answer to the summons, an arrest warrant may be issued (para. 4(5)) and the witness is liable to be committed to custody for up to a month or be fined up to £2,500 (para. 4(7)).

D10.40 Where evidence has been taken as a deposition under para. 4, para. 5(2) provides that the deposition may be read as evidence at the trial unless (under para. 5(3)) the trial judge orders that this should not be so or a party to the proceedings objects to the use of the deposition.

The Divisional Court considered this power in *R (CPS) v Bolton Magistrates' Court* [2003] EWHC 2697 (Admin), [2004] 1 WLR 835, granting a declaration that the procedure of taking a deposition from a witness who will not voluntarily make a statement is a 'proceeding in open court'. In the circumstances of a particular case, however, the justices may exceptionally exclude persons from the taking of the deposition or otherwise modify the procedure where that will assist in the reception of the evidence or is in the interests of justice to do so. There is, however, no basis for excluding the party seeking the deposition, which will include the CPS and representatives of the investigating authority. Kennedy LJ went on to hold (at [23]) that lawyers representing those sent for trial are entitled to be present unless there is some special reason for excluding them. Nonetheless, anyone seeking to cross-examine the witness should normally be told to reserve cross-examination for the Crown Court. However, in a case where the reluctant witness is likely to be unavailable at the Crown Court, or can perhaps be spared attendance there if one or two questions are asked at the earlier stage, it would be open to the justice to permit cross-examination.

This procedure is not available to the defence, since its object is to facilitate the gathering of evidence for the prosecution.

Discontinuance of the Prosecution Case

The prosecution may discontinue the case against the accused not only in the magistrates' court, but also, in the case of offences sent up to the Crown Court under the CDA 1998, s. 51, at any time before the indictment is preferred (Prosecution of Offences Act 1985, s. 23A; see **D3.59**). **D10.41**

Abuse of Process: the Discretion to Discharge an Accused

The fact that a magistrates' court has a duty under the CDA 1998, s. 51(1), to send the case to the Crown Court 'forthwith' does not necessarily preclude the court from exercising its jurisdiction to stay the proceedings as an abuse of process in an appropriate case, though such cases will be very rare (*R (Salubi) v Bow Street Magistrates' Court* [2002] EWHC 919 (Admin), [2002] 1 WLR 3073, per Auld LJ at [20]). For discussion of abuse of process, see **D3.66** ***et seq.*** **D10.42**

Statutory Materials

Crime and Disorder Act 1998, ss. 50A, 51, 51B, 51C, 51D, 51E, 52, 52A and 52B and sch. 3 **D10.43**

50A.—(1) Where an adult appears or is brought before a magistrates' court charged with an either-way offence (the 'relevant offence'), the court shall proceed in the manner described in this section.

(2) If notice is given in respect of the relevant offence under section 51B or 51C below, the court shall deal with the offence as provided in section 51 below.

(3) Otherwise—

(a) if the adult (or another adult with whom the adult is charged jointly with the relevant offence) is or has been sent to the Crown Court for trial for an offence under section 51(2)(a) or 51(2)(c) below—

(i) the court shall first consider the relevant offence under subsection (3), (4), (5) or, as the case may be, (6) of section 51 below and, where applicable, deal with it under that subsection;

(ii) if the adult is not sent to the Crown Court for trial for the relevant offence by virtue of sub-paragraph (i) above, the court shall then proceed to deal with the relevant offence in accordance with sections 17A to 23 of the 1980 Act;

(b) in all other cases—

(i) the court shall first consider the relevant offence under sections 17A to 20 (excluding subsections (8) and (9) of section 20) of the 1980 Act;

(ii) if, by virtue of sub-paragraph (i) above, the court would be required to proceed in relation to the offence as mentioned in section 17A(6), 17B(2)(c) or 20(7) of that Act (*indication of guilty plea*), it shall proceed as so required (and, accordingly, shall not consider the offence under section 51 or 51A below);

(iii) if sub-paragraph (ii) above does not apply—

(a) the court shall consider the relevant offence under sections 51 and 51A below and, where applicable, deal with it under the relevant section;

(b) if the adult is not sent to the Crown Court for trial for the relevant offence by virtue of paragraph (a) of this sub-paragraph, the court shall then proceed to deal with the relevant offence as contemplated by section 20(9) or, as the case may be, section 21 of the 1980 Act.

(4) Subsection (3) above is subject to any requirement to proceed as mentioned in subsections (2) or (6)(a) of section 22 of the 1980 Act (certain offences where value involved is small).

(5) Nothing in this section shall prevent the court from committing the adult to the Crown Court for sentence pursuant to any enactment, if he is convicted of the relevant offence.

D10.44 51.—(1) Where an adult appears or is brought before a magistrates' court ('the court') charged with an offence and any of the conditions mentioned in subsection (2) below is satisfied, the court shall send him forthwith to the Crown Court for trial for the offence.

(2) Those conditions are—

(a) that the offence is an offence triable only on indictment other than one in respect of which notice has been given under section 51B or 51C below;

(b) that the offence is an either-way offence and the court is required under section 20(9)(b), 21, 22A(2)(b), 23(4)(b) or (5) or 25(2D) of the Magistrates' Courts Act 1980 to proceed in relation to the offence in accordance with subsection (1) above;

(c) that notice is given to the court under section 51B or 51C below in respect of the offence.

(3) Where the court sends an adult for trial under subsection (1) above, it shall at the same time send him to the Crown Court for trial for any either-way or summary offence with which he is charged and which—

(a) (if it is an either-way offence) appears to the court to be related to the offence mentioned in subsection (1) above; or

(b) (if it is a summary offence) appears to the court to be related to the offence mentioned in subsection (1) above or to the either-way offence, and which fulfils the requisite condition (as defined in subsection (11) below).

(4) Where an adult who has been sent for trial under subsection (1) above subsequently appears or is brought before a magistrates' court charged with an either-way or summary offence which—

(a) appears to the court to be related to the offence mentioned in subsection (1) above; and

(b) (in the case of a summary offence) fulfils the requisite condition,

the court may send him forthwith to the Crown Court for trial for the either-way or summary offence.

(5) Where—

(a) the court sends an adult ('A') for trial under subsection (1) or (3) above;

(b) another adult appears or is brought before the court on the same or a subsequent occasion charged jointly with A with an either-way offence; and

(c) that offence appears to the court to be related to an offence for which A was sent for trial under subsection (1) or (3) above,

the court shall where it is the same occasion, and may where it is a subsequent occasion, send the other adult forthwith to the Crown Court for trial for the either-way offence.

(6) Where the court sends an adult for trial under subsection (5) above, it shall at the same time send him to the Crown Court for trial for any either-way or summary offence with which he is charged and which—

(a) (if it is an either-way offence) appears to the court to be related to the offence for which he is sent for trial; and

(b) (if it is a summary offence) appears to the court to be related to the offence for which he is sent for trial or to the either-way offence, and which fulfils the requisite condition.

(7) to (9) [Cover the situation where child or young person is charged with adult: see **D24.46**.]

(10) The trial of the information charging any summary offence for which a person is sent for trial under this section shall be treated as if the court had adjourned it under section 10 of the 1980 Act and had not fixed the time and place for its resumption.

(11) A summary offence fulfils the requisite condition if it is punishable with imprisonment or involves obligatory or discretionary disqualification from driving.

(12) In the case of an adult charged with an offence—

(a) if the offence satisfies paragraph (c) of subsection (2) above, the offence shall be dealt with under subsection (1) above and not under any other provision of this section or section 51A below;

(b) subject to paragraph (a) above, if the offence is one in respect of which the court is required to, or would decide to, send the adult to the Crown Court under—

(i) subsection (5) above; or

(ii) subsection (6) of section 51A below,

the offence shall be dealt with under that subsection and not under any other provision of this section or section 51A below.

(13) The functions of a magistrates' court under this section, and its related functions under section 51D below, may be discharged by a single justice.

...

51B.—(1) A notice may be given by a designated authority under this section in respect of an indictable offence if the authority is of the opinion that the evidence of the offence charged— D10.45
(a) is sufficient for the person charged to be put on trial for the offence; and
(b) reveals a case of fraud of such seriousness or complexity that it is appropriate that the management of the case should without delay be taken over by the Crown Court.
(2) That opinion must be certified by the designated authority in the notice.
(3) The notice must also specify the proposed place of trial, and in selecting that place the designated authority must have regard to the same matters as are specified in paragraphs (a) to (c) of section 51D(4) below.
(4) A notice under this section must be given to the magistrates' court at which the person charged appears or before which he is brought.
(5) Such a notice must be given to the magistrates' court before any summary trial begins.
(6) The effect of such a notice is that the functions of the magistrates' court cease in relation to the case, except—
(a) for the purposes of section 51D below;
(b) as provided by regulations under section 19 of the Legal Aid, Sentencing and Punishment of Offenders Act 2012; and
(c) as provided by section 52 below.
(7) The functions of a designated authority under this section may be exercised by an officer of the authority acting on behalf of the authority.
(8) A decision to give a notice under this section shall not be subject to appeal or liable to be questioned in any court (whether a magistrates' court or not).
(9) In this section 'designated authority' means—
(a) the Director of Public Prosecutions;
(b) the Director of the Serious Fraud Office;
(c) [repealed]; or
(e) the Secretary of State.

51C.—(1) A notice may be given by the Director of Public Prosecutions under this section in respect of an offence falling within subsection (3) below if he is of the opinion— D10.46
(a) that the evidence of the offence would be sufficient for the person charged to be put on trial for the offence;
(b) that a child would be called as a witness at the trial; and
(c) that, for the purpose of avoiding any prejudice to the welfare of the child, the case should be taken over and proceeded with without delay by the Crown Court.
(2) That opinion must be certified by the Director of Public Prosecutions in the notice.
(3) This subsection applies to an offence—
(a) which involves an assault on, or injury or a threat of injury to, a person;
(b) under section 1 of the Children and Young Persons Act 1933 (cruelty to persons under 16);
(c) under the Sexual Offences Act 1956, the Protection of Children Act 1978 or the Sexual Offences Act 2003;
(d) of kidnapping or false imprisonment, or an offence under section 1 or 2 of the Child Abduction Act 1984;
(da) under section 1 or 2 of the Modern Slavery Act 2015;
(e) which consists of attempting or conspiring to commit, or of aiding, abetting, counselling, procuring or [intentionally encouraging or assisting] the commission of, an offence falling within paragraph (a), (b), (c), (d) or (da) above.
(4) Subsections (4), (5) and (6) of section 51B above apply for the purposes of this section as they apply for the purposes of that.
(5) The functions of the Director of Public Prosecutions under this section may be exercised by an officer acting on behalf of the Director.
(6) A decision to give a notice under this section shall not be subject to appeal or liable to be questioned in any court (whether a magistrates' court or not).
(7) In this section 'child' means—
(a) a person who is under the age of 17; or
(b) any person of whom a video recording (as defined in section 63(1) of the Youth Justice and Criminal Evidence Act 1999) was made when he was under the age of 17 with a view to its admission as his evidence in chief in the trial referred to in subsection (1) above.

51D.—(1) The court shall specify in a notice— D10.47
(a) the offence or offences for which a person is sent for trial under section 51 or 51A above; and

(b) the place at which he is to be tried (which, if a notice has been given under section 51B above, must be the place specified in that notice).

(2) A copy of the notice shall be served on the accused and given to the Crown Court sitting at that place.

(3) In a case where a person is sent for trial under section 51 or 51A above for more than one offence, the court shall specify in that notice, for each offence—

(a) the subsection under which the person is so sent; and

(b) if applicable, the offence to which that offence appears to the court to be related.

(4) Where the court selects the place of trial for the purposes of subsection (1) above, it shall have regard to—

(a) the convenience of the defence, the prosecution and the witnesses;

(b) the desirability of expediting the trial; and

(c) any direction given by or on behalf of the Lord Chief Justice with the concurrence of the Lord Chancellor under section 75(1) of the Senior Courts Act 1981.

D10.48 51E. For the purposes of sections 50A to 51D above—

(a) 'adult' means a person aged 18 or over, and references to an adult include a corporation;

(b) 'either-way offence' means an offence triable either way;

(c) an either-way offence is related to an indictable offence if the charge for the either-way offence could be joined in the same indictment as the charge for the indictable offence;

(d) a summary offence is related to an indictable offence if it arises out of circumstances which are the same as or connected with those giving rise to the indictable offence.

D10.49 52.—(1) Subject to section 4 of the Bail Act 1976, section 41 of the 1980 Act, section 115(1) of the Coroners and Justice Act 2009, regulations under section 22 of the 1985 Act and section 25 of the 1994 Act, the court may send a person for trial under section 51 or 51A above—

(a) in custody, that is to say, by committing him to custody there to be safely kept until delivered in due course of law; or

(b) on bail in accordance with the Bail Act 1976, that is to say, by directing him to appear before the Crown Court for trial.

(2) Where—

(a) the person's release on bail under subsection (1)(b) above is conditional on his providing one or more sureties; and

(b) in accordance with subsection (3) of section 8 of the Bail Act 1976, the court fixes the amount in which a surety is to be bound with a view to his entering into his recognisance subsequently in accordance with subsections (4) and (5) or (6) of that section,

the court shall in the meantime make an order such as is mentioned in subsection (1)(a) above.

(3) The court shall treat as an indictable offence for the purposes of section 51 or 51A above an offence which is mentioned in the first column of Schedule 2 to the 1980 Act (offences for which the value involved is relevant to the mode of trial) unless it is clear to the court, having regard to any representations made by the prosecutor or the accused, that the value involved does not exceed the relevant sum.

(4) In subsection (3) above 'the value involved' and 'the relevant sum' have the same meanings as in section 22 of the 1980 Act (certain offences triable either way to be tried summarily if value involved is small).

(5) A magistrates' court may adjourn any proceedings under section 51 or 51A above, and if it does so shall remand the accused.

(6) Schedule 3 to this Act (which makes further provision in relation to persons sent to the Crown Court for trial under section 51 or 51A above) shall have effect.

D10.50 52A.—(1) Except as provided by this section, it shall not be lawful—

(a) to publish in the United Kingdom a written report of any allocation or sending proceedings in England and Wales; or

(b) to include in a relevant programme for reception in the United Kingdom a report of any such proceedings,

if (in either case) the report contains any matter other than that permitted by this section.

(2) Subject to subsections (3) and (4) below, a magistrates' court may, with reference to any allocation or sending proceedings, order that subsection (1) above shall not apply to reports of those proceedings.

(3) Where there is only one accused and he objects to the making of an order under subsection (2) above, the court shall make the order if, and only if, it is satisfied, after hearing the representations of the accused, that it is in the interests of justice to do so.

(4) Where in the case of two or more accused one of them objects to the making of an order under subsection (2) above, the court shall make the order if, and only if, it is satisfied, after hearing the representations of the accused, that it is in the interests of justice to do so.

(5) An order under subsection (2) above shall not apply to reports of proceedings under subsection (3) or (4) above, but any decision of the court to make or not to make such an order may be contained in reports published or included in a relevant programme before the time authorised by subsection (6) below.

(6) It shall not be unlawful under this section to publish or include in a relevant programme a report of allocation or sending proceedings containing any matter other than that permitted by subsection (7) below—
- (a) where, in relation to the accused (or all of them, if there are more than one), the magistrates' court is required to proceed as mentioned in section 20(7) of the 1980 Act, after the court is so required;
- (b) where, in relation to the accused (or any of them, if there are more than one), the court proceeds other than as mentioned there, after conclusion of his trial or, as the case may be, the trial of the last to be tried.

(7) The following matters may be contained in a report of allocation or sending proceedings published or included in a relevant programme without an order under subsection (2) above before the time authorised by subsection (6) above—
- (a) the identity of the court and the name of the justice or justices;
- (b) the name, age, home address and occupation of the accused;
- (c) in the case of an accused charged with an offence in respect of which notice has been given to the court under section 51B above, any relevant business information;
- (d) the offence or offences, or a summary of them, with which the accused is or are charged;
- (e) the names of counsel and solicitors engaged in the proceedings;
- (f) where the proceedings are adjourned, the date and place to which they are adjourned;
- (g) the arrangements as to bail;
- (h) whether a right to representation funded by the Legal Services Commission as part of the Criminal Defence Service was granted to the accused or any of the accused.

(8) The addresses that may be published or included in a relevant programme under subsection (7) above are addresses—
- (a) at any relevant time; and
- (b) at the time of their publication or inclusion in a relevant programme.

(9) The following is relevant business information for the purposes of subsection (7) above—
- (a) any address used by the accused for carrying on a business on his own account;
- (b) the name of any business which he was carrying on on his own account at any relevant time;
- (c) the name of any firm in which he was a partner at any relevant time or by which he was engaged at any such time;
- (d) the address of any such firm;
- (e) the name of any company of which he was a director at any relevant time or by which he was otherwise engaged at any such time;
- (f) the address of the registered or principal office of any such company;
- (g) any working address of the accused in his capacity as a person engaged by any such company;

and here 'engaged' means engaged under a contract of service or a contract for services.

(10) Subsection (1) above shall be in addition to, and not in derogation from, the provisions of any other enactment with respect to the publication of reports of court proceedings.

(11) In this section—

'allocation or sending proceedings' means, in relation to an information charging an indictable offence—
- (a) any proceedings in the magistrates' court at which matters are considered under any of the following provisions—
  - (i) sections 19 to 23 of the 1980 Act;
  - (ii) section 51, 51A or 52 above;
- (b) any proceedings in the magistrates' court before the court proceeds to consider any matter mentioned in paragraph (a) above; and
- (c) any proceedings in the magistrates' court at which an application under section 25(2) of the 1980 Act is considered;

'publish', in relation to a report, means publish the report, either by itself or as part of a newspaper or periodical, for distribution to the public;

'relevant programme' means a programme included in a programme service (within the meaning of the Broadcasting Act 1990);

'relevant time' means a time when events giving rise to the charges to which the proceedings relate occurred.

D10.51 52B.—(1) If a report is published or included in a relevant programme in contravention of section 52A above, each of the following persons is guilty of an offence—

(a) in the case of a publication of a written report as part of a newspaper or periodical, any proprietor, editor or publisher of the newspaper or periodical;
(b) in the case of a publication of a written report otherwise than as part of a newspaper or periodical, the person who publishes it;
(c) in the case of the inclusion of a report in a relevant programme, any body corporate which is engaged in providing the service in which the programme is included and any person having functions in relation to the programme corresponding to those of the editor of a newspaper.

(2) A person guilty of an offence under this section is liable on summary conviction to a fine not exceeding level 5 on the standard scale.
(3) Proceedings for an offence under this section shall not, in England and Wales, be instituted otherwise than by or with the consent of the Attorney General.
(4) Proceedings for an offence under this section shall not, in Northern Ireland, be instituted otherwise than by or with the consent of the Attorney General for Northern Ireland.
(5) Subsection (11) of section 52A above applies for the purposes of this section as it applies for the purposes of that section.

...

SCHEDULE 3

D10.52 1. [A-G's power to make regulations.]

Applications for dismissal

2.—(1) A person who is sent for trial under section 51 or 51A of this Act on any charge or charges may, at any time—

(a) after he is served with copies of the documents containing the evidence on which the charge or charges are based; and
(b) before he is arraigned (and whether or not an indictment has been preferred against him),

apply orally or in writing to the Crown Court sitting at the place specified in the notice under section 51D(1) of this Act for the charge, or any of the charges, in the case to be dismissed.

(2) The judge shall dismiss a charge (and accordingly quash any count relating to it in any indictment preferred against the applicant) which is the subject of any such application if it appears to him that the evidence against the applicant would not be sufficient for him to be properly convicted.
(3) No oral application may be made under sub-paragraph (1) above unless the applicant has given to the Crown Court sitting at the place in question written notice of his intention to make the application.

...

(6) If the charge, or any of the charges, against the applicant is dismissed—

(a) no further proceedings may be brought on the dismissed charge or charges except by means of the preferment of a voluntary bill of indictment; and
(b) unless the applicant is in custody otherwise than on the dismissed charge or charges, he shall be discharged.

(7) [Power to make rules.]

Reporting restrictions

D10.53 3.—(1) Except as provided by this paragraph, it shall not be lawful—

(a) to publish in the United Kingdom a written report of an application under paragraph 2(1) above; or
(b) to include in a relevant programme for reception in the United Kingdom a report of such an application,

if (in either case) the report contains any matter other than that permitted by this paragraph.

(2) An order that sub-paragraph (1) above shall not apply to reports of an application under paragraph 2(1) above may be made by the judge dealing with the application.
(3) Where in the case of two or more accused one of them objects to the making of an order under sub-paragraph (2) above, the judge shall make the order if, and only if, he is satisfied, after hearing the representations of the accused, that it is in the interests of justice to do so.
(4) An order under sub-paragraph (2) above shall not apply to reports of proceedings under sub-paragraph (3) above, but any decision of the court to make or not to make such an order

may be contained in reports published or included in a relevant programme before the time authorised by sub-paragraph (5) below.

(5) It shall not be unlawful under this paragraph to publish or include in a relevant programme a report of an application under paragraph 2(1) above containing any matter other than that permitted by sub-paragraph (8) below where the application is successful.

(6) Where—
(a) two or more persons were jointly charged; and
(b) applications under paragraph 2(1) above are made by more than one of them,
sub-paragraph (5) above shall have effect as if for the words 'the application is' there were substituted the words 'all the applications are'.

(7) It shall not be unlawful under this paragraph to publish or include in a relevant programme a report of an unsuccessful application at the conclusion of the trial of the person charged, or of the last of the persons charged to be tried.

(8) The following matters may be contained in a report published or included in a relevant programme without an order under sub-paragraph (2) above before the time authorised by sub-paragraphs (5) and (6) above, that is to say—
(a) the identity of the court and the name of the judge;
(b) the names, ages, home addresses and occupations of the accused and witnesses;
(bb) where the application made by the accused under paragraph 2(1) above relates to a charge for an offence in respect of which notice has been given to the court under section 51B of this Act, any relevant business information;
(c) the offence or offences, or a summary of them, with which the accused is or are charged;
(d) the names of counsel and solicitors engaged in the proceedings;
(e) where the proceedings are adjourned, the date and place to which they are adjourned;
(f) the arrangements as to bail;
(g) whether a right to representation funded by the Legal Services Commission as part of the Criminal Defence Service was granted to the accused or any of the accused.

(9) The addresses that may be published or included in a relevant programme under sub-paragraph (8) above are addresses—
(a) at any relevant time; and
(b) at the time of their publication or inclusion in a relevant programme.

(9A) The following is relevant business information for the purposes of sub-paragraph (8) above—
(a) any address used by the accused for carrying on a business on his own account;
(b) the name of any business which he was carrying on on his own account at any relevant time;
(c) the name of any firm in which he was a partner at any relevant time or by which he was engaged at any such time;
(d) the address of any such firm;
(e) the name of any company of which he was a director at any relevant time or by which he was otherwise engaged at any such time;
(f) the address of the registered or principal office of any such company;
(g) any working address of the accused in his capacity as a person engaged by any such company;
and here 'engaged' means engaged under a contract of service or a contract for services.

(10) If a report is published or included in a relevant programme in contravention of this paragraph, the following persons, that is to say—
(a) in the case of a publication of a written report as part of a newspaper or periodical, any proprietor, editor or publisher of the newspaper or periodical;
(b) in the case of a publication of a written report otherwise than as part of a newspaper or periodical, the person who publishes it;
(c) in the case of the inclusion of a report in a relevant programme, any body corporate which is engaged in providing the service in which the programme is included and any person having functions in relation to the programme corresponding to those of the editor of a newspaper;
shall be liable on summary conviction to a fine not exceeding level 5 on the standard scale.

(11) Proceedings for an offence under this paragraph shall not, in England and Wales, be instituted otherwise than by or with the consent of the Attorney General.

(11A) [Northern Ireland.]

(12) Sub-paragraph (1) above shall be in addition to, and not in derogation from, the provisions of any other enactment with respect to the publication of reports of court proceedings.

(13) In this paragraph—
'publish', in relation to a report, means publish the report, either by itself or as part of a newspaper or periodical, for distribution to the public;
'relevant programme' means a programme included in a programme service (within the meaning of the Broadcasting Act 1990);
'relevant time' means a time when events giving rise to the charges to which the proceedings relate occurred.

Power of justice to take depositions etc.

D10.54 4.—(1) Sub-paragraph (2) below applies where a justice of the peace for any commission area is satisfied that—
(a) any person in England and Wales ('the witness') is likely to be able to make on behalf of the prosecutor a written statement containing material evidence, or produce on behalf of the prosecutor a document or other exhibit likely to be material evidence, for the purposes of proceedings for an offence for which a person has been sent for trial under section 51 or 51A of this Act by a magistrates' court for that area; and
(b) it is in the interests of justice to issue a summons under this paragraph to secure the attendance of the witness to have his evidence taken as a deposition or to produce the document or other exhibit.

(2) In such a case the justice shall issue a summons directed to the witness requiring him to attend before a justice at the time and place appointed in the summons, and to have his evidence taken as a deposition or to produce the document or other exhibit.

(3) If a justice of the peace is satisfied by evidence on oath of the matters mentioned in sub-paragraph (1) above, and also that it is probable that a summons under sub-paragraph (2) above would not procure the result required by it, the justice may instead of issuing a summons issue a warrant to arrest the witness and to bring him before a justice at the time and place specified in the warrant.

(4) A summons may also be issued under sub-paragraph (2) above if the justice is satisfied that the witness is outside the British Islands, but no warrant may be issued under sub-paragraph (3) above unless the justice is satisfied by evidence on oath that the witness is in England and Wales.

(5) If—
(a) the witness fails to attend before a justice in answer to a summons under this paragraph;
(b) the justice is satisfied by evidence on oath that the witness is likely to be able to make a statement or produce a document or other exhibit as mentioned in sub-paragraph (1)(a) above;
(c) it is proved on oath, or in such other manner as may be prescribed, that he has been duly served with the summons and that a reasonable sum has been paid or tendered to him for costs and expenses; and
(d) it appears to the justice that there is no just excuse for the failure,

the justice may issue a warrant to arrest the witness and to bring him before a justice at the time and place specified in the warrant.

(6) Where—
(a) a summons is issued under sub-paragraph (2) above or a warrant is issued under sub-paragraph (3) or (5) above; and
(b) the summons or warrant is issued with a view to securing that the witness has his evidence taken as a deposition,

the time appointed in the summons or specified in the warrant shall be such as to enable the evidence to be taken as a deposition before the relevant date.

(7) If any person attending or brought before a justice in pursuance of this paragraph refuses without just excuse to have his evidence taken as a deposition, or to produce the document or other exhibit, the justice may do one or both of the following—
(a) commit him to custody until the expiration of such period not exceeding one month as may be specified in the summons or warrant or until he sooner has his evidence taken as a deposition or produces the document or other exhibit;
(b) impose on him a fine not exceeding £2,500.

(8) A fine imposed under sub-paragraph (7) above shall be deemed, for the purposes of any enactment, to be a sum adjudged to be paid by a conviction.

(9) If in pursuance of this paragraph a person has his evidence taken as a deposition, the designated officer for the justice concerned shall as soon as is reasonably practicable send a copy of the deposition to the prosecutor and the Crown Court.

(10) If in pursuance of this paragraph a person produces an exhibit which is a document, the designated officer for the justice concerned shall as soon as is reasonably practicable send a copy of the document to the prosecutor and the Crown Court.

(11) If in pursuance of this paragraph a person produces an exhibit which is not a document, the designated officer for the justice concerned shall as soon as is reasonably practicable inform the prosecutor and the Crown Court of that fact and of the nature of the exhibit.

(12) In this paragraph—
'prescribed' means prescribed by Criminal Procedure Rules;
'the relevant date' means the expiry of the period referred to in paragraph 1(1) above.

Use of depositions as evidence

5.—(1) Subject to sub-paragraph (3) below, sub-paragraph (2) below applies where in pursuance of paragraph 4 above a person has his evidence taken as a deposition. **D10.55**

(2) Where this sub-paragraph applies the deposition may without further proof be read as evidence on the trial of the accused, whether for an offence for which he was sent for trial under section 51 or 51A of this Act or for any other offence arising out of the same transaction or set of circumstances.

(3) Sub-paragraph (2) above does not apply if—
(a) it is proved that the deposition was not signed by the justice by whom it purports to have been signed;
(b) the court of trial at its discretion orders that sub-paragraph (2) above shall not apply; or
(c) a party to the proceedings objects to sub-paragraph (2) above applying.

...

Power of Crown Court to deal with summary offence

6.—(1) This paragraph applies where a magistrates' court has sent a person for trial under section 51 or 51A of this Act for offences which include a summary offence. **D10.56**

(2) If the person is convicted on the indictment, the Crown Court shall consider whether the summary offence is related to the indictable offence for which he was sent for trial or, as the case may be, any of the indictable offences for which he was so sent.

(3) If it considers that the summary offence is so related, the court shall state to the person the substance of the offence and ask him whether he pleads guilty or not guilty.

(4) If the person pleads guilty, the Crown Court shall convict him, but may deal with him in respect of the summary offence only in a manner in which a magistrates' court could have dealt with him.

(5) If he does not plead guilty, the powers of the Crown Court shall cease in respect of the summary offence except as provided by sub-paragraph (6) below.

(6) If the prosecution inform the court that they would not desire to submit evidence on the charge relating to the summary offence, the court shall dismiss it.

(7) The Crown Court shall inform the designated officer for the magistrates' court of the outcome of any proceedings under this paragraph.

(8) If the summary offence is one to which section 40 of the Criminal Justice Act 1988 applies, the Crown Court may exercise in relation to the offence the power conferred by that section; but where the person is tried on indictment for such an offence, the functions of the Crown Court under this paragraph in relation to the offence shall cease.

(9) Where the Court of Appeal allows an appeal against conviction of an indictable offence which is related to a summary offence of which the appellant was convicted under this paragraph—
(a) it shall set aside his conviction of the summary offence and give the clerk of the magistrates' court notice that it has done so; and
(b) it may direct that no further proceedings in relation to the offence are to be undertaken;
and the proceedings before the Crown Court in relation to the offence shall thereafter be disregarded for all purposes.

(10) A notice under sub-paragraph (9) above shall include particulars of any direction given under paragraph (b) of that sub-paragraph in relation to the offence.

(11) ...

(12) An offence is related to another offence for the purposes of this paragraph if it arises out of circumstances which are the same as or connected with those giving rise to the other offence.

Procedure where no indictable-only offence remains

D10.57 7.—(1) Subject to paragraph 13 below, this paragraph applies where—
(a) a person has been sent for trial under section 51 or 51A of this Act but has not been arraigned; and
(b) the person is charged on an indictment which (following amendment of the indictment, or as a result of an application under paragraph 2 above, or for any other reason) includes no main offence.
(2) Everything that the Crown Court is required to do under the following provisions of this paragraph must be done with the accused present in court.
(3) The court shall cause to be read to the accused each remaining count of the indictment that charges an offence triable either way.
(4) The court shall then explain to the accused in ordinary language that, in relation to each of those offences, he may indicate whether (if it were to proceed to trial) he would plead guilty or not guilty, and that if he indicates that he would plead guilty the court must proceed as mentioned in sub-paragraph (6) below.
(5) The court shall then ask the accused whether (if the offence in question were to proceed to trial) he would plead guilty or not guilty.
(6) If the accused indicates that he would plead guilty the court shall proceed as if he had been arraigned on the count in question and had pleaded guilty.
(7) If the accused indicates that he would plead not guilty, or fails to indicate how he would plead, the court shall decide whether the offence is more suitable for summary trial or for trial on indictment.
(8) Subject to sub-paragraph (6) above, the following shall not for any purpose be taken to constitute the taking of a plea—
(a) asking the accused under this paragraph whether (if the offence were to proceed to trial) he would plead guilty or not guilty;
(b) an indication by the accused under this paragraph of how he would plead.
(9) In this paragraph, a 'main offence' is—
(a) an offence for which the person has been sent to the Crown Court for trial under section 51(1) of this Act; or
(b) an offence—
(i) for which the person has been sent to the Crown Court for trial under subsection (5) of section 51 or subsection (6) of section 51A of this Act ('the applicable subsection'); and
(ii) in respect of which the conditions for sending him to the Crown Court for trial under the applicable subsection (as set out in paragraphs (a) to (c) of section 51(5) or paragraphs (a) and (b) of section 51A(6)) continue to be satisfied.

D10.58 8.—(1) Subject to paragraph 13 below, this paragraph applies in a case where—
(a) a person has been sent for trial under section 51 or 51A of this Act but has not been arraigned;
(b) he is charged on an indictment which (following amendment of the indictment, or as a result of an application under paragraph 2 above, or for any other reason) includes no main offence (within the meaning of paragraph 7 above);
(c) he is represented by a legal representative;
(d) the Crown Court considers that by reason of his disorderly conduct before the court it is not practicable for proceedings under paragraph 7 above to be conducted in his presence; and
(e) the court considers that it should proceed in his absence.
(2) In such a case—
(a) the court shall cause to be read to the representative each remaining count of the indictment that charges an offence triable either way;
(b) the court shall ask the representative whether (if the offence in question were to proceed to trial) the accused would plead guilty or not guilty;
(c) if the representative indicates that the accused would plead guilty the court shall proceed as if the accused had been arraigned on the count in question and had pleaded guilty;
(d) if the representative indicates that the accused would plead not guilty, or fails to indicate how the accused would plead, the court shall decide whether the offence is more suitable for summary trial or for trial on indictment.

(3) Subject to sub-paragraph (2)(c) above, the following shall not for any purpose be taken to constitute the taking of a plea—
(a) asking the representative under this section whether (if the offence were to proceed to trial) the accused would plead guilty or not guilty;
(b) an indication by the representative under this paragraph of how the accused would plead.

9.—(1) This paragraph applies where the Crown Court is required by paragraph 7(7) or 8(2)(d) above to decide the question whether an offence is more suitable for summary trial or for trial on indictment. **D10.59**
(2) Before deciding the question, the court—
(a) shall give the prosecution an opportunity to inform the court of the accused's previous convictions (if any); and
(b) shall give the prosecution and the accused an opportunity to make representations as to whether summary trial or trial on indictment would be more suitable.
(3) In deciding the question, the court shall consider—
(a) whether the sentence which a magistrates' court would have power to impose for the offence would be adequate; and
(b) any representations made by the prosecution or the accused under sub-paragraph (2)(b) above,

and shall have regard to any allocation guidelines (or revised allocation guidelines) issued as definitive guidelines under section 122 of the Coroners and Justice Act 2009.
(4) Where—
(a) the accused is charged on the same occasion with two or more offences; and
(b) it appears to the court that they constitute or form part of a series of two or more offences of the same or a similar character;

sub-paragraph (3)(a) above shall have effect as if references to the sentence which a magistrates' court would have power to impose for the offence were a reference to the maximum aggregate sentence which a magistrates' court would have power to impose for all of the offences taken together.
(5) In this paragraph any reference to a previous conviction is a reference to—
(a) a previous conviction by a court in the United Kingdom, or
(aa) a previous conviction by a court in another member State of a relevant offence under the law of that State, or
(b) a previous conviction of a service offence within the meaning of the Armed Forces Act 2006.
(5A) For the purposes of sub-paragraph (5)(aa) an offence is 'relevant' if the offence would constitute an offence under the law of any part of the United Kingdom if it were done in that part at the time when the allocation decision is made.

10.—(1) This paragraph applies (unless excluded by paragraph 15 below) where the Crown Court considers that an offence is more suitable for summary trial. **D10.60**
(2) The court shall explain to the accused in ordinary language—
(a) that it appears to the court more suitable for him to be tried summarily for the offence;
(b) that he can either consent to be so tried or, if he wishes, be tried on indictment; and
(c) in the case of a specified offence (within the meaning of section 224 of the Criminal Justice Act 2003), that if he is tried summarily and is convicted by the court, he may be committed for sentence to the Crown Court under section 3A of the Powers of Criminal Courts (Sentencing) Act 2000 if the committing court is of such opinion as is mentioned in subsection (2) of that section.
(3) After explaining to the accused as provided by sub-paragraph (2) above the court shall ask him whether he wishes to be tried summarily or on indictment, and—
(a) if he indicates that he wishes to be tried summarily, shall remit him for trial to a magistrates' court acting for the place where he was sent to the Crown Court for trial;
(b) if he does not give such an indication, shall retain its functions in relation to the offence and proceed accordingly.

11.—(1) If the Crown Court considers that an offence is more suitable for trial on indictment, the court— **D10.61**
(a) shall tell the accused that it has decided that it is more suitable for him to be tried for the offence on indictment; and
(b) shall retain its functions in relation to the offence and proceed accordingly.

...

D10.62 13.—(1) This paragraph applies, in place of paragraphs 7 to 12 above, in the case of a child or young person who—

(a) has been sent for trial under section 51 or 51A of this Act but has not been arraigned; and
(b) is charged on an indictment which (following amendment of the indictment, or as a result of an application under paragraph 2 above, or for any other reason) includes no main offence.

(2) The Crown Court shall remit the child or young person for trial to a magistrates' court acting for the place where he was sent to the Crown Court for trial.

(3) In this paragraph, a 'main offence' is—

(a) an offence for which the child or young person has been sent to the Crown Court for trial under section 51A(2) of this Act; or
(b) an offence—
(i) for which the child or young person has been sent to the Crown Court for trial under subsection (7) of section 51 of this Act; and
(ii) in respect of which the conditions for sending him to the Crown Court for trial under that subsection (as set out in paragraphs (a) and (b) of that subsection) continue to be satisfied.

Procedure for determining whether offences of criminal damage etc. are summary offences

D10.63 14.—(1) This paragraph applies where the Crown Court has to determine, for the purposes of this Schedule, whether an offence which is listed in the first column of Schedule 2 to the 1980 Act (offences for which the value involved is relevant to the mode of trial) is a summary offence.

(2) The court shall have regard to any representations made by the prosecutor or the accused.

(3) If it appears clear to the court that the value involved does not exceed the relevant sum, it shall treat the offence as a summary offence.

(4) If it appears clear to the court that the value involved exceeds the relevant sum, it shall treat the offence as an indictable offence.

(5) If it appears to the court for any reason not clear whether the value involved does or does not exceed the relevant sum, the court shall ask the accused whether he wishes the offence to be treated as a summary offence.

(6) Where sub-paragraph (5) above applies—

(a) if the accused indicates that he wishes the offence to be treated as a summary offence, the court shall so treat it;
(b) if the accused does not give such an indication, the court shall treat the offence as an indictable offence.

(7) In this paragraph 'the value involved' and 'the relevant sum' have the same meanings as in section 22 of the 1980 Act (certain offences triable either way to be tried summarily if value involved is small).

Power of Crown Court, with consent of legally-represented accused, to proceed in his absence

D10.64 15.—(1) The Crown Court may proceed in the absence of the accused in accordance with such of the provisions of paragraphs 9 to 14 above as are applicable in the circumstances if—

(a) the accused is represented by a legal representative who signifies to the court the accused's consent to the proceedings in question being conducted in his absence; and
(b) the court is satisfied that there is good reason for proceeding in the absence of the accused.

(2) Sub-paragraph (1) above is subject to the following provisions of this paragraph which apply where the court exercises the power conferred by that sub-paragraph.

(3) If, where the court has decided as required by paragraph 7(7) or 8(2)(d) above, it appears to the court that an offence is more suitable for summary trial, paragraph 10 above shall not apply and—

(a) if the legal representative indicates that the accused wishes to be tried summarily, the court shall remit the accused for trial to a magistrates' court acting for the place where he was sent to the Crown Court for trial;
(b) if the legal representative does not give such an indication, the court shall retain its functions and proceed accordingly.

(4) If, where the court has decided as required by paragraph 7(7) or 8(2)(d) above, it appears to the court that an offence is more suitable for trial on indictment, paragraph 11 above shall apply with the omission of paragraph (a).

(5) Where paragraph 14 above applies and it appears to the court for any reason not clear whether the value involved does or does not exceed the relevant sum, sub-paragraphs (5) and (6) of that paragraph shall not apply and—
  (a) the court shall ask the legal representative whether the accused wishes the offence to be treated as a summary offence;
  (b) if the legal representative indicates that the accused wishes the offence to be treated as a summary offence, the court shall so treat it;
  (c) if the legal representative does not give such an indication, the court shall treat the offence as an indictable offence.

VOLUNTARY BILLS OF INDICTMENT

The Administration of Justice (Miscellaneous Provisions) Act 1933, s. 2(2)(b), provides that a bill of indictment may be preferred 'by the direction or with the consent of a judge of the High Court'. Obtaining a 'voluntary bill of indictment' simply means seeking an order from a High Court judge that the accused should stand trial in the Crown Court for the offence(s) set out in the application. The principal use of this exceptional procedure is to allow proceedings to be reinstituted where a charge has been dismissed under the CDA 1998, sch. 3, para. 2 (see **D10.23**), but fresh evidence against the accused has subsequently come to light. **D10.65**

Procedure for Obtaining a Voluntary Bill

CrimPR 10.9 (see Supplement, **R10.9**) applies 'where a prosecutor wants a High Court judge's permission to serve a draft indictment' (in other words, seeks a voluntary bill of indictment). The prosecutor must serve a written application on the court and (unless the judge otherwise directs) on the proposed defendant; if the prosecutor asks for a hearing, the application must explain why a hearing is needed (r. 10.9(2)). The application must attach (i) the proposed indictment; (ii) copies of the documents containing the evidence on which the prosecutor relies, including any written witness statements; (iii) a copy of any indictment on which the accused already has been arraigned, and (iv) if not contained in such an indictment, a list of any offence(s) for which the accused has already been sent for trial (r. 10.9(3)(a)). The application must also include (i) 'a concise statement of the circumstances in which, and the reasons why, the application is made', and (ii) a concise summary of the evidence contained in the documents which accompany the application, relating that evidence to each count in the proposed indictment (r. 10.9(3)(b)). Unless the application is made on behalf of the DPP or the Director of the SFO, the application must also contain a statement that, to the best of the prosecutor's knowledge, information and belief, (i) the evidence on which the prosecutor relies will be available at the trial, and (ii) the allegations contained in the application are substantially true (r. 10.9(3)(c)). **D10.66**

Under r. 10.9(4), a proposed defendant served with an application who wants to make representations to the judge must serve written representations on the court and on the prosecutor, as soon as practicable. If the proposed defendant asks for a hearing, the reason why a hearing is needed must be explained.

Rule 10.9(5) provides that the judge may determine the application without a hearing, or at a hearing (in public or in private), and may do so with or without receiving the oral evidence of any proposed witness. CrimPD II, para. 10B.5 (see Supplement, **CPD.10B**), states that prosecutors must follow the procedure set out in CrimPR Part 10, unless there are 'good reasons' for not doing so, in which case prosecutors should inform the judge that the procedures have not been followed and seek leave to dispense with all or any of them. The judge should not give such leave unless 'good reasons' are shown. Paragraph 10B.6 states that, as well as considering any written submissions, the judge may invite oral submissions from either party, or accede to a request for an opportunity to make such oral submissions, if the judge considers it necessary or desirable to receive such oral submissions in order to make a sound and fair decision on the application. Any such oral submissions should usually be made on notice to the other party and in open court.

The CCA 2013, sch. 17, para. 32, amended s. 2(2) of the 1933 Act so as to provide for deferred prosecution agreements (see **D12.106**). Once a deferred prosecution agreement has been approved, proceedings are commenced by seeking a voluntary bill of indictment from a Crown Court judge (not a High Court judge), without any involvement of a magistrates' court. Once the proceedings have been instituted in this way, they are automatically suspended. This suspension may only be lifted following the termination of the deferred prosecution agreement as a consequence of a breach of the agreement.

Finality of High Court Judge's Decision

D10.67 Where a High Court judge directs the preferment of a voluntary bill of indictment under the Administration of Justice (Miscellaneous Provisions) Act 1933, s. 2(2)(b), the Court of Appeal will not inquire into the correctness or otherwise of this decision, so long as it is clear that the judge was acting within his or her jurisdiction (*Rothfield* (1938) 26 Cr App R 103, per Humphreys J at p. 106). The issuing of a voluntary bill of indictment is not subject to judicial review (*Manchester Crown Court, ex parte Williams* (1990) 154 JP 589). In *Rothfield*, the Court of Appeal also held that a High Court judge's authorisation for the preferring of a bill is binding on a trial judge, and the latter has no jurisdiction to quash the indictment simply on the basis that the former, according to the defence, made a mistake (at p. 106). Moreover, it is clear from *Rothfield* that procedural irregularities do not necessarily invalidate the judge's decision to grant a voluntary bill.

Even though the decision of a High Court judge to issue a voluntary bill of indictment is not subject to judicial review, the decision of a prosecutor to seek a voluntary bill is susceptible to review, but only on very limited grounds, such as bad faith or personal malice on the part of the prosecutor (*Inland Revenue Commissioners, ex parte Dhesi* (1995) *Independent*, 14 August 1995).

D10.68 In *Muse* [2007] EWHC 2924 (QB), on an application for a voluntary bill of indictment, the CPS had decided not to rely on certain evidence. The judge found that there was insufficient evidence to put the defendants on trial. The CPS subsequently reconsidered the matter, and sought a voluntary bill of indictment in respect of the same incident on the basis of the evidence that it had chosen not to use at the previous hearing. It was held by Openshaw J that it would be wrong in principle for the prosecution to be able to get round a decision that it did not like by inviting another judge to take a different view of the same material that had been before the judge who had dismissed the charges. However, a voluntary bill may be granted to correct a mistaken decision by the CPS or to reflect a change of mind within the CPS. The power to do so should be used sparingly, in truly exceptional cases. Relevant factors include the public interest in putting defendants on trial where there is sufficient evidence to justify doing so and the offence is a serious one. On the other hand, given the desirability of finality in criminal matters, it would not usually be in the interests of justice that persons should have to face a second prosecution in relation to the same offence if the evidence relied on was in fact available at the earlier hearing, particularly when a deliberate decision had been taken not to rely on that evidence. Each case must be decided on its own facts.

Circumstances in which it is Appropriate to Apply for a Voluntary Bill

D10.69 CrimPD II, para. 10B.4 (see Supplement, **CPD.10B**), makes the point that the preferment of a voluntary bill is 'an exceptional procedure' and should be used only where 'good reason to depart from the normal procedure is clearly shown and only where the interests of justice, rather than considerations of administrative convenience, require it'.

Specific provision is made for the use of the voluntary bill procedure where a charge transferred to the Crown Court (under the CDA 1998, s. 51) has been dismissed (under the CDA 1998, sch. 3, para. 2; see **D10.23**) and the prosecution wish to seek a trial nonetheless; indeed, in such circumstances, further proceedings may be brought on the dismissed charge(s) only by means of the preferment of a voluntary bill of indictment (para. 2(6)).

In *Arfan* [2012] EWHC 2450 (QB), Nicol J noted (at [23]) that, where an application to dismiss a case sent to the Crown Court has been successful, caution should be exercised before a High Court judge grants leave to prefer a voluntary bill of indictment, and went on to say: **D10.70**

> Without attempting to give an exhaustive list, there may be circumstances which would justify the granting of leave if the judge who had dismissed the charge had taken the decision without regard to a relevant statutory provision or judicial authority, or had otherwise erred in law, or if the Crown had new evidence which made a significant difference to its case, or if the decision to dismiss lacked a rational foundation.

Thus, an application for a voluntary bill 'will only succeed if the Crown can show that the circumstances are exceptional' (at [25]). This follows the approach taken in earlier cases, such as *Davenport* [2005] EWHC 2828 (QB), where Pitchers J said that it would be 'wrong in principle for the prosecution to be able to get round a decision that they do not like by inviting another judge to take a different view of the same material that was before the judge who dismissed the charges'. His lordship went on to say that an obvious example of where a voluntary bill would be appropriate 'would be if the judge had not had a crucial authority or statutory provision drawn to his attention' (at [23]), or where 'the prosecution can produce fresh cogent evidence which was not before the judge who dismissed the charges', though in such a case it 'would still be necessary for the judge considering the voluntary bill to conclude that it was in the interests of justice for a voluntary bill to be preferred but he would be making a decision on new material and would not be being asked simply to take a different view from the one taken previously' (at [26]).

In *SFO v Evans* [2014] EWHC 3803 (QB), [2015] 1 WLR 3526, Fulford LJ, said (at [85]) that:

> Granting a voluntary bill of indictment is an exceptional course, and it will only be issued following a successful application to dismiss if (i) the court has made a basic and substantive error of law that is clear or obvious; or (ii) new evidence has become available that the prosecution could not put before the court at the time of the dismissal hearing which (along with any existing evidence) provides the prosecution with a sustainable factual basis for the charge; or (iii) there was a serious procedural irregularity... [T]his is not an exhaustive list because there will be other exceptional situations when it may be appropriate to grant a voluntary bill, for instance if the charges against the accused were dismissed on the basis of a technicality, particularly if it was one that the prosecution reasonably failed to anticipate.

His lordship went on to say (at [86]) that, whether a voluntary bill will be granted to correct a mistaken decision of the prosecution or to reflect a change of mind by the prosecuting authority:

> ... will depend on the nature and the extent of the prosecution's changed position, the reasons that have led to the new approach and the implications for the proceedings as a whole. Therefore, the court will need to consider carefully the prosecution's suggested justification against the background of the relevant procedural history. Furthermore, it is to be emphasised [that,] although the accused will always be prejudiced by the prosecution's application to revive dismissed criminal proceedings, his position will necessarily require careful consideration.

Evans was followed in *Environment Agency v Hennessy* [2016] EWHC 539 (QB), where it was held that a voluntary bill of indictment was appropriate because the Crown Court judge had made a 'fundamental error of law' in dismissing the original charge. Similarly, in *SFO v Barclays plc* [2018] EWHC 3055 (QB), [2020] 1 Cr App R 28 (481), Davis LJ reiterated (at [8]) that 'it should be an exceptional course to grant leave to prefer a voluntary bill'.

In *Gadd* [2014] EWHC 3307 (QB), Globe J considered the principles to be applied where a voluntary bill of indictment is sought in respect of charges which have been stayed as an abuse of process. His lordship granted the voluntary bill on the basis that, in the circumstances prevailing at the time of the application, it was not unfair for the defendant to be tried for the charges which had previously been stayed.

Section D11 The Indictment

INTRODUCTION

D11.1 The indictment is the document containing the charges against the accused on which the accused is arraigned at the commencement of a trial on indictment. The law on indictments is contained principally in the Indictments Act 1915, CrimPR Part 10 (see Supplement, **R10.1** *et seq.*), and CrimPD II, paras. 10A.1 to 10A.20 (see Supplement, **CPD.10A**).

The content of this section can be divided into four categories:

(a) rules as to the form of an indictment, which includes rules as to the layout of an indictment, who is responsible for its drafting and the time-limits relevant to its preferment (**D11.2** to **D11.12**);
(b) rules as to the composition of an indictment, in terms of the charges included in an indictment and their wording (**D11.13** to **D11.62**);
(c) rules as to the alteration of an indictment, whether by joinder of charges or offenders, severance or amendment (**D11.63** to **D11.108**);
(d) rules for objecting to an indictment, whether by a motion to quash or as a ground of appeal (**D11.109** to **D11.116**).

REQUIREMENT THAT AN INDICTMENT BE PREFERRED

The Rule

D11.2 The Administration of Justice (Miscellaneous Provisions) Act 1933, s. 2(2), provides that no draft indictment may be served unless:

(a) the accused has been sent for trial (pursuant to the CDA 1998, s. 51 or 51A);
(b) a High Court judge has directed or consented to the preferment of a voluntary bill of indictment (the procedure relating to which is in CrimPR 10.9 and CrimPD II, para. 10B; see **D10.66**);
(c) a Crown Court Judge has consented to the preferment of a bill of indictment following a declaration by the court approving a deferred prosecution agreement (pursuant to the CCA 2013, sch. 17, para. 8(1));
(d) the Court of Appeal has ordered a retrial.

An indictment may also be preferred where a prosecutor reinstitutes proceedings after custody time-limits have expired (see **D15.38**). Provision is also made for the preferring of the indictment in a case where there is a deferred prosecution agreement, which acts as the catalyst for the suspending of the proceedings pursuant to the terms of the agreement (see **D12.106**).

The CAJA 2009, s. 116, amended s. 2(1) of the 1933 Act, so that it reads:

> Subject to the provisions of this section, a bill of indictment charging any person with an indictable offence may be preferred by any person before the [Crown Court] and it shall thereupon become an indictment and be proceeded upon accordingly.

The effect of this amendment is to remove the previous prerequisite that an indictment came into being only once it was signed by a proper officer of the Crown Court. In *Lord Chancellor v McCarthy* [2012] EWHC 2325 (Admin) it was emphasised that an indictment that had been served pursuant to CrimPR Part 10 duly became 'the indictment' without the necessity for it to be signed. This was reiterated in *W (P)* [2016] EWCA Crim 745, [2016] 2 Cr App R 27 (351). This was further emphasised in *MJ* [2018] EWCA Crim 2485, [2019] 1 Cr App R 10 (122), when it was confirmed that the act of uploading such an indictment to the digital system is sufficient for that indictment to be preferred for the purposes of CrimPR 10.3 and 10.4.

Electronically Generated Indictments Under CrimPR 10.3, in the majority of cases a draft indictment will be generated electronically when the case is sent, based on the allegations before the magistrates' court, subject to substitution or amendment of the charges included by the prosecution. It was made clear in *MJ* [2018] EWCA Crim 2485, [2019] 1 Cr App R 10 (122) that a draft indictment, by being uploaded to the digital system, had been 'preferred', for the purposes of the Administration of Justice (Miscellaneous Provisions) Act 1933, s. 2, because CrimPR Part 10 had been complied with. While CrimPR 10.2 requires that a draft indictment should be served on the court and endorsed by a court officer and that when the draft indictment is endorsed, the date of receipt should be added (r. 10.2(7)(a)), it is clear that a failure to satisfy these requirements does not impugn the validity of an electronically served indictment. The officer of the Crown Court is required to endorse it, unless the court directs otherwise (r. 10.1(3)). It was stressed in *MJ* that it was the duty of prosecution and defence to regularise the position where more than one indictment had been uploaded by the time of trial and that, at trial, the court should inquire whether there were outstanding issues in relation to the indictment on which it was about to try an accused before proceeding to do so. D11.3

Problems with Compliance with this Rule The electronic generation of the vast majority of indictments and the discretion of the court to dispense with the requirement that an indictment be endorsed, pursuant to CrimPR 10.2(7), have arguably reduced the significance of the requirement to endorse an indictment, which had previously, been held to be a 'necessary condition precedent to the existence of a proper indictment' (*Morais* [1988] 3 All ER 161; *Clarke* [2008] UKHL 8, [2008] 2 All ER 665). D11.4

In any event, the authorities demonstrated that the question was whether the failure to sign the indictment in the proper manner was actually more than merely procedural. Examples of such procedural failures include:

(a) In *Jackson* [1997] 2 Cr App R 497, although the judge had directed in open court that the appropriate officer should sign the indictments, she had failed to comply with the judge's direction.
(b) In *Laming* (1989) 90 Cr App R 450, where the appropriate officer of the court signed the indictment on the front page rather than at the end, as was required by sch. 1 to the Indictment Rules 1971, the Court of Appeal held that it was nonetheless valid. The important fact was that the appropriate officer of the court had signed the indictment, intending thereby to validate it. The Court added, however, that any departure from the normal practice of signing indictments at the end was to be strongly discouraged.

Consequences of an Unsigned Indictment In *Ashton* [2006] EWCA Crim 794, [2007] 1 WLR 181, the Court of Appeal held that the approach to procedural failures in relation to the indictment in cases such as *Morais* [1988] 3 All ER 161, had been superseded by the decision in the House of Lords in *Soneji* [2005] UKHL 49, [2006] 1 AC 340. This approach was rejected by the House of Lords in *Clarke* [2008] UKHL 8, [2008] 2 All ER 665. Applying the reasoning D11.5

that had been adopted in *Soneji*, the questions to be asked, as identified by Lord Bingham, were as follows:

(a) What did Parliament intend to be the consequences of a failure to comply with the requirement in s. 2(1) that a draft indictment should be signed?
(b) What did Parliament intend to be the consequences of a trial proceeding on an unsigned draft indictment?

On the law at that time, Lord Bingham concluded that 'Parliament intended that there could be no valid trial on indictment if there was no indictment', and, following that approach, in *Leeks* [2009] EWCA Crim 1612, [2010] 1 Cr App R 5 (87) proceedings on the basis of an unsigned indictment were held to be invalid and a nullity.

However, those decisions were not followed in *MJ* [2018] EWCA Crim 2485, [2019] 1 Cr App R 10 (122). In each of two cases before the Court of Appeal, the applicant had been tried on the second bill of indictment to be uploaded to the digital case system (and in one case without any sending of certain charges on that indictment). The Court found that the failure to amend or arraign did not render the trial indictment a nullity. Each trial indictment, by being uploaded to the digital system, had been 'preferred', for the purposes of the Administration of Justice (Miscellaneous Provisions) Act 1933, s. 2, because CrimPR Part 10 had been complied with. Each applicant had therefore been tried on a valid indictment.

The Court of Appeal considered that a significant change had been achieved by the CAJA 2009, s. 116(1)(c), which addressed the consequences of procedural failures by inserting subsections (6ZA) to (6ZC) into s. 2 of the 1933 Act. The effect is that, where a draft indictment is served in accordance with s. 2(1) and (2), no objection may be taken to it after the commencement of the trial (i.e. after a jury is sworn or an accused pleads guilty) by reason of any failure to observe the rules relating to indictments. The Court observed that, pursuant to s. 2(6ZA) of the 1933 Act, no issue had been taken in either case as to the validity of the indictment before the trial, and that section precluded any challenge on appeal in such circumstances. The Court therefore considered whether the failure to arraign and/or to apply to amend undermined the safety of the conviction, and concluded that, in a case where it was accepted there was no prejudice to the accused, it did not. This, in combination with the discretion of the court (pursuant to CrimPR 10.2(7)) to dispense with the need for the indictment to be signed at all, may make technical objections based on the signing of the indictment less common.

RESPONSIBILITY FOR DRAFTING AN INDICTMENT

Ultimate Responsibility

D11.6 Ultimate responsibility for the indictment rests with counsel for the prosecution, who must ensure that it is in proper form before arraignment. This principle was affirmed by Watkins LJ, giving the judgment of the Court of Appeal in *Newland* [1988] QB 402, who said (at p. 409):

> It was the responsibility of counsel to ensure that the indictment was in proper form before arraignment. A return to that practice — it seems not to be followed generally — may in our view be a salutary thing for everyone concerned, and moreover relieve the staff of the Crown Court of any responsibility it may be felt they have in that respect, and also to have the result of there being fewer appeals to this court based on defective indictments.

Mechanics of Drafting Indictments

D11.7 Although at the time that Watkins LJ made the observations in *Newland* [1988] QB 402 (see **D11.6**) Crown Court staff drafted the bulk of indictments, invariably now the prosecuting authority prepares a schedule of charges drafted in the form of counts suitable for inclusion in an indictment. This schedule, in effect a draft indictment, is sent to the Crown Court, and as was made clear in *MJ* [2018] EWCA Crim 2485, [2019] 1 Cr App R 10 (122) the act of uploading such an indictment to the digital system is sufficient for that indictment to be preferred for the purposes of CrimPR 10.3 and 10.4. While, pursuant to CrimPR 10.2(7) there is an expectation that the Crown Court officer will check that there has been no contravention of the Administration of Justice (Miscellaneous Provisions) Act 1933, s. 2(2), before endorsing it, this is now largely a formality.

It remains, rather, the ultimate responsibility of counsel, once instructed, to ensure that the indictment is in proper form (*Moss* [1995] Crim LR 828), and (as was made clear in *MJ*) that the indictment on which an offender is to be tried has been properly preferred, amended and/or the subject of arraignment.

TIME-LIMIT FOR SERVING A BILL OF INDICTMENT

The Rule

Save in cases where the draft indictment has been generated automatically on the sending of the case for trial (pursuant to CrimPR 10.3), a draft indictment should be served on an appropriate officer of the Crown Court within 20 business days of the date on which: **D11.8**

(a) copies of documents are served where a person is sent for trial under the CDA 1998, s. 51 (CrimPR 10.4); or
(b) a High Court judge has consented to the preferment of a voluntary bill of indictment under r. 10.5 (the procedure relating to which is in CrimPR 10.9 and CrimPD II, para. 10B: see **D10.66**).

CrimPD II, para. 10A (see Supplement, **CPD.10A**), makes it clear that the draft indictment should be served more quickly than this period if the prosecution will be seeking to include counts on the indictment which differ from, or are additional to, the counts on the basis of which the accused was sent. Moreover, CrimPD I, para. 3A.16 (see Supplement, **CPD.3A**), requires the indictment to be served at least seven days before the PTPH, which itself takes place within 28 days of the case being sent to the Crown Court (CrimPD I, para. 3A.11).

Extension of the Time-limit CrimPR 10.2(8) permits the Crown Court to extend the time-limit, even after it has expired. Moreover, there are no specific rules as to the means by which an application for an extension should be made, or what such an application should contain. **D11.9**

Breaches of the Rule When r. 5 of the Indictments (Procedure) Rules 1971 still applied, it was held to be directory, not mandatory. Consequently, breach of the rule was not in itself a good ground of appeal, and the same principle applies to CrimPR 10.2. The effect of the Administration of Justice (Miscellaneous Provisions) Act 1933, s. 2(6ZA) to (6ZC), further underlines the lack of scope for an appeal based on such a breach. Case law under the old r. 5 is now of relevance only to the question of whether inordinate delay of a magnitude sufficient to prejudice the accused in the preparation of the defence might render a conviction unsafe or an application to extend the time-limit after its expiry ought to be granted. **D11.10**

Cases in relation to the form of the rule which simply provided that 'the bill of indictment must be preferred within 28 days of... committal or within such longer period as a judge of the Crown Court may allow' must now be considered in the light of these amendments.

These include *Sheerin* (1976) 64 Cr App R 68, in which defence counsel moved to quash an indictment preferred 21 days out of time, no application for an extension of time having been made. The trial judge, finding that S had not suffered any prejudice by reason of the delay, gave leave for preferment of a late bill and rejected the motion to quash. On appeal, Lawton LJ held: **D11.11**

(i) First, that the judge had had jurisdiction to grant the extension of time even though the application was not made until after the 28 days had elapsed (this is now expressly confirmed by r. 10.12(8)).

(ii) Secondly, as to the status of the rule, his lordship said (at p. 70): 'It is to be noted that the very title of the rules is "Procedure Rules" — that is rules for the guidance of courts in the administration of justice. They are not rules setting boundaries beyond which the courts cannot go.'
(iii) Thirdly, the judge had properly exercised his discretion in allowing late preferment since preparation of the indictment would have taken longer than the usual period.

In *Soffe* (1982) 75 Cr App R 133 and *Farooki* (1983) 77 Cr App R 257 the issue was the status of authorisation for an extension of time for preferment given by the chief clerk of the Crown Court concerned, not by a judge. Such breaches were found not to constitute a material irregularity in the course of the trial or in any way to invalidate the proceedings, and accordingly there were no valid grounds of appeal.

The approach in these three cases was specifically approved by the House of Lords in *Clarke* [2008] UKHL 8, [2008] 2 All ER 665 (at [14]) (see **D11.5**). They serve to underline the effect of the Administration of Justice (Miscellaneous Provisions) Act 1933, s. 2(6ZA) to (6ZC) (see **D11.10**).

D11.12 **Need for Compliance** The lack of effective sanction for breach of the time-limit for preferring an indictment should not, however, be treated by prosecutors as a licence to take as long as they like to draft the indictment, especially as its preferment is now part of a detailed timetable under CrimPD I, para. 3A. In *Sheerin*, Lawton LJ gave this warning (at p. 71):

> If there is inordinate delay in preferring a bill of indictment, which clearly has caused, or clearly is likely to cause prejudice to accused persons, then the judge may very well not exercise his discretion and leave the prosecution to take such course as they think fit. Prosecutors should not assume that they will always be granted leave to prefer a voluntary bill of indictment.

Similarly, in *Soffe* (1982) 75 Cr App R 133, Donaldson LJ (at pp. 136–7), 'first and foremost', emphasised 'that it is the duty of all concerned to take all reasonable steps to ensure that bills of indictment are preferred within the 28-day period'.

COUNTS WHICH MAY BE INCLUDED IN AN INDICTMENT

D11.13 These paragraphs deal with which charges may be included in the original draft of the indictment, rather than matters of joinder, severance or amendment to the indictment which may alter its content between the original drafting and the trial (which are dealt with at **D11.63 *et seq.***). The power to amend derives from the Indictment Act 1915, s. 5 (*Wells* (1995) 159 JP 243 and *Osieh* [1996] 1 WLR 1260; and see **D11.99**).

Charges Revealed by the Papers

D11.14 The Administration of Justice (Miscellaneous Provisions) Act 1933, s. 2(2)(a), allows a bill of indictment charging an offence to be preferred if the person charged has been sent for trial, pursuant to the CDA 1998, s. 51 and sch. 3, in each case in conjunction with proviso (i) to the subsection. The proviso is: 'where the person charged has been sent for trial, the bill of indictment against him may include, either in substitution for or in addition to any count charging an offence specified in the notice under section 57D(1) of the CDA 1998, any counts founded on material which, in pursuance of regulations made under paragraph 1 of schedule 3 to that Act, was served on the person charged, being counts which may lawfully be joined in the same indictment'. This position is reflected by CrimPR 10.2(4) (see Supplement, **R10.2**).

It follows that, subject to the rules on when counts and/or defendants are sufficiently closely linked to be properly joined in a single indictment (see **D11.63** and **D11.72**), a draft indictment may include charges for *any* indictable offence disclosed by the evidence served under the regulations for the service of the prosecution case after the accused has been sent. Usually the counts in the indictment simply follow the original charges.

Where the drafter chooses to include a count for an offence in respect of which the accused was not sent, the drafter must be careful to ensure that the offence is in fact disclosed by the statements, so as to ensure compliance with the proviso to s. 2(2)(i). The drafter must also ensure, pursuant to CrimPD II, para. 10A.10, that as much notice as possible of such charges is provided to the accused.

Application of the Proviso in s. 2(2)(i) Further points as to the effect of proviso (i) to the Administration of Justice (Miscellaneous Provisions) Act 1933, s. 2(2), are as follows: **D11.15**

(a) The prosecution may not rely on the proviso to s. 2(2) of the 1933 Act to prefer an indictment consisting *entirely* of counts for charges in respect of which the accused was not sent for trial, even where the accused has been sent on other charges and the offences charged in the indictment are disclosed by the evidence that was before the justices (*Lombardi* [1989] 1 All ER 992, which arose in the context of committal proceedings). The reasoning in *Lombardi* was that, in the absence of at least one count on the indictment for a 'committal' offence, the 'non-committal' counts cannot properly be said to be in addition to or in substitution for counts charging the offence in respect of which the accused was committed, as required by the terms of the proviso.

(b) The proviso may not be relied on to add counts to an indictment where that joinder in one indictment would have contravened what is now r. 3.21(4), on the joinder of counts. This was demonstrated in *Lombardi*, in which Lord Lane CJ said (at p. 77):

> Section 2(2) is clearly restrictive. Its primary purpose is to prevent indictments being preferred save after committal or alternative judicial leave. The proviso allows some relaxation, which is itself restricted by the final words 'being counts which may lawfully be joined in the same indictment'.
>
> It would, in our judgement, be contrary to the whole tenor of the section to allow the prosecution to prefer indictments in the way they here suggest without any reference to justices, judge or appellate court...
>
> ... charges in respect of which there has been no committal, even though based on evidence which was before the justices, can only be the proper subject of indictment where two conditions are satisfied. First, they must be in 'substitution' for or in addition to the counts in respect of which [the] defendant was committed...
>
> The second condition which has to be satisfied is that the new counts 'may lawfully be joined in the same indictment'. That must... mean the same indictment as that containing the charges on which the appellant was committed. That is clear from the whole context and also from the use of the word 'include'...
>
> In short, in the judgment of this court, the words of section 2(2) and its proviso are not apt to entitle the prosecution to prefer the second indictment.

(c) The proviso requires that any offence, other than one on which the accused was sent for trial, must be founded on the papers served under the regulations for the service of the prosecution case after the accused has been sent, but it does not require that such evidence must be conclusive (*Biddis* [1993] Crim LR 392, another case concerned with committal proceedings). In *Biddis*, it was argued that it was not permissible to add a count of possessing a firearm to the charge of robbery upon which D had been committed because a statement formally proving that it was a firearm within the meaning of the Firearms Act 1968, s. 57(1), was not included in the committal papers. The Court of Appeal held that evidence that the gun had been loaded and fired was sufficient evidence from which the jury could reasonably have inferred that it was an effective weapon.

Limitations to the Application of the Proviso There are two important limitations to objections to indictments on the basis that there has not been compliance with the proviso: **D11.16**

(a) Insofar as an indictment consists of separate counts against several accused who are individually charged (i.e. there is no joint count), the counts against each accused should be treated for purposes of proviso (i) as a separate indictment. Therefore, if two accused, D1 and D2, were separately sent for trial (e.g., because, although their offences are linked, one was not arrested until after the other had been sent for trial) and the prosecution then prefer a single indictment against them both, neither can successfully argue that the counts were preferred without authority simply because the offence alleged against the co-accused happened not to be disclosed by the material served on him or herself (*Groom* [1977] QB 6): see **D11.22**. This principle is now embodied in CrimPD II, para. 10A.5 (see Supplement, **CPD.10A**).

(b) Section 2(2) and its proviso do not apply to the amendment of an indictment, being concerned with the question of what offences can be included in the bill of indictment when it is *preferred*. The power to amend derives from the Indictments Act 1915, s. 5 (*Wells* (1995) 159 JP 243 and *Osieh* [1996] 1 WLR 1260; and see **D11.99**).

Counts for Summary Offences

D11.17 In addition to being able to indict the accused for those offences for which the accused has been sent for trial together with any other indictable offences disclosed by the material served on the accused, the drafter of an indictment has a limited power to include counts for certain summary offences.

The power is contained in the CJA 1988, s. 40, and arises when (s. 40(1)):

(a) the accused has been sent for trial for an indictable offence; and
(b) a summary offence to which s. 40 applies is either:
 (i) 'founded on the same facts or evidence as a count charging an indictable offence', or
 (ii) 'is part of a series of offences of the same or similar character as an indictable offence which is also charged'; and
(c) the facts or evidence relating to the summary offence were disclosed 'to a magistrates' court inquiring into the offence as examining justices', or are disclosed by material served on the accused as part of the procedure for sending indictable-only offences to the Crown Court under the CDA 1998, s. 51 and sch. 3 (see **D10**).

Where a count for a summary offence is included in an indictment by virtue of s. 40(1), it is tried exactly as if it were an indictable offence, but, if the accused is convicted, the maximum penalty that may be imposed is that which could have been imposed for the offence by a magistrates' court (s. 40(2)). In *Lewis* [2013] EWCA Crim 2596, [2014] 1 Cr App R 25 (345) it was emphasised that an indictment including offences pursuant to s. 40 remained valid even if the accused was acquitted of the indictable offence (reaffirmed in *Taylor* [2014] EWCA Crim 2411, [2015] RTR 11 (97)).

D11.18 **Criminal Justice Act 1988, s. 40**

(1) A count charging a person with a summary offence to which this section applies may be included in an indictment if the charge—
 (a) is founded on the same facts or evidence as a count charging an indictable offence; or
 (b) is part of a series of offences of the same or similar character as an indictable offence which is also charged,

 but only if (in either case) the facts or evidence relating to the offence are disclosed by material which, in pursuance of regulations made under paragraph 1 of Schedule 3 to the Crime and Disorder Act 1998 (procedure where person sent for trial under section 51 or 51A), has been served on the person charged.

(2) Where a count charging an offence to which this section applies is included in an indictment, the offence shall be tried in the same manner as if it were an indictable offence; but the Crown Court may only deal with the offender in respect of it in a manner in which a magistrates' court could have dealt with him.

(3) The offences to which this section applies are—
 (a) common assault;
 (aa) an offence under section 90(1) of the Criminal Justice Act 1991 (assaulting a prisoner custody officer);
 (ab) an offence under section 13(1) of the Criminal Justice and Public Order Act 1994 (assaulting a secure training centre custody officer);

(ac) an offence under paragraph 14 or 24 of Schedule 10 to the Criminal Justice and Courts Act 2015 (assaulting secure college custody officer);
(b) an offence under section 12(1) of the Theft Act 1968 (taking motor vehicle or other conveyance without authority etc.);
(c) an offence under section 103(1)(b) of the Road Traffic Act 1988 (driving a motor vehicle while disqualified);
(d) an offence [of criminal damage etc.] which would otherwise be triable only summarily by virtue of section 22(2) of [the MCA 1980]; and
(e) any summary offence specified under subsection (4) below.

Relevant Summary Offences The summary offences to which the CJA 1988, s. 40, applies are common assault, assaulting a prisoner custody officer or a secure training centre custody officer, taking a motor vehicle without the owner's consent, driving while disqualified and criminal damage where the value involved is the relevant sum or less (s. 40(3)). **D11.19**

For the purposes of s. 40(3), common assault includes the offence of battery (*Lynsey* [1995] 3 All ER 654), but common assault is not included as a lesser alternative to assault by beating unless added as a specific count (*Nelson* [2013] EWCA Crim 30, [2013] 1 WLR 2861).

Although included within the scope of s. 40, criminal damage is not, strictly speaking, a summary offence, even when the value involved is less than the relevant sum. The MCA 1980, s. 22, merely provides that, where it is clear that the value does not exceed the relevant sum of £5,000, the court 'shall proceed *as if* the offence were triable only summarily' (*Fennell* [2000] 1 WLR 2011; *Considine* (1980) 70 Cr App R 239). If the committing magistrates have not gone through the s. 22 procedure, the Court of Appeal has held that s. 40 will have no relevance, and the Crown Court is therefore not fettered by s. 40(2) to pass such sentence as could have been passed in a magistrates' court (*Alden* [2002] EWCA Crim 421, [2002] 2 Cr App R (S) 74 (326)).

However, the Court of Appeal came to the opposite view in *Gwynn* [2002] EWCA Crim 2951, [2003] 2 Cr App R (S) 41 (267). The distinction between the two cases lies in the stage at which the criminal damage count was added to the indictment. In *Gwynn* the count had been on the indictment from the outset, and the court had applied its mind to the s. 22 consideration of the value of the criminal damage, whereas in *Alden* the count had been added once the case was in the Crown Court and s. 22 did not therefore arise.

Preconditions in the Criminal Justice Act 1988, s. 40 As to the preconditions for including a count for a summary offence, the CJA 1988, s. 40(1), does *not* require the magistrates actually to have committed the accused for trial for the summary matter, providing that the facts relating to the summary offence have been disclosed 'to a magistrates' court inquiring into the offence as examining justices'. **D11.20**

The phrases 'founded on the same facts *or evidence* as a count charging an indictable offence' and 'part of a series of offences of the same or similar character as an indictable offence', are taken almost verbatim from the Indictment Rules 1971, r. 9 (now CrimPR 3.29(4) and 10.2(4)). This is borne out by *Plant* [2008] EWCA Crim 960, [2008] 2 Cr App R 27 (386) (see **D16.69**).

The Court of Appeal has provided guidance as to interpretation of the phrase:

(a) In *Bird* [1996] RTR 22, D was charged on an indictment containing two counts: (1) possession of an offensive weapon (triable either way) which was found in his car when he was stopped and (2) driving while disqualified (summary only), in relation to the fact that he was driving at all. The Court of Appeal, rejecting the argument that charge (2) was improperly joined, held that the two offences were committed at the same time as he drove along and were 'founded on the same facts or evidence'.
(b) In *Smith* [1997] QB 837, the Court of Appeal held that offences of driving a conveyance taken without authority and driving while disqualified were not offences of a similar character to dangerous driving (which was the only indictable offence in the indictment on which D was tried). Since the first two offences were not founded on the same facts as the third

offence, they were improperly joined to the indictment, and the convictions in respect of them were quashed (see **D11.64**).

D11.21 Section 40 of the CJA 1988 should be read in conjunction with the CDA 1998, s. 51(3) (see **D10.6**), which requires a magistrates' court to send the accused for trial for any either-way or summary offence with which the accused is charged and which appears to the court to be related to the offence being sent to the Crown Court under the CDA 1998, s. 51(1) (provided that, if the offence is a summary offence, it is punishable with imprisonment or disqualification from driving). In the case of children and young people, the CDA 1998, s. 51A (see **D24.42**), has a similar effect.

DUPLICATION OF INDICTMENTS

D11.22 Closely linked with the questions of authority to prefer an indictment and counts that may be included in an indictment (see **D11.13**) is the question of whether there may be more than one indictment outstanding against an accused for the same offence. The effect of the somewhat intricate case law is as follows:

(a) Ordinarily, a single sending for trial may be used as authority to prefer several indictments (see, e.g., *Follett* [1989] QB 338 per Lord Lane CJ at p. 344H). Similarly, if several accused are all sent for trial on one occasion, the prosecution may choose to indict them separately if, for example, the offences are not sufficiently linked for a single trial to be in the interests of justice or they wish to use the evidence of one accused against the others.
(b) An accused may have two or more indictments outstanding for the same offence (*Poole* [1961] AC 223). Thus, if D has been sent for trial separately for offences A and B, if offences A and B are connected as required by the rules on joinder of counts, the prosecution may serve a joint indictment for both offences. The existence of a prior indictment for offence A by itself is no bar to the later joint indictment but the prosecution will be required to elect before trial on which of the two they wish to proceed (see **D11.95**). The operation of the digital case system often results in multiple indictments. The court at the start of any trial was encouraged in *MJ* [2018] EWCA Crim 2486, [2019] 1 Cr App R 10 (122) to determine which indictment was to be used at trial, and that necessary formalities in relation to that indictment had been completed.
(c) Similarly, where two accused are separately sent for trial and it is then wished to have them tried together, the prosecution may prefer a joint indictment regardless of whether separate indictments have already been preferred against the two accused individually (*Groom* [1977] QB 6 and CrimPD II, para. 10A.5 (see Supplement, **CPD.10A**)).
(d) Equally, the prosecution may, where counts in an indictment are improperly joined, ask the judge for leave to prefer two or more fresh indictments out of time and then elect to proceed on those instead of on the original. The consequent duplication of counts between the original and fresh indictments is irrelevant (*Follett* [1989] QB 338 at p. 345C–D). The prosecution must, however, ensure that the fresh indictments are preferred before the original one is quashed.

GENERAL FORM OF AN INDICTMENT

Layout

D11.23 The layout of an indictment should substantially follow the form given in the CrimPR and the Indictments Act 1915. Save where generated electronically under CrimPR 10.3 (see Supplement, **R10.3**), the form must normally be one of those set out in the CrimPD (r. 10.2(16)). The basic requirements as to *the layout of an indictment* are as follows:

(a) Each offence charged should be set out in a separate paragraph or *count* (r. 10.2(1)). If there is more than one count, they should be numbered (r. 10.2(43)).

(b) Each count should be divided into a statement of offence and particulars of offence (r. 10.2(1)(a) and (b)).
(c) The statement of offence describes the offence shortly in ordinary language, and, if the offence is statutory, should specify by section and subsection the provision contravened (Indictments Act 1915, s. 3(1), and r. 10.2(1)(a)).
(d) The particulars of offence should give 'such particulars as may be necessary for giving reasonable information as to the nature of the charge' (Indictments Act 1915, s. 3(1)). This is supplemented by r. 10.2(1)(b) which states that there should be included 'such particulars of the conduct constituting the commission of the offence as to make clear what the prosecutor alleges against the defendant'.

In short, CrimPR Part 10 requires that the statement of offence make clear what legislation underlies the charge, and that the particulars make clear what the accused is alleged to have done. It follows that the rules now require less than the Indictment Rules 1971, r. 6, which required all the essential elements of the offence to be disclosed (r. 6(b)). This change was recognised by Lord Thomas CJ in *Clarke* [2015] EWCA Crim 350, [2015] 2 Cr App R 6 (74), when he said (at [18]): 'the sole question is whether the particulars make clear what the prosecutor alleges against the defendant'. It was not necessary to the particulars to identify the ingredients of the offence, provided that the offence was properly described in general terms. **D11.24**

Indictments Act 1915, s. 3

(1) Every indictment shall contain, and shall be sufficient if it contains, a statement of the specific offence or offences with which the accused person is charged, together with such particulars as may be necessary for giving reasonable information as to the nature of the charge.
(2) Notwithstanding any rule of law or practice, an indictment shall, subject to the provisions of this Act, not be open to objection in respect of its form or contents if it is framed in accordance with the rules under this Act.

Degree of Detail Required in the Particulars

In normal circumstances, the particulars of offence are drafted in a short form. Such a course is encouraged as a means to avoid complex, lengthy or unmanageable trials (*Cohen* (1992) *Independent*, 29 July 1992). **D11.25**

Such brevity does not prejudice the defence since the way the prosecution put their case and the evidence they intend to call will sufficiently emerge from the documents served. For example, in *Teong Sun Chuah* [1991] Crim LR 463, the appellants were convicted of obtaining by deception. One of the grounds of appeal was that no particulars were given of the false representations relied on in support of the charges. The Court of Appeal said that, although it was advantageous for particulars to be given of the false representations in such cases, it was plain in the present case what the particulars were. No injustice was done by failing to spell them out in advance.

However, it is established practice to give extended particulars where the offence charged is complicated. For example, in *Warburton-Pitt* (1991) 92 Cr App R 136, the prosecution's failure to particularise the facts upon which they relied in support of allegations of recklessness formed the basis of a successful appeal. The Court of Appeal said that particulars of the allegations of recklessness were needed because the case was a complicated one; there were a number of possible explanations for the incident.

A comparison of *Teong Sun Chuah* and *Warburton-Pitt* demonstrates that the test is: do the particulars provided, whether in the indictment or elsewhere, meet the requirement in r. 10.2(1)(b) that there should be clarity as to the nature of the prosecution case?

This test was reaffirmed by the Court of Appeal in *K* [2004] EWCA Crim 2685, [2005] 1 Cr App R 25 (408). The particulars of the offence needed to provide reasonable information as to the nature of the charge and as to the principal matters on which the prosecution relied. In the case of a conspiracy charge, the indictment needed to spell out the agreement alleged, but such further information as is provided to assist the defence does not thereby become an ingredient of the offence that must be proved and on which the jury in due course have to be unanimous. In *Chargot Ltd* [2008] UKHL 73, [2009] 1 WLR 1, similarly, the Supreme Court concluded that in a prosecution alleging breaches of the Health and Safety at Work etc. Act 1974 it was sufficient that the risk to the employee's health and safety was particularised, without further specifying the respects in which that risk was associated with his employment or identifying the cause of the accident in which the employee was injured.

Moreover, it is open to the defence to ask for additional particulars. One of the purposes of doing so is to anchor the prosecution to a particular means by which the charge may be made out (see, e.g., *Landy* [1981] 1 All ER 1172 and *Hancock* [1996] 2 Cr App R 554, and see also the comment on those decisions in *Clarke* [2015] EWCA Crim 350, [2015] 2 Cr App R 6 (74) (at [21])). In *Clarke*, an indictment for robbery was valid where the offence had been correctly described and the particulars supported the conviction of the offence and made the prosecution case clear. It was not necessary to specify the ingredients of the offence, such as whether a person had been put in fear or unlawful force had been used.

Components of the Particulars

D11.26 Rule 5(2) of the Indictment Rules 1971 made provision for the rules to include specimen forms of counts approved by the Lord Chief Justice. No such specimens were provided under the 1971 Rules, and the 2007 redraft removed even reference to them. Such authority as there is on drafting counts for specific offences is therefore derived from decided cases. In addition, the CPS has issued guidance as to how particulars for certain offences should be drafted, and has drafted model forms for such counts (see www.cps.gov.uk/prosecution-guidance). A suggested form of count for the major offences will also be found in the section of this work dealing with the offence in question.

The standard components of particulars are:

(a) the names of the defendants charged in the count;
(b) the date of the offence (or the dates of the period within which it occurred if the precise date is not known);
(c) the act constituting the offence (e.g., 'stole' such and such an item of property, or 'inflicted grievous bodily harm' on such and such a person);
(d) the name of the victim of the offence (e.g., the owner of the property stolen or the person wounded or assaulted); and
(e) the state of mind on the part of the accused which the prosecution must establish in order to secure a conviction.

Points of drafting procedure which apply generally, whatever the specific offence alleged, are considered below.

D11.27 **Names** A person named in an indictment (whether as accused, victim or otherwise) should be described by forenames and surname (see 2 Hale 175). Errors in stating names will not, however, affect the validity of the proceedings, provided that the misnamed person is identified with reasonable precision and the parties are not misled. Under r. 8 of the Indictment Rules 1971, it was sufficient where a person's name was not known to refer to a 'person unknown'. There seems no reason to depart from that practice under the new rules. Trading companies may be described by their corporate name, whether or not they are incorporated.

D11.28 **Date of the Offence** The count should state the date on which the offence occurred insofar as it is known. Normal practice is to give the day of the month, followed by the month, followed by the year (e.g., 'on 1st day of January 2020'). If the precise date is unknown, it is sufficient to allege that the offence occurred 'on or about' a specified date, or 'on a day unknown' before a specified date, or 'on a date other than the date in count one'. Where the formula 'on or about' a date is used, the evidence must show the offence to have been committed 'within some period that has a reasonable approximation to the date mentioned in the indictment' (per Sachs LJ in *Hartley* [1972] 2 QB 1 at p. 7).

An alternative permitted formulation is 'on a day unknown between' two specified dates. If the last-mentioned formula is adopted, the days specified should be those immediately before the earliest and immediately after the latest days on which the offence could have been committed.

See also **D11.51** on duplicity in relation to this formulation.

Materiality of Date If the evidence at trial as to date differs from that particularised in the count, that is not, as a rule, fatal to a conviction (*Dossi* (1918) 13 Cr App R 158; and see *Pritchett* [2007] EWCA Crim 586, in which *Dossi* was approved and it was held not to invalidate an indictment that the offence charged was in force for only part of the period mentioned in the indictment). **D11.29**

This position will be different where the allegation as to date is not merely procedural, but may determine the outcome of the case. For example, in some instances the date on which the act occurred will affect the age of the alleged victim, which may be material. This was the case in *Radcliffe* [1990] Crim LR 524, where, in a case of indecency with a child, the judge in summing-up said: 'The dates which are set out in the indictment ... are immaterial. The prosecution do not have to prove that any particular act happened between those dates. What you have to prove is that it happened.' The Court of Appeal criticised this direction because the jury may have been left with the belief that her age was immaterial and that they could convict even if she was over 14 at the time.

Avoiding Prejudice as to Dates The decision in *Wright v Nicholson* [1970] 1 All ER 12, provides authority for the proposition that where the defence may have been prejudiced in the preparation of their case by a divergence during the evidence from the date specified in the count, the trial may be adjourned to allow them to respond to the altered situation. Alternatively, it might be necessary to discharge the jury and have a second trial on an amended indictment. Failure to allow an adjournment could result in the quashing of any resultant conviction as being unsafe or unsatisfactory. **D11.30**

However, some caution is necessary in applying that decision in the present context because (a) the appeal was not against conviction on indictment but against the dismissal by the Crown Court of an appeal against summary conviction, and (b) the Divisional Court's reasoning was partly based on the faulty premise that the Crown Court had power to amend the information on which the magistrates had convicted the appellant.

Amendment of Dates Since divergence between a count and the evidence as to date is not in itself fatal to conviction, it may be unnecessary for the prosecution to apply for the indictment to be amended on such a divergence becoming apparent (*Dossi* (1918) 13 Cr App R 158; but see *Bonner* [1974] Crim LR 479, where the Court of Appeal apparently overlooked the point). However, as a matter of practice, it may be preferable to eliminate the divergence by an appropriate amendment, thus avoiding confusing the jury. **D11.31**

Continuous Offences

In most instances, the rule against duplicity (i.e. each count may allege only one offence, see **D11.45**) requires that a count must allege that the offence occurred on *one* day, not on several days. Were it to be otherwise, the only sensible interpretation of such an allegation would be that the accused had committed several distinct offences on different days. Although the prosecution are permitted to have one count for what are technically distinct criminal acts where those acts formed a single activity or transaction (e.g., pursuant to CrimPR 10.2(2)), the mention of more than one day (whether conjunctively or disjunctively) in the count is inconsistent with there having been a single activity on the accused's part. **D11.32**

The difference here is between an offence being committed once between a start and end date, and the offence having been committed repeatedly but separately on a number of days.

The exception to the general principle just stated is that where an offence is properly to be regarded as a continuing offence which may take place continuously or intermittently over a period of time, then a count may properly allege that it occurred on more than one day.

D11.33 **Enunciation of the Principle in *Hodgetts v Chiltern District Council*** The leading authority on drafting charges for continuous offences is *Hodgetts v Chiltern District Council* [1983] 2 AC 120, in which the House of Lords was concerned with the validity of an information under the Town and Country Planning Act 1971, s. 89(5), which created two offences, an initial one committed immediately where there was non-compliance with an enforcement notice requiring the subject of the notice to desist from a certain use of land, and a further offence committed by a person who had already been convicted of the initial offence and who still failed to desist from the prohibited use.

The argument for H was that s. 89(5) was separately breached on each day of the period during which an enforcement notice was ignored, and a separate information was required for each day. Rejecting this argument, Lord Roskill said (at p. 128, emphasis added):

> It is not an essential characteristic of a criminal offence that any prohibited act or omission, in order to constitute a single offence, should take place once and for all on a single day. It may take place, whether continuously or intermittently, over a period of time.
>
> … as respects non-compliance with a 'desist' notice, it is in my view clear that the initial offence (as well as the further offence) though it too may take place over a period, whether continuously or intermittently (e.g., holding a Sunday market), is a single offence and not a series of separate offences committed each day that the non-compliance prior to the first conviction for non-compliance continues.
>
> … in the instant case each information … charged the offence 'on and since' a specified date … I see no objection to [that wording], but it might be preferable if hereafter offences under the first limb of section 89(5) were charged as having been committed between two specified dates, the termini usually being on the one hand the date when compliance with the enforcement notice first became due and on the other hand a date not later than the date when the information was laid, or of course some earlier date if meanwhile the enforcement notice has been complied with. *Indictments frequently charge offences as having been committed between certain dates.* I see no reason in principle why the same practice should not be followed with these informations.

D11.34 **Application of the Principle** Other than in circumstances to which CrimPR 10.2(2) has application, the following points on drafting counts for continuous offences emerge from the above decision:

(a) Although *Hodgetts v Chiltern District Council* [1983] 2 AC 120 concerned an information for a summary offence, the italicised words in the quotation at **D11.33** make clear that the same principles apply to counts in an indictment.
(b) Determining whether an offence is properly to be treated as continuous will require detailed analysis of the offence-creating provision. In the absence of specific authority, the drafter of an indictment may have no means of knowing with certainty whether the offence for which the drafter is indicting the accused is continuous or not. In such cases, it may be preferable to avoid potential complications by stating that the offence occurred on one day (not on several), unless the continuation of the misconduct significantly adds to the gravity of the case.
(c) That said, conspiracy is a clear example of a continuous indictable offence. The offence begins when any two or more parties enter into the unlawful agreement and continues until it comes to an end. See, e.g.:
    (i) *Greenfield* [1973] 3 All ER 1050 (and see **D11.46**), where a count for conspiring to cause explosions between 1 January 1968 and July 1971 was held not to be bad for duplicity;
    (ii) *Landy* [1981] 1 All ER 1172, where the Court of Appeal, in indicating how the prosecution should have drafted a count for conspiracy to defraud a bank, suggested that

the particulars could have begun '[The defendants] *on divers days* between ... and ... conspired together and with ...'.

(d) Theft is clearly not a continuous offence. However, where the evidence is that the accused, on numerous separate occasions over a lengthy period, stole small sums or items of property, but it is not possible to particularise the exact days on which the appropriations occurred, it is possible to have a single count alleging that, on a day within the overall period, the accused stole all the relevant money or property. The cases on this point (known as the general deficiency cases) are considered at **B4.3** (see also the discussion of sample counts at **D11.36**). This problem may also be cured by CrimPR 10.2(2).

Effect of CrimPR 10.2(2) Rule 10.2(2) states: **D11.35**

> More than one incident of the commission of an offence may be included in a count if those incidents taken together amount to a course of conduct having regard to the time, place or purpose of commission.

Before this form of words was incorporated into the CrimPR, it had been argued that it was usually possible to allege only one incident per count, as to allege more than one incident in a count fell foul of the rule against duplicity (see **D11.45**).

Circumstances in which it is suggested to be appropriate to use r. 10.2(2) to charge a 'multiple offending count' are identified in CrimPD II, para. 10A.11 (see Supplement, **CPD.10A**):

> CrimPR 10.2(2) allows a single count to allege more than one incident of the commission of an offence in certain circumstances. Each incident must be of the same offence. The circumstances in which such a count may be appropriate include, but are not limited to, the following:
> (a) the victim on each occasion was the same, or there was no identifiable individual victim as, for example, in a case of the unlawful importation of controlled drugs or of money laundering;
> (b) the alleged incidents involved a marked degree of repetition in the method employed or in their location, or both;
> (c) the alleged incidents took place over a clearly defined period, typically (but not necessarily) no more than about a year;
> (d) in any event, the defence is such as to apply to every alleged incident without differentiation. Where what is in issue differs between different incidents, a single 'multiple incidents' count will not be appropriate, though it may be appropriate to use two or more such counts according to the circumstances and to the issues raised by the defence.

Counts which allege more than one incident can give rise to certain difficulties. One, which was identified in *Kidd* [1998] 1 All ER 42, is that the accused should be sentenced only for offences on which the accused has been indicted and of which the accused has been convicted. This is discussed further at **D20.52**.

In *Hartley* [2011] EWCA Crim 1299, [2012] 1 Cr App R 7 (91) Hughes LJ gave further guidance for multiple incident indictments. In particular:

(a) it is important to make clear where it is the case that what is charged is a course of conduct, and make clear the period over which it is charged;
(b) a verdict on the resultant charge must not be impossible to interpret, and so, where it is possible that there was one incident during the period encompassed by the course of conduct count, a count alleging that incident should also be included in the indictment (such a course may also avoid the difficulty of some jurors being sure of one incident and others being sure of another, a matter addressed in *Williams* [2012] EWCA Crim 2516);
(c) where specific incidents can be identified even 'exiguously' (e.g., 'the time the vase broke') it is appropriate for such a single incident to be indicted and particularised in such terms (the same approach was encouraged in *Hobson* [2013] EWCA Crim 819, [2013] 1 WLR 3733);
(d) where the period of time over which the course of conduct is said to have occurred is long, it should be addressed by a series of counts covering the period (e.g., on a yearly basis).

Further, in *A* [2015] EWCA Crim 177, [2015] 2 Cr App R (S) 12 (115) the Court of Appeal said that it was incumbent on the prosecution, in a case of alleged sustained sexual abuse, to ensure that there were either one or more broad course of conduct counts or a mix of individual and course of conduct counts to permit certainty as to the basis for sentence, whilst also taking care not to overburden the indictment.

Specimen or Sample Counts

D11.36 Where a person is accused of adopting a systematic course of criminal conduct, and where it is not appropriate to allege a continuous offence (see **D11.32**) or a multiple offending count (see **D11.35**), the prosecution sometimes proceed by way of specimen or sample counts. For example, where dishonesty over a period of time is alleged, a limited number of sample counts are included so as to avoid too lengthy an indictment.

D11.37 **Procedure for Specimen Counts** The practice which the prosecution ought to adopt in these circumstances is as follows:

(a) the defence should be provided with a list of all the similar offences of which it is alleged that those selected in the indictment are samples;
(b) evidence of some or all of these additional offences may in appropriate cases be led as evidence of system;
(c) in other cases, the additional offences need not be referred to until after a verdict of guilty upon the sample offence is returned (*DPP v Anderson* [1978] AC 964).

D11.38 **Potential Problems with Specimen Counts** Potential problems arise with specimen counts in relation to sentencing because the accused should not thereby be denied the right to be tried by a jury for offending for which the accused may ultimately be sentenced. This is discussed at **D20.56** *et seq*.

In any event, it is crucial that the accused should know the case he or she has to meet (*Evans* [1995] Crim LR 245). In *Rackham* [1997] 2 Cr App R 222, the Court of Appeal emphasised that the indictment had to be drafted in such a way as to enable the accused to know, with as much particularity as the circumstances would admit, what case the accused had to meet.

D11.39 **Split Trials** As an alternative to the use of specimen counts, ss. 17 to 21 of the DVCVA 2004 permit a court in certain circumstances to order that the trial of certain counts on an indictment take place before a jury in the normal way and that, if the jury convict the accused on those counts, the remainder should then be tried before a judge alone. These provisions are set out and discussed at **D13.81**.

The procedure, drafting and service of indictments are set out in CrimPD II, paras. 10A.15 to 10A.20 (see Supplement, **CPD.10A**). The key points are:

(a) the prosecution must identify when drafting the indictment which counts should be tried by the jury and which should be held in reserve for the judge;
(b) when such an indictment is served, it should be accompanied by an application for a preparatory hearing, because it is only at such a hearing that such a mode of trial may be ordered (see **D15.51**).

Place of the Offence

D11.40 Provided the conduct alleged against the accused constitutes an offence regardless of where it occurred, it is unnecessary for the particulars to specify venue. In *Wallwork* (1958) 42 Cr App R 153, the particulars alleged that the offence, in that case of incest, had been committed 'in the county of Sussex or elsewhere'. The Court of Criminal Appeal held that the indictment was not bad for duplicity as the venue need not have been mentioned at all. Lord Goddard CJ said (at pp. 156–7):

> So far as place is concerned, I think [counsel for the prosecution's] point is a perfectly good one, that incest is an offence wherever it is committed, and it matters not whether it is committed in one

> place or another, provided the prisoner knows the substance of the charge against him. It makes no difference whether the incest in this case was committed in Sussex or Surrey or any other place. ... There are cases ... in which it is necessary to indicate a particular place in the indictment, and an illustration [is] the offence of larceny on a ship which was at the time of the larceny in a harbour or in a creek or other place of anchorage ... where it would be necessary to show that the theft took place while the ship was in a harbour or some particular creek, and then it would be necessary to mention the name of the harbour or creek. But ... it is not necessary to refer to any place in the indictment in an offence of this description.

The example given in the above passage of instances where the place of offence should be particularised may be anachronistic, but current examples of the same requirement are burglary and dangerous driving. Counts for the former should state the building entered as a trespasser, and counts for the latter the roads or other public places where the driving took place. The reason, in both cases, is that, having regard to the definition of the offences, the place where the prohibited conduct occurred is an essential ingredient of the crime (see, e.g., *Miller* [2010] EWCA Crim 809, [2011] 1 Cr App R (S) 2 (7), where it was held that the indictment for burglary should specify if it was committed on domestic premises as this had an impact on the maximum penalty).

Allegations as to Money and Property

The Criminal Procedure Act 1851, s. 18, provides that: **D11.41**

> In every indictment in which it shall be necessary to make any averment as to any money or any note of the Bank of England or any other bank, it shall be sufficient to describe such money or bank note simply as money, without specifying any particular coin or bank note; and such allegation, so far as regards the description of the property, shall be sustained by proof of any amount of coin or of any bank note, although the particular nature of the bank note shall not be proved.

Where the offence alleged is one against property, the count must give reasonable particulars of the property concerned. This is normally done by stating what the property was, and who owned it. If that is not known, the count may read 'belonging to a person unknown'. The value of the property need not be stated.

Indicting Secondary Parties

When indicting a secondary party to an offence, namely an aider, abettor, counsellor or procurer, **D11.42**
there is no need to indicate, either in the statement of offence or particulars, that such was the party's role. This convenient rule flows from the Accessories and Abettors Act 1861, s. 8, which provides that:

> Whosoever shall aid, abet, counsel, or procure the commission of any indictable offence, whether the same be an offence at common law or by virtue of any Act passed or to be passed, shall be liable to be tried, *indicted*, and punished as a principal offender [emphasis added].

The usual practice is to take advantage of the 1861 Act and employ the same form of words in indicting a secondary party as would be used against a principal offender.

There is, however, no objection to an express allegation of aiding and abetting, and it may be preferable so to draft if the circumstances are such that the accused could not possibly have been guilty as a principal offender. In such cases, the precedent for a count against a principal offender may be adapted by prefixing the statement of offence with the words 'Aiding and abetting', and by inserting in the particulars 'aided and abetted [name of principal offender] to ...'.

Where the prosecution are unsure of the precise role played by the accused, it is permissible to allege aiding, abetting, counselling or procuring in the alternative in one count (*Ferguson v Weaving* [1951] 1 KB 814).

The normal practice of indicting secondary parties as if they were principals was criticised in **D11.43**
Maxwell [1978] 3 All ER 1140, where the particulars for an offence of doing an act with intent,

contrary to the Explosive Substances Act 1883, s. 3(a), alleged that D had planted a pipe bomb whereas in reality he had merely guided others to the scene where they planted it. The House of Lords dismissed D's appeal against conviction, but Viscount Dilhorne said, *obiter*, at p. 1352G:

> It is desirable that the particulars of the offence should bear some relation to the realities and where, as here, it is clear that the appellant was alleged to have aided and abetted the placing of the bomb and its possession or control, it would... have been better if the particulars of offence had made that clear.

Lords Hailsham of St Marylebone, Fraser and Edmund-Davies all commented to like effect; see, e.g., Lord Edmund-Davies at p. 1359G: 'However surprising and unreal such allegations might have sounded to a jury, ... it has to be said that such wording [of the count] was strictly in accordance with section 8 of the Accessories and Abettors Act 1861' (but see *Montague* [2013] EWCA Crim 1781).

Consequences of Errors

D11.44 What if the particulars of offence are incorrect? In *Moses* [1991] Crim LR 617, the Court of Appeal observed that particulars of offence were not like the words of a statute, such that failure of the facts proved to fall precisely within them was fatal. It seems that the test to apply in relation to incorrect particulars is whether the defence were prejudiced by the erroneous description of the offence (see also *Hancock* [1996] 2 Cr App R 554).

THE RULE AGAINST DUPLICITY

The Rule

D11.45 The ordinary rule is that each count in an indictment must allege only one offence. If a count alleges more than one offence, it is said to be bad for duplicity and should be quashed before arraignment.

D11.46 **Duplicity Revealed by the Wording of the Count** Whether or not a count is bad for duplicity is decided by looking at its wording without reference to the prosecution evidence as disclosed by the evidence served under the regulations for the service of the prosecution case after the accused has been sent for trial (*Greenfield* [1973] 3 All ER 1050, a case decided in the context of committal papers, followed in *Mintern* [2004] EWCA Crim 7).

This is illustrated by *Greenfield* itself, in which the appellants and others were charged in a count which alleged that they had conspired together to cause, by explosive substances, explosions in the UK. The prosecution relied on evidence of a series of explosions occurring in different parts of England which the jury were invited to conclude had all been the work of the same group.

On appeal, the defence argued that the conspiracy count was bad for duplicity because, as the trial progressed, the evidence was consistent with the existence of more than one conspiracy. The Court of Appeal held that, even if that were so, it did not affect the validity of the count, although it was essential that the jury should be directed to convict only if they found the offence charged proved. Lawton LJ said (at pp. 1155F–1156B):

> A conspiracy count is bad in law if it *charges* the defendants with having been members of two or more conspiracies. This is elementary law. ... [Count 1] referred to one conspiracy only... judges may be in doubt as to what they should consider before deciding whether a conspiracy count is bad for duplicity. They should look first at the count itself. In most cases it will be unnecessary to look at any other material. If particulars of the count have been requested and given, those too should be considered. ... If the prosecution has been requested to give particulars and has refused to do so, the judge may have to look at the depositions to discover the nature of the charge.
>
> Duplicity in a count is a matter of form; it is not a matter relating to the evidence called in support of the count.

Thus, leaving aside the exceptional case of the defence having asked for and been refused additional particulars of a count, the only matters to be considered by a judge determining whether a count is bad for duplicity are the form (i.e. wording) of the count and any additional particulars supplied by the prosecution. The evidence as disclosed on the served documents is irrelevant. In *Ali* [2011] EWCA Crim 1260, [2011] 3 All ER 1071 the Court of Appeal held that it was not appropriate to include two conspiracy charges in an indictment which were the same in law but factually different so as to gauge the jury's finding of fact for the purposes of sentence (see also **D19.83**). **D11.47**

If the evidence called at trial in fact establishes more than one offence but only one offence is charged in the count, then, subject to any possible amendment of the indictment, the accused will be entitled to an acquittal, not because the count was bad, but because the prosecution have failed to prove the accused guilty of the precise offence charged in the count, even though they may have proved the accused guilty of some other offence or offences (*Griffiths* [1966] 1 QB 589, which was considered more recently in *Mehta* [2012] EWCA Crim 2824 and *Shillam* [2013] EWCA Crim 160, where the judge had erred in directing that the defendants could be guilty of a conspiracy count where there was doubt as to whether they were all party to the same conspiracy).

Consideration of the Meaning of 'Offence' The proposition that a count must charge only one offence begs the question, what is an offence? The issue came before the House of Lords in *DPP v Merriman* [1973] AC 584. In that case two brothers (FM and JM) were charged in a joint count with wounding P with intent, where the evidence showed JM to have stabbed P both on his own and then with FM. In considering whether the judge had been correct to direct the jury that they should ignore any possibility that JM was acting in concert with FM, and should concentrate solely on whether he had personally stabbed P, the House of Lords considered the true import of the rule against duplicity. Lord Morris of Borth-y-Gest said (at p. 593A–E): **D11.48**

> It is ... a general rule that not more than one offence is to be charged in a count in an indictment. ... The question arises — what is an offence? ... I agree ... that it will often be legitimate to bring a single charge in respect of what might be called one activity even though that activity may involve more than one act. It must, of course, depend upon the circumstances. In the present case, it was not at any time suggested, and in my view could not reasonably have been suggested, that count 1 was open to objection because evidence was to be tendered that the respondent stabbed [P] more than once.

In a similar vein, Lord Diplock said (at p. 607C):

> The rule against duplicity, viz. that only one offence should be charged in any count of an indictment ... has always been applied in a practical, rather than in a strictly analytical, way for the purpose of determining what constituted one offence. Where a number of acts of a similar nature committed by one or more defendants were connected with one another, in the time and place of their commission or by their common purpose, in such a way that they could fairly be regarded as forming part of the same transaction or criminal enterprise, it was the practice, as early as the 18th century, to charge them in a single count of an indictment. Where such a count was laid against more than one defendant, the jury could find each of them guilty of one offence only: but a failure by the prosecution to prove the allegation, formerly expressly stated in the indictment but now only implicit in their joinder in the same count, that the unlawful acts of each were done jointly in aid of one another, did not render the indictment *ex post facto* bad or invalidate the jury's verdict against those found guilty.

The Test Derived from *DPP v Merriman* In summary, the conclusion in *DPP v Merriman* [1973] AC 584 was that a count is not to be held bad on its face for duplicity merely because its words are logically capable of being construed as alleging more than one criminal act. This applies whether a count is against one accused or several. **D11.49**

The test of whether it is proper to have a single count is: can the separate acts attributed to the accused fairly be said to form a single activity or transaction? (see **D11.57**). It follows from that test that, if the particulars of a count can sensibly be interpreted as alleging a single activity, it will not be bad for duplicity, even if a number of distinct criminal acts are implied.

This interpretation of the rule against duplicity clearly forms the basis for the rule permitting 'multiple offences' counts to be found in CrimPR 10.2(2). As the wording of that rule demonstrates, what is permitted is a count alleging a series of offences that amount to a course of conduct or, to use Lord Diplock's words, the same 'criminal enterprise' (see **D11.35**).

Practical Application of the Rule

D11.50 Thus, the rule against duplicity rests ultimately on common sense and pragmatic considerations of what is fair in all the circumstances. That being so, the rule is best understood in terms of past decisions on what is acceptable drafting practice, rather than by applying an artificial concept of what is a single offence. The guidelines below emerge from the cases.

D11.51 **Several Dates** Unless the offence charged is properly to be construed as a continuing offence (see **D11.32**), a count alleging that the accused committed criminal acts on more than one day is bad for duplicity.

For example, in *Thompson* [1914] 2 KB 99, the count charged alleged the commission of incest 'on divers days between the month of January, 1909, and the 4th day of October, 1910'. Although the Court of Criminal Appeal dismissed the appeal because the appellant had had ample notice of the precise dates on which the acts of incest were said to have occurred, it was common ground that the count was 'irregular' because it patently alleged more than one offence.

However, in *DPP v McCabe* [1992] Crim LR 885, a charge alleging that D stole 76 library books from South Glamorgan Library between two specified dates was held not to be bad for duplicity. The Divisional Court held that where there is appropriation of a number of articles, but no evidence as to when the individual appropriations took place, the prosecution is entitled to charge the appropriation of the aggregate number within a specified period.

D11.52 **Several Items of Property** A count for an offence against property may allege that several items were stolen, damaged, unlawfully possessed or otherwise subjected to the accused's criminal behaviour (per Lord Morris of Borth-y-Gest in the passage from *DPP v Merriman* [1973] AC 584, quoted at **D11.48**, and see *Wilson* (1979) 69 Cr App R 83). Provided there is nothing on the face of the count to indicate to the contrary, it will be presumed that, even if a separate criminal act is being alleged in respect of each item, those acts were so closely related as to form part of a single activity and are therefore properly charged in a single count.

A single count is appropriate if only one act is being alleged, albeit that the act was in respect of several items (e.g., *Thomas* (1800) 2 East PC 934, in which a count for uttering a number of forged receipts in one bundle was upheld). But the special circumstances of a case may make separate counts for each item necessary or desirable even if what is alleged against the accused is a single act or activity. For example, in *Bristol Crown Court, ex parte Willets* (1985) 149 JP 416, where the accused was charged with possession of five obscene videos, the Divisional Court said it would have been better to include five separate counts to allow the jury to consider the obscenity of each video individually (see also *Malhi* [1994] Crim LR 755).

D11.53 **Several Victims** Old cases provide examples of a single count naming more than one person as the victim of the offence (see, e.g., *Giddins* (1842) Car & M 634). Modern practice, however, is in general to have a separate count per victim (see, e.g., *Mansfield* [1977] 1 All ER 134, in which D was charged, *inter alia*, with seven counts of murder, a different victim being named in each count, even though all seven deaths resulted from a single fire allegedly started by D).

Even so, what is appropriate must depend ultimately on the facts of each case. For example:

(a) In *Shillingford* [1968] 2 All ER 200, the Court of Appeal said it was unnecessary to have two separate counts where it was alleged that D had administered a drug to enable both himself and another to have unlawful sexual intercourse with V. According to Salmon LJ: 'the essence of this offence consists in administering the drug, and ... accordingly in this particular case there was only one offence under the section ... In the view of this court, if there is only one administration there is only one offence, whether the administration was for the purpose of enabling one man or half a dozen men to have intercourse with the woman in question.'

(b) Similarly, in *Jemmison v Priddle* [1972] 1 QB 489, an information for taking and killing two red deer was held not to be bad for duplicity because the deer were shot within seconds of each other. In that case, however, there certainly could not have been any objection to two informations.

Count Alleging Acts or Omissions in the Alternative

A separate question is raised where the statutory provision creating an offence indicates that it may be committed either by one of a number of positive acts or by a failure to act in one of a number of ways. This problem was specifically addressed by the Indictment Rules 1971, r. 7, which permitted alternative means of committing an offence to be included in the count. Although CrimPR Part 10 does not replicate this rule, the principle remains that a count containing particulars framed in the alternative is not necessarily bad for duplicity, as is recognised for example by CrimPR 10.2(2) (set out at **D11.35**). However, if an enactment creates several offences and it is desired to charge two or more of those offences in the alternative, the indictment must contain a separate count for each. Furthermore, it is plain that a single section, subsection or paragraph of a statute may be construed as creating more than one offence (see, e.g., *Naismith* [1961] 2 All ER 735 at **D11.55**). What is required, therefore, is a correct assessment of whether a statutory provision is creating one offence that may be committed in a number of alternative ways, or is creating several separate offences. If the former, these statutory alternatives may be particularised as alternatives in one count; if the latter, the rule against duplicity applies and each alternative the prosecution wish to put before the jury must go into a separate count. **D11.54**

Application of the Rule as to Alternative Acts or Omissions It follows from the discussion at **D11.54** that decisions on whether an enactment creates one or several offences have consistently turned on whether, in defining the conduct prohibited, the enactment refers to a single act (or omission) or to several. If one act is referred to, the enactment will almost certainly be construed as creating one offence, even if the *mens rea* or other elements thereof are defined in the alternative; if more than one, it will be held that the enactment creates a separate offence for each separate act. **D11.55**

For example, in *Grout* [2010] EWCA Crim 1203, [2011] 1 Cr App R (S) 38 (472), the Court of Appeal concluded that where the section of the SOA 2003 under which the offender had been charged created four separate offences, some of which involved different penalties, it was necessary for the indictment to make clear which offence was alleged, and to have separate charges for the different offences where appropriate (see **B3.101**). This approach acccords with the observations of Ashworth J in *Naismith* [1961] 2 All ER 735. In determining whether an allegation under military law that D had 'caused grievous bodily harm to H with intent to do him grievous bodily harm or to maim, disfigure or disable him' was bad for duplicity, he said (at p. 954):

> It seems to this court that the proposition with which [counsel for the Crown] started his argument is the right approach. That approach is to keep in mind the distinction between a section creating two or more offences and a section creating one offence but providing that that offence may be committed in more than one way ... so far as the intents specified in section 18 are concerned, they are variations of method rather than creations of separate offences in themselves. It is probably true to say that the species of assault mentioned in that section, of which there are three, are each in themselves different offences, that is to say, wounding, causing grievous bodily harm and shooting, but that difference does not affect the result of this case in the least because the only act or species of assault alleged was causing grievous bodily harm.

D11.56 The number of offences an enactment is held to create, whether one or several, turns on a fine analysis of the enactment in question, as well as on pragmatic considerations of whether one or several counts would be fairer. This is illustrated by a comparison of *Thomson v Knights* [1947] KB 336 and *Mallon v Allon* [1964] 1 QB 385.

In *Thomson* it was held that a count for being in charge of a motor vehicle when unfit through drink or drugs (contrary to what is now s. 4 of the Road Traffic Act 1988) was valid because the section made criminal one act, namely being in charge of a vehicle, in two situations, namely when under the influence of drink or when under the influence of drugs.

By contrast, in *Mallon*, an information for admitting and allowing to remain in a licensed betting office a person apparently under 18 contrary to s. 5 of the Betting and Gaming Act 1960 (now repealed) was held bad because the enactment referred to two separate acts, first admitting a person on to licensed premises, and secondly allowing him to remain after he had got on to the premises (for further discussion of this topic see, e.g., **B4.162** and **B4.172**, and *Nicklin* [1977] 2 All ER 444, on the number of counts appropriate when the accused is charged with handling stolen goods).

'Quasi-duplicity'

D11.57 The foregoing discussion of the rule against duplicity demonstrates the distinction between an allegation that the accused has committed a number of distinct offences, which must always be put in separate counts, and an allegation merely that the accused committed a number of distinct criminal acts which formed part of one activity or transaction, which can properly go into a single count. The distinction was mentioned by both Lord Morris of Borth-y-Gest and Lord Diplock in their opinions in *DPP v Merriman* [1973] AC 584 (quoted at **D11.48**), but the leading authority is the Court of Appeal decision in *Wilson* (1979) 69 Cr App R 83, which incorporates the essential parts of the judgment of Lord Widgery CJ in *Jemmison v Priddle* [1972] 1 QB 489.

D11.58 **The Approach in *Wilson*** In *Wilson* (1979) 69 Cr App R 83, W was charged with theft. The issue was whether the indictment should have been split so as to have a separate count for the items allegedly stolen from different departments of two shops. Browne LJ (giving the judgment of the Court of Appeal) distinguished between duplicity in the full sense of the term and what he described as quasi-duplicity or divergence. He said (at p. 85):

> The word duplicity is used in a rather ambiguous sense ... First there is a case where it appears on the face of the indictment, or particulars of the indictment, that a count is charging more than one offence. It may sometimes be legitimate to look at the depositions in this context (see *Greenfield* [1973] 1 WLR 1151). That has been referred to in the course of the argument as true duplicity. Secondly, there is a case where, although the indictment is good on its face, it appears at the close of the prosecution case that the evidence establishes that more than one offence was committed on the occasion to which a particular count relates. Perhaps that is best described as divergence or departure, but it often seems to be called duplicity ... in whatever sense one uses the word duplicity, it is confined to those two situations. But even if a case is not within either the first or the second of those situations, there may be cases where, in the interests of justice, it may be right to make the prosecution split a count or elect on what particular charge they are going to proceed.

D11.59 Having reviewed the authorities (especially *Jemmison v Priddle* [1972] 1 QB 489), Browne LJ adopted what Lord Widgery CJ had said in *Jemmison v Priddle* as correctly stating the law ((1979) 69 Cr App R 83 at pp. 86–7):

> Lord Widgery CJ said this ... 'What is the principle which distinguishes between [cases where one count is appropriate and cases where there should be several counts]? ... one finds that the explanation is given in somewhat inappropriate language, namely, that the test is whether the acts were all one transaction. That is a phrase hallowed by time, but not, in my judgment, of particular assistance in dealing with a particular problem. I find more assistance from somewhat different language used by Lord Parker CJ in *Ware v Fox* [1967] 1 WLR 379.' Then Lord Widgery CJ quotes from what

> Lord Parker CJ had said at p. 381 … and went on: 'I think perhaps that the phraseology of Lord Parker is more helpful to me than the phraseology often found in the text books, and I think that what it means is this, that it is legitimate to charge in a single information one activity even though the activity may involve more than one act. One looks at this case [i.e., *Jemmison v Priddle*] and asks oneself what was the activity with which the appellant was being charged. It was the activity of shooting red deer without a game licence, and although as a nice debating point it might well be contended that each shot was a separate act, indeed that each killing was a separate offence, I find that all these matters, occurring as they must have done within a very few seconds of time and all in the same geographical location are fairly to be described as components of a single activity, and that made it proper for the prosecution in this instance to join them in a single charge.'

Browne LJ concluded that: 'Whether there is one or more offence disclosed is really a question of fact and degree' ((1979) 69 Cr App R 83 at p. 88). On the facts of *Wilson*, the appellant 'entirely failed to satisfy' the court that the counts complained of disclosed more than one offence.

Application of the *Wilson* Principle Thus, the principle emerging from *Wilson* (1979) 69 Cr App R 83 is simply that more than one criminal act may properly be alleged in one count if the acts formed a single activity. Whether there was one activity or several depends on the facts of each individual case. This is now reflected in CrimPR 10.2(2), save that the wording used there is that the acts 'amount to a course of conduct' rather than 'one activity'. **D11.60**

This approach was illustrated in *Iaquaniello* [2005] EWCA Crim 2029, where D was charged on an indictment containing a count of doing an act or a series of acts tending and intended to pervert the course of public justice. The Court of Appeal held that it was not duplicitous for a count to state, in this context, 'act or acts'. Where the particulars of offence alleged that the accused did an act or a series of acts tending, and intended, to pervert the course of justice, it was not duplicitous to particularise the acts within one count on the indictment.

Charging Offences Conjunctively in an Effort to Avoid the Rule against Duplicity

It has so far been assumed that the rule against duplicity will apply whether separate offences are alleged in one count as alternatives or conjunctively. That assumption is in line with the overwhelming weight of authority (the only exception being *Clow* [1965] 1 QB 598, which was fact-specific and in any event distinguished in *Mallon v Allon* [1964] 1 QB 385 (see **D11.56**)). The same rule should therefore apply whether a count is framed conjunctively or disjunctively. **D11.61**

Effect of Breach of the Rule against Duplicity

Where a count is bad on its face for duplicity, the defence should move to quash it before the accused is arraigned. Although the objection can be taken at a later stage (*Johnson* [1945] KB 419), the Court of Appeal has disapproved of the defence postponing the application to quash for purely tactical reasons (*Asif* (1982) 82 Cr App R 123), and this accords with the general duty of the defence to raise issues expeditiously (for which see **D4.6**). It is open to the prosecution to defeat a motion to quash by asking the judge to allow a suitable amendment of the indictment (see the Indictments Act 1915, s. 5(1), for the power to amend indictments at **D11.99**). **D11.62**

The procedure of applying to quash a count will be available only if it is a case of 'true' duplicity, namely that the wording of the count shows that two or more offences are being alleged. Such a motion must be determined solely by considering the wording of the indictment, without reference to the evidence. In a case of quasi-duplicity or divergence (see *Wilson* (1979) 69 Cr App R 83 and **D11.57**), which becomes apparent only after the evidence has been called, the defence should wait until the close of the prosecution case and then ask the judge to split the count.

Rejection by the trial judge of a motion to quash a count bad on its face for duplicity and/or rejection of an application to split a count open to objection for quasi-duplicity are plainly valid grounds of appeal. In *Donnelly* [1998] Crim LR 131, the Court of Appeal made it clear that cases of true duplicity and quasi-duplicity would be differently treated. In a case where the count was plainly duplicitous in form the appeal must be allowed, even if the point had not been taken at trial (though this does not necessarily follow, see *Thompson* [1914] 2 KB 99).

In cases of 'quasi duplicity', a motion to quash the indictment should be moved before the trial judge. If it was not, the appeal would fail unless it was accompanied by an allegation of incompetence by counsel.

The approach taken by the House of Lords in *Clarke* [2008] UKHL 8, [2008] 2 All ER 665 does not affect the principle that duplicity does not automatically result in the quashing of a count (*Marchese* [2008] EWCA Crim 389, [2009] 1 WLR 992).

JOINDER OF COUNTS IN AN INDICTMENT

The Rule

D11.63 The procedure for applications for joint trials is set out in CrimPR 3.29 and 3.30 (see Supplement, **R3.29** and **R3.30**). The circumstances in which the prosecution may lawfully join two or more counts against one accused in a single indictment are prescribed by CrimPR 3.29(4), which replaces the test formerly contained in r. 9 of the Indictment Rules 1971. The court may order separate trials unless 'the offences to be tried together (i) are founded on the same facts, or (ii) form or are part of a series of offences of the same or similar character'. That this is an exercise of the court's discretion in this respect, as set out in the Indictment Act 1915, s. 5(3), is underlined by the amendment to by SI 2018 No. 132 from a direction that the court must sever to a power that it may do so, and CrimPR 3.29(4) now states:

> Where the same indictment charges more than one offence, the court may exercise its power to order separate trials of those offences if of the opinion that—(a) the defendant otherwise may be prejudiced or embarrassed in his or her defence (for example, where the offences to be tried together are neither founded on the same facts nor form or are part of a series of offences of the same or a similar character); or (b) for any other reason it is desirable that the defendant should be tried separately for any one or more of those offences.

Application of the Rule

D11.64 Unsurprisingly, cases in which the application of the rule have been considered relate to r. 9 of the Indictment Rules 1971 rather than CrimPR 3.29(4). In particular, the leading case of *Newland* [1988] QB 402 must be read in the light of r. 3.29(4). In that case, D was charged in an indictment containing counts relating to drugs offences and assaults, which were entirely unconnected. At trial, when counsel for D submitted that the indictment was invalid, the judge held that he had power under s. 5(3) of the Indictments Act 1915 (see **D11.76**) to sever the indictment. The conclusions reached by the Court of Appeal, which have not all survived subsequent developments (in case law and under the CrimPR), were as follows:

(a) The power to sever under s. 5(3) applies only to a valid indictment (at p. 406C–D). It is at the least arguable that this aspect of the decision has been overtaken by CrimPR 3.29(4), which appears to recognise a power to sever without this qualification.

(b) The trial judge could have amended the indictment so as to delete either the drugs count or the assault counts. That having been done, the trial could validly have proceeded on what remained (at p. 406F). See also *Follett* [1989] QB 338.

(c) Given that no amendment had in fact been made, the unamended indictment was invalid by reason of the contravention of r. 9. Because it was capable of being rendered valid by an appropriate amendment, it was not a nullity (at p. 408C–D, applying *Bell* (1984) 78 Cr App R 305). But, even though the indictment itself was not a nullity, the fact of its being invalid was sufficient to render null the proceedings flowing from it (at p. 408E). This conclusion was disapproved in *Smith* [1997] QB 837. The Court of Appeal held that it was wrong to suggest that all proceedings flowing from an indictment containing a count improperly joined were a nullity (as opposed to the proceedings on the improperly joined count). *Smith* was approved and followed in *Lockley* [1997] Crim LR 455.

For a recent example of the application of CrimPR 3.29 (then CrimPR 2015, r. 3.21), see *Hamou* [2019] EWCA Crim 281, in which the Court of Appeal considered that joinder was inappropriate where one of those to be joined was absent, he had not been arraigned on the pre-joinder indictment, and evidence relating to him was prejudicial to the defendants who were present. In *Toner* [2019] EWCA Crim 447, the Court of Appeal observed that 'where the evidence on one count would be properly admissible on the other as evidence of bad character it is difficult to argue that the defendant would be "prejudiced or embarrassed in his defence" by having both counts or sets of counts on the same indictment' (at [13]).

First Limb of CrimPR 3.29(4): Charges Founded on the Same Facts

The first limb of r. 3.29(4) is clearly satisfied if the offences alleged in counts joined in one indictment arose out of a single incident or an uninterrupted course of conduct (see, e.g., *Mansfield* [1977] 1 All ER 134, where the indictment against D was held to be properly joined where it contained counts for arson and murder relating to the same fire). **D11.65**

Joinder where One Offence is a Precondition of the Second CrimPR 3.29(4), like its predecessor, is not restricted to offences that were committed contemporaneously or substantially contemporaneously with each other, as in *Mansfield* [1977] 1 All ER 134 (see **D11.65**), but extends to situations where later offences would not have been committed but for the prior commission of an earlier offence. **D11.66**

The leading authority is *Barrell* (1979) 69 Cr App R 250, where the appellants were charged jointly in counts 1 and 2 with affray and assault occasioning actual bodily harm, and W alone was charged in count 3 with attempting to pervert the course of justice. This third count related to an attempt by W to persuade the witness to counts 1 and 2 to 'modify' his evidence. On appeal it was submitted that count 3 did not arise from the same facts as counts 1 and 2. The argument was rejected by the Court of Appeal. Shaw LJ, giving the judgment of the Court, said (at pp. 252–3):

> The phrase 'founded on the same facts' does not mean that for charges to be properly joined in the same indictment, the facts in relation to the respective charges must be identical in substance or virtually contemporaneous. The test is whether the charges have a common factual origin. If the charge described by counsel as the subsidiary charge is one that could not have been alleged but for the facts which give rise to what he called the primary charge, then it is true to say for the purposes of rule 9 that those charges are founded, that is to say have their origin, in the same facts and can legitimately be joined in the same indictment.

If W had not been involved in the violence which gave rise to the charges of assault and affray, he would have had no motive for offering the witness a bribe. It followed that all three counts had a common factual origin and were properly joined in one indictment.

A factual connection between the counts is established by a coincidence of time and place. It is irrelevant that the accused's explanation is different for each offence (*Roberts* [2008] EWCA Crim 1304, [2009] 1 Cr App R 20 (273)). See also *Toner* [2019] EWCA Crim 447, as to the relevance of cross-admissibility between counts to their joinder.

Joinder of Mutually Destructive Counts Difficulty has arisen over whether the principle in *Barrell* (1979) 69 Cr App R 250 can properly be extended to counts that are mutually destructive, that is, the prosecution evidence is such that, if their case on one count is accepted, the accused cannot have committed the offence alleged in the other count and vice versa. **D11.67**

The House of Lords settled the point in *Bellman* [1989] AC 836. The case centred on representations which D had made to obtain money. If they were false, he had obtained the property by deception. If they were true, he had conspired to evade the prohibition on the importation of controlled drugs. The indictment contained counts both for conspiracy and for obtaining by deception.

On appeal, D relied 'upon the more fundamental proposition that under our adversarial procedure of trial in which the burden of establishing the guilt of the accused is placed on the prosecution, it can never be right for mutually contradictory counts to be contained in one indictment. He submitted that to do so would be contrary to the prosecution's duty of proving the case, unfair to the accused and an embarrassment for the jury' (at pp. 846H–847A). Lord Griffiths rejected the argument. There was nothing in the Indictments Act 1915 to support it; r. 9 of the Indictment Rules 1971 prima facie contradicted it, and no authority had been cited in which joinder had been refused on the ground that the facts of two counts were mutually destructive (at p. 849B–D). On the other hand, it had long been the practice to include in one indictment counts for stealing and handling the same property even though a conviction for theft would necessarily preclude a conviction for handling and vice versa (see *Shelton* (1986) 83 Cr App R 379 for approval of the practice).

D11.68 Moreover, there will be occasions when justice can be done only by drafting mutually contradictory counts. An example is provided by the facts of *Barnes* (1985) 83 Cr App R 38, where the indictment contained counts for perjury and wounding with intent, the case being that Barnes was either telling the truth at an earlier trial and so was guilty of wounding, or he was telling lies, in which case he was guilty of perjury. The Court of Appeal dismissed the appeal on the ground that, whether or not the joinder of the mutually destructive counts was lawful, there had on the facts been no miscarriage of justice.

In *Bellman*, Lord Griffiths, *obiter*, confirmed the legality of the joinder because the factual origin of both counts was the attack on the victim (at p. 850F–G). Furthermore, the joinder was necessary in the interests of justice since, had Barnes been tried separately for the two offences, he might have 'played the system' by obtaining an acquittal for perjury through testifying that he had indeed wounded the victim and then, at his later trial for wounding, he could have reversed his evidence, secure in the knowledge that he could not be prosecuted again for perjury.

D11.69 **Application of the Decision in *Bellman*** Although the decision in *Bellman* [1989] AC 836 puts beyond doubt the propriety of joining mutually destructive counts in one indictment, the prosecution will rarely wish to prefer such an indictment in practice, since it leaves open the risk that a jury will not be able to reach a verdict on either. (Certain sexual offences provide one exception, see **B3.1** and **B3.104**.)

As a matter of evidence, it is clear that if, at the end of the prosecution case, it is established that the accused has committed a crime but it is impossible to say which, the judge must direct the jury to acquit. Similarly, if, as in *Bellman* itself, there is evidence on which the jury could properly convict of either count, they must nonetheless be directed in the summing-up that, should they be left in doubt about which of the two offences the accused has committed, they are under a duty to acquit of both, even though they are sure the accused committed one or other. The various evidential problems that may arise from mutually destructive counts are discussed by Lord Griffiths in *Bellman* at p. 847. See further **D16.61**.

Second Limb of CrimPR 3.29(4): Series of Offences of the Same or a Similar Character

D11.70 The circumstances in which two or more offences may be said to amount to a series of offences of the same or similar character within the meaning of the second limb of what is now CrimPR 3.29(4) were considered by the House of Lords in *Ludlow v Metropolitan Police Commissioner* [1971] AC 29. The indictment against D contained counts for (a) attempted theft at a public house in Acton on 20 August and (b) robbery at a different public house in Acton on 5 September. The trial judge refused an application that the two charges should be tried separately, and D was convicted on both counts. The case was considered by the House of Lords, where Lord Pearson delivered the leading opinion. The main points emerging from this opinion are as follows.

(a) Two offences are capable of constituting a 'series' for the purposes of the Indictment Rules 1971, r. 9 (see p. 38E–G confirming the Court of Appeal decision in *Kray* [1970] 1 QB 125).
(b) In deciding whether offences exhibit the similarity demanded by the rule, the court should take into account both their legal and their factual characteristics (at p. 39B). The prosecution submission (that the phrase 'a similar character' means exclusively of a similar legal character) and the defence submission (that the phrase means exclusively of a similar factual character) were each rejected.
(c) To show the existence of a series of offences, the prosecution must be able to point to some nexus between them. This means 'a feature of similarity which in all the circumstances of the case enables the offences to be described as a series' (at p. 39D). A nexus is clearly established if the offences are so connected that the evidence of one would be admissible to prove the commission of the other in accordance with the rules on similar fact evidence, but this is not essential (at p. 39D–F, quoting with approval from *Kray* and *Clayton-Wright* [1948] 2 All ER 763, and see observations to the same effect in *Toner* [2019] EWCA Crim 447).
(d) On the facts of *Ludlow*, the offences were similar in law in that they each had the ingredient of actual or attempted theft. They were also similar in fact because they involved stealing or attempting to steal in neighbouring public houses at a time interval of only 16 days. A sufficient nexus was therefore present to make the offences a series of a similar character within the meaning of r. 9, even though the similarity was not nearly striking enough to bring them within the similar fact evidence rule (at p. 39H).

Application of the Principles in *Ludlow* The following cases are decisions on whether the degree of similarity between offences justified joinder under r. 9 of the Indictment Rules 1971, and thus by implication CrimPR 3.29(4): **D11.71**

(a) *Mansfield* [1977] 1 All ER 134, where three counts for arson were held to be properly joined since the offences were committed within a short space of time, and related to premises in the same geographical area, with each of which the accused had some connection.
(b) *Harward* (1981) 73 Cr App R 168, where it was held that an allegation relating to the handling of stolen goods could not be joined to an offence of conspiring to defraud banks by the use of stolen cheques and cheque cards. The only possible nexus between the charges, there being no factual similarity, was the element of dishonesty. However, the dishonesty in the conspiracy count related to D's involvement in fraudulent practices, whereas that in the handling count related to his state of mind when he received the goods. This was therefore insufficient.
(c) *McGlinchey* (1983) 78 Cr App R 282, where two counts for handling stolen goods were held to be properly joined. The only factual similarity between the offences seems to have been their closeness in time. (*McGlinchey* was applied in *Mariou* [1992] Crim LR 511.)
(d) *Marsh* (1985) 83 Cr App R 165, where the indictment included two pairs of counts for criminal damage and reckless driving and a fifth count of assault occasioning actual bodily harm, relating to a wholly separate incident. The joinder was held to be improper because (i) there was no legal similarity between criminal damage and reckless driving on the one hand and assault on the other, and (ii) the common factual element of violence was insufficient by itself to provide a nexus.
(e) *Baird* [1993] Crim LR 778, where the indictment alleged two counts of indecent assault against two boys, the incidents having taken place nine years apart. Although there was no coincidence in time or place, there were similarities in the offences which, their lordships said, 'were truly remarkable'. They concluded that the judge was entitled to hold that the various counts could properly be joined under r. 9, and was justified in refusing to exercise his discretion to sever under the Indictments Act 1915, s. 5(3) (see **D11.76**).

(f) *C* (1993) *The Times*, 4 February 1993, where the accused was charged with rape and attempted rape. Although the counts were separated in time by 11 years, the victim in each case was the accused's daughter. It was held that the counts were properly joined.
(g) *Williams* [1993] Crim LR 533, where it was alleged that D had falsely imprisoned a girl of 13, having indecently assaulted her five days earlier. The Court of Appeal held that these were two separate incidents and the two offences were not of a similar character, despite an evidential nexus.
(h) *Ferrell* [2010] UKPC 20, [2011] 1 All ER 95, where it was held that offences of supplying drugs and money laundering were correctly joined, even where the laundering offences pre-dated the possession of the drugs that were the subject of the supply counts, because it was proper for the jury to infer that the money that was laundered was the proceeds of drugs.
(i) *Williams* [2017] EWCA Crim 281, [2017] 2 Cr App R 7 (65), where D was charged with assault on one former girlfriend and the rape of another. The Court of Appeal was required to consider the wider characteristics of the offence, including the fact that both offences involved violence against a particular category of person.

JOINDER OF ACCUSED

D11.72 Two or more accused may be joined in one indictment either as a result of being named together in one or more counts on the indictment, or as a result of being named individually in separate counts, albeit that there is no single count against them all. The procedure for applications for joint trials is set out in CrimPR 3.29 and 3.30 (see Supplement, **R3.29** and **R3.30**).

Joint Counts

D11.73 All parties to a joint offence may be indicted for it in a single count. In drafting the count:

(a) There is no need to distinguish between principal offenders and secondary parties (Accessories and Abettors Act 1861, s. 8: see **D11.42**).
(b) The count need not expressly allege that the unlawful acts of each accused were done in aid of the others, as that allegation is implicit in the drafting of a single count (*DPP v Merriman* [1973] AC 584 per Lord Diplock at p. 607C).

Where the prosecution seek to join an accused to an indictment following an order that the accused in question be retried pursuant to the Criminal Appeal Act 1968, s. 7(2), then, in addition to the considerations of general application to an application for joinder, there is added the need to consider if the accused would be substantially adversely affected, so that joinder would represent an abuse of process (*Booker* [2011] EWCA Crim 7, [2011] 1 Cr App R 26 (330)). That said, there is no prohibition on the addition of counts to an indictment in such circumstances, where it is fair to do so (*Feeley* [2012] EWCA Crim 720, [2012] 1 WLR 3133).

In *Marsh-Smith* [2015] EWCA Crim 1883 the issue was whether D should have been severed from his co-accused on a joint charge where one of the co-accused had implicated the appellant in interview. The Court of Appeal observed that the interests of justice were normally best served by allegations with a common thread being ventilated together, and this included issues between defendants, always assuming that injustice could be avoided by robust direction to the jury as to the uses to which parts of the evidence could, and could not, be put.

D11.74 **Possible Verdicts on Joint Counts** Notwithstanding that the accused have been charged in a single count, the jury may convict all or any of them on the basis that they committed the offence charged independently of the others. For example, in *DPP v Merriman* [1973] AC 584, Lord Diplock said (at p. 607F):

> ... whenever two or more defendants are charged in the same count of an indictment with any offence which men can help one another to commit it is sufficient to support a conviction against any and each of them to prove *either* that he himself did a physical act which is an

essential ingredient of the offence charged *or* that he helped another to do such an act, *and*, that in doing the act or in helping the other defendant to do it, he himself had the necessary criminal intent.

In short, if two accused, A1 and A2, are charged in a joint count the jury may (a) acquit both, or (b) convict both, or (c) acquit one and convict the other.

Should they convict both it will usually be on the basis implicit in the joint count that they helped each other to commit the crime, but the jury may equally convict both where the evidence suggests that they acted independently of each other if they are satisfied that each accused committed the offence.

Similarly, if there is a split verdict, the verdict against the convicted accused is not open to challenge on the ground that the jury must have found that the accused acted alone without assistance either from the acquitted co-accused or anybody else. The argument that to uphold convictions on a single count in the absence of proof of joint enterprise contravenes the rule against duplicity was rejected in *DPP v Merriman*.

Despite this, the prosecution are well advised only to draft a joint count where the evidence reveals a joint enterprise. If the co-defendants were acting without reference to each other, separate counts are preferable.

Separate Counts

The joining of two or more accused in one indictment notwithstanding the absence of a joint count against them is governed by the decision in *Assim* [1966] 2 QB 249. In that case, the indictment against the two accused, D1 and D2, contained two counts. The first alleged that D1 had maliciously wounded W, and the second alleged that D2, on the same day, had caused actual bodily harm to L. D1 and D2 both worked at the premises where the two assaults had allegedly occurred, a nightclub of which both the victims were customers. **D11.75**

On appeal, D1 argued that it was bad in law to charge two different people in one indictment with two different offences. Offenders could properly be joined in one indictment only as principals said to have jointly committed one offence, or as principals and accessories (see p. 251F–G for counsel's argument). A five-judge Court of Appeal extensively reviewed the authorities, and (in a judgment given by Sachs J) reached the following conclusions:

(a) Questions of joinder, whether of offences or offenders, are 'matters of practice on which the court has, unless restrained by statute, inherent power both to formulate its own rules and to vary them in the light of current experience and the needs of justice' (at p. 258F). On the assumption that the rule (now CrimPR 3.29(4)) covers only joinder of offences, the propriety of the joinder of offenders is unaffected either by the Indictments Act 1915 or by any other legislation, whether subordinate or primary, passed since then (at p. 258E). Subsequently, Lord Widgery CJ in *Camberwell Green Stipendiary Magistrate, ex parte Christie* [1978] QB 602, said that *Assim* should be accepted as laying down a principle that joinder of offenders is a matter of the practice of the courts.
(b) Since joinder of offenders is merely a matter of practice, errors in the application of the relevant rules, though amounting to an irregularity in the proceedings, will not deprive the trial court of jurisdiction. Consequently, the Court of Appeal is entitled to dismiss an appeal against conviction advanced on this ground if there has been no miscarriage of justice (at p. 259D–E), and especially where there has been a failure by the defence to object to the joint trial.
(c) Sachs J 'came to some general conclusions as to what would nowadays be an appropriate rule of practice on the basis that none of the rules of 1915 deal with the joinder of offenders'. In summary, joinder is appropriate if the offences separately alleged against the accused are, on the evidence, so closely related by time or other factors that the interests of justice are best served by a single trial. His lordship said (at p. 261B–F):

As a general rule it is, of course, no more proper to have tried by the same jury several offenders on charges of committing individual offences that have nothing to do with each other than it is to try before the same jury offences committed by the same person that have nothing to do with each other. Where, however, the matters which constitute the individual offences of the several offenders are upon the available evidence so related, whether in time or by other factors, that the interests of justice are best served by their being tried together, then they can properly be the subject of counts in one indictment and can, subject always to the discretion of the court, be tried together. Such a rule, of course, includes cases where there is evidence that several offenders acted in concert but is not limited to such cases.

Again, while the court has in mind the classes of case that have been particularly the subject of discussion before it, such as incidents which, irrespective of there appearing a joint charge in the indictment, are contemporaneous (as where there has been something in the nature of an affray), or successive (as in protection racket cases), or linked in a similar manner, as where two persons individually in the course of the same trial commit perjury as regards the same or a closely connected fact, the court does not intend the operation of the rule to be restricted so as to apply only to such cases as have been discussed before it.

(d) It was conceded by the appellant and accepted by the court that, where there is a joint count against two accused, that count may be followed by a separate count or counts against one or more of the accused even in relation to a distinct matter, provided that there is no breach of what is now r. 3.21(4) (at p. 257D, quoting *Cox* [1898] 1 QB 179). See also *Barrell* (1979) 69 Cr App R 250 at **D11.66**.

(e) On the facts of *Assim*, the joinder of D1 and D2 in one indictment was clearly proper, however narrowly any rule as to joinder of offenders might have been formulated (at p. 260G). Having regard to the rule of practice Sachs J had stated, the counts they faced were so closely related by time and other factors that indicting the accused jointly was the correct course.

SEVERANCE

D11.76 The court has the power to order the separate trial of accused or of offences that are properly joined in one indictment, pursuant to the Indictments Act 1915, s. 5(3). This is supplemented by:

(a) s. 5(4), which requires the court, following an order for severance under s. 5(3), to make such order for postponement of the trial as appears necessary and expedient; and

(b) s. 5(5), which provides that the procedure on the separate trial of a count following an order under s. 5(3) shall be the same in all respects as if the count had been preferred in a separate indictment.

The power to sever an indictment contained in s. 5(3) was held to apply only to valid indictments in *Newland* [1988] QB 402. However, the combined effect of CrimPR 3.29(4) and the decisions of the Court of Appeal in *Smith* [1997] QB 837 and *Lockley* [1997] Crim LR 455 have altered the effect upon the indictment where a count has been improperly joined (see **D11.64**). The procedure for such applications is set out in CrimPR 3.29 (see Supplement, **R3.29**).

D11.77 **Indictments Act 1915, s. 5**

(3) Where, before trial, or at any stage of a trial, the court is of opinion that a person accused may be prejudiced or embarrassed in his or her defence by reason of being charged with more than one offence in the same indictment, or that for any other reason it is desirable to direct that the person should be tried separately for any one or more offences charged in an indictment, the court may order a separate trial of any count or counts of such indictment.

(4) Where, before trial, or at any stage of a trial, the court is of opinion that the postponement of the trial of a person accused is expedient as a consequence of the exercise of any power of the court under this Act to amend an indictment or to order a separate trial of a count, the court shall make such order as to the postponement of the trial as appears necessary.

(5) Where an order of the court is made under this section for the postponement of a trial—

(a) if such an order is made during a trial the court may order that the jury (if there is one) are to be discharged from giving a verdict on the count or counts the trial of which is postponed or on the indictment, as the case may be; and

(b) the procedure on the separate trial of a count shall be the same in all respects as if the count had been found in a separate indictment, and the procedure on the postponed trial shall be the same in all respects (if the jury has been discharged under para (a)) as if the trial had not commenced; and

(c) the court may make such order as to granting the accused person bail and as to the enlargement of recognisances and otherwise as the court thinks fit.

Severance of Counts on an Indictment

The proper exercise of the power was considered by Lord Pearson in *Ludlow v Metropolitan Police Commissioner* [1971] AC 29 (see also **D11.70**). Having held that the joinder of the counts against D for attempted theft and robbery was lawful, his lordship dealt with D's further argument that a single trial of the two offences inevitably prejudiced or embarrassed D in his defence since the jury heard evidence on count 1 that was inadmissible on count 2 and vice versa. Therefore, the trial judge should have ordered separate trials in exercise of the discretion given him by s. 5(3). In rejecting this argument Lord Pearson said (at pp. 40–2): **D11.78**

> Before the Indictments Act 1915, it was a tenable theory ... to say that any joinder of counts relating to distinct alleged offences was necessarily so prejudicial to the accused that such joinder ought not to be permitted. [His lordship then reviewed pre-1915 cases lending support to the theory.]
>
> In my opinion, this theory — that a joinder of counts relating to different transactions is in itself so prejudicial to the accused that such a joinder should never be made — cannot be held to have survived the passing of the Indictments Act 1915. No doubt the juries of that time were much more literate and intelligent than the juries of the late 18th and 19th centuries, and could be relied upon in any ordinary case not to infer that, because the accused is proved to have committed one of the offences charged against him, therefore he must have committed the others as well. I think the experience of judges in modern times is that the verdicts of juries show them to have been careful and conscientious in considering each count separately. Also in most cases it would be oppressive to the accused, as well as expensive and inconvenient for the prosecution, to have two or more trials when one would suffice. *At any rate, ... the manifest intention of the Act is that charges which either are founded on the same facts or relate to a series of offences of the same or a similar character properly can and normally should be joined in one indictment, and a joint trial of the charges will normally follow, although the judge has a discretionary power to direct separate trials under section 5(3).* If the theory were still correct, it would be the duty of the judge in the proper exercise of his discretion under section 5(3) to direct separate trials in every case where the accused was charged with a series of offences of the same or a similar character, and the manifest intention appearing from section 4 and [r. 9] would be defeated. *The judge has no duty to direct separate trials under section 5(3) unless in his opinion there is some special feature of the case which would make a joint trial of the several counts prejudicial or embarrassing to the accused and separate trials are required in the interests of justice.* In some cases the offences charged may be too numerous and complicated, ... or too difficult to disentangle, ... so that a joint trial of all the counts is likely to cause confusion and the defence may be embarrassed or prejudiced. In other cases objection may be taken to the inclusion of a count on the ground that it is of a scandalous nature and likely to arouse in the minds of the jury hostile feelings against the accused ...

Application of this Principle Thus, where counts for separate offences can be tried together (through compliance with CrimPR 3.29(4)), the trial judge is able to exercise discretion to order separate trials, if their joint trial would be prejudicial or embarrassing for some reason (r. 3.29(4)(a)), or if some other feature makes that course desirable (r. 3.29(4)(b)). Although they are not intended to be exhaustive, examples of such features or reasons might include the following: **D11.79**

(a) *The scandalous nature of the evidence as to one of the counts.* For example in *Laycock* [2003] EWCA Crim 1477, the Court of Appeal warned that prosecutors should be careful not to charge counts that would prejudice an accused unless there was a real purpose to be served. In that case, the prosecution were criticised for including in a firearms indictment a count which showed that D had been sentenced to a previous sentence of imprisonment with the result that he was prohibited from possession of a firearm.

(b) *The number and/or complexity of the counts.* This may result in difficulties for a jury in disentangling evidence on one count from that on the other count or counts. In this regard, special considerations govern the trial of counts for sexual offences (see **D11.80**).

The fact that the accused wishes to give evidence in his or her own defence on one of the counts but not on the others is not, in the normal case, a sufficient reason for severance, even though non-severance will oblige the accused to choose between not testifying at all and being exposed to cross-examination about all the charges (*Phillips* (1987) 86 Cr App R 18). See also *Lanford v General Medical Council* [1990] 1 AC 13.

Severance of Multi-count Indictments for Similar Offences, such as Sexual Offences

D11.80 The CJA 2003, s. 101(1), created a number of gateways by which evidence of offences of a similar kind may be admissible as 'bad character' evidence in support of the offences charged in the indictment. If such cross-admissibility between allegations is established, it follows that those allegations ought to be tried together. This arises most commonly in cases where there are a number of allegations of sexual offending. To understand the application of s. 101(1) in this context, it is of assistance to identify how the law has developed in relation to the joint trial of a number of sexual offences.

In *DPP v Boardman* [1975] AC 421, the indictment contained counts that D, the headmaster of a boarding-school, had (a) committed buggery on S, a 16-year-old pupil, and (b) had incited H, a 17-year-old pupil, to commit buggery on D. The primary question for the House of Lords was whether the trial judge correctly directed the jury that the evidence of one count was admissible as corroborative evidence in relation to the other. Resolution of this issue involved the answering of two essential questions.

D11.81 **Is the Other Allegation Admissible?** The CJA 2003, s. 101(1), now has a considerable bearing on this question. Some assistance is still provided by *DPP v Boardman* [1975] AC 421, where Lord Cross of Chelsea said that the first question is whether the evidence of one count is admissible supporting evidence of another: 'if it is decided that the evidence is inadmissible and the accused is being charged in the same indictment with offences against the other men the charges relating to the different persons ought to be tried separately' (at p. 459D).

The reason why this approach was necessary is because 'it is asking too much of any jury to tell them to perform mental gymnastics of this sort. If the charges are tried together it is inevitable that the jurors will be influenced, consciously or unconsciously, by the fact that the accused is being charged not with a single offence against one person but with three separate offences against three persons.'

D11.82 **Has there been Contamination?** Even where the respective offences are otherwise admissible (e.g., as being mutually corroborative), the judge should consider whether there is material in the evidence served under the regulations for the service of the prosecution case after the accused has been sent for trial which suggests that the 'victims' colluded together to tell false stories. Again this should be considered as a preliminary issue.

If there is a real danger that that happened, separate trials should be ordered, but the judge should not use his imagination to invent a conspiracy to make false allegations where there is no evidence in the statements that such a conspiracy existed (see especially *Johannsen* (1977) 65 Cr App R 101, where it was held that the mere fact that four out of the five complainants knew each other gave rise to no more than a speculative possibility that they had collaborated, and there was accordingly no need to direct severance of the counts).

D11.83 **Limitations to the Impact of a Ruling on Severance in Such Cases** A decision as to severance does not represent a final decision on the admissibility of each incident alleged in the indictment as similar fact evidence to prove the others. Even where severance is refused, during the course of the ensuing trial it will still be necessary for the court to rule whether the evidence of one victim corroborates that of the other victims. If the court concludes, contrary to the provisional view taken at the application for severance stage, that each victim's evidence is relevant only to the offence against him, then either the jury must be directed accordingly in the summing-up or, more realistically, the jury should be discharged and severance ordered at that stage.

Conversely, if the court initially ordered severance, the prosecution could still ask to be allowed to lead evidence of the other incidents in support of whichever incident the jury is trying. Detailed guidance from Scarman LJ on how trial judges should approach applications for severance and problems of similar fact evidence in multi-count sexual cases will be found in *Scarrott* [1978] 1 QB 1016 at pp. 1027–8. See also *N (H)* [2011] EWCA Crim 730 and *Adams* [2019] EWCA Crim 1363.

Application of *Boardman* beyond Indictments for Sexual Offences It might have been thought that the arguments that Lord Cross used in *DPP v Boardman* [1975] AC 421 to justify his dictum that, in cases involving sexual offences, the indictment should be severed if the evidence of one victim could not be used as corroboration of the evidence of the other victims, would apply with equal force whatever the nature of the offence charged. However, the Court of Appeal in subsequent cases has refused to extend the principles stated in *Boardman* and *Scarrott* [1978] 1 QB 1016 beyond multi-count indictments for sexual offences. **D11.84**

Where there is a multi-count indictment for some other type of offence, the principles in *Ludlow v Metropolitan Police Commissioner* [1971] AC 29 apply (see **D11.70**). Accordingly, the judge should order separate trials only if there is a special feature in the case likely to cause the defence prejudice or embarrassment.

(a) In *McGlinchey* (1983) 78 Cr App R 282, the Court of Appeal held that two counts for handling stolen goods on dates approximately six weeks apart were properly joined in one indictment even though there was manifestly no striking similarity between the offences. The Court approved the judge's exercise of discretion against severance, applying *Ludlow* and distinguishing *Boardman.*
(b) In *Cannan* (1991) 92 Cr App R 16, the Court of Appeal made it clear that, even where an indictment charged a series of sexual offences, the judge had a discretion whether to sever. The indictment in C's case included three sets of offences which were evidentially separate. The Court of Appeal rejected the submission that the judge should have followed 'the general modern practice in sexual cases', and severed the counts in the absence of striking similarity. Lord Lane CJ said (at p. 23):

> It may well be that often the judge in sexual cases will order severance ... But the fact remains that the Indictments Act 1915 gives the judge a discretion, and ... that is not a matter with which this Court will interfere, unless it is shown that the judge has failed to exercise his discretion upon the usual and proper principles ...

Consideration of the *Boardman* Approach In *DPP v P* [1991] 2 AC 447, Lord Mackay (at p. 462) made the following comment about the issue of whether, in the absence of striking similarity, there should have been joinder: **D11.85**

> ... the evidence referred to is admissible if the similarity is sufficiently strong, or there is other sufficient relationship between the events described in the evidence of the other young children of the family and the abuse charged, that the evidence, if accepted, would so strongly support the truth of that charge that it is fair to admit it notwithstanding its prejudicial effect. It follows that the answer to the second question is no, provided there is a relationship between the offences of a kind which I have just described.

On one interpretation, this could be taken to mean that the rule on joinder in cases of multiple sexual offences is the same as for admissibility, namely that the offences should constitute similar fact evidence in order to be tried together. However, in *Christou* [1997] AC 117, the House of Lords considered the words used by Lord Mackay, and stated that

D

Part D Procedure

they were *obiter*. The approach to the question of severance in *Cannan* (1991) 92 Cr App R 16 was endorsed.

Consideration must also be given to the cross-admissibility of different offences because the evidence of one is relevant to a 'matter in issue' with respect to another, pursuant to the CJA 2003, s. 101(1)(d). For example, in *McAllister* [2008] EWCA Crim 1544, [2009] 1 Cr App R 10 (129), the Court of Appeal considered the admissibility of evidence of robbery A in support of robbery B. The evidence of robbery A was relevant to an important matter in issue between the parties, namely whether D was guilty of robbery B. Moses LJ observed (at [14]):

> Asking a jury to look at evidence relating to a number of allegations as a whole in order to cast light on the evidence relating to an individual offence is not asking a jury to consider a propensity to commit an offence; on the contrary, it is merely asking the jury to recognise that the evidence in relation to a particular offence on an indictment may appear stronger and more compelling when all the evidence, including evidence relating to other offences is looked at as a whole.

In *Freeman* [2008] EWCA Crim 1863, [2009] 2 All ER 18 the Court of Appeal found counts in the indictment to be properly joined where the evidence in relation to any count met the criteria for admissibility in relation to the others under the CJA 2003. (See also *AB* [2011] EWCA Crim 3331, *Adams* [2019] EWCA Crim 1363 and **F13.59**.)

The court has a discretion as to severance, with which the appellate courts should interfere only on grounds of *Wednesbury* unreasonableness. In exercising discretion, the essential task of the trial judge was to achieve a fair resolution of the issues. That required fairness to the accused but also to the prosecution and those involved in it. Among the factors which the judge might consider were:

(a) how discrete or interrelated were the facts giving rise to the counts;
(b) the impact of ordering two or more trials on the accused and his or her family, on the victims and their families, and on press publicity; and
(c) importantly, whether directions the judge could give to the jury would suffice to secure a fair trial if the counts were tried together.

(See also *Dixon* (1991) 92 Cr App R 43, *F* [1996] Crim LR 257, *O'Brien* [2000] Crim LR 863, *Thomas* [2006] EWCA Crim 2442 and *N (H)* [2011] EWCA Crim 730.)

Discretion to Order Separate Trials of Accused

D11.86 The court has a discretion to order separate trials of accused who have properly been joined in one indictment pursuant to CrimPR 3.29(4) and in accordance with the principles stated in *Ludlow v Metropolitan Police Commissioner* [1971] AC 29 (see **D11.70**). The existence of the discretion was acknowledged by Sachs J in *Assim* [1966] 2 QB 249. His lordship said (at p. 261B–C):

> Where… the matters which constitute the individual offences of the several offenders are upon the available evidence so related… that the interests of justice are best served by their being tried together, then they can properly be the subject of counts in one indictment and can, *subject always to the discretion of the court*, be tried together [emphasis added].

Although that was said in the context of an indictment which did not contain a joint count, it has never been doubted that the discretion may be exercised as much in respect of accused charged in a joint count as in respect of those charged in separate counts on one indictment. The discretion may be attributed either to the court's inherent power to control its own proceedings or to the power to sever contained in the Indictments Act 1915, s. 5(3).

D11.87 **Guidance as to the Exercise of the Discretion** Because severance of the trial of jointly indicted accused is a matter of discretion, the way in which the discretion is exercised is unlikely to provide a successful ground of appeal (see **D11.113**). Guidance on ordering separate trials does, however, emerge from the decided cases. The following propositions summarise that guidance.

(a) Where the accused are charged in a joint count, the arguments in favour of a joint trial are very strong. These arguments include:
   (i) severance will necessitate much or all of the prosecution evidence being given twice before different juries and increase the risk of inconsistent verdicts;
   (ii) even if the accused are expected to blame each other for the offence (i.e. will run 'cut-throat' defences), the interests of the prosecution and the public in a single trial will generally outweigh the interests of the defence in not having to call each accused before the same jury to give evidence for him or herself which will incriminate the other (*Grondkowski* [1946] KB 369; *Moghal* (1977) 65 Cr App R 56; *Edwards* [1998] Crim LR 756; *Crawford* [1997] 1 WLR 1329).
(b) Where the prosecution case against one accused (D1) includes evidence that is admissible against D1 but not against the co-accused (D2), there is no obligation to order severance simply because the evidence in question might prejudice the jury against D2. However, the judge should balance the advantages of a single trial against the possible prejudice to D2, and should consider especially how far an appropriate direction to the jury is really likely to ensure that they take into account the evidence only for its proper purpose of proving the case against D1 (*Lake* (1976) 64 Cr App R 172; *B* [2004] EWCA Crim 1254, [2004] 2 Cr App R 34 (570); *Miah* [2011] EWCA Crim 945, [2012] 1 Cr App R (S) 11 (47)).
(c) Where a joint trial of numerous accused would lead to a very long and complicated trial, the judge should consider whether a number of shorter trials, each involving only some of the accused, might make for a fairer and more efficient disposition of the issues. This reason for severance is tied up with the rule against overloading indictments, which is considered at **D11.91**.
(d) There may be some distinction to be drawn between cases where the accused are jointly charged in a single count and those where they allegedly committed separate offences which were nonetheless sufficiently linked to be put in one indictment. In the latter situation, the cases against the accused are unlikely to be as closely intertwined as when a joint offence is alleged, and the public interest argument in favour of a single trial is correspondingly less strong. There should, therefore, be a greater willingness to order separate trials.

Presumption in Favour of Joint Trial The authorities cited above indicate that the decision whether to grant severance is one within the discretion of the trial judge, and that the decision should be in favour of joint trial unless the risk of prejudice is unusually great. Thus in *Josephs* (1977) 65 Cr App R 253, where the same issue arose as in *Lake* (1976) 64 Cr App R 172, Lord Widgery CJ said (at p. 255, emphasis added): **D11.88**

> ... it is a very rare thing for this court to interfere with the trial judge's decision about separate trials. Nothing is more peculiarly left to the trial judge as his concern with that particular point. *Of course we have jurisdiction to interfere where something has clearly gone wrong*, but it is very rare, and members of the court today cannot remember a case in which such an interference with the trial judge's decision was made.
>
> ... the fact that some of [a co-accused's] statements may rub off on the other accused ... is just one of those things that happens in the course of a multiple criminal trial. The advantages of having co-defendants tried together is so great that the right to order a separate trial will not be granted unless there is good reason for it.

See also *Marsh-Smith* [2015] EWCA Crim 1883 for an application of the same approach, discussed at **D11.73**.

Refusal of Severance as a Ground of Appeal In general, the Court of Appeal will interfere with the exercise of a discretion only if it can be shown that the trial judge took into account irrelevant considerations, or ignored relevant ones, or arrived at a manifestly unreasonable decision. This was illustrated in *Moghal* (1977) 65 Cr App R 56, where the appeal failed even though the members of the court indicated strongly that, had they been trying the case, they would not have acted as the trial judge had done. The test of whether to intervene is usually stated simply as: did the trial judge's decision cause unacceptable prejudice to the appellant such as might have led to a miscarriage of justice? (*Grondkowski* [1946] KB 369 and *Moghal* (1977) 65 Cr App R 56). **D11.89**

In a suitable case, however, the Court of Appeal has shown that it is willing to exercise its power to intervene where, to use the words of Lord Widgery CJ in *Josephs* (1977) 65 Cr App R 253, 'something has clearly gone wrong'.

(a) In *O'Boyle* (1991) 92 Cr App R 202, D1 was charged with conspiracy to supply cocaine. His co-defendant D2 alleged that he had acted under duress from D1. At trial, D1's confession to US investigators was excluded, but counsel for D2 sought to cross-examine D1 on its contents. On appeal, the Court of Appeal held that the trial judge should have ordered severance. The Court recognised that the trial judge had a discretion and that, generally, conspirators should be tried together. However, this was an exceptional case, where separate trials would have done little or no harm to the co-defendant or prosecution, while joint trial prejudiced the appellant. See also *Randle* [1995] Crim LR 331.
(b) In *Smith* (1966) 51 Cr App R 22, D and two others were prosecuted in relation to a large-scale theft. The evidence against the co-accused consisted largely of their admissions to the police, in which they also implicated D. The evidence directly admissible against D was scanty. The co-accused were acquitted and D alone convicted. Although the Court of Criminal Appeal accepted that the trial judge had correctly rejected an application for separate trials, the Court nevertheless held that the only explanation for D alone being convicted was that the jury must have been prejudiced against him by the material in the co-accused's statements, notwithstanding the judge's direction that those statements were evidence only against the co-accused (see the discussion of *Smith* in *Lake* (1976) 64 Cr App R 172 at p. 177).

D11.90 What the decisions in *Lake* and *Josephs* demonstrate is a distinction between ordinary prejudice occasioned by a joint trial and what Lord Widgery referred to as 'dangerous prejudice'. The former is almost bound to arise when co-accused run inconsistent defences and does not in general justify severing the indictment. The latter, exemplified by *Smith*, should be dealt with by severance. See also *Miah* [2011] EWCA Crim 945, [2012] 1 Cr App R (S) 11 (47).

Note that the situation may be different where the admissions made by one accused become admissible against another in the circumstances identified in *Hayter* [2005] UKHL 6, [2005] 2 All ER 209.

Overloading Indictments

D11.91 In drafting indictments and in ruling on applications to sever indictments, both the drafter and the court should have regard not only to what is permitted by the rules on joinder (discussed from **D11.63**) but also to whether the interests of justice are best served by one long trial or several shorter ones.

If a single indictment, containing numerous counts and/or accused, would result in an unduly long or complicated trial and place an unfair burden on the jury, the prosecution should opt for however many shorter indictments are necessary to cover the same ground, notwithstanding that a single indictment would be within the rules. Similarly, if the prosecution have not taken the initiative in this regard, the court should intervene to order separate trials, whether of counts or accused.

In *Wright* [1995] Crim LR 251, it was made clear that the mere length of a trial is not sufficient in itself to characterise convictions as unsafe. (See also *Kellard* [1995] 2 Cr App R 134.) The issue is therefore not that a trial can never be both long and fair, but that no jury ought to be required to try an overloaded indictment.

There are various sources of guidance in this regard, including the observations of Lord Judge CJ in *N [2010] EWCA Crim* 941, [2010] 2 Cr App R 14 (97) and the guidance related to cases of serious fraud (which are discussed in more detail in **D4** and **D15**).

Observations of the Court of Appeal Dicta on overloaded indictments are contained especially in *Novac* (1976) 65 Cr App R 107 and *Thorne* (1977) 66 Cr App R 6. D11.92

In *Novac*, there were some 19 counts against four accused (N, R, A-C and A). The major count was against N, R and A-C and alleged a conspiracy to procure males under 21 to commit acts of gross indecency. Further counts alleged specific offences such as living on the earnings of male prostitution, importuning in a public place and buggery or gross indecency with named persons. These had been committed both during the currency of the conspiracy and outside that period. The fourth accused (A) was not alleged to be a member of the conspiracy, but was charged with further indecency offences which had been uncovered during the police investigation.

Bridge LJ made observations about this complicated indictment (at p. 188): D11.93

> We cannot conclude this judgment without pointing out that ... most of the difficulties which have bedevilled this trial, which have led in the end to the quashing of all convictions except on the conspiracy and related counts, arose directly out of the overloading of the indictment ... the indictment of 19 counts against four defendants resulted ... in a trial of quite unnecessary length and complexity. If the specific offence counts against [N, R and A-C] and all the counts against [A] had been tried separately, the main trial of the conspiracy and related counts would have been reasonably manageable and the four separate trials would have been short and straightforward. Quite apart from the question whether the prosecution could find legal justification for joining all these counts in one indictment and resisting severance, the wider and more important question has to be asked whether in such a case the interests of justice were likely to be better served by one very long trial, or by one moderately long and four short separate trials.
>
> We answer unhesitatingly that whatever advantages were expected to accrue from one long trial, ... they were heavily outweighed by the disadvantages. A trial of such dimensions puts an immense burden on both judge and jury. In the course of a four or five-day summing-up the most careful and conscientious judge may so easily overlook some essential matter. Even if the summing-up is faultless, it is by no means cynical to doubt whether the average juror can be expected to take it all in and apply all the directions given. Some criminal prosecutions involve consideration of matters so plainly inextricable and indivisible that a long and complex trial is an ineluctable necessity. But we are convinced that nothing short of the criterion of absolute necessity can justify the imposition of the burdens of a very long trial on the court.

Much the same sentiments were expressed in *Thorne*, where the trial was even longer. The indictment related essentially to three separate armed robberies. In addition, there were counts for related conspiracies to rob, handling some of the proceeds, and conspiracy to pervert the course of justice by making threats against a potential prosecution witness. In all, there were ten counts and 14 accused, and the trial lasted nearly seven months. The Court of Appeal (Lawton LJ) commented that the indictment was undoubtedly overloaded, and the trial placed 'a burden on the judge which he should never be asked to bear' (at p. 14). D11.94

A further aspect of not overloading indictments arises when the conduct of the accused may either be charged in a number of distinct offences or brought under one charge. In those circumstances, the prosecution should have just one count for the obviously appropriate offence, because nothing is gained and much is lost in terms of simplicity of presentation to the jury if the indictment contains counts for all the offences of which the accused might possibly be guilty (*Staton* [1983] Crim LR 190). This is the situation in which CrimPR 10.2(2) comes into its own (see **D11.35**).

Putting the Prosecution to its Election Both *Novac* (1976) 65 Cr App R 107 and *Thorne* (1977) 66 Cr App R 6 were cases in which the complexity of the indictment was in part attributable to the combination of conspiracy and substantive charges. CrimPD II, para. 10A.4 (see Supplement, **CPD.10A**), addresses this problem: D11.95

Criminal Practice Directions, para. 10A.4

> Where an indictment contains substantive counts and one or more related conspiracy counts, the court will expect the prosecution to justify the joinder. Failing justification, the prosecution should be required to choose whether to proceed on the substantive counts or on the conspiracy counts. In any event, if there is a conviction on any counts that are tried, then those that have been postponed can remain on the file marked 'not to be proceeded with without the leave of the court or the Court of Appeal'. In the event that a conviction is later quashed on appeal, the remaining counts can be tried.

Special circumstances apply where there is a split between a trial by jury and a trial by judge alone pursuant to the DVCVA 2004, ss. 17 to 21 (see **D11.39** and CrimPD II, paras. 10A.15 to 10A.20) and where multiple offending counts are used pursuant to CrimPR 10.2(2) (see **D11.35** and CrimPD II, paras. 10A.11 to 10A.14).

D11.96 If a substantive count and a related conspiracy count are joined in the indictment, the prosecution must justify their inclusion. If their inclusion is not justified, the prosecution will have to decide on which counts they wish to proceed. It follows that a conspiracy count which adds nothing to the charge of a substantive offence has no place in the indictment (*Jones* (1974) 59 Cr App R 120; see *Watts* (1995) *The Times*, 14 April 1995).

If the prosecution elect to proceed upon the substantive charge, such an election is not necessarily irreversible. In *Findlay* [1992] Crim LR 372, for example, the prosecution, which had elected to proceed on substantive robbery counts, were permitted to reverse that election when the evidence necessary to sustain a conviction on those counts was later ruled inadmissible. The Court of Appeal dismissed the appeal, in view of the fact that there was no demonstrable prejudice to F.

D11.97 **Cases of Serious Fraud** The most striking instances of overloaded indictments have emerged in serious fraud cases.

One illustration is *Cohen* (1992) *Independent*, 29 July 1992 (the 'Blue Arrow' case), a case in which the indictment was long and complex, and in which the jury did not retire until the 184th day of the trial. The Court of Appeal said that the basic assumption that the jury determined guilt or innocence on evidence which they were able to comprehend and remember had been destroyed in that case. The prosecution had a heavy responsibility not to overload the indictment, but the ultimate responsibility lay with the trial judge, whose powers of severance should have been used at an early stage to overcome the problems of an overloaded indictment.

The prosecution's responsibility to ensure that the indictment was not overloaded was emphasised amongst the conclusions of the HM Crown Prosecution Service Inspectorate report, 'Review of the Investigation and Criminal Proceedings Relating to the Jubilee Line case' (June 2006). At paras. 1.30 to 1.32, the Review emphasised that the lack of particularisation in the conspiracy to defraud allegation relied on by the prosecution, and its reliance on broad inferences which necessitated detailed examination of a very considerable number of documents, resulted in a considerable lengthening of the trial without any material effect on the overall level of criminality. The Review underlined the importance of the prosecution ensuring at the outset that their allegations are particularised, focused and aimed at keeping the evidence and length of trial within reasonable bounds.

D11.98 **Reopening an Application for Severance** An application to sever the indictment may be made on more than one occasion. Sometimes the second application will be before the same judge but not necessarily so (e.g., where the first application was made at a pre-trial review; see **D15.46**).

In *Wright* (1989) 90 Cr App R 325, Judge G at the pre-trial review refused to sever a conspiracy count from an indictment which also contained a series of counts relating to substantive offences. Before the trial itself began, defence counsel applied again to sever, this time before Judge C, who rejected the submission on the ground that the matter had been concluded by Judge G. The Court of Appeal held that the question for the second judge was whether there had been a sufficient change to justify reopening the question. If there had not, he was not obliged to hear the same point argued again.

AMENDING THE INDICTMENT

Statutory Provision

D11.99 The power to amend an indictment, once it has been served, lies in the Indictments Act 1915, s. 5(1).

Indictments Act 1915, s. 5

(1) Where, before trial, or at any stage of a trial, it appears to the court that the indictment is defective, the court shall make such order for the amendment of the indictment as the court thinks necessary to meet the circumstances of the case, unless, having regard to the merits of the case, the required amendments cannot be made without injustice.

Extent of the Power to Amend

D11.100 The power to amend may be exercised both:

(a) in respect of formal defects in the wording of a count, for example when the statement of offence fails to specify the statute contravened or when the particulars do not disclose an essential element of the offence, and
(b) in respect of substantial defects such as divergences between the allegations in the count and the evidence foreshadowed in the material served under the regulations for the service of the prosecution case after the accused has been sent for trial or called at trial.

This was confirmed by the Court of Criminal Appeal in *Pople* [1951] 1 KB 53 at p. 54:

> The argument for the appellants appeared to involve the proposition that an indictment, in order to be defective, must be one which in law did not charge any offence at all and therefore was bad on the face of it. We do not take that view. In our opinion, any alteration in matters of description, and probably in many other respects, may be made in order to meet the evidence in the case so long as the amendment causes no injustice to the accused person.

It followed that the trial judge in *Pople* had been entitled to allow an amendment at the close of the prosecution case to make the property allegedly obtained by deception from a building society a cheque rather than the sum of money. Furthermore, there was no injustice to the accused because the matter in which the indictment was defective was 'the mere description of the thing obtained', while 'in substance, the charge was the same'.

D11.101 Similarly, in *Radley* (1973) 58 Cr App R 394, Lord Widgery CJ quoted with approval the passage from *Pople* quoted above, and held that an indictment may be defective if it merely fails to allege an offence disclosed by the material served when sending for trial. 'Defective', in the context of s. 5(1), is not restricted to defects in form, but 'has got a very much wider meaning' (at p. 401). Moreover, this wide meaning is acceptable because the power to amend is subject to the overriding limitation that it must not cause injustice (at p. 402). See also *Booker* [2011] EWCA Crim 7, [2011] 1 Cr App R 26 (330) for a restatement of the principle that the interests of justice should not be narrowly construed for these purposes.

The power to amend may be exercised in respect of voluntary bills of indictment preferred on the direction of a High Court judge just as it may be exercised in respect of 'ordinary' indictments preferred on the authority of a sending for trial (*Allcock* [1999] 1 Cr App R 227; *Wells*

[1995] 2 Cr App R 417 at p. 422; *Walters* (1979) 69 Cr App R 115 — all cases decided in the context of committal proceedings).

D11.102 **Limitation on Power to Amend** If the indictment is so defective as to be a nullity, it is not capable of amendment and there is a mistrial. An indictment is invalid from the outset in this way where, for example, it alleges an offence unknown to law. Where a count describes a known offence inaccurately, however, it is capable of amendment, subject to the usual considerations of prejudice to the defendant (*McVitie* [1960] 2 QB 483, applied in *Tyler* (1992) 96 Cr App R 332).

D11.103 **Amendment by Insertion of a New Count** As well as enabling amendments to be made to existing counts, s. 5(1) of the Indictments Act 1915 permits the insertion of an entirely new count into an indictment, whether in addition to or in substitution for the original counts (*Johal* [1973] QB 475), where Ashworth J said (at p. 481A), 'there is no rule of law which precludes amendment of an indictment after arraignment, either by addition of a new count or otherwise'.

The words 'after arraignment' appear in the sentence quoted because the main point at issue in that case was whether the amendment was made too late, but obviously the addition of a count before arraignment is even less open to objection than a subsequent addition. Where the addition is made after arraignment, it will be necessary to put the new counts to the accused to enable the accused to plead to them. Amendment can be made even after the close of the prosecution case, as occurred in *Rogers* [2014] EWCA Crim 1680, [2015] 1 WLR 1017 (amendment following successful submission of no case to answer as to certain counts on the indictment).

The amendment to an indictment can be so extensive that the question arises whether it amounts to the substitution of a fresh indictment. This was the issue in *Fyffe* [1992] Crim LR 442, where the Crown amended an 11-count indictment so that it contained 27 counts. It was submitted on appeal that the 27-count indictment was a fresh indictment and therefore the judge should have gone through the procedural steps of staying the 11-count indictment and granting the prosecution leave to prefer the 27-count indictment out of time, whereupon the defendants should have been arraigned once more. The appeal was dismissed since, for all material purposes, the 27 counts reproduced what had appeared in the 11 counts. No new allegations had been added; the amendments were of form rather than substance and it was not necessary to go through the process of re-arraignment.

D11.104 **Evidential Basis for the New Count** A further question arises as to whether it is necessary for the amendment to be founded on the material disclosed under the regulations for the service of the prosecution case after the accused has been sent for trial. According to the Court of Appeal in *Osieh* [1996] 1 WLR 1260, a case decided in the context of committal proceedings, it is not necessary. However, it was held in that case that the amendment *had* been founded on evidence disclosed at committal, and this approach ran counter to dicta in *Dixon* (1991) 92 Cr App R 43 and *Hall* [1968] 2 QB 788. In *Hall*, Lord Parker CJ said (at p. 792) that, granted that there was power to amend, the question is really 'whether the amendment asked for and granted was supported by evidence given at the committal proceedings'. The position has now been resolved in *Thompson* [2011] EWCA Crim 102, [2012] 1 Cr App R 12 (153). The Court of Appeal approved and adopted the approach in *Osieh*. The power to amend under s. 5 was held not to be limited by the evidence served at committal, and the question to be assessed before permission to amend is granted is whether or not the accused will be unfairly prejudiced by the amendment. The fact that an amendment raises for the first time something not foreshadowed in the documents may be a ground for not permitting the amendment, or permitting it only together with an adjournment (see Professor JC Smith, 'Adding Counts to an Indictment' [1996] Crim LR 889).

Timing of Amendment

The Indictments Act 1915, s. 5(1), makes clear that an indictment may be amended at any stage of a trial, whether before or after arraignment. This was demonstrated in the following cases: **D11.105**

(a) in *Johal* [1973] QB 475, where the insertion of the new counts occurred after arraignment but before the empanelling of the jury;
(b) in *Pople* [1951] 1 KB 53, where the amendment took the form of an alteration in the description of the property obtained by deception and was granted after the close of the prosecution case;
(c) in *Collison* (1980) 71 Cr App R 249, where the amendment was made after the jury had been out considering their verdict for over three hours — on appeal, counsel for C accepted 'that the words in section 5(1) of the Indictments Act 1915 "at any stage of a trial" do permit amendment even after the jury have gone into retirement if the circumstances otherwise justify it and no injustice is caused to the defendant' (at p. 253).

The later the amendment, the greater the risk of its causing injustice and therefore the less likely it is to be allowed. However, an indictment may be amended even at the stage of retrial, provided that no injustice is done (*Swaine* [2001] Crim LR 166; see also *B (JJ)* [2012] EWCA Crim 1440, adding an alternative count after D had given evidence was considered unfair, and *Feeley* [2012] EWCA Crim 720, [2012] 1 WLR 3133, adding counts to an indictment for a retrial was considered permissible). The procedure for amendment is contained in CrimPR 3.29 and 3.30 (see Supplement, **R3.29** and **R3.30**).

Risk of Injustice

The main consideration for a judge deciding whether to allow an amendment is the risk of injustice. If the amendment cannot be made without injustice, it must not be made, as the last clause of s. 5(1) of the Indictments Act 1915 makes clear. The timing of the amendment is a major factor in determining whether there will be injustice. Thus, in *Johal* [1973] QB 475, the Court of Appeal rejected the view in *Harden* [1963] 1 QB 8 that an amendment that substantially substitutes another offence for that originally charged could *never* be made after arraignment, but agreed that such amendments would usually cause injustice. Ashworth J said (at pp. 480G–481C): **D11.106**

> As a statement of principle, to be applied generally, this [i.e., the decision in *Harden*] is ... too wide. No doubt in many cases in which, after arraignment, an amendment is sought for the purpose of substituting another offence for that originally charged, or for the purpose of adding a further charge, injustice would be caused by granting the amendment. But in some cases (of which the present is an example) no such injustice would be caused and the amendment may properly be allowed ...
>
> In the judgment of this court there is no rule of law which precludes amendment of an indictment after arraignment, either by addition of a new count or otherwise ...
>
> On the other hand this court shares the view expressed in some of the earlier cases that amendment of an indictment during the course of a trial is likely to prejudice an accused person. The longer the interval between arraignment and amendment, the more likely it is that injustice will be caused, and in every case in which amendment is sought, it is essential to consider with great care whether the accused person will be prejudiced thereby.

Consideration of the Risk of Injustice Test On the facts of *Johal* [1973] QB 475, there was no injustice because the amendment was made immediately after arraignment, and 'the situation was to all intents and purposes the same as if application to amend had been made before arraignment'. In *Collison* (1980) 71 Cr App R 249, where the amendment was made after the jury had retired, there was still no injustice because the amendment merely removed a technical impediment to the jury convicting of the lesser offence (see also *Teong Sun Chuah* [1991] Crim **D11.107**

LR 463 for an example of amendment at a relatively late stage which was held to be acceptable since it caused no injustice).

On the other hand, in *Gregory* [1972] 2 All ER 861, the Court of Appeal criticised a late amendment to the particulars by the deletion of the allegation as to ownership where that was the central issue in the case and it could not be said that the allegation that the motor belonged to a named person was 'mere surplusage'. In *O'Connor* [1997] Crim LR 516, similarly, there was held to be a risk of injustice where the effect of an amendment made at the close of the prosecution case was to allow the prosecution to shift its ground significantly. The Court of Appeal held that the amendment was unfair, because the Crown's case had changed very significantly, and the appellant had been confronted with a different and more difficult case. It was for the prosecution to decide how to put their case, and they could not rely on the court granting leave to change it as the trial progressed. (The same approach was adopted in *B (JJ)* [2012] EWCA Crim 1440, where it was held that the addition of an alternative count after D had given evidence could be unfair.)

Procedure on Amendment

D11.108 In *Moss* [1995] Crim LR 828, it was stated that, where counsel seeks an amendment, counsel ought to ensure that there is a properly amended form of indictment before the judge, and that any order of the court is clear and is complied with. When amendment is allowed, a note of the order must be endorsed on the indictment (Indictments Act 1915, s. 5(2)). It should be noted that failure to make a proper application to amend is fatal to the amendment, but failure to endorse an amendment is not (*Leeks* [2009] EWCA Crim 1612, [2010] 1 Cr App R 5 (87)).

If necessary, an adjournment may be granted to allow the parties (in particular the defence) to deal with the altered position (s. 5(4)). Where the amendment comes during the course of a trial, there is power to discharge the jury from giving a verdict and order a retrial on the amended indictment (s. 5(5)(a)).

MOTION TO QUASH AN INDICTMENT

D11.109 Either party may move to quash either the whole indictment or a count thereof. The obvious time for doing so is before the accused is arraigned, although it would seem that the defence may make the application at any stage of the trial.

The effect of a successful application is that the accused may not be tried on the indictment (or particular count thereof to which the motion relates). However, this does not mean that the accused is thereby acquitted. Although the quashing of the indictment exhausts the effect of the sending on which it was founded (*Thompson* [1975] 2 All ER 1028), the prosecution may either institute fresh proceedings or apply for a voluntary bill of indictment.

Circumstances in which to Bring a Motion

D11.110 A motion to quash may be brought in any of three circumstances.

(a) Where the indictment is bad on its face (e.g., for duplicity or because the particulars of a count do not disclose an offence known to law, as in *Yates* (1872) 12 Cox CC 233).
(b) Where the indictment (or a count thereof) has been preferred otherwise than in accordance with the provisions of the Administration of Justice (Miscellaneous Provisions) Act 1933, s. 2. Such an indictment must be quashed because it is preferred without authority (*Lombardi* [1989] 1 All ER 992).
(c) Where the indictment contains a count for an offence in respect of which the accused was not sent for trial and the material served under the regulations for the service of the

prosecution case after the accused has been sent does not disclose a case to answer for that offence (*Jones* (1974) 59 Cr App R 120, a case decided in relation to committal documents).

Use of Such Motions by the Defence

Motions to quash are of little practical importance for the defence for three main reasons: **D11.111**

(a) the limited grounds on which they may be brought;
(b) the prosecution are often able to prevent a motion succeeding by making a suitable amendment to the indictment (e.g., splitting into two a count that the defence say should be quashed on grounds of duplicity);
(c) a successful motion results in the accused's discharge, not his acquittal.

However, such motions should not be ignored as a defence tool because failure to apply to quash may prejudice the chances of a successful appeal, since it may be argued that, if the defence at trial had felt themselves to be prejudiced by a defect in the indictment rendering it liable to be quashed, they would surely have made the appropriate application. The lack of a motion to quash may show that there was no miscarriage of justice (see, e.g., *Thompson* [1914] 2 KB 99 and *Donnelly* [1998] Crim LR 131).

Use of Such Motions by the Prosecution

Although motions to quash are most obviously a remedy available to the defence, the prosecution may wish to quash if they realise that an indictment they have preferred is invalid. The risk involved in adopting this course is that the sending on which the quashed indictment was founded may not be used as authority to prefer another indictment for the same offence (*Thompson* [1975] 2 All ER 1028 and dicta in *Newland* [1988] QB 402). The better course will usually be to ask the judge to stay (but not quash) the defective indictment and at the same time prefer a fresh indictment correcting the error in the original bill (*Follett* [1989] QB 338). **D11.112**

DEFECTS IN THE INDICTMENT AS A GROUND OF APPEAL

Where a trial proceeds on an unamended but defective indictment, there is an irregularity in the course of the trial which may result in the Court of Appeal finding that the conviction is unsafe (see, e.g., *Ayres* [1984] AC 447). **D11.113**

Decided cases do, however, show a marked reluctance on the part of the Court of Appeal to allow appeals on grounds of errors in the indictment. The precise reasoning varies. Sometimes it is said that the defect concerned a matter which was 'mere surplusage' (*Dossi* (1918) 13 Cr App R 158). Sometimes a distinction is drawn between an indictment which is a nullity and one which is merely defective (*McVitie* [1960] 2 QB 483; *Nelson* (1977) Cr App R 119).

The most helpful approach is that adumbrated by Lord Bridge in *Ayres*. He said (at pp. 460G–461B):

> In a number of cases where an irregularity in the form of the indictment has been discussed in relation to the application of the proviso a distinction, treated as of crucial importance, has been drawn between an indictment which is 'a nullity' and one which is merely 'defective'. For my part, I doubt if this classification provides much assistance in answering the question which the proviso poses. If the statement and particulars of the offence in an indictment disclose no criminal offence whatever or charge some offence which has been abolished, in which case the indictment could fairly be described as a nullity, it is obvious that a conviction under that indictment cannot stand. But if the statement and particulars of offence can be seen fairly to relate to and to be intended to charge a known and subsisting criminal offence but plead it in terms which are inaccurate, incomplete or otherwise imperfect, then the question whether a conviction on that indictment can properly be

affirmed under the proviso must depend on whether, in all the circumstances, it can be said with confidence that the particular error in the pleading cannot in any way have prejudiced or embarrassed the defendant.

Test on Appeal

D11.114 Normally, therefore, the crucial question is whether the defect has caused prejudice or embarrassment to the defence. This is illustrated by *Ayres* [1984] AC 447 itself. On the facts, the indictment faced by D 'did not charge him accurately with the only offence for which he could properly be convicted' (at p. 460C), because it charged a common-law conspiracy when he was in fact guilty of statutory conspiracy. Nonetheless, the House of Lords held that there had been no prejudice, because (at p. 462):

> The particulars of offence in this indictment left no one in doubt that the substance of the crime alleged was a conspiracy to obtain money by deception. The judge in summing up gave all the appropriate directions in relation to that offence ... the evidence amply proved that offence against the present appellant. The jury in returning a verdict of guilty must have been sure of his guilt of that offence. The judge passed a modest sentence comfortably below the maximum for that offence. The misdescription of the offence in the statement of offence as a common-law conspiracy to defraud had in the circumstances not the slightest practical significance ... there [cannot] possibly have been any actual miscarriage of justice.

Ayres was referred to in *Graham* [1997] 1 Cr App R 302, where the Court of Appeal made clear that a conviction would not be quashed because of a drafting or clerical error, or a discrepancy, omission or departure from good practice. A conviction would be unsafe only where the particulars did not support a conviction for the offence charged. See also *McKenzie* [2011] EWCA Crim 1550, [2011] 1 WLR 2807 and *Wilson* [2013] EWCA Crim 1780, [2014] QB 704, in which the Court of Appeal repeated that, even where there was a material irregularity in the drafting of the indictment on which an appellant had been convicted, where the error constituted a mis-labelling of the offence (whether it be a misdescription in the statement or particulars of the offence as to the source of criminality), that would not result in the indictment being a nullity and a conviction based on that indictment would be safe unless there was unfairness occasioned to the appellant by the error.

The test was expressed in *Walker* [2017] EWCA Crim 392, [2018] 1 Cr App R 19 (289) as the difference between 'purely technical defects' and 'fundamentally flawed in substance'.

Applications of the Test

D11.115 *Ayres* [1984] AC 447 is an extreme and somewhat questionable example of a defect in the indictment not resulting in a successful appeal. Appeals have also failed in the following cases notwithstanding the defects indicated below:

(a) *Thompson* [1914] 2 KB 99, where a count for incest was held to be bad for duplicity because it alleged offences 'on divers days' in a 21-month period;
(b) *McVitie* [1960] 2 QB 483, where the particulars omitted an essential ingredient of the offence charged (a breach of r. 5(1) of the Indictment Rules 1971);
(c) *Nelson* (1977) 65 Cr App R 119, where the statement of offence failed to specify the statute contravened (a breach of r. 6(a)(i) of the 1971 Rules);
(d) *Power* (1977) 66 Cr App R 159, where the statement of offence misdescribed the offence charged (a breach of r. 5(1) of the 1971 Rules);
(e) *Pritchett* [2007] EWCA Crim 586, where the indictment period commenced before the commencement date of the statute creating the offence;
(f) *Stocker* [2013] EWCA Crim 1993, [2014] 1 Cr App R 18 (247), where the statement of offence identified the wrong statute but the appeal failed on the basis that this was an error that could easily have been corrected at the time and occasioned no prejudice to the accused (see also *D* [2016] EWCA Crim 454, [2016] 2 Cr App R 18 (241) to similar effect);

(g) *Clarke* [2015] EWCA Crim 350 [2015] 2 Cr App R 6 (74), where the particulars of offence failed to specify the ingredients of the offence of robbery, but did make clear the nature of the prosecution allegation.
(h) *MJ* [2018] EWCA Crim 2485, [2019] 1 Cr App R 10 (122), where a second indictment had been uploaded to the digital case system without any application to amend or arraign, this did not undermine its validity if the procedure in CrimPR Part 10 for preferring an indictment had been followed.

In each of the above, the reasoning of the Court of Appeal was essentially that the indictment, although defective, was not null as it described an offence known to the law albeit in inaccurate terms; the accused, on the facts, had not been misled or prejudiced in the conduct of his defence by the error and the nature of the prosecution case was nevertheless apparent.

COURT'S DISCRETION TO PREVENT ABUSE OF PROCESS

The Crown Court has an inherent power to protect its process from abuse. This includes the capacity to protect against delays in prosecution but other forms of abuse of process have been recognised. For a full discussion of abuse of process, see **D3.66** ***et seq***. **D11.116**

Section D12 Arraignment and Pleas

INTRODUCTION

D12.1 This section addresses the issues which arise at the stage in proceedings when the accused is normally asked to plead to the indictment. Normal practice is for the accused to enter a plea personally when arraigned by the clerk. There are some circumstances in which arraignment should not occur. Those addressed here are circumstances in which the defendant is unfit to plead, or where a claim to autrefois acquit or autrefois convict is raised. Two further bars to arraignment arise where the court has no jurisdiction to proceed (which are addressed at **D12.51** and at **A8.1** to **A8.24**), or where the court orders a stay of proceedings before arraignment because the proceedings represent an abuse of the court's process (which is addressed at **D3.66** ***et seq.***).

Where an accused is arraigned, there are then a number of pleas available to him (not guilty, guilty to the offence charged, guilty to a lesser offence etc.) and a variety of possible consequences that can follow from arraignment, including the prosecution offering no evidence or asking for counts to lie on the file. It is at this stage that plea bargains become relevant. There are also, finally, situations where a plea may change. For convenience, deferred prosecution agreements, introduced by the CCA 2013, sch. 17, as an alternative to prosecution, are addressed at **D12.106** ***et seq.***

UNFITNESS TO PLEAD AND OTHER REASONS FOR FAILING TO PLEAD

D12.2 An accused may fail to plead to the indictment when arraigned in three situations:

(a) because the accused is mentally incapable of doing so, i.e. is unfit to plead;
(b) in the increasingly rare circumstances in which the accused is physically incapable, sometimes known as 'mute by visitation of God' (which will largely be addressed as a question of fitness to plead); or
(c) because the accused wilfully chooses to stay silent, known as 'mute of malice'.

In relation to the procedure by which a report can be obtained to investigate an accused's mental health, see CrimPD 1, para. 3P (see Supplement, **CPD.3P**).

Unfitness to Plead

D12.3 Whether or not an accused is fit to plead is determined in accordance with tests laid down by common law. The procedure to be followed when an accused might be unfit and the consequences of a finding of unfitness are contained in the Criminal Procedure (Insanity) Act 1964, ss. 4, 4A and 5, and CrimPR 25.10 (see Supplement, **R25.10**).

Test of Unfitness to Plead The leading case of *Pritchard* (1836) 7 C & P 303 concerned a deaf mute who was otherwise of sound mind. Alderson B's direction to the jury empanelled to determine whether D was fit to plead was in terms which Lord Parker CJ was later to say had become 'firmly embodied in our law' (*Podola* [1960] 1 QB 325 at p. 353). Alderson B said (7 C & P 303 at pp. 304–5): **D12.4**

> There are three points to be inquired into: First, whether the prisoner is mute of malice or not; secondly, whether he can plead to the indictment or not; thirdly, whether he is of sufficient intellect to comprehend the course of proceedings on the trial, so as to make a proper defence — to know that he might challenge [any jurors] to whom he may object — and to comprehend the details of the evidence... if you think that there is no certain mode of communicating the details of the trial to the prisoner, so that he can clearly understand them, and be able properly to make his defence to the charge; you ought to find that he is not of sane mind. It is not enough that he may have a general capacity of communicating on ordinary matters.

The elements of this test were helpfully enunciated in directions that the Court of Appeal approved in *M* [2003] EWCA Crim 3452. The following points emerge from the modern application of Alderson B's direction in *Pritchard*: **D12.5**

(a) An accused may be unfit to plead even though not insane within the meaning of the M'Naghten rules. The point was expressly decided in *Governor of Stafford Prison, ex parte Emery* [1909] 2 KB 81 (and see also Lord Parker CJ's judgment in *Podola* [1960] 1 QB 325 at p. 353). Similarly, loss of memory through hysterical amnesia does not amount to unfitness to plead if the accused will be able to comprehend the proceedings and communicate with legal advisers (*Podola*).

(b) It would logically follow that an accused may be unfit even though not suffering from any form of mental disorder, by reference to the definition in the Mental Health Act 1983, s. 37(1) (see **E22.2**). Conversely, a high degree of abnormality does not *ipso facto* render the accused unfit to plead (*Berry* (1977) 66 Cr App R 156 — finding of unfitness quashed because, although D was in a 'grossly abnormal mental state', the judge failed to direct the jury on the crucial issue of whether those abnormalities made him incapable of following the trial).

(c) The test of unfitness to plead is whether the accused will be able to comprehend the course of the proceedings so as to make a proper defence (*Pritchard*). Whether the accused can understand and reply rationally to the indictment is obviously a relevant factor, but the court must also consider whether the accused would be able to exercise the right to challenge jurors, understand details of the evidence as it is given, instruct legal advisers and give evidence in person. This includes consideration not only of whether an accused can give evidence but whether the accused can be cross-examined (*Orr* [2016] EWCA Crim 889, [2016] 2 Cr App R 32 (400)). The test is not adapted to circumstances where an accused can enter a plea of guilty but would not be fit to participate in a trial (*Marcantonio* [2016] EWCA Crim 14, [2016] 2 Cr App R 9 (81)). See also *Hamberger* [2017] EWCA Crim 273, [2017] 2 Cr App R 9 (81), where measures to permit a defendant to participate in a trial were considered.

(d) In assessing whether an accused is unfit to plead, it is essential that the court has regard to the facilities available to assist in effective participation despite any disability, such as the use of an intermediary or special measures. In *Walls* [2011] EWCA Crim 443, [2011] 2 Cr App R 6 (61), Thomas LJ enjoined (at [38]): 'save in clear cases, a court must rigorously examine evidence of psychiatrists adduced before them and then subject that evidence to careful analysis against the *Pritchard* criteria'. See also *Hamberger*.

(e) In applying those criteria, the court is required to assess the accused's capabilities in the context of the particular proceedings, by reference to the complexity or otherwise of the case and what the process will in fact demand of the accused (*Marcantonio*).

(f) An accused who can understand the course of the proceedings will be fit to plead even when acting against his or her own best interests as a consequence of a mental condition (*Robertson* [1968] 3 All ER 557 — paranoiac who might have made irrational objections to potential jurors, held fit to plead).

D12.6 **Burden of Proof** Following the evidence, the court must consider whether the accused is capable of understanding the proceedings so as to be able to:

(a) put forward a defence;
(b) challenge any juror to whom the accused has cause to object;
(c) give proper instructions to legal representatives; and
(d) follow the evidence.

If the issue was raised by the defence, the burden of proof is on them to establish on a balance of probabilities that the accused is unfit (*Robertson* [1968] 3 All ER 557); if raised by the prosecution, they bear the burden of proof beyond reasonable doubt (*Podola* [1960] 1 QB 325). Whilst it will normally be raised by the defence, the prosecution might wish to assert that the accused is unfit to plead either because of the general principle that prosecuting counsel should act as a 'minister of justice' assisting the court, or because in certain circumstances (e.g., where the offence charged requires proof of a specific or ulterior intent on the part of the accused) it may in practice be difficult to establish guilt if, at the time of trial, the accused is manifestly suffering from mental illness.

D12.7 **Procedure for Determining Unfitness to Plead** By reference to *Norman* [2008] EWCA Crim 1810, [2009] 1 Cr App R 13 (192) and CrimPR 25.10 (see Supplement, **R25.10**):

(a) Once the issue of fitness to plead has been raised, very careful case management is required to allow early resolution of the issue.
(b) Once full information is available, the court should consider carefully whether to postpone determination of the issue until immediately before the opening of the defence case at trial, or to proceed to an immediate determination.
(c) If the court determines the accused to be unfit, the court (pursuant to the Criminal Procedure (Insanity) Act, s. 4A(2)) is entitled to consider who is best placed to put the case for the accused. This is not necessarily the person who has been representing the accused until that point, as the responsibility of representing an unfit accused is different to that of representing an accused who is able to give instructions. The factors that the court needs to take into account are spelt out in CrimPR 25.10(3)(a).

D12.8 **Timing of Raising the Issue** Subject to a special procedure contained in the Criminal Procedure (Insanity) Act 1964, s. 4(2) (set out in full at **D12.16**), and the qualification in CrimPR 25.10(2) (see Supplement, **R25.10**), the issue must be determined as soon as it arises (s. 4(4)).

Section 4(2) of the 1964 Act permits the court to postpone consideration of unfitness until any time up to the opening of the defence case. The court must be of the opinion that, having regard to 'the nature of the supposed disability', postponement is 'expedient' and 'in the interests of the accused'. Such a postponement would be appropriate where there is a reasonable chance that the prosecution evidence may be subject to successful challenge without the need for the defence to be called upon (*Webb* [1969] 2 QB 278; *Burles* [1970] 2 QB 191).

In *Orr* [2016] EWCA Crim 889, [2016] 2 Cr App R 32 (400) the Court of Appeal explicitly found that D had been fit to participate in his trial up to the point of cross-examination and thereby implicitly determined that he was no longer able to participate fully thereafter. At that point, the procedure mandated by s. 4A cannot be avoided by the court's general discretion to order proceedings otherwise, however beneficial to the accused. In *Orr* the jury should not have been allowed to return a verdict, other than a verdict of acquittal, if they were not satisfied on the evidence already given in the trial that D did the act charged against him.

If an issue arises as to whether an accused is fit to be tried after the start of a trial, the jury already empanelled may determine whether the accused did the act alleged. This remains the case even where that jury is also determining the guilt or innocence of other accused. The same principle applies where the accused in question, who is charged with others, has been found unfit to plead before the start of the trial of those others (*B* [2008] EWCA Crim 1997, [2009] 1 Cr App R 19 (261)). Where it is discovered that the accused is unfit only after conviction, that court is required to proceed to sentence rather than embarking on a fitness to plead hearing (*Grant* [2008] EWCA Crim 1870).

The Issue of Fitness Under the DVCVA 2004, s. 22, the decision whether the accused is unfit to plead is taken by a judge alone, rather than by a jury as had been the case before. **D12.9**

The Criminal Procedure (Insanity) Act 1964, s. 4(6), lays down that the court may not determine the question of unfitness except on the evidence (written or oral) of two or more registered medical practitioners, at least one of whom must have been approved by the Secretary of State as having special experience in the diagnosis or treatment of mental disorder (see **D20.73** for the power of the court to remand an accused for the preparation of reports on the accused's mental condition under the Mental Health Act 1983, s. 35). Although such medical evidence is required, the judge is entitled to reject it and must assess it rigorously (*Walls* [2011] EWCA Crim 443, [2011] 2 Cr App R 6 (61) at [38]). The judge must, however, keep the issue under review (*M* [2006] EWCA Crim 2391). Such medical evidence is required before a determination of unfitness is reached. It is not required before an accused is found to be fit to plead (*Ghulam* [2009] EWCA Crim 2285, [2010] 1 WLR 891).

In *Ehi-Palmer* [2016] EWCA Crim 1844, after giving evidence D had been admitted to an inpatient unit as a result of a drug-induced psychosis, attested to in a report provided following the summing-up. The Court of Appeal held that the trial judge had been correct not to have found D unfit to plead on the basis of only one report, received after the close of the evidence, and had been right to proceed as if D had wilfully absented himself during the trial, given the self-induced nature of his difficulties.

Trial of the Facts Section 4A of the Criminal Procedure (Insanity) Act 1964 (which is set out in full at **D12.16**) applies where the court has determined that the accused is unfit to plead. As CrimPR 25.10(3)(b) makes clear, a jury is then sworn (if not sworn already) to determine whether the accused 'did the act or made the omission charged against him as the offence' (s. 4A(2)). If they are satisfied that the accused did, they must find accordingly (s. 4A(3)). If they are not so satisfied, they must acquit. If the question of fitness to plead was determined on or before arraignment, a jury must be empanelled to try the issue of whether the accused did the act or made the omission. If it was postponed under s. 4(2), the jury by whom the accused was being tried should also determine whether the accused did the act or made the omission (s. 4A(5)). **D12.10**

The purpose of this 'trial of the facts' is to ensure that the case against an accused who has been found unfit to plead is tested. It aims in this way to avoid the detention of innocent persons in hospital, merely because they are mentally unfit. It is also necessary to establish that the offence with which the unfit accused is charged is made out in law (*McKenzie* [2011] EWCA Crim 1550, [2011] 1 WLR 2807). The question for the jury (CrimPR 25.10(3)(c)(ii)) is not the guilt of the accused but whether the accused did the act or made the omission charged. Although the statute is silent on the standard of proof, it is clear that the test is 'beyond reasonable doubt' (*Chal* [2007] EWCA Crim 2647, [2008] 1 Cr App R 18 (247)).

CrimPR 25.10(3)(c) spells out that the normal trial procedure (set out at CrimPR 25.9) continues to apply, for example as to the making of a submission of no case to answer, and final representations being made to the jury on the accused's behalf. Given that the accused is not fit to give evidence, the warning as to the consequences of a defendant not giving evidence does not arise (CrimPR 25.10(3)(c)(iii)). The same rules of evidence apply to a trial of the facts as to a conventional criminal trial. Accordingly, the hearsay provisions (*Chal*: see **F17.1**) and the bad character provisions (*Creed* [2011] EWCA Crim 144 at **F13.1**) of the CJA 2003 continue to apply.

Relevance of the Mental Element of an Offence at the Trial of the Facts There is no all purpose answer to the question of whether it is necessary to prove the mental element of an offence in order to prove that the accused did the act, and it was recognised in *Wells* [2015] EWCA Crim 2, [2015] 1 WLR 2797 that the prosecution would be required to disprove issues relating to **D12.11**

self-defence, mistake or accident where there was objective evidence capable of raising them. That said, in *Antoine* [2001] 1 AC 340, the House of Lords considered that by using the word 'act' rather than 'offence' in the Criminal Procedure (Insanity) Act 1964, s. 4A(2), Parliament had made it clear that the jury were not to consider the mental ingredients of the offence, and thus in a 'trial of the facts', the defence of diminished responsibility could not be raised. Similarly in *Grant* [2001] EWCA Crim 2611, [2002] QB 1030, it was held that provocation could not be raised at the s. 4A hearing, since it inevitably required examination of D's state of mind, rather than whether he 'did the act charged'. Only exceptionally will it be possible for the intentions of the accused to be considered as part of the inquiry (see, e.g., *R (Young) v Central Criminal Court* [2002] EWHC 548 (Admin), [2002] 2 Cr App R 12 (178), where the *actus reus* of the offence was that D 'concealed' material facts contrary to the Financial Services Act 1986, s. 47(1), and *B* [2012] EWCA Crim 770, [2012] 2 Cr App R 15 (164), where the 'act' of voyeurism included the purpose of the voyeur).

In *Antoine*, the House of Lords (Lord Hutton) also observed that careful consideration would always have to be given to whether an accused found to be under a disability should be called to give evidence at the hearing under s. 4A(2). Applying that approach, the Court of Appeal in *Swinbourne* [2013] EWCA Crim 2329 concluded that the interview under caution of such an accused should not be adduced at the s. 4A hearing, there being grounds to doubt that he would have understood the caution or the interview process. However, in *Wells* [2015] EWCA Crim 2, [2015] 1 WLR 2797, Sir Brian Leveson P took the view that there would be circumstances where a jury might properly hear what was said in interview, albeit with an appropriate warning.

D12.12 **The ECHR Perspective** In *M* [2001] EWCA Crim 2024, [2002] 1 WLR 824, the Court of Appeal considered the above procedures in the light of the ECHR, Article 6. The Court held that the criminal charge provisions of Article 6 do not apply to proceedings under ss. 4 and 4A of the 1964 Act, since those proceedings cannot result in a conviction. In any event, they concluded that the procedure under ss. 4 and 4A constituted a fair procedure, providing an opportunity for investigation of the facts on behalf of a disabled person, so far as possible. It fairly balanced the public interest and the interest of the person alleged to have committed the act. In addition, their lordships stated that the defence were able to make an application to stay proceedings for abuse of process when it appeared necessary, and this could be either before arraignment or before any question of disability fell to be determined.

This decision was endorsed by the House of Lords in *H* [2003] UKHL 1, [2003] 2 Cr App R 2 (25); any orders made following a finding that the accused did the act in question were said not to be punitive, but to be made only for the purpose of protecting the public.

Consequences of a Finding of Unfitness

D12.13 Under the Criminal Procedure (Insanity) Act 1964, s. 5 (set out in full at **D12.16**), if the accused is found unfit to plead, and the jury determine that the accused did the act or made the omission as charged, the court may make one of the following orders:

(a) a hospital order, for admission to such hospital as the Secretary of State specifies — such an order may be made the subject of a restriction order without limit of time (see **E22.2**);
(b) a supervision order; or
(c) an order for the accused's absolute discharge.

In *Fairley* [2003] EWCA Crim 1625, it was emphasised that the only orders which the judge could make, following a finding that an accused who was unfit to plead had committed the act in question, were those set out in the statute. Moreover, before the court can make a supervision order in the case of an accused found to be unfit to plead and to have done the act charged against him, it must have evidence that the necessary arrangements for that supervision are in place, and such supervision is available (*City and County of Swansea v Swansea Crown Court* [2016] EWHC 1389 (Admin)).

In *Grant* [2001] EWCA Crim 2611, [2002] QB 1030, the Court of Appeal recognised that where an accused had been found unfit to plead to a charge of murder, the trial judge was compelled to make an order for admission to a hospital without limitation of time whether or not such an order was justified on the medical evidence, which was directed to the question of whether the accused was fit to plead.

Rights of the Victim Under the DVCVA 2004, s. 38, the victim of a sexual or violent offence has certain rights where an offence is committed by a person who is found not guilty by reason of insanity or who is subject to a finding under the Criminal Procedure (Insanity) Act 1964, ss. 4 and 4A ('the patient'). Where the court makes a hospital order with a restriction order, the probation board for the area must take all reasonable steps to ascertain whether the victim wishes to make representations about any conditions to which the patient should be subject. The victim is also entitled to receive information about any conditions to which the patient is to be subject in the event of discharge from hospital. This right was extended by the amendment of s. 38 by the Mental Health Act 2007, s. 48, so that the victim has the same entitlement to information from the hospital as from the probation board. **D12.14**

Reversing Such an Order In *R (Hasani) v Crown Court at Blackfriars* [2005] EWHC 3016 (Admin), [2006] 1 Cr App R 27 (427), D was found unfit to plead to serious offences against the person. A jury then determined that he had done the acts in question. The judge adjourned the matter to determine the issue of disposal. Before that issue could be determined, evidence was presented to show that D was capable of pleading. The judge then directed that D be arraigned. On judicial review, the judge's order was quashed, and the case was remitted to the Crown Court. The order to arraign was premature in that a fresh hearing on fitness to plead, in accordance with s. 4, had to be held first. There was nothing in the Criminal Procedure (Insanity) Act 1964 to preclude the holding of a second hearing on the issue of fitness to plead where the evidence justifies that course of action and there has been no final disposition of the case. In *McKenzie* [2011] EWCA Crim 1550, [2011] 1 WLR 2807 it was recognised that, if a finding following a determination that an accused is unfit is later quashed by the Court of Appeal, it is not possible to return a guilty verdict of another offence or to order a retrial. **D12.15**

In *Roberts* [2019] EWCA Crim 1270, [2019] 2 Cr App R 33 (402) the Court of Appeal made clear that a person who had been found unfit to plead was not competent to appeal against that finding, or the finding that the person had done the act alleged, albeit that those acting for the person in the proceedings could do so on the person's behalf. This is now reflected by CrimPR 39.1 to 39.2 (see Supplement, **R39.1** *et seq.*).

Procedure where Accused is Found Fit to Plead If the accused is found fit to plead before the calling of any prosecution evidence, the accused will thereafter be arraigned in the usual way and plead to the indictment. **D12.16**

Criminal Procedure (Insanity) Act 1964, ss. 4, 4A and 5

4.—(1) This section applies where on the trial of a person the question arises (at the instance of the defence or otherwise) whether the accused is under a disability, that is to say, under any disability such that apart from this Act it would constitute a bar to his being tried.

(2) If, having regard to the nature of the supposed disability, the court are of opinion that it is expedient to do so and in the interests of the accused, they may postpone consideration of the question of fitness to be tried until any time up to the opening of the case for the defence.

(3) If, before the question of fitness to be tried falls to be determined, the jury return a verdict of acquittal on the count or each of the counts on which the accused is being tried, that question shall not be determined.

(4) Subject to subsections (2) and (3) above, the question of fitness to be tried shall be determined as soon as it arises.

(5) The question of fitness to be tried shall be determined by the court without a jury.

(6) The court shall not make a determination under subsection (5) above except on the written or oral evidence of two or more registered medical practitioners at least one of whom is duly approved.

D

Part D Procedure

4A.—(1) This section applies where in accordance with section 4(5) above it is determined by a court that the accused is under a disability.

(2) The trial shall not proceed or further proceed but it shall be determined by a jury—
  (a) on the evidence (if any) already given in the trial; and
  (b) on such evidence as may be adduced or further adduced by the prosecution, or adduced by a person appointed by the court under this section to put the case for the defence,

whether they are satisfied, as respects the count or each of the counts on which the accused was to be or was being tried, that he did the act or made the omission charged against him as the offence.

(3) If as respects that count or any of those counts the jury are satisfied as mentioned in sub-section (2) above, they shall make a finding that the accused did the act or made the omission charged against him.

(4) If as respects that count or any of those counts the jury are not so satisfied, they shall return a verdict of acquittal as if on the count in question the trial had proceeded to a conclusion.

(5) Where the question of disability was determined after arraignment of the accused, the determination under subsection (2) is to be made by the jury by whom he was being tried.

5.—(1) This section applies where—
  (a) a special verdict is returned that the accused is not guilty by reason of insanity; or
  (b) findings have been made that the accused is under a disability and that he did the act or made the omission charged against him.

(2) The court shall make in respect of the accused—
  (a) a hospital order (with or without a restriction order);
  (b) a supervision order; or
  (c) an order for his absolute discharge.

(3) Where—
  (a) the offence to which the special verdict or the findings relate is an offence the sentence for which is fixed by law, and
  (b) the court have power to make a hospital order,

the court shall make a hospital order with a restriction order (whether or not they would have power to make a restriction order apart from this subsection).

(4) In this section—

'hospital order' has the meaning given in section 37 of the Mental Health Act 1983;
'restriction order' has the meaning given to it by section 41 of that Act;
'supervision order' has the meaning given in Part 1 of Schedule 1A to this Act.

Muteness

D12.17 If an accused stays silent when arraigned, the issue arises whether the silence is due to reasons beyond the accused's control or deliberate choice. In the former case, the accused is 'mute by visitation of God'; in the latter case, the accused is said to be 'mute of malice'.

D12.18 **Mute by Visitation of God** If the finding of the jury is that the accused is 'mute by visitation of God', the court has the option of adjourning for a short period in order that means of communicating may be found (e.g., through bringing an expert in sign language or lip-reading to court, and see also *Harris* (1897) 61 JP 792, where the jury found that D was mute as a result of a self-inflicted wound to his throat and the case was simply adjourned for the wound to heal).

Alternatively, if it seems that the muteness will be permanent and cannot be overcome, the jury should be asked to go on to consider whether the accused is unfit to plead (see **D12.4**; see also *Pritchard* (1836) 7 C & P 303 and *Governor of Stafford Prison, ex parte Emery* [1909] 2 KB 81). Therefore, a finding that the accused is mute by visitation of God is likely to be merely a stage en route to a finding of unfitness to plead, rather than a final determination in itself— indeed, the classic direction of Alderson B in *Pritchard* required the jury to consider in turn whether P was (a) mute of malice, (b) able to plead, and (c) able to comprehend the course of the proceedings.

D12.19 **Mute of Malice** Section 6(1)(c) of the CLA 1967 provides that:

> Where a person is arraigned on an indictment . . . if he stands mute of malice or will not answer directly to the indictment, the court may order a plea of not guilty to be entered on his behalf, and he shall then be treated as having pleaded not guilty.

The court may not itself conclude that a silent accused is mute of malice but must empanel a jury to determine the issue (*Schleter* (1866) 10 Cox CC 409), the burden of proof being on the prosecution to establish malice beyond reasonable doubt (*Sharp* [1960] 1 QB 357). The accused has no right of challenge in respect of the jurors so empanelled (*Paling* (1978) 67 Cr App R 299).

If the accused is found mute of malice, there is no objection to the jury that has made this finding going on to try the case, subject only to the general rule that a jury empanelled to try one issue may not try a second issue unless the trial of the latter commences within 24 hours of their empanelment to try the first (Juries Act 1974, s. 11).

In modern times, a silent accused will almost certainly be mute of malice. Should there be reasons beyond the accused's control leading to an inability to answer to the indictment, that will have been realised long before arraignment and steps will have been taken to overcome the problem (e.g., by the provision of an interpreter). Alternatively, if the accused is or may be unfit to plead, either the prosecution or defence will raise that issue with the judge before the indictment is put, thus avoiding the question of muteness arising as a separate issue lest the accused should be found fit to plead and then stay silent when arraigned.

AUTREFOIS ACQUIT AND AUTREFOIS CONVICT

The pleas of autrefois acquit and autrefois convict, together with the plea of pardon (see **D12.52**), are known as pleas in bar, because, if upheld, they bar any further proceedings on the indictment. The basic purpose of the two pleas is to protect the subject against repeated prosecutions for the same offence. Although a large body of case law has developed defining the precise circumstances in which the pleas may be relied on, in reality it will be very rare that a prosecution would occur where the proposed accused has already been acquitted or convicted of the offence that would be charged. In addition to domestic case law, it is relevant to consider the principle of double jeopardy enshrined in EU law by Article 54 of the Schengen Implementing Convention (CISA), which is one of the Schengen provisions which are binding on the UK. This is dealt with at **D12.30**. **D12.20**

There are a number of important statutory exceptions which will arise under the tainted acquittal provisions of the CPIA 1996, ss. 54 to 57, which are dealt with at **D12.38**, and the retrial provisions of the CJA 2003, ss. 75 to 97, which are dealt with at **D12.40**. Whilst not creating a form of autrefois, the CCA 2013, sch. 17, para. 11, provides that the prosecution will be prohibited from proceeding against an accused in respect of an offence that has been the subject of a deferred prosecution agreement (see **D12.106**) that has since expired.

Consideration of the pleas will involve asking: (a) what amounts to an acquittal or a conviction in this context? (b) precisely what is meant by being prosecuted twice for the same offence? and (c) what is the procedure to be followed on the pleas being raised?

Meaning of 'Acquittal' and 'Conviction' in Context of Autrefois Pleas

For an autrefois plea to succeed, the earlier conviction or acquittal relied on by the accused must have been by a court of competent jurisdiction and the proceedings must not have been *ultra vires*. This is illustrated in respect of autrefois convict by *Kent Justices, ex parte Machin* [1952] 2 QB 355, in which the Divisional Court quashed D's conviction on the ground that the correct procedure for determining mode of trial had not been complied with and the magistrates therefore acted *ultra vires*. Lord Goddard CJ stated that the prosecution were entitled to recharge D as he 'has never been technically in peril and he could now be tried over again' (at p. 360). An autrefois plea does not arise where the accused has previously been cautioned in relation to conduct for which the accused is then prosecuted, though this might give rise to a claim of abuse of process (*DPP v Alexander* [2010] EWHC 2266 (Admin), [2011] 1 WLR 653). **D12.21**

The same applies to *ultra vires* acquittals. For example, where magistrates purport to acquit an accused of an offence triable only on indictment, the accused cannot rely on the 'acquittal' to bar a trial on indictment (*West* [1964] 1 QB 15, and see also *Cardiff Magistrates' Court, ex parte Cardiff City Council* (1987) *The Times*, 24 February 1987). Similarly, in *DPP v Jarman* [2013] EWHC 4391 (Admin) the Administrative Court found that the dismissal of proceedings for want of prosecution did not constitute an acquittal for the purposes of a plea of autrefois. The Court found on the facts of the case that the plea would have been unlikely to succeed even if it had been available because, at the hearing at which the court dismissed the case, it did not consider the merits of the evidence.

Scope of the Pleas

D12.22 **At Common Law** The leading case is *Connelly v DPP* [1964] AC 1254, the facts of which are illustrative of the general principle. D and three others were jointly charged in two indictments, the first for murder and the second for armed robbery. The murder had occurred during the course of the indicted robbery and the issue considered by the House of Lords was whether, following D's acquittal for murder, his prosecution for robbery was precluded. At first instance, this plea was rejected, the jury following the judge's direction that the offence of murder could not be regarded as 'substantially or practically the same' as an offence of robbery with aggravation of a sum of money from a different employee. D was convicted of robbery, following a further trial.

D12.23 **The *Connolly* Nine Propositions** D appealed against conviction on the ground that his plea of autrefois acquit should have been upheld. The House of Lords dismissed the appeal. The speech of Lord Morris of Borth-y-Gest reviewed at length the old authorities and summarised their effect in nine propositions ([1964] AC 1254 at pp. 1305–6), which may be further summarised as follows:

(a) *A man may not be tried for a crime in respect of which he has previously been acquitted or convicted.* This is the straightforward and obvious application of autrefois, and covers cases where the offence charged in a count is identical in law and on the facts to a crime of which the accused has previously been acquitted or convicted.

(b) *A man cannot be tried for a crime in respect of which he could on some previous indictment have been convicted.* This is the corollary of the power of a jury to return a verdict of not guilty as charged but guilty of a lesser offence. The reasoning is that, where the jury on a certain count could have convicted of a lesser offence but failed to do so, they have impliedly acquitted the accused both of the offence charged and of the lesser offence. This appears to be the case whether or not the lesser alternative was actually left to the jury. Consequently, their verdict can be relied on to bar a later indictment for either or both offences. Lord Morris traced the principle back to Hale's *Pleas of the Crown* (1778), giving the example of an acquittal for murder barring any later indictment for manslaughter ([1964] AC 1254 at p. 1311) (see *Old Street Magistrates' Court, ex parte Davies* [1995] Crim LR 629).

(c) *A man cannot be tried for a crime which is in effect the same, or is substantially the same, as a crime of which he has previously been acquitted or convicted (or could have been convicted by way of alternative verdict).* Lord Morris (see pp. 1310–28) undertook a detailed survey of the decided cases which relate to when a count is to be regarded as alleging a crime that is substantially the same as one of which the accused has previously been acquitted or convicted. One clear example of the test being satisfied is provided by an accused being indicted for murder after having been acquitted of the alleged victim's manslaughter (*Wrote v Wigges* (1591) 4 Co Rep 45b; *Tancock* (1876) 34 LT 455).

The same will apply whenever proof of an offence of which the accused has already been acquitted is a necessary step towards proving the offence now charged. The strictness of the test is, however, illustrated by *Salvi* (1857) 10 Cox CC 481, where D, after being acquitted on a charge of wounding with intent to murder, was indicted for murder after his victim's death. His plea of autrefois failed because murder could be committed without there being an intention to murder. Therefore, the evidence on the second indictment would not necessarily have to be such as to support a conviction on the first (it could show merely an intention to do the victim grievous bodily harm).

(d) What must be considered is whether the crime or offence charged in the later indictment is the same, or is in effect or is substantially the same, as the crime charged in the former indictment and it is immaterial that the facts under examination or the witnesses being called in the later proceedings are the same as those in some earlier proceedings. The actual decision in *Connelly v DPP* provides the best illustration. The evidence called and facts relied on by the prosecution against C at the trial for robbery were precisely the same as they had called and relied on at the earlier trial for murder. But, despite the coincidence of prosecution facts and evidence at the two trials, the House of Lords were unanimous in holding that autrefois acquit did not avail.

Reconsideration of the Principles in *Beedie* The above analysis should now be considered in the light of the decision of the Court of Appeal in *Beedie* [1998] QB 356. D was prosecuted first for Health and Safety Act offences and then for manslaughter, both relating to the same death. At his trial for manslaughter, his counsel applied to stay the indictment, relying upon *Connelly*, but the judge refused. He was convicted and he appealed. The Court of Appeal considered the question of whether the second offence had to be the same as the first, or whether it was sufficient that it arose from the same facts, and stated the following principles: **D12.24**

(a) The House of Lords in *Connelly* had identified a narrow principle of autrefois. It was applicable only where the *same* offence was alleged in the second indictment. Rose LJ, delivering the judgment of the Court of Appeal in *Beedie*, quoted with approval Lord Devlin in *Connelly* (at p. 1340): 'For the doctrine to apply it must be the same offence both in fact and in law'.
(b) Importantly, however, judicial discretion should be exercised where the second offence arises out of the same or substantially the same set of facts as the first. In addition, there should be no sequential trials for offences on an ascending scale of gravity (relying on the principle in *Elrington* (1861) 1 B & S 688). As it was put in *Forest of Dean Justices, ex parte Farley* [1990] RTR 228 at p. 239, there is an 'almost invariable rule that when a person is tried on a lesser offence he is not to be tried again on the same facts for a more serious offence'.
(c) It was for the prosecution to show that there were special circumstances before the judge should allow the trial to proceed. In *Beedie*, a stay should have been ordered because the manslaughter allegation was based on substantially the same facts as the earlier summary prosecutions, it was a prosecution for an offence of greater gravity, and there were no special circumstances such as to allow the prosecution to proceed; the appeal was allowed (see also *South East Hampshire Magistrates' Court, ex parte CPS* [1998] Crim LR 422 and *Hartnett* [2003] EWCA Crim 345).

It follows that in such circumstances the plea of autrefois has in reality become a species of abuse of process. This was illustrated in *Cheong* [2006] EWCA Crim 524, in which it was held that, where an accused has not been acquitted or convicted in a foreign court but the prosecuting authority in that country has acted in some other way in relation to the charge now brought against him, the question for the court is whether the accused could not now receive a fair trial, or it would otherwise be unfair to try the accused. It was also illustrated by *Dwyer* [2012] EWCA Crim 10, where the Court of Appeal ruled that a conspiracy charge which relied in part on a substantive act to which D had pleaded guilty could not be stayed through a plea of autrefois convict, but could be stayed as an abuse of process.

Findings that Can Form Basis for Plea of Autrefois Acquit The following findings *do* amount to acquittals and therefore can found a plea of autrefois acquit: **D12.25**

(a) The quashing of a conviction by the Court of Appeal, provided it does not at the same time order a retrial (Criminal Appeal Act 1968, s. 2(3)).
(b) An acquittal by a foreign court of competent jurisdiction (*Aughet* (1919) 13 Cr App R 101). This was confirmed, *obiter*, by Lord Diplock in *Treacy v DPP* [1971] AC 537, when he said (at p. 562D) that the common-law doctrine of autrefois acquit and convict was 'a doctrine

which has always applied whether the previous conviction or acquittal based on the same facts was by an English court or by a foreign court'.

D12.26 **Findings that Cannot Form Basis for Plea of Autrefois Acquit** The following findings do *not* amount to acquittals and therefore cannot found a plea of autrefois acquit:

(a) Discharge of the accused at committal proceedings (*Manchester City Stipendiary Magistrate, ex parte Snelson* [1977] 2 All ER 62).
(b) Quashing of an indictment following a motion to quash. This point would not seem to be covered by specific authority but follows inevitably from the nature of the remedy, which is to prevent any proceedings on the indictment in question and, *ex hypothesi*, prevent the returning of a verdict (*Newland* [1988] QB 402).
(c) The withdrawal of a summons by the prosecution in the magistrates' court prior to the accused having pleaded to it (*Bedford and Sharnbrook Justices, ex parte Ward* [1974] Crim LR 109). The reason for this, as Nolan J observed in *Grays Justices, ex parte Low* [1990] QB 54 at p. 59A–B, is 'there has been no adjudication upon the merits of the charge in the original summons, and the defendant has not been put in peril of conviction upon it'.
(d) The prosecution offering no evidence and laying an alternative charge as in *Brookes* [1995] Crim LR 630, where D pleaded not guilty to a charge under the OAPA 1861, s. 20, and the prosecution offered no evidence and laid a charge under s. 18. The Court of Appeal approved the rejection of his plea of autrefois acquit (see also *Islington London Borough Council v Michaelides* [2001] EWHC Admin 468).
(e) The dismissal of an information under s. 15 of the MCA 1980 on account of the non- appearance of the prosecutor (*Bennett and Bond, ex parte Bennet* (1908) 72 JP 362 and *DPP v Jarman* [2013] EWHC 4391 (Admin) (see **D12.21**)) or where the information is so faulty in form and content that the accused could never have been in jeopardy on it (*DPP v Porthouse* (1988) 89 Cr App R 21; *Dabhade* [1993] QB 329).
(f) The dismissal of a charge, pursuant to the CDA 1998, s. 51.
(g) The prosecution serving notice of discontinuance under the Prosecution of Offences Act 1985, s. 23.
(h) The jury being discharged from giving a verdict.
(i) Reliance on evidence of an offence of which the accused has been acquitted as similar fact evidence (*Z* [2000] 2 AC 483).
(j) Where the provisions relating to tainted acquittals in the CPIA 1996, ss. 54 to 57, apply (see **D12.38**).

In *Fawcett* [2013] EWCA Crim 1399 the Court of Appeal rejected the contention that it had been an abuse of process to prosecute D for burglary when he had earlier pleaded guilty to offences of handling stolen goods relating to the same conduct on an indictment that had been preferred in error. The Court found that the guilty pleas to that indictment could be vacated and D arraigned on the proper burglary indictment without any injustice.

D12.27 **Findings that Can Form Basis for Plea of Autrefois Convict** The following findings *do* amount to convictions and therefore can found a plea of autrefois convict:

(a) A conviction by a foreign court will found autrefois convict, subject to the qualification that if an accused who now relies on the foreign conviction was found guilty and sentenced in his or her absence and there is no likelihood of the accused ever returning to the country concerned to serve the sentence, the plea will fail (*Thomas* [1985] QB 604).
(b) A prison adjudication proceeding that involved punishment by loss of liberty (*Robinson (Anthony)* [2017] EWCA Crim 936, [2018] QB 941).
(c) A plea of autrefois convict could only be based upon a complete adjudication against the accused, including the final disposal of the case by passing sentence or some other order such as an absolute discharge. This was the conclusion of the Privy Council in *Richards*

v The Queen [1993] AC 217. The underlying rationale of the plea was to prevent double punishment. But, if a finding of guilt was all that was necessary to support the plea in bar, an accused might escape punishment altogether. The Privy Council thereby concluded that two earlier decisions to the contrary, *Sheridan* [1937] 1 KB 223 and *Grant* [1936] 2 All ER 1156, were wrongly decided.

Findings that Cannot Form Basis for Plea of Autrefois Convict The following findings do *not* amount to convictions and therefore cannot found a plea of autrefois convict: **D12.28**

(a) The taking of an offence into consideration when passing sentence for other offences of which the offender has been convicted (*Nicholson* [1947] 2 All ER 535).
(b) A finding of contempt of court in civil proceedings (*Green* [1993] Crim LR 46, but note that the position in relation to non-molestation orders has changed as a result of the DVCVA 2004, s. 1 (see **B14.138**)).

It was formerly said that a finding of guilt in disciplinary proceedings does not amount to a conviction, albeit that the finding is followed by the imposition of a penalty (*Hogan* [1960] 2 QB 513). However, in *Robinson (Anthony)* [2017] EWCA Crim 936, [2018] QB 941, the Court of Appeal found that a prison adjudication proceeding which involved punishment by loss of liberty amounted to 'criminal proceedings' by a body of competent jurisdiction and the rule against double jeopardy applied.

A Note on Issue Estoppel A further question raised by the appeal in *Connelly v DPP* [1964] AC 1254, was whether the doctrine of issue estoppel applies in criminal cases, i.e. can either the prosecution or the defence prevent the other side reopening a question of fact if that question has already been decided in previous proceedings between the same parties? However, in *DPP v Humphrys* [1977] AC 1, it was held that issue estoppel has no place in criminal proceedings. There is a limited exception in the case of an application for habeas corpus (*Governor of Brixton Prison, ex parte Osman* [1991] 1 All ER 108). For full discussion of issue estoppel, see **F12.22 *et seq*.** **D12.29**

Double Jeopardy in EU Law

Allied to the concept of autrefois acquit is the principle of double jeopardy. The principle of double jeopardy in EU law, otherwise referred to as the *ne bis in idem* principle, is set out in Article 54 of the Schengen Implementing Convention (CISA), which is one of the Schengen provisions which are binding on the UK. Article 54 reads as follows: **D12.30**

> A person whose trial has been finally disposed of in one Contracting Party may not be prosecuted in another Contracting Party for the same acts provided that, if a penalty has been imposed, it has been enforced, is actually in the process of being enforced or can no longer be enforced under the laws of the sentencing Contracting Party.

A number of questions have arisen regarding the interpretation of Article 54, in particular on the definition of what constitutes 'same acts' and what is meant by a trial being 'finally disposed of'. The CJEU has adopted a purposive interpretation, emphasising the key aim of facilitating free movement in the Area of Freedom, Security and Justice as well as legal certainty for the accused.

'Finally Disposed of' The CJEU has found that the *ne bis in idem* principle applies to: the termination of prosecutions by the Public Prosecutor following out-of-court settlements with the accused (Joined cases C-187/01 and C-385/01 *Gözütok and Brügge* [2003] ECR I-1345); final decisions acquitting the accused for lack of evidence (Case C-150/05 *Van Straaten* [2006] ECR I-9327); and time-barred prosecutions (Case C-467/04 *Gasparini* [2006] ECR I-9199). It is also applicable to criminal proceedings against an accused whose trial for the same acts as those for which the accused faces prosecution was finally disposed of in another Contracting State, even though, under the law of the State in which the accused was convicted, the sentence which was imposed could never, on account of specific features of procedure such as those referred to in the main proceedings, have been directly enforced (Case C-297/07 *Bourquain* [2008] ECR I-9425). However, *ne bis in idem* **D12.31**

does not apply to a decision by which an authority of a Contracting State, after examining the merits of the case brought before it, makes an order (at a stage before the charging of a person suspected of a crime) suspending criminal proceedings, where the suspension decision does not, under the domestic law of that State, definitely bar further prosecution and therefore does not preclude new criminal proceedings in respect of the same acts in that State (Case C-491/07 *Turansky* [2008] ECR I-11039). In Case C-398/12 *M* [2015] 2 CMLR 2 (46), the Court found that a finding that there is no ground to refer a case to a trial court which precludes, in the Contracting State in which that order was made, the bringing of new criminal proceedings in respect of the same acts against the person to whom that finding applies, unless new facts and/or evidence against that person come to light, must be considered to be a final judgment, and thus precludes new proceedings against the same person in respect of the same acts in another Contracting State.

In Case C-486/14 *Kossowski* [2016] 1 WLR 4393, the investigation was closed in the absence of sufficient evidence, but D had not given a statement, and V and the hearsay witness were not interviewed during the investigation in order to verify the statements made by V because they lived abroad. Under these circumstances, the Grand Chamber found (at [48]) that a decision terminating criminal proceedings does not constitute a decision given after a determination has been made as to the merits of the case.

D12.32 **'Same Acts'** In a consistent line of case law, the CJEU has interpreted the phrase 'same acts' as based on the 'identity of the material acts, understood as the existence of a set of facts which are inextricably linked together, irrespective of the legal classification given to them or the legal interest protected' (Case C-436/04 *Van Esbroek* [2006] ECR I-2333; Case C-150/05 *Van Straaten* [2006] ECR I-9327; Case C-288/0 *Kretzinger* [2007] ECR I-6641). In a case involving money laundering, the CJEU reiterated that the acts in question must make up 'an inseparable whole', but added that, if the acts do not make up an inseparable whole, the fact that they were committed with the same criminal intention does not suffice (Case C-367/05 *Kraajenbrink* [2007] ECR I-619 at [29]). The interpretation of the concept of 'same acts' under the CISA is equally valid for the purposes of the EAW Framework Decision (Case C-261/09 *Mantello* [2013] All ER (EC) 312).

D12.33 **'Enforced'** In *Kretzinger* [2007] ECR I-6641 the CJEU confirmed that a penalty 'has been enforced' or is 'actually in the process of being enforced' if a suspended custodial sentence has been imposed. In Case C-129/14 *Spasic* (CJEU, 27 May 2014) the Court found that the enforcement condition set out in Article 54 of the CISA is compatible with Article 50 of the EU Charter of Fundamental Rights. Article 54 must be interpreted as meaning that the mere payment of a fine by a person sentenced by the self-same decision of a court of another Member State to a custodial sentence that has not been served is not sufficient to consider that the penalty 'has been enforced' or is 'actually in the process of being enforced' within the meaning of that provision.

Procedure on Autrefois Pleas

D12.34 The following procedural steps are involved in raising the plea of autrefois, although failure to observe the correct formalities in entering the plea does not prevent reliance on it (*Flatman v Light* [1946] KB 414).

(a) Under the Criminal Procedure Act 1851, s. 28, an accused may raise a plea of autrefois simply by claiming to have already been lawfully acquitted or convicted of the offence now charged. Where, however, the accused is legally represented, the correct procedure is for the plea to be entered in writing signed by counsel. A suggested form of words is, '[The accused] says that the Queen ought not further to prosecute the indictment against him because he has been lawfully acquitted/convicted of the offence charged therein'.
(b) The obvious time for pleading autrefois is before the indictment is put to the accused, but failure to do so then will not prevent the defence raising the issue at a later stage ('the plea may be raised at any time either as a plea in bar to the second indictment or at any stage in the proceedings': per Lord Hodson in *Connelly v DPP* [1964] AC 1254 at p. 1331).

(c) The prosecution either admit that the plea is good (in which case the accused is discharged) or join issue in writing.
(d) Alternatively, the court may raise the plea of its own motion (*Cooper v New Forest District Council* [1992] Crim LR 877).
(e) Once the plea has been entered and issue joined by the prosecution, the burden of proof is on the accused to make good the plea on the balance of probabilities (*Coughlan* (1976) 63 Cr App R 33).
(f) The parties are not restricted to the formal record of the earlier proceedings (which will establish only the date and place of conviction or acquittal, the wording of the charges and the name of the accused), but may call relevant evidence. In the absence of dispute, counsel should shorten the proceedings by reading to the court a brief statement of the relevant facts from (a) the previous trial, and (b) the statements in the present case on which they respectively intend to rely in argument (*Coughlan*).
(g) The issue is determined by the judge without empanelling a jury (CJA 1988, s. 122).
(h) If a plea of autrefois convict or acquit succeeds, it is a bar to any further proceedings on the indictment. If the plea fails, the indictment is put and the accused is entitled to plead not guilty to the general issue notwithstanding earlier unsuccessful reliance on autrefois (CLA 1967, s. 6(1): 'Where a person is arraigned on indictment . . . he shall in all cases be entitled to make a plea of not guilty in addition to any demurrer or special plea').

Statutory Provisions In addition to the procedure to deal with tainted acquittals (D12.38) and a procedure for the retrial of certain serious offences in the light of new evidence (D12.40), the common law on the ambit of autrefois is supplemented by two sets of statutory provisions. **D12.35**

Offences against the Person Act 1861 Sections 44 and 45 of the OAPA 1861 provide that, if justices, 'upon the hearing of any case of assault or battery upon the merits, *where the complaint was preferred by or on behalf of the party aggrieved*, shall deem the offence not to be proved, or shall find the assault or battery to have been justified, or so trifling as not to merit any punishment, and shall accordingly dismiss the complaint, they shall forthwith make out a certificate under their hands stating the fact of such dismissal and shall deliver such certificate to the party against whom the complaint was preferred' (s. 44, emphasis added). The obtaining of a s. 44 certificate of dismissal releases the party 'from all further or other proceedings, civil or criminal, *for the same cause*' (s. 45, emphasis added). **D12.36**

The italicised words indicate the main limitations on the scope of ss. 44 and 45. First, a certificate of dismissal may be granted only where the victim of the alleged offence is the prosecutor, rather than the CPS. Secondly, a certificate frees the recipient only from further proceedings 'for the same cause'.

Section 18 of the Interpretation Act 1978 Section 18 of the Interpretation Act 1978 states that: **D12.37**

> Where an act or omission constitutes an offence under two or more Acts, or both under an Act and at common law, the offender shall, unless the contrary intention appears, be liable to be prosecuted and punished under either or any of those Acts or at common law, but shall not be liable to be punished more than once for the same offence.

According to Humphreys J in *Thomas* [1950] 1 KB 26, the predecessor of s. 18 of the 1978 Act (s. 33 of the Interpretation Act 1889) 'added nothing and detracted nothing from the common law'. In particular, the prohibition on being punished more than once for the same offence did not protect an accused from being convicted and sentenced on successive occasions for different offences arising out of the same criminal act (conviction for wounding with intent no bar to later indictment for murder).

TAINTED ACQUITTALS

The provisions of the CPIA 1996, ss. 54 to 57, which relate to 'tainted acquittals', constitute a major exception to the availability of autrefois acquit. They enable the prosecution of an accused for a second time for a crime of which the accused has already been acquitted at trial, provided **D12.38** certain conditions are met. Sections 54 and 55 (set out below) lay down a procedure relating to tainted acquittals where the following conditions are met:

(a) an accused has been acquitted of an offence (s. 54(1)(a)); and
(b) a person has been convicted of an administration of justice offence involving interference with or intimidation of a juror or a witness or potential witness (s. 54(1)(b)); and
(c) the court convicting of the administration of justice offence certifies that there is a real possibility that, but for the interference or intimidation, the acquitted person would not have been acquitted, and that it would not be contrary to the interests of justice to proceed against the acquitted person (s. 54(2) and (5)); and
(d) the High Court grants an order quashing the acquittal after deciding that the four conditions set out in s. 55 are satisfied (s. 55 is set out below).

The provisions of ss. 54 to 57 apply in relation to acquittals in respect of offences alleged to have been committed on or after 15 April 1997. It should be emphasised that it is the *original* offence of which the defendant was acquitted which must be alleged to have been committed on or after that date (s. 54(7)).

The formalities relating to the tainted acquittal procedure are set out in CrimPR 27.2 (see Supplement, R27.2). Rule 27.2 makes it clear that the certification referred to in s. 54(2) must take place as soon as practicable after conviction.

D12.39 **Criminal Procedure and Investigations Act 1996, ss. 54 and 55**

54.—(1) This section applies where—
(a) a person has been acquitted of an offence, and
(b) a person has been convicted of an administration of justice offence involving interference with or intimidation of a juror or a witness (or potential witness) in any proceedings which led to the acquittal.

(2) Where it appears to the court before which the person was convicted that—
(a) there is a real possibility that, but for the interference or intimidation, the acquitted person would not have been acquitted, and
(b) subsection (5) does not apply,

the court shall certify that it so appears.

(3) Where a court certifies under subsection (2) an application may be made to the High Court for an order quashing the acquittal, and the Court shall make the order if (but shall not do so unless) the four conditions in section 55 are satisfied.

(4) Where an order is made under subsection (3) proceedings may be taken against the acquitted person for the offence of which he was acquitted.

(5) This subsection applies if, because of lapse of time or for any other reason, it would be contrary to the interests of justice to take proceedings against the acquitted person for the offence of which he was acquitted.

(6) For the purposes of this section the following offences are administration of justice offences—
(a) the offence of perverting the course of justice;
(b) the offence under section 51(1) of the Criminal Justice and Public Order Act 1994 (intimidation etc. of witnesses, jurors and others);
(c) an offence of aiding, abetting, counselling, procuring, suborning or inciting another person to commit an offence under section 1 of the Perjury Act 1911.

(7) This section applies in relation to acquittals in respect of offences alleged to be committed on or after the appointed day.

55.—(1) The first condition is that it appears to the High Court likely that, but for the interference or intimidation, the acquitted person would not have been acquitted.

(2) The second condition is that it does not appear to the Court that, because of lapse of time or for any other reason it would be contrary to the interests of justice to take proceedings against the acquitted person for the offence of which he was acquitted.

(3) The third condition is that it appears to the Court that the acquitted person has been given a reasonable opportunity to make written representations to the Court.

(4) The fourth condition is that it appears to the Court that the conviction for the administration of justice offence will stand.

(5) In applying subsection (4) the Court shall—
 (a) take into account all the information before it, but
 (b) ignore the possibility of new factors coming to light.
(6) Accordingly, the fourth condition has the effect that the Court shall not make an order under section 54(3) if (for instance) it appears to the Court that any time allowed for giving notice of appeal has not expired or that an appeal is pending.

RETRIAL PROVISIONS OF THE CRIMINAL JUSTICE ACT 2003

The CJA 2003 introduced a radical revision to the principles stated above. Sections 75 to 97 of the Act constitute the second major statutory exception to the rule against double jeopardy. In summary, they permit an accused to be retried for a 'qualifying' offence of which the accused has earlier been acquitted where there is new evidence of guilt, following an order of the Court of Appeal quashing that acquittal. **D12.40**

Application

As a starting point, the CJA 2003 defines the acquittals to which it has application. **D12.41**

(a) The new provisions apply to offences listed as 'qualifying offences' in the CJA 2003, sch. 5 (set out at **D12.48**). They are all serious offences, which in the main carry a maximum sentence of life imprisonment.
(b) The provisions apply to acquittals after trial on indictment in England and Wales (s. 75(1)) and to acquittals in proceedings outside the UK, of an offence that would have amounted to or included the commission of a qualifying offence in the UK or elsewhere (s. 75(4)).
(c) The meaning of 'acquittal' in s. 75(1) is extended by s. 75(2) so as to include any qualifying offence of which the accused could have been convicted on the original indictment as an alternative verdict (e.g., manslaughter where the original indictment was for murder). The implied acquittal of the alternative offence (manslaughter in the example) can be quashed by the same procedure as the express acquittal (for murder).
(d) Convictions, special verdicts of not guilty by reason of insanity and findings of unfitness to plead in alternative verdict offences are excluded from the procedure (s. 75(2)(a) to c)).

By virtue of s. 75(6), the procedure, with its removal of the freedom from double jeopardy, is made fully retrospective. The provisions apply equally to acquittals before and after the passing of the CJA 2003. It is of course possible that the retrospective nature of this provision may be subject to challenge under the ECHR, Article 7.

Application for a Quashing Order Section 76 of the CJA 2003 allows a prosecutor to apply to the Court of Appeal for an order to quash a person's acquittal for a qualifying offence or a lesser qualifying offence of which the person could have been convicted at that time. **D12.42**

The application to the Court of Appeal to quash the acquittal requires the personal written consent of the DPP (s. 76(3)). Before giving consent, the DPP must be satisfied (s. 76(4)):

(a) that there is evidence that meets the requirements of s. 78 (see **D12.45**);
(b) that it is in the public interest for the application to proceed; and
(c) that any trial would not run counter to our obligations under the Treaty on European Union relating to the principle of *ne bis in idem* (see **D12.30**).

The relevant Treaty obligations would appear to be apposite where a retrial is proposed for an offence already dealt with in another country of the EU. In such a case, the DPP would have to certify that such a course of action would not be contrary to the UK's obligations to the EU. In *Andrews* [2008] EWCA Crim 2908, [2009] 1 Cr App R 26 (347) the Court of Appeal approved the elucidation of the test by the then DPP, to the effect that consent would only be given to an application where the new evidence rendered a conviction highly probable. The Court also observed that the DPP's consent was not conclusive of the success of an application.

D12.43 **Notice** Notice of the application under the CJA 2003, s. 76(1) or (2), must be given to the Court of Appeal (s. 80(1)). The acquitted person must be served with a copy of the application within two days, and be charged with the offence in question. The acquitted person is entitled to attend and be represented at the hearing in the Court of Appeal. The procedure is set out in CrimPR 27.3 to 27.7 (see Supplement, **R27.3** *et seq.*).

Criteria

D12.44 The Court of Appeal must order a retrial if:

(a) 'there is new and compelling evidence in the case' (CJA 2003, s. 78); and
(b) 'it is in the interests of justice for an order to be made' (s. 79).

D12.45 **New Evidence** Under the CJA 2003, s. 78, evidence is 'new' if it was not adduced at the original trial of the acquitted person. This would include evidence that was available at the first trial, but not used. Reliance upon such evidence would raise questions about whether it would be in the interests of justice to order a retrial. Where the failure to use the evidence is because of a lack of diligence or expedition by the prosecutor, that is a factor relevant to the application of the interests of justice test (s. 79(2)(c)). But, as is pointed out in *Blackstone's Guide to the Criminal Justice Act 2003*, at p. 113, that formula is not apt to cover a tactical decision not to use the evidence in question first time round. The A-G, however, gave to the House of Lords (*Hansard*, HL col. 710 (4 November 2003)), on behalf of the government:

> . . . an undertaking, which I have agreed with the Director of Public Prosecutions, that where evidence was not adduced for tactical reasons, it would not be right to use it as a basis for an application . . . I hope that that will give some comfort. It will be reflected in guidance.

Section 78(5) makes clear that evidence that would have been inadmissible in the original proceedings could form the basis for an application for a retrial as 'new' evidence. It also applies to evidence that does not directly relate to the qualifying offence, but which would be admissible at a retrial of that offence, e.g., similar fact evidence (*Andrews* [2008] EWCA Crim 2908, [2009] 1 Cr App R 26 (347)).

The evidence is 'compelling' if the Court of Appeal considers it to be reliable and substantial and highly probative of the case against the accused. What is compelling will depend on the context of the previous trial. For example, if the identity of the offender was not in issue in the original trial, new evidence as to identification would not fit the evidence criterion so as to justify a retrial.

In *Miell* [2007] EWCA Crim 3130, [2008] 1 WLR 627, the new evidence upon which the prosecution sought to rely for the purposes of s. 78 was a confession which had been made after D had been convicted, and his subsequent conviction for perjury. The Court of Appeal carried out its own evaluation of the confession and, having concluded that it was unreliable, declined to treat it as 'new evidence'. See also *B and G* [2009] EWCA Crim 1077, where the Court of Appeal made clear that its assessment of whether evidence was compelling was different to a jury's assessment of whether it was persuasive; *Dobson* [2011] EWCA Crim 1255, [2011] 1 WLR 3230, where Lord Judge CJ made it clear that compelling evidence does not have to be irresistible; and *MH* [2015] EWCA Crim 585, for the application of the provisions in a case of fresh scientific evidence.

D12.46 **Interests of Justice** As to the interests of justice test in the CJA 2003, s. 79, the court will consider in particular whether a fair trial is unlikely (e.g., because of adverse publicity about the accused), the length of time since the alleged offence, and whether the police and prosecution have acted with due diligence and expedition with regard to the new evidence. The factors set out in s. 79 are not exhaustive, and the Court of Appeal can consider other relevant issues in determining whether a retrial would be in the interests of justice.

Dunlop [2006] EWCA Crim 1354, [2007] 1 WLR 1657 is illustrative. D had been acquitted, but subsequently not only confessed to the offence but had pleaded guilty to perjury in relation to his evidence at the original trial. The Court of Appeal held that far from it being contrary to the 'interests of justice' to retry him, treating his plea and confession as new evidence (pursuant to s. 78), the public would have been rightly outraged if any other course were taken. By contrast, in *Miell* [2007] EWCA Crim 3130, [2008] 1 WLR 627 (see **D12.45**), the Court of Appeal concluded that allowing D to be retried on the basis of his subsequent conviction for perjury would be contrary to the interests of justice, because in effect the burden would be on the accused to negate the impact of that conviction.

In *Andrews* [2008] EWCA Crim 2908, [2009] 1 Cr App R 26 (347), the Court of Appeal observed that it would usually only be in the interests of justice to grant an application where the prospects of conviction were 'very good', but went on to observe that considerations of double jeopardy are irrelevant to the assessment of an application.

Procedural Issues

Reporting restrictions may be imposed by the Court of Appeal in respect of matters surrounding the application for a retrial. The restrictions may last until the end of the retrial or to the point at which it is clear that the acquitted person can no longer be retried (CJA 2003, s. 82). An application for such an order is made in accordance with CrimPR 27.3 (see Supplement, **R27.3**). The restrictions may apply to any information in respect of the investigation and to the republication of matters previously published. An application to order or refuse a retrial can be the subject of an appeal to the Supreme Court on a point of law (s. 81). **D12.47**

If a retrial is ordered, it must be on an indictment preferred by the direction of the Court of Appeal (s. 84). Arraignment must take place within two months of the date on which the Court of Appeal ordered a retrial, unless it specifies a longer period. The period can be extended only if the Court of Appeal is satisfied that the prosecutor has acted with due expedition since the order was made, and that there is still good and sufficient reason to hold the retrial despite any additional lapse of time.

The procedure in respect of the retrial provisions was considered in *Re D (Acquitted person: Retrial)* [2006] EWCA Crim 828, [2006] 1 WLR 1998.

Relevant Statutory Extracts

Criminal Justice Act 2003, ss. 75 to 80 and 82 to 84 and sch. 5, part 1 **D12.48**

75.—(1) This Part applies where a person has been acquitted of a qualifying offence in proceedings—
- (a) on indictment in England and Wales,
- (b) on appeal against a conviction, verdict or finding in proceedings on indictment in England and Wales, or
- (c) on appeal from a decision on such an appeal.

(2) A person acquitted of an offence in proceedings mentioned in subsection (1) is treated for the purposes of that subsection as also acquitted of any qualifying offence of which he could have been convicted in the proceedings because of the first-mentioned offence being charged in the indictment, except an offence—
- (a) of which he has been convicted,
- (b) of which he has been found not guilty by reason of insanity, or
- (c) in respect of which, in proceedings where he has been found to be under a disability (as defined by section 4 of the Criminal Procedure (Insanity) Act 1964), a finding has been made that he did the act or made the omission charged against him.

(3) References in subsections (1) and (2) to a qualifying offence do not include references to an offence which, at the time of the acquittal, was the subject of an order under section 77(1) or (3).

(4) This Part also applies where a person has been acquitted, in proceedings elsewhere than in the United Kingdom of an offence under the law of the place where the proceedings were held, if the commission of the offence as alleged would have amounted to or included the commission (in the United Kingdom or elsewhere) of a qualifying offence.
(5) Conduct punishable under the law in force elsewhere than in the United Kingdom is an offence under that law for the purposes of subsection (4), however it is described in that law.
(6) This Part applies whether the acquittal was before or after the passing of this Act.
(7) References in this Part to acquittal are to acquittal in circumstances within subsection (1) or (4).
(8) In this Part 'qualifying offence' means an offence listed in Part 1 of Schedule 5.

76.—(1) A prosecutor may apply to the Court of Appeal for an order—
(a) quashing a person's acquittal in proceedings within section 75(1), and
(b) ordering him to be retried for the qualifying offence.
(2) A prosecutor may apply to the Court of Appeal, in the case of a person acquitted elsewhere than in the United Kingdom, for—
(a) a determination whether the acquittal is a bar to the person being tried in England and Wales for the qualifying offence, and
(b) if it is, an order that the acquittal is not to be a bar.
(3) A prosecutor may make an application under subsection (1) or (2) only with the written consent of the Director of Public Prosecutions.
(4) The Director of Public Prosecutions may give his consent only if satisfied that—
(a) there is evidence as respects which the requirements of section 78 appear to be met,
(b) it is in the public interest for the application to proceed, and
(c) any trial pursuant to an order on the application would not be inconsistent with obligations of the United Kingdom under Article 31 or 34 of the Treaty on European Union (as it had effect before 1 December 2009) or Articles 82, 83 or 85 of the Treaty on the Functioning of the European Union relating to the principle of *ne bis in idem*.
(5) Not more than one application may be made under subsection (1) or (2) in relation to an acquittal.

77.—(1) On an application under section 76(1), the Court of Appeal—
(a) if satisfied that the requirements of sections 78 and 79 are met, must make the order applied for;
(b) otherwise, must dismiss the application.
(2) Subsections (3) and (4) apply to an application under section 76(2).
(3) Where the Court of Appeal determines that the acquittal is a bar to the person being tried for the qualifying offence, the court—
(a) if satisfied that the requirements of sections 78 and 79 are met, must make the order applied for;
(b) otherwise, must make a declaration to the effect that the acquittal is a bar to the person being tried for the offence.
(4) Where the Court of Appeal determines that the acquittal is not a bar to the person being tried for the qualifying offence, it must make a declaration to that effect.

78.—(1) The requirements of this section are met if there is new and compelling evidence against the acquitted person in relation to the qualifying offence.
(2) Evidence is new if it was not adduced in the proceedings in which the person was acquitted (nor, if those were appeal proceedings, in earlier proceedings to which the appeal related).
(3) Evidence is compelling if—
(a) it is reliable,
(b) it is substantial, and
(c) in the context of the outstanding issues, it appears highly probative of the case against the acquitted person.
(4) The outstanding issues are the issues in dispute in the proceedings in which the person was acquitted and, if those were appeal proceedings, any other issues remaining in dispute from earlier proceedings to which the appeal related.
(5) For the purposes of this section, it is irrelevant whether any evidence would have been admissible in earlier proceedings against the acquitted person.

79.—(1) The requirements of this section are met if in all the circumstances it is in the interests of justice for the court to make the order under section 77.
(2) That question is to be determined having regard in particular to—
(a) whether existing circumstances make a fair trial unlikely;

(b) for the purposes of that question and otherwise, the length of time since the qualifying offence was allegedly committed;
(c) whether it is likely that the new evidence would have been adduced in the earlier proceedings against the acquitted person but for a failure by an officer or by a prosecutor to act with due diligence or expedition;
(d) whether, since those proceedings or, if later, since the commencement of this Part, any officer or prosecutor has failed to act with due diligence or expedition.

(3) In subsection (2) references to an officer or prosecutor include references to a person charged with corresponding duties under the law in force elsewhere than in England and Wales.

(4) Where the earlier prosecution was conducted by a person other than a prosecutor, subsection (2)(c) applies in relation to that person as well as in relation to a prosecutor.

80.—(1) A prosecutor who wishes to make an application under section 76(1) or (2) must give notice of the application to the Court of Appeal.

(2) Within two days beginning with the day on which any such notice is given, notice of the application must be served by the prosecutor on the person to whom the application relates, charging him with the offence to which it relates or, if he has been charged with it in accordance with section 87(4), stating that he has been so charged.

(3) Subsection (2) applies whether the person to whom the application relates is in the United Kingdom or elsewhere, but the Court of Appeal may, on application by the prosecutor, extend the time for service under that subsection if it considers it necessary to do so because of that person's absence from the United Kingdom.

(4) The Court of Appeal must consider the application at a hearing.

(5) The person to whom the application relates—
(a) is entitled to be present at the hearing, although he may be in custody, unless he is in custody elsewhere than in England and Wales or Northern Ireland, and
(b) is entitled to be represented at the hearing, whether he is present or not.

(6) For the purposes of the application, the Court of Appeal may, if it thinks it necessary or expedient in the interests of justice—
(a) order the production of any document, exhibit or other thing, the production of which appears to the court to be necessary for the determination of the application, and
(b) order any witness who would be a compellable witness in proceedings pursuant to an order or declaration made on the application to attend for examination and be examined before the court.

(7) The Court of Appeal may at one hearing consider more than one application (whether or not relating to the same person), but only if the offences concerned could be tried on the same indictment.

...

82.—(1) Where it appears to the Court of Appeal that the inclusion of any matter in a publication would give rise to a substantial risk of prejudice to the administration of justice in a retrial, the court may order that the matter is not to be included in any publication while the order has effect.

(2) In subsection (1) 'retrial' means the trial of an acquitted person for a qualifying offence pursuant to any order made or that may be made under section 77.

(3) The court may make an order under this section only if it appears to it necessary in the interests of justice to do so.

(4) An order under this section may apply to a matter which has been included in a publication published before the order takes effect, but such an order—
(a) applies only to the later inclusion of the matter in a publication (whether directly or by inclusion of the earlier publication), and
(b) does not otherwise affect the earlier publication.

(5) After notice of an application has been given under section 80(1) relating to the acquitted person and the qualifying offence, the court may make an order under this section only—
(a) of its own motion, or
(b) on the application of the Director of Public Prosecutions.

(6) Before such notice has been given, an order under this section—
(a) may be made only on the application of the Director of Public Prosecutions, and
(b) may not be made unless, since the acquittal concerned, an investigation of the commission by the acquitted person of the qualifying offence has been commenced by officers.

(7) The court may at any time, of its own motion or on an application made by the Director of Public Prosecutions or the acquitted person, vary or revoke an order under this section.

(8) Any order made under this section before notice of an application has been given under section 80(1) relating to the acquitted person and the qualifying offence must specify the time when it ceases to have effect.
(9) An order under this section which is made or has effect after such notice has been given ceases to have effect, unless it specifies an earlier time—
(a) when there is no longer any step that could be taken which would lead to the acquitted person being tried pursuant to an order made on the application, or
(b) if he is tried pursuant to such an order, at the conclusion of the trial.
(10) Nothing in this section affects any prohibition or restriction by virtue of any other enactment on the inclusion of any matter in a publication or any power, under an enactment or otherwise, to impose such a prohibition or restriction.
(11) In this section—
'programme service' has the same meaning as in the Broadcasting Act 1990,
'publication' includes any speech, writing, relevant programme or other communication in whatever form, which is addressed to the public at large or any section of the public (and for this purpose every relevant programme is to be taken to be so addressed), but does not include an indictment or other document prepared for use in particular legal proceedings,
'relevant programme' means a programme included in a programme service.

83.—(1) This section applies if—
(a) an order under section 82 is made, whether in England and Wales or Northern Ireland, and
(b) while the order has effect, any matter is included in a publication, in any part of the United Kingdom, in contravention of the order.
(2) Where the publication is a newspaper or periodical, any proprietor, editor or publisher of the newspaper or periodical is guilty of an offence.
(3) Where the publication is a relevant programme—
(a) any body corporate or Scottish partnership engaged in providing the programme service in which the programme is included, and
(b) any person having functions in relation to the programme corresponding to those of an editor of a newspaper,
is guilty of an offence.
(4) In the case of any other publication, any person publishing it is guilty of an offence.
(5) If an offence under this section committed by a body corporate is proved—
(a) to have been committed with the consent or connivance of, or
(b) to be attributable to any neglect on the part of,
an officer, the officer as well as the body corporate is guilty of the offence and liable to be proceeded against and punished accordingly.
(6) In subsection (5), 'officer' means a director, manager, secretary or other similar officer of the body, or a person purporting to act in any such capacity.
(7) If the affairs of a body corporate are managed by its members, 'director' in subsection (6) means a member of that body.
(8) [Applies only to Scotland.]
(9) A person guilty of an offence under this section is liable on summary conviction to a fine not exceeding level 5 on the standard scale.
(10) Proceedings for an offence under this section may not be instituted—
(a) in England and Wales otherwise than by or with the consent of the Attorney General, or
(b) [applies only to Northern Ireland].
(11) [Applies only to Northern Ireland.]

84.—(1) Where a person—
(a) is tried pursuant to an order under section 77(1), or
(b) is tried on indictment pursuant to an order under section 77(3),
the trial must be on an indictment preferred by direction of the Court of Appeal.
(2) After the end of 2 months after the date of the order, the person may not be arraigned on an indictment preferred in pursuance of such a direction unless the Court of Appeal gives leave.
(3) The Court of Appeal must not give leave unless satisfied that—
(a) the prosecutor has acted with due expedition, and
(b) there is a good and sufficient cause for trial despite the lapse of time since the order under section 77.

(4) Where the person may not be arraigned without leave, he may apply to the Court of Appeal to set aside the order and—
   (a) for any direction required for restoring an earlier judgment and verdict of acquittal of the qualifying offence, or
   (b) in the case of a person acquitted elsewhere than in the United Kingdom, for a declaration to the effect that the acquittal is a bar to his being tried for the qualifying offence.

(5) An indictment under subsection (1) may relate to more than one offence, or more than one person, and may relate to an offence which, or a person who, is not the subject of an order or declaration under section 77.

(6) Evidence given at a trial pursuant to an order under section 77(1) or (3) must be given orally if it was given orally at the original trial, unless—
   (a) all the parties to the trial agree otherwise,
   (b) section 116 applies, or
   (c) the witness is unavailable to give evidence, otherwise than as mentioned in subsection (2) of that section, and section 114(1)(d) applies.

(7) At a trial pursuant to an order under section 77(1), paragraph 5 of schedule 3 to the Crime and Disorder Act 1998 (use of depositions) does not apply to a deposition read as evidence at the original trial.

SCHEDULE 5

QUALIFYING OFFENCES FOR PURPOSES OF PART 10

PART 1

LIST OF OFFENCES FOR ENGLAND AND WALES

Offences Against the Person

Murder

1. Murder.

Attempted murder

2. An offence under section 1 of the Criminal Attempts Act 1981 of attempting to commit murder.

Soliciting murder

3. An offence under section 4 of the Offences against the Person Act 1861.

Manslaughter

4. Manslaughter.

Corporate manslaughter

4A. An offence under section 1 of the Corporate Manslaughter and Corporate Homicide Act 2007.

Kidnapping

5. Kidnapping.

Sexual Offences

Rape

6. An offence under section 1 of the Sexual Offences Act 1956 or section 1 of the Sexual Offences Act 2003.

Attempted rape

7. An offence under section 1 of the Criminal Attempts Act 1981 of attempting to commit an offence under section 1 of the Sexual Offences Act 1956 or section 1 of the Sexual Offences Act 2003.

Intercourse with a girl under thirteen

8. An offence under section 5 of the Sexual Offences Act 1956.

Incest by a man with a girl under thirteen

9. An offence under section 10 of the Sexual Offences Act 1956 alleged to have been committed with a girl under thirteen.

Assault by penetration

10. An offence under section 2 of the Sexual Offences Act 2003 (c. 42).

Causing a person to engage in sexual activity without consent

11. An offence under section 4 of the Sexual Offences Act 2003 where it is alleged that the activity caused involved penetration within subsection (4)(a) to (d) of that section.

Rape of a child under thirteen

12. An offence under section 5 of the Sexual Offences Act 2003.

Attempted rape of a child under thirteen

13. An offence under section 1 of the Criminal Attempts Act 1981 of attempting to commit an offence under section 5 of the Sexual Offences Act 2003.

Assault of a child under thirteen by penetration

14. An offence under section 6 of the Sexual Offences Act 2003.

Causing a child under thirteen to engage in sexual activity

15. An offence under section 8 of the Sexual Offences Act 2003 where it is alleged that an activity involving penetration within subsection (2)(a) to (d) of that section was caused.

Sexual activity with a person with a mental disorder impeding choice

16. An offence under section 30 of the Sexual Offences Act 2003 where it is alleged that the touching involved penetration within subsection (3)(a) to (d) of that section.

Causing a person with a mental disorder impeding choice to engage in sexual activity

17. An offence under section 31 of the Sexual Offences Act 2003 where it is alleged that an activity involving penetration within subsection (3)(a) to (d) of that section was caused.

Drugs Offences

Unlawful importation of Class A drug

18. An offence under section 50(2) of the Customs and Excise Management Act 1979 alleged to have been committed in respect of a Class A drug (as defined by section 2 of the Misuse of Drugs Act 1971).

Unlawful exportation of Class A drug

19. An offence under section 68(2) of the Customs and Excise Management Act 1979 alleged to have been committed in respect of a Class A drug (as defined by section 2 of the Misuse of Drugs Act 1971).

Fraudulent evasion in respect of Class A drug

20. An offence under section 170(1) or (2) of the Customs and Excise Management Act 1979 alleged to have been committed in respect of a Class A drug (as defined by section 2 of the Misuse of Drugs Act 1971).

Producing or being concerned in production of Class A drug

21. An offence under section 4(2) of the Misuse of Drugs Act 1971 alleged to have been committed in relation to a Class A drug (as defined by section 2 of that Act).

Criminal Damage Offences

Arson endangering life

22. An offence under section 1(2) of the Criminal Damage Act 1971 alleged to have been committed by destroying or damaging property by fire.

Causing explosion likely to endanger life or property

23. An offence under section 2 of the Explosive Substances Act 1883.

Intent or conspiracy to cause explosion likely to endanger life or property

24. An offence under section 3(1)(a) of the Explosive Substances Act 1883.

War Crimes and Terrorism

Genocide, crimes against humanity and war crimes

25. An offence under section 51 or 52 of the International Criminal Court Act 2001.

Grave breaches of the Geneva Conventions

26. An offence under section 1 of the Geneva Conventions Act 1957.

Directing terrorist organisation

27. An offence under section 56 of the Terrorism Act 2000.

Hostage-taking

28. An offence under section 1 of the Taking of Hostages Act 1982.

Conspiracy

29. An offence under section 1 of the Criminal Law Act 1977 of conspiracy to commit an offence listed in this Part of this Schedule.

OTHER PLEAS THAT MAY BE TAKEN AT ARRAIGNMENT

For convenience, three further objections that may be taken to the arraignment of the accused can briefly be addressed at this point. **D12.49**

Demurrer

This is 'an objection to the form or substance of the indictment, apparent on the face of the indictment' (per Cantley J in *Inner London Quarter Sessions, ex parte Metropolitan Police Commissioner* [1970] 2 QB 80 at p. 83G). The plea must be entered in writing, filed in the Crown Office, and a copy served on the opposite party, preferably prior to the accused being arraigned. **D12.50**

The scope of the remedy by demurrer is no wider than the scope of motions to quash. Lord Parker CJ said that he hoped that demurrer would now 'be allowed to die naturally' (at p. 85G). Similarly, Cantley J said that demurrers had been 'supplanted in practice by the safe and convenient procedures of motion to quash the indictment or motion in arrest of judgment' (a motion that the accused had been convicted of an offence not known to law) (at p. 83C). However, in *Cumberworth* (1989) 89 Cr App R 187, where the defence made a submission as to jurisdiction at the end of the prosecution evidence, the Court of Appeal stated, *obiter*, that it would have been more convenient procedurally to raise the point by way of demurrer at the outset of the trial, thus avoiding the necessity of hearing the evidence if the point were good.

The entry of a demurrer does not affect the accused's right to plead not guilty to the indictment should the demurrer fail (CLA 1967, s. 6(1)(a)).

Plea to the Jurisdiction

The purpose of this plea is to assert that the Crown Court has no jurisdiction to try the offence charged (e.g., because it is a summary offence or because it was committed abroad and does not come within the exceptional categories of 'foreign' offences that may be tried in England and Wales). Like a demurrer, the plea should be entered in writing prior to arraignment, although it is always open to the defence to take any jurisdictional point simply under a general not guilty plea (see, e.g., *Treacy v DPP* [1971] AC 537, where that was done, but see also *Cumberworth* (1989) 89 Cr App R 187 at **D12.50**, in which the Court of Appeal said that a jurisdiction point should be raised at the outset). **D12.51**

Pardon

This is the third special plea in bar (the other two being autrefois acquit and autrefois convict). It may be relied on where a pardon has been granted by the Crown on the advice of the Home Secretary in exercise of the royal prerogative of mercy. It must be pleaded at the first opportunity (i.e. before arraignment if the pardon has by then been granted). In modern times, the plea has become obsolete. **D12.52**

THE ARRAIGNMENT

Procedure on Arraignment

The procedure for arraignment is contained in CrimPR 3.32 (see Supplement, **R3.32**). The arraignment consists of the clerk of the court reading the indictment to the accused and asking whether the accused pleads guilty or not guilty to the counts contained therein. If there are several counts, a plea must be taken on each one separately immediately after it is read out (*Boyle* [1954] 2 QB 292); if, however, two counts are in the alternative and the accused pleads guilty **D12.53** to the first count, it is unnecessary to take a plea on the second (*Boyle*). If there is a joint indictment against several accused, normal practice is to arraign them together. Separate pleas must be taken from each of those named in any joint count.

The court is required, before arraignment, to confirm with the prosecution that the indictment represents the charges on which it wishes to proceed against the accused (CrimPR 3.32(1)).

The CDA 1998, ss. 57A to 57F, allow an accused in custody to be arraigned via live link rather than in person. CrimPD I, para. 3N.9 (see Supplement, **CPD.3N**), permits the same facility for those not in custody in appropriate circumstances (addressed to some extent at para. 3N.13). (As to the procedure to be adopted where an accused absents himself, see **D12.57** and **D12.70**.)

It is now standard practice to exclude the jurors in waiting from court until after the arraignment has been completed. This avoids the possibility of potential jurors being prejudiced by hearing the accused plead guilty to some but not all the counts on the indictment. After the jury have been sworn, they are told by the clerk the counts to which the accused has pleaded not guilty, no mention being made of any matters to which the accused has pleaded guilty nor of any co-accused who may have pleaded guilty.

Time for Arraignment

D12.54 **Time-limits** The Senior Courts Act 1981, s. 77(1), provides that rules of court are to prescribe the minimum and maximum periods which may elapse between a person being sent for trial and the beginning of the trial (defined by s. 77(3) as the time when the accused is arraigned). These limits are now set by CrimPR 3.32(5), which requires that arraignment should occur at least ten business days and at most 80 business days after sending.

By s. 77(2), the trial of a person sent for trial shall not begin within the minimum period prescribed by the rules unless the defence and the prosecution consent, and shall not begin after the maximum period unless a Crown Court judge orders otherwise.

D12.55 **Variations** It should be noted, however, that the Crown Court has an unfettered discretion to adjourn proceedings; there is thus no objection to the accused being arraigned and then the case being immediately adjourned to a later date if the parties are still not ready for trial.

Where the prosecution are seeking an order under the DVCVA 2004, s. 17 (see **D13.81**), for a trial of part of the indictment by a judge alone, they are required to prepare a split indictment with those charges which are to be tried by a jury in part one and the remaining counts in part two (CrimPD II, para. 10A.17: see Supplement, **CPD.10A**). At arraignment, the accused should be arraigned only on the counts in part one of the indictment, with arraignment on part two only to occur following conviction on part one (para. 14A.7).

D12.56 **Failure to Arraign within a Reasonable Period** While the absence of stated time-limits creates a change, under the former regime, leave for late arraignment was readily given (*Urbanowski* [1976] 1 All ER 679). The requirement under the ECHR, Articles 5(3) and 6(1), for a trial to be held within a reasonable period (see **A7.73**) is of obvious relevance.

Effect of Lack of Arraignment on the Validity of the Proceedings

D12.57 Failure by the court to have the accused arraigned does not necessarily render invalid subsequent proceedings on the indictment (*Williams* [1978] QB 373). Thus, the defence may waive the accused's right to be arraigned, either expressly or by simply remaining silent while the trial proceeds without arraignment. It was held in *K (John)* [2007] EWCA Crim 1339, where D absconded prior to arraignment, that by absenting himself he had waived his right to arraignment. It follows that D has also waived his right to be present for arraignment on an indictment which has been amended by the addition of a more serious count, even though he may have wished to plead guilty to the less serious alternative charge (*K (John)* at [19]).

A dictum of Edmund Davies LJ in *Ellis* (1973) 57 Cr App R 571 (at p. 575), that the 'only safe and proper course... is to say... that (apart from a few very special cases) it is an invariable requirement that the initial arraignment must be conducted between the clerk of the court and the accused person himself', should be understood in the context of the facts of that case, namely, the entry of a guilty plea.

On the facts of *Williams*, by contrast, D had always intended to plead not guilty and the trial proceeded in all respects as if he had so pleaded but in fact (through an administrative muddle) the indictment was never put. The pre-trial irregularity did not invalidate the proceedings and D's conviction was upheld despite lack of arraignment. This accords with the decisions of the Court of Appeal in *Ashton* [2006] EWCA Crim 794, [2007] 1 WLR 181 and of the House of Lords in *Clarke* [2008] UKHL 8, [2008] 2 Cr App R 2 (18), to the effect that a failure to follow the correct procedure as to arraignment is not necessarily fatal to proceedings thereafter (see also *MJ* [2018] EWCA Crim 2485, [2019] 1 Cr App R 10 (122)). The question to be considered is whether Parliament intended non-compliance to be fatal to the validity of proceedings thereafter, and, if not, whether the accused has been prejudiced as a result of the failure.

Further, the decision in *Williams* is without prejudice to the principle that a plea of guilty must be entered by the accused personally, the corollary of which is that a conviction on a guilty plea will be valid only if the accused has been properly arraigned (see **D12.72**).

PLEAS THAT MAY BE ENTERED ON ARRAIGNMENT

In the great majority of cases, the plea entered by the accused will be simply one of guilty or not guilty. It is sometimes open to the accused to plead not guilty as charged but guilty of an alternative (lesser) offence. **D12.58**

The only alternatives to such a plea arise in the circumstances addressed above where it is submitted that it would not be appropriate for the accused to be arraigned at all. This might apply in the case of a plea of autrefois acquit or autrefois convict (see **D12.20**), where there is some other obstacle (such as unfitness: see **D12.2**), or where there is a plea to the jurisdiction (see **D12.51**).

PLEA BARGAINING

The issues that arise under this heading are: **D12.59**

(a) the extent to which the judge may properly influence the accused's decision as to plea by indicating the probable sentence, and
(b) the propriety of bargains between the prosecution and defence involving the offering of no evidence in respect of certain charges in return for the accused pleading guilty to others.

Judicial Indications of Sentence

A plea of guilty must be entered voluntarily. If the accused is deprived of a genuine choice as to plea and in consequence purports to plead guilty, the plea is a nullity and the conviction will be quashed on appeal (see **D12.101**). This was stressed by the Court of Appeal in *Turner* [1970] 2 QB 321. The observations of the Court of Appeal in that case, designed to assist counsel and judges over what was referred to as 'the vexed question of plea bargaining' (at pp. 326E–327D), **D12.60** have now been superseded, following the decision in *Goodyear* [2005] EWCA Crim 888, [2005] 2 Cr App R 20 (281), by CrimPD VII, Sentencing, Part C (see Supplement, **CPD.VII.C**).

The *Goodyear* Approach

D12.61 The correct approach to judicial indications of sentence is set out in *Goodyear* [2005] EWCA Crim 888, [2005] 2 Cr App R 20 (281), restated in *Seddon* [2007] EWCA Crim 3022, [2008] 2 Cr App R (S) 30 (174) and *Ibori* [2013] EWCA Crim 815, [2014] 1 Cr App R (S) 15 (73), and endorsed in CrimPD VII, Sentencing, Part C (see Supplement, **CPD.VII.C**). CrimPR 3.31 sets out a detailed procedure for an application for an indication of the maximum sentence that would be passed if a guilty plea were entered (see Supplement, **R3.32**). Proper roles in the process are identified for the court, and those responsible for prosecuting and defending. The guidelines also demonstrate the need to take into account the review of any sentence then passed, either by way of an appeal by the defendant or a reference on behalf of the A-G. The importance of following the procedure was again emphasised by the Court of Appeal in *Ali* [2014] EWCA Crim 542. In summary, the guidance is as follows.

D12.62 **Responsibilities of the Court** (1) A court should not give an indication of sentence unless one has been sought by the accused.

(2) However, the court remains entitled to exercise the power to indicate that the sentence, or type of sentence, on the accused would be the same whether the case proceeds as a plea of guilty or goes to trial, with a resulting conviction. Where the sentence will vary according to plea, the court should only give an indication as to the sentence following a guilty plea. An indication as to sentence following trial may put undue pressure on the accused to plead (*Clark* [2008] EWCA Crim 3221). The court is also entitled in an appropriate case to remind the defence advocate that the accused is entitled to seek an advance indication of sentence (see also CrimPD VII, para. C.3: see Supplement, **CPD.VII.C**).

(3) Where an indication is sought, the court may refuse altogether to give an indication, or may postpone doing so, with or without giving reasons. The probability is that the judge would explain the reasons for deferral, and further indicate the circumstances in which, and when, he or she would be prepared to respond to a request for a sentence indication.

(4) Where the court has it in mind to defer an indication, the probability is that the judge would explain the reasons, and further indicate the circumstances in which, and when, he or she would be prepared to respond to a request for a sentence indication.

(5) If the court refuses to give an indication (as opposed to deferring it), it remains open to the defence to make a further request for an indication at a later stage. However, in such circumstances the court should not normally initiate the process, except where appropriate to indicate that the circumstances have changed sufficiently to permit a renewed application for an indication.

(6) Once an indication has been given (CrimPD VII, para. C.6), it is binding and remains binding on the judge who has given it, and it also binds any other judge who becomes responsible for the case. An indication may cease to be binding where guideline authority from the Court of Appeal alters the appropriate sentencing level (*Jalil* [2008] EWCA Crim 2910, [2009] 2 Cr App R (S) 40 (276)) or where a new definitive sentencing guideline is issued by the Sentencing Council. However, an indication remains binding even where D subsequently absconds and falls to be sentenced also for his failure to attend (*Davies* [2015] EWCA Crim 930, [2015] 2 Cr App R (S) 57 (404)).

(7) If, after a reasonable opportunity to consider his or her position in the light of the indication, the accused does not plead guilty, the indication will cease to have effect.

(8) Where appropriate, there must be an agreed, written basis of plea, otherwise the judge should refuse to give an indication (CrimPD VII, para. C.3).

Additional guidance was given in *A-G's Ref (No. 80 of 2005)* [2005] EWCA Crim 3367, when the Court of Appeal stated that:

(a) the principal feature of an appropriate indication of sentence is that an advance indication should be sought by the defence, and not promulgated by the judge;
(b) an indication should not be given that a trial would result in a much longer sentence compared to the one offered if the accused pleads guilty.

Responsibilities of the Defence (1) Subject to the court's power to give an appropriate reminder to the advocate for the accused, the process of seeking a sentence indication should normally be started by the defence. **D12.63**
(2) Whether or not such a reminder has been given, the accused's advocate should not seek an indication without signed written authority that the client wishes to seek an indication.
(3) The advocate is personally responsible for ensuring that the client fully appreciates that (a) he or she should not plead guilty unless he or she is guilty, (b) any sentence indication given by the court remains subject to the entitlement of the A-G (where it arises) to refer an unduly lenient sentence to the Court of Appeal, (c) any indication given by the court reflects the situation at the time when it is given and if a guilty plea is not tendered in the light of that indication, the indication ceases to have effect, and (d) any indication which may be given relates only to the matters about which an indication is sought.
(4) An indication should not be sought while there is any uncertainty between the prosecution and the defence about an acceptable plea or pleas to the indictment, or the factual basis relating to any plea.
(5) Any agreed basis should be reduced into writing before an indication is sought (see CrimPD VII, para. C.3, in this regard).
(6) Where there is a dispute about a particular fact which counsel for the accused believes to be effectively immaterial to the sentencing decision, the difference should be recorded for the court to consider.
(7) The court should never be invited to indicate levels of sentence which depend on possible different pleas.
(8) In the unusual event that the accused is unrepresented, the accused would be entitled to seek a sentence indication of his or her own initiative, but it would be wrong for either the court or prosecuting counsel to take any initiative in this regard that might too readily be interpreted as or subsequently argued to have been improper pressure.

Responsibilities of the Prosecution (1) As the request for indication comes from the defence, the prosecution are obliged to react to, rather than initiate the process. In doing so, the prosecution should act in accordance with CrimPR 3.31(4) (see Supplement, **R3.31**). **D12.64**
(2) If there is no final agreement about the plea to the indictment, or the basis of plea, and the defence nevertheless proceed to seek an indication, which the court appears minded to give, prosecuting counsel should remind the court that an indication of sentence should normally not be given until the basis of the plea has been agreed, or the judge has concluded that the case can be properly dealt with without the need for a *Newton* hearing (see **D20.8** and CrimPD VII, para. C.3).
(3) If an indication is sought, the prosecution should normally inquire whether the court is in possession of or has had access to all the evidence relied on by the prosecution, including any personal impact statement from the victim of the crime, as well as any information of relevant previous convictions recorded against the accused (CrimPD VII, para. C.4).
(4) If the process has been properly followed, it should not normally be necessary for counsel for the prosecution, before the court gives any indication, to do more than (a) draw the judge's attention to any minimum or mandatory statutory sentencing requirements, and, where applicable or where invited to do so (and as required by CrimPD VII, para. C.4), to any definitive sentencing guidelines of the Sentencing Council or any relevant guideline cases, and (b) where it applies, to remind the judge that the entitlement of the A-G to refer any eventual sentencing decision as unduly lenient is not affected.

(5) In any event, counsel should not say anything which may create the impression that the sentence indication has the support or approval of the Crown.

Further guidance is given to prosecutors through the A-G's Guidelines on the Acceptance of Pleas (see **appendix 2**) as to their part in any discussion on plea and sentence in chambers. Such discussions should take place only 'in the most exceptional circumstances'.

(a) Where they do take place, the prosecution advocate should if necessary remind the judge of the desirability of an independent record, and should make a full note, recording all decisions and comments. This note should be made available to the prosecuting authority.
(b) Where there is a discussion on plea and sentence and the prosecution advocate does not believe that the circumstances are exceptional, the prosecution advocate should remind the judge of the relevant decisions of the Court of Appeal and not take part in any discussion on sentence.
(c) The prosecution advocate should not say or do anything which might be taken to agree, expressly or by implication, with a particular sentence.
(d) In cases where s. 35 of the CJA 1988 applies, the prosecution advocate should indicate that the A-G may, if the A-G sees fit, seek leave to refer any sentence as unduly lenient (see **D28.3**).

D12.65 **The Indication Process** (1) It is anticipated that any sentence indication would normally be sought at the plea and case management hearing, following a written application (CrimPR 3.31(2)).
(2) In accordance with *A-G's Ref (No. 80 of 2005)* [2005] EWCA Crim 3367, a hearing involving an indication of sentence should normally take place in open court with a full recording of the entire proceedings, and both sides represented, in the presence of the accused (one of the exceptions is where an accused is unaware of being terminally ill).
(3) The court is most unlikely to be able to give an indication in complicated or difficult cases unless issues between the prosecution and the defence have been addressed and resolved. Therefore, in such cases, no less than seven days' notice of an intention to seek an indication should normally be given in writing to the prosecution and the court.
(4) If an application is made without notice when it should have been given, the court may conclude that any inevitable adjournment should have been avoided and that the discount for the guilty plea should be reduced accordingly.
(5) There should be very little need for the court to be involved in the discussions with the advocates, save to seek better information on any troubling aspect of the case. An opening by the Crown, or a mitigation plea by the defence, is not envisaged.
(6) The fact that notice has been given, and any reference to a request for a sentence indication, or the circumstances in which it was sought, would be inadmissible in any subsequent trial.
(7) Reporting restrictions should normally be imposed, to be lifted if and when the accused pleads or is found guilty.

It is clear from *Goodyear* [2005] EWCA Crim 888, [2005] 2 Cr App R 20 (281) that the Court of Appeal did not envisage a process by which the judge should give some kind of preliminary indication, leading to comments on it by counsel for the Crown, with the judge then reconsidering the indication, and perhaps raising it to a higher level, with counsel for the accused then making further submissions to persuade the judge, after all, to reduce the indication. Any indication which has been given lapses if the accused does not then plead guilty and cannot later bind the court (*Patel* [2009] EWCA Crim 1161).

The Court of Appeal has revisited the *Goodyear* procedure in two recent cases. In *Almilhin* [2019] EWCA Crim 220, [2019] 2 Cr App R (S) 45 (373) the Court held that a sentencing judge who had given an indication in accordance with the *Goodyear* procedure, was not required to further reduce the sentence to reflect personal mitigation advanced after the indication had been given; it was a matter for the judge's discretion. In *Utton* [2019] EWCA Crim

1341, [2020] 1 Cr App R (S) 7 (61), the Court repeated that a court was entitled, in an appropriate case, to resile from an indication given even after an accused had then pleaded guilty, providing that the proceedings remained fair to the accused. Moreover, if an accused did not take advantage of an indication within a reasonable period (by reference to the circumstances of the case), the accused could not later complain if the judge considered that the indication had ceased to have effect.

Indications where the Dangerous Offender Provisions Might Apply In *Kulah* [2007] EWCA Crim 1701, [2008] 1 Cr App R (S) 85 (494), the Court of Appeal provided guidance as to the approach a court should adopt when invited to give an indication in a case where the accused was charged with one or more specified offences within the CJA 2003, sch. 15, and might be liable to an indeterminate sentence pursuant to the CJA 2003, Part 12, if the accused was determined to be a dangerous offender (see **E4**). The court should make clear that the accused was charged with a specified offence and that the necessary material for an assessment as to dangerousness was not available. It followed that if, in due course, the accused was assessed to be dangerous, the determinate sentence indicated would in fact become the notional determinate term, and the actual length of the sentence was beyond the judge's control. See also *Seddon* [2007] EWCA Crim 3022, [2008] 2 Cr App R (S) 30 (174) and CrimPD VII, para. C.7. **D12.66**

Magistrates' Court It would be impracticable for these new arrangements to be extended to proceedings in magistrates' courts. Accordingly, for the time being, magistrates should confine themselves to the statutory arrangements in the CJA 2003, sch. 3. **D12.67**

References and Appeals against Sentence If the responsibilities of counsel for the prosecution have been addressed, the discretion of the A-G to refer a sentence is wholly unaffected by the advance sentence indication process. In such circumstances, the fact that a judge has given an indication of sentence before plea will not bind the Court of Appeal if the A-G appeals on the basis that the sentence is unduly lenient (*A-G's Ref (No. 40 of 1996)* [1997] 1 Cr App R (S) 357: see **D28.6**). **D12.68**

The accused's entitlement to apply for leave to appeal against sentence if, for example, insufficient allowance has been made for matters of genuine mitigation, is similarly unaffected.

Arrangements between Prosecution and Defence

It is common practice for the prosecution and defence to agree through counsel prior to arraignment that, in the event of the accused pleading guilty to parts of the indictment, the Crown will not seek to prove the accused guilty as charged. Such an arrangement may take the form of accepting a plea of guilty to a lesser offence, or of offering no evidence on counts to which the accused pleads not guilty, or of asking the judge to allow some counts to remain on the file marked not to be proceeded with. This is addressed in more detail at **D12.79**, **D12.82** and **D12.83** (as to the admissibility of a basis of plea as evidence in the trial of another, see *Mansfield* [2014] EWCA Crim 1846). See also the A-G's Guidelines on Plea Discussions in Cases of Serious or Complex Fraud (see **appendix 2**). The CCA 2013, sch. 17, introduced deferred prosecution agreements (see **D12.106**) under which, with court approval, the accused and the prosecution may reach an agreement resulting in the suspension of an indictment before arraignment if the accused complies with the requirements specified in the agreement. **D12.69**

PLEA OF NOT GUILTY

Entry of Plea of Not Guilty

Normal practice is for the accused to enter a plea of not guilty personally when arraigned by the clerk in the absence of any potential jurors (see **D12.1**). It is not, however, essential to the **D12.70** validity of a trial that the accused formally says the words 'not guilty' (*Williams* [1978] QB 373 at **D12.57**). If an accused wilfully stays silent when arraigned, or fails to give a direct answer to the charge, or enters a plea which purports to be one of guilty but is in fact ambiguous, the court may and should enter a plea of not guilty on the accused's behalf (CLA 1967, s. 6(1)(c), and CrimPR 25.9(1): see Supplement, **R25.9**).

Effect of Plea of Not Guilty

D12.71 A plea of not guilty puts the prosecution to proof of their entire case. The burden is therefore on them to satisfy the jury beyond reasonable doubt that the accused committed the *actus reus* of the offence (or aided, abetted, counselled or procured its commission), and that in doing so the accused had the necessary *mens rea*. Should the prosecution fail to adduce sufficient evidence as to *any* element of the offence, the accused is entitled to be acquitted on the judge's direction following a submission of no case to answer made at the close of the prosecution case.

The defence statement should have indicated in advance of trial those parts of the prosecution case which are disputed (see **D9.29**). Nevertheless defence counsel is still entitled to take advantage of any deficiency in the prosecution evidence (e.g., a witness not coming up to proof) and submit that there is no case to answer, whether or not the element of the offence of which evidence is lacking would otherwise have been contested.

The only method by which the prosecution may be released from their obligation to prove each essential element of the offence is if the defence have made formal admissions under s. 10 of the CJA 1967, or where a fact is presumed (see **F3.60** ***et seq.***) or judicially noticed (see **F1.4** ***et seq.***).

PLEA OF GUILTY

Requirement that Accused Plead Personally

D12.72 A plea of guilty must be entered by the accused personally. If counsel purports to plead guilty on behalf of an accused, the purported plea has no validity and the proceedings constitute a mistrial (*Ellis* (1973) 57 Cr App R 571). On appeal, the Court of Appeal will be obliged either to quash the conviction or to grant a writ of *venire de novo* (i.e. set the conviction aside but order that the accused be retried) (*Ellis*). In *Ellis*, defence counsel intervened during the arraignment to set out the basis on which D would plead guilty, and the judge proceeded to sentence. At no stage did D himself say he was guilty, although that was undoubtedly what he would have said had he been allowed to. On appeal, Edmund Davies LJ reviewed the authorities and then said (at pp. 574–5):

> ...great mischief would ensue if a legal representative was generally regarded as entitled to plead on an accused's behalf. It would open the door to dispute as to whether, for example, counsel had correctly understood and acted upon the instructions which the accused had given him, and, if a dispute of that kind arose, the consequential embarrassment and difficulty could be difficult in the extreme.
>
> We think that the only safe and proper course accordingly is to say... that (apart from a few very special cases) it is an invariable requirement that the initial arraignment must be conducted between the clerk of the court and the accused person himself or herself directly.

Edmund Davies LJ's dicta do not expressly distinguish between cases where the accused intends to plead guilty and those where the accused intends to plead not guilty or refuses to plead. As regards the latter, it is possible for a valid trial to take place despite the absence of a personal plea from the accused (see **D12.57**). As regards guilty pleas, however, there can be no derogation whatsoever from the rule that the plea must come from the mouth of the accused. This is confirmed by *Williams* [1978] QB 373, where Shaw LJ, giving the judgment of the Court of Appeal, said (at p. 378G): 'No qualification of or deviation from the rule that a plea of guilty must come from him who acknowledges guilt is... permissible. A departure from the rule in a criminal trial would therefore necessarily be a vitiating factor rendering the whole procedure void and ineffectual.' See also *Westminster City Council v Owadally* [2017] EWHC 1092 (Admin), [2017] 2 Cr App R 18 (223).

Effect of Plea of Guilty

If the accused pleads guilty (as CrimPR 25.4 makes clear: see Supplement, **R25.4**), the prosecution are released from their obligation to prove the case. There is no need to empanel a jury, and the accused stands convicted simply by virtue of the word that has come from his or her own mouth. The only evidence the prosecution then need call in the ordinary case is that of the accused's antecedents and criminal record (see **D20.45** to **D20.51**). **D12.73**

Exceptionally, there may be a dispute between the parties about the material facts of the offence. If the dispute is serious enough to have a significant effect on sentence, the prosecution must either call evidence in support of their own version at a so-called '*Newton* hearing' or allow sentence to be passed on the basis of the defence version (for *Newton* hearings, see **D20.8** to **D20.29**). However, even in such cases, the prosecution evidence goes to *how* the offence was committed, not whether it was committed, and the accused remains convicted by his or her own plea whatever the outcome of the *Newton* hearing. See *Padellec* [2012] EWCA Crim 1956 as to the need for the prosecution and court to be cautious about too readily accepting a basis of plea.

Adjournments Following Plea of Guilty

Once a plea of guilty has been entered, the court may forthwith commence the procedure leading up to the passing of sentence (for which see **D20.2**). It may, on the other hand, take the plea and then adjourn. Whether to adjourn is entirely at the discretion of the court. Common reasons for an adjournment are to obtain reports on the accused or to await the outcome of other proceedings outstanding with a view to the accused being sentenced on one occasion for all matters (see *Bennett* (1980) 2 Cr App R (S) 96, for the desirability of linking up outstanding charges). **D12.74**

By virtue of the Senior Courts Act 1981, s. 81(1)(c), on adjourning, the court may either commit the accused to custody or grant bail. Despite having been convicted, an accused who is remanded for inquiries or report at this stage still has a prima facie right to bail under the BA 1976, s. 4, although in practice bail is usually withdrawn if the accused has pleaded guilty to a serious offence.

MIXED PLEAS

Three scenarios fall to be considered under the head of mixed pleas, namely where an accused pleads guilty to some charges but not others, where an accused pleads guilty and the co-accused do not, and where an accused pleads guilty and gives evidence against those co-accused who have not. The procedure is set out in CrimPD VII, Sentencing, parts B to D (see Supplement, **CPD.VII.B** *et seq.*). **D12.75**

Mixed Pleas from an Accused

If an accused enters mixed pleas on a multi-count indictment and the prosecution are not prepared to accept those pleas, sentencing for the counts to which the accused has pleaded guilty should be postponed until after the accused has been tried on the not guilty counts. This is different from the situation of an accused who pleads guilty to a lesser offence, which is discussed at **D12.79**, or where an accused pleads on a factual basis that is not agreed (see CrimPD VII, para. B.11). **D12.76**

Mixed Pleas from Co-accused

D12.77 Where there are co-accused, one of whom pleads guilty and the other not guilty, normal practice is to adjourn sentencing the former until after the trial of the latter. In the event of a conviction, they can then both be sentenced together. The desirability of co-accused being sentenced on one occasion by the same judge has frequently been stressed. Separate sentencing may lead to unacceptable disparity in the ways they are respectively treated. Also, the judge will hear, during the course of the trial of the accused pleading not guilty, evidence indicating the gravity of the offence charged and the extent of each accused's role in it, which information may ultimately assist in sentencing the one pleading guilty.

The above principles were stated by Lord Goddard CJ in *Payne* [1950] 1 All ER 102, when he said:

> [Where several persons are indicted together, and one pleads guilty and the other or others not guilty] the proper course is to postpone sentence on the man who has pleaded guilty until the others have been tried and then to bring up all the prisoners to be dealt with together because by that time the court will be in possession of the facts relating to all of them and will be able to assess properly the degree of guilt of each.

A still stronger statement of the same principle occurs in the judgment of Boreham J in *Weekes* (1980) 74 Cr App R 161, where he said:

> Here are made manifest the difficulties that arise when persons involved with others are sentenced before the full facts have been heard, particularly where a trial is to take place, as it was to take place here.... There may be exceptions but generally it is clearly right, it is clearly fairer and it is better for both the public and all the defendants concerned, that all are sentenced at the same time by the same court whenever that is possible.

D12.78 **Practice where Accused Pleads Guilty and Gives Evidence for Prosecution against Co-accused** It is now clear that an accused turning Queen's evidence should not be sentenced until after the co-accused's trial. This clarity resulted from 'difficulties' arising in *Weekes* (1980) 74 Cr App R 161, to which Boreham J referred in the passage quoted in **D12.77**, namely that D1, one of four co-accused charged with armed robbery, was sentenced to seven years' imprisonment while a co-accused (D2) had been given only 12 months, a term described by the Court of Appeal as 'ludicrously light', before D1's trial by a different judge. At D1's appeal, Boreham J criticised the decision to sentence D2 separately (at p. 166):

> It may be... that [D2] was sentenced at that early stage by a different court because it had been made known that he was to give evidence on behalf of the Crown against the other three. If that was the reason... it is not sufficient reason.... it should be left to the judge who may sentence those who have pleaded not guilty to sentence all.

The clear statement in *Weekes* that an accused turning Queen's evidence should not be sentenced until after the co-accused's trial is in direct conflict with the dicta of Lord Goddard CJ in *Payne* [1950] 1 All ER 102. However, the reversal of the practice approved in *Payne* was signalled by two unreported cases in 1977, namely *Potter* (15 September 1977 unreported) and *Woods* (25 October 1977 unreported), before it was confirmed by *Weekes* and *Chan Wai-keung* [1995] 2 All ER 438. In *Coffey* (1976) 74 Cr App R 168, the principle that all should be sentenced at the end of any trial was held to apply when the accused who has pleaded guilty is going to testify for the co-accused, just as it applies when the accused is to testify for the prosecution. Even so, whether to sentence a co-accused pleading guilty forthwith or adjourn until after the co-accused's trial must, in the last resort, remain a question for the judge (*Palmer* (1994) 158 JP 138).

The SOCPA 2005, ss. 73 to 75 (see **E1.11**), demonstrate that the court may take into account the assistance the accused is going to provide to the 'investigator or prosecutor', e.g., by giving evidence or intelligence, when determining sentence, and should indicate that it has done so unless that would be contrary to the public interest (s. 73). However, if the accused then fails to provide the promised assistance, the prosecution may invite the court to review the sentence and the court may substitute a greater sentence for the sentence originally passed (s. 74, reversing *Stone* [1970] 2 All ER 594 on that point).

PLEA OF GUILTY TO A LESSER OFFENCE

Where the indictment contains a count on which, if the accused were to plead not guilty, the jury could find the accused not guilty as charged but guilty of an alternative (hereafter referred to as 'lesser') offence, the accused may enter a plea to the same effect, namely not guilty to the offence charged but guilty only of the lesser offence (CLA 1967, s. 6(1)(b)). **D12.79**

If the plea is accepted, the accused is treated as having been acquitted of the offence actually charged and the court proceeds to sentence the accused for the lesser offence (CLA 1967, s. 6(5)). The circumstances in which a jury have the power to return a verdict of guilty of a lesser offence are defined by legislation, chiefly subsections (2) to (4) of s. 6 of the 1967 Act, which are considered in detail at **D19.41** to **D19.68**.

The considerations relevant to the decision by the prosecution to either accept or reject the plea are considered below.

In *Soanes* (1948) 32 Cr App R 136, Lord Goddard CJ said, 'it must always be in the discretion of the judge whether he will allow [a plea of guilty to a lesser offence] to be accepted'. However, CrimPD VII, paras. B.2 to B.3, make clear that the prosecution are only bound to act in accordance with the judge's view if they have sought it. Therefore, if the prosecution refuse to call evidence to prove the accused guilty as charged, the court would have no real alternative but to accept the situation, subject to any proper question of professional misconduct. The judge can, in accordance with CrimPD VII, para. B.4, adjourn proceedings for further review of the prosecution's decision if satisfied that the proposed course may lead to serious injustice.

Moreover, in the analogous situation of the accused pleading to some counts on the indictment in exchange for the prosecution offering no evidence on others, the rule seems to be that the prosecution are bound by the judge's views of the bargain if, and only if, they have expressly asked the judge to approve it in advance (see **D12.89** and CrimPD VII, paras. B.2 to B.3). If they choose not to seek prior approval, they may accept the pleas even though the judge indicates in court that they ought to proceed on all counts (*Coward* (1979) 70 Cr App R 70; *Broad* (1978) 68 Cr App R 281).

Status of Original Plea in Event of Verdict of Not Guilty

In *Hazeltine* [1967] 2 QB 857, D, on being arraigned for wounding with intent contrary to s. 18 of the OAPA 1861, replied, 'Not guilty, but guilty to unlawful wounding'. The prosecution would not accept the plea, and a trial followed, during which D offered a defence of acting in reasonable self-defence. Although this was inconsistent with his original plea, almost no mention was made of it during the trial. When the jury then acquitted D, the judge proceeded to sentence D in accordance with his plea. That sentence had to be quashed on appeal as D had not been convicted of any offence. His original plea to unlawful wounding was impliedly withdrawn on the prosecution saying that it was not acceptable, and the jury's verdict implied an acquittal both in respect of the offence charged and in respect of the lesser included offence. **D12.80**

Salmon LJ explained the purpose and effect of the then equivalent of s. 6(1) of the CLA 1967 (s. 39(1) of the Criminal Justice Administration Act 1914). His lordship said (at p. 861A–F):

> Prior to that statutory provision, it was not possible for an accused to plead guilty to unlawful wounding when charged with wounding with intent but it was and always has been possible for a jury, when a man is charged with wounding with intent, to return a verdict of unlawful wounding...

> This court has no doubt but that section 39(1) of the Act of 1914 was introduced so as to remove this anomaly which resulted in the great waste of time and money to which I have referred. In the view of this court, however, that statutory provision did not get rid of the rule that there can be but one plea to one count should the trial proceed on that count. Accordingly if an accused pleads not guilty to wounding with intent but guilty to unlawful wounding and counsel for the prosecution or the judge takes the view that that plea ought not to be accepted and the trial proceeds, the plea of guilty to unlawful wounding is deemed to be withdrawn and the only plea is the plea of not guilty to wounding with intent. It is then for the jury to consider the evidence and at the end of the case to say either quite simply that the man is not guilty or that he is guilty of wounding with intent or that he is not guilty of wounding with intent but guilty to unlawful wounding.

Although couched in terms of wounding with intent and unlawful wounding, the above passage is obviously applicable whenever a plea of guilty to a lesser offence is rejected.

To avoid a repetition of the manifestly unsatisfactory result in *Hazeltine*, the Court of Appeal suggested that, in cases where the accused offers a defence that is inconsistent with an earlier plea to a lesser offence, the prosecution ought to call evidence of the plea and, if the accused testifies, cross-examine the accused about it (*Hazeltine* at p. 862F–G). There was no need to adopt a policy of always having separate counts for the greater and lesser offences. However, should the prosecution fail to adduce evidence of the plea, it is not open to the judge to repair the omission in the summing-up by informing the jury of what occurred (*Lee* [1985] Crim LR 798). Nor may the judge direct the jury to convict of the lesser offence as opposed to informing them that such a verdict is open to them (*Lee*, and see *Notman* [1994] Crim LR 518).

PROSECUTION OPTIONS ON PLEA OF NOT GUILTY OR MIXED PLEAS BEING ENTERED

D12.81 Apart from the obvious course of proceeding to a contested trial, there are two options available to the prosecution on the accused pleading not guilty, namely, to offer no evidence or to ask that the indictment remain on the court file. Similar responses are possible where an arraignment results in mixed pleas, with either only some of the accused pleading guilty, or with one accused entering guilty pleas to only some of the charges.

Each of these two options is addressed here. In addition, considerable guidance has been given, notably through guidelines handed down by the A-G and in the report of the Farquharson committee on the role of prosecuting counsel. This guidance is also addressed below.

Offering No Evidence

D12.82 **Criminal Justice Act 1967, s. 17**

> Where a defendant arraigned on an indictment or inquisition pleads not guilty and the prosecutor proposes to offer no evidence against him, the court before which the defendant is arraigned may, if it thinks fit, order that a verdict of not guilty shall be recorded without the defendant being given in charge to a jury, and the verdict shall have the same effect as if the defendant had been tried and acquitted on the verdict of a jury.

The obvious situation for reliance on s. 17 is if the prosecution have reviewed their evidence since the accused was sent for trial, and have concluded that they cannot properly ask a jury to convict. Alternatively, offering no evidence on some counts in an indictment may be part of an agreement with the defence under which the accused pleads guilty to other counts.

Whilst the plain wording of s. 17 gives the court a discretion to decline to order a verdict of not guilty to be entered even though the prosecution intimate that they do not wish to proceed, in the last resort, the prosecution cannot be forced by the court to call evidence.

In *Renshaw* [1989] Crim LR 811, the Court of Appeal stressed the importance of the judge listening to the reasons given by the prosecution for proposing to offer no evidence. If the judge fails to heed what the prosecution say, there will be no proper basis for approving or disapproving of their proposed course of action.

Letting Counts Lie on the File

As an alternative to offering no evidence, the prosecution may ask the judge to order that an indictment (or counts thereof) shall lie on the file, marked not to be proceeded with without leave of the court or of the Court of Appeal. Such a course is particularly appropriate where the accused pleads guilty to the bulk of the charges (whether contained in one indictment or several) but not guilty to some subsidiary charges. Leaving the latter on the file avoids the necessity of a trial, but also avoids the accused actually being acquitted on the 'not guilty' counts, which might seem inappropriate if the evidence against the accused is in fact strong. **D12.83**

Contrary to what was previously understood to be the position, there is no objection to an entire indictment remaining on the file, as opposed to merely dealing with some counts of a multi-count indictment in that way (e.g., in *Central Criminal Court, ex parte Raymond* [1986] 2 All ER 379, as a result of D's conviction on one count of a severed 14-count indictment, the trial judge ordered that both the remaining counts of the original indictment and all counts of a completely separate indictment should lie on the file).

The use and practical effect of the order is helpfully summarised by Woolf LJ in *Ex parte Raymond* (at pp. 714H–715B):

> [It is important] to analyse the nature of the order that an indictment should lie on the file.
>
> It starts off by having the same effect as an order for an adjournment but an adjournment which it is accepted may never result in a trial. Frequently the order is made to safeguard the position of the prosecution and the defence in case a defendant, who has been convicted, should appeal, it being the intention of the court if there is no appeal or if the appeal is unsuccessful the defendant should never stand trial. That the defendant can still stand trial is indicated by the limits on the discretion of the court (laid down by the House of Lords in *Connelly v DPP* [1964] AC 1254) to prevent the Crown proceeding with a prosecution if it wishes to do so. However, in the majority of cases where such an order is made, there will be no trial and there will certainly come a stage when either the prosecution would not seek a trial or if it did seek a trial, the court would regard it as so oppressive to have a trial that leave to proceed would inevitably be refused.

Challenge to an Order to Lie on the File Whether to order that counts lie on the file is a matter totally within the judge's discretion since there is no method by which either party can challenge the decision. There is no appeal to the Court of Appeal as that only arises once there has been a conviction. See *Mackell* (1981) 74 Cr App R 27, on the Court of Appeal's lack of jurisdiction to reverse an order that counts lie on the file, and Dunn LJ's dictum, quoted with approval in *Central Criminal Court, ex parte Raymond* [1986] 2 All ER 379, that 'there are certain matters upon which the trial judge should have the final say. It seems to us this is one of them.' **D12.84**

Moreover, it was made clear in *Ex parte Raymond* that there cannot be an application to the High Court for judicial review since a decision to leave counts on the file has been held to relate to a trial on indictment and so, by virtue of s. 29(3) of the Senior Courts Act 1981, is not eligible for review. The reasoning of the Court of Appeal was that an order to leave counts on the file effectively 'starts off by having the same effect as an order for an adjournment' (per Woolf LJ at p. 714H), and it was already recognised that decisions to adjourn were something on which 'the trial judge should have the final word' (per Lord Denning MR in *Sheffield Crown Court, ex parte Brownlow* [1980] QB 530).

In *Ex parte Raymond* D argued that a Crown Court judge should not order that counts lie on the file unless the defence agree to that course, and, in the absence of such agreement, the judge ought to require the prosecution to elect between proceeding to trial and offering no evidence. The Court of Appeal ultimately refused to state its view or give any guidance on when orders to lie on the file are appropriate. This reticence was because of its primary decision that it did not in any event have jurisdiction to review the decision of the court below.

D12.85 **Reversing an Order to Lie on the File** Before the Crown Court or Court of Appeal is likely to give leave for a count or indictment ordered to lie on the file to be tried, a significant change of circumstances will be required. This would most commonly arise where the accused's convictions on the other matters (i.e. the charges on the same or separate indictments to which the accused pleaded guilty or of which the accused was found guilty at the same time as the order to lie on the file was made) are quashed on appeal and a retrial sought (as was identified in *Central Criminal Court, ex parte Raymond* [1986] 2 All ER 379). See, however, *H* [2006] NICC 5, for other circumstances (relating to a complainant who had been unwilling to give evidence changing her stance) in which such an order was reversed (also by analogy *Gadd* [2014] EWHC 3307 (QB), where other similar allegations later came to light).

Accepting or Rejecting a Plea to a Lesser Offence

D12.86 As was addressed at **D12.79**, it is possible for an accused to plead guilty to a lesser offence than that charged in the indictment. The prosecution may refuse to accept a plea of guilty to a lesser offence. If so, the plea is deemed to be withdrawn and the case proceeds as if the accused had simply pleaded not guilty (*Hazeltine* [1967] 2 QB 857).

Criteria to be Applied by the Prosecution

D12.87 **Guidelines** The report of the Farquharson committee on the role of prosecuting counsel (May 1986), considered counsel's control over the acceptance of pleas (as endorsed and developed by the CPS and the Bar Council in 2002). The committee discussed the authorities, and also made the point that, in the reverse situation of the judge thinking that the evidence on the depositions does not warrant a conviction or that further proceedings would be unfair, the judge has no power to prevent the prosecution calling their evidence save in the very exceptional case of the proceedings amounting to an abuse of the process of the court.

D12.88 **General Rule** In accepting a plea of guilty to a lesser offence or guilty to some counts only on the indictment, prosecuting counsel is in reality making a decision to offer no evidence on a particular charge. Since the committee were of the opinion that counsel was undoubtedly entitled to offer no evidence on the indictment as a whole and could not be forced to call evidence against his or her will, it followed that counsel must also be entitled to decide to accept pleas to part only of the indictment.

D12.89 **The Three Qualifications** This general rule is, however, subject to three qualifications:

(a) If prosecuting counsel expressly asks for the court's approval of the proposed acceptance of certain pleas, he or she must abide by the court's decision (*Broad* (1978) 68 Cr App R 281). There is no obligation to seek such approval, but counsel might feel it right to do so where either it is desirable to reassure the public at large that the course proposed is being properly taken, or it has not been possible to reach agreement with the instructing solicitor about what ought to be done.

(b) In a case where the court's approval is not sought beforehand, it is nonetheless usual for counsel to explain in open court the reasons for accepting the plea. It is then open to the judge to express his or her views. If the judge, on the information available, is 'of the opinion that the course proposed by counsel would lead to serious injustice, he [or she] may decline to proceed with the case until counsel has consulted with either the [DPP] or the [A-G] as may be appropriate' (Farquharson, para. k). However, in the final analysis and once those steps have been taken, the judge has no power to prevent counsel taking the course counsel thinks fit — 'any attempt by him to do so would give the impression that he was stepping into the arena and pressing the prosecution case'. However, the committee expressed the opinion that 'the occasions when counsel felt it right to resist the judge's views would be rare'.

(c) Should the decision to accept proposed pleas fall to be taken during the course of the trial, prosecuting counsel's position remains as in (b) above until the close of the prosecution case. Following this, however, if the judge has either found there is a case to answer or if no submission to the contrary has been made, there is, *ex hypothesi*, a case for the accused to answer, and 'it would be an abuse of process for the prosecution to discontinue without leave'. But, even though the judge can rule that the case shall proceed, 'it would not be the duty of counsel to cross-examine the defence witnesses or address the jury if he was of the view that it would not be proper to convict'.

Consideration in *Grafton* The report of the Farquharson committee was referred to with approval in *Grafton* [1993] QB 101. In that case, there was a conflict of evidence between two prosecution witnesses. Having taken instructions, prosecution counsel said he would call no further evidence. However, the judge disagreed profoundly with this decision and proceeded to call the Crown's remaining witness himself. G was convicted, and appealed. The appeal was allowed on the basis that the decision whether to continue with the case or not had to be that of the prosecution. By proceeding as he did, the judge had ceased to appear impartial, but had become the adversary of the defendant. The Court of Appeal in *Grafton* also approved qualification (c) above. They added, however, that where the prosecution's case is complete, but the judge refuses leave to the Crown to discontinue, it was prosecution counsel's duty to remain in the case. If the prosecution counsel's view later changed (perhaps as a result of hearing the accused testify), he or she would then be free to cross-examine witnesses or address the jury. **D12.90**

Acceptance of a Plea to a Lesser Offence As to the circumstances in which it is appropriate to accept a plea to a lesser offence, Lord Goddard in *Soanes* (1948) 32 Cr App R 136 declined to lay down a 'hard and fast rule' but expressed the view that, 'where nothing appears on the depositions which can be said to reduce the crime from the more serious offence charged to some lesser offence for which a verdict may be returned, the duty of counsel for the Crown would be to present the offence charged in the indictment'. The possible effect on the prosecution witnesses of testifying at a contested trial (e.g., where the offence charged is of a sexual nature) and/or the reaction of the victim to the charge being reduced may also have a bearing on counsel's ultimate decision (see, e.g., *Coward* (1979) 70 Cr App R 70). **D12.91**

The Attorney-General's Guidelines The A-G's Guidelines on the Acceptance of Pleas stress that justice should be conducted in public, save in the most exceptional circumstances, and that this includes the acceptance of pleas by the prosecution. Prosecutors are directed to the guidance contained in the Code for Crown Prosecutors, and told that they should be prepared to explain in open court the reasons for accepting pleas to a reduced number of charges or less serious charges. **D12.92**

CHANGE OF PLEA

The final topic to be addressed in relation to the arraignment is the procedure to be followed, and criteria to be applied, where an accused seeks to change plea thereafter. Where the accused wishes to change plea from not guilty to guilty (see **D12.94**), this causes little difficulty. Where, however, the accused seeks to change plea from guilty to not guilty (see **D12.95**) more difficult considerations arise, not least because such a change represents an assertion that an accused has realised that he or she did not commit the offence after all. The considerations in this category also include issues as to whether a plea was ambiguous (see **D12.100**) or involuntary (see **D12.101**). The topic is addressed procedurally by CrimPR 25.5 (see Supplement, **R25.5**). **D12.93**

From Not Guilty to Guilty

The judge may allow the accused to change plea from not guilty to guilty at any stage prior to the jury returning their verdict. The procedure is that the defence ask for the indictment to be **D12.94** put again and the accused then pleads guilty. If the change of plea comes after the accused has been put in the charge of a jury, the jury should be directed to return a formal verdict of guilty. This was emphasised in *Heyes* [1951] 1 KB 29, where D changed his plea in the jury's presence but they were not asked to return a verdict, and the judge proceeded forthwith to sentence. On appeal, Lord Goddard CJ said:

> Once the jury had heard the appellant say that he wished to withdraw his plea and admit his guilt, the proper proceeding was for the court to ask them to return a verdict. It appears that counsel did suggest to the learned recorder that this was the proper course; but the recorder thought that it did not matter. It does matter because, once a prisoner is in charge of a jury, he can only be either convicted or discharged by the verdict of the jury.
>
> As there was no verdict of the jury here, the trial was a nullity to such an extent that the court could set aside the proceedings and order a retrial or *venire de novo* [but, in the circumstances of this case we] will merely quash the conviction.

In *Poole* [2001] EWCA Crim 2664, [2002] 1 WLR 1528, however, the accused changed her plea to guilty on the second day of the trial. The judge discharged the jury without entering any verdict, and proceedings continued as though the accused had pleaded guilty on arraignment, with an adjournment for reports. The accused then wished to vacate her plea of guilty and, when this was refused, appealed against conviction. The Court of Appeal held that the course taken was permissible and resulted in a valid conviction.

Although having the indictment put again with a view to a change of plea to guilty is a matter for the judge's discretion, it is difficult to envisage circumstances in which the judge would be unwilling to allow it to be done. As to the effect of such a change of plea upon the trial of a co-accused, see **D13.65** and the case of *Fedrick* [1990] Crim LR 403 dealt with there.

From Guilty to Not Guilty

D12.95 **Discretion to Allow a Change** The judge has a discretion to allow the accused to withdraw a plea of guilty at any stage before sentence is passed. This was confirmed in *Plummer* [1902] 2 KB 339, where the major question for the court was whether D's conviction on a guilty plea in relation to a conspiracy charge could be sustained in view of the acquittal of his five alleged co-conspirators. D was not sentenced until after the acquittal of the others, and, prior to sentence, asked to withdraw his plea. Wright J said (at p. 347):

> Another point is raised in this case, namely, whether the court had power to allow the appellant to withdraw his plea of guilty. There cannot be any doubt that the court had such power at any time before, though not after, judgment [i.e. sentence] and, as we infer that but for the erroneous opinion that there was no such power the withdrawal would have been allowed, this might of itself be a ground for a *venire de novo*.

Similarly, Bruce J held that the first-instance court clearly had a discretion to allow the change of plea; that, if it had exercised its discretion against the appellant, the appellate court might have had no power to interfere; but, in fact, the discretion was never exercised one way or the other and that had deprived the appellant of a chance of an acquittal, with the consequence that the conviction could not stand (at p. 349).

The existence of the discretion was indirectly confirmed by the House of Lords in *S v Recorder of Manchester* [1971] AC 481, when it held that, in the context of change of plea, there is no conviction until sentence has been passed, and therefore magistrates (like the Crown Court) can allow a change to not guilty provided they have not yet passed sentence.

Finally, in *Dodd* (1981) 74 Cr App R 50, the Court of Appeal unhesitatingly accepted the three following propositions from counsel for D, namely that: (a) the court has a discretion to allow a defendant to change a plea of guilty to one of not guilty at any time before sentence; (b) the discretion exists even where the plea of not guilty is unequivocal; and (c) the discretion must be exercised judicially (see p. 57).

Application of the Discretion The procedure for application to vacate a guilty plea is set out in CrimPR 25.5. The authorities make clear that the discretion now under consideration should be sparingly exercised in favour of the accused. Thus, in *McNally* [1954] 2 All ER 372, where D had indicated even in the magistrates' court an intention to plead guilty, could not possibly have misunderstood the nature of a straightforward charge and had unequivocally admitted guilt when the indictment was put to him, the Court of Criminal Appeal approved the trial judge's decision to refuse a change of plea. The same approach was more recently adopted in *Revitt v DPP* [2006] EWHC 2266 (Admin), [2006] 1 WLR 3172 and *Brahmbhatt* [2014] EWCA Crim 573. **D12.96**

Unrepresented Accused Even if the accused was unrepresented when he or she pleaded but instructs solicitors during an adjournment prior to sentencing and is advised by them that he or she has a defence, the court is not obliged to accede to a change of plea (*South Tameside Magistrates' Court, ex parte Rowland* [1983] 3 All ER 689). **D12.97**

In *Ex parte Rowland*, in considering such an application for a change of plea, the magistrates, 'rightly, balanced the instructions which the applicant had given to her solicitor after [the original plea] against the prospect that she was changing her story because of the possibility that she might be sentenced to a custodial sentence' (per Glidewell J at p. 692J). Furthermore, the magistrates 'were perfectly entitled to come to the conclusion to which they did come' (i.e. that fear of a custodial sentence was the real motivation for the change of plea), and thus were justified in exercising their discretion against D.

Glidewell J approved the advice given to the magistrates by their clerk that, 'to allow a change of plea was a matter for [the magistrates'] absolute discretion and that once an unequivocal plea had been entered the discretionary power should be exercised judicially, very sparingly and only in clear cases' (at p. 692A). However, the implication is that, had the magistrates thought the plea to have been entered under a misapprehension of law as to the nature of the offence, then their only proper course would have been to allow the application. Although *Ex parte Rowland* was a case concerning change of plea in the magistrates' court, there is no reason why the same principles should not apply in the Crown Court.

In *Revitt v DPP* [2006] EWHC 2266 (Admin), [2006] 1 WLR 3172, the accused had been unrepresented, but had been advised by the court legal adviser of the nature and seriousness of the charges and of their right both to legal representations and to advance disclosure before plea. Where the accused proceeded to enter a guilty plea, the Administrative Court found the plea to be both informed and unequivocal.

Represented Accused If the accused was represented when entering a plea of guilty, there would seem to be no absolute bar to the accused applying to withdraw the plea, but it will obviously be very difficult to convince the court that the plea was entered by a genuine mistake. This was demonstrated in *Drew* [1985] 2 All ER 1061, where Lord Lane CJ said (at p. 923C): 'only rarely would it be appropriate for the trial judge to exercise his undoubted discretion in favour of an accused person wishing to change an unequivocal plea of guilty to one of not guilty. Particularly this is so in cases where, as here, the accused has throughout been advised by experienced counsel.' **D12.98**

Provided the court at first instance recognised that it had a discretion to allow a change of plea and applied the correct principles in determining the application, the Court of Appeal will not interfere with the trial judge's exercise of discretion (*Dodd* (1981) 74 Cr App R 50 (see **D12.95**); *Cantor* [1991] Crim LR 481; *Anjum* [2004] EWCA Crim 977; *Towers* [2004] EWCA Crim 1128).

Double Change of Plea

Where D has changed his plea from not guilty to guilty, the judge still has a discretion to allow him to change back to not guilty (*Drew* [1985] 2 All ER 1061). The fact that the jury **D12.99** empanelled to try him as a result of the original not guilty plea formally found him guilty on hearing the change to guilty does not affect the existence of the judge's discretion. In *Drew*, Lord Lane CJ said (at p. 922C):

> There appears to this court no greater difficulty in altering the record following a jury's verdict than doing so upon a change of plea in any other situation. The jury's verdict where, as here, it is entered upon the direction of the judge, is essentially a formality. In our judgment, logic and good sense dictate that the trial judge should have the same power to allow a change of plea even where the verdict of guilty has been returned formally by the jury.

Ambiguous Pleas

D12.100 If an accused purports to enter a plea of guilty but, either at the time of pleading or subsequently in mitigation, qualifies it with words that suggest the accused may have a defence (e.g., 'Guilty, but it was an accident' or 'Guilty, but I was going to give it back'), then the court must not proceed to sentence on the basis of the plea but should explain the relevant law and seek to ascertain whether the accused genuinely intends to plead guilty.

If the plea cannot be clarified, the court should order a not guilty plea to be entered on the accused's behalf (CLA 1967, s. 6(1)(c): 'if [the accused] stands mute of malice *or will not answer directly to the indictment*, the court may order a plea of not guilty to be entered').

Should the court proceed to sentence on a plea which is imperfect, unfinished or otherwise ambiguous, the accused will have a good ground of appeal. Since the defect in the plea will have rendered the original proceedings a mistrial, the Court of Appeal will have the options either of setting the conviction and sentence aside and ordering a retrial (see, e.g., *Ingleson* [1915] 1 KB 512) or of simply quashing the conviction (see, e.g., *Field* (1943) 29 Cr App R 151). If the former course is chosen (i.e. there is to be a retrial), the court may either then and there direct that a not guilty plea be entered or order that the accused be re-arraigned in the court below (e.g., *Baker* (1912) 7 Cr App R 217).

Involuntary Pleas

D12.101 A plea of guilty must be entered voluntarily. If, at the time of pleading, the accused was subject to such pressure that there was no genuinely free choice between 'guilty' and 'not guilty', the plea is a nullity (*Turner* [1970] 2 QB 321). On appeal, the Court of Appeal will have the same options as it has when a plea is adjudged ambiguous, namely that it must quash the conviction and sentence but will be able, in its discretion, to issue a writ of *venire de novo* for a retrial as the original proceedings constitute a mistrial.

Pressure to plead may come from a number of sources: the court, defence counsel or other factors. Whatever the source, the effect is the same.

D12.102 **The Court** An example of this principle is provided by *Barnes* (1970) 55 Cr App R 100, where the judge, during a submission of no case to answer made in the absence of the jury but in D's presence, said that, having regard to the prosecution evidence, D was plainly guilty and was wasting the court's time by pleading not guilty. Despite this pressure, D did not change his plea. Allowing his appeal against conviction on other grounds, the court indicated that the judge's remarks were 'wholly improper', and, if D had pleaded guilty in consequence of them, the plea would have been null.

D12.103 **Defence Counsel** It is the duty of counsel to advise the client on the strength of the evidence and the advantages of a guilty plea as regards sentencing (see, e.g., *Herbert* (1991) 94 Cr App R 233 and *Cain* [1976] QB 496). Such advice may, if necessary, be given in forceful terms (*Peace* [1976] Crim LR 119).

Where an accused is so advised and thereafter pleads guilty reluctantly, the plea is not *ipso facto* to be treated as involuntary (*Peace*). It will be involuntary only if the advice was so very forceful as to take away the accused's free choice. Thus, in *Inns* (1974) 60 Cr App R 231, defence counsel, as he was then professionally required to do, relayed to D the judge's warning in chambers that, in the event of conviction on a not guilty plea, D would definitely be given a sentence of detention whereas if he pleaded guilty a more lenient course might be possible. This rendered the eventual guilty plea a nullity.

However, in the absence of a suggestion that counsel was acting as a conduit to pass on a threat or promise from the judge, it will be extremely difficult for an appellant to satisfy the court that the appellant was deprived by counsel's advice of a voluntary choice when pleading. Thus, in *Hall* [1968] 2 QB 788, D was charged with burglary and, alternatively, with handling some of the items stolen during that burglary. The prosecution were willing to accept a plea to the latter. Counsel advised D that, if he pleaded not guilty to both counts, he ran the risk of being convicted of the burglary itself since his defence would involve attacks on the character of prosecution witnesses and thus the revelation of his own bad character. If so convicted, he could expect to receive up to 12 years' imprisonment, whereas if he pleaded guilty to handling the maximum sentence would be five years.

Dismissing D's appeal, Lord Parker CJ said (at pp. 534–7):

> What the court is looking to see is whether a prisoner in these circumstances has a free choice; the election must be his, the responsibility his, to plead guilty or not guilty. At the same time, it is the clear duty of any counsel representing a client to assist the client to make up his mind by putting forward the pros and cons, if need be in strong language, to impress upon the client what the likely results are of certain courses of conduct.

His lordship then paraphrased the advice given by counsel:

> [Defence counsel], in the opinion of this court, was only doing his duty in setting forth the dangers, even, as [he] said, in strong language.
>
> ...anybody who has heard the evidence in this case and has understood the workings of the law and our procedure, could not fail to realise that the appellant has no grievance at all...and that his counsel performed his duty to the best of his ability. This court has no hesitation in those circumstances in dismissing the appeal.

See *McCarthy* [2015] EWCA Crim 1185 for 'a paradigm example of why some formality and distance was required between advocates and lay clients' but where the plea was nevertheless not permitted to be vacated.

The position will be different if the advice given by counsel is demonstrably wrong. For example, in *Sorhaindo* [2006] EWCA Crim 1429, the Court of Appeal held that, where D had erroneously been advised that his factual case afforded him no defence, he should have been permitted to vacate the guilty plea that he entered in reliance on this advice.

Guidance to Defence Counsel In *Turner* [1970] 2 QB 321 Lord Parker CJ said (at p. 326F) that: 'Counsel of course will emphasise that the accused must not plead guilty unless he has committed the acts constituting the offence charged'. However, it may be felt that, on occasions, realistic advice about the strength of the prosecution case and the sentencing discount for a guilty plea will effectively force an accused into a guilty plea however punctilious defence counsel may be in saying that the accused should plead guilty only if guilty. **D12.104**

Where an accused persists in pleading guilty notwithstanding telling counsel that he or she is in fact innocent, counsel may thus be forced to confine mitigation to the circumstances and background of the offender and any matters minimising the gravity of the offence which are apparent on the face of the prosecution statements.

Other Pressures Apart from cases where pressure has been brought to bear on the accused to plead guilty, there may be other situations where the accused's mind did not go with the plea and the accused is therefore entitled to have the conviction set aside. An example is *Swain* [1986] Crim LR 480, in which D changed his plea to guilty half-way through the prosecution case. He gave no coherent explanation to counsel at the time, but it was afterwards discovered that he had been under the influence of the drug LSD. Psychiatric evidence called before the Court of Appeal established that LSD can put the user into a state akin to schizophrenia where he drifts **D12.105**

in and out of a delusional world and makes irrational decisions. The Court held the change of plea to have been a nullity.

DEFERRED PROSECUTION AGREEMENTS

D12.106 The CCA 2013, sch. 17, introduced deferred prosecution agreements ('DPA') as an alternative to prosecution. Such an agreement, if complied with, involves an agreement between the accused and prosecution under which, if the accused abides by specified conditions during the currency of the agreement, the prosecution will be suspended and ultimately avoided.

These provisions were brought into force on 24 February 2014 by SI 2014 No. 258 and the first such agreement was entered into between the SFO and ICBC Standard Bank before Sir Brian Leveson on 30 November 2015 (who further addressed the criteria for making such an order in *SFO v XYZ Ltd* [2016] Lloyd's Rep FC 509). The third and largest DPA was approved in *SFO v Rolls-Royce plc* [2017] Lloyd's Rep FC 249. Sir Brian Leveson restated the role of the court in the DPA process, first in satisfying itself that such an agreement was likely to be in the interests of justice, and ultimately to ensure that the final agreement is open to public scrutiny. Changes to the company between the time of the conduct under consideration and the present were found to be relevant to whether a DPA was a fair and proportionate outcome.

D12.107 The stages in the process are set out in sch. 17 and CrimPR Part 11 (see Supplement, **R11.1** *et seq.*). In summary, these are as follows:

(a) A designated prosecutor (identified in sch. 17, para. 3(1) as the DPP, Director of the SFO or any other prosecutor to be so designated) reaches an agreement with an accused (which may be a body corporate, partnership or unincorporated association but not an individual: para. 4(1)). The power of the prosecutor cannot be delegated (save in the circumstances set out in para. 3(3)). Pursuant to para. 6, a Code has been published by the DPP and the Director of the SFO to regulate the circumstances in which DPAs will be countenanced, which lists factors relevant to the prosecutor's decision to initiate negotiations for a DPA (the Code is available via tinyurl.com/y8auq6q5). Such agreements are possible only where the accused is charged with an offence listed in sch. 17, part 2, and negotiations for such an agreement can only occur following the determination of the prosecutor that it is appropriate and after the prosecutor has communicated to this effect to the accused (Code, paras. 2.5 and 3.5).

(b) Under the terms of a DPA, the prosecutor will suspend the prosecution, with automatic effect from when the indictment is preferred in accordance with the Administration of Justice (Miscellaneous Provisions) Act 1933, s. 2(2)(a) (sch. 17, para. 2), if the accused will agree to comply with the requirements set out in para. 5(3) for the period identified (para. 5(2)). These requirements can include financial terms.

(c) Before a DPA can be agreed, the approval of the Crown Court must first be sought. It will be sought first in principle at a preliminary hearing conducted in private at which the court will be invited to agree that the draft DPA is 'likely to be in the interests of justice' and its terms are 'fair, reasonable and proportionate' (sch. 17, para. 7; Code, para. 10). Thereafter, once the terms of the DPA are finally agreed between the parties, the court must again be asked for a declaration to the same effect. Only then, and once the DPA is published by the prosecution, will it take effect (sch. 17, para. 8; Code, para. 11) so that, when the bill of indictment is preferred, the proceedings are automatically suspended (sch. 17, para. 2(2)). The Code addresses the content of the application to the court and the terms of the agreement at paras. 6 and 7 (note that CrimPD XIII, Listing B (see Supplement, **CPD.XIII.B**) makes provision for the judges who may deal with such cases).

(d) There is provision to vary the terms of the DPA whilst it is operative (sch. 17, para. 10; Code, para. 13). If the accused breaches the requirements of the DPA, the prosecution can apply to the court (sch. 17, para. 9(1); Code, para. 12). Such an application, if made before the expiry of the DPA, prevents its expiry (sch. 17, para. 11(4)). If, on the balance of probabilities, the accused is found to be in breach, the court can either invite the prosecution to suggest a remedy or terminate the DPA (para. 9(3)). Whatever finding the court makes must be published by the prosecution. Similarly, the prosecution must publish its reasons for not applying to the court even though it believes the accused to be in breach (para. 9(8)).

(e) Otherwise, the DPA expires when its term comes to an end. Thereafter, the prosecution cannot institute fresh proceedings for the offence that was identified in the DPA unless it is later discovered that the accused had provided false information or otherwise misled the prosecution (para. 11).

The offences listed in sch. 17, part 2, in relation to which a DPA may be entered into, are as follows: conspiracy to defraud; cheating the public revenue; offences under the Theft Act 1968, ss. 1, 17, 20 and 24A; offences under the Customs and Excise Management Act 1979, ss. 68, 167 and 170; offences under the Forgery and Counterfeiting Act 1981, ss. 1 to 5; offences under the Companies Act 1985, s. 450; offences under the Value Added Tax Act 1994, s. 72; offences under the FSMA 2000, ss. 23, 25, 85, 346, 397 and 398; offences under the POCA 2002, ss. 327 to 330 and 333A; offences under the Companies Act 2006, ss. 658, 680 and 993; offences under the Fraud Act 2006, ss. 1, 6, 7 and 11; offences under the Bribery Act 2010, ss. 1, 2, 6 and 7; offences under the Money Laundering Regulations 2007, reg. 45; and offences of failure to prevent tax evasion, contrary to the Criminal Finances Act 2017, ss. 45 and 46. A DPA may also be entered into in respect of any ancillary offence (as defined in para. 29) relating to a listed offence and the Secretary of State may amend the list by order.

Crime and Courts Act 2013, sch. 17

1.—(1) A deferred prosecution agreement (a 'DPA') is an agreement between a designated prosecutor and a person ('P') whom the prosecutor is considering prosecuting for an offence specified in Part 2 (the 'alleged offence').

(2) Under a DPA—

(a) P agrees to comply with the requirements imposed on P by the agreement;

(b) the prosecutor agrees that, upon approval of the DPA by the court (see paragraph 8), paragraph 2 is to apply in relation to the prosecution of P for the alleged offence.

2.—(1) Proceedings in respect of the alleged offence are to be instituted by the prosecutor in the Crown Court by preferring a bill of indictment charging P with the alleged offence (see section 2(2)(ba) of the Administration of Justice (Miscellaneous Provisions) Act 1933 (bill of indictment preferred with consent of Crown Court judge following DPA approval)).

(2) As soon as proceedings are instituted under sub-paragraph (1) they are automatically suspended.

(3) The suspension may only be lifted on an application to the Crown Court by the prosecutor; and no such application may be made at any time when the DPA is in force.

(4) At a time when proceedings are suspended under sub-paragraph (2), no other person may prosecute P for the alleged offence.

3.—(1) The following are designated prosecutors—

(a) the Director of Public Prosecutions;

(b) the Director of the Serious Fraud Office;

(c) any prosecutor designated under this paragraph by an order made by the Secretary of State.

(2) A designated prosecutor must exercise personally the power to enter into a DPA and, accordingly, any enactment that enables a function of a designated prosecutor to be exercised by a person other than the prosecutor concerned does not apply.

(3) But if the designated prosecutor is unavailable, the power to enter into a DPA may be exercised personally by a person authorised in writing by the designated prosecutor.

4.—(1) P may be a body corporate, a partnership or an unincorporated association, but may not be an individual.

(2) In the case of a DPA between a prosecutor and a partnership—

(a) the DPA must be entered into in the name of the partnership (and not in that of any of the partners);

(b) any money payable under the DPA must be paid out of the funds of the partnership.

(3) In the case of a DPA between a prosecutor and an unincorporated association—

(a) the DPA must be entered into in the name of the association (and not in that of any of its members);

(b) any money payable under the DPA must be paid out of the funds of the association.

5.—(1) A DPA must contain a statement of facts relating to the alleged offence, which may include admissions made by P.

(2) A DPA must specify an expiry date, which is the date on which the DPA ceases to have effect if it has not already been terminated under paragraph 9 (breach).

(3) The requirements that a DPA may impose on P include, but are not limited to, the following requirements—

(a) to pay to the prosecutor a financial penalty;
(b) to compensate victims of the alleged offence;
(c) to donate money to a charity or other third party;
(d) to disgorge any profits made by P from the alleged offence;
(e) to implement a compliance programme or make changes to an existing compliance programme relating to P's policies or to the training of P's employees or both;
(f) to co-operate in any investigation related to the alleged offence;
(g) to pay any reasonable costs of the prosecutor in relation to the alleged offence or the DPA.

The DPA may impose time limits within which P must comply with the requirements imposed on P.

(4) The amount of any financial penalty agreed between the prosecutor and P must be broadly comparable to the fine that a court would have imposed on P on conviction for the alleged offence following a guilty plea.

(5) A DPA may include a term setting out the consequences of a failure by P to comply with any of its terms.

6. [Requirement that the DPP and the Director of the SFO must jointly issue a Code of guidance for prosecutors.]

7.—(1) After the commencement of negotiations between a prosecutor and P in respect of a DPA but before the terms of the DPA are agreed, the prosecutor must apply to the Crown Court for a declaration that—

(a) entering into a DPA with P is likely to be in the interests of justice, and
(b) the proposed terms of the DPA are fair, reasonable and proportionate.

(2) The court must give reasons for its decision on whether or not to make a declaration under sub-paragraph (1).

(3) The prosecutor may make a further application to the court for a declaration under sub-paragraph (1) if, following the previous application, the court declined to make a declaration.

(4) A hearing at which an application under this paragraph is determined must be held in private, any declaration under sub-paragraph (1) must be made in private, and reasons under sub-paragraph (2) must be given in private.

8.—(1) When a prosecutor and P have agreed the terms of a DPA, the prosecutor must apply to the Crown Court for a declaration that—

(a) the DPA is in the interests of justice, and
(b) the terms of the DPA are fair, reasonable and proportionate.

(2) But the prosecutor may not make an application under sub-paragraph (1) unless the court has made a declaration under paragraph 7(1) (declaration on preliminary hearing).

(3) A DPA only comes into force when it is approved by the Crown Court making a declaration under sub-paragraph (1).

(4) The court must give reasons for its decision on whether or not to make a declaration under sub-paragraph (1).

(5) A hearing at which an application under this paragraph is determined may be held in private.

(6) But if the court decides to approve the DPA and make a declaration under sub-paragraph (1) it must do so, and give its reasons, in open court.

(7) Upon approval of the DPA by the court, the prosecutor must publish—

(a) the DPA,
(b) the declaration of the court under paragraph 7 and the reasons for its decision to make the declaration,
(c) in a case where the court initially declined to make a declaration under paragraph 7, the court's reason for that decision, and
(d) the court's declaration under this paragraph and the reasons for its decision to make the declaration,

unless the prosecutor is prevented from doing so by an enactment or by an order of the court under paragraph 12 (postponement of publication to avoid prejudicing proceedings).

9.—(1) At any time when a DPA is in force, if the prosecutor believes that P has failed to comply with the terms of the DPA, the prosecutor may make an application to the Crown Court under this paragraph.

(2) On an application under sub-paragraph (1) the court must decide whether, on the balance of probabilities, P has failed to comply with the terms of the DPA.
(3) If the court finds that P has failed to comply with the terms of the DPA, it may—
 (a) invite the prosecutor and P to agree proposals to remedy P's failure to comply, or
 (b) terminate the DPA.
(4) The court must give reasons for its decisions under sub-paragraphs (2) and (3).
(5) Where the court decides that P has not failed to comply with the terms of the DPA, the prosecutor must publish the court's decision and its reasons for that decision, unless the prosecutor is prevented from doing so by an enactment or by an order of the court under paragraph 12 (postponement of publication to avoid prejudicing proceedings).
(6) Where the court invites the prosecutor and P to agree proposals to remedy P's failure to comply, the prosecutor must publish the court's decisions under sub-paragraphs (2) and (3) and the reasons for those decisions, unless the prosecutor is prevented from doing so by an enactment or by an order of the court under paragraph 12 (postponement of publication to avoid prejudicing proceedings).
(7) Where the court terminates a DPA under sub-paragraph (3)(b), the prosecutor must publish—
 (a) the fact that the DPA has been terminated by the court following a failure by P to comply with the terms of the DPA, and
 (b) the court's reasons for its decisions under sub-paragraphs (2) and (3),
 unless the prosecutor is prevented from doing so by an enactment or by an order of the court under paragraph 12 (postponement of publication to avoid prejudicing proceedings).
(8) If the prosecutor believes that P has failed to comply with the terms of the DPA but decides not to make an application to the Crown Court under this paragraph, the prosecutor must publish details relating to that decision, including—
 (a) the reasons for the prosecutor's belief that P has failed to comply, and
 (b) the reasons for the prosecutor's decision not to make an application to the court,
 unless the prosecutor is prevented from doing so by an enactment or by an order of the court under paragraph 12 (postponement of publication to avoid prejudicing proceedings).

10.—(1) At any time when a DPA is in force, the prosecutor and P may agree to vary its terms if—
 (a) the court has invited the parties to vary the DPA under paragraph 9(3)(a), or
 (b) variation of the DPA is necessary to avoid a failure by P to comply with its terms in circumstances that were not, and could not have been, foreseen by the prosecutor or P at the time that the DPA was agreed.
(2) When the prosecutor and P have agreed to vary the terms of a DPA, the prosecutor must apply to the Crown Court for a declaration that—
 (a) the variation is in the interests of justice, and
 (b) the terms of the DPA as varied are fair, reasonable and proportionate.
(3) A variation of a DPA only takes effect when it is approved by the Crown Court making a declaration under sub-paragraph (2).
(4) The court must give reasons for its decision on whether or not to make a declaration under sub-paragraph (2).
(5) A hearing at which an application under this paragraph is determined may be held in private.
(6) But if the court decides to approve the variation and make a declaration under sub-paragraph (2) it must do so, and give its reasons, in open court.
(7) Where the court decides not to approve the variation, the prosecutor must publish the court's decision and the reasons for it, unless the prosecutor is prevented from doing so by an enactment or by an order of the court under paragraph 12 (postponement of publication to avoid prejudicing proceedings).
(8) Where the court decides to approve the variation the prosecutor must publish—
 (a) the DPA as varied, and
 (b) the court's declaration under this paragraph and the reasons for its decision to make the declaration,
 unless the prosecutor is prevented from doing so by an enactment or by an order of the court under paragraph 12 (postponement of publication to avoid prejudicing proceedings).

11.—(1) If a DPA remains in force until its expiry date, then after the expiry of the DPA the proceedings instituted under paragraph 2(1) are to be discontinued by the prosecutor giving notice to the Crown Court that the prosecutor does not want the proceedings to continue.
(2) Where proceedings are discontinued under sub-paragraph (1), fresh criminal proceedings may not be instituted against P for the alleged offence.

(3) But sub-paragraph (2) does not prevent fresh proceedings from being instituted against P in a case where, after a DPA has expired, the prosecutor finds that, during the course of the negotiations for the DPA—
  (a) P provided inaccurate, misleading or incomplete information to the prosecutor, and
  (b) P knew or ought to have known that the information was inaccurate, misleading or incomplete.
(4) A DPA is not to be treated as having expired for the purposes of sub-paragraph (1) if, on the expiry date specified in the DPA—
  (a) an application made by the prosecutor under paragraph 9 (breach) has not yet been decided by the court,
  (b) following an application under paragraph 9 the court has invited the parties to agree proposals to remedy P's failure to comply, but the parties have not yet reached an agreement, or
  (c) the parties have agreed proposals to remedy P's failure to comply following an invitation of the court under paragraph 9(3)(a) but P has not yet complied with the agreement.
(5) In the case mentioned in sub-paragraph (4)(a)—
  (a) if the court decides that P has not failed to comply with the terms of the DPA, or that P has failed to comply but does not take action under paragraph 9(3), the DPA is to be treated as expiring when the application is decided;
  (b) if the court terminates the DPA, the DPA is to be treated as not having remained in force until its expiry date (and sub-paragraph (1) therefore does not apply);
  (c) if the court invites the parties to agree proposals to remedy P's failure to comply, the DPA is to be treated as expiring when the parties have reached such an agreement and P has complied with it.
(6) In the case mentioned in sub-paragraph (4)(b), the DPA is to be treated as expiring when the parties have reached an agreement and P has complied with it.
(7) In the case mentioned in sub-paragraph (4)(c), the DPA is to be treated as expiring when P complies with the agreement.
(8) Where proceedings are discontinued under sub-paragraph (1), the prosecutor must publish—
  (a) the fact that the proceedings have been discontinued, and
  (b) details of P's compliance with the DPA,

  unless the prosecutor is prevented from doing so by an enactment or by an order of the court under paragraph 12 (postponement of publication to avoid prejudicing proceedings).

12. The court may order that the publication of information by the prosecutor under paragraph 8(7), 9(5), (6), (7) or (8), 10(7) or (8) or 11(8) be postponed for such period as the court considers necessary if it appears to the court that postponement is necessary for avoiding a substantial risk of prejudice to the administration of justice in any legal proceedings.

13.—(1) Sub-paragraph (2) applies where a DPA between a prosecutor and P has been approved by the Crown Court under paragraph 8.
(2) The statement of facts contained in the DPA is, in any criminal proceedings brought against P for the alleged offence, to be treated as an admission by P under section 10 of the Criminal Justice Act 1967 (proof by formal admission).
(3) Sub-paragraph (4) applies where a prosecutor and P have entered into negotiations for a DPA but the DPA has not been approved by the Crown Court under paragraph 8.
(4) Material described in sub-paragraph (6) may only be used in evidence against P—
  (a) on a prosecution for an offence consisting of the provision of inaccurate, misleading or incomplete information, or
  (b) on a prosecution for some other offence where in giving evidence P makes a statement inconsistent with the material.
(5) However, material may not be used against P by virtue of sub-paragraph (4)(b) unless evidence relating to it is adduced, or a question relating to it is asked, by or on behalf of P in the proceedings arising out of the prosecution.
(6) The material is—
  (a) material that shows that P entered into negotiations for a DPA, including in particular—
    (i) any draft of the DPA;
    (ii) any draft of a statement of facts intended to be included within the DPA;
    (iii) any statement indicating that P entered into such negotiations;
  (b) material that was created solely for the purpose of preparing the DPA or statement of facts.

Section D13 Juries

INTRODUCTION

This section deals with the various stages of the process by which a jury is empanelled to try an accused, and the handling of that jury thereafter. The main source of the law on jurors is the Juries Act 1974. Regard must also be had to CrimPR 25.6 to 25.9 and 26.1 to 26.5, and CrimPD VI, Part 26. Under the heading of the process for empanelment, this section addresses eligibility for jury service, the summoning of jurors, and the selection and empanelling of jurors for a particular case. Under the heading of jury management, this section addresses the conduct of jurors during a trial, and the judge's power to discharge the jury or individual jurors. The offences that may be committed by jurors who fail to heed the directions as to the proper performance of their role, inserted into the Juries Act 1974 by the CJCA 2015, are also addressed. **D13.1**

The rules governing retirement of the jury while they consider their verdict, and the verdicts they may return, are considered in **D19**.

In addition, this section considers the extent to which errors in the formation of the jury may ground an appeal, and recent legislative measures designed to replace juries with trials by judge alone in certain categories of cases (see **D13.75** *et seq.*).

ELIGIBILITY FOR JURY SERVICE AND DISQUALIFICATION

The basic rule is that all persons aged 18 to 75 who: **D13.2**

(a) are registered either as parliamentary or local government electors; and
(b) have been ordinarily resident in the UK for any period of at least five years since attaining the age of 13,

are eligible for jury service and are therefore under a duty to attend for service if summoned (Juries Act 1974, s. 1). CrimPD VI, para. 26B.1 (see Supplement, **CPD.26B**), states: 'The normal presumption is that everyone, unless ineligible or disqualified, will be required to serve when summoned to do so.'

There are a number of exceptions to this general rule. The first category is those who are disqualified from serving by the provisions of the Juries Act 1974, as amended by the CJCA 2015, s. 77 (see **D13.3**). The second category is those who are able to excuse themselves from serving, either as of right under the Act, or at the discretion of the appropriate court officer in accordance with CrimPD VI, paras. 26B.2 and 26C.1 to 26C.10 and the *Guidance for summoning officers when considering deferral and excusal applications* published by HM Courts and Tribunals Service. These include; persons with insufficient understanding of English; jurors with professional and public service commitments; and serving police officers, prison officers or employees of prosecuting agencies (see **D13.5**).

Ineligibility and Disqualification

Parts I and II of sch. 1 to the Juries Act 1974 set out those persons who are disqualified from jury service. **D13.3**

The Mental Health (Discrimination) Act 2013, s. 2, amended the 1974 Act so as to remove the blanket ineligibility that previously applied to mentally disordered persons and replace it with a more limited disqualification. As amended, the first group of disqualified persons, under sch. 1, part I, consists of those for the time being: (a) liable to be detained under the Mental Health Act 1983; (b) resident in a hospital on account of a mental disorder as defined in the 1983 Act (i.e. any disorder or disability of the mind); (c) under a guardianship order or community treatment order under the 1983 Act; or (d) who lack capacity within the meaning of the Mental Capacity Act 2005.

The other persons disqualified (as defined by part II of sch.1), either for life or for ten years, are either disqualified by reason of previous convictions or by virtue of being on bail in criminal proceedings. This now includes those who have committed any of the offences pursuant to the Juries Act 1974 itself (sch. 1, para. 6).

If a person serves on a jury while aware of being disqualified from so doing, the person commits a summary offence punishable with an unlimited fine (Juries Act 1974, s. 20(5)).

D13.4 **Juries Act 1974, s. 1 and sch. 1**

1.—(1) Subject to the provisions of this Act, every person shall be qualified to serve as a juror in the Crown Court, the High Court and the county court and be liable accordingly to attend for jury service when summoned under this Act if—

(a) he is for the time being registered as a parliamentary or local government elector and aged eighteen or over but under seventy six;
(b) he has been ordinarily resident in the United Kingdom, the Channel Islands or the Isle of Man for any period of at least five years since attaining the age of thirteen;
(c) [omitted by the Mental Health (Discrimination) Act 2013, s. 2]; and
(d) he is not disqualified for jury service.

(2) [Omitted by the Mental Health (Discrimination) Act 2013, s. 2.]
(3) The persons who are disqualified for jury service are those listed in Schedule 1.

SCHEDULE 1
PERSONS DISQUALIFIED FOR JURY SERVICE

PART 1
PERSONS SUBJECT TO MENTAL HEALTH ACT 1983 OR
MENTAL CAPACITY ACT 2005

1. A person for the time being liable to be detained under the Mental Health Act 1983.
1A. A person for the time being resident in a hospital on account of mental disorder as defined by the Mental Health Act 1983.
2. A person for the time being under guardianship under section 7 of the Mental Health Act 1983 or subject to a community treatment order under section 17A of that Act.
3. A person who lacks capacity, within the meaning of the Mental Capacity Act 2005, to act as a juror.
4. [Repealed.]

PART 2
OTHER PERSONS DISQUALIFIED FOR JURY SERVICE

5. A person who is on bail in criminal proceedings (within the meaning of the Bail Act 1976).
6. A person who has at any time been sentenced in the United Kingdom, the Channel Islands or the Isle of Man—
(a) to imprisonment for life, detention for life or custody for life,
(b) to detention during her Majesty's pleasure or during the pleasure of the Secretary of State,
(c) to imprisonment for public protection or detention for public protection,
(d) to an extended sentence under section 227 or 228 of the Criminal Justice Act 2003 or section 210A of the Criminal Procedure (Scotland) Act 1995, or
(e) to a term of imprisonment of five years or more or a term of detention of five years or more.

6A. A person who at any time in the last ten years has been convicted of—
(a) an offence under section 20A, 20B, 20C or 20D of this Act,

(b) an offence under paragraph 5A, 5B, 5C or 5D of Schedule 6 to the Coroners and Justice Act 2009 (equivalent offences relating to jurors at inquests), or
(c) an offence under paragraph 2, 3, 4 or 5 of Schedule 2A to the Armed Forces Act 2006 (equivalent offences relating to members of the Court Martial).

7. A person who at any time in the last ten years has—
(a) in the United Kingdom, the Channel Islands or the Isle of Man—
(i) served any part of a sentence of imprisonment or a sentence of detention, or
(ii) had passed on him a suspended sentence of imprisonment or had made in respect of him a suspended order for detention,
(b) in England and Wales, had made in respect of him a community order under section 177 of the Criminal Justice Act 2003, a community rehabilitation order, a community punishment order, a community punishment and rehabilitation order, a drug treatment and testing order or a drug abstinence order, or
(c) had made in respect of him any corresponding order under the law of Scotland, Northern Ireland, the Isle of Man or any of the Channel Islands or a service community order or overseas community order under the Armed Forces Act 2006.

8. For the purposes of this Part of this Schedule—
(a) a sentence passed (anywhere) in respect of a service offence within the meaning of the Armed Forces Act 2006 is to be treated as having been passed in the United Kingdom, and
(b) a person is sentenced to a term of detention if, but only if—
(i) a court passes on him, or makes in respect of him on conviction, any sentence or order which requires him to be detained in custody for any period, and
(ii) the sentence or order is available only in respect of offenders below a certain age,
and any reference to serving a sentence of detention is to be construed accordingly.

EXCUSAL FROM JURY SERVICE

Excusal as of Right

Certain narrowly defined groups are entitled to be excused from jury service even though they are eligible to serve and have been duly summoned to attend for service under the Juries Act 1974, s. 2. **D13.5**

There are two main categories:

(a) Section 8 of the Juries Act 1974 deals with those excusable by virtue of having served in the recent past.
(b) Section 9(2A) sets out the position with regard to full-time serving members of the armed forces. The Crown Court officer should (within certain limits set out in s. 9A(2A) and (2B)) excuse such members if their commanding officer certifies that their absence would be prejudicial to the efficiency of the service.

If a member of an excusable group is summoned, the onus is on that person to apply for excusal and satisfy an appropriate officer of the Crown Court of the person's membership of the group in question. There is also provision for the court itself to excuse the juror without the application first going through an officer (ss. 8(1) and 9(4)).

In addition, s. 9(3) provides that rules shall enable a juror refused excusal by an officer to appeal to the court against the refusal. CrimPR 26.1 (see Supplement, **R26.1**) requires the juror to give written notice of appeal to the appropriate officer, specifying the matters relied on as grounds for excusal. The juror must also be given an opportunity to make representations to the court. The appeal would normally be determined in chambers.

The courts have identified other categories of persons who, as a result of their occupation, may qualify for excusal. These include those employed by the prosecuting authority (*Abdroikov* [2007] UKHL 37, [2008] 1 Cr App R 21 (280) (see **D13.27**) and CrimPD VI, para. 26C.9 (see Supplement, **CPD.26C**)) and those who have publicly expressed strong views on criminal issues, such as writers and journalists (*Cornwall* [2009] EWCA Crim 2458).

D13.6 **Juries Act 1974, ss. 8 and 9**

8.—(1) If a person summoned under this Act shows to the satisfaction of the appropriate officer, or of the court (or any of the courts) to which he is summoned—

(a) that he has served on a jury, or duly attended to serve on a jury, in the prescribed period ending with the service of the summons on him, or

(b) that the Crown Court or any other court has excused him from jury service for a period which has not terminated, the officer or court shall excuse him from attending, or further attending, in pursuance of the summons.

(2) In subsection (1) above 'the prescribed period' means two years or such longer period as the Lord Chancellor may prescribe...

9.—(1) [Repealed.]

(2) If any person summoned under this Act shows to the satisfaction of the appropriate officer that there is good reason why he should be excused from attending in pursuance of the summons, the appropriate officer may, subject to section 9A(1A) of this Act, excuse him from so attending.

(2A) Without prejudice to subsection (2) above, the appropriate officer shall excuse a full-time serving member of Her Majesty's naval, military or air forces from attending in pursuance of a summons if—

(a) that member's commanding officer certifies to the appropriate officer that it would be prejudicial to the efficiency of the service if that member were to be required to be absent from duty, and

(b) subsection (2A) or (2B) of section 9A of this Act applies.

(2B) Subsection (2A) above does not affect the application of subsection (2) above to a full-time serving member of Her Majesty's naval, military or air forces in a case where he is not entitled to be excused under subsection (2A).

(3) [Power to make rules governing appeals against summonses.]

(4) Without prejudice to the preceding provisions of this section, the court (or any of the courts) before which a person is summoned to attend under this Act may excuse that person from so attending.

Discretionary Excusal

D13.7 Both CrimPD VI and the Juries Act 1974 make provision for persons summonsed for jury service to be excused. Section 9(2) of the 1974 Act permits a juror discretionary excusal wherever it can be shown to the satisfaction of the jury summoning officer that 'there is good reason why he should be excused from attending'. There is a right of appeal against the appropriate officer's refusal to excuse following the procedure set out in CrimPR 26.1 (see Supplement, **R26.1**). Excusal is dealt with in CrimPD VI, paras. 26B.3 and 26C.1 to 26C.10 (see Supplement, **CPD.26B** and **CPD.26C**). Excusal from service on a long trial is dealt with by CrimPR 26.4 (see Supplement, **R26.4**).

D13.8 **Proper Approach to a Discretionary Excusal** The test identified in *Guildford Crown Court, ex parte Siderfin* [1990] 2 QB 683 for whether and, if so, in what circumstances conscientious and/or religious objection to serving on a jury should entitle a juror to be excused is whether the applicant has established a good reason for excusal. A conscientious objection arising out of religious belief is unlikely *on its own* to amount to a good reason, since it will not outweigh the necessity of the observance of the public duty to perform jury service. 'Adherence to some kind of religious belief cannot be regarded as an unchallengeable right to excusal from jury service' (at p. 159F). But where the applicant's belief would stand in the way of her fulfilling her duty as a juror 'properly, responsibly and honestly', she should be excused.

As to procedure, although there is no right to be represented, the judge hearing the appeal has a discretion to allow it and, unless there is good reason to the contrary, an adjournment should be allowed for solicitors to be instructed (at p. 158G–H). Any application for excusal from jury service must first be independently considered by an appropriate officer; it is unacceptable for certain types of application to be automatically transferred to a judge.

SUMMONING FOR JURY SERVICE

D13.9 The procedure for summoning jurors is governed by s. 2 of the Juries Act 1974 and CrimPR 25.6 (see Supplement, **R25.6**). Responsibility for summoning jurors for service rests with the

Lord Chancellor (s. 2(1)). In making arrangements for the discharge of that duty, the Lord Chancellor is to have regard to the convenience of the persons summoned and the desirability of selecting jurors who live within reasonable daily travelling distance of the Crown Court location they are summoned to attend (s. 2(2)). Subject to that, a person may be required to attend for service anywhere in England and Wales (s. 2(3)). The summons may be served by ordinary post (s. 2(4)).

Basis for Selection

To enable the Lord Chancellor to perform duties in relation to the summoning of jurors, the Lord Chancellor must be provided with as many copies of published electoral registers as required (Juries Act 1974, s. 3). The copies must indicate those persons on the register who are either under 18 or aged 76 or over (i.e. ineligible for jury service by reason of age). The choice of those to be summoned is made on a random basis from amongst those who are (a) on the register and (b) of an eligible age. **D13.10**

It follows that a summons may be sent to a person who is ineligible on a ground other than age or who is disqualified by reason of previous convictions. Therefore, s. 2(5) provides that the summons for service shall be accompanied by a notice informing the person summoned of the categories of ineligible person, the possibility of being prosecuted for serving when ineligible or disqualified, and the right to apply for excusal from or deferral of jury service.

Panels of those Summoned

As well as summoning jurors, the Lord Chancellor is required to prepare panels (i.e. lists) of those persons who have been summoned (Juries Act 1974, s. 5(1)). The arrangement of and the information contained in the panels is a matter for the Lord Chancellor's discretion (s. 5(1)). At present the only information given is the names and addresses of those summoned and the dates and place of attendance. Parties to a case which will or may be tried by jury are entitled to reasonable facilities for inspecting the panel from which their jurors will be drawn (s. 5(2)). The right must be exercised before the close of the trial (s. 5(3)). **D13.11**

Praying a Tales

In the unlikely event that there will be insufficient jurors on the panel to form a complete jury to try an issue, the court may require any persons who are in the vicinity to be summoned without written notice for service (Juries Act 1974, s. 6(1)). This practice is known as '*praying a tales*'. The procedure for this process is set out in CrimPR 25.6(3) and (5), and requires the parties to be informed where this procedure has been adopted. **D13.12**

The names of persons so summoned are added to the panel, and the court then proceeds as if they had been on the panel in the first instance (s. 6(2)). The reference in s. 6 to 'making up' a full jury by means of additional panellists suggests that the jury must always include at least one person who was on the original panel. This interpretation is consistent with the decision in *Solomon* [1958] 1 QB 203 (jury consisting of jurors not on the original panel was held to be no jury at all).

Obligation Imposed by the Summons

Unless the person summoned has been excused from jury service under the provisions described above, an offence is committed if the person either fails to attend on a day covered by the summons, or, having attended, is then either not available when called on to serve or is unfit by reason of drink or drugs (Juries Act 1974, s. 20(1)). By s. 20(2), the offence is punishable either on summary conviction or as if it were a criminal contempt committed in the face of the court (i.e. the Crown Court judge may determine whether an offence has been committed without recourse to summary prosecution). The offence is punishable with a level 3 fine of up to £1,000. If the juror can show reasonable cause for the failure to attend etc. the juror is not liable to any **D13.13** penalty (s. 20(4)). In *Andrews* [2008] EWCA Crim 2394 the importance of a proper inquiry as to whether such reasonable cause existed was stressed.

Deferral of Jury Service

D13.14 Section 9A of the Juries Act 1974 provides that, if a juror who has been summoned shows to the satisfaction of the appropriate officer that there is good reason why the juror's attendance should be deferred, the officer shall vary the summons accordingly (s. 9A(1)). Obvious reasons for deferral are if the dates in the summons clash with the juror's holiday arrangements or business commitments. Attendance may be deferred only once in respect of one summons (s. 9A(2A)).

An application for deferral may be made direct to the court (s. 9A(4)), and, in any event, there is a right of appeal against the appropriate officer's refusal to defer (s. 9A(3) and CrimPR 26.1).

Reference to the Judge for Discharge of a Summons

D13.15 Should it appear to the appropriate officer of the court that a person attending for jury service in pursuance of a summons may be unable to act effectively as a juror on account of 'physical disability or insufficient understanding of English', that person may be brought before a judge who 'shall determine whether or not he should act as a juror and, if not, shall discharge the summons' (Juries Act 1974, ss. 9B and 10 and CrimPD VI, para. 26C.1).

Furthermore, by s. 2(5), an officer may 'at any time put or cause to be put to [a person summoned for jury service] such questions as the officer thinks fit in order to establish whether or not the person is qualified for jury service'. Under s. 20(5), knowingly or recklessly providing false answers to such questions is a summary offence punishable with a level 3 fine of up to £1,000.

D13.16 **Procedure** The procedure in relation to those who may be unable to act as jurors because of physical disability is governed by the Juries Act 1974, s. 9B. This states that the judge 'shall affirm the summons unless he is of the opinion that the person will not, on account of his disability, be capable of acting effectively as a juror, in which case he shall discharge the summons'.

In *Re Osman* [1996] 1 Cr App R 126, the Recorder of London, Sir Lawrence Verney, held at first instance that a person summoned to be a juror who was profoundly deaf should be discharged from jury service pursuant to s. 9B. The prospective juror could not follow the proceedings in court or the deliberations in the jury room without the assistance of an interpreter in sign language, and it would be an incurable irregularity in the proceedings for the interpreter to retire with the jury when they considered their verdict.

SELECTION OF JURY FOR A PARTICULAR CASE

D13.17 Once a jury panel has been selected by the process described above, the next stage is to select a jury for a particular case, pursuant to s. 11 of the Juries Act 1974. The procedure for selecting the jury is set out in CrimPR 25.6 (see Supplement, **R25.6**); r. 26.4 makes further provision relating to selection for long trials. Normally, a jury will be called to try the issue of the accused's guilt or innocence. However, they might alternatively be asked to determine whether an accused whom the court has found to be unfit to plead did the act alleged, or to try the issues mute by visitation of God or of malice (for which see **D12.10** and **D12.17**).

Ballot in Open Court

D13.18 **Juries Act 1974, s. 11**

(1) The jury to try an issue before a court shall be selected by ballot in open court from the panel, or part of the panel, of jurors summoned to attend at the place and time in question.

The 'ballot in open court' is conventionally conducted by the clerk of the court. Part of the jury panel which is sufficient to provide a full jury of 12, allowing for the possibility that some may be successfully challenged, is brought into the back of the court by an usher. These jurors are usually referred to as the 'jury in waiting'. The need for selection to be random so far as practicable was emphasised in *Salt* [1996] Crim LR 517 and *Tarrant* [1998] Crim LR 342. However, in *Jalil* [2008] EWCA Crim 2910, [2009] 2 Cr App R (S) 40 (276) it was held that a ballot remained valid where the prospective panel had been reduced to a final 12 by the use of a questionnaire provided to the original panel and then by earlier challenges to other jurors. The scope of questions that may be posed to a jury in waiting, identifying reasons for excusal of members of that panel from service on the jury, is addressed at CrimPD VI, para. 26D.1, together with a cautionary note as to its limitations at para. 26D.2.

The clerk is given the juror cards for each of the jurors in waiting (i.e. a card on which is printed the juror's name and address). The clerk selects cards at random, and reads out the names on them, inviting the jurors in waiting to step into the jury-box should their names be called (CrimPR 25.6(4)).

Once the jurors are in the box, the clerk informs the accused of the right to challenge jurors. The clerk then reads out the names again, pausing after each name so that the juror may take the juror's oath (or affirm). The form of oath is: 'I swear by almighty God that I will faithfully try the defendant[s] and give [a] true verdict[s] according to the evidence'. That form is not set out in CrimPD VI, paras. 26E.1 to 26E.3 (see Supplement, **CPD.26E**), because the form may vary according to the faith indicated by the juror to the court (para. 26E.2), but para. 26E.3 states that a solemn affirmation shall be permitted if the juror objects to being sworn and sets out the form of that declaration. Each juror must take the oath or affirm separately (s. 11(3)). See also **D12** in relation to jurors who are asked to decide whether a defendant, who is unfit to plead or stand trial, did the act alleged. In those circumstances the wording of the oath is different. The juror must swear or affirm 'that I will determine whether or not I am satisfied that the defendant did the acts charged against him and give a true verdict according to the evidence'.

Shadow Jurors Under CrimPR 25.6(6), in the case of a trial expected to last more than four weeks, as many as 14 jurors may be selected initially to allow for a need arising to discharge one or more of the 12 first selected for reasons that emerge during the prosecution opening address. The court must explain to the jurors the reason why 14 have been selected and will discharge any extra juror or jurors remaining by no later than the beginning of the prosecution evidence (r. 25.6(7)). **D13.19**

Anonymity of Jurors In *Comerford* [1998] 1 All ER 823, the Court of Appeal considered the decision of the trial judge that jurors should be identified by number, not by name, to reduce the risk of intimidation. Their lordships took the view that, as there was no mandatory requirement that names should be called, such a departure from the normal procedure did not render the trial a nullity, unless it made the proceedings unfair to D. It was made clear, however, that D could have exercised his right to ascertain the names of all the jurors forming the panel if he had so desired and it was said that it is 'highly desirable that in normal circumstances the usual procedure for empanelling a jury should be followed'. **D13.20**

Comerford [1998] 1 All ER 823 was considered in *Baybasin* [2013] EWCA Crim 2357, [2014] 1 Cr App R 19 (264), in which complaint was made that the jury had been selected following a ballot by number, and other measures had been adopted to protect the jury. The Court of Appeal considered that the measures, such as collecting the jury from a city-centre pick-up point and requiring them to remain in their room when not in court, did not affect the fairness of the trial and that ballot by numbers had not inhibited the accused's right of challenge. The Court did, however, observe that the permissible measures for jury management and selection were now those promulgated by the Criminal Procedure Rules Committee, and that local initiatives ought to be referred to that committee for its approval.

Warnings to the Jury on Empanelment In the light of the decision of the House of Lords in *Mirza* [2004] UKHL 2, [2004] 1 AC 1118 (see **D13.51**), the Court of Appeal issued *Practice Direction (Crown Court: Guidance to Jurors)* [2004] 1 WLR 665, which requires that the judge **D13.21**

warn the jury that they should raise any concerns about the behaviour of fellow jurors at the time, rather than waiting until the conclusion of the case. That Practice Direction is consolidated in CrimPD VI. At the start of every trial in the Crown Court the judge is under a duty to give the jury directions in the opening remarks, together with further reminders of those directions, consistent with the requirements set out in CrimPD VI, paras. 26G.1 to 26G.5 (see Supplement, **CPD.26G**). See also the *Crown Court Compendium* (July 2020), ch. 3, which gives extensive guidance on how a trial judge should give such directions. The directions are reinforced by providing the jurors with a document setting out their legal responsibilities as a juror.

As was restated in *Marshall* [2007] EWCA Crim 35, at the outset of the trial the judge should warn the jury: (a) that they must try the case on the evidence that they hear in court and on nothing else; (b) that they must not discuss the case with others outside court, such as members of their family; and (c) that they should not conduct their own private research, e.g., using the internet. See also *Thompson* [2010] EWCA Crim 1623, [2010] 2 Cr App R 27 (259) and *McDonnell* [2010] EWCA Crim 2352, [2011] 1 Cr App R 28 (347) for the special emphasis given to warnings on internet research and the collective responsibility of jurors. In *A-G v Davey* [2013] EWHC 2317 (Admin), [2014] 1 Cr App R 1 (1), it was suggested that handing the jury a notice setting out what they must and must not do and the penal consequences of any breach might be advisable, so that no juror can subsequently claim not to have understood what not to do and what the consequences might be; this practice is now embodied in CrimPR 26.3 (see Supplement, **R26.3**). Since March 2018 this has become common practice in all trials in the Crown Court, with each juror being handed a copy of the 'Jurors Notice' at the start of each trial, when the judge gives all relevant information and warnings to the jury.

There has been an increasingly robust response to failures to follow these instructions. See, e.g., the approach of the Court of Appeal to a breach of the internet injunction to jurors in *A-G v Dallas* [2012] EWHC 156 (Admin), [2012] 1 WLR 991 (see **B14.107**). With effect from 13 April 2015, the CJCA 2015, ss. 71 to 73, amended the Juries Act 1974 by adding s. 20A, which makes it an offence for jurors to undertake their own researches during the trial process, s. 20B, which makes it an offence for jurors to share such researches with other jurors, and s. 20C, which makes it an offence to engage intentionally in other forms of 'prohibited conduct'. For details of these offences, see **B14.133 *et seq.*** The prohibition on the use of the internet is further reinforced by the CJCA 2015, s. 69, which amended the Juries Act 1974 by adding s. 15A, which permits the court to require jurors to surrender electronic communication devices while at court, and by the CJCA 2015, s. 70, which grants court security officers the power to search jurors to enforce this prohibition. See also CrimPR 26.3.

CHALLENGING JURORS

D13.22 It is fundamental to the jury process that the jurors who try an accused are selected at random. That said, however, it is recognised that there will be circumstances in which the interests of justice require some intervention in that random selection process. The methods of replacing one or more of the prospective jurors called into the box as a result of the clerk's ballot with others from the jury in waiting are:

(a) for either the prosecution or defence to challenge for cause;
(b) for the prosecution to ask a juror to stand by;
(c) for the judge to exercise the discretionary power to remove a juror.

The procedure for objecting to potential jurors is now contained in CrimPR 25.8 (see Supplement, **R25.8**).

Challenges for Cause

D13.23 A challenge for cause may be made by either the prosecution or defence. It is either a challenge to the whole panel of jurors, known as a challenge 'to the array', or to an individual juror, known as a challenge 'to the polls'.

Challenges to the Array At common law either party could challenge the whole panel summoned for their case on the ground that the person responsible for the summoning acted improperly or was biased. Although this right is preserved by the Juries Act 1974, s. 12(6), it is now almost dormant. D13.24

Juries Act 1974, s. 12

(6) Without prejudice to subsection (4) above [right to challenge individual jurors], the right of challenge to the array, that is to say the right of challenge on the ground that the person responsible for summoning the jurors in question is biased or has acted improperly, shall continue to be unaffected by the fact that, since the coming into operation of section 31 of the Courts Act 1971 (which is replaced by this Act), the responsibility for summoning jurors for service in the Crown Court... has lain with the Lord Chancellor.

Historically, challenge to the array was made when the sheriff responsible for summoning the jury had an apparent interest in the outcome of the trial. More recently, such a challenge is more likely to relate to the racial or religious composition of the jury.

Specific malfeasance in the summoning was also a ground of challenge, as when jurors were summoned at the express request of prosecution or defence, or had been selected on grounds of their religion (see, e.g., *O'Doherty* (1848) 6 St Tr NS 831).

Racial or Religious Composition of the Jury In the absence of evidence of bias or improper conduct by the person responsible for summoning, the jury panel's being imbalanced racially or not reflecting the overall racial or religious composition of the catchment area from which jurors are summoned is *not* sufficient ground for challenge. See, e.g., *Danvers* [1982] Crim LR 680 and *Broderick* [1970] Crim LR 155, which were both approved by the Court of Appeal in *Ford* [1989] QB 868 (analysed at **D13.40**). The principle of these decisions will apply equally to other apparent imbalances in the jury panel (e.g., as to the proportion of men to women). D13.25

Challenges to the Polls D13.26

Juries Act 1974, s. 12

(4) The fact that a person summoned to serve on a jury is not qualified to serve shall be a ground of challenge for cause; but subject to that, and to the foregoing provisions of this section, nothing in this Act affects the law relating to challenge of jurors.

Thus, jurors who are too old or too young to be on a jury, or who have not been resident in the UK for a five-year period since attaining the age of 13, or who are not on the electoral roll, or who are disqualified by convictions may all be successfully challenged for cause (see **D13.3**).

In the absence of any challenge from the parties, a juror may in effect challenge him or herself by stating, if it be the case, that he or she is not qualified (*Cook* (1696) 13 St Tr 311). The summons sent to each juror is accompanied by a notice which sets out the ineligible and disqualified groups and warns the juror of the duty to inform the court if he or she comes within any of them.

Police Officers and Employees of Prosecuting Authorities as Jurors In *Abdroikov* [2007] UKHL 37, [2008] 1 Cr App R 21 (280), the House of Lords considered whether the Court of Appeal ([2005] EWCA Crim 1986, [2006] 1 Cr App R 1 (1)), had been correct to hold that the presence on a jury of a police officer, or a prosecuting solicitor, did not offend against the requirement for a fair trial. The House of Lords identified the appropriate question to be whether a fair-minded observer would perceive a possibility of bias, albeit unconscious, as inevitable when a juror was professionally committed to only one side of an adversarial trial process. In the case of an employee of the prosecuting authority, their lordships concluded that such a perception of bias did arise, and it was therefore not appropriate for such an employee to form part of a jury trying a case brought by his or her employer. In the case of police officers, however, a fair-minded observer would not conclude that there was a real possibility that such a person would be biased as a juror simply because of being involved in the administration of justice. The position would, however, be different if the juror had special knowledge either of the individuals D13.27

involved or the facts of the case (as was the case in *Pintori* [2007] EWCA Crim 1700), or where the credibility or reliability of police evidence was a central issue (as was the case in one of the conjoined appeals in *Abdroikov* itself).

The approach advocated by the House of Lords was applied in *Khan* [2008] EWCA Crim 531, [2008] 2 Cr App R 13 (161), and approved by the ECtHR in *Hanif v UK* (2012) 55 EHRR 16 (424) and *Armstrong v UK* [2014] ECHR 1368. It was stressed, for example in *Hanif*, that the right to be tried by an impartial tribunal would be infringed where the credibility of the police was in issue and a serving officer was part of the jury. See also *Yemoh* [2009] EWCA Crim 930 and *LL* [2011] EWCA Crim 65, [2011] 1 Cr App R 27 (338), where it was repeated that there needed to be a specific reason to exclude a serving/retired police officer from the jury, rather than there being any form of blanket prohibition, whereas the position of an employee of the prosecution authority was nearer to the latter position. This topic is addressed at CrimPD VI, para. 26C.6 (see Supplement, **CPD.26C**).

D13.28 **Fear of Bias** At common law a qualified juror could be challenged *propter affectum*, i.e. on the ground of some presumed or actual bias which would make the juror unsuitable to try the case. This ground of challenge is preserved by the last clause of s. 12(4). Most authorities on challenges to the polls *propter affectum* are old, and reflect the very different social and legal conditions of their time. The broad thrust of the decisions is that a juror is challengeable if the juror has expressed hostility to one side or the other (*O'Coigley* (1798) 26 St Tr 1191), has expressed a wish as to the outcome of the case, is related to a party, or has some other connection with a party (e.g., was the party's servant or agent).

In *Kray* (1969) 53 Cr App R 412, the defence wished to object to any jurors who had read newspaper articles which had reported not only that two of the accused before the court charged with murder had been convicted at an earlier trial for murder but also included 'a number of facts which were not in evidence at the trial and which were discreditable of those to whom they referred'. Lawton J, having criticised the newspapers for publishing these additional facts, then said (at p. 415, emphasis added):

> This does, in my judgment, lead to a prima facie presumption that anybody who may have read that kind of information might find it difficult to reach a verdict in a fair-minded way. It is, however, a matter of human experience... first, that the public's recollection is short, and, secondly, that the drama... of a trial almost always has the effect of excluding from recollection that which went before. A person summoned for this case would not... disqualify himself merely because he had read any of the newspapers containing allegations of the kind I have referred to; but the position would be different if, as a result of reading what he had, *his mind had become so clogged with prejudice that he was unable to try the case impartially*.

Insofar as a general principle may be extracted from the above passage, it seems to be that a juror may be challenged for cause if the juror's mind is so prejudiced that he or she is unable to try the case impartially, but merely having once been informed of matters discreditable to the accused will not necessarily occasion such prejudice.

Procedure for Challenging for Cause

D13.29 The Juries Act 1974, s. 12(1)(b), provides that 'any challenge for cause shall be tried by the judge before whom [the accused] is to be tried'.

D13.30 **Timing** The challenge must be entered after the juror's name has been drawn by ballot and before being sworn (s. 12(3)). Conventionally, a challenge is indicated simply by counsel for the challenging party saying the word 'challenge' as the juror is about to take the oath. Should the challenge not be made until after the juror has begun to take the oath the judge has a discretion to allow it but is not obliged to do so (*Harrington* (1977) 64 Cr App R 1).

It is clear from *Morris* (1991) 93 Cr App R 102, that the right to challenge for cause is limited to the time when the jury is sworn, and cannot be exercised during the course of the trial. M was accused of stealing from a Marks and Spencer store. During the trial, it was revealed that a juror was employed by that company. The judge refused to discharge the juror saying that the right way to deal with the matter was by a challenge for cause. The Court of Appeal, allowing the appeal, held that by the time the facts about the juror had emerged, it was too late for the defence to challenge for cause.

Process The burden of proof is on the challenging party, and the judge may order that the hearing be *in camera* or in chambers (CJA 1988, s. 118(2)). If the challenge is of any substance, it will be proper for it to be heard in the absence of the other jurors. The challenged juror should be kept outside the court except insofar as it is necessary to question him. The remaining jurors should leave the court, retiring to the jury room in the charge of the jury bailiff if they have already been sworn. A shorthand note of proceedings should in any event be taken, and the court's decision should be entered on the court record. The judge can hear evidence and question the juror concerned. Counsel may be allowed to ask questions directed to the ground on which the juror is challenged. **D13.31**

After hearing the evidence and any submissions, the judge will decide whether to allow the challenge. If the challenge is allowed, the juror is discharged and a fresh juror called as a replacement. If the challenge is rejected, the judge should tell the juror not to disclose any of the matters dealt with during the challenge to other jurors, and not to be influenced by the fact that the challenge was made.

Need for Prima Facie Evidence The main difficulty in challenging for cause is that, in marked contrast to the practice adopted in the USA of conducting preliminary questioning of the jury panel to establish a prima facie ground of challenge, the challenging party must provide prima facie evidence of the grounds at the time that the challenge is made. It is only *after* this that a juror may be asked questions on the *voir dire* to determine whether the challenge is well founded. **D13.32**

The initial requirement of prima facie evidence from the challenger was stated in *Dowling* (1848) 7 St Tr NS 382, and was confirmed by Lord Parker CJ in *Chandler (No. 2)* [1964] 2 QB 322, in which his lordship said (at p. 338):

> ... before any right to cross-examine the juror arose, the defendant would have had to lay a foundation of fact in support of his ground of challenge. It is no good his saying, 'I think this man is antagonistic'.... There must be a foundation of fact creating a prima facie case before the juror can be cross-examined.

Similarly, in *Broderick* [1970] Crim LR 155, where defence counsel unsuccessfully sought to cross-examine each member of the panel to determine whether he or she might be biased against D on racial grounds, the Court of Appeal held that it had never been the practice to allow potential jurors to be paraded for cross-examination in a fishing expedition, seeking possible grounds on which a challenge might subsequently be made.

In *Kray* (1969) 53 Cr App R 412 (see **D13.28**), defence counsel was permitted to examine each juror who came into the box to be sworn on whether the juror had read certain newspaper articles discreditable to the accused on the basis that the production of the offending articles was in itself sufficient to raise a prima facie ground of challenge.

Standing Jurors By

The Right This is a right possessed by the prosecution but not the defence (although in *Chandler (No. 2)* [1964] 2 QB 322 at p. 337, Lord Parker CJ observed that 'in an exceptional case the judge [could] in his discretion stand by a juror or allow the defendant to do so'). **D13.33**

CrimPR 25.8(3) provides that the prosecution must announce the exercise of its right before the juror completes the oath or affirmation.

Standing a juror by differs from challenging the juror for cause in that counsel need not give a reason for the stand-by. It differs from the peremptory challenges formerly available to the defence in that the juror is not conclusively removed from the jury but will be recalled to the jury-box should the entire jury panel be exhausted without a full jury being obtained, at which stage the prosecution must either accept the juror or show cause why that juror should not serve. (See the leading case of *Mason* [1981] QB 881, per Lawton LJ, giving the Court of Appeal's judgment to this effect (at pp. 890H–891A), but adding the rider that he expected that prosecuting counsel would act responsibly and would not request a stand-by unnecessarily (at p. 891C)).

D13.34 **Guidance as to the Use of the Right** Since *Mason* [1981] QB 881 was decided, the defence right of peremptory challenge, which was perceived as a counterbalance to the prosecution right of stand-by, has been abolished. The A-G's guidelines on the exercise by the Crown of its right of stand-by (see **appendix 2**) affirm the general principles that:

(a) members of a jury should be selected at random from the panel subject to any rule of law as to right of challenge by the defence; and
(b) the Juries Act 1974 identifies those classes of persons who *alone* are disqualified from or ineligible for service on a jury, and no other class of person may be so treated (para. 2).

Responsibility for ensuring that an individual does not serve on a jury if not competent to discharge the duties properly rests, first, with the appropriate court officer and, ultimately, with the trial judge. In the context of that legislative background, para. 5 of the guidelines defines the two situations in which it is appropriate for prosecuting counsel to use the right of stand-by as follows:

> (a) where a jury check authorised in accordance with the Attorney-General's guidelines on jury checks [see **D13.45** and **appendix 2**] reveals information justifying exercise of the right to stand by in accordance with para. 9 of the guidelines and the Attorney-General personally authorises the exercise of the right to stand by; or
> (b) where a person is about to be sworn as a juror who is manifestly unsuitable and the defence agree that, accordingly, the exercise by the prosecution of the right to stand by would be appropriate. An example of the sort of *exceptional* circumstances which might justify stand-by is where it becomes apparent that . . . a juror selected for service to try a complex case is in fact illiterate.

D13.35 On the assumption that the guidelines are loyally followed, the importance of the right of stand-by has been vastly reduced. Counsel will exercise the right only in the tiny minority of cases which involve national security or terrorism (para. 5(a)), or 'ordinary' cases where a juror is obviously unsuitable *and the defence agree* (para. 5(b)). Thus, the chief function of the right now seems to be to avoid the clumsy mechanics of a challenge for cause where the parties concur that a juror should not serve.

In addition to the example given in para. 5(b) itself, subject to defence consent, jurors could properly be stood by if, e.g., counsel has been informed that they are in fact disqualified by previous convictions, or if they know the accused or any witnesses in the case. The guidelines are presumably not meant to inhibit prosecuting counsel from challenging for cause on grounds of bias if counsel considers that a juror's previous convictions or other involvement with the police might make the juror so prejudiced against the Crown as to be unable to try the case fairly. Whether such a challenge would succeed is open to question.

The Court's Power to Exclude Jurors

D13.36 Even in the absence of a formal challenge from either party, the trial judge has a residual discretion to exclude from the jury a juror selected by the initial ballot. Existence of the discretion can be traced back to Lord Campbell CJ's judgment in *Mansell v The Queen* (1857) 8 E & B 54, and has since been confirmed by Lord Parker CJ (*Chandler (No. 2)* [1964] 2 QB 322 at p. 327), by Lawton LJ (*Mason* [1981] QB 881 at p. 887G–H) and, most recently, by Lord Lane CJ in *Ford [1989] QB 868*.

D13.37 **Reasons for Exclusion** The discretion may and should be exercised where an individual juror is obviously incompetent to act but, for whatever reason, counsel do not challenge or exercise the right of stand-by. It is then the court's duty to prevent the 'scandal and perversion of justice which would arise from compelling or permitting such a juryman to be sworn' (per Lord Campbell CJ in *Mansell v The Queen* (1857) 8 E & B 54, who then gave as specific examples for the judge's intervention cases where the juror was mentally or physically infirm, or insane or drunk, or preoccupied with the dangerous illness of a relative).

Lawton LJ in *Mason* [1981] QB 881, succinctly described modern practice by saying (at p. 887G–H):

> ... trial judges, as an aspect of their duty to see that there is a fair trial, have had a right to intervene to ensure that a competent jury is empanelled. The most common form of judicial intervention is when a judge notices that a member of the panel is infirm or has difficulty in reading or hearing; and nowadays jurors for whom taking part in a long trial would be unusually burdensome are often excluded from the jury by the judge.

In *Jalil* [2008] EWCA Crim 2910, [2009] 2 Cr App R (S) 40 (276) the Court of Appeal found that a court was entitled to exclude jurors from the ballot who fell within criteria that had formed the basis of a challenge for cause that had been made and upheld in relation to other potential jurors.

See also CrimPD VI, para. 26C.3 (see Supplement, **CPD.26C**).

Limitations However, judicial intervention should not extend beyond the kinds of situation mentioned above into a more systematic process which would undermine the random nature of jury selection or influence the overall composition of the jury (per Lord Lane CJ in *Ford* [1989] QB 868). In particular, the court has no power to discharge jurors on account of their religion, race or ethnic group in order to obtain a more diverse jury. Lord Lane said (at p. 872A) that the discretion to exclude a juror 'is to be exercised to prevent individual jurors who are not competent from serving. It has never been held to include a discretion to discharge a competent juror or jurors in an attempt to secure a jury drawn from particular sections of the community, or otherwise to influence the overall composition of the jury.' (See also the discussion of racially balanced juries at **D13.39**.) **D13.38**

Racial or Religious Balance of Jury

From time to time judicial intervention has been sought to ensure that at least some members of the jury come from the same ethnic group as the accused. Although examples from the case law refer to the racial composition of the jury, the same principles have equal application to attempts to affect the religious composition of the jury. They include: **D13.39**

(a) *Binns* [1982] Crim LR 522 (trial of black accused on charges relating to racial riot in Bristol);
(b) *Bansal* [1985] Crim LR 151 (trial of Asians for offences of violence committed when protesting against a National Front march);
(c) *McCalla* [1986] Crim LR 335 (black accused alleging that his admissions to robbery were extracted from him by racially prejudiced white police officers);
(d) *Danvers* [1982] Crim LR 680 (accused at Nottingham Crown Court objected to the jury panel because it was entirely white and he was anxious that there should be a substantial representation of black people on the jury; challenge failed, even though the black population in Nottingham apparently represented about 10 per cent of the total);
(e) *Broderick* [1970] Crim LR 155 (black accused wished to be tried by an all-black jury).

The precise form of judicial aid sought has varied from case to case. In *Binns*, counsel asked the judge to exercise the right to stand jurors by until a jury representing 'the corporate good sense of the community' had been obtained; in *Bansal* the application was to move the venue of trial to a racially mixed area, while in *Broderick* the defence wished to have the jury panel paraded and asked 'fishing' questions about their possible racial prejudice.

Judicial response to the applications has been equally varied. The judges in *Binns* and *Bansal* were basically sympathetic to the defence request (although in doubt about how far they could go in ordering a certain racial mix on the jury or jury panel). By contrast, Judge Mander in *McCalla* ruled that he had no power to order that a jury be racially balanced and, even if he had such power, he would not have chosen to exercise it because a jury should be selected at random subject only to the law on disqualified jurors and challenges for cause. Moreover, to allow interference with jury selection on racial grounds would open the way to further manipulation, e.g., on grounds of political view, sex, or religion, or for some similar reason.

D13.40 **Guidelines for Approaching the Issue** It is the latter view which has found favour with the Court of Appeal. In *Ford* [1989] QB 868, D appealed against his convictions on the ground that the trial judge had refused an application for a racially balanced jury. The main points established by Lord Lane CJ's judgment are as follows:

(a) A challenge to the array of jurors summoned must be on the ground of bias or other irregularity on the part of the summoning officer. Therefore, the racial composition of the jury panel cannot of itself found a challenge or justify the judge in discharging the panel and ordering the summoning of a new one (see *Danvers* [1982] Crim LR 680 and **D13.25**).
(b) Summoning of jurors is the responsibility of the Lord Chancellor. It is not the judge's function to alter the composition of the jury panel or give directions about the area from which it should be drawn. Woolf J's direction in *Bansal* [1985] Crim LR 151, to the effect that the panel should be drawn from a part of the court's catchment area in which a high proportion of Asians lived, was made without benefit of full argument and was wrong.
(c) Nor should the judge consider a complaint that the jury panel is not truly random because it contains a lower proportion of persons of a certain race or ethnic group than live in the court's catchment area for jurors, unless, of course, the disproportion can be attributed to bias or impropriety on the part of the summoning officer. If the disproportion may be due to maladministration in the procedures for summoning jurors, that must be corrected by *administrative*, not judicial intervention.
(d) The mere fact that a juror is of a particular race or holds a particular religious belief cannot found a challenge for cause by a party on the ground of bias.
(e) The judge may not use the power to stand by or discharge individual jurors selected in the ballot from the jury panel for the purpose of securing a jury of a certain racial mix. To do so would conflict with the principle of random jury selection. In effect, the judge would be altering the composition of the jury panel when no irregularity on the part of the summoning officer had been shown and upholding a challenge when there was no ground in law for it. The judge's intervention should be restricted to the exceptional circumstances indicated in *Mansell v The Queen* (1857) 8 E & B 54 (see **D13.37**). Insofar as the judge in *Binns* [1982] Crim LR 522 had been prepared to stand jurors by until a balanced jury had been obtained, he was in error.
(f) In short, there is not (as had been suggested in *Frazer* [1987] Crim LR 418 and *Bansal*) any principle that a jury should be racially balanced, and it is impermissible for the judge to use the residual discretionary powers over the composition of the jury as a device for obtaining such a balance.

In *Smith* [2003] EWCA Crim 283, [2003] 1 WLR 2229, the Court of Appeal considered the standing of *Ford* in the light of the HRA 1998 and the ECHR, Article 6. It held that the approach in *Ford* had not been superseded by the HRA 1998. Pill LJ said:

> We do not accept that it was unfair for the appellant to be tried by a randomly selected all white jury or that the fair-minded and informed observer would regard it as unfair. We do not accept that, on the facts of this case, the trial could only be fair if members of the defendant's race were present on the jury. It was not a case where a consideration of the evidence required knowledge of the traditions or social circumstances of a particular racial group.

For a recent re-affirmation of this approach see *Bridge* [2019] EWCA Crim 2220 at [41].

INVESTIGATION OF THE JURY PANEL

Effective challenging of jurors depends on the amount of information about the jury panel available to the parties. Section 5(2) and (3) of the Juries Act 1974 entitles the parties to inspect the jury panel before or during trial but such inspection will inform them only of the names and addresses of the panel members. It will not of itself yield material capable of founding a challenge for cause. **D13.41**

Proper Inquiries

There would seem to be no objection in theory to a party identifying the panellists summoned to the location of the Crown Court for the time when the party's case is listed to be heard and then making inquiries into their employment, background, attitudes etc. on the off chance that grounds for a challenge for cause may emerge. The party must, of course, take care not to infringe the general law on privacy or interfere with the jurors in a way which might amount to contempt of court or interference with the course of justice. In practice, the defence do not have the resources to conduct the kind of inquiries mentioned above. **D13.42**

Checks for Previous Convictions

The one inquiry that the prosecution are likely to make is into the criminal records of the panellists. This practice was approved by the Court of Appeal in *Mason* [1981] QB 881. In that case, the police provided prosecution counsel with the results of checks as to whether the panellists summoned had convictions. Counsel stood by certain jurors, some but not all of whom were disqualified by their convictions, without informing defence counsel of the reason. Lawton LJ, giving the judgment of the Court of Appeal, justified the police action as being part of their usual function of preventing crime, it being an offence to serve on a jury when disqualified by convictions (at p. 891D–F). **D13.43**

Further, the court could see no reason why the information obtained should not be communicated to prosecuting counsel who could then make such use of it as he considered fit. 'The practice of supplying prosecuting counsel with information about potential jurors' convictions has been followed during the whole of our professional lives.... It is not unlawful, and has not until recently been thought to be unsatisfactory' (at p. 891G). Prosecuting counsel is under no duty to transmit the information to the defence, although this may be done if so wished (at p. 891B–D).

Evolution since *Mason*

The decision in *Mason* that there is no objection to prosecution counsel standing a juror by if he or she has convictions which are not themselves such as warrant disqualification, has been effectively reversed by the A-G's guidelines on the matter (see below). However, the case remains good authority to justify the practice of 'vetting' jurors by running a preliminary check on their criminal records. **D13.44**

Following the decision in *Mason*, the Association of Chief Police Officers (ACPO) issued recommendations on when the police 'should undertake a check of the names of potential jurors against records of previous convictions'. This is now done automatically by HM Courts and Tribunals Service, and so the ACPO recommendations are no longer annexed to the present version of the A-G's guidelines (issued in 2012). Save when authorised by the A-G's guidelines (see **D13.45**), no further checks on jurors should be carried out, and the prosecution should only seek to stand a juror by either as result of such checks, or where the juror is 'manifestly unsuitable' for the particular case and the defence agree.

Jury Vetting

D13.45 Jury vetting by the police or prosecution is controlled by guidelines issued by the A-G (see **appendix** 2). In brief, they affirm that the provisions of the Juries Act 1974 on disqualified and ineligible jurors, and the powers under that Act to excuse or defer service, combined with majority verdicts (which prevent one perverse juror stopping the other jurors from reaching a verdict) will, in all normal cases, be sufficient to ensure the proper administration of justice without recourse to any investigation of the jury panel.

In two classes of case, however, the public interest may demand additional checks (para. 3). Those classes are (a) cases in which national security is involved and part of the evidence is likely to be heard *in camera*, and (b) terrorist cases (para. 4). In both types of case there is a risk that a juror's political views might be so extreme as to interfere with a fair assessment of the case or lead the juror to exert improper pressure on fellow jurors, while in security cases there is the additional risk of the juror either voluntarily or under pressure making improper use of evidence given *in camera* (para. 5).

To ascertain whether a juror might be unsuitable for the above reasons, it may be necessary to investigate the panel by checking the records of Police Special Branches. In security (but not in terrorist) cases the investigation may additionally involve the security services (para. 6). Such checks may be made *only* on the personal authority of the A-G, and are therefore known as 'authorised checks' (para. 7). If a chief officer of police considers that an authorised check is likely to be desirable, the officer should refer the matter to the DPP, who will make the appropriate application to the A-G (para. 7).

The result of any authorised check will be sent to the DPP, who in turn will decide how much of the information should be passed on to prosecuting counsel (para. 8). In any event, no right of stand-by should be exercised by counsel on the basis of information derived from an authorised check unless counsel has the personal authority of the A-G and unless the information affords 'strong reason for believing that a particular juror might be a security risk, be susceptible to improper approaches or be influenced in arriving at a verdict for the reasons given [in the guidelines]' (para. 9).

Where a juror is stood by, prosecuting counsel has discretion to disclose to the defence the information on which the stand-by was based, but is under no duty to do so (para. 10). If an authorised check suggests that a juror might be biased against the accused, the defence should be informed of that in general terms although it may not be possible to give them precise details of the information revealed by the check (para. 11). It will be apparent that authorised checks are a possibility in only a tiny proportion of trials. In the general run of criminal cases, there will either be no check at all on the jury panel or there will be a check only of their criminal records.

COMPOSITION OF THE JURY AS A GROUND OF APPEAL

D13.46 The Juries Act 1974, s. 18, governs the extent to which the defence may use as a ground of appeal against conviction errors in the way the jury panel was summoned or the particular jury for their case was selected or empanelled. The overall effect is to prevent the verdict being challenged unless the irregularity complained of was raised but not remedied at trial. Moreover, s. 18 prevents lack of qualification or unfitness on the part of an individual juror being a ground of appeal.

Juries Act 1974, s. 18

(1) No judgment after verdict in any trial by jury in any court shall be stayed or reversed by reason—
  (a) that the provisions of this Act about the summoning or empanelling of jurors, or the selection of jurors by ballot, have not been complied with, or
  (b) that a juror was not qualified in accordance with section 1 of this Act, or
  (c) that any juror was misnamed or misdescribed, or
  (d) that any juror was unfit to serve.

(2) Subsection (1)(a) above shall not apply to any irregularity if objection is taken at, or as soon as practicable after, the time it occurs, and the irregularity is not corrected.
(3) Nothing in subsection (1) above shall apply to any objection to a verdict on the ground of personation.

It should be noted that the saving in s. 18(2) applies only to appeals based on contraventions of the Act's provisions as to the summoning or empanelling of jurors or their selection by ballot. If objection to such an irregularity was taken when or as soon as practicable after it occurred and the court did not correct it, it may be relied on as a material irregularity in the course of the trial justifying the quashing of a conviction by virtue of s. 2(1) of the Criminal Appeal Act 1968. Section 18(2) will not assist in a case where the defence did not know of the irregularity in summoning etc. until after conviction, since it will not have been possible to object until a stage at which the Crown Court was *functus officio*.

Unfitness of a Juror

Save in the special case of impersonation of a juror, a juror's having been disqualified from or ineligible for jury service (Juries Act 1974, s. 18(1)(b)) or more generally unfit to serve (s. 18(1)(d)) cannot be a ground of appeal. The statutory provision follows the common law, for example: **D13.47**

(a) *Kelly* [1950] 2 KB 164, in which it was held that the only instances of convictions being quashed on account of a defect in a juror, that defect not having been raised at trial by means of a challenge for cause, were cases in which the juror actually summoned had been impersonated by another;
(b) *Tremearne* (1826) 5 B & C 254, in which the son of the juror called, who was not on the panel and was under age, answered for his father and served. The fact that the defence did not discover the defect in the juror until after conviction (and therefore could not have challenged for cause) is irrelevant to the application of s. 18 (see *Chapman* (1976) 63 Cr App R 75 and especially *Pennington* (1985) 81 Cr App R 217).

On a literal reading of s. 18 it is even possible to argue that, where a challenge was made at trial and wrongly rejected, the defence still cannot rely on the error on appeal. However, in such circumstances the proper ground of appeal would in fact be the judge's error of law in ruling against the challenge. Therefore, the appellant would not be caught by s. 18. See also *Tomar* [1997] Crim LR 682.

The broad and somewhat draconian effect of s. 18 is illustrated by the leading case of *Chapman* (1976) 63 Cr App R 75. After conviction, the defence learnt that one of the jurors who tried the case was deaf and had heard only half the evidence. The defence were prevented from submitting on appeal that deafness rendered the juror unfit to serve, and that there had therefore been a material irregularity in the course of the trial (pursuant to the Criminal Appeal Act 1968, s. 2(1)(c)) because s. 18(1)(d) expressly prevented any unfitness in a juror being used to reverse a verdict. Equally there had been no wrong decision on a question of law (for the purposes of s. 2(1)(b) of the 1968 Act), since no challenge had been made to the juror in the lower court. Accordingly, the only possible ground of appeal was the assertion that the verdict was unsafe (s. 2(1)(a)). On the facts of *Chapman*, the Court of Appeal concluded that the verdict was safe. The convictions were unanimous. Therefore, even on the assumption that, had he heard all the evidence, the deaf juror would have been for acquittal, the jury could and no doubt would have convicted by an 11–1 majority. Moreover, if the juror's incapacity had come to light during the course of the trial, the judge could simply have discharged him from the jury (see **D13.52**), allowing his colleagues to complete the trial and convict. **D13.48**

However, even though the argument failed on the facts, the Court of Appeal did indicate, *obiter*, that a juror's unfitness or lack of qualification was in principle a factor capable of rendering a conviction unsafe in conjunction with other circumstances.

Unfitness in General or in Particular

D13.49 It is unclear whether the terms of the Juries Act 1974, s. 18(1)(d), preventing a juror's unfitness to serve being used as the ground for reversing a verdict, apply only to an argument that the juror was unfit to serve on *any* jury or whether it extends to an argument that, although in general a qualified and competent juror, he or she was unfit to serve on the jury trying D because of bias arising out of knowledge of or previous dealings with D.

Whichever is the correct interpretation of s. 18 matters little, since common law, even before the passing of the 1974 Act, had made it virtually impossible to use subsequently discovered bias of a juror as a ground of appeal.

For example, in *Box* [1964] 1 QB 430, the foreman of the jury which had convicted the appellants gave evidence before the Court of Appeal that, at the time he served on the jury, he knew of the appellants' bad character. Lord Parker CJ adopted a dictum of Bankes J in *Syme* (1914) 10 Cr App R 284, to the effect that, unless the evidence shows the juror to have been determined *before* trial to come to a certain verdict regardless of the evidence, the court would not interfere.

Similarly, the foreman's knowledge of the appellant's bad character was not an automatic disqualification from serving on the jury, nor did it mean that he was unable to listen to the evidence and give the accused a fair trial in accordance with his oath. See also *Pennington* (1985) 81 Cr App R 217 and *Bliss* (1987) 84 Cr App R 1.

In practice it will be difficult if not impossible to satisfy the Court of Appeal that a juror was so biased against the accused before the case started as to be determined to convict whatever the evidence might turn out to be. These cases can be contrasted with decisions such as *Pintori* [2007] EWCA Crim 1700, in which a juror knew prosecution witnesses and this could justify a conclusion of bias on the part of the juror, thus rendering any resultant conviction unsafe.

DISCHARGE OF JURORS OR ENTIRE JURY

D13.50 CrimPR 25.7 sets out the procedure on the discharge of individual jurors or an entire jury before it has delivered its verdict (see Supplement, **R25.7**). The judge has a discretion to discharge jurors from the jury and allow the trial to continue to verdict with the remainder, provided that at least nine jurors remain. The judge also has a discretion to discharge the entire jury from giving a verdict, in which case the accused is not acquitted but may be retried before a fresh jury. CrimPD VI, paras. 26M.1 to 26M.26 (see Supplement, **CPD.26M**), cover jury irregularities; see in particular para. 26M.5.

Once a jury has been discharged the general rule is that it is *functus officio* and cannot be reconvened to return a verdict, even if it is realised almost immediately after the order for discharge that the order was made in error (*Russell* (1984) 148 JP 765). In *Follen* [1994] Crim LR 225, it was stated that there was no fixed rule of law that once the judge had discharged the jury that order could not be set aside, but it would be only in very rare circumstances that this should be done (see *S* [2005] EWCA Crim 1987, for an example of such circumstances). In *Aylott* [1996] 2 Cr App R 169, the Court of Appeal adopted a more flexible approach, and stated that the underlying principle was to ensure that proceedings were fair and to do justice in the particular case (see **D19.77** for more detail).

There are three situations that should be considered in this context. First, where the jury themselves identify a problem; secondly, where there is a problem with a particular juror; and, thirdly, where the problem extends to the jury as a whole.

In each of these situations the test to be applied is the same, either where there is or may be bias or prejudice against the accused or misbehaviour that risks injustice, namely 'a high degree of need'. This approach is analysed below, together with consideration of how any alleged bias or misconduct can be investigated, and how any ultimate decision as to whether or not to discharge the jury can thereafter be reviewed on appeal. In cases where a juror encounters personal difficulties with continued service (addressed by CrimPD VI, paras. 26H.1 to 26H.3): 'All such applications should be dealt with sensitively and sympathetically and the trial judge should always seek to meet the interests of justice without unduly inconveniencing any juror' (para. 26H.3).

Jury Monitoring Itself

The House of Lords in *Mirza* [2004] UKHL 2, [2004] 1 AC 1118, decided in effect that if after verdict a juror raises a concern about a fellow juror's behaviour, the courts will not investigate such behaviour (see **D19.31**). As a result of the views expressed by Lord Hope and Lord Hobhouse, the Court of Appeal issued *Practice Direction (Crown Court: Guidance to Jurors)* [2004] 1 WLR 665, which is consolidated at CrimPD VI, paras. 26G.1 to 26G.4 (see Supplement, **CPD.26G**, and **D13.21**). Note especially para. 26G.3vi. **D13.51**

As was made clear in *Adams* [2007] EWCA Crim 1, [2007] 1 Cr App R 34 (449), it is implicit in this approach that the Court of Appeal can hear evidence from jurors to resolve an issue of alleged jury bias when this is raised on appeal, although anyone seeking to interview jurors with a view to investigating such an issue should first obtain the Court of Appeal's leave. It was made clear that this course would only be countenanced in rare and exceptional cases (a recent example of such investigation is *Hambleton* [2009] EWCA Crim 13). Equally, a court at first instance would be entitled to question jurors in relation to any alleged impropriety. In *Thompson* [2010] EWCA Crim 1623, [2010] 2 Cr App R 27 (259), it was restated that an investigation of the jury was permissible only where there was a suggestion of a complete repudiation of the jury's oath, or a risk that extraneous material had entered the jury's deliberations (see *OKZ* [2010] EWCA Crim 2272 as an example of self-monitoring by a jury, where one juror reported pre-judgment by another).

For a recent example of a jury raising a concern about a fellow juror's misconduct, see *KK* [2019] EWCA Crim 1634, [2020] 1 Cr App R 29 (515). In that case a juror wrote to the judge reporting a fellow juror (J9) on day 78 of a particularly complex trial involving allegations of serious sexual offences committed by a number of defendants. J9 had informed his fellow 11 jurors of research showing that one of the defendants (NK) had a significant previous conviction which had not been placed before the jury. The judge immediately separated J9 from the other 11 jurors. Despite submissions to the contrary, the judge refused to conduct further detailed inquiries into J9's behaviour and refused applications on behalf of other defendants that the jury should be questioned whether any other research had been carried out. Instead, the jury, as a whole, were asked to state what information they had received from J9 in relation to any defendant. Subsequently, the judge asked the foreman, in the presence of the remaining ten jurors, to indicate whether they wished to report any other matters—the answer was 'no'. Further, the jury indicated that they had not reached any verdict concerning NK. Following this the judge discharged J9, and also discharged the remaining 11 jurors from reaching verdicts in relation to NK. The judge refused to discharge the jury from reaching verdicts concerning other defendants, in response to submissions that there was a perception of, if not actual, bias. The judge was satisfied that there had been no contamination by J9's information concerning NK's previous sexual offence. Subsequently, the jury reached mixed verdicts of guilty and not guilty against other defendants. One of the grounds of appeal was that the judge's investigations into the misconduct by J9 and his subsequent instructions to the remaining 11 jurors were inadequate. This was rejected by the Court of Appeal, following the approach in *Thompson*. During the trial, the other defendants had put in their previous character, to show either no previous convictions for sexual matters or previous good character. The trial judge had had regard to CrimPD V, paras. 26M.1 to 26M.26 (see Supplement, **CPD.26M**), in reaching his decision and the Court was satisfied that the subsequent convictions were safe.

Discharge of Individual Jurors

Juries Act 1974, s. 16 **D13.52**

(1) Where in the course of a trial of any person for an offence on indictment any member of the jury dies or is discharged by the court whether as being through illness incapable of

> continuing to act or for any other reason, but the number of its members is not reduced below nine, the jury shall nevertheless ... be considered as remaining for all the purposes of that trial properly constituted, and the trial shall proceed and a verdict may be given accordingly.

Section 16(1) is without prejudice to the judge's power to discharge the entire jury if the judge considers it preferable to do that (for which see **D13.57**), rather than continuing with reduced numbers (s. 16(3)). Discharge of jurors is *not* dependent on the consent of the parties.

In a case where the jury must consider more than one verdict, the judge retains the power to discharge a juror even after one or more of the verdicts has been given. The reasoning is that the trial (and the accompanying power to discharge) continues in respect of those counts on which the verdict has not been delivered (*Wood* [1997] Crim LR 229).

D13.53 **Judicial Discretion to Discharge a Juror** Section 16(1) does not define the circumstances in which the judge may or should discharge a juror beyond implying that it may be on account of illness making the juror incapable of continuing to act or 'any other reason'. In *Hambery* [1977] QB 924, D's trial exceeded its estimate and was not likely to finish until after the weekend. The judge explained the position to the jury, one of whom indicated that she was due to go on holiday that weekend. After a short discussion with counsel, during which defence counsel raised no express objection, the judge discharged the juror in reliance on s. 16.

On appeal, Lawton LJ held (p. 927D–H) that the extent of the jurisdiction to discharge a juror is a matter of common law, since s. 16 does not confer the power but merely sets out the consequences of exercising it. At common law a jury could be discharged 'in cases of evident necessity' (*Blackstone's Commentaries*, 1857 edn, and see also Erle CJ's judgment in *Winsor v R* (1866) LR 1 QB 390, where he refers (at p. 394) to 'a high degree of need ... such as ... might be denoted by the word necessity'). At that time and until 1925, if one juror had to be discharged then so had the whole jury (i.e. there was no power to continue with a reduced jury). Therefore, the present test for jurisdiction to discharge a juror must be the same as the old test for discharging the whole jury, namely, has an evident necessity for it arisen?

D13.54 Although no specific guidance is given as to what may constitute an 'evident necessity', CrimPD VI, paras. 26H.1 to 26H.3 (see Supplement, **CPD.26H**), address the discharge of a juror for personal reasons, and the test set out at para. 26H.2 is that 'the judge must exercise his or her discretion according to the interests of justice and the requirements of each individual case'. It would seem to be a fairly elastic concept and is certainly not limited to illness or other cause making it literally impossible for the juror to continue to act.

Trial by jury depends on the willing co-operation of the public, and 'if the administration of justice can be carried on without inconveniencing jurors unduly it should be' (*Winsor*, at p. 930C–G). Therefore, in the circumstances that had arisen in *Winsor*, the judge both had jurisdiction to discharge the juror and could not be criticised for the way he exercised his discretion.

In *S* [2009] EWCA Crim 104 the Court of Appeal described the test for discharge of a juror where there was potential for prejudice as being whether the presence of that juror might deprive the accused of a fair jury deliberation (see also *F* [2009] EWCA Crim 805).

D13.55 **Discharge for Misconduct** Misconduct by a juror often necessitates discharge of the whole jury; however, it should be borne in mind that, depending on the precise circumstances, the judge might be able to deal with the problem by discharging only the juror guilty of the misconduct. See **D13.66** for fuller consideration of misconduct on the part of a juror.

D13.56 **Direction to the Remaining Jurors** Once a juror has been discharged, the remainder of the jury should be directed to have no further contact with that juror during their remaining service (CrimPD VI, para. 26M.26). Where a juror had to be discharged while the jury was in retirement, the Court of Appeal considered it wholly unrealistic to direct the remaining jurors to ignore any views expressed by the departed juror. Those views became part of the fabric of opinions under consideration (*Carter* [2010] EWCA Crim 201, [2010] 1 WLR 1577).

Discharge of the Entire Jury

The judge has a discretion to discharge the whole jury from giving a verdict. If the judge does so, the accused is not acquitted but may be retried on the same indictment before a fresh jury (*Winsor v R* (1866) LR 1 QB 390). According to *Blackstone's Commentaries* (1857 edn), a jury should not be discharged unless an 'evident necessity' for it has arisen. In *Winsor v R*, Erle CJ gave some further limited guidance on the subject, which may be summarised as follows: **D13.57**

(a) a jury should not be discharged unless a high degree of need for it arises;
(b) whether to discharge is purely a matter for the judge's discretion; and
(c) if the judge exercises the discretion wrongly by discharging the jury when that ought not to have been done, the appellate courts are powerless to correct the error (the extent of appellate review of the discharge of a jury, or the refusal to accede to an application for discharge, is addressed at **D13.72**).

These points must be read subject to the authorities set out at **D13.58** and **D13.66** which identify the proper approach of the court to possible bias or prejudice by a juror or jury and to alleged misconduct on the part of jurors.

Test for Bias or Prejudice

In *Sander v UK* [2000] Crim LR 767, the ECtHR emphasised the need for any allegation of bias to be looked at from an objective, as well as a subjective, standpoint. The question, in other words, is not only whether the jury which tried the accused can be shown to be biased, but also whether 'there were sufficient guarantees to exclude any objectively justified or legitimate doubts as to the impartiality of the court'. **D13.58**

D, a British national of Asian origin, had been tried in the Crown Court for conspiracy to defraud. During the trial, the judge received a note from a juror referring to racist remarks and jokes by other jurors. The judge directed the jury to disregard their prejudices and try the case solely on the evidence. The judge subsequently received a letter from the jury refuting the allegation of racial bias, and a letter from another juror apologising for making jokes and denying racial bias. The judge decided not to discharge the jury and D was found guilty. The appeal was dismissed by the Court of Appeal (see also *Agera* [2017] EWCA Crim 740, [2017] 2 Cr App R 22 (277)).

The ECtHR held that the allegations contained in the note were capable of causing objective legitimate doubts about the impartiality of the court, and these doubts were not dispelled by the jury's letter or the judge's directions. Article 6(1) of the ECHR had been violated. (See also *Montgomery v HM Advocate* [2003] 1 AC 641.) **D13.59**

In *Porter v Magill* [2001] UKHL 67, [2002] 2 AC 357, the House of Lords considered the question of bias in relation to the courts generally, and approved the test derived from *Re Medicaments and Related Classes of Goods (No. 2)* [2001] 1 WLR 700: would a fair-minded and informed observer conclude that there was a real possibility, or real danger (the two being the same) that the tribunal was biased (see **D3.32**).

This test, which is in accordance with that adopted by the ECtHR in *Sander*, was applied by the Court of Appeal in *Poole* [2001] EWCA Crim 2664, [2002] 1 WLR 1528; *Brown* [2001] EWCA Crim 2828 and *Mason* [2002] EWCA Crim 385, [2002] 2 Cr App R 38 (628). In *Szypusz v UK* [2010] ECHR 1323 the ECtHR said that the impartiality of a jury must be subjectively and objectively beyond doubt. In some cases where an issue arose this could only be achieved by discharge, in others lesser safeguards might achieve the same objective.

In *Abdroikov* [2007] UKHL 37, [2008] 1 Cr App R 21 (280), it was held that a fair-minded and informed observer, in determining whether there was a real possibility of bias on the part of a juror, would draw a distinction between the unconscious bias to which any member of the public might be subject and a specific bias that would result from a particular juror being professionally committed to one party to the proceedings, or from having special knowledge either of individuals involved in the case or as to the facts of the case apart from those provided by the evidence (see also **D13.27**). In *Khan* [2008] EWCA Crim 531, [2008] 2 Cr App R 13 (161), the Court of Appeal drew a distinction between partiality to a party and partiality to a witness. This distinction was approved and applied in *Cornwall* [2009] EWCA Crim 2458 and *A-G of Cayman Islands v Tibbetts* [2010] UKPC 8, [2010] 3 All ER 95.

If an issue arises as to whether a member of the jury has knowledge which makes him or her unsuitable to sit on that jury, the test in *Porter v Magill* must be applied in order to determine whether or not the requirements of fairness have been met and, in making that determination, there is no need to distinguish between the position under Article 6 and the position at common law (see *Burcombe* [2010] EWCA Crim 2818 and *LL* [2011] EWCA Crim 65, [2011] 1 Cr App R 27 (338) as examples of the application of that test). In *Pouladian-Kari* [2013] EWCA Crim 158, the Court of Appeal rejected the submission that a juror who had identified that he had experience relevant to a crucial issue in the case could nevertheless try the case only on the evidence.

In *Hewgill* [2011] EWCA Crim 1778 the Court of Appeal applied the test for bias set out in *Re Medicaments* where there was evidence that an accused on bail had spoken to jurors during a luncheon adjournment. The Court concluded that, whilst undesirable, that would not have made a material difference to the jury's deliberations, and a fair-minded, independent and informed observer would conclude that the jury would have been able to reach their verdict without taking any such conversation into account. This approach was then followed in *Mears* [2011] EWCA Crim 2651, where the Court concluded that the independent observer could not come to such a view where a juror had been in contact with her fiancé, sitting in the public gallery, during the trial and thus aware of those aspects of the proceedings that took place in the absence of the jury (see also *Ahmed* [2014] EWCA Crim 619).

Grounds for Discharge

D13.60 The decided cases deal with four main situations in which the question arises of the discharge of a jury, or in certain circumstances one juror. These are:

(a) when the jury cannot agree on their verdict (as discussed at **D19.84** ***et seq.***);
(b) when they may have been inadvertently prejudiced against the accused;
(c) when one or more of their number has misconducted themselves; and
(d) when they acquire or possess personal knowledge of the accused or the accused's bad character.

In addition, there is the related situation in which an application may be made for the discharge of the jury when the misconduct in question is that of the accused.

Accidental Prejudice

D13.61 It may be necessary for a jury to be discharged where prejudicial material is inadvertently adduced. The way in which this most commonly arises is if a witness refers to the accused's bad character during a trial where character has not been put in issue.

D13.62 **The Principle** Whether or not to discharge the jury is a matter for the judge's discretion. The test is whether any conviction would be unsafe in view of the revelation (*Lawson* [2005] EWCA Crim 84, [2007] 1 Cr App R 20 (277), followed in *Dicks* [2013] EWCA Crim 429). This involves consideration of the nature of the prejudicial material, the circumstances in which it was revealed, the strength of the respective cases and the extent to which the harm is otherwise remediable.

How the judge should act will depend on the facts of the particular case, and the court 'will not lightly interfere with' what the judge does (see Sachs LJ's judgment in *Weaver* [1968] 1 QB 353 at p. 359G).

In *Weaver*, the accused's previous convictions were revealed during incautious cross-examination of the police officer who had interviewed him. Sachs LJ said that every decision turned on its own facts and depended especially on 'the nature of what has been admitted into evidence, the circumstances in which it has been admitted and what, in the light of the circumstances of the case as a whole, is the correct course' (at p. 360B). The factors which particularly weighed against discharge were (a) that defence counsel had himself been responsible for inviting the answers which he then complained of, and (b) the degree of prejudice had been minimised by the judge's wise summing-up.

By contrast, in *Blackford* (1989) 89 Cr App R 239 the appellant was convicted of possessing cannabis with intent to supply after a police officer in cross-examination had gratuitously revealed that he had a previous conviction for a similar offence. The Court of Appeal concluded that this had been 'a deliberate attempt by the police to queer the appellant's pitch'. In those circumstances, the trial judge should have discharged the jury and ordered a retrial.

Revelation by a Co-accused Should an improper indication that one accused may be of bad character come from a co-accused, the Court of Appeal will be particularly loath to interfere with the trial judge's exercise of discretion against discharging the jury. In *Sutton* (1969) 53 Cr App R 504, Fenton Atkinson LJ (giving the Court of Appeal's judgment) said (at pp. 512–3): **D13.63**

> We have considered this matter with some anxiety, but...in all the circumstances of this case the judge was justified in exercising his discretion in the manner in which he did, and we would certainly be slow to lay down as a general rule that where one co-defendant says something of this nature about his co-accused, a judge must automatically allow a fresh trial, because it would simply make it too easy if a trial is not going well for one co-accused to say something which would secure his co-accused the advantages, if they are advantages, of a new trial.... there was an exercise of discretion by the trial judge, and the court is always slow to interfere with such an exercise of discretion.

Similarly, the fact that one accused changes plea during a trial does not necessarily require the discharge of the jury continuing to try the co-accused (*Sookram* [2011] UKPC 5).

Dealing with Prejudicial Revelation Where the accused is represented by counsel and prejudicial matters are accidentally disclosed, it would seem that counsel must take the initiative and apply at trial for the jury to be discharged. If counsel fails to do so, any appeal is liable to be dismissed, even if the circumstances were such that, had an application for discharge been made, it would probably have been granted (*Wattam* [1942] 1 All ER 178). **D13.64**

It is different if the accused is unrepresented. Should circumstances then arise in which an application for discharge might succeed, the judge is under a duty so to inform the accused. Failure to do so will be a material irregularity in the course of the trial necessitating the quashing of any conviction (*Featherstone* [1942] 2 All ER 672). However, provided the accused is invited to consider applying for discharge, no complaint may be made if the judge, in the proper exercise of his or her discretion, then decides to rule against the application (*Featherstone*).

Other Forms of Accidental Prejudice Other cases illustrate the same principle, namely that it is proper for a judge to exercise his or her discretion to discharge the jury when they inadvertently learn something to the accused's potential detriment. For example: **D13.65**

(a) Discovery that the accused faces further charges:
   (i) In *Dubarry* (1977) 64 Cr App R 7, while a jury trying D on one charge were considering their verdict, at least one member of the jury probably saw D being tried on another charge. The Court of Appeal held that the jury should have been discharged.
   (ii) In *Hutton* [1990] Crim LR 875, an order was made under the Contempt of Court Act 1981, s. 4(2), banning publication of the proceedings because further trials were pending. The copy of the order pinned to the court door and read by a juror published this fact. The Court of Appeal held that as the juror who read the order might well have discussed it with his fellow jurors, potential prejudice resulted directly from the irregularity.
   (iii) In *Wilson* (1995) *The Times*, 24 February 1995, the Court of Appeal held that there was a real danger of bias where one of the jurors was the wife of a prison officer at the prison where the accused were held on remand.

(b) Where matters are heard during the trial which, albeit not evidence against the accused, cannot be ignored by the jury:

(i) In *Fedrick* [1990] Crim LR 403, D1's co-accused, D2, changed his plea to guilty during the course of the trial. The prosecution had opened the case on the basis that D1 and D2 were 'in cahoots'. The judge emphasised to the jury that D2's plea of guilty made no difference to D1's position both at the time and in his summing-up. The Court of Appeal held that the jury could not properly consider D1's case in isolation from D2's. They should therefore have been discharged and a fresh trial held.

(ii) In *Boyes* [1991] Crim LR 717, as the judge concluded his summing-up on charges of rape and indecent assault, the complainant's mother shouted from the public gallery, 'When is it going to come out about the other five girls he has attacked?' The judge told the jury not to pay any attention to the outburst. The Court of Appeal criticised the judge's failure to inquire of the jury whether they had heard the outburst. If they had, one could hardly think of more damaging and prejudicial evidence being taken to the jury room. It was only after such inquiry, with the help of counsel and a very careful contemplation by the judge, that he could decide what to do. He should have considered a fresh trial. His failure to do so was a serious irregularity.

(iii) In *Maguire* [1997] 1 Cr App R 61, the judge told a defence witness who had refused to answer certain questions that he was to be arrested for contempt of court and would be dealt with at the end of the day. Defence counsel made an application to the judge to discharge the jury on the basis that D had been severely prejudiced. The judge refused, and directed the jury in due course that the arrest of the witness was not to affect their approach to the evidence, had nothing to do with D, and was to be ignored. The Court of Appeal held that the judge should have dealt with the witness in the absence of the jury; the direction given to the jury was not an adequate remedy as it could not have dispelled the inevitable prejudice which had been created.

(iv) In *Brown* [2006] EWCA Crim 827, [2006] 2 Cr App R (S) 107 (699), the Court of Appeal held that an assessment of the consequences of the jury hearing inadmissible material, whether by oversight or deliberate deployment, did not start with the presumption that the jury would be discharged. The same approach was taken in *Lawson* [2005] EWCA Crim 84, [2007] 1 Cr App R 20 (277). See *Mitcham v R* [2009] UKPC 5 for the proper approach to the jury hearing inadmissible material.

(v) Similarly, in *Tufail* [2006] EWCA Crim 2879, where the judge had inadvertently disclosed matters to the jury during his summing-up that had not been adduced during the trial, the Court of Appeal held that the factors to be considered in deciding whether this necessitated the discharge of the jury were (a) the nature of the judge's actions to cure the slip, (b) the strength of the case against the accused, and (c) the degree to which the jury were or may have been influenced by it.

(c) Where publicity or comment on issues relating to the accused's case are reported at a time when they may have an effect on the jury. For example, in *McCann* (1991) 92 Cr App R 239, M and others were tried for conspiracy to murder Mr King, who was then Secretary of State for Northern Ireland, and others. They elected not to give evidence. During the closing stages of the trial, the Home Secretary announced in the House of Commons the government's intention of changing the law on the right to silence. That night, in televised interviews, Mr King himself and Lord Denning expressed in strong terms their view that in terrorist cases a failure to answer questions or give evidence was tantamount to guilt. Although the Court of Appeal afforded great weight to the trial judge's exercise of discretion, its powers to review were not confined to cases of errors of principle or lack of material upon which the judge could properly have arrived at his decision. If necessary, it must examine anew the relevant facts and circumstances, and exercise a discretion by way of review if it considered that the failure to discharge the jury might have resulted in injustice. In this case there was a real risk that the jury had been influenced by the statements and the only way in which justice could be done and be seen to be done was by discharging the jury and ordering a retrial.

(d) Where there has been a material change in circumstances to the detriment of the accused which cannot otherwise be rectified:
   (i) In *Ricketts* [1991] Crim LR 915, the trial judge gave leave for the statement of S to be read, on the basis that S's absence was caused by fear. After the jury had retired, S arrived, and the judge saw him in chambers, without informing counsel. Apparently S denied that he had failed to appear because he was frightened. The judge told S that his evidence had been read and was not in dispute and that he was free to go. The judge gave no indication to counsel that S had denied staying away through fear. D was convicted and appealed. The Court of Appeal held that S's evidence had been given prominence on a false basis, i.e. that it was so damning that D or someone on his behalf would seek violent revenge if he testified. In those circumstances, an application to discharge the jury could not properly have been resisted.
   (ii) In *Robson* [1992] Crim LR 655, the trial judge decided to direct the jury on a different basis to that on which the parties had presented the evidence. The Court of Appeal found that the fresh issue raised by the judge did not merely introduce a new interpretation of the evidence. It opened up the possibility of conviction on a different factual basis from that put forward by the Crown, and one which had not been fully explored. That resulted in unfairness to the defence, and was a material irregularity. The best course would have been to discharge the jury.

Misconduct by a Juror

The judge has discretion to allow the jury to separate (Juries Act 1974, s. 13). It is standard practice to allow them to separate both for luncheon and overnight adjournments. The discretion of the judge to allow the jury to separate was extended by the CJPO 1994, s. 43, which allows the judge to permit separation even after the jury have retired to consider their verdict. **D13.66**

Inevitably, the jury will have the opportunity to speak about the case with those who are not of their number, and to undertake researches of their own. However, they should be warned on the first occasion they separate that that is something they must not do (see the guidance in the *Crown Court Compendium* (July 2020), ch. 21-2, and *A-G v Davey* [2013] EWHC 2317 (Admin), [2014] 1 Cr App R 1 (1)).

Most cases coming before the Court of Appeal on discharge of the jury due to misconduct concern allegations that, in defiance of the warning, one or more jurors spoke to others about the case, or made their own researches. For example: **D13.67**

(a) In *Davis* [2001] 1 Cr App R 8 (115), the foreman of the jury was found to have visited the scene of the crime during the trial, and the Court of Appeal held that this was a serious material irregularity.
(b) In *Karakaya* [2005] EWCA Crim 346, [2005] 2 Cr App R 5 (77), the Court of Appeal stated that a juror should not conduct private research for material that might have a bearing on the trial. If such material were obtained or privately used, two fundamental linked rules were violated: the first was of open justice, and the second was that the prosecution and defence were entitled to a fair opportunity to address all material considered by the jury when reaching their verdict. See also *Thompson* [2010] EWCA Crim 1623, [2010] 2 Cr App R 27 (259) in relation to improper internet activity.
(c) In *Marshall* [2007] EWCA Crim 35, the Court of Appeal recommended that the judge should warn the jury, at the outset of the trial, that they must try the case on the evidence that they heard in court and on nothing else, which meant that they should not conduct their own private research, e.g., using the internet.

See also *A-G v Dallas* [2012] EWHC 156 (Admin), [2012] 1 WLR 991 and CrimPD VI, paras. 26M.5 to 26M.13 (see Supplement, **CPD.26M**). Jurors who engage in their own researches may also be guilty of offences under the Juries Act 1974, ss. 20A and 20B (see **B14.133** ***et seq.***). In *McDonnell* [2010] EWCA Crim 2352, [2011] 1 Cr App R 28 (347), where a juror had brought the results of his researches to the jury room, the question was whether the jury might be influenced to reach its verdict on the basis of that material, which had not been addressed by the parties in court.

Juror's Personal Knowledge of a Witness, the Accused or of the Accused's Bad Character

D13.68 A further situation in which the judge will have to consider discharge either of the whole jury or of an individual juror is when it comes to light that a juror knows either the accused or a witness in the case. The problem is particularly acute where the juror may know the accused to be of bad character. The following propositions summarise the Court of Appeal's decisions relating to a juror's possible bias on account of knowledge of the accused's character.

(a) A juror who knows the accused or who knows from hearsay of the accused's bad character ought not to sit on the jury, and should ask to be excused from service. Failure to disqualify him or herself on account of knowledge of the accused is 'quite improper' (per Lord Parker CJ in *Box* [1964] 1 QB 430 at p. 435, for which see **D13.49**). Depending on the facts of the particular case, previous contact with a witness may not disqualify the juror, but in reality if the juror has any previous acquaintance with the accused, however slight, it is safer for that juror to be removed.

(b) If the defence are aware at the time the jury is empanelled that a juror is open to objection for the reasons stated in (a) they should obviously challenge for cause or (more simply) ask prosecuting counsel to stand the juror by. Although the Court of Appeal has stated that a juror is not automatically disqualified by knowledge of the accused's previous convictions (see per Lord Parker CJ in *Box*), those statements are in the context of cases where the relevant facts were not known to the defence until after the time for challenging had passed. They do not, it is submitted, cast doubt on the fundamental proposition that a person who knows facts detrimental to the accused should not be on the jury.

(c) Where a juror's possible knowledge of the accused is not brought to the court's attention until after the trial has commenced, the judge must consider discharging the individual juror and/or the entire jury. For example, in *Hood* [1968] 2 All ER 56, defence counsel informed the judge that H's wife, who had just given evidence for the defence, had recognised a jury member as a person who lived in the same road as her mother and would consequently know about her husband's previous convictions. The Court of Appeal confirmed that (a) a juror is not automatically disqualified by knowledge of the accused's previous convictions, and (b) that the Court of Appeal will not inquire into what occurred in the jury room. Moreover, the judge was right not to address questions to the juror himself about the allegations but should have heard evidence from the wife.

(d) If a juror's knowledge of or bias against the accused does not come to the defence's attention until after conviction, an appeal is most unlikely to succeed since the appellant will have to show that the juror had made up his or her mind before the trial started to convict the accused regardless of the evidence (*Box* [1964] 1 QB 430).

(e) See also *Eaton* [2020] EWCA Crim 595, where a judge refused an application to discharge the jury from reaching verdicts where limited evidence showed that one of the jurors had a distant link to one of the defendants who had given evidence which was damaging to his co-defendants. Although the judge discharged that particular juror, on the basis that there may have been a perception of bias, he concluded that, on the facts, there was no actual bias. The trial judge had closely followed the requirements set out in CrimPD V, paras. 26M.1 to 26M.26, and on the facts of the case there was no actual bias. Accordingly, the subsequent appeal against conviction failed.

Similar issues may arise where a juror has knowledge of the area of activity that is the subject of the allegations, as was highlighted in *Pouladian-Kari* [2013] EWCA Crim 158.

Misconduct of the Accused

D13.69 In more recent times, the Court of Appeal has made clear that action by the accused, albeit that it may serve to prejudice the jury, will not, of itself, form the basis for the discharge of the jury. For example, in *Russell* [2006] EWCA Crim 470, the Court of Appeal considered whether misconduct by D during the course of the trial might result in the discharge of the jury. D, who was being tried for attempted murder, leapt from the dock and attacked the judge. Once the incident was over, the defence advocate asked the judge to discharge the jury on the basis that they had witnessed the attack and could no longer try D impartially. The judge refused to do so. The Court of Appeal dismissed the appeal. D's conduct was manipulative and intended to abort the trial. To continue with the trial was neither unfair, nor capable of being seen to be unfair.

Investigation of Misconduct

The procedure to be followed in investigating any alleged misconduct is set out in CrimPD VI, paras. 26M.5 to 26M.18 (see Supplement, **CPD.26M**), by reference to the following steps: (i) consider isolating juror(s), (ii) consult with advocates, (iii) consider appropriate provisional measures (which may include surrender/seizure of electronic communications devices and taking the accused into custody), (iv) seek to establish basic facts of jury irregularity, (v) further consult with advocates, (vi) decide what to do in relation to conduct of trial and (vii) consider ancillary matters, such as contempt proceedings. **D13.70**

In *Blackwell* [1995] 2 Cr App R 625, the Court of Appeal emphasised that the judge has a duty to investigate if there is any realistic suspicion that any juror has been approached or pressured or otherwise tampered with. Such investigation will probably include questioning of individual jurors or even the jury as a whole. Questioning must be directed to the possibility that the jury's independence has been compromised, rather than to their deliberations on the issues in the case (see also *Oke* [1997] Crim LR 898 and *Appiah* [1998] Crim LR 134, and the standard direction on the need to preserve the privacy of the jury room).

In *Orgles* [1994] 4 All ER 533, the point at issue was whether the recorder at trial had acted correctly in questioning individual jurors, who had complained of dissension in the jury room. The Court of Appeal held that the procedure adopted by the recorder of initially questioning the two jurors separately was wrong and amounted to an irregularity. The circumstances giving rise to an inference that an individual juror or jurors could not fulfil their duties normally arose externally. It was usual in that situation to question the individual juror in open court so that the trial judge might make inquiries without jeopardising the continued participation of the whole jury (see also *Davey* [2017] EWCA Crim 1062).

Occasionally, however, the circumstances were internal to the jury, whether through individual characteristics or through interaction with fellow jury members. In the latter circumstances, the problem was not the capacity of one or more individuals to carry out their duties, but the capacity of the jury as a whole. The appropriate course therefore was for the jury as a whole to be asked in open court as to their capacity to continue with the trial. Thereafter, it would be a matter for the judge's exercise of discretion as to whether no order was made, the whole jury was discharged or individual jurors up to three in number were discharged. See also *Farooq* [1995] Crim LR 169 and *Burland* [2013] EWCA Crim 518.

Consultation with the Parties After making such inquiries as are appropriate, CrimPD VI, paras. 26M.10 and 26M.22, invite the judge to consult the parties before discharging a juror. However, discharge is not dependent on their consent (see **D13.52**) and it is not absolutely essential even to consult them (see *Richardson* [1979] 3 All ER 247, where the court received a telephone message from a juror that her husband had died during an overnight adjournment and the judge discharged her without any consultation with counsel; the conviction was nonetheless upheld). **D13.71**

In *Bryan* [2001] EWCA Crim 2550, members of the jury were overheard discussing the case on a bus, and referring to one elderly juror who had considered the accused guilty throughout the trial. The judge decided not to discharge the jury, but told them that the discussion was scandalous and a possible contempt of court, and directed them to return verdicts based on the evidence, and not on prejudice. The Court of Appeal suggested the following steps should be taken where there was a major crisis of that sort:

(a) the judge should organise a pause for consideration — the jury could be told to cease deliberating and to await the ruling of the court as to when they would be asked to continue their deliberations;
(b) counsel and the judge should then adjourn for half an hour or so to allow proper consideration of the steps to take;
(c) the judge should then hear submissions from counsel, and, if necessary, rise to consider what to do.

See CrimPD VI, paras. 26M.10 to 26M.13, for the procedure for such consultation (see Supplement, **CPD.26M**).

Appellate Review of the Exercise of the Discretion to Discharge

D13.72 In *Winsor v R* (1866) LR 1 QB 390, it was made clear that the decision whether to discharge is purely a matter for the judge's discretion; and if the judge exercises this discretion wrongly by discharging the jury when this ought not to have been done, the appellate courts are powerless to correct the error.

In *Hambery* [1977] QB 924, Lawton LJ reviewed the earlier authorities (especially *Winsor v R*), and concluded that the view that discharge was solely a matter for the trial judge should be understood as referring only to discharge of the entire jury (at pp. 928F–929E). A decision to discharge one juror and continue with the remainder is a matter that may be raised on appeal. If the judge acted capriciously, that would be a material irregularity in the course of the trial which could lead to the quashing of any conviction (at p. 929F).

However, that the decision to discharge the jury is unlikely to be interfered with on appeal was confirmed in *Gorman* [1987] 2 All ER 435. D, who was convicted at a retrial following the jury at his first trial being discharged, appealed on the ground that a note from the first jury to the judge was to the effect that they were deadlocked, with a split 9–3 in favour of acquittal. The judge simply told counsel that the jury were split and would be incapable of reaching a verdict, without revealing the numbers, and, with counsels' agreement, the jury were discharged. After D's conviction at the retrial, the defence discovered by chance the proportions in which the first jury had been split and argued on appeal that the judge had exercised his discretion to discharge the jury improperly. The Court of Appeal concluded that the law remained as stated in *Winsor v R*, namely that, if the first jury had as a matter of fact been discharged, a court hearing an appeal against the second jury's verdict had no power to review the propriety or otherwise of the discharge.

The position is different should the judge be invited to discharge the jury and refuse to do so. If the accused is then convicted, the accused may appeal on the basis that continuing with the original jury casts doubt on the safety of the conviction. Such cases have given rise to a considerable amount of authority on when judges ought to discharge juries, although, as it is a matter for discretion, the appellate court is unlikely to interfere save in extreme cases.

D13.73 **Risk of Contamination** In *Barraclough* [2000] Crim LR 324, the jury were discharged because they had come to know, as a result of the evidence, of the fact that D had previous convictions, in circumstances in which that information should not have been revealed. The judge discharged the jury, who were in their first week of jury service, and a new jury were empanelled on the following day. On appeal it was argued that the retrial should have been delayed until there was an entirely new panel of jurors or that the first jury should have been discharged from further service. The Court of Appeal dismissed the appeal, in view of the fact that the court centre in question was a large one, with a panel of jurors at any one time of over 200, and in the light of the clear warning delivered by the trial judge.

As to the general issue of contamination and retrials, their lordships took the view that in smaller court centres, where there was a greater likelihood of jurors meeting, the court might have to consider discharging the first jury from further attendance or delaying the retrial for, say, a fortnight. In larger court centres, there should be no such problem. Defence counsel should in any event raise any concerns about contamination at the time that the first jury was discharged. If counsel did not, it would not ordinarily be open to an accused to raise the point on appeal.

ISSUES THAT MAY BE TRIED BY ONE JURY

Subject to the exceptions mentioned below, a jury may try only one issue; that is, once it has brought in a verdict on the issue for which it was empanelled, it must be split up with the individual jurors going back into the pool of jurors in waiting with a view to being selected by ballot for further juries. **D13.74**

The exceptional cases in which a jury may be kept together to try a second issue are: (a) where the trial of the second issue begins within 24 hours from the time when the jury was constituted, and (b) where the trial of an issue of unfitness to plead has been postponed until the end of the prosecution evidence and the judge directs that the jury empanelled to try the general issue shall also try unfitness (Juries Act 1974, s. 11(5)) (see **D12.8**). Even where it is decided that a jury shall try a second issue, the court may order individual members of it to be replaced by others selected by ballot from the jury panel (s. 11(6)).

Juries Act 1974, s. 11

(4) Subject to subsection (5) below, the jury selected by any one ballot shall try only one issue (but any juror shall be liable to be selected on more than one ballot).

(5) Subsection (4) above shall not prevent—

(a) the trial of two or more issues by the same jury if the trial of the second or last issue begins within 24 hours from the time when the jury is constituted, or

...

(c) in a criminal case beginning with a special plea, the trial of the accused on the general issue by the jury trying the special plea.

(6) In the cases within subsection (5)(a) [and (b)] above the court may, on the trial of the second or any subsequent issue, instead of proceeding with the same jury in its entirety, order any juror to withdraw, if the court considers that he could be justly challenged or excused, or if the parties to the proceedings consent, and the juror to replace him shall . . . be selected by ballot in open court.

An important corollary of the rule that a jury may try only one issue is that, if an accused is charged in two or more separate indictments, there must be a separate trial for each indictment (*Crane v DPP* [1921] 2 AC 299), and, subject to s. 11(5)(a), a fresh jury must be empanelled for each trial. A purported trial by one jury of two indictments is a nullity (*Crane*) and that is so even if the parties consented to the course adopted (*Dennis* [1924] 1 KB 867).

JUDGE-ONLY TRIALS ON INDICTMENT

The CJA 2003, ss. 43 to 50, introduced for the first time in England and Wales the concept of trial on indictment without a jury. There were two different sets of circumstances: fraud trials and jury tampering. In addition, the DVCVA 2004 introduced judge-only trials in the case of sample counts. **D13.75**

Fraud Trials

The CJA 2003, s. 43, gave the prosecution the right to apply for a trial in the Crown Court to take place without a jury (i.e. in front of a judge sitting alone) in the case of serious or complex fraud. However, s. 43 was never brought into force and has been repealed by the Protection of Freedoms Act 2012, s. 113 and sch. 10, part 10, without any replacement provision. **D13.76**

Jury Tampering

Where there is a danger of jury tampering, the prosecution will be able to apply for the trial to be conducted without a jury. Further, where the jury has been discharged in the course of a trial **D13.77** because of jury tampering, the prosecution will be able to apply for it to continue without a jury. 'Jury tampering' is likely to include threatened or actual harm to, or intimidation or bribery of, a jury or any of its members, or their family or friends or property. For the prosecution's application to be granted in respect of a trial which has yet to take place, the court must be satisfied that two conditions are fulfilled:

(a) there is evidence of a real and present danger that jury tampering would take place (CJA 2003, s. 44(4)); and
(b) there is so substantial a risk of jury tampering that it is necessary in the interests of justice for the trial to be conducted without a jury, notwithstanding any steps (e.g., police protection) that might reasonably be taken to prevent the risk (s. 44(5)).

In *T* [2009] EWCA Crim 1035, [2009] 2 Cr App R 25 (412), the Court of Appeal considered these provisions, concluding that they were 'unequivocal and unambiguous'. If the conditions are met, the court has no alternative to a non-jury trial. The court must be satisfied that the conditions are met to the criminal standard. The risk to be considered in s. 44(4) may arise at any stage of the trial process and, in weighing up the steps that might be taken to avoid a risk of tampering for the purposes of s. 44(5), the court may have regard to the cost and feasibility of the measures and their impact on the jury subjected to them (see also *S (K)* [2009] EWCA Crim 2377, [2010] 1 Cr App R 20 (285); *JSM* [2010] EWCA Crim 1755, [2011] 1 Cr App R 5 (42); *S (K) (No. 2)* [2010] EWCA Crim 1756, [2011] 1 Cr App R 6 (46)). There is no requirement that the material on the basis of which the court exercises its powers under s. 44 must be disclosed to the accused. Equally, there is no requirement that the eventual trial judge should have to consider all that material (*Twomey* [2011] EWCA Crim 8, [2011] 1 Cr App R 29 (356)).

In *McManaman* [2016] EWCA Crim 3, [2016] 1 WLR 1096, the Court of Appeal stressed the importance of the judge acting as soon as there was sufficient material to form a conclusion that there had been tampering, rather than waiting for any police investigation to have concluded. The Court also stressed that there was no need for there to be a proven link between the tampering and the accused, especially as tampering was often likely to have been undertaken by a third party.

D13.78 **The Court's Decision** Where the trial is already under way and the judge is minded to discharge the jury in accordance with common-law powers because jury tampering appears to have occurred, the judge must hear representations from the defence and the prosecution as to how to proceed. In *T* [2009] EWCA Crim 1035, [2009] 2 Cr App R 25 (412), the Court of Appeal concluded that it would be appropriate for a court to reach its decision in reliance on sensitive material not disclosed to the defence. If the judge decides to discharge the jury, the trial may be ordered to continue without a jury if the judge is satisfied that this would be fair to the defendant. Alternatively, the judge may terminate the trial, and has the option of ordering that the retrial is to take place without a jury. Again, the judge must be satisfied that the danger of jury tampering is such as to make trial without jury necessary in the interests of justice, notwithstanding any steps that could be taken to prevent jury tampering (s. 46(5)). In *T* the Court of Appeal stressed that the preferred option would be for the judge to continue to hear the case alone, rather than to order a retrial. If a retrial is ordered, it does not have to be heard before the original judge who made that order (see also *S (K)* [2009] EWCA Crim 2377, [2010] 1 Cr App R 20 (285)). In *Guthrie* [2011] EWCA Crim 1338, [2011] 2 Cr App R 20 (260), Lord Judge CJ emphasised that the jurisdiction under s. 46 adds to, but does not replace, the court's existing powers to deal with jury difficulties.

D13.79 **Right of Appeal** There is a right of appeal to the Court of Appeal by both the defence and the prosecution against any decision made by the court at a preparatory hearing on any application for a trial without a jury (s. 45(5)). There is also a right of appeal against any order to continue a trial in the absence of a jury, or for a retrial to be conducted in the absence of a jury (s. 47).

Application Where a court orders a trial to be conducted or continued without a jury, the trial will proceed in the usual way, except that functions which a jury would have performed will be performed by the judge alone. If the accused is convicted, the judge will have to give reasons for the conviction (s. 48). D13.80

Criminal Justice Act 2003, ss. 44 to 48

44.—(1) This section applies where one or more defendants are to be tried on indictment for one or more offences.

(2) The prosecution may apply to a judge of the Crown Court for the trial to be conducted without a jury.

(3) If an application under subsection (2) is made and the judge is satisfied that both of the following two conditions are fulfilled, he must make an order that the trial is to be conducted without a jury; but if he is not so satisfied he must refuse the application.

(4) The first condition is that there is evidence of a real and present danger that jury tampering would take place.

(5) The second condition is that, notwithstanding any steps (including the provision of police protection) which might reasonably be taken to prevent jury tampering, the likelihood that it would take place would be so substantial as to make it necessary in the interests of justice for the trial to be conducted without a jury.

(6) The following are examples of cases where there may be evidence of a real and present danger that jury tampering would take place—

(a) a case where the trial is a retrial and the jury in the previous trial was discharged because jury tampering had taken place,

(b) a case where jury tampering has taken place in previous criminal proceedings involving the defendant or any of the defendants,

(c) a case where there has been intimidation, or attempted intimidation, of any person who is likely to be a witness in the trial.

45.—(1) This section applies—

(a) [Repealed]

(b) to an application under section 44.

(2) An application to which this section applies must be determined at a preparatory hearing (within the meaning of the 1987 Act or Part 3 of the 1996 Act).

(3) The parties to a preparatory hearing at which an application to which this section applies is to be determined must be given an opportunity to make representations with respect to the application.

(4) In section 7(1) of the 1987 Act (which sets out the purposes of preparatory hearings) for paragraphs (a) to (c) there is substituted—

'(a) identifying issues which are likely to be material to the determinations and findings which are likely to be required during the trial,

(b) if there is to be a jury, assisting their comprehension of those issues and expediting the proceedings before them,

(c) determining an application to which section 45 of the Criminal Justice Act 2003 applies,'.

. . .

(10) In this section—

'the 1987 Act' means the Criminal Justice Act 1987,

'the 1996 Act' means the Criminal Procedure and Investigations Act 1996.

46.—(1) This section applies where—

(a) a judge is minded during a trial on indictment to discharge the jury, and

(b) he is so minded because jury tampering appears to have taken place.

(2) Before taking any steps to discharge the jury, the judge must—

(a) inform the parties that he is minded to discharge the jury,

(b) inform the parties of the grounds on which he is so minded, and

(c) allow the parties an opportunity to make representations.

(3) Where the judge, after considering any such representations, discharges the jury, he may make an order that the trial is to continue without a jury if, but only if, he is satisfied—

(a) that jury tampering has taken place, and

(b) that to continue the trial without a jury would be fair to the defendant or defendants;

but this is subject to subsection (4).

(4) If the judge considers that it is necessary in the interests of justice for the trial to be terminated, he must terminate the trial.

(5) Where the judge terminates the trial under subsection (4), he may make an order that any new trial which is to take place must be conducted without a jury if he is satisfied in respect of the new trial that both of the conditions set out in section 44 are likely to be fulfilled.

(6) Subsection (5) is without prejudice to any other power that the judge may have on terminating the trial.

(7) Subject to subsection (5), nothing in this section affects the application of section 44 in relation to any new trial which takes place following the termination of the trial.

47.—(1) An appeal shall lie to the Court of Appeal from an order under section 46(3) or (5).

(2) Such an appeal may be brought only with the leave of the judge or the Court of Appeal.

(3) An order from which an appeal under this section lies is not to take effect—

(a) before the expiration of the period for bringing an appeal under this section, or

(b) if such an appeal is brought, before the appeal is finally disposed of or abandoned.

(4) On the termination of the hearing of an appeal under this section, the Court of Appeal may confirm or revoke the order.

(5) Subject to rules of court made under section 53(1) of the Senior Courts Act 1981 (power by rules to distribute business of Court of Appeal between its civil and criminal divisions)—

(a) the jurisdiction of the Court of Appeal under this section is to be exercised by the criminal division of that court, and

(b) references in this section to the Court of Appeal are to be construed as references to that division.

48.—(1) The effect of an order under section 44 or 46(5) is that the trial to which the order relates is to be conducted without a jury.

(2) The effect of an order under section 46(3) is that the trial to which the order relates is to be continued without a jury.

(3) Where a trial is conducted or continued without a jury, the court is to have all the powers, authorities and jurisdiction which the court would have had if the trial had been conducted or continued with a jury (including power to determine any question and to make any finding which would be required to be determined or made by a jury).

(4) Except where the context otherwise requires, any reference in an enactment to a jury, the verdict of a jury or the finding of a jury is to be read, in relation to a trial conducted or continued without a jury, as a reference to the court, the verdict of the court or the finding of the court.

(5) Where a trial is conducted or continued without a jury and the court convicts a defendant—

(a) the court must give a judgment which states the reasons for the conviction at, or as soon as reasonably practicable after, the time of the conviction, and

(b) the reference in section 18(2) of the Criminal Appeal Act 1968 (notice of appeal or of application for leave to appeal to be given within 28 days from date of conviction etc.) to the date of the conviction is to be read as a reference to the date of the judgment mentioned in paragraph (a).

(6) Nothing in this Part affects the requirement under section 4A of the Criminal Procedure (Insanity) Act 1964 that any question, finding or verdict mentioned in that section be determined, made or returned by a jury.

Sample Counts

D13.81 A further avenue by which the prosecution can seek trial on indictment without a jury is opened up by the DVCVA 2004, s. 17. In essence, it is for the jury to try sample counts, with the remaining counts in the indictment capable of being tried by a judge sitting alone.

The application by the prosecution may be acceded to by the judge if the following conditions are fulfilled:

(a) the number of counts in the indictment is such that a trial of them all by jury would be impracticable;

(b) each count to be tried by the jury can be regarded as a sample of counts that could for their part be tried by a judge alone; and

(c) it is in the interests of justice to grant the order sought.

The judge should have regard to any steps that might be taken to facilitate a jury trial, but not if that might result in the defendant receiving a lesser sentence.

Domestic Violence, Crime and Victims Act 2004, ss. 17 and 18 **D13.82**

17.—(1) The prosecution may apply to a judge of the Crown Court for a trial on indictment to take place on the basis that the trial of some, but not all, of the counts included in the indictment may be conducted without a jury.

(2) If such an application is made and the judge is satisfied that the following three conditions are fulfilled, he may make an order for the trial to take place on the basis that the trial of some, but not all, of the counts included in the indictment may be conducted without a jury.

(3) The first condition is that the number of counts included in the indictment is likely to mean that a trial by jury involving all of those counts would be impracticable.

(4) The second condition is that, if an order under subsection (2) were made, each count or group of counts which would accordingly be tried with a jury can be regarded as a sample of counts which could accordingly be tried without a jury.

(5) The third condition is that it is in the interests of justice for an order under subsection (2) to be made.

(6) In deciding whether or not to make an order under subsection (2), the judge must have regard to any steps which might reasonably be taken to facilitate a trial by jury.

(7) But a step is not to be regarded as reasonable if it could lead to the possibility of a defendant in the trial receiving a lesser sentence than would be the case if that step were not taken.

(8) An order under subsection (2) must specify the counts which may be tried without a jury.

(9) For the purposes of this section and sections 18 to 20, a count may not be regarded as a sample of other counts unless the defendant in respect of each count is the same person.

18.—(1) An application under section 17 must be determined at a preparatory hearing.

(2) Section 7(1) of the 1987 Act and section 29(2) of the 1996 Act are to have effect as if the purposes there mentioned included the purpose of determining an application under section 17.

(3) Section 29(1) of the 1996 Act is to have effect as if the grounds on which a judge of the Crown Court may make an order under that provision included the ground that an application under section 17 has been made.

(4) The parties to a preparatory hearing at which an application under section 17 is to be determined must be given an opportunity to make representations with respect to the application.

(5) Section 9(11) of the 1987 Act and section 35(1) of the 1996 Act are to have effect as if they also provided for an appeal to the Court of Appeal to lie from the determination by a judge of an application under section 17.

(6) In this section—

'preparatory hearing' means a preparatory hearing within the meaning of the 1987 Act or Part 3 of the 1996 Act;

'the 1987 Act' means the Criminal Justice Act 1987;

'the 1996 Act' means the Criminal Procedure and Investigations Act 1996.

Section D14 Special Measures and Anonymity Orders

SPECIAL MEASURES FOR WITNESSES: GENERAL

Introduction

D14.1 Since the YJCEA 1999, the prevailing ethos is that the orthodox procedures of the adversarial trial must be adapted to the needs of all child and other vulnerable witnesses, including those with physical or mental disabilities, appearing in the criminal and civil courts (*Barker* [2010] EWCA Crim 4 at [42]; CrimPR 3.8(3) and (6) and 3.13 (see Supplement, **R3.8** and **R3.13**); CrimPD I, paras. 3D.1, 3D.2 and 3E.4 (see Supplement, **CPD.3D**)). Advocates must adapt to the witness, not the other way round (*Lubemba* [2014] EWCA Crim 2064, [2015] 1 WLR 1579 at [45]). Yet 21 years after the full panoply of special measures were introduced by the YJCEA 1999, three highly critical reports have found that vulnerable people are still unable to participate effectively in the criminal system (J Plotnikoff and R Woolfson, *Falling Short? A Snapshot of Young Witness Policy and Practice* (NSPCC, February 2019, tinyurl.com/y55hemwz); Sir Nicholas Blake, *Understanding Courts* (JUSTICE, 2019, tinyurl.com/y3w9sgwy); HH Peter Rook QC, *Prosecuting Sexual Offences* (JUSTICE, 2019, tinyurl.com/yb86vjj2)).

The Equality Act 2010 demands substantive equality for every person appearing in court to ensure their full participation, and provides that the court has safeguarding responsibilities in respect of children and vulnerable adults, often discharged through judicial discretion. The Bar Standards Board (BSB) has published a list of competencies which every barrister is expected to have from the outset in order to act in youth proceedings, defined as all cases heard in the youth court and cases involving defendants under 18 in the magistrates' courts, Crown Court or higher courts (*Youth Proceedings Competences* (February 2017)). These specialist competencies must now be registered with the Board as part of the practising certificate application in order to practise in the youth court (*BSB Handbook*, rS59). The *Equal Treatment Bench Book* (March 2020), with comprehensive chapters and appendices on child, disabled, and other vulnerable witnesses, including in modern slavery cases, is essential reading for advocates, as is the expanding range of toolkits on The Advocate's Gateway (www.theadvocatesgateway.org), endorsed as representing best practice by CrimPD I, para. 3D.7, and in *Lubemba* [2014] EWCA Crim 2064, [2015] 1 WLR 1579 at [40]. The *Crown Court Compendium* (July 2020), chs. 3-6, 3-7, 10-5, and appendix IV, and the *Equal Treatment Bench Book* (March 2020), ch. 2, provide useful summaries of procedures and considerations for the evidence of children and vulnerable witnesses, including ground rules hearings (GRH).

The family court's consent is not required for any child, even a ward of the court, to be interviewed by police or security services, or to be called as a witness in a criminal trial in this jurisdiction (*Re a Ward of Court* [2017] EWHC 1022 (Fam), [2017] Fam 369). Consent is required for a ward to testify in another jurisdiction, a factor being the availability of special measures there (*Re X (Worship) (Foreign Proceedings: Child's Evidence* [2019] EWHC 91 (Fam) at [22])]. This stance has been made possible by the wide availability of special measures in the criminal courts of England and Wales.

Under the YJCEA 1999, s. 53(3) (see **F4.21** ***et seq.***), all witnesses regardless of age (or disability) are presumed competent. If that competence is put in issue, it need only be demonstrated that the witness can understand questions and give answers that can be understood, competence being 'witness, trial and issue specific' (*IA* [2013] EWCA Crim 1308 at [70]). This minimal test has resulted in younger children and adults with mental disorders or severe impairments being witnesses in circumstances that once would have been unthinkable (see, e.g., *Watts* [2010] EWCA Crim 1824 and *F* [2013] EWCA Crim 424, [2013] 1 WLR 2143; *Equal Treatment Bench Book* (March 2020), ch. 5). The YJCEA 1999, ss. 16 to 30, modify the orthodox trial process for witnesses who are in fear, suffering from a physical or mental disability, or are complainants of sexual offences, as well as witnesses aged under 18, to enable them to provide their best evidence. This section addresses the availability and use of special measures directions (SMDs) for witnesses in these categories. In general, the statutory regime of SMDs has been found to be compliant with the ECHR, Article 6; residual issues of compliance are noted below.

This section also considers witness anonymity orders made under the CAJA 2009 (see **D14.72** ***et seq.***). For investigation anonymity orders, see **D1.210**.

The Court of Appeal has stressed that the wide range of special measures has not altered the court's responsibility for the fairness of the trial; trial judges are expected to deal with specific communication problems faced by any defendant or witness as part of their ordinary control of the judicial process (*Cox* [2012] EWCA Crim 549, [2012] 2 Cr App R 6 (63) at [29]; *F* [2013] EWCA Crim 424, [2013] 1 WLR 2143). Whilst the statutory regime is comprehensive in its application to non-defendant witnesses, it does not oust this residual inherent jurisdiction to make ad hoc modifications to the orthodox procedures for a particular non-eligible witness in the interests of justice (YJCEA 1999, s. 19(6); CrimPR 3.5(1)). This has provided the route to special measures for vulnerable defendants who were initially excluded from the statutory regime, including access to intermediaries. That residual inherent jurisdiction has been viewed as limited, and not extending to permitting a witness to testify by live link or by video-recorded interview in circumstances not covered by the YJCEA 1999 (*Ukpabio* [2007] EWCA Crim 2108, [2008] 1 WLR 728; *H* [2003] EWCA Crim 1208). The failure to cater for physically disabled defendants is an obvious gap in the statutory scheme: see *Hamberger* [2017] EWCA Crim 273, [2017] 2 Cr App R 9 (81) at [36], holding that video link is only available to mentally disordered defendants under the YJCEA 1999, s. 33A, and not to one unable to attend court due to a physical disability. The current view of the Court of Appeal appears to be that wherever a statute makes specific but limited provision for defendants' participation in the trial, that ousts the residual jurisdiction to make other provision. However, the issue could be revisited in light of : the Equality Act 2010, the *Equal Treatment Bench Book* (March 2020), ch. 3, paras. 66 to 67, 87 to 88, and the UN Convention on the Rights of Persons with Disabilities (which have not yet been argued in this context); active case management powers including facilitating participation of the defendant (CrimPR 1.1(2)(a) to (e), 3.8(3)(b) and 3.13(c)(v); CrimPD I, para. 3D.2), and using technology (CrimPR 3.2(2)(h)). See Supplement, **R3.2**, and *Clark* [2015] EWCA Crim 2192, [2016] 1 Cr App R (S) 52 (332) at [19]–[22]).

The litmus test of the special measures regime appears in s. 19(2), requiring the court to consider which measures will 'maximise the quality of the evidence'. For witnesses under 18, the test in s. 19(2) is presumed to be satisfied by playing their recorded interviews with the police as their evidence-in-chief, and by cross-examination via video link (s. 21(2)). In certain circumstances this presumption can be displaced. In all other cases, s. 19(2) requires that the measures be tailored to the needs of the individual witness and defendant, and CrimPD I, para. 3D.2, and CrimPD V, paras. 18A.1 and 18A.2 (see Supplement, **CPD.18A**), now encourage flexibility in devising a combination of appropriate special measures. This is a response to the common practice of police and prosecutors ignoring the wording and spirit of s. 19(2), operating on assumptions that the presumptive measures must be used without evaluating witnesses' specific needs and preferences, and without considering early special measures strategy meetings. **D14.2**

Range of Special Measures Available

D14.3 The YJCEA 1999, Part II, ch. I, ss. 16 to 33, as amended by the CAJA 2009, Part 3, ch. 3 (ss. 98 to 104 and sch. 14: SI 2011 No. 1452), provide for a range of special measures which a court can direct in respect of vulnerable and intimidated witnesses. Additional measures to guarantee the anonymity of witnesses are in the CAJA 2009, Part 3, ch. 2 (see **D14.82** ***et seq.***), replacing the Criminal Evidence (Witness Anonymity) Act 2008. This package of measures is available in both the Crown Court and the magistrates' courts, including the youth court. Amendments providing limited access to intermediaries to child and other vulnerable defendants (under the CAJA 2009, s. 104) have not yet been, and probably will not be, implemented. For the staged implementation of pre-trial cross examination under s. 28, see **D14.46**.

The range of statutory special measures currently available is:

(a) *screening* the witness from the accused (YJCEA 1999, s. 23);
(b) giving evidence by *live link*, accompanied by a supporter (s. 24) (for other uses of live link, see **D15.96**);
(c) giving evidence in *private*, available where sex offences or modern slavery, servitude, forced labour or human trafficking are charged (Modern Slavery Act 2015, s. 46(3)) or where there is a concern that the witness may be intimidated (YJCEA 1999, s. 25);
(d) ordering the *removal of wigs and gowns* while the witness gives evidence (s. 26);
(e) *video recording of evidence-in-chief* (s. 27);
(f) *video recording of cross-examination and re-examination* where the evidence-in-chief of the witness has already been video-recorded (s. 28) (see **D14.46**);
(g) examination through an *intermediary* for a young or incapacitated witness (s. 29);
(h) provision of *aids to communication* for a young or incapacitated witness (s. 30); and
(i) a *witness anonymity* order (CAJA 2009, Part 3, ch. 2), which may be preceded by an *investigation anonymity* order applying to the police investigation and pre-trial procedures such as disclosure (part 3, chapter 1: see **D1.210**).

D14.4 Practitioners should also bear in mind other protective procedures, such as:

- orders under the YJCEA 1999, s. 46, for restrictions on reporting and public access to protect a fearful or distressed adult witness's identity, where such an order is likely to improve the quality of that witness's testimony or cooperation (see **D3.139** and CrimPD I, para. 5B.33; see Supplement, **CPD.5B**);
- complainant anonymity in sex offence cases (Sexual Offences (Amendment) Act 1992, s. 1(1): see **D3.138**);
- the prohibition in the YJCEA 1999, ss. 34 to 38, on cross-examination by the accused in person of (i) child complainants of or witnesses to sexual offences, offences of violence, cruelty, kidnapping, false imprisonment or abduction, and (ii) adult complainants in sexual offence cases (see **F7.3** and CrimPD V, para. 23A); and
- the use of pre-trial depositions of children or young persons under the CYPA 1933, s. 43 (see **D16.38**).

The *Equal Treatment Bench Book* (March 2020), chs. 2 to 4, make detailed suggestions for flexibly and creatively adapting special measures to accommodate the individual witness's particular needs and preferences. More guidance can be found in *Achieving Best Evidence in Criminal Proceedings* (March 2011) ('*ABE 2011*') and on the CPS and Ministry of Justice web sites. A new edition of *ABE* was completed in February 2016, and was referenced in the 2016 edition of this work. However, the Ministry of Justice cancelled the new edition, and so the seriously outdated *ABE 2011* (which does not deal with questioning trafficking and modern slavery complainants, or s. 28 pre-trial recorded cross-examination) continues to apply; practitioners should be aware of its shortcomings (for a list of the gaps and expected updates, see L Hoyano, 'ABE 2016/19 Has Gone AWOL' [May 2020] Counsel 38). A new edition is expected to be published in 2020.

Eligibility Categories: General

The measures apply with equal force to both prosecution and defence witnesses (YJCEA 1999, s. 19(1)). Different provisions apply in the case of an accused (see **D14.21**). The categories of eligibility are discussed in detail at **D14.13** ***et seq***. In summary, they are: **D14.5**

- all witnesses under the age of 18 at the time of the hearing or video recording;
- vulnerable witnesses affected by a mental or physical impairment;
- witnesses in fear or distress about testifying;
- adult complainants of sexual offences, or of offences under the Modern Slavery Act 2015, ss. 1 (slavery, servitude and forced or compulsory labour) and 2 (human trafficking); and
- any witness in a case involving a 'relevant offence', currently defined to include homicide offences and other offences involving a firearm or knife.

For witnesses who are not automatically eligible (i.e. those affected by mental or physical impairment or in fear or distress about testifying), the court must determine whether the quality of the evidence would be diminished by the witness's condition (ss. 16(1)(b) and 17(1); see **D14.51** and **D14.52**), taking into account any views of the witness (ss. 16(4) and 17(3)), before making a declaration of eligibility. Adult complainants of sexual offences (s. 17(4)) and witnesses in 'relevant offence' cases have an unqualified right to opt out of special measures (s. 17(5)). After the declaration of eligibility is made, the court must consider which special measures will maximise the quality of the witness's evidence; for all child witnesses, this is presumed to be the consequence of the 'primary rule' measures (discussed at **D14.14**).

Testifying through an intermediary and aids to communication are not available for witnesses eligible only by reason of fear or intimidation.

Procedure Relating to Special Measures Directions

The ethos of active and effective case management (CrimPR Parts 3 and 18, and, especially, CrimPD I, paras. 3D to 3G (see Supplement, **CPD.3D** ***et seq.***)) is crucial where young or vulnerable or intimidated witnesses are involved. A revised protocol between HM Courts and Tribunals Service, the CPS and the National Police Chiefs' Council, issued in July 2018, requires, *inter alia*, that in any case in the Crown Court or magistrates' courts where a prosecution or defence witness aged under ten at the time the incident is reported to police has provided an evidential statement or ABE interview, a provisional trial date must be set no more than eight weeks from the date of plea, absent exceptional circumstances. The prosecution should ensure compliance with this requirement, which is widely disregarded. Where the implications of the Covid-19 pandemic make compliance impossible, the prosecution should seek a priority listing as a fixture for such trials. **D14.6**

A SMD application is required, unless the primary rule requires the court to order special measures, in which case the party calling that witness must notify the court of the witness's eligibility. If a witness wishes to opt out of the primary rule, the party adducing the testimony must provide the court with any relevant information to evaluate that choice (CrimPR 18.9; CrimPD I, para. 3D.3). A court of its own motion may raise whether a direction should be given (YJCEA 1999, s. 19(1)(b)).

CrimPR Part 18 (see Supplement, **R18.1** ***et seq.***) governs the procedure for applying for SMDs and witness anonymity orders in both the Crown Court and magistrates' courts. The procedure for applications for defendant's evidence directions is contained in rr. 18.14 to 18.17 (although rr. 18.3 to 18.7 also apply). The procedure is analogous to that described below, but see also **D14.21**. The procedure on applications for witness anonymity orders (rr. 18.18 to 18.22) is dealt with at **D14.72** ***et seq.***

Applications Applications must be in writing and be made as soon as reasonably practicable, and in any event within 20 business days after a not guilty plea in a magistrates' court, or ten business days after a not guilty plea in the Crown Court (CrimPR 18.3: see Supplement, **R18.3**). The time-limit applies to defence as well as prosecution witnesses. Time-limits are expected to be respected and the parties must be fully prepared (CrimPD I, para. 3A.2: see **D14.7**

D

Part D Procedure

Supplement, **CPD.3A**). Late applications must explain any delay (r. 18.5). *Ex parte* applications are not permitted (r. 18.3(b)); if there is material which the applicant does not want revealed to another party then the redaction procedures in r. 18.12 must be followed. The closed list of exceptions to the rule barring further case management hearings before the trial after the PTPH includes cases involving a vulnerable witness, and where the defendant is a child or otherwise under a disability or requires special assistance (CrimPD I, para. 3A.21(d) and (e)).

CrimPR 18.10 (see Supplement, **R18.10**) requires the applicant to provide an expanded list of supporting material, to:

(a) explain the basis on which the witness is eligible for assistance;
(b) explain (where the witness is not a child: r. 18.9) why special measures would be likely to improve the quality of the witness's evidence;
(c) set out the measure(s) sought;
(d) report any views that the witness has expressed about the proposed measures;
(e) where a child witness or a qualifying witness does not want the primary rule to apply, provide the information that the court may need to assess the witness's views;
(f) where the live link is proposed, identify any supporter and explain why that person is appropriate, including the witness's views;
(g) where video-recorded evidence is to be submitted, identify the date and duration of the recording and what material is to be edited, if any (see also CrimPD V, para. 16B; see Supplement, **CPD.16B**); and
(h) attach any other material relied upon.

An applicant seeking a hearing must explain why one is needed (r. 18.10(i)). Practitioners should strive to ensure that witnesses and defendants eligible for SMDs have pre-trial familiarisation visits to the court *before* the SMD application, so that the witness and advocate can make an informed choice (*Momodou (Practice Note)* [2005] EWCA Crim 177, [2005] 1 WLR 3442 at [62]; CrimPD I, para. 3G.2 (see Supplement, **CPD.3G**)). The witness is entitled to practise speaking using the live link and to see screens in place (CrimPD V, para. 18B.4; see Supplement, **CPD.18B**), but few child witnesses receive this entitlement. Arrangement should also be made for vulnerable defendants to practise with the live link (CrimPD I, para. 3G.4) (see **D15.103**).

D14.8 **Opposed Applications** Any response opposing an application, or variation or discharge of an order, must be in writing and served on all parties within ten business days of receipt of the application (CrimPR 18.13); again material may be redacted under r. 18.12. CrimPR 18.13(4) requires that the respondent explain why issue is taken with:

(a) the witness's eligibility for special measures; or
(b) the effect of the proposed measure(s) on the quality of the evidence; or
(c) their effect on the effective testing of that evidence; or
(d) where video-recorded evidence is proposed, the reasons why it is not in the interests of justice for the recording or part of it to be admitted.

Where an intermediary appointment is opposed, the assessor of the witness's or defendant's needs should attend the hearing.

D14.9 **The Ruling** The court may decide an unopposed application without a hearing. Opposed applications may be heard in public or private (CrimPR 18.8); but the ruling granting, refusing, varying or discharging a SMD must be made at a public hearing before the witness gives evidence (YJCEA 1999, s. 20(5); CrimPR 18.4(3)). The decision may be taken in the absence of the applicant or any respondent who has had at least ten business days in which to make representations. CrimPR 18.4(2) requires the court to determine an application promptly, and *allow a party sufficient time to notify* the witness of the court's decision, and to comply with any applicable requirements under the code of practice under the DVCVA 2004, s. 32. The SMD is binding from the time it is made until the proceedings have been determined by a verdict, or abandoned, in relation to each accused (YJCEA 1999, s. 20(1)).

Procedure Following the Ruling The applicant is responsible for informing the witness of the court's decision and the arrangements as soon as reasonably practicable (CrimPR 18.4(1)). **D14.10**

Variation or Discharge of a Ruling A party may apply in writing to discharge or vary a SMD, or to review a denial of a SMD, only if there has been a material change in circumstances since the order (YJCEA 1999, s. 20(2)(a) and (3); CrimPR 18.11). The court may also so act of its own motion, without that constraint (usually after informal representations by a party). The SMD may be altered only if it is in the interests of justice to do so. **D14.11**

Jury Direction Where a special measure has been used, the judge in a trial on indictment is required to give a warning to ensure that the measure does not prejudice the accused (YJCEA 1999, s. 32). The *Crown Court Compendium* (July 2020), chs. 3-1, para. 25, and 3-6, paras. 10 to 11, advise the judge to explain that special measures are commonplace and are the way Parliament has decided such witnesses should give evidence, and that the use of special measures does not reflect on the defendants or their case. Chapter 3-7, paras. 3 to 6, provide a model explanation to juries regarding the use of intermediaries for prosecution witnesses and defendants. At the same time as the statutory warning, the judge should direct the jury in general terms that limitations have been placed on the defence advocate in cross-examination (*YGM* [2018] EWCA Crim 2458 at [21]). Nevertheless, it is inappropriate for advocates to undermine a SMD by suggesting to the jury that its use is relevant to weighing the witness's evidence (*Garland* [2008] EWCA Crim 3276). **D14.12**

A special measures warning need not be repeated in summing up if it was given when the witness gave evidence, when it was more likely to make an impression on the jury (*Brown* [2004] EWCA Crim 1620). An omission to give a direction altogether is not necessarily an error warranting quashing a conviction (*R* [2010] EWCA Crim 2741).

ESTABLISHING ELIGIBILITY FOR SPECIAL MEASURES

Child Witnesses

Deemed Eligibility A child witness is defined as being under 18 years old at the time of the hearing or, if the witness has surpassed the maximum age by that date, under 18 when the video interview took place, the latter being described as a 'qualifying witness' (YJCEA 1999, s. 22(1)(a); CrimPD I, para. 3D.1). A complainant whose age is uncertain is presumed to be under 18 in regard to charges of slavery, servitude, forced labour and human trafficking offences, sexual offences (as defined by the YJCEA 1999, s. 62), and offences under the Protection of Children Act 1978, s. 1, and the CJA 1988, s. 160 (both concerning indecent photographs of children); this implemented Directive 2011/92/EU ([2011] OJ L335/1). The YJCEA 1999, s. 33(5) and (6), were amended by the Special Measures for Child Witnesses (Sexual Offences) Regulations 2013 (SI 2013 No. 2971) and by the Modern Slavery Act 2015, s. 46(4). **D14.13**

It is vital to appreciate that all child witnesses are automatically eligible for special measures, including defence witnesses other than a child defendant, and so, subject to what is said at **D14.15**, it is generally not open to an opposing party to contend that a particular child does not need special procedures because they would not maximise the quality of the child's evidence. The House of Lords held in *Camberwell Green Youth Court, ex parte D* [2005] UKHL 4, [2005] 1 WLR 393 that the deemed eligibility rule for child witnesses does not contravene the ECHR, Article 6.

Automatic eligibility notwithstanding, the individual child's needs must be evaluated at the earliest opportunity in the investigation, using the detailed guidance in *ABE 2011*, paras. 2.44 to 2.59, and apps. D and E, and The Advocate's Gateway toolkits. In complex cases, and those involving very young or especially vulnerable children, the police should seek early investigative advice from the CPS, before the ABE interview is conducted, to consider whether an intermediary should evaluate the child's communication skills and identify any issue about competence, to minimise the need for further interviews (see the statutory Code of Practice for Victims of Crime (2015, being updated) and *ABE 2011*, Boxes 2.1 and 2.7). Until its replacement on 4 April 2016, CrimPD I, para. 3F.5, had stated that assessment should be considered for all witnesses aged under 18; moreover, for children aged 11 years and under, it should be presumed that an intermediary assessment was appropriate before trial. However, the replacement paras. 3F.5 and 3F.25 revoked this advice concerning both those aged under 18 and this presumption for children aged 11 and under, 'in light of the scarcity of intermediaries'. The new Directions state that the appropriateness of assessment must be decided with care 'to ensure their availability for those witnesses and defendants who are most in need', so the decision must be made on a case-by-case basis. It remains unclear how the witnesses and defendants 'most in need' will be identified without an assessment, nor how prioritisation under the rationing regime is to be done by the court without information as to the availability of intermediaries at the expected date of trial. There is also tension between the April 2016 CrimPD and the *Equal Treatment Bench Book* (March 2020), which notes that 'although the decision whether to use an intermediary is ultimately the judge's, it is important to remember that the extent of communication difficulties can sometimes be hidden, and that despite best intentions, advocates do not necessarily have the required expertise either to diagnose difficulty, or to adapt their questioning' (p. 41). The *Equal Treatment Bench Book* recommends that 'all young witnesses should ideally have an intermediary assessment as, no matter how advanced they appear, their language comprehension is likely to be less than that of an adult witness' (ch. 2, para. 98), and that an intermediary assessment should be considered because the majority of young witnesses across all ages are unable to recognise a problematic question, or may be reluctant to say so to a questioner in a position of authority (ch. 2, para. 97). The *Equal Treatment Bench Book* also suggests arguments to counter opposition to an intermediary appointment (ch. 2, para. 101). Research cited by the BSB shows that six in ten children in the youth justice system have a communication disability, and one third of children in custody have identified special educational needs (*Youth Proceedings Competences* (BSB, February 2017), at p. 8). See also the *Youth Court Bench Book* (August 2017), paras. 11, 29, 33 to 37 and Table at p. 21.

D14.14 **The 'primary rule'** The 'primary rule' provides for the admission of any video interview and the use of live link for any non-video testimony. The regime originally included a category of children 'in need of special protection' (i.e. witnesses to charges of sexual or violent offences) for whom the primary rule was mandatory, but this rigidity created difficulties where the child preferred to testify in court. The CAJA 2009, s. 100, abolished the special protection category while retaining the primary rule, but making it apply presumptively to *all* witnesses under 18, regardless of the nature of the offence charged.

D14.15 **Flexibility in Use of SMDs for Child Witnesses** Under the CAJA 2009, s. 100, the trial court has greater flexibility in tailoring special measures to the needs of the individual child witness to facilitate best evidence, so this must now be the paramount consideration for the applicant, subject to Covid-19 court arrangements. The court may disapply the primary rule where it is satisfied that compliance would be unlikely to maximise the quality of the child's evidence so far as practicable, in which case it should consider the other optional special measures (YJCEA 1999, s. 21(4)(c)). Another reform introduced by the CAJA 2009, s. 100, enables the child to opt out of the primary rule in whole or in part (YJCEA 1999, s. 21(4)(ba)); the court must be satisfied that testifying in court would not diminish the quality of the child's evidence. The court must have regard to a non-exclusive set of factors. In practice the opt-out is most often exercised regarding the live link (see **D14.38**).

Exactly what each measure entails should be explained and demonstrated to the witness and carers during a court visit (which ideally the advocate tendering the witness should attend if the witness has particular communication difficulties). If a visit is not possible before the application, it may become necessary to apply to vary the direction after the visit, subject to Covid-19 court arrangements. In more complex cases, the prosecuting advocate should hold a special measures meeting with the witness, making full notes of the discussion for disclosure to the defence. Advocates are responsible at the PTPH for explaining the child's needs, such as the best time of day to schedule testimony, concentration span and other welfare concerns, and for checking that those circumstances have not changed by trial.

If the child testifies in chief other than through a pre-recorded interview, the court must be alive to the witness's needs and difficulties (*Turner* [2012] EWCA Crim 1786, [2013] 1 Cr App R 25 (327)). In *Turner*, the Court of Appeal approved the trial judge's solution where the witness was too embarrassed to vocalise what had happened; as there was no dispute that such sexual activity had occurred, that part of her statement was adduced under the CJA 2003, s. 114.

Adult Witnesses with Physical or Mental Impairment

The applicant for a declaration of eligibility (YJCEA 1999, s. 16(2); see **D14.51**) must file material under CrimPR 18.10 (see **D14.7**) establishing that the witness: **D14.16**

(a) is affected by a mental disorder within the meaning of the Mental Health Act 1983 (i.e. 'any disorder or disability of the mind': s. 1(2));
(b) otherwise has a significant impairment of intelligence and social functioning; or
(c) has a physical disability or is suffering from a physical disorder (not otherwise defined).

The *Equal Treatment Bench Book* (March 2020), appendix B, contains a useful glossary of physical and mental disabilities and illnesses.

The applicant must also satisfy the court that the quality of the evidence would be diminished by the witness's condition (s. 16(1)(b)). The court should also take into account, but is not bound by, the witness's wishes regarding eligibility (s. 16(4)).

Practitioners should be alert to the possibility that their witness may suffer from a mental impairment, as research shows that such people frequently are not identified by anyone in the criminal justice system as being in need of special measures; they often have adopted coping mechanisms to conceal their impairment. A useful set of prompts to identify and question such witnesses appears in *Vulnerable and Intimidated Witnesses: A police service guide* (March 2011, tinyurl.com/yxd942to), in *ABE 2011*, para. 2.69, and in The Advocate's Gateway Toolkit 10. Police should seek advice from the CPS before the *ABE* interview about areas to be covered and special measures for the interview. In complex cases, early special measures strategy meetings should be held with the prosecuting advocate and those who know the witness well to identify difficulties and solutions, such as an intermediary, keeping full notes for disclosure purposes. If competence may be in issue, reports identifying the specific difficulties and how they could be ameliorated during testimony must be collected as early as possible. A court visit must be arranged for the witness to experience the measures in practice (CrimPD I, para. 18B.4), subject to Covid-19 court arrangements. Advocates are responsible at the PTPH for identifying the witness's needs, such as the best time of day to testify, concentration span and ways to detect its lapse, any medication or other care required, and other welfare concerns. The appropriateness of the measures ordered should be kept under review, including at trial, as circumstances may change, requiring an application for variation.

It might be easier for a disabled or very young witness to testify by video link from a remote location; contact the local Police and Crime Commissioner to ascertain their availability. Consideration should also be given to using remote live links whenever there is a risk of confrontation with defence supporters (*Equal Treatment Bench Book* (March 2020), ch. 2, para. 65).

Adult Complainants of Sexual Offences

Such complainants are effectively *presumed* to be in fear or distress about testifying, and are not subject to the threshold criteria for fearful adult witnesses, being deemed to be eligible for special measures unless they decline (YJCEA 1999, s. 17(4)). This applies to any offence under the SOA 2003, Part 1, or any relevant superseded offence (YJCEA 1999, s. 62(1)). See also **D14.29**. **D14.17**

As with child witnesses, the specific special measures likely to maximise the quality of the evidence of adult vulnerable or intimidated witnesses must normally be considered for each individual with full consultation during a court visit, without any default assumptions, subject to Covid-19 court arrangements. A combination of measures is now possible after the CJA 2009 amendments, e.g., playing the video interview as evidence-in-chief with cross-examination of the witness in court behind a screen.

Witnesses in Slavery, Servitude or Human Trafficking Cases

D14.18 Witnesses in relation to offences under the Modern Slavery Act 2015, s. 1 (slavery, servitude, forced or compulsory labour) or s. 2 (human trafficking) (see **B22.6**) are deemed to be eligible for special measures unless they decline to be so considered (YJCEA 1999, s. 17(4)). See also **D14.13** where there is doubt about whether a witness might be under 18.

Intimidated and Other Special Witnesses

D14.19 **Witnesses in Fear or Distress about Testifying** For a witness to be eligible for a SMD under the YJCEA 1999, s. 17(1), the court must be satisfied that the quality of the evidence is likely to be diminished by the witness's fear or distress in connection with testifying. The application must give detailed grounds, and attach supporting evidence under CrimPR 18.10(a) and (h). The court is required by s. 17(2) to take into account the following factors:

(a) the nature and alleged circumstances of the offence;
(b) the age of the witness;
(c) so far as relevant, the witness's:
- social and cultural background and ethnic origins,
- domestic and employment circumstances, and
- religious beliefs or political opinions;

(d) any behaviour towards a witness on the part of:
- the accused,
- the accused's family or associates, or
- any other person likely to be an accused or witness.

The court must also consider any views expressed by the witness (s. 17(3)).

It may be appropriate to hold a *voir dire* and call the witness to testify to establish eligibility; it does not matter that other witnesses in the same circumstances are prepared to testify without special measures (*Brown* [2004] EWCA Crim 1620). In *Brown* it was also held that, although s. 17(2) required the court to consider the factors in s. 17(2)(a) to (d), it was entitled to find eligibility solely having regard to the nature and circumstances of the offence, regardless of the witness's age or any particular vulnerability. The overall question for the trial court under s. 17 is fairness to the accused and to the witnesses, and the Court of Appeal is unlikely to interfere with its answer.

D14.20 **Witnesses to Relevant Offences Involving Knives or Guns** The CAJA 2009, s. 99, amended the YJCEA 1999, s. 17, to make witnesses in proceedings for 'any relevant offence' automatically eligible for special measures. A 'relevant offence' is defined in sch. 1A to the YJCEA 1999 (in sch. 14 to the CAJA 2009). The categories of offences specified in sch. 1A are murder and manslaughter; offences under the OAPA 1861, ss. 18, 20, 38 and 47; the Prevention of Crime Act 1953, ss. 1 and 1A; the FA 1968, ss. 1 to 5, 16 to 21A and 24A; the CJA 1988, ss. 139, 139A and 139AA; and the VCRA 2006, ss. 28, 32 and 36. However, a number of these offences are to be treated as specified offences only if a knife or gun was involved. Complainants of slavery, servitude and human trafficking are automatically eligible (see **D14.18**).

Note that *all* witnesses involved in such cases, including police officers, are automatically eligible for a SMD unless they decline, without any proof of intimidation or other ground for concern about whether they can give their best evidence using the orthodox procedures.

Child and Other Vulnerable Defendants

D14.21 The YJCEA 1999 expressly excluded the accused from access to special measures (ss. 16(1) and 17(1)). The resulting disparity in treatment between child defendants and other child witnesses was particularly evident in youth courts. After pressure from the Law Lords and the ECtHR

(*Camberwell Green Youth Court, ex parte D* [2005] UKHL 4, [2005] 1 WLR 393; *SC v UK* (2005) 40 EHRR 10 (226)), Parliament moved to give limited access to special measures to child and vulnerable adult defendants, in 2007, permitting them to use live link (YJCEA 1999, ss. 33A, 33B, 33C). Under the CAJA 2009, s. 104 (inserting ss. 33BA and 33BB into the YJCEA 1999: not yet in force), they were to have access to intermediaries for their testimony, but this measure will probably not be implemented (see **D14.24**). Other special measures available to child witnesses are still not directly applicable to child defendants who testify, as the YJCEA 1999, ss. 17(1) and 19(1), have not been repealed. This gives rise to questions about compliance with the equality of arms test in the ECHR, Article 6(3)(d).

While practical difficulties such as the constraints of the courtroom available cannot be ignored, they also do not override the demands of the ECHR, Article 6, 'which does not settle for an inadequate best effort' (*H* [2006] EWCA Crim 853 at [42]). As noted at **D14.1**, the case management rules introduced in 2015 reinforced the court's duty to facilitate the participation of the defendant (CrimPR 3.8(3) to (7)). CrimPD I, para. 3E.4, emphasises that defendants, like all other witnesses, should be enabled to give the best evidence they can. CrimPD I, paras. 3D, 3E, 3F and especially 3G.1 to 3G.14 (see Supplement, **CPD.3G**), govern the treatment of vulnerable defendants in the Crown Court and magistrates' courts, adopting procedures analogous to those in use in youth courts. The overriding principle is that all possible steps should be taken to assist a vulnerable defendant to comprehend the proceedings and engage fully with the defence, adapting the ordinary trial process as necessary (see also CrimPD I, paras. 3D.2 and 3G.9 to 3G.12). The welfare of a young defendant must be considered (CYPA 1933, s. 44), as must CrimPR Parts 1 and 3 (the overriding objective and the court's powers of case management). Defence advocates should be fully familiar with CrimPD V, paras. 18A.1 and 18A.2 (see Supplement, **CPD.18A**), and The Advocate's Gateway toolkit on vulnerable defendants, to assist the court in fulfilling its obligations to a child or other vulnerable defendant. The PTPH form requires the judge to give reasons for departing from the CrimPD (*Grant-Murray* [2017] EWCA Crim 1228 at [227]). The court must always consider at the PTPH whether a young defendant should be seated outside the dock (*Grant-Murray* at [157]–[158]). The advice at **D14.15, D14.16** and **D14.50** about handling witnesses applies equally to defendants. CrimPR 3.8(6) provides that facilitating participation of any person includes giving directions for the appropriate treatment and questioning of the defendant as well as other witnesses. The detailed directions on ground rule hearings apply equally to the defendant as to other vulnerable witnesses (CrimPD I, paras. 3E.1 to 3E.6; see Supplement, **CPD.3E**). CrimPD I, para. 3N.11 (see Supplement, **CPD.3N**), requires that a defence witness be provided with the same facilities and treatment as a prosecution witness. Subject to Covid-19 court arrangements, plans should be made for a vulnerable defendant to make a pre-trial familiarisation visit to the court, including practising using the live link, accompanied by an intermediary where one is to be used at trial (CrimPD I, paras. 3G.2 to 3G.4). See **D14.22** ***et seq.*** for the effect of changes to the CrimPD which constrain this approach to facilitating the effective participation of vulnerable defendants. As to the inference which may be drawn, under the CJPO 1994, s. 35, from the failure of a vulnerable defendant to give evidence, see **F20.46**. See also CrimPD I, paras. 3N.13 to 3N.15, concerning the use of remote live link for pre-trial proceedings and sentencing of youth defendants in the youth court, magistrates' court or Crown Court.

Eligibility of Defendant for Live Link The YJCEA 1999, s. 33A, allows the Crown Court or a magistrates' court, on application by the defence, to direct that the accused testify via a 'live link'. The court must be satisfied that it would be in the interests of justice, and also that the live link would enable the accused to participate more effectively as a witness, whether by improving the quality of the accused's evidence or otherwise, because: **D14.22**

(a) if the accused is under the age of 18, 'his ability to participate effectively . . . as a witness giving oral evidence is *compromised* by his level of intellectual ability or social functioning' (s. 33A(4), emphasis added); or

(b) if the accused is aged 18 or over, he or she is *unable* to participate effectively in the proceedings as a witness giving oral evidence because he or she has a mental disorder (within the meaning of the Mental Health Act 1983) or a 'significant impairment of intelligence and social function' (s. 33A(5)).

Explanatory Notes accompanying the 2006 amendment stated that the presumption remains that adult defendants should give evidence in court. The Notes explained that 'the lower threshold for child defendants recognises that it may be more common for them to experience difficulties during the trial through limited intelligence and social development, than it would be for adults' but went on to emphasise that s. 33A(4) 'is aimed at juvenile defendants with a low level of intelligence or a particular problem in dealing with social situations, and is not intended to operate merely because an accused is a juvenile and is nervous, for example'.

D14.23 Under CrimPR 18.15, an applicant for a 'defendant's evidence direction' must explain how the proposed direction meets these prescribed conditions. An application for live link must identify a person to accompany the accused while testifying and explain why that person is appropriate. See also CrimPD I, para. 3G.11, and CrimPD V, paras. 18B.1 to 18B.5. If the layout of a particular courthouse means that a defendant could have access to the live link room only through the area reserved for witnesses, the defence advocate should make inquiries about alternative live link venues such as police stations before making the application.

Section 33A(6) provides that the accused must give all evidence in accordance with the live link direction, including any cross-examination. However, the court has discretion to discharge a direction if it is in the interests of justice (s. 33A(7)), such as where the accused finds that testifying via live link is more difficult than expected.

D14.24 **Eligibility of Defendant for an Intermediary** The Crown Court and magistrates' courts may deploy inherent powers to direct that the defendant be assisted by an intermediary (*R (C) v Sevenoaks Youth Court* [2009] EWHC 3088 (Admin), [2010] 1 All ER 735 at [15]–[17]; *Head* [2009] EWCA Crim 1401; *R (TP) v West London Youth Court* [2005] EWHC 2583 (Admin), [2006] 1 All ER 477; CrimPD I, paras. 3F.3 to 3F.4: see Supplement, **CPD.3F**). If the Legal Aid Agency does not authorise payment of the intermediary, then the trial court may direct payment from Central Funds (CrimPD I, para. 3F.16). Expert reports in support of applications for an intermediary appointment should address not only the vulnerabilities of and the difficulties experienced by the defendant, but also the way in which those factors potentially relate to the particular proceedings (*Thomas* [2020] EWCA Crim 117, [2020] 4 WLR 66 at [55]). The possibility of appointing an intermediary is a relevant consideration in assessment of fitness to plead under the *Pritchard* criteria (*Roberts* [2019] EWCA Crim 1270, [2019] 2 Cr App R 33 (402) at [10]). Until it was replaced in April 2016, CrimPD I, para. 3F.3, provided that the court could order that an intermediary accompany the defendant throughout the trial and, where necessary, in preparation for trial, to assist the defendant in understanding what is taking place. However, para. 3F.5 now provides that 'in light of the scarcity of intermediaries' they should be reserved for the defendants and witnesses 'most in need'. In 2011, the Witness Intermediary Service ceased assisting defence solicitors through its matching service in locating an appropriate intermediary for a defendant (although it would do so for other defence witnesses). However, in *R (OP) v Secretary of State for Justice* [2014] EWHC 1944 (Admin), [2014] 1 Cr App R 7 (70) the Divisional Court held (at [16]–[17]) that the withholding of access of vulnerable defendants to the Witness Intermediary Service, and to professionally regulated registered intermediaries acting in that capacity for their testimony, breached equality of arms with Crown witnesses under the ECHR, Article 6. The Ministry of Justice abandoned its application for leave to appeal; it appears that the onus is on defence advocates to seek access to the Register in each case. Defence solicitors, police and the courts may now contact Intermediaries for Justice (www.intermediaries-for-justice.org) which operates an online defence referral system.

Practitioners should be vigilant to identify defendants with comprehension difficulties which could warrant an application for an intermediary. The assessment may conclude that there is no need for an intermediary's assistance at trial, instead recommending ground rules for conduct of the trial (as in *Grant-Murray* [2017] EWCA Crim 1228 at [140]; Communicourt, which specialises in vulnerable defendants, does not recommend an intermediary attend trial in 24 per cent of its assessments). Those ground rules should take account of how all evidence is led throughout the trial to enable the defendant to understand and participate in the proceedings (see **D15.47**). In *R (AS) v Great Yarmouth Youth Court* [2011] EWHC 2059 (Admin), Mitting J held that magistrates had acted irrationally in denying an intermediary to a defendant with ADHD, notwithstanding that he was not wholly incapable of communicating his testimony, underlining the entitlement of a defendant with communication difficulties, like any other witness, to give best evidence. Where an appropriate intermediary is not available for a defendant assessed as being in need of one, the trial judge must make an informed assessment as to whether it is possible nonetheless to have a fair trial by adapting procedures, e.g., by taking frequent breaks to enable defence counsel to summarise the evidence and take instructions, and ensuring that *all* questions to *all* witnesses are phrased simply (*Cox* [2012] EWCA Crim 549, [2012] 2 Cr App R 6 (63) at [21] and [29]–[30]; *Thomas* [2020] EWCA Crim 117, [2020] 4 WLR 66 at [53]–[54]). Where an intermediary refuses to attend court for evidence only, having recommended an intermediary appointment throughout the trial, a summary of relevant parts of the report can be admitted as hearsay evidence to assist the jury in evaluating the defendant's responses in interview and in court (*Pringle* [2019] EWCA Crim 1722 at [87], [107]–[108], discussing *Beards* [2016] EW Misc B143 (CC) 23 May 2016, and *Biddle* [2019] EWCA Crim 86, [2019] 2 Cr App R 20 (209), discussed at **D14.25**).

The CAJA 2009, s. 104 (not in force), inserts new ss. 33BA and 33BB into the YJCEA 1999 to provide statutory authorisation for the defendant to testify assisted by an intermediary. Section 33BA sets out parallel criteria for eligibility for an intermediary as for the live link for adult and child defendants, which are more stringent than for other witnesses. The Law Commission has urged that they not be implemented as enacted because they do not adequately protect the child or disabled defendant's right to participate effectively in the trial (*Unfitness to Plead*, Law Com No. 364 (January 2016), vol. 1, at para. 2.65).

Compliance with the ECHR, Article 6 The differential eligibility criteria as between child defendants and ordinary child witnesses, and as between child and adult defendants, have been criticised as potentially contravening the ECHR, Article 6(3)(d) (see L Hoyano, 'Coroners and Justice Act 2009 — (3) Special Measures Directions Take Two: Entrenching Unequal Access to Justice?' [2010] Crim LR 345). The risk of unfairness due to inequality of arms was noted by Rafferty LJ in *R (OP) v Secretary of State for Justice* [2014] EWHC 1944 (Admin), [2014] 1 Cr App R 7 (70) at [46]. The Law Commission has stated that a statutory entitlement to an intermediary in appropriate circumstances is 'essential' to rectify the inequity of the comparative positions of defence and prosecution witnesses, to ensure compliance with the Equality Act 2010, s. 20, and the UN Convention on the Rights of Persons with Disabilities, Articles 12(3) and 13, and to provide a proper framework, provision and funding for what has become a practical reality through the exercise of inherent jurisdiction (*Unfitness to Plead*, Law Com No. 364 (January 2016), vol. 1, at paras. 2.31 to 2.37). The proposed entitlement would encompass intermediary assistance both for the giving of evidence and for as much of the wider trial proceedings as necessary for the defendant to have a fair trial (at paras. 2.62 to 2.69). In contrast, the April 2016 amendment to CrimPD I, para. 3F.12, states that, because the court should adapt the trial process to address a defendant's communication needs, the court 'will rarely exercise its inherent powers to direct appointment of an intermediary', and para. 3F.13 emphasises that 'directions to appoint an intermediary for a defendant's evidence will thus be *rare*, but for the entire trial *extremely rare*' (emphasis added). This admonition for judicial restraint in the appointment of defence intermediaries was reinforced by Lord Thomas CJ in *Rashid* [2017] EWCA Crim 2, [2017] 1 Cr App R 25 (383) at [73]–[82] (and by Hallett VP in *Biddle* [2019] EWCA Crim 86 at [48]; also *Thomas* [2020] EWCA Crim 117, **D14.25**

[2020] 4 WLR 66 at [42]), emphasising that competent advocates have undergone specific training for vulnerable witnesses and are capable of doing what is needed to ensure that a defendant is fully able to participate in every aspect of the trial. The same, however, could be said of any advocate dealing with a prosecution witness. Moreover, these provisions do not address the valuable work a defence intermediary can provide outside the courtroom in assisting the defence advocate to communicate with the client, a role which has now been judicially acknowledged by Fulford VP in *Thomas* at [43], so the necessity of obtaining informed instructions also should be addressed in an application. The *Equal Treatment Bench Book* (March 2020) notes that 'the vulnerable person is likely to need help not only during hearings but also away from court for the purpose of giving instructions and considering advice and options' (ch. 2, para. 84). The Court of Appeal has noted that applications for defence intermediaries call upon trial judges to make fact-sensitive decisions which require not only an assessment of the relevant circumstances of the defendant, but also of the factual complexity, legal and procedural difficulty, and length, of the particular trial (*Thomas* at [34]–[43]). In *Thomas*, Fulford VP noted (at [47]) that *Pringle* [2019] EWCA Crim 1722 provided 'an object lesson as to the type of pitfalls that need to be avoided' where a defendant without an intermediary struggled to respond to cross-examination. So the CrimPD's 'rarity' injunction should not be treated as a prohibition. This softened position signalled by *Thomas* is further borne out by *TI v Bromley Youth Court* [2020] EWHC 1204 (Admin), where Sharpe P explained the 'rarity' injunction as referring to all cases coming before the courts, where most defendants do not require an intermediary's assistance, making an appointment 'rare': '[i]t does not follow that there is a high hurdle to overcome for the appointment of an intermediary if one is necessary for the effective participation of a defendant in the trial process' (at [39]). The President explained the application of *Thomas* to the Youth Court: its specialist jurisdiction and experience in dealing with vulnerable young people with complex needs does not mean that the judge should not be assisted by an intermediary if required to enable a young person to engage with the trial process (at [38]); where the evidence demonstrates that the defendant lacks the capacity to participate unaided in the trial process, it is incumbent on the judge to explain how the court will enable the defendant effectively to participate in the proceedings despite that evidence (at [43]).

Importantly, no equivalent 'rarity' injunction applies to any vulnerable prosecution or defence witness in the CrimPD, raising anew the issue of equality of arms found to have been breached in *R (OP) v Secretary of State for Justice* [2014] EWHC 1944 (Admin), [2014] 1 Cr App R 7 (70); see Laura Hoyano and Angela Rafferty QC, 'Rationing Defence Intermediaries under the April 2016 Criminal Practice Direction' [2017] Crim LR 93. Notwithstanding the successful human rights challenge in *R (OP), in TI v Bromley Youth Court* [2020] EWHC 1204 (Admin) at [27]–[33] and [39], Sharpe P emphasised that applications should not seek to challenge the adequacy of the current regime of special measures for defendants against international norms, but rather should closely scrutinise the particular circumstances of the specific applicant, applying the current principles.

With effect from 1 October 2018 para. 3F.12 adds that 'where a defendant is vulnerable or for some other reason experiences communication or hearing difficulties, such that he or she needs more help to follow the proceedings than her or his legal representatives readily can give having regard to their other functions on the defendant's behalf, then the court should consider sympathetically any application for the defendant to be accompanied throughout the trial by a support worker or other appropriate companion who can provide that assistance'. There is no reference to any remuneration of the support worker.

The appointment of intermediaries for vulnerable defendants has become an even more fraught issue due to the policy of some intermediary providers that they will not accept instructions solely for testimony where the assessment recommends an intermediary's assistance throughout the trial, the rationale being that it is contrary to their professional function to ensure effective participation (Intermediaries for Justice, *Evidence Only?*, tinyurl.com/y5a5v26u). In *Biddle* [2019] EWCA Crim 86, Hallett VP described this policy as 'wrong' and stated that if intermediaries accept instructions to assess possibly vulnerable defendants, they also accept that they will abide by the trial judge's directions as to the duration of that appointment. The serious difficulties caused for defendants where intermediaries are unwilling to accept defence instructions on this judicially prescribed basis can be seen in *Pringle* [2019] EWCA Crim 1722. A possibility mooted by the Court of Appeal in *Pringle* was to issue a witness summons to the intermediary to attend for the defendant's testimony; however, an intermediary is not a witness for any party to the proceedings.

SPECIAL MEASURES AVAILABLE FOR WITNESSES

Video-recorded Evidence-in-chief

Section 27 of the YJCEA 1999 permits a video-recorded interview with a police officer (or social worker) to constitute the evidence-in-chief of an eligible witness, provided that the witness is available for cross-examination at trial. Specific issues relating to particular classes of witness are noted below. **D14.26**

ECHR Compliance As the ECHR, Article 6, does not require face-to-face confrontation, it does not matter that the accused was not present during the recording of the video interview, provided that the defence has an adequate and proper opportunity to challenge and question the witness at some stage (*Camberwell Green Youth Court, ex parte D* [2005] UKHL 4, [2005] 1 WLR 393 at [12]–[15] and [49]–[53]). The statutory discretion to exclude all or part of the video interview in the interests of justice adequately protects the defence's rights under Article 6 (*Camberwell Green Youth Court, ex parte D* at [33] and [45]–[46]). However, the YJCEA 1999, s. 27(4), contemplates the possibility that a video interview be admitted even where the witness does not appear at trial for cross-examination and, unless the hearsay provisions of the CJA 2003, ss. 114 to 117, apply (and subject to *Al-Khawaja and Tahery v UK* (2012) 54 EHRR 23 (807): see **F17.89**), it is possible that this would breach Article 6. (See *Riat* [2012] EWCA Crim 1509, [2013] 1 All ER 349 for the steps to be followed should such a hearsay application be made.) **D14.27**

Defence Witnesses The use of video-recorded interviews as evidence-in-chief is available in principle to all vulnerable and intimidated witnesses apart from the accused, whether called by the prosecution or the defence. Since the primary rule applies to all child witnesses regardless of who calls them (YJCEA 1999, ss. 16(1), 21(3) and 22), and *requires* that they have their evidence-in-chief recorded on video, and this is expected to be conducted before trial (by an interviewer trained in ABE), one of several logistical difficulties is that the prosecution might be able to improve their case if they were to have access to the defence video evidence before trial through the defence application for a SMD. This difficulty was met by the Crown Court (Special Measures Directions and Directions Prohibiting Cross-examination) Rules 2002 (SI 2002 No. 1688), r. 8(6) and (7), which provided that any video recording that the accused proposed to tender in evidence need not be sent to the prosecution until the close of the prosecution case at trial. Those provisions were not replicated in the CrimPR. However, r. 18.12 does provide for an applicant to withhold information relating to a special measures application from the other parties, and the Rules Committee apparently expected that this provision would apply to defence video interviews, if the conditions there identified were met. If the court concludes that they are, the normal sequence of events would follow and the prosecution would not see that defence evidence unless and until the defence decided to rely upon it as part of the defence case. **D14.28**

Adult Complainants of Sexual Offences The measures available to adult complainants of sexual offences under the YJCEA 1999 included having a video-recorded interview admitted as evidence-in-chief where this was determined to be likely to maximise the quality of the complainant's evidence. Because the measure was not being used for such witnesses, CAJA 2009 amendments have made the video interview *presumptively* admissible in the Crown Court on the basis that it *will* maximise the quality of the witness's evidence so far as practicable (in the same way as child witnesses), unless the court is not satisfied of this, or otherwise concludes that its admission is not in the interests of justice (YJCEA 1999, s. 22A(8) and (9)). A video interview is a prerequisite to invocation of s. 28 for such witnesses in the three **D14.29**

D

Part D Procedure

Crown Courts where that measure is available (s. 28(1)). Prosecutors should scrutinise the video interview to satisfy themselves that it provides the complainant's best direct evidence. In magistrates' courts, however, the original provisions continue to govern, so that the prosecution must establish that the video interview is likely to maximise the quality of an adult complainant's evidence. Defence arguments that they are entitled to viva voce examination-in-chief so as to exploit any discrepancies with the video are likely to be given short shrift (*Davies* [2011] EWCA Crim 1177).

D14.30 **Availability for Cross-examination** A precondition to the admission of a recorded interview as evidence-in-chief is that the witness must be available for cross-examination at trial, whether in the ordinary way or with the use of special measures, unless the parties agree that it is unnecessary to call that witness (YJCEA 1999, s. 27(4) and (5); *Lubemba* [2014] EWCA Crim 2064, [2015] 1 WLR 1579 at [47]). It has become more common for the police to video interview prosecution witnesses with failing health or difficulties with memory retention, and if that witness is no longer able to testify by the time of trial, the video interview can be admitted under the CJA 2003, s. 116(2)(b) (see **F17.8** and *Sed* [2004] EWCA Crim 1294, [2004] 1 WLR 3218). This may also be relevant for an intimidated or otherwise reluctant witness who refuses to testify at trial (*Burton* [2011] EWCA Crim 1990), but only if the court finds the admission of the video to be in the interests of justice having regard to its contents, the risk of unfairness to any party, and the availability of special measures at trial to assist that witness (CJA 2003, s. 116(2)(e) and (4)).

D14.31 **Witnesses Not Eligible for SMDs** The police may choose to record interviews with so-called 'significant witnesses', defined in police guidance such as the Murder Investigation Manual (ACPO 2006). But, unless the case involves a relevant offence within the meaning of the YJCEA 1999, sch. 1A (see **D14.20**), such witnesses are not entitled to special measures and there is no statutory provision for these interviews to be used as evidence-in-chief. However, the interview transcript can be used for the purposes of a statement under the CJA 1967 (see **D16.36**), and the defence might ask the court for permission to play some or all of the recording (*ABE 2011*, paras. 1.25 to 1.28, 2.133 to 2.138).

D14.32 **Admissibility of the Video Interview** The conduct of an interview eligible to serve as evidence-in-chief is governed by *ABE 2011* (see in particular chs. 2 and 3). Any significant failure by an interviewer to comply with the guidance is just one factor to be taken into account in deciding whether to exclude all or part of the recording in the interests of justice under s. 27(2) (*G v DPP* [1998] QB 919). The guidance is not intended to be a legally enforceable code, and most instances of non-compliance can be dealt with in summing-up as being relevant to weight; only if there is real prejudice to the defendant should an interview be ruled entirely inadmissible (*F* [2011] EWCA Crim 940 at [8]–[14]). The test is: 'could a reasonable jury properly directed be sure that the witness had given a credible and accurate account on the video tape regarding the central issues in the case against the accused, notwithstanding any breaches?' (*Hanton* [2005] EWCA Crim 2009; *K* [2006] EWCA Crim 74, [2006] 2 All ER 552; *Krezolek* [2014] EWCA Crim 2782, [2015] 2 Cr App R (S) 2 (12) at [52]–[53]). This assessment must not subject children's accounts to forensic analysis as if they were 'miniature adults' (*Krezolek* at [51]–[53]). The same principle seems to apply to an intermediary assisting a witness in an ABE interview, but the intermediary must be given latitude to tailor the guidance to the individual witness and the circumstances of the case, providing a full written record of intermediary involvement (*IA* [2013] EWCA Crim 1308 at [52]). While the trial judge may consider other evidence corroborating the video evidence in ruling on its admissibility, considerable care should be taken (*K*, explaining dicta in *G v DPP*). It is not necessary that the witness have an independent recollection of events entirely apart from the video interview for it to be admitted, as that would defeat the purpose of the pre-trial recorded interview as a special measure (*R* [2010] EWCA Crim 2469 at [21]–[22]).

D14.33 **Editing the Interview** An application to tender a video interview as evidence-in-chief must indicate, in addition to the information specified in CrimPR 18.10, whether all or only parts are to be adduced. In deciding under the YJCEA 1999, s. 27(2), whether to exclude part of a recording in the interests of justice, the court must consider whether any prejudice to the accused which might result from its admission is outweighed by the desirability of showing the whole, or substantially the whole, of the recording (s. 27(3)). Statements which are excised typically include hearsay, allegations of bad character against the suspect, answers to questions in breach of other rules of evidence or *ABE* (see *C* [2012] EWCA Crim 2380, holding that a flawed identification by the child witness should have been excluded) and irrelevant material. Frequently, the interviews are rambling, lengthy and difficult to follow, and advocates should consider editing to remove irrelevant or repetitive material and facts not in issue, so that the resulting evidence focuses on the live issues. The recording must be edited in accordance with the court's ruling and the edited version is then served on the court officer and on the parties (CrimPD V, para. 16B.2: see Supplement, **CPD.16B**). If a problem with the editing of the video delays a trial, the court can make a wasted costs order (para. 16B.4), so it is incumbent on advocates before trial to check the edited videotape and transcript to ensure compliance with the editing order (*ABE 2011*, paras. 5.3 and 5.6). The Court of Appeal has stressed that it is of the greatest importance that an agreement between prosecution and defence as to the editing of an ABE interview should be adhered to by advocates and the court over the course of the trial, unless there is very good reason to depart from it, for example where the prosecution have been unfairly taken by surprise by cross-examination, and need to use excised portions in rebuttal (*M (A)* [2012] EWCA Crim 899, [2013] 1 Cr App R 17 (243)).

Refreshing Memory from a Video Recording The witness is entitled to refresh his or her memory by viewing the (edited) video interview *before* (but preferably not immediately before) testifying (*R* [2010] EWCA Crim 2469 at [21]–[22]; CrimPD V, para. 18C.4 (see Supplement, **CPD.18C**)). See also **F6.16** and the CJA 2003, s. 139. The court should inquire at the PTPH about how and where refreshing will be done, on a case-by-case basis, requiring that any viewing be monitored by a person (usually the officer in the case) who will report to the court anything said by the witness (CrimPD V, para. 18C.3). Witnesses' particular needs must be considered, taking into account their concentration span. An intermediary may advise the court as to how memory refreshment should take place, and may be present to facilitate communication, but should not act as an independent person designated to take a note and report to the court if anything is said (CrimPD V, paras. 18C.1 and 18C.4). In exceptional circumstances, such as those involving very young children or children with learning disabilities, the prosecutor should consider making a video recording of the refreshment process (*ABE 2011*, para. 4.51); this was done in *Barker* [2010] EWCA Crim 4 where the complainant was then aged four. If the video is ruled inadmissible, or if the witness wishes to give viva voce evidence-in-chief, guidance should be sought from the court at the PTPH on an acceptable alternative method of memory refreshing (CrimPD V, para. 18C.2). **D14.34**

CrimPD V was amended with effect from 2 April 2018 to provide that the witness should be asked by the prosecutor or by the court whether and when the witness had reviewed the interview, and whether the witness had anything to correct or add, before cross-examination. If so, the prosecutor should lead that evidence before cross-examination, after proper notice to the defence (CrimPD V, para. 18C.4). This replaces the previous practice of asking the witness to confirm if the statements in the *ABE* interview are true, because this is thought to be confusing (*Key Changes Amendment No. 6*, para. 4).

Playing the Video Interview Several practical matters arise. **D14.35**

(a) There is no legal requirement for the witness to be present when the video is played for the jury or trial bench (CrimPD V, para. 18C.4).
(b) The defendant must have the opportunity to examine the video and any exhibits in circumstances which allow confidential discussion with legal advisers (*R (L)* [2010] EWCA Crim 2552, [2011] 3 All ER 969).
(c) Unless the parties otherwise agree, a recording adduced in Crown Court proceedings should be produced and proved by the interviewer or another witness who was present at the interview (CrimPD V, para. 16B.3: see Supplement, **CPD.16B**).

(d) Where a video-recorded interview with a child aged 14 or over is admitted under the YJCEA 1999, s. 27, the oath should be administered before the start of further questioning (see *Simmonds* [1996] Crim LR 816 at **F4.31**).

(e) The court may allow a jury to have a transcript of a recording while it is played if it will assist them to follow the evidence and they are instructed to use it only for that limited purpose (*Welstead* [1996] 1 Cr App R 59). Problems have arisen where the jury have been permitted, whether deliberately or inadvertently, to retain the transcripts during deliberations. Guidelines propounded in *Popescu* [2010] EWCA Crim 1230 and reiterated in *Sardar* [2012] EWCA Crim 134 require that transcripts be withdrawn from the jury once the video has been played except in very exceptional circumstances; if they are retained during cross-examination, then they must be retrieved at the conclusion of that testimony. The jury are not permitted to retire with the transcript unless the defence positively want the jury to have it for very good reasons which the judge must explain to the jury, ensuring that the cross-examination and re-examination of the witness is fully summed up. See also the *Crown Court Compendium* (July 2020), ch. 3-6, paras. 7 to 8.

(f) Where the jury during deliberations request that the video be replayed, the judge should ascertain the reasons for the request. If the jury wish to be reminded of the content of the testimony, a summary from the judge's notes will likely suffice; however it may be appropriate to replay the recording where the jury wish to see the manner in which the witness testified (*Mullen* [2004] EWCA Crim 62, [2004] 2 Cr App R 18 (290)). The jury must be cautioned not to give the video interview disproportionate weight and must be reminded of the oral cross-examination and re-examination of that witness (*Rawlings* [1995] 1 All ER 580; *W* [2011] EWCA Crim 1142); however, provided that the additional caution to the jury achieves balance and perspective, failure to adhere to the precise terms used in *Rawlings* does not create an unfair trial (*M* [2015] EWCA Crim 1848 at [22] and [27]). See also the *Crown Court Compendium* (July 2020) ch. 3-6, para. 9.

D14.36 **Supplementary Questions in Chief** The YJCEA 1999 originally imposed strict limitations on supplementary questions and evidence. The CAJA 2009, s. 103(2), relaxes these strictures: leave of the court will be required only where the matter has already been dealt with in the interview. Permission for supplementary questions will be given if it is in the interests of justice. This should be dealt with at the PTPH (*Crown Court Compendium* (July 2020), ch. 10-5, para. 16(4)).

D14.37 **Issues Related to Testimonial Competence** The trial judge will normally form a view as to the competence of the witness from the video recording, but if an issue is raised by the opponent of that evidence then the trial judge should investigate by asking the witness appropriate questions (*MacPherson* [2005] EWCA Crim 3605, [2006] 1 Cr App R 30 (459): see **F4.24**). It is imperative that any judicial assessment take place in the presence of the parties, if need be with the assistance of an expert, and the availability of special measures to assist the witness should be considered (*Lubemba* [2014] EWCA Crim 2064, [2015] 1 WLR 1579 at [48]). See also **D14.13** about collecting evidence of competence for very young or mentally impaired witnesses.

Live Link Testimony

D14.38 A SMD for live link for the evidence of an eligible witness is authorised by the YJCEA 1999, s. 24. See also CrimPD V, paras. 18B.1 to 18B.5 (see Supplement, **CPD.18B**). In this context, references to a live link are to 'a live television link or other arrangements whereby a witness, whilst absent from the courtroom or other place where the proceedings are being held, is able to see and hear a person there and to be heard and seen' by the judge, jury, justices, legal representatives, and any interpreter for the accused (s. 24(8)). Usually the witness testifies from a live link room in the courthouse, but a remote location should be considered for particularly young or disabled witnesses likely to be intimidated by the court building. Where a live link direction has been given, cross-examination must be conducted by live link, unless the court directs otherwise because it is in the interests of justice, and either there has been a material change in circumstances since the live link order was granted, or the court acts of its own motion (s. 24(2), (3) and (4)).

Dispensing with the Primary Rule for a Child Witness The CAJA 2009 modified the rigid and mandatory 'primary rule' regime (see **D14.14**), enabling the child to opt out of application of the primary rule in whole or in part (YJCEA 1999, s. 21(4)(ba)). This means that, subject to Covid-19 court arrangements, the child can opt to testify in the courtroom, either with or without a screen, rather than using the live link. The court must be satisfied that testifying in court would not diminish the quality of the child's evidence (s. 21(4)(ba)). CrimPR 18.9(2)(b) requires a party adducing the child's evidence to provide the court with information to enable it to assess the witness's views, which is likely to address the following mandatory statutory factors (s. 21(4C)), as well as any other relevant factors in the particular circumstances: **D14.39**

(a) the child's age and maturity;
(b) the child's ability to understand the consequences of giving evidence in court rather than through the live link;
(c) the child's relationship with the accused, if any;
(d) the child's social and cultural background and ethnic origins; and
(e) the nature and alleged circumstances of the offence charged.

Factor (b) will require careful handling of the witness familiarisation process (see **D14.14**), especially as it may well be difficult for first-time witnesses to predict how they will find the experience of testifying.

Witness Supporters

The CAJA 2009, s. 102(1), amended the YJCEA 1999, s. 24(1A), so as to give statutory standing to the routine practice of having a witness supporter in the live link room. The trial judge is required to consider the witness's wishes in the choice of supporter, the reasons for that choice being stated in the application (CrimPR 18.10(f)). There is now increased flexibility in the selection of an appropriate supporter, who can be anyone known to or trusted by the witness who is not a party to the proceedings and who has no detailed knowledge of the evidence (CrimPD V, para. 18B.2). *ABE 2011* provides guidance on the boundaries to the supporter role (paras. 4.21 to 4.29 and app. L (National Standards for the Court Witness Supporter in the Live Link Room)). The court usher should be present to ensure compliance with the judge's directions (CrimPD V, para. 18B.3). Paragraph 18B.5 authorises the court to allow a witness supporter to be present if a child elects to testify in the courtroom. **D14.40**

Screens

The YJCEA 1999, s. 23, allows the witness to testify behind a screen so that the witness cannot see the accused. The witness must be able to be seen by the judge, jury or justices, the legal representatives and any interpreter or other person appointed to help (s. 23(2)), a requirement which may be impossible to meet with Covid-19 social distancing of jurors, making the live link the sole feasible measure. If there are two representatives, it is sufficient if the witness can be seen by one of them (s. 23(3)). Occasionally a witness requests a screen rather than live link because it has the incidental effect of preventing the accused from seeing the witness testify. CrimPD V, para. 18A.2 (see Supplement, **CPD.18A**), notes that, if the witness wishes, the court may authorise that the accused and the public be prevented from seeing the live link screen, as would happen if the witness used a screen while testifying in the courtroom. Note, however, that the Court of Appeal has held that the right of the accused to see his or her accusers should be denied only in rare circumstances such as where the witness has been intimidated or where there is an anonymity order (*Taylor* [1995] Crim LR 253; *Watford Magistrates' Court, ex parte Lenman* [1993] Crim LR 388). Absent such circumstances, even where the witness testifies from behind a screen, a video camera can be discreetly positioned so as to enable the accused to see the witness while the screen prevents the witness from seeing the accused. The Court of Appeal has observed that, **D14.41** where it is important that the accused be able to see the witness, e.g., to determine whether the accused recognises the witness and whether the witness might have some motive or reason wrongly to implicate the accused in the offence charged, then the live link rather than a screen should be used (*Pope* [2010] EWCA Crim 2113). However, circumstances might justify screening the witness from the defendant, as where the witness does not want the defendant or the defendant's associates to see the witness's current physical appearance.

Removal of Wigs and Gowns

D14.42 In the Crown Court the trial judge should consider whether robes and wigs should be worn, taking into account the wishes of both a vulnerable accused and any vulnerable witness (CrimPD I, para. 3G.12: see Supplement, **CPD.3G**).

Intermediaries

D14.43 Intermediaries are independent of the parties and owe their duty to the court (CrimPD I, para. 3F.1: see Supplement, **CPD.3F** and the *Crown Court Compendium* (July 2020), ch. 3-7). Contrary to occasional practice, an intermediary should not be sworn as a witness at a GRH (ch. 10-5, para. 15). Intermediaries should not be asked to provide expert opinion or testimony (ch. 3-7, paras. 4(1) and 9(3); *Mahomud* [2019] EWCA Crim 667 at [24]) or an opinion regarding the reliability of a witness, or as to the defendant's fitness to plead, as their role is to assist communication of evidence (CrimPD I, para. 3F.1). See however *Boxer* [2014] EWCA Crim 1684 at [24], approving the provision to the jury of an intermediary's assessment report, to give them the full picture. An intermediary can be used at trial even if the ABE interview was conducted without one. The Court of Appeal has approved the use of intermediaries for profoundly disabled witnesses incapable of speech (*Watts* [2010] EWCA Crim 1824). For less disabled witnesses, experience has shown that one of the most useful functions of intermediaries is to assist the trial judge and counsel in establishing what types of questions are likely to cause misunderstanding, and thus avert them (cited with approval in *Cox* [2012] EWCA Crim 549, [2012] 2 Cr App R 6 (63) at [28]). Even though the YJCEA 1999, s. 29, makes it clear that an intermediary can assist a witness to communicate by explaining questions and answers, this happens very rarely in practice; advocates usually put their questions directly to the witness, with the intermediary intervening only where miscommunication is likely to have occurred. Practitioners should consult the detailed procedural guidance to understand the role of intermediaries in *The Registered Intermediary Procedural Guidance Manual* (2015) and also the toolkit 'Intermediaries Step-By-Step' (2015) on The Advocate's Gateway (www.theadvocatesgateway.org). Appendix E of *ABE 2011* advises on how to elicit testimony from very young, disabled or psychologically disturbed children.

Particular care is required to ensure that intermediaries assisting defendants do not jeopardise their impartiality through their close contact with them, and that transparency as to their involvement is observed at all times (*Piggin*, unreported ruling of the Recorder of London, March 2015, at [29]–[33]; *Unfitness to Plead*, Law Com No. 364 (January 2016), vol. 1, at paras. 2.56 to 2.57 and 2.73). The same is true for intermediaries assisting complainants (*Christian* [2015] EWCA Crim 1582 at [28]–[41]).

D14.44 The use of an intermediary for the video-recorded interview must be approved by the court retrospectively. The intermediary must make a declaration before the video-recorded interview begins, and again before examination of the witness at trial, in the form prescribed by CrimPR 18.7. When an intermediary is used at trial, the judge or magistrates and at least one legal representative for both the prosecution and the defence must be able to see and hear the witness giving evidence, and be able to communicate with the intermediary (YJCEA 1999, s. 29(3)).

The intermediary's written assessment will greatly assist the 'ground rules' discussion between advocates and the trial judge, which the intermediary should also attend (CrimPR 3.8(7)(a); CrimPD I, para. 3F.27); however the ground rules will usually extend well beyond the communication issues involving the intermediary, such as timing of breaks, and these are for the trial judge to enforce, not the intermediary (*Piggin*). The intermediary can provide valuable assistance to all advocates in formulating appropriate questions, and it is appropriate for them to consult the intermediary privately in preparing cross-examination; it is increasingly common for the court to direct that advocates provide their draft questions to the intermediary in advance of cross-examination. During cross-examination, the intermediary should invite the judge to ask counsel to rephrase any questions which do not comply with the ground rules; ultimately the burden rests on the court to ensure the effective participation of a vulnerable person, not on the intermediary (*Grant-Murray* [2017] EWCA Crim 1228 at [199]; *Equal Treatment Bench Book* (March 2020), ch. 2, para. 87).

Responsibility for the Intermediary Register and the Witness Intermediary Scheme Matching Service has been moved to the NCA. The Register and the Service are available for defence as well as prosecution witnesses and, following the judgment in *R (OP) v Secretary of State for Justice* [2014] EWHC 1944 (Admin), [2015] 1 Cr App R 7 (70) (at [16]–[17]), should also be available to defendants' legal advisers. Finding an appropriate intermediary for a particular witness or defendant is now facilitated through the online portal Intermediaries for Justice (www.intermediaries-for-justice.org). See further **D14.24**, and CrimPD I, para. 3F.16, regarding funding of intermediaries.

Communication Aids

Communication aids, such as sign and symbol boards or electronic communication devices, can be authorised under the YJCEA 1999, s. 30, to overcome physical or developmental difficulties with understanding or answering questions (for examples of use, see *Watts* [2010] EWCA Crim 1824 and the *Equal Treatment Bench Book* (March 2020) ch. 2, paras. 112 to 114). Communication aids will usually be used with an intermediary to ensure accurate communication with the court. Aids can be devised to meet a witness's cognitive needs, such as pictures or other visual prompts to enable the witness to recall sequences of events. In cases of profound impairment it may be necessary to have a caregiver familiar with the witness interpret signals (*Watts* at [35]). **D14.45**

Pre-trial Cross-examination

Section 28 of the YJCEA 1999 was brought into force on 30 December 2013 (SI 2013 No. 3236), but only for the purposes of Crown Court proceedings in Kingston-upon-Thames, Leeds and Liverpool to enable pilot schemes to proceed in respect of witnesses under 16 at the time of the hearing (partial implementation of s. 16(1)(a)), or under an incapacity (s. 16(1)(b)). The success of those pilot schemes has meant that pre-trial cross-examination for child witnesses and those with significant impairments of mental or physical health is gradually being rolled out across England and Wales. Section 28 came formally into force in the three pilot areas on 2 January 2017 (Youth Justice and Criminal Evidence Act 1999 (Commencement No. 15) Order 2016 (SI 2016 No. 1201)), for witnesses aged 16 or 17 at the time of hearing; this expands the category of eligible witnesses to fulfil the full terms of s. 16(1)(a) in those areas. The Youth Justice and Criminal Evidence Act 1999 (Commencement No. 16) Order 2019 (SI 2019 No. 947), with effect from 3 June 2019, extended s. 28 to s. 16(1) witnesses (under 18 or incapacity) to Crown Courts at Bradford, Carlisle, Chester, Durham, Mold and Sheffield. As of 24 February 2020, s. 28 is available in Crown Courts in Aylesbury, Oxford, Reading, Northampton, Leicester, Bristol, Wolverhampton, Portsmouth and Swansea (SI 2020 No. 155). The original pilot courts of Leeds, Liverpool and Kingston-upon-Thames are now empowered to use s. 28 in further pilots for adult complainants in sexual or modern slavery proceedings, or if they are witnesses in proceedings relating to other offences, provided they do not wish to opt out. **D14.46**

Procedures for Pre-trial Cross-examination The *Crown Court Compendium* (July 2020), appendix IV, describes comprehensively the procedural mechanics adopted for national roll-out of s. 28; advocates must absorb their detail and adhere to them to the letter. Incremental **D14.47**

implementation of s. 28 means that it will be necessary for advocates to check for a statutory instrument for a particular Crown Court. Eligibility will reflect the full range of s. 16(1) and (2) (eligibility based on age or incapacity), namely that the witness:

(a) is aged under 18 at the time of the special measures hearing; or
(b) has
  (i) a mental disorder within the meaning of the Mental Health Act 1983, or
  (ii) a significant impairment of intelligence and social functioning, or
  (iii) a physical disability or physical disorder,

and the quality of the witness's evidence is likely to be diminished as a consequence. In terms of the last criterion, s. 28 aims to put the jury in the best position to receive evidence at its sharpest, clearest and, consequently, fairest, in the interests of justice (*Benn-Landale* [2017] EWCA Crim 1321 at [12]).

Advocates should be aware of a joint protocol between the police and CPS dealing with the identification of eligible witnesses, and of the appropriate package of special measures, including a s. 27 ABE interview which is a prerequisite to s. 28. The prosecutor must formally notify the magistrates' court at the first hearing that the case is eligible for s. 28 special measures. Investigators and prosecutors are required to commence the disclosure process at the start of the investigation, using the *Judicial Protocol on Disclosure of Unused Material in Criminal Proceedings* (November 2013, currently under review by the National Disclosure Improvement Plan) and, if applicable, the *2013 Protocol and Good Practice Model: Disclosure of Information in Cases of Alleged Child Abuse and Linked Criminal and Care Directions Hearings* (October 2013, tinyurl.com/ybfvcalv). See also the *CPS Disclosure Manual* (14 December 2018, tinyurl.com/y4samxgy).

Strict case management, including frequent reporting of progress and any difficulties, will govern all s. 28 cases (CrimPD V, paras. 18E.12, 18E.27, 18E47; *Crown Court Compendium* (July 2020), appendix IV), displacing the *Protocol between the Association of Chief Police Officers, the Crown Prosecution Service and Her Majesty's Courts and Tribunals Service to expedite cases involving witnesses under 10 years*, sections 8.6 and 10.2. The case management timetable requires, *inter alia*, early identification by the defence of the core issues in dispute, before a formal defence statement is due to be served (CrimPD V, para. 18E.18), and prosecution disclosure within 50 days of sending (*Crown Court Compendium* (July 2020), appendix IV, para. 18E.21). See also the checklist for s. 28 hearings in the revised PTPH form. The ABE interview transcript and any intermediary assessment must be served on the court and the defence at least seven days prior to the PTPH. Applications for extensions of time for service of disclosure by either party will generally be refused, subject to judicial discretion (para. 18E.22). Applications for third party disclosure must be made promptly and any difficulty notified to the court. Paragraph 18E.25 recommends a single point of contact in each relevant agency to facilitate speedy disclosure; advocates should ascertain whether there are any local protocols. Counsel should also consider whether a defendant with communication difficulties will require the presence of an intermediary at the s. 28 hearing, bearing in mind the judicial guidance in *Thomas* [2020] EWCA Crim 117, [2020] 4 WLR 66 and *TI v Bromley Youth Court* [2020] EWHC 1204 (Admin) (see **D14.25**).

D14.48 **Ground Rules Hearing** The GRH will usually be soon after the deadline for service of the defence statement, with the s. 28 proceeding about one week later (para. 18E.22). The same intermediary (if any) must attend the GRH and the s. 28 hearing unless the court otherwise directs. Advocates must be familiar with the annex to CrimPD V, para. 18E (see Supplement, **CPD.18E**) (as well as CrimPD I, paras. 3E.1 *et seq.* (see Supplement, **CPD.3E**) and the relevant toolkits at the Advocate's Gateway), and in particular the required preparation by the defence, including completion of the GRH form (para. 18E.27), the receipt of full instructions (making early rapport-building with the defendant advisable), and the submission of cross-examination questions in writing for the court to consider and edit, if appropriate. Advocates must be prepared to discuss how to put the case to the witness and any restrictions thereon, and how any restrictions should be explained to the jury (para. 18E.27). The court will stipulate the timing and likely duration of the cross-examination (subject to the defence right to a fair trial), having regard to the needs of the witness, which in the case of a young child will usually be in the morning (para. 18E.24; *Crown Court Compendium* (July 2020), appendix IV, para.18E.64). Discussion should include how any exhibits or documents will be handled (appendix IV, para. 18E.37(ii)). In the Crown Court, the July 2018 *Protocol* for witnesses under ten, para. 10.3 (see **D14.6**), expects the court to consider whether a ground rules hearing is necessary; if so, the CrimPD procedure described above will apply. The default position is likely to be that a GRH is required (*Crown Court Compendium* (July 2020), appendix IV, paras. 18E.21(vii), 18E.22). Appeals from the youth court involving a Class 2B offence require a directions hearing to consider special measures, ground rules and appropriate adjustments for the hearing of the trial (CrimPD XIII, para. G.3(xii), with effect from 1 April 2019; see Supplement, **CPD.XIII.G**).

Practice Notes for Pre-trial Cross-examination See also **D14.50**. **D14.49**

- Advocates are admonished to 'master' the toolkits available through The Advocate's Gateway.
- The judge presiding over the s. 28 hearing has wide discretion over how it is conducted, provided that the rights of the defence to a fair trial are respected, especially under the ECHR, Article 6(3)(d).
- CrimPD V requires continuity of defence representation at the GRH, the s. 28 hearing and the trial itself (paras. 18E.34, 18E.59, 18E.60), so advocates must be particularly conscious of the tight timetable in order to avert returned briefs due to (foreseeably) part-heard trials. The resident judges of both courts involved in such a timetable clash must be notified to resolve difficulties, the starting point being that the s. 28 hearing takes priority (para. 18E.60; *Crown Court Compendium* (July 2020), appendix IV, paras. 18E.34, 18E.59; *PMH* [2018] EWCA Crim 2452, [2019] 1 Cr App R 27 (356) at [17]).
- Listing: All PTPHs must be listed before full-time judges authorised to deal with s. 28 cases by the resident judge. It is 'essential' that the same judge preside over the GRH and the s. 28 hearing, but any other judge may be allocated to the trial, including recorders (para. 18E.62; CrimPD XIII, Listing E (see Supplement, **CPD.XIII.E**); *Crown Court Compendium* (July 2020), appendix IV, para. 18E.62). Due to the limited availability of recording facilities, the s. 28 hearing takes precedence over other hearings and will be listed as the first matter in the morning, usually concluding before lunchtime (para. 18E.64). Time must be allowed for the witness to meet the judge and advocates. In the pilots, the usual length of cross-examination for a child witness was up to 15 minutes. Advocates should consider using remote recording facilities (currently underused), which can be much easier for the vulnerable witness than attending court; such arrangements require thinking ahead as to the use of documents and exhibits.
- If the prosecution wish to ask supplementary questions in examination-in-chief under the YJCEA 1999, s. 27(5)(b) and (7), this should be dealt with at the GRH.
- The statutory 'deeming provisions' in the YJCEA 1999 relating to s. 28 are referred to as 'assumptions' in CrimPD V, para. 18E.19 (see Supplement, **CPD.18E**). However s. 28 is a 'primary rule' measure for witnesses under 18 unless they choose to opt out, with the court's concurrence, under the YJCEA 1999, s. 21(4)(ba). Hence pre-trial cross-examination is deemed to be likely so far as practicable to improve the quality of the child's evidence (ss. 19(2) and 21(2)). Consequently it is likely to be difficult to identify viable grounds upon which to oppose a s. 28 application for a witness under 18.
- For an adult witness, the threshold questions for the defence to consider in challenging a s. 28 application will be the existence and extent of any mental disorder or impairment of intelligence and social functioning; whether the quality of the evidence would be diminished by the witness's condition (YJCEA 1999, ss. 16(1)(b), 17(2)); and whether pre-trial cross-examination would be likely to maximise the quality of that witness's testimony (s. 19(2)).
- Before deciding to oppose a prosecution application under s. 28 for an eligible witness, the defence advocate should consider the advantages to the defence of the procedure. In

particular: the possibility of the prosecution withdrawing or downgrading the charges if the complainant fails to come up to proof; or of an early guilty plea to all or some charges (but note that the recorded cross-examination is deemed to be the first day of trial for the purpose of a one-tenth reduction in sentence, applying the Sentencing Council's definitive guideline, *Reduction in Sentence for a Guilty Plea*, para. D2; see Supplement, **SG5-5**; *Crown Court Compendium* (July 2020), appendix IV, para. 18E.46); or the relative ease of raising points with the court without a jury being present or having to be sent out. (For additional considerations, see L Hoyano, 'Variations on a Theme by Pigot' [2000] Crim LR 250 at pp. 265–9.)

- Although CrimPD V focuses on applications by the prosecution for s. 28, it should be noted that defence witnesses other than the accused are also eligible for pre-trial cross-examination on grounds of age or incapacity (YJCEA 1999, s. 16(1) and (2)). This might be appropriate where a defence witness is gravely ill or has a condition associated with mental deterioration. Like ABE interviews for defence witnesses, this sets up distinct logistical issues which must be addressed by the PTPH judge.
- The s. 28 process is dependent upon prompt and full disclosure, and possessors of documents have been summoned by the designated judge in pilot areas, to account to the court in person for their tardiness.
- It is recommended that a test video of a few minutes' duration be conducted to ensure that the witness is fully visible, allowing for some bodily movement (see *PMH* [2018] EWCA Crim 2452, [2019] 1 Cr App R 27 (356) where no one present at the hearing realised that the witness's face was partially obscured during the whole of the recording). Advocates should immediately request a Quickcode and PIN from the court's listings office for access to the recording before the trial continues.
- Given the strict case management involved in prompt disclosure of issues in dispute and evidence from all likely sources, applications to reopen cross-examination of a witness conducted under the s. 28 procedure, on the basis that it was not possible for the defence through reasonable diligence to have been made aware of relevant and significant material or matter before the original recording (s. 28(5)), are likely to be subjected to especially intense scrutiny by the trial court and the Court of Appeal. One significant change may be where the Crown elects to add a count to the indictment after the s. 28 cross-examination, raising issues which had not been the subject of cross-examination at that hearing; nevertheless, if the disputed fact had been in evidence through that witness in her ABE interview before then, the conviction may still be safe notwithstanding the trial judge's refusal to permit further cross-examination (*Benn-Landale* [2017] EWCA Crim 1321 at [13]–[20]).
- In all the cases heard in the pilot areas, the defence were enabled with assistance from the court to put their case appropriately, in whole or in part, to the witness, even those as young as four years of age. Advocates will not be permitted to put their case in a way that the witness will not understand or which may be distressing. Advocates should consider very carefully how this can be done before the GRH, and not assume that they will be dispensed from doing so (*RK* [2018] EWCA Crim 603; *Crown Court Compendium* (July 2020), appendix IV, pp. 25-8 to 25-9). The manner in which the challenge can be put will be witness-specific, and in some circumstances, if the defence case is apparent to the jury, the judge may agree it is not necessary.
- In multi-handed cases, the standard practice is for the court to appoint one advocate to put the main points of dispute to the witness (see also CrimPD I, para. 3E.5 (see Supplement, **CPD.3E**), *Jonas* [2015] EWCA Crim 562 at [31], and **D14.50**); it is essential that the same ground is not covered by more than one advocate. All advocates before the GRH should be prepared to inform the judge of any specific issues pertaining only to their lay clients, so that a ruling may be obtained as to whether and how those points should be put to the witness.
- The usual requirement by the CPS that advocates meet the witness will apply in s. 28 cases for intimidated witnesses, but not necessarily for vulnerable witnesses. The CPS have

special guidance for s. 28 cases, *Speaking to Witnesses at Court* (March 2018, tinyurl.com/y6usqaj9), para. 4, which is intended to be 'bespoke' according to the needs of the witness. The GRH may ascertain that it is more appropriate for the judge and prosecuting and defence advocates to meet the witness together, where the guidance can be applied.

- Advocates should also be prepared to be very flexible in how they approach the s. 28 hearing. Provided that the defendant can see and hear the proceeding and communicate with his or her advocate, there are no prescribed rules for the physical arrangements for other participants. In cases where a witness allegedly has been filmed during commission of the alleged offence, or where the witness is very young, it may be appropriate for the trial judge and one or both advocates to be in the recording room, so that direct eye contact may be maintained without the interpolation of technology. Defence counsel in the pilots have been known to sit on the floor and play with very young children while conducting effective cross-examination. Flexibility and creativity are the bywords for s. 28 hearings.
- In cases of young children and witnesses with significant impairments of mental functioning, the judge at the GRH will require that all questions be submitted to the judge in writing in advance of the GRH, and to the intermediary if there is one. The *Crown Court Compendium* (July 2020) now requires that the defence also provide their draft questions to the prosecution (ch. 10-5, para. 14).
- Questions in cross-examination often produce unexpected answers. The better practice is not for the advocate to carry on immediately with unscripted questions, but rather to ask for a pause in the hearing to enable consultation with the judge, and any intermediary, as to the appropriate form of follow-through.
- In the first appellate ruling regarding s. 28, *RL* [2015] EWCA Crim 1215, the Court of Appeal rejected a leave application which contended that the ground rules had excessively restricted follow-through on answers; counsel had been able to put his case of fabrication and manipulation by the complainants' father, to challenge their veracity and to make his forensic points in addressing the jury. However, if the judge were to adhere strictly to questions previously agreed at the GRH, and not allow any follow-through on relevant points, this could raise the issue of compliance with the right to challenge a witness under the ECHR, Article 6(3)(d) (see the Scottish case of *MacLennan v HM Advocate* [2015] HCJAC 128 at [26]).
- As noted earlier, CrimPD V, para. 18E.27, recommends that the GRH address how any restrictions on cross-examination be explained to the jury. In *RL* (at [10]), the Court of Appeal approved the following passage in the trial judge's summing up: 'So far as [the] Defendant is concerned you must also bear in mind the difficulty which [defence counsel] had in cross-examination of the children. It is not possible to cross-examine children in the same way as you would an adult, it necessarily has to be more simple and inevitably cannot be as incisive as cross-examination of an adult. So please bear that disadvantage in mind.' The same type of direction is advisable in any case where cross-examination has been restricted due to the witness's intrinsic characteristics, regardless of whether s. 28 has been used. See also the *Crown Court Compendium* (July 2020), ch. 10-5, paras. 8 to 10 and appendix IV draft direction; *Wills* [2011] EWCA Crim 1938, [2012] 1 Cr App R 2 (16); *Edwards* [2011] EWCA Crim 3028; *Mahomud* [2019] EWCA Crim 667 at [26]. *PMH* [2018] EWCA Crim 2452, [2019] 1 Cr App R 27 (356) recommends (at [21]) that the limitations be explained to the jury in s. 28 cases *before* the pre-recorded cross-examination is played, and then reiterated in the summing-up, including in any written directions to the jury; this is good practice even where viva voce cross-examination is conducted at trial (*YGM* [2018] EWCA Crim 2458 at [21]; see **D14.51**). It is wholly inappropriate for defence advocates to complain in their closing speeches of perceived unfairness of restrictions imposed by a GRH ruling on cross-examination and of the s. 28 procedure (*Le Brocq v Liverpool Crown Court* [2019] EWCA Crim 1398, [2019] 4 WLR 108 at [62]–[64]; see also *Mahomud* [2019] EWCA Crim 667 at [26] for the boundaries of acceptable comment relating to the use by a co-defendant of an intermediary in a cutthroat case).

Evidence in Private for Sex and Intimidation Cases

D14.50 Under the YJCEA 1999, s. 25, where the proceedings relate to a sexual offence (see **D14.17**), a slavery or human trafficking case (see **D14.18**) or there are reasonable grounds to believe that a person other than the accused has sought or will seek to intimidate the witness, the court may permit a witness to give evidence in private. However, the accused, legal representatives and any interpreter or other person appointed to assist the witness cannot be excluded from the court under s. 25. Any order to close the court must provide for a nominated representative of a news gathering or reporting organisation to attend. The court retains inherent jurisdiction to close the court or to limit the numbers of people in the public gallery, e.g., in proceedings involving a vulnerable defendant (CrimPR 6.6 to 6.8 and 50.3; CrimPD I, paras. 3G.13 and 3G.14). In *Richards* (1999) 163 JP 246, the Court of Appeal held that s. 25 did not conflict with the ECHR, Article 6(1), as it expressly permits departure from the principle of trial in public where 'publicity would prejudice the interests of justice'.

Statutory Provisions on Special Measures

D14.51 **Youth Justice and Criminal Evidence Act 1999, ss. 16 to 30 and 33A to 33C**

16.— (1) For the purposes of this chapter a witness in criminal proceedings (other than the accused) is eligible for assistance by virtue of this section—
(a) if under the age of 18 at the time of the hearing; or
(b) if the court considers that the quality of evidence given by the witness is likely to be diminished by reason of any circumstances falling within subsection (2).
(2) The circumstances falling within this subsection are—
(a) that the witness—
(i) suffers from mental disorder within the meaning of the Mental Health Act 1983, or
(ii) otherwise has a significant impairment of intelligence and social functioning;
(b) that the witness has a physical disability or is suffering from a physical disorder.
(3) In subsection (1)(a) 'the time of the hearing', in relation to a witness, means the time when it falls to the court to make a determination for the purposes of section 19(2) in relation to the witness.
(4) In determining whether a witness falls within subsection (1)(b) the court must consider any views expressed by the witness.
(5) In this chapter references to the quality of a witness's evidence are to its quality in terms of completeness, coherence and accuracy; and for this purpose 'coherence' refers to a witness's ability in giving evidence to give answers which address the questions put to the witness and can be understood both individually and collectively.

D14.52 17.—(1) For the purposes of this chapter a witness in criminal proceedings (other than the accused) is eligible for assistance by virtue of this subsection if the court is satisfied that the quality of evidence given by the witness is likely to be diminished by reason of fear or distress on the part of the witness in connection with testifying in the proceedings.
(2) In determining whether a witness falls within subsection (1) the court must take into account, in particular—
(a) the nature and alleged circumstances of the offence to which the proceedings relate;
(b) the age of the witness;
(c) such of the following matters as appear to the court to be relevant, namely—
(i) the social and cultural background and ethnic origins of the witness,
(ii) the domestic and employment circumstances of the witness, and
(iii) any religious beliefs or political opinions of the witness;
(d) any behaviour towards the witness on the part of—
(i) the accused,
(ii) members of the family or associates of the accused, or
(iii) any other person who is likely to be an accused or a witness in the proceedings.
(3) In determining that question the court must in addition consider any views expressed by the witness.
(4) Where the complainant in respect of a sexual offence or an offence under section 1 or 2 of the Modern Slavery Act 2015 is a witness in proceedings relating to that offence (or to that offence and any other offences), the witness is eligible for assistance in relation to those proceedings by

virtue of this subsection unless the witness has informed the court of the witness's wish not to be so eligible by virtue of this subsection.

(5) A witness in proceedings relating to a relevant offence (or to a relevant offence and any other offences) is eligible for assistance in relation to those proceedings by virtue of this subsection unless the witness has informed the court of the witness's wish not to be so eligible by virtue of this subsection.

(6) For the purposes of subsection (5) an offence is a relevant offence if it is an offence described in Schedule 1A.

(7) The Secretary of State may by order amend Schedule 1A.

18.— (1) For the purposes of this chapter— **D14.53**

(a) the provision which may be made by a special measures direction by virtue of each of sections 23 to 30 is a special measure available in relation to a witness eligible for assistance by virtue of section 16; and

(b) the provision which may be made by such a direction by virtue of each of sections 23 to 28 is a special measure available in relation to a witness eligible for assistance by virtue of section 17;

but this subsection has effect subject to subsection (2).

(2) Where (apart from this subsection) a special measure would, in accordance with subsection (1)(a) or (b), be available in relation to a witness in any proceedings, it shall not be taken by a court to be available in relation to the witness unless—

(a) the court has been notified by the Secretary of State that relevant arrangements may be made available in the area in which it appears to the court that the proceedings will take place, and

(b) the notice has not been withdrawn.

(3) In subsection (2) 'relevant arrangements' means arrangements for implementing the measure in question which cover the witness and the proceedings in question.

(4) The withdrawal of a notice under that subsection relating to a special measure shall not affect the availability of that measure in relation to a witness if a special measures direction providing for that measure to apply to the witness's evidence has been made by the court before the notice is withdrawn.

(5) [Power of Secretary of State to amend so as to alter special measures available.]

19.— (1) This section applies where in any criminal proceedings— **D14.54**

(a) a party to the proceedings makes an application for the court to give a direction under this section in relation to a witness in the proceedings other than the accused, or

(b) the court of its own motion raises the issue whether such a direction should be given.

(2) Where the court determines that the witness is eligible for assistance by virtue of section 16 or 17, the court must then—

(a) determine whether any of the special measures available in relation to the witness (or any combination of them) would, in its opinion, be likely to improve the quality of evidence given by the witness; and

(b) if so—

(i) determine which of those measures (or combination of them) would, in its opinion, be likely to maximise so far as practicable the quality of such evidence; and

(ii) give a direction under this section providing for the measure or measures so determined to apply to evidence given by the witness.

(3) In determining for the purposes of this chapter whether any special measure or measures would or would not be likely to improve, or to maximise so far as practicable, the quality of evidence given by the witness, the court must consider all the circumstances of the case, including in particular—

(a) any views expressed by the witness; and

(b) whether the measure or measures might tend to inhibit such evidence being effectively tested by a party to the proceedings.

(4) A special measures direction must specify particulars of the provision made by the direction in respect of each special measure which is to apply to the witness's evidence.

(5) In this chapter 'special measures direction' means a direction under this section.

(6) Nothing in this chapter is to be regarded as affecting any power of a court to make an order or give leave of any description (in the exercise of its inherent jurisdiction or otherwise)—

(a) in relation to a witness who is not an eligible witness, or

(b) in relation to an eligible witness where (as, for example, in a case where a foreign language interpreter is to be provided) the order is made or the leave is given otherwise than by reason of the fact that the witness is an eligible witness.

D14.55 20.— (1) Subject to subsection (2) and section 21(8), a special measures direction has binding effect from the time it is made until the proceedings for the purposes of which it is made are either—

(a) determined (by acquittal, conviction or otherwise), or

(b) abandoned, in relation to the accused or (if there is more than one) in relation to each of the accused.

(2) The court may discharge or vary (or further vary) a special measures direction if it appears to the court to be in the interests of justice to do so, and may do so either—

(a) on an application made by a party to the proceedings, if there has been a material change of circumstances since the relevant time, or

(b) of its own motion.

(3) In subsection (2) 'the relevant time' means—

(a) the time when the direction was given, or

(b) if a previous application has been made under that subsection, the time when the application (or last application) was made.

(4) Nothing in section 24(2) and (3), 27(4) to (7) or 28(4) to (6) is to be regarded as affecting the power of the court to vary or discharge a special measures direction under subsection (2).

(5) The court must state in open court its reasons for—

(a) giving or varying,

(b) refusing an application for, or for the variation or discharge of, or

(c) discharging, a special measures direction and, if it is a magistrates' court, must cause them to be entered in the register of its proceedings.

(6) [Provision as to rules of court.]

D14.56 21.— (1) For the purposes of this section—

(a) a witness in criminal proceedings is a 'child witness' if he is an eligible witness by reason of section 16(1)(a) (whether or not he is an eligible witness by reason of any other provision of section 16 or 17);

(b) [repealed]; and

(c) a 'relevant recording', in relation to a child witness, is a video recording of an interview of the witness made with a view to its admission as evidence-in-chief of the witness.

(2) Where the court, in making a determination for the purposes of section 19(2), determines that a witness in criminal proceedings is a child witness, the court must—

(a) first have regard to subsections (3) to (4C) below; and

(b) then have regard to section 19(2);

and for the purposes of section 19(2), as it then applies to the witness, any special measures required to be applied in relation to him by virtue of this section shall be treated as if they were measures determined by the court, pursuant to section 19(2)(a) and (b)(i), to be ones that (whether on their own or with any other special measures) would be likely to maximise, so far as practicable, the quality of his evidence.

(3) The primary rule in the case of a child witness is that the court must give a special measures direction in relation to the witness which complies with the following requirements—

(a) it must provide for any relevant recording to be admitted under section 27 (video recorded evidence-in-chief); and

(b) it must provide for any evidence given by the witness in the proceedings which is not given by means of a video recording (whether in chief or otherwise) to be given by means of a live link in accordance with section 24.

(4) The primary rule is subject to the following limitations—

(a) the requirement contained in subsection (3)(a) or (b) has effect subject to the availability (within the meaning of section 18(2)) of the special measure in question in relation to the witness;

(b) the requirement contained in subsection (3)(a) also has effect subject to section 27(2);

(ba) if the witness informs the court of the witness's wish that the rule should not apply or should apply only in part, the rule does not apply to the extent that the court is satisfied that not complying with the rule would not diminish the quality of the witness's evidence; and

(c) the rule does not apply to the extent that the court is satisfied that compliance with it would not be likely to maximise the quality of the witness's evidence so far as practicable (whether because the application to that evidence of one or more other special measures available in relation to the witness would have that result or for any other reason).

(4A) Where as a consequence of all or part of the primary rule being disapplied under subsection (4)(ba) a witness's evidence or any part of it would fall to be given as testimony in court, the court must give a special measures direction making such provision as is described in section 23 for the evidence or that part of it.

(4B) The requirement in subsection (4A) is subject to the following limitations—

(a) if the witness informs the court of the witness's wish that the requirement in subsection (4A) should not apply, the requirement does not apply to the extent that the court is satisfied that not complying with it would not diminish the quality of the witness's evidence; and

(b) the requirement does not apply to the extent that the court is satisfied that making such a provision would not be likely to maximise the quality of the witness's evidence so far as practicable (whether because the application to that evidence of one or more other special measures available in relation to the witness would have that result or for any other reason).

(4C) In making a decision under subsection (4)(ba) or (4B)(a), the court must take into account the following factors (and any others it considers relevant)—

(a) the age and maturity of the witness;

(b) the ability of the witness to understand the consequences of giving evidence otherwise than in accordance with the requirements in subsection (3) or (as the case may be) in accordance with the requirement in subsection (4A);

(c) the relationship (if any) between the witness and the accused;

(d) the witness's social and cultural background and ethnic origins;

(e) the nature and alleged circumstances of the offence to which the proceedings relate.

(5) to (7) [Repealed.]

(8) Where a special measures direction is given in relation to a child witness who is an eligible witness by reason only of section 16(1)(a), then—

(a) subject to subsection (9) below, and

(b) except where the witness has already begun to give evidence in the proceedings,

the direction shall cease to have effect at the time when the witness attains the age of 18.

(9) Where a special measures direction is given in relation to a child witness who is an eligible witness by reason only of section 16(1)(a) and—

(a) the direction provides—

(i) for any relevant recording to be admitted under section 27 as evidence-in-chief of the witness, or

(ii) for the special measure available under section 28 to apply in relation to the witness, and

(b) if it provides for that special measure to so apply, the witness is still under the age of 18 when the video recording is made for the purposes of section 28,

then, so far as it provides as mentioned in paragraph (a)(i) or (ii) above, the direction shall continue to have effect in accordance with section 20(1) even though the witness subsequently attains that age.

22.— (1) For the purposes of this section— D14.57

(a) a witness in criminal proceedings (other than the accused) is a 'qualifying witness' if he—

(i) is not an eligible witness at the time of the hearing (as defined by section 16(3)), but

(ii) was under the age of 18 when a relevant recording was made;

(b) [repealed]; and

(c) a 'relevant recording', in relation to a witness, is a video recording of an interview of the witness made with a view to its admission as evidence-in-chief of the witness.

(2) Subsections (2) to (4) and (4C) of section 21, so far as relating to the giving of a direction complying with the requirement contained in section 21(3)(a), apply to a qualifying witness in respect of the relevant recording as they apply to a child witness (within the meaning of that section).

22A.— (1) This section applies where in criminal proceedings relating to a sexual offence (or to a sexual offence and other offences) the complainant in respect of that offence is a witness in the proceedings. D14.58

(2) This section does not apply if the place of trial is a magistrates' court.

(3) This section does not apply if the complainant is an eligible witness by reason of section 16(1)(a) (whether or not the complainant is an eligible witness by reason of any other provision of section 16 or 17).

(4) If a party to the proceedings makes an application under section 19(1)(a) for a special measures direction in relation to the complainant, the party may request that the direction provide for any relevant recording to be admitted under section 27 (video recorded evidence in chief).

(5) Subsection (6) applies if—
(a) a party to the proceedings makes a request under subsection (4) with respect to the complainant, and
(b) the court determines for the purposes of section 19(2) that the complainant is eligible for assistance by virtue of section 16(1)(b) or 17.
(6) The court must—
(a) first have regard to subsections (7) to (9); and
(b) then have regard to section 19(2);
and for the purposes of section 19(2), as it then applies to the complainant, any special measure required to be applied in relation to the complainant by virtue of this section is to be treated as if it were a measure determined by the court, pursuant to section 19(2)(a) and (b)(i), to be one that (whether on its own or with any other special measures) would be likely to maximise, so far as practicable, the quality of the complainant's evidence.
(7) The court must give a special measures direction in relation to the complainant that provides for any relevant recording to be admitted under section 27.
(8) The requirement in subsection (7) has effect subject to section 27(2).
(9) The requirement in subsection (7) does not apply to the extent that the court is satisfied that compliance with it would not be likely to maximise the quality of the complainant's evidence so far as practicable (whether because the application to that evidence of one or more other special measures available in relation to the complainant would have that result or for any other reason).
(10) In this section 'relevant recording', in relation to a complainant, is a video recording of an interview of the complainant made with a view to its admission as the evidence-in-chief of the complainant.

D14.59 23.— (1) A special measures direction may provide for the witness, while giving testimony or being sworn in court, to be prevented by means of a screen or other arrangement from seeing the accused.
(2) But the screen or other arrangement must not prevent the witness from being able to see, and to be seen by—
(a) the judge or justices (or both) and the jury (if there is one);
(b) legal representatives acting in the proceedings; and
(c) any interpreter or other person appointed (in pursuance of the direction or otherwise) to assist the witness.
(3) Where two or more legal representatives are acting for a party to the proceedings, subsection (2)(b) is to be regarded as satisfied in relation to those representatives if the witness is able at all material times to see and be seen by at least one of them.

D14.60 24.— (1) A special measures direction may provide for the witness to give evidence by means of a live link.
(1A) Such a direction may also provide for a specified person to accompany the witness while the witness is giving evidence by live link.
(1B) In determining who may accompany the witness, the court must have regard to the wishes of the witness.
(2) Where a direction provides for the witness to give evidence by means of a live link, the witness may not give evidence in any other way without the permission of the court.
(3) The court may give permission for the purposes of subsection (2) if it appears to the court to be in the interests of justice to do so, and may do so either—
(a) on an application by a party to the proceedings, if there has been a material change of circumstances since the relevant time, or
(b) of its own motion.
(4) In subsection (3) 'the relevant time' means—
(a) the time when the direction was given, or
(b) if a previous application has been made under that subsection, the time when the application (or last application) was made.
(5) to (7) [Repealed.]
(8) In this chapter 'live link' means a live television link or other arrangement whereby a witness, while absent from the courtroom or other place where the proceedings are being held, is able to see and hear a person there and to be seen and heard by the persons specified in section 23(2)(a) to (c).

25.— (1) A special measures direction may provide for the exclusion from the court, during the giving of the witness's evidence, of persons of any description specified in the direction. **D14.61**

(2) The persons who may be so excluded do not include—

(a) the accused,

(b) legal representatives acting in the proceedings, or

(c) any interpreter or other person appointed (in pursuance of the direction or otherwise) to assist the witness.

(3) A special measures direction providing for representatives of news gathering or reporting organisations to be so excluded shall be expressed not to apply to one named person who—

(a) is a representative of such an organisation, and

(b) has been nominated for the purpose by one or more such organisations, unless it appears to the court that no such nomination has been made.

(4) A special measures direction may only provide for the exclusion of persons under this section where—

(a) the proceedings relate to a sexual offence or an offence under section 1 or 2 of the Modern Slavery Act 2015; or

(b) it appears to the court that there are reasonable grounds for believing that any person other than the accused has sought, or will seek, to intimidate the witness in connection with testifying in the proceedings.

(5) Any proceedings from which persons are excluded under this section (whether or not those persons include representatives of news gathering or reporting organisations) shall nevertheless be taken to be held in public for the purposes of any privilege or exemption from liability available in respect of fair, accurate and contemporaneous reports of legal proceedings held in public.

26. A special measures direction may provide for the wearing of wigs or gowns to be dispensed with during the giving of the witness's evidence.

27.— (1) A special measures direction may provide for a video recording of an interview of the witness to be admitted as evidence-in-chief of the witness. **D14.62**

(2) A special measures direction may, however, not provide for a video recording, or a part of such a recording, to be admitted under this section if the court is of the opinion, having regard to all the circumstances of the case, that in the interests of justice the recording, or that part of it, should not be so admitted.

(3) In considering for the purposes of subsection (2) whether any part of a recording should not be admitted under this section, the court must consider whether any prejudice to the accused which might result from that part being so admitted is outweighed by the desirability of showing the whole, or substantially the whole, of the recorded interview.

(4) Where a special measures direction provides for a recording to be admitted under this section, the court may nevertheless subsequently direct that it is not to be so admitted if—

(a) it appears to the court that—

(i) the witness will not be available for cross-examination (whether conducted in the ordinary way or in accordance with any such direction), and

(ii) the parties to the proceedings have not agreed that there is no need for the witness to be so available; or

(b) any Criminal Procedure Rules requiring disclosure of the circumstances in which the recording was made have not been complied with to the satisfaction of the court.

(5) Where a recording is admitted under this section—

(a) the witness must be called by the party tendering it in evidence, unless—

(i) a special measures direction provides for the witness's evidence on cross-examination to be given otherwise than by testimony in court, or

(ii) the parties to the proceedings have agreed as mentioned in subsection (4)(a)(ii); and

(b) the witness may not without the permission of the court give evidence in chief otherwise than by means of the recording as to any matter which, in the opinion of the court, is dealt with in the witness's recorded testimony.

(6) Where in accordance with subsection (2) a special measures direction provides for part only of a recording to be admitted under this section, references in subsections (4) and (5) to the recording or to the witness's recorded testimony are references to the part of the recording or testimony which is to be so admitted.

(7) The court may give permission for the purposes of subsection (5)(b) if it appears to the court to be in the interests of justice to do so, and may do so either—

(a) on an application by a party to the proceedings, or

(b) of its own motion.

(8) [Repealed.]

(9) The court may, in giving permission for the purposes of subsection (5)(b), direct that the evidence in question is to be given by the witness by means of a live link.

(9A) If the court directs under subsection (9) that evidence is to be given by live link, it may also make such provision in that direction as it could make under section 24(1A) in a special measures direction.

(10) A magistrates' court inquiring into an offence as examining justices under section 6 of the Magistrates' Courts Act 1980 may consider any video recording in relation to which it is proposed to apply for a special measures direction providing for it to be admitted at the trial in accordance with this section.

(11) Nothing in this section affects the admissibility of any video recording which would be admissible apart from this section.

D14.63 28.— (1) Where a special measures direction provides for a video recording to be admitted under section 27 as evidence in chief of the witness, the direction may also provide—

(a) for any cross-examination of the witness, and any re-examination, to be recorded by means of a video recording; and

(b) for such a recording to be admitted, so far as it relates to any such cross-examination or re-examination, as evidence of the witness under cross-examination or on re-examination, as the case may be.

(2) Such a recording must be made in the presence of such persons as [the Criminal Procedure Rules] or the direction may provide and in the absence of the accused, but in circumstances in which—

(a) the judge or justices (or both) and legal representatives acting in the proceedings are able to see and hear the examination of the witness and to communicate with the persons in whose presence the recording is being made, and

(b) the accused is able to see and hear any such examination and to communicate with any legal representative acting for him.

(3) Where two or more legal representatives are acting for a party to the proceedings, subsection (2)(a) and (b) are to be regarded as satisfied in relation to those representatives if at all material times they are satisfied in relation to at least one of them.

(4) Where a special measures direction provides for a recording to be admitted under this section, the court may nevertheless subsequently direct that it is not to be so admitted if any requirement of subsection (2) or [the Criminal Procedure Rules] or the direction has not been complied with to the satisfaction of the court.

(5) Where in pursuance of subsection (1) a recording has been made of any examination of the witness, the witness may not be subsequently cross-examined or re-examined in respect of any evidence given by the witness in the proceedings (whether in any recording admissible under section 27 or this section or otherwise than in such a recording) unless the court gives a further special measures direction making such provision as is mentioned in subsection (1)(a) and (b) in relation to any subsequent cross-examination, and re-examination, of the witness.

(6) The court may only give such a further direction if it appears to the court—

(a) that the proposed cross-examination is sought by a party to the proceedings as a result of that party having become aware, since the time when the original recording was made in pursuance of subsection (1), of a matter which that party could not with reasonable diligence have ascertained by then, or

(b) that for any other reason it is in the interests of justice to give the further direction.

(7) Nothing in this section shall be read as applying in relation to any cross-examination of the witness by the accused in person (in a case where the accused is to be able to conduct any such cross-examination).

D14.64 29.— (1) A special measures direction may provide for any examination of the witness (however and wherever conducted) to be conducted through an interpreter or other person approved by the court for the purposes of this section ('an intermediary').

(2) The function of an intermediary is to communicate—

(a) to the witness, questions put to the witness, and

(b) to any person asking such questions, the answers given by the witness in reply to them,

and to explain such questions or answers so far as necessary to enable them to be understood by the witness or person in question.

(3) Any examination of the witness in pursuance of subsection (1) must take place in the presence of such persons as Criminal Procedure Rules or the direction may provide, but in circumstances in which—
   (a) the judge or justices (or both) and legal representatives acting in the proceedings are able to see and hear the examination of the witness and to communicate with the intermediary, and
   (b) (except in the case of a video recorded examination) the jury (if there is one) are able to see and hear the examination of the witness.
(4) Where two or more legal representatives are acting for a party to the proceedings, subsection (3)(a) is to be regarded as satisfied in relation to those representatives if at all material times it is satisfied in relation to at least one of them.
(5) A person may not act as an intermediary in a particular case except after making a declaration, in such form as may be prescribed by Criminal Procedure Rules, that he will faithfully perform his function as intermediary.
(6) Subsection (1) does not apply to an interview of the witness which is recorded by means of a video recording with a view to its admission as evidence-in-chief of the witness; but a special measures direction may provide for such a recording to be admitted under section 27 if the interview was conducted through an intermediary and—
   (a) that person complied with subsection (5) before the interview began, and
   (b) the court's approval for the purposes of this section is given before the direction is given.
(7) Section 1 of the Perjury Act 1911 (perjury) shall apply in relation to a person acting as an intermediary as it applies in relation to a person lawfully sworn as an interpreter in a judicial proceeding; and for this purpose, where a person acts as an intermediary in any proceeding which is not a judicial proceeding for the purposes of that section, that proceeding shall be taken to be part of the judicial proceeding in which the witness's evidence is given.

30. A special measures direction may provide for the witness, while giving evidence (whether by testimony in court or otherwise), to be provided with such device as the court considers appropriate with a view to enabling questions or answers to be communicated to or by the witness despite any disability or disorder or other impairment which the witness has or suffers from. **D14.65**

. . .

33A.—(1) This section applies to any proceedings (whether in a magistrates' court or before the Crown Court) against a person for an offence. **D14.66**
(2) The court may, on the application of the accused, give a live link direction if it is satisfied—
   (a) that the conditions in subsection (4) or, as the case may be, subsection (5) are met in relation to the accused, and
   (b) that it is in the interests of justice for the accused to give evidence through a live link.
(3) A live link direction is a direction that any oral evidence to be given before the court by the accused is to be given through a live link.
(4) Where the accused is aged under 18 when the application is made, the conditions are that—
   (a) his ability to participate effectively in the proceedings as a witness giving oral evidence in court is compromised by his level of intellectual ability or social functioning, and
   (b) use of a live link would enable him to participate more effectively in the proceedings as a witness (whether by improving the quality of his evidence or otherwise).
(5) Where the accused has attained the age of 18 at that time, the conditions are that—
   (a) he suffers from a mental disorder (within the meaning of the Mental Health Act 1983) or otherwise has a significant impairment of intelligence and social function,
   (b) he is for that reason unable to participate effectively in the proceedings as a witness giving oral evidence in court, and
   (c) use of a live link would enable him to participate more effectively in the proceedings as a witness (whether by improving the quality of his evidence or otherwise).
(6) While a live link direction has effect the accused may not give oral evidence before the court in the proceedings otherwise than through a live link.
(7) The court may discharge a live link direction at any time before or during any hearing to which it applies if it appears to the court to be in the interests of justice to do so (but this does not affect the power to give a further live link direction in relation to the accused).
The court may exercise this power of its own motion or on an application by a party.
(8) The court must state in open court its reasons for—
   (a) giving or discharging a live link direction, or
   (b) refusing an application for or for the discharge of a live link direction,

and, if it is a magistrates' court, it must cause those reasons to be entered in the register of its proceedings.

D14.67 33B.—(1) In section 33A 'live link' means an arrangement by which the accused, while absent from the place where the proceedings are being held, is able—

(a) to see and hear a person there, and

(b) to be seen and heard by the persons mentioned in subsection (2),

and for this purpose any impairment of eyesight or hearing is to be disregarded.

(2) The persons are—

(a) the judge or justices (or both) and the jury (if there is one),

(b) where there are two or more accused in the proceedings, each of the other accused,

(c) legal representatives acting in the proceedings, and

(d) any interpreter or other person appointed by the court to assist the accused.

[Sections 33BA and 33BB, inserted by the CAJA 2009, s. 104, are not yet in force and are not included here.]

D14.68 33C. Nothing in this Chapter affects—

(a) any power of a court to make an order, give directions or give leave of any description in relation to any witness (including an accused), or

(b) the operation of any rule of law relating to evidence in criminal proceedings.

BEST PRACTICE IN QUESTIONING CHILD AND OTHER VULNERABLE WITNESSES

D14.69 CrimPD I, para. 3E.4 (see Supplement, CPD.3E), states that enabling young and/or vulnerable people to give the best evidence they can 'may mean departing radically from traditional cross-examination'. The Court of Appeal has emphasised that there is nothing inherently unfair in restricting the scope, structure and nature of cross-examination or in requiring questions to be submitted in advance, in any case involving a child witness or one with a mental disability or disorder, observing that far from prejudicing the defence, it is the experience of many trial judges that the practice ensures that defence advocates ask focused, and often more effective, questions (*Dinc* [2017] EWCA Crim 1206; see also *Wills* [2011] EWCA Crim 1938, [2012] 1 Cr App R 2 (16) and *E* [2011] EWCA Crim 3028).

Yet there continues to be widely expressed criticism of the way in which advocates question young children and other vulnerable witnesses, including adult complainants of sexual offences, damaging public confidence in the criminal justice system and potentially deterring valid complaints. Lord Judge CJ in *Barker* [2010] EWCA Crim 4 noted (at [42]) that 'the competency test is not failed because the forensic techniques of the advocate (in particular in relation to cross-examination) or the processes of the court (for example, in relation to the patient expenditure of time) have to be adapted to enable the child to give the best evidence of which he or she is capable' (see also *F* [2013] EWCA Crim 424, [2013] 1 WLR 2143 regarding how not to conduct a competency examination). In September 2014 the Lord Chancellor announced plans for compulsory training for all advocates involved in sexual assault cases. Although the proposed regulation has been abandoned, a programme of cascaded training in the handling of vulnerable witnesses has been delivered since 2017 by the Inns of Court, the Circuits, Chambers, and the Law Society. In *Grant-Murray* [2017] EWCA Crim 1228, Lord Burnett CJ observed (at [226]) that '[i]t would be difficult to conceive of an advocate being competent to act in a case involving young witnesses or defendants unless the advocate had undertaken [that] specific training'. Hallett VP has recently recommended to judges conducting pre-trial and ground rules hearings that they check with the instructed advocates to ensure they have undergone the necessary training (*Biddle* [2019] EWCA Crim 86 at [27]; also *RT* [2020] EWCA Crim 155 at [40]–[41]).

For useful guidance for questioning witnesses in categories of vulnerability such as autism see The Advocate's Gateway (www.theadvocatesgateway.org), including guidance on GRH (CrimPD I, paras. 3E.1 to 3E.6; see Supplement, **CPD.3E**). See the *Equal Treatment Bench Book* (March 2020), ch. 2, paras. 115 to 125 on GRHs, and paras. 126 to 141, 143 to 157, on planning to question child and adult witnesses with communication needs, and effective participation by young defendants, including questions about third party material, and annexes A and B to the NSPCC/Nuffield *Good Practice Guidance in Managing Young Witness Cases and Questioning Children* (July 2009). Advocates can expect the court not to be tolerant of poor practice given these resources, now endorsed by CrimPD I, paras. 3D.5 to 3D.8 (see Supplement, **CPD.3D**). Best practice continues to evolve with the benefit of experience, and advocates and judges are expected to keep themselves up-to-date (*YGM* [2018] EWCA Crim 2458 at [21]).

CrimPD I, para. 3E.1, instructs the judiciary to stop over-rigorous or repetitive cross-examination of a child or vulnerable witness. Many trial judges now intercept questions that are not purely factual in nature.

In January 2012, the Judicial College issued a Bench Checklist for Young Witness Cases (see tinyurl.com/y7nbvjme), which requires all advocates to adapt their questions to a child's developmental stage, 'enabling *this* child's "best evidence"' (emphasis in original). The court has a duty to enforce the ground rules during cross-examination, including ensuring that the tenor, tone, language and duration of the questioning is developmentally appropriate to the particular child, to prevent questioning that is irrelevant, repetitive, oppressive or intimidating, and to be alert to possible difficulties in understanding (see also CrimPD I, para. 3E.1).

The ground rules discussion for any case involving a young or disabled or mentally disordered witness who might have difficulty in understanding questions must address the scope of cross-examination, even if the s. 28 procedure is not used, and even if questions are not directed to be reduced to writing (*Usayi* [2017] EWCA Crim 1394 at [38]; *Dinc* [2017] EWCA Crim 1206). The 2019 and 2020 versions of the *Crown Court Compendium* seem to reflect a change of judicial view since *Usayi* (decided in July 2017), in requiring that questions be reduced to writing. 'Before the GRH the defence advocate must serve on the court and on the Prosecution a copy of the list of proposed questions to be put to the young or vulnerable witness, together with a copy of the Defence Statement', and the prosecution must also submit any proposed questions for supplementary examination-in-chief (ch. 10-5, paras. 14, 16(9)). In *LeBrocq v Liverpool Crown Court* [2019] EWCA Crim 1398, [2019] 4 WLR 108 at [6], Lord Burnett CJ observed: 'whether the evidence is being video-recorded or whether cross-examination proceeds at the trial the modern and accepted way of dealing with cross-examination of a child witness is generally for the questions to be approved in advance by the judge to ensure that the witness is treated appropriately but without any compromise of the fairness of the trial.' The GRH must address how the defence case is to be put to the witness, bearing in mind the jury direction mandated by *Barker* that the defence case need not be put in detail in cross-examination of younger children. CrimPD I, para. 3E.4, provides that the court may dispense with the normal practice of 'putting the case', and impose clearly defined restrictions on the advocate's cross-examination, where there is a risk of a young or otherwise vulnerable witness failing to understand, becoming distressed, or acquiescing to leading questions. Limitations on content do not necessarily affect the safety of the conviction as there are usually ways in which a defence case and any relevant material can be put fully and fairly before a jury without confronting a vulnerable witness (*YGM* [2018] EWCA Crim 2458 at [24]). Prosecution and defence advocates must address with the court how matters which otherwise would have been put to a witness should be handled in closing speeches. The Court of Appeal has recently noted, with disapproval, 'an increasing practice of defence advocates to decide they will not cross-examine a vulnerable, especially a child, witness' (*RK* [2018] EWCA Crim 603 at [27]). Hallett VP cautioned prosecutors to think very carefully before agreeing to that course, as should the trial judge (at [29]). If a child is assessed as competent and the judge agrees with this assessment, the child should be expected to be called and cross-examined, with the benefit of special measures. The Court concluded (at [27]): 'although this court has in the past doubted the *right* to put every aspect of the defence D14.70

case to a vulnerable witness whatever the circumstances, it has not questioned the general *duty* to ensure the defence case is put fully and fairly and witnesses challenged, where that is possible' (emphasis in original). If the defence has not been directed at the GRH to submit questions in advance, then requiring an advocate to do so partway through cross-examination is an exceptional course unless the witness is shown to have difficulty understanding the questions; distress is not a sufficient ground to confine cross-examination (*G (S)* [2017] EWCA Crim 617, [2017] 4 WLR 119; *Dinc* [2017] EWCA Crim 1206).

The GRH must explore how the trial judge will explain to the jury the ways in which the defence has been constrained in dealing with the vulnerable witness. The Court of Appeal has recently determined that best practice is that these limitations should be explained in general terms before the cross-examination (or before the s. 28 recording is played), and any specific issues of content which the cross-examiner could not explore should be directed after the cross-examination is completed, and then reiterated in the summing-up (including any written directions) (*YGM* [2018] EWCA Crim 2458 at [21]).

D14.71 Impeachment of a vulnerable witness's credibility in cross-examination using a previous inconsistent statement should be addressed in advance. One solution is for the advocate or judge to point out important inconsistencies after (instead of during) the witness's testimony (*Rehman* [2017] EWCA Crim 106 at [50]–[52]); the judge should also remind the jury of these during summing-up, disregarding any trivial inconsistencies (para. 3E.4). Counsel should also consider the use of agreed statements of fact under the CJA 1967, s. 10, for matters which could particularly distress a vulnerable witness, such as previous sexual behaviour evidence. In *Dinc* [2017] EWCA Crim 1206, Hallett VP noted that '[t]he combination of admissions and focussed cross examination can produce a powerful defence case; more powerful than a defence advocate putting to a witness a whole series of propositions only to be met with the answers: "No", "I don't understand" or "I don't remember" '. In multi-handed trials defence advocates will be treated as a group and, if necessary, topics and issues will be divided amongst them at the GRH to prevent over-rigorous or repetitive cross-examination of a vulnerable witness (*Jonas* [2015] EWCA Crim 562 at [31]; CrimPD I, para. 3E.5). Advocates must consider whether the subject matter of cross-examination as to credit as a collateral issue requires a bad character application under the CJA 2003, s. 100 (*Jonas* at [37]). Body maps should be provided for the witness's use in sexual offence trials; advocates should never ask a witness (or intermediary) to point to his or her own body (CrimPR 3.8(7)(b)(vii); CrimPD I, para. 3E.6).

In *F (S)* [2011] EWCA Crim 1844, [2012] QB 703 at [36]–[41], Lord Judge CJ reinforced the authority of *Galbraith* [1981] 2 All ER 1060 (see **D16.54** ***et seq.***), with its emphasis on the constitutional primacy of the jury as the fact-finding body responsible for judging the credibility of the complainant, regardless of the nature of the case. These dicta are of particular force to child or vulnerable adult complainants (*Watts* [2010] EWCA Crim 1824 at [48]–[49], [54]). An application for a directed verdict is likely to succeed only where the complainant's evidence is so unsatisfactory, contradictory or transparently unreliable that no jury properly directed could convict (*F (S)* at [36]), which is likely to be a significantly higher threshold than heretofore.

WITNESS ANONYMITY ORDERS

D14.72 One measure which has received considerable attention from both Parliament and the courts is the protection for a witness afforded by anonymity. The House of Lords in *Davis* [2008] UKHL 36, [2008] 1 AC 1128 unanimously held that the burgeoning practice of according anonymity to prosecution witnesses who claimed to be intimidated, endorsed by the Court of Appeal in *Davis* [2006] EWCA Crim 1155, [2006] 4 All ER 648, breached both the common law's and the ECHR's precepts of a fair trial.

Within a month Parliament responded to *Davis* with the Criminal Evidence (Witness Anonymity) Act 2008 (replaced by Part 3, ch. 2, of the CAJA 2009 as of 1 January 2010), which introduced a new procedure for witness anonymity orders. Sections 86 to 90 of the 2009 Act largely replicate ss. 2 to 5 and 7 of the 2008 Act, and thus decisions under the 2008 Act are still relevant. Lord Judge CJ comprehensively analysed the new statutory regime in *Mayers* [2008] EWCA Crim 2989, [2009] 2 All ER 145. He stressed that 'an anonymity order should be regarded as the special measure of last practicable resort' (reiterated in respect of the 2009 Act in *Donovan* [2012] EWCA Crim 2749, and in CrimPD V, para. 18D.2: see Supplement, **CPD.18D**); nevertheless it represented Parliament's view as to how best to address the countervailing interests of the accused, the victim and the public, warranting the conclusion (perhaps dubiously) that such an order therefore complied with the ECHR, Article 6. A witness anonymity order protects the identity of the witness from disclosure in the proceedings (CAJA 2009, s. 86), although (like a SMD) it cannot include screening of the witness from the judge or jury (s. 86(4)). The CAJA 2009, s. 87, restricts the power to make an anonymity order to criminal proceedings where the accused is charged with 'an offence to which the proceedings relate', and so the common law discussed in *Davis* remains relevant to cases falling outwith its provisions (*R (B) v Westminster Magistrates' Court* [2014] UKSC 59, [2015] AC 1195 at [47]–[50], [62]–[73], holding that anonymous evidence is receivable in extradition proceedings where it is fair to receive it, confirming the pre-*Davis* case of *R (Al-Fawwaz) v Governor of Brixton Prison* [2001] UKHL 69, [2002] 1 AC 556). **D14.73**

Procedure

An application for a witness anonymity order may be made by either the prosecution or defence pursuant to the CAJA 2009, s. 87, in a magistrates' court, the Crown Court and the Court of Appeal (s. 97). The procedure is set out in CrimPR 18.18 to 18.22 (see Supplement, **R18.18** ***et seq.***) and CrimPD V, paras. 18D.1 to 18D.26 (see Supplement, **CPD.18D**), with new CrimPDs in force from 1 October 2018 focusing on practical arrangements to ensure anonymity when the witness attends court. In summary: **D14.74**

(a) The application must be served on all parties and contain nothing that might identify the witness (CrimPR 18.19(1)). It should specify the measures proposed, explain how they comply with s. 88 and why no lesser measures will suffice, such as an admission of the relevant facts (now a common practice; consider *Greenwood* [2004] EWCA Crim 1388, [2005] 1 Cr App R 7 (99)), a hearsay statement under the CJA 2003, s. 116, an order restricting public access, a SMD under the YJCEA 1999, s. 19, or witness protection measures (r. 18.19(1)(b) to (d)). The required supporting documentation is the statement of the witness whose anonymity is sought, any disclosure relating to that witness, and a defence statement or other available particulars of the defence case (r. 18.19(1)(e)). The Court of Appeal in *Mayers* [2008] EWCA Crim 2989, [2009] 2 All ER 145 made clear that the prosecution's disclosure obligations in relation to an anonymous witness 'go much further than the ordinary duties of disclosure', adding that disclosure must be 'complete' and 'full and frank'. Any failures in disclosure will be very closely scrutinised (*Okuwa* [2010] EWCA Crim 832). Disclosure is now governed by the Judicial Protocol on Disclosure and the A-G's Guidelines on Disclosure (see **D9**), CrimPR Part 15, and CrimPD IV, para. 15A.1 (unused material; see Supplement, **CPD.15A**). In the case of a defence application, the court should notify the DPP (CrimPR 18.20). A respondent prosecutor must assist the court with all available material relevant to the considerations, beyond the requirements of the CPIA 1996 (CrimPD V, para 18D.7).
(b) The accused (or other opposing party) is then afforded ten business days to respond to the application (CrimPR 18.22(2)), and is required actively to assist the court (CrimPD V, para. 18D.7). In *Mayers* the Court of Appeal stressed the importance of detailed defence statements, both to anonymity applications and to disclosure in relation to anonymous witnesses: 'the defence statement provides the benchmark against which the disclosure process

must be examined'. Where the application has been made by the defence, and the response is thus from the prosecution, additional disclosure obligations arise at that stage (r. 18.22(6)).

(c) At the hearing, the applicant should provide the court, but not the other parties, with the information redacted from the application, and either identify the witness or state why it is not possible to identify him (r. 18.19(2)). An oral hearing will be held only where sought (rr. 18.19(1)(f) and 18.22(2)(c)); if there is none, the applicant must reveal the witness's identity to the court before calling him (r. 18.19(4)).

(d) Any hearing usually takes place in private, and may be held in the absence of the accused or the accused's representative (r. 18.18(1); CrimPD V, para. 18D.10). The court's overriding obligation is to ensure that the proceedings are fair (*Mayers* [2008] EWCA Crim 2989, [2009] 2 All ER 145), and no order can be made without giving each party the opportunity to make representations (r. 18.18(2)), even if there is no hearing (r. 18.18(1)). The application will be recorded and the audiotape stored securely as for any public interest ruling application (CrimPR 5.5(2); see Supplement, **R5.5**). The record must correlate witness and order without jeopardising anonymity (CrimPD V, para. 18D.20).

(e) The court may also use its common-law power to ask the A-G to consider appointing a special advocate (*H* [2004] UKHL 3, [2004] 2 AC 134 at [21]–[22]), adapting the procedures as needed from public interest immunity applications (*Mayers* at [10]). See now CrimPD V, para. 18D.14, which emphasises that such appointment would always be exceptional and a course of last resort. For examples of special advocates cross-examining the witness claiming anonymity on a *voir dire*, see *Nazir* [2009] EWCA Crim 213 and *Chisholm* [2010] EWCA Crim 258.

(f) On a prosecutor's application, the court is likely to be assisted by the attendance of a senior investigator or other person of comparable authority who is familiar with the case (CrimPD V, para. 18D.12).

(g) The court exceptionally may invite the applicant to present the proposed witness to be questioned by the court in order to satisfy itself that the three conditions prescribed by the Act (see **D14.75**) are met, ensuring that the arrangements protect the witness's identity (CrimPD V, para. 18D.13).

(h) On an application by a defendant, it is not permissible under s. 87(3) for the defence to attempt to place disclosure of the identity of the proposed witness under conditions, such as a 'ring of confidentiality', as this would prevent the prosecution from discharging their onerous responsibility to investigate and disclose the antecedents of the proposed witness and to ensure that any application or order is consistent with a fair trial (*Sardar* [2016] EWCA Crim 1616, [2017] 1 WLR 917 at [34]–[37]). This requirement of an unfettered disclosure by the defence is consistent with the right to a fair trial because there is no obligation on the defendant equivalent to that on the prosecution to disclose material that may tend to cast doubt on the credibility, reliability, or accuracy of the witness's evidence (*Sardar* at [37]).

(i) In *C* [2008] EWCA Crim 3228 the Court of Appeal stressed that anonymity orders should not be made the subject of interlocutory appeals, as only at trial can their impact be assessed.

(j) During the trial, the court and the parties (especially the applicant) are expected to keep under review whether the conditions for making an anonymity order are met, and whether there is a case for discharge or variation (CrimPD V, paras. 18D.20 and 18D.21).

(k) If the application is refused, consideration must be given to whether the witness to whom the application related can be compelled to give evidence despite any risk to their safety, and what special measures could support them to give their evidence (CrimPD V, para. 18D.21).

(l) Should the application be granted, the judge, assisted by the court staff, should consider nine enumerated practical arrangements (confidentially recorded) to ensure that the witness's anonymity will not be compromised (CrimPD V, paras. 18D.19, 18D.26).

The A-G has issued guidelines arising from the Act: *The Prosecutor's Role in Applications for Witness Anonymity Orders* (30 November 2012) (see **appendix 2**), and the DPP has also issued guidance, *The Director's Guidance on Witness Anonymity* (December 2009, updated 28 February 2013, tinyurl.com/y7dpoba9).

Criteria

An anonymity order can be granted only if three stipulated conditions are satisfied (CAJA 2009, s. 88) to the highest standard, probability not sufficing (*Mayers* [2008] EWCA Crim 2989, [2009] 2 All ER 145 at [38]). These conditions require that the measures be: **D14.75**

(a) *necessary* (*Condition A*);
(b) that in all the circumstances the order's effect would be consistent with the defendant receiving a *fair trial* (*Condition B*); and
(c) that the witness's testimony is so important that it is in the *interests of justice* for the witness to testify and he or she would not do so if the order was not made, or alternatively there would be *real harm to the public interest* if the witness were to testify without the order (*Condition C*).

In *Mayers* Lord Judge CJ suggested that the proper starting point for trial judges is Condition C. It was stressed in *Mayers* that each of the three preconditions must be satisfied before an order can be made. However, the force of this admonition arguably was undermined by *Willett* [2011] EWCA Crim 2710, [2012] 2 Cr App R (S) 18 (76), where D knew the identity of the witness as he was a cell-mate during a disclosed specified period, so Condition A (necessity) appeared not to be met. The Court of Appeal nevertheless held that the trial judge's direction 'was entirely apt to prevent the jury from holding [the witness's] anonymity against the appellant and to get them to concentrate on the evidence actually given by the witness'. If, as the Court of Appeal said, the standard directions ensure that no prejudice arises from the witness's anonymity, then the stringent wording of the conditions seem of little protection to the defence (*Willett* at [45]–[46]; *Nazir* [2009] EWCA Crim 213).

Necessity In relation to Condition A there are three bases on which an anonymity order may be necessary. The first two are based upon the necessity of protecting the safety of the witness or another person or to prevent serious damage to property (s. 88(3)(a) and (6)). It was held in *Mayers* that the oral evidence of the witness must be important, and the threat to his or her safety must be real; reluctance to give evidence is insufficient. The threat to the witness need not come from the accused. In *Powar* [2009] EWCA Crim 594, [2009] 2 Cr App R 8 (120), the Court of Appeal rejected witness relocation as a practical alternative to anonymity in most cases. The ground of prevention of 'any serious damage to property' is controversial as it is contrary to the position of the Council of Europe (Committee of Experts, *Intimidation of Witnesses and the Rights of the Defence*, Recommendation No. R (97) 13, adopted by the Council of Europe Committee of Ministers on 10 September 1997). This ground may engage Article 6 issues since all of the ECtHR decisions approving witness anonymity were predicated on their rights to personal safety under Articles 2, 3 and 8. The Court of Appeal in *Mayers* interpreted this ground as requiring a 'serious risk' of serious damage to property (at [28]–[29]). **D14.76**

A third and distinct form of necessity is a generic ground of preventing 'real harm to the public interest, affecting any activities or safety of persons involved in them' (s. 88(3)(b)). This is less controversial, as before the Act there had been a regular practice for security, undercover and test purchase officers to testify using a pseudonym, with the benefit of a screen, and sometimes voice modulation, but with the jury and defence fully aware that these witnesses were officers acting in the course of their duties and using a pseudonym (*Mayers* at [35]; *Jack* [1998] EWCA Crim 1206). A witness anonymity order for such vital intelligence and law-enforcement assets can usually be readily justified because it is not normally germane to the defence for the purposes of cross-examination to know the witness's true identity, and any matters of criticism can be directed to the witness using the name by which the accused knew the witness (if at all) (*Mayers* at [30]–[35]). See also *Khan* [2010] EWCA Crim 1692 regarding Condition B.

Relevant Considerations Section 89(2) provides guidance as to the considerations to which a court should have regard in assessing whether the three conditions are met: **D14.77**

(a) the defendant's general right to know the witness's identity;
(b) the extent to which the witness's credibility is in issue;

(c) whether the evidence might be the 'sole or decisive' evidence implicating the defendant (see the discussion of *Al-Khawaja v UK* (2012) 54 EHRR 23 (807) at **D14.78**);
(d) whether the evidence could be properly tested without the witness's identity being disclosed (*Donovan* [2012] EWCA Crim 2749, where the Court of Appeal held that the jury had been prevented from hearing admissible and substantive material relevant to the question whether either witness granted anonymity might have been lying);
(e) whether there is any reason to believe the witness has a tendency to be dishonest or any motive for dishonesty in the circumstances of the case, having regard to any relationship between the witness and the defendant or the defendant's associates, and any prior convictions; and
(f) whether it would be reasonably practicable to protect the witness by any other means (see the list in CrimPR 18.19(1)(d)).

The weight to be given to any relevant factor is for the trial judge, and that decision can be challenged on appeal only in extreme cases (*Taylor* [2010] EWCA Crim 830). *Mayers* emphasised that s. 89(1)(b) meant that the list was not exhaustive, and that no consideration outweighed the others. This is significant because the list includes the right of an accused to confront his or her accuser, *and* the status of the anonymous evidence as the 'sole and decisive' evidence against the accused, both being heavily stressed in *Davis* [2008] UKHL 36, [2008] 1 AC 1128.

D14.78 **Sole or Decisive Evidence** In *Davis* [2008] UKHL 36, [2008] 1 AC 1128 the Law Lords considered the consistent ECtHR jurisprudence that an accused could not have a fair trial under the ECHR, Article 6, where the evidence was based solely or to a decisive extent on the testimony of an anonymous witness (e.g., *Doorson v Netherlands* (1996) 22 EHRR 330 at [76]; *Kostovski v Netherlands* (1989) 12 EHRR 434 at [42], [44]; *Lucà v Italy* (2003) 36 EHRR 46 (807) at [40]), a position adopted by the Council of Europe (Committee of Experts, *Intimidation of Witnesses and the Rights of the Defence*, Recommendation No. R (97) cl. 13). Lord Bingham (at [25]) and Lord Brown (at [64]) regarded the 'sole or decisive' test as a rule, whereas Lord Mance (at [89] and [96]–[97]) and Lord Carswell (at [59]) considered it to be a more flexible, but nonetheless important, principle to be weighed in the balance. The latter position was adopted by the Grand Chamber in *Al-Khawaja and Tahery v UK* (2012) 54 EHRR 23 (807): while those cases involved hearsay evidence, the majority's dicta explained that the reasoning also applied to anonymous witnesses (e.g., at [139] and [141]), and this was confirmed by the 4th Section of the ECtHR in *Ellis v UK* (2012) 55 EHRR SE3 (8) at [75]. The Grand Chamber described 'sole or decisive' as a 'rule' which should be applied flexibly, seemingly an oxymoron (for analysis see L Hoyano, 'What is Balanced on the Scales of Justice? In Search of the Essence of the Right to a Fair Trial' [2014] Crim LR 4). That flexibility requires consideration of the strength of any corroborating evidence for that testimony, and strong procedural safeguards which permit a fair and proper assessment of its reliability. The Grand Chamber elucidated the meaning of 'decisive', which Lord Phillips had found problematic in *Horncastle* [2009] UKSC 14, [2010] 2 AC 373; it is to be narrowly understood as 'indicating evidence of such significance or importance as is likely to be determinative of the outcome of the case' (at [131]). It is therefore likely that the three conditions and enumerated factors in the English anonymous witness legislation would prima facie meet this test; the fairness of any particular anonymous witness order must, like all other cases under Article 6, be considered in retrospect in the context of the whole trial as it unfolded. In *Ford* [2010] EWCA Crim 2250 and *Fox* [2010] EWCA Crim 1280, the Court of Appeal ruled inadmissible hearsay evidence from unidentified declarants. There must be adequate counterbalancing measures to protect the accused's rights for the admission of the evidence to comply with Article 6 (*Pesukic v Switzerland* [2012] ECHR 2031). See also *Horncastle v UK* (2015) 60 EHRR 31 (1331).

Range of Protective Measures

D14.79 Section 86(2) of the CAJA 2009 sets out a non-exclusive list of measures to protect the identity of the witness, including withholding or redacting the witness's name or other identifying details, use of a pseudonym, screen, and voice modulation. No questions may be asked of the witness of any specified description which might lead to the witness's identification, potentially imposing a major constraint on cross-examination. Thus the defence must anticipate what questions might be asked in cross-examination and make submissions at the application stage that the anonymity order would not be consistent with a fair trial, such that Condition B would not be satisfied.

Variation or Discharge of an Order

The court is required to keep any anonymity order under review. Any party may seek to discharge or vary it (CAJA 2009, s. 91), the procedure mirroring that employed for the original application (CrimPR 18.21; see Supplement, **R18.21**). A witness anonymity order may also be discharged or varied after the proceedings have come to an end (s. 92), or by an 'appeal court' in an appeal by the accused (s. 93). Such a variation or discharge may equally be ordered of the court's own motion (s. 91(2)(b)). The Court of Appeal has held that, where Condition C continues to be satisfied (see s. 88, and **D14.75**), it would be grossly unfair to a witness who has already testified to revoke the anonymity order because of what transpired later in the trial (*Taylor* [2010] EWCA Crim 830). **D14.80**

Jury Directions

Where testimony has been given anonymously, the judge in a trial on indictment must warn the jury to ensure that the order does not prejudice the accused (CAJA 2009, s. 90). Directions approved by the Court of Appeal have instructed jurors not to speculate as to the reasons why the witness testified under conditions of anonymity and, where the inference is almost inevitable, to deny specifically that the reason is attributable to the accused (*Nazir* [2009] EWCA Crim 213). The *Crown Court Compendium* (July 2020), ch. 3-8, para. 5(2), requires the trial judge to highlight the disadvantages faced by the defendant due to not knowing the witness's identity. It may be difficult, however, for such admonitions to protect against adverse inferences; the more the disadvantage is emphasised, the more juries are likely to think that the risk to the witness must be very high indeed, and attribute that threat to the defence, to warrant the trial judge ordering a procedure which the judge acknowledges prejudices the defence's right to make full answer and defence. *Willett* [2011] EWCA Crim 2710, [2012] 2 Cr App R (S) 18 (76) (at [45]–[46]) shows the Court of Appeal's faith in the efficacy of jury directions to cure prejudice even where the original anonymous witness order was not warranted in the first place (see **D14.75**). **D14.81**

The Court of Appeal has suggested that a witness anonymity warning given when the witness gives evidence should be repeated when summing-up (*Okuwa* [2010] EWCA Crim 832).

Statutory Provisions on Anonymous Witnesses

Coroners and Justice Act 2009, ss. 86 to 90 **D14.82**

86.—(1) In this Chapter a 'witness anonymity order' is an order made by a court that requires such specified measures to be taken in relation to a witness in criminal proceedings as the court considers appropriate to ensure that the identity of the witness is not disclosed in or in connection with the proceedings.

(2) The kinds of measures that may be required to be taken in relation to a witness include measures for securing one or more of the following—
   (a) that the witness's name and other identifying details may be—
      (i) withheld;
      (ii) removed from materials disclosed to any party to the proceedings;
   (b) that the witness may use a pseudonym;
   (c) that the witness is not asked questions of any specified description that might lead to the identification of the witness;
   (d) that the witness is screened to any specified extent;
   (e) that the witness's voice is subjected to modulation to any specified extent.

(3) Subsection (2) does not affect the generality of subsection (1).

(4) Nothing in this section authorises the court to require—
(a) the witness to be screened to such an extent that the witness cannot be seen by—
(i) the judge or other members of the court (if any), or
(ii) the jury (if there is one);
(b) the witness's voice to be modulated to such an extent that the witness's natural voice cannot be heard by any persons within paragraph (a)(i) or (ii).
(5) In this section 'specified' means specified in the witness anonymity order concerned.

D14.83 87.—(1) An application for a witness anonymity order to be made in relation to a witness in criminal proceedings may be made to the court by the prosecutor or the defendant.
(2) Where an application is made by the prosecutor, the prosecutor—
(a) must (unless the court directs otherwise) inform the court of the identity of the witness, but
(b) is not required to disclose in connection with the application—
(i) the identity of the witness, or
(ii) any information that might enable the witness to be identified,
to any other party to the proceedings or his or her legal representatives.
(3) Where an application is made by the defendant, the defendant—
(a) must inform the court and the prosecutor of the identity of the witness, but
(b) (if there is more than one defendant) is not required to disclose in connection with the application—
(i) the identity of the witness, or
(ii) any information that might enable the witness to be identified,
to any other defendant or his or her legal representatives.
(4) Accordingly, where the prosecutor or the defendant proposes to make an application under this section in respect of a witness, any relevant material which is disclosed by or on behalf of that party before the determination of the application may be disclosed in such a way as to prevent—
(a) the identity of the witness, or
(b) any information that might enable the witness to be identified,
from being disclosed except as required by subsection (2)(a) or (3)(a).
(5) 'Relevant material' means any document or other material which falls to be disclosed, or is sought to be relied on, by or on behalf of the party concerned in connection with the proceedings or proceedings preliminary to them.
(6) The court must give every party to the proceedings the opportunity to be heard on an application under this section.
(7) But subsection (6) does not prevent the court from hearing one or more parties in the absence of a defendant and his or her legal representatives, if it appears to the court to be appropriate to do so in the circumstances of the case.
(8) Nothing in this section is to be taken as restricting any power to make rules of court.

D14.84 88.—(1) This section applies where an application is made for a witness anonymity order to be made in relation to a witness in criminal proceedings.
(2) The court may make such an order only if it is satisfied that Conditions A to C below are met.
(3) Condition A is that the proposed order is necessary—
(a) in order to protect the safety of the witness or another person or to prevent any serious damage to property, or
(b) in order to prevent real harm to the public interest (whether affecting the carrying on of any activities in the public interest or the safety of a person involved in carrying on such activities, or otherwise).
(4) Condition B is that, having regard to all the circumstances, the effect of the proposed order would be consistent with the defendant receiving a fair trial.
(5) Condition C is that the importance of the witness's testimony is such that in the interests of justice the witness ought to testify and—
(a) the witness would not testify if the proposed order were not made, or
(b) there would be real harm to the public interest if the witness were to testify without the proposed order being made.
(6) In determining whether the proposed order is necessary for the purpose mentioned in subsection (3)(a), the court must have regard (in particular) to any reasonable fear on the part of the witness—
(a) that the witness or another person would suffer death or injury, or
(b) that there would be serious damage to property,if the witness were to be identified.

89.—(1) When deciding whether Conditions A to C in section 88 are met in the case of an application for a witness anonymity order, the court must have regard to— **D14.85**

(a) the considerations mentioned in subsection (2) below, and

(b) such other matters as the court considers relevant.

(2) The considerations are—

(a) the general right of a defendant in criminal proceedings to know the identity of a witness in the proceedings;

(b) the extent to which the credibility of the witness concerned would be a relevant factor when the weight of his or her evidence comes to be assessed;

(c) whether evidence given by the witness might be the sole or decisive evidence implicating the defendant;

(d) whether the witness's evidence could be properly tested (whether on grounds of credibility or otherwise) without his or her identity being disclosed;

(e) whether there is any reason to believe that the witness—

(i) has a tendency to be dishonest, or

(ii) has any motive to be dishonest in the circumstances of the case,

having regard (in particular) to any previous convictions of the witness and to any relationship between the witness and the defendant or any associates of the defendant;

(f) whether it would be reasonably practicable to protect the witness by any means other than by making a witness anonymity order specifying the measures that are under consideration by the court

90.—(1) Subsection (2) applies where, on a trial on indictment with a jury, any evidence has been given by a witness at a time when a witness anonymity order applied to the witness. **D14.86**

(2) The judge must give the jury such warning as the judge considers appropriate to ensure that the fact that the order was made in relation to the witness does not prejudice the defendant.

D

Part D Procedure

Section D15 Trial on Indictment: General Matters and Pre-trial Procedure

INTRODUCTION

D15.1 Once the accused has pleaded not guilty to the charges (see **D12**), the accused is at the centre of a procedural framework, now governed by the CrimPR (see Supplement, **R3.1** *et seq.*) and CrimPD I, Part 3 (see Supplement, **CPD.3A** *et seq.*), that is designed to prepare the case for trial. That framework was overhauled under the banner of Better Case Management, giving effect to the recommendations of Sir Brian Leveson's *Review of Efficiency in Criminal Proceedings* (see also **D4**). The aim is to reduce the number of hearings and to maximise engagement by participants in the process through 'robust' case management.

This section addresses those matters of general preliminary application to trials on indictment, the conduct of hearings pre-trial, and the obligations and safeguards imposed by rules at the pre-trial stage. For special measures and anonymity of witnesses, see **D14**.

PLACE OF TRIAL

D15.2 The first issue that arises is the location in which the case is to be tried. Following on from this is the question of transfer of cases between Crown Court centres.

Venue of Trial

D15.3 This is primarily regulated by the Senior Courts Act 1981, s. 75, which empowers the Lord Chief Justice to regulate both the location of the Crown Court to which an accused is initially sent and the nature of the tribunal before the trial will ultimately take place (i.e. High Court judge, circuit judge or recorder). Proceedings in advance of trial can in large measure be undertaken through the use of live link and telephone facilities, in accordance with CrimPD I, paras. 3N.1 *et seq.* (see Supplement, **CPD.3N**), so that the parties and judge are not necessarily in the same place before trial (para. 3N.8).

Senior Courts Act 1981, s. 75

(1) The cases or classes of cases in the Crown Court suitable for allocation respectively to a judge of the High Court, circuit judge, recorder or district judge (magistrates' court), and all other matters relating to the distribution of Crown Court business, shall be determined in accordance with directions given by or on behalf of the Lord Chief Justice with the concurrence of the Lord Chancellor.

(2) Subject to section 74(1) [which requires that when hearing an appeal the Crown Court shall normally consist of a professional judge together with at least two justices of the peace], the cases or classes of cases in the Crown Court suitable for allocation to a court comprising justices

> of the peace (including those by way of trial on indictment which are suitable for allocation to such a court) shall be determined in accordance with directions given by or on behalf of the Lord Chief Justice with the concurrence of the Lord Chancellor.

In addition, the MCA 1980, s. 7, provides that, when specifying the particular location of the Crown Court to which an accused should be sent for trial, a magistrates' court must have regard, *inter alia*, to the directions given by the Lord Chief Justice under s. 75(1) of the Senior Courts Act 1981. CrimPD XIII contains detailed guidance on listing; para. E deals with the allocation of business within the Crown Court (see Supplement, **CPD.XIII.E**). CrimPD I, para. 3A.4, requires the prosecution to provide the court at the outset of proceedings with 'sufficient information' to permit an informed view on, amongst other things, venue.

Transfer of Cases between Locations of the Crown Court

Section 76(1) of the Senior Courts Act 1981 provides that the Crown Court may give directions altering the place of any trial on indictment, varying either the venue specified in a notice under the CDA 1998, s. 51D(1), or any earlier decision of the Crown Court itself. Such a change can be brought about in a number of ways: **D15.4**

(a) an officer of the Crown Court may give such directions on behalf of the court (s. 76(2));
(b) either party, if dissatisfied with the place of trial that has been fixed, may apply to the Crown Court for a variation (s. 76(3)), such application to be heard in open court by a High Court judge (s. 76(4)).

The place of trial specified in notices of transfer under s. 4 of the CJA 1987 can be varied in the same way (s. 76(2A)); see also CrimPD XIII, Listing, para. F (see Supplement, **CPD.XIII.F**).

Reasons for Transfer Section 76 provides no assistance as to how the powers it gives are to be exercised. The power given to listing officers of the Crown Court by s. 76(2) to switch a trial from one court centre to another is exercised principally on administrative rather than judicial grounds. **D15.5**

Section 76(1) does contain the qualification that it is 'Without prejudice to the provisions of this Act about the distribution of Crown Court business'. It follows that, on an application by a party under s. 76(3) for variation of the venue, the High Court judge determining the application is entitled to consider any factors not originally taken into account. Such additional factors may include the possible prejudice to the accused of being tried in the area where the offence was allegedly committed if the nature of the charge has provoked exceptional public hostility.

However, in the light of the Court of Appeal's decision in *Ford* [1989] QB 868 (see **D13.40**), it would be inappropriate to vary the trial venue with a view to obtaining a multiracial jury panel (see also *Bansal* [1985] Crim LR 151).

Senior Courts Act 1981, s. 76 **D15.6**

(1) Without prejudice to the provisions of this Act about the distribution of Crown Court business, the Crown Court may give directions, or further directions, altering the place of any trial on indictment, whether by substituting some other place for the place specified in a notice under section 51D(1) of the Crime and Disorder Act 1998 (a 'section 51D notice') or by varying a previous decision of the Crown Court.
(2) Directions under subsection (1) may be given on behalf of the Crown Court by an officer of the court.
(2A) Where a preparatory hearing has been ordered under section 7 of the Criminal Justice Act 1987, directions altering the place of trial may be given under subsection (1) at any time before the time when the jury are sworn.
(2B) The reference in subsection (2A) to the time when the jury are sworn includes the time when the jury would be sworn but for the making of an order under Part 7 of the Criminal Justice Act 2003.

(3) The defendant or the prosecutor, if dissatisfied with the place of trial specified in a section 51D notice or as fixed by the Crown Court, may apply to the Crown Court for a direction, or further direction, varying the place of trial; and the court shall take the matter into consideration and may comply with or refuse the application, or give a direction not in compliance with the application, as the court thinks fit.

(4) An application under subsection (3) shall be heard in open court by a judge of the High Court.

CUSTODY TIME-LIMITS

D15.7 Section 22 of the Prosecution of Offences Act 1985 (set out at **D15.38**) was introduced to remedy the manifest inadequacy of the provisions then available to ensure that trials on indictment begin within a reasonable time. It empowers the Secretary of State to make regulations fixing:

(a) the maximum period available to the prosecution to complete any preliminary (pre-trial) stage of proceedings for an offence; and/or

(b) the maximum period for which an accused may be kept in custody while awaiting completion of such a stage.

Periods Applicable

D15.8 The regulations may prescribe an *overall time-limit* within which the prosecution must complete the stage of the proceedings in question (Prosecution of Offences Act 1985, s. 22(1)(a)). However, no overall time-limits currently apply.

Alternatively or additionally, the regulations may prescribe a *custody time-limit*, that being the maximum period for which the accused may be remanded in custody while the stage is being completed (s. 22(1)(b)).

D15.9 **Time-limits** The regulations in question, the Prosecution of Offences (Custody Time Limits) Regulations 1987 (SI 1987 No. 299), only impose custody time-limits. These are as follows:

(a) *Between first appearance and committal.* By reg. 4(2) and (4), the maximum period for which an accused charged with an indictable offence may be held in the custody of the magistrates' court between first appearance and committal proceedings is 70 days.

(b) *Between first appearance and summary trial.* If the offence is triable either way and the court determines to try the case summarily, the maximum period in custody between first appearance and the court beginning to hear evidence for the prosecution is again 70 days, unless the decision for summary trial is taken within 56 days, in which case the limit is reduced to 56 days (reg. 4(2) and (3)). In the case of a summary offence, the maximum period is 56 days (reg. 4(4A)).

(c) *Between committal and trial on indictment.* By reg. 5(3)(a), the maximum period for which an accused committed for trial to the Crown Court may be held in custody between 'committal' and the start of trial is 112 days.

(d) *Multiple committals.* If a single indictment is preferred containing counts in respect of which the accused was committed for trial on two or more different occasions, the 112-day limit applies separately in relation to each offence (reg. 6(4)). See also **D15.10**.

(e) *Section 51 sending.* Where the accused has been sent for trial under the CDA 1998, s. 51, the maximum period is 182 days between the date on which the accused is sent to the Crown Court and the start of the trial. From this maximum must be deducted any period during which the accused was held in custody by the magistrates (reg. 5(6B)).

(f) *Retrial directed by the Court of Appeal.* Where an indictment is preferred by direction of the Court of Appeal, following the ordering of a retrial, the 112-day limit applies from that preferment (reg. 5(2)(b) and (3)(b)). See also *Leeds Crown Court, ex parte Whitehead* (17 June 1999 unreported, DC).

(g) *Voluntary bill.* Where proceedings are by way of a voluntary bill of indictment the 112-day period runs from the date of preferment of the bill (reg. 5(3)(b)).

Separate Time-limits for Each Offence

Each offence with which the accused is charged attracts its own time-limit (*Wirral District Magistrates' Court, ex parte Meikle* (1990) 154 JP 1035). In this case, M was charged with five different offences at different dates, being held in custody from the date of the first charge. In view of the fact that the 1987 Regulations repeatedly refer to 'offence' in the singular, the Divisional Court had no difficulty in concluding that each offence attracts its own custody time-limit. **D15.10**

Meaning of Separate Offences In *R (Wardle) v Leeds Crown Court* [2001] UKHL 12, [2002] 1 AC 754, D was originally charged with murder, but the prosecution offered no evidence on that charge and preferred a charge of manslaughter on the day that the original custody time-limit was due to expire. On appeal, the House of Lords considered the question: what constitutes the charging of an offence, such as to trigger a fresh custody time-limit? It concluded: **D15.11**

(a) the word 'offence' in reg. 4 could not be read as including an alternative offence of which the accused could be found guilty under the CLA 1967;
(b) the situation would be different if the new charge was simply a restatement of the original charge with different particulars — it had to be a different offence in law to attract a fresh custody time-limit; and
(c) the bringing of a fresh charge would be an abuse of process if the prosecution could not demonstrate, on the facts of the case, that it was justified and had not been brought solely with a view to obtaining the substitution of a fresh custody time-limit.

Definition of Terms

Inevitably the main concern of practitioners and the courts is the consequences of a time-limit expiring and applications being made to extend it. Before approaching these issues, however, it is of assistance to define some of the relevant terminology. **D15.12**

Committal References to 'committal' in this context should be taken to include sending for trial under the CDA 1998, s. 51, and the giving of a notice of transfer under either the CJA 1987, s. 4, or the CJA 1991, s. 53 (subject to specific variations in such cases). **D15.13**

Regulations under the Prosecution of Offences Act 1985, s. 22, have application not only to the time between committal and arraignment, but also to the time between the accused being charged and committal (for offences triable on indictment) or the time between charge and the commencement of summary trial (in other cases). Section 22 is thus relevant to the timing both of committal and summary trial, as well as to the timing of arraignment.

Preliminary Stage of Proceedings The general effect of s. 22 of the Prosecution of Offences Act 1985 is that the Secretary of State may by regulation impose time-limits in respect of any specified 'preliminary stage' of proceedings for an offence (s. 22(1)). The regulations may relate to any type of offence, whether triable only on indictment, triable either way or summarily. 'Preliminary stage' is defined as *not* including anything after the start of trial. **D15.14**

Start of a Trial on Indictment As far as trial on indictment is concerned, the 'start of trial' is defined as the point when a jury is sworn, or the court accepts a plea of guilty (Prosecution of Offences Act 1985, s. 22(11A)). **D15.15**

This is significant in cases where a preparatory hearing is held, whether for a long or complex case (in accordance with the CPIA 1996, s. 30: see **D15.51** ***et seq.***) or for a serious or complex fraud (in accordance with the CJA 1987, s. 8). Under each of those sections, the beginning of the preparatory hearing is deemed to be the beginning of the trial, and therefore custody time-limits will cease to operate from that moment.

In *Re Kanaris* [2003] UKHL 2, [2003] 1 WLR 443, the House of Lords considered the consequences of the removal of the protection of the custody time-limits regime where a preparatory hearing took place. Lord Hope said:

> . . . a judge who is minded to order a preparatory hearing in a long and complex case should be careful not to deprive an accused who is in custody of the protection of the statutory custody time-limit until it has become necessary for him to do so.

He indicated that the judge could, where appropriate, exercise powers under the CPIA 1996, s. 31(4) to (7) (see **D15.58**), before the preparatory hearing begins to permit effective case management whilst preserving the accused's right to the protection of the statutory custody time-limit.

D15.16 **Start of a Summary Trial** As far as summary trial is concerned, the start of trial is 'when the court begins to hear evidence for the prosecution at trial' or accepts a plea of guilty (Prosecution of Offences Act 1985, s. 22(11B)). There is an exception where the court begins to consider whether to exercise its power, under the Mental Health Act 1983, s. 37(3), to make a hospital order without convicting the accused.

D15.17 **Meaning of Custody** As far as custody time-limits are concerned, 'custody' includes:

(a) local authority accommodation or youth detention accommodation to which a juvenile is committed by virtue of the LASPO 2012, s. 91 (Prosecution of Offences Act 1985, s. 22(11));
(b) the detention of a youth charged with an indictable offence — in *Stratford Youth Court, ex parte S* (1998) 162 JP 552, the Divisional Court held that the 56-day custody time-limit imposed for completion of preliminary stages in indictable offences applied to a young person charged with robbery because, in the case of a young person, it was an offence triable either way;
(c) where an accused is unable to provide a surety and so remains in custody, under the terms of the MCA 1980, s. 128 (*Re Ofili* [1995] Crim LR 880).

In *Peterborough Crown Court, ex parte L* [2000] Crim LR 470, the Divisional Court held that the whole period during which the accused was remanded in custody for the offence in question should be taken into account when calculating the relevant period for custody time-limits. There was no basis on which part of the period could be disregarded on the basis that the accused was also serving a custodial sentence for an unrelated matter.

Effect of Expiry of Custody Time-limit

D15.18 If a custody time-limit expires before completion of the stage of proceedings in question, the accused must be granted bail, in relation at least to the offence to which the limit relates. This is made clear by reg. 6(6), which states that, where the Crown Court is notified that the 112-day time-limit between 'committal' and the start of the trial is about to expire in a certain case, it must bail the accused as from the expiry of the limit, subject to a duty to attend for trial. The regulations do not expressly deal with the procedure for bailing an accused who has the benefit of the 70-day time-limit between charge and committal or summary trial.

D15.19 **Grant of Bail** The regulations may make provision for the BA 1976 and the MCA 1980 to apply in cases where the accused is bailed as a result of a custody time-limit's expiry with such modifications as the Secretary of State considers necessary (Prosecution of Offences Act 1985, s. 22(2)(d)).

In the case of the BA 1976, its application to accused persons in respect of whom custody time-limits have expired is modified in that:

(a) they are automatically entitled to bail;
(b) on granting bail, the court may not require sureties or the deposit of security; and

(c) following the grant of bail, they may not be arrested without warrant merely on the ground that a police officer believes they are unlikely to surrender to custody (reg. 8).

Other conditions, such as curfew, residence or reporting to a police station, may nevertheless be imposed as in other cases, and the rule that actual or feared breach of such conditions is a ground for arrest without warrant (BA 1976, ss. 3(6) and 7(3)(b)) applies to an accused bailed on expiry of a time-limit just as it applies to an accused granted bail in any other circumstances (see also **D7.43**).

Procedure for Imposing Conditions Regulation 6 requires the prosecution to give notice to the appropriate court and the accused stating whether they intend to ask the court to impose conditions on the bail of an accused in respect of whom a custody time-limit is about to expire. In response to such an indication, the defence must give either: **D15.20**

(a) written notice of a wish to be represented at the hearing of the application;
(b) written notice that the accused does not object to the proposed conditions; or
(c) a written statement of the accused's reasons for objecting.

It is the prosecution's duty to arrange for the accused to be brought before the court within the two days preceding expiry of a custody time-limit (reg. 6(1)(b)).

Where the accused acquires the right to bail as a result of the expiry of a custody time-limit, that right continues until the start of the trial. The decision to the contrary, *Croydon Crown Court, ex parte Lewis* (1994) 158 JP 886, no longer represents the law.

Limits on the Effect of Expiry Beyond the grant of bail, the expiry of the custody time-limit otherwise has no effect on the proceedings. This was illustrated in *Sheffield Magistrates' Court, ex parte Turner* [1991] 2 QB 472. D had been unlawfully detained, contrary to the Prosecution of Offences Act 1985, s. 22, for a period culminating in his committal for trial. Although the Divisional Court granted a declaration relating to his period of unlawful detention, it was held that this had no effect on the validity of the committal, the fresh custody time-limit, laid down by reg. 5(3), which commenced on that date, or the lawfulness of his detention thereafter. **D15.21**

Consequences of Absconding

Escape from custody during the running of a custody time-limit automatically leads to the regulations imposing the time-limit being disregarded (Prosecution of Offences Act 1985, s. 22(5)). Similarly, if an accused has been released in consequence of the expiry of a custody time-limit and then fails to attend court in answer to bail, the earlier expiry of the limit is disregarded and the question, once the accused has been arrested, of whether to bail again or remand in custody is therefore entirely in the discretion of the court (s. 22(5)). **D15.22**

Criteria for Extension

The criteria for the extension of a custody time-limit, as set out in the Prosecution of Offences Act 1985, s. 22(3), are that the court must be satisfied (i) that there was good and sufficient cause, and (ii) that the Crown had acted with all due diligence and expedition (the need for 'diligence' was added by the CDA 1998). The authorities since 1985 have provided considerable assistance both in general terms as to the proper approach of the appropriate court to an application, and more specifically as to the proper meaning and ambit of the two criteria. **D15.23**

General Guidance In *Manchester Crown Court, ex parte McDonald* [1999] 1 All ER 805, Lord Bingham CJ set out the principles underlying the custody time-limit provisions in the Prosecution of Offences Act 1985, s. 22, and gave guidance upon the practicalities of interpreting the tests laid down by the statute. As far as the fundamental principles of the provisions are concerned, he emphasised the presumption of liberty set out in the ECHR, Article 5(3): 'Everyone arrested or detained [for trial] ... shall be entitled to trial within a reasonable **D15.24**

time or to release pending trial'. With that provision in mind, the overriding purposes of the statutory provisions were said to be:

(a) to ensure that the periods for which unconvicted defendants are held in custody are as short as is reasonably and practically possible;
(b) to oblige the prosecution to prepare cases for trial with due diligence and expedition; and
(c) to give the court power to control any extension of the maximum period for which any defendant may be held awaiting trial.

The main points of practical guidance which emerge from *ex parte McDonald* are:

(1) It is for the prosecution to satisfy the court on the balance of probabilities that the statutory conditions are met.
(2) The necessary standard is that of a competent prosecutor conscious of his duty to bring the case to trial as quickly as is reasonably and fairly possible.
(3) In judging whether this standard was met, the court should consider the nature and complexity of the case, the preparation necessary, the conduct of the defence, the extent to which the prosecutor was dependent on others outside his control and other relevant factors.
(4) What amounts to good and sufficient cause is a matter for the court on the facts of the case.
(5) Staff shortages and sickness will be inadequate reasons for extension. The unavailability of a judge or a courtroom may be good and sufficient cause, but such cases should be approached with 'great caution'.
(6) The court should state the reasons for its decision.
(7) Once the court had heard full argument and decided, the Divisional Court would be most reluctant to disturb its decision, and would do so only on the familiar grounds which support an application for judicial review.

See also *R (Raeside) v Luton Crown Court* [2012] EWHC 1064 (Admin), [2012] 1 WLR 2777.

Good and Sufficient Cause

D15.25 Factors that have been held not to amount to a good and sufficient cause for the extension of a time-limit include the following.

(1) *The seriousness of the offence charged.* For example, in *Governor of Winchester Prison, ex parte Roddie* [1991] 2 All ER 931, the Divisional Court held that the seriousness of the offence could not represent a good and sufficient cause, because Parliament had provided the same time-limit for all offences except treason. The more serious the charge, the more important it was for the police to get on with preparing the case.
(2) *Public protection.* For example, in *Central Criminal Court, ex parte Abu-Wardeh* [1997] 1 All ER 159, the Divisional Court held that the protection of the public was, in itself, an insufficient ground for the extension of a custody time-limit, disagreeing with *Luton Crown Court, ex parte Neaves* (1993) 157 JP 80. In *Birmingham Crown Court, ex parte Bell* [1997] 2 Cr App R 363, the Divisional Court accepted that, although protection of the public might not be enough in itself to constitute good and sufficient cause, where protection of prosecution witnesses was an issue, that might be capable in conjunction with other factors of giving rise to good and sufficient cause.
(3) *Factors that may be relevant to an application for bail.* For example, in *Sheffield Crown Court, ex parte Headley* [2000] Crim LR 374, the Divisional Court stated that it was wrong for a judge in considering an application to extend custody time-limits to take account of matters relevant to the grant of bail under the BA 1976. The custody time-limits regime was a separate and additional safeguard for those in custody, over and above that provided by the BA 1976. Parliament could not have intended that Bail Act considerations could be determinative of a custody time-limit application (see also *R (Eliot) v Reading Crown Court* [2001] EWHC Admin 464, [2002] 1 Cr App R 3 (32)).

Unavailability of a Judge or Courtroom Several cases have turned upon the question of whether the fact that there is no judge or courtroom in which a case may be tried can constitute good and sufficient cause for the grant of an extension. In *Norwich Crown Court, ex parte Cox* (1993) 97 Cr App R 145, the Divisional Court made it plain that, in appropriate circumstances, the lack of a judge and courtroom is capable of constituting the necessary 'good and sufficient cause'. Mann LJ stated that it 'must depend upon the facts of that instant case including, in particular, whether a trial date has been specified'. However, in *R (Miah) v Crown Court at Snaresbrook* [2006] EWHC 2873 (Admin), it was made clear that listing difficulties had to be exceptional to justify an extension; difficulties caused by the pressure of work on a Crown Court in routine cases would not be sufficient. D15.26

The court must consider what measures had been taken to address the listing difficulties; if it was clear that the difficulties were systemic, rather than particular to the case, they would represent routine difficulties and would not therefore be sufficient (*Kalonji v Crown Court at Wood Green* [2007] EWHC 2804 (Admin)). It is incumbent on the court to make inquiries as to whether an earlier trial date is possible, either at that court centre or elsewhere (*Preston Crown Court, ex parte Barraclough* [1999] Crim LR 973). This involves the court in satisfying itself that the court staff responsible for fixing the date for trial have fulfilled their duties scrupulously (*Leeds Crown Court, ex parte Wilson* [1999] Crim LR 378).

The approach adopted in these cases culminated in the decision of the Divisional Court in *R (McAulay) v Coventry Crown Court* [2012] EWHC 680 (Admin), [2012] 1 WLR 2766. The Court restated that unavailability of a court could only exceptionally represent a good and sufficient cause. However, the Court went further. There is a need to keep court resources under review, and to take steps to address a shortfall in those resources. Such a shortfall will 'rarely, if ever' provide proper grounds for an extension of a custody time-limit, and detailed evidence will be required to establish the necessary 'good and sufficient cause' in such circumstances. See also *R (Raeside) v Luton Crown Court* [2012] EWHC 1064 (Admin), [2012] 1 WLR 2777.

The Divisional Court has also addressed the issue of whether the availability of counsel could represent a good and sufficient cause for the extension of a custody time-limit in *Campbell-Brown v Central Criminal Court* [2015] EWHC 202 (Admin), [2015] 1 Cr App R 34 (516). The Court concluded that it could, for example, in the case of 'the trial of a vulnerable defendant who trusts one particular barrister who is well-known to him; or linked fraud trials with common counsel' (per Jay J at [66]). However, the Court also observed that the extension of custody time-limits should be addressed at the time that a trial date was fixed outwith the existing limit, rather than after the decision as to listing had already been made.

Convenience of Defence and Witnesses In *White v DPP* [1989] Crim LR 375, the Divisional Court found that the reason for the extension of the time-limit in D's case, namely that the defence had successfully applied for an adjournment to consider the prosecution statements that had only just been served on them, could permit an extension. The reasonable requirement of the defence to consider the papers was capable of being a good and sufficient cause for extension of time, although each case must turn on its own facts. Their lordships did not necessarily agree with the Crown Court judge's approach, namely, that he had to be satisfied beyond reasonable doubt of the existence of good cause before granting an extension (see **D15.32**). See also *O'Dowd v UK* (2012) 54 EHRR 8 (187). The absence or illness of the accused is itself a ground for extension (s. 22(3)(a)(i)). D15.27

In *Central Criminal Court, ex parte Bennett* (1999) *The Times*, 25 January 1999, the illness of a prosecution witness, which prevented the trial from taking place, was held to amount to a good and sufficient cause. Likewise, the unexpected non-availability of a prosecution witness may suffice (*Leeds Crown Court, ex parte Redfearn* [1999] COD 437). The fact that a witness is a professional investigator does not make his convenience irrelevant (*Leeds Crown Court, ex parte Wilson* [1999] Crim LR 378).

Due Expedition

D15.28 In *Norwich Crown Court, ex parte Parker* (1992) 96 Cr App R 68, the Divisional Court said that all concerned with the prosecution were not required to act as though this were their only task at hand; 'all due expedition' meant the expedition appropriate in the circumstances, one of those circumstances being the custody time-limit. In *Governor of Winchester Prison, ex parte Roddie* [1991] 2 All ER 931, however, it was made clear that due expedition had to be measured against some objective yardstick or it would defeat the Act's objects. Therefore, the fact that the police were understaffed and suffered delays in the receipt of typing and scientific evidence did not mean there was due expedition.

The following factors have relevance to the assessment of this question.

D15.29 (a) *The stage of the proceedings to which the time-limit relates.* In considering whether the prosecution had acted with all due expedition, the judge ought to consider the matter by reference to the presence or absence of all due expedition at the stage to which the custody time-limit relates (*Birmingham Crown Court, ex parte Bell* [1997] 2 Cr App R 363). For example, in *Central Criminal Court, ex parte Behbehari* [1994] Crim LR 352, the Divisional Court held that, in determining whether the prosecution had acted with 'all due expedition', the court should take into account whether papers were served on the defence in time to allow adequate consideration of the type of committal. See also *R (CPS) v Ipswich Crown Court* [2010] EWHC 1515 (Admin).

By extension of the same principle, however, the due expedition of the prosecution should be assessed in relation to matters they were obliged to carry out, rather than additional burdens they had assumed (*Southwark Crown Court, ex parte DPP* [1999] Crim LR 394). The decision of the Divisional Court in *R (Hughes) v Woolwich Crown Court* [2006] EWHC 2191 (Admin) underlines the fact that the due expedition of the prosecution in complying with its duties of disclosure will be judged from the time that the obligation in fact arises, rather than necessarily when the formal requirements of the service of a defence statement have been completed (see also *R (Alexander) v Isleworth Crown Court* [2009] EWHC 85 (Admin) for consideration of due expedition in the context of obtaining psychiatric evidence on the issue of fitness to plead and *R (Clarke) v Lewes Crown Court* [2009] EWHC 805 (Admin) in relation to the obtaining of expert evidence more generally).

D15.30 (b) *Who is responsible for any delay.* The other consideration to which the court should have regard is whether the lack of expedition is actually the fault of the prosecution, or whether it is caused by some third party and beyond the prosecution's control. The most obvious third party in this context is the independent science service. In *Central Criminal Court, ex parte Johnson* [1999] 2 Cr App R 51, the Divisional Court recognised that the prosecution would not have failed to show due expedition where delay had been caused by the independent science service, providing that all reasonable steps had been taken to ensure that the evidence in question was provided in proper time. This includes the obligation to make the laboratory aware of the trial date and time-limit. In *R (Holland) v Leeds Crown Court* [2002] EWHC 1862 (Admin), failure to inform the laboratory of the time constraints was fatal to a claim to due expedition.

Similarly, delay occasioned by the non-availability of a prosecution witness will translate into a failure by the prosecution to act with due expedition only where it could not be shown that the prosecution had taken reasonable steps in the circumstances to ensure the attendance of the witness. However, the prosecution cannot be expected to 'nursemaid' their witnesses at all times (*Leeds Crown Court, ex parte Redfearn* [1999] COD 437).

Where the delay to proceedings is the result of, or substantially contributed to by, the conduct of the accused, the court is entitled to take that into account in weighing up whether the prosecution has acted with all due diligence (*O'Dowd v UK* (2012) 54 EHRR 8 (187)).

Link between Due Expedition and the Need for an Extension

In *Leeds Crown Court, ex parte Bagoutie* (1999) *The Times*, 31 May 1999, Lord Bingham CJ emphasised that the requirement of due expedition was not disciplinary in intention. It aimed to protect the accused from being kept in prison awaiting trial longer than was justifiable. Parliament had intended to insist that prosecutors could not seek extensions where the need for the extension was attributable to their own failure to act with due expedition. Hence, if the court was satisfied that there was good and sufficient cause for the extension, but was not satisfied that the prosecution had acted with all due expedition, it was not obliged to refuse the application if it concluded that the prosecution's failure had neither caused nor contributed to the need for the extension. **D15.31**

In *R (Gibson) v Winchester Crown Court* [2004] EWHC 361 (Admin), [2004] 1 WLR 1623, the Divisional Court held that a judge may properly extend custody time-limits even where the prosecution had not acted with all due diligence, if the prosecution's failure is not itself a cause for the required extension.

Applying the Criteria

In *White v DPP* [1989] Crim LR 375, the Divisional Court expressed doubt over the Crown Court judge's approach to the extension of the custody time-limit in D's case, namely that he had to be satisfied beyond reasonable doubt of the existence of good cause before granting an extension. In *Governor of Canterbury Prison, ex parte Craig* [1991] 2 QB 195, Watkins LJ (giving the judgment of the Divisional Court) referred (at p. 132) to the doubt expressed in *White v DPP* and stated: **D15.32**

> In our view, the standard to be applied is that of the balance of probabilities. That is the standard for determining bail applications. It should apply equally, we think, to related interlocutory questions of the sort here in question.

The onus, then, is on the prosecution to satisfy the court as to the criteria for extension.

In *Wildman v DPP* [2001] EWHC Admin 14, the Divisional Court stated that the prosecution 'have to enable the defendant to test the matters which are relied upon by the Crown'. If the material on which they rely includes oral evidence, the defence must be given an opportunity to cross-examine (*R (DPP) v Havering Magistrates' Court* [2001] 3 All ER 997). However, it is for the prosecution to decide what evidence to call in support of their application, and the defence cannot insist on a witness being called purely to allow the witness to be criticised (*R (Rippe) v Chelmsford Crown Court* [2001] EWHC Admin 1115).

Crown Court applications for extension of a time-limit may and normally would be determined by a Crown Court judge in chambers. In *Leeds Crown Court, ex parte Briggs (No. 1)* [1998] 2 Cr App R 413, the Divisional Court stated that the Crown Court judge dealing with an application should give reasons for granting an extension.

Procedure for Seeking an Extension of Time-limits

At any time before the expiry of a time-limit, the Crown Court, if the accused has already been committed for trial, or the magistrates' court, in other cases, may extend the limit if satisfied of two matters (Prosecution of Offences Act 1985, s. 22(3)): **D15.33**

(a) that 'the prosecution has acted with all due diligence and expedition', and
(b) that there is 'good and sufficient cause for doing so'.

Instances of 'good and sufficient cause' are given in s. 22(3)(a)(i) and (ii), but they are clearly meant to be no more than examples.

An already extended limit may be further extended (s. 22(3)).

The criteria for the extension of the time-limit are discussed in more detail below. As to the timing of the application, in *Campbell-Brown v Central Criminal Court* [2015] EWHC 202

(Admin), [2015] 1 Cr App R 34 (516) the Divisional Court observed that the extension of custody time-limits should be addressed at the time that a trial date was fixed outwith the existing limit (in that case to accommodate the convenience of counsel), rather than after the decision as to listing had already been made. Further procedural guidance relating to custody time-limit extensions is contained in CrimPD XIII, Listing F.4 (see Supplement, **CPD.XIII.F**).

D15.34 **Notice Requirement** By reg. 7 of the Prosecution of Offences (Custody Time Limits) Regulations 1987 and CrimPR 14.18(2) (see Supplement, **R14.18**), an application for extension may be made orally or in writing. Notice of the intention to make the application must be given to the defence and the court not less than five days before an application to the Crown Court and not less than two days before an application to a magistrates' court. Notice may, however, be dispensed with if the court is satisfied that it is not practicable for the prosecution to give it in the time specified (reg. 7(4) and CrimPR 14.18(3)).

The effect of a failure by the prosecution to give proper notice was considered in *Governor of Canterbury Prison, ex parte Craig* [1991] 2 QB 195. It was held in that case that the justices still had a discretion under s. 22(3) of the Prosecution of Offences Act 1985 to extend a time-limit 'at any time before . . . expiry'. Hence they could extend the time-limit despite the prosecution's failure to show that it had been impracticable to give the accused two days' notice of an application for extension.

In *R (Haque) v Central Criminal Court* [2003] EWHC 2457 (Admin), the Divisional Court considered the import of the opening words of s. 22(3): 'The appropriate court may, at any time before the expiry of a time-limit imposed by the regulations, extend, or further extend, that limit'. It was held that they had to be construed as meaning before the expiry of a time-limit imposed by the regulations *as extended, if appropriate* by the court. They did not mean that the application could only be made within the 182 days provided for in reg. 6B following the date on which the accused first appeared in the magistrates' court.

D15.35 **Use of a Chronology** In *Chelmsford Crown Court, ex parte Mills* (2000) 164 JP 1, Lord Bingham CJ said that when a contested application was made for an extension, turning wholly or partly on whether the prosecution had acted with all due expedition, the judge should be given a detailed chronology (preferably agreed), showing the dates of all material events and orders. When the judge ruled on such an application, reasons should be given for the decision, which need not be long or elaborate.

Appeals

D15.36 **From the Magistrates' Court to the Crown Court** Following an application to a magistrates' court for extension of a time-limit, the party against whom the magistrates' decision goes may appeal to the Crown Court (Prosecution of Offences Act 1985, s. 22(7) and (8)). An appeal by the prosecution against refusal to extend must be commenced before the actual expiry of the limit, but, provided that is done, the limit is deemed not to have expired until after the determination of the appeal (s. 22(9)).

CrimPR 14.19 sets out the procedure to be followed on such appeals, in particular, the requirement for notice to the court and the other party and the contents of the notice. Appeals against magistrates' decisions on applications to extend are matters that may and normally would be determined by a Crown Court judge in chambers.

D15.37 **From the Crown Court to the Divisional Court** The mechanism of a challenge to the decision of the Crown Court to grant an extension of time-limits will depend on its basis.

(a) If it is on the basis that there was insufficient evidence to justify that decision, the challenge should be made by way of appeal by case stated to the Divisional Court. In that way, the Crown Court judge will be able to set out clearly the facts found and the material on which the findings were based (*Central Criminal Court, ex parte Behbehari* [1994] Crim LR 352).

(b) In other circumstances, it will be appropriate for a challenge to the decision to be by way of judicial review. In such a case, the requirement for promptness under the Civil Procedure Rules, Part 54, will not always be satisfied by commencing proceedings within the three-month period set out therein, but will depend on the circumstances of the case. In *R (Siraju) v Crown Court at Snaresbrook* [2001] EWHC Admin 638, it was stated that a delay which makes it impossible for the matter to be reconsidered by the Crown Court before the original time-limit expires will normally be fatal to a judicial review application.

The exercise of the power to extend a time-limit cannot be used as a ground of appeal should the accused ultimately be convicted (s. 22(10)).

Statutes on Custody Time-limits

Prosecution of Offences Act 1985, ss. 22 and 22B **D15.38**

22.—(1) The Secretary of State may by regulations make provision, with respect to any specified preliminary stage of proceedings for an offence, as to the maximum period—
- (a) to be allowed to the prosecution to complete that stage;
- (b) during which the accused may, while awaiting completion of that stage, be—
  - (i) in the custody of a magistrates' court; or
  - (ii) in the custody of the Crown Court; in relation to that offence.

(2) [Permissible content of the regulations.]

(3) The appropriate court may, at any time before the expiry of a time limit imposed by the regulations, extend, or further extend that limit; but the court shall not do so unless it is satisfied—
- (a) that the need for the extension is due to—
  - (i) the illness or absence of the accused, a necessary witness, a judge or a magistrate;
  - (ii) a postponement which is occasioned by the ordering by the court of separate trials in the case of two or more accused or two or more offences; or
  - (iii) some other good and sufficient cause; and
- (b) that the prosecution has acted with all due diligence and expedition.

(4) Where, in relation to any proceedings for an offence, an overall time limit has expired before the completion of the stage of the proceedings to which the limit applies, the appropriate court shall stay the proceedings.

(5) Where—
- (a) a person escapes from the custody of a magistrates' court or the Crown Court before the expiry of a custody time limit which applies in his case; or
- (b) a person who has been released on bail in consequence of the expiry of a custody time limit—
  - (i) fails to surrender himself into the custody of the court at the appointed time; or
  - (ii) is arrested by a constable on a ground mentioned in section 7(3)(b) of the Bail Act 1976 (breach, or likely breach, of conditions of bail);

the regulations shall, so far as they provide for any custody time limit in relation to the preliminary stage in question, be disregarded.

(6) Subsection (6A) below applies where—
- (a) a person escapes from the custody of a magistrates' court or the Crown Court; or
- (b) a person who has been released on bail fails to surrender himself into the custody of the court at the appointed time;

and is accordingly unlawfully at large for any period.

(6A) The following, namely—
- (a) the period for which the person is unlawfully at large; and
- (b) such additional period (if any) as the appropriate court may direct, having regard to the disruption of the prosecution occasioned by—
  - (i) the person's escape or failure to surrender; and
  - (ii) the length of the period mentioned in paragraph (a) above,

  shall be disregarded, so far as the offence in question is concerned, for the purposes of the overall time limit which applies in his case in relation to the stage which the proceedings have reached at the time of the escape or, as the case may be, at the appointed time.

(6B) Any period during which proceedings for an offence are adjourned pending the determination of an appeal under Part 9 of the Criminal Justice Act 2003 shall be disregarded, so far as the offence is concerned, for the purposes of the overall time limit and the custody time limit which applies to the stage which the proceedings have reached when they are adjourned.

(7) Where a magistrates' court decides to extend, or further extend, a custody or overall time limit, or to give a direction under subsection (6A) above, the accused may appeal against the decision to the Crown Court.
(8) Where a magistrates' court refuses to extend, or further extend, a custody or overall time limit, or to give a direction under subsection (6A) above, the prosecution may appeal against the refusal to the Crown Court.
(9) An appeal under subsection (8) above may not be commenced after the expiry of the limit in question; but where such an appeal is commenced before the expiry of the limit the limit shall be deemed not to have expired before the determination or abandonment of the appeal.
(10) Where a person is convicted of an offence in any proceedings, the exercise, in relation to any preliminary stage of those proceedings, of the power conferred by subsection (3) above shall not be called into question in any appeal against that conviction.
(11) In this section—

'appropriate court' means—

(a) where the accused has been sent for trial or indicted for the offence, the Crown Court; and
(b) in any other case, the magistrates' court specified in the summons or warrant in question or, where the accused has already appeared or been brought before a magistrates' court, a magistrates' court for the same area;

'custody' includes local authority accommodation or youth detention accommodation to which a person is remanded under section 91 of the Legal Aid, Sentencing and Punishment of Offenders Act 2012, and references to a person being committed to custody shall be construed accordingly;

'custody of the Crown Court' includes custody to which a person is committed in pursuance of—

(a) section 43A of the Magistrates' Courts Act 1980 (magistrates' court dealing with a person brought before it following his arrest in pursuance of a warrant issued by the Crown Court); or
(b) section 52 of the Crime and Disorder Act 1998 (provisions supplementing section 51);

'custody of a magistrates' court' means custody to which a person is committed in pursuance of section 128 of the Magistrates' Courts Act 1980 (remand);

'custody time limit' means a time limit imposed by regulations made under subsection (1)(b) above or, where any such limit has been extended by a court under subsection (3) above, the limit as so extended;

'preliminary stage', in relation to any proceedings, does not include any stage after the start of the trial (within the meaning given by subsections (11A) and (11B) below);

'overall time limit' means a time limit imposed by regulations made under subsection (1)(a) above or, where any such limit has been extended by a court under subsection (3) above, the limit as so extended; and

'specified' means specified in the regulations.

(11ZA) For the purposes of this section, proceedings for an offence shall be taken to begin when the accused is charged with the offence or, as the case may be, an information is laid charging him with the offence.
(11A) For the purposes of this section, the start of a trial on indictment shall be taken to occur at the time when a jury is sworn to consider the issue of guilt or fitness to plead or, if the court accepts a plea of guilty before the time when a jury is sworn, when that plea is accepted; but this is subject to section 8 of the Criminal Justice Act 1987 and section 30 of the Criminal Procedure and Investigations Act 1996 (preparatory hearings).
(11AA) The references in subsection (11A) above to the time when a jury is sworn include the time when that jury would be sworn but for the making of an order under Part 7 of the Criminal Justice Act 2003.
(11B) For the purposes of this section, the start of a summary trial shall be taken to occur—

(a) when the court begins to hear evidence for the prosecution at the trial or to consider whether to exercise its power under section 37(3) of the Mental Health Act 1983 (power to make hospital order without convicting the accused), or
(b) if the court accepts a plea of guilty without proceeding as mentioned above, when that plea is accepted.

(12) For the purposes of the application of any custody time limit in relation to a person who is in the custody of a magistrates' court or the Crown Court—

(a) all periods during which he is in the custody of a magistrates' court in respect of the same offence shall be aggregated and treated as a single continuous period; and

(b) all periods during which he is in the custody of the Crown Court in respect of the same offence shall be aggregated and treated similarly.

(13) For the purposes of section 29(3) of the Senior Courts Act 1981 (High Court to have power to make prerogative orders in relation to jurisdiction of Crown Court in matters which do not relate to trial on indictment) the jurisdiction conferred on the Crown Court by this section shall be taken to be part of its jurisdiction in matters other than those relating to trial on indictment.

22B.—(1) This section applies where proceedings for an offence ('the original proceedings') are stayed by a court under section 22(4) or 22A(5) of this Act.

(2) If—

(a) in the case of proceedings conducted by the Director, the Director or a Chief Crown Prosecutor so directs;

(b) in the case of proceedings conducted by the Director of the Serious Fraud Office, the Commissioners of Inland Revenue or the Commissioners of Customs and Excise, that Director or those Commissioners so direct; or

(c) in the case of proceedings not conducted as mentioned in paragraph (a) or (b) above, a person designated for the purpose by the Secretary of State so directs,

fresh proceedings for the offence may be instituted within a period of three months (or such longer period as the court may allow) after the date on which the original proceedings were stayed by the court.

(3) Fresh proceedings shall be instituted as follows—

(a) where the original proceedings were stayed by the Crown Court, by preferring a bill of indictment;

(b) where the original proceedings were stayed by a magistrates' court, by laying an information.

(4) Fresh proceedings may be instituted in accordance with subsections (2) and (3)(b) above notwithstanding anything in section 127(1) of the Magistrates' Courts Act 1980 (limitation of time).

(5) Where fresh proceedings are instituted, anything done in relation to the original proceedings shall be treated as done in relation to the fresh proceedings if the court so directs or it was done—

(a) by the prosecutor in compliance or purported compliance with section 3, 4 or 7A of the Criminal Procedure and Investigations Act 1996; or

(b) by the accused in compliance or purported compliance with section 5 or 6 of that Act.

(6) Where a person is convicted of an offence in fresh proceedings under this section, the institution of those proceedings shall not be called into question in any appeal against that conviction.

PRE-TRIAL AND PLEA AND TRIAL PREPARATION HEARINGS

Since the introduction of the CrimPR, a considerably greater emphasis has been placed on case management (see **D4** for a full discussion). At the forefront of this development is the court's active role in ensuring that, by the time a case reaches trial, all necessary preparation has been completed, and completed as efficiently and expeditiously as possible. 'Better Case Management' is a series of complementary initiatives, implementing Sir Brian Leveson's *Review of Efficiency in Criminal Proceedings*, and given effect under the umbrella of CrimPD I, paras. 3A.1 to 3A.28 (see Supplement, **CPD.3A**). The parties to proceedings are required to engage fully in court-led pre-trial case management, which is designed to identify those cases that will not go to trial at as early a stage as possible, and to ensure the efficient and expeditious dispatch of those that do. The two major Better Case Management hearings to give effect to these objectives are the early guilty plea scheme and the PTPH. **D15.39**

Use of Live Links and Telephone Facilities for Pre-trial Hearings

CrimPD I, paras. 3N.1 to 3N.17 (see Supplement, **CPD.3N**), address the use of live link and telephone technology for the conduct of pre-trial hearings. CrimPD I, para. 3N.1, makes clear that: 'Where it is lawful and in the interests of justice to do so, courts should exercise their statutory and other powers to conduct hearings by live link or telephone'. It is recognised that hearings that would in any event be public can properly be conducted via non-secure means such as Skype or Facetime (CrimPD I, para. 3N.4). **D15.40**

Courts are enjoined to direct the use of such facilities in the circumstances listed in CrimPR 3.2(4) and (5) (see Supplement, **R3.2**), and further guidance as to when such use is 'appropriate' is provided in CrimPD I, para. 3N.4 (and includes, wherever such facilities are available and can operate satisfactorily, their suitability for administrative hearings and where the satisfactory participation of the accused can be achieved). The parties are required to alert the court to any reason why such facilities should not be used (para. 3N.3, with further guidance at paras. 3N.5 to 3N.6). It is emphasised at para. 3N.8 that there is no bar to the parties and the judge being in different locations for the purposes of a live link application for a 'virtual hearing' (see also **D15.3**). Further guidance on establishing and using live links is provided in the annex to CrimPD I.

Sections 57A to 57E of the CDA 1998 permit an accused who is in police or prison custody to appear at any preliminary hearing via a live link, including preparatory hearings, early guilty plea, and PTPH. The accused is thereby deemed to be present at the hearing. CrimPR 3.2(4) (see Supplement, **R-8**) strongly encourages the use of live links where the technology is available and where the accused can participate effectively. CrimPD I, para. 3N.9, extends this facility, where appropriate, to those on bail. Factors that the court should consider include the importance of the accused understanding the proceedings.

The Coronavirus Act 2020, s. 54 and sch. 24, have made temporary modifications to the CDA 1998, ss. 57A to 57B and sch. 3A, to give the court power to direct 'live link' attendance at 'preliminary hearings'. For full details, see the Special Supplement at **D15.40A** ***et seq.***

See also **D15.96** for live links for witnesses.

Impact of Directions by the Magistrates' Court

D15.41 The first stages of case management for cases reaching the Crown Court will already have been undertaken in the magistrates' court, giving effect to CrimPR Part 3 (see Supplement, **R3.1** ***et seq.***) and CrimPD I, paras 3A.1 to 3A.15 (see Supplement, **CPD.3A**).

The objective is for the court to identify those cases that will result in guilty pleas by asking the accused for an indication as to plea at his first appearance (CrimPD I, para. 3A.1), and to make directions, governing the preparation of the case by the parties, to ensure that the matters set out have been addressed before the first hearing at the Crown Court.

The process at this stage is dependent on the initial details of the prosecution case, provided in accordance with CrimPR 8.2 (see Supplement, **R8.2**), and addresses the matters identified in r. 8.3 and CrimPD I, para. 3A.4. This information is intended to permit an accused to indicate his plea, and for the court to proceed by the correct route from that indication. Where a not guilty plea is anticipated in relation to an accused on bail, more extensive information is required at this stage (CrimPD I, para. 3A.12).

Where a magistrates' court sends a case to the Crown Court for trial, the magistrates' court must set a date for a PTPH at the Crown Court (see **D10.22**) if a guilty plea has been indicated for an offence triable only on indictment (CrimPD I, para. 3A.10), or no guilty plea is indicated (para. 3A.11). The PTPH must be held within 28 days of sending (para. 3A.11). Paragraph 3A.16 states that an indictment should be lodged at least seven days in advance of the PTPH. Note the need to have the necessary consent for prosecution before the case is sent to the Crown Court (see *Welsh* [2015] EWCA Crim 906, [2016] 1 Cr App R 8 (113) and **D2.17**).

Parties will be expected to have communicated with each other by the time of any first hearing and must report to the court on that communication; parties are expected to continue thereafter to communicate with each other and with the court officer (CrimPD I, para. 3A.2).

CrimPD I, para. 3P.5, makes clear that the timetable for the obtaining and service of reports as to the mental health of the accused should be incorporated into the wider timetable for trial preparation rather than operating independently of it.

Time for Service of Case Under the Crime and Disorder Act 1998 (Service of Prosecution Evidence) Regulations 2005 (SI 2005 No. 902: see **D10.19**), the period allowed for the service of the case is 50 days when the accused is in custody (8 days + 42 days) and 70 days when the accused is on bail (28 days + 42 days). **D15.42**

Digital Case System Following a roll-out in February 2016, under the Digital Case System (DCS), new CPS cases sent to the Crown Court (save for limited categories) are paperless, with the evidential and administrative material accessed from an electronic file instead. This does not apply to other prosecution agencies. **D15.43**

Preliminary Hearings Generally

CrimPD I, paras. 3A.15 to 3A.28 (see Supplement, **CPD.3A**), provide a comprehensive and detailed guide to the procedure to be adopted as regards case progression and preliminary hearings. **D15.44**

Where a deferred prosecution agreement is proposed (see **D12.106**) then, under the CCA 2013, sch. 17, para. 7, a preliminary hearing must occur at which the court will be invited to declare that it is 'likely to be in the interests of justice' that the prosecution and accused enter into a deferred prosecution agreement and that the proposed terms of the agreement are 'fair, reasonable and proportionate'.

Note the need to have the necessary consent for prosecution prior to any such hearing (see *Welsh* [2015] EWCA Crim 906, [2016] 1 Cr App R 8 (113) and **D2.18**).

Pre-trial Hearings

The CPIA 1996, ss. 39 to 43, and especially ss. 39 and 40, promote the efficient conduct of trials on indictment. They complement the rules for PTPH and preparatory hearings (see **D15.47** and CrimPR 3.21). Otherwise, such hearings occur where a guilty plea is anticipated, it is required for reasons of effective case management or to set ground rules for a vulnerable witness or defendant (r. 3.21(1)(c)). **D15.45**

Criminal Procedure and Investigations Act 1996, ss. 39 and 40

39.—(1) For the purposes of this Part a hearing is a pre-trial hearing if it relates to a trial on indictment and it takes place—
(a) after the accused has been sent for trial for the offence and
(b) before the start of the trial.
(2) For the purposes of this Part a hearing is also a pre-trial hearing if—
(a) it relates to a trial on indictment to be held in pursuance of a bill of indictment preferred under the authority of section 2(2)(b) or (ba) of the Administration of Justice (Miscellaneous Provisions) Act 1933 (bill preferred by direction of Court of Appeal or by direction or with consent of a judge), and
(b) it takes place after the bill of indictment has been preferred and before the start of the trial.
(3) For the purposes of this section the start of a trial on indictment occurs at the time when a jury is sworn to consider the issue of guilt or fitness to plead or, if the court accepts a plea of guilty before the time when a jury is sworn, when that plea is accepted; but this is subject to section 8 of the Criminal Justice Act 1987 and section 30 of this Act (preparatory hearings).
(4) The references in subsection (3) to the time when a jury is sworn include the time when that jury would be sworn but for the making of an order under Part 7 of the Criminal Justice Act 2003.

40.—(1) A judge may make at a pre-trial hearing a ruling as to—
(a) any question as to the admissibility of evidence;
(b) any other question of law relating to the case concerned.
(2) A ruling may be made under this section—
(a) on an application by a party to the case, or
(b) of the judge's own motion.
(3) Subject to subsection (4), a ruling made under this section has binding effect from the time it is made until the case against the accused or, if there is more than one, against each of them is disposed of; and the case against an accused is disposed of if—
(a) he is acquitted or convicted, or
(b) the prosecutor decides not to proceed with the case against him.

(4) A judge may discharge or vary (or further vary) a ruling made under this section if it appears to him that it is in the interests of justice to do so; and a judge may act under this subsection—
(a) on an application by a party to the case, or
(b) of the judge's own motion.
(5) No application may be made under subsection (4)(a) unless there has been a material change of circumstances since the ruling was made or, if a previous application has been made, since the application (or last application) was made.
(6) The judge referred to in subsection (4) need not be the judge who made the ruling or, if it has been varied, the judge (or any of the judges) who varied it.
(7) For the purposes of this section the prosecutor is any person acting as prosecutor, whether an individual or a body.

D15.46 **Procedure** Such hearings should normally be in public, and their outcome published if held in private (CrimPR 3.21(3)). As these are pre-trial hearings, they can therefore be conducted by a judge who will not be the eventual trial judge. They differ from preparatory hearings in long or complex cases (see **D15.52**) in this respect. Restrictions on the reporting of pre-trial rulings are contained in the CPIA 1996, ss. 41 and 42. There are no exemptions in respect of the publication of formal details, such as the name, address and occupation of the accused (again, in contrast with the position in relation to preparatory hearings).

Plea and Trial Preparation Hearings

D15.47 Save in cases where a preparatory hearing is required (discussed at **D15.51**), the major pre-trial Crown Court hearing will be the PTPH. The objective, expressed in CrimPD I, para. 3A.21, is that normally it should be the only pre-trial hearing. Its purpose, where an accused has indicated a guilty plea either in the magistrates' court at the time his case was sent or where such an indication has been given between that time and the PTPH, is for sentencing to occur (para. 3A.17). Otherwise, it is to ensure that all steps necessary for the proper preparation of a case for trial have been taken or are properly timetabled for future attention.

D15.48 **Material for the Hearing** The time allowed for the conduct of the PTPH must be sufficient for effective trial preparation, including the service of the prosecution case, the preferring of the indictment, the service of a defence statement and the making of any application to dismiss. The steps to be followed in relation to a PTPH are set out in detail in CrimPD I, paras. 3A.16 to 3A.20 (see Supplement, **CPD.3A**) and CrimPR 3.21 (see Supplement, **R3.21**).

CrimPR 3.21 requires the judge at the hearing to be satisfied of the following: (a) the defendant understands that credit will be given for a guilty plea; (b) what the defendant's plea is or is to be; (c) the defendant understands that if there is a trial, this can take place in the defendant's absence, and the consequences in relation to bail if the defendant were to fail to attend court.

Where an accused has been remanded in custody and sent to the Crown Court without the prior provision of initial details of the prosecution case, the material which is required for an accused on bail (para. 3A.12) has to be provided at least seven days in advance of the PTPH. Beyond that, the prosecution must have served sufficient evidence by the hearing 'to enable to court to case manage effectively without the need for a further case management hearing' (para. 3A.20), save in those cases to which para. 3A.21 applies (see **D15.50**). Moreover, CrimPD I, para. 3P6, envisages a further case management hearing where it is necessary to set a timetable for obtaining evidence as to the mental health or capacity of an accused (see para. 3P7 for the stages of that process).

D15.49 **The Form** The form to be used at a PTPH is that which appears in CrimPD, annex F, and is available via tinyurl.com/hwf3otl. The information required by the PTPH form must be available to the court at the PTPH, and it must have been discussed between the parties in advance. The prosecutor must provide details of the availability of likely prosecution witnesses so that a trial date can immediately be arranged if there is no guilty plea (CrimPD I, para. 3A.20).

The matters of case preparation that are addressed in the form are also addressed in other parts of this book. These include:

(a) orders in relation to witnesses, such as special measures (see **D14.1**) and witness summonses (see **D15.92**);
(b) orders as to disclosure (see **D9** and **D15.69**, including guidance as to large-scale digital storage issues: see *R* [2015] EWCA Crim 1941, [2016] 1 WLR 1872, discussed at **D15.62**); and
(c) outstanding legal issues, including applications under the bad character and hearsay provisions of the CJA 2003 (see **F13**, **F15** and **F17**).

In *Diedrick* [1997] 1 Cr App R 361, the appeal concerned the actions of the trial judge in questioning D about what he thought was a lie which D had told in the form submitted at what was then a plea and directions hearing. The Court of Appeal observed that what was said at the hearing was not expected to form part of the material for trial, and it would rarely be appropriate to refer to it. Where the trial judge was considering the use of such material, counsel should be allowed to address the judge first.

In *Newell* [2012] EWCA Crim 650, [2012] 1 WLR 3142 the Court of Appeal made clear that matters recorded on the form on behalf of the accused should not then ordinarily be used as evidence against the accused through the exercise of the court's discretion under the PACE 1984, s. 78, even though it is prima facie admissible as an admission by an agent, which is an exception to the hearsay rule. That was predicated, however, on there having been compliance by the accused with the CrimPR, and with the 'cards on the table' approach to proactive case management now required (discussed at **D4**).

Valiati v DPP [2018] EWHC 2908 (Admin), [2019] 1 Cr App R 17 (216) upheld that approach. The content of the form was technically admissible, subject to the exercise of the PACE 1984, s. 78, but it was essential that the parties were open in their answers at a hearing such as a PTPH, and that no party ambushed another subsequent to such a pre-trial hearing, and such candour was more likely where the answers given were not liable to be admitted in evidence at a later stage.

Subsequent Hearings CrimPD I, para. 3A.21, states that after the PTPH there will be no further case management hearing before the trial unless a condition listed in CrimPR 3.21(1)(c) is met and the court so directs, in order to further the overriding objective. Paragraph 3A.21 goes on to set out the types of cases in which it might be considered usual for a direction at the PTPH to include a direction for a further hearing. If a further case management hearing is directed, an accused held in custody will not usually be expected to attend in person, unless the court otherwise directs (para. 3A.22). Again, the provision for live links (see **D15.40**) will apply. Parties will be required to complete Effective Trial monitoring forms (para. 3A.25). If a party fails to comply with a case management direction, identified by case progression monitoring and the completion of monitoring forms, that party may be required to attend the court to explain the failure (para. 3A.23). Courts should maintain a record whenever a party to the proceedings has failed to comply with a direction made by the court (para. 3A.26). Non-compliance hearings may be conducted via live link or telephone (para. 3A.27). **D15.50**

As far as possible, case progression should be managed without a hearing in the courtroom, using electronic communication (para. 3A.24).

PREPARATORY HEARINGS

Preparatory hearings are a key pre-trial part of the criminal process in complex cases, the aims of which are very much in keeping with the case management ethos described above, namely the early identification of the issues and the tailoring of the trial process to those issues. Such **D15.51** hearings may be held in long and complex cases (pursuant to the CPIA 1996: see **D15.52**) and in serious fraud cases (pursuant to the CJA 1987).

Statutory Basis for a Preparatory Hearing

D15.52 The CJA 1987 provides for special 'preparatory hearings' in serious cases of fraud. The relevant provisions are contained in ss. 7 to 11. Similarly, ss. 28 to 38 of the CPIA 1996 (see **D15.63**) contain provisions for preparatory hearings in other types of long or complex case. In each case, the statutory regime is supplemented by CrimPR 3.22 to 3.26 (see Supplement, **R3.22** ***et seq.***).

D15.53 **Initiating a Preparatory Hearing** By s. 7(1) of the CJA 1987, if it appears to a Crown Court judge that the evidence on an indictment 'reveals a case of fraud of such seriousness or complexity that substantial benefits are likely to accrue from a [preparatory] hearing', the judge may order such a hearing. See also *Quillan* [2015] EWCA Crim 538, [2015] 1 WLR 4673, discussed at **D15.54**, in which the Court observed that there might also be special circumstances where a trial would be very long and costly and where a ruling on a point of law might determine whether a trial was required at all. Under both the CJA 1987 and the CPIA, the decision to hold a preparatory hearing may be made by a Crown Court judge at any time before a jury is sworn, on the application of any of the parties or by the court of its own motion. The court's discretion should not be narrowly applied (*VJA* [2010] EWCA Crim 2742). CrimPR 3.22 to 3.26 (see Supplement, **R3.22** ***et seq.***) lay down deadlines for the defence or prosecution to apply for a preparatory hearing and sets out the procedure for determining any such application. Rule 3.24 also covers the situation where a prosecutor seeks an order for a trial to be conducted with a judge sitting alone, within the terms of the CJA 2003, s. 43 or 44 (see **D13.75** ***et seq.***).

D15.54 **Test for Holding a Hearing** The purposes of the hearing are: (a) to identify the issues which are likely to be material to the verdict of the jury; (b) to assist their comprehension of those issues; (c) to expedite the proceedings before the jury; (d) to assist the judge's management of the trial; (e) to consider questions as to the severance or joinder of charges (CJA 1987, s. 7(1)(a) to (e)).

A preparatory hearing can be held, within the scope of the CPIA 1996, only if the case appears to the judge to be complex, serious or likely to lead to a lengthy trial. Where there is no material upon which the judge can properly come to the conclusion that the case will be complex, serious or lengthy, there is no power to hold a preparatory hearing. In such a case, there will be no jurisdiction to entertain an interlocutory appeal under these provisions (*Ward* [2003] EWCA Crim 814, [2003] 2 Cr App R 20 (315)). The real test for holding such a hearing is whether an issue of importance to the conduct of the trial ought to be resolved, on appeal if necessary, at an early stage (see also *VJA* [2010] EWCA Crim 2742, where the Court of Appeal said that the purposes of a preparatory hearing should be interpreted broadly).

In *I* [2009] EWCA Crim 1793, [2010] 1 WLR 1125, the Court of Appeal essentially concluded that preparatory hearings were only of value where such an interlocutory appeal might be required. However, although that approach was endorsed to some extent in *R* [2015] EWCA Crim 1941, [2016] 1 WLR 1872, it was not followed in *R* [2013] EWCA Crim 708, [2014] 1 Cr App R 5 (33), where the Court of Appeal expressly rejected the possibility of interlocutory appeal as a reason to hold such a hearing, and it was qualified in *Quillan* [2015] EWCA Crim 538, [2015] 1 WLR 4673. In *Quillan*, the Court considered that there might also be special circumstances where a trial would be very long and costly and where a ruling on a point of law in relation to the legal basis on which a count on the indictment was founded might determine whether a trial was required at all.

D15.55 **Status of a Preparatory Hearing** The preparatory hearing is in fact a stage of the trial itself and may be used in order to settle various issues without requiring the jury to attend (CJA 1987, s. 8, and CPIA 1996, s. 30).

In *Southwark Crown Court, ex parte Commissioners for Customs and Excise* [1993] 1 WLR 764, the Divisional Court held that a change of judge after a preparatory hearing could only be accepted in exceptional circumstances. However, the Court of Appeal in *I* [2009] EWCA Crim 1793, [2010] 1 WLR 1125 made clear that it was sufficient that there was a compelling reason to change, rather than anything more exceptional.

It is possible for a judge to conduct separate preparatory hearings in respect of different accused who are charged in the same indictment (*Re Kanaris* [2003] UKHL 2, [2003] 1 WLR 443). Each accused is charged jointly and severally, and may thus be dealt with individually if the interests of justice so require.

Matters that May be Addressed during a Preparatory Hearing

The purpose of a preparatory hearing is set out in the CPIA 1996, s. 29(2), and may be summarised as: **D15.56**

(a) identifying material issues for the jury;
(b) assisting them to understand those issues;
(c) expediting proceedings before them;
(d) helping the judge to manage the trial; and
(e) considering questions as to the severance or joinder of charges.

The same purposes are identified in the CJA 1987, s. 7(1) (see **D15.54**). Any question as to the admissibility of evidence and any other question of law relating to the case may be determined at the preparatory hearing (CJA 1987, s. 9(3)). According to *Re Gunawardena* [1990] 2 All ER 447, however, that power is in fact confined to questions related to the purposes of the preparatory hearing, as now outlined in s. 7(1)(a) to (e). See also CrimPR 3.23 and 3.24.

Disclosure Among the powers available to the court at a preparatory hearing is the power to order the prosecutor and the defence to make disclosure in advance of the hearing (CPIA 1996, s. 31(4) to (7)), in addition to any disclosure already made as a result of the general duties on the parties (see **D9**). **D15.57**

Similarly, either before or at the preparatory hearing, the judge may, under the CJA 1987, s. 9(4) (and the CPIA 1996, s. 31(4)), order the prosecution to do any or all of the following:

(a) supply the court and the accused with a 'case statement' specifying (i) the principal facts of the prosecution case; (ii) the witnesses who will speak to those facts; (iii) any exhibits relevant thereto; (iv) any proposition of law on which the prosecution propose to rely; and (v) the relevance of the aforementioned to any of the counts in the indictment;
(b) prepare their evidence and other explanatory material in a form that appears to the judge to be likely to aid comprehension by the jury (and to supply it in that form to the court and the accused);
(c) give the court and the accused notice of matters which, in their view, ought to be agreed (including, where appropriate, the truth of the contents of relevant documents);
(d) amend the case statement in the light of objections from the defence.

Once an order to the prosecution to supply a case statement has been complied with, the judge may, under the CJA 1987, s. 9(5), and the CPIA 1996, s. 31(5), order the defence to do any or all of the following:

(a) give the court and the prosecution a written statement setting out in general terms the nature of the defence and indicating the principal matters on which they take issue with the prosecution;
(b) give the court and the prosecution notice of any objection they have to the prosecution case statement;
(c) inform the court and the prosecution of any point of law (including one of admissibility of evidence) which they wish to take and the authorities on which they will be relying; or

(d) give the court and the prosecution a notice stating the extent to which they are prepared to agree the documents and other matters which the prosecution have asked to have admitted, together with the reason for any refusal to agree.

Once the prosecution have received the defence case statement, they are entitled to make use of it by re-interviewing their own witnesses and asking them questions which arise from that statement. The judge has no power to forbid the prosecution from doing so or to prescribe the way in which they may carry out such re-interviews (*Nadir* [1993] 4 All ER 513).

In *H* [2007] UKHL 7, [2007] 2 AC 270, the House of Lords held that an order or ruling in relation to disclosure under the CPIA 1996, s. 8, did not fall within the purposes for which a preparatory hearing may be held, and therefore could not form the basis for an interlocutory appeal (see also **D15.59**). However, the requirement that the court is 'both entitled and obliged' robustly to case manage the disclosure process (per Sir Brian Leveson P in *R* [2015] EWCA Crim 1941, [2016] 1 WLR 1872 at [39]–[48]) makes orders as to disclosure an inevitable and important part of any such hearing.

Legal Rulings

D15.58 The court may also make rulings as to any question of law relating to the case, including questions as to the admissibility of evidence (CPIA 1996, s. 31(3)), but its powers in this respect may be circumscribed by the principle in *Re Gunawardena* [1990] 2 All ER 447. In that case, it was held that the power to make binding rulings in a preparatory hearing in a serious fraud case was limited by implication to the purposes for which preparatory hearings may be ordered, as set out in s. 29(2) (see **D15.56**). Applying that decision, in *VJA* [2010] EWCA Crim 2742 it was emphasised that the court should only make rulings that would serve a useful trial purpose within the ambit of s. 29.

Applications of this principle include the following.

(a) **The indictment:** In *G* [2001] EWCA Crim 442, [2002] 1 WLR 200, the trial judge at the preparatory hearing considered the management of the trial of three accused for conspiracy to cheat. He ruled that the indictment related only to one particular 'cell' of the alleged conspiracy, and therefore, only evidence which related to the narrower conspiracy would be admissible. It was held that the purpose of the ruling fell within s. 7(1)(a) since it was 'identifying issues which are likely to be material to the verdict of the jury'. Further, the judge's purpose was pro-active case management to ensure that the jury were not over-burdened. Moreover, applications relating to joint or separate trial are specifically identified in CrimPR 3.29 as a matter to be addressed at a pre-trial hearing, and preparatory hearings are not excluded from its ambit.

(b) In *van Hoogstraaten* [2003] EWCA Crim 3642, where the prosecution appealed against the ruling of the judge which was, in effect, to quash the indictment, by contrast, the Court of Appeal held that the ruling in question lay outside the scope of the CPIA 1996, s. 29(2), and it therefore had no jurisdiction to entertain an appeal.

(c) **Available defences:** In *Shayler* [2001] EWCA Crim 1977, [2001] 1 WLR 2206, the Court of Appeal held that the judge at a preparatory hearing could rule on whether a particular defence (in this case, duress/necessity) was available to an accused as a matter of law. See also *S Ltd* [2009] EWCA Crim 85, [2009] 2 Cr App R 11 (171) as to the propriety of determining the availability of a defence at a preparatory hearing on the basis of the defence case statement.

(d) **Admissibility:** In *Claydon* [2001] EWCA Crim 1359, [2004] 1 WLR 1575, the Court of Appeal held that the purpose of 'expediting the proceedings before the jury' must include '*questions* of evidence such as typically arise' under s. 78 of the PACE 1984. Following *Gunawardena*, however, the judge's rulings as to abuse of process would not be subject to appeal because they did not come within the listed purposes of a preparatory hearing, but any resolution of the anomaly 'must be left to a higher court'. An attempt at such a resolution came in *H* [2007] UKHL 7, [2007] 2 AC 270 (see (f) below).

(e) *R* (2000) *The Independent*, 10 April 2000, in which, similarly, the Court of Appeal held that it had jurisdiction to hear an appeal brought pursuant to s. 35, in respect of evidence sought to be excluded under the PACE 1984, s. 78.

(f) **Disclosure:** *H* UKHL 7, [2007] 2 AC 270, in which it was held that because an order as to disclosure, following an application under the CPIA 1996, s. 8, did not fall within the purposes of a preparatory hearing, it could not form the subject of an appeal. However, there was nothing to prevent a judge dealing with a preparatory hearing from addressing issues of disclosure at the same time and, in effect, in parallel.

Note, however, that in *H* considerable doubts were cast on the correctness of *Re Gunawardena, Claydon* and *van Hoogstraaten*. Applying that decision, in *VJA* [2010] EWCA Crim 2742 it was emphasised that the court should only make rulings relating specifically to the matters identified in s. 29. **D15.59**

However, CrimPR Part 3 addresses applications for a stay for abuse of process (r. 3.28) or the joinder or severance of the indictment (r. 3.29) as matters to be addressed before trial, and there is no suggestion in these rules that they do not operate within the ambit of a preparatory hearing, as they do in the context of other pre-trial hearings.

Where an order made pursuant to s. 29 is varied by the Court of Appeal following an interlocutory appeal (pursuant to s. 35) but the position is later altered by a subsequent decision of the Court of Appeal to the effect that its earlier decision was incorrect, the judge who originally made the order is entitled to vary it so as to accord with that second Court of Appeal decision (*Rowe* [2007] EWCA Crim 635, [2007] QB 975).

Status of Rulings Made at a Preparatory Hearing Subject to the possibility of being varied on appeal to the Court of Appeal (see **D15.64**), an order or ruling made at the preparatory hearing will have effect at the trial unless it then appears to the judge, on application by a party, that the interests of justice require the order or ruling to be varied or discharged (CJA 1987, s. 9(10), and CPIA 1996, s. 31(11)). See **D15.59** and *Rowe* [2007] EWCA Crim 635, [2007] QB 975 as to the effect of Court of Appeal decisions on such rulings. **D15.60**

The sanction for a party departing at trial from his case as disclosed at the preparatory hearing and/or failing to comply with an order made at the hearing is that the judge may comment on the departure or failure and the jury may draw such inferences as appear to them proper (CJA 1987, s. 10(1), and CPIA 1996, s. 34). The judge may also give leave to comment to any of the other parties, but, in deciding whether such leave is appropriate, must have regard to the extent of the departure from the case as earlier disclosed and the justification for it (CJA 1987, s. 10(2), and CPIA 1996, s. 34(2)). Save as allowed under the statutory regime, no mention may be made to the jury of any information about the defence case disclosed at the preparatory hearing.

Reporting Restrictions Restrictions on reporting preparatory hearings are contained in the CPIA 1996, s. 37, although certain formal details (e.g., the names, ages, home addresses and occupations of the accused and witnesses, and the offence(s) charged) may be published by virtue of s. 37(9). The court has power to lift the restrictions (s. 37(3)). **D15.61**

The Fraud Protocol At such hearings, it is important to consider the aspirations behind the *Protocol for the Control* and Management of Heavy Fraud and other Complex Criminal Cases, the Crown Court disclosure in document-heavy cases initiative that forms part of Better Case Management and the guidance as to the disclosure process in large cases, especially large-scale digital disclosure exercises (*R* [2015] EWCA Crim 1941, [2016] 1 WLR 1872). **D15.62**

The Protocol seeks to achieve this, in conjunction with the CrimPR and CrimPD, by encouraging continuous case management by judges presiding over trials which may last more than eight weeks. The Protocol includes guidance covering the following areas.

(a) There should be initial consideration of the length of trial, requiring the prosecution team to justify the length of trial where it will exceed eight weeks (para. 1(iv)) and to notify the court and others where the case is likely to exceed that length (para. 1(v)). The trial judge is also expected to 'consider what steps should be taken to reduce the length of the trial, while still ensuring that the prosecution has the opportunity of placing the full criminality before the court' (para. 3(vi)(b)).
(b) Early appointment of a trial judge is required where the case will last more than four weeks, who will then 'manage the case from cradle to grave' (para. 2). The judge will require a more detailed knowledge of the case than would normally be the case (para. 3(i)(b)).
(c) Case management issues are highlighted, including the matters that should be addressed at directions hearings (para. 3(iii)), with a short preliminary hearing followed by a full case management hearing attended by trial counsel. Prior to that hearing, both prosecution and defence will have identified their cases and at the preliminary hearing there should be 'a real dialogue between the judge and all advocates for the purpose of identifying the focus of the prosecution case, the common ground and the real issues in the case' (para. 3(iv)(b)).
(d) On disclosure, there should be a timetable for structured disclosure which prevents the defence solicitors spending 'a disproportionate amount of time and incur[ring] disproportionate costs trawling through a morass of documents' (para. 4(iii)). In relation to the latter, this requirement is now addressed comprehensively in *R* [2015] EWCA Crim 1941, [2016] 1 WLR 1872.

In cases involving large-scale digital disclosure exercises, the essential guidance provided in *R* was:

(a) the prosecution is and must be in the driving seat at the stage of initial disclosure, and should produce a Disclosure Management Document identifying the overall disclosure strategy, selection of software tools and search terms and means of addressing potential privilege issues;
(b) there must be prompt and proactive dialogue between the parties, with defence statements playing a valuable role where there has been actual or purported initial disclosure, as to which the courts should not employ a counsel of perfection as to the nature and extent of initial disclosure;
(c) the process of disclosure has to be subject to robust case management, with the court prepared to give orders and directions even at the initial disclosure stage; the aim of this process being to drive the disclosure process efficiently to expeditious resolution of the case.

D15.63 Selected Statutory Provisions Governing Preparatory Hearings

Criminal Procedure and Investigations Act 1996, ss. 29 to 32 and 34

29.—(1) Where it appears to a judge of the Crown Court that an indictment reveals a case of such complexity, a case of such seriousness or a case whose trial is likely to be of such length, that substantial benefits are likely to accrue from a hearing—
(a) before the time when the jury are sworn, and
(b) for any of the purposes mentioned in subsection (2),
he may order that such a hearing (in this Part referred to as a preparatory hearing) shall be held.

(1A) A judge of the Crown Court may also order that a preparatory hearing shall be held if an application to which section 45 of the Criminal Justice Act 2003 applies (application for trial without jury) is made.

(1B) An order that a preparatory hearing shall be held must be made by a judge of the Crown Court in every case which (whether or not it falls within subsection (1) or (1A)) is a case in which at least one of the offences charged by the indictment against at least one of the persons charged is a terrorism offence.

(1C) An order that a preparatory hearing shall be held must also be made by a judge of the Crown Court in every case which (whether or not it falls within subsection (1) or (1A)) is a case in which—

(a) at least one of the offences charged by the indictment against at least one of the persons charged is an offence carrying a maximum of at least 10 years' imprisonment; and
(b) it appears to the judge that evidence on the indictment reveals that conduct in respect of which that offence is charged had a terrorist connection.

(2) The purposes are those of—
(a) identifying issues which are likely to be material to the verdict of the jury;
(b) assisting their comprehension of any such issues;
(c) expediting the proceedings before the jury;
(d) assisting the judge's management of the trial;
(e) considering questions as to the severance or joinder of charges.

[(2) The purposes are those of—
(a) identifying issues which are likely to be material to the determinations and findings which are likely to be required during the trial,
(b) if there is to be a jury, assisting their comprehension of those issues and expediting the proceedings before them,
(c) determining an application to which section 45 of the Criminal Justice Act 2003 applies,
(d) assisting the judge's management of the trial,
(e) considering questions as to the severance or joinder of charges.]

(3) In a case in which it appears to a judge of the Crown Court that evidence on an indictment reveals a case of fraud of such seriousness or complexity as is mentioned in section 7 of the Criminal Justice Act 1987 (preparatory hearings in cases of serious or complex fraud)—
(a) the judge may make an order for a preparatory hearing under this section only if he is required to do so by subsection (1B) or (1C);
(b) before making an order in pursuance of either of those subsections, he must determine whether to make an order for a preparatory hearing under that section; and
(c) he is not required by either of those subsections to make an order for a preparatory hearing under this section if he determines that an order should be made for a preparatory hearing under that section;

and, in a case in which an order is made for a preparatory hearing under that section, requirements imposed by those subsections apply only if that order ceases to have effect.

(4) An order that a preparatory hearing shall be held may be made—
(a) on the application of the prosecutor,
(b) on the application of the accused or, if there is more than one, any of them, or
(c) of the judge's own motion.

(5) The reference in subsection (1)(a) to the time when the jury are sworn includes the time when the jury would be sworn but for the making of an order under Part 7 of the Criminal Justice Act 2003.

(6) In this section 'terrorism offence' means—
(a) an offence under section 11 or 12 of the Terrorism Act 2000 (offences relating to proscribed organisations);
(b) an offence under any of sections 15 to 18 of that Act (offences relating to terrorist property);
(c) an offence under section 38B of that Act (failure to disclose information about acts of terrorism);
(d) an offence under section 54 of that Act (weapons training);
(e) an offence under any of sections 56 to 59 of that Act (directing terrorism, possessing things and collecting information for the purposes of terrorism and inciting terrorism outside the United Kingdom);
(f) an offence in respect of which there is jurisdiction by virtue of section 62 of that Act (extra-territorial jurisdiction in respect of certain offences committed outside the United Kingdom for the purposes of terrorism etc.);
(g) an offence under Part 1 of the Terrorism Act 2006 (miscellaneous terrorist related offences);
(h) conspiring or attempting to commit a terrorism offence;
(i) incitement to commit a terrorist offence.

(7) For the purposes of this section an offence carries a maximum of at least 10 years' imprisonment if—
(a) it is punishable, on conviction on indictment, with imprisonment; and
(b) the maximum term of imprisonment that may be imposed on conviction on indictment of that offence is 10 years or more or is imprisonment for life.

(8) For the purposes of this section conduct has a terrorist connection if it is or takes place in the course of an act of terrorism or is for the purposes of terrorism.

(9) In subsection (8) 'terrorism' has the same meaning as in the Terrorism Act 2000 (see section 1 of that Act).

[*Note:* The version of s. 29(2) displayed in square brackets is in force only in respect of applications under the CJA 2003, s. 44 (jury tampering). Section 29(6)(i) is to be read as a reference to an offence under Part 2 of the SCA 2007: see SCA 2007, s. 63 and sch. 6, para. 29.]

30. If a judge orders a preparatory hearing—
(a) the trial shall start with that hearing, and
(b) arraignment shall take place at the start of that hearing, unless it has taken place before then.

31.—(1) At the preparatory hearing the judge may exercise any of the powers specified in this section.
(2) The judge may adjourn a preparatory hearing from time to time.
(3) He may make a ruling as to—
(a) any question as to the admissibility of evidence;
(b) any other question of law relating to the case;
(c) any question as to the severance or joinder of charges.
(4) He may order the prosecutor—
(a) to give the court and the accused or, if there is more than one, each of them a written statement (a case statement) of the matters falling within subsection (5);
(b) to prepare the prosecution evidence and any explanatory material in such a form as appears to the judge to be likely to aid comprehension by a jury and to give it in that form to the court and to the accused or, if there is more than one, to each of them;
(c) to give the court and the accused or, if there is more than one, each of them written notice of documents the truth of the contents of which ought in the prosecutor's view to be admitted and of any other matters which in his view ought to be agreed;
(d) to make any amendments of any case statement given in pursuance of an order under paragraph (a) that appear to the judge to be appropriate, having regard to objections made by the accused or, if there is more than one, by any of them.
(5) The matters referred to in subsection (4)(a) are—
(a) the principal facts of the case for the prosecution;
(b) the witnesses who will speak to those facts;
(c) any exhibits relevant to those facts;
(d) any proposition of law on which the prosecutor proposes to rely;
(e) the consequences in relation to any of the counts in the indictment that appear to the prosecutor to flow from the matters falling within paragraphs (a) to (d).
(6) Where a judge has ordered the prosecutor to give a case statement and the prosecutor has complied with the order, the judge may order the accused or, if there is more than one, each of them—
...
(b) to give the court and the prosecutor written notice of any objections that he has to the case statement;
...
(7) Where a judge has ordered the prosecutor to give notice under subsection (4)(c) and the prosecutor has complied with the order, the judge may order the accused or, if there is more than one, each of them to give the court and the prosecutor a written notice stating—
(a) the extent to which he agrees with the prosecutor as to documents and other matters to which the notice under subsection (4)(c) relates, and
(b) the reason for any disagreement.
(8) A judge making an order under subsection (6) or (7) shall warn the accused or, if there is more than one, each of them of the possible consequence under section 34 of not complying with it.
(9) If it appears to a judge that reasons given in pursuance of subsection (7) are inadequate, he shall so inform the person giving them and may require him to give further or better reasons.
(10) An order under this section may specify the time within which any specified requirement contained in it is to be complied with.
(11) An order or ruling made under this section shall have effect throughout the trial, unless it appears to the judge on application made to him that the interests of justice require him to vary or discharge it.

32.—(1) This section applies where—
(a) a judge orders a preparatory hearing, and
(b) he decides that any order which could be made under section 31(4) to (7) at the hearing should be made before the hearing.

(2) In such a case—
(a) he may make any such order before the hearing (or at the hearing), and
(b) section 31(4) to (11) shall apply accordingly.

34.—(1) Any party may depart from the case he disclosed in pursuance of a requirement imposed under section 31.

(2) Where—
(a) a party departs from the case he disclosed in pursuance of a requirement imposed under section 31, or
(b) a party fails to comply with such a requirement,

the judge or, with the leave of the judge, any other party may make such comment as appears to the judge or the other party (as the case may be) to be appropriate and the jury or, in the case of a trial without a jury, the judge may draw such inference as appears proper.

(3) In doing anything under subsection (2) or in do anything under it the judge shall have regard—
(a) to the extent of the departure or failure, and
(b) to whether there is any justification for it.

(4) Except as provided by this section, in the case of a trial with a jury no part—
(a) of a statement given under section 31(6)(a), or
(b) of any other information relating to the case for the accused or, if there is more than one, the case for any of them, which was given in pursuance of a requirement imposed under section 31,

may be disclosed at a stage in the trial after the jury have been sworn without the consent of the accused concerned.

APPEALS FROM PREPARATORY HEARINGS

There are provisions for appealing from rulings made by the judge at a preparatory hearing to the Court of Appeal and, ultimately, the Supreme Court (see the CPIA 1996, ss. 35 and 36, and the CJA 1987, s. 9(11)). Leave to appeal is required from either the judge or the court (ibid.). **D15.64**

Where leave to appeal has been granted, the preparatory hearing may continue, but it cannot be concluded until the appeal has been determined or abandoned (s. 35(2); s. 9(13)). The Court of Appeal may confirm, reverse or vary the decision appealed against (s. 35(3); s. 9(14)).

The Court of Appeal only has jurisdiction to entertain appeals from orders that the Crown Court was entitled to make within a preparatory hearing (though the pool of orders which may be appealed has potentially been dramatically increased by *H* [2007] UKHL 7, [2007] 2 AC 270: see **D15.59**).

CrimPR Part 37 (see Supplement, **R37.1** *et seq.*) contains the relevant procedural rules in relation to an appeal from a preparatory hearing to the Court of Appeal, and Part 43 (see Supplement, **R43.1** *et seq.*) addresses appeals to the Supreme Court in this context.

The Rules

Notice of Appeal An application for leave to the judge of the Crown Court who made the decision to be appealed should be made within two days of the relevant decision. Unless the application for leave is made on the same occasion that the relevant decision is given, the appellant must give written notice of the application (and specify the grounds upon which it is made) to the Crown Court officer and all the parties affected by the decision (r. 37.4(1)). **D15.65**

Under r. 37.2(1) and (2), notice of appeal or an application to the Court of Appeal for leave to appeal must be served on the Registrar, the Crown Court officer and all parties to the preparatory hearing affected by the order or ruling to be appealed. It must be served no later than five days after either the date of the decision to be appealed or the determination or withdrawal of any application for leave has been made to the judge of the Crown Court.

By implication and in accordance with the rationale of the Court of Appeal in *PY* [2019] EWCA Crim 17, [2019] 1 Cr App R 22 (297) it would be possible for the prosecution to give notice of their intention to appeal by email.

If written notice of appeal was given to the Crown Court, a copy of it must accompany the notice or application for leave to appeal which is served on the Registrar (r. 37.3(2)(g)). The notice of appeal must (r. 37.3(2)):

(a) specify any question of law to which the appeal relates and include any facts which are necessary for the consideration of that point of law;
(b) summarise the arguments to be advanced before the Court of Appeal;
(c) list any authorities which are to be cited in argument; and
(d) if the judge of the Crown Court has given leave to appeal against his ruling, the notice must refer to that and must set out the grounds on which leave was granted.

The notice should be accompanied by any documents or other things which are necessary for the proper determination of the appeal or application as the case may be (r. 37.3(2)(v)).

D15.66 **Response to a Notice of Appeal** If the respondent wishes to oppose the appeal then, within five days of receipt of the notice, the respondent must serve written notice to that effect in the form set out in the CrimPD. The notice must be served on the Registrar and must state the date on which the appellant's notice was received, summarise the response to the arguments to be advanced by the appellant and set out any authorities the respondent proposes to rely on. Copies must also be served on the Crown Court officer, the appellant and any other parties directly affected by the decision (r. 37.5).

D15.67 **Role of the Court** The powers of a single judge of the Court of Appeal are set out in CrimPR 37.6 and may be exercised as though they were being exercised by the full court. Thus the single judge may give leave to appeal under the appropriate section, extend the time-limit for service of the notice of application and opposition, and give leave for a person in custody to attend a hearing. Any application refused by a single judge can be renewed before the full Court under r. 37.7 by means of service of a written notice.

D15.68 **Criminal Procedure and Investigations Act 1996, ss. 35 and 36**

> 35.—(1) An appeal shall lie to the Court of Appeal from any ruling of a judge under section 31(3), from the refusal by a judge of an application to which section 45 of the Criminal Justice Act 2003 applies or from an order of a judge under section 43 or 44 of that Act which is made on the determination of such an application but only with the leave of the judge or of the Court of Appeal.
> (2) The judge may continue a preparatory hearing notwithstanding that leave to appeal has been granted under subsection (1), but the preparatory hearing shall not be concluded until after the appeal has been determined or abandoned.
> (3) On the termination of the hearing of an appeal, the Court of Appeal may confirm, reverse or vary the decision appealed against.
> **36.** …
> (2) The judge may continue a preparatory hearing notwithstanding that leave to appeal has been granted under Part II of the Criminal Appeal Act 1968, but the preparatory hearing shall not be concluded until after the appeal has been determined or abandoned.

Section 9(11), (13) and (14) of the CJA 1987, which creates a right of appeal in serious and complex fraud cases, is in identical terms to the CPIA 1996, s. 35. It is possible to challenge the ruling of the Court of Appeal in such an interlocutory appeal by a further appeal to the Supreme Court.

PRE-TRIAL PROVISION OF INFORMATION: PROSECUTION OBLIGATIONS

D15.69 Regardless of whether the trial is preceded by a preliminary or preparatory hearing, certain obligations rest upon the parties to disclose information about the evidence they intend to call or other material which is in their possession but which they do not intend to use at trial.

Service of Evidence to Be Called

The defence at trial on indictment are entitled to know in advance of trial the evidence the prosecution intend to call. Most if not all the evidence will in fact have been disclosed by the statements or depositions. If the prosecution wish to call additional evidence, they are under a duty to serve notice of it. D15.70

In *Owens and Owens* [2006] EWCA Crim 2206, the Court of Appeal held that, even where a court had ordered that evidence would only be admissible if served before a certain date, it retained the discretion to vary that order to admit evidence served later.

Disclosure of Information Not Intended to Be Used as Evidence

The prosecution's duty to be fair to the defence extends to disclosing information which will not be part of their case and might even contradict their case, and of which the defence might otherwise be unaware. This obligation is now set out in the CPIA 1996, Part I (see **D9** for details). D15.71

Custody Record etc.

By PACE Code C, para. 2.4, the defence are entitled to a copy of the custody record which the custody officer is required to keep in respect of each person detained at a police station (see **appendix 1**). Failure to supply a copy would be a breach of the Code and might lead to the exclusion of evidence through exercise of the court's discretion under the PACE 1984, s. 78 (see **F2.9**). Similarly, if the accused was stopped in the street and searched under the powers given to the police by the PACE 1984, s. 1, the defence are entitled to a copy of the record of search (see s. 2(9)). D15.72

PRE-TRIAL PROVISION OF INFORMATION: DEFENCE OBLIGATIONS

Historically, there was no general obligation on the defence to disclose the nature of their case, or the evidence they proposed to call before trial. The position altered radically with the implementation of the CPIA 1996, Part I (see **D9** for details), which applies to alleged offences for which no criminal investigation began before 1 April 1997 (see **D9.4**) and is addressed in the Judicial Protocol on the Disclosure of Unused Material in Criminal Cases, issued in December 2013 (see **D9**). In *R* [2015] EWCA Crim 1941, [2016] 1 WLR 1872 the importance of defence co-operation and engagement with the disclosure process from its initial stages was stressed (see **D15.62**). D15.73

Defence Statement

Under the CPIA 1996, s. 5, once the prosecution case has been served the defence are required to provide the court and prosecution with a defence statement, setting out in general terms the nature of the defence, and indicating the principal matters on which they take issue with the prosecution. The requirements are defined by s. 6A (see **D9.29** and the Judicial Disclosure Protocol, para.17; see **appendix 4**). Where a preparatory hearing is held in a case of serious fraud, the defence may similarly be ordered to supply a written statement setting out the nature of the defence (CJA 1987, s. 9(5)). D15.74

Expert Evidence

By the PACE 1984, s. 81, rules may require any party to proceedings before the court to disclose to the other parties any expert evidence which the party proposes to adduce. CrimPR Part 19 and the robust provisions of CrimPD V, Part 19 (see Supplement, **R19.1** *et seq.* and **CPD.19A** *et seq.*), contain the rules that apply under this power. D15.75

D15.76 **Application** The rules apply to both the prosecution and defence, but those relating to service have less relevance to the prosecution because prosecution expert evidence (like the ordinary prosecution evidence) will normally be disclosed by other means. For example, the statement that experts are required to make as to their understanding of the rules (CrimPR 19.4(j) and (k), and CrimPD V, para, 19B.1; see Supplement, **R19.4** and **CPD.19B**) is not limited to experts instructed for the defence.

D15.77 **Content of the Rules** CrimPR 19.3 sets out the procedure for a party to seek to have a summary of an expert's conclusions admitted as a fact and the steps to be taken where a party seeks to have expert evidence admitted when it is not agreed. On request, a copy of the record of any 'examination, measurement, test, or experiment' on which the finding or opinion is based must be supplied or, if it is more practicable, reasonable opportunity to inspect such a record must be allowed; the duty also applies to anything on which the procedure was carried out (r. 19.3(3)(d)). Once expert opinion has been served, the court may direct a meeting of experts to discuss the issues and to prepare a statement of those matters on which they agree and disagree (r. 19.6(2), supplemented by CrimPD V, paras. 19C.1 to 19C.8). Alternatively, where several defendants give notice that they will seek to rely on expert opinion going to the same issue, the court may direct that only one expert should be instructed on their joint behalf (r. 19.7).

D15.78 **Breaches of the Rules** Failure to comply with the rules means that the expert evidence will be admissible at trial only with leave of the court or agreement of every other party (CrimPR 19.3(4)). The court retains the power to extend time-limits for compliance with these rules, even after their expiry (r. 19.9(1)). In *Ensor* [2009] EWCA Crim 2519, [2010] 1 Cr App R 18 (255), the Court of Appeal stressed that the CrimPR obliged the parties to give notice of their reliance on an expert, and to serve the report of that expert, at the earliest practicable moment; failure to do so entitled the trial judge to exclude that report (see also **F11.46**). (See also *Writtle v DPP* [2009] EWHC 236 (Admin) and **D4**).

PRE-TRIAL DISCLOSURE OF THIRD-PARTY MATERIAL

D15.79 Another important area of pre-trial disclosure relates to material in the possession of third parties. This will include records held by health and education authorities, or financial institutions. Although applications for such material may commonly be made on behalf of the accused, under para. 51 of the A-G's Guidelines: Disclosure of information for criminal proceedings (set out at **appendix** 4), the prosecution is placed under an obligation to obtain material in the hands of third parties which might be relevant to the prosecution case. Such disclosure is addressed in the Judicial Protocol on the Disclosure of Unused Material in Criminal Cases, issued in December 2013 (see **D9**).

In either event, the mechanism for securing disclosure of third-party material, unless it is volunteered, is through the issuing of a witness summons for the production of documents, pursuant to the Criminal Procedure (Attendance of Witnesses) Act 1965, s. 2A. These provisions are set out at **D15.94**, and this topic is addressed in more detail at **D9.70**.

PRIVATE MEETING BETWEEN JUDGE AND COUNSEL

D15.80 Before or during the trial, counsel may, with the judge's agreement, see the judge privately about the case. The basic principles are contained in Lord Parker CJ's observations in *Turner* [1970] 2 QB 321 at p. 324, modified in the light of the decision of the five-judge Court of Appeal in *Goodyear* [2005] EWCA Crim 888, [2005] 2 Cr App R 20

(281) (see also **D12.61** and CrimPD VI, para. 26N.1: see Supplement, **CPD.26N**). The guidance is as follows.

(a) Freedom of access between counsel and judge is essential. This is because there may be matters calling for communication or discussion which cannot, in the interests of the client, be mentioned in open court.
(b) It is imperative that so far as possible justice be administered in open court. Counsel should therefore ask to see the judge only when it is felt to be really necessary. Equally, the judge should be careful to treat communications made out of court as private only when fairness to the accused so requires. In *Llewellyn* (1978) 67 Cr App R 149, the Court of Appeal criticised a trial judge who had asked counsel to come to see him so that they could discuss whether the trial should proceed on a single count for conspiracy or on two conspiracy counts as in the indictment or on charges of substantive offences. The issues should have been aired publicly and a full shorthand note taken which, *inter alia*, might assist the Court of Appeal should the judge's decision later be challenged on appeal.
(c) Any private discussion that does take place should be between the judge and both prosecuting and defence counsel, regardless of who asked for the meeting. If in court, the defence solicitor should also be allowed to attend if so wished.
(d) In *Goodyear*, Lord Woolf CJ made it clear (at [67]) that private meetings between judge and counsel should not act as a vehicle for plea bargaining.

Recording the Meeting Where such a meeting occurs it is essential that a record is made. In *Smith* [1990] 1 All ER 634, Russell LJ put it this way (at p. 1314B–C): **D15.81**

> Of course, on the authority of the well known case of *Turner* [1970] 2 QB 321, in some circumstances it is permissible for counsel to see the judge in his room to ascertain his reaction to possible sentencing options open to him. But that should never occur, as has been said on almost innumerable occasions in this court, in the absence of a shorthand note-taker or, alternatively, in the absence of some recording device.

His lordship went on to quote with approval the words of Mustill LJ in *Harper-Taylor* (1988) 138 NLJ 80 at pp. 80–1, which encapsulate the problems posed by 'unnecessary visits to the judge's room':

> A first principle of criminal law is that justice is done in public, for all to see and hear. By this standard a meeting in the judge's room is anomalous: the essence, and indeed the purpose, being that neither the defendant nor the jury nor the public are there to hear what is going on. Undeniably, there are circumstances where the public must be excluded. Equally, the jury cannot always be kept in court throughout. The withdrawal of the proceedings into private, without even the defendant being there, is another matter. It is true, as this court stated in *Turner* [1970] 2 QB 321 at p. 326, that there must be freedom of access between counsel and the judge when there are matters calling for communications or discussions of such a nature that counsel cannot in the interests of his client mention them in open court. Criminal trials are so various that a list of situations where an approach to the judge is permissible would only mislead; but it must be clear that communications should never take place unless there is no alternative.
>
> Apart from the question of principle, seeing the judge in private creates risks of more than one kind, as the present case has shown. The need to solve an immediate practical problem may combine with the more relaxed atmosphere of the private room to blur the formal outlines of the trial. ... in particular, there is a risk that counsel and solicitors for the other parties may hear something said to the judge which they would rather not hear, putting them into a state of conflict between their duties to their clients, and their obligation to maintain the confidentiality of the private room.
>
> The absence of the defendant is also a potential source of trouble. He has to learn what the judge has said at second hand, and may afterwards complain (rightly or not) that he was not given an accurate account. Equally, he cannot hear what his counsel has said to the judge, and hence cannot intervene to correct a misstatement or an excess of authority...

PRESENCE OF THE ACCUSED AT TRIAL

The Principle

D15.82 As a general principle, an accused should be present throughout the trial. The attendance of the accused at the Crown Court is secured by the magistrates remanding in custody or on bail when the case is sent for trial. If, having been bailed, the accused fails to attend on the day notified as the day of trial, a bench warrant may be issued forthwith for the accused's arrest under the BA 1976, s. 7 (see **D7.98**).

The accused must be present at the commencement of a trial on indictment in order to plead. It is then the almost invariable practice for the accused to be present throughout the trial. The implication of this rule is that the accused must not only be physically present, but must have the proceedings interpreted if that is necessary (*Kunnath v The State* [1993] 4 All ER 30). CrimPR 25.2(1)(b) (see Supplement, **R25.2**) provides that the court must not proceed if the accused is absent, unless the court is satisfied that the accused has waived the right to attend and the trial will still be fair despite the accused's absence.

By extension, this also means that the judge ought not to deal with matters which constitute part of the trial proceedings in the absence of counsel for the defence. For example, in *Coolledge* [1996] Crim LR 748, an appeal was allowed because the judge inquired of a witness in chambers and in the absence of defence counsel as to the reason why he had failed to attend court to give evidence. The Court of Appeal held that counsel should not have been excluded since the procedure went beyond a mere inquiry, and affected the conduct of the trial itself, which was therefore tainted.

Exceptions to the Principle

D15.83 Notwithstanding this general rule, the accused's presence may be dispensed with in exceptional circumstances (per Lord Reading CJ in *Lee Kun* [1916] 1 KB 337 at p. 341). The situations in which the court may be justified in proceeding without the accused are as follows.

(a) as a result of the misbehaviour of the accused (see **D15.86**);
(b) where his absence is voluntary;
(c) when the accused is too ill to attend;
(d) following the death of the accused.

Each of these circumstances and various related matters is considered below.

D15.84 **Principles to be Considered** In *Hayward* [2001] EWCA Crim 168, [2001] QB 862, the Court of Appeal considered the principles which the trial judge ought to apply when dealing with an absent defendant, and summarised them as follows.

(a) An accused has, in general, a right to be present at the trial and a right to be legally represented.
(b) Those rights can be waived, separately or together, wholly or in part, by the accused:
  (i) they may be wholly waived if, knowing or having the means of knowledge as to when and where the trial is to take place, the accused is deliberately and voluntarily absent and/or withdraws instructions from legal representatives;
  (ii) they may be waived in part if, being present and represented at the outset, the accused, during the course of the trial, behaves in such a way as to obstruct the proper course of the proceedings and/or withdraws instructions from legal representatives.
(c) The trial judge has a discretion as to whether a trial should take place or continue in the absence of an accused and/or the accused's legal representatives. The judge is required to warn the defendant at the PTPH of the risk of the trial continuing in the defendant's absence (CrimPR 3.21(2); see Supplement, **R3.21**).

(d) That discretion must be exercised with great care and it is only in rare and exceptional cases that it should be exercised in favour of a trial taking place or continuing, particularly if the accused is unrepresented.
(e) In exercising that discretion, fairness to the defence is of prime importance but fairness to the prosecution must also be taken into account. The judge must have regard to all the circumstances of the case including, in particular:
    (i) the nature and circumstances of the accused's behaviour in being absent from the trial or disrupting its continuation, and, in particular, whether the behaviour was deliberate, voluntary and such as plainly waived the right to appear;
    (ii) whether an adjournment might result in the accused being caught or attending voluntarily and/or not disrupting the proceedings;
    (iii) the likely length of such an adjournment;
    (iv) whether the accused, though absent, is, or wishes to be, legally represented at the trial or has waived the right to representation;
    (v) the extent to which the absent accused's legal representatives are able to present the defence;
    (vi) the extent of the disadvantage to the accused in not being able to give his or her account of events, having regard to the nature of the evidence;
    (vii) the risk of the jury reaching an improper conclusion about the absence of the accused (but see (f) below);
    (viii) the seriousness of the offence to the accused, victim and public;
    (ix) the general public interest and the particular interest of victims and witnesses that a trial should take place within a reasonable time of the events to which it relates;
    (x) the effect of delay on the memories of witnesses;
    (xi) where there is more than one accused and not all have absconded, the undesirability of separate trials, and the prospects of a fair trial for the defendants who are present.
(f) If the judge decides that a trial should take place or continue in the absence of an unrepresented accused, the judge must ensure that the trial is as fair as the circumstances permit. In particular, reasonable steps must be taken, both during the giving of evidence and in the summing-up, to expose weaknesses in the prosecution case and to make such points on behalf of the accused as the evidence permits. In summing-up the judge must warn the jury that absence is not an admission of guilt and adds nothing to the prosecution case.

D15.85 The clear emphasis in *Hayward* was on the need for caution before proceeding to try a defendant in his absence. In view of the need to ensure compliance with the ECHR, Article 6, that caution is entirely proper. For the same reason, it is entirely proper that the focus in determining whether to proceed should be upon the accused's right to attend the trial and be represented at it.

The principles outlined by the Court of Appeal in *Hayward* were considered and commended by the House of Lords in *Jones* [2002] UKHL 5, [2003] 1 AC 1. Lord Bingham endorsed the Court of Appeal's guidelines with two reservations:

(1) the seriousness of the offence should not be considered — the principles would be the same whether the offence was serious or minor; and
(2) even if the accused absconded voluntarily, it would generally be desirable that the accused should be represented. It was emphasised that it was a step to be taken with 'great caution and close regard to the overall fairness of the proceedings'. In *Amrouchi* [2007] EWCA Crim 3019, relying on those observations, Hughes LJ said it was a step that should only be taken when it was 'unavoidable'.

In *Lopez* [2013] EWCA Crim 1744, the Court of Appeal observed that the decision to proceed with a trial in the absence of an accused was one that had to be approached with the utmost care and that such a course should be adopted only in rare cases and only after consideration had been given to all relevant matters and in particular the fairness of the trial. Where D's defence involved the retraction of admissions made to the police in interview, his presence at his trial was of importance. In *R (Drinkwater) v Solihull Magistrates' Court* [2012] EWHC 765 (Admin) the Administrative Court emphasised that expedition should not be a reason to continue a trial in the absence of the accused.

In a multi-handed case where one defendant was voluntarily absent, the impact of evidence relevant to that defendant being adduced in the trial of others had to be considered, and the possibility of severing the absent defendant to avoid prejudice to others considered (*Hanou* [2019] EWCA Crim 281, [2019] 4 WLR 149).

CrimPD III, para. 14E.1, also addresses trials in the absence of the accused (see Supplement, **CPD.14E**). See also *Rebihi* [2012] EWCA Crim 2481 for the proper direction that should be given to the jury if the trial is to continue in the absence of the accused.

D15.86 **Misbehaviour of the Accused** If the accused behaves in an unruly fashion in the dock, e.g., by shouting out, or is apparently trying to intimidate jurors or witnesses, and thereby makes it impracticable for the hearing to continue, the judge may order that the accused be removed from court and that the trial proceed in the accused's absence (*Lee Kun* [1916] 1 KB 337).

In practice, the judge would warn the accused before taking the extreme step of barring from court, and it may be appropriate to permit a return to the dock at a later stage if the accused undertakes not to repeat the unruly behaviour. Unruly behaviour may also be deterred by the threat of holding the accused to be guilty of a contempt in the face of the court (see **B14.89**). An accused should not be handcuffed in the dock unless there is a real risk of violence or escape and there is no alternative to visible restraint (*Horden* [2009] EWCA Crim 388, [2009] 2 Cr App R 24 (406)).

Similarly, if the accused refuses to be brought into court from the cells, the trial judge is entitled to proceed without the accused where the right to be present has been unequivocally waived (*Smith* [2006] EWCA Crim 2307). As is made clear at CrimPR 25.2(1)(b), and was repeated in *Hussain* [2018] EWCA Crim 1785, the discretion to continue in the absence of the accused is to be approached with great caution and with close regard to the fairness of the proceedings. It may often be better to allow time to cool off, and to continue the trial in the accused's presence.

D15.87 **Voluntary Absence of the Accused** If the accused, having been present for the commencement of his trial, later goes voluntarily absent, either by escaping from custody or by failing to surrender having been bailed by the court for the period of an adjournment, the judge has a discretion to complete the trial in the accused's absence (*Jones (No. 2)* [1972] 2 All ER 731). Should the accused be convicted, sentence may also be passed in the accused's absence (*Jones (No. 2)*). In *Simms* [2016] EWCA Crim 9, it was held that the same principle applied where D had voluntarily rendered himself incapable of participation in the trial through intoxication (or through a self-induced drug psychosis: *Ehi-Palmer* [2016] EWCA Crim 1844).

Whether to proceed in the accused's absence must, however, be a matter for the judge's discretion. In *Amrouchi* [2007] EWCA Crim 3019, the Court of Appeal identified questions relevant to the exercise of that discretion including whether (a) D had deliberately absented himself and (b) there were reasonable steps that could be taken to secure his attendance.

In *Hanou* [2019] EWCA Crim 281, [2019] 4 WLR 149, the Court of Appeal restated that a trial can proceed in the absence of an accused who has not been arraigned, however, the court was first required to be satisfied that the accused had waived the right to be arraigned. If the indictment had been amended after the accused had absconded, it could not necessarily be assumed that the accused had waived the right to be arraigned on that amended indictment, although this also depended on a fact-specific analysis.

The alternative is to discharge the jury from giving a verdict, thus allowing a retrial to take place before a different jury once the accused's presence has been secured. This exercise of discretion involved more than an assessment of the adequacy of the evidence to explain the accused's absence, and required an assessment of fairness (*R (Rathor) v Southampton Magistrates' Court* [2018] EWHC 3278 (Admin)). Whether or not the court proceeds in the accused's absence, the judge may and almost certainly will issue a warrant for his arrest under the BA 1976, s. 7 (see **D7.98**).

Absent Defendant's Legal Representatives The position of defence legal representatives when a trial continues in the absence of an accused who has absconded was considered in *Shaw* [1980] 2 All ER 433. The accused's instructions are not deemed to have been withdrawn and counsel and solicitor are not therefore automatically required to withdraw from the case. Whether counsel should continue to act and to what extent are essentially matters for counsel having regard to the guidance given in the Code of Conduct of the Bar (per Kilner Brown J in *Shaw* at p. 1529G). Counsel can advance existing instructions and even fresh instructions provided by the offender after having absconded (*Pomfrett* [2009] EWCA Crim 1939, [2010] 2 Cr App R 28 (281)). **D15.88**

In *Kepple* [2007] EWCA Crim 1339, the Court of Appeal said that counsel was entitled to cross-examine witnesses in the continuation of the trial of an absent accused, providing he considered that he had sufficient instructions to do so, as long as he did not suggest what the absent accused's account would have been.

Where an accused absconds and is convicted in his absence, the limited circumstances in which his legal representatives (assuming they have chosen not to withdraw) may give notice of appeal on his behalf are dealt with in **D26.14**.

Sickness of the Accused If the accused's absence from court is for reasons beyond the accused's control, the trial may *not* continue in the absence of the accused unless the accused consents (see, e.g., the dicta of Williams J in *Abrahams* (1895) 21 VLR 343, adopted by Roskill LJ in *Jones (No. 2)* [1972] 2 All ER 731) or if the case can be fully presented, including the accused's own written evidence, without unfairness (*Hamberger* [2017] EWCA Crim 273, [2017] 2 Cr App R 9 (81)). **D15.89**

The obvious and common example of involuntary absence is sickness. Thus, should the accused become ill during the course of the trial, the judge must either adjourn the case until the accused recovers or discharge the jury (*Howson* (1981) 74 Cr App R 172; *Kaur* [2013] EWCA Crim 590). If the court is not satisfied with the adequacy of the evidence of illness it should provide an opportunity for further evidence to be provided before continuing the trial in the acccused's absence, and must always have regard to fairness (*R (Rathor) v Southampton Magistrates' Court* [2018] EWHC 3278 (Admin)). Possible exceptions to this proposition include:

(a) As mentioned in *Howson*, if there are several accused and one falls sick, the trial may continue in that accused's absence provided that the evidence and proceedings relate entirely to the cases against the co-accused and have no possible bearing on the absent accused's case.
(b) Where D's voluntary ingestion of drugs makes his participation in the trial impossible, the situation may well be otherwise (*Simms* [2016] EWCA Crim 9).
(c) Where D had a heart condition preventing his attendance but it was considered that his counsel were able to argue his case effectively and he was given the opportunity to give written evidence (*Hamberger*).

The decision in *Howson* also indicates that it is not enough for an accused to be physically present if too unwell to pay proper attention to the proceedings and give instructions to legal representatives. However, in *F* [2018] EWCA Crim 2693, the judge was found to have been correct to continue with the trial of an elderly hospitalised defendant by reference to factors such as the long delays in bringing the case to trial; the many adjournments which had already been granted; the interests of witnesses, including the complainant; and, crucially, whether the appellant's counsel was fully instructed and able to represent his interests without him being present.

Death of the Accused Where the accused dies before the trial is completed, formal evidence of death should be given, and endorsed upon the indictment. This may, for example, be the **D15.90**

evidence of the officer in the case that the officer has seen and identified the remains of the person named in the indictment. If such evidence is not available, other evidence such as a certified copy of the entry in the register of deaths will suffice. The endorsement of the indictment in such circumstances renders it of no legal effect. In such circumstances, the court has no discretion to take verdicts already reached but not delivered by the jury (*Turk* [2017] EWCA Crim 391, [2017] 2 Cr App R 2 (14)).

ATTENDANCE OF WITNESSES

Securing the Attendance of Witnesses

D15.91 In most cases, it is the responsibility of the police to secure the attendance of prosecution witnesses, and that of the defence solicitor to ensure that defence witnesses attend. The steps taken will depend on the sensitivity of the witness and whether there is a fixed date for trial, or whether the case is in a warned list in which case an accused, for example, would need to keep in daily contact with his solicitors during the period in which his case might be called on.

D15.92 **Compelling Attendance** Where the prosecution or defence wish to secure the attendance of a witness but are not satisfied that the witness will attend voluntarily, they can apply for a witness summons. The procedure is set out in the Criminal Procedure (Attendance of Witnesses) Act 1965, ss. 2 to 3, which are set out at **D15.94**, and CrimPR 17.3 to 17.4 (see Supplement, **R-17.3** ***et seq.***

The same provisions are used to secure the production of documents, rather than the attendance of a witness, as evidence. The use of the provisions for this purpose is particularly pertinent to the disclosure of material in the possession of third parties, which is discussed at D15.79 and **D9.71**.

D15.93 **Punishment for Failure to Attend** A person who 'without just excuse' disobeys a witness order or summons requiring the person to attend court is guilty of contempt of the court that the person fails to attend (Criminal Procedure (Attendance of Witnesses) Act 1965, s. 3(1)). The person may be summarily punished as if having committed a contempt in the court's face (ibid.); it is desirable and appropriate for the judge who issued the warrant to deal in person with the witness (*Yusuf* [2003] EWCA Crim 1488, [2003] 2 Cr App R 32 (488)). The maximum penalty is three months' imprisonment (s. 3(2)). It was stressed in *Popat* [2008] EWCA Crim 1921 that it is disobedience of a summons which represents the contempt, and there is no requirement for an arrest warrant to have been issued in addition.

The existence of a 'just excuse' will not be lightly inferred. Witnesses are required to submit even to very substantial inconvenience in their business and private lives. Culpable forgetfulness can certainly never amount to a 'just excuse' (*Lennock* (1993) 97 Cr App R 228). However, the prosecution must prove beyond reasonable doubt that proper notification of the trial date was given (*Abdulaziz* [1989] Crim LR 717).

In *Wang* [2005] EWCA Crim 476, no witness summons had been issued at the time when D was warned that he might be needed at the Crown Court on a particular date. The Court of Appeal quashed his conviction. Nevertheless, the Court indicated that, if D had been warned that the prosecution would obtain a witness summons, and had gone to ground to evade it, a conviction under s. 3 of the 1965 Act, or at common law, might have been sustainable. This approach was approved in *Popat*.

In *R (H) v Wood Green Crown Court* [2006] EWHC 2683 (Admin), [2007] 1 WLR 1670, it was made clear that a witness may be remanded for as long as there is a real possibility that the witness may be required to give evidence, or further evidence, as the case may be.

Criminal Procedure (Attendance of Witnesses) Act 1965, ss. 2 to 3 D15.94

2.—(1) This section applies where the Crown Court is satisfied that—

(a) a person is likely to be able to give evidence likely to be material evidence, or produce any document or thing likely to be material evidence, for the purpose of any criminal proceedings before the Crown Court, and

(b) it is in the interests of justice to issue a summons under this section to secure the attendance of that person to give evidence or to produce the document or thing.

(2) In such a case the Crown Court shall, subject to the following provisions of this section, issue a summons (a witness summons) directed to the person concerned and requiring him to—

(a) attend before the Crown Court at the time and place stated in the summons, and

(b) give the evidence or produce the document or thing.

(3) A witness summons may only be issued under this section on an application; and the Crown Court may refuse to issue the summons if any requirement relating to the application is not fulfilled.

(4) Where a person has been sent for trial, for any offence to which the proceedings concerned relate, an application must be made as soon as is reasonably practicable after service on that person, in pursuance of regulations made under paragraph 1 of Schedule 3 to the Crime and Disorder Act 1998, of the documents relevant to that offence.

(5) [Repealed.]

(6) Where the proceedings concerned relate to an offence in relation to which a bill of indictment has been preferred under the authority of section 2(2)(b) of the Administration of Justice (Miscellaneous Provisions) Act 1933 (bill preferred by direction of Court of Appeal, or by direction or with consent of judge) an application must be made as soon as is reasonably practicable after the bill was preferred.

(6A) Where the proceedings concerned relate to an offence that is the subject of a deferred prosecution agreement within the meaning of Schedule 17 to the Crime and Courts Act 2013, an application must be made as soon as reasonably practicable after the suspension of the proceedings is lifted under paragraph 2(3) of that Schedule.

(7) to (10) [Require compliance with the CrimPR and specify matters which may be covered by them.]

2A. A witness summons which is issued under section 2 above and which requires a person to produce a document or thing as mentioned in section 2(2) above may also require him to produce the document or thing—

(a) at a place stated in the summons, and

(b) at a time which is so stated and precedes that stated under section 2(2) above, for inspection by the person applying for the summons.

2B.—(1) If—

(a) a document or thing is produced in pursuance of a requirement imposed by a witness summons under section 2A above,

(b) the person applying for the summons concludes that a requirement imposed by the summons under section 2(2) above is no longer needed, and

(c) he accordingly applies to the Crown Court for a direction that the summons shall be of no further effect,

the court may direct accordingly.

(2) and (3) [Require compliance with the CrimPR and specify matters which may be covered by them.]

2C.—(1) If a witness summons issued under section 2 above is directed to a person who—

(a) applies to the Crown Court,

(b) satisfies the court that he was not served with notice of the application to issue the summons and that he was neither present nor represented at the hearing of the application, and

(c) satisfies the court that he cannot give any evidence likely to be material evidence or, as the case may be, produce any document or thing likely to be material evidence,

the court may direct that the summons shall be of no effect.

(2) For the purposes of subsection (1) above it is immaterial—

(a) whether or not Criminal Procedure Rules require the person to be served with notice of the application to issue the summons;

(b) whether or not Criminal Procedure Rules enable the person to be present or represented at the hearing of the application.

(3) In subsection (1)(b) above 'served' means—
(a) served in accordance with Criminal Procedure Rules, in a case where such rules require the person to be served with notice of the application to issue the summons;
(b) served in such way as appears reasonable to the court to which the application is made under this section, in any other case.
(4) The Crown Court may refuse to make a direction under this section if any requirement relating to the application under this section is not fulfilled.
(5) to (7) [Require compliance with the CrimPR and specify matters which may be covered by them.]
(8) Where a direction is made under this section that a witness summons shall be of no effect, the person on whose application the summons was issued may be ordered to pay the whole or any part of the costs of the application under this section.
(9) [Taxation and payment of costs.]
2D. For the purpose of any criminal proceedings before it, the Crown Court may of its own motion issue a summons (a witness summons) directed to a person and requiring him to—
(a) attend before the court at the time and place stated in the summons, and
(b) give evidence, or produce any document or thing specified in the summons.
2E.—(1) If a witness summons issued under section 2D above is directed to a person who—
(a) applies to the Crown Court, and
(b) satisfies the court that he cannot give any evidence likely to be material evidence or, as the case may be, produce any document or thing likely to be material evidence,
the court may direct that the summons shall be of no effect.
(2) The Crown Court may refuse to make a direction under this section if any requirement relating to the application under this section is not fulfilled.
(3) and (4) [Require compliance with the CrimPR and specify matters which may be covered by them.]
3.—(1) Any person who without just excuse disobeys a witness summons requiring him to attend before any court shall be guilty of contempt of that court and may be punished summarily by that court as if his contempt had been committed in the face of the court.
(1A) Any person who without just excuse disobeys a requirement made by any court under section 2A above shall be guilty of contempt of that court and may be punished summarily by that court as if his contempt had been committed in the face of the court.
(2) No person shall by reason of any disobedience mentioned in subsection (1) or (1A) above be liable to imprisonment for a period exceeding three months.

The relevant rules are to be found in CrimPR Part 17 (see Supplement, **R17.1** ***et seq.***).

D15.95 Section 4 of the Act describes the powers available to ensure compliance with a witness summons.

Criminal Procedure (Attendance of Witnesses) Act 1965, s. 4

(1) If a judge of the Crown Court is satisfied by evidence on oath that a witness in respect of whom a witness summons is in force is unlikely to comply with the summons, the judge may issue a warrant to arrest the witness and bring him before the court before which he is required to attend:
Provided that a warrant shall not be issued under this subsection unless the judge is satisfied by such evidence as aforesaid that the witness is likely to be able to give evidence likely to be material evidence or produce any document or thing likely to be material evidence in the proceedings.
(2) Where a witness who is required to attend before the Crown Court by virtue of a witness summons fails to attend in compliance with the summons, that court may—
(a) in any case, cause to be served on him a notice requiring him to attend the court forthwith or at such time as may be specified in the notice;
(b) if the court is satisfied that there are reasonable grounds for believing that he has failed to attend without just excuse, or if he has failed to comply with a notice under paragraph (a) above, issue a warrant to arrest him and bring him before the court.
(3) A witness brought before a court in pursuance of a warrant under this section may be remanded by that court in custody or on bail (with or without sureties) until such time as the court may appoint for receiving his evidence or dealing with him under section 3 of this Act; and where a witness attends a court in pursuance of a notice under this section the court may direct that the notice shall have effect as if it required him to attend at any later time appointed by the court for receiving his evidence or dealing with him as aforesaid.

Live Link

The use of a live link for the evidence of a witness is permitted by the YJCEA 1999, s. 24, the CJA 1988, s. 32, and the CJA 2003, s. 51. **D15.96**

In the context of the YJCEA 1999, references to live links are references to 'a live television link or other arrangements whereby a witness, whilst absent from the courtroom or other place where the proceedings are being held, is able to see and hear a person there and to be heard and seen' by the judge, jury, justices, legal representatives, and interpreter for the accused (s. 24(8)). As to live links under the YJCEA 1999, see **D14.38**.

The procedure relating to live link directions other than in the context of 'special measures' is now set out in CrimPR 18.23 to 18.26 (see Supplement, **R18.23** ***et seq.***). The application must be made using part B of the prescribed form. Under r. 18.23, the court may decide whether to give or discharge a direction at a hearing or without a hearing and in a party's absence if that party is the applicant or has had at least ten business days in which to make representations. Under r. 18.24, an applicant for a live link direction must identify the place from which the witness will give evidence and, if that place is in the UK, explain why it would be 'in the interests of the efficient or effective administration of justice for the witness to give evidence by live link'. If the applicant wants the witness to be accompanied by another person while giving evidence, that person must be named and the application must explain why it is appropriate for the witness to be accompanied. See also r. 18.10(f). See the Special Supplement at **D15.40A** ***et seq.*** for details of temporary modifications made by the Coronavirus Act 2020 to the rules relating to live links.

Live Links for Overseas Witnesses The CJA 1988, s. 32, provides for the use of live links for witnesses who are overseas. **D15.97**

Criminal Justice Act 1988, s. 32

(1) A person other than the accused may give evidence through a live television link in proceedings to which subsection (1A) applies if—
  (a) the witness is outside the United Kingdom;
  (b) [repealed];
  but the evidence may not be so given without the leave of the court.

(1A) This subsection applies—
  (a) to trials on indictment, appeals to the criminal division of the Court of Appeal and hearings of references under section 9 of the Criminal Appeal Act 1995;
  (b) to proceedings in youth courts, appeals to the Crown Court arising out of such proceedings and hearings of references under section 11 of the Criminal Appeal Act 1995 so arising.

Such links are now available at all trials in the Crown Court.

Further Use of Live Links in the Interests of Justice The CJA 2003, s. 51, allows a court to permit witnesses, other than the accused, to give evidence through a 'live link' from another location in the UK, rather than just from overseas. This will usually be via a closed circuit television link, but is defined in such a way as to include any technology with a similar effect, such as video conferencing facilities or the internet. **D15.98**

The court may authorise the use of a live link only if:

(a) it is in the interests of the efficient or effective administration of justice for the witness to give evidence in this way (e.g., because the witness works in a different part of the country and can give evidence from the place of work via a live link); and
(b) notification has been received that the necessary facilities are available in the area where the criminal proceedings are to take place (the assumption is that the parties will ensure that there are facilities in the location from which the witness will give evidence).

Where a direction for a live link has been given, that means that the witness must give all his evidence in that way, so that cross-examination must also be conducted by live link. If it is in the interests of justice to do so, the court can rescind a direction for a live link.

Although the CJA 2003, s. 51, sought to increase the availability of live links, their availability remained under statutory control. Accordingly, it was not permissible for a court to permit a witness to give evidence by telephone where such a link was not available (*Hampson* [2012] EWCA Crim 1807, [2014] 1 Cr App R 4 (28)).

The use of live links for pre-trial hearings, as opposed to witness evidence at trial, is addressed in CrimPD I, paras. 3N.1 *et seq.* (see Supplement, **CPD.3N**) (see also **D15.3** and **D15.40**).

CONTACT WITH WITNESSES, WITNESS COACHING AND FAMILIARISATION

D15.99 An important aspect of the handling of witnesses is consideration of what contact it is appropriate for counsel, and others involved in either the prosecution or defence team, to have with them. This also involves consideration of the prohibition on witnesses being rehearsed by the party that is to call them, which potentially competes with the need to ensure that a witness is able to give his evidence in the best possible way, is not distracted by a lack of familiarity with his surroundings in court, and receives proper support from those responsible for his welfare through what can be a very stressful experience.

Contact between Counsel and Witnesses

D15.100 Contact with witnesses was addressed in detail in the Code of Conduct. The Code has now been replaced by the BSB Handbook. Insofar as this addresses the issue, it may be summarised as follows:

(a) There is no longer a general rule preventing a barrister from having contact with any witness. Under the Written Standards that operated under the old Code, a barrister could have contact with a witness whom the barrister expected to call and examine in chief, with a view to introducing him or herself, explaining the court's procedure, and answering any questions about it which the witness might have. CPS guidance still indicates that a prosecuting barrister has a positive responsibility to ensure that a witness facing unfamiliar court procedures is put as much at ease as possible, particularly when that witness is nervous, vulnerable or apparently the victim of criminal conduct.

(b) Although the BSB Handbook provides only limited guidance, in a contested case in the Crown Court it is generally inappropriate for a barrister to *interview* any potential witness. Interviewing includes discussing the substance of the witness's evidence, or the evidence of other witnesses. The practice set out in the Code for Pre-Trial Witness Interviews (Written Standards, para. 6.3.2) remains useful (if not enforceable) guidance.

(c) To the extent that general disclosure obligations require (in the absence of any specific requirement in the BSB Handbook), where a barrister has interviewed a potential witness, that fact should be disclosed to all the other parties in the case before the witness is called.

(d) Counsel must not rehearse, practise or coach any witness, in relation either to the evidence itself or to the way in which to give it (BSB Handbook, rC9.4), as was made clear in *Momodou (Practice Note)* [2005] EWCA Crim 177, [2005] 1 WLR 3442, where the extent of permissible witness familiarisation was set out (see **D15.103**).

D15.101 **Prosecution Counsel** The proper handling of witnesses has become an important part of the role of the prosecutor, not least since the introduction of CPS Standards in this regard. Prosecuting counsel should not confer with any investigator witness unless the latter has a supervisory responsibility in the investigation (e.g., as officer in the case), and should not confer with or receive factual instructions directly from investigators on matters which may be in dispute.

Defence Counsel The interlocking matters of conferences, counsel being attended at court by his professional client, and the seeing of witnesses are dealt with in various provisions of the Code of Conduct of the Bar, which may be summarised as follows: **D15.102**

(a) Provided that the interests of justice and of the lay client will not be prejudiced, counsel may agree with his professional client that attendance by the latter's representative may be dispensed with (BSB Handbook, rC17).
(b) Although, in general, counsel should not interview witnesses or discuss their evidence with them, there may be extraordinary circumstances in which departure from this principle is unavoidable. In *Fergus* (1994) 98 Cr App R 313 Steyn LJ stated (at p. 323) that, since defence solicitors had failed to see the alibi witnesses in order to ask why they had remembered the events of the day in question, counsel should have seen them himself.

Witness Familiarisation

In *Momodou (Practice Note)* [2005] EWCA Crim 177, [2005] 1 WLR 3442, the Court of Appeal made clear that, while familiarisation of witnesses with the court and procedure is legitimate, it must be carefully regulated. Judge LJ stated (at [61] and [62]): **D15.103**

> There is a dramatic distinction between witness training or coaching, and witness familiarisation. Training or coaching for witnesses in criminal proceedings (whether for prosecution or defence) is not permitted. This is the logical consequence of well-known principle that discussions between witnesses should not take place, and that the statements and proofs of one witness should not be disclosed to any other witness. (See [*Richardson* [1971] 2 QB 484, *Arif* (1993) *The Times*, 17 June 1993, *Skinner* (1994) 99 Cr App R 212] and *Shaw* [2002] EWCA Crim 3004.) The witness should give his or her own evidence, so far as practicable uninfluenced by what anyone else has said, whether in formal discussions or informal conversations. The rule reduces, indeed hopefully avoids any possibility, that one witness may tailor his evidence in the light of what anyone else said, and equally, avoids any unfounded perception that he may have done so. These risks are inherent in witness training. Even if the training takes place one-to-one with someone completely remote from the facts of the case itself, the witness may come, even unconsciously, to appreciate which aspects of his evidence are perhaps not quite consistent with what others are saying, or indeed not quite what is required of him. An honest witness may alter the emphasis of his evidence to accommodate what he thinks may be a different, more accurate, or simply better remembered perception of events. A dishonest witness will very rapidly calculate how his testimony may be 'improved'. These dangers are present in one-to-one witness training. Where however the witness is jointly trained with other witnesses to the same events, the dangers dramatically increase. Recollections change. Memories are contaminated. Witnesses may bring their respective accounts into what they believe to be better alignment with others. They may be encouraged to do so, consciously or unconsciously. They may collude deliberately. They may be inadvertently contaminated. Whether deliberately or inadvertently, the evidence may no longer be their own. Although none of this is inevitable, the risk that training or coaching may adversely affect the accuracy of the evidence of the individual witness is constant. So we repeat, witness training for criminal trials is prohibited.
>
> This principle does not preclude pre-trial arrangements to familiarise witness with the layout of the court, the likely sequence of events when the witness is giving evidence, and a balanced appraisal of the different responsibilities of the various participants. Indeed such arrangements, usually in the form of a pre-trial visit to the court, are generally to be welcomed. Witnesses should not be disadvantaged by ignorance of the process, nor when they come to give evidence, taken by surprise at the way it works. None of this however involves discussions about proposed or intended evidence. Sensible preparation for the experience of giving evidence, which assists the witness to give of his or her best at the forthcoming trial is permissible. Such experience can also be provided by out of court familiarisation techniques. The process may improve the manner in which the witness gives evidence by, for example, reducing the nervous tension arising from inexperience of the process. Nevertheless the evidence remains the witness's own uncontaminated evidence. Equally, the principle does not prohibit training of expert and similar witnesses in, for example, the technique of giving comprehensive evidence of a specialist kind to a jury, both during evidence-in-chief and in cross-examination, and, another example, developing the ability to resist the inevitable pressure

of going further in evidence than matters covered by the witnesses' specific expertise. The critical feature of training of this kind is that it should not be arranged in the context of nor related to any forthcoming trial, and it can therefore have no impact whatever on it.

D15.104 **Familiarisation by Outside Agency** The Court of Appeal in *Momodou (Practice Note)* [2005] EWCA Crim 177, [2005] 1 WLR 3442, went on to give guidance (at [63]–[65]) as to the way in which any familiarisation process ought to be regulated, where it was by an outside agency rather than, as is routine, through the Witness Service. The guidance was as follows:

(a) The CPS should be consulted where prosecution witnesses were involved, and the proposed programme should be put in writing.
(b) Where the defence engaged in such a process, counsel's advice should be sought and the trial judge should be informed.
(c) The familiarisation process should be supervised by a barrister or solicitor, preferably by an organisation accredited for the purpose by the Bar Council and Law Society.
(d) None of those involved should have personal knowledge of the matters in issue, and the material used should not bear any similarity to the issues in the case. Nothing should be done to play on or trigger the witnesses' recollection of events.
(e) Any discussion of the criminal proceedings in question must be stopped and advice given about why it is not permissible.
(f) Careful records should be kept of the programme, those present and those responsible for the process. The records should be handed to the CPS and, in relation to defence witnesses, to the court.
(g) Barristers and solicitors were professionally obliged to see that this guidance was followed.

Section D16 Trial on Indictment: The Prosecution Case

INTRODUCTION

Following a plea of not guilty (see **D12**) and the empanelling of a jury (see **D13**), the trial proper commences with the prosecution case. This falls into two parts, namely (a) counsel's opening speech, and (b) the evidence. It should be noted that CrimPD VI, paras. 25A.2 to 25A.3 (see Supplement, **CPD.25A**), also provide for the defence to set out the issues in the case (CrimPR 25.9(2)(c); see Supplement, **R25.9**) and for the trial judge to give legal directions to the jury at the outset of the trial. **D16.1**

If some evidence that forms the basis for the prosecution case is agreed by the accused, it may therefore be read or summarised in the form of admitted evidence. Other evidence is subjected to challenge on behalf of the accused, either through cross-examination of witnesses called or through objection being taken to the admissibility of evidence. The ultimate challenge to the validity of the prosecution case can be mounted at its conclusion, namely a submission of no case to answer.

Where a ruling of the court has fundamentally undermined the prosecution case, for example where evidence is excluded or where the court upholds a submission of no case to answer, the prosecution now has a right of appeal, pursuant to the provisions of the CJA 2003, Part IX. Because these provisions operate either during or at the conclusion of the prosecution case, they are addressed at the conclusion of this section.

First, however, it is important to consider the obligations that the law, and professional ethics, impose on those who prosecute.

DUTIES AND ROLE OF PROSECUTION COUNSEL

Introduction

The manner in which prosecution counsel should conduct themselves in a criminal trial and the duties resting upon them are set out in dicta in Court of Appeal, the Code of Conduct in the BSB Handbook and the recommendations of the Farquharson committee on the role of prosecuting counsel. **D16.2**

Ministers of Justice In *Puddick* (1865) 4 F & F 497, Crompton J said (at p. 499) that prosecution counsel 'are to regard themselves as ministers of justice, and not to struggle for a conviction' (see also per Avory J in *Banks* [1916] 2 KB 621 at p. 623). Some of the implications this has on the prosecutor's role are identified in the introductory paragraphs of the Farquharson report: **D16.3**

> There is no doubt that the obligations of prosecution counsel are different from those of counsel instructed for the defence in a criminal case or of counsel instructed in civil matters. His duties are wider both to the court and to the public at large. Furthermore, having regard to his duty to present the case for the prosecution fairly to the jury, he has a greater independence of those instructing

> him than that enjoyed by other counsel. It is well known to every practitioner that counsel for the prosecution must conduct his case moderately, albeit firmly. He must not strive unfairly to obtain a conviction; he must not press his case beyond the limits which the evidence permits; he must not invite the jury to convict on evidence which in his own judgement no longer sustains the charge laid in the indictment. If the evidence of a witness is undermined or severely blemished in the course of cross-examination, prosecution counsel must not present him to the jury as worthy of a credibility he no longer enjoys.... Great responsibility is placed upon prosecution counsel and although his description as a 'minister of justice' may sound pompous to modern ears it accurately describes the way in which he should discharge his function.

In *Gonez* [1999] All ER (D) 674, the Court of Appeal endorsed the description of prosecuting counsel as a minister of justice, stating that it was incumbent on counsel not to be betrayed by personal feelings, not to excite emotions or to inflame the minds of the jury, and not to make comments which could reasonably be construed as racist and bigoted. Counsel was to be clinical and dispassionate.

D16.4 **Relationship of Prosecution Counsel with Those Instructing Him or Her** As the Farquharson committee stated in the passage quoted at **D16.3**, prosecution counsel is recognised as enjoying greater independence from those instructing him or her, whether it be the CPS or other prosecuting agency or private prosecutor, than does defence counsel from the instructing solicitor or lay client.

The committee helpfully summarised their views in the following propositions:

(a) It is the duty of prosecution counsel to read the instructions delivered expeditiously and to advise or confer with those instructing him or her on all aspects of the case well before its commencement.
(b) A solicitor who has briefed counsel to prosecute may withdraw instructions before the commencement of the trial up to the point when it becomes impracticable to do so, if the solicitor disagrees with the advice given by counsel or for any other proper professional reason.
(c) While remaining instructed it is for counsel to take all necessary decisions in the presentation and general conduct of the prosecution.
(d) Where matters of policy fall to be decided after the point indicated in (b) above (including offering no evidence on the indictment or on a particular count, or the acceptance of pleas to lesser counts), it is the duty of counsel to consult those instructing him or her, as their views at this stage are of crucial importance.
(e) In the rare case where counsel and the instructing solicitor are unable to agree on a matter of policy, it is (subject to (g) below) for prosecution counsel to make the necessary decisions.
(f) Where counsel has taken a decision on a matter of policy with which the instructing solicitor has not agreed, then it would be appropriate for the A-G to require counsel to submit a written report of all the circumstances, including reasons for disagreeing with those who instructed him or her.
(g) When counsel has had the opportunity to prepare the brief and to confer with those instructing him or her, but at the last moment before trial unexpectedly advises that the case should not proceed or that pleas to lesser offences should be accepted, and the instructing solicitor does not accept such advice, counsel should apply for an adjournment if instructed so to do.
(h) Subject to the above, it is for prosecution counsel to decide whether to offer no evidence on a particular count or on the indictment as a whole and whether to accept pleas to a lesser count or counts.

Provisions of the Code of Conduct of the Bar Relating to Prosecuting Counsel

D16.5 The CPS and the General Council of the Bar issued Guidelines in 2002 on the application of the Farquharson principles and, where appropriate, these were incorporated in the Code of Conduct of the Bar, and are now to be found in the BSB Handbook.

The status of the Code of Conduct of the Bar was explained as follows in *McFadden* (1975) 62 Cr App R 187, by James LJ (at p. 190):

> The Bar Council issues statements from time to time to give guidance to the profession in matters of etiquette and procedure. A barrister who conforms to the Council's rulings knows that he cannot be committing an offence against professional discipline. But such statements, although they have strong persuasive force, do not bind the courts. If therefore a judge requires a barrister to do, or refrain from doing, something in the course of a case, the barrister may protest and may cite any relevant ruling of the Bar Council, but since the judge is the final authority in his own court, if counsel's protest is unavailing, he must either withdraw or comply with the ruling or look for redress in a higher court.

Prosecution Counsel's Duties Until 6 January 2014, Written Standards issued under the 8th edition of the Code of Conduct addressed the duties of prosecuting counsel. The Code has now been replaced by the BSB Handbook which does not include comparable specific guidance. The observations of Avory J in *Banks* [1916] 2 KB 621, and the Farquharson committee (see **D16.3**) remain as guidance. **D16.6**

Core Obligations Under the new Code, the core obligations of counsel, including prosecution counsel, are set out at rC3: **D16.7**

1. you must not knowingly or recklessly mislead or attempt to mislead the *court*;
2. you must not abuse your role as an advocate;
3. you must take reasonable steps to avoid wasting the *court's* time;
4. you must take reasonable steps to ensure that the *court* has before it all relevant decisions and legislative provisions;
5. you must ensure that your ability to act independently is not compromised.

Documents Coming into Counsel's Possession In *Tompkins* (1977) 67 Cr App R 181, prosecution counsel used a note from the accused to defence counsel, which had been inadvertently dropped, as a previous inconsistent statement during cross-examination. The Court of Appeal upheld the conviction since, although the note was privileged as a communication between client and legal adviser, the doctrine of privilege merely protects a party from the obligation of producing a document and does not determine its admissibility or the use which may be made of it should it come into the hands of the other side. Moreover, even if the note had been inadmissible in itself, that would not have prevented counsel asking questions based upon it without directly revealing its contents to the jury. **D16.8**

EARLY PROVISION OF LEGAL DIRECTIONS

From the very outset of the trial (and even, where necessary, before the case is opened), it is important to recognise the possible need for the judge to provide legal direction to the jury. CrimPD VI, para. 26K.8 (see Supplement, **CPD.26K**), states that 'the court is required to provide directions about the relevant law at any time that will assist the jury to evaluate the evidence'. It suggests that 'the judge may provide an early direction prior to any evidence being called, prior to the evidence to which it relates or shortly thereafter'. Such early direction should be given where it will assist the jury as to 'their approach to the evidence', or the evaluation of a part of the evidence (para. 26K.9), and examples that are provided in the CrimPD include an early direction as to concepts such as joint enterprise, consent or *mens rea*, in relation to identification evidence, or as to expert, hearsay or bad character evidence (para. 26K.10). Additionally, the judge will provide instruction to the jury as to the rules governing their task at the start of the trial (CrimPD VI, para. 26G.3; see Supplement, **CPD.26G**). **D16.9**

OPENING SPEECH

CrimPD VII, para. 25A.1 (see Supplement, **CPD.25A**), states that 'the purpose of the prosecution opening is to help the jury understand what the case concerns, not necessarily to present a detailed account of all the prosecution evidence due to be introduced'. **D16.10**

CrimPR 25.9(2)(b) invites the prosecution to identify the issues in the case as well as providing a concise outline of the evidence which the prosecution propose to call. In the same way, pursuant to CrimPR 25.9(2)(c), the judge may invite defence counsel concisely to identify what is in issue, in order to assist the jury, following the prosecution opening (CrimPD VII, para. 25A.4) (see also **D16.16** and **D17.7**).

The following are matters that may affect the style and content of a prosecution opening speech.

Emotive Language

D16.11 In addressing the jury, prosecuting counsel's role is that of a minister of justice who ought not to strive over-zealously for a conviction (see **D16.3**). Counsel should therefore avoid using emotive language liable to prejudice the jury against the accused. Avory J's oft-quoted description in *Banks* [1916] 2 KB 621 was given in relation to observations by prosecution counsel 'calculated to prejudice the jury'. The use of emotive language was criticised by his lordship as being 'not in good taste or strictly in accordance with the character which prosecuting counsel should always bear in mind' (see also *Solloway* [2019] EWCA Crim 454 as an example of inappropriate language from a prosecutor).

Submissions as to Law

D16.12 The extent to which the prosecutor deals with points of law that may arise during the trial or possible defences which the accused is likely to raise is a matter for discretion, depending on the circumstances of the particular case. In *Lashley* [2005] EWCA Crim 2016, Judge LJ stated (at [13]):

> The presumption should be that an opening address by counsel for the Crown should not address the law, save in cases of real complication and difficulty where counsel believes and the trial judge agrees that the jury may be assisted by a brief and well-focused submission.

If counsel deals with a matter of law, it is usual to remind the jury that matters of law are ultimately for the judge, and that counsel's remarks should therefore be disregarded insofar as they differ from the judge's directions. Such directions can be given at the beginning of a trial, or indeed at any other appropriate stage (CrimPD VI, para. 25A.3).

Omission of Inadmissible Evidence or Evidence Objected to by Defence

D16.13 If defence counsel has intimated that there is an objection to some of the prosecution evidence, no reference should be made to that evidence in opening. If the opening speech cannot be made coherently without reference to the disputed evidence, the judge should be invited to determine whether or not the evidence is admissible as a preliminary issue. See also **D16.43**.

Whether reference in opening to evidence which turns out to be inadmissible or which for any other reason is not called, represents a ground for quashing an accused's conviction depends on the extent to which the accused is prejudiced by it (*Jackson* [1953] 1 All ER 872). A relevant consideration is how the irregularity was dealt with in the summing-up.

In fact, both defence counsel and the judge are likely to point out to the jury that what prosecuting counsel has said is simply not evidence. If the defence, as a result of prosecuting counsel's improper remarks, applied unsuccessfully for the jury to be discharged, the refusal to discharge may be used as a ground of appeal. However, the Court of Appeal is generally reluctant to interfere with a trial judge's exercise of discretion in respect of discharging a jury (see **D13.50** ***et seq.***).

References to Plea of Guilty by Co-accused

D16.14 Where the allegation against the accused on trial relates to the accused's actions in concert with another who has pleaded guilty, presentation of the evidence against the accused on trial will involve reference to the actions of that other. To prevent speculation by the jury and provided the defence consent, the jury may be told in opening of the co-accused's plea. It has been implied that they may be told of it even if the defence do not consent. In *Moore* (1956) 40 Cr App R 50, Lord Goddard CJ said (at pp. 53–4):

> When two people are indicted together for a criminal offence and one pleads guilty and the other does not, it is the commonest thing in the world to tell the jury, as was done in this case, 'You must not pay any attention to the fact that the other man has pleaded guilty'. Even if the plea has not been taken in the presence of the jury, it is very difficult to avoid telling the jury in some way that the other person has pleaded guilty.

The admissibility of convictions of persons other than the accused on trial (including guilty pleas by co-accused) is now governed by the PACE 1984, s. 74(1) (see **F12.6**), and is subject to s. 78 of the same Act (exclusion of evidence on grounds of unfairness) (see **F2.7**). Therefore, if it is necessary to address this issue in opening, it should be ventilated at the outset. Unless and until the judge rules the evidence of the co-accused's guilty plea to be admissible, the co-accused's absence from the dock should be dealt with by a formula such as: 'X, of whom you may hear mention in the course of this case, is not before you and is none of your concern'.

Defence Statements

Under s. 6E(4) of the CPIA 1996, the court has the power to provide a jury with copies of a defence statement served pursuant to that Act. This power is discussed in more detail at **D9**. In the context of the prosecution opening its case, or adducing evidence thereafter as part of its case, there will be circumstances, such as in relation to proving that notice had been given of a since rejected alibi, where the jury would be entitled to receive a copy of the defence statement to help them, using the wording of s. 6E(5), 'to understand the case or to resolve any issue in the case'. **D16.15**

DEFENCE OPENING STATEMENT OF THE ISSUES

CrimPR 25.9(2)(c) allows the judge to ask the defence to set out their position on the issues, where it will assist with the jury's understanding and focus on the issues, or to provide the jury with the defence statement in the alternative. CrimPD VII, paras. 25A.2 to 25A.6 (see Supplement, **CPD.25A**), provide further guidance and include a statement that 'such identification of issues at this stage is not to be treated as a substitute for or extension of the summary of the defence case' and indicate that a court will usually invite the defence to address the jury but retains a discretion not to do so. **D16.16**

WITNESSES THE PROSECUTION SHOULD CALL OR TENDER

General Rule: Witnesses on Back of Indictment

Having opened the case, prosecuting counsel calls witnesses and reads out any written statements admissible under exceptions to the rule against hearsay. The rules relating to witness statements are set out in CrimPR Part 16 (see Supplement, **R16.1** *et seq.*). Although counsel has a discretion not to call a witness on the back of the indictment, as a matter of practice the statements of all witnesses whose statements have been served should be called or read and counsel must exercise the discretion in a proper manner and not for what Lord Thankerton described in *Adel Muhammed El Dabbah v A-G for Palestine* [1944] AC 156 as 'some oblique motive' (e.g., unfairly so as to surprise or prejudice the defence). **D16.17**

Rationale for the Rule The rationale for the above rule is that service of the statement of a witness is an indication that the prosecution will call that witness and will secure the attendance of the witness at trial, and therefore the defence do not need to approach that witness themselves for a statement. Thus, to avoid the defence being taken by surprise and prejudiced by the loss of evidence of potential value to their case, the prosecution are in general obliged to call the witness at the trial. **D16.18**

It follows that the rule has no application to witnesses whose statements have never formed part of the prosecution case, but were served upon the defence as unused material. The prosecution is under no duty to call such witnesses to give evidence (*Richardson* (1994) 98 Cr App R 174).

D16.19 **Exceptions to the Rule** The general rule is subject to the following exceptions:

(a) *Witness to be read.* A witness on the back of the indictment need not be called or even brought to court if the prosecution anticipate being able to read the witness's statement, e.g., by virtue of the CJA 1967, s. 9 (see **D22.41**), or the CJA 2003, ss. 116 and 117 (see **F17.7** ***et seq.***).

(b) *Witness not credible.* Prosecuting counsel has a discretion not to call a witness whose name is on the back of the indictment if the witness no longer appears to counsel to be a credible witness, worthy of belief (*Oliva* [1965] 3 All ER 116). This exception presupposes that something has occurred between the case being sent and trial to cast doubt on the witness's veracity. In *Oliva*, the prosecution declined to call the victim of an alleged offence who had made a statement to the police naming D as the culprit which he had later retracted. The Court of Criminal Appeal dismissed D's appeal, holding that the prosecution's duty extended only to calling witnesses who appeared capable of belief. As a result of his volte-face, the victim could no longer be regarded as creditworthy and, in the circumstances, prosecuting counsel had a discretion not to call him which he exercised properly.

(c) *Unhelpful but credible evidence.* The ruling of Park J in *Nugent* [1977] 3 All ER 662, and the Privy Council cases of *Seneviratne v R* [1936] 3 All ER 36 and *Adel Muhammed El Dabbah v A-G for Palestine* [1944] AC 156, have lent some support to the proposition that the prosecution need not call a witness, even though they regard the witness as capable of belief, if the anticipated evidence would be likely to confuse the jury about the nature of the prosecution case. However, in *Balmforth* [1992] Crim LR 825, the Court of Appeal held that, once the prosecution had decided that a witness on the back of the indictment was capable of belief, they must call that witness.

The Reality of the Prosecution's Obligation

D16.20 The problems which arose in *Nugent* [1977] 3 All ER 662, and earlier similar cases, over which side should call witnesses were the result of a misguided view that the prosecution at committal proceedings were under a duty to tender the evidence of *all* witnesses who appeared to be (a) credible and (b) capable of giving evidence relevant to the case. If the prosecution are not obliged to use all the evidence favouring their own case at the outset (*Epping and Harlow Justices, ex parte Massaro* [1973] QB 433), there can be no obligation to call evidence or tender statements helpful to the defence (see also **D16.25**).

The prosecution's duty is rather to inform the defence of all unused material, including statements containing evidence which contradicts the prosecution case and/or lays the foundation for a defence (see **D15.71**). Provided that is done, the defence will be able to interview the witnesses and arrange for them to be at the Crown Court to testify as defence witnesses if necessary (see also *Russell-Jones* [1995] 3 All ER 239 and *Brown* [1997] 1 Cr App R 112).

D16.21 **Mixed Statements** A grey area still remains where the prosecution have a number of statements broadly agreeing with each other but differing on points of detail, some being more helpful to the defence than others. In such cases, the better practice may be to include all the statements in the material served on the accused under the regulations for the service of the prosecution case after the accused has been sent, and, subject to any later doubts as to credibility, all the statement-makers should then be called by the prosecution at trial (see also *Witts* [1991] Crim LR 562). Where there is a duty on the prosecution to call or tender a witness, reading the statement of the witness may be an acceptable alternative (*Armstrong* [1995] Crim LR 831).

In *Cairns* [2002] EWCA Crim 2838, [2003] 1 WLR 796, the issue was whether the Crown was entitled to call a witness, rather than whether it was obliged to do so. The Crown called a witness who, they submitted, was worthy of belief in respect of Dl and D2, but not in respect of D3 (their co-accused). The Court of Appeal held that there was no known principle requiring the prosecution to regard the whole of a witness's evidence to be reliable before calling that witness. It was not uncommon for part of a witness's evidence to be accepted by a jury and another part rejected. The Crown had acted properly, as had the judge, in admitting the evidence of the witness in question. See also *Hengari-Ajufo* [2016] EWCA Crim 1913, in which the Court of Appeal stressed that the prosecution, by calling a witness, should not be taken to accept as true everything that witness says (and see also *Smith* [2019] EWCA Crim 1151, in which the principles for mixed statements were restated).

Duty to Have the Witnesses at Court

Where the prosecution intend not to call a witness whose name appears on the back of the indictment, they nonetheless have a duty to ensure that the witness is present at court for the trial so that the defence may call that witness if they wish (per Lord Parker CJ in *Oliva* [1965] 3 All ER 116 at p. 1035: 'The prosecution must of course have in court the witnesses whose names are on the back of the indictment, but there is a wide discretion in the prosecution as to whether they should call them'). **D16.22**

The above-stated rule as to attendance of witnesses does not apply if they are absent for reasons beyond the prosecution's control. The considerations relevant to the exercise of the judge's discretion in such cases were summarised by Geoffrey Lane J in giving the judgment of the Court of Appeal in *Cavanagh* [1972] 2 All ER 704. His lordship said (at p. 679B–F):

> The prosecution must take all reasonable steps to secure the attendance of any of their witnesses who are not the subject of a conditional witness order or whom the defence might reasonably expect to be present...
>
> If, however, it proves impossible, despite such steps, to have the witnesses present, the court may in its discretion permit the trial to proceed provided that no injustice will be done thereby. What considerations will affect the exercise of the court's discretion will vary infinitely from case to case. Would the defence wish to call the witness if the prosecution did not? What are the chances of securing the witness's attendance within a reasonable time? Are the prosecution prepared to proceed in his absence? If so, to what extent would the evidence of the absent witness have been likely to assist the defendant? If the absent witness can be procured, will other witnesses by then have become unavailable?

Does the Judge Have Power to Require the Prosecution to Call a Witness?

The authorities on the prosecution's duty to call witnesses are inconclusive as to whether, in the last resort, the judge may force counsel to call a witness unwillingly. In *Oliva* [1965] 3 All ER 116 at p. 1036, Lord Parker CJ stated the position thus: **D16.23**

> If the prosecution appear to be exercising that discretion [not to call a witness] improperly, it is open to the judge of trial to interfere and in his discretion in turn to invite the prosecution to call a particular witness, and if they refuse there is the ultimate sanction in the judge himself calling that witness.

The implication of the dictum is that the judge can 'invite' rather than compel the calling of a witness by prosecution counsel. Counsel has the right to refuse the invitation, but must be aware that, in that case, the judge could call the witness of his or her own motion. A contrary view was taken in *Sterk* [1972] Crim LR 391, where the Court of Appeal held that the trial judge should have ordered the prosecution at least to tender a witness on the back of the indictment for cross-examination by the defence. Certainly, pursuant to CrimPR 3.13(c) (see Supplement, **R3.13**), the Court's case management powers include requiring identification of the witnesses to be called and the timetabling and arrangements for them. Moreover, CrimPR 16.4(5) (see Supplement, **R16.4**) gives the court power to require a witness to give evidence in person on application or 'on its own initiative'. It is not clear how far these powers will allow a court to adopt the approach identified in *Sterk*.

Tendering a Witness

As an alternative to calling and examining a witness in the normal way, it is open to prosecuting counsel to tender a witness for cross-examination. Counsel merely calls the witness, establishes the witness's name and address, and then invites the defence to ask any questions they wish. **D16.24**

Additional Evidence

D16.25 The prosecution at trial on indictment are not confined to using solely the evidence that was included when its case was served pursuant to the Crime and Disorder Act 1998 (Service of Prosecution Evidence) Regulations 2005 (SI 2005 No. 902) (see **D10.19**). Under the old procedure (MCA 1980, s. 6), they were not obliged to use at committal all the evidence then available to them, and by extension they are not obliged to serve the whole of their case at the outset (*Epping and Harlow Justices, ex parte Massaro* [1973] QB 433; see **D16.20**). If, however, they intend to call evidence at trial additional to the evidence so served, whether that be evidence which was not then available or evidence which they simply chose not to adduce, they are required to give the defence notice of their intention.

They must also supply a copy of the statement of the additional witness or, as the case may be, a copy of the further statement made by a witness already relied upon, complying with the formal requirements of the CJA 1967, s. 9. If the defence do not object within five business days, it will then be possible to read the statement as evidence at the trial without calling the witness (see also CrimPR 16.4: Supplement, **R16.4**).

D16.26 **Response to the Service of Additional Evidence** In *Wright* (1934) 25 Cr App R 35, the ground of appeal was that the prosecution called a witness to produce two specimens of handwriting, and then invited the jury to compare these specimens with the writing on a certain envelope in order to prove that the handwriting was that of the witness. Apart from objecting to the lack of evidence from a handwriting expert, the defence contended that they had not been notified of the intention to put the specimens into evidence. Avory J said (at p. 40):

> At most that is a grievance and cannot affect the admissibility of the evidence put before the jury, and, if the appellant or his counsel thought that he was being prejudiced by having had no notice and really desired to call expert evidence to deal with the question of handwriting, he could have applied for an adjournment, but he did not do so.

Thus, the sanction requiring the prosecution to give timely notice of additional evidence is the knowledge that, in the absence of such notice, the trial may have to be adjourned until it has been served and the defence have had time to consider their response to it. Alternatively, if an adjournment is undesirable in the circumstances, the judge could exercise his or her discretion and exclude the evidence under the PACE 1984, s. 78, on the ground that to admit it would be unfair in view of the lack of notice.

SUPPLYING INCONSISTENT STATEMENTS TO THE DEFENCE

D16.27 As is clear from the discussion above, the prosecution is absolved from calling witnesses whose statements are inconsistent with the broad thrust of its case only if those statements have otherwise been made available to the defence. The prosecution's duty is now set out in the CPIA 1996 (see **D16.29**).

The prosecution duty of disclosure may cover (a) potential witnesses whom they do not intend to call, and (b) statements made by intended prosecution witnesses additional to the material served when the accused was sent for trial.

Common-law Duty

D16.28 Whether or not the CPIA 1996 provisions apply, the common law has long identified circumstances in which inconsistent statements should be disclosed. In *Clarke* (1930) 22 Cr App R 58, where the issue was whether an identification of the accused was correct, the Court of Criminal Appeal were critical of prosecution counsel's refusal to disclose an earlier description given by the witness. If there had been any serious discrepancy between the description and testimony, the court 'would have had seriously to consider whether any miscarriage of justice had been caused by this attitude which was unfortunately assumed by the learned counsel for the prosecution'.

Clarke was confirmed in *Liverpool Juvenile Court, ex parte R* [1988] QB 1, where the prosecution failed to disclose a previous inconsistent statement of the complainant. The Divisional Court held that the failure amounted to a breach of the rules of natural justice.

Disclosure where the Criminal Procedure and Investigations Act 1996 Applies

Pursuant to the disclosure regime contained in the CPIA 1996, the prosecution must disclose material which is 'capable of undermining the case for the prosecution against the accused or of assisting the case for the accused' (s. 3(1)(a)). Beyond this, the prosecution have a continuing duty to keep disclosure under review (s. 9). If material becomes 'capable of undermining the case for the prosecution against the accused or of assisting the case for the accused', it must be disclosed 'as soon as reasonably practicable' (s. 9(2)). **D16.29**

Similar considerations apply to material which 'might be reasonably expected to assist the accused's defence as disclosed by the defence statement given under section 5' (s. 9(5)). For further details, see **D9**.

Use of a Witness Summons for a Disclosed Witness

The defence are not entitled to a witness summons under s. 2 of the Criminal Procedure (Attendance of Witnesses) Act 1965 ordering the person summonsed to attend court and produce statements in his or her possession made by anticipated prosecution witnesses, with a view to the contents of the statements being used in cross-examination of those anticipated witnesses at the accused's trial (*Cheltenham Justices, ex parte Secretary of State for Trade* [1977] 1 All ER 460). See **D15.94** for the text of s. 2 of the 1965 Act. **D16.30**

EXAMINATION AND CROSS-EXAMINATION OF A WITNESS

Examination-in-Chief

A variety of issues arise in relation to the calling of a witness by the prosecution. The first stage is for the witness to take the oath or affirmation (which is dealt with at **F4.31** *et seq*.). Thereafter, circumstances which may arise, and which are dealt with elsewhere, include: **D16.31**

(a) the use of the special measures provisions contained in the YJCEA 1999, Part II, ch. I (see **D14**);
(b) the use of television live links where the witness is outside the UK, pursuant to the CJA 1988, s. 32 (see **D15.96**), or in the circumstances set out in the CJA 2003, s. 51 (see **D15.98**);
(c) the restriction on the use of leading questions (see **F6.15**);
(d) the rules in relation to memory refreshing, especially pursuant to the CJA 2003, s. 139 (see **F6.16**);
(e) the rules relating to the handling of hostile witnesses, as developed from the Criminal Procedure Act 1865, s. 3 (see **F6.52**).

CrimPR 25.11 (see Supplement, **R25.11**) deals with live witness evidence, including arrangements for where the witness should wait before giving evidence and the sequence of evidence when a witness is called. A witness waiting to give evidence must not wait inside the courtroom, unless that witness is a party or an expert witness (r. 25.11(2)(a)). But see *Carty* [2011] EWCA *Crim 2087, where the* presence of a witness in court in advance of her giving evidence was not of itself a reason to exclude her evidence. The court has power to limit the duration of witnesses' evidence, and their evidence-in-chief (CrimPR 3.13(d); see Supplement, **R3.13**).

Use of an Interpreter A decision whether an interpreter should be allowed to assist a witness to give evidence is a matter for the court to decide. The court is not bound to accept the assertion of a witness that an interpreter is necessary. It can investigate the need itself, and having been told that a witness has some command of English, the court may take the opportunity to **D16.32**

assess the limits of the comprehension and fluency of the witness before permitting the use of an interpreter (*Sharma* [2006] EWCA Crim 16, [2006] 2 Cr App R (S) 63 (416)).

Cross-examination

D16.33 Cross-examination of witnesses called by the prosecution on behalf of the accused gives rise to a number of issues. The court has power to limit the cross-examination as part of its case management of evidence at trial (CrimPR 3.13(d)). Limitations are also imposed on the scope of proper cross-examination by a number of sources, which include the following.

(a) The limitations imposed by statute, e.g., the restrictions on cross-examination by an accused in person, contained in the YJCEA 1999, ss. 34 and 35 (discussed at **F7.3** *et seq.*), and as to the sexual history of a complainant to whom s. 41 of that Act applies see **F7.28**.
(b) The duty of the court to restrain lengthy cross-examination on matters not in issue, or which is otherwise unnecessarily prolonging the proceedings (*Kalia* (1974) 60 Cr App R 200), coupled with the court's discretion to limit cross-examination (CrimPR 3.13(d)) and/or to set a timetable for the evidence of witnesses (CrimPR 3.13(b)).
(c) The limitations imposed by the BSB Handbook, discussed below.

In addition, in cases where a video recording of a witness's evidence-in-chief has been admitted under the YJCEA 1999, s. 27, the court may direct that cross-examination also be recorded in advance of trial, pursuant to s. 28 (see F7).

D16.34 **Limits of Proper Cross-examination** Counsel is required to consider not only whether a proposed question is legally permissible but whether it is ethically justified. Counsel must, therefore, 'not make statements or ask questions merely to insult, humiliate or annoy a witness or any other person' (BSB Handbook, rC7)).

Counsel must not suggest that a witness or other person is guilty of crime, fraud or misconduct or attribute to another person the crime or conduct of which counsel's lay client is accused unless such allegations go to a matter in issue (including the credibility of the witness) which is material to the lay client's case, and appear to be supported by reasonable grounds. A witness should never be impugned in a speech by counsel unless counsel has first given the witness an opportunity in cross-examination to answer the allegation (BSB Handbook, rC7).

A limitation on defence counsel's unfettered discretion to cross-examine about the issues and impugn the witness's character in the process was suggested by Lord Goddard CJ in *O'Neill* (1950) 34 Cr App R 108, when he criticised defence counsel for his cross-examination, saying that it was 'quite wrong and improper conduct on the part of counsel' to make charges against the police (or any other prosecution witnesses) if counsel did not intend to call evidence in support of those charges. A distinction had to be drawn between proper and temperate cross-examination as to credit (where one was bound by the witness's answer) and the kind of allegations made by counsel.

READING STATEMENTS AS EVIDENCE AT THE TRIAL ON INDICTMENT

D16.35 The subject-matter of this heading might equally be regarded as one of the exceptions to the rule against hearsay evidence and therefore be allocated to the evidence part of this work. However, it is considered here as it also has crucial implications for the procedural question of which witnesses should attend at trial.

Written Statements in Criminal Proceedings

D16.36 The CJA 1967, s. 9, provides for the admissibility of written statements in criminal proceedings (its terms are set out at **D22.42**). CrimPR 16.4 and CrimPD V, paras. 16A.1 to 16A.6, set out the procedure (see Supplement, **R16.4** and **CPD.16A**).

In trials on indictment, it applies where the prosecution wish to adduce evidence additional to that served in accordance with the procedure when the case was sent, or by way of a notice of additional evidence thereafter (for which, see also CrimPD I, paras. 3B.1 to 3B.5: see Supplement, **CPD.3B**). The party proposing to tender the statement in evidence must serve a copy of it on each of the other parties. If one of those parties serves notice on the party wishing to use the statement that he or she objects to it going into evidence, the statement cannot be read at the trial. The Deregulation Act 2015, s. 80, amended the CJA 1967, s. 9, so as to replace the seven-day period in which such objection had to be made with provision for time-limits to be set by the CrimPR, though, subject to special circumstances, the time-limit is set by r. 16.4 at five business days.

In effect, s. 9 statements are admissible only if all the parties agree. Even if a statement is admissible under s. 9, the court may require that the maker attend to give evidence, e.g., where the defence dispute the contents of the statement but failed to object through an oversight (provision for which is made by s. 9(4) and CrimPR 16.4(4)). **D16.37**

Where objection had been taken it remains open for the prosecution to seek to read the statement. Under the procedure set out in the CPIA 1996, sch. 2, para. 1(4), the court was able to permit such a course where it was in the interests of justice.

In the Parliamentary debate on the subject at that time, it was stated by the government that it was anticipated that the courts, in applying the 'interests of justice' test, would turn for guidance to the CJA 1988, s. 26 (see Baroness Blatch, *Hansard*, HL col. 951 (26 June 1996)). That section referred to the admissibility of certain hearsay statements under the CJA 1988, ss. 23 and 24 (now replaced by the CJA 2003, ss. 116 and 117). Although s. 26 itself has been repealed, the test under the CJA 2003 retains some of the features of the 1988 Act (see **F17.7**).

In considering whether the admission of such a statement under the 2003 Act would be in the interests of justice, the court must have regard to its contents, the risk of unfairness to the accused resulting from the inability to controvert the statement, and any other circumstances which may appear to be relevant.

In any event, a trial judge will no doubt be extremely wary about overruling the objections of the defence, and thus denying the accused the right to see those who are giving evidence against the accused, let alone the right to cross-examine them. Any suspicion that objections were overruled for reasons which were less than compelling would be contrary to well-established principle and, in addition to the normal channels for challenge, would be likely to lead to the prospect of a challenge based upon the ECHR, Article 6(3)(d) (see **A7** and **D30.9**).

Depositions of Children or Young People

Where a justice has taken a deposition out of court from a child or young person under the provisions of the CYPA 1933, s. 42, the deposition (subject to certain conditions) is admissible in any proceedings in respect of any of the offences mentioned in sch. 1 to the Act (s. 43). Schedule 1 lists numerous specific sexual offences, and also refers to 'any other offence involving bodily injury to a child or young person'. The child or young person may have been the victim of the offence but the power applies to depositions from those other than victims. **D16.38**

The conditions of the admissibility of such a deposition are:

(a) that attendance at court would involve serious danger to the child or young person's life or health;
(b) that the deposition is signed by the justice by or before whom it purports to have been taken; and
(c) that, if the deposition is to be admitted against the accused, reasonable notice was given of the intention to take it and the accused (or legal representative) had the opportunity of cross-examining the deponent.

Evidence as to the effect of attending court on the child or young person's health must be provided by a duly qualified medical practitioner (see also CrimPD I, para. 3D.3).

Address of Witness

D16.39 By virtue of CrimPR 25.11(2)(c), unless it is necessary for evidential purposes, witnesses should not be required to disclose their address in open court. Where the address is relevant, the witness may choose to write it down for the record.

Agreed Facts

D16.40 As an alternative to the reading of witness statements, facts derived from such witness statements or otherwise may be presented as agreed evidence. These facts, which are admitted by all parties to be true, are presented pursuant to the CJA 1967, s. 10 (see **F1.2**). Such admissions should be reduced to writing, and provided to the jury providing they are relevant to the issues that they are to determine and do not contain inadmissible material (*Pittard* [2006] EWCA Crim 2028 and CrimPR 25.13).

OBJECTIONS TO PROSECUTION EVIDENCE

Standard Procedure

D16.41 Where the defence intend to object to the admissibility of prosecution evidence disclosed on the statements relied on by the prosecution (hereafter referred to as 'disputed evidence'), the standard procedure is as follows.

(a) Pursuant to CrimPR 16.4(4) (see Supplement, **R16.4**) the defence should notify the prosecution of their objection to its introduction in evidence.
(b) Further or alternatively, defence counsel should inform prosecution counsel of the objection before the latter opens the prosecution case to the jury. In the opening, prosecution counsel therefore makes no mention of the disputed evidence (as to circumstances where the admissibility issue ought to be resolved before the case starts, see **D16.43**).
(c) At the point at which the admissibility falls to be considered, the jury will withdraw to allow the matter to be resolved by the judge alone (see **D16.42**).
(d) If the admissibility of the disputed evidence raises collateral factual issues as to how it was obtained, it may be necessary to adduce evidence about those facts before the judge in the absence of the jury. This is known as a trial 'on the *voir dire*' because the witnesses testify on a special form of oath (see **F4.32**). Both prosecution and defence are entitled to call witnesses at this stage. However, their evidence (whether in chief or in cross-examination) should be limited to matters relevant to the admissibility of the disputed evidence. For the application of this rule to the admissibility of confessions, see the PACE 1984, s. 76(2), and *Brophy* [1982] AC 476 (see **F18.8** and **F18.73**).
(e) Whether or not there has been evidence on the *voir dire*, the parties make their representations to the judge about the admissibility of the disputed evidence.
(f) The judge then announces findings on any factual issues arising on the *voir dire* and rules on whether the disputed evidence should be admitted or not, in the light of the findings of fact, the relevant law on admissibility of evidence and any discretionary power to exclude material which is legally admissible (considerations applicable to this determination are set out at **D16.47**).
(g) The jury return to court. If the judge ruled against the disputed evidence, the jury will know nothing about it (as to the editing of evidence consequent on such a ruling, see **D16.51**). If it is ruled admissible, the defence are still entitled to cross-examine on matters they raised on the *voir dire*, although at this stage the cross-examination goes to the weight, if any, that the jury should attach to the disputed evidence, not to its admissibility.
(h) The judge retains the discretion to review a determination on admissibility at a later stage (*Watson* [1980] 2 All ER 293, see **D16.48**).

This procedure, and the extent to which it is appropriate to depart from it in certain circumstances, is discussed below.

Presence of Jury in Court during Determination of Question of Admissibility

In *Hendry* (1988) 88 Cr App R 187, where the jury had retired for the *voir dire* contrary to the wishes of the defence, the Court of Appeal refused to follow earlier decisions in *Anderson* (1929) 21 Cr App R 178 and *Ajodha v The State* [1982] AC 204. It was held that the judge had the ultimate discretion as to whether or not the jury retired, as their presence could defeat one of the fundamental objectives of the *voir dire* procedure, namely, to prevent the jury knowing of potentially inadmissible evidence. **D16.42**

In *Mitchell* [1998] AC 695, the Privy Council stressed that the judge should give no explanation of the outcome of the *voir dire* to the jury, as to do so would risk unfair prejudice to the accused.

Determination of Question of Admissibility as a Preliminary Issue

Where the evidence to which the defence indicate an objection is vital to the prosecution case, such that the prosecution case cannot sensibly be opened without reference to it, the question of admissibility may be determined as a preliminary issue. **D16.43**

In *Hammond* [1941] 3 All ER 318, the Court of Criminal Appeal, while stating that the appropriate time for determining admissibility of evidence is normally immediately prior to the evidence being called, also indicated that that practice should not be regarded as invariable. Humphreys J (giving the principal judgment) said (at p. 320, emphasis added):

> The ordinary practice in such a case, if there is any objection on the part of the counsel for the defence to the admissibility of a piece of evidence, is that he should inform the prosecution of that fact beforehand, and that that piece of evidence should not be opened to the jury. This court desires to reiterate that what was said by this court in *Cole* (1941) 28 Cr App R 43 is a good practice which should be adhered to, certainly in most cases. *The court cannot lay down as a rule of practice that in no case should the judge decide to hear in advance arguments as to the admissibility of evidence.* There may be cases in which it is convenient, and in which it cannot possibly result in any harm in its being done.

Although for some purposes a trial begins with the arraignment of the accused (see, e.g., the Senior Courts Act 1981, s. 77, which deals with time-limits for commencement of trial), it is arguable that, in general, there is no trial in being until a jury has been sworn and therefore no question connected with the trial (such as whether evidence is admissible) can validly be determined. In deference to this argument, it seems to be the practice to empanel a jury *before* considering objections to evidence (or any other question of law).

Circumstances in which a *Voir Dire* Hearing is Necessary

Most authorities on the procedure for objecting to evidence concern disputed confessions and the holding of a trial on the *voir dire* to determine their admissibility. However, the procedure is not limited to such circumstances. For example, in *Minors* [1989] 2 All ER 208, Steyn J stated that the trial within a trial procedure ought to be adopted where there is a disputed issue as to the admissibility of a computer printout (for further instances, see **F1.43**). **D16.44**

However, the Court of Appeal in *Flemming* (1987) 86 Cr App R 32, warned against resorting to the procedure unnecessarily. D appealed against his conviction for robbery on the grounds that (a) the identification evidence against him was unsatisfactory and should have been excluded, and (b) the judge was wrong to conclude that he had signed notes of his interview with the police on those pages which contained admissions. The Court of Appeal upheld the rulings of the trial judge but stated that he should have made them without himself hearing evidence on the *voir dire*. The issue of whether the accused had signed the relevant pages of the interview notes was one solely for the jury, the question being whether a confession had been made at all, not whether (assuming it had been made) it had been improperly obtained. As to the identification evidence, the judge could consider the exercise of his discretion to exclude it by reading the depositions and inviting argument from counsel. There was no need to call the witnesses before the judge.

Objecting to Evidence without a *Voir Dire*

D16.45 The *voir dire* procedure is designed to assist the defence by preventing the jury hearing possibly inadmissible evidence unless and until the judge rules it admissible. It therefore seems logical that the defence should not be forced to adopt the procedure if they consider that the accused's interests will be better served by having the possibly inadmissible evidence, and any evidence of how it was obtained, adduced before both judge and jury as part of the general case.

The tactical reason sometimes advanced for not wanting a hearing on the *voir dire* is that, if the judge in fact rules the disputed evidence admissible, the prosecution witnesses may have to be asked the same questions before the jury as they were asked before the judge, albeit that the cross-examination before the jury goes to the weight of the evidence, not its admissibility. Having had a 'dry run' before the judge, the witnesses are likely to give a better account of themselves before the jury than they would have done had the questions come as a surprise.

In *Ajodha v The State* [1982] AC 204, the Privy Council affirmed the defence's right to have evidence ruled inadmissible even though they do not seek to exclude it by means of the standard *voir dire* procedure. See **F18.66** for details.

D16.46 There are a number of qualifications of this general principle:

(a) If the defence elect not to have a *voir dire*, they are usually entitled to a ruling from the judge on the admissibility of the confession at the close of all the evidence, rather than at the end of the prosecution case (*Jackson* [1985] Crim LR 442). The judge should exclude a confession of his or her own motion only in a totally exceptional case where the prosecution's own evidence makes it quite clear that the confession was improperly obtained. Otherwise, the judge should not rule or be asked to rule on the confession's admissibility until the close of *all* the evidence, both prosecution and defence. This considerably reduces the attractiveness to the defence of forgoing the normal procedure, since their decision on whether or not to call evidence will have to be taken at a time when they still do not know whether the jury will ultimately be directed to ignore the accused's confession.

(b) In *Cunningham* [1985] Crim LR 374, the Court of Appeal took a liberal attitude to the prosecution being allowed to reopen their case when the defence evidence had raised matters relevant to the admissibility of a confession where there had not been a hearing on the *voir dire*. In that case, it was put to the police officers who had taken a confession statement from C that it was the result of earlier inducements by officers whom the prosecution chose not to call. After C gave evidence repeating what had been put in cross-examination, the trial judge allowed the prosecution to reopen their case so as to call the officers named by C. The Court of Appeal held that it would have been an affront to the course of justice to have done otherwise.

See also **D16.49** for the effect of ss. 76 and 78 of the PACE 1984 (admissibility of confessions and unfairly obtained evidence) on the timing of such applications.

Guidance on *Voir Dire* Procedure where Objection to Evidence Taken under Police and Criminal Evidence Act 1984, s. 78

D16.47 Guidance has been given in *Keenan* [1990] 2 QB 54, on the appropriate procedure for asking the judge to rule under the PACE 1984, s. 78, that evidence obtained in breach of the PACE codes of practice should be excluded because its reception would have such an adverse effect on the fairness of the proceedings that it ought not to be admitted.

The Court of Appeal distinguished between three categories of case:

(a) Cases where a breach of the code is apparent from the custody record or statements of the prosecution witnesses, e.g., where (as in *Keenan* itself) there has been a breach of ss. 11 and 12 of PACE Code C relating to the contemporaneous noting of interviews with a suspect and/or showing the suspect the officer's note. In this situation, it ought only to be necessary for prosecution counsel to make an admission as to the breach, after which there may be legal argument about the consequences for admissibility.

(b) Cases where there may be a prima facie breach which the prosecution seeks to justify, e.g., if access to a solicitor has been refused but the prosecution seek to justify that refusal on grounds such as the risk of interference with evidence if access had been allowed. In such cases, it will clearly be necessary for the prosecution to call evidence on the *voir dire* to explain away the prima facie breach, after which the accused may choose to testify in rebuttal.

(c) Alleged breaches which can be established only by evidence from the accused personally, e.g., cases of alleged oppression or where the accused claims to be a person at risk not given the extra protection provided for in PACE Code C. Here, the accused will have to take the initiative by giving evidence on the *voir dire* to establish the breach.

In *Keenan*, Hodgson J thought that cases under (c) would be rare, and that in situations (a) and (b) it would be unlikely that the accused would want to testify in rebuttal. His lordship also said that the trial judge was obliged to give his ruling on whether admission of the evidence would be unfair in ignorance of what the defence's response to the evidence would be if it were admitted. That might seem unsatisfactory, but was simply a consequence of the overall structure of a criminal trial. The judgment helpfully summarises many of the earlier cases dealing with similar issues.

Reviewing a Determination as to Admissibility

Prior to the enactment of the PACE 1984, the court was entitled to reconsider a ruling as to the admissibility of evidence where fresh evidence later emerged before the jury which cast doubt on its correctness. This was held in *Watson* [1980] 2 All ER 293, in which Cumming-Bruce LJ adopted the following passage from *Cross on Evidence* (5th edn, 1979, p. 720), as correctly stating the law: **D16.48**

> The judge retains his control over the evidence ultimately to be submitted to the jury throughout the trial. Accordingly, if, having admitted a confession as voluntary on evidence given in the absence of the jury, the judge concludes, in the light of subsequent evidence, that the confession was not voluntary, he may either direct the jury to disregard it, or, where there is no other sufficient evidence against the accused, direct an acquittal or, presumably, direct a new trial.

However, his lordship went on to say that 'the occasions on which a judge should allow counsel to invite him to reconsider a ruling already made are likely to be extremely rare' (p. 995D).

Effect of the Police and Criminal Evidence Act 1984 The general principle stated in *Watson* (i.e. that a trial judge may in exceptional circumstances be invited to reconsider the decision to admit disputed evidence) was no doubt intended to apply to any disputed evidence, whatever its nature, and not just to possibly inadmissible confessions. However, the position in respect of confession evidence has again been complicated by the wording of the PACE 1984, ss. 76 and 78. **D16.49**

In *Sat-Bhambra* (1988) 88 Cr App R 55, the Court of Appeal held that s. 76 (mandatory exclusion of a confession on grounds of oppression or unreliability) applies only *before* the confession has gone into evidence. Accordingly, if it is sought to exclude evidence in reliance on them, the objection must always be made *before* the disputed evidence is adduced.

There was consequently also no statutory obligation on the judge to reconsider the earlier ruling. However, under s. 82(3) of the 1984 Act (preservation of discretionary powers to exclude evidence), the judge could still take whatever steps were necessary to prevent injustice, whether by directing the jury to disregard the evidence they had heard, commenting on its weight in the light of changed evidence, or even discharging them. But he was not, as the appellant contended, *obliged* to discharge them.

Equally, if the defence do not ask for a *voir dire* but nonetheless evidence is adduced in the course of either the prosecution or defence cases which suggests that a confession was obtained in a manner prohibited by s. 76 or otherwise unfairly, the judge can be invited to exercise residual common-law powers and either direct the jury to ignore the confession or discharge them from giving a verdict.

D16.50 The relevant paragraphs from the Court of Appeal's judgment ((1988) 88 Cr App R 55 at p. 62) are set out below:

> In *Watson* [1980] 1 WLR 991, decided before the 1984 Act, it was held that a judge who has second thoughts about the voluntariness of a statement which he has earlier ruled admissible upon the *voir dire* may, where it is appropriate so to do, change his opinion as to its admissibility, and may take such steps as are necessary to put matters right, by, for example, directing the jury to disregard it or discharging the jury.
>
> The words of section 76 are crucial: 'proposes to give in evidence' and 'shall not allow the confession to be given' are not . . . appropriate to describe something which has happened in the past. They are directed solely to the situation before the statement goes before the jury. Once the judge has ruled that it should do so, section 76 (and section 78, for the same reasons) ceases to have effect. The judge, whatever his change of mind may be, is no longer acting under section 76 as the appellant contends. To that extent the decision in *Watson* does not survive the wording of the 1984 Act.
>
> That does not mean that the judge is powerless to act. He has the power, if only under section 82(3), to take such steps as are necessary, depending on the circumstances, to prevent injustice. He may, if he thinks that the matter is not capable of remedy by a direction, discharge the jury; he may direct the jury to disregard the statement; he may by way of direction point out to the jury matters which affect the weight of the confession and leave the matter in their hands. He is not, as is the submission here, obliged to discharge the jury and to order a new trial.
>
> If a defendant wishes under section 76 to exclude a confession, the time to make his submission to that effect is before the confession is put in evidence and not afterwards.

Editing of Prosecution Evidence

D16.51 Where the prosecution evidence as foreshadowed in the statements relied on by the prosecution contains material which is of such prejudicial effect that the jury clearly ought not to hear it, the practice is for the parties to 'edit' the evidence by agreement before it is called. This practice was recognised by the Court of Appeal in *Weaver* [1968] 1 QB 353. Sachs LJ indicated (at pp. 357G–358A) that the best way for such editing to take place is for the evidence to appear 'unvarnished' in the committal statements. Counsel can then confer at trial to ensure that 'the editing is done in the right way and to the right degree'. If necessary the judge can also play a part in the process.

CrimPD V, paras. 16A.1 to 16A.6 (see Supplement, **CPD.16A**), contain detailed instructions on the treatment of statements served as part of the prosecution case where some of the material contained therein may be inadmissible or unduly prejudicial. Three options are set out:

(a) A composite statement can be prepared to replace several earlier statements made by a witness (para. 16A.2).

(b) A completely fresh statement can be prepared for a witness to sign, omitting those parts of the first statement which are inadmissible or prejudicial (para. 16A.3(b)). The circumstances in which this is the preferred option are set out at para. 16A.4.

(c) Where the prosecution decide that it is unnecessary to have a new statement, the procedure to be adopted is that the *original* of the witness's statement should be tendered to the court unmarked in any way but, on the *copies* served on the defence and provided to the court, the passages on which the prosecution do not propose to rely should either be bracketed or lightly struck out. The striking out should not be done in such a way as to obscure what is being deleted.

Paragraph 16A.3(a) states that the following note should be attached to the foot of the frontispiece or index to the bundle when served: 'The prosecution does not propose to adduce evidence of those passages of the attached copy statements which have been struck out and/or bracketed (nor will it seek to do so at the trial unless a notice of further evidence is served)'.

A difficulty may arise where the jury ask to see the original of an edited document. They may be told that there are technical reasons why this cannot be permitted. Although this is not altogether satisfactory, it may be the only way of dealing with an inherent problem. **D16.52**

SUBMISSION OF NO CASE TO ANSWER

After the prosecution have closed their case, the defence may submit that the evidence does not disclose a case to answer in respect of any or all the counts on the indictment. The procedure for the making of such an application is dealt with at **D16.66**, along with the consequences of such a submission (see **D16.69**). The first issue, however, is the test to be applied. **D16.53**

The Test to Be Applied

The leading authority on the test a trial judge should apply in determining whether there is a case to answer is *Galbraith* [1981] 2 All ER 1060. In the course of his judgment in that case, Lord Lane CJ said (at p. 1042B–D): **D16.54**

> How then should the judge approach a submission of 'no case'? (1) If there is no evidence that the crime alleged has been committed by the defendant, there is no difficulty. The judge will of course stop the case. (2) The difficulty arises where there is some evidence but it is of a tenuous character, for example because of inherent weakness or vagueness or because it is inconsistent with other evidence. (a) Where the judge comes to the conclusion that the prosecution evidence, taken at its highest, is such that a jury properly directed could not properly convict upon it, it is his duty, upon a submission being made, to stop the case. (b) Where however the prosecution evidence is such that its strength or weakness depends on the view to be taken of a witness's reliability, or other matters which are generally speaking within the province of the jury and where on one possible view of the facts there *is* evidence upon which a jury could properly come to the conclusion that the defendant is guilty, then the judge should allow the matter to be tried by the jury...
>
> There will of course, as always in this branch of the law, be borderline cases. They can safely be left to the discretion of the judge.

First Limb As Lord Lane remarked, the first limb of the test set out in *Galbraith* [1981] 2 All ER 1060, does not cause any conceptual problems. The test of there being 'no evidence that the crime alleged has been committed by the defendant' is intended to convey the same meaning as the words of Lord Parker CJ in his *Practice Direction (Submission of No Case)* [1962] 1 WLR 227, when he told magistrates that submissions of no case to answer at summary trial should be upheld, *inter alia*, if 'there has been no evidence to prove an essential element in the alleged offence'. **D16.55**

Such cases may arise, for example, where an essential prosecution witness has failed to come up to proof, or where there is no direct evidence as to an element of the offence and the inferences which the prosecution ask the court to draw from the circumstantial evidence are inferences which, in the judge's view, no reasonable jury could properly draw (see further **D22.52**). However, judges should take care to avoid taking into account defence evidence which is yet to be called and potential defences which have not yet been made out in assessing this limb of the test (*C* [2007] EWCA Crim 1862).

Second Limb The second limb of the test in *Galbraith* [1981] 2 All ER 1060, is far less straightforward, and has to be understood in the context of the practice that developed after the passing of the Criminal Appeal Act 1966, s. 4(1)(a) (now Criminal Appeal Act 1968, s. 2(1)), of inviting the judge to hold that there was no case to answer because a conviction on the prosecution evidence would be 'unsafe'. That form of submission reflected the power given to the Court of Appeal by first the 1966 and then the 1968 Act to quash a conviction on the basis **D16.56**

that it was, in the court's opinion, 'unsafe or unsatisfactory' (but, since the Criminal Appeal Act 1995, Part I, came into force, simply 'unsafe').

This approach inevitably involves the court considering the *quality* and *reliability* of the evidence, rather than its legal sufficiency, and therefore involved the court carrying out the assessment of evidence and witnesses that would otherwise be the exclusive prerogative of the jury. The judgment in *Galbraith* makes clear that it is not appropriate to argue on a submission of no case that it would be unsafe for the jury to convict, which would be an invitation for the judge to impose his or her own views of the witnesses' veracity (see especially p. 1041B–C).

However, the second limb of the *Galbraith* test does leave a residual role for the court as assessor of the reliability of the evidence. The court is empowered by the second limb of the *Galbraith* test to consider whether the prosecution's evidence is too inherently weak or vague for any sensible person to rely on it. Thus, if the witness undermines his or her own testimony by conceding uncertainty about vital points, or if what the witness says is manifestly contrary to reason, the court is entitled to hold that no reasonable jury properly directed could rely on the witness's evidence, and therefore (in the absence of any other evidence) there is no case to answer.

D16.57 **Reliability of Evidence under the Second Limb** It is often central to the application of the test in *Galbraith* [1981] 2 All ER 1060 to undertake an assessment of the reliability of the evidence adduced by the prosecution. This was illustrated in *Shippey* [1988] Crim LR 767, where the trial judge (Turner J) found there was evidence to support the prosecution's assertions, but that the evidence as a whole contained 'really significant inherent inconsistencies'. On a literal view of *Galbraith* and *Barker* (1975) 65 Cr App R 287, the case should therefore have gone to the jury for them to weigh the inconsistencies, but Turner J took a more robust view. He said that 'taking the prosecution case at its highest' did not mean 'taking out the plums and leaving the duff behind'. It was for the judge to assess the evidence and, if it was 'self-contradictory and out of reason and all common sense', then the judge could properly conclude that it was 'inherently weak and tenuous' within the meaning of the second limb of the *Galbraith* test.

However, it has since been emphasised, in *Pryer* [2004] EWCA Crim 1163, *Silcock* [2007] EWCA Crim 2176, and most comprehensively in *Christou* [2012] EWCA Crim 450, that *Shippey* should not be elevated from a decision on specific facts into a legal principle. The proper test to be applied remains that enunciated in *Galbraith*, and the decision in *Shippey* merely illustrates the requirement that the court consider the evidence as a whole, including both its weaknesses and strengths.

D16.58 **Proper Approach to a Submission of No Case to Answer** The following propositions are advanced as representing the position that has now been reached on determining submissions of no case to answer:

(a) If there is no evidence to prove an essential element of the offence, a submission must obviously succeed.
(b) If there is some evidence which, taken at face value, establishes each essential element, the case should normally be left to the jury.
(c) If, however, the evidence is so weak that no reasonable jury properly directed could convict on it, a submission should be upheld. Weakness may arise from the sheer improbability of what the witness is saying, from internal inconsistencies in the evidence or from its being of a type which the accumulated experience of the courts has shown to be of doubtful value (especially in identification evidence cases, which are considered in **D16.59**).
(d) The question of whether a witness is lying is nearly always one for the jury, save where the inconsistencies are so great that any reasonable tribunal would be forced to the conclusion that it would not be proper for the case to proceed on the evidence of that witness alone.

Having identified those general principles, it is appropriate to consider various particular types of evidence and categories of cases. (For a striking example of a court's failure to follow proper procedure and an early intervention by the trial judge which led to the 'acquittal' being declared a nullity in the Court of Appeal, see *D* [2012] EWCA Crim 2181.)

Identification Cases

The correct approach to submissions of no case to answer in prosecutions turning upon identification evidence was laid down by the Court of Appeal in *Turnbull* [1977] QB 224 (see **F19.2** and **F19.18**), namely that, if the quality of the identification evidence on which the prosecution case depends is poor and there is no other evidence to support it, the judge should direct the jury to acquit (pp. 229H–230A). However, supporting evidence capable of justifying leaving a case to the jury, even where the identifying evidence is poor, need not be corroboration in the strict sense (p. 230B–D). **D16.59**

Although *Turnbull* predates *Galbraith* [1981] 2 All ER 1060, there is no suggestion that the principles in it have been affected by the later decision. In fact, the obligation on the trial judge to uphold a submission if the identifying evidence is poor and there is no supporting evidence may be regarded as the clearest example of the application of the second limb of the *Galbraith* test (*Daley v The Queen* [1994] 1 AC 117).

Confession Cases

In *MacKenzie* (1992) 96 Cr App R 98, the Court of Appeal laid down special guidance for trial judges considering a submission of no case to answer in confession cases. Cases depending solely or mainly on confessions, like cases depending mainly upon identification evidence, had given rise to miscarriages of justice. Accordingly, a court should, in the interests of justice, take the initiative and withdraw the case from the jury where the following conditions applied: **D16.60**

(a) the prosecution case depended wholly upon confessions;
(b) the accused suffered from a significant degree of mental handicap; and
(c) the confessions were unconvincing to a point where a jury properly directed could not properly convict upon them.

Confessions might be unconvincing, for example, because they lacked the incriminating details to be expected of a guilty and willing confessor, because they were inconsistent with other evidence, or because they were otherwise inherently improbable. See also *Wood* [1994] Crim LR 222.

Mutually Destructive Counts

Where two counts in an indictment are mutually destructive (e.g., alternative counts for theft and handling of the same goods), it may be possible to submit that no reasonable jury properly directed could be sure of which of the two counts the accused is guilty, and therefore they must be directed to acquit of both. **D16.61**

The problem arose in *Bellman* [1989] AC 836, a case chiefly important for the House of Lords' decision that mutually destructive counts may be joined in one indictment (see **D11.67**). In the course of reaching that conclusion, the House also considered whether in such cases the judge ought to have upheld a submission of no case in respect of all counts. Lord Griffiths said (at pp. 847G–848G):

> There are, of course, rare situations in which it is clear that the accused has committed a crime but the state of the evidence is such that it is impossible to say which crime he has committed. In such circumstances no prima facie case can be established to support either crime and neither crime can be left to the jury. The classic example arises where a man has given contradictory evidence on oath on two occasions. It is obvious that one statement must be false but in the absence of any evidence to indicate which statement was false it cannot be proved on which occasion the perjury was committed: see *Harris* (1822) 5 B & Ald 926…
>
> An accused is always entitled to have the counts in the indictment considered separately by the judge at the end of the prosecution's evidence and if there is insufficient evidence to provide a prima facie case on any count to have that count withdrawn from the jury.

The situation in *Bellman* was different from that in the perjury example cited by Lord Griffiths. There being prima facie case sufficient in relation to both alternatives, it was a matter for the jury to decide at the end of all the evidence which of the two possible hypotheses based upon the prosecution evidence was the correct one. See also *Tsang Ping-nam v The Queen* [1981] 1 WLR 1462.

Prima Facie Case against Two Accused

D16.62 Analogous problems to those discussed in **D16.61** arise where there are co-accused and the evidence establishes that one or other committed the offence charged but it is impossible to say which.

In such cases, and assuming there is no evidence of joint enterprise, both are clearly entitled to be acquitted on a submission of no case. Lord Griffiths stated the principle succinctly in his judgment in *Bellman* [1989] AC 836 (at p. 849A): 'It, of course, goes without saying that if the evidence shows that one of two accused must have committed a crime but it is impossible to go further and say which of them committed it, both must be acquitted: see *Lane* (1985) 82 Cr App R 5'. The same point had earlier been made by Lord Goddard CJ in *Abbott* [1955] 2 QB 497 at p. 503.

This approach was restated by the Court of Appeal in *Banfield* [2013] EWCA Crim 1394, which held that, where two accused were charged with murder, as opposed to conspiracy to murder, and the evidence was inconclusive as to whether the killing had been the responsibility of one, the other or both, the trial judge ought to have stopped the case against both. However, whether the evidence really does leave the question of which accused committed the offence in total doubt or whether there is evidence just capable of pointing to one or the other as the person responsible will depend on close analysis of the evidence in the particular case (compare *Gibson* (1984) 80 Cr App R 24, *Lane* (1986) 82 Cr App R 5, *Aston* (1992) 94 Cr App R 180 and *S* [1996] Crim LR 346, all of which involved injuries to young children where it was difficult to determine which of the two parents was responsible).

D16.63 The position in this regard has been significantly altered by the DVCVA 2004, which delays consideration of a submission of no case to answer in cases where, for example, one of two parents may have been responsible for the death of their child, until the conclusion of all the evidence (see **D16.68**).

A similar problem arises where evidence is as consistent with the guilt of a third party as with that of the accused. This was illustrated in *Grant* [2008] EWCA Crim 1890, where the only evidence against D was the presence of his DNA. The scientific analysis identified the DNA of D and of at least one other and was therefore as consistent with that other being responsible for the offence. The Court of Appeal concluded that the trial judge should have found that there was no case to answer.

Cases Based upon Inferences Drawn from Circumstantial Evidence

D16.64 There has been a degree of debate as to the proper approach to a submission of no case where the prosecution contends that guilt is proved, in whole or in part, by the drawing of certain inferences from circumstantial evidence. In the past, it was argued on the basis of *Moore* (20 August 1992 unreported) and *R (Inland Revenue Commissioners) v Crown Court at Kingston* [2001] EWHC Admin 581, [2001] 4 All ER 721, that a case to answer would only be made out where the prosecution could exclude any alternative inference being drawn from that circumstantial evidence. It is now clear that this is not the case.

On the proper application of the test in *Galbraith* [1981] 2 All ER 1060, the prosecution are not required to show that the jury could not reasonably reach any alternative inference contended for. The question is whether it is properly open to the jury to reach the inferences contended for by the prosecution.

This was the conclusion of Tuckey LJ, giving the judgment of the Court of Appeal in *Bokkum* (7 March 2000 unreported), at [32]:

> Read literally the passage in *Moore* would mean that in any case dependent on circumstantial evidence the judge would be required to withdraw the case from the jury if some inference other than guilt could reasonably be drawn from the facts proved. We do not think that the Court intended to say this and if it did it is contrary to what was said in *Galbraith*. The approach suggested may be appropriate in a case such as *Moore* where the inference of guilt is sought to be drawn from a single fact, but this is much more difficult in a case such as the instant case where the Crown rely on a combination of facts. The judge will, of course, withdraw the case if he considers that it would be unsafe for the jury to conclude that the defendant is guilty on the totality of the circumstantial evidence adduced, but if he concludes that it is open to them to convict then Galbraith requires the judge to leave the decision to them.

This statement of principle was specifically approved by the Court of Appeal in *Edwards* [2004] EWCA Crim 2102 at [84], and the same approach was adopted in *Jabber* [2006] EWCA Crim 2694 at [21] and *Goring* [2011] EWCA Crim 2, where it was emphasised that there was a case to answer where, on a reasonable assessment of the evidence, the jury were entitled (rather than bound) to reach conclusions consistent with guilt.

The same approach was adopted in *R (Boota) v Gwent Magistrates' Court* [2012] EWHC 3550 (Admin) and *Goddard* [2012] EWCA Crim 1756. In *Goddard*, Aikens LJ said (at [36]):

> We think that the legal position can be summarised as follows: (1) in all cases where a judge is asked to consider a submission of no case to answer, the judge should apply the 'classic' or 'traditional' test set out by Lord Lane CJ in *Galbraith*. (2) Where a key issue in the submission of no case is whether there is sufficient evidence on which a reasonable jury could be entitled to draw an adverse inference against the defendant from a combination of factual circumstances based upon evidence adduced by the prosecution, the exercise of deciding that there is a case to answer *does* involve the rejection of all realistic possibilities consistent with innocence. (3) However, most importantly, the question is whether a reasonable jury, not *all* reasonable juries, could, on one possible view of the evidence, be entitled to reach that adverse inference. If a judge concludes that *a* reasonable jury could be entitled to do so (properly directed) on the evidence, putting the prosecution case at its highest, then the case must continue; if not it must be withdrawn from the jury.

See also *Lewis (Dean Malcolm)* [2017] EWCA Crim 1734 for a recent application of this approach.

Silence in Interview

The CJPO 1994, s. 34(2)(c), permits the court, in considering whether the accused has a case to answer, to take into account the fact that the accused failed to answer questions in interview. However s. 38(3) makes clear that a submission of no case cannot be rejected solely on the basis of such silence (see **F20.8**). **D16.65**

Moreover, as was demonstrated in *Broadhead* [2006] EWCA Crim 1705, care has to be taken to be sure that the accused is relying on facts not mentioned in interview rather than simply putting the prosecution to proof before inferences can be relied upon at the close of the prosecution case, and therefore before the accused has given evidence.

Procedure on a Submission of No Case

Jury to be Kept in Ignorance of the Submission Submissions of no case should be made in the absence of the jury, and should not be referred to in their presence thereafter if they are unsuccessful. This was made clear by the Court of Appeal in *Smith* (1986) 85 Cr App R 197. In that case, in which identification evidence was relied on, the judge told the jury during the summing-up that, if he had not thought there was sufficient evidence of identification, he would have withdrawn the case from them. Watkins LJ said (at p. 200 emphasis added): **D16.66**

> That is an improper observation for a judge to make to a jury. Submissions [of no case to answer] are made in the absence of the jury. There is very good reason for that as all who take part in trials

> know. The question as to whether or not there is a sufficiency of evidence is one which is exclusively for the judge following submissions made to him *in the absence of the jury*. His decision *should not be revealed* to the jury lest it wrongly influences them. There is a risk that they might convict because they think the judge's view is a sufficient indication that the evidence is strong enough for that purpose.

In *Crosdale v The Queen* [1995] 2 All ER 500, it was emphasised that a trial judge should ask a jury to withdraw during a submission of no case to answer since it was a matter for the judge alone whether there was sufficient evidence to go before the jury.

D16.67 **Timing of a Submission** Almost invariably, the proper time for making a submission of no case is after the prosecution have called their evidence (*Leadbeater* [1988] Crim LR 463). The only exceptions to this rule are cases where either (a) there is an objection to the jurisdiction of the court (see, e.g., *DPP v Doot* [1973] AC 807, in which the question was whether an offence of conspiracy had been committed inside or outside the jurisdiction), or (b) where there is an agreed statement of facts and the judge is effectively being asked whether what undoubtedly happened amounts to the offence charged. The trial judge cannot rule that there is no case to answer before the conclusion of the prosecution case unless all parties agree to this (*N Ltd* [2008] EWCA Crim 1223, [2008] 1 WLR 2684).

D16.68 **Timing of a Submission: Special Provision under the Domestic Violence, Crime and Victims Act 2004** A different procedure is to be followed where the accused is charged in the same proceedings with an offence of murder or manslaughter and with an offence under the DVCVA 2004, s. 5 (causing or allowing the death of a child or a vulnerable adult: see **B1.77**), in respect of the same death. The question whether there is a case for the accused to answer on the charge of murder or manslaughter must not then be considered before the close of all the evidence. If the accused ceases to be charged with the offence under s. 5, then whether there is a case to answer on the murder or manslaughter charge is to be considered before the accused ceases to be so charged (s. 6). Although s. 6(4) changes the timing for a submission of no case to answer, it does not otherwise change the approach to such a submission (*Ikram* [2008] EWCA Crim 586, [2008] 2 Cr App R 24 (347)).

A similar procedure applies by virtue of the DVCVA 2004, s. 6A. The Domestic Violence, Crime and Victims (Amendment) Act 2012 amends the DVCVA 2004, s. 5, so as to extend it to cover causing or allowing a child or vulnerable adult to suffer serious physical harm. Where the accused is charged with such an offence and a relevant offence (i.e. an offence under the OAPA 1861, s. 18 or 20, or attempted murder), the question whether there is a case for the accused to answer on the relevant offence must not then be considered before the close of all the evidence.

D16.69 **Procedure Following a Successful Submission** As already indicated, the procedure upon the judge upholding a submission on all counts of the indictment is for the jury to return to court, so that one of their number can be asked to stand as foreman and, on the judge's direction, formally return a verdict of not guilty.

If the submission has succeeded on some counts but failed on others, the defendant should be regarded during the rest of the trial as no longer being charged on the former (*Plain* [1967] 1 All ER 614). However, in those circumstances no verdict is taken until the end of the trial when the jury both announce their decision on the counts for which there was a case and, on the judge's direction, find the accused not guilty on the remainder of the indictment.

It was made clear in *Carson* (1990) 92 Cr App R 236, and restated in *Livesey* (2007) 1 Cr App R 35 (462), that the court can direct a verdict of not guilty on the only charge indicted but permit the trial to continue in relation to any statutory alternative summary offence. In *Plant* [2008] EWCA Crim 960, [2008] 2 Cr App R 27 (386), it was made clear that a successful submission in relation to the indictable offence on an indictment did not require the remaining summary offence, joined under the CJA 1988, s. 40, to be remitted to a magistrates' court.

Initiative for a Submission It is defence counsel's responsibility to make a submission of no case to answer should the circumstances warrant it (*Juett* [1981] Crim LR 113). In general, the trial judge is neither required nor even entitled to intervene if no submission is made. Exceptionally, however, the interests of justice may demand that the judge take the initiative and suggest that there may not be a case to answer. In such exceptional cases and assuming there was not in fact enough evidence to go to the jury at the end of the prosecution case, the Court of Appeal will quash the conviction, notwithstanding that defence counsel did not make a submission (*Juett*). **D16.70**

Stopping the Case before the End of the Trial

Jury May Acquit at Any Time At common law a jury are entitled to decide at any stage after the prosecution have closed their case that they do not need to hear any further evidence or argument but may wish to acquit forthwith. Although the judge may 'remind' them that this course is open to them, the judge should not go further and issue an invitation to them to acquit (*Kemp* [1995] 1 Cr App R 151, approving the observations of Roskill LJ in *Falconer-Atlee* (1973) 58 Cr App R 348 at p. 357). The judge must make it absolutely clear to the jury that, although they may acquit at this stage, they may not convict. **D16.71**

In *Speechley* [2004] EWCA Crim 3067, [2005] 2 Cr App R (S) 15 (75), counsel for the defence had, when opening the defence at trial, sought to remind the jury of their right to acquit. The judge ruled that he could not do so. The Court of Appeal held that the common-law right of the jury to acquit after the conclusion of the prosecution case was exercisable only where they had been invited to do so by the trial judge. If a jury were invited by counsel, or sought of their own motion, to return a verdict before the judge asked them to do so, the jury should be directed that it was the judge's duty to ensure that justice was done and that it was not open to them to return a verdict until the judge had invited them to do so (see also *Collins* [2007] EWCA Crim 854 and *H (S)* [2010] EWCA Crim 1931, [2011] 1 Cr App R 14 (182)).

Submission at the Close of the Evidence In *Boakye* (12 March 1992 unreported), Steyn LJ pointed out that, as a matter of principle, the judge was entitled to hold that there was no case to answer even at the end of the defence case: **D16.72**

> [Counsel for the Crown] has made a submission to us that it was not appropriate to make a submission of no case to answer at the end of the defence case. In our judgment a judge is entitled, even at that late stage, if no evidence is available on a count or if there is no evidence of that count upon which a reasonable jury could convict, to rule that there is no case to go before the jury. The contrary proposition would be a startling one. It would contemplate that the judge might be powerless to prevent a real miscarriage of justice in a case where there was a sudden change in the strength of the prosecution case as a result of cogent evidence emerging in the defence case. We rule without any doubt that it was within the power of the judge to make the ruling that was requested of him.

In *Anderson* (1998) *Independent*, 13 July 1998, the Court of Appeal, similarly, stated that, although it was more usual for defence counsel to make a submission of no case to answer at the close of the prosecution case, a trial judge is not precluded from entertaining and ruling on such a submission at the close of the defence case.

The reasoning of the Court of Appeal in *Brown* [1998] Crim LR 196 reinforces this approach. Their lordships stated that throughout the trial the judge has a duty not to allow a jury to consider evidence on which they could not safely convict. The judge should not invite them to acquit since, if they convicted, the accused would be left with a sense of grievance. But if, at the conclusion of the evidence, the trial judge is of the opinion that no reasonable jury properly directed could safely convict, the matter should be raised for discussion with counsel even if no submission of no case to answer is made. If, having heard submissions, the judge is of the same opinion, the case should be withdrawn from the jury. See also *Brown* [2001] EWCA Crim 961, [2002] 1 Cr App R 5 (46).

For the special rule where an accused is charged with murder/manslaughter or causing serious injury to a child, together with an offence under the DVCVA 2004, s. 5, see **D16.68**.

D

Part D Procedure

APPEALS BY THE PROSECUTION AGAINST ADVERSE RULINGS

D16.73 Before the introduction of the CJA 2003, the prosecution's ability to challenge a ruling adverse to its position which either terminated a case entirely or excluded evidence in such a way as to fundamentally undermine its ability to continue was extremely limited. It had a right to appeal against rulings made at a preparatory hearing (see **D15.64**) and, after the termination of a prosecution, it was possible for the A-G to refer a point of law to the Court of Appeal, pursuant to the CJA 1977, s. 36, with a view to clarifying the law for the future.

Part 9 of the CJA 2003 (ss. 57 to 74) introduced provision for appeals by the prosecution against rulings of the Crown Court in relation to trial on indictment. These can be divided into two broad categories:

(a) appeals against terminating rulings (ss. 58 to 61);
(b) appeals against evidentiary rulings which significantly weaken the prosecution case (ss. 62 to 67).

Application

D16.74 Pursuant to the Criminal Justice Act 2003 (Commencement No. 8 and Transitional and Saving Provisions) Order 2005 (SI 2005 No. 950), a terminating ruling may be the subject of a s. 58 appeal only where proceedings were committed or sent for trial after the date of its commencement (4 April 2005). The provisions relating to s. 62 evidentiary ruling appeals have not yet come into force.

Rulings Adverse to the Prosecution

D16.75 Section 58 of the CJA 2003 permits the prosecution to challenge rulings of the Crown Court which would otherwise bring proceedings in a particular case to an end, in such a way that, if the ruling in question was found to have been in error, it would be possible for the proceedings to continue. By virtue of s. 58(6), the prosecution may appeal in relation only to certain counts of the indictment. Moreover, s. 58(7) allows the prosecution to appeal other rulings made during the course of the trial in addition to the court's ruling in response to a submission of no case to answer. Such an appeal requires leave either from the trial judge or the Court of Appeal (s. 57(4)). Arguably the wording of s. 58 does not limit the use of such appeals only to terminatory rulings, but it was designed for such rulings.

The Court of Appeal has provided guidance on a number of occasions as to the scope of s. 58.

(a) In *Clarke* [2007] EWCA Crim 2532, [2008] 1 Cr App R 33 (403), the Court accepted that the prosecution could appeal against the refusal of an adjournment to allow them to secure the attendance of the principal witness, without whose evidence the case was unsustainable.
(b) In *Y* [2008] EWCA Crim 10, [2008] 1 Cr App R 34 (411), the Court recognised that a ruling as to the admissibility of evidence was capable of both representing an evidential ruling (within the meaning of s. 62) and a terminating ruling (within s. 58) where its effect was to make the continuation of the case impossible.
(c) In *R* [2008] EWCA Crim 370, the Court went one step further, and found that even a ruling as to the exclusion of evidence which was less obviously determinative of the prosecution case could be made the subject of an appeal under s. 58 if the prosecution chose to make it a terminating ruling by entering into an acquittal agreement, pursuant to s. 58(8). This approach was confirmed in *O* [2008] EWCA Crim 463 and *F* [2009] EWCA Crim 1639.

Consideration of an Appeal

D16.76 The rules applicable to appeals from both forms of preparatory hearing are contained in CrimPR Part 38 (see Supplement, **R38.1** *et seq.*). The process involves a series of stages, which are dealt with below.

Adjournment The first step to be taken in relation to such an appeal is for the prosecution, pursuant to the CJA 2003, s. 58(4), either to inform the court that it intends to appeal or to request an adjournment (s. 58(4)(a)(ii)) to consider whether or not to appeal against the ruling of the court. In the latter event the prosecution must, in accordance with CrimPR 38.2, make the request to the judge of the court immediately following the relevant ruling. In *CPS v C* [2009] EWCA Crim 2614 the Court of Appeal underlined that these were the only options as to timing. See also *Mian* [2012] EWCA Crim 792, [2010] 2 Cr App R 9 (103). It was made clear in *PY* [2019] EWCA Crim 17, [2019] 1 Cr App R 22 (297), that there was no requirement for the notification by the prosecution of their intention to appeal to be made orally in court. The procedural time-limits in s. 58, and in CrimPR 38.2, were to avoid undue delay, and it was wholly consistent with this for it to be possible for the prosecution to give notice of their intention to appeal, or to request an adjournment to consider whether to appeal, by email. Any such email would have to go to the parties and the court, and would have properly to address the formalities contained in s. 58 (see **D16.87**). D16.77

The court must grant the adjournment (s. 58(5)), which will normally be until the next business day (r. 38.2(2)). While the general rule was that where the court grants the adjournment for the prosecution to consider their position permitted by s. 58(5)), this would be until the next business day (CrimPR 38.2(2)), there will be cases where the factual position and the interests of justice require and permit a longer adjournment. In *H* [2008] EWCA Crim 483, it was made clear that the reference in CrimPR 38.2(2)(b) to the 'general rule' that an adjournment of 24 hours be permitted connoted exceptions, although there would have to be 'a real justification for an extension of time at all and that expedition is always required' (at [12]) (see also *SA* [2019] EWCA Crim 144, where it was made clear that there can, within the meaning of the section, be more than one adjournment).

Announcing the Decision to Appeal Following the adjournment (if any) or immediately after the ruling, the prosecutor must inform the judge whether there is an intention to appeal. This notification may be made by email (*PY* [2019] EWCA Crim 17, [2019] 1 Cr App R 22 (297)), but the formalities in the CJA 2003, s. 58 (see **D16.87**), would still have to be met. Any such email would have to go to the parties and the court. D16.78

If the prosecutor does intend to appeal, the prosecutor must either serve a notice of appeal on the court, the Registrar and the accused (which must take place either by the next day if the appeal is expedited or within five days if it is not (r. 38.3)) or apply orally (or by email, see *PY*) to the judge for leave to appeal (CJA 2003, s. 57(4)).

In *P* [2016] EWCA Crim 745, [2016] 2 Cr App R 27 (351) the Court of Appeal made clear that the prosecution, in advancing a terminating ruling appeal, were limited to matters and counts on the indictment that they had indicated at the time that they informed the Court that they were going to appeal in accordance with the CJA 2003, s. 58(6)(b).

The judge must hear representations from the defence before deciding whether to grant leave, but must make the decision on the same day as the oral application for leave is made unless it is in the interests of justice to take longer (CrimPR 38.5). In *Ali-Ali* [2008] EWCA Crim 2186, [2009] 1 Cr App R 21 (279) the Court of Appeal said that, before leave was granted, consideration should be given to whether the appeal was in the interests of justice, in the sense that the Court of Appeal would allow the prosecution of the accused to proceed.

Prosecutor's Undertaking Crucially, when appealing against a terminating ruling, the prosecution must undertake to offer no evidence against the accused in the event that the appeal is either abandoned or refused (s. 58(8)). In *Arnold* [2008] EWCA Crim 1034, [2008] 1 WLR 2881 the Court of Appeal emphasised that the giving of this undertaking is an essential prerequisite of any appeal (see also *CPS v C* [2009] EWCA Crim 2614 and *T (N)* [2010] EWCA Crim 711, [2010] 2 Cr App R 12 (84)). A ruling that is to be subject to appeal ceases to have effect once notice has been given (s. 58(11)). In *H (S)* [2010] EWCA Crim 1931, [2011] 1 Cr D16.79

App R 14 (182) the Court of Appeal criticised a judge at first instance for proceeding to invite the jury to acquit following notification that the prosecution sought to appeal against his ruling that there was no case to answer.

D16.80 **Expediting an Appeal** Section 59 of the CJA 2003 permits an appeal to be expedited, in the discretion of the trial judge. When the prosecutor signals an intention to appeal, the prosecutor must also make oral representations as to whether the appeal should be expedited. Before deciding the issue, the judge must hear representations from the defence and any interested party (CrimPR 38.6). This decision is significant because, if the appeal is not expedited, the court may decide to discharge the jury rather than adjourn the case to allow the appeal to be heard (s. 59(3)).

Any decision by the judge to expedite an appeal may be reversed by the judge at any time before notice of appeal or application for leave to appeal is served on the Crown Court in accordance with CrimPR 38.6(3), or by the Court of Appeal thereafter. The reasons for the reversal of that decision must be provided in writing to the prosecutor, defence and any interested party.

D16.81 **Documentation** Usually a notice of appeal or application for leave to appeal must be served by the prosecutor on the Registrar, the Crown Court officer, the accused and any interested party. If the judge decides to expedite the appeal, that notice must be served on the day after the prosecutor states an intention to appeal. In any other case, the prosecutor has five days (CrimPR 38.3). If the appeal or application is resisted, the necessary documentation must be served on the other parties on the next day if the appeal is expedited and otherwise within five days (r. 38.7). There are special rules for appeals which relate to rulings as to the disclosure of material over which public interest immunity is claimed in r. 38.8.

D16.82 **Conduct by the Court of Appeal** Rule 38.9 sets out the powers of a single judge in relation to such appeals. The options available to the Court of Appeal in relation to such an appeal are set out in the CJA 2003, s. 61, namely that it may either confirm the ruling at first instance (in which case it orders the acquittal of the accused), reverse it or vary it. If either of the latter options is taken, the orders that the Court of Appeal may then make are that (i) the Crown Court trial resume, (ii) a fresh trial take place, or (iii) if the defendant could not receive a fair trial if option (i) or (ii) is taken, the accused be acquitted (s. 61(4) and (5), as amended by the CJIA 2008, s. 44).

Evidentiary Rulings

D16.83 Once the relevant provisions come into force, the prosecution may appeal one or more 'qualifying' evidentiary rulings pursuant to the CJA 2003, s. 62. Such rulings are rulings as to the admissibility or exclusion of prosecution material (s. 62(9)), made at any time before the opening of the defence case (s. 62(2)) where the accused is charged with a 'qualifying offence'.

D16.84 **Qualifying Offences** These offences are defined in the CJA 2003, sch. 4, and can be summarised as follows:

(a) offences against the person, including murder, manslaughter, offences under the OAPA 1861, s. 18 and kidnap;
(b) sexual offences, including rape;
(c) drugs offences relating to Class A drugs;
(d) robbery with the use of a firearm or imitation firearm;
(e) arson endangering life and offences contrary to the Explosives Substances Act 1883, ss. 2 and 3;
(f) war crimes and terrorist offences.

D16.85 **Procedure** The CrimPR do not yet provide a procedural framework for such appeals, although it is likely to mirror that in Part 37 which relates to s. 58 appeals. The first step, as with terminating ruling appeals, is for the prosecution to inform the court that it seeks to appeal against an identified ruling (CJA 2003, s. 62(5)). Leave to appeal, which may be granted by either the trial judge or the Court of Appeal (s. 57(4)), will be granted only if the ruling, or the rulings taken together, '*significantly* weakens the prosecution's case' (s. 63). Again the issue of expedition of appeal is to be determined by the trial judge, and is subject to review (see **D16.80**).

Conduct of the Court of Appeal The options available to the Court of Appeal in relation to such an appeal are set out in the CJA 2003, s. 61, namely that it may either confirm the ruling at first instance, reverse it or vary it. It may only reverse the ruling if the conditions in s. 67 are satisfied. The orders that it may make are those set out in s. 66(2). See *F* [2009] EWCA Crim 1639 as to the relationship between ss. 58 and 67. **D16.86**

Statutory Extracts on Prosecution Appeals

Criminal Justice Act 2003, ss. 57 to 66 **D16.87**

57.—(1) In relation to a trial on indictment, the prosecution is to have the rights of appeal for which provision is made by [part 9].

(2) But the prosecution is to have no right of appeal under this Part in respect of—

(a) a ruling that a jury be discharged, or

(b) a ruling from which an appeal lies to the Court of Appeal by virtue of any other enactment.

(3) An appeal under this Part is to lie to the Court of Appeal.

(4) Such an appeal may be brought only with the leave of the judge or the Court of Appeal.

58.—(1) This section applies where a judge makes a ruling in relation to a trial on indictment at an applicable time and the ruling relates to one or more offences included in the indictment.

(2) The prosecution may appeal in respect of the ruling in accordance with this section.

(3) The ruling is to have no effect whilst the prosecution is able to take any steps under sub-section (4).

(4) The prosecution may not appeal in respect of the ruling unless—

(a) following the making of the ruling, it—

(i) informs the court that it intends to appeal, or

(ii) requests an adjournment to consider whether to appeal, and

(b) if such an adjournment is granted, it informs the court following the adjournment that it intends to appeal.

(5) If the prosecution requests an adjournment under subsection (4)(a)(ii), the judge may grant such an adjournment.

(6) Where the ruling relates to two or more offences—

(a) any one or more of those offences may be the subject of the appeal, and

(b) if the prosecution informs the court in accordance with subsection (4) that it intends to appeal, it must at the same time inform the court of the offence or offences which are the subject of the appeal.

(7) Where—

(a) the ruling is a ruling that there is no case to answer, and

(b) the prosecution, at the same time that it informs the court in accordance with sub-section (4) that it intends to appeal, nominates one or more other rulings which have been made by a judge in relation to the trial on indictment at an applicable time and which relate to the offence or offences which are the subject of the appeal,

that other ruling, or those other rulings, are also to be treated as the subject of the appeal.

(8) The prosecution may not inform the court in accordance with subsection (4) that it intends to appeal, unless, at or before that time, it informs the court that it agrees that, in respect of the offence or each offence which is the subject of the appeal, the defendant in relation to that offence should be acquitted of that offence if either of the conditions mentioned in subsection (9) is fulfilled.

(9) Those conditions are—

(a) that leave to appeal to the Court of Appeal is not obtained, and

(b) that the appeal is abandoned before it is determined by the Court of Appeal.

(10) If the prosecution informs the court in accordance with subsection (4) that it intends to appeal, the ruling mentioned in subsection (1) is to continue to have no effect in relation to the offence or offences which are the subject of the appeal whilst the appeal is pursued.

(11) If and to the extent that a ruling has no effect in accordance with this section—

(a) any consequences of the ruling are also to have no effect,

(b) the judge may not take any steps in consequence of the ruling, and

(c) if he does so, any such steps are also to have no effect.

(12) Where the prosecution has informed the court of its agreement under subsection (8) and either of the conditions mentioned in subsection (9) is fulfilled, the judge or the Court of Appeal must order that the defendant in relation to the offence or each offence concerned be acquitted of that offence.

(13) In this section 'applicable time', in relation to a trial on indictment, means any time (whether before or after the commencement of the trial) before the time when the judge starts his summing-up to the jury.

(14) The reference in subsection (13) to the time when the judge starts his summing-up to the jury includes the time when the judge would start his summing-up to the jury but for the making of an order under Part 7.

59.—(1) Where the prosecution informs the court in accordance with section 58(4) that it intends to appeal, the judge must decide whether or not the appeal should be expedited.

(2) If the judge decides that the appeal should be expedited, he may order an adjournment.

(3) If the judge decides that the appeal should not be expedited, he may—

(a) order an adjournment, or

(b) discharge the jury (if one has been sworn).

(4) If he decides that the appeal should be expedited, he or the Court of Appeal may subsequently reverse that decision and, if it is reversed, the judge may act as mentioned in subsection (3)(a) or (b).

60.—(1) This section applies where the prosecution informs the court in accordance with section 58(4) that it intends to appeal.

(2) Proceedings may be continued in respect of any offence which is not the subject of the appeal.

61.—(1) On an appeal under section 58, the Court of Appeal may confirm, reverse or vary any ruling to which the appeal relates.

(2) Subsections (3) to (5) apply where the appeal relates to a single ruling.

(3) Where the Court of Appeal confirms the ruling, it must, in respect of the offence or each offence which is the subject of the appeal, order that the defendant in relation to that offence be acquitted of that offence.

(4) Where the Court of Appeal reverses or varies the ruling, it must, in respect of the offence or each offence which is the subject of the appeal, do any of the following—

(a) order that proceedings for that offence may be resumed in the Crown Court,

(b) order that a fresh trial may take place in the Crown Court for that offence,

(c) order that the defendant in relation to that offence be acquitted of that offence.

(5) But the Court of Appeal may not make an order under subsection (4)(c) in respect of an offence unless it considers that the defendant could not receive a fair trial if an order were made under subsection (4)(a) or (b).

(6) Subsections (7) and (8) apply where the appeal relates to a ruling that there is no case to answer and one or more other rulings.

(7) Where the Court of Appeal confirms the ruling that there is no case to answer, it must, in respect of the offence or each offence which is the subject of the appeal, order that the defendant in relation to that offence be acquitted of that offence.

(8) Where the Court of Appeal reverses or varies the ruling that there is no case to answer, it must in respect of the offence or each offence which is the subject of the appeal, make any of the orders mentioned in subsection (4)(a) to (c) (but subject to subsection (5)).

62.—(1) The prosecution may, in accordance with this section and section 63, appeal in respect of—

(a) a single qualifying evidentiary ruling, or

(b) two or more qualifying evidentiary rulings.

(2) A 'qualifying evidentiary ruling' is an evidentiary ruling of a judge in relation to a trial on indictment which is made at any time (whether before or after the commencement of the trial) before the opening of the case for the defence.

(3) The prosecution may not appeal in respect of a single qualifying evidentiary ruling unless the ruling relates to one or more qualifying offences (whether or not it relates to any other offence).

(4) The prosecution may not appeal in respect of two or more qualifying evidentiary rulings unless each ruling relates to one or more qualifying offences (whether or not it relates to any other offence).

(5) If the prosecution intends to appeal under this section, it must before the opening of the case for the defence inform the court—
  (a) of its intention to do so, and
  (b) of the ruling or rulings to which the appeal relates.
(6) In respect of the ruling, or each ruling, to which the appeal relates—
  (a) the qualifying offence, or at least one of the qualifying offences, to which the ruling relates must be the subject of the appeal, and
  (b) any other offence to which the ruling relates may, but need not, be the subject of the appeal.
(7) The prosecution must, at the same time that it informs the court in accordance with subsection (5), inform the court of the offence or offences which are the subject of the appeal.
(8) For the purposes of this section, the case for the defence opens when, after the conclusion of the prosecution evidence, the earliest of the following events occurs—
  (a) evidence begins to be adduced by or on behalf of a defendant,
  (b) it is indicated to the court that no evidence will be adduced by or on behalf of a defendant,
  (c) a defendant's case is opened, as permitted by section 2 of the Criminal Procedure Act 1865 (c. 18).
(9) In this section—
'evidentiary ruling' means a ruling which relates to the admissibility or exclusion of any prosecution evidence,
'qualifying offence' means an offence described in Part 1 of Schedule 4.
(10) [Secretary of State's power to amend part 1 of sch. 4.]
(11) Nothing in this section affects the right of the prosecution to appeal in respect of an evidentiary ruling under section 58.

63.—(1) Leave to appeal may not be given in relation to an appeal under section 62 unless the judge or, as the case may be, the Court of Appeal is satisfied that the relevant condition is fulfilled.
(2) In relation to an appeal in respect of a single qualifying evidentiary ruling, the relevant condition is that the ruling significantly weakens the prosecution's case in relation to the offence or offences which are the subject of the appeal.
(3) In relation to an appeal in respect of two or more qualifying evidentiary rulings, the relevant condition is that the rulings taken together significantly weaken the prosecution's case in relation to the offence or offences which are the subject of the appeal.

64.—(1) Where the prosecution informs the court in accordance with section 62(5), the judge must decide whether or not the appeal should be expedited.
(2) If the judge decides that the appeal should be expedited, he may order an adjournment.
(3) If the judge decides that the appeal should not be expedited, he may—
  (a) order an adjournment, or
  (b) discharge the jury (if one has been sworn).
(4) If he decides that the appeal should be expedited, he or the Court of Appeal may subsequently reverse that decision and, if it is reversed, the judge may act as mentioned in subsection (3)(a) or (b).

65.—(1) This section applies where the prosecution informs the court in accordance with section 62(5).
(2) Proceedings may be continued in respect of any offence which is not the subject of the appeal.

66.—(1) On an appeal under section 62, the Court of Appeal may confirm, reverse or vary any ruling to which the appeal relates.
(2) In addition, the Court of Appeal must, in respect of the offence or each offence which is the subject of the appeal, do any of the following—
  (a) order that proceedings for that offence be resumed in the Crown Court,
  (b) order that a fresh trial may take place in the Crown Court for that offence,
  (c) order that the defendant in relation to that offence be acquitted of that offence.
(3) But no order may be made under subsection (2)(c) in respect of an offence unless the prosecution has indicated that it does not intend to continue with the prosecution of that offence.

Section D17 Trial on Indictment: The Defence Case

INTRODUCTION

D17.1 Assuming any submission of no case to answer has been rejected (see **D16.53**), the next stage following the close of the prosecution case is for the defence to call such evidence as they choose. This section briefly considers the various potential aspects of a defence case, from opening to the decision to call either the accused or any defence witnesses. Special considerations arise where the accused is representing him or herself (see **D17.17**). First, however, it is necessary to assess briefly the professional duties of defence counsel.

DUTIES AND ROLE OF DEFENCE COUNSEL

General Principle

D17.2 Defence counsel is not subject to the constraints of impartiality that apply to prosecuting counsel (addressed at **D16.2**). Subject to the duty resting on any barrister not deliberately to mislead the court, and to the rules of professional conduct generally, defence counsel may use all proper means to secure the acquittal or lenient sentencing of the lay client (as is made clear at rC16 of the BSB Handbook).

In presenting the accused's defence, counsel should not be influenced by personal opinions of its truth. This cardinal principle was stated by the Court of Appeal in *McFadden* (1975) 62 Cr App R 187, which was to the effect that:

> It is the duty of counsel when defending an accused on a criminal charge to present to the court, fearlessly and without regard to his personal interests, the defence of that accused. It is not his function to determine the truth or falsity of that defence, nor should he permit his personal opinion of that defence to influence his conduct of it. No counsel may refuse to defend because of his opinion of the character of the accused nor of the crime charged. That is a cardinal rule of the Bar, and it would be a grave matter in any free society were it not. Counsel also has a duty to the court and to the public. This duty includes the clear presentation of the issues and the avoidance of waste of time, repetition and prolixity. In the conduct of every case counsel must be mindful of this public responsibility.

More recently, in *Ebanks v The Queen* [2006] UKPC 16, [2006] 1 WLR 1827, the Privy Council stressed the duty of defence counsel to put the client's case irrespective of whether the accused would ultimately give evidence, that decision being one for the accused alone.

As the approach of the Court of Appeal in *Newell* [2012] EWCA Crim 650, [2012] 1 WLR 3142 illustrates, an advocate has authority to act, in the course of his or her profession, in a manner incidental to the execution of the express authority vested in the advocate by the client. This means that the advocate is deemed to be the client's agent when giving an undertaking, or identifying the issues in the case, e.g., on a plea and case management form, with the result that any such undertaking or statement is potentially admissible as evidence against the client.

Becoming a Witness

Occasionally, the question will arise as to whether it is proper for defence counsel to be called as a witness on behalf of the client. In *Jaquith* [1989] Crim LR 563, the Court of Appeal provided guidance for the Bar Council and the Law Society as to the circumstances in which this should occur, which included the following: **D17.3**

(a) No advocate should give evidence in a criminal trial if doing so can possibly be avoided.
(b) If an advocate does give evidence, the advocate should thereafter take no further part in the trial. It follows that, unless there is a leader, there must be a retrial.
(c) Counsel should be able to anticipate before the trial whether it will be necessary to give evidence personally. If it will be, counsel should withdraw.
(d) If the giving of evidence by an advocate causes real embarrassment or prevents proper cross-examination by other counsel, a retrial should be ordered.

In *Wood* [1996] 1 Cr App R 207, the Court of Appeal said that the rule should be enforced that a member of the Bar giving evidence could no longer act as counsel in the same case. The comment was made in response to a ground of appeal which concerned the tone of voice used by the trial judge and the physical expression of views by sighing, shrugging his shoulders and raising his eyebrows in a way that was said to be hostile to the defence. Their lordships' view was that they could not act on such information unless it was either agreed between counsel or supported by evidence.

Professional Embarrassment

The Court of Appeal has identified other circumstances in which it would be inappropriate for counsel to act. These include the following: **D17.4**

(a) It is generally undesirable for husband and wife, or other partners living together, to appear as advocates against each other in a contested criminal matter (*Batt* [1996] Crim LR 910).
(b) It is undesirable for counsel to prosecute an accused whom counsel had previously defended. The Conduct Rules in the BSB Handbook refer (at rC21.4) to the risk that a barrister may have confidential information or special knowledge disadvantageous to a former client. In *Dann* [1997] Crim LR 46, it was made clear that it was the *risk* which was material.

Rules of Conduct for the Bar

Until 6 January 2014, the conduct of defence counsel was regulated by the written standards issued under the 8th edition of the Code of Conduct. Those are now superseded by the Conduct Rules in the BSB Handbook. Matters of relevance to defence counsel in the Conduct Rules include the following: **D17.5**

(a) Counsel should be satisfied, if briefed to represent more than one accused, that no conflict of interest is likely to arise (rC17).
(b) In the cross-examination of witnesses, rC7 is of central importance. It requires that the advocate 'must not make statements or ask questions merely to insult, humiliate or annoy a witness or any other person'. The advocate must put any 'serious allegation' to a witness and must not make a serious allegation against any person, or suggest that a person is guilty of a crime with which the accused is charged unless there are 'reasonable grounds for the allegation' and the other requirements in rC7.3 are met.
(c) The fact that the accused confesses to counsel that the accused did commit the offence charged does not bar counsel from appearing or continuing to appear for the defence on a not guilty plea (rC3.5 and gC9–10). Counsel may properly take objections to the

competency of the court, the form of the indictment and the admissibility of any evidence, and may test the prosecution's evidence, but may not call evidence or advance an affirmative defence inconsistent with the confession.

Other Issues

D17.6 The interlocking matters of conferences, counsel being attended at court by a professional client, and the seeing of witnesses are dealt with in various provisions of the BSB Handbook, and are summarised at **D15.99** ***et seq***. See also *Anderson* [2010] EWCA Crim 2553, where the need for proper notes of all consultations between defence counsel and client to be completed and retained was emphasised.

As to the duties of counsel in relation to the decision of a defendant to give evidence, and the implications of the CJPOA 1994, s. 35, see **D17.12** ***et seq***.

DEFENCE OPENING SPEECH

D17.7 If the defence intend to call evidence as to the facts of the case other than, or in addition to, the evidence of the accused, defence counsel has the right to an opening speech at the beginning of the defence case (*Hill* (1911) 7 Cr App R 1; CrimPR 25.9(2)(g)). If, however, the only defence evidence is to come from the accused (or from the accused and character witnesses) then counsel does not have an opening speech (see the Criminal Evidence Act 1898, s. 2) save where, pursuant to r. 25.9(2)(c), the judge invites defence counsel concisely to identify what is in issue, in order to assist the jury, following the prosecution opening. CrimPD VI, para. 25A.4 (see Supplement, **CPD.25A**), while acknowledging that the defence are not entitled to address the jury, indicates that the advantages of inviting the defence to do so are such that 'usually the court should extend such an invitation'.

In an opening speech, defence counsel may both outline the anticipated defence case and criticise the evidence already given for the prosecution (*Randall* (1973) *The Times*, 11 July 1973). However, the speech should not make assertions of fact that are not to be proved by evidence that is to come.

THE DEFENCE CASE

D17.8 Because the burden of proof is on the prosecution, the defence are never obliged to call evidence, and more particularly the defence are not obliged to call the accused, since the accused is a competent but not compellable witness (Criminal Evidence Act 1898, s. 1(1)). Most defence witnesses are governed by the same rules and considerations as prosecution witnesses (discussed at **D16.31**). The only additional limitation is the duty of the court to stop evidence being given where it is irrelevant to the issues in the case (*Brown* [1998] 2 Cr App R 364), or where the court is being used as a political sounding board (*King* (1973) 57 Cr App R 696).

Order of Defence Evidence

D17.9 The accused should normally be called before any other defence witnesses (PACE 1984, s. 79; Criminal Evidence Act 1898, s. 2; CrimPR 25.9(2)(h)). The rationale for this rule is that, whilst witnesses are normally kept out of court until they testify, the accused has the right to be present throughout the trial, and therefore would otherwise have the opportunity to adjust his or her evidence to accord with that of the witnesses. The court has a discretion to depart from this usual rule (PACE 1984, s. 79), for example to allow a witness whose evidence was not substantially disputed to testify out of the normal order if circumstances made that convenient (*Morrison* (1911) 6 Cr App R 159 and *Smith* [1968] 2 All ER 115). In contrast, psychiatric expert evidence in relation to an accused ought to follow on after the prosecution's evidence of the offence and any evidence from the offender (*Sutton* [2008] EWCA Crim 3129). Character witnesses must *always* be called after the accused unless there are other witnesses as to the facts (Criminal Evidence Act 1898, s. 2).

Police and Criminal Evidence Act 1984, s. 79

If at the trial of any person for an offence—
(a) the defence intends to call two or more witnesses to the facts of the case; and
(b) those witnesses include the accused,
the accused shall be called before the other witness or witnesses unless the court in its discretion otherwise directs.

Criminal Evidence Act 1898, s. 2

Where the only witness to the facts of the case called by the defence is the person charged, he shall be called as a witness immediately after the close of the evidence for the prosecution.

A witness waiting to give evidence must not wait inside the courtroom, unless that witness is a party or an expert witness (CrimPR 25.11(2)(a)). But see *Carty* [2011] EWCA Crim 2087, where the Court of Appeal declined to exclude the potentially helpful evidence of a defence witness who had been in court during the prosecution case.

The Accused as a Witness

The special evidential rules relating to the accused as a witness, for example, the application of the rule against self-incrimination and the circumstances in which the accused may be cross-examined as to character, are fully discussed in **Part F**. Mentioned below are some further points of a specifically procedural nature concerning evidence from the accused. **D17.10**

Evidence from the Witness Box Subject to a contrary direction from the court, an accused who chooses to testify should give evidence from the witness-box, not the dock (Criminal Evidence Act 1898, s. 1(4), and see **F4.11**). The obvious situation in which the court might exercise its discretion against allowing the accused physically to enter the witness-box is when there is a perceived risk of violence that can be controlled more easily if the accused remains in the dock while testifying (*Symonds* (1924) 18 Cr App R 100). See also **D15.96** in relation to the use of live links for the accused, and see CrimPR 3.8(5) and 18.14 (see Supplement **R3.8** and **R18.14**) and CrimPD V, paras. 18A.1 to 18A.2 (see Supplement, **CPD.18A**). **D17.11**

Decision to Call the Accused The decision whether to testify or not is for the accused. **D17.12**

The Court of Appeal has stated that, when the accused decides not to go into the witness box, it should be the invariable practice of counsel to have that decision recorded and to cause the accused to sign the record giving a clear indication (a) of the fact of having, of his or her own accord, decided not to give evidence, and (b) that the accused has done that bearing in mind the advice, regardless of what it was, given by counsel (*Bevan* (1994) 98 Cr App R 354; *Ebanks v The Queen* [2006] UKPC 16, [2006] 1 WLR 1827; *Anderson* [2010] EWCA Crim 2553; *Good* [2016] EWCA Crim 1869). There is no right, even in cases to which the DVCVA 2004, s. 6, applies (see **B1.78**), for an accused to give evidence twice (*Ikram* [2008] EWCA Crim 586, [2008] 2 Cr App R 24 (347)).

Failure to advise the accused properly about the advisability of testifying may, in appropriate circumstances, constitute grounds for the Court of Appeal to decide that a conviction is unsafe and unsatisfactory (*Clinton* [1993] 2 All ER 998, but see also *Good* [2016] EWCA Crim 1869; for further detail, see **D26.24**).

Failure to Give Evidence Since s. 35 of the CJPO 1994 became law, it is particularly important that the accused should be advised whether to give evidence, since an inference may be drawn from a failure to do so. Section 35 is addressed at **F20.42**, and the procedure which the court should adopt is laid down in CrimPR 25.9(2)(d) and CrimPD VI, paras. 26P.1 to 26P.5 (see Supplement, **PD-71**). In considering a comparable provision in the Cayman Islands, the Privy **D17.13**

Council considered that the failure to follow this procedure was an irregularity, but not always a material one (*Wright v The Queen* [2016] UKPC 18). If it were to be demonstrated that counsel had failed to take instructions from the accused at all, resulting in the accused's failure to give evidence, this might represent a material irregularity (*MacLeod v The Queen* [2017] UKPC 1).

In particular, para. 26P.2 states that, unless defence counsel has indicated that the accused will give evidence, the court is required to ask:

> Have you advised your client that the stage has now been reached at which he may give evidence and, if he chooses not to do so or, having been sworn, without good cause refuses to answer any question, the jury may draw such inferences as appear proper from his failure to do so?

The approach of the court where the accused is unrepresented is addressed at **D17.17**.

ALIBI EVIDENCE

D17.14 Prior to the commencement of the CPIA 1996, Part I, alibi evidence and expert opinion evidence were the only types of evidence of which the defence were required to warn the prosecution in advance. That old regime, pursuant to the CJA 1967, s. 11, applies to offences for which the investigation commenced before 1 April 1997.

For later offences, the duty to give specific notice of alibi has been replaced by the wider duties placed on the defence by the CPIA 1996, ss. 5 to 6E (see **D9.29** ***et seq.***). The consequences flowing from a defence failure to comply with its duty to notify an alibi now relate not to a potential impediment to the calling of alibi evidence, but to the fact that comment may be made or permitted or inferences drawn in relation to a notice of alibi that is served, or the failure to serve one. (Disclosure of expert evidence is addressed at **D9.68**.)

Meaning of 'Alibi'

D17.15 The definition of 'alibi' in the CPIA 1996 is provided by s. 6A(3) (see **D9.33**), namely 'evidence tending to show that by reason of the presence of the accused at a particular place or in a particular area at a particular time he was not, or was unlikely to have been, at the place where the offence is alleged to have been committed at the time of its alleged commission'.

It follows that it is only evidence putting the accused at a certain place at the time of the commission of the offence that creates an obligation on the defence to give particulars of alibi if the accused claims to have been elsewhere (*Lewis* [1969] 2 QB 1).

In *Fields* [1991] Crim LR 38, the Court of Appeal found that a letter from D's solicitor, claiming that D was 25 miles away from the scene of the crime at the time he was allegedly first seen by the witness who later identified him as a participant in the offence, did amount to a notice of alibi. This was because the letter contained a claim as to where D had been and that tended to show that D could not have been at the scene of the robbery when it took place.

Similarly, evidence may amount to an alibi even though it comes from the accused only and is to the effect that, at the relevant time, the accused was alone at a location other than the scene of the crime (*Jackson* [1973] Crim LR 356).

However, the term 'alibi' presupposes that the offence alleged was committed at a particular place and time. Therefore, failure by the defence to notify the prosecution that D was not where they claimed him to be on one day during the period of three weeks over which the offence allegedly occurred did not mean that an alibi notice was necessary (*Hassan* [1970] 1 QB 423).

In *Johnson* [1995] 2 Cr App R 1, it was held that 'evidence in support of an alibi' must be evidence that the defendant was at some place or in a particular area other than the place where the offence was allegedly committed. D's instructions to his legal representatives were that he had not been present at the club where the offence was committed on the night in question. He was unable to say where he had been, since his arrest took place almost three months later. The Court of Appeal held that the trial judge was wrong to rule that an alibi notice was necessary in those circumstances.

The duty of defence disclosure under the CPIA 1996, s. 5, is addressed at **D9.29**.

Obligation to Consult Accused about Calling Alibi Evidence

Defence counsel is under a duty to consult the accused before deciding not to call alibi evidence. In *Irwin* [1987] 2 All ER 1085, D's defence was alibi and at his first trial evidence of alibi was called. At the retrial, counsel decided, without consulting D, not to call those witnesses. On appeal, it was held that failure to consult D about the non-calling of the alibi witnesses was a material irregularity. According to Michael Davies J at p. 906, it is not necessarily vital to consult the client immediately before the alibi witnesses are or, as the case may be, are not called, but it is essential to have discussed the matter thoroughly at some stage. If the client declines to accept counsel's advice that the witnesses should not be called, then counsel should either act on the client's instructions or ask to be discharged from the case (p. 905C–D). If the client accepts counsel's advice, it is preferable to have that confirmed by the client in writing (p. 906C). **D17.16**

TREATMENT BY COURT OF UNREPRESENTED ACCUSED

If an accused is not legally represented, the court will, as a matter of practice, seek to give the accused such assistance in conducting his or her defence as may seem appropriate. The CrimPD includes reference to a defendant providing assistance to the jury as to the issues in the case after the prosecution opening (CrimPD VI, para. 25A.2; see Supplement, **CPD.25A**), but only if the court invites the defendant to do so by reference to considerations as to whether the issues are already clear, the prosecution has already fairly identified them, or there is a risk that the defendant might suffer injustice or prejudice in trying to do so (CrimPD VI, para. 25A.4). **D17.17**

Alternatively, where the accused dismisses counsel and/or solicitors during the course of the trial (or they withdraw during trial) and the accused remains entitled to public funding, the judge may grant an adjournment for the accused to be represented (*Chambers* [1989] Crim LR 367; *Sansom* [1991] 2 QB 130), though there is no requirement that the court must do so.

Accused's Right to Give or Call Evidence

The accused should always be told by the court at the end of the prosecution case of the right to give evidence in person, to call witnesses in his or her defence (whether or not the accused goes into the witness-box), or to stay silent and call no evidence. Failure to give the accused this information may lead to any conviction being quashed (*Carter* (1960) 44 Cr App R 225). **D17.18**

It is particularly important that an unrepresented accused should be informed of the inferences which may be drawn from a failure to give evidence, pursuant to the CJPOA 1994, s. 35 (see **F20.42**). The court is obliged to address the accused, pursuant to CrimPD VI, para. 26P.5 (see *Supplement*, **CPD.26P**), in the following terms:

> You have heard the evidence against you. Now is the time for you to make your defence. You may give evidence on oath, and be cross-examined like any other witness. If you do not give evidence or, having been sworn, without good cause refuse to answer any question, the jury may draw such inferences as appear proper. That means they may hold it against you. You may also call any witness or witnesses whom you have arranged to attend court. Afterwards you may also, if you wish, address the jury by arguing your case from the dock. But you cannot at that stage give evidence. Do you now intend to give evidence?

Restrictions on the Accused

D17.19 CrimPR 25.11(6) (see Supplement, **R25.11**) recognises the role of the trial judge in asking questions of witnesses on behalf of an unrepresented defendant in that defendant's interests. Beyond that, there are limitations on what such a defendant can do personally.

Since the YJCEA 1999, ss. 34 to 39 (see **F7.3**) came into effect, certain restrictions have applied. Unrepresented defendants are prohibited from cross-examining complainants and child witnesses in trials for certain offences. The courts also have the power to prohibit cross-examination of witnesses by unrepresented defendants if satisfied that the circumstances of the witness and the case merit it, and that a prohibition would not be contrary to the interests of justice. There are provisions for the appointment of representatives to conduct cross-examinations on behalf of unrepresented defendants. By way of guidance as to the role of such a representative, in *Abbas v CPS* [2015] EWHC 579 (Admin), [2015] 2 Cr App R 11 (183) the Divisional Court said that a s. 38 advocate did not have a free-ranging remit to conduct the trial on the defendant's behalf. Rather the advocate was under a statutory duty to be in a position to properly conduct a cross-examination, which might include a pre-trial application to admit bad character evidence or for disclosure, if relevant to the cross-examination. The important point was that s. 38 advocates must ensure that their duties accorded with the words of the statute.

For the position as to cross-examination by an unrepresented accused and related matters, see also *Brown* [1998] 2 Cr App R 364, which is dealt with at **F7.3**. The procedure on an application for a prohibition on cross-examination of a particular witness is specified by CrimPR 23.4 (see Supplement, **R23.4**).

Section D18 Trial on Indictment: Procedure between Close of Defence Case and Retirement of Jury

INTRODUCTION

This section addresses the progress of a trial on indictment following the closing of the defence case. This involves consideration of the potential reopening of either the defence or, more usually, the prosecution case thereafter, discussion between the court and counsel of the law relevant to the case, the closing speeches of counsel, and the judge's summing-up, though the order of these is now addressed by CrimPD VI, para. 26K.16 (see **D18.21**). The *Crown Court Compendium* is now the primary source of guidance in relation to the judge's summing-up. **D18.1**

REOPENING OF PROSECUTION CASE

The general principle is that once prosecuting counsel has stated that the case is closed the prosecution may not adduce any further evidence (see Tindal CJ in *Frost* (1839) 4 St Tr NS 85 at col. 386). The exceptions, described below, cannot be listed exhaustively, but as a general rule the court's discretion to admit fresh evidence after the close of the prosecution case must be exercised with great caution (*Munnery* (1991) 94 Cr App R 164). See also CrimPR 25.9(2)(i) (see Supplement, **R25.9**). **D18.2**

Matters which Arise *Ex Improviso*

Where a matter arises *ex improviso* in the course of the defence case which no human ingenuity could have foreseen, the judge may allow the prosecution to adduce evidence on the point to rebut that which has been led by the defence (see also **F6.5** ***et seq.***). This includes instances where matters are raised in defence counsel's closing submissions which had not been foreshadowed in the cross-examination of prosecution witnesses. The justification for this is that CrimPR 3.3 imposes a duty on the defence to identify the issues at an early stage; if they choose not to do so, the prosecution should be allowed to address them (*Malcolm v DPP* [2007] EWHC 363 (Admin), [2007] 2 Cr App R 1 (1)). **D18.3**

Evidence Becoming Available to the Prosecution Only after Close of Case

If evidence unexpectedly becomes available to the prosecution between the close of their case and the judge's summing-up, they may exceptionally be given leave to call it even though the issue to which it relates does not arise *ex improviso* (*Doran* (1972) 56 Cr App R 429). For further discussion, see **F6.6**. **D18.4**

Evidence of a Purely Formal Nature Inadvertently Omitted

It has been held that an omission to call evidence of a purely formal nature, the lack of which leaves a technical gap in the prosecution case, may be repaired by allowing them to reopen (*McKenna* (1956) 40 Cr App R 65). However, the circumstances in which this is appropriate are narrowly confined and should not be used as a device for rescuing the prosecution when they **D18.5** have failed to prepare or prove their case properly. *McKenna* should be contrasted with *Central Criminal Court, ex parte Garnier* [1988] RTR 42, in which the Divisional Court found that the court should not have adjourned during submissions as to evidential sufficiency to allow the prosecution to obtain evidence that went beyond the purely formal, the need for which had not arisen *ex improviso*. See further **F6.7**.

Evidence to Rebut Answers in Cross-examination as to Credit

D18.6 Although a witness's answers to questions going only to his or her credit are generally final, there are important exceptions to the rule, notably where the question related to a previous conviction, a previous inconsistent statement, possible bias or a reputation for untruthfulness (see **F7.48** ***et seq.***). It follows that, where the accused or other defence witness is asked in cross-examination a question going to his or her credit and the question is such that the witness's answer is *not* final because it comes within one of these exceptions, the prosecution must be allowed to reopen their case to adduce evidence to rebut a denial given in cross-examination.

Time for Reopening Prosecution Case

D18.7 As to the latest stage at which the prosecution may be permitted to reopen their case, assuming one of the exceptional situations applies, the majority of the decided cases contemplate the additional evidence being called either during or, more probably, at the end of the defence case. However, in *Flynn* (1958) 42 Cr App R 15, the judge gave the prosecution leave to call a witness to rebut an alibi raised *ex improviso* by the defence after closing speeches but before the summing-up (see also *Lawson v Stafford Magistrates' Court* [2007] EWHC 2490 (Admin), in which the prosecution were permitted an adjournment to obtain further evidence following the defence closing speech).

Use in Cross-examination of Unproved Material

D18.8 The rule that the prosecution must adduce all the material on which they intend to rely as part of their case extends to the use they may make of statements or admissions not earlier proved in evidence in cross-examination.

For example in *Kane* (1977) 65 Cr App R 270, prosecuting counsel was criticised for cross-examining D about 'off the record' answers he had given to police officers, and which had not been adduced in evidence as part of the prosecution's case. This prohibition was particularly acute in cases like *Kane*, where there were issues as to the admissibility of the evidence, or *Phillipson* [1990] 91 Cr App R 226, where the material had neither been served nor disclosed before the prosecution sought to use it. See also *Pershad* [2014] EWCA Crim 692, where the Court of Appeal considered that material used in cross-examination should have been disclosed.

A distinction has been drawn between cases such as *Kane*, where the cross-examination on fresh material goes to the issues in the case, and cases where the cross-examination goes only to the credit of the defence witness (*Halford* (1978) 67 Cr App R 318). However, it will often be difficult, if not impossible, to determine the borderline between cross-examination as to credit and cross-examination on the issues.

REOPENING OF DEFENCE CASE

D18.9 The judge may allow the defence to reopen their case at any stage before the jury retire to consider their verdict. This is made clear by CrimPR 25.9(6) (see Supplement, **R25.9**), but the principles to be applied are elucidated by earlier authority, for example:

(a) In *Morrison* (1911) 6 Cr App R 159, defence evidence was permitted which had only just then come to light after counsel's closing speeches.
(b) In *Hussain* [2010] EWCA Crim 1327 the considerations relevant to the re-opening of the defence case to call a latterly available witness included the delay that would be occasioned

by those seeking to call the witness needing to take a proof from him and instructions from the defendant, co-defendants needing to consider the evidence, and the re-casting of legal directions already given to the jury.

(c) In *Sanderson* [1953] 1 All ER 485, the defence were allowed to call a witness even after the end of the summing-up. The Court of Appeal said that 'it was not a course one would wish to be taken often but, on the particular facts of this case, we think that there is no objection to what was done here. The learned recorder was fully justified in the course he took'.

However, once the jury retire to consider their verdict, evidence must never be received, whether it is favourable to the defence or the prosecution (CrimPR 25.9(6) and *Owen* [1952] 2 QB 362).

JUDGE CALLING OR RECALLING A WITNESS

CrimPR 16.4(5) (see Supplement, **R16.4**) identifies the discretion of a court to require a witness to give live evidence 'on its own initiative'. In fact, it has long been recognised that the judge has a discretion to call a witness whom neither the prosecution nor defence have chosen to call (*Wallwork* (1958) 42 Cr App R 153). The power should be sparingly exercised (*Roberts* (1984) 80 Cr App R 89), and used only where it is necessary in the interests of justice. **D18.10**

Calling a Witness the Prosecution Fail to Call

One appropriate situation for the judge taking such a course is where the prosecution have wrongly refused to call a witness originally served as part of their case (see dicta to that effect in *Oliva* [1965] 3 All ER 116, and **D16.19**). If the witness is likely to be adverse to the defence and the prosecution have already closed their case, the judge should not use power so as to circumvent the restrictions on the prosecution reopening their case (*Cleghorn* [1967] 2 QB 584). If the defence want the judge to call such a witness, the judge has greater latitude in the exercise of discretionary powers and any conviction is unlikely to be quashed even if the evidence turns out to be in some respects adverse to the defence (*Tregear* [1967] 2 QB 574). **D18.11**

Consequences of Such Action

The parties require leave to cross-examine a witness called by the judge, but such leave should be given if the witness's evidence has been adverse to the party wishing to put questions (*Cliburn* (1898) 62 JP 232). Moreover, an adjournment may then be necessary to enable a cross-examining party to call his or her own evidence in rebuttal (*Coleman* (1987) *The Times*, 21 November 1987). **D18.12**

DISCUSSION OF THE RELEVANT LAW

Prior to summing-up, or the first part of the summing-up if it is split (as advocated in CrimPD VI, para. 26K16, see **D18.21**), the court will almost always invite counsel, in the absence of the jury, to make representations on how certain aspects of the case should be dealt with. This is especially important where there might otherwise be misunderstanding or doubt as to how points of law and evidence which have arisen during the course of the case should be dealt with (*N* [1998] Crim LR 886; *Wright* [2000] Crim LR 510). **D18.13**

Such a discussion should take place before speeches, which are required to be 'consistent with' directions already provided to the jury in a split summing-up (CrimPD VI, para. 26K.18; see Supplement, **CPD.26K**).

Only in very exceptional circumstances would it be appropriate for the court to discuss the law with counsel after concluding the summing-up and before the jury's retirement (*Cocks* (1976) 63 Cr App R 79). The course adopted by the judge in *Charles* [1976] 1 WLR 248, of asking counsel to intervene in the course of the summing-up and correct any errors as they arose, was criticised by the Court of Appeal as it detracted from the authority of what the judge was saying.

Assisting the Court

D18.14 Counsel is under a duty to bring all relevant authorities to the court's attention even if some are unfavourable to counsel's own argument. Further, any procedural irregularity must be brought to the attention of the court during the hearing and not reserved to be raised on appeal (e.g., where a juror is seen speaking to a witness).

The duties outlined so far apply equally to prosecution and defence counsel (see also **D16.2** and **D17.2** respectively). In *Smith* [1994] Crim LR 458, one of the grounds of appeal was the fact that contact with a child witness during her evidence was alleged to be irregular. The Court of Appeal said that counsel should have raised the matter at the time with the judge, in the absence of the jury. Failure to do so was reprehensible. See, for more detail, **D18.23**.

CLOSING SPEECHES

D18.15 Subject to one exception, both the prosecution and defence have the right to a closing speech in which they may sum up their respective cases, criticise the opposition's case and comment upon the evidence. The court should intervene to seek clarification or correction of something said in a speech at its conclusion, or at a convenient break, rather than interrupting counsel in the presence of the jury (*Tuegel* [2000] 2 All ER 872).

Order of Speeches

D18.16 CrimPR 25.9(2)(j) and (k) address the order of speeches, and make clear that the prosecution speech is made first (Watkins J summarised the case law and statutory provisions that underline this rule in *Bryant* [1979] QB 108 at pp. 113–18).

Restrictions on Prosecution Closing Speeches

D18.17 In *Mondon* (1968) 52 Cr App R 695, the Court of Appeal held that the prosecution lost the right to make a closing speech where the accused was unrepresented and either called no evidence at all or was himself the only witness (apart from character witnesses). However, in *Stovell* [2006] EWCA Crim 27, the Court of Appeal concluded (per Rose LJ at [36]):

> ... in the light of the procedural and evidential changes which have taken place since the decision of this Court in *Mondon*, we are by no means satisfied that in all cases, particularly when a defendant has been represented substantially throughout the trial and there are issues arising during the defence upon which the jury would be assisted by comment from prosecuting counsel, it is necessarily inappropriate for prosecuting counsel to make a second speech.

Mondon was approved in *Rabani* [2008] EWCA Crim 2030. The position is now made clear in CrimPR 25.9(2)(j) (see Supplement, **R25.9**), which provides that the prosecutor may make final representations where the accused is represented or has called at least one witness (other than the accused) to give evidence in person about the facts of the case or where the court so permits. This approach was approved in *Cojan* [2014] EWCA Crim 2512, [2015] 2 Cr App R 20 (294), where the Court of Appeal said that rather than there being a hard and fast rule, it is 'an issue of balance and fairness'.

Even where prosecuting counsel is entitled to make a closing speech, this does not mean that the right should be exercised as a matter of course. In particular, if the accused is legally represented but does not give or call any evidence, the normal practice is for prosecuting counsel *not* to sum up the case. This was confirmed by Watkins J in *Bryant* [1979] QB 108 at p. 117D, who said that the prosecution's right to make a speech in such circumstances:

> ... should only rarely be necessary to use save possibly in long and complex cases and whenever used should bear, as should the majority of speeches by prosecuting and defence counsel, the becoming hallmark of brevity.

In *Hoggard* [1995] Crim LR 747, it was emphasised that the prosecution had the statutory right, by virtue of the Criminal Procedure Act 1865, s. 2, to make a closing speech where the defendant was represented. The length of the speech should, however, be commensurate with the number and complexity of the issues. In a case where the defence relied on self-serving statements made in interviews, or allegations put in cross-examination to witnesses, it would generally be in order for the prosecution to make a closing speech in order to deal with them.

In *Tahir* [1997] Crim LR 837, the Court of Appeal held that prosecuting counsel should not be deprived of the right to make a closing speech in relation to a represented defendant where the co-defendant was unrepresented. In such circumstances, however, the speech must focus on the evidence relating to the represented defendant.

Limitations as to Content

Neither counsel in a closing speech should allude to alleged facts or other matters which have not been the subject of evidence (see a resolution of the judges dated 26 November 1881, adopted in *Shimmin* (1882) 15 Cox CC 122). Neither should the jury be invited to add a recommendation of mercy to their verdict should it be one of guilty (*Black* [1963] 3 All ER 682). In *Ekaireb* [2015] EWCA Crim 1936 Lord Thomas CJ deprecated (at [59]–[62]) the practice of advocates making personal criticism of their opponents in closing addresses; this was a practice that 'judges must ensure ceases immediately and not be repeated in any case'. **D18.18**

Prosecution Counsel In *Gonez* [1999] All ER (D) 674, the Court of Appeal emphasised that prosecutors must remember their role as a minister of justice in relation to the terms in which they make their speeches (see **D16.3**, and *Solloway* [2019] EWCA Crim 454). In *Ramdhanie* [2005] UKPC 47, [2006] 1 WLR 796, the Privy Council upheld an appeal based upon an improper closing speech by the prosecutor, which contained emotive and unjustified comments on the defence case, insinuations of additional unadduced incriminating material and a number of passages where the prosecutor improperly vouched for the soundness of the prosecution's case. **D18.19**

Prosecuting counsel should not comment to the jury on the potentially serious consequences to police officers of their evidence being disbelieved, even where a police officer has raised the matter in evidence (*Gale* [1994] Crim LR 208).

Equally, prosecution counsel is not entitled to abandon or attack the credit of the prosecution's own witness (unless leave has been given to treat the witness as hostile) and counsel should not invite inferences contrary to the evidence that has been called (*Pacey* (1994) *The Times*, 13 March 1994; *Cairns* [2002] EWCA Crim 2838, [2003] 1 WLR 796) Although in *Cairns* it was made clear that the prosecution should regard the whole of a witness's evidence as reliable before calling that person as a witness (see **D16.21**).

Pursuant to the PACE 1984, s. 80A, the prosecution should not comment on the failure of the accused's spouse or civil partner to give evidence. However, prosecution counsel is entitled to comment on the failure of the accused to answer questions in interview, or to give evidence (see **F20.41**). Similarly, pursuant to the CPIA 1996, s. 11(5), the prosecution may make 'such comment as appears appropriate', providing that the court grants leave, about the failure of the accused to serve a defence statement, or as to divergence between that statement and the accused's evidence (see **D9**).

Defence Counsel In delivering the closing speech defence counsel is not confined to putting forward the client's version of events. Hypotheses may be advanced which go beyond this version of events, always provided that other evidence has been called which supports such hypotheses (*Bateson* (1991) *The Times*, 10 April 1991). **D18.20**

Defence counsel should not refer to the likely consequences of a conviction in terms of punishment since sentencing is no concern of the jury (*A-G for South Australia v Brown* [1960] AC 432). See also *Edgington* [2013] EWCA Crim 2185, [2014] 1 Cr App R 24 (334) (at [20]–[30]).

For the position as to comment by counsel on the defendant's failure to give evidence, see **F20.41**. Defence counsel is obviously entitled to comment upon his or her own client's failure to give evidence. Counsel is also, in a case where a co-accused runs a defence which conflicts with that of the accused he or she represents, entitled to comment upon the co-accused's not having entered the witness-box (*Wickham* (1971) 55 Cr App R 199). The judge has no power to prevent or restrict such comment, but, if it seems to the judge to have been unfair, may comment upon it personally (*Wickham*).

In *Ekaireb* [2015] EWCA Crim 1936 Lord Thomas CJ approved the observations of his predecessor in *Farooqi* [2013] EWCA Crim 1649, [2014] 1 Cr App R 8 (69) as to the duties of defence counsel in presenting the client's case, and the duty of a trial judge to ensure that the defence case is accurately put before the jury even if this requires intervention in defence counsel's speech.

SUMMING-UP

Preliminary and General Matters

D18.21 The trial judge's summing-up conventionally falls into two parts, namely, a direction on the law (see **D18.25**) and a summary of the evidence (see **D18.36**). CrimPR 25.14(3) (see Supplement, R25.14) sets out the appropriate steps to be followed on summing-up. CrimPD VI, para. 26K.16 (see Supplement, **CPD.26K**), encourages the court to split the summing-up so as to address the law before speeches and then turn to the facts after speeches have been made. The use of written directions is also strongly advocated (see **D18.24**). The Court of Appeal has stressed the desirability of using the *Crown Court Compendium* as an invaluable resource in terms of guidance and draft directions (*G* [2018] EWCA Crim 1393, [2018] 2 Cr App R 26 (413); *Miah* [2018] EWCA Crim 563).

The Court of Appeal has also discouraged courts from commencing a summing-up, or addressing an important aspect of one, at a late hour or just before the weekend (*Rimmer* [1983] Crim LR 250).

Where the judge does not provide the summing-up (or parts of it) in writing, both counsel should take as full a note of the summing-up as is possible. This is especially important where any sentence is likely to be short. A good note may avoid delay caused by waiting for a transcript and thus expedite an appeal (*Campbell* [1976] Crim LR 508).

D18.22 **Correcting Errors** Where the judge discovers an error in the summing-up, whether as a result of representations by counsel (see **D18.23**) or otherwise, the error should be expressly acknowledged, the jury told to disregard it, and the judge should then go on to give the correct direction (*Cole* [1993] Crim LR 300). In *Kilbane* [2003] EWCA Crim 607, the judge was alerted in the absence of the jury to a misdirection as to the burden of proof in cases covered by the MDA 1971, s. 28. When the jury returned, the judge gave a correct direction, but described it as an attempt to 'clarify' and 'repeat' what she had previously said. The Court of Appeal quashed the conviction, quoting Salmon LJ in *Moon* [1969] 3 All ER 803:

> Such a misdirection could be corrected only in the plainest terms. The court must repeat the direction given, acknowledge that it was wrong, tell the jury to put out of their minds all they had heard from the court... and then direct them on the law in clear terms incapable of being misunderstood.

D18.23 **Duties of Counsel in Relation to the Summing-up** Prosecuting counsel is under a duty to attend carefully to the summing-up and draw any possible errors (whether of fact or law) to the judge's attention at its close (*Donoghue* (1987) 86 Cr App R 267). Moreover, the court is entitled to rely on such assistance (*McVey* [1988] Crim LR 127).

Beyond the duties described at **D18.14**, defence counsel has traditionally been able to remain silent, if that was considered to be in the best interests of the client (*Curtin* [1996] Crim LR 831, relying upon *Cocks* (1976) 63 Cr App R 79 and see also *Edwards* (1983) 77 Cr App R 5). However, this position has since been eroded. For example:

(a) It is the duty of both prosecution and defence counsel to alert the judge to evidence on which the jury could find provocation, before the summing-up, and, if the judge agrees, remind him or her that statute requires the judge to leave the remaining issues to the jury (*Cox* [1995] 2 Cr App R 513).

(b) Defence counsel is under a duty to request a good character direction, if the accused was entitled to one, rather than making complaint later if one is not given (*Gilbert v The Queen* [2006] UKPC 15, [2006] 1 WLR 2108; and see *Hunter* [2015] EWCA Crim 631, [2015] 2 Cr App R 9 (116)).

However, in *Holden* [1991] Crim LR 478, the Court of Appeal made it clear that the dismissal of an appeal would not be automatic where defence counsel had failed to correct an error.

Written Directions

In virtually all cases, under CrimPR 25.14(3)(b) and (4), the judge should provide the jury with a written list of questions (a route to verdict), written legal directions and such other material as will assist them in their task, for example, setting out the legal issues which must be proved in order to reach their verdict. CrimPD VI, para. 26K.11, encourages the use of written directions in this way, which it describes as a 'written route to verdict'. Before providing the jury with the written route to verdict, the judge should submit them to counsel, so that they can make suggestions and can base their closing speeches upon the issues raised in the proposed directions. While failure by counsel to comment on such draft directions is not necessarily fatal to an appeal based on any misdirection, such failure is likely to affect the weight accorded to the deficiency (*Gammans* (13 November 1998 unreported)). **D18.24**

While in *Lawson* [1998] Crim LR 883 it was said that the judge was entitled to decline to provide the jury with written directions, even where they have been requested, it is now clear from CrimPD VI, Part 26K, and more recent pronouncements of the Court of Appeal that cases where written directions would not be required are very few, and that their provision should be the 'norm' (*Atta-Dankwa* [2018] EWCA Crim 320, [2018] 2 Cr App R 16 (248); *PP* [2018] EWCA Crim 1300). (The *Crown Court Compendium* (July 2020), ch. 1-8, describes the argument in favour of giving written directions as 'overwhelming' and gives further guidance on their use.)

The jury should then be given the written list at the start of the summing-up, so that the judge can take them through the directions one by one, as each point is dealt with. See *McKechnie* (1992) 94 Cr App R 51 and *Taxquet v Belgium* (2012) 54 EHRR 26 (933).

Standard Directions

As Lord Hailsham observed in *Lawrence* [1982] AC 510 (at p. 519), a summing-up should be 'custom-built to make the jury understand their task in relation to a particular case'. Which legal directions are necessary will therefore vary and what is set out here is a survey of the standard directions which may be required. CrimPD VI, para. 26K.17, provides a useful checklist of directions that could form part of part one of a split summing-up. **D18.25**

From the 1970s onwards, the Judicial Studies Board issued specimen directions in relation to the applicable law, and these are now found in the *Crown Court Compendium*. The Court of Appeal continues to encourage the use of these standard forms through which directions on frequently recurring matters of law may be given (see, e.g., *G* [2018] EWCA Crim 1393, [2018] 2 Cr App R 26 (413); *Miah* [2018] EWCA Crim 563), though they are suggested as guidelines only, and judges should adapt them to the circumstances of the particular case. In the foreword to the *Crown Court Bench Book*, the predecessor to the *Crown Court Compendium* published in March 2010, Lord Judge CJ said that its 'objective has been to move away from the perceived rigidity of specimen directions towards a fresh emphasis on the responsibility of the individual judge, in an individual case, to craft directions appropriate to that case'. As the *Crown Court Compendium* provides guidance, rather than scripted text for legal directions, it follows that the case law as to the appropriate form of directions on legal topics becomes more important.

In *Hayes* [2010] EWCA Crim 773, Hughes LJ, responding to a submission that the trial judge's direction did not conform to a Judicial Studies Board model direction, stated (at [12]):

> That... it needs to be said as clearly as possible, is not and never can be by itself a ground of appeal. The Judicial Studies Board does not issue directions or orders to judges. It is a forum within which they can compare their practices. The so-called model directions which are in any event about to be supplemented by additional sample directions are no more than that. They are examples which may be helpful to judges in framing a direction which is tailored to the individual case. It is fundamentally to misunderstand the nature of the Judicial Studies Board and the materials provided by it to treat any of its materials as carrying any force of law at all.... it is important that it should be understood what the significance is and more importantly what the significance is not of model directions issued by the Board.

D18.26 **Direction as to the Functions of Judge and Jury** At the beginning of the summing-up, the judge must direct the jury as to their respective roles and hence the different status of the two parts of the summing-up: that part relating to law, in relation to which the judge is the final arbiter, and that relating to fact (summarising the evidence before them). See also the *Crown Court Compendium* (July 2020), ch. 4. As regards the facts, the jury are the judges (*Wootton* [1990] Crim LR 201). Therefore, if, in the course of the summing-up, the judge expresses a certain view as to the facts or as to the significance of a piece of evidence but the jury disagree; or mention of certain evidence which they consider important is omitted; or, conversely, something which they consider unimportant is stressed — in all such eventualities, it is the *jury's* view which matters.

D18.27 **Burden and Standard of Proof** Every summing-up must contain at least a direction to the jury as to the burden and standard of proof, and as to the ingredients of the offence or offences which the jury are called upon to consider (*McVey* [1988] Crim LR 127; *Crown Court Compendium* (July 2020), ch. 5). Thus, if the judge fails properly to direct the jury as to the prosecution (a) having the burden of proof and (b) having to discharge that burden beyond reasonable doubt or so that the jury are sure, a conviction is liable to be quashed (see *Donoghue* (1987) 86 Cr App R 267 on the burden of proof and *Edwards* (1983) 77 Cr App R 5 on the standard of proof) (see also **F3.48**). Judges were warned of the risks of deviating from this core direction, even in answer to a question from a jury as to the meaning of 'sure', in *JL* [2017] EWCA Crim 621.

In *Bowditch* [1991] Crim LR 831, the Court of Appeal stressed that in cases involving injuries to a small child it was essential that a very clear direction should be given as to the burden of proof. This was to counteract any tendency on the part of the jury, albeit subconsciously, to succumb to their emotions. Where the statute under which an accused was being prosecuted imposed an evidential burden upon the accused, good sense dictated that in appropriate circumstances the court should seek agreement that this burden had been discharged so that only the prosecution's burden needed to be left to the jury (*Malinina* [2007] EWCA Crim 3228).

D18.28 **Separate Consideration of Counts and Defendants** Where there is more than one count on the indictment, the jury should be directed to give separate consideration to each of them (*Lovesey* [1970] 1 QB 352; *Crown Court Compendium* (July 2020), ch. 6-1). For the same reason, the judge should also summarise the evidence on a count by count rather than a witness by witness basis (*Robson* [2007] EWCA Crim 3362). In *Adams* [2019] EWCA Crim 1363 the Court of Appeal emphasised that where an accused faced multiple counts, the jury should be given clear direction as to whether, and if so in what way, evidence relating to one count was admissible in relation to consideration of any other. Where there was no cross-admissibility between counts this had to be made clear.

Similarly, where there is more than one accused on trial, the jury should be directed to consider the case for and against each separately (*Smith* (1935) 25 Cr App R 119). Where the allegation against the accused is one of joint participation, a direction of the kind suggested in the *Crown Court Compendium* (July 2020), chs. 7-3 and 7-4, may be appropriate (see also **A4.10**).

Ingredients of Offence Appellate decisions reveal a tension between the need for the trial judge to direct the jury as to the ingredients of the offence charged on the one hand, and tailoring such directions to the actual issues in the particular case on the other. D18.29

The first of these approaches is exemplified in *McVey* [1988] Crim LR 127, in which the Court of Appeal made clear that it was insufficient for the judge simply to spell out the issue in the case. He was required to direct the jury as to the elements of the offence charged. The same approach was adopted in *James* [1997] Crim LR 598.

The second approach was advocated by Diplock LJ in *Mowatt* [1968] 1 QB 421, when he stated that the function of a summing-up was not to give a jury a general dissertation on some aspect of the criminal law, but to isolate the issues for the jury's consideration. Similarly, in *Lawrence* [1982] AC 510, Lord Hailsham of St Marylebone LC remarked (at pp. 519F–520A):

> The purpose of a direction to a jury is not best achieved by a disquisition on jurisprudence or philosophy or a universally applicable circular tour round the area of law affected by the case. The search for universally applicable definitions is often productive of more obscurity than light.... A direction to a jury should be custom built to make the jury understand their task in relation to a particular case. Of course it must include references to the burden of proof and the respective roles of jury and judge. But it should also include a succinct but accurate summary of the issues of fact as to which a decision is required, a correct but concise summary of the evidence and arguments on both sides, and a correct statement of the inferences which the jury are entitled to draw from their particular conclusions about the primary facts.

Failure to Answer Questions or Give Evidence Pursuant to the CJPO 1994, ss. 34 and 35, the jury are entitled to draw such inferences as they deem appropriate from the failure of the defendant to answer questions in interview (s. 34) or failure to give evidence (s. 35). Guidance as to the proper form of direction that should be given was provided in *Cowan* [1996] QB 373 and is contained in the *Crown Court Compendium* (July 2020), ch. 17-5. Although not expected to identify every fact in relation to which an inference may be drawn, the judge is required to identify significant facts relied on and to remind the jury of any reason for silence advanced by the accused (*Lowe* [2007] EWCA Crim 833). D18.30

A number of limitations to the requirement for a s. 34 direction have been recognised:

(a) No inferences should be drawn from the silence in interview of an accused who does not give or call evidence, and has not advanced a positive case (*Moshaid* [1998] Crim LR 420).
(b) Where an accused's account had changed between interview and trial, this was a matter on which comment could be made without the need for a formal direction under s. 34 (*Maguire* [2008] EWCA Crim 1028).

Where such inferences should not be drawn, the jury should be specifically directed to that effect (*McGarry* [1999] 1 Cr App R 377).

This topic is discussed in more detail at **F20.9**, **F20.24** and **F20.31**.

Failure to Call a Witness In *Wright* [2000] Crim LR 510, the Court of Appeal emphasised the dangers of comment on the failure of the defence to call certain witnesses in the summing-up, since such comments could so easily detract from the realisation that the burden of proof must be upon the prosecution. Such comment has been held to be justified, however, where the prosecution could have had no means of knowing that the witness could have any relevant evidence to give before the defence case (*Gallagher* [1974] 3 All ER 118) or the witness was one only the defence could have called, such as the accused's solicitor (*Wilmot* (1988) 89 Cr App R 341). See also *Khan* [2001] EWCA Crim 486 and the application of that decision in *Campbell* [2009] EWCA Crim 1076 and *Seaton* [2010] EWCA Crim 1980, [2011] 1 Cr App R 2 (7). D18.31

D18.32 **Other Standard Directions** Other commonly given directions include ones concerning:

(a) the proper approach to circumstantial evidence (see **F1.22**, *Stephens and Clarke* (95/1758/S2 unreported) and the *Crown Court Compendium* (July 2020), ch. 10-1);
(b) evidence of lies by the defendant (see **F1.25** for the direction set out in *Lucas* [1981] QB 720, *Burge* [1996] 1 Cr App R 163 and the *Crown Court Compendium* (July 2020), ch. 16-3);
(c) identification evidence (see **F19.9** for the direction set out in *Turnbull* [1977] QB 224 and the *Crown Court Compendium* (July 2020), ch. 15), but note that such a direction is not required where the identifying witness retracts the identification (*Davis* [2006] EWCA Crim 2015) — see also *Ley* [2006] EWCA Crim 3063, [2007] 1 Cr App R 25 (325), in which the Court of Appeal held that a judge was not required to direct a jury to acquit if they rejected evidence which was potentially supportive of a weak identification;
(d) trial in the absence of the accused (see **D15.83** and the *Crown Court Compendium* (July 2020), ch. 3-3);
(e) the limited admissibility of interviews of co-defendants (see **F18.80** and the decisions in *Rhodes* (1959) 44 Cr App R 23 and *Hayter* [2005] UKHL 6, [2005] 2 Cr App R 3 (37)) — see also *Knowlden* (1981) 77 Cr App R 94, in relation to the warning that should be given to the jury where one accused gives evidence adverse to another;
(f) pleas of co-accused (*Dixon* (2000) 164 JP 721: see **D12.77**);
(g) the need for corroboration and care warnings (see **F5.2** for the former and **F5.5**, the CJPO 1994, s. 32, and *Makanjuola* [1995] 3 All ER 730, for the latter; see also the *Crown Court Compendium* (July 2020), ch. 10-2);
(h) the need for a warning in relation to a witness who may be tainted by improper motives (see *Beck* [1982] 1 All ER 807 and **F5.14**);
(i) expert evidence (following *Stockwell* (1993) 97 Cr App R 260, the jury should be directed that they are not bound to accept expert opinion; see also **F11.42** and the *Crown Court Compendium* (July 2020), ch. 10-3); and
(j) the approach to evidence of good or bad character (see *Vye* (1993) 97 Cr App R 134, *Aziz* [1996] 1 AC 41 and in particular *Campbell* [2007] EWCA Crim 1472, [2007] 1 WLR 2798, in which the Court of Appeal emphasised that the judge should explain the relevance of bad character evidence to the jury on the facts of the case, rather than by following any set direction) (see also **F13** and **F14** and the *Crown Court Compendium* (July 2020), chs. 11 and 12).

Defences

D18.33 There is an obligation on the trial judge to give the legal directions which apply to the defence advanced on behalf of the accused. Common defences and partial defences to which this applies include:

(a) self-defence (see *Palmer* [1971] AC 814, *Lobell* [1957] 1 QB 547, *Harvey* [2009] EWCA Crim 469, the *Crown Court Compendium* (July 2020), ch. 18-1 and **A3.55**);
(b) alibi (see *Anderson* [1991] Crim LR 361, the *Crown Court Compendium* (July 2020), ch. 18-2 and **F3.44**) — where an alibi is demonstrated or accepted to be false, a *Lucas*-type direction is appropriate, see *Lesley* [1996] 1 Cr App R 39;
(c) loss of control (*Stewart* [1995] 4 All ER 999); and
(d) diminished responsibility (see *Terry* [1961] 2 QB 314 and **B1.18**).

Where an accused is unrepresented, the judge should also remind the jury to bear in mind the difficulties for the accused of representing him or herself at trial (*De Oliveira* [1997] Crim LR 600, and see *Johnson* [2013] EWCA Crim 2001).

D18.34 **Alternative Defences** The jury should not generally be directed on matters which are not issues in the case. Nonetheless, there are occasions when the jury should be directed as to a defence which has not been raised by the evidence or by counsel. The following cases provide examples:

(a) In *Watson* [1992] Crim LR 434, D was charged with buggery, which he denied. The Court of Appeal found that, although the defence of accident had not been raised, there was a duty on the judge to spell out that penetration must have been deliberate (but see *Johnson* [1994] Crim LR 376, where the Court of Appeal concluded to the contrary).

(b) In *Phillips* [1999] All ER (D) 1372, D was charged with unlawful wounding contrary to the OAPA 1861, s. 20. The prosecution case was that D had deliberately attacked the victim with a knife and inflicted wounds upon her by way of retribution. D's case was that the wounding had been accidental. The trial judge summed up on the basis that the defence was accident, mentioning self-defence only to dismiss it. The Court of Appeal held that the judge ought to have left the defence of self-defence to the jury.

Invisible Burden This burden arises where a potential defence has not been raised on the accused's behalf, but there is a cogent, rather than speculative, evidential basis for its consideration (*Bonnick* (1978) 66 Cr App R 266). In such circumstances there is a burden upon the judge to raise such an alternative defence in the summing-up. Circumstances in which this may arise include cases where self-defence is lurking in the background (see *Kachikwu* (1965) 52 Cr App R 538 and S Doran, 'Alternative Defences: the "invisible burden" on the trial judge' [1991] Crim LR 878). **D18.35**

The Facts

In addition to directing the jury on the law, the judge should remind them of and comment upon the evidence. Despite suggestions to the contrary in *Attfield* [1961] 3 All ER 243, it is clear that a summary of the evidence is necessary in almost all cases. For example: **D18.36**

(a) In *Brower* [1995] Crim LR 746, it was made clear that in the majority of cases, it was necessary for the judge to sum up on the facts in order to assist the jury and ensure a fair trial. It was incumbent on the judge to define the issues and remind the jury of the evidence they had heard, albeit very recently.

(b) In *Amado-Taylor* [2000] 2 Cr App R 194, it was held to be a procedural irregularity for a judge to sum up without a review of the facts. There were exceptions where this was not required, such as where a case was short and simple. But the closing speeches of counsel were no substitute for a judicial and impartial view of the facts from the trial judge, whose duty it was to focus the attention of the jury upon the issues which he identified.

(c) In *Reynolds* [2019] EWCA Crim 2145, [2020] 1 Cr App R 20 (348) the Court of Appeal stressed that, since the jury's verdict was not reasoned, the summing-up provides the record of the facts on which that verdict was founded and, in a long case, was needed to provide a 'rational consideration of the evidence' (at [55]).

The Analysis Involved In very simple cases, it might suffice for the judge to sum up the facts by reading out an abbreviated version of his or her note of the evidence. However, if the trial has been at all complex, judges are exhorted to assist the jury by analysing the evidence and relating it to the various issues raised (*Gregory* [1993] Crim LR 623). Merely reading a note of the evidence in such cases has been criticised, not least because it 'must bore the jury to sleep' (see pp. 339–41 of Lawton LJ's judgment in *Charles* (1976) 68 Cr App R 334). **D18.37**

Similarly, in the passage from Lord Hailsham's speech in *Lawrence* [1982] AC 510 quoted at **D18.29**, reference is made to the desirability of the summing-up including a '*succinct* but accurate summary of the issues of fact as to which a decision is required, a correct but *concise* summary of the evidence and arguments on both sides, and a correct statement of the inferences which the jury are entitled to draw from their particular conclusions about the primary facts' (*emphasis added*). Such a succinct and focused summary of the evidence is of particular importance at the end of a long and complex trial, as it is required to provide the jury with a rational consideration of the evidence (*D* [2007] EWCA Crim 2485).

Summarising the Defence Case Crucially, in *Curtin* [1996] Crim LR 831, the Court of Appeal stated that it was part the judge's duty to identify the defence. The way in which this is done will depend on the circumstances of the case, however the following propositions apply: **D18.38**

(a) Where the accused has given evidence, it will be desirable to summarise that evidence.

(b) Where the accused has given evidence and answered questions in interview, it may be appropriate to draw attention to consistencies and inconsistencies between the two.
(c) When an accused is interviewed at length but does not give evidence, the judge has to decide how, fairly and conveniently, to place the interview before the jury.
(d) When the accused has done neither, it will usually be appropriate to remind the jury of counsel's speech.

Moreover, it is desirable for the judge to give an overview of the defence case, in addition to weaving the defence case into the chronology of the prosecution evidence (*Pomfrett* [2009] EWCA Crim 1939, [2010] 2 Cr App R 28 (281)). As to the extent of the trial judge's duty to summarise the defence case where no evidence has been called for the defence, see *Singh-Mann* [2014] EWCA Crim 717, in which Fulford LJ said (at [90]):

> ...it is clear that when a defendant has said little or nothing in interview and has elected not to give or call evidence, ordinarily the limit of the judge's duty is simply to remind the jury of 'such assistance, if any, as (defence) counsel had been able to extract from the Crown's witnesses in cross-examination' and any 'significant points made in defence counsel's speech'. In this context, it is to be stressed that in order to present a defence to the charges the defendant is not compelled to give or to call evidence; instead, he is entitled to rely on evidence presented by the prosecution or by his co-accused when advancing arguments for the jury's consideration as to whether the prosecution has established his guilt. The rehearsal of this material by the judge does not necessarily have to be extensive or detailed — indeed, frequently it will be sufficient merely to identify the central submissions and the evidence that underpins them — but the judge must generally ensure that the jury receives a coherent rehearsal of the main arguments that are being advanced by the accused.

These observations were approved and applied by the Court of Appeal in *Lunkulu* [2015] EWCA Crim 1350.

On the question of whether defence counsel has a duty to draw the judge's attention to a failure to deal adequately with the defence, see **D18.23**.

D18.39 **Judicious Judicial Comment** It is the judge's duty to state matters 'clearly, impartially and logically', and not to indulge in inappropriate sarcasm or extravagant comment (*Berrada* (1989) 91 Cr App R 131). Similarly, in *Marr* (1989) 90 Cr App R 154, the Court of Appeal stressed that observance of the accused's right to have the case presented fairly is never more important than when 'the cards seem to be stacked most heavily against the defendant' (p. 156). Lord Lane CJ added: 'however distasteful the offence, however repulsive the defendant, however laughable his defence, he is nevertheless entitled to have his case fairly presented to the jury both by counsel and by the judge' (p. 156).

However, provided it is emphasised to the jury that they are entitled to ignore opinions, the judge may comment on the evidence in a way which indicates his or her own views. Robust comments to the detriment of the defence case are permitted (e.g., *O'Donnell* (1917) 12 Cr App R 219, in which the judge described the accused's story as a 'remarkable one'), providing the judge is not so critical as effectively to withdraw the issue of guilt or innocence from the jury (*Canny* (1945) 30 Cr App R 143, in which the judge repeatedly told the jury that the defence case was absurd; see also *Green* [2017] EWCA Crim 1774, [2018] 1 Cr App R 14 (218) and *Marchant* [2018] EWCA Crim 2606, [2019] 4 WLR 20).

D18.40 **Advancing an Alternative Basis for Conviction** The question sometimes arises whether the judge is confined, when summarising the case against the accused, to the same basis as that on which the prosecution has put its case. In *Japes* [1994] Crim LR 605, the Court of Appeal said that a judge was not bound by the way in which the Crown opened its case. As the evidence developed, it might become apparent that the offence may have been committed on a somewhat different factual basis. If so, the judge was not debarred from putting that basis before the jury to consider, so long as the accused was not disadvantaged or prejudiced by this course of action (see however *Falconer-Atlee* (1973) 58 Cr App R 348, where the judge was criticised for leaving the case to the jury on a new basis). In *Singh* [2011] EWCA Crim 2992 the Court of Appeal concluded that a trial judge had been entitled to advance a potential co-conspirator who was not particularised in the indictment, or advanced by the prosecution, where the jury would otherwise have been left with 'an incomplete range of options'.

Where the judge intends to direct the jury on a new legal basis, it is important that the parties should be given an opportunity to consider and if necessary to argue the point (*Ramzan* [1998] 2 Cr App R 328; see also *Taylor* [1998] Crim LR 582). This should be done in advance of closing speeches (*Reynolds* [2019] EWCA Crim 2145, [2020] 1 Cr App R 20 (348)), and, in appropriate cases, the judge should give the defence the opportunity to call further evidence (*Powell* [2006] EWCA Crim 685).

As to leaving lesser alternative counts to the jury, see **D19.41**.

Summing-up Amounting to Direction

Application of the principle that the judge should not dictate the jury's verdict through excessively robust comment during the summing-up (see **D18.39**) becomes difficult where the defence case amounts to an admission of guilt. Even in such circumstances, however, the judge must not take the issue of guilt away from the jury. **D18.41**

In *DPP v Stonehouse* [1978] AC 55, one of the issues was whether the admitted facts established an attempt to obtain property by deception or merely established acts which were preparatory to such an attempt. Having ruled as a matter of law that the facts proved did constitute an attempt, the judge so directed the jury. The majority of the House of Lords held that, even where any reasonable jury properly directed on the law must upon the facts reach a verdict of guilty, the trial judge should nevertheless leave the issues of fact to them.

The same approach was adopted in *Thompson* [1984] 3 All ER 565. The judge directed the jury that there 'could not be room for any doubt at all' about the elements of the offence being made out, and that he (the judge) had already ruled that the offence was within the jurisdiction of the court. The Court of Appeal held that the judge's direction amounted to an irregularity in the course of the trial.

In *Wang* [2005] UKHL 9, [2005] 2 Cr App R 8 (136), the House of Lords considered a number of authorities on the certified question of law: 'In what circumstances, if any, is a judge entitled to direct a jury to return a verdict of guilty?' Their lordships concluded unanimously that there were no such circumstances. This was the case even where a burden of proof lay on the defence. No matter how inescapable a judge might consider a conclusion to be, in the sense that any other conclusion would be perverse, it remained the judge's duty to leave the decision to the jury, and not to dictate what the verdict should be.

The decision in *Wang* was applied in *Caley-Knowles* [2006] EWCA Crim 1611, [2006] 1 WLR 3181 to two cases in which judges had directed the jury to convict. In each case the judge, in doing so, had made clear that the matter was being taken out of the hands of the jury. The Court of Appeal emphasised that it would be a significant misdirection and material irregularity for the decision to be taken away from the jury in that way. However, providing it is clear at all times that the verdict is the sole province of the jury, comment from the judge short of a direction to convict was permissible.

Appointment of a Foreman

At the end of the summing-up, the judge should advise the jury to appoint one of their number to be their foreman. The foreman will act as their spokesman and, in due course, announce their verdict. **D18.42**

Unanimity

Finally, the judge should invite the jury to retire and to seek to reach a unanimous decision. However, a failure on the part of the judge to give the jury the direction that their verdicts must **D18.43** be unanimous will not necessarily render a conviction unsafe (*Georgiou* (1969) 53 Cr App R 428; see also *Daly* [1999] Crim LR 88).

To anticipate jury questions about the possibility of a majority verdict, the judge should direct the jury, at this stage, to try to reach a unanimous verdict. If the time should come when the judge can accept a verdict which is not the verdict of them all, a further direction will be given (CrimPD VI, para. 26Q.1 (see Supplement, **CPD.26Q**)). The judge should not, however, indicate the precise period which must elapse before a majority verdict becomes a possibility (*Thomas* [1983] Crim LR 745). If this is done, it will not necessarily be improper, e.g., where the effect is to alleviate anxiety or uncertainty which the jury may be feeling (*Guthrie* (1994) *The Times*, 23 February 1994; *Porter* [1996] Crim LR 126). For the appropriate directions to be given in relation to majority verdicts and verdicts of guilt as to an alternative offence, see **D19.35** and **D19.41**.

D18.44 **Unanimity as to the Basis of a Guilty Verdict** Where the prosecution have put their case on more than one basis, it may be necessary to tell the jury that, in order to convict, they must be unanimous not only as to the accused being guilty but also as to the basis of that guilt. For example, in *Brown* (1983) 79 Cr App R 115, the prosecution alleged the obtaining of property by the use of two different deceptions by D. The Court of Appeal held that the jury should have been directed that, if they were not unanimous that D used both deceptions, they should at least all agree as to which one he used.

In *Mitchell* [1994] Crim LR 66, the Court of Appeal stated that the following principles were to be derived from the cases:

(a) Where several matters were set out in a single count, the judge must consider whether to give the jury a direction that they must all be agreed on the particular ingredient which they rely on to find the accused guilty (*Brown*).
(b) Such a direction will be necessary only comparatively rarely. In the great majority of cases (particularly where dishonesty is alleged and where the allegations stand or fall together), it will be unnecessary and may serve only to confuse the jury (*Price* [1991] Crim LR 465 and *More* (1988) 86 Cr App R 234).
(c) In an appropriate case, where there was a realistic danger that the jury might return a verdict of guilty on the basis that some of them found one ingredient proved and others found another ingredient proved, a direction should be given that they must be unanimous as to the proof of the ingredient which demonstrated that offence.

D18.45 **Limitations to this Principle** The Court of Appeal has sought to limit the need for a direction that the jury should be unanimous as to the ingredients that should be proved in a number of cases, examples of which are mentioned below:

(a) In *Jones* (1999) *The Times*, 17 February 1999, the Court of Appeal held that the considerations in *Brown* did not have any application to the circumstances where a verdict of manslaughter was returned as an alternative to murder. Provided a jury were agreed that an accused was guilty of manslaughter, in the sense that they were sure that the accused perpetrated an unlawful act which caused the death of the deceased, there was no need for unanimity as to the basis of that verdict (see **B1.35**).
(b) In *Giannetto* [1997] 1 Cr App R 1, the Court of Appeal stated that there were two cardinal principles involved in the proposition that a jury must find each essential element in an offence proved. First, the jury must be agreed upon the basis on which they found an accused guilty. Second, an accused must know what case he or she had to meet. Where the Crown alleged that on the evidence the accused must have committed the offence either as principal or as secondary offender, and made it equally clear that they could not say which, the basis on which the jury had to be unanimous was that the accused, having the necessary *mens rea*, by whatever means caused the result which was criminalised by the law (see *Smith* [1997] 1 Cr App R 14, about the application of these principles to an offence of affray; see also *Tirnaveanu* [2007] EWCA Crim 1239, [2007] 2 Cr App R 23 (295)).

(c) In *D* [2001] 1 Cr App R 13 (194), D was charged with indecent assaults on his daughter allegedly committed over a three-year period, in some instances in a variety of ways. The Court of Appeal held that where a number of different matters were set out in a single count, the judge should consider whether the jury should be given a direction that they should all be agreed upon the particular ingredient upon which they relied in order to find the accused guilty of the offence charged. Circumstances requiring such a direction would be rare but, where there was a realistic danger that the jury might not appreciate that they must all be agreed on the particular ingredient on which they relied to find their guilty verdict, a direction must be given that they should be unanimous as to the proof of that ingredient (see also *Carr* [2000] 2 Cr App R 149, *Boreman* [2000] Crim LR 409 and *Turner* [2000] Crim LR 325).

(d) In *Smith* [2014] EWCA Crim 2163, [2015] 1 WLR 937, D was charged with possession of a firearm with intent either to endanger life himself or to allow another to endanger life. The jury were not required to be sure which of these scenarios applied, provided they were sure it was one or the other.

(e) In *Aviss* [2014] EWCA Crim 2210, D was charged with failure to disclose the existence of four creditors in the context of bankruptcy. The Court of Appeal rejected the submission, by reference to *Brown,* that the jury had to agree on the identity of the creditor; it was sufficient for them to agree that he had failed to disclose creditors.

Section D19 Trial on Indictment: Procedure Relating to Retirement of the Jury and Verdict

INTRODUCTION

D19.1 This section addresses the practices and procedures that are engaged with the retirement of the jury to consider its verdict. It also considers the different forms of verdict that can be reached, the directions appropriate to them, and the consequences where the jury conclude that no verdict can be reached.

RETIREMENT OF THE JURY

Basic Rules

D19.2 The principle that governs the keeping of the jury during the period between the close of the judge's summing-up and their returning to court to announce their verdict was succinctly stated by James LJ in *Alexander* [1974] 1 All ER 539 at p. 426H: 'once the jury retires to consider their verdict it should not separate, one from another and from the jury bailiffs. They must remain in the charge of the court through the bailiffs throughout.' The purpose of this is to ensure that nobody interferes with the jury while they are considering their verdict.

The Need to Retire

D19.3 In *Rankine* [1997] Crim LR 757, the Court of Appeal considered that there was nothing in the decided cases to render it wrong for a judge to ask a jury if they wished to consider their verdict without retiring, but stressed the danger that the jury might feel under pressure, and said that such a course would be appropriate only in rare circumstances.

Timing of Retirement

D19.4 Until the CJPO 1994, s. 43, amended the Juries Act 1974, s. 13, to permit a jury in retirement to part company at the end of the normal court day, the rule was that if the summing-up concludes late in the day, the jury should not begin to consider their verdict until the following day. While this is no longer such a strong prohibition, there remains a good argument (as was held in *Birch* (1992) *The Times*, 27 March 1992) that, in a serious case, especially one involving more than one defendant and a number of verdicts, it is undesirable that a jury should be sent out after 3 p.m. unless there are exceptional circumstances. In *Senna (Amin)* [2018] EWCA Crim 789, [2018] 4 WLR 84, the Court of Appeal observed that it was appropriate for a jury to commence retirement late in the day when it was made clear to them before they retired that there was no expectation that they would reach a verdict that day, and that they were under no pressure of time (see also *Akano* (1992) *The Times*, 3 April 1992, where retirements continuing until late in the evening were disapproved).

The decision as to whether the jury should retire late in the afternoon, or wait until the next morning, is one which the judge should take. It should not be left to the jury to decide (*Hawkins* (1994) 98 Cr App R 228).

Custody of the Jury Bailiff

Immediately before the jury retire, one or more court ushers takes an oath to escort the jurors to some 'private and convenient place' where [he] will not 'suffer anybody to speak to them about the trial this day, nor will [he] speak to them [himself] without leave of the court, except if it be to ask them if they are agreed upon their verdict'. An usher who has so sworn is thereafter referred to as a 'jury bailiff'. **D19.5**

At all times during their retirement the jury must be in the custody of a jury bailiff in the sense that the bailiff must be near enough to the room where they are to ensure that no non-juror enters the room or otherwise communicates with them.

Communication with the Jury Once the bailiff has escorted the jury to their room, the bailiff must not enter it 'unless he is expressly ordered by the court to make a communication to, or inquiry of, the jury, and except in special circumstances and at the express order of the court no other persons should have any communication with the jury' (see para. 4(29)(i) of the Court Manual issued by the Lord Chancellor's office on the creation of the Crown Court). **D19.6**

This wording was adopted by James LJ in his judgment in *Lamb* (1974) 59 Cr App R 196, finding it to have been a material irregularity for the clerk of court to have entered the jury room to tell the jury that they should continue to seek unanimity, they having sent a message via the bailiff asking if they could return a majority verdict. It was further stated that: 'If it be the practice in any Crown Court for directions of this kind between judge and jury to be communicated through the medium of court officers, that practice should cease'.

Similarly, in *Davis (No. 2)* (1960) 44 Cr App R 235, the introduction of a shorthand writer into the jury room and, in *Rose* [1982] 2 All ER 536, the clerk entering the jury room to deliver a message from the judge indicating how much longer the latter was prepared to give them to reach a verdict, were both material irregularities. The correct procedure for answering jury questions has been laid down by the Court of Appeal in, *inter alia*, *Gorman* [1987] 2 All ER 435, and is considered at **D19.18**. In *Szypusz v UK* [2010] ECHR 1323 it was held by the ECtHR that it was not a breach of proper procedure for a police officer to be present with a jury in retirement to control the operation of video equipment.

The jury bailiffs are themselves strictly limited in the communication which they can make with the jury. In *Brown* (1989) *The Times*, 25 October 1989, it was stressed that their fundamental duty was to prevent approaches by outsiders and preserve the integrity of the deliberative process. As to an extraordinary breach of the limitation on communication between the jury bailiff and the jury in retirement, and the obstruction of communication between such a jury and the trial judge, see *Mole* [2013] EWCA Crim 2420.

Consequences of a Lapse of Custody If the jury leave the custody of the jury bailiff, it constitutes a material irregularity in the course of the trial which will almost certainly necessitate the quashing of any conviction. For example: **D19.7**

(a) In *Neal* [1949] 2 KB 590, the jury (with the judge's permission) left the court building in order to buy lunch at a restaurant. The conviction was quashed because, even assuming the circumstances justified the judge in allowing the jury to leave the court precincts, it was essential that the bailiff went with them. In his absence, there was no way of knowing who might have spoken to them about the case. It should be noted that the Juries Act 1974, s. 15, now permits the jury to purchase reasonable refreshment at their own expense during the course of their retirement.
(b) In *Ketteridge* [1915] 1 KB 467, where one of the jurors by mistake did not go to the jury room on retirement but left the court and was on his own for some 15 minutes before rejoining his colleagues, there was a breach both of the rule that the jury must not separate (see **D19.8**) and of the rule that the jurors must remain in a bailiff's custody.

Separation of Jury after Retirement By the Juries Act 1974, s. 13, the judge may permit the jury to separate, even after they have retired to consider their verdict. In *Oliver* [1996] 2 Cr App R 514, the Court of Appeal considered the directions which the judge ought to give the jury **D19.8**

when allowing them to separate during consideration of their verdict, and stated that the jury ought to be told (without any prescription as to the words to be used):

(a) to decide the case on the evidence and the arguments seen and heard in court, and not on anything seen or heard outside the court;
(b) that the evidence had been completed and it would be wrong for any juror to seek or receive further evidence or information of any sort about the case;
(c) not to talk to anyone about the case save to the other members of the jury and then only when they were deliberating in the jury room;
(d) not to allow anyone to talk to them about the case unless that person was a juror and he or she was in the jury room deliberating about the case; and
(e) on leaving the court, to set the case on one side until they retired to the jury room to continue the process of deliberating about their verdict.

It would be desirable for the direction to be given in full on the first dispersal by the jury, and for a brief reminder to be given at each subsequent dispersal. Further directions might be necessary in particular circumstances. Directions relating to access to exhibits are addressed by CrimPD VI, paras. 26L.1 to 26L.3 (see Supplement, **CPD.26L**).

In *Edwards* [2004] All ER (D) 324 (Nov), the Court of Appeal made it clear that a failure by the judge to direct a jury not to discuss the case with anyone or any outsider did not make a subsequent conviction unsafe. The whole of the circumstances had to be considered, including the absence of any suggestion that any such discussion had taken place, and the strength of the evidence against the defendant.

D19.9 **Keeping the Jury in a Hotel** Rather than allowing the jury to separate and go home at the end of a court day, in appropriate cases arrangements can be made to keep them at a hotel overnight. When this happens, the judge should direct the jury, before they leave court, that their deliberations should not continue at the hotel, but should await their return to court the next day (*Tharakan* [1995] 2 Cr App R 368).

D19.10 **'Evident Necessity' Exception** Lord Goddard CJ in *Neal* [1949] 2 KB 590, stated that, by way of exception to the rule that the jury must not separate other than with the permission of the judge, a juror could be separated from the rest in a case of 'evident necessity'. The examples he gave of 'evident necessity' were if the juror were 'taken ill or wishe[d] to relieve himself'. It is submitted that the juror must remain in the custody of a jury bailiff while absent from the jury room.

D19.11 **Consequences of Improper Separation** The consequences of improper separation of the jury depend upon the extent to which the rule is breached. This is illustrated by a comparison of the Court of Appeal's decisions in *Alexander* [1974] 1 All ER 539, on the one hand, and *Ketteridge* [1915] 1 KB 467 and *Goodson* [1975] 1 All ER 760, on the other.

In *Alexander*, just after the jury had retired, one of them returned alone to court in order to collect the exhibits. Although the judge had by then risen, defence counsel was still in court, and he told the juror to return to the jury room. Upon the judge being informed what had occurred, the jury were brought back to court; the facts of the incident were confirmed, and they were simply given the exhibits they wanted. James LJ acknowledged that whilst this constituted a procedural irregularity, it did not amount to a *material* irregularity, and there was no possible prejudice to the accused (see also *Farooq* [1995] Crim LR 169).

In *Ketteridge*, where the separation was for a much more substantial period and the separated juror had been out of the control of the court, the conviction was quashed. Similarly, in *Goodson* [1975] 1 All ER 760, a juror was allowed by the bailiff to leave the jury room and speak to unidentified persons on the telephone. He was prevented from returning to the jury room and discharged. On appeal, it was held that what occurred was a material irregularity which had deprived the appellant of a potential voice in the jury room. The Court of Appeal did not rule on whether the judge had the power to discharge a juror even after the jury have retired (see also *Chandler* [1993] Crim LR 394).

Prohibition of Further Evidence Once Jury Enclosed

CrimPR 25.9(6) (see Supplement, **R25.9**) makes clear that which had long been an absolute rule that once the jury have retired to consider their verdict no further evidence may be adduced before them. The proper approach was well put in *Owen* [1952] 2 QB 362, when Lord Goddard CJ said (at p. 369): **D19.12**

> . . . we think it right to lay down that once the summing-up is concluded, no further evidence ought to be given. The jury can be instructed in reply to any question they may put on any matter on which evidence has been given, but no further evidence should be allowed.

Even where a pertinent request for further evidence is made, the jury 'ought to have been told that the prosecution had laid before them such evidence as they had thought fit and the evidence could not now be reopened' (p. 369).

Cases suggesting some relaxation of the rule have to be read in the light of r. 25.9(6); for example:

(a) In *Khan* [2008] EWCA Crim 1112 the Court of Appeal accepted that it had been subject to some relaxation, and upheld a conviction where evidence had been admitted late, by agreement with the defence.
(b) In *Hallam* [2007] EWCA Crim 1495, the Court accepted that there were circumstances in which material would be put before the jury at the request of the accused on the basis that it advanced or purported to advance his case.
(c) In *Kaul* [1998] Crim LR 135, the Court observed that, although the introduction of fresh evidence after a jury had retired should almost invariably lead to the discharge of that jury, in certain circumstances the defence might properly invite the judge to continue with the trial. Where defence counsel took that risk, it did not necessarily bar the way to an appeal on the basis of the irregularity.

The Extent of the Prohibition As CrimPR 25.9(6) also makes clear, the prohibition only starts once the jury have actually retired. Thus, for example, in *Sanderson* [1953] 1 All ER 485, the defence were allowed to call a witness who arrived while the judge was addressing the jury. In a case such as *Sanderson*, however, where evidence is available at the moment the judge finishes the remarks and before the jury have actually retired, there would seem to be no rule of law preventing further evidence, provided it is adduced before the jury retire, and subject to the judge's discretion. **D19.13**

The prohibition must be distinguished from the situation where the jury retires with exhibits, including CCTV material, to examine during their retirement, which is addressed by CrimPD VI, para. 26L.3 (see Supplement, **CPD.26L**).

The prohibition on evidence after retirement applies to documents as it does to oral evidence. For example:

(a) In *Davis* (1975) 62 Cr App R 194, it was a material irregularity for the jury to be supplied, inadvertently, with a copy of a police statement from a witness which had not been exhibited although it had been used by defence counsel in cross-examination.
(b) In *Hulme* [2006] EWCA Crim 2899, [2007] 1 Cr App R 26 (334), it had been an error to allow the jury to retire with a previous inconsistent statement from a hostile witness, even where it had been admitted in evidence pursuant to the CJA 2003, s. 119 (see also the CJA 2003, s. 122, at **F6.25**).
(c) In *Thomas* (3 February 1987 unreported) it was held to have been quite wrong to have provided the jury with a map during their retirement, no map having been exhibited in evidence.

Provision of Tools/Measuring Equipment etc. Furthermore, if the jury ask to be supplied with tools or measuring equipment, great care must be taken to ensure that their intention is **D19.14**

not to conduct a private experiment germane to the issues in the case. In *Stewart* (1989) 89 Cr App R 273, the Court of Appeal held that the trial judge had erred in permitting the jury, at their request but without asking them why, to have a pair of scales. The case was one in which the weight of a quantity of drugs allegedly concealed in a holdall was highly relevant. In *Maggs* (1990) 91 Cr App R 243 Lord Lane CJ agreed that equipment that was required or designed to enable a jury to carry out unsupervised scientific experiments, such as the scales in *Stewart*, was not permissible. However, a magnifying glass or a ruler or a tape-measure were the kind of objects which any person might normally have in a pocket when called to serve on a jury, and therefore there could be no objection to using them in the jury room (see also *Crees* [1996] Crim LR 830).

In *Wallace* [1990] Crim LR 433, the usher supplied the jury in retirement with a dictionary, at their request, but without informing the judge. The jury had not understood what the judge had said about 'grievous' in 'grievous bodily harm'. After seeing the dictionary, they requested further guidance from the judge. The Court of Appeal held that it was an irregularity but not, in the circumstances, a material irregularity such as to lead to the quashing of the convictions.

In *McNamara* [1996] Crim LR 750, the Court of Appeal held that a request from the jury that the accused stand up in the dock and turn around (presumably so that they could perform a dock identification by comparison with video films seen during the trial) should have been treated as a request for further evidence, and was thus impermissible.

D19.15 **Jury's Own Specialist Knowledge or Researches** In *Fricker* (1999) *The Times*, 13 July 1999, the prohibition on new evidence after the jury's retirement was applied to specialist knowledge in the possession of one of the jurors. The Court of Appeal held that the trial judge had been wrong to rule that the jury had been entitled to take such specialist knowledge into account. It represented entirely new evidence, which neither party had had an opportunity to test. In these circumstances, it would have been appropriate to discharge the jury.

In *Marshall* [2007] EWCA Crim 35, evidence was found in the jury room, at the conclusion of the trial, which showed that at least one of the jurors had carried out research on the internet into the offences charged and the possible sentences they might attract. The Court of Appeal found this to be an irregularity but not, on the facts, a material one. However, Hughes LJ did observe (at [15]):

> ... the case underlines the importance of the direction which is conventionally given to jurors at the outset of the trial (and was given to this jury) to the general effect that the golden rule which they must apply is to try the case on the evidence alone which is what they hear in court and nothing else. That can, without drawing attention to any particular risks, conveniently be given in a form which reminds them first of the general rule, secondly of its application in a prohibition on discussion of the case with family, friends or anybody else, and quite often conveniently also with a reminder that private research, whether in the library or on the Internet, should be abjured.

See also the guidance in CrimPD VI, paras. 26M.5 to 26M.27 (see Supplement, **CPD.26M**), and the *Crown Court Compendium* (July 2020), ch. 2-4, for the approach to be adopted by the court; see also *A-G v Dallas* [2012] EWHC 156 (Admin), [2012] 1 WLR 991 for the penalties for disobedience by a juror of the injunction against research on the internet.

Repetition of Existing Evidence

D19.16 It is, of course, only new evidence which the jury may not have after retirement. The jury may be provided with items that have been exhibited in court. If the jury, after retirement, asks for any exhibits, the matter should be dealt with in open court. Counsel should be given an opportunity to ensure that the exhibits can properly go before the jury (*Ellis* (1991) 95 Cr App R 52; and see also *Devichand* [1991] Crim LR 446). In *Asgodom* [2012] EWCA Crim 2054, the fact that the electronic equipment in the jury room afforded a clearer CCTV image than the equipment used in court did not result in the jury having any new material in their retirement, and thus no unfairness flowed from this.

Application of this Rule to Tape Recordings In *Emmerson* (1991) 92 Cr App R 284, complaint was made on appeal that the trial judge had refused to provide the jury with the tape of E's interviews, which had been played at trial. The Court of Appeal held that the tape was evidence, becoming an exhibit on production by the officer, regardless of whether it was played during the trial. In *Riaz* (1991) 94 Cr App R 339, it was suggested that, if the jury ask to hear an exhibited tape, the better practice would be for the judge to order the court to reassemble, so that the jury could hear it in open court. The dictum to the contrary in *Emmerson* was disapproved. (For further detail on jury requests for tapes, see *Sardar* [2012] EWCA Crim 134 and **F8.56**.) **D19.17**

In relation to replaying evidence that was adduced at trial of an *ABE* interview of a complainant, three requirements were identified in *Rawlings* [1995] 2 Cr App R 222: (a) the replaying should occur in court with the parties present, (b) the jury should be warned to guard against giving the replayed evidence disproportionate weight and (c) the jury should also be reminded of relevant cross-examination in order to maintain balance. Providing the effect of these three requirements was met by a judge, failure to follow them exactly would not result in unfairness (*M (A)* [2015] EWCA Crim 1848).

In contrast, where CCTV or other audio/visual material has been adduced as part of the trial, the jury are entitled to view that material again in retirement, with equipment provided where possible to allow them to do that in their retiring room (CrimPD VI, para.26L.3; see Supplement, **CPD.26L**). The logical extension of the rule relating to the provision of measuring equipment (see **D19.14**) would permit them to use features of that equipment to slow down or zoom footage they have already watched.

Questions from the Jury

The jury are permitted to ask questions of the judge during their retirement. The normal method of so doing is to pass a note to the jury bailiff who takes it to the judge. In *Zulhayir* [2010] EWCA Crim 2272, the Court of Appeal stressed the need to time and date such notes. The procedure to be adopted in answering such questions was set out in *Gorman* [1987] 2 All ER 435. The object of the procedures is: (a) to remove any suspicion of private or secret communication between the court and jury, and (b) to enable the judge to assist the jury properly on any matter of law or fact which appears to be troubling them (per Lord Lane CJ at p. 546C; for the facts, see **D13.72**). **D19.18**

Lord Lane set out three propositions to assist judges who receive a note from a jury who have retired to consider their verdict (at pp. 550H–551B):

> First of all, if the communication raises something unconnected with the trial, for example a request that some message be sent to a relative of one of the jurors, it can simply be dealt with without any reference to counsel and without bringing the jury back to court.
>
> Secondly, in almost every other case a judge should state in open court the nature and content of the communication which he has received from the jury and, if he considers it helpful so to do, seek the assistance of counsel. This assistance will normally be sought before the jury is asked to return to court, and then, when the jury returns, the judge will deal with their communication.
>
> Exceptionally if, as in the present case, the communication from the jury contains information which the jury need not, and indeed should not, have imparted, such as details of voting figures... then, so far as possible the communication should be dealt with in the normal way, save that the judge should not disclose the detailed information which the jury ought not to have revealed.

In *Inns* [2018] EWCA Crim 1081, [2019] 1 Cr App R 5 (61) the Court of Appeal reminded judges that they should normally share the content of jury questions with counsel, and invite their view, before answering them.

D19.19 **Notes Not Relating to the Trial** As to the first proposition, the implication is that, since the jury's note does not concern the trial itself, it need not even be read in open court. Presumably any answer which needs to be given may be conveyed via the jury bailiff. However, to avoid any possible complaint, it is as well to inform defence counsel of what has occurred (*Connor* (1985) *The Times*, 26 June 1985; *Brown* [1998] Crim LR 505). As to the proper approach to notes relating to problems in the jury room, see **D13.70**.

D19.20 **Notes Relating to the Trial** Requiring notes connected with the trial to be read in open court, reflects a consistent line of authority going back to *Green* [1950] 1 All ER 38, in which Lord Goddard CJ said, 'any communication between a jury and the presiding judge must be read out in court, so that both parties, the prosecution and the defence, may know what the jury are asking and what is the judge's answer' (see also *Furlong* [1950] 1 All ER 636, *Townsend* [1982] 1 All ER 509 and *Rose* [1982] 2 All ER 536). In *Kachikwu* (1968) 52 Cr App R 538 at p. 541, it was further said by Winn LJ that, whenever a jury note is received, immediate steps should be taken to show it to counsel before it is put in the court archives. Whether to ask counsel for assistance about how the note should be answered is within the judge's discretion.

D19.21 **Answering a Note** In *Gorman* [1987] 2 All ER 435 (see **D19.18**), it was envisaged that the jury should return to court to be given the answer to any note, however simple the answer. However, earlier authorities indicate that this is a matter for the judge's discretion, and that there is no objection in principle to an answer being communicated by a note taken in by the jury bailiff, provided both the jury's note and the answer given are read out in open court. Thus, in *Lamb* (1974) 59 Cr App R 196, James LJ said (at p. 199):

> The practice should be that, on the court being informed by the jury bailiff of the jury's wish to make a request of the court or to communicate something to the court, the request or communication should either be delivered in writing to the court and the contents and any reply to be delivered through the bailiff, made known in public in court before delivery, or, the jury should be brought back into court to make the request themselves and the judge should answer their request in court.

D19.22 **Answering Only the Question Asked** The jury's usual aim in asking a question of the judge will be to seek assistance on a matter which is troubling them. As *Gascoigne* [1988] Crim LR 317 shows, the judge's response should be within strict limits, particularly as far as any new issue is concerned. In that case the judge, in answering a jury note, proceeded spontaneously to give a direction as to an issue which the prosecution had never raised. The Court of Appeal observed that it would seldom be proper for a trial judge to open up spontaneously with a jury, after they had deliberated for some time, an issue which had not been referred to in the trial or the summing-up.

It might be proper to give a supplementary direction, where a matter canvassed at trial had accidentally been omitted from the summing-up. If this were done, it must be carried out with the utmost caution. It was very much more difficult to envisage any occasion where an entirely new basis for conviction should be volunteered at such a late stage. If, in a very exceptional case, such a direction were to be volunteered, counsel must be given an opportunity to make submissions.

D19.23 **Exceptions to this Requirement** There are two exceptions to the rule that the judge should only answer the question which the jury has asked.

(1) Where the jury's question reveals that they have forgotten or failed to understand a crucial point, it is incumbent on the judge to remind them of it. In *Wickramaratne* [1998] Crim LR 565, it was apparent from the jury's question that they had failed to take the standard direction on the burden of proof on board. The Court of Appeal said that the trial judge should have reminded the jury in forcible terms of that important direction.
(2) Where the jury's question indicates that they are considering an irrelevant matter. The following cases provide examples:
   (a) Where the jury ask the judge if they are allowed to recommend leniency, the Court of Appeal have held that the judge must tell them that they must try the case on the evidence according to their oath and leave questions of penalty to the judge (*Sahota* [1979]

Crim LR 678; *Langham* [1996] Crim LR 430). The reason for this is that the jury might have been influenced by the fact that they could add a rider recommending leniency to come to a verdict which they might not otherwise have done.

(b) In *Thanki* (1991) 93 Cr App R 12, a note from the jury indicated that they suspected a diary, on which T relied, to be concocted. This had never been suggested by the prosecution. The court held that the accused should have been given an opportunity to meet this line of reasoning (presumably by means other than the production of evidence, in view of the prohibition on new evidence after the jury retires: see **D19.12**).

Notes Recording Voting Numbers Lord Lane CJ's third proposition (at **D19.18**) arose directly out of the ground of appeal in *Gorman* [1987] 2 All ER 435. The jury at G's first trial were discharged from giving a verdict after sending a note to the judge indicating that their 'voting' was split 9–3 for an acquittal. The judge simply told counsel that he had received a note that the jury were split, there was no prospect of them reaching a verdict, and, with counsels' agreement, the jury was discharged. The Court of Appeal concluded that there had been no irregularity in not revealing the content of the note, since the proportions in which the jury are split should not be revealed in open court, and the general rule that a jury note should be read out must therefore be qualified. In such circumstances, a judge should do as the judge did in *Gorman*, namely, give the gist of the note (i.e. the jury are split and unlikely to agree even if given more time) but keep secret that which the jury ought not to have communicated. **D19.24**

Status of a Jury Note A note from any juror is taken to be a note from the jury as a whole, and it was not appropriate to make inquiries as to which juror had written a particular note. This was stressed in *Obellim* [1997] 1 Cr App R 355. In that case a question from the jury caused the judge to suspect that its author might have previous convictions. The judge, without seeking the views of defence counsel, instigated inquiries into the identity of the juror in question, with a view to ascertaining whether he should have been disqualified from jury service. The Court of Appeal said that the only proper check the judge should have made was as to whether the proper inquiries had been made before the juror was called to jury service, and defence counsel should have been informed before even that check. **D19.25**

Consequences of Breach of the *Gorman* Procedure The consequences of failing to observe the procedures described above depend upon the gravity of the breach. It will only represent a material irregularity if it 'goes to the root of the case'. This is illustrated by a comparison of the Court of Appeal's decisions in *Green* [1950] 1 All ER 38 and *Furlong* [1950] 1 All ER 636. **D19.26**

(a) In *Green*, the jury's question and the judge's answer were never read in court at any stage and the judge could not even remember what the question had been about. This was a material irregularity.
(b) In *Furlong* the respective communications were publicly read, albeit after the verdict, and the answer the judge had given was clearly correct. No such irregularity was found.

Investigation of the Jury's Retirement

What occurs in the jury room during the course of the jury's deliberations is privileged. This is reinforced by the Juries Act 1974, s. 20D, which makes it an offence 'to disclose information about statements made, opinions expressed, arguments advanced or votes cast by members of a jury in the course of their deliberations in proceedings... or... to solicit or obtain such information' (see **B14.137**). Exceptions permit the judge to seek disclosure in order properly to regulate proceedings (s. 20E) and to permit alleged irregularities in the way the jury reached their verdict to be investigated either as a criminal offence or when a ground of appeal (s. 20F). **D19.27**

Inquiries Covered by the Prohibition In *Miah* [1997] 2 Cr App R 12, it was emphasised that the barrier to the Court of Appeal receiving material relating to the jury's deliberations was to be found in the common-law authorities (including *Ellis v Deheer* [1922] 2 KB 113 at p. 121) rather than in the Contempt of Court Act 1981. **D19.28**

Thompson [1962] 1 All ER 65 demonstrates strikingly the absolute nature of the rule that the Court of Appeal will not, metaphorically speaking, enter the jury room. The proposed ground of appeal was that the jury foreman had read to his colleagues a list of T's previous convictions which had somehow come into his possession. The Court of Criminal Appeal simply refused leave for the evidence of the irregularity to be adduced before them, because it would have breached the privacy of the jury room (see also *Schofield* [1993] Crim LR 217).

The decision in *Box* [1964] 1 QB 430, where the complaint also related to a juror's prior knowledge of the accused's character, demonstrates that if the bias can be established without calling evidence of the juror's conduct in the jury room the appeal is not invalid *ab initio* (see also **D13.49** and **F9.22**).

The prohibition applies to attempts to obtain information about proceedings in the jury room by the defence (*Mickleburgh* [1995] 1 Cr App R 297), the prosecution (*McCluskey* (1994) 98 Cr App R 216), or the court (*Schot* [1997] 2 Cr App R 383). Inquiries may be embarked upon only with the consent of the court, which, as the trial judge is *functus officio* after sentence, means the Court of Appeal (*McCluskey*).

D19.29 **Inquiries Outside the Prohibition** The prohibition does not extend to events outside the jury room, for example, in the hotel at which a jury is accommodated overnight. For example, in *Young* [1995] QB 324, some of the jurors met in a group and sought the assistance of a Ouija board as to the guilt of the accused. The Court of Appeal held that it could inquire into the incident, as it was not in the course of the jury's deliberation.

The Proper Approach to an Investigation

D19.30 The procedure for investigation of any jury irregularity is addressed in CrimPD VI, paras. 26M.41 to 26M.58 (see Supplement, **CPD.26M**). This procedure must be considered in accordance with the observations as to the confidentiality of jury deliberations of the House of Lords in *Mirza* [2004] UKHL 2, [2004] 1 AC 1118, and *Smith and Mercieca* [2005] UKHL 12, [2005] 2 Cr App R 10 (160).

D19.31 **The Approach in *Mirza*** Their lordships considered two conjoined cases in which letters after the trial indicated irregularities in the jury's deliberations. The Court of Appeal had dismissed both appeals on the basis that evidence as to what had been said by the jurors in private was inadmissible and contravened the Contempt of Court Act 1981, s. 8. Their lordships came to the following conclusions:

(a) The common-law principle prohibiting intrinsic evidence of jury deliberations was in accordance with the ECHR, Article 6. In so doing, they looked at the rationale for the rule of confidentiality, and concluded that it underpinned the independence and impartiality of the jury as a whole.
(b) Consequently, confidentiality reinforced the values in Article 6, and provided essential assistance for the jury to operate as a collective body impartially, and independently of outside influences.
(c) Section 8 of the Contempt of Court Act 1981 did not affect the duty of the trial court and the Court of Appeal to investigate any irregularity in the conduct of the jury within the limits of the common law so as to ensure that the accused received a fair trial.

Their lordships went on to advise that certain measures should be taken to strengthen the jury system. Jurors should be told to inform the court clerk or the judge in writing (either individually or collectively) if anything improper came to their notice. They should be reminded that what was said during their deliberations was confidential to them and could not be repeated or discussed outside the jury room. Their duty of confidentiality continued after the verdict. CrimPD VI, para. 26G.3 (see Supplement, **CPD.26G**), refers to the relevant directions.

D19.32 **The Approach in *Smith and Mercieca*** After the jury had retired and considered its verdict over some period of time, one of its members alleged in some detail that some jurors were disregarding the judge's directions on the law, were indulging in speculation contrary to his instructions and were engaging in a process of horse-trading, whereby some jurors were being pressed to return a guilty verdict on some counts in return for acquittal on others. The judge, with the agreement of counsel, gave the jury a further direction.

On appeal, it was suggested, *inter alia*, that the judge should have carried out an investigation into the alleged irregularities in the jury room. The Court of Appeal (prior to the judgment of the House of Lords in *Mirza* [2004] UKHL 2, [2004] 1 AC 1118) held that he was precluded from doing so by the Contempt of Court Act 1981, s. 8(1). As a result, the judge was faced with the alternative of discharging the jury or giving a further direction, and could not be criticised for choosing the latter course, particularly since counsel had agreed to it.

On appeal to the House of Lords, it was held that the judge was not obliged as a matter of law in these circumstances to investigate events in the jury room. The common-law prohibition against inquiring into such events certainly extended to matters connected with the subject-matter of the jury's deliberations, and nothing in the opinions in *Mirza* casts doubt upon that basic proposition. Further, their lordships were of the opinion that it would not have been appropriate for the judge to question the jurors about the content of the letter, given that such a course of action would have been likely to make the situation worse. The judge was left with a choice of discharging the jury or giving them a further direction emphasising their duties. He was entitled to adopt the latter course, providing that the direction given was sufficiently comprehensive and emphatic.

In *Adams* [2007] EWCA Crim 1, [2007] 1 Cr App R 34 (449), the Court of Appeal identified the approach that should be taken where, on appeal, it was necessary to make inquiries of the jury. It was stressed that such a course was exceptional (see also **D13.51**).

Relationship of Jury Room Restrictions to Freedom of Expression

In *A-G v Scotcher* [2005] UKHL 36, [2005] 2 Cr App R 35 (573), D was prosecuted under the Contempt of Court Act 1981, s. 8(1). He had served on a jury which convicted the defendants by a majority. The day after the end of the trial, he wrote to their mother informing her of the discussions which had taken place in the jury room, which he felt would show that the verdict was unsafe. **D19.33**

The Divisional Court held that it was not a defence for a juror to show that he had disclosed the jury's deliberations with the bona fide aim of preventing a miscarriage of justice. The House of Lords, which dismissed his appeal, held that D had been in contempt of court in writing to a third party but he would have been entitled to communicate with the Crown Court, the jury bailiff or the clerk of the court, or to have raised the matter directly with the Court of Appeal. Although the appellant's right to freedom of expression under the ECHR, Article 10(1), had been engaged, it was subject to a restriction which was prescribed by law and necessary in a democratic society for preventing the disclosure of information received in confidence. The rule governing the secrecy of jury deliberations was a crucial and legitimate feature of English trial law, with the result that the limitation placed on the juror's freedom of expression was justified.

TYPES OF VERDICT

Before considering the method by which the jury return their verdict, it is necessary to consider the different types of verdict available to them. As was made clear at **D18.43**, CrimPD VI, para. 26K.1 (see Supplement, **CPD.26K**), instructs judges that they 'should' direct the jury on unanimous verdicts. In circumstances identified below, a jury may return a verdict that represents the view only of the majority (see **D19.35**), or return a verdict in relation to an offence in the alternative to the one charged (see **D19.41**). In *Hopkinson* [2013] EWCA Crim 795, [2014] 1 Cr App R 3 (22), the Court of Appeal repeated that the taking of special verdicts, by which the jury were required to indicate the basis for their finding of guilt, should only be used in the context of a trial for murder where there were a number of alternative defences, such as loss of control or diminished responsibility available, and even then only rarely. **D19.34**

MAJORITY VERDICTS

D19.35 At common law, the verdict of a jury had to be unanimous. This was qualified by what is now the Juries Act 1974, s. 17 (set out at the end of **D19.40**). By s. 17(1) some majority verdicts are permissible, subject to certain conditions being satisfied. The procedure for taking majority verdicts is set out in CrimPR 25.14(5) (see Supplement, **R25.14**) and CrimPD VI, paras. 26Q.1 to 26Q.9 (see Supplement, **CPD.26Q**).

Time Requirement

D19.36 A majority verdict may not be accepted unless the jury have been considering their verdict for such period as the court considers reasonable having regard to the nature and complexity of the case, being in any event a period of not less than two hours (Juries Act 1974, s. 17(4)). Any period during which the jury return to court to ask a question of or receive a communication from the judge should be included when computing the two hours (*Adams* [1969] 3 All ER 437).

Time spent not actually deliberating, for example in making their way to the jury room and electing a foreman, is catered for by CrimPD VI, para. 26Q.3 (see Supplement, **CPD.26Q**), which states that the jury should be allowed at least two hours and ten minutes for deliberation before the majority direction is given. CrimPD. VI, para. 26Q.7 addresses the considerations to be applied by a trial judge as to when to take any unanimous verdicts before giving the majority direction for the remaining counts.

D19.37 **Application of the Time Requirement** It is unusual for judges to invite a majority verdict at the earliest moment permitted. However, the time allowed before the majority verdict procedure is set in motion is a matter for the trial judge's discretion, depending largely on the complexity of the case. This is demonstrated by cases such as the following.

In *Wright* (1974) 58 Cr App R 444, following a five-day trial for murder, the judge had the jury back after a bare two hours, told them he could now accept a majority verdict, and asked them to retire for a short time to consider the matter. This was clearly a breach of the *Practice Direction* guidance then applicable, but that is directory only, not mandatory (see **D19.40**). On appeal the majority conviction was found to be lawful because (a) there had been no breach of the Juries Act 1974, s. 17, itself, and (b) the judge had not unjustifiably rushed the jury into a majority verdict. Although the case had been relatively long, the issue was a very simple one, namely whether the jury were satisfied that W's confession to the police had been genuine. In the circumstances, allowing the jury a longer time to reach unanimity would not have helped.

In *Rose* [1982] 2 All ER 536, the Court of Appeal indicated that a period of two hours and 40 minutes was 'a little soon' for the majority verdict direction in a murder trial which had lasted for 15 days.

Minimum Number for Acceptable Majority

D19.38 By the Juries Act 1974, s. 17(1), the minimum majorities permissible are 11–1 or 10–2, or (in the case of a jury from which one or more of the original jurors have been discharged) 10–1 or 9–1. A jury reduced to nine must be unanimous.

Statement of Size of Majority and Minority in Open Court

D19.39 If (and only if) the verdict is guilty, the foreman of the jury must state in open court the number of jurors who respectively agreed to and dissented from the verdict (Juries Act 1974, s. 17(3)).

Since stating the size of a majority for conviction is expressed as a precondition of the court accepting the verdict, failure to comply with s. 17(3) will result in any purported conviction being quashed (*Barry* [1975] 2 All ER 760; *Austin* [2002] EWCA Crim 1796). However, it is sufficient for compliance with s. 17(3) if, as happened in *Pigg* [1983] 1 All ER 56, the foreman states the number in the majority leaving the size of the minority to be inferred by the simplest of arithmetic. In *Pigg*, Lord Brandon of Oakbrook (with whose speech all the other Law Lords concurred) stated the position thus (at p. 13G–H, emphasis added):

> . . . compliance with the requirement of section 17(3) of the Act of 1974 is mandatory before a judge can accept a majority verdict of guilty; but the precise form of words used by the clerk of the court when asking questions of the foreman of the jury, and the precise form of words used by the latter in answer to such questions, *as long as they make it clear to an ordinary person how the jury was divided*, do not constitute any essential part of that requirement.

Effect of Failure to Comply

The effect of non-compliance with the procedures described above varies depending on whether the non-compliance amounts to a breach of the Juries Act 1974, s. 17, or is merely a breach of CrimPD VI, paras. 26Q.1 to 26Q.9 (see Supplement, **CPD.26Q**). **D19.40**

In the former case, since the court's power to accept a majority verdict depends entirely upon the statutory provision, any conviction must be quashed (*Barry* [1975] 2 All ER 760; *Pigg* [1983] 1 All ER 56).

If, on the other hand, there has been failure to comply with paras. 39Q.1 to 39Q.9 and nothing more, the conviction may stand since the direction is (as the name implies) directory not mandatory (*Wright* (1974) 58 Cr App R 444; *Shields* [1997] Crim LR 758). The Court of Appeal has, however, stressed the importance of following the directions closely (*Georgiou* (1969) 53 Cr App R 428). The Court of Appeal in *Arthur* [2013] EWCA Crim 1852 underlined the importance of following the Judicial Studies Board wording for a majority direction, so that no pressure was placed on, or perceived to be placed on, the jury when that direction was given. The trial judge had erroneously included words in his direction that had the effect of giving a partial *Watson* direction as part of the majority direction. Such a merging of the two directions was undesirable (but see *Scully* [2013] EWCA Crim 2288 where a contrary conclusion was reached).

Juries Act 1974, s. 17

(1) Subject to subsections (3) and (4) below, the verdict of a jury in proceedings in the Crown Court . . . need not be unanimous if—
  (a) in a case where there are not less than 11 jurors, 10 of them agree on the verdict; and
  (b) in a case where there are 10 jurors, nine of them agree on the verdict.

. . .

(3) The Crown Court shall not accept a verdict of guilty by virtue of subsection (1) above unless the foreman of the jury has stated in open court the number of jurors who respectively agreed to and dissented from the verdict.

(4) No court shall accept a verdict by virtue of subsection (1) . . . above unless it appears to the court that the jury have had such period of time for deliberation as the court thinks reasonable having regard to the nature and complexity of the case; and the Crown Court shall in any event not accept such a verdict unless it appears to the court that the jury have had at least two hours for deliberation.

VERDICT OF GUILTY OF AN ALTERNATIVE OFFENCE

It is sometimes open to a jury to find the accused not guilty of the offence alleged in a count but guilty of some other alternative offence. This is commonly referred to as a verdict of guilty of a lesser offence. **D19.41**

At common law, a jury could find an accused guilty of a lesser offence if the definition of the greater offence charged necessarily included the definition of the lesser. However, the enactment of a number of statutory provisions has considerably broadened the situations in which alternative verdicts are now permitted. Although the decision of the House of Lords in *Saunders* [1988] AC 148 demonstrates that there is still a residual role for the common law to play, this discussion of alternative verdicts proceeds on the basis that the law is now to be found in statute.

General Rule

D19.42 The general provision on the availability of alternative verdicts is contained in the CLA 1967, s. 6(3), which provides as follows:

> Where, on a person's trial on indictment for any offence except treason or murder, the jury find him not guilty of the offence specifically charged in the indictment, but the allegations in the indictment amount to or include (expressly or by implication) an allegation of another offence falling within the jurisdiction of the court of trial, the jury may find him guilty of that other offence or of an offence of which he could be found guilty on an indictment specifically charging that other offence.

There are thus two principal situations covered by s. 6(3). One is where the offence charged *expressly* includes an allegation of another indictable offence; the other is where it *impliedly* includes such an allegation.

Express Allegation of Another Offence

D19.43 To determine whether a count expressly includes an allegation of another offence it is necessary to apply a 'blue-pencil test'. This involves striking from the particulars of the count in the indictment the allegations that the prosecution evidence cannot or may not be able to sustain and, if what remains is a valid count for another offence, that alternative may be left for the jury's consideration (*Lillis* [1972] 2 QB 236).

For example, in *Lillis*, the particulars of a count for burglary contrary to the Theft Act 1968, s. 9(1)(b), alleged that D, on a certain date, entered part of a building, and stole therein a lawnmower. However, the complaint of the owners was not that D had taken the mower in the first place but that he had failed to return it when he should have done. Although a submission of no case to answer on the charge of burglary inevitably succeeded, the judge held that there was a case to answer for theft by keeping, and he left that alternative verdict to the jury, who convicted. On appeal, the Court of Appeal applied the 'blue-pencil test', notionally striking from the count those allegations the prosecution could not prove. What remained were the particulars: 'D stole a lawn-mower'. As this was sufficient to satisfy the Indictment Rules 1971 for a count of theft, the alternative verdict had been open to the jury.

The *Lillis* test was approved by the House of Lords in their decision in *Metropolitan Police Commissioner v Wilson* [1984] AC 242.

Implied Allegation of another Offence

D19.44 There have been two distinct tests promulgated by the appellate courts for determining when a count impliedly includes an allegation of another offence. The first test was laid down by Sachs LJ in *Springfield* (1969) 53 Cr App R 608 ('the *Springfield* test'), and the second, less restrictive test was laid down by Lord Roskill in *Metropolitan Police Commissioner v Wilson* [1984] AC 242 ('the *Wilson* test').

D19.45 **The *Springfield* Test** Sachs LJ's test in *Springfield* (1969) 53 Cr App R 608 was that a count for offence A impliedly contains an allegation of offence B if, and only if, the commission of offence B is a necessary step towards committing offence A. There were two qualifications to this test:

(a) the court was entitled to look only at the wording of the count and the legal definitions of the offence in the count and the suggested alternative — therefore, if there was any possibility in law that the accused could have committed the 'count' offence without committing the alternative, the latter could not be left to the jury;
(b) it was irrelevant that the prosecution case was that the accused had in fact committed both offences.

Application of the *Springfield* Test Since it has been overtaken by the *Wilson* test, applications of the *Springfield* test are now of limited assistance. However, those cases which would still be decided the same way include the following. **D19.46**

(a) In *Hodgson* [1973] QB 565, it was held that a jury may, on a count of rape, convict of indecent assault. This is because the allegation of rape impliedly includes both an allegation of an assault and an allegation of indecency. This has application only where the victim is under 16 and the accused cannot rely on consent as a defence, otherwise consent would be a complete defence to the charge and no alternative would be needed.
(b) In *McCready* [1978] 3 All ER 967, it was held that, on a count for causing grievous bodily harm with intent contrary to the OAPA 1861, s. 18, the jury may not convict either of malicious wounding contrary to s. 20 of the Act or of any form of assault. This is because harm can be caused within the meaning of s. 18 without there having been either an application of force or a wounding. On the other hand, if the count under s. 18 is for wounding, the alternatives mentioned above would be open to the jury since an assault is a necessary step towards a wounding, while an allegation of wounding with intent to do grievous bodily harm expressly includes an allegation of malicious wounding.

The *Wilson* Test The *Springfield* test was disapproved by Lord Roskill in *Metropolitan Police Commissioner v Wilson* [1984] AC 242. The question raised in that case was whether a count for inflicting grievous bodily harm impliedly includes an allegation of assault occasioning actual bodily harm. An allegation that grievous bodily harm occurred obviously and probably expressly includes an allegation that there was actual bodily harm (p. 259C). But do the words 'inflicting harm' impliedly include assault? The crucial passage from Lord Roskill's speech is at pp. 260H–261B: **D19.47**

> The critical question is, therefore, whether it being accepted that a charge of inflicting grievous bodily harm contrary to section 20 [of the Offences Against the Person Act 1861] may not necessarily involve an allegation of assault, but may nonetheless do so, and in very many cases will involve such an allegation, the allegations in a section 20 charge 'include either expressly or by implication' allegations of assault occasioning actual bodily harm. If 'inflicting' can, as the cases show, include 'inflicting by assault', then even though such a charge may not necessarily do so, I do not for myself see why on a fair reading of section 6(3) these allegations do not at least impliedly *include* 'inflicting by assault'. That is sufficient for present purposes though I also regard it as also a possible view that those former allegations *expressly* include the other allegations.

Lord Roskill then held that the reasoning in *Springfield* should no longer be followed. Instead the test is that an allegation of the latter offence is impliedly included in the count where commission of the offence alleged in a count may involve commission of another offence, even if it is possible in law for the one offence to be committed without commission of the other.

Applications of the *Wilson* Test Applications of the *Wilson* test include: **D19.48**

(a) In *Metropolitan Police Commissioner v Wilson* [1984] AC 242 itself, the House of Lords restored W's conviction for assault occasioning actual bodily harm on a count alleging inflicting grievous bodily harm contrary to the OAPA 1861, s. 20 (the Court of Appeal, applying the *Springfield* test, had quashed the conviction).
(b) Similarly, in *Jenkins* (which was heard with *Wilson*), a conviction for actual bodily harm was restored on a count alleging burglary contrary to the Theft Act 1968, s. 9(1)(b), in that J, having entered a building as a trespasser, inflicted grievous bodily harm on a person therein.
(c) In *Savage* [1992] 1 AC 699, the House of Lords held that a verdict of assault occasioning actual bodily harm is a permissible alternative verdict on a count alleging unlawful wounding contrary to the OAPA 1861, s. 20.
(d) In *Whiting* (1987) 85 Cr App R 78, the Court of Appeal held that on a count for burglary contrary to the Theft Act 1968, s. 9(1)(b), where the allegation is that the accused, having entered as a trespasser, stole certain property, the jury may convict of entry as a trespasser with intent to steal contrary to s. 9(1)(a).

(e) In *Mandair* [1995] 1 AC 208, the House of Lords held that 'causing' grievous bodily harm contrary to the OAPA 1861, s. 18, was wide enough to include any action that could amount to inflicting grievous bodily harm under s. 20. *Metropolitan Police Commissioner v Wilson* was applied, and *Field* (1993) 97 Cr App R 357 overruled.

(f) In *Morrison* [2003] EWCA Crim 1722, [2003] 1 WLR 1859, the Court of Appeal held that an allegation of attempted murder necessarily involves an allegation of attempt to cause grievous bodily harm, since the act of killing inevitably involves causing serious injury.

Specific Statutory Provisions Relating to Alternative Verdicts

D19.49 The CLA 1967, s. 6(3), is supplemented by a number of other provisions prescribing the alternative verdicts which may be returned on counts for certain specific offences.

D19.50 **Murder** Section 6(2) of the CLA 1967 provides that:

> On an indictment for murder a person found not guilty of murder may be found guilty—
> (a) of manslaughter, or of causing grievous bodily harm with intent to do so; or
> (b) of any offence of which he may be found guilty under an enactment specifically so providing, or under section 14(2) of this Act; or
> (c) of an attempt to commit murder, or of an attempt to commit any other offence of which he might be found guilty; but may not be found guilty of any offence not included above.

Paragraph (b) of the subsection preserves the effect of the Infanticide Act 1938, s. 1(2) (upon the trial of a woman for murder or manslaughter of her newly born child the jury may convict of infanticide), and of the Infant Life (Preservation) Act 1929, s. 2(2) (upon a trial for, *inter alia*, murder of a child the jury may convict of child destruction).

D19.51 **Assisting Offenders** By the CLA 1967, s. 4(2), if the jury are satisfied that the offence with which the accused is charged (or some other offence of which the accused might be found guilty on that charge) has been committed by someone, but they find the accused not guilty of it, they may, by way of alternative verdict, find the accused guilty of assisting whoever the offender was contrary to s. 4(1) of the Act.

It has been held that, where it can be foreseen that a charge under s. 4(1) might be a proper way of dealing with the accused's case, the prosecution should not invoke s. 4(2) to put the matter before the jury but should have a separate count for assisting an offender (*Cross* [1971] 3 All ER 641). If, however, the possibility of a conviction under s. 4(1) only arises during the course of the case, then the prosecution are entitled to rely on s. 4(2), although they should still apply to amend the indictment to add an appropriate count before the evidence has been completed so that the defence have a fair opportunity of dealing with the new allegation (*Cross* and see also *Vincent* (1972) 56 Cr App R 281).

D19.52 **Attempts** By the CLA 1967, s. 6(4), 'any allegation of an offence shall be taken as including an allegation of attempting to commit that offence'. It follows that, whenever charged with a completed indictable offence, the accused may be convicted of an attempt to commit that offence. Moreover, when s. 6(3) is read in conjunction with s. 6(4), the accused may be convicted of an attempt to commit any other completed offence of which he or she could be found guilty on the count.

Conversely, under the second limb of s. 6(4), if the accused is charged merely with an attempt (or with any assault or other act preliminary to an offence, such as assault with intent to rob) but the evidence in fact establishes the completed offence, the accused may be convicted as charged. The court retains the discretion to discharge the jury or otherwise act with a view to the preferment of an indictment for the completed offence.

D19.53 **Driving Offences** The Road Traffic Offenders Act 1988, s. 24, makes provision for the alternative verdicts which may be returned where a person is tried for certain offences contrary to the Road Traffic Act 1988 (see **C2.8**).

Offences under the Public Order Act 1986 By the Public Order Act 1986, s. 7, if a jury find the accused not guilty on a count for either violent disorder (contrary to s. 2 of the Act) or affray (contrary to s. 3), they may (without prejudice to the CLA 1967, s. 6(3)) find the accused guilty of the summary offence of threatening behaviour contrary to s. 4 of the 1986 Act. **D19.54**

In addition, because the offences under ss. 1, 2 and 3 of the 1986 Act (riot, violent disorder and affray) are in descending order of gravity, s. 6(3) of the CLA 1967 would have the result that a count under s. 1 will expressly or impliedly include an allegation of offences under the other two sections. Similarly, a count under s. 2 will include an allegation under s. 3.

Taking a Motor Vehicle without the Owner's Consent If, on a count for theft, the jury are not satisfied that the accused committed the offence charged, but it is proved that the accused committed an offence under the Theft Act 1968, s. 12(1) (taking a motor vehicle without the owner's consent etc.), they may convict the accused of the latter offence (Theft Act 1968, s. 12(4)). **D19.55**

Common Assault Until the CJA 1988, s. 40, came into force, a person charged under the OAPA 1861, s. 47, with assault occasioning actual bodily harm could be convicted, as an alternative, of common assault. This followed from the CLA 1967, s. 6(3), and was the case whether or not there was a specific allegation of common assault as an alternative in the indictment. **D19.56**

By the CJA 1988, s. 40 (see **D11.17**), common assault became a summary offence. As a result, in *Mearns* [1991] 1 QB 82, it was held that common assault was not within the jurisdiction of the Crown Court, unless a specific count alleging that offence was added to the indictment. The position is now covered by the DVCVA 2004, s. 11 (see **D19.57**).

Other Offences Listed in the CJA 1988, s. 40 In *Mearns* [1991] 1 QB 82, it was suggested that all the offences listed in s. 40 were excluded as alternative offences, unless specific counts were added. The position was altered, however, as a result of the DVCVA 2004, s. 11. This inserted subsections (3A) and (3B) in s. 6 of the CLA 1967, which provide that an offence falls within the jurisdiction of the Crown Court if it is an offence to which s. 40 of the CJA 1988 applies, even if a count specifying it is not included in the indictment. **D19.57**

Judge's Judgment in Directing Jury as to Alternative Offences

The judge in summing-up is not obliged to direct the jury about the option of finding the accused guilty of an alternative offence, even if that option is available to them as a matter of law. If, however, the possibility that the accused is guilty only of a lesser offence has been obviously raised by the evidence, the judge should, in the interests of justice, leave the alternative to the jury. This is the case even if neither prosecution nor defence counsel wishes the alternative offence to be left to the jury (*Coutts* [2006] UKHL 39, [2007] 1 Cr App R 6 (60), followed in *Brown* [2014] EWCA Crim 2176, but see *Brown* [2011] EWCA Crim 1606). It is important for the court to leave an alternative which does not require proof of specific intent where such intent was required for the charge on the indictment (*Hodson* [2009] EWCA Crim 1590; *Foster* [2009] EWCA Crim 2214; *Johnson* [2013] EWCA Crim 2001). The court should not take the initiative to add an alternative charge after the accused has given evidence (*B (JJ)* [2012] EWCA Crim 1440). **D19.58**

Considerations Relevant to the Exercise of that Judgment The judge's Judgment in relation to alternative verdicts is usually invoked to protect the accused against being prejudiced by the unexpected introduction at a late stage of the trial of a suggestion that the accused is guilty on a charge that has never been expressly preferred and which there has been no fair opportunity of countering in the course of the defence. Thus, in *Metropolitan Police Commissioner v Wilson* [1984] AC 242, Lord Roskill rejected the defence argument that the extension of the availability of alternative verdicts implied in the abandonment of the *Springfield* test (see **D19.45**) might result in injustice by referring to the judge's discretion. His lordship said (at p. 261F): **D19.59**

> If it be said that [our conclusion in this case] exposes the defendant to the risk of conviction on a charge which would not have been fully investigated at the trial on the count in the indictment, the answer is that a trial judge must always ensure, before deciding to leave the possibility of conviction of another offence to the jury under section 6(3) [of the CLA 1967], that that course will involve no risk of injustice to the defendant and that he has had the opportunity of fully meeting that alternative in the course of his defence.

The proper approach to the exercise of the judge's discretion in this regard is further illustrated in a number of appellate decisions. In *M* [2019] EWCA Crim 1094, the Court of Appeal identified factors relevant to the judgment as to whether a lesser alternative should be left (see **D19.64**).

D19.60 **Exercise of the Discretion in *Fairbanks*** The exercise of the judge's discretion in relation to alternative verdicts was further considered by the Court of Appeal in *Fairbanks* [1986] 1 WLR 1202, in the context of the defence wanting the alternative of careless driving to be left to the jury at a trial for causing death by reckless driving. The judge had declined the request and the jury were directed to put out of their minds categories of bad driving other than recklessness. The jury, having sent a note indicating that they might have wanted to convict of careless driving, found D guilty as charged. On appeal, having reviewed the earlier authorities (*Vaughan* (1908) 1 Cr App R 25; *Naylor* (1910) 5 Cr App R 19; *Parrott* (1913) 8 Cr App R 186), Mustill LJ said that an alternative offence should be left to the jury 'only if that is in the interests of justice' (at p. 1205H).

D19.61 The application of this test involved a number of possibilities:

(a) Since justice serves the interests of the public as well as those of the accused, there will be cases where, on the evidence, the accused *ought* to be convicted of at least the lesser offence and it would be wrong for the jury to acquit entirely merely because they cannot be sure that the accused is guilty as charged (at p. 1206D). In such cases the alternative should be left.
(b) Where, on the other hand, the lesser verdict simply did not arise given the way the case had been presented to the court (e.g., the defence was one of alibi), or where it might have arisen had a certain line of questioning been pursued but that had not in fact happened and the possible alternative had therefore ceased to be a live issue, it will be wrong to direct the jury about the alternative.
(c) Similarly, if the possible alternative is very trivial by comparison with the offence charged, introducing it will be an unnecessary and undesirable complication.

Applying those principles to the facts of *Fairbanks*, the judge erred by failing to direct the jury that they could return a verdict of careless driving. A verdict of not guilty of causing death by reckless driving but guilty of driving without due care and attention was a verdict at which a 'conscientious jury could properly arrive on the evidence', and it should have been available to them notwithstanding that they might use it as a bolt-hole to avoid facing up to the hard decision of whether the accused had been reckless. (See also *M* [2019] EWCA Crim 1094, at **D19.64**.)

D19.62 **Exercise of the Discretion in *Maxwell*** The decision in *Fairbanks* was approved by the House of Lords in *Maxwell* [1990] 1 All ER 801. D, who was charged with robbery, asserted that he was guilty of burglary, but denied that he had intended any violence to the victims. The prosecution declined to apply to amend the indictment to include a count of burglary and the judge directed the jury that they were not entitled to bring in a verdict in relation to burglary. The jury could have been directed that they were entitled to bring in a verdict of guilty to the even lesser charge of theft, but the judge did not deal with that possibility.

On appeal to the House of Lords, it was held that:

(a) the prosecution were entitled, on the evidence, to take the view that the jury should not be distracted by an inappropriate alternative count of burglary;
(b) the judge had been entitled to accept that view;
(c) the judge had been entitled to decline to leave the alternative of theft to the jury since it was relatively trifling, and the essential issue was: did D intend violence to be used?

Lord Ackner, with whose reasons the other Law Lords agreed, stated the test, in cases where the judge has failed to leave an alternative offence to the jury, as follows (at p. 408F):

> ... the court, before interfering with the verdict, must be satisfied that the jury may have convicted out of a reluctance to see the defendant get clean away with what, on any view, was disgraceful conduct. If they are so satisfied then the conviction cannot be safe or satisfactory.

Maxwell was followed in *Cambray* [2006] EWCA Crim 1708, [2007] RTR 10 (128).

Exercise of the Discretion in *Coutts* The Court of Appeal and House of Lords judgments in *Coutts* [2005] EWCA Crim 52, [2005] 1 WLR 1605 and [2006] UKHL 39, [2007] 1 Cr App R 6 (60) clash. **D19.63**

D was charged with murder. His defence was that the death had been a tragic accident. The parties agreed that it would be unfair to direct the jury on manslaughter, and the trial judge did not direct the jury on manslaughter. D was convicted, and appealed on the basis that the judge should have directed the jury on manslaughter. The House of Lords allowed the appeal.

Lord Bingham, with whom the other Law Lords agreed, stated that, while the murder count against the appellant was clearly a strong one, no appellate court could be sure that a jury to whom the alternative count had been left, would not have convicted of manslaughter. He stated the principle in this way:

> The public interest in the administration of justice is, in my opinion, best served if in any trial on indictment the trial judge leaves to the jury, subject to any appropriate caution or warning, but irrespective of the wishes of trial counsel, any obvious alternative offence which there is evidence to support. I would not extend the rule to summary proceedings since, for all their potential importance to individuals, they do not engage the public interest to the same degree. I would also confine the rule to alternative verdicts obviously raised by the evidence: by that I refer to alternatives which should suggest themselves to the mind of any ordinarily knowledgeable and alert criminal judge, excluding alternatives which ingenious counsel may identify through diligent research after the trial. Application of this rule may in some cases benefit the defendant, protecting him against an excessive conviction. In other cases it may benefit the public, by providing for the conviction of a lawbreaker who deserves punishment. A defendant may, quite reasonably from his point of view, choose to roll the dice. But the interests of society should not depend on such a contingency... Nor, with respect, is it an objection that the jury's task would have been more complicated had a manslaughter direction been given. Compared with many directions given to juries, a manslaughter direction in this case would not have been complicated. But even if it would, that cannot be relied on as a reason for not leaving to the jury a verdict which they should on the facts have considered. If juries are to continue to command the respect of the public, they must be trusted to understand the issues raised even by a case of some complexity. For reasons already given, the wishes of counsel cannot override the judge's duty.

Doubt was cast, in the course of the opinions delivered by members of the House of Lords in *Coutts*, on the test for an appellate court to apply, as set out in *Maxwell* [1990] 1 All ER 801 (see **D19.62**). Lord Hutton said that 'that approach is an unsatisfactory one and should no longer be taken'. As Lord Roger put it: **D19.64**

> Since the appeal court cannot inquire into what went on in the jury room, it is very far from clear how they are meant to satisfy themselves in any given case that a jury may have convicted out of a reluctance to see the defendant get clean away.

Coutts was applied by the Court of Appeal in *Foster* [2007] EWCA Crim 2869, [2008] 1 Cr App R 38 (470). It was emphasised that it would not always be appropriate for an alternative verdict to be left to the jury. It would depend on considerations of fairness, including the potential disadvantage to the accused if no alternative verdict was available, and the proportionality of the alternative verdict to the conduct alleged.

In *M* [2019] EWCA Crim 1094 the Court of Appeal, having considered *Coutts* [2006] UKHL 39, [2007] 1 Cr App R 6 (60), made clear that there was no requirement that a lesser alternative always be left to the jury whenever it was a possibility. It involved consideration of factors such as the evidence adduced or to be adduced at trial, whether the leaving of an alternative will assist or complicate the jury's task, and whether the leaving of the alternative will be fair to the accused or otherwise.

D19.65 **Consideration of the ECHR** The need for the judge to exercise his or her discretion in such a way as to ensure that the accused is not prejudiced by the unexpected introduction of an alternative offence has been underlined by the ECtHR in *Pelissier and Sassi v France* (2000) 30 EHRR 715. In that case, the defendants, who had been acquitted of the substantive offence of criminal bankruptcy, were convicted on the prosecution's appeal of aiding and abetting the substantive offence. It was not contested that the French court had the power so to do, but it had violated the ECHR, Article 6, by doing so without the possibility having been properly raised in advance of the judgment.

D19.66 **Discussion in Advance with Counsel** At the very least, a judge intending to leave an alternative verdict to the jury should warn counsel beforehand and should give them the opportunity of making representations about the propriety or otherwise of the proposed course (*Hazell* [1985] RTR 369). Counsel should also have an opportunity to address the jury about the alternative verdict, assuming it is to be left (*Hazell*).

In appropriate cases, giving the defence a fair opportunity to deal with an alternative verdict will involve drawing counsel's attention to the possibility of such a verdict before the close of defence evidence. In *Harris* (1993) *The Times*, 22 March 1993, for example, Steyn LJ in the Court of Appeal stated that it was appropriate to leave an alternative offence to the jury only if the accused had a full opportunity to meet the revised case so as to ensure no prejudice. See also *Griffiths* [2005] EWCA Crim 237.

It is generally assumed that, if the judge does not direct the jury about an alternative verdict or even (as in *Fairbanks* [1986] 1 WLR 1202) expressly tells them to ignore the possibility, they will be guided by the judge and either find the accused guilty as charged or acquit. However, in *Carter* [1964] 2 QB 1, a conviction for a lesser offence was upheld where prosecuting counsel had told the jury that the verdict was available but the judge made no reference to it in summing-up. In order to avoid criticism for flouting the judge's authority, it would seem advisable for counsel first to raise the issue in the absence of the jury after the close of the evidence.

Procedure where the Jury are Unable to Agree that the Accused is Not Guilty as Charged

D19.67 The CLA 1967, ss. 4(2) and 6(2) and (3), make it a precondition of the jury convicting of an alternative offence that they should first find the accused not guilty of the offence specifically charged in the indictment. Where they cannot so agree, the clear wording of the legislation demonstrates that they are not entitled to return a verdict of guilty of the lesser offence. This could lead to the absurd result that the jury would be discharged from giving any verdict whatsoever when they are agreed that the accused is guilty of something.

The solution to this problem reached by the cases is by no means satisfactory. It was held in *Collison* (1980) 71 Cr App R 249 that if the possibility of an alternative verdict arose under the CLA 1967, s. 6(3) (the general provision), the judge, upon being informed that the jury cannot agree as to the greater offence but are agreed on the lesser, could and should amend the indictment by adding a separate count for the lesser offence. A verdict could then be taken on the added count and the jury discharged from giving a verdict on the other.

In *Foster* [2007] EWCA Crim 2869, [2008] 1 Cr App R 38 (470), the Court of Appeal considered the circumstances in which it would be appropriate to add counts to an indictment in relation to potential alternative verdicts. The Court observed that the indictment represented a statement of the charges on which the prosecution, rather than the court, sought a conviction, and that substantial amendment to the indictment at a very late stage in proceedings was liable to obscure the issues relied on by the parties and complicate the jury's task.

Role of the Common Law in the Light of *Saunders* In *Saunders* [1988] AC 148, in contrast to *Collison* (1980) 71 Cr App R 249, it was the effect of the CLA 1967, s. 6(2), that was in issue. The indictment charged murder only, but it became apparent towards the end of the jury's retirement that they had concluded that D was at least guilty of manslaughter. The judge took a verdict of guilty of manslaughter, although no separate count for manslaughter had been added, and discharged the jury from giving a verdict in respect of murder. The House of Lords held that an additional count of manslaughter was unnecessary. Prior to the enactment of the CLA 1967, alternative verdicts of manslaughter on a charge of murder had always been allowed by common law. The provisions of the Act did not abrogate the common law but were merely intended to deal with a procedural problem highlighted in *DPP v Nasralla* [1967] 2 AC 238, namely, whether the judge could ask for a verdict as to manslaughter if the jury had initially announced a verdict of not guilty *simpliciter*. Section 6(2) confirmed that this was possible. However, in situations not covered by s. 6(2), the common law continued to apply. **D19.68**

Although the interpretation of s. 6(2) adopted in *Saunders* [1988] AC 148, avoided the necessity of quashing S's conviction for manslaughter and ordering a retrial, it does seem surprising that the common law on alternative verdicts should have survived legislation which was apparently intended to define with some precision when such verdicts are, and when they are not, available. With respect, the decision in *Saunders* was convenient but ought to be confined to its special facts, and this appears to have been the view of the Court of Appeal in *Foster* [2007] EWCA Crim 2869, [2008] 1 Cr App R 38 (470).

Where problems similar to those in *Collison* arise, it is safer to deal with them by means of adding a count rather than invoking the court's purported residual powers at common law.

RETURNING THE VERDICT

General Procedure

The jury's verdict is delivered in open court, in the presence of the accused (and this cannot occur if the accused has died during the jury's retirement: *Turk* [2017] EWCA Crim 391, [2017] 2 Cr App R 2 (14)). The invariable practice is for the person the jury have selected to be their foreman to state in response to questions from the clerk of court whether they find the accused guilty or not guilty. The procedure is set out in CrimPR 25.14 and CrimPD VI, para. 26Q (see Supplement, **R25.14** and **CPD.26Q**). **D19.69**

The jury are entitled to return a partial verdict in the sense of finding an accused guilty on one count but not on others, or finding one accused guilty but another not. They are also entitled to find an accused guilty in respect of some only of the allegations set out in the particulars of a count, as when a count for theft specifies several items as the subject-matter of the charge and the jury are satisfied that the accused stole some of them but are left in doubt as to others (see *Furlong* [1950] 1 All ER 636, where the jury sent a note asking the judge if they could return such a verdict and the Court of Criminal Appeal held that the judge's affirmative answer was undoubtedly correct, even though the method by which he had communicated the answer was at fault).

Unanimity of the Verdict Unless a juror indicates dissent at the time, it is conclusively presumed that they all agree with the verdicts announced on their behalf, and the Court of Appeal will not breach the privacy of the jury room by hearing evidence that the necessary unanimity was lacking (*Roads* [1967] 2 QB 108, and see also *Lalchan Nanan v The State* [1986] AC 860, in which, on appeal from the Court of Appeal of Trinidad and Tobago in a capital case, the Privy Council held that the court below had rightly refused to read affidavits from four jurors to the effect that they had not realised the need for unanimity and had wished to acquit the appellant). **D19.70**

See also *Ul Hamid* [2016] EWCA Crim 449, [2016] 2 Cr App R 29 (377), in which the unanimous verdict of the jury was upheld where two jurors later revealed their previously unspoken disagreement with the majority.

If the jury return to court apparently with a verdict prior to their having been given the majority verdict direction, the first question the foreman is asked is whether they have reached a verdict (or verdicts) on which they are all agreed (CrimPD VI, para. 26Q.2; see **D19.73** and Supplement, **CPD.26Q**). If the foreman indicates that they have reached unanimous verdicts, he or she is then asked in respect of each count on the indictment and each accused charged in a count what the jury's verdict is. Where there is an indictment with multiple counts, CrimPD VI, para. 26Q.7 (and CrimPR 25.14), gives the trial judge discretion not to take any unanimous verdicts before giving a majority direction in relation to other counts or defendants where no such unanimous verdict has been reached.

D19.71 **Verdicts on Alternative Counts** The general rule that there should be verdicts on each count is subject to the qualification that, where a jury wish to convict on one of two counts which are in the alternative, it is preferable to take a verdict only on that count and discharge them from giving a verdict on the other. This is because the Court of Appeal will then, in appropriate circumstances, be able on appeal to substitute for the jury's verdict a verdict of guilty of the alternative count, whereas if the jury are allowed formally to acquit the accused of the alternative their verdict on that must stand, even though the conviction on the other count has to be quashed (see *Seymour* [1954] 1 All ER 1006, *Melvin* [1953] 1 QB 481 and *Roma* [1956] Crim LR 46, and also the Criminal Appeal Act 1968, s. 3, for the Court of Appeal's power to substitute for the actual verdict a conviction for another offence of which the jury could lawfully have convicted the appellant on the indictment).

Having regard to the above considerations, the procedure normally adopted where counts are in the alternative is for the clerk to ask the foreman whether the jury find the accused guilty on *either* of the counts. If the answer is yes, the foreman is asked on which count they wish to convict; a verdict is taken on that count, and the judge discharges them from giving a verdict on the other. If the answer is no, not guilty verdicts are taken on each count.

D19.72 **Verdicts on Counts of Descending Gravity** A rather different problem arises where counts are not strict alternatives, but they arise out of the same facts and are of differing degrees of gravity (e.g., counts for wounding with intent to cause grievous bodily harm and malicious wounding contrary to ss. 18 and 20 of the OAPA 1861).

It is usual in such cases for the judge in summing-up to tell the jury to consider first the more serious count and only to go on to consider the lesser one if they are not satisfied as to the former. Similarly, when verdicts are taken, the foreman will be asked first for the verdict on the graver count. If it is guilty, the jury will be discharged from giving a verdict on the other; if it is not guilty, a verdict is also taken on the lesser count.

It would not be proper in such cases to allow the jury to convict on both counts because the lesser count really merges into the greater. For example in *Harris* [1969] 2 All ER 599, where D was convicted of both buggery and indecent assault on a boy of 14, the latter offence consisting in playing with the victim's private parts immediately prior to the act of buggery. Edmund Davies LJ (giving the Court of Appeal's judgment) said:

> There is no suggestion of any indecent assault upon [the victim] except that which formed the preliminary to and was followed very shortly thereafter by the commission of the full act of buggery. It does not seem to this court right or desirable that one and the same incident should be made the subject-matter of distinct charges, so that hereafter it may appear to those not familiar with the circumstances that two entirely separate offences were committed. Were this permitted generally, a single offence could frequently give rise to a multiplicity of charges and great unfairness could ensue. We accordingly allow the application for leave to appeal against the conviction of indecent assault, which really merges into the conviction for the graver charge.

Although his lordship appears to criticise even the formulating of distinct charges based on one incident, the actual mischief was in allowing the jury, once they had convicted of buggery, to go on to convict of the lesser charge also. They should simply have been discharged from giving a verdict in respect of indecent assault.

Where the jury were mistakenly asked for their verdict on the lesser count first, but this error was corrected and the proper procedure then followed, their conviction on the more serious count remained valid (*Fernandez* [1997] 1 Cr App R 123 and see *McEvilly* [2008] EWCA Crim 1162).

Procedure for Taking Majority Verdicts

Majority verdicts are discussed at **D19.35**. The procedure for taking majority verdicts is set out at CrimPD VI, paras. 26Q.2 to 26Q.7 (see Supplement, **CPD.26Q**). The main features of the procedure are as follows. **D19.73**

(a) If the jury return to court in a period in which it is considered that they should be trying to reach a unanimous verdict (and certainly where they return in less than two hours and ten minutes), the clerk of the court asks the foreman if they have reached a verdict on which they are all agreed. If the answer is yes, the verdict is taken; if the answer is no, they are sent back to their room with a direction to continue to try to achieve unanimity.
(b) If the jury return or are sent for after that period has elapsed, the clerk similarly asks the foreman if they have reached a verdict on which they are all agreed. If the answer at this stage is no, the judge directs the jury that a majority verdict can now be accepted, and tells them the size of the permissible majorities. However, the judge must also tell them that, when they again retire, they should make a further attempt to reach a unanimous verdict, and only if that last attempt at unanimity fails should they come back with a majority decision.
(c) Upon the jury returning to court after the majority verdict direction has been given, the clerk asks the foreman whether they have reached a verdict on which the required majority of them are agreed. If the answer is yes, they are asked for the verdict. A verdict of not guilty should be accepted without more ado. If the verdict is guilty, the foreman should be further asked whether it was unanimous or by a majority and, if the latter, how many agreed and how many dissented.

Correcting a Verdict

It occasionally happens that a jury return a verdict and then realise that they have been misunderstood. **D19.74**

Where the Verdict is Incorrect In such cases, the trial judge may allow them to correct their verdict (unless they have been discharged and have dispersed). **D19.75**

This was demonstrated in *Andrews* (1985) 82 Cr App R 148, in which the Court of Appeal held that a jury does have power to alter a verdict from not guilty to guilty provided it acts promptly (*Parkin* (1824) 1 Mood CC 45; *Vodden* (1853) Dears CC 229). Whether such an alteration should be allowed is in the discretion of the trial judge, taking into account especially:

(a) the length of time which has elapsed between the original verdict and the moment when the jury express a wish to change;
(b) the apparent reason for the mistake, for example, as in *Andrews* itself, that the jury were mistakenly waiting for a further question from the court clerk; and
(c) the necessity to ensure that justice is done both to the prosecution and to the defence.

In *Andrews*, the accused had been discharged but this was *not* fatal to allowing a change of verdict. However, if the jury had been discharged, and certainly if they had been allowed to disperse, it would then have been too late to rectify the mistake.

Equally, if the jury had heard anything since returning the original verdict that might have affected their earlier thinking, that would preclude any alteration (*Tantram* [2001] EWCA Crim 1364).

In *Austin* [2002] EWCA Crim 1796, the Court of Appeal stated that, where a verdict was given in the sight and hearing of the entire jury without any dissent by any member of it, there was a presumption that they had all assented to it, albeit that such a presumption could be rebutted.

D19.76 **Correcting an Incomplete Verdict** An alteration to the verdict may also be allowed where the original one was not so much incorrect as incomplete. For example, in *Carter* [1964] 2 QB 1 the jury, which had not been directed by the judge about the possibility of finding the accused guilty of a lesser offence (although prosecuting counsel had referred to it), initially found the accused simply not guilty. After the accused had been discharged, it became clear that the jury had wished to convict of the lesser offence and the accused were then recalled for the verdict to be completed and sentence passed. The conviction was upheld.

D19.77 **Otherwise Rectifying the Verdict** Although the general rule is that, once the jury has been discharged, it is *functus officio* (see **D13.50**), there are circumstances in which it can be reconvened in order to rectify its verdict. Examples of such circumstances include the following cases.

(a) In *Aylott* [1996] 2 Cr App R 169, the judge discharged the jury because of a mistaken belief that they were unable to reach a verdict. When he received a further note from the jury which made it clear that they had already reached verdicts, he took the verdicts, as a result of which D was convicted of murder. On appeal it was held that a judge was entitled in certain circumstances to set aside the discharge which he had ordered, for example, in *Aylott* the discharge had been based on a fundamental mistake. The underlying principle was to ensure that proceedings were fair and to do justice in the particular case.

(b) In *Maloney* [1996] 2 Cr App R 303, a guilty verdict was taken by the court on Friday afternoon, without asking how many jurors had agreed with the verdict and how many dissented. To rectify this mistake, the jury was reconvened the following Monday and asked about the figures. The Court of Appeal held that the discharge of the jury did not prevent the court carrying out the rectifying procedure. Nor were the lapse of time and the fact that the jury had dispersed fatal, in view of the CJPO 1994, s. 43, which permitted the jury to separate after retirement. There was no suggestion that they had deliberated further after the dispersal, nor that the numbers given as to the size of the majority were incorrect. The position would have been different if the jury had had to deliberate further, or, perhaps, if the verdict was being altered from not guilty to guilty.

Power of Judge to Refuse to Accept Verdict

D19.78 In general, a judge is obliged to accept the jury's verdict however much the judge may disagree with it (*Robinson* [1975] QB 508, following *Lester* (1938) 27 Cr App R 8). The exceptions to the general rule were succinctly stated by Lord Parker CJ in *Harris* [1964] Crim LR 54. The *Criminal Law Review*'s paraphrase of his lordship's judgment reads:

> Where a single verdict is ambiguous, or two verdicts are inconsistent, or the verdict is one which cannot on the indictment or in the circumstances be lawfully returned, the judge is entitled, unless the jury insist, to refuse to accept the first verdict and ask the jury to reconsider the matter and if they change their verdict to record only the second verdict.

Similarly, in *Robinson* [1975] QB 508, James LJ said (at p. 512F):

> ...once the jury has returned a verdict, then the judge cannot say 'I will not have it', provided, of course, it is a verdict that is not ambiguous and provided it is a verdict that can properly be returned upon the indictment they have been considering.

D19.79 **Three Categories of Verdicts that a Judge Can Refuse** Thus, there are three categories of case in which the first verdict need not be accepted:

(a) *The original verdict is one which the jury cannot lawfully return on the indictment.* An example would be a verdict of guilty of a lesser offence when such a verdict does not, in the circumstances of the case, come within any of the statutory provisions allowing a jury to convict the accused of something other than that with which the accused is expressly charged in the indictment (see **D19.41**).

(b) *The original verdict is ambiguous.* In such cases the judge should ask whatever questions are necessary to resolve the ambiguity (*Hawkes* (1931) 22 Cr App R 172) and may, if necessary, give a supplementary direction on the law before taking a final verdict (*Sweetland* (1957) 42 Cr App R 62). If the judge proceeds to sentence on a purported verdict of guilty which remains ambiguous, both conviction and sentence will have to be quashed (*Hawkes*).

(c) *Inconsistency in the verdict.* If the individual verdicts on a number of counts or in respect of several accused are inconsistent with each other, having regard to the nature of the evidence that has been adduced, the judge may ask the jury to reconsider their decision. The judge should only do so, however, if the verdicts are *necessarily* inconsistent (*Durante* [1972] 1 WLR 1612; *Fanning* [2016] EWCA Crim 550, [2016] 2 Cr App R 19 (259)). If there is a possible, albeit unlikely, view of the evidence on which the verdicts can be justified, the judge should accept them without further query. An example of this third category is the case of *Burrows* [1970] Crim LR 419. D1, D2 and another were jointly charged with theft of a purse and D2 alone was charged in the alternative with handling it. The judge declined to accept the jury's initial verdict, acquitting all three of theft but convicting D2 of handling, because that acquittal implied that they were not satisfied that the goods in question had ever been stolen. Further discussion revealed a misunderstanding by the jury, and when this was corrected the jury found D1 guilty of theft. On appeal, it was held that the judge should have accepted the original verdicts, because they were not necessarily inconsistent *inter se* since the jury might have been sure that *either* D1 or the third co-accused had stolen the purse but the jury might have been unable to attribute responsibility to one or the other (see also *Fletcher* [2017] EWCA Crim 1778 and *McDonald* [2018] EWCA Crim 798).

If the judge legitimately refuses to accept the jury's first verdict and in consequence they return a proper second verdict, it is the latter which is the operative decision. If the jury, notwithstanding the judge's intervention, persist in returning inconsistent verdicts, the inconsistency may be a good ground of appeal.

Supplementary Questions about the Verdict

It is not in general good practice to ask the jury questions about the basis on which they have returned a verdict of guilty (per Humphreys J in *Larkin* [1943] KB 174). Where the prosecution evidence is such that two or more views of the facts consistent with guilt are tenable, on one of which the accused's culpability is greater than on the other, it is the judge's responsibility to decide what the circumstances of the offence were for the purposes of sentencing (*Solomon* (1984) 6 Cr App R (S) 120; *Stosiek* (1982) 4 Cr App R (S) 205). Asking the jury to refine their verdict may merely lead to confusion. **D19.80**

Circumstances in which Supplementary Questions May be Asked The one recognised exception to this principle is in cases where the accused is charged with murder and the jury have been left two or more alternative bases on which they might find the accused guilty of manslaughter and not guilty of murder. This is because exactly why the accused was found guilty of manslaughter (whether it was on grounds of loss of control or diminished responsibility and, if the latter, its cause) is of crucial importance to sentence (*Matheson* [1958] 2 All ER 87; *Frankum (1983) 5 Cr App R (S) 259*; *Solomon* (1984) 6 Cr App R (S) 120 per Beldam J at p. 126). **D19.81**

There is, however, no absolute requirement to ask supplementary questions even in these circumstances. In *Cawthorne* [1996] Crim LR 526, the Court of Appeal stressed that whether or not the judge asked the jury to indicate the basis of the verdict was a matter for his discretion; following the verdict, he was entitled to sentence on the basis of the facts which he had heard in evidence. In *Hopkinson* [2013] EWCA Crim 795, [2014] 1 Cr App R 3 (22), the Court of Appeal repeated that the taking of special verdicts should only be used in the context of a trial for murder where there were a number of alternative defences, and even then only rarely.

D19.82 **Procedure for Supplementary Questions** Because the jury are entitled to decline to answer any supplementary question, beyond delivering their verdict, a judge who intends to ask a jury the basis of a guilty verdict should warn them of that intention before they retire (*Heckstall-Smith* [1989] Crim LR 742). After any such warning, if they convict, they should then be asked the supplementary question immediately after returning the main verdict and before they separate (*Heckstall-Smith*).

In complicated cases, it may be a 'sensible precaution' to write the questions down for the jury. In *Frankum* (1983) 5 Cr App R (S) 259, Dunn LJ approved the course adopted by the trial judge in the case who gave the jury a list of questions as follows: 'First, do you think it more probable than not that the accused was suffering from diminished responsibility? If so, you should find him guilty of manslaughter. If you find him guilty of manslaughter, you will be asked (1) is that on the ground of diminished responsibility, and (2) if so, do you think the abnormality (a) arose as a result of inherent causes, (b) was induced by injury from the toxic effects of [a drug D was taking for a peptic ulcer] or (c) was both?'

D19.83 **Factual Basis for Sentence** Subject to the discussion above and **D19.41**, in general, having summed up the case to the jury on one factual basis, the judge is entitled to assume that they will acquit or convict on that basis and not on some alternative view of the facts which may theoretically have been open on the evidence but was not a live issue during the trial (*Heckstall-Smith* [1989] Crim LR 742). Where the jury do attempt to indicate, while sentence is being passed, that the factual basis on which the judge is doing so is different from that which they found proved, the judge may refuse to hear what they wish to say (*Ekwuyasi* [1981] Crim LR 574).

Jury Must Not Be Pressurised

D19.84 The jury should be given as much time as they reasonably need to reach a verdict, and must not be pressurised into agreeing against their better judgement. As Cassels J said in *McKenna* [1960] 1 QB 411 (at p. 422): 'It is a cardinal principle of our criminal law that in considering their verdict ... a jury shall deliberate in complete freedom, uninfluenced by any promise, unintimidated by any threat.'

The pressure in *McKenna* itself was extreme, in that the jury were told by the judge that, if they did not reach a verdict within the next ten minutes, they would have to be 'kept all night'. That was at least capable of conveying the impression that they would be kept in their jury room.

Even a much gentler indication of a time-limit may result in unacceptable pressure on the jury. In *Duggan* [1992] Crim LR 513, the jury made it known at 3.52 p.m. that, as some of them had child care commitments, they wished to sit until they had reached a verdict. The judge said that he was prepared to wait until 5 p.m. if it would help. The Court of Appeal held that the judge's intimation of a time-limit was likely to put some of the jury under pressure, in view of their earlier indication of commitments and the fact that it was clear that they would have to spend the night in a hotel if they could not agree.

Measures which did not exert such pressure were entirely within the discretion of a trial judge. So, in *Brown* [2016] EWCA Crim 523, where the jury, which had already received a majority direction, sent a note stating that they were deadlocked, the trial judge was entitled to call them back to court and to tell them to continue to seek to reach a unanimous or majority verdict.

D19.85 **Proper Discussion of Timing with the Jury** Provided the principle in *McKenna* [1960] 1 QB 411 is not breached, there is no objection to the jury being asked if there is any reasonable prospect of their reaching agreement and being told that if there is not the judge will discharge them, while if there is they may have as much time as they want (*Modeste* [1983] Crim LR 746).

Any communication between the judge and jury about the chances of a verdict being reached should take place in open court and should not be conducted by, for example, the clerk going into the jury room with a message (*Rose* [1982] 2 All ER 536). Where the jury request more time to deliberate, the judge may be obliged to allow more time; in any event, the judge is fully justified in permitting it (*Turner* [1994] Crim LR 287).

Wharton [1990] Crim LR 877 emphasises the importance of the judge inquiring of the jury in open court as to the prospect of a verdict being reached. In that case, the jury retired to consider their verdict at 3 p.m., received the majority direction at 5.34 p.m. and sent a note saying that they had reached a verdict 9–3 at 6.10 p.m. The course then adopted by the judge, with counsel's concurrence, of sending the jury a message asking them to continue their deliberations, was held to represent a material irregularity. Where the jury are unable to reach a verdict, the judge should reassemble them in court and ascertain from the foreman in open court at first hand what prospect there is of reaching a verdict.

When giving a majority direction, the judge should not refer to the possibility of another trial taking place if the jury cannot agree, as to do so might put undue pressure on them to reach agreement (*Boyes* [1991] Crim LR 717).

Saturday Sitting In *Duffin* [2003] EWCA Crim 3064, the Court of Appeal considered the circumstances in which the jury might be asked to consider their verdict on a Saturday. At the trial of the defendant for possession with intent to supply Class A drugs, the jury was sent out at 3.54 p.m. on the Friday of the last day of their scheduled sitting. At 6.07 p.m. the judge told them they were under no pressure to deliver a verdict, and asked them to retire and consider whether they wished to continue their deliberations or return the following day. Majority verdicts of guilty were returned at 7.31 p.m. The appeal of the accused on the ground that the jury had been placed under improper pressure to deliver the verdicts was allowed. Occasionally, a Saturday sitting might be desirable and practicable but, if it was, the proper course was to determine whether the jury had commitments for the following day. Given the lateness of the hour and the fact that the only options had been to stay late or return the following day, the jury had been put under pressure to deliver the verdicts. **D19.86**

Encouraging the Jury to Reach a Verdict

Watson [1988] QB 690 raised the vexed question of whether a judge is entitled to use a form of words encouraging the jury to listen to each other's views and thus, if possible, reach agreement. In particular, the Court of Appeal considered the appropriateness in modern circumstances of a direction approved in *Walhein* (1952) 36 Cr App R 167, which drew attention to the cost and inconvenience caused by a jury not being able to agree. Lord Lane CJ's judgment in *Watson* starts from the proposition that (at p. 700A–B): **D19.87**

> ...a jury must be free to deliberate without any form of pressure being imposed upon them, whether by way of promise or of threat or otherwise. They must not be made to feel that it is incumbent upon them to express agreement with a view they do not truly hold simply because it might be inconvenient or tiresome or expensive for the prosecution, the defendant, the victim or the public in general if they do not do so.

Experience had shown that the *Walhein* direction potentially put too much pressure on jurors who happened to be in the minority to concur with the majority. There was, however, no reason why a jury should not be directed as follows (at p. 700F–G):

> Each of you has taken an oath to return a true verdict according to the evidence. No one must be false to that oath, but you have a duty not only as individuals but collectively. That is the strength *of the jury system*. Each of you takes into the jury-box with you your individual experience and wisdom. Your task is to pool that experience and wisdom. You do that by giving your views and listening to the views of the others. There must necessarily be discussion, argument and give and take within the scope of your oath. That is the way in which agreement is reached. If, unhappily, [ten of] you cannot reach agreement you must say so.

It is solely a decision for the trial judge, in the exercise of his or her discretion, whether to give the above direction and, if so, at what time to do so (as was restated in *Pinches* [2010] EWCA Crim 2000).

D19.88 **Timing of a '*Watson*' Direction** In *Watson* [1988] QB 690, it was held that the direction was probably best given as part of the summing-up or as a last resort should the jury have had the majority verdict direction but still be unable to reach the minimum majority required (at pp. 700H–701A). The Court of Appeal have indicated, in any event, that, once a jury has retired, a *Watson* direction should never be given before the majority direction (*Atlan* [2004] EWCA Crim 1798) but, equally, should not be given at the same time as a majority direction (*Buono* (1992) 95 Cr App R 338).

D19.89 **Form of the Direction** If the direction is given, individual variations in its wording may prove dangerous and should if possible be avoided (*Watson* [1988] QB 690). In *Atlan* [2004] EWCA Crim 1798, it was stressed that, if a *Watson* direction is given, it should be made clear that any 'give and take' should be within the scope of the juror's oath. The Court of Appeal suggested that it was just as dangerous to omit words from the *Watson* direction as to add them (see also *Morgan* [1997] Crim LR 593).

JURY UNABLE TO AGREE ON A VERDICT

D19.90 If the jury cannot agree on a verdict, the judge discharges them from giving a verdict. As always when the jury are discharged, the accused is not acquitted but may be retried by a different jury. Whether to ask for a retrial is in the discretion of the prosecution. In the absence of exceptional reasons to the contrary, it is the practice to have a retrial following failure by one jury to agree. If a second jury also fail to agree, the prosecution would not usually seek a third trial but instead offer no evidence.

This convention was examined in *Henworth* [2001] EWCA Crim 120, [2001] 2 Cr App R 4 (47), and it was stated that it should not be elevated into a proposition of law. In some cases, a further trial might be proper, e.g., if a jury had been tampered with, or some cogent piece of evidence for the Crown had since been discovered. Whether it was an abuse of process for the prosecution to seek a further trial must depend on the facts, including:

(a) the overall period of the delay and the reasons for it;
(b) the results of the previous trials;
(c) the seriousness of the offence; and (possibly)
(d) the extent to which the case against the defendant had changed since previous trials.

D19.91 In *Bell* [2010] EWCA Crim 3, [2010] 1 Cr App R 27 (407) the Court of Appeal confirmed that no rule of law forbids a second retrial in cases where juries in the first two trials have failed to reach a verdict. Where no verdict can be reached at a first retrial, it is initially for the prosecutor to judge whether, taking account of all relevant considerations, the public interest is better served by offering no evidence or by seeking a further retrial. The judge must then consider whether or not the proposed second retrial would be oppressive and unjust. A second retrial should be 'confined to the very small number of cases in which the jury is being invited to address a crime of extreme gravity which has undoubtedly occurred (as here) and in which the evidence that the defendant committed the crime (again, as here), on any fair minded objective judgment remains very powerful' (see also *Bowe v The Queen* [2001] UKPC 19 and *Benguit* [2005] EWCA Crim 1953). Moreover, in *Burton* [2015] 1 Cr App R 7, [2015] 1 Cr App R 7 (97), the Court of Appeal again emphasised the 'strictly limited' number of cases in which a third trial should be permitted.

Section D20 Trial on Indictment: Sentencing Procedure

INTRODUCTION

This section describes the procedure which applies following, as appropriate, a verdict or a plea of guilty, and which regulates the sentencing of the offender. First, there is a need to ascertain the basis of facts, which is of particular importance where the offender has pleaded guilty and the court has therefore not had the opportunity to form a view of the evidence at trial. Secondly, there is a need to consider the character of the offender, to obtain such pre-sentence reports as are appropriate, and to consider such mitigation as is advanced on the offender's behalf, before either sentencing or adjourning sentence in one of a number of ways. This topic is addressed by CrimPR 25.16 (see Supplement, **R25.16**) and the *Crown Court Compendium, Part II: Sentencing*. **D20.1**

Although sentencing procedure is essentially the same in both the Crown Court and magistrates' courts, it is the former that is considered here. For ways in which the summary procedure differs, see **D23**. See also **Part E** as to the sentences that are available, and the procedures and guidelines that apply to them.

Note that the Sentencing Act 2020 will bring into operation the Sentencing Code which simplifies the law of sentencing and procedure, removing multiple layers of redundant or unnecessary provisions and updating the language. Once the Code is in force an offender will automatically be sentenced under the current law, subject to necessary exceptions to safeguard defendants' fundamental rights, thereby making the sentencing process easier, clearer and simpler to understand.

ASCERTAINING THE FACTS OF THE OFFENCE

Where the offender pleads guilty, the first stage of a sentencing hearing is for prosecuting counsel to summarise the facts of the offence (CrimPR 25.16(3)). As well as assisting the court, this informs the offender and the public of how the prosecution put their case. As to the provision of necessary financial and other information relevant to sentence, CrimPD VII, paras. Q.1 to Q.6 (see Supplement, **CPD.VII.Q**), are also relevant. **D20.2**

It will normally be unnecessary for the facts to be opened at the conclusion of a contested trial. However, in the event of split pleas by co-defendants, the sentencing of the offender who pleaded guilty will normally be adjourned until the conclusion of the trial of the accused who pleaded not guilty. If the latter is convicted, the facts will still have to be summarised for the benefit of the one who pleaded guilty.

Duties of the Prosecutor in Relation to Sentencing

D20.3 By convention, the prosecution adopt a neutral attitude at the sentencing stage, not seeking to influence the court in favour of a heavy sentence. The following points may also be made about the role of prosecution counsel at the sentencing stage.

(a) Prosecution counsel can only provide evidence of the impact on the victim of the offence for which the offender is to be sentenced if it accords with the relevant guidelines (see **D20.4**).
(b) Where the possibility arises of the court making an ancillary order in conjunction with the main sentence (e.g., compensation under the PCC(S)A 2000, s. 130, deprivation of property under s. 143 of the same Act, confiscation of the proceeds of crime, or forfeiture of prohibited articles such as drugs or offensive weapons), counsel is required to address this.
(c) Prosecution counsel is under a general duty to assist the court to avoid appealable error. According to the standards applicable to criminal cases, this goes beyond ensuring that the judge does not exceed the court's maximum powers and extends to ensuring the court is aware of all relevant statutory provisions, sentencing guidelines and additional guidance from the Court of Appeal (see **D20.6**).
(d) Prosecution counsel will in some cases prepare a 'plea and sentence document' which identifies the aggravating and mitigating factors of the offence and the relevant statutory provisions and sentencing guidelines (Addendum to the A-G's Guidelines on the Acceptance of Pleas and the Prosecutor's Role in the Sentencing Exercise); see also CrimPD VII, para. Q.3, concerning the need for the defence, where possible, to agree the identification of aggravating and mitigating features).

In *Maxwell* [2017] EWCA Crim 1233, [2018] 1 Cr App R 5 (76) it was emphasised that these obligations are not limited to the prosecution. While ultimately the sentencing judge was responsible for ensuring that the sentence passed met all relevant technical requirements, it was also the duty of all counsel to provide appropriate assistance to ensure that this occurred.

Victim Personal Statements

D20.4 The court is frequently provided with an account from the victim of the offence for which the offender is to be sentenced, which can then be taken into account by the court when it passes sentence.

In *Hobstaff* (1993) 14 Cr App R (S) 632, the Court of Appeal stressed that allegations made by prosecuting counsel as to the effect of the offence upon the victim must be backed up by potentially admissible evidence. Such evidence should be made in a proper form, such as a witness statement, and served in advance on the defence and the court. Defence counsel would exercise a careful judgement as to how it should be dealt with and the court would not be influenced by prosecution information alone (see also *A-G's Ref (No. 2 of 1995)* [1996] 1 Cr App R (S) 274).

In *H (Indecent Assault)* (1999) *The Times*, 18 March 1999, the Court of Appeal emphasised that where the prosecution does provide a statement from the victim, the sentencer should approach it with some care. Since it would ill behove the offender to attempt to investigate such a statement, it would necessarily reflect one side of the case only.

In *Perks* [2001] 1 Cr App R (S) 19 (66), the Court of Appeal laid down guidelines for the courts to take into account in considering 'victim personal statements' for the purpose of sentencing (see **E1.30** for details). The main points of *Perks* are now summarised in CrimPD VII, paras F.1 to F.3 (see Supplement, **CPD.VII.F**), and in particular, '[i]n all cases it will be appropriate for a VPS to be referred to in the course of the sentencing hearing and/or in the sentencing remarks'.

Code of Practice for Victims of Crime (the 'Victims' Code')

D20.5 The Ministry of Justice's Code of Practice for Victims of Crime (October 2015) sets out the information, support and services that victims of crime are entitled to receive at every stage of the process from reporting a crime to post-trial support. The Code entitles the victim to give and receive information that is relevant to sentence, affords victims of crime the opportunity to prepare a victim personal statement which they may either read or have read, subject to the discretion of the court, and also an entitlement to be informed promptly of the outcome of the sentence and whether any aspect of the case is the subject of an appeal.

Counsel's Duty to Assist the Court

All counsel appearing in sentence cases must make themselves aware of any legal limitations on the court's sentencing powers and any relevant guidelines as to sentence so as to be in a position to assist the judge if necessary (*Panayioutou* (1989) 11 Cr App R (S) 535). **D20.6**

In *Komsta* (1990) 12 Cr App R (S) 63, it was emphasised that there was a positive obligation on counsel, both for the prosecution and the defence, to ensure that no order is made which the court has no power to make. See also *Reynolds* [2007] EWCA Crim 538, [2007] 2 Cr App R (S) 87.

In *Cain* [2006] EWCA Crim 3233, [2007] 2 Cr App R (S) 25 (135), the Lord Chief Justice observed:

> It is of course the duty of a judge to impose a lawful sentence, but sentencing has become a complex matter and a judge will often not see the papers very long before the hearing and does not have the time for preparation that advocates should enjoy. In these circumstances a judge relies on the advocates to assist him with sentencing. It is unacceptable for advocates not to ascertain and be prepared to assist the judge with the legal restrictions on the sentence that he can impose on their clients.
>
> This duty is not restricted to defence advocates. We emphasise the fact that advocates for the prosecution also owe a duty to assist the judge at the stage of sentencing. It is not satisfactory for a prosecuting advocate, having secured a conviction, to sit back and leave sentencing to the defence. Nor can an advocate, when appearing for the prosecution for the purpose of sentence on a plea of guilty, limit the assistance that he provides to the court to the outlining of the facts and details of the defendant's previous convictions.
>
> The advocate for the prosecution should always be ready to assist the court by drawing attention to any statutory provisions that govern the court's sentencing powers. It is the duty of the prosecuting advocate to ensure that the judge does not, through inadvertence, impose a sentence that is outside his powers. The advocate for the prosecution should also be in a position to offer to draw the judge's attention to any relevant sentencing guidelines or guideline decisions of this court.

Factual Basis for Sentence

The great majority of summaries of the facts provided by the prosecution raise no procedural problems whatsoever. However, a considerable body of law has developed dealing with the proper approach to that minority of cases in which there is a dispute about the facts of the offence, in the sense that the prosecution version of how the offence was committed differs from that advanced by the defence in mitigation, albeit that the offender is clearly guilty on either version. This will arise in particular where the defence advance a written factual basis of plea which is not accepted by the prosecution or the court. Under CrimPR 25.16(4) (see Supplement, **R26.16**) the court may give directions for determining the facts on the basis of which sentence must be passed; the principles to be applied are discussed at **D20.8** ***et seq***. Prosecution counsel is under a duty to alert the court as to the possible use of this procedure where there is a dispute as to the factual basis for sentence (*Hughes* [2011] EWCA Crim 556). **D20.7**

DISPUTES ABOUT THE FACTS FOLLOWING A PLEA OF GUILTY

Newton Hearings

In *Newton* (1982) 77 Cr App R 13, although N pleaded guilty to sexual offences, there was considerable dispute between the prosecution and defence as to whether the sexual acts alleged had been consensual. The Court of Appeal indicated three ways in which the judge, in a case where there is such a sharp divergence on the facts of the offence, 'can approach his difficult task of sentencing'. Lord Lane CJ said (at p. 15): **D20.8**

> It is in certain circumstances possible to obtain the answer to the problem from a jury. For example, when it is a question of whether the conviction should be under section 18 or section 20 of the

> Offences against the Person Act 1861, the jury can determine the issue on a trial under section 18 by deciding whether or not the necessary intent has been proved by the prosecution…
>
> The second method which could be adopted by the judge in these circumstances is himself to hear the evidence on one side and another, and come to his own conclusion, acting so to speak as his own jury on the issue which is the root of the problem.
>
> The third possibility in these circumstances is for him to hear no evidence but to listen to the submissions of counsel and then come to a conclusion. But if he does that,… where there is a substantial conflict between the two sides, he must come down on the side of the defendant. In other words where there has been a substantial conflict, the version of the defendant must so far as possible be accepted.

General Approach

D20.9 The basic propositions set out in *Newton* have since been analysed and refined. In particular, in *Underwood* [2004] EWCA Crim 2256, [2005] 1 Cr App R 13 (178), the Court of Appeal gave guidelines on the approach that the sentencer ought to take where an offender pleads guilty on a specific basis that the prosecution may not accept. In summary, and renumbered, they are as follows:

(1) The offender should be sentenced as far as possible on a basis that accurately reflects the facts of the individual case.

(2) If the resolution of the facts in dispute may matter to the sentencing decision, the responsibility for alerting the prosecutor to the areas of dispute rests with the defence (see also **D20.10**).

(3) The prosecution should not be taken by surprise and should if necessary take time to reflect, consult and consider their position and the interests of justice.

(4) Whatever view is formed by the prosecution on any proposed basis of plea is deemed to be conditional on the judge's acceptance of it.

(5) The prosecution may agree the offender's account of the disputed facts. If so, the agreement should be reduced to writing and signed by both advocates (see also **D20.14**).

(6) The agreement should be available to the court before the prosecution's opening and if possible before the judge is invited to approve the acceptance of plea, or in any event before the sentencing hearing begins.

(7) If the agreed basis of plea is not signed by advocates for both sides, or it is not legible, the judge is entitled to ignore it.

(8) If the prosecution rejects the offender's version, the areas of dispute should be identified in a document that focuses the attention of the court on the precise facts which are in dispute.

(9) The most difficult situation arises when the prosecution lack the evidence positively to dispute the offender's account. In many cases, for example, the matter in issue is outside the knowledge of the prosecution. The prosecution's position may be that they have no evidence to contradict the defence assertions, but that does not mean that the truth of matters outside their own knowledge should be agreed. In those circumstances, particularly if the facts relied upon arise from the offender's personal knowledge and depend on the offender's own account of the facts, the prosecution should only agree that account if it is supported by other material. Neither the prosecution nor the judge is bound to agree facts merely because the prosecution cannot gainsay the offender's account.

(10) Whether or not the basis of plea is agreed, the judge is not bound by any such agreement, and is entitled to insist that any evidence relevant to the facts in dispute should be called. The judge is responsible for the sentencing decision and may order a *Newton* hearing to ascertain the truth about disputed facts (see also **D20.15**).

(11) The prosecution and defence should call any relevant evidence. Where the issue arises from facts that are within the exclusive knowledge of the offender, the defence should be willing to call evidence from the offender, failing which, subject to any explanation put forward, the judge may draw an appropriate inference.

(12) An adjournment for these purposes is often unnecessary bearing in mind the offender will almost invariably be present.

(13) The judge should direct him or herself on the burden and standard of proof in accordance with ordinary principles.
(14) A *Newton* hearing has the following limitations:
  (a) some issues require a verdict from a jury, e.g., intent (see **D19.81**);
  (b) a judge cannot make findings of fact and sentence that are inconsistent with the pleas to the counts on the indictment;
  (c) where a number of persons are charged with a joint enterprise, the seriousness and context are always relevant;
  (d) matters of mitigation are not normally dealt with in a *Newton* hearing, but where there is no evidence to support an offender's account other than a bare contention, the judge is entitled to invite defence counsel to call the offender to give evidence;
  (e) where the impact of the dispute on the eventual sentencing decision is minimal, a *Newton* hearing is unnecessary — the judge will rarely be concerned with minute differences about events on the periphery (see also **D20.18**);
  (f) the judge is entitled to decline to hear evidence about disputed facts if the offender's case is absurd or obviously untenable, but the judge should explain why that conclusion was reached (see also **D20.20**).
(15) If issues on a *Newton* hearing are resolved in the offender's favour, the credit due for a guilty plea should not be reduced.
(16) If the offender is disbelieved or obliges the prosecution to call evidence from a witness causing unnecessary and inappropriate distress, thereby demonstrating no insight into the consequences of the offence and no genuine remorse for it, the judge may reduce the discount for a guilty plea, particularly if it has been tendered at a very late stage.
(17) There might be an exceptional case in which the normal entitlement to credit for a guilty plea is wholly dissipated by the *Newton* hearing, in which case the judge should give reasons (see **D20.28**).

Certain of the more important aspects of these guidelines are analysed below. *Underwood* was specifically endorsed by the Court of Appeal in *Temple* [2008] EWCA Crim 2511 and *Nicholls v DPP* [2013] EWHC 4365 (Admin).

In *Sheard* [2013] EWCA Crim 1161, the Court of Appeal expressed concern that the sentencing judge had been invited to resolve a factual dispute as to whether or not certain aggravating features were present without hearing any live evidence.

Duty of the Offender's Legal Representatives

It is the responsibility of defence solicitors and counsel to notify the prosecution, and the court, that a plea of guilty will be put forward on the basis that the offender disputes the prosecution version of the facts (*Hughes* [2011] EWCA Crim 556). The court should then be informed, ideally at the outset of the hearing and at the latest during mitigation, not merely that there is a dispute but that the defence wish to see it resolved in a *Newton* hearing (*Gardener* [1994] Crim LR 301). The Court of Appeal would not normally consider an argument that the sentencer had failed to order a hearing unless the possibility of such a hearing was raised unequivocally and expressly in the Crown Court (see also *A-G's Refs (Nos. 3 and 4 of 1996)* [1997] 1 Cr App R (S) 29). **D20.10**

Power of Court to Direct a Hearing

Ultimately, the decision as to whether or not a *Newton* hearing is required is for the court. As a result, such a hearing may arise even where prosecution and defence are agreed on the facts on which the plea is based. The judge is under a duty to hold a *Newton* hearing if an application of the principles stated in **D20.9** leads to that conclusion, whatever the position of the parties may be. **D20.11**

In *Smith* (1986) 8 Cr App R (S) 169, for example, the judge offered defence counsel a *Newton* hearing to resolve an important factual issue, but counsel declined. The judge then proceeded to sentence on a basis adverse to S. In the Court of Appeal, where the term was reduced, Peter Pain J quoted from Goff LJ in *Williams* (1983) 5 Cr App R (S) 134:

> . . . the question whether an issue should be tried does not depend upon the consent of counsel for the appellant or the accused person as the case may be. It is entirely a matter for the decision of the court in any particular case, although the court may of course hear submissions from counsel on the propriety of ordering such an issue to be tried. The question whether counsel for a party agrees or does not agree to the trial of the issue is a matter of no materiality, the decision being entirely within the control of the court.

See also *Myers* [1996] 1 Cr App R (S) 187.

The court is entitled to decline to hear evidence at a *Newton* hearing where D's version of events is absurd or clearly unreliable (*Mula* [2017] EWCA Crim 32, [2017] 4 WLR 124) (see **D20.20**) but where a *Newton* hearing is to be held, the judge should avoid giving any impression that a conclusion has already been reached as to the plausibility of the defence version (*Satchell* [1997] 2 Cr App R (S) 258).

The Crown Court has the power to hold a *Newton* hearing even where such a hearing has already taken place in the magistrates' court which committed the offender for sentence. However, there ought to be good reason for it to reopen a factual dispute that has already been resolved elsewhere (*R (Gillan) v Crown Court at Winchester* [2007] EWHC 380 (Admin), [2007] 1 WLR 2214).

D20.12 **Factual Disputes Revealed by the Pre-sentence Report** One way in which the court may be alerted to a factual dispute which may have a bearing on the eventual sentence is where the offender presents to the author of the pre-sentence report a factual account which is at variance with the prosecution case. In such circumstances, the court can initiate a *Newton* hearing (see, e.g., *Oakley* [1998] 1 Cr App R (S) 100, where the Court of Appeal held that the sentencer should have heard evidence to resolve the conflict, whether or not the prosecution or defence asked for a *Newton* hearing). However, in *Tolera* [1999] 1 Cr App R 29, the Court of Appeal emphasised that the initiative rested with the defence where it was asking the court to sentence on a basis other than that disclosed by the prosecution case. If the offender wished to rely on the account which was given to the probation officer and which conflicted with the prosecution case, defence counsel should draw the relevant paragraphs to the attention of the court and ask that it be treated as the basis of sentence. The prosecution should be alerted to the fact that such a request would be made. A *Newton* hearing could then follow.

D20.13 **Dispute Arising in Ancillary Proceedings** The court may also be alerted to a material factual dispute during proceedings ancillary to sentencing, such as confiscation. In *McNulty* [1994] Crim LR 385, for example, the court's inquiry as to whether a confiscation order should be made in respect of the proceeds of drug trafficking, raised doubts as to D's basis of plea of non-commercial supply. The judge therefore embarked on a *Newton* hearing, in which he found that D had been dealing commercially. The Court of Appeal held that it was proper to hold a *Newton* hearing in these circumstances, and upheld the sentence and the confiscation order. In such a situation, it is important to ensure that the *Newton* hearing is governed by the criminal rules of evidence and procedure, regardless of the assumptions and standard of proof which may govern an inquiry under the POCA 2002 (see **E19.11**).

Written Basis of Plea

D20.14 An offender who pleads guilty on a particular basis (e.g., accepting only a limited version of the allegations made by the prosecution), should set out the basis of the plea in a written form so that it is unequivocal and unambiguous. If it is not, the judge is entitled to ignore it (*Mula* [2017] EWCA Crim 32, [2017] 4 WLR 124, and see *Tolera* [1999] 1 Cr App R 29). Where the court does not accept a basis of plea, it must make this clear before proceeding to sentence (*Lucien* [2009] EWCA Crim 2004). See also CrimPR 3.31 (see Supplement, **R3.31**) as to applications for indications as to sentence.

Response to an Agreed Basis of Plea In *Beswick* [1996] 1 Cr App R (S) 343, the Court of Appeal dealt with the situation where agreement had been reached between prosecution and defence counsel as to the facts upon which a plea of guilty was to be based, and the judge declined to give effect to that agreement. **D20.15**

Their lordships set out five principles for the guidance of the court in such cases:

(1) Whenever the court has to sentence an offender it should seek to do so on a basis which is true. The prosecution should not, therefore, lend itself to any agreement with the defence which was founded on an unreal and untrue basis.
(2) When that had happened, the judge was entitled to direct a *Newton* hearing in order to determine the true factual basis for sentence.
(3) Such a decision did not create a ground upon which an offender should be allowed to vacate a plea of guilty, provided that the offender does continue to admit guilt.
(4) The decision that there should be a trial of an issue meant that the judge was entitled to expect the assistance of prosecuting counsel in presenting evidence, and in testing any evidence called by the defence. The agreement which the prosecution has previously entered into with the defence must be viewed as conditional on the approval of the judge. If the judge's approval is not forthcoming, the defence cannot seek to hold the prosecution to the agreement.
(5) Before embarking on the trial of an issue, the judge might consider whether there is any part of the agreement by which the prosecution should be bound. Counsel should also consider which issues are to be tried, and which of the prosecution statements are relevant to them.

Guidance on the issues arising where the basis of a plea is the subject of an agreement between prosecution and defence is to be found in *Underwood* [2004] EWCA Crim 2256, [2005] 1 Cr App R 13 (178) (see **D20.9** and points (1), (4), (5), (6), (7), (8) and (10) in particular).

Longer-than-commensurate Sentence

In *Oudkerk* [1994] Crim LR 700, it was held that, where the imposition of a longer-than-commensurate sentence under the PCC(S)A 2000, s. 80(2)(b) (now repealed), was contemplated, the sentencing court must resolve by a *Newton* hearing any important issue going to the application of that provision. Similar situations may arise in relation to the application of the CJA 2003, ss. 224 to 236, and, in particular, a finding that an offender is 'dangerous' on the basis of particular conduct (see **E4.1** ***et seq.***). **D20.16**

Where *Newton* Hearing Unnecessary

Change of Plea Some difficulty arises where the offender enters a guilty plea only after some evidence has been given at trial by prosecution witnesses. In *Mottram* (1981) 3 Cr App R (S) 123, it was held that the judge should then hear evidence from the offender (and, presumably from any requested witnesses called upon), before deciding on the version of the facts which would form the basis for sentence. The totality of the evidence received on the point relevant to sentence can then be treated as a *Newton* hearing (see also *Archer* [1994] Crim LR 80). **D20.17**

Insignificant Disputes The principles in *Newton* (1982) 77 Cr App R 13, apply only where the dispute between prosecution and defence is 'substantial' (see the words of Lord Lane's judgment quoted at **D20.8**). It follows that, where the judge's sentence would be the same whichever version of the facts was accepted, there is no obligation on the judge to hear evidence but a decision can be made one way or the other simply on the basis of counsel's representations. This was illustrated in *Bent* (1986) 8 Cr App R (S) 19, where the factual dispute did not go to the gravamen of the charge. In cases such as *Bent*, a judge should sentence on the assumption that the defence version is correct, and expressly say so (see dicta to that effect by Lincoln J in *Hall* (1984) 6 Cr App R (S) 321 at p. 324). **D20.18**

Further guidance on this topic is to be found in *Underwood* [2004] EWCA Crim 2256, [2005] 1 Cr App R 13 (178) (see **D20.9** and point (14)(e) in particular).

D20.19 **Extraneous Matters** There is no requirement to hold a *Newton* hearing where the matter that is not accepted relates to extraneous mitigation which is outside the prosecution's knowledge (the 'reverse *Newton*' situation). For this see **D20.81** and *Underwood* [2004] EWCA Crim 2256, [2005] 1 Cr App R 13 (178) at **D20.9**, especially point (9).

D20.20 **Defence Version Manifestly Absurd** The guidance in *Newton* (1982) 77 Cr App R 13 requires a sentencer either to hear evidence about a significant dispute as to the facts of the offence or to accept the defence version 'so far as possible'. The implication is that the defence account may be so implausible that a judge ought not to be obliged to waste time by hearing evidence before rejecting it.

Such an interpretation of *Newton* has been confirmed by subsequent decisions, in particular *Hawkins* (1985) 7 Cr App R (S) 351. In that case, D accepted that he had acted as the get-away driver in a joint offence of burglary but he only became aware of the full facts at a very late stage. The judge declined to hear evidence about the facts but sentenced on the prosecution version that D had been a knowing participant throughout. The Court of Appeal dismissed D's appeal because the suggestion that 'he was driving the car around to keep the engine warm or to look for a lavatory for himself, whilst unknown to him his colleagues were burgling a house was an incredible assertion'. The judge did not have to trouble himself with evidence.

The same approach was taken in *Bilinski* (1987) 86 Cr App R 146, and in *Walton* (1987) 9 Cr App R (S) 107 at p. 109 where Kennedy J said, 'the words used by this court in *Newton* (1982) 77 Cr App R 13 do not mean that in every case a judge must hear evidence before he rejects a version of the facts put forward in mitigation, but which for good reason he regards as untenable... The judge was fully entitled [in the circumstances of this case] to reject the submission that was put forward [in mitigation] out of hand during the course of argument.'

D20.21 **Evidence of the Offender Incredible** Similar reasoning applies to the case where the offender gives an account on oath at the *Newton* hearing. The fact that the burden of proof is upon the prosecution does not inevitably lead to the conclusion that the offender's testimony must automatically be accepted in the absence of direct evidence to the contrary. If the offender's account on oath is incredible, the judge is entitled to reject it whether or not the prosecution call evidence. Thus, in *Kerr* (1980) 2 Cr App R (S) 54, D, who pleaded guilty to importing cannabis through Heathrow, gave evidence that, until almost the moment of leaving the plane, he had thought the packets in his luggage to be samples of marble, not drugs. It was held that the judge was entitled to reject that explanation even though the prosecution called no evidence and did not even cross-examine D.

D20.22 **Restrictions on the Court's Right to Reject the Offender's Account** The judge's view that the defence version is manifestly absurd must, however, be in accordance with the facts. This was illustrated in *Costley* (1989) 11 Cr App R (S) 357. The prosecution alleged that D, who had pleaded guilty to inflicting grievous bodily harm, had used a piece of wood as a weapon. However, D claimed he had been provoked, and even then had only used his fists. In sentencing (without first hearing evidence), the judge said: 'I find as a fact that the attack was totally unprovoked by anything [V] said or did.... I reject your explanation for the use of violence as being wholly incredible'. The Court of Appeal held that it was not open to the judge to come to these conclusions, and upheld the appeal against sentence. In a case where the sentencer is faced with a substantial conflict on issues such as this, a *Newton* hearing should be held. Where the court feels unable to accept the defence account, it should make that clear, and indicate why (*Tolera* [1999] 1 Cr App R 29).

Procedure

D20.23 **Burden and Standard of Proof** In a *Newton* hearing, the burden of proof is on the prosecution to satisfy the judge beyond reasonable doubt that their version of events is the correct one. This was demonstrated in *Ahmed* (1984) 80 Cr App R 295, where the issue between prosecution and defence was whether D was a mere courier or a dealer. The trial judge, after hearing evidence from D, decided against his account and sentenced accordingly. On appeal, the defence argument that the judge had misdirected himself as to the standard of proof failed. Parker LJ observed:

> If it be right that in the absence of evidence the submissions of the defence should be accepted and that the other two possible courses are to have the matter (where circumstances permit) determined by a jury or the judge, then it must in our view follow that the defence version of the facts must be accepted, unless a jury or the judge, as the case may be, is sure that it is wrong.

In *Kerrigan* (1993) 14 Cr App R (S) 179, it was said that it was better for the judge to direct himself openly as to the relevant standard and onus of proof, although the failure to do so was not fatal in every case.

Calling Evidence Once the judge has decreed that there should be a *Newton* hearing, the hearing itself follows normal adversarial lines (per May LJ in *McGrath* (1983) 5 Cr App R (S) 460 at p. 463). The parties are given the opportunity to call such evidence as they wish and to cross-examine the witnesses called by the other side. The roles of the parties, and the court, do require consideration. **D20.24**

Role of the Prosecution Where the basic facts are not in dispute, the prosecution are not obliged to call any evidence, and the judge is then entitled to draw any appropriate inferences, so long as expressly mindful of the burden and standard of proof (*Mirza* (1993) 14 Cr App R (S) 64). The prosecution are still required to participate, whether or not they have material to dispute the defence account. In *Tolera* [1999] 1 Cr App R 29, the Court of Appeal suggested that, in questioning the offender, the prosecutor should adopt the role of *amicus curiae*, exploring matters which the court wished to be explored. The prosecution should not leave the questioning to the judge. **D20.25**

Role of the Defence On the other hand, the defence cannot be forced to call evidence or otherwise participate, but may simply observe while the prosecution seek to establish their version to the judge's satisfaction. A defendant cannot, however, by declining to give evidence, frustrate the exercise which the judge has undertaken so as to ground a subsequent complaint that there has been no *Newton* hearing (*Mirza* (1993) 14 Cr App R (S) 64). **D20.26**

Role of the Court In order for the judge to avoid giving the impression of having come to conclusions in advance, it will be preferable for judicial questioning to wait until the offender has been examined by defence counsel, and cross-examined by counsel for the prosecution (*Myers* (1996) 1 Cr App R (S) 187). In assessing the evidence, the judge must, as the tribunal of fact, observe the directions which would have been given to the jury for their guidance. This was illustrated in *Gandy* (1989) 11 Cr App R (S) 564. D had pleaded guilty to violent disorder. On the completion of the trial of his co-offender, a *Newton* hearing was held to determine identification evidence relating to D's role. The Court of Appeal held that, during that *Newton* hearing, it was important that the judge should have approached the matter and directed himself as if he were a jury. In particular this required the court: **D20.27**

(a) to go through the steps which *Turnbull* [1977] QB 224 required the judge to set out when directing a jury;
(b) to consider the admissibility of identification evidence which breached the PACE 1984 codes of practice; and
(c) to consider the reliability of other aspects of the evidence, e.g., discrepancies between the contemporaneous descriptions and D's appearance.

Hence it appears that, in the context of a *Newton* hearing: (a) the rules of evidence should be strictly followed, and (b) the judge should clearly express and apply appropriate legal directions as the trier of fact.

Consequences of a *Newton* Hearing

D20.28 **Loss of Mitigation for a Guilty Plea** In *Underwood* [2004] EWCA Crim 2256, [2005] 1 Cr App R 13 (178) (see **D20.9**), the Court of Appeal set out guidance as to the extent to which the offender should receive credit for a guilty plea where a *Newton* hearing is necessary (see also *Stevens* (1986) 8 Cr App R (S) 291; *Jauncey* (1986) 8 Cr App R (S) 401; and *Williams* [1991] Crim LR 150). The main points are:

(a) If issues on a *Newton* hearing are resolved in the offender's favour, the credit due for a guilty plea should not be reduced.
(b) If the offender is disbelieved or obliges the prosecution to call evidence from a witness causing unnecessary and inappropriate distress, thereby demonstrating no insight into the consequences of the offence and no genuine remorse for it, the judge may reduce the discount for a guilty plea, particularly if it has been tendered at a very late stage.
(c) There might be an exceptional case in which the normal entitlement to credit for a guilty plea is wholly dissipated by the *Newton* hearing, in which case the judge should give reasons.

If the judge mentions the prospect of loss of mitigation prior to holding a *Newton* hearing, it is important to be careful to avoid giving the impression of having decided against the offender's version in advance (*Satchell* (1997) 2 Cr App R (S) 258). See also *Elicin* [2008] EWCA Crim 2249, [2009] 1 Cr App R (S) 98 (561).

Appeals in *Newton* Hearing Cases

D20.29 The Court of Appeal does have power to interfere with the decision of the sentencing judge as to the facts of the offence arrived at following a *Newton* hearing (*A-G's Refs (Nos. 3 and 4 of 1996)* (1997) 1 Cr App R (S) 29). However, there are important limitations (per Parker LJ in *Ahmed* (1984) 80 Cr App R 295):

(a) if the judge has properly expressed and applied appropriate legal directions as to the burden and standard of proof, the Court of Appeal will exercise its power only in 'exceptional cases' where 'no reasonable jury [properly] directed could have reached the judge's conclusion';
(b) if the offender gave evidence at the *Newton* hearing, the occasions on which interference is justified will be 'rare indeed', bearing in mind the trial judge's advantage in having seen the demeanour etc. of the offender when testifying.

In an appropriate case, however, the Court of Appeal will depart from findings of fact made by a judge in a *Newton* hearing (see, e.g., *Gandy* (1989) 11 Cr App R (S) 564, discussed in **D20.27**). In appropriate cases, the Court of Appeal can itself hold a *Newton* hearing (*Guppy* [1994] Crim LR 614).

DISPUTES ABOUT THE FACTS FOLLOWING A VERDICT OF GUILTY

General Principle

D20.30 Where the offender is convicted following a trial, it is for the sentencer to form a view as to the facts of the offence established by the evidence, and to sentence accordingly. In general, the jury should not be asked to supplement a verdict of guilty by stating the factual basis on which they reached their decision (*Stosiek* (1982) 4 Cr App R (S) 205; *Solomon* (1984) 6 Cr App R (S) 120).

There is a recognised exception to this principle, relating to a verdict of guilty of manslaughter (see **D19.81**). Although *Cranston* (1993) 14 Cr App R (S) 103 appears to give some encouragement to this becoming a wider practice, Dr. Thomas's commentary on that case at [1992] Crim LR 831 correctly identifies the inevitable problems with such a course. A number of propositions emerge from the cases.

Court Not Bound to Accept the Version Most Favourable to the Offender

The court is not obliged to accept the version of events most favourable to the defence consistent with the jury's verdict. For example, in *Solomon* (1984) 6 Cr App R (S) 120, the court was held to be entitled, in a case where D2 was found not guilty of attempted murder but guilty of causing grievous bodily harm with intent, to sentence on the basis that D2 had deliberately caused grievous bodily harm with the shot gun, even though he had not intended to kill, despite D1's evidence being to a contrary effect (see also *McGlade* (1990) 12 Cr App R (S) 105). **D20.31**

Giving the Offender the Benefit of the Doubt

The court should, however, be 'extremely astute' to give to the offender the benefit of any doubt about the facts of the offence (per Watkins LJ in *Stosiek* (1982) 4 Cr App R (S) 205). In *Stosiek*, D was sentenced for assaulting a plain-clothes police officer occasioning him actual bodily harm on the basis that D realised at the time of the assault that his victim was an officer. The Court of Appeal reduced the sentence because the alternative basis that D had over-reacted to what he took to be a minor assault by an ordinary member of the public was a 'reasonable possibility', and should therefore have been accepted in preference to the unfavourable alternative hypothesis. **D20.32**

In *Efionayi* (1995) 16 Cr App R (S) 380, the defendants were convicted of wilful neglect of a child over a 14-day period. The jury were directed that they could convict if satisfied that any neglect had occurred within the period specified in the count. After they convicted, the judge sentenced on the basis that the neglect covered the whole 14 days. The Court of Appeal allowed the appeal against sentence, stating that the judge should have taken the jury's verdict to relate to the shorter period and sentenced accordingly. The Court observed that, to prevent this problem, the indictment could easily have been amended to secure the jury's finding on the point. Where there was more than one possible interpretation of the verdict and the sentencing judge was able to reach a conclusion, to the criminal standard, as to the factual basis on which to pass sentence, the judge was entitled to sentence on that basis. Otherwise, the interpretation most favourable to the offender should be adopted (*King (Dwayne)* [2017] EWCA Crim 128, [2017] 2 Cr App R (S) 6 (25)).

The Basis Must be Consistent with the Verdict

The court must not adopt a view of the facts which is adverse to the offender and inconsistent with the jury's verdict, even if that verdict is difficult to understand. Thus, in *Hazelwood* (1984) 6 Cr App R (S) 52, D was acquitted of assault with intent to resist arrest but convicted of common assault in the alternative. His sentence was reduced: 'the court has...to have respect for the jury's verdict and must avoid concluding or indeed suspecting that the appellant was in fact resisting arrest' (per Stephen Brown LJ). This is really an aspect of the broader principle (see **D20.41**) that an offender must be sentenced only in relation to offences proved or admitted, or offences taken into consideration (or exceptionally, in relation to wider criminal conduct where the offender accepts that the indictment does not reflect the totality of the offending). **D20.33**

Impact of any Expressed Jury Opinion

If the jury indicate on their own initiative a view of the facts which is relevant to sentence, the judge is not bound by that view when deciding upon sentence. In *Mills* [2003] EWCA Crim 2397, [2004] 1 Cr App R (S) 57 (332), D was sentenced on the basis of knowledge of importing drugs with a high value, notwithstanding a note that had been submitted by the jury, stating that their verdict of guilty was based on a view that D genuinely believed that the imported goods were not drugs but were prohibited. The Court of Appeal agreed that the sentencing judge was not bound by the jury's finding, and dismissed the appeal. **D20.34**

Newton Hearing Following a Trial

D20.35 The court can hold a *Newton* hearing after the jury has returned a verdict of guilty (*Finch* (1993) 14 Cr App R (S) 226). This would be appropriate where an issue material to sentence was not properly canvassed during the trial because it was not relevant to guilt. In *Finch* itself, it was held that a *Newton* hearing should have been held to determine whether or not D had been entrapped, because it could, if true, amount to substantial mitigation, whilst not in law constituting a defence.

Ascertaining Facts by Verdict of Jury

D20.36 In *Newton* (1982) 77 Cr App R 13, the third alternative method of identifying the factual basis for sentence to which Lord Lane referred was to obtain the answer from a jury (see **D20.8**). The method for achieving this is to include a count on the indictment which will indicate how, in the jury's view, the primary offence to which the offender pleads guilty was committed. For example, in *Gandy* (1989) 11 Cr App R (S) 564 (see **D20.27** for the facts), where the issue was whether D, charged with violent disorder, had caused a particular injury, the Court of Appeal felt 'some regret that the Crown had not seen fit in the circumstances of this case to include a specific count against [the appellant] for either wounding with intent under section 18 of the Offences against the Person Act 1861 or alternatively under section 20 of that Act for unlawful wounding' (see also *Efionayi* (1995) 16 Cr App R (S) 380 and **D20.32**).

In *Dowdall* (1992) 13 Cr App R (S) 441, however, the Court of Appeal held that the jury should be used to decide the issue only where the difference in the versions of the facts alleged by the prosecution and the defence reflects different offences. In that case, in which D was charged with theft, the prosecution had amended the indictment to reflect two possible means of appropriation: finding and taking. On appeal, the Court held that the count should not have been split in two as the alternative averments added in each case were immaterial to guilt. The right course where sentence turned on which version was right was for the judge either to adopt D's version or to try the issue in a *Newton* hearing. Similarly, in *Ali* [2011] EWCA Crim 1260, [2011] 2 Cr App R 22 (285), the Court of Appeal deprecated the suggestion of having two legally identical but factually different conspiracy charges on the same indictment as a means of identifying the factual basis for sentence.

ASCERTAINING THE FACTS OF THE OFFENCE WHERE ONE OFFENDER PLEADS GUILTY AND THE OTHER NOT GUILTY

D20.37 The rule that, if there has been a not guilty plea followed by a verdict of guilty, it is for the judge to decide for sentencing purposes how the offence was committed on the basis of the evidence heard during the course of the trial, and the rule that, if the offender pleads guilty, the judge must accept the defence version of the facts unless satisfied at a *Newton* hearing that the prosecution version is correct, come into conflict with each other when one offender pleads guilty and the co-defendant not guilty.

The Court of Appeal has wavered in its approach to the problem. In *Taggart* (1979) 1 Cr App R (S) 144 and *Depledge* (1979) 1 Cr App R (S) 183, it was held that, when sentencing the offender who pleaded guilty, the judge could take into account the evidence heard at the co-defendant's trial. However, in *Michaels* (1981) 3 Cr App R (S) 188, the judge was criticised for taking a view of the facts adverse to the appellants without having all the witnesses who had testified at the trial of their co-accused recalled for cross-examination. The Court of Appeal has since been afforded the opportunity of resolving the conflict between the earlier authorities on two occasions, namely in *Smith* (1988) 87 Cr App R 393 and *Mahoney* (1993) 14 Cr App R (S) 291.

The Approach in *Smith*

In *Smith* (1988) 87 Cr App R 393, *Taggart* and *Depledge* were preferred to *Michaels*. D pleaded guilty to conspiracy to obtain property by deception. At their trial, certain of his co-accused offered the defence that they acted under duress stemming from D. When the time came to sentence, the judge indicated that he had taken a preliminary view that D was the ringleader in the enterprise, albeit that the jury had rejected the co-accused's claim that they had been subjected to duress by him. None of the evidence called at the trial was recalled but D was offered the opportunity to testify in his own defence that he was not the ringleader. **D20.38**

The Court of Appeal upheld the sentence and said that the judge had handled the procedural problem 'impeccably'. His primary task when sentencing was to decide what had been the facts of the conspiracy and, in doing that, he *was* entitled to take into account evidence he had heard at the trial of the co-accused and even witness statements. There was no need to have the witnesses recalled for cross-examination by the offender pleading guilty. To hold otherwise might have led to a situation where the judge felt constrained to sentence one conspirator on a view of the facts which he had rejected when sentencing a co-conspirator. It was, however, necessary for D himself to be offered the opportunity of giving evidence about the extent of his involvement. The judge had done that more than once, and the appeal was accordingly dismissed.

Difficulties with *Smith* The decision in *Smith* (1988) 87 Cr App R 393, while understandable as a pragmatic solution to a difficult problem, may lead to a sense of unfairness being felt by an offender who is sentenced on a view of the facts which is not accepted and which the defence team have not been able to test. In *Smith*, counsel was present in court during the trial of the co-accused, holding a noting brief. Thus, the defence at least knew what had been said against D. However, counsel had no standing to cross-examine the witnesses who impugned his client, and D himself never heard the evidence on the basis of which he was sentenced. **D20.39**

A further anomaly appears when one compares the approach outlined in *Smith* with that adopted in a case such as *Gandy* (1989) 11 Cr App R (S) 564 (see **D20.27**). In *Gandy*, a *Newton* hearing was held in relation to D, who had pleaded guilty, at the end of the trial of others. In that *Newton* hearing the judge was required to follow the rules which would govern the use of evidence in a jury trial. Clearly, there is no equivalent protection for the offender where the *Smith* procedure is concerned. The resultant distinction exacerbates the sense of unfairness already referred to (see also *Winter* [1997] Crim LR 66).

The Approach in *Mahoney*

In *Mahoney* (1993) 14 Cr App R (S) 291, the Court of Appeal favoured the approach suggested in *Michaels*, although neither that case nor *Taggart* nor *Depledge* was referred to. Twenty-one prisoners were indicted in relation to a prison riot. There were two trials, and D pleaded guilty to the lesser offence of violent disorder and was sentenced at the end of the second trial. The Court of Appeal reduced D's sentence, stating (Leonard J at p. 293): **D20.40**

> A further submission is made that in this case what happened was that the learned judge heard the evidence in the first trial and in the second trial which led to acquittal, and that in large part he passed sentence upon the appellant on the basis of that material. The problem about that was that the appellant was neither present at, nor represented at, either of those two trials. It was, in our view, wrong therefore, for the learned judge to pay regard to what he had heard in those trials when he was passing sentence upon the appellant.
>
> It is quite clear that the judge formed the view that the prosecution had been somewhat supine in accepting the pleas to violent disorder at the threshold of the second trial. That seems to be the point of his observation about his sentencing on the basis of the facts rather than the title of the offence. If there were matters which were in dispute, the learned judge should either have adopted the course which he indicated at the earlier stage and have sentenced on the basis of what the appellant through his counsel was accepting to be the appropriate facts of the case, or alternatively, if there was a need to resolve the dispute, it should have been resolved by means of a *Newton* hearing.

DUTY TO MAKE SENTENCE CONFORM TO FACTS CONSISTENT WITH VERDICT

D20.41 The above heading may seem a statement of the obvious. It is, however, a cardinal principle of sentencing, confirmed by *Ralf* (1989) 11 Cr App R (S) 121. It has a number of implications for determining the facts of the offence, which are addressed below.

Respecting the Verdict

D20.42 First, as explained immediately above, the sentencer must respect the jury's verdict when determining the facts of the offence and not pass a sentence appropriate to a more serious charge of which the offender has been acquitted (*Gillespie* [1998] 2 Cr App R (S) 61). Similarly, if the prosecution accept a plea to a lesser offence or to one of several counts, the judge must be careful to sentence for that only and not for the more serious matters left on the file (*Booker* (1982) 4 Cr App R (S) 53). The Court of Appeal emphasised this in *Stubbs* (1988) 89 Cr App R 53, saying 'the court must abide loyally by the plea which had been tendered'.

Not Inflating the Offending

D20.43 Secondly, the judge must not sentence on the basis that the offender has committed other similar offences on other occasions, even if the circumstances of the offence charged or admissions made by the offender when being questioned by the police strongly indicate that it was not a 'one-off' occurrence (*Reeves* (1983) 5 Cr App R (S) 292; *Ayensu* (1982) 4 Cr App R (S) 248). This is subject to the major exception that the defence may concede that the counts in the indictment are merely samples of a continuing course of conduct or ask for other offences to be taken into consideration (see **D20.52**).

Similarly, the judge must not, under the pretence of determining the facts of the offence at a *Newton* hearing, in effect find the offender guilty of an offence more serious than that charged (*Courtie* [1984] AC 463; *Druce* (1993) 14 Cr App R (S) 691).

Secondary Offending

D20.44 Difficult problems also arise where the prosecution version of the facts of the offence on the indictment (the primary offence) implies that the offender is guilty of an additional offence (the secondary offence) not charged.

There are some cases which seem to suggest that, provided the secondary offence is of no greater gravity than the primary offence, the judge may (subject to the need for a *Newton* hearing) sentence on the basis that the latter did indeed involve commission of the former as alleged by the prosecution. This is illustrated in the cases of *Ribas* (1976) 63 Cr App R 147 and *Rubinstein* (1982) 4 Cr App R (S) 202, which concerned, respectively, counts for importing controlled drugs and conspiracy to cultivate controlled drugs. The question arose whether the sentencers were right to reject the defence mitigation that the drugs were intended only for personal consumption, given that there was no count on either indictment for possession with intent to supply or conspiracy to supply. The Court of Appeal in both cases upheld the judges' approach.

These cases may be contrasted with *Lawrence* (1981) 3 Cr App R (S) 49, where D pleaded guilty to cultivating cannabis and the Court of Appeal held that the sentencer had to 'banish from his mind' the possibility that D was growing the cannabis in order to sell it. *Lawrence* was considered and applied in *O'Prey* [1999] 2 Cr App R (S) 83, where the Court of Appeal stressed that it was not permissible for the sentencer to sentence for criminality not reflected in the indictment (for the solution being to add a count to the indictment to reflect the secondary offence, see **D20.36**).

However, in other circumstances the Court of Appeal has positively exhorted sentencers to take into account other offences in this way. For example in *Boswell* [1984] 3 All ER 353, in the course of giving guidelines on sentencing for causing death by reckless driving, Lord Lane CJ said that an aggravating feature conclusive towards a custodial sentence was if the offender's driving had involved other offences, whether formally charged or not. In *Khan* [2009] EWCA Crim 389, [2010] 1 Cr App R (S) 1 (1), the Court of Appeal concluded that account could be taken of conduct relevant to the offence charged which had been scrutinised at trial.

EVIDENCE OF CHARACTER AND ANTECEDENTS

Requirement for Evidence of Character and Antecedents

After the prosecution summary of the facts, or immediately after the jury's verdict of guilty if it was a not guilty plea, it is the responsibility of the prosecution to adduce evidence about the offender's character and antecedents in accordance with CrimPD II, paras. 8A.2 and 8A.6 to 8A.8 (see Supplement, **CPD.8A**). **D20.45**

Procedure for Giving Antecedents

Evidence of the offender's antecedents will usually be presented by prosecuting counsel, provided that the defence has agreed that the antecedents are not in dispute. Where evidence is disputed, an officer may give evidence, taking the *voir dire* oath (see **F4.32**), in effect, reading from the antecedents and previous convictions forms. The normal rules of evidence are relaxed in that counsel may ask leading questions. Moreover, the antecedents will not necessarily have been prepared by the officer giving the evidence or contain matters personally known to the officer. In fact, most of the information may have come from the offender, either on the occasion of the present arrest or in the course of previous dealings with the police. An officer giving such evidence may be cross-examined. **D20.46**

Contents of Antecedents

The prosecution are not necessarily restricted to the basic and essentially uncontroversial form of antecedents specifically sanctioned by CrimPD II, paras. 8A.2 and 8A.6 to 8A.8. Further guidance has been provided as to what may or may not be included in the presentation of antecedents. **D20.47**

(a) It must not contain allegations of a generalised nature which are prejudicial to the offender and, by their very nature, incapable of proof (*Van Pelz* [1943] KB 157).
(b) In exceptional cases, it may be proper to adduce additional information about the offender's involvement in gangland crime and organised prostitution (*Wilkins* (1977) 66 Cr App R 49) or position in a chain of criminals supplying drugs (*Robinson* (1969) 53 Cr App R 314). As to whether it is proper to adduce evidence of the offender's criminal associates, in *Bibby* [1972] Crim LR 513 the Court of Appeal ruled that it was unfair but Lord Goddard CJ in *Crabtree* [1952] 2 All ER 974 could see nothing wrong with such evidence provided that the officer could give it from first-hand knowledge.
(c) Such allegations are likely to be challenged by the defence, and, in the event of challenge, it is essential that the prosecution prove what they allege in accordance with the ordinary rules of criminal evidence.
(d) 'Evidence' from the antecedents officer based on hearsay is inadmissible, even if it takes the form of recounting information supplied by colleagues (*Wilkins*). This reflects a principle first stated in *Campbell* (1911) 6 Cr App R 131 that, whenever antecedents evidence is challenged by the defence, the onus is on the prosecution to prove their case by strict evidence. If they fail to do so, the judge should ignore the challenged allegation and state that it will be ignored (see also *Sargeant* (1974) 60 Cr App R 74).

If the prosecution anticipate that the antecedents will be disputed by the defence, it is good practice to give the defence notice of the proposed evidence (see dicta in both *Robinson* and *Wilkins*).

Proof of the Offender's Convictions

D20.48 Like any other disputed part of the antecedents, if the offender disputes a previous conviction alleged at the antecedents stage, it must either be proved in accordance with the strict rules of evidence or ignored. For the methods of proving a previous conviction, see **F12**. If the offender has a long record, it is rare for it to be given in full. The judge will indicate which convictions are necessary to read.

Spent Convictions

D20.49 The Rehabilitation of Offenders Act 1974, as applied to criminal proceedings by CrimPD V, paras. 21A.1 to 21A.3 (see Supplement, **CPD.21A**), restricts the circumstances in which it is proper to refer to 'spent convictions'. The Act was subject to substantial amendment by the LASPO 2012, s. 139, replacing the original periods set out in the 1974 Act.

Where an offender is sentenced to 48 months' imprisonment or less for an offence, the conviction becomes spent upon the expiry of the 'rehabilitation period'. That period runs from the date of completion of the sentence (i.e. the entire sentence, not just the custodial element) and varies in length depending upon the sentence imposed (e.g., 12 months for a community order, 24 months for a custodial sentence up to six months, 48 months for a sentence up to 30 months, seven years for a sentence up to 48 months). Sentences over four years are not subject to a rehabilitation regime. Commission of a further offence during the rehabilitation period for an earlier one usually means that neither conviction becomes spent until the rehabilitation date for the later one. Thus, recidivist offenders rarely enjoy the advantages of their convictions becoming spent. For further details of periods of rehabilitation, see **E24**; for evidential considerations, see **F13.96**.

D20.50 **Proper Approach to Spent Convictions** The main function of the Rehabilitation of Offenders Act 1974 is to protect a person with spent convictions from having to reveal his or her record in civil proceedings or when applying for a job. Indeed, s. 7(2) provides that the protection against questions relating to spent convictions afforded by s. 4(1) of the Act does *not* apply to evidence given in criminal proceedings. However, CrimPD V, paras. 21A.1 to 21A.3, give guidance on how the criminal courts should deal with spent convictions. See further **E24.1** and **F13.96**.

Breach of Court Orders

D20.51 If the present conviction apparently puts the offender in breach of an existing court order such as a suspended sentence (for which see **E6.11**) or a conditional discharge (for which see **E12.5**), it will be necessary that the breach be put. If there is a denial, the matter must be proved by strict evidence. Upon the breach being admitted or proved, prosecuting counsel should, if possible, be able to give the court details of the offence in respect of which the order breached was made.

SENTENCING FOR MATTERS OF WHICH THE OFFENDER HAS NOT BEEN CONVICTED

D20.52 It is a basic principle of sentencing to sentence only for those crimes of which the offender has been convicted and not for anything else (see **D20.43**).

There are three identifiable exceptions to this principle where a sentencer may properly be influenced by other offences not officially before the court. These are as follows:

(a) taking into account a less serious secondary offence which has not been charged but the commission of which is implicit in, and represents an aggravating feature of, the more serious primary offence (see *Rubinstein* (1982) 4 Cr App R (S) 202 at **D20.44**);
(b) if the offender expressly asks for the other offences to be taken into consideration (see **D20.53**); and

(c) if the prosecution case is that the offences on the indictment are merely samples of a continuing course of conduct and the defence accept that to be so (see **D20.56**).

Taking Other Offences into Consideration

This is a common practice. It is based upon convention rather than statute or common law. It requires the co-operation of the police, the court and, most importantly, the offender. It operates to the benefit of both the police and the offender. The police are enabled to clear up numerous offences which might otherwise remain unsolved. The offender is able to 'wipe the slate completely clean' at a minimal cost in terms of increased sentence. The definitive sentencing guideline, *Offences Taken into Consideration*, applies in relation to all offenders whose cases are dealt with on or after 11 June 2012 (see Supplement, **SG3-1**). **D20.53**

Normal Practice The normal procedure involves the following stages. **D20.54**

(a) The police, having arrested and obtained admissions from a suspect for a certain offence, will then invite the suspect to tell them about other crimes committed.
(b) Depending on the suspect's response, a list is then drawn up of the other offences.
(c) The suspect is charged with a limited number of offences, is prosecuted in the normal way, and pleads guilty.
(d) At some time before the sentencing exercise, the offender is served with the list of the other offences and asked to sign it to acknowledge committing them. The offender may, of course, accept some but not all of the offences.
(e) Copies of the list (the 't.i.c.s') are then given to the defence and included in prosecuting counsel's brief.
(f) At a convenient moment during counsel's summary of the facts of the offence to which the offender has pleaded guilty, the court is told that the offender wishes to have other offences taken into consideration. The court is given the original of the signed list.
(g) The offender then confirms the offences are admitted and that the court is invited to take them into consideration.
(h) The court then decides whether to comply with the offender's request. Assuming that it does, prosecuting counsel gives brief details of the offences, and the sentencing process thereafter continues in the normal way. When passing sentence, the judge should state expressly that certain other offences were taken into consideration.

Although the t.i.c. procedure is geared for offenders expected to plead guilty, there is no objection to adapting it for an offender pleading not guilty. Thus, in anticipation of a guilty verdict, the police might prepare a t.i.c. list and then use an adjournment between conviction and sentence to invite the offender to sign the list.

Assessment of the Procedure A number of matters arise in relation to the t.i.c. procedure: **D20.55**

(a) Since the offender is never charged with or convicted of the t.i.c.s, the court's powers of sentence are limited to the maximum for the offences on the indictment of which the offender has been convicted, whether by way of guilty plea or jury verdict (hereafter referred to as 'the conviction offences'). This is not a significant restriction since it is rare that a court would wish to impose a sentence nearing the maximum penalties. The exception to this limitation is that the court may order the offender to pay compensation for a matter taken into consideration, and to that extent may sentence directly for the offence (PCC(S)A 2000, s. 130(1)(a)).
(b) An offence should not be taken into consideration if it carries endorsement of the licence and discretionary or obligatory disqualification where the conviction offences are non-endorsable (*Collins* [1947] KB 560; *Simons* (1953) 37 Cr App R 120). Otherwise, the offender would escape even endorsement whereas, had the t.i.c. offence been prosecuted in the normal way, the court would have been obliged to endorse in the absence of special reasons and might have chosen also to disqualify.

(c) Offences should not be taken into consideration unless the offender clearly requests the sentencer to do so and admits commission of the offences (*Griffiths* (1932) 23 Cr App R 153). In *Walsh* (8 March 1973 unreported), Scarman J stressed the importance of the offender understanding what is being done, admitting the offences and genuinely wanting them taken into consideration.
(d) It is not necessary to read the list out in full. It is sufficient if the judge confirms the offender has signed the list containing a specified number of offences, agrees to having committed them, and confirms a wish to have them borne in mind when sentence is passed for the offences on the indictment.
(e) The judge always has a discretion whether to comply with a request to take an offence into consideration. It is important not to take into consideration an offence which the offender is willing to admit if the public interest requires that the offence be dealt with by indictment (*McLean* (1910) 6 Cr App R 26). Further, it would be bad practice to take offences into consideration which are either more serious than or of a completely different type from the conviction offences.
(f) The fact that an offence has been taken into consideration does not entitle the offender formally to rely on autrefois convict in a subsequent prosecution for the same offence (*Nicholson* [1947] 2 All ER 535). However, in the absence of quite exceptional circumstances, the prosecution would not consider instituting proceedings for a matter that they know to have been taken into consideration by a court on a previous occasion.
(g) In passing sentence, the judge may increase the penalty somewhat because of the t.i.c.s. However, the amount of the increase will almost certainly be considerably less severe than it would have been had the offences taken into consideration been separately prosecuted.

As to the difficulties with which a court is presented where the offences to be taken into consideration are more serious than the offence on the indictment, see *Lavery* [2008] EWCA Crim 2499, [2009] 3 All ER 295.

Sample Offences

D20.56 As an alternative to following strictly the procedure for taking other offences into consideration, the prosecution may invite the judge to treat the offences on the indictment of which the offender has been convicted, or to which the offender has pleaded guilty, as samples of a continuing course of conduct. (See **D11.36** for detail on the implications of sample counts when considering the indictment.)

This is an attractive course where the offender appears to have committed a large number of similar offences over a protracted period. Although there is no reason, in such a case, why a list of t.i.c.s should not be prepared as described in **D20.53**, the list can become inordinately long (see, e.g., *Sequeira* (1982) 4 Cr App R (S) 65, where, in respect of an offender who had claimed social security benefit for four years when ineligible, the t.i.c. procedure resulted in a list of 150 offences). See also CrimPD VII, Sentencing B (see Supplement, **CPD.VII.B**).

D20.57 **Sentencing for Sample Offences Following a Guilty Plea** It is generally accepted that where the offender pleads guilty and the defence agree with the prosecution that the offences on the indictment are merely samples, the court may sentence on that basis even though the offender does not formally ask for other offences to be taken into consideration.

Such an approach was approved in *Huchison* [1972] 1 All ER 936 per Phillimore LJ at p. 400C:

> Of course, there are cases where the prosecution puts forward a count as a sample count, and in those cases it is well understood that if that course is taken and the defence are notified, a judge is entitled to deal with the whole matter on the basis that the offence in fact was repeated more than once, or that there were other similar incidents.

If, however, the defence dispute the other occasions on which similar offences were allegedly committed, the judge should sentence the offender only for those occasions which are admitted, whether by way of guilty plea or by asking for a limited number of other occasions to be taken into consideration. This, again, was demonstrated in *Huchison*. The Court of Appeal held that where it became obvious that the defence denied the suggestion that the offence on the indictment was a sample one, the judge's options were either to sentence D strictly for the one act that was admitted, or to adjourn so that counts for the other occasions could be added to the indictment.

Huchison has been followed in *McKenzie* (1984) 6 Cr App R (S) 99 (sentence reduced for seven cheque card offences involving loss to the victims of £640 because the judge had apparently sentenced on the basis denied by the defence that the counts on the indictment were samples of continuing conduct in which £11,000 had been obtained), and *Ralf* (1989) 11 Cr App R (S) 121 (sentence for assault on a child reduced because the judge referred to the appellant having caused various injuries to the child over and above those she actually admitted).

Sentencing for Sample Offences Following a Trial Where the offender pleads not guilty to the offences on the indictment but is found guilty, more recent authorities support the proposition that the offender should not be sentenced as if found guilty of other offences not included in the indictment even if the prosecution had described them as 'specimens'. This is the view adopted in *Burfoot* (1990) 12 Cr App R (S) 252. The offender ought not to be deprived of the right to jury trial because offences are omitted from the indictment. **D20.58**

In *Clark* [1996] 2 Cr App R (S) 351, the Court of Appeal followed the reasoning in *Burfoot* and in *McKenzie* (1984) 6 Cr App R 99. Their lordships said that the weight of authority supported the proposition that, where an offender was convicted on a single count, the sentencer must not sentence this person on the basis of being guilty of further offences of a similar nature unless the offender admitted that this was so.

In *Canavan* [1998] 1 Cr App R 79, Lord Bingham CJ stated that a court could not base its decision as to sentence on the commission of offences not forming part of the offence for which the offender was to be sentenced.

In *Clifford* [2014] EWCA Crim 2245, [2015] 1 Cr App R (S) 32 (242), the Court of Appeal said that it would be inappropriate to sentence an offender to a greater sentence on the basis of material adduced as bad character evidence at trial.

An alternative to the above procedure is now set out in the DVCVA 2004, s. 17. This allows the prosecution to apply for trial by jury on sample counts, with the judge trying the remaining counts alone (see **D13.81** for details).

REPORTS ON THE OFFENDER

After the prosecution summary of the facts and antecedents evidence, the court considers any reports that have been prepared on the offender. These may include pre-sentence reports, medical and psychiatric reports and assessments for suitability for a community sentence. In many cases, it will have been necessary to delay sentencing to allow such reports to be prepared (see **D20.62** and **D20.111**). **D20.59**

Judicial Promise of Non-custodial Sentence on Adjournment for Reports

Where the court adjourns for reports in circumstances which justifiably lead the offender to expect that, if the report turns out to be favourable, the sentence will be non-custodial, the court is bound by the implied promise it has given. Consequently, if the report is indeed favourable, a custodial sentence should not be passed, and will be quashed on appeal, however deserved it would otherwise have been. **D20.60**

The principle was first stated in *Gillam* (1980) 2 Cr App R (S) 267. D, a serving prisoner, appeared to be sentenced for offences for which the possibility of receiving a further prison term was very high. However, the judge adjourned so that D's suitability for community service could be assessed, and ordered that, upon the expiry of his present sentence, D should be released on bail. The Court of Appeal's judgment observed that the main purpose of the adjournment was 'to ascertain whether community service was available for such a person as [D] and whether he was a fit subject to perform that service'. In the event, although D was assessed suitable for community service he received a sentence of imprisonment.

The Court of Appeal allowed the appeal for the following reasons (per Watkins LJ at p. 269, emphasis added):

> ... an important principle of sentencing is involved in this case. All the signs, when the appellant first appeared before the deputy circuit judge, ... pointed to the imposition of an immediate prison sentence. For reasons best known to himself he decided against that course but to request the production of a report with a view to considering whether or not this man should perform community service. There was, therefore, created in the appellant's mind an expectation, not unnaturally, of performing that service if the probation officer and others who were called upon to assist in the production of the report were disposed to recommend such a course to the court. It was recommended. *When a judge in these circumstances purposely postpones sentence so that an alternative to prison can be examined and that alternative is found to be a satisfactory one in all respects the court ought to adopt the alternative.* A feeling of injustice is otherwise aroused.

D20.61 **Application of the *Gillam* principle** The decision in *Gillam* has been followed in a number of cases since, in which reports prepared on offenders during adjournments were favourable, and the custodial sentences ultimately imposed had to be quashed. These included:

(a) *Ward* (1982) 4 Cr App R (S) 103 (three-week adjournment so that D could stay at a probation hostel with a view to the making of a probation order with a condition of residence at the hostel);
(b) *McMurray* (1987) 9 Cr App R (S) 101 (four-week adjournment so that D could attend a day assessment centre);
(c) *Wilkinson* (1988) 9 Cr App R (S) 468, the facts of which were similar to *Ward*, where the sentencing judge conceded that the judge who adjourned for social inquiry reports had, by so doing, more or less promised a non-custodial disposition, but said that the offence was so serious that he (the sentencing judge) was not prepared to incur public wrath by such a lenient course — the Court of Appeal held that, in the circumstances, there was no option but to honour the first judge's implied promise, whatever the public reaction.

D20.62 **Adjournment for Reports Not Binding the Judge** However, there is no rule that adjourning for reports *inevitably* carries the implication that the sentence will be non-custodial if the report so recommends. The application of the *Gillam* principle depends upon 'there having been something in the nature of a promise, express or implied, that if a particular proposal is recommended, it will be adopted' (per Croom-Johnson J in *Moss* (1983) 5 Cr App R (S) 209).

Thus, if the judge makes it clear when adjourning that all sentencing options are open and that no promise of a non-custodial sentence is being made, then even if the report is generally favourable and recommends such a course, the offender can have no complaints about the recommendation being rejected. That was held in *Horton* (1985) 7 Cr App R (S) 299, where the judge, on adjourning for reports, said that he thought that an immediate custodial sentence would be the likely conclusion. One reason for the judge adjourning in *Horton* was the fact that the offender was under 21 (there then being a statutory requirement for a report in respect of such offenders).

The combination of such a statutory requirement and the principle in *Gillam's* case creates a difficulty for the judge who may well feel it necessary to obtain a report to comply with the statutory provisions. Silence about the sentencer's ultimate intentions may be construed as an implied promise to pass a non-custodial sentence but equally the judge ought not to give the impression that a custodial sentence is inevitable. It may be thought that the judge in *Horton* steered a judicious middle course, indicating that custody was probable but leaving open the possibility that something truly exceptional in the reports might result in a change of decision. See also *Norton* (1989) 11 Cr App R (S) 143.

In *Renan* (1994) 15 Cr App R (S) 722, the Court of Appeal said that the silence of the judge when adjourning for a pre-sentence report should never be taken as an indication that a non-custodial sentence would be passed, even when the offender was granted bail. It was the duty of counsel in these circumstances to warn the defendant that the grant of bail did not mean that custody would be avoided.

Committal for Sentence The *Gillam* principle also applies when the Crown Court is dealing with a committal for sentence or appeal from a magistrates' court. In both cases, if the ordering of reports by the court below created a reasonable expectation of a non-custodial sentence, the Crown Court is bound by the lower court's implied promise (*Rennes* (1985) 7 Cr App R (S) 343; *Gutteridge v DPP* (1987) 9 Cr App R (S) 279). **D20.63**

Effect of an Adjournment for Inquiries It need not be an adjournment for reports which creates the expectation of a non-custodial sentence. In *McMillan* (1988) 10 Cr App R (S) 205, counsel addressed the Crown Court judge on the basis that sentence might be deferred in view of the fact that employment was available to D. The judge adjourned for an hour to allow confirmation that the employment was still open to be obtained. The Court of Appeal held that D's hopes had been raised by the judge's actions, resulting in a sense of grievance when a custodial sentence was nevertheless imposed. See also *Jackson* [1996] Crim LR 355. **D20.64**

Effect of Judicial Indications as to Sentence Another situation in which the offender might have a legitimate expectation of a non-custodial sentence is where the judge has indicated that such a sentence will be passed. The procedure set out in *Goodyear* [2005] EWCA Crim 888, [2005] 2 Cr App R 20 (281), is now to be found in CrimPD VII, para. C.1 (see Supplement, **CPD.VII.C**: see also **D12.61**). In particular, unless the same type of sentence would be passed irrespective of plea, only an indication as to sentence following a guilty plea should be given, and while such an indication remains binding both on the judge who gives it and any other judge with subsequent conduct of the case, the indication will cease to have effect if, after a reasonable period, the offender does not plead guilty. It follows that the proper approach is that set out in **D12**. **D20.65**

The fact that a judge gave an indication of sentence before plea will not bind the Court of Appeal if the A-G appeals against the sentence as unduly lenient (*A-G's Ref (No. 40 of 1996)* [1997] 1 Cr App R (S) 357: see **D28.6**).

Pre-sentence Report

Meaning The term 'pre-sentence report' is defined by the CJA 2003, s. 158(1), as a report which: **D20.66**

(a) with a view to assisting the court in determining the most suitable method of dealing with an offender, is made or submitted by an appropriate officer [defined in subsection (2)]; and
(b) contains information as to such matters, presented in such manner, as may be prescribed by rules made by the Secretary of State.

The report is usually in writing but, by s. 158(1A) and (1B) (as inserted by the CJIA 2008, s. 12), may be given orally in open court in certain circumstances.

Preparation of the Report Pre-sentence reports on adults are compiled by probation officers. In the cases of children under 13, reports are prepared by local authority social workers. In the cases of those aged 13 to 16 inclusive, responsibility is shared between the probation service and social services, precise arrangements varying from area to area (CYPA 1969, ss. 9 and 34(3)). **D20.67**

Circumstances in which a Report Must Be Obtained The CJA 2003 places an obligation on the court to obtain a pre-sentence report in two circumstances. **D20.68**

(a) Under s. 156(3)(a), the court 'shall obtain and consider a pre-sentence report' in determining whether a custodial sentence should be imposed. This is not obligatory, however, where

D

Part D Procedure

the court is of the opinion that it is unnecessary and the offender is over 18. In the case of a child or young person, a pre-sentence report is obligatory unless the court considers it unnecessary (s. 156(4)) and in reaching that decision it has considered any existing pre-sentence report relating to the offender and takes account of the information therein (s. 156(5): see **E1.26**).

(b) Under s. 156(3)(b), the court is required to obtain and consider a pre-sentence report before forming an opinion as to the suitability of an offender for various types of community sentence (for further details, see **E8.6**).

D20.69 **Circumstances in which a Report May Be Prepared** It is the duty of the probation service or, as the case may be, youth offending team to prepare a report if one is requested by the court. Alternatively, the probation service may take the initiative and prepare a report without being asked to do so if:

(a) it is anticipated that the offender will plead guilty and is either aged 30 or less;
(b) the conviction will put the offender in breach of a suspended sentence or other court order; or
(c) the offender has recently been in contact with the probation service, or medical reports are also being prepared.

The probation service will be reluctant to prepare a report if the offender indicates a not guilty plea, both because it will be wasted effort in the event of an acquittal and also because one of the main purposes of a report is to assess the offender's attitude to the offence and that cannot be done if there is a denial of having committed it. Where the court desires a report and one has not already been prepared, it will be necessary to adjourn unless a 'stand down' report can be compiled within the court day. It may be made a condition of bail that the offender co-operates in the preparation of the report (BA 1976, s. 3(6): see **D7.63**).

D20.70 **Procedure on Receiving Pre-sentence Report** A copy of the pre-sentence report must be given either to the offender or to a legal representative and to the prosecutor. In the case of an unrepresented offender aged under 18, the report need not be given personally but must be given to a parent or guardian if present. Where the offender is aged under 18 and disclosure either to the offender or any parent or guardian would be likely to create a risk of significant harm to the offender, the copy provided need not be a complete copy of the report (CJA 2003, s. 159(2) and (3)).

A copy of the report may be withheld from the prosecutor if the prosecutor is not of a prescribed description and the court considers it inappropriate to disclose it (s. 159(4)). The prescribed description of a prosecutor for these purposes is contained in the Pre-Sentence (Prescription of Prosecutors) Order 1998 (SI 1998 No. 191).

The probation officer who prepared the report is not usually present in court when the report is submitted, but may give evidence about it on request. The report is not read out in full in open court, but counsel may refer to passages of it in mitigation.

D20.71 **New Disclosures in a Pre-sentence Report** In *Cunnah* [1996] 1 Cr App R (S) 393, the Court of Appeal stressed that when fresh and highly relevant material appeared in a pre-sentence report it must be discussed with counsel. This is particularly important, as was the case in *Cunnah*, where pleas had been entered on a limited basis.

Medical and Psychiatric Reports

D20.72 It is a precondition of the making of a hospital order under the Mental Health Act 1983, s. 37(1) (or an interim hospital order under s. 38), that the court be satisfied on the written or oral evidence of two medical practitioners that the offender is suffering from a mental disorder within the meaning of the Act such as to warrant the making of an order (see **E22.2**). Equally, a report from at least one medical practitioner is required before a custodial sentence is passed on a mentally disordered offender (CJA 2003, s. 157). The procedure for the obtaining of medical reports in relation to an offender (and the funding arrangements for such reports) are contained in CrimPD I, paras. 3P.1 to 3P.17 (in particular, the timetable at paras. 3P.6 to 3P.7, the commissioning of a report at para. 3P.11 and the funding arrangements at para. 3P.15; see Supplement, **CPD.3P**).

Where a medical report is to be tendered in evidence under the provisions of the Mental Health Act 1983, s. 54(3)(a) requires that a copy be given to the offender's 'authorised person' (normally counsel or solicitor). If the offender is unrepresented, the gist of the report should be disclosed although the offender is not entitled to a copy; in the case of a child or young person, the substance of the report must be disclosed to any parent or guardian present in court (s. 54(3)(b)). The medical practitioner who made the report may be required to attend for cross-examination (s. 54(3)(c)).

Power to Remand to Obtain a Report A magistrates' court has various powers in relation to obtaining such a report: **D20.73**

(a) When remanding an offender in custody the court may, in appropriate cases, request the prison medical service to prepare a report.
(b) If a magistrates' court is satisfied that the offender 'did the act or made the omission charged', it has the power to remand the offender for up to three weeks in custody or four weeks on bail for a medical examination to be made and report prepared (PCC(S)A 2000, s. 11(1) and (2)). A remand under s. 11(1) and (2) may be ordered notwithstanding that the offender is unconvicted. If the offender is granted bail, it *must* be made a condition of the bail that the offender co-operate in the preparation of the reports (s. 11(3)).

No specific provisions govern the obtaining of medical reports by the Crown Court. If none have been prepared as a result of proceedings in the court below, the court may exercise its inherent power to adjourn so as to give the opportunity for a report to be made.

Remand to Hospital The courts have been given the power, under the Mental Health Act 1983, s. 35, to remand any accused or convicted persons to hospital, for the preparation of reports on their mental condition (see below). This may arise either on the court's own motion or at the initiative of defence solicitors. There are special requirements for medical evidence in the case of mentally disordered offenders. It was emphasised by the Divisional Court in *R (M) v Kingston Crown Court* [2014] EWHC 2702 (Admin), [2015] 1 Cr App R 3 (27) that the purpose of an order under s. 35 was to inform the court as to issues relating to fitness to plead and disposal, not to compel the assessment of the offender for evidential purposes at the behest of the prosecution. **D20.74**

Mental Health Act 1983, s. 35

(1) Subject to the provisions of this section, the Crown Court or a magistrates' court may remand an accused person to a hospital specified by the court for a report on his mental condition.
(2) For the purposes of this section an accused person is—
  (a) in relation to the Crown Court, any person who is awaiting trial before the court for an offence punishable with imprisonment or who has been arraigned before the court for such an offence and has not yet been sentenced or otherwise dealt with for the offence on which he has been arraigned;
  (b) in relation to a magistrates' court, any person who has been convicted by the court of an offence punishable on summary conviction with imprisonment and any person charged with such an offence if the court is satisfied that he did the act or made the omission charged or he has consented to the exercise by the court of the powers conferred by this section.
(3) Subject to subsection (4) below, the powers conferred by this section may be exercised if—
  (a) the court is satisfied, on the written or oral evidence of a registered medical practitioner that there is reason to suspect that the accused person is suffering from mental disorder; and
  (b) the court is of the opinion that it would be impracticable for a report on his mental condition to be made if he were remanded on bail;

but those powers shall not be exercised by the Crown Court in respect of a person who has been convicted before the court if the sentence for the offence of which he has been convicted is fixed by law.

(4) The court shall not remand an accused person to a hospital under this section unless satisfied, on the written or oral evidence of the approved clinician who would be responsible for making the report or of some other person representing the managers of the hospital, that arrangements have been made for his admission to that hospital and for his admission to it within the period of seven days beginning with the date of the remand; and if the court is so satisfied it may, pending his admission, give directions for his conveyance to and detention in a place of safety.

Other Reports

D20.75 Before passing a community sentence, the court must normally be satisfied, on the basis of a report from a probation officer (or social worker of a local authority social services department) that the offender is a suitable person to perform work under a community order (CJA 2003, s. 148 and s. 156: see **E8.2** and **E1.27**). An assessment for suitability for a community penalty is usually ordered in conjunction with a pre-sentence report.

Various other types of report may also be before the court. In particular, in the cases of children and young people, detailed reports by social workers may be prepared during the period of a remand in care prior to sentence. There may also be a report from the child or young person's school, dealing with attendance, behaviour, performance etc. The CJA 2003, s. 161, permits the drug testing of offenders before any community penalty is imposed upon them.

In *AXN* [2016] EWCA Crim 590, [2016] 2 Cr App R (S) 33 (341) the Court of Appeal provided guidance as to the approach the police ought to take when an offender seeks confidential confirmation of assistance provided to the police, and/or where the police did not consider it appropriate to provide such confirmation. Where such police confirmation through a 'text' was not available, the court should be slow to adjourn for that purpose.

MITIGATION OF SENTENCE

D20.76 The final stage in the sentencing process before the sentence is pronounced is the presentation of defence mitigation. CrimPR 25.16(6) (see Supplement, **R25.16**) provides that before passing sentence the court must give the offender an opportunity to make representations and introduce evidence relevant to sentence and, where the offender is under 18, the court may give parents, guardians or other supporting adults, if present, such an opportunity as well.

According to Comyn J in *Gross v O'Toole* (1982) 4 Cr App R (S) 283, the presentation of defence mitigation is 'purported to be the province of the most junior of counsel' but 'is in fact amongst the most difficult tasks any barrister can ever face'. The plea in mitigation usually consists solely of a speech by defence counsel. As a matter of discretion, counsel may additionally call witnesses to speak to the offender's generally good character or to explain why, in their view, the offender's criminal conduct occurred.

Legal Representation at the Sentencing Stage

D20.77 Unrepresented offenders may, of course, put forward mitigation on their own behalf. However, if the court is considering a custodial disposition it is generally desirable that the mitigation should be professionally presented. This is especially so if the offender is either young or has not previously been given a custodial sentence.

D20.78 **Statutory Requirement for Representation** Section 83 of the PCC(S)A 2000, which applies to both the Crown Court and magistrates' courts, provides that (a) adult offenders who have not previously been sentenced to imprisonment and (b) offenders aged under 21 whether or not they have previously lost their liberty shall not be sentenced to imprisonment or, as the case may be, one of the custodial sentences available for the offenders aged under 21 unless they are legally represented. The exception to that requirement is where the offender was granted representation under the LASPO 2012, Part 1, but it was withdrawn because of the offender's own conduct, or where it was withdrawn or refused because of financial ineligibility or where (having been informed of the right to apply for such representation and having the opportunity to do so) the offender has refused or failed to do so (s. 83(3)). See also CrimPR 25.2(1)(c) (see Supplement, **R25.2**).

Section 83 extends to the passing of suspended sentences of imprisonment, but a suspended sentence which has not taken effect is ignored for purposes of deciding if an offender has previously had a prison sentence (s. 83(5)). Section 83(4) lays down that a person having legal assistance after conviction and before sentence is to be treated as legally represented.

Consequences of Breach Failure to comply with the s. 83(1) requirement has been held to have differing consequences depending upon the court in error. If the failure occurred in the magistrates' court, the Crown Court, on appeal, must pass a sentence which the lower court could *lawfully* have passed, and therefore it must replace the custodial sentence with a non-custodial one (*Birmingham Justices, ex parte Wyatt* [1976] 3 All ER 897). If, however, the Crown Court was the sentencing court and the appeal is to the Court of Appeal, the latter may uphold the sentence below if they consider that it was the right one in all the circumstances (*McGinlay* (1975) 62 Cr App R 156; *Hollywood* (1990) 154 JP 705; *Wilson* [1995] Crim LR 510). **D20.79**

Powers of Criminal Courts (Sentencing) Act 2000, s. 83 **D20.80**

(1) A magistrates' court on summary conviction, or the Crown Court on committal for sentence or on conviction on indictment, shall not pass a sentence of imprisonment on a person who—
(a) is not legally represented in that court, and
(b) has not been previously sentenced to that punishment by a court in any part of the United Kingdom,
unless he is a person to whom subsection (3) below applies.
(2) A magistrates' court on summary conviction, or the Crown Court on committal for sentence or on conviction on indictment, shall not—
(a) pass a sentence of detention under section 90 or 91 below,
(b) pass a sentence of custody for life under section 93 or 94 below,
(c) pass a sentence of detention in a young offender institution, or
(d) make a detention and training order,
on or in respect of a person who is not legally represented in that court unless he is a person to whom subsection (3) below applies.
(3) This subsection applies to a person if either—
(a) representation was made available to him for the purposes of the proceedings under Part 1 of the Legal Aid, Sentencing and Punishment of Offenders Act 2012 but was withdrawn because of his conduct or because it appeared that his financial resources were such that he was not eligible for such representation;
(aa) he applied for such representation and the application was refused because it appeared that his financial resources were such that he was not eligible for such representation; or
(b) having been informed of his right to apply for such representation and having had the opportunity to do so, he refused or failed to apply.
(4) For the purposes of this section a person is to be treated as legally represented in a court if, but only if, he has the assistance of counsel or a solicitor to represent him in the proceedings in that court at some time after he is found guilty and before he is sentenced.
(5) For the purposes of subsection (1)(b) above a previous sentence of imprisonment which has been suspended and which has not taken effect under section 119 below... shall be disregarded.
(6) In this section 'sentence of imprisonment' does not include a committal for contempt of court or any kindred offence.

Requirement to Prove Mitigation

Although normally a plea in mitigation consists solely of a speech by counsel, exceptionally, counsel may also decide to call evidence in order to establish the facts being advanced in mitigation. Whether to call evidence and, if so, whether to call it before, in the middle or at the end of **D20.81**

Part D Procedure

the speech is a matter for counsel (per Comyn J in *Gross v O'Toole* (1982) 4 Cr App R (S) 283). Having made the decision, the advocate 'cannot…easily…go back on it' (at p. 285).

The requirement to prove mitigation should not be confused with the resolution of a factual dispute as to the circumstances of the offence in a *Newton* hearing (see **D20.8** ***et seq.***). The cases appear to draw a distinction between 'true *Newton*' situations, where the dispute is about the immediate circumstances of the offence, and what have been described by Dr. Thomas in his case commentaries in the *Criminal Law Review* as 'reverse *Newton*' situations. In the latter, the dispute is about extraneous matters about which the prosecution witnesses are unlikely to have any knowledge. Since these matters would not have formed part of the prosecution case, or be within the prosecution's knowledge, and may well be within the peculiar knowledge of the offender, the rule is that the onus of satisfying the judge rests on the defence.

D20.82 **Applicable Principles** The general principles as to proving mitigation were stated by the Divisional Court in *Gross v O'Toole* (1982) 4 Cr App R (S) 283. D's mitigation, in relation to offering his services as a taxi driver, was that he had offered his services gratuitously. This mitigation was rejected by the court. The Divisional Court rejected the argument that the court ought not to have rejected a substantial part of the mitigation without giving an opportunity for affirmative evidence to be called. The decision whether to call evidence or rely solely on his or her own submissions was one for the defence advocate. Ormrod LJ said:

> …if an advocate is going to put forward in mitigation something which is, on the face of it, quite inconsistent with the other information that the magistrates have so far as sentence is concerned, e.g. the list of previous convictions, it really is for the defending advocate to indicate that he wishes to make good the submission…he takes the chance himself if he does not offer to call evidence…
>
> I do not think [the magistrates] were obliged to tell the defending advocate that they did not accept his mitigation, because I do not think anyone in court, least of all the defending advocate, could have supposed for a moment that they would accept his mitigation.

Comyn J, in a supplementary judgment, slightly qualified Ormrod LJ's remarks by stating that if, on a significant point on which there is room for some doubt, the magistrates do in fact doubt what the advocate is saying, they ought to indicate that expressly before mitigation is concluded to give the advocate an opportunity to remedy it. However, both their lordships clearly accepted the basic premise that it is for the defence to establish its own mitigation to the court's satisfaction, and whether they do that by a speech or evidence or both is essentially a matter for them, not the court.

D20.83 **Court's Discretion to Reject Such Evidence** It follows from the principles stated in *Gross v O'Toole* (1982) 4 Cr App R (S) 283, that the court may reject matters advanced in mitigation even if the offender or other defence witnesses testify in support of those facts and no contradictory evidence is adduced by the prosecution (*Kerr* (1980) 2 Cr App R (S) 54).

This has been demonstrated in a number of cases.

(a) In *Ogunti* (1987) 9 Cr App R (S) 325, following D's guilty plea to possessing heroin with intent to supply, the court was held to be entitled to disbelieve counsel's mitigation to the effect that D had acted under duress. The Court of Appeal held that it was a 'reverse *Newton*' situation and the onus of proving the facts rested on the defence. The judge was entitled to draw reasonable inferences from the statements of the witnesses (e.g., as to the value of the drugs and the skilful way they were hidden in D's car), and therefore reject the defence account of the nature of D's involvement.
(b) In *Guppy* [1994] Crim LR 614, the Court of Appeal held that, where extraneous matters of mitigation were raised, a burden of proof rested upon the offender to the civil standard. Their lordships did state, however, that in the general run of cases the sentencer would readily accept the accuracy of defence counsel's statements.
(c) In *Broderick* (1993) 15 Cr App R (S) 476, it was held that the mitigation alleging duress went to matters outside the prosecution's knowledge so that *Newton* principles did not apply.

However, in *Tolera* [1999] 1 Cr App R 29, the Court of Appeal held that there was an onus on the prosecution to rebut the appellant's explanation about being under a degree of compulsion, falling short of duress, to carry the heroin which was the subject of the charge.

Content of Mitigation

Guidance on matters of mitigation within the knowledge of the defence is provided by *Underwood* [2004] EWCA Crim 2256, [2005] 1 Cr App R 13 (178) (see **D20.9** and points (9), (11) and (14)(d) in particular). Guidance has similarly been provided in relation to other aspects of mitigation. **D20.84**

Mitigation Following Conviction Where counsel delivers a plea in mitigation after a trial and a verdict of guilty, it is generally unrealistic to reiterate in strong terms the client's innocence and at the same time ask for leniency. Where the advocate takes a more realistic course, and mitigates on the basis of acceptance of the jury's verdict, this should not be taken as an admission of guilt on behalf of the client, so as to undermine a subsequent appeal (*Wu Chun-piu v The Queen* [1996] 1 WLR 1113). **D20.85**

Citing of Sentencing Guidelines Advocates are expected to be able to address the relevant definitive sentencing guidelines issued by the Sentencing Council (bearing in mind that several may be relevant in relation to the same sentencing exercise) and to be prepared to argue for appropriate categorisation within the guideline. Where there are applicable guidelines it will be the exception rather than the rule to cite authorities which pre-date them (*Tongue* [2007] EWCA Crim 561). **D20.86**

For offences without a specific guideline the *General Guideline: Overarching Principles* (see Supplement, **SG2-1**) is used for all offenders sentenced on or after 1 October 2019, mandating a general approach to sentencing based on concepts of harm, culpability, aggravating and mitigating factors. For these offences there will be a residual value in citing guideline cases of the Court of Appeal, if any.

Judicial Indications as to Sentence Where the judge is contemplating imposing a sentence which defence counsel might not be anticipating, the judge is under a duty in fairness to the offender to give notice of what is being considered so that defence counsel can then make submissions on that issue. **D20.87**

(a) In *Scott* (1989) 11 Cr App R (S) 249, the judge disqualified D for life without giving his counsel the opportunity to make submissions on that aspect of the sentence; the Court of Appeal reduced the disqualification.
(b) In *Woods* (1989) 11 Cr App R (S) 551, the Court of Appeal said that if the judge intended to impose a separate custodial sentence for an offence under the BA 1976 it is important to invite submissions from counsel (see also *O'Brien* (1995) 16 Cr App R (S) 556).
(c) In *Metcalfe* [2009] EWCA Crim 374, [2009] 2 Cr App R (S) 85 (568), it was indicated that where the court is minded not to make a direction in respect of time spent on remand in custody, pursuant to the CJA 2003, s. 240, submissions should be invited on behalf of the offender.

Derogatory Assertions in Mitigation

There are two restrictions placed on the content of mitigation where that involved derogatory assertions, which in turn impose obligations on prosecution counsel. These are contained in the BSB Handbook Conduct Rules and the CPIA 1996. **D20.88**

Code of Conduct Defence counsel 'must not make statements or ask questions merely to insult, humiliate or annoy a witness or any other person' (Conduct Rules, rC7.1). **D20.89**

Criminal Procedure and Investigations Act 1996 The CPIA 1996, ss. 58 to 61, allow the judge to impose reporting restrictions on false or irrelevant assertions made during a speech in mitigation. There is power to make a full order where there are substantial grounds for believing **D20.90**

that the assertion is derogatory to a person's character, and either false or irrelevant to the proceedings. Whilst considering the matter, the court is empowered to make an interim order, provided that there is a real possibility that a full order will be made. The powers do not apply if the assertion has been made earlier in proceedings, e.g., at trial. Full orders may be revoked at any time by the court, and if not revoked will cease to have effect after one year. It is an offence to publish or broadcast in breach of a full or interim order, rendering the offender liable to a fine on summary conviction not exceeding level 5 on the standard scale.

D20.91 **Criminal Procedure and Investigations Act 1996, s. 58**

(1) This section applies where a person has been convicted of an offence and a speech in mitigation is made by him or on his behalf before—
 (a) a court determining what sentence should be passed on him in respect of the offence, or
 (b) a magistrates' court determining whether he should be committed to the Crown Court for sentence.
(2) This section also applies where a sentence has been passed on a person in respect of an offence and a submission relating to the sentence is made by him or on his behalf before—
 (a) a court hearing an appeal against or reviewing the sentence, or
 (b) a court determining whether to grant leave to appeal against the sentence.
(3) Where it appears to the court that there is a real possibility that an order under subsection (8) will be made in relation to the assertion, the court may make an order under subsection (7) in relation to the assertion.
(4) Where there are substantial grounds for believing—
 (a) that an assertion forming part of the speech or submission is derogatory to a person's character (for instance, because it suggests that his conduct is or has been criminal, immoral or improper), and
 (b) that the assertion is false or that the facts asserted are irrelevant to the sentence,
 the court may make an order under subsection (8) in relation to the assertion.
(5) An order under subsection (7) or (8) must not be made in relation to an assertion if it appears to the court that the assertion was previously made—
 (a) at the trial at which the person was convicted of the offence, or
 (b) during any other proceedings relating to the offence.
(6) Section 59 has effect where a court makes an order under subsection (7) or (8).
(7) An order under this subsection—
 (a) may be made at any time before the court has made a determination with regard to sentencing;
 (b) may be revoked at any time by the court;
 (c) subject to paragraph (b), shall cease to have effect when the court makes a determination with regard to sentencing.
(8) An order under this subsection—
 (a) may be made after the court has made a determination with regard to sentencing, but only if it is made as soon as is reasonably practicable after the making of the determination;
 (b) may be revoked at any time by the court;
 (c) subject to paragraph (b), shall cease to have effect at the end of the period of 12 months beginning with the day on which it is made;
 (d) may be made whether or not an order has been made under subsection (7) with regard to the case concerned.
(9) For the purposes of subsections (7) and (8) the court makes a determination with regard to sentencing—
 (a) when it determines what sentence should be passed (where this section applies by virtue of subsection (1)(a));
 (b) when it determines whether the person should be committed to the Crown Court for sentence (where this section applies by virtue of subsection (1)(b));
 (c) when it determines what the sentence should be (where this section applies by virtue of subsection (2)(a));
 (d) when it determines whether to grant leave to appeal (where this section applies by virtue of subsection (2)(b)).

PRONOUNCEMENT OF SENTENCE

D20.92 After the defence mitigation, the judge pronounces sentence, often immediately upon the close of defence counsel's address, although in complex cases the sentence will often be adjourned briefly or overnight, whether for reflection or to allow for the presence of other interested parties at the passing of sentence itself.

Giving Reasons

Section 174 of the CJA 2003 (see **E1.23** for the full text) creates an obligation on the judge to give reasons for, and explain the effects of, the sentence passed, save where the sentence is fixed by law or is otherwise mandatory (s. 174(3)). See also CrimPR 25.16(7)(b) (see Supplement, **R25.16**). In summary: **D20.93**

(a) The court must explain in non-technical terms its reasons for deciding on the sentence passed (s. 174(2)).
(b) The court must explain the effect of the sentence, and the consequences of non-compliance (s. 174(3)).

Statutory obligations to give reasons are also imposed by the following:

(a) PCC(S)A 2000, s. 130(3) — a court with power to make a compensation order in an offender's case must explain its reasons for not doing so.
(b) RTOA 1988, s. 47(1) — where the court does not order disqualification or endorsement on account of special reasons or hardship.

CrimPR 25.16(7) **25.16** provides:

> When the court has taken into account all the evidence, information and any report available, the court must —
> (a) as a general rule pass sentence at the earliest opportunity;
> (b) when passing sentence
>   (i) explain the reasons;
>   (ii) explain to the defendant its effect, the consequences of any failure to comply with any order or pay any fine, and any power that the court may have to vary or review the sentence, unless the defendant is absent or the defendant's ill-health or disorderly conduct makes such an explanation impracticable, and
>   (iii) give any explanation in terms the defendant, if present, can understand (with help if necessary); and
> (c) deal with confiscation, costs and any behaviour order.

CrimPD VII, para. F.3(d) provides that '[i]n all cases it will be appropriate for a VPS to be referred to in the course of the sentencing hearing and/or in the sentencing remarks'.

Pursuant to the CJA 2003, s. 240ZA, the court is no longer required to identify the allowance that it has made to the sentence for the time spent by the offender in custody on remand as this is done administratively. Ancillary duties may include explicitly deducting any time which arises from the offender having been on a qualifying curfew and tag; and both considering a compensation order and giving reasons if one is not made. The need for a judge to say what degree of credit was being afforded for an offender's guilty plea was emphasised in *Hacatoroglu* [2015] EWCA Crim 1122, [2015] 2 Cr App R (S) 67 (468). Moreover, it is essential that the reasoning underlying a sentence is articulated orally in public, even after the court has taken time to consider and to reduce those reasons to writing (*Billington* [2017] EWCA Crim 618, [2017] 2 Cr App R (S) 22 (171)).

Court of Appeal Guidance In *Billington* [2017] EWCA Crim 618, [2017] 2 Cr App R (S) 22 (171), the Court of Appeal described the public articulation of reasons for sentence as 'crucial'. In that case a sentence was passed on one date, with detailed reasons being supplied in writing to the parties after some days. The Court considered this was insufficient to comply with the important public duty involved in the sentencing exercise. **D20.94**

Nevertheless the failure by the sentencing court to give reasons when required to do so does not invalidate the sentence (*McQueen* (1989) 11 Cr App R (S) 305). Where the sentencer does give reasons and they indicate an error of principle in the way the task was approached, the Court of Appeal will sometimes reduce the sentence even though the penalty was not in itself excessive. Although the extent of discount for guilty plea should normally be expressed, a failure by the judge to do so does not oblige the Court of Appeal to interfere with what is otherwise an appropriate sentence (*Wharton* (2001) *The Times*, 27 March 2001).

In *Chin-Charles* [2019] EWCA Crim 1140, [2020] 1 Cr App R (S) 6 (40) a powerful constitution of the Court of Appeal (Lord Burnett CJ, Hallett VP, and Rafferty LJ) sought to redress the balance of what were perceived to be ever-lengthening sentence remarks by reassuring judges that succinct remarks focused on the essentials would suffice in many cases:

> 6. . . . The key to the nature of sentencing remarks is the use of the terms 'in ordinary language' and 'in general terms'. The offender is the first audience because he or she must understand what sentence has been passed, why it has been passed, what it means and what might happen in the event of non-compliance. If the offender understands, so too will those with an interest in the case, especially the victim of any offence and witnesses, the public and press.
>
> . . .
>
> 10. The sentence must be located in the guidelines. In general, the court need only identify the category in which a count sits by reference to harm and culpability, the consequent starting point and range, the fact that adjustments have been made to reflect aggravating and mitigating factors, where appropriate credit for plea (and amount of credit) and the conclusion. It may be necessary briefly to set out what prompts the court to settle on culpability and harm, but only where the conclusion is not obvious or was in issue, and also to explain why the court moved from the starting point.
>
> 11. Findings of fact should be announced without, in most cases, supporting narrative.
>
> 12. If in play, a finding of dangerousness contrary to statute must be recorded. Supporting facts should be set out only when essential to an understanding of the finding, not as a matter of course.
>
> 13. Victim personal statements might merit brief reference . . . Limited brief reference to the contents of reports will be apt only if essential to an understanding of the court's decision.

The judgment has been met with mixed responses, including significant academic criticism (see, e.g., [2019] Crim LR 893). Analysis of published sentencing remarks by High Court judges reveals little alteration of approach or scope. It may be thought that the judgment was intended to anticipate the televising of sentencing hearings by the senior judiciary and may be read as an exhortation for them to keep sentencing remarks appropriate to that medium. However, in these more serious cases, as well as all others, the sentencing exercise is an important moment for offender, victims, those with a special interest in the case and the wider public. The judge's careful and authoritative explanation as to why the particular sentence has been arrived at — including the legal and factual basis that drives it — will in some cases be a more telling event than the declaration of the sentence itself. Despite the unarguable experience and authority of the members of the Court in *Chin-Charles*, it remains to be seen whether the case will mark a significant change in sentencing practice.

VARIATION OF SENTENCE

D20.95 By the PCC(S)A 2000, s. 155(1) and CrimPR 28.4 (see Supplement, **R28.4**), a sentence imposed or other order made by the Crown Court when dealing with an offender may be varied or rescinded within 56 days of being passed or made. The judge who makes the variation must be the judge who originally passed sentence; if, however, the judge was accompanied by justices on the first occasion, they need not be present for the variation (s. 155(4) and see *Morrison* [2005] EWCA Crim 2705).

The power to vary may not be exercised in relation to any sentence or order if an appeal against it (or application for leave to appeal against it) has been determined (s. 155(1A)).

Extent of the Power to Vary

The power in the PCC(S)A 2000, s. 155, may be used to replace one form of sentence with a quite different form. This was illustrated in: **D20.96**

(a) *Sodhi* (1978) 66 Cr App R 260, where the Crown Court, upon learning that D had been diagnosed by psychiatrists as suffering from paranoid psychosis and was dangerous, substituted for a six-month prison sentence a hospital order plus restriction order without time-limit; and
(b) *Iqbal* (1985) 7 Cr App R (S) 35, in which an unlawful sentence of 30 months' youth custody passed on a 16-year-old was replaced by an equivalent term of detention under what is now the PCC(S)A 2000, s. 91(3).

The Court of Appeal upheld both variations, saying in *Sodhi* that the word 'varied' in s. 155(1) has a wide meaning and the court's power is therefore not restricted to changing the length of a sentence. The section may also be used to add an extra order to the sentence already passed (*Reilly* [1982] QB 1208).

This provision may be used to make a correction to the period which the court has allowed for time spent in custody on remand pursuant to the CJA 2003, s. 240 (see **D20.93**).

The Court may use the power to impose either a more punitive or more lenient sentence and to correct a sentence that is, on reflection, considered to have been wrong in principle (*O'Connor* [2018] EWCA Crim 1417, [2018] 2 Cr App R (S) 49 (397)).

Increasing the Sentence by Variation

The obvious use of the power in the PCC(S)A 2000, s. 155, is to correct minor errors made by the court when passing sentence. It is also clear that the power may be used to benefit the offender by reducing the sentence if, on reflection, the judge considers that the original sentence was too harsh. Decisions also show that the power may be used to increase a sentence substantially in appropriate circumstances. **D20.97**

(a) In *Newsome* [1970] 2 QB 711, the sentencer had overlooked legislation then in force which obliged the court to suspend any sentence of imprisonment it passed on the appellants unless the term thereof exceeded six months. The Court of Appeal held that he had jurisdiction to increase the sentence to address this problem because he had always intended to pass a short, immediate custodial sentence, and the increase he ordered was virtually the minimum necessary to achieve his original object.
(b) In *Grice* (1977) 66 Cr App R 167, a more restrictive view was taken of the court's power to vary sentence. The sentencer had varied a suspended sentence to make the term one of immediate imprisonment where D had during the period for variation breached an undertaking given to the court pre-sentence. The Court of Appeal restored the original sentence, holding that only in exceptional circumstances (such as in *Newsome*) should s. 155 be used to make a substantial increase in penalty.
(c) In *Reilly* [1982] QB 1208, the sentencer initially declined to make a criminal bankruptcy order when he passed sentence. He was then persuaded to make the order, and varied the sentence accordingly. Kerr LJ, giving the Court of Appeal's judgment, held that *Grice* had to be considered in the light of *Sodhi* (1978) 66 Cr App R 260 and dicta of the House of Lords in *Menocal* [1980] AC 598, in which Lord Edmund-Davies said that, contrary to *Grice*, the statutory power to vary is not 'restricted to mere slips of the tongue or slips of the memory'. It was therefore clear 'almost beyond argument' that the judge in *Reilly* had jurisdiction to change his mind and add the criminal bankruptcy order (see also *Warren* [2017] EWCA Crim 226, [2017] 2 Cr App R (S) 5 (18)).
(d) In *Hart* (1983) 5 Cr App R (S) 25, the sentencer became aware that he had been induced to pass a sentence of six months' imprisonment suspended for 18 months by a false story which D had invented to gain a lenient sentence. Unfortunately, the sentencer did not vary the sentence within the prescribed period. However, Lord Lane CJ said: 'the learned judge was

D

Part D Procedure

absolutely correct... to take this opportunity to review the sentence, had he done it within the stipulated time. Where someone makes it known after the event that he, as this appellant put it, has "conned the court", in other words told lies to the court and has thereby escaped his just punishment, is one of the plain cases for which [section 155(1)] is designed.'

D20.98 **Correct Approach to Upward Variation** General guidance was given in *McLean* (1988) 10 Cr App R (S) 18, where the sentencer had passed a sentence of three years' imprisonment on the strength of D's promise that he had turned over a new leaf, but had varied his sentence to four years' imprisonment when he then promptly escaped from custody. The Court of Appeal held that the judge did have power to increase the sentence.

In the course of argument, McCullough J put to counsel that the proper approach of the court was to ask: (i) Did D's conduct create an exceptional situation? (ii) If it did, was the judge reasonably entitled to take the view that the exceptional situation undermined the whole basis upon which the sentence was passed? If the answer to both questions was yes, then the judge could properly exercise the wide discretion given by the statute to increase the sentence. In delivering the court's judgment, Woolf LJ confirmed that this was the correct approach (at p. 22).

The upshot of the above cases seems to be that the Crown Court may increase sentence by a variation under s. 155(1), even to the extent of substituting an immediate custodial sentence for a suspended one, where additional argument put before the court (as in *Reilly* [1982] QB 1208) or information that the original sentence was passed on an incorrect factual basis (as in *Hart* (1983) 5 Cr App R (S) 25 and *McLean*) justifies such variation. It is clear from *McLean* that the principle advanced in *Grice* (1977) 66 Cr App R 167 remains good law: namely, that variations to the detriment of the offender are justified only in exceptional circumstances.

More recently, in *Reynolds* [2007] EWCA Crim 538, [2007] 2 Cr App R (S) 87, the Court of Appeal held that the power to vary could be used within the variation period to increase sentence when the impact of the CJA 2003, ch. 5, (in that the offence was a 'specified' offence, or that a 'specified' offence was a 'serious' offence) had not originally been appreciated. If a sentence is rescinded in such circumstances, the court may then adjourn sentence, e.g., to allow a report to be prepared to address the question of dangerousness, even if that results in sentencing finally occurring after the end of the period.

Procedure for Variation of Sentence

D20.99 **Presence of the Offender** CrimPR 28.4(4) (see Supplement, **R28.4**) indicates that an offender should normally be present for a variation of sentence. This accords with the earlier approach in both *May* (1981) 3 Cr App R (S) 165 and *Cleere* (1983) 5 Cr App R (S) 465, where it was held that the offender has a right to be present when the sentence is varied, and that variations made in the absence of the respective appellants and without their having the benefit of legal representation should be quashed.

This was slightly qualified in *Shacklady* (1987) 9 Cr App R (S) 258, where Rose J, quoting a sentence from Watkins LJ's judgment in *Cleere*, stated the principle to be that 'the defendant or his counsel must have an opportunity to address the court' (at p. 261). Accordingly, a variation made in the absence of the offender but with counsel in attendance on the offender's behalf was upheld. This exception is specifically included at r. 28.4(4)(b). A variation in the absence of the offender is also permissible where it is either sought by the defence, or involves a reduction in sentence (r. 28.4(4)(a)). It follows that the approach in *McLean* (1988) 10 Cr App R (S) 18 (see **D20.98**) would still be permitted. D's sentence was increased from three to four years after his escape from custody and hence in his absence (voluntary on his part, unavoidable from the court's point of view). The judge heard representations from D's counsel on the occasion when he varied sentence. With the obvious exception of such circumstances, it is submitted that a genuine increase by variation should not be made unless both the offender and counsel are present.

Hearing in Open Court CrimPR 28.4(2)(b) permits a variation to be made either in public or private. In terms of guidance as to approach, in *Dowling* (1988) 88 Cr App R 88, it was stressed that any variation of sentence should take place in open court. In that case, the judge purported to vary the sentence, as a result of a query from his clerk, without returning to court, or discussing the matter with counsel. The Court of Appeal emphasised that where the 'judge is minded to vary a sentence he has passed or even to clarify a doubt or ambiguity as to the effect of it, he should do so in open court'. Only in this manner would all those concerned hear the final decision from the judge directly, and in such a way that a shorthand note would be available. The court may rescind a sentence on one occasion, and then resentence at a later date, provided that the whole process is completed within the variation period (*Dunham* [1996] 1 Cr App R (S) 438). **D20.100**

Variations outside the 56-day Period

A sentence may not be varied outside the period specified in the PCC(S)A 2000, s. 155(1) (*Menocal* [1980] AC 598, where the House of Lords quashed an order which was not added to the original sentence until after the expiry of the time for variation). *Menocal* was followed in *Hart* (1983) 5 Cr App R (S) 25 and *Hudson* [2011] EWCA Crim 906, [2011] 2 Cr App R (S) 116 (666). The period cannot be extended by rescinding the original sentence within the time-limit, and then not sentencing until after the time-limit has expired (*Stillwell* (1991) 94 Cr App R 65). CrimPR 28.4 does not alter the position in this regard. **D20.101**

Correcting Rather than Varying A distinction is drawn, however, between varying the sentence by changing its length, adding an order to it or replacing it with a different type of disposition and merely correcting a technical defect in the sentence as originally announced. For example, in *Saville* [1981] QB 12, the Court of Appeal upheld the correction of the terms of a criminal bankruptcy order because the Crown Court has an inherent jurisdiction, apart from the statutory jurisdiction, to remedy mistakes in its record and the correction or variation was of such a minor nature that it was appropriate to exercise the inherent jurisdiction. Correcting technical defects does not include varying the reference to the legislation under which a confiscation order has been made (*Bukhari* [2008] EWCA Crim 2915, [2009] 2 Cr App R (S) 18 (113)). **D20.102**

DEFERRING SENTENCE

Purpose of Deferring Sentence

Under the PCC(S)A 2000, ss. 1 to 1D (set out at **D20.110**), the purpose for which sentence may be deferred is to enable the court, when it does deal with the offender, to have regard to: **D20.103**

(a) his conduct after conviction (including, where appropriate, the making by him of reparation for his offence), or
(b) any change in his circumstances (s. 1(1)).

The court must fix the date to which sentence is deferred, the maximum period allowed being six months (s. 1(4)). Subject to an exception mentioned below, sentence may be deferred only once (s. 1(4)).

Deferment requires the offender's consent and the court must be satisfied that exercise of the power would be in the interests of justice (s. 1(3)). The court dealing with the offender after the period of deferment may approach the case in any way the deferring court could have done (s. 1D(2)(a)). By s. 1D(2)(b), that includes, where sentence was deferred by a magistrates' court, committing the offender for sentence under s. 3. Where a magistrates' court defers sentence and then commits under s. 3, the Crown Court may also defer sentence, that being the exception to the rule that sentence may be deferred only once (s. 1D(3)).

Where there is a requirement to make a referral order on a young offender (see **E10.5**), the court may not defer passing sentence.

D20.104 **Requirements that May be Imposed** The most important requirement imposed on an offender when sentence is deferred is to return on the specified day. Upon deferring sentence, the court does not bail the offender but a failure to appear on the deferment date may lead to a warrant being issued for the offender's arrest (PCC(S)A 2000, s. 1(7)).

The requirements imposed by the court when deferring sentence may include reparative and other activity to be undertaken during the period of deferment. When the court comes to impose sentence at the end of the period of deferment, it is able to have regard to the conduct of the offender and any change in the offender's circumstances or attitude. In this context, 'conduct' includes reference to how well the offender has complied with any requirements imposed by the court. The CJA 2003, s. 204(3), allows a curfew to be imposed as a condition of a deferred sentence; the court may include a further curfew as a condition of a community order imposed at the conclusion of the deferred period, although it ought then to take the earlier period of curfew into account (*Ali* [2011] EWCA Crim 2747).

The court may appoint a supervisor to monitor the offender's compliance with the requirements imposed, who may be a probation officer. Those requirements may include one as to residence (s. 1A). If the court is satisfied that the offender has failed to comply with one or more requirements, it may deal with the offender before the end of the period of deferment (s. 1B). The offender may in any event be dealt with before the end of the period of deferment if found to have committed a further offence (s. 1C).

D20.105 **Challenge to a Deferred Sentence** A deferred sentence may, in appropriate circumstances, be referred by the A-G to the Court of Appeal for review (see **D28.7**), as an unduly lenient sentence (*A-G's Ref (No. 22 of 1992)* (1993) 97 Cr App R 275; *A-G's Ref (No. 101 of 2006)* [2006] EWCA Crim 3335).

Appropriate Circumstances for Deferring

D20.106 In *George* [1984] 3 All ER 13, Lord Lane CJ gave some indication of when it may be appropriate to defer sentence. He referred especially to cases where the improvement in the offender's conduct or steps which the court wishes to see taken are not sufficiently specific to be made the subject of a requirement in a probation order, but nonetheless the court wishes to see what progress is made by the offender before sentencing (p. 1085G–H). However, deferment should not be used either as an easy option when the sentencer's intentions could in fact be achieved by other means (*George*, at p. 1086A) or where it imposes such a restriction on the offender's freedom of action that another order was more appropriate (*Skelton* [1983] Crim LR 686).

Recommended Procedure when Deferring Sentence

D20.107 Lord Lane CJ in his judgment in *George* [1984] 3 All ER 13, gave guidance on the procedure which should be adopted when deferring sentence. The chief points to be noted are:

(a) When deferring sentence the court must make it clear to the offender the particular purposes under the PCC(S)A 2000, s. 1(1), that it has in mind, and the conduct that is expected of the offender during deferment. The court should also make it clear that it is deferring sentence as opposed to merely adjourning (*Fairhead* [1975] 2 All ER 737).
(b) A careful note should be made by the court of what the offender is told. Ideally, the offender should also be given a written note of the conduct expected.
(c) The court eventually passing sentence should:
  (i) ascertain the purpose of the deferment and any requirement as to conduct then imposed;
  (ii) determine whether the offender has substantially conformed (or attempted to conform) with the proper expectations of the deferring court.

(d) In order to decide whether the offender has lived up to expectations, the sentencing court will almost certainly require an up-to-date pre-sentence report. To avoid unnecessary delay, it may be appropriate to order the report when sentence is deferred. If the offender has conformed with the sentencing court's expectations then, depending on the terms of the deferment, a non-custodial sentence may be expected; if not, the sentencing court should state with precision in what respects the offender has failed. Failure to do so may lead to any custodial sentence being quashed because of the appearance given that the sentencing court merely disagrees with the original decision to defer as opposed to being genuinely disappointed in the offender's conduct (*Glossop* (1981) 3 Cr App R (S) 347).

The above procedure is recommended in part because the judge who passes sentence need not necessarily be the judge who deferred sentence, and it is therefore necessary to ensure as far as possible that the former knows how the latter was thinking. However, whenever possible, both the judge who deferred sentence and counsel who then represented the offender should make themselves available for the eventual sentencing (*Gurney* [1974] Crim LR 472; *Ryan* [1976] Crim LR 508).

(e) Every effort should be made to sentence the offender on the date to which sentence was deferred (per Lord Lane CJ in *Anderson* (1983) 78 Cr App R 251). In exceptional circumstances, however, the court may adjourn to a later date, even if that is more than six months after the original deferment (*Ingle* [1974] 3 All ER 811). In *Anderson* the Court of Appeal held that the Crown Court had not been deprived of its jurisdiction to sentence by reason of the delay, but the sentence eventually passed should reflect how stale the offence had become.

Custodial Sentence after Deferment

As indicated by Lord Lane CJ in *George* [1984] 3 All ER 13, the tacit understanding between the court and the offender when sentence is deferred is that, if the offender substantially conforms (or, at least, tries to conform) with the deferring court's proper expectations, the sentencing court will pass a favourable, often non-custodial sentence. It follows that, although conviction for further offences during a deferment period will almost certainly lead to a custodial sentence (see, e.g., *Hope* (1980) 2 Cr App R (S) 6), merely staying out of trouble does not guarantee the opposite. For example, in *Smith* (1976) 64 Cr App R 116, where sentence was deferred to see if D could (a) work regularly and (b) reduce his alcohol consumption, the Court of Appeal upheld an eventual custodial sentence because D had done neither of those things, even though he had avoided further offending. **D20.108**

There are qualifications to this approach:

(a) where the offender falls short of the deferring court's expectations in only a minor way, this should not be used as a justification for a custodial sentence (*Smith* (1979) 1 Cr App R (S) 339);
(b) offences which were allegedly committed during the period of deferment but which are unresolved by the time the period expires should not influence the sentencer in any way unless and until the offender has been convicted of the later alleged offences (*Aquilina* [1990] Crim LR 134).

Sentencing before the End of the Deferment Period

Once sentence has been deferred, the court may not proceed to sentence until the deferment period has expired, unless either it revokes the order for deferment within 56 days by virtue of the PCC(S)A 2000, s. 155(1) (see **D20.95**), or s. 1C applies (*McQuaide* (1974) 60 Cr App R 239). **D20.109**

The effect of the latter provision is that, if an offender is convicted of an offence (the subsequent offence) during a deferment period, the court passing sentence for the subsequent offence may also sentence for the deferment offence (s. 1C(3)). This does not apply if sentence was deferred by the Crown Court and the sentencing court for the subsequent offence is a magistrates' court (proviso (a) to s. 1C(3)).

In the converse case of the Crown Court sentencing for the subsequent offence, sentence having been deferred by a magistrates' court, the Crown Court's powers in respect of the deferment offence are limited to those of a magistrates' court (proviso (b)). Apart from the possibility of the court that sentences an offender for a subsequent offence also sentencing for the deferment offence, conviction for a subsequent offence during a deferment period always entitles the *deferring* court to sentence forthwith for the deferment offence, even though the deferment period has not expired (s. 1C(1)).

D20.110 **Powers of Criminal Courts (Sentencing) Act 2000, ss. 1 to 1D**

1.—(1) The Crown Court or a magistrates' court may defer passing sentence on an offender for the purpose of enabling the court, or any other court to which it falls to deal with him, to have regard in dealing with him to—

(a) his conduct after conviction (including, where appropriate, the making by him of reparation for his offence); or

(b) any change in his circumstances;

but this is subject to subsections (3) and (4) below.

(2) Without prejudice to the generality of subsection (1) above, the matters to which the court to which it falls to deal with the offender may have regard by virtue of paragraph (a) of that subsection include the extent to which the offender has complied with any requirements imposed under subsection (3)(b) below.

(3) The power conferred by subsection (1) above shall be exercisable only if—

(a) the offender consents;

(b) the offender undertakes to comply with any requirements as to his conduct during the period of the deferment that the court considers it appropriate to impose; and

(c) the court is satisfied, having regard to the nature of the offence and the character and circumstances of the offender, that it would be in the interests of justice to exercise the power.

(4) Any deferment under this section shall be until such date as may be specified by the court, not being more than six months after the date on which the deferment is announced by the court; and, subject to section 1D(3) below, where the passing of sentence has been deferred under this section it shall not be further so deferred.

(5) Where a court has under this section deferred passing sentence on an offender, it shall forthwith give a copy of the order deferring the passing of sentence and setting out any requirements imposed under subsection (3)(b) above—

(a) to the offender,

(b) where an officer of a local probation board has been appointed to act as a supervisor in relation to him, to that board,

(ba) where an officer of a provider of probation services has been appointed to act as a supervisor in relation to him, to that provider, and

(c) where a person has been appointed under section 1A(2)(b) below to act as a supervisor in relation to him, to that person.

(6) Notwithstanding any enactment, a court which under this section defers passing sentence on an offender shall not on the same occasion remand him.

(7) Where—

(a) a court which under this section has deferred passing sentence on an offender proposes to deal with him on the date originally specified by the court, or

(b) the offender does not appear on the day so specified,

the court may issue a summons requiring him to appear before the court at a time and place specified in the summons, or may issue a warrant to arrest him and bring him before the court at a time and place specified in the warrant.

(8) Nothing in this section or sections 1A to 1D below shall affect—

(a) the power of the Crown Court to bind over an offender to come up for judgment when called upon; or

(b) the power of any court to defer passing sentence for any purpose for which it may lawfully do so apart from this section.

1ZA.—(1) Without prejudice to the generality of paragraph (b) of section 1(3), the requirements that may be imposed under that paragraph include restorative justice requirements.

(2) Any reference in this section to a restorative justice requirement is to a requirement to participate in an activity—

(a) where the participants consist of, or include, the offender and one or more of the victims,

(b) which aims to maximise the offender's awareness of the impact of the offending concerned on the victims, and
(c) which gives an opportunity to a victim or victims to talk about, or by other means express experience of, the offending and its impact.
(3) Imposition under section 1(3)(b) of a restorative justice requirement requires, in addition to the offender's consent and undertaking under section 1(3), the consent of every other person who would be a participant in the activity concerned.
(4) For the purposes of subsection (3), a supervisor appointed under section 1A(2) does not count as a proposed participant.
(5) Where a restorative justice requirement is imposed under section 1(3)(b), the duty under section 1(5) (to give copies of order) extends to every person who would be a participant in the activity concerned.
(6) In a case where there is such a restorative justice requirement, a person running the activity concerned must in doing that have regard to any guidance that is issued, with a view to encouraging good practice in connection with such an activity, by the Secretary of State.
(7) In this section 'victim' means a victim of, or other person affected by, the offending concerned.

1A.—(1) Without prejudice to the generality of paragraph (b) of section 1(3) above, the requirements that may be imposed by virtue of that paragraph include requirements as to the residence of the offender during the whole or any part of the period of deferment.
(2) Where an offender has undertaken to comply with any requirements imposed under section 1(3)(b) above the court may appoint—
(a) an officer of a local probation board or an officer of a provider of probation services, or
(b) any other person whom the court thinks appropriate,
to act as a supervisor in relation to him.
(3) A person shall not be appointed under subsection (2)(b) above without his consent.
(4) It shall be the duty of a supervisor appointed under subsection (2) above—
(a) to monitor the offender's compliance with the requirements; and
(b) to provide the court to which it falls to deal with the offender in respect of the offence in question with such information as the court may require relating to the offender's compliance with the requirements.

1B.—(1) A court which under section 1 above has deferred passing sentence on an offender may deal with him before the end of the period of deferment if—
(a) he appears or is brought before the court under subsection (3) below; and
(b) the court is satisfied that he has failed to comply with one or more requirements imposed under section 1(3)(b) above in connection with the deferment.
(2) Subsection (3) below applies where—
(a) a court has under section 1 above deferred passing sentence on an offender;
(b) the offender undertook to comply with one or more requirements imposed under section 1(3)(b) above in connection with the deferment; and
(c) a person appointed under section 1A(2) above to act as a supervisor in relation to the offender has reported to the court that the offender has failed to comply with one or more of those requirements.
(3) Where this subsection applies, the court may issue—
(a) a summons requiring the offender to appear before the court at a time and place specified in the summons; or
(b) a warrant to arrest him and bring him before the court at a time and place specified in the warrant.

1C.—(1) A court which under section 1 above has deferred passing sentence on an offender may deal with him before the end of the period of deferment if during that period he is convicted in Great Britain of any offence.
(2) Subsection (3) below applies where a court has under section 1 above deferred passing sentence on an offender in respect of one or more offences and during the period of deferment the offender is convicted in England and Wales of any offence ('the later offence').
(3) Where this subsection applies, then (without prejudice to subsection (1) above and whether or not the offender is sentenced for the later offence during the period of deferment), the court which passes sentence on him for the later offence may also, if this has not already been done, deal with him for the offence or offences for which passing of sentence has been deferred, except that—
(a) the power conferred by this subsection shall not be exercised by a magistrates' court if the court which deferred passing sentence was the Crown Court; and

(b) the Crown Court, in exercising that power in a case in which the court which deferred passing sentence was a magistrates' court, shall not pass any sentence which could not have been passed by a magistrates' court in exercising that power.

(4) Where a court which under section 1 above has deferred passing sentence on an offender proposes to deal with him by virtue of subsection (1) above before the end of the period of deferment, the court may issue—

(a) a summons requiring him to appear before the court at a time and place specified in the summons; or

(b) a warrant to arrest him and bring him before the court at a time and place specified in the warrant.

1D.—(1) In deferring the passing of sentence under section 1 above a magistrates' court shall be regarded as exercising the power of adjourning the trial conferred by section 10(1) of the Magistrates' Courts Act 1980, and accordingly sections 11(1) and 13(1) to (3A) and (5) of that Act (non-appearance of the accused) apply (without prejudice to section 1(7) above) if the offender does not appear on the date specified under section 1(4) above.

(2) Where the passing of sentence on an offender has been deferred by a court ('the original court') under section 1 above, the power of that court under that section to deal with the offender at the end of the period of deferment and any power of that court under section 1B(1) or 1C(1) above, or of any court under section 1C(3) above, to deal with the offender—

(a) is power to deal with him, in respect of the offence for which passing of sentence has been deferred, in any way in which the original court could have dealt with him if it had not deferred passing sentence; and

(b) without prejudice to the generality of paragraph (a) above, in the case of a magistrates' court, includes the power conferred by section 3 below to commit him to the Crown Court for sentence.

(3) Where—

(a) the passing of sentence on an offender in respect of one or more offences has been deferred under section 1 above, and

(b) a magistrates' court deals with him in respect of the offence or any of the offences by committing him to the Crown Court under section 3 below,

the power of the Crown Court to deal with him includes the same power to defer passing sentence on him as if he had just been convicted of the offence or offences on indictment before the court.

(4) Subsection (5) below applies where—

(a) the passing of sentence on an offender in respect of one or more offences has been deferred under section 1 above;

(b) it falls to a magistrates' court to determine a relevant matter; and

(c) a justice of the peace is satisfied—

(i) that a person appointed under section 1A(2)(b) above to act as a supervisor in relation to the offender is likely to be able to give evidence that may assist the court in determining that matter; and

(ii) that person will not voluntarily attend as a witness.

(5) The justice may issue a summons directed to that person requiring him to attend before the court at the time and place appointed in the summons to give evidence.

(6) For the purposes of subsection (4) above a court determines a relevant matter if it—

(a) deals with the offender in respect of the offence, or any of the offences, for which the passing of sentence has been deferred; or

(b) determines, for the purposes of section 1B(1)(b) above, whether the offender has failed to comply with any requirements imposed under section 1(3)(b) above.

ADJOURNMENTS

D20.111 Apart from its power under the PCC(S)A 2000, s. 1, to defer passing sentence for up to six months, the Crown Court has inherent jurisdiction at common law to adjourn before sentencing an offender. In other words, it need not sentence on the occasion on which an offender pleads guilty or is found guilty.

Although there are no express limitations on the grounds for adjourning or the length of the adjournment, by analogy with the decision in *Arthur v Stringer* (1986) 84 Cr App R 361, it would be improper to adjourn solely because the offender is slightly too young for the form of sentence the court considers desirable in this case and adjourning will allow the offender to attain the minimum age necessary. The discretion vested in the court to adjourn has to be exercised judicially. It cannot be said to have been exercised judicially if the only reason for exercising it was to ensure that the offender had reached the age of 21 by the time of sentence, thus enabling the court to pass a sentence of imprisonment.

During the period of the adjournment, the offender may be remanded in custody or granted bail at the court's discretion (see the Senior Courts Act 1981, s. 81(1)(c), for the power to grant bail).

Maximum Length

As to the maximum period for an adjournment, analogous guidance is provided by the MCA 1980, s. 10(3), which restricts an adjournment after conviction to a maximum of three weeks at a time if the offender is remanded in custody, four weeks if granted bail. Although the subsection does not directly apply to the Crown Court when dealing with an offender convicted on indictment, it is an indication of the kind of periods Parliament considers appropriate for post-conviction adjournments, at least where the ultimate sentence is likely to be relatively short. **D20.112**

Where the Crown Court is dealing with an offender who has appealed against conviction and/or sentence in the magistrates' court, the higher court is directly bound by the provisions of s. 10(3) since the appeal takes the form of a rehearing, and the Crown Court's powers are therefore no greater than those of the magistrates (*Arthur v Stringer* (1986) 84 Cr App R 361).

Binding Over

A final power possessed by the Crown Court, analogous to adjourning, is to bind the offender over to come up for judgment if called upon to do so. Although in form a postponement of sentence, this is used more as a means of avoiding sentencing an offender if, exceptionally, the court does not want to impose a penalty but the ordinary alternatives to a penalty (such as a conditional discharge or a probation order) are inappropriate to meet the court's concerns in the particular circumstances of the case. The understanding is that, if the offender does not reoffend and complies with any conditions the court imposes, there will be no requirement, in practice, to return before the court. **D20.113**

Section D21 Summary Trial: General and Preliminary Matters

INTRODUCTION

D21.1 This section and the two sections which follow examine the procedure for summary trial, concentrating on those respects in which it differs from trial on indictment. It should be read in conjunction with **D5** and **D6**, which deal with the proceedings in a magistrates' court prior to the commencement of trial (or the sending of the case to the Crown Court).

JURISDICTION TO TRY CASES SUMMARILY

Basis of Jurisdiction

D21.2 The jurisdiction of a magistrates' court to try cases summarily is set out in the MCA 1980, s. 2. See also **D3.22** and **D3.23**. Under s. 2:

(a) A magistrates' court has jurisdiction to try any summary offence (s. 2(1)).
(b) A magistrates' court has jurisdiction to try an either-way offence provided only that the procedure for determining allocation (mode of trial) contained in the MCA 1980, ss. 18 to 22A, resulted in a decision for summary trial (s. 2(3)).

D21.3 **Magistrates' Courts Act 1980, s. 2**

(1) A magistrates' court has jurisdiction to try any summary offence.
(2) A magistrates' court has jurisdiction under sections 51 and 51A of the Crime and Disorder Act 1998 in respect of any offence committed by a person who appears or is brought before the court.
(3) Subject to—
  (a) sections 18 to 22A, and
  (b) any other enactment (wherever contained) relating to the mode of trial of offences triable either way,

a magistrates' court has jurisdiction to try summarily any offence which is triable either way.

Determining the Place of the Trial

D21.4 The Courts Act 2003, s. 30(3), empowers the Lord Chancellor (with the concurrence of the Lord Chief Justice) to give directions as to the distribution and transfer of magistrates' courts business. Where a person is charged with an offence, the prosecution decide which court that person should appear before and this decision will have to take account of any such directions (s. 30(4)).

The approach usually adopted is that a case should normally be heard either at a magistrates' court in the local justice area where the offence is alleged to have been committed, or where the person charged with the offence resides.

Transfer of Cases between Magistrates' Courts

It sometimes proves necessary, or desirable, to transfer cases from one magistrates' court to another. The MCA 1980, s. 27A, contains a general power to effect such a transfer at any stage in the proceedings. This power may be exercised by the court of its own motion, or on the application of one of the parties to the case. Where the court is minded to transfer a case, it should invite representations from all parties before doing so. There is to be no appeal from a decision on transfer. **D21.5**

Magistrates' Courts Act 1980, s. 27A

(1) Where a person appears or is brought before a magistrates' court—
 (a) to be tried by the court for an offence, . . .
 the court may transfer the matter to another magistrates' court.
(2) The court may transfer the matter before or after beginning the trial. . . .
(3) But if the court transfers the matter after it has begun to hear the evidence and the parties, the court to which the matter is transferred must begin hearing the evidence and the parties again.
(4) The power of the court under this section to transfer any matter must be exercised in accordance with any directions given under section 30(3) of the Courts Act 2003.

In addition to the general power conferred by s. 27A, there are specific statutory provisions relevant to sentencing hearings and remand hearings: **D21.6**

(a) By virtue of the PCC(S)A 2000, s. 10(1), where a magistrates' court has convicted an offender of an offence (the 'instant offence') and is then informed that the offender also stands convicted in another magistrates' court of another offence for which sentence has yet to be passed, it may remit the offender to that other court to be dealt with for the instant offence. This power applies only if (i) the offender is aged 18 or over, (ii) the other court consents to the case being remitted, and (iii) the instant offence is either imprisonable or punishable with disqualification from driving (s. 10(1) and (2)). The provisions of the MCA 1980, s. 128 (power to remand in custody or on bail and maximum period for remands in custody), apply where a case is remitted to another court just as they would apply if the court were adjourning with a view to the offender being brought back before the same court (PCC(S)A 2000, s. 10(3)(a)). Once the case has been remitted, the other court may deal with the case as if all the proceedings before the convicting court had in fact taken place before itself (s. 10(3)(b)). This includes the power to remit the offender to a third magistrates' court (s. 10(4)) or even back to the original convicting court (s. 10(5)). It will be noted that s. 10 applies only if the person to be remitted has already been convicted (though not sentenced or committed for sentence) in *both* the courts concerned.

(b) To avoid inconveniently long journeys from prison to court for remand hearings, a magistrates' court may order that, for any subsequent remands, the accused is to be brought before an alternate magistrates' court nearer to the prison where the accused is on remand (s. 130(1)). While the order under s. 130(1) is in force, the alternate court exercises all the powers relating to any further remand (whether in custody or on bail) and the granting of legal aid which would otherwise fall to be exercised by the original court (s. 130(3)). The order ceases to have force when the alternate court, when making a further remand in custody, either orders that the accused be brought before the original court at the end of the remand, or it grants the accused bail (s. 130(4)).

THE SUMMONS APPLICATION OR WRITTEN CHARGE

Contents of the Charge

D5.1 *et seq.* set out the various ways of commencing criminal proceedings, including the written charge and requisition (for public prosecutions) and applying for the issue of a summons (private prosecutions); D5.14 *et seq.* discuss the content of the written charge or application for a summons. **D21.7**

CrimPR Part 7 (see Supplement, **R7.1** *et seq.*) deals with the procedure on starting a prosecution in a magistrates' court.

Rule against Duplicity

D21.8 A charge should allege only one offence. However, under CrimPR 7.2(9) a single document may contain more than one application for a summons or more than one written charge. This means that an accused who appears before a magistrates' court may face more than one charge.

However, each application or written charge should allege only one offence; if it alleges more than one offence it may be 'duplicitous'. In *Carrington Carr v Leicestershire County Council* (1994) 158 JP 570, it was said that there are five situations where a charge may be duplicitous:

(a) where two or more discrete offences are charged conjunctively in one charge (e.g., where a single charge alleges both dangerous driving and careless driving);
(b) where two offences are charged disjunctively or in the alternative in one charge (e.g., where a single charge alleges dangerous driving or careless driving);
(c) where an offence is capable of being committed in more ways than one (e.g., driving under the influence of drink or drugs) and both ways are referred to in one charge;
(d) where a single offence is charged in respect of an activity but the activity involved more than one act; and
(e) where a single activity is charged but a number of particulars are relied on by the prosecution to prove the offence (e.g., a single act of obtaining by deception where the deception involved several misrepresentations).

In the latter two situations, it is submitted that a single charge may well be appropriate by virtue of CrimPR 7.3(2) (see **D21.9**). However, if the accused wishes to admit some, but not all, of the allegations (or wishes to raise different defences to different allegations), separate charges will be necessary.

The rule against duplicity was considered in *Euro Foods Group v Cumbria County Council* [2013] EWHC 2659 (Admin). However, it is respectfully submitted that the case should not be regarded as authoritative as the court mistakenly applied r. 12 of the Magistrates' Courts Rules 1981, rather than CrimPR 7.3.

See also **D11.45** *et seq.* for discussion of the rule against duplicity in the context of indictments.

D21.9 **Whether One or More than One Act is Being Alleged** Under CrimPR 7.3(2), more than one incident of the commission of the offence may be included in the allegation if those incidents, taken together, amount to a course of conduct (having regard to the time, place or purpose of commission). This mirrors r. 10.2(2), which applies to indictments (see **D11.32**). Whether more than one offence is being alleged in a single charge depends on the facts of the particular case.

In *Heaton v Costello* (1984) 148 JP 688, for example, the charge alleged theft of a bottle of cider, a pair of trousers and a cardigan from a supermarket. It was held that the appropriate test in such cases is whether the various acts can properly and fairly be described, having regard to all the circumstances of the case, as forming part of one activity. The present charge was held not to be bad for duplicity, since all the items were stolen on one visit to the supermarket (even though the way in which the theft had been committed had not been the same for all three items, in that the theft of the cider was effected by switching price labels and the theft of the clothing by walking through the checkouts without paying).

Another example is *Barton v DPP* [2001] EWHC Admin 223, where a single charge alleged theft of a total of £1,338.23. The prosecution case was that on 94 separate occasions, D had taken small amounts of cash from the till. D gave no specific explanation for the individual takings and put forward the same defence for all. The charge was held not be duplicitous. Indeed, to bring 94 separate charges would rightly have been regarded as oppressive. *Barton* was approved by the Court of Appeal in *Tovey* [2005] EWCA Crim 530, [2005] 2 Cr App R (S) 100 (606) and *Lunn* [2017] EWCA Crim 34, [2017] 2 Cr App R 5 (42) (cases concerning indictments).

By contrast, in *Ministry of Agriculture, Fisheries and Food v Nunn Corn (1987) Ltd* [1990] Crim LR 268, a charge was held to be duplicitous because it alleged more than one victim of the offence (different purchasers of seeds). However, it is submitted that this should not be seen as an invariable rule. In most cases the fact that there are separate victims will indeed mean that there were separate offences (e.g., theft of an item belonging to A and theft of an item belonging to B will necessarily be separate offences). However, there may be circumstances where a single offence can be committed against more than one victim (e.g., a single act of fraud might cause loss to more than one victim).

Whether a Statutory Provision Creates One or More than One Offence An important issue that may arise when the question of duplicity is under consideration is whether the statutory provision in question creates a single offence or more than one offence. This is a matter of statutory interpretation, but case law offers a guide to the approach taken by the courts. **D21.10**

In *Surrey Justices, ex parte Witherick* [1932] 1 KB 450, for example, a single charge alleging driving without due care and attention or without reasonable consideration (contrary to what is now the RTA 1988, s. 3) was held to be duplicitous because the section creates two separate offences, one of driving without due care and the other of driving without reasonable consideration. Accordingly, they must be alleged in separate charges, not as alternatives in a single charge.

By contrast, in *Thomson v Knights* [1947] KB 336, a single charge that alleged driving when unfit through drink or drugs (contrary to what is now the RTA 1988, s. 4) was held not to be duplicitous, since the section created a single offence of driving when in a 'self-induced state of incapacity, whether that incapacity was due to drink or drugs', not two separate offences of driving while unfit through drink, and driving while unfit through drugs.

AMENDMENT OF THE CHARGE

Before (or even during the course of) a summary trial it may become apparent that the charge is defective, either in the sense that it does not comply with CrimPR Part 7 (see **D21.7**), or in the sense that there is a discrepancy between the particulars alleged in it and the prosecution evidence adduced at trial. The MCA 1980, s. 123, greatly limits the extent to which any such defect may be used as a ground for objecting to the proceedings, but at the same time requires the court to grant an adjournment if a variation between the offence charged and the evidence adduced may have misled the defence. **D21.11**

Magistrates' Courts Act 1980, s. 123

(1) No objection shall be allowed to any information or complaint, or to any summons or warrant to procure the presence of the defendant, for any defect in it in substance or in form, or for any variance between it and the evidence adduced on behalf of the prosecutor or complainant at the hearing of the information or complaint.

(2) If it appears to a magistrates' court that any variance between a summons or warrant and the evidence adduced on behalf of the prosecutor or complainant is such that the defendant has been misled by the variance, the court shall, on the application of the defendant, adjourn the hearing.

(3) In the application of this section to proceedings conducted in accordance with section 16A—

(a) a reference in subsection (1) or (2) to evidence adduced on behalf of the prosecutor at a hearing is to be read as a reference to evidence placed before the court on behalf of the prosecutor, and

(b) subsection (2) is to be read as if for the words from 'has been misled' to the end there were substituted 'is likely to have been misled by the variance, the court shall treat the written charge as not being appropriate for trial in accordance with section 16A'.

D

Part D Procedure

If read literally, the wording of s. 123 requires the magistrates' court to ignore any defect, however gross it might be, save to the extent of granting the defence an adjournment in the circumstances set out in s. 123(2). The appellate courts have not, however, allowed s. 123 to have such a sweeping effect. Lord Widgery CJ in *Garfield v Maddocks* [1974] QB 7, at p. 12, summarised the correct approach thus:

> Those extremely wide words, which on their face seem to legalise almost any discrepancy between the evidence and the information, have in fact always been given a more restricted meaning, and in modern times the section is construed in this way, that if the variance between the evidence and the information is slight and does no injustice to the defence, the information may be allowed to stand notwithstanding the variance which occurred. On the other hand, if the variance is so substantial that it is unjust to the defendant to allow it to be adopted without a proper amendment of the information, then the practice is for the court to require the prosecution to amend in order to bring their information into line. Once they do that, of course, there is provision in [s. 123(2)] whereby an adjournment can be ordered in the interests of the defence if the amendment requires him to seek an adjournment.

In *New Southgate Metals Ltd v London Borough of Islington* [1996] Crim LR 334, the Divisional Court held that there are three types of error which can occur in a charge:

(a) an error 'so fundamental that it cannot be rescued by any appropriate and reasonable amendment': this will cause the prosecution to fail immediately;
(b) a 'defect that is substantial enough to require amendment': the magistrates have power to allow amendment (subject to granting an adjournment if the defence are placed at any disadvantage by the amendment) — if such an error is not corrected, any conviction obtained upon the defective charge is at risk of being quashed by the Divisional Court;
(c) an error that is 'so trivial that no amendment is required' where the defence were always aware of the true basis of the complaint: the conviction may be upheld even without amendment of the charge.

In *New Southgate Metals Ltd*, the charge referred to the wrong statute. The Divisional Court held that this error was capable of amendment, since the factual particulars of the offence were accurately set out in the charge, and the error to be one that was 'trivial in nature and in no way misled or disadvantaged the defence'.

Minor Defects which Do Not Require Amendment

D21.12 In *Sandwell Justices, ex parte West Midlands Passenger Transport Executive* [1979] RTR 17, the Divisional Court held that a variation between the charge (which alleged that the company had put a vehicle on the road with a defective rear nearside tyre) and the evidence (which was that it was a defective rear offside tyre) was so trivial that, even in the absence of the amendment which was in fact made, the conviction would have been upheld. It was clear that the company was always aware of which tyre was the subject of the complaint, and had in fact brought it to court for inspection at the hearing.

Defects which Require Amendment but which Are Not Incurable

D21.13 In such cases, if an amendment is sought and allowed, the court must go on to consider whether the defence have been misled by the original error and, if they have, it should grant an adjournment. Failure by the prosecution to ask for the amendment, or failure by the court to grant an adjournment, may lead to any conviction being quashed by the Divisional Court. In *Meek v Powell* [1952] 1 KB 164, for example, the charge referred to a repealed section of an Act which had later been re-enacted in identical terms; it was held that the justices could have allowed the charge to be amended (granting an adjournment if sought), or they could have dismissed it, allowing the prosecution to commence fresh proceedings under the correct Act, but it was not open to them to convict in the absence of such an amendment.

Similarly, in *DPP v Short* [2001] EWHC Admin 885, the charge alleged that D 'used' a vehicle with excess alcohol (rather than 'drove') under the RTA 1988, s. 5. At the end of the evidence, the prosecution invited the justices to exercise their power under the MCA 1980, s. 123, to amend the charge to substitute 'drove' for 'used', thus bringing the charge within the wording of the RTA 1988, s. 5. The magistrates refused to allow the charge to be amended. The Divisional Court said that, taking account of the express reference to s. 5 of the 1988 Act, it could not be said that the charge disclosed an offence not known to law. The Court went on to say that the MCA 1980, s. 123, confers a wide discretion on justices to amend a charge, and that discretion should ordinarily be exercised in favour of amendment unless so amending would result in injustice to an accused. In the present case, no injustice would have been caused to D by the proposed amendment, since he was fully aware of the case against him. It followed that the justices had erred in refusing the prosecution amendment.

Similarly, in *Foster v DPP* [2013] EWHC 2039 (Admin), D was charged with an offence allegedly committed on 18 April. In fact, the offence with which he was charged was such that it could not have been committed before the period of 28 days from 28 March had expired. It followed that D could not be guilty of the offence charged. Wilkie J said (at [23]) that:

> ... a discrepancy of [this] nature ... where the information on the basis of which the defendant before the magistrates had been brought to court does not disclose any offence at all, must be of sufficient substance that it requires amendment in order for the magistrates properly then to try the information. It would be an extremely odd set of circumstances if the magistrates could lawfully try a case and convict someone of an offence where the statement of the offence does not in fact, on the evidence, on any view, disclose the commission of the offence of which they convict the defendant.

The amendment can, in an appropriate case, change the offence with which the accused is charged. In *R (James) v DPP* [2004] EWHC 1663 (Admin), for example, D was charged with supplying a Class B drug. At the close of her case, it was submitted on her behalf that the evidence, although demonstrating an attempt to supply the drug, did not demonstrate an actual supply. The prosecution, relying on s. 123, applied to amend the charge to allege an offence of attempting to supply a Class B drug (contrary to the CAA 1981). Issues arose as to whether the justices were right to allow the amendment after the close of the defence case and whether they were right not to hold fresh mode of trial proceedings after allowing the amendment. The Divisional Court held that there is no fetter on the justices relying on the very wide wording of s. 123 to substitute a different offence, even where that offence arises under a different Act of Parliament, provided that no injustice is caused to the accused in so doing. There is, said the Court, no reason why magistrates' courts should apply different principles to the Crown Court, which has the power to make such amendments. In the present case, the Court decided that D had suffered no prejudice. The Court also ruled that, where there is no such injustice to the accused, there is no requirement on the magistrates to restart the mode of trial procedure when the charge is amended to substitute one offence for another. D21.14

Where the effect of the amendment would be to replace one offence with a different one, a key question is how similar those offences are. For example, in *Wyllie v CPS* [1988] Crim LR 753, a charge under what is now the RTA 1988, s. 7 (failure to provide a specimen of urine for analysis), was amended to allege failure to provide a specimen of blood; the Divisional Court said the amendment was permissible because, on the facts of the particular case, the evidence would have been the same under whichever limb of s. 7 the case was prosecuted.

In *R (Thornhill) v Uxbridge Magistrates' Court* [2008] EWHC 508 (Admin), on the other hand, D had been asked to provide a specimen of urine, it being accepted that a medical reason precluded him from providing a specimen of breath; he refused to comply and was charged with failing to provide a specimen of breath. The prosecution later sought to amend the charge to allege failure to provide a specimen of urine. The six-month time-limit for commencing proceedings in respect of the failure to supply a specimen of urine had expired. Silber J held that there is a distinct difference between a failure to provide a specimen of urine and one of breath, and so the decision of the justices to permit the amendment of the charge was quashed. However, in *Williams v DPP* [2009] EWHC 2354 (Admin), Thomas LJ noted (at [19]) that the CPS did not appear and were not represented in *Thornhill*, and so it is of limited value as an authority; in any event, the question whether the offence arises out of the same or substantially the same facts is a factual question. On this basis, it is submitted that *Thornhill* should not be followed. In *Crann v CPS* [2013] EWHC 552 (Admin), Foskett J pointed out (at [23]) that '[e]very case depends upon its own facts, the essential question being whether the principles appropriate to the question of whether the discretionary exercise involved in deciding whether to grant the amendment to the charge were observed'.

D21.15 In the case of summary offences, an important question is whether or not the six-month time-limit for commencing a prosecution (MCA 1980, s. 127: see **D21.17**) has expired: if it has not, there is nothing to stop the prosecution simply starting the proceedings again, and this is a strong factor in favour of allowing an amendment to the existing charge. However, the fact that the time-limit has expired is not necessarily fatal to an application to amend the existing charge.

In *Newcastle-upon-Tyne Justices, ex parte John Bryce (Contractors) Ltd* [1976] 1 WLR 517, the justices permitted the amendment of a charge which had originally alleged *permitting* the use of an overladen lorry so as to allege its actual *use*. It was held that, even though the amendment was more than six months from the date of the alleged offence, and even though it substituted a different offence for that originally charged ('use' and 'permitting use' were two separate offences), nonetheless the amendment was permissible. The defence were not misled or taken by surprise, since the nature of the prosecution case had always been apparent from the statement of facts on the summons.

The relevant principles were set out in *Scunthorpe Justices, ex parte McPhee* (1998) 162 JP 635, where D had originally been charged with robbery, but the CPS subsequently agreed to accept pleas of guilty to theft and common assault. The justices granted an application to amend the charge to allege theft, but refused to allow an amendment to charge common assault (since the six-month time-limit (under the MCA 1980, s. 127) for the summary offence of common assault had elapsed). Dyson J, giving the judgment of the Divisional Court, said:

> (1) The purpose of the six-month time limit imposed by s. 127 of the 1980 Act is to ensure that summary offences are charged and tried as soon as reasonably practicable after their alleged commission.
> (2) Where an information has been laid within the six-month period it can be amended after the expiry of that period.
> (3) An information can be amended after the expiry of the six-month period, even to allege a different offence or different offences provided that:
> (i) the different offence or offences allege the 'same misdoing' as the original offence; and
> (ii) the amendment can be made in the interests of justice.
>
> ... The phrase 'same misdoing' ... should not be construed too narrowly. I understand it to mean that the new offence should arise out of the same (or substantially the same) facts as gave rise to the original offence ...
>
> Once they are satisfied that the amended offence or offences arise out of the same or substantially the same facts as the original offence, the justices must go on to consider whether it is in the interests of justice to allow the amendment. In exercising their discretion the justices should pay particular regard to the interests of the defendant. If an amendment will result in a defendant facing a significantly more serious charge, that should weigh heavily — perhaps conclusively — against allowing the amendment after the six-month time limit has expired.

These conditions were met in the instant case, and the information could have been amended accordingly.

This approach was applied in *Thames Magistrates' Court, ex parte Stevens* (2000) 164 JP 233, where D was charged with assault occasioning actual bodily harm (OAPA 1861, s. 47). The prosecution subsequently indicated that they wished to withdraw the s. 47 charge and replace it with a charge alleging the summary offence of common assault (CJA 1988, s. 39). However, it was more than six months since the commission of the offence. The Divisional Court held that the magistrate had correctly concluded that what was being sought by the prosecution was an amendment of the original charge rather than the laying of a new charge. The MCA 1980, s. 127, therefore did not prevent the court from dealing with the charge of common assault. The magistrate, in considering whether the amendment was in the interests of justice, had taken proper account of the fact that: (i) the case against D was, to all intents and purposes, the same after the amendment as before; (ii) D had not been misled or prejudiced by the amendment; (iii) she knew the case against her; (iv) she had not been deprived by the amendment of any defence; (v) the evidence to be adduced by the prosecution was not different after the amendment; and (vi) the effect of the amendment was in fact to reduce the gravity of the original charge.

In *Shaw v DPP* [2007] EWHC 207 (Admin), however, the justices allowed a charge to be amended to allege a different offence that carried imprisonment, whereas the original one did not. Significantly, the amendment introduced the new charge outside the six-month time-limit imposed by s. 127 of the 1980 Act. The Divisional Court held that the substitution of a new offence with a significantly heavier penalty, especially one where the accused faces the possibility of a custodial sentence, should have led the justices to reach the conclusion that it was not in the interests of justice to allow such an amendment.

It should be emphasised that an amendment which seeks to replace an indictable-only or either-way offence with a summary offence can be permitted (even if arising out of the 'same misdoing') only if the proceedings for the original offence were commenced within six months of the alleged commission of that offence.

In *Dougall v CPS* [2018] EWHC 1367 (Admin), [2018] 2 Cr App R 24 (372), Holroyde LJ said (at [22]) that if no proceedings are commenced within the period of six months following the offence, 'but an indictable offence is later charged and then subsequently amended to charge a summary offence, that amendment does not avoid the consequence of the statutory time limit [in the MCA 1980, s. 127]'.

Fundamental Defects that Cannot be Rescued by Amendment

Some errors are so fundamental that, despite the breadth of the wording of s. 142, they cannot be remedied by amendment. For example, it has been held that a charge which names the wrong person cannot be amended to cure the defect. In *Marco (Croydon) Ltd v Metropolitan Police* [1984] RTR 24, for example, it was held that magistrates were not entitled to allow the amendment of the name of the defendant company from 'A J Bull Ltd' to the correct name of 'Marco (Croydon) Ltd, trading as A & J Bull Containers'. Similarly, in *R (J Sainsbury plc) v Plymouth Magistrates' Court* [2006] EWHC 1749 (Admin), the charge named the defendant company as 'J Sainsbury plc (trading as Sainsburys Supermarket Ltd)'. J Sainsbury plc asserted that it was not the proper defendant, since the correct names of the relevant companies were in fact 'J. Sainsbury plc' and 'Sainsbury's Supermarkets Ltd' (the former was the holding company for the latter, and it was the latter which ran the business at the store in question). The prosecution applied under the MCA 1980, s. 123, to substitute J Sainsbury Supermarkets Ltd as defendant. The district judge acknowledged that the two companies were two separate legal entities, but allowed the amendment notwithstanding that the time-limit for bringing a prosecution had since expired. The Divisional Court, however, held that the proper defendant had not been before the court and so the effect of the decision of the district judge was impermissibly to prefer a charge out of time. D21.16

Where the correct defendant is not before the court, the only remedy for the prosecution in the case of an irremediable defect is to start the proceedings afresh (which, in the case of a summary offence, is possible only if less than six months have elapsed since the commission of the offence). There must then be an adjournment so that a fresh summons or requisition can be served on the new defendant (*Greater Manchester Justices, ex parte Aldi GmbH & Co. KG* (1995) 159 JP 717). However, where the accused is misnamed but nonetheless appears before the court, this may have the effect of waiving the error and rendering amendment permissible (see *Allan v Wiseman* [1975] RTR 217, where the wrong surname was used but the right person was nonetheless before the court). The relevant authorities were reviewed by the Divisional Court in *Platinum Crown Investments Ltd v North East Essex Magistrates' Court* [2017] EWHC 2761 (Admin), [2018] 1 Cr App R 25 (361). The charges and summonses referred to Platinum Crown Ltd. That company was in fact defunct. The defendant should have been identified as Platinum Crown Investments Ltd. The question was whether the name of the company could be amended under the MCA 1980, s. 123, even though the six-month time limit applicable under s. 127 had expired. Treacy LJ considered *R (Essence Bars Ltd) v Wimbledon Magistrates' Court* [2016] EWCA Civ 63, [2016] 1 WLR 3265, and (at 35]) said that this decision 'shows that a degree of factual inquiry is necessary before the court can distinguish between a mistake as to identity (which cannot be corrected out of time) and a mis-statement of name (which may be corrected out of time)'. His lordship went on to say that 'the local authority always intended to prosecute PCIL', and both PCIL and its director (who also faced charges) were aware of that fact prior to the application for a summons. On the first court appearance, when the director attended and entered not guilty pleas, 'it is clear that he must have intended to enter pleas on behalf of PCIL' (at [37]). It followed that this involved 'a mistake or mis-statement of name in circumstances where there could be no reasonable doubt as to the identity of the defendant entertained by the court or indeed by the defendant itself' (at [38]). Accordingly, the magistrates were entitled to permit amendment of the name of the company, notwithstanding the expiry of the statutory time-limit (at [39]).

TIME-LIMIT FOR STARTING PROCEEDINGS FOR SUMMARY OFFENCES

General Rule

D21.17 A magistrates' court may not try an accused for a *summary* offence unless the application for a summons was served on the magistrates' court within six months of the time when the offence was allegedly committed (MCA 1980, s. 127(1); see **D21.20**). Section 127(2)(a) makes it clear that s. 127(1) does not apply to indictable offences (which term includes either-way offences).

Section 127 refers to the laying of an information (i.e. applying for a summons) but does not make it clear when time starts to run in the case of proceedings brought by the written charge and requisition procedure established by the CJA 2003, s. 29 (see **D5.4**). In *Brown v DPP* [2019] EWHC 798 (Admin), the Divisional Court held that, where a prosecution is initiated by the written charge and requisition process, the written charge must be issued within the six months permitted by s. 127. For these purposes, 'the written charge can be regarded as issued only when the document comprising the written charge is completed, with all relevant details and in the form needed for service. Provided that is done within six months of the relevant offence, the written charge will have been issued in time' (per Irwin LJ, at [20]). Irwin LJ added that if, following issue within the permitted time-limit, 'there is an inordinate or unwarranted or unjustified but significant delay before such a written charge is served, that should not and cannot go without remedy. The remedy is abuse of process' (see **D21.21** ***et seq.***). His lordship suggested that, as a matter of practice, both issue and service should be completed before six months from the relevant offence, 'so as to put paid to any suggestion of such unwarranted delay' (at [22]).

In *Atkinson v DPP* [2004] EWHC 1457 (Admin), [2005] 1 WLR 96, it was held that, where there is uncertainty as to whether proceedings were started in time, the question should be determined according to the criminal standard of proof and the magistrates should decline to hear the matter unless satisfied so that they are sure that the proceedings were commenced within the statutory time-limit.

As regards either-way offences, there is no time-limit within which proceedings must be started, unless it is one of the exceptional offences for which there is statutory limitation on the time for taking proceedings on indictment, in which case that limitation applies equally to summary proceedings (s. 127(2) and (4)). **D21.18**

Even where a statute creates an either-way offence and then appears to impose a time-limit in respect of summary proceedings (but not proceedings on indictment), the limitation is overridden by the MCA 1980, s. 127(2). In *Kemp v Liebherr (Great Britain) Ltd* [1987] 1 All ER 885, a prosecution under the Health and Safety at Work etc. Act 1974 was commenced more than six months after evidence justifying a prosecution had become available to the prosecutor. By s. 34(3) of the Act, summary proceedings for contravening the Act apparently had to be commenced within six months of obtaining the evidence. The Divisional Court held that the proceedings were nonetheless within time since, on a true construction of the Act, the offence charged was triable either way and, therefore, s. 34(3) was effectively negated by the MCA 1980, s. 127(2). Similarly in *Thames Metropolitan Stipendiary Magistrate, ex parte Horgan* [1998] QB 719, a provision in the Companies Act 1985 which prescribed a different time-limit to that laid down in s. 127 in respect of 'offences triable by a magistrates' court' was held to refer only to summary offences, and so did not apply to an either-way offence that was to be tried summarily.

Start of Time-limit

The time-limit under the MCA 1980, s. 127, begins to run from the date of the commission of the offence. Where a statute creates a *continuing* summary offence, a prosecution can be brought at any time until six months have elapsed from the date when the offence ceased to be committed (*British Telecommunications plc v Nottinghamshire County Council* [1999] Crim LR 217; *Hertfordshire County Council v National Grid Gas plc* [2007] EWHC 2535 (Admin), [2008] 1 WLR 2562). **D21.19**

Some statutes which create offences specify different periods within which the prosecution must be commenced, or different starting points for that period; some statutes specify alternative periods, usually one with a start date based on the date of the commission of the offence and the other based on the date when the commission of the offence came to light or when the prosecuting authority has sufficient evidence on which to proceed. In *Woodward* [2017] EWHC 1008 (Admin), the Divisional Court considered the Animal Welfare Act 2006, s. 31. This requires the application for a summons to be made within six months of 'the date on which evidence which the prosecutor thinks is sufficient to justify the proceedings comes to his knowledge' (s. 31(1)(b)), with a longstop date of three years from the commission of the offence (s. 31(1)(a)). Hickinbottom LJ reviewed the case law on this topic and (at [23]) helpfully summarised the law thus:

(a) The relevant date is the date upon which the prosecutor considers that, upon the available evidence, it is in the public interest to prosecute the particular individual(s); this requires not merely consideration of whether there is a prima facie case, but also whether it is in the public interest for such a prosecution to be brought (see also *Letherbarrow v Warwickshire County Council* [2014] EWHC 4820 (Admin), at [17], per Bean LJ).
(b) The prosecutor is entitled to reasonable time, even after the primary evidence has been gathered in, and even after the prosecutor has decided that there is or may be a prima facie case against someone or even identified individuals, to carry out this consideration (see also *Riley v CPS* [2016] EWHC 2531 (Admin), [2017] 1 WLR 505, at [17], per Gross LJ).
(c) However, this decision cannot be avoided or delayed by the mere 'shuffling of papers', or by information being suppressed so as to extend the time-limit (see also *RSPCA v Johnson* [2009] EWHC 2702 (Admin), at [33], per Pill LJ).

(d) Section 31 applies to all prosecutors, not just those who have a statutory power to prosecute, and so it applies equally to private prosecutors (see also *Lamont-Perkins v RSPCA* [2012] EWHC 1002 (Admin), at [26], per Wyn Williams J).
(e) A distinction must be drawn between investigators and prosecutors; the prosecutor is the individual who is given responsibility for making the important decision whether to prosecute (see also *Letherbarrow*, at [19] and *Riley*, at [15]).
(f) Where there is an issue as to whether the prosecution was commenced in time, it is for the prosecutor to show, to the criminal standard of proof, that there has been compliance with s. 31(1)(b); if not, the prosecution is invalid.
(g) The prosecutor may establish that the prosecution was commenced in time either by the issue of a certificate under s. 31(2) or by adducing evidence showing who made the decision that a prosecution was justified and when (*Letherbarrow*, at [20]).
(h) Where reliance is placed upon a certificate, it must comply strictly with the statutory requirements and must do so on its face, since deficiencies cannot be remedied by reference to extrinsic evidence (see also *Azam v Epping Forest District Council* [2009] EWHC 3177 (Admin), at [25](3), per Scott Baker LJ, and *RSPCA v King* [2010] EWHC 637 (Admin), at [9], per Toulson LJ).
(i) A valid certificate is determinative of the matter unless the certificate is inaccurate on its face (i.e. plainly wrong on its face and patently misleading), or else can be shown to be fraudulent (see also *Azam* at [25](4) and (5)).
(j) A certificate can be issued at any time until the close of the prosecution case, and if a certificate is defective, there is no reason in principle why a new certificate cannot be issued.
(k) Where there is no certificate to be relied upon (because either none was issued, or any certificate issued was defective), the court must determine whether the prosecution was brought within the time required by s. 31(1)(b) (*Azam* at [25](1)), considering all the available evidence, including documents such as reports, even if not supported by a statement (*Letherbarrow* at [20]–[23]).

In *Downes v RSPCA* [2017] EWHC 3622 (Admin), [2018] 2 Cr App R 3 (25), the Divisional Court reiterated the court's reluctance to go behind a s. 31 certificate. Knowles J (at [10]) said:

> [T]he circumstances in which it will be proper to try to go behind the certificate are likely to be few and far between, and I would encourage magistrates and District Judges to deal robustly with suggestions that certificates are wrong so as to be susceptible to challenge. Before the point can be argued, it seems to me that the defence must make clear that there is a *prima facie* case for undermining the certificate. Given that ... s. 31(2)(a) provides the certificate is to be conclusive, I consider that it will seldom be proper to open up a lengthy evidential inquiry into the decision-making process leading to the laying of an information. If it were otherwise, then the presumptively conclusive nature of a s. 31 certificate would be undermined.

It should be noted that the Road Traffic Offenders Act 1988, s. 6(3), is in very similar terms to the Animal Welfare Act 2006, s. 31, and so the principles enunciated in the case law on s. 31 are of wider application.

In *Chesterfield Poultry Ltd v Sheffield Magistrates' Court* [2019] EWHC 2953 (Admin), [2020] 1 Cr App R 26 (419), the Divisional Court considered a statutory instrument with the same provision regarding time-limits. Males LJ said (at [23]):

> The provision for a prosecutor's certificate to be conclusive evidence does...require a strict approach. A conclusive evidence provision prevents the court, subject to very limited exceptions, from enquiring whether the fact certified is or is not correct. Accordingly, if it is to be given conclusive effect, the certificate must comply strictly with the statutory requirements for such a certificate.

His Lordship then made a number of general points (at [31]):

> (1) The decision which the prosecutor has to make is not merely whether the evidence amounts to a prima facie case, but also whether it is in the interests of justice to bring proceedings...
> (2) This requires careful consideration, so that a prosecutor is entitled to a reasonable time to make the decision even after evidence amounting to a prima facie case has been obtained...

(3) There is a well-established distinction between an investigator and a prosecutor. In the context of animal welfare, the FSA is the investigator and the CPS is the prosecutor, but evidence coming to the prosecutor's knowledge refers to the knowledge of the individual prosecutor to whom the case is allocated ...

(4) The burden is on the prosecution to show that the proceedings have been commenced in time. This may be done in either of two ways, namely (a) by relying on a prosecutor's certificate or alternatively (b) by adducing evidence of fact as to the knowledge of the relevant prosecutor ...

(5) When the prosecution relies on a certificate, it must comply strictly with the statutory requirements and must do so on its face, in the sense that deficiencies cannot be remedied by reference to extrinsic evidence ...

(6) A certificate which does comply with those requirements 'is determinative of the matter unless the certificate is inaccurate on its face (i.e. plainly wrong on its face and patently misleading), or can be shown to be fraudulent' ...

(7) A defective certificate is a nullity. However, where a defective certificate is issued, there is nothing to prevent the prosecutor from subsequently issuing a further certificate which will be conclusive evidence of the relevant date if it complies with the statutory requirements ...

(8) Where there is no valid certificate, the court must determine on all the available evidence whether the prosecution was brought in time ...

Males LJ (at [70]–[71]) went on to reject the submission that if, on the evidence available, it is clear that the prosecutor's certificate mis-states the date when sufficient evidence came to the prosecutor's knowledge, that would mean that the certificate was 'plainly wrong' and that it would be an abuse of process for the proceedings to continue. His lordship said:

> [W]hether a certificate is 'plainly wrong' must be determined, in the absence of fraud, by reference to the face of the certificate and without regard to extraneous evidence. Absent fraud, a certificate which is valid on its face is conclusive evidence of the relevant date. If it were possible to circumvent this principle by dressing up a challenge to the certificate as an abuse of process argument, the purpose of the time bar provisions would be frustrated.
>
> Abuse of process may have a role to play in an appropriate case. That may be so, even in a case where there is a conclusive certificate, for example if a prosecutor's failure to apply his or her mind to the sufficiency of evidence led to a delay which impacted on the fairness of the proceedings. That, no doubt, is the kind of consideration which courts have had in mind in emphasising that the conclusive evidence provisions must not be manipulated to deprive a defendant of the benefit of a time-bar defence and are 'not a charter for paper-shuffling' ... But abuse of process is and should remain a separate question concerned with the fairness of the procedure and of the trial.

For the position where the charge is amended after the expiry of the time-limit so as to allege a different offence, see *Scunthorpe Justices, ex parte McPhee* (1998) 162 JP 635 at **D21.15**.

Magistrates' Courts Act 1980, s. 127 **D21.20**

(1) Except as otherwise expressly provided by any enactment and subject to subsection (2) below, a magistrates' court shall not try an information ... unless the information was laid ... within six months from the time when the offence was committed ...

(2) Nothing in—
 (a) subsection (1) above; or
 (b) subject to subsection (4) below, any other enactment (however framed or worded) which, as regards any offence to which it applies, would but for this section impose a time-limit on the power of a magistrates' court to try an information summarily or impose a limitation on the time for taking summary proceedings,

shall apply in relation to any indictable offence.

(3) Without prejudice to the generality of paragraph (b) of subsection (2) above, that paragraph includes enactments which impose a time-limit that applies only in certain circumstances (for example, where the proceedings are not instituted by or with the consent of the Director of Public Prosecutions or some other specified authority).

(4) Where, as regards any indictable offence, there is imposed by any enactment (however framed or worded, and whether falling within subsection (2)(b) above or not) a limitation on the time for taking proceedings on indictment for that offence no summary proceedings for that offence shall be taken after the latest time for taking proceedings on indictment.

DISCRETION NOT TO PROCEED ON ACCOUNT OF DELAY

Effect of Delay

D21.21 Even where proceedings were commenced within time, a magistrates' court has a discretion to refuse to try a case, and so to acquit the accused without trial, if there has been delay amounting to an abuse of the process of the court (*Brentford Justices, ex parte Wong* [1981] QB 445). Delay as a possible abuse of process is dealt with fully at **D3.66** ***et seq.***

Where the delay is deliberate, it is likely to amount to an abuse of process, as in *Brentford Justices, ex parte Wong*, where the prosecutor deliberately delayed in effecting service of the summons in order to gain more time in which to decide whether or not to continue the case against the accused.

Where deliberate delay in bringing the case to court cannot be shown, the defence may nonetheless apply for the magistrates to exercise their discretion not to proceed if (i) there has been inordinate or unconscionable delay due to the prosecution's inefficiency, and (ii) prejudice to the defence from the delay is either proved or to be inferred (per Lloyd LJ in *Gateshead Justices, ex parte Smith* (1985) 149 JP 681). If, however, the delay was in part attributable to the accused's own conduct, an application to stay is unlikely to succeed.

D21.22 **Delay in Service of Summons or Requisition** There is no specific time-limit within which the summons (or requisition) must be served once an application for a summons has been made (or a written charge issued). However, excessive delay in effecting service could amount to an abuse of process, giving the court the power to dismiss the case. For example, in *Watford Justices, ex parte Outrim* [1983] RTR 26, the summons was served almost two years after issue. It was held that when service of the summons is delayed so long as to produce substantial prejudice to an accused or to be unconscionable, the justices have a discretion to decline to proceed to hear the case. Where the accused has not tried to evade service or in any way contributed to the failure to effect service (e.g., by giving a wrong address or by failing to leave a forwarding address), there is a clear inference that something had gone wrong with the process serving procedures, and in such circumstances the justices are entitled and, in appropriate cases, bound to refuse to proceed with the case.

D21.23 **Application to Summary Offences and Either-way Offences** The discretion to halt the proceedings applies both to proposed trials of summary offences and to summary trials of offences triable either way. However, it is submitted that the discretion to stay the proceedings is more likely to be exercised in respect of summary offences since Parliament, by enacting the MCA 1980, s. 127, has indicated that proceedings for summary offences should take place within a reasonably short period, and delays in bringing the accused before the court effectively thwart Parliament's intention.

DISCLOSURE BY THE PROSECUTION

Advance Warning of the Prosecution Case

D21.24 Under CrimPR Part 8 (see Supplement, **R8.1** ***et seq.***), the prosecution must serve on the court, and (if requested) on the accused, 'initial details' of the prosecution case. These details must include a summary of the circumstances of the offence and, if the accused is not in custody at the time of the first hearing, any witness statements that the prosecutor has available and considers material to plea, or to the allocation of the case for trial, or to sentence (see **D5.20**).

While the Divisional Court, in *Stratford Justices, ex parte Imbert* [1999] 2 Cr App R 276, ruled that the right to a fair trial guaranteed by the ECHR, Article 6, did not necessarily require the prosecution to disclose the statements of their witnesses to the defence prior to a summary trial, the Court made the point that it is desirable that prosecution witness statements should be furnished to defendants in magistrates' court cases in all but the most exceptional cases. It is indeed the current practice of the CPS to provide to the defence all evidence upon which they propose to rely in a summary trial in sufficient time to allow proper consideration of that evidence before the trial.

Disclosure under the CPIA 1996

The position relating to disclosure of 'unused' material under the CPIA 1996 in summary trials is dealt with at **D9.37**. In brief, the prosecution are obliged to disclose to the defence any unused material that might reasonably be considered capable of undermining the case for the prosecution against the accused or of assisting the case for the accused (CPIA 1996, s. 3). **D21.25**

The main difference between disclosure under the CPIA in the magistrates' court, as against the Crown Court, is that in the magistrates' court the provision of a 'defence statement' is voluntary, not mandatory (CPIA 1996, s. 6). If, however, the defence choose to serve a defence statement, it must fulfil the requirements that are applicable to defence statements (set out in s. 6A), and adverse inferences can be drawn (under s. 11) if it does not comply with those requirements or if, for example, the accused serves the defence statement late or puts forward a different case at trial. The only advantage of serving a defence statement in the magistrates' court is that it triggers a further check by the prosecution (under s. 7A) to see if they have any previously undisclosed material which might assist the accused's defence as set out in the defence statement. If the defence statement would not add anything to what the accused said when interviewed by the police (and so the prosecution are already aware of the nature of the defence case), it is submitted that there is little to be gained from serving a defence statement where the case is to be heard by a magistrates' court.

It should be noted that the obligation on the defence, under the CPIA 1996, s. 6C, to give to the prosecution details of any proposed defence witnesses is mandatory whether the trial is to take place in the Crown Court or in a magistrates' court.

SECURING THE ATTENDANCE OF WITNESSES: WITNESS SUMMONSES

The attendance of witnesses for purposes of criminal proceedings in magistrates' courts may be secured by the issue of a summons or warrant under the MCA 1980, s. 97 (see **D21.32**), which applies equally to proposed prosecution and proposed defence witnesses. It provides that, where a magistrate is satisfied that: **D21.26**

(a) any person within the jurisdiction is likely to be able to give material evidence, or produce any document or thing likely to be material evidence, for purposes of a summary trial, and
(b) it is in the interests of justice to issue a summons to secure the attendance of that person to give evidence or produce the document or thing,

the magistrate may issue a summons requiring the person to attend before the court on the date specified in the summons (s. 97(1)). A similar power is given to justices' clerks by the Justices' Clerks Rules 2005 (SI 2005 No. 545), sch. 1, para. 2.

If a magistrate (but not a clerk) is also satisfied by evidence on oath that it is probable that a summons issued under s. 97(1) would not procure the witness's attendance, an arrest warrant may be issued instead (s. 97(2)).

Should a person summoned under s. 97(1) fail to attend as required, the court may issue an arrest warrant (s. 97(3)). It must, however, be satisfied that: **D21.27**

(a) the witness is indeed likely to be able to give material evidence or produce a material document or thing;

(b) the witness has been duly served with the summons and been paid or tendered a reasonable sum for costs and expenses; and
(c) there is no just excuse for the failure to attend.

Requirement (a) must be established by evidence on oath; requirement (b) may be established either by evidence on oath or in such other manner as is prescribed. By virtue of CrimPR Part 4 (see Supplement, **R4.1** *et seq.*), a witness summons may be served in one of the following ways:

(a) by handing it to individual (r. 4.3(1)(a));
(b) by leaving it at, or sending it by first class post to, an address where it is reasonable to believe that the individual will receive it (r. 4.4(1) and (2)(a)).

It should be noted that the Criminal Procedure (Attendance of Witnesses Act 1965), s. 3, which provides that a person who, without just excuse, disobeys a witness summons is guilty of contempt of court, applies to magistrates' courts as well as the Crown Court (see **D15.94**).

Material Evidence

D21.28 The power to issue a witness summons is conditional upon the magistrate being satisfied that the witness will be able to give or produce material evidence. In *Peterborough Magistrates' Court, ex parte Willis* (1987) 151 JP 785, it was held that a witness summons should not be issued to enable someone to find out whether the witness can give any material evidence, as there has to be material before the court on which it may be satisfied that the witness is likely to be able to give material evidence. The Divisional Court added that, when it reviews a s. 97 order, it will consider only the material before the magistrates who issued the summons.

Similarly, where the summons is to produce a document or thing, the applicant must be able to show that the item to be produced would be admissible evidence and not, for example, material subject to legal professional privilege (*Derby Magistrates' Court, ex parte B* [1996] AC 487). Moreover, the court will not allow s. 97 to be used for 'fishing expeditions' (*R (Cunliffe) v Hastings Magistrates' Court* [2006] EWHC 2081 (Admin)).

In *Reading Justices, ex parte Berkshire County Council* [1996] 1 Cr App R 239, Simon Brown LJ summarised the key principles governing such applications as follows (at pp. 246–7):

(i) to be material evidence documents must be not only relevant to the issues arising in the criminal proceedings, but also documents admissible as such in evidence;
(ii) documents which are desired merely for the purpose of possible cross-examination are not admissible in evidence and, thus, are not material for the purposes of s. 97;
(iii) whoever seeks production of documents must satisfy the justices with some material that the documents are 'likely to be material' in the sense indicated, likelihood for this purpose involving a real possibility, although not necessarily a probability;
(iv) it is not sufficient that the applicant merely wants to find out whether the third party has such material documents. This procedure must not be used as a disguised attempt to obtain discovery.

Procedure

D21.29 CrimPR Part 17 deals with witness summonses, warrants and orders (see Supplement, **R17.1** *et seq.*). Rule 17.2 provides that the court may issue (or withdraw) a witness summons, warrant or order with or without a hearing, and that any hearing under Part 17 must be in private unless the court otherwise directs. Under r. 17.3(1), a party seeking a witness summons (or warrant) must apply as soon as practicable after becoming aware of the grounds for doing so. It should also be noted that, under the MCA 1980, s. 97(2B), an application for a witness summons (whether made by the defence or the prosecution) may be refused if the magistrate or clerk is not satisfied that the application has been made as soon as reasonably practicable after the accused pleaded not guilty. Rule 17.3(2) requires the applicant to explain:

(i) what evidence the proposed witness can give or produce;
(ii) why it is likely to be material evidence; and
(iii) why it would be in the interests of justice to issue a summons … or warrant …

The application may be made orally (unless r. 17.5 applies — see below) except where the court directs otherwise (r. 17.3(3)). Where the application is in writing, it has to be in the prescribed form (r. 17.4).

Rule 17.5 applies where the application is for a witness summons requiring the proposed witness to produce in evidence a document or thing, or to give evidence about information apparently held in confidence, that relates to another person. Under r. 17.5(4), the court must not issue a witness summons in such a case unless everyone served with the application has had at least ten business days in which to make representations, and the court is satisfied that it has been able to take adequate account of the duties and rights, including rights of confidentiality, of the proposed witness and of any person to whom the proposed evidence relates.

Under r. 17.6, a person served with an application for a witness summons requiring production of a document or thing may object to its production on the ground that either it is not likely to be material evidence, or the duties or rights (including rights of confidentiality) of the proposed witness or of any person to whom the document or thing relates outweigh the reasons for issuing a summons. Under r. 17.6(2), the court may require the proposed witness to make the document or thing available for the objection to be assessed. **D21.30**

Rule 17.7 makes provision for the withdrawal of a witness summons or warrant. The party who applied for it may seek its withdrawal on the ground that it is no longer needed; the witness (or any person to whom the evidence relates) may seek its withdrawal on the grounds that he or she was not aware of the application for it, and either the witness cannot give or produce evidence likely to be material evidence, or the witness's duties or rights (including rights of confidentiality) outweigh the reasons for the issue of the summons or warrant (r. 17.7(1)).

Failure to Testify

A witness who attends the magistrates' court but refuses without just excuse to take the oath (or affirm) or to give evidence (or to produce a document or thing) may be imprisoned for up to one month and/or fined up to £2,500 (MCA 1980, s. 97(4)). This applies whether the witness attended court voluntarily or in answer to a summons or was brought there following execution of a warrant. **D21.31**

Statutory Provision on Witness Summonses and Warrants

Magistrates' Courts Act 1980, s. 97 **D21.32**

(1) Where a justice of the peace is satisfied that—
  (a) any person in England or Wales is likely to be able to give material evidence, or produce any document or thing likely to be material evidence, at the summary trial of an information ... by a magistrates' court, and
  (b) it is in the interests of justice to issue a summons under this subsection to secure the attendance of that person to give evidence or produce the document or thing,

the justice shall issue a summons directed to that person requiring him to attend before the court at the time and place appointed in the summons to give evidence or to produce the document or thing.

(2) If a justice of the peace is satisfied by evidence on oath of the matters mentioned in subsection (1) above, and also that it is probable that a summons under that subsection would not procure the attendance of the person in question, the justice may instead of issuing a summons issue a warrant to arrest that person and bring him before such a court as aforesaid at a time and place specified in the warrant...

(2A) A summons may also be issued under subsection (1) above if the justice is satisfied that the person in question is outside the British Islands but no warrant shall be issued under subsection (2) above unless the justice is satisfied by evidence on oath that the person in question is in England or Wales.

(2B) A justice may refuse to issue a summons under subsection (1) above in relation to the summary trial of an information if he is not satisfied that an application for the summons was made by a party to the case as soon as reasonably practicable after the accused pleaded not guilty.

(2C) In relation to the summary trial of an information, subsection (2) above shall have effect as if the reference to the matters mentioned in subsection (1) above included a reference to the matter mentioned in subsection (2B) above.

(3) On the failure of any person to attend before a magistrates' court in answer to a summons under this section, if—

(a) the court is satisfied by evidence on oath that he is likely to be able to give material evidence or produce any document or thing likely to be material evidence in the proceedings; and

(b) it is proved on oath, or in such other manner as may be prescribed, that he has been duly served with the summons, and that a reasonable sum has been paid or tendered to him for costs and expenses; and

(c) it appears to the court that there is no just excuse for the failure, the court may issue a warrant to arrest him and bring him before the court at a time and place specified in the warrant.

(4) If any person attending or brought before a magistrates' court refuses without just excuse to be sworn or give evidence, or to produce any document or thing, the court or justice, as the case may be, may commit him to custody until the expiration of such period not exceeding one month as may be specified in the warrant or until he sooner gives evidence or produces the document or thing or impose on him a fine not exceeding £2,500 or both.

(5) A fine imposed under subsection (4) above shall be deemed, for the purposes of any enactment, to be a sum adjudged to be paid by a conviction.

PRE-TRIAL HEARINGS

D21.33 CrimPD I, para. 3A.5 (see Supplement, **CPD.3A**), requires that, if the accused is charged with an indictable (including either-way) offence and is in custody, the magistrates' court should, at the first hearing, proceed 'at once' with the allocation of the case for trial (if it is an either-way offence) and, if so required, with the sending of the accused to the Crown Court for trial. If the offence is a summary one or an either-way offence that is allocated for summary trial, the magistrates should 'forthwith' give such directions as are necessary, either (on a guilty plea) to prepare for sentencing or for a trial (para. 3A.6).

If the accused is on bail, para. 3A.7 requires that the case must be listed for the first hearing 14 days after charge (or the next available court date thereafter) if the prosecutor anticipates a guilty plea 'which is likely to be sentenced in the magistrates' court'. Where it is anticipated that the accused will plead not guilty, or that the case is likely to be sent for trial or committed for sentence to the Crown Court, the case must be listed for the first hearing 28 days after charge (or the next available court date thereafter).

Where the accused pleads guilty or indicates a guilty plea in a magistrates' court, the court should consider whether a pre-sentence report is necessary (para. 3A.8). Paragraph 3A.9 requires that, where a magistrates' court is considering committal for sentence, or the accused has indicated an intention to plead guilty in a matter which is to be sent to the Crown Court, the magistrates' court should request a pre-sentence report for use by the Crown Court if the magistrates' court considers that there is a realistic alternative to a custodial sentence, the accused may satisfy the criteria for classification as a dangerous offender or there is some other appropriate reason for doing so.

The CDA 1998, s. 50, makes provision for pre-trial hearings. It provides that where the accused has been charged with an offence at a police station, the magistrates' court before which the accused appears for the first time in relation to that charge may consist of a single justice (s. 50(1)). At a hearing under s. 50, the accused is asked whether he or she wishes to be provided with legal aid (s. 50(2)(a)); if the accused does so wish, the necessary arrangements for an application must be made and, where appropriate, legal aid obtained (s. 50(2)(b)) and, if necessary, the hearing may be adjourned for this purpose under s. 50(4A)(a). On adjourning the hearing, the magistrate may remand the accused in custody or on bail (s. 50(3)(b)). Under s. 50(4), an early administrative hearing may be conducted by a justices' clerk (or an assistant clerk who has been specifically authorised by the justices' clerk for that purpose), but the clerk is not empowered to remand the accused in custody or, without the consent of the prosecutor and the accused, to remand the accused on bail on conditions other than those (if any) previously imposed.

Section 50(1) makes it clear that s. 50 applies only where the accused was charged at the police station, and so does not apply where the accused is granted police bail and is then charged by the CPS using the written charge and requisition procedure. However, there is nothing to prevent magistrates' courts operating a system of early administrative hearings in all cases where a not guilty plea is expected.

Preparation for Trial Hearings

By virtue of CrimPR 3.16 (see Supplement, **R3.16**), a magistrates' court must conduct a 'preparation for trial hearing' (unless the accused is sent for trial in the Crown Court or enters a written guilty plea, or the single justice procedure applies). The court may conduct one or more further pre-trial case management hearings if (i) the court anticipates a guilty plea; or (ii) it is necessary to conduct such a hearing in order to give directions for an effective trial; or (iii) such a hearing is required to set ground rules for the conduct of the questioning of a witness or defendant (r. 3.16(1)). At a preparation for trial hearing, 'the court must give directions for an effective trial' (r. 3.16(2)). Under r. 3.16(3), if the accused is present, the court must: (a) satisfy itself that the accused understands that credit will be received for a guilty plea; (b) take a plea from the accused (or, if no plea can be taken, find out whether the accused is likely to plead guilty or not guilty); and (c) unless the accused pleads guilty, satisfy itself that the accused understands that, at the trial, (i) he or she will have the right to give evidence after the court has heard the prosecution case; (ii) if the accused does not attend, the trial is likely to take place in his or her absence; and (iii) if released on bail, failure to attend court when required to do so is an offence which may lead to arrest and punishment, and that bail may be withdrawn. The court is also required to ascertain the name, date of birth and nationality of the accused (r. 3.16(5)). These hearings will usually take place in public (r. 3.16(4)). **D21.34**

Pre-trial Rulings

The MCA 1980, s. 8A (see **D21.37**), applies to cases that are to be tried summarily where the accused has entered a not guilty plea (s. 8A(1)). For these purposes, a pre-trial hearing is a hearing that takes place before the court begins to hear evidence from the prosecution at the trial (or, in those cases where fitness to plead is an issue, before the court considers whether to exercise its power under the Mental Health Act 1983, s. 37(3), to make a hospital order without convicting the accused (s. 8A(2)). At a pre-trial hearing, the magistrates may decide any question as to the admissibility of evidence and any other question of law relating to the case (s. 8A(4)). Such rulings may be made only if the court has given the parties an opportunity to be heard and it appears to the court that it is in the interests of justice to make the ruling (s. 8A(3)(b) and (c)). If the accused is unrepresented, he or she must be given the chance to apply for legal aid (s. 8A(5)). Pre-trial rulings may be made on the application of the defence or prosecution, or of the court's own motion (s. 8A(6)). **D21.35**

Under s. 8B(1), a pre-trial ruling is binding until the case against the accused (or, where there is more than one, against each of them) is disposed of. The case is disposed of if the accused is acquitted or convicted, or the prosecutor decides not to proceed with the case, or the case is dismissed (s. 8B(2)). However, under s. 8B(3), the court may (on application by a party or of its own motion) discharge or vary a pre-trial ruling provided it appears to the court that it is in the interests of justice to do so, and the court has given the parties an opportunity to be heard. A party can apply for the ruling to be discharged or varied only if there has been a material change of circumstances since the ruling was made or, if there has been a previous application under s. 8B, since that application was made (s. 8B(5)).

In *R (CPS) v Gloucester Justices* [2008] EWHC 1488 (Admin), MacKay J, considering the power of the magistrates' court to vary the pre-trial ruling of its own motion, made the point that it is difficult to accept that it could be in the interests of justice for the court to annul or discharge its own ruling without a compelling reason to do so, such as changed circumstances or fresh evidence; it is not sufficient that a different bench reaches a different conclusion on the same material (at [12]). In *Jones v South East Surrey Local Justice Area* [2010] EWHC 916 (Admin), Cranston J noted (at [11]) that, before the introduction of ss. 8A and 8B into the MCA 1980, *Newham Juvenile Court, ex parte F (a minor)* [1986] 3 All ER 17 had recognised a similar rule in common law. Cranston J quoted from the judgment of Simon Brown LJ in *Newham* (at p. 946B): 'Once a decision has been made after proper inquiry and consideration of all relevant factors, it cannot be reversed merely by re-examining the case afresh on the same material'. In *Newham*, McCullough J (at p. 947D–E) had also said that review of a decision 'will be permissible if a change of circumstances has occurred since the original decision was taken' or 'if circumstances are brought to the attention of the court which, although existing when the original decision was taken, were not then drawn to the attention of the court'. Cranston J also referred to *Acton Youth Court, ex parte DPP* [2002] Crim LR 75, where Laws LJ (at [25] and [26]) had said that it is 'necessary for the efficacious administration of justice to take a strict approach to the power of a lower court to revisit and revoke an order earlier made by itself' but that 'there must be some power to do so in the interests of justice'; that power arises where there is 'a change of relevant circumstances' but 'cases in which an earlier existing circumstance, not drawn to the attention of the court at the first hearing, would justify the court in later overturning its first decision would be most infrequent'. Cranston J (at [24] and [25]) assumed (having heard no argument to the contrary) that the common-law rule remains, but would be relevant only to those cases where ss. 8A and 8B do not apply (those sections 'bite' only once the decision has been made that a summary trial will occur).

There is no provision for appeals against rulings under s. 8A. However, an error of law in such a ruling could form the basis of an appeal by way of case stated (under the MCA 1980, s. 111), once there has been a final determination of the proceedings in the magistrates' court (see, e.g., *Miller v DPP* [2018] EWHC 262 (Admin), [2018] RTR 19 (278)). See **D29.17** ***et seq***.

Reconsideration of Allocation

D21.36 Under the MCA 1980, s. 25, where the magistrates have accepted jurisdiction in the case of an either-way offence, the prosecution may ask the magistrates (before the start of the summary trial) to reconsider that decision (on the ground that the magistrates' sentencing powers are inadequate to deal with the offence if the accused is convicted); under the MCA 1980, s. 8B(6)(a), any pre-trial ruling in respect of such an offence is discharged when the case is sent to the Crown Court for trial (so, unsurprisingly, the Crown Court would not be bound by that ruling).

Statutory Provisions on Pre-trial Hearings and Rulings

D21.37 **Magistrates' Courts Act 1980, ss. 8A and 8B**

8A.—(1) For the purposes of this section a hearing is a pre-trial hearing if—
- (a) it relates to an information—
  - (i) which is to be tried summarily, and
  - (ii) to which the accused has pleaded not guilty, and
- (b) it takes place before the start of the trial.

(2) For the purposes of subsection (1)(b), the start of a summary trial occurs when the court begins—
- (a) to hear evidence from the prosecution at the trial, or
- (b) to consider whether to exercise its power under section 37(3) of the Mental Health Act 1983 (power to make hospital order without convicting the accused).

(3) At a pre-trial hearing, a magistrates' court may make a ruling as to any matter mentioned in subsection (4) if—
(a) the condition in subsection (5) is met,
(b) the court has given the parties an opportunity to be heard, and
(c) it appears to the court that it is in the interests of justice to make the ruling.
(4) The matters are—
(a) any question as to the admissibility of evidence;
(b) any other question of law relating to the case.
(5) The condition is that, if the accused is not legally represented—
(a) the court must ask whether he wishes to be provided with representation for the purposes of the proceedings under Part 1 of the Legal Aid, Sentencing and Punishment of Offenders Act 2012, and
(b) if he does, the necessary arrangements must be made for him to apply for it and, where appropriate, obtain it.
(6) A ruling may be made under this section—
(a) on an application by a party to the case, or
(b) of the court's own motion.
(7) For the purposes of this section and section 8B, references to the prosecutor are to any person acting as prosecutor, whether an individual or body.

8B.—(1) Subject to subsections (3) and (6), a ruling under section 8A has binding effect from the time it is made until the case against the accused or, if there is more than one, against each of them, is disposed of.
(2) The case against an accused is disposed of if—
(a) he is acquitted or convicted,
(b) the prosecutor decides not to proceed with the case against him, or
(c) the information is dismissed.
(3) A magistrates' court may discharge or vary (or further vary) a ruling under section 8A if—
(a) the condition in section 8A(5) is met,
(b) the court has given the parties an opportunity to be heard, and
(c) it appears to the court that it is in the interests of justice to do so.
(4) The court may act under subsection (3)—
(a) on an application by a party to the case, or
(b) of its own motion.
(5) No application may be made under subsection (4)(a) unless there has been a material change of circumstances since the ruling was made or, if a previous application has been made, since the application (or last application) was made.
(6) A ruling under section 8A is discharged in relation to an accused if—
(a) the magistrates' court sends him to the Crown Court for trial for the offence charged in the information, or
(b) a count charging him with the offence is included in an indictment by virtue of section 40 of the Criminal Justice Act 1988.

Reporting Restrictions Applicable to Pre-trial Hearings

Section 8C of the MCA 1980 imposes restrictions on reporting of pre-trial hearings in order to avoid prejudicing the right to a fair trial. The publishing of anything other than the basic factual information permitted by s. 8C(7) is prohibited — unless the court orders that reporting restrictions should not apply — until such time as the case against the accused is disposed of. Section 8C(7) permits the publication of the identity of the court and the names of the justices; the names, ages, home addresses and occupations of the accused and witnesses; the offence(s) with which the accused is charged; the names of counsel and solicitors in the proceedings; where the proceedings are adjourned, the date and place to which they are adjourned; any arrangements as to bail; whether legal aid was granted. **D21.38**

The power to lift the reporting restrictions is conferred by s. 8C(3). Where the court is minded to order that the reporting restrictions do not apply and the accused (or one of the accused) objects to the making of an order removing the restrictions, the court may make the order if (and only if) satisfied, after hearing representations from (each of) the accused, that it is in the interests of justice to do so (s. 8C(4)(a) and (5)(a)).

Breach of these reporting restrictions is a summary offence punishable under s. 8D (i.e. with an unlimited fine). Under s. 8D(6), proceedings for this offence require the consent of the A-G.

CASE MANAGEMENT

D21.39 CrimPD I, para. 3A.3 (see Supplement, **CPD.3A**), states that, in all cases to be tried in a magistrates' court or youth court, the 'Preparation for Effective Trial form' ('PET form') authorised for use must be used, adding that the form, and the notes which accompany it, provide a timetable for the effective preparation of a case and a list of all the matters that the court should consider in giving directions for trial. Where the accused intends to plead not guilty, the defence must normally complete the relevant parts of the form before (or, with the court's permission, during) the first hearing. The form requires the parties (in particular, the defence) to identify, with a significant level of detail, the issues in the case. When a defendant indicates a not guilty plea but has not completed the relevant sections of the trial preparation form, the justices' legal adviser must either ensure that the form is completed or, in appropriate cases, assist the court to obtain and record the essential information on the form (CrimPD VI, para. 24A.10: see Supplement, **CPD.24A**).

The admissibility of any admissions made by the accused in such forms was considered in *R (Firth) v Epping Justices* [2011] EWHC 388 (Admin), [2011] 1 WLR 1818, where it was held that the magistrates were entitled to treat an assertion of self-defence in the case management form as an admission by the defence that D was present at the scene of the offence. However, this decision must be seen in the light of *Newell* [2012] EWCA Crim 650, [2012] 1 WLR 3142. In that case, the issue was whether a trial judge in the Crown Court was right to admit as evidence a previous inconsistent statement in the form which had to be completed prior to the Plea and Case Management Hearing (the precursor to the PTPH). The Court of Appeal held that the statement in the form was prima facie admissible, but the judge ought to have excluded it under the PACE 1984, s. 78. Sir John Thomas P went on to consider the position in magistrates' courts and said (at [35]) that:

> The Trial Preparation Form ... should be completed at the first hearing. It provides for the making of admissions or the acknowledgement that matters are not in issue. Where admissions are made in that way they will be admissible at the trial. Where statements are made on the form which are not made under the section relating to admissions, such statements should be made without the risk that they would be used at trial as statements of the defendant admissible in evidence against the defendant, provided the advocate follows the letter and the spirit of the Criminal Procedure Rules.

The potential admissibility of the PET form that is used in magistrates' courts was considered in *Valiati v DPP* [2018] EWHC 2908 (Admin), [2019] 1 WLR 1221, which concerned two unrelated appeals. In each case, information on the PET form had been taken into account by the magistrates' court even though no formal application had been made by the prosecution to admit the information on the PET form, nor had the defence been alerted to the evidential use to which the PET form would be put so that representations could be made about it. The Divisional Court held that, in both cases, the magistrates' court had erred in taking account of information in the PET form. Sir Brian Leveson P (at [41]) concluded that, 'if circumstances arise in which it is sought to argue that the information provided on a PET form should have evidential significance, an appropriate application must be made' to admit the evidence as hearsay, so that the accused has the opportunity to oppose the application and/or apply for the evidence to be excluded under the PACE 1984, s. 78. His lordship emphasised (at [40]) that the outcome of the two appeals was not to be taken to minimise the importance of the PET form in the magistrates' court, or the PTPH form in the Crown Court, nor was is it to 'discourage the identification of issues, leading to appropriate admissions thereby reducing the time which a trial necessarily takes up' or to 'imply that what is contained in information provided to the court by way of case management cannot be used to prevent "game-playing" '. Indeed, earlier in his judgment (at [16]), his lordship said that:

> ... requiring a defendant to identify the issues does not offend the twin principles that the prosecution must prove its case and that a defendant is not obliged to inculpate himself. In that regard, if the defence is to put the prosecution to proof, that is what must be indicated: this does not involve the presentation of a positive case. Where such a case is thereafter sought to be presented, such an attempt could demonstrate that the defendant is not acting in the spirit of the CrimPR and applications by the prosecution can be considered accordingly. If there is a failure to comply and what then appears to the court to be the creation of a trap for the prosecution, in addition to the possible approaches described by CPD 24B.4, it could be open to the prosecution to seek to rely on the CJA 2003 s. 118 and, subject to PACE s. 78, the admission of hearsay.

Valiati does not depart from the decision of the Court of Appeal in *Newell*, that the contents of case management forms can be adduced as evidence only where the defence have not conducted their case in accordance with the letter and spirit of the Rules. Rather, it emphasises the importance of the prosecution making a formal application to admit the contents of the case management form as hearsay evidence and of the defence having the opportunity to oppose that application and/or invoke s. 78 to have that evidence excluded if its admission would result in unfairness. It remains the case that applications to admit into evidence what is said in PET forms (or PTPH forms in the Crown Court) should not be made (or accepted) as a matter of routine.

Essential Case Management: Applying the Criminal Procedure Rules

In December 2009, Leveson LJ (then Senior Presiding Judge for England and Wales) issued guidance to magistrates' courts in a document entitled *Essential Case Management: Applying the Criminal Procedure Rules*. Where the accused pleads not guilty, the parties must, from the start, identify the disputed issues and tell the court what they are; if the parties do not supply this information, the court must require them to do so. The 'live' evidence at the trial should be confined to those issues, and so only witnesses 'who are really needed in relation to genuinely disputed, relevant issues should be required to attend'. Moreover, the court's directions must include a timetable for the progress of the case, and the parties are required to warn the court 'promptly' if any problems (e.g., relating to witnesses) are anticipated. **D21.40**

In *R (Drinkwater) v Solihull Magistrates' Court* [2012] EWHC 765 (Admin), Sir John Thomas P said (at [49]) that 'in any case in the magistrates' court where a trial is likely to be other than a short one, it should be the ordinary practice for a timetable for the conduct of a trial to be set at the time the trial date is fixed and the estimate made'. His lordship went on to say (at [50]) that, in setting the timetable:

> ... the court should scrutinise the reasons why it is said a witness is necessary and the time examination and cross-examination would take. It is also important in setting a timetable to have regard to the nature of the issues and the fact that the trial is a summary trial; any estimate of more than a day in the Magistrates' Courts should be scrutinised with the utmost rigour. Parties must realise that a summary trial requires a proportionate approach. If a timetable for the trial is not set, it is difficult to have any real confidence that the estimate is accurate.

In *DPP v Radziwilowicz* [2014] EWHC 2283 (Admin), Sir Brian Leveson P referred (at [8]) to a judicially-led initiative known as 'Stop Delaying Justice!', the aim of which is that 'all contested trials in the magistrates' court will be fully case managed in the first hearing and disposed of, by way of trial or otherwise, at the second'. His lordship noted that 'such a course might be adopted if the initial or advanced disclosure contains all of the likely available evidence of note' and the 'prosecution evidence is not challenged and the only evidence, if any, will be that of the defendant'. However, his lordship emphasised (at [9]) that the 'real issue' is the 'fairness of the proceedings to all parties'.

Standard Case Preparation Time-limits

D21.41 The PET form contains a summary of applicable time-limits (some of which are not in fact prescribed by the CrimPR but are regarded as standard directions). Those time-limits are as follows:

Written admissions (CJA 1967, s. 10; CrimPR 24.6): the parties must serve any written admissions of agreed facts within 14 days of the date when the accused pleads not guilty.

Defence statement (CPIA 1996, s. 6): any defence statement must be served within 14 days of the prosecutor complying (or purporting to comply) with the duty of disclosure imposed by the CPIA 1996, s. 3 (Criminal Procedure and Investigations Act 1996 (Defence Disclosure Time Limits) Regulations 2011 (SI 2011 No. 209), reg. 2(2)).

Details of defence witnesses (CPIA 1996, s. 6C): details of any defence witness must be notified within 14 days of the prosecutor complying (or purporting to comply) with the duty of disclosure imposed by the CPIA 1996, s. 3 (Criminal Procedure and Investigations Act 1996 (Defence Disclosure Time Limits) Regulations 2011 (SI 2011 No. 209), reg. 2(2)).

Application for disclosure (CPIA 1996, s. 8): the accused must serve any application for prosecution disclosure as soon as reasonably practicable after the prosecutor complies (or purports to comply) with the duty of disclosure imposed by the CPIA 1996, s. 3 (and a defence statement must be served before an application can be made under s. 8); the prosecutor must serve any representations in response within ten business days thereafter (CrimPR 15.5(5)(b)).

D21.42 *Witness statements* (CJA 1967, s. 9; CrimPR 16.4): the accused must serve any defence witness statement to be read at trial at least 14 days before the trial, and any objection to a witness statement being read at trial must be made within five business days of service of the statement.

Measures to assist a witness or defendant to give evidence (CrimPR Part 18): any application for special or other measures must be served within 20 business days of the date when the accused pleads not guilty (r. 18.3(a)(i)), and any representations in response must be served within ten business days after that (r. 18.13(2)(b)).

Cross-examination where defendant not represented (YJCEA 1999, ss. 34 to 36; CrimPR Part 23): the prosecutor must serve any application to prohibit cross-examination by the defendant in person as soon as reasonably practicable (r. 23.4), and any representations in response must be served within ten business days thereafter (r. 23.7).

Expert evidence (CrimPR Part 19): if either party relies on expert evidence, the expert's report must be served within 28 days of the date when the accused pleads not guilty (although r. 19.3(3)(b) merely says 'as soon as practicable').

D21.43 *Hearsay evidence* (CrimPR Part 20): the prosecutor must serve any notice to introduce hearsay evidence within 20 business days of the date when the accused pleads not guilty, and the accused must serve any notice to introduce hearsay evidence as soon as reasonably practicable (r. 20.2(3)(a)). Any application to determine an objection to hearsay evidence must be served within ten business days of service of the notice or evidence (r. 20.3(2)(c)(i)).

Bad character evidence (CrimPR Part 21): the prosecutor must serve any notice to introduce evidence of the defendant's bad character within 20 business days of the date when the accused pleads not guilty (r. 21.4(3)(a)), and any application to determine an objection to that notice must be served within ten business days after that. Any application to introduce evidence of a non-defendant's bad character must be served within ten business days of prosecution disclosure (r. 21.3(3)(b)), and any notice of objection to that evidence must be served within ten business days after that (r. 21.3(4)(a)).

Previous sexual behaviour evidence (YJCEA 1999, s. 41; CrimPR Part 22): the accused must serve any application for permission to introduce evidence of a complainant's previous sexual behaviour within ten business days of prosecution disclosure (r. 22.4(1)(b)), and the prosecutor must serve any representations in response within ten business thereafter (r. 22.6(2)(b)).

Points of law: any skeleton argument must be served at least 14 days days before the trial, and any skeleton argument in reply must be served within seven days thereafter.

Trial readiness: the parties must certify readiness for trial at least 14 days before the trial, confirming which witnesses will give evidence in person, and the trial time estimate.

TRIAL OF CHARGES

Discretion Not to Try a Charge

Save in cases where there has been inordinate delay amounting to an abuse of the process of the court (see **D21.21**), magistrates are almost always obliged to hear the prosecution evidence. In *Birmingham Justices, ex parte Lamb* [1983] 3 All ER 23, the Divisional Court held that the justices erred in refusing to try charges for reasons such as the relative triviality of the charge, the apparent frailty of the prosecution evidence insofar as it had been disclosed, and the long period that would elapse before the court would have time to hear the case on the basis of a not guilty plea. McNeill J said (at p. 344D): **D21.44**

> [T]he law does not permit cases, on grounds of supposed injustice, to be dismissed out of hand without hearing any evidence. The justices can reflect their sense of injustice at the end of the prosecution case if they are not satisfied that the offence has been made out. They can reflect it at the end of the whole of the evidence by acquitting the defendant or, if they feel obliged to convict, they can reflect it by imposing such a penalty as reflects their view of the case.

It is submitted that this statement may be too wide insofar as it suggests that magistrates may *never* dismiss a charge without a hearing, since they may do so where there has been unconscionable delay or where the proceedings otherwise amount to an abuse of process (*Horseferry Road Magistrates' Court, ex parte Bennett* [1994] 1 AC 42). However, this jurisdiction is confined to cases where the accused could not receive a fair trial (*R (CPS) v City of London Magistrates' Court* [2006] EWHC 1153 (Admin) at [28]). See **D3.71**.

Apparent bad faith on the part of the prosecutor has also been held sufficient to justify dismissal without hearing (see *Sherwood v Ross* [1989] Crim LR 576, where a private prosecution was brought apparently as a bargaining counter in negotiations over a civil claim). **D21.45**

Discretion to Try Charges Separately

Where an accused faces several charges, or there are several accused charged with separate offences, the decision whether the charges or accused should be tried together or separately is one for the magistrates (*Chief Constable of Norfolk v Clayton* [1983] 2 AC 473). In *Clayton*, Lord Roskill set out the practice which should be adopted in such cases. His lordship said (at pp. 491G–492E): **D21.46**

> ... I see no compelling reason why your lordships should not say that the practice in magistrates' courts in these matters should henceforth be analogous to the practice prescribed in *Assim* [1966] 2 QB 249 in relation to trials on indictment. Where a defendant is charged on several informations and the facts are connected ..., I can see no reason why those informations should not, if the justices think fit, be heard together. Similarly, if two or more defendants are charged on separate informations but the facts are connected, I can see no reason why they should not, if the justices think fit, be heard together ... Of course, when this question arises, justices will be well advised to inquire both of the prosecution and of the defence whether either side has any objection to all the informations being heard together. If consent is forthcoming on both sides, there is no

> problem. If such consent is not forthcoming, the justices should then consider the rival submissions and ... rule as they think right in the overall interests of justice ... Absence of consent, either express where the defendant is present or represented and objects or necessarily brought about by his absence or the absence of representation, should no longer in practice be regarded as a complete and automatic bar to hearing more than one information at the same time or informations against more than one defendant charged on separate informations at the same time when in the justices' view the facts are sufficiently closely connected to justify this course and there is no risk of injustice to defendants by its adoption. Accordingly, the justices should always ask themselves whether it would be fair and just to the defendant or defendants to allow a joint trial. Only if the answer is clearly in the affirmative should they order joint trial in the absence of consent by or on behalf of the defendant.

The above passage implies that where all parties (including the prosecution) are in favour of a joint trial, the court should automatically agree to that course. In the case of both prosecution and defence being *against* a joint trial, the ultimate decision is still one for the magistrates, but they should be slow to exercise their discretion in favour of ordering a joint trial when all the parties want separate trials (*Highbury Corner Magistrates' Court, ex parte McGinley* (1986) 150 JP 257, per Lloyd LJ).

Successive Trials by Same Bench

D21.47 If an accused who is charged with two or more offences applies successfully for the offences to be tried separately, the question then arises whether the bench that decided in favour of separate trials may properly hear any or all of the cases. This is part of the broader question of whether knowledge that the accused faces more than one charge in their court should disqualify magistrates on the ground of possible bias (see also D3.35). The proper approach is to apply the usual test for bias, namely whether the fair-minded and informed observer, having considered the facts, would conclude that there was a real possibility that the tribunal was biased (per Lord Hope in *Porter v Magill* [2001] UKHL 67, [2002] 2 AC 357 at [103]). In *Sandwich Justices, ex parte Berry* (1982) 74 Cr App R 132, Donaldson LJ, at p. 134, said that the question whether an accused who is to be tried by justices in more than one trial is entitled to a fresh bench of justices for each trial is essentially a matter for the discretion of the justices. However, his lordship observed that there may well be cases in which there would be 'real problems' in the justices approaching the trial of a subsequent charge 'in a proper and impartial manner or, alternatively, at least of their appearing to do so'. In such a case, the magistrates ought to refuse to adjudicate upon the second or subsequent charges (which should be tried by another bench).

Alternative Charges

D21.48 It is possible for an accused to be charged with offences which are alternatives, in the sense that the two charges are based on the same facts and the prosecution seek a conviction on one or the other. One offence will be more serious than the other, and the prosecution present their case on the basis that the accused is guilty of the more serious offence or, alternatively, if not guilty of that offence then the accused is guilty of the lesser offence. In such a case, the accused should not be convicted of both offences, since that would effectively mean being convicted twice for the same wrong, which is unfair (per Laws LJ in *R (Dyer) v Watford Magistrates' Court* [2013] EWHC 547 (Admin), at [11]). See D22.72.

Charges against Two or More Defendants Jointly

D21.49 A single charge may be brought against two or more defendants who allegedly committed an offence jointly. The principles governing such cases are analogous to those governing trial of joint counts in a trial on indictment. The justices may convict either or both, whether on the basis that they did indeed commit the offence jointly or on the basis that they acted independently of each other. Thus, the acquittal of one does not prevent the conviction of the other (see, e.g., *Barsted v Jones* (1964) 124 JP 400). As at trial on indictment (see **D11.86**), there is a discretion to order separate trials where two or more defendants are charged jointly. However, it is submitted that a joint trial will generally be preferable.

SPECIAL PLEAS IN THE CONTEXT OF SUMMARY TRIALS

Double Jeopardy

There is no special procedure for pleading autrefois acquit or autrefois convict at summary trial. However, a previous acquittal or conviction for the same matter is as much a bar to summary proceedings as it is to proceedings on indictment (*Connelly v DPP* [1964] AC 1254, per Lord Morris of Borth-y-Gest at p. 1320). The issue may be raised simply on a not guilty plea. For detailed discussion of the autrefois doctrine, see **D12.20** ***et seq***. **D21.50**

The question most frequently raised by autrefois arising out of summary proceedings is whether there has been a genuine acquittal or, as the case may be, conviction by magistrates acting properly within their jurisdiction. If there has not, the accused is said never to have been in jeopardy and is therefore unable to rely on autrefois. The withdrawal of a charge before a plea is entered does *not* found autrefois, whereas the dismissal of the charge following a not guilty plea and the offering of no evidence normally does. However, a distinction is drawn between cases where, for whatever reason, no evidence is offered and those where the proceedings in the magistrates' courts are so flawed that the accused was never in danger of a valid conviction. In the latter type of case, a purported acquittal (or conviction) does not prevent the magistrates re-trying the accused for the same offence (see *Dabhade* [1993] QB 329, where it was confirmed that fresh proceedings may be brought if (but only if) the accused was never in jeopardy of a valid conviction). Thus, where magistrates purport to acquit the accused without giving the prosecution the opportunity to call evidence, the purported acquittal is liable to be quashed and the autrefois doctrine will not prevent fresh proceedings for the same offence being instituted (*Dorking Justices, ex parte Harrington* [1984] AC 743). For example, in *DPP v Jarman* [2013] EWHC 4391 (Admin), the prosecutor failed to attend and the magistrates dismissed the case for want of prosecution under s. 15. Fresh proceedings were then instituted. Griffith Williams J (at [30]) reiterated that the scope of autrefois acquit 'is narrowly confined to those cases where the accused is put in peril of conviction for the same offence as that with which he is then charged'. This requires that 'the court must be in a position to conduct a hearing and so it follows that there must be a prosecutor to prosecute and a defendant to defend unless, of course, the defendant has wilfully absented himself or herself and so the trial proceeds in his or her absence' (at [31]). In *Jarman*, D 'was in no way in peril because, while the court was competent to try him and there was a valid charge upon which he was to be tried, the dismissal was not on the merits; there was no prosecutor and the magistrates had heard no evidence' (at [32]).

In *J (JF)* [2013] EWCA Crim 569, [2014] QB 561, the Court of Appeal undertook a detailed analysis of the scope of the autrefois doctrine. After consideration of *Connelly v DPP*, Sir John Thomas P (at [23]) concluded that 'the scope of autrefois is narrow and the offence, as well as the facts, must be the same for the plea of autrefois to apply'. Moreover, a key question is whether the accused was ever 'in peril' of being convicted on the earlier occasion. So far as magistrates' court cases are concerned, his lordship gave an example (at [45]) of where an accused would be at peril for the purposes of autrefois, namely a case where the court sets a date for trial, the accused attends, the prosecutor unsuccessfully applies for an adjournment of the trial (with the effect that the magistrates are entitled to proceed with the trial), and the prosecution then offer no evidence, with the result that the accused is acquitted by the magistrates. His lordship went on (at [50]) to rule that the accused can be 'in peril' only when the magistrates' court hearing is for the purpose of determining whether the accused is guilty (which can be the first hearing when the plea is put, but is more likely to be the date fixed for the summary trial).

Unfitness to Plead

D21.51 There is no specific procedure by which a person's fitness to plead may be determined in the magistrates' court (and the Criminal Procedure (Insanity) Act 1964, ss. 4 and 4A, apply only to trial on indictment). If the accused is thought to be suffering from a mental disability such as to be unable to comprehend the course of the proceedings or make a proper defence to the charge (i.e. the accused would be found unfit to plead if facing trial on indictment — see **D12.2** ***et seq.***), the defence have the following options:

(a) Assuming the offence is triable either way, the accused may elect trial on indictment and have the question of fitness determined in the Crown Court. Indeed, it would be open to the justices to decline jurisdiction on the basis that the Crown Court is the more appropriate forum for a case where fitness to plead is an issue.
(b) Assuming there is to be a summary trial, the accused may plead not guilty (or a not guilty plea may be entered on behalf of the accused), thereby putting the prosecution to proof of their case. If the definition of the offence requires the prosecution to prove *mens rea*, and especially if the offence involves a specific intent, the accused's mental condition may make it difficult for the prosecution to discharge their burden. Moreover, the common-law defence of insanity is available to an accused in a summary trial (*Horseferry Road Magistrates' Court, ex parte K* [1997] QB 23 at p. 46; *R (Singh) v Stratford Magistrates' Court* [2007] EWHC 1582 (Admin), [2007] 1 WLR 3119).
(c) The defence may invite the court to make a hospital order under the Mental Health Act 1983, s. 37(3), without convicting the accused (see **D21.54**). Section 37(3) enables magistrates to achieve a result very similar to that which follows upon an accused being found unfit to plead to an indictment: if the court is satisfied that the accused did the act or made the omission charged, the court may, if it thinks fit, make such a hospital order without convicting the accused. This provision should be read in conjunction with the PCC(S)A 2000, s. 11(1), which provides that if, on the summary trial of an offence punishable with imprisonment, the court is satisfied that the accused did the act or made the omission charged, but thinks that there ought to be an inquiry into his or her physical or mental condition before appropriate disposal is decided, the court must adjourn the case to enable a medical examination and report to be made (see **D21.53**).

D21.52 The same principles are to be followed in respect of a young person facing trial in the youth court (*R (P) v Barking Youth Court* [2002] EWHC 734 (Admin), [2002] 2 Cr App R 19 (294); *G v DPP* [2012] EWHC 3174 (Admin)). For detailed guidance on the approach to be taken, see *CPS v P* [2007] EWHC 946 (Admin), [2008] 1 WLR 1005 (see **D24.94**).

In *R (Singh) v Stratford Magistrates' Court*, the Divisional Court considered the effect of the Mental Health Act 1983, s. 37(3) (see **D21.54**). Hughes LJ (at [39]–[41]) said that a magistrates' court has the power, in an appropriate case, to try the issue of insanity and pronounce its conclusion upon it, without convicting or acquitting the accused, provided that the conditions for making an order under s. 37(3) are met. However, if satisfied that there is no purpose in resolving the issue of insanity, and if a s. 37(3) order is going to be made, the court can deal with the case without trying that issue. If it is clear that no s. 37(3) order is going to be possible on the medical evidence whatever happens then, in the absence of some other compelling factor, the case must proceed to trial. Before embarking on a case in which s. 37(3) may be applied, magistrates should make it clear that it is a possibility and should invite submissions from the parties upon the course to be adopted. In particular, careful consideration must be given to any reason advanced why the issue of insanity should be tried. Such an application should be resolved having regard to the interests of justice, which include, but are not limited to, justice to the accused.

Powers of Criminal Courts (Sentencing) Act 2000, s. 11 **D21.53**

(1) If, on the trial by a magistrates' court of an offence punishable on summary conviction with imprisonment the court—
   (a) is satisfied that the accused did the act or made the omission charged, but
   (b) is of the opinion that an inquiry ought to be made into his physical or mental condition before the method of dealing with him is determined,

   the court shall adjourn the case to enable a medical examination and report to be made, and shall remand him.

(2) An adjournment under subsection (1) above shall not be for more than three weeks at a time where the court remands the accused in custody, nor for more than four weeks at a time where it remands him on bail.

(3) Where on an adjournment under subsection (1) above the accused is remanded on bail, the court shall impose conditions under paragraph (d) of section 3(6) of the Bail Act 1976 and the requirements imposed as conditions under that paragraph shall be or shall include requirements that the accused—
   (a) undergo medical examination by a registered medical practitioner or, where the inquiry is into his mental condition and the court so directs, two such practitioners; and
   (b) for that purpose attend such an institution or place, or on such practitioner, as the court directs and, where the inquiry is into his mental condition, comply with any other directions which may be given to him for that purpose by any person specified by the court or by a person of any class so specified.

Mental Health Act 1983, s. 37 **D21.54**

(3) Where a person is charged before a magistrates' court with any act or omission as an offence and the court would have power, on convicting him of that offence, to make a [hospital order], then, if the court is satisfied that the accused did the act or made the omission charged, the court may, if it thinks fit, make such an order without convicting him.

Adjournment for Reports It will be noted that the power to order medical reports under the PCC(S)A 2000, s. 11(1), and the power to make a hospital order under the Mental Health Act 1983, s. 37(3), both depend merely upon the court being satisfied that the accused committed the *actus reus* of the offence charged. Therefore, in a case where the accused is apparently suffering from mental illness or impairment, the court may cause a not guilty plea to be entered on behalf of the accused and hear the prosecution evidence. Assuming that evidence establishes the *actus reus*, the court may then adjourn for reports. If, on the basis of those reports, the medical criteria for the making of a hospital order are satisfied, the court may make such an order *without convicting the accused*. For details about the preconditions for a hospital order and, in particular, the need for reports from medical practitioners confirming that the accused is suffering from a mental disorder as defined by the Mental Health Act 1983, see **E22.2**. **D21.55**

Either-way Offences Where the accused is charged with an either-way offence a further difficulty arises, namely that the magistrates' court will not have jurisdiction to commence summary trial of the offence unless the accused consents to summary trial. *Ex hypothesi*, the accused is unlikely to be in a fit state to give consent. In *Lincoln (Kesteven) Justices, ex parte O'Connor* [1983] 1 WLR 335, D was charged with assault occasioning actual bodily harm. His mental state was such that he was incapable of consenting to summary trial. The Divisional Court held that a trial is *not* a necessary precondition of the court being satisfied for the purposes of s. 37(3) that the accused committed the *actus reus* of the offence. In an exceptional case such as **D21.56**

the instant one, where D was legally represented and everybody agreed that he had assaulted V, the justices could conclude without evidence that the offence had occurred. Therefore, they had jurisdiction to make a hospital order. It is, however, clear that the magistrates have no jurisdiction under s. 37(3) to make a hospital order in respect of a person charged with an indictable-only offence (*Chippenham Magistrates' Court, ex parte Thompson* (1996) 160 JP 207).

Section D22 Summary Trial: The Course of the Trial

PLEAS WHICH MAY BE TENDERED

Pleas that May Be Tendered

A summary trial begins with the taking of the plea from the accused (MCA 1980, s. 9(1)). The allegation is read to the accused, the procedure at the hearing is explained, the accused is asked if he or she has been advised about the potential effect on sentence of a guilty plea, and is then asked to enter a plea of guilty or not guilty (CrimPR 24.2(2)). **D22.1**

An accused who pleads guilty may be convicted without evidence being heard (s. 9(3); CrimPR 24.7); if the accused pleads not guilty, the court will proceed to try the case (or adjourn to a later date for the trial to take place). If a plea of not guilty was entered on a previous occasion, the accused must be asked to confirm that plea (r. 24.3(2)).

The requirement to record a conviction following a guilty plea is without prejudice to the requirement to hold a *Newton* hearing (*Newton* (1982) 77 Cr App R 13) if there is a substantial variation between the prosecution and defence versions of the facts of the offence (see **D23.7**).

In the absence of a guilty plea, the court is under a duty to hear evidence and either convict the accused or dismiss the charge (s. 9(2)). **D22.2**

Magistrates' Courts Act 1980, s. 9

(1) On the summary trial of an information, the court shall, if the accused appears, state to him the substance of the information and ask him whether he pleads guilty or not guilty.
(2) The court, after hearing the evidence and the parties, shall convict the accused or dismiss the information.
(3) If the accused pleads guilty, the court may convict him without hearing evidence.

Alternative Offences

The only pleas which may be entered are guilty or not guilty. Unlike the Crown Court, a magistrates' court has no power to return a verdict of not guilty as charged but guilty of a lesser offence (*Lawrence v Same* [1968] 2 QB 93, overruled on a different point in *Chief Constable of Norfolk v Clayton* [1983] 2 AC 473), and it follows that a plea to like effect is not an option available to the accused even if the prosecution would be willing to accept it. However, in a case where a plea to something other than the offence charged would be acceptable to the parties, the procedural difficulty may be overcome simply by charging the accused with the lesser offence (assuming, if it is a summary offence, the six-month time-limit under the MCA 1980, s.127, has not expired). The accused may then plead guilty to the new charge in exchange for the prosecution offering no evidence on the original one (see also **D22.8**). Whether or not a new charge should be added is a matter for the prosecution; the court has no power to add a charge if that course of action is opposed by the prosecution (*R (Morales) v Kettering Magistrates' Court* [2013] EWHC 1922 (Admin)). **D22.3**

Plea of Guilty

D22.4 The same basic principles govern guilty pleas at summary trial as govern such pleas at trial on indictment (see **D12.72** ***et seq.***). It is essential that the plea be *unequivocal*. CrimPR 24.7(1)(b) says that the court must be satisfied that the guilty plea 'represents a clear acknowledgement of guilt'. If, when the charge is put, the accused does not answer directly or qualifies what purports to be a guilty plea with words suggesting that he or she is really putting forward a defence, then the court must try to resolve the ambiguity. If the plea remains ambiguous, the court must reject it and hear evidence before convicting or acquitting. The concept of an equivocal plea has been extended to pleas which, although unambiguous when made, are thrown into doubt by something which occurs between plea and sentence (e.g., the presentation of mitigation which is inconsistent with guilt, as in *Durham Quarter Sessions, ex parte Virgo* [1952] 2 QB 1). It has also been extended to pleas entered under duress (*Huntingdon Crown Court, ex parte Jordan* [1981] QB 857). One reason why justices must be careful to ensure that a purported plea of guilty is unequivocal is that, if they convict and sentence on an equivocal plea, the accused may appeal to the Crown Court against conviction, notwithstanding the general rule in the MCA 1980, s. 108, that a person who pleads guilty in the magistrates' court may appeal only against sentence (see **D29.4**). If the Crown Court finds the plea to have been equivocal, it remits the case to the lower court with a binding direction to hear the evidence on a not guilty plea (*Plymouth Justices, ex parte Hart* [1986] QB 950).

D22.5 Where the accused is present, a guilty plea must be entered by the accused personally, not by a legal representative acting on his or her behalf (*Westminster City Council v Owadally* [2017] EWHC 1092 (Admin), [2017] 2 Cr App R 18 (223)). The position is less clear where the accused does not appear in person but is, by virtue of the MCA 1980, s. 122, deemed to be present because he or she is legally represented (unless, for example, the accused is on bail, in which case s. 122 does not apply). In *Owadally*, Gross LJ said (at [45](v)) that, where s. 122 applies, 'it may be doubtful whether a legal representative can enter a binding guilty plea in the absence of the accused'. The reason for this doubt comes from *Williams* [1978] QB 373, a case concerning guilty pleas in the Crown Court, where Shaw LJ (at p. 378) said that: 'No qualification of or deviation from the rule that a plea of guilty must come from him who acknowledges guilt is thus permissible. A departure from the rule in a criminal trial would therefore necessarily be a vitiating factor rendering the whole procedure void and ineffectual.' However, an argument to the contrary would be that, if Parliament allows a party (so long as the party is not under a duty to be present) to appear through a legal representative, the purpose of allowing that to happen is negated if the representative cannot enter a plea on behalf of a client. It is therefore submitted that s. 122 ought to be construed as permitting a duly appointed representative to enter a guilty plea on behalf of a client who is deemed to be present by virtue of being represented.

Where the accused is a corporation, a duly appointed 'representative' of the corporation may, *inter alia*, consent to summary trial (where the offence is triable either way) and enter a plea of guilty or not guilty (MCA 1980, sch. 3, para. 2(b) and (c)).

Plea of Not Guilty

D22.6 A not guilty plea will normally be entered by the accused personally. If, however, the accused is absent and the court decides to proceed in his or her absence, or the accused remains silent when asked to plead, or enters an ambiguous plea, then the court simply hears the evidence in accordance with the requirement of the MCA 1980, s. 9(2), as if there had been a not guilty plea.

The options open to the prosecution (other than proceeding to summary trial) where an accused does not plead guilty are as follows.

D22.7 **Withdrawal of Summons** The prosecution may, with the leave of the court, withdraw the summons (*Redbridge Justices, ex parte Sainty* [1981] RTR 13). If the prosecution are not in a position to prove guilt on the day appointed for the hearing, or for any other reason do not wish to proceed forthwith to trial, they may prefer to withdraw the summons (rather than offering no evidence or asking for an adjournment), since such withdrawal avoids there being a verdict of not guilty. Consequently, a fresh summons may later be obtained in respect of the same offence, and the accused will not be able to rely upon autrefois acquit to prevent the trial on that summons proceeding.

That withdrawal of a summons is not equivalent to an acquittal was confirmed in *Grays Justices, ex parte Low* [1990] 1 QB 54. Nolan J said (at p. 59A–B):

> [T]he withdrawal of a summons with the consent of the justices will not of itself operate as a bar to the issue of a further summons in respect of the same charge where there has been no adjudication upon the merits of the charge in the original summons, and the defendant has not been put in peril of conviction upon it.

It is submitted that the same principles apply to prosecutions commenced by way of charge at the police station and to prosecutions brought under the written charge and requisition procedure: the prosecution can avert a not guilty verdict by withdrawing the charge and then re-prosecuting.

Offering No Evidence Once the accused has entered a plea of not guilty, the option of asking for the summons to be withdrawn ceases to be open to the prosecution. Therefore, if they are not ready to proceed on the date that has been fixed for trial, the only course available to them is to ask for an adjournment. If the adjournment is refused, they must either call whatever evidence they do have at court or, if that evidence would plainly be insufficient for a conviction, offer no evidence. **D22.8**

Other situations where it may be appropriate for the prosecution to offer no evidence are where the accused has pleaded guilty to one offence and the prosecution do not wish to proceed with another (related) charge, or where new evidence exonerating the accused has come to light, or where the CPS have reviewed the evidence and have decided that there is insufficient prospect of securing a conviction to merit continuing the proceedings.

Where the charge is dismissed following the prosecution deciding to offer no evidence, this counts as an acquittal for the purpose of the doctrine of autrefois acquit. In *R (A) v South Staffordshire Youth Court* [2006] EWHC 1200 (Admin), D was charged with assault occasioning actual bodily harm. He pleaded not guilty. The prosecution subsequently preferred the more serious charge of inflicting grievous bodily harm and offered no evidence in respect of the lesser charge, which was formally dismissed by the court. During the trial of the grievous bodily harm charge, the prosecutor concluded that he would not be able to establish that charge and offered D the opportunity to plead guilty to the original lesser charge. The question at issue was whether the court had jurisdiction to reopen the case on the charge of occasioning actual bodily harm. It was held that, in a case where a not guilty verdict is entered in the Crown Court under the CJA 1967, s. 17 (which provides that where the prosecutor offers no evidence, the court may order that a verdict of not guilty be recorded without the need for a verdict from a jury), an accused is entitled to rely on the defence of *autrefois acquit* if charged again with that offence. This principle applies equally where a magistrates' court dismisses a charge pursuant to the MCA 1980, s. 27 (which provides that where, on the summary trial of an either-way offence the court dismisses the charge, the dismissal has the same effect as an acquittal on indictment), since s. 27 is, for all practical purposes, the same as s. 17. The court was therefore *functus officio* and the decision to proceed on the lesser charge was wrong. **D22.9**

Change of Plea

A magistrates' court may allow an accused to change plea from guilty to not guilty at any stage before sentence is passed (*S (an infant) v Recorder of Manchester* [1971] AC 481). Lord Upjohn, at p. 507, observed that 'this discretionary power is one which should only be exercised in clear cases and very sparingly'. **D22.10**

The procedure for seeking permission to change plea is set out in CrimPR 24.10 (see Supplement, **R24.10**). The accused must apply, in writing (unless the court directs otherwise), as soon as practicable after becoming aware of the reasons for making an application to change plea, explaining why it would be unjust not to allow withdrawal of the guilty plea, and identifying any evidence the defence wish to call. The application must also say whether the accused is waiving legal professional privilege.

Whether to accede to an application for a change of plea is in the court's discretion and there is no automatic rule that an accused who was unrepresented when the plea was entered is entitled to change that plea upon obtaining legal representation during the period of an adjournment before sentence (*South Tameside Magistrates' Court, ex parte Rowland* [1983] 3 All ER 689). The question for the bench is whether the original plea was unequivocal and entered with a proper understanding of what the charge entailed. If it was, then the magistrates are entitled to refuse any application to change.

D22.11 In *Revitt v DPP* [2006] EWHC 2266 (Admin), [2006] 1 WLR 3172, the Divisional Court applied the guidance given in *S v Recorder of Manchester*, holding that if, after an unequivocal plea of guilty has been made, it becomes apparent that the accused did not appreciate the elements of the offence to which the guilty plea related, then it is likely to be appropriate to permit withdrawal of that plea (per Lord Phillips CJ (at [17])). Similarly, if the facts relied upon by the prosecution do not add up to the offence charged, justice will normally demand that the accused be permitted to withdraw the guilty plea (at [18]). His lordship added (at [19]) that the onus lies on a party seeking to vacate a guilty plea to demonstrate that justice requires that this should be permitted.

In *Wilson v CPS* [2020] EWHC 820 (QB), the Divisional Court reiterated (at [31]) that the jurisdiction to vacate a plea of guilty 'should be exercised sparingly and only in clear cases'. However, if it is established that the accused pleaded guilty without understanding elements of the offence, or without intending to admit guilt of what was alleged, then it may be appropriate to allow withdrawal of the guilty plea. Legal representation may be relevant: it will be more difficult to justify a change of plea where the accused was represented by experienced criminal representations (at [32]). However, if there has been improper pressure to plead guilty (going beyond forceful but appropriate advice), the court may allow a guilty plea to be vacated; moreover, incorrect legal advice that a certain factual basis would not amount to a defence may enable to the guilty plea to be set aside. The Court said (at [33]) that, in such circumstances, 'the plea would have been entered into in circumstances amounting to a mistake', enabling the rescinding of the guilty plea under the MCA 1980, s. 142 (see **D22.76**).

If the court permits a change of plea from guilty to not guilty in the case of an either-way offence, it must go on to allow the accused to consider afresh whether to consent to summary trial and so the allocation procedure should be repeated (*Bow Street Magistrates' Court, ex parte Welcombe* (1992) 156 JP 609; see also **D6.32**).

Once the court has passed sentence, it is *functus officio*, although a conviction based upon a guilty plea may be set aside by appealing to the Crown Court on the basis that the plea was equivocal.

A magistrates' court has an unfettered discretion to allow a change of plea from not guilty to guilty at any time before a verdict is returned.

FAILURE OF PARTIES OR WITNESSES TO APPEAR

Power to Adjourn

D22.12 If the one or both of the parties is absent, or witnesses fail to attend, the court must consider what action to take. If the trial does not proceed on the appointed day, the court may adjourn the case (under the MCA 1980, s. 10(1)). Under s. 10(2), the court may either set the date for the hearing to resume when it adjourns the case or, unless it also remands the accused (in which case a date must be fixed), leave the time and place to be determined. The trial can resume only where the court is satisfied that the parties have had adequate notice;

if the accused was not present when the case was adjourned, it will therefore be necessary to send the accused an adjournment notice. For detailed discussion of adjournments, see **D5.22** *et seq*.).

Failure of Accused to Appear

These paragraphs should be read in conjunction with **D5**, which deals with adjournments and with the options available to a magistrates' court upon non-appearance in answer to a summons or requisition, and **D7**, which deals with bail. **D22.13**

Trial in the Absence of the Accused: Powers and Procedure Under the MCA 1980, s. 11(1)(b), if, at the time and place appointed for the trial, the prosecutor appears but the accused does not, and the accused has attained the age of 18, the court *must* proceed in the absence of the accused 'unless it appears to the court to be contrary to the interests of justice to do so'. Thus, where an adult accused is absent, assuming he or she is aged 18 or over, the general rule is that the court will proceed as if the accused were present and, unless a plea was entered on an earlier occasion, had pleaded not guilty; the court must give reasons if it does not do so (CrimPR 24.12(3)). However, where proceedings were commenced by summons or by written charge and requisition then (unless the accused has appeared on a previous occasion in answer to the summons or requisition) it must be proved to the satisfaction of the court that the summons (or requisition) was served on the accused a reasonable time before the hearing (MCA 1980, s. 11(2); CrimPR 24.12(3)(b)(i)). Proof of service of a summons or requisition is governed by CrimPR Part 4 (see **D5.16**). **D22.14**

Where the case has previously been adjourned (under the MCA 1980, s. 10(1)), it is necessary to satisfy the court that the accused has had 'adequate notice' of the adjournment date (MCA 1980, s. 10(2)) or, as it is expressed in CrimPR 24.12(3)(b)(ii), 'reasonable notice' of when and where the hearing would resume. If the accused does not appear and the conditions for proceeding in his or her absence are satisfied, a not guilty plea is entered on behalf of the accused (CrimPR 24.12(3). The burden is then on the prosecution to prove the case to the normal criminal standard, whether by calling oral evidence or by reading statements served on the accused under the CJA 1967, s. 9 (such statements are admissible in the absence of objection from the defence — positive consent is not required: see s. 9(2)(d)). Should the prosecution evidence turn out to be insufficient, the court is of course obliged to acquit the accused. Assuming, however, that the case is proved, the court may either proceed immediately to sentence or, in certain circumstances, it may adjourn to give the accused notice to attend for sentencing (MCA 1980, s. 10(3)).

Where a written charge is to be tried using the single justice procedure (see **D22.33**), s. 11 does not apply (s. 11(8)).

Where the proceedings were instituted by summons or by the issue of a written charge and requisition, the MCA 1980, s. 11(3) and (4), restrict the power of the court to pass a custodial sentence, or impose a disqualification, upon an offender who is absent (see **D23.10**). **D22.15**

Either-way Offences The power to conduct a trial in the absence of the accused applies both to either-way and summary offences. However, if the proceedings are for an either-way offence, the trial cannot proceed in the absence of the accused unless, at an earlier hearing, he or she consented to summary trial. It will normally be necessary for the accused to have attended in person for the determination of mode of trial (see **D6.9**). Assuming the accused has already consented to summary trial, the actual trial may then take place in the absence of the accused in the event of failure to attend. **D22.16**

Determining Whether to Proceed to Trial in Accused's Absence Section 11(2A) makes it clear that 'the court shall not proceed in the absence of the accused if it considers that there is an acceptable reason for his failure to appear'; however, s. 11(6) provides that the court is not required to inquire into the reasons for the accused's failure to appear before deciding whether to proceed in his or her absence. Section 11(7) requires the court to state in open court its **D22.17**

reasons for not proceeding in the absence of an accused who has attained the age of 18 and who fails to attend (see also CrimPR 24.12(3)).

CrimPD VI, para. 24C.17 (see Supplement, **CPD.24C**), makes the point that, in 'marked contrast to the position in the Crown Court' (as to which, see **D15.87** ***et seq.***), in magistrates' courts proceeding in the absence of an accused who fails to attend is the 'default position' where the accused is aware of the date of trial and no acceptable reason is offered for absence. The court is 'not obliged to investigate if no reason is offered'. In assessing where the interests of justice lie, the court will take into account all factors, including: (i) 'such reasons for absence as may be offered'; (ii) the 'reliability of the information supplied in support of those reasons'; (iii) the date on which the reasons for absence became known to the accused, and what action the accused took in response to those reasons. Paragraph 24C.17 adds that, where the accused provides a medical note to excuse non-attendance, the court must consider CrimPD I, paras. 5C.1 to 5C.6 (see **D22.18**), and 'give reasons if deciding to proceed notwithstanding'.

An example of involuntary absence may be found in *R (Davies) v Solihull Justices* [2008] EWHC 1157 (Admin). After his case had been called on, it was discovered that D had been excluded from the court building by the security staff because of disorderly behaviour. The justices ruled that D had, by virtue of his conduct, voluntarily absented himself from the hearing of his case, and that he should be tried in his absence. Underhill J ruled that D's misbehaviour did not justify excluding him from his own trial. Moreover, the justices erred in treating him as being voluntarily absent, since he had wanted to be in court but was prevented by the exclusion. While it could be said that the exclusion was his own fault, that was not the same as it being his own choice; the position was no different than if he had committed an offence on the way to court and then been arrested (and so unable to attend court), as had happened in *R (R) v Thames Youth Court* [2002] EWHC 1670 (Admin). In that case, the district judge had formed the view that D had brought his arrest on himself and should therefore be regarded as having excluded himself deliberately from court. Pitchford J said (at [27]) that the district judge was wrong to take that approach.

D22.18 **Adjournment Sought on Medical Grounds** The principles applicable where an adjournment is sought on the basis that the accused is unfit to attend were helpfully summarised by Sharp J in *R (Killick) v West London Magistrates' Court* [2012] EWHC 3864 (Admin) (at [17]):

1. The overriding principle is that the court should not proceed to hear a case in the defendant's absence without satisfying itself that the claim for an adjournment may properly be rejected and that no unfairness will thereby be done …
2. The discretion to commence a trial in the absence of a defendant should be exercised with the utmost care and caution. Where a defendant to a criminal charge wishes to resist it and is shown by medical evidence to be unfit to attend court to do so, either as a result of involuntary illness or incapacity, it would be very rarely, if indeed ever, right for the court to exercise its discretion in favour of commencing the trial, or to proceed to hear the case in his absence, at any rate unless the defendant is represented and asks that the trial should begin …
3. If a court asked for an adjournment on medical grounds, suspects the grounds to be spurious or believes them to be inadequate, the court should ordinarily express its doubts and thereby give the defendant an opportunity to resolve those doubts …
4. A court considering an application to adjourn will need carefully to distinguish between genuine reasons for the defendant not being present and those reasons which are spuriously advanced or designed to frustrate the process. However, if the court comes to the conclusion that either of the latter is the case, it should say so. It cannot simply be inferred that a court has come to that conclusion unless that is clearly stated by the magistrates …
5. If a conclusion is open to the court reasonably on the material before it either to the effect that an excuse given is spurious or there is a truly compelling and exceptional reason for proceeding notwithstanding a good excuse for non-attendance, the court has the power to do so. This however will be an exceptional case …

CrimPD I, para. 5C.3 (see Supplement, **CPD.5C**), emphasises that the court 'is not absolutely bound by a medical certificate' and may require the medical practitioner who provided the certificate to give evidence or may exercise its discretion to disregard a certificate which it finds 'unsatisfactory'.

Paragraph 5C.4 goes on to state that the circumstances in which the court may find a medical certificate 'unsatisfactory' include cases where the certificate indicates that the accused is unfit to attend work (rather than to attend court), where the nature of the ailment (e.g., a broken arm) does not appear to be capable of preventing attendance at court, or where the accused is certified as suffering from stress, anxiety, or depression and there is no indication of recovery within a realistic timescale. Paragraph 5C.5 stipulates that a medical certificate should set out the 'exact nature' of the ailment from which the accused is suffering and (unless it is self-evident) why that ailment prevents attendance at court; the certificate must also give an indication as to when the accused is likely to be able to attend court, or a date when the certificate expires.

It should be noted that CrimPD III, para. 14B.2 (see Supplement, **CPD.14B**), requires that an accused who is on bail and who will be unable for medical reasons to attend court should obtain a certificate from a GP (or hospital doctor, as the case may be) in advance of the hearing. Without a medical certificate, or if an unsatisfactory certificate is provided, the court is likely to consider that the accused has failed to surrender to bail (para. 14B.3). In such a case, the trial may proceed in the absence of the accused (see **D22.14**).

However, a note of caution was sounded in *R (Rathor) v Southampton Magistrates' Court* [2018] EWHC 3278 (Admin), where D did not attend court on the date fixed for trial. He supplied a medical certificate which stated that he had suspected food poisoning, but which did not address the question of whether he was well enough to attend his trial on the following day. The district judge refused to adjourn the trial. Quashing the decision, Andrews J (at [13]) noted that 'the court cannot simply rely on the adequacy or otherwise of the medical certificate'; the judge was obliged also 'to consider whether it would be contrary to the interests of justice to refuse the adjournment'. In the present case, there was no evidence that any consideration was properly given to the consequences for D of not being present 'in a case which turned on one man's word against another's'.

Warrant for Arrest Under the MCA 1980, s. 13(1), where the court, instead of proceeding in the absence of the accused, adjourns or further adjourns the trial, it has the option of issuing an arrest warrant, provided that the offence in question is punishable with imprisonment, or the court, having convicted the accused, proposes to impose a disqualification (s. 13(3) (adults) and s. 13(3A) (children and young people)). For this provision to apply, it must be proved to the satisfaction of the court that the summons or requisition was served on the accused within a reasonable time before the trial (s. 13(2A)), unless the current adjournment is a second or subsequent adjournment of the trial, the accused was present on the last occasion when the trial was adjourned and the date for the present hearing was fixed then (s. 13(2B)). **D22.19**

If the accused appears to be evading service of the summons or requisition, and the offence is an indictable one, it is open to the prosecution to start proceedings again by seeking an arrest warrant. The MCA 1980, s. 1(6), provides that: 'Where the offence charged is an indictable offence, a warrant under this section may be issued at any time notwithstanding that a summons has, or a written charge and requisition have, previously been issued.'

If the accused is currently on bail and fails to attend court, an arrest warrant may, in any event, be issued under the BA 1976, s. 7(1).

Declaration that the Accused Did Not Know of the Proceedings

The provisions as to service of a summons or requisition, and the possibility of trial in absence, make it possible for an accused to be tried and sentenced when, in fact, he or she knew nothing of the proceedings. The MCA 1980, s. 14(1) (see **D22.21**), therefore provides a procedure by which a conviction in absence may be set aside. The accused must make a statutory declaration of ignorance of the summons (or requisition) or of the proceedings until after the court had begun to try the case. The declaration must specify the date on which the accused first had knowledge of the proceedings, and must be served on the court within 21 days thereof. The effect of a timely statutory declaration is to make void the summons (or requisition) and all subsequent **D22.20** proceedings, although the charge itself is unaffected. Consequently, the prosecution may serve a fresh summons (or requisition) for the same offence, even if it is a summary offence and more than six months have elapsed since the date of commission. Under s. 14(3), the court may allow a statutory declaration to take effect even though it is served out of time if, in the circumstances, it appears to the court that it was not reasonable for the accused to serve the declaration within the 21 days permitted. The accused may appear before the court in person to make a statutory declaration, or may send the declaration to the court office by registered letter or recorded delivery (s. 14(2)). The procedure established by s. 14 is summarised in CrimPR 44.2 (see Supplement, R44.2).

D22.21 **Magistrates' Courts Act 1980, s. 14**

(1) Where a summons has been issued under section 1 above and a magistrates' court has begun to try the information to which the summons relates, then, if—
  (a) the accused, at any time during or after the trial, makes a statutory declaration that he did not know of the summons or the proceedings until a date specified in the declaration, being a date after the court has begun to try the information; and
  (b) within 21 days of that date the declaration is served on the designated officer for the court,

without prejudice to the validity of the information, the summons and all subsequent proceedings shall be void.

(2) For the purposes of subsection (1) above a statutory declaration shall be deemed to be duly served on the designated officer if it is delivered to him, or left at his office, or is sent in a registered letter or by the recorded delivery service addressed to him at his office.

(3) If on the application of the accused it appears to a magistrates' court (which for this purpose may be composed of a single justice) that it was not reasonable to expect the accused to serve such a statutory declaration as is mentioned in subsection (1) above within the period allowed by that subsection, the court may accept service of such a declaration by the accused after that period has expired; and a statutory declaration accepted under this subsection shall be deemed to have been served as required by that subsection.

(4) Where any proceedings have become void by virtue of subsection (1) above, the information shall not be tried again by any of the same justices.

Failure of Prosecutor to Appear

D22.22 If the prosecutor does not appear for the trial (but the accused is present), the court may, at its discretion, either (a) dismiss the charge, or (b) adjourn the trial, or (c) proceed in the prosecutor's absence (MCA 1980, s. 15(1)). Section 15 is supplemented by CrimPR 24.12(2), which provides that, where the prosecutor is absent, the court may, if it has already received evidence, deal with the case as if the prosecutor were present; otherwise, the court should inquire into the reasons for the prosecutor's absence and, if satisfied there is no good reason, may exercise its power to dismiss the allegation.

It follows that the option of proceeding in the absence of the prosecutor is available only if the court has received evidence on a previous occasion (i.e. the case was adjourned part-heard after prosecution evidence sufficient to raise a case to answer had been adduced — if that has not been done, the court obviously cannot proceed in the prosecutor's absence because there will be no one with standing to call the evidence).

Should the court decide to adjourn, it may not remand the accused in custody unless he or she (a) has been brought from custody, or (b) cannot be remanded on bail because of failure to find sureties (s. 15(2)).

The power to dismiss the charge has not been conferred for punitive purposes. The justices must not, therefore, exercise their power to dismiss where they know that a prosecutor is on the way to court, and that the case is otherwise ready to be presented (*Hendon Justices, ex parte DPP* [1994] QB 167); nor should the power be invoked where the prosecutor is present but unable to proceed because of the absence of the prosecution file (*DPP v Shuttleworth* [2002] EWHC 621 (Admin)). In *DPP v Jarman* [2013] EWHC 4391 (Admin), the prosecutor failed to attend and the magistrates dismissed the case for want of prosecution under the MCA 1980, s. 15. Griffith Williams J said (at [36]) that:

> While the overriding objective [in CrimPR Part 1] includes... the requirement to deal with cases efficiently and expeditiously, the... power to dismiss proceedings pursuant to s 15 of the Act must not... be used, save in the most exceptional cases, to, in effect, punish the prosecution for its inefficiency.

Where a magistrates' court dismisses a charge under s. 15 without consideration of the merits of the case because of the non-attendance of the prosecutor, there is no rule of law which prevents the court dealing with an identical charge subsequently preferred against the same accused; the question to be decided is whether the new charge amounts to an abuse of process, and so the court must consider what prejudice would be caused by the preferment of that new charge (*Holmes v Campbell* (1998) 162 JP 655).

Failure of Both Parties to Appear

Should neither the prosecutor nor the accused appear for the trial (or adjourned trial) of an information, the court may either dismiss the charge or — if evidence has been received on a previous occasion — proceed in their absence (MCA 1980, s. 16). **D22.23**

Appearance by Legal Representative

The parties to proceedings in magistrates' courts may be represented by legal representatives (MCA 1980, s. 122(1) (see **D22.26**)). Alternatively, they may conduct their case in person. It is not the practice to grant persons other than the parties or their legal representatives a right of audience, unless statute expressly allows for alternative representation in a particular category of case. However, where a party wishes to have the assistance of a friend, the friend may sit by the party, advise during the course of the hearing, suggest questions or points for argument etc., although the friend will not be permitted actually to ask questions of witnesses or address the court (*McKenzie v McKenzie* [1971] P 33). See **D3.121**. **D22.24**

The nature of the assistance permitted was examined by the Court of Appeal in *Leicester City Justices, ex parte Barrow* [1991] 2 QB 260. Watkins LJ, giving the judgment of the court, confirmed that a party was entitled to have someone attend as a friend, to take notes, to quietly make suggestions, and to give advice. His lordship said (at p. 289), that litigants have the right to present their own case and, in doing so, have such assistance as may be thought necessary, subject to the right of the court to intervene; the accused does not have to seek the leave of the court to exercise that right. Nevertheless, the court should be informed of the fact that a party would be accompanied by an adviser; and, if the assistance was unreasonable in nature or degree, was provided for an improper purpose or was in any way inimical to the administration of justice, the court could restrict the use of that assistance.

Where a party does not attend court but is represented by a legal representative, the party is deemed not to be absent (s. 122(2)). The prosecution is customarily conducted by a Crown Prosecutor, or counsel or a solicitor acting on behalf of the CPS. If the accused chooses not to attend but to be legally represented, the legal representative may cross-examine the prosecution witnesses, make submissions and speeches, and even call witnesses other than the accused, just as if the accused were present. Furthermore, the effect of s. 122(2) is that the presence of the legal representative precludes the issue of a warrant for the accused's arrest under s. 13 (warrants for arrest where the court adjourns instead of proceeding in the absence of the accused). However, s. 122(3) limits the effect of this deeming provision to the extent that a represented party is *not* deemed to be present if the party's presence was required to 'satisfy any provision of any enactment or any condition of a recognizance expressly requiring his presence'. Consequently, an arrest warrant may be issued for an accused who fails to surrender to custody in answer to bail whether or not he or she is legally represented in court (see the BA 1976, s. 3(1), which provides **D22.25** that a person granted bail in criminal proceedings shall be under a duty to surrender to custody, and s. 7(1) which empowers the court to issue a bench warrant upon failure to do so). Similarly, the terms of the MCA 1980, s. 23, make it clear that proceedings to determine allocation require the actual presence of the accused save in the exceptional circumstances defined in the section.

D22.26 **Magistrates' Courts Act 1980, s. 122**

(1) A party to any proceedings before a magistrates' court may be represented by a legal representative.
(2) Subject to subsection (3) below, an absent party so represented shall be deemed not to be absent.
(3) Appearance of a party by a legal representative shall not satisfy any provision of any enactment or any condition of a recognisance expressly requiring his presence.

Absence of a Witness

D22.27 CrimPD VI, para. 24C.20 (see Supplement, **CPD.24C**), says that, where the court is asked to adjourn because a witness has failed to attend, the court must:

(i) 'rigorously investigate' the steps taken to secure the attendance of that witness, the reasons given for absence, and the likelihood of the witness attending should the case be adjourned;
(ii) consider the relevance of the witness to the case, and whether their witness statement can be agreed (under the CJA 1967, s. 9; see **D22.41**) or admitted as hearsay (under the CJA 2003, s. 114(1)(d), see **F17.3**));
(iii) in the case of a defence witness, consider whether proper notice has been given of the intention to call that witness (under the CPIA 1996, s. 6C, see **D9.34**);
(iv) consider whether the absent witness could be heard later in the trial;
(v) where other witnesses have attended and the court has determined that the absent witness is required, 'consider hearing those witnesses who are present and adjourning the case part-heard, provided the next hearing can be held conveniently in a matter of days or weeks, not months, to avoid having to recall all the witnesses'.

In *R (Parashar) v Sunderland Magistrates' Court* [2019] EWHC 514 (Admin), a request to vacate the trial date was made on the basis that the defence expert was not available on the date in question. The application was refused even though the result would have been that the magistrates' court would have had to decide between the evidence of two experts, one of whom was present and the other was not. Bean LJ said (at [46]) that, 'the decision to fix a date for a trial at which the prosecution expert could attend and the defence expert (whose report had been served in good time) could not was clearly wrong. If the trial had proceeded on that basis the defendant's ability to present his defence would have been seriously compromised and the trial would inevitably have been unfair.' Concurring, Simler J (at [49]) said:

> There is a high public interest in summary trials taking place quickly and on the day set for trial, and in adjournments not being granted absent compelling reasons. But it is also necessary as a matter of fairness and in the interests of justice, where a defence request to vacate a trial date is made, to consider whether, if it is not granted, the defendant will be able fully to present his defence, and if he will not be able to do so, the degree to which the defence will be compromised.

Plea of Guilty by Post

D22.28 To avoid the inconvenience of putting the prosecution to proof in cases where the accused does not wish to contest the charge but is unwilling to attend court to plead guilty, the MCA 1980, s. 12 (see **D22.32**), sets out a procedure allowing the accused to plead guilty by post.

D22.29 **Procedure** The procedure applies to proceedings for summary offences started by means of summons or requisition in a magistrates' court (s. 12(1)) or, where the accused is aged 16 or 17, in a youth court (s. 12(2)). Where a written charge is to be tried using the single justice procedure (see **D22.33**), s. 12 does not apply (s. 11(8)). Whether to give the accused the option of pleading by post is at the discretion of the prosecutor. The main steps in the procedure are:

(a) With the written charge, the prosecutor serves (i) a notice summarising the effect of s. 12, (ii) a summary of the evidence on which the prosecution case is based and/or a copy of the written witness statements under the CJA 1967, s. 9, and (iii) details of any information about the accused, relevant to sentence, which will be made available to the court. If the witness statements are served, they are admissible as evidence unless the accused objects. If the accused fails to plead guilty by post or to attend court to plead not guilty, and so fails to object to the use of the witness statements as evidence, the court can proceed to try the case in the absence of the accused, the prosecution case being based upon the witness statements already served. In *Rymer v DPP* [2010] EWHC 1848 (Admin), [2011] 1 WLR 188, Hooper LJ (at [68]) expressed the view that failure to use the form prescribed is unlikely to result in a conviction based on a postal plea of guilty being quashed, provided that the notice contains a sufficient statement of the effect of s. 12.

(b) The prosecutor notifies the court that the above documents have been served (s. 12(1)(b)).

(c) To take advantage of the procedure, the accused (or the accused's legal representative) must notify the court in writing of the desire to plead guilty without attending court (s. 12(4)). A form is normally enclosed with the summons for the purpose. On the form (or in an accompanying letter), the accused may state any mitigating circumstances for the court's attention. Provided the notification is received before the actual hearing, it does not matter that it arrives after the return date specified in the summons or requisition (*Norham and Islandshire Justices, ex parte Sunter Bros Ltd* [1961] 1 All ER 455). If the offence is endorsable, the accused must also send his or her driving licence, plus a statement of date of birth and sex (RTOA 1988, ss. 7 and 8).

(d) If the court is satisfied that all the above has been done, it may proceed to hear and dispose of the case as if the accused had appeared and pleaded guilty (MCA 1980, s. 12(5)). The prosecutor may, but need not, be present (s. 12(5)). The notification of a guilty plea, the statement of facts served by the prosecution or (unless the court otherwise directs) the written statement or statements under the CJA 1967, s. 9, and any statement submitted in mitigation must be read out in open court (s. 12(7) to (7B)).

(e) The court is not obliged to hear and dispose of the case on a plea of guilty by post simply because the parties have chosen to adopt the procedure. The magistrates may, in their discretion, decide that the case is not appropriate for such disposal. If so, they must adjourn so that (at the resumed hearing) the case may be dealt with as if the plea had never been notified (s. 12(9)). The adjournment notice sent to the accused must state the reason for the adjournment (s. 12(10)). Alternatively, the magistrates may accept the plea, hear the statement of facts and mitigation, and then decide that the accused ought to be given an opportunity to attend before sentence is pronounced. If so, they adjourn after convicting. Again, the notice of adjournment must specify the reason for it (s. 12(10)). It should be borne in mind that a sentence of imprisonment, or disqualification from driving, cannot be imposed in the absence of the accused. If the court is minded to impose such a sentence, the accused will be summoned to attend on a later occasion (MCA 1980, s. 11(3) and (4)).

(f) At any time before the hearing, the accused may withdraw the plea of guilty by post simply by giving written notice to that effect to the court (s. 12(6)). The magistrates have jurisdiction at the hearing itself to allow a change of plea, enabling an accused who earlier pleaded guilty by post to contest the matter (*Bristol Justices, ex parte Sawyers* [1988] Crim LR 754).

This procedure is summarised in CrimPR 24.8 and 24.14(4) (see Supplement, **R24.8** and **R24.14**).

D22.30 **Where Accused Attends Court after Plea of Guilty by Post** The MCA 1980, s. 12A, makes provision for the application of s. 12 where the accused appears in court. If the accused has indicated a wish to plead guilty by post but nevertheless appears before the court, the court may (if the accused consents) proceed as if the accused were absent. Similarly, if the accused has not indicated a wish to plead guilty by post, but attends court and indicates a wish to plead guilty, the court may (with the consent of the accused) proceed as if the accused were absent and had indicated an intention to plead guilty by post. Where the court proceeds as if the accused were absent, the prosecution summary of the facts of the case must not go beyond the statement served on the accused when given the option of pleading guilty by post. However, if the accused is in fact present in court, he or she must be given the opportunity to make an oral submission with a view to mitigation of sentence.

In *Rymer v DPP* [2010] EWHC 1848 (Admin), [2011] 1 WLR 188, D chose to plead guilty by post, his written plea of guilty was accepted at a hearing in his absence, and a conviction was recorded; the court then adjourned the case to consider whether he should be disqualified from driving. At the adjourned hearing, before sentence had been passed, D informed the court that he wished to plead not guilty. The Divisional Court held that he had no automatic right to plead not guilty; rather, he had to show a good reason why he should be allowed to change his plea.

D22.31 **DVLA Printout** The 'pleading guilty by post' system is used most commonly for driving offences, and so the RTOA 1988, s. 13, makes provision for a printout from the DVLA to be admissible as evidence of previous convictions for traffic offences without the need to give the defendant advance notice of intention to refer to these previous convictions (see C2.20).

Statutory Material

D22.32 **Magistrates' Courts Act 1980, s. 12**

(1) This section shall apply where—
   (a) a summons has been issued requiring a person to appear before a magistrates' court, other than a youth court, to answer to an information for a summary offence, not being—
      (i) [repealed]
      (ii) an offence specified in an order made by the Secretary of State by statutory instrument; and
   (b) the designated officer for the court is notified by or on behalf of the prosecutor that the documents mentioned in subsection (3) below have been served upon the accused with the summons.
(2) The reference in subsection (1)(a) above to the issue of a summons requiring a person to appear before a magistrates' court other than a youth court includes a reference to the issue of a summons requiring a person who has attained the age of 16 at the time when it is issued to appear before a youth court.
(3) The documents referred to in subsection (1)(b) above are—
   (a) a notice containing such statement of the effect of this section as may be prescribed;
   (b) either of the following, namely—
      (i) a concise statement of such facts relating to the charge as will be placed before the court by the prosecutor if the accused pleads guilty without appearing before the court, or
      (ii) a copy of such written statement or statements complying with subsections (2)(a) and (b) and (3) of section 9 of the Criminal Justice Act 1967 (proof by written statement) as will be so placed in those circumstances; and
   (c) if any information relating to the accused will or may, in those circumstances, be placed before the court by or on behalf of the prosecutor, a notice containing or describing that information.

(4) Where the designated officer for the court receives a notification in writing purporting to be given by the accused or by a legal representative acting on his behalf that the accused desires to plead guilty without appearing before the court—
(a) the designated officer for the court shall inform the prosecutor of the receipt of the notification; and
(b) the following provisions of this section shall apply.
(5) If at the time and place appointed for the trial or adjourned trial of the information—
(a) the accused does not appear; and
(b) it is proved to the satisfaction of the court, on oath or in such manner as may be prescribed, that the documents mentioned in subsection (3) above have been served upon the accused with the summons,
the court may, subject to section 11(3) and (4) above and subsections (6) to (8) below, proceed to hear and dispose of the case in the absence of the accused, whether or not the prosecutor is also absent, in like manner as if both parties had appeared and the accused had pleaded guilty.
(6) If at any time before the hearing the designated officer for the court receives an indication in writing purporting to be given by or on behalf of the accused that he wishes to withdraw the notification—
(a) the designated officer for the court shall inform the prosecutor of the withdrawal; and
(b) the court shall deal with the information as if the notification had not been given.
(7) Before accepting the plea of guilty and convicting the accused under subsection (5) above, the court shall cause the following to be read out before the court by the clerk of the court, namely—
(a) in a case where a statement of facts as mentioned in subsection (3)(b)(i) above was served on the accused with the summons, that statement;
(aa) in a case where a statement or statements as mentioned in subsection (3)(b)(ii) above was served on the accused with the summons and the court does not otherwise direct, that statement or those statements;
(b) any information contained in a notice so served, and any information described in such a notice and produced by or on behalf of the prosecutor;
(c) the notification under subsection (4) above; and
(d) any submission received with the notification which the accused wishes to be brought to the attention of the court with a view to mitigation of sentence.
(7A) Where the court gives a direction under subsection (7)(aa) above the court shall cause an account to be given orally before the court by the clerk of the court of so much of any statement as is not read aloud.
(7B) Whether or not a direction under paragraph (aa) of subsection (7) above is given in relation to any statement served as mentioned in that paragraph the court need not cause to be read out the declaration required by section 9(2)(b) of the Criminal Justice Act 1967.
(8) If the court proceeds under subsection (5) above to hear and dispose of the case in the absence of the accused, the court shall not permit—
(a) any other statement with respect to any facts relating to the offence charged; or
(b) any other information relating to the accused,
to be made or placed before the court by or on behalf of the prosecutor except on a resumption of the trial after an adjournment under section 10(3) above.
(9) If the court decides not to proceed under subsection (5) above to hear and dispose of the case in the absence of the accused, it shall adjourn or further adjourn the trial for the purpose of dealing with the information as if the notification under subsection (4) above had not been given.
(10) In relation to an adjournment on the occasion of the accused's conviction in his absence under subsection (5) above or to an adjournment required by subsection (9) above, the notice required by section 10(2) above shall include notice of the reason for the adjournment.
(11) No notice shall be required by section 10(2) above in relation to an adjournment—
(a) which is for not more than 4 weeks; and
(b) the purpose of which is to enable the court to proceed under subsection (5) above at a later time.

TRIAL ON THE PAPERS BY A SINGLE JUSTICE

D22.33 The MCA 1980, s. 16A, enables a single justice to try certain cases 'on the papers'. This procedure is limited to cases where a person who has attained the age of 18 is charged with a summary offence that does not carry imprisonment. In such a case, the prosecution may serve on the accused a written charge and requisition and also a single justice procedure notice. If that is done, the single justice procedure will apply unless the accused serves a written notice indicating a desire either to plead not guilty or not to be dealt with under the single justice procedure notice. If the accused fails to respond to the documents which were served, the single justice procedure can still be used even though the accused has not admitted the offence (see s. 16A(1)(d)).

Where s. 16A applies, the court acting under this section may be composed of a single justice (s. 16A(11)). The court tries the case in the absence of the parties; if a party appears, the court must proceed as if that party were absent (s. 16A(7)). If the accused has served on the court written notification stating a desire to plead guilty and to be tried in accordance with s. 16A, the court may try the charge as if the accused had pleaded guilty (s. 16A(8)). The court therefore hears no oral evidence but considers only the documents served on the court by the prosecution and the accused (s. 16A(3)). The court may disregard a written submission if it has not been served within the prescribed period (s 16A(5)). The court is not required to conduct any part of the proceedings in open court (s. 16A(6)). Under s. 16B, if the court decides, before the accused is convicted of the offence, that it is not appropriate to proceed under s. 16A, the case will be adjourned, and a summons will be issued requiring the accused to appear before a magistrates' court for the trial.

Similarly, under s. 16C, if the court decides, after the accused has been convicted of the offence, that it is not appropriate to proceed under s. 16A, the court must adjourn the case and issue a summons requiring the accused to appear before a magistrates' court to be dealt with. Under s. 16C(2), if a magistrates' court which has been proceeding under s. 16A, having convicted the accused, proposes to order disqualification from driving, the court must give the accused the opportunity to make representations about the proposed disqualification; if the accused indicates a wish to make such representations, the court may not continue to proceed under s. 16A (and so must adjourn and issue a summons requiring the attendance of the offender).

Where a case has been adjourned under s. 16B or 16C, the court which hears the case when it resumes will be composed in the usual way (namely, at least two lay justices, as required by the MCA 1980, s. 121(1), or a district judge).

Where the case is being dealt with under s. 16A, the powers of the court as regards sentence are limited by the MCA 1980, s. 121(5A): the court may (for example) discharge the offender (conditionally or absolutely) or impose a fine, and may make a number of ancillary orders (such as compensation and disqualification from driving), but cannot impose a community order or a custodial sentence.

The procedure to be followed is summarised in CrimPR 24.9 (see Supplement, **R24.9**).

THE COURSE OF THE TRIAL

Active Case Management: Applying the Criminal Procedure Rules

D22.34 In *R (Drinkwater) v Solihull Magistrates' Court* [2012] EWHC 765 (Admin), Sir John Thomas P said (at [47]) that it is 'self-evident that proceedings in the magistrates' courts ought to be simple, speedy and summary. That requires close attention to the Criminal Procedure Rules and active case management before *and during* the trial' (emphasis added). His lordship went on to emphasise the importance of setting a timetable (see **D21.40**) and added that, at the commencement of the trial, the court 'should check with the parties that the timetable and the estimates remain valid. If there is any variation which lengthens the estimate, the court should make every effort to see if the trial can still be accommodated that day by sitting late or otherwise' (at [51]). Moreover, once the trial has started, 'the court must actively manage the trial, keeping an eye on progress in relation to the timetable' (at [52]). His lordship noted (at [54]) that if a magistrates' court case cannot be concluded on time, the magistrates may not be available to continue the hearing the following day. The consequential delay is 'plainly inimical to the principles of speedy and summary justice', making it 'essential that the closest attention is paid to timetabling, that the case is actively managed and concluded within the estimate'.

In *R (Hassani) v West London Magistrates' Court* [2017] EWHC 1270 (Admin), the Divisional Court emphasised the importance of complying with the CrimPR. Echoing the words of Auld LJ in *Gleeson* [2003] EWCA Crim 3357, [2004] 1 Cr App R 29 (406) (at [36]), Irwin LJ said (at [9]–[11]):

> The criminal law is not a game to be played in the hope of a lucky outcome . . . [The CrimPR] are there to . . . preclude game playing and ensure that the courts only have to address real issues with some substance . . . Time wasting, extension of hearings and taking hopeless points in the hope of wearing down an opponent or the court are neither proper nor legitimate ways in which to conduct a case . . . Courts must be aware of such behaviour and employ firm case management to prevent it.

Attention is drawn (at [12]) to the effect on the defence of the duty to co-operate in the achievement of the overriding objective:

> If the defence are going to suggest that some document or some piece of service is missing, they must do so early. If they do not, then it is open to the court to find that the point was raised late, and any direction then sought to produce a document or to apply for an adjournment may properly be refused.

His lordship concluded (at [18]) that this judgment was 'an intentional reminder to criminal courts that active case management using the Criminal Procedure Rules is their duty. Increased rigour and firmness is needed.'

The stages of the summary trial itself are set out in CrimPR 24.3. The Coronavirus Act 2020, s. 53 and sch. 23, have made temporary modifications to the CJA 2003, ss. 51 to 56 and sch. 3A, to give the court power to direct live link attendance by certain participants at 'eligible criminal proceedings'. The CJA 2003, sch. 3A, para. 2, permits certain eligible criminal proceedings to be conducted wholly as video proceedings. This includes summary trials, but only where a single justice notice has been served on the accused under the MCA 1980, s. 16A and the parties agree to the proceedings being conducted wholly as video proceedings (see the Special Supplement, **D3.124G**).

Witnesses Waiting to Testify

CrimPR 24.4(2)(a) stipulates that, in the absence of a direction to the contrary, a witness who is waiting to give evidence must (unless either a party to the proceedings or an expert witness) wait outside the courtroom. **D22.35**

In *Carty* [2011] EWCA Crim 2087, Mackay J noted (at [10]) that, while the PACE 1984, s. 78, might operate so as to give the court a discretion to exclude the evidence of a prosecution witness if that witness's earlier presence in court might lead to the creation of an adverse effect on the fairness of the trial, this provision would not apply in the case of a witness called by a co-accused (as had occurred in that case).

Start of the Trial

If a plea was not entered on an earlier occasion, the accused is asked to enter a plea. If the accused entered a not guilty plea on an earlier occasion, he or she will be asked to confirm that plea (CrimPR 24.3(1)). **D22.36**

CrimPD VI, para. 24A.11 (see Supplement, **CPD.24A**), states that, immediately prior to the commencement of the trial, the authorised court officer must summarise for the court the agreed and disputed issues, together with the way in which the parties propose to present their cases. This will usually be based on the contents of the PET form that the parties are required to complete. If it is done by way of a 'pre-court briefing', it should be confirmed in court or agreed with the parties.

THE PROSECUTION CASE

Opening Speech

D22.37 Assuming the accused pleads not guilty, the prosecution representative has the right to make an opening speech (CrimPR 24.3(3)(a)). CrimPD VI, para. 24B.1 (see Supplement, **CPD.24B**), notes that the purpose of the prosecutor's summary of the prosecution case is to explain briefly what the case is about (including any relevant legislation or case law relevant to the particular case) and that it will not usually be necessary, or helpful, to present a detailed account of all the prosecution evidence that will be adduced. In *L and B v DPP* [1998] 2 Cr App R 69, the case had been adjourned for a month after the main prosecution witnesses had given evidence. At the resumed hearing, the justices invited the prosecutor to deliver a second speech in order to remind them of evidence which they were having difficulty remembering. On appeal to the Divisional Court, the appellants contended that the prosecution should not have been allowed to address the justices again. The Divisional Court dismissed the appeal. There was nothing unfair in the prosecutor being asked to remind the court of evidence which had been given, subject to the safeguard that the defence should invariably be asked to address the court in reply, to correct any errors or draw attention to any differences of recollection.

D22.38 CrimPR 24.3(3)(b) states that, in order to help the members of the court to understand the case and resolve any issue in it, the court (immediately after the prosecution opening) may invite the accused 'concisely to identify what is in issue'. CrimPD VI, para. 24B.2, notes that the purpose of this is to provide the court with 'focus as to what it is likely to be called upon to decide', so that the justices will be 'alert to those issues from the outset and can evaluate the prosecution evidence that they hear accordingly'.

D22.39 CrimPD VI, para. 24B.3, makes the point that the justices will, in most cases, already be aware of what has been declared to be in issue (from the PET form and any summary of issues provided at the start of the trial; see **D22.36**). It follows that a party who has nothing of substance to add should say so. Paragraph 24B.4 contains an important warning that, if the accused refuses to identify the issues at the case management stage, 'the court may limit the proceedings on the day of trial' in accordance with CrimPR 3.13(d), which empowers the court to limit the questioning of witnesses and the duration of any stage of the hearing. Moreover, 'any significant divergence from the issues identified at case management at this late stage may well result in the exercise of the court's powers under CrimPR 3.5(6), the powers to impose sanctions'.

Witnesses whom the Prosecution Must Call

D22.40 After the opening speech (if any), the prosecutor must call evidence (CrimPR 24.3(3)(c)). Where a prosecution witness attends court to give evidence in a summary trial, the prosecutor is obliged to call that witness to give evidence if the defence so requests, or at least tender the witness for cross-examination (*Wellingborough Magistrates' Court, ex parte Francois* (1994) 158 JP 813). If, as should happen, the prosecutor serves a bundle of witness statements on the defence prior to summary trial, the prosecution must call as witnesses all the people whose statements have been served, unless any of the exceptions which relate to Crown Court trials are applicable (see **D16.20**). Otherwise, the prosecutor retains an unfettered discretion until the case starts, and the outline of the evidence is given to the court in the opening speech. If the prosecution choose not to call a particular witness, the court cannot compel the prosecutor to call that witness. However, if the court is satisfied that the prosecution are so conducting the case that the accused cannot obtain a fair trial, the court has the power to dismiss the case as an abuse of process. Moreover, in an appropriate case, the justices may call the witness themselves (*Haringey Justices, ex parte DPP* [1996] QB 351, per Stuart-Smith LJ at pp. 359–60); however, it is submitted that it will rarely be appropriate to do so, given the need for the justices to show impartiality in the proceedings.

WRITTEN EVIDENCE AT SUMMARY TRIAL: CRIMINAL JUSTICE ACT 1967, s. 9

A party wishing to tender a written statement as evidence at a summary trial rather than calling the maker of the statement may make use of the provisions of the CJA 1967, s. 9 (see **D22.42**). CrimPR Part 16 (see Supplement, **R16.1** *et seq.*) governs the use of witness statements under the CJA 1967, s. 9. The main points about s. 9 are that: **D22.41**

(a) The statement must (at the beginning) contain the name and (if under 18) the age of the maker (r. 16.2(a)). It must be signed by the maker, and must contain a declaration that it is true to the best of his or her knowledge and belief, and that it is made knowing that, if it is tendered in evidence, the maker might be prosecuted for wilfully stating in it anything he or she knew to be false or did not believe to be true (s. 9(2)(a) and (b); r. 16.2(b) and (d)). In *Wood v DPP* [2010] EWHC 1769 (Admin), Mitting J ruled that the fact that the declaration on the statement referred to two pages, when there were in fact three, did not render the statement inadmissible.

(b) A copy of the statement (together with a copy of any documentary exhibit it refers to) must be served on each of the other parties (s. 9(2)(c); r. 16.4(1)). If, within five business days of service, any of them serves a counter-notice objecting to the statement being put in evidence, it may not be used (s. 9(2)(d) and (2A); r. 16.4(4)). Even where the copy statement was served more than a week before the hearing and no objection to its being read was indicated, the court may, of its own volition or on the application of a party, require the maker of the statement to attend and give oral evidence (s. 9(4)(b)).

(c) Where a statement is admitted in evidence under s. 9, it is either read in full to the court or, at the court's discretion, parts of it may be summarised (s. 9(6); CrimPR 24.5). Rule 24.5(2) requires that, where a written statement is tendered in accordance with s. 9, the court must read the statement, and (unless the court directs otherwise), if any members of the public, or reporters, are present, each relevant part of the statement must be read or summarised aloud.

A s. 9 statement is *not* to be taken conclusively to be true, but is merely 'admissible as evidence to the like extent as oral evidence to the like effect' by the maker would be admissible (s. 9(1)). It follows that if the defence fail to serve a notice objecting to the admissibility of the statement, they are not precluded at trial from adducing evidence inconsistent with it (*Lister v Quaife* [1983] 2 All ER 29). However, if there are differences between the defence case and the contents of a proposed s. 9 statement, then a notice should be served objecting to the statement. In the event of failure to give such notice and defence witnesses then contradicting the statement, the prosecution should ask for an adjournment so that the maker of the statement can be called. The court ought not only to agree to the adjournment but should also consider ordering that the costs thrown away be paid by the defence whatever the eventual outcome of the case (*Lister v Quaife* at pp. 54H–55A). In any event, the prosecution should hesitate before making use of the s. 9 procedure in respect of evidence that is central to their case (per Stephen Brown J, at p. 55E).

(d) CrimPD V, para. 16A.5 (see Supplement, **CPD.16A**), notes that, where statements are to be tendered under s. 9 in the course of summary proceedings and the statement contains evidence which is inadmissible or prejudicial, that evidence should not be excised by means of striking out or bracketing (a method that would otherwise be permissible) and so there will be a need to prepare fresh statements excluding any inadmissible or prejudicial material.

D22.42 **Criminal Justice Act 1967, s. 9**

(1) In any criminal proceedings a written statement by any person shall, if such of the conditions mentioned in the next following subsection as are applicable are satisfied, be admissible as evidence to the like extent as oral evidence to the like effect by that person.

(2) The said conditions are—

(a) the statement purports to be signed by the person who made it;

(b) the statement contains a declaration by that person to the effect that it is true to the best of his knowledge and belief and that he made the statement knowing that, if it were tendered in evidence, he would be liable to prosecution if he wilfully stated in it anything which he knew to be false or did not believe to be true;

(c) before the hearing at which the statement is tendered in evidence, a copy of the statement is served, by or on behalf of the party proposing to tender it, on each of the other parties to the proceedings; and

(d) none of the other parties or their solicitors, within the relevant period, serves a notice on the party so proposing objecting to the statement being tendered in evidence under this section:

Provided that the conditions mentioned in paragraphs (c) and (d) of this subsection shall not apply if the parties agree before or during the hearing that the statement shall be so tendered.

(2A) For the purposes of subsection (2)(d), 'the relevant period' is—

(a) such number of days, which may not be less than seven, from the service of the copy of the statement as may be prescribed by Criminal Procedure Rules, or

(b) if no such number is prescribed, seven days from the service of the copy of the statement.

...

(4) Notwithstanding that a written statement made by any person may be admissible as evidence by virtue of this section—

(a) the party by whom or on whose behalf a copy of the statement was served may call that person to give evidence; and

(b) the court may, of its own motion or on the application of any party to the proceedings, require that person to attend before the court and give evidence.

[(5) and (5A) Applications before trial under subsection (4)(b) above to courts other than a magistrates' court.]

...

(7) Any document or object referred to as an exhibit and identified in a written statement tendered in evidence under this section shall be treated as if it had been produced as an exhibit and identified in court by the maker of the statement.

Formal Admissions

D22.43 Where a party introduces into evidence a fact admitted by another party or the parties jointly admit a fact (e.g., where a formal admission is made — usually by the accused — under the CJA 1967, s. 10 (see **F1.2**)), a written record must, unless the court otherwise directs, be made of the admission (CrimPR 24.6).

OBJECTIONS TO PROSECUTION EVIDENCE

D22.44 The procedure to be followed where the defence object, during the course of a summary trial, to proposed prosecution evidence (or have some other preliminary point of law to argue before the magistrates) raises the difficulty that the magistrates are the judges of both fact and law. Especially if the issue is one of admissibility of evidence, there is a danger that the magistrates will learn the nature of the evidence in the course of hearing arguments about its admissibility. Should they then rule it inadmissible, they may have difficulty in ignoring it when reaching a verdict. This problem is mitigated to some extent by the availability of pre-trial rulings (see **D21.35**) but these will not avail where issues of admissibility are raised for the first time during the course of trial itself.

The stage of the trial at which the magistrates rule upon a question of admissibility of evidence (or other incidental issue) is a matter for their discretion (*F v Chief Constable of Kent* [1982] Crim LR 682). However, delaying the determination of a question of admissibility of a confession until after the conclusion of the prosecution evidence may be unfair to the defence, in that the accused will not be able to give evidence about alleged irregularities in the obtaining of the confession unless he or she testifies (thus becoming exposed to cross-examination about the general issues). Moreover, in taking the decision what evidence to call, the defence advocate ought to know whether crucial evidence, such as a confession, is to be part of the case against the accused. These special considerations were recognised by Lord Lane in the following passage from his judgment in *F v Chief Constable of Kent* (quoted in *Epping and Ongar Justices, ex parte Manby* [1986] Crim LR 555 and *A v DPP* (2000) 164 JP 317, at [4]), where the admissibility of a confession was at issue:

> It is impossible to lay down any general rule as to when magistrates should announce their decision on this type of point, and indeed when the point itself should be taken. Every case will be different. Some sort of preliminary point, for instance with regard to the admissibility of a document or something like that, can plainly, with the assistance of the clerk, be decided straight away. Other points... may require a decision at a later stage of the case, possibly after further argument. It may be that in some cases the defendant will be entitled to know what the decision of the justices with regard to the admissibility of a confession is at the close of the prosecution case in order to enable him to know what proper course he should take with regard to giving evidence and calling evidence and so on.

It is submitted that, where a confession is the main evidence against the accused, so that without **D22.45**
it there might not be a case to answer, the interests of justice dictate that admissibility should be determined as a preliminary issue. In *ADC v Chief Constable of Greater Manchester* (14 March 1983 unreported, DC), quoted in *Halawa v Federation against Copyright Theft* [1995] 1 Cr App R 21 at p. 27, Goff LJ said:

> The proper approach of magistrates is to proceed in accordance with the justice of the case. I recognise that in very many cases it would indeed be proper for magistrates to deal with the issue of admissibility of a confession before the close of the prosecution case. To give a very simple and perhaps extreme example, if the only evidence before magistrates is the evidence of a confession and nothing else, then as a matter of common justice, the magistrates ought to deal with the issue of the admissibility of that confession as a preliminary point, before the close of the prosecution case, so that the defendant can then decide whether to make a submission of no case to answer.

Police and Criminal Evidence Act 1984, s. 78

Whereas under the PACE 1984, s. 76 (see **D22.47**), the court is obliged to hear evidence **D22.46**
about the obtaining of the confession (as the prosecution have to *prove* that the confession was not obtained in the manner forbidden by s. 76), where the admissibility of prosecution evidence falls to be considered under the general exclusionary power in s. 78, the court has a discretion to hear evidence on the issue of admissibility but is not obliged to do so (and so may rule on the matter following submissions on behalf of the parties). It remains a matter for the justices' discretion when they determine admissibility. In *Vel v Chief Constable of North Wales* (1987) 151 JP 510, Lloyd LJ said that, in some cases, the justices should deal with an application to exclude evidence when it arises, but in other cases they may leave the decision until the end of the hearing. Nonetheless, his lordship said that it was impossible to lay down any general rule, other than that 'the object should always be to secure a trial which is fair and just to both sides'. In *Halawa v Federation Against Copyright Theft* [1995] 1 Cr App R 21, the Divisional Court said that, in most cases, it is generally better for the magistrates to hear all the prosecution evidence (including the disputed evidence) before considering an application to exclude evidence under s. 78 (per Gibson LJ at p. 34). This does of course leave the justices with the very difficult (some might say impossible) task

of putting from their minds prejudicial evidence that they have heard but then decide is inadmissible.

Police and Criminal Evidence Act 1984, s. 76

D22.47 Where the defence object to the admissibility of a confession on the basis of the PACE 1984, s. 76, the terms of s. 76 require that the court shall not admit the confession unless satisfied that it was not obtained by oppression or by words or conduct likely to render a confession unreliable. It follows that magistrates (just like the Crown Court) are obliged to hear evidence on the obtaining of the confession. In *Liverpool Juvenile Court, ex parte R* [1988] QB 1 at pp. 10–11, Russell LJ summarised the position regarding s. 76 as follows:

> 1. The effect of section 76(2) of the Police and Criminal Evidence Act 1984 is that in summary proceedings justices must now hold a trial within a trial if it is represented to them by the defence that a confession was or may have been obtained by either of the improper processes appearing in subparagraphs (a) or (b) of section 76(2).
> 2. In such a trial within a trial the defendant may give evidence confined to the question of admissibility and the justices will not be concerned with the truth or otherwise of the confession.
> 3. In consequence of paragraphs 1 and 2 above, the defendant is entitled to a ruling upon admissibility of a confession before, or at, the end of the prosecution case.
> 4. There remains a discretion open to the defendant as to the stage at which an attack is to be made upon an alleged confession. A trial within a trial will only take place before the close of the prosecution case if it is represented to the court that the confession was, or may have been, obtained by one or other of the processes set out in subparagraphs (a) or (b) of section 76(2). If no such representation is made the defendant is at liberty to raise admissibility or weight of the confession at any subsequent stage of the trial. For the avoidance of doubt, I consider that 'representation' is not the same as, nor does it include, cross-examination. Thus the court is not required to embark upon, nor is the defence bound to proceed upon, a *voir dire* merely because of a suggestion in cross-examination that the alleged confession was obtained improperly.
> 5. It should never be necessary to call the prosecution evidence relating to the obtaining of a confession twice.

It should be noted that the fourth proposition would seem to be at odds with the case law on challenging confessions at trials on indictment (see **D16.47** and **F18.63** and especially *Sat-Bhambra* (1988) 88 Cr App R 55, where it was held that an application to exclude evidence should be made before that evidence has been adduced).

Best Practice

D22.48 Given that magistrates are triers of both law and fact, it is submitted that the best practice is to consider questions of admissibility *before* the evidence in question is adduced. That way, the magistrates will be aware of the nature of the disputed evidence, but not its precise content, unless they rule it admissible. This approach is the one that is most consistent with achieving a fair trial, as it does not require the magistrates to try to put from their minds evidence that they have heard prior to ruling that evidence inadmissible, if such be the case. If magistrates hear evidence and then, having heard it, rule it inadmissible, there remains a perception of a risk that the magistrates may, perhaps unconsciously, allow their ultimate decision to be influenced by that evidence despite ruling it inadmissible.

'Dock Identifications'

D22.49 One particular element of some prosecution cases is the use of the so-called 'dock identification' (see **F6.38** and **F19.6**). Where the identity of the accused as the person who committed the offence is in issue, asking a witness who has not previously identified the accused at an identification parade or video identification procedure 'do you see the person who committed the offence in court today?' is undesirable. This is because the safeguards built into the out-of-court identification procedures are not available when the witness is asked to identify the accused in the dock during the trial, and because the accused is at a great disadvantage — the eyes of the witness are bound to go to the person sitting in the dock. Whether a dock identification should be admitted in the exercise of discretion is for the justices to decide (*North Yorkshire Trading Standards Department v Williams* (1995) 159 JP 383; *Barnes v DPP* [1997] 2 Cr App R 505).

In *Karia v DPP* [2002] EWHC 2175 (Admin), D appealed against conviction for a number of motoring offences on the ground that the magistrates should not have allowed the police officer who had stopped the vehicle to make a 'dock identification' of him, and that an identification parade should have been held. He argued that the decision in *Barnes v DPP* permitting dock identifications in such cases was incompatible with the HRA 1998. Stanley Burnton J said (at [29]) that the aim of a dock identification in such cases is usually to avoid an unmeritorious dismissal of a prosecution case resulting from a failure to make a purely formal identification of the accused. Moreover, in *Karia*, D had not notified the prosecution that identity was in issue, and so the dock identification was not unfair because there was no basis on which the police could have considered that it would be useful to hold an identification procedure (at [33]). As far as the human rights point was concerned, his lordship said (at [40]) that a requirement that the issues should be made known to the court before or during the proceedings cannot infringe the ECHR, Article 6; moreover, a requirement that an accused should indicate before or at the trial what are the issues in the trial does not infringe the right to silence. On this basis, it would appear that dock identifications are to be ruled out only where the accused has already indicated that identity is in issue in the case. In *Holland v HM Advocate* [2005] UKPC D 1, [2005] HRLR 25, the Privy Council confirmed that there is no basis, except perhaps in an extreme case, for regarding dock identifications as inadmissible *per se*.

'SPECIAL MEASURES' DIRECTIONS

D22.50 The court has power to make arrangements for vulnerable witnesses and accused both under its inherent jurisdiction and under the YJCEA 1999. These powers include powers to protect witness anonymity and are dealt with fully at **D14**.

The special measures available under the YJCEA 1999, s. 19, which are those most commonly used in the magistrates' court, include:

(a) screening the witness from the accused (s. 23);
(b) giving evidence by live link (s. 24), although the significance of this provision is reduced by the CJA 2003, s. 51, which enables a court to permit witnesses, other than the accused, to give evidence through a live link in criminal proceedings, and by the YJCEA 1999, s. 33A, which enables the accused to testify via a 'live link' in prescribed circumstances;
(c) giving evidence in private, in a sexual case or where there are reasonable grounds for believing that someone other than the accused has sought, or will seek, to intimidate the witness (s. 25);
(d) video recording of evidence-in-chief (s. 27);
(e) video recording of cross-examination and re-examination where the evidence-in-chief of the witness has been video recorded (s. 28);
(f) examination through an intermediary (s. 29);
(g) provision of aids to communication to enable the witness to testify despite any disability, disorder or other impairment (s. 30).

The procedure for making (and opposing) applications for special measures directions is set out in CrimPR Part 18 (see Supplement, **R18.1** *et seq.*).

Position of Justices Following Application

D22.51 Justices who have ruled on an application for special measures are not disqualified from hearing the case against the accused. In *KL and LK v DPP* [2001] EWHC Admin 1112, the prosecution made an application for the use of screens in relation to a prosecution witness, on the grounds that she would feel intimidated having to give evidence in D's presence and had been intimidated. The question to be decided was whether the justices should withdraw from the case after hearing the application. Richards J said (at [13]) that:

> ... there can be no objection in principle to justices continuing to hear a case after listening to and ruling on an application for the witness to be screened from a defendant. The fact that evidence or submissions adverse to the defendant are advanced in support of such an application does not necessarily prevent fair-minded consideration of the case after the application has been determined, whether it has been allowed or refused.

It is submitted that the same approach should be taken with regard to any other applications for special measures.

SUBMISSION OF NO CASE TO ANSWER

D22.52 Under CrimPR 24.3(3)(d) (see Supplement, **R24.3**) the magistrates may acquit the accused on the ground that the prosecution evidence is insufficient for any reasonable court properly to convict. They may do so following an application by the defence or on their own initiative but, in either case, the prosecutor must be given an opportunity to make representations. Thus, at the close of the prosecution evidence, the defence may submit that there is no case to answer (see **D16.53** for the position in trial on indictment).

Rule 24.3(3)(d) sets out the basis for the decision, namely that no reasonable court could properly convict. Thus, the decision depends not on whether the justices *would* at that stage convict or acquit but on whether the evidence is such that a reasonable tribunal *might* convict. If a reasonable tribunal might convict on the evidence so far laid before it, there is a case to answer. The submission should therefore succeed if a conviction would be perverse, in the sense that no reasonable bench could convict.

In *DPP v LB* [2019] EWHC 825 (Admin), the Divisional Court emphasised the importance of the prosecutor's right to make representations if a submission of no case to answer is made.

There is no obligation on justices to give reasons for rejecting a submission of no case to answer (*Moran v DPP* [2002] EWHC 89 (Admin), per Maurice Kay LJ at [16]).

Credibility of Prosecution Witnesses

D22.53 An important issue is the extent to which justices may have regard to the credibility of prosecution witnesses when considering a submission of no case to answer. In the Crown Court, the test to be applied by the judge when ruling on a submission of no case (set out in *Galbraith* [1981] 2 All ER 1060) is whether the prosecution evidence is so tenuous that, even taken at its highest, a jury properly directed could not properly convict on it. The requirement that the Crown Court judge should 'take the prosecution evidence at its highest' is intended to leave questions of credibility to the jury. In *Barking and Dagenham Justices, ex parte DPP* (1995) 159 JP 373, the Divisional Court said that questions of credibility should, except in the clearest of cases, not normally be taken into account by justices considering a submission of no case. Nonetheless, it is submitted that some justices may well take the pragmatic view that it would be inappropriate for them to go through the motions of hearing defence evidence if they have already formed the view that the prosecution evidence is so unconvincing that they will not be able to convict on it in any event. However, the general principle remains that, so long as the necessary minimum amount of prosecution evidence has been adduced so as to raise a case on which a reasonable tribunal *could* convict, the justices should allow the trial to run its course rather than acquitting on a submission.

Prosecution Right of Reply

When the justices are provisionally minded to uphold the submission of no case to answer, they should first call on the prosecution to address them (*Barking and Dagenham Justices, ex parte DPP* (1995) 159 JP 373), so that the prosecutor has an opportunity to address the court to show why the case should not be dismissed. This means that the prosecution have the right to reply to the defence submission that there is no case to answer unless, having heard the defence submission, the magistrates decide to rule that there is a case to answer and indicate this fact to the prosecutor. The importance of the prosecutor's right of reply was emphasised in *DPP v LB* [2019] EWHC 825 (Admin). **D22.54**

Reopening the Case following a Submission

In some cases, the deficiency in the prosecution case which is highlighted by the defence submission of no case to answer may be cured by allowing the prosecution to reopen their case, rather than upholding the submission of no case to answer and acquitting the accused. In *Hughes v DPP* [2003] EWHC 2470 (Admin), Stanley Burnton J said (at [16]) that when, on a submission of no case to answer, a point is raised which has no bearing on the merits of the prosecution, and the defect in the prosecution case is one of omission (and probably oversight), the magistrates should normally exercise their discretion to permit the prosecution to reopen their case so that such evidence can be given, particularly where the fact in question is likely to be uncontroversial. Indeed, if necessary, the magistrates should consider inviting the prosecution to recall the relevant witness. It is submitted that it may well be appropriate for the justices to allow the prosecution to reopen their case, and thus adduce evidence that was inadvertently omitted, even if the missing evidence has a more direct bearing on the merits of the prosecution case. If the defect in the prosecution case is one that could be cured simply and speedily by allowing them to reopen their case and recall a witness, it may well be that the interests of justice require that the prosecution be given the chance to remedy the defect. It is difficult to see how the defendant would be prejudiced by this decision. However, if the reopening of the prosecution case would require an adjournment, and thus cause delay in the disposal of the case, the balance of the interests of justice might require that the submission be upheld and the defendant acquitted. **D22.55**

In *Tuck v Vehicle Inspectorate* [2004] EWHC 728 (QB), the Divisional Court considered another case in which magistrates had permitted the prosecution to repair omissions in their evidence after they had closed their case, following a submission of no case to answer. MacKay J, in a judgment with which Kennedy LJ agreed, summarised the principles applicable as follows (at [15]):

> (1) The discretion to allow the case to be reopened is not limited to matters arising [unexpectedly] or mere technicalities, but is a more general discretion.
> (2) The exercise of this discretion should not be interfered with by a higher court unless its exercise was wrong in principle or perverse.
> (3) The general rule remains that the prosecution must finish its case once and for all and the test to be applied is narrower than consideration of whether the additional evidence would be of value to the tribunal. The discretion will only be exercised on the rarest of occasions.
> (4) The discretion must be exercised carefully having regard to the need to be fair to the defence, and giving consideration to the question of whether any prejudice will be caused.
> (5) The courts have in the past differed as to whether the mere loss of a tactical advantage can constitute such prejudice.
> (6) Criminal procedure while adversarial is not a game, and the overall interests of justice include giving effect to the requirement that a prosecution should not fail through inefficiency, carelessness or oversight.
> (7) Of particular significance is the consideration of whether there is any risk of prejudice to the accused.

D22.56 In *Smith v DPP* [2008] EWHC 771 (Admin), following a submission of no case to answer, a district judge permitted the prosecution to recall their main witness. Dyson LJ (at [5]) said that: 'Prosecuting authorities should not be encouraged to believe that they can reopen a case to adduce evidence which was available to them but which they did not adduce before a case was closed. Sloppiness would result if it were thought that omissions could routinely be made good by the Crown at a later stage in the proceedings. On the other hand, the interests of the defendant must be balanced against the public interest in ensuring that those who have committed crimes should be convicted.' In the instant case, the judge's decision to allow the Crown to reopen their case was not a 'plainly wrong' exercise of his discretion. The witness in question had already given evidence that the person who committed the offence was D, and the judge was entitled to permit the prosecution to strengthen their case by allowing the witness to give evidence to meet a point made in the course of the submission of no case to answer.

R (Payne) v South Lakeland Magistrates' Court [2011] EWHC 1802 (Admin) provides another example of a case where the prosecution were permitted to reopen their case. D was charged with driving a motor vehicle on a road at a speed in excess of the speed limit but, through an oversight on the part of the prosecution, no evidence of the speed of the vehicle was adduced. The magistrates adjourned the hearing to enable the prosecutor to cure this deficiency in the prosecution evidence. On appeal, Pitchford LJ said (at [38]–[40]) that no prejudice would be caused to D by such an adjournment 'because he had not attended trial and had no intention of giving evidence, and accordingly of contesting the matter on the merits'. Moreover, '[i]t is not in the public interest that cases should be decided upon the vagaries of forensic mistakes made by lawyers, provided no prejudice is done by delay or for other specific reasons'.

D22.57 **Ambushes Not Permitted** From the perspective of professional conduct and ethics, it is also noteworthy that, in his judgment in *Hughes v DPP* [2003] EWHC 2470 (Admin) (see **D22.55**), Stanley Burnton J said (at [16]) (echoing comments made by Auld LJ in *Gleeson* [2003] EWCA Crim 3357, [2004] 1 Cr App R 29 (406)) that: 'Ambushes of the kind attempted in this case are to be discouraged and discountenanced. Criminal proceedings are not a game: their object is to achieve a fair determination of the innocence or guilt of the defendant.' A similar point was made in *R (DPP) v Chorley Magistrates' Court* [2006] EWHC 1795 (Admin), where Thomas LJ gave a warning (at [26]) that the defence must raise issues as early as possible in the case:

> If a defendant refuses to identify what the issues are, one thing is clear: he can derive no advantage from that or seek . . . to attempt an ambush at trial. The days of ambushing and taking last-minute technical points are gone. They are not consistent with the overriding objective of deciding cases justly, acquitting the innocent and convicting the guilty.

In *R (CPS) v Norwich Magistrates' Court* [2011] EWHC 82 (Admin), the prosecution opened the case (a charge of assault) by stating that identification was not in dispute (the section of the case management form completed by the defence raised the issue of self-defence). At the close of the prosecution case, the defence made a submission of no case to answer based on the lack of adequate identification. The prosecution sought to call additional evidence, but the magistrates refused to allow this. The Divisional Court said that the decision of the magistrates was wrong. Richards LJ said (at [22]):

> . . . if the defence was going to take a positive point on identification, it was incumbent on it to flag the point at an early stage, not to wait until the close of the prosecution case before raising it for the first time in a submission of no case. It should have been expressed during the case management process and included in terms in the trial information form. That is all the more obvious in the environment in which the parties now operate by reference to the Criminal Procedure Rules and *the overriding objective.* Even if there had been an omission to deal with it at that earlier stage, it ought to have been raised very clearly when the prosecuting advocate opened the case by telling the magistrates that there was no issue over identification. It was not appropriate, as it seems to me, simply to sit tight and to raise it at the end of the prosecution case by way of a submission of no case.

His lordship concluded, at [25], that 'the decision to refuse the prosecution application to re-open ran counter to the overriding objective..., was plainly contrary to the interests of justice and lacked any reasonable basis'.

Reconsidering the Decision In *Steward v DPP* [2003] EWHC 2251 (Admin), [2004] 1 WLR 592, the justices acceded to a submission of no case to answer. The prosecutor then pointed out that the reasons given by the magistrates contained an error of fact. The justices reviewed their decision, and concluded that there was a case to answer. D, who was subsequently convicted, appealed by way of case stated on the basis that the justices had been acting *functus officio* by proceeding to hear the case after reaching a finding of no case to answer. The Divisional Court held that the justices were entitled to reopen a case, despite having acceded to a submission of no case to answer, where an error in the reasons has been identified by the prosecution and the accused agrees that there was an error. In those circumstances, the process of adjudication has not been completed and the justices are not *functus officio*. The case was said to be distinguishable from *Essex Justices, ex parte Final* [1963] 2 QB 816 (where it was held that justices should not reopen a case once they have reached their decision), as that case had been reopened in order to hear further submissions on the evidence, whereas in the present case the error was identified immediately, and the justices admitted it and rectified it; also, the earlier case was decided at a time when it was less common for justices to give reasons for accepting a submission of no case to answer, and so errors in their reasoning were less likely to be immediately apparent (per Maurice Kay J at [10] and [11]). **D22.58**

DEFENCE CASE AND SPEECHES

If a submission of no case to answer is not made, or is unsuccessful, the defence then have the opportunity to present evidence to the court. CrimPR 24.3 (see Supplement, **R24.3**) makes no reference to an opening speech by the defence, and established practice is that the defence have no right to make an opening speech prior to calling their evidence in a summary trial, although it should be borne in mind that, after the prosecutor's opening speech, the court may, under r. 24.3(3)(b), invite the accused concisely to identify what is in issue', in order to help the members of the court to understand the case. **D22.59**

After the close of the prosecution case (and after any submission of no case to answer has been rejected), the accused may introduce evidence (r. 24.3(3)(f)).

The CJPOA 1994, s. 35(2) (and CrimPR 24.3(3)(e)), require the court to explain that the accused is entitled to give evidence and to point out the potential effect, namely adverse inferences being drawn, under s. 35 (see **F20.42**), if the accused does not testify or refuses to answer any questions while testifying. In *Radford v Kent County Council* (1998) 162 JP 697, however, the magistrates failed to warn D that adverse inferences could be drawn if he failed to testify. Nonetheless, in their stated case, the justices said that 'we drew no inferences whatsoever from the failure of the appellant to give evidence, but simply were aware that the evidence for the prosecution was not rebutted by evidence from or on behalf of the appellant'. The Divisional Court held that, although the warning of the consequences of not testifying is very important, the failure to give the warning in the particular case did not render D's conviction unsafe.

It should be also be borne in mind that the restrictions on an accused cross-examining witnesses in cases involving alleged sexual offences (YJCEA 1999, ss. 34 to 39) apply equally in magistrates' courts. The procedural aspects are contained in CrimPR Part 23 (see Supplement, **R23.1** *et seq.*). See **D17.19**. **D22.60**

If the accused is going to call other witnesses, the accused should give evidence first unless the court otherwise directs (PACE 1984, s. 79).

Evidence in Rebuttal

D22.61 CrimPR 24.3(3)(g) provides that, after any evidence called by the defence, 'a party may introduce further evidence if it is then admissible', for example to rebut evidence that has already been adduced. Although this provision refers to 'a party', it is submitted that it is generally the prosecution who will seek to adduce rebuttal evidence (bearing in mind that the defence will have adduced any evidence on which they wish to rely after the close of the prosecution case).

Rebuttal evidence may be appropriate if something has arisen *ex improviso* (i.e. something that could not reasonably have been foreseen) during the course of the defence case (see **F6.4**), or where the evidence which the prosecution seek to adduce is intended to remedy a technical deficiency in their case. In those circumstances, the justices may allow the prosecution case to be reopened (*Price v Humphries* [1958] 2 QB 353; *Hammond v Wilkinson* (2001) 165 JP 786). However, the power to allow the prosecution to reopen their case can go beyond such technical difficulties. For example, in *James v South Glamorgan County Council* (1994) 99 Cr App R 321, the main prosecution witness had not arrived but the trial proceeded nonetheless; after the prosecution case had been closed and while the defendant was giving evidence, the witness arrived. It was accepted by the magistrates that the witness had a good reason for being late and the prosecution were allowed to call him as a witness. It was held by the Divisional Court that, since the evidence had not been available at the proper time and there was no unfairness to D (not least because there was no suggestion that D's case would have been differently conducted had the evidence of the witness been given when it ought to have been), the decision of the magistrates was correct.

D22.62 Similarly, in *Khatibi v DPP* [2004] EWHC 83 (Admin), Nelson J said (at [17]) that the discretion to admit evidence after the close of the prosecution case is not confined to the well-established exceptions of rebuttal and mere formality. The discretion must, however, be exercised with great caution. The magistrates should bear in mind the strictly adversarial nature of the English criminal process, whereby the cases for the prosecution and the defence are presented consecutively in their entirety. The normal order of events should not be departed from substantially unless justice really demands such a course of action. His lordship added (at [18]) that, in deciding whether to exercise their discretion to permit the calling of evidence after the close of the prosecution case, the magistrates must look carefully at the interests of justice overall, and in particular the risk of any prejudice to the defendant.

Another example is *R (Lawson) v Stafford Magistrates' Court* [2007] EWHC 2490 (Admin), where D was charged with driving in excess of the speed limit. During his closing submissions, defence counsel raised for the first time the issues that the prosecution had to satisfy the court that the signs indicating the limit complied with the relevant regulations and that the speed measuring device should be tested. The justices invited the prosecution to apply for the case to be adjourned part-heard so that these evidential issues could be addressed. The defence contended that the justices erred in encouraging an adjournment. The Divisional Court held that D had sought to ambush the prosecution and the magistrates were entitled to adjourn the case to receive further evidence. Aikens J (at [32]) pointed out that, in a pre-trial hearing before magistrates, an accused or the accused's lawyer should be specifically asked what issues are being taken by the defence. His lordship went on to say (at [34]) that 'magistrates have a jurisdiction to adjourn a trial to permit the prosecution to rectify a deficiency in evidence which is only identified by the defence at a very late stage, after the close of the prosecution case'. His lordship explained (at [39]) that:

> [T]he courts' power to allow a case to be re-opened is a power which must be exercised rarely and having regard to the need to be fair to the defendant. A court must bear in mind the question of whether any prejudice to the defendant will be caused by a case being re-opened. However those points do not detract from the legal proposition that justices are entitled to hear evidence after the case has been closed where special circumstances exist.

Closing Speeches

CrimPR 24.3(3)(h) provides that (after the defence have adduced any evidence they wish and after any rebuttal evidence), the prosecutor 'may make final representations in support of the prosecution case' (i.e. a closing speech) if the accused is represented or (whether represented or not) the accused has called evidence other than his or her own testimony. Under r. 24.3(3)(i), the accused may then 'make final representations in support of the defence case' (in other words, make a closing speech). Thus, if any prosecution representations are made, the accused is given the chance to reply, and so will always have the last word before the magistrates consider their verdict. **D22.63**

Rule 24.3(4), makes it clear that, if a party wishes to introduce evidence or make representations after the specified opportunity to do so under r. 24.3(3), the court is entitled to refuse to receive any such evidence or representations. It is submitted that the court should refuse to receive additional evidence or representations save in the most exceptional circumstances.

Rebuttal Evidence after Magistrates Have Retired to Consider Verdict In *Khatibi* [2004] EWHC 83 (Admin), Nelson J pointed out (at [20]) that it has 'generally been accepted that an application to call further evidence cannot succeed after the bench has retired to consider its verdict'. It is therefore only in the rarest of cases that further evidence may be adduced once the justices have retired to consider their verdict. In *Webb v Leadbetter* [1966] 2 All ER 114, one of two prosecution witnesses failed to arrive. The one available witness was called. The prosecution case closed. D gave evidence and his case closed. The justices had retired to consider their decision when they were informed that the second prosecution witness, whose car had broken down, had arrived. They returned to court and allowed the prosecution to call him. His evidence corroborated that of the first prosecution witness. D was convicted. The Divisional Court held that, although justices have a discretion to allow further evidence to be called in particular circumstances, the manner of the exercise of that discretion depends on the stage of the case. In the absence of 'special circumstances' (per Lord Parker CJ) or even 'very special circumstances' (per Winn LJ), they should not allow evidence to be called after they have retired. In the instant case, such circumstances were absent and so the further evidence had been wrongly admitted. **D22.64**

This decision was followed in *R (Traves) v DPP* [2005] EWHC 1482 (Admin), where D was charged with driving whilst disqualified. At the trial, the prosecution failed to produce the memorandum of conviction which was necessary in order to prove that D had been disqualified. The defence made a submission of no case to answer. The justices retired to consider their decision but, before they returned to court to announce their decision, they were informed that the prosecution now had the evidence that had been lacking. The prosecution sought, and were granted, leave to reopen their case. The prosecution produced evidence of the disqualification and the defendant was convicted. The Divisional Court held that the moment of retiring to consider the decision is a critical point, after which only very special circumstances could allow further evidence to be called. In the instant case, there existed no such very special circumstances and so the conviction was quashed.

However, in *Malcolm v DPP* [2007] EWHC 363 (Admin), [2007] 1 WLR 1230, the Divisional Court took a broader of view of what would amount to 'special circumstances', enabling the case to be reopened even after the justices had retired to consider their verdict. D had been charged with driving with excess alcohol. In her closing speech, defence counsel submitted that there had been no warning, as required by the RTA 1988, s. 7(7), that a failure to provide a specimen might render D liable to prosecution and that, accordingly, there was no admissible evidence of the analysis of alcohol in her breath. The magistrates retired to consider the submissions. They returned to court and gave their conclusions that the case would have to be dismissed because of **D22.65** the lack of admissible evidence of the proportion of alcohol in the appellant's breath. Before they formally dismissed the case, however, counsel for the prosecution requested, and was granted, leave to recall the officer in charge of the breath test procedure. The Divisional Court reiterated the test established by *Webb v Leadbetter*, that special circumstances are required before they can receive further evidence after they have retired to consider their verdict. However, Stanley Burnton J, with whom Maurice Kay LJ agreed, said (at [31]):

> [Counsel for the appellant's] submissions, which emphasised the obligation of the prosecution to prove its case in its entirety before closing its case, and certainly before the end of the final speech for the defence, had an anachronistic, and obsolete, ring. Criminal trials are no longer to be treated as a game, in which each move is final and any omission by the prosecution leads to its failure. It is the duty of the defence to make its defence and the issues it raises clear to the prosecution and to the court at an early stage... Even in a relatively straightforward trial such as the present, in the magistrates' court (where there is not yet any requirement of a defence statement or a pre-trial review), it is the duty of the defence to make the real issues clear at the latest before the prosecution closes its case. In *Pydar Justices, ex parte Foster* [1995] 160 JP 87 at 90B Curtis J. commented on the submission that a defending advocate was entitled to 'keep his powder dry'. He said:
>
> Without any doubt whatsoever, it is the duty of a defending advocate properly to lay the ground for a submission, either by cross examination or, if appropriate, by calling evidence.
>
> That was not done in this case.

The court concluded that there were, therefore, special circumstances entitling the magistrates to allow the case to be reopened. Moreover, Stanley Burnton J added (at [39]) that, 'I respectfully disagree with the decision of Bean J in *Traves*. In my judgment it was wrongly decided.' His lordship appears to be saying that Bean J should have decided that the facts in that case did, in fact, disclose 'special circumstances'.

CrimPR 24.3(4)(b) makes it clear that the court must not receive additional evidence or representations after it has announced its verdict, thus preserving the principle of finality.

SEEING THE MAGISTRATES IN PRIVATE

D22.66 The bench has an inherent discretion to hear representations in private during the course of a trial (*Nottingham Magistrates' Court, ex parte Furnell* (1996) 160 JP 201). However, given the magistrates' role as fact finders, that discretion must be exercised with even greater caution than in the case of Crown Court trial. In any event, all parties should be made aware of what is happening and be represented (except where there is an issue of public interest immunity to be heard on an *ex parte* basis) and a contemporaneous note should be taken.

DECISION ON THE ISSUE OF GUILT

Manner of Arriving at and Announcing Decision

D22.67 **Adverse Inferences** The adverse inference provisions of the CPIA 1996, s. 11 (see **D9.47**), apply to summary trials. An adverse inference may be drawn if the accused decides to serve a defence statement (which, in magistrates' court proceedings, is voluntary, under s. 6) but does so late, or (for example) presents at trial a case that is inconsistent with the case set out in the defence statement, or relies on a matter that was not disclosed in the defence statement. Similarly, the adverse inference provisions contained in the CJPO 1994, s. 34 (see **F20.4**), apply to summary trials where the accused failed to mention when questioned matters on which the defence subsequently relies. In *T v DPP* [2007] EWHC 1793 (Admin), the Divisional Court summarised the approach to be taken in a case where a magistrates' court is considering whether to draw adverse inferences in such a case. The justices should ask themselves three questions (per Hughes LJ at [26]):

(1) Has the defendant relied in his defence on a fact which he could reasonably have been expected to mention in his interview, but did not? If so, what is it?
(2) What is his explanation for not having mentioned it?
(3) If that explanation is not a reasonable one, is the proper inference to be drawn that he is guilty?

Use of Personal Knowledge In reaching their decision on questions of fact, it is open to magistrates to use their personal local knowledge. However, they should inform the prosecution and the defence that they are doing so, so that those representing the parties have the opportunity of commenting upon the knowledge which the magistrates claim to have (*Bowman v DPP* [1991] RTR 263; *Norbrook Laboratories (GB) Ltd v Health and Safety Executive* [1998] EHLR 207). In *Gibbons v DPP* (12 December 2000 unreported), the appellants were charged with assault. They said they had been acting in self-defence. An eye-witness gave evidence that the appellants were responsible. After the closing speeches had been made, the district judge had cause to visit the place where the alleged offence had occurred. While there, he checked the site of the assault, the distance the witness was located from the attack and whether her view would have been obstructed. The Divisional Court held that the matters checked were all critical issues at the trial. At the very least, the district judge should have informed the parties of his intention of taking a view, so that they could have had the opportunity to make submissions as to where the witness had actually been located. It followed that there had been a defect in the trial process; the convictions were quashed and a retrial ordered. **D22.68**

Connected with this is the possibility of the justices visiting the scene of the crime as part of the trial process. In *M v DPP* [2009] EWHC 752 (Admin), [2009] 2 Cr App R 12 (181), it was said (per Leveson LJ at [31]) to be critical that, before a court embarks on a 'view', it is determined with absolute clarity what will happen on the view, who should stand where, what objects (if any) should be placed where, and who should do what.

Majority Decisions In the event of disagreement, a lay bench reaches its decisions (including a decision to acquit or convict) by a majority. Where the bench is even-numbered, the chairman does *not* have a casting vote. Therefore, in the event of the justices being equally divided, it will be necessary for the case to be adjourned for rehearing before a differently constituted court (*Redbridge Justices, ex parte Ram* [1992] QB 384). **D22.69**

Assuming there is the possibility of a majority, justices are under a duty to reach a decision. In both *Bridgend Justices, ex parte Randall* [1975] Crim LR 287 and *Bromley Justices, ex parte Haymills (Contractors) Ltd* [1984] Crim LR 235, benches of three magistrates pronounced themselves unable to decide on the charge against the accused and remitted the case for rehearing by another bench. In each case, the Divisional Court ordered the original justices to reach a decision, saying that if two of them were unhappy about convicting then the prosecution had failed to prove its case and the finding would have to be one of not guilty.

When announcing the decision in open court, the chair does not state whether it is unanimous or by a majority.

Duty to Give Reasons CrimPR 24.3(5) provides that the court, if it convicts the accused (or makes a hospital order instead of doing so), must give 'sufficient reasons to explain its decision'. However, the justices are not required to state their reasons in the form of a judgment or to give reasons in any elaborate form (*McKerry v Teesdale and Wear Valley Justices* (2000) 164 JP 355, per Lord Bingham, at [23]). If a party wishes to obtain more detailed reasons, a request can be made to the magistrates to state a case. In *R (McGowan) v Brent Justices* [2001] EWHC Admin 814, the Divisional Court confirmed that *McKerry v Teesdale and Wear Valley Justices* is still good law following the coming into force of the HRA 1998. Tuckey LJ (at [18]), said that 'the essence of the exercise in a criminal case such as this is to inform the defendant why he has been found guilty. That can usually be done in a few simple sentences.' However, **D22.70**

great care must be taken when formulating those reasons. For example, in *JS (A Child) v DPP* [2017] EWHC 1162 (Admin), [2017] 2 Cr App R 17 (214), D was charged with the offence of tampering with a motor vehicle. The magistrates convicted him, saying that D 'did not say anything to persuade us that he did not tamper with the moped' and they were therefore 'sure' that he was guilty. The conviction was quashed. The words used by the magistrates created the impression that they had convicted D because he had not proved his innocence (thus reversing the burden of proof).

If the court acquits the accused, it may (but is not required to) give an explanation of its decision (CrimPR 24.3(6)(a)).

Guilty of a Lesser Offence

D22.71 The justices are restricted to reaching a decision of guilty or not guilty on the charge actually before them. They have no power to find an accused not guilty as charged but guilty of a lesser offence (*Lawrence v Same* [1968] 2 QB 93). This applies even when a jury, on an equivalently worded count for an either-way offence, would be entitled (under the CLA 1967, s. 6(3); see **D19.41** ***et seq.***) to return an alternative verdict. Thus, in *Lawrence v Same*, a purported summary conviction for common assault on a charge of unlawful wounding was quashed. It would have been otherwise had there been two separate charges, and the court had decided to convict only on the lesser offence.

There are, however, a number of exceptions to this rule. For example, the RTOA 1988, s. 24, enables magistrates, whenever trying certain driving offences, to find the accused not guilty of the offence charged, but guilty of another specified driving offence (e.g., convicting the accused of careless driving instead of dangerous driving, even though the only charge before the court is one of dangerous driving; see also **C2.8**). Similarly, the Theft Act 1968, s. 12A(5), provides that an accused who is charged with aggravated vehicle taking may instead be convicted of the lesser offence of vehicle taking contrary to s. 12; s. 12A(5) applies to summary trials as well as to trials on indictment (*R (H) v Liverpool City Youth Court* [2001] Crim LR 487).

D22.72 **Alternative Offences** If the accused is charged with alternative offences at the outset and pleads not guilty to both, the magistrates should not convict of both offences. In *R (Dyer) v Watford Magistrates' Court* [2013] EWHC 547 (Admin), D was charged with an offence under the POA 1986, s. 4, and also with the racially aggravated form of the offence under the CDA 1998, s. 31(1)(a). Before trial, he offered to plead guilty to the s. 4 offence, but that offer was rejected by the prosecution. Following trial, he was convicted of both offences. The Divisional Court declined to follow its earlier decisions in *DPP v Gane* (1991) 155 JP 846 and *R (CPS) v Blaydon Youth Court* [2004] EWHC 2296 (Admin) (where it had been held that it was open to the magistrates' court to convict D of both offences in similar circumstances), and quashed the conviction on the lesser charge. The Court held that it was 'unfair and disproportionate' for an accused to be convicted twice for a single wrong, since a person's criminal record should record what that person had done, no more and no less (per Laws LJ, at [11]). In such a case, the magistrates should adjourn the lesser charge at the end of the trial but before conviction so that, if an appeal succeeded against conviction on the greater charge, a conviction on the lesser offence might thereafter properly be recorded against the accused (at [12]); in other words, the court gives no verdict on the lesser alternative and adjourns that lesser charge, without setting a date, under the MCA 1980, s. 10, so that the lesser charge can be brought back, if appropriate, if the accused appeals successfully against the conviction for the more serious offence (per Hickinbottom J at [14]). In *Henderson v CPS* [2016] EWHC 464 (Admin), [2016] 1 WLR 1990, the Divisional Court rejected submissions that *Dyer* was wrongly decided. Simon LJ said (at [16]):

> As a matter of principle where there are two charges which are properly characterised as alternatives ... there should not be findings of guilt on both charges; and it is not open to a magistrates' court to make a finding of guilt on an alternative underlying offence having made a finding of guilt on the aggravated offence.

It follows that what his lordship described as the 'underlying offence' (the less serious offence) should be adjourned, without setting a date, under the MCA 1980, s. 10. The Court of Appeal expressed agreement with this approach in *Nelson* [2016] EWCA Crim 1517, [2017] 1 Cr App R 11 (123), so long as the two charges can properly be regarded as 'genuine' or 'true' alternatives, in that they 'overlap in terms of their ingredients'.

SETTING ASIDE A CONVICTION FOR REHEARING BEFORE DIFFERENTLY CONSTITUTED BENCH

General

The MCA 1980, s. 142(2) (see **D22.79**), enables an accused who was convicted in a magistrates' court (whether as a result of a guilty plea or of a finding of guilty after a trial) to ask the magistrates to set the conviction aside. This application can be considered by the same magistrates who convicted the accused or by a different bench. If the conviction is set aside, the case is reheard by different magistrates from those who convicted. **D22.73**

An application under s. 142(2) may be appropriate if, for example, the magistrates made an error of law or there was some defect in the procedure which led to the conviction. In *Croydon Youth Court, ex parte DPP* [1997] 2 Cr App R 411 at p. 416, McCowan LJ said that the purpose of s. 142(2) is most accurately described as a 'power to rectify mistakes', and that it is generally and correctly regarded as a 'slip rule'. Similarly, in *Zykin v CPS* [2009] EWHC 1469 (Admin), Bean J quoted from *R (Holme) v Liverpool Magistrates' Court* [2004] EWHC 3131 (Admin), and said (at [16]) that s. 142 'does not confer a wide and general power on a magistrates' court to re-open a previous decision on the grounds that it is in the interests of justice to do so'; rather, it is 'a power to be used in a relatively limited situation, namely one which is akin to mistake or the slip rule'.

The limited scope of s. 142(2) was emphasised in *DPP v Chajed* [2013] EWHC 188 (Admin), [2013] 2 Cr App R 6 (60). Hickinbottom J, with whom Laws LJ agreed, said (at [25]) that, where there has been a simple mistake (or something akin to such), s. 142 enables a magistrates' court to rectify it, if necessary by directing the case be reheard by different justices. However, once a guilty verdict has been pronounced by magistrates, it does not enable a convicted accused to make further submissions with a view to persuading the bench to change its mind and substitute a not guilty verdict. If the magistrates have reached the wrong decision on the merits of submissions which have been made to them, the appropriate course for the accused is to appeal to the Crown Court or by way of case stated to the High Court.

CrimPR 44.3(2) (see Supplement, **R44.3**) provides that the court may exercise its power to set aside a conviction under s. 142 on application by a party, or on its own initiative. An application under s. 142 may be dealt with in a public or private hearing, or without a hearing. Under r. 44.3(3), the court must not exercise its power in the absence of a party unless the court makes a decision proposed by that party, or the party has agreed in writing to that decision, or the party has had an opportunity to make representations at a hearing. Rule 44.3(4) states that an application for a conviction to be set aside should be made in writing as soon as reasonably practicable after the conviction, and should be served on the court and on each other party. The application must explain why the conviction should be set aside, and must identify any witness that the accused wants to call, and any other proposed evidence.

The wording of s. 142(2) makes it clear that it is not a general 'slip rule'. It applies only after conviction, enabling the court to set that conviction aside. It follows that s. 142 cannot be used to set aside a pre-trial ruling. Pre-trial rulings take effect pursuant to the MCA 1980, s. 8A; such rulings may be varied if (and only if) there has been a material change of circumstances since the ruling was made (s. 8B). See *R (Poskitt) v Reading Magistrates' Court* [2018] EWHC 984 (Admin), [2018] 2 Cr App R 17 (256).

Accused Convicted in Absence

D22.74 In *Gwent Magistrates' Court, ex parte Carey* (1996) 160 JP 613, the Divisional Court held that magistrates have a broad discretion in deciding whether to reopen a case under the MCA 1980, s. 142 (see **D22.79**), when an accused has been convicted in his or her absence. They are entitled to have regard to the fact that the failure to attend the original hearing was the accused's own fault and that witnesses would be inconvenienced if a retrial were to be ordered. Henry LJ also said that the magistrates were entitled to take account of the apparent strength of the prosecution case, although little weight should be given to it, since an apparently strong case can collapse during the course of a trial. His lordship also pointed out that the magistrates, by refusing to reopen the case, were not 'finally shutting out the defendant from the judgment seat' because the accused still has an unfettered right of appeal to the Crown Court under s. 108.

Where it transpires that the accused's absence was involuntary, the conviction should be quashed. In *R (Killick) v West London Magistrates' Court* [2012] EWHC 3864 (Admin), for example, it was held that a magistrates' court erred in refusing to set aside a conviction under s. 142 where D had been tried in his absence despite medical evidence which suggested that he was unfit to attend court.

D22.75 In *R (Morsby) v Tower Bridge Magistrates' Court* [2007] EWHC 2766 (Admin), D had been remanded in custody and so failed to attend his trial for another offence, of which he was convicted in his absence. He applied unsuccessfully under s. 142 to rescind his conviction and reopen the trial. It was held that the magistrates' court had placed substantially too much weight on D's failure to communicate with the court from prison. The interests of justice clearly required the rescission of the claimant's conviction and a retrial in his presence. Similarly, in *R (Blick) v Doncaster Magistrates' Court* [2008] EWHC 2698 (Admin), notice of the trial date was sent to D's last known address. In the meantime, she had moved address but had not informed the magistrates' court of her change of address. She was convicted in her absence. The refusal by the magistrates' court to reopen the case was quashed by the Divisional Court because the magistrates' court had been wrong to take the question of whether D had acted with 'all due diligence' as the primary test of whether to make the order under s. 142(2) and had also erred in taking account of the cost to the 'public purse'.

More recently, in *R (Rathor) v Southampton Magistrates' Court* [2018] EWHC 3278 (Admin), D did not attend court on the date fixed for trial. He supplied a medical certificate which stated that he had suspected food poisoning but which did not address the question of whether he was well enough to attend his trial on the following day. The district judge refused to adjourn the trial, and D was convicted in his absence. D subsequently sought to have the conviction set aside under s. 142, and supplied a certificate from his GP confirming that he was unfit to attend court on the day of the trial. The district judge refused to set the conviction aside. Andrews J, quashing the refusal to set the conviction aside, ruled that, if the magistrates' court 'had simply asked itself whether it was in the interests of justice for the case to be reopened in circumstances such as this, then it would have come to only one conclusion, since plainly it was': the fresh evidence established that D's non-attendance at trial was involuntary (at [21]). Moreover, D was not at fault for the fact that this information was not available at the time, since he could not be held responsible for the fact that his GP had not yet managed to attend to him (at [22]).

Use of s. 142 where Accused Pleaded Guilty

D22.76 In *R (Williamson) v City of Westminster Magistrates' Court* [2012] EWHC 1444 (Admin), [2012] 2 Cr App R 24 (299), D pleaded guilty in the magistrates' court but subsequently said that he did so on the basis of incompetent advice from his solicitor. Burnett J said (at [31]) that the purpose of the MCA 1980, s. 142, as originally enacted, was to enable the magistrates' court itself to correct mistakes so as to avoid the need for parties to appeal to the Crown Court, or to the High Court by way of case stated, or to bring judicial review proceedings; despite subsequent amendment, the power 'remains rooted in the concept of correcting mistakes and errors. It is not a power equivalent to an appeal to the Crown Court or the High Court, nor is it a general power of review.' His lordship noted that, in *Croydon Youth Court, ex parte DPP*, McCowan LJ had said (at p. 417) that, 'It would be wholly wrong...for it to be possible to employ s. 142(2) as a method of a defendant obtaining a re-hearing as a substitute for an appeal to the Crown Court which he cannot pursue because he has unequivocally pleaded guilty'. However, Burnett J said (at [36]) that the court accepted 'that there may be circumstances in which s. 142(2) could be used to allow an unequivocal guilty plea to be set aside'. His lordship suggested that a case in which a guilty plea was entered to an offence unknown to law would be an example, since it would 'fall comfortably within the language of mistake'. Other examples 'include cases where a jurisdictional bar was not appreciated by the defendant relating, for example, to a time limit or the identity of a prosecutor'. His lordship added that the court would not exclude the possibility that s. 142(2) 'would be apt to deal with a case in which circumstances developed after a guilty plea and sentence which led the prosecution to conclude that the conviction should not be sustained'. Nonetheless, the Divisional Court went on to hold that the circumstances relied upon in the present case, even if they were established, did not bring the case within the ambit of s. 142(2).

Delay

There is no time-limit for making an application under s. 142. However, where an accused applies under s. 142(2) for the trial to be reheard, delay in making the application is a relevant consideration for the magistrates in deciding whether or not to grant that application (*Ealing Magistrates' Court, ex parte Sahota* (1998) 162 JP 73). **D22.77**

Prosecution Role

Where a magistrates' court sets aside a conviction under the MCA 1980, s. 142, the court cannot require the Crown to pursue a prosecution (*R (Rhodes-Presley) v South Worcestershire Magistrates' Court* [2008] EWHC 2700 (Admin)). If the prosecution do not wish to proceed with a retrial, it may be necessary to list the matter before the magistrates; the prosecution will offer no evidence and the magistrates will then have no option but to dismiss the case with a verdict of not guilty (per Ouseley J at [9] and [10]). **D22.78**

Statutory Basis for Setting Aside for Rehearing

Magistrates' Courts Act 1980, s. 142 **D22.79**

(2) Where a person is convicted by a magistrates' court and it subsequently appears to the court that it would be in the interests of justice that the case should be heard again by different justices, the court may so direct.

(2A) The power conferred on a magistrates' court by subsection (2) above shall not be exercisable in relation to a conviction if—
- (a) the Crown Court has determined an appeal against—
  - (i) the conviction; or
  - (ii) any sentence or order imposed or made by the magistrates' court when dealing with the offender in respect of the conviction; or
- (b) the High Court has determined a case stated for the opinion of that court on any question arising in any proceeding leading to or resulting from the conviction.

(3) Where a court gives a direction under subsection (2) above—
- (a) the conviction and any sentence or other order imposed or made in consequence thereof shall be of no effect; and
- (b) section 10(4) above shall apply as if the trial of the person in question had been adjourned.

ROLE OF AUTHORISED COURT OFFICERS

Introduction

D22.80 To give effect to the Courts and Tribunals (Judiciary and Functions of Staff) Act 2018, CrimPR 2.2 (see Supplement, **R2.2**) now refers to an 'authorised court officer', instead of justices' clerk, and the term 'justices' legal adviser' is replaced by 'a person authorised under section 28 of the Courts Act 2003 to give advice about law to justices of the peace'; r. 2.4 now refers to 'authorised court officers'. The qualifications and appointment of authorised court officers are described at **D3.28**.

D22.81 The statutory functions of authorised court officers are set out in the Courts Act 2003, s. 28(1), which empowers the Lord Chief Justice to authorise a person:

(a) to give advice to justices of the peace about matters of law (including procedure and practice) on questions arising in connection with the discharge of their functions, including questions arising when the person is not personally attending on them, and
(b) to bring to the attention of justices of the peace, at any time when the person thinks appropriate, any point of law (including procedure and practice) that is or may be involved in any question so arising.

CrimPR 24.14 (see Supplement, **R24.14**) provides a further summary of the duties of authorised court officers. These include: drawing the court's attention, before the hearing begins, to the prosecution allegations, what is agreed and what is in dispute, and what the parties have said about how they expect to present their cases; whenever necessary, giving the court legal advice (and, if necessary, attending the members of the court outside the courtroom to give such advice, so long as the parties are informed of any advice given outside the courtroom); assisting the court in the formulation of its reasons and the recording of those reasons; assisting the accused if unrepresented; and assisting the court by making a note of the substance of any oral evidence or representations, marking as inadmissible any parts of written statements introduced in evidence that are ruled inadmissible; ensuring that a record is kept of the court's decisions and the reasons for them, and making any announcement (other than of the verdict or sentence).

CrimPD VI, para. 24A.5 (see Supplement, **CPD.24A**), provides a list of matters on which the authorised court officer may legitimately advise the magistrates:

(a) questions of law;
(b) questions of mixed law and fact;
(c) matters of practice and procedure;
(d) the process to be followed at sentence and the matters to be taken into account, together with the range of penalties and ancillary orders available, in accordance with the relevant sentencing guidelines;
(e) any relevant decisions of the superior courts or other guidelines;
(f) the appropriate decision-making structure to be applied in any given case; and
(g) other issues relevant to the matter before the court.

The authorised court officer is also required to assist the court, where appropriate, as to the formulation of reasons and the recording of those reasons (para. 24A.6). The court officer may also ask questions of witnesses and the parties in order to clarify the evidence and any issues in the case, and must ensure that every case is conducted justly (para. 24A.13).

Duties of Authorised Court Officer with Regard to Questions of Law

D22.82 The role of the authorised court officer is to *advise* on law, practice and procedure. Since the magistrates are the ultimate arbiters of both law and fact there is no obligation on them to adopt the court officer's advice on law, but it is accepted practice that they should in fact do so.

If the court officer forms the view that the justices have reached a decision that is wrong, he or she has no power to ignore their order and treat it as a nullity (*Liverpool Magistrates' Court, ex parte Abiaka* (1999) 163 JP 497).

When a point of law arises during the course of proceedings, any advice given by the authorised court officer to the magistrates should be given publicly in open court. Moreover, CrimPD VI, para. 24A.14 (see Supplement, **CPD.24A**), requires that the court officer must provide the parties with an opportunity to respond to any advice given.

In *Chichester Justices, ex parte DPP* [1994] RTR 175 at p. 178, Morland J said that, if the court officer who advises the justices is not the one who was present in court when the parties made their submissions on the point of law at issue, it is essential that the court officer should hear informal submissions on the relevant law from the parties before advising the justices.

Retirement of Court Officer with Bench

CrimPR 24.14(2)(b) says that the authorised court officer must give the court legal advice and may, if necessary, attend the members of the court outside the courtroom to give such advice; however, the parties must be informed of any advice given outside the courtroom. **D22.83**

The court officer should not leave the courtroom with the justices when they retire to consider their verdict. If the magistrates require assistance from the court officer, he or she should join them only when asked to do so and should return to the courtroom once the advice has been given, so as to avoid giving the impression that he or she is participating improperly in the decision-making process (*Eccles Justices, ex parte Farrelly* (1993) 157 JP 77). CrimPD VI, para. 24A.15, states that, where the justices request their court officer to join them in the retiring room, this request should be made in the presence of the parties in court. Moreover, any legal advice given to the justices in their retiring room should be regarded as provisional, and the court officer should then repeat the substance of the advice in open court and give the parties an opportunity to make representations on the correctness of that provisional advice; the court officer should state in open court whether the provisional advice is confirmed or has been varied (and, if so, how).

It is submitted, however, that this procedure may legitimately not be followed if the substance of the advice is simply repeating advice already given in open court, and on which the parties have already had the chance to make submissions. However, if the authorised court officer advises the justices after they have retired to consider their decision and in doing so cites authority which was not cited in open court, he or she should inform the advocates in the case and give them the opportunity to make further submissions to the magistrates (*W v W* (1993) *The Times*, 4 June 1993). **D22.84**

Authorised Court Officer to Play No Part in Decisions on Questions of Fact

CrimPD VI, para. 24A.12 (see Supplement, **CPD.24A**), makes it clear that the authorised court officer must play no part in making findings of fact (but may assist the bench by reminding them of the evidence, and clarifying the issues which are to be determined). Contravention of this rule may lead to judicial review of the court's decision (see, e.g., *Stafford Justices, ex parte Ross* [1962] 1 All ER 540, where the conviction was quashed because, while D was giving evidence in his own defence, the court officer handed the bench a note which, in effect, argued that the evidence ought not to be believed). **D22.85**

So far as sentencing is concerned, the authorised court officer should be careful not to go beyond advising on the range of penalties available and any relevant guidelines, and should certainly not advocate a certain type of disposal, as this would be to interfere with a decision which is for the bench alone.

In *R (Murchison) v Southend Magistrates' Court* [2006] EWHC 569 (Admin), the justices had retired to consider their verdict. They reached their decision and then sought advice on the compilation of reasons. After the court officer had done so, she informed the justices of D's antecedents. The justices then returned to court and gave their verdict. D was convicted. Immediately afterwards, the justices announced that they had seen the antecedents and were minded to adjourn sentence for a pre-sentence report. Judicial review of the conviction was sought on the ground that the justices had been made aware of D's antecedents before they had announced their decision in open court. The Divisional Court dismissed the appeal because the magistrates had not known of D's previous convictions until after they had concluded their deliberations and had reached a reasoned decision. However, it was said that, as a matter of procedure, 'no advice should be offered . . ., provisional or otherwise, on sentence until the magistrates have returned to court, announced their decision on conviction, heard about the accused's antecedents and listened to counsel's submissions' (per Hallett LJ at [20]). Her ladyship added that authorised court officers 'should only attend upon the bench … when called upon to do so; and then only to assist with matters arising at that stage' and that (given the possibility that in the instant case the court officer went into the retiring room with a copy of the appellant's previous convictions in her hand) court officers should ensure that any such documentation is left elsewhere when they retire to give the justices legal advice (at [21]).

Noting the Evidence

D22.86 CrimPR 24.14(3)(b)(i) says that the authorised court officer must assist the court by making a note of the substance of any oral evidence or representations. The importance of note-taking was emphasised in *L v DPP* [2007] EWHC 1843 (Admin), [2008] 1 Cr App R 8 (131), where Collins J (at [27]) said that, 'it is desirable that a note should be taken by someone . . . which is capable of being used as a formal note of the evidence if there is any later dispute as to what was or was not said in the course of evidence at the hearing'. Auld LJ echoed this sentiment (at [37]), saying, 'It is clearly important that adequate notes are made, even in comparatively minor cases …, going, albeit briefly, to the basis upon which the prosecution case is opened, the salient features of the evidence on both sides, and to any submissions as to law … '.

Role of Authorised Court Officer where Accused is Unrepresented

D22.87 Under CrimPR 24.2(2)(b) (see Supplement, **R24.2**) the authorised court officer (or the justices themselves) must explain the allegation, and what procedure will be adopted at the hearing, in terms the accused can understand. Moreover, r. 24.4(6) states that the authorised court officer (or the court) may ask a witness questions and, in particular, where the accused is not represented, ask any question necessary in the accused's interests. Rule 24.14(3)(a) provides that the authorised court officer must 'assist' an unrepresented defendant. However, the court officer must discharge the duty to assist unrepresented parties to present their case without appearing to become an advocate for the party concerned (CrimPD VI, para. 24A.16: see Supplement, **CPD.24A**). In *Simms v Moore* [1970] 2 QB 327 at pp. 332–3, Lord Parker CJ gave guidance which may be summarised as follows:

(1) In general neither the court nor the authorised court officer should take an active part in the proceedings except to clear up ambiguities in the evidence.
(2) So far as examining witnesses is concerned, this should never be done if the party concerned is legally represented or where a party, even though unrepresented, is competent to and desires to examine the witnesses him or herself.
(3) Where an unrepresented party is not competent, through a lack of knowledge of court procedure or rules of evidence or otherwise, to examine the witnesses properly, the court can at its discretion permit the authorised court officer to do so.
(4) When this is permitted, there is no reason why the authorised court officer should not do so by reference to a proof of evidence or witness statement, provided always that an opportunity is given to the other side to see it or to have a copy.

(5) Where notes of evidence have to be or are taken, care should be taken not to use the proof or statement as the basis of the notes. The best course is for it to be arranged that someone else, possibly a member of the court itself, should take the note.
(6) Generally, the discretion in the court should be so exercised that examination of witnesses by the court officer should be permitted only when there are reasonable grounds for thinking that thereby the interests of justice would be best promoted, care being taken to see that nothing is done which conflicts with the rules of natural justice or the principle that justice must manifestly be seen to be done.

Thus, it is common practice for the authorised court officer to explain to an unrepresented accused the purpose of cross-examination and, if the accused still seems incapable of doing it properly, to frame suitable questions on the accused's behalf. Moreover, under r. 24.3(3)(e), at the close of the prosecution case, the court officer (or the justices) must explain that the accused has the right to give evidence, and also the potential effect of not doing so at all, or of refusing to answer a question while doing so (namely the drawing of adverse inferences).

Section D23 Sentencing in the Magistrates' Court

INTRODUCTION

D23.1 The procedure to be followed between a plea or verdict of guilty and the court pronouncing sentence in the Crown Court is described in **D20**. Sentencing procedure in the magistrates' courts follows the same basic pattern. The following paragraphs, which should be read in conjunction with **D20** and with **Part E** (which deals with sentencing generally), focus on topics of particular relevance to magistrates' courts.

The duty on the court, under the CAJA 2009, s. 125, to follow any relevant sentencing guidelines, unless satisfied that it would be contrary to the interests of justice to do so, applies to all courts, including magistrates' courts. The *Magistrates' Court Sentencing Guidelines* (see Supplement, **SG10-1** *et seq.*), which are updated regularly, cover most of the offences that are regularly encountered in magistrates' courts, and include some very useful general explanatory material.

ADJOURNMENTS PRIOR TO SENTENCE

D23.2

Magistrates' Courts Act 1980, s. 10

(3) A magistrates' court may, for the purpose of enabling inquiries to be made or of determining the most suitable method of dealing with the case, exercise its power to adjourn after convicting the accused and before sentencing him or otherwise dealing with him; but, if it does so, the adjournment shall not be for more than four weeks at a time unless the court remands the accused in custody and, where it so remands him, the adjournment shall not be for more than three weeks at a time.

It is apparent from the words 'at a time' that, although the maximum period for adjournment after conviction is four weeks on bail or three weeks in custody, the court is not obliged to sentence at the end of the first such adjournment but may, if necessary, adjourn again. A common reason for adjourning the case prior to passing sentence will be to enable the preparation of a pre-sentence report, especially if the court is considering a custodial sentence or a community order (since a report will normally be required in such cases by virtue of the CJA 2003, s. 156). Where an offender is granted bail for a post-conviction adjournment, the court may impose a condition that the offender be available for the purpose of enabling inquiries or a report to be made to assist the court in dealing with the offender for the offence (BA 1976, s. 3(6)(d)), provided that it appears to be necessary to do so for the purpose of enabling inquiries or a report to be made (BA 1976, sch. 1, part 1, para. 8(1A)).

D23.3 There is some overlap between the MCA 1980, s. 10(3), and the PCC(S)A 2000, s. 11, which empowers magistrates to adjourn for medical reports once they are satisfied that the accused committed the *actus reus* of the offence. If magistrates have convicted, they must *ex hypothesi* be satisfied as to the *actus reus*, and may therefore adjourn under s. 11. However, the chief value of s. 11 is not so much at the post-conviction stage (as the magistrates may adjourn for medical reports under the general power conferred by the MCA 1980, s. 10(3)) but before conviction, when the obtaining of suitable reports and recommendations may enable the court to make a hospital or guardianship order without finding the accused guilty. Where the court adjourns under the PCC(S)A 2000, s. 11, and grants bail to the accused, it *must* make it a condition of bail that the accused undergo a medical examination by either one or two duly qualified medical practitioners (s. 11(3)).

In December 2009, Leveson LJ (then Senior Presiding Judge for England and Wales) issued guidance to magistrates' courts in a document entitled *Essential Case Management: Applying the Criminal Procedure Rules* (see also **D21.40**). That document says that where the accused pleads guilty, the court should (unless committing for sentence) pass sentence on the same day 'if at all possible'. Where a pre-sentence report is needed, 'it may be that a report prepared for earlier proceedings will be sufficient or a "fast delivery" report (oral or written) may be prepared that day'. Moreover, where a *Newton* hearing is needed, the court should identify the disputed issue and 'if possible, determine it there and then or, if it really cannot be decided, give directions... to ensure that the next hearing is the last'. The importance of avoiding delay is emphasised by CrimPR 24.11(9)(a), which says that once account has been taken of all relevant information, and any report that may be available, the court must, as a general rule, pass sentence there and then. **D23.4**

Keeping Sentencing Options Open

Where the court does not pass sentence immediately, the magistrates must be careful not to create an expectation that the accused will ultimately be sentenced in that court if they wish the option of committal for sentence to the Crown Court to remain open (see **D23.35**) or that the sentence will or will not take a particular form. In *Nottingham Magistrates' Court, ex parte Davidson* [2000] 1 Cr App R (S) 167, Lord Bingham CJ (at p. 169), set out the following principle: **D23.5**

> If a court at a preliminary stage of the sentencing process gives to a defendant any indication as to the sentence which will or will not be thereafter passed upon him, in terms sufficiently unqualified to found a legitimate expectation in the mind of the defendant that any court which later passes sentence upon him will act in accordance with the indication given, and if on a later occasion a court, without reasons which justify departure from the earlier indication, and whether or not it is aware of that indication, passes a sentence inconsistent with, and more severe than, the sentence indicated, the court will ordinarily feel obliged, however reluctantly, to adjust the sentence passed so as to bring it into line with that indicated.

This dictum was cited with approval in *Thornton v CPS* [2010] EWHC 346 (Admin), [2010] 2 Cr App R (S) 65 (434). In that case, Aikens LJ went on to say (at [49]) that:

> ...it is imperative that magistrates do not put themselves in a position which binds the hands of another bench on the question of sentence unless they are absolutely certain that it is the right course to take. Forms can be used, and forms of words used, to ensure that no expectation about sentence, legitimate or otherwise, is engendered in the mind of defendants or their advisers. If those forms and words are used correctly, then unnecessary and expensive expeditions to this court will be avoided.

His lordship also referred to the dictum of Wilkie J in *Nicholas v Chester Magistrates' Court* [2009] EWHC 1504 (Admin) (at [13]), that the court would 'thoroughly deprecate the practice, if such it be, of one bench to adjourn sentencing for reports and in so doing giving an indication as to the type of sentence which it would be appropriate to pass where that bench is not reserving sentence to itself'. He explained that, by so doing, the effect (save in an exceptional case) is to fetter the discretion of the sentencing court and that 'should only be done where the bench reserves to itself the sentence, or in a case where it is absolutely obvious that a certain type of sentence should be considered or should not be considered'.

PRESENTING THE FACTS, CHARACTER AND ANTECEDENTS

The procedure to be followed before sentence is passed in a magistrates' court is essentially the same as in the Crown Court. CrimPR 24.11(3) (see Supplement, **R24.11**) requires the **D23.6** prosecutor to summarise the prosecution case, if the sentencing court has not heard evidence (i.e. if the offender has pleaded guilty, or there has been an adjournment after the offender was convicted following a trial); r. 24.11(3) then requires the prosecutor to identify any offence(s) to be taken into consideration, and to provide information relevant to sentence (including any aggravating or mitigating factors, relevant legislative provisions, and any guidelines or guideline cases). The prosecutor must also draw the court's attention to any statement of the effect of the offence on the victim, the victim's family or others (i.e. any victim personal statement).

Under r. 24.11(4), the offender must provide details of financial circumstances. Rule 24.11(7) requires the court, before passing sentence, to give the offender an opportunity to make representations and introduce evidence relevant to sentence. Thus, there will be an opportunity for a plea in mitigation to be made on behalf of the offender.

The court which passes sentence need not be composed of the justices who convicted the offender (or who sat at an earlier post-conviction hearing when the case was adjourned) but, where the court which is to pass sentence consists of, or includes, justices who were not sitting when the offender was convicted, the court must 'make such inquiry into the facts and circumstances of the case as will enable the justices who were not sitting when the offender was convicted to be fully acquainted with those facts and circumstances' (MCA 1980, s. 121(7)). This will invariably be done through the summary of the relevant facts presented by the prosecutor (prior to any plea in mitigation by the defence).

Newton Hearings

D23.7 Under CrimPR 24.11(5), an accused who pleads guilty but wants to be sentenced on a different basis to the facts put forward by the prosecution must set out that basis in writing (identifying exactly what is in dispute). The court may invite the parties to make representations about whether the dispute is material to sentence (in the sense that the sentence would differ depending on whether it is based on the prosecution version or the defence version of the facts). If the court decides that it is a material dispute, the court will invite 'such further representations or evidence as it may require' and then decide the dispute. Although the CrimPR appear to suggest that, where the difference in versions put forward by the parties is significant (in that it would make a difference to the sentence passed), the court has a choice of hearing further representations or evidence, it is submitted that magistrates should follow the procedure laid down in *Newton* (1982) 77 Cr App R 13, and (if they are unwilling simply to accept the defence version of events) hear evidence (i.e. hold a *Newton* hearing) and then make findings of fact and sentence accordingly. Indeed, cases where it is possible to resolve such a factual dispute without hearing evidence are likely to be very rare, since the decision is likely to involve the court assessing the credibility of the evidence adduced by the parties.

Where there are co-accused, and one pleads not guilty and the other pleads guilty but on a factual basis that the prosecution do not accept, the magistrates should 'almost invariably' adopt the procedure applicable in the Crown Court by virtue of *Smith (Patrick)* (1988) 87 Cr App R 393, namely for the *Newton* hearing in respect of the person who has pleaded guilty to take place after the conclusion of the trial of the accused who pleaded not guilty (see *KK v DPP* [2016] EWHC 1976 (Admin), [2016] 4 WLR 162, per Lord Thomas CJ at [30]). In that case, it was held that the district judge had erred in hearing the trial and the *Newton* hearing together (and taking account of the evidence of the accused who had pleaded guilty when deciding to convict the accused who had pleaded not guilty). The effect of following the procedure laid down in *Smith* is that the evidence in the trial of the co-accused can be taken into account in the subsequent *Newton* hearing, which should generally be conducted by the same judge or bench which heard the trial. However, Lord Thomas CJ observed that there may be 'very rare cases' where it might not be appropriate to follow the approach laid down in *Smith*. In *KK v DPP*, for example, the issue to be determined at the *Newton* hearing was whether the robbery had involved the use of a knife. The co-accused had been convicted following trial, and the district judge, in giving reasons for the conviction, made an express finding that a knife had been used. It followed that it would not have been appropriate for the same judge to conduct the *Newton* hearing of the other accused.

Newton hearings are considered in more detail at **D20.8**.

ADJUDICATION ON AND PRONOUNCEMENT OF SENTENCE

Majority Decision

As with any adjudication of a magistrates' court, the decision as to sentence may be by a majority of those sitting. In the event of an equal division, the court should adjourn under the MCA 1980, s. 10 (adjournments after conviction and before sentence), for the matter to be reconsidered at the resumed hearing. **D23.8**

Reasons and Explanation

CrimPR 24.11(9)(b) (see Supplement, **R24.11**) requires that, when passing sentence, the court must (unless neither the offender nor any member of the public is present) explain the reasons for deciding on that sentence. Unless the offender is absent, or the offender's ill-health or disorderly conduct makes it impracticable to do so, the court must also explain the effect of the sentence, the consequences of failing to comply with any requirements imposed, and any power that the court has to vary or review the sentence (r. 24.11(9)(c)). The court must also consider exercising any power it has to make a costs or other order (r. 24.11(9)(e)). It should also be noted that the CJA 2003, s. 174(2), requires the court to give reasons for deciding on the sentence it has imposed; s. 174(3) requires the court to explain to the offender the effect of the sentence and the effects of non-compliance with any order that forms part of the sentence (see **E1.23**). The court must identify any relevant definitive sentencing guidelines and explain how it has discharged its duty to follow those guidelines; where the court did not follow any such guidelines because it was satisfied that it would be contrary to the interests of justice to do so, it must state why (s. 174(6)). **D23.9**

SENTENCING IN ABSENCE

The power in the MCA 1980, s. 11(1), to proceed in the accused's absence extends to passing sentence in the accused's absence, once the court has found the case proved. However, this is qualified by s. 11(3) to (5A): **D23.10**

Magistrates' Courts Act 1980, s. 11

(3) In proceedings to which this subsection applies, the court shall not in a person's absence sentence him to imprisonment or detention in a young offender institution or make a detention and training order or an order under paragraph 8(2)(a) or (b) of Schedule 12 to the Criminal Justice Act 2003 that a suspended sentence shall take effect.

(3A) But where a sentence or order of a kind mentioned in subsection (3) is imposed or given in the absence of the offender, the offender must be brought before the court before being taken to a prison or other institution to begin serving his sentence (and the sentence or order is not to be regarded as taking effect until he is brought before the court).

(4) In proceedings to which this subsection applies, the court shall not in a person's absence impose any disqualification on him, except on resumption of the hearing after an adjournment under section 10(3) above; and where a trial is adjourned in pursuance of this subsection the notice required by section 10(2) above shall include notice of the reason for the adjournment.

(5) Subsections (3) and (4) apply to—
(a) proceedings instituted by an information, where a summons has been issued; and
(b) proceedings instituted by a written charge.
(5A) Subsection (4) does not apply in relation to proceedings adjourned under section 16C(3)(a) because of section 16C(2) (adjournment of a section 16A trial because the accused indicates a wish to make representations).

The effect of these provisions is that, where the proceedings were started by written charge and requisition (or, in the case of a private prosecution, by the issue of a summons), the court must adjourn the sentencing hearing if the offender is absent and either (a) the court is considering the imposition of a custodial sentence, or (b) the court is considering the imposition of a disqualification and the hearing has not previously been adjourned to give the offender an opportunity to attend (see also CrimPR 24.11(10)(a)). Although the prohibition in s. 11(4) (which is qualified in certain cases to which the 'trial by single justice' procedure applies under the MCA 1980, s. 16A: see **D22.33**) will, in the majority of cases, be relevant to proposed disqualification from driving, it extends to any form of disqualification that a magistrates' court may order (see **E21**). While s. 11(3) appears to prohibit the imposition of a custodial sentence if the offender is absent, s. 11(3A) goes on to provide that, if the court does pass a custodial sentence in the absence of the offender, that sentence cannot take effect until he or she has been brought before the court. In any event, these provisions do not apply where the proceedings were started by the offender being charged at a police station, and so do not apply where the accused was bailed to return to the court (s. 11(5)).

A disqualification imposed in contravention of s. 11(4) will be a nullity and liable to be quashed (*Llandrindod Wells Justices, ex parte Gibson* [1968] 2 All ER 20).

D23.11 Where an accused is represented by counsel or solicitor, the deeming provision in the MCA 1980, s. 122 (see **D22.24**), presumably has the effect of allowing the normally prohibited sentences to be passed even though the offender is not physically present, but in practice the court would almost certainly adjourn rather than proceed in the absence of the offender. In any event, as a result of s. 122(3), s. 122 does not apply where the offender is on bail and therefore under a duty to attend court.

Where an absent offender is being sentenced for a summary offence, the court may take account of any previous convictions, provided notice of intention to cite the convictions was served on the offender at least seven days prior to the hearing (MCA 1980, s. 104). This restriction on the use of previous convictions does not apply to sentencing for either-way offences or to sentencing in a youth court.

Warrants

D23.12 Depending on the penalty they have in mind, magistrates may consider it undesirable to proceed to sentence in the offender's absence. If so, they will adjourn. They may also be able to issue a warrant for the offender's arrest under the MCA 1980, s. 13(1). The same basic conditions apply to issuing a warrant at the post-conviction stage as apply before conviction (i.e. where the proceedings were commenced by way of summons or written charge and requisition, it must be proved that the summons or requisition was served on the accused a reasonable time before the trial or adjourned trial, or else the accused was present in court when the case was adjourned to the present date). However, following conviction, the powers of the court are widened in that it may issue a warrant even though the offence is non-imprisonable, provided it is proposing to impose a disqualification on the offender (s. 13(3)(b)).

In cases where the accused has entered a plea of guilty by post, there is no power to issue a warrant if either the magistrates decide to adjourn rather than accept the plea, or, having convicted, they adjourn before sentence (e.g., because they are considering disqualification) (s. 13(4)). However, if the court has adjourned once without issuing a warrant in such a case and the accused fails to appear for the adjourned hearing, then (subject to proof that the adjournment notice was duly served) a warrant may be issued.

Attendance at Sentencing Hearings via Live Link

The CDA 1998, ss. 57D and 57E, enable the court to direct that an accused in custody may appear at sentencing hearings via a 'live link' from the place at which he or she is being held. Section 57D deals with preliminary hearings which turn into sentencing hearings because the accused pleads guilty (see **D5.38**). Section 57E deals with other sentencing hearings. Under s. 57E(2), where it is likely that an offender who has been convicted will be held in custody during the sentencing hearing, the court may direct that the offender attend via a live link. Under s. 57E(4), such a direction may be given by the court of its own motion or following an application from either party, and may include subsequent sentencing hearings in relation to that offence. A direction may be given only if the court is satisfied that it is not contrary to the interests of justice to do so (s. 57E(5)). The court may, if it is in the interests of justice to do so, rescind the live link direction, either of its own motion or on the application of either party (s. 57E(6)). Under s. 57E(7), the offender can give oral evidence via the live link under s. 57E only if the court is satisfied that it is not contrary to the interests of justice for the offender to give evidence in that way. If the court refuses an application for (or for the rescinding of) a live link direction under s. 57E, it must state its reasons in open court and, in the case of a magistrates' courts, must record the reasons in the court register (s. 57E(8)). **D23.13**

RESTRICTIONS ON MAGISTRATES' COURTS' POWERS OF SENTENCE

Offences Triable Either Way

The maximum sentence that magistrates may currently impose upon an offender summarily convicted of an either-way offence listed in the MCA 1980, sch. 1, is six months' imprisonment and/or a fine of any amount (PCC(S)A 2000, s. 78; MCA 1980, s. 32(1) and (2)). The Legal Aid, Sentencing and Punishment of Offenders Act 2012 (Fines on Summary Conviction) Regulations 2015 (SI 2015 No. 664) make specific provision for maximum fines for a large number of specific offences. The effect is that an either-way offence is punishable with a fine of any amount unless specific provision is made for that offence in the 2015 Regulations. The six-month ceiling on magistrates' powers of imprisonment contained in s. 78(1) may be expressly excluded. Thus, if an offence-creating enactment simply provides that the maximum term on summary conviction for an offence triable either way shall be nine months' imprisonment, the effect of s. 78(1) is to reduce the maximum to six months, but, if it provides that 'notwithstanding anything in section 78(1) of the PCC(S)A 2000, the maximum term shall be nine months', then s. 78(1) is overridden and the maximum is indeed nine months. **D23.14**

By virtue of the MCA 1980, s. 34(3), if the statute creating the offence empowers the court to impose a custodial sentence on the offender but makes no mention of a fine, then (unless this provision is expressly excluded), the court may, instead of imposing a custodial sentence, impose a fine of any amount if the offence is triable either way, or £1,000 (level 3) if the offence is a summary one. **D23.15**

Summary Offences

The maximum sentence of imprisonment (if any) for a summary offence is six months or that prescribed by the statute creating the offence, whichever is the less (PCC(S)A 2000, s. 78(1)). Again, this is subject to the six-month ceiling in s. 78(1) being expressly overridden by any **D23.16** other enactment. The maximum fine for a summary offence is whatever the offence-creating provision specifies; fines are usually fixed by reference to a level on the standard scale of fines rather than by reference to a specific sum of money (see **E15.9** for the standard scale of fines). The offence-creating provision will indicate whether a fine may be imposed in addition to any sentence of imprisonment or only as an alternative thereto. When magistrates are dealing with an offender for several summary offences punishable with fines at levels 1 to 4, there is no restriction on the aggregate fine that may be imposed.

Aggregate Prison Terms

D23.17 Magistrates sentencing an offender for several offences and imposing imprisonment for two or more of them may make the terms concurrent or consecutive (MCA 1980, s. 133(1)). This is subject to the maximum *aggregate* term that a magistrates' court may impose on one occasion for more than one summary offence, which is six months (proviso to s. 133(1)). In *Garthwaite* [2019] EWCA Crim 2357, Holroyde LJ said (at [26]) that the effect of s. 133(1) was that:

> ... a magistrates' court, sentencing a person to two or more terms of imprisonment for summary offences, can only pass an aggregate term not exceeding 6 months. It can however order that aggregate term to run consecutively to another sentence imposed by another court. In that situation it is not limited to a maximum of 6 months' imprisonment including the earlier sentence imposed by another court.

Where a magistrates' court is sentencing for two or more either-way offences, the maximum aggregate term of imprisonment becomes 12 months (s. 133(2)).

Where magistrates have power to deal with an offender for breach of a suspended sentence, they may (if they choose to activate part or all of the suspended term) make it run consecutively to any term of imprisonment they impose for the offences that put the offender in breach (CJA 2003, sch. 12, para. (9)(1)(b)). In such a case, the aggregate of the suspended term and the terms for the present offences may exceed the aggregate normally permitted by s. 133(1) and (2) (*Chamberlain* (1992) 13 Cr App R (S) 525). It follows that, if the offender is in breach of a six-month suspended sentence and has been convicted of two either-way offences, the magistrates' court could impose six months on each 'breach' offence to run consecutively, and activate the suspended sentence, also to run consecutively, thereby making a total aggregate sentence of 18 months.

Criminal Damage Cases

D23.18 Where magistrates deal with a charge of criminal damage under the special procedure in the MCA 1980, s. 22, as if it were a summary offence (see **D6.20**) and the accused is convicted, their powers of sentencing are restricted to three months' imprisonment or to a fine at level 4 (currently £2,500, see **E15.9**). If, on the other hand, they conclude that the value involved in the offence exceeded the relevant sum (£5,000) and therefore adopt the usual procedure for determining mode of trial, the maximum sentence, should there be a summary conviction, is that which may be imposed for any other either-way offence listed in sch. 1 to the MCA 1980 (i.e. six months' imprisonment and/or a fine of any amount).

Compensation Orders

D23.19 Where the offender has attained the age of 18, there is no limit on the amount of compensation that a magistrates' court may order in respect of each offence.

Detention in a Young Offender Institution

D23.20 A magistrates' court may impose a sentence of detention in a young offender institution on an offender aged 18 to 20. The court's powers are limited to the same extent as are their powers to imprison offenders who have attained the age of 21.

Where the offender is under the age of 18 (at the date of conviction), a youth court may impose a detention and training order, for which the maximum duration is 24 months (12 months' custody and 12 months' supervision in the community). See E7.15.

Non-custodial Sentences

The powers of magistrates' courts as regards non-custodial sentences, including community orders, are identical to those of the Crown Court. **D23.21**

Provisions of the Magistrates' Courts Act 1980 and the Powers of Criminal Courts (Sentencing) Act 2000 Relating to Magistrates' Sentencing Powers

Magistrates' Courts Act 1980, ss. 32 and 133 **D23.22**

32.—(1) On summary conviction of any of the offences triable either way listed in Schedule 1 to this Act a person shall be liable to imprisonment for a term not exceeding six months or to a fine not exceeding the prescribed sum or both, except that—

(a) a magistrates' court shall not have power to impose imprisonment for an offence so listed if the Crown Court would not have that power in the case of an adult convicted of it on indictment;

...

(2) For any offence triable either way which is not listed in Schedule 1 to this Act, being an offence under a relevant enactment, the maximum fine which may be imposed on summary conviction shall by virtue of this subsection be the prescribed sum unless the offence is one for which by virtue of an enactment other than this subsection a larger fine may be imposed on summary conviction.

(3) Where, by virtue of any relevant enactment, a person summarily convicted of an offence triable either way would, apart from this section, be liable to a maximum fine of one amount in the case of a first conviction and of a different amount in the case of a second or subsequent conviction, subsection (2) above shall apply irrespective of whether the conviction is a first, second or subsequent one.

(4) Subsection (2) above shall not affect so much of any enactment as (in whatever words) makes a person liable on summary conviction to a fine not exceeding a specified amount for each day on which a continuing offence is continued after conviction or the occurrence of any other specified event.

(5) Subsection (2) above shall not apply on summary conviction of any of the following offences:—

(a) offences under section 5(2) of the Misuse of Drugs Act 1971 (having possession of a controlled drug) where the controlled drug in relation to which the offence was committed was a Class B or Class C drug;

(b) offences under the following provisions of that Act, where the controlled drug in relation to which the offence was committed was a Class C drug, namely—

(i) section 4(2) (production, or being concerned in the production, of a controlled drug);

(ii) section 4(3) (supplying or offering a controlled drug or being concerned in the doing of either activity by another);

(iii) section 5(3) (having possession of a controlled drug with intent to supply it to another);

(iv) section 8 (being the occupier, or concerned in the management, of premises and permitting or suffering certain activities to take place there);

(v) section 12(6) (contravention of direction prohibiting practitioner etc. from possessing, supplying etc. controlled drugs); or

(vi) section 13(3) (contravention of direction prohibiting practitioner etc. from prescribing, supplying etc. controlled drugs).

[(6) Any power by subordinate instrument to restrict the amount of fine which may be imposed on summary conviction for an either-way offence shall not be affected by subsection (2) above.]

(7) [Repealed.]

(8) In subsection (5) above 'controlled drug', 'Class B drug' and 'Class C drug' have the same meaning as in the Misuse of Drugs Act 1971.

D

Part D Procedure

(9) In this section—

'fine' includes a pecuniary penalty but does not include a pecuniary forfeiture or pecuniary compensation;

'the prescribed sum' means £5,000 or such sum as is for the time being substituted in this definition by an order in force under section 143(3) below;

'relevant enactment' means an enactment contained in the Criminal Law Act 1977 or in any Act passed before, or in the same session as, that Act.

(10) Section 85 of the Legal Aid, Sentencing and Punishment of Offenders Act 2012 (removal of limit on certain fines on conviction by magistrates' court) makes provision that affects the application of this section.

133.—(1) Subject to section 265 of the Criminal Justice Act 2003, a magistrates' court imposing imprisonment or a sentence of detention in a young offender institution on any person may order that the term of imprisonment or detention in a young offender institution shall commence on the expiration of any other term of imprisonment or detention in a young offender institution imposed by that or any other court; but where a magistrates' court imposes two or more terms of imprisonment or detention in a young offender institution to run consecutively the aggregate of such terms shall not, subject to the provisions of this section, exceed six months.

(2) If two or more of the terms imposed by the court are imposed in respect of an offence triable either way which was tried summarily otherwise than in pursuance of section 22(2) above [criminal damage triable only summarily if the value involved did not exceed £5,000], the aggregate of the terms so imposed and any other terms imposed by the court may exceed six months but shall not, subject to the following provisions of this section, exceed 12 months.

(2A) In relation to the imposition of terms of detention in a young offender institution subsection (2) above shall have effect as if the reference to an offence triable either way were a reference to such an offence or an offence triable only on indictment.

(3) The limitations imposed by the preceding subsections shall not operate to reduce the aggregate of the terms that the court may impose in respect of any offences below the term which the court has power to impose in respect of any one of those offences.

(4) Where a person has been sentenced by a magistrates' court to imprisonment and a fine for the same offence, a period of imprisonment imposed for non-payment of the fine, or for want of sufficient [goods] to satisfy the fine, shall not be subject to the limitations imposed by the preceding subsections.

(5) For the purposes of this section a term of imprisonment shall be deemed to be imposed in respect of an offence if it is imposed as a sentence or in default of payment of a fine adjudged to be paid by the conviction or for want of sufficient [goods] to satisfy such a sum.

Powers of Criminal Courts (Sentencing) Act 2000, s. 78

(1) A magistrates' court shall not have power to impose imprisonment, or detention in a young offender institution, for more than six months in respect of any one offence.

(2) Unless expressly excluded, subsection (1) above shall apply even if the offence in question is one for which a person would otherwise be liable on summary conviction to imprisonment or detention in a young offender institution for more than six months.

(3) Subsection (1) above is without prejudice to section 133 of the Magistrates' Courts Act 1980 (consecutive terms of imprisonment).

(4) Any power of a magistrates' court to impose a term of imprisonment for non-payment of a fine, or for want of sufficient distress to satisfy a fine, shall not be limited by virtue of subsection (1) above.

(5) In subsection (4) above 'fine' includes a pecuniary penalty but does not include a pecuniary forfeiture or pecuniary compensation.

(6) In this section 'impose imprisonment' means pass a sentence of imprisonment or fix a term of imprisonment for failure to pay any sum of money, or for want of sufficient distress to satisfy any sum of money, or for failure to do or abstain from doing anything required to be done or left undone.

(7) Section 132 of the Magistrates' Courts Act 1980 contains provision about the minimum term of imprisonment which may be imposed by a magistrates' court.

VARIATION OF SENTENCE UNDER THE MAGISTRATES' COURTS ACT 1980, s. 142

The MCA 1980, s. 142(1) (see **D23.28**), allows a magistrates' court to vary or rescind its decision as to sentence if it is in the interests of justice to do so. The power is similar to that in respect of setting aside a conviction (see **D22.73**). The magistrates can reopen the case under s. 142 regardless of whether the accused pleaded guilty or was found guilty. However, s. 142 cannot operate where the accused was acquitted (*Coles v East Penwith Justices* (1998) 162 JP 687, where the Divisional Court held that there was no power under s. 142(1) to revoke a defendant's costs order where the prosecution had withdrawn the charges). **D23.23**

Guidance on the use of s. 142(1) was given in *Holme v Liverpool City Justices* [2004] EWHC 3131 (Admin). D pleaded guilty to dangerous driving, a pedestrian having sustained serious injuries. A community sentence was imposed. The magistrates agreed to a request from the CPS to reopen the case under s. 142, on the basis that the original counsel for the prosecution had not addressed the extent of the pedestrian's injuries and that the difference between the sentence imposed and the custodial sentence that would probably have been imposed had the court known all the facts offended the principles of justice. On appeal to the Divisional Court, Collins J (at [30]) said that: **D23.24**

> ... the power under s. 142 is to be used in a relatively limited situation, namely one which is akin to mistake or, as the court says, the slip rule. But there is no reason, on the face of it, to limit it further. It seems to me that if a court has been misled into imposing a particular sentence, and it is discovered that it has been so misled, then the sentence may properly be said to have been imposed because of a mistake; the mistake being the failure of the court to appreciate a relevant fact. That may well give power to the court to exercise the jurisdiction conferred by s. 142, but it does not indicate that that power should necessarily be used.

It follows that s. 142 can be used to increase sentence only in exceptional circumstances. His lordship went on (at [33]) to say that the sort of case which is appropriate for use of the power under s. 142 is one 'where the mistake is quickly identified and it is accepted on all sides that a mistake had been made'. At [42]–[43], his lordship said that it was possible to envisage circumstances in which the failure of the court to be aware of factors which would be relevant to sentence could properly mean that it would be appropriate to resort to s.142, but:

> ... it would only be in very rare circumstances that it would be appropriate to resort to s. 142 to consider an increase in sentence, particularly if that increase... brought the possibility of custody as opposed to another form of disposal.

The facts of the instant case, said the court, did not come anywhere near justifying such a use of s. 142.

In *Zykin v CPS* [2009] EWHC 1469 (Admin), Bean J quoted from *Holme* and said (at [16]) that s. 142 'does not confer a wide and general power on a magistrates' court to reopen a previous decision on the grounds that it is in the interests of justice to do so'; rather, it is 'a power to be used in a relatively limited situation, namely one which is akin to mistake or the slip rule'. In *R (Williamson) v City of Westminster Magistrates' Court* [2012] EWHC 1444 (Admin), [2012] 2 Cr App R 24 (299) (see **D22.76**), Burnett J said (*obiter*), at [31], that it could be contended that it would be in the interests of justice to substitute a new sentence on the ground that the one originally imposed was manifestly excessive. However, his lordship said that s. 142(1) 'cannot be read as conferring a power to substitute a new sentence in the same way as an appellate court might'. His lordship went on to reiterate that it is a power to rectify mistakes, not something broader (at [32]). **D23.25**

The power under s. 142 should not be used to punish an offender who has misbehaved in the dock after pronouncement of sentence by increasing what was first announced (*Powell* **D23.26**

(1985) 7 Cr App R (S) 247, a case which in fact concerned misbehaviour by an offender at the Crown Court).

In *R (Trigger) v Northampton Magistrates' Court* [2011] EWHC 149 (Admin), it was held to have been inappropriate for the magistrates to exercise their powers under s. 142 to increase a sentence originally imposed some 20 months earlier. Ramsey J said (at [33]) that the 'wide power and absence of any time limit in s. 142 must however be exercised taking account of the principle of finality of sentencing'. Moreover, although s. 142 gives the magistrates jurisdiction to vary or rescind the sentence so as to impose a sentence that could have been imposed at the date of the original sentence, 'it must be borne in mind that it would not usually be in the interests of justice to increase a sentence imposed earlier unless the power is exercised speedily after the date of the original sentence'.

Procedure

D23.27 CrimPR 28.4(2) (see Supplement, **R28.4**) states that the court may exercise its power to vary or rescind a sentence on application by a party, or on its own initiative. An application under s. 142 may be dealt with in a public or private hearing, or without a hearing. Under r. 28.4(3), a party seeking a variation in sentence under s. 142 must apply in writing as soon as reasonably practicable after the sentence has been passed, explaining why that sentence should be varied and specifying the variation that the applicant proposes. The application must be served on the court and on each other party. Under r. 28.4(4), the court cannot vary the sentence in the absence of the offender unless the court is making the variation which the offender has proposed, or the effect of the variation is that the offender is not dealt with more severely under the sentence as varied than before; otherwise the offender must be given the opportunity to make representations at a hearing.

CrimPD VII, para. S.3 (see Supplement, **CPD.VII.S**), states that 'the court retains a discretion to convene a hearing, in the exercise of which discretion due regard must be had to the overriding objective and to the importance of dealing with criminal cases in public, in accordance with the principle of open justice'.

Paragraph S.4 emphasises that the making of the decision to vary sentence, and the reasons for that decision, must always be announced at a public hearing, even if only briefly and even if the parties are absent on that occasion. The paragraph goes on to state that, while the decision itself must be made, and the reasons for that decision formulated, by the sentencing court itself, the public announcement may be made by a differently constituted court if it would be impracticable for the sentencing court to sit in public for the purpose within a reasonable time. However, it is respectfully suggested that it is only in Crown Court cases where the variation decision must be made by the judge who passed the original sentence (as clearly required by the PCC(S)A 2000, s. 155(4); see **D20.95**). Section 142 of the 1980 Act does not have an equivalent provision to s. 155(4) of the 2000 Act, and so an application for variation does not have to be made to the same justices who passed the sentence. It follows that, in the case of a sentence passed by a magistrates' court, an application under s. 142 should be made to the magistrates' court where sentence was passed but the court to whom the application is made does not have to be constituted in the same way as the court which passed sentence (i.e. the application may be made to a different bench of magistrates at that court).

D23.28 **Magistrates' Courts Act 1980, s. 142**

(1) A magistrates' court may vary or rescind a sentence or other order imposed or made by it when dealing with an offender if it appears to the court to be in the interests of justice to do so; and it is hereby declared that this power extends to replacing a sentence or order which for any reason appears to be invalid by another which the court has power to impose or make.

(1A) The power conferred on a magistrates' court by subsection (1) above shall not be exercisable in relation to any sentence or order imposed or made by it when dealing with an offender if—

(a) the Crown Court has determined an appeal against—

(i) that sentence or order;

(ii) the conviction in respect of which that sentence or order was imposed or made; or

(iii) any other sentence or order imposed or made by the magistrates' court when dealing with the offender in respect of that conviction (including a sentence or order replaced by that sentence or order); or

(b) the High Court has determined a case stated for the opinion of that court on any question arising in any proceeding leading to or resulting from the imposition or making of the sentence or order.

[(2), (2A) and (3) Relate to setting aside a conviction: see **D22.79**.]

(4) [Repealed.]

(5) Where a sentence or order is varied under subsection (1) above, the sentence or other order, as so varied, shall take effect from the beginning of the day on which it was originally imposed or made, unless the court otherwise directs.

COMMITTAL FOR SENTENCE

Powers to Commit for Sentence

As an alternative to passing sentence themselves, magistrates may, in some circumstances, commit the offender to the Crown Court to be sentenced. The major powers to commit for sentence are as follows: **D23.29**

(a) PCC(S)A 2000, s. 3: general power to commit an adult offender who is summarily convicted of an either-way offence.
(b) PCC(S)A 2000, s. 3A: power to commit an adult offender who is summarily convicted of an either-way offence in a case where the 'dangerous offender' provisions of the CJA 2003 are applicable.
(c) PCC(S)A 2000, s. 4: power to commit an adult offender who indicates a guilty plea at a 'plea before venue' hearing and who has also been sent for trial for one or more related offences.
(d) CJA 2003, sch. 12, paras. 8(6) and 11(2): power to commit an offender who is in breach of a requirement under a Crown Court suspended sentence and power to commit an offender convicted of an offence committed during the operational period of a Crown Court suspended sentence, respectively.
(e) PCC(S)A 2000, s. 13(5): power to commit an offender convicted of an offence committed during the period of Crown Court conditional discharge.
(f) CJA 2003, sch. 8, para. 9(6): power to commit an offender who is in breach of a Crown Court community order to be dealt with for that breach.
(g) PCC(S)A 2000, s. 6: supplementary power to commit offenders who are being committed under the PCC(S)A 2000, ss. 3 to 4A, or 13(5), or the CJA 2003, sch. 12, para. 11(2), to be sentenced also for other matters that would otherwise fall to be dealt with by the magistrates.
(h) POCA 2002, s. 70: power to commit to the Crown Court with a view to a confiscation order being considered under s. 6 of that Act (see **E19** for discussion of confiscation orders).

It should be noted that these committal provisions will appear in the Sentencing Code when it is implemented.

Committal under the Powers of Criminal Courts (Sentencing) Act 2000, s. 3

The PCC(S)A 2000, s. 3 (see **D23.41**), applies where a magistrates' court has convicted an offender of one or more either-way offences and the court takes the view that the seriousness of the offence(s) is such that its sentencing powers are inadequate. In such a case, the magistrates' court may commit the offender (in custody or on bail) to the Crown Court to be sentenced. The Crown Court can then pass sentence on the offender as if convicted on indictment, and so the limitations on the magistrates' sentencing powers do not apply (s. 5). **D23.30**

Limitations on the Power to Commit under s. 3

Scope of s. 3 Although the PCC(S)A 2000, s. 3(1), refers to an adult being convicted of an either-way offence 'on the summary trial' of that offence, s. 3 applies not just to cases where the **D23.31**

accused pleads not guilty but is found guilty by the court, but also to cases where the accused indicates a plea of guilty at the plea before venue hearing. Support for this interpretation can be found in the wording of the MCA 1980, s. 17A(6), which provides that, if the accused (at a plea before venue hearing) indicates a guilty plea, the court shall proceed as if the proceedings constituted from the beginning the summary trial of the information, and the accused pleaded guilty to it.

D23.32 **Nature of the Offence** The offender must have been convicted of an either-way offence (not a summary offence). Furthermore, the MCA 1980, s. 17D(2)(b), provides that the power to commit for sentence contained in the PCC(S)A 2000, s. 3 (or s. 4), does not apply when an offender is convicted of an offence of criminal damage which the magistrates dealt with as if it were a summary offence because the value involved did not exceed £5,000 (see **D6.20** for the special procedure for criminal damage charges).

Reason for Committal under s. 3

D23.33 In order to commit to the Crown Court for sentence under the PCC(S)A 2000, s. 3, the magistrates must be of the opinion that the offence(s) are so serious that the appropriate sentence exceeds their powers. Committal for sentence under s. 3 may be appropriate where, for example, the accused is revealed as having a record of relevant previous convictions (the CJA 2003, s. 143, indicates that each previous conviction may be treated as an aggravating factor), or the accused asks for further offences to be taken into consideration ('TICs' may result in an increase in the sentence eventually passed).

In *Sheffield Crown Court, ex parte DPP* (1994) 15 Cr App R (S) 768, and *Dover Justices, ex parte Pamment* (1994) 15 Cr App R (S) 778, the Divisional Court held that the power of the magistrates to commit for sentence under what is now s. 3 is unfettered. There is therefore nothing unreasonable or illogical about permitting a court to form one view at the stage of deciding on the appropriateness of summary trial, and a different view at the stage of deciding to commit for sentence. In *North Sefton Magistrates' Court, ex parte Marsh* (1994) 16 Cr App R (S) 401, the Divisional Court confirmed that the decision to commit for sentence under s. 3 does not have to be based on information received by the court after the decision to try the accused summarily.

D23.34 It should be noted that the Sentencing Council's definitive guideline, *Allocation* (see Supplement, **SG1-1**), states that either-way offences should be tried summarily unless the outcome would *clearly* be a sentence in excess of the court's powers for the offence(s) concerned (after taking into account personal mitigation and any potential reduction for a guilty plea). This means that, unless the case is patently too serious for their sentencing powers, magistrates should offer the accused the option of summary trial and, in the event of a finding of guilt, commit under s. 3 if they decide (at that stage) that their sentencing powers are inadequate. The guideline specifically notes that, given its power to commit for sentence, the magistrates' court may (in cases with 'no factual or legal complications') retain jurisdiction notwithstanding that the likely sentence might exceed its powers.

In *Wirral Magistrates' Court, ex parte Jermyn* [2001] 1 Cr App R (S) 137 (485), it was held that a decision to commit for sentence is not the sort of decision for which reasons must be given, as any person so committed has the opportunity to make full representations to the sentencing court in due course as to the appropriate penalty (per Penry-Davey J at [39]).

D23.35 **Legitimate Expectation** The discretion of the magistrates to commit for sentence is subject to the general principle of 'legitimate expectation' (see **D23.5**). If the offender has been led to believe, whether expressly or by implication, that the magistrates will pass sentence, the offender should not subsequently be committed for sentence, whether by the same or a differently constituted bench. For example, in *Horseferry Road Magistrates' Court, ex parte Rugless* (2000) 164 JP 311, D indicated a guilty plea at the 'plea before venue' hearing; the court ordered a pre-sentence report, stating that all sentencing options were to remain open with the exception of committal to the Crown Court for sentence. At the next hearing, D was committed to the

Crown Court for sentence. The Divisional Court held that D had a 'legitimate expectation' that he would be sentenced in the magistrates' court. The subsequent decision to commit him for sentence was in breach of this legitimate expectation; accordingly, it was appropriate to quash the decision to commit for sentence. Similarly, in *Wirral Magistrates' Court, ex parte Jermyn* [2001] 1 Cr App R (S) 137 (485), it was clear that D had been warned of the court's power to commit, but the warning gave the impression that the court was satisfied, on the material that it had, that the matter should remain in the magistrates' court and that would change only if new material emerged; no such material did emerge and so D had a legitimate expectation that he would be sentenced in the magistrates' court.

The burden is on the offender to show that there was a 'clear and unequivocal representation' that sentence would be determined by the magistrates (*Sheffield Magistrates' Court, ex parte Ojo* (2000) 164 JP 659). **D23.36**

Moreover, the expectation must be a *legitimate* one. In *R (White) v Barking Magistrates' Court* [2004] EWHC 417 (Admin), D was charged with production of cannabis contrary to the MDA 1971, s. 4(2). The charges related to a large-scale production operation. When he appeared before the justices, they adjourned the matter for a pre-sentence report to be prepared. At the next hearing they committed him to the Crown Court for sentence. He applied for judicial review of the decision to commit, contending that, at the first hearing, the justices had created a legitimate expectation that they would deal with sentence themselves. It was held that, although an expectation had been created by the justices at the earlier hearing that they would not commit D to the Crown Court, that expectation would not be fulfilled, since it would have been an unreasonable decision by the justices. Given the gravity of the offending, it would have been unreasonable, and therefore unlawful, for the justices not to have committed D for sentencing in the Crown Court. In *R (Harrington) v Bromley Magistrates' Court* [2007] EWHC 2896 (Admin), Mitting J (at [12]) said that he could not conceive of circumstances in which a *properly given* (emphasis added) indication could be gone back on by a subsequent decision without that decision being held to be irrational or unlawful. Likewise, in *Nicholas v Chester Magistrates' Court* [2009] EWHC 1504 (Admin), Wilkie J (at [10]) said that 'no judicial review would lie on the basis of legitimate expectation if the legitimate expectation was founded on a decision of a bench which was so unreasonable as to be perverse or such that no reasonable bench properly directing itself could have reached'.

Magistrates sometimes use the phrase 'keeping all options open' when adjourning for a pre-sentence report, in an effort to avoid arousing the expectations of the accused. In *Norwich Magistrates' Court, ex parte Elliott* [2000] 1 Cr App R (S) 152, Otton LJ said (at p. 159) that: **D23.37**

> ... care should be taken that nothing is said or done which might indicate to the accused that committal has been ruled out. If the court wishes to retain the discretion to commit to the Crown Court it should say so. For the court properly to retain the discretion to commit for sentence in such circumstances, it is necessary for it to make absolutely clear to the accused that the decision whether or not to commit for sentence has not been taken, and would only be taken at the adjourned hearing ... [However,] the mere fact of adjourning for pre-sentence reports, without more, cannot amount to a promise by the court that the subsequent justices will not commit the defendant to the Crown Court for sentence.

However, in *Feltham Justices, ex parte Rees* [2001] 2 Cr App R (S) 1 (1), the justices invited D's solicitor to mitigate before them and then adjourned for the preparation of a pre-sentence report; at the time of the adjournment they stated that they were leaving 'all options open' but did not say that committal to the Crown Court was one of those options. This was held to have given rise to a legitimate expectation that the justices themselves would pass sentence (and that the phrase 'all options open' meant that a custodial sentence was a possibility). Rose LJ (at [12]) said that, 'if justices have in mind that one of the options which is open to them is to commit for sentence, they should specifically say so'. Elias J, in a short concurring judgment, said (at [14]–[15]):

> If the legitimate expectation is not to be created in those circumstances, it is incumbent on the justices to make it absolutely clear to the accused that the decision whether or not to commit for sentence has not been taken, and that he might yet be sent for sentence before the Crown Court. The simple issue in this case is whether the words 'all options open' did make it absolutely clear that the defendant might be sent to the Crown Court for sentence. In my judgment, they did not …

If the Crown Court does pass sentence on an offender who has been committed for sentence despite the magistrates having adjourned for reports in circumstances giving rise to a legitimate expectation that the sentence would be non-custodial if the reports should be favourable, the Crown Court (on committal for sentence) is as much precluded from imposing a custodial sentence as the magistrates would have been (*Rennes* (1985) 7 Cr App R (S) 343, applying the general principle in *Gillam* (1980) 2 Cr App R (S) 267).

Guilty Plea at 'Plea before Venue' and Committal for Sentence

D23.38 Guidance on several issues that may arise in this context was given by the Divisional Court in *Warley Magistrates' Court, ex parte DPP* [1999] 1 WLR 216. The Court held as follows:

(a) The magistrates must have regard to the reduction in sentence on a plea of guilty when deciding whether the punishment which they would have power to inflict would be adequate.

(b) Where the gravity of the offence is such that, even when allowance has been made for the indicated plea, it is obvious that whatever may be the mitigation the punishment should be greater than the magistrates' court has power to impose, then the court should be prepared to commit the offender to the Crown Court for sentence without seeking any pre-sentence report or hearing in full any mitigation which the offender may wish to advance. However, if that course is to be adopted, the offender should be told what the court has in mind, and the offender (or legal representative) should be allowed to make brief submissions in opposition to that course. If the court is persuaded by the submission to change its mind, it should invite the prosecutor to make submissions in reply.

(c) In other cases (i.e. where, after allowance has been made for the plea of guilty, it appears that the court sentencing powers are, or may be, adequate), the hearing should proceed as usual. If a court, initially minded to commit at an early stage of the proceedings, is persuaded not to adopt that course at that stage, it can keep the option open by saying that the option of committal remains available, and then arranging for the preparation of a pre-sentence report. If, at the end of the hearing, whether or not to commit for sentence remains a live issue, the court should seek assistance from the prosecution and from the offender or his or her representative in relation to that issue.

(d) If the accused indicates a plea of guilty but there is a dispute as to the facts which must be resolved before sentence can be passed, necessitating a *Newton* hearing (see **D20.8** ***et seq.***):
   (i) if the magistrates consider that, whatever the outcome of the *Newton* hearing, they will have adequate powers of sentencing, they should proceed to hold a *Newton* hearing;
   (ii) if the magistrates consider that, whatever the outcome, the offender will have to be committed for sentence, it is clearly preferable to leave the Crown Court to conduct the *Newton* hearing;
   (iii) if the decision as to whether or not to commit for sentence turns, or may turn, on the outcome of the *Newton* hearing, the magistrates' court should proceed to conduct the *Newton* hearing.

(e) If a magistrates' court does conduct a *Newton* hearing and then commits to the Crown Court, it should record its findings for the benefit of the Crown Court, but it is open to the offender to seek to challenge those findings in the Crown Court (which may conduct a fresh *Newton* hearing) if he or she can point to some significant development, such as the discovery of important further evidence, having occurred since the magistrates' court reached its conclusion.

Bail In *Rafferty* [1999] 1 Cr App R 235, the Court of Appeal considered the question whether a committal for sentence should be on bail or in custody where the accused indicates a plea of guilty in the 'plea before venue' procedure. Thomas J said (at p. 237) that: D23.39

> ... in most cases where a plea of guilty is made at the plea before venue, it will not be usual to alter the position as regards bail or custody. In the usual case, when a person who has been on bail pleads guilty at the plea before venue, the usual practice should be to continue bail, even if it is anticipated that a custodial sentence will be imposed by the Crown Court, unless there are good reasons for remanding the defendant in custody. If the defendant is in custody, then after entering a plea of guilty at the plea before venue, it would be unusual, if the reasons for remanding him in custody remained unchanged, to alter the position.

It should be borne in mind, however, that there is no statutory presumption in favour of bail, since the BA 1976, s. 4, does not apply where an offender is being committed for sentence.

Challenging the Decision to Commit or to Refuse to Commit

If an offender is aggrieved at a decision to commit for sentence to the Crown Court, there is little that can be done about it. The Crown Court has power to remit the case back to the magistrates' court only if the committal is plainly invalid (e.g., s. 3 is invoked by the magistrates in respect of an offence which is triable only summarily); in any other case, the committal can be challenged only by means of an application for judicial review before the Divisional Court (*Sheffield Crown Court, ex parte DPP* (1994) 15 Cr App R (S) 768; *Bahbahani* [2018] EWCA Crim 95, [2018] QB 1099, at [30]). However, such a challenge would succeed only if the committal were irrational in the *Wednesbury* sense that no reasonable bench of magistrates could have decided to commit the offender for sentence. D23.40

However, two points should be noted. First, it is by no means inevitable that the Crown Court will in fact impose a sentence which is more severe than the sentence which the magistrates' court could have imposed. Secondly, there is the option of appealing to the Court of Appeal against the sentence imposed by the Crown Court (under the Criminal Appeal Act 1968, s. 10) if that sentence is in fact excessive.

If the prosecution are unhappy with a decision *not* to commit for sentence, judicial review may be available. However, the Divisional Court will interfere with such decisions only where they are properly categorised as 'truly astonishing' (*Warley Magistrates' Court, ex parte DPP* [1999] 1 All ER 251 at 225, per Kennedy LJ; *R (DPP) v Devizes Magistrates' Court* [2006] EWHC 1072 (Admin), per Maurice Kay LJ at [25]).

Powers of Criminal Courts (Sentencing) Act 2000, s. 3 D23.41

(1) Subject to subsection (4) below, this section applies where on the summary trial of an offence triable either way a person aged 18 or over is convicted of the offence.
(2) If the court is of the opinion—
  (a) that the offence or the combination of the offence and one or more offences associated with it was so serious that the Crown Court should, in the court's opinion, have the power to deal with the offender in any way it could deal with him if he had been convicted on indictment,
  (b) [repealed]
  the court may commit the offender in custody or on bail to the Crown Court for sentence in accordance with section 5(1) below.
(3) Where the court commits a person under subsection (2) above, section 6 below (which enables a magistrates' court, where it commits a person under this section in respect of an offence, also to commit him to the Crown Court to be dealt with in respect of certain other offences) shall apply accordingly.
(4) This section does not apply in relation to an offence as regards which this section is excluded by section 17D or 33 of the Magistrates' Courts Act 1980 (certain offences where value involved is small).
(5) The preceding provisions of this section shall apply in relation to a corporation as if—
  (a) the corporation were an individual aged 18 or over; and
  (b) in subsection (2) above, paragraph (b) and the words 'in custody or on bail' were omitted.

Committal for Sentence under the Powers of Criminal Courts (Sentencing) Act 2000, s. 4

D23.42 The PCC(S)A 2000, s. 4(1) and (2) (see **D23.44**), provide that, where the accused has indicated a guilty plea to an either-way offence (and so is deemed to have pleaded guilty to it) and is also sent for trial for one or more related offences, the magistrates may commit the offender to the Crown Court for sentence in respect of the either-way offence to which he or she has pleaded guilty. For the purposes of these provisions, one offence is related to another if the charges for them could be joined (under CrimPR 3.29(4): see **D11.63**) in the same indictment if both charges were to be tried in the Crown Court (s. 4(7)). Thus, the two charges must be founded on the same facts or must be, or be part of, a series of offences of the same or a similar character.

Section 4(4) provides that, where the magistrates' court has committed an offender for sentence pursuant to s. 4(2), the Crown Court can exceed the sentencing powers of the magistrates' court in respect of the either-way offence so committed only if either:

(a) the magistrates stated that they considered their sentencing powers were inadequate to deal with the offender for that offence (and so they also had power to commit the offender for sentence under s. 3); or
(b) the offender is convicted by the Crown Court of one or more of the related offences.

D23.43 If the magistrates take the view that their sentencing powers are adequate to deal with the offence in respect of which the offender has indicated a guilty plea, then only s. 4 allows them to commit the offender to the Crown Court for sentence for that offence. On the other hand, if the magistrates take the view that their sentencing powers are not adequate to deal with that offence, they have two options: they can either commit for sentence for that offence under s. 3, or they can commit for sentence under s. 4 but indicate that they took the view that their sentencing powers were inadequate and so could have invoked s. 3. When committing an offender for sentence the court should state whether it is doing so under s. 3 or s. 4.

In *S* [2012] EWCA Crim 2031 Thirlwall J said (at [21]) that where an offender is committed for sentence under s. 4, the magistrates must consider whether their powers would be sufficient in respect of the matter which is being committed for sentence. If they do not consider that their sentencing powers would be sufficient, it is imperative that they observe the requirements of the statute and state in open court that the court has power to commit the offender under s. 3. If that is not done, the Crown Court will be able to exceed the powers of a magistrates' court in respect of the offence committed for sentence under s. 4 only where there is a conviction in the Crown Court in respect of at least one matter which was sent for trial.

It is submitted that, to avoid the risk of inadvertently fettering the powers of the Crown Court following a s. 4 committal, the best practice is to use s. 3 where the magistrates' sentencing powers are not adequate and to use s. 4 only where their powers are adequate.

D23.44 **Powers of Criminal Courts (Sentencing) Act 2000, s. 4**

(1) This section applies where—
(a) a person aged 18 or over appears or is brought before a magistrates' court ('the court') on an information charging him with an offence triable either way ('the offence');
(b) he or (where applicable) his representative indicates under section 17A, 17B or 20(7) of the Magistrates' Courts Act 1980 that he would plead guilty if the offence were to proceed to trial; and
(c) proceeding as if section 9(1) of that Act were complied with and he pleaded guilty under it, the court convicts him of the offence.

(1A) But this section does not apply to an offence as regards which this section is excluded by section 17D of that Act (certain offences where value involved is small).

(2) *If the court has sent the offender to the* Crown Court for trial for one or more related offences, that is to say, one or more offences which, in its opinion, are related to the offence, it may commit him in custody or on bail to the Crown Court to be dealt with in respect of the offence in accordance with section 5(1) below.

(3) If the power conferred by subsection (2) above is not exercisable but the court is still to determine to, or to determine whether to, send the offender to the Crown Court for trial under section 51 or 51A of the Crime and Disorder Act 1998 for one or more related offences—
 (a) it shall adjourn the proceedings relating to the offence until after it has made those determinations; and
 (b) if it sends the offender to the Crown Court for trial for one or more related offences, it may then exercise that power.

(4) Where the court—
 (a) under subsection (2) above commits the offender to the Crown Court to be dealt with in respect of the offence; and
 (b) does not state that, in its opinion, it also has power so to commit him under section 3(2) or, as the case may be, section 3A(2) above,

 section 5(1) below shall not apply unless he is convicted before the Crown Court of one or more of the related offences.

(5) Where section 5(1) below does not apply, the Crown Court may deal with the offender in respect of the offence in any way in which the magistrates' court could deal with him if it had just convicted him of the offence.

(6) Where the court commits a person under subsection (2) above, section 6 below (which enables a magistrates' court, where it commits a person under this section in respect of an offence, also to commit him to the Crown Court to be dealt with in respect of certain other offences) shall apply accordingly.

(7) For the purposes of this section one offence is related to another if, were they both to be prosecuted on indictment, the charges for them could be joined in the same indictment.

(8) In reaching any decision under or taking any step contemplated by this section—
 (a) the court shall not be bound by any indication of sentence given in respect of the offence under section 20 of the Magistrates' Courts Act 1980 (procedure where summary trial appears more suitable); and
 (b) nothing the court does under this section may be challenged or be the subject of any appeal in any court on the ground that it is not consistent with an indication of sentence

Hearing in the Crown Court following a Committal under the Powers of Criminal Courts (Sentencing) Act 2000, s. 3 or s. 4

Procedural Issues Committal under the PCC(S)A 2000, s. 3, will be to the most convenient location of the Crown Court, having regard to any relevant local direction on the matter. The Crown Court, when hearing a s. 3 committal, comprises a circuit judge or recorder. **D23.45**

Before proceeding to hear the case, the Crown Court should confirm that the person before it has indeed been committed for sentence by the magistrates' court. This is usually done by asking the offender if he or she admits that fact. In the absence of such admission, the prosecution must prove the committal by formal evidence. That evidence might come from a certified copy of the magistrates' court register or from someone present in the magistrates' court at the time of the committal. Once the committal has been admitted or proved, the procedure before sentence is passed is exactly the same as when there is a guilty plea, with a prosecution summary of the facts and a plea in mitigation on behalf of the offender.

Where the offender indicates an appeal against conviction in the lower court, the sentencing proceedings should be adjourned until the conclusion of the appeal (*Faithful* [1950] 2 All ER 1251). If, however, the court inadvertently disposes of the committal for sentence in ignorance of the fact that the offender is appealing against conviction, the appeal should be heard nonetheless and, if it succeeds, the sentence passed on the committal will simply fall with the conviction (*Croydon Crown Court, ex parte Bernard* [1981] 3 All ER 106).

Where the offender asked the lower court to take other offences into consideration, he or she is not bound to take the same course in the Crown Court (i.e. the normal procedure for taking offences into consideration should be followed in the Crown Court and, in the absence of a request to consider the other matters, they must be ignored (*Davies* (1981) 72 Cr App R 262).

D23.46 **Powers of Crown Court** The PCC(S)A 2000, s. 5, provides that, following a committal for sentence under s. 3 or (subject to the restrictions discussed above) s. 4, the Crown Court may deal with the offender as if just convicted on indictment.

Powers of Criminal Courts (Sentencing) Act 2000, s. 5

(1) Where an offender is committed by a magistrates' court for sentence under section 3, 3A or 4 above, the Crown Court shall inquire into the circumstances of the case and may deal with the offender in any way in which it could deal with him if he had just been convicted of the offence on indictment before the court.

(2) In relation to committals under section 4 above, subsection (1) above has effect subject to section 4(4) and (5) above.

(3) Section 20A(1) of the Magistrates' Courts Act 1980 (which relates to the effect of an indication of sentence under section 20 of that Act) shall not apply in respect of any specified offence (within the meaning of section 224 of the Criminal Justice Act 2003)—
   (a) in respect of which the offender is committed under section 3A(2) above; or
   (b) in respect of which—
      (i) the offender is committed under section 4(2) above; and
      (ii) the court states under section 4(4) above that, in its opinion, it also has power to commit the offender under section 3A(2) above.

D23.47 ***Newton* hearings** If a *Newton* hearing took place at the magistrates' court, the Crown Court should adopt the outcome. In *Warley Justices, ex parte DPP* [1999] 1 WLR 216, Kennedy LJ said (at p. 224) that it may be that the offender will seek to challenge the magistrates' findings in the Crown Court, but added 'I would not expect him to be allowed to do so unless he could point to some significant development, such as the discovery of important further evidence, having occurred since the magistrates' court reached its conclusion'. A similar point was made in *Gillan v DPP* [2007] EWHC 380 (Admin), [2007] 1 WLR 2214, where the court considered the question: 'Where magistrates have determined the factual basis for sentencing at a *Newton* hearing, and then commit the defendant for sentence in the Crown Court, does the duty of the Crown Court to inquire into the circumstances of the case include a power to hear evidence in a second *Newton* hearing to determine afresh the factual basis on which the defendant shall be sentenced?' Forbes J, giving the judgment of the Divisional Court said (at [28]–[29]):

> I am completely satisfied that the Crown Court does have jurisdiction to hold a further *Newton* hearing if it is in the interests of fairness and justice to do so... However, the fact that the Crown Court has jurisdiction or a power to hold a further *Newton* hearing does not mean, ipso facto, that it should accede to an application to do so in any case where it is apparent that the magistrates have already conducted such a hearing and made clear findings of fact as part of their perfectly proper decision-making with regard to committing the defendant to the Crown Court for sentence. Essentially, the matter is a question for the discretion of the judge, in the proper exercise of which he or she must be fully mindful of his or her obligation to carry out a proper inquiry into the circumstances of the case... I would not expect the judge in the Crown Court to exercise his discretion in favour of allowing a defendant to re-open the magistrates' findings of fact unless the defendant was able to point to some significant development or matter, such as (but not confined to) the discovery of important further evidence having occurred since the Magistrates' Court reached its conclusion on the facts. In saying that, I would not wish it to be thought that I was laying down any absolute or strict formula as to how the judge should exercise his or her discretion in any particular case. Everything will depend upon the facts and circumstances of the particular case; each case must be considered individually.

If the divergence between prosecution and defence versions becomes apparent for the first time at the Crown Court (or no *Newton* hearing was held at the magistrates' court), the Crown Court should, of course, hold a *Newton* hearing to determine the issue (*Munroe v DPP* (1988) 152 JP 657).

D23.48 **Age of Offender** In *Robson* [2006] EWCA Crim 1414, [2007] 1 Cr App R (S) 54, the Court of Appeal considered the position where the offender has attained an age of relevance to sentencing powers during the period between the magistrates' court and Crown Court proceedings.

In that case, a 17-year-old offender was convicted of sexual assault and was committed to the Crown Court for sentence under the PCC(S)A 2000, s. 3C (part of the 'dangerous offender' provisions established by the CJA 2003). When he appeared for sentencing, he had attained the age of 18. The Court of Appeal considered whether the age of an offender committed to the Crown Court for sentence is to be treated, for the purpose of sentence, differently from the age of an offender convicted after trial. The latter must be sentenced on the basis of age at the date of conviction, whether convicted following a guilty plea or a guilty verdict (*Danga* [1992] QB 476; *Robinson* [1993] 2 All ER 1). The Court held that, at least for the purposes of the sentencing regime created for dangerous offenders by the CJA 2003 (see E4), the matter should be decided on the basis of the wording of the relevant statutory provisions. For dangerous offenders, these refer to age at the date of conviction (not sentence), and so the relevant date for sentence purposes is the date of the conviction, not the date of the Crown Court appearance following committal for sentence.

Given that the PCC(S)A 2000, s. 89(1), provides that a sentence of imprisonment may not be passed on a person 'if he is aged under 21 when *convicted* of the offence', it would seem that the use of the word 'convicted' requires the court to pass a sentence appropriate to the age at the date of conviction, not the date of sentence, and so an offender who attains the age of 21 between conviction in the magistrates' court and appearance in the Crown Court for sentence should be sentenced as if under 21, and therefore is not eligible for a sentence of imprisonment.

Other Committal Powers

Dangerous Offenders The PCC(S)A 2000, s. 3A, enables a magistrates' court which convicts an adult defendant to commit him or her to the Crown Court for sentence when the criteria for an extended sentence under the 'dangerous offender' provisions of the CJA 2003 would appear to be met (see E4). It is submitted that s. 3A applies both following an indication of a guilty plea at a plea before venue hearing and where the accused is found guilty following a summary trial. **D23.49**

Powers of Criminal Courts (Sentencing) Act 2000, s. 3A

(1) This section applies where on the summary trial of a specified offence triable either way a person aged 18 or over is convicted of the offence.
(2) If, in relation to the offence, it appears to the court that the criteria for the imposition of a sentence under section 226A of the Criminal Justice Act 2003 would be met, the court must commit the offender in custody or on bail to the Crown Court for sentence in accordance with section 5(1) below.
(3) Where the court commits a person under subsection (2) above, section 6 below (which enables a magistrates' court, where it commits a person under this section in respect of an offence, also to commit him to the Crown Court to be dealt with in respect of certain other offences) shall apply accordingly.
(4) In reaching any decision under or taking any step contemplated by this section—
 (a) the court shall not be bound by any indication of sentence given in respect of the offence under section 20 of the Magistrates' Courts Act 1980 (procedure where summary trial appears more suitable); and
 (b) nothing the court does under this section may be challenged or be the subject of any appeal in any court on the ground that it is not consistent with an indication of sentence.
(5) Nothing in this section shall prevent the court from committing an offender convicted of a specified offence to the Crown Court for sentence under section 3 above if the provisions of that section are satisfied.
(6) In this section, references to a specified offence are to a specified offence within the meaning of section 224 of the Criminal Justice Act 2003.

Committal for Sentence in Respect of Breach of a Crown Court Order

An offender can be committed to the Crown Court to be dealt with if in breach of certain Crown Court orders, and an offender who has been convicted in a magistrates' court of an offence committed during the currency of certain Crown Court orders can also be committed for sentence. **D23.50**

Conditional Discharge

D23.51 The PCC(S)A 2000, s. 13(5), provides that an offender who is convicted by a magistrates' court of an offence committed during the period of conditional discharge imposed by the Crown Court may be committed (in custody or on bail) to the Crown Court to be dealt with.

Community Order

D23.52 The CJA 2003, sch. 8, para. 9(6), provides that, where a community order was made by the Crown Court and a magistrates' court would otherwise have the power to deal with the offender for breach of the order (because, under para. 7(1)(b), the order included a direction that any failure to comply with the requirements of the order was to be dealt with by a magistrates' court), it may instead commit the offender (in custody or on bail) to be dealt with by the Crown Court.

Suspended Sentence Order

D23.53 The CJA 2003, sch. 12, para. 8(6), deals with failure to comply with community order requirements under a suspended sentence order. It provides that, where a suspended sentence order was made by the Crown Court and a magistrates' court would otherwise have the power to deal with the offender for breach of the order (because, under para. 6(1)(b), the order included a direction that any failure to comply with the community requirements of the order was to be dealt with by a magistrates' court), it may instead commit the offender (in custody or on bail) to be dealt with by the Crown Court.

The CJA 2003, sch. 12, para. 11(2), deals with offences committed during the operational period of a suspended sentence. It provides that, where an offender is convicted by a magistrates' court of any offence and the court is satisfied that the offence was committed during the operational period of a suspended sentence passed by the Crown Court, the magistrates' court may, if it thinks fit, commit the offender (in custody or on bail) to the Crown Court. If it does not do so, it must inform the Crown Court of the conviction.

D23.54 Guidance on the effect of some of the committal powers under the CJA 2003 was given by the Court of Appeal in *Majury* [2007] EWCA Crim 2968. The Court emphasised that the CJA 2003, sch. 12, para. 8(6), applies only to a breach of a suspended sentence order with which the magistrates themselves can deal (i.e. in the case of a suspended sentence order made by the Crown Court, where the breach comprises a failure to comply with a community requirement and the Crown Court directed when the sentence was passed that failures to comply should be dealt with by the magistrates' court); para. 8(6) does not apply to breach of a suspended sentence when the sentence was passed by the Crown Court and the breach is comprised in the commission of a further offence. Furthermore, para. 11(2) does not apply to the 'new' offences committed in breach of the suspended sentence. If the offender is committed to the Crown Court, the Crown Court can deal with the breach under sch. 12, para. 8(1)(b) (see para. 11(1)). If the offender is not committed to the Crown Court, but the Crown Court receives notice of the breach, it can take its own enforcement proceedings by issuing a summons or an arrest warrant under para. 12(1). Paragraph 11(2) does not of itself give the Crown Court power to deal with the offences committed during the operational period of the suspended sentence; rather, it is the means by which the breach of the suspended sentence is brought before the Crown Court to be dealt with under para. 8(1)(b). If the justices want the Crown Court to deal with the original offence and the 'new' offences, and the latter are triable either way, the justices should decide whether the powers of the Crown Court to sentence for the new offences should be those of the Crown Court or of the magistrates' court. If the former, the committal of those offences would take place under the PCC(S)A 2000, s. 3; if the latter, committal would be under s. 6 of that Act (see **D23.55**).

Committal under the Powers of Criminal Courts (Sentencing) Act 2000, s. 6

D23.55 The PCC(S)A 2000, s. 6 (see **D23.61**), gives a power to commit for sentence which may be used to supplement a committal under the provisions listed in s. 6(4), which include committal for sentence under the PCC(S)A 2000, ss. 3 to 4A; committal for sentence in respect of the breach of a conditional discharge imposed by the Crown Court (under the PCC(S)A 2000, s. 13(5)); and committal to be dealt with for breach of a suspended sentence imposed by the Crown Court (under the CJA 2003, sch. 12, para. 11(2)).

These committal powers are referred to below as 'primary' committal powers.

By virtue of the PCC(S)A 2000, s. 6(2), when a magistrates' court exercises a 'primary' committal power in respect of an indictable offence (in this context, an either-way offence), it may also commit the offender to the Crown Court to be dealt with in respect of any other offence of which he or she stands convicted (whether summary or indictable) that the magistrates' court has jurisdiction to deal with as regards sentence. Section 6(2) expressly states that, provided the committing court would be able to deal with the matter if it were not to commit, the power to commit arises even if the conviction was by a different court.

To take the example of a magistrates' court which has decided to commit an offender under s. 3, for one either-way offence, a committal under s. 6 might (for instance) relate to:

(a) another, less serious, either-way offence of which the magistrates have convicted the offender on the same occasion;
(b) a summary offence of which they have convicted the offender on the same occasion.

The reason a committal under s. 3 for the secondary offence would be inappropriate in situation (a) is that, because the offence is not sufficiently serious, the magistrates' powers of sentencing for it are adequate. In situation (b), a committal under s. 3 would be inappropriate simply because that section does not extend to summary offences.

By virtue of s. 6(3), where the offence in respect of which the 'primary' power of committal arises is a *summary* offence, the magistrates may also commit the offender for sentence in respect of (a) any other offence carrying imprisonment or disqualification from driving of which their court has convicted the offender, or (b) breach of a suspended sentence passed on the offender by that or another magistrates' court. In *Qayum* [2010] EWCA Crim 2237, the Court of Appeal noted that s. 6(3) gives the magistrates a 'secondary' power to commit for sentence in respect of a breach of a suspended sentence order, but only where the 'relevant offence' (i.e. the offence in respect of which the 'primary' power of committal is being exercised) is itself summary only. In fact, the primary power of committal will, in practice, nearly always relate to an indictable offence, and so s. 6(3) is of little practical significance. **D23.56**

The other use of s. 6 is where a summary conviction puts the offender in breach of a suspended sentence passed by the Crown Court and the magistrates consider that, although the breach should be committed to the Crown Court under the CJA 2003, sch. 12, para. 11(2), the offence giving rise to the breach is not in itself serious enough to warrant committal under s. 3. The court should then commit the offender under para. 11(2), for possible activation of the suspended sentence, and under s. 6, for sentence for the present offence (*Majury* [2007] EWCA Crim 2968). **D23.57**

It should be noted that s. 6 applies only where the committal is under one of the enactments specified in s. 6(4). In *Ayhan* [2011] EWCA Crim 3184, [2012] 1 WLR 1775, D was committed for sentence to the Crown Court in respect of three offences, one of which was triable either way and two of which were summary only. The memorandum of conviction stated that all three committals were made under the PCC(S)A 2000, s. 3. However, s. 3 applies only to either-way offences. In fact, the summary offences had been committed under s. 6 (see **D23.55**). The Court of Appeal held that 'the essential question is not what power the memorandum of conviction records the justices to have used, but the power they actually used' (per Lord Judge CJ, at [16]). The correct approach 'was to examine the question whether the magistrates' court was vested with the necessary jurisdiction to commit to the Crown Court. If it was, then an omission from, or an inaccuracy in, the memorandum of conviction about the statutory powers which were **D23.58** exercised, or which were available to be exercised, did not affect the validity of the committal' (at [18]). His lordship went on to hold (at [22]) that 'provided the power of the magistrates' court to commit for sentence was properly exercised in respect of one or more either-way offences in accordance with s. 3 of the 2000 Act, a mistake in recording the statutory basis for a committal of summary-only offences does not invalidate the committal. The principle is that thereafter the Crown Court must abide by the sentencing powers available to the magistrates' court in relation to the summary only offences. If that principle is not followed, then the sentences must be reduced to sentences which fall within the jurisdiction of the magistrates.' *Ayhan* was followed in *Luff* [2013] EWCA Crim 1958, where the committal purported to be under s. 6, but the Court of Appeal held that the reference to s. 6 was a mistake, and that the committal should be treated as having been under s. 4.

Section 6 must be invoked at the hearing where the 'primary' power is exercised. In *Garthwaite* [2019] EWCA Crim 2357, D had committed three sets of offences. The first set included an either-way offence, for which he was committed to the Crown Court for sentence under s. 3 of the 2000 Act; the remaining charges in that group were summary offences, and these offences were (correctly) committed to the Crown Court for sentence under s. 6. The two other groups of offences — all summary offences — came before the magistrates' court a few days later. The magistrates' court purported to commit those offences to the Crown Court under s. 6 (on the basis of the earlier s. 3 committal). Had all three groups of offences been before the magistrates' court at the same time, all the summary offences could have been committed to the Crown Court under s. 6 when the either-way offence was committed under s. 3. However, as Holroyde LJ noted (at [14]–[15]), s. 6 confers a power which is 'necessarily ancillary' to the magistrates' court committing 'the relevant offence' to the Crown Court for sentence. At the second hearing in the magistrates' court, there was no 'relevant offence', because none of the offences in the two groups of offences was, at that hearing, being committed for sentence under any of the enactments mentioned in s. 6(4) of the 2000 Act.

It should also be noted that the power to commit for sentence under s. 6 applies only where the defendant has been committed for *sentence* in respect of one or more other offences, under one of the 'primary' powers in the 2000 Act; it does not apply where an accused has been sent for trial in respect of other offences (see *James* [2017] EWCA Crim 1367, where a number of offences were sent to the Crown Court for trial under the CDA 1998, s. 51, and the magistrates mistakenly purported to commit D for sentence under the PCC(S)A 2000, s. 6, in respect of three summary offences to which he had pleaded guilty). Similarly, in *Ross* [2020] EWCA Crim 210, [2020] RTR 19 (225), D pleaded guilty to a number of offences but not guilty to one either-way offence. The magistrates sent D to the Crown Court for trial in respect of the either-way offence to which he had pleaded not guilty, and purported to use s. 6 to commit him for sentence in respect of the offences to which he had pleaded guilty. This was an error, as the either-way offence had been committed for trial, not sentence. The Divisional Court noted that one of the offences to which D had pleaded guilty was triable either way, and therefore could have been committed for sentence under the PCC(S)A 2000, s. 4 (see **D23.42**); the Court deemed the committal for that offence to have been under s. 4 (thereby validating the committal for the summary offences under s. 6). These cases demonstrate the care that has to be taken in identifying which committal powers are available in the particular circumstances of the case at hand.

Powers of Crown Court following Committal for Sentence under the Powers of Criminal Courts (Sentencing) Act 2000, s. 6

D23.59 Following a committal under the PCC(S)A 2000, s. 6, the Crown Court may deal with the offender in respect of the offence(s) so committed in any way the magistrates' court might have done (s. 7; see **D23.61**). The Crown Court's sentencing powers for an offence committed under s. 6 are thus identical to those of the magistrates' court. This limitation on the Crown Court's powers reveals the basic purpose of a committal under s. 6, namely to enable one court to deal with an offender for all matters outstanding rather than have the sentencing function split between the Crown Court and the magistrates' court. The purpose of s. 6 is *not* to expose the offender to risk of greater punishment than the lower court could inflict.

In *Morgan* [2012] EWCA Crim 1939, Irwin J tentatively raised the possibility (at [23]) that, when a person is committed to the Crown Court for breach of a suspended sentence, the effect of s. 7(2) might be to give that court untrammelled powers of sentence in respect of all matters committed to it, including any offences constituting the breach of that suspended sentence. However, his lordship regarded that as doubtful. The Court of Appeal went on to reject this suggestion even more emphatically in *Bateman* [2012] EWCA Crim 2518, [2013] 1 WLR 1710, where Moore-Bick LJ said (at [20]) that, when considering the proper interpretation of s. 7(2), it had to be borne in mind that s. 7(1) and (2) are both concerned with committals under s. 6 (committal of a person to the Crown Court to be dealt with in respect of an associated offence), and that subsection (2) must be read in the context of subsection (1), to which it provides an exception. His lordship noted that committal to be dealt with for breach of a suspended sentence imposed by the Crown Court takes place under the CJA 2003, sch. 12, para. 11(2), not under the PCC(S)A 2000, s. 6. It follows that, when s. 7(2) refers to committal under s. 6 to be dealt with by the Crown Court in respect of a suspended sentence, it must be referring to a suspended sentence previously imposed by a magistrates' court. This provision enables the Crown Court to exercise the powers under sch. 12, paras. 8 and 9, which could otherwise have been exercised by the magistrates themselves, and ensures that, on committal to the Crown Court under s. 6, a person is not exposed to a more severe penalty than could have been imposed by the magistrates.

Where the offender is in breach of a suspended sentence imposed by the Crown Court, and the breach is because of the commission of an either-way offence, the magistrates' court should consider carefully whether its sentencing powers are adequate in respect of the offence which constituted the breach. As Irwin J said in *Morgan* (at [26]), if the magistrates consider that the gravity of the offence which constitutes the breach, together with any associated matters, is such as to justify committal under s. 3 (on the basis that their sentencing powers are inadequate), then the offence(s) should be committed pursuant to s. 3, rather than s. 6, so that the Crown Court powers are those contained in s. 5, not those contained in s. 7 (a point echoed by Moore-Bick LJ in *Bateman*, at [31]). **D23.60**

Powers of Criminal Courts (Sentencing Act) 2000, ss. 6 and 7 **D23.61**

6.—(1) This section applies where a magistrates' court ('the committing court') commits a person in custody or on bail to the Crown Court under any enactment mentioned in subsection (4) below to be sentenced or otherwise dealt with in respect of an offence ('the relevant offence').

(2) Where this section applies and the relevant offence is an indictable offence, the committing court may also commit the offender, in custody or on bail as the case may require, to the Crown Court to be dealt with in respect of any other offence whatsoever in respect of which the committing court has power to deal with him (being an offence of which he has been convicted by that or any other court).

(3) Where this section applies and the relevant offence is a summary offence, the committing court may commit the offender, in custody or on bail as the case may require, to the Crown Court to be dealt with in respect of—

(a) any other offence of which the committing court has convicted him, being either—

(i) an offence punishable with imprisonment; or

(ii) an offence in respect of which the committing court has a power or duty to order him to be disqualified under section 34, 35 or 36 of the Road Traffic Offenders Act 1988 (disqualification for certain motoring offences); or

(b) any suspended sentence in respect of which the committing court has under paragraph 11(1) of Schedule 12 to the Criminal Justice Act 2003 power to deal with him.

(4) The enactments referred to in subsection (1) above are—

(a) the Vagrancy Act 1824 (incorrigible rogues);

(b) sections 3 and 4 [3 to 4A] above (committal for sentence for offences triable either way);

(c) section 13(5) below (conditionally discharged person convicted of further offence);

. . . and

(e) paragraph 11(2) of Schedule 12 to the Criminal Justice Act 2003 (committal to Crown Court where offender convicted during operational period of suspended sentence).

7.—(1) Where under section 6 above a magistrates' court commits a person to be dealt with by the Crown Court in respect of an offence, the Crown Court may after inquiring into the circumstances of the case deal with him in any way in which the magistrates' court could deal with him if it had just convicted him of the offence.

(2) Subsection (1) above does not apply where under section 6 above a magistrates' court commits a person to be dealt with by the Crown Court in respect of a suspended sentence, but in such a case the powers under paragraphs 8 and 9 of Schedule 12 to the Criminal Justice Act 2003 (power of court to deal with suspended sentence) shall be exercisable by the Crown Court.

(3) Without prejudice to subsections (1) and (2) above, where under section 6 above or any enactment mentioned in subsection (4) of that section a magistrates' court commits a person to be dealt with by the Crown Court, any duty or power which, apart from this subsection, would fall to be discharged or exercised by the magistrates' court shall not be discharged or exercised by that court but shall instead be discharged or may instead be exercised by the Crown Court.

(4) Where under section 6 above a magistrates' court commits a person to be dealt with by the Crown Court in respect of an offence triable only on indictment in the case of an adult (being an offence which was tried summarily because of the offender's being under 18 years of age), the Crown Court's powers under subsection (1) above in respect of the offender after he attains the age of 18 shall be powers to do either or both of the following—

(a) to impose [an unlimited fine];

(b) to deal with the offender in respect of the offence in any way in which the magistrates' court could deal with him if it had just convicted him of an offence punishable with imprisonment for a term not exceeding six months.

Section D24 Trial of Children and Young People

INTRODUCTION

Aims of the Youth Justice System

The CDA 1998, s. 37(1), provides that: 'It shall be the principal aim of the youth justice system to prevent offending by children and young persons'. Section 37(2) goes on to require that: 'In addition to any other duty to which they are subject, it shall be the duty of all persons and bodies carrying out functions in relation to the youth justice system to have regard to that aim'. However, the CYPA 1933, s. 44(1), provides that 'every court in dealing with a child or young person who is brought before it, either as an offender or otherwise, shall have regard to the welfare of the child or young person'. **D24.1**

Terminology: 'Adult', 'Child' and 'Young Person' **D24.2**

(a) *Adult.* In the context of criminal procedure and mode of trial, an 'adult' is any person aged 18 or over. In the context of sentencing, however, 'adult' is sometimes used to mean those aged 21 or over, since it is at that age that an offender currently becomes liable to imprisonment.
(b) *Child.* By the CYPA 1933, s. 107(1), 'child' (when used in that Act) means a person under the age of 14 years. The CYPA 1969, s. 70(1), contains a similar provision in respect of most of the provisions of that Act, while the CYPA 1963, s. 65(3), provides that the 1963 Act shall be construed 'as one with' the 1933 Act.
(c) *Young person.* The definition sections referred to in (c) above also define 'young person' as a 'person who has attained the age of 14 years and is under the age of 18 years'. Thus, a distinction has to be drawn between children (aged under 14) and young persons (aged 14 to 17 inclusive).

Youth Offending Teams

Pursuant to the CDA 1998, s. 39, each local authority must establish a youth offending team ('YOT'). The YOT must comprise: **D24.3**

(a) a probation officer;
(b) a person with experience of social work in relation to children, nominated by the director of children's services appointed by the relevant local authority;
(c) a police officer;
(d) a person nominated by a Clinical Commissioning Group or Local Health Board any part of whose area lies within the local authority's area; and
(e) a person with experience in education nominated by the relevant director of children's services appointed by the relevant local authority.

Other people may be co-opted on to the YOT (e.g., housing officers and people with experience of dealing with drugs and alcohol misuse). The functions of the YOT are to co-ordinate the provision of youth justice services for all those in the authority's area who need them, and to carry out such functions as are assigned to it in the local authority's 'youth justice plan'. The plan (made under the CDA 1998, s. 40) sets out how youth justice services in the area are to be provided and funded, and the functions of the YOTs in that area. The YOT is able to ascertain the needs of each young offender, identifying the specific problems that make that young person offend and measuring the risk that the young person poses to others. This enables the YOT to identify suitable programmes to address the needs of the young person in order to prevent further offending.

Prosecuting Children and Young People

D24.4 Detailed guidance on prosecuting children and young people from the perspective of the CPS is available on its web site, under the heading 'youth offenders' (tinyurl.com/ydfwhno3). That guidance makes reference to *Chief Constable of Kent, ex parte L* (1991) 93 Cr App R 416, where it was held that the discretion of the CPS to continue or to discontinue criminal proceedings against a child or young person is reviewable by the Divisional Court, but only where it can be demonstrated that the decision was made regardless of or clearly contrary to a settled policy of the DPP evolved in the public interest (see generally **D2.21**). This means that Crown Prosecutors have to be careful to follow the guidance contained in the Code for Crown Prosecutors and, in particular, the guidance on 'youth offenders'. In *R (E) v DPP* [2011] EWHC 1465 (Admin), [2012] 1 Cr App R 6 (68), the Divisional Court considered a decision to prosecute a 14-year-old girl for the alleged sexual abuse by her of her two younger sisters and emphasised the importance of the decision-maker considering, in a case where the alleged offender and the victim are both under 18, what is in the best interests and welfare of both the accused and the victim.

D24.5 **Age of Criminal Responsibility** There is an irrebuttable presumption that a person who is under the age of ten cannot be guilty of a criminal offence (CYPA 1933, s. 50). There used to be a rebuttable presumption that a child aged between ten and 14 was incapable of committing an offence (*doli incapax*). This presumption (which could be rebutted by evidence that the child knew that he or she was doing wrong) was, however, abolished by the CDA 1998, s. 34. In *JTB* [2009] UKHL 20, [2009] 1 AC 1310, the issue was whether the effect of s. 34 had been to abolish the defence of *doli incapax* altogether in the case of a child aged between 10 and 14 years, or merely to abolish the presumption that the child has that defence, thereby leaving it open to the child to prove that, at the material time, he or she was *doli incapax*. The House of Lords ruled that, by enacting s. 34, Parliament intended to abolish both the presumption and the defence of *doli incapax*. The trial judge's ruling, that D (aged 12) was precluded by s. 34 from raising the issue of *doli incapax*, was therefore upheld.

Court of First Appearance

D24.6 The first court appearance by a child or young person in respect of an alleged offence will be in the youth court unless the case is an exceptional one where the first appearance is in the adult magistrates' court. Those exceptional cases are where:

(a) the child or young person is jointly charged with an adult; or
(b) the child or young person is charged with aiding and abetting an adult to commit an offence (or vice versa); or
(c) the child or young person is charged with an offence which arises out of circumstances which are the same as (or connected with) those which resulted in the charge faced by an adult accused.

CrimPD I, para. 3N.13 (see Supplement, **CPD.3N**), states that it will usually be appropriate for the child or young person to be produced in person at court (rather than appearing via a live link where that would otherwise be permissible), to ensure proper engagement.

Bail

The BA 1976 (with the presumption in favour of bail in s. 4) applies to persons under the age of 18 (s. 2(2)). The criteria for granting bail are virtually the same as for adults. There are, however, a number of important differences. First, a child or young person can be refused bail where this is necessary for his or her own 'welfare', not just if necessary for his or her own 'protection', as is the case with adults (BA 1976, sch. 1, part 1, para. (3)). Secondly, a parent or guardian may be asked to act as a surety not only for the accused's attendance at court (the function of the surety in the case of adult defendants) but also for compliance with any other conditions of bail which the court may impose (BA 1976, s. 3(7)). In *R (B) v Brent Youth Court* [2010] EWHC 1893 (Admin), Wilkie J ruled that the requirement imposed by the CYPA 1933, s. 44, to have regard to the 'welfare' of a defendant under the age of 18, requires the court to consider whether, notwithstanding the restrictions on repeated bail applications contained in the BA 1976, sch. 1, part IIA (see **D7.70**), it should nonetheless consider substantively a further bail application in order to have regard to the welfare of the child or young person. **D24.7**

The most significant difference between adults and those under the age of 18 is in what happens if bail is withheld, whether before or after conviction. Where children or young people are refused bail, they are remanded to local authority accommodation or to youth detention accommodation under the LASPO 2012, ss. 91 to 107 (see **D7.131**).

Allocation (Mode of Trial)

The normal rules governing allocation (sometimes known as 'mode of trial') do not apply where the accused is under the age of 18. Most children and young people are tried and sentenced in *youth courts*. By virtue of the CYPA 1933, s. 45, youth courts are magistrates' courts. It follows that trial in the youth court is merely a form of summary trial (even though there are special rules governing the procedure to be followed by youth courts). However, the youth court has jurisdiction to try offences which, in the case of an adult, are triable only on indictment (with the exception of homicide and certain firearms offences). Whereas an adult may never be tried summarily for an offence triable only on indictment and always has the right to elect trial on indictment for an offence triable either way, an accused under the age of 18 may (and usually will) be tried summarily for an indictable offence, whatever the accused's wishes as to mode of trial may be. In other words, an accused under the age of 18 has no right to elect a Crown Court trial. If a child or young person is sent to the Crown Court for trial, it is because the *magistrates* have decided that they should not accept jurisdiction — the most the accused may do is to make representations for or against staying in the youth court. **D24.8**

In summary:

(a) a child or young person either *must* be tried in the Crown Court if charged:
  - (i) with homicide, or
  - (ii) with certain offences to which mandatory minimum sentence provisions (e.g. the FA 1968, s. 51A) apply, if applicable in the instant case;

(b) a child or young person *may* be tried in the Crown Court if charged:
  - (i) with an offence to which the PCC(S)A 2000, s. 91, applies (offences carrying at least 14 years' imprisonment in the case of an adult, together with those specified in s. 91 itself), or
  - (ii) *with an offence which falls* within the ambit of the 'dangerous offender' provisions of the CJA 2003 (see **E4**), or
  - (iii) alongside an adult accused;

(c) a child or young person may be tried in an adult magistrates' court if charged alongside an adult accused.

The procedure for determining where the child or young person will be tried in those cases where allocation is an issue is discussed at **D24.19** *et seq.*

TRIAL OF CHILDREN AND YOUNG PEOPLE IN THE YOUTH COURT

D24.9 As we have seen, the youth court has jurisdiction to try offences which would be triable only on indictment in the case of an adult. Most accused under the age of 18 are therefore tried in the youth court.

Constitution and Operation of the Youth Court

D24.10 The CYPA 1933, s. 45, sets out the framework under which lay magistrates and district judges are authorised to hear youth court cases. Under s. 45(2), a justice of the peace is not qualified to sit as a member of a youth court unless authorised to do so under s. 45(3). Under s. 45(3), authorisation is given by the Lord Chief Justice, with concurrence of the Lord Chancellor. These personal authorisations are valid throughout England and Wales. A magistrate can be given authorisation for particular proceedings (set out in the authorisation) or for all youth court proceedings (s. 45(3)).

Under the Justices of the Peace Rules 2016 (SI 2016 No. 709), r. 30, in order to be authorised, the justice must have completed the relevant training courses. This is to ensure that, given the specific knowledge and understanding that is required in youth court cases, only trained and suitable magistrates sit in youth courts.

D24.11 **Composition of the Youth Court** The composition of the youth court mirrors the composition of the adult magistrates' court, and so will comprise no more than three lay justices or a district judge (magistrates' courts). See also **D3.25**.

D24.12 **Exclusion of Public** The public are excluded from the courtroom of a youth court. By virtue of the CYPA 1933, s. 47(2), together with CrimPR 24.2(1)(c), the only persons permitted to be present in the youth court are:

(a) members of the court and court officials;
(b) parties to the case before the court and their legal representatives (lawyers cannot enter the courtroom if a case they are appearing in is not being dealt with at that time);
(c) witnesses and other persons directly concerned in that case (witnesses are allowed to remain in court once they have given evidence);
(d) bona fide representatives of news gathering or reporting organisations (but note the reporting restrictions set out below);
(e) anyone else directly involved in the case (e.g., probation officers or social workers involved in the case); and
(f) such other persons as the court may specially authorise to be present.

The position in the youth court should be contrasted with those cases where a child or young person is appearing as an accused, or as a witness, in an adult magistrates' court or the Crown Court — in those courts, the public has the right to be present unless the court takes the exceptional step of sitting in private.

Trial in Absence of Accused

D24.13 The MCA 1980, s. 11(1)(a), provides that if, at the time and place appointed for the trial, the prosecutor appears but the accused does not, and the accused is under 18 years of age, the court *may* proceed in the absence of the accused. The presumption that the court should do so unless it appears to the court to be contrary to the interests of justice applies only where the accused has attained the age of 18 (see **D22.17**). CrimPD VI, para. 24C.19 (see Supplement, **CPD.24C**), identifies a number of matters that should be taken into account when deciding whether it is in the interests of justice to proceed in the absence of an accused who is under the age of 18, including:

(a) trial in absence 'can and sometimes does result in acquittal and that it is in nobody's interests to delay an acquittal';
(b) if convicted, the accused can 'ask that the conviction be re-opened in the interests of justice, for example if absence was involuntary' (under the MCA 1980, s. 142(2); see **D22.74** ***et seq.***);
(c) if convicted, the accused has a right to a rehearing on appeal to the Crown Court under the MCA 1980, s. 108 (see **D29.2** ***et seq.***);
(d) the 'age, vulnerability, or experience' of the accused;
(e) whether a parent or guardian is present;
(f) the interests of any co-accused;
(g) the interests of any witnesses who have attended, including the age of any such witness;
(h) the 'nature of the evidence and whether memories of relevant evidence are liable to fade'; and
(i) how soon an adjourned trial can be accommodated in the court list.

Whether the court decides to proceed in the absence of the accused or to adjourn the trial, it must give reasons for the decision.

Media Reports

Restrictions on what can be reported are contained in the CYPA 1933, s. 49 (as amended by the YJCEA 1999, sch. 2, para. 3). Under s. 49(1), no matter relating to any child or young person concerned in youth court proceedings (or appeals from youth court proceedings) shall, while that child or young person is under the age of 18, be included in any publication if it is likely to lead members of the public to identify that person as someone concerned in the proceedings. For these purposes, a person is 'concerned in the proceedings' if the person is the accused or a witness (s. 49(4)). The protected information includes the person's name and address, the identity of any school or other educational establishment attended, and the identity of any place of work; the restriction also applies to any 'still or moving picture' of that person (s. 49(3A)). **D24.14**

For these purposes, 'publication' is defined very widely, and includes 'any speech, writing, relevant programme or other communication in whatever form, which is addressed to the public at large or any section of the public' (s. 49(3)).

It should be noted that the restrictions imposed by s. 49 apply only while the person in question remains under the age of 18. Breach of the restrictions imposed by s. 49 is a summary offence, punishable with a fine of any amount (s. 49(9)).

Lifting the Restrictions The court may lift the ban on publicity to the extent it considers necessary either to avoid injustice to the child or young person (CYPA 1933, s. 49(5)(a)) or, in the case of an accused who is unlawfully at large, where it is necessary to do so for the purpose of apprehension (s. 49(5)(b)). However, s. 49(5)(b) applies only to a child or young person who is charged with, or convicted of, a violent or sexual offence or an offence punishable in the case of an adult with imprisonment for 14 years or more; moreover, the power conferred by s. 49(5)(b) may be exercised only upon the application of the DPP (this includes Crown Prosecutors), and notice of the application must be given to any legal representative of the accused (s. 49(7)). **D24.15**

The court may also lift the ban on publicity where a child or young person has been convicted of an offence, if it is satisfied that it is in the public interest to do so (s. 49(4A)). Before doing so, it must afford an opportunity to the parties to make representations (s. 49(4B)). In *McKerry v Teesdale and Wear Valley Justices* [2000] EWCA Crim 3553, the Divisional Court recognised that there was a tension between the young person's right to privacy and the 'hallowed principle that justice is administered in public, open to full and fair reporting of the proceedings in court' (per Lord Bingham CJ at [19]). His lordship stressed that the power to dispense with anonymity under s. 49(4A) had to be exercised with 'very great care, caution and circumspection', adding that it would be 'wholly wrong' for any court to dispense with a child or young person's prima facie right to anonymity as an additional punishment, and that it was also very difficult to see any place for 'naming and shaming'. The court must be satisfied that the statutory criterion, that it was in the public interest to dispense with the reporting restrictions, is satisfied. His lordship observed that this will very rarely be the case, and justices making an order under s. 49(4A) must be clear *why* it is in the public interest to dispense with the restrictions (at [19]). His lordship added that, in weighing up the public interest, it is entirely proper for the justices to ask a reporter present in court if he or she wishes to say anything ([22]).

The power to lift the reporting restrictions may be exercised by a single justice (s. 49(8)).

It should be borne in mind that the rule on publicity in the youth court is the reverse of that which applies in the adult magistrates' court and the Crown Court, where the media are permitted to identify a child or young person concerned in proceedings unless an order to the contrary is made under the YJCEA 1999, s. 45 (see **D24.79**). In the youth court, on the other hand, the child or young person must not be identified unless the court gives permission.

Attendance of Parent or Guardian

D24.16 The CYPA 1933, s. 34A(1), provides that if the accused is aged under 16, the court *must* (and if the accused is aged 16 or 17, the court *may*) require a parent or guardian to 'attend at the court during all the stages of the proceedings, unless and to the extent that the court is satisfied that it would be unreasonable to require such attendance, having regard to the circumstances of the case'. 'Guardian' is defined as any person who, in the opinion of the court, has for the time being 'the care of the child or young person' (CYPA 1933, s. 107). 'Parent' is not defined in the 1933 Act but, by the Adoption Act 1976, s. 39, includes the adopter of an adopted child. In cases where the local authority has parental responsibility, their representative, rather than, or in certain cases as well as, the parent must (or may) be required to attend (CYPA 1933, s. 34A(2)).

Course of the Trial in a Youth Court

D24.17 The course of a trial in the youth court is essentially the same as the course of a trial in an adult magistrates' court. CrimPR Part 24 (see Supplement, **R24.1** *et seq.*), which applies to trials in both adult magistrates' courts and youth courts, governs the procedure.

As a matter of terminology, the words 'conviction' and 'sentence' are not to be used in connection with children and young people who are tried summarily (CYPA 1933, s. 59). They are replaced by, respectively, the terms 'finding of guilt' and 'order made on a finding of guilt' (CrimPR 24.1(2)). This applies both to proceedings in the youth court and to proceedings against children and young people in the adult magistrates' court. It does not, however, apply to proceedings on indictment.

The procedure in the youth court is intended to be less formal than in the adult magistrates' court. So, for example, the accused sits on a chair, not in a dock, and usually has a parent or guardian sitting nearby; the accused and any young witnesses are addressed by their first names; the oath taken by witnesses is to 'promise' (not 'swear') to tell the truth (CYPA 1963, s. 28(1)).

Detailed guidance for youth court justices, and for practitioners appearing in the youth court, is contained in the Judicial College's *Youth Court Bench Book* (August 2017, tinyurl.com/y9f79mgl). This makes the important point (at para. 6) that one of the key differences between youth and adult courts 'is that the magistrates talk directly to the child or young person and their parent/guardian'. Paragraph 8 goes on to say that, in the event of a finding of guilt, 'magistrates should be encouraged to talk directly to the child or young person. This encourages the child or young person to confront their behaviour, take responsibility for it and its consequences. Magistrates should also engage with the parent/guardian of the child or young person as they may be affected by the proceedings.'

Statutory Provisions Relating to Youth Court Procedure

Children and Young Persons Act 1933, ss. 34A, 47, 49 and 59 D24.18

34A.—(1) Where a child or young person is charged with an offence or is for any other reason brought before a court, the court—

(a) may in any case; and

(b) shall in the case of a child or a young person who is under the age of sixteen years,

require a person who is a parent or guardian of his to attend at the court during all the stages of the proceedings, unless and to the extent that the court is satisfied that it would be unreasonable to require such attendance, having regard to the circumstances of the case.

(2) In relation to a child or young person for whom a local authority have parental responsibility and who—

(a) is in their care; or

(b) is provided with accommodation by them in the exercise of any functions (in particular those under the Children Act 1989) which are social services functions within the meaning of the Local Authority Social Services Act 1970 or the Social Services and Well-being (Wales) Act 2014,

the reference in subsection (1) above to a person who is a parent or guardian of his shall be construed as a reference to that authority or, where he is allowed to live with such a person, as including such a reference.

In this subsection 'local authority' and 'parental responsibility' have the same meanings as in the Children Act 1989.

47.—(1) Youth courts shall sit as often as may be necessary for the purposes of exercising any jurisdiction conferred on them by or under this or any other Act.

(2) No person shall be present at any sitting of a youth court except—

(a) members and officers of the court;

(b) parties to the case before the court, their legal representatives, and witnesses and other persons directly concerned in that case;

(c) bona fide representatives of newspapers or news agencies;

(d) such other persons as the court may specially authorise to be present.

. . .

49.—(1) No matter relating to any child or young person concerned in proceedings to which this section applies shall while he is under the age of 18 be included in any publication if it is likely to lead members of the public to identify him as someone concerned in the proceedings.

(2) The proceedings to which this section applies are—

(a) proceedings in a youth court;

(b) proceedings on appeal from a youth court (including proceedings by way of case stated);

(c) proceedings in a magistrates' court under Schedule 2 to the Criminal Justice and Immigration Act 2008 (proceedings for breach, revocation or amendment of youth rehabilitation orders); and

(d) proceedings on appeal from a magistrates' court arising out of any proceedings mentioned in paragraph (c) (including proceedings by way of case stated).

(3) In this section 'publication' includes any speech, writing, relevant programme or other communication in whatever form, which is addressed to the public at large or any section of the public (and for this purpose every relevant programme shall be taken to be so addressed), but does not include an indictment or other document prepared for use in particular legal proceedings.

(3A) The matters relating to a person in relation to which the restrictions imposed by subsection (1) above apply (if their inclusion in any publication is likely to have the result mentioned in that subsection) include in particular—

(a) his name,

(b) his address,

(c) the identity of any school or other educational establishment attended by him,

(d) the identity of any place of work, and

(e) any still or moving picture of him.

(4) For the purposes of this section a child or young person is 'concerned' in any proceedings if he is—

(a) a person against or in respect of whom the proceedings are taken, or

(b) a person called, or proposed to be called, to give evidence in the proceedings.

(4A) If a court is satisfied that it is in the public interest to do so, it may, in relation to a child or young person who has been convicted of an offence, by order dispense to any specified extent with the restrictions imposed by subsection (1) above in relation to any proceedings before it to which this section applies by virtue of subsection (2)(a) or (b) above, being proceedings relating to—

(a) the prosecution or conviction of the offender for the offence;

(b) the manner in which he, or his parent or guardian, should be dealt with in respect of the offence;

(c) the enforcement, amendment, variation, revocation or discharge of any order made in respect of the offence;

(d) where an attendance centre order is made in respect of the offence, the enforcement of any rules made under section 221(1)(d) or (e) of the Criminal Justice Act 2003; or

(e) where a detention and training order is made, the enforcement of any requirements imposed under section 103(6)(b) of the Powers of Criminal Courts (Sentencing) Act 2000.

(4B) A court shall not exercise its power under subsection (4A) above without—

(a) affording the parties to the proceedings an opportunity to make representations; and

(b) taking into account any representations which are duly made.

(5) Subject to subsection (7) below, a court may, in relation to proceedings before it to which this section applies, by order dispense to any specified extent with the requirements of this section in relation to a child or young person who is concerned in the proceedings if it is satisfied—

(a) that it is appropriate to do so for the purpose of avoiding injustice to the child or young person; or

(b) that, as respects a child or young person to whom this paragraph applies who is unlawfully at large, it is necessary to dispense with those requirements for the purpose of apprehending him and bringing him before a court or returning him to the place in which he was in custody.

(6) Paragraph (b) of subsection (5) above applies to any child or young person who is charged with or has been convicted of—

(a) a violent offence,

(b) a sexual offence, or

(c) an offence punishable in the case of a person aged 21 or over with imprisonment for fourteen years or more.

(7) The court shall not exercise its power under subsection (5)(b) above—

(a) except in pursuance of an application by or on behalf of the Director of Public Prosecutions; and

(b) unless notice of the application has been given by the Director of Public Prosecutions to any legal representative of the child or young person.

(8) The court's power under subsection (4A) or (5) above may be exercised by a single justice.

(9) If a publication includes any matter in contravention of subsection (1) above, the following persons shall be guilty of an offence and liable on summary conviction to [an unlimited fine]—

(a) where the publication is a newspaper or periodical, any proprietor, any editor and any publisher of the newspaper or periodical;

(b) where the publication is a relevant programme—

(i) any body corporate or Scottish partnership engaged in providing the programme service in which the programme is included; and

(ii) any person having functions in relation to the programme corresponding to those of an editor of a newspaper;

(c) in the case of any other publication, any person publishing it.

(9A) Where a person is charged with an offence under subsection (9) above it shall be a defence to prove that at the time of the alleged offence he was not aware, and neither suspected nor had reason to suspect, that the publication included the matter in question.

(9B) If an offence under subsection (9) above committed by a body corporate is proved—

(a) to have been committed with the consent or connivance of, or

(b) to be attributable to any neglect on the part of,

an officer, the officer as well as the body corporate is guilty of the offence and liable to be proceeded against and punished accordingly.

(9C) In subsection (9B) above 'officer' means a director, manager, secretary or other similar officer of the body, or a person purporting to act in any such capacity.

(9D) If the affairs of a body corporate are managed by its members, 'director' in subsection (9C) above means a member of that body.

(9E) Where an offence under subsection (9) above is committed by a Scottish partnership and is proved to have been committed with the consent or connivance of a partner, he as well as the partnership shall be guilty of the offence and shall be liable to be proceeded against and punished accordingly.

(10) In any proceedings under schedule 7 to the Powers of Criminal Courts (Sentencing) Act 2000 (proceedings for varying or revoking supervision orders) before a magistrates' court other than a youth court or on appeal from such a court it shall be the duty of the magistrates' court or the appellate court to announce in the course of the proceedings that this section applies to the proceedings; and if the court fails to do so this section shall not apply to the proceedings.

(11) In this section—

'legal representative' means an authorised advocate or authorised litigator, as defined by section 119(1) of the Courts and Legal Services Act 1990;

'picture' includes a likeness however produced;

'relevant programme' means a programme included in a programme service, within the meaning of the Broadcasting Act 1990;

'sexual offence' means an offence listed in part 2 of Schedule 15 to the Criminal Justice Act 2003;

'specified' means specified in an order under this section;

'violent offence' means an offence listed in part 1 of Schedule 15 to the Criminal Justice Act 2003;

and a person who, having been granted bail, is liable to arrest (whether with or without a warrant) shall be treated as unlawfully at large.

...

59. The words 'conviction' and 'sentence' shall cease to be used in relation to children and young persons dealt with summarily and any reference in any enactment ... to a person convicted, a conviction or a sentence shall, in the case of a child or young person, be construed as including a reference to a person found guilty of an offence, a finding of guilt or an order made upon such finding, as the case may be.

DETERMINING PLACE OF TRIAL OF CHILDREN AND YOUNG PEOPLE

Most trials involving accused under the age of 18 take place in the youth court. However, there are cases where a child or young person may, or must, be tried in an adult court (either an adult magistrates' court or the Crown Court). The law on place of trial for accused under the age of 18 is to be found (somewhat confusingly) in a combination of statutory sources, including the CYPA 1933, s. 46, the CYPA 1963, s. 18, and the MCA 1980, ss. 24 and 29. In summary, there are five circumstances in which the trial of a child or young person either may or must take place in the Crown Court: **D24.19**

(a) where the child or young person is accused of homicide (i.e. murder or manslaughter) the case *must* be heard in the Crown Court; or

(b) where the child or young person is charged with a firearms offence where the FA 1968, s. 51A, applies (or using someone to mind a weapon under the VCRA 2006, s. 29(3)), and had attained the age of 16 at the date of the alleged offence, the case *must* be heard in the Crown Court; or

(c) where the child or young person is accused of an offence to which the PCC(S)A 2000, s. 91, applies (i.e. an offence carrying at least 14 years' imprisonment in the case of an adult or one specified in s. 91 itself), the case *may*, depending on whether or not a sentence in excess of two years is likely to be appropriate, be heard in the Crown Court; or

(d) where the child or young person is charged with a 'specified' offence as defined by the CJA 2003, s. 224 (and so falls within the ambit of the 'dangerous offender' provisions of that Act), the case *may* be heard in the Crown Court, depending on whether the accused can properly be regarded as a dangerous offender; or

(e) where the child or young person is charged alongside an adult who is to be tried in the Crown Court, the child or young person *may* also be sent to the Crown Court for trial, but only if it is necessary in the interests of justice to do so.

There is only one situation where the trial of a child or young person may take place in an adult magistrates' court, namely where the child or young person is charged alongside an adult who is being tried in the magistrates' court.

Trial on Indictment

D24.20 The MCA 1980, s. 24(1), provides that, unless a child or young person is sent to the Crown Court for trial, he or she must be tried summarily.

Magistrates' Courts Act 1980, s. 24

(1) Where a person under the age of 18 years appears or is brought before a magistrates' court on an information charging him with an indictable offence he shall, subject to sections 51 and 51A of the Crime and Disorder Act 1998 and to sections 24A and 24B below, be tried summarily.

The MCA 1980, s. 24(1), must be read in conjunction with the CDA 1998, ss. 51 and 51A. Section 51(7) deals with cases where there is an adult co-accused. Section 51A deals with those cases in which either a child or young person must be tried on indictment or else the magistrates have a discretion to send him or her to the Crown Court for trial. Section 51A(2) and (3) require the court to send the child or young person forthwith to the Crown Court for trial where charged with:

(a) homicide; or
(b) a firearms offence where there is a mandatory minimum sentence (FA 1968, s. 51A), or an offence under the VCRA 2006, s. 29(3) (minimum sentences in certain cases of using someone to mind a weapon);
(c) an offence to which the provisions of the PCC(S)A 2000, s. 91, apply *and* the court considers that it ought to be possible to sentence the accused to detention under that section in the event of being convicted of the offence; or
(d) the offence is a 'specified' offence (under the CJA 2003, s. 224) *and* it appears to the court that, if the accused is found guilty of the offence, the criteria for the imposition of a sentence under the CJA 2003, s. 226B (extended sentence for certain violent or sexual offences) would be met.

The functions of the court under s. 51A can be exercised by a single justice (s. 51A(11)).

Homicide Cases

D24.21 The term 'homicide' is not defined but obviously includes murder and manslaughter; however, it does not include causing death by dangerous driving, as that offence falls within the ambit of the PCC(S)A 2000, s. 91 (see **D24.27**). Under the DVCVA 2004, s. 6(5), an offence under s. 5 of that Act of causing or allowing a person's death is an offence of homicide for these purposes. Where a child or young person is charged with homicide, there is no determination of allocation, since the case *must* be sent to the Crown Court.

Firearms Offences

D24.22 Under the CDA 1998, s. 51A(2) and (3), a child or young person *must* be sent to the Crown Court for trial on any charge where, if convicted, he or she would be subject to the mandatory minimum sentence under the FA 1968, s. 51A (see **E5.9**). These minimum sentence provisions apply only where the offender had attained the age of 16 when the offence was committed (FA 1968, s. 51A(1)(b)). The court must impose a term of detention of at least three years if the offender was under 18 at the date of the offence (s. 51A(5)(a)(ii)), unless the court is of the opinion that there are exceptional circumstances relating to the offence or to the offender which justify its not doing so (s. 51A(2)). Where these requirements would be satisfied if the accused were to be convicted, he or she will be sent to the Crown Court for trial. If the accused pleads guilty or is found guilty in the Crown Court, the sentence imposed by virtue of the FA 1968, s. 51A, takes the form of a sentence of long-term detention under the PCC(S)A 2000, s. 91. The position is similar where the accused is charged with an offence to which the VCRA 2006, s. 29(3) (using someone to mind a weapon), is applicable. Again, the minimum age is 16 (at the date of the offence) and the minimum sentence, in the absence of exceptional circumstances, is three years in the case of an offender who is under the age of 18 at the date of conviction.

Mandatory Sentences Generally It should be noted that the mandatory minimum sentences for a third class A drug trafficking conviction (PCC(S)A 2000, s. 110) or third domestic burglary (s. 111) do not apply to children and young people as the third offence must be committed after the offender has attained the age of 18. **D24.23**

'Plea before Venue' Procedure for Children and Young People

The MCA 1980, ss. 24A to 24D (see **D24.26**), apply a procedure similar to that contained in ss. 17A to 17C of that Act (the 'plea before venue' hearing) to cases involving an accused who is under the age of 18. **D24.24**

The plea before venue procedure set out in s. 24A applies where the court would otherwise be required to send a child or young person to the Crown Court for trial by virtue of the CDA 1998, s. 51(7) or (8) (cases where there is an adult co-accused), or s. 51A(3)(b), (4), or (5) (cases falling within the ambit of the PCC(S)A 2000, s. 91, see **D24.27** ***et seq.***). However, s. 24A does not apply where a child or young person is charged with an offence listed in the CDA 1998, s. 51A(12), namely homicide or cases where the requirements of the FA 1968, s. 51A(1), or the VCRA 2006, s. 29(3), would apply if the child or young person were convicted of the offence. It follows that, except in the cases which fall within s. 51A(12), a plea before venue hearing must take place where there is a possibility of the child or young person being tried in the Crown Court because he or she is charged alongside an adult or where the offence is one to which the PCC(S)A 2000, s. 91, applies.

In those cases, the child or young person is invited to indicate an intention to plead guilty or not guilty (s. 24A(6)). If the accused indicates that an intention to enter a guilty plea, a guilty plea is deemed to have been entered at that point (s. 24A(7)). The magistrates then proceed to the sentencing stage; if the offence is one to which the PCC(S)A 2000, s. 91, applies, the magistrates may commit the offender to the Crown Court for sentence under the PCC(S)A 2000, s. 3B (see **D24.58**), if they take the view that their sentencing powers are insufficient. If the accused indicates a not guilty plea (or gives no indication as to intended plea), the magistrates proceed to determine allocation (s. 24A(8) and (9)). Thus, if the case is one to which s. 91 of the 2000 Act applies, the magistrates go on to consider whether it ought to be possible to impose a sentence of detention under that section if the accused is found guilty of it; if the case is one where the child or young person is charged alongside an adult who is to be tried in the Crown Court, the magistrates go on to consider whether it is necessary in the interests of justice for the child or young person to be sent to the Crown Court for trial as well.

Section 24B enables the plea before venue procedure to be determined in the absence of a child or young person who is legally represented, and the court considers that, because of the accused's disorderly conduct before the court, it is not practicable for proceedings to be conducted in his or her presence, and the court considers that it should proceed in the absence of the accused. In such cases, the legal representative is invited to enter a plea on behalf of the accused (and an indication by the representative of an intended guilty plea is deemed to be a plea of guilty under s. 24B(2)(c)). **D24.25**

Proceedings under s. 24A or 24B can be adjourned. Where the accused is present, the adjournment may take the form of a remand, either in custody or on bail (s. 24C). The functions of the magistrates' court under ss. 24A to 24C may be exercised by a single justice (s. 24D(1)).

Magistrates' Courts Act 1980, ss. 24A to 24D **D24.26**

24A.—(1) This section applies where—

(a) a person under the age of 18 years appears or is brought before a magistrates' court on an information charging him with an offence other than one falling within section 51A(12) of the Crime and Disorder Act 1998 ('the 1998 Act'); and

(b) but for the application of the following provisions of this section, the court would be required at that stage, by virtue of section 51(7) or (8) or 51A(3)(b), (4) or (5) of the 1998 Act to determine, in relation to the offence, whether to send the person to the Crown Court for trial (or to determine any matter, the effect of which would be to determine whether he is sent to the Crown Court for trial).

(2) Where this section applies, the court shall, before proceeding to make any such determination as is referred to in subsection (1)(b) above (the 'relevant determination'), follow the procedure set out in this section.

(3) Everything that the court is required to do under the following provisions of this section must be done with the accused person in court.

(4) The court shall cause the charge to be written down, if this has not already been done, and to be read to the accused.

(5) The court shall then explain to the accused in ordinary language that he may indicate whether (if the offence were to proceed to trial) he would plead guilty or not guilty, and that if he indicates that he would plead guilty—

(a) the court must proceed as mentioned in subsection (7) below; and

(b) (in cases where the offence is one mentioned in section 91(1) of the Powers of Criminal Courts (Sentencing) Act 2000) he may be sent to the Crown Court for sentencing under section 3B or (if applicable) 3C of that Act if the court is of such opinion as is mentioned in subsection (2) of the applicable section.

(6) The court shall then ask the accused whether (if the offence were to proceed to trial) he would plead guilty or not guilty.

(7) If the accused indicates that he would plead guilty, the court shall proceed as if—

(a) the proceedings constituted from the beginning the summary trial of the information; and

(b) section 9(1) above was complied with and he pleaded guilty under it,

and, accordingly, the court shall not (and shall not be required to) proceed to make the relevant determination or to proceed further under section 51 or (as the case may be) section 51A of the 1998 Act in relation to the offence.

(8) If the accused indicates that he would plead not guilty, the court shall proceed to make the relevant determination and this section shall cease to apply.

(9) If the accused in fact fails to indicate how he would plead, for the purposes of this section he shall be taken to indicate that he would plead not guilty.

(10) Subject to subsection (7) above, the following shall not for any purpose be taken to constitute the taking of a plea—

(a) asking the accused under this section whether (if the offence were to proceed to trial) he would plead guilty or not guilty;

(b) an indication by the accused under this section of how he would plead.

24B.—(1) This section shall have effect where—

(a) a person under the age of 18 years appears or is brought before a magistrates' court on an information charging him with an offence other than one falling within section 51A(12) of the Crime and Disorder Act 1998;

(b) but for the application of the following provisions of this section, the court would be required at that stage to make one of the determinations referred to in paragraph (b) of section 24A(1) above ('the relevant determination');

(c) the accused is represented by a legal representative;

(d) the court considers that by reason of the accused's disorderly conduct before the court it is not practicable for proceedings under section 24A above to be conducted in his presence; and

(e) the court considers that it should proceed in the absence of the accused.

(2) In such a case—

(a) the court shall cause the charge to be written down, if this has not already been done, and to be read to the representative;

(b) the court shall ask the representative whether (if the offence were to proceed to trial) the accused would plead guilty or not guilty;

(c) if the representative indicates that the accused would plead guilty the court shall proceed as if the proceedings constituted from the beginning the summary trial of the information, and as if section 9(1) above was complied with and the accused pleaded guilty under it;

(d) if the representative indicates that the accused would plead not guilty the court shall proceed to make the relevant determination and this section shall cease to apply.

(3) If the representative in fact fails to indicate how the accused would plead, for the purposes of this section he shall be taken to indicate that the accused would plead not guilty.
(4) Subject to subsection (2)(c) above, the following shall not for any purpose be taken to constitute the taking of a plea—
(a) asking the representative under this section whether (if the offence were to proceed to trial) the accused would plead guilty or not guilty;
(b) an indication by the representative under this section of how the accused would plead.

24C.—(1) A magistrates' court proceeding under section 24A or 24B above may adjourn the proceedings at any time, and on doing so on any occasion when the accused is present may remand the accused.
(2) Where the court remands the accused, the time fixed for the resumption of proceedings shall be that at which he is required to appear or be brought before the court in pursuance of the remand or would be required to be brought before the court but for section 128(3A) below.

24D.—(1) The functions of a magistrates' court under sections 24A to 24C above may be discharged by a single justice.
(2) Subsection (1) above shall not be taken as authorising—
(a) the summary trial of an information (other than a summary trial by virtue of section 24A(7) or 24B(2)(c) above); or
(b) the imposition of a sentence,
by a magistrates' court composed of fewer than two justices.

Cases Falling within the Powers of Criminal Courts (Sentencing) Act 2000, s. 91

The CDA 1998, s. 51A, must be read in conjunction with the PCC(S)A 2000, s. 91 (see **D24.37**), which provides for the punishment of children and young people who are convicted on indictment of certain serious offences. Section 91 empowers the Crown Court to order that a child or young person be detained for a period not exceeding the maximum sentence of imprisonment which may be imposed on an adult offender for the offence in question. It applies only in the following cases: **D24.27**

(a) where a child or young person who has attained the age of ten is convicted of an offence which carries at least 14 years' imprisonment in the case of an adult offender;
(b) where a child or young person who has attained the age of ten is convicted of an offence under the SOA 2003, ss. 3, 13, 25 or 26.

This provision is necessary because of the relatively limited ambit of the normal custodial sentence for young offenders, namely the detention and training order: this order is limited to a total of 24 months (12 months' custody, followed by 12 months' supervision); where the offender is under the age of 15, a detention and training order can be imposed only if the child or young person is a 'persistent offender'; moreover, a detention and training order is not available where the offender is under the age of 12. Section 91 achieves two key objectives: (a) it enables the Crown Court to pass a longer term of detention than would otherwise be possible (given the 24-month limit on the duration of the detention and training order); and (b) it enables the Crown Court to impose a term of detention where otherwise no detention would be possible (in the case of an offender under the age of 12, or an offender under the age of 15 who is not a persistent offender). (It should be noted that the provisions contained in s. 91 will appear in the Sentencing Code when it is implemented.)

Scope of s. 91 The power to impose a sentence under s. 91 applies (a) where a child or young person is convicted of an offence to which s. 91 applies, and is then committed to the Crown Court for sentence under the PCC(S)A 2000, s. 3B (see **D24.58**), and (b) where a child or young person is sent to the Crown Court for trial, under the CDA 1998, s. 51A(2) and (3)(b), in respect of an offence to which s. 91 applies, and is then convicted of that offence. This means that if the child or young person, at the 'plea before venue' hearing, indicates a not guilty plea to such an offence, the magistrates must consider whether, if the child or young person is found guilty of the offence, it 'ought to be possible' to impose a sentence under s. 91; if so, the accused must be sent to the Crown Court for trial. **D24.28**

In *AM* [1998] 1 WLR 363 at p. 372, Lord Bingham CJ confirmed that, where a child or young person is charged with more than one offence, and the PCC(S)A 2000, s. 91, applies to one or some, but not all, of those offences, the court may, when considering the seriousness of the offence(s) to which s. 91 applies, consider the seriousness of the combination of all offences, since they are 'associated offences' within the meaning of the PCC(S)A 2000, s. 161(1). However, in the event of conviction, the Crown Court may order long-term detention only in respect of those offences to which s. 91 applies.

Where a child or young person appears before a youth court charged with a number of offences and is sent to the Crown Court in respect of some (but not all) of them, the youth court is not required to adjourn proceedings in respect of the other offences (MCA 1980, s. 10(3A)).

Deciding Allocation where s. 91 Applies

D24.29 The Sentencing Council's definitive guideline, *Sentencing Children and Young People* (with effect from 1 June 2017; see Supplement, **SG8-1**), says that, in a case to which s. 91 applies, before deciding whether to send the case to the Crown Court or retain jurisdiction in the youth court, the court should hear submissions from the prosecution and defence (para. 2.10). However, *evidence* about the gravity of the offence (as opposed to representations) is not appropriate at this stage (*South Hackney Juvenile Court, ex parte RB and CB* (1983) 77 Cr App R 294).

When a youth court is deciding whether to send a child or young person to be tried in the Crown Court in a case where s. 91 applies, the court is entitled to know about any previous findings of guilt (*R (Tullet) v Medway Magistrates' Court* [2003] EWHC 2279 (Admin).

It must be emphasised that the child or young person has no right to elect Crown Court trial. Where the trial takes place is a matter for the magistrates, who will take account of the representations made by the prosecution and defence in coming to their decision.

In *R (W) v Brent Youth Court* [2006] EWHC 95 (Admin), Smith LJ pointed out (at [9]) that, where several accused are charged together and all are under 18, the court must consider the position of each one separately 'even if this results in one defendant being tried in the youth court and others in the Crown Court'. It follows that (in contrast to cases involving adult accused, where CrimPR 9.2(6) and (7) apply) one child or young person cannot be sent to the Crown Court for trial merely because another co-accused under the age of 18 is being sent there (*R (W and M) v Oldham Youth Court* [2010] EWHC 661 (Admin)).

D24.30 The justices must take into account the sentencing practice of the Crown Court (and the Court of Appeal) in relation to s. 91. As Stanley Burnton J observed in *R (D) v Sheffield Youth Court* [2003] EWHC 35 (Admin), when deciding whether it considers that it ought to be possible to impose a sentence pursuant to s. 91, the youth court 'must consider the sentencing powers of the Crown Court and the guidance that has been given as to their exercise. If, on the basis of that guidance, there is no real possibility of such a sentence, [sending the accused to the Crown Court] is inappropriate' (at [39]). His lordship added (at [40]) that, in making its decision, the youth court should take into account any undisputed facts put forward as mitigation (such as the good character of the accused). However, contentious mitigation should be ignored: if the case is sent to the Crown Court and the accused convicted, mitigation will be a matter for that court.

Guidance on the Decision-making Process in s. 91 Cases

D24.31 In deciding whether it ought to be possible for the Crown Court to pass a sentence under s. 91, the court must consider the *range* of sentences that would be appropriate. In *CPS v Newcastle-upon-Tyne Youth Court* [2010] EWHC 2773 (Admin), Langstaff J said (at [18]) that the question is not what sentence is likely, but rather what sentence is 'realistically possible', bearing in mind the available range.

D24.32 The Sentencing Council's definitive guideline, *Sentencing Children and Young People*, states that: 'The test to be applied by the court is whether there is a real prospect that a sentence in excess of two years' detention will be imposed' (para. 2.8). This confirms the effect of cases such as *R (M and W) v West London Youth Court* [2004] EWHC 1144 (Admin), where Leveson J (at [16]) expressed the appropriate test thus:

> Whether there is a real prospect that a custodial sentence of, or in excess of, 2 years might be required, or is there any unusual feature of this case which might justify a sentence of less than two years, pursuant to section 91(3), for which purpose the absence of a power to impose a detention and training order because the offender is under the age of 15 is not an unusual feature?

In *R (H) v Southampton Youth Court* [2004] EWHC 2912 (Admin), [2005] 2 Cr App R (5) 30 (171), it was emphasised that offenders under 18, and in particular those under 15, should be tried in the youth court, with Crown Court jurisdiction being reserved for the most serious crimes. It would only be in exceptional cases that an offender aged between 12 and 14 should be sent for trial to the Crown Court. Leveson J summarised the relevant principles as follows (at [33]–[35]):

> The general policy of the legislature is that those who are under 18 years of age, and in particular children of under 15 years of age, should, wherever possible, be tried in the youth court. It is that court which is best designed to meet their specific needs. A trial in the Crown Court with the inevitably greater formality and greatly increased number of people involved (including a jury and the public) should be reserved for the most serious cases.
>
> It is a further policy of the legislature that, generally speaking, first-time offenders aged 12 to 14 and all offenders under 12 should not be detained in custody and decisions as to jurisdiction should have regard to the fact that the exceptional power to detain for grave offences should not be used to water down the general principle. Those under 15 will rarely attract a period of detention and, even more rarely, those who are under 12.
>
> In each case the court should ask itself whether there is a real prospect, having regard to his or her age, that this defendant whose case they are considering might require a sentence of, or in excess of, two years or, alternatively, whether although the sentence might be less than two years, there is some unusual feature of the case which justifies declining jurisdiction, bearing in mind that the absence of a power to impose a detention and training order because the defendant is under 15 is not an unusual feature.

The definitive guideline reiterates that the youth court is the court which is best designed to meet the specific needs of young people, and so a trial in the Crown Court, with the inevitably greater formality and greater number of people involved (including a jury and the public), should be reserved for the most serious cases (at para 2.1). The guideline goes on to state (at para. 2.10) that children and young people should be sent for trial or committed for sentence to the Crown Court only if the offence in question is 'of such gravity that a custodial sentence substantially exceeding two years is a realistic possibility'. The guideline requires the court to bear in mind that detention and training orders are not available for offenders aged ten or 11, or for those who are aged 12 to 14 but who are not persistent offenders (suggesting a presumption against invoking s. 91 in such cases).

In *R (CPS) v Redbridge Youth Court* [2005] EWHC 1390 (Admin), the Divisional Court (at [11]), adopting counsel's summary of the legal framework, said that the power to make an order for detention is a 'long-stop reserved for very serious offences'. The youth court should start with a strong presumption against sending a young defendant to the Crown Court unless it is satisfied that it is clearly required. A magistrates' court should therefore not decline jurisdiction unless the offence and the circumstances surrounding it and the offender are such as to make it more than a vague or theoretical possibility that a sentence of detention for a long period might be passed under s. 91. Section 91 is primarily applicable to cases of such gravity that the court is or might be considering a sentence of at least two years, and there must be a real possibility of such a sentence. D24.33

If the accused is charged with an offence to which s. 91 applies, the only question for the youth court is whether it considers that, if the accused is found guilty of the offence, it ought to be possible to impose a sentence pursuant to s. 91. Once it so considers, the youth court has no discretion in the matter. In *R (D) v Sheffield Youth Court* [2003] EWHC 35 (Admin), Stanley Burnton J said (at [38]):

> Section 24(1) unambiguously requires the youth court to commit to the Crown Court if the conditions for the exercise of the power to commit are satisfied: the words are 'the Court shall commit the accused for trial'. Parliament has decided that the Crown Court is the suitable venue for the trial of persons under the age of 18 if the conditions expressly laid down by section 24(1) are satisfied.

D24.34 **Power to Commit for Sentence** In *R (DPP) v South Tyneside Youth Court* [2015] EWHC 1455 (Admin), [2015] 2 Cr App R (S) 59 (411), the Divisional Court considered the effect of the PCC(S)A 2000, s. 3B, which had been amended so as to enable committal for sentence to the Crown Court whether the offender pleads guilty or is found guilty after a trial. Sir Brian Leveson P observed that, because s. 3B (as amended) 'means that the youth court is not making a once and for all decision at the point of allocation, the "real prospect" assessment requires a different emphasis' (see also **D24.57**). One consequence is that the requirement to take the prosecution case at its highest (*R (W) v Oldham Youth Court* [2010] EWHC 661 (Admin) at [15], per Langstaff J) is no longer necessary. Sir Brian Leveson P continued (at [31]):

> [T]here will, of course, be cases in which the alleged offending is so grave that a sentence of or [in] excess of two years will be a 'real prospect' irrespective of particular considerations in relation either to the offence or the offender's role in it: such cases are, however, likely to be rare. [At] the time of allocation and determination of venue, the court will doubtless take the views of the prosecution and defence into account; these views could include representations as [to] the value of privacy of the proceedings or, alternatively, the desire for a jury trial. Subject to such submissions, however, in most cases whether there is such a 'real prospect' will generally be apparent only when the court has determined the full circumstances of the offence and has a far greater understanding of the position of the offender. Since the youth court now has the option of committing a defendant for sentence after conviction if the court considers that the Crown Court should have the power to impose a sentence of detention pursuant to s. 91(3) of the 2000 Act, it will generally be at that point when the assessment can and should be made. In that way, the observations in *Southampton Youth Court* (at [33]) that Crown Court trial for a youth 'should be reserved for the most serious cases' remain entirely apposite.

The Sentencing Council's definitive guideline, *Sentencing Children and Young People*, makes a similar point (at para. 2.10), that:

> In most cases it is likely to be impossible to decide whether there is a real prospect that a sentence in excess of two years' detention will be imposed without knowing more about the facts of the case and the circumstances of the child or young person. In those circumstances the youth court should retain jurisdiction and commit for sentence if it is of the view, having heard more about the facts and the circumstances of the child or young person, that its powers of sentence are insufficient.

The guideline also requires that, where the court decides that the case is suitable to be dealt with in the youth court, it must warn the accused that all available sentencing options remain open in the event of a finding of guilt, including committal to the Crown Court for sentence.

In *R (B) v Norfolk Youth Court* [2013] EWHC 1459 (Admin), Cox J said (at [50]) that 'a trial in the Crown Court should be reserved for those most serious and ... exceptional cases, which truly merit the description "grave crimes"'. Her ladyship added that to fall within that definition an offence would have to be 'so serious that it necessitated the exceptional course of declining jurisdiction for such crimes. The exceptional power to detain for grave crimes should not be used to water down the general principle that a child ... should stand trial in the youth court, which is, for him, the appropriate place of trial.'

D24.35 It is possible for a child or young person who is charged with rape to be tried in a youth court. In *W v Warrington Magistrates' Court* [2009] EWHC 1538 (Admin), the Divisional Court upheld the decision of a circuit judge to try a rape case in the youth court, sitting as a district judge. Nonetheless, Pill LJ (at [34]) emphasised that the court must apply the statutory test in the MCA 1980, s. 24(1)(a), adding that 'Parliament has seen fit to grant a right to a Crown

Court hearing (including trial by jury) to young offenders in certain circumstances and that cannot be defeated administratively. There will be alleged sexual offences involving very young defendants where committal to the Crown Court is the correct decision.'

CrimPD XIII, annex 2 (see Supplement, **CPD.XIII.x2**), states that, where possible, cases involving sexual offences which fall within the ambit of s. 91 should be listed before a district judge who has been authorised to hear cases involving serious sexual offences, to decide whether the case should be sent to the Crown Court for trial. If the case is retained in the youth court, and the offence involves actual or attempted penetrative activity, the case must be tried by an authorised district judge; in other cases, the district judge must consider whether the case is so serious and/or complex that it should be tried by an authorised district judge, or whether it can be heard by any district judge or any youth court bench.

Challenging the Decision to Send a Child or Young Person to the Crown Court

The appropriate means of challenging a decision to send a child or young person to the Crown Court is by way of judicial review. In *AH* [2002] EWCA Crim 2938, an application to stay the proceedings as an abuse of process was made at the start of the trial, on the ground that the case should not have been sent for trial. It was held that the appropriate forum for challenging the decision to send for trial is the Divisional Court (by way of an application for judicial review) rather than by making an abuse of process application in the Crown Court (per Mance LJ at [13]). **D24.36**

It might be thought that the Divisional Court would apply the well-known *Wednesbury* irrationality test to any challenge to a decision to send for trial. However, it is clear from *R (W) v Thetford Youth Court* [2002] EWHC 1252 (Admin), [2003] 1 Cr App R (S) 67 (323); *R (W) v Southampton Youth Court* [2002] EWHC 1640 (Admin), [2003] 1 Cr App R (S) 87 (455) and *R (D) v Sheffield Youth Court* [2003] EWHC 35 (Admin) that the test is less restrictive than that. As Stanley Burnton J put it in the latter case (at [41]):

> The test to be applied by the High Court on judicial review of a decision of a youth court under s. 24(1) is: in the judgment of the High Court, was the decision of the youth court wrong? ... It is not sufficient for the High Court to consider that it would have made a different decision under s. 24(1) to that of the youth court. Only if the High Court is satisfied that the original decision was wrong may it interfere.

Where a youth court intends to send a child or young person to the Crown Court for trial with a view to the imposition of a sentence of detention under the PCC(S)A 2000, s. 91, in the event of conviction the court should give reasons for its decision (*R (C) v Balham Youth Court* [2003] EWHC 1332 (Admin), [2004] 1 Cr App R (S) 22 (143), per Scott Baker LJ at [14]).

It should be noted that, even if a child or young person is tried and convicted in the Crown Court, the Crown Court is not obliged to pass a sentence of detention under s. 91. The Crown Court retains the power to deal with the offender in any way that the youth court could have done.

Challenging a Refusal to Send a Child or Young Person to the Crown Court

If the justices refuse to send the accused to the Crown Court in a case where a sentence under s. 91 of the 2000 Act would be available, the procedure to be used to challenge that decision should be an application for judicial review (and not the seeking of a voluntary bill of indictment). In *R (DPP) v Camberwell Youth Court* [2004] EWHC 1805 (Admin), [2005] 1 WLR 810, the Divisional Court said that, in order that the matter can be dealt with within the sort of timescale that would be involved in seeking a voluntary bill of indictment, an expedited hearing of the application for judicial review should be sought (by completing Form N463). It follows that if, without adequate explanation, an application for a voluntary bill is made, the court will probably refuse consent on the basis that no good reason has been shown to depart from the normal procedure, and the interests of justice do not require it (per Kennedy LJ at [36]). **D24.37**

Powers of Criminal Courts (Sentencing Act) 2000, s. 91

(1) Subsection (3) below applies where a person aged under 18 is convicted on indictment of—

(a) an offence punishable in the case of a person aged 21 or over with imprisonment for 14 years or more, not being an offence the sentence for which is fixed by law; or

[(b) an offence under section 3 of the Sexual Offences Act 2003 (in this section, 'the 2003 Act') (sexual assault); or

(c) an offence under section 13 of the 2003 Act (child sex offences committed by children or young persons); or

(d) an offence under section 25 of the 2003 Act (sexual activity with a child family member); or

(e) an offence under section 26 of the 2003 Act (inciting a child family member to engage in sexual activity)].

(1A) Subsection (3) below also applies where—

(a) a person aged under 18 is convicted on indictment of an offence—

(i) under subsection (1)(a), (ab), (aba), (ac), (ad), (ae), (af) or (c) of section 5 of the Firearms Act 1968 (prohibited weapons), or

(ii) under subsection (1A)(a) of that section,

(b) the offence was committed after the commencement of section 51A of that Act and for the purposes of subsection (3) of that section at a time when he was aged 16 or over, and

(c) the court is of the opinion mentioned in section 51A(2) of that Act (exceptional circumstances which justify its not imposing required custodial sentence).

(1B) Subsection (3) below also applies where—

(a) a person aged under 18 is convicted on indictment of an offence under the Firearms Act 1968 that is listed in section 51A(1A)(b), (e) or (f) of that Act and was committed in respect of a firearm or ammunition specified in section 5(1)(a), (ab), (aba), (ac), (ad), (ae), (af) or (c) or section 5(1A)(a) of that Act;

(b) the offence was committed after the commencement of section 30 of the Violent Crime Reduction Act 2006 and for the purposes of section 51A(3) of the Firearms Act 1968 at a time when he was aged 16 or over; and

(c) the court is of the opinion mentioned in section 51A(2) of the Firearms Act 1968.

(1C) Subsection (3) below also applies where—

(a) a person aged under 18 is convicted of an offence under section 28 of the Violent Crime Reduction Act 2006 (using someone to mind a weapon);

(b) section 29(3) of that Act applies (minimum sentences in certain cases); and

(c) the court is of the opinion mentioned in section 29(6) of that Act (exceptional circumstances which justify not imposing the minimum sentence).

(2) …

(3) If the court is of the opinion that neither a youth rehabilitation order nor a detention and training order is suitable, the court may sentence the offender to be detained for such period, not exceeding the maximum term of imprisonment with which the offence is punishable in the case of a person aged 21 or over, as may be specified in the sentence.

(4) Subsection (3) above is subject to (in particular) section 152 and 153 of the Criminal Justice Act 2003.

(5) Where—

(a) subsection (2) of section 51A of the Firearms Act 1968, or

(b) subsection (6) of section 29 of the Violent Crime Reduction Act 2006,

requires the imposition of a sentence of detention under this section for a term of at least the term provided for in that section, the court shall sentence the offender to be detained for such period, of at least the term so provided for but not exceeding the maximum term of imprisonment with which the offence is punishable in the case of a person aged 18 or over, as may be specified in the sentence.

Dangerous Offenders

D24.38 **Extended Sentences** The CDA 1998, s. 51A(2) and (3)(d), stipulate that, where the offence is a 'specified offence' (within the meaning of the CJA 2003, s. 224) *and* it appears to the court that, if the child or young person is found guilty of the offence, the criteria for the imposition of an extended sentence under s. 226B of that Act would be met, the court must send the accused forthwith to the Crown Court for trial for that offence.

Offences that come within the definition of 'specified offence' for these purposes are listed in the CJA 2003, sch. 15. Section 226B applies where the court takes the view 'that there is a significant risk to members of the public of serious harm occasioned by the commission by the offender of further specified offences'. If the appropriate custodial term for the present offence is at least four years, the court may impose an extended sentence, so that the offender is under licence, following release from custody, for an extended period, for the purpose of protecting members of the public from serious harm occasioned by the commission by the offender of further specified offences (see **E4**). Where a child or young person is charged with an offence to which these provisions apply, the court must therefore consider whether the criteria for imposing a sentence under s. 226B are likely to be met and, if so, must send the accused to the Crown Court for trial.

In *R (DPP) v East Surrey Youth Court (Ghanbari, interested party)* [2005] EWHC 2929 (Admin), [2006] 1 WLR 2543, the Divisional Court considered the guidance on the dangerous offender provisions of the CJA 2003, given by the Court of Appeal in *Lang* [2005] EWCA Crim 2864, [2006] 1 WLR 2509. Rose LJ emphasised (at [17]) the need highlighted in *Lang*, in relation to those under 18, to be 'particularly rigorous before concluding that there is a significant risk of serious harm by the commission of further offences'. The Sentencing Council's definitive guideline, *Sentencing Children and Young People* (see Supplement, **SG8-1**), states (at para. 2.5): **D24.39**

> A 'significant risk' is more than a mere possibility of occurrence. The assessment of dangerousness should take into account all the available information relating to the circumstances of the offence and may also take into account any information regarding previous patterns of behaviour relating to this offence and any other relevant information relating to the child or young person. In making this assessment it will be essential to obtain a pre-sentence report.

The guideline goes on to say (at para. 2.7) that in 'anything but the most serious cases it may be impossible for the court to form a view as to whether the child or young person would meet the criteria of the dangerous offender provisions without greater knowledge of the circumstances of the offence and the child or young person. In those circumstances jurisdiction for the case should be retained in the youth court.' Thus, unless it is abundantly clear at the outset that the accused can properly be regarded as 'dangerous', the youth court should accept jurisdiction. If, following a guilty plea or a finding of guilt, the dangerousness criteria appear to be met, the offender should be committed for sentence under the PCC(S)A 2000, s. 3C.

The CPS guidance on 'youth offenders' (see **D24.4**) similarly suggests that there will be few cases in which it will be appropriate to send a child or young person to the Crown Court for trial under the 'dangerous offender' provisions, and that such power should be exercised only where (a) there is sufficient information (which will usually include a risk assessment in a recent pre-sentence report) about the nature and circumstances of the offender, the offence and any pattern of behaviour of which the offence forms part, to enable the court to assess the offender as dangerous, and (b) it is in the interests of justice for the accused to be tried on indictment. The guidance goes on to say that 'prosecutors should usually recommend summary trial on the basis that the youth court is the appropriate tribunal for youth trials', and that trial on indictment is unnecessary as the youth can be committed for sentence under the PCC(S)A 2000, s. 3C (see **D24.61**), if (having heard all the facts about the offence and the offender) the court decides that a sentence under the dangerous offender provisions may be necessary. On this basis, sending a child or young to the Crown Court for trial is described as an 'exceptional' course of action. **D24.40**

Life Sentences The CJA 2003, s. 226, provides that, if (i) a person under the age of 18 is convicted of a serious offence (defined by s. 224 as an offence which is listed in sch. 15 and which carries a life sentence); (ii) the offence is one in respect of which the offender would be liable to a sentence of detention for life under the PCC(S)A 2000, s. 91; (iii) the court is of the opinion that there is a significant risk to members of the public of serious harm occasioned by the commission by the offender of further specified offences; and (iv) the court considers that the seriousness of the offence, or of the offence and any associated offences, **D24.41**

is such as to justify the imposition of a sentence of detention for life, then the court must impose a sentence of detention for life under the PCC(S)A 2000, s. 91. Determination of allocation in such cases therefore takes place in the same way as other cases which fall within the ambit of s. 91.

Related Offences

D24.42 The CDA 1998, s. 51A(4), provides that, where a magistrates' court sends a child or young person to the Crown Court for trial under s. 51A(2), the court may also send the accused for trial for any other related indictable or summary offence with which he or she is charged. Where the related offence is a summary one, it can be sent to the Crown Court only if it is punishable with imprisonment or disqualification from driving.

D24.43 The CDA 1998, sch. 3, para. 13, applies where a person under 18 has been sent to the Crown Court for trial under s. 51A (or, in a case where there is an adult co-accused, under s. 51(7)) but, as a result of an amendment to the indictment or a successful application (under para. 2) for the main charge to be dismissed, the indictment includes no 'main' offence (i.e. an offence for which the accused was sent to the Crown Court for trial under s. 51A(2), or an offence for which he or she was sent for trial under s. 51(7) (adult co-accused)). In such a case, the Crown Court must remit the accused to a magistrates' court (in this context, this includes a youth court) acting for the place where the accused was sent to the Crown Court for trial.

D24.44 **Crime and Disorder Act 1998, s. 51A**

(1) This section is subject to sections 24A and 24B of the Magistrates' Courts Act 1980 (which provide for certain offences involving children or young persons to be tried summarily).

(2) Where a child or young person appears or is brought before a magistrates' court ('the court') charged with an offence and any of the conditions mentioned in subsection (3) below is satisfied, the court shall send him forthwith to the Crown Court for trial for the offence.

(3) Those conditions are—

(a) that the offence falls within subsection (12) below;

(b) that the offence is such as is mentioned in subsection (1) of section 91 of the Powers of Criminal Courts (Sentencing) Act 2000 (other than one mentioned in paragraph (d) below in relation to which it appears to the court as mentioned there) and the court considers that if he is found guilty of the offence it ought to be possible to sentence him in pursuance of subsection (3) of that section;

(c) that notice is given to the court under section 51B or 51C below in respect of the offence;

(d) that the offence is a specified offence (within the meaning of section 224 of the Criminal Justice Act 2003) and it appears to the court that if he is found guilty of the offence the criteria for the imposition of a sentence under section 226B of that Act would be met.

(4) Where the court sends a child or young person for trial under subsection (2) above, it may at the same time send him to the Crown Court for trial for any indictable or summary offence with which he is charged and which—

(a) (if it is an indictable offence) appears to the court to be related to the offence mentioned in subsection (2) above; or

(b) (if it is a summary offence) appears to the court to be related to the offence mentioned in subsection (2) above or to the indictable offence, and which fulfils the requisite condition (as defined in subsection (9) below).

(5) Where a child or young person who has been sent for trial under subsection (2) above subsequently appears or is brought before a magistrates' court charged with an indictable or summary offence which—

(a) appears to the court to be related to the offence mentioned in subsection (2) above; and

(b) (in the case of a summary offence) fulfils the requisite condition,

the court may send him forthwith to the Crown Court for trial for the indictable or summary offence.

(6) Where—

(a) the court sends a child or young person ('C') for trial under subsection (2) or (4) above; and

(b) an adult appears or is brought before the court on the same or a subsequent occasion charged jointly with C with an either-way offence for which C is sent for trial under subsection (2) or (4) above, or an either-way offence which appears to the court to be related to that offence,

the court shall where it is the same occasion, and may where it is a subsequent occasion, send the adult forthwith to the Crown Court for trial for the either-way offence.

(7) Where the court sends an adult for trial under subsection (6) above, it shall at the same time send him to the Crown Court for trial for any either-way or summary offence with which he is charged and which—
  (a) (if it is an either-way offence) appears to the court to be related to the offence for which he was sent for trial; and
  (b) (if it is a summary offence) appears to the court to be related to the offence for which he was sent for trial or to the either-way offence, and which fulfils the requisite condition.

(8) The trial of the information charging any summary offence for which a person is sent for trial under this section shall be treated as if the court had adjourned it under section 10 of the 1980 Act and had not fixed the time and place for its resumption.

(9) A summary offence fulfils the requisite condition if it is punishable with imprisonment or involves obligatory or discretionary disqualification from driving.

(10) In the case of a child or young person charged with an offence—
  (a) if the offence satisfies any of the conditions in subsection (3) above, the offence shall be dealt with under subsection (2) above and not under any other provision of this section or section 51 above;
  (b) subject to paragraph (a) above, if the offence is one in respect of which the requirements of subsection (7) of section 51 above for sending the child or young person to the Crown Court are satisfied, the offence shall be dealt with under that subsection and not under any other provision of this section or section 51 above.

(11) The functions of a magistrates' court under this section, and its related functions under section 51D below, may be discharged by a single justice.

(12) An offence falls within this subsection if—
  (a) it is an offence of homicide; or
  (b) each of the requirements of section 51A(1) of the Firearms Act 1968 would be satisfied with respect to—
    (i) the offence; and
    (ii) the person charged with it,

  if he were convicted of the offence; or
  (c) section 29(3) of the Violent Crime Reduction Act 2006 (minimum sentences in certain cases of using someone to mind a weapon) would apply if he were convicted of the offence.

Crime and Disorder Act 1998, sch. 3, para. 13 **D24.45**

(1) This paragraph applies, in place of paragraphs 7 to 12 above, in the case of a child or young person who—
  (a) has been sent for trial under section 51 or 51A of this Act but has not been arraigned; and
  (b) is charged on an indictment which (following amendment of the indictment, or as a result of an application under paragraph 2 above, or for any other reason) includes no main offence.

(2) The Crown Court shall remit the child or young person for trial to a magistrates' court acting for the place where he was sent to the Crown Court for trial.

(3) In this paragraph, a 'main offence' is—
  (a) an offence for which the child or young person has been sent to the Crown Court for trial under section 51A(2) of this Act; or
  (b) an offence—
    (i) for which the child or young person has been sent to the Crown Court for trial under subsection (7) of section 51 of this Act; and
    (ii) in respect of which the conditions for sending him to the Crown Court for trial under that subsection (as set out in paragraphs (a) and (b) of that subsection) continue to be satisfied.

Where a Child or Young Person is Charged with an Adult

D24.46 The CDA 1998, s. 51(7), applies where an adult is sent for trial under s. 51 and a person under 18 appears before the court (whether on the same or a subsequent occasion) charged jointly with an adult who has been sent for trial for the same or a related offence. It provides that the court shall, 'if it considers it necessary in the interests of justice to do so', send the child or young person forthwith to the Crown Court for trial for the indictable offence. By virtue of s. 51(8), the child or young person may also be sent for trial for any related offences (though if a related offence is a summary offence this provision will apply only if it is punishable with imprisonment or involves obligatory or discretionary disqualification from driving).

Crime and Disorder Act 1998, s. 51

(7) Where—

(a) the court sends an adult ('A') for trial under subsection (1), (3) or (5) above; and

(b) a child or young person appears or is brought before the court on the same or a subsequent occasion charged jointly with A with an indictable offence for which A is sent for trial under subsection (1), (3) or (5) above, or an indictable offence which appears to the court to be related to that offence,

the court shall, if it considers it necessary in the interests of justice to do so, send the child or young person forthwith to the Crown Court for trial for the indictable offence.

(8) Where the court sends a child or young person for trial under subsection (7) above, it may at the same time send him to the Crown Court for trial for any indictable or summary offence with which he is charged and which—

(a) (if it is an indictable offence) appears to the court to be related to the offence for which he is sent for trial; and

(b) (if it is a summary offence) appears to the court to be related to the offence for which he is sent for trial or to the indictable offence, and which fulfils the requisite condition.

(9) Subsections (7) and (8) above are subject to sections 24A and 24B of the Magistrates' Courts Act 1980 (which provide for certain cases involving children and young persons to be tried summarily).

D24.47 **Determining Allocation** Assuming that the child or young person indicates an intention to plead not guilty, the court will invite representations from the prosecution and defence on the issue of whether or not it is 'necessary in the interests of justice' to send the child or young person to the Crown Court for trial.

In coming to their decision on this question, the justices must balance what may well be conflicting interests. On one hand, it is desirable that there should be a joint trial (to avoid prosecution witnesses having to give their evidence twice, to avoid the risk of inconsistent verdicts, and to avoid the risk of disparity in the sentences which are passed in the event of conviction). On the other hand, a child or young person may well find appearing in the Crown Court an unduly traumatic experience.

In *R (DPP) v East Surrey Youth Court (Ghanbari, interested party)* [2005] EWHC 2929 (Admin), [2006] 1 WLR 2543, the Divisional Court said that, when deciding whether to send a child or young person for trial in the Crown Court, justices should bear in mind the policy of the legislature that those who are under 18 should, wherever possible, be tried in a youth court, which is designed for their specific needs. When an accused under the age of 18 is jointly charged with an adult, an exercise of judgement is called for by the youth court when assessing the competing presumptions in favour of (i) joint trial of those jointly charged, and (ii) the trial of young defendants in the youth court. Factors relevant to that judgement will include the age and maturity of the young defendant, the comparative culpability in relation to the offence and the previous convictions of the two and whether the trial can be severed without either injustice or undue inconvenience to witnesses (per Rose LJ at [17]). It is submitted that the younger the child or young person and the less serious the charge, the more reluctant the justices should be to send the accused to the Crown Court. Moreover, if it is alleged by the prosecution that the child or young person played only a minor role in the offence, it is likely to be more appropriate to deal with him or her separately.

D24.48 The Sentencing Council's definitive guideline, *Sentencing Children and Young People* (see Supplement, SG8-1), states that the proper venue for the trial of any child or young person is normally the youth court. Subject to statutory restrictions, that remains the case where a child or young person is charged jointly with an adult. When the interests of justice test must be considered because the adult is sent for trial to the Crown Court, the court should conclude that the child or young person must be tried separately in the youth court unless it is in the interests of justice for there to be a joint trial (para. 2.11). The guideline gives examples (at para. 2.12) of factors that should be considered when deciding whether it is in the interests of justice to send the child or young person to the Crown Court (rather than having a trial in the youth court):

- whether separate trials will cause injustice to witnesses or to the case as a whole (bearing in mind the possibility of video recorded testimony under the YJCEA 1999, ss. 27 and 28);
- the age of the child or young person (the younger the child or young person, the greater the desirability of trial in the youth court);
- the age gap between the child or young person and the adult (a substantial gap in age militates in favour of the child or young person being tried in the youth court);
- the lack of maturity of the child or young person;
- the relative culpability of the child or young person compared with the adult and whether the alleged role played by the child or young person was minor;
- the lack of previous convictions recorded against the child or young person.

The guideline also notes that the court should bear in mind that the youth court now has a general power to commit for sentence following conviction pursuant to the PCC(S)A 2000, s. 3B (so long as the offence is one to which s. 91 of the 2000 Act applies). In appropriate cases, this will permit the same court to sentence adult and young offenders who have been tried separately (para. 2.13).

No Power to Remit to Youth Court In *R (W (a minor)) v Leeds Crown Court* [2011] EWHC 2326 (Admin), [2012] 1 WLR 2786, the Divisional Court ruled that, where an adult and a child or young person are charged together and the adult is to be tried in the Crown Court, and the magistrates decide that it is necessary in the interests of justice for the child or young person to be tried in the Crown Court as well, the Crown Court has no power to remit the child or young person back to the youth court for trial. This is so even if, for example, the adult pleads guilty in the Crown Court and so the child or young person will be tried alone in the Crown Court. **D24.49**

Procedure where Child or Young Person is Not Sent with Adult to the Crown Court for Trial If the child or young person indicates a plea of guilty, and is thereby deemed to have pleaded guilty, the magistrates will consider whether their sentencing powers are adequate. Those powers are to make any one or more of the following orders (PCC(S)A 2000, s. 8(8)): **D24.50**

(a) absolute discharge;
(b) conditional discharge;
(c) a fine (up to £1,000 for an offender who has attained the age of 14; up to £250 for one who has not: PCC(S)A 2000, s. 135);
(d) requiring the offender's parents to enter into a recognizance to keep proper control of him or her.

An adult magistrates' court is also able to make a referral order under the PCC(S)A 2000, s. 16(1).

If these powers are not appropriate, the justices will remit the child or young person to the youth court to be sentenced (PCC(S)A 2000, s. 8(6)).

If the case is one where, in the youth court, a referral order would be mandatory under the PCC(S)A 2000, s. 16(2), the adult magistrates' court may, but is not obliged to, remit the case to the youth court (s. 8(7)).

If, on the other hand, the child or young person pleads not guilty, the adult magistrates' court may either try the accused or remit him or her for trial to the youth court (MCA 1980, s.

29(2)). In the absence of a good reason to the contrary (e.g. the prosecution wishing to offer no evidence), it is submitted that the child or young person should normally be remitted to the youth court for trial.

D24.51 **Procedure where Adult Co-accused is Tried Summarily** Where the child or young person is jointly charged with an adult who is to be tried summarily (i.e. the offence is a summary one, or an either-way offence where the adult defendant and the justices both agreed to summary trial), the procedure is as follows. If the child or young person indicates a plea of not guilty at the plea before venue hearing, the adult court *must* try him or her (CYPA 1933, s. 46(1)(a)). If the child or young person indicates a guilty plea at the plea before venue hearing, or is subsequently found guilty, the magistrates will remit him or her to the youth court for sentence if the sentences which the adult court can impose (see **D24.50**) are inappropriate. If, on the other hand, the adult pleads guilty and the child or young person pleads not guilty, the adult magistrates' court *may* try the child or young person under the MCA 1980, s. 29(2), or else remit him or her to the youth court for trial. Although the magistrates could theoretically try the child or young person (even though the adult has pleaded guilty, so that there will be no trial of the adult), it is much more likely that they will remit the child or young person to the youth court for trial. There is little justification for trying a child or young person alone in the adult magistrates' court. If the child or young person pleads guilty (or the adult court does try the child or young person and he or she is found guilty), the adult court will remit the child or young person to the youth court if none of the sentences which the adult court can impose are appropriate.

Where the child or young person is charged with aiding and abetting the adult or the adult is charged with aiding and abetting the child or young person, the adult magistrates' court has a discretion to try them both if they both plead not guilty (CYPA 1933, s. 46(1)(b); CYPA 1963, s. 18(a)). Similarly, if the adult and child or young person are charged with offences which arise out of the same circumstances and both plead not guilty, the adult magistrates' court may either try the child or young person or remit him or her to the youth court for trial (CYPA 1963, s. 18(b)). If the adult pleads guilty and the child or young person pleads not guilty, the magistrates are likely to remit the child or young person to the youth court for trial; if the adult magistrates' court tries and convicts the child or young person, he or she will be remitted to the youth court for sentence if the magistrates' sentencing powers are inappropriate.

D24.52 **Where the PCC(S)A 2000, s. 91, Applies and There Is an Adult Co-accused** There will be cases where a child or young person and an adult are charged with an offence to which the PCC(S)A 2000, s. 91, applies, and so the CDA 1998, ss. 51(7) and 51A(2), are both relevant. If the adult is sent to the Crown Court for trial, the question of whether a sentence under s. 91 would be appropriate in the event of the child or young person being convicted of the offence will be highly relevant to the decision whether to send the child or young person to the Crown Court for trial. As both defendants will be appearing in the adult magistrates' court, it will be that court which takes the decision on where the child or young person is to be tried. The adult court has no power to remit the child or young person to the youth court for that court to decide mode of trial (*Tottenham Youth Court, ex parte Fawzy* [1999] 1 WLR 1350).

D24.53 **Separate Trials** CrimPD I, para. 3G.1 (see Supplement, **CPD.3G**), says that if a 'vulnerable defendant, especially one who is young, is to be tried jointly with one who is not', the court should consider at the Plea and Trial Preparation Hearing, or the Preparation for Trial in a magistrates' court, whether the vulnerable defendant should be tried alone; however, the court should so order only 'if satisfied that a fair trial cannot be achieved by use of appropriate special measures or other support for the defendant'. If a vulnerable defendant is tried jointly with one who is not, the court should consider modifications to the trial process to accommodate the needs of the vulnerable defendant.

If the offence with which the adult and child or young person are charged is one which falls within the ambit of the PCC(S)A 2000, s. 91, or the 'dangerous offender' provisions of the CJA

2003, but the court orders that the adult and the child or young person be tried separately, the child or young person would still be tried in the Crown Court (with its procedures modified as appropriate). However, if the offence does not fall within the scope of these provisions, it seems anomalous that the child or young person should still be tried in the Crown Court even though separately from the adult. Nevertheless, this would seem to be inevitable, as there is currently no statutory power enabling the Crown Court to remit the child or young person to the youth court for trial in such a case.

Varying the Decision on Allocation

The MCA 1980, s. 25, which enables the prosecution to apply to the magistrates' court to reverse a decision in favour of summary trial, applies only where the accused has attained the age of 18, and so is inapplicable in the case of children and young people. **D24.54**

Challenging the Decision to Try a Case Summarily

Where the decision of the justices to try the case summarily is alleged to be unreasonable, the appropriate remedy for the prosecution is to seek judicial review (*Inner London Youth Court, ex parte DPP* (1997) 161 JP 178). **D24.55**

In *R (D) v Sheffield Youth Court* [2008] EWHC 601 (Admin), D (who was aged 17) appeared in an adult magistrates' court charged with offences falling under the PCC(S)A 2000, s. 91, and was jointly charged with adults. The magistrates' court allowed D to enter pleas of guilty to all charges against him and then remitted him to the youth court to be dealt with there. Richards LJ said (at [18]) that he did not think that it was Parliament's intention that failure to consider the matters set out in what is now the CDA 1998, ss. 51(7) and 51A(2), should render subsequent steps invalid. It followed that, despite the failure of the court to consider the relevant statutory provisions, there had been a valid acceptance of summary jurisdiction by the magistrates' court; equally, the subsequent decision to remit the case to the youth court was valid. His lordship added that the failure of the magistrates' court to proceed in the way that it should have done did not empower the youth court subsequently to reopen the matter under the MCA 1980, s. 142; it was too late for the matter to be reopened in that way.

COMMITTAL FOR SENTENCE

Three powers of committal for sentence under the PCC(S)A 2000 are relevant to children and young people: s. 3B (which applies where the accused pleads guilty to, or is found guilty of, an offence to which s. 91 applies); s. 3C (which applies where the accused pleads guilty to, or is found guilty of, an offence for which an extended sentence under the CJA 2003, s. 226B, may be imposed); and s. 4A (which applies where the accused is sent for trial for one or more offences but also indicates a guilty plea for one or more other offences). **D24.56**

Committal under the Powers of Criminal Courts (Sentencing) Act 2000, s. 3B

The PCC(S)A 2000, s. 3B (see **D24.58**), provides that, where a person under 18 is convicted (whether following a guilty plea at the 'plea before venue' hearing or a finding of guilt after summary trial) of an offence which falls within the ambit of the PCC(S)A 2000, s. 91, and the court is of the opinion that the offence (together with any associated offences) is such that the Crown Court should have power to deal with the offender under s. 91, then the court may commit the offender (in custody or on bail) to the Crown Court for sentence. **D24.57**

Sir Brian Leveson P, in *R (DPP) v South Tyneside Youth Court* [2015] EWHC 1455 (Admin), [2015] 2 Cr App R (S) 59 (411), noted (at [31]) that the current version of s. 3B (which enables committal for sentence after trial and not just after a guilty plea, as was formerly the case) means that the court is 'not making a once and for all decision' at the point deciding whether the case should be tried in the youth court or in the Crown Court. He added that it will generally be after conviction (when the court 'has determined the full circumstances of the offence and has a far greater understanding of the position of the offender') that the assessment of whether there is a 'real prospect' that a sentence under s. 91 is appropriate 'can and should be made'.

D24.58 Section 3B(3) provides that, where a child or young person is committed for sentence under s. 3B(2), s. 6 of the 2000 Act (which enables a magistrates' court to commit the offender to the Crown Court to be dealt with in respect of other offences) is applicable.

Powers of Criminal Courts (Sentencing) Act 2000, s. 3B

(1) This section applies where on the summary trial of an offence mentioned in section 91(1) of this Act a person aged under 18 is convicted of the offence.

(2) If the court is of the opinion that—

(a) the offence; or

(b) the combination of the offence and one or more offences associated with it, was such that the Crown Court should, in the court's opinion, have power to deal with the offender as if the provisions of section 91(3) below applied, the court may commit him in custody or on bail to the Crown Court for sentence in accordance with section 5A(1) below.

(3) Where the court commits a person under subsection (2) above, section 6 below (which enables a magistrates' court, where it commits a person under this section in respect of an offence, also to commit him to the Crown Court to be dealt with in respect of certain other offences) shall apply accordingly.

Committal for Sentence: Related Offences Sent for Trial

D24.59 The PCC(S)A 2000, s. 4A, applies where a person under 18 is charged with an offence to which s. 91 of the 2000 Act applies and, at the 'plea before venue' hearing, indicates an intention to plead guilty. Under s. 4A(2), if the court has sent the offender to the Crown Court for trial for one or more offences that are related to the s. 91 offence, it may commit the offender (in custody or on bail) to the Crown Court to be dealt with in respect of the s. 91 offence. Under s. 4A(4), if the magistrates commit the s. 91 offence to the Crown Court for sentence but do not state that, in their opinion, the case is one where it ought to be possible to impose detention under s. 91, the Crown Court cannot impose detention under s. 91 for that offence (and so is limited to the sentences that could be imposed by the youth court) unless the child or young person is convicted by the Crown Court of one or more of the related offences. This provision thus mirrors the PCC(S)A 2000, s. 4, which is applicable to adult offenders.

Powers of Criminal Courts (Sentencing) Act 2000, s. 4A

(1) This section applies where—

(a) a person aged under 18 appears or brought before a magistrates' court ('the court') on an information charging him with an offence mentioned in subsection (1) of section 91 below ('the offence');

(b) he or his representative indicates under section 24A or (as the case may be) 24B of the Magistrates' Courts Act 1980 (child or young person to indicate intention as to plea in certain cases) that he would plead guilty if the offence were to proceed to trial; and

(c) proceeding as if section 9(1) of that Act were complied with and he pleaded guilty under it, the court convicts him of the offence.

(2) If the court has sent the offender to the Crown Court for trial for one or more related offences, that is to say one or more offences which, in its opinion, are related to the offence, it may commit him in custody or on bail to the Crown Court to be dealt with in respect of the offence in accordance with section 5A(1) below.

(3) If the power conferred by subsection (2) above is not exercisable but the court is still to determine to, or to determine whether to, send the offender to the Crown Court for trial under section 51 or 51A of the Crime and Disorder Act 1998 for one or more related offences—

(a) it shall adjourn the proceedings relating to the offence until after it has made those determinations; and

(b) if it sends the offender to the Crown Court for trial for one or more related offences, it may then exercise that power.

(4) Where the court—
    (a) under subsection (2) above commits the offender to the Crown Court to be dealt with in respect of the offence; and
    (b) does not state that, in its opinion, it also has power so to commit him under section 38(2) or, as the case may be, section 3C(2) above,

section 5A(1) below shall not apply unless he is convicted before the Crown Court of one or more of the related offences.

(5) Where section 5A(1) below does not apply, the Crown Court may deal with the offender in respect of the offence in any way in which the magistrates' court could deal with him if it had just convicted him of the offence.

(6) Where the court commits a person under subsection (2) above, section 6 below (which enables a magistrates' court, where it commits a person under this section in respect of an offence, also to commit him to the Crown Court to be dealt with in respect of certain other offences) shall apply accordingly.

(7) Section 4(7) above applies for the purposes of this section as it applies for the purposes of that section.

Committal for Sentence: Dangerous Offenders

The PCC(S)A 2000, s. 3C (see **D24.61**), enables committal for sentence of dangerous young offenders. Where a person under 18 is convicted of an offence specified in the CJA 2003, s. 224, and it appears to the court that the criteria for the imposition of a sentence under s. 226B would be met, the court must commit the offender (in custody or on bail) to the Crown Court for sentence (s. 3C(2)). The power to commit for sentence under s. 3C can be exercised whether the accused pleaded guilty or was found guilty. According to Pitchford LJ in *R (BW) v Caernarfon Youth Court* [2013] EWHC 1466 (Admin) (at [18]–[19]), this is to take account of the fact that: **D24.60**

> ... there may become available to the court, either in the course of evidence or upon the production of pre-sentence reports, information which drives the tribunal to alter its opinion as to the seriousness of the offences committed, and the risk for the future of repetition. For that reason, the court is given a residual power in very exceptional circumstances to commit to the Crown court for sentence, notwithstanding the original acceptance of summary jurisdiction.

The offender can also be committed (under the PCC(S)A 2000, s. 6) to be sentenced for other offences that the magistrates would otherwise be dealing with (s. 3C(3)). Section 3C(4) makes it clear that s. 3C does not prevent the court from committing a specified offence to the Crown Court for sentence under s. 3B (committal in the case of offences that fall within s. 91) if the provisions of that section are satisfied.

Powers of Criminal Courts (Sentencing) Act 2000, s. 3C **D24.61**

(1) This section applies where on the summary trial of a specified offence a person aged under 18 is convicted of the offence.

(2) If, in relation to the offence, it appears to the court that the criteria for the imposition of a sentence under section 226B of the Criminal Justice Act 2003 would be met, the court must commit the offender in custody or on bail to the Crown Court for sentence in accordance with section 5A(1) below.

(3) Where the court commits a person under subsection (2) above, section 6 below (which enables a magistrates' court, where it commits a person under this section in respect of an offence, also to commit him to the Crown Court to be dealt with in respect of certain other offences) shall apply accordingly.

(4) Nothing in this section shall prevent the court from committing a specified offence to the Crown Court for sentence under section 3B above if the provisions of that section are satisfied.

(5) In this section, references to a specified offence are to a specified offence within the meaning of section 224 of the Criminal Justice Act 2003.

Powers of Crown Court Following Committal for Sentence

The PCC(S)A 2000, s. 5A, provides that, where an offender is committed for sentence under s. 3B, 3C or 4A, the Crown Court may deal with the offender as if he or she had just been convicted of the offence on indictment. It should be noted, however, that in *Robson* [2006] EWCA **D24.62**

Crim 1414, [2007] 1 All ER 506, the Court of Appeal ruled that the Crown Court is required to pass sentence on the basis of the age of the offender at the date of conviction (not the age of appearance before the Crown Court).

Powers of Criminal Courts (Sentencing) Act 2000, s. 5A

(1) Where an offender is committed by a magistrates' court for sentence under section 3B, 3C or 4A above, the Crown Court shall inquire into the circumstances of the case and may deal with the offender in any way in which it could deal with him if he had just been convicted of the offence on indictment before the court.

(2) In relation to committals under section 4A above, subsection (1) above has effect subject to section 4A(4) and (5) above.

Relationship between the Powers of Criminal Courts (Sentencing) Act 2000 and Dangerous Offender Provisions

D24.63 The existence of the power of committal for sentence conferred by the PCC(S)A 2000, s. 3C, necessitates consideration of the relationship between s. 91 of that Act and the dangerous offender provisions (CJA 2003, s. 226B). If the offence is a 'specified offence' (as defined by the CJA 2003, s. 224(1) — i.e. an offence specified in sch. 15 to that Act), the youth court must send the child or young person to the Crown Court (under the CDA 1998, s. 51A(3)(d)) if the justices are of the opinion that the Crown Court will take the view that there is a significant risk to members of the public of serious harm occasioned by the commission by the offender of further specified offences. If the offence is a 'serious offence' (as defined by s. 224(2) — i.e. an offence specified in sch. 15 and punishable with a life sentence), the youth court must similarly send the child or young person to the Crown Court for trial (under the CDA 1998, s. 51A(3)(b)) if the justices are of the opinion that it ought to be possible to impose a sentence under the PCC(S)A 2000, s. 91 (in this case, to a sentence of detention for life pursuant to the CJA 2003, s. 226) because the Crown Court would take the view that there is a significant risk to members of the public of serious harm occasioned by the commission by the offender of further specified offences.

D24.64 There are, essentially, three categories of offence:

(1) Offences which fall within s. 91 but which are not 'specified offences' under s. 224: the court follows the plea before venue procedure (under the MCA 1980, s. 24A), and may commit the accused to the Crown Court for sentence, under the PCC(S)A 2000, s. 3B, if he or she pleads guilty or is found guilty.

(2) Offences which are 'specified offences' but which do not fall within s. 91: the justices must decide whether it appears to them that the criteria for the imposition of a sentence under the CJA 2003, s. 226B, are satisfied. If the justices take the view that the criteria are satisfied, they must send the accused to the Crown Court for trial. If the justices take the view that the criteria are not satisfied, they will try the case summarily. If they try the case and convict the accused, and decide at that stage that the criteria are, in fact, satisfied (they will, of course, have much more information by that stage), they must commit the offender to the Crown Court for sentence under the PCC(S)A 2000, s. 3C(2).

(3) Offences that are both 'specified' offences and fall within s. 91: the justices will go through the 'plea before venue' procedure. If the accused indicates a guilty plea, he or she may be committed for sentence either under s. 3B, on the basis that the justices are of the opinion that the Crown Court should have power to impose detention under s. 91 (a test that depends on the seriousness of the offence), or under s. 3C, on the basis that it appears to the court that the criteria for the imposition of a sentence under s. 226B would be met (a test that depends largely on there being a significant risk of future serious harm). If the accused indicates an intention to plead not guilty (or gives no indication), the justices must decide whether to try the case *summarily or to send the accused* for trial in the Crown Court. If the justices take the view that the Crown Court ought to be able to pass a sentence under s. 91 or that the accused is likely to satisfy the criteria for a sentence under s. 226B, they must send the accused for trial in the

Crown Court. If the justices decide to try the case themselves and they find the accused guilty, they will be able to commit him or her to the Crown Court for sentence under s. 3C (if they decide, at that stage, that the criteria for a sentence under s. 226B are met) or under s. 3B (if they decide that the Crown Court ought to have power to deal with the offender under s. 91). If the offender is committed for sentence under s. 3B or s. 3C, the Crown Court has power to impose any sentence it could have imposed had the offender been convicted on indictment.

MODE OF TRIAL AND PROCEDURE FOR PERSONS CLOSE TO 18TH BIRTHDAY

This part of the section deals with the various provisions relevant to persons who are close to their 18th birthday at the time of the proceedings against them. Some of the relevant case law was decided at a time when the determining event was the accused's 17th birthday, and so it needs to be borne in mind that the coming into force of the CJA 1991, s. 68, made the 18th birthday the watershed at which an accused becomes an adult. **D24.65**

Determining Age

By the CYPA 1933, s. 99(1) (see **D24.67**), where a person apparently under 18 is brought before a court, the court is to make 'due inquiry' as to the person's age and must take into account such evidence on the matter as may be forthcoming at the hearing of the case. However, any order or judgment of the court is not invalidated by subsequent proof that the person's age was incorrectly stated; the person is deemed for the purposes of the 1933 Act to be whatever age he or she is presumed or declared to be by the court (s. 99(1)). The court is entitled to accept what the person (or the person's parent or guardian, if present) says on the matter, although in cases of doubt it may ask for further inquiries to be undertaken. The MCA 1980, s. 150(4), makes similar provision in respect of age-dependent powers granted to magistrates by that Act. For the purposes of the PCC(S)A 2000, a person's age 'shall be deemed to be that which it appears to the court ... after considering any available evidence' (s. 164(1)). **D24.66**

In *R (M) v Hammersmith Magistrates' Court* [2017] EWHC 1359 (Admin), D claimed to be 16, but the youth court held him to be 18. In reaching that decision, the court had received no evidence on the question of the claimant's age. The Divisional Court held that the youth court had erred. Irwin LJ (at [16]) said that, in cases where there is a real doubt as to the claimed age of the accused, the proper course is to require an age assessment to be conducted (usually through a youth offending team).

Children and Young Persons Act 1933, s. 99 **D24.67**

(1) Where a person, whether charged with an offence or not, is brought before any court otherwise than for the purposes of giving evidence, and it appears to the court that he is a child or young person, the court shall make due inquiry as to the age of that person, and for that purpose shall take such evidence as may be forthcoming at the hearing of the case, but an order or judgment of the court shall not be invalidated by any subsequent proof that the age of that person has not been correctly stated to the court, and the age presumed or declared by the court to be the age of the person so brought before it shall, for the purposes of this Act, be deemed to be the true age of that person, and, where it appears to the court that the person so brought before it has attained the age of 18 years, that person shall for the purposes of this Act be deemed not to be a child or young person.

[(2) to (4) deal with proof of age of the victim of an offence where the charge alleges that he was a child or young person.]

Magistrates' Courts Act 1980, s. 150

(4) Where the age of any person at any time is material for the purposes of any provision of this Act regulating the powers of a magistrates' court, his age at the material time shall be deemed to be or to have been that which appears to the court after considering any available evidence to be or to have been his age at that time.

Discovery of True Age during Proceedings

D24.68 The statutory presumption in the MCA 1980, s.150(4), that an accused is whatever age he or she is declared to be by the court, prevents judgments or orders of the court (in particular, findings of guilt and sentences) being disturbed should it be discovered, after the conclusion of the proceedings, that the court was misled as to age. The presumption cannot assist where it emerges during the course of the proceedings that the court's initial view about age was erroneous. However, proviso (c) of the CYPA 1933, s. 46(1), gives an adult magistrates' court which has embarked upon the trial of an accused in the belief that he or she was an adult the discretion to complete the hearing even if it should appear to the court during the course of the proceedings that the accused is in fact under 18. Conversely, s. 48(1) of the 1933 Act provides that:

> A youth court sitting for the purpose of hearing a charge against a person who is believed to be a child or young person may, if it thinks fit to do so, proceed with the hearing and determination of the charge notwithstanding that it is discovered that the person in question is not a child or young person.

Accused Attaining the Age of 18 During Proceedings

D24.69 **Relevant Date** In *Islington North Juvenile Court, ex parte Daley* [1983] 1 AC 347, the House of Lords had to consider at what stage of the proceedings an accused charged with an either-way offence must attain the relevant age (then 17, now 18) in order to be entitled to elect trial by a jury. Lord Diplock, with whom the other Law Lords agreed, held (at p. 364) that 'the only appropriate date at which to determine whether an accused person has attained an age which entitles him to elect to be tried by jury for offences which … are triable either way is the date of his appearance before the court on the occasion when the court makes its decision as to the mode of trial'. In that case, D was 16 when he made his first appearance in the juvenile [youth] court (when the case was simply adjourned). By the time he next appeared, he had attained the age of 17 and so had become an adult according to the law at the time. The effect of the decision of the House of Lords was that he was entitled to elect trial by jury, because he became an adult before mode of trial was determined. Similarly, in *Uxbridge Youth Court, ex parte H* (1998) 162 JP 327, D was 17 (at a time when 17, not 18, was the relevant age) when arrested and charged but, by the time he made his first appearance at the youth court, he had turned 18. The Divisional Court held that the youth court did not have jurisdiction to deal with D, since he had attained the age of 18 (and so was an adult) by the time of his first court appearance.

D24.70 The reference by Lord Diplock in *Ex parte Daley* to the moment when the youth court 'makes its decision as to the mode of trial' is problematic because, in the great majority of cases, there is no separate occasion on which mode of trial for a child or young person is determined — the accused is simply asked to plead guilty or not guilty. Therefore, it is submitted that Lord Diplock must be taken as having meant that the right of a person who attains the relevant age during the currency of proceedings to be tried on indictment for an indictable offence depends either upon the person's age when mode of trial is determined, or — if there is no express determination of mode of trial — upon his or her age when the court is ready for the charge to be put. If the accused is under the age of 18 on the occasion of entering a plea, there is no right to elect trial on indictment, even if the matter is forthwith adjourned for trial at a later date and the accused attains that age before any evidence is heard.

D24.71 The corollary of *Ex parte Daley* is that, where the offence charged is triable only on indictment in the case of an adult, an accused must go to the Crown Court for trial if he or she attains the age of 18 before a plea is taken. In *Ford* [2018] EWCA Crim 1751, for example, D was charged with wounding with intent, an indictable-only offence. He was aged 17 when he first appeared in the youth court, but the case was simply adjourned on that occasion. At the next hearing, he had attained the age of 18. The youth court took his plea and then committed him to Crown

Court for sentence. On appeal, it was held that, because he was charged with an indictable-only offence, the only route available to the youth court was to send him to the Crown Court for trial; the youth court had no jurisdiction to take his plea.

It also follows that, if the accused is charged with an either-way offence and is 17 at the date of the first appearance in the youth court but attains the age of 18 before the court is ready to take a plea, the court may decline jurisdiction if it considers that the charge is too serious for summary trial, and the accused may elect Crown Court trial; any summary trial would take place in the adult magistrates' court, not the youth court.

Additional Charges after Accused Attains the Age of 18

Where an accused against whom proceedings have properly been commenced in the youth court attains the age of 18 and is then charged with an additional matter, the latter charge may not be heard in the youth court (*Chelsea Justices, ex parte DPP* [1963] 3 All ER 657). That applies regardless of whether the youth court is able to retain jurisdiction over the original charge. **D24.72**

TRIAL OF CHILDREN AND YOUNG PEOPLE ON INDICTMENT

The procedure for trying a person under 18 on indictment is identical to that for trying an adult, subject to certain modifications, which are discussed below. **D24.73**

Reporting Restrictions

The YJCEA 1999, s. 45 (see **D24.79**), applies to proceedings in the Crown Court and in adult magistrates' courts, but not to youth court proceedings (which are covered by the CYPA 1933, s. 49). **D24.74**

Under s. 45(3), the court may direct that no matter relating to any person concerned in the proceedings shall, while the person is under the age of 18, be included in any publication if it is likely to lead members of the public to identify him or her as a person concerned in the proceedings. For these purposes, a person is 'concerned in the proceedings' if he or she is the accused or a witness (s. 45(7)). The protected information includes the person's name and address, the identity of any school or other educational establishment attended, and the identity of any place of work; the restriction also applies to any 'still or moving picture' of the person (s. 45(8)).

It should be noted that a direction under s. 45(3) applies only to information likely to enable the person in question to be identified; that it applies only while that person is under the age of 18; and that it applies to 'any publication' (and so includes, for example, social media). Although orders under s. 45 apply only while the person concerned is under the age of 18, s. 45A confers an additional power, in specified circumstances, to make a lifelong reporting restriction in respect of a victim or witness who is under 18 during the proceedings (see **D3.139**).

Publication of matter in contravention of a direction given under s. 45(3) is a summary offence punishable with a fine of any amount (s. 49(5)). Where an order under s. 45(3) is breached, the proper course is for the judge to report the matter so that proceedings for the summary offence created by s. 49(5) may be taken, not to treat it as a contempt of court (*Tyne Tees Television Ltd* (1997) *The Times*, 20 October 1997, decided in the context of the CYPA 1933, s. 39, which now applies only in civil proceedings). **D24.75**

Criteria for Making an Order It is submitted that much of the case law on whether reporting restrictions under the CYPA 1933, s. 39, would be appropriate is equally applicable to orders under the YJCEA 1999, s. 45, given the similarity between the two provisions. **D24.76**

In *Central Criminal Court, ex parte S* (1999) 163 JP 776, for example, the Divisional Court held that there must be a good reason for making an order preventing identification of a child or young person who appears before an adult court. The Court said that, in deciding whether to make such an order, the weight which the court should attach to the various factors relevant to the decision might be different at differing stages of the proceedings. For example, after the person has been convicted, it might be appropriate to place greater weight on the interest of the public in knowing the identity of those who have committed serious crimes.

In considering the range of factors that may be considered by a court when determining whether to impose reporting restrictions, some useful guidance comes from the judgment of Simon Brown LJ in *Winchester Crown Court, ex parte B* [1999] 1 WLR 788 at p. 790 (that decision was not followed in *Manchester Crown Court, ex parte H and D* [2000] 2 All ER 166, but this was on a point that does not affect what is said below):

> (i) In deciding whether to impose or thereafter to lift reporting restrictions, the court will consider whether there are good reasons for naming the defendant. (ii) In reaching that decision, the court will give considerable weight to the age of the offender and to the potential damage to any young person of public identification as a criminal before the offender has the benefit or burden of adulthood. (iii) By virtue of s. 44 of the Act of 1933, the court must 'have regard to the welfare of the child or young person.' (iv) The prospect of being named in court with the accompanying disgrace is a powerful deterrent and the naming of a defendant in the context of his punishment serves as a deterrent to others. These deterrents are proper objectives for the court to seek. (v) There is a strong public interest in open justice and in the public knowing as much as possible about what has happened in court, including the identity of those who have committed crime. (vi) The weight to be attributed to the different factors may shift at different stages of the proceedings and, in particular, after the defendant has been found, or pleads, guilty and is sentenced. It may then be appropriate to place greater weight on the interest of the public in knowing the identity of those who have committed crimes, particularly serious and detestable crimes. (vii) The fact that an appeal has been made may be a material consideration.

In *R (Y) v Aylesbury Crown Court* [2012] EWHC 1140 (Admin), Hooper LJ said that an accused who applies for the imposition of reporting restrictions will have to satisfy the court that there is a 'good reason' to do so. This reason will usually be based on the accused's welfare (since this must be taken into account under the CYPA 1933, s. 44). The court must also have regard to the public interest, and to the ECHR, Article 10. This includes the possible public interest in 'knowing the outcome of proceedings in court' and in the 'valuable deterrent effect that the identification of those guilty of at least serious crimes may have on others'. So far as Article 10 is concerned, the Court adopted the words of the document entitled 'Reporting Restrictions in the Crown Court' (2016, tinyurl.com/lluexdb: see **D3.128**), namely that 'any order restricting publication must be necessary, proportionate and there must be a pressing social need for it' (at [29]). The Court went on to say that, prior to conviction, the accused's welfare is likely to take precedence over the public interest but, after conviction, the age of the accused and the seriousness of the crime of which he or she has been convicted will be particularly relevant; moreover, the judge may permit the publication of some details but not all (at [46]–[47]). His lordship concluded that where the factors favouring a restriction on publication and the factors favouring publication are very evenly balanced, the court should make an order restricting publication.

In *Cornick* [2014] EWHC 3623 (QB), Coulson J noted (at [10]) that 'in the vast majority of cases, a defendant in a criminal case can be expected to be named, unless there is an absolute necessity for anonymity'. Referring to the ECHR, his lordship went on to say (at [12]) that the onus is on the party seeking an order for anonymity 'to establish, either by way of Article 2 or by way of Article 8, that the rights of the Press and public under Article 10 should be trumped by the welfare of the child'. Accordingly, there had to be 'a good reason' for making an order for anonymity. His lordship added (at [14]) that it is only the child or young person whose interests can be considered in the balancing exercise: save for any indirect impact on the child or young person, the effect of identification on his or her family is not a relevant consideration.

Excepting Directions The court may (at the time the direction is given under s. 45(3) or subsequently) make an 'excepting direction', which dispenses, to any extent specified, with the restrictions imposed by a direction under s. 45(3), if it is satisfied either that it is 'necessary in the interests of justice' to do so (s. 45(4)) or that the effect of the restrictions imposed under s. 45(3) 'is to impose a substantial and unreasonable restriction on the reporting of the proceedings', and that 'it is in the public interest to remove or relax that restriction' (s. 45(5)). An 'excepting direction' cannot be given under s. 45(5) solely on the basis that the proceedings have been determined in any way or have been abandoned. **D24.77**

When deciding whether to make a direction under s. 45(3), or an 'excepting direction', the court must have regard to the welfare of the person in question (s. 45(6)).

In *Markham* [2017] EWCA Crim 739, [2017] 2 Cr App R (S) 30 (249), the Court of Appeal upheld the lifting, post conviction, of reporting restrictions in respect of a horrific murder case. The offenders were both aged 15. Sir Brian Leveson P noted (at [83]) that when a person under 18 is tried on indictment in the Crown Court, 'there is a strong presumption that justice takes place in open, and the press may report the proceedings'. His lordship went on to observe that no new material had been put before the Court of Appeal to justify the conclusion that lifting anonymity would cause harm to either appellant; nor was there any evidence before the Court that reporting their identities would adversely affect their future rehabilitation. Account was also taken of the fact that the appellants would remain in custody for a considerable time after the restrictions expired in any event, when they attained the age of 18. The Court (at [90]) held that the lifting of reporting restrictions pursued a legitimate aim and was a reasonable and proportionate measure, properly balancing the welfare of the appellants (and other factors identified in the ECHR, Article 8) against the Article 10 rights of the press and the interests of the public.

Markham was followed in *Aziz* [2019] EWCA Crim 1568, where the Court of Appeal identified a number of key points (at [40]):

(1) The general approach to be taken is that reports of proceedings should not be restricted unless there are reasons to do so which outweigh the legitimate interests of the public in receiving fair and accurate reports of criminal proceedings and knowing the identity of those in the community who have been guilty of criminal conduct and may, therefore, present a danger or threat to the community in which they live . . .
(2) The fact that the person before the court is a child or young person will normally be a good reason for restricting reports of the proceedings in the way permitted by the legislation; and it will only be in rare cases that a direction under s. 45(3) will not be given or, having been given, will be discharged . . .
(3) Very great weight must be given to the welfare of such a child or young person. Power to dispense with anonymity must be exercised with very great care, caution and circumspection; the court must be clear in its mind why it is in the public interest to dispense with the restrictions, which will very rarely be the case . . .
(4) It is not the case, however, that the welfare of the child or young person will always trump other considerations. Even in the youth court, where the regime requires that proceedings should be held in private, with the public excluded, the court has power to lift restrictions. When a juvenile is tried on indictment in the Crown Court there is a strong presumption that justice takes place in open and the press may report the proceedings . . .

In the instant case, which concerned offences of murder and rape that were 'exceptionally serious and shocking in their planning' (at [43]), neither the experts nor the authors of the pre-sentence report were able to provide cogent evidence that identification of D would cause or risk significant harm to his health or wellbeing (at [46]). The Court also rejected the criticism that the judge erred in proceeding on the assumption that anonymity would necessarily fall away when D reached the age of 18 (at [48]), as the facts of the case were very far removed from those in which an injunction against all the world (*contra mundum*) to preserve anonymity could be made. As the Court pointed out, in *RXG v Ministry of Justice* [2019] EWHC 2026 (QB), [2020] 2 WLR 635 (at [32]–[35]), it was made clear that such injunctions are exceptional (indeed, as the Court observed, the jurisdiction had been exercised on only four occasions, in each case to protect the new identities of notorious offenders). The exceptional nature of such orders was again emphasised in *DXB v Persons Unknown* [2020] EWHC 134 (QB), where the Divisional Court concluded (at [114]) that the claimant had demonstrated that, if his anonymity was not extended, this would give rise to an interference with his right to private and family life under Article 8. However, the curtailment of the claimant's (and his family's) right to respect for their private and family life was justified by the 'compelling public interest in open justice'.

D24.78 **Appeals against Orders** In *Lee* [1993] 2 All ER 170 at pp. 110–11 (per Lloyd LJ), the Court of Appeal summarised the position in relation to appeals against a decision to impose reporting restrictions:

(a) a member of the press who is aggrieved by an order should go back to the Crown Court in the event of a change of circumstances, or should appeal to the Court of Appeal (under the CJA 1988, s. 159);
(b) an accused who is aggrieved by the withholding or discharging of an order should go back to the Crown Court in the event of a change of circumstances or challenge the validity of the order by seeking judicial review;
(c) if an accused indicates an intention to apply to the Divisional Court, the Crown Court has the power to make a temporary order or grant a stay of the order discharging the direction, pending a decision of the Divisional Court.

D24.79 **Youth Justice and Criminal Evidence Act 1999, s. 45**

(1) This section applies (subject to subsection (2)) in relation to—
(a) any criminal proceedings in any court (other than a service court) in England and Wales or Northern Ireland; and
(b) any proceedings (whether in the United Kingdom or elsewhere) in any service court.
(2) This section does not apply in relation to any proceedings to which section 49 of the Children and Young Persons Act 1933 applies.
(3) The court may direct that no matter relating to any person concerned in the proceedings shall while he is under the age of 18 be included in any publication if it is likely to lead members of the public to identify him as a person concerned in the proceedings.
(4) The court or an appellate court may by direction ('an excepting direction') dispense, to any extent specified in the excepting direction, with the restrictions imposed by a direction under subsection (3) if it is satisfied that it is necessary in the interests of justice to do so.
(5) The court or an appellate court may also by direction ('an excepting direction') dispense, to any extent specified in the excepting direction, with the restrictions imposed by a direction under subsection (3) if it is satisfied—
(a) that their effect is to impose a substantial and unreasonable restriction on the reporting of the proceedings, and
(b) that it is in the public interest to remove or relax that restriction;
but no excepting direction shall be given under this subsection by reason only of the fact that the proceedings have been determined in any way or have been abandoned.
(6) When deciding whether to make—
(a) a direction under subsection (3) in relation to a person, or
(b) an excepting direction under subsection (4) or (5) by virtue of which the restrictions imposed by a direction under subsection (3) would be dispensed with (to any extent) in relation to a person,
the court or (as the case may be) the appellate court shall have regard to the welfare of that person.
(7) For the purposes of subsection (3) any reference to a person concerned in the proceedings is to a person—
(a) against or in respect of whom the proceedings are taken, or
(b) who is a witness in the proceedings.

(8) The matters relating to a person in relation to which the restrictions imposed by a direction under subsection (3) apply (if their inclusion in any publication is likely to have the result mentioned in that subsection) include in particular—
   (a) his name,
   (b) his address,
   (c) the identity of any school or other educational establishment attended by him,
   (d) the identity of any place of work, and
   (e) any still or moving picture of him.

(9) A direction under subsection (3) may be revoked by the court or an appellate court.

(10) An excepting direction—
   (a) may be given at the time the direction under subsection (3) is given or subsequently; and
   (b) may be varied or revoked by the court or an appellate court.

(11) In this section 'appellate court', in relation to any proceedings in a court, means a court dealing with an appeal (including an appeal by way of case stated) arising out of the proceedings or with any further appeal.

Attendance of Parent or Guardian

The CYPA 1933, s. 34A (power of court to order attendance by the accused's parent or guardian), applies to proceedings in the Crown Court (and in adult magistrates' courts) in the same way as it applies in proceedings in the youth court (see **D24.16**). **D24.80**

TRIAL OF CHILDREN AND YOUNG PEOPLE IN ADULT MAGISTRATES' COURTS

The exceptional circumstances in which a person under 18 is to be tried summarily in an adult magistrates' court rather than a youth court are set out in the CYPA 1933, s. 46 (see **D24.83**), and the CYPA 1963, s. 18 (see **D24.84**). Their effect is as follows: **D24.81**

(a) Where an adult and a child or young person are charged jointly with an offence, and both plead not guilty to that offence, the trial must take place in the adult magistrates' court (first proviso to the CYPA 1933, s. 46(1)). If, however, the child or young person has pleaded not guilty and either (i) the adult has pleaded guilty, or (ii) the adult is sent to the Crown Court for trial but the magistrates decide that it is not necessary in the interests of justice for the child or young person to be sent to the Crown Court as well, then the child or young person may be remitted to the youth court for trial (by virtue of the MCA 1980, s. 29(2); see **D24.85**). Whether to remit the accused in these circumstances is a matter for the adult court's discretion, but it is submitted that it would normally be appropriate to remit the child or young person for trial in the youth court. The phrase 'jointly charged' usually means two (or more) persons named in the same charge because they are alleged to have committed the offence together. However, the phrase is sometimes to be given a broader meaning. In *Peterborough Magistrates, ex parte Allgood* (1995) 159 JP 627, it was held that if, arising out of the same circumstances, one accused is charged with driving a motor vehicle taken without the owner's consent and the other is charged with allowing himself to be carried in that motor vehicle, then the two accused may properly be regarded (even though charged with separate offences) as being jointly charged.

(b) Where an adult is charged with aiding, abetting, causing, procuring, allowing or permitting a person under 18 to commit an offence, and at the same time the child or young person is charged with the offence as principal offender, the adult magistrates' court may, in its discretion, hear the charge against the child or young person (second proviso to the CYPA 1933, s. 46(1)). The same applies in the reverse situation (where a person under 18 is charged with aiding, abetting etc. an adult: CYPA 1963, s. 18). The normal practice, however, is simply to join aiders and abettors with the principal offender in a single charge (i.e. as if they are all principal offenders, as permitted by the Accessories and Abettors Act 1861, s. 8), in which event the first proviso to the CYPA 1933, s. 46(1), applies. Thus, the situation envisaged by the second proviso will rarely arise.

(c) Where a person under 18 is charged separately from but at the same time as an adult, and the charge against one arises out of circumstances which are the same as or linked with the charge against the other, then the adult court may try the charge against the child or young person (CYPA 1963, s. 18). It is not entirely clear whether, when referring to a child or young person and an adult being charged at the same time, the second proviso to the CYPA 1933, s. 46(2), and the CYPA 1963, s. 18, are referring to the moment when proceedings are commenced or to the time when the accused appear before the court. The latter construction would, however, appear more appropriate.

(d) Where it becomes apparent during the course of proceedings before an adult magistrates' court that an accused who had been thought to be over 18 is in fact under 18, the adult court may, if it thinks fit, complete the hearing (third proviso to the CYPA 1933, s. 46(1)). Similarly, the CYPA 1933, s. 46(1A), provides that, where a plea of guilty by post is received from a person who is in fact under 18 but the court has no reason to be aware of his or her true age, then the offender shall be deemed to be an adult.

It will be noted that in situation (a) the adult magistrates' court is obliged to try both the child or young person and the adult together unless the MCA 1980, s. 29 (see **D24.85**), comes into play, whereas in situations (b) to (d), whether to try the child or young person or remit him or her to the youth court is in the court's discretion. It should also be noted that the fact that a child or young person will ultimately have to be tried before the youth court does not prevent him or her from being brought before an adult court for purposes of a bail application and remand (CYPA 1933, s. 46(2)).

Summary Trial Procedure for Children and Young People Tried in an Adult Magistrates' Court

D24.82 The procedure in an adult magistrates' court when a person under 18 is being tried is the same as the procedure for trial of an adult. CrimPR Part 24 applies to all summary trials, whether in a youth court or an adult magistrates' court.

Where a child or young person is tried in an adult magistrates' court, the automatic reporting restrictions contained in the CYPA 1933, s. 49, do not apply. However, the court has a discretion to impose reporting restrictions under the YJCEA 1999, s. 45, to prevent identifying details of the child or young person being published (see **D24.74**).

Under the CYPA 1933, s. 34A(1), a parent or guardian must (if the accused is under 16), or may (if the accused is 16 or 17) be ordered to attend each hearing in the case unless, and to the extent that, it would be unreasonable to require such attendance (see **D24.16**).

D24.83 **Children and Young Persons Act 1933, s. 46**

(1) Subject as hereinafter provided, no charge against a child or young person, and no application whereof the hearing is by rules made under this section assigned to youth courts, shall be heard by a magistrates' court which is not a youth court: Provided that—
  (a) a charge made jointly against a child or young person and a person who has attained the age of 18 years shall be heard by a magistrates' court other than a youth court, and
  (b) where a child or young person is charged with an offence, the charge may be heard by a magistrates' court which is not a youth court if a person who has attained the age of 18 years is charged at the same time with aiding, abetting, causing, procuring, allowing or permitting that offence; and
  (c) where in the course of any proceedings before any magistrates' court other than a youth court it appears that the person to whom the proceedings relate is a child or young person, nothing in this subsection shall be construed as preventing the court, if it thinks fit so to do, from proceeding with the hearing and determination of those proceedings.

(1A) If a notification that the accused desires to plead guilty without appearing before the court is received by the designated officer for a court in pursuance of section 12 of the Magistrates' Courts Act 1980 and the court has no reason to believe that the accused is a child or young person, then, if he is a child or young person he shall be deemed to have attained the age of 18 for the purposes of subsection (1) of this section in its application to the proceedings in question.

(2) No direction, whether contained in this or any other Act, that a charge shall be brought before a youth court shall be construed as restricting the powers of any justice or justices to entertain an application for bail or for a remand, and to hear such evidence as may be necessary for that purpose.

Children and Young Persons Act 1963, s. 18 D24.84

Notwithstanding section 46(1) of [the CYPA 1933] . . . a magistrates' court which is not a youth court may hear an information against a child or young person if he is charged—

(a) with aiding, abetting, causing, procuring, allowing or permitting an offence with which a person who has attained the age of 18 is charged at the same time; or

(b) with an offence arising out of circumstances which are the same as or connected with those giving rise to an offence with which a person who has attained the age of 18 is charged at the same time.

Magistrates' Courts Act 1980, s. 29 D24.85

(1) Where—

(a) a person under the age of 18 ('the juvenile') appears or is brought before a magistrates' court other than a youth court on an information jointly charging him and one or more other persons with an offence; and

(b) that other person, or any of those other persons, has attained that age,

subsection (2) below shall have effect notwithstanding proviso (a) in section 46(1) of the Children and Young Persons Act 1933 (which would otherwise require the charge against the juvenile to be heard by a magistrates' court other than a youth court).

In the following provisions of this section 'the older accused' means such one or more of the accused as have attained the age of 18.

(2) If—

(a) the court proceeds to the summary trial of the information in the case of both or all of the accused, and the older accused or each of the older accused pleads guilty; or

(b) the court—

(i) in the case of the older accused or each of the older accused, proceeds to inquire into the information as examining justices and either commits him for trial or discharges him; and

(ii) in the case of the juvenile, proceeds to the summary trial of the information,

then, if in either situation the juvenile pleads not guilty, the court may before any evidence is called in his case remit him for trial to a youth court acting for the same place as the remitting court or for the place where he habitually resides.

(3) A person remitted to a youth court under subsection (2) above shall be brought before and tried by a youth court accordingly.

(4) Where a person is so remitted to a youth court—

(a) he shall have no right of appeal against the order of remission; and

(b) the remitting court may give such directions as appear to be necessary with respect to his custody or for his release on bail until he can be brought before the youth court.

(5) The preceding provisions of this section shall apply in relation to a corporation as if it were an individual who has attained the age of 18.

VULNERABLE DEFENDANTS: ADAPTATIONS TO NORMAL TRIAL PROCESS

Various adaptations to the trial process are applicable if the trial of a person under the age of 18 is to take place in the Crown Court or in a magistrates' court. D24.86

Ensuring Fairness of the Trial Process

In *V v UK* (2000) 30 EHRR 121, the ECtHR scrutinised the procedure adopted for the murder trial of two children in the Crown Court, and held that the right of the two accused to a fair trial under the ECHR, Article 6(1), had been violated. The ECtHR stated that it is essential that a young child charged with a serious offence attracting high levels of media interest (as was the case here) should be tried in such a way as to reduce as far as possible any feelings of D24.87

intimidation. It considered that the formality and ritual of the Crown Court must at times have seemed incomprehensible and intimidating for a child aged 11. Moreover, there was evidence that certain of the modifications to the courtroom, in particular the raised dock which was designed to enable the accused to see what was going on, had the adverse effect of increasing their sense of discomfort during the trial, since they felt exposed to the scrutiny of the press and public. Further, there was evidence that the post-traumatic stress disorder suffered by the accused, combined with the lack of any therapeutic work since the offence, had limited their ability to instruct lawyers or testify in their own defence. The ECtHR found that they were unable to follow the trial or take decisions in their own best interests. They were therefore unable to participate effectively in the criminal proceedings against them and were, in consequence, denied a fair hearing in breach of Article 6(1).

It should be emphasised that the ECtHR did not find that trial of children and young people in the Crown Court is necessarily unfair, only that appropriate adaptations to the procedure must be made to accommodate the needs of the young defendant.

CrimPD I, paras. 3G.7 to 3G.14 (see Supplement, **CPD.3G**), set out the special arrangements which should be made where a vulnerable defendant is being tried; this includes a child or young person being tried in the Crown Court or in an adult magistrates' court.

D24.88 Possible modifications include:

(a) arranging for the accused to visit, out of court hours and before the trial, the courtroom in which that hearing is to take place, to enable familiarisation;
(b) if the possibility of the accused testifying via a live link is being considered, there should be an opportunity to have a practice session;
(c) putting appropriate reporting restrictions in place;
(d) ensuring, so far as possible, that all the participants are on the same, or almost the same, level;
(e) allowing the accused to sit with family members and with another suitable supporting adult such as a social worker, and in a place which permits easy, informal communication with the legal representatives;
(f) ensuring that each step of the trial is explained in language that the accused can understand;
(g) conducting the trial according to a timetable which takes full account of the accused's ability to concentrate, including frequent and regular breaks;
(h) ensuring that the trial is conducted in simple, clear language that the accused can understand and that examination-in-chief and cross-examination are conducted using questions that are short and clear;
(i) in the Crown Court, not wearing robes and wigs;
(j) having no recognisable police presence in the courtroom save for good reason;
(k) if necessary, restricting attendance by members of the public in the courtroom to a small number (e.g., those with an immediate and direct interest in the outcome of the case) and restricting the number of reporters attending in the courtroom to such number as is judged practicable and desirable.

Additionally, in cases where there is a young or vulnerable defendant (or witness), it may be necessary to hold a 'ground rules' hearing to lay down rules for the questioning of that defendant or witness (see CrimPR 3.8 and CrimPD I, paras. 3E.1 to 3E.6: see Supplement, **R-15** and **CPD.3E**). It may also be necessary to make use of an intermediary (CrimPD I, paras. 3F.11 to 3F.18: see Supplement, **CPD.3F**).

In *TI v Bromley Youth Court* [2020] EWHC 1204 (Admin), a refusal to appoint an intermediary was quashed by the Divisional Court. Dame Victoria Sharp P noted (at 23]) that the 'essential point' is that any accused in any criminal proceedings must have a fair trial; an accused who cannot participate effectively in the proceedings, whether in whole or in part, will not have a fair trial. Moreover, a court must be 'vigilant to consider how issues of concentration and understanding' may affect such an accused's ability to participate in the trial. Also, where the accused is under 18, the court must take account of the duty, under the CYPA 1933, s. 44(1), to 'have regard to the welfare of the child or young person'. Her ladyship made the point (at [38]) that, although the youth court is accustomed to dealing with vulnerable young people with complex needs, 'that does not mean that... the youth court cannot be assisted by another professional such as an intermediary if the needs of the individual require such assistance'. Moreover, while the appointment of an intermediary will be 'rare', it does not follow from this 'that there is a high hurdle to overcome for the appointment of an intermediary if one is necessary for the effective participation of a defendant in the trial process'.

Ways of helping to ensure 'effective participation' by the accused were set out by Scott Baker LJ in *R (P) v West London Youth Court* [2005] EWHC 2583 (Admin), [2006] 1 WLR 1219 (at [26]): **D24.89**

> i) keeping the [accused's] level of cognitive functioning in mind;
> ii) using concise and simple language;
> iii) having regular breaks;
> iv) taking additional time to explain court proceedings;
> v) being proactive in ensuring the [accused] has access to support;
> vi) explaining and ensuring the [accused] understands the ingredients of the charge;
> vii) explaining the possible outcomes and sentences;
> viii) ensuring that cross-examination is carefully controlled so that questions are short and clear and frustration is minimised.

In *SC v UK* (2005) 40 EHRR 10 (226), the ECtHR said that the right of an accused to effective participation in the trial generally includes the right to hear and follow the proceedings. In the case of a child, it is essential that he or she be dealt with in a manner which takes full account of age, level of maturity and intellectual and emotional capacities, and that steps are taken to promote the child's ability to understand and participate in the proceedings, including conducting the hearing in such a way as to reduce as far as possible any feelings of intimidation and inhibition (at [28]). **D24.90**

SC v UK was considered in *R (P) v West London Youth Court* [2005] EWHC 2583 (Admin), [2006] 1 WLR 1219, where the main issue was whether the intellectual capacity of D (who was aged 15 but had a mental age of eight) was such that he could not effectively participate in the proceedings. It was held that neither youth nor limited intellectual capacity necessarily leads to a breach of Article 6. What is crucial is whether the tribunal hearing the case (in that case, a youth court) is able to adapt its procedures so that the defendant can effectively participate in the proceedings. Scott Baker LJ ruled (at [7]) that the district judge had correctly directed himself that the minimum requirements for a fair trial for D were: **D24.91**

> (i) he had to understand what he is said to have done wrong; (ii) the court had to be satisfied that the juvenile when he had done wrong by act or omission had the means of knowing that was wrong; (iii) he had to understand what, if any, defences were available to him; (iv) he had to have a reasonable opportunity to make relevant representations if he wished; (v) he had to have the opportunity to consider what representations he wished to make once he had understood the issues involved. He had therefore to be able to give proper instructions and to participate by way of providing answers to questions and suggesting questions to his lawyers in the circumstances of the trial as they arose.

In a similar vein, Openshaw J said in *R (C) v Sevenoaks Youth Court* [2009] EWHC 3088 (Admin), [2010] 1 All ER 735 (at [17]): **D24.92**

> ... when trying a young child, and most particularly a child ... with learning and behavioural difficulties, ... the Youth Court has a duty under its inherent powers and under the Criminal Procedure Rules to take such steps as are necessary to ensure that he has a fair trial, not just during the proceedings, but beforehand as he and his lawyers prepare for trial. He must be given such help as he needs to understand the case against him; he must be helped to give his own side of the story as his proof of evidence is drawn up; it may be that he needs help to speak to his lawyers, let alone to the court; he will need help to follow the case as it proceeds ... he will need particular help to decide if he is to give evidence, and if so he will need help to do so. It is in the highest degree unlikely that this level

> of help can be given by a lawyer, however kind and sympathetic she may be. He needs someone to befriend and to help him, both during the trial itself and in preparation for it. In short, he needs an intermediary. ... Moreover, the court will have to adapt its procedures to ensure that the hearing is fair ... by using simple language, by taking breaks, by taking any and all such steps as are necessary. Experienced justices sitting in youth courts are well able to ensure the fairness of the proceedings.

In *Dixon* [2013] EWCA Crim 465, [2014] 1 WLR 525, Treacy LJ emphasised (at [97]) the need for the judge to take an active role throughout the proceedings to ensure that the accused is actively participating in the proceedings.

The importance of advocates being properly trained in the handling of vulnerable witnesses and defendants was underlined by the Court of Appeal in *Grant-Murray* [2017] EWCA Crim 1228 (at [226]):

> We would like to emphasise that it is, of course, generally misconduct to take on a case where an advocate is not competent. It would be difficult to conceive of an advocate being competent to act in a case involving young witnesses or defendants unless the advocate had undertaken specific training. That consequence should help focus the minds of advocates on undertaking such training, whilst the Regulators engage on the process of making such training compulsory.

Advocates dealing with young defendants or witnesses should make sure they are familiar with the relevant 'toolkits' that are available on the Advocate's Gateway web site (www.theadvocatesgateway.org/toolkits). Of particular relevance are toolkits 1 (*Ground rules hearings and the fair treatment of vulnerable people in court*), 6 (*Planning to question a child or young person*) and 8 (*Effective participation of young defendants*).

For the range of special measures available for young defendants, see **D14.26** ***et seq.***

D24.93 **Legal Aid** A child or young person being tried in the youth court in a serious or complex case may be represented by two lawyers: a solicitor and an advocate (a barrister or a solicitor with higher rights). Legal aid for representation by two lawyers may be sought by making an application for an 'assigned advocate'. Such an application can be made only if the accused is charged with an indictable offence. The application must be made in writing to the court hearing the case (see the Criminal Legal Aid (Determinations by a Court and Choice of Representative) Regulations 2013 (SI 2013 No. 614), reg. 11). The decision as to whether to grant the certificate is made by the magistrates or district judge. The application must explain why the case is 'unusually grave or difficult' in comparison to a 'usual case' of its type (reg. 16).

FITNESS TO PLEAD

D24.94 In *CPS v P* [2007] EWHC 946 (Admin), [2008] 1 WLR 1005, the Divisional Court considered the procedure to be adopted in cases where a youth court is required to consider the question whether the accused is fit to plead. In particular, Smith LJ considered whether there should ever be a stay before evidence is heard, saying (at [51]):

> [N]otwithstanding the fact that the youth court is a creature of statute (like any other magistrates' court) it has an inherent jurisdiction to stay proceedings as an abuse of process at any stage. The jurisdiction is limited to matters directly affecting the fairness of the trial of the particular defendant concerned and does not extend to the wider supervisory jurisdiction for upholding the rule of law, which is vested in the High Court ... However ... it will be in only exceptional cases that it should be exercised, on the ground of one or more of the capacity issues, before any evidence is heard.

Her ladyship then addressed the weight to be accorded to medical evidence in such cases (at [52] and [53]):

> Medical evidence ... will rarely provide the whole answer to the question of whether the child ought to be tried for a criminal offence. This is an issue which the court has to decide, not the doctors, although of course the medical evidence may be of great importance. But, the medical evidence must almost always be set in the context of other evidence relating to the child, which may well

> bear upon the issues of his understanding, mental capacity and ability to participate effectively in a trial ... The court must be willing, in an appropriate case, to disagree with and reject the medical opinion. It is the court's opinion of the child's level of understanding which must determine whether a criminal trial proceeds.
>
> ... [I]n most cases, the medical evidence should be considered as part of the evidence in the case and not as the sole evidence on a freestanding application. Although the medical evidence might on its own appear quite strong, when other matters are considered the court might conclude that the defendant's understanding and ability to take part in the trial are greater than were suggested by the doctors and that, with proper assistance from his legal adviser and suitable adjustments to the procedure of the court, the trial can properly proceed to a conclusion.

Smith LJ also emphasised (at [54]–[57]) the need to keep the issue of capacity under review and, as part of that review process, to consider whether the case was one where the court should simply make a finding of fact whether the accused committed the *actus reus* of the offence (thus enabling a disposal under the Mental Health Act 1983 rather than convicting the accused): **D24.95**

> [T]he court has a duty to keep under continuing review the question of whether the criminal trial ought to continue. If at any stage the court concludes that the child is unable to participate effectively in the trial, it may decide to call a halt. However, the court may consider that it is in the interests of the child that the trial should continue ...
>
> If the court decides that it should call a halt to the criminal trial on the ground that the child cannot take an effective part in the proceedings, it should then consider whether to switch to a consideration of whether the child has done the acts alleged ... That process is part of the protective jurisdiction contemplated by the 1983 Act and the child's article 6 rights are not even engaged.
>
> The decision as to whether or not to switch to fact-finding is one for the discretion of the court ... I consider that proceedings should be stayed as an abuse of process before fact-finding only if no useful purpose at all could be served by finding the facts.
>
> If the court decides to find the facts and finds that the defendant did the acts alleged, it would then consider whether to seek further medical evidence with a view to making an order under the Mental Health Act 1983. If the court finds that the defendant did not do the acts alleged, the proceedings would be brought to an end by a finding of not guilty.

In *G v DPP* [2012] EWHC 3174 (Admin), Pitchford LJ emphasised (at [31]) that the discretion whether to conduct an inquiry as to whether the accused was guilty of the facts with which he or she was charged, without making a finding of guilt, depends upon the court's assessment of whether it is necessary to do so in the particular circumstances of the case.

SENTENCING POWERS AND PROCEDURE IN THE YOUTH COURT

Sentencing Powers Generally

All the sentences and other orders provided for by statute for use in respect of offenders under the age of 18 are at the disposal of the youth court following conviction of a child or young person, with the exception of long-term detention under the PCC(S)A 2000, which is available only to the Crown Court. There is detailed discussion of the sentencing options available in respect of young offenders in **Part E** of this work. In brief, the principal sentences are as follows: **D24.96**

(a) detention and training orders (see **E7.15** for details);
(b) fines (see **E15**) — in the case of young offenders, fines are limited by virtue of the MCA 1980, s. 24(3) and (4), to a maximum of £1,000 in the case of offenders who are aged 14 to 17, and a maximum of £250 where the offender is aged 10 to 13 (or the maximum specified for the offence, if less);
(c) youth rehabilitation orders under the CJIA 2008, s. 1 (see **E9.2**);
(d) referral orders and reparation orders (see **E10** and **E11** for details); and
(e) absolute and conditional discharges (see **E12** for details).

The youth court can also make ancillary orders, such as a compensation order. By virtue of the PCC(S)A 2000, s. 131(1), the maximum amount of compensation that can be ordered in respect of an offence where the offender is under the age of 18 is £5,000. Where such an offender is convicted of several offences, there is no restriction on the aggregate sum of compensation (i.e. the offender may be ordered to pay up to £5,000 for each offence). Where a young offender asks for offences to be taken into consideration, compensation may be ordered in respect of those offences but the total amount ordered must not exceed the maximum which could be ordered for the offence(s) of which he or she has actually been convicted (s. 131(2)).

The youth court is also empowered to make certain orders against the parents of a young offender, namely binding the parents over or making a parenting order (see E14 for details).

Procedure before Sentence in the Youth Court

D24.97 Under CrimPR 24.11(7), before the court passes sentence on a young offender, it must give the parent, guardian or other supporting adult, if present, an opportunity to make representations and introduce evidence relevant to sentence (as well as giving the offender an opportunity to do so).

CrimPD I, para. 3N.14 (see Supplement, **CPD.3N**), notes that it will rarely be appropriate for a young offender to be sentenced via a live link where this would otherwise be permissible (unless, for example, the offender is already serving a custodial sentence, or is detained in a secure establishment a long way from the court).

D24.98 **Preparation of Reports** The responsibility for preparing reports on young offenders rests primarily on the local authority in whose area the offender resides (CYPA 1969, s. 9), although in the cases of offenders who have attained the age of 13, the task may be undertaken by probation officers (see s. 34(3) of the 1969 Act and SI 1970 No. 1882).

Children and Young Persons Act 1969, ss. 9 and 34

9.—(1) Where a local authority bring proceedings for an offence alleged to have been committed by a young person or are notified that any such proceedings are being brought, it shall be the duty of the authority, unless they are of opinion that it is unnecessary to do so, to make such investigations and provide the court before which the proceedings are heard with such information relating to the home surroundings, school record, health and character of the person in respect of whom the proceedings are brought as appear to the authority likely to assist the court.

(2) If the court mentioned in subsection (1) of this section requests the authority aforesaid to make investigations and provide information or to make further investigations and provide further information relating to the matters aforesaid, it shall be the duty of the authority to comply with the request.

34. …

(3) In the case of a person who has attained such age as the Secretary of State may by order specify, an authority shall, without prejudice to subsection (2) of section 9 of this Act, not be required by virtue of subsection (1) of that section to make investigations or provide information which it does not already possess with respect to his home surroundings if, by direction of the justices or local probation board acting for any relevant area, arrangements are in force for information with respect to his home surroundings to be furnished to the court in question by an officer of a local probation board.

Sending to Another Youth Court

D24.99 Instead of itself sentencing an offender who pleads or is found guilty before it, a youth court may remit the offender to the youth court for the area where he or she habitually resides, and that court may then deal with the offender as if it had just convicted him or her (PCC(S)A 2000, s. 8(2) and (3)). The receiving court has all the powers that it would have had if it had dealt with the matter in the first place. It can, for example, accept a change of plea during the course of proceedings (*Stratford Youth v Court, ex parte Conde* [1997] 1 WLR 113).

Sentencing Powers where Accused Attains the Age of 18 after Finding of Guilt

Children and Young Persons Act 1963, s. 29 D24.100

Where proceedings in respect of a young person are begun for an offence and he attains the age of 18 before the conclusion of the proceedings, the court may deal with the case and make any order which it could have made if he had not attained that age.

Where an offender pleads or is found guilty when still under 18 but attains the age of 18 during an adjournment before sentence, the court may deal with the offender as if he or she remained under that age. In *Aldis v DPP* [2002] EWHC 403 (Admin), [2002] 2 Cr App R (S) 88 (400), D attained the age of 18 before sentence. It was held that the justices were entitled, pursuant to s. 29, to impose a detention and training order even though D had attained the age of 18 prior to the sentencing hearing, provided he was under 18 at the date when the court decided whether they were obliged to try the case summarily. This decision should be seen in light of the fact that the relevant age for determining the type of sentence is the date of conviction, not the date when sentence is passed (*Danga* [1992] QB 476; *Robson* [2006] EWCA Crim 1414, [2007] 1 All ER 506), and so the effect of the CYPA 1963, s. 29, is not quite as anomalous as it may at first seem.

Remission to an Adult Magistrates' Court The PCC(S)A 2000, s. 9(1), gives the youth court a discretionary power to remit a child or young person to an adult magistrates' court once he or she reaches the age of 18. The adult magistrates' court may then 'deal with the case in any way in which it would have power to deal with it if all proceedings relating to the offence which took place before the youth court had taken place before [the adult court]' (s. 9(2)(b)). There is no right of appeal against the order of remission (s. 9(4)). D24.101

In *R (Denny) v Acton Youth Court* [2004] EWHC 948 (Admin), [2004] 1 WLR 3051, a 17-year-old was charged with attempted robbery. He entered a plea of not guilty at the youth court. By the time the matter came on for trial and he was found guilty, he was 18. The justices in the youth court adjourned sentence and remitted him to the adult magistrates' court pursuant to s. 9. The Divisional Court held that the order remitting the case to the adult court was unlawful: youth courts should never remit an offender to a magistrates' court for sentence in relation to an offence which, in the case of an adult, is triable only on indictment (per Maurice Kay LJ at [9]). It was also held (at [14]) that, provided the adult court has not reached the stage of considering sentence, it is possible for the youth court to rescind a remittal to an adult magistrates' court under the MCA 1980, s. 142(1), since a remittal under s. 9 is an 'order made when dealing with an offender'.

Powers of Criminal Courts (Sentencing) Act 2000, s. 9

(1) Where a person who appears or is brought before a youth court charged with an offence subsequently attains the age of 18, the youth court may, at any time after conviction and before sentence, remit him for sentence to a magistrates' court (other than a youth court).

Determining Sentences Available where Offender Attains Age of 18 The type of sentence is generally fixed by the offender's age at the date of conviction (*Danga* [1992] QB 476). This was confirmed in *Robson* [2006] EWCA Crim 1414, [2007] 1 All ER 506, where D was aged 17 when he was convicted of sexual assault. The youth court committed him to the Crown Court for sentence under the PCC(S)A 2000, s. 3C. When he appeared for sentencing, he had attained the age of 18. The Court of Appeal held that, as a matter of statutory construction, the age of the offender for the purpose of determining which of the statutory 'dangerous offender' regimes under the CJA 2003 (see **E4**) applies, is the offender's age at the date of conviction. The Court reached this conclusion on the basis that the relevant provisions refer to cases where 'a person aged 18 or over is *convicted*' and where 'a person aged under 18 is *convicted*'. The use of the word 'convicted', rather than 'sentenced', was held to be determinative of the question of which date is relevant. Where appropriate, however, the court should have regard to the offender's age at the date when the offence was committed when considering the severity of the penalty to impose. D24.102

Where an offender crosses a relevant age threshold between the date of commission of the offence and the date of conviction, the starting point is the sentence that would have been appropriate if the offender had been sentenced at the date of the commission of the offence (*Ghafoor* [2002] EWCA Crim 1857, [2003] 1 Cr App R (S) 84 (428), per Dyson LJ at [31]). In *Bowker* [2007] EWCA Crim 1608, [2008] 1 Cr App R (S) 72 (412), the Court of Appeal emphasised that the principle that the offender's culpability should be judged by reference to age at the time of the offence is only a starting point: the sentence that would have been imposed at the time of the commission of the offence is a 'powerful' factor, but is not the sole or determining factor. In *Amin* [2019] EWCA Crim 1583, [2020] 1 Cr App R (S) 36 (263) the Court of Appeal noted (at [13]) the importance of taking into account the definitive guideline, *Sentencing Children and Young People* (see Supplement, **SG8-1**), section 6 of which gives guidance on sentencing where a significant age threshold has been crossed between the commission of an offence and sentence. Section 6.2 states that, in such situations, the court should 'take as its starting point the sentence likely to have been imposed on the date at which the offence was committed'. Moreover, when this occurs, the court has to take into account the purpose of sentencing *adult* offenders set out in the CJA 2003, s. 142 (see **E1.1**). Section 6.3 goes on to say that, 'where any significant age threshold is passed, it will rarely be appropriate that a more severe sentence than the maximum that the court could have imposed at the time the offence was committed should be imposed. However, a sentence at or close to the maximum may be appropriate.'

SENTENCING PROCEDURE AND POWERS IN THE CROWN COURT

Sentencing Powers Generally

D24.103 The Crown Court has the same powers as the youth court when sentencing a young offender (see **D24.96**) save that a referral order is not available in the Crown Court, and that the Crown Court may impose a sentence of detention under the PCC(S)A 2000, s. 91.

Remission to the Youth Court

D24.104 Save in cases of homicide, where a child or young person has been convicted on indictment, the Crown Court 'shall unless satisfied that it would be undesirable to do so', remit the case to a youth court acting for the place where the offender was sent for trial' (PCC(S)A 2000, s. 8(2); see **D24.107**)). The youth court may then deal with the offender as if he or she had been tried and found guilty by the youth court (s. 8(3)). There is no appeal against an order under s. 8(2), although the sentence eventually passed by the youth court may be appealed to the Crown Court (or the Divisional Court, if wrong in law) in the usual way (s. 8(5)). The Crown Court may remit the offender to the youth court in custody or on bail (s. 8(4)(a)).

The obligation imposed on the Crown Court by s. 8(2) to remit a child or young person convicted before it to the youth court for sentence 'unless satisfied that it would be undesirable to do so' might seem to be a major fetter on the power of the Crown Court to deal with young offenders. However, s. 8(2) has been interpreted so as to give the Crown Court an almost unfettered discretion to retain the sentencing function for itself if it so wishes. Guidance on the application of s. 8 was given by Lord Lane CJ in *Lewis* (1984) 79 Cr App R 94 at p. 99. His lordship indicated that reasons for *not* remitting include:

(a) that, in a case where the young offender pleaded not guilty and was convicted, the Crown Court judge who presided at the trial will be better informed about the facts of the offence and general nature of the case than the youth court could hope to be;
(b) that, in a case where an adult and a person under 18 have been jointly tried on indictment and both convicted, sentencing the child or young person in the Crown Court will avoid

the risk of unacceptable disparity in sentencing that would arise if the child or young person were to be remitted to the youth court;
(c) that remitting would cause delay, unnecessary duplication of proceedings and extra expense.

Lord Lane did suggest (ibid.) that it may become desirable to remit the case where a report must be obtained and the Crown Court judge will be unable to sit when the report becomes available, but added that this situation should be avoided wherever possible. It is submitted that, in virtually any case, the Crown Court will be able to justify a decision not to remit on the basis of one or more of the reasons put forward by Lord Lane.

The Sentencing Council's definitive guideline, *Sentencing Children and Young People* (see Supplement, **SG8-1**), notes that when considering whether remittal to the youth court for sentence is 'undesirable', the court should balance the need for expertise in the sentencing of young offenders with the benefits of sentence being imposed by the court which has determined guilt (para. 2.15). Paragraph 2.16 states that 'particular attention' should be given to cases where the child or young person is being tried in the Crown Court only because he or she was charged with an adult offender (the implication being that the Crown Court should be more ready to remit the child or young person to the youth court in such a case). The guideline also makes the point that a referral order (see **E10**) is not available in the Crown Court (since the PCC(S)A 2000, s. 16, applies only where a youth court or other magistrates' court is dealing with a person aged under 18 for an offence). **D24.105**

Cases where the Powers of Criminal Courts (Sentencing) Act 2000, s. 91, Applies

Where the PCC(S)A 2000, s. 91, applies, the Crown Court is not obliged to pass a sentence of detention under s. 91. The Crown Court retains the power to deal with the offender in any way that the youth court could have done. It will generally be undesirable for the Crown Court to remit the case to the youth court for sentence under the PCC(S)A 2000, s. 8(2), since the youth court will already have expressed the view that the case is too serious for its powers (*Allen* (1999) 163 JP 841). **D24.106**

Powers of Criminal Courts (Sentencing) Act 2000, s. 8 **D24.107**

(1) Subsection (2) below applies where a child or young person (that is to say, any person aged under 18) is convicted by or before any court of an offence other than homicide.
(2) The court may and, if it is not a youth court, shall unless satisfied that it would be undesirable to do so, remit the case—
 (a) if the offender was sent to the Crown Court for trial under section 51 or 51A of the Crime and Disorder Act 1998, to a youth court acting for the place where he was committed for trial or sent to the Crown Court for trial;
 (b) in any other case, to a youth court acting either for the same place as the remitting court or for the place where the offender habitually resides;
 but in relation to a magistrates' court other than a youth court this subsection has effect subject to subsection (6) below.
(3) Where a case is remitted under subsection (2) above, the offender shall be brought before a youth court accordingly, and that court may deal with him in any way in which it might have dealt with him if he had been tried and convicted by that court.
(4) A court by which an order remitting a case to a youth court is made under subsection (2) above—
 (a) may, subject to section 25 of the Criminal Justice and Public Order Act 1994 (restrictions on granting bail), give such directions as appear to be necessary with respect to the custody of the offender or for his release on bail until he can be brought before the youth court; and
 (b) shall cause to be transmitted to the designated officer for the youth court a certificate setting out the nature of the offence and stating—
  (i) that the offender has been convicted of the offence; and
  (ii) that the case has been remitted for the purpose of being dealt with under the preceding provisions of this section.
(5) Where a case is remitted under subsection (2) above, the offender shall have no right of appeal against the order of remission, but shall have the same right of appeal against any order of the court to which the case is remitted as if he had been convicted by that court.

SENTENCING PROCEDURE AND POWERS IN THE ADULT MAGISTRATES' COURT

D24.108 The powers of the adult magistrates' court to deal with an offender under the age of 18 are restricted by the PCC(S)A 2000, s. 8(6) to (8) (see **D24.109**). Under s. 8(6), the magistrates must remit the offender to the youth court to be sentenced unless the case is one where the court is required by the PCC(S)A 2000, s. 16(2), to refer the offender to a youth offender panel (in which event the court may, but need not, remit the case to the youth court) or where the magistrates' court's very limited sentencing powers are appropriate. Those powers are set out at D24.50.

Where the offender is remitted to the youth court, the remittal must be either to the youth court acting for the same place as the remitting court or to the court for the place where the offender habitually resides (see s. 8(2)). The remitting court may grant the offender bail (s. 8(4)(a)).

D24.109 **Powers of Criminal Courts (Sentencing) Act 2000, s. 8**

(6) Without prejudice to the power to remit any case to a youth court which is conferred on a magistrates' court other than a youth court by subsections (1) and (2) above, where such a magistrates' court convicts a child or young person of an offence it must exercise that power unless the case falls within subsection (7) or (8) below.

(7) The case falls within this subsection if the court would, were it not so to remit the case, be required by section 16(2) below to refer the offender to a youth offender panel (in which event the court may, but need not, so remit the case).

(8) The case falls within this subsection if it does not fall within subsection (7) above but the court is of the opinion that the case is one which can properly be dealt with by means of—
(a) an order discharging the offender absolutely or conditionally, or
(b) an order for the payment of a fine, or
(c) an order (under section 150 below) requiring the offender's parent or guardian to enter into a recognisance to take proper care of him and exercise proper control over him,

with or without any order that the court has powers to make when absolutely or conditionally discharging an offender.

Section D25 Behaviour Orders: Civil Injunctions, CBOs, CPNs, PSPOs, Closure Notices, Closure Orders, SCPOs, VOOs, STROs, KCPOs and SPOs

ANTI-SOCIAL BEHAVIOUR, CRIME AND POLICING ACT 2014

The ABCPA 2014 received Royal Assent on 13 March 2014. The civil injunction in Part 1 replaced the stand-alone ASBO, and the criminal behaviour order (CBO) in Part 2 replaced the 'post-conviction' ASBO (CRASBO). Chapter 1 of Part 4 created the community protection notice (CPN). Chapter 2 of Part 4 created the public spaces protection order (PSPO). Chapter 3 of Part 4, entitled 'Closure of premises associated with nuisance or disorder etc.', replaced closure orders under Parts 1 and 1A of the ASBA 2003 with a regime for issuing closure notices and for making closure orders. These changes were substantial and not merely cosmetic. They came about as a result of governmental dissatisfaction with the suite of powers available in the CDA 1998 and the ASBA 2003 to tackle anti-social behaviour. **D25.1**

The Explanatory Notes state that of the 14 parts to the Bill, Part 1 'makes provision for a civil injunction to prevent nuisance and annoyance', Part 2 'makes provision for an order on conviction to prevent behaviour which causes harassment, alarm or distress' and Part 4 'covers the new powers to deal with community protection and makes provision for a CPN, a public spaces protection order and provisions to close premises associated with nuisance and annoyance'. On 24 December 2017, the Home Office published updated *Statutory guidance for frontline professionals* ('the Statutory Guidance') on the approach that should be taken to applications for the aforementioned orders. This Statutory Guidance replaced and updated the original guidance that was issued in July 2014 shortly before the ABCPA 2014 came into force. **D25.2**

CIVIL INJUNCTIONS

The provisions of Part 1 of the ABCPA 2014 (ss. 1 to 21) introduced the civil injunction and came into force on 23 March 2015. Section 1(1) of the CDA 1998 ('stand-alone ASBOs') was repealed from that date save where a stand-alone ASBO was applied for before that date, made before that date or anything has been done in connection with such an application or order before that date, in which case, by virtue of s. 21(2) of the ABCPA 2014, the provisions of the CDA 1998 will continue to apply to such an application or order. However, as of 23 March 2015, no application can be made under the CDA 1998 to vary the terms of an existing stand-alone ASBO by extending the period of the order or by extending any of its provisions (s. 21(4)). If any stand-alone ABSOs are still in force by 23 March 2020, s. 21(5)(a) provides that those orders will be treated as if they were civil injunctions and so any application to vary or discharge them will need to be made under Part 1 of the ABCPA 2014 and not under s. 1 of the CDA 1998. For the relevant provisions of the CDA 1998, see D25.21 of the 2015 edition of this work. Reporting restrictions under s. 49 of the CYPA 1933 do not apply to applications under Part 1 of the ABCPA 2014 (s. 17). **D25.3**

Power to Make Civil Injunctions

D25.4 An application for a civil injunction must be made to a youth court where the respondent is under 18 years of age (s. 1(8)(a)) or to the High Court or the county court in any other case (s. 1(8)(b)). A person's age is treated for the purposes of Part 1 as being that which it appears to the court to be after considering any available evidence (s. 20(2)). Applications to the youth court are governed by the Magistrates' Courts (Injunctions: Anti-Social Behaviour) Rules 2015 (SI 2015 No. 423). By contrast, applications to the High Court and the county court are governed by Part 65, ch. VIII, of the Civil Procedure Rules. Applications to the High Court or to the county court fall outside the scope of this work. An application for a civil injunction does not involve the determination of a criminal charge and so Article 6(2) and (3) of the ECHR are not engaged (*Jones v Birmingham City Council* [2018] EWCA Civ 1189, [2018] 2 Cr App R 23 (353)).

Rule 15 of the 2015 Rules and s. 18(2) and (3) of the ABCPA 2014 provide that a youth court may, on application, give permission for an application for a civil injunction against a person aged 18 or over to be made to the youth court if an application to the youth court has been made, or is to be made, for an injunction against a person aged under 18 *and* the youth court thinks it would be in the interests of justice for the applications to be heard together. Rule 16 provides that, where a respondent attains the age of 18 after the commencement of the proceedings under Part 1, the proceedings must remain in the youth court, subject to the exercise of the court's discretion under r. 16(3) to transfer the application to the High Court or to the county court, having regard in particular to (a) the stage which the proceedings have reached, (b) the circumstances of the applicant and the respondent, and (c) the need to ensure fairness between the applicant and the respondent. The application for a civil injunction can only be made against an identified individual or individuals (*Wolverhampton City Council v Persons Unknown* [2018] EWHC 3777 (QB) at [2]).

Application Procedure

D25.5 An application for a civil injunction can be made only by a local authority, a housing provider, the chief officer of police for a police area, the chief constable of the British Transport Police Force, Transport for London, Transport for Greater Manchester, the Environment Agency, the Natural Resources Body for Wales, the Secretary of State (in certain defined circumstances) and the Welsh Ministers (also in certain defined circumstances) (s. 5(1)).

The 2015 Rules state that an application to the youth court must (i) be made by way of complaint in writing (r. 2), (ii) be supported by evidence of the matters of which the court must be satisfied under s. 1 of the ABCPA 2014, and (iii) state the terms of the injunction applied for (r. 3).

An application for a civil injunction may be made without notice being given to the respondent (s. 6(1)). Rule 3(2) of the 2015 Rules provides that any without-notice application must state the reason why it is necessary for the application to be made without notice. If an application is made without notice, the court must either (a) adjourn the proceedings and grant an interim civil injunction under s. 7, (b) adjourn the proceedings without granting an interim civil injunction, or (c) dismiss the application (s. 6(2)). An interim civil injunction can last until the final hearing of the application or until further order if the court thinks it just to grant it on that basis (s. 7(2)). Further, an interim civil injunction may contain any prohibitions or requirements that can be included in a civil injunction (see **D25.10**), including a power of arrest (see **D25.11**), save that, where the respondent was not given notice of the hearing at which the court proposes to make an interim civil injunction, the court cannot impose a term in the interim order that would have the effect of requiring the respondent to participate in particular activities (s. 7(3)). For cases where an interim civil injunction was granted in the High Court, see *Chief Constable of Bedfordshire Police v Golding* [2015] EWHC 1875 (QB) and *Birmingham City Council v Afsar (No.3)* [2019] EWHC 1560 (QB).

Prior Consultation

A person applying for a civil injunction under s. 1 must, before doing so, (a) consult the local youth offending team about the application, if the respondent will be aged under 18 when the application is made, and (b) inform any other body or individual the applicant thinks appropriate of the application, save that neither (a) nor (b) apply to a without-notice application (s. 14(1)). Where the court adjourns a without-notice application under s. 6, before the date of the first on-notice hearing, the applicant must (a) consult the local youth offending team about the application, if the respondent will be aged under 18 on that date, and (b) inform any other body or individual the applicant thinks appropriate of the application (s. 14(2)). The duty to consult also applies when an application is made to vary or discharge a civil injunction (see **D25.13**). **D25.6**

Under s. 1 of the CDA 1998, on an application for a stand-alone ASBO, a failure by the applicant to consult the person against whom it is seeking the order during the decision-making process was held not to be a breach of that person's rights under the ECHR, Article 6 or 8, since that person could resist the application in court (*Wareham v Purbeck District Council* [2005] EWHC 358 (Admin)). This is likely to be the position under Part 1 of the ABCPA 2014 as well.

Statutory Test

The court may grant a civil injunction against a respondent (who must be aged ten or over) if two conditions are met (ABCPA 2014, s. 1(1)). The first condition is that the court is satisfied, on the balance of probabilities, that the respondent has engaged or threatens to engage in anti-social behaviour (s. 1(2)). The second condition is that the court considers it just and convenient to grant the injunction for the purpose of preventing the respondent from engaging in anti-social behaviour (s. 1(3)). **D25.7**

At the final hearing to decide whether these conditions are met, special measures under Part II, ch. I, of the YJCEA 1999 (see **D14.3**) will apply with the amendments set out in s. 16 of the ABCPA 2014. Where an application is made to the youth court, the court will be sitting in its civil capacity. Hearsay is admissible and the Civil Evidence Act 1995 and the Magistrates' Courts (Hearsay Evidence in Civil Proceedings) Rules 1999 (SI 1999 No. 681) must be complied with. As to the weight to be attached to hearsay evidence, see *Moat Housing Group-South Ltd v Harris* [2005] EWCA Civ 287, [2006] QB 606.

It is important to note that in deciding whether to make a civil injunction under s. 1, the court may take account of conduct occurring up to six months before 23 March 2015 (s. 21(7)). This seems to mean that any anti-social behaviour on the part of the respondent that occurred before 23 September 2014 cannot be taken into account by the court in deciding whether the condition in s. 1(2) is satisfied, but see **D25.17**. Conduct occurring after the application is made but not determined will be admissible (*Birmingham City Council v Dixon* [2009] EWHC 761 (Admin), [2010] 1 WLR 32).

Meaning of 'Anti-social Behaviour'

The meaning of 'anti-social behaviour' is set out in s. 2(1). It means (a) conduct that has caused, or is likely to cause, harassment, alarm or distress to any person, (b) conduct capable of causing nuisance or annoyance to a person in relation to that person's occupation of residential premises (but only where the applicant is a housing provider, a local authority, or the chief officer of police), or (c) conduct capable of causing housing-related nuisance or annoyance to any person. **D25.8**

In s. 1(1)(a) of the CDA 1998, 'anti-social behaviour' meant behaving 'in a manner that caused or was likely to cause harassment, alarm or distress to one or more persons not of the same household as himself'. That definition is broadly the same as the definition under s. 2(1)(a) of the ABCPA 2014 and so the authorities relating to it will continue to be relevant.

In *R (Mills) v Birmingham Magistrates' Court* [2005] EWHC 2732 (Admin), an ASBO imposed upon an habitual shoplifter from chain stores was quashed as her conduct did not cause harassment, alarm or distress, nor was it likely to. In *Perry v Humberside Police* [2012] EWHC 3226 (Admin) a former journalist had started an online blog about his local community. He claimed that various figures in his village had been guilty of corruption and perverting the course of justice. The police applied for a stand-alone ASBO against him and the magistrates' court imposed a ten-year order. The Divisional Court quashed the ASBO. The Court held that the fact that a blog may contain material that is untrue or even defamatory could justify the civil courts in granting an injunction but, in deciding whether the statutory criteria for the purposes of imposing an ASBO were made out, the district judge put far too much weight upon the fact that the allegations made in the blog were uncorroborated. The Court found that:

> ... the District Judge far too readily accepted the assertion made by each of the complainants that they had suffered harassment, alarm or distress. More is required than repeating this mantra in each witness statement ... the entries on the blog and the physical contacts such as there were between the appellant and those whom he targeted were offensive and tiresome, it is even possible that they could properly be described as amounting to anti-social behaviour but I do not think that the high threshold set by the statutory criteria was met at all.

In *R (Gosport Borough Council) v Fareham Magistrates' Court* [2006] EWHC 3047 (Admin), [2007] 1 WLR 634, the Divisional Court held that, in order to show that behaviour 'caused' harassment, alarm or distress within the meaning of s. 1(1)(a) of the CDA 1998, it would probably be necessary for a court to hear evidence from one of the harassed, alarmed or distressed victims. In contrast, the alternative formulation in s. 1(1)(a), 'or was likely to cause', enables police witnesses to demonstrate that there were potential victims present, who were likely to have been caused harassment, alarm or distress (per Bean J at [20]). On this approach, the behaviour of the respondent must take place in such a way that it was likely to be witnessed and likely to cause harassment, alarm or distress. The Court of Appeal in *Hashi* [2014] EWCA Crim 2119, [2015] 1 Cr App R (S) 17 (135) (a CRASBO case), endorsed the view of Bean J in *Gosport* and added (at [9]–[10]):

> ... the words 'was likely to cause' do not require the prosecution to prove that the offending behaviour was actually witnessed. As Bean J observed in *Gosport*, it would be sufficient to justify the imposition of an ASBO if there were people in the vicinity of someone whose behaviour otherwise crossed the statutory threshold. To hold otherwise would be to require the prosecution to prove that those nearby did not happen to be, by chance, looking in the opposite direction at the material time.
>
> On this approach, behaviour under the Act must take place in circumstances where it was: (i) likely to be witnessed; and (ii) likely, if witnessed, to cause harassment, alarm or distress.

'Likely' in this context means more probable than not (*Chief Constable of Lancashire v Potter* [2003] EWHC 2272 (Admin)).

There is nothing in the plain language of the statute to suggest that Parliament intended to exclude 'protest' from the definition of 'anti-social behaviour' in order to protect a person's legitimate right to protest. As Warby J explained in *Birmingham City Council v Afsar (No.3)* [2019] EWHC 1560 (QB) at [32]:

> ...there is no reason to doubt that in passing the legislation Parliament intended to confer power to seek and to grant injunctions to prohibit anti-social utterances and assemblies of all kinds, in any case where it is shown that this is necessary and proportionate in pursuit of one of the legitimate aims identified in Articles 10(2) and 11(2) [of the ECHR].

Just and Convenient to Grant an Injunction

D25.9 Part 1 of the ABCPA 2014 offers no guidance on what the words 'just and convenient' mean in s. 1(3). The equivalent test in s. 1(1)(b) of the CDA 1998 in respect of stand-alone ASBOs was one of necessity ('such an order is necessary to protect relevant persons from further anti-social acts by him'). It is clear from the Statutory Guidance that the decision to lower the threshold was a deliberate one and so it is very unlikely that the courts will interpret 'just' in such a way as to re-introduce a 'necessary' requirement. Instead, the courts may well equate the 'just and convenient' test with the 'helpfulness' test in s. 22(4) in relation to CBOs (see **D25.23**), which is itself taken from s. 14A(2) of the Football Spectators Act 1989 (football banning orders: see **E21.3**). Where an interim injunction is made under the ABCPA 2014, s. 7, before the hearing at which the court will determine whether to grant a final injunction, and the conduct complained of ceases following the making of the interim injunction, it does not follow that it would be unjust to make a final injunction because in all likelihood the conduct only stopped because of the interim injunction and not for reasons unrelated to it (*Reigate and Banstead Borough Council v Walsh* [2017] EWHC 2221 (QB)).

Where a person's rights under the ECHR, Articles 10 and 11, are engaged the court will have to be satisfied that the granting of an injunction in the terms sought is necessary and proportionate in pursuit of one of the legitimate aims identified in those Articles (*Birmingham City Council v Afsar (No.3)* [2019] EWHC 1560 (QB)). The availability of an alternative remedy, such as a PSPO, does not mean the court should decline to grant a civil injunction (*Birmingham City Council v Sharif* [2019] EWHC 1268 (QB) at [27] and *Birmingham City Council v Afsar (No.3)* at [34]).

Terms of a Civil Injunction

A civil injunction may, for the purpose of preventing the respondent from engaging in anti-social behaviour, prohibit the respondent from doing anything described in the injunction *and* require the respondent to do anything described in the injunction (s. 1(4)). The prohibitions and requirements that comprise the civil injunction must, so far as is practicable, be such as to avoid (a) any interference with the times, if any, at which the respondent normally works or attends school or other educational establishment, and (b) any conflict with the requirements of any other court order or injunction to which the respondent may be subject (s. 1(5)). **D25.10**

The civil injunction must either specify the period for which it has effect or state that it has effect until further order (s. 1(6)). Where the civil injunction is granted before the respondent turns 18, the period of the civil injunction must be specified and it must be no more than 12 months (s. 1(6)). Particular prohibitions or requirements can be effective for different periods, and the civil injunction may specify what those periods are (s. 1(7)).

Where a civil injunction includes a requirement, the injunction must specify the person (whether an individual or an organisation) that is to be responsible for supervising compliance with the requirement (s. 3(1)). Before the court can include a requirement in the terms of the civil injunction, it must receive evidence about the suitability and enforceability of the requirement from the supervisor or from a person representing the supervisor, where the supervisor is an organisation (s. 3(2)). Before including two or more requirements in a civil injunction, the court must consider their compatibility with each other (s. 3(3)). In relation to a requirement, the supervisor has a duty (a) to make any necessary arrangements in connection with the requirements for which the person has responsibility, (b) to promote the respondent's compliance with the relevant requirements, and (c) if the supervisor considers that the respondent has complied with all relevant requirements or has failed to comply with a relevant requirement, to inform the person who applied for the injunction and the appropriate chief officer of police (s. 3(4)). A respondent subject to a requirement in a civil injunction must keep in touch with the supervisor in relation to the requirement, in accordance with any instructions given by the supervisor from time to time, and notify the supervisor of any change of address. These obligations on the respondent have effect as requirements of the injunction (s. 3(6)).

A civil injunction may have the effect of excluding the respondent from the place where the respondent normally lives but only if aged 18 or over and the other conditions in s. 13 are met.

Power of Arrest

D25.11 A court may attach a power of arrest to a prohibition or requirement if the court thinks that either (a) the anti-social behaviour in which the respondent has engaged or threatens to engage consists of or includes the use or threatened use of violence against other persons, or (b) there is a significant risk of harm to other persons from the respondent; but the power to attach a power of arrest does not arise where the requirement has the effect of requiring the respondent to participate in particular activities (s. 4(1)). 'Harm' includes serious ill-treatment or abuse, whether physical or not (s. 20(1)). If the court attaches a power of arrest to a prohibition or a requirement in a civil injunction, the injunction may specify a period for which the power is to have effect which is shorter than that of the prohibition or requirement to which it relates (s. 4(2)).

Where a power of arrest attaches to a term of a civil injunction, a constable may arrest the respondent without warrant if the constable has reasonable cause to suspect that the respondent is in breach of the term (s. 9(1)). A constable who arrests a person under s. 9(1) must inform the person who applied for the civil injunction (s. 9(2)). A person who is arrested under s. 9(1) must, within the period of 24 hours beginning with the time of the arrest, be brought before (a) a judge of the High Court or a judge of the county court if the injunction was granted by the High Court, (b) a judge of the county court if the injunction was granted by the county court or the injunction was granted by a youth court but the respondent is aged 18 or over, or (c) a justice of the peace if neither (a) nor (b) applies (s. 9(3)). The judge before whom a person is brought may remand the person if the matter is not disposed of straight away (s. 9(5)). Where the respondent is brought before a justice of the peace, the justice must remand the respondent to appear before the youth court that granted the injunction (s. 9(6)). Schedule 1 has effect in relation to s. 9 (s. 11).

Issue of Arrest Warrant

D25.12 If a person who applied for a civil injunction thinks that the respondent is in breach of any of its provisions, the person may apply for the issue of a warrant for the respondent's arrest (s. 10(1)). The application must be made to (a) a judge of the High Court if the injunction was granted by the High Court, (b) a judge of the county court if the injunction was granted by the county court or the injunction was granted by a youth court but the respondent is aged 18 or over, or (c) a justice of the peace if neither (a) nor (b) applies (s. 10(2)). A judge or justice may issue a warrant only if the judge or justice has reasonable grounds for believing that the respondent is in breach of a provision of the injunction (s. 10(3)). A warrant issued by a particular court must require the respondent to be brought before that court, except where the warrant is issued by a justice of the peace but the respondent is aged 18 or over when brought before the court, in which case the respondent must be brought before the county court (s. 10(4) to (6)). A constable who arrests a person under a warrant issued under s. 10 must inform the person who applied for the injunction (s. 10(7)). If the respondent is brought before a court but the matter is not disposed of straight away, the court may remand the respondent (s. 10(8)). Schedule 1 has effect in relation to s. 10 (s. 11).

Variation or Discharge

D25.13 The court may vary or discharge a civil injunction on the application of the person who applied for the injunction or the respondent (s. 8(1)). Rule 6 of the 2015 Rules sets out the procedure for making an application to vary or discharge a civil injunction. In this context, 'the court' means the court that granted the civil injunction except where that court was the youth court and the respondent is aged 18 or over, in which case 'the court' means the county court (s. 8(2)). The power to vary a civil injunction includes a power (a) to include an additional prohibition or requirement in the civil injunction, or to extend the period for which an existing prohibition or requirement has effect, or (b) to attach a power of arrest, or to extend the period for which a power of arrest has effect (s. 8(3)). If the court dismisses an application to vary or discharge a civil injunction, the party that made the application may make no further application without either the consent of the court or the agreement of the other party (s. 8(4)). There does not appear to be a power in s. 8 to extend the period of the civil injunction itself. It follows that if the injunction is made for five years and one of the requirements in the injunction is made for three years, an application can be made to extend the period of the requirement to five years but an application cannot be made to extend the period of the injunction or to extend the period of the requirement beyond five years.

Appeal

Where the youth court makes a decision under Part 1 of the ABCPA 2014 (which can include a decision whether to make or not to make a civil injunction, whether to vary or not to vary a civil injunction, whether to discharge or not to discharge a civil injunction etc.) an appeal lies to the Crown Court (s. 15(1)). In a similar vein to appeals against stand-alone ASBOs, an appeal against a decision of the youth court under Part 1 will be by way of a full rehearing. **D25.14**

Appellate proceedings in the Crown Court will be civil in character too and so the Crown Court Rules 1982 (SI 1982 No. 1109) will apply. Pursuant to r. 7, an appeal shall be commenced by the giving of notice not later than 21 days after the day on which the decision to be appealed against was made. There is no requirement in r. 7 for the grounds of appeal to be identified in the notice, as there was when any appeal was made against the making of a stand-alone ASBO. There is power under r. 7(5) for the Crown Court to extend the time for service of the notice of appeal, even after the 21-day period has expired, provided the application for an extension of time is submitted to the court in writing and sets out the reason or reasons why an extension is required (r. 7(6)). In *R (Birmingham City Council) v Birmingham Crown Court* [2009] EWHC 3329 (Admin), [2010] 1 WLR 1287, the Divisional Court considered out-of-time appeals to the Crown Court against stand-alone ASBOs. It held that appellants must say why time should be extended, giving the reasons for delay and, if they are able to, why the proposed respondent would not be prejudiced by an extension of time.

On an appeal to the Crown Court under s. 15(1), the Crown Court may make (a) whatever orders are necessary to give effect to its determination of the appeal, or (b) whatever incidental or consequential orders appear to it to be just (s. 15(2)). An order of the Crown Court made on an appeal under s. 15 (other than one directing that an application be reheard by the youth court) is to be treated for the purposes of s. 8 (variation or discharge) as an order of the youth court (s. 15(3)).

In the case of stand-alone ASBOs, it was possible to bring judicial review proceedings against the decision of the magistrates' court to make or to refuse to make an ASBO, or to appeal that decision to the Crown Court by way of case stated. That will remain the position for civil injunctions too. In *R (W) v Acton Youth Court* [2005] EWHC 954 (Admin), the Divisional Court held that, in a claim for judicial review, it is not enough for the claimant to demonstrate that there were some errors in procedure, or that the terms of the order can be criticised (since the remedy for such complaints where the order is made by a magistrates' court was by way of appeal to the Crown Court); to succeed in having the order quashed by judicial review the claimant must demonstrate that the process before the magistrates was so flawed that the making of the order amounted to an excess of jurisdiction (per Pitchers J at [26]).

Breach

A respondent who breaches the terms of a civil injunction does not commit a criminal offence. **D25.15**
Instead, the youth court can deal with such a respondent under the powers contained in the ABCPA 2014, sch. 2. In brief, if the youth court is satisfied beyond reasonable doubt that a respondent aged under 18 is in breach of a provision of a civil injunction, it may make in respect of that respondent either a supervision order (under sch. 2, part 2) or a detention order (under sch. 2, part 3). A supervision order can contain supervision requirements, activity requirements,

curfew requirements and electronic monitoring requirements. A detention order is an order that the person in respect of whom it is made be detained for a period specified in the order in whatever youth detention accommodation (either a secure training centre, a young offender institution or secure accommodation) the Secretary of State decides. The period of the detention order may not exceed three months, not counting the day on which the order is made. The procedure for seeking either a supervision order or a detention order is set out in r. 10 of the 2015 Rules.

CRIMINAL BEHAVIOUR ORDERS

D25.16 The provisions of Part 2 of the ABCPA 2014 (ss. 22 to 33) introduced the CBO, and came into force on 20 October 2014. At the same time, para. 24(a) of sch. 11(1) to the ABCPA 2014 repealed s. 1C of the CDA 1998 (CRASBOs). By virtue of s. 33(1) of the ABCPA 2014, that repeal does not (a) prevent a CRASBO made under s. 1C of the CDA 1998 from being made in connection with criminal proceedings begun before 20 October 2014, (b) apply when such an order was made in connection with criminal proceedings begun before that date, or (c) apply in relation to anything done in connection with such an order.

The ABCPA 2014 does not define 'criminal proceedings' or indicate at what time such proceedings should be treated as commencing for the purpose of the transitional provisions. The position appears to be as follows (*Simsek* [2015] EWCA Crim 1286):

(a) where criminal proceedings were commenced before 20 October 2014 and the defendant was convicted before that date, the court can make a CRASBO but not a CBO;
(b) where criminal proceedings were commenced before 20 October 2014 and the defendant is convicted after that date, the court can make either a CRASBO or a CBO;
(c) where criminal proceedings are commenced after 20 October 2014, the court can make a CBO but not a CRASBO.

Where a CRASBO was made before 20 October 2014, the power to vary or discharge it will remain as set out in s. 1C of the CDA 1998. However, s. 33(3) of the ABCPA 2014 makes it plain that, if an application is made to vary a CRASBO after 20 October 2014, the court seised of the application cannot extend either the period of the CRASBO or the period of any term of the CRASBO. Moreover, s. 33(5) provides that any CRASBOs still in force by 20 October 2019 will be governed from that date onwards by the sections in Part 2 of the ABCPA 2014 as if the CRASBO were in fact a CBO. For the power to vary or discharge a CRASBO under s. 1C of the CDA 1998, see D25.30 of the 2015 edition of this work.

It should be noted that when the Sentencing Act 2020 comes into force these provisions will be repealed and replaced. For the new provisions see Part 11, ch. 1, of the Act.

Power to Make CBOs

D25.17 The Crown Court, the magistrates' court and the youth court will be able to make CBOs under s. 22 of the ABCPA 2014 whenever an offender is convicted of an offence (s. 22(1)). However, in *Khan (Kamran)* [2018] EWCA Crim 1472, [2018] 1 WLR 5419, the Court of Appeal said (at [19] and [20]): 'We are still in the early days of CBOs and the case law is not yet fully developed . . . We do not believe that it was the intention of Parliament that criminal behaviour orders should become a mere matter of box-ticking routine . . . such orders are not lightly to be imposed: the court should proceed with a proper degree of caution and circumspection.' The type of offence committed by the offender is immaterial for the purposes of s. 22, as is the date of its commission. This position stands in marginal contrast to that established by s. 1C of the CDA 1998, under which a CRASBO could be made only following the offender's conviction for a 'relevant offence' (meaning one committed after the Police Reform Act 2002 came into force) and in respect of behaviour occurring after (but not before) the commencement date. Under the ABCPA 2014, where an offender is convicted of an offence committed before

20 October 2013, the offender's behaviour at the time that offence was committed cannot form the basis of the court's decision to make a CBO. Instead, the prosecution would have to rely on evidence (not necessarily adduced at trial) of D's behaviour after 20 October 2013. Although that appears to be the effect of s. 33(5), in relation to a similarly worded provision in the ABCPA 2014, s. 27, concerning the making of civil injunctions, Holroyde J held in *Birmingham City Council v Pardoe* [2016] EWHC 3119 (QB) that such a provision does not operate so as to exclude the court from taking into account evidence of a person's behaviour which occurred before a certain date, provided that behaviour assists the court in deciding whether any behaviour on the part of the person occurring after that date amounted to anti-social behaviour, and, moreover, the behaviour of the person where it occurred before that date can also be taken into account in deciding whether it would be just and convenient to grant the civil injunction.

A CBO can be imposed only where the offender receives a 'sentence ... in respect of the offence' or 'an order discharging the offender conditionally' (s. 22(6)). It follows that where the offender receives an absolute discharge or is bound over to keep the peace, s. 22 is not engaged and the court cannot make a CBO in respect of that person (see para. 136 of the Explanatory Note to the Bill).

The court does not have to impose a CBO at the same time that it sentences the offender. It can adjourn the hearing of an application for a CBO until after sentencing (s. 23(3)) but, as the original Statutory Guidance pointed out at p. 27, the 'court cannot consider an application for a CBO at a hearing after the offender has been sentenced unless the court has adjourned proceedings from the sentence date for the application to be considered'. If the offender is sentenced and then some days or weeks later the prosecution serve an application for a CBO, the court will be *functus officio* and unable to consider the application. If the application for a CBO is adjourned, and at the next hearing the offender fails to attend notwithstanding the fact that adequate notice was given of the time and place of the adjourned proceedings (s. 23(5)), the court may (a) further adjourn the proceedings, or (b) issue a warrant for the offender's arrest, and (c) if in addition the offender has been previously informed that if he does not appear at the adjourned hearing the court may hear the application in his or her absence, hear the application in the offender's absence (s. 23(4)).

The Court of Appeal, having quashed a restraining order, held that the Criminal Appeal Act 1968, s. 11(3), permits it to impose a CBO instead (*AD* [2019] EWCA Crim 1339, [2020] 1 Cr App R (S) 21 (165) at [77]). The Court of Appeal went on to hold that any application to discharge or vary a CBO made by that Court would have to be made in the Crown Court and not in the Court of Appeal (at [81)]).

Applying for a CBO

The court cannot make a CBO of its own motion but only on the application of the prosecution (ABCPA 2014, s. 22(7)). This is in contrast to the position under s. 1C(3) of the CDA 1998, where the court could make a CRASBO if the prosecution asked it to *or* if the court itself thought it appropriate to do so. If the prosecution expressly decline to invite the court to make a CBO, the court will be powerless to make one. The Statutory Guidance contemplates that the prosecution can either apply for a CBO 'at its own initiative or following a request from a council or the police'. **D25.18**

The CPS have published legal guidance on applications for CBOs. The current version was released in December 2017. The CPS Guidance stresses at the outset that the CBO 'is aimed at tackling the most serious and persistent offenders where their behaviour has brought them before a criminal court', which is an expression borrowed from the Statutory Guidance.

The prosecution must find out the views of the local youth offending team (YOT), as defined in s. 22(10), before applying for a CBO if the offender will be under the age of 18 when the application is made (s. 22(8)). According to para. 138 of the Explanatory Note to the Bill,

Parliament envisages that the police or the local authority will consult the YOT and inform the prosecution of the views expressed by them. The YOT cannot veto the application for a CBO but clearly if the team members voice strong opposition to the making of any CBO the prosecution will take that on board before deciding whether to press ahead with an application. The Explanatory Note goes on to recommend that children or young people who will be affected by the order should be given the chance to express their views in line with their rights under the UN Convention on the Rights of the Child. In fact, there is no mention in the Statutory Guidance, so far as CBOs are concerned, to indicate that the views of affected children or young people (in particular the offender) should be canvassed before the application is made. The Statutory Guidance does suggest that aside from the mandated consultation with the YOT, the police or the local authority might wish to consult with 'local organisations that have come into contact with the individual, such as schools and colleges of further education, providers of probation services and social services, mental health services, housing providers or others'. The Statutory Guidance adds that the views of these agencies should be considered before the police or the local authority invite the prosecution to consider applying for a CBO. In June 2015, the Youth Justice Board published guidance to YOT Practitioners on the ABCPA 2014, including Part 2.

Procedural Requirements

D25.19 CrimPR Part 31 (see Supplement, **R31.1** *et seq.*) sets out the procedure to be followed when making an application for a CBO. Rule 31.3 provides that, where the prosecution want the court to make a CBO, they must serve notice of that intention on the court, the offender and 'any person on whom the order would be likely to have a significant adverse effect'. The prosecution must serve the notice 'as soon as practicable (without waiting for a verdict)'. It would be a mistake to assume, therefore, that as a matter of routine the prosecution should simply wait until conviction before serving an application for a CBO. The application must be served as soon as practicable whatever position has been reached in the criminal proceedings. The notice must summarise the relevant facts, identify the evidence on which the prosecution rely in support of the application, attach any written statement that the prosecutor has not already served and specify the order the prosecutor wants the court to make. If the prosecution wish to rely on evidence not served during the criminal proceedings, they must serve that evidence along with the notice. It does not matter whether that evidence would be admissible in the criminal proceedings (s. 23(2)). Once the prosecution have complied with their obligation to serve the notice and any necessary accompanying document on the defence, the defence must respond 'as soon as reasonably practicable (without waiting for the verdict)', notifying the court and the prosecution of the defence position in relation to the application and identifying any evidence and attaching any witness statement the defence would wish to rely on in the proceedings for a CBO which has not already been served. Where the offender opposes the application for a CBO, the court will set the matter down for a contested hearing. The court cannot make a CBO unless the offender has had an opportunity to consider what order is proposed and why and the evidence in support of the application, and an opportunity to make representations.

In *Lima* [2010] EWCA Crim 284, a failure to comply with the relevant rule resulted in procedural unfairness and was one of the reasons the Court of Appeal quashed the CRASBO. Mackay J said (at [8]): 'This case illustrates in our judgment the need for observance of such rules where an order significantly restricting the liberty of a person is envisaged.' In contrast, a failure to follow the rules did not render it 'unfair' to uphold a CBO made against the appellant in *Asfi* [2016] EWCA Crim 1236. There had been a lengthy discussion with the judge ahead of sentencing about the appropriate terms to be included in a CBO and so while no written notice of the prosecution's intention to seek a CBO upon conviction had been given, in breach of the rules, that breach caused no injustice to the appellant.

Reporting Restrictions

Where the application for a CBO is made against an offender who is under the age of 18, the CYPA 1933, s. 49 (restrictions on reports of proceedings in which children and young persons are concerned), does not apply in respect of the offender (s. 23(8)(a)) but s. 39 of that Act (power to prohibit publication of certain matters) does apply (s. 23(8)(b)). Section 39 was considered in the context of CRASBOs in *R (T) v St Albans Crown Court* [2002] EWHC 1129 (Admin). Elias J was of the view that where a CRASBO has been imposed, that is a factor which reinforces the general public interest in the public disclosure of court proceedings for two reasons. First, disclosure of the identity of the individuals may make an order efficacious; secondly, the very purpose of CRASBOs is to protect the public from individuals who have committed acts of anti-social behaviour. In each case the balance must be struck between the desirability of public disclosure and the need to protect the welfare of the child. In *R (K) v Knowsley MBC* [2004] EWHC 1933 (Admin), the Divisional Court endorsed Elias J's approach and said it applied equally to interim CRASBOs. However, the court recognised that the fact that the order was an interim one meant that the allegations against the defendant were unproven (and might or might not be proven at a full hearing) and that was a very important consideration in deciding where the balance lies. **D25.20**

In *R (Stanley, Marshall and Kelly) v Metropolitan Police Commissioner* [2004] EWHC 2229 (Admin), the Divisional Court gave guidance on post-CRASBO publicity and its dissemination. When questions of publicity arise in such cases, the police and local authorities should recognise that those subject to the orders might have their rights under the ECHR, Article 8(1), infringed; they should consider whether the publicity that is envisaged is necessary and proportionate to the authorities' legitimate aims. Whether publicity is intended to inform, to reassure, to assist in enforcing the existing orders by policing, to inhibit the behaviour of those against whom the orders have been made or to deter others, it is unlikely to be effective unless it includes photographs, names and at least partial addresses. Those responsible for publicity must therefore leave no room for misidentification. As to the remainder of the content of any publicity, that must depend upon the facts of the case. If residents have been exposed to criminal behaviour for years and orders have been obtained by reference to that behaviour and in order to bring it to an end, there is no reason why publicity material should not say so. It must not assert that those against whom orders have been made have been convicted of any crime, since CRASBO proceedings were civil, not criminal (per Kennedy LJ at [40]).

As a result of the *Stanley* case, the Home Office issued detailed guidance, *Publicising Anti-social Behaviour Orders*, in October 2005. This guidance makes the point that 'each individual case should be judged on its merits as to whether or not to publicise the details of an individual subject to an ASBO' and that the decision-making process should aim to consider and record several key factors:

(a) the need for publicity;
(b) a consideration of the human rights of the public;
(c) a consideration of the human rights of those against whom ASBOs are made;
(d) what the publicity should look like and whether it is proportionate to the aims of the publicity.

Special Measures

Chapter I of Part II of the YJCEA 1999 (special measures directions in the case of vulnerable and intimidated witnesses: see **D14.3**) applies to CBO proceedings (s. 31(1)) with certain modifications specified in s. 31(2). By virtue of CrimPR 31.3(6), the rules about special measures contained in Part 18 apply too, with the exception of the time-limit in r. 18.3(a). Where the prosecution seek special measures in respect of a witness in proceedings for a CBO, they must serve the application for special measures at the same time that they serve the written application for the CBO. Such special measures can include the physical screening of a witness, enabling evidence to be given in private or the use of a video-recorded interview (see para. 146 of the Explanatory Note). **D25.21**

Evidence

D25.22 For the purposes of deciding whether to make a CBO, the court may consider evidence led by the prosecution and evidence led by the offender (s. 23(1)). At the hearing of the application, the court is permitted to receive hearsay evidence, which should be understood as a reference to evidence consisting of hearsay within the meaning of s. 1(2) of the Civil Evidence Act 1995 and *not* as a reference to hearsay evidence within the meaning of s. 115 of the CJA 2003. This will include bad character evidence as well (see para. 139 of the Explanatory Note). This is because proceedings on an application for a CBO are civil in nature notwithstanding the fact that the court will apply the criminal standard of proof. Any party (whether prosecution or defence) that wishes to adduce hearsay evidence in the proceedings must serve notice of their intention to do so. That notice must identify the evidence that is said to be hearsay, identify the person who made the hearsay statement (or explain why that person is not identified) and explain why that person will not be called to give oral evidence (CrimPR 31.6(1)). Where one party applies to adduce hearsay evidence, the other party must apply in writing not more than five business days after receiving the notice if it wishes to cross-examine the maker of the hearsay statement (r. 31.7). The court can determine that application with or without holding a hearing for that purpose. Instead of applying to cross-examine the maker of the hearsay statement, the other party can apply within the same seven-day period if it wishes to 'challenge the credibility or consistency of' the maker of the hearsay statement. In response, the party seeking to adduce the hearsay evidence can then call the maker of the statement to give oral evidence if it so chooses (r. 31.8). These provisions are intended to replicate in large measure the regimes in the Civil Evidence Act 1995, ss. 2 to 5, and the Magistrates' Courts (Hearsay Evidence in Civil Proceedings) Rules 1999, rr. 3 to 5.

Statutory Test

D25.23 The court may make a CBO on the application of the prosecution if, but only if, two conditions are satisfied (ABCPA 2014, s. 22(1)). The first is that the court is satisfied to the criminal standard that 'the offender has engaged in behaviour that causes or was likely to cause harassment, alarm or distress to any person' (s. 22(3)). The second is that 'the court considers that making the order will help in preventing the offender from engaging in such behaviour' (s. 22(4)).

As to the first of these conditions, there does not have to be 'a link between the criminal behaviour which led to the conviction and the anti-social behaviour' for this condition to be satisfied (see p. 30 of the Statutory Guidance). In other words, it may be that the evidence relied on and served by the prosecution in support of the application for a CBO is wholly different to the evidence relied on to convict the offender. In such a case, the conviction (and the evidence to support it) will be no more than a springboard for the prosecution to reach s. 22 and invoke the court's jurisdiction to make a CBO. Section 33(5) makes it plain that, in considering whether the first condition is satisfied, the court can take into account behaviour of the offender stretching back to a point in time no further than one year before the commencement date of Part 2 (i.e. to 20 October 2013). Any behaviour on the part of the offender that occurred before that date would, it seems, be inadmissible in any application for a CBO, subject to the commentary at **D25.17**. There is no limitation in s. 22(3) on the category of person who is caused or who was likely to have been caused harassment, alarm or distress. Unlike CRASBOs, therefore, a CBO can be sought even where that person is a member of the same household as the offender. For considerations of the circumstances in which the first condition might be satisfied, see **D25.8**.

As to the second of these conditions, the court must determine whether making a CBO in the terms sought by the prosecution will (*not* may) assist in preventing the offender from engaging in further anti-social behaviour. This is a much weaker test than that set out in s. 1C(2)(b) of the CDA 1998, where the court had to be satisfied that a CRASBO was 'necessary to protect persons in any place in England and Wales' from further anti-social acts by the offender. In certain instances, a CRASBO was held to be unnecessary because the sentence imposed by the court offered sufficient protection for those who could be affected by the offender's continuing anti-social behaviour (*R (F) v Bolton Crown Court* [2009] EWHC 240 (Admin)). The Court of Appeal has ruled that a CRASBO was not necessary where D's mental impairment meant that he would be unable to comply with its terms (*R (Cooke) v DPP* [2008] EWHC 2703 (Admin), (2008) 172 JP 596). In *Humphreys v CPS* [2019] EWHC 2794 (Admin), [2020] 1 Cr App R (S) 39 (283) the Divisional Court endorsed *Cooke* and held that where an offender is *capable* of understanding the terms of a CBO but *incapable* of complying with them, 'so that the only effect of the order will be to criminalise behaviour over which he has no control', that 'will indicate that the order will not be helpful and will not satisfy the second condition' (at 24]).

In respect of the second condition there is no burden of proof on the prosecution to demonstrate to any standard that the imposition of a CBO would be helpful. Instead, the exercise for the court 'remains one of judgment and evaluation' (*DPP v Bulmer* [2015] EWHC 2323 (Admin), [2015] 1 WLR 5159 at [32]; *Browne-Morgan* [2016] EWCA Crim 1903, [2017] 1 Cr App R (S) 33 (279) at [15] and *Khan (Kamran)* [2018] EWCA Crim 1472, [2018] 1 WLR 5419 at [20]). In *Bulmer*, Beatson LJ stressed (at [35]) that the courts 'should proceed with a proper degree of caution and circumspection because such orders are not lightly to be imposed, satisfaction to the criminal standard is not required in what is an evaluative exercise'.

It is difficult to imagine circumstances in which a CBO would not be a helpful way of preventing anti-social behaviour in the future, especially as the court may be inclined to view the terms of the CBO as a useful accompaniment to any sentence received by the offender. Arguments from the defence to the effect that the sentence alone is a sufficient safeguard against further harassing behaviour by the offender will be met with the response that provided the CBO adds *something* to the protection afforded to the public by the sentence then the second condition for making a CBO will be satisfied, and that is likely to be true in most cases. In *Bulmer*, the Court of Appeal emphasised that the focus of the CBO regime remains the prevention of anti-social behaviour and so the 'helpfulness' condition does not mean that the proposed order must contain requirements that are intended to assist the defendant to overcome some affliction that drives anti-social behaviour (such as alcoholism): it is enough that the proposed order will be helpful in preventing the defendant's anti-social behaviour from causing harassment, alarm or distress to members of the public. Even if the risk of the defendant breaching the CBO is high, this does not mean that a CBO would be an unhelpful way of preventing the defendant from engaging in anti-social behaviour (*Barclay* [2011] EWCA Crim 32, [2011] 2 Cr App R (S) 67 (385) at [33]).

Section 14A(2) of the Football Spectators Act 1989 (see E21.3) contains broadly the same test as set out in s. 22(4) of the ABCPA 2014: 'If the court is satisfied that there are reasonable grounds to believe that making a banning order would help to prevent violence or disorder at or in connection with any regulated football matches, it must make such an order in respect of the offender.' The weight of authority under s. 14A suggests that an order can be 'helpful' even where there is no evidence to suggest that the offender's conduct is likely to be repeated (*R (White) v Blackfriars Crown Court* [2008] EWHC 510 (Admin), [2008] 2 Cr App R (S) 97 (542); *Curtis* [2009] EWCA Crim 1225, [2010] 1 Cr App R (S) 31 (193)). By contrast, the decision of the Court of Appeal in *Doyle* [2012] EWCA Crim 955, [2013] 1 Cr App R (S) 36 (197) indicates that such orders should only be made where there *is* a danger of repetition.

It is clear from a consideration of the two aforementioned conditions that there is no requirement in s. 22 or elsewhere in Part 2 of the ABCPA 2014 that the offender must be a persistently anti-social individual before a CBO can be made.

Terms of a CBO

Section 1C(2) of the CDA 1998 empowered the court to incorporate into a CRASBO any terms 'which prohibit the offender from doing anything described in the order'. The focus under the CDA was on prohibiting the offender from engaging in anti-social behaviour by imposing suitable restrictions. Section 22(5) of the ABCPA 2014, on the other hand, retains the **D25.24** power of the court to impose restrictions on the offender but complements that with a further power to impose mandatory requirements on the offender too. Thus, a CBO can include both positive and negative obligations. A CBO does not have to include both (*DPP v Bulmer* [2015] EWHC 2323 (Admin), [2015] 1 WLR 5159 at [23]). Any prohibitions or restrictions included in a CBO, so far as is practicable, must not interfere with the offender's work or schooling or with the operation of any other order or injunction imposed by any other court (s. 22(9)). In *Janes* [2016] EWCA Crim 676, [2016] 2 Cr App R (S) 27 (256), D was a self-employed gardener who committed two offences of fraud by significantly over-charging elderly customers for his services. He was convicted following a trial and the court proceeded to impose a CBO against him for a period of ten years with conditions that prohibited him from soliciting work by knocking on people's doors, dropping leaflets through their letterboxes etc. On appeal against the CBO, D argued that these prohibitions violated the ABCPA 2014, s. 22(9), because they amounted to an unwarranted interference with his work. The Court of Appeal dismissed the appeal. McCombe LJ noted that the second pre-condition for making a CBO is that it will help to prevent the offender from engaging in behaviour that caused, or was likely to cause, harassment, alarm or distress to any person. This does not require the prosecution to prove that there has been a sustained course of such conduct by the offender. The prohibition in s. 22(9) does not preclude the court from imposing a prohibition that interferes with the times at which the offender normally works, and such prohibitions may be necessary where the offender's work is the vehicle for harassing behaviour.

The Statutory Guidance suggests (at p. 31) that, before inviting the court to impose prohibitions or requirements, the prosecution should consider with care 'the impact on any caring responsibilities the [offender] may have and, in the event that the [offender] has any disability, whether he or she is capable of complying with the proposed' terms. It is beyond doubt that the terms of the CBO, whether they be prohibitions or requirements, must be 'reasonable, proportionate, realistic, practical, clear and enforceable' (*Boness* [2005] EWCA Crim 2395, [2006] 1 Cr App R (S) 120 (690); *Bulmer* at [36] and [46]). In *P (Shane Tony)* [2004] EWCA Crim 287, [2004] 2 Cr App R (S) 63 (343), Henriques J said (at [34]) that 'the terms of the order must be precise and capable of being understood by offender', 'the findings of fact giving rise to the making of the order must be recorded', 'the order must be explained to the offender' and 'the exact terms of the order must be pronounced in open court and the written order must accurately reflect the order as pronounced'. In *Khan (Kamran)* [2018] EWCA Crim 1472, [2018] 1 WLR 5419, the Court of Appeal held (at [14]) that when considering the proposed terms of a CBO it is essential that the guidance given in *Boness* should be borne in mind. The Court also endorsed (at [17]) the four requirements set out in *P (Shane Tony)* and the observations of the Court in *Bulmer* to the effect that the order must be tailored to the specific circumstances of the person on whom it is to be imposed and that assessments of proportionality are intensively fact-sensitive. The Court added (at [15]):

> Because an order must be precise and capable of being understood by the offender, a court should ask itself before making an order 'are the terms of this order clear so that the offender will know precisely what it is that he is prohibited from doing?' Prohibitions should be reasonable and proportionate; realistic and practical: and be in terms which make it easy to determine and prosecute a breach. Exclusion zones should be clearly delineated (generally with the use of clearly marked maps . . .) and individuals whom the defendant is prohibited from contacting or associating with should be clearly identified. In the case of a foreign national, consideration should be given for the need for the order to be translated.

One illustration of an unclear, unrealistic and impractical term can be found in *M v DPP* [2007] EWHC 1032 (Admin). The Divisional Court quashed a term in a CRASBO ('not to knowingly associate with a person or persons while such person or persons are engaged in attempting or conspiring to commit any criminal offence in England and Wales') on the basis that the clause involved the exercise of a value judgement on the part of D who might have to take an instant decision as to whether those with whom he was associated were about to commit a crime and that could not be right. Similarly, in *Maguire* [2019] EWCA Crim 1193, [2019] 2 Cr App R (S) 55 (447), the Court of Appeal quashed a term in a CBO that required D to notify the police when he formed a relationship with a female because it was 'hopelessly vague' (at [21]). In doing so the Court re-emphasised how important it is that the provisions of behaviour orders such as the CBO are 'policeable' in the sense that they must be clear and comprehensible to the defendant, to the police and to the public.

As to the sorts of terms that could be included in a CBO, para. 135 of the Explanatory Note to the Bill suggests that 'prohibitions could include not being in possession of a can of spray paint in a public place, not entering a particular area, or not being drunk in a public place. The requirements in an order could include attendance at a course to educate offenders on alcohol and its effects.' In *Asfi* [2016] EWCA Crim 1236, the Court of Appeal endorsed a prohibition in these terms: not to 'congregate in a public place in a group of two or more persons in a manner causing or likely to cause any person to fear for their safety'. The Statutory Guidance suggests (at p. 31) that requirements could include, by way of example, attendance at an anger management course where an offender finds it difficult to respond without violence, youth mentoring, a substance misuse awareness session where an offender's anti-social behaviour occurred when drinking or using drugs, or a job readiness course to help the offender get employment and move away from the circumstances that led to anti-social behaviour.

Section 24 of the ABCPA 2014 contains a number of provisions that relate specifically to the inclusion in CBOs of requirements rather than prohibitions. Before the court can impose a requirement on an offender, the person (whether an individual or an organisation) responsible for monitoring the offender's compliance with the requirement will need to be identified (s. 24(1)) so that the supervisor or its representative can provide the court with evidence about the suitability and enforceability of the requirement before it is imposed (s. 24(2)). The Explanatory Note suggests (at para. 140) that the supervisor could be 'the local authority, recognised providers of substance misuse recovery or dog training providers for irresponsible dog owners'. The supervisor must be named in the CBO itself and is entreated by s. 24(4) to make any necessary arrangements to further the offender's compliance with the requirements, to promote the offender's compliance with the requirements and to notify the prosecution and the chief officer of police if the offender either fails to comply with a requirement or complies with all the requirements, assuming in the latter instance that the requirements are not continuous ones. By virtue of s. 24(6), where a requirement is included in a CBO, the offender is obliged to keep in touch with the supervisor in relation to that requirement in accordance with any instructions handed down by the supervisor from time to time and to notify the supervisor of any change in the offender's address. These obligations are treated as if they were terms of the CBO, so a failure to comply with them will amount to a breach of the order. **D25.25**

Duration

A CBO takes effect on the day it is made (ABCPA 2014, s. 25(1)). If on the day the CBO is made, the offender is already subject to an existing CBO, the court can order that the new CBO will take effect on the day the old CBO expires (s. 25(2)). The period of the CBO must be set out in the CBO itself (s. 25(3)). Where the offender is under 18 at the time the CBO is made, the CBO must be for not less than one year and for not more than three years (s. 25(4)). In any other case, the CBO must be either for a fixed period of not less than two years or for an indefinite period, i.e. until further order (s. 25(5): see para. 141 of the Explanatory Note). For an example of the rare circumstances in which an indefinite order may be appropriate, see *Avery* [2009] EWCA Crim 2670, [2010] 2 Cr App R (S) 33 (209), where 'a group had pursued a course of reprehensible conduct where they were messianic in their fervour about the cause of animal rights and where they had shown no real remorse at any stage and were likely to repeat their offending'. For an example where an indefinite order was held to be inappropriate, see *West* [2013] EWCA Crim 1309. With a CBO, the court can impose different periods for particular **D25.26** prohibitions and requirements so the overall 'package' can be tailored to suit the individual offender's case (s. 25(6)).

Section 28 provides for the periodical review of CBOs made against those aged under 18. Reviews must be held every 12 months. That period starts from the date the order was made, or from the date it was subsequently varied. The chief officer of police for the force where the offender is living or appears to be living is the person responsible for carrying out the review. According to the Statutory Guidance (at p. 32), the chief officer of police 'may invite any other person or body to participate in the review. This could include youth offending teams, educational establishments or other organisations who have been working with the young person.' The review must include a consideration of the offender's progress on the order, the adequacy of the support available to help the offender to comply with its terms and any other matters relevant to a consideration of whether the order should be varied or discharged. The ABCPA 2014 does not say what the consequences of the review should be, but the Statutory Guidance indicates that if the conclusions of the review are that the CBO should be varied or discharged then the chief officer of police will invite the prosecution to make the appropriate application under s. 27 (see **D25.27**). Reviews must be carried out within each successive 12-month period so long as the offender remains under the age of 18 and the CBO remains in force. If the end of the next 12-month period occurs on a date beyond the offender's 18th birthday, there is no obligation for the chief officer of police to hold a review.

Variation or Discharge

D25.27 The court which makes a CBO is empowered under s. 27(1) of the ABCPA 2014 to vary or discharge the order on the application of either the prosecution or the offender. Where a magistrates' court imposes a CBO the Crown Court has no power to vary it and nor would the judge in the Crown Court be able to acquire such a power by reconstituting him or herself as a district judge pursuant to the Courts Act 2003, s. 66 (*Potter* [2019] EWCA Crim 461, [2019] 2 Cr App R (S) 5 (36)). The power to vary an order includes the power to add further prohibitions or requirements, and to extend the period for which the existing prohibitions or requirements have effect (s. 27(4)). Where an application to vary or discharge a CBO is dismissed, the unsuccessful party (whether the prosecution or the offender) can make no further applications under s. 27 without either the consent of the court or the agreement of the other party (s. 27(2) and (3)). This ensures that neither the prosecution nor the offender can keep revisiting the same application again and again in the hope that a different composition of the court might accede to it.

The procedure for seeking a variation or discharge of a CBO is set out in CrimPR 31.5 (see Supplement, **R31.5**). The party seeking a variation or discharge must apply in writing as soon as practicable after becoming aware of the grounds for doing so, explaining what material circumstances have changed since the order was made and why the CBO should be varied or discharged as a result. If that party wishes the court to consider any particular evidence in support of the application, it should serve that evidence along with the written application. The court may decide an application with or without a hearing but (a) the court cannot dismiss the application unless the applicant has had an opportunity to make representations at a hearing, and (b) the court cannot allow an application unless everyone who should have been served with a copy of the application has had at least ten business days to make representations.

Breach

D25.28 An offender who without reasonable excuse either (a) does anything he or she is prohibited from doing by a CBO, or (b) fails to do anything he or she is required to do by a CBO, commits an offence (ABCPA 2014, s. 30(1)). The maximum sentence on summary conviction is six months' imprisonment and/or a fine and the maximum sentence on conviction on indictment is five years' imprisonment and/or a fine (s. 30(2)). The court cannot impose a conditional discharge following such a conviction (s. 30(3)). For those offenders aged under 18 who breach the terms of a CBO, proceedings will be held in the youth court where the maximum sentence is a two-year detention and training order (Statutory Guidance, at p. 32).

Where an offender aged under 18 is prosecuted for breaching the terms of a CBO, s. 49 of the CYPA 1933 (reporting restrictions) does not apply in respect of that person but s. 45 of the YJCEA 1999 (power to restrict reporting) does apply (s. 30(5)). If the court does exercise its power to give a direction under s. 45 of the YJCEA 1999 it must give its reason for doing so (s. 30(6)).

Reasonable Excuse

The meaning of the phrase 'reasonable excuse' in the context of s. 1C of the CDA 1998 was **D25.29** considered by the Court of Appeal in *Nicholson* [2006] EWCA Crim 1518, [2006] 1 WLR 2857. The Court ruled that forgetfulness on the part of the accused, or a misunderstanding of the terms of the CRASBO, *may* be capable of constituting a defence of reasonable excuse (per Auld LJ at [15]). Where a person is incapable of complying with the terms of the CBO, that should amount to a reasonable excuse (*Humphreys v CPS* [2019] EWHC 2794 (Admin), [2020] 1 Cr App R (S) 39 (283) at [24]). Where the accused appears before the Crown Court and raises a defence of reasonable excuse, it is a matter for the jury to resolve (*Nicholson*, at [17]). In *Charles* [2009] EWCA Crim 1570, [2010] 4 All ER 553, the Court of Appeal considered the question of where the burden lies when the defence raise 'reasonable excuse' and said that it cannot have been intended by Parliament to place any burden of proof on the defendant. The Court held that the burden of disproving reasonable excuse rests on the prosecution where the defendant has raised the issue on the evidence before the court and that the CDA 1998 is perfectly workable on the basis that it imposes only an evidential burden on the defendant, but leaves the legal burden on the prosecution. The question of what is the nature of the mental element that a prosecutor must prove when a defendant is prosecuted for beach of a CRASBO was considered in *B v DPP* [2012] EWHC 72 (Admin), [2012] 1 WLR 2357. The Divisional Court found that the relevant provisions of the CDA 1998 do not require the Crown to prove a specific mental element on the part of a defendant at the time the acts which constitute the breach of a CRASBO were committed. However, if the issue of reasonable excuse arises in any given case, a defendant can raise his or her state of mind at the time of the alleged breach since state of mind will usually be relevant to the issue of reasonable excuse. Applying *Nicholson*, the Court held that, as the effect of the provisions of the CDA 1998 was to criminalise conduct that would otherwise not be criminal, it would not be right, on principle, to exclude matters that go to a defendant's state of mind (such as forgetfulness or a misapprehension about the meaning of the order or an accidental breach).

The question of the raising of arguments as to the validity of clauses in a CRASBO in the context of proceedings for breach (rather than on appeal from the making of the order) was considered in *DPP v T* [2006] EWHC 728 (Admin), [2007] 3 All ER 471. On the particular facts the Divisional Court ruled that the wide provision 'not to act in an anti-social manner' without further definition or limitation should never again be included in a CRASBO (see also *Heron v Plymouth City Council* [2009] EWHC 3562 (Admin)). It held that the normal rule in relation to an order of the court is that it must be treated as valid and be obeyed unless and until it is set aside. Even if the order should not have been made in the first place, a person may be liable for any breach of it committed before it is set aside. Moreover, the person against whom a CRASBO is made has a full opportunity to challenge that order on appeal or to apply to vary it. Accordingly, insofar as any question does arise as to the validity of such an order, there is no obvious reason why the person against whom the order was made should be allowed to raise that issue as a defence in subsequent breach proceedings rather than by way of appeal against the original order (per Richards LJ at [27]). His lordship went on to say (at [35]):

> ... although it is alleged that the relevant provision of the ASBO is unduly wide and uncertain and unnecessary for the purpose of protecting against further anti-social acts, we very much doubt whether that could be said to go to the validity of the order. The magistrates' court plainly had jurisdiction under the Crime and Disorder Act 1998 to make an ASBO. It seems to us that if the

> court was in error in including a provision in these terms... that did not have the consequence of taking the order outside the court's jurisdiction; and if the order was within the court's jurisdiction, it would remain valid even if there were errors in it that were open to correction on appeal. With great respect to the Divisional Court in *R (W)*, we do not accept that because an order is 'plainly too wide' it is also 'plainly invalid'.

Where the court is concerned that one or more of the terms of the ASBO is drafted too widely, Richards LJ indicated (at [37]) that the court may:

> ... consider whether the relevant provision lacked sufficient clarity to warrant a finding that the respondent's conduct amounted to a breach of the order; whether the lack of clarity provided a reasonable excuse for non-compliance with the order; and whether, if a breach was established, it was appropriate in the circumstances to impose any penalty for the breach.

Sentencing

D25.30 The definitive sentencing guideline for breach of a CRASBO (see Supplement, **SG17-1**) applies to adult and young offenders, although very different principles are set out in respect of each. The same guidelines will apply to breaches of CBOs. Seriousness is determined in the same way for both categories of offender: two aspects of culpability need to be considered, namely the degree to which the offender intended to breach the order and the degree to which the offender intended to cause the harm that resulted or could have resulted. The original conduct that led to the making of the order is also a relevant consideration. Offender mitigation is relevant, particularly if the offender has a low level of understanding due to mental health issues or learning disabilities. The sentencing ranges and starting points apply to first time offenders convicted after a trial. Importantly, in this context, 'first time offender' means somebody who does not have a conviction for breach of a CBO.

The guideline identifies three starting points for adults according to the nature of the failure and harm, each starting point having a defined range, which is adjusted according to the non-exhaustive list of aggravating and mitigating features. Offender mitigation is considered after the court has reached a provisional sentence based on its assessment of offence seriousness. The range is a Band B fine to two years' custody. For the application of the guideline where there were repeated breaches of a CRASBO which did not involve harassment, alarm or distress, see *Savage* [2012] EWCA Crim 1678, where the Court of Appeal reduced a sentence of 18 months to one of 12 months. In *Lamb* [2005] EWCA Crim 3000, [2006] 2 Cr App R (S) 11 (84), Leveson J said (at [19]) that, where breaches of CRASBOs do not involve harassment, alarm or distress, community penalties, rather than custody, should be considered in order to help offenders learn to live within the terms of the ASBO to which they are subject. In those cases when there is no available community penalty (as where offenders refuse to co-operate), custodial sentences which are necessary to maintain the authority of the court should be kept as short as possible.

The sentencing framework for persons aged under 18 is significantly different and is summarised at annex C of the guideline. A youth without any previous convictions will usually be subject to a referral order. In most other cases, the appropriate sentence will be a community sentence, although a fine or reparation order may be appropriate where the breach involved no harassment, etc. Custody should be used only as a measure of last resort and, even where the custody threshold is crossed, the court should normally impose a community penalty. Where a custodial sentence is considered to be unavoidable, the starting point is a four-month detention and training order, with a range of up to 12 months. But see also the definitive sentencing guideline, *Sentencing Children and Young People* (see Supplement, **SG8-1**), which post-dates the guideline.

D25.31 What is the position where the offender breaches the terms of an order by committing an offence where the maximum sentence for that offence is less than five years' imprisonment on indictment? Is the sentencing court bound to have regard to the lower maximum sentence for that offence when sentencing the offender for the breach? In *Morrison* [2005] EWCA Crim

2237, [2006] 1 Cr App R (S) 85 (488), the Court of Appeal held that, if a breach of a CRASBO consists of no more than the commission of an offence for which a maximum penalty is prescribed by statute, it is wrong in principle to pass a sentence for that breach calculated by reference to the five-year maximum for breach of a CRASBO; the tariff is determined by the statutory maximum for the offence in question. There may, however, be exceptional cases in which it can properly be said that the vice of the breach of an order, although it amounts to an offence, goes beyond that offence, e.g., repeated offences of criminal damage directed against a particular and perhaps vulnerable victim or group of victims. However, in *Lamb* [2005] EWCA Crim 3000, [2006] 2 Cr App R (S) 11 (84), Leveson J said (at [16]) that the view expressed in *Morrison* 'appears to ignore the impact of anti-social behaviour on the wider public which was the purpose of the legislation in the first place' and also 'means that anti-social behaviour short of a criminal offence could be more heavily punished than anti-social behaviour that coincidentally was also a criminal offence'. He said that the contrary approach taken in *Tripp* [2005] EWCA Crim 2253 and *Braxton* [2004] EWCA Crim 1374, [2005] 1 Cr App R (S) 36 (167) was to be preferred. In *Tripp*, Clarke J said (at [7]) that, where breach of a CRASBO consists of conduct which is itself a criminal offence, the potential sentence may be far longer than the maximum for that basic offence; in *Braxton*, Leveson J had made the point (at [17]) that the offender in that case had to understand that misconduct that the offender might consider trivial was, because of the persistence of that conduct, now to be treated seriously, specifically to protect the public. In *Stevens* [2006] EWCA Crim 255, [2006] 2 Cr App R (S) 68 (453), the Court of Appeal did not consider it was wrong in principle for a sentence of imprisonment to be imposed in respect of breach of a CRASBO, where the conduct amounting to that breach constituted an offence for which the statutory maximum sentence was a fine.

Interim CBOs

By the time a conviction is returned against the offender, the court should be in receipt of the prosecution's written application for a CBO and the defence response in accordance with CrimPR Part 31 (see Supplement, **R31.1** *et seq*.). If the court decides to proceed to sentence immediately it can either determine the application at the same time or adjourn the hearing of the application to some later date. Alternatively, the court could adjourn sentencing to some later date and either determine the application immediately or adjourn the hearing of the application to some later date, which could be the date for sentencing but would not have to be so. If the court, by whatever route, adjourns hearing the application for a CBO beyond the date of conviction, it can make an interim CBO to last until the final hearing of the application or until further order 'if the court thinks it just to do so' (s. 26(2)). It follows, as annex C.16 to the White Paper suggests, that 'an interim order would be available at conviction (if the court adjourned for sentencing)'. **D25.32**

Section 26(3) disapplies certain provisions of ss. 22 and 25, with the effect that the court can make an interim CBO of its own motion and in circumstances where the prosecution has not sought the views of the YOT in a case where the offender is under 18. Under CrimPR 31.2(2), the court can make an interim CBO even though the offender has not had an opportunity to (a) consider what order is proposed and why, (b) consider the evidence served in support of the application for the order, or (c) make representations about whether the order should be made, provided the offender is present when the interim CBO is made and is handed a document recording the terms of the interim order not more than five business days after it is made.

Appeals

Part 2 of the ABCPA 2014 does not on its face afford to an offender a right of appeal to the Crown Court against the making of a CBO in the magistrates' court or the youth court. However, there is a right of appeal to the Crown Court under the MCA 1980, s. 108(3) (see **D29.2**). That will be an appeal by way of rehearing. The prosecution have no right of appeal against the refusal of the magistrates' court or the youth court to make a CBO but they would be able to appeal **D25.33** by way of case stated or bring a claim for judicial review of that decision. Where the CBO is made by the Crown Court, an appeal by the offender will be to the Court of Appeal, Criminal Division, despite the civil nature of the order (*P (Shane Tony)* [2004] EWCA Crim 287, [2004] 2 Cr App R (S) 63 (343)).

Individual Support Orders

D25.34 Individual support orders (ISOs), made under the CDA 1998, ss. 1AA and 1AB, are aimed at preventing further anti-social behaviour where either a stand-alone ASBO or a CRASBO has been made against a person under the age of 18. The Anti-social Behaviour, Crime and Policing Act 2014 (Commencement No. 8, Saving and Transitional Provisions) Order 2015 (SI 2015 No. 373) repealed ss. 1AA and 1AB of the CDA 1998 from 23 March 2015. Pursuant to s. 21(1)(e) and (3) of the ABCPA 2014, this repeal does not apply in relation to an ISO made in connection with a stand-alone ASBO when the ISO was made before 23 March 2015 and nor does it apply to anything done in connection with such an order. As from 23 March 2015, such an ISO cannot be varied by extending its period or the period of any of its provisions (s. 21(4)). On 23 March 2020, if such an ISO is still in force, Part 1 of the ABCPA 2014 will have effect, with any necessary modifications, as if the provisions of the ISO were provisions of a civil injunction. Pursuant to s. 33(3)(a) of the ABCPA 2014, in respect of ISOs made in connection with CRASBOs, the repeal does not (a) prevent an ISO from being made in connection with criminal proceedings begun before 20 October 2014, (b) apply in relation to an ISO which is made in connection with criminal proceedings begun before that day, or (c) apply in relation to anything done in connection with such an order (s. 33(1)). As from 20 October 2014, an ISO made in connection with a CRASBO cannot be varied in such a way as to extend its period or the period of any of its provisions (s. 33(3)). As of 20 October 2019, any ISOs made in connection with a CRASBO that are still in force will be treated as if their provisions were terms of a CBO (s. 33(4)). For a discussion of ISOs, see D25.45 in the 2015 edition of this work.

Parenting Orders

D25.35 The provisions of s. 9 of the CDA 1998 provide that (a) where a person under the age of 16 is convicted of an offence and receives a sentence other than a referral order, the court must make a parenting order if the relevant condition in s. 8 is satisfied (s. 9(1)(a)), and (b) where a civil injunction is made against a person under the age of 16, the court must make a parenting order if the relevant condition is satisfied (s. 9(1B)) (see E14.3 *et seq*).

Intervention Orders

D25.36 Intervention orders may be attached to a stand-alone ASBO by virtue of the CDA 1998, s. 1G. The Anti-social Behaviour, Crime and Policing Act 2014 (Commencement No. 8, Saving and Transitional Provisions) Order 2015 (SI 2015 No. 373) repealed s. 1G of the CDA 1998 on 23 March 2015. Pursuant to s. 21(1)(f) of the ABCPA 2014, this repeal does not apply in relation to (a) an application for an intervention order made before 23 March 2015, (b) an intervention order (whether made before or after that date) applied for before that date, or (c) anything done in connection with such an application or order (s. 21(2)). As from 23 March 2015, such an intervention order cannot be varied by extending its period or the period of any of its provisions (s. 21(4)). On 23 March 2020, if such an intervention order is still in force, Part 1 of the ABCPA 2014 will have effect, with any necessary modifications, as if the provisions of the intervention order were provisions of a civil injunction. For a discussion of intervention orders, see D25.49 of the 2015 edition of this work.

COMMUNITY PROTECTION NOTICES

D25.37 The Anti-social Behaviour, Crime and Policing Act 2014 (Commencement No. 7, Saving and Transitional Provisions) Order 2014 (SI 2014 No. 2590) brought ch. 1 (community protections notices) of Part 4 (community protection) of the ABCPA 2014 into force on 20 October 2014.

The Statutory Guidance (at pp. 38–46) addresses the regime for issuing CPNs (s. 56(1)) and states (at p. 39) that the CPN 'is intended to deal with particular, ongoing problems or nuisances which negatively affect the community's quality of life by targeting those responsible'.

Issuing a CPN

The power to issue a CPN can be exercised by an authorised person, which includes a constable, the relevant local authority or a person designated by the relevant local authority (ABCPA 2014, s. 53(1)). Paragraph 1ZB of sch. 4 to the Police Reform Act 2002 extends that power to community support officers in certain circumstances. An authorised person may issue a CPN to an individual aged 16 or over, or a body, if satisfied on reasonable grounds that (a) the conduct of the individual or body is having a detrimental effect, of a persistent or continuing nature, on the quality of life of those in the locality, and (b) the conduct is unreasonable (s. 43(1)). 'Conduct' includes a failure to act (s. 57). **D25.38**

Conduct on, or affecting, premises that a particular person owns, leases, occupies, controls, operates or maintains, is treated as conduct of that person (s. 44(1)). 'Premises' includes any land (s. 57) and 'owner', in relation to premises, means a person (other than a mortgagee not in possession) entitled to dispose of the fee simple of the premises, whether in possession or in reversion, and a person who holds or is entitled to the rents and profits of the premises under a lease that (when granted) was for a term of not less than three years (s. 57). Conduct on, or affecting, premises occupied for the purposes of a government department is treated as conduct of the Minister in charge of the department (s. 44(2)). The conduct of one person cannot be treated as the conduct of another person if that other person cannot reasonably be expected to control or affect it (s. 44(3)).

A CPN may be issued to a person by (a) handing it to the person, (b) leaving it at the person's proper address, or (c) sending it by post to the person at that address (s. 53(1)). Special rules exist where the person is a body corporate (s. 55(2)) or a partnership (s. 55(3)). Where the occupier or owner of premises is unascertainable, the authorised person can, in certain circumstances, post the CPN on the premises (s. 45).

Terms of a CPN

A CPN is a notice that imposes any of the following requirements on the individual or body issued with it: **D25.39**

(a) a requirement to stop doing specified things,
(b) a requirement to do specified things, or
(c) a requirement to take reasonable steps to achieve specified results (s. 43(3)).

The CPN may specify periods within which, or times by which, requirements under (b) or (c) are to be complied with (s. 43(8)). The only requirements that may be imposed are ones that are reasonable to impose in order (a) to prevent the detrimental effected referred to in s. 43(1) from continuing or recurring, or (b) to reduce that detrimental effect or to reduce the risk of its continuance or recurrence (s. 43(4)). An authorised person (A) may issue a CPN to an individual or body (B) only where B has been given a written warning that the notice will be issued unless B's conduct ceases to have the detrimental effect referred to in s. 43(1), and A is satisfied that, despite B having had enough time to deal with the matter, B's conduct is still having that *effect (s. 43(5))*. A person issuing a CPN must before doing so inform any body or individual the person thinks appropriate (s. 43(6)). A CPN must identify the conduct referred to in s. 43(1) and explain the effect of ss. 46 to 51 of the ABCPA 2014.

Appeals

A person issued with a CPN may appeal to a magistrates' court against the notice on any of the grounds set out in s. 46(1). These include procedural grounds (that there is a material defect **D25.40** or error in the notice or that it was issued to the wrong person) and substantive grounds (the conduct complained of did not take place or did not have a detrimental effect on the quality of life of those in the locality etc.). An appeal must be made within the period of 21 days beginning with the day on which the person is issued with the notice (s. 46(2)). Until an appeal is determined or withdrawn, the requirements in the CPN remain in effect unless the court orders otherwise (s. 46(3)). In determining the appeal, the magistrates' court will be exercising its civil jurisdiction. The magistrates' court hearing an appeal must quash the notice, modify the notice (e.g., by extending a period specified in it) or dismiss the appeal (s. 46(4)).

In *Stannard v CPS* [2019] EWHC 84 (Admin), [2019] 1 WLR 3229, the Divisional Court held that while the 21-day time-limit in which to appeal against the issuing of a CPN could not be extended, the power to issue a CPN carried with it a power on the part of the police to vary or discharge a CPN at any time. In other words, even if a person who was made subject to a CPN was out of time to challenge the decision to issue it, the person could still approach the police and seek a variation or discharge of the CPN. If the police refused then it would be possible, in theory, to seek judicial review of the decision not to vary or discharge the CPN.

Remedial Action

D25.41 Where a person issued with a CPN (the defaulter) fails to comply with a requirement of the notice, the relevant local authority may take action (s. 47(1)). In taking action, the local authority may have work carried out to ensure that the failure is remedied, but only on land that is open to the air (s. 47(2)). As regards premises other than land open to the air, the local authority can issue the defaulter with a notice specifying the work the local authority intends to carry out to ensure that the failure is remedied along with the costs of that work and inviting the defaulter to consent; if consent is forthcoming, the local authority can carry out the work (s. 47(3)). If the work is carried out and the local authority issues a notice to the defaulter confirming that it has been carried out and specifying the amount it cost the local authority to carry out that work, the defaulter will be liable to pay that sum to the local authority (s. 47(6)). A person issued with such a notice may appeal to the magistrates' court within the period of 21 days beginning with the day on which the notice was issued on the ground that the amount specified in the notice is excessive (s. 47(7)). On hearing an appeal, the magistrates' court can confirm the amount or substitute a lesser amount (s. 47(8)).

Offence

D25.42 A person issued with a CPN who fails to comply with it commits an offence (s. 48(1)). On summary conviction the maximum penalty is a fine not exceeding level 4 on the standard scale, in the case of an individual, or an unlimited fine in the case of a body (s. 48(2)). A person does not commit an offence if (a) the person took all reasonable steps to comply with the notice, or (b) there is some other reasonable excuse for the failure to comply with it (s. 48(3)). As to the reasonable excuse defence in relation to CBOs, see **D25.29**. In *Stannard v CPS* [2019] EWHC 84 (Admin), [2019] 1 WLR 3229, the Divisional Court held that the existence of an automatic right of appeal against the issuing of a CPN, coupled with the possibility of bringing a claim for judicial review against the refusal of the police to vary or discharge the CPN, provided a defendant with effective remedies for a CPN that contained unreasonable terms. In these circumstances it had not been Parliament's intention to permit those charged with breaching the terms of a CPN to be able to raise the reasonableness and/or legality of the terms of the CPN at a criminal trial.

When an offender is convicted under s. 48, the magistrates' court may make whatever order it thinks appropriate for ensuring that what the CPN requires to be done is done (s. 49(1)). In particular, the magistrates' court may require the offender (a) to carry out specified work or (b) to allow specified work to be carried out by or on behalf of the local authority (s. 49(2)). An order in the terms of (b) cannot authorise the person carrying out the work to enter the offender's home without the offender's consent, although this does not prevent an offender who fails to give that consent from being in breach of the order (s. 49(4)). This means that if the court makes an order in those terms and the offender refuses to consent to the work being carried out the offender will be in breach of the order and in contempt of court. If the remedial work is carried out and notice of the costs is given to the offender, he or she will be liable to pay those costs, subject to an appeal to the magistrates' court if the sum claimed is excessive (s. 46(6) and (7)).

Seizure/Forfeiture of Items

If a justice of the peace is satisfied on information on oath that there are reasonable grounds for suspecting that an offence under s. 48 has been committed and that there is an item used in the commission of the offence on premises specified in the information, he or she may issue a warrant authorising any constable or designated person to enter the premises within 14 days from the date of issue of the warrant to seize the item (s. 51(1)). A constable or designated person may use reasonable force to execute the warrant (s. 51(3)). The item can be retained for 28 days after it is seized unless within that period criminal proceedings for a s. 48 offence (in the commission of which the item is alleged to have been used) are commenced, in which case the item can be retained until those proceedings have been finally determined (s. 51(4)). D25.43

Where a person is convicted of a s. 48 offence, the magistrates' court may order the forfeiture of any item that was used in the commission of the offence (s. 50(1)). A forfeiture order may require a person in possession of the item to hand it over as soon as reasonably practicable to a constable or to a person employed by a local authority or designated by a local authority under s. 53(1)(c) (s.50(2)). A forfeiture order may require the item to be destroyed or to be disposed of in whatever way the order specifies (s. 50(3)).

Fixed Penalty Notice

An authorised person may issue a fixed penalty notice to anyone who that person has reason to believe has committed an offence under s. 48 (s. 52(1)). The amount of the fixed penalty cannot be more than £100 (s. 52(7)). D25.44

PUBLIC SPACES PROTECTION ORDERS

The Anti-social Behaviour, Crime and Policing Act 2014 (Commencement No. 7, Saving and Transitional Provisions) Order 2014 (SI 2014 No. 2590) brought chapter 2 (public spaces protection orders) of Part 4 (community protection) of the ABCPA 2014 into force on 20 October 2014. D25.45

The Statutory Guidance addresses the regime for issuing PSPOs (at pp. 47–56) and states (at p. 48) that PSPOs 'are intended to deal with a particular nuisance or problem in a particular area that is detrimental to the local community's quality of life, by imposing conditions on the use of that area which apply to everyone. They are intended to help ensure the law-abiding majority can use and enjoy public spaces, safe from anti-social behaviour.'

Nature of PSPOs

A local authority may make a PSPO if satisfied on reasonable grounds that two conditions are met (s. 59(1)). The first condition is that either (a) activities carried on in a public place within the authority's area have had a detrimental effect on the quality of life of those in the locality, or (b) it is likely that activities will be carried on in a public place within that area and that they will have such an effect (s. 59(2)). The expression 'those in the locality' is not confined to those who regularly visit or work in the locality. Depending on the facts of the case it could extend to occasional visitors as well (*Dulgheriu v Ealing London Borough Council* [2019] EWCA Civ 1490, [2020] 1 WLR 609 at [48]). The second condition is that the effect, or likely effect, of the activities (a) is, or is likely to be, of a persistent or continuing nature, (b) is, or is likely to D25.46

be, such as to make the activities unreasonable, and (c) justifies the restrictions imposed by the notice (s. 59(3)). A public place means any place to which the public or any section of the public has access, on payment or otherwise, as of right or by virtue of express or implied permission (s. 74(1)).

A PSPO must identify the public place referred to in the first condition (the restricted area). A PSPO (a) prohibits specified things being done in the restricted area, (b) requires specified things to be done by persons carrying on specified activities in that area, or (c) does both of those things (s. 59(4)). The only prohibitions or requirements that may be imposed in a PSPO are ones that are reasonable to impose in order (a) to prevent the detrimental effect referred to in s. 59(2) from continuing, occurring or recurring, or (b) to reduce that detrimental effect or to reduce the risk of its continuance, occurrence, or recurrence (s. 59(5)). A prohibition or requirement may be framed (a) so as to apply to all persons, or only to persons in specified categories, or to all persons except those in specified categories, (b) so as to apply at all times, or only at specified times, or at all times except those specified, or (c) so as to apply in all circumstances, or only specified circumstances, or in all circumstances except those specified (s. 59(6)).

A PSPO may not have effect for a period of more than three years (s. 60(1)) but the local authority may extend that period before it expires in certain circumstances (s. 60(2)). Powers exist for the local authority to vary and discharge PSPOs (s. 61) and restrictions are also in place to ensure that certain types of restrictions cannot be imposed in PSPOs, especially in relation to prohibitions on the consumption of alcohol (s. 62) and restrictions on public rights of way over highways (s. 64). An interested person (meaning an individual who lives in the restricted area or who regularly works in or visits that area) may apply to the High Court to question the validity of the PSPO or to seek a variation of the PSPO on certain grounds as identified in s. 66.

In *Dulgheriu v Ealing London Borough Council* [2018] EWHC 1667 (Admin), [2018] 4 All ER 881, D made a PSPO around an abortion clinic to prevent pro-life supporters from congregating outside the entrance. The claimants brought a challenge to the order under the ABCPA 2014, s. 66, which was essentially by way of judicial review of the decision to issue the PSPO. The Court concluded that while the imposition of the PSPO had significantly interfered with the rights of activists under Articles 9, 10 and 11 of the ECHR, on the evidence available to D it had been entitled to conclude that the making of the order had been necessary in a democratic society to protect the privacy and dignity of the users of the clinic. The Court of Appeal dismissed an appeal against this decision ([2019] EWCA Civ 1490, [2020] 1 WLR 609).

Offence

D25.47 It is a summary offence, attracting a fine not exceeding level 3 on the standard scale, for a person without reasonable excuse (a) to do anything that the person is prohibited from doing by a PSPO or (b) to fail to comply with a requirement to which the person is subject under a PSPO (s. 67(1) and (2)). As to the meaning of 'reasonable excuse', see **D25.29**. A person does not commit an offence by failing to comply with a prohibition or requirement that the local authority did not have power to include in the PSPO (s. 67(3)) and nor does a person commit an offence by consuming alcohol in breach of a PSPO (s. 67(4)). Instead of prosecution for the s. 67(1) offence, a constable or an authorised person may issue an 'offender' with a fixed penalty notice (s. 68).

CLOSURE NOTICES AND CLOSURE ORDERS

D25.48 The ASBA 2003, Part 1 (s. 1 (closure notices), s. 2 (closure orders)), and the Crime and Courts Act 2013 (Application and Modification of Certain Enactments) Order 2014 (SI 2014 No. 1704) governed the 'crack house' closure order regime. The ASBA 2003, Part 1A (s. 11A (closure notices) and s. 11B (closure orders)), governed closure orders in relation to premises associated with persistent disorder and nuisance. Both Part 1 and Part 1A were repealed by para. 4(1) of sch. 11 to the ABCPA 2014 with effect from 20 October 2014 and replaced with a new regime in Part 3, ch. 4 (closure of premises associated with nuisance or disorder etc.), of the ABCPA 2014.

The Statutory Guidance addresses the regime for issuing closure notices and making closure orders (at pp. 57–61) and states (at p. 58) that '[t]he closure power is a fast, flexible power that can be used to protect victims and communities by quickly closing premises that are causing nuisance or disorder'.

Closure Notices

A police officer of at least the rank of inspector, or the local authority, may issue a closure notice if satisfied on reasonable grounds (a) that the use of particular premises has resulted, or (if the notice is not issued) is likely soon to result, in nuisance to members of the public, or (b) that there has been, or (if the notice is not issued) is likely soon to be, disorder near those premises associated with the use of those premises, and that the notice is necessary to prevent the nuisance or disorder from continuing, recurring or occurring (s. 76(1)). 'Premise' includes any land or other place (whether enclosed or not) and any outbuildings that are, or are used as, part of premises (s. 92(1)). A closure notice prohibits access to the premises for either 24 hours (extendable by a further 24 hours) (s. 77(1)) or, where the notice is issued by a police officer of at least the rank of superintendent or is issued by a local authority and signed by its chief executive officer or delegate, for 48 hours (s. 77(2)). A closure notice cannot prohibit access to the premises by people who habitually live on the premises or the owner of the premises (s. 76(4)). In deciding whether to issue a closure notice, the person with the power to issue the notice may take into account things that happened before 20 October 2014 and which would have given rise to the power to issue a closure notice under s. 40 of the ASBA 2003 or s. 161 of the Licensing Act 2003. **D25.49**

A closure notice must identify the premises, explain the effect of the notice, state that failure to comply with the notice is an offence, state that an application will be made for a closure order under s. 80, specify when and where the application will be heard, explain the effect of a closure order and give information about the names of, and means of contacting, persons and organisations in the area that provide advice about housing and legal matters (s. 76(5)). A closure notice may be issued only if reasonable efforts have been made to inform people who live on the premises (whether habitually or not) and any person who has control of or responsibility for the premises or who has an interest in them, that the notice is going to be issued (s. 76(6)). In *R (Qin) v Metropolitan Police Commissioner* [2017] EWHC 2750 (Admin), the Divisional Court held that before issuing a closure notice the police were not obliged to consult those who are likely to be affected by the notice. Section 76(6) imposes an obligation on the police to make reasonable efforts to inform certain people that a closure notice is to be issued but it does not oblige the police to consult with those people before issuing the notice. On the facts of *Qin*, there had been substantial compliance with s. 76(6) in any event.

If, during the effective period of the closure notice, the relevant police officer or the local authority is no longer satisfied that either of the two conditions necessary for the issuing of the notice is met, then the officer or authority must issue a cancellation notice (cancelling the closure notice) or a variation notice (altering the closure notice so that it does not apply to a part of the premises) (s. 78(1) to (3)). Section 79 sets out the provisions governing the service of closure notices on those affected by them.

Closure Orders

Whenever a closure notice has been issued and not cancelled, an application must be made to a magistrates' court for a closure order (s. 80(1)). The application must be heard not later than 48 hours after service of the closure notice (s. 80(3)). The court may make a closure order if it is satisfied (a) that a person has engaged, or (if the order is not made) is likely to engage, in **D25.50** disorderly, offensive or criminal behaviour on the premises, (b) that the use of the premises has resulted, or (if the order is not made) is likely to result, in serious nuisance to members of the public, or (c) that there has been, or (if the order is not made) is likely to be, disorder near those premises associated with the use of those premises, and that the order is necessary to prevent the behaviour, nuisance or disorder from continuing, recurring or occurring (s. 80(5)). 'Criminal behaviour' means behaviour that constitutes a criminal offence (s. 92(1)). 'Offensive behaviour' means behaviour by a person that causes or is likely to cause harassment, alarm or distress to one or more persons not of the same household as that person (s. 92(1)). A court deciding whether to make a closure order may take into account things that happened before 20 October 2014 and which would have given rise to the power to make an order under s. 2 or s. 11B of the ASBA 2003.

In *R (Qin) v Metropolitan Police Commissioner* [2017] EWHC 2750 (Admin) D issued closure notices under s. 76 in relation to a number of massage parlours, which the police believed were operating as brothels. The district judge refused to make closure orders because the police had failed to prove the alleged criminal conduct to the appropriate standard and also refused to order compensation or costs in favour of the claimants. They sought to challenge those decisions by judicial review and an appeal by way of case stated. One of the issues the Divisional Court had to consider was whether, and if so to what extent, non-compliance on the part of the police with the procedural requirements for issuing a closure notice should affect the exercise of the discretion to grant compensation and costs when the lower court refuses to make a closure order. The Court held (at [54]) that in an application for a closure order the magistrates should not generally consider the validity of the closure notice. On a prosecution for breaching the terms of the closure notice the position will be different, however, because a defendant would be entitled to raise the invalidity of the notice in the defence (see **D25.57**). It followed that any shortcomings in the closure notice should not affect the jurisdiction of the magistrates to make a closure order. The issuing of the closure notice merely triggers the jurisdiction to make a closure order, but the validity of the notice is generally not relevant to the exercise of that jurisdiction (at [57]) and so the magistrates should not delay considering whether to make a closure order while those affected by the closure notice pursue a challenge to it by way of judicial review.

Burden of Proof

D25.51 As with closure orders under the ASBA 2003, the burden of proof is on the applicant (*R (Cleary) v Highbury Corner Magistrates' Court* [2006] EWHC 1869 (Admin), [2007] 1 All ER 270). The standard of proof is the normal civil standard. In *Chief Constable of Merseyside Police v Harrison* [2006] EWHC 1106 (Admin), [2007] QB 79 the High Court distinguished closure orders from CRASBOs, which required a criminal standard of proof, describing them as 'less adverse to the interests' of individuals than CRASBOs. However, in *Cleary* (at [7]), the Court emphasised that, since a closure order may dispossess a person from his or her home, the ECHR, Article 8, is of central importance, and a court must be satisfied that it is necessary and proportionate to make such an order. The civil standard of proof is plainly coloured by these considerations. It should be borne in mind, however, that Article 8 does not require the police to have considered less draconian measures before seeking a closure order (*Leary v Chief Constable of West Midlands* [2012] EWHC 639 (Admin)), but in deciding whether it would be proportionate to make a closure order the existence of less restrictive statutory powers available to the local authority could be relevant, although the justice were not required of their own motion to identify what those powers were in circumstances where neither party had drawn them to their attention (*Taylor v Solihull Metropolitan Borough Council* [2020] EWHC 412 (Admin) at [49]).

Application Procedure

D25.52 An application for a closure order is a civil matter and, as with civil injunction hearings in the youth court, hearsay is admissible. Consequently, the Civil Evidence Act 1995 and the

Magistrates' Courts (Hearsay Evidence in Civil Proceedings) Rules 1999 apply. In *R (Cleary) v Highbury Corner Magistrates' Court* [2006] EWHC 1869 (Admin), [2007] 1 All ER 270 the Divisional Court emphasised the importance of a fair hearing in compliance with the ECHR, Article 6, recognising that the first hearing held within 48 hours may well not be effective in order to achieve that aim. The evidence relied upon by the police ought to be served before the first hearing and, if it is not fully served by then, the Court made plain that fairness requires that it is served well in advance of an adjourned hearing.

The Court in *Cleary* also reiterated the dangers of relying upon hearsay evidence, identified in *Moat Housing Group-South Ltd v Harris* [2005] EWCA Civ 287, [2006] QB 606, and pointed out that the statutory timetable in the ASBA 2003 (as with the timetable in s. 80 of the ABCPA 2014) was at odds with the usual entitlement to 21 days' notice of reliance on hearsay under the Magistrates' Courts (Hearsay Evidence in Civil Proceedings) Rules 1999. The Rules do provide for a shortening of that notice period but they certainly could not be complied with in the case of the first hearing. The Court suggested that, if hearsay evidence was to be relied upon, the police should make any application to reduce the notice period at the first hearing.

The magistrates' court may adjourn the hearing of an application for a closure order for a maximum of 14 days to enable those who would be affected by the making of a closure order to show that such an order should not be made (s. 81(3)). In circumstances where an adjournment for that purpose is granted, the court may order that the closure notice remains in force until the final hearing (s. 81(4)).

Duration

The period of a closure order must not exceed three months (s. 80(6)). A closure order may prohibit access to the premises by anyone, at any time and in any circumstances (s. 80(7)). Further, a closure order may be made in respect of the whole or any part of the premises and may include provision about access to a part of the building or structure of which the premises form part (s. 80(8)). **D25.53**

Where a closure order is made, an application for an extension of the order may be made at any time before the order is due to expire (s. 82(1)). A police officer or local authority may make an application for an extension only if satisfied on reasonable grounds that it is necessary for the period of the order to be extended to prevent the occurrence, recurrence or continuance of (a) disorderly, offensive or criminal behaviour on the premises, (b) serious nuisance to members of the public resulting from the use of the premises, or (c) disorder near the premises associated with the use of the premises, and if also satisfied that either the police (where the applicant is the local authority) or the local authority (where the applicant is a police officer) has been consulted about the intention to make an application (s. 82(3)). For the proper approach to similar extensions under Part 1 of the ASBA 2003, see *R (Smith) v Crown Court at Snaresbrook* [2008] EWHC 1282 (Admin), [2009] 1 All ER 547. In *R (Longato) v Camberwell Green Magistrates' Court* [2009] EWHC 691 (Admin), the High Court held that a defendant had a right to be on notice of a hearing to extend an order and that such notice is required by the MCA 1980, s. 55(3), and the Magistrates' Courts Rules 1981, r. 99. A failure to do so was an irregularity and a real injustice and the claimant was entitled to have the order quashed by way of judicial review.

Appeal

Under the ABCPA 2014, s. 84, an appeal to the Crown Court lies against a decision of a magistrates' court (a) to make or not to make a closure order, (b) to extend or not to extend a disclosure order, and (c) not to order (under s. 81) the continuation in force of the closure notice issued by a constable (s. 84(1) to (3)). An appeal must be made within 21 days beginning with the date of the decision to which it relates (s. 84(5)). On an appeal, the Crown Court may make whatever order it thinks appropriate (s. 84(6)). **D25.54**

Such appeals are 'as of right' and by way of full rehearing, do not require permission and, as such, do not require the appellant to specify the grounds of appeal. In *R (Errington) v Metropolitan Police Authority* [2006] EWHC 1155 (Admin), Collins J said that Crown Courts should give such appeals priority and hear them in a matter of days. In *Hampshire Police Authority v Smith* [2009] EWHC 174 (Admin), [2010] 4 All ER 316 the Divisional Court held that the appeal notice must be issued within 21 days, not that it must be heard within that period. The primary issue on appeal was whether the time for service of the notice could be extended in accordance with r. 7(5) of the Crown Court Rules 1982. The Court held that r. 7(5) did not apply to a notice of appeal issued under the ASBA 2003, s. 6(2). There was a clear and unqualified statutory time-limit which provided an appellant with a significant period of time in which to issue a notice of appeal and the statute made no provision for extension. In *R (Longato) v Camberwell Green Magistrates' Court* [2009] EWHC 691 (Admin) it was held that Parliament had intentionally not given a general power to magistrates to reopen hearings in civil cases (MCA 1980, s. 142 did not apply) and no such power existed at common law.

Discharge

D25.55 Just as a closure order can be extended before it expires, so an application can be made for it to be discharged before it expires (s. 83(1)). The magistrates' court may not make an order discharging the closure order unless satisfied that the closure order is no longer necessary to prevent the occurrence, recurrence or continuance of (a) disorderly, offensive or criminal behaviour on the premises, (b) serious nuisance to members of the public resulting from the use of the premises, or (c) disorder near the premises associated with the use of the premises (s. 83(7)).

Powers of Entry

D25.56 An 'authorised person' may enter premises in respect of which a closure order is in force and do anything necessary to secure the premises against entry (s. 85(1)); a person may be authorised for this purpose, in the case of a closure order made on an application by the police, by the chief officer of police for the area or, in the case of a closure order made on a local authority application, by that authority (s. 85(2)). Such a person may use reasonable force to achieve his or her objectives under s. 85(1) (s. 85(3)).

Offences

D25.57 A person who, without reasonable excuse, remains on or enters premises in contravention of a closure notice (including a notice continued in force under s. 81) commits an offence (s. 86(1)). A person who, without reasonable excuse, remains on or enters premises in contravention of a closure order also commits an offence (s. 86(2)). A person who, without reasonable excuse, obstructs a person acting under s. 79 (service of closure notices) or s. 85(1) (entering or securing premises subject to a closure order) also commits an offence (s. 86(3)). For the meaning of 'reasonable excuse' in the context of the offence of breaching a CBO, see **D25.29**. In *R (Errington) v Metropolitan Police Authority* [2006] EWHC 1155 (Admin), Collins J expressed the view (at [23]) that an invalid notice may afford a defence to any criminal charge under parts 1 and 1A of the ASBA 2003. See, to similar effect, *R (Qin) v Metropolitan Police Commissioner* [2017] EWHC 2750 (Admin), but note also the opposite view in *Stannard v CPS* [2019] EWHC 84 (Admin), [2019] 1 WLR 3229, discussed at **D25.42**.

A person who is convicted under s. 86(1) or (3) is liable to imprisonment for a period not exceeding three months and/or a fine (s. 86(4)). A person who is convicted under s. 86(2) is liable to imprisonment for a period not exceeding six months and/or a fine (s. 86(5)).

SERIOUS CRIME PREVENTION ORDERS

D25.58 The SCA 2007, Part 1, introduced the serious crime prevention order (SCPO). These orders are civil orders available upon application to the High Court (SCA 2007, s. 1) and upon conviction for a 'serious offence' in the Crown Court (s. 19). They are designed to protect the public by preventing, restricting or disrupting involvement in serious crime. SCPOs can include extensive restrictions and requirements (s. 5). An order may endure for a period of up to five years (s. 16). Prohibitions, restrictions and requirements can also be placed on bodies corporate, partnerships and unincorporated associations (s. 5(3)). The SCA 2007 provides for general safeguards (ss. 6 to 10) as well as information safeguards (ss. 11 to 15).

Powers of the High Court

In order to impose a SCPO, the High Court (a) must be satisfied (see **D25.67** as to standard of proof) that a person ('the respondent') has been involved in serious crime (whether in England and Wales or elsewhere); and (b) must have reasonable grounds to believe that the order would protect the public by preventing, restricting or disrupting involvement by the person in serious crime in England and Wales (SCA 2007, s. 1(1)(a) and (b)). When the court is considering such an order, it is concerned with future risk. There must be a real, or significant risk (not a bare possibility) that the defendant will commit further serious offences (*Hancox* [2010] EWCA Crim 102, [2010] 4 All ER 537 at [9]). **D25.59**

An order under s. 1 may contain such prohibitions, restrictions or requirements, and such other terms, as the court considers appropriate for the purpose of protecting the public by preventing, restricting or disrupting involvement by the person concerned in serious crime in England and Wales (s. 1(3)). In *Hancox* the Court of Appeal indicated that, although not couched in terms of necessity, this phrase is no different in practice. Hughes LJ said (at [10]) 'that it is not enough that the order *may* have some public benefit in preventing, restricting or disrupting involvement by the defendant in serious crime; the interference which it will create with the defendant's freedom of action must be justified by the benefit; the provisions of the order must be commensurate with the risk'. Further, his lordship said that much of what the Court of Appeal said in relation to ASBOs in *Boness* [2005] EWCA Crim 2395, [2006] 1 Cr App R (S) 120 (690) (see **D25.24**) applies to SCPOs, in particular the test of proportionality, the emphasis on the order being practicable and enforceable, the test of precision and certainty and the fact that the order is preventative not punitive. See *Silk* [2010] EWCA Crim 3140 for an example of a requirement that the Court of Appeal found was too widely framed and consequently capable of being unjust or leading to unintended breaches. In *Strong* [2017] EWCA Crim 999, the Court of Appeal considered the decision in *Hancox* and concluded that on the facts of that case the restrictions on the appellant's ownership of electronic communication devices were reasonable and proportionate. Further, in *McGrath* [2017] EWCA Crim 1945, the Court of Appeal emphasised that the terms of a SCPO 'must be practical, enforceable and precise . . . as well as being proportionate and must be restricted to those which are absolutely necessary' (at [12]).

The powers of the court in respect of an order under s. 1 are subject to the safeguards set out in ss. 6 to 15 (s. 1(4): see **D25.62** for the safeguards).

Involvement in Serious Crime A person is treated as 'involved in serious crime' in any of three circumstances. First, if the person has a conviction for a serious offence (SCA 2007, s. 2(1)(a) and (2)(a)). A list of serious offences is set out in sch. 1, part 1, to the Act and includes drug trafficking, drug importation, people trafficking, arms trafficking, prostitution and child sex, money laundering, fraud, public revenue offences, blackmail, armed robbery, bribery, copyright offences, environmental offences and certain terrorism offences. An offence can be treated as if it were specified in sch. 1 if, in the particular circumstances of the case, the court considers it to be sufficiently serious to be so treated (s. 2(2)(b)), as to which, see *Brown* [2016] EWCA Crim 1437. In *Batchelor* [2010] EWCA Crim 1025, [2011] 1 Cr App R (S) 25 (169) the Court of Appeal said that 'serious crime' is not restricted to offences committed by multiple offenders in the context of organised crime or offences committed with a high degree of sophistication: there is nothing in the Act which suggests that the restrictions cannot be applied to a single offender (in this case a man convicted of numerous offences of dishonesty). The single test is whether **D25.60**

there are reasonable grounds to believe that the order would prevent, restrict or disrupt the offender's involvement in serious crime. See also *Mangham* [2012] EWCA Crim 973, [2013] 1 Cr App R (S) 11 (62).

Secondly, a person can be involved in serious crime if he or she has facilitated the commission by another person of such an offence (s. 2(1)(b)).

Thirdly, a person is involved if 'he has conducted himself in a way that was likely to facilitate the commission by himself or another person of a serious offence in England and Wales (whether or not such an offence was committed)' (s. 2(1)(c)). In applying s. 2(1)(c), the court must ignore acts that the respondent can show to be reasonable and, subject to that exception, it must also ignore the respondent's intention or any other aspect of mental state at the time the offence was committed (s. 4(2) and (3)).

Criminal conduct which takes place outside the jurisdiction may be taken into account (ss. 1(1)(a) and 2(4) and (5)).

D25.61 **Prohibitions, Restrictions and Requirements** Non-exhaustive examples of the type of provision that may be made by a SCPO are contained in the SCA 2007, s. 5. A SCPO may include, *inter alia*, prohibitions or restrictions on an individual's financial dealings, working arrangements, access to premises (including the individual's dwelling) and travel arrangements. It may also regulate the means by which an individual communicates or associates with others, and may require the individual to answer certain questions and produce certain documents, for example, in relation to financial, property or business dealings.

Section 5A (verification and disclosure of information) provides that where information is provided to a law enforcement officer in response to an information requirement imposed by a SCPO, the law enforcement officer may, for the purpose of checking the accuracy of the information or discovering the true position, disclose the information to any person who the officer reasonably believes may be able to contribute to doing either of those things (s. 5A(2)). Any other person may disclose information to the law enforcement officer or the person referred to in s. 5A(2) for the purpose of contributing to doing either of the things mentioned in s. 5A(2). The law enforcement officer may also disclose this information for the purpose of (a) the prevention, detection, investigation or prosecution of criminal offences, whether in the UK or elsewhere, or (b) the prevention, detection or investigation of conduct for which penalties other than criminal penalties are provided under the law of any part of the UK or of any country or territory outside the UK (s. 5A(4)).

D25.62 **Safeguards** The SCA 2007 provides general safeguards in relation to the making of SCPOs in ss. 6 to 10.

By s. 6, individuals under the age of 18 may not be the subject of an order. By s. 8, an order whether in the Crown Court or High Court may be made only on an application by the DPP or the Director of the SFO. The High Court must, on an application by a third party, give that person an opportunity to make representations in the proceedings about the decision it is making, if the making, varying or discharging of an order (or a decision not to vary or discharge an order) would be likely to have a significant adverse effect on that person (s. 9(1) to (3)); a similar duty applies to the Crown Court under s. 9(4) but this does not extend to the discharge of a SCPO (it has no power to discharge). A court which is considering an appeal against an order must also, on application by a person, give that person an opportunity to make such representations, if that person was given an opportunity to make representations in the proceedings which are the subject of the appeal (s. 9(5)).

A person is bound by an order (or a variation of an order) if the person is represented at the proceedings at which the order (or the variation) is made or if a notice setting out the terms of the order has been served (s. 10).

Information safeguards are created by ss. 11 to 15. A person may not be required by a SCPO to answer questions, or provide information, orally (s. 11). An order cannot override legal professional privilege, except it does not prevent an order that requires a lawyer to provide the name and address of one of his or her clients (s. 12).

Powers of the Crown Court

The Crown Court has a power to impose a SCPO where a person has been convicted of a serious offence in England and Wales either in the Crown Court or in a case where a magistrates' court has committed the matter for sentence (SCA 2007, s. 19(1)). The Crown Court may impose an order on the same basis as the High Court (see **D25.59**). It can make an order in addition to sentencing the person in relation to the offence or conditionally discharging the person (s. 19(7)). In accordance with s. 19(6), such an order is also subject to the safeguards in ss. 6 to 15 (see **D25.62**). Proceedings in relation to SCPOs can be adjourned even after sentencing (s. 36(3)(b)). **D25.63**

In *Seale* [2014] EWCA Crim 650, the Court of Appeal emphasised (at [12]) that SCPOs 'can only be made for the statutory purpose: they are designed to be preventative rather than punitive; they must be necessary and proportionate; and they must be enforceable'. In *Hall* [2014] EWCA Crim 2046, [2015] 1 Cr App R (S) 16 (127), the defendants argued that, because they had been sentenced to long terms of imprisonment and because the conditions to be imposed on their licences following their release would last longer than the terms of any SCPO, it was unnecessary for such an order to be made. The Court of Appeal rejected this argument. In the Court's view (at [32]), Parliament must have intended that the regime under Part 1 of the SCA 2007 'added to the licence regime otherwise it would not have been enacted'.

Duration and Discharge

A SCPO may not be in force for more than five years from the date it is specified to come into force, although different provisions of the order can come into force at different times (s. 16(1) to (4)). The court is not prevented from making a new order to the same or similar effect, either after an order or any of its provisions has expired or in anticipation of an earlier order or provision ceasing to be in force (s. 16(5) and (6)), but if the court makes a SCPO when there is already an existing SCPO in force, the court must discharge the earlier order (s. 19(2A)). **D25.64**

The High Court, unlike the Crown Court, also has the power, on application, to discharge an order in certain circumstances (s. 18).

Variation

The High Court has the power, on application, to vary an order, if it has reasonable grounds to believe that such a variation would protect the public by preventing, restricting or disrupting involvement by the person in serious crime in England and Wales (s. 17(1)). An application to vary (which includes a power to extend the order, subject to the overriding five-year limit) may be made by the authority which applied for the original order (s. 17(3)(a)). The subject of the order may apply to vary only if there has been a change of circumstances (s. 17(3)(b)(i) and (4)). A person significantly adversely affected by the order may apply to vary only if the person has had or applied to have an opportunity to make representations in earlier proceedings and there has been a change of circumstances, or if the person has not so applied but it was reasonable not to have done so (s. 17(3)(b)(ii), (5), (6) and (7)); such a person cannot make an application for the order to be more onerous (s. 17(5)(c)). **D25.65**

The Crown Court also has power, on application, to vary an order already in existence when it is dealing with a person convicted of a serious crime (SCA 2007, s. 20(2)). Section 21 gives it a similar power of variation when it is dealing with a person convicted of an offence under s. 25 (failing to comply with a SCPO). Instead of varying the existing SCPO, the Crown Court can also discharge the existing SCPO and replace it with a new order. Further, the Crown Court may vary an order made or varied by the High Court (s. 22(1)) and the High Court may vary or discharge an order made or varied by the Crown Court (s. 22(2)). A decision by the Crown Court not to make or vary an order under s. 19 does not prevent a subsequent application to the High Court to make or vary an order in relation to the same offence (s. 22(4)).

As to the interrelationship between orders made in the High Court and the Crown Court, see s. 22.

Extension

D25.66 Section 22E applies where a person subject to a SCPO is charged with a serious offence or an offence under s. 25 of failing to comply with a SCPO (s. 22E(1)). The relevant applicant authority may make an application under s. 22E to the Crown Court for it to vary the SCPO so that it continues in effect until one of four events occur (if the order would otherwise cease to have effect before then) (s. 22E(3)). Those four events are (a) following the person's conviction of the new offence, (i) the SCPO is varied under s. 20 or 21, (ii) a new SCPO is made under s. 19 or 21, or (iii) the court deals with the person for the offence without varying the SCPO or making a new one, (b) the person is acquitted of the offence, (c) the charge is withdrawn, or (d) proceedings in respect of the charge are discontinued or an order is made for the charge to lie on the file (s. 22E(4)). An order under s. 22E can be made only if the SCPO is still in force and the court has reasonable grounds for believing that the order would protect the public by preventing, restricting or disrupting involvement by the person in serious crime (s. 22E(5)).

Standard of Proof

D25.67 Proceedings in the High Court and the Crown Court are civil proceedings (SCA 2007, ss. 35 and 36). These sections also make plain that the standard of proof is the civil standard.

Application Procedure

D25.68 The Civil Procedure Rules 1998 (SI 1998 No. 3132), Part 77, makes provision for applications in the High Court for or relating to SCPOs.

The Crown Court, when exercising its jurisdiction in relation to SCPOs, is a criminal court for the purposes of procedure rules and practice directions (s. 36(4)). CrimPR Part 31 applies to SCPOs by virtue of r. 31.1 (see Supplement, **R31.1** *et seq*.).

Appeals

D25.69 An appeal from a High Court decision relating to a SCPO is to the Court of Appeal (SCA 2007, s. 23). Section 24 makes provision for appeals from the Crown Court; such appeals require the leave of the Court of Appeal or to be certified fit for appeal by the sentencing judge. On an appeal to the Court of Appeal from a decision of the Crown Court to make a SCPO pursuant to the SCA 2007, s. 19, the powers of the Court of Appeal are set out in the Serious Crime Act 2007 (Appeals under Section 24) Order 2008 (SI 2008 No. 1863). By art. 4(1), the Court of Appeal is limited to a review of the decision of the Crown Court unless it considers that it would be in the interests of justice to hold a rehearing. The Court of Appeal will allow an appeal in such circumstances where the decision of the Crown Court was either wrong or unjust because of a serious procedural or other irregularity that occurred in the Crown Court (art. 4(2)).

Criminal Offences

D25.70 A failure, without reasonable excuse, to comply with a SCPO is an either-way offence (SCA 2007, *s*. 25). A person guilty of such an offence is liable, on summary conviction, to imprisonment for a term not exceeding six months and/or an unlimited fine and, on conviction on indictment, to imprisonment for a term not exceeding five years and/or a fine (s. 25(1) and (2) and sch. 13, para. 4). *Koli* [2012] EWCA Crim 1869, [2013] 1 Cr App R (S) 6 (39), described by the Court of Appeal as 'a ground-breaking case', was the first to consider the appropriate sentence for breach of a SCPO. The Court set out the following as relevant factors:

(a) the lapse of time between the imposition of the original order and the date of the breach;
(b) any history of non-compliance and the issue as to whether non-compliance has been repeated and has come in the face of warnings and requests for information;
(c) whether the non-compliance was inadvertent or deliberate;
(d) whether the breach was related to the commission of further serious offences and might lead to the conclusion that the failure to comply added to the risk that the particular subject of the order was likely to commit further offences; and
(e) any harm caused by non-compliance for breach.

On the particular facts, the concurrent two-year sentences of imprisonment for two convictions for failure to notify in relation to possession of mobile phones and a motor vehicle, following a trial, were reduced to 12 months concurrent. The Court held that recall to prison following breach of D's licence conditions (mirroring the terms of his SCPO) relating to the original sentence for money laundering offences did not obviate the need for a criminal court to impose a punishment upon breach of a SCPO imposed at the time of the original sentence. See also *Place* [2017] EWCA Crim 884.

The court before which a person is convicted of an offence under s. 25 may also order the forfeiture of anything in the person's possession at the time of the offence which the court considers to have been involved in the offence (s. 26). Where a company, partnership, etc. has been convicted of this offence, the DPP or the Director of the SFO may, if it is considered to be in the public interest, petition for its winding up under the Insolvency Act 1986 (s. 27).

VIOLENT OFFENDER ORDERS

The CJIA 2008, Part 7, introduced another behaviour order, the violent offender order (VOO), which can be applied for by a chief officer of police by way of complaint in a magistrates' court (s. 100). The person to whom an application relates must be given notice of any such application and of the hearing a reasonable time before the hearing (s. 105). The Magistrates' Courts (Violent Offender Orders) Rules 2009 (SI 2009 No. 2197) require that an application for a VOO must be in the form set out in sch. 1. *A Guide to Violent Offender Orders* (2009) has been published by the Home Office. **D25.71**

Statutory Test

A VOO can be made only if the court is satisfied that the person is a 'qualifying offender' *and* that the person has since the relevant conviction acted in such a way as to make it necessary to make a VOO for the purpose of protecting the public from the risk of serious violent harm (CJIA 2008, s. 101(3)). In deciding whether an order is necessary, the court is specifically required by s. 101(4) to have regard to whether the person would be subject to any other measure which operated to protect the public. **D25.72**

The risk of serious violent harm may be to the public in general or specified members of it and must be a *current* risk of serious physical or psychological harm caused by that person committing one or more specified offences (s. 98(2): see D25.73 for the meaning of 'specified offence'). A VOO made under s. 101 must be in the form set out in sch. 2 to the Magistrates' Courts (Violent Offender Orders) Rules 2009.

Qualifying Offenders

A 'qualifying offender' means a person who is aged 18 or over who comes within the CJIA 2008, s. 99(2) *or* (4). A person comes within s. 99(2) if convicted of a specified offence, regardless of whether the conviction occurred before or after the commencement of Part 7; the person must **D25.73** also have either received a custodial sentence of at least 12 months for that offence or received a hospital order (with or without a restriction order). A person also comes within s. 99(2) if (i) the person has been found not guilty of a specified offence by reason of insanity *and* received a hospital order (with or without a restriction order) or a supervision order (s. 99(2)(b) and (3)) or (ii) if the person has been found to have been under a disability and to have done the act charged in relation to a specified offence *and* has received a hospital order (with or without a restriction order) or a supervision order (s. 99(2)(c) and (3)).

The term 'specified offence' is defined in s. 98(3) to mean manslaughter, soliciting murder, wounding with intent to cause grievous bodily harm, malicious wounding, attempted murder, conspiracy to murder and relevant service offences (specified at s. 98(4)).

Under s. 99(4), a person could still qualify for a VOO if the conviction for the equivalent of a specified offence was obtained outside England and Wales, i.e. the offence would have to have constituted an offence in the country in question as well as have constituted a specified offence or an offence of murder if it had been committed in England and Wales (a 'relevant offence') (s. 99(5)). An offence is an act punishable under the law of the particular country, however it is described in that law (s. 99(6)). Additionally, just as with convictions in England and Wales, the offender would either have to have received a sentence of imprisonment of at least 12 months or the equivalent of a hospital order (s. 99(4)(a)) or the court would have had to have made the equivalent findings and disposals in relation to insanity and fitness to plead (s. 99(4)(b) and (c)). Rule 4 of the Magistrates' Courts (Violent Offender Orders) Rules 2009 provides that a defendant who wishes to serve a notice under s. 99(7) (denying that an act done outside England and Wales would have constituted a specified offence if it had been done in England and Wales) must do so no later than three days before the hearing date for the application under s. 100.

Terms of a VOO

D25.74 A qualifying offender may be made subject to such prohibitions, restrictions or conditions (as authorised by the CJIA 2008, s. 102), 'as the court making the order considers necessary for the purpose of protecting the public from the risk of serious violent harm caused by the offender' (s. 98(1)(a)). Section 102(1) authorises prohibitions, etc. that prevent the offender from going to a particular place or premises (the person can be prevented altogether or have specified access); from attending a specified event (e.g., a wedding or a football match); from having any contact or a specified description of contact with an individual (a person could therefore, for example, be prohibited from face-to-face contact but not be restricted in relation to telephone contact). The Secretary of State has power to amend s. 102(1) by order.

Any of the provisions, etc. in a VOO may also relate to conduct in Scotland or Northern Ireland (s. 102(2)). Presumably a court would have to find it necessary for a prohibition, etc. to so extend and so specify.

Duration

D25.75 A VOO cannot be made so as to come into force when a person is in custody for any offence, is on licence or is subject to a hospital order or a supervision order (CJIA 2008, s. 101(5)). VOOs can be made for a period of not less than two years and not more than five years, unless renewed or discharged (s. 98(1)(b)). The minimum term of a VOO is two years from the date it came into force, unless discharged. Either the offender or the chief officer of police that applied for the VOO (or, if different, the chief officer of police for the area in which the offender resides or is intending to reside) can apply to the appropriate court to vary, renew or discharge a VOO (s. 103). An order can be renewed for a period of up to five years (s. 103(1)(b)). Reading s. 98(1)(b) together with s. 103(1)(b) suggests that a VOO is indefinitely renewable, as long as each period of renewal is for no more than five years. However, before a court can renew or vary so as to impose *additional* prohibitions etc., it must be satisfied of the necessity in accordance with s.

103(5). Each prohibition etc. must be necessary for the purpose specified and can only be of a kind authorised by s. 102.

VOOs are available on an interim basis (IVOOs) (s. 104) if it appears to the court that the person to whom the application relates is a qualifying offender and that it would be likely to make a VOO if it was determining the full application and that it is 'desirable' to act before the full application is heard 'with a view to securing the immediate protection of the public from the risk of serious violent harm caused by P' (s. 103(3)). There is no specific limit on the duration of an IVOO but it will have effect 'only for such period as is specified in the order' (s. 104(6)(a)).

Section 104(8) makes the VOO variation and discharge powers in s. 103 applicable to IVOOs, but not the renewal powers. An application for an IVOO must be in the form set out in sch. 1 to the Magistrates' Courts (Violent Offender Orders) Rules 2009 (see r. 2) and an IVOO must be in the form set out in sch. 3. Under r. 3, an application for the variation, discharge or renewal of a VOO (or an IVOO) must be made in writing and must specify the reason why the applicant believes the court should vary, discharge or renew the order, as the case may be.

Notification Requirements

Any person subject to a VOO will also be subject to complex notification requirements, broadly similar to the requirements which apply to offenders convicted of sex offences (CJIA 2008, ss. 107 to 122). These requirements are automatic once a VOO or IVOO is in force (s. 107(1)), although those subject to IVOOs are not subject to the periodic notification requirements in s. 110. See the Criminal Justice and Immigration Act 2008 (Violent Offender Orders) (Notification Requirements) Regulations 2009 (SI 2009 No. 2019). **D25.76**

Appeals

A person subject to a VOO or an IVOO can appeal against the making of the order to the Crown Court (CJIA 2008, s. 106(1)). Such a person can also appeal to the Crown Court against the making or refusal to make an order under s. 103 (namely, the variation, renewal or discharge of a VOO) (s. 106(2)). As s. 103 applies in relation to the variation or discharge of an IVOO (s. 104(8)), an appeal will also lie to the Crown Court against the variation or discharge, or refusal to vary or discharge, an IVOO. **D25.77**

The Crown Court has wide powers on appeal. It can make such orders as may be necessary to give effect to its determination as well as such incidental or consequential orders as appear to it to be just (s. 106(3)). Any order made by the Crown Court on appeal from a magistrates' court is treated, for the purposes of any application to vary, renew or discharge, as an order of the magistrates' court from which the appeal was brought (s. 106(4)).

Criminal Offences

There are three types of offences provided for by the CJIA 2008, s. 113, all of which attract the same penalty. A failure, without reasonable excuse, to comply with any prohibition, restriction or condition contained in a VOO or failure, without reasonable excuse, to comply with various notification requirements is an either-way offence as is knowingly providing false information in relation to notification requirements (s. 113(1) to (3)). **D25.78**

A person guilty of any of these offences is liable, on summary conviction, to imprisonment for a term not exceeding six months and/or an unlimited fine and, on conviction on indictment, to imprisonment for a term not exceeding five years and/or a fine (s. 113(7) and sch. 27, para. 31).

SLAVERY AND TRAFFICKING RISK ORDERS

The Modern Slavery Act 2015, ss. 23 to 29, enable a magistrates' court to make a slavery and trafficking risk order (STRO) against a person (the defendant) on an application by a chief **D25.79** officer of police, an immigration officer, the Director of the NCA or the Gangmasters and Labour Abuse Authority (s. 23(1)). The court may make such an order only if it is satisfied to the civil standard that the defendant has acted in a way which means that (a) there is a risk that the defendant will commit a slavery or human trafficking offence, as listed in sch. 1 to the 2015 Act, and (b) it is necessary to make the STRO for the purpose of protecting persons generally, or particular persons, from the physical or psychological harm which would be likely to occur if the defendant committed such an offence (s. 23(2)).

Procedure

D25.80 An application under s. 23(1) should be made by complaint (s. 23(4)). Where the defendant is under 18, the complaint should be made to the youth court and that court rather than the magistrates' court will determine the application (s. 23(5)). In determining the application, the court may take into account acts of the defendant which occurred before s. 23 came into force (s. 23(8)).

Nature and Effect of Order

D25.81 A STRO prohibits the defendant from doing anything described in the order (s. 24(1)). The order may contain only those prohibitions which the court is satisfied are necessary for the purpose of protecting persons generally, or particular persons, from the physical or psychological harm which would be likely to occur if the defendant committed a slavery or human trafficking offence (s. 24(2)). The prohibitions in the order may prevent the defendant from doing things in any part of the world (s. 24(3)). A prohibition may have effect for a fixed period of at least two years or may have effect until further order (s. 24(4)) and, where an order contains more than one prohibition, individual prohibitions may last for differing lengths of time (s. 24(5)). Where the order contains a prohibition on foreign travel, as defined in s. 25(2), that prohibition must be for a fixed period of not more than five years (s. 25(1)) but may be extended in five-yearly increments if necessary (s. 27). Where the prohibition on foreign travel precludes the defendant from travelling to *any* country outside the UK, the STRO must require the defendant to surrender all passports at a police station (s. 25(4)). Thus, STROs may, in specified circumstances, contain requirements as well as or in addition to prohibitions. By virtue of s. 26, the court making the order may require the defendant to notify certain 'relevant matters' to a person specified in the order. These relevant matters include the defendant's name and address (s. 26(4)). The Secretary of State is required to issue guidance on the use of the powers in ss. 23 to 29 (s. 33). The current guidance was issued in April 2017.

Variation, Renewal, Discharge and Appeal

D25.82 Either the applicant or the defendant may make a complaint to the court seeking the variation, renewal or discharge of the STRO (s. 27). In addition, a defendant may appeal to the Crown Court against the making of a STRO and also against the making of an order under s. 27, or the refusal to make such an order (s. 28).

Offence

D25.83 person who, without reasonable excuse, does anything that is prohibited by a STRO, or fails to do anything required by a STRO, commits an offence. The maximum sentence on conviction on indictment is a term of imprisonment not exceeding five years; on summary conviction, the maximum is six months' imprisonment and/or a fine (s. 30).

KNIFE CRIME PREVENTION ORDERS

D25.84 Part 2 of the Offensive Weapons Act 2019 introduced the knife crime prevention order (KCPO), although those provisions are not yet in force nationwide. In March 2020, the government announced that from 6 April 2020 the provisions will be piloted in certain areas for a period of 14 months. By virtue of s. 70(1) the Act comes into force on such day as the Secretary of State may by regulations appoint subject to s. 31(2), (3) and (5). Section 31(1) provides that the Secretary of State may exercise the power in s. 70(1) so as to bring all the provisions of Part 2 into force for all purposes and in relation to the whole of England and Wales only if the conditions in subsections (2) and (3) are met, and those conditions require the Secretary of State to pilot the introduction of KCPOs in relation to one or more specified areas in England and Wales. It follows that before Part 2 can be brought into force nationwide, the Secretary of State must trial KCPOs in specified areas to be chosen and then lay before Parliament a report on the operation of that pilot. Once in force, Part 2 allows a court to make a KCPO either on conviction or otherwise than on conviction.

KCPOs Otherwise than on Conviction

Sections 14 to 18 of the Offensive Weapons Act 2019 govern applications for KCPOs made otherwise than on conviction. An application for a KCPO can only be made by a relevant chief officer of police, the chief constable of the British Transport Police Force or the chief constable of the Ministry of Defence Police (s. 15(1)). For these purposes a chief officer of police is a relevant chief officer of police if the defendant lives in the chief officer's police area or the chief officer believes that the defendant is in, or is intending to come to, the chief officer's police area (s. 15(2)). **D25.85**

The application for a KCPO can be made in respect of a defendant aged 12 or over (s. 14(1)). Where the defendant is under 18 years of age the application should be made to the youth court, but where the defendant is 18 or over the application should be made to the magistrates' court (s. 14(10)). Where the defendant is a youth, the applicant must consult the youth offending team in whose area it appears the defendant lives before making the application (s. 15(5)) unless the application is to be made without notice to the defendant.

The court may make a KCPO where it is satisfied on the balance of probabilities that, on at least two occasions in the relevant period, the defendant had a bladed article with him or her without good reason or lawful authority in a public place in England and Wales, on school premises or on further education premises (s. 14(3)). The 'relevant period' means the period of two years ending with the day on which the order is made but, importantly, an event may be taken into account only if it occurred after the coming into force of s. 14 (s. 14(4)). This means that when Part 2 is brought into force the applicant for a KCPO will be unable to rely on any events that took place before Part 2 was brought into force in seeking to persuade the court that the statutory test for making a KCPO is met. The expressions 'public place', 'school premises' and 'further educational institution' are defined in s. 14(10).

Without prejudice to the generality of s. 14(3), a person has good reason for having a bladed article with him or her in a place mentioned in that subsection if that person has the article for use at work, for educational purposes, for religious reasons or as part of any national costume (s. 14(5)). This provision can be contrasted with the CJA 1988, s. 139(5), which contains the offence of having a bladed article in a public place (see **B12.177**). It is a defence for such a person to prove that there was a good reason or a lawful excuse for having that article in a public place. Without prejudice to the generality of those defences, s. 139(5) provides that it will be a defence for a person to prove that the article was for use at work, for religious reasons or as part of any national costume. For the purposes of Part 2 of the Offensive Weapons Act 2019 that list is replicated but with the additional factor that it will be a good reason for the defendant to have a bladed article if it is for educational purposes, which is not a defence specifically recognised in the CJA 1988 provisions.

In addition to the test in s. 14(3), the court can only make a KCPO if it thinks it is necessary to protect the public in England and Wales from the risk of harm involving a bladed article, to protect any particular members of the public in England and Wales (including the defendant) from such a risk or to prevent the defendant from committing an offence involving a bladed article (s. 14(6)). It is noteworthy that the risk of harm to members of the public does not have to be a risk that emanates from the defendant. The test is one of necessity and so it will be a harder test for the applicant to meet than the 'just and convenient' test that applies when a person seeks a civil injunction under the ABCPA 2014, s. 1(1) (see **D25.9**). Given the lower hurdle for obtaining a civil injunction rather than a KCPO, it remains to be seen whether applicants will apply for the former rather than the latter.

An application for a KCPO can be made without notice to the defendant (s. 16(1)). In circumstances where the defendant is a youth and the application is made without notice, there is no requirement for the applicant to consult the youth offending team before making the application (s. 16(2)). Where an application without notice is made, the court must either dismiss the application, adjourn the proceedings and make an interim KCPO, or adjourn the proceedings without making an interim KCPO (s. 16(3)). If the court takes one of the first two courses of action then the duty on the part of the applicant to consult the youth offending team in the case of a juvenile defendant must be complied with before the adjourned hearing (s. 16(4)). Sections 17 and 18 contain provisions concerned with the making of interim KCPOs pending a final hearing. In broad terms the court has the power to make an interim KCPO whether the application was made on notice or without notice.

KCPOs on Conviction

D25.86 Where a defendant aged 12 or over is convicted of an offence that was committed after the Offensive Weapons Act 2019, s. 19, comes into force, and the court is satisfied on the balance of probabilities that the offence is a relevant offence, then the court will have jurisdiction to consider making a post-conviction KCPO (s. 19(1)). An offence is a relevant offence if it involves violence or the threat of violence, the bladed article was used by the defendant or another person to commit the offence or the defendant or another person who committed the offence had a bladed article with him or her when the offence was committed (s. 19(10)). Where the defendant is aged under 18, the prosecutor must consult the youth offending team in whose area the defendant appears to live before inviting the court to make a KCPO (s. 20(1)).

Where it has jurisdiction to do so, the court may make a KCPO against the convicted defendant if two conditions are met. The first is that the prosecutor applies for a KCPO, and so the court cannot make a KCPO of its own motion (s. 19(3)). The second is that the court thinks it is necessary to make a KCPO to protect the public in England and Wales from the risk of harm involving a bladed article, to protect any particular members of the public in England and Wales (including the defendant) from such a risk or to prevent the defendant from committing an offence involving a bladed article (s. 19(4)). As with non-conviction KCPOs the test here is one of necessity, which can be contrasted with the helpfulness test that applies whenever the court is invited to make a CBO under the ABCPA 2014, s. 22 (see **D25.23**). Given the stricter test for KCPOs it remains to be seen whether prosecutors who wish the court to impose a behaviour order on a convicted defendant will opt for a CBO or a KCPO.

The court can only make a post-conviction KCPO in addition to a sentence imposed in respect of the offence or where the defendant has been conditionally discharged for the offence. It follows that the court cannot make a KCPO where it discharges the defendant absolutely (s. 19(7)). In deciding whether the statutory test for making a KCPO is met the court may consider evidence led by the prosecution and by the defence (s. 19(8)), and is not limited to considering only such evidence as was admitted during the trial that led to conviction, or such evidence as would have been admissible if there had been a trial (s. 19(9)). It will be open to the court to take account of any material placed before it by either party without the need to consider whether that material would have been admissible as evidence in any trial. This will include evidence of bad character and hearsay.

Provisions of KCPOs

Whether the KCPO that has been applied for is a non-conviction KCPO or a post-conviction KCPO is irrelevant when it comes to considering the sorts of requirements and prohibitions that can be contained in it. The only requirements and prohibitions that can be contained in KCPOs are those which the court thinks are necessary to protect the public in England and Wales from the risk of harm involving a bladed article, to protect any particular members of the public in England and Wales (including the defendant) from such a risk or to prevent the defendant from committing an offence involving a bladed article (s. 21(1)). Although not strictly a restriction on the ability of the court to insert certain requirements or prohibitions into a KCPO, the court is required, so far as is practicable, to avoid any terms that conflict with a defendant's religious beliefs or that interfere with the defendant's work or attendance at any educational establishment (s. 21(8)). **D25.87**

Section 21(2) and (4) provide examples of the sorts of requirements and prohibitions that can be included in a KCPO. They are very broad and include terms directing where the defendant can or cannot be at certain times and on certain days, with whom the defendant can and cannot associate, what activities the defendant can and cannot undertake and what articles the defendant can or cannot carry in public places. Of course these are just illustrative examples. Provided a particular requirement or prohibition sought by the prosecution satisfies the necessity test in s. 21(1), the court will have the power to impose it.

Where a KCPO or an interim KCPO imposes a requirement on a defendant, the order must specify the person who will be responsible for supervising the defendant's compliance with that requirement (s. 22(1)), and before the court inserts that requirement into the KCPO it must receive evidence from the supervisor about the suitability and enforceability of the requirement (s. 22(3)). Once the requirement is included in the KCPO the supervisor becomes subject to a number of responsibilities, which include promoting the defendant's compliance with the requirement and informing the police where there has been non-compliance (s. 22(5)). Moreover, a defendant who is subject to a requirement in a KCPO must keep in touch with the supervisor and notify any change of address (s. 22(7)). Those obligations on the part of the defendant are treated as if they were terms of the KCPO itself so a failure to comply with them will amount to a breach of the order (s. 22(8)).

Duration

A KCPO generally takes effect on the day it is made (s. 23(1)), but where the defendant is in custody (whether on remand or serving a sentence of imprisonment) or on licence, the court can order that the KCPO will not take effect until the defendant is released or ceases to be subject to licence (s. 23(6) and (7)). A KCPO must specify the period for which it has effect, which must be a fixed period of at least six months and not more than two years (s. 23(3)). Where a KCPO contains a number of prohibitions or requirements they do not have to have the same duration (s. 23(8)), provided, of course, that none of them is fixed to last longer than the period of the KCPO itself. Where a KCPO is imposed upon a defendant, s. 24 provides that within a period of three days from the making of the order the defendant must notify the police of certain personal information that is set out in that section. A failure to do so without reasonable excuse is a separate offence (s. 25). **D25.88**

Review, Variation, Discharge, Appeals and Breach

D25.89 Where a court has made a KCPO it can order the defendant to attend periodic reviews that will be listed before the court (s. 26). Section 27 contains a suite of powers that allow the court to vary, renew or discharge a KCPO. Section 28 provides that a defendant against whom a non-conviction KCPO has been made by the youth court or the magistrates' court can appeal to the Crown Court, and the person whose application for a KCPO was refused by the youth court or the magistrates' court has a similar right of appeal. To like effect, the applicant or the defendant can appeal to the Crown Court against a decision of the youth court or magistrates' court arising out of an application to vary, renew or discharge a KCPO. Section 29 provides that where a person breaches the terms of a KCPO or an interim KCPO without reasonable excuse, an offence is committed. The maximum sentence on conviction on indictment is two years' imprisonment or a fine or both. A conditional discharge is not available as a sentence for a defendant found to have breached such an order (s. 29(4)).

STALKING PROTECTION ORDERS

D25.90 The Stalking Protection Act 2019 came into force on 20 January 2020. The Act makes provision for orders to protect persons from risks associated with stalking and for connected purposes. Section 1 provides that a chief officer of police may apply to a magistrates' court by way of complaint for a stalking protection order (SPO) in respect of a defendant if it appears to the chief officer that the defendant has carried out acts associated with stalking, the defendant poses a risk associated with stalking to another person and there is reasonable cause to believe the proposed order is necessary to protect another person from such a risk, whether or not the other person was the victim of the acts already referred to. For these purposes it does not matter whether the acts were carried out by the defendant before s. 1 came into force or whether they were even carried out in a part of the UK (s. 1(5)). Section 2A of the Protection from Harassment Act 1997 contains examples of acts that are associated with stalking (see B2.194). A risk associated with stalking may be in respect of physical or psychological harm to the other person and may arise from acts which the defendant knows or ought to know are unwelcome to the other person even if, in other circumstances, the acts would appear harmless in themselves (s. 1(4)).

A magistrates' court can only make a SPO if it is satisfied that the defendant has carried out acts associated with stalking, the defendant poses a risk associated with stalking to another person and there is reasonable cause to believe the proposed order is necessary to protect another person from such a risk, whether or not the other person was the victim of the acts already referred to (s. 2(1)). A magistrates' court may include any prohibition or requirement in a SPO provided the court is satisfied that such a term is necessary to protect the other person from a risk associated with stalking (s. 2(2)). Such terms as the court deems appropriate for inclusion in an SPO should, so far as is practicable, not conflict with the defendant's religious beliefs nor interfere with the defendant's work or attendance at an educational establishment (s. 2(5)). A prohibition or requirement in a SPO has effect in all parts of the UK unless the order states otherwise (s. 2(4)).

The court can direct that the SPO should continue until further order or be for a fixed period, and if the latter the period must be for at least two years. Different periods may be specified in relation to different prohibitions and requirements in the SPO (s. 3). Either the applicant or the defendant can apply to the magistrates' court to vary, renew or discharge an SPO (s. 4). The court has the power to impose an interim SPO before the application has been finally determined (s. 5). Both the applicant and the defendant have a right of appeal to the Crown Court against the decision of the magistrates' court in relation to the granting, variation, renewal or discharge of a SPO (s. 7). A defendant who breaches the terms of a SPO without reasonable excuse commits an offence that carries a maximum sentence of five years' imprisonment (s. 8). A defendant who is made subject to a SPO or an interim SPO becomes subject to the notification requirements in s. 9 which oblige the defendant to notify the police of certain matters set out in that section within a specified period of time. A failure, without reasonable excuse, to comply with the notification requirements is a separate criminal offence that also carries a maximum sentence of five years' imprisonment (s. 11).

Section D26 Appeal to the Court of Appeal (Criminal Division) Following Trial on Indictment

BASES OF JURISDICTION OF THE COURT OF APPEAL (CRIMINAL DIVISION)

Statutory Bases

D26.1 The vast majority of appeals against conviction and sentence are disposed of by the Court of Appeal (Criminal Division) under its statutory jurisdiction. Section 15(2) of the Senior Courts Act 1981 enables the exercise of the statutory powers conferred under the following legislative provisions, amongst others:

Criminal Appeal Act 1968, ss. 1 and 2	Jurisdiction to determine appeals against conviction on indictment.
Criminal Appeal Act 1968, ss. 9 and 11	Jurisdiction to determine appeals against sentence passed following conviction on indictment.
Criminal Appeal Act 1968, ss. 10 and 11	Jurisdiction to determine appeals against sentence passed on a committal for sentence.
Criminal Justice Act 1972, s. 36	Jurisdiction to give an opinion on a point of law referred to the court by the A-G following an acquittal on indictment.
Criminal Justice Act 1987, s. 9(11)–(14)	Jurisdiction to determine appeals against rulings made at preparatory hearings in serious fraud cases.
Criminal Justice Act 1988, ss. 35 and 36	Jurisdiction to increase sentence on a reference by the A-G following an unduly lenient sentence for an offence triable only on indictment.
Criminal Appeal Act 1995, s. 9	Jurisdiction to determine appeals on a reference by the CCRC.

There is no power for the Court of Appeal (Criminal Division) to hear an appeal against a refusal to make a football banning order (*Boggild* [2011] EWCA Crim 1928, [2012] 1 Cr App R (S) 81 (457): see **E21.7**).

Venire de Novo

In addition to its statutory jurisdiction, the Court of Appeal retains the power to deal with appeals by way of a writ of *venire de novo*. The power has its origins in the jurisdiction of the Court for Crown Cases Reserved, a forerunner of the modern Court of Appeal (Criminal Division). In essence, the power is exercised when there has been such a fundamental irregularity in procedure that no valid trial has taken place. In *Rose* [1982] AC 822, the House of Lords referred with approval to an article by Sir Robin Cooke (published at (1955) 71 LQR 100) in which he identified categories of procedural irregularity which had been found sufficient to ensure that the trial was in effect a nullity and hence justify the issue of a writ of *venire de novo*. The categories identified were as follows: **D26.2**

(a) where there was error as to the true plea of the defendant or some doubt about the nature of the plea, whether guilty or not guilty;
(b) where there was misjoinder of defendants (*Crane v DPP* [1921] 2 AC 299);
(c) where there was failure to take the verdict of the jury on a change of plea from not guilty to guilty (*Hancock* (1931) 23 Cr App R 16);
(d) where there was some irregularity in the committal proceedings (*Gee* [1936] 2 KB 442);
(e) where there was personation of a juror (*Wakefield* [1918] 1 KB 216);
(f) where there was denial of the right to challenge a juror (*Williams* (1925) 19 Cr App R 67); and
(g) where the judge was unqualified to act as such.

When *Rose* was before the Court of Appeal, Lord Lane CJ added an eighth category of case in which retrials had historically been ordered, namely when the verdict of the jury was so ambiguous or ill-expressed that no judgment could properly be given on it. His reasoning was approved in the House of Lords.

The effect of the procedure is that the Court orders a retrial. In *Bahbahani* [2018] EWCA Crim 95, [2018] QB 1099, the Court of Appeal emphasised that its power to issue a writ of *venire de novo* is confined to appeals following trial on indictment. In *Stromberg* [2018] EWCA Crim 561, [2019] QB 14, the Court of Appeal emphasised that its jurisdiction to hear appeals against conviction is a single jurisdiction created by statute. If the Court ordered the issue of a writ of *venire de novo*, it was not exercising a separate jurisdiction. Instead, it was using a particular remedy pursuant to its jurisdiction. Consequently, an application for a writ of *venire de novo* must be made within an application for leave to appeal under the Criminal Appeal Act 1968 and comply with that Act's leave provisions and time limits.

ALLOCATION OF BUSINESS

Matters Dealt with by the Full Court

Under the Senior Courts Act 1981, s. 55, a court consisting of an uneven number of judges no fewer than three is required to determine (a) an appeal against conviction, (b) a review of a sentence under the CJA 1988, Part IV (A-G's references), (c) an appeal against a finding under the Criminal Procedure (Insanity) Act 1964, s. 4 (unfitness to plead), that a person is under a disability, (d) an application for leave to appeal a verdict of not guilty by reason of insanity or a finding under s. 4 of the 1964 Act which has not previously been refused by a single judge, and (e) an application for leave to appeal to the Supreme Court. **D26.3**

Ordinarily, a court sitting to deal with any of the above hearings will comprise just three judges. But, exceptionally, five or even seven judges will sit when the matter to be decided is very important and would benefit from the authority of such a court or where there have been conflicting decisions of the Court of Appeal on the same point (*Newsome* [1970] 2 QB 711).

Matters Dealt with by a Two-judge Court

By virtue of s. 55(4) of the Senior Courts Act 1981, a court comprised of two judges may deal with any matter other than those mentioned at **D26.3**. **D26.4**

Matters Dealt with by a Single Judge

D26.5 Sections 31 and 44 of the Criminal Appeal Act 1968 set out the matters which may be dealt with by a single judge. CrimPR 36.5 sets out the procedure governing the renewal before the full court of any application refused by the single judge (see **D27.10** and, for the full text, see Supplement, **R36.5**).

DECIDING OUTCOME OF APPEAL AND GIVING JUDGMENT

D26.6 The Court of Appeal may determine an appeal by majority decision. If a two-judge court is equally divided then, under the Senior Courts Act 1981, s. 55(5), the case must be reargued before a reconstituted court comprised of an uneven number of judges. A case is finally determined once the decision has been announced in open court, even if no reasons have yet been given, as it is then properly binding on the judges (*Coates* [2004] EWCA Crim 2253, [2005] 1 Cr App R 14 (199)). Consequently in *Steele* [2006] EWCA Crim 2000, [2007] 1 WLR 222, it was held that when the Court circulated the transcript of its judgment in advance of handing it down, the appeal was determined even though, when the judgment was handed down, not all members of the original constitution were present. The handing down of the judgment was merely its formal promulgation. The Senior Courts Act 1981, s. 59 stipulates that only one judgment should ordinarily be delivered by the Court of Appeal in any particular case, save where the case involves an issue of law and the Presiding Judge deems it convenient for two judgments to be delivered.

APPEAL AGAINST CONVICTION

Statutory Basis of Appeal against Conviction

D26.7 **Criminal Appeal Act 1968, s. 1**

(1) Subject to subsection (3) below a person convicted of an offence on indictment may appeal to the Court of Appeal against his conviction.
(2) An appeal under this section lies only—
  (a) with the leave of the Court of Appeal; or
  (b) if, within 28 days of the date of the conviction, the judge of the court of trial grants a certificate that the case is fit for appeal.

Unless the trial judge certifies that a case is fit for appeal, leave to appeal to the Court of Appeal is required (see **D26.8**). CrimPD III, paras. 14H.1 to 14H.4 (see Supplement, **CPD.14H**), give guidance as to the circumstances in which a certificate of fitness to appeal should be granted. Such a certificate of fitness to appeal against conviction or sentence should be issued only in exceptional circumstances. The certificate removes the need for leave to appeal to be granted by the Court of Appeal but it does not commence the appeal; advocates still need to follow the procedure under CrimPR Part 39 (see D27.2).

Appeal against Conviction with Leave

D26.8 Unless the trial judge has granted a certificate that the case is fit for appeal, any would-be appellant needs leave to appeal. Written grounds of appeal must be submitted within 28 days of the conviction. The initial decision either to grant or refuse leave is usually taken on the papers by the single judge (Criminal Appeal Act 1968, s. 31(2)(a)), but sometimes the decision as to leave may be made by a two-judge or full court at the discretion of the Registrar of Criminal Appeals ('the Registrar'). The need for expedition is sometimes a reason for holding such a leave hearing. Such a hearing will also often take place when an unlawful sentence has been passed and the sentence will inevitably need adjusting.

If leave is refused by the single judge, the applicant is entitled to renew the application before a two-judge or full court under s. 31(3).

Appeal against Conviction following a Plea of Guilty

The fact that a plea of guilty has been entered does not preclude an appeal against the resultant conviction. If the conviction is found to be unsafe despite the plea of guilty (see **D26.15**), it will be quashed. However, the fact that an appellant was fit to plead, had received expert advice, had been aware of what he or she was doing and had intended to plead guilty would be highly relevant to the consideration of the safety of the conviction (*Lee* [1984] 1 All ER 1080). The most common basis upon which an unequivocal plea of guilty is challenged is where there has been an incorrect ruling on a point of law by the trial judge which allows the appellant no escape from a guilty verdict. But if an appellant has simply been influenced to enter a plea of guilty because of a decision to admit evidence which meant that the prospects of acquittal were hopeless, the conviction would not normally be held to be unsafe (*Chalkley* [1998] QB 848). That aspect of the judgment in *Chalkley* was approved in *Togher* [2001] 3 All ER 463, and found reflection in *Hanson* [2005] EWCA Crim 824, [2005] 1 WLR 3169, where Rose V-P observed that it was highly unlikely that an appeal would be entertained when a defendant pleaded guilty following a decision to admit evidence of bad character. **D26.9**

The Court of Appeal may also quash a conviction arising from a guilty plea following the admission of fresh evidence on appeal under the Criminal Appeal Act 1968, s. 23 (*Swain* [1986] Crim LR 480).

A conviction may also be held to be unsafe when the guilty plea which led to it flowed from inappropriate legal advice (see, e.g., *McCarthy* [2015] EWCA Crim 1185, where a conviction for a lesser offence was substituted). For an unsuccessful appeal on this basis see *Oliver* [2016] EWCA Crim 1053. The Court of Appeal ruled that D had received realistic advice and the case against him had been overwhelming. The Court of Appeal considered the effect of inappropriate legal advice in *Sadighpour* [2012] EWCA Crim 2669, [2013] 1 WLR 2725. D had pleaded guilty to an offence of possessing a false identity document contrary to the Identity Documents Act 2010, s. 4, without being advised as to a possible defence under the Immigration and Asylum Act 1999, s. 31. The Court observed that in *Boal* (1992) 95 Cr App R 272 it was indicated that a guilty plea might be set aside on appeal in such a situation if the circumstances are such that the Court regards the conviction as unsafe. But it was an exceptional course to be taken only when the Court believes that the overlooked defence would quite probably have succeeded and therefore concludes that an injustice has been done. The approach in *Boal* was adopted in *Dastjerdi* [2011] EWCA Crim 365. The Court in *Sadighpour* noted that in *Mohamed* [2010] EWCA Crim 2400, [2011] 1 Cr App R 35 (432), the Court of Appeal had cited *Boal* but spoken in terms of there being 'no reasonable prospect of a defence under section 31 succeeding'. The Court concluded that if it asked itself whether the defence would quite probably succeed or whether it put the question in terms of there being a reasonable prospect of a s. 31 defence succeeding, it was quite satisfied that the appellant would not satisfy either test. See also *Mateta* [2013] EWCA Crim 1372, [2014] 1 All ER 152 (discussed in detail at **B22.86**) as to inappropriate advice on this type of defence.

Single Right of Appeal

If an appeal is unsuccessful (either because leave is refused or leave is granted and the appeal is dismissed), there is usually no opportunity for a further appeal even if the point to be argued is that new or fresh evidence has arisen (*Pinfold* [1988] QB 462). **D26.10**

Two minor caveats to that rule were acknowledged in *Pinfold*:

(a) where the appeal has been abandoned, the Court of Appeal may in exceptional circumstances treat the abandonment as a nullity (*Medway* [1976] QB 779); and
(b) if the dismissal of the first appeal involved some procedural irregularity which led to injustice for the appellant, the court may treat the dismissal as a nullity.

In *Yasain* [2015] EWCA Crim 1277, [2016] QB 146 it was acknowledged that, where an appeal had been heard and the decision recorded in the relevant records, there was ordinarily no jurisdiction to rehear an appeal, but the Court of Appeal could exceptionally rehear such an appeal if: (i) its previous ruling was a nullity; or (ii) a defect in the earlier procedure might have led to real injustice. The Court also noted that the Civil Division could exercise an implicit power to reopen a concluded appeal and assumed a similar implicit power. For further guidance on the relevant procedure to be followed when seeking to reopen an appeal following a final determination see *Hockey* [2017] EWCA Crim 742, [2017] 2 Cr App R 23 (288), which is now reflected in CrimPR 36.15 (see Supplement, **R36.15**). For a recent example of the Court of Appeal allowing an application to treat abandonment as a nullity see *Riley* [2017] EWCA Crim 243.

Unless either of those caveats apply, an unsuccessful appellant's only remedy is to ask the CCRC to refer the case back to the Court of Appeal (see **D28.9**). See also *Mohammed* [2004] EWCA Crim 2889.

In *CC* [2019] EWCA Crim 2101, [2020] 1 Cr App R 15 (258) the Court of Appeal approved the approach of the Court in *Yasain* to applications to reopen a decision of the Court of Appeal. Thus, save for decisions that are a nullity, the usual exercise of the Court's jurisdiction is to be confined to correcting 'procedural errors' that are clear and undisputed and when there is no alternative effective remedy. The Court said that it did not wish to close the door entirely on exceptional circumstances, when the lack of an alternative effective remedy, or some other reason, may lead the Court to reopen a decision in order to avoid a manifest injustice. The Court agreed with the observation of Gross LJ in *Gohil* [2018] EWCA Crim 140, [2018] 1 Cr App R 30 (432) at [128] to the effect that 'although the jurisdiction to re-open concluded proceedings has not been removed by the availability of recourse to the CCRC, that will almost invariably be the proper route'. The Court decided that applications to reopen a decision of the Court of Appeal should be sent by the Registrar straight to the full court (constituted of three judges). The applications should be dealt with on paper, without a hearing, unless the court orders otherwise. The Court observed that such a process would require no amendment of the Criminal Procedure Rules.

Right of Appeal Vests only in the Convicted Person

D26.11 Section 1(1) of the Criminal Appeal Act 1968 confers a right of appeal only on a person convicted on indictment. However, s. 44A provides that the Court of Appeal may allow an approved person to begin or continue an appeal on behalf of a deceased appellant (see, e.g., *Whelan* [1997] Crim LR 659).

Directions Concerning Loss of Time and Frivolous and Vexatious Appeals

D26.12 Section 29 of the Criminal Appeal Act 1968 enables the Court of Appeal to direct that all or part of the time an applicant for leave to appeal has spent in custody since the commencement of the appeal proceedings shall not count in relation to the sentence the applicant is required to serve. CrimPD IX, paras. 39E.1 and 39E.2 (see Supplement, **CPD.13E**), govern the procedure for directions in relation to loss of time served after service of the notice of appeal and include a reminder of the warning given by the Court of Appeal in *Hart* [2006] EWCA Crim 3239, [2007] 1 Cr App R 31 (412) that it may order that time be lost even where counsel has advised that there are good grounds for appeal. In *Fortean* [2009] EWCA Crim 437, the Court of Appeal ordered that six weeks of the time spent by D in custody should not count towards his sentence after he had renewed his application for leave to appeal against conviction following the refusal of leave by the single judge. It was emphasised that the fact that counsel or solicitors have associated themselves with such a renewal will be relevant, but it will not necessarily avoid such an order if there was no justification for continuing the case. A single judge refusing permission under s. 31 is now asked to identify on Form SJ cases without merit where the court should consider using the power under s. 29 should the refused application be renewed to the full court. There is also a box for the applicant to indicate why such an order should not be made, whether or not an indication has been given by the single judge. In *Brind* [2008] EWCA Crim 934, the Court of Appeal listed five renewed applications for leave to appeal together in order to reiterate its powers under s. 29. The Vice-President stated that, where the single judge had indicated on Form SJ that the application was without merit, the would-be applicant must expect that the Court will order that the time served should not count.

D26.13 The Court of Appeal revisited the question of when it is appropriate to make orders for loss of time or costs against an applicant in *Gray* [2014] EWCA Crim 2372, [2015] 1 Cr App R (S) 27 (197). Hallett V-P noted that the Court has the power to award costs against any applicant under the Prosecution of Offences Act 1985, s. 18, and a loss of time order can be made under s. 29 or s. 31(2)(h) of the 1968 Act. Hallett V-P also remarked that CrimPD IX, paras. 39E.1 and 39E.2 (see Supplement, **CPD.39E**), repeat previous warnings about loss of time orders and state that the fact that an application is renewed on the advice of counsel will not necessarily prevent a loss of time order. Hallett V-P concluded by saying (at [10]):

> ... in every case where the court is presented with an unmeritorious application, consideration should be given to exercising these powers. The single judge should consider whether to initial the box, and if the application is renewed, the Full Court (be it a two or three judge court) should consider whether or not to make a loss of time order or costs order. If it decides to exercise the power, a statement to this effect would suffice:
>
> > 'Despite being warned of the court's power to make a loss of time order, the applicant chose to pursue a totally unmeritorious application which has wasted the time of the court. Such applications hamper the court's ability to process meritorious applications in a timely fashion.'

The Court went on to make loss of time orders in respect of all of the applicants. See also *James* [2018] EWCA Crim 285, [2018] 1 Cr App R 33 (528).

By virtue of s. 20 of the 1968 Act, the Court may summarily dismiss an appeal or application for leave to appeal without either of the parties being called on to attend if it considers the appeal to be frivolous or vexatious. A ground of appeal is 'frivolous or vexatious' if it is so unmeritorious that there is no realistic prospect of it succeeding after full argument (*Taylor* [1979] Crim LR 649). In *Achogbuo* [2014] EWCA Crim 567, [2014] 2 Cr App R 7 (94) Lord Thomas CJ emphasised that the Court of Appeal would consider exercising the power under s. 20 more frequently if unmeritorious cases were appealed. *Achogbuo* was considered to be an example of an appeal being brought, based on alleged incompetence of the lawyers acting at trial, without 'due diligence' and involved the Court referring the circumstances to the Solicitors Regulation Authority.

The loss of time procedure has been held to comply with the ECHR, Articles 5 and 6 (*Monnell v UK* (1988) 10 EHRR 205).

For a recent example of the Court of Appeal making a loss of time order see *Munt* [2019] EWCA Crim 2085.

Appellant who Absconds

D26.14 The Court of Appeal may consider and determine the appeal of a person who has absconded. In *Charles* [2001] EWCA Crim 129, [2001] 2 Cr App R 15 (233), the Court expressed the view that it might be contrary to the ECHR, Article 6, if the appeal of a person was shut out solely because the person had absconded.

The approach taken in *Charles* was approved in *Okedare* [2014] EWCA Crim 228, [2014] 1 WLR 4071 where Hallett V-P said (at [31]–[33]):

> ... *we are satisfied that* the practice should be: applications from absconders should not be treated as ineffective per se. If there are grounds for believing an absconder has given authority to appeal, expressly or impliedly, or the case is one where the Court might wish to intervene in the interests of justice, the Court should proceed as normal. The application should be put before the single judge. The single judge may adjourn the application for more information, grant/refuse leave or refer the application to the full Court as usual.
>
> If the single judge is satisfied there is no authority to pursue an application for leave and the application is not one the Court would wish to entertain, she or he has the power to treat the application as

ineffective and time will continue to run. However, we would expect orders declaring an application ineffective and orders staying applications brought on behalf of absconders to be the exception rather than the norm at this stage.

However, it remains the professional responsibility of the lawyer to highlight the fact their client has absconded for the benefit of the Criminal Appeal Office and the single judge. He must provide a full account of the circumstances of the absconding (with updates if necessary) coupled with an explanation for the basis for the assertion of authority and/or any reason why the Court would wish to entertain the application.

In approving such an approach, the Court saw no reason to distinguish between appeals against conviction and sentence. Moreover, if leave to appeal has been granted, it is a matter for the full Court to decide whether to hear the case on the merits or stay the appeal.

DETERMINATION OF APPEALS AGAINST CONVICTION

Statutory Basis of Determination of Appeal

D26.15 **Criminal Appeal Act 1968, s. 2**

(1) Subject to the provisions of this Act, the Court of Appeal—
  (a) shall allow an appeal against conviction if they think that the conviction is unsafe; and
  (b) shall dismiss such an appeal in any other case.

Safety Test

D26.16 By virtue of s. 2 of the Criminal Appeal Act 1968, the principal question for the Court of Appeal in the determination of an appeal against conviction is whether the conviction is unsafe.

Prior to the amendment of s. 2 by the Criminal Appeal Act 1995, it provided that the Court of Appeal should allow an appeal if it was of the view that the conviction was unsafe or unsatisfactory, or that the judgment of the court of trial should be set aside because of an error of law, or that there had been a material irregularity in the course of the trial. Even if the point in issue concerning a point of law or material irregularity was decided in favour of the appellant, the Court could exercise the proviso and dismiss the appeal if it was satisfied that no miscarriage of justice had occurred. Despite the change in wording, the authorities which developed in relation to the application of the earlier version of s. 2 are relevant to the operation of the provision as now amended and the consideration of the ultimate question of the safety of the conviction.

D26.17 The classic analysis of the Court's powers under the old s. 2 was set out in *Cooper* [1969] 1 QB 267, where Lord Widgery said (at p. 271C–G):

> [This is] a case in which every issue was before the jury and in which the jury was properly instructed, and, accordingly, a case in which this court will be very reluctant indeed to intervene. It has been said over and over again throughout the years that this court must recognise the advantage which a jury has in seeing and hearing the witnesses, and if all the material was before the jury and the summing-up was impeccable, this court should not lightly interfere. Indeed, until the passing of the Criminal Appeal Act 1966 [which somewhat widened the court's powers to quash a conviction] it was almost unheard of for this court to interfere in such a case.
>
> However, now our powers are somewhat different, and we are indeed charged to allow an appeal against conviction if we think that the verdict of the jury should be set aside on the ground that under all the circumstances of the case it is unsafe or unsatisfactory. That means that in cases of this kind the court must in the end ask itself a subjective question, whether we are content to let the matter stand as it is, or whether there is not some lurking doubt in our minds which makes us wonder whether an injustice has been done. This is a reaction which may not be based strictly on the evidence as such; it is a reaction which can be produced by the general feel of the case as the court experiences it.

Despite the comments by the Court in *F* [1998] Crim LR 307 to the effect that there was no need to add to the simple words of the new section and the concept of lurking doubt was inappropriate, *Cooper* was regularly used as guidance for the approach to be taken in relation to the issue of whether or not a conviction is safe, and the Court continued to refer to the test (see, e.g., *Litchfield* [1998] Crim LR 507). As Professor Sir John Smith pointed out in his commentary on *F*, the repealed words 'or unsatisfactory' played no part in the decision in *Cooper*, and that case has not been overruled. The scope of the continuing applicability of the concept of 'lurking doubt' was considered in *Pope* [2012] EWCA Crim 2241, [2013] 1 Cr App R 14 (214), where Lord Judge CJ observed (at [14]):

> As a matter of principle, in the administration of justice when there is trial by jury, the constitutional primacy and public responsibility for the verdict rests not with the judge, nor indeed with this court, but with the jury. If therefore there is a case to answer and, after proper directions, the jury has convicted, it is not open to the court to set aside the verdict on the basis of some collective, subjective judicial hunch that the conviction is or may be unsafe. Where it arises for consideration at all, the application of the 'lurking doubt' concept requires reasoned analysis of the evidence or the trial process, or both, which leads to the inexorable conclusion that the conviction is unsafe. It can therefore only be in the most exceptional circumstances that a conviction will be quashed on this ground alone, and even more exceptional if the attention of the court is confined to a re-examination of the material before the jury.

It follows from *Pope* (and other cases) that the Court of Appeal (unlike its continental European counterparts) is concerned with the safety of the conviction and not with innocence. If there is a case to answer and if the jury, after proper directions, has convicted (on admissible evidence) then, in the absence of material not considered by the jury, an appeal against conviction will not succeed save in the most exceptional circumstances. The public responsibility for the verdict rests with the jury. It follows that the trial judge's role in deciding whether there is sufficient admissible evidence upon which a jury could properly convict of a count charged in the indictment is vital if miscarriages of justice are to be avoided. Likewise if, on any count, there is more than one factual route to verdict, the trial judge's role in deciding whether there is sufficient admissible evidence to convict on each of those routes is similarly vital. The approach taken in *Pope* was followed in *Davies* [2013] EWCA Crim 1592.

In *Cooper* [2019] EWCA Crim 43 the Court of Appeal relied on grounds advanced on a 'cumulative basis' (at [1]) when quashing the appellant's conviction.

In *Mullen* [2000] QB 520, an appeal was based upon the circumstances in which the appellant was brought to trial. The English authorities had colluded with their Zimbabwean counterparts to ensure M's deportation from Zimbabwe to England in a manner which amounted to an abuse of process. The Court held that abuse of process could still amount to a ground for the quashing of a conviction under the new wording of s. 2. Any safe conviction must of necessity be lawful and, if a trial should never have taken place, the conviction could not be safe.

In *Smith* [1999] 2 Cr App R 238, the Court dealt with an appeal which was based on a contention that the trial judge had been wrong to reject a submission of no case to answer. After the judge had rejected the submission, D gave evidence and admitted his guilt. Prior to the amendment of s. 2, the Court could have quashed the conviction if it thought that the rejection of the submission of no case was erroneous. Faced with the question of whether the change in the wording had changed that position, the Court held that it had not and, even though D had admitted his guilt, the conviction was quashed. **D26.18**

The test applied by the Court is different to that applied by the trial judge on a submission of no case to answer (*Arobieke* [1988] Crim LR 314).

So far as 'fresh evidence' cases are concerned, the classic statement relating to the old s. 2 is to be found in *Stafford v DPP* [1974] AC 878 where Lord Kilbrandon approved *Cooper* and summarised the test to be applied by each member of the appellate court as: 'Have I a reasonable doubt, or perhaps even a lurking doubt, that this conviction may be unsafe or unsatisfactory?' Their lordships rejected the central submission by the appellants that the consideration by the Court **D26.19** should be of the likely effect that the fresh evidence would have had on the minds of the jury; the test was no different in a fresh evidence case than in any other appeal against conviction.

In *Ahmed* [2010] EWCA Crim 2899, the Court of Appeal restated its role in deciding whether fresh evidence renders a conviction unsafe. Hughes LJ emphasised that the responsibility for deciding whether fresh material renders a conviction unsafe is on the Court, which must make up its own mind. It must consider the nature of the issue before the jury and such information as it can gather as to the reasoning process through which the jury will have been passing. The Court is likely to ask itself by way of check what impact the fresh material might have had on the jury. But Hughes LJ observed that, in most cases of arguably relevant fresh evidence, it will be impossible to be 100 per cent sure that it might not possibly have had *some* impact on the jury's deliberations, since *ex hypothesi* the jury have not seen the fresh material. The most important question for the Court is whether the fresh material causes it to doubt the safety of the guilty verdict. Hughes LJ pointed out that the Court had had the advantage of seeing the analysis of *Pendleton* [2001] UKHL 66, [2002] 1 Cr App R 34 (441) and *Dial* [2005] UKPC 4, [2005] 1 WLR 1660 made by a different constitution of the Court in *Burridge* [2010] EWCA Crim 2847, [2011] 2 Cr App R (S) 27 (148) (at [99]–[101]) and agreed with it. In *Dial* it was held that where fresh evidence is under consideration the primary question is for the Court itself and is not what effect the fresh evidence would have had on the mind of the jury. Moreover, both in *Stafford v DPP* and in *Pendleton*, the House of Lords rejected the proposition that the jury impact test was determinative, explaining that it was only a mechanism in a difficult case for the Court to 'test its view' as to the safety of a conviction. To similar effect see *Noye* [2011] EWCA Crim 650. For more recent restatements of the relevant principles see *Garland* [2016] EWCA Crim 1743, [2017] 4 WLR 117 and *Pabon* [2018] EWCA Crim 420. In *Park* [2020] EWCA Crim 589, having reviewed the relevant authorities, the Court of Appeal reaffirmed the conclusions reached in *Noye* and *Garland* and said (at [178]):

> In the result, we have concluded that the law in relation to the Court's approach to non-disclosure appeals and fresh evidence appeals is the same and is both settled and clear. The ultimate question is not . . . the jury impact test — which is simply a way in which the court can test its view as to the safety of the conviction in a difficult case. Rather, the ultimate question is whether the non-disclosure and/or fresh evidence relied on in this appeal causes us to doubt the safety of the conviction.

Charlton [2016] EWCA Crim 52 contains an important analysis of the principles to be applied when it is argued that a conviction may be unsafe because of the involvement of investigating police officers whose conduct in other cases may cast doubt on their methods and integrity.

D26.20 The Criminal Evidence (Witness Anonymity) Act 2008 provides (in s. 11) that, where a court is considering an appeal in a case where the trial ended before commencement (21 July 2008), it may not treat the conviction as unsafe solely on the ground that the trial court had no power to make an anonymity order in relation to a witness. It must, however, treat the conviction as unsafe if the anonymity order was not one that the trial court could have made had the 2008 Act (or its successor provision in the CAJA 2009, Part 3, ch. 2: see the CAJA 2009, sch. 22, para. 17) been in force and, as a result of the order, the accused did not receive a fair trial. (See D14.72 for witness anonymity orders generally.)

COMMONLY OCCURRING ERRORS RAISED ON APPEAL

D26.21 Exhaustive consideration of the many errors and irregularities which can found a successful appeal against conviction is not possible within this section and regard should be had to other parts of this work dealing with matters of procedure and substantive law. Nevertheless, it is possible to identify commonly occurring errors, some of which are dealt with below.

Wrongful Admission or Exclusion of Evidence

D26.22 The wrongful exclusion of admissible evidence or wrongful inclusion of inadmissible evidence will lead to the quashing of a conviction if the error means that the conviction is unsafe. That remains true even if the appellant's advocate failed to object to the admission of the evidence when it was adduced. But the fact that the advocate did not object to the evidence will be a factor in determining whether its admission was sufficiently prejudicial to render the conviction unsafe (*Stirland v DPP* [1944] AC 315; *Mustafa* (1977) 65 Cr App R 26). See also *T* [2012] EWCA Crim 2358.

Erroneous Exercise of Discretion

The Court of Appeal has often said that it will not interfere to quash a conviction on the basis of an erroneous exercise of discretion save in very limited circumstances (*Grondkowski* [1946] KB 369; *Selvey v DPP* [1970] AC 304; *Moghal* (1977) 65 Cr App R 56). The prospects of an appeal succeeding in relation to a matter in the judge's discretion are much improved if there has been a failure to exercise the discretion or a failure to take relevant factors into account, or the judge has taken irrelevant factors into account in the exercise of his or her discretion (*Sullivan* [1971] 1 QB 253; *Quinn* [1996] Crim LR 516). Occasionally, the Court of Appeal has suggested a wider approach to its function of reviewing the exercise of the judge's discretion. In *McCann* (1991) 92 Cr App R 239, the Court said that the review was not limited to cases in which a trial judge had erred in principle or where there was no material on which the decision reached could properly have been arrived at. If necessary, the Court could examine afresh the relevant facts and circumstances in order to exercise a discretion by way of review where the judge's ruling may have resulted in injustice to the appellants. **D26.23**

Conduct of Lawyers

Errors on the part of advocates may lead to a conviction being found to be unsafe. If the decision of the advocate is taken in good faith, having weighed the competing considerations and having consulted the client where appropriate, the Court of Appeal is much less likely to interfere than where the decision is taken in defiance of instructions and without reference to the client (*Clinton* [1993] 2 All ER 998). **D26.24**

A number of formulations of the test for determining when an advocate's conduct is sufficient to lead to the quashing of a conviction have found favour at different times. That the advocate's conduct must be flagrantly incompetent was said to be necessary in *Ensor* [1989] 2 All ER 586, while in *Richards* [2000] All ER (D) 900, the Court held that the test to be applied in relation to the conduct of the lawyer was that contained in *Associated Provincial Picture Houses Ltd v Wednesbury Corporation* [1948] 1 KB 223, i.e. the *Wednesbury* unreasonableness test.

The Court of Appeal has recognised the difficulties associated with such tests and, in *Clinton*, stressed that the real test to be applied was not the extent or quality of the advocate's incompetence but whether the conduct affected the safety of the conviction in accordance with s. 2(1) of the Criminal Appeal Act 1968. In *Scollan* [1999] Crim LR 566, the Court approved that approach and said that the position had been unaffected by the amendment of s. 2(1) by the Criminal Appeal Act 1995 (see **D26.15**). Similarly, in *Nangle* [2001] Crim LR 506, the Court emphasised that a test requiring flagrant incompetence might not be appropriate in the light of the ECHR, Article 6. What mattered was whether the appellant had had a fair trial; if the conduct of the lawyers was such that that requirement had not been met, the Court might have to intervene. In *Boodram v State of Trinidad and Tobago* [2001] UKPC 20, [2002] 1 Cr App R 12 (103), the Privy Council observed that, if the conduct of an appellant's lawyers was such that the appellant had been denied due process, the conclusion would be that the appellant had not had a fair trial and the conviction should be quashed without the need for an investigation of the impact of the lawyers' failings on the outcome of the trial.

See also *Ekaireb* [2015] EWCA Crim 1936, where the main focus of the complaint concerning the conduct of trial counsel was his closing speech. The Court quoted with approval the dictum of Buxton LJ in *Day* [2003] EWCA Crim 1060 (at [15]): 'in order to establish lack of safety in an incompetence case the appellant has to go beyond the incompetence and show that the incompetence led to identifiable errors or irregularities in the trial, which themselves rendered the process unfair or unsafe'. The Court observed that there had not previously been a case in which a closing speech formed the basis of a successful appeal against conviction and refused the appeal.

D26.25 Guidance as to the procedure to be followed by an advocate when dealing with an appeal involving criticism of counsel was issued by the Bar Council and approved by Lord Taylor CJ in December 1995. The guidance was quoted with approval by Judge LJ in *Doherty* [1997] 2 Cr App R 218, and the importance of advocates following that guidance was emphasised in *Nasser* (1998) *The Times*, 19 February 1998. Paragraph A2-7.2 of the *Guide to Commencing Proceedings in the Court of Appeal Criminal Division* (August 2018) describes the waiver procedure which is required of an applicant when grounds of appeal criticising the conduct of lawyers are advanced. See also *Achogbuo* [2014] EWCA Crim 567, [2014] 2 Cr App R 7 (94), where Thomas LJ stated (at [16]):

> Before applications are made to this court alleging incompetent representation which is based upon an account given by a convicted criminal, we expect lawyers to take proper steps to ascertain by independent means, including contacting the previous lawyers, as to whether there is any objective and independent basis for the grounds of appeal.

See also *Kanu* [2014] EWCA Crim 67, and *McCook* [2014] EWCA Crim 734, [2016] 2 Cr App R 30 (388), in which Lord Thomas CJ stated (at [11]) that all counsel dealing with an appeal who have replaced trial counsel are required to 'go to . . . counsel who have previously acted to ensure that the facts are correct'. This means, in practice, that counsel with conduct of the appeal should send their advice and grounds and any other relevant documents to previous counsel and ask them whether the contents are correct. In *Roberts* [2016] EWCA Crim 71, [2016] 2 Cr App R (S) 14 (98) it was confirmed that this duty even applies in an application for leave to appeal against sentence. The Court of Appeal reiterated the duty on counsel in *Grant-Murray* [2017] EWCA Crim 1228.

Rejection of Submission of No Case to Answer

D26.26 The wrongful rejection of a submission of no case to answer at the close of the prosecution case will lead to the conclusion that a conviction is unsafe (*Abbott* [1955] 2 QB 497). That can be so even when the appellant has given evidence and admitted guilt in cross-examination (*Smith* [1999] 2 Cr App R 238). The failure of an experienced advocate to make a submission of no case will not preclude the quashing of a conviction on the basis that there was in fact no case to answer, but the Court of Appeal will presume that the advocate had reason to not make the submission and will look at the whole of the evidence in making its decision. The Court will not ordinarily interfere if a submission would have succeeded but was not made, and evidence of guilt emerged later in the trial (*Juett* [1981] Crim LR 113).

Defects in the Indictment

D26.27 There are a number of different challenges to the safety of a conviction which can be made by reference to defects in the indictment.

Where the indictment charges an offence not known to law, the conviction will be quashed (*DPP v Bhagwan* [1972] AC 60). That will be the case even if the accused pleads guilty or no point is taken at trial (*Whitehouse* (1977) 65 Cr App R 33).

Where the indictment is preferred and signed without jurisdiction, the proceedings will be a nullity (*Thompson* (1975) 61 Cr App R 108, but see *Ashton* [2006] EWCA Crim 794, [2007] 1 WLR 181). A bill of indictment must be duly signed by the proper officer of the court for it to be a valid indictment. Without such an indictment, there could be no valid trial on indictment (*Clarke* [2008] UKHL 8, [2008] 2 Cr App R 2 (18)). But see **D11.5** and the CAJA 2009, s. 116. See also *J* [2018] EWCA Crim 2485, [2019] 1 Cr App R 10 (122) where trials proceeded on indictments that had been uploaded to the Crown Court Digital Case System but had not been formally amended and the defendants had not been arraigned on them. The Court of Appeal dismissed the appeals against conviction, observing that although the proper course would have been for the original indictments to have been amended and for the defendants to have been re-arraigned, those procedural errors had not resulted in any unfairness to the defendants, nor had they otherwise called into question the safety of their convictions.

Where an indictment is duplicitous, a conviction may be quashed if the duplicity results in the conviction being unsafe (*Cain* [1983] Crim LR 802; *Levantiz* [1999] 1 Cr App R 465). That is so whether objection was taken at trial or not (*Molloy* [1921] 2 KB 364).

When counts are improperly joined or included in an indictment contrary to CrimPR 3.29(4) (see **D11.63**), the Administration of Justice (Miscellaneous Provisions) Act 1933, s. 2(2), or the CJA 1988, s. 40, the conviction may be quashed. If the joinder of counts falls foul of s. 2(2) of the 1933 Act, the conviction will be quashed subject to the caveat that application must be made at trial to quash the indictment. In *Morry* [1946] KB 153, the appellant had been unrepresented at trial but the trial judge raised the point and that was held to be sufficient. In *Nisbet* [1972] 1 QB 37, the Court of Appeal expressed the *obiter* view that it had inherent jurisdiction to quash added or substituted counts if they might result in injustice even though they were founded on the committal papers and no objection was taken at trial. If counts are improperly joined contrary to CrimPR 10.2 or s. 40, the conviction in relation to the wrongly joined count will be quashed (*Smith* [1997] 1 Cr App R 390).

For a review of the authorities on the effects of misjoinder, see *McGrath* [2013] EWCA Crim 1261.

For the effect of proceeding on an indictment in respect of allegations which are time-barred see *Walker* [2017] EWCA Crim 392, [2018] 1 Cr App R 19 (289).

Inconsistent Verdicts and Jury Irregularities

The Court of Appeal will quash a conviction based on apparently inconsistent verdicts only if those verdicts are such that no reasonable jury applying its mind to the evidence could have reached the conclusions that it did (*Durante* [1972] 3 All ER 962, adopting the judgment of Devlin J in *Stone* (13 December 1954 unreported)). For examples of the importance of the scrutiny of the facts of a case in the application of this rule, see *Drury* (1971) 56 Cr App R 104; *Kirby* (1972) 56 Cr App R 758; *Grizzle* [1991] Crim LR 553; *McKechnie* (1991) 94 Cr App R 51; *Harrison* [1994] Crim LR 859; *Aldred* [1995] Crim LR 160; *Malashev* [1997] Crim LR 587; *G* [1998] Crim LR 483; *Hayward* [2000] Crim LR 189; *B & Q plc* [2005] EWCA Crim 2297; *Burke* [2006] EWCA Crim 3122; *W* [2009] EWCA Crim 476 and *S* [2014] EWCA Crim 927. **D26.28**

In *Fanning* [2016] EWCA Crim 550, [2016] 2 Cr App R 19 (259), the Court of Appeal reasserted that the test to be applied in determining whether a conviction should be quashed is that set out in *Durante* and *Stone*, and stated that it is necessary on appeal to demonstrate the verdicts were not merely inconsistent but were so inconsistent as to demand interference on appeal.

In *P* [2018] EWCA Crim 2492, the appellant's convictions were quashed because they were by a majority of nine to two. By virtue of the Juries Act 1974, s. 17(1), when a jury is only 11 in number any majority verdict must be one on which at least ten of the jury are agreed. When there are only ten jurors remaining, the verdict must be one on which at least nine are agreed.

Misconduct by jurors in various forms can lead to the quashing of a conviction by the Court of Appeal. For example, in *Young* [1995] QB 324 a number of jurors consulted a Ouija board whilst in retirement. The Court of Appeal quashed the conviction, taking the view that there was a real danger that some jurors may have been influenced by it and that D was thereby prejudiced (see **D19.29**). Many cases of juror misconduct have centred on the downloading of information from the internet, which, following the implementation of the CJCA 2015, s. 71, is now a criminal offence (see **D13.67** and **D19.15**). In *Karakaya* [2005] EWCA Crim 346, [2005] 2 Cr App R 5 (77) a juror had downloaded material from the internet which prejudiced D and concerned matters to which the prosecution would not have been able to refer. The Court of Appeal quashed the conviction.

CrimPD VI, paras. 26M.1 to 26M.58 (see Supplement, **CPD.26M**), contain detailed guidance as to the procedure to be followed should any irregularity emerge.

Conduct of the Trial Judge

D26.29 Excessive judicial intervention during the course of the evidence of the accused has sometimes led to the quashing of a conviction. In *Hulusi* (1974) 58 Cr App R 378, Lawton LJ summed up the principle underlying such appeals (at p. 385):

> It is a fundamental principle of an English trial that, if an accused gives evidence, he must be allowed to do so without being badgered and interrupted. Judges should remember that most people go into the witness-box, whether they be witnesses for the Crown or the defence, in a state of nervousness. They are anxious to do their best. They expect to receive a courteous hearing, and when they find, almost as soon as they get into the witness-box and are starting to tell their story, that the judge of all people is intervening in a hostile way, then, human nature being what it is, they are liable to become confused and not to do as well as they would have done had they not been badgered and interrupted.

Conduct other than interruption which prevents justice being done to the defence case can also give rise to a successful ground of appeal against conviction (*Barnes* (1970) 55 Cr App R 100). In *Alves* [1997] 1 Cr App R 78, the Court of Appeal held that dismissive remarks about the prospects of acquittal, albeit in the absence of the jury, when D was in the course of giving evidence, would have the same inhibiting effect on an accused as interruption, and quashed the conviction. In *Cordingley* [2007] EWCA Crim 2174, the Court expressed the view that exchanges between the judge and counsel betrayed a rudeness and discourtesy on the judge's part of which he should be ashamed. The judge had also delayed a change of clothes for D after he had withdrawn his bail. The Court observed that the safety of a conviction does not simply depend on the strength of evidence the jury hears, but also on the observance of due process. It was an inescapable effect of the judge's conduct that D must have been inhibited in the course of his defence. In *Cole* [2008] EWCA Crim 3234, the Court quashed a conviction for dangerous driving when the trial judge had not only made inappropriate interventions, but had treated defence counsel's questions and submissions with hostility. It culminated in his sending a note to defence counsel headed '6P's'. The 6P's were explained in bold as 'Prior Planning Prevents Piss Poor Performance'. See also *Lashley* [2005] EWCA Crim 2015; *Harirbafan* [2008] EWCA Crim 1967; *Copsey* [2008] EWCA Crim 2043; *Michel* [2009] UKPC 41, [2010] 1 WLR 879; *Malcolm* [2011] EWCA Crim 2069; *Meall* [2011] EWCA Crim 2526; *Myers* [2018] EWCA Crim 2191 and *Marchant* [2018] EWCA Crim 2606, [2019] 4 WLR 20.

APPROACH OF COURT OF APPEAL TO COMMONLY OCCURRING ERRORS IN SUMMING-UP

D26.30 Plainly, errors in the summing-up may found a successful appeal against conviction if the error leads to the conclusion that the conviction is unsafe.

Misdirection on Law

D26.31 A misdirection as to law will lead to the quashing of a conviction only if that misdirection causes the conviction to be unsafe. Thus, in *Edwards* (1983) 77 Cr App R 5 and *Donoghue* (1987)

86 Cr App R 267, the Court of Appeal dismissed the appeals despite the judge having failed to direct the jury as to the standard and burden of proof respectively. In each case the Court observed that the evidence against D was very strong and justified the exercise of the proviso which then applied under s. 2(1) of the Criminal Appeal Act 1968. By contrast, in *James* [1997] Crim LR 598, the Court quashed a conviction for robbery where the trial judge had failed to direct the jury that it was necessary for the force used to be for the purpose of stealing. That direction was crucial to distinguish between robbery and theft. See also *Vinall* [2011] EWCA Crim 2652, [2012] 1 Cr App R 29 (400).

Wrongful Withdrawal of Issues from the Jury

In *Sheaf* (1925) 19 Cr App R 46, Avory J said 'When we once arrive at the conclusion that a vital question of fact has not been left to the jury, the only ground on which we can affirm a conviction is that there has been no miscarriage of justice, on the ground that if the question had been left to the jury, they must necessarily have come to the conclusion that the appellant was guilty'. Thus, if a judge fails to direct a jury as to an issue of fact going to an element of the offence, the conviction may be quashed if it is, as a result, unsafe. **D26.32**

Where the evidence on a particular issue is agreed, it can be appropriate for a judge to direct a jury that they may draw an adverse inference against the accused on that issue. But if the judge removes all issues of fact and law from the jury so that they are effectively directed to convict, the conviction is highly likely to be quashed (*Stonehouse* [1978] AC 55). That is not inevitably so if a not guilty verdict from a properly directed jury would have been perverse (*Thompson* [1984] 3 All ER 565).

Misdirection on Facts

A misstatement or omission of a fact in the course of the summing-up may lead to the quashing of a conviction if the fact was of such importance that, if it had been correctly stated, the jury may not have reached the same verdict. In *Bateson* [1969] 3 All ER 1372, the Court of Appeal quashed the conviction where the judge told the jury that D had first mentioned his defence when the trial had commenced. The Court took the view that it was at least 'on the cards' that the jury would have acquitted if the facts had been correctly stated to them. Conversely in *Wright* [1974] 58 Cr App R 444, the Court dismissed an appeal when the misdirection as to facts was not sufficiently central. Scarman LJ said (at p. 452): **D26.33**

> At the end of the day, when the appellant's case is not that the judge erred in law but that the judge erred in his handling of the facts, the question must be, first of all, was there error, and secondly, if there was, was it significant error which might have misled the jury? If this court has a lurking doubt it is its duty to quash the conviction as unsafe, but this court... has reached the clear conclusion that this verdict was safe and satisfactory.

Improper Comment on Facts or Defence Case

A judge is entitled to comment on the facts and express an opinion as to those facts, so it is rare that an appeal will be successful when it is based on such judicial comments. It is only when a judge exhibits blatant unfairness and pro-prosecution bias that the conviction will be imperilled. In *Canny* (1945) 30 Cr App R 143, the conviction was quashed when the judge repeatedly described the defence case as absurd. Similarly, in *Berrada* (1989) 91 Cr App R 131, the conviction was quashed when the judge described allegations put by the defence to a prosecution witness as 'really monstrous' and 'wicked'. **D26.34**

Comment on Failure of Accused to Testify

A direction on the failure of an accused to testify is an important one and an error as to that direction may give rise to an arguable ground of appeal. Detailed consideration of the appropriate direction to the jury can be found at **F20.41**. **D26.35**

Comment on the Accused's Character

D26.36 Detailed consideration of the elements of directions as to character may be found at **F13**. An inappropriate direction may lead to the quashing of a conviction. In *Hunter* [2015] EWCA Crim 631, [2015] 1 WLR 5367 (see **F14.3**), the Court of Appeal observed that, where an accused is entitled to a good character direction and the judge fails to give it in proper form, the conviction will not be quashed as a matter of course. An appellate court should interfere only if, on the facts, it was not properly open to the judge to reach the conclusions he or she did.

EFFECT OF SUCCESSFUL APPEAL AGAINST CONVICTION

D26.37 **Criminal Appeal Act 1968, ss. 2 and 7**

2.—(2) In the case of an appeal against conviction the court shall, if they allow the appeal, quash the conviction.

(3) An order of the Court of Appeal quashing a conviction shall, except when under section 7 below the appellant is ordered to be retried, operate as a direction to the court of trial to enter, instead of the record of conviction, a judgment and verdict of acquittal.

7.—(1) Where the Court of Appeal allow an appeal against conviction and it appears to the court that the interests of justice so require, they may order the appellant to be retried.

(2) A person shall not under this section be ordered to be retried for any offence other than—

(a) the offence of which he was convicted at the original trial and in respect of which his appeal is allowed as mentioned in subsection (1) above;

(b) an offence of which he could have been convicted at the original trial on an indictment for the first mentioned offence; or

(c) an offence charged in an alternative count of the indictment in respect of which no verdict was given in consequence of his being convicted of the first-mentioned offence.

Decision to Order a Retrial

D26.38 Under s. 2(2) of the Criminal Appeal Act 1968, the Court of Appeal may quash a conviction and order that the court of trial enter a verdict of not guilty against the accused. Alternatively, the Court may order a retrial of the successful appellant under s. 7.

The factors which the Court will take into account when deciding whether or not to order a retrial will include the length of time which has elapsed between the appellant's original conviction and the successful appeal and the extent to which any fresh evidence received undermines the strength of the case against the appellant (*Saunders* (1974) 58 Cr App R 248; *Flower* [1966] 1 QB 146; *McIlkenny* (1991) 93 Cr App R 287).

Occasionally, a retrial will not be ordered because of considerable publicity surrounding the alleged offences which is adverse to the defendant (*Taylor* (1994) 98 Cr App R 361). But, it is submitted, an application that the appellant should not be retried because of prejudicial publicity is highly unlikely to succeed. The Court of Appeal will allow such an application only if it is satisfied on the balance of probabilities that, as a result of the publicity, one or all of the verdicts returned by a jury would be unsafe. The Court may take account of the time between the publicity and the retrial and can seek to minimise its effect by a change of trial venue and suitable questions to the jury (*Stone* [2001] EWCA Crim 297, [2001] Crim LR 465).

In *Maxwell* [2010] UKSC 48, [2011] 2 Cr App R 31 (448), a case involving serious prosecutorial misconduct, the Supreme Court ruled (by a majority) that the Court of Appeal was entitled to order a retrial notwithstanding the abuse of process that had been revealed to have taken place prior to the original trial. The 'interests of justice' test in s. 7 called for an exercise of judgement and in the instant case (involving a grave crime and an admission of guilt) it would be wrong to override the exercise by the Court of Appeal of its discretion.

D26.39 Section 8 includes a number of procedural requirements to be followed when a retrial is ordered. The most important of those requirements are as follows:

(a) a new indictment must be preferred by the Court of Appeal;
(b) arraignment must be within two months of the quashing of the conviction unless the Court allows longer;
(c) at any time after the two months has elapsed, the appellant may apply for the order for retrial to be set aside and for a verdict of not guilty to be entered;
(d) upon receipt of such an application, the Court may quash the order for retrial or may allow late arraignment — the Court will allow late arraignment only if the prosecution have acted with due expedition and there is good and sufficient cause that the retrial take place despite the delay following the order for a retrial.

In *Horne* [1992] Crim LR 304, the prosecution papers were lost and, as a result, D was not arraigned within the two-month time-limit. The prosecution were held not to have acted with due expedition despite an early trial date being set down. In *Jones* [2002] EWCA Crim 2284, [2003] 1 Cr App R 20 (313), an adjourned date for the arraignment was set down outside the two-month period without the prosecution noticing the difficulties that listing would produce. The Court of Appeal held that the prosecution had acted with due expedition but if the applicable test had been of due diligence (as in relation to custody time-limits), the position would have been different. Defence lawyers were also criticised for failing to draw the difficulties to the attention of the prosecution so that they could comply with the order of the court.

The procedure to be followed when making an application to arraign more than two months after the Court ordered a retrial, or when the accused wants such an order to be set aside more than two months after that order, is set out in CrimPR 39.14 (see Supplement, **R39.14**).

Partially Successful Appeal: Substituting Verdict

Criminal Appeal Act 1968, s. 3 **D26.40**

(1) This section applies on an appeal against conviction, where the appellant has been convicted of an offence to which he did not plead guilty and the jury could on the indictment have found him guilty of some other offence, and on the finding of the jury it appears to the Court of Appeal that the jury must have been satisfied of facts which proved him guilty of the other offence.
(2) The Court may, instead of allowing or dismissing the appeal, substitute for the verdict found by the jury a verdict of guilty of the other offence, and pass such sentence in substitution for the sentence passed at the trial as may be authorised by law for the other offence, not being a sentence of greater severity.

Section 3 allows the Court of Appeal to substitute a verdict of guilty for an offence other than that of which the appellant was convicted if it appears to the Court that:

(a) the jury could on the indictment have found the appellant guilty of the substituted offence, the allegation of which was expressly or impliedly included in the allegation in the particular count in the indictment, and
(b) the jury must have been satisfied of facts which proved the appellant guilty of the substituted offence (*Graham* [1997] 1 Cr App R 302).

Section 3 applies to two broad categories of cases. The first is where the appellant was tried and convicted on a single count but the evidence was such that the jury could have convicted of the substituted offence. For example, in *Spratt* [1980] 2 All ER 969, following a conviction for murder, fresh evidence as to diminished responsibility allowed the substitution of a conviction for manslaughter.

The second category of case is where there are counts charged in the alternative and the jury have convicted on a count which is not supported by the evidence. The Court may substitute the alternative count provided the jury have not already entered a not guilty count in relation to that count (*Seymour* [1954] 1 All ER 1006; but see also *Smythe* (1980) 72 Cr App R 8 for a minor variation of the rule).

For illustration of the care that must be taken with the application of s. 3 in practice, see *Shields* [2011] EWCA Crim 2343, [2012] 1 Cr App R 9 (113).

Section 3A provides that, if the Court quashes a conviction produced by a guilty plea, in circumstances where the appellant could have pleaded guilty to or been convicted of another offence and it appears to the Court that the plea of guilty indicates an admission by the appellant of acts which would make him or her guilty of the other offence, the Court may substitute a plea of guilty to that offence without allowing or dismissing the appeal. The Court may then proceed to sentence for that offence but may not pass a more grave sentence than that originally passed.

In *Lawrence* [2013] EWCA Crim 1054, [2014] 1 WLR 106, the Court of Appeal said that s. 3A has to be construed strictly; its operation must be confined to cases where the guilty plea inevitably involves an admission to the alternative offence. Any other approach would involve the Court in making a decision as to whether a defence was available and that could not be permitted given the importance of the right to jury trial. In *Lawrence*, a wrongly entered guilty plea to possession of a prohibited weapon could not be substituted with a conviction for possessing a firearm without a certificate contrary to the FA 1968, s. 1(1)(a), as the indictment alleging possession of the prohibited weapon did not, and did not need to, allege the absence of a firearm certificate so there could not have been a conviction on that indictment of the offence sought to be substituted. However, in *White* [2014] EWCA Crim 714, [2014] 2 Cr App R 14 (194) the Court of Appeal allowed substitution of conviction for appropriate offences notwithstanding that the indictment on which the appellant had been convicted was wholly flawed.

Sentence when Appeal Allowed on Part Only of an Indictment

D26.41 If an appellant has been convicted in the Crown Court of a number of offences and the Court of Appeal quashes some of the convictions but not others, the Court is entitled to resentence on the counts of which the offender remains convicted and may even increase the sentence on those counts (*Hewgill* [2011] EWCA Crim 1778). The power, which arises under the Criminal Appeal Act 1968, s. 4, is limited to the extent that the Court may not pass a sentence of greater totality or severity than that which was originally passed by the Crown Court. The Court of Appeal may resentence even on those counts for which the Crown Court imposed no separate penalty (*O'Grady* (1941) 28 Cr App R 33; *Dolan* (1975) 62 Cr App R 36).

RIGHT OF APPEAL AGAINST SENTENCE

Statutory Basis of Appeal against Sentence

D26.42 The right to appeal against sentence is statutory and derives from the Criminal Appeal Act 1968. Section 9 governs appeals against sentence following conviction on indictment. Appeals from sentences imposed in the Crown Court following summary conviction are covered by s. 10. The definition of sentence for the purposes of the sections is to be found in s. 50.

Whether the appeal lies under s. 9 or s. 10, the appellant must, by virtue of s. 11, either have leave to appeal from the Court of Appeal or the sentencing judge must certify that the case is fit for appeal against sentence. CrimPD III, paras. 14H.1 to 14H.4 (see Supplement, **CPD.14H**), deal with the certification of fitness for appeal against sentence. Paragraph 14H.3 directs that a sentencing judge should not certify an appeal against sentence 'merely in the light of mitigation to which, in his opinion, he has given due weight'. The reality in practice is that certificates of appeal against sentence are rarely applied for and are even less seldom granted. Paragraphs 14H.5 and 14H.6 govern the grant of bail pending appeal following the issue of a certificate of fitness for appeal. Bail can only be granted in the Crown Court within 28 days of the conviction or sentence which is to be the subject of the appeal and may not be granted if an application for bail has already been made to the Court of Appeal. The procedure for bail to be granted by a judge of the Crown Court pending an appeal is governed by CrimPR Part 14. The length of time likely to elapse before the appeal is heard is not relevant to the decision as to the grant of a certificate. However, if a judge issues a certificate, it may be one factor to take into account in deciding whether to grant bail. If the judge does grant bail, a condition of residence in line with the practice of the Court of Appeal should be considered (CrimPD III, para. 14H.6).

Sentence Following Conviction on Indictment

Criminal Appeal Act 1968, ss. 9 and 50 **D26.43**

9.—(1) A person who has been convicted of an offence on indictment may appeal to the Court of Appeal against any sentence (not being a sentence fixed by law) passed on him for the offence, whether passed on his conviction or in subsequent proceedings.

(1A) In subsection (1) of this section, the reference to a sentence fixed by law does not include a reference to an order made under subsection (2) or (4) of section 269 of the Criminal Justice Act 2003 in relation to a life sentence (as defined in section 277 of that Act) that is fixed by law.

(2) A person who on conviction on indictment has also been convicted of a summary offence under paragraph 6 of Schedule 3 to the Crime and Disorder Act 1998 (power of Crown Court to deal with summary offence where person sent for trial for indictable-only offence) may appeal to the Court of Appeal against any sentence passed on him for the summary offence (whether on his conviction or in subsequent proceedings) under subsection (7) of that section or sub-paragraph (4) of that paragraph.

50.—(1) In this Act, 'sentence', in relation to an offence, includes any order made by a court when dealing with an offender including, in particular—

(a) a hospital order under Part III of the Mental Health Act 1983, with or without a restriction order;

(b) an interim hospital order under that Part;

(bb) a hospital direction and a limitation direction under that Part;

(c) a recommendation for deportation;

(ca) a confiscation order under Part 2 of the Proceeds of Crime Act 2002 (but not a determination under section 10A of that Act);

(cb) an order which varies a confiscation order made under Part 2 of the Proceeds of Crime Act 2002 if the varying order is made under section 21, 22 or 29 of that Act (but not otherwise);

(cc) a direction under section 20(3) or 21(3) of the Crime (Sentences) Act 1997 (extended supervision for sexual or violent offenders);

(d) a confiscation order under the Drug Trafficking Act 1994 other than one made by the High Court;

(e) a confiscation order under Part VI of the Criminal Justice Act 1988;

(f) an order varying a confiscation order of a kind which is included by virtue of paragraph (d) or (e) above;

(g) an order made by the Crown Court varying a confiscation order which was made by the High Court by virtue of section 19 of the Act of 1994;

(h) a declaration of relevance within the meaning of section 23 of the Football Spectators Act 1989; and

(i) an order under section 129(2) of the Licensing Act 2003 (forfeiture or suspension of personal licence).

(1A) Section 14 of the Powers of Criminal Courts (Sentencing) Act 2000 (under which a conviction of an offence for which an order for conditional or absolute discharge is made is deemed not to be a conviction except for certain purposes) shall not prevent an appeal under this Act, whether against conviction or otherwise.

(2) Any power of the Criminal Division of the Court of Appeal to pass a sentence includes a power to make a recommendation for deportation in cases where the court from which the appeal lies had power to make such a recommendation.

(3) An order relating to a requirement to make a payment under regulations under section 23 or 24 of the Legal Aid, Sentencing and Punishment of Offenders Act 2012 is not a sentence for the purposes of this Act.

A person convicted on indictment may appeal to the Court of Appeal against *any* sentence passed for the offence, unless it is one fixed by law (i.e. the life sentence for murder) (s. 9(1)). Under s. 9(2) **D26.44**

D

Part D Procedure

as it applied prior to the abolition of committals, if an offender is convicted on indictment and pleads guilty to an additional offence which was committed or transferred to the Crown Court by the magistrates under the CJA 1988, s. 41, the offender's right of appeal extended to the sentence for that matter also. The appeal is available if the sentence is passed at the time of the conviction or later. Thus, the right of appeal exists if an offender is resentenced for an offence following subsequent offending. Equally, if an offender is convicted of drug trafficking offences and is subsequently made the subject of a confiscation order, the offender may appeal against the confiscation order (*Neal* [1999] Crim LR 509).

Section 50(1) of the 1968 Act states that 'sentence' includes any order made by a court when dealing with an offender'. The definition therefore covers not only the penalty but also many orders made ancillary to that sentence. Thus an order to pay costs (*Hayden* [1975] 2 All ER 558) or compensation (see the numerous cases such as *Vivian* [1979] 1 All ER 48) may be the subject of appeal to the Court of Appeal. Other ancillary orders which have been held to be part of the sentence for the purposes of an appeal are restitution orders under the Theft Act 1968, s. 28 (*Parker* [1970] 2 All ER 458); orders binding an offender over to come up for judgment if required to do so (*Williams* [1982] 3 All ER 1092); and orders revoking a parole licence (*Welch* [1982] 2 All ER 824). Section 50(1) also specifically provides that hospital orders under Part III of the Mental Health Act 1983 (whether with or without a restriction order) and recommendations for deportation are part of the sentence.

Although by virtue of s. 9(1) it is not possible to appeal against the mandatory life sentence for murder, it is possible to appeal against the minimum term set by the court or against a whole life term (s. 9(1A)). Such appeals are routinely heard by the Court of Appeal. Moreover, the period specified in respect of a discretionary life sentence under s. 82A of the PCC(S)A 2000 is susceptible to appeal. An appeal can be instituted against either the failure of a sentencer to specify a period (*Hollies* (1995) 16 Cr App R (S) 463), or against the actual period which the sentencer fixes (*D* (1995) 16 Cr App R (S) 564). (For details of s. 82A, see **E4.25**.)

Sentence Following Summary Conviction and Crown Court Disposal

D26.45 **Criminal Appeal Act 1968, s. 10**

(1) This section has effect for providing rights of appeal against sentence when a person is dealt with by the Crown Court (otherwise than on appeal from a magistrates' court) for an offence of which he was not convicted on indictment.

(2) The proceedings from which an appeal against sentence lies under this section are those where an offender convicted of an offence by a magistrates' court—
   (a) is committed by the court to be dealt with for his offence at the Crown Court; or'
   (b) having been made the subject of an order for conditional discharge or a youth community order within the meaning of the Powers of Criminal Courts (Sentencing) Act 2000 or a community order within the meaning of the Criminal Justice Act 2003 or given a suspended sentence, appears or is brought before the Crown Court to be further dealt with for his offence.

(3) An offender dealt with for an offence at the Crown Court in a proceeding to which subsection (2) of this section applies may appeal to the Court of Appeal against any sentence passed on him for the offence by the Crown Court.

D26.46 The right of appeal against a sentence imposed by the Crown Court for which the offender was summarily convicted is governed by s. 10. The appeal arises when (a) an offender is committed for sentence (e.g., under the PCC(S)A 2000, s. 3 or s. 6), or (b) having been made the subject of an order for conditional discharge or a community order or given a suspended sentence of imprisonment, the offender breaches the order or suspended sentence by a subsequent conviction and falls to be dealt with by the Crown Court for the breach (s. 10(2)(a) and (b)). Although such cases are dealt with relatively infrequently, there are two main situations in which such matters come before the Crown Court, namely:

(a) the offender is summarily convicted of an offence which puts him or her in breach of an order mentioned in s. 10(2)(b) that was made by a magistrates' court and the convicting magistrates' court decides to commit the offender for sentence in respect of the subsequent offence and also decides to commit the offender to be dealt with for the breach;

(b) the offender is summarily convicted of an offence which puts him or her in breach of a relevant order previously made by the Crown Court following committal for sentence for a summary conviction. In such a case, the magistrates' court may either commit the offender to be dealt with for the breach or may decline to commit but, in the latter case, the Crown Court may secure the attendance of the offender before it by the appropriate process.

The previous limitation of the right of appeal to a sentence imposing a term of imprisonment of six months or more has been removed by the CJA 2003, s. 319. Thus any offender committed to the Crown Court for sentence may institute an appeal against the sentence imposed.

Powers of the Court of Appeal when Determining an Appeal against Sentence

Criminal Appeal Act 1968, s. 11 D26.47

(1) Subject to subsection (1A) below, an appeal against sentence, whether under section 9 or section 10 of this Act, lies only with the leave of the Court of Appeal.

(1A) If, within 28 days of the date on which sentence was passed, the judge who passed it grants a certificate that the case is fit for appeal under section 9 or 10 of this Act, an appeal lies under this section without the leave of the Court of Appeal.

(2) Where the Crown Court, in dealing with an offender either on his conviction on indictment or in a proceeding to which section 10(2) of this Act applies, has passed on him two or more sentences in the same proceeding..., being sentences against which an appeal lies under section 9(1) or section 10, an appeal or application for leave to appeal against any one of those sentences shall be treated as an appeal or application in respect of both or all of them.

(2A) Where following conviction on indictment a person has been convicted under section 41 of the Criminal Justice Act 1988 of a summary offence an appeal or application for leave to appeal against any sentence for the offence triable either way shall be treated also as an appeal or application in respect of any sentence for the summary offence and an appeal or application for leave to appeal against any sentence for the summary offence shall be treated also as an appeal or application in respect of the offence triable either way.

(2B) If the appellant or applicant was convicted on indictment of two or more offences triable either way, the references to the offence triable either way in subsection (2A) above are to be construed, in relation to any summary offence of which he was convicted under section 41 of the Criminal Justice Act 1988 following the conviction on indictment, as references to the offence triable either way specified in the notice relating to that summary offence which was given under subsection (2) of that section.

(3) On an appeal against sentence the Court of Appeal, if they consider that the appellant should be sentenced differently for an offence for which he was dealt with by the court below may—

   (a) quash any sentence or order which is the subject of the appeal; and

   (b) in place of it pass such sentence or make such order as they think appropriate for the case and as the court below had power to pass or make when dealing with him for the offence;

but the court shall so exercise their powers under this subsection that, taking the case as a whole, the appellant is not more severely dealt with on appeal than he was dealt with by the court below.

(3A) Where the Court of Appeal exercise their power under paragraph (a) of subsection (3) to quash a confiscation order, the Court may, instead of proceeding under paragraph (b) of that subsection, direct the Crown Court to proceed afresh under the relevant enactment.

(3B) When proceeding afresh pursuant to subsection (3A), the Crown Court shall comply with any directions the Court of Appeal may make.

(3C) The Court of Appeal shall exercise the power to give such directions so as to ensure that any *confiscation* order made in respect of the appellant by the Crown Court does not deal more severely with the appellant than the order quashed under subsection (3)(a).

(3D) [Defines confiscation order and relevant enactment by reference to the Drug Trafficking Offences Act 1986, the CJA 1988, the Drug Trafficking Act 1994 and the POCA 2002.]

(4) [Repealed.]

(5) [Concerns the position where the Court of Appeal quashes an interim hospital order but does not replace it with its own sentence.]

(6) [Repealed.]

(7) For the purposes of this section, any two or more sentences are to be treated as passed in the same proceeding if—
(a) they are passed on the same day; or
(b) they are passed on different days but the court in passing any one of them states that it is treating that one together with the other or others as substantially one sentence.

D26.48 Upon appeal against sentence, the Court of Appeal may quash the sentence and substitute any other sentence or order that it deems appropriate, provided that the substituted sentence could lawfully have been passed by the Crown Court and provided also that the appellant is not dealt with more severely when the case is viewed as a whole. The Court may not impose a mandatory sentence where a Crown Court has failed to impose one or if it would mean treating the appellant more severely (*Reynolds* [2007] EWCA Crim 538, [2007] 2 Cr App R (S) 87 (553)).

As the Court must look at the position as a whole when deciding whether the substituted sentence would constitute treating the appellant more severely, it follows that, if the offender was sentenced for two or more matters, the Court may increase the sentence for one of them and adjust the others accordingly (see, e.g., *McKenna* (1985) 7 Cr App R (S) 348).

In *Rogers* [2016] EWCA Crim 801, [2016] 2 Cr App R (S) 36 (370), the Court of Appeal approved *Caines* [2006] EWCA Crim 2915, [2007] 1 WLR 1109 and re-emphasised the limitations on the use of 'update material' and 'fresh evidence' in appeals against sentence. Lord Thomas CJ explained that material the Court will hear without an application under the Criminal Appeal Act 1968, s. 23 (see **D27.24**), will include updated pre-sentence and prison reports on conduct in prison after sentence. (The Court will also receive an updated text, but the circumstances in which such material will be received are likely to be highly unusual, for the reasons explained in *AXN* [2016] EWCA Crim 590, [2016] 2 Cr App R (S) 33 (341)). However, it will not include fresh psychiatric or psychological evidence in support of an argument that a finding of dangerousness ought not to have been made or a hospital order should have been made. If an appellant seeks to introduce material of that type, the Court will apply the provisions of s. 23 (*Hughes* [2009] EWCA Crim 841, [2010] 1 Cr App R (S) 25 (146); *Vowles* [2015] EWCA Crim 45, [2015] 1 WLR 5131). Lord Thomas CJ observed that compliance with s. 23 is necessary for two reasons. First, it is incumbent on those acting for an offender to call all the evidence before the sentencing court and, therefore, persuasive evidence is required to explain why it was not all called. Second, the court must consider whether it is in the interests of justice that it should be admitted notwithstanding that failure. If the advocate in the Court of Appeal did not represent the offender at the trial or sentencing hearing, that advocate must obtain information from the advocate previously instructed as to why the evidence was not called (*Caines* at [40]). The Court also observed that it may conduct a *Newton* hearing, or a hearing analogous to that, in respect of certain alleged facts which were disputed matters of mitigation. In such a case, the evidential burden lies on the offender to establish those facts, on the balance of probabilities. However, it was established in *Ahmed* (1984) 6 Cr App R (S) 391, that a court will not interfere save in the rarest of cases with findings of a judge on a *Newton* hearing where the judge has properly directed him or herself.

D26.49 Infrequently, the relative severity of a substituted sentence to the original sentence is not immediately obvious. Examples of such situations include:

(a) '"Taking the case as a whole" means taking together the totality of the matters in respect of which the appellant was being dealt with in the court below on the day he was sentenced' (per Glidewell J in *Sandwell* (1984) 80 Cr App R 78 at p. 81). In *Sandwell*, S pleaded guilty on the same day to two offences charged in separate indictments, and was sentenced for each to, *inter alia*, 12 months' disqualification to run consecutively. There is no power to impose consecutive disqualifications and so those disqualifications fell to be quashed, but the Court of Appeal varied the sentence to two years' disqualification for each offence to run concurrently.
(b) A sentence of life imprisonment may not be substituted for a sentence of imprisonment for a fixed term of years (*Whittaker* [1967] Crim LR 431).

(c) An immediate custodial term may not normally be imposed in place of a suspended sentence (*Peppard* (1990) 12 Cr App R (S) 88, following *McCabe* (1988) 10 Cr App R (S) 134). But see *Waters* [2008] EWCA Crim 2538 and *Maughan* [2011] EWCA Crim 787, [2011] 2 Cr App R (S) 89 (493).
(d) A hospital order coupled with a restriction order for an indefinite period has been held to be no more severe than a sentence of three years' imprisonment (*Bennett* [1968] 2 All ER 753, cited with approval in *Crozier* (1990) 12 Cr App R (S) 206). Furthermore, a hospital order without restriction was substituted for a sentence of Borstal training (*Marsden* [1968] 2 All ER 341). It would appear that the rationale underlying those decisions is that, in contrast to a custodial term, a hospital order is intended to be a remedial treatment and not a punishment.
(e) A fine in combination with a custodial term may properly be substituted for a reduced custodial term (*Walton* (29 August 1989 unreported)). D had been sentenced by the court below to four months' imprisonment. He served 11 days in custody and was then released on bail. At the appeal, such term of imprisonment as would allow immediate release was substituted, with the addition of a fine of £1,000.
(f) A period of disqualification from driving may be imposed or increased where a sentence of imprisonment is reduced (*Ardani* (1983) 77 Cr App R 302). Conversely, in *McLaren* (1983) 5 Cr App R (S) 332, D's fine was increased but his period of disqualification was reduced.

Commonly Occurring Grounds of Appeal against Sentence

D26.50 From the existing case law, it is possible to identify a number of heads of appeal against sentence which have emerged. What follows is a summary of the more conspicuous of those heads of appeal.

D26.51 **Sentence Wrong in Law** The Court of Appeal will intervene when the sentence imposed on an appellant could not legally be passed. A simple example is *Corcoran* (1986) 8 Cr App R (S) 118, in which a youth convicted summarily was sentenced to three years' detention, ostensibly in accordance with s. 53(3) of the CYPA 1933 but following committal for sentence. As s. 53(3) detention could be imposed only following conviction on indictment, the Court of Appeal was forced to substitute the maximum available sentence in the youth court of 12 months' youth custody, despite observing that a sentence of three years was richly deserved.

D26.52 **Sentence Wrong in Principle or Manifestly Excessive** The Court of Appeal will interfere with a sentence if it is of the view that it was outside the broad range of appropriate penalties. The fact that a sentence is merely severe will not be sufficient. In *Nuttall* (1908) 1 Cr App R 180, Channell J said: 'This court will…be reluctant to interfere with sentences which do not seem to it to be wrong in principle, though they may appear heavy to individual judges'. Likewise, in *Gumbs* (1926) 19 Cr App R 74, Lord Hewart CJ stated:

> …this court never interferes with the discretion of the court below merely on the ground that this court might have passed a somewhat different sentence; for this court to revise a sentence there must be some error in principle.

If a sentence is not of the appropriate form (e.g., because an offender was not eligible for the custodial sentence imposed), the more appropriate description is that the sentence is 'wrong in principle'. Equally, an inappropriate combination of sentences can be most appropriately described as 'wrong in principle' (*Socratous* (1984) 6 Cr App R (S) 33, in which the imposition of a short custodial term combined with a probation order was held to be wrong in principle).

D26.53 That a sentence passed is 'manifestly excessive' is the basis that is most commonly used in the modern appeal process. An appeal will succeed only if the sentence was excessive in the sense of being outside the appropriate range for the offence and offender in question, as opposed to being merely more than the Court of Appeal itself would have passed. For example in *Withers* [1983] Crim LR 339, the principal submission was that a sentence of nine months' imprisonment for stealing £1,000 from employers was too long by three months. The Court held that a sentence of six months would not have been wrong, but to reduce the sentence by such a small amount would have been 'tinkering' with the judge's decision and the appeal was dismissed. Although the sentence was 'excessive' in one sense, it was not so excessive as to be outside the appropriate range. Equally, where a sentence was not manifestly excessive at the time that it was passed, the Court of Appeal will not interfere with the level of that sentence just because the 'tariff' for that offence is reduced after the sentence is passed or legislation alters the level of sentence to be imposed (*Graham* [1999] 2 Cr App R (S) 312).

By virtue of the CAJA 2009, s. 125(1), a judge must follow sentencing guidelines and may disregard any authority which precedes the guideline (see **E1.3**).

D26.54 **Judge's Remarks when Sentencing** If the judge's sentencing remarks tend to reveal that irrelevant factors have been taken into account in deciding the appropriate sentence to impose on the appellant, the Court of Appeal may allow the appeal and substitute a different sentence. But if the Court takes the view that the sentence was appropriate despite the flaws in the decision-making by the judge, it may nonetheless uphold the sentence. Examples of circumstances in which the judge's sentencing remarks might lead to a reduction in sentence include where the judge implies that the sentence has been increased because the offender elected trial on indictment, pleaded not guilty, or made attacks on the character of prosecution witnesses (*Skone* (1966) 51 Cr App R 165; *Scott* (1983) 5 Cr App R (S) 90; *Doab* [1983] Crim LR 569).

D26.55 **Procedural Errors** The failure of a judge to follow the correct procedure may lead to a variation in the sentence by the Court of Appeal. But that is by no means necessarily the case. The failure of a sentencing judge to secure a pre-sentence report before passing sentence in circumstances where one was required will not necessarily lead to a reduction in sentence, but the Court of Appeal will secure such a report before dealing with the appeal. Similarly, where information about an offender's antecedents has been inappropriately given to the court of sentence, the Court may either reduce the sentence or maintain it as the correct sentence in all the circumstances (*Wilkins* (1977) 66 Cr App R (S) 49; *Van Pelz* [1943] KB 157). The failure of the judge to hold a *Newton* hearing when asked to do so is more likely to result in a reduction in sentence, as the sentencing judge may well have proceeded on a basis adverse to the defendant (see *Costley* (1989) 11 Cr App R (S) 357 and **D20.22**).

D26.56 **Sense of Grievance** The Court of Appeal will intervene when the appellant has a justifiable sense of grievance at the sentence imposed following events preceding sentence. In practice, this principle applies most often when a sentencing judge orders pre-sentence reports and indicates that, if the reports are satisfactory, a non-custodial sentence will be passed, but then proceeds to send the offender into custody despite positive reports (*Gillam* (1980) 2 Cr App R (S) 267; *Ward* (1982) 4 Cr App R (S) 103). Moreover, if an indication of a non-custodial sentence is given privately to an advocate and a guilty plea follows, any subsequent judge will be bound by the indication of the first judge (*Moss* (1983) 5 Cr App R (S) 209). But if a judge indicates that the fact of ordering reports should not be taken as any indication that a non-custodial sentence would eventually be passed, or indicates that he or she is 'making no promises', then the Court will not be moved to vary the sentence imposed if a custodial sentence follows, as the appellant's hopes could not be said to have been legitimately raised (*Horton* (1985) 7 Cr App R (S) 299).

D26.57 **Disparity of Sentence** There has been some inconsistency in the approach taken by the Court of Appeal to the question of the circumstances in which a difference in sentence between co-accused can form a ground of appeal against sentence. In *Stroud* (1977) 65 Cr App R 150, Scarman LJ stated that disparity can never in itself be a sufficient ground of appeal. Instead, the question for the Court of Appeal is simply whether the sentence received by the appellant was wrong in principle or manifestly excessive. If it was not, the appeal should be dismissed, even though a co-offender was, in the Court's view, treated with undue leniency. To reduce the heavier sentence would simply result in two, rather than one, over-lenient penalties. Decisions in the same vein include *Brown* [1975] Crim LR 177, *Hair* [1978] Crim LR 698 and *Weekes* (1980) 74 Cr App R 161.

By contrast, in *Fawcett* (1983) 5 Cr App R (S) 158, the Court held that, where an offender had received a sentence which itself was not objectionable but, for no apparent good reason, was more severe than that of his co-accused, the Court could intervene if the disparity was serious. Lawton LJ said that the question to be asked is:

> ... would right-thinking members of the public, with full knowledge of all the relevant facts and circumstances, learning of this sentence consider that something had gone wrong with the administration of justice?

(See also *Wood* (1983) 5 Cr App R (S) 381 and *Sigston* [2004] EWCA Crim 1548.)

In more recent cases the Court has followed the approach in *Fawcett* (but see *Tate* (2006) 150 SJ 1192, for an example of a case following the line of reasoning in *Stroud*).

The fact that offenders who are sentenced at roughly the same time as an appellant in the same Crown Court have received more lenient sentences for comparable offences can never be relied on as a ground of appeal. The Court will not allow such comparisons to be made (*Large* (1981) 3 Cr App R (S) 80).

Failure to Distinguish between Offenders The failure of the court of sentence to distinguish between offenders when one has powerful mitigation and the other does not can give rise to a successful ground of appeal against sentence. See, e.g., *Fraser* (1982) 4 Cr App R (S) 254. **D26.58**

APPEAL AGAINST VERDICT OF NOT GUILTY BY REASON OF INSANITY

Criminal Appeal Act 1968, ss. 12 and 13 **D26.59**

12. A person in whose case there is returned a verdict of not guilty by reason of insanity may appeal to the Court of Appeal against the verdict—
(a) with the leave of the Court of Appeal; or
(b) if, within 28 days of the date of the verdict, the judge of the court of trial grants a certificate that the case is fit for appeal.

13.—(1) Subject to the provisions of this section, the Court of Appeal—
(a) shall allow an appeal under section 12 of this Act if they think that the verdict is unsafe; and
(b) shall dismiss such an appeal in any other case.
(2) [Repealed.]
(3) Where apart from this subsection—
(a) an appeal under section 12 of this Act would fall to be allowed; and
(b) none of the grounds for allowing it relates to the question of the insanity of the accused,
the Court of Appeal may dismiss the appeal if they are of opinion that, but for the insanity of the accused, the proper verdict would have been that he was guilty of an offence other than the offence charged.
(4) Where an appeal under section 12 of this Act is allowed, the following provisions apply—
(a) if the ground, or one of the grounds, for allowing the appeal is that the finding of the jury as to the insanity of the accused ought not to stand and the Court of Appeal are of opinion that the proper verdict would have been that he was guilty of an offence (whether the offence charged or any other offence of which the jury could have found him guilty), the court—
(i) shall substitute for the verdict of not guilty by reason of insanity a verdict of guilty of that offence; and
(ii) shall, subject to subsection (5) below, have the like powers of punishing or otherwise dealing with the appellant, and other powers, as the court of trial would have had if the jury had come to the substituted verdict; and
(b) in any other case, the Court of Appeal shall substitute for the verdict of the jury a verdict of acquittal.

D26.60 As with appeals against other findings in the Crown Court, leave is required to appeal a finding of not guilty by reason of insanity unless the judge certifies that the case is fit for appeal. Equally, just as s. 2 of the 1968 Act stipulates that the Court of Appeal will allow an appeal against conviction only if the verdict is unsafe, the Court takes the same approach under s. 12 to any appeal against a finding of not guilty by reason of insanity.

If the basis for allowing the appeal is that the appellant is not insane, the Court will substitute a finding of guilt of the appropriate offence and sentence accordingly. If the Court reaches the view that the appeal should be allowed on grounds which are not related to the insanity of the appellant, but which grounds undermine the safety of the conviction (such as fresh evidence showing that the appellant did not commit the offence), a verdict of not guilty will be recorded. If the Court reaches the view that a verdict of not guilty would not have been appropriate, but findings that the appellant did the act or omission charged and was under a disability were appropriate, it may make any of the orders which could have been made by the court of sentence (s. 14).

The *Guide to Commencing Proceedings in the Court of Appeal Criminal Division* (August 2018) provides valuable guidance as to the procedure to be followed upon an appeal against a verdict of not guilty by reason of insanity (see D9 of the guide).

APPEAL AGAINST FINDING OF UNFITNESS TO PLEAD

D26.61 **Criminal Appeal Act 1968, s. 15**

(1) Where there has been a determination under section 4 of the Criminal Procedure (Insanity) Act 1964 of the question of a person's fitness to be tried, and there have been findings that he is under a disability and that he did the act or made the omission charged against him, the person may appeal to the Court of Appeal against either or both of those findings.

(2) An appeal under this section lies only—
   (a) with the leave of the Court of Appeal; or
   (b) if, within 28 days from the date of the finding that the accused did the act or made the omission charged, the judge of the court of trial grants a certificate that the case is fit for appeal.

Section 15 enables the Court of Appeal to quash a finding of unfitness to plead. If the finding was made after arraignment and the Court is of the view that the appellant should have been acquitted, the Court may order the acquittal of the appellant. In other cases, following the finding that the appellant is fit to plead, the Court will ensure that the appellant is brought to trial. See also *Norman* [2008] EWCA Crim 1810, [2009] 1 Cr App R 13 (192). Guidance as to the procedure to be followed on an appeal against a finding of unfitness to plead or that the accused did the act or made the omission charged is set out at D8 of the *Guide to Commencing Proceedings in the Court of Appeal Criminal Division* (August 2018). An important lacuna in the powers of the Court is that it cannot order a retrial of the facts; if the Court decides that the jury's finding as to the facts is unsafe, it must order acquittal.

In *Roberts (Alfred)* [2019] EWCA Crim 1270, [2019] 2 Cr App R 33 (402), the Court of Appeal addressed a number of procedural points which might arise in an appeal against a finding of unfitness to plead. While no statistics are kept, the Court observed that it is estimated that the Criminal Appeal Office receives around a dozen applications for leave to appeal each year with regard to ss. 4 and 4A determinations. Those applications are often combined and many are prepared by defendants acting in person. The points the Court addressed included:

(1) An individual who has been adjudged unfit to be tried under the Criminal Procedure (Insanity) Act 1964, s. 4, is not competent to appeal in person against that ruling or any subsequent ruling under s. 4A. A person appointed by the court to present the defence case may pursue the appeal on the individual's behalf. As a matter of professional obligation, it is the duty of the appointed person to consider whether an appeal might properly lie against either determination or against the ultimate disposal. If the appointed person is of the opinion that there is no arguable ground of appeal and declines to settle a notice of appeal there

can be no valid appeal. The accused will not be competent to pursue an appeal in person nor instruct fresh counsel or solicitors to pursue an appeal on his or her behalf. Best practice in such circumstances would be for the Criminal Appeal Office first to check with the person appointed in the Crown Court to establish that no arguable grounds of appeal were identified as available. The papers should then be referred to the single judge for review and to consider whether to give any procedural direction that such a person be appointed. The single judge will reject the application without such a direction if no arguable grounds can be found. There is no right of renewal to the full court. By rejecting the application in that way, the single judge will be finding that the application is to be rejected on the ground that it is ineffective by reason of lack of mental capacity on the part of the defendant to pursue it. However, in any event, the single judge will no doubt give reasons in respect of the grounds actually sought to be advanced. If, after considering the papers, the single judge is of the view that there may potentially be arguable grounds, then the single judge may direct that fresh counsel be appointed to consider whether there are viable grounds of appeal and settle them if there are such grounds. If fresh counsel concludes that there are no viable grounds to be advanced, the case will be referred back to the single judge, who will inevitably reject the application.

(2) The accused cannot meaningfully waive privilege. The appointed representative or fresh counsel will decide in each case whether privilege will be waived, acting in the best interests of the accused and in accordance with the normal obligations to the court.

(3) There is no jurisdictional objection to appeals against a s. 4 and/or a s. 4A determination being brought under the standard Form NG applicable to all proposed appeals against conviction and sentence. However, it may be appropriate to review the contents of the form of appeal to be used in such cases.

(4) An advocate appointed to deal with such a case may be remunerated from central funds.

CrimPR 39.2 (see Supplement, **R39.2**) was amended to take account of this with effect from 6 April 2020.

APPEAL AGAINST CONVICTION: SUBSTITUTION OF FINDING OF INSANITY OR UNFITNESS TO PLEAD

Under s. 6 of the Criminal Appeal Act 1968, the Court of Appeal may quash a conviction on the basis that the offender should have been found not guilty by reason of insanity or unfit to plead. In such circumstances, the Court may then make any appropriate order which would have been available to the court of sentence. **D26.62**

JUDICIAL REVIEW OF ORDERS RESTRICTING OPEN JUSTICE

Section 159 of the CJA 1988 allows for appeals to the Court of Appeal (Criminal Division) against orders made by the Crown Court restricting reporting in relation to a trial on indictment (or public access to the trial: see **D3.122** ***et seq.***). **D26.63**

It appears that the Court of Appeal has no power to grant an order which would act to restrict reporting or access when the Crown Court has refused to make such an order (*Lee* [1993] 2 All ER 170).

Section D27 Procedure on Appeal to the Court of Appeal (Criminal Division)

THE RULES AND THE GUIDE

D27.1 The procedure for appealing to the Court of Appeal (Criminal Division) is governed by relevant sections of the Criminal Appeal Act 1968 combined with CrimPR Parts 36 to 42 (see Supplement, **R36.1** *et seq.*). Part 36 sets out general rules applicable to appeals to the Court of Appeal (Criminal Division); in Parts 37 to 42 the same general framework forms the basis for the procedure adopted in the different types of appeal dealt with in those parts. The rules also provide for the forms to be used. Part 39, read in conjunction with Part 36, deals with appeals against conviction and sentence under the Criminal Appeal Act 1968. Part 42 governs appeals under the POCA 2002.

Appeals under the CJA 2003, sch. 22, are dealt with under the Criminal Justice Act 2003 (Mandatory Life Sentences: Appeals in Transitional Cases) Order 2005 (SI 2005 No. 2798).

The *Guide to Commencing Proceedings in the Court of Appeal Criminal Division* ('the Guide') was issued in October 2008. The Guide provides a good deal of useful practical advice and was last updated in August 2018.

This section deals with the procedure for appealing against conviction and the procedure for appealing against sentence.

NOTICE OF APPEAL AND NOTICE OF APPLICATION FOR LEAVE TO APPEAL

D27.2 **Criminal Appeal Act 1968, s. 18**

(1) A person who wishes to appeal under this Part of this Act to the Court of Appeal, or to obtain the leave of that court to appeal, shall give notice of appeal or, as the case may be, notice of application for leave to appeal, in such manner as may be directed by rules of court.

(2) Notice of appeal, or of application for leave to appeal, shall be given within 28 days of the conviction, verdict or finding appealed against, or in the case of appeal against sentence, from the date on which sentence was passed or, in the case of an order made or treated as made on conviction, from the date of the making of the order.

(3) The time for giving notice under this section may be extended, either before or after it expires, by the Court of Appeal.

D27.3 Notice of appeal (if the trial judge has granted a certificate that the case is fit for appeal) or notice of application for leave to appeal (required in all other cases) must be lodged in the prescribed manner. Under s. 18(2), the notice must be lodged within 28 days of either conviction or sentence, depending on which is being appealed. By virtue of s. 18A, the same rule applies in respect of cases of contempt of court. If a conviction is the subject of appeal, then time runs from the date of conviction and not sentence (if the sentence hearing takes place at a later date) (*Long* (1997) 161 JP 769). CrimPR 39.2(1) (see Supplement, **R39.2**) requires an applicant to serve the Form NG, signed grounds of appeal and accompanying forms directly on the Registrar of Criminal Appeals. Electronic service on the Registrar's office is encouraged. Advocates are reminded that the appeal documents should not be uploaded to the Digital Case System, but if reliance is to be placed on trial documents which are uploaded to the Digital Case System the location of the documents should be identified in order that the Criminal Appeal Office may access them (para. A2-3 of the Guide). CrimPR 39.3 sets out the numerous required contents of a notice of appeal.

CrimPD IX, paras. 39A.1 to 39A.7 (see Supplement, **CPD.39A**), govern the provision of notice of appeal to the prosecuting authority and the giving of notice by the prosecuting authority should it wish to be heard.

The Guide encourages prompt action on the part of counsel and solicitors in the event of a conviction. At para. A1-1, the Guide states that, immediately following the conclusion of the case, the legal representatives should see the defendant and advocates should orally express their final view as to the prospects of an appeal against conviction and/or sentence. If there are reasonable grounds of appeal, they should be drafted, signed and sent to instructing solicitors as soon as possible. The solicitors should then immediately send a copy to the accused.

CrimPD IX, para. 39B.6 (see Supplement, **CPD.39B**), specifies target times within which appeals should be heard. The target times run from when the case is received by the listing officer; for an appeal against sentence the target time is 28 days, whilst for an appeal against conviction it is 63 days rising to 80 days where a witness is to attend. **D27.4**

Paragraph 39B.2 stipulates that the listing of matters before the Court of Appeal takes precedence over all lower courts and, wherever possible, the Crown Court should have regard to that when arranging to release an advocate to attend the Court of Appeal.

GROUNDS OF APPEAL

Drafting and Contents of Grounds of Appeal

At para. A3-1 of the Guide, it is stated that grounds of appeal should be sufficiently detailed to enable the Registrar and the Court of Appeal to identify clearly the matters relied on. Paragraph A3-2 lists the requirements for a notice as set out in CrimPR 39.3(1) and para. A3-3 covers the level of detail in the grounds which is required by CrimPR 39.3(2). Paragraph A3-4 explains that a separate list of authorities must be provided which should contain the appellant's name and refer to the relevant paragraph numbers in each authority. **D27.5**

Advice with Grounds

Paragraph A3-3 of the Guide points out that the Court of Appeal requires the grounds of appeal and relevant facts to be set out in one document. Counsel should not submit separate grounds and advice. The purpose of the document is to enable the single judge easily to identify the facts and issues in the case, and its intended readership is not the lay or professional client (para. A3-4). **D27.6**

Perfection and Variation

The grounds of appeal first lodged may be varied or amplified within such time as the Court of Appeal will allow (CrimPR 36.3: see Supplement, **R36.3**). Section A8 of the Guide deals with the process of perfection of grounds of appeal. When grounds of appeal are lodged, it is necessary to identify any transcripts which are needed to perfect the grounds of appeal. If the Registrar agrees, the transcripts are secured and sent to counsel. When the Registrar's office sends **D27.7** the transcripts, counsel has 14 days within which to perfect the grounds. In the absence of any response from counsel, the grounds are placed before the single judge. If counsel does not wish to perfect the grounds, the transcript should be returned with a note to that effect (para. A8-4). If counsel is not able to perfect the grounds within 14 days, it is advisable to contact the office of the Registrar as soon as possible. The purpose of perfection of the grounds is two-fold: first, to save judicial time by enabling the Court to identify the relevant parts of the transcript; secondly, to enable counsel to reconsider the grounds in the light of the transcript. Paragraph A8-1 suggests that the perfected grounds should comprise a fresh document which includes references to the appropriate part of the transcript by page number and letter. If, having read the transcript, the advocate forms the view that the appeal is no longer arguable, the solicitors should be informed of that in an appropriate advice (para. A8-4). The Registrar should also be informed but not sent a copy of the advice. If the advocate advises abandonment and the applicant for leave continues with the appeal, the applicant is at risk of a direction that time served does not count (see **D26.12**). It should be noted that an applicant may be at risk of a loss of time order or costs even when advised by lawyers that the grounds of appeal are arguable (see **D26.12**).

Duty of Counsel with Regards to Grounds of Appeal

D27.8 Paragraph A3-6 of the Guide states that 'Advocates should not settle or sign grounds unless they consider that they are properly arguable'. Counsel should not settle grounds he or she is unable to support just because 'instructed' to do so by a lay client. It is not unknown for counsel to be criticised for grounds of appeal that the Court of Appeal considers improper. In *Morson* (1976) 62 Cr App R 236, grounds of appeal drafted by counsel suggested that the summing-up was unfair and amounted to a direction to convict. Scarman LJ said that the description of the summing-up was a travesty and that the Court deplored the fact that that ground of appeal was advanced.

Appellant Drafting Notice and Grounds of Appeal

D27.9 An appeal may be conducted in person, without the benefit of legal representation. The necessary forms are available to prospective appellants in custody as well as those who are at liberty. However, the unrepresented applicant who has had the benefit of negative advice as to the prospects of success of his or her appeal runs an increasing risk of a direction that any time served in custody between the commencement of appeal proceedings and their conclusion not count towards time served (see **D26.12**).

LEAVE TO APPEAL

Procedure for Obtaining Leave to Appeal

D27.10 Ordinarily, once the grounds have been perfected, the case is referred to a single judge for the consideration of whether leave to appeal should be granted. In determining whether or not to grant leave, the single judge may be assisted by having the prosecution's response to the grounds. Consequently, under CrimPR 39.6 (see Supplement, **R39.6**) the Registrar or single judge may direct that the prosecution respond to the grounds within Form RN. The A-G and the Registrar have agreed guidance on the types of cases and/or issues where the Registrar should consider either directing or inviting a party to serve a response in Form RN before leave is considered (para. A9-3 of the Guide). As examples, the Registrar might direct a response within Form RN in cases where the grounds advanced concern issues of public interest immunity, allegations of jury irregularity, criticism of the conduct of the judge and complex frauds.

Sometimes, the single judge or Registrar may refer the case to a full court to determine the issues of leave and the prosecution will be asked to attend. If the full court grants leave, the court may then forthwith proceed to a substantive hearing of the appeal. Such a course may be taken, for example, where a procedural error has been identified (para. A10-1 of the Guide).

The far more usual procedure is for the single judge to consider the issue of leave on the papers. If the application for leave is refused, the applicant has ten business days to notify the intention to renew the application before the Court (CrimPR 36.5). The time for notification may be extended either before or after that period has expired upon application by the applicant (rr. 36.3 and 36.4), but the applicant must have good reason for not being able to comply with the deadline. That reason cannot be to do with the merits of the case. If the applicant has received misleading advice as to the need to notify the renewal from prison, that is capable of being sufficient (*Doherty* [1971] 3 All ER 622).

If the single judge grants leave on a particular ground without deciding the issue of leave in respect of the other grounds, the appellant is free to argue the other grounds at the substantive hearing of the appeal. But if the single judge grants leave on one ground but refuses leave on others, the appellant must renew the application for leave in relation to those other grounds, having previously informed the respondents and the Registrar's office of that intention, before the appellant is allowed to argue them at the substantive hearing (*Cox* [1999] 2 Cr App R 6). **D27.11**

A renewed application for leave to appeal is heard by the Court. The Court will be comprised of at least two judges and usually three. The applicant has no right to attend, so if in custody the applicant will not be present. Even though legal aid is not available for representation at such hearings, it is common for counsel to provide their services free of charge (and for applications to be fully argued) and for counsel to submit written skeleton arguments for renewed applications for leave to appeal. If counsel is to appear on behalf of an applicant at a renewed application for leave, whether on a privately paid or pro bono basis, the Court of Appeal Office should be informed of that in writing as soon as possible (para. A15-3 of the Guide). Where counsel does not appear, renewed applications for leave to appeal are often placed in a 'non-counsel list'. Such hearings then simply involve the calling on of the case followed by one member of the Court giving judgment in the case.

Extension of Time for Leave to Appeal

Although the time period for lodging the notice of application for leave to appeal is 28 days, that period may be extended either before or after its expiry (Criminal Appeal Act 1968, s. 18(3)). The period may be extended either by the Registrar or the single judge; its extension is a matter of discretion. An appellant is usually required to show good reason for the extension of time to be granted (*Ramsden* [1972] Crim LR 547; *Burley* (1994) *The Times*, 9 November 1994). Any application for an extension of time in which to serve an application for leave to appeal or notice of appeal must be supported with reasons as to why the application or notice was not served in time. (*Wilson* [2016] EWCA Crim 65). It is not sufficient simply to tick the relevant box requesting an extension of time. Paragraph A6-5 of the Guide stipulates that any application for an extension of time must be made at the time of the serving of the application or notice and not before. In exceptional circumstances, the Court of Appeal will allow an extension even where the period of delay is inordinate and unexplained because, if the appeal has merit, the refusal might lead to a reference to the CCRC, with all the attendant delay and cost associated (*King* [2000] Crim LR 835). There is no incompatibility with the ECHR in imposing time-limits on appeal proceedings provided that they are not too short or too rigorously enforced (*Ballinger* [2005] EWCA Crim 1060, [2005] 2 Cr App R 29 (433)). If the appellant has commenced an appeal against sentence and subsequently seeks to commence an appeal against conviction, the Court will usually allow an extension of time so as to avoid any difficulties associated with resolving an appeal against sentence before the conviction appeal is resolved (*Mitchell* [1977] 2 All ER 168; *Childs* [2014] EWCA Crim 1884). **D27.12**

TRANSCRIPTS

By virtue of CrimPR 39.3(1) (see Supplement, **R39.3**), the notice of appeal is now required to indicate which transcripts will be required for the resolution of the appeal. Those transcripts may include, for example, the evidence of particular witnesses and rulings on issues of law. The **D27.13**

Registrar will usually provide those transcripts; if there is any disagreement as to the need for them, the Registrar may refer the matter to the single judge for resolution (para. A7-3 of the Guide). Given the cost associated with the provision of a transcript, counsel should request one only if it is essential for the conduct of the appeal (*Flemming* (1987) 86 Cr App R 32 and para. A7-3 of the Guide). In *Lifely* (1990) *The Times*, 16 July 1990, the Court of Appeal said that transcripts of submissions made by counsel to the trial judge were costly and time-consuming to prepare and were usually unnecessary. At para. A7-1 of the Guide it is pointed out that, in publicly funded conviction cases, transcripts of the summing-up and proceedings up to and including verdict are invariably obtained. In sentence cases which follow a guilty plea, a transcript of the prosecution opening of the facts is usually obtained. Paragraph A7-4 points out that the cost of unnecessary transcripts may be ordered to be paid by the appellant.

BAIL PENDING APPEAL

Bail by the Court of Appeal

D27.14 **Criminal Appeal Act 1968, s. 19**

(1) The Court of Appeal may, subject to section 25 of the Criminal Justice and Public Order Act 1994, if they think fit,—
  (a) grant an appellant bail pending the determination of his appeal; or
  (b) revoke bail granted to an appellant by the Crown Court under paragraph (f) of section 81(1) of the Senior Courts Act 1981 or paragraph (a) above; or
  (c) vary the conditions of bail granted to an appellant in the exercise of the power conferred by either of those paragraphs.
(2) The powers conferred by subsection (1) above may be exercised—
  (a) on the application of an appellant; or
  (b) if it appears to the registrar of criminal appeals of the Court of Appeal . . . that any of them ought to be exercised, on a reference to the court by him.

D27.15 The Court of Appeal may grant bail to an appellant under s. 19 and an application about bail and any conditions may be made by either the appellant or respondent. CrimPR 39.8(2) requires that any application must be by way of Form B and must be served on the Registrar (unless the application is with the notice of appeal) and the other party to enable the Crown to make representations about the application and any conditions (para. A13-2 of the Guide). If bail is granted, it is the practice of the Court of Appeal to require a condition of residence (para. A13-4).

D27.16 In *Watton* (1978) 68 Cr App R 293, the Court of Appeal said that the question that the Court should ask itself is whether there are exceptional circumstances which drive the Court to the conclusion that justice can only be done with the granting of bail. The strength of the grounds of appeal will be a relevant factor in the decision as to whether to grant bail. Equally, the likely length of time before the appeal is heard will be relevant depending on how long the appellant has to serve. If an appellant is granted bail but the appeal is unsuccessful, the appellant will be returned to custody.

CrimPR 39.9 and 39.10 (see Supplement, **R39.9** and **R39.10**) contain detailed provisions as to the imposition of conditions of bail and the forfeiture of any sureties. Under s. 19(1)(b) and (c) the Court may vary or revoke bail previously granted by the Court of Appeal or the Crown Court.

The Registrar may vary bail in certain circumstances (see **D27.35**).

Bail Granted by the Crown Court

D27.17 **Senior Courts Act 1981, s. 81**

(1) The Crown Court may, subject to section 25 of the Criminal Justice and Public Order Act 1994, grant bail to any person—
  (a) [bail following sending to the Crown Court: see D7];

(b) who is in custody pursuant to a sentence imposed by a magistrates' court, and who has appealed to the Crown Court against his conviction or sentence; or
(c) who is in the custody of the Crown Court pending the disposal of his case by that court; or
(d) who, after the decision of his case by the Crown Court, has applied to that court for the statement of a case for the High Court on that decision; or
(e) who has applied to the High Court for a quashing order to remove proceedings in the Crown Court in his case into the High Court, or has applied to the High Court for leave to make such an application; or
(f) to whom the Crown Court has granted a certificate under section 1(2) or 11(1A) of the Criminal Appeal Act 1968 or under subsection(1B) below; or
(g) who has been remanded in custody by a magistrates' court on adjourning a case under section 11 of the Powers of Criminal Courts (Sentencing) Act 2000 (remand for medical examination), section 52(5) of the Crime and Disorder Act 1998 (adjournment of proceedings under section 51 etc) or—
 (i) [repealed];
 (ii) section 10 (adjournment of trial);
 (iia) section 17C (intention as to plea: adjournment);
 (iii) section 18 (initial procedure on information against adult for offence triable either way); or
 (iiia) section 24C (intention as to plea by child or young person: adjournment);
 of the Magistrates' Courts Act 1980;
(h) in respect of whom a judge of the Crown Court is required to make a decision pursuant to section 115(3) of the Coroners and Justice Act 2009 (bail decisions in murder cases to be made by Crown Court judge);

and the time during which a person is released on bail under any provision of this subsection shall not count as part of any term of imprisonment or detention under his sentence.

(1A) The power conferred by subsection (1)(f) does not extend to a case to which section 12 or 15 of the Criminal Appeal Act 1968 (appeal against verdict of not guilty by reason of insanity or against findings that the accused is under a disability and that he did the act or made the omission charged against him) applies.

(1B) A certificate under this subsection is a certificate that a case is fit for appeal on a ground which involves a question of law alone.

(1C) The power conferred by subsection (1)(f) is to be exercised—
(a) where the appeal is under section 1 or 9 of the Criminal Appeal Act 1968, by the judge who tried the case; and
(b) where it is under section 10 of that Act, by the judge who passed the sentence.

(1D) The power may only be exercised within twenty-eight days from the date of the conviction appealed against, or in the case of appeal against sentence, from the date on which sentence was passed or, in the case of an order made or treated as made on conviction, from the date of the making of the order.

(1E) The power may not be exercised if the appellant has made an application to the Court of Appeal for bail in respect of the offence or offences to which the appeal relates.

(1F) It shall be a condition of bail granted in the exercise of the power that, unless a notice of appeal has previously been lodged in accordance with subsection (1) of section 18 of the Criminal Appeal Act 1968—
(a) such a notice shall be so lodged within the period specified in subsection (2) of that section; and
(b) not later than 14 days from the end of that period, the appellant shall lodge with the Crown Court a certificate from the registrar of criminal appeals that a notice of appeal was given within that period.

(1G) If the Crown Court grants bail to a person in the exercise of the power, it may direct him to appear—
(a) if a notice of appeal is lodged within the period specified in section 18(2) of the Criminal Appeal Act 1968 at such time and place as the Court of Appeal may require; and
(b) if no such notice is lodged within that period, at such time and place as the Crown Court may require.

(1H) Where the Crown Court grants a person bail under subsection (1)(g) it may direct him to appear at a time and place which the magistrates' court could have directed and the recognisance of any surety shall be conditioned accordingly.

D

Part D Procedure

(1J) The Crown Court may only grant bail to a person under subsection(1)(g) if the magistrates' court which remanded him in custody has certified under section 5(6A) of the Bail Act 1976 that it heard full argument on his application for bail before it refused the application.

(2) Provision may be made by rules of court as respects the powers of the Crown Court relating to bail, including any provision—

(a) except in the case of bail in criminal proceedings (within the meaning of the Bail Act 1976), allowing the court instead of requiring a person to enter into a recognisance, to consent to his giving other security;

(b) allowing the court to direct that a recognisance shall be entered into or other security given before a magistrates' court or a justice of the peace, or, if the rules so provide, a person of such other description as is specified in the rules;

(c) prescribing the manner in which a recognisance is to be entered into or other security given, and the persons by whom and the manner in which the recognisance or security may be enforced;

(d) authorising the recommittal, in such cases and by such courts or justices as may be prescribed by the rules, of persons released from custody in pursuance of the powers;

(e) making provision corresponding to sections 118 and 119 of the Magistrates' Courts Act 1980 (varying or dispensing with requirements as to sureties, and postponement of taking recognisances).

(3) Any reference in any enactment to a recognisance shall include, unless the context otherwise requires, a reference to any other description of security given instead of a recognisance, whether in pursuance of subsection (2)(a) or otherwise.

(4) The Crown Court, on issuing a warrant for the arrest of any person, may endorse the warrant for bail, and in any such case—

(a) the person arrested under the warrant shall, unless the Crown Court otherwise directs, be taken to a police station; and

(b) the officer in charge of the station shall release him from custody if he, and any sureties required by the endorsement and approved by the officer, enter into recognisances of such amount as may be fixed by the endorsement:

Provided that in the case of bail in criminal proceedings (within the meaning of the Bail Act 1976) the person arrested shall not be required to enter into a recognisance.

(5) A person in custody in pursuance of a warrant issued by the Crown Court with a view to his appearance before that court shall be brought forthwith before—

(a) if the person is charged with murder or with murder and one or more other offences, the Crown Court, and

(b) in any other case, either the Crown Court or a magistrates' court.

(6) A magistrates' court shall have jurisdiction, and a justice of the peace may act, under or in pursuance of rules under subsection (2) whether or not the offence was committed, or the arrest was made, within the court's area, or the area for which he was appointed.

D27.18 Section 81(1) of the Senior Courts Act 1981 provides that the Crown Court may grant bail to any person to whom it has granted a certificate under ss. 1(2) or 11(1A) of the Criminal Appeal Act 1968.

Section 81 also provides for the means by which the Crown Court may exercise the power. The Court of Appeal may revoke or vary bail granted by the Crown Court (Criminal Appeal Act 1968, s. 19(1)(b) and (c)). CrimPD III, paras. 14H.1 to 14H.4 (see Supplement, **CPD.14H**), give guidance both on the granting of certificates that a case is fit for appeal and on the consequent granting of bail (see **D26.7**). Bail can only be granted in the Crown Court within 28 days of the conviction or sentence which is to be the subject of the appeal and may not be granted if an application for bail has already been made to the Court of Appeal. The procedure for bail to be granted by a judge of the Crown Court pending an appeal is governed by CrimPR Part 14. The Crown Court judge should use the Criminal Appeal Office Form BC (Crown Court Judge's Order granting bail). The length of the period which might elapse before the hearing of any appeal is not relevant to the granting of a certificate but, if the judge does decide to grant a certificate, it is one factor in the decision whether also to grant bail (CrimPD III, para. 14H.6). In *Harries* [2007] EWCA Crim 820, the Court of Appeal cautioned that a Crown Court judge should grant a certificate of appeal only where there was an unresolved issue of law or where there were clear reasons for considering that an appeal would be allowed. In the instant case, the judge expressly declined to give any view as to the substance of the grounds of appeal when granting a certificate; if he had sought the assistance of the prosecution as to the grounds advanced, he might have realised that the appeal was extremely unlikely to succeed. For additional cases where the Court of Appeal has emphasised the exceptional nature of any decision to grant a certificate of appeal, see *Bansal* [1999] Crim LR 484, *Inskip* [2005] EWCA Crim 3372 and *Matthews* [2014] EWCA Crim 2757.

Suspension of Other Sentences Pending Appeal

The Court of Appeal may suspend the disqualification of a driver pending appeal (RTOA 1988, s. 40(2)). By virtue of s. 30(1) and (2) of the Criminal Appeal Act 1968, an order for the restitution of property to a person made by the Crown Court under the PCC(S)A 2000, s. 148, shall, unless the Court of Appeal directs to the contrary in a case in which, in its opinion, title to the property is not in dispute, be suspended until there is no further possibility of an appeal which might result in the order being varied or set aside. In determining whether there is any possibility of an appeal, the power of a court to give leave to appeal out of time is to be disregarded. Thus, a restitution order will take effect 28 days from sentence if no notice of application for leave to appeal is given but, if notice is given, it will be suspended until determination of the appeal unless the Court of Appeal gives a direction to the contrary because title to the property does not appear to be disputed. The Court may annul or vary the order for restitution even though the conviction is not quashed (s. 30(2)). Under the PCC(S)A 2000, s. 132(1), compensation orders are treated for the purposes of the Criminal Appeal Act 1968, s. 30, in the same way as restitution orders. **D27.19**

PRESENCE OF THE APPELLANT AT THE APPEAL

Criminal Appeal Act 1968, s. 22 **D27.20**

(1) Except as provided by this section, an appellant shall be entitled to be present, if he wishes it, on the hearing of his appeal, although he may be in custody.
(2) A person in custody shall not be entitled to be present—
 (a) where his appeal is on some ground involving a question of law alone; or
 (b) on an application by him for leave to appeal; or
 (c) on any proceedings preliminary or incidental to an appeal; or
 (d) where he is in custody in consequence of a verdict of not guilty by reason of insanity or of a finding of disability,
 unless the Court of Appeal give him leave to be present.
(3) The power of the Court of Appeal to pass sentence on a person may be exercised although he is for any reason not present.
(4) The Court of Appeal may give a live link direction in relation to a hearing at which the appellant is expected to be in custody but is entitled to be present (by virtue of subsection (1) or leave given under subsection (2)) at any time before the beginning of that hearing.
(5) For this purpose—
 (a) a 'live link direction' is a direction that the appellant (if he is being held in custody at the time of the hearing) is to attend the hearing through a live link from the place at which he is held; and
 (b) 'live link' means an arrangement by which the appellant is able to see and hear, and to be seen and heard by, the Court of Appeal (and for this purpose any impairment of eyesight or hearing is to be disregarded).
(6) The Court of Appeal—
 (a) must not give a live link direction unless the parties to the appeal have had the opportunity to make representations about the giving of such a direction; and
 (b) may rescind a live link direction at any time before or during any hearing to which it applies (whether of its own motion or on the application of a party).

An appellant who is not in custody has the right to be present at his or her appeal. The position in respect of appellants in custody is governed by CrimPR 39.11 (see Supplement, **R39.11**). An appellant has the right to attend a hearing in public unless either (a) the hearing is preliminary **D27.21** or incidental to an appeal (including an application for permission) or (b) the party is in custody by virtue of a verdict of not guilty by reason of insanity or a finding of disability. An appellant may be present for the purposes of s. 22 via live link (s. 22(4) to (6)). Under s. 22(2)(a), if an appellant is in custody and the ground of appeal is concerned with only a point of law, the appellant is not entitled to be present for the hearing.

If an appellant is not in custody or bailed to appear at the hearing, there is no requirement for the appellant to be present at the hearing. If the appellant is not present, but has been given notice of the hearing, the Court of Appeal may proceed in his or her absence. If an appellant absconds before the hearing of the appeal, the Court may adjourn the appeal, find against the appellant in his or her absence or, exceptionally, agree to hear the appeal on its merits (*Flower* [1966] 1 QB 146; *Carter* (1994) 98 Cr App R 106).

By virtue of CrimPR 39.12, if the Court decides an appeal affecting sentence in a party's absence, it may vary that decision if it failed to take account of something because of that party's absence. A party who seeks such a variation must serve a written application on the Registrar no more than five business days after the decision (if the party was represented at the appeal hearing) or no more than five business days after the Registrar serves the decision (if the party was not represented at the hearing).

HEARING OF AN APPEAL

Practice in Usual Case

D27.22 CrimPR 36.7 (see Supplement, **R36.7**) requires the Registrar to give as much notice as reasonably practicable of the date on which the Court will hear any appeal or application. The notice must be served on (a) the parties, (b) any party's custodian, and (c) any other party the Court requires to be notified. As is made plain in r. 36.7(3), notice should not ordinarily be given of public interest immunity hearings. If a representation order is to be granted for an appellant for any hearing, it is normally granted either by the Registrar or by the single judge at the same time as leave to appeal is given. In most cases, a representation order will be granted only if the single judge grants leave. The representation order is usually limited to an advocate, but if necessary it will be extended to provide for the services of a solicitor. The Registrar will forward the necessary papers to counsel and will try to agree a date for the hearing with counsel's clerk. It is usual for various dates to be offered to counsel's clerk. Traditionally, the respondent was not usually represented at an appeal against sentence. However, it is increasingly common for the respondent to be present. Moreover, the respondent will frequently submit a 'Respondent's Notice' setting out a reply to the applicant's grounds of appeal. At an appeal against conviction, the respondent is invariably represented. CrimPD IX, paras. 39B.1 to 39B.4, govern the usual procedure for the listing of an appeal against conviction or sentence (see Supplement, **CPD.39B**).

The use of case summaries by the Criminal Appeal Office is governed by CrimPD IX, paras. 39G.1 to 39G.7 (see Supplement, **CPD.39G**). Under para. 39F.1, advocates must ensure that the Court and any other party has a single document containing all of the points that are to be argued. On an appeal against conviction, a skeleton argument must be served if the appeal notice 'does not sufficiently outline the grounds of the appeal, particularly where a complex or novel point of law has been raised'. On a sentencing appeal, a skeleton argument 'may be helpful if a complex issue is raised'.

The service of skeleton arguments is governed by para. 39F.2: the 'appellant's skeleton argument, if any, must be served no later than 21 days before the hearing date, and the respondent's skeleton argument, if any, no later than 14 days before the hearing date', unless otherwise directed. Any skeleton argument should contain a numbered list of the points the advocate intends to argue and should be as succinct as possible (para. 68F.3). In *Brandford* [2016] EWCA Crim 1794, [2017] 1 Cr App R 14 (197), the Court of Appeal expressed concern over the length of written submissions from counsel, both in that case and more generally.

CrimPD XII, para. D.17 (see Supplement, **CPD.XII.D**), now states that directions may provide for the number of pages, or the number of words, to which a skeleton argument is to be confined. In the absence of such directions, skeleton arguments must:

i. not normally exceed 15 pages (excluding front sheets and back sheets) and be concise;
ii. be presented in A4 page size and portrait orientation, in not less than 12 point font and in 1.5 line spacing;
iii. define the issues;
iv. be set out in numbered paragraphs;
v. be cross-referenced to any relevant document in any bundle prepared for the court;
vi. be self-contained and not incorporate by reference material from previous skeleton arguments;
vii. not include extensive quotations from documents or authorities.

In *Erskine* [2009] EWCA Crim 1425, [2009] 2 Cr App R 29 (461), Lord Judge CJ referred to the aphorism of Viscount Falkland in 1641 to the effect that if it is not *necessary* to refer to a previous decision of the Court, it is *necessary* not to refer to it. Similarly, if it is not *necessary* to include a previous decision in the bundle of authorities, it is *necessary* to exclude it. If it is necessary to cite an authority within a skeleton argument, CrimPD XII, para. D.18, now requires that the author state the proposition of law the authority demonstrates, and identify but not quote the parts of the authority that support the proposition. If more than one authority is cited in support of a given proposition, para. D.19 stipulates that the skeleton argument must briefly state why. **D27.23**

Receipt of Evidence by the Court of Appeal

Criminal Appeal Act 1968, s. 23 **D27.24**

(1) For purposes of an appeal or an application for leave to appeal under this part of this Act [appeals against conviction and/or sentence and references to the Court of Appeal by the Home Secretary] the Court of Appeal may, if they think it necessary or expedient in the interests of justice—
 (a) order the production of any document, exhibit or other thing connected with the proceedings, the production of which appears to them necessary for the determination of the case;
 (b) order any witness to attend for examination and be examined before the Court (whether or not he was called in the proceedings from which the appeal lies); and
 (c) receive any evidence which was not adduced in the proceedings from which the appeal lies.
(1A) The power conferred by subsection (1)(a) may be exercised so as to require the production of any document, exhibit or other thing mentioned in that subsection to—
 (a) the Court;
 (b) the appellant;
 (c) the respondent.
(2) The Court of Appeal shall, in considering whether to receive any evidence, have regard in particular to—
 (a) whether the evidence appears to the Court to be capable of belief;
 (b) whether it appears to the Court that the evidence may afford any ground for allowing the appeal;
 (c) whether the evidence would have been admissible in the proceedings from which the appeal lies on an issue which is the subject of the appeal; and
 (d) whether there is a reasonable explanation for the failure to adduce the evidence in those proceedings.
(3) Subsection (1)(c) above [power to receive evidence of any witness if tendered] applies to any evidence of a witness (including the appellant) who is competent but not compellable, and applies also to the appellant's husband or wife where the appellant makes an application for that purpose and the evidence appeal lies except on such an application.

At any appeal against conviction, the Court of Appeal may admit evidence which is relevant to that appeal by virtue of s. 23. Section 23(1)(b) has been amended by the CJIA 2008, sch. 8, so as to extend the power of the Court (or a judge or the Registrar) to issue a witness order to anyone whom it is thought may be able to give relevant evidence. The former qualification that the witness was compellable in the proceedings below has been repealed. The principal effect of this amendment is that both jurors and, subject to waiver of privilege, legal representatives can be compelled to appear at the hearing of an appeal. In appropriate cases, evidence may be **D27.25** introduced in the interests of justice at the request of the respondents and is not limited to rebuttal of fresh evidence adduced by the appellant (*Hanratty* [2002] EWCA Crim 1141, [2002] 2 Cr App R 30 (419)). However, it will not be admitted where its purpose is to advance a basis for conviction not argued previously and not put before the jury (*Fitzgerald* [2006] EWCA Crim 1565). The admission of evidence under s. 23 is a matter of discretion. The Court will admit evidence if it is necessary or expedient in the interests of justice (s. 23(1)). The factors listed in s. 23(2) are not preconditions for the admission of evidence, but are merely factors to take into account in deciding whether evidence should be received. As Lord Judge CJ observed in *Erskine* [2009] EWCA Crim 1425, [2009] 2 Cr App R 29 (461) (at [39]), '[v]irtually by definition, the decision whether to admit fresh evidence is case and fact specific. The discretion to receive fresh evidence is a wide one focusing on the interests of justice.' In *Brown* [2016] UKPC 6, Lord Toulson indicated that, while there may be exceptional cases in which the interests of justice would require evidence of an alternative defence to be received, what cannot be permissible is to advance one defence at trial and then, after conviction, seek to advance an alternative defence, such as diminished responsibility, on appeal, endorsing Lord Judge's statement in *Erskine* that 'there is one trial, and that trial must address all relevant issues relating to guilt and innocence'.

For observations on the relevance of s. 23 to the admissibility of psychiatric reports on appeal against sentence, see *Beesley* [2011] EWCA Crim 1021, [2012] 1 Cr App R (S) 15 (71). For the applicability of s. 23 to applications for third-party disclosure on appeal, see *Doski* [2011] EWCA Crim 987. In *Cleobury* [2012] EWCA Crim 17, the Court of Appeal restated its view on the role of expert evidence on appeal. The renewed application for permission to appeal was based upon the contents of a report from an expert which was secured post-conviction and sought to criticise the way in which DNA evidence was dealt with at trial. The Court observed (at [15]) that it has become not uncommon to try to persuade the Court to reconsider the DNA evidence given at trial by adducing a new report. While there are occasions when this is justified, such as where there has been an advance in DNA science, it is for the defence to call their expert evidence at trial and it is not the function of the Court of Appeal to permit expert evidence to be re-litigated on appeal. For a summary of the principles to be applied by the Court of Appeal when deciding whether or not to receive expert evidence under s. 23, and an example of the application of those principles, see *Chattoo* [2012] EWCA Crim 190. See also *Meachen* [2009] EWCA Crim 1701. In *George* [2014] EWCA Crim 2507, [2015] 1 Cr App R 15 (183), the Court of Appeal quashed the conviction on the basis of the impact advances in the science of gunshot residue detection might have had on the trial judge's summing-up. See *Choudhry* [2017] EWCA Crim 1325 and *Challen* [2019] EWCA Crim 916 for examples of the admission of fresh medical evidence. The Court of Appeal reiterated the principles to be applied and refused to admit fresh evidence which was argued to be relevant to a potential partial defence of diminished responsibility in *Foy* [2020] EWCA Crim 270.

For the application of s. 23 to sentence appeals, see **D26.48**.

In *Smith* [2013] EWCA Crim 2388, [2014] 2 Cr App R 1 (1) the Court of Appeal strongly criticised 'a growing and unwelcome tendency of convicted defendants to dismiss their original counsel and then to bring in new counsel to criticise their predecessors'. The Court described this as an attempt to circumvent the restriction on calling fresh evidence contained in s. 23 and deplored this strategy.

D27.26 **Capable of Belief** The Court of Appeal will often make a judgement as to whether the evidence is capable of belief before actually hearing it. Thus the Court gives an indication as to whether or not the evidence appears to be capable of belief. Matters which will be important in that consideration will include the contents of any statement produced and the compatibility of those contents with the evidence at trial, along with any explanation as to how the evidence came to light. In *Sale* [2000] 2 Cr App R 431, Rose LJ said that fresh evidence falls into three categories. *First*, evidence which is plainly capable of belief; there is no difficulty with such evidence and the Court will ordinarily receive it. Second, evidence which is plainly incapable of belief; such evidence again presents no difficulty and the Court will usually not receive such evidence. The third type of evidence is that which is possibly capable of belief; it may be necessary for the Court to hear the witness *de bene esse* (provisionally receiving the evidence in order to determine its admissibility) and that course is frequently followed. See *Patel* [2010] EWCA Crim 1858 for a practical application of the test in respect of an application to admit affidavits as fresh evidence.

Capable of Founding a Ground of Appeal Even if fresh evidence potentially fulfils all the other criteria in the Criminal Appeal Act 1968, s. 23, it is necessary that it is capable of founding an arguable ground of appeal before it can be admitted. For example, an appellant may produce evidence of a statement by the complainant which was inconsistent with the evidence given by the complainant at trial. Unless the inconsistency of the statement is of sufficient magnitude to be capable of disturbing the safety of the conviction, it will not be admissible. See *Aslam* [2014] EWCA Crim 1292 and *Kingston* [2014] EWCA Crim 1420. **D27.27**

Admissible in the Proceedings from which the Appeal Lies Plainly, evidence which would not have been admissible at the trial proceedings cannot form the basis of a successful appeal against conviction. The importance of that point has been most keenly felt in appeals involving misconduct by police officers which only comes to light after conviction (*Twitchell* [2000] 1 Cr App R 373). **D27.28**

Reasonable Explanation for the Failure to Adduce the Evidence In *Stafford and Luvaglio (No. 1)* (1969) 53 Cr App R 1, Edmund-Davies LJ said 'public mischief would ensue and legal process could become indefinitely prolonged were it the case that evidence produced at any time will generally be admitted by this court when verdicts are being reviewed'. That warning against the potential dangers of admitting fresh evidence is indicative of a general reluctance on the part of the Court of Appeal to admit evidence without a reasonable explanation for the failure to adduce the evidence at trial. Nevertheless, it should always be borne in mind that the ultimate test for admission of evidence under the Criminal Appeal Act 1968, s. 23, is whether it is in the interests of justice. In exceptional circumstances, the Court will admit fresh evidence even when there is no reasonable explanation for the failure to adduce it at trial. For a highly unusual and stark example of the admission of such evidence leading to the quashing of a conviction, see *Solomon* [2007] EWCA Crim 2633. For an example of the operation of this factor in relation to the receipt of fresh medical evidence, see *Moyle* [2008] EWCA Crim 3059. **D27.29**

An appellant will not have a reasonable explanation for failing to adduce evidence at trial if the appellant has taken a decision not to call particular evidence following advice from lawyers (*Hampton* (2004) *The Times*, 13 October 2004). Similarly, it will not assist an appellant that alibi witnesses have not been called because the lawyers had been unable to trace them, if the appellant could have made the lawyers aware of information which would have enabled them to trace the witnesses in good time (*Beresford* (1971) 56 Cr App R 143). If witnesses could genuinely not be found in time for trial, that may amount to a reasonable explanation. But before the Court will admit the evidence, it is likely to be necessary for each person involved in the process of finding and taking a proof of evidence from the witnesses to serve a statement of truth about their role in that process (*Gogana* (1999) *The Times*, 12 July 1999; *James* [2000] Crim LR 571).

Procedure for Calling Evidence

CrimPR 39.3 (see Supplement, **R39.3**) requires that an appellant who wishes the Court of Appeal to exercise its power to receive evidence should so indicate within the notice of appeal. It may be made by the Registrar or a single judge (s. 31(2); see **D27.34**). The decision to receive the evidence is for a court and not a single judge or the Registrar. Indeed, even an order under s. 23(4) that the witness be examined by an officer of the court prior to determination of the appeal is one that only a court can make. **D27.30**

By virtue of s. 23(4), if the Court of Appeal thinks it necessary or expedient in the interests of justice, the Court may order that the examination of any witness be conducted before any judge, officer of the court or other person appointed by the Court for the purpose. The deposition may then be admitted as evidence before the Court, so avoiding the need for oral evidence (s. 23(4)).

D27.31 Whilst the rules do not specify the precise way in which a witness's evidence should be given, the usual route is the same as that adopted in first instance proceedings. The witness is examined in chief by the party tendering the witness's evidence, cross-examined by the opposite party and then, if need be, re-examined and questioned directly by the Court. The procedure followed by the Court of Appeal will more often than not be a matter for the Court, and so it may commence the questioning of the witness and allow the parties to ask any appropriate additional questions. Where the appellant is allowed to call evidence, the prosecution may be allowed to call their own evidence in rebuttal. See *Lee* [1984] 1 All ER 1080, for a case where the Court contemplated hearing virtually the whole of the prosecution and defence cases in order to determine an appeal against conviction where D had pleaded guilty at the Crown Court. The Court of Appeal noted that there were exceptional circumstances and stipulated that it was not to provide a precedent for the hearing of such extensive evidence.

REVIEW OF PUBLIC INTEREST IMMUNITY

D27.32 In *McDonald* (2004) *The Times*, 8 November 2004, the Court of Appeal set out the principles that applied to a review of a trial judge's conduct of a public interest immunity hearing.

(a) The approach was to be the same whether the hearing had been on notice or not. The principles regarding the appointment of special counsel or the need for a judge to recuse himself are the same in both cases.
(b) The Court of Appeal would have to review all the material with the prosecution present. A prosecution summary by itself is not sufficient. However, such a summary is usually desirable, especially where the material is voluminous.
(c) The review of the material should be carried out by a court of the same constitution as hears the substantive appeal.
(d) The review is to take place sufficiently in advance of the substantive hearing to permit special counsel to be appointed and prepared if the need arises.
(e) In the majority of cases where the material can be read in an hour or two and where there are no listing difficulties, the review should take place in the first week of that constitution of the court sitting, with the substantive hearing following in the third week.
(f) Where the public interest immunity material is unusually voluminous, special listing arrangements have to be made over a longer time-scale.

ABANDONING AN APPEAL

D27.33 CrimPR 36.13 (see Supplement, **R36.13**) governs the abandonment of an appeal. An appellant may abandon an appeal without permission before a hearing by serving a notice of abandonment on the Registrar and any respondent, but at any hearing may only abandon an appeal or application with the permission of the Court (r. 36.13(2)). The appellant must serve the notice of abandonment (Form A) on the Registrar's office and any respondent. The form must be signed by, or on behalf of, the appellant (r. 36.13(3)). The Registrar must date the form and serve it on the appellant, the custodian of the appellant, the officer of the Crown Court and any other party upon whom the notice of appeal was served. The proceedings are then deemed to have been dismissed or refused (r. 36.13(4)). Abandonment of the appeal does not preclude the making of a loss of time order or the award of costs against the appellant. Once an appeal has commenced, the appellant may still abandon the appeal but needs the leave of the Court of Appeal (*De Courcy* [1964] 3 All ER 251).

If an appellant abandons the appeal, it may be reinstated with the leave of the Court. Any application for the reinstatement of an abandoned appeal or application must be made in writing to the Registrar, setting out the reasons for the application (r. 36.13(5)). The Court will allow such a reinstatement if it is of the view that the abandonment was a nullity because, for example, of fraud, mistake or erroneous advice. The important question will be whether the appellant's mind goes with the abandonment. If the appellant cannot show that it did not, the abandonment will not be held to be a nullity. In *Grant* [2005] EWCA Crim 2018, correspondence between D and his lawyers culminated in his lawyers advising that if they did not hear from him within seven days they would abandon the appeal. Because of a delay in the post, caused by D being transferred between prisons, he had no opportunity to communicate a change of mind about his appeal. The Court held that by virtue of D's original letter his mind had gone with the notice and the abandonment was therefore not a nullity.

In *Smith* [2013] EWCA Crim 2388, [2014] 2 Cr App R 1 (1), the Court of Appeal revisited the question of when an abandonment of appeal was a nullity because it came about as a result of wrong legal advice. Following a review of relevant authorities, the Court observed (at [58]) that:

> From this review of the law we derive four propositions which are relevant to the present case:
> i) A notice of abandonment of appeal is irrevocable, unless the Court of Appeal treats that notice as a nullity.
> ii) A notice of abandonment is a nullity if the applicant's mind does not go with the notice which he signs.
> iii) If the applicant abandons his appeal after and because of receiving incorrect legal advice, then his mind may not go with the notice which he signs. Whether this is the case will depend upon the circumstances.
> iv) Incorrect legal advice for this purpose means advice which is positively wrong. It does not mean the expression of opinion on a difficult point, with which some may agree and others may disagree.

APPLICATIONS TO A SINGLE JUDGE

Criminal Appeal Act 1968, ss. 31 and 44 D27.34

31.—(1) There may be exercised by a single judge in the same manner as by the Court of Appeal and subject to the same provisions—
- (a) the powers of the Court of Appeal under this Part of this Act specified in subsection (2) below;
- (aa) the power to give leave under section 14(4B) of the Criminal Appeal Act 1995;
- (b) the power to give directions under section 4(4) of the Sexual Offences (Amendment) Act 1976; and
- (c) the powers to make orders for the payment of costs under sections 16 to 18 of the Prosecution of Offences Act 1985 in proceedings under this Part of this Act.

(2) The powers mentioned in subsection (1)(a) above are the following—
- (a) to give leave to appeal;
- (b) to extend the time within which notice of appeal or of application for leave to appeal may be given;
- (c) to allow an appellant to be present at any proceedings;
- (ca) to give a live link direction under section 22(4);
- (d) to order a witness to attend for examination;
- (e) to exercise the powers conferred by section 19 of this Act [bail pending determination of appeal];
- (f) to make orders under section 8(2) of this Act and discharge or vary such orders [orders relating to procedure on a retrial];
- [(g) repealed];
- (h) to give directions under section 29(1) of this Act [directions for loss of time];
- (i) to make orders under s. 23(1)(a).

(2ZA) The power of the Court of Appeal to renew an interim hospital order made by them by virtue of any provision of this part may be exercised by a single judge in the same manner as it may be exercised by the Court.

(2A) The power of the Court of Appeal to suspend a person's disqualification under section 40(2) of the Road Traffic Offenders Act 1988 may be exercised by a single judge in the same manner as it may be exercised by the court.

(2B) The power of the Court of Appeal to grant leave to appeal under section 159 of the Criminal Justice Act 1988 [appeals against orders restricting publicity] may be exercised by a single judge in the same manner as it may be exercised by the court.

(2C) The power of the Court of Appeal, under section 130 of the Licensing Act 2003, to suspend an order under section 129 of that Act may be exercised by a single judge in the same manner as it may be exercised by the Court.

(2D) The power of the Court of Appeal to grant leave to appeal under section 9(11) of the Criminal Justice Act 1987 may be exercised by a single judge in the same manner as it may be exercised by the Court.

(2E) The power of the Court of Appeal to grant leave to appeal under section 35(1) of the Criminal Procedure and Investigations Act 1996 may be exercised by a single judge in the same manner as it may be exercised by the Court.

(2F) The powers of the Court of Appeal to make, discharge or vary a witness anonymity order under Chapter 2 of Part 3 of the Coroners and Justice Act 2009 may be exercised by a single judge in the same manner as they may be exercised by the Court.

(3) If the single judge refuses an application on the part of an appellant to exercise in his favour any of the powers above specified, the appellant shall be entitled to have the application determined by the Court of Appeal.

44.—(1) There may be exercised by a single judge—

(a) the powers of the Court of Appeal under this Part of this Act—
  (i) to extend the time for making an application for leave to appeal;
  (ii) to make an order for or in relation to bail; and
  (iii) to give leave for a person to be present at the hearing of any proceedings preliminary or incidental to an appeal; and

(b) their powers to make orders for the payment of costs under sections 16 and 17 of the Prosecution of Offences Act 1985 in proceedings under this Part of this Act,

but where the judge refuses an application to exercise any of the said powers the applicant shall be entitled to have the application determined by the Court of Appeal.

(2) The power of the Court of Appeal to suspend a person's disqualification under section 40(3) of the Road Traffic Offenders Act 1988 may be exercised by a single judge, but where the judge refuses an application to exercise that power the applicant shall be entitled to have the application determined by the Court of Appeal.

The single judge may be either a judge of the High Court or a Lord Justice of Appeal. The functions of the single judge are ordinarily carried out by a High Court judge. By virtue of ss. 31 and 44, a single judge may exercise a number of powers in the same manner as the Court of Appeal. It should be noted that the single judge may order a witness to attend for examination, but it is a matter for the Court as to whether the evidence will be received (*Ahmed* [1996] Crim LR 339).

In *Hyde* [2016] EWCA Crim 1031, [2016] 2 Cr App R (S) 39 (416), the Court of Appeal dealt with the question of whether, in respect of appeal against sentence, the single judge is entitled, if he or she considers that some of the grounds of appeal are arguable and some not, to grant leave to appeal on limited grounds only. Davis LJ summarised the position (at [32]) as follows:

(1) The Single Judge is entitled to grant leave to appeal against sentence on limited grounds or against part of a sentence only.

(2) The limited basis on which leave to appeal is granted should be made unambiguously clear on the form SJ.

(3) It is a matter for the discretion and evaluation of the Single Judge (where not refusing leave outright on all grounds) as to whether to grant leave to appeal on limited grounds or whether to grant leave to appeal generally.

(4) If an applicant desires to pursue those grounds for which leave to appeal has been refused by the Single Judge he is required to renew his application in the usual way within the prescribed time limit.

(5) Where the Single Judge has granted leave, either generally or on a limited basis, leave from the Full Court is required to advance a further ground formulated since the Single Judge's decision.

(6) If limited leave is granted by the Single Judge together with a Representation Order, that funding is limited to the ground(s) identified as arguable by the Single Judge. It will only extend to arguing renewed grounds of appeal if the Full Court subsequently grants leave on the renewed grounds.

(7) No different approach is called for where one element of the sentence relates to a Bail Act offence....

(8) Where a sentence requires to be corrected in order to put right an unlawful element of the sentence, but the totality of the sentence will not arguably be affected by correction of such error and there are no other grounds considered arguable and there is no other complexity, the Single Judge ordinarily should grant leave to appeal on that part of the sentence only, withholding a grant of representation order; the matter will then be dealt with by the Full Court as a non-counsel application. If in such a case any other grounds have been raised and rejected by the Single Judge the applicant is then required to renew in the usual way if he wishes to pursue those grounds.

APPLICATIONS TO THE REGISTRAR

Criminal Appeal Act 1968, s. 31A D27.35

(1) The powers of the Court of Appeal under this Part of this Act which are specified in subsection (2) below may be exercised by the registrar.
(2) The powers mentioned in subsection (1) above are the following—
 (a) to extend the time within which notice of appeal or of application for leave to appeal may be given;
 (aa) to give a live link direction under section 22(4);
 (b) to order a witness to attend for examination;
 (c) to vary the conditions of bail granted to an appellant by the Court of Appeal or the Crown Court;
 (d) to make orders under section 23(1)(a).
(3) No variation of the conditions of bail granted to an appellant may be made by the registrar unless he is satisfied that the respondent does not object to the variation; but, subject to that, the powers specified in that subsection are to be exercised by the registrar in the same manner as by the Court of Appeal and subject to the same provisions.
(4) If the registrar refuses an application on the part of an appellant to exercise in his favour any of the powers specified in subsection (2) above, the appellant shall be entitled to have the application determined by a single judge.
(5) In this section 'respondent' includes a person who will be a respondent if leave to appeal is granted.

The powers exercisable by the Registrar in connection with appeals are set out in s. 31A of the Criminal Appeal Act 1968. Under CrimPR 36.2 (see Supplement, **R36.2**), the Registrar must fulfil the duty of active case management under r. 3.2 (see **D4.7**). In fulfilling that duty, the Registrar may exercise (subject to the direction of the Court) any of the powers of case management in rr. 3.5 (the Court's general powers of case management), 3.9(3) (requiring a certificate of readiness) and 3.10 (requiring a party to identify intentions and anticipated requirements).

With effect from 6 April 2020, revisions to CrimPR 2.4 and 2.5 (see Supplement, **R2.4** and **R2.5**) enable an authorised court officer to exercise functions of the Registrar. Subject to CrimPR 2.4, an authorised court officer may exercise any function of the criminal division of the Court of Appeal that may be exercised by the Registrar of Criminal Appeals, and any other judicial function of the Registrar. Where an authorised court officer exercises a function of the court the same provision as that made by ss. 31A(4) or 31C(3), as the case may be, of the Criminal Appeal Act 1968 applies as if that function had been exercised by the Registrar; and CrimPR 36.5 (Renewing an application refused by a judge or the Registrar) applies.

Section D28 Reference to the Court of Appeal (Criminal Division) by the Attorney-General and Criminal Cases Review Commission

REFERENCES BY THE ATTORNEY-GENERAL

Reference on a Point of Law Following Acquittal

D28.1 **Criminal Justice Act 1972, s. 36**

(1) Where a person tried on indictment has been acquitted (whether in respect of the whole or part of the indictment) the Attorney-General may, if he desires the opinion of the Court of Appeal on a point of law which has arisen in the case, refer that point to the court, and the court shall, in accordance with this section, consider the point and give their opinion on it.

(2) For the purpose of their consideration of a point referred to them under this section the Court of Appeal shall hear argument—

(a) by, or by counsel on behalf of, the Attorney-General; and

(b) if the acquitted person desires to present any argument to the court, by counsel on his behalf or, with the leave of the court, by the acquitted person himself.

(3) Where the Court of Appeal have given their opinion on a point referred to them under this section, the court may, of their own motion or in pursuance of an application in that behalf, refer the point to the Supreme Court if it appears to the court that the point ought to be considered by the Supreme Court.

(4) If a point is referred to the Supreme Court under subsection (3) of this section, the Supreme Court shall consider the point and give its opinion on it accordingly.

(5) Where, on a point being referred to the Court of Appeal under this section or further referred to the Supreme Court, the acquitted person appears by counsel for the purpose of presenting any argument to the Court of Appeal or the Supreme Court, he shall be entitled to his costs, that is to say to the payment out of central funds of such sums as are reasonably sufficient to compensate him for expenses properly incurred by him for the purpose of being represented on the reference or further reference; and any amount recoverable under this subsection shall be ascertained, as soon as practicable, by the registrar of criminal appeals or, as the case may be, such officer as may be prescribed by [Supreme Court Rules].

. . .

(7) A reference under this section shall not affect the trial in relation to which the reference is made or any acquittal in that trial.

D28.2 Section 36 provides for the reference of a point of law to the Court of Appeal by the A-G. The use of the power is confined to circumstances following the acquittal of an accused where the A-G requires the opinion of the Court of Appeal on a point of law. There is no provision for the referral of points of law that do not arise from proceedings resulting in an acquittal. In *A-G's Reference (No. 1 of 1975)* [1975] QB 773, Lord Widgery stated that the procedure should not be used simply for very heavy questions of law but should be used for short but important points requiring a quick ruling. With the advent of the prosecution powers to appeal terminating rulings under the CJA 2003 (see **D16.75**) the use of this procedure has reduced substantially.

Whatever the opinion of the Court of Appeal, the acquittal is unaffected. Nevertheless, the acquitted defendant is entitled to be represented at the hearing (s. 36(5)).

The process of referral of a point of law by the A-G is governed by CrimPR Part 41 (see Supplement, **R41.1** *et seq.*).

The *Guide to Commencing Proceedings in the Court of Appeal Criminal Division* (August 2018) provides valuable guidance as to the procedure to be followed upon an A-G's reference of a point of law on an acquittal (see D8 of the Guide).

Section 36 provides for the further referral of the point of law to the Supreme Court following the judgment of the Court of Appeal. The point may be referred to the Supreme Court upon application by the parties or on the Court of Appeal's own motion. The procedure for the making of an application for a reference to the Supreme Court is governed by CrimPR Part 43 (see Supplement, **R43.1** *et seq.*).

Given the emergence of prosecution powers of interlocutory appeal on points of law under s. 58 of the CJA 2003, the s. 36 procedure is now much less significant.

Reference for Review of Sentence

Criminal Justice Act 1988, Part IV (ss. 35 and 36) **D28.3**

35.—(1) A case to which this Part of this Act applies may be referred to the Court of Appeal under section 36 below.

(2) Subject to rules of court, the jurisdiction of the Court of Appeal under section 36 below shall be exercised by the criminal division of the Court, and references to the Court of Appeal in this Part of this Act shall be construed as references to that division.

(3) This Part of this Act applies to any case—
- (a) of a description specified in an order under this section; or
- (b) in which sentence is passed on a person—
  - (i) for an offence triable only on indictment; or
  - (ii) for an offence of a description specified in an order under this section.

(4) and (5) [Order-making power and procedure.]

(6) In this Part of this Act 'sentence' has the same meaning as in the Criminal Appeal Act 1968, except that it does not include an interim hospital order under Part III of the Mental Health Act 1983, and 'sentencing' shall be construed accordingly.

36.—(1) If it appears to the Attorney-General—
- (a) that the sentencing of a person in a proceeding in the Crown Court has been unduly lenient; and
- (b) that the case is one to which this Part of this Act applies,

he may, with the leave of the Court of Appeal, refer the case to them for them to review the sentencing of that person; and on such a reference the Court of Appeal may—
  - (i) quash any sentence passed on him in the proceeding; and
  - (ii) in place of it pass such sentence as they think appropriate for the case and as the court below had power to pass when dealing with him.

(2) Without prejudice to the generality of subsection (1) above, the condition specified in paragraph (a) of that subsection may be satisfied if it appears to the Attorney-General that the judge—
- (a) erred in law as to his powers of sentencing; or
- (b) failed to pass a sentence required by—
  - (zi) section 1(2B) or 1A(5) of the Prevention of Crime Act 1953;
  - (i) section 51A(2) of the Firearms Act 1968;
  - (ia) section 139(6B), 139A(5B) or 139AA(7) of this Act;
  - (ii) section 110(2) or 111(2) of the Powers of Criminal Courts (Sentencing) Act 2000;
  - (iii) section 224A, 225(2) or 226(2) of the Criminal Justice Act 2003; or
  - (iv) under section 29(4) or (6) of the Violent Crime Reduction Act 2006.

(3) For the purposes of this Part of this Act any two or more sentences are to be treated as passed in the same proceeding if they would be so treated for the purposes of section 11 of the Criminal Appeal Act 1968.

(3A) Where a reference under this section relates to a case in which the judge made an order specified in subsection (3B), the Court of Appeal shall not, in deciding what sentence is appropriate for the case, make any allowance for the fact that the person to whom it relates is being sentenced for a second time.

(3B) The orders specified in this subsection are–
- (a) an order under section 269(2) of the Criminal Justice Act 2003 (determination of minimum term in relation to mandatory life sentence);
- (b) an order under section 82A(2) of the Powers of Criminal Court (Sentencing) Act 2000 (determination of minimum term in relation to discretionary life sentences and certain other sentences).

(4) No judge shall sit as a member of the Court of Appeal on the hearing of, or shall determine any application in proceedings incidental or preliminary to, a reference under this section of a sentence passed by himself.

(5) Where the Court of Appeal have concluded their review of a case referred to them under this section the Attorney-General or the person to whose sentencing the reference relates may refer a point of law involved in any sentence passed on that person in the proceeding to the Supreme Court for its opinion, and the Supreme Court shall consider the point and give its opinion on it accordingly, and either remit the case to the Court of Appeal to be dealt with or itself deal with the case.

(6) A reference under subsection (5) above shall be made only with the leave of the Court of Appeal or the Supreme Court; and leave shall not be granted unless it is certified by the Court of Appeal that the point of law is of general public importance and it appears to the Court of Appeal or the Supreme Court (as the case may be) that the point is one which ought to be considered by the Supreme Court.

(7) For the purpose of dealing with a case under this section the Supreme Court may exercise any powers of the Court of Appeal.

D28.4 The scope of the power to refer now extends beyond indictable-only offences to include a number of offences, and combinations of offences, set out in the Criminal Justice Act 1988 (Reviews of Sentencing) Order 2006 (SI 2006 No. 1116), sch. 1 (see D28.7). An offence is deemed to be triable only on indictment for the purposes of s. 35 if it is so for an adult and it is irrelevant that a youth can be tried summarily on such an allegation (*W* (1993) *The Times*, 16 March 1993). It is for the A-G to consider whether leave should be sought for a reference to the Court of Appeal on the basis that the sentence was unduly lenient and if appropriate to apply for leave. The procedure to be followed is set out in the CJA 1988, sch. 3, supplemented by CrimPR Part 41 (see Supplement, **R41.1** *et seq.*). If leave is granted, the reference proceeds according to the facts before the sentencing judge, and the Court of Appeal will not alter the sentence on the grounds of new material that was not before the sentencing judge, but will decide whether the sentence was unduly lenient on the basis of what was before the sentencing judge (*A-G's Ref (No. 19 of 2005)* [2006] EWCA Crim 785). However, if the Court concludes that the sentence was unduly lenient, it may receive fresh material, either favourable or adverse to the offender, in reaching its conclusions as to the correct new sentence (*A-G's Ref (No. 74 of 2010)* [2011] EWCA Crim 873).

Guidance as to the procedure to be followed on an A-G's reference of an unduly lenient sentence is set out in the *Guide to Commencing Proceedings in the Court of Appeal Criminal Division* (August 2018), at D7.

Double Jeopardy

D28.5 When the Court of Appeal increases a sentence under the reference procedure, its practice has often been to allow some discount on the sentence it would consider appropriate because of what is usually termed the 'double jeopardy' of an offender having to wait before knowing if the sentence is to be increased. In *A-G's Refs (Nos. 14 and 15 of 2006)* [2006] EWCA Crim 1335, [2007] 1 Cr App R (S) 40 (215), the Court gave some guidance as to the relevance and applicability of such double jeopardy. The effect of the principle will vary significantly according to the circumstances. Where an offender has a substantial part of a long determinate sentence remaining to be served or is serving a discretionary life sentence, the principle has limited effect, if any, because the anxiety occasioned by the process will consequently be less keenly felt. Where, however, an offender had completely served a custodial sentence, was close to release, had a custodial sentence substituted for a non-custodial sentence or was very young, the discount for double jeopardy should be near the upper end of the range, at about 30 per cent. In *A-G's Ref (No. 38 of 2013)* (*Hall*) [2013] EWCA Crim 1450, [2014] 1 Cr App R (S) 61 (394), the Court explicitly stated that the question of discount did not arise when an offender was in custody and was aware that the A-G intended to refer the sentence to the Court of Appeal.

Additional Matters Taken into Account on Reference The following additional points apply to references under the CJA 1988, s. 35. D28.6

(a) If an indication of sentence is given to an offender by the sentencing judge, the Court of Appeal will take that into account but is not necessarily bound by it. In *A-G's Refs (Nos. 86 and 87 of 1999)* [2001] 1 Cr App R (S) 141 (505), an indication was given by the judge before trial that a non-custodial sentence would be imposed whether D pleaded guilty or proceeded to a contested trial. The indication was repeated after a finding of guilty. That indication plainly could have had no effect on any decision made by D as to plea and so would be no bar to the increase of sentence under the reference procedure (cf. *A-G's Ref (No. 44 of 2000)* [2001] 1 Cr App R 27 (416), relevance of prosecution representations to the accused).
(b) By virtue of s. 35(6), a 'sentence' for the purposes of the reference procedure has the same meaning as in the Criminal Appeal Act 1968, s. 50 (see **D26.43**) (except that it does not include an interim hospital order under Part III of the Mental Health Act 1983) and thus is any order made by a court when dealing with an offender.
(c) The Court of Appeal will act in relation to a sentence only if it is unduly lenient and not simply lenient. The test to be applied is whether the sentence was outside the range which the judge, applying his or her mind to all relevant factors, could reasonably consider appropriate (*A-G's Ref (No. 4 of 1989)* [1990] 1 WLR 41).
(d) The Court of Appeal's decision following the reference may be the subject of appeal to the Supreme Court by the A-G or the offender. That appeal must be by leave of either the Court of Appeal or the Supreme Court and must concern a point of law of public importance.

Reviewable Sentences and Procedure: Statutory Provisions

Criminal Justice Act 1988 (Reviews of Sentencing) Order 2006 (SI 2006 No. 1116), sch. 1 D28.7

1. Any case tried on indictment—
   (a) following a notice of transfer given under section 4 of the Criminal Justice Act 1987 (notices of transfer and designated authorities) by an authority designated for that purpose under subsection (2) of that section; or
   (b) in which one or more of the counts in respect of which sentence is passed relates to a charge which was dismissed under section 6(1) of the Criminal Justice Act 1987 (applications for dismissal) and on which further proceedings were brought by means of preferment of a voluntary bill of indictment.

1A. Any case tried on indictment—
   (a) following a notice given under section 51B of the Crime and Disorder Act 1998 (notices in serious or complex fraud cases); or
   (b) following such a notice, in which one or more of the counts in respect of which sentence is passed relates to a charge—
      (i) which was dismissed under paragraph 2 of Schedule 3 to the Crime and Disorder Act 1998 (applications for dismissal); and
      (ii) on which further proceedings were brought by means of the preferment of a voluntary bill of indictment.

2. Any case in which sentence is passed on a person for one of the following offences:
   (a) an offence under section 16 of the Offences against the Person Act 1861 (threats to kill);
   (b) an offence under section 5(1) of the Criminal Law Amendment Act 1885 (defilement of a girl between 14 and 17);
   (c) an offence under section 1 of the Children and Young Persons Act 1933 (cruelty to persons under 16) or section 20 of the Children and Young Persons Act (Northern Ireland) 1968 (cruelty to persons under 16);
   (d) an offence under section 6 of the Sexual Offences Act 1956 (unlawful sexual intercourse with a girl under 16), section 14 or 15 of that Act (indecent assault on a woman or on a man), section 52 of the Offences against the Person Act 1861 (indecent assault upon a female), or Article 21 of the Criminal Justice (Northern Ireland) Order 2003 (indecent assault on a male);
   (e) an offence under section 1 of the Indecency with Children Act 1960 or section 22 of the Children and Young Persons Act (Northern Ireland) 1968 (indecent conduct with a child);
   (f) an offence under section 4(2) or (3) (production or supply of a controlled drug), section 5(3) (possession of a controlled drug with intent to supply) or section 6(2) (cultivation of cannabis plant) of the Misuse of Drugs Act 1971;

D

Part D Procedure

(g) an offence under section 54 of the Criminal Law Act 1977 or Article 9 of the Criminal Justice (Northern Ireland) Order 1980 (inciting a girl under 16 to have incestuous sexual intercourse);
(h) an offence under section 50(2) or (3), section 68(2) or section 170(1) or (2) of the Customs and Excise Management Act 1979, insofar as those offences are in connection with a prohibition or restriction on importation or exportation of either:
(i) a controlled drug within the meaning of section 2 of the Misuse of Drugs Act 1971, such prohibition or restriction having effect by virtue of section 3 of that Act; or
(ii) an article prohibited by virtue of section 42 of the Customs Consolidation Act 1876 but only insofar as it relates to or depicts a person under the age of 16;
(i) offences under sections 29 to 32 of the Crime and Disorder Act 1998 (racially or religiously aggravated assaults; racially or religiously aggravated criminal damage; racially or religiously aggravated public order offences; racially or religiously aggravated harassment etc);
(j) an offence under section 4 of the Asylum and Immigration (Treatment of Claimants, etc.) Act 2004 (trafficking people for exploitation);
(k) an offence under section 71 of the Coroners and Justice Act 2009 (slavery, servitude and forced or compulsory labour).
(l) an offence under section 1 (slavery, servitude and forced or compulsory labour), 2 (human trafficking) or 4 (committing an offence with intent to commit a human trafficking offence) of the Modern Slavery Act 2015.

3. To the extent that Part IV of the Criminal Justice Act 1988 does not apply by virtue of section 35(3)(b)(i), any case in which sentence is passed on a person for an offence under one of the following sections of the Sexual Offences Act 2003:
(a) section 3 (sexual assault);
(b) section 4 (causing a person to engage in sexual activity without consent);
(c) section 7 (sexual assault of a child under 13);
(d) section 8 (causing or inciting a child under 13 to engage in sexual activity);
(e) section 9 (sexual activity with a child);
(f) section 10 (causing or inciting a child to engage in sexual activity);
(g) section 11 (engaging in sexual activity in the presence of a child);
(h) section 12 (causing a child to watch a sexual act);
(i) section 14 (arranging or facilitating commission of a child sex offence);
(j) section 15 (meeting a child following sexual grooming etc);
(k) section 25 (sexual activity with a child family member);
(l) section 47 (paying for sexual services of a child);
(m) section 48 (causing or inciting sexual exploitation of a child);
(n) section 49 (controlling a child in relation to sexual exploitation);
(o) section 50 (arranging or facilitating sexual exploitation of a child);
(p) section 52 (causing or inciting prostitution for gain);
(q) section 57 (trafficking into the UK for sexual exploitation);
(r) section 58 (trafficking within the UK for sexual exploitation);
(s) section 59 (trafficking out of the UK for sexual exploitation);
(sa) section 59A (trafficking people for sexual exploitation);
(t) section 61 (administering a substance with intent).

4.—(1) Any case in which sentence is passed on a person for—
(a) attempting to commit a relevant offence;
(b) inciting the commission of a relevant offence; or
(c) an offence under section 44 or 45 of the Serious Crime Act 2007 (encouraging or assisting an offence) in relation to a relevant offence.

(2) In this paragraph, 'a relevant offence' means an offence set out in paragraph 2(a) to (h), (j) or (k) or paragraph 3.

Criminal Justice Act 1988, sch. 3

D28.8 REVIEWS OF SENTENCING — SUPPLEMENTARY

1. Notice of an application for leave to refer a case to the Court of Appeal under section 36 above shall be given within 28 days from the day on which the sentence, or the last of the sentences, in the case was passed.
2. If the registrar of criminal appeals is given notice of a reference or application to the Court of Appeal under section 36 above, he shall—
(a) take all necessary steps for obtaining a hearing of the reference of application; and

(b) obtain and lay before the court in proper form all documents, exhibits and other things which appear necessary for the proper determination of the reference or application.

3. Rules of court may enable a person to whose sentencing such a reference or application relates to obtain from the registrar any documents or things, including copies or reproductions of documents, required for the reference or application and may authorise the registrar to make charges for them in accordance with scales and rates fixed from time to time by the Treasury.

4. An application to the Court of Appeal for leave to refer a case to the Supreme Court under section 36(5) above shall be made within the period of 14 days beginning with the date on which the Court of Appeal conclude their review of the case; and an application to the Supreme Court for leave shall be made within the period of 14 days beginning with the date on which the Court of Appeal conclude their review or refuse leave to refer the case to the Supreme Court.

5. The time during which a person whose case has been referred for review under section 36 above is in custody pending its review and pending any reference to the Supreme Court under subsection (5) of that section shall be reckoned as part of the term of any sentence to which he is for the time being subject.

6. Except as provided by paragraphs 7 and 8 below, a person whose sentencing is the subject of a reference to the Court of Appeal under section 36 above shall be entitled to be present, if he wishes it, on the hearing of the reference, although he may be in custody.

7. A person in custody shall not be entitled to be present—

(a) on an application by the Attorney-General for leave to refer a case; or

(b) on any proceedings preliminary or incidental to a reference,

unless the Court of Appeal give him leave to be present.

8. The power of the Court of Appeal to pass sentence on a person may be exercised although he is not present.

9. A person whose sentencing is the subject of a reference to the Supreme Court under section 36(5) above and who is detained pending the hearing of that reference shall not be entitled to be present on the hearing of the reference or of any proceeding preliminary or incidental thereto except where an order of the Supreme Court authorises him to be present, or where the Supreme Court of Appeal, as the case may be, give him leave to be present.

10. The term of any sentence passed by the Court of Appeal or Supreme Court under section 36 above shall, unless they otherwise direct, begin to run from the time when it would have begun to run if passed in the proceeding in relation to which the reference was made.

11. (1) Where on a reference to the Court of Appeal under section 36 above or a reference to the Supreme Court under subsection (5) of that section the person whose sentencing is the subject of the reference appears by counsel for the purpose of presenting any argument to the Court of Appeal or the Supreme Court, he shall be entitled to the payment out of central funds of such funds as are reasonably sufficient to compensate him for expenses properly incurred by him for the purpose of being represented on the reference; and any amount recoverable under this paragraph shall be ascertained, as soon as practicable, by the registrar of criminal appeals or, as the case may be, under Supreme Court Rules.

(2) Sub-paragraph (1) has effect subject to—

(a) sub-paragraph (3), and

(b) regulations under section 20(1A)(d) of the Prosecution of Offences Act 1985 (as applied by this paragraph).

(3) A person is not entitled under sub-paragraph (1) to the payment of sums in respect of legal costs (as defined in section 16A of the Prosecution of Offences Act 1985) incurred in proceedings in the Court of Appeal.

(4) Subsections (1A) to (1C) and (3) of section 20 of the Prosecution of Offences Act 1985 (regulations as to amounts ordered to be paid out of central funds) apply in relation to funds payable out of central funds under sub-paragraph (1) as they apply in relation to amounts payable out of central funds in pursuance of costs orders made under section 16 of that Act.

12. [Northern Ireland.]

REFERENCE BY THE CRIMINAL CASES REVIEW COMMISSION

The 'CCRC' was created by the Criminal Appeal Act 1995. Under s. 9, the CCRC may at any time refer a conviction on indictment or any sentence imposed in relation to that conviction (unless it is a sentence fixed by law) to the Court of Appeal. Under s. 11, the CCRC may refer any summary **D28.9** conviction or associated sentence to the Crown Court. For the CCRC to refer a case, there must be a real possibility that the Court of Appeal or Crown Court will quash the original conviction or sentence. The reference will ordinarily only be made in respect of an argument or information not available in the court of first instance or on appeal (s. 13). However, in exceptional circumstances, the CCRC may refer a case without any such development in the proceedings (s. 14).

Under CrimPR 39.5 (see Supplement, **R39.5**), when a reference is made, the Registrar must serve the reference on the appellant and must treat it as the notice of appeal unless a notice of appeal is given under r. 39.2 (see **D27.3**). The reference or notice must then be served on the respondent. The respondent may then serve a respondent's notice and must do so if it wishes to make representations or is directed to serve a respondent's notice by the court or Registrar (r. 39.6(2)).

Sections 17 to 21 set out the investigative powers of the CCRC. Under s. 17, the CCRC may require any public body to produce any document or information. Section 18A, inserted by the Criminal Cases Review Commission (Information) Act 2016 with effect from 12 July 2017, provides for the Crown Court, on an application by the CCRC, to order any person to give the CCRC access to a document or other material that is in the person's possession or control if it thinks that the document or other material may assist the CCRC in the exercise of any of its functions.

D28.10 In *Cottrell* [2007] EWCA Crim 2016, [2007] 1 WLR 3262, Sir Igor Judge P (as he then was) said that it is not open to the CCRC lawfully to apply a policy based on the decision in *R (Director of Revenue and Customs Prosecutions) v CCRC* [2006] EWHC 3064 (Admin), [2007] 1 Cr App R 30 (395). The practice of the court must be addressed and evaluated in every case. Just as the court will not normally allow an application for an extension of time for leave to appeal in a change of law case, a conviction should not normally be referred on the basis of a change of law. In the final analysis, however, it is for the CCRC to exercise its own independent and fact-specific judgement whether to refer a case, provided it gives proper weight to the law and practice of the court. The Criminal Appeal Act 1968, s. 16C, empowers the Court of Appeal to dismiss an appeal following a reference by the CCRC in respect of a conviction or special verdict if (i) the only ground for allowing it would be that there has been a change in the law since the date of the conviction; and (ii) had the reference not been made but the appellant had sought an extension of time within which to seek leave to appeal on the ground of the development of the law, the court would not think such an extension appropriate. Giving the judgment of the court in *Tierney* [2009] EWCA Crim 2220, Lord Judge CJ respectfully invited the CCRC to continue to have regard to *Cottrell* in respect of appeals based on a change in law.

In *Johnson* [2016] EWCA Crim 1613, [2017] 1 Cr App R 12 (136), the Court of Appeal considered a number of applications for exceptional leave to appeal out of time which followed in the wake of *Jogee* [2016] UKSC 8, [2017] AC 387. Perhaps mindful of the large number of potential appeals related to the decision in *Jogee* that the CCRC would have to consider, the Court reinforced the importance of s. 16C and stated that it would be for the applicant to show that a substantial injustice would be done, and that was a high threshold. The Court concluded (at [21]) that: 'In determining whether that high threshold has been met, the court will primarily and ordinarily have regard to the strength of the case advanced that the change in the law would, in fact, have made a difference'. As a good example of the way in which that principle might operate, the Court said, when dealing with the application for leave of *Hall* (at [191]): 'Can it therefore be said that there is a sufficiently strong case that the defendant would not have been convicted of murder if the law had been explained to the jury as set out in Jogee? We do not consider that there is and therefore we do not consider that a substantial injustice would be done. We refuse leave.' It should be noted that the Court did not think that the age of the case should make a difference to the assessment of whether exceptional leave to appeal should be granted. In accordance with s. 16C, the CCRC will be required to approach the question of whether to refer a case to the Court of Appeal with this decision in mind.

The test laid down in *Johnson* was subsequently applied in *Ordu* [2017] EWCA Crim 4, [2017] 1 Cr App R 21 (319).

An unsuccessful attempt to certify a point of law of public importance arising out of the *Johnson* approach to substantial injustice was made in *Garwood* [2017] EWCA Crim 59, [2017] 1 Cr App R 30 (451). As is explained at **D30.3**, that challenge necessarily failed because the parties seeking certification of the point had not secured leave to appeal to the Court of Appeal in the first place. Further attempts to certify a question in respect of *Johnson* were made in *Towers* [2019] EWCA Crim 664 and *Mitchell* [2018] EWCA Crim 2687. Both cases were references by the CCRC and so the parties were able legitimately to seek certification because they were appellants for the purposes of Part 1 of the Criminal Appeal Act 1968. However, in both cases the Court of Appeal refused to certify any point of law. Giving the judgment of the Court in *Towers*, Sir Brian Leveson P said:

> 11. Thus, the decision in *Johnson* is founded on established principles which . . . the Supreme Court in *Jogee* fully recognised; *Johnson* does no more than reflect them. To adopt the argument advanced . . . would be fundamentally to change practice. More particularly . . . it would rob the requirement of substantial injustice of meaning.
>
> 12. It is the responsibility of the Court of Appeal (Criminal Division) . . . to apply the principles identified by the Supreme Court and to refer back to that Court cases where a point of law of general public importance is identified. The argument which [counsel] wishes to deploy is not a point of law of general public importance . . . Rather, he wishes to relitigate, in the context of [*Jogee*], the practical application in relation to past convictions (and . . . past pleas of guilty) of the principles identified in *Jogee* (and other cases) despite the Supreme Court having given this court the clearest of steers.

A distinction between 'change of law' cases, and those involving a subsequent definition of an aspect of the law (where previously there had been none) was drawn by the Court of Appeal in *Rowe* [2008] EWCA Crim 2712. In the latter type of case, the issues dealt with in *Cottrell* did not arise. The appellant in *Rowe* had been convicted of the possession of indecent images of children. His conviction was prior to the judgment of the Court of Appeal in *Porter* [2006] EWCA Crim 560, [2006] 1 WLR 2633 and followed a summing-up by the trial judge which was inconsistent with *Porter* in respect of the possession of deleted images on a computer. Giving the judgment of the court, Lord Judge CJ explained (at [21]): **D28.11**

> Before the decision in *Porter* this court had not addressed the problem of possession of indecent images of children in the context of items deleted from a computer or computers in a defendant's possession. *Porter* explained the principles. It is binding upon us. It is not suggested that it was wrongly decided or decided per incuriam. If, following his application, the appellant had been granted leave to appeal, whether by the single judge, or, following refusal by the single judge, if he had applied to this court, we must assume that the principles now explained in *Porter* would have been decided in this case some time before *Porter* was decided. Until *Porter* was decided, however, the law had simply not been defined.

The CCRC was therefore justified in referring the conviction.

In *R (Dowsett) v CCRC* [2007] EWCA Crim 1923, the Divisional Court held that the CCRC is not required to refer a case to the Court of Appeal (Criminal Division) simply because the Strasbourg Court has ruled that there has been a breach of the ECHR. The Court of Appeal does not automatically quash convictions in such cases and so the CCRC should apply the test set out in the Criminal Appeal Act 1995, s. 13(1)(a), and refer a case only if there is a real possibility that the conviction would not be upheld. **D28.12**

By the CJA 2003, s. 315, leave from the Court of Appeal is required if an appellant is to argue any grounds additional to those upon which the CCRC has referred the case to the Court of Appeal.

See *Siddall* [2006] EWCA Crim 1353, for the timetable suggested by the Court of Appeal for the progress of an appeal referred by the CCRC.

The CCRC publishes a wide range of policy and procedure guidance which may be accessed via www.ccrc.gov.uk.

Section D29 Challenging Decisions of Magistrates' Courts and of the Crown Court in its Appellate Capacity

ROUTES OF CHALLENGE OF DECISIONS OF MAGISTRATES' COURTS

D29.1 A person aggrieved by a decision of the magistrates' court has three means of challenge to that decision available. They are as follows:

(a) appeal to the Crown Court;
(b) appeal to the High Court by way of case stated;
(c) application to the High Court for judicial review.

Any person convicted by a magistrates' court may appeal against either the conviction and/or sentence. If the offender pleaded guilty in the magistrates' court then the offender may also appeal against conviction (in the limited circumstances set out in **D29.4**) and sentence to the Crown Court. An appeal to the High Court by way of case stated or an application for judicial review is available to either party in the magistrates' court if they are aggrieved at the outcome of proceedings. An appeal by way of case stated or application for judicial review is heard by a Divisional Court of the Queen's Bench Division of the High Court.

APPEAL TO THE CROWN COURT

D29.2 **Magistrates' Courts Act 1980, s. 108**

(1) A person convicted by a magistrates' court may appeal to the Crown Court—
 (a) if he pleaded guilty, against his sentence;
 (b) if he did not, against the conviction or sentence.

(1A) Section 14 of the Powers of Criminal Courts (Sentencing) Act 2000 (under which a conviction of an offence for which a conditional or absolute discharge is made is deemed not to be a conviction except for certain purposes) shall not prevent an appeal under this section, whether against conviction or otherwise.

(2) A person sentenced by a magistrates' court for an offence in respect of which an order for conditional discharge has been previously made may appeal to the Crown Court against the sentence.

(3) In this section 'sentence' includes any order made on conviction by a magistrates' court, not being—
 (a) [repealed by Criminal Justice Act 1982, sch. 16]
 (b) an order for the payment of costs;
 (c) an order under section 37(1) of the Animal Welfare Act 2006 (which enables a court to order the destruction of an animal); or
 (d) an order made in pursuance of any enactment under which the court has no discretion as to the making of the order or its terms;

and also includes a declaration of relevance, within the meaning of section 23 of the Football Spectators Act 1989.

(4) Subsection (3)(d) above does not prevent an appeal against a surcharge imposed under section 161A of the Criminal Justice Act 2003.
(5) Subsection (3) does not prevent an appeal against an order under section 21A of the Prosecution of Offences Act 1985 (criminal courts charge).

Appeals against Conviction and Sentence

Appeals to the Crown Court are governed by the MCA 1980, s. 108, and CrimPR Part 34. The Criminal Procedure (Amendment) Rules 2016 (SI 2016 No. 120) amended r. 34.7 to widen its application beyond applications to introduce further evidence so as to cover applications about case management, or any other question of procedure, or the introduction or admissibility of evidence, or any other question of law that has not been determined before the hearing of the appeal begins (see Supplement, **R34.7**). **D29.3**

Additionally, r. 34.11 on the composition of a panel to hear an appeal was substituted to allow for greater flexibility in the hearing of appeals (see Supplement, **R34.11**), especially during the course of case management (when it is permissible for no justices to be involved).

It remains the case that, generally, an appeal from the youth court must be heard by a judge or recorder of the Crown Court sitting with two lay justices (one man and one woman) who are authorised to sit in the youth court. Exceptionally, the Crown Court may include only one justice of the peace and need not include both a man and a woman if the presiding judge decides that the hearing of the appeal will otherwise be unreasonably delayed or one or more of the justices who started hearing the appeal is absent (r. 34.11(1) and (2)).

The broad definition of 'sentence' contained within s. 108(3) mirrors that in the equivalent provision for the Court of Appeal (Criminal Division) in s. 50 of the Criminal Appeal Act 1968.

Appeal against Conviction Following Plea of Guilty

Generally, if a plea of guilty is entered in the magistrates' court, no appeal against the resulting conviction is available to the Crown Court. There are exceptions to that rule as follows: **D29.4**

(a) *When a plea is equivocal when made.* A plea is equivocal when made if a defendant enters a plea of guilty but, by additional comment following the plea, suggests that he or she is not guilty and has a defence. For example, if on a charge of assault a defendant pleads guilty but adds that it was self-defence, then the plea is equivocal. The usual practice would then be for the clerk of the court to explain any necessary matters of law to the defendant and retake the plea. If the defendant then unambiguously pleads guilty the court may proceed to sentence, but if the plea remains equivocal, the court enters a not guilty plea. If the court does not follow that procedure and the Crown Court is satisfied on appeal that the plea was equivocal, the case will be remitted back to the magistrates' court for a fresh plea to be entered. The magistrates' court is required to co-operate with any investigation by the Crown Court into whether or not the plea is equivocal. Such co-operation extends to the provision of affidavits explaining the circumstances in which the guilty plea came to be entered (*Rochdale Justices, ex parte Allwork* [1981] 3 All ER 434). If, having conducted a proper inquiry into whether the initial plea was equivocal, the Crown Court remits the proceedings with a direction that a trial take place, the magistrates' court must comply with that direction (*Plymouth Justices, ex parte Hart* [1986] QB 950).
(b) *When a plea is subsequently shown to be equivocal.* The usual circumstances in which an unambiguous plea of guilty subsequently becomes equivocal are when material emerges in mitigation which undermines the unambiguous nature of the plea. On appeal on such a basis, the Crown Court should remit the case for trial (*Durham Quarter Sessions, ex parte Virgo* [1952] 2 QB 1; *Blandford Justices, ex parte G* [1967] 1 QB 82).
(c) *When a plea is entered under duress.* Plainly, any plea entered under duress is not a true plea and the Crown Court may remit a case back to the magistrates' court for trial if a plea of guilty has been entered under duress. In *Huntingdon Justices, ex parte Jordan* [1981] QB 857, D had

pleaded guilty to shoplifting under duress from her husband. Her defence to the shoplifting allegations would similarly have been one of duress. The Divisional Court held that the Crown Court had jurisdiction to remit the case for trial in such circumstances if they were made out.

(d) *When autrefois convict or acquit arises.* The Crown Court in its appellate capacity may examine a plea in bar of autrefois convict or acquit even where the defendant has pleaded guilty in an entirely unambiguous way in the magistrates' court (*Cooper v New Forest District Council* [1992] Crim LR 877).

(e) *When a reference is made by the CCRC.* Under s. 11 of the Criminal Appeal Act 1995, the CCRC may refer any conviction in the magistrates' court to the Crown Court irrespective of whether the conviction arose from a plea of guilty or following a trial. Thus all of the bases of challenge to a conviction following a guilty plea in the Crown Court are available through the CCRC.

Appeal against Binding Over

D29.5 Under s. 1(1) of the Magistrates' Courts (Appeals from Binding Over Orders) Act 1956, any person who feels aggrieved at being bound over by the magistrates may appeal that binding over order to the Crown Court. The appeal is by way of rehearing, and so if the facts which led to the binding over are not accepted by the appellant, they must be proved to the satisfaction of the court (*Shaw v Hamilton* [1982] 2 All ER 718).

Procedure on Appeal to the Crown Court

D29.6 CrimPR 34.2(1) and (3) (see Supplement, **R34.2**) require notice of appeal to be given in writing to the relevant magistrates' court officer and every other party within 15 business days of sentence being passed or sentence being deferred. The appellant has 15 business days from the date of sentence, even if that is after the date of conviction, to appeal only against conviction. The time-limit is also 15 business days where the appeal is against an order, or failure to make an order. That is to be contrasted with the position in respect of an appeal against conviction from the Crown Court to the Court of Appeal (Criminal Division) (see **D27.2**). The notice should state whether the appeal is against conviction or sentence or an order or failure to make an order. The notice of appeal must also summarise the issues and in an appeal against conviction must specify the witnesses whom the appellant will want to question and state how long the trial lasted in the magistrates' court and how long the appeal is likely to take. In an appeal against a finding that the appellant insulted someone or interrupted proceedings in the magistrates' court, the magistrates' court's written findings of fact and the appellant's response to those findings must be attached to the notice. Any notice must also stipulate whether the appellant has asked the magistrates' court to reconsider the case and identify all those upon whom the notice has been served. Under r. 34.10(d), the Crown Court may allow an appeal notice to be in a form other than the specified form, or to be presented orally. If a notice is served within time, no leave to appeal is required. By virtue of r. 34.3 an application for an extension of time must be served with the appeal notice and must explain why the appeal notice is late. Under r. 34.10(a), the Crown Court may shorten or extend (even after it has expired) any time-limit under Part 34. Rule 34.7 applies where a party wants to introduce further evidence relating to bad character or previous sexual history, or hearsay evidence or evidence involving the use of special measures; notice of an application to introduce such evidence must be made not more than 14 days after service of the appeal notice.

Bail pending appeal is dealt with at **D29.16**.

An appeal is heard by a circuit judge or recorder who must normally sit with two lay magistrates who were not involved with the original proceedings (Senior Courts Act 1981, s. 74). Prior to the hearing, the defence may request a copy of the clerk's notes of evidence of the summary trial. Any request the appellant might make for a copy should be 'viewed sympathetically' (per Lord Lane CJ in *Clerk to Highbury Corner Justices, ex parte Hussein* [1986] 1 WLR 1266).

Hearing Under s. 79(3), the appeal proceeds by way of complete rehearing. Thus, at an appeal against conviction, counsel for the respondent (i.e. the prosecution) makes an opening speech and calls evidence, after which counsel for the appellant may make a submission of no case to answer. If that fails, defence evidence is called, counsel makes a closing speech, and the court announces its decision. The parties may call evidence which has only become available to them since the trial, or evidence they decided not to use in the magistrates' court. The information on which the appellant was convicted may not be amended by the Crown Court (*Garfield v Maddocks* [1974] QB 7). In *Swansea Crown Court, ex parte Stacey* [1990] RTR 183, it was held that the judge erred in allowing a prosecution application to amend the information in respect of the date of the alleged offences. Equally, the Crown Court cannot strike out an amendment made by the magistrates (*Fairgrieve v Newman* (1985) 82 Cr App R 60). **D29.7**

An appeal against sentence is, in essence, a fresh sentencing hearing. The prosecution open the facts and antecedents of the appellant, and defence counsel then mitigates. The court then decides the sentence to be imposed. When dealing with an appeal against sentence, the Crown Court should not ask itself whether the sentence was within the discretion of the magistrates (as would be the appropriate question in judicial review proceedings) but should consider whether, in the light of all the matters which the Crown Court had heard, the sentence passed by the magistrates was the correct one. If what the court thinks is the appropriate sentence differs significantly from the sentence imposed by the magistrates, the appeal should be allowed and the sentence of the Crown Court substituted for that of the magistrates (*Swindon Crown Court, ex parte Murray* (1998) 162 JP 36). The Crown Court is not entitled to increase the sentence on appeal from the magistrates' court on the basis that the magistrates ought to have committed the offender to the Crown Court for sentence in the first place (*R (Lees-Sandey) v Chichester Crown Court* (2004) *The Times*, 15 October 2004). The Crown Court may, however, increase the sentence to the maximum that could be imposed by the magistrates' court.

If a defendant pleads guilty in the magistrates' court but disputes the version of events put forward by the prosecution, and the magistrates decide to accept the defendant's version of events without hearing evidence, the Crown Court hearing an appeal against sentence is not bound by that action. As the appeal is a rehearing, the court may determine the appeal and hence pass a different sentence on a different factual basis to that which formed the basis of the sentence imposed by the magistrates' court. However, if the Crown Court intends to decide the appeal on a different factual basis, the court should inform the appellant of that intention in clear terms and give the opportunity of a *Newton* hearing (*Bussey v DPP* [1999] 1 Cr App R (S) 125). **D29.8**

Reasons for Decision Reasons for the decision of the Crown Court should be given by the judge presiding over the hearing. The reasons should include a statement of the main contentious issues in the case and how the court had resolved them. A refusal to give reasons might amount to a denial of natural justice (*Harrow Crown Court, ex parte Dave* [1994] 1 All ER 315). The duty to provide reasons exists whether the court allows or dismisses the appeal against conviction (*Inner London Crown Court, ex parte Lambeth London Borough Council* [2000] Crim LR 303). If reasons are not given the decision of the Crown Court will usually be vitiated, but that is not an unqualified rule. If, for example, the reasons are obvious, the failure to set them out will not necessarily be fatal (*Kingston Crown Court, ex parte Bell* (2000) 164 JP 633). In *Snaresbrook Crown Court, ex parte Input Management Ltd* (1999) 163 JP 533, the Divisional Court defined the obligation to give reasons, holding that the reasons given by the Crown Court should enable the defendant: (i) to see the nature of the criminality found to exist by the court; and (ii) to properly consider whether there are grounds for a further appeal to the Divisional Court by way of case stated. **D29.9**

Powers of the Crown Court on Appeal

The powers of the Crown Court when disposing of an appeal are set out in the Senior Courts Act 1981, s. 48. The decision of the Crown Court may be a majority decision. This means that **D29.10** the lay justices can out-vote the judge. The lay justices must, however, accept any decisions on questions of law made by the judge.

Section 48(2) provides that, following an appeal from the magistrates' court, the Crown Court:

(a) may confirm, reverse or vary any part of the decision appealed against, including a determination not to impose a separate penalty in respect of an offence; or
(b) may remit the matter with its opinion thereon to the authority whose decision is appealed against; or
(c) may make such other order in the matter as the court thinks just, and by such order exercise any power which the said authority might have exercised.

Section 48(4) and (5) further provide that:

(4) ... if the appeal is against a conviction or a sentence, the preceding provisions of this section shall be construed as including power to award any punishment, whether more or less severe than that awarded by the magistrates' court whose decision is appealed against, if that is a punishment which that magistrates' court might have awarded.
(5) This section applies whether or not the appeal is against the whole of the decision.

Thus, s. 48 allows the Crown Court to:

(a) quash the conviction;
(b) remit the case to the magistrates' court (e.g., in the case of an equivocal plea);
(c) vary the sentence imposed by the magistrates (this includes the power to increase the sentence, but not beyond the maximum sentence which the magistrates' court could have passed: s. 48(4)).

D29.11 Under the Criminal Appeal Act 1995, s. 11(5), if a reference to the Crown Court is made by the CCRC, the Crown Court has no power to increase the sentence.

If a defendant's hopes of a non-custodial sentence are legitimately raised as a result of an indication given by magistrates that favourable pre-sentence reports would be likely to result in a non-custodial sentence, the Crown Court should not impose or uphold a custodial sentence. Whilst the appeal proceedings constitute a complete rehearing, the expectation created in the appellant should be respected (*Isleworth Crown Court, ex parte Irvin* [1992] RTR 281).

In *Portsmouth Crown Court, ex parte Ballard* (1989) 154 JP 109, it was held that the Crown Court had no power to impose a sentence consecutive to one imposed *after* the date of imposition of the sentence being appealed.

An unsuccessful appellant may be required to pay the prosecution's costs (Prosecution of Offences Act 1985, s. 18(1)(b) (see **D33.24**), and CrimPR Part 45). A successful appellant may be awarded costs (s. 16(3)) as may a private prosecutor (s. 17(1) and (2)), but there is no provision for a public prosecutor to be awarded costs from the public purse.

Abandonment of Appeal

D29.12 **Magistrates' Courts Act 1980, s. 109**

(1) Where notice to abandon an appeal has been duly given by the appellant—
 (a) the court against whose decision the appeal was brought may issue process for enforcing that decision, subject to anything already suffered or done under it by the appellant; and
 (b) the said court may, on the application of the other party to the appeal, order the appellant to pay to that party such costs as appear to the court to be just and reasonable in respect of expenses properly incurred by that party in connection with the appeal before notice of the abandonment was given to that party.
(2) In this section 'appeal' means an appeal from a magistrates' court to the Crown Court, and the reference to a notice to abandon an appeal is a reference to a notice shown to the satisfaction of the magistrates' court to have been given in accordance with rules of court.

CrimPR 34.9 (see Supplement, **R34.9**) sets out the procedure for abandonment of an appeal under the MCA 1980, s. 109. The appellant may abandon the appeal by giving notice in writing to that effect to the magistrates' court, to the appropriate officer of the Crown Court and to the prosecution and to any other party to the appeal (r. 34.9(1)(a)). The appeal may be abandoned without permission if it is done before the hearing commences. Once the hearing has started, the appeal may be abandoned only with the permission of the Crown Court. As with a notice of appeal, under r. 34.10(d), the Crown Court may allow the notice of abandonment to be given in a form other than that specified or to be given orally. The Crown Court has a discretion to award costs in an appeal from a magistrates' court in all cases (even where a timely notice of abandonment has been served). **D29.13**

An appeal cannot be abandoned simply by an appellant failing to attend or failing to instruct an advocate. Upon the abandonment of an appeal, the Crown Court has no power to increase sentence (*Gloucester Crown Court, ex parte Betteridge* (1997) 161 JP 721). Once an appeal has been abandoned, the Crown Court has no power to reinstate the appeal unless the abandonment was a nullity (*Knightsbridge Crown Court, ex parte Commissioners of Customs and Excise* [1986] Crim LR 324).

Proceeding in the Absence of the Parties

If an appellant fails to attend at the appeal hearing when required but is represented by an advocate, the Crown Court should hear the appeal. It is not open to the Crown Court to treat the non-attendance as an effective abandonment of the appeal (*R (Hayes) v Chelmsford Crown Court* [2003] EWHC 73 (Admin)). **D29.14**

Where neither party appears or is represented, the proper course is to dismiss the appeal (*Croydon Crown Court, ex parte Clair* [1986] 2 All ER 716).

Enforcement of Orders of Crown Court on Appeal

Magistrates' Courts Act 1980, s. 110 **D29.15**

After the determination by the Crown Court of an appeal from a magistrates' court the decision appealed against as confirmed or varied by the Crown Court, or any decision of the Crown Court substituted for the decision appealed against, may, without prejudice to the powers of the Crown Court to enforce the decision, be enforced—

(a) by the issue by the court by which the decision appealed against was given of any process that it could have issued if it had decided the case as the Crown Court decided it;

(b) so far as the nature of any process already issued to enforce the decision appealed against permits, by that process;

the decision of the Crown Court shall have effect as if it had been made by the magistrates' court against whose decision the appeal is brought.

Bail Pending Appeal

Under the MCA 1980, s. 113, bail may be granted pending appeal to the Crown Court in respect of either conviction or sentence. The BA 1976 does not apply so there is no right to bail. Under the Senior Courts Act 1981, s. 81(1), an appellant refused bail by the magistrates may apply to the Crown Court for bail. It is no longer possible to apply to the High Court for bail pending appeal if the Crown Court refuses bail. CrimPR 34.2(4) (see Supplement, **R34.2**) requires that the notice of appeal to the Crown Court (see **D29.6**) must stipulate whether the appellant wishes the magistrates' court or Crown Court to hear an application for bail. **D29.16**

APPEAL TO DIVISIONAL COURT BY WAY OF CASE STATED

Principles of Appeal by Way of Case Stated

Magistrates' Courts Act 1980, ss. 111 to 114 **D29.17**

111.—(1) Any person who was a party to any proceeding before a magistrates' court or is aggrieved by the conviction, order, determination or other proceeding of the court may question the proceeding on the ground that it is wrong in law or is in excess of jurisdiction by applying to the justices composing the court to state a case for the opinion of the High Court on the question of law or jurisdiction involved; but a person shall not make an application under this section in respect of a decision against which he has a right of appeal to the High Court or which by virtue of any enactment passed after 31st December 1879 is final.

(2) An application under subsection (1) above shall be made within 21 days after the day on which the decision of the magistrates' court was given.

(3) For the purpose of subsection (2) above, the day on which the decision of the magistrates' court is given shall, where the court has adjourned the trial of an information after conviction, be the day on which the court sentences or otherwise deals with the offender.

(4) On the making of an application under this section in respect of a decision any right of the applicant to appeal against the decision to the Crown Court shall cease.

(5) If the justices are of opinion that an application under this section is frivolous, they may refuse to state a case, and, if the applicant so requires, shall give him a certificate stating that the application has been refused; but the justices shall not refuse to state a case if the application is made by or under the direction of the Attorney-General.

(6) Where justices refuse to state a case, the High Court may, on the application of the person who applied for the case to be stated, make an order of mandamus requiring the justices to state a case.

112.—(1) Any conviction, order, determination or other proceeding of a magistrates' court varied by the High Court on an appeal by case stated, and any judgment or order of the High Court on such an appeal, may be enforced as if it were a decision of the magistrates' court from which the appeal was brought.

(2) [Family court variations.]

113.—(1) Where a person has given notice of appeal to the Crown Court against the decision of a magistrates' court or has applied to a magistrates' court to state a case for the opinion of the High Court, then, if he is in custody, the magistrates' court may, subject to section 25 of the Criminal Justice and Public Order Act 1994, grant him bail.

(2) If a person is granted bail under subsection (1) above, the time and place at which he is to appear (except in the event of the determination in respect of which the case is stated being reversed by the High Court) shall be—

(a) if he has given notice of appeal, the Crown Court at the time appointed for the hearing of the appeal;

(b) if he has applied for the statement of a case, the magistrates' court at such time within 10 days after the judgment of the High Court has been given as may be specified by the magistrates' court;

and any recognisance that may be taken from him or from any surety for him shall be conditioned accordingly.

(3) Subsection (1) above shall not apply where the accused has been committed to the Crown Court for sentence under section 37 above or section 3 of the Powers of Criminal Courts (Sentencing) Act 2000.

(4) Section 37(6) of the Criminal Justice Act 1948 (which relates to the currency of a sentence while a person is released on bail by the High Court) shall apply to a person released on bail by a magistrates' court under this section pending the hearing of a case stated as it applies to a person released on bail by the High Court under section 22 of the Criminal Justice Act 1967.

114. Justices to whom application has been made to state a case for the opinion of the High Court on any proceeding of a magistrates' court shall not be required to state the case until the applicant has entered into a recognisance, with or without sureties, before the magistrates' court, conditioned to prosecute the appeal without delay and to submit to the judgment of the High Court and pay such costs as that court may award; and (except in any criminal matter) a justices' clerk shall not be required to deliver the case to the applicant until the applicant has paid him the fees payable for the case and for the recognisances to the designated officer for the court.

D29.18 Appeal from the magistrates' court by way of case stated is provided for in the MCA 1980, s. 111(1), and the procedure is governed by ss. 111 to 114 of that Act, CrimPR Part 35 (see Supplement, **R35.1** *et seq.*) and the Civil Procedure Rules, Part 52. The appeal is to a Divisional Court of the Queen's Bench Division of the High Court. The essence of the procedure is an appeal on a point of law which is identified in a document known as the 'case'. The case is initially drafted by the justices' clerk in conjunction with the bench whose decision is being appealed.

Features of the 'case stated' process which emerge from s. 111 include:

(a) The remedy is available to both the prosecution and defence.
(b) The remedy operates only in relation to an error of law or a decision taken in excess of jurisdiction. A decision as to a question of fact will ordinarily not give rise to an appeal by way of case stated but may do so if the finding of fact is alleged to be such that no reasonable bench could have properly reached that factual conclusion on the evidence (*Bracegirdle v Oxley* [1947] KB 349; *Braintree District Council v Thompson* [2005] EWCA Civ 178). In *Oladimeji v DPP* [2006] EWHC 1199 (Admin), the Divisional Court stated that any defendant who believes that the justices should not have arrived at a finding for which there was evidence because, for example, it was against the weight of the evidence, has a remedy in an appeal to the Crown Court and not to the High Court. Under s. 111(4), any appellant who employs the case stated procedure forfeits the right to appeal to the Crown Court. In *K v CPS* [2013] EWHC 1678 (Admin) the Divisional Court observed that questions framed by a district judge such as 'Was I right to assert that criminal proceedings are about a search for the truth?' should never form part of a case stated as they are not the proper subject of s. 111.
(c) The remedy is available only after the final determination of proceedings in the magistrates' court. If trial proceedings are adjourned the procedure cannot be employed during the period of adjournment (*Streames v Copping* [1985] QB 920, affirmed in *Downes v RSPCA* [2017] EWHC 3622 (Admin), [2018] 2 Cr App R 3 (25)).
(d) The remedy is available in respect of errors made in relation to sentence as well as conviction. Such appeals have often been successfully established by the prosecution where the court has wrongly held that there were 'special reasons' for not disqualifying a driver (see, e.g., *Haime v Walklett* [1983] RTR 512). A defendant may use the case stated procedure if the bench has passed a sentence which is so far beyond the usual level of sentence for such an offence that it is 'harsh and oppressive' (*Tucker v DPP* [1992] 4 All ER 901).

Procedure on Appeal by Way of Case Stated

By virtue of the MCA 1980, s. 111(2) and (3), an application to state a case must be made within 21 days of the 'day on which the court sentences or otherwise deals with the offender'. CrimPR Part 35 (see Supplement, **R35.1** *et seq.*) provides a more uniform procedure for an application to state a case whether it be from the magistrates' court or from the Crown Court under the Senior Courts Act 1981, s. 28 (see **D29.37**). Rule 35.2 governs the initial application for the court to state a case for the opinion of the High Court. The application must made be in writing no more than 21 days after the decision sought to be appealed. However, in *Woolls v North Somerset Council* [2016] EWHC 1410 (Admin), Jeremy Baker J took the view that a court has some discretion to extend the time-limit if the interests of justice so require. That finding is in contrast to the more restrictive view previously taken in *Michael v Gowland* [1977] 1 WLR 296 and *Chief Constable of Cleveland v Vaughan* [2009] EWHC 2831 (Admin). Any apparent conflict between *Woolls* and the earlier cases was resolved in *Mishra v Colchester Magistrates' Court* [2017] EWHC 2869 (Admin), [2018] 1 Cr App R 24 (346), where the Divisional Court said that *Woolls* should not be followed and there is no discretion to extend the statutory time-limit set out in s. 111(2). **D29.19**

The only substantial change effected by the revision of Part 35 in the practice to be adopted in magistrates' courts is that, by virtue of r. 35.2(1)(b), notice must now be given to the other parties as well as the court officer of the intention to apply to state a case. The other parties may then make representations. Notice to the other parties as well as the court officer was always previously required when applying to the Crown Court to state a case. Rule 35.2(2) requires that the application must specify the decision in issue, as well as the proposed question(s) of law or jurisdiction on which the opinion of the High Court will be sought. It must also indicate the proposed grounds of appeal and include any application for bail pending appeal and the suspension of any disqualification pending appeal (where such suspension can be ordered). Under r. 35.2(3), any party wishing to make representations on the application must serve them on the court officer and any other parties within ten business days of service of the application for a case to be stated. The court may determine the application without a hearing (r. 35.2(4)).

The bench may refuse to state a case on the basis that it is frivolous. Frivolous, in this context, has been defined as 'futile, misconceived, hopeless or academic' and it should be rare that the magistrates' court reach such a conclusion *(Mildenhall Magistrates' Court, ex parte Forest Heath District Council* (1997) 161 JP 401). If the court refuses to state a case, it must serve notice of the decision on each party. If the applicant asks for written reasons, those written reasons must be served on each party no more than 15 business days after the request (CrimPR 35.2(5)).

The applicant may challenge the decision to refuse to state a case by way of judicial review. Upon the applicant doing so, the Divisional Court may quash the decision to refuse to state a case and decide to proceed to a substantive hearing of the case stated application, using the affidavit evidence provided by the parties as the 'case stated'. Such procedure has the advantage that the Divisional Court does not have to wait for the case to be returned to the magistrates' court for a case to be stated before quashing a conviction (*Reigate Justices, ex parte Counsell* (1983) 148 JP 193; *Ealing Justices, ex parte Woodman* [1994] Crim LR 372). In *Blackfriars Crown Court, ex parte Sunworld Ltd* [2000] 2 All ER 837, the Divisional Court said that if the court below has given a reasoned judgment which contains all the necessary findings of fact and identifies the points of law in question in its refusal to state a case, the single judge should grant permission for judicial review if it considers the point to be arguable. In that way, the need for a case to be stated is obviated.

Under s. 114 of the MCA 1980, if a magistrates' court does state a case, it may require an applicant to enter into a recognizance to prosecute the appeal without delay and pay any costs ultimately awarded against him or her by the High Court.

D29.20 **Preparation of Case Stated** If the court decides to state a case then, unless a magistrates' court directs otherwise or the court includes a district judge, a justices' legal adviser must give the court legal advice and, if the court so requires, assist it by preparing and amending a draft case (CrimPR 35.4). Rule 35.3(4) (see Supplement, **R35.3**) provides that the draft case must specify the decision in issue as well as the question(s) of law or jurisdiction on which the opinion of the High Court will be sought. It must also include a succinct summary of the nature and history of the proceedings, the court's relevant findings of fact and the relevant contentions of the parties. If a question to be asked of the High Court is whether there was sufficient evidence on which the court reasonably could reach a finding of fact, the draft case must specify the relevant finding of fact and include a summary of the evidence on which the court reached that finding. The draft case must not include any further account of the evidence received by the court (r. 35.3(5)). In *Wheeldon v CPS* [2018] EWHC 249 (Admin) the Divisional Court made clear that on an appeal by way of case stated, the court can only consider the facts stated in the case. The court will not go behind the stated case.

D29.21 **Service and Representations** CrimPR 35.3(2) requires the court officer to serve notice of a decision to state a case on each party as well as notice of any recognizance ordered by the court. That notice having been given then, unless the court directs otherwise, the court officer must serve a draft case on each party no more than 15 business days after the court's decision to state a case (r. 35.3(3)). Any party wishing to make representations about the content of the draft case, or proposing a revised draft, must serve its representations or revised draft on each party and the court officer no more than 15 business days after the service of the draft case. As with the drafting of a case, the court may require the justices' legal adviser to amend and complete the case (r. 35.4(2)). By virtue of r. 35.3(7), the court must state the case not more than 15 business days after the time for service of representations has expired. The case stated must identify the court that stated it and the court office for that court (r. 35.3(8)). The court officer must serve the case stated on each party (r. 35.3(9)). A failure to comply with the time-limits set out for the various participants is not necessarily fatal to an application. Rule 35.5 provides that the court may extend a time-limit even after it has expired. Any party seeking such an extension must make an application when serving either the application or representations for which the extension is needed and explain the delay. Within ten days of receiving the case, under para. 2.2 of *Civil Procedure Rules Practice Direction 52E*, the applicant or legal representative must lodge it at the Administrative Court Office. Paragraph 2.4 requires the applicant to serve the appellant's notice and accompanying documents on the respondents within four days of their being lodged at the Divisional Court. The time for lodging the case may be extended by the Divisional Court, but without such an extension the claim may be struck out if the applicant fails to lodge within ten days.

Whilst the time-limits applying after an application for the magistrates to state a case has been made may be extended (or shortened), the initial 21-day time-limit within which an application must be made cannot be varied as it is prescribed by statute. If the application arrives late when sent by post, the 21-day time-limit is met if the application would have arrived on time in the normal course of events (*P and M Supplies (Essex) Ltd v Hackney London Borough Council* (1990) 154 JP 814).

Amendment of Case Where there is a difference between an earlier draft of the case and the final version, the Divisional Court will act on the final version (*Thomas* [1990] Crim LR 269). On an appeal by way of case stated, the court is confined to the facts set out in the case. Thus if any party wishes to add any evidential matter to the case, he or she should seek to have the case amended either by agreement with the other party and the lower court or by application to the Divisional Court under the Senior Courts Act 1981, s. 28A(2) (*Skipaway Ltd v Environment Agency* [2006] EWHC 983 (Admin)). **D29.22**

Bail Pending Appeal

An appellant by way of case stated who has been sentenced to a term of immediate custody may be granted bail pending appeal by the magistrates' court under the MCA 1980, s. 113. If granted bail, the appellant must surrender to the magistrates' court no later than ten days after the final determination of the appeal. The exact date on which the surrender must take place will be fixed by the magistrates' court after the appeal. If refused bail, the appellant may apply to a judge in chambers in the High Court under the CJA 1967, s. 22. The procedure for an application for bail to the High Court in such circumstances is set out in the Rules of the Supreme Court, ord. 79, r. 9. **D29.23**

Determination by Divisional Court of an Appeal by Way of Case Stated

The Divisional Court which hears an application by way of case stated will be comprised of at least two judges, and often three. If a two-judge court cannot agree, the appeal is unsuccessful (see the *obiter* remarks of Scrutton LJ in *Flannagan v Shaw* [1920] 3 KB 96 at p. 107). No evidence is called at the hearing as all evidence which needs to be referred to will be contained in the stated case (see **D29.17**). Instead the appeal is conducted by way of submissions from the parties. If the facts contained within the case give rise to a point of law which was not argued before the magistrates but would have provided the defendant with a defence, the court may consider the point provided no further evidence is necessary (*Whitehead v Haines* [1965] 1 QB 200). **D29.24**

Under s. 28A(3) of the Senior Courts Act 1981, the court may 'reverse, affirm or amend' the decision of the magistrates' court, or remit the case with its opinion, or make any other order (including an order as to costs) as it sees fit. Thus the Divisional Court may quash an acquittal with a direction that the magistrates' court convicts and sentences. Alternatively, the court may simply substitute a conviction for the previous acquittal and proceed to sentence. Similarly, if the appeal concerns sentence only, the court may substitute the appropriate sentence.

An appellant may abandon an appeal by way of case stated without leave (*Collet v Bromsgrove District Council* (1996) 160 JP 593).

The Divisional Court is entitled to order a retrial before the same bench or a different bench where a fair trial is still possible (*Griffith v Jenkins* [1992] 2 AC 76).

APPLICATION FOR JUDICIAL REVIEW

Prerogative Orders Generally

D29.25 The High Court polices the decision-making of inferior public bodies by way of judicial review. Consequently, decisions of the magistrates' court and some of those of the Crown Court (those which are not concerned with matters relating to trial on indictment) are susceptible to review. The High Court does so by means of prerogative orders, foremost of which are quashing orders, mandatory orders and prohibiting orders.

The application for judicial review is dealt with by a Divisional Court of the Queen's Bench Division of the High Court.

The granting of prerogative orders is discretionary and the Divisional Court will sometimes withhold relief despite it being open to the court to grant it where fairness and the due administration of justice demand it. Undue delay on behalf of the applicant for judicial review may sometimes result in the withholding of relief. In *Neath and Port Talbot Justices, ex parte DPP* [2000] 1 WLR 1376, the Divisional Court identified the principal factors to be taken into account in considering whether delay should lead to a refusal of relief. They are:

(a) the seriousness of the offence;
(b) the nature of the evidence in the case (and in particular the extent to which the quality of the evidence would be affected by delay);
(c) the extent of any contribution by the defendant to the error of the magistrates' court;
(d) the extent of any contribution by the defendant to any delay in the review process;
(e) the extent to which the complainant would be justifiably aggrieved by the abandonment of the proceedings;
(f) the extent to which the defendant would be justifiably aggrieved by the continuation of the proceedings.

D29.26 Rule 54.5(1) of the Civil Procedure Rules provides that a claim form must be filed promptly and, in any event, not later than three months after the grounds to make the claim first arose. But a judicial review claim will not necessarily be regarded as being in time merely because it is made within a three-month period. Instead, the claim form must be lodged promptly, and applications for judicial review have been rejected as being out of time where delay has occurred within the three-month period (see, e.g., *Independent Television Commission, ex parte TV NI Ltd* (1991) *The Times*, 30 December 1991).

The Divisional Court has also refused relief when the defendant had an appeal to the Crown Court available (*Peterborough Justices, ex parte Dowler* [1996] 2 Cr App R 561). But in *Hereford Magistrates' Court, ex parte Rowlands* [1998] QB 110, Lord Bingham CJ emphasised the importance of the supervisory jurisdiction of the High Court in ensuring continued high standards in magistrates' courts, and concluded that the existence of a right to appeal to the Crown Court, particularly if unexercised, should not ordinarily preclude permission for judicial review, nor substantive relief in a proper case.

D29.27 The principal grounds upon which judicial review may be sought are:

(a) error of law on the face of the record — i.e. an error disclosed by the court records;
(b) excess of jurisdiction;
(c) breach of natural justice.

The concept of breach of natural justice has frequently been litigated and has been widely drawn. It has been held to include:

(i) failing to give the accused adequate time to prepare a defence (*Thames Magistrates' Court, ex parte Polemis* [1974] 2 All ER 1219);

(ii) failing to grant an adjournment to allow for the attendance of a witness (*Bracknell Justices, ex parte Hughes* [1990] Crim LR 266; and see *R (Parashar) v Sunderland Magistrates' Court* [2019] EWHC 514 (Admin) for a detailed examination of the authorities bearing on this issue);
(iii) the prosecution failing to call or disclose the statement of a witness who might assist the defence (*Leyland Justices, ex parte Hawthorn* [1979] QB 283);
(iv) the prosecution failing to disclose the previous convictions of prosecution witnesses (*Knightsbridge Crown Court, ex parte Goonatilleke* [1986] QB 1);
(v) making an order as to costs against a defendant without inquiring as to the defendant's means (*Newham Justices, ex parte Samuels* [1991] COD 412).

The proceedings in the magistrates' court must ordinarily be concluded before any application for judicial review. Interlocutory decisions by the magistrates' court are not generally amenable to review (*Greater Manchester Justices, ex parte Aldi GmbH & Co. KG* [1995] RTR 207), but it is possible to review a decision as whether proceedings should commence (*R (Hoar-Stevens) v Richmond-upon-Thames Magistrates* [2003] EWHC 2660 (Admin); *Rochford Justices, ex parte Buck* (1979) 68 Cr App R 114). A detailed analysis of the circumstances in which an application to judicially review an interlocutory decision of the magistrates' court is appropriate is found in *R (Parashar) v Sunderland Magistrates' Court* [2019] EWHC 514 (Admin). **D29.28**

Whilst it is possible to challenge a sentence by way of judicial review, it is not usually appropriate and the defendant should seek a remedy through appeal to the Crown Court unless there are clear and substantial grounds for proceeding by way of review (*Allen v West Yorkshire Probation Service* [2001] EWHC Admin 2; *Tucker v DPP* [1992] 4 All ER 901). Both of these cases were appeals by way of case stated but the court made it clear that judicial review was also inappropriate.

Quashing Orders

Quashing orders are used to nullify decisions and orders made by the magistrates' court, such as decisions to commit for sentence and convictions. Its use in respect of acquittals is more limited than in the case stated procedure because of the double jeopardy principle. Even if the prosecution are prejudiced to the extent that, had the defence had been similarly prejudiced it would have required the quashing of the conviction, review will still not be available. That principle was reaffirmed by the House of Lords in *Dorking Justices, ex parte Harrington* [1984] AC 743, but an important exception to the rule was established. In simple terms, the rule will not apply where the magistrates acquit where they have no jurisdiction to do so. If that occurs, the acquittal is a nullity and a quashing order may be made. Such a situation may come about when the magistrates acquit in respect of an indictable-only offence (*West* [1964] 1 QB 15) or a defendant is acquitted of an either-way offence when the correct mode of trial procedures have not been followed (*Cardiff Magistrates' Court, ex parte Cardiff City Council* (1987) *The Times*, 24 February 1987), or the magistrates' court, in the absence of good reason, acquits without listening to any of the prosecution witnesses available at court (*Hendon Justices, ex parte DPP* [1994] QB 167). **D29.29**

Excess of Jurisdiction When a magistrates' court acts in excess of jurisdiction, the Divisional Court may issue a quashing order. In *Kent Justices, ex parte Machin* [1952] 2 QB 355, a conviction was quashed when magistrates failed to explain to D the possibility that he could be committed for sentence before he consented to summary trial. **D29.30**

Judicial review is rarely the most appropriate means of challenge to a sentence imposed by the magistrates but it can in very limited circumstances be used to challenge a sentence passed in excess of jurisdiction. In *St Albans Crown Court, ex parte Cinnamond* [1981] QB 480, the Divisional Court extended the concept of excess of jurisdiction to include a sentence that was so harsh that no reasonable tribunal, properly understanding its powers, could have passed it. Not surprisingly, the courts have repeatedly sought to confine the applicability of *Ex parte Cinnamond* to very limited circumstances. In *Croydon Crown Court, ex parte Miller* (1986) 85

Cr App R 152, it was said that the sentence would have to appear in all the circumstances to be, by any acceptable standard, truly astonishing. Whilst in *Truro Crown Court, ex parte Adair* [1997] COD 296, Lord Bingham CJ questioned whether the sentence needed to be truly astonishing but asserted that it needed to fall clearly outside the broad area of the lower court's sentencing discretion.

D29.31 **Breach of Rules of Natural Justice** A number of decisions of magistrates' courts have been quashed where a magistrate or clerk has an interest of either a pecuniary or non-pecuniary nature such as to give rise to a reasonable suspicion of bias. In addition, procedural irregularities have often led to the quashing of decisions on the grounds of breach of natural justice (see **D29.25**).

D29.32 **Error of Law** An error of law made by a magistrates' court is amenable to review. As an example, in *Southampton Justices, ex parte Green* [1976] QB 11, the Court of Appeal quashed an order made by the magistrates that D should forfeit the surety provided as the decision-making process was wrong in law. So far as the exercise of discretion on questions of law is concerned, the court will apply the test in *Associated Provincial Picture Houses Ltd v Wednesbury Corporation* [1948] 1 KB 223 (*Re Proulx* [2001] 1 All ER 57).

Mandatory Orders

D29.33 A mandatory order is issued to compel a magistrates' court to comply with its obligations and usually flows from an order quashing the original decision. One may be issued where the magistrates' court has wrongly refused jurisdiction (*Rochford Justices, ex parte Buck* (1978) 68 Cr App R 114; *Wells Street Stipendiary Magistrate, ex parte Seillon* [1978] 3 All ER 257). In matters of discretion, if the magistrates' court overlooked the fact that it had a discretionary power, or applied the wrong principles in deciding whether or not to exercise it, the Divisional Court will issue a mandatory order requiring the court to consider or reconsider the matter, applying the correct principles as stated by the High Court (*Highgate Justices, ex parte Lewis* [1977] Crim LR 611). The court will not be required to exercise the power in a particular way unless it is clear that that would be the only conclusion to which a reasonable tribunal directing itself properly could come.

Prohibiting Orders

D29.34 A prohibiting order prevents a magistrates' court from taking a particular course of action which would be in excess of its jurisdiction (*Hatfield Justices, ex parte Castle* [1981] 3 All ER 509).

Procedure on Application for Judicial Review

D29.35 The procedure to be followed on an application for judicial review is governed by the Senior Courts Act 1981, s. 31, along with Part 54 of the Civil Procedure Rules and the *Part 54 Practice Direction*. The Judicial Review Pre-Action Protocol usually requires that a claimant for judicial review write to the proposed defendant explaining the basis of the challenge. Such a letter gives the decision-maker an opportunity to reverse the decision before proceedings are started. But a decision by a court will normally be a final decision and so the court will not be able to reverse that decision as it will often be *functus officio*. The Protocol recognises that in such circumstances a letter before claim is not necessary. If an interim decision of a court is to be challenged, the court will not be *functus officio* and the court should be put on notice that an application for judicial review will be made. The claimant should then apply for an adjournment in order to bring the judicial review proceedings (*Streames v Copping* [1985] QB 920). If the application for an adjournment is refused, the Administrative Court may stay the magistrates' court proceedings as interim relief under para. 6.4 of the Pre-Action Protocol.

Any claimant for judicial review requires permission to pursue the claim. The issue of permission is usually resolved on the papers by the single judge. If permission is granted, the matter proceeds to a substantive hearing.

(a) The first stage of the process is to submit a claim form. As well as the matters that normally must appear in a claim form (Civil Procedure Rules, r. 8.2), r. 54.6 provides that the claimant has to identify interested parties and must state the remedy sought. The claim form has to be accompanied by the documents required by the *Part 54 Practice Direction* which supplements Part 54. Paragraph 5.6 of the *Practice Direction* provides that the claim form must include or be accompanied by a detailed statement of the claimant's grounds for bringing the claim for judicial review, a statement of the facts relied upon, and a time estimate for the hearing. The statement of facts and the grounds to be relied on are usually drafted by counsel if the claimant is legally represented. The claim form must also be accompanied by any written evidence in support of the claim (or in support of any application to extend time), a copy of any order that the claimant seeks to have quashed, an approved copy of the lower court's reasons for reaching the decision under challenge, copies of any documents on which the claimant proposes to rely, copies of any relevant statutory material, and a list of essential documents for reading in advance by the court (with page references to the passages relied on) (para. 5.7). The prosecution must always be named as an interested party where the claim is for judicial review of a decision of a magistrates' court or the Crown Court (para. 5.2). Not more than 21 days after the service of the claim form the defendant must file an acknowledgement of service. The acknowledgement of service must be served on the claimant, and on any other person named in the claim form, not later than seven days after it is filed. If the person serving it intends to contest the claim, the acknowledgement of service must set out a summary of the grounds for contesting the claim, known as 'summary grounds of resistance', and must state the name and address of anyone whom the person filing it considers to be an interested party.

(b) The court will generally consider the question of permission without a hearing (para. 8.4) Where there is a hearing, neither the defendant nor any other interested party need attend the hearing unless the court directs otherwise (para. 8.5). The court will not usually make an order for costs where the defendant or any interested party does attend a hearing (para. 8.6). The single judge will grant permission if the claimant's application for judicial review discloses an arguable case. Rule 54.12 provides that, if the court (without a hearing) refuses permission to proceed or gives permission that is subject to conditions or on certain grounds only, the court will serve its reasons for making the order along with the order itself. Under r. 54.12, 'the claimant may not appeal but may request the decision to be reconsidered at a hearing' (and must file a request for such a hearing within seven days of the service of the court's reasons for the decision). If the court decides that the application is 'wholly without merit', such a renewed application is not possible. Any renewed application will be before a Divisional Court in a criminal cause or matter. Neither the defendant, nor anyone else served with the claim form, may apply to set aside an order giving the claimant permission to proceed (r. 54.13).

(c) Once permission has been granted, the defendant (and anyone else served with the claim form who wishes to contest the claim or support it on additional grounds) must serve detailed grounds for resisting the claim (or supporting it on additional grounds), and any written evidence, within 35 days after the service of the order granting permission.

(d) The court may decide the claim for judicial review without a hearing where all the parties agree (r. 54.18). In all other circumstances, the claimant must file and serve a skeleton argument not less than 21 working days before the date of the hearing of the judicial review claim (para. 15.1 of the *Practice Direction*). Under para. 15.2, the defendant (and any other party wishing to make representations at the hearing) must file and serve a skeleton argument not less than 14 working days before the date of the hearing. The skeleton arguments must contain a list of issues, a list of the legal points to be taken (together with any relevant authorities), a chronology of events, a list of essential reading by the court in advance of the hearing and a list of persons referred to.

(e) The claimant must have the court's permission to rely on grounds other than those for which the court gave permission to proceed (r. 54.15). The claimant must give notice no later than seven clear days before the hearing to any person served with the claim form if he or she intends to rely on additional grounds at the hearing of the claim for judicial review.

(f) The usual procedure followed at the hearing is one of legal argument supported by affidavits or witness statements. However, it is possible for oral evidence to be called if necessary.

Bail Pending Judicial Review

D29.36 In contrast to the position in respect of appeals by way of case stated, the magistrates' court has no power to grant bail pending an application for judicial review. Bail may be secured through an application to the High Court under s. 37(1)(d) of the CJA 1948.

ROUTES TO CHALLENGE DECISIONS OF THE CROWN COURT ACTING IN ITS APPELLATE CAPACITY

Appeal by way of Case Stated

D29.37 **Senior Courts Act 1981, s. 28**

(1) Subject to subsection (2), any order, judgment or other decision of the Crown Court may be questioned by any party to the proceedings, on the ground that it is wrong in law or is in excess of jurisdiction, by applying to the Crown Court to have a case stated by that court for the opinion of the High Court.
(2) Subsection (1) shall not apply to—
  (a) a judgment or other decision of the Crown Court relating to trial on indictment; or
  (b) any decision of that court under the Local Government (Miscellaneous Provisions) Act 1982 which, by any provision of any of those Acts, is to be final.
(3) Subject to the provisions of this Act and to rules of court, the High Court shall, in accordance with section 19(2), have jurisdiction to hear and determine—
  (a) any application, or any appeal (whether by way of case stated or otherwise), which it has power to hear and determine under or by virtue of this or any other Act; and
  (b) all such other appeals as it had jurisdiction to hear and determine immediately before the commencement of this Act.
(4) In subsection (2)(a) the reference to a decision of the Crown Court relating to trial on indictment does not include a decision relating to a requirement to make a payment under regulations under section 23 or 24 of the Legal Aid, Sentencing and Punishment of Offenders Act 2012.

D29.38 In common with applications by way of case stated from the magistrates' court, an application to appeal by way of case stated from the Crown Court may be made in respect of an error of law or where it is alleged that the Crown Court acted in excess of jurisdiction. There can be no challenge on the basis that a decision is against the weight of the evidence. Similarly, as with appeals by way of case stated from the magistrates' court, the proceedings in the Crown Court must have been finally decided before the case stated procedure may be employed (*Loade v DPP* [1990] 1 QB 1052). By virtue of s. 28(1)(a), no appeal by way of case stated is possible in respect of matters relating to trial on indictment (see **D29.40** for the meaning of 'relating to trial on indictment'). The means of challenge is plainly available in respect of any decision of the Crown Court relating to an appeal against conviction or sentence from the magistrates' court.

The procedure to be followed upon an application to the Crown Court to state a case is governed by CrimPR Part 35 (see Supplement, **R35.1** *et seq.*). Rule 35.2 governs the initial application for the court to state a case for the opinion of the High Court. The application must be made in writing no more than 21 days after the decision sought to be appealed and must be served on each party and the court officer. In contrast to the position when applying to the magistrates' court to state a case (see **D29.21**), an extension to the 21 days allowed for the application may be made at the time of the application (r. 35.2(2)(d)(i)). In common with the procedure in the magistrates' court, r. 35.2(2) requires that the application must specify the decision in issue as well as the proposed question(s) of law or jurisdiction on which the opinion of the High Court will be sought. It must also indicate the proposed grounds of appeal and include any application for bail pending appeal and the suspension of any disqualification pending appeal (where such suspension can be ordered). Under r. 35.2(3), a party wishing to make representations on the application must serve them on the court officer and any other parties within ten business days of service of the application for a case to be stated. The court may determine the application without a hearing (r. 35.2(4)). If the court refuses to state a case, it must serve notice of the decision on each party. If the applicant asks for written reasons, those written reasons must be served on each party no more than 15 business days days after the request (r. 35.2(5)).

If the court decides to state a case then r. 35.3(2) requires the court officer to serve notice of that decision on each party as well as notice of any recognizance ordered by the court. In contrast to the position in the magistrates' court, the applicant must then serve a draft case on each party and the court officer no more than 15 business days after the court's decision to state a case (r. 35.3(3)). The draft case must specify the decision in issue as well as the question(s) of law or jurisdiction on which the opinion of the High Court will be sought. It must also include a succinct summary of the nature and history of the proceedings, the court's relevant findings of fact and the relevant contentions of the parties (r. 35.3(4)). Any party wishing to make representations about the content of the draft case, or proposing a revised draft, must serve its representations or revised draft on each party and the court officer no more than 15 business days after the service of the draft case. By virtue of r. 35.3(7), the court must state the case no more than 15 business days after the time for service of representations has expired. The court officer must serve the case stated on each party (r. 35.3(9)). Time-limits may be shortened or extended in accordance with r. 35.5. **D29.39**

Under s. 81(1)(d) of the Senior Courts Act 1981, bail pending appeal by way of case stated from the Crown Court may be granted by the Crown Court.

Application for Judicial Review

By virtue of s. 29(3) of the Senior Courts Act 1981, it is possible to challenge a decision of the Crown Court by way of judicial review provided that that decision does not concern a matter relating to trial on indictment. In *Re Smalley* [1985] AC 622, the House of Lords held that the phrase 'relating to trial on indictment' covered all decisions relating to the conduct of the trial. It has thus been held that the decision to stay any part of an indictment as an abuse of process is a matter relating to trial on indictment (*Ashton* [1994] AC 9), as is an order that counts should lie on the file in the usual way (*Central Criminal Court, ex parte Raymond* [1986] 2 All ER 379), a decision as to the order in which indictments are tried (*Southwark Crown Court, ex parte Ward* [1996] Crim LR 123) and decisions as to disclosure (*Chester Crown Court, ex parte Cheshire County Council* [1996] Crim LR 336). It has also been held that the decision to hold a trial on the issue of fitness to plead is a matter relating to trial on indictment (*Bradford Crown Court, ex parte Bottomley* [1994] Crim LR 753) as is the imposition of a mandatory life sentence (*R (Lichniak) v Secretary of State for the Home Department* [2001] EWHC Admin 294, [2002] QB 296). **D29.40**

Matters which do not relate to trial on indictment include forfeiture of a surety (*Re Smalley*), forfeiture of property used in the course of an offence belonging to a third party (*Maidstone Crown Court, ex parte Gill* [1986] 1 All ER 129), binding over of an acquitted accused (*Inner London Crown Court, ex parte Benjamin* (1986) 85 Cr App R 265) and restrictions on the publication of the identity of a convicted youth (*Leicester Crown Court, ex parte S (A Minor)* [1993] 2 All ER 659).

Under s. 81(1)(e) of the 1981 Act, bail may be granted pending judicial review of a decision of the Crown Court.

If a defendant convicted in the magistrates' court appeals to the Crown Court, any further appeal to the High Court on a point of law should be by way of case stated and not judicial review (*Gloucester Crown Court, ex parte Chester* [1998] COD 365).

NO POWER OF JUDICIAL REVIEW OVER DECISIONS OF THE HIGH COURT

D29.41 There is no power available to the High Court to judicially review the decisions of the High Court. In that vein, the decision of a judge of the High Court on an application for leave to prefer a voluntary bill of indictment is not amenable to judicial review (*Manchester Crown Court, ex parte Williams* (1990) 154 JP 589).

CHOICE BETWEEN JUDICIAL REVIEW AND CASE STATED

D29.42 Both judicial review and the case stated procedure set aside the decision of the court below, and a choice must be made as to which route to pursue. In *R (P) v Liverpool City Magistrates* [2006] EWHC 887 (Admin), Collins J stated:

(a) the normal route for an appeal against a decision of justices where it is alleged there has been an error of law is by way of case stated;
(b) it would be wrong to seek judicial review where case stated was appropriate, merely in order to avoid the more stringent time-limit;
(c) however, judicial review is more appropriate where there is an issue of fact to be raised and decided which the justices did not decide themselves;
(d) judicial review may also be appropriate where it is alleged that there has been unfairness or bias in the conduct of the case by the justices but, where it is alleged that there has been a misdirection or an error of law, case stated is the appropriate remedy.

In *North Essex Justices, ex parte Lloyd* [2001] 2 Cr App R (S) 15 (86), the Divisional Court said that judicial review should be pursued where the inferior court has acted in excess of jurisdiction.

Judicial review is the only remedy available where the defence wish to challenge a committal for sentence, as the case stated procedure is not available where there has not been a final determination of the case.

D29.43 In *Essen v DPP* [2005] EWHC 1077 (Admin), Sedley LJ said that the authorities restricting appeal by way of case stated to those where there has been a final determination 'could usefully be revisited'. This was borne partly out of a concern that an appellant might be left without a remedy. If the interlocutory decision had been made more than 21 days before the final determination of the case, the case stated procedure would not be available. In addition, on one view, the court lacks jurisdiction to undertake judicial review of interlocutory decisions of justices (a view based on *Rochford Justices, ex parte Buck* (1979) 68 Cr App R 114). But it is submitted that the rule is not without exception. In *R (Watson) v Dartford Magistrates' Court* [2005] EWHC 905 (QB), it was held that the normal rule is that the High Court should not interfere with interlocutory rulings made by justices; but if the prosecution would say at the end of the trial that it was too late for the defendant to complain, there is no fetter on the High Court intervening.

APPEAL FROM THE DIVISIONAL COURT

D29.44 Any appeal from the High Court in a criminal cause or matter, either in relation to an appeal by way of case stated or a judicial review, is direct to the Supreme Court (see **D30.5**). For a full, recent explanation of the origins and meaning of the phrase 'criminal cause or matter' see *Belhaj v DPP* [2018] UKSC 33, [2018] 3 WLR 435 (see **B30.5**).

Section D30 Appeals to the Supreme Court and the Role of the Court of Justice of the European Union and the European Court of Human Rights

APPEAL TO THE SUPREME COURT

The Supreme Court, established under the Constitutional Reform Act 2005, s. 23, replaced the House of Lords as the highest court of the UK. **D30.1**

The Supreme Court Rules (SI 2009 No. 1603) govern practice and procedure.

From the Court of Appeal (Criminal Division)

Criminal Appeal Act 1968, ss. 33 and 34 **D30.2**

33.—(1) An appeal lies to the Supreme Court, at the instance of the defendant or the prosecutor, from any decision of the Court of Appeal on an appeal to that court under Part I of this Act or Part 9 of the Criminal Justice Act 2003 or section 9 (preparatory hearings) of the Criminal Justice Act 1987 or section 35 of the Criminal Procedure and Investigations Act 1996 or section 47 of the Criminal Justice Act 2003.

(1A) [Repealed by the SCA 2007, sch. 8, para. 144.]

(1B) An appeal lies to the Supreme Court, at the instance of the acquitted person or the prosecutor, from any decision of the Court of Appeal on an application under section 76(1) or (2) of the Criminal Justice Act 2003 (retrial for serious offences).

(2) The appeal lies only with the leave of the Court of Appeal or the Supreme Court; and leave shall not be granted unless it is certified by the Court of Appeal that a point of law of general public importance is involved in the decision and it appears to the Court of Appeal or the Supreme Court (as the case may be) that the point is one which ought to be considered by the Supreme Court.

(3) Except as provided by this Part of this Act and section 13 of the Administration of Justice Act 1960 (appeal in cases of contempt of court), no appeal shall lie from any decision of the criminal division of the Court of Appeal.

(4) In relation to an appeal under subsection (1B), references in this Part to a defendant are references to the acquitted person.

34.—(1) An application to the Court of Appeal for leave to appeal to the Supreme Court shall be made within the period of 28 days beginning with the relevant date; and an application to the Supreme Court for leave shall be made within the period of 28 days beginning with the date on which the application for leave is refused by the Court of Appeal.

(1A) In subsection (1), 'the relevant date' means—

(a) the date of the Court of Appeal's decision, or

(b) if later, the date on which the Court gives reasons for its decision.

(2) The Supreme Court or the Court of Appeal may, upon application made at any time by the defendant or, in the case of an appeal under section 33(1B), by the prosecutor, extend the time within which an application may be made by him to the Supreme Court or the Court of Appeal under subsection (1) above.

(3) An appeal to the Supreme Court shall be treated as pending until any application for leave to appeal is disposed of and, if leave to appeal is granted, until the appeal is disposed of; and for purposes of this Part of this Act an application for leave to appeal shall be treated as disposed of at the expiration of the time within which it may be made, if it is not made within that time.

Sections 33 and 34 of the Criminal Appeal Act 1968 allow either the prosecution or defence to appeal a decision of the Court of Appeal to the Supreme Court, but only if the Court of **D30.3**

Appeal or the Supreme Court itself considers that the appeal involves a point of law of general public importance which should be considered by the Supreme Court. In addition, the Court of Appeal must certify that the appeal involves a question concerning a point of law of general public importance. An application to the Court of Appeal for leave to appeal to the Supreme Court must be made by the party seeking to appeal no more than 28 days after the decision, or the date on which the court gives the reasons for its decision, whichever is later. Time begins to run on the day of the decision and not the day following the decision.

CrimPR Part 43 (see Supplement, **R43.1** *et seq.*) governs the making of an application to the Court of Appeal for permission to appeal or refer a case to the Supreme Court. Form SC must be served on the Registrar and all the parties. The Supreme Court has no power to grant representation orders and an application for appropriate representation before the Supreme Court should be made to the Court of Appeal.

Where the Court of Appeal is of the view that the prospective appeal raises no point of law of public importance, it may decide so on the papers (*Daines* [1961] 1 All ER 290). A refusal to allow oral submissions will not amount to a violation of a person's rights under the ECHR, Article 6 (*Steele* [2006] EWCA Crim 2000, [2007] 1 WLR 222). A refusal by the Court of Appeal to certify a question cannot be appealed. In *Dunn* [2010] EWCA Crim 1823, [2011] 1 WLR 958, the Court of Appeal concluded that the fact that whether an appeal that has failed before it raises a point of law of public importance is decided by the Court itself does not offend either Article 6 or Article 14 of the ECHR.

In *Garwood* [2017] EWCA Crim 59, [2017] 1 Cr App R 30 (451) the Court of Appeal considered whether there is jurisdiction to grant a certificate in circumstances when leave to appeal against conviction and sentence has been refused by the Court of Appeal. As a matter of statutory construction, the Court decided that the Criminal Appeal Act 1968 provided for an appeal to the Supreme Court only by appellants and not applicants. Therefore it was not open to the Court of Appeal to certify a question when an applicant had been refused leave to appeal to the Court of Appeal. The consequence of that first refusal is that applicants never attain the status of appellants (unless a renewed application for leave to appeal is made and the Court grants leave but dismisses the appeal). Moreover, the Court decided that the authorities of *Stafford* (1969) 53 Cr App R 1, *Mealey* (1974) 60 Cr App R 59, and *Moulden* [2004] EWCA Crim 2715, [2005] 1 Cr App R (S) 121 (691) and [2005] EWCA Crim 374, which had been decided to similar effect, were binding on the Court.

D30.4 If the Court of Appeal certifies a question but leave to appeal to the Supreme Court is refused, the party may apply for leave to the Supreme Court within 28 days of the day on which the Court of Appeal gives reasons for its refusal of leave.

If the Court of Appeal decides an appeal on one ground but leaves others undecided and the Supreme Court hears the appeal of that decision, the Supreme Court may either rule on those grounds as if it were the Court of Appeal or may remit them back to the Court of Appeal for its decision. In *Mandair* [1995] 1 AC 208, the House of Lords stated that the undecided grounds of appeal should be identified and written submissions should be made as to whether and how the House of Lords should dispose of them and the principle is equally applicable to appeals to the Supreme Court.

Practice Direction 12 of the Supreme Court Practice Directions provides comprehensive instruction in respect of appeals to the Supreme Court concerning criminal proceedings.

From the High Court in a Criminal Cause or Matter

D30.5 Section 1(1)(a) of the Administration of Justice Act 1960 provides that any appeal from the High Court in a criminal cause or matter is direct to the Supreme Court, leapfrogging the Court of Appeal. In a similar leave process to that operating in the Court of Appeal (see **D30.2**), the Divisional Court must certify that the appeal involves a point of law of general public importance, and leave to appeal must be granted by either the Divisional Court or the Supreme Court. For a comprehensive review by the Supreme Court of the authorities relating to the phrase 'criminal cause or matter' see *R (Belhaj) v DPP* [2018] UKSC 33, [2018] 3 WLR 435. The majority (Baroness Hale, Lord Mance and Lord Sumption; Lord Wilson and Lord Lloyd-Jones dissenting) held that the phrase 'criminal cause or matter', read as a whole, spoke for itself. A 'cause' was a proceeding, civil or criminal, actual or prospective, before a court. A 'matter' was something wider, namely a particular legal subject-matter, albeit arising in a different proceeding. That is the reason why a 'criminal cause or matter' extended to a judicial review in the High Court of a decision made in relation to actual or prospective criminal proceedings.

THE COURT OF JUSTICE OF THE EUROPEAN UNION

Treaty on the Functioning of the European Union (TFEU), Article 267 **D30.6**

(1) The Court of Justice of the European Union shall have jurisdiction to give preliminary rulings concerning:
  (a) the interpretation of the Treaties;
  (b) the validity and interpretation of acts of the institutions, bodies, offices or agencies of the Union;
(2) Where such a question is raised before any court or tribunal of a Member State, that court or tribunal may, if it considers that a decision on the question is necessary to enable it to give judgment, request the Court to give a ruling thereon.
(3) Where any such question is raised in a case pending before a court or tribunal of a Member State against whose decisions there is no judicial remedy under national law, that court or tribunal shall bring the matter before the court.
(4) If such a question is raised in a case pending before a court or tribunal of a Member State with regard to a person in custody, the Court of Justice of the European Union shall act with the minimum of delay.

From the end of the transition period of the UK's withdrawal from the EU, the CJEU will no **D30.7** longer have general jurisdiction over the UK. That change will therefore take effect in relation to any acts which take place on or after 1 January 2021. Until then, in principle, the CJEU assumes full jurisdiction to give preliminary rulings in the field of EU criminal law, with the limits to its jurisdiction set out by Article 35(2) of the EU Treaty (under the old third pillar) being abolished. This means it is open to UK courts to bring references to Luxembourg. The only exception is Article 276 of the TFEU, according to which the Court will have 'no jurisdiction to review the validity or proportionality of operations carried out by the police or other law-enforcement services of a Member State or the exercise of the responsibilities incumbent upon Member States with regard to the maintenance of law and order and the safeguarding of internal security'. Article 267 is more fully discussed at **A9.9**.

In *Plymouth Justices, ex parte Rogers* [1982] QB 863, it was held that a magistrates' court has **D30.8** the power to make a reference to the CJEU and the Divisional Court will not interfere with the exercise of the justices' discretion to make such a reference unless they act unreasonably in doing so, or misdirect themselves. Nevertheless, the Divisional Court advised that justices should exercise considerable caution before making such a reference. If a magistrates' court erred in the interpretation of community law, that could always be corrected by the higher courts. When making a reference, the form of the question to be answered is very important and the higher courts will normally be in a better position to assess the appropriateness of the question and assist in formulating it appropriately.

So far as the Crown Court is concerned, the House of Lords stated in *Henn* [1981] AC 850 (per Lord Diplock at p. 904):

> ... in a criminal trial upon indictment it can seldom be a proper exercise of the presiding judge's discretion to seek a preliminary ruling before the facts of the alleged offence have been ascertained, with the result that the proceedings will be held up for nine months or more in order that at the end of the trial he may give to the jury an accurate instruction as to the relevant law, if the evidence turns out in the event to be as was anticipated at the time the reference was made — which may not always be the case. It is generally better, as the judge himself put it, that the question be decided by him in the first instance and reviewed thereafter if necessary through the hierarchy of the national courts.

The procedure to be adopted in an application for a reference by the Crown Court is set out in CrimPR Part 44 (see Supplement, **R44.1** *et seq.*). It is supplemented by CrimPD IX, paras. 44A.1 to 44A.7 (see Supplement, **CPD.44A**), which set out the relevant persons to whom the order for reference should be addressed, as well as the required contents of any backsheet to the order. In addition, the matters which need to be included within any application for the Court to apply its urgent preliminary ruling procedure are identified.

THE EUROPEAN COURT OF HUMAN RIGHTS

D30.9 An individual has the power to petition the ECtHR if the individual feels that his or her human rights under the ECHR have been violated (see A7).

In order that a complaint be admissible before the ECtHR, the applicant must have exhausted all domestic remedies. The applicant is not required, however, to have pursued points which have no chance of success. Thus in *V v UK* (2000) 30 EHRR 121, the Court was concerned with the case of two boys convicted of the murder of James Bulger. The Court ruled that Article 6 requires a specially adapted procedure for the trial of juveniles in the Crown Court which promotes the welfare of the young defendant, respects D's right to privacy and enables D to understand and take part fully in the proceedings. The Court rejected an argument by the UK government that the complaint was inadmissible because the boys had not exhausted all domestic remedies as they had failed to argue in the domestic courts that their inability to understand and participate fully in the proceedings meant that they were in effect unfit to plead. The Court observed that the government could not point to one example where such an application had been successful.

In addition, the petition must raise an issue which is not substantially the same as one upon which the Court (or, when it existed, the Commission) has already ruled and, equally, the petition cannot have been submitted to another 'procedure of international investigation or settlement'.

D30.10 Under Article 35, the petition must be brought within six months of the date when the final decision is taken. That date was defined in *Greenock Ltd v UK* (1985) 42 DJR 33, as the date of a final decision taken in the exhaustion of an effective and sufficient domestic remedy, or from the date of the act or decision complained of where that act or decision finally determines the applicant's position in the domestic jurisdiction. Since 2014, the ECtHR has required strict adherence to formalities of the application process required under r. 47 of the Court's rules (see tinyurl.com/yaqthm2p).

The Court sits in committees of three judges, chambers of seven judges and, exceptionally, in Grand Chambers of 17 judges. The parties are required to file written evidence within certain time-limits and, if the Court considers it necessary, an oral hearing at which the applicant is represented takes place. The decision of the Court may be by way of majority. The Court can compel any State which is in breach of the ECHR to make 'just satisfaction', and if it finds that the State's laws are incompatible with the Convention, can impose a duty on the State to rectify the position.

Section D31 Extradition

INTRODUCTION

Extradition involves one territory making a request to another for the surrender of a person accused of an offence to stand trial, or for a convicted person to be sentenced or serve a custodial sentence. Extradition is governed by the Extradition Act 2003. **D31.1**

A foreign territory can be designated as a category 1 or category 2 territory by order of the Secretary of State (ss. 1 and 69). Part 1 of the Act governs requests from a category 1 territory and Part 2 governs requests from a category 2 territory. Part 3 governs requests made by the UK and is not dealt with in this section.

Part 1 Warrants

Part 1 (ss. 1 to 68) implements the EU Council Framework Decision on the European Arrest Warrant (EAW) and the surrender procedures between Member States (2002/584/JHA, [2002] OJ L190/1) and the EU-Norway/Iceland Surrender Agreement. (See also **A9.13**.) It applies to requests received from a category 1 territory (currently EU Member States, Norway, Iceland and Gibraltar) and is intended to allow surrender based on the mutual recognition of arrest warrants issued by Member States (*Office of the King's Prosecutor, Brussels v Cando Armas* [2005] UKHL 67, [2006] 2 AC 1). The EAW form is in the annex to the Framework Decision. The UK has left the EU and at the end of the transition period (at the time of writing 31 December 2020), EU Member States will be re-designated as category 2 territories. **D31.2**

If questions of interpretation arise in dealing with EAWs, the Extradition Act 2003 must be read subject to the common-law presumption that it was intended to give effect to the UK's obligations under the Framework Decision, but this is itself subject to the language of the Act (*Assange v Swedish Prosecution Authority* [2012] UKSC 22, [2012] 2 AC 471 at [217]). There are a number of decisions of the CJEU on its interpretation (see **A9.13**). The UK is subject to the jurisdiction of the CJEU, allowing a reference to be made to the CJEU for a preliminary ruling on the interpretation of the Framework Decision until the end of the transition period which is at the time of writing 31 December 2020 (see **A9.11**, *Cretu v Local Court of Suceava, Romania* [2016] EWHC 353 (Admin), [2016] 1 WLR 3344 at [12]–[17] and *Auzins v Prosecutor General's Office of the Republic of Latvia* [2016] EWHC 802 (Admin), [2016] 4 WLR 75 at [42]).

The NCA has been designated to receive Part 1 warrants which it will certify if the requirements in s. 2 are met (see **D31.13**). The NCA must not issue a certificate in an accusation case if it is clear that a judge would find extradition to be disproportionate (as to proportionality, see **D31.33**). The NCA must apply the guidance in CrimPD XI, paras. 50A.1 to 50A.5 (see Supplement, **CPD.50A**), discussed in *Miraszewski v District Court in Torun, Poland* [2014] EWHC 4261 (Admin), [2015] 1 WLR 3929 at [18]–[19] and [26]–[28] (see also **D31.33**).

Part 2 Requests

D31.3 Part 2 (ss. 69 to 141) applies to requests from category 2 territories. Article 3 of the Extradition Act 2003 (Designation of Part 2 Territories) Order 2003 (SI 2003 No. 3334) designates certain category 2 territories so that they do not have to provide evidence to justify the issue of an arrest warrant or evidence of a case to answer.

The Secretary of State must issue a certificate under s. 70 (certifying the request has been made in the approved way) if a valid request is received (s. 70(3) to (7): see **D31.16**) for extradition from a category 2 territory, unless s. 70(2) applies (s. 70(1)). Where (i) there are competing requests for extradition, (ii) the person requested is a refugee or (iii) the person requested has been granted leave to enter or remain because removal to the requesting territory would be a breach of the ECHR, Article 2 or 3, the Secretary of State may refuse to issue a certificate (s. 70(2); see also *District Court in Ostroleka v Dytlow* [2009] EWHC 1009 (Admin)). Once the Secretary of State has issued a certificate, the request and the certificate must be sent to the appropriate judge and the Secretary of State may not thereafter consider whether the extradition is compatible with rights under the ECHR (s. 70(9) to (11)).

First instance extradition hearings in England and Wales will only be dealt with at Westminster Magistrates' Court by an 'appropriate judge' who is designated by the Lord Chief Justice (ss. 67 and 139). The CPS ordinarily acts on behalf of the requesting territory.

ARREST AND INITIAL HEARING

Part 1

D31.4 A person wanted on a certified EAW may be arrested under s. 3. At an initial hearing the judge must decide if the arrested person has been given a copy of the EAW and may discharge the person if this has not happened (s. 4(2) and (4)). The judge must also find as a question of fact whether the person has been brought before the judge as soon as practicable; if this test is failed, the person must be discharged (s. 4(3) and (5): see *Nikonovs v Governor of HM Prison Brixton* [2005] EWHC 2405 (Admin), [2006] 1 All ER 927 at [21] as to the meaning of 'practicable').

Section 5 deals with provisional arrest when a EAW has not yet been issued or certified and it is rarely used in practice; it requires production before the appropriate judge within 48 hours of arrest (s. 6(2)). A certified Part 1 warrant must be produced at the hearing unless an extension of a further 48 hours is granted. The provisions on discharge are similar to those for a certified EAW (s. 6(6) and (7)).

At the hearing, the judge must decide on the balance of probabilities whether the person present is the person named in the EAW (s. 7(2) and (3); see *Lumenica v Government of Albania* [2012] EWHC 3802 (Admin)). If not so satisfied, the judge must order the person's discharge (s. 7(4)). The judge has the same powers as when hearing a summary trial. Delays in the grant of legal aid which are not the fault of the requested person or legal advisers cannot be held against the requested person (*Stopyra v District of Lublin, Poland* [2012] EWHC 1787 (Admin), [2013] 1 All ER 187 at [46]).

The judge's powers under s. 7(6) do not include the power under the MCA 1980, s. 142 (see **D22.73**), to reopen cases to correct mistakes (*R (Klimeto) v City of Westminster Magistrates' Court* [2012] EWHC 2051 (Admin), [2013] 1 WLR 420).

D31.5 Issues arising under ss. 4, 6 and 7 cannot be reopened after the initial hearing (*Stanczyk v Circuit Court in Katowice* [2010] EWHC 3651 (Admin)).

If the person is not discharged, the consent procedure is explained and consent to extradition is requested. A person may consent at any time (s. 45). Consent is irrevocable and must be given before the judge in writing (ss. 8(3)(c) and 45). Consent results in an immediate extradition order and the loss of any right of appeal. Once consent is given, a person should be removed within ten days but this period can be extended (s. 47; see **D31.46**).

Once consent has been dealt with, the judge will ordinarily ask if there are any issues regarding the validity of the warrant, the extradition offence, bars, proportionality or human rights to be raised at the extradition hearing (see **D31.12**). **D31.6**

If the case is to be contested, the hearing must be set within 21 days of the arrest (s. 8(1)(a) and (4)). It is not unusual for the extradition hearing to open immediately before adjourning to a future date. If the extradition hearing does not begin within 21 days, the person may apply to be discharged or the judge may order discharge of his or her own motion unless reasonable cause is shown for the delay (s. 8(7) and (8); see *Asliturk v HM Prison Wandsworth* [2010] EWHC 1720 (Admin)). Section 8(5) allows a party to apply to the judge for the period to be extended; an application to fix a later date for the extradition hearing may be made on the day on which the hearing is set to begin.

Part 2

Under Part 2 an arrest may take place on a warrant issued by an appropriate judge (s. 71) if the Secretary of State has certified a request and sent the required documents to the judge (s. 70) or under a provisional warrant (s. 74). A person arrested under Part 2 must be brought before the appropriate judge and given a copy of the arrest warrant as soon as practicable (ss. 72 and 74). Discharge for failing to produce the person as soon as practicable is mandatory but discharge for failure to serve the warrant is discretionary. Provisional arrest is more common under Part 2 than under Part 1. **D31.7**

The question of identity is decided at the extradition hearing. The person must be informed either of the contents of the request for extradition (s. 72(7)(a)) or that the person is accused of an offence or alleged to be unlawfully at large after conviction if arrested provisionally (s. 74(7)(a)). The consent procedure is explained and consent to extradition is requested. The procedure is the same as for Part 1 (see **D31.5**), except that a person who consents has the case sent to the Secretary of State (ss. 127 and 128; see **D31.40**).

If the arrest is under a provisional warrant, the judge must fix a date by which the certified extradition request must be received, failing which the person's discharge must be ordered (s. 74(10) and (11)). Most category 2 territories have 45 days in which to send the request but territories designated by art. 4 of the Extradition Act 2003 (Designation of Part 2 Territories) Order 2003 have longer. The extradition hearing must begin within two months of the first appearance of a person arrested under s. 71 or two months from the day on which the certified extradition request is received by the judge following provisional arrest (s. 76). If the extradition hearing has not begun within the required period and no extension has been granted, the requested person can apply for discharge (ss. 75(4), 76(4) and (5)). It is common practice for the judge to open the hearing before the end of the required period and then adjourn; the judge has the same power to adjourn as when hearing a summary trial (see **D31.4**). **D31.8**

Bail

Once the initial hearing is completed, the requested person must be remanded on bail or in custody. Normal considerations in relation to bail apply (see **D7**). There is no presumption in favour of bail for a convicted person (s. 198(5)). A person denied bail by a magistrates' court or granted bail subject to conditions may seek bail or seek to vary the conditions in the High Court (CJA 1967, s. 22(1A)). The High Court may be reluctant to allow an application unless there have been two unsuccessful applications in the magistrates' court. The CPS, on behalf of the requesting territory, may appeal a decision to grant bail to the High Court provided that it opposed the grant of bail before the magistrates' court (Bail (Amendment Act) 1993, s. 1(1A) and (3)). **D31.9**

Request for Temporary Transfer or Contact with Prosecutor

In Part 1 accusation cases, s. 21B provides a mechanism to allow the temporary transfer of a requested person to the requesting territory or for the requested person to speak with the **D31.10** prosecutor or investigator. This process requires the consent of the requested person and requesting territory (*Duncan v Presiding Magistrate, Malaga, Spain* [2015] EWHC 3466 (Admin), [2016] 1 WLR 1351).

Domestic Criminal Proceedings

D31.11 If a person arrested under Part 1 or Part 2 is charged with an offence in the UK and the judge either is aware of this before the extradition hearing begins or becomes aware of it during the extradition hearing, the judge must adjourn proceedings until the UK proceedings have concluded (ss. 8A, 22, 76A, 88 and 214) (see *Auzins v Prosecutor General's Office of the Republic of Latvia (No. 2)* [2017] EWHC 48 (Admin), [2017] 1 WLR 2981, which considers when UK proceedings are treated as concluded).

If a person arrested under Part 1 or Part 2 is serving a sentence of imprisonment in the UK, the proceedings may be adjourned for up to six months until the person is released (ss. 8B, 23, 76B and 89). If the court is informed after the extradition hearing that a person has been charged with an offence or is serving a sentence in the UK then similar provisions will apply so that the court may order that extradition is not to be carried out (*Auzins*).

THE EXTRADITION HEARING

Order of Consideration of Issues

D31.12 Part 1 and Part 2 hearings involve similar steps. The Divisional Court in *Lagocki v Regional Court in Szczecin, Poland* [2015] EWHC 3641 (Admin) considered the power of the judge to proceed with an extradition hearing in the absence of a requested person. Issues to be considered include the following:

- any challenge to the validity of the EAW or request (see **D31.13** and **D31.16**) — the issue of identity is also dealt with for Part 2 requests (see **D31.17**);
- whether the conduct identified in the warrant or request amounts to an extradition offence or offences (see **D31.18**) and, if it does, what bars arise (see **D31.21**);
- whether extradition is compatible with the person's rights under the ECHR and, for Part 1 accusation cases, whether it is proportionate (see **D31.33**);
- whether the requested person is entitled to an adjournment or discharge on the basis that extradition would be unjust or oppressive due to physical or mental condition (see **D31.36**);
- whether, in a Part 2 accusation case, the evidence is sufficient to require an answer by the person (a prima facie case: see **D31.32**), unless the requesting territory has been designated by the Secretary of State (see **D31.3**);
- in a conviction case, whether the person was present when convicted and, if not, whether the person was deliberately absent — if not deliberately absent, the person must be entitled to a retrial and for a Part 2 request the evidence must provide a prima facie case unless the requesting territory has been designated (see **D31.31** and **D31.32**).

If any of these requirements are not met or if a bar is made out, the person will be discharged. Otherwise, at the conclusion of the extradition hearing, extradition is ordered for a Part 1 case (s. 21(3); *Zubkovs v Court in Riga, Latvia* [2012] EWHC 3331 (Admin) confirms that the extradition hearing finishes when extradition is ordered) or a Part 2 case is sent to the Secretary of State (s. 87(3)). At the extradition hearing the judge has the same powers as a magistrates' court hearing a summary trial, including the power to adjourn (ss. 9(1) and 77). The judge's powers under ss. 9(1) and 77(1) do not include the power under the MCA 1980, s. 142 (see D22.73), to reopen cases to correct mistakes (*R (Klimeto) v City of Westminster Magistrates' Court* [2012] EWHC 2051 (Admin), [2013] 1 WLR 420). The requesting territory must prove that the warrant or request is valid, contains conduct which amounts to an extradition offence and that the prima facie case requirement (if applicable) and provisions relating to convictions in absence are satisfied. Unless otherwise specified, matters must be proved to the criminal standard (s. 206).

Validity of Part 1 Warrant

A warrant which does not satisfy the requirements of s. 2 is not a valid Part 1 warrant, and the judge must order the person's discharge (*Office of the King's Prosecutor, Brussels v Cando Armas* [2005] UKHL 67, [2006] 2 AC 1; *Lacorre v High Instance Court of Paris* [2008] EWHC 2871 (Admin)). A warrant is valid only if issued by a judicial authority. The NCA, as the designated authority, must certify that the foreign judicial authority has the function of issuing EAWs in the category 1 territory (s. 2(7) and (8); *Ministry of Justice, Republic of Lithuania v Bucnys* [2013] UKSC 71, [2014] AC 480 at [33]). **D31.13**

It is for the judge to determine whether the person or body that has issued the EAW has the quality of being a 'judicial authority'; 'judicial authority' embraces courts, judges, magistrates and public prosecutors (*Bucnys* at [34]), and see also Joined Cases C-508/18 and C-82/19 PPU *OG and PI* (CJEU, 27 May 2019) which consider public prosecutors and, in a conviction case, a Ministry of Justice could be a judicial authority if certain conditions are satisfied (at [66]). *Ziri v Head of the International Police Cooperation Division National Police Board* [2012] EWHC 3329 (Admin) considered the position of police authorities.

The contents of the warrant are to be assessed at the time the warrant is certified by the designated authority and any defects can be remedied before this time (*Dhar v National Office of the Public Prosecution Service, The Netherlands* [2012] EWHC 697 (Admin)).

A warrant must contain a statement that the person is accused of an offence and sought for prosecution or is convicted and sought for the execution or imposition of a sentence (s. 2(2), (3) and (5)).

A Part 1 warrant may deal with both accusations and convictions (*Pomiechowski v District Court in Legnica, Poland* [2012] EWHC 3161 (Admin), [2013] 1 WLR 2653). A warrant which seeks the person's return for questioning and not prosecution is invalid (*Vey v Office of the Public Prosecutor of the County of Montlucon* [2006] EWHC 760 (Admin); see also **D31.22**). Whether a person is wanted for prosecution is a question of fact, requiring a purposive construction and a 'cosmopolitan' approach rather than a parochial English one (*Re Ismail* [1999] 1 AC 320). The prosecution process may allow questioning to occur after surrender or for the investigation to continue (*R (Miguel Meizoso-Gonzales) v Juzgado de Instruccion Cinco de Palma de Mallorca* [2010] EWHC 3655 (Admin)). The purpose for which extradition is requested must be clear from an examination of the EAW as a whole and only if the wording of the warrant is equivocal should the court consider other evidence as a last resort (*Asztaslos v Szekszard City Court Hungary* [2010] EWHC 237 (Admin), [2011] 1 All ER 1027).

In an accusation case, the Part 1 warrant must include particulars of the domestic arrest warrant or any other enforceable judicial decision having the same effect on which the Part 1 warrant is based (s. 2(4)(b) and see *Goluchowski v District Court in Elblag, Poland* [2016] UKSC 36, [2016] 1 WLR 2665 at [28]). The Part 1 warrant must also contain sufficient particulars of the circumstances in which the offence was committed, including the time and place at which the offence was committed and the provisions of law of the requesting territory that have been contravened (s. 2(4)(c)). The Divisional Court has stated that the only distinction between accusation and conviction warrants, in terms of the particulars to be included in the warrant, is that circumstances are alleged in an accusation case but established in a conviction case (*King v Public Prosecutors of Villefranche Sur Saone, France* [2015] EWHC 3670 (Admin) at [18] and see s. 2(6)(b)). **D31.14**

A conviction warrant may state that the sentence for another offence has been 'merged' into the offence for which particulars are provided and return is sought. In *Edutanu v Iasi Court of Law* [2016] EWHC 124 (Admin), [2016] 1 WLR 2933, the Divisional Court considered whether a conviction warrant which does not give particulars of the other offence is invalid because it fails to comply with s. 2(6)(b) (see also **D31.27**). The level of detail that must be provided in a warrant will depend on the circumstances and complexity of the conduct alleged; a broad omnibus description, such as 'conspiracy to defraud' will not suffice (*Von der Pahlen v Government of Austria* [2006] EWHC 1672 (Admin)). A conviction warrant must contain details of a domestic warrant if this is the basis for the Part 1 warrant which is issued to secure the requested person's surrender for sentencing (s. 2(6)(c); *Goluchowski* at [27]). However, if the requested person has been sentenced to an immediate sentence of imprisonment, there is no requirement for a domestic warrant to be referred to (*Goluchowski* at [29]). *Goluchowski* considers a number of different scenarios where a sentence of imprisonment is imposed after conviction which does not take immediate effect and assesses in each scenario what is required for compliance with s. 2(6).

A warrant must contain particulars of the sentence that may be imposed on conviction or sentencing for each offence (s. 2(4)(d) and (6)(d)) or particulars of the sentence that has been imposed if the person has been sentenced (s. 2(6)(e)). See *Taylor v Public Prosecutors Office, Berlin, Germany* [2012] EWHC 475 (Admin) at [15] for an illustration of a failure in this respect. If the warrant deals with more than one sentence, it may provide the aggregate sentence (*Pilecki v Circuit Court of Legnica, Poland* [2008] UKHL 7, [2008] 1 WLR 325; see also **D31.27**). If the sentences are aggregated after the EAW is issued, this does not affect the validity of the warrant (*Zakrzewski v Regional Court in Lodz, Poland* [2013] UKSC 2, [2013] 1 WLR 324).

D31.15 The Supreme Court has stated that the validity of a Part 1 warrant depends on whether it contains the particulars required by s. 2 and not whether these particulars are correct (*Zakrzewski v Regional Court in Lodz, Poland* at [8]; see, however, the discussion in *Goluchowski* at [37]–[48]). Therefore the validity is also unaffected if particulars which are initially correct become incorrect. However, if the particulars required by s. 2 are or have become incorrect, the court can consider whether this amounts to an abuse of process (*Zakrzewski* at [11]–[13]; see **D31.37**). If the warrant does not include some of the particulars required by s. 2, the requesting territory can supply this information so that it is a valid Part 1 warrant but only if this involves filling a lacuna rather than where there has been a wholesale failure to provide the necessary particulars (*Alexander v Public Prosecutor's Office, Marseille District Court of First Instance* [2017] EWHC 1392 (Admin), [2018] QB 408 at [73]–[75]; see *M v Preliminary Investigation Tribunal of Napoli, Italy* [2018] EWHC 1808 (Admin) where the court found the warrants were wholly deficient). The Administrative Court has made clear that if further information is provided by the requesting territory it 'is to be treated as if it were incorporated into, and thus part of, the EAW' (*Litwinczuk v Circuit Court in Szczecin, Poland* [2019] EWHC 2745 (Admin)). In *Imre v District Court in Szolnok (Hungary)* [2018] EWHC 218 (Admin) the Divisional Court considered whether an accusation EAW is still valid if the requested person is convicted before the extradition process is concluded.

If the warrant is a valid Part 1 warrant, the judge will decide whether the offence in the warrant is an extradition offence (s. 10; see **D31.18**). If so, then bars to extradition are considered (s. 11; see **D31.21**).

Part 2 Requests

D31.16 Section 70 governs the validity of requests under Part 2 (see **D31.3**). Section 70 requires that a request contain similar statements to those required for a Part 1 warrant (see **D31.13**), i.e. that a person is accused and wanted for prosecution or convicted and sought for the imposition or service of a sentence. The request must be made by an appropriate authority or representative of that territory (s. 70(5) to (7)).

Part 2 imposes additional requirements for the initial stages of the extradition hearing (s. 78(2)). The judge must decide if the documents supplied include:

(a) the request and certificate;
(b) particulars of the person whose extradition is requested;
(c) particulars of the offence specified in the request;
(d) a warrant for the arrest of an accused person; or

(e) a certificate of conviction and sentence, if already sentenced, for a person alleged to be unlawfully at large after conviction.

A discharge must be granted if the judge has not been provided with these documents or if they do not include the required information. The level of detail required in a Part 2 request is the same as for a Part 1 warrant (*Dudko v Government of the Russian Federation* [2010] EWHC 1125 (Admin); see **D31.14**).

If the judge is satisfied on the balance of probabilities that the person before the court is the person who is the subject of the request (s. 78(4)(a) and (5)), the judge goes on to consider if the offence in the request is an extradition offence (s. 78(4)(b); see **D31.18**). A Part 2 request can be supplemented by further information to establish an extradition offence (*Norris v Government of the USA* [2008] UKHL 16, [2008] 1 AC 920 at [85]). Finally, the judge must decide if the request and certificate have been served on the requested person (s. 78(4)(c)). **D31.17**

If any of these conditions is not met, s. 78(6) demands a discharge. Otherwise the bars to extradition are considered under s. 79 (see **D31.21**).

EXTRADITION OFFENCE

An extradition offence is a criminal offence (*Director of the SFO v O'Brien* [2014] UKSC 23, [2014] AC 1246 at [34]) and is defined in ss. 64 and 65 for Part 1 and ss. 137 and 138 for Part 2. There are separate but similar definitions for accusation and conviction cases. There are a number of categories of extradition offence and conduct may satisfy more than one category. The judge is not concerned with the criminal law or the ingredients of the offence in the requesting territory when considering extradition offences. **D31.18**

In most Part 1 cases, extradition offences fall within s. 64(3) and (5) or s. 65(3) and (5) (although for Iceland and Norway ss. 64(5) and 65(5) do not apply).

For an offence to fall within s. 64(5) or 65(5):

(a) the conduct must have occurred within the requesting territory;
(b) no part of it can have occurred within the UK;
(c) the framework list on the EAW (which has 32 categories of offences: see *Jama v Senior Public Prosecutor Gera, Germany* [2013] EWHC 3276 (Admin), [2014] 1 WLR 1843 for the approach when considering the categories) must be ticked (*Dabas v High Court of Justice, Madrid* [2007] UKHL 6, [2007] 2 AC 31) or a separate certificate provided; and
(d) the conduct must be punishable under the law of the requesting territory with at least three years' imprisonment in an accusation case or a sentence of at least four months' imprisonment must have been imposed in a conviction case.

There is no equivalent category for Part 2 as dual criminality is required in all circumstances.

For an offence to fall within s. 64(3) or 65(3):

(a) the conduct must have occurred within the requesting territory;
(b) the conduct must have constituted an offence if it had taken place in the UK ('the dual criminality requirement'); and
(c) it must be punishable under the law of the requesting territory with at least 12 months' imprisonment in an accusation case or a sentence of at least four months' imprisonment must have been imposed in a conviction case (a sentence of 120 days is not sufficient: *Chorazewicz v Regional Court in Ostroleka, Poland* [2014] EWHC 2781 (Admin)).

Sections 137(3) and 138(3) make similar provision for accused and convicted persons in Part 2 cases if the conduct would have constituted an offence if it had taken place in the UK. There is an additional requirement for Part 2 in that the conduct must also be punishable with imprisonment for 12 months in the UK.

D31.19 If conduct which takes place outside the requesting territory brings about an intended effect within that territory then it will be treated as having occurred in the requesting territory (*Office of the King's Prosecutor, Brussels v Cando Armas* [2005] UKHL 67, [2006] 2 AC 1; *Lacorre v High Instance Court of Paris* [2008] EWHC 2871 (Admin); *Tesler v Government of the USA* [2011] EWHC 52 (Admin)).

It must be shown that the conduct would, if it had taken place in the UK, have constituted the *actus reus* of a UK offence (*Hertel v Government of Canada* [2010] EWHC 2305 (Admin)). If necessary, the *mens rea* of the UK offence can be inferred from the conduct described in the warrant or request (*Zak v Regional Court of Bydgoszcz, Poland* [2008] EWHC 470 (Admin)). If an essential element for the UK offence is missing from the offence for which extradition is sought then the dual criminality requirement may be satisfied if the court concludes that that ingredient would be the inevitable corollary of proving the matters alleged to constitute the foreign offence (*Cleveland v Government of the USA* [2019] EWHC 619 (Admin) at [83]). The information in a warrant may be supplemented by further information provided by the requesting territory (*Dabas v High Court of Justice, Madrid* [2007] UKHL 6, [2007] 2 AC 31 at [49]). In *Biri v High Court in Miskolc, Hungary* [2018] EWHC 50 (Admin), [2018] 4 WLR 50, the Divisional Court considered that it is necessary to return to the practice of drafting English charges in all but the most straightforward of cases and the Criminal Procedure Rules have been amended to reflect this (CrimPR 50.4; see Supplement, **R50.4**). This would allow the court to consider whether the requirement for dual criminality is satisfied and provide certainty as to what conduct extradition is being ordered for (at [42]).

However, when considering dual criminality the court cannot take into account evidence put forward by the requested person contradicting the extradition request but it can do so if considering whether the fairness or accuracy of the description of the extradition offence gives rise to an abuse of process (*Government of the USA v Shlesinger* [2013] EWHC 2671 (Admin); see D31.15 and D31.37).

D31.20 There are additional definitions of 'extradition offence' in ss. 64, 65, 137 and 138 which deal with extra-territorial offences or International Criminal Court offences.

The Extradition Act 2003 (Multiple Offences) Order 2003 (SI 2003 No. 3150) amends the Act to deal with warrants or requests for more than one offence; unless the context requires otherwise, any reference in the Act to an offence is to be construed as a reference to offences.

BARS TO EXTRADITION

D31.21 Section 11 in Part 1 and s. 79 in Part 2 require the judge to decide if there are any bars to extradition. The bars most frequently relied on are double jeopardy, extraneous considerations and the passage of time.

No Prosecution Decision

D31.22 For Part 1 cases, under s. 12A, the judge will decide if there are reasonable grounds to believe that the competent authorities in the requesting territory have made decisions to charge and try the requested person. If those decisions have not been made and this is not solely because of the requested person's absence, extradition will be barred unless the requesting territory can prove, to the criminal standard, that the decisions have been made or that any failure is solely caused by the requested person's absence (*Kandola v Generalstaatwaltschaft Frankfurt, Germany* [2015] EWHC 619 (Admin), [2015] 1 WLR 5097 at [32]; *Puceviciene v Lithuanian Judicial Authority* [2016] EWHC 1862 (Admin), [2016] 1 WLR 4937 at [13]–[16] and [51]). Evidence emanating from the requesting territory can be admissible in extradition proceedings even if its alleged effect is to undermine clear statements in a EAW to the effect that decisions to charge and try have been made (*Cimieri v Court of Agrigento, Italy* [2017] EWHC 3048 (Admin), [2018] 1

WLR 2833 at [25], see also *Litwinczuk v Circuit Court in Szczecin, Poland* [2019] EWHC 2745 (Admin)). If there is evidence which raises an issue as to whether these decisions have been taken, *Puceviciene* (at [23] and [52]–[56]) suggests the procedure to be followed. The Divisional Court stated that the court in *Kandola* was wrong to consider that mutual legal assistance might be relevant in assessing whether any failure to make the required decisions was caused solely by the requested person's absence (*Puceviciene* at [66]–[81]). In *Doci v Court of Brescia, Italy* [2016] EWHC 2100 (Admin), the Divisional Court stated that an intention to decide to charge or to try is not sufficient as a decision is required (at [35]). However, the Court said that forming a firm and settled intention may amount to a decision and, if so, this is how it should be analysed and described (the principles in *Puceviciene* and *Doci* were summarised in *Fenton v Court of Palma De Mallorca, Spain* [2017] EWHC 1161 (Admin) at [16]–[18]).

Double Jeopardy

By virtue of ss. 12 and 80, double jeopardy will bar extradition if any rule of law in this jurisdiction, including the abuse of process jurisdiction, would result in the requested person's discharge (see **A9.23** and **D12.30**). *Hamburg Public Prosecutor's Office v Altun* [2011] EWHC 397 (Admin) and *Osaikhwuwuomwan v Court of Ancona, Italy* [2012] All ER (D) 25 (Oct) involve a successful invocation of this bar. **D31.23**

Extraneous Considerations

Extraneous considerations will bar extradition by virtue of ss. 13 and 81 if: **D31.24**

(a) the warrant or request is issued for the purpose of prosecuting or punishing the requested person on account of race, religion, nationality, gender, sexual orientation or political opinions (to be proved on the balance of probabilities); or
(b) there is a 'reasonable chance' that if extradited the requested person might be prejudiced at the trial or punished, detained or restricted in his or her personal liberty for one of the same reasons (*Fernandez v Government of Singapore* [1971] 2 All ER 691).

The requested person must show a causal link between the issue of the warrant or request or the specific harm that the person asserts will be suffered and one of the extraneous considerations.

Passage of Time

Passage of time will bar extradition if it would make the person's extradition unjust or oppressive (ss. 14 and 82). *Zengota v Circuit Court of Zielona Gora, Poland* [2017] EWHC 191 (Admin), [2017] 1 WLR 3103 considers how the court should approach this bar if there are a number of offences dealt with in different EAWs. In a conviction case, time will be considered from when the requested person became unlawfully at large (i.e. from the time the person became liable to arrest without further order or judicial process: *Wisniewski v Regional Court in Wroclaw, Poland* [2016] EWHC 386 (Admin), [2016] 1 WLR 3750 at [52]; *Konecny v District Court in Brno-Venkov, Czech Republic* [2019] UKSC 8, [2019] 1 WLR 1586 considers the potential unfairness of the application of this bar to persons convicted in their absence with a right to a retrial). The requested person cannot, except in the most exceptional circumstances, rely on the delay which results after becoming a 'fugitive' (*Gomes v Government of Trinidad and Tobago* [2009] UKHL 21, [2009] 1 WLR 1038 at [26]–[29]). The prosecution must establish this status to the criminal standard (*Gomes* at [27]) and the court has considered that a person who breaches the terms of a suspended sentence knowing that the sentence may be implemented is a fugitive from the time of the breach (*Wisniewski* at [60]–[62]). A requested person who lawfully remains in his or her established country of residence without taking any positive steps to evade or avoid arrest once aware of a domestic arrest warrant issued in another country is not a fugitive (*Pillar-Neumann v Public Prosecutor's Office of Klagenfurt, Austria* [2017] EWHC 3371 (Admin) at [68]–[73]; see also *De Zorzi v Attorney General Appeal Court of Paris (France)* [2019] EWHC 2062 (Admin), [2019] 1 WLR 6249). **D31.25**

Injustice under ss. 14 and 82 relates to prejudice at trial on return. The requesting territory is presumed to be able to protect against an unjust trial and the requested person must prove a fair trial is impossible (*Gomes* at [35]–[36]). Oppression relates to changes in a person's circumstances. It requires more than hardship, which is a common result of extradition, and the seriousness of the offence is relevant (*Kakis v Government of the Republic of Cyprus* [1978] 2 All ER 634).

Age

D31.26 Age is a bar in relation to a Part 1 warrant only. Section 15 makes it clear that age acts as a bar only where the person has not attained the age required in the UK for the conduct complained of to be a criminal offence (e.g., the person was under the age of ten at the time — see Case C-367/16 *Piotrowski* (CJEU, 23 January 2018)).

Speciality

D31.27 Speciality is dealt with in s. 17, for Part 1 warrants, and by the Secretary of State for Part 2 cases. It is very difficult to argue as a bar for Part 1 cases because all category 1 territories are signatories to the Framework Decision which provides for speciality protection under Article 27. See *Brodziak v Circuit Court in Warsaw, Poland* [2013] EWHC 3394 (Admin), where whether aggregate sentences imposed for extradition and non-extradition offences would breach the speciality protection was considered, and *Edutanu v Iasi Court of Law* [2016] EWHC 124 (Admin), [2016] 1 WLR 2933, which examined speciality for conviction warrants which state that the sentence for another offence has been 'merged' into the offence for which particulars are provided and return is sought.

Forum

D31.28 Extradition will be barred in accusation cases if a substantial measure of the alleged criminal conduct occurred in the UK and if the judge decides, taking account only of the matters specified in s. 19B (for Part 1 warrants) or s. 83B (for Part 2 requests), that it would not be in the interests of justice. However, if the judge receives a prosecutor's certificate, the judge must not find extradition is barred (ss. 19C and 83C). A requested person who has been convicted but will have the right to a retrial cannot rely on the forum bar (*Bagri v Public Prosecutor, Bordeaux Court of First Instance* [2014] EWHC 4066 (Admin) at [39]). The court will take into account the requested person's connections with the UK (*Love v Government of the USA* [2018] EWHC 172 (Admin), [2018] 1 WLR 2889 at [40]–[41]). In *Dibden v Tribunal de Grande Instance de Lille, France* [2014] EWHC 3074 (Admin) the Divisional Court held (at [25]) that there is no hierarchy of importance in terms of the matters to be considered and so the weight to be accorded to each matter may vary in each case. The judge only has to ask whether each specified matter relating to the interests of justice is present in the case (*Atraskevic v Prosecutor General's Office, Republic of Lithuania* [2015] EWHC 131 (Admin), [2016] 1 WLR 2762). Therefore, if no prosecutor has formed or expressed a belief as to the appropriateness of a prosecution in the UK, which is one of the specified matters, the court cannot compel the CPS to form or express such a belief (at [37]) and the absence of a belief is a neutral factor (*Scott v Government of the USA* [2018] EWHC 2021 (Admin), [2019] 1 WLR 774). An indication by the CPS that there was no current intention to prosecute did not involve the expression of a belief as to whether the UK is the most appropriate jurisdiction in which a prosecution should take place (*Carpenter v Pre-trial Investigation Court Milan, Italy* [2019] EWHC 211 (Admin) at [38]). Evidence of any 'belief' should be provided in a document akin to a 'decision letter', which is used in immigration proceedings, providing reasons for the belief and identifying the prosecutor holding this belief (*Shaw v Government of the USA* [2014] EWHC 4654 (Admin) at [58]). In *Dibden* the Divisional Court held (at [35]) that the prosecutor's belief, if one has been expressed, should be reviewed only if it is irrational, but in *Piotrowicz v Regional Court in Gdansk, Poland* [2014]

EWHC 3884 (Admin) the Court accepted that inquiries to establish the basis of the belief may be appropriate and the prosecutor's belief may be based on factors wider than those set out in the statute (*Wyatt v Government of the USA* [2019] EWHC 2978 (Admin)).

Additional Potential Bars

By virtue of s. 83, hostage-taking considerations may act as a bar to extradition in respect of Part 2 requests. Sections 18, 19 and 19A provide that extradition may be barred in the case of Part 1 warrants where the person to whom the EAW refers has previously been extradited to or transferred to the UK and the consent of the territory from which the person was previously extradited is required for further onward extradition and has not been given. **D31.29**

Procedure where No Bars to Extradition

For Part 1 cases, if there are no bars to extradition and the person has not been convicted, human rights and proportionality must be considered next (s. 11(5); see **D31.33**). If the requested person has been convicted, the judge must consider s. 20 (see **D31.31**). **D31.30**

For Part 2 cases, if there are no bars to extradition and the person has not been convicted, the judge will consider whether there is a prima facie case (see **D31.32**). If the requested person has been convicted, the judge must consider s. 85 (see **D31.31**).

CONVICTION IN ABSENCE

For Part 1 cases, if the person has been convicted the judge must proceed under s. 20. If the person was not present when convicted, the judge will consider if the person was deliberately absent. In considering whether the person was deliberately absent the court will consider Article 4a of the Framework Decision (see *Stryjecki v District Court in Lublin, Poland* [2016] EWHC 3309 (Admin) at [50], which summarises the relevant case law and *Foster-Taylor v Prosecutor General's Office of Florence* [2019] EWHC 2938 (Admin) at [49] which considers the approach if there have been a number of judicial decisions with only some given in the person's absence). If the requesting territory proves, to the criminal standard, that the requested person was deliberately absent, s. 20(4) provides that the judge will proceed to consider human rights under s. 21 (see **D31.33**). See also *Mitoi v Government of Romania* [2006] EWHC 1977 (Admin). **D31.31**

If the person was not deliberately absent, the judge must decide if the person has the right to a retrial or review amounting to a retrial with the features set out in s. 20(8) (s. 20(5); see *Ogreanu v Italian Judicial Authority* [2020] EWHC 1254 (Admin), at [14]). That right must be automatic and not involve any exercise of discretion (*Bohm v Romanian Judicial Authority* [2011] EWHC 2671 (Admin)). However, it can involve the application of the law to the facts in accordance with a criminal code which requires a requested person to make an application for a retrial on return in order to obtain it (*Nastase v Office of the State Prosecutor, Trento, Italy* [2012] EWHC 3671 (Admin)). If there is no right to a retrial, the person must be discharged. Otherwise the judge will go on to consider human rights (see **D31.33**).

For Part 2 cases, if the requested person has been convicted, the questions in s. 85 (which is identical to s. 20) must be considered. If the person was present when convicted or was deliberately absent from the trial, the judge will continue to consider human rights (see **D31.33**). Otherwise, if the requested person is not discharged, the judge will continue to consider the prima facie case under s. 86 (which is similar to s. 84; see **D31.32**).

PRIMA FACIE CASE

Under s. 84(1), in a Part 2 case, the judge must consider if there is sufficient evidence to make a case requiring an answer if the requested person was appearing at a summary trial, unless the **D31.32** requesting territory has been designated under the Extradition Act 2003 (Designation of Part 2 Territories) Order 2003, art. 4 (see **D31.3**). See also *Governor of Pentonville Prison, ex parte Alves* [1993] AC 284. The procedure is akin to the old contested committal procedure, but the judge will also consider evidence called on behalf of the requested person (*Devani v Republic of Kenya* [2015] EWHC 3535 (Admin) at [49]). Section 84(2) to (4) deal with the admissibility of evidence (*Tudor v United Arab Emirates* [2012] EWHC 1098 (Admin), *Patel v India* [2013] EWHC 819 (Admin) and *Shankaran v India* [2014] EWHC 957 (Admin), which also confirms that on appeal the High Court should form its own assessment as to whether a prima facie case is made out (at [18])). If there is a prima facie case or the judge is not required to consider this because the requesting territory has been designated, the judge will consider human rights under s. 87 (see **D31.33**).

HUMAN RIGHTS AND PROPORTIONALITY

D31.33 The final consideration at an extradition hearing is whether a person's extradition would be compatible with Convention rights as defined by the HRA 1998, s. 1 (ss. 21 and 87). See **A7** for human rights generally. For Part 1 accusation cases, the court will also have to consider proportionality (s. 21A). Section 21A sets out a number of specified matters which the judge must take into account when deciding whether extradition would be disproportionate: the seriousness of the conduct, the likely penalty if convicted and the possibility of the requesting territory taking less coercive measures. See *Duncan v Presiding Magistrate, Malaga, Spain* [2015] EWHC 3466 (Admin), [2016] 1 WLR 1351, which considers how a judge should deal with a request pursuant to s. 21B for temporary transfer or contact with a representative of the requesting territory (see **D31.10**). See CrimPD XI, paras. 50A.1 to 50A.5 (see Supplement, **CPD.50A**), for guidance as to how to approach the assessment of the seriousness of the conduct, which is in the first instance to be judged against domestic standards, but this provides a 'floor rather than a ceiling' (*Miraszewski v District Court in Torun, Poland* [2014] EWHC 4261 (Admin), [2015] 1 WLR 3929 at [28]), and if there is an issue about seriousness the requesting territory must demonstrate that it is sufficiently serious (*Rinkevicius v Prosecutor General's Office, Lithuania* [2018] EWHC 145 (Admin)). In considering the likely penalty on conviction, the judge may consider domestic sentencing practice if no specific information has been provided by the requesting territory (at [38]). The judge must weigh the relevant factors but may give differential weight to them (at [33]).

It is often alleged that violations will take place following extradition and the approach for these prospective violations differs in some respects from that which is applied in the domestic context. Articles 3, 5, 6 and 8 of the ECHR are those most commonly relied on in extradition cases to show a prospective violation.

There is a rebuttable presumption that a Member State of the Council of Europe will fulfil its obligations under the ECHR (see discussion in *Yilmaz v Government of Turkey* [2019] EWHC 272 (Admin) at [15]–[18]). However, the presumption is rebutted if the ECtHR has issued a pilot judgment against a requesting territory identifying systemic or structural problems of wider significance (*Shmatko v Russian Federation* [2018] EWHC 3534 (Admin) at [36]). Diplomatic assurances may be given by a requesting territory to try to establish that there is no risk of a violation of a Convention right. In *Othman (Abu Qatada) v UK* (2012) 55 EHRR 1 (1) the ECtHR considered the detailed process which a court should go through to assess the quality of any diplomatic assurances which are given and whether they can be relied upon. In *Szalai v Tribunal of Veszpre, Hungary* [2019] EWHC 934 (Admin) the Divisional Court held that a court should exercise very considerable caution when asked by an appellant to admit and to evaluate evidence relating to an alleged breach of an assurance given to foreign authorities or courts (at [38]). The Court would have to be satisfied that the evidence was manifestly credible, directly relevant to the issue to be decided and of real importance for the purpose of that decision (at [44]).

A requested person must demonstrate substantial grounds for believing that there is a real risk of receiving treatment which would breach Article 3 if extradited (*Harkins v UK* (2012) 55 EHRR 19 (561); see also Joined Cases C-404/15 and C-659/15 *Aranyosi* [2016] QB 921, discussed at **A9.13**, in which the CJEU considered how to deal with Article 3 in the context of prison conditions in other EU Member States). A strong presumption of a violation of Article 3 arises when the personal space available to a detainee is less than three square metres and this presumption will normally only be capable of being rebutted if three specified factors are cumulatively met (*Muršić v Croatia* (2017) 65 EHRR 1 (1) at [138]; see *Scerbatchi v First District Court of Bucharest, Romania* [2018] EWHC 3612 (Admin) at [40], which considers the extent of diplomatic assurances that may be required to meet a potential violation of Article 3). Country guidance issued in an asylum case should be treated as an authoritative starting point (*Lutsyuk v Government of Ukraine*, at [15]–[16] and [24]). However, not every form of ill-treatment will be sufficient to reach the minimum level of severity necessary to bar extradition (*Harkins* at [129]–[131]). Article 3 may be violated if a person who is ill is not fit to travel (*Bobbe v Regional Court in Bydgoszcz, Poland* [2017] EWHC 3161 (Admin)) or could be detained after extradition and would not receive appropriate medical care (*Aswat v UK* (2014) 58 EHRR 1 (1) at [50]; see also *AM (Zimbabwe) v Secretary of State for the Home Department* [2020] UKSC 17, [2020] 2 WLR 1152). Alleged or feared Article 3 ill-treatment by non-State actors in the requesting territory will prevent extradition only where it can be shown that the requesting State will fail to provide reasonable protection (*R (Bagdanavicius) v Secretary of State for the Home Department* [2005] UKHL 38, [2005] 2 AC 668). **D31.34**

In *Othman (Abu Qatada)*, the ECtHR confirmed that Article 5 could be relied on to prevent extradition if there was a real risk of a flagrant violation which might involve, for example, arbitrary detention for many years without any intention to bring a person to trial (at [232]–[233]). A real risk of a civil commitment order being made in the USA might, in some circumstances, lead to a flagrant violation of Article 5 (*Government of the USA v Giese* [2015] EWHC 2733 (Admin) and [2015] EWHC 3658 (Admin), [2016] 4 WLR 10).

It must normally be assumed that the EU Member States will be capable of providing the sufficient minimum safeguards for a fair trial required by Article 6 (*Symeou v Public Prosecutor's Office at the Court of Appeals Patras, Greece* [2009] EWHC 897 (Admin), [2009] 1 WLR 2384). Extradition will violate Article 6 if the requested person has suffered or there is a real risk of suffering a flagrant denial of justice (Case C-216/18 PPU *Minister for Justice and Equality v LM* [2019] 1 WLR 1004). A flagrant denial of justice means a trial which is manifestly contrary to the provisions of Article 6 or the principles it embodies. This must be more than the mere irregularities or lack of safeguards in the trial procedures such as might result in a breach of Article 6 if occurring within a Contracting State itself (*Othman (Abu Qatada)* at [258]–[261], and see, e.g., *Government of Rwanda v Nteziryayo* [2017] EWHC 1912 (Admin)).

It is very difficult to show that extradition will involve a violation of Article 8; hardship alone will not suffice. It is only if there is some quite exceptionally compelling feature or combination of features that interference with the private and family life which results from extradition will be disproportionate to the objective that extradition serves (*Norris v Government of the USA (No. 2)* [2010] UKSC 9, [2010] 2 All ER 267 at [56]). The court may consider the gravity of the offence (*Norris* at [63]), the potential violation of the Article 8 rights of other family members (*Norris* at [64]) and the length of any sentence left to serve (*Wysocki v Polish Judicial Authority [2010] EWHC* 3430 (Admin)). The Supreme Court considered the Article 8 rights of children, which would be affected by the extradition of a parent in *HH v Deputy Prosecutor of the Italian Republic, Genoa* [2012] UKSC 25, [2013] 1 AC 338. The Court reiterated that the rights of the children are a primary consideration to be taken into account as part of a balancing exercise. See also *RT v Circuit Court in Tarnobrzeg, Poland* [2017] EWHC 1978 (Admin), [2017] 4 WLR 137, in which the Divisional Court considered the relationship between extradition proceedings and Family Court proceedings. Culpable delay which has caused a substantial delay to **D31.35** the execution of a EAW may be relevant to an assessment for Article 8 (*Oreszczynski v Krakow District Court, Poland* [2014] EWHC 4346 (Admin) at [11]).

The Divisional Court in *Polish Judicial Authorities v Celinski* [2015] EWHC 1274 (Admin), [2016] 1 WLR 551 cautioned (at [14]) against the citing of fact-specific Article 8 decisions and summarised (at [7]–[13]) the approach that should be taken by a court when considering Article 8.

If the judge finds that extradition is compatible with the requested person's rights under the ECHR, the judge will order extradition (Part 1 case) or the case will be sent to the Secretary of State (Part 2 case) (see **D31.40**).

PHYSICAL OR MENTAL CONDITION

D31.36 Extradition may be barred or the proceedings adjourned if the requested person's physical or mental condition makes it unjust or oppressive to extradite (ss. 25 and 91). Unjust and oppressive have the same meanings as for the passage of time bar (*Government of the Republic of South Africa v Dewani* [2012] EWHC 842 (Admin), [2013] 1 WLR 82 at [74]; see **D31.25**). In *Magiera v District Court of Krakow, Poland* [2017] EWHC 2757 (Admin) the Divisional Court considered the approach to be adopted if the medical conditions of a requested person are raised as a bar (this approach would also apply to an Article 3 assessment of prison conditions; see **D31.35**). Adequate medical evidence must be provided (*Jervis v Office of the Public Prosecutor of the Court of Appeals, Rennes* [2008] EWHC 2011 (Admin)). Only a very high risk that the requested person will commit suicide whatever steps are taken will be sufficient to bar extradition (*Mazurkiewicz v Rzeszow Circuit Court* [2011] EWHC 659 (Admin)). Amongst the factors to be considered is what might happen to a requested person after extradition (*Government of South Africa v Dewani* [2014] EWHC 153 (Admin), [2014] 1 WLR 3220 at [50]). If there is a genuine and legitimate dispute between medical experts as to a requested person's fitness to plead or stand trial, this is normally an issue which the court in the requesting State should determine as part of the trial process, although the English court can consider whether in a particular case this would result in unjustness or oppression (*Edwards v Government of the USA* [2013] EWHC 1906 (Admin), [2013] 4 All ER 871 at [54]–[58]). However, it might be unjust and oppressive to order the extradition of a person who was agreed to be unfit to stand trial at the time of the extradition proceedings if there was a prospect that the person might remain permanently unfit. In these circumstances the court would need to consider whether an undertaking to allow the person's return, if still likely to remain unfit after a reasonable time for further treatment, should be required from the requesting territory (*Dewani* at [60]).

ABUSE OF PROCESS

D31.37 Courts have an implied jurisdiction to order a person's discharge if extradition would constitute an abuse of process (see also asylum discussed at **D31.38**). In *R (Government of the USA) v Bow Street Magistrates' Court* [2006] EWHC 2256 (Admin), [2007] 1 WLR 1157 the Divisional Court set out the steps to be followed where abuse of process is alleged as the judge should be alert to the possibility of it being raised as a delaying tactic:

(a) no steps should be taken to investigate an alleged abuse of process unless the judge is satisfied that there is proper reason to believe that an abuse may have taken place — this requires the acts of alleged abuse to be identified with particularity;
(b) the judge must consider whether that conduct, if established, could amount to an abuse of process;
(c) he must consider whether there are reasonable grounds for believing that such conduct may have occurred.

If the judge is satisfied that these preliminary criteria are fulfilled, extradition should not be acceded to unless the judge is satisfied that such abuse has not occurred.

The requested person must prove the abuse on the balance of probabilities and the judge may ask for whatever information or evidence is required from the requesting territory to determine this issue.

Misconduct or bad faith by the police of the requesting State in the investigation of the case or the preparation of evidence for trial will not amount to an abuse (*Symeou v Public Prosecutor's Office at the Court of Appeals Patras, Greece* [2009] EWHC 897 (Admin), [2009] 1 WLR 2384). See *Belbin v Regional Court of Lille, France* [2015] EWHC 149 (Admin) at [43]–[44] for the approach to alleged conduct of the prosecutor or the requesting judicial authority. If the statements in a Part 1 warrant are inaccurate or incomplete, this may amount to an abuse of process (see **D31.15**). In *Camaras v Baia Mare Local Court Romania* [2016] EWHC 1766 (Admin), [2018] 1 WLR 1174 the Divisional Court examined how abuse of process might apply if a requesting territory made a further extradition request after the requested person had been discharged for the same offences (at [13]–[35]) (see also *Jasvins v General Prosecutor's Office Latvia* [2020] EWHC 602 (Admin)).

ASYLUM

Extradition cannot take place until the final determination of any asylum claim (ss. 39 and 121). For Part 1 cases, extradition can take place if it is to a safe third country (s. 40). Where a person has refugee status in respect of the requesting territory, extradition would constitute an abuse of process (*District Court in Ostroleka v Dytlow* [2009] EWHC 1009 (Admin)). In *VB v Westminster Magistrates' Court* [2014] UKSC 59, [2015] AC 1195 the Supreme Court considered the relationship between extradition proceedings and asylum claims. **D31.38**

PROCEDURAL MATTERS

If extradition is contested, an adjournment may be allowed by the judge for the case to be prepared (for delays arising from the processing of legal aid applications, see **D31.4**). Best practice should be followed when a requested person is a litigant in person (*Weszka v Regional Court in Poznan, Poland* [2017] EWHC 168 (Admin) at [21]–[24]). CrimPR Part 50 (see Supplement, **R50.1** ***et seq.***) makes specific provision for extradition proceedings. CrimPD XI, para. 50A.1(v) (see Supplement, **CPD.50A**), makes clear that 'any skeleton argument must comply with the requirements of these Practice Directions and, if applicable, of the court'. The court will case manage proceedings, requiring early identification of issues by the defence who will be expected to particularise the issues to be raised and any evidence to be relied on (*R (Government of the USA) v Bow Street Magistrates' Court* [2006] EWHC 2256 (Admin), [2007] 1 WLR 1157 at [77]). If a person is remanded in custody, and is not serving a sentence in the UK, the case will be reviewed every 28 days. **D31.39**

Section 202 provides for the admission of documents in authenticated or unauthenticated form (s. 202(5)). In *Kotsev v Sofia District Public Prosecutor's Office (A Bulgarian Judicial Authority)* [2018] EWHC 3087 (Admin), the Court cautioned that judges should not attempt to decide issues of foreign law for themselves without assistance from the requesting territory (at [52]). Evidence may be given through a television link by witnesses who are outside the UK (Evidence Through Television Links (England and Wales) Order 2013 (SI 2013 No. 1598)).

A judge hearing extradition proceedings has no power to order a closed material hearing or otherwise limit the disclosure of evidence on which a requested person wants to rely (*VB v Westminster Magistrates' Court* [2014] UKSC 59, [2015] AC 1195). A judge does have the power to admit anonymous witness evidence to determine whether the extraneous considerations bar applies, whether extradition would be incompatible with the requested person's Convention rights or whether a prima facie case is established (at [72]–[73]). However, the judge must ensure that the proceedings will nonetheless be fair and may wish to apply the same principles set out in the CAJA 2009 (see **D14.75**), which allows for the admission of anonymous evidence in criminal prosecutions.

The rules of disclosure in criminal proceedings do not apply to extradition cases. In Part 1 cases, the only documents ordinarily served are the EAW and certificate, a witness statement from the arresting police officer and antecedents. In Part 2 cases, the certificate and request will be served which should contain more detail and must include evidence if the territory is not designated. When acting for the requesting territory, the CPS has a duty of candour to disclose evidence or information that severely undermines or destroys its case (*R (Raissi) v Secretary of State for the Home Department* [2008] EWCA Civ 72, [2008] QB 836). The duty of candour that the CPS owe to disclose evidence or information that severely undermines or destroys their case may mean that the CPS will have to withdraw if their duty to the court conflicts with their duty to the requesting territory (*Atraskevic v Prosecutor General's Office, Republic of Lithuania* [2015] EWHC 131 (Admin), [2015] 4 All ER 770 at [20]). The Divisional Court considered the use of reporting restrictions in extradition proceedings in *Short v Falkland Islands* [2020] EWHC 439 (Admin), [2020] 4 WLR 68 (see also *BM v Republic of Ireland (No. 2)* [2020] EWHC 648 (Admin), [2020] 4 WLR 70).

SECRETARY OF STATE

D31.40 Where a judge sends a Part 2 case to the Secretary of State, he or she must consider if any of the bars under ss. 94 to 96A apply (death penalty, speciality or earlier extradition or transfer to the UK). A requested person has four weeks from the day the case is sent to the Secretary of State to make representations indicating that any of these bars apply (s. 93(5) and (6)). If the Secretary of State finds none apply, an order for extradition will be made under s. 93(4).

APPEALS

D31.41 Sections 26 to 34 govern appeals under Part 1 and ss. 103 to 116 govern appeals under Part 2. CrimPR Part 50 (see Supplement, **R50.1** *et seq.*) governs the procedure on extradition appeals. The decision of the judge can be subject to judicial review if the decision did not address the facts and circumstances of the case and was tantamount to a nullity (*R (Lazarov) v Westminster Magistrates' Court* [2018] EWHC 3050 (Admin)). An appeal to the High Court may be on a question of law or fact and can be brought by the requesting territory or the requested person. Permission is required and r. 50.17(4) states that permission will be granted if the court finds a ground of appeal to be reasonably arguable; r. 50.22 deals with renewing an application orally if permission is refused on the papers and the grounds for renewal must explain why the refusal was wrong (*Opalfvens v Public Prosecutor Antwerp, Belgium* [2015] EWHC 2808 (Admin) at [14]). For Part 2 cases, an appeal by the requested person cannot be heard until after the Secretary of State has made the decision and can be against the decision of the judge or the Secretary of State or both.

The approach to be adopted by the appeal court is clear for the passage of time bar (*Surico v Public Prosecutor of the Public Prosecuting Office of Bari, Italy* [2018] EWHC 401 (Admin) at [31]; see **D31.25**); the forum bar (*Love v Government of the USA* [2018] EWHC 172 (Admin), [2018] 1 WLR 2889 at [26]; see **D31.28**); the ECHR, Article 8 (*Polish Judicial Authorities v Celinski* [2015] EWHC 1274 (Admin), [2016] 1 WLR 551 at [19]–[24]; see **D31.35**) and physical or mental condition (*Surico* at [31]; see **D31.36**). The Divisional Court has considered how to approach challenges to factual findings in *Ioskevich v Government of the Russian Federation* [2018] EWHC 696 (Admin) at [37]–[41].

Orders made by the High Court must be complied with as otherwise the court may not permit evidence to be relied on or arguments to be advanced (*McIntyre v Government of the USA* [2014] EWHC 1886 (Admin), [2015] 1 WLR 507 at [66]). The High Court has considered in what circumstances it is appropriate for the court to administratively stay appeals in order to await a Supreme Court judgment or decision on whether to grant permission to appeal (*Miroslav Czach and Tadeusz Weszka v Poland* [2016] EWHC 1993 (Admin)).

Notice of Application for Leave to Appeal

Notices of application for leave to appeal must be filed at the High Court and served on the respondent (and any interested party) within seven days for Part 1 and 14 days for Part 2 (ss. 26(4) and 103(9) and CrimPR 4.11). Permission to appeal is required and, if the notice of application for leave to appeal is given after the prescribed period, the High Court must still allow the application to be dealt with if the person has done everything reasonably possible to ensure that the notice was given as soon as it could be given (see *Szegfu v Court of Pecs, Hungary* [2015] EWHC 1764 (Admin), [2016] 1 WLR 322, which considers a notice served by a requested person, and *Public Prosecutor's Office of the Appeal Court of Eastern Crete, Greece v Andrew* [2018] EWHC 441 (Admin), which considers a notice served electronically by a requesting territory). The Act provides that the notice must be given in accordance with the rules of court and these rules permit breaches of the requirements in the rules to be remedied (*R (Aldhouse) v Royal Government of Thailand* [2012] EWHC 191 (Admin)). The 14-day period for Part 2 begins from the date the Secretary of State informs the requested person, or the person's solicitors, of the extradition order. The court can make an order for extradition which will not take effect for a period of time to allow time for communication between the requested person, requesting territory and the court about specified issues (see, e.g., *BS v Court of First Instance Brussels, Belgium* [2017] EWHC 571 (Admin) at [62]–[64] and *PA v Criminal Court Coimbra, Portugal* [2017] EWHC 331 (Admin) at [72]). **D31.42**

Fresh Evidence

In order to adduce fresh evidence on appeal, that evidence must not have been available at the extradition hearing and it must be decisive (*Szombathely City Court v Fenyvesi* [2009] EWHC 231 (Admin), [2009] 4 All ER 324). 'Not available' means that it was not at the disposal of the party wishing to adduce it and it could not have been obtained with reasonable diligence, and includes where the requested person's mental health prevented giving proper instructions about the person's symptoms (*Baranik v NCA* [2019] EWHC 3520 (Admin) at [43]). The admissibility of fresh evidence does not extend to situations where the appellant seeks more favourable expert evidence (*Undrits v Northern Circuit Prosecutor's Office, Estonia* [2009] EWHC 3430 (Admin)). It may be possible to admit evidence that was available in order to avoid a breach of rights under the ECHR, but only if this new evidence would be decisive (*Plotkowski v Regional Court in Elblag, Poland* [2012] EWHC 375 (Admin)); see also *PA v Criminal Court Coimbra, Portugal* [2017] EWHC 331 (Admin) at [13]–[19], which deals with the admission of evidence if children may be affected). **D31.43**

The court can admit evidence in support of the extradition decision of the judge (*FK v Stuttgart State Prosecutor's Office, Germany* [2017] EWHC 2160 (Admin) at [39]).

New Issue

If an issue was available to be raised by a requested person on the evidence adduced at the extradition hearing, the requested person will, in general if not always, be entitled to raise that issue on appeal even though it was not raised at that hearing (*R (Adedeji) v Public Prosecutor's Office, Germany* [2012] EWHC 3237 (Admin) at [10]). However, the authorities on this point are not settled (*Koziel v District Court in Kielce, Poland* [2011] EWHC 3781 (Admin)). *Jones v Government of the USA* [2012] EWHC 2332 (Admin) considered whether an issue which was abandoned in the magistrates' court could be revived on appeal. **D31.44**

Further Appeal or Remedy

D31.45 An appeal under Part 1 or Part 2 from the decision of the High Court lies to the Supreme Court, with leave (ss. 32 and 114) and only if the High Court has certified a point of law of public importance (ss. 32(4) and 114(1)). The Court can reopen a final determination of an appeal or an application for permission to appeal under CrimPR 50.27, which was considered in *Government of the USA v Bowen* [2015] EWHC 1873 (Admin), but there is no right to an oral hearing (*Zibala v Prosecutor General's Office, Republic of Latvia* [2019] EWHC 816 (Admin)). The Court can also use this provision to consider a challenge following a remittal to the appropriate judge after an appeal (*Chawla v Government of India* [2020] EWHC 102 (Admin), [2020] 1 WLR 1609 at [36]; *Dempsey v Government of the USA* [2020] EWHC 603 (Admin)). However, this does not allow an appeal to be reopened in a Part 1 case after a person has been extradited (*Seprey-Hozo v Law Court of Miercurea CIUC, Romania* [2016] EWHC 2902 (Admin), [2016] 4 WLR 181). An appeal under s. 108 can be brought on human rights grounds at any time before physical removal. The High Court will consider the appeal only if it is necessary to do so to avoid real injustice and the circumstances are exceptional and make it appropriate to consider the appeal (s. 108(7)). For guidance as to how applications will be dealt with, see *McIntyre v Government of the USA* [2014] EWHC 1886 (Admin), [2015] 1 WLR 507 at [11].

The time within which the appeal must be heard (ss. 31 and 113) can be extended in the interests of justice, and does not require exceptional circumstances (*Wright v City of Westminster Magistrates' Court* [2011] EWHC 515 (Admin)).

POST-HEARING MATTERS

Time-limit for Removal

D31.46 If a person does not seek to appeal an order for extradition under Part 1, the person must be removed within ten days of the expiry of the seven-day period allowed for giving notice of application for leave to appeal or any later date fixed by the judge after an application by the requesting territory (s. 35(3)). If not removed within this period, the person can seek to be discharged, unless reasonable cause is shown for the delay (s. 35(5); see *Jane v Westminster Magistrates' Court* [2019] EWHC 394 (Admin), [2019] 4 WLR 95). The requesting territory can seek an extension of time from the judge (s. 35(4)(b); see *Cosar v Governor of HM Prison Wandsworth* [2020] EWHC 1142 (Admin)). Similar provisions apply under s. 36 following unsuccessful appeals to the High Court or Supreme Court. Any application for discharge under s. 35 or 36 must be made to the appropriate judge in the magistrates' court (*Kasprzak v Warsaw Regional Court, Poland* [2011] EWHC 100 (Admin)).

Part 2 makes similar provision for removal and a right to seek discharge if not removed within 28 days following the expiry of the 14-day period allowed to lodge a notice of application for leave to appeal against the Secretary of State's order for extradition where none is brought (s. 117), or following an unsuccessful appeal (s. 118; see *R (Tajik) v City of Westminster Magistrates' Court* [2012] EWHC 3347 (Admin), [2013] 2 All ER 602).

Section D32 Public Funding

INTRODUCTION

The primary source of the law on public funding in criminal matters is the LASPO 2012, as supplemented by various statutory instruments, and the standard crime contract 2017 issued by the Legal Aid Agency (LAA). The LASPO provisions apply to any advice and assistance, advocacy assistance or representation order dated on or after 1 April 2013. Any order dated before 1 April 2013 continues throughout the life of the case (which may include long delayed confiscation proceedings) under the previous law as set out in earlier editions of this work. **D32.1**

Grant of legal aid in criminal cases is, in all but a small minority of cases, authorised by the LAA and applications should be made electronically.

ADVICE AND ASSISTANCE, ADVOCACY ASSISTANCE AND REPRESENTATION ORDERS

Grant of Right to Advice and Assistance and Advocacy Assistance

Sections 13 and 15 of the LASPO 2012 provide for the provision of advice and assistance to those held in custody and to those involved in criminal investigations. This includes advice to those detained and to volunteers at the police station or other place where a constable is present. Advice and assistance and advocacy assistance are available to those appearing in a magistrates' court, or at armed forces custody hearings, in relation to warrants of further detention; applications to vary pre-charge bail; and applications by the police, under the PCA 2017, to extend the time that a person remains on bail (Criminal Legal Aid (Standard Crime Contract) (Amendment) Regulations 2017 (SI 2017 No. 311)). **D32.2**

Detailed provisions appear in the standard crime contract 2017. The contract also provides for advocacy assistance to court duty solicitors and representatives in virtual courts. The Criminal Legal Aid (Remuneration) Regulations 2013 (SI 2013 No. 435), reg. 8 and sch. 4, contain provisions for payment for this work.

Grant of Right to Representation

The LAA funds individuals and other legal persons who are granted the right to representation in accordance with the LASPO 2012, s. 16. The provisions for legal persons who are not individuals are contained in Part 6 of the Criminal Legal Aid (General) Regulations 2013 (SI 2013 No. 9) and in the Legal Aid (Financial Resources and Payment for Services) (Legal Persons) *Regulations* 2013 (SI 2013 No. 512). **D32.3**

Section 16 of the LASPO 2012 provides for representation to be made available to an individual, including in relation to any kind of criminal proceedings, and enabling an appeal to the Crown Court to be resisted otherwise than in an official capacity. Where the right is granted, it includes representation for any related bail or other preliminary or incidental proceedings (s. 16(3)). Under s. 14 the term 'criminal proceedings' is defined as including:

(a) proceedings before a court for dealing with an individual accused of an offence,

D

Part D Procedure

(b) proceedings before a court for dealing with an individual convicted of an offence, including proceedings in respect of a sentence or order,
(c) proceedings for dealing with an individual under the Extradition Act 2003,
(d) proceedings for binding an individual over to keep the peace or to be of good behaviour under s. 115 of the Magistrates' Courts Act 1980 and for dealing with an individual who fails to comply with an order under that section,
(e) proceedings on an appeal brought by an individual under s. 44A of the Criminal Appeal Act 1968 (appeal in case of death of appellant),
(f) proceedings on a reference under s. 36 of the Criminal Justice Act 1972 on a point of law following the acquittal of an individual on indictment,
(g) proceedings for contempt committed, or alleged to have been committed, by an individual in the face of a court, and
(h) such other proceedings, before any court, tribunal or other person, as may be prescribed.

Section 14 enables other proceedings to be brought within the ambit of legal funding by deeming those proceedings to be criminal proceedings.

Remuneration for representation is provided by the Criminal Legal Aid (Remuneration) Regulations 2013. Schedule 1 defines the advocates' graduated fee scheme and sch. 2 that for litigators. The current figures for advocates are set out in the Criminal Legal Aid (Remuneration) (Amendment) (No. 2) Regulations 2018 (SI 2018 No. 1323, in force from 31 December 2018). Those for litigators are set out in the Criminal Legal Aid (Remuneration) (Amendment) Regulations 2016 (SI 2016 No. 313, in force from 31 March 2016).

D32.4 The Criminal Legal Aid (General) Regulations 2013, reg. 9, prescribes certain proceedings as criminal proceedings for the purposes of s. 14(h).

Criminal Legal Aid (General) Regulations 2013, reg. 9

(a) civil proceedings in a magistrates' court arising from a failure to pay a sum due or to obey an order of that court where such failure carries the risk of imprisonment;
(b) proceedings under sections 14B, 14D, 14G, 14H, 21B and 21D of the Football Spectators Act 1989 in relation to banning orders and references to a court;
(c) proceedings under section 5A of the Protection from Harassment Act 1997 in relation to restraining orders on acquittal;
(d) and (e) [repealed];
(f) proceedings in relation to parenting orders made under section 8(1)(b) of the Crime and Disorder Act 1998 where an order under section 22 of the Anti-social Behaviour, Crime and Policing Act 2014 or a sexual harm prevention order under section 103A of the Sexual Offences Act 2003 is made;
(g) proceedings under section 8(1)(c) of the Crime and Disorder Act 1998 in relation to parenting orders made on the conviction of a child;
(h) proceedings under section 9(5) of the Crime and Disorder Act 1998 to discharge or vary a parenting order made as set out in sub-paragraph (f) or (g);
(i) proceedings under section 10 of the Crime and Disorder Act 1998 in relation to an appeal against a parenting order made as set out in sub-paragraph (f) or (g);
(j) proceedings under Part 1A of Schedule 1 to the Powers of Criminal Courts (Sentencing) Act 2000 in relation to parenting orders for failure to comply with orders under section 20 of that Act;
(ja) proceedings in a youth court (or on appeal from such a court) in relation to the breach or potential breach of a provision of an injunction under Part 1 of the Anti-social Behaviour, Crime and Policing Act 2014 where the person who is subject to the injunction is aged under 14;
(k) proceedings under sections 80, 82, 83 and 84 of the Anti-social Behaviour, Crime and Policing Act 2014 in relation to closure orders made under section 80(5)(a) of that Act where a person has engaged in, or is likely to engage in behaviour that constitutes a criminal offence on the premises;
(ka) proceedings under paragraph 3 of Schedule 2 to the Female Genital Mutilation Act 2003 in relation to female genital mutilation protection orders made other than on conviction and related appeals;
(kb) proceedings under paragraph 6 of Schedule 2 to the Female Genital Mutilation Act 2003 in relation to female genital mutilation protection orders made under paragraph 3 of that Schedule;

(l) proceedings under sections 20, 22, 26 and 28 of the Anti-social Behaviour Act 2003 in relation to parenting orders—
  (i) in cases of exclusion from school; or
  (ii) in respect of criminal conduct and anti-social behaviour;
(m) proceedings under sections 97, 100 and 101 of the Sexual Offences Act 2003 in relation to notification orders and interim notification orders;
(n) proceedings under sections 103A, 103E, 103F and 103H of the Sexual Offences Act 2003 in relation to sexual harm prevention orders;
(o) [repealed];
(p) proceedings under sections 122A, 122D, 122E and 122G of the Sexual Offences Act 2003 in relation to sexual risk orders;
(q) [repealed];
(r) proceedings under section 13 of the Tribunals, Courts and Enforcement Act 2007 on appeal against a decision of the Upper Tribunal in proceedings in respect of—
  (i) a decision of the Financial Conduct Authority;
  (ia) a decision of the Prudential Regulation Authority
  (ii) a decision of the Bank of England; or
  (iii) a decision of a person in relation to the assessment of any compensation or consideration under the Banking (Special Provisions) Act 2008 or the Banking Act 2009;
(s) proceedings before the Crown Court or the Court of Appeal in relation to serious crime prevention orders under sections 19, 20, 21 and 24 of the Serious Crime Act 2007;
(t) proceedings under sections 100, 101, 103, 104 and 106 of the Criminal Justice and Immigration Act 2008 in relation to violent offender orders and interim violent offender orders;
(u) proceedings under sections 26, 27 and 29 of the Crime and Security Act 2010 in relation to—
  (i) domestic violence protection notices; or
  (ii) domestic violence protection orders;
(ua) proceedings under sections 14(1)(b) and (c), 15 and 20 to 22 of the Modern Slavery Act 2015 in relation to slavery and trafficking prevention orders;
(ub) proceedings under sections 23 and 27 to 29 of the Modern Slavery Act 2015 in relation to slavery and trafficking risk orders;
(uc) proceedings under Part 2 of the Offensive Weapons Act 2019 in relation to a knife crime prevention order or an interim knife crime prevention order;
(ud) proceedings under sections 1, 4, 5 and 7 of the Stalking Protection Act 2019 in relation to stalking protection orders and interim stalking protection orders; and
(v) any other proceedings that involve the determination of a criminal charge for the purposes of Article 6(1) of the European Convention on Human Rights.

Regulation 19 of the General Regulations identifies certain proceedings as incidental so that they are included within a grant of representation: **D32.5**

(a) proceedings in the Crown Court, following committal for sentence by a magistrates' court;
(b) proceedings to quash an acquittal under the CPIA 1996, s. 54 (tainted acquittals: see **D12.38**); and
(c) proceedings for confiscation and forfeiture in connection with criminal proceedings.

Regulation 20 deals with proceedings that are not to be regarded as incidental and so justify a separate representation order, defined as:

(a) proceedings for applications for judicial review or habeas corpus in relation to criminal proceedings; and
(b) proceedings for dealing with an individual who is alleged to have failed to comply with an order of the magistrates' court or the Crown Court.

Applying for a Representation Order in a Magistrates' Court and the Crown Court

Section 17 of the LASPO 2012 provides for the determination of applications for a representation order in a magistrates' court or Crown Court. Responsibility (save in exceptional circumstances) in the Crown Court for making that determination rests with the LAA. Application should be made electronically on form CRM14e. **D32.6**

Magistrates have no power to grant representation, save when considering an appeal against the refusal of representation. Representation is applied for using the prescribed form (CRM14) and submitting it to the LAA, along with any proof of means required for those who are not passported (form CRM15).

The Crown Court has very limited power to grant a representation order and may do so only on oral application under the Criminal Legal Aid (Determinations by a Court and Choice of Representative) Regulations 2013 (SI 2013 No. 614). Regulation 6 states that a representation order may only be granted in proceedings:

(a) which are described in the LASPO 2012, s. 14(g) (contempt in the face of the court);
(b) which arise out of an alleged failure to comply with an order of the Crown Court and it appears to the court that there is no time to instruct a provider; or
(c) where the individual is brought before the court under the Senior Courts Act 1981, s. 81, in pursuance of a Crown Court warrant.

There is no means test for these applications. Any other order of the Crown Court will be invalid (Criminal Legal Aid (General) Regulations 2013, reg. 3). The Crown Court may consider appeals against the refusal of a representation order in those situations where the interests of justice merits test is not automatically met.

D32.7 The decision whether or not to grant a representation order is to be determined by a two-stage test, incorporating a merits test 'according to the interests of justice' and an assessment of means.

Legal Aid, Sentencing and Punishment of Offenders Act 2012, s. 17

(2) In deciding what the interests of justice consist of for the purposes of such a determination, the following factors must be taken into account—
  (a) whether, if any matter arising in the proceedings is decided against the individual, the individual would be likely to lose his or her liberty or livelihood or to suffer serious damage to his or her reputation,
  (b) whether the determination of any matter arising in the proceedings may involve consideration of a substantial question of law,
  (c) whether the individual may be unable to understand the proceedings or to state his or her own case,
  (d) whether the proceedings may involve the tracing, interviewing or expert cross-examination of witnesses on behalf of the individual, and
  (e) whether it is in the interests of another person that the individual be represented.

In respect of proceedings in the Crown Court on indictment (Criminal Legal Aid (General) Regulations 2013, reg. 24(1)) or following a committal for sentence (reg. 19(2)), the interests of justice test is deemed met. Appeals to the Crown Court are not automatically covered (reg. 24(2)). In assessing whether the accused is likely to lose his or her liberty, regard must be had to the facts alleged by the prosecution, rather than the maximum penalty that could theoretically be imposed (*Highgate Justices, ex parte Lewis* [1977] Crim LR 611). So it is not enough that the offence carries a custodial sentence: the court must consider whether a custodial sentence might be imposed in the particular case. The LAA pays particular regard to sentencing guidelines and a defendant's list of previous convictions. In *Liverpool City Magistrates, ex parte McGhee* [1993] Crim LR 609, the Divisional Court rejected the contention that what is now called an unpaid work requirement could be regarded as a sentence which deprives the accused of liberty. However, Rose LJ added that the list of criteria (in what is now the LASPO 2012, s. 17) is not exhaustive, and so the possibility of a community punishment order (now a community order with a relevant requirement) may be a factor in deciding whether to make a representation order.

In *R (Punatar) v Horseferry Road Magistrates' Court* [2002] EWHC 1196 (Admin), an application for representation submitted at the end of court proceedings was refused because the prosecution substituted a charge for a non-imprisonable offence in place of an imprisonable one. The Divisional Court held that representation should have been granted due to the fact that when the solicitor decided to attend court the offence that was charged at that time merited representation. It was wrong to apply hindsight.

The factor which includes expert cross-examination of witnesses means expert cross-examination of witnesses, not cross-examination of expert witnesses (*Liverpool City Magistrates, ex parte McGhee*). In *Scunthorpe Justices, ex parte* S (1998) *The Times*, 5 March 1998, the Divisional Court considered that refusal of legal aid to an accused aged 16 who sought to challenge whether a police officer had acted in the execution of his duty was irrational. The expertise needed to cross-examine police witnesses, and to find, select and proof defence witnesses, was beyond an accused aged 16.

In *R (GKR Law Solicitors) v Liverpool Magistrates' Court* [2008] EWHC 2974 (Admin) the Divisional Court held that it was appropriate to grant representation to D in relation to a special reasons hearing, where a witness in the case was D's 12-year-old son. The child was a witness entitled to and requiring special measures and consideration would need to be given to video-interviewing the young witness in order to ensure best evidence is given; such measures would be outside D's competence and resources.

In *R (Matara) v Brent Magistrates' Court* [2005] EWHC 1829 (Admin), D was charged with failure to provide a specimen of breath. He made an application for legal aid. It was argued that he would be unable to understand the court proceedings because his understanding of English was inadequate; the Court's response was that an interpreter would be provided. On appeal, it was held that at least one of the 'interests of justice' criteria in what is now s. 17 of the LASPO 2012 was met, making the refusal of legal aid unreasonable to a degree which entitled the Divisional Court to intervene. The availability of an interpreter did not meet the point that it was D's case that he was unable to understand what was being said at the time of his arrest, a point which lay at the heart of his defence. It went to his ability to state his own case and the overall fairness of the trial. The decision to refuse legal aid was therefore quashed and the case remitted to a differently constituted bench for reconsideration.

In *Chester Magistrates' Court, ex parte Ball* (1999) 163 JP 813 it was indicated that any defendant of previous good character pleading not guilty to a charge equal to, or more significant than, s. 5 of the Public Order Act 1986 in terms of nature and seriousness might be granted legal aid regardless of social or professional standing, because there might be damage to the defendant's reputation. It is unlikely that this principle will assist in relation to applications for legal aid in respect of non-imprisonable road traffic or regulatory offences.

In *Gravesend Magistrates' Court, ex parte Baker* (1977) 161 JP 765 the defendant was charged with driving with excess alcohol and put forward special reasons based on spiked drinks. The Court held that the applicant should be granted legal aid because a scientific expert would be required and the assistance of a solicitor would be necessary to identify witnesses, take proper proofs and extract the defence from the defendant in the witness box.

In *Oates* [2002] EWCA Crim 1071, [2002] 1 WLR 2833, it was held that legal assistance by way of a representation order will not, save in exceptional circumstances, be granted on a renewed application for permission to appeal against conviction following refusal by the single judge; this is not contrary to the right of an accused to 'defend himself... through legal assistance of his own choosing' under the ECHR, Article 6(3)(c).

Assistance on the application of the 'interests of justice' test is given in *Guidance on the Consideration of Defence Representation Order Applications* (LAA, January 2020).

Financial eligibility for a grant of representation is determined under Part 3 of the Criminal Legal Aid (Financial Resources) Regulations 2013 (SI 2013 No. 471), as amended by SI 2013 No. 2791 in relation to the magistrates' court and, in relation to applications made on or after 27 January 2014, the Crown Court. A means assessment is carried out following submission of information on forms CRM14 and, if appropriate, CRM15. Applicants who fall into one or more of the following categories will automatically pass the means test assessment: **D32.8**

(i) under the age of 18;
(ii) directly or indirectly in receipt of a 'qualifying benefit'.

A qualifying benefit means any of the following (or their equivalent benefit payable in Northern Ireland):

(a) income support;
(b) income-based jobseeker's allowance;

(c) guarantee credit;
(d) income-related employment and support allowance; and
(e) universal credit.

In magistrates' courts, legal aid is either granted or refused on financial grounds. In the Crown Court, legal aid may, because of the applicant's means, be granted without a contribution, granted with a contribution, or be refused. In both jurisdictions Form CRM16 may be used to reapply for legal aid in cases of hardship. This enables the private client costs of the case to be taken into account by the LAA when determining means eligibility.

In the Crown Court a financial eligibility test applies to (i) appeals from a magistrates' court, (ii) proceedings sent or transferred to the Crown Court, (iii) proceedings following a voluntary bill of indictment and (iv) proceedings remitted for trial by the Court of Appeal. The test does not apply to committals for sentence (to which the magistrates' court rules apply) or proceedings on breach of the terms of a Crown Court order (Criminal Legal Aid (Contribution Orders) Regulations 2013 (SI 2013 No. 483), reg. 6, and Criminal Legal Aid (Financial Resources) Regulations 2013, reg. 30). Because of the drafting of reg. 6 of the Criminal Legal Aid (Contribution Orders) Regulations 2013, the means test applies to prescribed proceedings in the Crown Court but not, in defined circumstances, to proceedings under reg. 9(f), (g), (h) and (s) of the Criminal Legal Aid (General) Regulations 2013.

An individual granted representation with a contribution for the Crown Court may be called upon to pay contributions from income and, if convicted, from capital under the Criminal Legal Aid (Contribution Orders) Regulations 2013, as amended by SI 2013 No. 2792. If the individual is acquitted, contributions are returned with interest. The differently worded Criminal Defence Service (Contribution Orders) Regulations 2009 (SI 2009 No. 3328) were interpreted in *R (Flannigan) v Director of Legal Aid Casework* [2018] EWHC 1927 (Admin).

Where a defendant is charged at the Crown Court with more than one offence and is convicted of one or more, but not all, such offences, and wishes to limit the extent of legal aid contributions, an application for apportionment should be made to the trial judge (within 21 days) under reg. 26 of the Criminal Legal Aid (Contribution Orders) Regulations 2013. Regulation 29 does not provide any additional discretion to the Director of Legal Aid Casework (*R (Khan) v Director of Legal Aid Casework* [2018] EWHC 3198 (Admin)).

For those appearing in the Crown Court to recover, on acquittal, from central funds, an application for legal aid must have been made and refused (Prosecution of Offences Act 1985, s. 16A(5A)). This is the case however inevitable such a refusal may be.

There are duties of disclosure upon providers (overriding legal privilege) contained in reg. 5 of the Criminal Legal Aid (General) Regulations 2013 where there is a failure by a client without good reason to comply with the requirements to provide information or documents, or a statement is made which the provider knows or believes to be false. This confirms the Legal Aid (Disclosure of Information) Regulations 2013 (SI 2013 No. 457). The LAA must not disclose privileged information for the purposes of criminal investigations or proceedings if it relates to the defence of an individual or legal person.

Applying for a Representation Order in the Courts above the Crown Court

D32.9 Provision for the grant of legal aid in the High Court (for instance on an appeal by way of case stated), Court of Appeal and Supreme Court is made by the Criminal Legal Aid (Determinations by a Court and Choice of Representative) Regulations 2013. The merits test is deemed to be satisfied in these courts under reg. 21 of the Criminal Legal Aid (General) Regulations 2013.

Criminal Legal Aid (Determinations by a Court and Choice of Representative) Regulations 2013, regs. 7 and 8

7.—*(1) On the application of an individual*, the High Court may make a determination under section 16 of the Act as to whether an individual qualifies for representation for the purposes of criminal proceedings before the High Court in relation to an appeal by way of case stated from a decision of the magistrates' court or the Crown Court.

(2) On the application of an individual, or of its own motion, the High Court may make a determination under section 16 of the Act as to whether an individual qualifies for representation for the purposes of proceedings before the High Court, or proceedings before the Supreme Court on appeal from the High Court, described in—
(a) section 14(a) to (g) of the Act, other than proceedings under paragraph (1); or.
(b) regulation 9(r) of the General Regulations
8.—(1) On the application of an individual, or of its own motion, the Court of Appeal may make a determination under section 16 of the Act as to whether an individual qualifies for representation for the purposes of any criminal proceedings before the Court of Appeal, or criminal proceedings before the Supreme Court on appeal from the Court of Appeal.
(2) A determination made in accordance with paragraph (1)—
(a) must not be made until service of an appeal notice in respect of the proceedings has taken place; and.
(b) may specify the stage of the proceedings at which the determination is to take effect.

In the higher courts there is no means test as to financial eligibility. The duties of these courts to make costs orders are contained in the Criminal Legal Aid (Recovery of Defence Costs Orders) Regulations 2013 (SI 2013 No. 511). They do not apply to those under 18 years of age or those with incomes below the specified limits. Where any such court is considering the making of a recovery of costs order, it must have regard to the extent to which the Crown was successful (*R (Baybasin) v Woolwich Crown Court* [2015] EWHC 1327 (Admin)).

Regulation 8(2)(b) of the Criminal Legal Aid (Determinations by a Court and Choice of Representative) Regulations 2013 provides that the Court of Appeal may specify the stage of the proceedings at which the determination is to take effect. In *K* (2005) *The Times*, 15 February 2005, the Court of Appeal emphasised that (under earlier provisions) when a court grants a representation order for an appeal, the representation order only covers work on, and attendance or appearance at, the hearing in respect of the grounds upon which the court has granted leave to appeal. It does not cover any work, preparation or time in court that is done or spent pertaining to any renewed application in respect of a ground on which leave to appeal has been refused. If, on a renewed application made at the same time as an appeal, leave is granted, the practice of the court is exactly the same as applies when a renewed application is made separately. **D32.10**

Nature of Representation

The Criminal Legal Aid (Determinations by a Court and Choice of Representative) Regulations 2013 (SI 2013 No. 614), Part 3, sets out the details of: **D32.11**

- the process of an application (regs. 10 to 12);
- which litigator may be chosen and the procedure where a person appearing in proceedings heard at the same time has already chosen a litigator (reg. 13);
- whether there may be a transfer of the case to another litigator (regs. 14 and 15 and see **D32.14**);
- whether and when an advocate may be chosen (regs. 16 to 18);
- the number of advocates that may be chosen (regs. 19 to 23).

The Process of Application

Criminal Legal Aid (Determinations by a Court and Choice of Representative) Regulations 2013, regs. 10 to 12 **D32.12**

10. This Part makes provision in relation to the right, conferred by section 27(4) of the Act (choice of provider of services etc), of an individual who qualifies for representation for the purposes of criminal proceedings by virtue of a determination under section 16 of the Act (representation for criminal proceedings), in accordance with Part 2 of these Regulations or Part 5 of the General Regulations, to select a representative.
11.—(1) The relevant court may make a determination under this Part only if it has considered an application made in accordance with paragraph (2)
(2) For the purposes of paragraph (1), an application must—
(a) be made by the individual seeking the determination;
(b) be in writing; and

(c) specify what the relevant court is being asked to determine and the grounds upon which it is being asked to do so.

(3) When it makes a determination under this Part, the relevant court must give reasons.

12. In relation to any criminal proceedings described in section 14(a) to (f) and (h) of the Act (criminal proceedings), the right of an individual conferred by section 27(4) of the Act does not include the right to select a provider unless the provider—

(a) is employed by the Lord Chancellor to provide criminal legal aid;

(b) is permitted to provide criminal legal aid to the individual under the arrangements the Lord Chancellor has made with the provider; or

(c) is representing the individual before the Court of Appeal in an appeal against a decision of the Upper Tribunal in proceedings in respect of a decision of—

(i) the Financial [Conduct] Authority;

(ia) a decision of the Prudential Regulation Authority;

(ii) the Bank of England; or

(iii) a person in relation to the assessment of any compensation or consideration under the Banking (Special Provisions) Act 2008 or the Banking Act 2009.

Choice of Litigator

D32.13 **Criminal Legal Aid (Determinations by a Court and Choice of Representative) Regulations 2013, reg. 13**

13.—(1) Subject to paragraph (2), in relation to any criminal proceedings involving co-defendants, the right of an individual conferred by section 27(4) of the Act does not include the right to select a provider who is not also instructed by the individual's co-defendant (or by one of the individual's co-defendants, if there are more than one) unless the relevant court or the Director determines that—

(a) there is a conflict of interest between the individual and that co-defendant; or.

(b) there is likely to be a conflict of interest between the individual and that co-defendant.

(2) Paragraph (1) does not apply where the provider selected by the individual is an advocate.

(3) In this regulation 'co-defendants' means defendants whose cases are to be heard together.

Transfer of Representation

D32.14 The rules on transfer of representation orders distinguish between the situations where the client wishes to transfer and those where the litigator is under a professional duty to withdraw. The procedures for such applications are set out in CrimPR 46.3 (see Supplement, **R46.3**).

In *R (Sanjari) v Crown Court at Birmingham* [2015] EWHC 2037 (Admin), [2015] 2 Cr App R 30 (415), the Divisional Court refused an application for a transfer that 'lacked the objectivity, independent judgment and high standards of professional conduct that a court on such an application is entitled to expect of a solicitor' (at [38]). Lord Thomas CJ remarked (at [43]) that a defendant 'must appreciate that the provision of a representation order does not give him a right to act in any way he chooses. It comes with conditions which are necessary in the interests of justice, with which each defendant must comply.'

The Court approved the following statement (at [35]):

> This court will insist on strict compliance with the provisions of Regulation [14]. The grounds of the application and full particulars need to be specified by the existing representatives. Next, the substantial compelling reason under [paragraph 3], if relied on, needs to be specified so that I can identify it. It will not generally be sufficient to allege a lack of care or competence of existing representatives ... only in extremely rare cases, and where full particulars are given in the application, will a general ground of loss of confidence or incompetence be entertained. It must further be pointed out that it will not be sufficient simply to say that there is a breakdown in the relationship between solicitor and client. Many breakdowns are imagined rather than real or as a result of proper advice.

Criminal Legal Aid (Determinations by a Court and Choice of Representative) Regulations 2013, regs. 14 and 15

14.—(1) Subject to paragraph (2), where an individual has selected a provider in criminal proceedings, the right conferred by section 27(4) of the Act does not include a right to select a provider in place of the original provider.

(2) The relevant court may determine that the individual can select a provider in place of the original provider in the circumstances set out in paragraphs (3) or (4).
(3) The circumstances are that the relevant court determines that—
(a) there has been a breakdown in the relationship between the individual and the original provider such that effective representation can no longer be provided by the original provider; or
(b) there is some other compelling reason why effective representation can no longer be provided by the original provider.
(4) The circumstances are that the relevant court determines that—
(a) the original provider—
(i) considers there to be a duty to withdraw from the case in accordance with the provider's professional rules of conduct; or
(ii) is no longer able to represent the individual through circumstances outside the provider's control; and
(b) the original provider has supplied the relevant court with details as to—
(i) the nature of any such duty to withdraw from the case; or
(ii) the particular circumstances that render the provider unable to represent the individual.

15.—(1) Paragraph (2) applies where, in relation to an individual—
(a) a determination is withdrawn in accordance with regulation 26 of the General Regulations or regulation 9 of these Regulations; and
(b) a subsequent determination under section 16 of the Act that the individual qualifies for representation is made in respect of the same proceedings.
(2) Subject to paragraph (3), the right of an individual conferred by section 27(4) of the Act does not include a right to select a provider other than the provider named in the original representation order.
(3) The relevant court may determine that the individual can select a provider other than the provider named in the original representation order if that court determines that there are good reasons why a different provider should be selected.

Choice, Nature and Number of Advocates

A representation order for failure to pay a confiscation order may not be extended to assigned counsel under reg. 16 as it is not an indictable offence (*Taylor v City of Westminster Magistrates' Court* [2009] EWHC 1498 (Admin)). **D32.15**

Criminal Legal Aid (Determinations by a Court and Choice of Representative) Regulations 2013, regs. 16 and 17

16.—(1) Subject to paragraph (2), in relation to any criminal proceedings before a magistrates' court, the right of an individual conferred by section 27(4) of the Act does not include a right to select an advocate.
(2) The relevant court may determine that the individual can select an advocate if—
(a) the proceedings relate to an extradition hearing under the Extradition Act 2003 or an indictable offence; and
(b) the relevant court determines that because there are circumstances which make the proceedings unusually grave or difficult, representation by an advocate would be desirable.

17.—(1) Subject to paragraph (2), where an individual is entitled to select an advocate in accordance with regulation 16, the right of an individual conferred by section 27(4) of the Act does not include a right to select a Queen's Counsel or more than one advocate.
(2) The relevant court may determine that the individual can select a Queen's Counsel or more than one advocate if the individual is—
(a) the subject of an extradition hearing under the Extradition Act 2003; and
(b) the relevant court determines that the individual could not be adequately represented except by a Queen's Counsel or more than one advocate.

In *Z* (9 October 2008 unreported, Leeds Crown Court), general guidance was given in relation to the grant of a certificate for two counsel in criminal cases.

(a) The fact that the prosecution were represented by two counsel had little bearing on whether the defence ought to have the same number.
(b) It is not enough that a case should involve substantial, complex or novel issues of law; the fundamental question for the court was why the case could not be presented by a single advocate.
(c) The identity of the proposed second advocate is not relevant.

(d) It will not usually be appropriate to decide on the level of representation until the prosecution case and defence case statement have been served.
(e) The application should state with some precision the work to be done by the second advocate and the reason why it cannot be done by a single advocate alone.
(f) The court expects both advocates to be present throughout the entire case, save where the trial judge grants a leave of absence.
(g) It is imperative that defendants receive the most appropriate representation; in cases where the criteria are met for leading counsel and junior that is the application that should be made. The financial benefit that comes from being a leading junior should not cloud that decision-making. The same principles apply to the use of inexperienced juniors.
(h) The court has the power to keep the need for two counsel under review and can amend the certificate at any time should it be appropriate to do so.

In *A-G's Ref (No. 82a of 2000)* [2002] EWCA Crim 215, [2002] 2 Cr App R 24 (342), the Court of Appeal held that the principle of equality of arms does not require that, where the Crown instructs leading counsel and the defence is being funded at public expense, the accused is entitled to be represented by leading counsel as well.

Criminal Legal Aid (Determinations by a Court and Choice of Representative) Regulations 2013, regs. 18 to 23

18.—(1) Subject to paragraphs (2) to (6), in relation to any criminal proceedings that are not before a magistrates' court, the right of an individual conferred by section 27(4) of the Act does not include a right to select a Queen's Counsel or more than one advocate.

(2) The relevant court may determine that an individual can select a Queen's Counsel if that individual's case involves substantial novel or complex issues of law or fact which could not be adequately presented except by a Queen's Counsel, and either—
(a) the exceptional condition is met; or
(b) the counsel condition is met.

(3) The relevant court may determine that an individual can select two junior advocates if that individual's case involves substantial novel or complex issues of law or fact which could not be adequately presented by a single advocate, including a Queen's Counsel alone, and either—
(a) the exceptional condition is met; or
(b) the prosecution condition is met.

(4) The relevant court may determine that an individual can select a Queen's Counsel and a junior advocate if that individual's case involves substantial novel or complex issues of law or fact which could not be adequately presented except by a Queen's Counsel assisted by a junior advocate and either—
(a) the exceptional condition is met; or
(b) the counsel condition and the prosecution condition are met.

(5) The relevant court may determine that an individual can select three advocates if the proceedings relate to a prosecution brought by the Serious Fraud Office and the relevant court determines that three advocates are required to represent the individual.

(6) If the proceedings described in paragraph (5) are in the Crown Court, that court must also determine that the individual's case involves substantial novel or complex issues of law or fact which could not be adequately presented by two junior advocates, or by a Queen's Counsel assisted by a junior advocate, and either—
(a) the exceptional condition is met; or
(b) the prosecution condition is met.

(7) In this regulation—

'the counsel condition' means, in relation to particular criminal proceedings, that a Queen's Counsel or senior Treasury Counsel has been instructed on behalf of the prosecution;

'the exceptional condition' means, in relation to particular criminal proceedings, that the individual's case is exceptional compared with the generality of cases involving similar offences;

'the prosecution condition' means, in relation to particular criminal proceedings, any of the following circumstances—

(a) two or more advocates have been instructed on behalf of the prosecution and the relevant court is satisfied that the individual will be, or will be likely to be, prejudiced if they too are not represented by two or more advocates;

(b) the number of prosecution witnesses exceeds 80;
(c) the number of pages of prosecution evidence exceeds 1000;
and
'prosecution evidence' means all witness statements, documentary and pictorial exhibits and records of interview with the individual and with any other defendants which form part of the served prosecution documents or are included in any notice of additional evidence.

19.—(1) A determination that an individual is entitled to select a Queen's Counsel or more than one advocate under regulation 18 may only be made by the following judges—
(a) subject to paragraph (2), in the course of a trial or a preliminary hearing, pre-trial review or plea and directions hearing, the judge who has been assigned as the trial judge;
(b) where a trial judge has not been assigned, by—
(i) a High Court judge; or
(ii) subject to paragraph (2), a resident judge of the Crown Court or, in the absence of a resident judge, a judge nominated by a resident judge of the Crown Court for the purpose of making such a determination; or
(c) where the proceedings are in the Court of Appeal, by the Registrar of Criminal Appeals, a High Court judge or a judge of the Court of Appeal.
(2) A determination made by a judge referred to in paragraph (1)(a) or (b)(ii) does not take effect unless it is approved by a presiding judge of the circuit or by a judge nominated by a presiding judge of the circuit for the purpose of giving such approval.

20. Nothing in regulation 18 permits an individual to select more than one Queen's Counsel.

21. For the purposes of making a determination under regulation 18, the relevant court may require from any advocate already assigned to the individual a written opinion on the representation needed to adequately present the case.

22.—(1) The Director may, upon the sending for trial of an individual, determine that the individual can select a Queen's Counsel without a junior advocate if the proceedings are a trial for murder.
(2) The Director may, upon receipt of a notice of an individual's case under section 51B of the Crime and Disorder Act 1998, determine that the individual can select a Queen's Counsel with one junior advocate if the prosecution is brought by the Serious Fraud Office.

23.—(1) The right of an individual conferred by section 27(4) of the Act does not include a right to select—
(a) two junior advocates, unless the relevant court determines that the individual could not be adequately represented by a junior advocate and a noting junior;
(b) a Queen's Counsel assisted by a junior advocate, unless the relevant court determines that the individual could not be adequately represented by a Queen's Counsel assisted by a noting junior;
(c) three junior advocates, unless the relevant court determines that the individual could not be adequately represented by two junior advocates and a noting junior;
(d) two junior advocates and a noting junior, unless the relevant court determines that the individual could not be adequately represented by a junior advocate and two noting juniors;
(e) a Queen's Counsel assisted by two junior advocates, unless the relevant court determines that the individual could not be adequately represented by a Queen's Counsel assisted by a junior advocate and a noting junior; or
(f) a Queen's Counsel assisted by a junior advocate and a noting junior, unless the relevant court determines that the individual could not be adequately represented by a Queen's Counsel assisted by two noting juniors.
(2) In this regulation 'noting junior' means a junior advocate whose instructions include (but are not limited to) taking a note of the proceedings.

An individual who faces proceedings that fall within the definition of very high cost criminal cases ('VHCC') does not have the absolute right to choose a representative to act for him or her. Only litigators, and in most cases advocates, who are accredited to carry out VHCC work may act in such proceedings. There is an obligation to report possible VHCC cases to the LAA under the Criminal Legal Aid (Remuneration) Regulations 2013 (SI 2013 No. 435), reg. 12, which also provides a sanction. **D32.16**

Criminal Legal Aid (Remuneration) Regulations 2013, reg. 12

(1) A litigator who has conduct of a case which is, or is likely to be classified as, a Very High Cost Case, must notify the Lord Chancellor in writing as soon as practicable.
(2) Where a litigator fails to comply with this regulation without good reason, and as a result there is a loss to public funds, the Lord Chancellor may refuse payment of the litigator's costs up to the extent of such loss.

(3) The Lord Chancellor must not refuse payment under paragraph (2) unless the litigator has been given a reasonable opportunity to show why the payment should not be refused.

The Criminal Legal Aid (Remuneration) Regulations 2013, reg. 2, defines a very high cost case as:

. . . a case in which a section 16 determination has been made and which the Director classifies as a Very High Cost Case on the grounds that—

(a) in relation to fees claimed by litigators—
   (i) if the case were to proceed to trial, the trial would in the opinion of the Director be likely to last for more than 40 days and the Director considers that there are no exceptional circumstances which make it unsuitable to be dealt with under an individual case contract for Very High Cost Cases made by the Lord Chancellor under section 2(1) of the Act; or
   (ii) if the case were to proceed to trial, the trial would in the opinion of the Director be likely to last no fewer than 25 and no more than 40 days and the Director considers that there are circumstances which make it suitable to be dealt with under an individual case contract for Very High Cost Cases made by the Lord Chancellor under section 2(1) of the Act;
(b) in relation to fees claimed by advocates, if the case were to proceed to trial, the trial would in the opinion of the Director be likely to last for more than 60 days and the Director considers that there are no exceptional circumstances which make it unsuitable to be dealt with under an individual case contract for Very High Cost Cases made by the Lord Chancellor under section 2(1) of the Act.

Appeals against Refusal of Representation

D32.17 Where an applicant for the grant of a representation order is refused, the provisions for appeal are contained in the Criminal Legal Aid (General) Regulations 2013.

Criminal Legal Aid (General) Regulations 2013, regs. 28 to 30

28. Where an individual remains dissatisfied following a review under regulation 27, that individual may appeal to a court in accordance with regulations 29 and 30 against the decision that the interests of justice do not require, or no longer require, representation to be made available.

29.—(1) In relation to a determination by the Director under section 16 of the Act that the interests of justice do not require, or no longer require, representation to be made available before the magistrates' court, the appeal lies to the magistrates' court.

(2) The court must either—
   (a) affirm the determination; or
   (b) decide that the interests of justice require representation to be made available, or to continue to be made available, to an individual for the purposes of criminal proceedings.

(3) Where the court makes a decision under paragraph (2)(b), the individual may apply to the Director for a determination.

(4) Where an individual applies to the Director under paragraph (3)—
   (a) if the individual states in writing, verified by a statement of truth, that the individual's financial resources have not changed since the date of the individual's original application for a determination, so as to make the individual financially ineligible for representation under section 21 of the Act (financial resources) and regulations made under that section, the Director must make a determination that the individual qualifies for representation; or
   (b) if the individual's financial resources may have so changed since the date of the individual's original application, the Director—
      (i) must determine whether the individual qualifies for representation in accordance with section 21 of the Act and regulations made under that section; and
      (ii) if the individual does so qualify, must make the determination accordingly.

(5) In this regulation—
'magistrates' court' means the magistrates' court in which the proceedings in respect of which an individual is seeking a determination under section 16 of the Act are taking place, or are to take place, and includes a single justice and a District Judge (magistrates' court); and

'statement of truth' means a declaration provided in accordance with regulations made under section 21 of the Act (financial resources).

30.—(1) In relation to a determination by the Director that the interests of justice do not require, or no longer require, representation to be made available in a case in the Crown Court, the appeal lies to an officer of the Crown Court ('the officer').

(2) The officer may refer the appeal to a judge of the Crown Court.

(3) The officer or the judge may—

(a) affirm the determination; or

(b) decide that the interests of justice require representation to be made available, or to continue to be made available, to an individual for the purposes of criminal proceedings.

(4) Where the officer or a judge makes a decision under paragraph (3)(b), the Director must make a determination reflecting that decision and record the determination in a representation order.

FUNDING OF JUDICIAL REVIEW, APPEAL BY WAY OF CASE STATED AND CERTAIN CIVIL AND CONTEMPT PROCEEDINGS

Work undertaken in relation to judicial review of criminal proceedings is not treated as being incidental to those proceedings. **D32.18**

However, appeals by way of case stated are covered within the definition of criminal proceedings. Verbal or written advice following conviction and, if appropriate, an application for representation in the High Court is treated as incidental to the lower court proceedings and should be claimed as part of representation in those proceedings.

If there is no representation order in force, advice and assistance can be given in the appeals and review class of work under the terms of the standard crime contract 2017 (as amended).

The POCA 2002 contains a range of civil measures designed to deprive criminals of the proceeds from criminal conduct. Cases involving earlier legislation continue to have effect in appropriate cases. Limited funding under civil legal aid is available and can be undertaken by providers working under the standard crime contract 2017 as 'Associated Civil Work'. **D32.19**

To be eligible for civil legal aid, the type of work must appear in sch. 1 to the LASPO 2012 and not be excluded. Judicial review and habeas corpus are covered subject to exclusions but only work related to the following sections of the POCA 2002 is covered: ss. 41, 47M, 54(3), 62, 67A, 72, 73, 361, 362, 369 and 375 (public funding is not available in relation to cash forfeiture in the magistrates' court).

Civil legal aid is available, including for advocacy (Legal Aid, Sentencing and Punishment of Offenders Act 2012 (Amendment of Schedule 1) (Advocacy Exceptions) Order 2014 (SI 2014 No. 3305)), for civil proceedings in the youth court in relation to civil injunctions (under the ABCPA 2014) and gang injunctions (under the PCA 2009). This extends to appeals to the Crown Court in such proceedings (SI 2014 No. 3305). **D32.20**

Where there is a contempt of court (other than in the face of the court) in the county court (*Brown v London Borough of Haringey* [2015] EWCA Civ 483, [2017] 1 WLR 542), the High Court (*King's Lynn and West Norfolk Council v Bunning* [2013] EWHC 3390 (QB), [2015] 1 WLR 531) or the Court of Appeal (*Devon County Council v Kirk* [2016] EWCA Civ 1221, [2017] 4 WLR 36), and whether the proceedings are criminal, civil or family, criminal legal aid is available as of right under the Criminal Legal Aid (General) Regulations 2013, reg. 9(v)). The work must be undertaken by a firm with a standard crime contract or an individual case contract. Respondents to committal proceedings in courts other than the magistrates' court are entitled to non-means-tested legal aid (*H v T* [2018] EWHC 1310 (Fam), [2018] 4 WLR 122, approved by *Re O (Committal: Legal Representation)* [2019] EWCA Civ 1721, [2019] 4 WLR **D32.21**

140, considering the Criminal Legal Aid (Financial Resources) Regulations 2013 (SI 2013 No. 471), reg. 17). Applications for legal aid in the High Court should be made to the Nottingham Office of the Legal Aid Agency; applications in relation to the Court of Appeal are made to that court (*All England Lawn Tennis Club (Championships) Ltd v McKay* [2019] EWHC 3065 (QB), [2020] 1 WLR 216).

D32.22 Criminal legal aid is also available on the same basis for breach of an anti-social behaviour injunction, which is treated as a contempt of court.

TOPPING UP CRIMINAL LEGAL AID FEES

D32.23 Once legal aid has been granted, the LASPO 2012, s. 28, provides:

> (2) A person who provides services under arrangements made for the purposes of this Part must not take any payment in respect of the services apart from—
> (a) payment made in accordance with the arrangements, and
> (b) payment authorised by the Lord Chancellor to be taken.

The standard crime contract issued by the LAA (specification, para. 8.43) allows for payment, provided that an application for prior authority to incur that expenditure has been refused and express authority has been obtained from the client, to:

(a) prepare, obtain or consider any report, opinion or further evidence, whether provided by an expert witness or otherwise; or
(b) obtain or prepare any transcripts or recordings of any criminal investigation or proceedings, including police questioning; or
(c) instruct counsel other than where an individual is entitled to counsel (as may be determined by the court) in accordance with the Criminal Legal Aid (Determinations by a Court and Choice of Representative) Regulations 2013, regs. 16 and 17. (This paragraph is wider than the Criminal Legal Aid (Remuneration) Regulations 2013, reg. 9, which restricts payments to (a) and (b), but appears to amount to an authority within the LASPO 2012, s. 28. Regulations 16 and 17 apply only in relation to magistrates' court proceedings.)

These provisions were considered in *Banfield* [2014] EWCA Crim 1824, which held that a case is 'legally aided' where an advocate has been granted a representation order and the litigator cannot recover private remuneration for the work covered in the same case.

Section D33 Costs

POWERS TO AWARD COSTS

The power of the courts to award costs in criminal proceedings is contained in ss. 16 to 21 of the Prosecution of Offences Act 1985, supplemented by the Costs in Criminal Cases (General) Regulations 1986 (SI 1986 No. 1335). The Prosecution of Offences Act 1985, s. 16, deals with limited costs out of central funds in favour of an acquitted accused, known as 'defendant's costs orders'; s. 17 deals with prosecution costs out of central funds; s. 18 with orders that a convicted accused pay prosecution costs; s. 19 with awards of costs in other circumstances (such as when a party to proceedings incurs costs as a result of an unnecessary or improper act or omission by another party, and in relation to witnesses, intermediaries and certain advocacy services); s. 19A with orders that legal or other representatives pay any wasted costs; and s. 19B with awards of costs against third parties. A detailed commentary on the costs in criminal cases is contained in the *Practice Direction (Costs in Criminal Proceedings)* [2015] EWCA Crim 1568, as amended by *Practice Direction (Costs in Criminal Proceedings) 2015 Amendment No. 1* [2016] EWCA Crim 98. CrimPR Part 45 sets out the procedural rules in relation to a wide range of costs orders, including those described in this section. **D33.1**

While an application under the CJPA 2001, s. 59, in relation to property seized by the police is an application in a criminal cause or matter, there is no jurisdiction to make an order for costs as the Crown Court Rules 1982 no longer apply to such proceedings and there is no inherent jurisdiction to do so, and there is no other statutory authority (*R (Chaudhury) v Crown Court at Bristol (No. 2)* [2015] EWHC 723 (Admin), [2016] 1 WLR 631).

Costs as a Sanction

CrimPR 3.5(6) (see Supplement, R3.5) provides for sanctions in respect to breach of the rules: **D33.2**

> If a party fails to comply with a rule or a direction, the court may—
> (a) fix, postpone, bring forward, extend, cancel or adjourn a hearing;
> (b) exercise its powers to make a costs order; and
> (c) impose such other sanction as may be appropriate.

Costs of a Witness Summons

Under the Criminal Procedure (Attendance of Witnesses) Act 1965, s. 2, there is a power to award costs to a person who successfully applies to set aside an order for a witness summons. This power was considered in *DLA Piper UK LLP v BDO LLP* [2013] EWHC 3970 (Admin), [2014] 1 WLR 4425. The Divisional Court held that the statute had a lacuna: no costs could be awarded to a party who successfully resists the original application for a summons but costs may be awarded to a successful applicant to set aside such an order provided that person was not notified of the original application. The Court stated that there is no inherent jurisdiction to make a costs order and no order could be made against the solicitors acting as they had not been guilty of any act or omission that would have justified a wasted costs order. **D33.3**

Costs in the High Court

D33.4 Costs from Central Funds are not available for a successful case stated in the Administrative Court because of the provisions of the Prosecution of Offences Act 1986, s. 16A.

The same applies to a successful application to discharge an extradition order (Extradition Act 2003, s. 62B). The civil costs regime does not apply because the Prosecution of Offences Act 1986, s. 16A, displaces the general discretion in the Senior Courts Act 1981, s. 28A(3), and the exceptional circumstances set out in *Murphy v Media Protection Services Ltd* [2012] EWHC 529 (Admin) do not apply to a routine road traffic matter (*Lord Howard of Lympne v DPP* [2018] EWHC 100 (Admin), [2019] RTR 4 (33)). In *Darroch v Football Association Premier League Ltd* [2016] EWHC 1220 (Admin), [2017] 4 WLR 6, the Court of Appeal held, *obiter*, that there was no power under the Senior Courts Act 1981, s. 51(1), for the Divisional Court to grant a third party costs order in relation to cases in the magistrates' court or Crown Court, on either a case stated or application for judicial review to quash a conviction. In *R (Bahbahani) v Ealing Magistrates' Court* [2019] EWHC 1385 (Admin) the Administrative Court confirmed that only in exceptional circumstances should the civil, rather than the criminal, costs regime apply to appeals by way of case stated or judicial review proceedings.

However, in *Hunt* [2020] EWHC 1292 (Admin), [2020] 4 WLR 81, the Court held that, in exceptional circumstances, a claimant may recover, as incidental costs in judicial review proceedings, the costs of an intervention in criminal proceedings which decided the very point in issue.

The Court of Appeal has no power to make a defendant's costs order in respect of legal costs save in limited circumstances relating to a defendant who has been found not guilty by reason of insanity, or has been found unfit to stand trial, or having been found unfit to stand trial, has been found to have done the act or made the omission alleged. The Court can award an amount in respect of legal costs in relation to the costs of an individual defendant in proceedings in the court below. On an appeal under the CJA 1987, s. 9(11) (appeals against orders or rulings at preparatory hearings), and on applications by the A-G, the Court of Appeal may not make an order for payment of costs from central funds. Personal expenses may be awarded (Prosecution of Offences Act 1985, s. 16(4A)).

Costs of a Special Advocate

D33.5 The costs of a special advocate, appointed to deal with disclosure, should be met by the party claiming public interest immunity (*Re R (Closed Material Procedure: Special Advocates: Funding)* [2017] EWHC 1793 (Fam), [2018] 1 WLR 163).

Indemnity Insurance

D33.6 In the context of an indemnity agreement, 'criminal proceedings' includes work done during the criminal investigation, and the contract is not invalidated by the doctrine *ex turpi causa*, which does not apply to the costs of representation in criminal proceedings, but only to the payment of any penalty imposed (*Coulson v News Group Newspapers Ltd* [2012] EWCA Civ 1547).

ENTITLEMENT TO RECOVER COSTS

D33.7 Solicitors must check the funding methods available to clients or risk losing their entire costs. In *McDaniel & Co. (a firm) v Clarke* [2014] EWHC 3826 (QB), [2014] 6 Costs LR 963, trade union funding would have been available for the claim but the claimant was not advised of its availability. As a consequence, the bill of costs tendered to the claimant was assessed at nil. The same principle applies in criminal cases, where eligibility under legal aid and relevant insurance policies, whether home or director and officer, must be considered.

DEFENDANT'S COSTS ORDERS

Jurisdiction to Make a Defendant's Costs Order

In any of the situations listed below the appropriate court may make a defendant's costs order in favour of a successful accused or, as the case may be, appellant. The effect of a defendant's costs order is that the defence costs are paid out of central funds (see CrimPR 45.4; Supplement, **R45.4**). However, this entitlement under the Prosecution of Offences Act 1985, s. 16, was substantially reduced by the LASPO 2012, as was the value of the orders which continue to be available, limiting them to legal aid rates. **D33.8**

The Prosecution of Offences Act 1985, s. 16A, defines the circumstances in which an individual who is a successful defendant but not in receipt of legal aid may recover reasonably incurred costs. Costs may be awarded only to individuals and, except in Supreme Court proceedings, not to companies or other bodies. Any recovery is always limited to legal aid rates (Costs in Criminal Cases (General) Regulations 1986, reg. 7(7)). That limitation on rates also applies to expert's fees in the proceedings (s. 16A(10)).

If a defendant is successful in a case sent or transferred to the Crown Court, the proceedings are instituted by voluntary bill, or are remitted to the Crown Court by the Court of Appeal, recovery of costs is conditional upon the defendant having applied for and having been refused legal aid.

These rules also apply to applications by the A-G to the Court of Appeal, extradition proceedings and Courts Martial.

Under the Prosecution of Offences Act 1985, s. 16(1), where an information is not proceeded with, or the accused is acquitted after a trial, the court with the power to make a defendant's costs order is the court which acquits the accused. The fact that the court would not have tried the case because the information was laid out of time does not prevent the court from making a defendant's costs order (*Patel v Blakey* [1988] RTR 65). The phrase 'not proceeded with' is wide enough to encompass proceedings that have been stayed as an abuse of process (*R (R E Williams and Sons) v Hereford Magistrates' Court* [2008] EWHC 2585 (Admin)). This would also extend to proceedings that were discontinued as a result of the defendant receiving a police caution (*R (Stoddard) v Oxford Magistrates' Court* [2005] EWHC 2733 (Admin)), or being bound over to keep the peace (*Emohare v Thames Magistrates' Court* [2009] EWHC 689 (Admin)). There is power to award costs in relation to pre-charge work, e.g., in relation to providing advice and assistance at a police station provided that the advice was related to the proceedings (*R (Hale) v North Sefton Justices* [2002] EWHC 257 (Admin)). In *Liverpool Magistrates' Court, ex parte Abiaka* (1999) 163 JP 497, the Divisional Court held that s. 16(1) gave power to any constitution of the magistrates' court to make a defendant's costs order, and was not confined to the same constitution of justices who had dismissed the case. **D33.9**

Under s. 16(2) of the Prosecution of Offences Act 1985, where an accused is not tried for an offence for which he or she has been sent for trial (or in respect of which notice of transfer has been given), or the accused is tried on indictment and acquitted on any count in the indictment, the Crown Court has jurisdiction to make a defendant's costs order, not only to allow for costs during those proceedings but also in respect of proceedings in the lower court.

Under s. 16(3) of the 1985 Act, where an accused convicted in the magistrates' court appeals against conviction and it is set aside by the Crown Court, or the accused appeals against sentence and is awarded a less severe punishment by the Crown Court, the Crown Court may make a defendant's costs order (subject to the legal aid cap).

An order under s. 16 is based on the indemnity principle. Section 16(6) provides that:

> A defendant's costs order shall, subject to the following provisions of this section, be for the payment out of central funds, to the person in whose favour the order is made, of such amount as the court considers reasonably sufficient to compensate him for any expenses *properly incurred by him* in the proceedings. (emphasis added)

Thus the defendant must have a liability to meet the costs involved. *Miller* [1983] 1 WLR 1056 confirms that such a liability may exist even though the costs had initially been met by a third party, such as an employer, insurance company or trade union, and that a liability to repay may be assumed in the absence of evidence that there was indeed no such liability.

A court may revisit a defendant's costs order where there had been a material non-disclosure, and then revoke an order where a claim has been fraudulently inflated (*Patel (Hitendra)* [2016] EWCA Crim 2001, [2017] 1 Costs LR 77).

In relation to both appeals by way of case stated and judicial review proceedings, the criminal costs rules under the Prosecution of Offences Act 1985, s. 16, should apply, and not the civil costs regime, unless there are exceptional circumstances requiring a different course (*R (Bahbahani) v Ealing Magistrates' Court* [2019] EWHC 1385 (Admin), where an interested party had sought, but failed, to recover the higher costs available under the Senior Courts Act 1981, s. 51).

Orders in Civil Proceedings in Magistrates' Courts

D33.10 There is no power to award costs under the Prosecution of Offences Act 1985, s. 16, in respect of proceedings commenced by way of complaint (as opposed to charge, requisition or information), such as alleged breaches of community orders or civil proceedings under the POCA 2002. Costs in those proceedings, when properly claimable, are governed by the MCA 1980, s. 64, if the case proceeds to a conclusion, or by the Courts Act 1971, s. 52, if the case is not proceeded with. Both sections are to be interpreted in the same way (*Chief Constable of Warwickshire Police v Young* [2014] EWHC 4213 (Admin); *Chief Constable of Warwickshire Police v MT* [2015] EWHC 2303 (Admin)) and require the court to determine the amount of the costs that it thinks are just and reasonable. The principles were established in *Bradford Metropolitan District Council v Booth* (2000) 164 JP 485:

1. Section 64(1) confers a discretion upon a magistrates' court to make such order as to costs as it thinks just and reasonable. That provision applies both to the quantum of the costs (if any) to be paid, but also as to the party (if any) which should pay them.
2. What the court will think just and reasonable will depend on all the relevant facts and circumstances of the case before the court. The court may think it just and reasonable that costs should follow the event, but need not think so in all cases...
3. Where a complainant has successfully challenged before justices an administrative decision made by a police or regulatory authority acting honestly, reasonably, properly and on grounds that reasonably appeared to be sound, in exercise of its public duty, the court should consider, in addition to any other relevant fact or circumstances, both (i) the financial prejudice to the particular complainant in the particular circumstances if an order for costs is not made in his favour; and (ii) the need to encourage public authorities to make and stand by honest, reasonable and apparently sound administrative decisions made in the public interest without fear of exposure to undue financial prejudice if the decision is successfully challenged.

Those principles were considered in *R (Perinpanathan) v City of Westminster Magistrates' Court* [2010] EWCA Civ 40, [2010] 1 WLR 1508 (see **D8.25**), where it was made clear that there is not the normal presumption that the unsuccessful party will pay the successful party's costs. This was the case even when there had been no active investigation, as an explanation for the presence of the moneys was required (*Bennett v Chief Constable of Merseyside* [2018] EWHC 3591 (Admin)). Indeed such an order will not usually be made unless the authority had acted dishonestly or unreasonably (see, e.g., *Chief Constable of Sussex v Taylor* [2013] EWHC 1616 (Admin) where the police had pursued an allegation of blackmail which had resulted in an acquittal in criminal proceedings).

Proper Approach to Making of a Defendant's Costs Order

D33.11 The Prosecution of Offences Act 1985, s. 16, merely empowers courts to make defendants' costs orders but gives no guidance on when and how the power should be exercised. Such guidance is, however, provided by the *Practice Direction (Costs in Criminal Proceedings)* [2015] EWCA Crim 1568, as amended by *Practice Direction (Costs in Criminal Proceedings) 2015 Amendment No. 1* [2016] EWCA Crim 98.

The *Practice Direction* applies whenever a magistrates' court, the Crown Court, Divisional Court or the Court of Appeal considers an award of costs in criminal proceedings. Paragraph 2.1.1 makes it clear that magistrates' courts may make defendant's costs orders, whether sending the proceedings to the Crown Court for trial or dealing summarily with an offence. In deciding whether to make an order, magistrates' courts should take into account the same factors as the Crown Court (see below).

Paragraphs 2.1.1 (magistrates' courts) and 2.2.1 (Crown Court) of the *Practice Direction* stipulate that, where s. 16 of the Act applies, an order should normally be made 'unless there are positive reasons for not doing so'. An example for not making an order is that 'the defendant's own conduct has brought suspicion on himself and has misled the prosecution into thinking that the case against him was stronger than it was'; in such a case, 'the defendant can be left to pay his own costs'. In *R (Rees) v Snaresbrook Crown Court* [2012] EWHC 3879 (Admin) the Divisional Court expressed the view *obiter* that this was not an exclusive list and thought an order might also be refused if, though acquitted, the defendant had committed perjury or relied on an ambush defence. Paragraph 2.1.1 (magistrates' courts) makes it clear that the decision whether to make an order under s. 16 'is a matter in the discretion of the court in the light of the circumstances of each particular case', effectively reducing the scope for challenging a refusal to make an order under s. 16. Paragraphs 2.1.1 and 2.2.1 state that the court, if it declines to make a costs order, should explain that the reason for not making an order does not involve any suggestion that the defendant is guilty of any criminal conduct but that the order is being refused because of a particular positive reason, which should be specifically identified. Paragraph 2.4.3 of the *Practice Direction* provides that where the Court of Appeal has jurisdiction to make an order under s. 16, it will have in mind the principles applied by the Crown Court in relation to acquitted defendants.

When considering whether the defendant brought the prosecution on him or herself, the court is entitled to rely on a statement of facts from the prosecution. Thus, the court does not have to hear oral evidence on this matter (*Mooney v Cardiff Justices* (2000) 164 JP 220). **D33.12**

In *R (Stoddard) v Oxford Magistrates' Court* [2005] EWHC 2733 (Admin), the defendants were charged with selling alcohol to an under-age purchaser. After considerable delay, the prosecution indicated that they were willing to conclude the proceedings by way of a formal caution, and the defendants accepted that offer. The charges were subsequently dismissed, with the prosecution offering no evidence. The defendants applied for a defendant's costs order under s. 16, but the application was refused. The Divisional Court held that a caution is not to be equated with a conviction. Although by accepting a formal caution a defendant is acknowledging having committed the alleged offence, and the existence of the caution can be drawn to the attention of a court on a subsequent occasion, it can be distinguished from a conviction since a defendant does not receive a criminal record, there is no penalty, and no risk of publicity. It follows that, where a prosecution is withdrawn following the acceptance by the accused of a caution, the defendant stands acquitted for the purposes of the making of a defendant's costs order under s. 16.

In *R (Spiteri) v Basildon Crown Court* [2009] EWHC 665 (Admin) the applicant successfully reviewed a refusal to make a defendant's costs order on the grounds that he was acquitted on a 'technicality'. It was held that a costs order could not be refused on the sole ground that the applicant had brought the proceedings upon himself, as more was required, such as the defendant having misled the prosecution as to the strength of the case against him. A similar point arose in *Dowler v MerseyRail* [2009] EWHC 558 (Admin), where the Divisional Court ruled that courts should give reasons for a refusal contemporaneously with the ruling. **D33.13**

In *R (Harry A Coff Ltd) v Environment Agency* [2003] EWHC 1305 (Admin), a district judge declined to make a defendant's costs order under s. 16 on the ground that the amount sought was unreasonable on its face and the court should not allow costs that reflect extravagance. The Divisional Court held that the district judge was wrong to refuse to make a defendant's costs order on this basis. What had been asked for was an order for costs to be assessed. It would therefore be for the person subsequently assessing the costs to determine whether the costs claimed were excessive. Where the Crown would not accept a proposal from the defence to be bound over to keep the peace until it became apparent, on the day of trial, that the complainant would not give evidence, it was wrong for the judge to limit the amount of the defendant's costs order to the cost of that day alone (*Newcombe v CPS* [2013] EWHC 2160 (Admin)).

Costs should not be denied merely because the prosecution acted properly in bringing the case. See, e.g., *Birmingham Juvenile Court, ex parte H* (1992) 156 JP 445, where the defence solicitor admitted that the prosecution was not malicious, but the Divisional Court held that this was no reason for the justices to refuse to make a defendant's costs order.

D33.14 The ECHR can also be relevant to the way in which costs applications are dealt with. In *Hussain v UK* (2006) 43 EHRR 22 (437), counsel for the Crown informed the court that a key witness did not want to give evidence and that the prosecution did not feel that she ought to be compelled to give evidence; accordingly, they offered no evidence. D was duly acquitted. An application was made for a defendant's costs order under s. 16. The trial judge stated that there was compelling evidence against D on the court papers and that the court was not going to exercise its discretion to make an order for costs in D's favour. The ECtHR noted the presumption of innocence enshrined in the ECHR, Article 6(2), and that there was no conduct by D which could have brought him within the sort of cases in which a costs order might be refused, and no suggestion that he was in any way responsible for the non-attendance of the witness. The only natural interpretation which could be put on the trial judge's words was that the court was refusing the order because it was of the view that, although D had been acquitted, he was in fact guilty of the offence. That was incompatible with the presumption of innocence. For a detailed review of the ECHR jurisprudence, see *Ashendon v UK* (2012) 54 EHRR 13 (433).

D33.15 **Partial Acquittal** Paragraphs 2.1.1 and 2.2.2 of the *Practice Direction*, as amended so as to take full account of amendments to the Prosecution of Offences Act 1985, deal with the situation where an accused is acquitted on some but not all charges or counts. The Prosecution of Offences Act 1985, s. 16(2)(b), expressly allows a defendant's costs order to be made in such cases. Paragraph 2.2.2 provides that the court may order that only part of the costs incurred be paid (see also s. 16(7) of the Act). The court 'should make whatever order seems just having regard to the relative importance of the two charges and the conduct of the parties generally'. The same approach applies in magistrates' courts (para. 2.1.1).

D33.16 **Costs on Crown Court Appeal** Paragraph 2.2.3 of the *Practice Direction*, as amended, points out that the Crown Court may make a defendant's costs order in favour of a successful appellant. In *R (Barrington) v Preston Crown Court* [2001] EWHC Admin 599, D was convicted in the magistrates' court of failing to provide a breath specimen. There was an appeal to the Crown Court. At the Crown Court, the prosecution offered no evidence after a crucial witness failed to attend. The conviction was quashed. However, the judge refused an application for a defendant's costs order. On review, it was held that, having regard to the fact that the case collapsed not because of anything D had said or done, or any misleading behaviour on her part, but simply because a prosecution witness had failed to attend court, an application for a defendant's costs order should have been successful. Similarly, in *R (Cunningham) v Exeter Crown Court* [2003] EWHC 184 (Admin), [2003] 2 Cr App R (S) 64 (374), the Divisional Court reiterated that, where the Crown Court allows an appeal from the magistrates' court, the successful defendant should be awarded costs under s. 16 unless there are positive reasons for not doing so. Where the court takes the view that there are such reasons for not awarding costs, it should set out its reasons for coming to that view (albeit briefly, but in sufficient detail that the defendant can see the basis for the decision). In *R (Pluckrose) v Snaresbrook Crown Court* [2009] EWHC 1506 (Admin) the Divisional Court ruled it appropriate to deny costs to a successful appellant whose appeal had been allowed as an act of mercy.

Effect of Defendant's Costs Order

D33.17 The effect of a defendant's costs order is that the accused or appellant is paid costs out of central funds. 'Proceedings' include any there may have been in a court below that making the costs order (see the definition of 'proceedings' in s. 21(1)). Thus, where the Crown Court on trial on indictment or appeal from the magistrates makes a defendant's costs order, the order will cover the costs of the sending proceedings or summary trial. Paragraph 1.3.1 of the *Practice Direction* provides that, where the court is sitting in an appellate capacity, the order 'will include the costs incurred in the proceedings in the lower courts unless for good reason the court directs that such costs are not included in the order'.

The term 'costs' covers only expenses properly incurred in the proceedings; it cannot include expenses that do not relate directly to the proceedings themselves, such as loss of earnings (see para. 1.3.1 of the *Practice Direction*). Paragraph 1.3.1 goes on to note that where the party in whose favour the costs order is made is funded by legal aid, he or she will only recover 'personal costs' (Prosecution of Offences Act 1985, s. 21(4A)(a)).

If the accused agrees, the amount payable under s. 16(6) may be fixed forthwith, or it may be taxed (*Practice Direction (Costs in Criminal Proceedings)* [2015] EWCA Crim 1568, para. 1.4.1). Courts will generally decline to award a fixed sum with respect to costs unless it is both modest and not contentious. In either case the claim must be determined in accordance with regulations made by the Lord Chancellor (s. 16(9)(b)). The relevant provisions are Part III (regs. 4 to 13) of the Costs in Criminal Cases (General) Regulations 1986. These provide in essence that the 'appropriate authority' (or officers appointed to act on the appropriate authority's behalf) shall consider the claim for costs submitted by or on behalf of the accused, and shall allow costs not exceeding prescribed maxima in respect of work that appears to have been actually and reasonably done and disbursements that have been actually and reasonably incurred (reg. 7). Regulation 7(6), which applies to legal proceedings involving individuals who are not eligible for legal aid, provides that, in such proceedings, if the amount of an award out of central funds is not fixed by the court, any amount payable in respect of legal costs must be calculated in accordance with rates or scales or other provision made by the Lord Chancellor, whether or not that results in the fixing of an amount that the appropriate authority considers reasonably sufficient or necessary to compensate the person. The amount payable is calculated at the current appropriate legal aid rates. The 'appropriate authority' is (a) the Registrar in the case of Court of Appeal proceedings; (b) the Master of the Crown Office in the case of Divisional Court proceedings; (c) an officer appointed by the Lord Chancellor in the case of Crown Court and magistrates' court proceedings. Save in relation to magistrates' court proceedings, an applicant (i.e. any person in whose favour an order for costs out of central funds has been made) who is dissatisfied with the appropriate authority's decision as to the amount of the costs payable may first apply for redetermination by the authority. If the result of that is unsatisfactory, there is an appeal to a costs judge, and a further appeal to the High Court if a point of principle of general importance is involved (regs. 9 to 12). The procedure on appeal to the High Court against the decision of a costs judge is set out in the *Practice Direction (Costs in Criminal Proceedings)* [2015] EWCA Crim 1568, para. 5.5. The above provisions for redetermination and appeal do not apply where the costs determined are in respect of magistrates' courts proceedings (see reg. 9), but the decision of the justices' clerk may be challenged by judicial review in accordance with the usual principles governing such applications. **D33.18**

The requirement that the payment be reasonably sufficient to compensate the defendant was met when the lawyers dealt with the matter proportionately and when approval was given at each stage by insurers notwithstanding that an estimate was exceeded. The full recovery of costs in such circumstances did not offend the indemnity principle (*Orrow* [2011] 3 Costs LR 519). **D33.19**

R (McCormick) v Liverpool City Magistrates' Court [2001] 2 All ER 705 concerned costs incurred before legal aid was granted. D did not have the means to pay those costs. It was held that costs are incurred by an accused for the purpose of s. 16(6) if the accused is contractually obliged to pay for them; there is no requirement to prove that those costs had in fact been, or were likely to be, paid. Agency fees may be claimed as a disbursement when a reasonable payment can be recovered, subject to the statutory limits now in place. However they may also be claimed, at appropriate fee earner rates, as profit costs and are required to be so claimed by the Standard Crime Contract 2017. The decision in *Murray* [2013] 5 Costs LR 867 suggesting otherwise is inconsistent with a series of earlier decisions (*Duxbury* [1997] Costs LR (Core Vol) 423; *Pullum*

[1997] Costs LR (Core Vol) 413; *Smith and Graham v Lord Chancellor* [1999] All ER (D) 957). The decision in *Murray* fails to acknowledge that the issue is the contractual liability accepted by the client to the principal firm and not the liability incurred by that firm.

Murray confirms that a former senior solicitor, requalified as a barrister, may recover hourly remuneration at the rate appropriate to a senior solicitor.

Orders for Less than the Full Costs Incurred

D33.20 By the Prosecution of Offences Act 1985, s. 16(6A), where the court making a defendant's costs order is of the opinion that there are circumstances making it inappropriate for the accused to recover the full amount of the costs that would otherwise be assessed payable under s. 16(6), it shall assess what amount would be just and reasonable and specify it in the order. One obvious situation for fixing the costs at less than the full amount is where an accused is acquitted on some but not all the counts on the indictment (see **D33.13**).

In *Dudley Magistrates' Court, ex parte Power City Stores Ltd* (1990) 154 JP 654, where D wanted to recover the cost of employing leading counsel, the Divisional Court held that, in calculating the amount of costs to be paid under s. 16, the officer doing the assessment has to carry out a two-stage test. First, it must be considered whether the expenses claimed were properly incurred by the defendant. If so, the second step is to ask what amount would be reasonably sufficient to compensate the defendant for those costs. The test is whether the defendant acted reasonably in instructing that counsel. There are cases in which junior counsel or a solicitor could conduct the case, but in which it is reasonable to instruct leading counsel. In *R (Hale) v North Sefton Justices* [2002] EWHC 257 (Admin) it was held that the question was whether D had acted reasonably in the circumstances by instructing a solicitor at a particular hourly rate, not whether he could have instructed a more junior solicitor. In that case, the justices' clerk had applied the statutory criterion of reasonable sufficiency in s. 16(6) to the wrong issue, namely the quality of representation, rather than the costs incurred.

Order in Favour of a Publicly Funded Accused

D33.21 By the Prosecution of Offences Act 1985, s. 21(4A)(a), the costs of a publicly funded accused shall *not*— for purposes of a defendant's costs order — be taken to include any costs of representation under the LASPO 2012, Part 1 (legal aid). It follows that a defendant's costs order will generally be pointless in the case of such an accused since all the legal costs properly incurred on the accused's behalf will have been defrayed out of legal aid, and there will be nothing left on which the order can bite. A costs order will, however, be appropriate if, for example, the accused was not aided until a late stage of the proceedings and paid for the costs of early representation privately, or if there were unusual expenditures incurred on the accused's behalf which were not authorised by the Legal Aid Agency. That an order can be made in relation to costs incurred before legal aid was granted is confirmed by *Gittins* [2007] EWCA Crim 806, [2007] 4 Costs LR 549.

The effect of s. 21(4A)(a) is that, save in a minority of exceptional cases, defendant's costs orders are relevant only to accused who have paid for their defences privately or who have been allowed to 'top up' legal aid fees (see **D32.23**). In *Lamb* [2011] 6 Costs LR 1092 D was allowed costs even though a representation order, held by his previous solicitors, had in error not been formally discharged. However, where the same firm continues to act privately for a client who has the benefit of a representation order, the effect of the Criminal Legal Aid (Remuneration) Regulations 2013 (SI 2013 No. 435), reg. 9, is that payment cannot be recovered from central funds for legal expenses incurred until the representation order is withdrawn notwithstanding the agreement of the client (*McCatty* [2013] 5 Costs LR 863). Every accused can, as a result of a defendant's costs order, become entitled to an allowance for travelling and subsistence, as if the accused had been a witness.

In *Brewer v Secretary of State for Justice* [2009] EWHC 987 (QB), [2009] 3 All ER 861 the Divisional Court held that a publicly funded defendant was able to recover payments made to a third party for professional services as out-of-pocket expenses. Whether such payments would be recoverable depended upon (i) the profession of the person instructed and the services provided, (ii) the reason why it was necessary and reasonable to incur the expenditure, and (iii) why the work was not paid for under the representation order in force. In cases where the expenditure claimed was outside the norm, the person claiming should assist the court by providing full details of the heads of expenditure.

Appeals and Reviews in Relation to Defence Costs Orders

If a magistrates' court refuses to make a defence costs order, an application may be made by way of judicial review. In some circumstances this will also apply to a Crown Court appeal from the lower court. In *R (DPP) v Aylesbury Crown Court* [2017] EWHC 2987 (Admin), [2018] 1 Cr App R 22 (325) it was held, qualifying *Hunter v Crown Court at Newcastle* [2013] EWHC 191 (Admin), [2014] QB 94, that the High Court will consider applications for judicial review, notwithstanding the Senior Courts Act 1981, s. 29(3), in relation to orders for costs made during a trial on indictment when the decision raises issues going to jurisdiction of sufficient gravity to take the case out of the jurisdiction of the Crown Court. In *R (DPP) v Aylesbury Crown Court* the Divisional Court held that there was no jurisdiction under the Prosecution of Offences Act 1985, s. 19, to order the Crown to meet the costs of the defence because of any failure by an expert instructed by the prosecution. **D33.22**

There is, however, no right of appeal to the Court of Appeal.

PROSECUTION COSTS

Power to Make Order for Prosecution Costs from Central Funds

Subject to what follows, the Prosecution of Offences Act 1985, s. 17(1), provides that the court may award a prosecutor such amount out of central funds as it considers reasonably necessary to compensate for any expenses properly incurred in the proceedings (see CrimPR 45.4; Supplement, **R45.4**). This applies whether or not the accused is convicted, but applies only to proceedings in respect of an indictable offence (whether tried summarily or on indictment) and proceedings before a Divisional Court in respect of a summary offence (s. 17(1)(a) and (b)). An important restriction on the ambit of s. 17(1) is that no order may be made in favour of a public authority (s. 17(2)), which term is defined by s. 17(3) as comprising a police force, the CPS, local authorities and any other authority appointed by the Crown or financed by money voted by Parliament. Thus, s. 17(1) is of potential value in prosecutions brought by private individuals or organisations. Where the subsection does potentially apply, an order *should* be made unless there is good reason for not doing so; e.g., the proceedings have been instituted or continued without good cause (see *Practice Direction (Costs in Criminal Proceedings)* [2015] EWCA Crim 1568, para. 2.6.1). It appears that other proper out of pocket expenses should be recovered as expenses properly incurred (and cf. *Brewer v Secretary of State for Justice* [2009] EWHC 987 (QB), [2009] 3 All ER 861 at **D33.21**). Even so, an express application must be made, rather than assuming that the court will automatically order costs of its own motion (para. 2.6.1). **D33.23**

The principles to be applied when a court is considering an application for prosecution costs under s. 17 were summarised in *R (Wollenberg) v Crown Court at Southwark* [2020] EWHC 1915 (Admin) at [8]:

(i) the general rule is that costs should be paid from central funds, unless a lesser sum is appropriate; the amount of costs to be paid are those that the court considers to be reasonably sufficient to compensate the prosecutor for any expenses properly incurred;
(ii) there is a discretion to decline to make an order if, for example, the prosecution was started or continued unreasonably;
(iii) or there is some other good reason for not doing so; examples include where proceedings have been instituted or continued without good cause or there has been misconduct;
(iv) whilst those examples are given in the Practice Direction and in the rules, they are not determinative of the extent of the discretion upon whether to refuse costs to the prosecution. The touchstone is objective reasonableness and proper conduct. Therefore, if the prosecution have behaved unreasonably and/or improperly then the court may refuse to award costs from central funds. Whether the private prosecutor's conduct of the prosecution can be reasonably described as unreasonable or improper is essentially a fact specific question: each case will depend on its own facts.

The judge held that the refusal in *Wollenberg* was not such as to raise issues going to jurisdiction of sufficient gravity to allow the High Court to intervene in relation to a trial on indictment (see **D33.22**).

Regulations 4 to 13 of the Costs in Criminal Cases (General) Regulations 1986 apply to assessment of prosecutors' costs out of central funds as they apply to costs under defendant's costs orders. Under earlier regulations, it was held that a private prosecutor could not claim for the time spent in preparation and presentation of the prosecution, although the prosecutor was entitled to recover travelling and secretarial expenses (*Stockport Magistrates' Court, ex parte Cooper* (1984) 149 JP 261). Legal expenses can be recovered when a private prosecutor is represented; these are paid at private client rates. The Criminal Cases Unit of the Legal Aid Authority has issued guidance confirming that the costs of investigation should not be recovered.

In *Zinga (Costs) (Practice Note)* [2014] EWCA Crim 1823, [2015] 1 Cr App R 2 (14) the Court of Appeal carried out a review of the amounts properly payable from central funds to a private prosecutor. It emphasised that the hourly rates used may be subject to competitive bids to enable the market to set the appropriate rate.

Issues surrounding the quantum of costs payable to private prosecutors were considered in *Fuseon Ltd v Senior Courts Costs Office* [2020] EWHC 126 (Admin). The Administrative Court acted in its inherent jurisdiction to put right 'real injustice', as the Senior Courts Costs Office had refused to grant a certificate that the case involved a point of general importance. Reviewing earlier authorities the Court held that the prosecutor had made sufficient efforts to find a suitably qualified local firm of solicitors to bring the case. The test was not whether a local firm might competently have conducted the case but rather whether it was reasonable in the circumstances to instruct a London firm, with the higher hourly rates involved. While all parties accepted that in accordance with the decision in *Supreme Court Taxing Office, ex parte John Singh and Co.* [1997] 1 Costs LR 49, the court could stand back and review the overall cost of the prosecution, it was wrong to limit the claim only to the costs that would have been incurred had the matter been brought by the CPS. The private prosecutor had contacted the police and CPS who declined to take on the matter. The right of private persons to bring a prosecution was an important constitutional principle and the Regulations should be interpreted to protect their financial position.

In appeal proceedings, prosecutors bringing an unsuccessful appeal, but one that clarified the relevant law, should receive only part of their costs (*RSPCA v McCormick* [2016] EWHC 928 (Admin), [2016] 1 WLR 2641).

In *Murphy v Media Protection Services Ltd* [2012] EWHC 529 (Admin), [2013] Costs LR 16 a private prosecutor was denied costs recovery as the prosecution was essentially advanced to protect commercial interests (satellite broadcast of football matches) and the litigation had been conducted in a manner indistinguishable from litigation in the civil courts where a substantial sum of money is involved.

In *Somaia* [2019] EWHC 1227 (QB) the Divisional Court confirmed that a private prosecutor cannot recover the costs of enforcing a confiscation order in the High Court because the Prosecution of Offenders Act 1985, s. 17, does not apply to civil proceedings even if they are consequential on criminal proceedings.

Order that the Accused Pay Prosecution Costs

D33.24 The Prosecution of Offences Act 1985, s. 18(1) and (2), and the Costs in Criminal Cases (General) Regulations 1986, reg. 14, authorise the making of orders that a convicted accused or unsuccessful appellant or person in breach of a court order, prison licence or post-release supervision shall pay costs to the prosecutor, or where the appellant is unsuccessful in the Court of Appeal to the prosecutor or other named third party (see CrimPR 45.5 and 45.6; Supplement, **R45.5** and **R45.6**). In addition, reg. 14 provides, *inter alia*, that the Prosecution of Offences Act 1985, s. 18, is to apply to proceedings in the Crown Court on committals for sentence (including committals to be dealt with for breach of a suspended sentence, probation order or conditional discharge) just as it applies to trials on indictment. In short, the Crown Court when dealing with the committed offender may order him or her to pay costs.

In *Hamilton-Johnson v RSPCA* [2000] 2 Cr App R (S) 390, the issue was whether the Crown Court had jurisdiction to order a defendant who appealed unsuccessfully from the magistrates' court to the Crown Court to pay to the prosecutor sums by way of costs which the magistrates had refused to award to the prosecutor. The Court of Appeal (Civil Division) concluded that the Crown Court had the requisite jurisdiction to make such an order, but should hesitate before doing so as the magistrates would be far better placed to decide the issue.

In *Constantine* [2010] EWCA Crim 2406, [2011] 1 WLR 1086 the Court of Appeal held that prosecution costs ought not to be ordered until any issue of confiscation under the POCA 2002 had been resolved, but this was effectively overruled in *Darroch v A-G for the Isle of Man* [2019] UKPC 31, where the Privy Council held that the time-limit of 28 days in the POCA 2002, s. 15(4), for the making of a costs order when confiscation proceedings have been postponed, cannot be extended. In *D Ltd v A* [2017] EWCA Crim 1604, a private prosecutor recovered, against individual defendants, the costs of a successful appeal to the Court of Appeal against a terminating ruling. The Court commented that the sums involved should not differ substantially from those incurred by a public prosecutor and had to take account of each defendant's individual financial circumstances. The sums were to be paid at the end of the trial.

Amount of Order against the Defendant for Prosecution Costs

When a court makes an order under the Prosecution of Offences Act 1985, s. 18, for the payment of prosecution costs, it orders the payment of an amount that it considers 'just and reasonable'. That sum must be specified in the order (s. 18(3)). The court may not delegate (e.g., to a justices' clerk or Crown Court officer) the duty of determining what the accused should pay (*Bunston v Rawlings* [1982] 2 All ER 697), although it may seek assistance from the Criminal Cases Unit of the Legal Aid Authority or Registrar of Criminal Appeals (*Practice Direction (Criminal Proceedings: Costs)* [2015] EWCA Crim 1568, para. 1.2.4). While the CPS publish average costs for proceedings brought by them, other prosecutors and claimants must justify the amount claimed and its connection to the particular prosecution; they cannot rely on a general agreement with the court (*R (Nicolson) v Tottenham Magistrates* [2015] EWHC 1252 (Admin)). In *Rahal* [2017] EWCA Crim 1779 the Court of Appeal confirmed that where a local authority properly brought proceedings for obtaining services (a tenancy) by deception, it should be paid its reasonable costs, and was not limited to rates published by the CPS. However, the use of two counsel in this case was not reasonable. **D33.25**

The prosecution should, if possible, be able to inform the court of the costs that have been incurred at each stage of the relevant proceedings, thus enabling the court to make an appropriate order. Where the prosecution are unable to provide a figure forthwith, the court should adjourn for inquiries to be made by an appropriate officer.

When seeking an order for costs against a defendant, the prosecution must give notice to the defendant of their intention to apply for such an order (*Emmett* (1999) *The Times*, 15 October 1999).

In *Associated Octel Ltd* [1997] 1 Cr App R (S) 435, the Court of Appeal held that the costs of the prosecution for the purposes of s. 18(1) might include the costs of the prosecuting authority in carrying out investigations. In *Octel*, the offence was both investigated and prosecuted by the Health and Safety Executive. The position would be different where different bodies investigated and prosecuted (e.g., the police and the CPS respectively). It would not seem to be 'just and reasonable' for the court to order the defendant to pay the prosecution in respect of costs for which it was not liable.

In *Balshaw v CPS* [2009] EWCA Crim 470, [2009] 1 WLR 2301 the Court of Appeal held that the proposition in *Associated Octel Ltd* [1997] 1 Cr App R (S) 435 should not be taken too far and that the CPS need not show a contractual liability to the third party to pay costs. In that case the prosecution made clear that it was intended that they would be reimbursing the police for costs occasioned in relation to a forensic accountant's report. The Court held:

> Since the CPS was, thereby, acknowledging its obligation to pay any award of those fees to the police in respect of the report and the report formed an important part of the CPS's presentation of the case, the judge was correct to conclude that the order was just and reasonable.

As to the procedure to be adopted in cases where the prosecution seeks an order requiring the defendant to pay costs, the Court of Appeal observed that:

(a) the prosecution should serve on the defence, at the earliest time, full details of its costs, so as to give the defence a proper opportunity to consider them and make representations on them, if appropriate;
(b) if the defendant, once served with a schedule of the prosecution's costs, wished to dispute the whole or any part of the schedule, he should give proper notice to the prosecution of the objections which it was proposed to make and should at least make it clear to the court what the objections were — in some exceptional cases, a full hearing would need to be held for the objections to be resolved, as there was no provision for the taxation of the prosecution's costs in a criminal case.

It was confirmed in *R (Donovan) v Burnley Crown Court* [2014] EWHC 742 (Admin) that the costs of housing animals pending an appeal cannot amount to investigation costs (and so be costs of the case) within the meaning of *Associated Octel*, but that there is a specific power under the Animal Welfare Act 2006, s. 21, to apply to the court for directions as to expenses arising pending appeal.

D33.26 In *Bow Street Stipendiary Magistrate, ex parte Multimedia Screen Ltd* (1998) *The Times*, 28 January 1998, D sought judicial review of a costs order requiring him to pay £15,000 although he had made only a tiny profit from the offence of which he was convicted. The Divisional Court held that the prosecution had had to do a lot of research and so the order was appropriate. In most cases, precise assessment of prosecution costs will be irrelevant, since the principles discussed below as to the exercise of the court's discretion in the making of orders will result in the amount the accused is required to pay being well below the actual costs, however restrictively interpreted.

Section 18(1) is subject to two specific qualifications. First, where a person is, on summary conviction, fined £5 or less, no order for costs may be made 'unless in the particular circumstances of the case [the court] considers it right to do so'. Secondly, where a child or young person is convicted before a magistrates' court, the amount of any costs the child or young person is ordered to pay shall not exceed the amount of any fine imposed (s. 18(5)). It is submitted that, where a child or young person is dealt with by means other than a fine, the costs that may be awarded against the child or young person are entirely discretionary and not subject to any statutory upper limit.

Proper Approach to Orders that the Accused Pay Prosecution Costs

D33.27 Paragraph 3.4 of the *Practice Direction (Costs in Criminal Proceedings)* [2015] EWCA Crim 1568 states that an order should be made under the Prosecution of Offences Act 1985, s. 18, where the court is satisfied that the offender or appellant has the means and ability to pay. This is the fundamental principle governing costs against the accused and merely confirms pre-existing case law; in *Mountain* (1978) 68 Cr App R 41, Lawton LJ said that when imposing financial penalties, including costs, the court must have regard to the means of a convicted person. Similarly, in *Nottingham Justices, ex parte Fohmann* (1986) 84 Cr App R 316, the Divisional Court quashed an order by magistrates that D pay a fine of £400 (for offences of obtaining by deception by turning back the odometers on cars he was selling at auction) and prosecution costs of £600, since he was in receipt of benefit and, even if able to maintain the rate of £10 per week ordered by the court, would have taken two years to pay the combined fine and costs. Glidewell LJ indicated that the amount of costs ordered should not exceed that which the offender can reasonably pay within a year. The case also illustrates that the propriety or otherwise of the decision on costs must be viewed in the light of the overall financial orders made by the court, in particular, any fines or compensation the offender is required to pay. This principle was clearly stated by Phillimore LJ in *Whalley* (1972) 56

Cr App R 304 at p. 305: 'This Court takes the view that whenever a court is imposing a financial penalty, or making an order in regard to costs, it must have regard to the means of the individual.'

To make an order such that a sale would be required of a matrimonial home being used by an adult child with Asperger's syndrome was unreasonable (*Pegley* [2012] EWCA Crim 2583).

Although *Ex parte Fohmann* remains important for its statement of principle, the suggested time-limit of a year for payment of costs may no longer be appropriate in view of the Court of Appeal having held that fines and compensation may now be fixed at amounts requiring payment by instalments over a two or even three-year period (see **E15.21** and **E16.8**). In *Reilly* [2017] EWCA Crim 2240 the Court of Appeal held, reducing the payment period at the same rate from 50 to 30 months, that while there is no strict limit to the period over which costs orders should be payable, there is a need to impose periods which are proportionate only. The Magistrates' Court Sentencing Guidelines recommend payment periods dependent on the band in which the fine is fixed.

In deciding whether the offender has sufficient means to pay an order for costs, mortgage debts should be taken into account (*Ghadami* [1998] 1 Cr App R (S) 42).

In *Northallerton Magistrates' Court, ex parte Dove* [2000] 1 Cr App R (S) 136, the Divisional Court gave the following series of guidelines on the imposition of costs.

(1) The order to pay costs should never exceed the sum which the offender is able to pay, and which it is reasonable to expect the offender to pay, having regard to his or her means and any other financial order imposed.
(2) Nor should it exceed the sum which the prosecutor has actually and reasonably incurred.
(3) The purpose of such an order is to compensate the prosecutor and not to punish the offender, e.g., for exercising the constitutional right to defend him or herself.
(4) Any costs ordered should not in the ordinary way be grossly disproportionate to any fine imposed. Where the fine and the costs exceeded the sum which the offender could reasonably be ordered to pay, the costs should be reduced, rather than the fine.
(5) An offender facing a fine or an order as to costs should disclose to the magistrates the data relevant to his or her financial position, so that they can assess what the offender can reasonably afford to pay. Failure to make such disclosure could lead the court to draw reasonable inferences as to the offender's means.
(6) The court should give the offender a fair opportunity to adduce any relevant financial information and make submissions prior to the determination of any financial order.

In *Nuthoo* [2010] EWCA Crim 2383, [2011] 1 Costs LR 87 the Court of Appeal added the following guideline (at [12]):

> . . . a costs order is to be enforced as if it had been adjudged to be paid on conviction in the magistrates' court . . . ; that it is the duty of the court to consider the defendant's means . . . ; that it is the court that has the power to allow an individual to pay by instalments . . . ; that in default of payment, imprisonment will be imposed, in this case up to a maximum of six months . . . ; and that therefore, in order to avoid sending an offender to prison by the back door, and to ensure that the length of time over which the order would be paid is not oppressive, the amount and length of time for payment must be just, albeit that a period of up to three years for payment in an appropriate case is not necessarily too long.

Applying paras. 3.6 and 3.7 of the *Practice Direction (Costs in Criminal Proceedings)* [2015] EWCA Crim 1568, in *Adedeji* [2019] EWCA Crim 804, [2019] 4 WLR 136, the Court of Appeal held that the following guidelines should be applied:

(a) The prosecution must serve full details of its costs in good time so that the defence may make appropriate representations.
(b) The costs must be broadly proportionate to the financial sanction imposed and must not exceed the actual costs incurred.
(c) The decision should take into account that the prosecution may be seeking to defer costs such as staff wages that were routine and would have been incurred in any event.

D

Part D Procedure

D33.28 **Plea** A plea of guilty does not preclude the making of an order for costs. However, combined with other factors such as the offender's limited means, it may persuade the court not to make an order or to make one for considerably less than the actual costs (*Matthews* (1979) 1 Cr App R (S) 346). The weight to be attached to the plea in this context will depend, *inter alia*, on the stage at which it was entered and the gravity of the case (*Maher* [1983] QB 784).

D33.29 **Remainder of the Sentence** Where the offender is given an immediate custodial sentence it is unusual to impose an order for costs, if only because the offender will for the time being have no income out of which to make the required payments. But, again, it is ultimately a matter for the court's discretion. Thus, if there is good reason to suppose that the offender has substantial capital assets (in particular if they are the proceeds of crime), an order may properly be made (see, e.g., *Maher* [1983] QB 784). Where the sentence is non-custodial, one line of authority suggests that any order for costs should not be out of proportion to the penalty proper. The Court of Appeal has considered on a number of occasions the question whether the court should make an order for the payment of prosecution costs which is larger than the fine imposed for the offence itself. For example, in *Whalley* (1972) 56 Cr App R 304, an order to pay the whole costs of prosecuting a drink-driving offence, for which W had been disqualified and fined £20, was reduced to an order to pay costs not exceeding £50. Similarly, in *Firmston* (1984) 6 Cr App R (S) 189, costs of £400 ordered following D's conviction on indictment for theft from a shop were reduced to £100 because he had been given an absolute discharge for the offence itself. These cases were cited in *Boyle* [1995] Crim LR 514, in which the Court of Appeal nonetheless decided to follow instead the case of *Bushell* (1980) 2 Cr App R (S) 77. Their lordships upheld an order to pay £1,000 prosecution costs where D had been fined £250 after electing trial on indictment when the case could conveniently have been tried summarily; in such a case, which was otherwise appropriate for an order for him to pay prosecution costs, D could properly be ordered to pay costs on the Crown Court scale. In a level 1 fine case a costs order for £6,871 was grossly disproportionate notwithstanding the complexity of prosecuting the case and a late guilty plea (*R (Middleton) v Cambridge Magistrates' Court* [2012] EWHC 2122 (Admin).

D33.30 **Conduct of the Defence** At least in theory, an offender who is found guilty on indictment of an either-way offence should not be punished in costs for having exercised the constitutional right to trial by jury (*Hayden* [1975] 2 All ER 558). However, any order made will inevitably reflect the fact that the more expensive method of trial was chosen (*Hayden*, and see also *Bushell* (1980) 2 Cr App R (S) 77 where orders to pay £250 costs against each of two accused were upheld because, even though the offence was merely one of obtaining services worth £21 and the fines imposed were only £100, they had elected Crown Court trial in a matter eminently suitable for summary disposition and thus greatly increased the costs incurred by the prosecution). The exercise of the court's discretion may also be affected by the accused having chosen to plead not guilty when the prosecution case was manifestly strong and the accused must have known all along that he or she was guilty (see dicta in *Singh* (1982) 4 Cr App R (S) 38 where an order of £400 costs against D following conviction on indictment for a minor assault occasioning actual bodily harm was upheld partly because he had 'extravagantly' elected trial on indictment when there was 'really no need in the circumstances' to do so). The relevance of the reasonableness of the defence (albeit disbelieved) to costs was also referred to, *obiter*, by Lawton LJ in *Mountain* (1978) 68 Cr App R 41 (at pp. 43–4, emphasis added):

> In many cases at the trial the accused says, as he is entitled to say and frequently is justified in saying, that there has been some mistake on the part of the prosecution witnesses; that they have confused themselves in thinking that they saw something which they did not see, that their memories have failed them or that the accused has some explanation for what at first sight seems to be criminal conduct. *In that class of case it may be unfair to make an order that the accused should pay the costs of the prosecution.* But there are other kinds of cases which come before the Crown Court where the defence is that everybody except the accused is telling lies and that the prosecution's case is virtually a concocted one....
>
> It is in that kind of case that courts are entitled to make an order that the accused should pay the costs of the prosecution.

Conduct of the Prosecution Where a minor case is in the Crown Court through the prosecution's choice, they cannot expect to recover their full costs from the accused. In *Hall* (1988) 10 Cr App R (S) 456, H was willing to plead guilty to careless driving. The case went to the Crown Court because the prosecution insisted on a charge of reckless (now 'dangerous') driving. In the Crown Court, H pleaded guilty to careless driving, and the Crown offered no evidence on the reckless driving charge. H was conditionally discharged and ordered to pay £372 prosecution costs. On appeal, the order was reduced to £25 (the amount appropriate to a guilty plea in the magistrates' court at the time). See also *Clark* (1993) 14 Cr App R (S) 360. **D33.31**

Apportionment between Co-defendants Where there is more than one accused, each should be liable only for that portion of the prosecution's costs which is attributable to him or her. In *Ronson* [1991] Crim LR 794, the appellant and two co-defendants were each ordered to pay a third of the prosecution costs (£440,000 each). The fourth defendant was unable to pay. On appeal, the Court of Appeal held that the right approach was to see what would be a reasonable estimate of the cost of trying each defendant alone. That could not be done here. It was not right that the three defendants who could pay should bear the burden of the fourth. The costs of each defendant were reduced from a third to a quarter. Thus, the court should divide the total amount payable between the number of defendants (not just those who are able to pay) so that each defendant pays only his or her own share of the costs and does not subsidise a defendant who cannot pay (see also *D Ltd v A* [2017] EWCA Crim 1604). However, in *Harrison* (1993) 14 Cr App R (S) 419, the Court of Appeal upheld an order made against only one of a number of defendants, who was the principal offender (the other defendants having played relatively minor roles in the offences) and had the means to pay the amount ordered. In *Durose* [2004] EWCA Crim 2188, it was argued by counsel that the court had power to make an order for costs which imposed joint and several liability. The court did not hear full argument on the point but said that their 'instinctive reaction' was that that is not an appropriate kind of order to make in a criminal case. The point was left open for decision in a later case. That the correct question was to ask, in relation to each defendant, what would have been the costs had the defendant been tried alone was confirmed in *R (Gray) v Aylesbury Crown Court* [2013] EWHC 500 (Admin), [2014] 1 WLR 818, but subject to an overriding discretion if no figures could easily be identified. **D33.32**

APPEALS ON COSTS

Neither party has a right of appeal to the Crown Court in respect of a costs order made by a magistrates' court: the prosecution have no right of appeal to the Crown Court, and the MCA 1980, s. 108(3)(b), precludes a defence appeal to the Crown Court against a costs order. However, it was held in *Hamilton-Johnson v RSPCA* [2000] 2 Cr App R (S) 390, that the Crown Court does have jurisdiction on an appeal to make an order as to costs incurred before the conclusion of the magistrates' court proceedings (either under the Prosecution of Offences Act 1985, s. 18(1), or the Senior Courts Act 1981, s. 48(2)). But, following an unsuccessful appeal against conviction, the Crown Court should hesitate to modify the magistrates' costs order. If the prosecutor wishes to seek an increase in the costs the defendant has to pay, the prosecutor should give written notice to this effect to the defendant, so that the defendant is aware of the possible consequences of pursuing an appeal against conviction. **D33.33**

Coleman [2016] EWCA Crim 1665, [2017] 4 WLR 29 confirms that where a defendant's means have declined so that the defendant can no longer afford to pay an order for prosecution costs, the Court of Appeal will not interfere. There is no procedure similar to a certificate of inadequacy. Rather the matter should be dealt with during enforcement proceedings in the magistrates' court as that court has considerable power to enforce, vary or remit the amount due (MCA 1980, Part III, and Crim PR Part 30). If a party wishes to appeal a final order in judicial review proceedings it must meet the requirements in *R (RA) v DPP* [2017] EWHC 714 (Admin), [2017] 2 Costs LR 323, especially if it did not participate in the proceedings. It must give a good reason for that, act promptly on learning of the final order, and show a real prospect of success.

ORDERS AGAINST A PARTY TO PAY COSTS THROWN AWAY

D33.34 The Prosecution of Offences Act 1985, s. 19(1) and (2), empower the Lord Chancellor to make regulations by virtue of which a party to criminal proceedings may be ordered to pay costs thrown away as a result of the party's 'unnecessary or improper act or omission' (see CrimPR 45.8; Supplement, **R45.8**). Section 19 cannot be construed as conferring a discretion to make a costs order in favour a person who is not a party to criminal proceedings, nor can it be read as a provision giving a general discretion to make a costs order based on the outcome of proceedings. As a result, journalists who had successfully resisted an application for a production order could not recover their costs (*Channel 4 Television Corporation v Metropolitan Police Commissioner* [2019] 1 Costs LR 67). Regulation 3 of the Costs in Criminal Cases (General) Regulations 1986 provides that, before making such an order, the court shall hear the parties concerned, and shall take into account any other order as to costs which has been made in the proceedings (reg. 3(2)). Conversely, when the time comes to make a general order as to costs, the court shall take into account any order that has already been made under reg. 3 (reg. 3(4)). The amount to be paid by the 'guilty' party must be specified in the order (reg. 3(3)). In the case of a child or young person who has been convicted of an offence, any sum ordered to be paid by a magistrates' court under reg. 3 shall not exceed the amount of any fine imposed (reg. 3(5)). If, during the period of an adjournment, the prosecution serves a notice of discontinuance, the court retains jurisdiction to determine applications for costs (*DPP v Denning* [1991] 2 QB 532). Save when there is a notice of discontinuance, an order for costs under the Prosecution of Offences Act 1985, s. 19, cannot be made once the case has concluded (*Quayum v DPP* [2015] EWHC 1660 (Admin)).

For an order as to costs to be made under reg. 3, there must be a causal relationship between the unnecessary or improper act, and the incurring of the costs to be paid under the order (*Wood Green Crown Court, ex parte DPP* [1993] 2 All ER 656). The court in *DPP v Denning* defined an act as unnecessary or improper if events would not have occurred if the party had conducted itself properly. A mere mistake without repetition can be grounds for a costs order under s. 19. If additional costs arise from the prosecution not conducting the case properly, it is not an answer to be unsure whether the fault lies with the CPS or the police as the prosecution's responsibility is indivisible. However, s. 19 contains a discretion not a duty and, where there is a satisfactory explanation, no order should be made (*R (Singh) v Ealing Magistrates' Court* [2014] EWHC 1443 (Admin)).

The test set out in *DPP v Denning* was doubted in *R (DPP) v Crown Court at Sheffield* [2014] EWHC 2014 (Admin), [2014] 1 WLR 4639. The Divisional Court held that a judge has no jurisdiction to use s. 19 as a means of impugning the prosecutorial discretion given to the DPP, but suggested *obiter* that the test under s. 19 as to what was improper or unnecessary was more demanding than that in *DPP v Denning* and should meet the level set in *Ridehalgh v Horsefield* [1994] Ch 205 (see **D33.44**). However, that case was concerned with the costs jurisdiction against representatives rather than a party to the proceedings, and in *R (DPP) v Aylesbury Crown Court* [2017] EWHC 2987 (Admin), [2018] 1 Cr App R 22 (325) the Divisional Court accepted that Parliament had chosen different wording for the two provisions so that they must have a different meaning, preferring the reasoning in *DPP v Denning* and *Evans v SFO* [2015] EWHC 263 (QB), [2015] 1 WLR 3595 (see **D33.35**).

D33.35 The conflict of authority was considered in *Evans v SFO*. Hickinbottom J held that the principles established in cases on s. 19A and the wasted cost jurisdiction could not be carried over and applied to s. 19, and set out (at [148]) the following principles:

i) When any court is considering a potential costs order against any party to criminal proceedings, it must clearly identify the statutory power(s) upon which it is proposing to act; and thus the relevant threshold and discretionary criteria that will be applicable.

ii) In respect of an application under section 19 of the 1985 Act, a threshold criterion is that there must be 'an unnecessary or improper act or omission' on the part of the paying party, i.e. an act or omission which would not have occurred if the party concerned had conducted his case properly or which could otherwise have been properly avoided.
iii) In assessing whether this test is met, the court must take a broad view as to whether, in all the circumstances, the acts of the relevant party were unnecessary or improper.
iv) Recourse to cases concerning wasted costs applications under section 19A or its civil equivalent, such as *Ridehalgh*, will not be helpful. Similarly, in wasted costs applications under section 19A, recourse to cases under section 19 will not be helpful.
v) The section 19 procedure is essentially summary; and so a detailed investigation into (e.g.) the decision-making process of the prosecution will generally be inappropriate.
vi) Each case will be fact-dependent; but cases in which a section 19 application against a public prosecutor will be appropriate will be very rare, and generally restricted to those exceptional cases where the prosecution has acted in bad faith or made a clear and stark error as a result of which a defendant has incurred costs for which it is appropriate to compensate him. The court will be slow to find that such an error has occurred. Generally, a decision to prosecute or similar prosecutorial decision will only be an improper act by the prosecution for these purposes if, in all the circumstances, no reasonable prosecutor could have come to that decision.

All the relevant jurisprudence was considered in *Cornish* [2016] EWHC 779 (QB) and the following principles were found to be relevant (at [16]): **D33.36**

(a) Simply because a prosecution fails, even if the defendant is found to have no case to answer, does not of itself overcome the threshold criteria of s. 19...
(b) Improper conduct means an act or omission that would not have occurred if the party concerned had conducted his case properly...
(c) The test is one of impropriety, not merely unreasonableness... The conduct of the prosecution must be starkly improper such that no great investigation into the facts or decision-making process is necessary to establish it...
(d) Where the case fails as a matter of law, the prosecutor may be more open to a claim that the decision to charge was improper, but even then, that does not necessarily follow because 'no one has a monopoly of legal wisdom, and many legal points are properly arguable'...
(e) It is important that s. 19 applications are not used to attack decisions to prosecute by way of a collateral challenge, and the courts must be ever vigilant to avoid any temptation to impose too high a burden or standard on a public prosecuting authority in respect of prosecution decisions...
(f) In consequence of the foregoing principles, the granting of a s. 19 application will be 'very rare' and will be 'restricted to those exceptional cases where the prosecution has made a clear and stark error as a result of which a defendant has incurred costs for which it is appropriate to compensate him'.

The wording in (f) should be contrasted with that in *DPP v Denning* [1991] 2 QB 532, which established the principle at (b) above that 'improper does not necessarily connote some grave impropriety'. It should be noted that both *Evans v SFO* and *Cornish* were concerned with the total costs of a failed prosecution. However, more common is the situation where a party fails to comply with a particular court order, or individual hearings are unnecessary, or it should only have been necessary to carry out part of the work, had the 'guilty' party conducted itself to the standard required by *DPP v Denning* [1991] 2 QB 532.

These principles are likely to result in more orders where unnecessary expense is incurred for one of those reasons. It is suggested that a failure to comply with a court order will normally be improper.

The principles in *Evans v SFO* and *Cornish* apply to private prosecutions. While there will likely be more room for questioning the initiation and conduct of a private prosecution, neither the loss or withdrawal of the proceedings will be enough to justify an order (*R (Haigh) v City of Westminster Magistrates' Court* [2017] EWHC 232 (Admin), [2017] 1 Costs LR 175).

In *Leicester Crown Court, ex parte Commissioners of Customs and Excise* (2001) *The Times*, 23 February 2001, the prosecution had refused to disclose some documents and there was an **D33.37** application to stay the trial as an abuse of process. The prosecution offered no evidence and the judge ordered verdicts of not guilty to be recorded. The judge ordered the prosecution to pay the defence costs incurred. The Divisional Court held that, under reg. 3 of the Costs in Criminal Cases Regulations 1986, the judge must:

- consider whether there had been an unnecessary or improper act or omission by, or on behalf, of the prosecution;
- determine whether the costs that were incurred by the defendants were as a result of that unnecessary or improper act or omission;
- decide whether, as a matter of discretion, to order all or part of the costs to be paid by the party in default.

It is implicit in the last stage that, before an order can be made, the judge is required to identify the costs incurred as a result of the unnecessary or improper act or omission.

Having performed those exercises, the judge must specify the amount to be paid. In the present case, the judge had not complied with reg. 3. However, as the decision was not one made without jurisdiction, since the judge was entitled to make a costs order once seised of the issue of whether the relevant documents had been disclosed, the High Court had no jurisdiction to reconsider the judge's decision on an application for judicial review in relation to a case heard on indictment.

A party cannot be liable for any costs arising from a failure by an expert witness instructed by the party. Under CrimPR 19.2 (see Supplement, **R19.2**) the duty of an expert witness is owed to the court (*R (DPP) v Aylesbury Crown Court* [2017] EWHC 2987 (Admin), [2018] 1 Cr App R 22 (325)).

In *DPP v Bury Magistrates' Court* [2007] EWHC 3256 (Admin) the Divisional Court considered the position of a party to proceedings who had failed, in accordance with the duty under CrimPR Part 3, to report the opposing party for breach of the rules. An adjournment could have been avoided if the breach had been reported. The Court held that, when assessing the quantum of any loss, a court would consider taking into account the failings of the party seeking to claim a loss.

Where a defendant was prosecuted and convicted of an offence that did not exist, costs under reg. 19 were awarded from the time the prosecution were put on notice that they should identify the basis for the prosecution and were at risk as to costs if they failed to do so. In *Najib and Sons Ltd v CPS* [2018] EWCA Crim 1554, [2018] 4 WLR 144 that occurred at the oral hearing for leave to appeal. When quashing a magistrate's decision to issue a summons in a private prosecution, the High Court should:

(a) determine the cost in the court below;
(b) make a full order when the claimant received all the remedies sought, notwithstanding that there was no determination on one ground;
(c) make an order on an indemnity basis where there was a breach of the fundamental duty of candour and the claim was continued on an inappropriate basis (*R (Kay) v Leeds Magistrates' Court* [2018] EWHC 2842 (Admin), [2018] 6 Costs LR 1317.

In *R (Holloway) v Harrow Crown Court* [2019] EWHC 1731 (Admin), [2020] 1 Cr App R 8 (171) a private prosecutor was held to be at risk of a finding of improper conduct under the Prosecution of Offences Act 1986, s. 19, when he sought no legal advice and did not approach the police before bringing criminal proceedings. It might lead to an inference of a wish to proceed whatever the prospects of success and without an objective analysis of the sufficiency of the evidence.

While the court may not delegate the making of the order for a specific amount, it may seek assistance from the Criminal Cases Unit of the Legal Aid Authority or Registrar of Criminal Appeals. The parties must provide assistance (*Practice Direction (Costs in Criminal Proceedings) 2015 Amendment No. 1* [2016] EWCA Crim 98, para. 4.1.6).

WITNESS EXPENSES AND FEES FOR COURT-APPOINTED LAWYERS

Section 19(3) of the Prosecution of Offences Act 1985 empowers the Lord Chancellor to make regulations authorising the payment out of central funds of (a) witness expenses, (b) the cost of obtaining medical reports, (c) the fees of an interpreter, (d) the proper fee or costs of a person appointed under the Criminal Procedure (Insanity) Act 1964, s. 4A, to put the case for the defence and (e) the fees, costs and expenses of a legal representative appointed under the YJCEA 1999, s. 38(4), to cross-examine a witness where the Act prevents a defendant undertaking that cross-examination in person. Part V of the Costs in Criminal Cases (General) Regulations 1986 (regs. 15 to 25) deals with such payments, including setting the rates for general expert and professional witnesses. An anomaly arises in the Court of Appeal because the costs will be limited to legal aid rates if the appeal succeeds but not if it fails (Prosecution of Offences Act 1985, s. 16A(4)). **D33.38**

Roberts [2019] EWCA Crim 1270, [2019] 2 Cr App R 33 (402) confirms that an order in favour of legal representatives of costs under the Prosecution of Offences Act 1985, s. 19(3), is appropriate at the Crown Court and in the Court of Appeal once a defendant has been found unfit to plead under the Criminal Procedure (Insanity) Act 1964, s. 4. Legal aid should not be granted in those circumstances.

By reg. 16(1), the expenses properly incurred by the witness or, as the case may be, maker of a medical report, or interpreter required because of the accused's lack of English, are to be allowed out of central funds unless the court directs otherwise. This applies whatever the outcome of the proceedings and regardless of whether the witness etc. is required by the prosecution or defence. A non-expert witness (other than police or prison officers) is entitled to travelling expenses, a subsistence allowance and a loss allowance (e.g., for loss of earnings) (see reg. 18). Payment of professional witnesses, experts, suppliers of medical reports and interpreters is dealt with in regs. 19 and 20. If a defendant's costs order is made in favour of the accused, a subsistence allowance and travelling expenses may also be allowed, but the accused is not entitled to compensation for loss of earnings (reg. 23). See also paras. 2.5.1 and 2.5.2 of the *Practice Direction (Costs in Criminal Proceedings)* [2015] EWCA Crim 1658. Regulation 16 also provides for the payment of the fees of any intermediary required to assist the defendant.

Appointment of Legal Representative by the Court

An appointment may be made by the court under the Criminal Procedure (Insanity) Act 1964, s. 4A, or the YJCEA 1999, s. 38. In the latter case, CrimPR 23.2(10) (see Supplement, **R23.2**) provides that the appointment terminates at the conclusion of the cross-examination of the witness. In *Andrews* [2016] EWHC 1937 (Comm), [2016] 4 Costs LR 705 the costs judge held that cross-examination of a witness continues until such time as any such witness might be recalled, noting that trials involving defendants in person tend to be chaotic. **D33.39**

Section 40 of the YJCEA 1999 provides for such payments to be allowed in accordance with regulations and the Costs on Criminal Cases (General) Regulations 1986, Part IIIA, confirms that payments will be made out of central funds. Because the legal aid cap does not apply to this provision, the costs of court-appointed lawyers are paid at private client rates. In *Abbas v CPS* [2015] EWHC 579 (Admin), [2015] 2 Cr App R 11 (183) the Divisional Court considered the extent of the work that can be carried out by a lawyer appointed to cross-examine under the YJCEA 1999, s. 38 (see **F7.3**). It was held that such work extends beyond the mere cross-examination and includes necessary preparatory work — not only meeting the defendant to identify the issues and reading the papers but dealing with issues at pre-trial hearings around disclosure and bad character as these are relevant to effective cross-examination. That position is reinforced by CrimPR 23.7 (see Supplement, **R23.7**). The Court accepted that an appointee may remain at court pro bono once cross-examination is complete.

COSTS AGAINST LEGAL REPRESENTATIVES

D33.40 An order to pay costs may be made against a legal representative (as distinct from a party) by virtue of the inherent jurisdiction of the Crown Court (in the case of a solicitor) or under the Prosecution of Offences Act 1985, s. 19A (in respect of a solicitor or a barrister) (see CrimPR 45.9: Supplement, **R45.9**). Orders for the payment of wasted costs may be made against individual solicitors as well as against their firm (*Whitworth* [2014] EWCA Crim 1387).

The Crown Court has inherent jurisdiction to order that solicitors pay personally any costs thrown away by them or their staff's improper act or omission (see para. 4.6.1 of the *Practice Direction (Costs in Criminal Proceedings)* [2015] EWCA Crim 1568). Such an order may not be made unless reasonable notice is given and the solicitor has a reasonable opportunity of being heard in reply (para. 4.6.2). This power should be used only in exceptional circumstances and not where a statutory power would be available (para. 4.6.3). In *Holden and Co. v CPS* [1990] 2 QB 261, it was held that mistake, error of judgement or mere negligence were not sufficient to trigger such an order. The court's jurisdiction arose only where there was a serious dereliction of the solicitor's duty to the court. The primary object of such an order was to reimburse a litigant for costs incurred because of the solicitor's default, but there were also punitive and deterrent elements in the order.

The power to order legal representatives to pay costs has been extended by the Prosecution of Offences Act 1985, s. 19A. A magistrates' court, the Crown Court or the Court of Appeal may disallow costs or order the legal representative concerned to meet the whole or part of any wasted costs. Wasted costs are costs which are incurred as a result of any improper, unreasonable or negligent act or omission by the representative or the representative's employee, or which the court considers it unreasonable to expect a party to pay in the light of such act or omission occurring after the costs were incurred (s. 19A(3)). The test is therefore extended to cover negligence, in addition to improper or unreasonable acts or omissions. An order under s. 19A may only be made against the representative of a party to criminal proceedings. Criminal proceedings do not, for these purposes, include either applications for papers after the conclusion of a criminal case or contempt proceedings (*Re Soni (Appeal against a Wasted Costs Order)* [2019] EWCA Crim 1304, [2019] 4 WLR 103).

Procedure and Practice in Making Order

D33.41 The procedure for the exercise of the power is laid down in regs. 3A to 3D of the Costs in Criminal Cases (General) Regulations 1986. These require the court to specify the amount of the wasted costs order, and allow the representative and any party to the proceedings to make representations. The hearing should normally be in chambers, with a shorthand writer present. The court should give reasons for its order, which it may announce in public. Paragraph 4.2.2 of the *Practice Direction (Costs in Criminal Proceedings)* [2015] EWCA Crim 1568 says that judges in criminal cases have more direct responsibility for costs than their civil counterparts and so should keep the question of costs in the forefront of their mind at every stage of the case. They ought to be prepared to take the initiative themselves without any prompting from the parties. Paragraph 4.2.4 provides that judges contemplating making a wasted costs order should bear in mind the guidance given by the Court of Appeal in *Re a Barrister (Wasted Costs Order) (No. 1 of 1991)* [1993] QB 293, and para. 4.2.5 goes on to refer to the additional guidance given by the Court of Appeal in *Re P (a Barrister) (Wasted Costs Order)* [2001] EWCA Crim 1728, [2002] 1 Cr App R 19 (207).

D33.42 In *Re a Barrister (Wasted Costs Order) (No. 1 of 1991)*, the Court of Appeal considered an order made against defence counsel in the Crown Court. The trial judge purported to 'disallow such part of the brief fee which would otherwise have been payable on the partial trial as exceeds what would be the proper enhanced refresher for the retrial'. The order was based upon a finding that the barrister was guilty of an 'unreasonable act or omission'. On appeal by the barrister, the Court of Appeal held that the order was *ultra vires* and fatally flawed, since it did not specify the amount of the wasted costs. In any event, the barrister was not, their lordships held, guilty of any unreasonable act or omission such as could found a wasted costs order. They went on to lay down the following guidelines as to the practice to be adopted in deciding upon a wasted costs order:

1 There is a clear need for any judge or court intending to exercise the wasted costs jurisdiction to formulate carefully and concisely the complaint and grounds upon which such an order might be sought. Those measures were draconian, and, as in contempt proceedings, the grounds must be clear and particular.
2 Where necessary a transcript of the relevant part of the proceedings under discussion should be available. And, in accordance with the rules, a transcript of any wasted costs hearing must be made.
3 A defendant involved in a case where such proceedings are contemplated should be present if, after discussion with counsel, it is thought that his interests might be affected. And he should certainly be present and represented if the matter might affect the course of his trial. Regulation 3B(2) [of the Costs in Criminal Cases (General) Regulations 1986] furthermore requires that before a wasted costs order is made 'the court shall allow the legal or other representative and any party to the proceedings to make representations'. There may be cases where it may be appropriate for counsel for the Crown to be present.
4 A three-stage test or approach is recommended when a wasted costs order is contemplated:
   (i) Has there been an improper, unreasonable or negligent act or omission?
   (ii) As a result, have any costs been incurred by a party?
   (iii) If the answers to (i) and (ii) are yes; should the court exercise its discretion to disallow or order the representative to meet the whole or any part of the relevant costs, and if so what specific sum is involved?
5 It is inappropriate to propose any deal or settlement... that the representative might forgo fees. The judge should formally state his complaint, in chambers, and invite the representative to make his own comments. After any other party has been heard the judge should give his formal ruling. Discursive conversations such as took place in the present case may be unfair and should certainly not take place.
6 As is indicated above the judge must specify the sum to be disallowed or ordered. Alternatively, the relevant available procedure should be substituted, should it be impossible to fix the sum.

Further guidance was given in *Re P (a Barrister) (Wasted Costs Order)* [2001] EWCA Crim 1728, [2002] 1 Cr App R 19 (207), where the Court of Appeal reiterated that the crucial questions in determining whether to make a wasted costs order were those set out in 4(i) to (iii) above, and stated that the standard of proof to be applied was on the balance of probability. Generally, it would be appropriate for any application in respect of costs to be heard by the trial judge. It was, however, open to the trial judge to decline to consider such an application if, for example, the judge was personally embarrassed by the appearance of bias. It was only in the most exceptional circumstances that it would be appropriate to pass the matter to another judge, and the fact that, in the proper exercise of judicial functions, a judge had expressed views in relation to the conduct of a lawyer against whom an order was sought did not of itself normally constitute bias or the appearance of bias so as to necessitate a transfer. **D33.43**

If criticism is made by the court of a litigator, not only must an amount in issue be specified, but notice of the wasted costs hearing must be given to the litigator. An advocate instructed to represent a defendant is not thereby instructed to represent the litigator in question (*Reeves & Co. Solicitors* [2011] EWCA Crim 819, [2011] 4 Costs LR 616).

In *Ridehalgh v Horsefield* [1994] Ch 205, the Court of Appeal gave guidance on the discretion to make a wasted costs order in favour of one party to litigation against the legal representative of the other. Sir Thomas Bingham MR made it clear that the judgment was applicable to criminal as well as civil courts, and made the following points. **D33.44**

(a) 'Improper' covered, but was not confined to, conduct which would ordinarily justify serious professional penalty. It was not limited to significant breach of the relevant code of professional conduct. It included conduct which was improper according to the consensus of professional, including judicial, opinion, whether it violated the letter of a professional code or not.

(b) 'Unreasonable' described conduct which was vexatious, i.e. designed to harass the other side rather than advance the resolution of the dispute. Conduct could not be described as unreasonable simply because it led to an unsuccessful result, or because other more cautious legal representatives would have acted differently. The acid test was whether the conduct permitted of a reasonable explanation. If it did, the course adopted might be regarded as optimistic and reflecting on a practitioner's judgment, but it was not unreasonable.
(c) 'Negligent' should be understood in an untechnical way to denote failure to act with the competence reasonably expected of ordinary members of the profession. It was not a term of art and did not necessarily involve an actionable breach of the legal representative's duty to his or her own client.
(d) A legal representative was not acting improperly, unreasonably or negligently simply by acting for a party who pursued a claim or defence which was plainly doomed to fail.
(e) However, a legal representative could not lend assistance to proceedings which were an abuse of process, and was not entitled to use litigious procedures for purposes for which they were not intended, for example, by issuing proceedings for reasons unconnected with success in the action, pursuing a case which was known to be dishonest or knowingly conniving at incomplete disclosure of documents.
(f) Any judge considering making a wasted costs order must make full allowance for the fact that an advocate in court often had to make decisions quickly and under pressure.
(g) Legal professional privilege might be relevant. If so, only the client could waive privilege. Judges should make full allowance for the inability of respondent lawyers to tell the whole story. Where there was room for doubt, the respondent lawyers were entitled to the benefit of it. It was only when, with all allowance made, a lawyer's conduct of proceedings was quite plainly unjustifiable, that it would be appropriate to make the order.
(h) When a solicitor sought the advice of counsel, that was not an abdication of professional responsibility. The solicitor had to apply his or her mind to the advice received. But the more specialised the advice, the more reasonable it was likely to be to accept it.
(i) A threat to apply for a wasted costs order should not be used as a means of intimidation. However, if one side considered that the conduct of the other was improper, unreasonable or negligent and likely to cause a waste of costs, it was not objectionable to alert the other side to that view.
(j) In the ordinary way, such applications were best left until after the end of the trial.
(k) As to procedure, the respondent lawyer should be told very clearly what he or she was said to have done wrong. No formal process of discovery would be appropriate. Elaborate pleadings should in general be avoided. The Court of Appeal could not imagine circumstances in which the applicant could interrogate the respondent lawyer or vice versa. The legal representative must have opportunity to show cause why an order should not be made, but this did not mean that the burden was on the legal representative to exculpate him or herself.

Paragraph 4.2.7 of the *Practice Direction (Costs in Criminal Proceedings)* [2015] EWCA Crim 1568 says that the court may postpone the making of a wasted costs order to the end of the case if it appears more appropriate to do so, e.g., where there may be conflict between the legal representatives as to the apportionment of blame, or the legal representative concerned is unable to make full representations because of a possible conflict with his or her duty to the client. Paragraph 4.2.6 confirms that while the court must make the order, it may seek assistance from the Criminal Cases Unit of the Legal Aid Authority and the Registrar of Criminal Appeals.

In Re Joseph Hill Solicitors (Wasted Costs Order) [2013] EWCA Crim 1728, [2014] 1 WLR 786 the Court of Appeal emphasised (at [46]) that 'the power to make a wasted costs order can be valuable but this case, and others recently before this Court, demonstrate that it should be reserved only for the clearest cases otherwise more time, effort and cost goes into making and challenging the order than was alleged to have been wasted in the first place'. The Court declined to make an order because, although the solicitors had failed to lodge an alibi notice in good time, they had been acting in accordance with the standard, now identified as mistaken, practice of the profession. In

Le Brocq v Liverpool Crown Court [2019] EWCA Crim 1398, [2019] 4 WLR 108 the Court of Appeal held that the costs (often at private client rates) of investigating a wasted costs issue should always be borne in mind and be proportionate, However, if that became an overriding consideration, the jurisdiction would lose its purpose when an investigation was necessary and an adjournment might be required.

The reference to 'criminal proceedings' in the Prosecution of Offences Act 1985, s. 19A(1), is wide enough to include proceedings relating to the issue of a witness summons. A local authority attending to answer an application for disclosure of social services files relating to the complainant in a criminal case is a party to criminal proceedings, and can be the beneficiary of a wasted costs order (*Re A Solicitor (Wasted Costs Order)* [1996] 1 FLR 40). **D33.45**

Paragraph 4.2.8 of the *Practice Direction* stipulates that a wasted costs order should normally be made regardless of the fact that the client of the legal representative concerned is funded by Criminal Legal Aid. However, where the court is minded to disallow substantial costs arising from criminal legal aid, it may, instead of making a wasted costs order, make observations to the determining authority that work may have been unreasonably done in accordance with para. 4.3.1.

Paragraph 4.5.1 notes that the Administrative Court is governed by a different regime, namely making a wasted costs order under the Senior Courts Act 1981, s. 51(6), and has to comply with the Civil Procedure Rules, r. 46.8 (which contains similar provisions as to giving the legal representative a reasonable opportunity to attend a hearing to give reasons why the court should not make such an order).

In *R (Hide) v Staffordshire County Council* [2007] EWHC 2441 (Admin) the Divisional Court declined to order wasted costs when the effect of the order being made would be the bankruptcy of the advocate.

Examples of Conduct Justifying Order for Wasted Costs

In *Re a Barrister (Wasted Costs Order) (No. 4 of 1992)* (1994) *The Times*, 15 March 1994, the Court of Appeal held that a barrister who practised at home without a clerk must not rely wholly on instructing solicitors to notify him of the dates and times of his cases. He was responsible for keeping abreast of listing details and should have adopted a system which enabled him to do so. **D33.46**

In *Rodney (Wasted Costs Order)* (9 December 1996 unreported), counsel failed to appear before the Court of Appeal due to an error by a junior clerk. Counsel was liable for the actions of a clerk in chambers in the same way as a solicitor was vicariously liable on a wasted costs order for the actions of a clerk in the solicitor's firm.

In *Re A Barrister (Wasted Costs Order No. 4 of 1993)* (1995) *The Times*, 21 April 1995, the Court of Appeal held that a judge should not impose such a draconian penalty as a wasted costs order without taking into account the daily demands of practice and the difficulties associated with time estimates.

In *Re a Firm of Solicitors (Wasted Costs Order)* [1999] All ER (D) 728, D, who was on trial in the Crown Court, was unhappy with his barrister and wished to dispense with her services. Defence counsel suggested that this should be put in writing, and when the court had risen, the experienced solicitor's clerk took a statement from D to that effect. Whilst the clerk was reading the statement back to D, the usher brought the jury past them. It was later contended that some of them must have heard what was said, and the jury had to be discharged. The judge made a wasted costs order, which was upheld by the Court of Appeal. The question was whether taking those instructions at a place where he knew the jury was likely to appear and then being oblivious to their appearance constituted negligence on the part of the clerk. In the circumstances, he had been negligent.

In *Re Boodhoo (Wasted Costs Order)* [2007] EWCA Crim 14, [2007] 4 All ER 762, the Court of Appeal held that it was not unreasonable for a solicitor to withdraw from proceedings in circumstances where a client had warned in advance that he would not attend the trial, and no instructions in relation to continuing to act in the client's absence had been obtained.

D33.47 In *SVS Solicitors* [2012] EWCA Crim 319, [2012] 3 Costs LR 502 the Court of Appeal upheld a wasted costs order made against solicitors who were complicit in their client's breach of the CrimPR and manipulation of the criminal process to suit the client's own ends. The Court observed that in such circumstances a solicitor should withdraw from the case in the event that a client refuses to comply properly with the obligations imposed by rules governing criminal procedure. To avoid difficulties in such a situation, solicitors will normally list the case for mention.

It is not negligent, but perfectly proper, for the defence to withhold from the Crown relevant documents undermining the prosecution case until after the Crown has established that there is a case to answer (*Reeves & Co. Solicitors* [2011] EWCA Crim 819, [2011] 4 Costs LR 616).

In *Henrys Solicitors* [2012] EWCA Crim 1480 the requirements for a wasted costs order were met where an advocate accepted instructions in two cases on the same day in geographically distant Crown Courts when there was a real risk that a hold-up at the first court might result in wasted costs being incurred in the second. However, Pitchford LJ did remark (at [9]) that it was not the case that 'because an advocate fails to appear at the listed time on the listed day that a wasted costs order will follow'.

A wasted costs order cannot be made in favour of defence solicitors as they are not a party to the proceedings. The effect is that, while a privately paying client may recover wasted costs, a firm with the benefit of a representation order cannot do so (*R (CPS) v Bolton Crown Court* [2013] EWHC 3570 (Admin), [2013] 1 WLR 1880).

Rights of Appeal

D33.48 **Costs in Criminal Cases (General) Regulations 1986 (SI 1986 No. 1335), reg. 3C**

(1) A legal or other representative against whom the wasted costs order is made may appeal—
 (a) in the case of an order made by a magistrates' court, to the Crown Court, and
 (b) in the case of an order made at first instance by the Crown Court, to the Court of Appeal.

AWARDS OF COSTS AGAINST THIRD PARTIES

D33.49 The Prosecution of Offences Act 1985, s. 19B, enables costs to be awarded against third parties where there has been serious misconduct by a third party (see CrimPR 45.10; Supplement, **R45.10**). See also para. 4.7 of the *Practice Direction (Costs in Criminal Proceedings)* [2015] EWCA Crim 1568.

The Costs in Criminal Cases (General) Regulations 1986, reg. 3F(1), provides that if (a) there has been serious misconduct (whether or not constituting a contempt of court) by a third party; and (b) the court considers it appropriate, having regard to that misconduct, to make a third-party costs order against him or her, the court may order the third party to pay all or part of the costs incurred or wasted by any party as a result of that misconduct. Under reg. 3F(2), the court may make a third-party costs order at any time during or after the proceedings, either on the application of any party or of its own initiative. This is qualified by reg. 3F(3), which stipulates that the court may make a third-party costs order during the proceedings only if it decides that there are good reasons to do so, rather than making the order after the proceedings; the parties to the proceedings, and the third party, must be allowed to make representations on the issue of the timing of the order.

D33.50 *Regulation 3F(4) requires the court*, before making a third-party costs order, to allow the third party, and any party to the proceedings, to make representations; the court is also empowered to hear evidence.

Under reg. 3G, where a party applies to the court for a third-party costs order or the court decides that it might make a third-party costs order of its own initiative, the third party must receive written notice of the application; this written notice must include details of the alleged misconduct of the third party. If the third party or any other party does not attend the hearing, the court may proceed in his or her absence if satisfied that the party has been duly served with notice of the hearing; if an order is made, it can be set aside if it is later shown that the third party did not receive notice (reg. 3G(8)).

Regulation 3H makes provision for appeals against third-party costs orders. In the case of an order made by a magistrates' court, the appeal lies to the Crown Court; in the case of an order made at first instance by the Crown Court, the appeal lies to the Court of Appeal. The appeal has to be instituted (with written notice to the court that made the order, stating the grounds of appeal) within 21 days of the order being made. This time-limit may be extended where there is good reason (reg. 3H(4)). Under reg. 3H(6), the appeal court may affirm, vary or revoke the order, as it thinks fit.

The Regulations were considered in *Allied Language Solutions* [2013] EWCA Crim 319, [2013] 1 WLR 3820 following difficulties in obtaining interpreters. The Court of Appeal held that, for there to be serious misconduct, there must be a history of failure to address an underlying issue.

Section E1 Sentencing: General Provisions

PURPOSES OF SENTENCING

The CJA 2003, s. 142, sets out a list of the purposes of sentencing. E1.1

Criminal Justice Act 2003, s. 142

(1) Any court dealing with an offender in respect of his offence must have regard to the following purposes of sentencing—
  - (a) the punishment of offenders,
  - (b) the reduction of crime (including its reduction by deterrence),
  - (c) the reform and rehabilitation of offenders,
  - (d) the protection of the public, and
  - (e) the making of reparation by offenders to persons affected by their offences.

Section 142(2) limits the scope of this by stating that s. 142(1) does not apply in relation to an offender who is aged under 18 at the time of conviction. Section 142A of the 2003 Act specifies the purposes of sentencing in relation to offenders aged under 18, but is not in force. The relevant provisions for young offenders are the CDA 1998, s. 37, which states that the principal purpose of the youth justice system 'is to prevent offending by children and young persons', and the statutory duty under the CYPA 1933, s. 44, to 'have regard to the welfare of the child or young person'. Section 142(1) does not apply where the offence is fixed by law (murder); where the sentence falls to be imposed under the Prevention of Crime Act 1953, s. 1(2B) or 1A(5), the PCC(S)A 2000, s. 110(2) or 111(2), the FA 1968, s. 51A(2), the CJA 1988, s. 139(6B), 139A(5B) or 139AA(7), or the VCRA 2006, s. 29(4) or (6) (all prescribed minimum sentences: see **E5**), or under the CJA 2003, ss. 224A, 225(2) or 226(2) (dangerous offenders: see **E4**); or in relation to the making of a hospital order (with or without restriction), an interim hospital order, a hospital and limitation direction (as to which, see **E22**). Section 142(3) states that 'sentence' includes any order made by a court when dealing with an offender in respect of an offence, and so clearly extends to ancillary orders as well as custodial, community, and financial penalties. The Court of Appeal in *Sellafield Ltd* [2014] EWCA Crim 49 made it clear that the purposes of sentencing listed in s. 142 are equally applicable to corporate offenders.

The Sentencing Council's *General Guideline: Overarching Principles*, applicable to all offenders aged 18 or over and to organisations sentenced on or after 1 October 2019 irrespective of the date of the offence, states that: 'The court should consider which of the five purposes of sentencing it is seeking to achieve through the sentence that is imposed. More than one purpose might be relevant and the importance of each must be weighed against the particular offence and offender characteristics when determining sentence' (see Supplement, SG2-3). E1.2

SENTENCING GUIDELINES

The CAJA 2009, Part 4 (ss. 118 to 136 and sch. 15), created a Sentencing Council for England and Wales. Section 120 requires the Council to prepare sentencing guidelines, which may be general in nature or limited to a particular offence, particular category of offence, or particular category of offender. By s. 121, the sentencing guidelines should specify the 'offence range' appropriate for E1.3

a court to impose on an offender convicted of that offence and, if the guidelines describe different categories of case, specify for each category a 'category range' within the offence range. The guidelines should also specify the 'starting point' within the offence range or within each category range.

Coroners and Justice Act 2009, s. 125

(1) Every court—
(a) must, in sentencing an offender, follow any sentencing guidelines which are relevant to the offender's case, and
(b) must, in exercising any other function in relation to the sentencing of offenders, follow any sentencing guidelines which are relevant to the exercise of that function,
unless the court is satisfied that it would be contrary to the interests of justice to do so.

E1.4 Where a court is deciding what sentence to impose, and there are in place applicable 'offence-specific guidelines' structured in the way described in s. 121, the duty imposed on the court under s. 125(1)(a) includes in all cases a duty to impose a sentence which is within the offence range, and a duty to decide which of the categories most resembles the offender's case in order to identify the sentencing starting point, but nothing in s. 125 imposes on the court a duty to impose a sentence which is within the category range (s. 125(2) and (3)). The duty to decide which category most resembles the offender's case does not apply if none of the categories sufficiently resembles the offender's case (s. 125(4)). The duty on the court to impose a sentence which is within the offence range is subject to the CJA 2003, s. 144 (reduction in sentence for guilty pleas), the SOCPA 2005, ss. 73 and 74 (assistance by defendants: reduction of sentence), and any rule of law as to the totality of sentences (s. 125(5)). The duty imposed by s. 125(1) is also subject to the CJA 2003, ss. 148(1) and (2), 152, 153, 164(2), 224A and 269 and sch. 21, and the various statutory provisions prescribing specific sentences considered in **E5**. Finally, nothing in s. 125 is to be taken as restricting any power which enables a court to deal with a mentally disordered offender in the manner it considers to be most appropriate in all the circumstances (s. 125(7): see *PS* [2019] EWCA Crim 2286, [2020] 2 Cr App R (S) 9 (56) and **E1.33**). Section 125(2) to (5) also apply for the purpose of determining the notional determinate term in relation to an offence (s. 126).

The duty to 'follow any sentencing guideline' is a duty to pass a sentence which falls within the 'offence range' for that offence, as specified in the relevant guideline. A court may choose not to follow a particular guideline (by imposing a sentence which falls outside the offence range) if it would be 'contrary to the interests of justice' to pass a sentence which is within the offence range. A good example of a judge taking this course (and sentence being upheld by the Court of Appeal) is *Maxwell* [2019] EWCA Crim 130. It is not permissible to ignore, or to depart from, a sentencing guideline because the judge dislikes the effect of the guideline (*Taylor* [2012] EWCA Crim 630, [2012] 2 Cr App R (S) 98 (581); *Umoh* [2013] EWCA Crim 1260). Nor is it permissible to depart from a guideline because a judge prefers the earlier case law, since earlier case law is superseded by the guideline (*Healey* [2012] EWCA Crim 1005, [2013] 1 Cr App R (S) 33 (176)). However, in *Thornley* [2011] EWCA Crim 153, [2011] 2 Cr App R (S) 62 (361) Lord Judge CJ said that the 'interests of justice' required a court considering a sentencing guideline to take into account any subsequent statutory changes and the effect of appellate case law on a sentencing guideline: 'guidelines are not tramlines ... nor are they ring-fenced' (at [13]). In *Dyer* [2013] EWCA Crim 2114, [2014] 2 Cr App R (S) 11 (61), Leveson LJ said that the role of the Court of Appeal was to interpret the guidelines and provide practical illustrations of their operation, including examples where departure from them might be appropriate. His lordship further observed that an appeal against sentence on the basis of alleged disparity with a sentence imposed on a co-defendant, or on a defendant sentenced in a different case, was effectively precluded where the relevant guideline(s) had been followed and applied. In *Thelwall* [2016] EWCA Crim 1755, Lord Thomas CJ said that our sentencing system 'now proceeds on the basis of guidelines, not case law', and so the citation before a sentencing judge, or the Court of Appeal, of appellate decisions which were simply illustrations of the operation of a sentencing guideline on particular facts was unlikely to be of assistance. The only exception to that principle was where the Court had said something to clarify the terms of the guideline. In *Blackshaw*

[2011] EWCA Crim 2312, [2012] 1 WLR 1126 the Court of Appeal considered a number of sentences imposed in the context of widespread public disorder across cities and towns which occurred during the summer of 2011. Lord Judge CJ said that the sentencing guidelines in place at that time had not contemplated the exceptional context of such disorder and that sentences above the normal ranges indicated in the guidelines had been appropriate and inevitable.

The CAJA 2009, sch. 22, part 4, contains transitional provisions following the setting up of the Sentencing Council. In particular, para. 28(2) refers to 'existing guidelines', which means any definitive guideline of the Sentencing Guidelines Council or any guidelines issued by the Court of Appeal before the SGC came into being and which have not been superseded. By art. 7 of the commencement order (SI 2010 No. 816), 'existing guidelines' are to be treated as guidelines issued by the Sentencing Council under s. 120 of the 2009 Act. **E1.5**

Definitive guidelines of the SGC and the Sentencing Council are all set out in edited form in the Supplement. If the court is to sentence an offender for an offence for which no definitive guideline exists, the court should apply the Sentencing Council's *General Guideline: Overarching Principles* (see Supplement, **SG2-3**). **E1.6**

Appellate judges have stressed that it is the duty of counsel to bring any sentencing guidelines to the attention of the sentencer, in case they might otherwise be overlooked. In *Maxwell* [2017] EWCA Crim 1233, [2018] 1 Cr App R 5 (76) Treacy LJ said that while judges had the primary responsibility for getting things right, they were entitled to expect proper assistance from counsel.

It is clear that the duty to 'follow' a relevant sentencing guideline applies only to the final or definitive guideline. The Court of Appeal in several cases, including *Connelly* [2017] EWCA Crim 1569, [2018] 1 Cr App R (S) 19 (127) and *Smythe* [2019] EWCA Crim 90, [2019] 2 Cr App R (S) 7 (46), has stressed that draft guidelines, or material in a consultation paper, should not be used by sentencing courts. It is only when a guideline becomes definitive that courts should use it as a sentencing guide. In *Hodgkins* [2016] EWCA Crim 360, [2016] 2 Cr App R (S) 13 (95), the Court of Appeal said, in a case where the Sentencing Council's definitive guideline on *Theft Offences* had come into force after the date of sentence but before the hearing of the appeal, that it was not appropriate for the Court of Appeal to refer to that guideline.

Sentencing guidelines are not retrospective in effect and, if a guideline reduces sentencing levels for a particular category of offence, no right of appeal lies for an offender sentenced before that guideline came into effect (*Boakye* [2012] EWCA Crim 838, [2013] 1 Cr App R (S) 2 (6)). Conversely, if the guideline increases sentencing levels, and an offender is sentenced for an offence committed before that guideline came into effect, the ECHR, Article 7, is not engaged because sentencing guidelines are instruments of practice rather than law (*Bao* [2007] EWCA Crim 2781, [2008] 2 Cr App R (S) 10 (61)).

The decision of the Court of Appeal in *A-G's Refs (Nos. 15, 16 and 17 of 2012) (Lewis)* [2012] EWCA Crim 1414, [2013] 1 Cr App R (S) 52 (289) provides a valuable summary of the proper judicial approach to Sentencing Council guidelines. According to Hallett LJ, the guidelines set out a series of eight steps for the sentencing process, not all of which will be necessary in every case but which should be followed sequentially. Step One is the determination of the offence category, to which there are two aspects: culpability and harm. The court should determine culpability and harm by reference *only* to the factors listed there. The judge must do his or her best to reach a fair assessment of the overall offending, namely culpability and harm, before proceeding to Step Two. The judge should declare his or her conclusions on Step One in the sentencing remarks, for the benefit of the offender, those advising the offender, and in the event of appeal. At Step Two, the judge should use the corresponding starting point to reach a sentence within the category ranges which follow. The starting point applies to all offenders irrespective of plea or previous convictions. The judge should then factor in any aggravating or mitigating features and adjust the sentence within the range. The Council emphasises that the list of aggravating and mitigating factors is non-exhaustive. In some cases, having considered these factors it may be appropriate to move outside the identified category range. If that is so, the judge should explain the reasoning (*Datsun* [2013] EWCA Crim 964, [2014] 1 Cr App R (S) 25 (137)). In cases where the offender is regarded as being at the very top of the highest range it may be justifiable for the court to depart from the guideline.

The Court of Appeal in *Bush* [2017] EWCA Crim 137, [2017] 1 Cr App R (S) 49 (393) made observations as to the terminology to be used in relation to sentencing guidelines. It was noted that the term 'starting point' had been used by different judges to mean different things. It would be of assistance if that term was confined to mean the figure provided by the relevant guideline at Step Two, rather than the figure reached at the end of Step Two after adjustment has been made for aggravating and mitigating factors. That was better described as 'the appropriate figure for sentence following a contested trial'.

A valuable template to assist judges in constructing their sentencing remarks in accordance with sentencing guidelines is provided in the *Crown Court Compendium: Sentencing* (December 2019), app. S II.

SERIOUSNESS OF OFFENCE

Determining the Seriousness of an Offence

E1.7 **Criminal Justice Act 2003, s. 143**

(1) In considering the seriousness of any offence, the court must consider the offender's culpability in committing the offence and any harm which the offence caused, was intended to cause or might foreseeably have caused.

The Sentencing Council's *General Guideline: Overarching Principles* (see Supplement, **SG2-1** ***et seq.***), applicable to all offenders aged 18 or over and to organisations sentenced on or after 1 October 2019 irrespective of the date of the offence, states that: 'The seriousness of an offence is assessed by considering the culpability of the offender and the harm caused by the offending.… Once a provisional sentence is arrived at the court should take into account factors that may make the offence more serious and factors which may reduce seriousness or reflect personal mitigation.'

REQUIRED REDUCTIONS IN SENTENCE

Reduction in Sentence for Guilty Plea

E1.8 **Criminal Justice Act 2003, s. 144**

(1) In determining what sentence to pass on an offender who has pleaded guilty to an offence in proceedings before that or another court, a court must take into account—
  (a) the stage in the proceedings for the offence at which the offender indicated his intention to plead guilty, and
  (b) the circumstances in which this indication was given
(2) In the case of an offender who—
  (a) is convicted of an offence the sentence for which falls to be imposed under a provision mentioned in subsection (3), and
  (b) is aged 18 or over when convicted
  nothing in that provision prevents the court, after taking into account any matter referred to in subsection (1) of this section, from imposing any sentence which is not less than 80 per cent of that specified in that provision.
(3) The provisions referred to in subsection (2) are—
  section 1(2B) or 1A(5) of the Prevention of Crime Act 1953;
  section 110(2) of the Sentencing Act;
  section 111(2) of the Sentencing Act;
  section 139(6B), 139A(5B) or 139AA(7) of the Criminal Justice Act 1988[;
  section 8(2) of the Offensive Weapons Act 2019].
(4) In the case of an offender who—

(a) is convicted of an offence the sentence for which falls to be imposed under a provision mentioned in subsection (5), and
(b) is aged 16 or 17 when convicted,
nothing in that provision prevents the court from imposing any sentence that it considers appropriate after taking into account any matter referred to in subsection (1) of this section.

(5) The provisions referred to in subsection (4) are—
section 1(2B) or 1A(5) of the Prevention of Crime Act 1953;
section 139(6B), 139A(5B) or 139AA(7) of the Criminal Justice Act 1988[;
section 8(2) of the Offensive Weapons Act 2019].

The references in s. 144(3) and (5) to the Offensive Weapons Act 2019, s. 8(2), will come into effect from a date to be appointed.

The Sentencing Council guideline, *Reduction in Sentence for a Guilty Plea* (see Supplement, **SG5-1**), applies to all individual offenders aged 18 and over and to organisations in cases where the 'first hearing' (see **E1.9**) was on or after 1 June 2017. The guideline applies to magistrates' courts and the Crown Court. For offenders aged under 18 the Sentencing Council guideline, *Sentencing Children and Young People* (see Supplement, **SG8-1**), sets out similar principles and also applies where the 'first hearing' was on or after 1 June 2017. *Reduction in Sentence for a Guilty Plea* replaces an earlier guideline of the same name with effect from that date.

The guideline explains that 'although a guilty person is entitled not to admit the offence and to put the prosecution to proof of its case, an acceptance of guilt (a) normally reduces the impact of the crime upon victims, (b) saves victims and witnesses from having to testify, and (c) is in the public interest in that it saves public time and money' (part B, Key Principles). Reduction for plea is a separate matter from remorse and other aspects of mitigation, and is separate from any reduction which may be appropriate to reflect assistance to the prosecuting or enforcement authorities. The guideline makes it clear that the benefits of a guilty plea 'apply regardless of the strength of the evidence against an offender', and so 'the strength of the evidence should *not* be taken into account when determining the level of reduction'. This is an important change from the earlier guideline, where a reduced discount was often given in such cases. The guideline applies only to the punitive elements of the sentence, and has no impact on ancillary orders, including orders of disqualification from driving.

The guideline (part C: The Approach) indicates that the court should determine the appropriate sentence for the offence(s) in accordance with any offence-specific sentencing guideline, determine the level of reduction for a plea of guilty, state the amount of that reduction, apply the reduction, and then follow any further steps in the offence-specific guideline to determine the final sentence. The CJA 2003, s. 174(7), states that where, as a result of taking into account any matter referred to in s. 144(1), the court imposes a punishment on the offender which is less severe than it otherwise would have imposed, it must state that fact. In *Beckford* [2018] EWCA Crim 2997, [2019] 1 Cr App R (S) 53 (449), the Court of Appeal stressed that 'a judge should, when a defendant has pleaded guilty, indicate whether he is giving credit [and] how much credit is afforded' (at [13]). Where multiple offences are being sentenced on the same occasion clarity requires that the proper reduction is made in respect of each sentence, rather than the sentences being totalled and the reduction applied to the total, even if arithmetically this would produce the same final sentence (see, e.g., *Smith* [2020] EWCA Crim 466). The Court of Appeal in *Parsons* [2019] EWCA Crim 1451, [2020] 1 Cr App R (S) 8 (69), said that there was a duty on both prosecuting and defence counsel to alert the court as to any arithmetical error made by the judge as to the credit to be afforded for a guilty plea. **E1.9**

The guideline (part D: Determining the Level of Reduction) indicates that the maximum level of reduction in sentence for a guilty plea is one third, which is applicable (subject to the exceptions indicated below) where a guilty plea is indicated at the 'first stage of proceedings'. The first stage 'will normally be the first hearing at which a plea or indication of plea is sought and recorded by the court'. Where the plea of guilty is indicated after the first stage of proceedings 'the maximum level of reduction is one-quarter' (again subject to the exceptions below). The reduction 'should be decreased from one-quarter to a maximum of one-tenth on the first day of trial', and the reduction 'should normally be decreased further, even to zero, if the guilty plea is entered during the course of the trial'. It should be noted that in the Crown Court the one third reduction should not normally be given at the PTPH, unless the defendant has indicated guilt in the magistrates' court. An unequivocal indication of guilt in the magistrates' court justifies a full one-third reduction, even if the defendant has made no admissions at the police interview (*Shuli* [2020] EWCA Crim 181). If the words 'G indication' are entered in the plea box on the Better Case Management form in the magistrates' court, that demonstrates the defendant's intention and entitles the defendant to a full reduction (*Handley* [2020] EWCA Crim 361). If, however, 'G likely' is entered in the box then the defendant is keeping options open, and is not so entitled (*Davids* [2019] EWCA Crim 553, [2019] 2 Cr App R (S) 33 (243)). There is no sliding scale between the reductions of one third and one quarter. While it is possible to take a guilty plea into account by reducing a custodial sentence to a community sentence, or reducing a community sentence to a fine (see Part E: Applying the Reduction), it was held in *Hussain* [2018] EWCA Crim 780, [2018] 2 Cr App R (S) 12 (89) that it is wrong to suspend a prison sentence to reflect a plea of guilty. If a custodial sentence is justified for the offence the judge should first adjust it to reflect plea, and only then decide if there are grounds to justify suspension.

The following exceptions (set out in Part F of the guideline) apply to the general scheme of reduction for a guilty plea. By para. F1, where the court is 'satisfied that there were particular circumstances which significantly reduced the defendant's ability to understand what was alleged or otherwise made it unreasonable to expect the defendant to indicate a guilty plea *sooner than was done*, a reduction of one third should still be made. In considering whether this exception applies sentencers should distinguish between cases in which it is necessary to receive advice and/or have sight of evidence in order to understand whether the defendant is in fact and law guilty of the offence(s) charged, and cases in which a defendant merely delays guilty plea(s) in order to assess the strength of the prosecution evidence and the prospects of conviction or acquittal.' This appears to be an exception designed to be limited to cases where the defendant genuinely cannot know whether he or she is guilty of the offence charged. Such an exception was identified on the facts in *Markham* [2017] EWCA Crim 739, [2017] 2 Cr App R (S) 30 (249), where the defendants (both aged 14) admitted in interview that they had intended to kill the victim, but in each case it was necessary to order psychiatric reports to determine whether a partial defence of diminished responsibility might be available. The Court of Appeal said that the case was very unusual and must not be taken as indicating that full credit would normally be appropriate where a defence of diminished responsibility was pursued. By contrast, in *Reid* [2017] EWCA Crim 1523, [2018] 1 Cr App R (S) 8 (45) the defendant pleaded guilty 17 days before her trial and was given a reduction of 10 per cent. On appeal defence counsel submitted a series of emails purporting to show that the plea had been delayed while awaiting legal advice, but the Court of Appeal said that the emails did not show a clear decision to accept guilt, and nothing had been communicated to the prosecution or to the court. That was well short of the situation contemplated in the guideline. Also, in *Gorman* [2018] EWCA Crim 423 the judge gave a discount of 10 per cent for a guilty plea tendered on the first day of trial. The Court of Appeal heard that discussions had taken place between the prosecution and the defence over plea at an earlier stage, but no unconditional offer to admit guilt was made. Singh LJ said (at [19]) that, on that basis, the case that a larger discount should have been given 'cannot possibly get off the ground'. A similar case is *West* [2019] EWCA Crim 497, [2019] 2 Cr App R (S) 27 (209). By contrast, in *Ball* [2019] EWCA Crim 1260, a reduction of 25 per cent should have been given where D at the PTPH had clearly indicated an intention to plead guilty, but the plea was not formally entered because the prosecution required additional time to review the terms of the indictment.

By para. F2, '[i]n circumstances where an offender's version of events is rejected at a *Newton* hearing or special reasons hearing, the reduction which would have been available at the stage of proceedings the plea was indicated should normally be halved. Where witnesses are called during such a hearing, it may be appropriate further to decrease the reduction.' This exception differs from earlier guidance by indicating an appropriate level of adjustment, rather than simply leaving the matter to the discretion of the sentencer. In *Beckford* [2018] EWCA Crim 2997, [2019] 1 Cr App R (S) 53 (449), however, the Court of Appeal upheld the judge's decision to afford no credit at all to a defendant who had pleaded guilty on the day of trial, where a *Newton* hearing with witnesses was required, and the defendant's version of the facts was 'roundly disbelieved'. By para. F3, 'if an offender is convicted of a lesser or different offence from that originally charged, and has earlier made an unequivocal indication of a guilty plea to this lesser offence or different offence to the prosecution and the court, the court should give the level of reduction that is appropriate to the stage in the proceedings at which this indication ... was made ...'. The fourth exception (para. F4) refers to the minimum sentence under the FA 1968, s. 51A. The Court of Appeal decided in *Jordan* [2004] EWCA Crim 3291, [2005] 2 Cr App R (S) 44 (266) that s. 51A did not permit any reduction below that minimum to reflect a guilty plea (see further **E5.13**). The fifth exception (para. F5) refers to the special rule in relation to reduction for a guilty plea in the case of various prescribed minimum custodial sentences (see **E5**). In those circumstances the reduction for guilty plea must not produce a final sentence which is less than 80 per cent of the required minimum sentence (and see *Gray* [2007] EWCA Crim 979, [2007] 2 Cr App R (S) 78 (494)). It is clear from *Darling* [2009] EWCA Crim 1610, [2010] 1 Cr App R (S) 63 (420) that if the judge has found that it would be unjust in all the circumstances to impose the minimum required sentence, the limited reduction permissible under s. 144(2) no longer applies.

For the application of a guilty plea to setting the minimum term in murder cases, see the guideline (see Supplement, **SG2-11**) and **E3.2**, and for application of the guilty plea to setting the specified period under the PCC(S)A 2000, s. 82A, see **E4.30**.

It is important to note that various observations in the pre-guideline case of *Caley* [2012] EWCA Crim 2821, [2013] 2 Cr App R (S) 47 (305), concerning the propriety of giving an enhanced discount for a late plea in certain serious and complex cases, are not reflected in the sentencing guideline. Those observations must now be regarded as wrong. It is clear that a reduction of one third is now the maximum permitted, whatever may have been the practice prior to the current guideline (*Jhurry* [2018] EWCA Crim 2799, [2019] 1 Cr App R (S) 40 (274)). In *Hoddinott* [2019] EWCA Crim 1462, [2020] 1 Cr App R (S) 26 (204), a case of conspiracy to supply two types of Class A drugs, the Court of Appeal reaffirmed that the maximum reduction for plea was one third, but added that if a defendant in a multi-handed case is the first to plead guilty, and by doing so has encouraged others to plead guilty, that might provide mitigation prior to credit being given for the plea. Whether such an adjustment should be made was fact-specific. **E1.10**

According to the Court of Appeal in *Alkidir* [2019] EWCA Crim 330, 'the Sentencing Council guilty plea guideline is not to be usurped by extraneous considerations' (at [26]). In that case D should not have been denied the proper credit for his plea as a means of ensuring that he served a sentence of at least 12 months and became eligible for deportation (see **E20.1**). Similarly, it is wrong to reduce the appropriate credit for a guilty plea so as to ensure that the sentence does not fall below four years, making the defendant eligible for the imposition of an extended sentence (*Nsumbu* [2017] EWCA Crim 1046, [2017] 2 Cr App R (S) 51 (425)). It is also wrong to withhold or reduce credit for a guilty plea because the defendant has given false evidence in support of another in a trial (*Lawless* [1998] 2 Cr App R (S) 176; *Wilson* [2018] EWCA Crim 449, [2018] 2 Cr App R (S) 7 (55)).

Reduction in Sentence for Assistance by Offender

The SOCPA 2005, s. 73, makes provision for reduction in an offender's sentence to reflect assistance given or offered to the authorities by that offender. Any reduction on this ground is separate from and additional to the appropriate discount for pleading guilty (*Wood* [1997] 1 Cr App R (S) 347). These two matters require separate consideration at Steps Three and Four in the Sentencing Council guidelines. A helpful overview of the provisions and general guidance on their practical effect is provided by the Court of Appeal in *P* [2007] EWCA Crim 2290, [2008] 2 Cr App R (S) 5 (16). **E1.11**

Serious Organised Crime and Police Act 2005, s. 73

(1) This section applies if a defendant—
 (a) following a plea of guilty is either convicted of an offence in proceedings in the Crown Court or is committed to the Crown Court for sentence, and
 (b) has, pursuant to a written agreement made with a specified prosecutor, assisted or offered to assist the investigator or prosecutor in relation to that or any other offence.

(2) In determining what sentence to pass on the defendant the court may take into account the extent and nature of the assistance given or offered.

(3) If the court passes a sentence which is less than it would have passed but for the assistance given or offered, it must state in open court—
 (a) that it has passed a lesser sentence than it would otherwise have passed, and
 (b) what the greater sentence would have been.

(4) Subsection (3) does not apply if the court thinks that it would not be in the public interest to disclose that the sentence has been discounted; but in such a case the court must give written notice of the matters specified in paragraphs (a) and (b) of subsection (3) to both the prosecutor and the defendant.

(5) Nothing in any enactment which—
 (a) requires that a minimum sentence is passed in respect of any offence or an offence of any description or by reference to the circumstances of any offender (whether or not the enactment also permits the court to pass a lesser sentence in particular circumstances), or
 (b) in the case of a sentence which is fixed by law, requires the court to take into account certain matters for the purposes of making an order which determines or has the effect of determining the minimum period of imprisonment which the offender must serve (whether or not the enactment also permits the court to fix a lesser period in particular circumstances),

affects the power of a court to act under subsection (2).

(6) If, in determining what sentence to pass on the defendant, the court takes into account the extent and nature of the assistance given or offered as mentioned in subsection (2), that does not prevent the court from also taking account of any other matter which it is entitled by virtue of any other enactment to take account of for the purposes of determining—
 (a) the sentence, or
 (b) in the case of a sentence which is fixed by law, any minimum period of imprisonment which an offender must serve.

Section 73(7) provides that, where a court thinks that it would not be in the public interest to state in open court that a discount has been given, the CJA 2003, s. 174 (which requires the court to explain its reasons), does not apply to the extent that the explanation would reveal that a discount has been given for that reason. Further, the CJA 2003, s. 270, which requires the court to give reasons for its selection of the minimum term in a case of murder, is qualified to the same extent.

Section 74 provides for a subsequent review of a sentence passed (a) on an offender who received a discounted sentence under s. 73 on the basis of a written agreement to assist the prosecutor which was not fulfilled, or (b) on an offender who received a discounted sentence at the time, but has since given or offered to give by way of a written agreement further assistance, or (c) on an offender who did not receive a discounted sentence within s. 73(2) but has subsequently by way of a written agreement given or offered to give assistance (s. 74(2)). The case may be referred back to the court by which the sentence was passed if the offender is still serving the sentence and the specified prosecutor thinks it is in the interests of justice to do so (s. 74(3)). The Supreme Court in *Re Loughlin* [2017] UKSC 63, [2018] 1 Cr App R (S) 21 (135) held that a specified prosecutor had an unfettered discretion when deciding whether to refer a defendant for resentencing under the SOCPA 2005, s. 74, where that offender had been given a lower sentence after entering into an assisting offender agreement. It was a prerequisite to consideration of whether to refer the sentence that the defendant had knowingly *failed to comply with the agreement*. Once that had been established, the prosecutor had to decide whether it was in the interests of justice to make the reference. The section imposed no explicit constraint on how the prosecutor should approach that question, and there was no justification for implying a fetter on that discretion. A case so referred must, if possible, be heard by the judge who passed the sentence (s. 74(4)). Section 74 has no application in murder cases if the offender did not plead guilty to the offence for which he or she was sentenced (s. 74(13)). See further *Z* [2015] EWCA Crim 1427, [2016] 1 Cr App R (S) 15 (107).

Extent of Discount Sections 73 and 74 of the SOCPA 2005 are silent as to the appropriate extent of any reduction to reflect actual or promised assistance by the offender. There are a number of long-standing Court of Appeal authorities which, according to *P* [2007] EWCA Crim 2290, [2008] 2 Cr App R (S) 5 (16), are still relevant despite the introduction of the statutory scheme. The decision in *Sinfield* (1981) 3 Cr App R (S) 258 establishes that, where an offender has given significant assistance to the police or prosecuting authorities, especially where it leads to the apprehension of other offenders or the prevention of other offences, the offender may expect a discount, possibly a substantial one, from the sentence. The level of discount will depend on the quality, quantity, accuracy and timeliness of the information given, the offender's willingness to testify if required, and the extent to which co-operation with the authorities has put the offender or the offender's family at serious risk of reprisal. In general, the greater the nature of the criminality revealed by the offender, the greater the consequent risks to the offender and family. The discount should be set at a level appropriate to show to offenders that it was worthwhile to provide such assistance (*Sivan* (1988) 10 Cr App R (S) 282). This created a difficulty in *Dougall* [2010] EWCA Crim 1048, [2011] 1 Cr App R (S) 37 (227), where D had provided very considerable assistance in the context of offences involving large-scale corruption. In view of the relatively low custodial sentence which would have been appropriate on a guilty plea without such assistance, the Court of Appeal said that it was appropriate in this case to reward the co-operation by suspending the sentence. While it was said in *Wood* (1987) 9 Cr App R (S) 238 that, in a case where a discount had been given for assistance, that fact should be made clear in open court, there are many cases where such a course would put the informant in greater danger. The statutory scheme in s. 73(4) preserves the possibility of dealing with a difficult and sensitive matter other than in open court. In *A and B* [1999] 1 Cr App R (S) 52, the Court of Appeal reviewed earlier authorities and restated the applicable general principles. It was there noted that the Court of Appeal might on occasion increase the level of discount which had been granted by the trial judge, on the basis of later information which showed that the material provided by the offender had turned out to be of greater value to the authorities than initially had been thought. Section 74 provides for any such adjustment to be carried out by bringing the matter back before the sentencer, rather than by way of an appeal against sentence. For consideration of sentence reviews under s. 74, see *Blackburn* [2007] EWCA Crim 2290, [2008] 2 Cr App R (S) 5 (16) and *D* [2010] EWCA Crim 1485, [2011] 1 Cr App R (S) 69 (424). E1.12

Alongside the provisions of the SOCPA 2005 considered above, less formal arrangements (for consideration of a 'text') which existed well before 2005 are still in place, and in practice are used more frequently than the statutory scheme. In *X* [1999] 2 Cr App R 125 the Court of Appeal said that adjustment to a sentence may be made by a judge where the defendant claimed to have assisted the authorities and that assertion was supported by the police in the form of a confidential report (a 'text'), which should be provided in a standard format and signed by a senior police officer. If the content of the text is not in dispute the judge should make no open reference to it when passing sentence, but simply say that all information about the defendant has been taken into account when determining sentence. For guidance in cases where the defendant's claim to have assisted the authorities is in dispute, or where the police have declined to provide a 'text', see *AXN* [2016] EWCA Crim 590, [2016] 2 Cr App R (S) 33 (341). E1.13

In *Campbell* [2018] EWCA Crim 802, [2018] 2 Cr App R (S) 24 (222) the Court of Appeal noted that credit should be given where a defendant has given material assistance to the authorities in relation to a serious crime, even where that assistance fell outside the terms of the SOCPA regime and had not been the subject of a 'text'.

AGGRAVATING FACTORS

Previous Convictions

E1.14 **Criminal Justice Act 2003, s. 143**

(2) In considering the seriousness of an offence ('the current offence') committed by an offender who has one or more previous convictions, the court must treat each previous conviction as an aggravating factor if (in the case of that conviction) the court considers that it can reasonably be so treated having regard, in particular, to—
(a) the nature of the offence to which the conviction relates and its relevance to the current offence, and
(b) the time that has elapsed since the conviction.

The Sentencing Council's definitive guidelines list previous convictions as an aggravating feature. The Court of Appeal in *Darrigan* [2017] EWCA Crim 169, [2017] 1 Cr App R (S) 50 (397) dealt with a case in which D fell to be sentenced for an offence of wounding with intent, the commission of which pre-dated a number of other matters for which he had already been convicted and sentenced. The Court made it clear that convictions accrued after the instant offence was committed were not previous convictions for the purposes of s. 143 and could not be taken to aggravate the seriousness of the instant offence. Although relevant and recent previous convictions clearly aggravate the offence, it is wrong to impose a sentence wholly disproportionate to the seriousness of the latest offence purely on the basis of a bad record (*Byrne* [2012] EWCA Crim 418; *Bailey* [2013] EWCA Crim 1779). In *Chamberlin* [2017] EWCA Crim 39, [2017] 1 Cr App R (S) 46 (369), a case of theft from a shop by a persistent offender, the Court of Appeal said that sentencers may, in the light of previous convictions, depart from the level of sentence indicated by the sentencing guideline. The Court referred to the *Theft* guideline, including the aggravating feature of 'relevant recent convictions [which] may justify an upward adjustment, including outside the category range' (see Supplement, **SG33-3**). In the case of a persistent offender, with whom the range of sentencing methods have been tried and failed, and where there is no current prospect of reform or rehabilitation, punishment and deterrence come to the fore. However, it is not inevitable that the sentence must be longer than the last sentence imposed, and the sentence length must still be proportionate to the offence itself, aggravated as it is by the previous convictions. See also *Brooks* [2017] EWCA Crim 1066, where *Chamberlin* was followed and approved.

The various definitive sentencing guidelines issued by the Sentencing Council specify sentence starting points which make no assumption as to the offender's criminal record, and may well require adjustment upwards or downwards to take account of the presence or absence of relevant recent convictions.

Section 143(4) makes it clear that 'previous conviction' in this context means a previous conviction by a court in the UK or a previous conviction of a service offence within the meaning of the Armed Forces Act 2006 or a previous conviction in another EU Member State of a 'relevant offence'. By s. 143(5), this does not prevent the court from treating a previous conviction by a court outside the UK as an aggravating factor in any case where the court considers it appropriate to do so. At the end of the transition period following the UK's departure from the EU in accordance with the European Union (Withdrawal) Act 2018 (on 31 December 2020), the Criminal Justice (Amendment etc.) (EU Exit) Regulations (SI 2019 No. 780) will amend s. 143 so that references to previous convictions in a Member State are omitted from the section.

The provision of information on antecedents in the Crown Court and magistrates' courts is dealt with in CrimPD II, paras. 8A.1 to 8A.8 (see Supplement, **CPD.8A**).

Increase in Sentence for Offending on Bail

E1.15 The CJA 2003, s. 143(3), states: 'In considering the seriousness of any offence committed while the offender was on bail, the court must treat the fact that it was committed in those circumstances as an aggravating factor'. This is particularly so where the offence committed on bail is of the same type as the offence for which bail was granted (*Jeffrey* [2003] EWCA Crim 2089, [2004] 1 Cr App R (S) 25 (179)). While s. 143(3) is expressed in mandatory terms, it must be set against the established sentencing principle that consecutive sentences are appropriate where one offence is committed while the offender is on bail in respect of another (see **E2.19**). Operation of these rules together might result in a disproportionately severe sentence.

Increase in Sentence for Racial or Religious Aggravation

The CJA 2003, s. 145, states that where a court is considering the seriousness of an offence other than one under the CDA 1988, ss. 29 to 32, if the offence was racially or religiously aggravated, the court must treat that fact as an aggravating factor on sentence and must state in open court that the offence was so aggravated. As to the need for the court to make a determination of this issue where the presence of the aggravating factor is disputed, see *DPP v Giles* [2019] EWHC 2015 (Admin), [2020] 1 Cr App R (S) 20 (156) at **E1.19**. **E1.16**

For the definition of 'racial or religious aggravation', see **B11.145**. In *Morrison* [2001] 1 Cr App R (S) 5 (12), the Court of Appeal said that the appropriate additional punishment to reflect racial aggravation would depend on all the circumstances, but in that case approved the enhancement by two years of a nominal sentence of four and a half years for burglary committed in circumstances of racial aggravation.

Section 145 is of general application in sentencing, except that it does *not* apply where the court is imposing sentence for one of the racially or religiously aggravated offences under the CDA 1998, ss. 29 to 32 (certain aggravated assaults, aggravated criminal damage, certain aggravated public order offences, or aggravated harassment: see **B11.145**). The racially or religiously aggravated forms of these offences carry higher maximum penalties. The cases of *Saunders* [2000] 1 Cr App R (S) 548 and *Kelly* [2001] EWCA Crim 170, [2001] 2 Cr App R (S) 73 (341) provide guidance in sentencing cases involving racial aggravation. They are both cases of racially aggravated actual bodily harm and are considered at **B2.34**. Nor, at least generally, does s. 145 apply where the offender has been convicted of the basic offence where a racially or religiously aggravated version exists. In *McGillivray* [2005] EWCA Crim 604, [2005] 2 Cr App R (S) 60 (366), D pleaded guilty to assault occasioning actual bodily harm. The racially aggravated version of that offence had originally been charged as well, but no evidence was adduced on that count and a verdict of not guilty was entered. The judge passed a sentence of three years' imprisonment on the basis that the assault had been racially aggravated. The Court of Appeal said that it had not been open to the judge to sentence on that basis, since D had not been convicted of the racially aggravated form of the offence. The sentence was reduced to two years, a sentence appropriate for the basic offence. However, in *O'Leary* [2015] EWCA Crim 1306, [2016] 1 Cr App R (S) 11 (66) the Court of Appeal upheld the decision of the judge to treat an offence of unlawful wounding as racially aggravated by virtue of s. 145 even though the offence of unlawful wounding has a racially aggravated form which was not charged. The Court distinguished *McGillivray* by pointing out that in *O'Leary* there had been a contested trial during which evidence had clearly emerged as to the racial motivation behind the offending.

Increase in Sentence for Offence with a Terrorist Connection

Under the C-TA 2008, s. 30, when considering the seriousness of an offence specified in sch. 2 to that Act, if it appears to the sentencing court that the offence has or may have a terrorist connection, the court must determine whether that is the case and, if the court so determines it must treat that fact as an aggravating factor and must state in open court that the offence was so aggravated. As to the need for the court to make a determination of this issue where the presence of the aggravating factor is disputed, see *DPP v Giles* [2019] EWHC 2015 (Admin), [2020] 1 Cr App R (S) 20 (156) at **E1.19**. **E1.17**

Increase in Sentence for Offence Committed against an Emergency Worker

E1.18 By the Assaults on Emergency Workers (Offences) Act 2018, with effect from 13 November 2018, if the court is dealing with an offence listed in s. 2(3) to the Act and the offence was committed against an 'emergency worker' (as defined in s. 3) at a time when that person was acting in the exercise of functions as an emergency worker, or at a time when that person was not at work but was carrying out functions which, if done in work time, would have been in the exercise of functions as an emergency worker, the court must treat that fact as an aggravating feature of the offence and must state in open court that the offence is so aggravated. The listed offences are the OAPA 1861, ss. 16, 18, 20, 23, 28, 29 and 47, the SOA 2003, s. 3, manslaughter, kidnapping, and an ancillary offence in relation to any of those offences. Nothing, however, prevents a court from treating that fact as an aggravating factor of an offence which is not listed in s. 2(3). As to the need for the court to make a determination of this issue where the presence of the aggravating factor is disputed, see *DPP v Giles* [2019] EWHC 2015 (Admin), [2020] 1 Cr App R (S) 20 (156) at **E1.19**.

Increase in Sentences for Aggravation Related to Disability, Sexual Orientation or Transgender Identity

E1.19 The CJA 2003, s. 146, applies where the court is considering the seriousness of an offence committed in any of the following circumstances (s. 146(2)):

(a) that, at the time of committing the offence, or immediately before or after doing so, the offender demonstrated towards the victim of the offence hostility based on—
  (i) the sexual orientation (or presumed sexual orientation) of the victim, or
  (ii) a disability (or presumed disability) of the victim, or
  (iii) the victim being (or being presumed to be) transgender

or

(b) that the offence is motivated (wholly or partly)—
  (i) by hostility towards persons who are of a particular sexual orientation, or
  (ii) by hostility towards persons who have a disability or a particular disability, or
  (iii) by hostility towards persons who are transgender.

The court must treat the fact that the offence was committed in any of those circumstances as an aggravating factor, and must state in open court that the offence was committed in such circumstances (s. 146(1) to (3)). It is immaterial whether or not the offender's hostility is based, to any extent, on any other factor (s. 146(4)). 'Disability' means 'any physical or mental impairment' (s. 146(5)). References to being transgender include references to being transsexual, or undergoing, proposing to undergo or having undergone a process or part of a process of gender reassignment (s. 146(6)). In *DPP v Giles* [2019] EWHC 2015 (Admin), [2020] 1 Cr App R (S) 20 (156), the Divisional Court held that in circumstances where, on the prosecution version of the facts, the offence is aggravated by hostility towards the victim based upon actual or presumed sexual orientation, it was difficult to think of circumstances in which a higher sentence would not thereby be justified. If the presence of the aggravating factor was disputed by the defence a *Newton* hearing may well be necessary to resolve the matter but, even if this is considered to be unnecessary, the sentencing court would generally be bound to hold a hearing to determine whether the relevant circumstances existed at the time of the offence so that the required statement in open court that the offence was so aggravated could be made. To decline to make that finding would frustrate the purpose of s. 146(3). It is submitted that the reasoning in *DPP v Giles* must apply equally to other statutory aggravating factors within the CJA 2003, s. 146 (disability, and transgender identity), as well as to statutory aggravating factors referred to in **E1.16** (racial or religious aggravation), **E1.17** (offence with a terrorist connection) and **E1.18** (offence committed against an emergency worker).

It was held in *B* [2013] EWCA Crim 291, [2013] 2 Cr App R (S) 69 (443), that an assault committed because the offender believed the victim to be a paedophile was not an offence aggravated by hostility towards the 'sexual orientation (or presumed sexual orientation) of the victim'; s. 146 was not designed to cover such a case.

General Aggravating Factors

Criminal Justice Act 2003, s. 156 E1.20

(1) In forming any such opinion as is mentioned in section 148(1) or (2)(b), section 152(2) or section 153(2), or in section 1(4)(b) or (c) of the Criminal Justice and Immigration Act 2008 (youth rehabilitation orders with intensive supervision and surveillance or fostering), a court must take into account all such information as is available to it about the circumstances of the offence or (as the case may be) of the offence and the offence or offences associated with it, including any aggravating or mitigating factors.
(2) In forming any such opinion as is mentioned in section 148(2)(a), the court may take into account any information about the offender which is before it.

The *General Guideline: Overarching Principles* (see Supplement, **SG2-4**), sets out a list of aggravating factors relevant to sentencing. Some of these reflect higher culpability on the part of the offender, others reflect a more than usually serious degree of harm. Aggravating factors affecting the seriousness of the offence should always be taken into account when deciding, *inter alia*, whether an offence is 'serious enough' to warrant a community sentence (CJA 2003, s. 148(1)) or 'so serious that neither a fine alone nor a community sentence can be justified' (s. 152(2)). Each of the Sentencing Council's definitive guidelines sets out at Step Two a non-exhaustive list of aggravating factors to be taken into account when sentencing for the particular offence.

Lies told by the offender, whether at police interview or during trial, are not an aggravating factor for sentence (*Lowndes* [2013] EWCA Crim 1747, [2014] 1 Cr App R (S) 75 (471)). An offender's public denunciation of allegations made by the victim could amount to an aggravating factor (*A-G's Ref (No. 38 of 2013) (Hall)* [2013] EWCA Crim 1450, [2014] 1 Cr App R (S) 61 (394)) but protestations of innocence falling short of denunciation could not do so (*Clifford* [2014] EWCA Crim 2245, [2015] 1 Cr App R (S) 32 (242)).

MITIGATION

General Mitigating Factors

Criminal Justice Act 2003, s. 166 E1.21

(1) Nothing in—
  (a) section 148 (imposing community sentences),
  (b) section 152, 153 or 157 (imposing custodial sentences),
  (c) section 156 (pre-sentence reports and other requirements),
  (d) section 164 (fixing of fines),
  (e) paragraph 3 of Schedule 1 to the Criminal Justice and Immigration Act 2008 (youth rehabilitation order with intensive supervision and surveillance), or
  (f) paragraph 4 of Schedule 1 to that Act (youth rehabilitation order with fostering),

  prevents a court from mitigating an offender's sentence by taking into account any such matters as, in the opinion of the court, are relevant in mitigation of sentence.

The CJA 2003, s. 166(2), states that even though the offence, or the combination of the offence and one or more offences associated with it, was so serious that a community sentence could not normally be justified for the offence, the court may, after taking matters of personal mitigation into account, pass a community sentence. The *General Guideline: Overarching Principles* (see Supplement, **SG2-4**), sets out a list of mitigating factors relevant to sentencing. Some of these reflect significantly lower culpability on the part of the offender, others that the harm caused by the offence is less than usually serious. Each of the Sentencing Council's definitive guidelines sets out at Step Two a non-exhaustive list of mitigating factors to be taken into account when sentencing for the particular offence.

The weight to be given to mitigation is a matter within the discretion of the court and, in particular, the serious nature of the offence may mean that little weight can be given to what would otherwise be regarded as significant personal mitigation. The definitive guideline, *Imposition of Community and Custodial Sentences* (see Supplement, **SG9-1**), provides that the following factors indicate that it may be appropriate to suspend a custodial sentence: (i) realistic prospect of rehabilitation, (ii) strong personal mitigation, and (iii) immediate custody will result in significant harmful impact upon others. See further **E6.3**.

In *Seed* [2007] EWCA Crim 254, [2007] 2 Cr App R (S) 69 (436), the Court of Appeal stressed that good character and a clean record can be important personal mitigation. Other standard features of personal mitigation include remorse, youth/immaturity, old age (*Clarke* [2017] EWCA Crim 393, [2017] 2 Cr App R (S) 18 (140)), serious illness of the offender (*Bernard* [1997] 1 Cr App R (S) 135; *Hall* [2013] EWCA Crim 82, [2013] 2 Cr App R (S) 68 (434)), significant delay since the offence was committed, where this is not the fault of the offender (*Beattie-Milligan* [2019] EWCA Crim 2367, [2020] 2 Cr App R (S) 10 (75)), significant pressure on the offender (short of duress) to commit the offence (*Lingu* [2013] EWCA Crim 825, [2014] 1 Cr App R (S) 21 (120)), determination to address addiction or offending behaviour, and meritorious conduct unrelated to the offence (see, e.g., *Alexander* [1997] 2 Cr App R (S) 74). Serious adverse impact of a custodial sentence on persons other than the offender (such as young children of a single parent) may be taken into account at the discretion of the court (*Petherick* [2012] EWCA Crim 2214, [2013] 1 WLR 1102; *Humphries* [2013] EWCA Crim 1748; *Vincent* [2017] EWCA Crim 333).

The CJA 2003, s. 166(3), states that nothing prevents a court:

(a) from mitigating any penalty included in an offender's sentence by taking into account any other penalty included in that sentence, and
(b) in the case of an offender who is convicted of one or more other offences, from mitigating his sentence by applying any rule of law as to the totality of sentences.

The CAJA 2009, s. 125(5)(c), states that the duty on a court to follow sentencing guidelines (see **E1.3**) is 'subject to any rule of law as to the totality of sentences'.

The definitive sentencing guideline, *Totality* (see Supplement, **SG4-1**) applies. See further **E2.22**.

PREVALENCE

E1.22 The seriousness of an individual case should be judged on its own dimensions of harm and culpability, rather than as part of a collective social harm. It is legitimate for the overall approach to sentencing levels for particular offences to be guided by their cumulative effect. However, it would be wrong to further penalise individual offenders by increasing sentence length for committing an individual offence of that type. This principle has been endorsed by the Court of Appeal in many cases including *Oosthuizen* [2005] EWCA Crim 1978, [2006] 1 Cr App R (S) 73 (385); *Bondzie* [2016] EWCA Crim 552, [2016] 2 Cr App R (S) 28 (261) and *Khalid* [2017] EWCA Crim 592. Cases espousing a different approach, such as *Tatomir* [2015] EWCA Crim 2167, may be regarded as out of line.

There may be exceptional circumstances that lead a court to decide that local prevalence should influence sentencing levels. It is essential that sentencers both have supporting evidence from an external source to justify claims that a particular crime is prevalent in their area and are satisfied that there is a compelling need to treat the offence more seriously than elsewhere. Such evidence may be supplied by the local Criminal Justice Board or emerge from a 'community impact statement'. See **E1.29**. There was a comprehensive restatement of the principle, and the practical requirements which go with it, in *Bondzie* [2016] EWCA

Crim 552, [2016] 2 Cr App R (S) 28 (261), a drug supply case. Treacy LJ made it clear that sentencing guidelines already took the collective social harm of offending into account. It was not open to a judge to increase a sentence for prevalence based on the judge's personal view that there was 'too much of this sort of thing going on in this area'. On the contrary, there had to be evidence provided to the court by a responsible body or senior police officer, which had to be before the court in the specific case being considered, with the relevant statements or reports having been made available to the Crown and defence in good time so that meaningful representations could be made in connection with that material and, even if such material was provided, the judge would only be entitled to treat prevalence as an aggravating factor if the judge was satisfied that the level of harm caused in the particular locality was significantly higher than that caused elsewhere. The judge would need to be satisfied that the circumstances could be described as exceptional and that it was just and proportionate to increase the sentence for such factors. Since *Bondzie* the Court has stressed that if a judge is minded to pass a deterrent sentence for local prevalence reasons, not only is it necessary that the appropriate evidence be received, but also that the evidence does actually demonstrate a particular local problem. In *Duncanson* [2016] EWCA Crim 1537 there was a community impact statement, and in *Johncock* [2016] EWCA Crim 2218 evidence was received from a senior police officer as to the scale of the local drug supply problem, but in each case the Court of Appeal was unimpressed, saying that these reports 'showed an all-too-familiar picture of the effects of drug dealing, but not a situation which was so different to elsewhere in the country'. The Court of Appeal in *Ntim* [2019] EWCA Crim 311, dealing with a case where very serious injury had been caused by the use of a knife, said that the judge had been entitled in his sentencing remarks to express grave concern about the level of knife crime across the country, but that it was better for judges to avoid using the term 'prevalence' save in those cases where an uplift for exceptional local conditions was being considered in accordance with the principles set out in *Bondzie*.

DUTY TO GIVE REASONS FOR, AND EXPLAIN EFFECT OF, SENTENCE

Criminal Justice Act 2003, s. 174 E1.23

(1) A court passing sentence on an offender has the duties in subsections (2) and (3).
(2) The court must state in open court, in ordinary language and in general terms, the court's reasons for deciding on the sentence.
(3) The court must explain to the offender in ordinary language—
  (a) the effect of the sentence,
  (b) the effects of non-compliance with any order that the offender is required to comply with and that forms part of the sentence,
  (c) any power of the court to vary or review any order that forms part of the sentence, and
  (d) the effects of failure to pay a fine, if the sentence consists of or includes a fine.
(4) [Matters which may be covered by the CrimPR.]
(5) Subsections (6) to (8) are particular duties of the court in complying with the duty in subsection (2).
(6) The court must identify any definitive sentencing guidelines relevant to the offender's case and
  (a) explain how the court discharged any duty imposed on it by section 125 of the Coroners and Justice Act 2009 (duty to follow guidelines unless satisfied it would be contrary to the interests of justice to do so);
  (b) where the court was satisfied it would be contrary to the interests of justice to follow the guidelines, state why.
(7) Where, as a result of taking into account any matter referred to in section 144(1) (guilty pleas), the court imposes a punishment on the offender which is less severe than the punishment it would otherwise have imposed, the court must state that fact.
(8) Where the offender is under 18 and the court imposes a sentence that may only be imposed in the offender's case if the court is of the opinion mentioned in—

(a) section 1(4)(a) to (c) of the Criminal Justice and Immigration Act 2008 and section 148(1) of this Act (youth rehabilitation order with intensive supervision and surveillance or with fostering), or
(b) section 152(2) of this Act (discretionary custodial sentence),

the court must state why it is of that opinion.

E1.24 The importance of articulating in open court the sentence imposed, and the reasons for that sentence, was emphasised in *Billington* [2017] EWCA Crim 618, [2017] 2 Cr App R (S) 22 (171). Although the practice of giving written reasons for sentence was commended by the Court of Appeal, Treacy LJ said (at [34]) that nonetheless it had been a 'serious failure' for the judge not to give oral reasons for sentence in court. The judge should announce in open court what sentence has been imposed upon each and every count (*Whitwell* [2018] EWCA Crim 2311, [2019] 1 Cr App R (S) 29 (198)).

In *Chin-Charles* [2019] EWCA Crim 1140, [2020] 1 Cr App R (S) 6 (40), the Court of Appeal noted that in recent years there has been a tendency for judges to craft very detailed sentencing remarks with an eye to the Court of Appeal, rather than to provide those remarks 'in ordinary language and general terms' to ensure that the offender understands the nature and effect of the sentence. Lord Burnett CJ said that this tendency, understandable but unnecessary, has led to sentencing remarks becoming longer and longer. This should be avoided. The sentence must be located in the guidelines, and the remarks should identify the category in which the offence sits by reference to harm and culpability, the consequent starting point and range, the adjustments which have been made to reflect aggravating and mitigating factors and, where appropriate, the credit which has been given for a guilty plea. Findings of fact may be announced in most cases without supporting narrative. A finding of dangerousness must be recorded, but supporting facts set out only when essential to an understanding of that finding. Limited and brief reference to a victim personal statement may be apt, but only if essential to an understanding of the court's decision. See further CrimPR 25.16(7) (see Supplement, **R25.16**).

Failure to Comply

E1.25 No consequence of any failure to comply with these requirements is specified in the CJA 2003, s. 174. Lord Taylor CJ said in *Baverstock* (1993) 14 Cr App R (S) 471 (at p. 475) that statutory provisions were 'not to be treated as a verbal tightrope for judges to walk' and that even if judges made a mistake and failed to explain something they should have explained, the Court of Appeal would not interfere with the resultant sentence 'unless it is wrong in principle or excessive'. In *Giga* [2008] EWCA Crim 703, [2008] 2 Cr App R (S) 112 (638), where the judge made a mistake when explaining to D how long he could expect to serve in custody, the Court of Appeal said that such an error did not make the sentence unfair, nor did it found the basis for an appeal. The decisions in *Bright* [2008] EWCA Crim 462, [2008] 2 Cr App R (S) 102 (578) and *Bhayani* [2015] EWCA Crim 352 are to the same effect.

REPORTS

Pre-sentence Reports

E1.26 **Criminal Justice Act 2003, ss. 156 and 158**

156.—(1) [See **E1.20**.]
(2) [See **E1.20**.]
(3) Subject to subsection (4), a court must obtain and consider a pre-sentence report before—
(a) in the case of a custodial sentence, forming any such opinion as is mentioned in section 152(2), section 153(2), section 225(1)(b), section 226(1)(b), section 226A(1)(b) or section 226B(1)(b), or
(b) in the case of a community sentence, forming any such opinion as is mentioned in section 148(1) or (2)(b), or in section 1(4)(b) or (c) of the Criminal Justice and Immigration Act

2008, or any opinion as to the suitability for the offender of the particular requirement or requirements to be imposed by the community order or youth rehabilitation order.

(4) Subsection (3) does not apply if, in the circumstances of the case, the court is of the opinion that it is unnecessary to obtain a pre-sentence report.

(5) In a case where the offender is aged under 18, the court must not form the opinion mentioned in subsection (4) unless—

(a) there exists a previous pre-sentence report obtained in respect of the offender, and

(b) the court has had regard to the information contained in that report, or, if there is more than one such report, the most recent report.

(6) No custodial sentence or community sentence is invalidated by the failure of a court to obtain and consider a pre-sentence report before forming an opinion referred to in subsection (3), but any court on an appeal against such a sentence—

(a) must, subject to subsection (7), obtain a pre-sentence report if none was obtained by the court below, and

(b) must consider any such report obtained by it or by that court.

(7) Subsection (6)(a) does not apply if the court is of the opinion—

(a) that the court below was justified in forming an opinion that it was unnecessary to obtain a pre-sentence report, or

(b) that, although the court below was not justified in forming that opinion, in the circumstances of the case at the time it is before the court, it is unnecessary to obtain a pre-sentence report.

(8) In a case where the offender is aged under 18, the court must not form the opinion mentioned in subsection (7) unless—

(a) there exists a previous pre-sentence report obtained in respect of the offender, and

(b) the court has had regard to the information contained in that report, or, if there is more than one such report, the most recent report.

(9) References in subsections (1) and (3) to a court forming the opinions mentioned in sections 152(2) and 153(2) include a court forming those opinions for the purposes of section 224A(3).

(10) The reference in subsection (1) to a court forming the opinion mentioned in section 153(2) includes a court forming that opinion for the purposes of section 226A(6) or 226B(4).

158.—(1) In this Part 'pre-sentence report' means a report which—

(a) with a view to assisting the court in determining the most suitable method of dealing with an offender, is made or submitted by an appropriate officer, and

(b) contains information as to such matters, presented in such manner, as may be prescribed by rules made by the Secretary of State.

(1A) Subject to any rules made under subsection (1)(b) and to subsection (1B), the court may accept a pre-sentence report given orally in open court.

(1B) But a pre-sentence report that—

(a) relates to an offender aged under 18, and

(b) is required to be obtained and considered before the court forms an opinion mentioned in section 156(3)(a),

must be in writing.

(2) In subsection (1) 'an appropriate officer' means—

(a) where the offender is aged 18 or over, an officer of a local probation board or an officer of a provider of probation services, and

(b) where the offender is aged under 18, an officer of a local probation board or an officer of a provider of probation services, a social worker of a local authority or a member of a youth offending team.

The normal requirement (as stated in s. 156(3)) is that the court should obtain a pre-sentence report before making a decision to impose a custodial or community sentence. The court has discretion to dispense with that requirement whenever it appears to the court to be 'unnecessary *to obtain one* (s. 156(4)). This discretion is, however, subsequently narrowed (in s. 156(5)) in respect of offenders who are under the age of 18. Section 156(6) provides that no sentence shall be invalidated by failure of the court to comply with these requirements, but, on appeal against a custodial or community sentence passed without the court having obtained and considered a pre-sentence report, the appellate court must obtain and consider one unless s. 156(7) and (8) apply. **E1.27**

CrimPD I, paras. 3A.8, 3A.9 and 3A.17 (see Supplement, **CPD.3A**), set out the criteria to be applied by the justices in deciding whether to order a report in a case in which a guilty plea has been entered or indicated in the lower court prior to the matter being sent to the Crown Court and, in the event of a report not being ordered, the circumstances in which the defence may make an application to the Crown Court to be considered administratively prior to the sentence hearing. In these circumstances a report should be ordered if the court considers that (a) there is a realistic alternative to a custodial sentence, or (b) the defendant may satisfy the criteria for classification as a dangerous offender, or (c) there is some other appropriate reason for doing so. The Sentencing Council definitive guideline, *Imposition of Community and Custodial Sentences* (see Supplement, **SG9-1**), provides guidance on the circumstances in which a pre-sentence report should be ordered by a court. In particular, the guidance is that '[i]deally a pre-sentence report should be completed on the same day to avoid adjourning the case'. The judge's decision to dispense with a report was upheld in *Jamous* [2015] EWCA Crim 1720, where the judge had presided over the trial and, in full possession of the material facts, had decided that custody was inevitable. In *Townsend* [2018] EWCA Crim 875, [2018] 2 Cr App R (S) 30 (278) the Court of Appeal upheld the judge's decision to proceed to sentence without the benefit of a pre-sentence report in a case where the offender had pleaded guilty in the magistrates' court to supplying Class A drugs. The Court observed that it was the role of the defence advocate to gather relevant information about the defendant, and to construct the plea in mitigation. It was not for the Probation Service to do that work. Their role was to offer a realistic alternative to custody, to deal with the question of dangerousness, or to deal with something specific within their area of expertise. In *Allen* [2019] EWCA Crim 1772, the Court of Appeal said that to make a finding on the issue of dangerousness without the benefit of a pre-sentence report requires 'careful justification' and that to obtain a report in such circumstances was 'usually the better course'. In this case, however, the judge's decision not to order a report was upheld, because the judge had presided over the trial and that, together with the facts of the offence, gave him a proper basis for making that finding. A pre-sentence report should usually be obtained in a case where the defence argues that, exceptionally, a minimum sentence provision should not be applied (*Woofe* [2019] EWCA Crim 2249, [2020] 2 Cr App R (S) 6 (37)).

E1.28 The CJA 2003, s. 159, deals with disclosure of a pre-sentence report, other than a report given orally in court, (a) to the offender or the offender's legal representative, (b) if the offender is under 18, to any parent or guardian of the offender who is present in court (unless information in the report would be likely to create a significant risk of harm to the offender, in which case a complete copy of the report need not be given to the offender, or to the parent or guardian) and (c) to the prosecutor (unless the court considers that it would be inappropriate for the prosecutor to be given it).

The CJA 2003, s. 160, applies where a report (other than a pre-sentence report) is made by a probation officer or a member of the youth offending team with a view to assisting the court (except a youth court) in deciding how best to deal with an offender. It provides for disclosure of the contents of the report to the defence.

Community Impact Statements

E1.29 A community impact statement may be prepared by the police (CrimPD VII, para. H.6: see Supplement, **CPD.VII.H**). They are documents designed to express the specific crime concerns of a local community. They must be tendered in evidence as a witness statement, and served in good time upon the defendant. HM Courts and Tribunals Service produces a standard form for this purpose. In *Brzezinkski* [2012] EWCA Crim 198, [2012] 2 Cr App R (S) 62 (364) the Crown Court was provided with a report on the deleterious psychological effects (including increased fear of crime) on the local community of graffiti sprayed on local railway property. The judge used the report as the basis for imposing sentence on a persistent sprayer of graffiti. Sentence was upheld on appeal. *Wicks* [2013] EWCA Crim 1414, [2014] 1 Cr App R (S) 57 (355) is another example. D had installed a hydroponic unit for cannabis cultivation in an outbuilding. The prosecution presented a community impact statement suggesting that cannabis cultivation was associated with violence directed at cannabis producers and sometimes at those wrongly believed to be producers. The Court of Appeal upheld the sentence, saying that the judge had been entitled to rely on the material to find that there was a particular local problem. In *Haworth* [2018] EWCA Crim 1232 a sentence of 18 months' imprisonment for possession of cocaine with intent to supply drugs at a music festival was upheld. The judge had been entitled to rely on a 'detailed and evidence-based community impact statement' as to the efforts made by the police and local music festival organisers to prevent people in possession of drugs from gaining entry to festivals. In *Ardic* [2019] EWCA Crim 1836, [2020] 1 Cr App R (S) 59 (457), a case involving the throwing of a corrosive substance, the Court of Appeal said that the judge had been entitled to take into account a community impact statement provided by a senior Metropolitan Police officer relating to the year-on-year increase in corrosive liquid attacks in London, and the level of public concern over offending of that type. By contrast in *Ali* [2018] EWCA Crim 2359, [2019] 1 Cr App R (S) 27 (182), a case of causing death by dangerous driving, the Court of Appeal felt that the information in the report was too general to be of much value, and should not have been relied upon. In *Skelton* [2014] EWCA Crim 2409, [2015] 1 Cr App R (S) 34 (265), the Court deprecated the use of a statement made by a police officer as to D's level of involvement in drug-dealing in the locality. The Court said that this had been a singular misuse of impact statements, which should be limited to expressing the effect of particular crimes upon a particular community and should not be used as character assassination of offenders. For the proper approach to dealing with matters of local offence prevalence see *Bondzie* [2016] EWCA Crim 55, [2016] 2 Cr App R (S) 28 (261) at **E1.22**.

Victim Personal Statements

CrimPD VII, paras. F.1 to F.3 (see Supplement, **CPD.VII.F**), and the decisions of the Court of Appeal in *Perkins* [2013] EWCA Crim 323, [2013] 2 Cr App R (S) 72 (460) and, in the context of victims who have incurred psychological harm, *Chall* [2019] EWCA Crim 865, [2019] 2 Cr App R (S) 44 (344), together provide guidance on the relevance of victim personal statements placed before the sentencer on the impact which the offence had on the victim or, in a case where the victim had died, the impact on surviving close family. According to Lord Judge CJ in *Perkins*, properly formulated statements provide real assistance for the court. They provide a practical way of ensuring that the court will consider the evidence of the victim about the personal impact of the offence. The process is not an opportunity for the victim to suggest, or discuss, the type or level of sentence to be imposed. The distinction is important. Victims must be provided with information which makes it clear that they *may* make a statement but are under no obligation to do so. A judge must not assume that the absence of a victim personal statement indicates an absence of harm (*Chall*). **E1.30**

Further guidance is as follows: **E1.31**

(a) Except where inferences can properly be drawn from the nature of, or circumstances surrounding, the offence, the court must not make assumptions unsupported by evidence about the effects of an offence on the victim. The judge must act on evidence, which may include evidence given during the trial, and the demeanour of the victim. Relevant evidence will often come, and may exclusively come, from the victim personal statement. The court is not prevented from acting on it merely because it comes from such a statement (*Chall*).
(b) If an offence has had a particularly damaging or distressing effect upon the victim, this should be made known to and be taken into account by the court when passing sentence (said to be an 'elementary principle of sentencing' in *Nunn* [1996] 2 Cr App R (S) 136; see also *Doe* (1995) 16 Cr App R (S) 718).
(c) The statement constitutes evidence and must be treated as such. It must be in a formal witness statement, compliant with the requirements of the CrimPD, served on the offender's legal advisers in time for instructions to be taken, and for any objection to the use of the statement, or part of it, if necessary, to be prepared. Responsibility for presenting it lies with the prosecution. If the statement relates to a time when the victim's injuries were fresh, but there is no information about the extent to which the injury had given rise to continuing problems, the CrimPD permits the serving of a further statement, in proper form, at any

time prior to the disposal of the case. The statement may be challenged in cross-examination and it may give rise to disclosure obligations. It may be used after conviction to deploy an argument that the credibility of the victim is open to question (*Perkins* at [9]). That right will very rarely be exercised, for a number of reasons, including the risk that cross-examination may increase psychological harm suffered by the victim (*Chall*).

In *Mohammed* [2018] EWCA Crim 1995, at the sentencing hearing V read out his victim personal statement describing serious and ongoing injury to his eye occasioned by D's assault. After sentence the matter was reconvened under the slip rule for the defence to adduce evidence from V's Facebook account, showing him at social events and on holiday since the date of the injury, and records from V's ophthalmology clinic showing that V had recovered and had been discharged from his treatment. Sentence was reduced in light of these matters.

(d) Evidence of the victim alone should be approached with care, the more so if it related to matters which the defence could not realistically be expected to investigate. The judge must keep in mind that the intensely personal nature of a victim personal statement may sometimes require caution as to whether the harm suffered may unintentionally have been overstated. The statement may be couched in very emotional terms, but the judge must make a dispassionate assessment (*Chall*).

(e) The opinions of the victim and the victim's close relatives on the appropriate level of sentence should not be taken into account (see also *Perkins*). The court must pass what it judged to be the appropriate sentence having regard to the circumstances of the offence and of the offender. It could not accede to a plea for vengeance by the relatives, and had to be very cautious about paying attention to pleas for mercy. This was, however, subject to two exceptions:

  (i) where the sentence passed on the offender was aggravating the victim's distress, the sentence might be moderated to some degree 'as an act of mercy' (examples are *Nunn* and *Roche* [1999] 2 Cr App R (S) 105); and

  (ii) where the victim's forgiveness or unwillingness to press charges provided evidence that his or her physical or mental suffering must be very much less than would normally be the case (examples are *Hutchinson* (1994) 15 Cr App R (S) 134 and *Mills* [1998] 2 Cr App R (S) 229). (In *A-G's Ref (No. 38 of 2013) (Hall)* [2013] EWCA Crim 1450, [2014] 1 Cr App R (S) 61 (394), some victims of sexual offences committed by D wrote to the Court of Appeal to say that they were content with the original sentence(s). Lord Judge CJ said that these views could not determine what was appropriate, and the total sentence was increased from 15 months to 30 months.)

(f) The court should consider whether it is desirable in its sentencing remarks to refer to the evidence provided on behalf of the victim. In selecting any passages for quotation in open court the advocate and judge must be very sensitive to the position of the victim, and the need to respect the victim's privacy (*Perkins* at [11]).

(g) Where the author of a victim personal statement wishes to read out that statement in open court, that wish should be complied with wherever possible. The matter was for the court to decide, however, and there should not be delay or adjournment in order to accede to the victim's request (CrimPD VII, para. F.3).

E1.32 CrimPD VII, paras. G.1 to G.3 (see Supplement, **CPD.VII.G**), deal with sentencing issues arising in relation to the proper treatment of bereaved families. CrimPD VII, paras. I.1 to I.10 (see Supplement, **CPD.VII.I**), deal with impact statements tendered on behalf of a business rather than an individual.

Mentally Disordered Offenders

E1.33 The Sentencing Council's definitive guideline, *Sentencing Offenders with Mental Disorders, Developmental Disorders, or Neurological Impairments* (see Supplement, **SG7-1**), applies, with effect from 1 October 2020, in relation to adult offenders who at the time of the offence and/or at the time of sentence have a disorder such as one of those listed in annex A to the guideline. For matters relating to reports, see annex B.

The CJA 2003, s. 157(1), states that in any case where an offender is or appears to be mentally disordered, the court must obtain and consider a medical report before passing a custodial sentence other than one fixed by law. This is subject to s. 157(2), which states that the court need not order such a report if, in the circumstances of the case, it is of the opinion that it is unnecessary to do so. Section 157(6) defines 'medical report'. A medical report is distinct from a pre-sentence report, and s. 157(7) clearly states that the ordering of a medical report does not displace the need to order a pre-sentence report under s. 156. As to the ordering of a medical report for sentencing purposes see CrimPD VII, paras. R.1 to R.16 (see Supplement, **CPD.VII.R**).

Section 166(5) provides that nothing in the sections mentioned in s. 166(1)(a) to (d) (see **E1.21**) is to be taken as requiring a court to pass a custodial sentence, or any particular custodial sentence, on a mentally disordered offender, or as restricting any power (under the Mental Health Act 1983 or otherwise) which enables a court to deal with such an offender in the manner it considers to be the most appropriate in all the circumstances. 'Mentally disordered', in relation to a person, means suffering from a mental disorder within the meaning of the Mental Health Act 1983 (s. 166(6)).

The Court of Appeal in *PS* [2019] EWCA Crim 2286, [2020] 2 Cr App R (S) 9 (56) (decided prior to the Sentencing Council's guideline), considered the proper approach to sentencing offenders who suffered from autism or other mental health conditions or disorders. The Court held that such matters may be relevant to sentencing in the following ways:

(a) They might be relevant to the assessment of the offender's culpability. In some cases D's condition or disorder might have little or no effect on sentencing outcome, but in others it might be substantial. A concise explanation of those choices should be included in the judge's sentencing remarks.
(b) They might be relevant to the decision about the type of sentence imposed, in particular a disposal under the Mental Health Act 1983. If a custodial sentence was necessary, mental health conditions and disorders might be relevant to sentence length and to the question of suspension. The court would be assisted by a pre-sentence report and by appropriate psychiatric or psychological reports. The younger the offender, and the more serious the offence, the more likely it was that the court would need the assistance of expert reports. It was important, when such reports were commissioned, that the issues to which they were relevant should be clearly identified. As with all matters of case preparation, early identification of the real issues was important.
(c) They might be relevant to the issue of whether D qualified as a dangerous offender.
(d) They might need to be taken into account in ensuring that the effect of the sentence was clearly understood by D and in ensuring that D was capable of fulfilling the requirements of a community order or ancillary order.

Section E2 Custodial Sentences: General Provisions

AVAILABLE CUSTODIAL SENTENCES

E2.1 By the PCC(S)A 2000, s. 76(1), the term 'custodial sentence' means (a) a sentence of imprisonment, (b) a sentence of detention under the PCC(S)A 2000, s. 90 or 91, (bb) a sentence of detention for public protection under the CJA 2003, s. 226, (bc) a sentence of detention under the CJA 2003, s. 226B or 228, (c) a sentence of custody for life under the PCC(S)A 2000, s. 93 or 94, (d) a sentence of detention in a young offender institution, or (e) a detention and training order. The term 'sentence of imprisonment' does not include a committal for contempt of court or any kindred offence (s. 76(2)).

Offenders aged under 21 at the date of conviction cannot be sentenced to imprisonment (PCC(S)A 2000, s. 89(1)). Those under 21 cannot be committed to prison for any reason, such as non-payment of a fine, but if a person under 21 is remanded in custody, committed in custody for sentence, or sent in custody for trial under the CDA 1998, s. 51 or 51A, the peson may be committed to prison for the period before the case is disposed of (PCC(S)A 2000, s. 89(2)).

MAXIMUM CUSTODIAL SENTENCES

E2.2 Maximum prison terms for indictable offences and offences triable either way are almost always laid down by statutes creating those offences. Maximum terms are indicated in respect of each of the offences dealt with in **Part B**. Where a person is convicted on indictment of an offence against any enactment and is liable to be sentenced to imprisonment, but the sentence is not limited to a specified term or life by any enactment, the maximum prison sentence available is two years (PCC(S)A 2000, s. 77). This provision does not apply to common-law offences, for which the penalty which may be imposed by the Crown Court is not subject to any limitation except that it must not be disproportionate to the actual offence committed (*Higgins* [1952] 1 KB 7). For sentencing by magistrates' courts, and by the Crown Court when exercising the powers of a magistrates' court, see **E2.5**.

There are special rules in respect of statutory conspiracies and attempts, as to which see **A5.44** and **A5.72** respectively.

Changes to Maximum Sentences

E2.3 The effect of statutory changes to maximum sentences is as follows. Unless there is clear provision to the contrary, where an offender falls to be sentenced for an offence committed before an increase in the relevant maximum sentence, the offender should be sentenced on the basis of the old maximum. Article 7 of the ECHR states that no heavier penalty shall be imposed than the one applicable at the time the offence was committed (*Welch v UK* (1995) 20 EHRR 247). When the offence is charged as having been committed on a day unknown between specified dates and the maximum sentence was increased between those dates, the lower maximum applies (*Street* [1997] 2 Cr App R (S) 309; *Cairns* [1998] 1 Cr App R (S) 434). If the maximum penalty is reduced between the time of commission of the offence and the date of conviction then, in the absence of guidance from the relevant provision or commencement order, it seems that the sentencing court should infer the intention of Parliament in a common-sense way (*A-G's Ref (No. 48 of 1994)* (1995) 16 Cr App R (S) 980; *Shaw* [1996] 2 Cr App R (S) 278). The Court of Appeal in *Forbes* [2016] EWCA Crim 1388, [2016] 2 Cr App R (S) 44 (472) considered the approach to sentencing of 'historic' or 'cold' cases, especially sexual offences committed many years ago but only recently brought to conviction. Lord Thomas CJ confirmed the continuing importance of guidance in *H* [2012] EWCA Crim 149, [2012] 2 All ER 340, as codified by the Sentencing Council in the definitive guideline on *Sexual Offences - Historic* (see Supplement, **SG31-37**). The offender must be sentenced in accordance with the regime applicable at the date of sentence. The fact that attitudes have changed is of no moment. The sentence that can be passed is limited to the maximum sentence available at the time of the commission of the offence, unless the maximum has been reduced, when the lower maximum will be applicable (see also **B3.373**).

Abiding by the Maximum

In *Bridger* [2018] EWCA Crim 1678, [2018] 2 Cr App R (S) 44 (369) the Court of Appeal upheld the maximum sentence of ten years on D, a prison officer, convicted (with ten others) of conveying prohibited articles into a prison. The Court said that the offending deserved the maximum sentence, being a case of the utmost gravity, where D had been convicted after a trial, the matter was aggravated by breach of trust, and personal mitigation was very limited. The Court stated that 'the maximum sentence permitted by statute is reserved not for the worst possible case which can realistically be conceived, but for cases which in the statutory context are truly identified as cases of the utmost gravity' (at [26]). *Mahmood* [2017] EWCA Crim 1449 was a case of dangerous driving where the maximum sentence of two years was upheld by the Court of Appeal. The Court said that a maximum sentence should be reserved for those cases which exemplify the most serious criminality for that offence. But that principle did not mean that a judge considering whether to impose a maximum sentence had to imagine unlikely worst possible kinds of case. Instead, the judge should consider the worst type of offence which comes before the court and ask whether the particular case being dealt with comes within the broad band of that type. Where the maximum sentence is relatively low, that band may be wide (and see to the same effect *Wilkinson* [2019] EWCA Crim 258, [2019] 2 Cr App R (S) 10 (70), also a case of dangerous driving, and *Saxton* [2018] EWCA Crim 1976, a case of wounding or inflicting grievous bodily harm (see **B2.65**)). The statutory maximum should not normally be imposed where there is significant mitigation. An example is *R (McElroy) v Lewes Combined Court* [2014] EWHC 2518 (Admin), where the Administrative Court quashed the maximum sentence of six months' imprisonment for a battery, imposed by the Crown Court on appeal, where D was a man of good character. The Court said that the sentence was so severe as to amount to an error of law, and reduced it to two months. **E2.4**

Limits on Imprisonment: Magistrates' Courts and the Crown Court when Limited to Magistrates' Courts' Powers

General limits on the power of magistrates' courts to impose imprisonment are specified by the PCC(S)A 2000, s. 78, and the MCA 1980, s. 32. The minimum prison sentence which may be imposed is one of five days (MCA 1980, s. 132) and the maximum is six months in respect of any one offence (PCC(S)A 2000, s. 78(1)) unless a shorter maximum term is provided by statute. The six-month limit does not, however, apply to imprisonment for non-payment of a fine (see **E15.11**). The maximum aggregate term which magistrates can impose is six months, unless two of the terms are imposed for offences triable either way, in which case the maximum aggregate term is 12 months (MCA 1980, s. 133). These provisions also apply to the sentence of detention in a young offender institution but not to the detention and training order. For more detailed treatment of the sentencing powers of a magistrates' court, see **D23**. Magistrates' courts are, of course, subject to the criteria for determining both the imposition and length of a custodial sentence (see **E2.7** and **E2.9**). **E2.5**

Care must be taken when sentencing in the Crown Court in the situation where either-way offences have resulted in acquittal or have not been proceeded with, and the defendant falls to be sentenced only for one or more summary offences (such as common assault or an offence of criminal damage below the £5,000 threshold). The Crown Court is limited to a maximum of six months' imprisonment for common assault and to three months' imprisonment for the criminal damage and, by the MCA 1980, s. 133, to a maximum aggregate custodial sentence of six months, less any appropriate reduction for a guilty plea. A salutary case is *Moore* [2015] EWCA Crim 1621, where sentences of three months' imprisonment were imposed consecutively for four offences of common assault, producing a total of 12 months, which was then suspended for 18 months. On appeal the sentence was (with 'no enthusiasm at all') reduced on appeal to four months' imprisonment imposed concurrently on each count, and then suspended. In *Hester-Wox* [2016] EWCA Crim 1397, [2016] 2 Cr App R (S) 43 (463), D pleaded guilty to several summary-only offences, commission of which had placed him in breach of a suspended sentence imposed by the Crown Court. The Divisional Court held that while the Crown Court was limited to a total of six months when dealing with the summary offences, the judge had been entitled to activate the suspended sentence for six months consecutively, making a total of 12 months. See also *Brindle* [2019] EWCA Crim 813, where, in a case of domestic assault, the Court of Appeal reduced a total sentence of 12 months for two offences of common assault and one of criminal damage to a total of five months, so that the sentence no longer infringed the MCA 1980, s. 133, but ordered a five-months term for breach of a Family Court non-molestation order to run consecutively to that total.

A magistrates' court having power to imprison a person may instead order detention within the precincts of the court-house or at any police station until such hour, not later than 8 p.m. on the day on which the order is made, as the court directs (MCA 1980, s. 135(1)). Such order shall not operate to deprive the person of a reasonable opportunity of returning home on the same day (s. 135(2)).

RESTRICTIONS ON IMPOSING CUSTODIAL SENTENCES

Persons Not Legally Represented

E2.6 The PCC(S)A 2000, s. 83(1), states that a magistrates' court on summary conviction, or the Crown Court on committal for sentence or on conviction on indictment, shall not pass a sentence of imprisonment on a person who (a) is not legally represented in that court, and (b) has not been previously sentenced to that punishment by a court in any part of the UK unless he or she is a person to whom s. 83(3) applies. A previous suspended sentence does not count for this purpose, unless that sentence was later activated (s. 83(5)). Section 83(3) applies to a person if either '(a) representation was made available to him for the purposes of the proceedings under [the LASPO 2012] but was withdrawn because of his conduct or because it appeared that his financial resources were such that he was not eligible for such representation, or (aa) he applied for such representation and the application was refused because it appeared that his financial resources were such that he was not eligible for such representation, or (b) having been informed of his right to apply for such representation and having had the opportunity to do so, he refused or failed to apply'.

Section 83(2) extends the effect of these provisions on imprisonment to custodial sentences other than imprisonment: (a) detention under the PCC(S)A 2000, s. 90 or 91, (b) custody for life under the PCC(S)A 2000, s. 93 or 94, (c) detention in a young offender institution and (d) the detention and training order. In relation to the custodial sentences referred to in s. 83(2), in contrast to the wording of s. 83(1), the restriction applies whether or not the offender has previously received a custodial sentence. Section 83(2) does not mention the extended sentence under the CJA 2003, s. 226A or 226B, but it is submitted that this exclusion is a legislative oversight.

For the purposes of s. 83, 'a person is to be treated as legally represented if, but only if, he has the assistance of counsel or a solicitor to represent him in the proceedings in that court at some time after he is found guilty and before he is sentenced' (s. 83(4)).

A custodial sentence passed contrary to the provisions of s. 83 is unlawful, but may be substituted by a lawful sentence on appeal (*Howden* [2006] EWCA Crim 1691, [2007] 1 Cr App R (S) 31 (164); *Henry* [2013] EWCA Crim 1415, [2014] 1 Cr App R (S) 55 (347)); see also **D20.79**.

General Restrictions

Criminal Justice Act 2003, s. 152 **E2.7**

(1) This section applies where a person is convicted of an offence punishable with a custodial sentence other than one—
  (a) fixed by law, or
  (b) falling to be imposed under a provision mentioned in subsection (1A).

(1A) The provisions referred to in subsection (1)(b) are—
  (a) section 1(2B) or 1A(5) of the Prevention of Crime Act 1953;
  (b) section 51A(2) of the Firearms Act 1968;
  (c) section 139(6B), 139A(5B) or 139AA(7) of the Criminal Justice Act 1988;
  (d) section 110(2) or 111(2) of the Sentencing Act;
  (e) section 224A, 225(2) or 226(2) of this Act;
  (f) section 29(4) or (6) of the Violent Crime Reduction Act 2006.

(2) The court must not pass a custodial sentence unless it is of the opinion that the offence, or the combination of the offence and one or more offences associated with it, was so serious that neither a fine alone nor a community sentence can be justified for the offence.

The definitive sentencing guideline, *Imposition of Community and Custodial Sentences* (see Supplement, **SG9-1**), states that the clear intention of this 'threshold test' is to reserve prison as a punishment for the most serious offences, but that there is no general definition of where the custody threshold lies. The circumstances of the individual offence and the factors assessed by offence-specific guidelines will determine whether an offence is so serious that neither a fine alone nor a community sentence can be justified. The guideline also states that 'Passing the custody threshold does not mean that a custodial sentence should be deemed inevitable'.

Section 152(3) deals with the exceptional situation where a court may pass a custodial sentence on an offender who has failed to express willingness to comply with a requirement proposed to be included in a community order and where the requirement requires an expression of such willingness. Requirements which require the offender's expression of willingness to comply are a mental health treatment requirement (s. 207(3)(c)), a drug rehabilitation requirement (s. 209(2)(d)), and an alcohol treatment requirement (s. 212(3)).

Two or More Offences Where the offender stands convicted of two or more offences the court, in deciding whether custody is justified under s. 152(2), must consider the seriousness of the sum of the offences, provided that these are 'associated' with one another. Section 161(1) of the 2000 Act specifies when one offence is to be regarded as associated with another. **E2.8**

Powers of Criminal Courts (Sentencing) Act 2000, s. 161

(1) For the purposes of this Act, an offence is associated with another if—
  (a) the offender is convicted of it in the proceedings in which he is convicted of the other offence, or (although convicted of it in earlier proceedings) is sentenced for it at the same time as he is sentenced for that offence; or
  (b) the offender admits the commission of it in the proceedings in which he is sentenced for the other offence and requests the court to take it into consideration in sentencing him for that offence.

In *Baverstock* [1993] 2 All ER 32, D was dealt with for two offences; the second having been committed while D was on bail in respect of the first. D was sentenced for the two offences on the same occasion; hence, they were 'associated' for the purposes of s. 161(1). It is clear from the case of *Godfrey* (1993) 14 Cr App R (S) 804 that, where a sentencer is sentencing for a new offence and at the same time revokes a community sentence which had earlier been passed on the offender and resentences for that offence, or where the sentencer passes a sentence for an offence in respect of which a conditional discharge had earlier been granted, the new offence and the earlier offence are associated offences. In *Crawford* (1993) 98 Cr App R 297, it was held that, where D had been committed to the Crown Court in respect of an offence of theft which placed him in breach of a suspended sentence imposed for an earlier offence of theft, the two offences were not associated offences. *Crawford* was followed and applied in *Cawley* (1994) 15 Cr App R (S) 25. Where an offender has been convicted in respect of a number of charges which are represented as 'sample counts', offences which are not included in the indictment, nor formally taken into consideration, are not associated offences (*Canavan* [1998] 1 Cr App R (S) 79; *Hartley* [2011] EWCA Crim 1957, [2012] 1 Cr App R (S) 28 (166)). See further **D20.56**.

LENGTH OF SENTENCE

General Provision

E2.9 **Criminal Justice Act 2003, s. 153**

(1) This section applies where a court passes a custodial sentence other than one fixed by law or imposed under section 224A, 225 or 226.
(2) Subject to the provisions listed in subsection (3), the custodial sentence must be for the shortest term (not exceeding the permitted maximum) that in the opinion of the court is commensurate with the seriousness of the offence, or the combination of the offence and one or more offences associated with it.
(3) The provisions referred to in subsection (2) are—
 (a) sections 1(2B) and 1A(5) of the Prevention of Crime Act 1953;
 (b) section 51A(2) of the Firearms Act 1968;
 (c) sections 139(6B), 139(5B) and 139AA(7) of the Criminal Justice Act 1988;
 (d) sections 110(2) and 111(2) of the Sentencing Act;
 (e) sections 226A(4) and 226B(2) of this Act;
 (f) section 29(4) or (6) of the Violent Crime Reduction Act 2006.

The wording in s. 153(2) is a clear reflection of the well-established principle that, when it is necessary to impose a custodial sentence, that sentence should be as short as possible to achieve the goals of that sentence. The definitive guideline, *Imposition of Community and Custodial Sentences* (see Supplement, **SG9-1**), says that when assessing what is the shortest term commensurate with the seriousness of the offence, the court should not take into account any licence or post-sentence supervision requirements which may be imposed upon the offender's release.

Section 153(2) states that the court may have regard to 'the combination of the offence and one or more offences associated with it' when determining the length of a custodial sentence. The PCC(S)A 2000, s. 161(1) (see **E2.8**), defines when one offence may be regarded for these purposes as 'associated with' another.

The provisions listed in s. 153(3) are the extended sentence (see **E4.10** and **E4.13**) and the prescribed custodial sentences (see **E5**).

E2.10 **Dealing with Several Offences** Where the offender is being sentenced for several offences, this approach could lead to a total sentence which is disproportionate to the overall seriousness of the offending behaviour. The CJA 2003, s. 166(3)(b), declares that nothing shall prevent a court 'in a case of an offender who is convicted of one or more other offences, from mitigating his sentence by applying any rule of law as to the totality of sentences'. This provision gives statutory recognition to the totality principle. For discussion of that principle, see **E1.21**.

Where a court is dealing with an offender for several offences, one (or more) of which is (or are) so serious that only custody can be justified but the remainder of which are not so serious, the court is not precluded from passing custodial sentences for the lesser offences. However, those sentences should normally be ordered to run concurrently with the sentences for the more serious offences and should not increase the length of the overall term (*Oliver* [1993] 2 All ER 9).

E2.11 **Considering Shorter Period** In *Kefford* [2002] EWCA Crim 519, [2002] 2 Cr App R (S) 106 (495), Lord Woolf CJ said that the overcrowding of the prison system was a matter of grave concern and that all courts should heed the message, which was 'imprisonment only when necessary and for no longer than necessary'. See also *Mills* [2002] EWCA Crim 26, [2002] 2 Cr App R (S) 52 (229), with respect to the female prison population, and *Seed* [2007] EWCA Crim 254, [2007] 2 Cr App R (S) 69 (436). In *Manning* [2020] EWCA Crim 592, [2020] 4 WLR 77, Lord Burnett

CJ said that the impact of the Covid-19 emergency on prisons was well known. In accordance with established principles any court will take account of the likely impact of a custodial sentence upon an offender and, where appropriate, upon others as well. Judges and magistrates should remember that the impact of a custodial sentence upon an offender is likely to be heavier during the current emergency than it otherwise would be. Those in custody are confined to their cells for much longer than would normally be the case — up to 23 hours a day — and they are unable to receive visits. Applying ordinary principles, where a court is satisfied that a custodial sentence must be imposed, the likely impact of that sentence continues to be relevant as to the length of the sentence and whether it can be suspended. In *Jones* [2020] EWCA Crim 764, the Court of Appeal considered a sentence of eight months' imprisonment imposed just six days before the Covid-19 lockdown. Having noted that the judge imposing the sentence would clearly have been unaware of the impending change to prison conditions, and referring to Lord Burnett's comments in *Manning*, the Court reduced the sentence from eight months to six months.

Time Remanded in Custody to Count as Time Served

Criminal Justice Act 2003, s. 240ZA **E2.12**

(1) This section applies where—
  (a) an offender is serving a term of imprisonment in respect of an offence, and
  (b) the offender has been remanded in custody (within the meaning given by section 242) in connection with the offence or a related offence.
(2) It is immaterial for that purpose whether, for all or part of the period during which the offender was remanded in custody, the offender was also remanded in custody in connection with other offences (but see subsection (5)).
(3) The number of days for which the offender was remanded in custody in connection with the offence or a related offence is to count as time served by the offender as part of the sentence. But this is subject to subsections (4) to (6).
(4) If, on any day on which the offender was remanded in custody, the offender was also detained in connection with any other matter, that day is not to count as time served.
(5) A day counts as time served—
  (a) in relation to only one sentence, and
  (b) only once in relation to that sentence.
(6) A day is not to count as time served as part of any automatic release period served by the offender (see section 255B(1)).
(7) For the purposes of this section a suspended sentence—
  (a) is to be treated as a sentence of imprisonment when it takes effect under paragraph 8(2)(a) or (b) of schedule 12, and
  (b) is to be treated as being imposed by the order under which it takes effect.

Section 240ZA has the effect of crediting periods of remand in custody automatically, so that it is **E2.13** not necessary for sentencers to give any direction that time served on remand in custody should count towards sentence. Section 240ZA applies to sentences of imprisonment, detention in a young offender institution, detention under the PCC(S)A 2000, s. 91, custodial sentences for certain offenders of particular concern, and extended sentences of imprisonment or detention. It should be noted, however, that s. 240ZA does not apply to the detention and training order, so it remains necessary when imposing a detention and training order to take into account any period spent in custody on remand (PCC(S)A 2000, s. 101(8): see **E7.23**). Also, in respect of sentences where the law requires the setting of a specified period under the PCC(S)A 2000, s. 82A (life sentence where that sentence is not fixed by law), s. 82A(3)(b) of that Act requires the court, when fixing the specified period, to take into account the effect which s. 240ZA would have had if a determinate sentence had instead been imposed (see **E4.29**). In fixing the minimum term applicable in a case of murder, the court is similarly required by s. 269(3)(b) to take into account the effect of s. 240ZA (see **E3.2**).

As Treacy LJ observed in *Bhayani* [2015] EWCA Crim 352 (at [56]), 'granting of credit for time spent on remand... is now a purely administrative function of the prison service'. However, in cases where the offender has spent a substantial period in custody on remand, that matter may still be relevant to the court when deciding whether further punishment is justified or whether, in effect, the offender has already served the sentence in custody on remand. See, e.g., *Barrett* [2010] EWCA Crim 365, [2010] 2 Cr App R (S) 86 (551) and *Maughan* [2011] EWCA Crim 787, [2011] 2 Cr App R (S) 89 (493) at **E6.4**. If the appropriate sentence is one of six months' imprisonment and the offender has spent three months on remand, the sentence of six months should be imposed but no further punishment (whether by way of immediate custody or a suspended sentence) is necessary. To this extent, at least, it remains important for accurate information to be before the court as to the number of days spent on remand, so that an explanation can be given in open court as to the sentence passed and its practical effect. For offences committed on or after 1 February 2015, where a custodial sentence of more than one day but less than two years is imposed, D will be subject to supervision and licence requirements (see the CJA 2003, s. 256AA, and **E2.26**). Also, where a court imposes an immediate custodial sentence and disqualifies the offender from driving for the same offence, the court is required to add an extension period to the discretionary period of disqualification. See the RTOA 1988, s. 35A, and **C7.36**. The Court of Appeal in *Needham* [2016] EWCA Crim 455, [2016] 2 Cr App R (S) 26 (219) said that if an offender had spent a significant period on remand it was open to the court to avoid injustice by reducing the discretionary period accordingly, although a precise arithmetical calculation was not required. Care should be taken not thereby to infringe any applicable minimum period of disqualification.

E2.14 The effect of s. 240ZA(4) and (5) is that, if a prisoner is released from custody on licence but is recalled following a further offence, time on remand in respect of the further offence does not count as time to be deducted from a custodial sentence imposed for the new offence. In *Phillips* [2015] EWCA Crim 427, [2015] 2 Cr App R (S) 9 (96) the Court of Appeal said that, while the judge dealing with the new offence had discretion to adjust the custodial term to make some allowance to reflect the time spent on remand for the new offence, this was a 'residual discretion to correct injustice', for example where there had been 'excessive delay'. Ordinarily no reduction should be made, since to do so would undermine the clear words of the statute. See also *Elkington* [2015] EWCA Crim 659 and *Mayo* [2015] EWCA Crim 628.

Section 242(2) explains that 'remanded in custody' means (a) 'remanded in or committed to custody by order of a court', or (b) 'remanded to youth detention accommodation' under the LASPO 2012, s. 91(4), or (c) 'remanded, admitted or removed to hospital' under the Mental Health Act 1983. It does not apply to any committal in default of payment of any sum of money, other than one adjudged to be paid on a conviction (s. 242(1)). It does not include time spent in police detention. It does not include time on remand spent by a person under 18 in local authority accommodation under the LASPO 2012, s. 91(3) (*A* [2019] EWCA Crim 106, [2019] 2 Cr App R (S) 11 (75)). There is a residual power to adjust sentence to avoid injustice in a case where the defendant has spent time awaiting trial in restrictive conditions falling outside the definition of 'remanded in custody' in s. 242(2), but it is clear from the authorities that such power should only be used exceptionally (*Prenga* [2017] EWCA Crim 2149, [2018] 1 Cr App R (S) 41 (287); *Keeley* [2018] EWCA Crim 2089, [2019] 1 Cr App R (S) 13 (97); *A* [2019] EWCA Crim 106, [2019] 2 Cr App R (S) 11 (75)). The Court of Appeal in *Al Daour* [2011] EWCA Crim 2392 said that although police detention did not come within the terms of s. 242(2), it was not necessarily wrong to adjust sentence length to take account of an extended period in police detention (in that case under the TA 2000). In *Watson* [2000] 2 Cr App R (S) 301, the Court of Appeal said that it was right to take into account a period of 11 months that the offender had spent on remand in a bail hostel under restrictive conditions, although the Court stressed that a period in a bail hostel was not to be equated with a period on remand in custody.

E2.15 **Extradited Prisoners** The CJA 2003, s. 243, provides that in the case of an extradited prisoner the court must specify in open court the number of days for which the prisoner was kept in custody abroad while awaiting extradition, and that s. 240ZA applies to days specified in this way as if they were days for which the prisoner was remanded in custody. There is no power in the court to disallow these days. In *R (Shields-McKinlay) v Secretary of State for Justice* [2019] EWCA Civ 1954, [2020] QB 521, the Court of Appeal (Civil Division) confirmed the decision of the Administrative Court that the wording of the section was clear, and the days could not be credited unless so specified in open court. If the requirement had been overlooked the only remedy, once the slip rule period had expired, was to appeal the sentence. In *Hughes* [2020] EWCA Crim 266, the Court of Appeal corrected the sentencing judge's failure to specify in open court the number of days D had spent in custody awaiting extradition, but said that now the decision in *Shields-McKinlay* was established and understood, applications to correct errors must be made promptly and late applications would not routinely be granted.

Crediting Periods of Remand on Bail

The CJA 2003, s. 240A, states that, where an offender has been remanded on bail and that bail was subject both to a 'qualifying curfew condition' (requiring that person to remain at one or more specified places for a total of not less than nine hours in any given day) and an 'electronic monitoring condition' (imposed under the BA 1976, s. 3(6ZAA)), the court must normally direct that the 'credit period' is to count as time served by the offender as part of the sentence. It is the responsibility of the court to make this direction, unlike the adjustment for time spent on remand in custody, which under s. 240ZA does not require an order of the court. The credit period under s. 240A is calculated by taking the following five steps, as set out in s. 240A(3). Step 1 is to add the day on which the offender's bail was first subject to the relevant conditions (even if these did not apply for the whole day) and the number of other days on which the offender's bail was subject to these conditions (excluding the last day if part of that day was spent in custody). Step 2 is to deduct the number of days on which the offender was also subject to any requirement of electronic monitoring of a curfew requirement, or was on temporary release. Step 3 is to deduct any days during which the offender broke either or both of the conditions. Step 4 is to divide the result by two, and Step 5 is to round up the figure to the nearest whole number, if necessary. Subject to s. 240A(3A) and (3B), the court must direct that the credit period is to count as time served. Subsection (3A) states that a day of the credit period counts as time served in relation to only one sentence, and only once in relation to that sentence, and subsection (3B) says that a day of the credit period is not to count as time served as part of any automatic release period served by the offender (s. 255B(1)). The sentencer should state in open court the number of days on which the offender was subject to the conditions and the number of days which the court deducted under each of Steps 2 and 3 (s. 240A(8)). As with s. 240ZA, the term 'imprisonment' must be taken to apply to sentences of detention in a young offender institution, extended sentences of imprisonment or detention in a young offender institution, and determinate sentences of detention under the PCC(S)A 2000, s. 91. Again in line with s. 240ZA, a suspended sentence counts as a sentence of imprisonment for these purposes if it takes effect in consequence of breach. However, in *Williams* [2018] EWCA Crim 2396, where D had spent almost a year on a qualifying curfew, for which he was entitled to credit, and where the proper sentence for the offence was three months, it was held to be wrong to pass a sentence of three months suspended for 15 months with requirements. The Court of Appeal varied the sentence to three months' immediate custody, allowing D's immediate release. **E2.16**

The Court of Appeal in *Hoggard* [2013] EWCA Crim 102, [2014] 1 Cr App R (S) 42 (239) said that, in a case where the judge intends to direct that the full credit period during which an offender has been on bail subject to a qualifying curfew condition should count as time served but where there is uncertainty over the number of days involved, the judge should use the following form of words: **E2.17**

> The defendant will receive full credit for half the time spent under curfew qualified under the provisions of section 240A. On the information before me the total period is XX days (subject to the deduction of XX days that I have directed under Step(s) 2 and /or (3) making a total of XX days), but if this period is mistaken this court will order an amendment of the record for the correct period to be recorded.

If the above form of words is used, any error can be corrected in the court office even after the expiry of the 56 days allowed under the slip rule, provided the parties were agreed. If they were not agreed, the court would decide the issue. It is essential that every court which imposes a curfew and tagging condition uses the relevant Court Service form. Solicitors and counsel must ask the defendant whether he or she had been subject to curfew and tagging and, if the answer was 'yes', to find out, from the court record, for which periods. The sentencing judge should also inquire in every case whether the defendant had spent time on a qualifying curfew (*Thorsby* [2015] EWCA Crim 1, [2015] 1 WLR 2901; *Marshall* [2015] EWCA Crim 1999, [2016] 1 Cr App R (S) 45 (282)). In *Hoggard* itself, under Step 1 there was a period of 94 days. There was nothing to require a reduction from that period under Step 2. Under Step 3 the probation service said that the defendant had broken either or both of the relevant conditions on a total of eight of the 94 days. The breaches were denied. The net period in dispute was therefore four days. To resolve the dispute would have required an adjournment, the attendance of the prosecution, and probably the calling of evidence. The Court concluded that, in the circumstances of this case, such proceedings would amount to a disproportionate use of time and expense. Accordingly the issue was resolved in the defendant's favour. Having applied Steps 4 and 5 the Court ordered that 47 days should count towards the service of the sentence. The Court of Appeal in *Hoggard* also said that in future it would scrutinise with great care applications for extension of time for appeal where the sole complaint is an error of calculation relating to s. 240A. See further *Marshall* for the adopted procedure of the Court of Appeal.

Whether credit should be given, and if so how much, if a lengthy and onerous period of remand on bail falls outside the terms of s. 240A, is a matter for the sentencing judge. In *Monaghan* [2009] EWCA Crim 2699, [2010] 2 Cr App R (S) 50 (343), the Court indicated that a period of time spent by the offender subject to an electronically monitored curfew of *less* than nine hours should not normally occasion a reduction, but that the court should consider giving some modest credit where the offender had spent a significant period of time subject to those conditions. In *Whitehouse* [2019] EWCA Crim 970, [2019] 2 Cr App R (S) 48 (396), D had been on bail for 20 months and subject to a curfew between 7 p.m. and 5 a.m. as well as residence and reporting conditions. This was not a qualifying curfew because it had not been electronically monitored, but the Court of Appeal said that the conditions had been 'highly restrictive' and reduced the otherwise appropriate sentence of four years by a period of nine months.

E2.18 **Effect of Time on Remand on Suspended Sentence or Community Sentence** For the relevance of time spent on remand before the imposition of a suspended sentence, see **E6.4**. For the relevance of time spent on remand before the imposition of a community sentence, see **E8.3**.

Concurrent and Consecutive Determinate Custodial Sentences

E2.19 Where an offender is to be sentenced for more than one offence, the court should impose separate sentences for each offence, unless one of the offences is to be marked with 'no separate penalty'. Sentences of imprisonment or detention in a young offender institution may run concurrently or consecutively. The court should make it clear which sentence relates to which count and whether the sentences are concurrent or consecutive. If it fails to do so, it is presumed that the sentences are concurrent. Where a court passes a determinate custodial sentence on a person who is already serving one or more such sentences, it must make clear whether the fresh sentence is to be served concurrently with or consecutively to the existing sentence or sentences. It is unlawful to pass a sentence partly concurrent with and partly consecutive to another sentence (*Salmon* [2002] EWCA Crim 2088, [2003] 1 Cr App R (S) 85 (414)). There is no power to antedate the commencement of a sentence (PCC(S)A 2000, s. 154; *AJ* [2013] EWCA Crim 908; *Babiak* [2017] EWCA Crim 160, [2017] 1 Cr App R (S) 52 (407)), so the new sentence takes effect from the date on which it is imposed, unless the sentencer specifies a later date.

It is important to note that a court imposing a determinate custodial sentence must not direct that the new sentence shall commence on the expiration of any other custodial sentence from which D has been released on licence (CJA 2003, s. 265), whether or not D has been recalled from that licence (*McStravick* [2018] EWCA Crim 1207, [2018] 2 Cr App R (S) 26 (237); *Owusu* [2018] EWCA Crim 1959). See further *Costello* [2010] EWCA Crim 371, [2010] 2 Cr App R (S) 94 (608), where the Court of Appeal held that it is wrong in principle in such a case to pass a sentence which is disproportionate to the most recent offence in an attempt to ensure that the offender serves more than the remainder of the licence period of the original offence.

Guidance on Use of Concurrent Sentences For guidance on the imposition of concurrent determinate sentences, see the definitive sentencing guideline, *Totality* (see Supplement, **SG4-1**). The guideline states that *concurrent sentences* will ordinarily be concurrent where: **E2.20**

(a) offences arise out of the same incident or facts, or
(b) there is a series of offences of the same or similar kind, especially when committed against the same person.

Where concurrent sentences are to be passed the sentence should reflect the overall criminality involved. The sentence should be increased to reflect the presence of the associated offences.

Guidance on Use of Consecutive Sentences For guidance on the imposition of consecutive determinate sentences imposed on the same sentencing occasion, see the definitive sentencing guideline, *Totality* (see Supplement, **SG4-1**). The guideline states that *consecutive sentences* will ordinarily be appropriate where: **E2.21**

(a) offences arise out of unrelated facts or incidents.
(b) offences are of the same or similar kind but the overall criminality will not sufficiently be reflected by concurrent sentences;
(c) one or more offence(s) qualifies for a statutory minimum sentence and concurrent sentences would improperly undermine that minimum.

The guideline states that it is not permissible to impose consecutive sentences for offences committed at the same time in order to evade the statutory maximum penalty. Where consecutive sentences are to be passed, the judge should add up the sentences for each offence and consider if the aggregate length is just and appropriate.

In respect of the imposition of a determinate sentence upon an offender who is currently serving a determinate sentence, the Sentencing Council definitive guideline, *Totality* (see Supplement, **SG4-5**), sets out the proper approach for sentencing, distinguishing between cases where the new offence was (a) committed before the original sentence was imposed, and (b) committed after the original sentence was imposed.

Totality Principle The Sentencing Council definitive guideline, *Totality* (see Supplement, **SG4-5**), states that the principle of totality comprises two elements: **E2.22**

(a) All courts, when sentencing for more than a single offence, should pass a total sentence which reflects all the offending behaviour before it, and is just and proportionate. That is so whether the sentences are structured as concurrent or consecutive. Therefore, concurrent sentences will ordinarily be longer than a single sentence for a single offence.
(b) It is usually impossible to arrive at a just and proportionate sentence for multiple offending simply by adding together notional single sentences. It is necessary to address the offending behaviour, together with the factors personal to the offender as a whole.

In *Raza* [2009] EWCA Crim 1413, [2010] 1 Cr App R (S) 56 (354), the Court of Appeal said that where consecutive sentences are imposed, and one is a prescribed minimum sentence, the principle of totality must not be applied in a way that undermines the intention of Parliament in setting the minimum sentence. See, however, *Sparkes* [2011] EWCA Crim 880, [2011] 2 Cr App R (S) 107 (614), where the Court of Appeal, in order to preserve totality, chose to adjust a prescribed minimum sentence, rather than consecutive sentences imposed for other offences. In *Hardy* [2019] EWCA Crim 2247, [2020] 1 Cr App R (S) 61 (475), D received consecutive sentences for two unrelated offences, the first being a sentence of three years and four months for possession with intent to supply Class A drugs and the second attracting the minimum sentence of five years for possession of a disguised firearm. The judge said that to reduce the sentence for the drug dealing matter to reflect totality would undermine the purpose of the minimum sentence. On appeal, however, the Court of Appeal said that the judge was in error, that the 'principle of totality is of general application', and the sentence for the drugs offence was accordingly reduced by six months. See further the definitive sentencing guideline, *Totality* (see Supplement, **SG4-1**). For consideration of the extent, if any, to which a custodial sentence might be adjusted for totality to take account of a custodial sentence imposed on the offender by a foreign court for similar related offending see *Bazegurore* [2020] EWCA Crim 375. See further **A9.24**.

Determinate Custodial Sentences and Early Release Provisions

E2.23 In the case of determinate sentences of imprisonment, detention in a young offender institution, or detention under the PCC(S)A 2000, s. 91, there is normally a duty on the Secretary of State to release the offender on licence once *one half* of the sentence has been served (CJA 2003, s. 244). The licence remains in force until the expiry of the sentence (s. 249). There is an exception in relation to sentences of imprisonment or detention in a young offender institution imposed under s. 236A upon certain offenders of 'particular concern' (see s. 244A and **E4.31**).

Different early release provisions apply in relation to extended sentences under the CJA 2003, s. 226A or 226B (see s. 246A and **E4.12**). A different regime applies to the detention and training order (see **E7.22**).

The early release and licence provisions in ss. 244 and 249 are made subject to ss. 256AA to 256C (inserted by the ORA 2014), which apply where an offender is serving a sentence of imprisonment or detention in a young offender institution which is for a term of more than one day but less than two years, and provided that the sentence was imposed for an offence committed on or after 1 February 2015. See further **E2.26**.

In respect of a determinate custodial sentence of imprisonment or detention in a young offender institution (but not detention under s. 91) imposed for a specified violent offence or a specified sexual offence listed in sch. 15 to the CJA 2003 (see **E4.4**) for which the maximum penalty is life imprisonment, and where the sentence imposed is one of seven years or more, with effect from 1 April 2020 the Release of Prisoners (Alteration of Relevant Proportion of Sentence) Order 2019 (SI 2020 No. 158) amends the automatic release point from *one half* to *two thirds* of the sentence. The change made by the 2019 Order applies to offenders sentenced on or after that date.

As from 26 February 2020 the Terrorist Offenders (Restriction of Early Release) Act 2020 inserts into the CJA 2003 a new s. 247A (eligibility for release on licence of terrorist prisoners) and a new sch. 19ZA, with the effect that, for offenders serving a determinate sentence of imprisonment, detention in a young offender institution, or detention under s. 91, who were (a) convicted of an offence specified in sch. 19ZA, part 1 (offences under counter-terrorism legislation), or (b) convicted of an offence specified in sch. 19ZA, part 2, and who were determined by the court to have had a terrorist connection under the C-TA 2008, s. 30, the offender must first be considered for early release by the Parole Board at the *two-thirds* point of the sentence (rather than being released automatically at the half-way point of the sentence). The Board may direct the offender's release at that point, but only if satisfied that it is no longer necessary for the protection of the public that the offender should be confined. The change made by the 2020 Act applies to offenders who are serving such a sentence at the commencement date and who have not been released on licence, as well as to offenders so sentenced on or after that date.

Relevance to Sentence of Early Release Provisions etc.

E2.24 In *Round* [2009] EWCA Crim 667, [2010] 2 Cr App R (S) 45 (292), the Court of Appeal confirmed the long-standing principle that matters of early release, licence and home detention curfew should normally be left out of account when imposing sentence. The same point was made in *A-G's Ref (No. 27 of 2013) (Burinskas)* [2014] EWCA Crim 334, [2014] 1 WLR 4209, in relation to statutory changes to early release from an extended sentence. It was held to have been wrong in *Lewis* [2019] EWCA Crim 1778, [2020] 1 Cr App R (S) 29 (221), for a judge when imposing a prison sentence on a serving prisoner in Scotland to adjust that sentence to take account of different early release provisions in Scotland. In *Al-Buhairi* [2003] EWCA Crim 2922, [2004] 1 Cr App R (S) 83 (496), and in *Alkazraji* [2004] EWCA Crim 204, [2004] 2 Cr App R (S) 55 (291), the Court of Appeal held that it was not proper for a judge to adjust sentence to take account of the fact that the offender may be released early on the home detention curfew scheme. Older authorities suggest, however, that a judge is entitled to adjust sentence length to avoid a seriously adverse effect upon an offender's release date (*Cozens* [1996] 2 Cr App R (S) 321; *Harrison* [1998] 2 Cr App R (S) 174).

The CJA 2003, s. 174 (**E1.23**), places a duty on the sentencer to explain to the offender the effect of the sentence 'in ordinary language and general terms'. In *Bright* [2008] EWCA Crim 462, [2008] 2 Cr App R (S) 102 (578) and in *Giga* [2008] EWCA Crim 703, [2008] 2 Cr App R (S) 112 (638), the Court of Appeal said that a judge's error, when explaining in open court the effect of early release provisions upon the offender's sentence, in no way invalidated that sentence or provided grounds for saying that the sentence was wrong in principle.

The sentencer should not recommend that an offender serve a custodial sentence at a specified prison, since it may not always be possible for this to be arranged (*Lancaster* (1995) 16 Cr App R (S) 184). The fact that a prisoner will be required to serve a sentence in isolation for the prisoner's own protection is not normally a relevant consideration when passing sentence (*Kay* (1980) 2 Cr App R (S) 284; *Parker* [1996] 2 Cr App R (S) 275). An exceptional case is *Holmes* (1979) 1 Cr App R (S) 233.

Sentences of 12 Months or More: Licence Conditions

By the CJA 2003, s. 238, where the court imposes a determinate sentence of imprisonment or detention in a young offender institution (but not a sentence of detention under the PCC(S)A 2000, s. 91, or the CJA 2003, s. 226B) of 12 months or more on an offender for any offence, the part of the sentence to be served after release from custody will be subject to prescribed standard conditions, and may be made subject to further conditions. Those further conditions are determined shortly before release of the offender by the Secretary of State, but the court, at the time of passing sentence, may make recommendations as to the content of those further conditions (s. 238(1)). The Secretary of State must have regard to any such recommendation (s. 238(2)). The conditions that the Secretary of State may attach to a licence are to be prescribed by order (s. 250), and the sentencer will wish to bear these in mind when making a recommendation at the point of sentence. A recommendation made by the sentencer as to licence conditions is not to be treated as part of the sentence (s. 238(3)), and so cannot be the subject of an appeal against sentence. **E2.25**

Sentences of More than One Day but Less than Two Years: Breach of Supervision Requirement

Where an offender is released from a sentence of imprisonment or a sentence of detention in a young offender institution of more than one day but less than two years, and that sentence was imposed for an offence committed on or after 1 February 2015, the offender will be on licence from the point at which the requisite custodial period (one half of the sentence) has been served until the expiry of the sentence and will then be subject to a further period of supervision which will begin at the expiry of the sentence and end on the expiry of the period of 12 months beginning immediately after the offender has served the requisite custodial period (CJA 2003, s. 256AA). This means that, for a six-month sentence of imprisonment, the offender is released at the half-way point, is under licence for three months and subject to supervision for nine months. For a 12-month sentence of imprisonment, the offender is released at the half-way point, is on licence for six months and under supervision for six months. During the licence period the offender is subject to recall to custody for breach of the terms of the licence. During the supervision period the offender must comply with requirements specified by the Secretary of State. If the offender breaches a requirement of supervision imposed under s. 256AA, the **E2.26** offender will be brought before the appropriate magistrates' court to be dealt with for the breach (s. 256AC). If it is proved to the satisfaction of the court that the person has failed without reasonable excuse to comply with a supervision requirement, the court may:

(a) order the person to be committed to prison (or in the case of a person under the age of 21, to a young offender institution) for a period not exceeding 14 days;
(b) order the person to pay a fine not exceeding level 3 on the standard scale; or
(c) make an order (a 'supervision default order'), imposing on the person (i) an unpaid work requirement (as defined by the CJA 2003, s. 199) or (ii) a curfew requirement (as defined by the CJA 2003, s. 204).

The Sentencing Council definitive guideline, *Breach Offences* (see Supplement, **SG15-1**), applies to offenders sentenced on or after 1 October 2018, irrespective of the date of the offence.

A person dealt with under s. 256AC may appeal to the Crown Court. The Offender Rehabilitation Act 2014, sch. 19A, makes provision about requirements of supervision default orders and about the breach, revocation and amendment of supervision default orders.

Section E3 Mandatory Life Sentences

INTRODUCTION

An offender aged 21 and over who is convicted of murder (but not related offences such as attempted murder or conspiracy to murder) must be sentenced to imprisonment for life (Murder (Abolition of Death Penalty) Act 1965, s. 1(1)). For an offender aged under 21 on the date of conviction, the equivalent sentence is custody for life (see the PCC(S)A 2000, s. 93, and **E3.11**). If, however, the offender who is convicted of murder was aged under 18 when the offence was committed, irrespective of his or her age at the date of conviction, the sentence is one of detention at Her Majesty's pleasure (see the PCC(S)A 2000, s. 90, and **E3.12**). **E3.1**

MURDER: LIFE IMPRISONMENT

The CJA 2003, ss. 269 to 277 and schs. 21 and 22, provide a statutory scheme for the setting of minimum terms in murder cases. These provisions apply to all cases in which a court passes a mandatory life sentence for murder. This applies to sentences of life imprisonment for murder, detention at Her Majesty's pleasure under the PCC(S)A 2000, s. 90, and custody for life imposed for murder committed by an 18, 19 or 20-year-old offender under the PCC(S) A 2000, s. 93. By the CJA 2003, s. 269(2), the court must normally make an order that the early release provisions of the Crime (Sentences) Act 1997, s. 28(5) to (8), are to apply to the offender as soon as he or she has served the part of the sentence which is specified in the order. That part is to be such as the court considers appropriate, taking into account (a) the seriousness of the offence, or the combination of the offence and any one or more offences associated with it, and (b) the effect of any direction which it would have given under the CJA 2003, s. 240ZA (crediting periods of remand in custody) or of any direction which it would have given under s. 240A (crediting of periods of remand on certain types of bail), if it had sentenced the offender to a term of imprisonment (s. 269(3)). If the offender was aged 21 or over when the offence was committed, the court may, however, because of the seriousness of the offence, order that the early release provisions are not to apply (s. 269(4)). An order under s. 269(4) would have the effect of imposing a 'whole life' minimum term. A judge fixing the minimum term to be served as part of the mandatory life sentence for murder is concerned with the seriousness of the offence itself, and not the dangerousness of the offender. The element of public protection is provided by the indeterminate nature of the life sentence and becomes the responsibility of the Parole Board once the minimum term has been served (*Leigers* [2005] EWCA Crim 802, [2005] 2 Cr App R (S) 104 (654); *Jones* [2005] EWCA Crim 3115, [2006] 2 Cr App R (S) 19 (121)). In considering the seriousness of an offence under s. 269(3) or (4), the court must have regard to (a) the 'general principles' set out in sch. 21 and (b) any guidelines relating to offences in general which are relevant to the case and are not incompatible with the provisions of sch. 21 (s. 269(5)). Any court making an order under s. 269(2) or (4) must, in compliance with the duty under s. 174(2) to state its reasons for deciding on the order made, state in open court, in ordinary language, its reasons; in particular, which of the starting points in sch. 21 it has chosen and its reasons for doing so and its reasons for any departure from that starting point (s. 270). See further CrimPD VII, paras. M.1 to M.14 (see Supplement, **CPD.VII.M**). **E3.2**

Schedule 21 Principles

E3.3 Schedule 21 sets out a detailed scheme of 'general principles' for determination of the minimum term in relation to mandatory life sentences. Schedule 21 applies to secondary parties to murder as well as principal offenders (*A-G's Ref (No. 24 of 2008) (Sanchez)* [2008] EWCA Crim 2936, [2009] 2 Cr App R (S) 41 (289)). It should be noted that, for the purposes of sch. 21, 'child' means a person under 18 years of age, 'minimum term' means the part of the sentence to be specified by the sentencer under s. 269(2), and 'whole life order' means an order under s. 269(4). Section 28 of the CDA 1998 (meaning of 'racially or religiously aggravated') applies for the purposes of sch. 21 as it does for ss. 29 to 32 of the 1998 Act (see **B11.145**), and for the purposes of sch. 21 an offence is aggravated by sexual orientation if it is committed in circumstances mentioned in the CJA 2003, s. 146(2)(a)(i) or (b)(i), is aggravated by disability if it is committed in circumstances mentioned in s. 146(2)(a)(ii) or (b)(ii) and, an offence is aggravated by transgender identity if it is committed in circumstances mentioned in s. 146(2)(a)(iii) or (b)(iii) (see **E1.19**).

In *Oakes* [2012] EWCA Crim 2435, [2013] 2 All ER 30, a five-strong Court of Appeal, having regard to the decision of the ECtHR in *Vinter v UK* (2012) 55 EHRR 34 (1003), said that a whole life order is not incompatible with the ECHR, Article 3. The Grand Chamber of the ECtHR held in *Vinter v UK* (2016) 63 EHRR 1 (1) that for a sentence of life imprisonment to be compatible with Article 3 there must be provision for the possibility of review and release. A five-strong Court of Appeal in *A-G's Ref (No. 69 of 2013) (McLoughlin)* [2014] EWCA Crim 188, [2014] 3 All ER 73, however, found that the power of the Secretary of State conferred by the Crime (Sentences) Act 1997, s. 30, to release any life sentence prisoner exceptionally on compassionate grounds satisfied that requirement, so that English law was compliant with the ECHR and judges should continue to impose the whole life order in the rare circumstances in which it was appropriate to do so. The ECtHR in *Hutchinson v UK* (2015) 61 EHRR 13 (393) said that it was now satisfied that the Secretary of State's power to release was sufficient to comply with Article 3, and so there had been no violation of Article 3 in that case (decision upheld by the Grand Chamber in *Hutchinson v UK* [2017] ECHR 65).

E3.4 **Criminal Justice Act 2003, sch. 21, paras. 4 to 11**

Starting points

4.—(1) If—

(a) the court considers that the seriousness of the offence (or the combination of the offence and one or more offences associated with it) is exceptionally high, and

(b) the offender was aged 21 or over when he committed the offence,

the appropriate starting point is a whole life order.

(2) Cases that would normally fall within sub-paragraph (1)(a) include—

(a) the murder of two or more persons, where each murder involves any of the following—

(i) a substantial degree of premeditation or planning,

(ii) the abduction of the victim, or

(iii) sexual or sadistic conduct,

(b) the murder of a child if involving the abduction of the child or sexual or sadistic motivation,

(ba) the murder of a police officer or prison officer in the course of his or her duty,

(c) a murder done for the purpose of advancing a political, religious, racial or ideological cause, or

(d) a murder by an offender previously convicted of murder.

5.—(1) If—

(a) the case does not fall within paragraph 4(1) but the court considers that the seriousness of the offence (or the combination of the offence and one or more offences associated with it) is particularly high, and

(b) the offender was aged 18 or over when he committed the offence,

the appropriate starting point, in determining the minimum term, is 30 years.

(2) Cases that (if not falling within paragraph 4(1)) would normally fall within sub-paragraph (1)(a) include—

(a) *[repealed]*

(b) a murder involving the use of a firearm or explosive,

(c) a murder done for gain (such as a murder done in the course or furtherance of robbery or burglary, done for payment or done in the expectation of gain as a result of the death),

(d) a murder intended to obstruct or interfere with the course of justice,
(e) a murder involving sexual or sadistic conduct,
(f) the murder of two or more persons,
(g) a murder that is racially or religiously aggravated or aggravated by sexual orientation, disability or transgender identity, or
(h) a murder falling within paragraph 4(2) committed by an offender who was aged under 21 when he committed the offence.

5A.—(1) If—
(a) the case does not fall within paragraph 4(1) or 5(1),
(b) the offence falls within sub-paragraph (2), and
(c) the offender was aged 18 or over when the offender committed the offence,
the offence is normally to be regarded as sufficiently serious for the appropriate starting point, in determining the minimum term, to be 25 years.

(2) The offence falls within this sub-paragraph if the offender took a knife or other weapon to the scene intending to—
(a) commit any offence, or
(b) have it available to use as a weapon,
and used that knife or other weapon in committing the murder.

6. If the offender was aged 18 or over when he committed the offence and the case does not fall within paragraph 4(1), 5(1) or 5A(1), the appropriate starting point, in determining the minimum term, is 15 years.

7. If the offender was aged under 18 when he committed the offence, the appropriate starting point, in determining the minimum term, is 12 years.

Aggravating and mitigating factors

8. Having chosen a starting point, the court should take into account any aggravating or mitigating factors, to the extent that it has not allowed for them in its choice of starting point.

9. Detailed consideration of aggravating or mitigating factors may result in a minimum term of any length (whatever the starting point), or in the making of a whole life order.

10. Aggravating factors (additional to those mentioned in paragraph 4(2), 5(2)) and 5A(2) that may be relevant to the offence of murder include—
(a) a significant degree of planning or premeditation,
(b) the fact that the victim was particularly vulnerable because of age or disability,
(c) mental or physical suffering inflicted on the victim before death,
(d) the abuse of a position of trust,
(e) the use of duress or threats against another person to facilitate the commission of the offence,
(f) the fact that the victim was providing a public service or performing a public duty; and
(g) concealment, destruction or dismemberment of the body.

11. Mitigating factors that may be relevant to the offence of murder include—
(a) an intention to cause serious bodily harm rather than to kill,
(b) lack of premeditation,
(c) the fact that the offender suffered from any mental disorder or mental disability which (although not falling within section 2(1) of the Homicide Act 1957) lowered his degree of culpability,
(d) the fact that the offender was provoked (for example by prolonged stress),
(e) the fact that the offender acted to any extent in self-defence or in fear of violence,
(f) a belief by the offender that the murder was an act of mercy, and
(g) the age of the offender.

The Criminal Justice Act 2003 (Mandatory Life Sentence: Determination of Minimum Term) Order 2010 (SI 2010 No. 197), inserted para. 5A, which applies in relation to a sentence imposed for an offence of murder committed on or after 2 March 2010. The CAJA 2009, *sch. 21, para. 52,* made amendments to para. 11 consequential on the changes in the law on provocation which apply only in relation to offences committed on or after 4 October 2010. The LASPO 2012, s. 65(9), amended para. 5(2)(g) by the insertion after 'aggravated by sexual orientation' of the phrase 'disability or transgender identity', and is applicable to sentences for murder committed on or after 3 December 2012. The CJCA 2015, s. 27, inserted para. 4(2)(ba) and repealed para. 5(2)(a), and is applicable to sentences for murder committed on or after 13 April 2015.

E3.5 Paragraph 12 states that nothing in sch. 21 restricts the application of the CJA 2003, s. 143(2) (previous convictions: see **E1.14**), s. 143(3) (commission of an offence while on bail: see **E1.15**) or s. 144 (reduction in sentences for guilty pleas: see **E1.8**). Detailed guidance as to the procedure for passing a mandatory life sentence under s. 269 and sch. 21 can be found in CrimPD VII, paras. M.1 to M.14 (see Supplement, **CPD.VII.M**). The definitive sentencing guideline, *Reduction in Sentence for a Guilty Plea* (see **E1.8** and, for the text, see Supplement, **SG5-1**), is applicable when setting the minimum term to be served in a mandatory life sentence. The guideline states that the maximum reduction for plea is one sixth or five years, whichever is less. While the reduction for a guilty plea can have no direct effect on a whole life minimum term, the offender's guilty plea is a factor to bear in mind when considering whether a whole life minimum term is appropriate. In *Peters* [2005] EWCA Crim 605, [2005] 2 Cr App R (S) 101 (627), the Court of Appeal said that where the offender clearly accepts responsibility for the killing, in considering whether the offender has pleaded guilty at the first reasonable opportunity, there are some cases where that opportunity would not arise until the accused has obtained advice on possible defences from leading counsel. Although now expressed in different terms, see para. F1 in the revised sentencing guideline (and especially *Markham* [2017] EWCA Crim 739, [2017] 2 Cr App R (S) 30 (249)).

Appeal

E3.6 Since the sentence for murder is a mandatory sentence, there is no appeal against it. By the Criminal Appeal Act 1968, s. 9(1A), however, an offender may appeal against an order specifying a minimum term made under the CJA 2003, s. 269(2), or against an order under s. 269(4) that the early release provisions are not to apply. The A-G may refer an order specifying a minimum term under s. 269(2) to the Court of Appeal under the CJA 1988, s. 36(3A), which states that the Court of Appeal 'shall not, in deciding what order under that section is appropriate for the case, make any allowance for the fact that the person to whom it relates is being sentenced for a second time'. For consideration of the now largely outdated practice of adjustment of sentence for so-called 'double jeopardy', see **D28.5**.

Court of Appeal Guidance

E3.7 Guidance on the operation of these provisions for the setting of minimum terms in murder cases can be found in a series of Court of Appeal decisions, the most prominent of which are *Peters* [2005] EWCA Crim 605, [2005] 2 Cr App R (S) 101 (627); *Jones* [2005] EWCA Crim 3115, [2006] 2 Cr App R (S) 19 (121) and *Height* [2008] EWCA Crim 2500, [2009] 1 Cr App R (S) 117 (656). Taken together, these cases show that while judges must pay close attention to the scheme of sch. 21, to identify the correct starting point and relevant aggravating and mitigating factors, there is considerable flexibility within the scheme, which requires the exercise of judicial discretion. In *Jones*, the Court of Appeal pointed out the huge gap which exists between the specified starting points, which could only provide 'a very broad framework' for the sentencing exercise, and in *Kolman* [2018] EWCA Crim 2624, [2019] 1 Cr App R (S) 33 (220), the Court said that the 'starting points were merely markers on a continuum graph, rather than step changes' (at [22]). In *A-G's Ref (No. 12 of 2008)* [2008] EWCA Crim 1060, [2009] 1 Cr App R (S) 18 (97), where the murder involved a prolonged and very violent attack on an elderly man, the case was before the Court of Appeal on the question whether the murder was committed in the furtherance of gain, and hence attracted a 30-year starting point. The Court of Appeal criticised the way in which the sentencing hearing had adopted a somewhat 'mechanistic or arithmetical approach', and said that looking at the seriousness of the case as a whole, the appropriate minimum term was 22 years. On the other hand, it was held in *Davies* [2008] EWCA Crim 1055, [2009] 1 Cr App R (S) 15 (79) that, if the presence of a particular feature of the murder (such as whether it involved sexual or sadistic conduct, attracting a 30-year rather than a 15-year starting point) is in issue, that circumstance must be proved according to the criminal standard. See also *Healy* [2008] EWCA Crim 2853, [2009] 2 Cr App R (S) 3 (10), which states that a court is entitled to draw its own conclusions from the facts and is not limited by a lack of other charges on the indictment. It is well established that in a case where the offender is to be sentenced for other offences as well as murder, the judge when setting the minimum term should take into account the totality of the offending. See, e.g., *Bailey-Mascoll* [2019] EWCA Crim 406.

Care must be taken not to 'double count' an aggravating factor which is already catered for in a specified starting point (see sch. 21, para. 8). In *Markham* [2017] EWCA Crim 739, [2017] 2 Cr App R (S) 30 (249) the Court of Appeal confirmed that the intention to kill (rather than to cause grievous bodily harm) was written into all the starting points within sch. 21, including the 12-year starting point for offenders aged under 18, and it was 'an error of statutory construction' to treat the intention to kill *per se* as aggravating the offence. However, factors such as premeditation and planning were always, on the facts, potential aggravating factors. The list of aggravating and mitigating features is not exhaustive. The Court of Appeal in *Wilson* [2018] EWCA Crim 1352, [2018] 2 Cr App R (S) 25 (228) upheld a minimum term of 20 years in a case of murder where D had stabbed his wife to death. The Court said that a proven background of domestic violence which had culminated in the murder was a 'distinct aggravating circumstance' and it was not necessary that it be the subject of a separate charge and conviction. The relative weight to be accorded to each, or to any particular combination, of those features, will vary greatly, depending on the circumstances of the case, and sch. 21, para. 9, indicates that 'detailed consideration' of aggravating and mitigating factors may result in a final minimum term of 'any length', which seems to accord the judge a good deal of discretion. In *Blue* [2008] EWCA Crim 769, [2009] 1 Cr App R (S) 2 (6) it was accepted by the Court of Appeal that the judge had been entitled to find that the murder had been aggravated by a racial element but not sufficiently to make the 'huge leap' from a 15-year to a 30-year starting point. In *Kolman* [2018] EWCA Crim 2624, [2019] 1 Cr App R (S) 33 (220), prosecution and defence agreed that the appropriate starting point was 15 years, the criteria for cases of 'particularly high seriousness' not having been met. The judge disagreed, taking the view that 'sadistic conduct' was involved in the prolonged beating over two to three hours which eventually caused the vulnerable victim's death, and the starting point was 30 years. The Court of Appeal agreed with the judge, but said that the case was unusual and most instances of beatings causing death would attract the lower starting point. In *Peters*, it was noted that, although sch. 21, para. 11(a), treats as a mitigating factor an intention to cause grievous bodily harm rather than to kill, there would be circumstances where the absence of that intention would provide little or no mitigation (a clear example of this is *Cameron* [2010] EWCA Crim 1282, [2011] 1 Cr App R (S) 24 (163)). The same was true of para. 11(e), where the offender had, to some extent, acted in self-defence. **E3.8**

In upholding a whole life minimum term in *Coonan* [2011] EWCA Crim 5 the Court of Appeal considered sch. 21, para. 11(c) and said that, even though an element of mental disturbance was intrinsic to the murders committed, the jury had rejected the defence of diminished responsibility at trial and the sentencing judge should not impose a sentence which reflected a defence that had been rejected. In *Inglis* [2010] EWCA Crim 2637, [2011] 1 WLR 1110 the Court considered a case of 'mercy killing', where the relevant aggravating features included para. 10(a), (b) and (d) factors but where specific mitigating features included para. 11(f) factors. Lord Judge CJ said that the 'prescriptive statutory regime' in relation to murder had on occasions caused difficulty and dilemma, and that on the facts the specific aggravating factors should not be taken to aggravate the murder. If it were otherwise the express mitigating factor would be deprived of any practical effect. The minimum term was reduced from nine years to five years. In *Height* [2008] EWCA Crim 2500, [2009] 1 Cr App R (S) 117 (656), the offenders were implicated in the murder of D2's wife. D2 had recruited D1 to carry out the murder. The judge imposed a 30-year starting point on D1, since his motive for murder was financial gain, while D2's motive was not financial but, rather, to dispose of his wife. The Court of Appeal said that, taken literally, para. 6 seems to suggest that any case falling outside the specified criteria attracts a 15-year starting point. However, according to Lord Judge CJ, the scheme was not to be interpreted **E3.9** rigidly in that way. It was hard to imagine a case in which one offender, acting for gain, should be subject to a different starting point to the offender who agreed to pay him. The appropriate starting point for each offender was 30 years. In *Lovell* [2018] EWCA Crim 19, [2018] 1 Cr App R (S) 48 (364), it was argued that the judge had wrongly chosen the 30-year starting point for a murder involving the use of a firearm because D was not the person who had used the gun. Rejecting the argument, the Court of Appeal confirmed that the language of sch. 21, para. 5, was sufficient to cover an offender involved in a joint enterprise and was not confined to the person who actually pulls the trigger.

E3.10 In *Malasi* [2008] EWCA Crim 2505, [2009] 1 Cr App R (S) 51 (276) the Court of Appeal considered the principles applicable when sentencing an offender, aged 16, for two murders committed 15 days apart. It was held that the judge should have regard to the provisions of sch. 21 in respect of each murder, assessing all relevant factors, aggregate the minimum terms arrived at and then make an appropriate adjustment for totality. In *Miah* [2011] EWCA Crim 945, [2012] 1 Cr App R (S) 11 (47), where two murders arose out of the same facts and the offenders were aged 21 and 14 (with the younger one being the 'prime mover and leader'), the Court of Appeal said that the Act required for each offender the fixing of a single overall minimum term, and that the judge had correctly taken account of all relevant factors. In *Markham* [2017] EWCA Crim 739, [2017] 2 Cr App R (S) 30 (249), where two murders arose from the same facts and the offenders were both aged 14, the Court of Appeal endorsed the judge's detailed reasoning in arriving at minimum terms of 21 years in each case before adjustment for plea, but made no specific reference to the reasoning in *Malasi*.

Guidance on the meaning and application of para. 5A was provided by the Court of Appeal in *Kelly* [2011] EWCA Crim 1462, [2012] 4 All ER 687, where the Court dealt with several appeals in relation to it. The Court considered the phrase 'took the knife or other weapon to the scene', as well as particular problems arising from a joint enterprise where only one of the offenders carried a knife. In *Dillon* [2015] EWCA Crim 3, [2015] 1 Cr App R (S) 62 (434), following an earlier altercation, D opened his own front door to V and stabbed him in the chest, killing him. The Court, noting comments in *Kelly* that if the case was only just within para. 5A a minimum term of less than 25 years might well be justified, reduced the minimum term to 20 years. See also *Ali* [2017] EWCA Crim 2321 and *Somers* (3 October 2018 unreported, CA). In *Beckford* [2014] EWCA Crim 1299, [2014] 2 Cr App R (S) 34 (285), the Court of Appeal said that the judge had been entitled to find that D had taken a weapon to the scene when he had driven a motor vehicle at V, knocking him off his bike and killing him.

MURDER: OFFENDERS UNDER 21

E3.11 For an offender convicted of murder who is aged under 21 at the date of conviction, the mandatory sentence is custody for life under the PCC(S)A 2000, s. 93, unless the offender was under 18 when the offence was committed, in which case the mandatory sentence is detention at Her Majesty's pleasure.

Guidance on the setting of a minimum term for the sentence of custody for life is now set out in the CJA 2003, ss. 269 to 277 and schs. 21 and 22 (see **E3.2**). It should be noted that an offender aged 18, 19 or 20 cannot attract a 'whole life' starting point but may, in a case where the seriousness of the offence is 'particularly high', attract a starting point of 30 years. Otherwise, the starting point is 15 years. In *Peters* [2005] EWCA Crim 605, [2005] 2 Cr App R (S) 101 (627) it was said (at [11]) that 'although the passage of an eighteenth or twenty-first birthday represents a significant moment … it does not necessarily tell us very much about the individual's true level of maturity, insight and understanding'. It has also been noted in *Matthew* [2005] EWCA Crim 2399, [2006] 1 Cr App R (S) 88 (505) that there should be no sudden postponement or acceleration of sentence levels due to age — there are 'no cliff edges'. See also *Martin* [2009]

EWCA Crim 1182, [2010] 1 Cr App R (S) 38 (226); *Clarke* [2018] EWCA Crim 185, [2018] 1 Cr App R (S) 52 (401) and *Quartey* [2019] EWCA Crim 374.

MURDER: DETENTION AT HER MAJESTY'S PLEASURE

The PCC(S)A 2000, s. 90, prescribes a mandatory sentence of detention at Her Majesty's pleasure for murder committed by an offender who was under 18 at the time of the offence, irrespective of age at the date of conviction. It is confined to murder cases (*Abbott* [1964] 1 QB 489). A person so sentenced will be detained in such place and under such conditions as the Secretary of State may direct or may arrange (s. 92). In *V v UK* (1999) 30 EHRR 121 a challenge to the effect that the sentence of detention at Her Majesty's pleasure was severely disproportionate and in breach of the ECHR, Article 3, and unlawful under Article 5 was rejected by the ECtHR. The same conclusion was reached by the Court of Appeal in *Parchment* [2003] EWCA Crim 2428, and further confirmed by that Court in *Grant-Murray* [2017] EWCA Crim 1228. **E3.12**

Guidance on the setting of a minimum term for the sentence of detention at Her Majesty's pleasure is now set out in the CJA 2003, ss. 269 to 277 and schs. 21 and 22 (see **E3.2**). It should be noted that an offender who was aged under 18 when the offence was committed cannot attract a 'whole life' starting point or a starting point of 30 or 15 years. The starting point is always 12 years. Even so, the final minimum term may be above or below 12 years, and the court is entitled to take into account express features identified in one or more of the adult starting points in sch. 21 as well as relevant aggravating and mitigating factors (*A-G's Ref (No. 126 of 2006) (H)* [2007] EWCA Crim 53, [2007] 2 Cr App R (S) 59 (362); *Markham* [2017] EWCA Crim 739, [2017] 2 Cr App R (S) 30 (249)). In *DM* [2019] EWCA Crim 1354, [2020] 1 Cr App R (S) 17 (138), the Court of Appeal dismissed appeals by two offenders, both aged 14 at the time of the murder. In relation to D1 the minimum term was 14 years and six months and in relation to D2 the minimum term was 14 years. The Court of Appeal noted that the starting point of 12 years applies to all offenders aged under 18. Given that the starting point is lower than the adult starting point, and much lower when, as in this case, the murder has been committed with a knife taken to the scene for use as a weapon, it must be borne in mind that the age of a young offender has already been taken into account to a significant degree by the terms of the CJA 2003, sch. 21. The extent to which any further reduction can be made on grounds of the offender's particularly young age will depend on all the circumstances. In *Cornick* [2015] EWCA Crim 110, [2015] 1 Cr App R (S) 69 (483), a 15-year-old student planned the murder of his teacher and, having taken two knives to school with him, attacked her from behind, stabbing her numerous times. The killing was staged in front of D's classmates. The Court of Appeal upheld a minimum term of 20 years notwithstanding D's youth, ongoing adjustment disorder, guilty plea and previous good character. In *Aziz* [2019] EWCA Crim 1568, D was aged 16 at the time of the offence. He raped and murdered a 14-year-old girl. A minimum term of 19 years for the murder, with a concurrent sentence of ten years for the rape, was upheld on appeal. The Court of Appeal said that there were six aggravating factors in the case, including planning, sexual motivation, vulnerability of V, and weapon brought to the scene, as against four mitigating factors, including lack of previous convictions, youth, unstable upbringing and a degree of mental instability. Lord Burnett CJ said (at [25]) that these factors do not lead to 'a rigid arithmetical increase or decrease in a minimum term, but require a subtle evaluation by the sentencing judge'. The resulting minimum term was 'long in the context of a 16 year old' (at [29]) but not manifestly excessive.

Section E4 Life Sentences, Extended Sentences and Custodial Sentences for Certain Offenders of 'Particular Concern'

OVERVIEW OF PROVISIONS

General

E4.1 Sections 224 and 225 to 229 of, and schs. 15 and 15B to, the CJA 2003, provide measures for sentencing 'dangerous offenders', principally the discretionary life sentence and the extended sentence. These sentences require, *inter alia*, a finding by the court that the offender is 'dangerous', in that the offender poses a 'significant risk to members of the public of serious harm occasioned by the commission by him of further specified offences'. There are two other closely related sentences, the 'life sentence for the second listed offence' (s. 224A) and the custodial sentence for 'certain offenders of particular concern' (s. 236A), although for neither of these sentences must the 'dangerousness test' be passed. The practical operation of all these sentences requires an understanding of the criteria of eligibility for each, as well as an understanding of the different early release provisions which apply.

Sentence Indications

E4.2 Where a defendant is charged with a specified offence to which the dangerous offender provisions may apply, the judge should be very cautious about giving a sentence indication in accordance with *Goodyear* [2005] EWCA Crim 888, [2005] 3 All ER 117 (see **D12.61**). There are obvious practical difficulties in giving such an indication where relevant reports are not available and the issue of dangerousness has still to be determined by the judge. In *Kulah* [2007] EWCA Crim 1701, [2008] 1 All ER 16, the Court of Appeal said that there would be some cases where the assessment of dangerousness would be manifest based on the nature of the offence and the antecedent history, but the great majority of cases would not be clear cut. A judge who had not been provided with reports might well feel disinclined to give an indication.

Offence Classification

E4.3 Section 224 of the CJA 2003 defines 'specified offence', 'serious offence', and 'serious harm' for the purposes of these provisions. 'Specified offences' are those violent, sexual, or terrorism offences which are listed in sch. 15 (s. 224(1)). All the offences listed in sch. 15 carry a maximum penalty of two years' imprisonment or more. A 'serious offence' is defined as a specified violent, sexual or terrorism offence which (apart from s. 224A) is punishable in the case of a person aged 18 or over by (i) imprisonment for life, or (ii) imprisonment for a determinate period of ten years or more (s. 224(2)). 'Serious harm' means death or serious personal injury, whether physical or psychological (s. 224(3)).

E4.4 **Offences Listed in sch. 15** The *specified violent offences* listed in part 1 to sch. 15 are manslaughter, kidnapping, false imprisonment and offences under the following enactments: OAPA 1861, ss. 4, 16, 18, 20 to 23, 27 to 32, 35, 37, 38 and 47; Explosive Substances Act 1883, ss. 2, 3 and 4; Infant Life (Preservation) Act 1929, s. 1; CYPA 1933, s. 1; Infanticide Act 1938, s. 1; FA 1968, ss. 16, 16A, 17(1), 17(2) and 18; Theft Act 1968, ss. 8 and 9 (where the burglary is committed with intent to inflict grievous bodily harm, or to do unlawful damage), 10 and 12A (involving an accident which caused the death of any person); Criminal Damage Act 1971, s. 1 (arson) and 1(2); Taking of Hostages Act 1982, s. 1; Aviation Security Act 1982, ss. 1 to 4; Mental Health Act 1983, s. 127; Prohibition of Female Circumcision Act 1985, s. 12; POA 1986, ss. 1 to 3; CJA 1988, s. 134; RTA 1988, ss. 1, 3ZC and 3A; Aviation and Maritime Security Act 1990, ss. 1 and 9 to 13; Channel Tunnel (Security) Order 1994 (SI 1994 No. 570), Part 2; Protection from Harassment Act 1997, s. 4 or 4A; CDA 1998, ss. 29, 31(1)(a) and 31(1)(b); International Criminal Court Act 2001, ss. 51 and 52; Female Genital Mutilation Act 2003, ss. 1 to 3; DVCVA 2004, s. 5; TA 2006, ss. 5, 6, 9, 10 and 11; Modern Slavery Act 2015, ss. 1 and 2. With effect from 12 April 2019 when the C-TBSA 2019 came into force, offences in the TA 2000, ss. 54, 56, 57 and 59 and offences in the A-TCSA 2001, ss. 47, 50 and 113 were moved from part 1 to part 3 of sch. 15. Paragraph 64 of sch. 15 also makes it clear that aiding, abetting, counselling, procuring, conspiring or attempting to commit or inciting any of the specified violent offences or encouraging or assisting them within the meaning of the SCA 2007 are also covered. Attempt, conspiracy, or incitement to commit murder are also listed, as is encouraging or assisting murder within the meaning of the SCA 2007.

The *specified sexual offences* listed in part 2 to sch. 15 are: SOA 1956, ss. 1 to 7, 9 to 11, 14 to 17, 19 to 29, 32 and 33A; Mental Health Act 1959, s. 128; Indecency with Children Act 1960, s. 1; SOA 1967, ss. 4, 5 and 9; Theft Act 1968, s. 9 (burglary with intent to commit rape); CLA 1977, s. 54; CEMA 1979, s. 70 (in relation to goods prohibited under the Customs Consolidation Act 1876, s. 42); Protection of Children Act 1978, s. 1; CJA 1988, s. 160; SOA 2003, ss. 1 to 19, 25, 26, 30 to 41, 47 to 50, 52, 53, 57 to 59A, 61 to 67, 69 and 70; Modern Slavery Act 2015, s. 2 (where that offence constitutes sexual exploitation). Paragraph 153 of sch. 15 makes it clear that aiding, abetting, counselling, procuring, conspiring or attempting to commit or inciting any of the specified sexual offences or encouraging or assisting them within the meaning of the SCA 2007 are also covered.

The *specified terrorism offences* listed in part 3 to sch. 15 are: TA 2000, ss. 11, 12, 54, 56, 57, 58, 58A, 58B and 59; A-TCSA 2001, ss. 47, 50 and 113; TA 2006, ss. 1, 2, 5, 6, 8, 9, 10 and 11. Aiding, abetting, counselling, procuring, conspiring or attempting to commit or inciting any of the specified terrorism offences or encouraging or assisting them within the meaning of the SCA 2007 are also covered. It is important to note that, with effect from 12 April 2019 when the C-TBSA 2019 came into force, the offences in the TA 2000, ss. 54, 56, 57 and 59 and in the A-TCSA 2001, ss. 47, 50 and 113 were moved from part 1 to part 3 of sch. 15. The other offences listed in part 3 were added from that date. These amendments to sch. 15 apply to the CJA 2003, s. 225 (life sentence) and s. 226 (detention for life) only where the relevant offence was committed on or after 12 April 2019. As far as the extended sentence is concerned, the effect of these amendments is to provide a maximum permitted extension period of eight years for offenders sentenced for an offence listed in part 3, irrespective of the date of the offence.

IMPRISONMENT OR DETENTION FOR LIFE FOR SERIOUS OFFENCE

Life Sentence for Serious Offence

Criminal Justice Act 2003, s. 225 E4.5

(1) This section applies where—
   (a) a person aged 18 or over is convicted of a serious offence committed after the commencement of this section, and
   (b) the court is of the opinion that there is a significant risk to members of the public of serious harm occasioned by the commission by him of further specified offences.

(2) If—
   (a) the offence is one in respect of which the offender would apart from this section be liable to imprisonment for life, and

(b) the court considers that the seriousness of the offence, or of the offence and one or more offences associated with it, is such as to justify the imposition of a sentence of imprisonment for life,

the court must impose a sentence of imprisonment for life.

[(3), (3A) to (3C) and (4) repealed.]

(5) An offence the sentence for which is imposed under this section is not to be regarded as an offence the sentence for which is fixed by law.

E4.6 For the meaning of 'serious offence' and 'serious harm', see **E4.3**. For amendments made to sch. 15 by the inclusion of a new part 3 containing 'specified terrorism offences', see **E4.4**. In s. 225(1), '18 or over' means '18 or over at the date of conviction' (*Bennett* [2019] EWCA Crim 629, [2019] 2 Cr App R (S) 39 (280)). In the case of a person aged 18, 19 or 20 at the date of conviction the court must impose a sentence of custody for life rather than imprisonment for life.

In *J* [2012] EWCA Crim 132, [2012] 2 Cr App R (S) 73 (416), Lord Judge CJ stressed that the decision whether to impose an indeterminate sentence was made at sentencing, and at that point the court must form its opinion whether there was a significant risk to members of the public of serious harm occasioned by the offender committing any further specified offences. On the issue of public safety, the decision made at sentencing was required to address the future. Before a sentence of life imprisonment can be imposed under the CJA 2003, s. 225, a judge must first consider under s. 225(2) whether the offence carries life imprisonment as its maximum sentence and whether the seriousness of the offence itself justifies a discretionary life sentence. If not, a sentence of life imprisonment should not be imposed, and the judge should consider whether the criteria for the imposition of an extended sentence pursuant to s. 226A were established (*A-G's Ref (No. 27 of 2013) (Burinskas)* [2014] EWCA Crim 334, [2014] 1 WLR 4209, applied in *Younas* [2017] EWCA Crim 1, [2017] 1 Cr App R (S) 44 (348) and *Kavanagh* [2018] EWCA Crim 728)).

Following abolition of the sentence of imprisonment for public protection by the LASPO 2012, guidance on the future use of the discretionary life sentence was given by the Court of Appeal in *Saunders* [2013] EWCA Crim 1027, [2014] 1 Cr App R (S) 45 (258). Lord Judge CJ said that, in cases which, prior to the implementation of the LASPO 2012, would have required a sentence of imprisonment for public protection, the discretionary life sentence will arise for consideration where the necessary level of public protection cannot be achieved by the extended sentence. The 'denunciatory' element, previously identified to distinguish between the circumstances in which a life sentence rather than imprisonment for public protection should be imposed, is no longer apposite. Although the denunciatory element of the sentencing decision may continue to justify the passing of a discretionary life sentence, its absence does not preclude such an order. As every judge appreciates, however, the life sentence remains the sentence of last resort. The Court of Appeal in the leading case of *Burinskas* endorsed what was said in *Saunders*. Lord Thomas CJ said that although the provisions of s. 225 remained the same, the statutory context was fundamentally changed by the LASPO 2012, and it was inevitable that life sentences under s. 225 would be imposed more frequently than before. Cases decided before 2012 were now of limited value. For an example of a discretionary life sentence upheld for a series of armed robberies, see *Meddlicott* [2016] EWCA Crim 55.

Discretionary Life Sentence for Offence not Listed in sch. 15

E4.7 The Court in *Saunders* confirmed that a court retains power to impose a sentence of life imprisonment for any offence which carries that maximum penalty, even though the offence in question is not listed in sch. 15 to the CJA 2003 and the court is therefore not considering whether to pass a life sentence under s. 225. Neither the CJA 2003 nor the LASPO 2012 removed that power. Although the occasions on which a court might impose a discretionary life sentence on an offender who did not fall within the dangerous offender provisions of the CJA 2003 would be rare, one example might be an offender who had committed repeated offences of very serious drug supply. The Court of Appeal in *Ali* [2019] EWCA Crim 856, [2019] 2 Cr App R (S) 43 (333), upheld a discretionary life sentence for an offence not listed in sch. 15 in respect of an offender convicted of playing a leading role in a conspiracy to import prohibited firearms, contrary to the CLA 1977, s. 1. The Court confirmed that the appropriate criteria to determine the applicability of a life sentence in such a case were (i) that the offender had been convicted of a very serious offence, and (ii) there were good grounds for believing that the offender may remain a serious danger to the public for a period which cannot be reliably estimated at the date of sentence. The Court said (at [54]) that the judge had been 'entitled to the view that the appellant was dangerous in the ordinary meaning of the word, rather than as defined in the 2003 Act'.

Detention for Life for Serious Offence

Criminal Justice Act 2003, s. 226 E4.8

(1) This section applies where—
  (a) a person aged under 18 is convicted of a serious offence committed after the commencement of this section, and
  (b) the court is of the opinion that there is a significant risk to members of the public of serious harm occasioned by the commission by him of further specified offences.
(2) If—
  (a) the offence is one in respect of which the offender would apart from this section be liable to a sentence of detention for life under section 91 of the Sentencing Act, and
  (b) the court considers that the seriousness of the offence, or of the offence and one or more offences associated with it, is such as to justify the imposition of a sentence of detention for life,

  the court must impose a sentence of detention for life under that section.
[(3), (3A) and (4) repealed.]
(5) An offence the sentence for which is imposed under this section is not to be regarded as an offence the sentence for which is fixed by law.

For the meaning of 'serious offence' and 'serious harm', see **E4.3**. For amendments made to sch. 15 by the inclusion of a new part 3 containing 'specified terrorism offences', see **E4.4**. In s. 226(1), 'under 18' means 'under 18 at the date of conviction' (*Bennett* [2019] EWCA Crim 629, [2019] 2 Cr App R (S) 39 (280)). A sentence imposed under this provision is one of detention for life under the PCC(S)A 2000, s. 91.

In *Lang* [2005] EWCA Crim 2864, [2006] 2 All ER 410, the Court of Appeal said that when sentencing young offenders it was important to bear in mind that they may change and develop in a shorter time than an adult. This, together with their level of maturity, may be highly relevant when assessing future conduct and whether that may give rise to a significant risk of serious harm. See further *Frota* [2007] EWCA Crim 2602 and *Kehoe* [2008] EWCA Crim 819, [2009] 1 Cr App R (S) 9 (41). E4.9

EXTENDED SENTENCE

Extended Sentence: Persons 18 or Over

Criminal Justice Act 2003, s. 226A E4.10

(1) This section applies where—
  (a) a person aged 18 or over is convicted of a specified offence (whether the offence was committed before or after this section comes into force),
  (b) the court considers that there is a significant risk to members of the public of serious harm occasioned by the commission by the offender of further specified offences,
  (c) the court is not required by section 224A or 225(2) to impose a sentence of imprisonment for life, and
  (d) condition A or B is met.
(2) Condition A is that, at the time the offence was committed, the offender had been convicted of an offence listed in Schedule 15B.
(3) Condition B is that, if the court were to impose an extended sentence of imprisonment, the term that it would specify as the appropriate custodial term would be at least 4 years.
(4) The court may impose an extended sentence of imprisonment on the offender.
(5) An extended sentence of imprisonment is a sentence of imprisonment the term of which is equal to the aggregate of—
  (a) the appropriate custodial term, and
  (b) a further period (the 'extension period') for which the offender is to be subject to a licence.

(6) The appropriate custodial term is the term of imprisonment that would (apart from this section) be imposed in compliance with section 153(2).
(7) The extension period must be a period of such length as the court considers necessary for the purpose of protecting members of the public from serious harm occasioned by the commission by the offender of further specified offences, subject to subsections (7A) to (9).
(7A) The extension period must be at least 1 year.
(8) The extension period must not exceed—
(a) 5 years in the case of a specified violent offence, and
(b) 8 years in the case of a specified sexual offence or a specified terrorism offence.
(9) The term of an extended sentence of imprisonment imposed under this section in respect of an offence must not exceed the term that, at the time the offence was committed, was the maximum term permitted for the offence.

E4.11 For the meaning of 'specified offence' and 'serious harm', see **E4.3**. Section 226A was inserted by the LASPO 2012 with effect from 3 December 2012, but it is irrelevant whether the offence was committed before or after that date (s. 226A(1)). Section 226A(7A) was inserted by the Offender Rehabilitation Act 2014, s. 8, with effect from 1 February 2015; that amendment does not apply to an offence committed before that date. Note that, by virtue of the LASPO 2012, sch. 21, para. 36, s. 226A is modified so that, in the case of an offender aged at least 18 but under 21, the reference in s. 226A(1)(c) to imprisonment for life is to be read as a reference to custody for life and other references to imprisonment are to be read as references to detention in a young offender institution. For amendments made to sch. 15 by the inclusion of a new part 3 containing 'specified terrorism offences', see **E4.4**. In s. 226A, '18 or over' means '18 or over at the date of conviction' (*Bennett* [2019] EWCA Crim 629, [2019] 2 Cr App R (S) 39 (280)).

The offender must pass the 'dangerousness test' (see **E4.19**). An extended sentence of imprisonment (or detention in a young offender institution if the offender is aged 18, 19 or 20) can only be passed where (Condition A) the offender has previously been convicted of an offence listed in sch. 15B, or (Condition B) the appropriate custodial term, proportionate to the seriousness of the offence, is at least four years. Clearly, if the offender qualifies for an extended sentence by virtue of Condition A the custodial term imposed may be for less than four years. Condition A applied in *Wagstaff* [2017] EWCA Crim 1601, [2018] 1 Cr App R (S) 16 (95), where an extended sentence of six years, with a custodial term of 18 months and an extension period of four and half years, was upheld for an offence of causing a child to engage in sexual activity, an offence listed in sch. 15B. Because D had a like offence on his record, Condition A applied and a custodial term of much less than four years could properly be imposed. Condition B applied in *Gwilym* [2018] EWCA Crim 377, where an extended sentence of five years, with a custodial term of four years and an extension period of one year, was upheld for an offence of occasioning actual bodily harm. In that case the threshold of four years was reached by aggregating the sentence for that offence with the sentence for a separate racially aggravated common assault. See further **E4.22**. In the leading case of *A-G's Ref (No. 27 of 2013) (Burinskas)* [2014] EWCA Crim 334, [2014] 1 WLR 4209, Lord Thomas CJ said that even if all the above criteria are met, imposition of the sentence is discretionary. If there is a finding of dangerousness a life sentence or an extended sentence will usually be appropriate but the option of a determinate sentence should not be forgotten. In *Bourke* [2017] EWCA Crim 2150, [2018] 1 Cr App R (S) 42 (298) it was said that before proceeding to pass an extended sentence a judge should explain, even briefly, why a determinate sentence would not suffice (see also *Griffith* [2018] EWCA Crim 1953), although in *O'Callaghan* [2018] EWCA Crim 94 the Court of Appeal said that while giving such an explanation was 'technically preferable', a failure to do so in the context of otherwise carefully constructed sentencing remarks did not make the sentencing process flawed.

To the custodial term there must always be added the appropriate extension period, the maximum being five years for a specified violent offence, or eight years for a specified sexual offence *or a specified terrorism offence*. The length of the extension period is a matter for judicial assessment in each case, and is that which the court considers necessary to reduce the future danger posed by the particular offender. According to the Court of Appeal in *ARD* [2017] EWCA Crim 1882, [2018] 1 Cr App R (S) 23 (163), the length of the extension period is not to be determined by the age of the defendant or lack of previous convictions save in so far as they were indicators as to the degree of harm the defendant posed into the future and for how long the defendant would pose that harm. Further, in *Phillips* [2018] EWCA Crim 2008, [2019] 1 Cr App R (S) 11 (85), the Court of Appeal said that the purpose of the licence period was preventive rather than punitive, and so was not tied to the seriousness of the offence. It should be no longer than necessary for the relevant purpose, and should not be such as to crush the offender. The judge should be guided by what realistically can be achieved within the licence period (including the availability of accredited programmes within prison) to secure the offender's rehabilitation and to prevent reoffending. The total term of an extended sentence of imprisonment (or detention in a young offender institution) must not exceed the maximum penalty for the offence. An extended sentence of seven and a half years' imprisonment was therefore held to be unlawful in *Hayes* [2016] EWCA Crim 663, [2016] 2 Cr App R (S) 24 (208) where the maximum penalty for the offence was five years. The Court of Appeal in *Thompson* [2018] EWCA Crim 639, [2018] 2 Cr App R (S) 19 (164), however, has made it clear that, in the unusual circumstances which justify the passing of consecutive extended sentences, the total extended licence may properly exceed the maximum licence period for a single offence.

The extended sentence, as amended by the LASPO 2012, is more onerous than the version originally created by the CJA 2003, when release from the sentence was at the half way point of the custodial term. By the CJCA 2015, s. 4, any offender sentenced to an extended sentence on or after 13 April 2015 (irrespective of the date of the offence) will serve at least two-thirds of the custodial term. Extended sentence prisoners will be released only upon the recommendation of the Parole Board at some point between the two-thirds point and end point of the custodial term. The Court in *Burinskas* considered argument that the changes made by the LASPO 2012 to early release from an extended sentence created an anomaly in that the first opportunity for release occurred sooner for a life sentence prisoner than for a prisoner serving an extended sentence. In one of the appeals heard in that case the sentencing judge had reduced the custodial term in an extended sentence by one year to reflect the fact that time to be served had been increased. The Court said that this adjustment should not have been made since, other than when fixing the minimum term in a life sentence case under s. 82A, a judge should disregard early release provisions. The differential sentencing and early release provisions relating to the extended sentence, when compared to those applicable to the life sentence, or to a determinate sentence, survived challenge before the Supreme Court in respect of the ECHR, Articles 5 and 14, in *R (Stott) v Secretary of State for Justice* [2018] UKSC 59, [2018] 3 WLR 1831. The Court held, considering the extended sentencing package as a whole, that the early release provisions were justified as a proportionate means of achieving the government's legitimate aims. Although D had been treated differently on the grounds of 'other status' within Article 14, there was an objective justification for that difference in treatment. **E4.12**

Extended Sentence: Persons under 18

Criminal Justice Act 2003, s. 226B **E4.13**

(1) This section applies where—
- (a) a person aged under 18 is convicted of a specified offence (whether the offence was committed before or after this section comes into force),
- (b) the court considers that there is a significant risk to members of the public of serious harm occasioned by the commission by the offender of further specified offences,
- (c) the court is not required by section 226(2) to impose a sentence of detention for life under section 91 of the Sentencing Act, and
- (d) if the court were to impose an extended sentence of detention, the term that it would specify as the appropriate custodial term would be at least 4 years.

(2) The court may impose an extended sentence of detention on the offender.

(3) An extended sentence of detention is a sentence of detention the term of which is equal to the aggregate of—
- (a) the appropriate custodial term, and
- (b) a further period (the 'extension period') for which the offender is to be subject to a licence.

(4) The appropriate custodial term is the term of detention that would (apart from this section) be imposed in compliance with section 153(2).

(5) The extension period must be a period of such length as the court considers necessary for the purpose of protecting members of the public from serious harm occasioned by the commission by the offender of further specified offences, subject to subsections (5A) to (7).

(5A) The extension period must be at least 1 year.

(6) The extension period must not exceed—

(a) 5 years in the case of a specified violent offence, and

(b) 8 years in the case of a specified sexual offence or a specified terrorism offence.

(7) The term of an extended sentence of detention imposed under this section in respect of an offence may not exceed the term that, at the time the offence was committed, was the maximum term of imprisonment permitted for the offence in the case of a person aged 18 or over.

E4.14 For the meaning of 'specified offence' and 'serious harm', see **E4.3**. Note that, by virtue of the LASPO 2012, sch. 21, para. 36, s. 226B is modified so that the reference in s. 226B(7) to '18' is to be read as a reference to '21'. It is irrelevant whether the offence was committed before or after s. 226B came into force (s. 226B(1)). For amendments made to sch. 15 by the inclusion of a new part 3 containing 'specified terrorism offences', see **E4.4**. In s. 226B, 'under 18' means 'under 18 at the date of conviction' (*Bennett* [2019] EWCA Crim 629, [2019] 2 Cr App R (S) 39 (280)).

The offender must pass the 'dangerousness test' (see **E4.19**). An extended sentence of detention can be passed only where the appropriate custodial term, proportionate to the seriousness of the offence, is at least four years. There is no equivalent provision in s. 226B to that of Condition A in s. 226A, so it follows that the custodial term under s. 226B must always be for at least four years. To the custodial term there must always be added the appropriate extension period, the maximum being five years for a specified violent offence, or eight years for a specified sexual offence or a specified terrorism offence. The length of the extension period is a matter for judicial assessment in each case, and is that which the court considers necessary to reduce the future danger posed by the particular offender. According to the Court of Appeal in *ARD* [2017] EWCA Crim 1882, [2018] 1 Cr App R (S) 23 (163), the length of the extension period is not to be determined by the defendant's age or lack of previous convictions save in so far as they were indicators as to the degree of harm the defendant posed into the future and for how long the defendant would pose that harm. The total term of an extended sentence of detention must not exceed the maximum penalty for the offence. A person sentenced to be detained under s. 226B is liable to be detained in such place as may be determined by the Secretary of State (s. 235).

Although s. 226B was not directly in issue in *A-G's Ref (No. 27 of 2013) (Burinskas)* [2014] EWCA Crim 334, [2014] 1 WLR 4209, the early release provisions in respect of ss. 226A and 226B are identical, and it is submitted that the decision (considered at **E4.6**) is equally applicable to s. 226B, subject to (a) the non-availability of the sentence of life for the second listed offence where D is aged under 18 and (b) the adjustments which need to be made to sentencing when dealing with offenders aged under 18.

Life Sentence for Second Listed Offence

E4.15 The CJA 2003, s. 224A, provides for the sentence of life imprisonment for the second listed offence.

Criminal Justice Act 2003, s. 224A

(1) This section applies where—

(a) a person aged 18 or over is convicted of an offence listed in Part 1 of Schedule 15B,

(b) the offence was committed after this section comes into force, and

(c) the sentence condition and the previous offence condition are met.

(2) The court must impose a sentence of imprisonment for life unless the court is of the opinion that there are particular circumstances which—

(a) relate to the offence, to the previous offence referred to in subsection (4) or to the offender, and

(b) would make it unjust to do so in all the circumstances.

(3) The sentence condition is that, but for this section, the court would, in compliance with sections 152(2) and 153(2), impose a sentence of imprisonment for 10 years or more, disregarding any extension period imposed under section 226A.
(4) The previous offence condition is that—
  (a) at the time the offence was committed, the offender had been convicted of an offence listed in Schedule 15B ('the previous offence'), and
  (b) a relevant life sentence or a relevant sentence of imprisonment or detention for a determinate period was imposed on the offender for the previous offence.
(5) A life sentence is relevant for the purposes of subsection (4)(b) if—
  (a) the offender was not eligible for release during the first 5 years of the sentence, or
  (b) the offender would not have been eligible for release during that period but for the reduction of the period of ineligibility to take account of a relevant pre-sentence period.
(6) An extended sentence imposed under this Act (including one imposed as a result of the Armed Forces Act 2006) is relevant for the purposes of subsection (4)(b) if the appropriate custodial term imposed was 10 years or more.
(7) Any other extended sentence is relevant for the purposes of subsection (4)(b) if the custodial term imposed was 10 years or more.
(8) Any other sentence of imprisonment or detention for a determinate period is relevant for the purposes of subsection (4)(b) if it was for a period of 10 years or more.
(9) An extended sentence or other sentence of imprisonment or detention is also relevant if it would have been relevant under subsection (7) or (8) but for the reduction of the sentence, or any part of the sentence, to take account of a relevant pre-sentence period.
(10) For the purposes of subsections (4) to (9)—
'extended sentence' means—
  (a) a sentence imposed under section 85 of the Sentencing Act or under section 226A, 226B, 227 or 228 of this Act (including one imposed as a result of section 219A, 220, 221A or 222 of the Armed Forces Act 2006), or
  (b) an equivalent sentence imposed under the law of Scotland, Northern Ireland or a member state (other than the United Kingdom);
'life sentence' means—
  (a) a life sentence as defined in section 34 of the Crime (Sentences) Act 1997, or
  (b) an equivalent sentence imposed under the law of Scotland, Northern Ireland or a member state (other than the United Kingdom);
'relevant pre-sentence period', in relation to the previous offence referred to in subsection (4), means any period which the offender spent in custody or on bail before the sentence for that offence was imposed;
'sentence of imprisonment or detention' includes any sentence of a period in custody (however expressed).
(11) An offence the sentence for which is imposed under this section is not to be regarded as an offence the sentence for which is fixed by law.
(12) Where an offence is found to have been committed over a period of two or more days, it must be taken for the purposes of subsections (1)(b) and (4)(a) to have been committed on the last of those days,

For offences listed in sch. 15B, see **E4.17**. At the date when the UK leaves the EU in accordance with the European Union (Withdrawal) Act 2018, the Criminal Justice (Amendment etc.) (EU Exit) Regulations will amend s. 224A(10) so that references to sentences imposed in a Member State are omitted. Section 224A came into force on 3 December 2012 and the sentence is available for offenders whose offence was committed on or after that date. The relevant sentence is life imprisonment if the offender is aged 21 and over, and custody for life if aged 18, 19 or 20. Section 224A(10) incorporates the definition of 'life sentence' which is to be found in the Crime (Sentences) Act 1997, s. 34, which defines life sentence to include imprisonment for public protection. There are probably very few examples of offenders who fall within the criteria in s. 224A but who would not attract a discretionary life sentence under s. 225 (see **E4.5**) in any event. However, to qualify for a discretionary life sentence the offender must pass the 'dangerousness' test. This is *not* a requirement for the life sentence under s. 224A. Even if all the conditions in s. 224A apply, the court may still avoid passing the 'life sentence for second listed offence' if there are particular circumstances relating to either the current offence or the past offence, or to the **E4.16** offender, which 'would make it unjust to do so in all the circumstances'. This formula is the same as that which applies in the prescribed minimum sentences in relation to drug trafficking and domestic burglary (PCC(S)A 2000, ss. 110 and 111): see **E5.1** and **E5.4**.

E4.17 The offences listed in part 1 of sch. 15B are: manslaughter; offences under the OAPA 1861, ss. 4, 18, 28 and 29; FA 1968, ss. 16, 17(1) and 18; Theft Act 1968, s. 8 (where at some time during the commission of the offence the offender had in his possession a firearm or imitation firearm); Protection of Children Act 1978, s. 1; TA 2000, ss. 54, 56, 57 and 59; A-TCSA 2001, ss. 47, 50 and 113; SOA 2003, ss. 1, 2, 4 to 12, 14, 15, 25 and 26 (if D is over 18), 47 to 50 and, where the offence is punishable with life imprisonment, 30, 31, 34, 35 and 62; DVCVA 2004, s. 5; TA 2006, ss. 5, 6, 9, 10 and 11; Explosive Substances Act 1883, ss. 2, 3 and 4; Modern Slavery Act 2015, ss. 1 and 2. Also included are attempts to commit any of these offences, conspiracy to commit a listed offence or murder, incitement to commit a listed offence or murder, an offence under the SCA 2007 in relation to which a listed offence or murder is the offence which the person intended or believed would be committed, and aiding, abetting, counselling or procuring the commission of a listed offence.

The offences listed in part 2 of sch. 15B are murder, and any offence that was abolished before the coming into force of sch. 15B and which would, if committed on the relevant day, have constituted an offence specified in part 1.

It should be noted that the new offence must be listed in *part 1* of sch. 15B, while the previous offence can be listed anywhere in the schedule. This is to allow for the inclusion within the previous conviction of the offence of murder and repealed offences (such as under the Sexual Offences Act 1956) which have been replaced with broadly equivalent offences. At the date when the UK leaves the EU in accordance with the European Union (Withdrawal) Act 2018, the Criminal Justice (Amendment etc.) (EU Exit) Regulations will amend sch. 15B so that references to previous convictions in a Member State are omitted from the schedule.

E4.18 Several of the offences in part 1 are not punishable with life imprisonment *per se*, but only become so as one of the two relevant offences under s. 224A. Many of the sexual offences carry maximum terms of ten or 14 years. The offence under the Protection of Children Act 1978, s. 1, is included and has a maximum of ten years. The offence of robbery (which does carry life imprisonment) is included, but only where, at some time during the commission of the offence, the offender had in his possession a firearm or imitation firearm within the meaning of the FA 1968. This particular formulation has caused difficulty under earlier provisions. In *Gore* [2010] EWCA Crim 369, [2010] 2 Cr App R (S) 93 (590), the Court of Appeal held that the offence of robbery committed in the circumstances so described included involvement by D in a joint enterprise robbery in the course of which one of his co-defendants had been in possession of a firearm.

The Court of Appeal in *A-G's Ref (No. 27 of 2013) (Burinskas)* [2014] EWCA Crim 334, [2014] 1 WLR 4209 provided guidance in respect of this sentence. Lord Thomas CJ said (at [43]) that, where s. 224A might be relevant, it could be tempting for the judge to move straight to consideration of that provision before deciding whether the offender qualifies as a dangerous offender. That temptation should be resisted. The proper approach is:

(a) Consider the issue of dangerousness. If the offender is *not* dangerous, and s. 224A does not apply, a determinate sentence should be passed. (It should be noted that, although the relevant provision was not in force when *Burinskas* was decided, the court *must* also consider whether s. 236A (custodial sentence for certain offenders of particular concern) applies: see **E4.31**.) If the offender is *not* dangerous, but the conditions in s. 224A are satisfied, then (subject to s. 224A(2)(a) and (b)) a life sentence for the second listed offence *must* be imposed.
(b) If the offender *is* dangerous, consider whether the seriousness of the offence(s) justifies a discretionary life sentence. If a discretionary life sentence is justified then it *must* be passed. If s. 224A also applies, the judge should record that fact, in open court. If a discretionary life sentence is not imposed then the judge should consider s. 224A. If it applies then (subject to the terms of that section) a life sentence *must* be imposed under that section.

In *Fernandez* [2014] EWCA Crim 2405, [2015] 1 Cr App R (S) 35 (268), D received a life sentence under s. 224A for two armed robberies and a further attempted armed robbery, having many previous convictions including other armed robberies for one of which he had served a sentence of 11 years. The judge took a notional sentence of 17 to 18 years, reduced it to 13 years to take account of the guilty plea, and set the minimum term at eight years. On appeal the Court of Appeal rejected an argument that because D had remained conviction-free for ten years before the current offences that rendered the automatic life sentence unjust, but said that the minimum term should have been set at half the notional determinate term, and varied it to six and a half years.

ASSESSMENT OF DANGEROUSNESS

Section 229 of the CJA 2003 deals with the necessary evidence base for the assessment of dangerousness required for the court to establish whether, under any of ss. 225, 226, 226A and 226B, the offender poses a 'significant risk to members of the public of serious harm occasioned by the commission by him of further specified offences'. Section 229 is not relevant where the court is considering the application of s. 224A (life sentence for the second listed offence). **E4.19**

Section 229 applies where '(a) a person has been convicted of a specified offence; and (b) it falls to a court to assess... whether there is a significant risk to members of the public of serious harm occasioned by the commission by him of further such offences'. In making that assessment, the court:

(a) must take into account all such information as is available to it about the nature and circumstances of the offence,
(aa) may take into account all such information as is available to it about the nature and circumstances of any other offences of which the offender has been convicted by a court anywhere in the world,
(b) may take into account any information which is before it about any pattern of behaviour of which any of the offences mentioned in paragraph (a) or (aa) forms part, and
(c) may take into account any information about the offender which is before it.

In the leading case of *Lang* [2005] EWCA Crim 2864, [2006] 2 All ER 410, Rose LJ said that the requirement that a risk be 'significant' means more than a possibility — it must be 'noteworthy, of considerable amount or importance'. A wide variety of information will need to be considered before such an assessment is made by the court. The court will rely upon the pre-sentence report and the details of the offender's previous convictions, where relevant. In *Mayers* [2018] EWCA Crim 1552, [2019] 1 Cr App R (S) 1 (1), the Court of Appeal said that it was normal, or usual, to obtain a pre-sentence report to assist in the determination of the issue of dangerousness. In a multi-handed case the sentencer must consider the issue of dangerousness in respect of each offender separately, and information in a pre-sentence report will often be of assistance in determining that question. A psychiatric report would be appropriate in some cases, but should be clearly directed to the issue of dangerousness. In *Pluck* [2006] EWCA Crim 1394, [2007] 1 Cr App R (S) 9 (43) the Court of Appeal commented that reports before the courts were not binding on the sentencer but, if the judge was minded to depart from the conclusion set out in a report, counsel should be warned in advance. It would only rarely be appropriate for a judge to permit cross-examination of the author of a pre-sentence report on the assessment of risk (*S* [2006] EWCA Crim 2389, [2006] 2 Cr App R (S) 35 (224)). Wherever possible the prosecution should be in a position to describe to the court the facts of any previous specified offences on the record. If there is doubt over the accuracy of the facts or circumstances of previous convictions of the offender, it may be necessary, according to *Samuels* (1995) 16 Cr App R (S) 856, to adjourn to investigate the context of an earlier offence, but it may be possible to proceed on the information before the court or to infer the seriousness of past offences from the sentences which had been imposed for them. It is clear that in the assessment **E4.20** of dangerousness it is not just previous *specified* offences which are relevant. The court may have regard to offences on the record which are not specified offences, especially where they indicate an escalating pattern of seriousness. Indeed, it is not a prerequisite to a finding of dangerousness that the offender has any previous convictions. A first offender might qualify. In *Bourke* [2017] EWCA Crim 2150, [2018] 1 Cr App R (S) 42 (298) the Court of Appeal confirmed that there was nothing wrong in principle with the judge finding that dangerousness was established on the basis of a single incident. Nor is it necessary that serious harm (or indeed any harm) has been caused by the offender in the course of past offences, since that may have been simply a matter of good fortune — a public protection sentence may properly be imposed where there is a significant risk of serious harm from such offences in the future (see further *Johnson* [2006] EWCA Crim 2486, [2007] Cr App R (S) 112 (674)). The Court of Appeal in *Pedley* [2009] EWCA Crim 840, [2009] 1 WLR 2517 said that there was no justification for trying to redefine the 'significant risk of serious harm' test in terms of numerical probability. Each case must be determined on its own facts, but that did not mean that the sentence was too uncertain to comply with the ECHR, Article 5(1). According to the Court of Appeal in *Chowdhury* [2016] EWCA Crim 1341, [2016] 2 Cr App R (S) 41 (452), sentencers should be careful when reaching a finding of dangerousness in relation to young people, especially where there is no pattern of offending. Young people are more likely to act impulsively, more likely to be responsive to any sentence imposed, and more likely to change.

E4.21 In *Lang*, Rose LJ said that since the CJA 2003 defines 'serious harm' as 'death or serious personal injury, whether physical or psychological', and that was a phrase familiar to courts from earlier legislation, earlier guidance might be helpful. His lordship said that the fact that the further offence that is foreseen is a 'serious offence' does not automatically mean that commission of such an offence would result in 'serious harm', and if the offence foreseen is not a 'serious offence', it will be rare that there is a 'significant risk of serious harm'. The Court of Appeal in *Dobson* [2018] EWCA Crim 2402 said that repetitive violent offending at a relatively low level did not of itself give rise to a significant risk of serious harm in the future. In *Terrell* [2007] EWCA Crim 3079, [2008] 2 All ER 1065, a case where D had pleaded guilty before the magistrates to making indecent photographs of a child and had been committed to the Crown Court for sentence, the Court of Appeal said that, although there was a clear risk that D might reoffend in a similar way in future, there was no evidence that his offending would escalate to photographing children or to child abuse. It could not therefore be shown that D represented a 'significant risk... of serious harm', where 'serious harm' meant death or serious personal injury, the latter phrase being deliberately coloured by the associated word 'death'. The decision in *Terrell* has been followed in several later cases, including *Hayes* [2016] EWCA Crim 663, [2016] 2 Cr App R (S) 24 (208) and *Jones* [2018] EWCA Crim 1733, [2019] 1 Cr App R (S) 2 (16). The Court of Appeal in *Lang* confirmed that risk to 'members of the public' was a general term, and should not be construed so as to exclude any particular group, such as prison officers or staff in mental hospitals. Such a risk can properly be made out where the risk is specific to a small group of individuals, or perhaps just to one potential victim (*Hashi* (1995) 16 Cr App R (S) 121, approved and applied in *Laverick* [2015] EWCA Crim 1059, [2015] 2 Cr App R (S) 62 (434)). In the context of an offence of engaging in conduct in preparation for acts of terrorism, contrary to the TA 2006, s. 5(1), the Court of Appeal confirmed in *A-G's Ref (No. 323 of 2016) (Abdallah)* [2016] EWCA Crim 1868, [2017] 1 Cr App R (S) 29 (204) that 'members of the public' can include non-UK citizens who would not be within the UK at a time when the anticipated risk might materialise.

In applying s. 229 the court will be relying upon the facts of the offence (especially where these have emerged in some detail during the course of a contested trial), the offender's previous record, normally the contents of a pre-sentence report, and the contents of any other relevant report, such as a psychiatric report. The Court of Appeal confirmed in *Lavery* [2008] EWCA Crim 2499, [2009] 3 All ER 295 that the sentencer was entitled to have regard to offences which the offender had asked to have taken into consideration. Other material may be taken into account, as in *Hillman* [2006] EWCA Crim 690, [2006] 2 Cr App R (S) 85 (565), where the judge properly had regard to a synopsis of material prepared by the prosecution containing details of earlier alleged misconduct by D which had resulted in the making of an anti-social behaviour order against him. The Court of Appeal said that although the incidents referred to in the synopsis had not been tested in adversarial judicial proceedings, they could be regarded as 'hard information' and could be relied upon. In *Considine* [2007] EWCA Crim 1166, [2008] 3 All ER 621, the Court of Appeal confirmed that the word 'information' in s. 229 was not restricted in its meaning to 'evidence', and that relevant information bearing on the offender's dangerousness in a particular case might include material adverse to the offender but which had not been proved by criminal conviction. In *Lang*, the Court of Appeal said that the sentencer should be careful to give reasons for all conclusions, particularly for the finding of whether there is a significant risk. Reasons should include reference to the information which has been taken into account. If the sentencer is minded to come to a different conclusion from the report(s) presented, it would be wise to alert counsel so that representations can be made on the issue. See further the CJA 2003, s. 174, at **E1.23**.

In *Chowdhury* [2016] EWCA Crim 1341, [2016] 2 Cr App R (S) 41 (452), the Court of Appeal said that it will not normally interfere with a finding of dangerousness unless it can be shown that the sentencer has failed to apply the correct principles, or has reached a conclusion to which he or she was not entitled to come on the evidence. In *Howlett* [2019] EWCA Crim 1224, [2020] 1 Cr App R (S) 14 (123), the Court of Appeal said (at [27]) that 'it will be a rare case in which an appellate court, which has not conducted the trial and seen the offender, would overturn on sentence an exercise of judicial discretion in relation to an assessment of dangerousness'. In *Johnson* [2006] EWCA Crim 2486, [2007] Cr App R (S) 112 (674), on an application by the A-G arguing that the judge had erred in not making a finding of dangerousness, the Court of Appeal said that it was for the applicant to show that the judge's decision could not properly have been reached had he identified the relevant principles and applied his mind to the facts. Even so, in *A-G's Ref (No. 5 of 2011) (Troninas)* [2011] EWCA Crim 1244, [2012] 1 Cr App R (S) 20 (103) and again in *Smith* [2017] EWCA Crim 252, [2017] 2 Cr App R (S) 2 (5) the Court of Appeal, without finding that the judge had erred in the manner set out in *Johnson*, increased a determinate sentence to an extended sentence on the basis of commission of a very serious sexual offence by an offender of otherwise good character for reasons that 'simply cannot be fathomed [which] suggests something dangerous and unpredictable within this offender [and] there cannot be confidence that another serious event might not occur in the future' (per Treacy LJ in *Smith* at [25]). For consideration of the circumstances in which the Court of Appeal might consider new reports on an offender attempting to challenge an assessment of dangerousness made by a sentencing judge, see *Beesley* [2011] EWCA Crim 1021, [2012] 1 Cr App R (S) 15 (71).

Multiple Offences and Concurrent and Consecutive Terms

Life Sentence The Sentencing Council definitive guideline, *Totality* (see Supplement, SG4-7), sets out the proper approach for sentencing in each of the following circumstances: (a) imposing multiple life sentences on the same occasion and using multiple offences to calculate the minimum term for an indeterminate sentence; (b) imposing a life sentence where the offender is already serving an existing determinate sentence; (c) imposing a life sentence where the offender is already serving an existing indeterminate sentence; and (d) ordering a determinate sentence to run consecutively to an indeterminate sentence. In *Baker* [2020] EWCA Crim 176, [2020] 2 Cr App R (S) 23 (166), the Court of Appeal said that it was not unlawful, nor necessarily wrong, to impose an extended sentence on an offender serving a life sentence. In *Jeter* [2015] EWCA Crim 1804, a life sentence was imposed on an offender already serving a life sentence. The judge concluded that the appropriate minimum term for the new offence was 13 years, but he passed a life sentence with a minimum term of 34 years to ensure that the overall minimum term would be extended by 13 years. The Court of Appeal approved that approach. In *Mohammed* [2019] EWCA Crim 2095, [2020] 1 Cr App R (S) 65 (503), the judge imposed a life sentence on an offender already serving an extended sentence, and the Court of Appeal said that the judge had **E4.22**

been entitled to increase the minimum term, but this should have been calculated so as to run from the two-thirds point of the custodial term of the extended sentence rather than from the end of that custodial term. The minimum term was accordingly reduced from 13 years to nine years.

E4.23 **Extended Sentence Using Multiple Offences to Calculate the Custodial Term** See the Sentencing Council definitive guideline, *Totality* (see Supplement, **SG4-6**).

In relation to the extended sentence, in *Pinnell* [2010] EWCA Crim 2848, [2011] 2 Cr App R (S) 30 (168) it was held that where the condition that the custodial term be at least four years applies, and a person has been convicted of a specified offence and one or more associated non-specified offences none of which taken alone would justify a four-year custodial term, the seriousness of the aggregate offending must be considered. If a four-year custodial term results from aggregating the shortest terms commensurate with the seriousness of each offence, then that four-year term can be imposed in relation to the specified offence. In *D* [2014] EWCA Crim 2340, [2014] 1 Cr App R (S) 23 (168) the Court of Appeal said that an extended sentence could be passed only for one specified offence, or concurrently on two or more of them. Associated non-specified offences should attract concurrent determinate sentences, or no separate penalty. The Court also said that, when imposing an extended sentence in a multiple offence case, the judge should always identify the specified offence which has triggered the extended sentence, and clearly link that to the relevant custodial term and extension period. These principles were applied in *Smith* [2015] EWCA Crim 1627, where a mix of concurrent and consecutive extended sentences, which the Court of Appeal said was unlawful, was varied on appeal to a single extended sentence of 12 years, with a custodial term of eight years and a four-year extension period, concurrent determinate sentences being imposed on other counts.

E4.24 **Extended Sentence to Run Consecutively, or Consecutively to a Determinate Sentence** In *Pinnell* [2010] EWCA Crim 2848, [2011] 2 Cr App R (S) 30 (168) the Court of Appeal said that there was no objection in principle to imposing consecutive extended sentences, or to imposing an extended sentence consecutive to a determinate sentence, although this should be done only where there was a particular reason for doing so. The extension periods in the case of consecutive extended sentences will themselves be consecutive (and see further *Thompson* [2018] EWCA Crim 639, [2018] 2 Cr App R (S) 19 (164), making it clear that in the unusual circumstances which justify the passing of consecutive extended sentences, the total extended licence may properly exceed the maximum licence period for a single offence). On the other hand, there is no reason why an extended sentence cannot run consecutively to a determinate sentence, irrespective of the time order in which the offences were committed. This was the approach recommended in *Francis* [2014] EWCA Crim 631 and applied in *Watkins* [2014] EWCA Crim 1677, [2014] 1 Cr App R (S) 6 (41), where the Court of Appeal varied the original sentence to a determinate sentence of 15 years with a consecutive extended sentence of 14 years with an extension period of six years. The authorities were comprehensively reviewed in *Ulhaqdad* [2017] EWCA Crim 1216, [2017] 2 Cr App R (S) 46 (397), where the Court of Appeal confirmed that when sentencing on the same occasion it is better practice for the determinate sentence to be passed first, followed by the extended sentence. However, the imposition of the extended sentence first, followed by the determinate sentence, is not in itself unlawful, and the Court had been provided with information from the prison service indicating that their practice when calculating the offender's release date was to aggregate the custodial terms, so that it made no practical difference which way round the sentences were imposed. Even so, in the instant case the Court restructured the sentence so that the extended sentence followed the determinate sentence. The Court also confirmed that it was permissible to pass consecutive extended sentences, although in such a case the explanation of the sentences was likely to be complex and great care was needed (see also *Watkins* [2014] EWCA Crim 1677, [2014] 1 Cr App R (S) 6 (41)). Finally, if an offender is currently serving an extended sentence, there is nothing unlawful in the imposition of a consecutive determinate sentence (see also *Hibbert* [2015] EWCA Crim 167, [2015] 2 Cr App R (S) 15 (159)).

PERIOD SPECIFIED UNDER THE POWERS OF CRIMINAL COURTS (SENTENCING) ACT 2000, s. 82A

Powers of Criminal Courts (Sentencing) Act 2000, s. 82A **E4.25**

(1) This section applies if a court passes a life sentence in circumstances where the sentence is not fixed by law.
(2) The court shall, unless it makes an order under subsection (4) below, order that the provisions of section 28(5) to (8) of the Crime (Sentences) Act 1997 (referred to in this section as the 'early release provisions') shall apply to the offender as soon as he has served the part of his sentence which is specified in the order.
(3) The part of his sentence shall be such as the court considers appropriate taking into account—
(a) the seriousness of the offence, or of the combination of the offence and one or more offences associated with it;
(b) the effect that the following would have if the court had sentenced the offender to a term of imprisonment—
(i) section 240ZA of the Criminal Justice Act 2003 (crediting periods of remand in custody);
(ii) section 246 of Armed Forces Act 2006 (equivalent provision for service courts);
(iii) any direction which the court would have given under section 240A of the Criminal Justice Act 2003 (crediting periods of remand on bail subject to certain types of condition), and.
(c) the early release provisions as compared with section 244(1) of the Criminal Justice Act 2003.
(4) If the offender was aged 21 or over when he committed the offence and the court is of the opinion that, because of the seriousness of the offence or the combination of the offence and one or more offences associated with it, no order should be made under subsection (2) above, the court shall order that the early release provisions shall not apply to the offender.

It was emphasised in *Andrews* [2015] EWCA Crim 883, [2015] 2 Cr App R (S) 40 (317) that the imposition of a life sentence is designed to protect the public from the risk posed by the offender, whereas the period specified under s. 82A is meant to reflect the degree of punishment, retribution and deterrence appropriate for the offence, aside from the question of public protection. The specified period should not therefore be lengthened with a view to protecting the public. The effect of specifying part of the sentence under s. 82A is that the life sentence prisoner will not become eligible to be considered for early release until the expiry of that period. If the court is of the view that because of the seriousness of the offence or offences no order should be made under s. 82A(2), it should make an order under s. 82A(4) to the effect that the early release provisions shall not apply to the offender. In *Oakes* [2012] EWCA Crim 2435, [2013] 2 All ER 30 the Court of Appeal said that such an order (referred to in the judgment as a 'whole life order') is reserved for the most exceptional discretionary life sentence cases. While stopping just short of saying that a whole life order was limited to cases of murder, the Court said that whole life orders outside the context of murder would be 'very rare indeed'. See further *Andrews* [2015] EWCA Crim 883, [2015] 2 Cr App R (S) 40 (317). **E4.26**

Some of the cases referred to below relate to earlier versions of these provisions but, it is submitted, still represent the law.

Procedure

CrimPD VII, para. L.1 (see Supplement, **CPD.VII.L**), indicates that the sentencer should specify the relevant period, save in the very exceptional case where he or she considers that the offence is so serious that imprisonment for life is justified by that alone, irrespective of the risk to the public. In that case, this should be stated in open court when passing sentence. A decision not to specify the relevant period may be the subject of an appeal (*Hollies* (1995) 16 Cr App **E4.27**

R (S) 463). When specifying the relevant period, the judge should have regard to the specific terms of the section, and should indicate the reasons for the decision. Before specifying the relevant period, the sentencer should permit counsel for the defence to address the court on the appropriate length of the relevant part. An order made under s. 82A may be the subject of an appeal (*McBean* [2001] EWCA Crim 1891, [2002] 1 Cr App R (S) 98 (430)) or might constitute an unduly lenient sentence (*A-G's Ref (No. 82 of 2000)* [2001] EWCA Crim 65, [2001] 2 Cr App R (S) 60 (289)).

Section 82A(3)(a)

E4.28 In *A-G's Ref (No. 3 of 2004)* [2004] EWCA Crim 1532, [2005] 1 Cr App R (S) 52 (230), the Court of Appeal emphasised that, when having regard to the seriousness of the offence (or the combination of the offence and other offences associated with it), the section permitted the sentencer to look at the totality of the associated offences, rather than just the offence for which the indeterminate sentence was being passed, and to consider whether the sentences for the associated offences would have been consecutive to the main sentence if an indeterminate sentence had not been given. In a case where the offender falls to be sentenced on the same occasion for more than one serious specified offence, or for one or more serious specified offence and one or more specified offence, such sentences should take effect concurrently rather than consecutively but the seriousness of the totality of the offences should be reflected in the length of the period selected by the judge under s. 82A. The Sentencing Council definitive guideline, *Totality* (see Supplement, **SG4-7**), sets out the proper approach for sentencing when imposing multiple life sentences on the same occasion, or using multiple offences to calculate the minimum term for an indeterminate sentence.

Section 82A(3)(b)

E4.29 This subsection refers to the CJA 2003, ss. 240ZA and 240A (effect of time spent in custody on remand or under qualifying curfew: see **E2.12** and **E2.16**). Section 82A(3)(b) requires the sentencer to make an appropriate adjustment for the matters referred to in s. 82A(3)(b). This is so even though s. 240ZA operates automatically to deduct time spent in custody on remand from a determinate custodial sentence, since under s. 82A the court is fixing the length of the specified period within an indeterminate sentence and not the length of a determinate sentence. According to the Court of Appeal in *Marklew* [1999] 2 All ER 939, the sentencer should normally give full credit under s. 82(3)(b) for the period spent by the defendant on remand. *Marklew* also indicates, however, that there may be some circumstances in which the giving of full credit to the offender would not be appropriate. It is submitted that, now that time spent on remand in custody is deducted automatically from a determinate sentence by virtue of the CJA 2003, s. 240ZA, the circumstances in which a judge might refuse full credit when fixing the specified period under s. 82A would be very rare.

Section 82A(3)(c)

E4.30 A sentencer exercising power under s. 82A is required to take into account the fact that under the CJA 2003, s. 244, a prisoner who has received a determinate sentence is entitled to be released after serving one half of the sentence. In *Marklew* [1999] 2 All ER 939, Thomas J stated that sentencers should make clear what the determinate sentence would have been and should then normally fix the specified period at *one half* of the notional term. In fixing the notional determinate sentence, appropriate allowance should be made for a guilty plea, applying the relevant guideline. The principle of setting the specified period at *one half* of the notional determinate sentence has been followed and applied in many subsequent cases (see, e.g., *Szczerba* [2002] EWCA Crim 440, [2002] 2 Cr App R (S) 86 (387)). The rationale, according to Pill LJ in *West* [2001] 1 Cr App R (S) 30 (103), is that an indeterminate sentence prisoner should be in no worse a position on an application for early release than a determinate sentence prisoner. The Court of Appeal in *A-G's Ref (No. 27 of 2013) (Burinskas)* [2014] EWCA Crim 334, [2014] 1 WLR 4209 noted that the first opportunity for release from custody occurs sooner for a life sentence prisoner than for a prisoner serving an extended sentence (who must serve two-thirds of the custodial term before being first considered for early release), but held that sentencers must not seek to correct any perceived anomaly by adjusting the specified period under s. 82A for that reason. Section 82A(3)(c) refers to the CJA 2003, s. 244(1), which is solely concerned with release from a determinate sentence. A highly exceptional case is *Rossi* [2014] EWCA Crim 2081, [2015] 1 Cr App R (S) 15 (120), where the Court of Appeal agreed that setting the specified period at one half was 'a conventional rule of practice', but upheld the judge's decision requiring D (who had served two earlier life sentences) to serve two thirds of the notional sentence applicable to his third life sentence.

CUSTODIAL SENTENCE FOR CERTAIN OFFENDERS OF 'PARTICULAR CONCERN'

Section 236A of the CJA 2003 provides that, where a person is convicted of an offence listed in sch. 18A to that Act (whenever the offence was committed), the offender was aged 18 or over when the offence was committed and the court does not impose a sentence of imprisonment for life or an extended sentence under s. 226A, if the court imposes a sentence of imprisonment or detention in a young offender institution for the offence (or for the offence and one or more offences associated with it), the term of the sentence must be the aggregate of (a) 'the appropriate custodial term' and (b) a further period of one year for which the offender is to be subject to a licence (s. 236A(1) and (2)). The 'appropriate custodial term' is the term that 'in the opinion of the court, ensures that the sentence is appropriate' (s. 236A(3)). The total custodial sentence (including the licence period) must not exceed the maximum for the offence (s. 236A(4)). The Court of Appeal in *Powell* [2018] EWCA Crim 1074, [2018] 2 Cr App R (S) 34 (303) clarified the position that, if an offender is to be sentenced for a number of offences and in respect of one or more of those offences an extended sentence has been imposed, it is unlawful to pass a sentence under the CJA 2003, s. 236A, for any of the other offences. **E4.31**

Section 244A of the CJA 2003 is the provision which sets out arrangements for early release of an offender serving a sentence imposed under s. 236A. That makes it clear that, subject to an exception for certain terrorist offenders which is explained below, the offender must first be considered for release by the Parole Board at the half-way point of the custodial term. The Board may direct the offender's release at that point, but only if satisfied that it is not necessary for the protection of the public that the offender should be confined. If the Parole Board does not direct release at that point, the Board must again consider the matter not more than two years later. The offender must in any event be released when the whole of the custodial term has been served. An offender who is not released before the end of the custodial term will still then be subject to the one-year period of licence which was ordered by the court under s. 236A. As from 26 February 2020, the Terrorist Offenders (Restriction of Early Release) Act 2020 amends the CJA 2003, s. 244A, with the effect that, for an offender sentenced as an offender of particular concern under s. 236A having been convicted of an offence specified in sch. 19ZA, part 1 (offences under counter-terrorism legislation), or convicted of an offence specified in sch. 19ZA, part 2, and who was determined by the court to have had a terrorist connection under the C-TA 2008, s. 30, the offender must first be considered for early release by the Parole Board at the *two-thirds* point (rather than the half-way point) of the custodial term. The Board may direct the offender's release at that point, but only if satisfied that it is no longer necessary for the protection of the public that the offender should be confined. The change made by the 2020 Act applies to qualifying terrorist offenders serving such a sentence at the commencement date, and who have not been released on licence, as well as to offenders so sentenced on or after that date.

The offences listed in sch. 18A are offences under the SOA 2003, ss. 5 (rape of a child under 13) and 6 (assault of a child under 13 by penetration) and offences under the following provisions where the offence has a terrorist connection: OAPA 1861, ss. 4, 28 and 29; Explosive Substances Act 1883, ss. 2, 3 and 4; TA 2000, ss. 11, 12, 54, 56, 57, 58, 58A and 59; A-TCSA 2001, ss. 47, 50 and 113; TA 2006, ss. 1, 2, 5, 6, 8, 9, 10 and 11. It should be noted that the offences under the TA 2000, ss. 11 and 12, and the TA 2006, ss. 1, 2 and 8, were inserted into sch. 18A by the C-TBSA 2019. Also included are aiding, abetting, counselling or procuring the commission of an offence specified above ('a relevant offence'), attempt or conspiracy to commit a relevant offence, or an offence under Part 2 of the SCA 2007 in relation to which a relevant offence is the offence (or one of the offences) which the person intended or believed would be committed. If the offence has a terrorist connection, attempt or conspiracy to commit murder is also included, as is an offence under Part 2 of the SCA 2007 in relation to which murder is the offence (or one of the offences) which the person intended or believed would be committed.

It is important to note that where an offence was abolished before the coming into force of s. 236A but, if committed on the day on which the offender was convicted of the offence, it would have constituted one of the offences specified above, that offence is also included. This of course means that 'historic' cases involving rape or penetration of a child under 13 are covered by this provision.

For the purposes of sch. 18A, an offence has a 'terrorist connection' if a court has determined under the C-TA 2008 that the offence has such a connection (sch. 18A, para. 24).

Comprehensive guidance on imposition of a sentence under s. 236A was provided by the Court of Appeal in *LF* [2016] EWCA Crim 561, [2016] 2 Cr App R (S) 30 (271), also referred to as *Fruen*, where Treacy LJ noted that judges and practitioners had misapplied, or failed to apply, the relevant provisions in a significant number of cases. The Court provided a checklist of points to be considered when deciding if a case fell within s. 236A, and how such a sentence should be expressed. A sentence imposed under s. 236A should always be expressed as a single term, comprising the custodial element and a further one-year licence period. If the offender was to be sentenced under s. 236A for more than one qualifying offence, each such offence had to be expressed in that way. If the s. 236A sentences were to run concurrently, the overall custodial term for those offences plus the one-year licence period had to be stated by the judge. If the s. 236A sentences were to run consecutively, the total custodial term for those offences, as well as the total licence period, had to be stated. Where a determinate sentence and a s. 236A sentence are to run consecutively, the latter should follow the former (*LF*; *Clarke* [2017] EWCA Crim 572, [2017] 2 Cr App R (S) 18 (140)).

For detailed consideration of the powers of the Court of Appeal to substitute a sentence under s. 236A in circumstances where such a sentence should have been imposed by the sentencing court but where that requirement was overlooked at the time, see *A* [2020] EWCA Crim 948 and earlier authorities considered therein.

Section E5 Prescribed Custodial Sentences

MINIMUM CUSTODIAL SENTENCES FOR CLASS A DRUG OFFENCES

Section 110 of the PCC(S)A 2000 provides that where: **E5.1**

(a) a person is convicted of a Class A drug trafficking offence committed after 30 September 1997;
(b) at the time when that offence was committed he was aged 18 or over and had been convicted in any part of the UK of two other Class A drug trafficking offences (or equivalent offence in another EU Member State committed after 15 August 2010); and
(c) one of those offences was committed after he had been convicted of the other,

the Crown Court shall impose a custodial sentence for a term of at least seven years, unless the court is of the opinion that there are particular circumstances which relate to any of the offences or to the offender which would make it unjust to do so in all the circumstances (s. 110(2) and (2A)). At the date when the UK leaves the EU in accordance with the European Union (Withdrawal) Act 2018, the Criminal Justice (Amendment etc.) (EU Exit) Regulations will amend s. 110 so that references to previous convictions outside the UK are omitted.

Section 110 applies *only* to *Class A* drug trafficking offences. A drug trafficking offence is: **E5.2**

(a) producing, supplying or possessing with intent to supply (MDA 1971, s. 4(2), 4(3) and 5(3)) (but *not* simple possession);
(b) assisting in or inducing the commission outside the UK of an offence punishable under a corresponding law (MDA 1971, s. 20);
(c) an offence under the Customs and Excise Management Act 1979, s. 50(2), 68(2) or 170;
(d) manufacturing or supplying a scheduled substance (Criminal Justice (International Cooperation) Act 1990, s. 12);
(e) having possession etc. of a controlled drug on a ship (Criminal Justice (International Cooperation) Act 1990, s. 19);
(f) inciting, attempting or conspiring to commit any of these offences or aiding abetting, counselling or procuring the commission of any of them.

Nothing in s. 110 prevents a hospital order being imposed on an offender in an appropriate case (*Mental Health Act 1983, s. 37(1A)*). In *Harvey* [2000] 1 Cr App R (S) 368, Lord Bingham CJ said that the object of the provision plainly was to require courts to impose a sentence of at least seven years in cases where otherwise they would not, or might not, have done so. His lordship declined to indicate what might amount to circumstances 'which would make it unjust' to impose the prescribed sentence, but for subsequent examples see *Pearce* [2004] EWCA Crim 2129, [2005] 1 Cr App R (S) 73 (364) (supply of single wrap of heroin); *Turner* [2005] EWCA Crim 2363, [2006] 1 Cr App R (S) 95 (565) (personal dealing); *McDonagh* [2006] EWCA Crim 2742, [2006] 1 Cr App R (S) 111 (647) (age of previous convictions); and *Reid* [2008] EWCA Crim 212, [2008] 2 Cr App R (S) 68 (363) (no drugs in fact supplied). By contrast, in *Lucas* [2011] EWCA Crim 2806, [2012] 2 Cr App R (S) 14 (57), it was held not to be unjust to impose the minimum sentence where D had committed the earlier offences when aged 15 and 17 and the third offence when aged 18. The Court of Appeal noted that D was a young man who had been drawn into the drug culture and who had not served a custodial sentence before, and that s. 110 could be 'harsh', but 'perfectly normal circumstances' such as these could not amount to 'particular circumstances' for circumventing its operation. *Lucas* was followed in *Usherwood* [2018] EWCA Crim 1156, [2018] 2 Cr App R (S) 39 (337). It was further endorsed in *Marland* [2018] EWCA Crim 1770, [2018] 2 Cr App R (S) 51 (411), where the Court of Appeal said that s. 110 was intended to have deterrent effect, that 'normal circumstances' could not amount to 'particular circumstances', and that one way of testing whether a sentence would be unjust in the particular circumstances is whether the sentence under s. 110 is 'markably more severe' than the sentence to be derived from the Sentencing Council guideline. *Marland* was applied in *McDonald* [2020] EWCA Crim 56, [2020] 2 Cr App R (S) 13 (91), where it was held that an agreed basis of plea confirming social supply of drugs on a third qualifying drug offence was not in itself enough to bring D within the exception to the required minimum term. A very helpful summary of the general approach to be taken on these matters can be found in *Woofe* [2019] EWCA Crim 2249, [2020] 2 Cr App R (S) 6 (37), where the Court said that if the defence sought to persuade the judge that the minimum sentence should not be imposed, a pre-sentence report should usually be obtained.

In a case where either of the earlier Class A drug trafficking offences was dealt with by way of an absolute discharge or conditional discharge without subsequent breach, the conviction for that offence is a conviction for limited purposes only (see the PCC(S)A 2000, s. 14, and **E12.6**) and, it is submitted, would not count as a qualifying conviction for the purposes of s. 110.

For consecutive sentences imposed on the same sentencing occasion where one sentence is a prescribed custodial sentence, see *Raza* [2009] EWCA Crim 1413, [2010] 1 Cr App R (S) 56 (354) at **E5.10**.

Guilty Plea

E5.3 Where the offender has pleaded guilty, the sentencing court is required to take into account the stage at which the offender indicated an intention to plead guilty and the circumstances in which this indication was given (CJA 2003, s. 144 ; see also the definitive guideline, *Reduction in Sentence for a Guilty Plea*, para. F5 (see Supplement, **SG5-7**)). Section 144(2) and (3) state that in the case of an offence coming within s. 110 the court may not impose a sentence which would be less than 80 per cent of the minimum sentence specified (and see *Gray* [2007] EWCA Crim 979, [2007] 2 Cr App R (S) 78 (494)). Eighty per cent of seven years produces a sentence slightly less than five years and eight months. If the sentencer has taken a starting point which is higher than the minimum sentence, a sentence reduction of one third to reflect a timely guilty plea may be perfectly appropriate, always provided that the final sentence is not less than 80 per cent of the minimum sentence (*Gray*). The Sentencing Council definitive guideline, *Drug Offences* (see Supplement, **SG23-1**) is, therefore, incorrect in stating that where the minimum sentence provision applies 'the discount for an early guilty plea must not exceed 20 per cent'. In *Darling* [2009] EWCA Crim 1610, [2010] 1 Cr App R (S) 63 (420) the Court of Appeal held that, where the sentencing judge is of the opinion that there are particular circumstances which would make it unjust to impose the minimum sentence, the limited reduction permissible for a guilty plea no longer applies and the judge may in an appropriate case reduce sentence to reflect a guilty plea to a sentence which is less than 80 per cent of the minimum sentence specified.

MINIMUM CUSTODIAL SENTENCES FOR DOMESTIC BURGLARY

E5.4 Section 111 of the PCC(S)A 2000 provides that where:

(a) a person is convicted of a domestic burglary committed after 30 November 1999;
(b) at the time when the domestic burglary was committed the person was aged 18 or over and had been convicted in England and Wales of two other domestic burglaries; and

(c) one of those other burglaries was committed after the person had been convicted of the other, and both of them were committed after 30 November 1999,

the Crown Court shall impose a custodial term of at least three years except where the court is of the opinion that there are particular circumstances which relate to any of the offences or the offender which would make it unjust to do so in all the circumstances.

The CAJA 2009, sch. 17, para. 10(3), amended s. 111 so as to provide for the treatment of previous convictions elsewhere in the UK or in another EU Member State. The amendment took effect from 15 August 2010. A previous domestic burglary which took place outside England and Wales is a relevant offence for the purposes of s. 111 only if it was committed after that date. At the date when the UK leaves the EU in accordance with the European Union (Withdrawal) Act 2018, the Criminal Justice (Amendment etc.) (EU Exit) Regulations will amend s. 111 so that references to previous convictions outside the UK are omitted.

For the purposes of s. 111, 'domestic burglary' means a burglary committed in respect of a building or part of a building which is a dwelling (s. 111(5)), and it must always be established that each of the relevant burglaries was in fact a domestic burglary (*Miller* [2010] EWCA Crim 809, [2011] 1 Cr App R (S) 2 (7)). For these purposes s. 111 and the Theft Act 1968, s. 9, should be read together and as a whole (*Coleman* [2013] EWCA Crim 544, [2013] 2 Cr App R (S) 79 (514)). People who live in narrow boats or caravans should attract the same protection conferred by s. 111 as people who live in more conventional housing. In *Flack* [2013] EWCA Crim 115, [2013] 2 Cr App R (S) 56 (366) the Court of Appeal said that if, on the current charge of burglary, it was in dispute whether the property was a dwelling or not, the matter should be resolved by a jury asked to consider alternative counts on the indictment, and not by a *Newton* hearing after conviction. **E5.5**

An attempt to commit a domestic burglary is not a qualifying offence (*Maguire* [2002] EWCA Crim 2689, [2003] 2 Cr App R (S) 10 (40)), nor is a conspiracy to burgle (*Mayo* [2015] EWCA Crim 628). In a case where either of the earlier domestic burglaries was dealt with by way of an absolute discharge or conditional discharge without subsequent breach, the conviction for that offence is a conviction for limited purposes only (see the PCC(S)A 2000, s. 14, and **E12.6**) and, it is submitted, would not count as a qualifying conviction for the purposes of s. 111. 'Custodial sentence' means imprisonment or detention in a young offender institution (s. 111(6)). Nothing in s. 111 prevents a hospital order being imposed on an offender in an appropriate case (Mental Health Act 1983, s. 37(1A)).

In *Andrews* [2010] EWCA Crim 2332, [2013] 2 Cr App R (S) 5 (26), and again in *Silvera* [2013] EWCA Crim 1764, the Court of Appeal has stressed that, when a judge is sentencing a 'three-strikes' burglary case, the three-year prescribed sentence in s. 111 should not be adopted as the sentencing starting point. The proper approach is to apply the Sentencing Council definitive guideline in the usual way, but then to cross-check that the resulting sentence does not infringe the rule in s. 111 (or, if it does, to consider whether there are particular circumstances relating to any of the offences or to the offender which would make imposition of the minimum sentence unjust). **E5.6**

In *McInerney* [2003] EWCA Crim 3003, [2003] 1 All ER 1089, Lord Woolf CJ said at [16]:

> It may be helpful to give examples of the type of situation where a three year sentence may be unjust. The sentence could be unjust if two of the offences were committed many years earlier than the third offence, or if the offender has made real efforts to reform or conquer his drug addiction, but some personal tragedy triggers the third offence, or if the first two offences were committed when the offender was not yet 16. As we read s. 111 it gives the sentencer a fairly substantial degree of discretion as to the categories of situations where the presumption can be rebutted.

The prescribed sentence was found to be unjust in *Stone* [2011] EWCA Crim 2823, [2012] 2 Cr App R (S) 12 (50), where D reached through an open window and stole a box containing items worth £60. He had two previous convictions for domestic burglary, committed 11 years and six years earlier, and there was personal mitigation. His sentence was reduced to eight months' imprisonment. The prescribed sentence was held to be unjust in *Taylor* [2014] EWCA Crim 1611, [2014] 2 Cr App R (S) 85 (658), where the first of the two earlier burglaries committed by the 19-year-old offender had been committed at his mother's house when he was aged 13 and he had been sentenced to a supervision order, and also in *Fletcher* [2015] EWCA Crim 1709, [2016] 1 Cr App R (S) 28 (173), where the latest offence was theft of a games console from an unlocked bedroom in a bedsit and the two earlier burglaries were nine years and 11 years old. In *Mahon* [2017] EWCA Crim 102, the prescribed sentence was unjust where the latest burglary was of lesser harm, with nothing taken, and D's drug and alcohol abuse was now being properly addressed.

In *Sparkes* [2011] EWCA Crim 880, [2011] 2 Cr App R (S) 107 (614), where D was made subject to the prescribed sentence, imposed consecutively to a sentence of five years which he was serving for similar other offences, it was held to be unjust to pass the prescribed sentence because the overall sentence would infringe totality (see also *Dixon* [2017] EWCA Crim 1363). For consecutive sentences imposed on the same sentencing occasion, where one sentence is a prescribed custodial sentence, see *Raza* [2009] EWCA Crim 1413, [2010] 1 Cr App R (S) 56 (354) at **E5.10**.

Sequence of Offences

E5.7 The key considerations in the PCC(S)A 2000, s. 111, are the dates on which the qualifying offences were committed and the dates on which the offender was convicted. The sequence must be (a) commission, then conviction, (b) commission, then conviction, (c) commission, then conviction; s. 111 would not bite in a case where the offender commits a third domestic burglary before being convicted of the second (*Hoare* [2004] EWCA Crim 191, [2004] 2 Cr App R (S) 50 (261)). 'Convicted' must be distinguished from 'sentenced'. So, commission of a third domestic burglary at a time when the offender is on bail awaiting sentence for a second domestic burglary does trigger the operation of the section (*Webster* [2003] EWCA Crim 3597, [2004] 2 Cr App R (S) 25 (126)). Section 111 can operate in an uneven way, so that one offender will infringe the provision after having been convicted of just three domestic burglaries, while another might have been convicted of (or had taken into consideration) many more such offences without yet having infringed it.

A finding of guilt in a youth court is equivalent to a conviction and counts for these purposes (*Frost* [2001] 2 Cr App R (S) 26 (124)). It is unclear whether an earlier spent conviction for domestic burglary counts as a qualifying conviction. It is submitted that such a conviction does count, but that the fact that the conviction was spent may be a particular circumstance relating to that offence making the imposition of the prescribed sentence unjust in all the circumstances.

Guilty Plea

E5.8 Where the offender has pleaded guilty, the sentencing court is required to take into account the stage at which the offender indicated an intention to plead guilty and the circumstances in which this indication was given (CJA 2003, s. 144; see also the definitive guideline, *Reduction in Sentence for a Guilty Plea*, para. F5 (see Supplement, **SG5-7**)). Section 144(2) and (3) state that in the case of an offence coming within s. 111, the court may not impose a sentence which would be less than 80 per cent of the minimum sentence specified (and see *Gray* [2007] EWCA Crim 979, [2007] 2 Cr App R (S) 78 (494); *Darling* [2009] EWCA Crim 1610, [2010] 1 Cr App R (S) 63 (420), and the discussion at **E5.3**). Eighty per cent of three years produces a sentence of just less than two years and five months. If the sentencer has taken a starting point which is higher than the minimum sentence, a sentence reduction of one third to reflect a timely guilty plea may be perfectly appropriate, always provided that the final sentence is not less than 80 per cent of the minimum sentence (*Gray*). The Sentencing Council definitive guideline,

Domestic Burglary (see Supplement, **SG19-3**), is, therefore, incorrect in stating that where the minimum sentence provision applies 'the discount for an early guilty plea must not exceed 20 per cent'. In *Nelson* [2013] EWCA Crim 2410, D fell within the provisions of s. 111, but had availed himself of an early guilty plea scheme at the Crown Court. The Court of Appeal said that, in all the circumstances of the case, the proper starting point was four years and three months, from which a full one third discount for plea could be given without infringing the rule in s. 144(2). Had a lower starting point (close to three years) been appropriate, then there would have been a clash between s. 144(2) and the offender's expectation of a full discount under the early guilty plea scheme. In such circumstances, it is submitted that the statutory provision must take precedence.

MINIMUM CUSTODIAL SENTENCES FOR FIREARMS OFFENCES

Section 51A of the FA 1968 provides for minimum custodial sentences for certain firearms offences committed on or after 22 January 2004. For details of the offences listed in s. 51A, see **B12.61**, **B12.90** ***et seq.*** and **B13.83**. **E5.9**

Firearms Act 1968, s. 51A

(1) This section applies where—
 (a) an individual is convicted of
  (i) an offence under s. 5(1)(a), (ab), (aba), (ac), (ad), (ae), (af) [(ag), (ba)] or (c) of this Act, or
  (ii) an offence under s. 5(1A)(a) of this Act, or
  (iii) an offence under any of the provisions of this Act listed in subsection (1A) in respect of a firearm or ammunition specified in section 5(1)(a), (ab), (aba), (ac), (ad), (ae), (af), [(ag), (ba)] or (c) or section 5(1A)(a) of this Act, and
 (b) the offence was committed after the commencement of this section and at a time when he was aged 16 or over.
(1A) The provisions are—
 (za) section 5(2A) (manufacture, sale or transfer of firearm, or possession etc. for sale or transfer);
 (a) section 16 (possession of firearm with intent to injure);
 (b) section 16A (possession of firearm with intent to cause fear of violence);
 (c) section 17 (use of firearm to resist arrest);
 (d) section 18 (carrying firearm with criminal intent);
 (e) section 19 (carrying a firearm in a public place);
 (f) section 20(1) (trespassing in a building with firearm).
(2) The court shall impose an appropriate custodial sentence (or order for detention) for a term of at least the required minimum term (with or without a fine) unless the court is of the opinion that there are exceptional circumstances relating to the offence or to the offender which justify its not doing so.
(3) Where an offence is found to have been committed over a period of two or more days, or at some time during a period of two or more days, it shall be taken for the purposes of this section to have been committed on the last of those days.

Subsections (1)(a)(iii) and (1A) apply only in relation to offences committed on or after 6 April 2007 (VCRA 2006, s. 30). Subsection (1A)(za) was added by the ABCPA 2014, s. 108, and has effect only in relation to offences committed on or after 14 July 2014. The references in s. 51A(1)(a)(i) and (iii) to the offences under s. 5(1)(ag) or (ba) are inserted by the Offensive Weapons Act 2019 and will come into effect from a date to be appointed. This change applies only to an offence committed after the date that amendment is brought into force.

In *A-G's Ref (No. 114 of 2004)* [2004] EWCA Crim 3238, [2005] 2 Cr App R (S) 6 (24), the Court of Appeal made it clear that s. 51A applies only where one of the listed offences is proved or admitted. Although the offender in that case might properly have been charged with an offence under the FA 1968, s. 5, no such count had been included on the indictment and so the minimum sentence did not apply. In *A-G's Ref (Nos. 48 and 49 of 2010)* [2010] EWCA Crim 2521, [2011] 1 Cr App R (S) 122 (706) it was held that, although s. 51A did not extend to a conspiracy or an attempt to commit any of the offences there set out, the specified minimum sentence was a highly relevant though not determining factor in sentencing for an inchoate offence.

E5.10 The minimum sentences specified in s. 51A are (a) five years' imprisonment (or detention in a young offender institution for those aged 18 to 20) in the case of an offender aged 18 or over when convicted, and (b) three years' detention under the PCC(S)A 2000, s. 91, for an offender aged at least 16 but under 18 when convicted (s. 51A(4)), always provided that the offender was at least 16 when the offence was committed (s. 51A(1)(b)). Nothing in s. 51A prevents a hospital order being imposed on an offender in an appropriate case (Mental Health Act 1983, s. 37(1A)). See *McEneaney* [2005] EWCA Crim 431, [2005] 2 Cr App R (S) 86 (531).

In *Raza* [2009] EWCA Crim 1413, [2010] 1 Cr App R (S) 56 (354), the Court of Appeal said that, where an offender is being sentenced for a number of offences, one of which is subject to a prescribed minimum custodial sentence, the principle of totality applies and the sentencer must pass an overall term which is proportionate to the overall offending, but that principle must not be applied in such a way which waters down the intended impact of the minimum sentence. See also *Moutouna* [2018] EWCA Crim 2491. Similar considerations apply where an offender already serving a prescribed minimum custodial sentence is made subject to a further custodial sentence to run consecutively to it (*Chaplin* [2015] EWCA Crim 1491, [2016] 1 Cr App R (S) 10 (63)).

Exceptional Circumstances Proviso

E5.11 The 'exceptional circumstances' proviso in the FA 1968, s. 51A(2), is differently worded from the 'particular circumstances' proviso in the PCC(S)A 2000, ss. 110 (see **E5.1**) and 111 (see E5.4). It is important to note, however, that the minimum sentence for the firearms offences listed in the FA 1968, s. 51A, applies to *all* such offences, whereas ss. 110 and 111 apply only to repeat offenders.

There is currently no sentencing guideline for firearms offences, although the Sentencing Council has consulted upon a draft guideline, a process which ended on 14 January 2020. Until a definitive guideline is made available, the proper approach is for the judge to consider the questions in *Avis* [1998] 1 Cr App R 420 (at **B12.138**), which will identify the appropriate sentencing bracket and should also assist on the issue of whether there are 'exceptional circumstances'. According to the Court of Appeal in *Boyle* [2018] EWCA Crim 2035, [2019] 1 Cr App R (S) 9 (65), the sentencer should determine sentence length in accordance with the relevant principles and then check whether the provisional sentence infringes the prescribed minimum sentence. A holistic approach should be taken, as required by *Rehman* [2005] EWCA Crim 2056, [2006] 1 Cr App R (S) 77 (404). The important case of *Rogers* [2016] EWCA Crim 801, [2016] 2 Cr App R (S) 36 (370) (dealing with the appellant Beaman) states that if D wishes to rely on exceptional circumstances, these should be set out on D's behalf in writing, and signed by D's advocate, and the procedure should follow that of a *Newton* hearing. The prosecution should state whether they are agreed or not. If they are not agreed, D can decide whether to seek a hearing, with the consequence that if D is disbelieved some of the credit for plea will be lost. If the circumstances are agreed by the prosecution, but the judge does not approve that agreement, D must decide whether to have a hearing. The judge must determine the matters to the criminal standard of proof and the burden is on the Crown to disprove D's account. If the Crown fails to do so, the judge must proceed on the basis that D's version is correct. It does not, however, follow that the judge, even if he or she accepts D's version, will find that it amounts to exceptional circumstances. The hurdle for D, in establishing exceptional circumstances, remains a high one. On the other hand, it does not follow that rejection of D's basis of plea is determinative against there being exceptional circumstances. All matters, including D's mental and physical health, must be considered together (*Nancarrow* [2019] EWCA Crim 470, [2019] 2 Cr App R (S) 4 (30)). The importance of compliance with the procedure in *Rogers* has been emphasised in several later cases, including *Dawson* [2017] EWCA Crim 2244 and *Hussain* [2019] EWCA Crim 362, [2019] 2 Cr App R (S) 8 (52).

The Court of Appeal has given some indication of the factors which might amount to 'exceptional circumstances' in respect of this provision, building on the early declaration in *Jordan* [2004] EWCA Crim 3291, [2005] 2 Cr App R (S) 44 (266) that such cases would be 'rare'. General guidance was given in *Rehman*. The Court of Appeal said that, in determining whether the case involved 'exceptional circumstances', it was necessary to look at the case as a whole. Sometimes there would be a single isolated factor that would amount to an exceptional circumstance, but in other cases it would be the collective impact of all the relevant circumstances. Lord Woolf CJ said that s. 51A was capable of causing considerable injustice, especially bearing in mind that possession of a prohibited firearm was an absolute offence. Reading s. 51A in the light of the HRA 1998, s. 3, his lordship said that the circumstances would be 'exceptional' if it would mean that to impose the minimum sentence would result in an arbitrary and disproportionate sentence.

In *Rehman* itself, the Court of Appeal held that the judge had erred in not finding exceptional circumstances in the case, where D's background (in particular his previous good character), his early plea of guilty, his ignorance of the unlawfulness of the weapon (he had purchased it as a collector's model), and the fact that there was just one weapon, taken together amounted to exceptional circumstances. The sentence was reduced from five years to one year, allowing D's immediate release. In *A-G's Ref (No. 37 of 2013) (Culpeper)* [2013] EWCA Crim 1466, [2014] 1 Cr App R (S) 62 (411), the Court of Appeal increased a sentence of two years' imprisonment to five years. D was in possession of a Browning self-loaded pistol containing ammunition. It was accepted that he had stored the gun for a few days because he owed money to his drug suppliers, who had forced him to store the gun, as well as drugs, at his home. The Court of Appeal said the factors in this case fell 'well short' of exceptional. Being subjected to pressure of that kind was not unusual. *Culpeper* was approved in *A-G's Ref (No. 115 of 2015) (Greenfield)* [2016] EWCA Crim 765, [2016] 2 Cr App R (S) 23 (201), where Hallett LJ stressed that exceptional circumstances will only be found in 'rare cases', and that judges should not be swayed by sympathy for the offender. Exceptional circumstances were found in *Stoker* [2013] EWCA Crim 1431, [2014] 1 Cr App R (S) 47 (286), where D, a man of good character, admitted possession of a stun gun disguised as a mobile phone. The weapon could not be fired, and D was unaware that possession of it was illegal. **E5.12**

The Court of Appeal in *Nancarrow* [2019] EWCA Crim 470, [2019] 2 Cr App R (S) 4 (30), helpfully identified from the case law the following eight principles as to the application of s. 51A (at [19]):

(1) 'The purpose of the mandatory minimum term is to act as a deterrent...';
(2) 'Circumstances are *exceptional*... if to impose five years' imprisonment would amount to an arbitrary and disproportionate sentence...';
(3) courts should not accept too readily that the circumstances of the offence or the offender are exceptional—the circumstances must be '*truly* exceptional';
(4) a holistic approach should be taken;
(5) the court should always have regard to the questions set out in *Avis*;
(6) the circumstances of the offender are important, such as where the offender is unfit to serve a five-year sentence or where such a sentence would have a significantly adverse effect on the offender's health;
(7) 'Each case is fact-specific'; and
(8) unless the judge is clearly wrong on the issue of whether exceptional circumstances exist or not, the Court of Appeal will not readily interfere.

In *Bartell* [2020] EWCA Crim 625, [2020] 4 WLR 79, the Court of Appeal said that the judge had been 'clearly wrong' in finding exceptional circumstances in a case where D explained that he converted blank firearms as a hobby, the resulting lethal weapons were not sold or distributed, and he had no connection with violence or organised crime, a basis of plea accepted by the prosecution. The sentence of 30 months was increased to five years, the Court commenting on the need for deterrence and accepting that 'in some cases the sentence will be a harsh sentence'.

In *Antoine* [2014] EWCA Crim 1971, [2015] 1 Cr App R 8 (81), an earlier 'inexplicable' charging decision by the prosecution, which led to D serving a sentence of four months' detention for possession of the same firearm without a certificate, before being charged with the FA 1968, s. 5, offence arising from the same facts, amounted to exceptional circumstances. In *Ospina* [2017] EWCA Crim 1509, the same charging mistake was made, but this time the error was discovered while D was remanded in custody awaiting sentence for possession of the firearm without a certificate, and the proper charge was then preferred. The sentencing judge rejected the suggestion that the charging error amounted to exceptional circumstances, and the Court of Appeal agreed.

Guilty Plea

E5.13 In contrast to the PCC(S)A 2000, ss. 110(2) and 111(2), there is no reference in the CJA 2003, s. 144 (reduction of sentence on plea of guilty), to the FA 1968, s. 51A, as limiting the extent to which the offender's guilty plea can affect the sentence imposed. It was established in *Jordan* [2004] EWCA Crim 3291, [2005] 2 Cr App R (S) 44 (266) and confirmed in *El Sheikh* [2015] EWCA Crim 718 that the appropriate reduction for a guilty plea should be given, provided that the final sentence does not fall below the prescribed minimum of five years. This would allow a full one third reduction from a starting point of seven and a half years or more. See the definitive guideline, *Reduction in Sentence for a Guilty Plea*, para. F4 (see Supplement, **SG5-7**). It was also made clear in *Jordan* that if the court finds that there are 'exceptional circumstances' in the case then sentence is at large and the appropriate reduction for plea should always be given. An example is *Antoine* [2014] EWCA Crim 1971, [2015] 1 Cr App R 8 (81). In *Bexley* [2019] EWCA Crim 1018, the Court of Appeal said that in the context of this minimum sentence provision it was important that the judge explain whether credit had been given for a guilty plea, and how much credit had been afforded.

MINIMUM CUSTODIAL SENTENCES FOR USING SOMEONE TO MIND A WEAPON

E5.14 The VCRA 2006, s. 28 (see **B12.221**), creates an offence where an offender aged 16 or over at the date of the offence uses another person to look after, hide or transport a dangerous weapon for the offender under arrangements or in circumstances that facilitate, or are intended to facilitate, the weapon's being available to the offender for an unlawful purpose. By the VCRA 2006, s. 29, where at the time of the conviction the offender was aged 18 or over and the dangerous weapon in respect of which the offence was committed was a firearm mentioned in s. 5(1)(a) to (af) or (c) or s. 5(1A)(a) of the FA 1968 (firearms possession of which attracts a minimum sentence), the court must impose a term of imprisonment (or detention in a young offender institution) of not less than five years, unless it is of the opinion that there are exceptional circumstances relating to the offence or to the offender which justify its not doing so. If the offender is aged under 16 or 17 at the time of conviction, the court must impose a sentence of detention under the PCC(S)A 2000, s. 91, of not less than three years, unless it is of the opinion that there are exceptional circumstances relating to the offence or to the offender which justify its not doing so. From a date to be appointed the VCRA 2006, s. 29, is amended by the Offensive Weapons Act 2019 so that the reference to 'mentioned in section 5(1)(a) to (af) or (c)' is replaced by 'specified in section 5(1)(a) to (ag) or (ba)'. This change applies only to an offence committed after the date that amendment is brought into force.

Statutory Aggravating Factor

Where a court is considering the seriousness of an offence under the VCRA 2006, s. 28, and the offender was aged 18 or over and used a person to look after etc. the weapon who was under 18, the court must treat that fact as increasing the seriousness of the offence (s. 29(11)). The judge should state in open court that the offence was so aggravated (s. 29(12)). See by analogy the decision in *DPP v Giles* [2019] EWHC 2015 (Admin), [2020] 1 Cr App R (S) 20 (156), considered at **E1.19**. **E5.15**

Guilty Plea

In contrast to the PCC(S)A 2000, ss. 110(2) and 111(2), there is no reference in the CJA 2003, s. 144 (reduction of sentence on plea of guilty), to the VCRA 2006, s. 28, as limiting the extent to which the offender's guilty plea can affect the sentence imposed. By analogy with the decisions in *Jordan* [2004] EWCA Crim 3291, [2005] 2 Cr App R (S) 44 (266) and *El Sheikh* [2015] EWCA Crim 718 (considered at **E5.13**), it seems clear that the full reduction for a guilty plea should be given, provided that the final sentence does not fall below the prescribed minimum of five years. **E5.16**

MINIMUM CUSTODIAL SENTENCE FOR THREATENING WITH OFFENSIVE WEAPON IN PUBLIC

The Sentencing Council definitive guideline, *Bladed Articles and Offensive Weapons* (see Supplement, **SG14-1**), applies in relation to sentences imposed on or after 1 June 2018, regardless of the date of the offence. There are separate guidelines for offenders aged 18 and over, and for offenders aged under 18. Step Three in the guideline deals with minimum terms. **E5.17**

Section 1A(1) of the Prevention of Crime Act 1953 provides that a person is guilty of an offence if that person (a) has an offensive weapon with him or her in a public place, (b) unlawfully and intentionally threatens another person with the weapon, and (c) does so in such a way that there is an immediate risk of serious physical harm to that other person. For consideration of this offence and for pending changes to the offence definition when the Offensive Weapons Act 2019 is brought into force, see **B12.171**.

Prevention of Crime Act 1953, s. 1A

(4) A person guilty of an offence under this section is liable—
- (a) on summary conviction, to imprisonment for a term not exceeding 12 months or to [an unlimited fine], or to both;
- (b) on conviction on indictment, to imprisonment for a term not exceeding 4 years or to a fine, or to both.

(5) Where a person is aged 16 or over is convicted of an offence under this section, the court must impose an appropriate custodial sentence (with or without a fine) unless the court is of the opinion that there are particular circumstances which—
- (a) relate to the offence or to the offender, and
- (b) would make it unjust to do so in all the circumstances.

(6) In this section 'appropriate custodial sentence' means—
- (a) in the case of a person who is aged 18 and over when convicted, a sentence of imprisonment for a term of at least 6 months;
- (b) in the case of a person who is aged at least 16 but under 18 when convicted, a detention and training order of at least 4 months.

(7) In considering whether it is of the opinion mentioned in subsection (5) in the case of a person aged under 18, the court must have regard to its duty under section 44 of the Children and Young Persons Act 1933.

This provision was inserted by the LASPO 2012, s. 142. It was the view of the Court of Appeal in *Whyte* [2018] EWCA Crim 2437, [2019] 1 Cr App R (S) 35 (234), that, notwithstanding the CJA 2003, s. 189 (power to suspend sentence of imprisonment), the reference in s. 1A(6)(a) to 'sentence of imprisonment' must mean 'sentence of immediate imprisonment'. A detention and training order (under s. 1A(6)(b)) cannot be suspended. Where s. 1A(5) applies and the offender is aged 18 or over when convicted and the offender has pleaded guilty, the sentencing court is required to take into account the stage at which the offender indicated an intention to plead guilty but the court may not impose a sentence which is less than 80 per cent of the minimum sentence specified. See the CJA 2003, s. 144(2) and (3), and the definitive guideline, *Reduction in Sentence for a Guilty Plea*, para. F5 (see Supplement, **SG5-7**). See also *Gray* [2007] EWCA Crim 979, [2007] 2 Cr App R (S) 78 (494); *Darling* [2009] EWCA Crim 1610, [2010] 1 Cr App R (S) 63 (420) and the discussion at **E5.3**. Where s. 1A(5) applies and the offender is aged 16 or 17 when convicted and the offender has pleaded guilty, the normal principles applicable to reduction for a guilty plea apply (CJA 2003, s. 144(2) and (4)). For the CYPA 1933, s. 44, see **E1.1**. It should be noted that, under s. 1A(6)(b), a detention and training order of four months is the shortest term which may lawfully be imposed. The 'particular circumstances' proviso at s. 1A(5)(a) and (b) is very similarly worded to the equivalent provisions in the PCC(S)A 2000, ss. 110 and 111 (see **E5.1** and **E5.4**).

MINIMUM CUSTODIAL SENTENCE FOR THREATENING WITH ARTICLE WITH BLADE OR POINT OR OFFENSIVE WEAPON

E5.18 The Sentencing Council definitive guideline, *Bladed Articles and Offensive Weapons* (see Supplement, **SG14-1**), applies in relation to sentences imposed on or after 1 June 2018, regardless of the date of the offence. There are separate guidelines for offenders aged 18 and over, and for offenders aged under 18. Step Three in the guideline deals with minimum terms.

Section 139AA(1) of the CJA 1988 provides that a person is guilty of an offence if that person (a) has an offensive weapon with him or her in a public place or on school premises, (b) unlawfully and intentionally threatens another person with the weapon, and (c) does so in such a way that there is an immediate risk of serious physical harm to that other person. For consideration of this offence and for pending changes to the offence definition when the Offensive Weapons Act 2019 is brought into force, see **B12.189**.

Criminal Justice Act 1988, s. 139AA

(6) A person guilty of an offence under this section is liable—
  (a) on summary conviction, to imprisonment for a term not exceeding 12 months or to [an unlimited fine], or to both;
  (b) on conviction on indictment, to imprisonment for a term not exceeding 4 years or to a fine, or to both.

(7) Where a person is aged 16 or over is convicted of an offence under this section, the court must impose an appropriate custodial sentence (with or without a fine) unless the court is of the opinion that there are particular circumstances which—
  (a) relate to the offence or to the offender, and
  (b) would make it unjust to do so in all the circumstances.

(8) In this section 'appropriate custodial sentence' means—
  (a) in the case of a person who is aged 18 and over when convicted, a sentence of imprisonment for a term of at least 6 months;
  (b) in the case of a person who is aged at least 16 but under 18 when convicted, a detention and training order of at least 4 months.

(9) In considering whether it is of the opinion mentioned in subsection (7) in the case of a person aged under 18, the court must have regard to its duty under section 44 of the Children and Young Persons Act 1933.

This provision was inserted by the LASPO 2012, s. 142. It was the view of the Court of Appeal in *Whyte* [2018] EWCA Crim 2437, [2019] 1 Cr App R (S) 35 (234), that, notwithstanding the

CJA 2003, s. 189 (power to suspend sentence of imprisonment), the reference in s. 139AA(6)(a) to 'sentence of imprisonment' must mean 'sentence of immediate imprisonment'. A detention and training order cannot be suspended. Where s. 139AA(7) applies and the offender is aged 18 or over when convicted and has pleaded guilty, the sentencing court is required to take into account the stage at which the offender indicated an intention to plead guilty but the court may not impose a sentence which is less than 80 per cent of the minimum sentence specified. See the CJA 2003, s. 144(2) and (3), and the definitive guideline, *Reduction in Sentence for a Guilty Plea*, para. F5 (see Supplement, **SG5-7**). See also *Gray* [2007] EWCA Crim 979, [2007] 2 Cr App R (S) 78 (494); *Darling* [2009] EWCA Crim 1610, [2010] 1 Cr App R (S) 63 (420) and the discussion at **E5.3**. Where s. 139AA(7) applies and the offender is aged 16 or 17 when convicted and the offender has pleaded guilty, the normal principles applicable to reduction for a guilty plea apply (CJA 2003, s. 144(2) and (4)). For the CYPA 1933, s. 44, see **E1.1**. It should be noted that, under s. 139AA(8)(b), a detention and training order of four months is the shortest term which may lawfully be imposed. The 'particular circumstances' proviso at s. 139AA(7) is very similarly worded to the equivalent provisions in the PCC(S)A 2000, ss. 110 and 111 (see **E5.1** and **E5.4**).

MINIMUM CUSTODIAL SENTENCE FOR REPEAT OFFENCES INVOLVING OFFENSIVE WEAPONS ETC.

The Sentencing Council definitive guideline, *Bladed Articles and Offensive Weapons* (see Supplement, **SG14-1**), applies in relation to sentences imposed on or after 1 June 2018, regardless of the date of the offence. There are separate guidelines for offenders aged 18 and over, and for offenders aged under 18. Step Three in the guideline deals with 'minimum terms — second or further relevant offence'. **E5.19**

With effect from 17 July 2015 (SI 2015 No. 1463), the CJCA 2015, s. 28(2), amended the Prevention of Crime Act 1953, s. 1 (prohibition on the carrying of offensive weapons without lawful authority or reasonable excuse: see **B12.142**), by inserting subsections (2A) to (2G).

Prevention of Crime Act 1953, s. 1

(2A) Subsection (2B) applies where—
- (a) a person is convicted of an offence under subsection (1) committed after this subsection is commenced, and
- (b) when the offence was committed, the person was aged 16 or over and had at least one relevant conviction (see section 1ZA).

(2B) Where this subsection applies, the court must impose an appropriate custodial sentence (with or without a fine) unless the court is of the opinion that there are particular circumstances which—
- (a) relate to the offence, to the previous offence or to the offender, and
- (b) would make it unjust to do so in all the circumstances.

(2C) In this section 'appropriate custodial sentence' means—
- (a) in the case of a person who is aged 18 or over when convicted, a sentence of imprisonment for a term of at least 6 months;
- (b) in the case of a person who is aged at least 16 but under 18 when convicted, a detention and training order of at least 4 months.

(2D) In considering whether it is of the opinion mentioned in subsection (2B) in the case of a person aged 16 or 17, the court must have regard to its duty under section 44 of the Children and Young Persons Act 1933 (general considerations).

Subsections (2E) to (2G) concern appeals, offences committed over two or more days and transitional provision.

Section 1ZA of the 1953 Act (inserted by the CJCA 2015, s. 28(3)) provides that for these purposes 'relevant conviction' means a conviction under s. 1 or 1A of the 1953 Act, or under the CJA 1988, s. 139, 139A or 139AA, whenever such offence was committed. From a date to be appointed, 'relevant conviction' also includes a conviction under the Offensive Weapons

Act 2019, s. 6. At the date when the UK leaves the EU in accordance with the European Union (Withdrawal) Act 2018, the Criminal Justice (Amendment etc.) (EU Exit) Regulations will amend s. 1ZA so that references to previous convictions outside the UK are omitted. It is submitted that an earlier conviction which was dealt with by way of a discharge does not count for this purpose: see the PCC(S)A 2000, s. 14, at **E12.6**.

It was the view of the Court of Appeal in *Whyte* [2018] EWCA Crim 2437, [2019] 1 Cr App R (S) 35 (234), that, notwithstanding the CJA 2003, s. 189 (power to suspend sentence of imprisonment), the reference in s. 1(2C)(a) to 'sentence of imprisonment' should be read to mean 'sentence of immediate imprisonment'. A detention and training order (under s. 1(2C)(b)) cannot be suspended. Where s. 1(2B) applies and the offender is aged 18 or over when convicted and has pleaded guilty, the sentencing court is required to take into account the stage at which the offender indicated an intention to plead guilty but the court may not impose a sentence which is less than 80 per cent of the minimum sentence specified. See the CJA 2003, s. 144(2) and (3), and the definitive guideline, *Reduction in Sentence for a Guilty Plea*, para. F5 (see Supplement, **SG5-7**). See also *Gray* [2007] EWCA Crim 979, [2007] 2 Cr App R (S) 78 (494); *Darling* [2009] EWCA Crim 1610, [2010] 1 Cr App R (S) 63 (420) and the discussion at **E5.3**. Where s. 1(2B) applies and the offender is aged 16 or 17 when convicted and has pleaded guilty, the normal principles applicable to reduction for a guilty plea apply (CJA 2003, s. 144(2) and (4)). For the CYPA 1933, s. 44, see **E1.1**. It should be noted that, under s. 1(2c)(a), a detention and training order of four months is the shortest term which may lawfully be imposed. The 'particular circumstances' proviso at s. 1(2B) is very similarly worded to the equivalent provisions in the PCC(S)A 2000, ss. 110 and 111 (see **E5.1** and **E5.4**).

With effect from 17 July 2015, equivalent amendments were made by the CJCA 2015, s. 28(5), to the CJA 1988, s. 139 (offence of having article with blade or point in public place: see **B12.174**). Subsections (6A) to (6G) were inserted in s. 139 and the CJA 1988, s. 139A, was amended by the insertion of subsections (5A) to (5G). Section 139AZA provides that for these purposes 'relevant conviction' means a conviction under the Prevention of Crime Act 1953, s. 1 or 1A, or under the CJA 1988, s. 139, 139A or 139AA, whenever such offence was committed, and, from a date to be appointed, 'relevant conviction' includes a conviction under the Offensive Weapons Act 2019, s. 6.

MINIMUM CUSTODIAL SENTENCE FOR REPEAT OFFENCES INVOLVING HAVING CORROSIVE SUBSTANCE

E5.20 From a date to be appointed the Offensive Weapons Act 2019, s. 6, creates an offence of having a corrosive substance in a public place (see **B12.232**). The offence is punishable on indictment with imprisonment for a term not exceeding four years. From a date to be appointed s. 8 provides for a minimum custodial sentence for repeat offending:

Offensive Weapons Act 2019, s. 8

(1) This section applies where—
   (a) a person is convicted of an offence under section 6(1) by a court in England and Wales, and
   (b) when the offence was committed, the person—
      (i) was aged 16 or over, and
      (ii) had at least one relevant conviction (see section 9).

(2) The court must impose an appropriate custodial sentence (with or without a fine) unless the court is of the opinion that there are particular circumstances which—
   (a) relate to the offence, to the previous offence or to the offender, and
   (b) would make it unjust to do so in all the circumstances.

(3) An 'appropriate custodial sentence' is—
   (a) in the case of a person who is aged 18 or over when convicted, a sentence of imprisonment for a term of at least 6 months;

(b) in the case of a person who is aged 16 or 17 when convicted, a detention and training order of at least 4 months.

(4) In the case of a person aged 16 or 17, in considering whether it is of the opinion mentioned in subsection (2) the court must have regard to its duty under section 44 of the Children and Young Persons Act 1933 (general considerations).

Subsections (5) to (9) concern appeals, offences committed over two or more days and transitional provisions.

Section 9 of the 2019 Act provides that for these purposes 'relevant conviction' means a conviction for an offence under the PCA 1953, s.1 or 1A, or under the CJA 1988, s. 139, 139A or 139AA, or under the Offensive Weapons Act 2019, s. 6, whenever such offence was committed. It is submitted that an earlier conviction which was dealt with by way of a discharge does not count for this purpose (see the PCC(S)A 2000, s. 14, at **E12.6**).

By analogy with the view expressed by the Court of Appeal in *Whyte* [2018] EWCA Crim 2437, [2019] 1 Cr App R (S) 35 (234) (see **E5.19**), notwithstanding the CJA 2003, s. 189 (power to suspend sentence of imprisonment), the reference in the Offensive Weapons Act 2019, s. 8(3)(a), to 'sentence of imprisonment' should be read to mean 'sentence of immediate imprisonment'. A detention and training order (under s. 8(3)(b)) cannot be suspended. Where s. 8(2) applies and the offender is aged 18 or over when convicted and has pleaded guilty, the sentencing court is required to take into account the stage at which the offender indicated an intention to plead guilty but the court may not impose a sentence which is less than 80 per cent of the minimum sentence specified. See the CJA 2003, s. 144(2) and (3), and, by analogy, the definitive guideline, *Reduction in Sentence for a Guilty Plea* (see Supplement, **SG5-7**). See also *Gray* [2007] EWCA Crim 979, [2007] 2 Cr App R (S) 78 (494); *Darling* [2009] EWCA Crim 1610, [2010] 1 Cr App R (S) 63 (420) and the discussion at **E5.3**. Where s. 8(2) applies and the offender is aged 16 or 17 when convicted and has pleaded guilty, the normal principles applicable to reduction for a guilty plea apply (CJA 2003, s. 144(2) and (4)). For the CYPA 1933, s. 44, see **E1.1**. It should be noted that under the Offensive Weapons Act 2019, s. 8(3)(b), a detention and training order of four months is the shortest term which may lawfully be imposed. The 'particular circumstances' proviso at s. 8(2) is very similarly worded to the equivalent provisions in the PCC(S)A 2000, ss. 110 and 111 (see **E5.1** and **E5.4**).

Section E6 Suspended Sentences

POWER TO IMPOSE SUSPENDED SENTENCES

E6.1 The power to impose a suspended sentence under the CJA 2003 applies to sentences of imprisonment and to sentences of detention in a young offender institution. The suspended sentence is available where a court imposes a determinate custodial sentence of not more than two years. Sentences of less than 14 days cannot be suspended. Detention and training orders cannot be suspended.

E6.2 **Criminal Justice Act 2003, s. 189**

(1) If a court passes a sentence of imprisonment for a term of at least 14 days but not more than 2 years, it may make an order providing that the sentence of imprisonment is not to take effect unless—
(a) during a period specified in the order for the purposes of this paragraph ('the operational period') the offender commits another offence in the United Kingdom (whether or not punishable with imprisonment), and
(b) a court having power to do so subsequently orders under paragraph 8 of schedule 12 that the original sentence is to take effect.

(1A) An order under subsection (1) may also provide that the offender must comply during a period specified in the order for the purposes of this subsection ('the supervision period') with one or more requirements falling within section 190(1) and specified in the order.

(1B) Where an order under subsection (1) contains provisions under subsection (1A) it must provide that the sentence of imprisonment will also take effect if—
(a) during the supervision period the offender fails to comply with a requirement imposed under subsection (1A), and
(b) a court having power to do so subsequently orders under paragraph 8 of Schedule 12 that the original sentence is to take effect.

(2) Where two or more sentences imposed on the same occasion are to be served consecutively, the power conferred by subsection (1) is not exercisable in relation to any of them unless the aggregate of the terms of the sentences does not exceed 2 years.

(3) The supervision period (if any) and the operational period must each be a period of not less than six months and not more than two years beginning with the date of the order.

(4) Where an order under subsection (1) imposes one or more community requirements, the supervision period must not end later than the operational period.

(5) A court which passes a suspended sentence on any person for an offence may not impose a community sentence in his case in respect of that offence or any other offence of which he is convicted by or before the court or for which he is dealt with by the court.

(6) Subject to any provision to the contrary contained in the Criminal Justice Act 1967, the Sentencing Act, or any enactment or instrument made under any enactment after 31st December 1967, a suspended sentence which had not taken effect under paragraph 8 of Schedule 12 is to be treated as a sentence of imprisonment for the purposes of all enactments and instruments made under enactments.

(7) In this Part—
(a) 'suspended sentence order' means an order under subsection (1),
(b) 'suspended sentence' means a sentence to which a suspended sentence order relates, and
(c) 'community requirements' in relation to a suspended sentence order means a requirement imposed under subsection (1A).

E6.3 A suspended sentence cannot be ordered unless all the statutory provisions as to the imposition of a sentence of immediate imprisonment have been observed. Before a suspended sentence can be passed, the court must take account of the relevant provisions of the CJA 2003, ss. 152 and 153, which must be complied with before any custodial sentence is passed (see **E2.7** and

E2.9). The power to impose a suspended sentence in a magistrates' court is limited in the same way in which magistrates' powers to impose prison sentences are limited (see **E2.5**).

The definitive sentencing guideline, *Imposition of Community and Custodial Sentences* (see Supplement, **SG9-1**), applies. The guideline states that 'a suspended sentence must not be imposed as a more severe form of community order. Sentencers should be clear that they would impose an immediate custodial sentence if the power to suspend were not available. If not, a non-custodial sentence should be imposed.' The guideline also makes it clear that a custodial sentence that is suspended should be for the same term that would have applied if the sentence was to be served immediately. As far as the operational period is concerned, the guideline says that 'the time for which a sentence is suspended should reflect the length of the sentence; up to 12 months might normally be appropriate for a suspended sentence of up to six months'.

A number of factors are indicated in the guideline which should be weighed when considering whether it is possible to suspend the sentence.

The factors indicating that it would not be appropriate to suspend a custodial sentence are:

'offender presents a risk/danger to the public';
'appropriate punishment can only be achieved by immediate custody'; and
'history of poor compliance with court orders'.

The factors indicating that it may be appropriate to suspend a custodial sentence are:

'realistic prospect of conviction';
'strong personal mitigation'; and
'immediate custody will result in significant harmful impact on others'.

In addition to these considerations it is important to note that in *Manning* [2020] EWCA Crim 592, [2020] 4 WLR 77, Lord Burnett CJ said the following:

> The impact of the [Covid-19] emergency on prisons is well known. The current conditions in prisons represent a factor which can properly be taken into account in deciding whether to suspend a sentence.

Where the court is about to impose a custodial sentence which is within the range which may in law be suspended it is important that the judge expressly considers suspension by reference to those factors set out in the guideline. The Court of Appeal has made this point on several occasions, a recent example being *Evans* [2019] EWCA Crim 2358, a case of causing death by careless driving. Further, in *Montaut* [2019] EWCA Crim 2252, [2020] 2 Cr App R (S) 7 (45), the Court said that the judge should have considered the factors set out in the guideline in a case where the sentence was custody for two years and one month, especially where there had been some disagreement over the basis of plea but no *Newton* hearing had been held. Decisions on whether to suspend a custodial sentence are inevitably very fact-specific, but *Tharmaratnam* [2017] EWCA Crim 887, [2017] 2 Cr App R (S) 36 (318) (although a decision of a two-judge court) provides useful assistance. The Court of Appeal upheld a sentence of 12 months' imprisonment for an OAPA 1861, s. 20, 'glassing', although the 42-year-old offender was of previous good character, and he ran a small family business the future of which would be placed in jeopardy by immediate custody. Edis J said (at [12]) that:

> Where a factor from Table 1 is found, then a sentence will not normally be suspended, but where a factor in Table 2 is present it may be. In this case the only Table 1 factor that is arguably present is that 'appropriate punishment can only be achieved by immediate custody'. This involves an assessment of the seriousness of the offence in the usual way. The judge regarded an offence of glassing to the face using a heavy glass which broke as an offence which required immediate custody. That being so, the Table 2 factors, all of which were present, gave rise to a discretion. The guideline does not say that where one or all of those is found a sentence must or should or will normally be suspended. The guideline simply says that it may be — in other words the judge has a discretion. This court will only interfere with a decision of that kind where it is plainly wrong in principle or results in a sentence which is manifestly excessive.

This analysis was endorsed in *Hussain* [2019] EWCA Crim 1542, [2020] 1 Cr App R (S) 32 (235). The Court rejected a submission that if all Table 2 factors were present there was then a presumption in favour of suspension, and added that the factors identified in the guideline were not an exhaustive list of what might be relevant matters in any given case. Where a different balance of considerations applies to co-defendants, it may be appropriate to impose an immediate custodial sentence on one and to suspend sentence on another (see, e.g., *Seferi* [2012] EWCA Crim 1404, [2013] 1 Cr App R (S) 63 (350)). The absence of a plea of guilty is not a good reason for failing to consider whether sentence should be suspended (*Kumwenda* [2018] EWCA Crim 2856, [2019] 1 Cr App R (S) 44 (301)).

E6.4 Any period spent by the offender in custody on remand will be deducted automatically in the event of activation of the suspended sentence. This is set out in the CJA 2003, s. 240ZA(7), which states that a suspended sentence:

(a) is to be treated as a sentence of imprisonment when it takes effect under paragraph 8(2)(a) or (b) of schedule 12, and
(b) is to be treated as being imposed by the order under which it takes effect.

The sentencer has no discretion in the operation of this provision. Thus it would be otiose for a judge, when passing a suspended sentence, to say that in the event of breach, days served on remand will not count. However, the Court of Appeal has taken the view that, if an offender has spent a significant period in custody on remand, and has in fact served the equivalent of the appropriate custodial sentence, it is wrong to impose additional custody, whether immediate or suspended. Thus in *Maughan* [2011] EWCA Crim 787, [2011] 2 Cr App R (S) 89 (493), the Court said that where D had spent the equivalent of a 13-month sentence on remand it was wrong to pass a sentence of six months' imprisonment suspended for two years. The sentence should have been constructed in a way which would have given D the benefit of the time served on remand. It is submitted that this case remains good law after the insertion of s. 240ZA by the LASPO 2012. See also *Hinds* [2018] EWCA Crim 749 and *Dawes* [2019] EWCA Crim 848, [2020] 1 Cr App R (S) 1 (1).

A comparable approach was taken in *Williams* [2018] EWCA Crim 2396, where D had not spent time on remand but had spent 331 days on a qualifying curfew (the equivalent of 166 days on remand, or just short of 11 months' imprisonment). The offence itself merited three months' imprisonment, and the Court of Appeal said that it had been wrong in principle to impose a sentence of three months suspended for 15 months with community requirements. D was entitled to receive credit against his sentence under the CJA 2003, s. 240A (see **E2.16**), so a suspended sentence could not be justified, and the sentence was varied to imprisonment for three months which, in effect, had already been served.

Consecutive Terms

E6.5 Section 189(2) of the CJA 2003 (as amended) states that where two or more sentences imposed on the same occasion are to be served consecutively, the power to suspend sentence is not exercisable in relation to any of the sentences unless the aggregate of the terms does not exceed two years.

Combining with Other Sentences or Orders

E6.6 An immediate prison sentence and a suspended sentence should not be imposed on the same occasion (by analogy with *Sapiano* (1968) 52 Cr App R 674), nor should a suspended sentence be imposed on an offender currently serving a term of imprisonment (by analogy with *Butters* (1971) 55 Cr App R 515). A court which passes a suspended sentence on an offender must not on the same occasion impose a community sentence in respect of that offence or any other offence for which the offender is dealt with by the court (CJA 2003, s. 189(5)). It is submitted that a suspended sentence cannot be combined with a discharge when sentencing for a single offence (see **E12.4**) but a discharge could be given for one offence when a suspended sentence was passed in respect of another offence sentenced on the same occasion. A fine may be combined with a suspended sentence, but it is improper to combine them when a fine standing alone would have been the proper sentence. In *Butt* [2018] EWCA Crim 1617, [2019] 1 Cr App R (S) 4 (27), the Court of Appeal observed that a fine might properly be added to a suspended sentence where a confiscation order is not contemplated, there is no obvious victim to whom compensation can be awarded, and the offender has (or will have) resources from which a fine can be paid. It is particularly apt when the offending is related to a defendant's business or employment, when dealing with offenders with substantial means, or when the sentence allows an offender to continue in well-remunerated work. There is no restriction on imposing ancillary provisions such as compensation orders, restitution orders, or deprivation orders, at the same time as a suspended sentence.

IMPOSITION OF REQUIREMENTS

It is lawful to impose a suspended sentence without including a community requirement (CJA 2003, s. 189(1A)). Section 190(1) lists the requirements with which the court may order the offender to comply during the supervision period of the suspended sentence. These are: **E6.7**

(a) an unpaid work requirement (as defined by s. 199),
(aa) a rehabilitation activity requirement (s. 200A),
(b) [repealed],
(c) a programme requirement (s. 202),
(d) a prohibited activity requirement (s. 203),
(e) a curfew requirement (s. 204),
(f) an exclusion requirement (s. 205),
(g) a residence requirement (s. 206),
(ga) a foreign travel prohibition requirement (s. 206A),
(h) a mental health requirement (s. 207),
(i) a drug rehabilitation requirement (s. 209),
(j) an alcohol treatment requirement (s. 212),
(ja) an alcohol abstinence and monitoring requirement (s. 212A),
(k) [repealed],
(l) in a case where the offender is aged under 25, an attendance centre requirement (s. 214), and
(m) an electronic monitoring requirement (s. 215).

Section 212A provides for the alcohol abstinence and monitoring requirement which, following a lengthy period of piloting and assessment in accordance with the LASPO 2012, s. 77, was brought fully into force from 19 May 2020 by SI 2020 No. 478. Even so, such a requirement may not be made unless necessary local arrangements, as specified by the Secretary of State, are in place (s. 212A(6)).

The electronic monitoring requirement may be imposed as a means of securing compliance with one or more other requirements or, since 1 April 2019, as a free-standing requirement.

For details of these requirements, see **E8.11** to **E8.26**.

Whenever the court passes a suspended sentence which contains two or more different requirements, it must consider whether, in the circumstances of the case, the requirements are compatible with each other (s. 190(5)). Power to insert such requirements is made subject to the court ensuring, so far as possible, that they avoid any conflict with the offender's religious beliefs, or with the requirements of any other relevant order to which the offender may be subject, and avoid interference with the times, if any, at which the offender normally works or attends school or any other educational establishment (s. 217). The court must also be satisfied that local facilities exist, and that local arrangements are in place, for the carrying out of relevant requirements (s. 218). A suspended sentence must specify the local justice area in which the offender will reside (s. 216(1)). **E6.8**

Restrictions on Imposition of Requirements

The court cannot make an unpaid work requirement unless satisfied that the offender is a suitable person to perform such work (CJA 2003, s. 199(3)). The court cannot make a rehabilitation activity requirement unless the responsible officer obtains the agreement of any person other than the offender whose co-operation is necessary to comply with the requirement (s. 200A(10)). The court cannot insert a programme requirement unless the relevant programme has been accredited by the Secretary of State (s. 202(1) and (2)). The court cannot insert a **E6.9** prohibited activity requirement unless it has consulted an officer of a provider of probation services (s. 203(2)). The court cannot insert a mental health requirement unless the court is satisfied that the mental condition of the offender is such as requires and is susceptible to treatment and does not warrant the making of a hospital or guardianship order, that arrangements have been made for the treatment to be carried out, and that the offender has consented to the inclusion of the mental health requirement into the suspended sentence (s. 207(3)). The court may not insert a drug rehabilitation requirement unless it is satisfied that the offender is dependent on, or has a propensity to misuse, a controlled drug and that the dependency or propensity is such as requires and may be susceptible to treatment, that arrangements can be made for the treatment to be carried out, that the requirement has been recommended by the responsible officer, and that the offender has expressed willingness to comply with the requirement (s. 209(2)). The court may not impose an alcohol treatment requirement unless it is satisfied that the offender is dependent on alcohol, that the dependency is such as requires and may be susceptible to treatment, that arrangements can be made for the treatment to be carried out, and that the offender has expressed willingness to comply with the requirement (s. 212(2)). The court may not include an alcohol abstinence and monitoring requirement unless the consumption of alcohol by the offender is an element of the offence, or the consumption of alcohol contributed to the commission of the offence and the court is satisfied that the offender is not dependent on alcohol, the court does not include in the order an alcohol treatment requirement, and the court has been notified that arrangements for monitoring of such a requirement are locally available (s. 212A(9) to (12)).

If the suspended sentence contains a curfew requirement or an exclusion requirement, the court *must* also include an electronic monitoring requirement, as defined by s. 215 of the Act, *unless* the court is unable to do so because there is some person, other than the offender, whose co-operation is required but who does not consent (s. 215(2)), or because electronic monitoring arrangements are not available in the local area (s. 218(4)), or because, in the particular circumstances of the case, the court considers it inappropriate to do so.

If the suspended sentence contains an unpaid work requirement, a programme requirement, a prohibited activity requirement, a residence requirement, a mental health treatment requirement, a drug rehabilitation requirement, an alcohol treatment requirement, an alcohol abstinence and monitoring requirement, or an attendance centre requirement, the court *may* also require the licence to contain an electronic monitoring requirement, unless the court is unable to do so because there is some person, other than the offender, whose co-operation is required but who does not consent (s. 215(2)), or because electronic monitoring arrangements are not available in the local area (s. 218(4); see **E6.7**).

POWER TO PROVIDE FOR REVIEW

E6.10 Section 191(1) of the CJA 2003 confers a discretion on the court to provide that a suspended sentence that imposes one or more community requirements is made subject to periodic review, at review hearings, at specified intervals of time. The court may order the offender to attend those hearings, and it may order an officer of a provider of probation services, before each review, to provide to the court a report on the offender's progress under the suspended sentence. If the offender is subject to a suspended sentence which contains a drug rehabilitation requirement, such requirement will already be subject to court review hearings under the CJA 2003, s. 210, so s. 191(2) provides that in those circumstances the suspended sentence cannot be subject to review under s. 191(1). A review hearing is conducted by the court responsible for the order, and s. 191(3) to (5) specify which court is responsible for review of the suspended sentence in particular situations.

Section 192 describes what is to happen at the review hearings. Section 192(1) permits the court to amend any community requirement of the suspended sentence order, after consideration of the report from the review officer. This is limited by s. 192(2) which explains that the court cannot amend the order by adding a requirement of a different kind unless the offender consents to that new requirement, but it can impose a requirement of the same kind. The offender's consent is always required before the court amends a drug rehabilitation requirement, an alcohol treatment requirement, or a mental health treatment requirement (s. 192(2)(b)).

Under s. 192(4), if on the basis of the report from the review officer the court is of the opinion that the offender is making satisfactory progress, it can dispense with the next pending review hearing, or may amend the order so that subsequent reviews can be held by considering the papers rather than by a full hearing. The court may order the offender to attend a review hearing if progress is no longer satisfactory, or it may adjust the intervals of time between review hearings (s. 192(5) and (7)).

BREACH, COMMISSION OF FURTHER OFFENCE AND AMENDMENT

General

Section 193 refers to the CJA 2003, sch. 12, which contains provisions relating to (a) the breach and amendment of the community requirements of suspended sentence orders, and (b) the effect of the offender being convicted of a further offence during the operational period of the suspended sentence. The Sentencing Council definitive guideline, *Breach Offences* (see Supplement, **SG15-1**), applies to offenders sentenced on or after 1 October 2018, irrespective of the date of the offence. **E6.11**

By para. 4, if the responsible officer is of the opinion that the offender has failed without reasonable excuse to comply with any of the community requirements of the suspended sentence, the officer must give a *warning* describing the circumstances of the failure, stating that the failure is unacceptable, and informing the offender that if within the next 12 months he or she again fails to comply with any requirement of the order, the offender will be brought back before the court. The responsible officer need not give a warning if a previous warning was given within the preceding 12 months or if the matter is referred to an enforcement officer. By para. 5, if there has been a warning, and within 12 months there is a further failure without reasonable excuse to comply, the responsible officer must refer the matter to an enforcement officer. The enforcement officer is then under a duty 'to consider the matter and, where appropriate, to cause an information to be laid' before the appropriate court in respect of the failure to comply (para. 5A). In *West Yorkshire Probation Board v Robinson* [2009] EWHC 2517 (Admin), [2010] 4 All ER 1110, the Divisional Court said that the plain purpose of the warning provisions was to provide the probation officer with a discretion which could be exercised just once. If there is a further breach within the 12-month period, the matter must come back before the court. The Court also noted that when the information is laid there is nothing in the legislation to prevent the probation service from setting out details of the breach which prompted the warning as well as details of the second breach. Paragraphs 6 and 7 deal with the arrangements with respect to an alleged failure to comply, for issue of a summons or warrant by a magistrates' court or by the Crown Court. The information must be laid before the operational period of the suspended sentence has expired, although there is no requirement that the court hear the matter before then (*West Yorkshire Probation Board v Cruickshanks* [2010] EWHC 615 (Admin), [2011] 1 WLR 2154).

Powers Available to Deal with Breach

Paragraph 8 of sch. 12 to the CJA 2003 describes the powers of the court when it deals with an offender where, under para. 8(1)(a), it is proved to the satisfaction of the court that the offender has failed without reasonable excuse to comply with any of the community requirements of the suspended sentence order or where, under para. 8(1)(b), an offender is convicted of an offence committed during the operational period of a suspended sentence order (other than one which has already taken effect). It is submitted that the court is required to proceed under para. 8(1)(a) or (b) even if, by the time the court comes to deal with the breach, the operational period of the suspended sentence has come to an end. If the new offence is a summary-only offence the Crown Court is limited to magistrates' court powers in dealing with it. It is submitted that if the new offence is dealt with by **E6.12** way of a discharge, it does not count as a conviction for an offence committed within the operational period of a suspended sentence (see, by analogy, *Moore* [1995] QB 353). The Sentencing Council definitive guideline, *Breach Offences* (see Supplement, SG15-1) applies to all offenders aged 18 and over sentenced on or after 1 October 2018, irrespective of the date of the offence.

Criminal Justice Act 2003, sch. 12, para. 8

(2) The court must consider [the offender's] case and deal with him in one of the following ways—
 (a) the court may order that the suspended sentence is to take effect with the original term unaltered,
 (b) the court may order that the suspended sentence is to take effect with the substitution for the original term of a lesser term,
 (ba) the court may order the offender to pay a fine of an amount not exceeding £2,500,
 (c) in the case of a suspended sentence order that imposes one or more community requirements, the court may amend the order by doing any one or more of the following—
  (i) imposing more onerous community requirements which the court could include if it were then making the order,
  (ii) subject to subsections (3) and (4) of section 189, extending the supervision period, or
  (iii) subject to subsection (3) of that section, extending the operational period[,]
 (d) in the case of a suspended sentence order that does not impose any community requirements, the court may, subject to section 189(3), amend the order by extending the operational period.

(3) The court must make an order under sub-paragraph (2)(a) or (b) unless it is of the opinion that it would be unjust to do so in view of all the circumstances, including the matters mentioned in sub-paragraph (4); and where it is of that opinion the court must state its reasons.

(4) The matters referred to in sub-paragraph (3) are-
 (a) the extent to which the offender has complied with any community requirements of the suspended sentence order, and
 (b) in a case falling within sub-paragraph (1)(b) the facts of the subsequent offence.

It should be noted that, where the offender is before the court in respect of breach of a suspended sentence order, the court *must* deal with the offender in one of the ways listed in para. 8; it is *not permissible* simply to revoke the order, or to revoke it and resentence (*Clarke* [2018] EWCA Crim 2201), or to make no order with respect to it. Paragraph 8(3) requires that the suspended sentence be activated *in whole or in part* unless it would be unjust to do so; it does not require that it be activated in whole unless it would be unjust to do so (see *McDonagh* [2017] EWCA Crim 2193, where the provision was misapplied). If the suspended sentence is activated it may be ordered to run consecutively or concurrently to any custodial sentence imposed for the offence which has triggered the breach (para. 9). The usual approach is to pass a consecutive sentence, but subject to the restriction in the CJA 2003, s. 265, on imposing a custodial sentence to commence on the expiration of a prison sentence from which the offender has been released on licence (see further E2.21). There is no power under para. 8(2) for the court dealing with a breach to impose a custodial term longer than that originally suspended (a point noted in *Cassidy* [2010] EWCA Crim 3146, [2011] 2 Cr App R (S) 40 (240)). In *Phipps* [2007] EWCA Crim 2923, [2008] 2 Cr App R (S) 20 (114), the Court of Appeal observed that the power of the court to impose custody when dealing with breach of a requirement attached to a suspended sentence was thereby more restricted than its power when dealing with breach of a requirement in a community order. The Court of Appeal in *Levesconte* [2011] EWCA Crim 2754, [2012] 2 Cr App R (S) 19 (80), held that, where D had committed a further offence and the suspended sentence was activated in full, it was wrong to impose a longer sentence for the new offence simply by virtue of its having been committed in breach of the suspended sentence. To do so would be to punish D twice for the same matter. In *Maunder* [2015] EWCA Crim 778, [2015] 2 Cr App R (S) 26 (247), D had failed to comply with the supervision requirement, and had also committed a new offence during the operational period of the suspended sentence. In addition to imposing a custodial sentence for the new offence the judge activated the suspended sentence in part and then added a further three months for the failure to comply. The Court of Appeal said the three months sentence was unlawful, the judge having, in effect, activated the suspended sentence twice. In *Bostan* [2018] EWCA Crim 494, [2018] 2 Cr App R (S) 15 (112), D was sentenced to 18 months' imprisonment suspended for 24 months, the 18 months being composed of consecutive terms of nine months, six months and three months. The judge imposed an immediate custodial sentence for a new offence committed in breach of the suspended sentence and purported to activate the three-month term within the suspended sentence while leaving the remaining 15 months hanging over D's head. The Court of Appeal said that the approach was unlawful. If a suspended sentence is activated in part the effect is to replace the whole of it with an immediate sentence with a reduced term.

Under s. 240ZA(7) (set out at E6.4), the days spent by the offender on remand before the suspended sentence was imposed are deducted automatically in the event of activation of the suspended sentence following breach. The sentencer has no discretion in the matter. It is otiose for a judge passing a suspended sentence to indicate to the offender that the sentence has been suspended because of the time spent on remand, but that those days will not count in the event of breach. The judge activating the suspended sentence has no power to prevent the days on remand being deducted automatically. See *Archer v Governor of Low Newton Prison* [2014] EWHC 2407 (Admin). **E6.13**

The Sentencing Council definitive guideline *Breach Offences* (see Supplement, **SG15-1**) applies to all offenders aged 18 and over sentenced on or after 1 October 2018, irrespective of the date of the offence. The guideline distinguishes between the approach to be taken where (a) breach is in the form of conviction for a further offence committed during the operational period of the suspended sentence and (b) failure to comply with a community requirement during the supervision period. In respect of (a) the guideline states that 'the facts/nature of the new offence is the primary consideration' and sets out four categories of breach and the approach which may be taken, subject to the question whether activation of the sentence in whole or in part would be unjust in all the circumstances. Relevant factors include any strong personal mitigation, whether there is a realistic prospect of rehabilitation, or whether immediate custody will result in significant impact on others. The guideline states that in considering this question 'only new and exceptional factors/circumstances not present at the time the suspended sentence order was imposed should be taken into account'. Apart from the most serious cases, the court should apply an appropriate reduction to the activated sentence to reflect unpaid work or curfew requirements completed. See on this last point *Bell* [2019] EWCA Crim 2079. **E6.14**

In respect of (b) the court must take into account 'the extent to which the offender has complied' with the suspended sentence order, and sets out three categories of breach and the approach which may be taken, subject to the question whether activation of the sentence in whole or in part would be unjust in all the circumstances. The relevant factors listed above are repeated, as is the need to take into account only 'new and exceptional' matters.

Amendment of Requirements

Paragraphs 13 to 19 of sch. 12 to the CJA 2003 deal with various forms of amendment to community requirements in a suspended sentence order which may be made by an appropriate court on application by the offender or an officer of a provider of probation services: **E6.15**

(a) to cancel a community requirement if it is in the interests of justice to do so (including the offender making good progress) (para. 13), or
(b) because of a change in the offender's residence (para. 14), or
(c) to amend a community requirement by cancelling or replacing it with another requirement (para. 15), or
(d) to change a treatment requirement on the report of a medical practitioner (para. 16), or
(e) for drug rehabilitation reviews to take place without a hearing (para. 17), and
(f) to extend beyond 12 months the period for completion of unpaid work (para. 18).

It was pointed out in *West Yorkshire Probation Board v Cruickshanks* [2010] EWHC 615 (Admin), [2011] 1 WLR 2154, that no extension can be granted by a court on an application under para. 18 where to do so would entail the supervision period ending later than the operational period of the order — a situation not permitted by s. 189(4).

Section E7 Custodial Sentences: Detention and Custody of Offenders under 21

GENERAL RESTRICTIONS

E7.1 For the restrictions on imposing custodial sentences on persons aged under 21, see **E2.1** (on the restriction on imposing a sentence of imprisonment) and **E2.6** (on the requirement as to legal representation). According to the Sentencing Council definitive guideline, *Sentencing Children and Young People* (see Supplement, **SG8-1**), when sentencing a defendant aged under 18 a court must have regard to the principal aim of the youth justice system (to prevent offending by children and young people) and the welfare of the child or young person. While the seriousness of the offence will be the starting point, sentencing should be individual and focused on the child or young person, as opposed to offence-focused (paras. 1.1 and 1.2). Further, domestic and international laws dictate that a custodial sentence should always be a measure of last resort for children and young people and statute provides that a custodial sentence may only be imposed when the offence is so serious that no other sanction is appropriate (para. 1.3).

DETERMINING THE AGE OF THE OFFENDER

E7.2 **Powers of Criminal Courts (Sentencing) Act 2000, s. 164**

> (6) For the purposes of any provision of this Act which requires the determination of the age of a person by the court or the Secretary of State, his age shall be deemed to be that which it appears to the court or (as the case may be) the Secretary of State to be after considering any available evidence.

When a court imposes a sentence on an assumption of the offender's age made under s. 164(1), the sentence is not rendered unlawful when it is discovered subsequently that the assumption was incorrect (*Brown* (1989) 11 Cr App R (S) 263). Notwithstanding s. 164, if there is uncertainty over whether the person before the court is under 18, the CYPA 1933, s. 99, applies, and the court 'shall make due inquiry as to the age of that person'. This issue arose in *Steed* (1990) 12 Cr App R (S) 230, where the magistrates had 'deemed' D, from his physical appearance, to be over 18, and then committed him to the Crown Court. He pleaded guilty at the Crown Court, but at sentence asserted that he was aged 15. The judge sentenced him as an 18-year-old. The Court of Appeal said that the court should have adjourned for full inquiries to be made. In more recent cases it has been made clear that age determinations must not be made by a simple visual assessment in court, but must be carried out by the local authority in accordance with the requirements in *R (B) v Merton London Borough Council* [2003] EWHC 1689 (Admin), [2003] 4 All ER 280. See further *AH* [2013] EWCA Crim 344 and *L* [2013] EWCA Crim 991, [2013] 2 Cr App R 23 (247). The latter case also states that if, at the end of a *Merton*-compliant determination, D's age remains in doubt, and there are reasons to believe that D is under 18, then D must be presumed to be under that age.

In *Danga* [1992] QB 476, where D was aged 20 when convicted but aged 21 when sentenced, it was held that the relevant age of the offender, for the purposes of the PCC(S)A 2000, s. 96(1), was the age at the date of conviction. In *Robinson* [1993] 2 All ER 1 it was held, following *Danga*, that, in determining whether an offender was eligible for a sentence under s. 91, the relevant age was the age of the offender at the time of conviction rather than at the time of sentence.

E7.3 The definitive guideline, *Sentencing Children and Young People* (see Supplement, **SG8-8**), provides guidance at paras 6.1 to 6.3 on sentencing in cases where the young offender has crossed a significant age threshold between commission of an offence and date of sentence. It states that: 'When any significant age threshold is passed it will rarely be appropriate that a more severe sentence than the maximum that the court could have imposed at the time the offence was committed should be imposed. However, a sentence at or close to that maximum may be appropriate.' The guideline reflects a principle first recognised in *Ghafoor* [2002] EWCA Crim 1857, [2003] 1 Cr App R (S) 84 (428), where D, who was 17 when the offence was committed but 18 when convicted, pleaded guilty to riot. It was noted that the maximum penalty for the offence was ten years' detention in a young offender institution but, had D been convicted when still 17, the maximum penalty would have been a detention and training order of 24 months, less an appropriate discount for guilty plea. The Court of Appeal stated that, when fixing the appropriate term of detention in a young offender institution, a powerful factor (although not a sole or determining factor) would be the term which D would have been likely to receive if he had been sentenced at the date of the commission of the offence. The sentence of four and a half years' detention in a young offender institution was reduced to 18 months. *Ghafoor* has been followed and applied in many cases including *Bowker* [2007] EWCA Crim 1608, [2008] 1 Cr App R (S) 72 (412); *Y* [2013] EWCA Crim 1175, [2014] 1 Cr App R (S) 39 (228) and *Stoke* [2020] EWCA Crim 162. In *Bowker* it was held that there was no infringement of the ECHR, Article 7(1), in a case where the sentence imposed on an 18-year-old offender was greater than the maximum sentence which could have been imposed on him at the time of the offence (when he was aged 17).

DETENTION IN A YOUNG OFFENDER INSTITUTION

Power to Order Detention

E7.4 **Powers of Criminal Courts (Sentencing) Act 2000, s. 96**

(1) Subject to sections 90, 93 and 94 above, where—
  (a) a person aged at least 18 but under 21 is convicted of an offence which is punishable with imprisonment in the case of a person aged 21 or over, and
  (b) the court is of the opinion that either or both of paragraphs (a) and (b) of section 79(2) above apply or the case falls within section 79(3),

the sentence that the court is to pass is a sentence of detention in a young offender institution.

It should be noted that the procedural provisions which must be complied with before a custodial sentence may lawfully be imposed upon an adult offender must also be complied with in respect of an offender aged under 21 (see **E2.7** and **E2.9**).

A sentence of detention in a young offender institution may be suspended, in accordance with the provisions of the CJA 2003, s. 189. To be eligible for suspension the sentence of detention in a young offender institution must be for at least 21 days and not more than two years. See **E6.1** and **E7.5**. While the definitive guideline, *Sentencing Children and Young People* (see Supplement, **SG8-8**), is concerned with sentencing offenders aged under 18, the Court of Appeal in *Clarke* [2018] EWCA Crim 185, [2018] 1 Cr App R (S) 52 (401), pointed out that: 'Reaching the age of 18 has many legal consequences but it does not present a cliff edge for the purposes of sentencing ... The youth and maturity of an offender will be factors that inform any sentencing decision, even if an offender has passed his or her eighteenth birthday.' These comments were endorsed by the Court of Appeal (Lord Burnett CJ presiding) in *Hobbs* [2018] EWCA Crim 1003, [2018] 2 Cr App R (S) 36 (312), and again in *A-G v Gordon* [2020] EWCA Crim 360, [2020] 4 WLR 49, where the Court said that the principles underpinning the sentencing of young offenders 'have continuing application even after offenders have turned 18'.

Time spent in custody on remand is deducted automatically from the term of detention in a young offender institution (CJA 2003, s. 240ZA: see **E2.12**). Time spent on bail subject to qualifying curfew and electronic monitoring conditions will normally be deducted by the sentencing court from a sentence of detention in a young offender institution (CJA 2003, 240A: see **E2.16**).

In the case of determinate sentences of detention in a young offender institution there is normally a duty on the Secretary of State to release the offender once *one half* of the sentence has been served (CJA 2003, s. 244). There is an exception in relation to sentences of detention in a young offender institution imposed upon certain offenders of 'particular concern' (see **E4.31**). Where an offender is released from a sentence of detention in a young offender institution of more than one day but less than two years, he or she will be made subject to a supervision period which will begin at the expiry of the sentence and end on the expiry of the period of 12 months beginning immediately after the requisite custodial period has been served (CJA 2003, s. 256AA, inserted by the ORA 2014, s. 2). If a requirement of supervision imposed under s. 256AA is breached, the offender will be brought before the appropriate magistrates' court to be dealt with for the breach (s. 256AC, inserted by the ORA 2014, s. 3). The court's powers on breach are set out at **E2.26**.

In respect of a sentence of detention in a young offender institution imposed for a specified violent offence or a specified sexual offence listed in sch. 15 to the CJA 2003 (see **E4.4**), and for which the maximum penalty is life imprisonment, and where the sentence imposed is one of seven years or more, with effect from 1 April 2020 the Release of Prisoners (Alteration of Relevant Proportion of Sentence) Order 2019 (SI 2020 No. 158) amends the automatic release point from half-way to *two thirds* of the sentence. The change made by the 2019 Order applies to offenders sentenced on or after that date. As from 26 February 2020 the Terrorist Offenders (Restriction of Early Release) Act 2020 inserts into the CJA 2003 a new s. 247A (eligibility for release on licence of terrorist prisoners) and a new sch. 19ZA, with the effect that, for offenders convicted of an offence specified in sch. 19ZA, part 1 (offences under counter-terrorism legislation), or convicted of an offence specified in sch. 19ZA, part 2, that schedule and who were determined by the court to have had a terrorist connection under the C-TA 2008, s. 30, the offender must first be considered for early release by the Parole Board at the *two-thirds* point (rather than being released automatically at the half-way point) of the sentence. The Board may direct the offender's release at that point, but only if satisfied that it is no longer necessary for the protection of the public that the offender should be confined. The change made by the 2020 Act applies to offenders serving such a sentence at the commencement date who have not been released on licence, as well as to offenders so sentenced on or after that date.

Minimum and Maximum Terms

E7.5 The PCC(S)A 2000, s. 97, provides for minimum and maximum terms for this sentence.

Powers of Criminal Courts (Sentencing) Act 2000, s. 97

(1) The maximum term of detention in a young offender institution that a court may impose for an offence is the same as the maximum term of imprisonment that it may impose for that offence.
(2) A court shall not pass a sentence for an offender's detention in a young offender institution for less than 21 days.
(3) [Repealed].

In *Dover Youth Court, ex parte K (A Minor)* [1999] 4 All ER 24, the Divisional Court held that, on a proper construction of the word 'sentence', s. 97(2) should be taken to refer to the sentence imposed for a particular offence, rather than to the total sentence produced by aggregating more than one custodial term.

Concurrent and Consecutive Sentences of Detention

Powers of Criminal Courts (Sentencing) Act 2000, s. 97 E7.6

(4) Where—
(a) an offender is convicted of more than one offence for which he is liable to a sentence of detention in a young offender institution, or
(b) an offender who is serving a sentence of detention in a young offender institution is convicted of one or more further offences for which he is liable to such a sentence,
the court shall have the same power to pass consecutive sentences of detention in a young offender institution as if they were sentences of imprisonment.
(5) Subject to section 84 above (restriction on consecutive sentences for released prisoners) where an offender who—
(a) is serving a sentence of detention in a young offender institution, and
(b) is aged 21 or over,
is convicted of one or more further offences for which he is liable to imprisonment, the court shall have the power to pass one or more sentences of imprisonment to run consecutively upon the sentence of detention in a young offender institution.

For concurrent and consecutive custodial sentences, see **E2.19**.

CUSTODY FOR LIFE

Powers of Criminal Courts (Sentencing) Act 2000, s. 94 E7.7

(1) Where a person aged at least 18 but under 21 is convicted of an offence—
(a) for which the sentence is not fixed by law, but
(b) for which a person aged 21 or over would be liable to imprisonment for life,
the court shall, if it considers that a sentence for life would be appropriate, sentence him to custody for life.

The criteria for the imposition for the sentence of custody for life, where it is imposed as a discretionary sentence, are those contained in the CJA 2003, ss. 152 and 153 (see **E2.7** and **E2.9**). Where a person aged 18, 19 or 20 on the date of conviction for an offence which is a 'serious offence' satisfies the requirements of the CJA 2003, s. 225 (see **E4.5**), the court must impose a sentence of custody for life. The PCC(S)A 2000, s. 82A, provides that a sentencer imposing a sentence of custody for life as a discretionary life sentence under s. 94 may specify that part of the sentence which must expire before the offender becomes eligible for consideration for early release. The sentencer should start by deciding what determinate sentence would have been appropriate if custody for life had not been imposed, and then specify a period which will normally be one half of that notional sentence as the part to be specified under s. 82A (*Marklew* [1999] 2 All ER 939). Credit should be given for relevant mitigating factors, such as the youth of the offender.

The Court of Appeal has stressed that custody for life is reserved for exceptional cases and should not be passed on the assumption that it is a more merciful disposal than a fixed-term sentence (*Hall* (1986) 8 Cr App R (S) 458; *Lynas* (1992) 13 Cr App R (S) 363). It appears that the criteria applicable to the use of discretionary life imprisonment in the case of an adult should also be applied in relation to custody for life, while having regard to the relative youth of the offender. E7.8

A sentence of custody for life was upheld in *Busby* (1992) 13 Cr App R (S) 291, where D, aged 18, pleaded guilty to rape of a girl aged three. He was not suffering from any mental illness but was described as 'flat and detached' and showed no remorse. He had committed two earlier assaults on young children and, in the light of that, it was held that the primary responsibility of the court was to protect the public.

DETENTION UNDER THE PCC(S)A 2000, s. 91

E7.9 **Powers of Criminal Courts (Sentencing) Act 2000, s. 91**

(1) Subsection (3) below applies where a person aged under 18 is convicted on indictment of—
 (a) an offence punishable in the case of a person aged 21 or over with imprisonment for 14 years or more, not being an offence the sentence for which is fixed by law; or
 (b) an offence under section 3 of the Sexual Offences Act 2003 (in this section, 'the 2003 Act') (sexual assault); or
 (c) an offence under section 13 of the 2003 Act (child sex offences committed by children or young persons); or
 (d) an offence under section 25 of the 2003 Act (sexual activity with a child family member); or
 (e) an offence under section 26 of the 2003 Act (inciting a child family member to engage in sexual activity).

(1A) Subsection (3) below also applies where—
 (a) a person aged under 18 is convicted on indictment of an offence—
  (i) under subsection (1)(a), (ab), (aba), (ac), (ad), (ae), (af) [(ag), (ba)] or (c) of section 5 of the Firearms Act 1968 (prohibited weapons), or
  (ii) under subsection (1A)(a) of that section,
 (b) the offence was committed after the commencement of section 51A of that Act and at a time when he was aged 16 or over, and
 (c) the court is of the opinion mentioned in section 51A(2) of that Act (exceptional circumstances which justify its not imposing required custodial sentence).

(1B) Subsection (3) below also applies where—
 (a) a person aged under 18 is convicted on indictment of an offence under the Firearms Act 1968 that is listed in section 51A(1A)(b), (e) or (f) of that Act and was committed in respect of a firearm or ammunition specified in section 5(1)(a), (ab), (aba), (ac), (ad), (af) or (c) or section 5(1A)(a) of that Act;
 (b) the offence was committed after the commencement of section 30 of the Violent Crime Reduction Act 2006 and for the purposes of section 51A(3) of the Firearms Act 1968 at a time when he was aged 16 or over; and
 (c) the court is of the opinion mentioned in section 51A(2) of the Firearms Act 1968.

(1C) Subsection (3) below also applies where—
 (a) a person aged under 18 is convicted of an offence under section 28 of the Violent Crime Reduction Act 2006 (using someone to mind a weapon);
 (b) section 29(3) of that Act applies (minimum sentences in certain cases); and
 (c) the court is of the opinion mentioned in section 29(6) of that Act (exceptional circumstances which justify not imposing the minimum sentence).

(2) [Repealed.]

(3) If the court is of the opinion that neither a youth rehabilitation order nor a detention and training order is suitable, the court may sentence the offender to be detained for such period, not exceeding the maximum term of imprisonment with which the offence is punishable in the case of a person aged 21 or over, as may be specified in the sentence.

(4) Subsection (3) above is subject to (in particular) sections 152 and 153 of the Criminal Justice Act 2003.

(5) Where—
 (a) subsection (2) of section 51A of the Firearms Act 1968, or
 (b) subsection (6) of section 29 of the Violent Crime Reduction Act 2006,
 requires the imposition of a sentence of detention under this section for a term of at least the required minimum term (within the meaning of that section), the court shall sentence the offender to be detained for such period, of at least that term but not exceeding the maximum term of imprisonment with which the offence is punishable in the case of a person aged 18 or over, as may be specified in the sentence.

The references in s. 91(1A)(a)(i) to the offences under s. 5(1)(ag) or (ba) are inserted by the Offensive Weapons Act 2019 and will come into effect from a date to be appointed. This change applies only to an offence committed after the date that amendment is brought into force.

E7.10 Valuable guidance in relation to this sentence may be found in the definitive guideline, *Sentencing Children and Young People* (see Supplement, **SG8-1**). If detention for two years or less is called for, it will normally be appropriate to make a detention and training order rather than an order under s. 91. It should be noted, however, that the detention and training order may be imposed on an offender aged under 15 only where he or she is a 'persistent offender'. There is no such restriction in relation to detention under s. 91. In *J-R* [2001] 1 Cr App R (S) 109 (377), two boys aged 14 were convicted of robbery. Neither qualified as a persistent offender, but the Court of Appeal endorsed sentences of 15 months and 30 months' detention under s. 91. Further, in *Q* [2012] EWCA Crim 296, [2012] 2 Cr App R (S) 54 (309) sentences of 18 months' detention under s. 91 were upheld in the case of three offenders aged 13 and 14 who had committed a robbery at a corner shop while armed with a handgun. Since none of the offenders was a persistent offender, the Court of Appeal agreed with the judge that a detention and training order was not available, and also agreed that a youth rehabilitation order would have been inappropriate on the facts. A further distinction between the two sentences is that the detention and training order is available only where the offender is aged 12 or over, whereas detention under s. 91 may be imposed on an offender aged ten or 11.

The powers to sentence under s. 91 are limited to the Crown Court; a youth court may not exercise them. If the young offender pleads guilty in the youth court at the plea before venue hearing, he or she may be committed by the magistrates to the Crown Court with a view to a sentence under s. 91 being imposed (PCC(S)A 2000, s. 3B). It is clear that the general policy of the legislation is that young offenders should, wherever possible, be dealt with in the youth court, and the matter should be committed to the Crown Court only where there is a real prospect, having regard to the age of the offender, that he or she might require a sentence of, or in excess of, two years. Two years is the maximum term for a detention and training order and hence the longest custodial sentence which the youth court can lawfully pass. If the young offender has not indicated a plea of guilty before the magistrates, and on the information before them the seriousness of the case merits a greater penalty than two years, the magistrates have power, under the CDA 1988, s. 51A, to commit the young offender to the Crown Court for trial if the magistrates are of the view that it 'ought to be possible' to sentence him or her to detention under s. 91. For any defendant appearing in the youth court for the first time on or after 13 April 2015, the PCC(S)A 2000, s. 3B, as amended by the CJCA 2015, s. 53, allows for a young defendant to be tried in the youth court in relation to an offence which falls within s. 91 and then be committed for sentence if the Crown Court 'should in the [youth] court's opinion have power to deal with the offender' under s. 91. In *R (DPP) v South Tyneside Youth Court* [2015] EWHC 1455 (Admin), [2015] 2 Cr App R (S) 59 (411), the Divisional Court noted that the first principle remains that young persons should, wherever possible, be tried in the youth court and that there was public concern over the propriety of trials in the Crown Court for those under the age of 18. The test of whether there was a 'real prospect' that the young offender would require a sentence in excess of two years was a sensible interpretation of the requirements of s. 51A of the CDA 1988, but it should be borne in mind that the youth court would no longer be making a once and for all decision at the point of allocation for trial. For a fuller exposition see **D24.30**, and see further the definitive guideline, *Sentencing Children and Young People* (see Supplement, **SG8-1**), paras. 2.8 to 2.10.

E7.11 Time spent in custody (or on remand in youth detention) is deducted automatically from a sentence imposed under s. 91 (see the CJA 2003, s. 240ZA, at **E2.12**), and half of the number of days spent on bail subject to a qualifying curfew should normally be deducted by the sentencing court from a sentence imposed under s. 91 (CJA 2003, s. 240A). The PCC(S)A 2000, s. 83 (restriction on imposing sentence where offender not legally represented), applies (see **E2.6**). As to an order of detention under s. 91 imposed upon an offender already serving a detention and training order, and vice versa, see the PCC(S)A 2000, s. 106A.

In the case of determinate sentences of detention under the PCC(S)A 2000, s. 91, there is normally a duty on the Secretary of State to release the offender once *one half* of the sentence has been served (CJA 2003, s. 244). As from 26 February 2020 the Terrorist Offenders (Restriction of Early Release) Act 2020 inserts into the CJA 2003 a new s. 247A (eligibility for release on licence of terrorist prisoners) and a new sch. 19ZA, with the effect that, for offenders convicted of an offence specified in sch. 19ZA, part 1 (offences under counter-terrorism legislation), or convicted of an offence specified in sch. 19ZA, part 2, and who were determined by the court to have had a terrorist connection under the C-TA 2008, s. 30, the offender must first be considered for early release by the Parole Board at the *two-thirds* point (rather than being released automatically at the half-way point) of the sentence. The Board may direct the offender's release at that point, but only if satisfied that it is no longer necessary for the protection of the public that the offender should be confined. The change made by the 2020 Act applies to offenders serving such a sentence at the commencement date who have not been released on licence, as well as to offenders so sentenced on or after that date.

Sentencing Principles

E7.12 Where a young offender has been convicted of more than one offence, and power to sentence the offender under s. 91 is available in respect of one of the offences but not the other(s), the court may order detention under s. 91 in respect of the offence for which it is available, but pass an overall term of detention which reflects the totality of the offending. In *Walsh* [1997] 2 Cr App R (S) 210, there were five offenders, all girls aged 14 or 15. They pleaded guilty to false imprisonment and unlawful wounding, committed while carrying out a sustained violent attack on another girl aged 14. Sentences of detention under s. 91 were imposed, for terms varying between three and a half years and three years, 11 months. It was argued on appeal that the sentences were wrong since the real gravamen of the offending lay in respect of the unlawful wounding, an offence for which s. 91 is not available. The Court of Appeal, however, held that the two offences were associated with each other (see **E2.8**) and s. 91 was available for the offence of false imprisonment. The approach taken in *Walsh* was endorsed in *AM* [1998] 1 All ER 874.

General guidance on the use of the PCC(S)A 2000, s. 91, was provided by Lord Bingham CJ in *AM* [1998] 1 All ER 874, in which it was made clear that it was not good sentencing practice to pass a sentence of detention under s. 91 simply because the maximum available sentence of youth custody (now a detention and training order) appeared to be on the low side for the particular offence committed. Lord Bingham also stated that, while a Crown Court sentencer should not exceed the 24-month limit without much careful thought, if it was concluded that a longer (even if not much longer) sentence was called for then the court should impose whatever it considered the appropriate period of detention under s. 91 to be. The definitive guideline, *Sentencing Children and Young People* (see Supplement, **SG8-1**), provides further guidance on sentencing young offenders under s. 91. The guideline says that where a custodial sentence is unavoidable and offence-specific guidelines for children and young people are available, the court should consult them. If there is no offence-specific guideline, the court may want to consider the equivalent adult sentencing guideline. It may be appropriate to apply a sentence broadly within the region of half to two-thirds of the appropriate adult sentence for those aged 15, 16 or 17 and allow a greater reduction for those aged under 15. This is only a rough guide. Emotional and developmental age and maturity of the child or young person is of at least equal importance as chronological age (para. 6.46). In *Moorhouse* [2019] EWCA Crim 2197, [2020] 1 Cr App R (S) 66 (509), the Court of Appeal said that while it was open to a judge to pass a sentence on a 15 or 16-year-old defendant in excess of two thirds of what would have been the appropriate sentence for a young adult or an adult, the judge should explain in the sentencing remarks why a reduction of one third or more was not being made.

E7.13 The Court of Appeal considered the application of the *Sentencing Children and Young People* guideline in *TLS* [2018] EWCA Crim 395. The Court approved a sentence under s. 91 on a 14-year-old convicted of wounding with intent and possession of a kitchen knife, but the term was reduced from five years to four. In *Moorhouse* the two defendants were part of a group which had committed a series of house burglaries and thefts from vehicles over an 11-week period. One of the defendants was just under 16 at the time of the offending; the other was just over 16. Sentences of seven years and six years' detention under s. 91 were reduced on appeal to six years and five years. The following cases pre-date the *Sentencing Children and Young People* guideline. In *Ratcliffe* [2008] EWCA Crim 471, [2008] 2 Cr App R (S) 79 (441), seven and a half years' detention under s. 91 was reduced to six years on appeal in respect of a youth aged 17 on a plea of guilty to criminal damage being reckless whether life would be endangered. He dropped a block of masonry on to a train, with the result that the driver was seriously injured and the train ran out of control for some distance. In *Z* [2008] EWCA Crim 753, [2008] 2 Cr App R (S) 108 (623), 42 months' detention under s. 91 was upheld on a 14-year-old boy who pleaded guilty to causing death by dangerous driving. D had taken a vehicle and driven it erratically around a residential estate in the afternoon. He lost control of the car, which mounted a pavement and hit a tree. The tree snapped and crushed a 19-month-old child in a baby buggy. D left the scene but was eventually traced. In *SP* [2009] EWCA Crim 1091, [2010] 1 Cr App R (S) 30 (186) a sentence of six years' detention under s. 91 was upheld on a 13-year-old boy convicted after a trial of the manslaughter of two people by setting fire to a building in which they were sleeping. The boy, who acted alongside his 17-year-old brother, was described as being of low intelligence, and his parents had shown little interest in him. The Court of Appeal said that the case had presented 'an extraordinarily difficult sentencing exercise'.

DETENTION FOR LIFE UNDER THE PCC(S)A 2000, s. 91

Where, by the CJA 2003, s. 226 (see **E4.8**), a person aged under 18 on the date of conviction for an offence which is listed in sch. 15 to the CJA 2003 and which carries a maximum sentence of life imprisonment in the case of an adult, has been found to be 'dangerous' and where the seriousness of the offence justifies a life sentence, the court must impose a sentence of detention for life under s. 91. The PCC(S)A 2000, s. 82A, provides that a sentencer imposing a sentence of detention for life may specify what part of the sentence must expire before the offender becomes eligible for consideration for early release. The sentencer should start by deciding what determinate sentence would have been appropriate if detention for life had not been imposed, and then specify a period which will normally be one half of that notional sentence as the part to be specified under s. 82A (see *Marklew* [1999] 2 All ER 939 and **E4.25**). It is well established that a life sentence is always a sentence of last resort, and that is especially so where the offender is aged under 18 (see **E4.9**). The Sentencing Council definitive guideline, *Sentencing Children and Young People* (see Supplement, **SG8-8**), states (at para. 6.59) that 'a sentence of detention for life should be used as a last resort when an extended sentence is not able to provide the level of public protection that is necessary'. **E7.14**

In *JM* [2002] EWCA Crim 1636, [2003] 1 Cr App R (S) 51 (245), a case decided before the CJA 2003, s. 226, came into force, a sentence of detention for life under s. 91 was upheld in the case of a boy of 14 convicted of causing grievous bodily harm with intent, who had a history of violent and disturbed behaviour. He had struck a man on the back of the head with a wooden stake, fracturing his skull and causing long-lasting injuries. It was accepted that D was likely to remain a serious danger to the community for the foreseeable future, and no confident prediction of improvement could be made. Taking a notional determinate sentence of seven years, a period of three and a half years was specified under the PCC(S)A 2000, s. 82A.

DETENTION AND TRAINING ORDERS

Sections 100 to 107 of the PCC(S)A 2000 provide for the detention and training order. The detention and training order is available to youth courts and to the Crown Court in respect of offenders aged under 18 who have been convicted of an offence punishable with imprisonment **E7.15** in the case of an adult. Where an offender is aged 17 at the date of conviction but is aged 18 or over when sentenced, the sentence takes effect as a detention and training order rather than a sentence of detention in a young offender institution (*Danga* (1992) 13 Cr App R (S) 408; *Hahn* [2003] EWCA Crim 825, [2003] 2 Cr App R (S) 106 (636)).

Powers of Criminal Courts (Sentencing) Act 2000, s. 100

(1) Subject to sections 90 and 91 above, sections 226 and 226B of the Criminal Justice Act 2003, and subsection (2) below, where—
   (a) a child or young person (that is to say, any person aged under 18) is convicted of an offence which is punishable with imprisonment in the case of a person aged 21 or over, and
   (b) the court is of the opinion that subsection (2) of section 152 of the Criminal Justice Act 2003 applies or the case falls within subsection (3) of that section, the sentence that the courts is to pass is a detention and training order.

(1A) Subsection (1) applies with the omission of paragraph (b) in the case of an offence the sentence for which falls to be imposed under these provisions—
   (a) section 1(2B) or 1A(5) of the Prevention of Crime Act 1953 (minimum sentence for certain offences involving offensive weapons);
   (b) section 139(6B), 139A(5B) or 139AA(7) of the Criminal Justice Act 1988 (minimum sentence for certain offences involving article with blade or point or offensive weapon).

(2) A court shall not make a detention and training order—
   (a) in the case of an offender under the age of 15 at the time of the conviction, unless it is of the opinion that he is a persistent offender;
   (b) in the case of an offender under the age of 12 at that time, unless—
      (i) it is of the opinion that only a custodial sentence would be adequate to protect the public from further offending by him; and
      (ii) the offence was committed on or after such date as the Secretary of State may by order appoint.

(3) A detention and training order is an order that the offender in respect of whom it is made shall be subject, for the term specified in the order, to a period of detention and training followed by a period of supervision.

For s. 90 (detention at Her Majesty's pleasure), see **E3.12**; for s. 91 (long-term detention), see **E7.14**. No day has yet been appointed for the purposes of s. 100(2)(b); it follows that a detention and training order cannot be imposed on an offender aged ten or 11 at date of conviction.

E7.16 Power to pass a detention and training order on a young offender aged under 15 at the time of conviction is limited to cases in which the offender qualifies as a 'persistent' offender. Section 100(4) states that, where the court makes a detention and training order on an offender aged under 15, it must state in open court that it is of the opinion mentioned in s. 100(2)(a) and, where applicable, (b)(i). This is in addition to the normal obligations on the sentencer to give reasons for imposing a custodial sentence. In *AD* [2001] 1 Cr App R (S) 59 (202), it was held that formal cautions on the record are relevant in determining persistence. Formal cautions for juveniles were replaced by reprimands and warnings under the CDA 1998, and by youth cautions under the LASPO 2012, but it is clear that these are to be regarded as relevant in the same way. The definitive guideline, *Sentencing Children and Young People* (see Supplement, **SG8-8**), provides guidance on the meaning of 'persistent offender' at paras. 6.4 to 6.10 . It indicates that a finding of persistence may be derived from previous convictions and from orders which require an admission or finding of guilt, such as restorative justice disposals and conditional cautions, but not penalty notices for disorder. The guideline says that a child or young person who has committed one previous offence cannot reasonably be classed as a persistent offender and should not necessarily be assumed to be one if he or she has committed two or more. If there have been three findings of guilt (or other orders requiring an admission of guilt) in the past 12 months for imprisonable offences of a comparable nature, the court could certainly justify classing the child or young person as a persistent offender. Also, if the child or young person is being sentenced on a single appearance for a series of separate, comparable offences committed over a short space of time, the court could justifiably consider the child or young person to be a persistent offender.

Duration of Order and Consecutive Orders

Powers of Criminal Courts (Sentencing) Act 2000, s. 101 E7.17

(1) Subject to subsections (2) and (2A) below, the term of a detention and training order made in respect of an offence (whether by a magistrates' court or otherwise) shall be 4, 6, 8, 10, 12, 18 or 24 months.
(2) The term of a detention and training order may not exceed the maximum term of imprisonment that the Crown Court could (in the case of an offender aged 21 or over) impose for the offence.
(2A) Where—
 (a) the offence is a summary offence,
 (b) the maximum term of imprisonment that a court could (in the case of an offender aged 18 or over) impose for the offence is 51 weeks,
the term of a detention and training order may not exceed six months.
(3) Subject to subsections (4) and (6) below, a court making a detention and training order may order that its term shall commence on the expiry of the term of any other detention and training order made by that or any other court.
(4) A court shall not make in respect of an offender a detention and training order the effect of which would be that he would be subject to detention and training orders for a term which exceeds 24 months.
(5) Where the term of the detention and training orders to which an offender would otherwise be subject exceeds 24 months, the excess shall be treated as remitted.
(6) A court making a detention and training order shall not order that its term shall commence on the expiry of the term of a detention and training order under which the period of supervision has already begun (under section 103(1) below).
(7) Where a detention and training order ('the new order') is made in respect of an offender who is subject to a detention and training order under which the period of supervision has begun ('the old order'), the old order shall be disregarded in determining—
 (a) for the purposes of subsection (4) above whether the effect of the new order would be that the offender would be subject to detention and training orders for a term which exceeds 24 months; and
 (b) for the purposes of subsection (5) above whether the term of the detention and training orders to which the offender would (apart from that subsection) be subject exceeds 24 months.

Subsection (2A) and the reference to it in subsection (1) were inserted by the CJA 2003, s. 298, which is not in force.

By s. 101(1), the term of a detention and training order must be for one of the specified periods set out in that subsection, the minimum period being four months and the maximum period 24 months. It follows that in a case where the court would otherwise have imposed a detention and training order for four months but there is a guilty plea or other significant mitigation (or the offender has spent a period of time on remand in custody: see **E7.23**), the court cannot impose a detention and training order at all. It was noted by the Divisional Court in *Inner London Crown Court, ex parte N and S* [2001] 1 Cr App R (S) 99 (343), that one effect of the introduction of detention and training orders had been to raise the custody threshold for young offenders. In *Ganley* [2001] 1 Cr App R (S) 17 (60), the Court of Appeal said that terms of less than four months could not be aggregated so as to reach the four-month minimum. Individual terms of less than four months would not comply with s. 101(1). Section 101(1) is expressed as being 'subject to' s. 101(2), which explains that when imposing such a sentence the court may not exceed the maximum term of imprisonment which the Crown Court could have imposed on an adult for that offence. It follows from this that, if the maximum sentence for an offence is three months' imprisonment, a detention and training order cannot be imposed at all. An example is the offence of interfering with a motor vehicle (see **B4.136**). Where a court is sentencing for a summary-only offence, the longest detention and training order it may impose is normally six months, because that is the maximum term which the Crown Court could impose for that offence. An exception is the offence of absconding, under the BA 1976, s. 6, where the maximum penalty in the Crown Court is 12 months. Otherwise, the maximum sentence of 24 months is available to the youth court as well as to the Crown Court, since the restrictions on E7.18

the imposition of imprisonment and detention in a young offender institution by magistrates' courts (see **E2.5**) are not applicable to the detention and training order.

E7.19 In accordance with general principles, the maximum sentence of 24 months should not normally be imposed where the offender has pleaded guilty or there is other significant mitigation (*Kelly* [2001] EWCA Crim 1030, [2002] 1 Cr App R (S) 11 (40) and *Dalby* [2005] EWCA Crim 1292, [2006] 1 Cr App R (S) 38 (216), but for an exceptional case see *T* [2011] EWCA Crim 2345). If, however, the offence for which the offender is being sentenced is one which would have attracted a sentence of long-term detention under PCC(S)A 2000, s. 91, for a term in excess of 24 months, it is certainly possible that (making due allowance for mitigation) the proper sentence is a detention and training order for 24 months. This approach was taken in *Fieldhouse* [2001] 1 Cr App R (S) 104 (361), where there was a guilty plea and a significant period on remand in custody. A more recent example is *Baker* [2019] EWCA Crim 471, where the Court of Appeal upheld a 24-month detention and training order on a 15-year-old boy who admitted an offence of wounding with intent, 'thus sparing him from a significantly longer sentence by way of section 91' (at [1]). Restricting the sentencing courts to the specific terms identified in s. 101(1) has given rise to practical difficulty. If the appropriate duration of a detention and training order would otherwise be, say, 18 months, but the offender enters a timely guilty plea and/or there is other significant mitigation, the court must reduce the term, at least to 12 months, to take such matters into account. There is no stopping point between 18 and 12 months.

The definitive guideline, *Sentencing Children and Young People* (see Supplement, **SG8-1**), says that where a custodial sentence is unavoidable and offence-specific guidelines for children and young people are available, the court should consult them. If there is no offence-specific guideline, the court may want to consider the equivalent adult sentencing guideline. It may be appropriate to apply a sentence broadly within the region of half to two-thirds of the appropriate adult sentence for those aged 15, 16 or 17 and allow a greater reduction for those aged under 15. This is only a rough guide. Emotional and developmental age and maturity of the child or young person is of at least equal importance as chronological age (para. 6.46). In *Moorhouse* [2019] EWCA Crim 2197, [2020] 1 Cr App R (S) 66 (509), the Court of Appeal said that while it was open to a judge to pass a sentence on a 15 or 16-year-old defendant in excess of two thirds of what would have been the appropriate sentence for a young adult or an adult, the judge should explain in the sentencing remarks why a reduction of one third or more was not being made.

E7.20 **Consecutive Orders** As far as consecutive detention and training orders are concerned, it is clear that the terms of each order must comply with the PCC(S)A 2000, s. 101(1) and (2), but the Court of Appeal has held in *Norris* [2001] 1 Cr App R (S) 116 (401) that it is not necessary for the total term to add up to one of the periods listed. When imposing consecutive detention and training orders for two summary-only offences, the youth court may exceed a total term of six months, although that is the maximum aggregate term of imprisonment which the Crown Court can impose, by virtue of the MCA 1980, s. 133 (*C v DPP* [2001] EWHC Admin 453, [2002] 1 Cr App R (S) 45 (189)). The effect of the PCC(S)A 2000, s. 106A, is to permit the imposition of a sentence of detention under s. 91 on an offender who is already subject to a detention and training order. If the offender has already been released on licence from the detention and training order, the s. 91 sentence must commence on the day on which it is passed. If not, the s. 91 sentence may, at the discretion of the court, commence on the day on which it is passed or at the time when the offender would have been released from the detention and training order. Section 106A also makes similar provision in respect of the imposition of a detention and training order on an offender who is already subject to a sentence of detention under s. 91.

E7.21 **Imposition of Excessive Term** If a term, or aggregate term, longer than 24 months is imposed by the court, the excess is automatically remitted (PCC(S)A 2000, s. 101(5)). It is therefore important for a sentencer always to make clear whether the sentence being imposed is a detention and training order or one of long-term detention under the PCC(S)A 2000, s. 91. See further *GF* [2000] 2 Cr App R (S) 364 and commentary.

Early or Delayed Release Ordinarily the period of detention and training shall be one half of the full term of the order (PCC(S)A 2000, s. 102(2)), although the Secretary of State retains a discretion to release a person before the half-way point, on compassionate or other grounds. There is also power, on application of the Secretary of State, for a youth court to order the delay of a person's release beyond the half-way point (s. 102(5)). For a rare example of an application under s. 102(5), see *R (X) v Ealing Youth Court* [2020] EWHC 800 (Admin). The second half of the order is the period of supervision, although again the Secretary of State retains power to provide by order that the period of supervision shall be curtailed (s. 103). Supervision will be carried out by an officer of a local probation board, a social worker of a local authority, or a member of a youth offending team. Where an offender serving a detention and training order is aged 18 or over at the half-way point of the order and the order is for less than 24 months, the offender is subject to a supervision period which will begin at the expiry of the term of the detention and training order and end on the expiry of the period of 12 months beginning immediately after the half-way point of the order (PCC(S)A 2000, s. 106B). E7.22

Requirement to Take into Account Period Spent on Remand

Powers of Criminal Courts (Sentencing) Act 2000, s. 101 E7.23

(8) In determining the term of a detention and training order for an offence, the court shall take account of any period for which the offender has been remanded—
  (a) in custody, or
  (b) on bail subject to a qualifying curfew condition and an electronic monitoring condition (within the meaning of section 240A of the Criminal Justice Act 2003),

in connection with the offence, or any other offence the charge for which was founded on the same facts or evidence.

(9) Where a court proposes to make detention and training orders in respect of an offender for two or more offences—
  (a) subsection (8) above shall not apply; but
  (b) in determining the total term of the detention and training orders it proposes to make in respect of the offender, the court shall take account of the total period (if any) for which he has been remanded in custody in connection with any of those offences, or any other offence the charge for which was founded on the same facts or evidence.

(10) Once a period of remand has, under subsection (8) or (9) above, been taken account of in relation to a detention and training order made in respect of an offender for any offence or offences, it shall not subsequently be taken account of (under either of those subsections) in relation to such an order made in respect of the offender for any other offence or offences.

It is important to note that, with respect to the detention and training order, the court *must* take into account any period for which the offender has been remanded in custody or was subject to a qualifying curfew. The CJA 2003, ss. 240ZA and 240A (see **E2.12** *et seq.*), do not apply to the detention and training order. Where a young offender has spent time in custody on remand or subject to a qualifying curfew prior to the imposition of a detention and training order, in order to achieve the same effect which the operation of s. 240ZA or 240A would have, it will be necessary for the sentencer to double the number of days spent on remand before deducting that total from the length of the order imposed (*Eagles* [2006] EWCA Crim 2368, [2007] 1 Cr App R (S) 99 (612), followed and applied in *J* [2012] EWCA Crim 1570, [2013] 1 Cr App R (S) 74 (412)). The definitive guideline, *Sentencing Children and Young People* (see Supplement, **SG8-8**), says that this is the 'accepted approach' (para. 6.53). The requirement on the court to make such reduction has caused difficulty in relation to the specified duration of a detention and training order, which must be for one of the seven periods set out in the PCC(S)A 2000, s. 101(1). In *Inner London Crown Court, ex parte I* (2000) *The Times*, 12 May 2000, the Divisional Court stated that the duty imposed by s. 101(8) was to 'take account' of the time spent on remand in custody, but this did not require the sentencer to make a 'one-for-one discount'. This general approach was confirmed by the Court of Appeal in *B* [2001] 1 Cr App R (S) 89 (303) E7.24

and by the Divisional Court in *Inner London Crown Court, ex parte N and S* [2001] 1 Cr App R (S) 99 (343).

Breach of Order

E7.25 Section 104 of the PCC(S)A 2000 provides powers in relation to breach of supervision requirements in a detention and training order. By s. 104(3), if it is proved to the satisfaction of a youth court acting for the relevant local justice area that the offender has failed to comply with supervision requirements specified in the order, the court may:

(a) order the offender to be detained in youth detention accommodation not exceeding the maximum period found under subsection (3A) as the court may specify;
(aa) order the offender to be subject to such period of supervision, not exceeding the maximum period found under subsection (3A), as the court may specify; or
(b) impose on the offender a fine not exceeding level 3 on the standard scale.

Subsection (3A) states that the relevant maximum period is the shorter of three months, and the period beginning with the date the breach was committed and ending with the last day of the term of the detention and training order. A failure occurring over two or more days is taken to have occurred on the first of those days (s. 104(3B)). The court may make an order under s. 104(3) before or after the end of the term of the detention and training order (s. 104(3C)), and a period of detention or supervision ordered under s. 104(3) begins on the date the order is made and may overlap to any extent with the period of supervision under the detention and training order. For appellate consideration of this provision see *McGeechan* [2019] EWCA Crim 235, [2019] 2 Cr App R (S) 12 (91).

Section 105 relates to the commission of a further imprisonable offence by the offender following release from a detention and training order but prior to that order coming to an end. The court, whether or not it passes any other sentence on the offender, may order the offender to be detained in youth detention accommodation from the date of the new order for the whole or part of the period between the date of commission of the new offence and the date at which the full term of the original order would have come to an end. Such an order may be made even where the offender is convicted of the new offence after the full term of the original order has come to an end, as long as the offence was committed within the supervision part of the order. The reinstated part of the sentence may be served before any sentence imposed for the new offence, or it may be served concurrently with that sentence, but the reinstated period shall be disregarded in determining the appropriate length of the new sentence. The decision in *McGeechan* establishes that s. 105 does not apply if the defendant has reached the age of 18 when the further imprisonable offence is committed. Once the defendant attains the age of 18 he or she becomes eligible for a sentence of detention in a young offender institution, and the PCC(S)A 2000, s. 106, requires that such sentence be imposed with immediate effect and concurrently with the period of breach detention, a provision consistent with the rule applicable to adult offenders who have been released from custody, as set out in the CJA 2003, s. 265 (see **E2.19**).

Section E8 Community Orders

POWER TO MAKE A COMMUNITY ORDER

If the offender is aged 18 or over at the date of conviction, the appropriate community sentence is a community order under the CJA 2003. The maximum length of a community order is three years. The Sentencing Council definitive guideline, *Imposition of Community and Custodial Sentences* (see Supplement, **SG9-1**), applies. **E8.1**

Criteria for the Imposition of Community Order

By the CJA 2003, s. 147, a 'community sentence' means a sentence that consists of or includes a 'community order' (as defined by s. 177) or 'a youth rehabilitation order'. By s. 177, a 'community order' is an order imposed on an offender aged 18 or over. The order will contain one or more requirements imposed by the court. These requirements are considered in detail at **E8.8**. A number of general provisions apply to the imposition of all community sentences. These are dealt with now, before turning to the details of the individual requirements. **E8.2**

Criminal Justice Act 2003, s. 148

(1) A court must not pass a community sentence on an offender unless it is of the opinion that the offence, or the combination of the offence and one or more offences associated with it, was serious enough to warrant such a sentence.

(2) Where a court passes a community sentence—

(a) the particular requirement or requirements forming part of the community order, or, as the case may be, youth rehabilitation order, comprised in the sentence must be such as, in the opinion of the court, is, or taken together are, the most suitable for the offender, and

(b) the restrictions on liberty imposed by the order must be such as in the opinion of the court are commensurate with the seriousness of the offence, or the combination of the offence and one or more offences associated with it.

(2A) Subsection (2) is subject to section 177(2A) (community orders: punitive elements) and to paragraph 3(4) of Schedule 1 to the Criminal Justice and Immigration Act 2008 (youth rehabilitation order with intensive supervision and surveillance).

(3) [Repealed.]

(4) Subsections (1) and (2)(b) have effect subject to section 151(2).

(5) The fact that by virtue of any provision of this section—

(a) a community sentence may be passed in relation to an offence; or

(b) particular restrictions on liberty may be imposed by a community order or youth rehabilitation order.

does not require a court to pass such a sentence or to impose those restrictions.

Section 149 deals with the situation where an offender was remanded in custody in connection with the offence (or any other offence the charge for which was founded on the same facts or evidence) before being convicted of, or pleading guilty to, it. It states that the sentencing court *'may have regard'* to any such period of remand when determining the restrictions on liberty to be imposed by a community order or youth rehabilitation order. This clearly confers discretion to take account of such period, rather than requiring the court to do so. 'Remanded in custody' has the meaning given in s. 242(2) (see **E2.14**). In *Hemmings* [2007] EWCA Crim 2413, [2008] 1 Cr App R (S) 106 (623), the maximum available penalty was six months, and D had spent the equivalent of that time on remand. The Court of Appeal quashed the community order imposed on sentence, saying that a community order was a form of punishment and, given the period spent on remand, further punishment was inappropriate. A conditional **E8.3** discharge was substituted. However, in *Rakib* [2011] EWCA Crim 870, [2012] 1 Cr App R (S) 1 (1), the Court of Appeal doubted *Hemmings*, and that case should now be regarded as confined to its particular facts. The Court in *Rakib* said that there were circumstances where a judge might properly make a community order on an offender who had spent even a substantial period of time on remand (173 days in that case) if there were strong rehabilitative or public protection (as opposed to punitive) reasons for a community disposal. *Rakib* was followed in *Pereira-Lee* [2016] EWCA Crim 1705, [2017] 1 Cr App R (S) 17 (122), but in the context of an offender who had spent a considerable period under a qualifying curfew rather than having spent time on remand. The Court of Appeal said that the judge had been entitled to pass the community order even though D had spent ten months under the qualifying curfew and a custodial sentence of five months would have been appropriate for the offence. The community order was upheld because it was in the public interest, and in D's own interest, that he should complete the programme recommended by the probation service. In the event of imposition of a custodial sentence following breach of the community order, remand days are deducted automatically from the custodial term (CJA 2013, s. 240ZA). It follows that it is no longer open to the judge imposing a community order to state that remand days will not count in the event of breach and resentencing.

E8.4 Section 150(1) provides that the power to make a community order or youth rehabilitation order is not available where the sentence for the offence:

(a) is fixed by law (murder);
(b) falls to be imposed under the FA 1968, s. 51A(2) (required custodial sentence for certain firearms offences);
(c) falls to be imposed under the PCC(S)A 2000, s. 110(2) or 111(2) (required custodial sentence for repeat Class A drug trafficking offences or repeat domestic burglaries);
(ca) falls to be imposed under the VCRA 2006, s. 29(4) or (6) (required custodial sentence in certain cases of using someone to mind a weapon);
(cb) falls to be imposed under the CJA 2003, s. 224A (life sentence for second listed offence); or
(d) falls to be imposed under the CJA 2003, ss. 225(2) or 226(2) (requirement to impose imprisonment for life or detention for life).

Section 150(2) provides that the power to make a community order is not exercisable in respect of an offence for which the sentence:

(a) falls to be imposed under the Prevention of Crime Act 1953, s. 1(2B) or 1A(5) (minimum sentence for certain offences involving offensive weapons), or

(b) falls to be imposed under the CJA 1988, s. 139(6B), 139A(5B) or 139AA(7) (minimum sentence for certain offences involving article with blade or point or offensive weapon).

Section 150 needs to be read in the light of the PCC(S)A 2000, s. 164, which makes it clear that any reference in that Act to a sentence falling to be imposed under these provisions is to be read in accordance with s. 305(4) of the CJA 2003. That subsection, in turn, says that a sentence falls to be imposed under s. 150(1)(b), (c) or (ca) or s. 150(2)(a) or (b) where it is required by the relevant provision but the court is *not* of the opinion mentioned therein. A sentence falls to be imposed under the CJA 2003, s. 224A or s. 225(2), if the court is obliged to pass a sentence of imprisonment for life, or, under s. 226(2), if the court is obliged to pass a sentence of detention for life. See further *Burns* [2009] EWCA Crim 1907.

E8.5 Section 150A restricts the power to make a community order by limiting it to (a) cases where the offence is punishable with imprisonment, or (b) in any other case, where s. 151 confers power to make such an order. Section 151 is not in force.

E8.6 **Reports** Section 156 of the CJA 2003 deals with pre-sentence reports and other requirements, with respect to community sentences. It is set out at **E1.26**. Whenever a court is considering whether to impose a community sentence, and what restrictions to put on the offender's liberty as part of that sentence, the court must take into account all the information available to it, including information about the offence and about the offender. Before imposing a community sentence, the sentencing court must normally obtain a pre-sentence report but the court need not obtain such a report if it considers it 'unnecessary' to do so. For guidance on the ordering of a pre-sentence report in this context see the Sentencing Council definitive guideline, *Imposition of Community and Custodial Sentences* (see Supplement, **SG9-1**), in particular the comments that 'in many cases a pre-sentence report will be pivotal in helping the court to decide whether to impose a community order', that 'it may be helpful to indicate to the National Probation Service the court's preliminary opinion as to which of the three sentencing ranges is relevant', but that 'ideally a pre-sentence report should be completed on the same day to avoid adjourning the case'.

Section 159 deals with disclosure of pre-sentence reports to the defence and the prosecution (see **E1.28**).

Section 160 applies where a report (other than a pre-sentence report) is made by an officer of a local probation board with a view to assisting any court in deciding how best to deal with an offender. This section provides for disclosure of the contents of that report to the defence (but not the prosecution).

Drug Testing Section 161 of the CJA 2003 provides for pre-sentence drug testing, but is not **E8.7** in force.

Community Order Requirements

Section 177 lists the requirements with which the court may order an offender aged 18 or over **E8.8** to comply during the course of a community sentence. They are:

(a) an unpaid work requirement (as defined in s. 199),
(aa) a rehabilitation activity requirement (s. 200A),
(b) [repealed],
(c) a programme requirement (s. 202),
(d) a prohibited activity requirement (s. 203),
(e) a curfew requirement (s. 204),
(f) an exclusion requirement (s. 205),
(g) a residence requirement (s. 206),
(ga) a foreign travel prohibition order requirement (s. 206A),
(h) a mental health treatment requirement (s. 207),
(i) a drug rehabilitation requirement (s. 209),
(j) an alcohol treatment requirement (s. 212),
(ja) an alcohol abstinence and monitoring requirement (s. 212A),
(k) [repealed],
(l) in a case where the offender is aged under 25, an attendance centre requirement (s. 214), and
(m) an electronic monitoring requirement (s. 215).

A number of general provisions apply, which are dealt with now, before turning to the details **E8.9** of the individual requirements. The CJA 2003, s. 177(2A), requires that, where the court makes a community order, the court must (a) include in the order at least one requirement imposed for the purpose of punishment, or (b) impose a fine for the offence in respect of which the community order is made, or (c) do both of those things, unless (by s. 177(2B)) there are exceptional circumstances which relate to the offence or to the offender which would make it unjust in all the circumstances for the court to impose punishment in the particular case and would make it unjust in all the circumstances to impose a fine for the offence concerned. Any community order must specify the local justice area in which the offender resides or will reside (s. 216(1)). The court must ensure, so far as practicable, that any requirement imposed in a community order is such as to avoid (a) any conflict with the offender's religious beliefs, or with the requirements of any other relevant order to which the offender may be subject, and (b) any interference with the times, if any, at which the offender normally works, attends school or any other educational establishment (s. 217(1)). The court which makes the relevant order must forthwith provide copies of the order to the offender and to the appropriate responsible officer (s. 219(1)), and to certain other persons affected by the order (s. 219(2) and sch. 14). There is also a general duty on the offender made subject to a community order to keep in touch with the responsible officer in accordance with such instructions as the offender may from time to time be given by that officer, and the offender must notify the officer of any change of address (s. 220). In respect of an offence committed on or after 1 February 2015, the ORA 2014, s. 18, amended the CJA 2003, s. 220, and inserted s. 220A, which creates a general duty on the offender to obtain permission before changing residence. A community order must specify a date (the 'end date'), not more than three years after the date of the order, by which all the requirements in it must have been complied with, but if a community order imposes two or more different requirements the order may specify a date by which each of those requirements must have been complied with, and the last of those days must be the same as the end date (s. 177(5) and (5A)). A community order ceases to be in force on the end date, but that is subject to s. 200(3) (duration of community order imposing unpaid work requirement): see **E8.11**. Before making a community order which contains two or more requirements, the court must consider whether, in the circumstances of the case, the requirements are compatible with each other (s. 177(6)). The Crown Court may include in the community order a direction that any breach is to be dealt with by the magistrates' court. If no such direction is made then any breach will be dealt with by the Crown Court (CJA 2003, sch. 8, paras. 5 to 8). In *Aslam* [2016] EWCA Crim 845, [2016] 2 Cr App R (S) 29 (267) the Court of Appeal said that it was unwise for a judge, when imposing a community order, to specify what the outcome would be in the event of breach of the order, since the nature of the breach and the extent of compliance with the requirements would always have to be taken into account.

E8.10 The definitive sentencing guideline, *Imposition of Community and Custodial Sentences* (see Supplement, **SG9-2**), provides that, 'The seriousness of the offence should be the initial factor in determining which requirements to include in a community order. Offence-specific guidelines refer to the three sentencing levels within the community order band based on offence seriousness (low, medium and high). The culpability and harm present in the offence(s) should be considered to identify which of the three sentencing levels within the community order band (low, medium or high) is appropriate.' Non-exhaustive examples of requirements that might be appropriate for each band are set out in the guideline.

E8.11 **Unpaid Work Requirement** The number of hours of unpaid work which may be ordered by the court under the CJA 2003, s. 199, must be not less than 40 and not more than 300 (s. 199(2)). Before inserting an unpaid work requirement into a community order, the court must, if it thinks necessary, hear from an appropriate officer that the offender is a suitable person to perform work under the requirement (s. 199(3)) and that local arrangements exist for the requirement to be carried out (s. 218(1)). The appropriate officer is an officer of the local probation board or an officer of a provider of probation services.

If the court makes community orders on the offender in respect of two or more offences of which the offender has been convicted on the same occasion and includes unpaid work requirements in each of them, the court may direct that the hours of work may run concurrently or consecutively, but the total number of hours must not exceed 300 (s. 199(5)). The work required should normally be completed within 12 months (s. 200(2)). A community order with a single requirement of unpaid work is always a community order for 12 months (*Khan* [2015] EWCA Crim 835, [2015] 2 Cr App R (S) 39 (313)), and completion of the hours in less than 12 months does not affect the legal status of the order. Unless revoked, a community order imposing an unpaid work requirement remains in force until the offender has worked under it for the number of hours specified (s. 200(3)). It is submitted that the effect of s. 200(3) is that a failure to complete the required number of hours within the normal 12 months places the offender in breach of the community order, and the probation service may then apply to the court either to initiate breach or to extend the 12-month period. The court may order an extension irrespective of whether the normal 12-month period under s. 200(2) has expired or whether the end date specified in the community order has passed (*National Probation Service v Crown Court at Blackfriars* [2019] EWHC 529 (Admin), [2019] 2 Cr App R (S) 24 (177)). The position is different in the case of an unpaid work requirement in a suspended sentence, as to which see **E6.15**.

Rehabilitation Activity Requirement In respect of an offence committed on or after 1 February 2015, the CJA 2003, s. 200A, provides for the rehabilitation activity requirement, which replaces the former activity requirement and supervision requirement. A rehabilitation activity requirement is a requirement that, during the relevant period, the offender must comply with any instructions given by the responsible officer to attend appointments or participate in activities or both. By s. 200A(11), the 'relevant period' means (i) in relation to a community order, the period for which the community order is in force, and (ii) in relation to a suspended sentence, the supervision period. Appointments and activities can take place at any time during the order. In *Lindsay* [2018] EWCA Crim 2171 the Court of Appeal noted that a rehabilitation activity requirement may be used solely as a means of ensuring compliance with instructions to attend supervision appointments. **E8.12**

The court does not prescribe the activities to be undertaken but must specify the maximum number of days the offender must complete. The activities include those which form part of an accredited programme (as set out in s. 202) and those whose purpose is reparative, such as restorative justice. 'Restorative justice' activities are defined in s. 200A(8) and (9). The responsible officer must obtain the agreement of any person other than the offender whose co-operation is necessary to comply with the requirement. The definitive sentencing guideline, *Imposition of Community and Custodial Sentences* (see Supplement, **SG9-2**), states that 'sentencers should ensure the activity length of a [rehabilitation activity requirement] is suitable and proportionate'.

Programme Requirement Section 202(1) of the CJA 2003 defines a programme requirement as a requirement that the offender must participate in an accredited programme at a specified place on a certain number of days. Section 202(3) and (6) provide that 'programme' means a systematic set of activities, and a programme requirement operates to require the offender, in accordance with instructions given by the responsible officer, to participate in the accredited programme as specified, on the number of days specified, and to comply with instructions given by the person in charge of that programme. Such programmes include those which address offending behaviour and cover topics such as anger management, sex offending, substance misuse and so on. It was held in *Price* [2013] EWCA Crim 1283, [2014] 1 Cr App R (S) 36 (216) that, while the responsible officer has a wide discretion as to the appropriate programme to follow and the place where it must be undertaken, the court is not relieved of the duty to specify that an accredited programme needs to be undertaken; failure to specify that a programme needed to be complied with, and to specify the number of days, rendered the order unlawful. **E8.13**

Prohibited Activity Requirement Section 203(1) of the CJA 2003 defines a prohibited activity requirement. The court can require an offender to refrain from taking part in certain activities, on a specified day or days (such as attending football matches), or over a specified period of time. The requirement may include forbidding the offender to contact a certain person, and may be that the offender does not possess, use or carry a firearm (s. 203(3)). Before inserting a prohibited activity requirement into a community sentence, the court must consult an officer of a local probation board or an officer of a provider of probation services. The primary purpose of a prohibited activity requirement is to prevent or reduce the risk of further offending, so the requirement should address, and be proportionate to, that risk (*Marney* [2016] EWCA Crim 1944). **E8.14**

E8.15 **Curfew Requirement** By the CJA 2003, s. 204, a curfew requirement is a requirement that the offender remain at a place specified by the court for certain periods of time. These periods of time must be not less than two hours and not more than 16 hours in any given day (s. 204(2)). An order might require the offender to be indoors at home between 5 p.m. and 9 a.m. A curfew requirement within a community order may not specify periods which fall outside the period of 12 months beginning with the date on which the order was made (s. 204(3)). Before inserting a curfew requirement into a community order, the court must obtain and consider information about the place proposed to be specified in the order, including information as to the attitude of persons likely to be affected by the enforced presence there of the offender (s. 204(6)). Where the court makes a community sentence which includes a curfew requirement, it *must* normally also impose an electronic monitoring requirement unless the court considers it inappropriate to do so (s. 177(3)). In *Finlay* [2015] EWCA Crim 328 the Court of Appeal said that the duration of a curfew requirement must be related to culpability and need. There was no justification on the facts for the imposition of an electronically monitored curfew for the maximum period of 12 months.

E8.16 **Exclusion Requirement** Under the CJA 2003, s. 205, an exclusion requirement is a requirement which prohibits an offender from entering a specified place, or places, or area (such as a specified town centre), during a period specified in the order. The order can exclude the offender from different places for different periods of time. It may also be used as a means of keeping the offender away from a specified person, in which case the person for whose protection the order is made should be given a copy of the requirement made by the court (s. 219 and sch. 14). An exclusion requirement cannot last longer than two years. The Secretary of State may by order amend the periods of time which can be specified in an exclusion requirement (s. 223(3)(b)). Where the court makes a community order which includes an exclusion requirement, it *must* normally also impose an electronic monitoring requirement unless the court considers it inappropriate to do so (s. 177(3)). Since the primary purpose of an exclusion requirement is to prevent, or at least reduce the risk of, further offending, such a requirement should be proportionate to the risk of further offending (*J* [2008] EWCA Crim 2002).

E8.17 **Residence Requirement** A residence requirement is a requirement that the offender resides at a place specified in the order for a specified period of time (CJA 2003, s. 206(2)). Before making such a requirement, the court must consider the home surroundings of the offender (s. 206(3)). A court may not specify residence at a hostel or other institution except on the recommendation of an officer of a local probation board or an officer of a provider of probation services (s. 206(4)).

E8.18 **Foreign Travel Prohibition Requirement** By inserting a foreign travel prohibition requirement (CJA 2003, s. 206 A) into a community order, the court will be able to prohibit the offender from travelling, on a day or days specified in the order, for a period specified, to any country or territory outside the British Islands, or to any specified country. A day so specified must not fall outside the period of 12 months from the date of the order, and a period so specified must not exceed 12 months from the date of the order.

E8.19 **Mental Health Treatment Requirement** The Sentencing Council's definitive guideline, *Sentencing Offenders with Mental Disorders, Developmental Disorders, or Neurological Impairments* (see Supplement, **SG7-1**), applies with effect from 1 October 2020. See annex C of the guideline. The mental health treatment requirement in the CJA 2003, s. 207, is a requirement that the offender must, during a period or periods specified in the order, submit to mental health treatment, by or under the direction of a registered medical practitioner or registered psychologist. The treatment may take the form of treatment as a resident patient in a hospital or care home within the meaning of the Care Standards Act 2000, treatment as a non-resident patient, or treatment under the direction of such registered medical practitioner or registered psychologist as may be specified (s. 207(2)). Before the court can insert a mental health treatment requirement, it must be satisfied that the mental condition of the offender (a) is such as requires and may be susceptible to treatment but (b) is not such as to warrant the making of a hospital order or a guardianship order. The court must also be satisfied that arrangements have been made or can be made for the treatment to be specified in the order, and that the offender has expressed willingness to comply with such an order (s. 207(3)). The supervising officer will supervise the offender only to the extent necessary for revoking or amending the order (s. 207(4)). For a case considering the requirement of willingness to comply with an order for treatment as a residential patient for two years, and where D suffered from severe autistic spectrum disorder, see *Wakefield Metropolitan District Council v DN* [2019] EWHC 2306 (Fam).

Section 208 deals with provision for the registered medical practitioner or chartered psychologist subsequently to change the place at which the offender is to receive treatment to a place where treatment can be better or more conveniently given. The registered medical practitioner or registered psychologist must notify in writing the responsible officer in advance, and the offender must consent to any such change.

Drug Rehabilitation Requirement By the CJA 2003, s. 209, the court may insert into a community sentence a drug rehabilitation requirement, which includes drug treatment and testing. It requires that, during a period specified in the order (the treatment and testing period), the offender must submit to treatment by or under the direction of a specified person having the necessary qualifications or experience and must provide samples, at such times and in such circumstances as are requested, to determine whether the offender has any drug in his or her body during that period (s. 209(1)). **E8.20**

Before imposing a drug rehabilitation requirement, the court must be satisfied that the offender is dependent on, or has a propensity to misuse, any controlled drug (as defined by the MDA 1971, s. 2) and that the dependency or propensity is such as requires and may be susceptible to treatment (s. 209(2)(a)). The court must also be satisfied that arrangements have been made or can be made for the proposed treatment (s. 209(2)(b)), and that the insertion of a drug rehabilitation requirement has been recommended to the court as being suitable for the offender by an officer of the local probation board or an officer of a provider of probation services (s. 209(2)(c)). The offender must express willingness to comply with the requirement (s. 209(2)(d)). There is no minimum period for the treatment and testing requirement. It may take the form of treatment as a resident in a specified institution or place, or treatment as a non-resident (s. 209(4)). The Secretary of State may by order amend the periods of time which can be specified in a drug rehabilitation requirement (s. 223(3)(c)).

It is submitted that Court of Appeal authorities relating to (the now repealed) drug treatment and testing orders under the PCC(S)A 2000 provide useful guidance as to the appropriate use of the drug rehabilitation requirement in a community order. In *A-G's Ref (No. 66 of 2003) (Boujettif)* [2003] EWCA Crim 3514, [2004] 2 Cr App R (S) 22 (106), the Court of Appeal said that 'judges should be alert to pass sentences which have a realistic prospect of reducing drug addiction whenever it is possible sensibly to do so' (at [14]). Many offences were committed by an offender under the influence of drugs, but the fact that the offender was so acting was not itself a reason for making an order; a necessary prerequisite was clear evidence that the offender was determined to come off drugs. Such an order was likely to have a better prospect of success early in a criminal career, but there would be exceptional cases. It would be very rare for the order to be appropriate for an offence involving serious violence or threat of violence with a lethal weapon, and the type of offence for which it would generally be appropriate would be an acquisitive offence carried out to obtain money for drugs. It might be appropriate even when a substantial number of offences had been committed, but was unlikely to be appropriate for a substantial number of serious offences which either involved violence or had a particularly damaging effect on the victim(s). **E8.21**

Section 210 states that the court may (and must if the treatment and testing period is more than 12 months) provide for the drug rehabilitation requirement to be reviewed periodically at intervals of not less than one month, provide for these reviews to be held by the court responsible for the order (a review hearing) and require the offender to attend each review hearing. An officer of a provider of probation services will provide a written report, which will include the results of the offender's drug tests, on the offender's progress under the requirement in advance **E8.22** of each review hearing (s. 210(1)). Section 211 sets out what is to happen at each review of a drug rehabilitation requirement. The court, after considering the review officer's report, may amend the requirement, but cannot do so unless the offender consents. If the offender does not consent to the proposed amendment to the requirement, the court may revoke the order and resentence the offender as if he or she had just been convicted (s. 211(3)). If it does so, the court must take into account the extent to which the offender has complied with the requirements of the order. If the court wishes it may impose a custodial sentence on the offender, provided the offence was punishable with imprisonment (s. 211(4)). If the offender's progress is satisfactory, the court can state that in future reviews can be on paper and without a hearing (s. 211(6)). If the offender's progress then becomes unsatisfactory and he or she is not present, the court can require the offender to attend in future (s. 211(7)). The court may also amend the order to provide for future review hearings (s. 211(8)).

E8.23 **Alcohol Treatment Requirement** By the CJA 2003, s. 212, the court may insert into a community order an alcohol treatment requirement. It requires that, during a period specified in the order, the offender must submit to treatment by or under the direction of a specified person having the necessary qualifications or experience with a view to the reduction or elimination of the offender's dependency on alcohol.

Before imposing an alcohol treatment requirement, the court must be satisfied that the offender is dependent on alcohol and that the dependency is such as requires and may be susceptible to treatment (s. 212(2)). The court must also be satisfied that arrangements have been made or can be made for the proposed treatment. The offender must express willingness to comply with the requirement (s. 212(3)). There is no minimum period for the alcohol treatment requirement. Treatment may take the form of treatment as a resident in a specified institution or place, or treatment as a non-resident or treatment by or under the direction of such person having the necessary qualification or experience (s. 212(5)).

E8.24 **Alcohol Abstinence and Monitoring Requirement** The CJA 2003, s. 212A, provides for the alcohol abstinence and monitoring requirement which, following a lengthy period of piloting and assessment in accordance with the LASPO 2012, s. 77, was brought fully into force from 19 May 2020 by SI 2020 No. 478. Even so, such a requirement may not be made unless necessary local arrangements, as specified by the Secretary of State, are in place (s. 212A(6)). By SI 2018 No. 210 the Secretary of State has prescribed that, in respect of the alcohol abstinence and monitoring requirement, such monitoring shall be carried out by means of a transdermal electronic tag, which is a device fitted to an offender to measure the level of alcohol contained in the offender's sweat. An alcohol abstinence and monitoring requirement may be imposed only if (i) the consumption of alcohol is an element of the offence for which the offender was convicted or was a factor that contributed to its commission, (ii) the offender is *not* dependent on alcohol, and (iii) an alcohol treatment requirement is not also imposed. The specified period must not exceed 120 days (s. 212A(2)).

E8.25 **Attendance Centre Requirement** Section 214 of the CJA 2003 provides for an attendance centre requirement to be inserted into a community order. An attendance centre requirement is available only in respect of offenders aged under 25 years (see s. 177 and the cross-heading before s. 214).

Under an attendance centre requirement in a community sentence, the offender must attend at an attendance centre specified in the relevant order for a specified number of hours which must be not less than 12 nor more than 36 (s. 214(2)). The offender must not be required to attend more than once on any single day or for more than three hours on any occasion (s. 214(6)). The court cannot make an attendance centre requirement unless satisfied that there is an attendance centre available locally (s. 218(3)) and that the attendance centre order specified is reasonably accessible to the offender (s. 214(3)). The responsible officer will notify the offender of the date and time required for the first attendance, and subsequent hours are fixed by the officer in charge of the attendance centre (s. 214(5) and (6)). Sections 221 and 222 set out the powers of the Secretary of State to continue to provide attendance centres and to regulate a number of aspects of their provision.

Electronic Monitoring Requirement Section 215(1)(a) of the CJA 2003 provides that the court passing a community sentence can order the electronic monitoring of the offender's compliance with any of the other requirements in the sentence. Where the court makes a community order which includes a curfew requirement or an exclusion requirement, it *must* also impose an electronic monitoring requirement, unless the court considers it inappropriate to do so (s. 177(3)), and it *may* do so in respect of any other requirement (s. 177(4)). The periods of electronic monitoring can be specified by the court in the order, or set by the responsible officer (s. 215(1)). If the court is proposing to include such a requirement but there is a person, other than the offender, without whose co-operation it will not be practicable to secure the monitoring, the requirement cannot be included without that person's consent (s. 215(2)). The court must ensure that electronic monitoring arrangements are available in the local area and that the necessary provision can be made under those arrangements (s. 218(4)). An electronic monitoring requirement imposed under s. 215(1)(a) may not be included in the order for the purposes of monitoring compliance with an alcohol abstinence and monitoring requirement, unless the electronic monitoring requirement is in place for the purpose of monitoring compliance with a different requirement in the order. No such restriction applies if the electronic monitoring requirement has been imposed by the court as a free-standing requirement under s. 215(1)(b). **E8.26**

Section 215(1)(b) provides that the court may, in the alternative to s. 215(1)(a) or in addition to it, order the electronic monitoring of the offender's whereabouts *otherwise* than for the purpose of securing compliance with other requirements under s. 215(1)(a). This means that electronic monitoring may be ordered as a free-standing requirement of a community order, a provision which was brought fully into force from 1 April 2019. The court must specify the duration of the period of electronic monitoring within the term of the order, and if there is a person, other than the offender, without whose co-operation it will not be practicable to secure the monitoring, the requirement cannot be included without that person's consent (s. 215(2)). The court must ensure that electronic monitoring arrangements are available in the local area and that the necessary provisions can be made under those arrangements (s. 218(4)).

ENFORCEMENT OF COMMUNITY ORDERS

Section 179 of the CJA 2003 introduces sch. 8 to that Act, which contains provisions dealing with breach, revocation and amendment of community orders, and the effect of the offender being convicted of a further offence. The Sentencing Council definitive guideline, *Breach Offences* (see Supplement, **SG15-2**), applies to offenders sentenced for breach of a community order on or after 1 October 2018, irrespective of the date of the offence. Conviction for a further offence does not constitute breach of a community order, but the guideline also provides guidance in relation to that matter. **E8.27**

Warning and Enforcement

By the CJA 2003, sch. 8, para. 5, if the responsible officer is of the opinion that the offender has failed without reasonable excuse to comply with any of the requirements of a community order, the officer must give a *warning* describing the circumstances of the failure, stating that the failure is unacceptable, and informing the offender that if within the next 12 months he or she again fails to comply with any requirement of the order, the offender will be brought back before the court. The responsible officer need not give a warning if a previous warning was given within the preceding 12 months or if the matter is referred to an enforcement officer. By para. 6, if there has been a warning, and within 12 months there is a further failure without reasonable excuse to comply, the responsible officer must refer the matter to an enforcement officer. The enforcement officer is then under a duty 'to consider the matter and, where appropriate, to cause an information to be laid' in respect of the failure to comply (para. 6A). Paragraphs 7 and 8 deal in detail with the arrangements for issue of summons or warrant by the justice of the peace or by the Crown Court. **E8.28**

In *West Yorkshire Probation Board v Robinson* [2009] EWHC 2517 (Admin), [2010] 4 All ER 1110 the Divisional Court said that the plain purpose of the warning provisions was to provide the probation officer with a discretion which could be exercised just once. If there is a further breach within the 12-month period, the matter must come back before the court. The court also noted that when the information is laid there is nothing in the legislation to prevent the probation service from setting out details of the breach which prompted the warning as well as details of the second breach. The mere fact that a defendant has lodged an appeal against conviction or against sentence does not amount to a reasonable excuse for non-compliance with a community order (*West Midlands Probation Board v Sadler* [2008] EWHC 15 (Admin), [2008] 3 All ER 1193).

Breach of Community Order

E8.29 The Crown Court may have included in the community order a direction that any breach of the order is to be dealt with by the magistrates' court. If no such direction is made, any breach will be dealt with in the Crown Court (CJA 2003, sch. 8, paras. 5 to 8). The CJA 2003, sch. 8, para. 9, describes the powers of a magistrates' court when dealing with a breach of a community order. The offender must be sentenced on the basis of his or her age when the original order was made. Any breach should either be admitted by the offender or be formally proved to the criminal standard of proof (*West Yorkshire Probation Board v Boulter* [2005] EWHC 2342 (Admin), [2006] 1 WLR 232) and the prosecution should be in a position to put before the court the facts of the original offence, at least in outline, as well as the facts of the breach (*Clarke* [1997] 2 Cr App R (S) 163). These two cases relate to community orders under earlier provisions, but it is submitted that they are equally applicable here. If it is proved to the satisfaction of the court before which the offender is brought that he or she has failed without reasonable excuse to comply with any of the requirements of the community order, the court *must* deal with the offender in one of the following ways (set out in para. 9(1)):

(a) by amending the terms of the community order so as to impose more onerous requirements which the court could include if it were then making the order;
(aa) by ordering the offender to pay a fine of an amount not exceeding £2,500;
(b) where the community order was made by a magistrates' court, by dealing with him, for the offence in respect of which the order was made, in any way in which the court could deal with him if he had just been convicted by it of the offence;
(c) where—
  (i) the community order was made by a magistrates' court,
  (ii) the offence in respect of which the order was made was not an offence punishable by imprisonment,
  (iii) the offender is aged 18 or over, and
  (iv) the offender has wilfully and persistently failed to comply with the requirements of the order,

  by dealing with him, in respect of that offence, by imposing a sentence of imprisonment or, in the case of a person aged at least 18 but under 21, detention in a young offender institution, for a term not exceeding 6 months.

The court *must* deal with the breach in one of the ways specified. There is no power to take 'no action' on breach. When dealing with the offender under para. 9(1), the magistrates' court must take into account the extent to which the offender has complied with the requirements of the community order (para. 9(2)). In dealing with an offender under para. 9(1)(a), the court may extend the duration of particular requirements (subject to statutory limitations on the maximum duration of particular requirements). The court may extend the duration of the order for up to six months beyond the original end date even if that involves the total duration of the order exceeding three years. Such an extension may be exercised only once (para. 9(3ZA), (3ZB) and (3ZC)). If the community order was made by the Crown Court, the magistrates' court may commit the offender in custody or release the offender on bail to appear before the Crown Court (para. 9(6)).

The Sentencing Council definitive guideline, *Breach Offences* (see Supplement, **SG15-2**), applies to offenders sentenced on or after 1 October 2018, irrespective of the date of the offence. In *Aslam* [2016] EWCA Crim 845, [2016] 2 Cr App R (S) 29 (267), the Court of Appeal said that a court dealing with breach must always consider the nature of the breach and the extent of compliance with the order. If the breach report indicated that the probation service wished to continue working with the offender, that should be given considerable weight.

Paragraph 10 describes the powers of the Crown Court when dealing with a breach of a com- **E8.30**
munity order. The offender must be sentenced on the basis of his or her age when the original order was made. Any breach should either be admitted by the offender or be formally proved to the criminal standard of proof (*West Yorkshire Probation Board v Boulter* [2005] EWHC 2342 (Admin), [2006] 1 WLR 232) and the prosecution should be in a position to put before the court the facts of the original offence, at least in outline, as well as the facts of the breach (*Clarke* [1997] 2 Cr App R (S) 163). These two cases relate to community orders under earlier provisions, but it is submitted that they are equally applicable here. If it is proved to the satisfaction of the court before which the offender is brought that he or she has failed without reasonable excuse to comply with any of the requirements of the community order, the court must deal with the offender in one of the following ways (set out in para. 10(1)):

(a) by amending the terms of the community order so as to impose more onerous requirements which the Crown Court could impose if it were then making the order; or
(aa) by ordering the offender to pay a fine of an amount not exceeding £2,500;
(b) by dealing with him, for the offence in respect of which the order was made, in any way in which he could have been dealt with for that offence by the court which made the order if the order had not been made; or
(c) where—
  (i) the offence in respect of which the order was made was not punishable with imprisonment,
  (ii) the offender is aged 18 or over,
  (iii) the offender has wilfully and persistently failed to comply with the requirements of the order,

  by dealing with him, in respect of that offence, by imposing a sentence of imprisonment or, in the case of a person aged at least 18 but under 21, detention in a young offender institution for a term not exceeding 6 months.

The court *must* deal with the breach in one of the ways specified. There is no power to take 'no action' on breach. When dealing with the offender under para. 10(1), the Crown Court must take into account the extent to which the offender has complied with the requirements of the community order (para. 10(2)). In dealing with an offender under para. 10(1)(a), the court may extend the duration of particular requirements (subject to statutory limitations on the maximum duration of particular requirements). The court may extend the duration of the order for up to six months beyond the original end date even if that involves the total duration of the order exceeding three years. Such an extension may be exercised only once (para. 10(3ZA), (3ZB) and (3ZC)). If the Crown Court proceeds under para. 10(1)(b) or (c), it must revoke the community order if it is still in force (para. 10(5)).

Since time served on remand is now deducted automatically from a custodial sentence under the CJA 2003, s. 240ZA (see **E2.12**), it is clear that the judge dealing with an offender for breach of a community order by revoking the order and imposing custody has no power to direct that the time spent on remand shall not count. The Sentencing Council definitive guideline, *Breach Offences* (see Supplement, **SG15-2**), applies to offenders sentenced on or after 1 October 2018, irrespective of the date of the offence. In *Aslam* [2016] EWCA Crim 845, [2016] 2 Cr App R (S) 29 (267) the Court of Appeal said that a court dealing with breach must always consider the nature of the breach and the extent of compliance with the order. If the breach report indicated that the probation service wished to continue working with the offender, that should be given considerable weight.

Revocation of Community Order

E8.31 Paragraphs 13 to 14 of sch. 8 to the CJA 2003 deal with revocation of a community order where, on application by the offender or an officer of a provider of probation services, having regard to changed circumstances since the order was made, it is in the interests of justice to revoke the order or to deal with the offender for the offence in some other way. These circumstances include the offender making good progress under the order or responding satisfactorily to the requirements in the order.

Paragraphs 21 to 23 deal with the powers of a magistrates' court and the Crown Court in circumstances where an offender subject to a community order has been convicted of a further offence. The power to deal with the offender depends upon the offender being convicted while the community order is still in force; it does not arise where the order has expired, even if the additional offence was committed while it was still current. If a magistrates' court is dealing with the subsequent offence, and the community order was made by a magistrates' court, the magistrates' court may revoke the community order, or revoke it and deal with the offender for that original offence in any way in which the offender could have been dealt with by the court for that offence (para. 21(2)). When dealing with the offender under para. 21(2), the magistrates' court must take into account the extent to which the offender has complied with the requirements of the community order (para. 21(3)). If the community order was made by the Crown Court, the magistrates' court may instead commit the offender in custody or release the offender on bail to appear before the Crown Court (para. 22(1)), but if that course is taken the magistrates should ensure that the offender is also committed in respect of the new offence (*De Brito* [2013] EWCA Crim 1134, [2014] 1 Cr App R (S) 38 (223)). If the Crown Court is dealing with the subsequent offence, it may revoke the community order, or revoke it and deal with the offender for that original offence in any way in which the offender could have been dealt with for the offence by the court which made the order (para. 23(2)). When dealing with the offender under para. 23(2), the Crown Court must take into account the extent to which the offender has complied with the requirements of the community order (para. 23(3)).

Amendment of Community Order

E8.32 Paragraphs 16 to 20 of sch. 8 to the CJA 2003 deal with various forms of amendment to requirements in a community order which may be made by an appropriate court, on application by the offender or an officer of a provider of probation services:

(a) because of a change in the offender's residence (para. 16), or
(b) for cancellation or replacement of certain requirements in the order (para. 17), or
(c) to change a treatment requirement on the report of a medical practitioner (para. 18), or
(d) for drug rehabilitation reviews to take place without a hearing (para. 19), or
(e) for amending the order by substituting a later end date than that originally specified under s. 177(5), which may have the effect of extending the order beyond the normal maximum of three years but not so as to extend the order by more than six months from the end date originally specified (para. 19A), and
(f) to extend the period of 12 months specified in s. 200(2) for completion of an unpaid work requirement (para. 20).

Section E9 Youth Rehabilitation Orders

INTRODUCTION

By the CJA 2003, s. 147, a 'community sentence' means a sentence which consists of or includes a 'community order' or a 'youth rehabilitation order'. For the general provisions relating to the imposition of any community sentence, especially the CJA 2003, ss. 148, 149 and 150, see **E8.2** *et seq.* A YRO is the appropriate community sentence for offenders aged under 18 when convicted. The maximum length of a YRO is three years. See the definitive guideline, *Sentencing Children and Young People*, paras 6.23 to 6.41 (see Supplement, **SG8-8**). **E9.1**

Criminal Justice and Immigration Act 2008, s. 1 **E9.2**

(1) Where a person aged under 18 is convicted of an offence, the court by or before which the person is convicted may in accordance with Schedule 1 make an order (in this part referred to as a 'youth rehabilitation order') imposing on the person any one or more of the following requirements—
(a) an activity requirement (see paragraphs 6 to 8 of Schedule 1),
(b) a supervision requirement (see paragraph 9 of that Schedule),
(c) in a case where the offender is aged 16 or 17 at the time of the conviction, an unpaid work requirement (see paragraph 10 of that Schedule),
(d) a programme requirement (see paragraph 11 of that Schedule),
(e) an attendance centre requirement (see paragraph 12 of that Schedule),
(f) a prohibited activity requirement (see paragraph 13 of that Schedule),
(g) a curfew requirement (see paragraph 14 of that Schedule),
(h) an exclusion requirement (see paragraph 15 of that Schedule),
(i) a residence requirement (see paragraph 16 of that Schedule),
(j) a local authority residence requirement (see paragraph 17 of that Schedule),
(k) a mental health treatment requirement (see paragraph 20 of that Schedule,
(l) a drug treatment requirement (see paragraph 22 of that Schedule),
(m) a drug testing requirement (see paragraph 23 of that Schedule),
(n) an intoxicating substance treatment requirement (see paragraph 24 of that Schedule), and
(o) an education requirement (see paragraph 25 of that Schedule).

(2) A youth rehabilitation order—
(a) may also impose an electronic monitoring requirement (see paragraph 26 of Schedule 1), and
(b) must do so if paragraph 2 of that Schedule so requires.

(3) A youth rehabilitation order may be—
(a) a youth rehabilitation order with intensive supervision and surveillance (see paragraph 3 of Schedule 1), or
(b) a youth rehabilitation order with fostering (see paragraph 4 of that Schedule)

(4) But a court may only make an order mentioned in subsection (3)(a) or (b) if—
(a) the court is dealing with the offender for an offence which is punishable with imprisonment,
(b) the court is of the opinion that the offence, or the combination of the offence and one or more offences associated with it, was so serious that, but for paragraph 3 or 4 of Schedule 1, a custodial sentence would be appropriate (or, if the offender was aged under 12 at the time of conviction, would be appropriate if the offender had been aged 12), and
(c) if the offender was aged under 15 at the time of conviction, the court is of the opinion that the offender is a persistent offender.

(5) Schedule 1 makes further provision about youth rehabilitation orders.

(6) This section is subject to—
(a) sections 148 and 150 of the Criminal Justice Act 2003 (restrictions on community sentences etc.), and
(b) the provisions of parts 1 and 3 of Schedule 1.

E9.3 Section 4 of the CJIA 2008 defines 'the responsible officer' in relation to a YRO. Section 5 sets out the duties of the responsible officer and the duties of the offender in respect of whom a YRO is in force.

Schedule 1, para. 30(1), states that a YRO takes effect on the day on which it is made, but that is subject to para. 30(1A) which provides that the court may order that the YRO take effect instead on a later date. Further, by para. 30(2), if ('in particular') a detention and training order is in force in respect of an offender, the court may order the YRO to take effect (a) when the period of supervision begins or (b) upon expiry of the term of the detention and training order. The phrase 'in particular' envisages that there are other (unspecified) circumstances in which a court may wish to order the YRO to take effect at a later date.

A court must not make a YRO in respect of an offender at a time when another YRO or a reparation order is in force without revoking the earlier order (para. 30(4)). Paragraph 31 deals with concurrent and consecutive YROs. A YRO must specify a date (the 'end date'), not more than three years after the date on which it is made, by which all the requirements in it must have been complied with (para. 32). Where a YRO imposes two or more different requirements, the YRO may specify a date by which each of those requirements must have been complied with, and the last of those days must be the same as the end date of the order. A YRO ceases to be in force at the end date, subject to para. 10(7), which creates an exception for a YRO with an unpaid work requirement (see **E9.8**). In the case of a YRO with intensive supervision and surveillance, the date by which that requirement must have been complied with must not be earlier than six months from the date of the making of the order.

E9.4 Paragraph 33 states that the order must specify the local justice area in which the offender resides or will reside. Paragraph 34 deals with provision of copies of the order. Paragraph 36 states that, where the Crown Court makes a YRO, it may include in the order a direction that further proceedings relating to the order be in a youth court, whether (a) in respect of breach or (b) on application for amendment or revocation of the order.

REQUIREMENTS

E9.5 Prior to making a YRO, a court must obtain and consider information about the family circumstances of the young person and the effect that a YRO would be likely to have on those circumstances (sch. 1, para. 28). Any requirement must (so far as practicable) avoid conflict with the young person's religious beliefs and avoid interference with times at which the young person would normally work or attend an educational establishment. Where an order contains more than one requirement (or more than one YRO is being made), the court must consider whether the requirements are compatible with each other (para. 29).

The definitive guideline, *Sentencing Children and Young People* (see Supplement, **SG8-8**), sets out a recommended approach to fixing the nature and extent of requirements in a YRO. The guideline indicates (at paras. 6.28 to 6.31) that there are three 'intervention levels'— standard, enhanced and intensive. The sentencing court will consider a pre-sentence report prepared by a member of the youth offending team, who will identify a recommended level of intervention for the court to consider.

Activity Requirement

E9.6 The CJIA 2008, sch. 1, paras. 6 to 8, provide that an activity requirement means a requirement that the offender must participate in an activity or activities, including residential exercises, at a place specified and for a number of days specified which (subject to one exception) must not exceed 90 days in total. The exception is where the court has made a YRO with intensive supervision and surveillance in which case an activity requirement may specify a number of days greater than 90 but not more than 180 (an extended activity requirement) (para. 3). A court may include an activity requirement only if it has consulted an appropriate officer and is satisfied both that it is feasible to secure compliance and that provision for the activities can be made (para. 8(3)). Where compliance with an activity requirement would involve the co-operation of a person other than the offender and the responsible officer, the court may not include such a requirement unless that other person consents.

Supervision Requirement

By the CJIA 2008, sch. 1, para. 9, a supervision requirement is a requirement to attend appointments as required by the responsible officer. This requirement lasts for the length of the order, a maximum of three years. **E9.7**

Unpaid Work Requirement

By the CJIA 2008, sch. 1, para. 10, an unpaid work requirement is a requirement for an offender aged 16 or 17 on the date of conviction to work a specified number of hours between 40 and 240. The work should normally be completed within 12 months. Paragraph 10(7) states that, unless revoked, a YRO with an unpaid work requirement remains in force until the offender has worked under it for the number of hours specified in it. See, by analogy, the case law applicable to community orders, at **E8.11**. The court must not impose such a requirement unless, after hearing (if the court thinks necessary) from an appropriate officer, it is satisfied that the offender is a suitable person to perform work under such a requirement and that provision can be made to perform work under such a requirement in the local area in which the offender resides or is to reside (para. 10(3)). **E9.8**

Programme Requirement

By the CJIA 2008, sch. 1, para. 11, a programme requirement is a requirement to participate in a programme, i.e. a systematic set of activities, at a specified place on a specified number of days. Where appropriate, this may include a requirement to reside at a specified place for a specified period. A court may include a programme requirement only if it is recommended by the appropriate officer and the court is satisfied that the programme is available to the offender at the place or places proposed. Where compliance with that requirement would involve the co-operation of a person other than the offender and the responsible officer, the court may not include such a requirement unless that other person consents. **E9.9**

Attendance Centre Requirement

By the CJIA 2008, sch. 1, para. 12, an attendance centre requirement is a requirement to attend an attendance centre for the specified period. This requires the young person to attend at the beginning of the period and then, during the period, to engage in an occupation or receive instruction as directed. For a young person aged 16 or over at the time of conviction, the minimum length is 12 hours and the maximum is 36 hours; at age 14 or 15, the minimum is 12 hours and the maximum is 24 hours; at age 13 or below, the maximum is 12 hours. A court may include an attendance centre requirement only where it has been notified that a place at a centre is available for the young person and it is satisfied that the centre is reasonably accessible. The first time at which the offender is required to attend is fixed by the responsible officer and subsequent hours are fixed by the officer in charge of the centre, but attendance must not involve attendance on more than one occasion in any one day or for more than three hours on any occasion. **E9.10**

Prohibited Activity Requirement

By the CJIA 2008, sch. 1, para. 13, a prohibited activity requirement is a requirement to refrain from specified activities on a specified day or days, or during a specified period. A court may include a prohibited activity requirement only if it has consulted an appropriate officer. The requirements that may be included include a requirement that the offender does not possess, use or carry a firearm. **E9.11**

Curfew Requirement

By the CJIA 2008, sch. 1, para. 14, a curfew requirement is a requirement to remain at a specified location for specified periods between two and 16 hours in any day. The periods may not fall outside 12 months beginning with the day on which the requirement is made. Before making a curfew **E9.12** requirement, a court must obtain and consider information about the place to be specified, and this must include information about the attitude of people likely to be affected by the enforced presence there of the offender. The court must also make an electronic monitoring requirement (see **E9.21**) unless the court considers it to be inappropriate or electronic monitoring is not available.

Exclusion Requirement

E9.13 By the CJIA 2008, sch. 1, para. 15, an exclusion requirement is a prohibition on entering a specified place during a specified period that must not exceed three months. The requirement may operate for different places on different days. The court must also make an electronic monitoring requirement (see **E9.21**) unless the court considers it to be inappropriate or electronic monitoring is not available.

Residence Requirement

E9.14 By the CJIA 2008, sch. 1, para. 16, a residence requirement is a requirement that the young person live with a specified person or in a specified place. The person named in the order must consent. If the court specifies a place where the offender must live, this is referred to as a 'place of residence requirement' and may be imposed only if the offender is aged 16 or over at the time of conviction. Before making a place of residence requirement the court must consider the home surroundings of the young person. It may not specify a hostel or institution as a place where an offender must reside except on the recommendation of an appropriate officer. Where the order requires residence at a specified place, it may also provide that it does not prohibit residence elsewhere with the prior approval of the responsible officer.

Local Authority Residence Requirement

E9.15 By the CJIA 2008, sch. 1, para. 17, a local authority residence requirement is a requirement to reside in accommodation provided by a local authority for a specified period. The period must not exceed six months, nor may it apply to a young person once that person attains the age of 18. The requirement may also state that the young person is *not* to reside with a specified person. This requirement may not be included unless the court is satisfied that the behaviour which constituted the offence was due to a significant extent to the circumstances in which the young person was living and that the requirement will assist in the young person's rehabilitation. Further, by para. 19, the young person must be legally represented when the court is considering whether to include this requirement, or representation was made available for the purposes of the proceedings under the LASPO 2012, Part 1 (legal aid), but was withdrawn because of the offender's conduct, or the offender has been informed of the right to apply for representation but has refused or failed to apply. Before a local authority residence requirement can be made the court must consult a parent or guardian of the offender (unless this is impracticable), and the local authority which is to receive the offender (para. 17(4)).

Mental Health Treatment Requirement

E9.16 By the CJIA 2008, sch. 1, para. 20, a mental health treatment requirement is a requirement for residential or non-residential treatment by or under the direction of a registered medical practitioner or a registered psychologist, for a period or periods specified in the order. A court must be satisfied that the offender's condition requires and may be susceptible to treatment, but is not such as to warrant the making of a hospital order or guardianship order. The court must be satisfied also that the necessary arrangements have or can be made and that the offender is willing to comply. Paragraph 21 provides for the possibility that, by arrangement of the medical practitioner or psychologist, and with the consent of the offender, the treatment may be provided or continued at an institution or place different from that specified in the order.

Drug Treatment Requirement

E9.17 By the CJIA 2008, sch. 1, para. 22, a drug treatment requirement is a requirement for residential or non-residential treatment with a view to reducing or eliminating the offender's dependency on (or propensity to misuse) controlled drugs as defined by the MDA 1971, s. 2. This requirement may be included only if arrangements can be made for the treatment, it has been recommended to the court by an appropriate officer and the young person has expressed willingness to comply. The court must be satisfied that the young person is dependent on (or has a tendency to misuse) controlled drugs and that the dependency is susceptible to treatment.

Drug Testing Requirement

By the CJIA 2008, sch. 1, para. 23, a drug testing requirement is a requirement to provide samples as directed, in order to find out whether there is a controlled drug in the young person's body during any treatment period. This requirement will operate alongside the drug treatment requirement. The court must specify the minimum number of samples in each month and may specify when, how, and what type of sample must be provided. As with the drug treatment requirement, it may be included only where the court has been notified that arrangements are in place to enable the testing to take place and the young person has expressed willingness to comply. **E9.18**

Intoxicating Substance Treatment Requirement

By the CJIA 2008, sch. 1, para. 24, an intoxicating substance treatment requirement is a requirement for residential or non-residential treatment with a view to reduce or eliminate the offender's dependency on (or propensity to misuse) intoxicating substances (i.e. alcohol and any other substance or product (but not a controlled drug), capable of being inhaled or otherwise used for the purpose of causing intoxication). This requirement may be included only if arrangements can be made for the treatment, it has been recommended to the court by an appropriate officer and the young person has expressed willingness to comply. The court must be satisfied that the young person is dependent on (or has a tendency to misuse) intoxicating substances and that the dependency is susceptible to treatment. **E9.19**

Education Requirement

By the CJIA 2008, sch. 1, para. 25, an education requirement is a requirement to comply during a period or periods specified in the order with 'approved education arrangements'. This means arrangements for the education of the offender which are made by the parent or guardian of the young person and approved by the local authority specified in the order. The court must consult the local authority and must be satisfied both that, in the view of the authority, suitable arrangements exist to provide full-time education suited to the young person and that such a requirement is necessary to secure the good conduct of the young person or to prevent further offending. The requirement cannot extend beyond compulsory school age. **E9.20**

Electronic Monitoring Requirement

By the CJIA 2008, sch. 1, para. 26, an electronic monitoring requirement is a requirement for electronic monitoring in order to secure compliance with another requirement in a YRO. The court must have been notified that arrangements are in place in the area and that provision can be made for the monitoring being proposed. Where compliance with the electronic monitoring requirement would involve the co-operation of a person other than the offender and the responsible officer, the court may not include such a requirement unless that other person consents. **E9.21**

Youth Rehabilitation Order with Intensive Supervision and Surveillance

The CJIA 2008, s. 1(3)(a), states that a YRO may be with intensive supervision and surveillance, but (by s. 1(4)) only if (a) the court is dealing with an offender for an offence which is punishable with imprisonment, (b) the court is of the opinion that the offence, or the combination of the offence and one or more offences associated with it was so serious that, but for para. 3 or 4 of sch. 1, a custodial sentence would be appropriate (or if the offender was aged under 12 at the time of conviction, would have been appropriate if the offender had been aged 12), and **E9.22**

(c) if the offender was aged under 15 at the time of conviction, the court is of the opinion that the offender is a persistent offender. By sch. 1, para. 3, a YRO with intensive supervision and surveillance may include an activity requirement, the maximum number of days being at least 90 but not more than 180. This is described as an extended activity requirement and the court must then also include a supervision requirement and a curfew requirement. The curfew must be accompanied by electronic monitoring unless the exceptions apply. Other requirements (but not the fostering requirement) may also be included subject to the general duty regarding compatibility and the statutory obligation to ensure that restrictions on liberty are commensurate with the seriousness of the offence(s). For an example of the application of these provisions, see *L* [2012] EWCA Crim 1336, [2013] 1 Cr App R (S) 56 (317).

As to the YRO with intensive supervision and surveillance, see the definitive guideline, *Sentencing Children and Young People* (see Supplement, **SG8-8**), at paras. 6.32 to 6.36.

Youth Rehabilitation Order with Fostering

E9.23 The CIJA 2008, s. 1(3)(b), states that a YRO may be with fostering, but only if the conditions set out in s. 1(4) are satisfied (see E9.22). In addition, by sch. 1, para. 4, the court must be satisfied that the behaviour which constituted the offence was due to a significant extent to the circumstances in which the young person was living and that the imposition of a fostering requirement would assist in the rehabilitation of the young person. The requirement may be included only where the court has been notified that arrangements are available in the area of the relevant local authority. Further, by para. 19, the young person must be legally represented when the court is considering whether to include this requirement, or representation was made available for the purposes of the proceedings under the LASPO 2012, Part 1 (legal aid), but was withdrawn because of the offender's conduct, or the offender has been informed of the right to apply for representation but has refused or failed to apply. Before a fostering requirement can be made the court must consult a parent or guardian of the offender (unless this is impracticable), and the local authority which is to receive the offender (para. 17(4)). A supervision requirement must also be made. The court must specify the period during which the young person must reside with a foster parent, which must not exceed 12 months nor operate after the young person has attained the age of 18.

See further the definitive guideline, *Sentencing Children and Young People* (see Supplement, **SG8-8**), at paras. 6.32 to 6.34 and 6.37 to 6.41.

BREACH, REVOCATION AND AMENDMENT OF ORDER

Warning and Enforcement

E9.24 Provisions on breach, revocation and amendment of community rehabilitation orders are to be found in the CJIA 2008, sch. 2. By para. 3, if the responsible officer is of the opinion that the offender has failed without reasonable excuse to comply with any of the community requirements of the suspended sentence, the officer must give a *warning* describing the circumstances of the failure, stating that the failure is unacceptable, and informing the offender that if within the next 12 months he or she again fails to comply with any requirement of the order, the offender will be brought back before the court. By para. 4, if there has been a warning, and within 12 months there is a further failure without reasonable excuse to comply, the responsible officer may issue a second warning. If there is a further failure within the original 12 months then the officer must cause an information to be laid before a magistrate, or before the Crown Court. Breach of a YRO is dealt with by the 'appropriate court', which is the Crown Court if the order was made *by that court and no direction* has been made under para. 36 of sch. 1 (para. 5(2) of sch. 2), or if the breach has been committed to the Crown Court by a magistrates' court (para. 7). Otherwise the appropriate court is a youth court if the offender is aged under 18 or a magistrates' court if the offender is aged 18 or over (para. 5(3)). Any breach should either be admitted by the offender or be formally proved to the criminal standard of proof (*West Yorkshire Probation Board v Boulter* [2005] EWHC 2342 (Admin), [2006] 1 WLR 232) and the prosecution should be in a position to put before the court the facts of the original offence, at least in outline, as well as the facts of the breach (*Clarke* [1997] 2 Cr App R (S) 163). These two cases relate to community orders under earlier provisions, but it is submitted that they are equally applicable to the YRO.

Breach of Youth Rehabilitation Order

The magistrates have power to deal with the offender on breach (CJIA 2008, sch. 2, para. 6(2)): **E9.25**

(a) by ordering payment of a fine not exceeding £2,500; or
(b) by amending the terms of the YRO so as to impose any requirement which could have been included in the order when it was made, in addition to, or in substitution for, any requirement or requirements already included in the order; or
(c) by dealing with the offender, for the offence in respect of which the order was made, in any way in which the court could have dealt with the offender for that offence (had the offender been before that court to be dealt with for it).

If the court proceeds under para. 6(2)(b), it must take into account the extent to which the offender has complied with the order (para. 6(4)). If the court is inserting an unpaid work requirement, and the order did not previously contain such a requirement, the minimum number of hours which may be specified is 20 (rather than 40 (para. 6(7)). If the original order did not contain an extended activity requirement or a fostering requirement, the court may not insert one upon breach. The court has power under para. 9(6A) to (6D) to amend the order, by extending its duration beyond three years, but not for a period of more than six months beyond the original end date. Such extension may be exercised only once.

If the court deals with the offender under para. 6(2)(c), it must revoke the original order (para. 6(11)).

If the court is proceeding under para. 6(2)(c) and the offender has wilfully and persistently failed to comply with the YRO, the court may impose a YRO with intensive supervision and surveillance even though the offence is non-imprisonable (para. 6(13)). If the original order is a YRO with intensive supervision and surveillance and the offence was punishable with imprisonment, the court may impose a custodial sentence (para. 6(14)). Further, if the original order is a YRO with intensive supervision and surveillance imposed following wilful and persistent breach of a YRO made for a non-imprisonable offence, the court may impose a detention and training order for four months.

The definitive guideline, *Sentencing Children and Young People* (see Supplement, **SG8-9**), states at para. 7.18 that '[t]he primary objective when sentencing for breach of a YRO is to ensure that the child or young person completes the requirements imposed by the court'. The guideline also states (at para. 7.17) that '[a] child or young person will almost certainly be considered to have "wilfully and persistently" breached a YRO where there have been three breaches that have demonstrated a lack of willingness to comply with the order that have resulted in an appearance before court'.

The powers of the Crown Court when dealing with breach are set out in the CJIA 2008, sch. 2, para. 8, and they are closely similar to those applicable in the magistrates' court.

By paras. 11 and 12 (dealing with the youth court and Crown Court respectively), if it appears to the appropriate court to be in the interests of justice to do so, having regard to circumstances which have arisen since the order was made, the appropriate court may on application by the offender or the responsible officer: **E9.26**

(a) revoke the order, or
(b) both revoke the order and deal with the offender, for the offence in respect of which the order was made, in any way in which it could have dealt with the offender for that offence (had the offender been before that court to be dealt with for it).

Circumstances in which the order may be revoked include where the offender has made good progress under the order.

An application for the amendment of the order may be made to the appropriate court by the offender or by the responsible officer (para. 13 in respect of the youth court and para. 14 in respect of the Crown Court). By para. 16A, the appropriate court may, on application by the offender or the responsible officer, amend the YRO by substituting a later date than the 'end date' originally specified under sch. 1, para. 32. The new date may fall more than three years after the date on which the order originally took effect, but must not fall outside the period of six months from the original end date. The appropriate court may, in the interests of justice and taking account of circumstances which have arisen since the order was made, extend beyond 12 months the period within which an unpaid work requirement must be completed (para. 17). See, by analogy, the case law applicable to community orders, at **E8.32**.

Section E10 Referral Orders

INTRODUCTION

E10.1 Under Part III of the PCC(S)A 2000, a youth court or, exceptionally, an adult magistrates' court, dealing with an offender under the age of 18 for whom this is the first conviction, is in certain circumstances required to sentence the young offender by ordering referral to a youth offender panel. In other circumstances the court has discretion to deal with the young offender in that way. The Crown Court has no power to make a referral order, whether directly, or by purporting to exercise the powers of a district judge under the Courts Act 2003, s. 66, to do so (*Dillon* [2017] EWCA Crim 2671, [2019] 1 Cr App R (S) 22 (155), followed and applied in *Koffi* [2019] EWCA Crim 300). The youth offender panel is composed of people with an interest or expertise in dealing with young people. The panel agrees a 'contract' with the offender and his or her family which is aimed at tackling the offending behaviour and its causes. The contract sets out certain requirements, which may include the young offender being required to apologise to, and carry out some form of reparation for, the victim of the offence, or to carry out community work, or to take part in family counselling or drug rehabilitation. These requirements are specified by the youth offender panel rather than the sentencing court. For further detail see the definitive guideline, *Sentencing Children and Young People* (see Supplement, **SG8-8**), at paras. 6.19 to 6.22.

REQUIREMENT TO REFER AND POWER TO REFER

E10.2 The circumstances which must exist before the court is *required* to make a referral order are set out in the PCC(S)A 2000, ss. 16 and 17(1). In respect of s. 16, they are as follows:

(a) that the youth court (or other magistrates' court) is dealing with an offender under the age of 18 where neither the offence nor any connected offence is one for which the sentence is fixed by law;
(b) the court is not proposing to pass a custodial sentence or make a hospital order in respect of the offence or any connected offence;
(c) the court is not proposing to grant an absolute or conditional discharge in respect of the offence;
(d) the compulsory referral conditions set out in s. 17 are satisfied; and
(e) the court has been notified by the Secretary of State that arrangements for the implementation of referral orders are available in the area in which the young offender resides or will reside.

E10.3 The compulsory referral conditions referred to are set out in s. 17. They are satisfied in relation to an offence if the offence is punishable with imprisonment and the offender:

(a) pleaded guilty to the offence and to any connected offence;
(b) has never been convicted by or before a court in the UK of any offence other than the offence and any connected offence, nor convicted by or before a court in another Member State of any offence.

E10.4 The circumstances which must exist before a court has *power* to make a referral order, but is not under a requirement to do so, are set out in ss. 16 and 17(2) and are satisfied in relation to an offence if:

(a) the offender is being dealt with by the court for the offence and one or more connected offences, whether or not any of them is an offence punishable with imprisonment;

(b) he pleaded guilty to at least one of the offences mentioned in (a) above, whether or not he has been previously found guilty of an offence.

According to the definitive guideline, *Sentencing Children and Young People* (see Supplement, **SG8-8**): 'As a referral order is a sentence that is only available upon pleading guilty there should be no further reduction of the sentence to reflect the guilty plea' (para. 5.15).

Making of Referral Orders

E10.5 The referral order must specify the relevant youth offending team responsible for implementing the order, require the offender to attend each of the appropriate meetings of the panel, and specify the period (the 'compliance period') during which the youth offender contract is to have effect. The minimum compliance period is three months and the maximum period is one year (s. 18(1)). The definitive guideline, *Sentencing Children and Young People* (see Supplement, **SG8-7**), provides guidance on the duration of a referral order. Paragraph 6.22 sets out a scale of offence seriousness ranging from 'low' to 'very high', with in each case a suggested length of referral order . When making the order, the court must explain to the young offender in ordinary language the effect of the order and the consequences which may follow if there is a failure to agree the terms of the contract or if the young offender breaches the terms of the contract (s. 18(3)). Where the court is dealing with the young offender for connected offences and is passing more than one referral order, the court may order that the specified periods of the orders shall run concurrently or consecutively to one another, but the total period shall not exceed 12 months (s. 18(4) to (7)). Where a court makes a referral order on an offender who is already subject to one, the court may direct that any youth offender contract under the new order is not to take effect until the earlier order is revoked or discharged (s. 18(3A).

In the case of a young offender who is under the age of 16 when the order is made, the court must, and in any other case may, make an order requiring the parent or guardian of the young offender (or a representative of a local authority where that local authority has parental responsibility and the young offender is in the authority's care or is provided by them with accommodation under any statutory provision) to attend the relevant meetings of the youth offender panel (s. 20(1) and (2)). This does not apply if the court is satisfied that in the circumstances of the case it would be unreasonable to require such attendance (s. 20(3)).

Mixing Referral Orders with Other Sentences or Orders

E10.6 There are very strict limitations on the mixing of a referral order with other sentences or orders. A referral order cannot be made where the court imposes a custodial sentence or hospital order on the offender for the offence or for any connected offence, or where it grants an absolute or conditional discharge for the offence (PCC(S)A 2000, s. 16(1)). Where the court makes a referral order for an offence, it must not at the same time deal with the offender for that offence in any of the 'prohibited ways', which are to impose any community sentence, fine, reparation order or conditional discharge or any requirement to attend a meeting under s. 1(2A) of the Street Offences Act 1959 (s. 19(4)). Where the court makes a referral order for an offence, it is required to deal with any associated offence either by making a referral order or by passing an absolute discharge, and it must not deal with any connected offence in any of the 'prohibited ways' (s. 19(3)). Whether in respect of the offence for which the referral order is made or for any connected offence, the court must not make an order binding over the young offender to keep the peace or binding over the parent or guardian of the young offender under s. 150. Finally, where there is a requirement rather than a power to make a referral order, the court may not defer passing sentence on the young offender, although other specified powers of adjournment, remand, remission for sentence and committal for sentence are unaffected (s. 19(7)). Notwithstanding all these restrictions, it would still be permissible for the court, at the same time as making a referral order, in an appropriate case to make a compensation order under s. 130, a restitution order under s. 148 (see **E17**) or a deprivation order under s. 143 (see **E18**).

By the CJA 2003, s. 324 and sch. 34, a court sentencing a young offender by referral order may at the same time make a parenting order under the CDA 1998, s. 8 (see **E14.1**).

BREACH, REVOCATION AND AMENDMENT OF REFERRAL ORDERS

Provisions for dealing with a young offender who is referred back to court in breach of a referral order, or is convicted while subject to a referral order, are set out in the PCC(S)A 2000, sch. 1. In the case of a young offender who is under the age of 18 when he or she appears in court having been referred back, the appropriate court is the youth court acting for the relevant local justice area and, if the young offender is 18 or over at that time, it is a magistrates' court acting for that area (para. 1). See the definitive guideline, *Sentencing Children and Young People* (see Supplement, **SG8-9**), at paras. 7.7 and 7.8. **E10.7**

Under the PCC(S)A 2000, ss. 27A and 27B, there is power to revoke referral orders and power to extend the contract period.

If it is proved to the satisfaction of the court that the youth offender panel was entitled to make the finding of breach of the referral order which resulted in the young offender being referred back to court, or that any discretion of the panel in that respect was exercised reasonably, the court may (provided that the young offender is present before it) revoke the referral order and may deal with the young offender in any other manner in which he or she could have been dealt with for that offence by the court which made the order (para. 5(5)(a)). The court must have regard to the circumstances of the referral back to court and, where a contract has taken effect, the extent of compliance with it (para. 5(5)(b)). The court may, on the other hand, decide not to revoke the referral order, either because the court does not endorse the decision of the panel to refer the order back to the court or for any other reason (para. 7). Alternatively, the court may, provided that the young offender is present in court, by para. 6A(2)(a), order the young offender to pay a fine not exceeding £2,500 or, by para. 6A(2)(b), extend the length of the period for which the contract has effect, but not so that the period becomes longer than 12 months. If the period has already expired (whether before or after the referral of the young offender back to court), the court may make an order under para. 6A(2)(a) but not para. 6A(2)(b).

Where an offender who is subject to a referral order is convicted of an offence in relation to which s. 16(1)(a) to (c) apply (see **E10.2**), the court dealing with the offence may sentence the offender for the new offence by extending the compliance period of the referral order (para. 10). The compliance period cannot be extended so as to exceed 12 months. Apart from cases falling within para. 10, the court will deal with the commission of a further offence under para. 14, which states that, unless the court sentencing for the new offence deals with the case by way of absolute or conditional discharge, the effect of dealing with the offender for the further offence is to revoke the referral order. The court may, if it is in the interests of justice, deal with the offender for the original offence in any other manner in which the offender could have been dealt with for that offence by the court which made the referral order (para. 14(3)). The court must have regard, where a contract has taken effect, to the extent to which the young offender has complied with its terms (para. 14(4)). See the definitive guideline, *Sentencing Children and Young People* (see Supplement, **SG8-9**), at paras 7.9 to 7.11. **E10.8**

The court which made the referral order may vary the youth offending team specified in the order because of the young offender's change of residence (s. 21(5)).

Section E11 Reparation Orders

POWER TO MAKE A REPARATION ORDER

E11.1 Under ss. 73 and 74 of the PCC(S)A 2000, the Crown Court and youth courts have power to impose a reparation order on an offender aged under 18 who is convicted of any offence except murder. See the definitive guideline, *Sentencing Children and Young People* (see Supplement, SG8-8), paras. 6.15 to 6.16.

E11.2 A reparation order is *not* a 'community sentence' within the meaning of the CJA 2003, s. 147.

Powers of Criminal Courts (Sentencing) Act 2000, ss. 73 and 74

73.—(1) Where a child or young person (that is to say, any person aged under 18) is convicted of an offence other than one for which the sentence is fixed by law, the court by or before which he is convicted may make an order requiring him to make reparation specified in the order—

(a) to a person or persons so specified; or

(b) to the community at large;

and any person so specified must be a person identified by the court as a victim of the offence or a person otherwise affected by it.

(2) An order under subsection (1) above is in this Act referred to as a 'reparation order'.

(3) In this section and section 74 below 'make reparation', in relation to an offender, means make reparation for the offence otherwise than by the payment of compensation; and the requirements that may be specified in a reparation order are subject to section 74(1) to (3).

(4) The court shall not make a reparation order in respect of the offender if it proposes—

(a) to pass on him a custodial sentence; or

(b) to make in respect of him a youth rehabilitation order or a referral order.

(4A) The court shall not make a reparation order in respect of the offender at a time when a youth rehabilitation order is in force in respect of him unless when it makes the reparation order it revokes the youth rehabilitation order.

(4B) Where a youth rehabilitation order is revoked under subsection (4A), paragraph 24 of Schedule 2 to the Criminal Justice and Immigration Act 2008 (breach, revocation or amendment of youth rehabilitation order) applies to the revocation.

(5) Before making a reparation order, a court shall obtain and consider a written report by an officer of a local probation board, an officer of a provider of probation services, a social worker of a local authority or a member of a youth offending team indicating—

(a) the type of work that is suitable for the offender; and

(b) the attitude of the victim or victims to the requirements proposed to be included in the order.

(6) The court shall not make a reparation order unless it has been notified by the Secretary of State that arrangements for implementing such orders are available in the area proposed to be named in the order under section 74(4) below and the notice has not been withdrawn.

(7) [Repealed.]

(8) The court shall give reasons if it does not make a reparation order in a case where it has power to do so.

74.—(1) A reparation order shall not require the offender—

(a) to work for more than 24 hours in aggregate; or

(b) to make reparation to any person without the consent of that person.

(2) Subject to subsection (1) above, requirements specified in a reparation order shall be such as in the opinion of the court are commensurate with the seriousness of the offence, or the combination of the offence and one or more offences associated with it.

(3) Requirements so specified shall, as far as practicable, be such as to avoid—

(a) any conflict with the offender's religious beliefs or with the requirements of any youth community order to which he may be subject; and

(b) any interference with the times, if any, at which he normally works or attends school or any other educational establishment.

(4) A reparation order shall name the local justice area in which it appears to the court making the order (or to the court amending under Schedule 8 to this Act any provision included in the order in pursuance of this subsection) that the offender resides or will reside.

(5) In this Act 'responsible officer', in relation to an offender subject to a reparation order, means one of the following who is specified in the order, namely—

(a) an officer of a local probation board or an officer of a provider of probation services (as the case may be);

(b) a social worker of a local authority;

(c) a member of a youth offending team.

...

(8) Any reparation required by a reparation order—

(a) shall be made under the supervision of the responsible officer; and

(b) shall be made within a period of three months from the date of the making of the order.

The wording of s. 73(2) indicates that the court may require reparation to be made to a person who is the victim of the offence, or to someone 'otherwise affected' by it. In a case of assault, this might include not just the victim of the assault but, instead or in addition, a bystander who suffered shock as a result of witnessing the assault. Section 74(2) makes it clear that the number of hours of work required of the young offender and, presumably, the nature of that work, must be such as in the opinion of the court are commensurate with the seriousness of the offence committed. A reparation order may be imposed without the court first obtaining a pre-sentence report but, by s. 73(5), before making a reparation order the court must obtain and consider a report from a probation officer, a social worker or a member of a youth offending team indicating the type of work which is suitable for the young offender, and the attitude of the victim, or victims, to the requirements to be included in the order. Before making a reparation order, the court must explain to the offender in ordinary language the effect of the order and of the requirements proposed to be included in it, the consequences which may follow if the offender fails to comply with any of those requirements, and that the order may be reviewed by the court on the application either of the offender or of the responsible officer (s. 73(7)). The consent of the offender to the making of the order is not required. Section 73(8) requires the court to give reasons why it has not made a reparation order in a case where it had power to do so. **E11.3**

Mixing Reparation Orders with Other Sentences or Orders

A reparation order cannot be combined with a custodial sentence, a youth rehabilitation order or a referral order, either for the same offence or, it is submitted, for different offences sentenced at the same time (s. 73(4) and (4A)). There is nothing to prevent a reparation order being combined with ancillary orders such as a compensation order or a deprivation order under s. 143. **E11.4**

BREACH AND REVOCATION OF REPARATION ORDERS

Arrangements for dealing with the offender's failure to comply with the terms of a reparation order are set out in the PCC(S)A 2000, sch. 8. See the definitive guideline, *Sentencing Children and Young People* (see Supplement, **SG8-9**), at paras 7.4 to 7.6. **E11.5**

Section E12 Absolute and Conditional Discharges

POWER TO GRANT ABSOLUTE AND CONDITIONAL DISCHARGES

E12.1 **Powers of Criminal Courts (Sentencing) Act 2000, s. 12**

(1) Where a court by or before which a person is convicted of an offence (not being an offence the sentence for which is fixed by law or falls to be imposed under a provision mentioned in subsection (1A)) is of the opinion, having regard to the circumstances including the nature of the offence and the character of the offender, that it is inexpedient to inflict punishment, the court may make an order either—
 (a) discharging him absolutely; or
 (b) if the court thinks fit, discharging him subject to the condition that he commits no offence during such period, not exceeding three years from the date of the order, as may be specified in the order.

(1A) The provisions referred to in subsection (1) are—
 (a) section 1(2B) or 1A(5) of the Prevention of Crime Act 1953;
 (b) section 51A(2) of the Firearms Act 1968;
 (c) section 139(6B), 139A(5B) or 139AA(7) of the Criminal Justice Act 1988;
 (d) section 110(2) or 111(2) of this Act;
 (e) section 224A, 225(2) or 226(2) of the Criminal Justice Act 2003;
 (f) section 29(4) or (6) of the Violent Crime Reduction Act 2006[;
 (g) section 8(2) of the Offensive Weapons Act 2019].

(2) Subsection 1(b) above has effect subject to section 66ZB(6) of the Crime and Disorder Act 1998 (youth cautions).

(3) An order discharging a person subject to such a condition as is mentioned in subsection (1)(b) above is in this Act referred to as 'an order for conditional discharge'; and the period specified in any such order is in this Act referred to as 'the period of conditional discharge'.

(4) [Repealed.]

(5) If (by virtue of section 13 below) a person conditionally discharged under this section is sentenced for the offence in respect of which the order for conditional discharge was made, that order shall cease to have effect.

A discharge is *not* a community sentence within the meaning of the CJA 2003, s. 147.

The reference in s. 12(1A)(g) to the Offensive Weapons Act 2019, s. 8(2), will come into effect from a date to be appointed. By s. 12(6), any court may, on making an order for conditional discharge, allow any person who consents to do so to give security for the good behaviour of the offender. When making such an order the court should specify the type of conduct from which the offender is to refrain (CrimPD VII, para. J.20; see Supplement, **CPD.VII.J**). Where a conditional discharge has been imposed on appeal, it shall be deemed, if made on appeal from a magistrates' court, to have been imposed by that court and, if made on appeal from the Crown Court or the Court of Appeal, to have been made by the Crown Court (s. 15(2)).

Use of Absolute Discharge

E12.2 The power to grant an absolute discharge is available to all criminal courts whatever the age of the offender and, apart from the exceptional cases in which the PCC(S)A 2000, s. 12(1) or (1A), *applies, whatever the offence committed*. Its imposition may reflect the triviality of the offence, the circumstances in which it came to be prosecuted, or special factors relating to the offender. Where an offence is dealt with by way of an absolute discharge, no surcharge is payable (see **E15.24**).

Use of Conditional Discharge

The power to grant a conditional discharge is available to all criminal courts whatever the age of the offender. The conditional discharge cannot be used in any of the cases set out in the PCC(S) A 2000, s. 12(1) or (1A) (see **E12.1**). By the CDA 1998, s. 66ZB(5) and (6), where (a) a person who has received two or more youth cautions is convicted of an offence committed within two years of the date of the last of those cautions or (b) a person who has received a youth conditional caution followed by a youth caution is convicted of an offence within two years of the date of the youth caution, the court must not deal with the offence by way of conditional discharge unless it is of the opinion that there are exceptional circumstances relating to the offence or the person that justify its doing so. A person convicted of breaching a prohibition in a sexual harm prevention order (SHPO) cannot be dealt with by way of a conditional discharge (SOA 2003, s. 103I(4)). **E12.3**

When a discharge is conditional, the sole condition is that the offender should commit no further offence during the period of the conditional discharge. No other condition or requirement may be inserted. The period of the conditional discharge is fixed by the court but must not exceed three years.

Combining Discharge with Other Sentences or Orders

A discharge cannot be combined with a punitive measure for the same offence (*Savage* (1983) 5 Cr App R (S) 216) except where permitted by statute. Thus a discharge cannot be combined with a custodial sentence, a community order or a fine (*Sanck* (1990) 12 Cr App R (S) 155). If, however, an offender is given a discharge for one of a number of offences, the court is free to exercise its normal powers of sentence with respect to the other offences (*Bainbridge* (1979) 1 Cr App R (S) 36). There are restrictions on the use of the discharge where the court is proposing to make a referral order (see **E10.6**). Section 12(7) and (8) of the PCC(S)A 2000 state that: **E12.4**

> (7) Nothing in this section shall be construed as preventing a court, on discharging an offender absolutely or conditionally in respect of any offence, imposing any disqualification on him or from making in respect of the offence an order under section 130, 143 or 148 below (compensation orders, deprivation orders and restitution orders) or from making in respect of the offence an unlawful profit order under section 4 of the Prevention of Social Housing Fraud Act 2013.
>
> (8) Nothing in this section shall be construed as preventing a court, on discharging an offender absolutely or conditionally in respect of an offence, from—
>
> (a) making an order under section 21A of the Prosecution of Offences Act 2015 (criminal courts charge), or
>
> (b) making an order for costs against the offender.

With respect to s. 12(8)(a) it should be noted that the criminal courts charge was effectively abolished with effect from 24 December 2015 by reducing the sum payable to £0. The wording of s. 12(7) permits the combination of a discharge with 'any disqualification'. Thus, for example, a discharge may be combined with an order for disqualification from driving. A discharge may be combined with an order to disqualify a person from acting as a company director or with a recommendation for deportation. It seems that a football banning order cannot be made where the offence has been dealt with by way of an absolute (but not a conditional) discharge (Football Spectators Act 1989, s. 14A(4) and (5)).

Section 12(7) makes no mention of confiscation orders (see **E19**). In *Varma* [2012] UKSC 42, [2013] 1 AC 463, the Supreme Court held that a confiscation order can be made on an offender who has been sentenced by way of a discharge.

BREACH OF CONDITIONAL DISCHARGE

A conditional discharge can be breached only by the conviction of the offender of a further offence committed during the period of the discharge (PCC(S)A 2000, s. 13(1)). The Sentencing **E12.5**

Council's definitive guideline, *Breach Offences* (see Supplement, **SG15-1**) is *not* applicable, but the Sentencing Council's definitive guideline *Sentencing Children and Young People* deals with breach of conditional discharge imposed upon on an offender aged under 18 (at para 7.1; see Supplement, **SG8-9**). A court dealing with the breach (the Crown Court if it made the conditional discharge, or the magistrates' court if it made it) may sentence the offender for the original offence in any manner in which it could have dealt with him or her if the offender had just been convicted before the court for that offence (s. 13(6)), but the Crown Court dealing with a person conditionally discharged by a magistrates' court is limited to the lower court's powers (s. 13(7)). One magistrates' court may deal with breach of a conditional discharge imposed by a different magistrates' court, but only with the consent of the original magistrates' court (s. 13(8)). Where an offender aged under 18 has been conditionally discharged by a magistrates' court in respect of an offence triable only on indictment in the case of an adult, and the offender has now attained the age of 18, the powers exercisable by the court under s. 13(6), (7) or (8) are to impose a fine for the original offence, or to deal with the offender in any way in which a magistrates' court could deal with him or her if it had just convicted the offender of an offence punishable with imprisonment for a term not exceeding six months (s. 13(9)). Sentencing for the original offence always terminates the conditional discharge itself, but any order for compensation or costs made at the time of the discharge remains valid (*Evans* [1963] 1 QB 979).

LIMITED EFFECT OF CONVICTION

E12.6 **Powers of Criminal Courts (Sentencing) Act 2000, s. 14**

(1) Subject to subsection (2) below, a conviction of an offence for which an order is made under section 12 above discharging the offender absolutely or conditionally shall be deemed not to be a conviction for any purpose other than the purposes of the proceedings in which the order is made and of any subsequent proceedings which may be taken against the offender under section 13 above.

(2) Where the offender was aged 18 or over at the time of his conviction of the offence in question and is subsequently sentenced (under section 13 above) for that offence, subsection (1) above shall cease to apply to the conviction.

(3) Without prejudice to subsections (1) and (2) above, the conviction of an offender who is discharged absolutely or conditionally under section 12 above shall in any event be disregarded for the purposes of any enactment or instrument which—

(a) imposes any disqualification or disability upon convicted persons; or

(b) authorises or requires the imposition of any such disqualification or disability.

(4) Subsections (1) to (3) above shall not affect—

(a) any right of any offender discharged absolutely or conditionally under section 12 above to rely on his conviction in bar of any subsequent proceedings for the same offence; or

(b) the restoration of any property in consequence of the conviction of any such offender; or

(c) . . .

An offender who has been discharged by the Crown Court or a magistrates' court may appeal against conviction, or sentence or any other ancillary order made in conjunction with the discharge (s. 14(6)).

It is submitted that the effect of s. 14 is that a previous conviction dealt with by way of an absolute discharge or a conditional discharge which was not subsequently breached does not count as a qualifying conviction for the purposes of s. 110 or 111 of the PCC(S)A 2000 (see **E5.1** and **E5.4**) or the Prevention of Crime Act 1953, s. 1(2A) to (2G) (see **E5.19**). Nor does it count as a conviction for a new offence committed within the operational period of a suspended sentence (see, by analogy, *Moore* [1995] QB 353).

Section E13 Binding Over

INTRODUCTION

This section deals with the power to bind over a person to keep the peace and the Crown Court's power to bind a person over to come up for judgment. The power to bind over a parent or guardian of an offender aged under 18 is dealt with at **E14.6**. **E13.1**

BINDING OVER TO KEEP THE PEACE

Power to Bind Over to Keep the Peace

Powers of a magistrates' court to bind over a person to keep the peace arise either on complaint (under the MCA 1980, s. 115) or of the court's own motion under common-law powers and pursuant to various statutes, most importantly the Justices of the Peace Act 1361. While an order under s. 115 can be made only after a full hearing of the complaint, where the court binds over of its own motion it may do so at any time before the conclusion of criminal proceedings, on withdrawal of the case by the prosecution, on a decision by the prosecution to offer no evidence, on an adjournment, or upon acquittal of the defendant. These powers, which are exercisable 'not by reason of any offence having been committed, but as a measure of preventive justice' (*Veater v Glennon* [1981] 2 All ER 304), may be used in a wide variety of situations, including as a sentencing option against a convicted offender. A person bound over to keep the peace may be made subject to a condition that the person shall not possess, use, or carry a firearm (FA 1968, s. 52(1)). Before imposing a binding over order the court must be satisfied so that it is sure that a breach of the peace involving violence, or an imminent threat of violence, has occurred, or that there is a real risk of violence in the future. Such violence might be perpetrated by the person to be bound over, or by a third party as a natural consequence of that person's conduct. When making an order binding over an individual to refrain from specified types of conduct or activities, the details of that conduct or those activities should be specified by the court in a written order, served on all relevant parties. The court should state its reasons (CrimPD VII, paras. J.2 to J.4: see Supplement, **CPD.VII.J**). **E13.2**

The person bound over is required to enter into a recognizance in an amount specified by the court, which will be forfeited if the person fails to keep the peace for a specified period. **E13.3**

Justices of the Peace Act 1968, s. 1

(7) It is hereby declared that any court of record having a criminal jurisdiction has, as ancillary to that jurisdiction, the power to bind over to be of good behaviour, a person who or whose case is before the court, by requiring him to enter into his own recognisances or to find sureties or both, and committing him to prison if he does not comply.

The Crown Court is a court of record (Senior Courts Act 1981, s. 45), so that both magistrates' courts and the Crown Court have powers to bind over offenders and others who are before the court. The Court of Appeal (Criminal Division) also possesses these powers (*Sharp* [1957] 1 QB 552). Those who may be bound over include an acquitted defendant (*Inner London Crown Court, ex parte Benjamin* (1986) 85 Cr App R 267), a defendant before the court in respect of whom the prosecution has been unable to proceed (*Lincoln Crown Court, ex parte Jude* [1998] 3 All ER 737), a witness before the court (*Sheldon v Bromfield*

Justices [1964] 2 QB 573), and a complainant (*Wilkins* [1907] 2 KB 380). On the other hand, the victim of an assault who is not a party to the proceedings and has not been called to give evidence cannot be bound over (*Swindon Crown Court, ex parte Pawitter Singh* [1984] 1 All ER 941), nor can a person who is the subject of a witness order, but who is in the event not required to give evidence (*Kingston-upon-Thames Crown Court, ex parte Guarino* [1986] Crim LR 325).

Bind Over: Procedural Requirements

E13.4 Where a court contemplates exercising its power to bind over a person, the court should give the person who would be subject to the order, and the prosecutor, the opportunity to make representations, both as to the making of the order and its terms. The court should also hear any admissible evidence the parties wish to call and which has not already been heard in the proceedings. Particularly careful consideration may be required where the individual who would be bound over is a witness in the proceedings (CrimPD VII, para. J.5). When fixing the amount of the recognizance courts should have regard to the individual's financial resources and should hear representations from the individual or legal representatives regarding finances. The court should fix the period of the recognizance and the sum of money to be forfeited upon breach at the time when it orders the bind over. There is no upper limit to the amount, save that it must be reasonable. A person may, therefore, be bound over in a sum which exceeds the maximum fine which could be exacted for the relevant offence (*Sandbach Justices, ex parte Williams* [1935] 2 KB 192).

The period for which the order may run is within the discretion of the court, but the length of the order should be proportionate to the harm sought to be avoided and should not generally exceed 12 months (CrimPD VII, para. J.4). Under the Magistrates' Courts (Appeals from Binding Over Orders) Act 1956, there is a right of appeal to the Crown Court against an order by a magistrates' court to enter into recognizances to keep the peace. Where the bind over is made by the Crown Court on sentence, an appeal lies to the Court of Appeal by virtue of Criminal Appeal Act 1968, s. 50(1).

Requirement for Additional Penalty

E13.5 It is unclear whether a convicted offender may be bound over to keep the peace without the passing of some other sentence. The wording of the Justices of the Peace Act 1968, s. 1(7) (see E13.3), indicates that the bind over is 'ancillary' to the court's criminal jurisdiction, and this may mean that a court should determine the penalty for the offence before the ancillary power of binding over to keep the peace is considered.

Refusal or Failure to Enter into Recognizance

E13.6 If there is any possibility that a person will refuse to enter into a recognizance, the court should consider alternatives to binding over (e.g., continuing with a prosecution). If there are no suitable alternatives and the person continues to refuse, the court may commit the person to custody. Before so acting the court should ensure that the person is given the opportunity to seek legal advice (CrimPD VII, paras. J.13 to J.15). In magistrates' courts, the power to impose custody derives from the Justices of the Peace Act 1968, s. 1(7), or the MCA 1980, s. 115(3). In the Crown Court this is a common-law power. Imprisonment cannot be imposed on a person who is under the age of 21 (PCC(S)A 2000, s. 89). Such a person may properly consent to be bound over even though refusal to consent could not lead to imprisonment (*Conlan v Oxford* (1983) 5 Cr App R (S) 237). A person aged between 18 and 20 inclusive who refuses to consent to be bound over by a magistrates' court may be detained under the PCC(S)A 2000, s. 108 (see *Howley v Oxford* (1985) 81 Cr App R 246 and E15.5). There is no power in these circumstances to order the detention of a person who is under the age of 18, but a magistrates' court may order such a person to attend at an attendance centre (s. 60(1)(b)).

Failure to Comply with Conditions of Order

Where there is an allegation of breach of a binding over order and this is contested, the court should be satisfied on the balance of probability that the defendant is in breach before making any order for forfeiture of the recognizance (CrimPD VII, para. J.9). If a person bound over by the Crown Court is adjudged to have failed to comply with the conditions of the order, the court may forfeit the whole or part of the recognizance, allow time for payment, direct payment by instalments or reduce or discharge the recognizance (PCC(S)A 2000, s. 139(1)), but it is not empowered to impose a prison term (*Finch* (1962) 47 Cr App R 58; *Gilbert* (1974) CSP D10–3A01). The Crown Court, when forfeiting a recognizance, must fix a term of imprisonment or detention, to be served in default (PCC(S)A 2000, s. 139(2)). See further **E13.4** and **E13.5**. **E13.7**

In a magistrates' court, a recognizance can be declared to be forfeit only by way of an order on complaint (MCA 1980, s. 120), by virtue of whichever power originally imposed the bind over. Such proceedings are civil in character, and require only the civil standard of proof (*Marlow Justices, ex parte O'Sullivan* [1984] QB 381), but the person concerned should be told the nature of the breach alleged and be given an opportunity to present evidence, call witnesses or give an explanation (*McGregor* [1945] 2 All ER 180). There is no right of appeal against an adjudication of forfeiture (*Durham Justices, ex parte Laurent* [1945] KB 33).

BINDING OVER TO COME UP FOR JUDGMENT

Powers to Bind Over to Come Up for Judgment

The common-law power to bind over to come up for judgment, which can be exercised only by the Crown Court, may be exercised in respect of any offence except one where the penalty is fixed by law. The effect of such an order is that the offender is bound over on recognizance on specified conditions. If one or more of the conditions is broken, the offender will be brought back before the court for sentence but, if none of the conditions is broken during the specified period, the offender will either not be sentenced for the offence, or will receive a nominal penalty. The *Crown Court Compendium: Sentencing* (December 2019), ch. S6-3, suggests that this power is most used where a person from another jurisdiction has committed an offence which is not of the most serious kind and has expressed a firm intention to return to his or her own country by a specified date. **E13.8**

A bind over to come up for judgment is in lieu of sentence, and it is therefore wrong to impose it in addition to a sentence for the offence (*Ayu* [1958] 3 All ER 636). An offender must consent to the making of the order, though consent would not be vitiated by a realistic expectation of a custodial sentence in the alternative (*Williams* [1982] 3 All ER 1092). If the Crown Court is considering binding over an individual to come up for judgment, the court should specify any conditions with which the individual is to comply in the meantime and not specify that the individual is to be of good behaviour. If the individual is not legally represented the court should explain the consequences of breach (CrimPD VII, paras. J.17 to J18).

If the offender is in breach of the order, the offender may forfeit the recognizance as well as being sentenced for the original offence. Where a person is brought back before the court on the ground that a recognizance has been broken, this must be proved beyond reasonable doubt (*McGarry* (1945) 30 Cr App R 187). The order is a 'sentence' made on conviction on indictment and an appeal lies to the Court of Appeal (Criminal Appeal Act 1968, s. 50(1); *Williams* [1982] 3 All ER 1092).

Section E14 Orders against Parents

PARENTING ORDERS

Power to Make Parenting Order

E14.1 Under the CDA 1998, s. 8(1), the Crown Court and youth courts have power to impose a parenting order on a parent or guardian of a child or young person where (a) a child safety order is made in respect of a child or the court determines, on an application under the CDA 1998, s. 12(6), that a child has failed to comply with any requirement included in such an order; (aa) a parental compensation order is made in relation to a child's behaviour; (b) an injunction is granted under the ABCPA 2014, s. 1, an order is made under s. 22 of that Act, or a SHPO is made in respect of child or young person; (c) a child or young person is convicted of an offence; or (d) a person is convicted of an offence under the Education Act 1996, s. 443 (failure to comply with school attendance order) or s. 444 (failure to secure regular attendance at school of registered pupil).

The focus in this section of this work is upon orders made following conviction. See the definitive guideline, *Sentencing Children and Young People* (see Supplement, **SG8-5**), at paras 3.1 to 3.4.

Before making a parenting order in any case the court must have been notified by the Secretary of State that arrangements for implementing such orders locally have been made.

Nature of Parenting Order

E14.2 **Crime and Disorder Act 1998, s. 8**

(4) A parenting order is an order which requires the parent—
- (a) to comply, for a period not exceeding twelve months, with such requirements as are specified in the order; and
- (b) subject to subsection (5) below, to attend, for a concurrent period not exceeding three months, such counselling or guidance sessions as may be specified in directions given by the responsible officer.

(5) A parenting order may, but need not, include such a requirement as is mentioned in subsection (4)(b) above in any case where a parenting order under this section or any other enactment has been made in respect of the parent on a previous occasion.

(6) The relevant condition is that the parenting order would be desirable in the interests of preventing—
- (a) in a case falling within paragraph (a), (aa) or (b) of subsection (1) above, any repetition of the kind of behaviour which led to the order being made or the injunction granted;
- (b) in the case falling within paragraph (c) of that subsection, the commission of any further offence by the child or young person;
- (c) in a case falling within paragraph (d) of that subsection, the commission of any further offence under section 443 or 444 of the Education Act 1996.

(7) The requirements that may be specified under subsection (4)(a) above are those which the court considers desirable in the interests of preventing any such repetition or, as the case may be, the commission of any such further offence.

(7A) A counselling or guidance programme which a parent is required to attend by virtue of subsection (4)(b) above may be or include a residential course but only if the court is satisfied—
- (a) that the attendance of the parent at a residential course is likely to be more effective than his attendance at a non-residential course in preventing any such repetition or, as the case may be, the commission of any such further offence, and

(b) that any interference with family life which is likely to result from the attendance of the parent at a residential course is proportionate in all the circumstances.

(8) [Meaning of 'responsible officer'.]

Requirements specified in s. 8(4)(a) might commonly include that the parent ensure that the child is accompanied to and from school each day, and is indoors by a certain hour in the evening. It is clear from s. 8(4)(b) and (5) that the court has no discretion to dispense with the requirement of attendance at counselling sessions, unless the parent has been the subject of a parenting order on a previous occasion. While s. 8 creates a power to impose a parenting order where the young offender is aged under 18, s. 9 goes further and places a duty on the court to make a parenting order where the young offender is aged under 16. If, however, the court is not satisfied that the 'relevant condition' is fulfilled (i.e. that the making of a parenting order would be desirable in the interests of preventing the commission of any further offence by the child or young person under 16) then the court must state in open court that it is not so satisfied, and why it is not (s. 9(1)).

By the CJA 2003, s. 324 and sch. 34, a youth court has power to make a parenting order at the same time as sentencing the young offender by referral order (see **E10**). If the offender is aged under 16, such that the youth court would normally be under a duty to impose a parenting order unless not satisfied that the 'relevant condition' is fulfilled, such a duty does *not* extend to cases where the youth court is considering whether to make a parenting order at the same time as sentencing the young offender by referral order.

Before making a parenting order the court need not obtain a pre-sentence report, but, by the CDA 1998, s. 9(2), before making a parenting order in a case where the young offender is aged under 16, the court must obtain and consider information about the young offender's family circumstances and the likely effect of the order on those circumstances. By s. 9(2A), if the court proposes to make a parenting order at the same time as sentencing the young offender by referral order, the court must obtain and consider a report by an appropriate officer indicating the requirements proposed to be included in the parenting order and indicating their desirability in preventing the commission of further offences by the young offender. Section 9(3) requires that before making a parenting order the court must explain to the parent in ordinary language the effect of the order and of the requirements proposed to be included in it, the consequences which may follow if the parent fails to comply with any of those requirements, and that the court has power to review the order on the application either of the parent or of the responsible officer. Requirements specified in, and directions given under, a parenting order shall, as far as practicable, be such as to avoid any conflict with the parent's religious beliefs and any interference with the times, if any, at which the parent normally works or attends an educational establishment (s. 9(4)). In *R (M) v Inner London Crown Court* [2003] EWHC 301 (Admin), the Divisional Court held that the making of parenting orders did not contravene the ECHR, Article 8, guaranteeing respect for private and family life. **E14.3**

Variation and Appeal

If, while the parenting order is in force, application is made to the court either by the responsible officer or by the parent, the court may, where appropriate, make an order discharging the parenting order or varying it by cancelling any provision included within it or by inserting in it any provision which could have been included in the order if the court had then the power to make it and were exercising that power (CDA 1998, s. 9(5)). If an application is made for the discharge of a parenting order and that application is dismissed, no fresh application for discharge can be made without the consent of the court which made the order (s. 9(6)). **E14.4**

A person in respect of whom a parenting order has been made by virtue of s. 8(1)(c) (commission of offence by offender aged under 18) has the same right of appeal against that order as if the offence that led to the making of the order were an offence committed by that person and the order were a sentence passed on that person for the offence (s. 10(4)).

Breach of Parenting Order

E14.5 If while a parenting order is in force the parent without reasonable excuse fails to comply with any requirement included in the order or specified in directions given by the responsible officer, the parent shall be liable on summary conviction to a fine not exceeding level 3 on the standard scale (CDA 1998, s. 9(7)). It would appear that in the absence of such failure to comply by the parent, commission of a further offence by the child does not constitute a breach of the parenting order.

BINDING OVER OF PARENT OR GUARDIAN OF OFFENDER AGED UNDER 18

E14.6 By the PCC(S)A 2000, s. 150(1), where a child or young person (a person aged under 18) is convicted of an offence the court may exercise its power to bind over his or her parent or guardian. Where the offender is aged under 16 when sentenced it shall be the duty of the court to bind over the parent or guardian of the young offender if it is satisfied that to do so would be desirable in the interests of preventing the commission by the young offender of further offences. If the court is not satisfied of that on the particular facts of the case, it should state in open court that it is not, and give reasons. Such an order cannot be made where the young offender has been sentenced by way of referral order (see **E10**).

By s. 150(2) and (3), the court is empowered to order the parent or guardian to enter into a recognizance (in a sum not exceeding £1,000) to take proper care of the offender and exercise proper control over the offender. The court should specify the actions which the parent or guardian is required to take (CrimPD VII, para. J.19: see Supplement, **CPD.VII.J**). Entry into the recognizance requires the consent of the parent or guardian, but if consent is refused and the court considers that refusal unreasonable, the parent or guardian may be punished by a fine not exceeding £1,000. A court which has passed a sentence which consists of or includes a youth rehabilitation order may include in the recognizance a provision that the young offender's parent or guardian ensure that the young offender complies with the requirements of that sentence. The maximum duration of the recognizance is until the offender reaches the age of 18, or for a period of three years, whichever is the shorter period (s. 150(4)).

In fixing the level of the recognizance, the court shall take into account, among other things, the means of the parent or guardian, whether doing so has the effect of increasing or reducing the level of the recognizance (s. 150(7)).

As far as forfeiture of the recognizance is concerned, s. 150(5) states that the MCA 1980, s. 120, shall apply in relation to a recognizance under s. 150 as it does to a recognizance to keep the peace (see **E13.7**). The court may order forfeiture of the whole, or part, of the recognizance, together with costs. A right of appeal against an order under s. 150 made by a magistrates' court is created by s. 150(8) and where the order is made by the Crown Court, a similar right applies under s. 150(9). A court may subsequently vary or revoke an order made under s. 150 on application by the parent or guardian, if it appears to be in the interests of justice to do so, having regard to any change in circumstances since the order was made (s. 150(10)).

FINANCIAL ORDER TO BE PAID BY PARENT OR GUARDIAN

E14.7 The parent or guardian of a child or young person may be ordered by the court to pay the fine, costs, compensation order or surcharge imposed upon a child or young person by virtue of the PCC(S)A 2000, s. 137. See the definitive guideline, *Sentencing Children and Young Persons* (see Supplement, **SG8-8**), at paras. 6.17 and 6.18.

Powers of Criminal Courts (Sentencing) Act 2000, s. 137

(1) Where—

(a) a child or young person (that is to say, any person aged under 18) is convicted of any offence for the commission of which a fine or costs may be imposed or a compensation order may be made, and

(b) the court is of opinion that the case would best be met by the imposition of a fine or costs or the making of such an order, whether with or without any other punishment, the court shall order that the fine, compensation or costs awarded be paid by the parent or guardian of the child or young person instead of by the child or young person himself, unless the court is satisfied—
   (i) that the parent or guardian cannot be found; or
   (ii) that it would be unreasonable to make an order for payment, having regard to the circumstances of the case.

Section 137(1A) provides that any surcharge (see **E15.24**) must be paid by the parent or guardian unless he or she cannot be found or it is unreasonable to require him or her to pay. Section 137(2) further provides that where a person under 18 would otherwise be required to pay a fine in respect of breach of a youth rehabilitation order, reparation order, an attendance centre order, attendance centre rules, or supervision requirements under a detention and training order, the court shall order the fine to be paid by the parent or guardian, subject to the same qualifications as appear in s. 137(1). The relevant provisions relating to the fixing of the level of a fine, costs etc. are to be read as if reference to the means of the offender were reference to the means of the parent or guardian (s. 138). The court may make a financial circumstances order with respect to the parent or guardian (s. 136(1)).

Section 137(3) states that in the case of a young person who has attained the age of 16 years, subsections (1) and (2) shall have effect as if, instead of imposing a duty, they conferred a power to make such an order. While an order under s. 137 may be made against a parent or guardian who has failed to attend court after having been required to do so, apart from such case no order should be made without giving the parent or guardian an opportunity of being heard (s. 137(4)). An appeal against an order made by a magistrates' court under s. 137 lies to the Crown Court (s. 137(6)) and an appeal against an order made by the Crown Court under s. 137 lies to the Court of Appeal (s. 137(7)).

E14.8 The court should not make an order under s. 137 against a parent or guardian without first considering the means of that parent or guardian (*Lenihan v West Yorkshire Metropolitan Police* (1981) 3 Cr App R (S) 42). It may be 'unreasonable' for the court to make an order under s. 137 in a case where the parent or guardian has done all that was reasonably possible to prevent the offending (*Sheffield Crown Court, ex parte Clarkson* (1986) 8 Cr App R (S) 454; *TA v DPP* [1997] 1 Cr App R (S) 1; *J-B* [2004] EWCA Crim 14, [2004] 2 Cr App R (S) 41 (211)). Assessment of the means of the parent or guardian, or assessment of the extent to which the parent or guardian has been neglectful of the offender, should be made on the basis of properly admissible evidence and not simply assumed from the pre-sentence report prepared upon the offender.

Section 137(8) provides that where a local authority has parental responsibility for a child or young person, and the child or young person is in the care of a local authority, or is provided with accommodation by it in the exercise of its social services functions, references to 'parent or guardian' should be construed as references to that local authority. In *D v DPP* (1995) 16 Cr App R (S) 1040, the Divisional Court held that a court should not make an order against the local authority in a case where the authority had done all that it reasonably and properly could to protect the public from the young offender and to keep the young offender from criminal ways; where the local authority so contends, it should be ready to provide evidence to the court of the steps which it has taken. In *Bedfordshire County Council v DPP* [1996] 1 Cr App R (S) 322, the Divisional Court further held that, before an order for payment by a local authority could be made, a causative link should normally be established between any fault proved on the part of the council and the offences committed. If no such causative fault was shown to the satisfaction of the court, it would be unreasonable to order compensation. 'Local authority' and 'parental responsibility' have the same meaning as in the Children Act 1989 (s. 137(9)).

Section E15 Fines and Surcharge

FINES IN THE CROWN COURT

Powers of Crown Court to Impose Fines

E15.1 **Criminal Justice Act 2003, s. 163**

> Where a person is convicted on indictment of any offence, other than an offence for which the sentence is fixed by law or falls to be imposed under section 110(2) or 111(2) of the Sentencing Act or under section 224A, 225(2) or 226(2) of this Act, the court, if not precluded from sentencing the offender by its exercise of some other power, may impose a fine instead of or in addition to dealing with him in any other way in which the court has power to deal with him, subject however to any enactment requiring the offender to be dealt with in a particular way.

Section 163 deals with the general power of the Crown Court to impose a fine on an offender convicted on indictment. In general, the Crown Court can impose a fine on an offender either instead of, or in addition to, dealing with the offender in any other way. There are some sentences which cannot be combined with a fine. A fine cannot be combined with a hospital order (Mental Health Act 1983, s. 37(8)), nor with a discharge when sentencing for a single offence (*McClelland* [1951] 1 All ER 557). There are also the exceptional cases, referred to in s. 163, where a fine is not available as a penalty.

E15.2 By the CLA 1977, s. 32(1), where a person convicted on indictment of any offence (whether triable only on indictment or either way) would, apart from that subsection, be liable to a fine not exceeding a specified amount, the person shall by virtue of that subsection be liable to a fine of any amount.

Powers of Criminal Courts (Sentencing) Act 2000, s. 139

> (1) Subject to the provisions of this section, if the Crown Court imposes a fine on any person or forfeits his recognisance, the court may make an order—
> (a) allowing time for the payment of the amount of the fine or the amount due under the recognisance;
> (b) directing payment of that amount by instalments of such amounts and on such dates respectively as may be specified in the order;
> (c) in the case of a recognisance, discharging the recognisance or reducing the amount due under it.

Power and Duty of Court to Fix Term in Default

E15.3 Although a term of imprisonment or detention to be served in default must be fixed in every case where the Crown Court imposes a fine or forfeits a recognizance (unless the offender is a limited company or is a person under 18 years of age), a failure to fix such a term does not invalidate the fine itself (*Hamilton* (1980) 2 Cr App R (S) 1). For the PCC(S)A 2000, s. 108, see **E15.5**, and for the table of maximum periods of imprisonment or detention in a young offender institution which may be fixed in default, see **E15.7**. The term which is fixed should relate to the whole sum, rather than to any instalment (*Power* (1986) 8 Cr App R (S) 8). Where fines are imposed in respect of more than one offence, the terms to be served in default may be ordered to run concurrently or consecutively and the court may order that the term(s) to be served in default may run concurrently or consecutively to any term of imprisonment or detention in a young offender institution to which the offender is sentenced at that time by the court or which he or she is currently serving (s. 139(5)). A term of imprisonment in default may be imposed consecutively to a maximum prison sentence imposed for the same offence (*Carver* [1955] 1 All ER 413). Consecutive custodial terms are, however, subject to the totality principle (see **E2.22**).

Where the Crown Court imposes a fine on committal for sentence from a magistrates' court, in circumstances where the powers of the Crown Court are limited to those of the magistrates' court, the Crown Court must specify the term to be served in default (s. 139(7)).

Powers of Criminal Courts (Sentencing) Act 2000, s. 139 **E15.4**

(2) Subject to the provisions of this section, if the Crown Court imposes a fine on any person or forfeits his recognisance, the court shall make an order fixing a term of imprisonment or of detention under section 108 above (detention of persons aged 18 to 20 for default) which he is to undergo if any sum which he is liable to pay is not duly paid or recovered.

(3) No person shall on the occasion when a fine is imposed on him or his recognisance is forfeited by the Crown Court be committed to prison or detained in pursuance of an order under subsection (2) above unless—
   (a) in the case of an offence punishable with imprisonment, he appears to the court to have sufficient means to pay the sum forthwith;
   (b) it appears to the court that he is unlikely to remain long enough at a place of abode in the United Kingdom to enable payment of the sum to be enforced by other methods; or
   (c) on the occasion when the order is made the court sentences him to immediate imprisonment, custody for life or detention in a young offender institution for that or another offence, or so sentences him for an offence in addition to forfeiting his recognisance, or he is already serving a sentence of custody for life or a term—
      (i) of imprisonment
      (ii) of detention in a young offender institution; or
      (iii) of detention under section 108 above.

Powers of Criminal Courts (Sentencing) Act 2000, s. 108 **E15.5**

(1) In any case where, but for section 89(1) above, a court would have power—
   (a) to commit a person aged at least 18 but under 21 to prison for default in payment of a fine or any other sum of money, or
   (b) to make an order fixing a term of imprisonment in the event of such a default by such a person, or
   (c) to commit such a person to prison for contempt of court or any kindred offence,

   the court shall have power, subject to subsection (3) below, to commit him to be detained under this section or, as the case may be, to make an order fixing a term of detention under this section in the event of default, for a term not exceeding the term of imprisonment.

(2) For the purposes of subsection (1) above, the power of a court to order a person to be imprisoned under section 23 of the Attachment of Earnings Act 1971 shall be taken to be a power to commit him to prison.

(3) No court shall commit a person to be detained under this section unless it is of the opinion that no other method of dealing with him is appropriate; and in forming any such opinion, the court—
   (a) shall take into account all such information about the circumstances of the default or contempt (including any aggravating or mitigating factors) as is available to it; and
   (b) may take into account any information about that person which is before it.

(4) Where a magistrates' court commits a person to be detained under this section, it shall—
   (a) state in open court the reason for its opinion that no other method of dealing with him is appropriate; and
   (b) cause that reason to be specified in the warrant of commitment and to be entered in the register.

There is no power to fix a term of detention under s. 108 in relation to an offender aged under 18 (*Basid* [1996] 1 Cr App R (S) 421; *Byas* (1995) 16 Cr App R (S) 869). It should be noted that, although s. 108(3) states that no court shall commit an offender to be detained unless 'no other method of dealing with him is appropriate', a sentence of detention under s. 108 is not a 'custodial sentence' for the purposes of the PCC(S)A 2000: s. 76(1) (see **E2.1**). The obligation in s. 83 (restriction on imposing custodial sentence on persons under 21 not legally represented), also does not apply in the present context.

E15.6 Where a court has power to commit a person aged at least 21 but under 25 to prison in default of payment of any sum of money, or a court would have power (but for the restrictions on imprisonment of young offenders and defaulters), to commit a person aged under 21 to prison in default of payment of any sum of money, or for failing to do or abstain from doing anything required to be done or left undone, the court may make an attendance centre order, requiring the offender to attend for such number of hours as may be specified (PCC(S)A 2000, s. 60(1)(b) and (c)). The aggregate number of hours of attendance must not be less than 12, except where the offender is aged under 14 and the court is of the opinion that 12 hours would be excessive having regard to age or other circumstances. The aggregate number of hours shall not exceed 12, except where the court is of the opinion, having regard to all the circumstances, that 12 hours would be inadequate, and in that case shall not exceed 24 hours (where the person is aged under 16) or 36 hours (where the person is aged 16 or over but under 21 or, where s. 60(1)(c) applies, under 25) (s. 60(3) and (4)). A person shall not be required to attend at an attendance centre more than once a day or for more than three hours on any occasion (s. 60(10)). If the defaulter pays the whole sum outstanding, the attendance centre order ceases to have effect, and payment of the sum outstanding shall reduce the number of hours proportionately (s. 60(12)).

Table of Maximum Periods in Default

E15.7 The periods set out in the following table are the maximum periods of imprisonment or detention to be served in default, applicable to the corresponding fine values (PCC(S)A 2000, s. 139(4)):

Not exceeding £200	7 days
Over £200, not exceeding £500	14 days
Over £500, not exceeding £1,000	28 days
Over £1,000, not exceeding £2,500	45 days
Over £2,500, not exceeding £5,000	3 months
Over £5,000, not exceeding £10,000	6 months
Over £10,000, not exceeding £20,000	12 months
Over £20,000, not exceeding £50,000	18 months
Over £50,000, not exceeding £100,000	2 years
Over £100,000, not exceeding £250,000	3 years
Over £250,000, not exceeding £1 million	5 years
Over £1 million	10 years

These are maximum periods, and the Crown Court has discretion to fix a shorter term within the appropriate bracket (*Szrajber* (1994) 15 Cr App R (S) 821). Where more than one fine is imposed, consecutive terms may be fixed. Where, exceptionally, a magistrates' court is empowered to fix a term in default of payment of a fine, the same periods apply, except that a default term in excess of 12 months cannot be exceeded (MCA 1980, sch. 4).

FINES IN THE MAGISTRATES' COURT

Powers of Magistrates' Court to Impose Fines

E15.8 With effect from 12 March 2015, when the LASPO 2012, s. 85, was brought into force (SI 2015 No. 504), limitations which had previously existed as to the maximum fine which could be imposed by a magistrates' court on a person aged 18 or over were removed. As from that date a 'relevant offence', whether a summary offence or an offence triable either way, previously punishable on summary conviction by a fine of £5,000 or more became punishable on or after that day by a fine of any amount (s. 85(1)). Nothing in s. 85(1) affects fines that may be imposed on a person aged under 18 (as to which see **E15.10**), or fines that may be imposed on a person convicted by a magistrates' court who is to be sentenced as if convicted on indictment.

A number of offences (mainly customs and revenue matters) where s. 85(1) has been disapplied and alternative provision made are set out in the Legal Aid, Sentencing and Punishment of Offenders Act 2012 (Fines on Summary Conviction) Regulations 2015 (SI 2015 No. 664), schs. 1 and 2. Revised maximum fines for other offences, where the maximum fine was formerly expressed as a proportion of £5,000, are set out in sch. 3. For offences where the maximum fine was previously expressed as a specified sum in excess of £5,000, the maximum fine becomes a fine of any amount (sch. 4). For offences where the maximum fine was previously expressed in some other way, see sch. 5.

Standard Scale of Maximum Fines for Summary Offences and Guideline Fines in Magistrates' Courts

The 'standard scale' of maximum fines for summary offences is contained in the CJA 1982, s. 37(2). The maximum fine which may be imposed for a summary offence is nearly always prescribed in the statute which creates the offence. If the statute refers only to punishment by means of imprisonment, there is an option to impose a level 3 fine instead (MCA 1980, s. 34(3)). **E15.9**

Level on the scale	*Amount of fine*
1	£200
2	£500
3	£1,000
4	£2,500
5	any amount

For offenders under 18, a special maximum fine applies (see **E15.10**).

The *Magistrates' Court Sentencing Guidelines* provide guideline fines for magistrates' courts expressed as one of three fine bands (A, B or C), although in some circumstances higher bands (D, E or F) may be used. Starting points and ranges are based upon percentage of relevant weekly income. For the applicable principles for fixing the level of a fine in a particular case, set out in the Explanatory Material in Part 5 of those Guidelines, see Supplement, **SG10-33** *et seq.*

FINING CHILDREN AND YOUNG PEOPLE

Under the PCC(S)A 2000, s. 135, where a person under 18 years of age is found guilty by a magistrates' court of an offence in respect of which the court would normally be empowered to impose a fine exceeding £1,000, the amount of the fine imposed shall not exceed £1,000. Section 135 also provides that, if the offender is under the age of 14 and the court could otherwise have imposed a fine exceeding £250, the amount of the fine imposed shall not exceed £250. **E15.10**

There is no limit upon the fine which may be imposed by a Crown Court upon a child or young person convicted on indictment.

See **E14.7** for the court's power to order that a fine be paid by a parent or guardian.

The definitive guideline, *Sentencing Children and Young People* (see Supplement, **SG8-8**), says that in practice many young people who offend have few financial resources, and a fine may not be the most appropriate disposal. A court should bear in mind that children and young people may have money that is specifically required for travel costs to school, college or apprenticeships and lunch expenses (paras. 6.17 and 6.18).

ENFORCEMENT OF FINES ETC.

E15.11 Enforcement of all fines is carried out by magistrates' courts, whether the fine was imposed in a magistrates' court or in the Crown Court. The procedure for enforcement of fines is contained in the MCA 1980, ss. 75 to 91, and the Courts Act 2003. Magistrates' courts are also responsible for enforcement of other financial orders imposed in a magistrates' court or in the Crown Court, including compensation orders and the surcharge, as specified in the Administration of Justice Act 1970, s. 41 and sch. 9, part 1. The magistrates' court which is responsible for enforcement is that court which imposed the fine or, if the fine was imposed by the Crown Court, the court specified in the fine order or, if none was specified, the court which committed the offender for trial or sentence to the Crown Court. If the offender is now residing in a different local justice area, a transfer of fine order may be made (MCA 1980, s. 89). When ordering a fine, the Crown Court must fix a term to be served in default (see E15.3) but a magistrates' court should not normally do so (ss. 82(3) and 77(2)).

When a fine is imposed it becomes due for payment immediately. The magistrates' court may, however, instead of requiring immediate payment, allow time for payment or order payment by instalments (s. 75(1)). Subsequently, further time may be given (s. 75(2)). If the court orders payment by instalments, default in any one instalment is taken to be a default in payment of all instalments then unpaid (s. 75(3)). By the Courts Act 2003, sch. 5, para. 12, the court must make a collection order in every case in which a fine or compensation order is imposed unless this would be impracticable or inappropriate. If an offender defaults on a collection order and is not already subject to an attachment of earnings order or order for deduction from qualifying state benefit, a fines officer must make an attachment of earnings order or make an order for benefit reduction. A court must in any event, unless it would be impracticable or inappropriate to do so, make an attachment of earnings order or order for deduction from qualifying state benefit whenever a compensation order has been imposed (sch. 5, para. 7A) or the court concludes that the offender is an existing defaulter and that the existing default cannot be disregarded (para. 8). In other cases, the court may make an attachment of earnings order or order for deduction from qualifying state benefit with the offender's consent (para. 9).

E15.12 If the offender fails to pay the whole or any part of the sum within the time allowed by the court, the magistrates' court may issue a summons or warrant requiring the offender to appear or issue a warrant to arrest the offender and bring him or her before the court to conduct a means inquiry to investigate the offender's ability to pay (MCA 1980, s. 83). The court may require that the offender produce evidence of income and outgoings. If the court orders the offender to produce a statement of means and the offender fails to do so, such failure is an offence punishable by a fine up to level 3 (s. 84(2)). If the offender knowingly or recklessly furnishes a statement which is false in a material particular, or knowingly fails to disclose any material fact, this is an offence punishable with imprisonment not exceeding four months, a fine not exceeding level 3, or both (s. 84(3)).

In the light of information received by the court at the means inquiry, the magistrates may grant further time to the offender for payment of the fine, or arrange payment by instalments, or reduce the amount of each instalment (s. 75). The court may remit the whole or any part of the fine having regard to any change in the offender's circumstances since conviction (s. 85(1)). This requirement may be satisfied where the defaulter's means have changed since the fine was imposed, or arrears have accumulated by the imposition of additional fines to the point where repayment of the total amount within a reasonable time becomes unlikely, or the defaulter is serving a period of imprisonment. There is no power to remit excise penalties, which include fines and back duty for using an untaxed vehicle. The court may also remit or reduce the fine where the fine was imposed in the absence of adequate information about the offender's means, either because the offender was convicted in his or her absence or failed to comply with an order to furnish information concerning his or her means. If the Crown Court imposed the fine, the magistrates may remit the fine in whole or in part only if they first obtain the consent of the Crown Court. It should be noted that the power to remit is restricted to fines and there is no equivalent power in respect of compensation orders (s. 85(4)).

The court may order the offender's *immediate imprisonment* (or, in the case of an offender aged 18 or over but under 21, detention under the PCC(S)A 2000, s. 108) for the term originally specified as being the time to be served in default or, if no such time was specified, a term specified by the court having regard to the table in the MCA 1980, sch. 4. This table corresponds to the first seven entries listed in the PCC(S)A 2000, s. 139(4), which is set out at **E15.7**. The period of commitment should be the shortest which in the view of the court is likely to succeed in obtaining payment, and the periods prescribed are to be regarded as maxima rather than the norm. The period of imprisonment may be suspended on condition that regular payments are made. Where such payments are not made the defaulter should be brought back before the court for consideration of whether the period of imprisonment should be implemented. An immediate committal to custody can be ordered only where the defaulter is already serving a custodial sentence (MCA 1980, s. 82(3)), if a means inquiry establishes that the defaulter has the means to pay immediately and the offence was punishable by imprisonment (s. 82(4)(a)), or where there has been a means inquiry and the court is satisfied that the default is due to wilful refusal or culpable neglect, and has considered or tried all other methods of enforcing payment and concluded that they are inappropriate or unsuccessful (s. 82(4)(b)).The other methods that the court is required to have considered or tried are money payment supervision order (s. 88), application for deduction from benefit, attachment of earnings order, distress warrant, the taking of civil proceedings, and, if the offender is aged under 25, an attendance centre order. **E15.13**

The requirement that the court must have 'considered or tried' all other methods of enforcement must be complied with and allows no room for the exercise of discretion (*Norwich Magistrates' Court, ex parte Tigger (formerly Lilly)* (1987) 151 JP 689). The warrant of commitment should state the grounds on which the court was satisfied that it was undesirable or impracticable to use the other methods of enforcement (*Oldham Justices, ex parte Cawley* [1997] QB 1). For an offender aged over 18 but under 21, the PCC(S)A 2000, s. 108(4), further requires the justices to specify in the warrant their reasons for concluding that detention is the only appropriate method of dealing with the defaulter (see **E15.5**). 'Wilful refusal', which means a deliberate defiance of the court order, or 'culpable neglect', which means a reckless disregard of the court order, must be established by proof beyond reasonable doubt (*South Tyneside Justices, ex parte Martin* (1995) *The Independent*, 20 September 1995).

FINES: SENTENCING PRINCIPLES

The CJA 2003, s. 162, provides that, where an individual has been convicted of an offence, the court may, before sentencing, make a 'financial circumstances order' with respect to the individual. Both magistrates' courts and the Crown Court may make such an order. Where a magistrates' court has been notified in accordance with the MCA 1980, s. 12(4), that an individual wishes to plead guilty without appearing before the court, the court also has power to make a financial circumstances order (s. 162(2)). A 'financial circumstances order' is an order requiring the relevant individual 'to give to the court, within such period as may be specified in the order, such a statement of his assets and other financial circumstances as the court may require' (s. 162(3)). An individual who, without reasonable excuse, fails to comply with a financial circumstances order is liable on summary conviction to a fine not exceeding level 3 (s. 162(4)), and if such individual makes, in pursuance of a financial circumstances order, a statement which **E15.14** the individual knows to be false in a material particular, is reckless as to its falsity or knowingly fails to disclose any material fact, the individual is liable on summary conviction to a fine not exceeding level 4 (s. 162(5)).

E15.15 Under the CJA 2003, s. 164, the following statutory principles are applicable to the fixing of fines, both in the Crown Court and in magistrates' courts.

Criminal Justice Act 2003, s. 164

(1) Before fixing the amount of any fine to be imposed on an offender who is an individual, a court must inquire into his financial circumstances.

(2) The amount of any fine fixed by a court must be such as, in the opinion of the court, reflects the seriousness of the offence.

(3) In fixing the amount of any fine to be imposed on an offender (whether an individual or other person), a court must take into account the circumstances of the case including, among other things, the financial circumstances of the offender so far as they are known, or appear, to the court.

(4) Subsection (3) above applies whether taking into account the financial circumstances of the offender has the effect of increasing or reducing the amount of the fine.

(4A) In applying subsection (3), a court must not reduce the amount of a fine on account of any surcharge it orders the offender to pay under section 161A, except to the extent that he has insufficient means to pay both.

(5) Where—

(a) an offender has been convicted in his absence in pursuance of section 11 or 12 of the Magistrates' Courts Act 1980 (non-appearance of accused),

(aa) an offender has been convicted in the offender's absence in proceedings conducted in accordance with section 16A of the Magistrates' Courts Act 1980 (trial by single justice on the papers), or

(b) an offender—

(i) has failed to furnish a statement of his financial circumstances in response to a request which is an official request for the purposes of section 20A of the Criminal Justice Act 1991 (offence of making false statement as to financial circumstances).

(ii) has failed to comply with an order under section 162(1) above, or

(iii) has otherwise failed to cooperate with the court in its inquiry into his financial circumstances,

and the court considers that it has insufficient information to make a proper determination of the financial circumstances of the offender, it may make such determination as it thinks fit.

For the MCA 1980, ss. 11 and 12, see **D22.14** and **D22.28** respectively. Section 164 is an important section concerned with fixing the amount of a fine. The court must inquire into the financial circumstances of an offender before fixing the amount of a fine. When determining the amount of the fine, the court must take into account the financial circumstances of the offender, the seriousness of the offence, and the circumstances of the case.

Proportionality to Gravity of Offence

E15.16 It is clear from s. 164(2) above that the first principle in relation to the use of the fine, whether in the Crown Court or in magistrates' courts, is that the selection of the fine as a sentence, and the determination of the appropriate level of any fine, should reflect the seriousness of the offence. A fine is an inappropriate penalty where the seriousness of the offence requires an immediate custodial sentence. An example is *A-G's Ref (No. 41 of 1994)* (1995) 16 Cr App R (S) 792, where fines totalling £350 had been imposed on the offender who had pleaded guilty to wounding with intent to cause grievous bodily harm. The Court of Appeal held that the sentence was 'absurd', and unduly lenient and substituted a custodial term of 30 months. On the other hand, there are cases which are not so serious as to justify a fine. In *Jamieson* (1975) 60 Cr App R 318, D, who had a clean record and substantial personal mitigation, was convicted of theft of a half bottle of whisky from a supermarket and fined £300. The Court of Appeal varied the sentence to a conditional discharge. It was held in *Karimu* [2017] EWCA Crim 1719 to have been wrong for the judge to impose a substantial fine on D, who was convicted of theft from a shop, because he had chosen to contest a 'hopeless case' and wasted the jury's time for two days. The Court of Appeal expressed some sympathy with the comments of the judge, but said that while those concerns might be relevant to an application for prosecution costs, they should not have affected the level of the fine imposed.

The imposition of the maximum available fine should be reserved for the most serious instances of the offence which are reasonably likely to occur. The existence of significant mitigation, such as the offender's guilty plea, should normally preclude the imposition of the maximum fine. In *Universal Salvage v Boothby* (1983) 5 Cr App R (S) 428, a company was fined for breach of regulations requiring it to have in its lorry proper equipment to record the journeys made. It was accepted that, in reliance on a letter from the relevant government department, the company had reasonably believed that the regulations were not applicable to them. Liability for the offence was strict, but the Divisional Court held that the circumstances provided considerable mitigation and that the imposition of the maximum fine on the company by the magistrates' court constituted an error of law.

Helpful guidance on the proper use of fines when imposed for several different offences **E15.17** was provided by the Court of Appeal in *Yorkshire Water Services* [2001] EWCA Crim 2635, [2002] 2 Cr App R (S) 13 (37), where the defendant company pleaded guilty to 17 counts of supplying water unfit for human consumption. The counts related to four separate incidents in which contaminated water was supplied, and a large number of households were affected. In reducing the total fine imposed from £119,000 to £80,000, Rougier J stated that the relevant considerations in setting the fine in a case of this sort were (1) the degree of culpability involved in the commission of the offence, (2) the damage done, considering both its spacial and temporal ambit together with the physical and economic ill effects, (3) the offender's previous record, including failure to heed warnings, (4) the need to strike a balance between a fitting punishment and avoiding counter-productive effects on the offending organisation, (5) the offender's plea, attitude, and performance after the event. In determining the appropriate fine, the court should determine the penalty for any one incident rather than 'tot up' the various manifestations of that incident. In *Chelmsford Crown Court, ex parte Birchall* (1989) 11 Cr App R (S) 510, the Divisional Court said that the application of a 'rigid formula' to the calculation of a fine was incorrect, even for a single offence, and it was wrong to apply it to each of ten offences and add the figures up: the courts had to consider all the circumstances and apply the principles of sentencing which were well known. The main importance of this decision is its clear endorsement of the application to fines of the totality principle. When fining in respect of a number of offences, the sentencer must review the total sentence and ensure that it remains proportionate to the totality of the offending, as well as being within the offender's capacity to pay. The CJA 2003, s. 166(3), reinforces this sentencing principle by stating that the court may mitigate the overall sentence 'by applying any rule of law as to the totality of sentences'.

Further guidance on the appropriate level of fines for particular offences may be obtained from the *Magistrates' Court Sentencing Guidelines* (see Supplement, **SG10-55** ***et seq.***).

Taking into Account Means of Offender

It is well established that while a fine is meant to be a punishment and it is perfectly proper for **E15.18** the offender to have to endure a degree of hardship in paying the fine, since 'one of the objects of the fine is to remind the offender that what he has done is wrong' (per Lord Lane CJ in *Olliver* (1989) 11 Cr App R (S) 10), the imposition of a fine which is quite beyond the means of the offender is wrong in principle.

Where the offender lacks the means to pay the level of fine which is proportionate to the **E15.19** seriousness of the offence, it is contrary to principle to impose a custodial sentence instead.

According to Roskill LJ in *Reeves* (1972) 56 Cr App R 366, where D had pleaded guilty to obtaining £600 by deception and had received a prison sentence of nine months, the comments made by the sentencer 'must plainly have indicated to the appellant... that he was being sent to prison not because the offence itself merited a sentence of immediate imprisonment but because he had not the financial wherewithal to pay a substantial fine. That... is, of course, completely wrong.'

Where the offender is well-off and paying the fine proportionate to the offence would cause little inconvenience, it is contrary to principle to impose a custodial sentence instead (*Gillies* [1965] Crim LR 64). It is, however, right to raise the level of the fine in such a case, so as to increase its impact on the offender, although the Court of Appeal in *Jerome* [2001] 1 Cr App R (S) 92 (316) said that there must remain some proportionality between the offence and the fine. In that case a fine of £10,000 imposed on a relatively affluent offender for handling stolen goods worth £2,739 was said to be manifestly excessive, and was reduced to £6,000. It should be noted that the CJA 2003, s. 164(4), makes it clear that the level of a fine should be adjusted upwards or downwards to take account of the offender's ability to pay. This does not, of course, affect the principle that an offender who is well-off should not be dealt with by financial penalty where the offence itself merits custody and an offender who is less well-off would have gone to prison (*Markwick* (1953) 37 Cr App R 125). The principle that a rich offender must not be permitted to 'buy his way out of prison' is a fundamental one, and it applies equally where the offender has family or friends who are able to meet a substantial fine (*Curtis* (1984) 6 Cr App R (S) 250).

In *Day* [2014] EWCA Crim 2683, [2015] 1 Cr App R (S) 53 (364), D was a very wealthy individual who admitted offences under the Wildlife and Countryside Act 1981; he had instructed his estate manager to carry out unauthorised works on a site of special scientific interest. A fine of £450,000, together with a similar figure for prosecution costs, was upheld by the Court of Appeal. The Court said that a proper assessment of harm and culpability had been made. The judge had proceeded on the assumption that D had assets of £300 million. Since that assumption was not challenged by the defence, the judge had been entitled to proceed as he did, but the Court said that it would have been preferable to have made a financial circumstances order requiring a detailed statement of D's assets and income covering a five-year period. In the case of a very wealthy individual, as with a large company, the fine should be paid immediately, or within a few days, unless there was cogent evidence that more time was required. The requirement that the court should adjust the level of the fine in accordance with the offender's means entails that the court should not assume that someone other than the offender will be paying the fine. In *Charambous* (1984) 6 Cr App R (S) 389, where a fine was imposed on a married woman who had limited income of her own, the Court of Appeal stressed that the fine must reflect the offender's means and was not a fine on the family.

In the case of a corporate offender, the court must take into account whether the corporation operates primarily for the purpose of making a profit for its shareholders, or whether a fine would have to be met from public funds and so might be said to harm the public. *Sellafield Ltd* [2014] EWCA Crim 49 provides a helpful analysis of how this issue should impact on sentence. If a defendant company wishes to make a submission as to its ability to pay a fine, it should supply copies of its accounts and other financial information to the court. Where such information has been withheld, the court is entitled to assume that the company is able to pay any fine the court is minded to impose (*F Howe and Sons (Engineers) Ltd* [1999] 2 All ER 249). The definitive sentencing guideline, *Health and Safety Offences, Corporate Manslaughter and Food Safety and Hygiene Offences*, provides guidance as to the appropriate financial information which should be provided to the court by a corporate defendant convicted of one of the offences within the guideline and the approach to be taken by the court in setting the appropriate level of fine. See, e.g., Step Two of the guideline on sentencing corporate manslaughter (see Supplement, **SG28-2**).

The Court of Appeal in *Tata Steel UK Ltd* [2017] EWCA Crim 704, [2017] 2 Cr App R (S) 29 (233) gave guidance in relation to imposition of a fine for two health and safety breaches committed by a 'very large organisation'. The starting point for the fine might warrant adjustment to reflect the true size of the organisation. In particular, an upwards adjustment might be called for in the case of a very large organisation so as to produce a proportionate fine, bringing home the message to management and shareholders of the need to comply with health and safety legislation. Then in accordance with the CJA 2003, s. 164, the financial circumstances of the offender must be taken into account. A downwards adjustment might be called for where an organisation had a small profit margin relative to its turnover, or where the business was loss-making. There was a reduction for an early guilty plea and totality must be taken into account. In the instant case Tata Steel UK was wholly owned by Tata Steel Europe and the ultimate parent company was Tata Steel Ltd. The Court of Appeal said that this was one of the exceptional cases within Step Two in the guideline where the resources of the parent company could properly be taken into account. The total fine was reduced to £1.5 million. **E15.20**

Sellafield Ltd [2014] EWCA Crim 49 and *Southern Water Services* [2014] EWCA Crim 120, [2014] 2 Cr App R (S) 29 (235) also provide good examples of the approach which a court should take to sentencing corporations (in these cases for breaches of environmental or health and safety regulations). Familiar issues of harm and culpability of the corporation determine the matter of offence seriousness. Culpability includes previous similar breaches of relevant regulations. See also *Thames Water Utilities Ltd* [2015] EWCA Crim 960, [2015] 1 WLR 4411, where the Court of Appeal noted that the usual starting points and ranges of fines expressly do not apply to 'very large' commercial organisations, such as the offending company, which pleaded guilty to environmental pollution through negligent discharge of untreated sewage. The company's record for such offences was not a good one and despite significant mitigation and a prompt guilty plea the fine of £250,000 imposed was not only upheld, but described as lenient.

Instalments Should Require Payment within a Reasonable Time

The *Magistrates' Court Sentencing Guidelines* state that 'normally a fine should be of an amount that is capable of being paid within 12 months' (see Supplement, **SG10-34**). In *Olliver* (1989) 11 Cr App R (S) 10, however, it was held by the Court of Appeal that the maximum time is not limited to 12 months. Lord Lane CJ said (at p. 15): **E15.21**

> . . . there is nothing wrong in principle in the period of payment being longer, indeed much longer than one year, providing it is not an undue burden and so too severe a punishment having regard to the nature of the offence and the nature of the offender. Certainly it seems to us that a two-year period will seldom be too long, and in an appropriate case three years will be unassailable, again of course depending on the nature of the offender and the nature of the offence.

There is an exception in relation to corporate defendants, where the fine may be payable over a substantially longer period than for an individual (*Rollco Screw and Rivet Co.* [1999] 2 Cr App R (S) 436).

Combining Fines with Other Sentences or Orders

For restrictions imposed by statute on combining a fine with certain custodial sentences see the CJA 2003, s. 163, at **E15.1**. Apart from those cases, there is no restriction on combining fines with imprisonment or other custodial sentences, whether in respect of the same offence or different offences sentenced on the same occasion, though this will not often be a desirable combination, since incarceration may well deprive the offender of the means to pay the fine. **E15.22**

E15.23 It is possible, whether sentencing for a single offence or for different offences sentenced on the same occasion, to combine a fine with a suspended prison sentence or a community order. The Court of Appeal in *Butt* [2018] EWCA Crim 1617, [2019] 1 Cr App R (S) 4 (27), said that this approach may be apt where the offending is related to the offender's business or employment, when dealing with offenders of substantial means, or where the sentence thereby allows an offender to continue in well-remunerated work. A fine cannot in law be combined with a discharge when sentencing for a single offence (*McClelland* [1951] 1 All ER 557), although it may be combined with a discharge when sentencing for different offences sentenced on the same occasion. A fine cannot be combined with a hospital order (Mental Health Act 1983, s. 37(8)).

A fine and a compensation order may be combined. The PCC(S)A 2000, s. 130(12), provides that, where the offender has insufficient means to pay both an appropriate fine and appropriate compensation, the court shall give preference to compensation. In a particular case this will mean that the level of the fine is reduced to enable the full compensation order to stand, or that no fine is ordered and the compensation order stands alone. Fines may be combined with other financial orders, such as an order to pay the costs of the prosecution, though the court must consider the total effect of the orders it is making, and should ensure that the whole sum is one that the offender can afford to pay. A fine may also be combined with a restitution order under the PCC(S)A 2000, s. 148(1), with a deprivation order under s. 143, and with a disqualification order, where the vehicle was used for the purposes of crime, under s. 147.

SURCHARGE

E15.24 When imposing sentence on an offender a magistrates' court or the Crown Court is normally required also to impose a surcharge.

Criminal Justice Act 2003, s. 161A

(1) A court when dealing with a person for one or more offences must also (subject to subsections (2) and (3)) order him to pay a surcharge.
(2) Subsection (1) does not apply in such cases as may be prescribed by an order made by the Secretary of State.
(3) Where a court dealing with an offender considers—
  (a) that it would be appropriate to make one or more of a compensation order, an unlawful profit order and a slavery and trafficking reparation order, but
  (b) that he has insufficient means to pay both the surcharge and appropriate amounts under such of those orders as it would be appropriate to make,

  the court must reduce the surcharge accordingly (if necessary to nil).
(4) For the purposes of this section a court does not 'deal with' a person if it—
  (a) discharges him absolutely, or
  (b) makes an order under the Mental Health Act 1983 in respect of him.
(5) In this section 'slavery and trafficking reparation order' means an order under section 8 of the Modern Slavery Act 2015, and 'unlawful profit order' means an unlawful profit order under section 4 of the Prevention of Social Housing Fraud Act 2013.

The Criminal Justice Act 2003 (Surcharge) (Amendment) Order 2020 (SI 2020 No. 310) specifies the amount of the surcharge applicable (see **E15.27**) but only in relation to offences committed on or after 14 April 2020. For an offence committed before that date, or when dealing with an offender for more than one offence any of which was committed before that date, the Criminal Justice Act 2003 (Surcharge) (Amendment) Order 2019 (SI 2019 No. 985) specifies the amount of the surcharge applicable, but only in relation to offences committed on or after 28 June 2019. For an offence committed before that date, or when dealing with an offender for more than one offence any of which was committed before that date, the Criminal Justice Act 2003 (Surcharge) Order 2016 (SI 2016 No. 389) specifies the amount of the surcharge applicable, but only in relation to offences committed on or after 8 April 2016. That Order revoked the Criminal Justice Act 2003 (Surcharge) Order 2012 (SI 2012 No. 1696), but only in relation to offences committed on or after 1 October 2012. For an offence committed before that date, or when dealing with an offender for more than one offence any of which was committed before that date, the Criminal Justice Act 2003 (Surcharge) (No. 2) Order 2007 (SI 2007 No. 1079) continues to apply. By the 2007 Order, a surcharge of £15 is payable in relation to a fine, but is not payable in respect of any other disposal. In *Bailey* [2013] EWCA Crim 1551, [2014] 1 Cr App R (S) 59 (376), the Court of Appeal held that where an offence was committed at some time shortly before or shortly after the commencement date of an Order changing the amount of the surcharge payable the court should take a view on the evidence as to the amount payable but not engage in lengthy (and costly) analysis. In the absence of a clear answer the defendant should be given the benefit of the doubt.

In *Stone* [2013] EWCA Crim 723, the Court of Appeal said that a surcharge order may be the subject of an appeal by the offender, the definition of 'sentence' in the Criminal Appeal Act 1968, s. 50(1), being wide enough to cover it. In the case of an application for leave to appeal a surcharge, the matter should be considered by the single judge on the papers. If leave to appeal on other grounds is given, the appeal will be listed before the full court. If the only ground upon which leave is given is the wrongful making of a surcharge order, the case will be listed as a non-counsel hearing. Pitchford LJ also pointed out that, if there is a failure by the sentencing court to impose a surcharge order when it should have done so, the Court of Appeal will normally be unable to remedy that omission since to do so would involve treating the offender more severely overall on sentence. If the court has overlooked the need to impose a surcharge that omission can, of course, be remedied within 56 days under the 'slip rule'. The Court in *Bailey* said that it was the duty of the advocates at the sentencing hearing to make sure that the correct surcharge sum was imposed, and this should be confirmed with the clerk if necessary. If there was a doubt the matter should be referred back to the court. If an error is made it should be possible for the record to be corrected well within the 56 days. **E15.25**

As indicated in *Bailey* and confirmed in *Abbott* [2020] EWCA Crim 516, the appropriate form of wording for judges to use in relation to the surcharge when making their sentencing remarks is as follows: **E15.26**

> The surcharge provisions apply to this case and the order can be drawn up accordingly.

This form of words is appropriate for use in all cases, and it is not necessary for the judge to state the relevant amount in open court.

A surcharge will not be payable in cases where the offender is dealt with by way of a disposal which is not set out in the schedule to the Order. The schedule (as amended by the 2020 Order) sets out the amounts payable as follows. **E15.27**

(Table 1) *If the offender was under 18 when the offence was committed*:

- conditional discharge, £17;
- fine, youth rehabilitation order, referral order or community order, £22;
- suspended sentence, £34;
- custodial sentence £34.

It should be noted that for offenders aged under 18, the PCC(S)A 2000, s. 137(1A), provides that any surcharge must be paid by the young offender's parent or guardian unless he or she cannot be found or it is unreasonable to require him or her to pay.

(Table 2) *If the offender was aged 18 or over when the offence was committed*:

- conditional discharge, £22;
- fine, 10 per cent of the value of the fine, rounded up or down to the nearest pound, which must be no less than £34 and no more than £190;
- community order, £95;

- suspended sentence where the term suspended is six months or less, £127;
- suspended sentence where the term suspended is more than six months, £156;
- imprisonment or detention in a young offender institution up to and including six months, £128;
- imprisonment or detention in a young offender institution imposed by the Crown Court for more than six months and up to and including 24 months, £156;
- imprisonment or detention in a young offender institution exceeding 24 months, £190;
- imprisonment or custody for life, £190.

(Table 3) *If the offender is not an individual (i.e. a corporate offender)*:

- conditional discharge, £22;
- fine, 10 per cent of the value of the fine, rounded up or down to the nearest pound, which must be no less than £34 and no more than £190.

If the offender is sentenced for more than one offence:

(a) the offender is only subject to the under 18 surcharge rate if all the offences were committed when the offender was under 18;
(b) in any case where the offender is made subject to two or more disposals of the same form the surcharge is paid once;
(c) if the offender is made subject to two or more different forms of disposal, the surcharge to be imposed is the higher or highest applicable amount.

E15.28 The duty to impose a surcharge is discharged when the court first sentences the offender. There is no power to order a second surcharge in circumstances where the court deals with the offender for a second time (e.g. when activating a suspended sentence, or taking action upon breach of a community or other order). If on that second occasion the court is dealing with the offender for a subsequent offence or offences, the surcharge payable on that occasion should be calculated only by reference to the new offence(s) (*Abbott* [2020] EWCA Crim 516, confirming *George* [2015] EWCA Crim 1096, [2015] 2 Cr App R (S) 58 (409)). No surcharge is payable in respect of an absolute discharge or a hospital order (s. 161A(4)). In *Poole* [2014] EWCA Crim 1641, [2015] 1 WLR 522, it was held that, where the Crown Court makes a hospital and limitation direction in accordance with the Mental Health Act 1983, s. 45A, the sentence is a sentence of imprisonment and not an order made under the 1983 Act. Accordingly the judge should impose the surcharge appropriate to the custodial sentence passed.

There is no power in the Crown Court to fix a default term when imposing a surcharge. The PCC(S)A 2000, s. 139, which requires the fixing of a default term for a fine, has not been amended to include the surcharge. There is no power to waive the imposition of the surcharge or to vary the sum to be paid, save by way of a reduction in the surcharge to enable a compensation order, an unlawful profit order or a slavery and trafficking prevention order to be paid (s. 161A(3)). This provision must be properly used, and it is not permissible for a judge simply to order that the surcharge 'be applied by way of compensation' (*Beckford* [2018] EWCA Crim 2997, [2019] 1 Cr App R (S) 53 (449)). The compensation order must first be imposed, and then the surcharge be reduced, if necessary to nil, in order for the compensation to be paid. There is, however, power to give the offender time to pay the surcharge, by virtue of the PCC(S) A 2000, s. 141. See further *Holden* [2013] EWCA Crim 2017. If the offender is of limited means and the court has imposed a fine, it may reduce that fine in order to allow the surcharge to be paid (see the CJA 2003, s. 164(4A), at **E15.15**).

Section E16 Compensation Orders

POWER TO MAKE COMPENSATION ORDERS

The power of the court to make compensation orders is governed by the PCC(S)A 2000, ss. 130 to 134. **E16.1**

Powers of Criminal Courts (Sentencing) Act 2000, s. 130

(1) A court by or before which a person is convicted of an offence, instead of or in addition to dealing with him in any other way, may, on application or otherwise, make an order (in this Act referred to as a 'compensation order') requiring him—
   (a) to pay compensation for any personal injury, loss or damage resulting from that offence or any other offence which is taken into consideration by the court in determining sentence; or
   (b) to make payments for funeral expenses or bereavement in respect of a death resulting from any such offence, other than a death due to an accident arising out of the presence of a motor vehicle on a road;

but this is subject to the following provisions of this section and to section 131 below.

(2) Where the person is convicted of an offence the sentence for which is fixed by law or falls to be imposed under a provision mentioned in subsection (2ZA), subsection (1) above shall have effect as if the words 'instead of or' were omitted.

(2ZA) The provisions referred to in subsection (2) are—
   (a) section 1(2B) or 1A(5) of the Prevention of Crime Act 1953;
   (b) section 51A(2) of the Firearms Act 1968;
   (c) section 139(6B), 139A(5B) or 139AA(7) of the Criminal Justice Act 1988;
   (d) section 110(2) or 111(2) of this Act;
   (e) section 224A, 225(2) or 226(2) of the Criminal Justice Act 2004;
   (f) section 29(4) or (6) of the Violent Crime Reduction Act 2006.

(2A) A court must consider making a compensation order in any case where this section empowers it to do so.

(3) A court shall give reasons, on passing sentence, if it does not make a compensation order in a case where this section empowers it to do so.

(4) Compensation under subsection (1) above shall be of such amount as the court considers appropriate, having regard to any evidence and to any representations that are made by or on behalf of the accused or the prosecutor.

The victim does not have to apply to the court before a compensation order can be made. In *Holt v DPP* [1996] 2 Cr App R (S) 314, the Divisional Court held that a compensation order could be made in respect of a victim of theft who had died before sentence was passed. There is no limit to the amount of compensation which the Crown Court or a magistrates' court may order, except that a compensation order shall not exceed £5,000 where a magistrates' court imposes such an order on an offender aged under 18 (s. 131(1) and (1A)). Nor is there a limit to the compensation (or total compensation) to be ordered for offences taken into consideration, except that a magistrates' court dealing with an offender aged under 18 cannot make a total compensation order in respect of the offences taken into consideration which exceeds £5,000 (s. 131(2)). In *Crutchley* (1994) 15 Cr App R (S) 627, followed in *Hose* (1995) 16 Cr App R (S) 682, the Court of Appeal held that where an offender pleads guilty on the basis of specimen counts, the amount of compensation is limited to the losses resulting from the offences charged. *Crutchley* was distinguished in *RCPO v Duffy* [2008] EWHC 848 (Admin), [2008] 2 Cr App R (S) 103 (593) on the ground that the offences charged were continuing rather than specimen charges. **E16.2**

According to the Sentencing Council definitive guideline, *Totality* (see Supplement, SG4-12), the court should make clear which amounts of compensation relate to which offences: the fixing of a **E16.3** 'global figure' is inappropriate, unless the offences were committed against the same victim. Where there are competing claimants for available funds, the total compensation available should normally be apportioned on a pro rata basis (*Miller* [1976] Crim LR 694), though in *Amey* [1983] 1 All ER 865 the court selected some claimants for compensation and excluded others. Where there are co-defendants, it is preferable to make separate orders against each of them (*Grundy* [1974] 1 All ER 292). It may be appropriate in a case of assault to reduce the compensation order to reflect a degree of provocation by the victim (*Flinton* [2007] EWCA Crim 2322, [2008] 1 Cr App R (S) 96 (575)).

A compensation order is part of the sentence of the court, and a decision by the trial judge not to make a compensation order, in accordance with s. 130(3), is a matter relating to trial on indictment and so not amenable to judicial review (*R (Faithfull) v Crown Court at Ipswich* [2007] EWHC 2763 (Admin), [2008] 3 All ER 749).

Nature of Payment

E16.4 **Liability for, and Evidence of, Injury, Loss or Damage** 'Any personal injury, loss or damage': it is not a prerequisite of making a compensation order that the offender would be civilly liable for the loss (*Chappell* (1984) 80 Cr App R 31), though this will generally be the case. The court may compensate distress and anxiety (*Bond v Chief Constable of Kent* [1983] 1 All ER 456; *Godfrey* (1994) 15 Cr App R (S) 536). 'Loss' may include a sum by way of interest (*Schofield* [1978] 2 All ER 705). An award may be made whenever it can fairly be said that a particular loss results from the offence (*Rowlston v Kenny* (1982) 4 Cr App R (S) 85), without having regard to technical issues of causation (*Thomson Holidays Ltd* [1974] QB 592). Thus in *Taylor* (1993) 14 Cr App R (S) 276, it was held to be appropriate to require D to pay compensation to a man who had been kicked in the course of an affray in which D and four others had accosted another group of men and a fight had developed. It could not be established that D had kicked V, but it was said to be 'artificial and unjust to look narrowly at the physical acts of each defendant'. A case which fell on the other side of the line was *Derby* (1990) 12 Cr App R (S) 502, where D1 had threatened V with a knife and D2 had seriously injured V by attacking him with a piece of wood. It was held that a compensation order for £4,000 made against D1 was improper, since D1 had clearly not been responsible for inflicting the injuries. This approach was followed in *Denness* [1996] 1 Cr App R (S) 159.

E16.5 Where there has been no damage or loss (e.g., where a stolen article is recovered and returned undamaged), no compensation order can be made (*Tyce* (1994) 15 Cr App R (S) 415); the issue is the loss to the victim rather than the benefit to the offender. Conversely, where there has been damage or loss to the victim, a compensation order is not precluded by the fact that the offender has made no profit from the offence. The amount of the victim's loss should either be agreed by the offender or established by evidence. The case of *Vivian* [1979] 1 All ER 48 is clear authority for this point. In *Horsham Justices, ex parte Richards* [1985] 2 All ER 1114, Neill LJ said (at p. 993), 'in my judgment the court has no jurisdiction to make a compensation order without receiving any evidence where there are real issues raised as to whether the claimants have suffered any, and if so what, loss'. The court should, however, hesitate to embark on a complex inquiry into the scale of loss, since compensation orders are designed to be used only in clear, straightforward cases (see **E16.14**).

In the case of an offence under the Theft Act 1968 or the Fraud Act 2006, where the property in question is recovered, any damage to the property occurring while it was out of the owner's possession is treated as having resulted from the offence, however and by whomsoever it was caused (PCC(S)A 2000, s. 130(5); *Quigley v Stokes* [1977] 2 All ER 317).

E16.6 **Motor Accidents** A compensation order may only be made in respect of injury, loss or damage (other than loss suffered by a person's dependants in consequence of the person's death) which was due to an accident arising out of the presence of a motor vehicle on a road, if:

(a) it is damage which falls within s. 130(5); or

(b) it is in respect of injury, loss or damage for which the offender is uninsured in relation to the use of the vehicle, and compensation is not payable under any arrangements to which the Secretary of State is a party (i.e. the Motor Insurers' Bureau Agreement) (s. 130(6)).

In the case of property damage, the Agreement does not cover the first £400 of the damage, and a compensation order up to that amount may be made in an appropriate case (*DPP v Scott* (1995) 16 Cr App R (S) 292). See further *Austin* [1996] 2 Cr App R (S) 191. If a compensation order is made in respect of such an accident, the compensation can include a sum representing the whole or part of any loss of or reduction in preferential rates of insurance attributable to the accident ('no claims' bonus) (s. 130(7)). A vehicle which is exempted from insurance (Road Traffic Act 1988, s. 144) is not uninsured for these purposes (s. 130(8)). In a motor accident case where there are real issues as to liability and quantum, the court should adhere to the general principle (see **E16.14**) that a compensation order should be made only in a clear case (*Stapylton* [2012] EWCA Crim 728, [2013] 1 Cr App R (S) 12 (68)).

Compensation for Loss Arising from Death A compensation order in respect of funeral expenses may be made for the benefit of anyone who incurred the expenses (s. 130(9)). A compensation order in respect of bereavement may only be made for the benefit of a person who could claim damages for bereavement under the Fatal Accidents Act 1976, s. 1A (i.e. the spouse of the deceased or, in the case of a deceased minor who was never married, his or her parents, or mother if the minor is illegitimate), and the amount of that compensation shall not exceed the sum specified in the Fatal Accidents Act 1976, s. 1A(3) (£12,980 where the cause of action arises after 1 April 2013) (s. 130(10)). **E16.7**

Offender's Means and Parental Liability

In determining whether to make a compensation order, and in determining the amount to be paid, it is the duty of the court to have regard to the offender's means so far as they appear or are known to the court (s. 130(11), and see **E16.12**). The court may allow the offender time to pay the sum due under the compensation order, or direct payment of the sum by instalments of such amounts and on such dates as the court may specify (PCC(S)A 2000, s. 141; MCA 1980, s. 75(1)). It was made clear in *York* [2018] EWCA Crim 2754, [2019] 1 Cr App R (S) 41 (283), that fixing the instalments by which the order is to be paid and the period over which the instalments should be paid is a matter for the sentencing court, and should not be left to the enforcing magistrates' court. **E16.8**

Where a child or young person is convicted of an offence and the court makes an order for compensation, it should, under the PCC(S)A 2000, s. 137, normally order the parent or guardian of the child or young person to pay the compensation order (see E14.7).

Payment, Discharge and Review

The victim of the offence shall not receive the compensation until there is no further possibility of an appeal on which the order could be varied or set aside (s. 132(1)). By s. 133, at any time before the offender has paid into court the whole of the money under the order, the magistrates' court having power to enforce the order may, on the application of the offender, discharge the order or reduce it, on the ground that: **E16.9**

(a) the injury, loss or damage in respect of which the order was made has been held in civil proceedings to be less than it was taken to be for the purposes of the order;
(b) that property, the loss of which was the subject of the order, has now been recovered;
(c) the means of the offender are insufficient to satisfy both the compensation order and a confiscation order made against the offender in the same proceedings under the CJA 1988, Part IV, or the POCA 2002, Part 2, an unlawful profit order under the Prevention of Social Housing Fraud Act 2013, s. 4, or a slavery and trafficking reparation order under the Modern Slavery Act 2015, s. 8 (or any combination of those orders); or
(d) the offender's means have suffered a substantial reduction, which was unexpected at the time of making the order.

Before the magistrates can act to discharge or reduce the order under (c) or (d), they must have the consent of the Crown Court if the Crown Court made the order.

Enforcement of Compensation Orders

E16.10 Enforcement of compensation orders is the function of the magistrates' courts. The maximum terms of imprisonment which a magistrates' court may impose in default of payment of compensation orders are specified in the MCA 1980, sch. 4. These are the same periods which apply in the case of fines, and which are set out in the table at **E15.7**, except that the magistrates have no power to specify a term in default in excess of 12 months. These are maximum terms, and the magistrates have discretion to fix a lower term. The Crown Court is not empowered to make an order fixing the term to be served in default of payment of a compensation order (in contrast to its duty to do so in respect of fines: *Komsta* (1990) 12 Cr App R (S) 63, and see **E15.3**). The maximum terms indicated in sch. 4 will thus normally also apply in default of compensation orders imposed by the Crown Court. Exceptionally, however, if the Crown Court makes a compensation order for an amount in excess of £20,000 and considers that a maximum default term of 12 months is inadequate, it may fix a longer period, not exceeding the term specified for the equivalent amount in the PCC(S)A 2000, s. 139(4). As with fines, part payment of the compensation order will result in a proportionate reduction in the term to be served in default.

COMPENSATION ORDERS: SENTENCING PRINCIPLES

Compensation Order Not Alternative to Sentence

E16.11 In *Inwood* (1974) 60 Cr App R 70, Scarman LJ said (at p. 73): 'Compensation orders were not introduced into our law to enable the convicted to buy themselves out of the penalties for crime. Compensation orders were introduced into our law as a convenient and rapid means of avoiding the expense of resort to civil litigation when the criminal clearly has means which would enable the compensation to be paid.' It follows from this important principle that the imposition of a compensation order should not affect the punishment imposed for the offence and, in particular, should not 'permit the offender to buy his way out of a custodial sentence'.

This principle is, however, subject to the PCC(S)A 2000, s. 130(12), which gives priority to the imposition of a compensation order over a fine. This, to some extent, permits the offender to 'buy his way out of the penalties for crime', by reducing the fine in order for compensation to be paid, but s. 130(12) does not affect sentences other than fines. Some watering down of the principle in *Inwood* (1974) 60 Cr App R 70 may be detected in other decisions of the Court of Appeal such as *Huish* (1985) 7 Cr App R (S) 272, but its importance was re-emphasised by Lord Taylor CJ in *A-G's Ref (No. 5 of 1993)* (1994) 15 Cr App R (S) 201.

Taking into Account Means of Offender

E16.12 In *York* [2018] EWCA Crim 2754, [2019] 1 Cr App R (S) 41 (283), the Court of Appeal said that the court must make inquiries about the offender's means, and the offender is required to give those details. The court must take that information into account and should not make an order unless it is realistic, in the sense that the offender has, or will have, the means to pay that order within a reasonable time. If the offender misleads the court into believing that he or she has the means to pay compensation, a subsequent appeal by the offender against the compensation order will not succeed (*Hayes* (1992) 13 Cr App R (S) 454; *Dando* [1996] 1 Cr App R (S) 155). The offender must pay the compensation, or serve the appropriate term in default of payment. If an offender 'has suffered a substantial reduction in his means which was unexpected at the time the order was made', the order may be reduced or discharged by a magistrates' court under the PCC(S)A 2000, s. 133. If the order was made by the Crown Court, the magistrates must obtain the consent of the Crown Court before proceeding (*Favell* [2010] EWCA Crim 2948).

There is no general principle that a compensation order should not be made where its effect would be to force the sale of the family or matrimonial home (*Maguire* (1992) 13 Cr App R (S) 332; *Martindale* [2014] EWCA Crim 1232), but if the making of a compensation order would have that effect the judge would of course take that fact into account. In a case where an offender has been made subject to both a confiscation order and a compensation order in accordance with the POCA 2002, s. 13, and the offender's share in the matrimonial home forms part of the available amount, the sale of the property is forced by the confiscation order and there can be no objection to compensation being paid from the assets thereby recovered (*Parkinson* [2015] EWCA Crim 1448, [2016] 1 Cr App R (S) 6 (24)).

Co-defendants may be required to pay different sums by way of compensation if their capacity to pay is different. See *Beddow* (1987) 9 Cr App R (S) 235, where D was one of two defendants who pleaded guilty to being carried in a vehicle taken without consent by a third defendant, who had fallen asleep at the wheel, causing the van to crash. D was conditionally charged and ordered to pay £300 in compensation. The other two defendants received a suspended sentence and a conditional discharge respectively, but neither was required to pay compensation. The Court of Appeal approved the sentences on the basis that D was the only one of the defendants who was in work and could afford to pay. A compensation order must not be imposed on the basis that persons other than the offender will pay, or contribute to, the order (*York* [2018] EWCA Crim 2754, [2019] 1 Cr App R (S) 41 (283)). It was held in *Carrington* [2014] EWCA Crim 425, [2014] 2 Cr App R (S) 41 (337), that it might be acceptable for an offender to borrow the money from a third party, but not if the reality was that the loan would not be repaid.

Compensation Should be Payable within Reasonable Time

The Court of Appeal in *York* [2018] EWCA Crim 2754, [2019] 1 Cr App R (S) 41 (283), said **E16.13**
that the court should make a compensation order only where it is satisfied that the offender will be able to discharge that order within a reasonable time. In general, long repayment periods should be avoided, but repayment over two or three years in an exceptional case would not be open to criticism. These comments are in line with earlier authority, especially *Olliver* (1989) 11 Cr App R (S) 10, where the Court of Appeal indicated that a fine (or compensation order) might properly be repaid over a period of up to three years. Lord Lane CJ said (at p. 15) that: 'Certainly it seems to us that a two-year period will seldom be too long, and in an appropriate case three years will be unassailable'.

Compensation Order Should be Made Only in Clear Case

In *Donovan* (1981) 3 Cr App R (S) 192, D pleaded guilty to taking a conveyance, having hired a **E16.14**
car for two days and failed to return it. The car had suffered no damage. D was fined £250, with £100 costs and £1,388 compensation, on the basis of the hire company's loss of use. Eveleigh LJ said that: 'A compensation order is designed for the simple, straightforward case where the amount of the compensation can be readily and easily ascertained.' Since the amount of damages in a civil case of loss of use 'is notoriously open to argument', the compensation order was quashed, and the hire company left to pursue its civil remedy if it wished to do so. In *Hyde v Emery* (1984) 6 Cr App R (S) 206, D pleaded guilty to three charges of obtaining unemployment benefit by false representation. There was a dispute over whether the sum claimed in compensation by the DHSS should be reduced by the amount of supplementary benefit which he could legitimately have claimed. Watkins LJ said in the Divisional Court that the magistrates should have declined to deal with the matter. See also *Briscoe* (1994) 15 Cr App R (S) 699, *White* [1996] 2 Cr App R (S) 58 and *Stapylton* [2012] EWCA Crim 728, [2013] 1 Cr App R (S) 12 (68).

A slightly different line was taken in *James* [2003] EWCA Crim 811, [2003] 2 Cr App R (S) 97 (574). D pleaded guilty to 20 counts of false accounting. The total sum involved was in dispute, but there was an agreed minimum loss of £8,000 to V. The Court of Appeal said that it was proper for a compensation order in that sum to be ordered, bearing in mind that the only realistic chance for V to receive any compensation from D was through the criminal court. In *Pola* [2009] EWCA

Crim 655, [2010] 1 Cr App R (S) 6 (32), the Court of Appeal upheld a compensation order in the sum of £90,000 made against a man convicted of failing to discharge a duty pursuant to the Health and Safety at Work Act etc. 1974, where a workman had been severely injured by the collapse of a wall. The Court noted that criminal courts had now developed more expertise in financial assessment from the experience of confiscation proceedings, and it might be that the very cautious approach adopted in the earlier authorities to the making of compensation orders needed some modification.

Combining Compensation Orders with Other Sentences or Orders

E16.15 Compensation orders may be imposed on an offender 'instead of or in addition to dealing with him in any other way' (PCC(S)A 2000, s. 130(1): see **E16.1**). It is expressly provided that a compensation order may be combined with a discharge (s. 12(7)).

The Sentencing Council definitive guideline, *Totality* (see Supplement, **SG4-12**), states that a compensation order may be combined with a sentence of immediate custody where the offender is clearly able to pay or has good prospects of employment on release from custody. It may, however, be undesirable for a compensation order to be hanging over the offender's head after release, and the order may be 'counterproductive, and force him back into crime to find the money' (*Inwood* (1974) 60 Cr App R 70). This principle has been stated on many occasions (see, e.g., *Clark* (1992) 13 Cr App R (S) 124; *Jorge* [1999] 2 Cr App R (S) 1) but there are exceptions, such as where the sentence is a short one and the offender's job will still be open upon release, or where there is clear evidence that the offender has sufficient assets to pay the compensation (*Love* [1999] 1 Cr App R (S) 484). While it is not wrong to combine a compensation order with a suspended sentence, and, indeed, that combination is positively encouraged by s. 118(5), regard should be had to the fact that if the offender is in breach of the suspended sentence, its activation may bring to an end any prospect of the payment of compensation (*McGee* [1978] Crim LR 370). It is contrary to principle to suspend a custodial sentence merely because of the offender's ability to pay compensation.

Where it would be appropriate both to impose a fine and to make a compensation order, but the offender has insufficient means to pay both, the court shall give preference to compensation, though it may impose a fine as well (s. 130(12)). This means that the fine should be reduced or, if necessary, dispensed with altogether, to enable the compensation to be paid. A compensation order may, thus, stand alone on sentence. If the offender has insufficient means to pay a surcharge imposed under the CJA 2003, s. 161A, as well as a compensation order, the surcharge should be reduced, if necessary to nil, to enable the compensation to be paid (s. 161A(3)).

Guidelines for Compensation

E16.16 Starting points for compensating physical and mental injuries commonly encountered in a magistrates' court are set out in the *Magistrates' Court Sentencing Guidelines* (see Supplement, **SG10-47**).

SLAVERY AND TRAFFICKING REPARATION ORDERS

E16.17 The Modern Slavery Act 2015, s. 8, creates a power to make a slavery and trafficking reparation order (STRO). The court (the Crown Court, or a magistrates' court which has power to make a confiscation order under the SOCPA 2005, s. 97) may make such an order against a person if that person has been convicted of an offence under s. 1, 2 or 4 of the 2015 Act and a confiscation order is made against that person in respect of the offence, even if the person has been sentenced for the offence before the confiscation order is made (s. 8(1)). A STRO may be made in addition to dealing with the person in any other way (s. 8(3)), except that a STRO and a compensation order under the PCC(S)A 2000, s. 130, cannot both be made in respect of the same offence (s. 10(1)). A STRO requires the person against whom it is made to pay compensation to the victim of a relevant offence for any harm resulting from that offence (s. 9(1)). The amount of compensation payable must not exceed the amount the person is required to pay under the confiscation order (s. 9(4)).

In determining whether to make a STRO, the court must have regard to the person's means (s. 8(5)). If the court considers that it would be appropriate both to impose a fine and to make a STRO but the person has insufficient means to pay both, the court must give preference to the STRO (s. 8(6)). In any case in which the court has power to make a STRO, it must consider whether to make one (whether or not an application is made) and if it does not make a STRO, give reasons why not (s. 8(7)). Further provisions in relation to STROs are provided by s. 10 of the Act.

Section E17 Restitution Orders

POWER TO MAKE RESTITUTION ORDERS

E17.1 A restitution order is designed to restore to a person entitled to them goods which have been stolen or otherwise unlawfully removed, or to restore to the person a sum of money representing the proceeds of the goods, out of money found in the offender's possession on apprehension. Either the Crown Court or a magistrates' court may make such an order. See further the *Crown Court Compendium: Sentencing* (December 2019), ch. S7-10.

Powers of Criminal Courts (Sentencing) Act 2000, s. 148

(1) This section applies where goods have been stolen, and either—
 (a) a person is convicted of any offence with reference to the theft (whether or not the stealing is the gist of his offence); or
 (b) a person is convicted of any other offence, but such an offence as is mentioned in paragraph (a) above is taken into consideration in determining his sentence.

(2) Where this section applies, the court by or before which the offender is convicted may on the conviction (whether or not the passing of sentence is in other respects deferred) exercise any of the following powers—
 (a) the court may order anyone having possession or control of the stolen goods to restore them to any person entitled to recover them from him; or
 (b) on the application of a person entitled to recover from the person convicted any other goods directly or indirectly representing the stolen goods (as being the proceeds of any disposal or realisation of the whole or part of them or of goods so representing them), the court may order those other goods to be delivered or transferred to the applicant; or
 (c) the court may order that a sum not exceeding the value of the stolen goods shall be paid, out of any money of the person convicted which was taken out of his possession on his apprehension, to any person who, if those goods were in the possession of the person convicted, would be entitled to recover them from him;

and in this subsection 'the stolen goods' means the goods referred to in subsection (1) above.

E17.2 For the purposes of s. 148, 'stealing' is widely construed to include not just theft and offences where theft is a constituent element, such as robbery and burglary, but also where the goods were obtained by blackmail or fraud (or deception where the act in question was prior to the commencement of the Fraud Act 2006), or were stolen goods handled following any of these offences (Theft Act 1968, s. 24(4)). A restitution order should not be made unless the evidence on which it is based (including available documents) is clear and has been given before sentence is imposed (PCC(S)A 2000, s. 148(5); *Church* (1970) 55 Cr App R 65). A restitution order should not be made where the question of title to goods is unclear. According to Woolf J:

> . . . the criminal courts are not the appropriate forum in which to satisfactorily ventilate complex issues as to the ownership of such money or goods. In cases of doubt it is better to leave the victim to pursue his civil remedies or, alternatively, to apply to the magistrates' court under the Police (Property) Act 1897. On the other hand, in appropriate cases where the evidence is clear, it is important that the court should make proper use of the power to order restitution since this can frequently avoid unnecessary expense and delay in the victim receiving the return of his property. (*Calcutt* (1985) 7 Cr App R (S) 385, at p. 390)

For obvious reasons, there is no requirement under these provisions that account should be taken of the offender's means: contrast compensation orders at **E16.12**.

If an order is made under s. 148(2)(a), it will be inappropriate to order restitution under s. 148(2)(b) or (c) in addition, since the person will thereby recover more than the value of the goods. Under s. 148(2)(a), the person in 'possession or control' need not be the offender, but may be an innocent purchaser. Where a person has, in good faith, bought the goods from the convicted person, or has, in good faith, lent money to the convicted person on the security of the goods, the court may order payment of compensation to that person out of money taken from the offender under s. 148(2)(c) (s. 148(4)). Such an order may be made with or without that person's application (s. 149(2)).

Under s. 148(2)(b), an application must be made by the person claiming, and may not relate to goods held by a third party. Application should be made in writing as soon as practicable and without waiting for the verdict (CrimPR 28.7: see Supplement, **R28.7**). Where the offender is no longer in possession of the goods, orders may be made under both s. 148(2)(b) and (c), with reference to the same goods, providing that the person does not thereby recover more than the value of the goods (s. 148(3)). **E17.3**

An order may be made under s. 148(2)(c) with or without an application being made (s. 149(2)). Again, where the offender is no longer in possession of the goods, orders may be made under both s. 148(2)(b) and (c), with reference to the same goods, providing that the person does not thereby recover more than the value of the goods (s. 148(3)).

Money seized from the offender after arrest may be the subject of an order (*Ferguson* [1970] 2 All ER 820, where £2,000, taken from D's safe deposit box 11 days after his arrest, was held to have been in his possession at the time of his apprehension). But it seems that money seized prior to the offender's arrest may not (*Hinde* (1977) 64 Cr App R 213, a case decided in relation to forfeiture orders but applicable by analogy here). There is no need to show that the money is the proceeds of the relevant offence; all that is necessary is that it be shown that the money belongs to the offender (*Lewis* [1975] Crim LR 353). It was also established in *Lewis* that, under s. 148(2)(c), a restitution order may be made against an offender for a greater sum than that received from the offence, provided that it is not for a sum greater than the total loss occasioned by the offence (in contrast to *Grundy* [1974] 1 All ER 292, which established that joint and several liability should not apply in relation to a compensation order).

An offender may appeal against a restitution order as against any other sentence. Such an order is, however, where made on conviction on indictment, subject to an automatic suspension for 28 days from the date of conviction (unless the trial court directs to the contrary on the ground that 'the title to the property is not in dispute': Criminal Appeal Act 1968, s. 30(1)) or, further, until the determination of any appeal. Where made by a magistrates' court, s. 149(4) provides that it is subject to an automatic suspension for 21 days from the date of conviction or, further, until the determination of any appeal (unless the court directs to the contrary as above).

COMBINING RESTITUTION ORDERS WITH OTHER SENTENCES OR ORDERS

A restitution order may be made in combination with any other sentence passed by the court. **E17.4**

Section E18 Deprivation and Forfeiture Orders

POWERS TO MAKE DEPRIVATION ORDERS UNDER THE PCC(S)A 2000, s. 143

Nature and Effect of Order

E18.1 The main power of the courts to order the forfeiture of property connected with the commission of an offence is created by the PCC(S)A 2000, s. 143(1). Other powers of forfeiture under specific statutes are considered at **E18.7**. The power under s. 143 may be exercised by the Crown Court or a magistrates' court, in respect of any offence. See further the *Crown Court Compendium: Sentencing* (December 2019), ch. S7-3.

Powers of Criminal Courts (Sentencing) Act 2000, s. 143

(1) Where a person is convicted of an offence and the court by or before which he is convicted is satisfied that any property which has been lawfully seized from him, or which was in his possession or under his control at the time when he was apprehended for the offence or when a summons in respect of it was issued—
   (a) has been used for the purpose of committing, or facilitating the commission of, any offence, or
   (b) was intended by him to be used for that purpose,

the court may (subject to subsection (5) below) make an order under this section in respect of that property.

(2) Where a person is convicted of an offence and the offence, or an offence which the court has taken into consideration in determining his sentence, consists of unlawful possession of property which—
   (a) has been lawfully seized from him, or
   (b) was in his possession or under his control at the time when he was apprehended for the offence of which he has been convicted or when a summons in respect of that offence was issued,

the court may (subject to subsection (5) below) make an order under this section in respect of that property.

(3) An order under this section shall operate to deprive the offender of his rights, if any, in the property to which it relates, and the property shall (if not already in their possession) be taken into the possession of the police.

(4) Any power conferred on a court by subsection (1) or (2) above may be exercised—
   (a) whether or not the court also deals with the offender in any other way in respect of the offence of which he has been convicted; and
   (b) without regard to any restrictions on forfeiture in any enactment contained in an Act passed before 29th July 1988.

(5) In considering whether to make an order under this section in respect of any property, a court shall have regard—
   (a) to the value of the property; and
   (b) to the likely financial and other effects on the offender of the making of the order (taken together with any other order that the court contemplates making).

(6) Where a person commits an offence to which this subsection applies by—
   (a) driving, attempting to drive, or being in charge of a vehicle, or
   (b) failing to comply with a requirement made under section 7 or 7A of the Road Traffic Act 1988 (failure to provide specimen for analysis or laboratory test or to give permission for such a test) in the course of an investigation into whether the offender had committed an offence while driving, attempting to drive or being in charge of a vehicle, or

(c) failing, as the driver of a vehicle, to comply with subsection (2) or (3) of section 170 of the Road Traffic Act 1988 (duty to stop and give information or report accident),

the vehicle shall be regarded for the purposes of subsection (1) above (and section 144(1)(b) below) as used for the purpose of committing the offence (and for the purpose of committing any offence of aiding, abetting, counselling or procuring the commission of the offence).

(7) Subsection (6) above applies to—
(a) an offence under the Road Traffic Act 1988 which is punishable with imprisonment;
(b) an offence of manslaughter; and
(c) an offence under section 35 of the Offences Against the Person Act 1861 (wanton and furious driving).

(8) Facilitating the commission of an offence shall be taken for the purposes of subsection (1) above to include the taking of any steps after it has been committed for the purpose of disposing of any property to which it relates or of avoiding apprehension or detection.

The effect of an order under s. 143 is to deprive the offender of his or her rights, if any, in the property (s. 143(3)), but it does not affect the rights of any other person, who may apply for recovery of the property (see **E18.3**). In *Hall* [2014] EWCA Crim 2413, [2015] RTR 9 (86), where D was convicted of dangerous driving, the judge made an order under s. 143 in respect of the car, saying that it would be sold to help defray prosecution costs. The order was quashed on appeal when it was found that the car belonged to D's father, who was in no way complicit in the offence. The power does not extend to real property, such as the offender's home (*Khan* (1982) 4 Cr App R (S) 298). Nor should an order be made where the property is subject to joint ownership (*Troth* (1980) 71 Cr App R 1, where it was said that deprivation orders should be confined to 'simple, uncomplicated cases'). This was the problem in *Kearney* [2011] EWCA Crim 826, [2011] 2 Cr App R (S) 106 (608), where D had committed six offences of making off without payment by filling his car with fuel and driving away without paying. The judge dealt with the matter by a community order together with an order depriving D of his rights in the vehicle. The deprivation order was quashed on appeal, it now having emerged that the car had been purchased on a hire purchase agreement. The power does not extend to property which was associated with an offence committed by some person other than the offender: s. 143(1)(a)(i) should be read as if the words 'by him' rather than 'by anyone' appeared after the word 'offence' (*Slater* [1986] 3 All ER 786; *Neville* (1987) 9 Cr App R (S) 222). The phrase 'facilitating the commission of, any offence' in s. 143 includes the taking of any steps after it has been committed for the purpose of disposing of any property to which it relates or of avoiding apprehension or detection (s. 143(8)). Section 143(6) and (7) make it clear that an offender's vehicle *shall* be regarded as having been used for the purpose of any offence specified therein. Section 143(6) and (7), however, in no way limit the courts' power to order forfeiture of an offender's car in respect of other offences under the general provision in s. 143(1). Where the making of a deprivation order is being considered, 'full and proper investigation' should be made (*Pemberton* (1982) 4 Cr App R (S) 328). In *Jones* [2017] EWCA Crim 2192, [2018] 1 Cr App R (S) 35 (248), D admitted possession of crack cocaine with intent to supply. His car had been stopped by the police, who found drugs in the car. A search of D's home revealed drugs paraphernalia and £4,600 in cash. In addition to a custodial sentence the judge made orders under s. 143 in respect of the car, mobile phones, the drugs paraphernalia and the cash. The Court of Appeal quashed the order in relation to the money. D had put forward an innocent explanation at police interview as to where the money had come from, and said that £400 of it belonged to his girlfriend. The Court noted that it was common practice in drugs supply cases, where cash has been recovered, for the court to make an order under s. 143 in preference to embarking on confiscation proceedings. Sometimes the court would order the money to be paid to an organisation tasked with combating drugs crime or supporting the rehabilitation of offenders. Even so, where there was an issue as to whether the order should be made, a proper formal procedure must be adopted. It had been open to the judge to find that D's account was untrue, and the money was in fact D's working capital for future drug dealing, but there had been no inquiry into the origins of that money, and so the order had not been made on a proper basis. **E18.2**

Dealing with Property

E18.3 The property is normally taken into the possession of the police, if not in their possession already, and the Police (Property) Act 1897 applies. The police have power under that Act to dispose of property where its ownership has not been ascertained and no court order has been made in respect of it. In relation to s. 143, the police have similar powers where no application has been made within six months or no such application has succeeded (s. 144(2)). No application for return of the property can be made after six months from the date of the deprivation order, and no order can be made unless the claimant satisfies the court either that the claimant had not consented to the offender having possession of the property or, where the order was made under the PCC(S)A 2000, s. 143(1)(a), that the claimant did not know, and had no reason to suspect, that the property was likely to be used for the purpose mentioned in s. 143(1) (s. 144(1)). By s. 25(1) of the UK Borders Act 2007, a court making an order under s. 143 of the PCC(S)A 2000 may order that the property be taken into the possession of the Secretary of State (rather than the police) where the court thinks that the offence relates to immigration or asylum or was committed for a purpose connected therewith.

E18.4 **Powers of Criminal Courts (Sentencing) Act 2000, s. 145**

(1) Where a court makes an order under section 143 above in a case where—
 (a) the offender has been convicted of an offence which has resulted in a person suffering personal injury, loss or damage, or
 (b) any such offence is taken into consideration by the court in determining sentence,
 the court may also make an order that any proceeds which arise from the disposal of the property and which do not exceed a sum specified by the court shall be paid to that person.

(2) The court may only make an order under this section if it is satisfied that but for the inadequacy of the offender's means it would have made a compensation order under which the offender would have been required to pay compensation of an amount not less than the specified amount.

No order can be made under this provision before the expiry of the six-month period mentioned above, or where a successful application has been made under the Police (Property) Act 1897 in respect of the property (s. 145(3)).

DEPRIVATION ORDERS: SENTENCING PRINCIPLES

Deprivation Order Affects Totality of Sentence

E18.5 See the PCC(S)A 2000, s. 143(5), at **E18.1**. In *Buddo* (1982) 4 Cr App R (S) 268, D pleaded guilty to burglary and assault. In addition to a total prison sentence of two years, D was deprived of his rights in a motor caravan in which he had driven to commit the burglary. The Court of Appeal was of the view that such an order could properly be made on the facts but that sentencers were 'not required to make such an order in every case in which a vehicle is used in the commission of a crime'. In this case, according to Park J, the deprivation order was 'overdoing the punishment', and the order was quashed. See also *Scully* (1985) 7 Cr App R (S) 119; *Priestley* [1996] 2 Cr App R (S) 144 and, in relation to deprivation of a computer, *Townsend-Johnson* [2010] EWCA Crim 1027.

Where the order would have a disproportionately severe impact upon the offender, it is also inappropriate. In *Tavernor* [1976] RTR 242, an order depriving D of his rights in a car, imposed in addition to a suspended prison sentence and a fine, was quashed in view of D's physical disability. See also *Highbury Corner Metropolitan Stipendiary Magistrate, ex parte Di Matteo* [1991] 1 All ER 102.

In a case where several offenders are equally implicated and receive comparable sentences, it is wrong to impose in addition a deprivation order upon one of them (*De Jesus* [2015] EWCA Crim 1118, [2015] 2 Cr App R (S) 44 (343), but see *Burgess* [2001] 2 Cr App R (S) 2 (5), where it was said that the principle can be taken so far but no further). This may be contrasted with the principle applicable to compensation orders, the object of which is to compensate the victim, rather than to punish the offender (see **E16.11**).

Combining Deprivation Orders with Other Sentences or Orders

A deprivation order may be combined with a compensation order, and provision is made under the PCC(S)A 2000, s. 145, to allow the sale of property connected with the offence in order to finance compensation for the victim where the means of the offender would otherwise have been inadequate to meet a compensation order. A deprivation order may be combined with a discharge (s. 12(7)). **E18.6**

OTHER STATUTORY POWERS TO MAKE FORFEITURE ORDERS

Many other statutes contain their own forfeiture provisions relating to offences committed under those statutes, or to property regulated under those statutes. The Misuse of Drugs Act 1971 includes a commonly used provision. **E18.7**

Misuse of Drugs Act 1971, s. 27

(1) Subject to subsection (2) below, the court by or before which a person is convicted of an offence under this Act or an offence falling within subsection (3) below or an offence to which section 1 of the Proceeds of Crime (Scotland) Act 1995 relates or a drug trafficking offence, as defined in Article 2(2) of the Criminal Justice (Confiscation) (Northern Ireland) Order 1990 may order anything shown to the satisfaction of the court to relate to the offence, to be forfeited and either destroyed or dealt with in such other manner as the court may order.

(2) The court shall not order anything to be forfeited under this section, where a person claiming to be the owner of or otherwise interested in it applies to be heard by the court, unless an opportunity has been given to him to show cause why the order should not be made.

(3) An offence falls within this subsection if it is an offence which is specified in—
- (a) paragraph 1 of Schedule 2 to the Proceeds of Crime Act 2002 (drug trafficking offences), or
- (b) so far as it relates to that paragraph, paragraph 10 of that Schedule.

Any personal property which relates to the offence may be forfeited, including money (*Beard* [1974] 1 WLR 1549), but s. 27 does not extend to intangibles, or to property situated outside the jurisdiction of the English courts (*Cuthbertson* [1981] AC 470). Nor, apparently, does s. 27 permit the forfeiture of real property such as a house (*Pearce* [1996] 2 Cr App R (S) 316). The property must be shown to relate to the offence of which the offender has been convicted; its relation to intended offences is insufficient (*Morgan* [1977] Crim LR 488; *Ribeyre* (1982) 4 Cr App R (S) 165; *Llewellyn* (1985) 7 Cr App R (S) 225; *Cox* (1986) 8 Cr App R (S) 384). Thus, where D was convicted of possession of cocaine, which was hidden in his car, a forfeiture order under s. 27 could not be made in respect of £1,489 also found in his possession and accepted to be the proceeds of drug dealing, since this was the proceeds of drugs other than those to which the conviction related (*Boothe* (1987) 9 Cr App R (S) 8). In *Boothe* an order made under the predecessor to the PCC(S)A 2000, s. 143 (see **E18.1**), for forfeiture of a car was upheld. It is clear that an order in relation to the car might have been made under s. 27 of the 1971 Act (*Bowers* (1994) 15 Cr App R (S) 315). If the offender disputes that property is related to the offence of which he or she has been convicted, the offender must be permitted to call evidence (*Churcher* (1986) 8 Cr App R (S) 94). Under s. 27(2), it seems that the court may order forfeiture notwithstanding such an application: contrast the position under the PCC(S)A 2000, s. 143, at **E18.1**. It may be assumed that the sentencing principles listed in relation to the PCC(S)A 2000, s. 143, also apply here. There is, however, under s. 27, no power to sell property to generate compensation. **E18.8**

For the power of forfeiture under the FA 1968 and power of seizure of offensive weapons, see **B12**. For powers of forfeiture in terrorism cases, see **B10.119**.

Where an offender is convicted of an offence under the Modern Slavery Act 2015, s. 2, there are powers of forfeiture in respect of vehicles, ships or aircraft used in connection with that offence.

Section E19 Confiscation Orders

GENERAL

Overview

E19.1 Part 2 of the Proceeds of Crime Act 2002 provides for the making of confiscation orders following conviction in criminal cases. (See **D8** for all other methods of asset recovery under the POCA 2002.) The purpose of a confiscation order is to recover from a defendant a sum of money not exceeding the value of his proceeds of crime. A confiscation hearing is mandatory in all cases if the prosecution apply for a determination (and do not withdraw their application). The parties may be required to exchange pleadings (see **E19.12**). The purpose of the confiscation hearing is to determine whether a defendant has benefited from criminal conduct and, if so, the value of that benefit (see **E19.46**). In determining these questions the court must, if the defendant has a 'criminal lifestyle', as defined, apply certain assumptions that property held or obtained (both currently and historically) should count as his benefit from criminal conduct (unless it would be unjust for those assumptions to be applied, see **E19.41**). If the court finds that the defendant has benefited in a particular sum, there is a duty to make a confiscation order in that sum, unless the defendant shows that the amount available to him is less than that sum (see **E19.81**). The duty to make a confiscation order is subject to exceptions, including where civil proceedings are anticipated and where to make the order would be 'disproportionate' (see **E19.61**).

Jurisdiction

E19.2 The POCA 2002 came into force on 24 March 2003. The basic framework is a merger and extension of the two similar but separate schemes contained in the Drug Trafficking Act 1994 for drug offences and in the CJA 1988 for other offences. The transitional arrangements specify that Part 2 shall not have effect where the index offence, or *any* of the offences, was committed before that date — in which case the earlier legislation should be applied. Where an offence occurs over a period, it is taken to have occurred on the earliest day in the period (Proceeds of Crime Act 2002 (Transitional Provisions, Savings and Amendment) Order (SI 2003 No. 333)). A defendant charged with a conspiracy which straddled the commencement date and who pleaded guilty on the basis that the first act admitted was after that date, but who did not suggest that the pleaded conspiracy dates were wrong, fell to be dealt with under the earlier legislation (*Evwierhowa* [2011] EWCA Crim 572, [2011] 2 Cr App R (S) 77 (442)). Where offences in an indictment straddle the material date and the prosecutor bases the confiscation application only upon offences committed after that date, it is permissible to proceed under the POCA 2002 (*McCool* [2018] UKSC 23, [2018] 1 WLR 2431, approving *Stapleton* [2008] EWCA Crim 1308, [2009] 1 Cr App R (S) 38 (209)). If the prosecutor wishes to proceed in respect of all such offences, careful consideration will need to be given to whether this is possible and, if so, how to proceed. In *McCool*, Lord Reed (with whom Lord Mance agreed), who gave the dissenting judgment, considered (at [150]–[152]) that the logic of Lord Hughes' judgment (with which Lady Black agreed) was that the prosecution could not so proceed since they would have to 'forego any confiscation proceedings in respect of pre-commencement offences' (though see [93], where Lord Hughes appears to say the opposite and envisages a single set of proceedings under the repealed legislation). By contrast Lord Reed understood Lord Kerr (who gave the other majority judgment) to be saying that it was possible for the prosecution so to proceed but there would have to be two sets of proceedings (one under the POCA 2002, the other under the repealed regime). Similarly, in a mixed indictment, where the defendant is convicted only of offences occurring after the relevant date, the appropriate regime is that of the POCA 2002 (*Onuigbo* [2014] EWCA Crim 65). Where there are two indictments, one relating to offences committed before 24 March 2003 and the other relating to offences all committed after that date, the court must treat them as separate proceedings and apply separate confiscation regimes (*Moulden* [2008] EWCA Crim 2648, [2009] 1 Cr App R 27 (362)). An order made under the incorrect legislation may be corrected on appeal by simple substitution (*McCool*, approving *Lazarus* [2004] EWCA Crim 2297, [2005] 1 Cr App R (S) 98 (552) and *Bukhari* [2008] EWCA Crim 2915, [2009] 2 Cr App R (S) 18 (113)).

The Prosecutor

A central actor in confiscation proceedings is 'the prosecutor', i.e. the legal person that has brought the criminal prosecution out of which the confiscation proceedings arise or that has assumed conduct of those proceedings. It means 'a person entitled to prosecute'. A decision to prosecute that is motivated by the possibility of receiving a percentage of any confiscation order may be abusive, as in the case of *Scott* [2019] EWCA Crim 205, [2020] 4 WLR 2 (but see, on the other side of the line, *Kombou v Wood Green Crown Court* [2020] EWHC 1529 (Admin)). A private prosecutor is entitled to bring confiscation proceedings even where that person has no financial or personal interest in the outcome (*R (Virgin Media Ltd) v Zinga* [2014] EWCA Crim 52, [2014] 1 Cr App R 27 (382)). In *Zinga*, in return for police assistance in prosecuting a company which had unlawfully sold equipment allowing free access to Virgin products, Virgin Media had undertaken to donate 25 per cent of any compensation to the police in return for assistance in the investigation of the offence. It did not matter that private prosecutors could not conduct financial investigations into a defendant's circumstances and supply the statement of information required by the POCA 2002. The Act distinguished between those who could investigate and those who could prosecute. The fact that a prosecutor may not possess investigative powers did not impair the ability to participate fully in confiscation proceedings provided that an appropriate officer, as defined by s. 378(1), assisted by exercising the investigatory powers. As the confiscation proceedings were for the sole benefit of the State, it could not be said that the agreement between Virgin Media and the police was an abuse of process, but it did run the risk of providing an incentive for the police to devote resources to assisting Virgin in its claim for compensation and gave rise to a perception of compromised police independence. It was not appropriate for the Court to comment upon the circumstances in which the police should assist in confiscation proceedings brought by private prosecutors, but such issues should be the subject of careful and very urgent consideration by those responsible for policing. E19.3

The Process: A Summary

Proceeds of Crime Act 2002, s. 6 E19.4

(1) The Crown Court must proceed under this section if the following two conditions are satisfied.
(2) The first condition is that a defendant falls within any of the following paragraphs—
  (a) he is convicted of an offence or offences in proceedings before the Crown Court;
  (b) he is committed to the Crown Court for sentence in respect of an offence or offences under section 3, 3A, 3B, 3C, 4, 4A or 6 of the Sentencing Act;
  (c) he is committed to the Crown Court in respect of an offence or offences under section 70 below (committal with a view to a confiscation order being considered).
(3) The *second condition* is that—
  (a) the prosecutor asks the court to proceed under this section, or
  (b) the court believes it is appropriate for it to do so.
(4) The court must proceed as follows—
  (a) it must decide whether the defendant has a criminal lifestyle;
  (b) if it decides that he has a criminal lifestyle it must decide whether he has benefited from his general criminal conduct;
  (c) if it decides that he does not have a criminal lifestyle it must decide whether he has benefited from his particular criminal conduct.

(5) If the court decides under subsection (4)(b) or (c) that the defendant has benefited from the conduct referred to it must—
(a) decide the recoverable amount, and
(b) make an order (a confiscation order) requiring him to pay that amount.
Paragraph (b) applies only if, or to the extent that, it would not be disproportionate to require the defendant to pay the recoverable amount.
(6) But the court must treat the duty in subsection (5) as a power if it believes that any victim of the conduct has at any time started or intends to start proceedings against the defendant in respect of loss, injury or damage sustained in connection with the conduct.
(6A) The court must also treat the duty in subsection (5) as a power if—
(a) an order has been made, or it believes an order may be made, against the defendant under section 4 (criminal unlawful profit orders) of the Prevention of Social Housing Fraud Act 2013 in respect of profit made by the defendant in connection with the conduct, or
(b) it believes that a person has at any time started or intends to start proceedings against the defendant under section 5 (civil unlawful profit orders) of that Act in respect of such profit.
(7) The court must decide any question arising under subsection (4) or (5) on a balance of probabilities.
(8) The first condition is not satisfied if the defendant absconds (but section 27 may apply).
(9) References in this Part to the offence (or offences) concerned are to the offence (or offences) mentioned in subsection (2).

E19.5 Under s. 6(2) an order may be made in the Crown Court against anyone (a) convicted of an offence in the Crown Court; (b) committed to the Crown Court for sentence; or (c) committed to the Crown Court for specific consideration of a confiscation order. Magistrates must commit a convicted defendant to the Crown Court 'with a view to a confiscation order being considered' if the prosecution so requests (s. 70). This includes summary offences (*Sumal & Sons (Properties) Ltd* [2012] EWCA Crim 1840, [2013] 1 WLR 2078). The magistrates themselves have no power to make confiscation orders (until such time as the Secretary of State may exercise the power under the SOCPA 2005, s. 97, to make provision for summary confiscation).

It is submitted that confiscation may not be pursued against a deceased defendant (cf. *Turk* [2017] EWCA Crim 391, [2017] 1 WLR 2919 at [14]). That possibility aside, a strict order of events must be followed after conviction or committal (for 'a useful guide', see *Whittington* [2009] EWCA Crim 1641, [2010] 1 Cr App R (S) 83 (545)).

The process starts when the prosecution asks for an inquiry or when 'the court believes it is appropriate' to hold one. This is a strict obligation. Absent exceptional circumstances it would be inappropriate for a judge to decline to proceed under s. 6 on the assumed basis that, were the matter to proceed to a final hearing, any resulting order would be disproportionate (*Parveaz* [2017] EWCA Crim 873).

The court must then decide whether D has a 'criminal lifestyle'. This depends upon the nature of the offence or offences of which D has been convicted in the current or earlier proceedings (see **E19.18**). There are then five stages.

E19.6 **Stage 1** The judge must determine whether D has a 'criminal lifestyle'. This determines whether the statutory assumptions apply and the approach to any tainted gifts that may have been made (see **E19.54**).

E19.7 **Stage 2** The judge must determine whether D has benefited from 'criminal conduct', that is whether D has obtained property or a pecuniary advantage as a result of or in connection with criminal conduct. There are two alternatives:

(i) if D has been found to have a criminal lifestyle, the court must determine whether D has benefited from 'his *general* criminal conduct'; or
(ii) if D does not have a criminal lifestyle, the court must determine whether D has benefited from 'his *particular* criminal conduct' (i.e. from the particular offence(s) of which D has been convicted and from any offences taken into consideration).

E19.8 **Stage 3** The judge must determine the value of D's proceeds of crime or benefit — 'the recoverable amount'. In calculating benefit from 'general criminal conduct', the judge must apply the relevant assumptions as to income and expenditure in the previous six years and as to property 'held' by D on conviction (unless D can show an assumption to be incorrect or that 'there would be a serious risk of injustice if an assumption were made').

Stage 4 The judge must make a confiscation order in that sum *unless* D can prove that the value of all D's existing assets, known as 'the available amount' (including the value of any gifts made to third parties), is less than the value of the benefit. If so, the 'available amount' becomes the 'recoverable amount', which is the amount of the confiscation order. At this stage the court is now able to make determinations as to D's interest in property which are binding on third parties (see **E19.57**). **E19.9**

Stage 5 This concerns the proportionality of the order contemplated at stage 4. The duty to make the order at stage 4 applies only if, or to the extent that, it would not be disproportionate to require D to pay the recoverable amount (s. 6(5)(b)). In other words, the court may reduce an order, or not make one at all, to avoid a disproportionate outcome. Proceedings may be stayed as an abuse of process. In *R (Secretary of State for Work and Pensions) v Croydon Crown Court* [2010] EWHC 805 (Admin), [2011] 1 Cr App R (S) 1 (1), the Divisional Court upheld a judge's refusal to make an order following an earlier unequivocal representation by the judge (to which the prosecution did not object) that confiscation proceedings would not follow if voluntary repayment was made. For the court to give an offender an inducement and then renege after the offender had acted to his or her disadvantage would damage the integrity of the criminal justice process. However, there ought to be no occasion to resort to this doctrine to prevent an allegedly disproportionate order, given that the court is now under a duty not to make such an order. **E19.10**

Procedure is governed by CrimPR 33.1 to 33.27 (see Supplement, **R33.1** *et seq.*).

The confiscation order may be made before sentence. Alternatively, the court may postpone the confiscation hearing for up to two years from the date of conviction and proceed first to sentence the defendant, but must not impose any financial orders or penalties in that period, such as a compensation order or fine (POCA 2002, s. 15). In 'exceptional circumstances' longer postponements are possible (see **E19.70**).

Information, Evidence and Proof

Proceeds of Crime Act 2002, ss. 16 to 18 **E19.11**

16.—(1) If the court is proceeding under section 6 in a case where section 6(3)(a) applies, the prosecutor must give the court a statement of information within the period the court orders.

(2) If the court is proceeding under section 6 in a case where section 6(3)(b) applies and it orders the prosecutor to give it a statement of information, the prosecutor must give it such a statement within the period the court orders.

(3) If the prosecutor believes the defendant has a criminal lifestyle the statement of information is a statement of matters the prosecutor believes are relevant in connection with deciding these issues—
 (a) whether the defendant has a criminal lifestyle;
 (b) whether he has benefited from his general criminal conduct;
 (c) his benefit from the conduct.

(4) A statement under subsection (3) must include information the prosecutor believes is relevant—
 (a) in connection with the making by the court of a required assumption under section 10;
 (b) for the purpose of enabling the court to decide if the circumstances are such that it must not make such an assumption.

(5) If the prosecutor does not believe the defendant has a criminal lifestyle the statement of information is a statement of matters the prosecutor believes are relevant in connection with deciding these issues—
 (a) whether the defendant has benefited from his particular criminal conduct;
 (b) his benefit from the conduct.

(6) If the prosecutor gives the court a statement of information—
 (a) he may at any time give the court a further statement of information;
 (b) he must give the court a further statement of information if it orders him to do so, and he must give it within the period the court orders.

(6A) A statement of information (other than one to which subsection (6B) applies) must include any information known to the prosecutor which the prosecutor believes is or would be relevant for the purpose of enabling the court to decide—
(a) whether to make a determination under section 10A, or
(b) what determination to make (if the court decides to make one).
(6B) If the court has decided to make a determination under section 10A, a further statement of information under subsection (6)(b) must, if the court so orders, include specified information that is relevant to the determination.
(7) If the court makes an order under this section it may at any time vary it by making another one.

17.—(1) If the prosecutor gives the court a statement of information and a copy is served on the defendant, the court may order the defendant—
(a) to indicate (within the period it orders) the extent to which he accepts each allegation in the statement, and
(b) so far as he does not accept such an allegation, to give particulars of any matters he proposes to rely on.
(2) If the defendant accepts to any extent an allegation in a statement of information the court may treat his acceptance as conclusive of the matters to which it relates for the purpose of deciding the issues referred to in section 16(3) or (5) (as the case may be).
(3) If the defendant fails in any respect to comply with an order under subsection (1) he may be treated for the purposes of subsection (2) as accepting every allegation in the statement of information apart from—
(a) any allegation in respect of which he has complied with the requirement;
(b) any allegation that he has benefited from his general or particular criminal conduct.
(4) For the purposes of this section an allegation may be accepted or particulars may be given in a manner ordered by the court.
(5) If the court makes an order under this section it may at any time vary it by making another one.
(6) No acceptance under this section that the defendant has benefited from conduct is admissible in evidence in proceedings for an offence.

18.—(1) This section applies if—
(a) the court is proceeding under section 6 in a case where section 6(3)(a) applies, or
(b) it is proceeding under section 6 in a case where section 6(3)(b) applies or it is considering whether to proceed.
(2) For the purpose of obtaining information to help it in carrying out its functions (including functions under section 10A) the court may at any time order the defendant to give it information specified in the order.
(3) An order under this section may require all or a specified part of the information to be given in a specified manner and before a specified date.
(4) If the defendant fails without reasonable excuse to comply with an order under this section the court may draw such inference as it believes is appropriate.
(5) Subsection (4) does not affect any power of the court to deal with the defendant in respect of a failure to comply with an order under this section.
(6) If the prosecutor accepts to any extent an allegation made by the defendant—
(a) in giving information required by an order under this section, or
(b) in any other statement given to the court in relation to any matter relevant to deciding
(i) the available amount under section 9, or
(ii) whether to make a determination under section 10A, or what determination to make (if the court decides to make one),

the court may treat the acceptance as conclusive of the matters to which it relates.
(7) For the purposes of this section an allegation may be accepted in a manner ordered by the court.
(8) If the court makes an order under this section it may at any time vary it by making another one.
(9) No information given under this section which amounts to an admission by the defendant that he has benefited from criminal conduct is admissible in evidence in proceedings for an offence.

E19.12 **Exchange of Information** The procedure has its own form of pleadings governed by CrimPR 33.13 (see Supplement, **R33.13**). First, the prosecution must serve a 'Statement of Information' outlining the matters that they believe are relevant to the various stages of the inquiry (POCA 2002, s. 16).

In return, D may be ordered to 'indicate... in a manner ordered by the court' the extent to which D accepts the allegations in the statement and, if D does not accept any allegation, 'to give particulars of any matters he proposes to rely on' (s. 17). If D fails 'in any respect' to comply with such an order, D may be treated as having accepted 'every allegation' in the statement apart from (a) those to which D has responded and (b) the basic allegation that D has benefited from criminal conduct (*Crutchley* (1994) 15 Cr App R (S) 627). If it was clear from the terms on which D consented to an order that D unambiguously accepted facts which justified the making of an order, a judge, provided that he or she was satisfied there had been an unambiguous acceptance of those facts from which D should not be permitted to resile, would be entitled to rely on the consent. This is not simply because D has consented but because the acceptance constitutes evidence upon which the judge is entitled to rely. Nevertheless, 'judges should be astute to ensure that agreements on the amount to be recovered were soundly based' (*Mackle* [2014] UKSC 5, [2014] AC 678). In reaching, under s. 6, its own determination of the 'recoverable amount', the court is not bound by any agreement between the parties as to the extent of D's property (*Kelly* [2016] EWCA Crim 1505).

The court also has a free-standing power at any time to order D to provide written information 'to help it in carrying out its functions' (s. 18). Typically, any such order is made at the start of the pleadings, even before the prosecution have served a statement under s. 16. Where the court is considering (a) whether to make a determination under s. 10A of the extent of D's interest in any property, or (b) is deciding what determination to make (see **E19.39**), it may order the prosecutor, D or an 'interested person' to provide information (ss. 16, 18 and 18A). An 'interested person' is a person (other than D) 'who the court thinks is or may be a person holding an interest in the property' (s. 18A(1)). Where there is a claim by an interested party, the court should be clear whether it is making a s. 10A determination, and give reasons (*Ghulam* [2018] EWCA Crim 1691, [2019] 1 WLR 534).

Failure to comply without reasonable excuse entitles the court to draw adverse inferences. These provisions may not be used to compel information from a third party such as a solicitor to provide information (*R (Dechert Solicitors) v Southwark Crown Court* [2001] EWHC Admin 477); but the court may be able to make an investigative order under the POCA 2002, Part 8 (see **D8.36** ***et seq.***).

Evidence and Proof The standard of proof is that of 'the balance of probabilities' (POCA 2002, s. 6(7)). (There may be one exception: where the prosecution can prove the obtaining of benefit *only* by proof of criminal offences outside the indictment, the criminal standard may apply (*Briggs-Price* [2009] UKHL 19, [2009] 1 AC 1026: see further below).) The prosecution carry the burden of proving both the fact that D has benefited from criminal conduct and the amount of D's benefit. However, in lifestyle cases, once the prosecution establish any relevant income, expenditure or interest in property that is attributable to D, there are mandatory, albeit rebuttable, assumptions to the effect that such income or property or expenditure should count as D's 'benefit'. Once the value of benefit is established, D carries the burden of proving that the available amount is less than that value. **E19.13**

It has been held that 'the ordinary rules of criminal evidence [do] not apply' to confiscation hearings (*Silcock* [2004] EWCA Crim 408, [2004] 2 Cr App R (S) 61 (323)). The hearsay provisions of the CJA 2003, while not strictly applicable, provide an appropriate framework for the determination of admissibility issues (*Clipston* [2011] EWCA Crim 446, [2011] 2 Cr App R (S) 101 (569)). Where the hearing has been preceded by a contested trial, the judge is entitled to form a personal view from the evidence (*Threapleton* [2001] EWCA Crim 2892, [2003] 3 All ER 458). If a *Newton* hearing is held to resolve a dispute of fact that is relevant to confiscation, the court should ensure that D is given an opportunity to give oral evidence, where that is necessary to ensure a fair hearing (*Morrow* [2019] NICA 71). However, in the confiscation proceedings, D is still entitled to challenge the evidence. This is so even where D has pleaded guilty and has declined a *Newton* hearing. The court must act with scrupulous fairness in making its assessment for the purposes of a confiscation order and afford D every opportunity to challenge evidence and to call witnesses (*Knaggs* [2009] EWCA Crim 1363, [2010] 1 WLR 435; *HM Advocate v McIntosh (No. 1)* [2003] UKPC D 1, [2003] 1 AC 1078; *Jenkins* (1990–91) 12 Cr App R (S) 582). Even so, an unqualified plea of guilty with no challenge to the prosecution opening on the basis of which D was content to be sentenced are circumstances that the judge is entitled to regard as powerful evidence contradicting assertions made in the confiscation proceedings. The judge may take account of discrepancies between D's evidence in the trial and D's evidence in the confiscation hearing (*O'Connell* [2005] EWCA Crim 1520). The judge may make additional and more extensive findings of fact than those upon which the verdict was based and is entitled to take into account all the evidence heard in the confiscation hearing provided that the judge acts consistently with the verdict and its factual basis (*Sangha* [2008] EWCA Crim 2562, [2009] 2 Cr App R (S) 17 (94)).

Where the evidence of a particular benefit derives solely from evidence of the commission of other offences, the ECHR, Article 6(1), requires proof of that offence to the criminal standard, but the extent of any benefit from such an offence may be proved to the civil standard (*Briggs-Price* [2009] UKHL 19, [2009] 1 AC 1026). *Briggs-Price* was distinguished in *Bagnall* [2012] EWCA Crim 677, [2013] 1 WLR 204, in which the Court of Appeal held that, in a case where the assumptions as to benefit were engaged, the prosecution were not required to prove the source of that benefit to the criminal standard, albeit that this involved allegations and evidence of other offences. *Briggs-Price* was distinguished on the basis that the 'issue in that case concerned the logically prior question of whether the defendant had been in possession of property in the past' and not its source (see also *Whittington* [2009] EWCA Crim 1641, [2010] 1 Cr App R (S) 83 (545)).

E19.14 **Effect of the Basis of a Guilty Plea** The agreed basis of a guilty plea, while relevant to sentence, will not necessarily limit the ambit of the confiscation inquiry. The prosecution should consider whether any sentencing concession might conflict with the assumptions of benefit which must ordinarily be applied in subsequent confiscation proceedings (see **E19.34**). 'What is unacceptable is for the concession to be made for part of the sentencing process, without qualification, but for reliance to be placed, tacitly, on the assumptions when it comes to the confiscation hearing' (*Lunnon* [2004] EWCA Crim 1125, [2005] 1 Cr App R (S) 24 (111)). In *Lunnon*, it had been accepted by the Crown that D had no prior involvement in drug trafficking. In those circumstances, to apply a mandatory assumption that D had previously benefited from drug trafficking would amount to 'injustice' and allow the court to disapply the assumption. The determining feature is the extent of the concession made by the prosecution rather than the fact that D's plea has been entered on a limited basis. In *Lazarus* [2004] EWCA Crim 2297, [2005] 1 Cr App R (S) 98 (552), the prosecution accepted a guilty plea to a drugs offence on the basis of limited involvement in the offence. The Court of Appeal nevertheless upheld a confiscation order that 'assumed' that monies passing through a bank account in previous years were the proceeds of drug trafficking. It held that the basis of the plea was not inconsistent with prior drug trafficking; the prosecution had never been invited to agree, as they had in *Lunnon*, that there had been no previous trafficking and D had known shortly after the acceptance of his plea that the prosecution were seeking to rely on the statutory assumptions and had the opportunity to rebut them. In *Green* [2007] EWCA Crim 1248, [2007] 3 All ER 751, the Crown and defence reached agreement that the extent of large-scale skunk trafficking was in fact greater than had been admitted by D in an earlier written basis of plea. The Court of Appeal held that, in the particular circumstances, the judge was not entitled to reject the agreed figures in favour of the basis of plea. The agreed figures provided a full account of the money gained (from skunk trafficking) whereas the basis of plea did not. Adopting the basis of plea had led the judge into error, in that he had assumed the existence of another source of income (from Class A drugs) for which there was no credible evidence. In *Bakewell* [2006] EWCA Crim 2, [2006] 2 Cr App R (S) 42 (277), the prosecution accepted a written basis of plea limiting the amount of D's payment for participation in a fraudulent evasion of duty. Significantly, they were not prepared to accept D's assertion that this was the extent of his benefit, and the confiscation proceedings could properly proceed on the basis that his benefit was not limited to the payment but was the value of the pecuniary advantage obtained in the evasion of duty.

E19.15 In most cases the prosecution are best advised to say no more than that they do not dispute a defence assertion for the purposes of sentence but that they cannot say what information may arise in the course of the confiscation inquiry (*Lazarus*).

E19.16 **Special Counsel** Frequently, the judge will have seen and reviewed material which has not been disclosed for reasons of public interest immunity. The material may be highly adverse to a defendant in subsequent confiscation proceedings and, in particular, damaging to credibility — e.g., information that the defendant has been a highly successful criminal for many years. In such a situation, the appointment of special counsel should be considered (*May* [2005] EWCA Crim 97, [2005] 3 All ER 523).

MAKING OF CONFISCATION ORDER

Stage One — Determining Criminal Lifestyle

Proceeds of Crime Act 2002, s. 75 **E19.17**

(1) A defendant has a criminal lifestyle if (and only if) the following condition is satisfied.
(2) The condition is that the offence (or any of the offences) concerned satisfies any of these tests—
    (a) it is specified in Schedule 2;
    (b) it constitutes conduct forming part of a course of criminal activity;
    (c) it is an offence committed over a period of at least six months and the defendant has benefited from the conduct which constitutes the offence.
(3) Conduct forms part of a course of criminal activity if the defendant has benefited from the conduct and—
    (a) in the proceedings in which he was convicted he was convicted of three or more other offences, each of three or more of them constituting conduct from which he has benefited, or
    (b) in the period of six years ending with the day when those proceedings were started (or, if there is more than one such day, the earliest day) he was convicted on at least two separate occasions of an offence constituting conduct from which he has benefited.
(4) But an offence does not satisfy the test in subsection (2)(b) or (c) unless the defendant obtains relevant benefit of not less than £5000.
(5) Relevant benefit for the purposes of subsection (2)(b) is—
    (a) benefit from conduct which constitutes the offence;
    (b) benefit from any other conduct which forms part of the course of criminal activity and which constitutes an offence of which the defendant has been convicted;
    (c) benefit from conduct which constitutes an offence which has been or will be taken into consideration by the court in sentencing the defendant for an offence mentioned in paragraph (a) or (b).
(6) Relevant benefit for the purposes of subsection (2)(c) is—
    (a) benefit from conduct which constitutes the offence;
    (b) benefit from conduct which constitutes an offence which has been or will be taken into consideration by the court in sentencing the defendant for the offence mentioned in paragraph (a).

The court must first decide whether D has a 'criminal lifestyle' (s. 6(4)(a)). This is a purely formulaic exercise by which D qualifies if one of the offences of which D has been convicted falls within the statutory catalogue in s. 75. **E19.18**

There are three sub-divisions:

(a) Offences specified in sch. 2 (including their inchoate forms and encouraging or assisting the commission of such an offence under the SCA 2007, s. 44). The specified offences fall under the following broad headings: (i) drug trafficking; (ii) money laundering; (iii) directing terrorism; (iv) people trafficking; (v) arms trafficking; (vi) counterfeiting; (vii) intellectual property; (viii) prostitution and child sex; (ix) blackmail. An offence under the Gangmasters (Licensing) Act 2004, s. 12, is also specified as are offences contrary to the Modern Slavery Act 2015, ss. 1 and 2.
(b) An offence that 'constitutes conduct forming part of a course of criminal activity'. To qualify, D must have been convicted of:
    (i) three or more other offences in the current proceedings, each of which was committed on or after 24 March 2003 and which constitutes conduct from which D has benefited (i.e. at least four offences in all), or
    (ii) such an offence on at least two separate occasions in the six years before the current proceedings were started.

A conviction for these purposes includes an offence taken into consideration. The total benefit from the offences or offences taken into consideration must be at least £5,000.

(c) An offence committed over a period of at least six months resulting in benefit of not less than £5,000. (This condition is not met where a conspiracy lasted for over six months but the individual defendant participated for a shorter period: *Bajwa* [2011] EWCA Crim 1093, [2012] 1 All ER 348. A count which specifies an offence as having been committed between 1 January and 31 December 2006 will not qualify as a 'lifestyle' offence if the evidence shows that the offence was actually committed over two months: *Odamo* [2013] EWCA Crim 1275, [2014] 1 Cr App R (S) 44 (252).)

Stage Two — Determination of Benefit from Criminal Conduct

E19.19 **Proceeds of Crime Act 2002, s. 76**

(1) Criminal conduct is conduct which—
  (a) constitutes an offence in England and Wales, or
  (b) would constitute such an offence if it occurred in England and Wales.
(2) General criminal conduct of the defendant is all his criminal conduct, and it is immaterial—
  (a) whether conduct occurred before or after the passing of this Act;
  (b) whether property constituting a benefit from conduct was obtained before or after the passing of this Act.
(3) Particular criminal conduct of the defendant is all his criminal conduct which falls within the following paragraphs—
  (a) conduct which constitutes the offence or offences concerned;
  (b) conduct which constitutes offences of which he was convicted in the same proceedings as those in which he was convicted of the offence or offences concerned;
  (c) conduct which constitutes offences which the court will be taking into consideration in deciding his sentence for the offence or offences concerned.
(4) A person benefits from conduct if he obtains property as a result of or in connection with the conduct.
(5) If a person obtains a pecuniary advantage as a result of or in connection with conduct, he is to be taken to obtain as a result of or in connection with the conduct a sum of money equal to the value of the pecuniary advantage.
(6) References to property or a pecuniary advantage obtained in connection with conduct include references to property or a pecuniary advantage obtained both in that connection and some other.
(7) If a person benefits from conduct his benefit is the value of the property obtained.

E19.20 At this stage the court must determine whether D has benefited from criminal conduct, which means conduct that either constitutes an offence in England and Wales or that would constitute an offence if it occurred here (s. 76(1)). D benefits from criminal conduct if D thereby 'obtains' property (see **E19.21**).

If D does not have a criminal lifestyle, the court must nevertheless determine the benefit of 'his *particular* criminal conduct' (s. 6(4)(c)). The inquiry is restricted to the offences that are proved or admitted in the current proceedings, including offences taken into consideration (s. 76(3)). The assumptions do not apply. If the conviction relates to conduct on a particular day, the benefit is strictly referable to property obtained as a result of the offence on that day, even if it was part of a longer course of conduct that was not pleaded (*Panalyi* [2019] EWCA Crim 413, [2019] 2 Cr App R (S) 21 (154)). If, on the other hand, D does have a criminal lifestyle, the court must determine D's benefit from 'his general criminal conduct' (s. 6(4)(b)). General criminal conduct is all D's criminal conduct regardless of when it occurred (s. 76(2)). In determining benefit from general criminal conduct in the period of six years prior to charge and subsequently, the court must apply the required assumptions (see **E19.34**). Where the prosecution have elected to proceed against only post-commencement offences (see **E19.2**), D's benefit from general criminal conduct may properly include property obtained as a result of pre-commencement offences on the indictment (*McCool* [2018] UKSC 23, [2018] 1 WLR 2431, per Lord Hughes at [93]). Note, however, that, where a confiscation order has been made in earlier proceedings based on D's general criminal conduct, no account may be taken in a subsequent application of any benefit obtained prior to the earlier order (*Chahal* [2014] EWCA Crim 101, [2014] 2 Cr App R (S) 35 (288)).

Obtaining A person benefits from criminal conduct 'if he obtains property as a result of or in connection with the conduct' (POCA 2002, s. 76(4)). If a person obtains a pecuniary advantage as a result of or in connection with conduct, the person is to be taken to obtain, as a result of or in connection with the conduct, a sum of money equal to the value of the pecuniary advantage (s. 76(5)) (see **E19.26**). **E19.21**

Property is 'obtained' by a person 'if he obtains an interest in it' (s. 84(2)(b)). An interest in land includes 'any legal estate or equitable interest or power' (s. 84(2)(f)); an interest in property other than land includes a right to possession (s. 84(2)(h)). Property is all property wherever situated and includes (a) money, (b) all forms of real or personal property, (c) things in action and other intangible or incorporeal property. Thus it has a wide definition which, it is submitted, is likely to include cryptocurrency (see the Commercial Court's conclusion in *AA v Persons Unknown* [2019] EWHC 3556 (Comm), [2020] 4 WLR 35, that cryptocurrency could be the subject of an interim proprietary injunction) (see also **E19.51** to **E19.52**). Property held or obtained abroad may nevertheless count as benefit, notwithstanding that no offence has been committed in that jurisdiction, provided such property was obtained as a result of or in connection with an offence committed within the UK (*McKinnon* [2004] EWCA Crim 395, [2004] 2 Cr App R (S) 46 (234)).

The burden of proving that D has obtained property and the amount of that property lies upon the prosecution to the civil standard of proof. There may possibly be an exception requiring proof to the criminal standard where the prosecution can *only* establish that D had obtained property in the past by proof of criminal offences other than those charged on the indictment (*Briggs-Price* [2009] UKHL 19, [2009] 1 AC 1026: see **E19.13**). However, this does not mean that, whenever the evidence upon which the prosecution rely to prove the obtaining of property implies the commission of offences, the prosecution must then necessarily prove the fact of the obtaining to the criminal standard: 'If the prosecution can prove that the defendant has obtained assets in the past other than by proof of previous criminal offences then the prosecution may do so on a balance of probabilities' (*Whittington* [2009] EWCA Crim 1641, [2010] 1 Cr App R (S) 83 (545) at [31]).

In an important review of confiscation principles, the House of Lords in *May* [2008] UKHL 28, [2008] 1 AC 1028, held that the phrase 'obtains' connotes 'a power of disposition or control'. Their lordships set out 'broad principles' which include the following: **E19.22**

> D ordinarily obtains property if in law he owns it, whether alone or jointly, which will ordinarily connote a power of disposition or control, as where a person directs a payment or conveyance of property to someone else. He ordinarily obtains a pecuniary advantage if (among other things) he evades a liability to which he is personally subject. Mere couriers or custodians or other very minor contributors to an offence, rewarded by a specific fee and having no interest in the property or the proceeds of sale, are unlikely to be found to have obtained that property. It may be otherwise with money launderers.

In *Jennings v CPS* [2008] UKHL 29, [2008] 1 AC 1046, the House applied *May*, holding that a defendant 'cannot, and should not, be deprived of what he has never obtained or its equivalent, because that is a fine' (at [13]). In particular, it is not sufficient that D is instrumental in the property being obtained as D's acts may contribute significantly to property being obtained without D obtaining it.

Crystallisation of Benefit The obtaining need only be momentary. The burglar caught in the act obtains what has momentarily been taken: 'Success or otherwise is irrelevant' (*Wilkes* [2003] EWCA Crim 848, [2003] 2 Cr App R (S) 105 (625) at [29]). Note, however, that in *Wilkes* the prosecutor did not assert that the benefit should include the value of the recovered goods, and an **E19.23**

order which did include their value would be disproportionate (*Waya* [2012] UKSC 51, [2013] 1 AC 294: see **E19.61**). By contrast, there will be cases where the criminal plan is far advanced but nothing has yet been obtained by D. In *Frost* [2009] EWCA Crim 1737, [2010] 1 Cr App R (S) 73 (485), a school business manager created false invoices which resulted in the local authority reclaiming VAT which was credited to the school bank account. Although he had been able to bring about the transfer into the school account dishonestly, the transfers fell short of creating a thing in action against the bank in his favour and, therefore, did not give him an interest in the property until he successfully extracted the money from that account. One should not 'confuse criminal liability and resulting benefit' (at [18]). A criminal plan may be disrupted prior to the crystallisation of any benefit, as where cigarettes were seized prior to the duty point, at which point the pecuniary advantage (the evaded duty) would have been obtained (*Bajwa* [2011] EWCA Crim 1093, [2012] 1 All ER 348). Likewise, no benefit is obtained if D withdraws from a conspiracy to rob prior to the robbery being carried out (*Byatt* [2006] EWCA Crim 904, [2006] 2 Cr App R (S) 116 (779)). In *Olubitan* [2003] EWCA Crim 2940, [2004] 2 Cr App R (S) 14 (70), D joined the conspiracy on the day that police action brought it to an end. The Court of Appeal stated (at [25]):

> We reject [the] extreme submission ... that, where there is a conspiracy, anyone who joins the conspiracy as a matter of law becomes liable for his proportion of the total amount by which the conspirators as a whole may have benefited. [The Act requires] findings of fact ... the court may often be entitled to make robust inferences if convicted defendants remain unhelpful as to which of them obtained what benefit as defined by the Act ... the section is not to be construed so that a person may be held to have obtained property or derived a pecuniary advantage when a proper view of the evidence demonstrates that he has not in fact done so.

E19.24 **Disposition or Control** In *May* [2008] UKHL 28, [2008] 1 AC 1028, the House of Lords held that an obtaining of property 'will ordinarily connote a power of disposition or control' (at [48]). In *Wilkinson* [2009] EWCA Crim 2733, D drove a stolen car which, following a test drive, he declined to purchase. He pleaded guilty to being in possession of criminal property. A confiscation order for the full value of the car was quashed. He had obtained the property for a limited time and a limited purpose and had no more control over the property than a courier or custodian would have had.

The statement in *May* (at [48]) that the approach to obtaining may not apply to 'money launderers' was examined in *Allpress* [2009] EWCA Crim 8, [2009] 2 Cr App R (S) 58 (399). A five-judge court considered whether a defendant convicted of money laundering obtained the entirety of the property being laundered. The five conjoined appeals respectively involved: couriers of cash derived from drug trafficking; a shopkeeper who had allowed the storage of cash at his shop knowing it was criminal property, and a partner in a law firm who had used a firm account to transfer funds obtained by another's criminal conduct. The Court of Appeal rejected the prosecution argument that money laundering cases constitute a 'special category'. A person was not to be regarded as holding an interest in property merely because the person was in manual possession. Even if a mere custodian of property were held to have a limited interest in the property, the relevant value would be the value of that interest, which if the property was being held purely for another would be nil. Accordingly, cases such as *Simpson* [1998] 2 Cr App R (S) 111, doubted in *May*, which held that a courier of cash obtains the whole amount carried, are no longer good law. However, in relation to the case involving the law firm, the bank account was that of D and his partners. Payment of money into that account gave rise to a thing in action in his favour, jointly with his partners. The starting point was therefore that that was his property (applying *Sharma* [2006] EWCA Crim 16, [2006] 2 Cr App R (S) 63 (416)). D had assisted another to retain control of the proceeds of that person's criminal conduct but, with that ultimate objective, had received funds in respect of which he had legal ownership and practical control. Note also *Roper* [2014] EWCA Crim 2476 and *Ilyas v Aylesbury District Council* [2008] EWCA Crim 1303, [2009] 1 Cr App R (S) 59 (316), where D had allowed the transfer of a house into her name as part of a fraudulent scheme by her family in which she subsequently transferred it back to the family. It was held that, where the legal title to real property is transferred as a result of or in connection with a fraudulent scheme, especially where the transferee is party to the scheme, he or she is generally in sufficient control of the title to meet the *May* test and is liable for the full value of the property.

Individual Benefit The Court of Appeal has emphasised that it is the individual defendant's benefit that matters, not the benefit of the wider criminal enterprise. In *Sivaraman* [2008] EWCA Crim 1736, [2009] 1 Cr App R (S) 80 (469), the manager of a service station accepted delivery of fuel on behalf of his employer without excise duty being paid. His benefit was not the duty evaded, since he was acting in his capacity as employee, albeit unlawfully, for which he was paid a fixed fee. Similarly, in *Clark* [2011] EWCA Crim 15, [2011] 2 Cr App R (S) 55 (319), D had assisted in the shipment of stolen cars abroad but, although an integral facilitator of the overall conspiracy, he was a bailee of the cars with nothing to link him to the original thefts or proceeds. By contrast, an employee with de facto control over an account through which money laundering was committed had benefited to the extent of the monies passing through the account, and not the commission paid to the employee (*Fulton* [2019] EWCA Crim 163, [2019] 4 WLR 123). **E19.25**

Pecuniary Advantage Evading tax on the basis of a false declaration or failure to declare a change in circumstances will amount to obtaining a pecuniary advantage (i.e. of the amount of the tax). However, legitimate trading profit which has not been declared for tax or national insurance purposes does not *per se* amount to criminal property (*Gabriel* [2006] EWCA Crim 229, [2007] 1 WLR 2272). Even so, 'these words do not mean more than that profits from legitimate trading can never without more give rise to criminal property' (*K (I)* [2007] EWCA Crim 491, [2007] 1 WLR 2262). Where the defendant has been proved to have cheated the Revenue, legitimate but undeclared cash receipts may amount to criminal property provided they represent 'in part' the tax of which the Revenue has been cheated. A defendant who cheats the Revenue, by diverting company income into a secret account for the defendant's own use, may obtain the whole amount and not just the amount of the evaded tax (*Foggon* [2003] EWCA Crim 270, [2003] 2 Cr App R (S) 85 (507); *William* [2013] EWCA Crim 1262). **E19.26**

A pecuniary advantage can be obtained by deferment of a debt or by evasion of payable duty. There has been considerable litigation respecting excise duty on imported goods. In *Smith* [2001] UKHL 68, [2002] 1 All ER 366, D fraudulently imported cigarettes by sea without paying the excise duty. The boat was intercepted before the cigarettes could be offloaded and sold. The House of Lords held that D had obtained a pecuniary advantage, notwithstanding the seizure of the cargo, and upheld a confiscation order in the amount of the duty evaded. The Supreme Court has ruled that the decision in *Smith* does not fall foul of principles of proportionality (*Waya* [2012] UKSC 51, [2013] 1 AC 294; see **E19.61**): in *Smith*, their lordships were not considering property held momentarily and returned but the pecuniary advantage of avoiding duty. (See also *Dimsey* [2000] 2 All ER 142, in relation to tax liability, potential double recovery and the use of offshore companies, and *Edwards* [2004] EWCA Crim 3358, [2005] 2 Cr App R (S) 37 (160), where the Court was informed that where a confiscation order is made, HMRC does not seek to recover the unpaid duty by way of civil proceedings.) It is irrelevant that cigarettes are counterfeit (*Varsani* [2010] EWCA Crim 1938, [2011] 1 Cr App R (S) 96 (575)).

In keeping with the decision in *May*, a person obtains a pecuniary advantage only if evading a liability to which the person is subject. Accordingly, playing an active part in the handling of goods to assist in their commercial realisation does not alone establish that a person has benefited from criminal activity (*Mackle* [2014] UKSC 5, [2014] AC 678). The defendant only obtains: **E19.27**

> ... a benefit by way of a pecuniary advantage in the form of the evasion of excise duty if he was himself under a liability for the payment of that duty which he dishonestly evaded. To help somebody else to evade the payment of duty payable by that other person, with intent to defraud, is no less criminal, but in confiscation proceedings the focus is on the benefit obtained by the relevant offender. An offender may derive other benefits from helping a person who is under a liability for

> the payment of duty to avoid that liability, e.g. by way of payment for the accessory's services, but that is another matter. In order to decide whether the offender has obtained a benefit in the form of the evasion of a liability, it is necessary to determine whether the offender had a liability which he avoided ... that turns on whether the appellant was liable for the payment of excise duty on the relevant goods under the relevant Regulations (*Chambers* [2008] EWCA Crim 2467).

Close attention should be paid to the legislation which imposes liability to pay duty, either jointly or severally, on persons connected with the dutiable goods. Under the Tobacco Products Regulations 2001, reg. 13(1) (now repealed), the question was whether a person held the goods at an excise duty point or had caused the goods to reach that point. The answer to that question was fact-specific and likely to depend on the person's role within the conspiracy. Thus, the loader of the lorry may not have caused goods to reach the excise point (*Mitchell* [2009] EWCA Crim 214, [2009] 2 Cr App R (S) 66 (463); *Khan* [2009] EWCA Crim 588) and nor may a person who merely handles smuggled cigarettes after importation (*Bell* [2011] EWCA Crim 6). By contrast, persons who had arranged for cigarettes to be fraudulently imported into the UK were regarded as having 'held' the cigarettes at the excise duty point despite the fact that their innocent agents were in physical possession of the cigarettes. The criminals exercised control over the cigarettes through their agents (*Taylor* [2013] EWCA Crim 1151). Liability to pay duty at an excise duty point is now governed by the Excise Goods (Holding, Movement and Duty Point) Regulations 2010 (SI 2010 No. 593), as interpreted by the Tribunal, e.g., *McKeown v HMRC* [2016] UKUT 479 (TCC), in which it was held that a driver of smuggled dutiable goods was 'holding' those goods at the duty point and liable to pay the duty. Benefit in these cases will include any unpaid VAT (*Redmond* [2011] EWCA Crim 203). Where a person is arrested prior to the cargo reaching the duty point and is not in constructive possession of the cargo because the bill of lading has been seized, the person may have an insufficient connection to the goods at the duty point to be liable for the duty (*Bajwa* [2011] EWCA Crim 1093, [2012] 1 All ER 348).

However, orders were upheld against the holders of bills of lading in *CPS v Doran* [2015] EWCA Crim 384, notwithstanding that HMRC had become aware of smuggled cigarettes at the port of entry and had maintained covert surveillance on their movements before subsequent seizure — there being no 'disconnection' as in *Bajwa*. Nor had they obtained the cigarettes themselves, the decision to opposite effect in *Waller* [2008] EWCA Crim 2037, [2009] 1 Cr App R (S) 76 (149) being 'clearly wrong' (*Ahmad* [2012] EWCA Crim 391, [2012] 2 All ER 1137; *Bagnall* [2012] EWCA Crim 677, [2013] 1 WLR 204).

No pecuniary advantage is obtained by a temporary and unrealised increase in the value of shares (*Rigby* [2006] EWCA Crim 1653, [2006] 1 WLR 3067).

Generally, much depends on the particular circumstances and a careful identification of what if anything has been obtained.

E19.28 'As a result of' To count as 'benefit' under the POCA 2002, it must have been obtained as a result of (or 'in connection with') the criminal conduct. The approach to deciding whether a causal connection is established has been considered in the context of so-called regulatory offending. The answer appears to depend upon the terms of the offence-creating provisions. In *Del Basso* [2010] EWCA Crim 1119, [2011] 1 Cr App R (S) 41 (268), the Court of Appeal upheld a finding that the total revenue of a park and ride facility operated in breach of an enforcement notice should count as 'benefit'. By contrast, in *Sumal & Sons (Properties) Ltd* [2012] EWCA Crim 1840, [2013] 1 WLR 2078, a company was convicted of owning rental property without a licence contrary to the Housing Act 2004. In circumstances where that Act did not affect the validity of a tenancy or licence and the right to recover rent remained enforceable, a confiscation order was quashed as the company was not unlawfully obtaining rent 'as a result of or in connection with' the statutory breach. The rationale appears to have been that the rent was received, not as a result of the criminal conduct, but as a result of the provision of accommodation (but cf. *Hussain* [2014] EWCA Crim 2344, in which rent obtained from a property let in breach of a planning enforcement notice was properly included in the benefit figure). The effect of *Sumal* is, however, confined to its statutory context. In *McDowell* [2015] EWCA Crim 173, [2015] 2 Cr App R (S) 14 (137), Pitchford LJ said (at [34]) that *Sumal* turned on 'a narrow but critical distinction … between an offence that prohibits and makes criminal the very activity admitted by the offender or proved against him (as in *del Basso*) and an offence comprised in the failure to obtain a licence to carry out an activity otherwise lawful (as in *Sumal*)'. In *Palmer* [2016] EWCA Crim 1049, [2017] 4 WLR 15, it was doubted that the distinction had any principled rationale (at [23]) but the focus must remain on whether, in the relevant statutory context, any benefit has been obtained from the criminal conduct (*Neuberg (No. 2)* [2016] EWCA Crim 1927, [2017] 4 WLR 58). Where property received by D through D's criminal conduct generates an income without D's interest in the property itself being diminished, such as investment interest or rent, the income may have been obtained as a result of the criminal conduct (*Pattison* [2007] EWCA Crim 1536, [2008] 1 Cr App R (S) 51 (287)). Rental income from a property obtained through mortgage fraud constitutes benefit (*Wootton* [2013] EWCA Crim 2522; *Oyebola* [2013] EWCA Crim 1052, [2014] 1 Cr App R (S) 58 (359)), as does an appropriate portion of the takings of a restaurant which employs illegal immigrants (*Xu* [2008] EWCA Crim 2372; *R (Chief Constable of the Greater Manchester Police) v City of Salford Magistrates' Court* [2008] EWHC 1651 (Admin), [2009] 1 WLR 1023).

Wages unlawfully earned by an illegal immigrant appear to count as 'benefit'. In *Paulet* [2009] EWCA Crim 288, D had pleaded guilty to obtaining a pecuniary advantage by deception. He was living unlawfully in the UK and had no entitlement to seek or find employment but he had obtained work using a counterfeit French passport and a false national insurance number. He deposited his wages into UK bank accounts. He argued that the money that he had earned from his employment was too remote from the criminal act to amount to a benefit under the Act, but the Court of Appeal was inclined to follow *Carter* [2006] EWCA Crim 416 and *King* [1987] QB 547 and to apply the test: 'Was the deception an operative cause of the obtaining of benefit'? On that basis D had benefited and a confiscation order was imposed. There must now be some uncertainty as to the correctness of this outcome as a result of the Supreme Court's approach to 'proportionality' in *Waya* [2012] UKSC 51, [2013] 1 AC 294 (see **E19.61**). (See also *Paulet v UK* (2015) 61 EHRR 39 (994), in which there was found to be a breach of the ECHR where the confiscation inquiry had failed to consider whether the order was proportionate.)

'In connection with' The full definition of 'benefit' goes beyond property which has been obtained '*as a result of*' criminal conduct. The POCA 2002 also catches property which has been obtained '*in connection with*' the defendant's criminal conduct (s. 76(4)). The Court of Appeal has considered that the test is met in the following circumstances: *Finch* (1993) 14 Cr App R (S) 226, where money was obtained by 'ripping-off' a drug dealer; *Randle and Pottle* [1991] COD 369, where profits were obtained from the sale of a book about the prison escape of the spy, George Blake, in which the defendants had participated. **E19.29**

However, this does not mean property which has been purchased simply in order to obtain the benefit — 'the cost of committing the offence' (unless in a criminal lifestyle case that expenditure is assumed to have been funded from previous criminal conduct; see **E19.34**). In *Ahmad* [2014] UKSC 36, [2015] AC 299, the two appellants were directors of second line buffer companies in a carousel MTIC fraud. The Supreme Court upheld identical orders against each for the full amount of the VAT loss to HMRC (£12.6 million), applying the principles in *May* [2008] UKHL 28, [2008] 1 AC 1028 (subject to individual enforcement: see **E19.27**). However, the Court of Appeal ([2012] EWCA Crim 391, [2012] 2 All ER 1137) earlier held that the two appellants' benefit could not include the value of the goods bought and sold in order to spin the carousel and, therefore, did not include the total amount of monies that passed through company bank accounts over which they had control (£92 million). On a proper construction of the Act, that was not property obtained 'in connection with' the criminal conduct: 'if the appellants had obtained the goods by theft or by fraud and sold them on, the resulting sale price would be a benefit. In this case the offence was cheating the revenue of the VAT, the selling or purported selling of the goods was a mechanism by which the fraud was committed and the necessary costs involved in the selling or purported selling were the costs of committing the offence' (at [59]).

Subsequent authority has distinguished *Ahmad*. In *Louca* [2013] Crim 2090, [2014] 2 Cr App R (S) 9 (49), it was held (at [13]) that where the criminal conduct is being knowingly concerned in the fraudulent evasion of duty on imported cigarettes by purchasing the goods after importation, D has obtained the value of the cigarettes 'either "as a result of" his criminal conduct or, at the very least "in connection with" his criminal conduct'. Note, however, that in that case D acquired the cigarettes for less than they were worth. A similar approach was applied in the context of the sale of counterfeit vodka (*Eddishaw* [2014] EWCA Crim 2783). In *Davy* [2003] EWCA Crim 781, [2003] 2 Cr App R (S) 101 (603), D had conspired to obtain and sell fake ecstasy tablets. The tablets were seized in transit and, accordingly, he had neither obtained any property nor derived any pecuniary advantage.

E19.30 **Piercing the Corporate Veil** There are three situations where the benefit obtained by a company may be treated as a benefit obtained by the individual criminal, namely (a) if D attempts to shelter behind a corporate veil to hide D's crime and benefits, (b) where D does an act in the name of the company that constitutes a criminal offence, and (c) where the business structure constitutes a device, cloak or sham in an attempt to disguise the true nature of a transaction (*Sale* [2013] EWCA Crim 1306, [2014] 1 WLR 663, and see *Boyle Transport (Northern Ireland) Ltd* [2016] EWCA Crim 19, [2016] 4 WLR 63). The principles should be applied with precision and in their proper factual context. In *Powell* [2016] EWCA Crim 1043, a company which controlled a composting facility had, contrary to its duty under environmental law, permitted its site to become heavily polluted. Two directors were convicted on the basis of their various consent, connivance or neglect. By avoiding the clean-up costs, paid for by public authorities, it was said the company had obtained a pecuniary advantage but, assuming this to be correct, the Court held that the same could not be said of the individual directors, in particular: (a) the company had not been used to pursue the directors' criminal purpose, rather the company pursued a lawful purpose (composting) in an illegal manner (so the directors could not be said to be sheltering behind the corporate façade: at [27]); (b) the directors' criminal liability was parasitic on that of the company (as distinct from the directors' criminal acts being done in the name of the company: at [27]); (c) the obligations under environmental law were imposed on the licensee company, not on its directors (so the directors were not using the corporate structure in a way to frustrate their own personal liability: at [30]).

E19.31 **Joint Benefit** Two or more defendants may obtain property jointly. In *May* [2008] UKHL 28, [2008] 1 AC 1028, it was argued that, in such a case, the court should nonetheless apportion benefit as between co-defendants. The House of Lords rejected the argument and determined that a 'division of the spoils' approach is not appropriate. This approach was upheld in *Ahmad* [2014] UKSC 36, [2015] AC 299, but the Supreme Court indicated (at [51]) that judges should be ready to investigate and make findings as to whether there were separate obtainings; while this may sometimes be too difficult or impossible, a court 'should never make a finding that there has been a joint obtaining from convenience, or worse, laziness'. Where there had been a genuine joint obtaining, confiscation orders must be made against each defendant for the whole of the benefit obtained. At the enforcement stage, a payment by one offender of an amount due under the confiscation order should go to reduce the amount payable by the others (*Ahmad* at [72]): 'To take the same proceeds more than once would not serve the aim of the legislation', would be disproportionate, and would violate the ECHR, Protocol 1, Article 1. Accordingly, each order had to provide that it was not to be enforced to the extent that any sum had been recovered in satisfaction of another confiscation order in respect of the same joint benefit (*Ahmad* at [74]).

Where property is obtained by one defendant on behalf of several defendants jointly, others who have joint control may be liable for the whole of the common pool. 'It does not matter that proceeds of sale may have been received by one conspirator who retains his share before passing on the remainder; what matters is the capacity in which he received them' (*Green* [2007] EWCA Crim 1248, [2007] 3 All ER 751 at [45]).

Where one defendant receives the benefit and then shares it with other members of the enterprise, for example by passing it through a bank account of which D is the sole signatory, D is treated as having obtained the whole amount of the benefit. The amount of D's benefit is not reduced by the share passed to the other members (*Sharma* [2006] EWCA Crim 16, [2006] 2 Cr App R (S) 63 (416)). In *Patel* [2000] 2 Cr App R (S) 10, a dishonest postmaster took cash from the till. The fact that he paid half the proceeds to an accomplice was irrelevant as he had obtained all the property. Whether proceeds of sale were initially received on the individual's own behalf or on behalf of the conspirators as a whole is a question of fact for the judge to decide on the evidence. **E19.32**

As Cranston J stated (at [19]–[20]), giving the judgment of the Court of Appeal in *Mahmood* [2013] EWCA Crim 325, [2013] 1 WLR 3146:

> Mere couriers or custodians and other minor contributors to a conspiracy who had been rewarded by a specific fee and had no interest in the property or proceeds of sale are unlikely to be found to have obtained the property ... even a person who played a more substantial role in a conspiracy could be found not to have obtained it ... conversely, a person does not have to be at the top of a conspiracy in order to have obtained the full value of the property ... what matters is the capacity in which a conspirator received the property, whether for his own personal benefit or on behalf of others or jointly on behalf of himself and others. The issue is not resolved by attaching a label to the person's position in the conspiracy, although the role a person played might assist in evaluating the available evidence.

Proceeds of Crime Act 2002, s. 10 **E19.33**

(1) If the court decides under section 6 that the defendant has a criminal lifestyle it must make the following four assumptions for the purpose of—
  (a) deciding whether he has benefited from his general criminal conduct, and
  (b) deciding his benefit from the conduct.
(2) The first assumption is that any property transferred to the defendant at any time after the relevant day was obtained by him—
  (a) as a result of his general criminal conduct, and
  (b) at the earliest time he appears to have held it.
(3) The second assumption is that any property held by the defendant at any time after the date of conviction was obtained by him—
  (a) as a result of his general criminal conduct, and
  (b) at the earliest time he appears to have held it.
(4) The third assumption is that any expenditure incurred by the defendant at any time after the relevant day was met from property obtained by him as a result of his general criminal conduct.
(5) The fourth assumption is that, for the purpose of valuing any property obtained (or assumed to have been obtained) by the defendant, he obtained it free of any other interests in it.
(6) But the court must not make a required assumption in relation to particular property or expenditure if—
  (a) the assumption is shown to be incorrect, or
  (b) there would be a serious risk of injustice if the assumption were made.
(7) If the court does not make one or more of the required assumptions it must state its reasons.
(8) The relevant day is the first day of the period of six years ending with—
  (a) the day when proceedings for the offence concerned were started against the defendant, or
  (b) if there were two or more offences and proceedings for them were started on different days, the earliest of those days.
(9) But if a confiscation order mentioned in section 8(3)(c) has been made against the defendant *at any time* during the period mentioned in subsection (8)—
  (a) the relevant day is the day when the defendant's benefit was calculated for the purposes of the last confiscation order;
  (b) the second assumption does not apply to any property which was held by him on or before the relevant day.
(10) The date of conviction is—
  (a) the date on which the defendant was convicted of the offence concerned, or
  (b) if there are two or more offences and the convictions were on different dates, the date of the latest.

E19.34 **Role of the Assumptions** Where the court determines that D has a criminal lifestyle, the assumptions in the POCA 2002, s. 10, that certain property is D's benefit from criminal conduct, are mandatory. The first three assumptions, relating to property transferred to or held by D and to expenditure made by D, cover the six years prior to charge and subsequently. However, where an earlier confiscation order has been made on the basis of general criminal conduct (or where the court was 'entitled' to make an extended order under earlier legislation), the relevant period commences on 'the day when the defendant's benefit was calculated for the purposes of the last such confiscation order' (POCA 2002, ss. 8(8) and 10(8) and (9); *Chahal* [2014] EWCA Crim 101, [2014] 2 Cr App R (S) 35 (288); *Barnett* [2011] EWCA Crim 2936). The assumptions are not triggered unless and until the prosecution have proved that property was transferred to or held by D, or that D incurred expenditure, but having done so such property is assumed to count towards D's benefit (*Whittington* [2009] EWCA Crim 1641, [2010] 1 Cr App R (S) 83 (545); *Mahmood* [2013] EWCA Crim 325, [2013] 1 WLR 3146). Following conviction, the ECHR, Article 6(2), has no application in relation to allegations made about D's character and conduct as part of the sentencing process, unless such accusations are of such a nature and degree as to amount to the bringing of a new 'charge' within the autonomous Convention meaning (*Benjafield* [2002] UKHL 2, [2003] 1 AC 1099). Accordingly, the use of the mandatory assumptions of fact and reverse burdens of proof in the determination of benefit and of the realisable amount do not engage, let alone breach, the specific protections of Article 6(2), including the presumption of innocence (*Grayson v UK* (2009) 48 EHRR 30 (722)).

E19.35 The first assumption is that any property transferred to D in the period since six years prior to the start of the proceedings was obtained (a) 'as a result of his general criminal conduct, and (b) at the earliest time he appears to have held it' (s. 10(2)). Proceedings start when a summons or warrant is issued, a written charge and requisition or single justice procedure notice is issued, a defendant is charged following arrest without warrant or a voluntary bill of indictment is preferred (s. 85). Property is transferred if 'an interest' in it is transferred or granted by another (s. 84(2)(c)).

E19.36 The second assumption is that any property held by D at any time after the date of conviction was obtained as a result of D's general criminal conduct at the earliest time D appears to have held it (s. 10(3)). It is irrelevant when D acquired the property (*Chrastny (No. 2)* [1991] 1 All ER 189). Where D holds property which has been purchased partly by means of a legitimate mortgage (i.e. not one fraudulently obtained), only the value of the equity should be treated as representing criminal proceeds (*Roach* [2008] EWCA Crim 2649) (and for other considerations in connection with fraudulently obtained mortgages, see **E19.45**).

E19.37 The third assumption is that any expenditure incurred by D at any time after the six-year period prior to the start of proceedings was met from property obtained by D as a result of D's general criminal conduct (s. 10(4)). In other words, once an item of expenditure is proved, the court must assume it was funded from property obtained as a result of earlier criminal conduct. In *Ernest* [2014] EWCA Crim 1312, the Court of Appeal left open the question whether it could ever be appropriate to use a cost of living index to infer expenditure of a given level. However, the fact of expenditure, classically in drugs cases, may be inferred from the circumstances:

> This is a perfectly proper inference to make, as a matter of common sense ... In relation to a large quantity of drugs of this sort, approaching the matter on the balance of probabilities where there is no alternative credible explanation, the inference is obvious: money would be required to pay for the drugs. Those who traffic in the drugs trade do not normally extend credit or trust to others involved (*Dellaway* [2001] 1 Cr App R (S) 77, explained in *Green* [2007] EWCA Crim 1248, [2007] 3 All ER 751).

E19.38 In *Barnham* [2005] EWCA Crim 1049, [2006] 1 Cr App R (S) 16 (83), D was convicted of two conspiracies to import drugs but no importation had actually occurred. The judge was entitled to infer, 'provided he keeps well in mind that the risk of serious injustice must be avoided', that D had in fact available to him quantities of drugs intended for importation and that those drugs had been paid for out of earlier trafficking. Moreover, where the judge concluded that D was the lead organiser, he was entitled to discount the possibility that other conspirators had contributed to the cost of the drugs.

The limits of the exercise were illustrated in *Williams* [2001] 2 Cr App R (S) 44 (206). The judge properly calculated drugs expenditure of nearly £500,000. However, treating this sum as profit from a notional earlier transaction, he then purported to work out the gross amount of *that* transaction. Deciding arbitrarily that the expenditure represented a 25 per cent profit on the earlier transaction, he multiplied the expenditure by four, making nearly £2 million, to which he then added the net benefit, making a total of nearly £2.5 million. The Court of Appeal quashed the order, observing:

> The mistake ... was to take the figure produced by the application of the proper approach, £484,437, and then to subject it to a series of further hypotheses for which there was no evidential basis, namely:
> (i) that it was the product of a particular form of drug trafficking i.e. wholesale supply,
> (ii) that it represented net profits of such activity and
> (iii) that a hypothetical quantity and value of drugs must have been required to be purchased during the preceding 6 years to enable such a net profit to be realised.

A finding or concession that a minder or courier had no beneficial interest in property such as drugs or that it is D's first such offence, should prevent any inference that D paid for the property (*J* [2001] 1 Cr App R (S) 79 (273); *Butler* (1993) 14 Cr App R (S) 537; *Johannes* [2001] EWCA Crim 2825, [2002] 2 Cr App R (S) 30 (109)). As Cranston J stated in *Mahmood* [2013] EWCA Crim 325, [2013] 1 WLR 3146 (at [26]):

> The section 10(4) assumption does not mean that, unless he can prove otherwise, each conspirator is treated as having incurred all of the expenditure. It may be that in the circumstances of a particular case the court can draw inferences that a particular member of the conspiracy met an expense of its operation. In other, and perhaps many cases, the natural inference will be that the conspirators will have contributed equally to such expenses. But without a finding that the defendant in question spent something, the section 10(4) assumption is not triggered.

The fourth assumption is that D is or was the only person with an interest in any property **E19.39**
which D is proven or assumed to have obtained (s. 10(5)). However, s. 10A allows the court to make a conclusive determination of the extent of D's interest where a third party may hold an interest in the property (for an illustration, see the first instance decision of Turner J in *Taylor* (9 February 2017 unreported)). The court may order Statements of Information relating to the issue from the prosecutor and D or from a person (other than D) who the court thinks is or may be a person holding an interest in the property (ss. 16(6A), 18(2) and 18A). The court must give a 'reasonable opportunity' to make representations to 'anyone who the court thinks is or may be a person holding an interest'. (For the deduction of third-party interests from the available amount, see **E19.57**.)

Defeating the Assumptions The assumptions must be applied unless one of a number **E19.40**
of reasons identified in the statute is engaged; a failure to explain why an assumption is to be disapplied may itself amount to an error of law (*Newhall* [2020] EWCA Crim 224). An assumption may not be made if D proves on the balance of probabilities that it is 'incorrect', e.g., by evidence of legitimate income (s. 10(6)(a)) (see, e.g., *Hesketh* [2006] EWCA Crim 2596). If the court finds an assumption to be incorrect, it must give reasons for its conclusion (s. 10(7)). It has been held by the ECtHR that the defence burden of proving that assets are probably legitimate is not incompatible with the ECHR, Article 6 (*Grayson v UK* (2009) 48 EHRR 30 (722)).

An assumption can be avoided when 'there would be a serious risk of injustice if the assumption **E19.41**
were made' (s. 10(6)(b)). 'It is putting it too high' to require D to prove injustice on the balance

of probabilities; 'the judge must avoid any real risk of injustice'; the court 'should step back and determine whether there is or might be a risk of serious or real injustice and, if there is or might be, then such an order should not be made' (*Benjafield* [2002] UKHL 2, [2003] 1 AC 1099).

In *Jones* [2006] EWCA Crim 2061, [2007] 1 WLR 7, the Court of Appeal expressly approved the following statement from an earlier edition of this work: the risk of injustice must arise from the operation of the assumptions in the calculation of benefit and not from eventual hardship in the making of a confiscation order. What is contemplated is some unjust contradiction in the process of assumption and an agreed factual basis for sentence (see **E19.14** and *Lunnon* [2004] EWCA Crim 1125, [2005] 1 Cr App R (S) 24 (111), *Lazarus* [2004] EWCA Crim 1125, [2005] 1 Cr App R (S) 98 (552) and *Bakewell* [2006] EWCA Crim 2, [2006] 2 Cr App R (S) 42 (277)) or in the process of assumption itself, e.g., in the double counting of income and expenditure.

There is no double penalty when drugs are both forfeited under the MDA 1971, s. 27 (see **E8.7**), and their value is counted as expenditure (*Dore*). In the case of forfeited cash, there should be no double counting if the Act is properly applied, since the confiscation order should be imposed before making any forfeiture order and once the confiscation order has been made there will be no cash remaining to forfeit (see **E19.67**).

E19.42 If the court is satisfied of a serious risk of injustice, it may temper the full force of the assumptions by making a percentage discount to guard against a 'remote possibility that a small part of the fund under consideration was in fact legitimate' (*Deprince* [2004] EWCA Crim 524, [2004] 2 Cr App R (S) 91 (483) at [20]).

Stage Three — Determination of the Recoverable Amount

E19.43 **Proceeds of Crime Act 2002, ss. 7 and 80**

7.—(1) The recoverable amount for the purposes of section 6 is an amount equal to pthe defendant's benefit from the conduct concerned.

(2) But if the defendant shows that the available amount is less than that benefit the recoverable amount is—
- (a) the available amount, or
- (b) a nominal amount, if the available amount is nil.

(3) But if section 6(6) or (6A) applies the recoverable amount is such amount as—
- (a) the court believes is just, but
- (b) does not exceed the amount found under subsection (1) or (2) (as the case may be).

(4) In calculating the defendant's benefit from the conduct concerned for the purposes of subsection (1), the following must be ignored—
- (a) any property in respect of which a recovery order is in force under section 266, or
- (b) any property which has been forfeited in pursuance of a forfeiture order under section 297A, and
- (c) any property in respect of which a forfeiture order is in force under section 298(2).

(5) If the court decides the available amount, it must include in the confiscation order a statement of its findings as to the matters relevant for deciding that amount.

80.—(1) This section applies for the purpose of deciding the value of property obtained by a person as a result of or in connection with his criminal conduct; and the material time is the time the court makes its decision.

(2) The value of the property at the material time is the greater of the following—
- (a) the value of the property (at the time the person obtained it) adjusted to take account of later changes in the value of money;
- (b) the value (at the material time) of the property found under subsection (3).

(3) The property found under this subsection is as follows—
- (a) if the person holds the property obtained, the property found under this subsection is that property;
- (b) if he holds no part of the property obtained, the property found under this subsection is any property which directly or indirectly represents it in his hands;

(c) if he holds part of the property obtained, the property found under this subsection is that part and any property which directly or indirectly represents the other part in his hands.

(4) The references in subsection (2)(a) and (b) to the value are to the value found in accordance with section 79.

Amount of Benefit This is critical, because 'the recoverable amount . . . is an amount equal to the defendant's benefit from the conduct concerned' (POCA 2002, s. 7(1)). The amount of the defendant's benefit is literally 'the value of the property obtained' (s. 76(7)). It follows that benefit does not mean profit. In other words, all the property obtained in accordance with the principles in *May* [2008] UKHL 28, [2008] 1 AC 1028 (see **E19.22**) is to be accounted and not merely the profit element. **E19.44**

No discount can be given to reflect income which the defendant would have derived from the loser had there been no misconduct — e.g., where D had falsely claimed income support, no account was to be taken of working families tax credit to which he would have been entitled but for his misrepresentations (*Richards* [2005] EWCA Crim 491, [2005] 2 Cr App R (S) 97 (583)).

Cases involving Mortgages Notwithstanding authorities to the contrary under earlier legislation, s. 79(3) (which caters for the individual valuation of each 'interest' held in property) requires real property to be valued by reference to the market value of the property less the value of any interest secured by a mortgage (*Waya* [2012] UKSC 51, [2013] 1 AC 294 at [69]). **E19.45**

In *Waya*, the Supreme Court distinguished the mechanics and legal implications of obtaining an unsecured loan from those of a normal mortgage transaction. In the latter, the advance is paid by the mortgage lender into the purchaser's solicitor's client account in trust for and to the order of the lender until paid over to the vendor's solicitor. The advance remains in the beneficial ownership of the lender until completion. The purchaser has no control over the disposal of the advance and it never comes into the purchaser's possession. D had obtained a £465,000 mortgage (60 per cent of the value) by false representations as to his means (but continued to meet the repayments); he had contributed £310,000 of his own funds towards the purchase (40 per cent of the value). The Court stated (at [53] and [78]):

> Mr Waya never in fact acquired anything but an equity of redemption, . . . the equity of redemption corresponding in value (at that point) to his untainted down-payment of £310,000. To conclude . . . that Mr Waya obtained £465,000 is a legally inaccurate account of the transaction, because the loan sum never became his or came into his possession. Under the tripartite contractual arrangements between vendor, purchaser and mortgage lender Mr Waya obtained property in the form of a thing in action which was an indivisible bundle of rights and liabilities, and it cannot be correct to fasten onto the rights and ignore the liabilities (the analysis would of course be different if the loan had ever been at the defendant's free disposal . . .) In short, what Mr Waya obtained was the right to have the mortgage advance applied in the acquisition of his flat, subject from the moment of completion to the mortgage lender's security, which ensured the repayment of the advance. This thing in action had no market value at or immediately after completion, as the equity of redemption (or in everyday speech, the equity) represented Mr Waya's down-payment. There will no doubt be other mortgage fraud cases in which this thing in action does have a value. One example would be the common case where false representations as to income and status of the borrower are accompanied by a dishonestly inflated valuation of the property which is being purchased. In such a case the fraud may not only have induced a larger loan than would otherwise have been made, but may well have induced a loan which is not fully secured as the lender believes. Another example might be the case where the property which the defendant is purporting to purchase does not exist, or is not really being purchased at all. In both these cases the thing in action has a real value to the defendant.
>
> . . . we consider that the benefit obtained by Mr Waya from his criminal behaviour was a thing in action with no immediate market value. It was an item of property but it had a very short life, since on completion it immediately came to be represented by a fractional 60 per cent share of the leasehold interest in the flat, subject to (the whole of) the mortgage, with the remaining 40% representing the untainted contribution.

In *Waya* the property had increased in value: 'In economic terms, his benefit was so much of any appreciation in value *as was attributable to the mortgage obtained by his dishonesty*. Immediately after completion this value was nil, but as the market value of the flat increased the benefit came to have a significant value, that is 60 per cent of the appreciation in the net value of the flat, *subject to the mortgage*' (emphasis added). The same approach should be taken in cases of 're-mortgage' (*Reid* [2018] EWCA Crim 628). In *Gor* [2017] EWCA Crim 3, the Court of Appeal explained that the principles in *Waya* (not a 'criminal lifestyle' case) had a limited role in a 'criminal lifestyle' case: the mere fact that it could be shown that some portion of the value of a property was attributable to mortgage fraud did nothing to rebut the statutory assumption that the entire value of the property was the proceeds of crime. Persons seeking to establish that a mortgage falls within the *Waya* principle would be well advised to lead evidence of the legal machinery of the mortgage transaction (cf. *Hockey* [2018] EWCA Crim 1419, where an absence of such evidence led to the dismissal of the appeal).

E19.46 **Valuation of Benefit** The 'basic rule' of valuation throughout the POCA 2002 is that the value of any property is its market value at the material time (s. 79(2)). If D and another person both hold interests in the same property, then it is the value of D's limited interest which is to be taken for the purposes of calculating D's benefit (s. 79(3); *Waya* [2012] UKSC 51, [2013] 1 AC 294; *Rose* [2008] EWCA Crim 239, [2008] 3 All ER 315). This does not mean that the value of a true owner's interest in property wipes out its value to D when D obtains it. In *Waya*, the Supreme Court rejected (at [68]) any construction of s. 79(3) which would lead to the conclusion that the value of stolen property was limited to the value of the thief's right to possess that property; such a construction would 'emasculat[e] POCA'.

The material time for valuing benefit 'is the time the court makes its decision' (s. 80(1)). Its value at that time is the *greater* of the following:

(a) its (market) value at the time it was obtained by D (adjusted for subsequent inflation); or
(b) if D still holds the property, its current market value or, if D no longer holds the property, the market value of any property that 'directly or indirectly represents' it, or a combination of both if D has converted only part of the property which was originally obtained (s. 80(2)).

Thus, if the market value of the property has declined since D obtained it, D's benefit is its original market value adjusted upwards for inflation (*Foxley* (1995) 16 Cr App R (S) 879). It is generally appropriate to apply the Retail Price Index rather than the Consumer Price Index (*Shepherd* [2014] EWCA Crim 179), though it is submitted that this general principle may not apply to a corporate defendant for which another of the various measures may be more suitable. The Court of Appeal has held that a defendant is not entitled to discount an increase in the market value of a property as a result of home improvements — 'value is the predominant approach' (*X* [2007] EWCA Crim 2498). Conversely, a worthless cheque has no value (*Johnson* (1990) 91 Cr App R 332).

The fraudulent purchase and subsequent sale of vehicles is a single process leading to a single benefit for these purposes. The judge should first look at the value of the vehicle when D obtained it and then go on to see whether there were any proceeds of sale in D's hands that exceeded (or were less than) the value of the vehicle when it was obtained. The benefit is the greater of the two values (*Scragg* [2006] EWCA Crim 2916, and see *X* [2007] EWCA Crim 2498).

Market value may vary according to whether goods have been obtained wholesale, e.g., by theft from containers in transit, or from a retail outlet (*Ascroft* [2003] EWCA Crim 2365, [2004] 1 Cr App R (S) 56 (326)). The market value of property obtained by a thief or handler is the amount it would have cost D to obtain the property legitimately or the economic value to the loser, rather than what D could get for the property if it was sold (*Rose* [2008] EWCA Crim 239, [2008] 3 All ER 315).

Overruling previous authority, the House of Lords held in *Islam* [2009] UKHL 30, [2009] 1 AC 1076, that it is consistent with both the language and the spirit of the statutory scheme to take account of the black market value of drugs when valuing the benefit obtained from their illegal importation, although such drugs had a nil market value after seizure for the purposes of assessing the amount available for confiscation. *Mejia* [2009] EWCA Crim 1940 concerned the importation of cocaine-impregnated fibre board which had been fashioned into ornate doors. It was argued that no market of any kind had been established for cocaine-impregnated doors and, in the absence of evidence as to the cost of extraction of the cocaine, there was no basis on which to determine the price that would be paid by a willing buyer. The Court of Appeal held that, had it been argued at trial that the relevant property was cocaine-impregnated doors, or that the true value was the invoice value of the doors or the purchase cost of the cocaine, the judge could have made relevant findings of fact. However, it was absurd to suggest that no value was to be attached to a product containing pure cocaine brought into the UK for the very purposes of extracting the cocaine and selling it on. The value of the cocaine was a reasonable indicator of the value of the doors. The relevant question was the market value of the property in the UK, not its cost at source. Even so, it may equally be argued on the basis of some of the dicta in *Islam* that, in drugs cases, the relevant market value will vary according to the position occupied by D in the supply chain. In other words, the market value of drugs held by a wholesale dealer will be their value 'at that time' and not their subsequent and greater street value. However, where a court is satisfied that the dealer intends to cut the drugs in his possession and to supply them at street level, the benefit is the retail value (*Elsayed* [2014] EWCA Crim 333, [2014] 1 WLR 3916). **E19.47**

Effect of Recovery or Forfeiture Order, Forfeiture Notice or Claim by Victim In calculating benefit, the court must ignore any property in respect of which proceedings under the POCA 2002, Part 5, have resulted in a recovery or forfeiture order or forfeiture notice in respect of cash (s. 297A) or a bank balance (s. 303Z9) (s. 7(4): see **E19.43**). The converse is true: for the purposes of Part 5 property is not recoverable if it has been taken into account in deciding a person's benefit (s. 308(9)). The combined effect of s. 7(4) and s. 308(9) appears not to have been considered in *Chatha* [2008] EWCA Crim 2597. In that case detained cash was included in the benefit figure, subsequently forfeited, and the Court of Appeal dismissed the appeal against the confiscation order. In the case of general criminal conduct, the court must deduct any benefit taken into account in previous confiscation orders (s. 8(3)). A court need not calculate the recoverable amount and make an order 'if it believes that any victim of the conduct has at any time started or intends to start proceedings against the defendant in respect of loss, injury or damage sustained in connection with the conduct' (s. 6(6): see **E19.4**). If it does decide to do so, the benefit is 'such amount as the court believes just'. Subsequent civil proceedings, e.g. a claim by Revenue and Customs for the recovery of the balance of unpaid duty not fully met by a confiscation order, will not necessarily amount to an abuse of process merely because Revenue and Customs did not disclose in the confiscation proceedings that they would or might institute civil action (*Revenue and Customs Commissioners v Crossman* [2007] EWHC 1585 (Ch), [2008] 1 All ER 483). The fact that criminal proceeds have been taken into account in the making of a confiscation order does not preclude an assessment to income tax payable on those proceeds (*Martin v HMRC* [2015] UKUT 0161). **E19.48**

Stage Four — Determination of the Available Amount

Proceeds of Crime Act 2002, s. 9 **E19.49**

(1) For the purposes of deciding the recoverable amount, the available amount is the aggregate of—
  (a) the total of the values (at the time the confiscation order is made) of all the free property then held by the defendant minus the total amount payable in pursuance of obligations which then have priority, and
  (b) the total of the values (at that time) of all tainted gifts.

(2) An obligation has priority if it is an obligation of the defendant—
  (a) to pay an amount due in respect of a fine or other order of a court which was imposed or made on conviction of an offence and at any time before the time the confiscation order is made, or
  (b) to pay a sum which would be included among the preferential debts if the defendant's bankruptcy had commenced on the date of the confiscation order or his winding up had been ordered on that date.
(3) 'Preferential debts' has the meaning given by section 386 of the Insolvency Act 1986.

E19.50 This is the 'bottom line' of confiscation. A court cannot (subject to the operation of the regime for 'tainted gifts') confiscate more than D is worth — 'the available amount'. The assessments, first of the amount of benefit and then of the available amount, are entirely separate exercises. The calculation of the available amount is simply a computation of D's realisable assets (including tainted gifts), regardless of their origins, illegitimate or not. Where an asset is jointly owned by defendants, the court must determine the extent of each owner's beneficial interest (*Gangar* [2012] EWCA Crim 1378, [2012] 4 All ER 972). The value is the normal sale price, not its 'forced sale' price, notwithstanding that the confiscation order might have to be paid within a maximum of three months (*Gor* [2017] EWCA Crim 3). Costs of sale may be deducted (*Cramer* (1992) 13 Cr App R (S) 390). If D proves on the balance of probabilities that D is worth less than the amount of his or her benefit, the 'available amount' becomes the 'recoverable amount' and, therefore, the amount of the order (s. 7(2)(a); see *Summers* [2008] EWCA Crim 872, [2008] 2 Cr App R (S) 101 (569); *A-G's Ref (No. 2 of 2008) (Winters)* [2008] EWCA Crim 2953). For the purpose of proving a lower available amount, it is open to D to show that the benefit obtained has been spent (*Yu* [2015] EWCA Crim 1076, [2015] 2 Cr App R (S) 75 (500)). Where D fails to establish that his or her assets are less than the benefit obtained, it is not necessary for the judge to make a specific finding that there are hidden assets (*Smith* [2011] EWCA Crim 2029). Where the judge is satisfied that there are hidden assets, it is for D to prove that their value is less than the benefit figure (*Siddique* [2005] EWCA Crim 1812; *Barnham* [2005] EWCA Crim 1049, [2006] 1 Cr App R (S) 16 (83); *Valentine* [2006] EWCA Crim 2717). That was so even if D's inability arose not from deceitfulness but simply from an inability to satisfy the court of D's true means. However, there was a balance to be struck. While the courts were right to treat with some scepticism assertions made by a defendant whose credibility, given his or her offending, might be deeply suspect, the absence of independent and credible corroborating evidence was not fatal as a proposition of law (despite the oft-cited dictum in *Walbrook* (1993) 15 Cr App R (S) 783 that generalised assertions will rarely be sufficient). While that absence might well prove fatal as a matter of fact, its impact was something that the judge had to take into account when considering the facts (*Glaves v CPS* [2011] EWCA Civ 69); there might be independent evidence not given by D that D is 'destitute' (*Lee* [2013] EWCA Crim 657 at [21]). Where the court concludes that D has not revealed the true extent of his or her assets, it is not bound to make an order in the full amount of the benefit figure — it must adopt 'a just and proportionate view of the facts as a whole' (*McIntosh* [2011] EWCA Crim 1501, [2011] 4 All ER 917). 'A confiscation order which, due to its magnitude, exceeds by far the likely assets of the defendant may operate as a disincentive to cooperate' (*Ahmad* [2012] EWCA Crim 391, [2012] 2 All ER 1137). Where D asserts that assets have been disposed of, D must provide positive evidence to that effect (*Druce* [2013] EWCA Crim 40). In drugs importation cases, notwithstanding that the benefit figure is calculated on wholesale values, when assessing what may be available, the court is entitled to have regard to the fact that drugs which had been successfully imported and sold had a higher retail value (*Soutter* [2011] EWCA Crim 3160).

E19.51 The ECtHR has held that D's burden of proving that the realisable assets are less than the benefit finding is not incompatible with Article 6 (*Grayson v UK* (2009) 48 EHRR 30 (722), approving decisions of the Court of Appeal in *Ripley* [2005] EWCA Crim 1453 and *Barnham* [2005] EWCA Crim 1049, [2006] 1 Cr App R (S) 16 (83)).

The 'available amount' is the aggregate of:

(a) the total value at the time of the order of 'all the free property then held by the defendant' (minus the total amount of any priority obligations), *and*
(b) the total value of all 'tainted gifts' (s. 9(1)).

The process of calculation is as follows:

(a) identify the free property in which D has an interest at the time of the order;
(b) calculate the total current market value of D's beneficial interests in that property;
(c) deduct the amount of D's priority obligations (i.e. fines, etc., and preferential debts);
(d) lastly, add the total value of any 'tainted gifts'.

Property is 'held' by a person 'if he holds an interest in it' (s. 84). Property, therefore, includes a beneficial interest in a deceased's estate under a will or upon intestacy, administered or not. This is so notwithstanding that the market value at the time of the confiscation order may be negligible where there have been no probate or letters of administration and no information as to the extent of the assets, it being open to the prosecutor to apply for a revaluation once the extent of the interest becomes established (*Walbrook*; *Re Maye* [2008] UKHL 9, [2008] 1 WLR 315).

When valuing D's beneficial interest in shared property, the fact that D's interest in the property cannot be realised without a court order or the consent of others does not mean that it has a nominal value only. Where property is subject to a trust, the court must proceed on the basis that D will, if necessary, obtain an order under the Trusts of Land and Appointment of Trustees Act 1996 for the sale of the whole property and that D will receive his or her due proportion of the proceeds (*Modjiri* [2010] EWCA Crim 829, [2010] 4 All ER 837). Free property will include an entitlement under a trust where trustees have an administrative power (such as a power of investment) which cannot preclude D's entitlement to such income as there is when income is produced by the invested assets, but it does not include a benefit under a trust where there is, by distinction, a dispositive power, such as the power of accumulation, which precludes any right to income at all until the trustees decide not to accumulate (*Walker* [2011] EWCA Crim 103, [2011] 2 Cr App R (S) 54 (309)). That case also held that a beneficial interest under a 'Friends Provident Children's Trust' is free property.

A pension fund is realisable property (*Ahmed v CPS* [2018] EWCA Civ 2543, [2019] 1 All ER 1003), but whether it has any realisable value depends upon whether the policy is capable of being surrendered before maturity. If it is not, the fund has no value as a realisable asset — bearing in mind, however, that the prosecution may apply for a reconsideration under s. 22 when the policy matures (*Chen* [2009] EWCA Crim 2669, [2010] 2 Cr App R (S) 34 (221); *Cornfield* [2006] EWCA Crim 2909, [2007] 1 Cr App R (S) 124 (771): see also, in respect of company pensions, *Silvester* [2009] EWCA Crim 2182). In *Chen*, the Court of Appeal distinguished *Ford* [2008] EWCA Crim 966, [2009] 1 Cr App R (S) 13 (68), which had held that, where a fund does have a surrender value, the available amount is the full value of the fund notwithstanding that the surrender value may be considerably less. The preferred view of the Court in *Chen* was that the available amount is the sum that D can actually realise, namely the surrender value. **E19.52**

Commission that had arisen from illegal conduct and was owed to D could not be treated as a realisable asset (*Najafpour* [2009] EWCA Crim 2723, [2010] 2 Cr App R (S) 38 (245)).

The fact that a bankruptcy order had been made against D when all D's assets were in the hands of the trustee in bankruptcy did not affect the judge's power to make a confiscation order. Whilst it might affect the enforcement of the confiscation order it would not affect the making of it. Under s. 102(8) of the CJA 1988, property held by a defendant included property held by a trustee in bankruptcy and it was therefore impossible to say that an order could not be made against a bankrupt. If the public interest was relevant, it would not be served if D was able to avoid an order by applying for his or her own bankruptcy when D was aware of the likelihood that a confiscation order would be made (*Shahid* [2009] EWCA Crim 831, [2009] 2 Cr App R (S) 105 (687)): presumably, this applies equally under the POCA 2002.

E19.53 Property is 'free' unless there is already a forfeiture or deprivation order in force or it is cash that has been detained under s. 297C or 297D (s. 82). Cash which is merely the subject of an application for summary forfeiture under s. 298(4) remains 'free property'. If the cash is then included in the recoverable amount, forfeiture under Part 5 is then prevented by s. 308(9). The purpose of s. 308(9) is plainly to achieve fairness, so that seized cash is not both used to make up the quantum of a recoverable amount *and* the amount available for forfeiture (*Weller* [2009] EWCA Crim 810, where Moses LJ said (at [19]) that a 'decision has to be made as to which process is going to be used').

Seizure under the Customs and Excise Management Act 1979, s. 139, of the instruments of crime, such as motor vehicles, may, if the seizure is not challenged, lead to their automatic forfeiture such that they no longer form part of the available amount (*Thacker* (1995) 16 Cr App R (S) 461).

The available amount must be reduced by the amount of any outstanding fine or other order made following a conviction at any time before the confiscation order is made (s. 9(2)(a)). A further discount must be given for any sum 'which would be included among the preferential debts' if D's bankruptcy had commenced or D's winding-up been ordered on the date of the confiscation order (s. 9(2)(b)). 'Preferential debt' has the same meaning as in s. 386 of the Insolvency Act 1986 and includes remuneration of employees and pension scheme contributions.

E19.54 **Tainted Gifts** The total value of 'all tainted gifts' must be added to the available amount (s. 9(1)(b)). D makes a gift if D transfers property to another for 'significantly less' consideration than its value at the time of the transfer (s. 78(1)). The discharge by payment of a lump sum as part of a divorce settlement, which was itself intended to discharge a mortgage, did not amount to a gift (*Rastelli* [2008] EWCA Crim 373). By contrast, a payment made to a spouse does not cease to be a gift simply because the spouse could be said to be providing a service by bringing up children; the 'consideration' must be capable of being ascribed a value in monetary terms (*Hayes* [2018] EWCA Crim 682, [2018] 2 Cr App R (S) 27 (239)).

The process of identifying whether a gift is 'tainted' varies according to whether D has been found to have a criminal lifestyle. Where D has a criminal lifestyle or where 'no court has made a decision', a gift is tainted if it was made since the start of the six-year period preceding the commencement of the proceedings (s. 77(2) and (9)). Alternatively, a gift is tainted, regardless of when it was made, if it is proved to consist of property obtained by D 'as a result of or in connection with his general criminal conduct' or of property in D's hands which represented such property 'in whole or part... directly or indirectly' (s. 77(3)). If D does not have a criminal lifestyle, any gift is tainted if made 'after the date on which the offence concerned was committed' (s. 77(5)), which is apt to include a gift made on the same day as the offence was committed, provided it was after the offence was committed (*Lehair* [2015] EWCA Crim 1324, [2015] 1 WLR 4811). Under the POCA 2002, a continuing offence is deemed to be committed 'on the first occasion when it is committed' (s. 77(6)).

E19.55 The value of the tainted gift is the value of 'the property given' so that in a transaction for consideration, the property given is the proportion of the whole that represents the gift element (s. 78(2)). The value of the property given is its market value. The market value is the greater of the following: (a) its value at the time it was given (adjusted for subsequent inflation); or (b) its value at the time of the confiscation order. If the recipient of the gift has retained none or only part of the property, its value is that of 'any property which directly or indirectly represents it in his hands' or a combination of the value of what has been retained and such property (s. 81).

It is important to establish whether D has in fact made a 'gift'. Where D makes a transfer without real ownership or control passing, that is not a 'gift' of any value, albeit D's beneficial interest in the property would be included within the available amount (*Richards* [2008] EWCA Crim 1841). For a useful illustration of transfers which were not, in fact, gifts, see *Re Somaia* [2017] EWHC 2554 (QB).

Corporate Veil Where a company has been used as a vehicle to commit offences (e.g., a fruit importing business through which drug trafficking is pursued), it may be appropriate, via the 'concealment principle', to identify the company's assets as being those of D (*Boyle Transport (Northern Ireland) Ltd* [2016] EWCA Crim 19, [2016] 2 Cr App R (S) 11 (43), following *Prest v Prest* [2013] UKSC 34, [2013] 2 AC 415) (and see **E19.30**). E19.56

Third-party Interests The court should first determine whether D has any beneficial interest in the property. Ordinary principles of property and trust law apply when determining a person's interest in property (*Larkfield Ltd v RCPO* [2010] EWCA Civ 521, [2010] 3 All ER 1173 at [31]), including separate corporate identity, the doctrine of 'sham' and the presumption that a registered owner is the beneficial owner of real property. See *Alom* [2012] EWCA Crim 736 at [23] ('where legal ownership is clearly expressed, it will be a rare outcome that beneficial ownership does not follow the same pattern'), *Jones v Kernott* [2011] UKSC 53, [2012] 1 AC 776 (where it is not possible to ascertain the intentions of the joint legal owners of the family home each party is entitled to such share as the court regards as 'fair' having regard to the whole course of dealings between them), and *CPS v Piper* [2011] EWHC 3570 (Admin) (see the useful summary at [7]). If the court does determine that D has such an interest, it should then go on to consider whether any other party's share is genuinely beneficial or whether it is a tainted gift (*Buckman* [1997] 1 Cr App R (S) 325). The genuineness of an encumbrance, such as a mortgage, is a question of fact to be determined on the evidence (*Ghori* [2012] EWCA Crim 1115; *Rowsell* [2011] EWCA Crim 1894; *Harvey* [1999] 1 Cr App R (S) 354). It is 'self-evident' that, in order to establish a third-party interest, there must be some evidence of when and how it was acquired (*Perrey* [2011] EWCA Crim 2316). The balance of a negative equity cannot be set off against the available amount (*Ghadami* [1998] 1 Cr App R (S) 42). E19.57

Frequently, D's share in the value of the family home will be included in the available amount. At this stage the fact that the home may need to be sold to meet the order, and innocent family members suffer hardship as a result, is irrelevant to 'the arithmetic exercise' of calculating D's worth (*Ahmed* [2004] EWCA Crim 2599, [2005] 1 All ER 128). The provisions are compatible with the ECHR (*Danison v UK* (1998) Appln. 45042/98, 7 September 1999). Arguments that the property ought not to be sold could, in an appropriate case, be pursued at the enforcement stage, on the basis of either the HRA 1998 or wider equitable principles (*Reynolds* [2017] EWCA Crim 57). In *Re Kone* [2017] EWHC 3763 (Admin), the High Court appointed a receiver over a family home, holding that any interference with the family's property rights was proportionate to the legitimate aim of the confiscation order.

An innocent partner or third party may be able to temper the harshness of the process in one of four ways. E19.58

First, at the earlier stage of determining the amount of benefit, the POCA 2002, s. 10A (see **E19.39**), allows the court to make a conclusive determination of the extent of D's interest in property which may be realised in satisfaction of the order, provided it has discharged the obligation to give a 'reasonable opportunity' to make representations to 'anyone who the court thinks is or may be a person holding an interest'. This obligation only applies where the court is making a s. 10A determination. If the court is not making such a determination there is no need to provide an opportunity to interested persons to make representations, and a failure to do so would not vitiate any confiscation order that is made. In such a case, the interests of any interested party, having not been taken into account in making the confiscation order, may be asserted at the enforcement stage (*Hilton* [2020] UKSC 29, [2020] 1 WLR 2945).

Secondly, at the enforcement stage (see **E19.73**), if the order is not met, and the prosecutor applies for permission to realise the property through the appointment of an enforcement receiver, the court is obliged to receive representations from affected third parties (s. 51(8)), unless the property is perishable or ought to be disposed of before its value diminishes (s. 51(8A)) (*Re Norris* [2001] UKHL 34, [2001] 3 All ER 961). A third party is ordinarily not entitled to make representations that are inconsistent with a properly conducted earlier determination of that party's interests under s. 10A (s. 51(8B). The rights under the ECHR, Article 8, of those affected are engaged and the court must consider whether, for example, the loss of the home is proportionate (*Ahmed*).

A tenant protected by contract or statute is not a 'person who has possession of realisable property' and may not be ordered to give up possession of property to the receiver under s. 51(5) (*Brittain (as Enforcement Receiver) v Noskova* [2009] EWHC 2884 (Admin)).

Thirdly, and similarly, where a management receiver has been appointed in the context of a restraint order over the property and the receiver wishes, for example, to realise part of the property to meet expenses, the court must give persons holding interests in the property a reasonable opportunity to make representations (s. 49(8)).

Fourthly, where there are concurrent matrimonial proceedings, it may be possible to order the transfer of property to the innocent partner as ancillary relief, thus taking that share out of the calculation of the available amount. In *Customs and Excise Commissioners v MCA* [2002] EWCA Civ 1039, [2003] 2 WLR 210, the prosecution sought to enforce an order by realising the home. The wife, who had filed for divorce before the offences occurred, sought its transfer to her as ancillary relief under the Matrimonial Causes Act 1973. It was held that it would be disproportionate to any legitimate public interest to force a sale of the home and that the appropriate course in these circumstances is to order the transfer of D's entire beneficial and legal interests to the wife (see also *CPS v Grimes*; *Grimes v Grimes* [2003] 2 FLR 510 (half the proceeds of sale ordered to the wife); *X v X* [2005] EWHC 296 (Fam), [2005] 2 FLR 487 (ancillary relief proceedings can be used as a shield for the wife but not to improve the husband's position)). Since the abolition by the POCA 2002 of the High Court jurisdiction over restraint and enforcement, there is no longer any dual procedure under which confiscation and matrimonial ancillary relief can be combined. The proper course is for the matrimonial aspects to be dealt with first (*Webber v CPS* [2006] EWHC 2893 (Fam), [2007] 1 WLR 1052). This should not be regarded as 'open season to collusive agreements between dishonest former spouses'. 'As a matter of justice and public policy', where the family assets are themselves tainted, they should not be distributed to satisfy ancillary relief claims. In *CPS v Richards* [2006] EWCA Civ 849, [2006] 2 FLR 1220, the Court of Appeal stated that, when conducting the discretionary balancing exercise in the family proceedings, 'the only decisive factor' is whether the assets are tainted as having been derived from crime. However, in *Stodgell v Stodgell* [2009] EWCA Civ 243, [2009] 2 FLR 244 (where, significantly, the ancillary application was for a lump sum and not a transfer of the family home), it was said (at [9]) that 'while non-complicity in the crime is a necessary condition for the wife to succeed in an ancillary relief claim as a matter of discretion where she is in competition with a confiscation order, such non-complicity is not a sufficient condition'.

E19.59 The confiscation regime does not permit the recovery of property belonging to a third party simply on grounds of public policy (*Gibson v RCPO* [2008] EWCA Civ 645, [2009] QB 348). In that case, the family home had been purchased in joint names before the offences began but, to the knowledge of D's wife, mortgage payments were met from their proceeds. Nevertheless, the Court of Appeal declined to hold that her guilty knowledge displaced her beneficial interest in the property (arising because the property was in joint names). The case could not be equated with the principle in *Richards* which involved the discretionary transfer of property; what the prosecution had sought here was for the court to take property from a person who already owned it. (Such property would now appear to be recoverable under the POCA 2002, Part 5.) In *CPS v Aquila Advisory Ltd* [2019] EWCA Civ 588, it was held that public policy could not be used to defeat a finding that persons, who had dishonestly acquired property from the company of which they were directors, held such property on trust for the company. In those circumstances the confiscation order could not be enforced against such property, since it was beneficially held by the company, not the directors.

Stage Five — Proportionality

ECHR, Protocol 1, Article 1 Article 1 encodes an entitlement to peaceful enjoyment of one's possessions. It states that 'No one shall be deprived of his possessions except in the public interest and subject to the conditions provided for by law and by the general principles of international law', but preserves 'the right of a State to enforce such laws as it deems necessary to control the use of property in accordance with the general interest or to secure the payment of taxes or other contributions or penalties'. **E19.60**

In a landmark decision, the Supreme Court decided that, in limited circumstances, the legislation is capable of leading to disproportionate results and, consequently, breaches of Article 1 (*Waya* [2012] UKSC 51, [2013] 1 AC 294). This has since been given statutory force in the POCA 2002, s. 6(5)(b), as amended by the SCA 2015 (see further **E19.4** and **E19.61**). It is important to note that the concept of proportionality is relevant for the purposes of calculating the amount of the order, not the benefit figure. In *Box* [2018] EWCA Crim 542, [2018] 4 WLR 134, the Court of Appeal suggested that the reference to 'disproportionate' in s. 6(5)(b) was the meaning of that word in 'UK domestic law' (and therefore it may have a meaning broader than in the ECHR context).

Proportionality and Abuse of Process Before the decision of a nine-judge Supreme Court in *Waya* [2012] UKSC 51, [2013] 1 AC 294, the Court of Appeal had occasionally had tentative recourse to the discretionary abuse of process jurisdiction in order to ameliorate some of the more 'draconian' features of benefit calculation. The Supreme Court has, instead, chosen the different, and arguably sounder, juridical route of 'proportionality'. It construed the terms of the ECHR, Protocol 1, Article 1, as applied by the HRA 1998, s. 3, so that, in limited circumstances, 'the judge should, if confronted by an application for an order which would be disproportionate, refuse to make it but accede only to an application for such sum as would be proportionate' (at [16]: see **E19.60**). The judgment further addresses this issue thus (at [12], [20]–[21] and [24]): **E19.61**

> It is clear law, and was common ground between the parties, that this imports, via the rule of fair balance, the requirement that there must be a reasonable relationship of proportionality between the means employed by the State in, inter alia, the deprivation of property as a form of penalty, and the legitimate aim which is sought to be realised by the deprivation ...
>
> The difficult question is when a confiscation order sought may be disproportionate. The clear rule as set out in the Strasbourg jurisprudence requires examination of the relationship between the aim of the legislation and the means employed to achieve it. The first governs the second, but the second must be proportionate to the first. Likewise, the clear limitation on the domestic court's power to read and give effect to the statute in a manner which keeps it Convention compliant is that the interpretation must recognise and respect the essential purpose, or 'grain' of the statute.
>
> ... The purpose of the legislation is plainly, and has repeatedly been held to be, to impose upon convicted defendants a severe regime for removing from them their proceeds of crime.... It does not, however, follow that its deterrent qualities represent the essence (or the 'grain') of the legislation. They are, no doubt, an incident of it, but they are not its essence. Its essence, and its frequently declared purpose, is to remove from criminals the pecuniary proceeds of their crime.
>
> ... it must clearly be understood that the judge's responsibility to refuse to make a confiscation order which, because disproportionate, would result in an infringement of the Convention right under ... (Article 1) ... is not the same as the re-creation by another route of the general discretion once available to judges but deliberately removed. An order which the judge would not have made as a matter of discretion does not thereby ipso facto become disproportionate. So to treat the jurisdiction would be to ignore the rule that the Parliamentary objective must, so long as proportionately applied, be respected.

The Court accepted the potential for disproportionate outcomes in cases such as *Morgan* [2008] EWCA Crim 1323, [2008] 4 All ER 890 and *Shabir* [2008] EWCA Crim 1809, [2009] 1 Cr App R (S) 84 (497), while stating (at [18]): 'the better analysis of such situations is that orders such as those there considered ought to be refused by the judge on the grounds that they would be wholly disproportionate and a breach of [Article 1]. There is no need to invoke the concept of abuse of process.' In *Morgan*, (a) D's crimes were limited to offences causing loss to one or more identifiable losers, (b) his benefit was limited to those crimes, (c) the loser had neither brought nor intended to bring civil proceedings to recover the loss, but (d) D either had repaid the loser or was ready, willing and able immediately to repay him the full amount of the loss. However, the Court of Appeal in *Morgan* opined (at [31]) that the position may be different where D had profited from the use of stolen monies or where, although D appears willing to make restitution, there is doubt whether it will be achieved. In *Shabir*, a pharmacist had inflated prescription claims. The net gain from his criminal conduct amounted to £464, whereas his statutory benefit was approximately £179,000 and his total benefit from general criminal conduct was £212,464.

E19.62 The Supreme Court in *Waya* went further: to take into account in a confiscation order the value of stolen goods returned intact to the owner where the burglar or handler is caught in the act would be disproportionate (see, e.g., *Wilkes* [2003] EWCA Crim 848, [2003] 2 Cr App R (S) 105 (625)), stating (at [32]):

> If … an order were sought independently of the lifestyle provisions and the concomitant assumptions, and to the extent that it were based solely on the momentary benefit of obtaining goods which had been restored intact to the true owners, that order would be disproportionate and ought not to be made: it would not serve the aim, or go with the grain, of the legislation. Such a defendant's proceeds of crime would already have been restored to the loser in their entirety. An order in the same sum again would simply impose an additional financial penalty upon him. If such a defendant deserves an additional financial penalty, as in some cases he may, it ought to be imposed openly by way of fine, and whether or not he is also sent to prison, providing he has the means to pay.

Moreover, their lordships stated (at [34]):

> There may be other cases of disproportion analogous to that of goods or money entirely restored to the loser. That will have to be resolved case by case as the need arises. Such a case might include, for example, the defendant who, by deception, induces someone else to trade with him in a manner otherwise lawful, and who gives full value for goods or services obtained. He ought no doubt to be punished and, depending on the harm done and the culpability demonstrated, maybe severely, but whether a confiscation order is proportionate for any sum beyond profit made may need careful consideration. Counsel's submissions also touched very lightly on cases of employment obtained by deception, where it may well be that difficult questions of causation may arise, quite apart from any argument based upon disproportion. Those issues were not the subject of argument in this case and must await an appeal in which they directly arise; moreover related issues are understood to be currently before the Strasbourg court.

The Court of Appeal has since quashed confiscation orders for the value of a stolen vehicle which was subsequently recovered intact — albeit in Ibiza (*Axworthy* [2012] EWCA Crim 2889). Note, however, that, if D obtained chattels as a result of criminal conduct and used them for a substantial period, thereby materially reducing their value, and the chattels were ultimately restored to their true owners, the court should not give credit for the residual value of those chattels. The court must focus on the property that D originally obtained. There was nothing in the wording of the POCA 2002 or the ECHR which required the court to deduct the residual value. A confiscation order based on the original value of the property would not be disproportionate (*Harvey* [2013] EWCA Crim 1104, [2014] 1 WLR 124). A confiscation order based on an amount of VAT which has been accounted for to HMRC is to that extent disproportionate (*Harvey* [2015] UKSC 73, [2017] AC 105).

An order was also quashed for the amount of property obtained by the forgery of a will where, although probate had been granted to D, the estate had yet to be distributed (*Hursthouse* [2013] EWCA Crim 517). In *Sale* [2013] EWCA Crim 1306, [2014] 1 WLR 663, D had corruptly given gifts to a Network Rail employee in order to procure contracts. An order in the sum of the total value of the contacts obtained was disproportionate. A proportionate order would be one which took account of the gross profit gained under the relevant contracts together with the value of the pecuniary advantage gained by obtaining a market share, excluding competitors and saving on the costs of preparing proper tenders. The value of that pecuniary advantage had not been assessed: 'In cases of this nature in the future, it was to be hoped that prosecutors would be alert to this aspect of the case, so that the real benefit or pecuniary advantage derived by the wrongdoer could be identified' (at [60]). (For examples of an application of these principles, see *Morgan* [2013] EWCA Crim 1307, [2014] 1 All ER 1208 and *Reynolds* [2017] EWCA Crim 1455, [2018] 4 WLR 33.) There is a 'clear distinction' between cases in which goods or services are provided by way of a lawful contract but the transaction is tainted by associated illegality, and cases where the entire undertaking is unlawful, as in *King* [2014] EWCA Crim 621, [2014] 2 Cr App R (S) 54 (437), where an order for the business turnover was upheld against a commercial car trader posing as a private seller in breach of consumer protection regulations, as the 'entire enterprise was characterised by deliberate misrepresentation' (at [33]). On the other hand, the fact that defendants had not acted dishonestly or in bad faith in committing, for example, an offence under the Trade Marks Act 1994 (a lifestyle offence) did not mean that an order applying the assumption of benefit to their gross profits was disproportionate: 'It is the proceeds which matter, not the blame' (*Hampshire County Council v Beazley* [2013] EWCA Crim 567, [2013] 1 WLR 3331 at [14]). Likewise, just because D could have earned income from property rental had he acted legitimately did not mean that it was disproportionate to recover the entirety of income he had in fact earned through criminal conduct (*Evangelou* (18 July 2019 unreported, CA)). The fact that the amount of a confiscation order based on general criminal conduct is 'vastly' greater than the financial penalty imposed does not itself mean the order is disproportionate, since those amounts are 'the product of two very different processes' (*Bahbahani* [2018] EWCA Crim 95, [2018] QB 1099).

Waya was distinguished in *Hussain v Brent London Borough Council* [2014] EWCA Crim 2344 (upholding a decision of the Crown Court to make an order based on rental income obtained in breach of an enforcement notice) and in *Chahal* [2015] EWCA Crim 816, in which the defendants had taken part in a series of fraudulent transactions as part of a wider 'missing trader' or 'carousel' fraud, and large sums of money had been paid into and out of their accounts in the furtherance of that fraud. While the sum of the benefit accruing to each defendant would inevitably be much higher than any net profit they might ever have made from cheating the revenue, the Court of Appeal could see no reason to reduce the calculation of those benefits in the interests of proportionality or justice:

> ... the entire series of transactions was bogus, and repeated bogus claims have been made on the Revenue. In our judgment it is in the public interest that in this case, the degree of benefit should be assessed in accordance with the POCA 2002 and requires no reduction on proportionality grounds.

For the correct approach to a confiscation order where a compensation order is also sought, see *Jawad* [2013] EWCA Crim 644, [2013] 1 WLR 3861 and **E19.68**.

The mandatory nature of the process makes the prosecution decision to invoke it critical and there must be an individual exercise of judgement in each case. As the Supreme Court noted in *Waya* [2012] UKSC 51, [2013] 1 AC 294 at [19], 'the Crown has an important preliminary function in ensuring that a disproportionate order is not sought. But the safeguard of the defendant's Convention right under [Article 1] not to be the object of a disproportionate order does not, and must not, depend on prosecutorial discretion.' **E19.63**

There may be a need to revisit dicta from various cases, such as *CPS v Nelson* [2009] EWCA Crim 1573, [2010] QB 678; *Del Basso* [2010] EWCA Crim 1119, [2011] 1 Cr App R (S) 41 (268); *Wilkinson* [2009] EWCA Crim 2733; *Mahmood* [2005] EWCA Crim 2168, [2006] 1 Cr App R (S) 96 (570) and *Farquhar* [2008] EWCA Crim 806, [2008] 2 Cr App R (S) 104 (601).

Tainted Gifts and Proportionality Any difficulty that D may have in retrieving the actual gift is immaterial to it being included in the available amount (*Smith* [2013] EWCA Crim **E19.64**

502, [2014] 1 WLR 898; *Tighe* [1996] 1 Cr App R (S) 314), subject to the possible impact of proportionality. In *Box* [2018] EWCA Crim 542, [2018] 4 WLR 134, drawing on the decision in *Johnson* [2016] EWCA Crim 10, [2016] 4 WLR 57, it was explained (at [21]): 'there may be some exceptional cases where the court is affirmatively satisfied on evidence which it is able to accept that making such an order will not recover the proceeds of crime and will simply lead to a sentence of imprisonment being served which the defendant in question can do nothing about'. Such an order would, held the Court of Appeal, be disproportionate. The Court added that it would be unlikely that a court could reach that 'affirmative' finding without 'oral evidence from [D] and called on her behalf, and without full disclosure of documents concerning the financial circumstances of all relevant persons' (at [22]). Where such evidence is given but only establishes that the donee is reluctant to restore a tainted gift, that would not establish disproportionality (*Morrison* [2019] EWCA Crim 351, [2019] 2 Cr App R (S) 25 (188)).

Confiscation Orders and Sentence

E19.65 **Proceeds of Crime Act 2002, ss. 13, 14 and 15**

13.—(1) If the court makes a confiscation order it must proceed as mentioned in subsections (2) and (4) in respect of the offence or offences concerned.

(2) The court must take account of the confiscation order before—
  (a) it imposes a fine on the defendant, or
  (b) it makes an order falling within subsection (3).

(3) These orders fall within this subsection—
  (a) an order involving payment by the defendant, other than . . . a priority order;
  (b) an order under section 27 of the Misuse of Drugs Act 1971 (forfeiture orders);
  (c) an order under section 143 of the Sentencing Act (deprivation orders);
  (d) an order under section 23 or 23A of the Terrorism Act 2000 (forfeiture orders).

(3A) In this section 'priority order' means any of the following—
  (a) a compensation order under section 130 of the Sentencing Act;
  (b) an order requiring payment of a surcharge under section 161A of the Criminal Justice Act 2003;
  (c) an unlawful profit order under section 4 of the Prevention of Social Housing Fraud Act 2013;
  (d) a slavery and trafficking reparation order under section 8 of the Modern Slavery Act 2015.

(4) Subject to subsection (2), the court must leave the confiscation order out of account in deciding the appropriate sentence for the defendant.

(5) Subsection (6) applies if—
  (a) the Crown Court makes both a confiscation order and one or more priority orders against the same person in the same proceedings, and
  (b) the court believes the person will not have sufficient means to satisfy all those orders in full.

(6) In such a case the court must direct that so much of the amount payable under the priority order (or orders) as it specifies is to be paid out of any sums recovered under the confiscation order; and the amount it specifies must be the amount it believes will not be recoverable because of the insufficiency of the person's means.

14.—(1) The court may—
  (a) proceed under section 6 before it sentences the defendant for the offence (or any of the offences) concerned, or
  (b) postpone proceedings under section 6 for a specified period.

(2) A period of postponement may be extended.

(3) A period of postponement (including one as extended) must not end after the permitted period ends.

(4) But subsection (3) does not apply if there are exceptional circumstances.

(5) The permitted period is the period of two years starting with the date of conviction.

(6) But if—
  (a) the defendant appeals against his conviction for the offence (or any of the offences) concerned, and
  (b) the period of three months (starting with the day when the appeal is determined or otherwise disposed of) ends after the period found under subsection (5),

the permitted period is that period of three months.

(7) A postponement or extension may be made—
  (a) on application by the defendant;

(b) on application by the prosecutor;
(c) by the court of its own motion.
(8) If—
(a) proceedings are postponed for a period, and
(b) an application to extend the period is made before it ends,
the application may be granted even after the period ends.
(9) The date of conviction is—
(a) the date on which the defendant was convicted of the offence concerned, or
(b) if there are two or more offences and the convictions were on different dates, the date of the latest.
(10) References to appealing include references to applying under section 111 of the Magistrates' Courts Act 1980 (statement of case).
(11) A confiscation order must not be quashed only on the ground that there was a defect or omission in the procedure connected with the application for or the granting of a postponement.
(12) But subsection (11) does not apply if before it made the confiscation order the court—
(a) imposed a fine on the defendant;
(b) made an order falling within section 13(3);
(c) made an order under section 130 of the Sentencing Act (compensation orders);
(ca) made an order under section 161A of the Criminal Justice Act 2003 (orders requiring payment of surcharge);
(d) made an order under section 4 of the Prevention of Social Housing Fraud Act 2013 (unlawful profit orders).

15.—(1) If the court postpones proceedings under section 6 it may proceed to sentence the defendant for the offence (or any of the offences) concerned.
(2) In sentencing the defendant for the offence (or any of the offences) concerned in the postponement period the court must not—
(a) impose a fine on him,
(b) make an order falling within section 13(3),
(c) make an order for the payment of compensation under section 130 of the Sentencing Act,
(ca) make an order for the payment of a surcharge under section 161A of the Criminal Justice Act 2003, or
(d) make an unlawful profit order under section 4 of the Prevention of Social Housing Fraud Act 2013.
(3) If the court sentences the defendant for the offence (or any of the offences) concerned in the postponement period, after that period ends it may vary the sentence by—
(a) imposing a fine on him,
(b) making an order falling within section 13(3),
(c) making an order for the payment of compensation under section 130 of the Sentencing Act,
(ca) make an order for the payment of a surcharge under section 161A of the Criminal Justice Act 2003, or
(d) making an unlawful profit order under section 4 of the Prevention of Social Housing Fraud Act 2013.
(4) But the court may proceed under subsection (3) only within the period of 28 days which starts with the last day of the postponement period.
(5) For the purposes of—
(a) section 18(2) of the Criminal Appeal Act 1968 (time limit for notice of appeal or of application for leave to appeal), and
(b) paragraph 1 of Schedule 3 to the Criminal Justice Act 1988 (time limit for notice of application for leave to refer a case under section 36 of that Act),
the sentence must be regarded as imposed or made on the day on which it is varied under subsection (3).
(6) If the court proceeds to sentence the defendant under subsection (1), section 6 has effect as if the defendant's particular criminal conduct included conduct which constitutes offences which the court has taken into consideration in deciding his sentence for the offence or offences concerned.
(7) The postponement period is the period for which proceedings under section 6 are postponed.

The judge may make a confiscation order before sentence or postpone the determination and proceed to sentence (s. 14(1)). When sentence follows the confiscation proceedings (which **E19.66** in practice is rare) the most basic principle of sentencing must still prevail — that a person cannot be sentenced for offences of which the person has not been convicted (or had taken into consideration), unless the person accepts that the offences are specimen examples of a wider course of conduct (*Bragazon* (1998) 10 Cr App R (S) 258; *Ayensu* (1982) 4 Cr App R (S) 248). It is, therefore, wrong to deny credit for having no previous convictions where the application of the assumptions has resulted in a finding of previous involvement in drug trafficking (*Callan* (1994) 15 Cr App R (S) 574). Even so, the sentencer may 'pay some regard to the evidence placed before him... in the same way as he might pay regard to general evidence placed before him' to find, for example, that this was not the first occasion on which D had offended (*Harper* (1989) 11 Cr App R (S) 240; *Thompson* [1997] 1 Cr App R (S) 289). Where the outcome of a confiscation inquiry does result in a conflict with other features of the case, the judge is entitled to hold a *Newton* hearing to resolve the conflict (*McNulty* (1994) 15 Cr App R (S) 606).

Relationship with Other Orders

E19.67 The interaction between confiscation orders and other sentencing powers is regulated by the POCA 2002, s. 13, as amended by the SCA 2015, s. 6, and the CJCA 2015, sch. 12. The effect of the confiscation order on the sentence varies according to the type of sentencing order. First, the court cannot make certain financial orders (fines, deprivation orders or forfeiture orders under the MDA 1971 or the TA 2000) without taking account of the confiscation order and reducing D's available means accordingly (s. 13(2) and (3)). Generally, however, the judge must 'leave the confiscation order out of account in deciding the appropriate sentence' (s. 13(4)), e.g., in deciding whether to impose a custodial sentence (*Rogers* [2001] EWCA Crim 1680, [2002] 1 Cr App R (S) 81 (337); *Andrews* [1997] 1 Cr App R (S) 279). A fine may not be appropriate when a court has sentenced D to imprisonment and made a confiscation order (*Hedley* (1989) 11 Cr App R (S) 298). The duty to make a confiscation order continues where the court makes an absolute or conditional discharge (*Varma* [2012] UKSC 42, [2013] 1 AC 463).

Secondly, the POCA 2002 has particular rules to ensure the primacy of 'priority orders' over confiscation. Priority orders are compensation orders, victim surcharge orders, unlawful profit orders under the Prevention of Social Housing Fraud Act 2013 or reparation orders under the Modern Slavery Act 2015. The court must still go through the initial process of making the confiscation order without taking account of the priority order. It must then compute the priority order without regard to the existence of the confiscation order. If 'the court (then) believes ... [D] will not have sufficient means to satisfy both the orders in full', it must order the shortfall in the priority order to be paid out of the confiscated sum (s. 13(5) and (6)). There is no general principle that a compensation order should not be imposed where satisfaction of that order will, prima facie, require the sale of the matrimonial or family home (*Parkinson* [2015] EWCA Crim 1448, [2016] 1 Cr App R (S) 6 (24), doubting *Beaumont* [2014] EWCA Crim 1664, [2015] 1 Cr App R (S) 1 (1)). If D does have sufficient assets, D can in theory be ordered to pay the money twice over, both as confiscation and compensation, and this was the position under the CJA 1988 (*Williams* [2001] 1 Cr App R (S) 140 (500)). However, the Court of Appeal in *Jawad* [2013] EWCA Crim 644, [2013] 1 WLR 3861, applying the approach of the Supreme Court in *Waya* [2012] UKSC 51, [2013] 1 AC 294, held that, before making such orders, the court should consider whether a confiscation order that includes the amount of the compensation amounts to disproportionate double-counting and, accordingly, to an infringement of the ECHR, Protocol 1, Article 1 (see further **E19.61**). Even so, as Hughes LJ, sitting in the Supreme Court, stated (at [21]):

> ... we do not agree that the mere fact that a compensation order is made for an outstanding sum due to the loser, and thus that the money *may* be restored, is enough to render disproportionate a POCA confiscation order which includes that sum. What will bring disproportion is the certainty of double payment.

Accordingly, the mere making of a compensation order did not mean that the confiscation order had to be reduced by that amount. Hughes LJ outlined a series of practical points (at [23]):

(a) If the defendant has control of his assets, he ought to be able to make repayment in the knowledge that, once he proves he has done so, credit would be given for it against a confiscation order. Repayment through solicitors on notice to the Crown should be sufficient.
(b) If repayment has not been made before the confiscation hearing, proof that his solicitors were in funds and willing to give an undertaking to repay on his behalf is likely to suffice.
(c) Where the defendant is not in control of his assets, similar principles should apply. If the assets are in the hands of the Crown, he can request repayment. If the assets are subject to a restraint order, he can apply for a variation of it for the purpose of repayment.
(d) In very few cases there might be occasion for a brief adjournment of a confiscation hearing for immediate arrangements for payment to be made but the court should not entertain a defendant's well-meaning intentions not backed by assurance of repayment.

Payment of a compensation order may be 'assured' on the facts even though it may not take place for some considerable time, as where it will be met from property which is restrained and to be realised to meet a confiscation order (*Davenport* [2015] EWCA Crim 1731, [2016] 1 WLR 1400).

An order for costs ought not to be made where the judge has assessed the available amount to be less than the benefit figure. The implication of such an assessment is that no further funds are available (*Ahmed* [1997] 2 Cr App R (S) 8; *Szrajber* [1994] 15 Cr App R (S) 821; *Hopes* (1989) 11 Cr App R (S) 38).

Postponement

Either the prosecution or defence may apply for a postponement or the court may order a postponement of its own motion (POCA 2002, s. 14(7)). The court has an unfettered discretion to postpone the determination for specified periods up to a maximum of two years from the date of conviction (or longer in exceptional circumstances) (s. 14(4) and (5)). If a determination is postponed, the judge may sentence in the meantime so long as various financial orders, such as orders for compensation, forfeiture or payment of a surcharge under the CJA 2003, s. 161A, are not made (s. 15(2)); these orders may be imposed after a postponed determination but only in the 28 days immediately following (and that period of 28 days may not be extended: *A-G for the Isle of Man v Darroch* [2019] UKPC 31, [2019] 1 WLR 4211). Even so, a postponed confiscation order is not invalidated simply by the making of such orders beforehand (*Guraj* [2016] UKSC 65, [2017] 1 WLR 22, and see *Sachan* [2018] EWCA Crim 2592, where the order erroneously imposed during the period of postponement was a compensation order which did not invalidate the subsequent confiscation order, and likewise *Bristowe* [2019] EWCA Crim 2005, [2020] 1 Cr App R (S) 58 (453), which concerned a 'victim surcharge'). Costs should not be awarded before making the confiscation order (*Threapleton* [2001] EWCA Crim 2892, [2003] 3 All ER 458; *Smart* [2003] EWCA Crim 258, [2003] 2 Cr App R (S) 65 (384)). E19.68

Numerous problems arose under earlier legislation when judges misapplied the mandatory postponement provisions. The question was whether, by failing to comply with such a provision, the court was thereby deprived of its jurisdiction to make a confiscation order. It is now unlikely that a procedurally incorrect order would be vulnerable to appeal. E19.69

First, orders are not to be quashed only on the ground that 'the procedure connected with the application for or the granting of a postponement' was defective (s. 14(11)).

Secondly, in *Guraj* [2016] UKSC 65, [2017] 1 WLR 22, the Supreme Court agreed (at [37]) that 'the courts will not wish to see the intention of Parliament defeated by technical points taken to stave off meritorious confiscation orders'. The decision in *Guraj* itself followed *Knights* [2005] UKHL 50, [2006] 1 AC 368, where the House of Lords held that flaws in the postponement procedure under the CJA 1988 would not invalidate a subsequent confiscation order if the judge has acted in good faith (see also *Ashton* [2006] EWCA Crim 794, [2007] 1 WLR 181). Subsequently, in *Iqbal* [2010] EWCA Crim 376, [2010] 1 WLR 1985, the Court of Appeal held that, where there had been an order for postponement but no return date set and the confiscation application was not then revived until after the expiry of the permitted two-year period, there was no jurisdiction to proceed. The decision in *Iqbal* was doubted in *T* [2010] EWCA Crim 2703 and does not survive the decision of the Supreme Court in *Guraj*.

There remains limited scope for arguing that an order ought not to be made because of a procedural failing. In *Guraj* the Supreme Court held (at [31]) that 'a failure to honour the procedure set down by the statute raises the very real possibility that it will be unfair to make an order, although the jurisdiction to do so remains, and that unless the court is satisfied that no substantial unfairness will ensue, an order ought not to be made'. This appears to be a reference to the possibility of staying proceedings as an abuse of process. In the event of a 'very long period of inactivity, the correct inference may well be that unfairness to the accused has ensued'. The Court explained that it may be possible to 'cure' unfairness, referring to the possibility of reducing the amount of a confiscation order or to the variation or quashing of a linked property order (where, for example, the procedural defect had led to unfairness by way of 'double counting'). In relation to the circumstances arising in *Iqbal*, the Court said (*obiter*, at [34]) that where the two-year period is exceeded where there are no exceptional circumstances 'it must be especially likely that unfairness will ensue'. It is submitted that where this is the case, the court would need to decide, first, whether there has been unfairness and, secondly, whether that unfairness can be cured. If it cannot, the court should not make an order, i.e. it must stay the proceedings as an abuse of process.

E19.70 **The Postponement Decision** A decision to postpone need not be expressed in any particular form of words. The fact that the judge has so decided may be inferred from the circumstances; e.g., where the intention to sentence first has been made plain and it was understood by all concerned that confiscation would be dealt with at a later date (*Tahir* [2006] EWCA Crim 792). Listing is a judicial function and listing officers make the necessary arrangements on behalf of the judiciary. A decision by the judge to put the date back because of the judge's unavailability constitutes a postponement. The decision is effected by the judge giving instructions to the list officer who fixes a new date (*Neish* [2010] EWCA Crim 1011, [2010] 1 WLR 2395).

The two-year period may be exceeded in 'exceptional circumstances' (s. 14(4)). The phrase 'must take its colour from the setting in which it appears' should not be strictly construed (*Soneji* [2005] UKHL 49, [2006] 1 AC 340). A judge had not erred in finding that there were 'exceptional circumstances' where there had been late filing of statements by the Crown and the defence, listing difficulties, and adverse weather conditions. Parliament had intended a broad interpretation of 'exceptional circumstances' and the failure to specify the period of postponement was not a bar to recovery as it was a procedural error (see *Johal* [2013] EWCA Crim 647, [2014] 1 WLR 146 and, for a further illustration in the context of a prosecutor's appeal, *Halim* [2017] EWCA Crim 33). Listing difficulties are capable of amounting to exceptional circumstances (*Soneji*; *Young* [2003] EWCA Crim 3481, [2004] 2 All ER 63; *Groombridge* [2003] EWCA Crim 1371, [2004] 1 Cr App R (S) 9 (84)).

The failure to refer expressly to 'exceptional circumstances' will not invalidate a postponement if it can be inferred that the court made an appraisal of the circumstances and had the appropriate test in mind, and if the order can be justified (*Chuni* [2002] EWCA Crim 453, [2002] 2 Cr App R (S) 82 (371); *Gadsby* [2001] EWCA Crim 1824, [2002] 1 Cr App R (S) 97 (423)). It is only if the timetable initially set makes it likely that the two-year period will be exceeded that the court must on the first occasion address itself to 'exceptional circumstances' (*Knights* [2005] UKHL 50, [2006] 1 AC 368).

The court may postpone the determination while D appeals against conviction. If the appeal takes more than two years, postponement for up to three months after the appeal is permitted (s. 14(6)). The court may grant a postponement without a hearing — presumably only where the parties agree (CrimPR 33.14; see Supplement, **R33.14**)).

Form of Order and Payment of Amount

The court must fix the recoverable amount. This is a fixed sum of money and therefore an order purporting to confiscate the equity of a particular property 'valued at not less than £26,000' is defective (*Jubb* [2001] EWCA Crim 2567, [2002] 2 Cr App R (S) 8 (24)). **E19.71**

The ordinary principle is that the order must be satisfied immediately (s. 11(1)). However, if D shows that time is needed to pay, D can be allowed a specified period of up to three months to meet the order. If D applies before the end of that period, it can be extended in exceptional circumstances to a maximum of six months from the date of the order. There is no inherent jurisdiction to extend time to pay further (*Revenue and Customs Prosecution Service v Kearney* [2007] EWHC 640 (Admin)).

A magistrates' court may order the release for the satisfaction of a confiscation order of money which has been seized under a 'relevant seizure power' (namely the PACE 1984 or the powers of seizure under the POCA 2002, s. 47V or 352) and is held in a bank account or which has been produced to an appropriate officer under a production order (POCA 2002, s. 67A).

ENFORCEMENT, RECONSIDERATION AND APPEALS

Compliance Orders

The POCA 2002, s. 13A, empowers the court to make 'such order as it believes is appropriate for the purpose of ensuring that the confiscation order is effective (a "compliance order")'. **E19.72**

The court must consider whether to make a compliance order (a) on the making of the confiscation order, and (b) if it does not make a compliance order then, at any later time on the application of the prosecutor. The court must, in particular, consider whether any restriction or prohibition on D's travel outside the UK ought to be imposed as part of the order. The court need not be satisfied that a compliance order is 'necessary' provided there is a 'proper reason' for making the order. In assessing whether an order is 'appropriate' the court must 'strike a balance' between the need to ensure that the confiscation order in question is effective and the impact upon the individual defendant if a travel restriction is made (*Pritchard* [2017] EWCA Crim 1267, [2017] 2 Cr App R (S) 54 (437)). In *Pritchard* a travel restriction was appropriate where D (who had committed drug trafficking offences, had international connections, including hidden assets overseas, and had failed to file tax returns) was able to maintain contact with his family overseas. The length of the order, which is a matter for the sentencing judge, will be informed by the circumstances, including the remaining period of imprisonment to be served, and an assessment of the period of time to ensure enforcement and the effectiveness of the confiscation order. An order of indefinite length would only be justified in an 'exceptional' case. A compliance order may be varied upon application by the prosecutor or any affected person (s. 13A(5)). Whereas, unlike the position in Scotland (s. 97C), there is no statutory mechanism for punishing a breach of a compliance order, it appears such breaches would be punishable as a contempt of court.

The new power to make compliance orders is likely to make it unnecessary to consider other ancillary orders for the purpose of enforcement, such as a financial reporting order within the framework of a SCPO (see **D25.58**) (which, in any event, should only be imposed where strictly justified by the circumstances: *Wright* [2008] EWCA Crim 3207, [2009] 2 Cr App R (S) 45 (313)).

Enforcement

A confiscation order is treated as a fine to be collected and enforced by a specified magistrates' court or, if none is specified, by the committing magistrates' court (POCA 2002, s. 35(2)). If the amount of the order is not paid in time, simple interest accrues on the unpaid amount for the **E19.73** period for which it remains unpaid (s. 12). For the enforcement of multiple confiscation orders which are referable to benefit that was obtained 'jointly', see **E19.31**.

E19.74 **Default Term** When making a confiscation order, the Crown Court must fix a term to be served in default. Failure to do so, however, will not invalidate the order (*Ellis* [1996] 2 Cr App R (S) 403). With effect from 1 June 2005, the scale of maximum terms is more severe than that applicable to fines and is contained in the POCA 2002, s. 35(2A):

Confiscation order value £10,000 or less	six months
Confiscation order value £10,001 to £500,000	five years
Confiscation order value £500,001 to £1 million	seven years
Confiscation order value more than £1 million	14 years

These are maximum terms and the court has a discretion up to the maximum period in the band. It is submitted that where the offending took place prior to 1 June 2015 the court should apply the maximum terms which pertained prior to the amendment, so as to avoid any impermissible retrospective effect (*Togher v RCPO* [2007] EWCA Civ 686, [2008] QB 476; *Jamil v France* [1995] 21 EHRR 65); the latter authorities were not addressed in *Malhi* [2016] EWCA Crim 2025, [2017] 4 WLR 27, where the Court of Appeal reached a contrary view in the absence of adversarial argument. As to the court's discretion, a number of principles emerge from the authorities, enumerated by Laws LJ in *Castillo* [2012] EWCA Crim 1007, [2012] 2 Cr App R (S) 36 (201) at [12]:

1. All the circumstances of the case have to be considered.
2. It is of the first importance to have in mind that the purpose of the default term is to secure payment of the confiscation order.
3. It is not the court's function to find an arithmetical match between the amount of the order and the length of the term, such that for any given band or bracket prescribed in the statute an order at the bottom of the band should attract a default term likewise at the bottom of the band, an order in the middle of the band should attract a term in the middle or an order at the top should attract a term at the top.
4. The court is not to be influenced by the overall totality of the sentence passed for the crime plus the default term.
5. But for any given band the court should have regard to the maxima: the maximum amount of a confiscation order within the band and the maximum default term within the band.
6. Given principle (5), and especially in a case…falling within the top band where there is no maximum confiscation order but only a maximum default term, regard must be had to the requirement of proportionality.

   …The purpose of the default term is not punishment for the achievement of retributive justice. It is rather to secure satisfaction of the confiscation order and so deprive the criminal of the fruits of his crime. In that endeavour, the demands of proportionality are much weaker than where the court is punishing the offender. Although retributive justice is by no means the only aim of sentencing, it remains a first condition of criminal punishment that the offender should get no more than his just deserts. Proportionality is thus at the centre of the process. By contrast, the ancillary regime of asset recovery is established on an altogether different footing. Its first condition is effectiveness.

In that case, the Court of Appeal substituted a nine-year term for the ten-year maximum where D was found to have £3 million in hidden assets.

The mechanism for enforcing the confiscation order, including the committal of an offender to prison, is based on that used in the enforcement of fines (POCA 2002, s. 35(2), requires the amount of the confiscation order to be treated as a fine for the purposes of the PCC(S) A 2000, s. 140(1) to (4), which, in turn, means the fine is to be enforced in accordance with the MCA 1980). The regime for enforcement of confiscation orders is, however, more severe than that for fines. By reason of the POCA 2002, s. 38(3), certain steps are not available to the magistrates' court, including the ability to extend time in which to pay and the ability to 'remit' fines. Moreover, 'serving that term does not prevent the confiscation order from continuing to have effect so far as any other method of enforcement is concerned' (s. 38(5)). Once half of the default period has been served, D must be released unconditionally unless the amount of the confiscation order is more than £10 million (CJA 2003, s. 258, as amended by the SCA 2015).

Default If D defaults, the magistrates must summons D and decide whether to commit D to prison (MCA 1980, s. 76). Where there has been a part payment, the default term ordered to be served must be reduced (s. 79(2)). In *Gibson v Secretary of State for Justice* [2018] UKSC 2, [2018] 1 WLR 629, the Supreme Court held that the reduction made must reflect the proportion paid of the original amount of the confiscation order (not including interest). For example, if a ten-year default term is fixed in respect of an order of £1 million and 50 per cent is paid, the term to be served is five years, regardless of the amount of accrued interest. The only means of enforcing the element of accrued interest is therefore civil enforcement (but note the power of the Crown Court to increase the default term where interest has accrued: POCA 2002, s. 39(5)). Instead of committing D, the court may decide to 'postpone the issue of the warrant until such time and on such conditions, if any, as the court thinks just' (MCA 1980, s. 77; see *DPP v Greenacre* [2007] EWHC 1193 (Admin), [2008] 1 WLR 438 and *Revenue and Customs Prosecution Service v Kearney* [2007] EWHC 640 (Admin)). Magistrates may postpone the issue of a warrant of commitment for a default term until after the expiry of a sentence imposed for separate offences (*RCPO v Taylor* [2010] EWHC 715 (Admin)). **E19.75**

A line of authority, ending in *R (Sanghera) v Birmingham Magistrates' Court* [2017] EWHC 3323 (Admin), has emphasised the MCA 1980, s. 82, and in particular the requirement that the court be satisfied, before it may commit a person to prison, that the default is due to 'the offender's wilful refusal or culpable neglect'. The court should be satisfied that no alternative means of enforcement is available before committing an offender; it may be unreasonable to do so when the sale of property has fallen through but the property remains saleable and the offender is co-operating in efforts to sell it (*Barnett v DPP* [2009] EWHC 2004 (Admin); *R (Joyce) v Dover Magistrates' Court* [2008] EWHC 1448 (Admin)). A failure to follow this process may result in the quashing of the committal (as in *R (Beach) v Folkestone Magistrates' Court* [2018] EWHC 2843 (Admin)), but the provision in the MCA 1980, s. 82(4) (see **E5.13**), that the court 'has considered or tried all other methods of enforcing payment of the sum and it appears to the court that they are inappropriate or unsuccessful' must be 'read with care ... It is enough for the court to have regard to other methods ... it is not a requirement before an order can be made that all other methods should have been tried and failed' (*Johnson v Birmingham Magistrates' Court* [2012] EWHC 596 (Admin) at [39]). There appears to be little guidance on how to approach committal for non-payment of orders based on 'tainted gifts' (which are, by definition, irrecoverable in law even if, in practice, the donee may be prevailed upon to return them). The POCA 2002 requires a default term to be fixed even where the order is based on such a gift, so the policy arguably favours imprisonment, even if it transpires the gift cannot be recovered. Such authority (*obiter*) as there is appears to suggest that in a tainted gift case, enforcing magistrates should consider alternative methods of enforcement, including whether the order could be satisfied through the appointment of a receiver (*L* [2010] EWHC 1531 (Admin)).

A refusal to adjourn where D faces lengthy imprisonment and is unrepresented may be contrary to common law and ECHR principles of fairness (*R (Agogo) v North Somerset Magistrates' Court* [2011] EWHC 518 (Admin)).

Proceedings to enforce an order by commitment to prison are part of the determination of a criminal charge within the meaning of the ECHR, Article 6(1), and must be determined 'within a reasonable time' (*Lloyd v Bow Street Magistrates' Court* [2003] EWHC 2294 (Admin), [2004] 1 Cr App R 11 (132); *Crowther v UK* (2005) *The Times*, 11 February 2005; *R (Syed) v City of Westminster Magistrates' Court* [2010] EWHC 1617 (Admin)). However, relevant to the evaluation would be the fact that D pursued 'every avenue of appeal available to him' (*R (Minshall) v Marylebone Magistrates' Court* [2008] EWHC 2800 (Admin), [2010] 1 WLR 590) or that D failed to engage with the process knowing that the prosecution intended **E19.76** to enforce the order (*Marsden v Leicester Magistrates' Court* [2013] EWHC 919 (Admin)). To date, the authorities do not address the question whether, in a suitable case, a sufficient remedy for delay might be a reduced period of detention, rather than no detention at all (applying by analogy *A-G's Ref (No. 2 of 2001)* [2001] EWCA Crim 1568, [2001] 1 WLR 1869). Where enforcement by way of a warrant for committal is stayed as a result of delay, it may not be appropriate to stay all enforcement action such as civil sanctions or compensation (*R (CPS) v Derby and South Derbyshire Magistrates' Court* [2010] EWHC 370 (Admin); *R (Joyce) v Dover Magistrates' Court* [2008] EWHC 1448 (Admin)).

Enforcement proceedings do not amount to the bringing of a fresh charge so as to breach the principle of speciality in extradition law (*R (Woolley) v Birmingham Magistrates' Court* [2010] EWHC 12 (Admin)).

E19.77 **Enforcement Receivers** If the order is not satisfied, the prosecution may ask the Crown Court (previously the High Court) to appoint an enforcement receiver (s. 50). The court may then confer powers on the receiver to: (a) take possession of realisable property; (b) manage 'or otherwise deal with' the property; (c) realise the property 'in such manner as the court may specify'; (d) bring, continue or defend legal proceedings (s. 51(2)). D is a party to the proceedings and is able to make appropriate applications, e.g., in relation to delay (*Re Dahner* [2010] EWHC 3397 (Admin)), and if D consents to an order it may, on conventional principles, be difficult for D to argue subsequently that the order should be set aside (*Khan* [2019] EWHC 2683 (Admin)). For third-party rights and representations, see **E19.57**. An order for costs out of central funds under the Prosecution of Offences Act 1985, s. 17, is not available to a private prosecutor in receivership proceedings in the High Court (*Re Somaia* [2019] EWHC 1227 (QB), [2019] 2 Cr App R 24 (253)).

E19.78 **Request for Assistance** Where the prosecutor believes that realisable property is situated outside the UK, a 'request for assistance' may be sent to the Secretary of State who may, in turn, forward the request to the relevant government (s. 74). A request for assistance asks the receiving country to apply the various co-operation treaties and, in particular, to prohibit anyone from dealing in the property and to ensure that the proceeds 'are applied in accordance with the law of the receiving country'. If property is realised abroad, the amount which D has been ordered to pay under the order is reduced accordingly.

Reconsideration

E19.79 **Variations** Confiscation orders may be varied within 56 days under the general 'slip-rule', particularly where further information comes to light (PCC(S)A 2000, s. 155; see *Miller* (1990) 12 Cr App R (S) 519). The only way for the prosecution to achieve a reduction of the benefit figure is to appeal the order to the Court of Appeal (*Oyebola* [2018] EWCA Crim 246). However, the POCA 2002 itself anticipates that the full extent of D's benefit or assets may not emerge for some considerable time or, alternatively, that D's assets actually amount to less than originally thought. Accordingly, the court retains powers to vary findings (a) as to the existence or amount of benefit for up to six years from conviction or (b) indefinitely as to the available amount. The court may give further time to pay the increased sum (*Escobar v DPP* [2008] EWHC 422 (Admin), [2009] 1 WLR 64). Procedure is governed by CrimPR 33.15 and 33.16 (see Supplement, **R33.15** and **R33.16**).

E19.80 **Uplift** As for reconsidering 'benefit', the prosecutor has six years from the date of conviction in which to ask the court to consider evidence of benefit which was previously 'not available'. Such an application may be made both where the court made no order, either because it did not proceed under the POCA 2002, s. 6 (s. 19), or did so proceed but concluded that D did not benefit (s. 20), and where the court made an order (s. 21). In re-assessing benefit, the application of the s. 10 assumptions is limited to property obtained or expenditure made after the date of conviction (ss. 19(5), 20(9) and 21(6)). Having identified the revised figure of benefit, if any, the court may fix the recoverable amount in such amount as 'the court believes is just'. In assessing what is 'just', the judge should consider the amount outstanding, the additional amount available, the passage of time since the original confiscation order and the impact on D, together with the legislative policy in favour of maximising the recovery of the proceeds of crime and after-acquired assets, even those acquired through legitimate work. The correct test on appeal is whether the new order is wrong in principle or manifestly excessive and not whether it is '*Wednesbury* unreasonable' (*Padda* [2013] EWCA Crim 2330, [2014] 1 WLR 1920).

As for reconsidering the 'available amount', the prosecutor (or a receiver) may apply at any point for reconsideration of the available amount (s. 22). Section 22 even catches property that has accrued to D after the date of the confiscation order and regardless of whether the prosecution can prove that it is the proceeds of crime (*Re Peacock* [2012] UKSC 5, [2012] 1 WLR 550 (substantial legitimate assets after release from prison); *Bates* [2006] EWCA Crim 1015, [2007] 1 Cr App R (S) 2 (9) (acquisition of equity in council house through exercise of 'right to buy' scheme); *John* [2014] EWCA Crim 1240, [2014] 2 Cr App R (S) 73 (569) (legitimate to increase order to reflect an award for general, but not specific, damages payable to D following a traffic accident); *Robinson* [2019] EWCA Crim 2204 (where a confiscation order is imposed as a result of negligent legal advice and, following civil proceedings, the lawyers are required to indemnify D against any increase in the confiscation order, the indemnity is itself property which may justify an increase in the amount of the confiscation order). The order may be increased to an amount that is 'just' (see above). This involves weighing up the relevant factors, the categories of which are not closed (*S* [2019] EWCA Crim 569: role as police informant properly taken into account in determining the 'just' amount). Where the court declines to increase an order it should give adequate reasons (*Mundy* [2018] EWCA Crim 105, [2018] 4 WLR 130). Note that the ECHR entitlement to 'a hearing within a reasonable time' applies to the reconsideration of the available amount notwithstanding that Parliament has stipulated no statutory time-limit. The issue of delay must be determined by reference to the entirety of the proceedings and not on the basis that the reconsideration proceedings are distinct and separate (*Re Saggar* [2005] EWCA Civ 174, [2005] 1 WLR 2693).

Inadequacy D, the prosecutor or an appointed receiver may apply to the Crown (previously the High Court) Court for the amount of the order to be reduced if the available amount is inadequate for payment in full (s. 23). An application does not provide an opportunity for D to make good deficiencies in the case presented at the time of the confiscation order (*Gokal v SFO* [2001] EWCA Civ 368; *Re McKinsley* [2006] EWCA Civ 1092, [2006] 1 WLR 3420; *R v Liverpool Magistrates' Court, ex parte Ansen* [1998] 1 All ER 692; *Rooney* [2007] EWCA Crim 236). The same appears not to apply to the Crown, which may, on D's application that his or her property has reduced, allege that at the time of the confiscation hearing, D did in fact have more assets than were then identified (*Adams v CPS* [2017] EWCA Civ 185, [2017] 1 WLR 3732). **E19.81**

The procedure is intended to be used only where there had been a genuine depletion in D's financial circumstances: it is a safety net intended to provide for post-confiscation order events. In *Najafpour* [2009] EWCA Crim 2723, [2010] 2 Cr App R (S) 38 (245), Elias LJ stated (at [12]):

> A typical example is where property is sold for less than its anticipated value. The intention of this provision is clear: it is to ensure that a defendant does not serve the period in default where it turns out that he is in fact unable to raise the money which the court anticipated he would be able to do when it imposed the confiscation order.

It is not open to D to challenge an earlier finding in the confiscation proceedings that D had hidden assets (*Younis* [2008] EWCA Crim 2950, [2009] 2 Cr App R (S) 34 (247)). However, there is no rule of law that the court cannot be persuaded that D was unable to pay the outstanding amount because of a worsening of financial circumstances unless D gives full disclosure of what had happened to the assets, including previously unidentified assets. In a case involving previously unidentified assets, D had to be allowed to try to persuade the court that the identified assets had reduced in value and that as a result D was unable to pay the amount outstanding. What the court made of D's evidence would be a matter of judgement and much would depend on the nature of the case (*Glaves v CPS* [2011] EWCA Civ 69; *Re O'Donoghue* [2004] EWCA Civ 1800; *Telli v RCPO* [2007] EWCA Civ 1385, [2008] 3 All ER 405).

E19.82 It may be difficult to secure a reduction of a confiscation order to the extent that it is based on a 'tainted gift'. Even where a tainted gift proves difficult to recover, the calculation of the 'recoverable amount' would include the value of the gift when given, and could not be reduced to reflect the apparent change of circumstances (*Johnson* [2016] EWCA Crim 10, [2016] 4 WLR 57).

The clarification of a third party's interest in property might be a post-confiscation order event, and the extent of such interest might have to be decided (*Re Norris* [2001] UKHL 34, [2001] 3 All ER 961). This principle may, exceptionally, permit a court to reduce an order based on D's consent, as where D's claim to own property is subsequently declared to be wrong in proceedings in the Chancery Division (*Yaseen* [2016] EWCA Crim 2139). However, D may not be entitled to rely on the fact of failure to recover funds placed with a third party in order to hide them; their irrecoverability could not, in the circumstances, be classed as a post-confiscation order event (*Re B* [2008] EWHC 3217 (Admin)).

Appeals

E19.83 A confiscation order or variation (apart from variations based upon inadequacy of the available amount: see *Ward* [2010] EWCA Crim 1932, [2011] 1 WLR 766) constitutes a sentence for the purposes of appeal (Criminal Appeal Act 1968, s. 50(1): see **D26.43**). Accordingly, D may appeal against the making or the amount of an order with the leave of the Court of Appeal. The Court may confirm, quash or vary the order.

An appeal against the making of an order under s. 10A (see **E19.39**) determining the extent of D's interest where a third party holds an interest in property may be made by the prosecutor or by 'a person who the Court of Appeal thinks is or may be a person holding an interest in the property', if the latter was not given a reasonable opportunity to make representations when the determination was made or if it appears to the Court of Appeal to be arguable that giving effect to the determination would result in a serious risk of injustice to the person (s. 31(4) to (7)). Appeals also lie by defendant or prosecutor against decisions whether or not to make compliance orders under s. 13A (s. 13B: see **E19.72**).

Where D has pleaded guilty on the basis of incorrect legal advice (e.g., as to the implications of admitting a 'lifestyle' offence), any resulting confiscation order should be set aside on appeal only 'in the most exceptional circumstances' and 'there would need to be a well-founded submission that the whole process was unfair' (*Ayankoya* [2011] EWCA Crim 1488; *Hirani* [2008] EWCA Crim 1463; *Kirman* [2010] EWCA Crim 614; *Perkes* [2010] EWCA Crim 101). This principle likewise applies to a case where D has consented to a particular sum of benefit arising from the statutory assumptions (*Morfitt* [2017] EWCA Crim 669). However, consent does not confer jurisdiction to make an order; the making of an order requires a deliberation by the judge. It would be manifestly unfair for D to be bound by consent when the only possible explanation was that it was given under a mistake of law (*Mackle* [2014] UKSC 5, [2014] AC 678).

Where the Court of Appeal quashes an order, it may, instead of substituting its own order, direct the Crown Court to proceed afresh so long as D is not dealt with more severely than under the order which is quashed (Criminal Appeal Act 1968, s. 11(3A)). Procedure is governed by the Proceeds of Crime Act 2002 (Appeals under Part 2) Order 2003 (SI 2003 No. 82). There is a single time-limit of 28 days for giving notice of appeal from the date of the decision sought to be appealed. This may be extended. The rules bring the procedural aspects broadly in line with the Criminal Appeal Act 1968 and the rules that formerly applied under the 1968 Act (CrimPR Part 42: see Supplement, **R42.1** *et seq*.). For the position as to extending time in order to avoid 'substantial injustice' in a 'change of law' case, see *Bestel* [2013] EWCA Crim 1305, [2014] 1 WLR 457 and *Neuberg (No. 2)* [2016] EWCA Crim 1927, [2017] 4 WLR 58.

The prosecutor has a general right of appeal under the POCA 2002, s. 31, 'in respect of' the making of a confiscation order and against a decision not to make an order. This requires leave.

The prosecutor may not appeal a decision not to reconsider a case (under ss. 19 and 20), nor a decision not to proceed against an absconder (under ss. 27 and 28). The parties may appeal further to the Supreme Court (s. 33).

MISCELLANEOUS

Absent Defendants

Inability to Attend There is in principle no reason why in an appropriate case the common-law principle that the judge has a discretion to continue proceedings in the absence of a defendant who is unable to attend (e.g., because of a long-standing illness) does not apply to confiscation proceedings (*Jones* [2002] UKHL 5, [2003] 1 AC 1; *Bhanji* [2011] EWCA Crim 1198). In the case of a person who is unwell and absent, if no order is made because of D's absence on account of illness, the effect of the POCA 2002, ss. 19 and 20, is that, when the case is reconsidered after D's recovery, it will only be possible to deploy the assumptions in relation to evidence which was not available to the prosecutor at the earlier time (*Ali* [2014] EWCA Crim 1658, [2015] 1 WLR 841). In *Gavin* [2010] EWCA Crim 2727, [2011] 1 Cr App R (S) 126 (731), in separate cases, G and T had been removed from the UK between the commencement and conclusion of confiscation proceedings; T was removed under a voluntary facilitated return scheme (the Home Office was unaware of the proceedings and he did not inform his solicitors of his pending removal) and G was unwillingly deported notwithstanding Home Office awareness of the proceedings. In T's case, the confiscation order was upheld on the basis that he had by implication consented to be absent. However, where, as in G's case, inability to attend arises because an arm of the State has prevented his attendance, the proceedings should not be continued: 'It cannot ... be in accordance with the [ECHR] for the State to deny a right to be present. It is an important safeguard in securing a fair trial, even in circumstances where his presence is not, on the facts, essential to secure that fairness. We consider this was a breach of Article 6' (at [37]). **E19.84**

Absconding Wilful absconding where there is a conviction triggers a specific scheme under the POCA 2002, ss. 27 and 28. Once D absconds, whether before or after conviction in the Crown Court, or after committal for sentence or committal for confiscation, the prosecution may apply to proceed in the normal way under s. 6. However, the court has a discretion rather than a duty to proceed and the price is a more limited form of inquiry. The court may proceed if it 'believes it is appropriate for it do so' (s. 27(3)) and the prosecution have taken reasonable steps to contact D. The court then proceeds as if D were present but the required assumptions and the provisions requiring defence disclosure must be ignored (s. 27(5)). 'Any person the court believes is likely to be affected by an order' is entitled to appear and to make representations; if D reappears following the making of an order, D can then do little other than to apply for a variation under s. 23 on the basis that the available amount is inadequate (see **E19.81**). If the prosecution had applied to proceed under s. 27 in D's absence but 'the court did not proceed', when D 'ceases to be an absconder' the prosecution may apply for a reconsideration under s. 19 within six years of the date of conviction if they have fresh evidence (s. 27(6) and (7) as amended). **E19.85**

There is a similar discretion to proceed where an unconvicted defendant absconds before the proceedings for the index offence(s) have been concluded (s. 28). Once three months have elapsed from the day that 'the court believes he absconded', a similarly modified form of inquiry can take place. If, on reappearance, D is 'tried and acquitted', the order must be discharged (s. 30(2)). Alternatively, the court may discharge the order if it finds either that there has been 'undue delay' in continuing the prosecution or that the prosecutor does not intend to continue with the prosecution (s. 30(4)). (It has also been held that s. 28 operates to permit the court to make an order under s. 6 where D has been convicted in his or her absence (*Okedare* [2014] EWCA Crim 1173, [2014] 1 WLR 4088).)

Compensation

E19.86 There are detailed provisions under which the court may order 'such compensation it believes is just' where there has been a 'serious default' by the prosecuting authorities (POCA 2002, s. 72). In order to qualify for compensation three conditions must be met: (a) a criminal investigation has been started but has not resulted in conviction (or the conviction is quashed on appeal); (b) there has been a serious default without which the investigation would not have continued; and (c) a person who held realisable property suffered loss in consequence of an order under Part 2. Procedure is governed by CrimPR 33.22 (see Supplement, **R33.22**). Where an order has been quashed out of time but monies have previously been paid to a receiver, the Courts Service has no liability to repay those monies (*R (Seago) v Her Majesty's Courts and Tribunal Service* [2012] EWHC 3490 (Admin)).

Confiscation and EU Law

E19.87 EU law has established a system of mutual recognition of confiscation orders. Under this system, a competent authority in one Member State is obliged in principle to recognise and execute a confiscation order issued by an authority in another Member State (see **A9.16**).

Under the Criminal Justice and Data Protection (Protocol No. 36) Regulations 2014 (SI 2014 No. 3141), reg. 11, if any of the property to which an application for a 'domestic confiscation order' (i.e. an order under the POCA 2002, s. 6) relates is property in a Member State other than the UK, the prosecutor may ask the Crown Court to make a certificate. The Crown Court may make a certificate if it makes a domestic confiscation order in relation to property in the other Member State. A certificate may be made in relation to confiscation orders made prior to 2 December 2014 (the date on which the 2014 Regulations came into force) and it is not necessary to show that the property in the other Member State is 'tainted' (i.e. traceable to property obtained through criminal conduct) (*Moss* [2019] EWCA Crim 501, [2019] 1 WLR 6033). The 2014 Regulations set out the subsequent procedure. They also set out the steps to be taken on receipt of an overseas confiscation order.

Section E20 Recommendation for Deportation

POWER TO RECOMMEND FOR DEPORTATION

The Secretary of State is empowered under the Immigration Act 1971 to order the deportation from the UK of persons who are not British citizens. A court may, on sentencing an offender, make a recommendation that the offender be deported, by virtue of that Act and the British Nationality Act 1981. The decision on deportation is taken by the Home Secretary, who is able to take account of a wider range of considerations than is the court, such as the political situation in the country to which the offender will go (*Nazari* [1980] 3 All ER 880). **E20.1**

Sections 32 to 39 of the UK Borders Act 2007 place the Secretary of State under a duty to make a deportation order in respect of a 'foreign criminal' unless certain exceptions apply. 'Foreign criminal' is defined in s. 32 as a person who is not a British citizen, is convicted in the UK of an offence, and who has either been sentenced to imprisonment for at least 12 months or who has committed an offence specified by the Secretary of State under the Nationality, Immigration and Asylum Act 2002 and who is subject to a period of imprisonment. The reference to 'imprisonment' for these purposes includes detention in a young offender institution and extends to any indeterminate sentence provided that it may last for at least 12 months. A suspended sentence does not count. It is also clear from s. 38 that there must be a single term of imprisonment of at least 12 months — it does not apply to a case in which two or more shorter terms run consecutively to total more than 12 months. As from the date of the departure of the UK from the EU, in accordance with the European Union (Withdrawal) Act 2018, the UK Borders Act 2007 is amended by the Immigration, Nationality and Asylum (EU Exit) Regulations (SI 2019 No. 745), which provide that, in s. 32, after 'British citizen' there is inserted 'or an Irish citizen', and s. 33 is amended so as to create an exception to automatic deportation for persons resident in the UK before exit day and where the offence occurred before that date.

The 2007 Act made no changes to the court's power to recommend deportation as such, but in practice the power is now greatly curtailed. It was held by the Court of Appeal in *Kluxen* [2010] EWCA Crim 1081, [2011] 1 WLR 218 that the issue of making a recommendation is now likely to arise only in the case of an offender receiving a short custodial sentence who has a long record of minor offending, or in cases involving the misuse of identity documents. Examples are *Junab* [2012] EWCA Crim 2660, [2013] 2 Cr App R (S) 23 (159) (offence involving false identification documents) and *Ul Haq* [2013] EWCA Crim 1478, [2014] 1 Cr App R (S) 52 (307) (repeated assaults involving sexual touching of women on public transport). The Court in *Mintchev* [2011] EWCA Crim 499, [2011] 2 Cr App R (S) 81 (465) held that, as a matter of principle, it was wrong to reduce to below 12 months an otherwise appropriate sentence so as to avoid the provisions of the UK Borders Act 2007. *Mintchev* was approved in *Alkidar* [2019] EWCA Crim 330, where the reverse situation occurred. The judge passed a custodial sentence of 20 months in order to give the authorities time to deport D but, in all the circumstances including time served on remand, no further punishment was appropriate. The Court of Appeal said that a judge was 'not entitled to reach a contrived result so as to defeat the operation of a statutory provision'. In *Gebru* [2011] EWCA Crim 3321, where the applicability of the dangerous offender provisions was in issue, the Court of Appeal noted the judge's sentencing remark that there was 'no point in considering the need for an extended sentence... because you will be deported automatically'. Hallett LJ said that the provisions described as 'automatic deportation' may not necessarily lead to deportation in every case, and so judges should not alter their sentence on that assumption. *Gebru* was considered and approved in *A-G's Ref (No. 41 of 2013) (M)* [2013] EWCA Crim 1729, [2014] 1 Cr App R (S) 80 (493); Pitchford LJ said that the sentencing court should make its decision on the risk posed by D without regard to the possibility that he would one day be deported.

E20.2 By the Immigration Act 1971, s. 3(6), a recommendation may be made in respect of any person who is not a British citizen, who is aged 17 or over, and who is convicted of an offence punishable with imprisonment as an adult. A 'British citizen' is a person who has a right of abode in the UK (see, for the definition, the British Nationality Act 1981, Part I), but, in addition, a Commonwealth citizen or a citizen of the Irish Republic shall not be recommended for deportation if that person was resident in the UK when the 1971 Act came into force, and has been ordinarily resident in the UK for at least the five years immediately prior to the date of conviction (s. 7(1)) (for the definition of 'Commonwealth citizen' see the British Nationality Act 1981, s. 37 and sch. 3). Section 6(2) provides that a court shall not make a recommendation for deportation unless the offender has been given at least seven days' written notice. This may require adjournment after conviction. If the court is considering making a recommendation for deportation, the defence should be given an opportunity to address the court on that matter (*Antypas* (1973) 57 Cr App R 207).

It is possible to make a recommendation for deportation against a person protected by Article 45 of the Treaty of Rome (national of an EU Member State), subject to the same principles which apply in respect of any other non-British subject who does not come within one of the exceptions to the Immigration Act 1971 (*Bouchereau* [1978] QB 732 (CJEC), considered in *Kluxen* [2010] EWCA Crim 1081, [2011] 1 WLR 218). Before exclusion and removal of an EU citizen can occur, the Secretary of State must ensure that the matters specified in Article 28 of Directive 2004/38/EC ([2004] OJ L158/77) have been taken into account (these include the period of time during which the person has resided in the territory, age, health, family links, level of social and economic integration etc.). The Immigration (European Economic Area) Regulations 2016 (SI 2016 No. 1052) make it clear that a host EU State must not expel an EU citizen who has a right of permanent residence in that State, if the person has lived in the host State for the previous ten years, or is under the age of 18, except on serious grounds of public policy, public security or public health.

E20.3 Before making a recommendation for deportation the sentencing court should always give careful consideration to the circumstances of the case, and full reasons for the decision to recommend deportation should always be given, in fairness to the offender and also to provide assistance to the Secretary of State who will have to make the final decision (*Nazari* [1980] 3 All ER 880; *Rodney* [1996] 2 Cr App R (S) 230). The Court of Appeal in *Ul Haq* [2013] EWCA Crim 1478, [2014] 1 Cr App R (S) 52 (307), while endorsing these requirements, said that a failure to give reasons did not necessarily mean that a recommendation should be quashed; the Court of Appeal could provide its own reasons if it considered deportation to be appropriate. See also *Bozat* [1997] 1 Cr App R (S) 270.

The Crown Court's common-law power to bind over an offender to come up for judgment has on occasion been used as a means of requiring an offender to leave the country indefinitely (see **E13**). Such power is not restricted by the Immigration Act 1971.

RECOMMENDATION FOR DEPORTATION: SENTENCING PRINCIPLES

Whether the Accused's Continued Presence in UK to Detriment of Community

E20.4 The principles set out below must be read in light of the changes made by the UK Borders Act 2007, ss. 32 to 39 (see **E20.1**).

In *Nazari* [1980] 3 All ER 880, Lawton LJ said (at p. 1373):

> This country has no use for criminals of other nationalities, particularly if they have committed serious crimes or have long criminal records. That is self-evident. The more serious the crime and the longer the record the more obvious it is that there should be an order recommending deportation. On the other hand, a minor offence would not merit an order.

The Court of Appeal in *Benabbas* [2005] EWCA Crim 2113, [2006] 1 Cr App R (S) 94 (550) reviewed a large number of authorities on the power to recommend deportation, and affirmed the continuing importance of the principles set out in *Nazari*. It was said that the required 'detriment to the community' had to be judged by reference to the public interest and the requirements of public policy. See also *Carmona* [2006] EWCA Crim 508, [2006] 1 WLR 2264 at **E20.6**.

Harshness of Foreign Regime Not to Be Considered

In *Nazari* [1980] 3 All ER 880, Lawton LJ said (at p. 1373): 'the courts are not concerned with the political systems which operate in other countries. ... The court has no knowledge of those matters over and above that which is common knowledge; and that may be wrong... It is for the Home Secretary to decide in each case whether an offender's return to his country of origin would have consequences which would make his compulsory return unduly harsh.' The principle in *Nazari* was reaffirmed in *Ukoh* [2004] EWCA Crim 3270, [2005] 2 Cr App R (S) 38 (231). **E20.5**

Likely Impact on Third Parties

Formerly it had been thought that the decision over whether to recommend deportation must engage with Convention rights, including the right to family life under Article 8 (*Boultif v Switzerland* (2001) 33 EHRR 50 (1179); *Mokrani v France* (2005) 40 EHRR 5 (123)). In the important case of *Carmona* [2006] EWCA Crim 508, [2006] 1 WLR 2264, however, the Court of Appeal preferred the view that, since the sentencing court was involved only in making a recommendation, and the final decision on deportation rested with the Secretary of State, the issue of engagement with Article 8, as well as the offender's rights under Articles 2 and 3, were for the Secretary of State and not the court. **E20.6**

Combining Recommendation with Other Sentences or Orders

A recommendation for deportation is ancillary to sentence. There is no statutory restriction upon combining a recommendation for deportation with any other sentence or order. Although a conviction followed by a discharge is treated as a conviction for limited purposes only (see **E12.6**), the Immigration Act 1971, s. 6(3), provides that, for the purposes of a recommendation for deportation, a person who has been found to have committed an offence 'shall ... be regarded as a person convicted of the offence'. **E20.7**

Section E21 Exclusions and Disqualifications

ALCOHOL-RELATED

Licensed Premises Exclusion

E21.1 **Licensed Premises (Exclusion of Certain Persons) Act 1980, s. 1**

(1) Where a court by or before which a person is convicted of an offence committed on licensed premises is satisfied that in committing that offence he resorted to violence or offered or threatened to resort to violence, the court may, subject to subsection (2) below, make an order (in this Act referred to as an 'exclusion order') prohibiting him from entering those premises or any other specified premises, without the express consent of the licensee of the premises or his servant or agent.

(2) An exclusion order may be made either—

(a) in addition to any sentence which is imposed in respect of the offence of which the person is convicted; or

(b) where the offence was committed in England or Wales, notwithstanding the provisions of sections 12 and 14 of the Powers of Criminal Courts (Sentencing) Act 2000 (cases in which absolute and conditional discharges may be made, and their effect), in addition to an order discharging him absolutely or conditionally; or

(c) [Scotland];

but not otherwise.

(3) An exclusion order shall have effect for such period, not less than three months or more than two years, as is specified in the order, unless it is terminated under section 2(2) below.

A licensed premises exclusion order may be made by the court either of its own motion, on the application of the victim or prosecutor or on the application of an interested third party made by way of representation to the prosecutor (*Penn* [1996] 2 Cr App R (S) 214).

E21.2 The expression 'licensed premises' means premises in respect of which there is in force a justices' on-licence. In *Grady* (1990) 12 Cr App R (S) 152, D pleaded guilty to assault occasioning actual bodily harm, after having been involved in an altercation in a public house, during which she pushed or punched the landlady, causing bruising to her back. The Court of Appeal quashed an order excluding D from entering licensed premises within the county of Norfolk for 12 months. It was said that exclusion orders were designed for those who might be described as making a nuisance of themselves in public houses, to the annoyance of other customers and possible danger to the licensee; it was inappropriate to make such an order in the case of a woman of mature years with a clean record. In *Arrowsmith* [2003] EWCA Crim 701, [2003] 2 Cr App R (S) 46 (301), D had head-butted a man in a public house, breaking his nose. The sentencer, in addition to passing a sentence of 12 months' imprisonment for the offence, made an exclusion order relating to 165 specified licensed premises within the borough where D resided. The Court of Appeal upheld the order on the particular facts of the case, but said that courts should not regard the decision as an invitation to draft overly wide exclusion orders.

Section 2 of the Act states that anyone who enters premises in breach of an exclusion order shall be guilty of an offence punishable on summary conviction with a fine not exceeding £200, or to imprisonment for one month or both. At the time of such conviction, the court shall consider whether the exclusion order should continue in force, and may terminate it, or vary it by deleting the name of any specified premises, if it thinks fit. There is no power to extend the order. By s. 4, a copy of any exclusion order, or order terminating or varying an exclusion order, shall be sent by the court to the licensee of the premises concerned.

FOOTBALL BANNING ORDERS

There are powers contained in the Football Spectators Act 1989 to exclude offenders who have been convicted of 'a relevant offence' from attendance at football matches. Where the court is satisfied that there are reasonable grounds to believe that a banning order would help to prevent violence or disorder at or in connection with any regulated football match(es), it *must* make a banning order (s. 14A(2)). Where these criteria are established, there is no discretion not to make an order (*Allen* [2011] EWCA Crim 3076). The order prohibits the offender from attending a regulated football match in the UK, and requires the offender to report when required to a police station when matches are being played outside the UK (s. 14(4)). It is not possible to make an order limited to particular matches or particular teams (*Doyle* [2012] EWCA Crim 995, [2013] 1 Cr App R (S) 36 (197); *Metropolitan Police Commissioner v Thorpe* [2015] EWHC 3339 (Admin), [2016] 1 Cr App R (S) 46 (291)). A banning order may include other requirements, and must require the offender to surrender his or her passport in connection with any match played outside the UK (s. 14E(3)). A banning order takes effect on the day when the order is made (s. 14F(1)). If the offender is sentenced to immediate imprisonment (including any form of detention), the banning order must be for at least six years and not more than ten years; if the offender is not sentenced to custody, the banning order must be for at least three years and not more than five years (s. 14F(3) and (4)). In *Gough v Chief Constable of Derbyshire* [2001] EWHC Admin 554, [2002] QB 459, the Divisional Court held that football banning orders were a lawful and proportionate restriction on a national citizen's freedom of movement under EU law. The court also held that such an order imposed after conviction was not a 'penalty' and accordingly there could be no infringement of the ECHR, Article 7, when, after conviction for a public order offence, the criminal court had imposed a ban for six years (twice the maximum ban available when the offence was committed). **E21.3**

Relevant Offences

The 'relevant offences' are listed in sch. 1 to the 1989 Act. A wide range of offences involving violence, possession of an offensive weapon, drunkenness, public disorder, damage to property and road traffic offences are 'relevant offences', but only if they were committed at or in connection with a football match, or when travelling to or from a football match (whether or not the match was actually attended by the offender). This is an important requirement, but much turns on the particular facts. Banning orders made under the Act were quashed in *Elliott* [2007] EWCA Crim 1002, [2007] 2 Cr App R (S) 68 (430), where a group of men who had attended a football match were later involved in violence in a public house but the violence was itself unrelated to the match. On the other hand, banning orders were upheld in *Parkes* [2010] EWCA Crim 2803, [2011] 2 Cr App R (S) 10 (54) even though some of those involved were supporters of neither club involved in the match in question. The applicable principles and case law are helpfully summarised in *Doyle* [2012] EWCA Crim 995, [2013] 1 Cr App R (S) 36 (197). The offences listed extend to any attempt or conspiracy, aiding, abetting, counselling or procuring the commission of such an offence and to encouraging or assisting such an offence within the meaning of the SCA 2007, Part 2. **E21.4**

Declaration of Relevance

In respect of a number of the offences listed in the Football Spectators Act 1989, sch. 1, before making a banning order the court is required to make a 'declaration that the offence related to a particular football match or matches' (a 'declaration of relevance'), which ordinarily requires that the prosecutor shall have given notice to the accused, at least five days before the first day of the trial, **E21.5** that it was proposed to show that the offence charged did relate to a particular football match or matches. Exceptionally, however, the court may make such a declaration in a case where the required notice has not been given, but only if the accused consents to waive the giving of full notice or the court is satisfied that the interests of justice do not require further notice to be given (s. 23). In *DPP v Beaumont* [2008] EWHC 523 (Admin), [2008] 2 Cr App R (S) 98 (549), it was suggested that a failure formally to state a declaration of relevance is not fatal to the proper making of a football banning order, provided that the court had the relevant considerations in mind before making the order.

Regulated Football Match

E21.6 The provisions as amended now relate to any 'regulated football match', which means 'an association football match (whether in the United Kingdom or elsewhere) which is a prescribed match or a match of a prescribed description' (Football Spectators Act 1989, s. 14(2)). 'Prescribed' means 'prescribed by an order made by the Secretary of State' (s. 22A(1)). The Football Spectators (Prescription Order) 2004 (SI 2004 No. 2409) describes the football matches both within and outside England and Wales which are regulated football matches. The 2004 Order was amended by SI 2010 No. 584 and SI 2013 No. 1709.

Miscellaneous Matters

E21.7 A magistrates' court or the Crown Court has power to make a banning order. Such an order can only be made in addition to a sentence imposed in respect of the relevant offence, or in addition to a conditional discharge for that offence (s. 14A(4)). A banning order may be made in combination with a conditional discharge notwithstanding the PCC(S)A 2000, s. 14 (s. 14A(5) and see **E12.6**). A banning order cannot be made where the offender has received an absolute discharge for the offence.

It is clear that a banning order may on the facts be justified on the basis of a single offence, without further evidence of repetition or propensity (*Hughes* [2005] EWCA Crim 2530, [2006] 1 Cr App R (S) 107 (632)), and in making such an order a court is entitled to take into account the potential deterrent effect of the order on persons other than the offender (*R (White) v Blackfriars Crown Court* [2008] EWHC 510 (Admin), [2008] 2 Cr App R (S) 97 (542)), followed in *Curtis* [2010] EWCA Crim 123, [2010] 1 Cr App R (S) 31 (193)).

For the purposes of deciding whether to make an order and whether the condition in s. 14A(2) (see **E21.3**) is satisfied, the court may consider evidence led by the prosecution and the defence (s. 14A(3A)) and it is immaterial whether that evidence would have been admissible in the proceedings (s. 14A(3B)). In *Boggild* [2011] EWCA Crim 1928, [2012] 1 Cr App R (S) 81 (457), Hughes LJ stated (at [20]) that 'it is palpably not the scheme of the Act to make a football banning order the inevitable consequence of a football related conviction'. But where the court is not satisfied as to the need to make an order in respect of a relevant offence, it must state that fact in open court and give its reasons (s. 14A(3)). On making a banning order, the court must explain the effect of that order to the offender in ordinary language (s. 14E(1)). The order requires the person to report initially at a specified police station within five days of the order being made (s. 14E(2)). There is power whereby the court may impose additional requirements on the person subject to the order in relation to any regulated football matches (s. 14G(1)). In particular, the court may make an order under the POA 1986, s. 35, requiring the offender to attend at a police station within seven days of the making of the order to have his or her photograph taken (s. 35(1)). This particular requirement, however, can be made by the court only where it has been requested by the prosecutor (s. 35(3)).

If a banning order has been in force for at least two-thirds of the period of the order, the person subject to it may apply to the court by which it was made to terminate it early (s. 14H).

A person subject to a banning order who fails to comply with any requirement imposed by the order is guilty of an offence punishable on summary conviction with imprisonment for a term not exceeding six months and/or an unlimited fine (s. 14J). The Sentencing Council definitive guideline, *Breach Offences* (see Supplement, **SG15-1**) applies to offenders aged 18 and over sentenced on or after 1 October 2018, irrespective of the date of the offence. The guideline says that in sentencing for 'other breach offences' (including this one), the court should refer to the sentencing approach in Step One of the guideline for breach of a criminal behaviour order to determine culpability and harm, and determine an appropriate sentence bearing in mind the maximum penalty for the offence.

DISQUALIFICATION OF COMPANY DIRECTOR

By the Company Directors Disqualification Act 1986, ss. 1 and 2, a court may make a disqualification order against an offender, convicted of an indictable offence, whether tried on indictment or summarily, in connection with the promotion, formation, management or liquidation or striking off of a company ('liquidation' was widely construed in *Georgiou* (1988) 87 Cr App R 207 and *Goodman* (1993) 14 Cr App R (S) 147, approving *Corbin* (1984) 6 Cr App R (S) 17), or in connection with the receivership or management of a company's property. This has the effect that the offender must not act as an insolvency practitioner nor, without the leave of the court, be a director of a company, a liquidator or administrator of a company, a receiver or manager of a company's property, or in any way, directly or indirectly, be concerned or take part in the promotion, formation or management of a company, for a specified period beginning with the date of the order. Such a disqualification has general effect; a court has no power to limit the order to a particular type of company (*Ward* [2001] EWCA Crim 1648). The purpose of the order is to protect the public from those who, for reasons of dishonesty, or naivety or incompetence, abuse their role and status as director (per Potter LJ in *Edwards* [1998] 2 Cr App R (S) 213). It is therefore essential for the sentencing judge to identify clearly the conduct of the offender which renders him or her unfit to be a company director (*Chandler* [2015] EWCA Crim 1825, [2016] 1 Cr App R (S) 37 (223)). **E21.8**

Length of Disqualification

The maximum period of disqualification which may be imposed by a magistrates' court is five years, and the maximum for the Crown Court is 15 years. There is no minimum period. The general principles applicable to company director disqualification were reviewed in the civil case of *Secretary of State for Business, Innovation and Skills v Rahman* [2017] EWHC 2468 (Ch), [2018] BCC 567, where it was confirmed that the disqualification brackets (of two to five years, six to ten years, and over ten years) set out in *Re Sevenoaks Stationery (Retail)* [1991] Ch 164 applied equally to civil and criminal cases, but this may overlook the fact that in a criminal case there is no equivalent to the two-year minimum disqualification period which applies in a civil case. Relevant sentencing factors include the duration of the offending, whether the offender had been dishonest throughout or had traded for a considerable period legitimately, the amount involved, the previous character of the offender, and whether there had been a prompt admission of guilt (*Cadman* [2012] EWCA Crim 611, [2012] 2 Cr App R (S) 88 (525)). **E21.9**

Disqualification for 15 years was appropriate in *Vanderwell* [1998] 2 Cr App R (S) 439 for a 'thoroughly dishonest fraudster' who pleaded guilty to managing a company while an undischarged bankrupt, obtaining property by deception and failing to keep proper accounts, and who had served an earlier prison sentence for fraud and received an earlier disqualification. See also *Atterbury* [1996] 2 Cr App R (S) 151, when disqualification for 12 years was imposed on D who had acted as a company director in contravention of an earlier disqualification order. Ten years' disqualification was upheld in *Sheikh* [2010] EWCA Crim 921, [2011] 1 Cr App R (S) 12 (99), for sophisticated dishonest activity carried out over a number of years. Seven years' disqualification was upheld in *Bott-Walters* [2005] EWCA Crim 243, [2005] 2 Cr App R (S) 70 (438), where D, the managing director of a company, had obtained £200,000 from another company by deception. Disqualification for five years was appropriate in *Theivendran* (1992) 13 Cr App R (S) 601 (managing a company whilst an undischarged bankrupt and obtaining excessive credit contrary to the Insolvency Act 1986) and in *Ashby* [1998] 2 Cr App R (S) 37. In

Victory [1999] 2 Cr App R (S) 102, two years' disqualification was reduced to 12 months in the case of a director who was 'careless to the point of incompetence' in keeping accounting records.

Breach Offence

E21.10 A contravention of a disqualification order is, in itself, a criminal offence punishable on indictment with up to two years' imprisonment and/or a fine, and on summary conviction with up to six months and/or a fine (Company Directors Disqualification Act 1986, s. 13). The Sentencing Council definitive guideline, *Breach Offences* (see Supplement, **SG15-1**), applies to offenders aged 18 and over sentenced on or after 1 October 2018, irrespective of the date of the offence. Where a disqualification order is made against a person who is already subject to one, the periods specified shall run concurrently (s. 1(3) and *Johnson* [1996] 2 Cr App R (S) 228).

DRIVING

Disqualification from Driving on Commission of an Offence

E21.11 By s. 146 of the PCC(S)A 2000, a court by or before which a person is convicted of an offence may, instead of or in addition to dealing with the offender in any other way, order the offender to be disqualified, for such period as it thinks fit, from holding or obtaining a driving licence (s. 146(1)). The power is made available to the Crown Court and magistrates' courts and applies in relation to any offence.

On a literal reading of s. 146, conviction for an offence may, without more, attract a period of disqualification from driving for such period as the court thinks fit. In *Cliff* [2004] EWCA Crim 3139, [2005] 2 Cr App R (S) 22 (118), D was convicted of affray. He was sentenced to 15 months' imprisonment together with a disqualification under s. 146 for two years. The Court of Appeal upheld the disqualification, saying that it was not necessary for the offence of conviction to be related in any way to the use of a motor vehicle. The Court added, however, that an order under s. 146 could not be made arbitrarily, and there must be sufficient reason for it. In this case, D had admitted that before the incident of affray he had driven his car while affected by drink or drugs or both. In *Bye* [2005] EWCA Crim 1230, [2006] 1 Cr App R (S) 27 (157), disqualification for 12 months under s. 146 in conjunction with a prison sentence of eight months was upheld by the Court of Appeal in a case where D got out of his car and attacked another motorist; in *Waring* [2005] EWCA Crim 1080, [2006] 1 Cr App R (S) 9 (56), disqualification for 18 months in conjunction with a prison sentence of four months for escape from lawful custody was upheld. In the latter case D had been stopped by the police, provided a positive breath test but, in the process of being taken to the police station, had jumped from the police car and escaped. He thereby avoided a second breath test and any possibility of being prosecuted for driving with excess alcohol. In *Griffin* [2019] EWCA Crim 563, [2019] 2 Cr App R (S) 32 (237), D admitted four counts of perverting the course of justice, where he had avoided penalty points and almost certainly a driving disqualification under the 'totting up' procedure by falsely entering the names of other persons on the notices of intended prosecution he received. Disqualification for three years under this provision was upheld in addition to a sentence of 16 months' imprisonment. In *Sofekun* [2008] EWCA Crim 2035, [2009] 1 Cr App R (S) 78 (460), an order under s. 146 was upheld where D had cannabis concealed within the bonnet of his car in small bags ready for supply. The Court of Appeal said that nothing in *Cliff* should be taken to have created any restrictions on the exercise of the power which cannot be found in the statutory provision itself. There is no power under s. 146 to order an offender to take an extended driving test on the expiry of the disqualification under the RTOA 1988, s. 36.

E21.12 **Totality** It is unclear whether an order made under s. 146 affects the totality of the sentence (by analogy with the power to order forfeiture of the offender's property under s. 143: see **E18.5**) or whether it should be regarded as an ancillary order (by analogy with compensation orders: see **E16.11**), imposition of which should not affect the punishment imposed for the offence. In

Sofekun the disqualification was viewed alongside the custodial sentence imposed in that case as 'part of an overall punitive sentence', and it is respectfully submitted that this is the better view.

Duty to Extend The CAJA 2009, s. 137 and sch. 16, provide for the extension of any driving disqualification imposed under s. 146 (or s. 147: see **E21.14**) in cases where the court also passes an immediate custodial sentence. In addition to the period of disqualification imposed under s. 146 (or s. 147), the court must order an extension period. The relevant extension period is the half-way point of a determinate custodial sentence, or two-thirds of the custodial term in the case of an extended sentence, or the conclusion of the minimum term in a life sentence. For guidance on the duty to extend, see *Needham* [2016] EWCA Crim 455, [2016] 2 Cr App R (S) 26 (219), discussed at **C7.36**. E21.13

Disqualification from Driving where Motor Vehicle Used for Committing or Facilitating Commission of an Offence

Section 147 of the PCC(S)A 2000 provides that the Crown Court may disqualify an offender from holding or obtaining a licence to drive a motor vehicle in cases where a motor vehicle has been used for the purpose of committing, or facilitating the commission of, the offence. This power is available: E21.14

(a) where a person is convicted before the Crown Court of an offence punishable on indictment with imprisonment for a term of two years or more, or where the offender has been convicted by a magistrates' court of such an offence and is committed under s. 3 of the 2000 Act to the Crown Court for sentence (s. 147(1)), or
(b) where a person is convicted before any court of common assault or any other offence involving assault (including an offence of aiding, abetting, counselling or procuring the commission of such an offence, or encouraging or assisting such an offence within the meaning of the SCA 2007, Part 2) (s. 147(2)),

and the Crown Court is satisfied that the motor vehicle was used (whether by the person convicted or by anyone else) for the purpose of committing, or facilitating the commission of the offence in question (s. 147(3)). Section 147(6) provides that facilitating the commission of an offence includes the taking of any steps after it has been committed for the purpose of disposing of any property to which it relates or of avoiding apprehension or detection.

In a case falling within s. 147, the Crown Court may order the person convicted to be disqualified, for such period as the court thinks fit, from holding or obtaining a licence (s. 147(3) and (4)), but there is no power under s. 147 to order the defendant to take an extended driving test on the expiry of the disqualification under the RTOA 1988, s. 36.

It should be noted that there is no requirement under s. 147 that the person convicted was the driver of the vehicle (*Skitt* [2004] EWCA Crim 3141, [2005] 2 Cr App R (S) 23 (122)), nor that the vehicle was directly involved in the commission of the offence, although use of the vehicle must at least have facilitated its commission (*Patel* (1994) 16 Cr App R (S) 756). If there is no causal link at all, an order under s. 147 cannot be made (*Parrington* (1985) 7 Cr App R (S) 18, although disqualification might now be ordered instead under s. 146 (see **E21.11**)). In *Gorry* [2018] EWCA Crim 1867, [2019] 1 Cr App R (S) 8 (59), the offenders received custodial sentences for conspiracy to burgle and conspiracy to steal, relating to high value motor cars. The Court of Appeal quashed orders of disqualification under s. 147, explaining that the power could only be exercised in respect of a conspiracy if the relevant vehicle had been used in the formation of the conspiracy itself, rather than used in furtherance of the conspiracy. It is submitted that the offenders in this case could properly have been disqualified under s. 146 instead (see **E21.11**).

Duty to Warn and Consider Effects Before disqualifying the offender, the court must warn counsel of the possibility of disqualification under s. 147, and counsel should be given an opportunity to address the court on that matter. Failure to warn may result in the disqualification being quashed on appeal (*Powell* (1984) 6 Cr App R (S) 354). A court imposing a E21.15

disqualification under s. 147 should take account of its likely effects on the offender's employment prospects (*Bowling* [2008] EWCA Crim 1148, [2009] 1 Cr App R (S) 23 (122)).

E21.16 **Duty to Extend** See **E21.13**.

CHILDREN AND VULNERABLE ADULTS

Barring Offenders from Regulated Activity Relating to Children and Vulnerable Adults

E21.17 By virtue of the Safeguarding Vulnerable Groups Act 2006 and the Safeguarding Vulnerable Groups Act 2006 (Commencement No. 3) Order 2009 (SI 2009 No. 39), there is a duty on a court to inform an offender that the Disclosure and Barring Service will bar him or her from working with children and/or vulnerable adults in any case where the court convicts the offender of a specified offence involving harm or a risk of harm to children or vulnerable adults.

E21.18 The reason for the requirement on the court is said to be to avoid a possible defence to a charge under s. 7(1) of the 2006 Act (offence of seeking to engage in, offering to engage in or engaging in a regulated activity from which barred), that D did not know he or she was barred from that activity (s. 7(3)).

E21.19 Judges are required to inform D, in a case where D has been convicted of a specified offence, that D either *will* be barred or (depending upon the offence of conviction) *may be* barred from working with children or with vulnerable adults, or both. D either '*will* or *may be*' barred because (depending upon the offence for which D is convicted) some offenders are barred without the right to make representations and some are barred with the right to make representation. CrimPR 28.3 (see Supplement, **R28.3**) states that the court 'must tell the defendant that [the notification] requirements apply, and under what legislation'. The *Crown Court Compendium: Sentencing* (December 2019), ch. S8-2, suggests the following as an appropriate form of words: 'The offence of which you have been convicted is one which will (or may) make you subject to barring from working with children or others. You will be told of the restrictions under the Safeguarding Vulnerable Groups Act 2006 by the Disclosure and Barring Service.' While the task of judges is simply to inform the offender, the Court of Appeal in *Lewis* [2016] EWCA Crim 1020, [2017] 1 Cr App R (S) 2 (5) said that a court making a sexual harm prevention order (SHPO) should avoid duplicating or interfering with the prohibitions placed upon the offender by virtue of the 2006 Act, and so before inviting the court to make a SHPO the prosecution should be in a position to ensure that duplication or interference between the two sets of restrictions is avoided.

E21.20 The specified offences can be found in the schedule to the Safeguarding Vulnerable Groups Act 2006 (Prescribed Criteria and Miscellaneous Provisions) Regulations 2009 (SI 2009 No. 37), as amended. The schedule lists the offences which will result in automatic inclusion on one or other (or both) lists, either with or without the right to make representations.

SEXUAL HARM PREVENTION ORDERS

E21.21 The SOA 2003, ss. 103A to 103K, provide power to impose a SHPO following conviction for a sexual offence which is listed in sch. 3 or sch. 5 to the Act. With effect from 8 March 2015 the earlier power to make a sexual offences prevention order (SOPO) following conviction for a sexual offence was repealed. A SOPO which was imposed before 8 March 2015 remains in place. Where a court in England and Wales makes a SHPO in relation to a person who is already subject to a SOPO, the SOPO ceases to have effect unless the court orders otherwise (s. 136ZB).

There are many similarities between SOPOs and SHPOs, so much of the case law relating to SOPOs continues to be relevant (see *McDonald* [2015] EWCA Crim 2119, [2016] 1 Cr App R (S) 48 (307) at **E21.25**). Whenever application is made for a SHPO the appropriate procedure as set out in CrimPR Part 31 (see Supplement, **R31.1** *et seq.*) should be complied with. In *Sokolowski*

[2017] EWCA Crim 1903, [2018] 1 Cr App R (S) 30 (216), the Court of Appeal noted that there had been many appeals against sentence involving SHPOs which did not conform to the statutory scheme, and there was no reasonable excuse for prosecution and defence counsel failing to appreciate the proper scope of such orders and their obligations to the court where an application for a SHPO was to be made.

Power to Make Order

By the SOA 2003, s. 103A, a court may make a SHPO in respect of a defendant where s. 103A(2) or (3) applies. The appropriate court may be the Crown Court, an adult magistrates' court, a youth court or the Court of Appeal. Section 103A(2) applies where the Crown Court or a magistrates' court deals with the defendant in respect of an offence listed in sch. 3 or 5 (or the defendant is found not guilty by reason of insanity or is found to be under a disability and has done the act charged) and the court is satisfied that it is necessary to make a SHPO for the purpose of (i) protecting the public or any particular members of the public from sexual harm from the defendant, or (ii) protecting children or vulnerable adults generally, or any particular children or vulnerable adults, from sexual harm from the defendant outside the UK. Section 103A(3) applies where an application is made by complaint to a magistrates' court for a SHPO in respect of D and it is proved that D is a qualifying offender and the court is satisfied that D's behaviour since conviction of an offence of the kind defined in s. 103B(2) and (3) means it is necessary to make a SHPO. Application under s. 103A(3) is not considered further here. **E21.22**

For the purposes of s. 103A(2), 'the public' means the public in the UK, 'sexual harm' means 'physical or psychological harm caused (a) by the person committing one or more offences listed in Schedule 3 or (b) (in the context of harm outside the United Kingdom) by the person doing, outside the United Kingdom, anything which would constitute an offence listed in Schedule 3 if done in any part of the United Kingdom' (s. 103B(1)). The subsection refers to 'sexual harm', whereas under the SOPO regime the term used was 'serious sexual harm', clearly signifying that the threshold for imposing a SHPO is lower than before. For the purposes of s. 103A, acts, behaviour, convictions and findings include those occurring before the commencement date (s. 103B(5)). In construing any reference to an offence listed in sch. 3, any condition subject to which an offence is so listed that relates (a) to the way in which the defendant is dealt with in respect of an offence so listed or a relevant finding (as defined by s. 132(9)) or (b) to the age of any person, is to be disregarded (s. 103B(9)). It should also be noted that under the SHPO regime a 'child' means a person aged under 18, whereas in relation to a SOPO it meant a person aged under 16. **E21.23**

Nature of Order

A SHPO prohibits the defendant from doing anything described in the order (s. 103C(1)). With the exception of a prohibition on foreign travel (which cannot exceed five years), a prohibition in a SHPO has effect (a) for a fixed period specified in the order for at least five years or (b) until further order (i.e. indefinitely) (s. 103C(2)). Some prohibitions in a SHPO may have effect until further order and some for a fixed period (s. 103C(3)). The Court of Appeal in *McLellan* [2017] EWCA Crim 1464, [2018] 1 Cr App R (S) 18 (107) said that a SHPO should not be made for an indefinite period unless the court was satisfied of the need to do so, and such an order should not be made without careful consideration. An indefinite SHPO would result in indefinite notification requirements: inadvertent extension of notification requirements was to be avoided. As a matter of good practice a court should explain, even if only briefly, the justification for making an indefinite SHPO. **E21.24**

The only prohibitions that may be included are those necessary for the purpose of (a) protecting the public or any particular members of the public from sexual harm from the defendant, or (b) protecting children or vulnerable adults generally, or any particular children or vulnerable adults, from sexual harm from the defendant outside the UK (s. 103C(4)). In the instructive case of *AB* [2019] EWCA Crim 2480, [2020] 1 Cr App R (S) 67 (515), D pleaded guilty to an offence of child abduction. He entered the house next door and took his neighbour's 17-month-old daughter to his own house, where he lived with his mother. The child's mother quickly realised what had happened, confronted D, and her daughter was released. D received a community order with a SHPO. The Court of Appeal quashed the SHPO. The offence of conviction is listed in sch. 5 rather than sch. 3 and the Court of Appeal was not satisfied that there was a sexual motivation to the offence and hence that a SHPO was necessary to protect the public or members of the public from sexual harm from D. Where a court makes a SHPO on a person already subject to one, the earlier order ceases to have effect (s. 103C(6)). A prohibition on foreign travel must be for a fixed period of not more than five years (s. 103D(1)), although the period may be extended on application to vary the order under s. 103E (s. 103D(3)).

E21.25 Court of Appeal decisions on the appropriate use of the SOPO have continuing relevance in relation to the SHPO. In *NC* [2016] EWCA Crim 1448, [2017] 1 Cr App R (S) 13 (87) the Court noted that the statutory provisions in relation to the SOPO were slightly different from those now relating to the SHPO in that the former referred to the need to protect the public from 'serious sexual harm' while the latter referred to 'sexual harm', but that with slight amendment the questions posed in the leading case of *Smith* [2011] EWCA Crim 1772, [2012] 1 All ER 451 remained relevant: (i) is the making of a SHPO necessary to protect the public from sexual harm through the commission of scheduled offences? (ii) if some order is necessary, are the terms imposed nevertheless oppressive? and (iii) overall, are the terms proportionate? In *McDonald* [2015] EWCA Crim 2119, [2016] 1 Cr App R (S) 48 (307) the Court stressed that a SHPO must not be made without proper consideration of the statutory requirements — a test of necessity for the imposition of the SHPO and a test of necessity for the inclusion of any prohibition within it. Judges were entitled to expect proper assistance from counsel on these matters. In *Smith* [2012] EWCA Crim 995, [2012] 1 All ER 451, Hughes LJ indicated (at [26]) that a draft order should be served on the court and the offender not less than two days before the hearing, and should be provided in electronic form to facilitate amendment. If counsel invite the judge to make such an order, appropriate material should be placed before the judge to show that the statutory requirements have been met. The Court of Appeal in *NC* endorsed that course of action, so that proper thought could be given to the draft order and amendments made, if required. In *Hemsley* [2010] EWCA Crim 225, [2010] 3 All ER 965 the Court of Appeal said that SOPOs should be clear on their face, capable of being complied with by the offender without unreasonable difficulty and/or the assistance of a third party, and free of the risk of unintentional breach. Such orders must be carefully drafted and, bearing in mind that they are often made against those of limited education, simplicity is a virtue. In *Pelletier* [2012] EWCA Crim 1060, the Court of Appeal said that the final version of the order must be approved and initialled by the judge and that it was sensible for a copy of the order to be given to the offender and that the offender should sign for it. In *Lewis* [2016] EWCA Crim 1020, [2017] 1 Cr App R (S) 2 (5), the Court said that a SHPO imposed on an offender convicted of an offence of viewing child pornography should only contain provisions preventing contact with children, or permitting only supervised contact with children, where there was a real risk that the offending would progress to contact offences. The Court of Appeal in *Franklin* [2018] EWCA Crim 1080 said that where there was no evidence that the defendant posed a risk to boys, as opposed to girls, a restriction in the SHPO in respect of 'any child' could not be justified. In *Begg* [2019] EWCA Crim 1578, [2020] 1 Cr App R (S) 30 (227), the Court of Appeal said that a prohibition in a SHPO that prevented D, who had admitted offences of possession of indecent images of children, from 'working paid or unpaid anywhere where there could be a child under 18 on the premises' was too vague, too prohibitive and too wide. In *Mortimer* [2010] EWCA Crim 1303, the Court of Appeal deleted or amended a number of prohibitions in an order relating to D's access to the internet, on the basis that the prohibitions were disproportionate and/or very difficult to enforce. The Court substituted provisions which prohibited owning any device with access to the internet without first notifying the monitoring officer, and prohibiting D from deleting from that device its history of internet use or refusing to show such history to a police officer on request. In *Thompson* [2009] EWCA Crim 3258, the Court of Appeal struck down a requirement purporting to allow the police unannounced access to

D's home to check his computer equipment and internet use. The Court of Appeal in *Parsons* [2017] EWCA Crim 2163, [2018] 1 Cr App R (S) 43 (307), said that in setting the terms of prohibitions under a SHPO the guidance given in *Smith* [2012] EWCA Crim 995, [2012] 1 All ER 451, remains sound and should be followed, but that in certain areas developments in technology and changes in everyday living call for an adapted and targeted approach. This is especially so in relation to the use of risk management monitoring software, and restrictions on cloud storage and encryption software. Examples of the approved wording of prohibitions relating to these matters can be found in the various appeals dealt with by the Court in *Parsons*. In *R (Richards) v Teesside Magistrates' Court* [2015] EWCA Civ 7, [2015] 1 Cr App R (S) 60 (412), the Court of Appeal confirmed that a SOPO could include a condition prohibiting D from leaving his home without wearing a location-monitoring device.

Variation, Renewal and Discharge

The defendant or the chief officer of police for the area in which the defendant resides (or is intending to reside) may apply to the Crown Court (if that court made the SHPO) or to the magistrates' court (if that court made the SHPO) for an order varying, renewing or discharging a SHPO (SOA 2003, s. 103E(1) and (2)). After hearing the application the court may make any order to vary, renew or discharge the SHPO as it considers appropriate. This may involve additional prohibitions but only if necessary for one of the purposes listed in s. 103C(4). A SHPO cannot be discharged before the end of five years from the making of the order without the consent of the defendant and, where the application is made by the chief officer of police for the area in which the defendant resides, that officer (s. 103E(7)), but this does not apply to a SHPO which contains a prohibition on foreign travel but no other prohibitions (s. 103E(8)). **E21.26**

The demarcation between appeals against sentence to the Court of Appeal in relation to a SHPO and applications to the Crown Court to vary or discharge the order was considered in some detail in *Spencer* [2013] EWCA Crim 2286, [2014] 2 Cr App R (S) 18 (127). Where variation is sought to the terms of an existing order a structured application should be made to the Crown Court, including clear evidence of the nature of the change of circumstances which forms the basis for the application. By contrast, any attack on the ambit of the original order (absent any change of circumstances) could only be considered by the Court of Appeal. It was further pointed out in *McLellan* [2017] EWCA Crim 1464, [2018] 1 Cr App R (S) 18 (107) that the power of the Crown Court on an application to 'discharge' a SHPO did not entail a consideration of whether the SHPO should have been made in the first place. The scope of the Crown Court's power to discharge the order was confined to whether, given the change in circumstances, it was now appropriate to bring it to an end. According to the Court of Appeal in *Parsons* [2017] EWCA Crim 2163, [2018] 1 Cr App R (S) 43 (307), although the Court in *McLellan* was dealing with a SOPO, the demarcation applied in exactly the same way to a SHPO. In *Cheyne* [2019] EWCA Crim 182, [2019] 2 Cr App R (S) 14 (105), there was an application to vary a SHPO by inserting a foreign travel prohibition. The Court noted that an application for a variation should be based on change of circumstances, including information about the offender which has come to light after the original order was made.

Notification Requirements

Where (a) the SHPO is made in respect of a defendant who was a relevant offender immediately before the making of the order, and (b) the offender would otherwise cease to be subject to the notification requirements (see **E23**) while the order has effect, the offender remains subject to the notification requirements (s. 103G(1)). Where the SHPO is made in respect of a defendant who was not a relevant offender immediately before the making of the order, the order causes the defendant to become subject to the notification requirements from the making of the order until the order (as renewed from time to time) ceases to have effect (s. 103G(2)). In relation to closely similar provisions on SOPOs, in *Hammond* [2008] EWCA Crim 1358, and again in **E21.27**

Smith [2012] EWCA Crim 995, [2012] 1 All ER 451, the Court of Appeal said that it would often though not always be appropriate to align the duration of an order with the applicable notification period set by the SOA 2003. In *McLellan* [2017] EWCA Crim 1464, [2018] 1 Cr App R (S) 18 (107) the Court of Appeal said that there was no requirement of principle that the duration of a SHPO should not exceed the duration of the applicable notification requirements. As explained in *Smith* [2012] EWCA Crim 995, [2012] 1 All ER 451, it all depended on the circumstances. While there was no need for the judge to give a specific warning where a SHPO of longer duration than the applicable notification period was contemplated, and the matter was best dealt by adherence to CrimPR Part 31, especially r. 31.3(5) (see Supplement, **R31.3**), which reflected the observations in *Smith*, all parties should be alert to the issue and 'inadvertent extension is to be avoided' (*Cole* [2019] EWCA Crim 1856).

Relationship with Other Forms of Restriction

E21.28 The relationship between the SOPO (now SHPO) and the dangerous offender regime was considered in *Terrell* [2007] EWCA Crim 3079, [2008] 2 All ER 1065, where the 21-year-old offender pleaded guilty before the magistrates' courts to four offences of making indecent photographs of a child and was committed to Crown Court for sentence. The Court of Appeal concluded that the dangerous offender provisions did not apply in this case. The Court noted that the court's discretion to make a SOPO (now SHPO) is prescribed by the SOA 2003 without reference to the dangerous offender provisions. The Court concluded that the restrictions which a court could impose under a prevention order would affect the question whether the dangerousness provisions had to be invoked in a particular case. It may be possible to avoid imposing such a sentence by imposing instead apt and effective conditions within a prevention order. Following an earlier division in the authorities as to whether an indeterminate sentence and a SOPO were mutually exclusive, it was settled in *Smith* [2012] EWCA Crim 995, [2012] 1 All ER 451 that the 'usual rule' was that an indeterminate sentence needed no SOPO. The Court in that case also noted that a SOPO (and by implication now a SHPO) should not duplicate or interfere with restrictions imposed by the sex offender notification provisions or with prohibitions placed on the offender by the Disclosure and Barring Service. Terms in SOPOs prohibiting activities likely to bring the offender into contact with children could be justified only as required beyond the restrictions placed upon the offender by the Disclosure and Barring Service : see, e.g., *Lewis* [2016] EWCA Crim 1020, [2017] 1 Cr App R (S) 2 (5), in relation to D's activities as a rugby coach, and *Begg* [2019] EWCA Crim 1578, [2020] 1 Cr App R (S) 30 (227). The Court of Appeal in *McLellan* [2017] EWCA Crim 1464, [2018] 1 Cr App R (S) 18 (107), dealt with a case where there was clear conflict between the terms of a SOPO and D's licence conditions following his release from custody, such that he was at risk of breaching the SOPO despite scrupulous compliance with his licence. The Court said that the conflict must be resolved, but that the proper route to deal with it lay in the Crown Court's power to vary the terms of its original order.

Appeal

E21.29 A defendant may appeal against the making of a SHPO under the SOA 2003, s. 103A(2)(a), as if the order were a sentence passed for the offence (s. 103H(1)).

Breach Offence

E21.30 A person who without reasonable excuse does anything that the person is prohibited from doing by a SHPO or a SOPO commits an offence punishable on summary conviction to imprisonment for a term not exceeding six months and/or a fine, and on conviction on indictment to imprisonment for a term not exceeding five years (s. 103I(3)). Where a person is convicted of such an offence, it is not open to the court to deal with it by way of a conditional discharge (s. 103I(4)). The Sentencing Council definitive guideline, *Breach Offences* (see Supplement, **SG15-1**), applies to offenders aged 18 and over sentenced on or after 1 October 2018 for breach of a SHPO (also applicable to breach of a SOPO and breach of a foreign travel order), irrespective of the date of the offence. In the pre-guideline case of *Simmonds* [2015] EWCA Crim 1068, [2015] 2 Cr App R (S) 60 (423) the Court of Appeal said that sentencing for breach of a SHPO or SOPO was highly fact-specific, but (i) a breach would be more serious if it involved harm, or risk of harm, to the particular section of the public that the order was designed to protect and (ii) although every breach was contemptuous, where the contempt was gross the culpability would be higher.

RESTRAINING ORDERS AND EUROPEAN PROTECTION ORDERS

A court which is sentencing or otherwise dealing with a person convicted of an offence may, as well as dealing with the offender in any other way, make a restraining order under s. 5 of the Protection from Harassment Act 1997. Further, under s. 5A of that Act, courts can in certain circumstances make a restraining order against a person who has been acquitted of the offence, provided that the court believes that a restraining order is necessary to protect another person from harassment, but a person against whom such an order is made under s. 5A has the same right of appeal against the order as if the person had been convicted of the offence in question before the court which made the order (s. 5A(5)). **E21.31**

Whenever a prosecution application is made for a restraining order, the appropriate procedure as set out in CrimPR Part 31 (see Supplement, **R31.1** *et seq.*) should be complied with.

Restraining Order on Conviction

By s. 5(1), a court sentencing a person convicted of an offence may (as well as sentencing or dealing with the person in any other way) make a restraining order. The order may, for the purpose of protecting the victim or victims of the offence (or any other person mentioned in the order) from further conduct which (a) amounts to harassment, or (b) will cause a fear of violence, prohibit the offender from doing anything described in the order (s. 5(2)). The order may have effect for a specified period or until further order (s. 5(3)). An order may be made for the protection of a named individual, or a group of individuals provided that the group is sufficiently clearly defined, or a limited company (*Buxton* [2010] EWCA Crim 2923, [2011] 1 WLR 857). In *AD* [2019] EWCA Crim 1339, [2020] 1 Cr App R (S) 21 (165), the Court of Appeal held that a restraining order which referred to the group of people to be protected as 'any child under 16 years old' was an insufficiently identifiable group of vulnerable persons to be lawful, and the order was quashed. On the particular facts of the case a criminal behaviour order was substituted. The order is a civil order and the civil standard of proof applies (*Major* [2010] EWCA Crim 3016, [2011] 1 Cr App R 25 (322)). **E21.32**

The order must be drafted in clear and precise terms so that there is no doubt as to its conditions, and may make reference to specific roads or addresses from which the offender is prohibited, if necessary by the inclusion of a map (*Debnath* [2005] EWCA Crim 3472, [2006] 2 Cr App R (S) 25 (169)). In considering the terms and extent of the restraining order, the court should have regard to proportionality with the seriousness of the offence. In *James* [2013] EWCA Crim 655, [2013] 2 Cr App R (S) 85 (542), D was convicted of assault upon his adult stepdaughter but the Court of Appeal quashed a restraining order which had been imposed in addition to a community order on the basis that it was clear from the jury's verdict that much of the complainant's evidence had been rejected, and it was not fair to impose a restraining order where most of the trouble was attributable to the complainant.

Restraining orders are commonly imposed following conviction for assault in a domestic context. In that context the Court of Appeal in *Khellaf* [2016] EWCA Crim 1297, [2017] 1 Cr App R (S) 1 (1), summarised the principles which should be taken into account when deciding whether to impose a restraining order:

(1) A court should take into account the views of the person to be protected by such an order. While there might occasionally be a case when an order can properly be made although the

subject of the order does not seek one, the views of the victim will be relevant. If the court does not have direct evidence it may be able to draw a proper inference as to those views. In normal circumstances the views of the victim should be obtained, and it is the responsibility of the prosecution to ensure that the necessary inquiries are made.

(2) An order should not be made unless the judge concludes that it is necessary to make an order in order to protect the victim.

(3) The terms of the order should be proportionate to the harm that it is sought to prevent.

(4) Particular care should be taken when children are involved to ensure that the order does not make it impossible for contact to take place between a parent and child if that is otherwise appropriate.

In *Herrington* [2017] EWCA Crim 889, [2017] 2 Cr App R (S) 38 (327), the complainant made it clear that she wished her relationship with D to continue, despite the obvious risk of violence against her. There was no evidence of lack of capacity, or duress. A restraining order, which had been 'made by the judge with the best of intentions and firmly based on a well-founded fear of harm' was quashed on appeal. See also *Brown* [2012] EWCA Crim 1152. In *Awan* [2019] EWCA Crim 1456, [2020] 1 Cr App R (S) 25 (198), the Court of Appeal quashed a restraining order without limit of time and which effectively prevented D from having contact with his children, and replaced it with an order for five years with a provision to permit arranged contact with the children. The Court said that the original order had been made with undue haste.

Restraining Order on Acquittal

E21.33 By s. 5A(1), a court before which a person is acquitted of an offence may, if it considers it necessary to do so to protect a person from harassment by the defendant, make an order prohibiting the defendant from doing anything described in the order. The order may have effect for a specified period or until further order (s. 5A(2)). The order is a civil order and the civil standard of proof applies (*Major* [2010] EWCA Crim 3016, [2011] 1 Cr App R 25 (322)). An order may be made for the protection of a named individual, or a group of individuals provided that the group is sufficiently clearly defined (*Smith* [2012] EWCA Crim 995, [2013] 2 Cr App R (S) 28 (191)). There is no principle that a restraining order made upon acquittal can be made only on undisputed facts, or can be used only rarely (*Major*). The relevant evidence will usually have emerged during the trial, but additional evidence can be heard on the matter.

A restraining order following an acquittal was upheld in *Thompson* [2010] EWCA Crim 2955, [2011] 2 Cr App R (S) 24 (131), where D was acquitted of assaulting a woman with whom he had a relationship, but the judge formed the view on the basis of evidence given at the trial that the order was necessary to protect the complainant from harassment. By contrast, in *K* [2011] EWCA Crim 1843, [2012] 1 Cr App R (S) 88 (523), a similar order was quashed on appeal. The prosecution had offered no evidence in respect of the charges against D and the limited information available to the judge did not provide a sound evidential basis for making the order. See also *Brough* [2011] EWCA Crim 2802, [2012] 2 Cr App R (S) 8 (30) and *Jose* [2013] EWCA Crim 939. The Court of Appeal in *Taylor* [2017] EWCA Crim 2209, [2018] 1 Cr App R (S) 39 (273), quashed a restraining order following D's acquittal in relation to a single count of burglary. After a function at a public house D had remained hidden within the premises overnight. The complainant was the landlady of the premises, who lived in the upstairs flat. D had set off the burglar alarm several times during the night in the course of his attempts to leave. The complainant made a victim personal statement indicating that she was fearful that D would return. The Court of Appeal quashed the restraining order. D was not previously known to the complainant, this was a one-off incident, and there was no evidence to suggest that he would pursue a course of conduct amounting to harassment in relation to her.

If the judge is considering making an order under s. 5A, time should be given to the parties to consider the appropriateness of the order and to make representations as to its terms. An order under s. 5A may be made following a finding of not guilty by reason of insanity. An order imposed in such a case was quashed in *Smith*, Hughes LJ saying that the order should not be used as an adjunct to the Mental Health Act 1983; further, the order had not been made to protect any named individual or individuals, and was not strictly 'necessary' within the meaning of s. 5A(1). In any case the appropriate procedure as set out in CrimPR Part 31 (see Supplement, **R31.1** *et seq.*) should be complied with.

Variation or Discharge of Restraining Order

Whether a restraining order is made under the Protection from Harassment Act 1997, s. 5 or 5A, the prosecutor, the defendant or any other person mentioned in the order may apply to the court which made the order for it to be varied or discharged by a further order (s. 5(4)). Any person mentioned in the order is entitled to be heard (s. 5(4A)). In an application under s. 5(4), the issue is whether circumstances have changed so that the restraining order is no longer necessary or appropriate. An application under s. 5(4) is not an appeal against the order. The Court of Appeal may decline to interfere on appeal with the terms of a restraining order if the proper remedy is an application to the court to vary or discharge the order (*Debnath* [2005] EWCA Crim 3472, [2006] 2 Cr App R (S) 25 (169)). The length of a restraining order may be extended (with or without limit of time) where circumstances have changed so as to justify it (*DPP v Hall* [2005] EWHC 2612 (Admin), [2006] 1 WLR 1000). When an order is varied following application under s. 5(4), it is better for a new order to be drawn up. **E21.34**

Breach of Restraining Order

Whether a restraining order is made under s. 5 or 5A, if without reasonable excuse D does anything which D is prohibited from doing under the order, D is guilty of an offence punishable, on conviction on indictment, with imprisonment for a term not exceeding five years and/or a fine, or on summary conviction to imprisonment for a term not exceeding six months and/or an unlimited fine (s. 5(5) and 5A(2)). **E21.35**

In relation to breach of a restraining order the Sentencing Council definitive guideline, *Breach Offences* (see Supplement, **SG15-6**), applies to all offenders aged 18 and over sentenced on or after 1 October 2018, irrespective of the date of the offence. That guideline supersedes the definitive guideline, *Breach of a Protective Order*, with effect from that date.

European Protection Order

The Criminal Justice (European Protection Order) (England and Wales) Regulations 2014 (SI 2014 No. 3300) provide for the making of a 'European protection order' where the Crown Court or a magistrates' court imposes a 'protection measure' in respect of a 'protected person' when dealing with a criminal cause or matter, in which one or more of the following prohibitions or restrictions are placed on an individual: **E21.36**

(a) a prohibition from entering certain localities, places or defined areas where the protected person resides or visits;
(b) a prohibition or restriction of contact with the protected person by any means (including by telephone, post, facsimile transmission or electronic mail);
(c) a prohibition or restriction preventing the individual from approaching the protected person whether at all or to within a particular distance.

In those circumstances the court which imposes the prohibition or restriction may also make a *European protection order* if the protected person is residing, or intends to reside, in a Member State other than the UK. The European protection order must not remain in force for longer than the protection measure itself (reg. 4(7)) or contain prohibitions or restrictions of a kind not contained in that protection measure (reg. 4(8)). A European protection order must be in the form set out in annex 1 to Directive 2011/99/EU ([2011] OJ L338/2), and must contain the specified information.

A European protection order would appear to be most likely to be used in conjunction with a restraining order under the Protection from Harassment Act 1997. It should be noted that at the end of the transition period following the UK's departure from the EU in accordance with the European Union (Withdrawal) Act 2018 (31 December 2020), the Criminal Justice (Amendment etc.) (EU Exit) Regulations 2019 (SI 2019 No. 780) will revoke the European Protection Order (England and Wales) Regulations 2014. CrimPR 31.9 and 31.10 deal with the European protection order. As from the same date these two rules will be revoked by the Criminal Procedure (Amendment) (EU Exit) Regulations 2019 (SI 2019 No. 908).

TRAVEL RESTRICTION ORDERS: DRUG TRAFFICKING OFFENDERS

E21.37 By the CJPA 2001, ss. 33 to 37, any criminal court (but, in practice, the Crown Court) is given power to impose a travel restriction order on an offender who is convicted of a drug trafficking offence committed after that date, and who has been sentenced by that court to a term of imprisonment for four years or more (s. 33(1)). The effect of the order is to restrict the offender's freedom to leave the UK for a period specified by the court, and it may require delivery up of the offender's passport (or 'travel authorisation'). The minimum duration of a travel restriction order is two years, starting from the date of the offender's release from custody. There is no maximum period prescribed in the legislation. The court must always consider whether such an order should be made and must give reasons where it does not consider such an order to be appropriate (s. 33(2)). According to Leveson LJ in *Shaw* [2011] EWCA Crim 98, given the terms of the statute it is not sufficient for the judge simply to assert that the offences did not contain a foreign element.

'Drug trafficking offence' is defined by s. 34. It may be noted that this is a different definition from that provided by the POCA 2002, sch. 2. Possession of a Class A drug with intent to supply is not within the section (*Whittle* [2007] EWCA Crim 539, [2007] 2 Cr App R (S) 88 (578); *Boland* [2012] EWCA Crim 1953). Section 35 provides for revocation and suspension of travel restriction orders. Section 36 creates various offences in relation to contravention of these orders.

E21.38 Guidance on the imposition of travel restriction orders was given by the Court of Appeal in *Mee* [2004] EWCA Crim 629, [2004] 2 Cr App R (S) 81 (434). The order was designed to prevent or reduce the risk of offending after the offender's release from prison. It was not confined to cases involving importation, but those were the cases in which it was most likely to be appropriate. The restriction on a person's freedom to travel was a significant restriction and should not be taken away for a number of years unless there were grounds for doing so. The length of the order should be that which was required to protect the public in the light of the assessment of risk of reoffending, taking into account the offender's age, previous convictions, family contacts and employment considerations. *Mee* was followed and applied in *Fuller* [2005] EWCA Crim 1029, [2006] 1 Cr App R (S) 8 (52), where a travel restriction order, imposed on a woman aged 25 who had pleaded guilty to importation of cocaine, was quashed on the basis that there was no significant risk of reoffending and that the order would prevent contact between D's child and his grandparents in Jamaica for a period of seven years. See also *Onung* [2006] EWCA Crim 2813, [2007] 2 Cr App R (S) 3 (9). If the travel restriction order is for four years or less it is open to the offender to apply to revoke or suspend the order after a period of two years. If the order is for a period between four and ten years, four years must elapse before such application is made.

RELATED ORDERS

Serious Crime Prevention Orders

E21.39 The SCA 2007, ss. 19 to 22, provide that the Crown Court has power to make an order known as a serious crime prevention order on a person aged 18 or over convicted of a serious offence (whether convicted in the Crown Court or committed for sentence) in addition to sentencing or conditionally discharging the person (s. 19). See **D25.58** for a full discussion of such orders.

Slavery and Trafficking Prevention Orders

The Modern Slavery Act 2015, ss. 14 to 22, make provision for the imposition of a slavery and trafficking prevention order (STPO). The Crown Court or a magistrates' court may make such an order against a person where it deals with the person in respect of (a) a conviction for a slavery or human trafficking offence (an offence under s. 1, 2 or 4 of the 2015 Act, or an offence under earlier legislation relating to trafficking for prostitution, trafficking for sexual exploitation, slavery, servitude and forced or compulsory labour, listed in sch. 1 to the Act); (b) a finding that the defendant is not guilty of such an offence by reason of insanity; or (c) a finding that the defendant is under a disability and has done the acts charged in respect of such an offence (s. 14(1)). The court may make the order only if satisfied that there is a risk that the person may commit a slavery or human trafficking offence, and it is necessary to make the order for the purpose of protecting persons generally, or particular persons, from the physical or psychological harm which would be likely to occur if the defendant committed such an offence (s. 14(2)). In December 2017 the Sentencing Council amended the definitive guideline on *Sexual Offences* in respect of offences of trafficking people for sexual exploitation (see Supplement, **SG31-23**), where prosecuted under the Modern Slavery Act 2015, s. 2. Guidance as to the making of slavery and trafficking prevention orders has been provided (see Supplement, **SG31-2**). **E21.40**

A STPO is an order prohibiting the defendant from doing anything described in the order (s. 17(1)), but the only prohibitions that may be included in a STPO are those which the court is satisfied are necessary for the purpose of protecting persons generally, or particular persons, from the form or forms of harm described in s. 14(2) (s. 17(2)). A prohibition in a STPO has effect for a fixed period specified in the order, of at least five years, or until further order (s. 17(4)). Some prohibitions may have effect for a fixed period and some until further order, and different periods may be specified for different prohibitions (s. 17(5)). A prohibition on foreign travel must be for a fixed period of not more than five years (s. 18(1)).

A magistrates' court may make a STPO on an application by a chief officer of police, an immigration officer or the Director of the NCA (s. 15). An interim order can be made pending determination of the application (s. 21).

Provisions dealing with variation, renewal and discharge of a STPO are set out in s. 20. Provisions dealing with appeals are set out in s. 22. Section 22(1) states that, where a STPO is made following a conviction for a slavery or human trafficking offence, the defendant may appeal against the order as if it were a sentence passed for the offence.

Section E22 Mentally Disordered Offenders

SENTENCING GUIDELINE

E22.1 The Sentencing Council's definitive guideline, *Sentencing Offenders with Mental Disorders, Developmental Disorders, or Neurological Impairments* (see Supplement, **SG7-1**), applies with effect from 1 October 2020 in relation to adult offenders who at the time of the offence and/or the time of sentence have a mental disorder, neurological impairment or developmental disorder, such as those listed in annex A to the guideline. Section 1 of the guideline deals with the general approach to be taken in such cases, section 2 deals with the assessment of culpability for the offence committed, and section 3 considers the range of disposals which may be appropriate in a particular case, including disposals specific to mental health. Annex A provides information on the main classes of mental disorders and presenting features, annex B deals with reports, and annex C considers the criteria applicable to relevant sentencing disposals and, where appropriate, the operation of release provisions.

HOSPITAL ORDERS

E22.2 An admission to a hospital by means of a hospital order has the same effect for most purposes as a compulsory civil commitment under Part II of the Mental Health Act 1983. The order lapses after six months, but may be renewed for a further six months and then at yearly intervals thereafter, where the responsible medical officer considers further detention necessary for the protection of the public or in the interests of the patient's health or safety (s. 20 and sch. 1). There is no limit to the number of renewals which might subsequently be made, but the patient may be discharged from hospital by way of various powers exercised by the responsible medical officer, the hospital managers, or the First-tier Tribunal (Mental Health). The purposes of a hospital order are rehabilitation of the patient and protection of the public; it is not concerned with punishment (*Fisher* [2019] EWCA Crim 1066).

Mental Health Act 1983, s. 37

(1) Where a person is convicted before the Crown Court of an offence punishable with imprisonment other than an offence the sentence for which is fixed by law, or is convicted by a magistrates' court of an offence punishable on summary conviction with imprisonment, and the conditions mentioned in subsection (2) below are satisfied, the court may by order authorise his admission to and detention in such hospital as may be specified in the order or, as the case may be, place him under the guardianship of a local social services authority or of such other person approved by a local social services authority as may be so specified.

(1A) In the case of an offence the sentence for which would otherwise fall to be imposed—

(za) under section 1(2B) or 1A(5) of the Prevention of Crime Act 1953,
(a) under section 51A(2) of the Firearms Act 1968,
(aa) under section 139(6B), 139A(5B) or 139AA(7) of the Criminal Justice Act 1988,
(b) under section 110(2) or 111(2) of the Powers of Criminal Courts (Sentencing) Act 2000,
(ba) under section 224A of the Criminal Justice Act 2003,
(c) under any of section 225(2) or 226(2) of the Criminal Justice Act 2003,
(d) under section 29(4) or (6) of the Violent Crime Reduction Act 2006 (minimum sentences in certain cases of using someone to mind a weapon)[, or]
(e) under section 8(2) of the Offensive Weapons Act 2019 (minimum sentences in certain cases of possession of corrosive substance),]

nothing in those provisions shall prevent a court from making an order under subsection (1) above for the admission of the offender to a hospital.

(1B) References in subsection (1A) above to a sentence falling to be imposed under any of the provisions mentioned in that subsection are to be read in accordance with section 305(4) of the Criminal Justice Act 2003.

(2) The conditions referred to in subsection (1) above are that—

(a) the court is satisfied, on the written or oral evidence of two registered medical practitioners, that the offender is suffering from mental disorder and that either—

(i) the mental disorder from which the offender is suffering is of a nature or degree which makes it appropriate for him to be detained in a hospital for medical treatment and appropriate medical treatment is available for him; or

(ii) in the case of an offender who has attained the age of 16 years, the mental disorder is of a nature or degree which warrants his reception into guardianship under this Act; and

(b) the court is of the opinion, having regard to all the circumstances including the nature of the offence and the character and antecedents of the offender, and to the other available methods of dealing with him, that the most suitable method of disposing of the case is by means of an order under this section.

See further the definitive guideline, *Sentencing Offenders with Mental Disorders, Developmental Disorders, or Neurological Impairments* (see Supplement, **SG7-1**), annex C, with effect from 1 October 2020. The reference in s. 37(1A)(e) to the Offensive Weapons Act 2019, s. 8(2), will come into effect from a date to be appointed.

There is no reference to a lower age limit for the imposition of a hospital order (as distinct from a guardianship order), so the lower age limit must be ten. At least one of the two medical practitioners referred to in s. 37(2) must be approved, for the purposes of s. 12, by the Secretary of State, as having special experience in the diagnosis or treatment of mental disorder (s. 54(1)). The Court of Appeal in *Clark* [2016] EWCA Crim 2192, [2016] 1 Cr App R (S) 52 (332) held that where, following the technical failure of a live link, the judge had received the view of a psychiatrist over the telephone, that did not constiture 'oral evidence' within the meaning of s. 37(2)(a) and, in any event, the evidence was not sworn. A hospital order may be appropriate, even though no causal link is established between the offender's mental disorder and the offence in respect of which the order is made (*Nafei* [2004] EWCA Crim 3238, [2005] 2 Cr App R (S) 24 (127)). In *Blackwood* (1974) 59 Cr App R 170, the Court of Appeal said that a court should not normally make a hospital order if the offender was not legally represented. Only a youth court may make a hospital order or guardianship order on a child or young person (PCC(S)A 2000, s. 8(6)). **E22.3**

Section 37(3) of the Mental Health Act 1983 deals with the power of a magistrates' court to make a hospital order, where the court is satisfied that the person did the act or made the omission charged, without proceeding to conviction. This power is to be very sparingly used (*Lincoln (Kesteven) Justices, ex parte O'Connor* [1983] 1 All ER 901).

A hospital order or guardianship order cannot be made unless the court is satisfied, on the written or oral evidence of the approved clinician who would be in charge of the offender's treatment, or of some other person representing the managers of the hospital, that arrangements have been made for the offender's admission to that hospital within 28 days of the date of the order (s. 37(4)). The health authorities are under no legal obligation to accept offenders from the courts (see, e.g., the comments of Field J in *Barker* [2002] EWCA Crim 1508, [2003] 1 Cr App R (S) 45 (212)). They are, however, under a legal obligation to supply information to the courts about the availability of beds in their regions for the admission of persons under hospital orders (s. 39). In an emergency or other special situation arising within the 28 days, the Secretary of State may give directions for the admission of the offender to a hospital different from that specified in the order (s. 37(5)). **E22.4**

The decision whether to make a hospital order under s. 37 or impose a sentence of imprisonment is within the discretion of the court (*Khelifi* [2006] EWCA Crim 770, [2006] 2 Cr App R (S) 100 (650)). If the medical evidence satisfies the condition in s. 37(2)(a), it is essential that the judge gives detailed consideration to all the factors set out in s. 37(2)(b) (*Vowles* [2015] EWCA Crim 45, [2015] 2 Cr App R (S) 6 (39)). The fact that the conditions in s. 37(2) are all made out does not, however, compel the making of a hospital order. The court must consider all options, including a hospital and limitation direction under s. 45A (see **E22.12**), and bear in mind the Secretary of State's power under

s. 47 to transfer from prison for treatment (*Vowles*; *Turner* [2015] EWCA Crim 1249). The welfare of the offender is always an important consideration, but must be assessed in light of the seriousness of the offence. In deciding on the most suitable disposal, the judge must bear in mind the importance wherever appropriate of including a penal element in the sentence. A disposal under s. 45A included a penal element, and in deciding whether a penal element was necessary the judge should assess the offender's culpability and the harm caused by the offence. A judge imposing a hospital order under s. 37 or s. 41 must explain why a penal element was inappropriate (see further *Edwards* [2018] EWCA Crim 595, [2018] 4 WLR 64). A hospital order was upheld in *Marshall* [2015] EWCA Crim 474, where the 30-year-old offender with previous convictions for violent and public order offences admitted involvement in football-related violent disorder. The medical reports agreed that D suffered from a learning disability associated with aggressive and irresponsible behaviour. He was a risk to others, and had a history of self-harming. The Court rejected the argument that D might remain in hospital for longer than the proportionate prison sentence, and said that the judge was entitled to conclude that a hospital order was the most suitable disposal.

By s. 37(8), when a hospital order or a guardianship order is made, the court shall not pass a sentence of imprisonment, make an order for detention, impose a fine, make a community order or a youth rehabilitation order in respect of the offence, or require a parent of a child or young person so dealt with to enter into a recognizance (see **E14.6**). A hospital order cannot be combined with a referral order (see **E10**). The court may, however, 'make any other order which the court has power to make apart from this section': this would include ancillary orders such as a compensation order. Where a hospital order or a guardianship order is made no surcharge is payable under the CJA 2003, s. 161A (see **E15.24**).

Interim Hospital Orders

E22.5 Section 38 provides for the making of an 'interim hospital order' for the purposes of establishing whether a convicted person is suitable to be the subject of a hospital order. The qualifying conditions are virtually the same as for the making of a hospital order under s. 37 (see **E22.2**), but the interim order is available to the court 'before making a hospital order or dealing with him in some other way'. One difference in the powers is that an interim order can be made only where one of the registered medical practitioners who give evidence is employed at the hospital where the person is to be detained. An interim hospital order is not a final disposal of the case; such an order may last for up to 12 weeks, renewable for further periods of not more than 28 days at a time, though in no case may it last for more than a total of 12 months. No minimum period is specified. Power to make an interim hospital order under s. 38 may also be exercised for the purposes of determining whether a person should be made subject to a hospital direction or a limitation direction under s. 45A (s. 45A(8): see **E22.12**). At the end of the interim period the court must make a final disposal of the case, and the interim order comes to an end. In a case where a court renews an interim hospital order, or where it finally disposes of the case by making a hospital order under s. 37, the offender need not appear before the court, provided that the offender is legally represented and the representative has had an opportunity of being heard (s. 38(2) and (6)). In *Vowles* [2015] EWCA Crim 45, [2015] 2 Cr App R (S) 6 (39), Lord Thomas CJ said (at [56]) that, although in some cases an interim order might be an appropriate course to take, a judge should think long and hard before doing so. There can be no closure for the victim of the offence until the final order is made, there are costs involved in bringing the case back to court, and there is acute pressure on the availability of secure beds.

GUARDIANSHIP ORDERS

E22.6 Guardianship orders are made under the Mental Health Act 1983, s. 37 (see **E22.2**). By s. 40(2) a guardianship order shall confer on the local authority or person named in the order as guardian, the same powers as a guardianship application made and accepted under Part II of the 1983 Act. These powers, in outline, are to determine place of residence, require attendance for treatment, occupation, education or training, and to require access to the patient in any place of residence for a doctor, social worker or other specified person (s. 8).

The relevant statutory provisions are similar to those which relate to the courts' powers to make hospital orders (s. 37(2)(a)(ii); see **E22.2**). In addition, by s. 37(6), a guardianship order cannot be made unless the relevant authority or person is willing to receive the offender into guardianship. Section 39A empowers a court which is minded to make a guardianship order to request the local social services authority to inform the court whether it would be willing to comply with the order and, if so, to give information about how it would exercise its powers under s. 40(2). A guardianship order lasts for six months, but may be renewed for a further six months and thereafter annually (s. 20). See further the definitive guideline, *Sentencing Offenders with Mental Disorders, Developmental Disorders, or Neurological Impairments* (see Supplement, **SG7-1**), annex C, with effect from 1 October 2020.

RESTRICTION ORDERS

Power to Make Restriction Orders

Mental Health Act 1983, s. 41 **E22.7**

(1) Where a hospital order is made in respect of an offender by the Crown Court, and it appears to the court, having regard to the nature of the offence, the antecedents of the offender and the risk of his committing further offences if set at large, that it is necessary for the protection of the public from serious harm so to do, the court may, subject to the provisions of this section, further order that the offender shall be subject to the special restrictions set out in this section; and an order under this section shall be known as 'a restriction order'.

(2) A restriction order shall not be made in the case of any person unless at least one of the registered medical practitioners whose evidence is taken into account by the court under section 37(2)(a) above has given evidence orally before the court.

A restriction order can only be made in conjunction with a hospital order. See further the definitive guideline, *Sentencing Offenders with Mental Disorders, Developmental Disorders, or Neurological Impairments* (see Supplement, **SG7-1**), annex C, with effect from 1 October 2020. For hospital orders, see **E22.2**.

The special restrictions applicable to a patient under a restriction order are set out in s. 41(3). In particular, powers under the 1983 Act to transfer or discharge the patient are exercisable only with the consent of the Secretary of State. Only the Crown Court may make a restriction order, though magistrates may commit an offender to the Crown Court, provided the offender is aged 14 or over, with a view to such a disposal (s. 43 and see *Avbunudje* [1999] 2 Cr App R (S) 189). If the magistrates' court commits the offender to the Crown Court, but the Crown Court decides not to make a restriction order, the Crown Court's powers of sentence are limited to those which the magistrates could have imposed, unless there is also in effect a general committal for sentence. **E22.8**

A restriction order cannot be made unless there is evidence that it is necessary to protect the public from serious harm, but in this context danger to a section of the public or a particular individual will suffice (*Courtney* (1987) 9 Cr App R (S) 404; *Kearney* [2002] EWCA Crim 2772, [2003] 2 Cr App R (S) 17 (85)). A court is not bound to accept the medical evidence for or against the imposition of a restriction order: it is ultimately a matter for the court (*Birch* (1989) 11 Cr App R (S) 202). There is no requirement for a causal connection between the disorder and the offence (*Birch*). Although decisions on the appropriateness of the inclusion of an order under s. 41 are highly fact-specific, the case of *Brooks* [2019] EWCA Crim 2004 is instructive. The Court of Appeal quashed a restriction order in that case, although recommended by both psychiatrists, where D, aged 34, pleaded guilty to offences involving possession of indecent images of children. Yip J said that the risk of serious harm was not made out by the risk of repetition of the index offences (applying *Terrell* [2007] EWCA Crim 3079, [2008] 2 Cr App R (S) 49 (292)), that other matters on D's record were 'relatively minor', and following their commission D had lived in the community for more than two years without coming to further notice.

Unlike a hospital order under s. 37, a restriction order does not lapse in the ordinary way unless renewed, but continues for as long as the restriction order is in place. If the restriction order is for a fixed period, at the end of that period the restrictions no longer apply but the hospital order continues in effect (s. 41(5)). It is regarded as imprudent apart from the most exceptional circumstances to impose a restriction for a fixed rather than an unlimited period (*Birch*; *Nwohia* [1996] 1 Cr App R (S) 170). Discharge of the patient occurs only when the First-tier Tribunal is satisfied that the patient's mental health poses no unacceptable risk to the public, and upon release the patient will be supervised by a mental health team led by a psychiatrist. Discharge will inevitably be conditional rather than absolute. Recall from an undischarged s. 41 restriction order can only be made on the basis of a relapse in the patient's mental health or a failure to comply with a mental health support package. Recall may be made by the responsible clinician and will be to hospital.

Sentencing Principles

E22.9 If the criteria within the Mental Health Act 1983, s. 41, are established, the sentencer may, but is not obliged to, make a restriction order. The alternative sentences are life imprisonment, an extended sentence, or a fixed-term sentence. In the decision of the House of Lords in *Drew* [2003] UKHL 25, [2004] 2 Cr App R (S) 24 (65) it was noted that offenders subject to hospital orders (with or without restriction) are entitled to release when their medical condition has been successfully treated, while release from a life sentence is a matter for the Parole Board, which can take into account all relevant matters of risk rather than just mental health. A life sentence thereby provided a greater degree of control over the offender.

E22.10 In making the choice between a hospital order, with or without restrictions, and a custodial sentence, the leading case of *Vowles* [2015] EWCA Crim 45, [2015] 2 Cr App R (S) 6 (39) holds that the court must consider all the evidence and not feel bound by medical opinion, and in considering whether a hospital order is the most suitable disposal the court must always have regard to the extent to which the offender requires treatment, the extent to which the offending is attributable to the mental condition, the extent to which punishment is necessary, and the need to protect the public, including the regime for deciding upon release and the nature of supervision after release.

E22.11 In a case where the judge concludes that a hospital order may be the correct disposal, consideration should still be given to whether the mental condition can be appropriately managed under a hospital and limitation direction. Hughes LJ in *A-G's Ref (No. 54 of 2011)* [2011] EWCA Crim 2276, [2012] 1 Cr App R (S) 106 (635), gave a detailed explanation of the relevant powers and difficult choices which a judge is required to make in this area of law. In making the choice between an indeterminate custodial sentence or a hospital order with restrictions, the 'absolutely crucial difference' between the two regimes is that under the former regime release is conditional upon the responsible authority being satisfied that the offender is no longer a risk to the public, while under the latter regime the responsible authority must be satisfied that the offender presents no danger arising from his or her medical condition. Release from the former regime is on licence, and the offender can be recalled if his or her behaviour shows that the offender is still a danger. On release from hospital, recall is available but only if the offender's medical condition relapses. The Court of Appeal in this case preferred custody to the hospital order imposed by the judge, partly because D had been living a criminal lifestyle and there was a clear risk that he would resume it on release. By contrast in *Fisher* [2019] EWCA Crim 1066, where D had admitted manslaughter on the grounds of diminished responsibility after he had stabbed and killed his mother, the Court of Appeal quashed the sentence of life imprisonment with a minimum term of two years, together with a hospital and limitation direction, and substituted a hospital order with a restriction order under s. 41. The Court said that D's responsibility for the killing was substantially diminished due to paranoid psychosis, and he had no history of violence. While the need to reflect a punitive element in the sentence may be an important consideration, in this case the minimum term would certainly be less than the treatment period necessary to reduce the risk posed by D, and he would have spent that period in hospital in the same conditions as under a hospital order. In *Westwood* [2020] EWCA Crim 598, also a case of diminished responsibility manslaughter, the Court of Appeal quashed an extended sentence of

21 years with a hospital direction under s. 45A and substituted a hospital order with a restriction order under s. 41. The judge had been wrong to assess D's retained responsibility under the relevant guideline as medium to high. It should have been assessed as low, in line with the psychiatric evidence, because the anger which underlay the offence was not extraneous to his mental illness but a manifestation of it. In *Ahmed* [2016] EWCA Crim 670, the Court of Appeal said that release arrangements following a hospital order might well provide better protection for the public because those responsible for monitoring the offender in the community had a higher level of expertise and resources than the probation service, but in *Edwards* [2018] EWCA Crim 595, [2018] 4 WLR 64, the Court distanced itself from that comment which, it said, was not of general application. Each case turned on its own facts.

HOSPITAL AND LIMITATION DIRECTIONS

Sections 45A and 45B of the Mental Health Act 1983 are designed to apply where the court has heard evidence that the offender is suffering from a mental disorder and the making of a hospital order is appropriate, but the court wishes to ensure that the offender upon completion of the period of treatment will thence be transferred to prison for the remainder of the sentence rather than being released from hospital. It was confirmed in *Poole* [2014] EWCA Crim 1641, [2015] 1 Cr App R (S) 2 (7) that a hospital direction under s. 45A *must* also include a limitation direction under s. 45B. These are sometimes referred to as constituting a 'hybrid' order. See further the definitive guideline, *Sentencing Offenders with Mental Disorders, Developmental Disorders, or Neurological Impairments* (see Supplement, **SG7-1**), annex C, with effect from 1 October 2020. **E22.12**

Section 45A applies where a person is convicted before the Crown Court of an offence the sentence for which is not fixed by law and the court considers making a hospital order before deciding to impose a sentence of imprisonment (s. 45A(1)). It was held by the Court of Appeal in *Fort* [2013] EWCA Crim 2332, [2014] 2 Cr App R (S) 24 (167) that 'sentence of imprisonment' in this context does not include the sentence of detention in a young offender institution, so that the power under s. 45A is limited to offenders aged 21 and over. The Court could find no good reason why the power was so limited, and recommended that it should be extended by Parliament to include young adult offenders. It was further held in *Poole* that, since a hospital and limitation direction was a sentence of imprisonment and not 'an order made under the MHA 1983', the surcharge appropriate to the custodial sentence was payable. **E22.13**

By s. 45A(2), the court must be satisfied on the written or oral evidence of two registered medical practitioners (at least one of whom must give oral evidence: s. 45A(4)) that:

(a) the offender is suffering from a mental disorder;
(b) the mental disorder from which the offender is suffering is of a nature or degree which makes it appropriate for him to be detained in a hospital for medical treatment; and
(c) appropriate medical treatment is available for him.

In these circumstances the court may make a 'hospital direction', which is a direction that, instead of being detained in prison, the offender be detained in a specified hospital. If the court makes a hospital direction it must also make a 'limitation direction', which is a direction that the offender is made subject to the restrictions set out in s. 41 of the 1983 Act (see **E22.7**). It was established in *Poole* that both directions must be made, even where on the facts of the case the criteria set out in s. 41 for imposing a restriction order are not made out.

If the offender ceases to require treatment prior to the expiration of the custodial sentence, the offender will be returned to prison. If the offender is still in hospital when the period during which or she is liable to be detained under sentence expires, the offender will continue to be detained in hospital, but as an unrestricted patient.

The court must also be satisfied on the written or oral evidence of the approved clinician who would have overall charge of the case, or of some other person representing the managers of the hospital, that arrangements have been made for the offender's admission to that hospital and for admission within the period of 28 days from the making of the order. The court may, pending admission within that period, give directions for the offender's detention in a place of safety (s. 45A(5)). A hospital and limitation direction given in respect of an offender has effect not only as regards the sentence of imprisonment imposed but also as regards any other sentence of imprisonment imposed on the same or a previous occasion (s. 45A(9)).

E22.14 Section 45B provides that, with respect to any person, a hospital direction shall have effect as a transfer direction and a limitation direction shall have effect as a restriction direction. While a person is subject to a hospital and limitation direction the responsible medical officer must supply to the Secretary of State a report on the offender at least every 12 months. In *Staines* [2006] EWCA Crim 15, [2006] 2 Cr App R (S) 61 (376), the Court of Appeal said that the hospital and limitation direction was appropriate for an offender for whom neither imprisonment nor a hospital order on its own was suitable, and the order carried the distinct advantage of addressing the offender's medical needs while also giving proper weight to the punishment and to safety of the public. In the leading case of *Vowles* [2015] EWCA Crim 45, [2015] 2 Cr App R (S) 6 (39), Lord Judge CJ said (at [54]) that in every case in which it appears to the judge that a hospital order (with or without a restriction order) may be an appropriate way of dealing with the case the court should first consider whether the case can appropriately be dealt with by a hospital and limitation direction. If it can, such an order should be made (remembering that this option is not available where the person is under the age of 21 at the time of conviction). The Court of Appeal in *Edwards* [2018] EWCA Crim 595, [2018] 4 WLR 64 emphasised that the decision in *Vowles* did not amount to a 'default setting' of imprisonment in these cases, as some had mistakenly assumed. The case must be one where a hospital order, with or without a restriction order, may be appropriate. If so, the court should step back and consider whether in all the circumstances a hospital and limitation direction would be more appropriate (neither a hospital order on its own nor imprisonment on its own being suitable). In deciding the penal element that was necessary the court should assess as best as it could the offender's culpability and the harm caused. In *Yuel* [2019] EWCA Crim 1693, [2020] 1 Cr App R (S) 42 (309), D had committed a series of rapes against a young woman in her home, and he had previous convictions for sexually assaulting young women. The Court of Appeal, following and applying the decision in *Edwards*, said that the judge had been correct to impose a 'hybrid order' under s. 45A, but, given the dangerousness of D, a determinate sentence of 11 years was increased to an extended sentence of 19 years. In *Jefferson* [2016] EWCA Crim 2023, [2017] 1 Cr App R (S) 38 (313), where D, who suffered from a psychotic illness, entered a shop and shouted racist abuse before stabbing V in the neck with a knife, the Court of Appeal upheld a sentence of life imprisonment with an order under s. 45A, saying that there was evidence to support the finding of dangerousness and a mental health disposal was also necessary.

Section E23 Notification Requirements under the Sexual Offences Act 2003

INTRODUCTION

A person is subject to the notification requirements of the SOA 2003 if convicted of an offence listed in sch. 3 to that Act, or found not guilty of such an offence by reason of insanity, or is found to be under a disability and to have done the act charged in respect of such an offence, or is cautioned in respect of such an offence (s. 80). A person subject to the notification requirements is referred to in the Act as a 'relevant offender'. The notification requirements are set out in s. 83. They are that the offender must, within the period of three days of the conviction, finding or caution, notify to the police the offender's date of birth, national insurance number, name (and any aliases), home address and any other address at which the offender regularly stays and provide any other information prescribed in regulations made by the Secretary of State. Subsequent changes to these details must also be notified to the police (s. 84). The Secretary of State has power to add further requirements. Additional requirements imposed by the Sexual Offences Act 2003 (Notification Requirements) (England and Wales) Regulations 2012 (SI 2012 No. 1876), that offenders should provide details of their bank, debit and credit card accounts, were upheld by the Divisional Court in *R (Prothero) v Secretary of State for the Home Department* [2013] EWHC 2830 (Admin), [2014] 1 WLR 1195. Powers of entry and search of the offender's home address were held to be compatible with Article 8 of the ECHR in *R (M) v Chief Constable of Hampshire* [2014] EWCA Civ 1651, [2015] 1 Cr App R 20 (263). Persons who were formerly subject to registration under the Sex Offenders Act 1997 are now made subject to the notification requirements under the SOA 2003 (s. 81). **E23.1**

The retrospective element in the notification requirements under the Sex Offenders Act 1997 was held by the European Commission on Human Rights not to breach the ECHR, Article 7(1), since registration under that Act was not a 'penalty' within the meaning of Article 7 (*Ibbotson v UK* (1999) 27 EHRR CD332). Although the requirements of the 1997 Act did not extend to offenders conditionally discharged (according to the House of Lords in *Longworth* [2006] UKHL 1, [2006] 1 All ER 887), the requirements of the 2003 Act do apply to such offenders (see **E23.4**). The Supreme Court held in *R (F (A Child)) v Secretary of State for the Home Department* [2010] UKSC 17, [2011] 1 AC 331 that the indefinite notification requirement under the Act, which contained no provision for review, was disproportionate and infringed Article 8. The Sexual Offences (Remedial) Order 2012 (SI 2012 No. 1883) inserted ss. 91A to 91E into the SOA 2003, to provide for the review of indefinite notification requirements. The Divisional Court in *R (NE) v Birmingham Magistrates' Court* [2015] EWHC 688 (Admin), [2015] 1 WLR 4771 held that, where an offender subject to indefinite notification requirements sought a review of those requirements, the burden of proof lay on the offender, on the balance of probabilities, to show that a continuation of the requirements was not necessary to protect the public from sexual harm.

The requirements of the 2003 Act are not an additional form of punishment, and so should not be taken into account when determining the sentence to be passed. See *A-G's Ref (No. 50 of 1997)* [1998] 2 Cr App R (S) 155. The provisions of the Act are automatic in their effect and, in principle, do not require the sentencer dealing with a case involving one of the listed offences to make reference to them, although informing the offender is required by CrimPR 28.3 (see Supplement, **R28.3**). The SOA 2003, s. 92, provides that, where a sentencer states in open court that an offender has been convicted of a listed offence and certifies those facts, the certificate is **E23.2** evidence of those facts. Notification requirements apply automatically, and so they cannot form the subject of an appeal before the Court of Appeal (*Longworth*). Similarly, certificates issued under the SOA 2003, s. 92, which recorded the fact of such a conviction, are not part of the sentence and could not be appealed, but they could be challenged by judicial review if wrongly issued (*Rawlinson* [2018] EWCA Crim 2825, [2019] 1 Cr App R (S) 51 (429)).

LISTED OFFENCES

E23.3 Offences listed in sch. 3 to the SOA 2003 are offences under:

SOA 1956, s. 1 (rape);
SOA 1956, s. 5 (intercourse with a girl under 13);
SOA 1956, s. 6 (intercourse with a girl under 16) if the offender was 20 or over;
SOA 1956, s. 10 (incest by a man) if the victim or other party was under 18;
SOA 1956, s. 12 (buggery) if the offender was 20 or over and the victim or other party was under 18;
SOA 1956, s. 13 (indecency between men) if the offender was 20 or over and the victim or other party was under 18;
SOA 1956, s. 14 (indecent assault on a woman) if the victim was under 18 or the offender was sentenced to at least 30 months' imprisonment or was admitted to hospital and subject to a restriction order;
SOA 1956, s. 15 (indecent assault on a man) if the victim was under 18 or the offender was sentenced to at least 30 months' imprisonment or was admitted to hospital subject to a restriction order;
SOA 1956, s. 16 (assault with intent to commit buggery) if the victim or other party was under 18;
SOA 1956, s. 28 (causing or encouraging the prostitution of, intercourse with, or indecent assault on, a girl under 16);
Indecency with Children Act 1960, s. 1 (indecent conduct towards young child);
Criminal Law Act 1977, s. 54 (inciting girl under 16 to have incestuous sexual intercourse);
Protection of Children Act 1978, s. 1 (indecent photographs of children) if the photographs showed persons under 16 and subject to age of offender and sentence imposed;
Customs and Excise Management Act 1979, s. 170 (penalty for fraudulent evasion of duty) in relation to indecent or obscene articles, if the prohibited goods included indecent photographs of persons under 16 and the offender was 18 or over or received a sentence of at least 12 months' imprisonment
CJA 1988, s. 160 (possession of indecent photograph of child) if the indecent photograph showed persons under 16 and the offender was 18 or over or received a sentence of at least 12 months' imprisonment;
SO(A)A 2000 (abuse of position of trust) if the offender was 20 or over;
SOA 2003, s. 1 or s. 2 (rape, assault by penetration);
SOA 2003, s. 3 (sexual assault) subject to age of offender and sentence imposed;
SOA 2003, s. 4, 5 or 6 (causing sexual activity without consent, rape of child under 13, assault of child under 13 by penetration);
SOA 2003, s. 7 (sexual assault of child under 13) where the offender was aged 18 or over or was sentenced to at least 12 months' imprisonment;
SOA 2003, ss. 8 to 12 (causing or inciting a child under 13 to engage in sexual activity; child sex offences committed by adults);
SOA 2003, s. 13 (child sex offences committed by children or young persons), if the offender was sentenced to at least 12 months' imprisonment;
SOA 2003, s. 14 (arranging or facilitating the commission of a child sex offence), where the offender was aged 18 or over or was sentenced to at least 12 months' imprisonment;
SOA 2003, s. 15 (meeting a child following sexual grooming);
SOA 2003, s. 15A (sexual communication with a child);
SOA 2003, ss. 16 to 19 (abuse of a position of trust), if the offender is imprisoned, detained in a hospital or receives a community sentence of at least 12 months;

SOA 2003, s. 25 or s. 26 (familial child sex offences) where the offender was aged 18 or over or was sentenced to at least 12 months' imprisonment;
SOA 2003, ss. 30 to 37 (offences against persons with a mental disorder impeding choice);
SOA 2003, ss. 38 to 41 (care workers for persons with mental disorder) subject to age of offender and sentence imposed;
SOA 2003, s. 47 (paying for sexual services of a child) where the victim was under 16 and where the offender was aged 18 or over or was sentenced to at least 12 months' imprisonment;
SOA 2003, s. 48 (causing or inciting sexual exploitation of a child) where the offender was aged 18 or over or was sentenced to at least 12 months' imprisonment;
SOA 2003, s. 49 (controlling a child in relation to sexual exploitation) where the offender was aged 18 or over or was sentenced to at least 12 months' imprisonment;
SOA 2003, s. 50 (arranging or facilitating sexual exploitation of a child) where the offender was aged 18 or over or was sentenced to at least 12 months' imprisonment;
SOA 2003, s. 61 (administering a substance with intent);
SOA 2003, s. 62 or s. 63 (committing an offence, or trespassing, with intent to commit a sexual offence) subject to age of offender and sentence passed and subject to age of intended victim;
SOA 2003, s. 64 or s. 65 (sex with an adult relative) subject to age of offender and sentence imposed;
SOA 2003, s. 66 (exposure), subject to age of offender, age of victim and sentence imposed;
SOA 2003, s. 67 (voyeurism), subject to age of offender and sentence imposed;
SOA 2003, s. 67A (voyeurism: additional offences), subject to the offence being committed for the purpose of sexual gratification, and subject to age of offender, age of victim, and sentence imposed;
SOA 2003, s. 69 or s. 70 (intercourse with animal or sexual penetration of corpse), subject to age of offender and sentence imposed;
CJIA 1998, s. 63 (possession of extreme pornographic images) where the offender was aged 18 or over and is sentenced in respect of the offence to imprisonment for a term of at least two years;
CAJA 2009, s. 62(1) (possession of prohibited images of children) where the offender was aged 18 or over and is sentenced in respect of the offence to imprisonment for a term of at least two years;
SCA 2015, s. 69 (possession of paedophile manual) where the offender was aged 18 or over and is sentenced in respect of the offence to imprisonment for a term of at least 12 months.
An attempt or conspiracy to commit the relevant offences or to encourage or assist the commission of such an offence within the meaning of the SCA 2007, Part 2 (sch. 3, para. 94).

NOTIFICATION PERIOD

The length of the notification period depends on the sentence which was imposed, and is set out in a table in s. 82(1) of the SOA 2003, which can be summarised as follows: **E23.4**

Description of relevant offender	*Notification period*
A person sentenced to imprisonment for life, imprisonment for public protection, imprisonment for a term of 30 months or more, or admitted to a hospital subject to a restriction order	Indefinite period
A person sentenced to imprisonment for a term of more than six months but less than 30 months	10 years
A person sentenced to imprisonment for a term of six months or less or admitted to hospital without being subject to a restriction order	7 years
A person cautioned	2 years
A person conditionally discharged	The period of the conditional discharge
A person of any other description	5 years

This table applies to sentences of detention in a young offender institution, detention and training orders, long-term detention under the PCC(S)A 2000, s. 91, and a sentence of custody for life, as it does to imprisonment (SOA 2003, s. 131). It should be noted that, if the person is under 18 on the relevant date, this table has effect as if for the periods of ten years, seven years, five years and two years there were substituted a reference to one half of those periods (s. 82(1)). There are special provisions for determining the notification period where consecutive or concurrent custodial terms have been imposed (s. 82(2)). In the case of an extended sentence it is the total sentence which counts for the purposes of s. 82(1), rather than just the length of the custodial term (*Begg* [2019] EWCA Crim 1578, [2020] 1 Cr App R (S) 30 (227)).

UNREASONABLE FAILURE TO COMPLY

E23.5 Unreasonable failure to comply with notification requirements or the deliberate provision of false information is an offence punishable on summary conviction with imprisonment for a term not exceeding six months, or a fine not exceeding the statutory maximum, or both; on conviction on indictment, the maximum penalty is five years' imprisonment (SOA 2003, s. 91). The Sentencing Council definitive guideline, *Breach Offences* (see Supplement, **SG15-1**), applies to offenders aged 18 and over sentenced on or after 1 October 2018 for failure to comply with notification requirements, irrespective of the date of the offence.

Section E24 Rehabilitation of Offenders

GENERAL PRINCIPLE

E24.1 Under the Rehabilitation of Offenders Act 1974, s. 4(1), after the passage of time convictions become 'spent' and a convicted person becomes 'rehabilitated'. When a conviction is spent, the offender is treated for a range of purposes as if never convicted or sentenced of the offence concerned. While s. 7(2) of the Act excludes from its scope the operation of criminal proceedings, CrimPD V, paras. 21A.1 to 21A.3 (see Supplement, **CPD.21A**), nonetheless require that spent convictions which appear on an offender's record should so far as practicable be marked as such, and that nobody should refer in open court to such spent convictions without the authority of the judge, which should only be given where the interests of justice so require. When passing sentence, the sentencer should make no reference to spent convictions unless it is necessary to do so to explain the sentence being passed. The guidance in CrimPD V, paras. 21A.1 to 21A.3, also applies in magistrates' courts, suitably adapted.

The Act's protection applies to all convictions, except those which result in an excluded sentence (see **E24.2**). 'Conviction' is given a broad meaning in the Act, but would not extend to cover a person bound over to keep the peace where that order was made at any time except at sentence. Offences in respect of which a conditional discharge is made do not count as convictions for a variety of purposes, but s. 1(4) of the Act provides that these are convictions which may be the subject of rehabilitation.

SENTENCES FALLING OUTSIDE THE SCOPE OF REHABILITATION

E24.2 Certain sentences fall outside the scope of the Rehabilitation of Offenders Act 1974, and an offender who has received such a sentence can never become rehabilitated with respect to that conviction. By s. 5(1), those sentences include:

(a) life imprisonment;
(b) imprisonment or detention in a young offender institution for a term exceeding 48 months;
(c) detention during Her Majesty's pleasure;
(d) detention under the PCC(S)A 2000, s. 91, for life or for a term exceeding 48 months;
(e) custody for life;
(f) imprisonment for public protection under the CJA 2003, s. 225, detention for public protection under the CJA 2003, s. 226, or an extended sentence under the CJA 2003, ss. 226A, 226B, 227 or 228.

REHABILITATION PERIODS

E24.3 Rehabilitation periods in respect of sentences not excluded by, s. 5(1) (see **E24.2**), are set out in a Table in s. 5(2). The Act was subject to substantial amendment when the LASPO 2012, s. 139, came into force on 10 March 2014. The original periods set out in the 1974 Act were replaced with the following periods. These periods have retrospective effect so that all convictions, whenever they were acquired by an offender, are now subject to the following rehabilitation periods. For custodial sentences the rehabilitation period runs from completion of the sentence, which means completion of the whole sentence including the licence period and not the date of release from the custodial part of the sentence.

Sentence	*End of rehabilitation period for adult offenders*	*End of rehabilitation period for offenders under 18 at date of conviction*
A custodial sentence of more than 30 months and up to, or consisting of, 48 months	The end of the period of 7 years beginning with the day on which the sentence (including any licence period) is completed	42 months beginning with the day on which the sentence (including any licence period) is completed
A custodial sentence of more than 6 months and up to, or consisting of, 30 months	The end of the period of 48 months beginning with the day on which the sentence (including any licence period) is completed	The end of the period of 24 months beginning with the day on which the sentence (including any licence period) is completed
A custodial sentence of 6 months or less	The end of the period of 24 months beginning with the day on which the sentence (including any licence period) is completed	The end of the period of 18 months beginning with the day on which the sentence (including any licence period) is completed
A fine	The end of the period of 12 months beginning with the date of the conviction in respect of which the sentence is imposed	The end of the period of 6 months beginning with the date of the conviction in respect of which the sentence is imposed
A compensation order	The date on which the payment is made in full	The date on which the payment is made in full
A community or youth rehabilitation order	The end of the period of 12 months beginning with the day provided for by or under the order as the last day on which the order is to have effect	The end of the period of 6 months beginning with the day provided for by or under the order as the last day on which the order is to have effect
A relevant order	The day provided for by or under the order as the last day on which the order is to have effect	The day provided for by or under the order as the last day on which the order is to have effect

A 'relevant order' means a conditional discharge, a bind over to keep the peace (where imposed on conviction), a hospital order with or without restrictions, a referral order or any order which imposes a disqualification, disability, prohibition or other penalty, but not a reparation order (s. 2(8)). It should be noted that, where no provision is made by or under a community or youth rehabilitation order or a relevant order for the last day on which the order is to have effect, the rehabilitation period for the order is to be the period of 24 months beginning with the date of conviction (s. 2(3)).

There is no rehabilitation period for: (a) an order discharging a person absolutely for an offence, or (b) any other sentence in respect of a conviction where the sentence is not dealt with in the Table, and, in such cases, references in the Act to any rehabilitation period are to be read as if the period of time were nil.

For the purposes of the Act, a suspended sentence of imprisonment counts as a sentence of immediate imprisonment of the same length. Two consecutive custodial sentences are aggregated for the purposes of the Act (s. 5(9)(b)). Where an offender receives more than one sentence or order in respect of a single offence, the relevant rehabilitation period is the longest of those applicable (s. 6(2)).

Effect of Further Conviction

A person who has been convicted can only become rehabilitated under the Rehabilitation of Offenders Act 1974 if the person is not reconvicted within the relevant rehabilitation period (s. 6(4)). If the person is reconvicted of anything other than a summary offence (s. 6(6)), the rehabilitation period for the first offence continues to run until the expiry of the period for the second offence. If an excluded sentence (see **E24.2**) is passed for the second offence, this excludes both convictions permanently from the possibility of rehabilitation. **E24.4**

The Protection of Freedoms Act 2012, ss. 92 to 101, provide for certain convictions and cautions to be disregarded and sch. 9, para. 134, amends s. 1 of the 1974 Act to provide that the 1974 Act has no application to them. Convictions and cautions within the scope of the Act are those that criminalised consensual homosexual acts between men over the age of consent, namely the SOA 1956, ss. 12 and 13. The provisions also cover corresponding offences which applied before the 1956 Act had effect as well as equivalent offences in service law. The PCA 2017, s. 165, further provides for the automatic pardoning of living persons who have been convicted or cautioned for one or more of those offences. Section 165 has effect from 31 January 2017.

Exceptions to the Act

The Rehabilitation of Offenders Act 1974 (Exceptions) Order 1975 (SI 1975 No. 1023) creates a large number of exceptions to the scope of the Act. It provides that, in respect of a range of occupations, any applicant seeking employment in the relevant occupation must declare any spent conviction. Important amendments were made to the 1975 Order by the Rehabilitation of Offenders Act 1974 (Exceptions) Order 1975 (Amendment) Order 2013 (SI 2013 No. 1198). That Order provides that for employment purposes a conviction falls within the scope of the 1974 Act if it was imposed for an offence other than one listed in art. 2A(5), it did not result in a custodial sentence, the person has not been convicted of any other offence at any time, and that 11 years have passed since the date of conviction (five and a half years if the offender was then under 18). Even if all these conditions apply, spent convictions must still be disclosed for a few specified forms of employment. In *R (T) v Chief Constable of Greater Manchester Police* [2014] UKSC 35, [2015] AC 49, the Supreme Court laid down the criteria that should be applied to determine whether schemes governing the retention, disclosure and use of records of this nature comply with the ECHR, Article 8. The Supreme Court also held in *Re Gallagher* [2019] UKSC 3, [2020] AC 185, that changes made to the Rehabilitation of Offenders Act 1974 and to the Police Act 1997 now meant that the provisions passed the legality test in relation to Article 8. Further, the 'carefully devised' categories within the legislation did not operate disproportionately except in two areas: (a) the so-called 'multiple conviction' rule under the 1997 Act (requiring disclosure of all matters on the record of a person with two or more convictions) and (b) the requirement of disclosure relating to warnings and reprimands for young offenders, which was disproportionate because the measures themselves were designed to avoid damaging effects later in life. Declarations of incompatibility were upheld in respect of P and Gallagher (multiple convictions) and G (reprimand). **E24.5**

Section F1 General Principles of Evidence in Criminal Cases

FACTS IN ISSUE

The facts in issue comprise: (a) the facts which the prosecution bear the burden of proving or disproving (in order to establish the guilt of the accused) and (b) the facts which, in exceptional cases, the accused bears the burden of proving (in order to succeed in the defence); see **F3.6** to **F3.36**. '[W]henever there is a plea of not guilty, everything is in issue and the prosecution have to prove the whole of their case, including the identity of the accused, the nature of the act and the existence of any necessary knowledge or intent' (*Sims* [1946] KB 531, per Lord Goddard CJ at p. 539). Thus the nature of the facts in issue in any given case is determinable by reference to the legal ingredients of the offence charged and any defence raised. Any fact which is formally admitted under the CJA 1967, s. 10, ceases to be in issue — it must be taken to have been proved and is not open to contradictory proof (see *Drummond* [2020] EWCA Crim 267 and cf. written statements admissible under the CJA 1967, s. 9; see **D22.41**). Under s. 10(1) of the Act, a formal admission may be made of 'any fact of which oral evidence may be given in any criminal proceedings', words which make it clear that the section cannot be used to admit what would otherwise fall to be excluded because, say, it is inadmissible hearsay (*Coulson* [1997] Crim LR 886). Although it has been held that s. 10(1) covers only facts and therefore cannot apply to the opinion of an expert (*Naylor* [2010] EWCA Crim 1188), a party who accepts another party's expert's conclusions may admit them as fact under s. 10 (CrimPR 19.3 (see Supplement, **R19.3**); considered at **F11.46**). **F1.1**

FORMAL ADMISSIONS

Criminal Justice Act 1967, s. 10 **F1.2**

(1) Subject to the provisions of this section, any fact of which oral evidence may be given in any criminal proceedings may be admitted for the purpose of those proceedings by or on behalf of the prosecutor or defendant, and the admission by any party of any such fact under this section shall as against that party be conclusive evidence in those proceedings of the fact admitted.
(2) An admission under this section—
  (a) may be made before or at the proceedings;
  (b) if made otherwise than in court, shall be in writing;
  (c) if made in writing by an individual, shall purport to be signed by the person making it and, if so made by a body corporate, shall purport to be signed by a director or manager, or the secretary or clerk, or some other similar officer of the body corporate;
  (d) if made on behalf of a defendant who is an individual, shall be made by his counsel or solicitor;
  (e) if made at any stage before the trial by a defendant who is an individual, must be approved by his counsel or solicitor (whether at the time it was made or subsequently) before or at the proceedings in question.
(3) An admission under this section for the purpose of proceedings relating to any matter shall be treated as an admission for the purpose of any subsequent criminal proceedings relating to that matter (including any appeal or retrial).
(4) An admission under this section may with the leave of the court be withdrawn in the proceedings for the purpose of which it is made or any subsequent criminal proceedings relating to the same matter.

F1.3 Ordinarily, written admissions should be put before the jury, provided at least that they are relevant to an issue before the jury and do not contain any material which should not go before the jury (*Pittard* [2006] EWCA Crim 2028). In court, a formal admission may be made by counsel or a solicitor *orally* (see s. 10(2)(b) and (d), and *Lewis* [1989] Crim LR 61). Whatever the manner of making a formal admission under s. 10 of the 1967 Act, it should be such that what has been admitted should appear clearly on the shorthand note (*Lennard* [1973] 2 All ER 831). It is also important that the jury are clear as to what has been formally admitted. In *Lewis* (1971) 55 Cr App R 386, in which counsel for D formally admitted every fact alleged in the prosecution's opening speech and the prosecution called no evidence, relying solely on admissions, leave to appeal against conviction was refused. The court added, however, that such a procedure should be adopted only rarely and with caution, because jurors, when considering the opening speech, might find it difficult to distinguish between law, mixed fact and law, and comment. Where a party introduces in evidence a fact admitted by another party, or parties jointly admit a fact, then unless the court otherwise directs, a written record must be made of the admission (CrimPR 24.6 (magistrates' court) and 25.13 (Crown Court); see Supplement, **R24.6** and **R25.13**). Section 10 will apply in the case of relevant facts in a written schedule which the parties agree to put before the jury; and will also apply to any such facts that were removed from the schedule, pending a judicial ruling on their admissibility, on their reinstatement following a judicial ruling in favour of admissibility (*Lunkulu* [2015] EWCA Crim 1350).

Formal admissions made with the benefit of advice are an important and cogent part of the evidence in a trial. If it is sought to resile from them, leave to withdraw them is unlikely to be given under s. 10(4) without cogent evidence from the accused and advisers that the admissions were made by reason of mistake or misunderstanding (*Kolton* [2000] Crim LR 761).

JUDICIAL NOTICE

Introduction

F1.4 Generally speaking, the doctrine of judicial notice allows the tribunal of fact to treat a fact as established, notwithstanding that no evidence has been adduced to establish it. The doctrine, however, takes three distinct forms. The first two, judicial notice without inquiry and judicial notice after inquiry, were defined and distinguished by Lord Sumner in *Commonwealth Shipping Representative v Peninsular and Oriental Branch Service* [1923] AC 191, at p. 212: 'Judicial notice refers to facts, which a judge can be called upon to receive and to act upon, either from his general knowledge of them, or from inquiries to be made by himself for his own information from sources to which it is proper for him to refer'. The phrase 'judicial notice' is also used, in a third sense, to refer to the use which may be made by jurors or magistrates of their personal knowledge of facts in issue or relevant to the facts in issue. This has been referred to as jury or magistrate notice. These three forms of judicial notice require separate analysis.

Judicial Notice without Inquiry at Common Law

F1.5 If a fact is sufficiently notorious or of such common knowledge that it requires no proof, the judge, without recourse to any extraneous sources of information, may take judicial notice of it and direct the jury to treat it as established, notwithstanding that it has not been established by evidence. Examples include: the fact that a fortnight is too short a period for human gestation (*Luffe* (1807) 8 East 193); the fact that the streets of London are full of traffic (*Dennis v AJ White & Co.* [1916] 2 KB 1, at p. 6); the fact that reconstructed trials with a striking degree of realism are among the popular forms of modern television entertainment (*Yap Chuan Ching (1976) 63 Cr App R 7*); and the fact that cocaine hydrochloride is a form of cocaine (*A-G for the Cayman Islands v Roberts* [2002] UKPC 18, [2002] 1 WLR 1842). In criminal cases, foreign law, being a question of fact generally calling for the evidence of an appropriately qualified expert, cannot be the subject of judicial notice (*Ofori* (1994) 99 Cr App R 219). There is one exception: the common law of Northern Ireland (*Re Nesbitt* (1844) 14 LJ MC 30 at p. 33).

Judicial Notice without Inquiry Pursuant to Statute

Judicial notice of a fact may be required by statute. The most important examples are the Evidence Act 1845, s. 2, and the Interpretation Act 1978, s. 3. Section 2 of the 1845 Act requires judicial notice to be taken of the fact that a judicial or official document purporting to have been signed by a judge was signed by that judge. **F1.6**

Evidence Act 1845, s. 2

> All courts, judges, justices, masters in Chancery, masters of courts, commissioners judicially acting, and other judicial officers, shall henceforth take judicial notice of the signature of any of the equity or common law judges of the superior courts at Westminster, provided such signature be attached or appended to any decree, order, certificate, or other judicial or official document.

Section 3 of the Interpretation Act 1978, as supplemented by s. 22(1) and sch. 2, para. 2, requires judicial notice to be taken of statutes of the UK (whether general, local and personal, or private) passed after 1850.

Interpretation Act 1978, s. 3

> Every Act is a public Act to be judicially noticed as such, unless the contrary is expressly provided by the Act.

Thus in the absence of express provision to the contrary, evidence is not required to prove either the contents of an Act passed after 1850 or that such an Act has been duly passed by both Houses of Parliament. At common law, the courts are bound to take judicial notice of Public Acts passed before 1850. Private Acts passed before 1850 require to be proved by the production of a Queen's Printer's or Stationery Office copy (see the Evidence Act 1845, s. 3, and the Documentary Evidence Act 1882, s. 2).

Statutory instruments may be proved by Queen's Printer's or Stationery Office copies (see *Ashley* (1967) 52 Cr App R 42 and the Documentary Evidence Act 1868, s. 2, at **F8.17**). There is no equivalent to the Interpretation Act 1978, s. 3, for judicial notice to be taken of statutory instruments, although some instruments have acquired such notoriety that judicial notice may be taken of them (*Jones* (1968) 54 Cr App R 63).

Judicial Notice after Inquiry

In a number of cases, judges have taken judicial notice of a fact only after referring to extraneous sources of information, such as certificates from ministers or officials, learned treatises, works of reference and expert witnesses. Such a judicial inquiry is distinct from proof by evidence in the normal way: the rules of evidence are inapplicable; the result of the inquiry is not open to evidence in rebuttal; and the result, except in the case of facts lacking constancy (e.g., the status of a foreign government), constitutes a legal precedent. The justification for judicial notice after inquiry is that some facts, although not sufficiently notorious to be the subject of judicial notice without inquiry, are readily demonstrable by reference to sources of virtually indisputable authority, or arise so frequently that proof in the normal way is undesirable because of the cost and the need for uniformity of decision. Judicial notice after inquiry has been taken of the following three kinds of fact: **F1.7**

(a) Facts of a political nature, such as relations between the government of the UK and a foreign state, the status of foreign sovereigns or governments, the membership of diplomatic suites, and the extent of territorial sovereignty. The source of information is usually a minister, whose certificate will be treated as an indisputably accurate source for reasons of public policy, namely the desirability of avoiding conflict between the courts and the executive. In *Bottrill, ex parte Kuechenmeister* [1947] KB 41, the Court of Appeal, treating as conclusive the certificate of the Foreign Secretary that Germany still existed as a State and German nationality as a nationality, and that His Majesty was still in a state of war with Germany, held that the applicant for a writ of *habeas corpus* was still an enemy alien. See also *Duff Development Co. Ltd v Government of Kelantan* [1924] AC 797; *Engelke v Musmann* [1928] AC 433; and *Carl Zeiss Stiftung v Rayner and Keeler Ltd (No. 2)* [1967] 1 AC 853.

(b) Facts which are readily demonstrable after reference to appropriate authoritative works of reference or learned treatises. Illustrations would be the day of the week on which a certain date fell, after reference to an almanac or diary; the longitude and latitude of a certain place, after reference to an atlas or other geographical work; and the date and location of a well-known historical event, after reference to an appropriate authoritative history. See *Read v Bishop of Lincoln* [1892] AC 644 and *R (HRH Sultan of Pahang) v Secretary of State for the Home Department* [2011] EWCA Civ 616.

(c) Customs and professional practices, after consultation with suitably qualified experts. See *Brandao v Barnett* (1846) 12 Cl & F 787 (the custom of bankers' lien); *Re Rosher* (1884) 26 Ch D 801 (conveyancers' practices); *Davey v Harrow Corporation* [1958] 1 QB 60 (ordnance surveyors' practices); and *Heather v P-E Consulting Group Ltd* [1973] 1 Ch 189 (accountants' practices).

A court is not entitled to take judicial notice of a fact simply on the basis that it has been proved in another case (per Lord Wright in *Lazard Brothers & Co. v Midland Bank* [1933] AC 289 at pp. 297–8, applied in *Jankowski v District Court Wroclaw (Poland)* [2016] EWHC 3792 (Admin), followed in *Krajewski v Circuit Law Court, Swidnica, Poland* [2016] EWHC 3241 (Admin)).

PERSONAL KNOWLEDGE OF COURT OR JURY

Judges

F1.8 It has been held that a judge may use personal knowledge of matters within the common knowledge of people in the locality. This principle derives from cases decided under the Workmen's Compensation Acts, under which county court judges sat as arbitrators and took into account, in assessing compensation, personal knowledge of the labour market, conditions of work, and wages (see, e.g., *Keane v Mount Vernon Colliery Co. Ltd* [1933] AC 309 and *Reynolds v Llanelly Associated Tinplate Co. Ltd* [1948] 1 All ER 140). See also, *sed quaere, Mullen v Hackney London Borough Council* [1997] 2 All ER 906.

Magistrates

F1.9 In *Wetherall v Harrison* [1976] QB 773, the issue was whether D had a reasonable excuse for failure to give a blood sample. D said that he had had a sort of fit, which the prosecution alleged had been simulated. One of the justices, a practising registered medical practitioner, gave his professional view on the matter to the other justices, who also drew on their own experience of wartime inoculations and the fear that they could create in certain cases. Dismissing the appeal, the Divisional Court held that justices, unlike judges, lack the ability to exclude certain factors from their consideration. In particular, if a magistrate is a specialist, whether doctor, engineer or accountant, 'it is not possible for him to approach the decision in the case as though he had not got that training, and . . . it would be a very bad thing if he had to' (at p. 777). One of the advantages of justices is that they bring a lot of varied experience into the court-room, and use it. Although it would be quite wrong for a justice to give evidence to himself or the other justices in contradiction of that which had been heard in court, he can employ his basic knowledge, for the benefit of himself and the other justices, in considering, weighing up and assessing the evidence given before the court.

'It has always been recognised that justices may and should — after all, they are local justices — take into consideration matters which they know of their own knowledge, and particularly matters in regard to the locality' (*Ingram v Percival* [1969] 1 QB 548 per Lord Parker CJ at p. 555). The appellant had been convicted of unlawfully using a net secured by anchors for taking salmon or trout in tidal waters. It was held that the justices were fully entitled to make use of their own knowledge that the place where the net was fixed was in tidal waters. See also *Paul v*

DPP (1989) 90 Cr App R 173 concerning a charge of soliciting a woman for the purposes of prostitution from a motor vehicle in a street in such manner or in such circumstances as to be likely to cause nuisance to other persons in the neighbourhood, contrary to the Sexual Offences Act 1985, s. 1(1). It was held that the justices, who had no evidence before them that anyone had actually been caused nuisance, were entitled to take into account two matters within their local knowledge: first, that the area in question was often frequented by prostitutes and that there was a constant procession of cars driving around the area at night; and secondly, that it was a heavily populated residential area. In *Field, ex parte White* (1895) 64 LJ MC 158, the issue being whether cocoa necessarily contains foreign ingredients, no evidence was adduced. The justices, relying on their own knowledge of the subject, found for D. Although Wills J observed that perhaps in future evidence should be heard on such a matter, the Divisional Court refused to disturb the justices' finding.

Jurors

The doctrine of judicial notice also applies to jurors in relation to matters coming within the sphere of their everyday knowledge and experience (*Rosser* (1836) 7 C & P 648, approved in *Jones* [1970] 3 All ER 1559). In *Jones* it was argued that it had not been proved that D had been given an opportunity to provide a specimen of breath for a breath test, because there had been no evidence to show that the device used, the Alcotest R80, was 'of a type approved by the Secretary of State' for the purposes of the Road Safety Act, 1967, s. 7. Rejecting this argument, Edmund Davies LJ said, at p. 20: 'the number of decided cases in which it has been proved that the Alcotest R80 device is of an approved type has by now become so large and so widely reported that, in our judgment, a court (including the jury) is entitled to take judicial notice of that fact, and its formal proof is accordingly no longer necessary'. **F1.10**

However, although jurors may use their *general* knowledge, they may not use their *personal* knowledge to supplement or contradict the evidence given in the case. The older authorities suggest that a juror with particular knowledge of a matter should be sworn as a witness and give evidence in the normal way (*Rosser* (1836) 7 C & P 648; *Manley v Shaw* (1840) Car & M 361; *Antrim Justices* [1895] 2 IR 603). A preferable solution, it is submitted, is the course adopted in *Blick* (1966) 50 Cr App R 280. In that case a juror passed a note to the judge to the effect that his own local knowledge contradicted the alibi evidence given by D. In consequence the judge allowed the prosecution to call evidence, relating to the matters contained in the note, to rebut the alibi. This decision was upheld by the Court of Criminal Appeal.

Each juror should receive written notice of the prohibitions against research into the case, disclosure of any such research to another juror and conduct suggesting that a juror intends to try the case otherwise than on the evidence (CrimPR 26.3, and see also CrimPD VI, para. 26G.3; see Supplement, **R26.3** and **CPD.26G**). As to ordering jurors to surrender electronic communication devices, see **D13.21**; and as to the offence, for a juror, of researching a case during a trial, see **B14.133**.

RELEVANCE

Relevance and Admissibility

The cardinal rule of the law of evidence is that, subject to the exclusionary rules, all evidence which is sufficiently relevant to the facts in issue is admissible, and all evidence which is irrelevant or insufficiently relevant to the facts in issue should be excluded. As to the former, however, evidence which is relevant may nonetheless be excluded if it is such that no reasonable jury, properly directed as to its defects, could place any weight on it (*Robinson* [2005] EWCA Crim 1940, [2006] 1 Cr App R 13 (221), a case concerning voice recognition evidence). As to the latter, inasmuch as an offence of strict liability involves no proof of *mens rea*, evidence of motive, intention or knowledge is inadmissible, being irrelevant to what the Crown has to prove and merely prejudicial to the accused (*Sandhu* [1997] Crim LR 288; and see also *Byrne* [2002] EWCA Crim 632, [2002] 2 Cr App R 21 (311)). **F1.11**

The Meaning of Relevance

F1.12 The classic formulation of relevance is to be found in Article 1 of Stephen's *Digest of the Law of Evidence* (12th edn, 1936), according to which the word signifies that 'any two facts to which it is applied are so related to each other that according to the common course of events one either taken by itself or in connection with other facts proves or renders probable the past, present or future existence or non-existence of the other'. *Nethercott* [2001] EWCA Crim 2535, [2002] Cr App R 7 (117) provides an example of a fact which was relevant to the past existence of another fact. D1's defence was that he had acted under duress as a result of threats by his co-accused D2. Evidence of the fact that D2 had subsequently attacked D1 with a knife was relevant to the defence because it made it more likely that D1, at the time of the offence, had genuinely feared for his safety.

On the question of relevance, Lord Simon of Glaisdale has said:

> Evidence is relevant if it is logically probative or disprobative of some matter which requires proof. I do not pause to analyse what is involved in 'logical probativeness', except to note that the term does not of itself express the element of experience which is so significant of its operation in law, and possibly elsewhere. It is sufficient to say, even at the risk of etymological tautology, that relevant (i.e., logically probative or disprobative) evidence is evidence which makes the matter which requires proof more or less probable. (*DPP v Kilbourne* [1973] AC 729, at p. 756.)

The question of relevance is typically a matter of degree to be determined, for the most part, by common sense and experience (*Randall* [2003] UKHL 69, [2004] 1 WLR 56, per Lord Steyn at [20]).

For some of the more frequently recurring examples of relevant evidence, see **F1.22** ***et seq***. In sexual cases, the relevance of evidence relating to the complainant's social media accounts, such as the content of Facebook messages to friends, whether they had been deleted, and if so, when and why, will depend on the precise circumstances of the case. Such evidence is most likely to be relevant in cases where the complainant and the accused were in a relationship or knew each other. In cases where there was no contact between them before or after the alleged crime, the fact that messages had been deleted is unlikely to be relevant, in the absence of any basis for suggesting that they contained material of assistance to the defence (*McPartland* [2019] EWCA Crim 1782, [2020] 1 Cr App R (S) 51 (383)). Concerning the evidential consequences if the complainant refuses to permit access to a potentially relevant device or deletes relevant material, see CB [2020] EWCA Crim 790 at **F7.46**.

Strict Application of the Test

F1.13 There is a long-standing practice on the part of the prosecution to make admissions in relation to facts that may point to a third party having committed the crime with which the accused is charged, such admissions being relevant and admissible material to weigh in the scales in deciding whether it might have been the third party and not the accused who committed the offence (*Greenwood* [2004] EWCA Crim 1388, [2005] 1 Cr App R 7 (99)). Such admissions were made in *Blastland* [1986] AC 41, but the test of 'logical probativeness' was strictly applied to exclude additional evidence relating to the state of mind of the third party. The appellant, D, was convicted of the buggery and murder of V, a boy. At the trial, D admitted that he had met V and engaged in sexual activity with him (including attempted buggery), but said that shortly afterwards he saw another man nearby and, fearing that he had been observed committing a serious offence, panicked and ran away. D's description of the other man corresponded closely to one M. D said that M must have committed both offences charged. There were formal admissions by the prosecution showing M to have been known to engage in the past in homosexual activities with adults but not with children. There were also both formal admissions and evidence relating to M's movements on the evening of V's murder. The defence sought leave to call a number of witnesses to give evidence that before V's body had been found, M had made statements to them that a boy had been murdered. The trial judge ruled that this evidence was inadmissible. Before the House of Lords, the appellant submitted that the statements made by M were admissible as original evidence to show M's state of mind, i.e. his knowledge of the murder before the body had been found. Lord Bridge, giving the judgment of the House, held that such evidence would only have been admissible if

M's state of mind had been either directly in issue itself or of direct and immediate relevance to an issue arising at the trial. The evidence had been properly rejected because the issue at the trial was whether D had committed the crimes, and what was relevant to that was not the fact of M's knowledge but how he had come by it; since he might have come by that knowledge in a number of different ways, there was no rational basis on which the jury could be invited to draw an inference as to the source of that knowledge. To do so would have been mere speculation. The evidence of what M said, therefore, could not be put before the jury to support the conclusion that he, rather than D, may have been the criminal. See also *Kearley* [1992] 2 AC 228 at **F16.16**, *Williams* [1998] Crim LR 494 and *Akram* [1995] Crim LR 50. However, in *Gadsby* [2006] EWCA Crim 3206, it was held, *obiter*, that evidence may be relevant if it is capable of increasing or diminishing the probability of facts indicating that some other person committed the crime (e.g., evidence that a person with the opportunity of committing the crime had a propensity to do so).

The strict approach taken in *Blastland* was also adopted in *T (AB)* [2006] EWCA Crim 2006, [2007] 1 Cr App R 4 (43). The complainant alleged that she had been sexually abused by the appellant, who was her uncle, and by her grandfather and her step-grandfather, but it was not alleged that they were acting in concert. The grandfather admitted the allegations against him but died before the matter reached court. The step-grandfather pleaded guilty to counts of indecently assaulting the complainant. It was held that evidence of the grandfather's admission and of the step-grandfather's guilty plea should not have been admitted, because it was not relevant, in itself, to the issue whether the appellant abused the complainant; and that while it was 'tempting' to say that it was relevant to the issue of her credibility, that would amount to a form of 'oath helping' which has never been permissible as a ground for admitting evidence.

Good Character

Evidence of the good character of a prosecution witness is generally inadmissible to bolster the witness's credibility, because it amounts to 'oath-helping' (see *Robinson* [1994] 3 All ER 346 at **F7.63**), but may be admissible if relevant to an issue in the case, for example: in a case of rape, the defence being consent, evidence of the complainant's disposition to resist any form of pre-marital sexual intimacy (*Amado-Taylor* [2001] EWCA Crim 1898); in a case of murder, the defence being self-defence, evidence of the deceased's non-violent disposition (*RG* [2002] EWCA Crim 1056); and, in a case of inflicting grievous bodily harm, the defence being self-defence accompanied by evidence that the complainant had started the violence making racially abusive comments, evidence to show that the complainant was not a racist (*Lodge* [2013] EWCA Crim 987). In *Mader* [2018] EWCA Crim 2454 the following propositions were said to be well established: **F1.14**

(1) Generally, evidence is not admissible simply to show that a prosecution witness has a good character in the sense that he or she is a generally truthful person who should be believed.
(2) However, evidence is admissible if it is relevant to an issue in the trial.
(3) The category of issues to which evidence of disposition may be relevant is not closed.
(4) If the evidence is admitted because 'issue-relevant', the judge should ensure that the effect of admitting it is not to water down the burden of proof on the prosecution and any good character direction given for the accused.

In *G (T)* [2017] EWCA Crim 1774, [2018] 1 Cr App R 14 (218), where D was of good character and the judge had given an appropriate good character direction, the Court of Appeal observed that unless a jury hear that a Crown witness is not of good character, they will no doubt assume that there is nothing to speak against the witness's credibility. As to this observation, it is respectfully submitted that in these circumstances the jury may well assume exactly the opposite, that the complainant is of bad character, on the reasoning that if the complainant were of good character then evidence to that effect would have been adduced in the same way that evidence of good character had been adduced on behalf of the accused. It is submitted that when an accused contradicts a prosecution witness on a relevant issue, both of them are of good character, evidence is given of the accused's good character and the jury are directed that it is relevant to the accused's credibility, then evidence of the good character of the prosecution witness should also be admissible and the jury should receive a direction that it is relevant to the witness's credibility accompanied by a rider, of the kind described in *Mader*, as to its limitations and effect.

Delayed Complaints

F1.15 In sexual cases, an appropriate direction may be required to counter the stereotypical assumption, on which the defence will often rely, that a late complaint is a false complaint (*D* [2008] EWCA Crim 2557). The delay may stem from shame, confusion, in the case of family abuse not knowing to whom a complaint should be made, feelings of personal blame, fear of not being believed, fear of the effect upon existing relationships, and so on (see *Miller* [2010] EWCA Crim 1578 and the *Crown Court Compendium* (July 2020), ch. 20-1). The direction should be crafted to reflect the facts of the case (*Smith* [2012] EWCA Crim 404) and should be discussed, in advance, with the advocates (*Miller* [2010] EWCA Crim 1578).

Demeanour of Victim

F1.16 In *Keast* [1998] Crim LR 748 (applied in *Venn* [2003] EWCA Crim 236) it was held that unless there is some concrete basis for regarding long-term demeanour and state of mind of a victim of sexual abuse as confirming or disproving the occurrence of such abuse, it cannot assist a jury bringing their common sense to bear on who is telling the truth. However, demeanour witnessed close in time to the event in question may have probative value, by analogy with the principle of *res gestae* (*Townsend* [2003] EWCA Crim 3173). See also *Zala* [2014] EWCA Crim 2181, considered at **F5.11**. Concerning the demeanour of complainants in sexual cases, see the *Crown Court Compendium* (July 2020), ch. 20-1, Examples 6 and 7.

Relevance in Drug Cases

F1.17 Concerning the offence of possession of drugs with intent to supply, evidence which is arguably relevant to the question of intent may fall to be excluded because of its prejudicial effect in indicating dealing in drugs in the past or generally. This principle and the following cases need to be read subject to the provisions in the CJA 2003, ss. 98 to 113, relating to the accused's bad character (see F13). However, it has been said that if the evidence would have been admissible before the 2003 Act, there would be 'something highly artificial' in the prosecution having to make an application under the Act (*Graham* [2007] EWCA Crim 1499). Under the principle, it has been held that evidence of the possession of weights and scales on which there are traces of the drug in question will be admitted (*Batt* [1994] Crim LR 592), but not evidence of past deposits in and withdrawals from savings accounts, because that can only found an inference of past drug dealing (*Gordon* [1995] 2 Cr App R 61). In *Batt* it was also held that evidence of the discovery of £150 in an ornamental kettle in B's house was inadmissible because it had nothing to do with intent to supply in future the drugs found, but had a highly prejudicial effect as evidence of propensity to supply or of past or future supplying generally. *Batt*, however, has not laid down a general principle that evidence of possession of money is never admissible (*Nicholas* [1995] Crim LR 942; *Okusanya* [1995] Crim LR 941). On one view the decision in *Batt* turned on the fact that the trial judge had failed to direct the jury as to how they could properly use the evidence of the money found (*Morris* [1995] 2 Cr App R 69). Alternatively, *Batt* should be seen as a case strictly confined to its own facts, bearing in mind that £150 was too small, and its hiding place too unremarkable, to be the hallmark of present drug dealing (*Okusanya*). In *Wright* [1994] Crim LR 55, it was held that drug traders needed to keep by them large sums of cash and therefore evidence of the discovery of £16,000 was capable of giving rise to an inference of dealing and tended to prove that the drugs found were for supply. In *Gordon* [1995] 2 Cr App R 61, it was held that evidence of the discovery of £4,200 was admissible subject to an appropriate direction. Similarly, in *Smith* [1995] Crim LR 940, it was held that evidence that in recent months £9,000 had been deposited in S's account, £2,100 of which could not be explained by legitimate transactions, was admissible, subject to an appropriate direction. The jury should be directed (a) that evidence of the discovery of money is relevant only if they reject any innocent explanation for it advanced by the accused, (b) that if there is any possibility of the money having been in the accused's possession for reasons other than drug dealing, then the evidence is not probative, but (c) that if they conclude that it indicates not merely past dealing but an on-going dealing in drugs, they may take into account the finding of it, together with the drugs, in considering the issue of intent to supply (*Grant* [1996] 1 Cr App R 73 and *Green* [2009] EWCA Crim 1688, where a similar direction was given on a charge of conspiracy to supply drugs; cf. *Antill* [2002] EWCA Crim 2114). The same principles apply where the prosecution relies on a list of names or drugs paraphernalia (*Lovelock* [1997] Crim LR 821; *Haye* [2002] EWCA Crim 2476). Such a direction, however, will not always need to be given in terms (*Malik* [2000] 2 Cr App R 8). The jury should also be directed not to treat it as evidence of propensity, i.e. not to pursue the line of reasoning that because of the past dealing the accused is likely to be guilty (*Simms* [1995] Crim LR 304; *Lucas* [1995] Crim LR 400). In *Guney* [1998] 2 Cr App R 242, the Court of Appeal declined to follow earlier authorities to the effect that, where possession of the drugs is in issue, evidence of possession of money or drugs paraphernalia can never be relevant to that issue (*Halpin* [1996] Crim LR 112; *Richards* [1997] Crim LR 499). It was held that, although evidence of possession of a large sum of cash or enjoyment of a wealthy lifestyle does not, on its own, prove possession, there are numerous sets of circumstances in which it may be relevant to that issue, not least to the issue of knowledge as an ingredient of possession. The real issue in the case was whether G was knowingly in possession of nearly five kilos of heroin or whether it had been 'planted', the defence having conceded that, if possession were to be proved, then it would be open to the jury to infer intent to supply. It was held that, in all the circumstances, evidence of the finding of nearly £25,000 in cash in the wardrobe of G's bedroom and in close proximity to the drugs was relevant to the issue of possession. *Guney* was applied in *Griffiths* [1998] Crim LR 567.

Illegal Importation Cases In cases of illegal importation of controlled drugs in which the accused denies any knowledge of how the drugs came to be in his or her possession, evidence of finding drugs in the accused's home is relevant and admissible because the jury are entitled to consider such a coincidence, which may go to rebut the defence raised (*Willis* (29 January 1979 unreported); *Peters* [1995] 2 Cr App R 77). The principle is not confined to couriers, but extends to those who claim to have been unknowingly involved in the importation of drugs, such as those meeting couriers at airports (*Groves* [1998] Crim LR 200). Evidence admissible to rebut such a defence includes evidence of the possession of drugs or drugs paraphernalia, and evidence suggesting a pattern of the accused having been involved in previous importations: see, as to the latter, *Ilomuanya* [2005] EWCA Crim 58, where the evidence relied on was held to be irrelevant because it neither established nor tended to suggest any such pattern. **F1.18**

Evidence of Marginal Relevance

Although it has been said that relevance is typically a matter of degree (*Randall* [2003] UKHL 69, [2004] 1 WLR 56, per Lord Steyn at [20]), it is probably more accurate to say that evidence is either relevant or not and, if relevant, has differing degrees of probative force. For example, evidence of facts which supply a motive for an accused to have committed a particular crime is generally admissible to show that it is more likely that the accused committed that crime (*Ball* [1911] AC 47, per Lord Atkinson at p. 68 and *Phillips* [2003] EWCA Crim 1379, [2003] 2 Cr App R 35 (528); but see also, in the case of offences of strict liability, *Sandhu* [1997] Crim LR 288). However, evidence of motive will be excluded if it is so remote from the offence charged that it can be said to be without any probative value at all (*Berry* (1986) 83 Cr App R 7). Similarly, on a charge of manslaughter against a doctor, although expert evidence of his skill as shown by his treatment of the case under investigation is admissible, expert evidence as to his skilful treatment of patients on other occasions is inadmissible (*Whitehead* (1848) 3 Car & Kir 202). **F1.19**

Evidence of marginal relevance may be excluded on the grounds that it would lead to a multiplicity of subsidiary issues, involving the court in a protracted investigation and distracting it from the main issue (*A-G v Hitchcock* (1847) 1 Exch 91 per Rolfe B at p. 105 and *Patel* [1951] 2 All ER 29, per Byrne J at p. 30). Similarly, questioning of a witness may be disallowed if it relates to matters too far removed from the issues in the case and is in the nature of a fishing expedition (*Haddock* [2011] EWCA Crim 303). On occasions, the effect of evidence which is technically admissible is so slight that it is wiser not to adduce it, especially if there is any danger of a contravention of the PACE 1984, s. 78 (see **F2.7**), i.e. where its admission would have such an adverse effect on the fairness of the proceedings that the court ought not to admit it (*Robertson* [1987] QB 920, per Lord Lane CJ at p. 928; and see also *Williams* [1990] Crim LR 409).

Evidence of Earlier Trial

F1.20 Where two trials arise out of the same transaction, evidence of the outcome of the first is generally inadmissible at the second, because the verdict in the first, whether reached on the same or different evidence, is usually irrelevant; some exceptional feature is needed before it will be considered relevant (*Hui Chi-ming v The Queen* [1992] 1 AC 34). See, as an illustration of such irrelevance, *Preko* [2015] EWCA Crim 42. The principle applies *a fortiori* if the first trial arose out of a different transaction (*Terry* [2004] EWCA Crim 3252, [2005] QB 996 at [34]). In *Golam-Rassoude* [2020] EWCA Crim 704, Mr and Mrs G-R were convicted on a retrial of converting or transferring criminal property, count 2 at the first trial. At the first trial they were acquitted on count 1, improper importation of Class A drugs. There was evidence that they had collected boxes containing the drugs and taken them to their home and that a co-accused A had collected and returned boxes from their home and given them large sums of cash which Mrs G-R had paid into various banks. It was held that, at the retrial, the prosecution were entitled to suggest that Mr and Mrs G-R knew that the boxes contained illegal drugs notwithstanding their acquittal at the first trial. It was further held that the defence were not entitled to adduce evidence of the acquittals. It did not prove that Mr and Mrs G-R did not know or suspect that the cash represented the proceeds of criminal conduct generally or drug dealing in particular. Cf. *Hajdarmataj* [2019] EWCA Crim 303 and *Terry* [2004] EWCA Crim 3252, [2005] QB 996. On one view, the rationale of the principle is that the evidence amounts to nothing more than evidence of the opinion of the first jury (*Hui-chi Ming v The Queen*), but by itself that would be a reason for never admitting evidence of a previous verdict. The true rationale, in the case of an earlier acquittal, is that in most cases it is impossible to be certain why a jury acquitted (*D* [2007] EWCA Crim 684), although the principle appears also to apply in the case of an acquittal following a ruling by a trial judge that there was insufficient evidence to go to the jury (see *Hudson* [1994] Crim LR 920 and cf. *Colman* [2004] EWCA Crim 3252, [2005] QB 996). The cases indicate that the 'exceptional feature' arises where there is a clear inference from the verdict that the jury rejected a witness's evidence because they did not believe him and his credibility is directly in issue in the second trial (*Hay* (1983) 77 Cr App R 70; *Cooke* (1986) 84 Cr App R 286; *Deboussi* [2007] EWCA Crim 684), as when it is alleged that an officer has fabricated an admission, the officer having given evidence of an admission in an earlier trial resulting in an acquittal by virtue of which his evidence can be shown to have been disbelieved (*Edwards* [1991] 2 All ER 226).

As to the relevance (and admissibility) of previous convictions or acquittals as evidence of the facts on which they were based, see **F12.6** ***et seq.***

DIRECT EVIDENCE

F1.21 Direct evidence is evidence of *facts in issue*. In the case of testimonial evidence, it is evidence about facts in issue of which the witness claims to have personal knowledge, for example, 'I saw the accused strike the victim'.

CIRCUMSTANTIAL EVIDENCE

Introduction

F1.22 Circumstantial evidence is to be contrasted with direct evidence (see **F1.21**). Circumstantial evidence is evidence of *relevant facts*, i.e. facts from which the existence or non-existence of facts in issue may be inferred. It does not necessarily follow that the weight to be attached to circumstantial evidence will be less than that to be attached to direct evidence. For example, the tribunal of fact is likely to attach more weight to a variety of individual items of circumstantial evidence, all of which lead to the same conclusion, than to direct evidence to the contrary coming from witnesses lacking in credibility.

Circumstantial evidence 'works by cumulatively, in geometrical progression, eliminating other possibilities' (*DPP v Kilbourne* [1973] AC 729 per Lord Simon at p. 758). Pollock CB, likening circumstantial evidence to a rope comprised of several cords, said:

> One strand of the cord might be insufficient to sustain the weight, but three stranded together may be quite of sufficient strength.
>
> Thus it may be in circumstantial evidence — there may be a combination of circumstances, no one of which would raise a reasonable conviction, or more than a mere suspicion; but the whole, taken together, may create a strong conclusion of guilt, that is, with as much certainty as human affairs can require or admit of. (*Exall* (1866) 4 F & F 922, at p. 929.)

However, although circumstantial evidence may sometimes be conclusive, it must always be narrowly examined, if only because it may be fabricated to cast suspicion on another. For this reason, it has been said that: 'It is also necessary before drawing the inference of the accused's guilt from circumstantial evidence to be sure that there are no other co-existing circumstances which would weaken or destroy the inference' (*Teper v The Queen* [1952] AC 480, per Lord Normand at p. 489). Nonetheless, there is no requirement, in cases in which the prosecution's case is based on circumstantial evidence, that the judge direct the jury to acquit unless they are sure that the facts proved are not only consistent with guilt but also inconsistent with any other reasonable conclusion (*McGreevy v DPP* [1973] 1 All ER 503).

Presumption of Fact

F1.23 Certain varieties of circumstantial evidence have arisen so frequently in practice as to attract the label 'presumption of fact'. For the presumption of continuance of life, see **F3.61**; for the presumption of intention, see **F3.62**; and for the presumption of guilty knowledge in cases of handling, theft etc., see **F3.63**. Although they have not attracted the label 'presumption of fact', other frequently recurring examples of circumstantial evidence include evidence of plans and acts preparatory to the commission of an offence (to show intention to commit the offence); evidence of opportunity; evidence of lack of opportunity, which may assist the accused, e.g., alibi evidence, or the prosecution, e.g., evidence that after arrest the accused had no opportunity to commit further offences and no offences similar to those with which the accused is charged were committed in the same area (*Wilson* [2008] EWCA Crim 1754); and evidence of identity, including evidence of physical idiosyncrasy, manner of vocal or written expression, fingerprints, DNA and tracker dog evidence (*Haas* (1962) 35 DLR (2d) 172 (British Columbia); *Pieterson* [1995] 1 WLR 293; *Sykes* [1997] Crim LR 752). Other typical examples of circumstantial evidence are dealt with below.

Motive

F1.24

> Surely in an ordinary prosecution for murder you can prove previous acts or words of the accused to show that he entertained feelings of enmity towards the deceased, and this is evidence not merely of the malicious mind with which he killed the deceased, but of the fact that he killed him. ... it is more probable that men are killed by those who have some motive for killing them than by those who have not. (*Ball* [1911] AC 47 per Lord Atkinson (during argument) at p. 68, affirmed in *Williams* (1986) 84 Cr App R 299.)

This classic statement remains good law and any doubt that may have been cast upon it in *Berry* (1986) 83 Cr App R 7 should be disregarded (*Phillips* [2003] EWCA Crim 1379, [2003] 2 Cr App R 35 (528) at [26]). Evidence of motive may be admissible notwithstanding that the motive is irrational and *Berry*, insofar as it suggests otherwise, has been disapproved (*Phillips* at [30]). Evidence of motive does not become irrelevant simply because others had the same motive. Thus, in the case of a feud between neighbouring families, the motive may be shared by members of a family, including the accused, but it is still relevant to show that the accused had a reason to do what is alleged (*Myers v R* [2015] UKPC 40, [2016] AC 314 at [45]).

Evidence of motive may be admissible notwithstanding that it reveals the accused's criminal disposition (*Williams*), provided that the evidence of bad character is admissible under the CJA 2003 (see **F13**). Evidence that the accused lacked a motive to commit the crime charged may be admissible to show the comparative improbability of the accused's having committed it (*Grant* (1865) 4 F & F 322). Evidence may also be adduced that someone else had such a motive, as in *Greenwood* [2004] EWCA Crim 1388, [2005] 1 Cr App R 7 (99) where, in the case of an undisputed murder, it was held that D was entitled to adduce evidence to show that V's ex-boyfriend was near the murder scene and appeared to have a motive. It does not follow from the foregoing, however, that evidence of motive (or its absence) is necessarily relevant to the facts in issue on a particular charge (see, e.g., *Graham-Kerr* (1989) 88 Cr App R 302 (the indecency of a photograph), applied in *Rowley* (1991) 94 Cr App R 95 (an act outraging public decency), and *H* [2005] EWCA Crim 732, [2005] 1 WLR 200 at **B3.58**; and compare *Court* [1989] AC 28).

Lies

F1.25 Lies told by the accused, on their own, do not make a positive case of any crime (*Strudwick* (1994) 99 Cr App R 326 at p. 331). However, they may indicate a consciousness of guilt and in appropriate circumstances may therefore be relied upon by the prosecution as evidence supportive of guilt, as in *Goodway* [1993] 4 All ER 894 where D's lies to the police as to his whereabouts at the time of the offence were used in support of the identification evidence adduced by the prosecution. In that case it was held that, whenever a lie told by an accused is relied on by the Crown or may be used by the jury to support evidence of guilt, as opposed merely to reflecting on the accused's credibility (and not only when it is relied on as corroboration or as support for identification evidence), a threefold *Lucas* ([1981] QB 720) direction should generally be given to the jury:

(a) The lie must be deliberate and must relate to a material issue.
(b) They must be satisfied that there was no innocent motive for the lie, reminding them that people sometimes lie, for example, in an attempt to bolster up a just cause, or out of shame or a wish to conceal disgraceful behaviour.
(c) The lie must be established by evidence other than that of the witness who is to be corroborated.

See also the *Crown Court Compendium* (July 2020), ch. 16-3, and *Taylor* [1994] Crim LR 680. In *Taylor* [1998] Crim LR 822, a trial for murder in which the only issue was provocation and D admitted that he had lied in saying that he had never had any contact with V, it was held that the jury should have been directed that the lies could support the case of murder only if they were sure that they were told to conceal the fact that D had murdered V, rather than merely to conceal his connection with the death, i.e. to avoid responsibility for deliberate murder rather than a provoked killing. Similarly, in *Reszpondek* [2010] EWCA Crim 2358 at [19], a murder trial in which there was evidence that D had told many lies and had been involved in acts of concealment of the death, it was held that this evidence could be used by the jury to support an inference of murder, provided that they were cautioned that the evidence could be accounted for by the fact that V's death might have resulted from manslaughter. See also *Bullen* [2008] EWCA Crim 4, [2008] 2 Cr App R 25 (364).

In *Goodway* it was also held that a direction need not be given where it is otiose as indicated in *Dehar* [1969] NZLR 763, i.e. where the rejection of the explanation given by the accused almost necessarily leaves the jury with no choice but to convict as a matter of logic. For an example, see *Barsoum* [1994] Crim LR 194 and cf. *Wood* [1995] Crim LR 154. See also *Gordon* [1995] Crim LR 306. Nor, it seems, does a judge need to give a *Lucas* direction where the accused has offered an explanation for lies and the judge has dealt with that explanation fairly in the summing-up (*Saunders* [1996] 1 Cr App R 463 at pp. 518–19).

The Four *Burge* Situations In *Burge* [1996] 1 Cr App R 163, the Court of Appeal held that a *Lucas* direction is usually required in four situations, which may overlap (Kennedy LJ at p. 173): F1.26

1. Where the defence relies on an alibi.
2. Where the judge considers it desirable or necessary to suggest that the jury should look for support or corroboration of one piece of evidence from other evidence in the case, and amongst that other evidence draws attention to lies told, or allegedly told, by the defendant.
3. Where the prosecution seek to show that something said, either in or out of the court, in relation to a separate and distinct issue was a lie, and to rely on that lie as evidence of guilt in relation to the charge which is sought to be proved.
4. Where although the prosecution have not adopted the approach to which we have just referred, the judge reasonably envisages that there is a real danger that the jury may do so.

The Court of Appeal held that the direction (if given) should, so far as possible, be tailored to the circumstances of the case, but that it will normally suffice to make two points: first that the lie must be admitted or proved beyond reasonable doubt, and secondly that the mere fact that the accused lied is not in itself evidence of guilt since defendants may lie for innocent reasons, so only if the jury are sure that the accused did not lie for an innocent reason can a lie support the prosecution case. The Court also stressed that the need for the direction arises only in cases where the prosecution say, or the judge envisages that the jury may say, that the lie is evidence against the accused, in effect using it as an implied admission of guilt. The direction is not needed in run-of-the-mill cases where the defence case is contradicted by the evidence of prosecution witnesses in such a way as to make it necessary for the prosecution to say that, insofar as the two sides are in conflict, the accused's account is untrue. Equally, a *Goodway* direction is not required simply because the jury may reject the evidence of an accused about a central issue in the case, because that situation is covered by the general direction on the burden and standard of proof (*Hill* [1996] Crim LR 419).

F1.27 As to the first situation identified in *Burge*, in *Lesley* [1996] 1 Cr App R 39 it was held that where evidence is adduced in support of an alibi, the Judicial Studies Board specimen direction (which then ended with the words 'An alibi is sometimes invented to bolster a genuine defence': see now the *Crown Court Compendium* (July 2020), ch. 18-2) should routinely be given. It was also held, however, that whether failure to do so renders a conviction unsafe depends on the facts of each case and the strength of the evidence. The accused had served an alibi notice but did not call the person named in it and gave no evidence in person. The prosecution inferentially invited the jury to conclude that the alibi was false and therefore evidence of guilt. Taking account of the fact that the chief prosecution witness was not altogether satisfactory, it was held that failure to give the direction rendered the verdict unsafe (cf. *Drake* [1996] Crim LR 109, in which the proviso was applied). See also *Peacock* [1998] Crim LR 681, in which D, when first interviewed, said that he had spent the evening of the robbery with his girlfriend, but at trial gave evidence that he had spent the evening with his former girlfriend and that what he had said initially was not a lie but a mistake. *Lesley* was distinguished in *Harron* [1996] 2 Cr App R 457, where it was held that the judge had not erred in failing to direct the jury that an alibi is sometimes falsified to bolster a genuine defence because the central issue in the case was whether the prosecution witnesses were lying or whether D was. Lies had not played a part in the way the Crown had put their case nor constituted a matter which the jury might have taken into account separate from their determination of the main issue, which turned upon the truthfulness of the witnesses. If they accepted the evidence for the Crown it necessarily involved a conclusion that D's evidence was untrue, and that he was lying. See also *Gultutan* [2006] EWCA Crim 207 and *House* [1994] Crim LR 682.

F1.28 As to the third situation identified in *Burge*, in *Genus* [1996] Crim LR 502, where the accused claimed to have been acting under duress and the prosecution case was that the accused had told lies to the police and in evidence on collateral issues (i.e. on issues not directly relevant to the question of duress) and that the jury should, by reason of those lies, disbelieve their account of acting under duress, it was held that the case cried out for a *Lucas* direction. *Zaman* [2017] EWCA Crim 1783, [2018] 1 Cr App R (S) 26 (177) was decided on the same basis as *Genus* [1996] Crim LR 502, but *Genus* was not cited. The prosecution case was that the evidence of D on the central facts in issue was confabulated and that he was an inherently untruthful man, as illustrated by the lies he had told in interview. It was held that the jury were entitled to assess D's credibility against his record of alleged lying and that a *Lucas* direction had been entirely appropriate.

F1.29 In *Robinson* [1996] Crim LR 417, where the judge in his summing-up gave considerable prominence to the issue whether D had lied about when his defence was first made known to the police, it was held that the case fell clearly within the fourth situation identified in *Burge*.

As to the fourth situation, the Court of Appeal is unlikely to be persuaded that there was a real danger of the jury treating a particular lie as evidence of guilt if defence counsel at the trial did not alert the judge to that danger and ask whether a direction should be given to meet it (per Kennedy LJ in *Burge* [1996] 1 Cr App R 163 at p. 174). The failure of defence counsel to raise the matter at the trial may also be taken into account in cases in which both the third and the fourth situations identified in *Burge* arise, and may lead the Court of Appeal to conclude that the matter was not a large or important feature of the case and that the absence of the usual direction did not make the conviction unsafe (*McGuinness* [1999] Crim LR 318).

F1.30 **Situations where a *Lucas* Direction is Unnecessary** A *Lucas* direction is required where a lie is directly related in some way to the offence charged (for example, a lie which amounts to a false alibi; see *Smith* [1995] Crim LR 305), or is relevant to the credibility of the accused but is also relied upon to support evidence of guilt (*Cooper* [2018] EWCA Crim 1454). If a lie is relevant only to the credibility of the accused, a direction is generally not required (*Landon* [1995] Crim LR 338) but may be appropriate in exceptional circumstances, for example where the lie figures largely in the case and there is a risk that the jury may think that the accused must be guilty because the accused lied (*Tucker* [1994] Crim LR 683). See also *Genus* [1996] Crim LR 502 and *Zaman* [2017] EWCA Crim 1783, [2018] 1 Cr App R (S) 26 (177), at **F1.28**. In *Odum-Toland* [2020] EWCA Crim 124, the case turned wholly on the jury's assessment of D's credibility as to his state of mind and the judge had directed the jury that a rejection of his explanation for a lie was not enough to prove the case against him. On this basis, it was held that a full *Lucas* direction, incorporating the rubric that people may lie for a number of reasons, was not required. In *Murray* [2016] EWCA Crim 1051, [2016] 4 WLR 142, where it was not suggested to the jury that a lie told in interview could be used to test D's honesty or as evidence of guilt, it was held that a *Lucas* direction was unnecessary and would have served only to confuse the jury. In *Middleton* [2001] Crim LR 251, it was said *per curiam* that if the question arises at trial whether a *Lucas* direction is required, it will generally be more useful to consider the application to the facts of the case of the principles derived from the many cases on the point, rather than to trawl through the cases themselves. The court stressed that the point of a *Lucas* direction is to warn against the 'forbidden reasoning' that lies necessarily demonstrate guilt. Where there is no risk of such forbidden reasoning on the part of the jury, a direction is unnecessary. See also, applying *Middleton*, *Williams* [2012] EWCA Crim 2516, where there was no risk of the forbidden reasoning and a *Lucas* direction might have advanced an aspect of the case against D which had not previously been put forward. According to *Middleton*, a direction is also generally unnecessary in relation to lies told by an accused in evidence, because the position is covered by the general directions on the burden and standard of proof. In cases where a direction could be given about a lie told in evidence, a judge may not be obliged to give a direction, especially if it would do more harm than good (*Nyanteh* [2005] EWCA Crim 686). In *Bhagchandka* [2016] EWCA Crim 700 it was held that: *Lucas* directions were introduced as a safeguard in cases where the Crown was relying upon lies told as a specific support for their case; they are not required in every case where a lie or potential lie, of whatever significance to the issues, can be extracted from the evidence; and there is danger from a defence point of view that to highlight a peripheral matter only serves to elevate its importance in the minds of the jury.

A *Lucas* direction is not likely to be required in the many cases of handling stolen goods in which the accused denies knowledge or belief that the goods were stolen, including those in which the accused gives different and inconsistent versions as to how the goods were obtained, and the Crown's case is that the accused is not telling the truth (*Barnett* [2002] EWCA Crim 454, [2002] 2 Cr App R 11 (168)).

It is usually unhelpful to give both a *Lucas* direction and a direction as to possible inferences under the CJPO 1994, s. 34 (see **F20.26** ***et seq.***). The judge should select and adapt the direction more appropriate to the facts and issues in the case. If the explanation given by an accused for failure to mention a fact is said to be a lie, a s. 34 direction alone will suffice. The explanation should be incorporated into that direction. In such a case, it would be unnecessary, confusing and unduly favourable to the defence for the judge to give the usual *Lucas* examples of innocent reasons for lying (*Hackett* [2011] EWCA Crim 380, [2011] 2 Cr App R 3 (35) and *Spottiswood* [2019] EWCA Crim 949, applying *Rana* [2007] EWCA Crim 2261).

Continuance of Events over Period of Time

Evidence of the speed at which someone was driving at a particular point in time may be admitted to prove the speed at which the person was driving a short time earlier or, as the case may be, later (see, respectively, *Dalloz* (1908) 1 Cr App R 258 and *Beresford v St Albans Justices* (1905) 22 TLR 1). **F1.31**

MULTIPLE ADMISSIBILITY

Evidence which is admissible in law for one purpose cannot be excluded because it is inadmissible for some other purpose (although if it is tendered by the prosecution it may be excluded as a matter of discretion). '[I]t often happens, both in civil and criminal cases, that evidence is tendered on several alternative grounds, and yet it is never objected that if on any ground it is admissible, that ground must not prevail, because on some other ground it would be inadmissible and prejudicial' (*Bond* [1906] 2 KB 389, per Jelf J at pp. 411–2). The principle has attracted the somewhat misleading label of 'multiple admissibility' (J.H. Wigmore, *Evidence in Trials at Common Law*, vol. 1 (revised by Peter Tillers) (1983), sect. 13). A typical example would be a case in which evidence of a confession which implicates both its maker and a co-accused is admitted in evidence against its maker, having been ruled inadmissible evidence against the co-accused. As to confessions implicating co-accused, see further **F18.80** and **F17.37**. **F1.32**

Where the principle applies, it has been said that 'it is usual for the judge (not always very successfully) to caution the jury against being biased by treating the evidence in the objectionable sense' (*Bond* [1906] 2 KB 389 per Jelf J at p. 412). Nowadays such a warning is often mandatory: see, e.g., *Gunewardene* [1951] KB 600 (a confession admissible for use only against its maker and not against any co-accused); *Flicker* [1995] Crim LR 493 (statements in which a confession is inextricably linked with material relating to the accused's propensity to offend); and *Norman* [2006] EWCA Crim 1662 (evidence of the discovery of drugs on a previous occasion inadmissible on the issue of intention to supply drugs subsequently found in the same place). In the case of a confession tendered by the prosecution and implicating both its maker and the co-accused, see also the *Crown Court Compendium* (July 2020), ch. 14-15, paras. 7 to 11. One solution is to edit the confession by omitting references to the co-accused or by replacing their names with letters of the alphabet or expressions such as 'another person' (see *Rogers* [1971] Crim LR 413; *Silcott* [1987] Crim LR 765; and generally **F18.90**). Alternatively, but only in exceptional circumstances, the judge may find it necessary to order separate trials for the accused (*Lake* (1976) 64 Cr App R 172).

CONDITIONAL ADMISSIBILITY

The relevance of a particular item of evidence may become apparent only if considered together with other evidence. However, because evidence is given in order and by one witness at a time, **F1.33** it often happens that the other evidence can only be adduced at a later stage. Prima facie, therefore, the first item of evidence is irrelevant, and for that reason inadmissible. In these circumstances, upon an undertaking by counsel to demonstrate the relevance of the first item by introducing the further evidence, the court may allow the first item of evidence to be admitted conditionally or *de bene esse*. If, notwithstanding the introduction of the further evidence, the first item remains irrelevant, the judge will direct the jury to disregard it. For example, in the case of a conspiracy, if the judge is satisfied that a statement was made by one conspirator that is reasonably open to the interpretation that it was made in furtherance of the common design, it is admissible in evidence against another party to the conspiracy, provided that the judge is also satisfied that there is sufficient further evidence beyond the statement itself to show that the other party was a party to the conspiracy. Admitting evidence of such a statement may be conditional upon the adduction of the further evidence. If it transpires that there is insufficient further evidence, or no such evidence, the statement should be disregarded (see generally **F17.70** *et seq*.). See also the cases on accusations made in the presence of the accused, the relevance of which depends on evidence of the accused's reaction to them (see Lords Atkinson and Reading in *Christie* [1914] AC 545 at pp. 554 and 565 respectively and **F18.99**). In an extreme case, where great prejudice may be caused to an accused, a warning by the judge may be insufficient, and it may be necessary for the judge to discharge the jury.

THE BEST EVIDENCE RULE

As an Inclusionary Rule

F1.34 In *Omychund v Barker* (1745) 1 Atk 21, in which depositions of Hindu witnesses were admitted in evidence, notwithstanding that they did not accept the authority of the Gospel, Lord Hardwicke said (at p. 49), '... there is but one general rule of evidence, the best that the nature of the case will admit'. This case suggests an inclusionary rule permitting the admission of the best evidence available in the circumstances of the case, but under the modern law of evidence, there exists no general rule to this effect.

As an Exclusionary Rule

F1.35 The best evidence rule is now all but defunct. In *Francis* (1874) LR 2 CCR 128, in which D was indicted for false pretences, in that he falsely represented a ring to be a diamond ring, evidence was admitted of his attempts on other occasions to obtain money on a cluster ring in order to prove guilty knowledge. Rejecting an argument that because the cluster ring itself was not produced in court, evidence of witnesses who saw it and swore to its being false had been improperly admitted, Lord Coleridge CJ said: 'No doubt if there was not admissible evidence that this ring was false it ought not to have been left to the jury; but though the non-production of the article may afford ground for observation more or less weighty, according to circumstances, it only goes to the weight, not to the admissibility, of the evidence'.

However, very occasionally reliance is placed upon the rule. In *Quinn* [1962] 2 QB 245, on a charge of keeping a disorderly house, arising out of the performance of allegedly indecent striptease acts, one of the accused sought to put in evidence a film made three months after the events complained of and purporting to depict the acts performed, together with evidence that the acts depicted in the film were identical to the acts performed. It was held that the evidence had been properly rejected. Ashworth J said (at p. 257), '... it was admitted that some of the movements in the film (for instance, that of a snake used in one scene) could not be said with any certainty to be the same movements as were made at the material time. In our judgment, this objection goes not only to weight, as was argued, but to admissibility: it is not the best evidence.' Compare *Thomas* [1986] Crim LR 682, a case of reckless driving in which a video recording of the route taken by D was ruled admissible to remove the need for maps and photographs and to convey a more accurate picture of the roads in question; and also *Metcalfe* [2016] EWCA Crim 681, [2016] 2 Cr App R 21 (297), where an expert called to give her opinion on how a deceased person had come to suffer injuries and be where she was found was allowed to use animations, being no more than an illustration of her opinion and not independent scientific evidence. See also *Moore* [2017] EWCA Crim 1304, at **F11.1**. The reasoning in *Quinn* [1962] 2 QB 245 is difficult to reconcile with the clear statement of Lord Denning MR in *Garton v Hunter* [1969] 2 QB 37. Referring to the best evidence rule, his lordship said (at p. 44):

> That old rule has gone by the board long ago. The only remaining instance of it that I know is that if an original document is available in your hands, you must produce it. You cannot give secondary evidence by producing a copy. Nowadays we do not confine ourselves to the best evidence. We admit all relevant evidence. The goodness or badness of it goes only to weight, and not to admissibility.

See also Ackner LJ in *Kajala v Noble* (1982) 75 Cr App R 149 at p. 152, *Governor of Pentonville Prison, ex parte Osman* [1990] 3 All ER 701 at p. 308 and *DPP v Sugden* [2018] EWHC 544 (Admin), [2018] 2 Cr App R 8 (101) at [23]; and cf. *Springsteen v Masquerade Music Ltd* [2001] EWCA Civ 563, discussed at **F8.4**. As to proof of the contents of documents, see **F8**.

QUESTIONS OF LAW AND FACT

In a Trial on Indictment: General Principles

As a general rule, questions of law (including practice) are for the judge, and questions of fact for the jury. In trials on indictment without a jury, the judge decides all questions of both law and fact and, if the accused is convicted, must give a judgment which states the reasons for the conviction (CJA 2003, s. 48(3) and (5)). Lay magistrates, when sitting with a judge in the Crown Court, are also judges of the court (Senior Courts Act 1981, ss. 8 and 73); they should participate in all questions to be determined by the court, including the factual aspect of any question relating to the admissibility of evidence, but must accept the ruling of the judge on any question of law (*Orpin* [1975] QB 283). In jury trials, questions of law for the judge include those relating to: **F1.36**

(a) where the court has determined that an accused is unfit to plead, whether the accused did the act or made the omission charged as the offence — see **D12.10**;
(b) challenges to jurors — see **D13.22** ***et seq.***;
(c) the discharge of a juror or the whole jury — see **D13.50** ***et seq.***;
(d) the competence of persons to give sworn or unsworn evidence — see **F4.2** ***et seq.***;
(e) the admissibility of evidence;
(f) the withdrawal of an issue from the jury;
(g) submissions of no case to answer — see **D16.53** ***et seq.***;
(h) the numerous issues on which the jury should be directed in the summing-up, such as the substantive law governing the charge, the burden and standard of proof, the use which the jury is entitled to make of the evidence adduced, the operation of any presumptions, the nature of, and any requirement for, corroboration, etc. — see further **D18.21** ***et seq.*** and **F5**; and
(i) matters ancillary to the trial itself, such as questions of bail, costs and leave to appeal.

Questions of fact for the jury include:

(a) whether the accused stands mute of malice or by visitation of God;
(b) the credibility of the witnesses called and the weight of the evidence adduced; and
(c) whether, applying the burden and standard of proof applicable to the case, they are satisfied as to the existence or non-existence of the facts in issue.

In jury trials, questions of fact which fall to be determined by the *judge* are whether the accused is fit to plead (see **D12.9**); the existence or non-existence of preliminary facts, i.e.

facts which must be proved or disproved as a condition precedent to the admissibility of certain types of evidence; the sufficiency of evidence (in deciding whether an issue should be withdrawn from the jury); and the evaluation of evidence adduced by the parties (for the purpose of commenting on its weight in summing up to the jury). There are also a number of special cases, dealt with below, in which questions of fact fall to be determined, either wholly or in part, by the judge.

F1.37 **Construction of Words** As a general rule, the construction of ordinary words in a statute is a question for the tribunal of fact (*Brutus v Cozens* [1973] AC 854 — 'insulting behaviour' under the Public Order Act 1936, s. 5; *Chambers v DPP* [1995] Crim LR 896 — 'disorderly behaviour' under the Public Order Act 1986, s. 5; *Feely* [1973] QB 530 — 'dishonestly' under the Theft Act 1968, s. 1(1); *Harris* (1968) 84 Cr App R 75 — 'knowledge or belief' under the Theft Act 1968, s. 22(1); *Garwood* [1987] 1 All ER 1032 — 'menaces' under the Theft Act 1968, s. 21(1); *Howard* [1993] Crim LR 213 — an 'explosive substance' under the OAPA 1861, s. 29; and *Kirk* [2006] EWCA Crim 725 — 'indecent or obscene' under the Postal Services Act 2000, s. 85(4)). Thus, although a judge is perfectly at liberty to direct a jury that it is not open to them to give to a word a particular meaning (being a meaning so unreasonable that if it were adopted and the accused convicted, the Court of Appeal would treat the verdict as perverse), normally the judge should not direct the jury as to the meaning of an ordinary word. The exceptions to this rule are: where the word has been used in a context which indicates that it is being used in an unusual sense (per Lord Reid in *Brutus v Cozens* [1973] AC 854 at p. 861); where it has acquired a special meaning as a result of the authorities (e.g., the word 'fraudulently' in the Larceny Act 1916, s. 1(1) — see *Feely* [1973] QB 530); and where it is capable of bearing two different meanings (e.g., the word 'substantially' in the Homicide Act 1957, s. 2(1)(b) — per Lord Hughes in *Golds* [2016] UKSC 61, [2016] 1 WLR 5231 at [27] and [38]).

When a statutory provision is dealing with a technical subject and can only be understood with the assistance of an expert, the words used must be given their ordinary and natural meaning to a person qualified to understand them, and evidence as to that meaning may be received from an appropriate expert (*Couzens* [1992] Crim LR 822).

As to the construction of *documents*, this is generally a matter of fact for determination by the jury, with the exception of binding agreements between parties and all forms of parliamentary and local government legislation, which are for the judge to construe as a matter of law. The City Code on Take-overs and Mergers sufficiently resembles legislation as to require construction of its provisions by a judge (*Spens* [1991] 4 All ER 421). However, if the legislation contains straightforward words which can be given their ordinary meaning, there will be nothing requiring any judicial interpretation as to their meaning and effect (*Pouladian-Kari* [2013] EWCA Crim 158).

F1.38 **Foreign Law** Questions relating to the law of any jurisdiction other than that of England and Wales are questions of fact to be determined, on the evidence adduced, by the judge alone.

Administration of Justice Act 1920, s. 15

> Where for the purpose of disposing of any action or other matter which is being tried by a judge with a jury in any court in England or Wales, it is necessary to ascertain the law of any other country which is applicable to the facts of the case, any question as to the effect of the evidence given with respect to that law shall, instead of being submitted to the jury, be decided by the judge alone.

Section 15 of the 1920 Act applies to criminal proceedings (*Hammer* [1923] 2 KB 786). As to the proof of foreign law, see **F8.22** and **F11.27**.

F1.39 **Autrefois Acquit or Convict** Where an accused pleads autrefois acquit or convict, it shall be for the judge, without the presence of a jury, to decide the issue (CJA 1988, s. 122). See also **D12.20** *et seq.*

Perjury The question whether a statement on which perjury is assigned was 'material' in the judicial proceeding in which it was made is a question of law to be determined by the court of trial (Perjury Act 1911, s. 11(6)). **F1.40**

Duty of Care in Cases of Manslaughter In a case of manslaughter by gross negligence, the existence of a duty of care or a duty to act, if in dispute, is a question of law, but the question whether the facts establish the existence of the duty is for the jury (*Evans* [2009] EWCA Crim 650, [2009] 1 WLR 1999). However, in the case of corporate manslaughter, whether a particular organisation owes a duty of care to a particular individual is a question of law and the judge must make any findings of fact necessary to decide that question (CMCHA 2007, s. 2(5); see **B1.72**). **F1.41**

In Summary Trials

In the case of proceedings presided over by lay justices, the justices decide all questions of both law and fact, but on questions of law, including the law of evidence, should seek and accept the advice of the justice's legal adviser. As to the duty and role of the legal adviser in a summary trial, see CrimPR 24.14 (see Supplement, **R24.14**) and CrimPD VI, paras. 24A.1 to 24A.18 (see Supplement, **CPD.24A**), and **D22.80** ***et seq***. In theory, district judges (magistrates' courts) are in the same position as lay justices. In practice, however, the district judge will be the more experienced lawyer, so that the occasions for asking for advice will be quite rare. **F1.42**

HEARINGS ON THE *VOIR DIRE*

General Principles

The hearing on the *voir dire*, or trial within a trial, is the procedure whereby the court determines disputed preliminary facts, i.e. facts which must be established as a condition precedent to the admission of certain items of evidence. The procedure is set out at **D16.41** to **D16.52** (trial on indictment) and **D22.44** (summary trial). **F1.43**

Concerning what evidence is admissible for the purpose of proving or disproving disputed preliminary facts, there is some authority to suggest that the judge is bound by the exclusionary rules of evidence which apply in relation to the admissibility of evidence at the trial proper. Thus, at common law, it has been held that it is wrong for a judge to determine the admissibility of a confession on the basis of the depositions (*Chadwick* (1934) 24 Cr App R 138). Most of the decisions concern specific statutory provisions governing the admissibility of evidence. In *O'Loughlin* [1988] 3 All ER 431, a decision on the conditions of admissibility imposed by the CJA 1925, s. 13(3) (now repealed), Kenneth Jones J ruled that in a criminal statute, unless other methods of proof are specified (e.g., 'by information or belief'), 'proof' means proof by admissible evidence. This principle applies to the proof of fear for the purposes of the CJA 2003, s. 116(2)(e) (see discussion at **F17.18**). However, concerning the preliminary facts in the CJA 2003, s. 117, relating to the compilation of business or other documents, in appropriate circumstances they may be inferred by the judge from the documents themselves (*O'Connor* [2010] EWCA Crim 2287).

In trials on indictment, the various matters which may fall to be determined in a hearing on the *voir dire* include the following: **F1.44**

(a) the competence of a witness (see **F4.2** and **F4.24**);
(b) the admissibility of a confession (see **F18.62** to **F18.74**) or some other variety of admissible hearsay, such as a statement made by someone who does not give evidence 'through fear' (see the CJA 2003, s. 116(2)(e), **F17.8** and *Shabir* [2012] EWCA Crim 2564 at [64], approved in *Harvey* [2014] EWCA Crim 54);
(c) the admissibility of a recording (see *Robson* [1972] 2 All ER 699 and **F8.53**);

(d) the admissibility of a statement contained in a document produced by a computer (see **F8.49**); and
(e) the admissibility of a plea of guilty against an accused who subsequently changes plea to not guilty (see **F18.3**).

Cases in which a Hearing on *Voir Dire* Usually Not Required

F1.45 A hearing on the *voir dire* is not normally required to determine the admissibility of evidence relating to an identification parade or, it is submitted, any other identification procedure. In *Walshe* (1980) 74 Cr App R 85 Boreham J said (at p. 87):

> ... those representing the applicant drew some close analogy between the admissibility of evidence of an identification parade and the admissibility of a voluntary statement. But those are very different matters. As soon as a statement is challenged the law places on the Crown the burden of showing that it is admissible by proving that it was voluntarily made. [See now the PACE 1984, s. 76(2).] That is a separate and different matter. Here there was no burden on the Crown to prove the admissibility of the evidence relating to the identification parade and what flowed from it. It was clearly admissible evidence and should have been admitted. Its quality is, of course, another matter, to be considered by the jury.

In *Beveridge* (1987) 85 Cr App R 255, it was argued on appeal that in the light of the PACE 1984, s. 78, *Walshe* could no longer stand. It was held, dismissing the appeal, that where a question arises under s. 78 as to the admissibility of identification parade evidence, although there may be rare occasions when it will be desirable to hold a trial within a trial, in general the judge should decide on the basis of the depositions, statements and submissions of counsel.

F1.46 In *Flemming* (1987) 86 Cr App R 32, a decision under the law prior to the 1984 Act, the appellant argued that identification evidence was inadmissible on the grounds, *inter alia*, that the identification at the police station was carried out in circumstances which contravened Home Office Circular No. 109 of 1978. It was submitted that the result was that the probative value of the evidence was minimal compared to its prejudicial effect, so that it would be unfair for the evidence to be admitted. The Court of Appeal held that it was quite unnecessary to hold a trial within a trial for this purpose. Woolf LJ (referring to one of the guidelines laid down by Lord Widgery CJ in *Turnbull* [1977] QB 224, at p. 229, namely that when, in the opinion of the judge, the quality of the identifying evidence is poor, the judge should withdraw the case from the jury unless there is other evidence which goes to support its correctness) said, at pp. 36–7:

> In the normal way the trial judge will make his assessment whether he needs to take the action referred to by the Lord Chief Justice either at the end of the case for the prosecution or after all the evidence in the case has been called. There may be exceptional cases where the position is so clear on the depositions that he can give a ruling at an earlier stage. However, the trial judge should not decide the matter by holding a preliminary trial, as in this case, before the evidence for the prosecution has been placed before the jury.
>
> It is, of course, true that the trial judge has a residual discretion to exclude evidence which is strictly admissible if he comes to the conclusion that its probative value is outweighed by its prejudicial effect, so that its admission would be unfair to the defendant. However, this residual discretion cannot justify the holding of trials within a trial as occurred here. Issues of this sort can be satisfactorily dealt with by the judge perusing the depositions, together with any facts that are common ground between the prosecution and the defence.

See also *Martin* [1994] Crim LR 218.

Application to Summary Trial

F1.47 There can be no question of a trial within a trial in proceedings before magistrates, because the function of the *voir dire* is to allow the tribunal of law to decide a point of law in the absence of the tribunal of fact, and magistrates are judges of both fact and law.

It is impossible to lay down any general rule as to when the question of admissibility should be determined by magistrates, or as to when their decision on it should be announced, every case being different (*F v Chief Constable of Kent* [1982] Crim LR 682). These principles, insofar as they relate to confessions, are subject to the statutory constraint of the PACE 1984, s. 76(2), and the decision in *Liverpool Juvenile Court, ex parte R* [1988] QB 1 (see **F1.48**). However, subject to this and other similar statutory constraints, there is still no general rule as to when admissibility should be determined and the decision on it announced. In *Epping and Ongar Justices, ex parte Manby* [1986] Crim LR 555, D, convicted as the proprietor of a firm on whose behalf an overweight vehicle had been driven, contested the admissibility of a certificate of a police officer to the effect that D had admitted responsibility for the vehicle (see **C2.17**), and sought leave to have the question resolved as a preliminary issue. It was held that the justices had not erred in refusing the application and admitting the evidence as providing a prima facie case for D to deal with later, if he saw fit.

Admissibility of Confession If, during the course of a summary trial, the defence, before the close of the prosecution case, challenge the admissibility of a confession under the PACE 1984, s. 76(2) (see **F18.8**), the magistrates are bound by the terms of that subsection to hold a trial within a trial (*Liverpool Juvenile Court, ex parte R* [1988] QB 1, considered in this and other related respects at **F18.64**, **F18.66**, **F18.67** and **F18.72**). When that happens, it is unnecessary to repeat the evidence in the trial proper, because magistrates are judges of both fact and law. **F1.48**

Challenging Admissibility under the PACE 1984, s. 78 Where the defence make a submission that the magistrates should exercise their discretion to exclude evidence under s. 78, they are not entitled to have that issue settled as a preliminary issue in a trial within a trial (*Vel v Chief Constable of North Wales* (1987) 151 JP 510). In *Halawa v Federation against Copyright Theft* [1995] 1 Cr App R 21, it was held that the duty of a magistrate, on an application under s. 78, is either to deal with the issue when it arises or to leave the decision until the end of the hearing, the objective being to secure a trial that is fair and just to both parties. Thus in some cases the accused will be given the opportunity to exclude the evidence before giving evidence on the main issues, because if denied that opportunity the accused's right to remain silent on the main issues will be impaired, but in most cases it is better for the whole of the prosecution case, including the disputed evidence, to be heard first, because under s. 78 regard should be had to 'all the circumstances' and fairness to the prosecution requires that the whole of its case, in this regard, be before the court. In deciding, the court may take account of the extent of the issues to be raised by the evidence of the accused in the trial within a trial. A trial within a trial may be appropriate if the issues are limited, but not if it is likely to be protracted and to raise issues which will need to be re-examined in the trial itself. **F1.49**

Where there is a s. 78 challenge to evidence of statements made by an accused, it is normally desirable in the interests of justice for the court to hear the evidence in question and to have canvassed in questioning any circumstances which it is said would render its admission unfair. Where the justices resolve to exclude it, they should then consider, after seeking the views of the parties, whether the substantive hearing should be conducted by a differently constituted bench (*DPP v Lawrence* [2007] EWHC 2154 (Admin), [2008] 1 Cr App R 10 (147) at [26]).

Section F2 Evidence Unlawfully, Improperly or Unfairly Obtained and the Discretion to Exclude Evidence

ADMISSIBILITY OF EVIDENCE OBTAINED UNLAWFULLY, IMPROPERLY OR UNFAIRLY

General Rule of Admissibility

F2.1 Where evidence has been obtained illegally, the court may exercise its power, in appropriate circumstances, to stay proceedings (see *Warren v A-G for Jersey* [2011] UKPC 10, [2012] 1 AC 22, considered at **D3.108**). However, where proceedings have not been stayed then, subject to the exceptions considered in **F2.2** to **F2.6**, evidence obtained unlawfully, improperly or unfairly is admissible as a matter of *law*. (Concerning the existence and extent of the *discretion* to exclude evidence thus obtained, see the PACE 1984, s. 78, at **F2.7** ***et seq.*** and the common-law discretion at **F2.36** ***et seq.***) In *Kuruma, Son of Kaniu v The Queen* [1955] AC 197, Lord Goddard CJ, on behalf of the Board, said (at p. 203):

> ... the test to be applied in considering whether evidence is admissible is whether it is relevant to the matters in issue. If it is, it is admissible and the court is not concerned with how the evidence was obtained. While this proposition may not have been stated in so many words in any English case there are decisions which support it, and in their lordships' opinion it is plainly right in principle.

Referring to this pronouncement in *Jeffrey v Black* [1978] QB 490, Lord Widgery CJ said (at p. 497): 'I have not the least doubt that we must firmly accept the proposition that an irregularity in obtaining evidence does not render the evidence inadmissible'. Evidence is admissible as a matter of law, therefore, if it has been obtained by any of the following means:

(a) Theft (*Leatham* (1861) 8 Cox CC 498 per Crompton J at p. 501).
(b) Unlawful search of persons (*Jones v Owen* (1870) 34 JP 759; *Kuruma, Son of Kaniu v The Queen* [1955] AC 197).
(c) Unlawful search of premises (*Jeffrey v Black* [1978] QB 490).
(d) The use of *agents provocateurs* (*Sang* [1980] AC 402).
(e) Eavesdropping (*Stewart* [1970] 1 All ER 689; *Keeton* (1970) 54 Cr App R 267; *Maqsud Ali* [1966] 1 QB 688; *Senat* (1968) 52 Cr App R 282).
(f) Invasion of privacy (*Khan* [1997] AC 558, in which evidence of an incriminating conversation was obtained by means of a secret electronic surveillance device). See also the RIPA 2000 and the IPA 2016 at **D1.198** ***et seq.*** and **F2.33** to **F2.35**.

In *Abdurahman* [2019] EWCA Crim 2239, [2020] 1 Cr App R 27 (439), the Court of Appeal, rejecting the apparent view to the contrary of the majority of the Grand Chamber in *Ibrahim v UK* [2016] ECHR 750, confirmed (at [111](d) and [121]) that under the Strasbourg jurisprudence the admission of evidence obtained unlawfully (including in particular real evidence discovered on the basis of an improperly conducted interview) is not necessarily unfair, save in the special case identified in *Gäfgen v Germany* (2009) 48 EHRR 13 (253) (see **F2.5**). The Court held that in this respect English law, under which facts discovered as a result of a coerced confession are, subject to the PACE 1984, s. 78, admissible in evidence, marches in step with the Convention (see *HM Advocate v P* [2011] UKSC 44 at [33]). See also **F18.86**, **A7.24** and **D1.62**.

Procedures for Obtaining Evidence Prescribed by Statute

Although in general the court is not concerned with how evidence is obtained, where it is a necessary step towards procuring a conviction for an offence that the evidence be obtained in accordance with a procedure prescribed by statute, evidence obtained other than in accordance with that procedure will not be admissible. See *Scott v Baker* [1969] 1 QB 659 (the procedure for providing a specimen in relation to an offence of drink driving), approved in *Spicer v Holt* [1977] AC 987 and distinguished in *Public Prosecution Service of Northern Ireland v Elliott* [2013] UKSC 32, [2013] 2 Cr App R 17 (180) (see **F3.70**); and contrast *Trump* (1979) 70 Cr App R 300, *Adams* [1980] QB 575 and *Tunbridge Wells Borough Council v Quietlynn Ltd* [1985] Crim LR 594. In *Murray v DPP* [1993] RTR 209, where D had not been warned, in accordance with the RTA 1988, s. 7(7), that a failure to provide a specimen of breath might make him liable to prosecution, it was held that evidence of the specimen taken from him should have been excluded. In *Twigg* [2019] EWCA Crim 1553, [2019] 1 WLR 6533, a healthcare professional, not complying with the RTA 1988, s. 7(3)(c), failed to advise the police that D's condition might be due to some drug. It was held that evidence of a blood sample taken from D was not automatically inadmissible. *Murray* was distinguished on the basis that under the RTOA 1988, s. 15(4), a sample is to be 'disregarded' if not obtained by consent and the Court in *Murray* considered that the failure to give the s. 7(7) warning vitiated consent. According to *Twigg*, *Murray* is not authority for the proposition that evidence of a specimen is automatically rendered inadmissible by *any* breach of *any* of the procedures associated with the obtaining of specimens under the RTA 1988, s. 7. **F2.2**

Confessions

If it is represented to the court that a confession made by an accused person was or may have been obtained by the means set out in the PACE 1984, s. 76(2), the court shall not allow the confession to be given in evidence against the accused, except to the extent that the prosecution prove to the court beyond reasonable doubt that the confession was not so obtained. Concerning the admissibility of both confessions and facts discovered in consequence of inadmissible confessions, see generally **F18**. **F2.3**

Evidence Obtained by Torture or Inhuman or Degrading Treatment

If it is represented to the court that a confession made by an accused was or may have been obtained by oppression, which is defined to include torture, the court shall not allow the confession to be given in evidence against the accused except insofar as the prosecution prove to the court beyond reasonable doubt that the confession (notwithstanding that it may be true) was not so obtained (see **F18.8** to **F18.10**). At common law, however, there is a broader general principle, established in *A v Secretary of State for the Home Department (No. 2)* [2005] UKHL 71, [2006] 2 AC 221, that evidence obtained by torture is inadmissible. In that case, according to Lord Bingham, as a matter of constitutional principle, evidence obtained by torturing another human being may not lawfully be admitted against a party to proceedings in a British court, irrespective of where, or by whom, or on whose authority the torture was inflicted. His lordship said (at [52]): **F2.4**

> The principles of the common law, standing alone... compel the exclusion of third party torture evidence as unreliable, unfair, offensive to ordinary standards of humanity and decency and incompatible with the principles which should animate a tribunal seeking to administer justice. But the principles of the common law do not stand alone. Effect must be given to the European Convention, which itself takes account of the all but universal consensus embodied in the Torture Convention.

The House of Lords did not clearly define torture for these purposes, but Lord Hoffmann (at [97]) expressed a preference for the definition adopted by Parliament in the CJA 1988, s. 134, namely the infliction of severe pain or suffering on someone by a public official in the performance or purported performance of official duties. The House also held that a conventional approach to the burden of proof was inappropriate in the context of a hearing before the Special Immigration Appeals Commission (SIAC) (in which, for example, the appellant may not see the statement or know what it says and may not know the name or identity of its author) and, by a majority, that the SIAC should refuse to admit the evidence if it concludes, on a balance of probabilities, that it was obtained by torture. However, it is submitted that in a criminal trial, if the defence can establish a prima facie case that evidence on which the prosecution seek to rely was obtained by torture, the burden should be on the prosecution to prove beyond reasonable doubt that it was not so obtained.

F2.5 Evidence obtained by inhuman or degrading treatment contrary to the ECHR, Article 3, and in breach of the privilege against self-incrimination, may also fall to be excluded (*Jalloh v Germany* (2007) 44 EHRR 32 (667)). Incriminating real evidence recovered as a direct result of torture should never be admitted, but evidence secured as an indirect result of statements made and obtained by inhuman treatment may be admitted if it is only accessory in securing a conviction and its admission does not compromise defence rights (*Gäfgen v Germany* (2009) 48 EHRR 13 (253)). See also **A7.86**. It is arguable that evidence should be excluded if obtained as a result of secret detention, but the argument for exclusion is not as strong as in relation to torture, there being no equivalent of the Torture Convention, Article 15, in relation to secret detention (*XX v Secretary of State for the Home Department* [2012] EWCA Civ 742, [2013] QB 656 at [39], *obiter*).

Privileged Documents

F2.6 If a document protected by legal professional privilege (or secondary evidence of it) has been obtained by the opponent of the party entitled to assert the privilege, the document (or secondary evidence of it) will be admissible in evidence. (However, see also the PACE 1984, ss. 9 and 10, and *R (A) v Central Criminal Court* [2017] EWHC 70 (Admin), [2017] 1 WLR 3567, considered at **F10.33**). This principle applies whether the document was obtained by the inadvertence of the party entitled to assert the privilege or by the wrongful act of the party's opponent (*Calcraft v Guest* [1898] 1 QB 759; *Tompkins* (1977) 67 Cr App R 181). In civil proceedings, the party in whom the privilege is vested may apply for an injunction to restrain the party's opponent from making any use of the confidential information obtained in the document (*Lord Ashburton v Pape* [1913] 2 Ch 469). However, the principle of *Lord Ashburton v Pape* cannot be used to prevent the prosecution from tendering relevant evidence in a public prosecution (see *Butler v Board of Trade* [1971] Ch 680, a decision which is consistent with the general rule that criminal courts are not concerned with the method by which the evidence they consider has been obtained). See also *K* [2009] EWCA Crim 1640, [2010] QB 343, considered at **F10.45**.

In *ITC Film Distributors Ltd v Video Exchange Ltd* [1982] Ch 431, one party to civil proceedings obtained by a trick in court privileged documents belonging to the other party. By that stage in the case there were difficulties in the way of granting injunctive relief under the principle established in *Lord Ashburton v Pape* [1913] 2 Ch 469. Warner J held that the public interest that litigants should be able to bring their documents into court without fear that they might be filched by their opponents required an exception to the rule in *Calcraft v Guest* [1898] 1 QB 759; and he observed that to obtain documents in such circumstances is probably a contempt of court which the court should not countenance by admitting the documents in evidence. It is submitted that if the same facts were to arise in a public prosecution rather than civil proceedings, then, notwithstanding the principles established in *Calcraft v Guest* and *Butler v Board of Trade* [1971] Ch 680, the result, on the reasoning employed by Warner J, should be the same.

PACE 1984, s. 78

Overview

F2.7 The most important discretionary power to exclude otherwise admissible prosecution evidence is contained in the PACE 1984, s. 78(1). (As to the common-law discretion founded on the duty of the judge or magistrates to ensure that every accused has a fair trial, see **F2.36** ***et seq.***)

Police and Criminal Evidence Act 1984, s. 78

(1) In any proceedings the court may refuse to allow evidence on which the prosecution proposes to rely to be given if it appears to the court that, having regard to all the circumstances, including

the circumstances in which the evidence was obtained, the admission of the evidence would have such an adverse effect on the fairness of the proceedings that the court ought not to admit it.

(2) Nothing in this section shall prejudice any rule of law requiring a court to exclude evidence.

Section 78 applies to evidence on which the prosecution *propose* to rely and therefore applications to exclude evidence under the section should be made before the evidence is adduced (and, if reference is to be made to it in the prosecution opening speech, before that speech): see, in the case of a confession, *Sat-Bhambra* (1988) 88 Cr App R 55, considered at **F18.67**, and, in the case of identification evidence, *Lashley* [2005] EWCA Crim 2016.

Section 78(1) is generally regarded as conferring a discretionary power. In *Jelen* (1989) 90 Cr App R 456 Auld J said, at pp. 464–5:

> . . . the decision of a judge whether or not to exclude evidence under section 78 of the 1984 Act is made as a result of the exercise by him of a discretion based upon the particular circumstances of the case and upon his assessment of the adverse effect, if any, it would have on the fairness of the proceedings. The circumstances of each case are almost always different, and judges may well take different views in the proper exercise of their discretion even when the circumstances are similar. This is not an apt field for hard case law and wellfounded distinctions between cases.

Similarly, it has been said that 'feel' for the case is usually the critical ingredient of the decision at first instance, which the Court of Appeal lacks, context is vital, and therefore citations from 'authority', in reality no more than observations of a fact-specific decision, are unnecessary (*Thompson* [2018] EWCA Crim 2082). However, strictly speaking s. 78(1) does not involve an exercise of discretion because, if a court decides that admission of the evidence in question would have such an adverse effect on the fairness of the proceedings that it ought not to admit it, it cannot logically exercise a discretion to admit it (per Auld LJ in *Chalkley* [1998] QB 848 at p. 874). Either way, the Court of Appeal has been loath to interfere with the decisions of trial judges under s. 78. It has been said that the Court of Appeal will intervene only if the judge has not exercised the discretion under s. 78 at all or has done so but in a *Wednesbury* unreasonable manner (*Associated Provincial Picture Houses Ltd v Wednesbury Corporation* [1948] 1 KB 223) and that where the Court of Appeal does intervene, it will exercise its own discretion (*O'Leary* (1988) 87 Cr App R 387 per May LJ at p. 391; *Quinn* [1995] 1 Cr App R 480 at p. 498; *Christou* [1992] QB 979; *Khan* [1997] Crim LR 508; *Dures* [1997] 2 Cr App R 247). However, it is submitted that the true test for the Court of Appeal should be whether the admission of the evidence in question renders the conviction unsafe, since that is now the only ground on which it may allow an appeal against conviction (see the Criminal Appeal Act 1968, s. 2(1), at **D26.15** ***et seq.***, and generally A Clarke, 'Safety or Supervision' [1999] Crim LR 108).

General Application

Section 78(1) may be used to attempt to exclude *any* evidence on which the prosecution propose **F2.8**
to rely: see, e.g., *O'Loughlin* [1988] 3 All ER 431 (depositions and documentary records); *Newell* • [2012] EWCA Crim 650, [2012] 1 WLR 3142, considered at **F17.67** (information provided by the defence on a plea and case management hearing (PCMH) form); *Mason* [1988] 3 All ER 481 (confessions); *Beveridge* (1987) 85 Cr App R 255 (identification parades); *Deenik* [1992] Crim LR 578 (voice identifications); and *McGrath v Field* [1987] RTR 349 (intoximeter readings).

Scope for Exclusion Wider Than at Common Law

Evidence open to exclusion at common law, i.e. (a) any admissible evidence which is likely to **F2.9**
have a prejudicial effect out of proportion to its probative value, and (b) admissions, confessions and other evidence obtained from the accused after the commission of the offence by improper or unfair means, and which might operate unfairly against the accused (*Sang* [1980] AC 402: see **F2.45**), may be excluded *either* at common law *or* pursuant to the PACE 1984, s. 78. In *Matto v Wolverhampton Crown Court* [1987] RTR 337 Woolf LJ said (at p. 346): 'Whatever is the right interpretation of s. 78, I am quite satisfied that it certainly does not

reduce the discretion of the court to exclude unfair evidence which existed at common law. Indeed . . . in any case where the evidence could properly be excluded at common law, it can certainly be excluded under s. 78.' An example is *O'Connor* (1986) 85 Cr App R 298, where A and B were jointly charged with having conspired to commit an offence. A pleaded guilty and B not guilty. At the trial of B the prosecution sought to admit the conviction of A under the PACE 1984, s. 74. The prejudicial effect of this evidence clearly outweighed its probative value, because A's admission of the offence charged might have led the jury to infer that B must have conspired with A, and therefore the common-law discretion to exclude could have been invoked. Instead, the Court of Appeal held that the evidence should have been excluded under s. 78. See also *Horne* [2020] EWCA Crim 487 and *Mattison* [1990] Crim LR 117, which are considered at **F12.13**. In *Daniels* [2010] EWCA Crim 2740, [2011] 1 Cr App R 18 (228), on the other hand, it was held that the fact that an accused has entered into an agreement pursuant to the SOCPA 2005, s. 73 (see **E1.11**), will not in itself call for exclusion of the accused's evidence under s. 78, even if it is of central importance; the dangers inherent in giving evidence against accomplices are met by giving the jury a proper warning (see **F5.13**). In *Mason* [1988] 3 All ER 481 Watkins LJ said that s. 78(1) 'does no more than to restate the power which judges had at common law before the 1984 Act was passed'. It is submitted that this view is erroneous in principle and inconsistent with the bulk of authority.

(a) Concerning the provisions of Part VIII of the PACE 1984, s. 82(3) expressly preserves the discretion to exclude which the court possessed at common law prior to the coming into force of the Act, and therefore Parliament, in enacting s. 78, must be taken to have extended the pre-existing discretion.
(b) Section 78(1), insofar as it may be used to exclude evidence obtained by improper or unfair means, is not confined, as is the common-law power described in *Sang* [1980] AC 402 at p. 437, see **F2.45**, to 'admissions, confessions and generally with regard to evidence obtained from the accused after the commission of the offence', but extends to any evidence on which the prosecution propose to rely.
(c) Nor, in relation to evidence obtained improperly or unfairly, is s. 78(1) necessarily confined, in the way that the common-law power apparently is, to cases in which those who obtained the evidence acted *mala fide* (*Fox* [1986] AC 281). See further **F2.48**.

Application to Evidence Obtained Unlawfully, Improperly or Unfairly

F2.10 The primary importance of s. 78 is not the degree of overlap with the common law, but the fact that it extends the common-law powers by reason of its potential for the exclusion of evidence obtained unlawfully, improperly or unfairly. Concerning evidence obtained by such means, the common-law powers are restricted to admissions, confessions and other evidence obtained from the accused after the commission of the offence (*Sang* [1980] AC 402: see **F2.45**). Section 78, however, is capable of application to *any* evidence obtained illegally or by improper or unfair means and on which the prosecution seek to rely, whether obtained from the accused, his or her premises or from any other source.

F2.11 **Procedure** As to procedure, the issue of unfairness may be raised by counsel for any accused against whom the evidence may be used (by the prosecution). Section 78(1) applies not to evidence which the prosecution have adduced, but to evidence on which the prosecution *propose* to rely. In *Harwood* [1989] Crim LR 285, in which a submission that evidence should be excluded under s. 78 was made *after* the evidence had been given, the Court of Appeal doubted whether s. 78 could in any circumstances entitle the judge to withdraw the evidence or to direct the jury to acquit when the judge had not been invited to refuse to allow the evidence to be given. However, where a judge has excluded evidence on which the prosecution propose to rely but, at some later stage in the trial, in the judge's opinion the balance of fairness shifts, there is then a discretion to reconsider the ruling and admit the evidence (*Allen* [1992] Crim LR 297).

It seems reasonable to suppose that if the court is prepared to entertain a submission that a particular item would have such an adverse effect on the fairness of the proceedings that the court ought not to admit it, argument should take place in the absence of the jury and, in cases in which evidence needs to be called as to the circumstances in which the evidence was obtained (because they are in dispute), there should be a hearing on the *voir dire*. In *Manji* [1990] Crim LR 512, D denied that he had made certain damaging admissions in a conversation with police officers and alleged that he had not been cautioned. On a defence application under s. 78 to exclude this evidence as having been obtained in breach of the Codes of Practice under the PACE 1984, the trial judge refused to hold a trial within a trial on the issue of whether D had been cautioned. It was held that the judge had erred. However, where a question arises under s. 78(1) as to the admissibility of identification parade evidence, it has been held that, although there may be rare occasions when it will be desirable to hold a trial within a trial, in general the judge should decide on the basis of the depositions, statements and submissions of counsel (*Beveridge* (1987) 85 Cr App R 255). See **F1.45**.

In *Anderson* [1993] Crim LR 447 it was acknowledged, *per curiam*, that it is not entirely clear under s. 78(1) where the burden of proof lies. It is submitted that, if there is no dispute as to the circumstances in which the evidence was obtained, there will be no issue of fact and no question of burden of proof will arise; if there is such a dispute, evidence is called for and, in accordance with the general rule, the burden should be on the prosecution to disprove beyond reasonable doubt the circumstances on which the accused relies. However, in *R (Saifi) v Governor of Brixton Prison* [2001] 4 All ER 168, which concerned the application of s. 78 in extradition proceedings, it was held that the absence from s. 78 of any suggestion that facts are to be proved to any particular standard is deliberate; that a magistrate may simply evaluate the evidence tendered both by the government and the accused as to the circumstances in which the evidence was obtained and may decide, on that evidence, the question of adverse effect on the fairness of the proceedings; and therefore that there is no need for a magistrate to make a specific finding in relation to every issue raised. **F2.12**

As to the procedure in summary trials, see **F1.47**.

Test for Exclusion Section 78(1) directs the court, in deciding whether to exercise the statutory discretion, to have regard to all the circumstances, including those in which the evidence was obtained. In some cases, of course, the submission to exclude under the subsection will *not* be based on the circumstances in which the evidence was obtained; see, e.g., the cases in which an application has been made under s. 78(1) to exclude evidence of the conviction of a person otherwise admissible under s. 74 of the 1984 Act, which are considered at **F12.6**. **F2.13**

In other cases, however, counsel will be fully justified in basing a submission to exclude on the circumstances in which the evidence was obtained, because it is implicit in the subsection that there can be circumstances in which the evidence was obtained which makes it have such an adverse effect on the fairness of the proceedings that the court ought not to admit it (*Matto v Wolverhampton Crown Court* [1987] RTR 337 per Woolf LJ). Thus, the court may have regard to any unlawful, improper or unfair conduct by means of which the evidence was obtained, including, in particular, conduct in breach of the ECHR or the provisions of the 1984 Act (or the Codes of Practice issued under the Act) relating to such matters as search, seizure, arrest, detention, treatment, questioning and identification. Even where the evidence in question was obtained by someone who is not 'charged with the duty of investigating offences' for the purposes of s. 67(9) of the 1984 Act, the principles underlying Code C may be of assistance in considering the discretion to exclude under s. 78(1) (*Smith* [1994] 1 WLR 1396). Useful guidance can be found in *Achieving Best Evidence in Criminal Proceedings: Guidance on interviewing victims and witnesses, and guidance on using special measures* (March 2011): see *Dunphy* (1993) 98 Cr App R 393, a decision on an earlier version of the guidance. However, breach of the

ECHR, the 1984 Act or the PACE codes etc. will not necessarily result in exclusion: every case must be determined on its own particular facts (*Parris* (1988) 89 Cr App R 65, per Lord Lane CJ at p. 72; *Khan* [1995] QB 27; *Keenan* [1990] 2 QB 54 per Hodgson J at p. 69). Equally, the fact that evidence has been obtained by 'oppressive' conduct will not automatically result in exclusion, because oppressive conduct, depending on its degree and actual or possible effect, may or may not affect the fairness of admitting particular evidence (*Chalkley* [1998] QB 848 at p. 874).

F2.14 **'The Fairness of the Proceedings'** In cases in which the court takes the view that there was serious or reprehensible conduct, and this results in exclusion, the decision should not be taken in order to discipline the police (*Mason* [1988] 3 All ER 481 per Watkins LJ; *Delaney* (1988) 88 Cr App R 338 per Lord Lane CJ at p. 341). The critical test under s. 78 is whether any impropriety affects the fairness of the proceedings: the court cannot exclude evidence under the section simply as a mark of its disapproval of the way in which it was obtained (per Auld LJ in *Chalkley*).

Thus if a sample of hair is obtained by an assault and not in accordance with the PACE 1984 and is then used to prepare a DNA profile which implicates the accused, the evidence will be admitted on the basis that the means used to obtain it have done nothing to cast doubt on its reliability and strength (*Cooke* [1995] 1 Cr App R 318; cf. *Nathaniel* [1995] 2 Cr App R 565). The same reasoning may also justify the admission in evidence of the fruits of an improper search (see *Stewart* [1995] Crim LR 500, where the entry involved a number of breaches of PACE Code B; and see also *McCarthy* [1996] Crim LR 818). The evidence should be excluded, however, where there is a real risk that the improper means used to obtain it have affected its reliability, and therefore the fairness of the trial, e.g., a case involving a complete flouting of Code B in which the accused claims that the property allegedly found must have been planted. (But see *Wright* [1994] Crim LR 55 at **F2.31**.) Equally, where officers are justified in delaying taking a suspect to a police station in order that a search may be conducted with the suspect's assistance, but abuse that opportunity to circumvent Code C by asking a series of questions, beyond those necessary to the search, on matters which properly ought to be asked under the rules of the Code applying at a police station, the answers may be excluded on the grounds of unfairness (*Khan* [1993] Crim LR 54, applied in *Raphaie* [1996] Crim LR 812).

F2.15 In *Quinn* [1990] Crim LR 581 Lord Lane CJ said:

> The function of the judge is therefore *to protect the fairness of the proceedings*, and normally proceedings are fair if a jury hears *all* relevant evidence which either side wishes to place before it, but proceedings may become unfair if, for example, one side is allowed to adduce relevant evidence which, for one reason or another, the other side cannot properly challenge or meet, or where there has been an abuse of process, e.g. because evidence has been obtained in deliberate breach of procedures laid down in an official code of practice.

In *Quinn*, identification evidence had come into existence abroad as a result of arrangements made by a foreign police force. A police officer went to a criminal court in Dublin, where D was on trial in respect of other offences committed in the Republic of Ireland, and identified D. It was held that, in the circumstances of the case, the judge had to have regard to such factors as (a) the possible cross-examination handicap to the defence; (b) the possibility of mistake being increased because of the way in which the identification was arranged and the fact that both the judge himself and the defence could warn the jury of the disadvantages of the procedure adopted and the consequent danger of relying upon the evidence; (c) the fact that D was deprived of the opportunity to stand on an identification parade or to consult a solicitor or to record what happened when the identification was carried out; (d) that D was not told of the identification at the time; and (e) the fact that the identification evidence did not stand alone but could be tested by other evidence. The Court of Appeal could find nothing to indicate that the trial judge had misdirected himself, had regard to irrelevant matters or failed to have regard to relevant matters. In *Konscol* [1993] Crim LR 950, the trial judge admitted evidence of an interview with D, containing lies, conducted by a Belgian customs officer. There was no dispute that D had said what was recorded, and the interview was conducted fairly according to Belgian law, but D was neither cautioned nor advised that he could have a lawyer present. The Court of Appeal dismissed the appeal and declined to lay down guidelines as to when a court should admit a statement made overseas according to rules which did not coincide with the provisions of the PACE 1984.

In *Mason* [1988] 3 All ER 481, D was convicted of arson. After arrest, D and his solicitor were **F2.16** told by police officers that D's fingerprint had been identified on glass from a bottle found at the scene of the crime. This was a deliberate falsehood designed to elicit a confession. The solicitor advised D to explain any involvement on his part in the incident, whereupon D confessed. There was no other prosecution evidence. Quashing the conviction, the Court of Appeal held that had the judge, in the exercise of the statutory discretion, taken into account the deceit practised on the solicitor, which he had failed to do, he would have been driven to exclude the confession. See also *Samuel* [1988] QB 615. *Mason* was distinguished in *DPP v Marshall* [1988] 3 All ER 683. On a charge of selling intoxicating liquor without a licence, evidence was adduced that officers, wearing plain clothes, and without announcing their office, had purchased liquor from the premises in question. It was held that this evidence could not have any effect on the fairness of the trial and therefore was not to be excluded under the PACE 1984, s. 78.

Prosecutions Founded on Entrapment The leading authority on the application of s. 78(1) to a **F2.17** prosecution founded on entrapment is the decision of the House of Lords in *A-G's Ref (No. 3 of 2000) (Looseley)* [2001] UKHL 53, [2001] 1 WLR 2060, from which the following propositions derive.

(a) Although in English law entrapment is not a substantive defence, where an accused can show entrapment, the court may stay the proceedings as an abuse of the court's process or it may exclude evidence pursuant to s. 78.
(b) Of these two remedies, the grant of stay, rather than the exclusion of evidence at the trial, should, as a matter of principle, normally be regarded as the appropriate response. A prosecution founded on entrapment would be an abuse of the court's process. Police conduct which brings about state-created crime is unacceptable and improper. To prosecute in such circumstances would be an affront to the public conscience.
(c) A decision on whether to stay criminal proceedings is distinct from a decision on the forensic fairness of admitting evidence (*Chalkley* [1998] 2 Cr App R 79 at p. 105). Thus if the court is not satisfied that a stay should be granted and the trial proceeds, the question under s. 78 is not whether the proceedings should have been brought but whether the fairness of the proceedings will be adversely affected by, for example, admitting the evidence of the *agent provocateur* or evidence which is available as a result of his or her activities (*Shannon* [2001] 1 WLR 51 at p. 68). However, if an application to exclude evidence under s. 78 is in substance a belated application for a stay, it should be treated as such and decided according to the principles appropriate to the grant of a stay.
(d) In deciding whether conduct amounts to state-created crime, the existence or absence of a predisposition on the part of the accused to commit the crime is not the criterion by which the acceptability of police conduct is to be decided, because predisposition does not make acceptable what would otherwise be unacceptable conduct on the part of the police or other law enforcement agencies. (But cf. *Moon* [2004] EWCA Crim 2872, where absence of disposition on the part of D to deal with or supply heroin was regarded as a critical factor.) A useful guide is to consider whether the police did no more than present the defendant with an unexceptional opportunity to commit a crime. The yardstick for the purposes of this test is, in general, whether the police conduct preceding the commission of the offence was no more than might have been expected from others in the circumstances. McHugh J had this approach in mind in *Ridgeway v The Queen* (1995) 184 CLR 19 at p. 92, when he said:

> The State can justify the use of entrapment techniques to induce the commission of an offence only when the inducement is consistent with the ordinary temptations and stratagems that are likely to be encountered in the course of criminal activity. That may mean that some degree of deception, importunity and even threats on the part of the authorities may be acceptable. But once the State goes beyond the ordinary, it is likely to increase the incidence of crime by artificial means.

Of its nature, the technique of providing an opportunity to commit a crime is intrusive. The greater the degree of intrusiveness, the closer will the courts scrutinise the reason for using it. On this, proportionality has a role to play. Whether a police officer can be said to have caused the commission of the offence, rather than merely providing an opportunity for the accused to commit it with a police officer instead of in secrecy with someone else, will usually be a most important factor, but not necessarily decisive. See, as illustrations of 'unexceptional opportunity to commit a crime', *Jones* [2010] EWCA Crim 925, [2010] 3 All ER 1186 and *Palmer* [2014] EWCA Crim 1681.

(e) Neither the judicial discretion conferred by s. 78, nor the court's power to stay proceedings as an abuse of the court, has been modified by the ECHR, Article 6, and the jurisprudence of the ECtHR. There is no appreciable difference between the requirements of Article 6, or the Strasbourg jurisprudence on Article 6, and the English law as it has developed in recent years. There is nothing in either the general principle applied by the ECtHR in *Teixeira de Castro v Portugal* (1998) 28 EHRR 101 or in the cluster of factors to which it attached importance which suggests any difference from the current English approach to entrapment.

(f) Ultimately, the overall consideration is always whether the conduct of the police or other law enforcement agency was so seriously improper as to bring the administration of justice into disrepute. In applying this test, the court has regard to all the circumstances of the case. The following circumstances are of particular relevance (for an illustration of how account may be taken of them, see *Moore* [2013] EWCA Crim 85).

(i) The nature of the offence. The use of proactive techniques is more appropriate in the case of some offences, e.g., dealing in unlawful substances, offences with no immediate victim (such as bribery), offences which victims are reluctant to report and conspiracies. The secrecy and difficulty of detection, and the manner in which the particular criminal activity is carried on, are relevant considerations.

(ii) The reason for the particular police operation and supervision. The police must act in good faith. Having reasonable grounds for suspicion is one way good faith may be established. It is not normally considered a legitimate use of police power to provide people not suspected of being engaged in any criminal activity with the opportunity to commit crimes. (See, e.g., *Ramanauskas v Lithuania* (2010) 51 EHRR 11 (303), where an officer acted on no more than *rumours* about a prosecutor's openness to bribery.) The principle is that the police should prevent and detect crime, not create it. Closely linked with the question whether the police were creating or detecting crime is the supervision of their activities. To allow police officers or controlled informers to undertake entrapment activities unsupervised carries great danger, not merely that they will try to improve their performances in court, but of oppression, extortion and corruption. The need for both reasonable suspicion and proper supervision is stressed in the Code of Practice for Covert Human Intelligence Sources. However, the requirement of reasonable suspicion does not necessarily mean that there must have been suspicion of the accused. The police may, in the course of a bona fide investigation into suspected criminality, provide an opportunity for the commission of an offence which is taken by someone to whom no suspicion previously attached (see, e.g., *Williams v DPP* [1993] 3 All ER 365). Sometimes random testing may be the only practicable way of policing a particular trading activity.

(iii) The nature and extent of police participation in the crime. The greater the inducement held out by the police, and the more forceful or persistent the police overtures, the more readily may a court conclude that the police overstepped the boundary. (In the absence of persuasion or pressure or the offer of a significant inducement, it will not generally amount to an abuse of process for an officer to so insinuate him or herself into the confidence of the accused as to offer an opportunity to commit a crime: see *M* [2011] EWCA Crim 648.) In assessing the weight to be attached to the police inducement, regard is to be had to the defendant's circumstances, including vulnerability. For the police to behave as would an ordinary customer of a trade, whether lawful or unlawful, being carried on by the accused will not normally be regarded as objectionable.

(iv) The accused's criminal record. This is unlikely to be relevant unless it can be linked to other factors grounding reasonable suspicion that the accused is currently engaged in criminal activity.

In *Syed* [2018] EWCA Crim 2809, [2019] 1 Cr App R 21 (267), detailed reasons were given (at [108]–[111]) for holding that, with the possible exception of burden of proof in relation to an application to stay proceedings as an abuse of the court's process (see **D3.103**), the Strasbourg jurisprudence on entrapment does not require a new approach different from that adopted in *Looseley*. *Looseley* remains compliant with the ECHR, Article 6. Efforts to construct differences on the basis of an unduly literal reading of some of the Strasbourg judgments are misplaced. Thus the reference to State agents acting in an 'essentially passive manner' in *Teixeira de Castro v Portugal* (1998) 28 EHRR 101 at [38] and *Ramanauskas v Lithuania* (2010) 51 EHRR 11 at [55] should not be taken to mean acting as no more than passive observers; and references to reasonable grounds for suspicion of a suspect (see, e.g., *Teixeira* at [38]) should not be taken to mean that such suspicion is always necessary.

Undercover Operations Where evidence has been obtained by illegal undercover operations, the court may, in appropriate circumstances, stay the proceedings (see *Warren v A-G for Jersey* [2011] UKPC 10, [2012] 1 AC 22, considered at **D3.108**). But where proceedings have not been stayed, the question arises whether to exclude the evidence obtained by the undercover operations. In *Smurthwaite* [1994] 1 All ER 898 it was held that the relevant factors, in deciding whether to exclude under the PACE 1984, s. 78, evidence obtained as a result of police undercover operations, *include* whether the undercover officer was acting as an *agent provocateur* in the sense that he was enticing D to commit an offence he would not otherwise have committed; the nature of any entrapment; whether the evidence consists of admissions to a completed offence or relates to the actual commission of an offence; how active the officer's role was in obtaining the evidence; whether there is an unassailable record of what occurred or whether it is strongly corroborated; and whether the officer abused his or her role to ask questions which ought properly to have been asked as a police officer and in accordance with the codes (see *Christou* [1992] QB 979 and *Bryce* [1992] 4 All ER 567 at **F2.25**). It was held that if in all the circumstances the evidence would have the adverse effect described in s. 78(1), the judge will exclude it. The factors recited in *Smurthwaite* also apply in the case of evidence obtained by undercover journalists acting not on police instructions, but on their own initiative (*Shannon* [2001] 1 WLR 51; *Shannon v UK* (2006) 42 EHRR 31 (660)). Section 78(1) cannot be circumvented by the police using, as *agents provocateurs*, informants who will not be called as witnesses. Thus if an informant, acting on police instructions, entraps an accused into committing an offence and the accused is then approached by an undercover police officer in whose presence the offence is committed, a submission may be made under s. 78(1) to exclude the officer's evidence notwithstanding that the officer's behaviour throughout cannot be criticised having regard to the relevant factors in *Smurthwaite* (*Smith* [1995] Crim LR 658; cf. *Mann* [1995] Crim LR 647). However, entrapment, whether direct or indirect, is not in itself sufficient to require exclusion under s. 78. The facts and circumstances amounting to entrapment may be taken into account (and in an appropriate case may prove decisive), but the principal focus must be the procedural fairness of the proceedings, the nature and reliability of the prosecution evidence and the **F2.18**

fullness and fairness of the opportunity available to the accused to deal with it (per Potter LJ in *Shannon* [2001] 1 WLR 51 at [38]; and see also *Governor of Pentonville Prison, ex parte Chinoy* [1992] 1 All ER 317).

F2.19 In *Smurthwaite*, the two appellants, D1 and D2, had been tried for soliciting to murder. In each case the person solicited was an undercover police officer posing as a contract killer, and the prosecution case depended upon secret tape recordings of meetings held between the undercover officer and the accused. In D1's case, the Court of Appeal was not persuaded that the officer was an *agent provocateur*. There was an element of entrapment and a trick, but (a) the tapes recorded not admissions about some previous offence but the actual offence being committed, (b) the tapes showed that D1 made the running and that the officer had taken a minimal role in the planning and had used no persuasion towards D1, (c) the tapes were an accurate and unchallenged record and (d) the officer had not abused his role to ask questions which ought properly to have been asked as a police officer. In these circumstances, the judge's decision not to exclude the evidence was upheld. The outcome was the same in D2's case: the facts were very similar and, although the first meeting between D2 and the officer was not recorded and there was a stark conflict of evidence as to what was said at that meeting, the existence of a total record was only one factor, and both the contents of the subsequent taped conversations and statements made by D2 in her formal police interviews supported the officer's account of the first meeting. In *Latif* [1996] 1 All ER 353, D was convicted of being knowingly concerned in the importation of drugs which had been brought into the country by an undercover customs officer. Although D had been lured into England by the deceit of an informer and both he and the undercover officer had possibly committed the offence of possessing heroin in Pakistan, the House of Lords upheld the trial judge's refusal to exclude the informer's evidence under s. 78. For further examples, see *Pattemore* [1994] Crim LR 836 (a police informant) and *Morley* [1994] Crim LR 919 (a reporter who informed the police).

F2.20 In *Williams v DPP* [1993] 3 All ER 365, plain-clothes officers, as part of an investigation into thefts from vehicles in Essex which was not directed at any specific individual, parked an insecure and unattended van, which appeared to contain a valuable load of cigarettes, in a busy street. Concealed officers later observed the accused removing cartons from the van. It was held that magistrates were entitled, in exercising their discretion under s. 78, to admit the police evidence. The officers were not acting as *agents provocateurs* and, following *DPP v Marshall* [1988] 3 All ER 683 (see **F2.16**) and the reasoning in *Christou* [1992] QB 979 (see **F2.25**), the trick was not applied to the accused: they voluntarily applied themselves to the trick. The argument that *Christou* could be distinguished, because in that case the police were seeking to obtain evidence of offences which had already been committed, was rejected. See also *Ealing London Borough Council v Woolworths plc* [1995] Crim LR 58, where a boy aged 11, acting on the instructions of trading standards officers, had purchased an 18-category video film. In *Nottingham City Council v Amin* [2000] 2 All ER 946, a taxi driver who was not licensed to ply for hire in a certain district, was flagged down there by plain-clothes officers who were then taken to their destination. A stipendiary magistrate used s. 78 to exclude the officers' evidence, having regard to the HRA 1998 and decisions of the ECtHR. On appeal, the respondent relied on *Teixeira de Castro v Portugal* (1998) 28 EHRR 101. In that case two undercover agents had instigated an offence and, since there was nothing to suggest that without their intervention it would have been committed, it was held that the intervention and use made of it at the trial amounted to a violation of the right to a fair trial under Article 6. (See also *Barkshire* [2011] EWCA Crim 1885.) Lord Bingham CJ distinguished the case on the basis that 'the facts…simply cannot lend themselves to the construction that this respondent was in any way prevailed upon or overborne or persuaded or pressured or instigated or incited to commit the offence'. Lord Bingham said (at pp. 1076–7):

> On the one hand it has been recognised as deeply offensive to ordinary notions of fairness if a defendant were to be convicted and punished for committing a crime which he only committed

> because he had been incited, instigated, persuaded, pressurised or wheedled into committing it by a law enforcement officer. On the other hand, it has been recognised that law enforcement agencies have a general duty to the public to enforce the law and it has been regarded as unobjectionable if a law enforcement officer gives a defendant an opportunity to break the law, of which the defendant freely takes advantage, in circumstances where it appears that the defendant would have behaved in the same way if the opportunity had been made by anyone else.

In *Looseley*, Lord Hoffmann made two important comments on this passage. First (at [54] and [55]), it was observed in relation to the final sentence that Lord Bingham obviously did not mean only that the accused would have responded in the same way to someone who was not a policeman, because the accused in such cases *ex hypothesi* is not aware of dealing with a policeman, and therefore such a condition would invariably be satisfied: **F2.21**

> What he meant was that the policemen behaved like ordinary members of the public in flagging the taxi down. They did not wave £50 notes or pretend to be in distress. The test of whether the law enforcement officer behaved like an ordinary member of the public works well and is likely to be decisive in many cases of regulatory offences committed with ordinary members of the public, such as selling liquor in unlicensed quantities (*DPP v Marshall* [1988] 3 All ER 683)... But ordinary members of the public do not become involved in large scale drug dealing, conspiracy to rob... or hiring assassins (... *Smurthwaite* [1994] 1 All ER 898). The appropriate standards of behaviour are in such cases more problematic. And even in the case of offences committed with ordinary members of the public, other factors may require a purely causal test to be modified.

Secondly (at [70]), Lord Hoffmann observed that when Lord Bingham said that the accused should not be 'incited, instigated, persuaded, pressurised or wheedled' into committing the offence, he was not intending each of those verbs to be given a disjunctive and technical meaning, but was intending to evoke a more general concept of conduct which causes the accused to commit the offence as opposed to giving the accused the opportunity to do so. 'No doubt a test purchaser who asks someone to sell him a drug is counselling and procuring, perhaps inciting the commission of an offence... But the fact that his actions are technically unlawful is not regarded in English law as a ground for treating them as an abuse of power: see *R v Latif* [1996] 1 All ER 353....' See also *East Riding of Yorkshire Council v Dearlove* [2012] EWHC 278 (Admin), [2012] RTR 29 (388) ('test purchase' by booking an unlicensed private hire vehicle).

Undercover Operations after Commission of the Offence As to evidence obtained by undercover operations *after* commission of the offence, although the PACE 1984, s. 78(1), does apply, each case must be decided on its own facts. In *Jelen* (1989) 90 Cr App R 456, D1, D2 and D3 were charged with conspiracy to commit false accounting. D1 pleaded guilty and after he was sentenced gave evidence for the prosecution in the case against D2 and D3. D1 had been the first to be arrested. He made admissions and implicated D2. That was the first that the police had heard of D2's involvement and their view was that they would have had to caution D2 if they had sought to question him then but that they had insufficient evidence upon which they could have arrested and charged him. They accordingly asked D1 if he would obtain some corroboration of what he had told them by arranging to have a recorded conversation with D2 without D2 knowing that it was being recorded. D1 then held such a conversation with D2 in the course of which D1 lied to D2, telling him that he had not said anything to the police. During the conversation, D2 made remarks from which his guilt could have been inferred. The trial judge admitted the evidence and the Court of Appeal held that although there was an element of entrapment, it could see no reason to disagree with the judge's conclusion. Cf. *H* [1987] Crim LR 47, which the Court distinguished. **F2.22**

In *Bailey* [1993] 3 All ER 513, two co-accused exercised their right to silence when interviewed by the police. They were charged, remanded in police custody and placed together in a bugged cell by officers who, in order to lull them into a false sense of security, pretended that they had been forced to put them in the same cell by an unco-operative custody officer. It was held that evidence of incriminating conversations between them, obtained by this police subterfuge, was **F2.23** admissible. Although the police were not entitled to question the accused further, they did not have to protect them from any opportunity to hold incriminating conversations, if they chose to do so, and there was nothing in the 1984 Act or PACE Code C to prohibit them from bugging a cell, even after an accused had been charged and had exercised the right to silence. The judge was therefore entitled to admit the evidence. See also *Mason* [2002] EWCA Crim 385, [2002] 2 Cr App R 38 (628) (where the surveillance constituted a breach of the right to privacy under the ECHR, Article 8), *Roberts* [1997] 1 Cr App R 217 (where another suspect asked to be put in a cell with D in order to get him to confess) and *Turner* [2013] EWCA Crim 642 (lawful covert surveillance in D's home).

Similarly, although the deliberate flouting of the PACE 1984, s. 30 (see **D1.20**), for the sole purpose of creating an opportunity for a covert recording before an interview under caution, may, depending upon the circumstances, result in exclusion under s. 78, the fairness of the proceedings will not be affected where, as in *King* [2012] EWCA Crim 805, the officers neither engaged the accused in conversation nor tricked them into believing that they must make some response to their arrest, but merely gave them an opportunity to speak together in the belief that they were not being overheard. See also *Plunkett* [2013] EWCA Crim 261, [2013] 1 WLR 3121, where it was held that, even if there had been a breach of the surveillance provisions of the RIPA 2000 or the PACE 1984, s. 30(1A), admissions covertly recorded were admissible because the breaches would have been minor given the seriousness of the crimes (aggravated burglary, false imprisonment and possession of a firearm) and the need to protect the victims of the crimes.

F2.24 In *Khan* [1997] AC 558, the police made a recording of an incriminating conversation relating to the importation of heroin, by means of a secret electronic surveillance device. The House of Lords held that the fact that evidence has been obtained in apparent or probable breach of the right to privacy set out in the ECHR, Article 8, or for that matter the law of a foreign country, is relevant to exercise of the s. 78 power, but the significance of such conduct is its effect, if any, upon the fairness of the proceedings. It therefore upheld the decision of the trial judge that the circumstances in which the evidence had been obtained, even if they constituted a breach of Article 8, did not require exclusion. In *Khan v UK* (2001) 31 EHRR 45 (1016), the ECtHR held that, although the recording was obtained in breach of Article 8, its use at the trial did not violate the right to a fair hearing under Article 6. The Court, repeating what it had said in previous judgments such as *Schenk v Switzerland*, held that the central question was whether the proceedings as a whole were fair. Noting that D had had the opportunity to challenge the admissibility of the evidence under s. 78, as well as its authenticity, the Court found that the use of the evidence did not conflict with the requirements of fairness guaranteed by Article 6(1). Similar conclusions have also been reached by the ECtHR in respect of evidence obtained in breach of Article 8 by the unlawful installation of a listening device in the applicant's home (*Chalkley v UK* (2003) 37 EHRR 30 (680)) and by the unlawful use of covert listening devices at a police station (*PG v UK* (2008) 46 EHRR 51 (1272)). See also *Mason* [2002] EWCA Crim 385, [2002] 2 Cr App R 38 (628) and *Khan* [2013] EWCA Crim 2230, involving a breach of both the surveillance provisions of the RIPA 2000 and Article 8. In *Perry v UK* (2004) 39 EHRR 3 (76) there are dicta (at [40]) to suggest that where personal data is recorded in breach of Article 8, its use at trial in a public court-room may also constitute a breach of Article 8. However, in *Button* [2005] EWCA Crim 516, where video evidence had been obtained in breach of Article 8, the proposition that the court was bound to exclude such evidence because otherwise it would act unlawfully was rejected on the basis that the court played no part in the covert surveillance, which had already occurred, and breach of Article 8 was subsumed by the Article 6 duty to ensure a fair trial. As to covert filming, see also *Loveridge* [2001] EWCA Crim 973, [2001] 2 Cr App R 29 (591) in which D was covertly and unlawfully filmed at court; *Marriner* [2002] EWCA Crim 2855, in which undercover journalists had made secret videos (as well as tape-recordings) of D; and *Rosenberg* [2006] EWCA Crim 6, where both D and the police were aware of surveillance carried out by the complainant but neither initiated nor encouraged by the police.

Khan v UK was distinguished in *Allan v UK* (2003) 36 EHRR 12 (143), in which it was held that the use of statements obtained in a way which effectively undermines a suspect's right to make a meaningful choice whether to speak to the authorities or remain silent infringed procedural rights inherent in the ECHR, Article 6. D was convicted of murder. He had been interviewed by officers on several occasions, but acting on legal advice had consistently refused to answer questions. H, an experienced informer, who had undergone coaching by police officers, was fitted with recording devices and placed in D's cell for the specific purpose of questioning him to obtain information about the murder. At the trial H gave evidence that D had admitted his presence at the scene of the murder. However, this conversation, which proved to be decisive evidence at trial, was not recorded on tape. The Court acknowledged that whether the right to silence is undermined to such an extent as to invoke Article 6 depends on the circumstances of the case, but was satisfied that evidence of the conversations with H had been obtained without sufficient regard to fair trial guarantees. The admissions allegedly made formed decisive evidence against him. They were not spontaneous but induced by persistent questioning of H who, at the instigation of the police, in effect interrogated D, but without any of the safeguards of a formal interview, including the issuing of a caution and the attendance of a solicitor. Compare *Bykov v Russia* [2010] ECHR 1517. When the case returned to the Court of Appeal (*Allan* [2004] EWCA Crim 2236), the conviction was quashed. It was held that H was a 'police stooge', an agent of the state carrying out the equivalent of interrogation after D had exercised a right of silence. The use of H to obtain admissions impinged on D's common-law right of silence and privilege against self-incrimination. The admission of H's evidence was in effect to allow the subversion of the provisions of PACE Code C serving to give procedural effect to the right to silence.

In *Christou* [1992] QB 979, the police set up a shop staffed by two undercover officers who purported to be willing to buy stolen jewellery. Transactions in the shop were recorded (on tape and video) in order to recover stolen property and obtain evidence against thieves and receivers. The accused, charged in consequence of the operation, sought to exclude evidence on the grounds that it had been obtained, without administering a caution in accordance with para. 10.1 of PACE Code C, by a trick designed to deprive them of their privilege against self-incrimination. The Court of Appeal, distinguishing *Payne* [1963] 1 All ER 848 (see **F2.44**) and *Mason* [1988] 3 All ER 481 (see **F2.16**), held that the accused had voluntarily applied themselves to the trick and this had resulted in no unfairness. It was further held that although the officers had grounds to suspect the accused of having committed an offence, para. 10.1 of PACE Code C was not intended to apply to the facts in question. It was designed to protect suspects who are vulnerable to abuse or pressure from officers, or who may believe themselves to be so. Where a suspect, even if not in detention, is being questioned by an officer acting as such, for the purpose of obtaining evidence, the parties are not on equal terms; the officer is perceived to be in a position of authority and the suspect may be intimidated or undermined. The accused, however, were not questioned by officers acting as such, conversation was on equal terms and there was no question of pressure or intimidation. *Christou* was applied in *Maclean* [1993] Crim LR 687, a very similar case in which a person suspected of the illegal importation of drugs 'applied himself to the trick', which was the opportunity of holding a conversation with a car salvage operator, who was in reality a customs officer. In *Cadette* [1995] Crim LR 229 a suspected drug courier, at the request of customs officers, telephoned C, pretended that she had not been arrested and tried to persuade C to come to the airport. Evidence of their conversation was admitted. It was held that although there comes a point when officers may move from following up available lines of inquiry in order to obtain evidence to a stage where they seek in effect to deprive a suspect of the protection afforded by the 1984 Act and Codes, the officers had not crossed the line. **F2.25**

In *Christou*, Lord Taylor CJ further held that it *would* be wrong for the police to adopt an undercover pose or disguise to enable them to ask questions about an offence uninhibited by PACE Code C and with the effect of circumventing it, and a judge could then exclude under s. 78. In that case, however, questions asked by the officers about the origin of the goods formed a part of their undercover pose as receivers — such information would prevent them from reselling the goods in the area from which they were stolen. See also *Lin* [1995] Crim LR 817, where an undercover officer was introduced to D not for the purpose of obtaining evidence about a past offence involving a stolen Inland Revenue cheque, but to discover D's future plans in relation to an on-going conspiracy to handle stolen cheques. It was held that a conversation about the Inland Revenue cheque was a necessary part of establishing the officer's credentials as a 'criminal'. The position was different in *Bryce* [1992] 4 All ER 567, where an undercover officer, in conversations with D about a car, asked how recently it had been stolen. D replied 'two to three days' and added 'we are having two a week away. Would you be interested in any others?' The Court of Appeal, quashing the conviction for handling, held that the evidence of these conversations should have been excluded. The questions were not necessary to the maintenance of the undercover pose. They went directly to the issue of guilty knowledge, they were disputed, there was no caution and there were no contemporary records.

F2.26 **Bad Faith** The common-law discretion to exclude evidence obtained unlawfully will not be exercised if those who obtained the evidence made a bona fide mistake as to their powers; but it may be exercised if such persons resorted to trickery, deception or oppression (*Fox* [1986] AC 281). Some of the authorities on the PACE 1984, s. 78, draw the same distinction, laying great stress on whether the police acted *mala fide*, *knowingly* exceeding their powers. In *Matto v Wolverhampton Crown Court* [1987] RTR 337, D was convicted of driving with excess alcohol. Police officers, when requesting a specimen of breath on D's property, realised that they were acting illegally. The specimen proved positive. D was then arrested and, at the police station, provided another positive specimen. The appeal was allowed on the grounds that, the officers having acted *mala fide* and oppressively, the Crown Court, had it directed itself properly, could have exercised its discretion under s. 78 to exclude the evidence. See also *Mason* [1988] 3 All ER 481, in which a *deliberate* deceit was practised on both D and his solicitor and *Canale* [1990] 2 All ER 187, in which it was held that had the trial judge directed his mind to breaches of the interview rules under PACE Code C which were 'flagrant', 'deliberate' and 'cynical', he would and should have concluded that the interviews should be excluded under s. 78.

F2.27 Other authorities, however, adopting an approach designed to protect the suspect from being denied his or her civil rights, make it clear that the statutory discretion may be exercised even in the absence of *deliberate* or *wilful* misconduct. Thus, in *DPP v McGladrigan* [1991] RTR 297, the Divisional Court held that the argument on *mala fides* originated from *Fox*, a case decided before the PACE 1984 came into force, and that s. 78(1) of the 1984 Act gave the courts a new and considerably wider discretion. The Court relied upon *Samuel* [1988] QB 615 to reject the argument that *mala fides* had to be established before the statutory discretion could be exercised. The Court also pointed out that, insofar as *Matto v Wolverhampton Crown Court* suggested that in breathalyser cases *Fox* still applied, it should be noted that the case was not only a successful appeal by D, but also preceded *Samuel*. See also *Brine* [1992] Crim LR 123. In *Foster* [1987] Crim LR 821, where no contemporaneous record of an interview had been made, there was no record of a reason for not having made such a record and D was not given the opportunity to read and sign the record of the interview, it was ruled that it was irrelevant whether the breaches were wilful or merely ignorant; in the absence of a contemporaneous record at the trial, D was deprived of the opportunity to demonstrate that his denial of the offence was not an afterthought but a denial which he made at the time of his arrest.

F2.28 In *Alladice* (1988) 87 Cr App R 380, a case in which D had been improperly denied the right of access to a solicitor pursuant to the PACE 1984, s. 58, Lord Lane CJ, giving the reserved judgment of the Court of Appeal, held that if the police had acted in bad faith, the court would have little difficulty in ruling any confession inadmissible under s. 78; but that if the police, albeit in good faith, had nevertheless fallen foul of s. 58, it was still necessary for the court to decide whether admission of the evidence would adversely affect the fairness of the proceedings to such an extent that the confession ought to be excluded. (On the facts, however, it was held that had the trial judge considered s. 78, he would not have been obliged to exclude the evidence because D was well able to cope with the interviews, understood the cautions that he had been given — at times exercising his right to silence — and was aware of his rights. Thus, if the solicitor had been present, his advice would have added nothing to the knowledge of his rights which D already had.) See also *Dunford* (1990) 91 Cr App R 150; *Parris* (1988) 89 Cr App R 68; *Walsh* (1989) 91 Cr App R 161; and *Anderson* [1993] Crim LR 447. In *Walsh*, Saville J, referring to breaches of s. 58 or the provisions of the Codes of Practice, said (at p. 163):

> ... although bad faith may make substantial or significant that which might not otherwise be so, the contrary does not follow. Breaches which are themselves significant and substantial are not rendered otherwise by the good faith of the officers concerned.

Significant and Substantial Breaches In *Quinn* [1990] Crim LR 581, *Walsh* (1989) 91 Cr App R 161 and *Keenan* [1990] 2 QB 54 were referred to with approval as authority for the general proposition that a significant and substantial breach of a PACE Code may well result in the exclusion of evidence obtained in consequence, even in the absence of bad faith. Whether a breach is 'significant and substantial' for these purposes is clearly a question of fact and degree. In *Sparks* [1991] Crim LR 128 (in which the proviso to s. 2(1) of the Criminal Appeal Act 1968 was applied), breaches of Code C (failure to caution and failure to keep a proper interview record) were held to be substantial. See also *Okafor* [1994] 3 All ER 741 (failure to caution, to remind of the right to legal advice and to make a contemporaneous record of interview); *Coelho* [2008] EWCA Crim 627 (failure to record in the original language a statement made other than in English and failure to provide an opportunity to the suspect to read a record and check its accuracy) and *Joseph* [1993] Crim LR 206 (failure to make contemporaneous record of interview), but cf. *Watson v DPP* [2003] EWHC 1466 (Admin). In *Pall* (1992) 156 JP 424, it was held that the absence of a caution was bound to be significant in most circumstances. However, an interview by an officer who genuinely does not believe that an offence has been committed does not call for a caution because its purpose is not to investigate any suspected criminal offence (Code C, para. 10.1, and *Shepherd* [2019] EWCA Crim 1062, [2019] 2 Cr App R 26 (282)). In *Ibrahim* [2008] EWCA Crim 880, [2008] 2 Cr App R 23 (311), where guidance was given on the application of s. 78 to 'safety interviews' carried out under the TA 2000, sch. 8, it was said that much will turn on the nature of the warning or caution given, if any. See also, concerning breaches of Code D, *Samms* [1991] Crim LR 197 (identification by confrontation: failure to show that it was impracticable to hold a parade or a group identification), *Marcus* [2004] EWCA Crim 3387 (failure in a video identification procedure to use images of persons bearing a sufficient resemblance to D) and *Preddie* [2011] EWCA Crim 312 (improper street identification that rendered valueless a subsequent video identification procedure). Contrast *Rajakuruna* [1991] Crim LR 458, where a breach of Code C (failure to inform a person not under arrest that the person is not obliged to remain with the officer) was held to be not significant or substantial. In appropriate circumstances, breach of the right to legal advice in the PACE 1984, s. 58, and in the ECHR, Article 6(3)(c), may result in the exclusion of evidence (see generally **F18.30** and, in the case of 'safety interviews', *Ibrahim v UK* [2016] ECHR 750, considered at **F18.38**). However, in the case of drink-driving offences the public interest requires that the obtaining of breath specimens should not be delayed to any significant extent in order to enable a suspect to take legal advice (*Campbell v DPP* [2002] EWHC 1314 (Admin); *Kennedy v CPS* [2002] EWHC 2297 (Admin)); and it is a question of fact and degree in any given case whether the custody officer acted without delay to secure the provision of legal advice and whether the person held in custody was permitted to consult a solicitor as soon as was practicable (*Kirkup v DPP* [2003] EWHC 2354 (Admin); *Whitley v DPP* [2003] EWHC 2512 (Admin)). Similarly, in the case of children, there is no reason to delay the obtaining of specimens in order for an appropriate adult to be present (*R (DPP) v B* [2002] EWHC 2976 (Admin)). **F2.29**

It is important to stress that the test for exclusion is not the seriousness of the breach *per se*, but the extent of any unfairness caused thereby (see **F2.13**). In *Ryan* [1992] Crim LR 187, it was **F2.30** argued that the judge's conclusion that there had been a major breach of the identification code (PACE Code D) should have sufficed to exclude the evidence. Rejecting this argument, the Court of Appeal pointed out that there had been occasions when there had been quite serious breaches but, it being established that this had not caused unjust prejudice to D, the judge had quite properly allowed the evidence in. In *Hoyte* [1994] Crim LR 215, a confession was admitted, despite a failure to caution, on the basis that the police had acted in good faith and, in the circumstances, there could have been no unfairness under s. 78. The outcome was the same in *Senior* [2004] EWCA Crim 454, [2004] 3 All ER 9, where customs officers had asked a series of preliminary 'routine' questions without first cautioning D, and also in *Devani* [2007] EWCA Crim 1926, [2008] 1 Cr App R 4 (65), where D was a solicitor and the questioning, which was not oppressive, took place in the presence of her principal. See also, applying *Senior*, *Rehman* [2006] EWCA Crim 1900. Similarly, in *Gill* [2003] EWCA Crim 2256, [2004] 4 All ER 681, evidence obtained in a 'Hansard' interview was admitted, despite a failure to caution, on the basis that the interviewers had not acted in bad faith and the interviewees knew that criminal proceedings were in prospect and must have known that they were not obliged to answer questions. See also *Law-Thompson* [1997] Crim LR 674 (confessions made by a mentally disordered accused in the absence of an appropriate adult).

F2.31 In *Wright* [1994] Crim LR 55, evidence of a search was admitted notwithstanding that a record of the search had not been made in D's custody record (contrary to s. 18(8) of the 1984 Act) and that there were said to have been breaches of PACE Code B (no communication had been made with D, he was not present at the search and no proper list had been made of the property). Noting that there had been no deliberate breach of Code B, it was held that the judge had taken into account the breach of s. 18(8) and the other matters could not have placed D at any disadvantage. See also *Khan* [1997] Crim LR 508 and *Sanghera* [2001] 1 Cr App R 20 (299), in both of which there could be no question as to the reliability of the evidence.

OTHER STATUTORY PROVISIONS

F2.32 Unlike the PACE 1984, s. 78(1), which is of general application, other statutory provisions empower the court, in the exercise of its discretion, to exclude specific types of otherwise admissible evidence. Thus the CJA 2003, s. 101(3), confers a discretion to exclude otherwise admissible evidence of the bad character of the accused, having regard to the particular factors set out in s. 101(4) (see **F13.15**) and appears to provide a protection *additional* to the PACE 1984, s. 78(1) (see *Highton* [2005] EWCA Crim 1985, [2005] 1 WLR 3472 at **F13.19**). Similarly, the CJA 2003, s. 126, confers a discretion to exclude otherwise admissible hearsay statements, whether adduced by the prosecution or defence (see in the case of defence evidence, *Drinkwater* [2016] EWCA Crim 16, [2016] 1 Cr App R 30 (471), considered at **F17.95**); and, in the case of evidence adduced by the prosecution, expressly preserves the power to exclude such evidence under s. 78(1) (see **F17.99** and s. 126(2) at **F17.94**).

INTERCEPTIONS OF COMMUNICATIONS

F2.33 The IPA 2016 sets out the extent to which certain investigatory powers may be used to interfere with privacy (s. 1(1)). It repeals and replaces the provisions of the RIPA 2000 relating to the interception of communications. It is an offence under the 2016 Act to intercept in the UK, without lawful authority, a communication in the course of its transmission by means of a public or private telecommunication system or a public postal service (s. 3(1)). Lawful authority may be granted by warrant or by one of the other means specified in s. 6.

F2.34 Under the IPA 2016, s. 56(1), significant restrictions apply to the use of intercepted material.

Investigatory Powers Act 2016, s. 56

(1) No evidence may be adduced, question asked, assertion or disclosure made or other thing done in, for the purposes of or in connection with any legal proceedings or Inquiries Act proceedings which (in any manner)—
  (a) discloses, in circumstances from which its origin in interception-related conduct may be inferred—
    (i) any content of an intercepted communication, or
    (ii) any secondary data obtained from a communication, or
  (b) tends to suggest that any interception-related conduct has or may have occurred or may be going to occur.

This is subject to Schedule 3 (exceptions).

'Interception-related conduct', for the purposes of s. 56(1), means, *inter alia*, conduct amounting to an offence of unlawful interception contrary to s. 3; a breach of the prohibition imposed by s. 9 (restriction on requesting interception by overseas authorities) or s. 10 (restriction on requesting assistance under mutual assistance agreements etc.); and the making of an application for a warrant, or the issue of a warrant, under Part 2, ch. 1, of the Act (s. 56(2)). It also includes any conduct taking place before s. 56(1) came into force and consisting of conduct that was an offence under the RIPA 2000, s. 1(1) or (2) (s. 56(4)). 'Intercepted communication', in s. 56, means any communication intercepted in the course of its transmission by means of a postal service or telecommunication system (s. 56(5)). In *Allsopp* [2005] EWCA Crim 703, a decision under the RIPA 2000, it was held that a conversation between two people face-to-face which is overhead by means of a listening device does not constitute a communication in the course of its transmission.

A blanket interception and recording of the telephone calls of prisoners at prisons will not constitute a breach of the IPA 2006. Under s. 49(1) and (2) of the Act, interception of a communication is authorised if it is in the exercise of a power conferred by or under the rules made under the Prison Act 1952, s. 47; and under the Prison Rules 1999, rr. 34 and 35A, the Secretary of State is empowered to impose restrictions and conditions on the telephone calls made by prisoners either across the entire prison estate or in relation to particular prisoners or classes of prisoners (see *Mahmood* [2013] EWCA Crim 2356, [2014] 1 Cr App R 31 (434), a decision under the RIPA 2000, s. 4(4), the statutory precursor to the IPA 2016, s. 49(1) and (2)). **F2.35**

DISCRETION TO EXCLUDE AT COMMON LAW

Nature of Discretion

Although there is no common-law authority to suggest that a criminal court has any power to *admit* as a matter of discretion evidence which is inadmissible under an exclusionary rule of law, it is well established that a judge, as part of his or her inherent power and overriding duty in every case to ensure that the accused receives a fair trial, always has a discretion to *exclude* otherwise admissible prosecution evidence if, in the judge's opinion, its prejudicial effect on the minds of the jury outweighs its true probative value. The classic description of the discretion is that of Lord du Parcq, delivering the reasons of the Board in *Noor Mohamed v The King* [1949] AC 182. Referring to cases in which the prosecution seek to admit similar-fact evidence, his lordship said (at p. 192): **F2.36**

> ... in all such cases the judge ought to consider whether the evidence which it is proposed to adduce is sufficiently substantial, having regard to the purpose to which it is professedly directed, to make it desirable in the interest of justice that it should be admitted. If, so far as that purpose is concerned, it can in the circumstances of the case have only trifling weight, the judge will be right to exclude it. To say this is not to confuse weight with admissibility. The distinction is

> plain, but cases must occur in which it would be unjust to admit evidence of a character gravely prejudicial to the accused even though there may be some tenuous ground for holding it technically admissible.

F2.37 The discretion developed on a case-by-case basis in relation to particular and different types of otherwise admissible evidence. In relation to similar fact evidence, for example, see *Harris v DPP* [1952] AC 694, at p. 707 (in which Viscount Simon cited and applied the passage from *Noor Mohamed v The King* set out above) and *DPP v Boardman* [1975] AC 421, at pp. 438, 441, 453, and 463. In relation to evidence otherwise admissible under the Theft Act 1968, s. 27(3), see *List* [1966] 3 All ER 710; *Herron* [1967] 1 QB 107; *Perry* [1984] Crim LR 680; and generally **F13.92** ***et seq***. Concerning exercise of the discretion in relation to identification evidence, see **F19**. See also *Eatough* [1989] Crim LR 289.

F2.38 In *Sang* [1980] AC 402, the House of Lords was firmly of the opinion that, notwithstanding its case-by-case development, the discretion is a general one. The cases, therefore, are not to be treated as a closed list of the situations in which the discretion may be exercised (see Viscount Dilhorne and Lord Salmon, at pp. 438 and 445 respectively). The cases are nothing more than examples of a single discretion founded on the duty of the judge to ensure that every accused person has a fair trial (per Lords Scarman and Fraser, at pp. 452 and 447 respectively). Lord Salmon said (at p. 445):

> I recognise that there may have been no categories of cases, other than those to which I have referred, in which technically admissible evidence proffered by the Crown has been rejected by the court on the ground that it would make the trial unfair. I cannot, however, accept that a judge's undoubted duty to ensure that the accused has a fair trial is confined to such cases. In my opinion the category of such cases is not and never can be closed except by statute.

Discretion to Exclude Only Prosecution Evidence

F2.39 The discretion may only be exercised to exclude evidence on which the prosecution, as opposed to any co-accused, proposes to rely. In *Lobban v The Queen* [1995] 2 All ER 602 (at p. 887), the Privy Council cited with approval the following description of this principle in Keane, *The Modern Law of Evidence* (3rd edn, 1994) at p. 36:

> There is no discretion to exclude, at the request of one co-accused, evidence tendered by another. Thus although . . . there is a discretion to exclude similar fact evidence tendered by the prosecution, such evidence, when tendered by an accused to show the misconduct on another occasion of a co-accused is, if relevant to the defence of the accused, admissible whether or not it prejudices the co-accused (see per Devlin J in *Miller* [1952] 2 All ER 667 (Winchester Assizes), approved in *Neale* (1977) 65 Cr App R 304). Similarly, there is no discretion to prevent an accused from cross-examining a co-accused about his previous convictions and bad character when, as a matter of law, he becomes entitled to do so...

See, in the case of evidence of bad character adduced by a co-accused, the CJA 2003, s. 101(1)(e), and *Musone* [2007] EWCA Crim 1237, [2007] 1 WLR 2467 at **F13.66** ***et seq***.

F2.40 In *Lobban v The Queen* itself, it was held that there is no discretion to exclude the exculpatory part of a 'mixed' statement (see **F18.93**) on which one co-accused wishes to rely on the grounds that it implicates another. D1 made a statement containing admissions as well as an exculpatory explanation, an integral part of which implicated D2, his co-accused. The prosecution tendered the statement against D1; it was no evidence against D2. Counsel for L submitted that the trial judge should have exercised his discretion to edit the statement to exclude the parts implicating D2. The Privy Council held that no such discretion existed. The discretionary power applies only to evidence on which the prosecution propose to rely. Although the prosecution had *tendered* the statement, they could not rely on it as evidence against D2 and the disputed material supported D1's defence. There was therefore no discretionary power to exclude the disputed material. However, in *Thompson* [1995] 2 Cr App R 589, at pp. 596–7, Evans LJ observed that where evidence is inadmissible against and prejudicial to an accused, but relevant to and therefore admissible for a co-accused, the only safeguard is the cumbersome device of separate trials, and it might be preferable to allow a discretion to exclude where the prejudice to the accused is substantial and the evidence of only limited benefit to the co-accused.

Exercise of Discretion as Basis of Appeal

Exercise of the discretion is a subjective matter, and each case must be decided in the context of its own particular facts (*Sang* [1980] AC 402, per Lords Fraser and Scarman, at pp. 450 and 456 respectively). In *Selvey v DPP* [1970] AC 304 Lord Guest went so far as to say (at p. 352): 'If it is suggested that the exercise of this discretion may be whimsical and depend on the individual idiosyncrasies of the judge, this is inevitable where it is a question of discretion'. It follows from this that the Court of Appeal will not lightly interfere with judicial exercise of the discretion. It was held that the Court of Appeal will not interfere unless: **F2.41**

(a) the judge has failed even to consider exercise of the discretion, in which case the appeal court may exercise its own discretion (*Cook* [1959] 2 QB 340); or
(b) 'he has erred in principle, or there is no material on which he could properly have arrived at his decision' (*Cook* per Devlin J, at p. 348, approved by Viscount Dilhorne in *Selvey v DPP* at p. 342 and applied in *Burke* (1985) 82 Cr App R 156).

Application to Summary Trial

In *Sang* [1980] AC 402, Lord Scarman made the following *obiter* observations relating to summary trials (at p. 456): **F2.42**

> The development of the discretion has, of necessity, been largely associated with jury trial. In the result, legal discussion of it is apt to proceed in terms of the distinctive functions of judge and jury. No harm arises from such traditional habits of thought, provided always it be borne in mind that the principles of the criminal law and its administration are the same, whether trial be (as in more than 90 per cent of the cases it is) in the magistrates' court or on indictment before judge and jury. The magistrates are bound, as is the judge in a jury trial, to ensure that the accused has a fair trial according to law; and have the same discretion as he has in the interests of a fair trial to exclude legally admissible evidence. No doubt, it will be rarely exercised. And certainly magistrates would be wise not to rule until the evidence is tendered and objection is taken.... They must wait and see what is tendered; and only then, if objection be taken, rule. When asked to rule, they should bear in mind that it is their duty to have regard to legally admissible evidence, unless in their judgment the use of the evidence would make the trial unfair.

Application to Evidence Obtained Unlawfully, Improperly or Unfairly

Cases before *Sang* Prior to *Sang* [1980] AC 402, the cases revealed an unbroken chain of dicta to the effect that in criminal proceedings the court has a general common-law discretion to exclude otherwise admissible prosecution evidence which has been obtained by improper or unfair means, e.g.: **F2.43**

(a) Evidence obtained 'by a trick' (*Kuruma, Son of Kaniu v The Queen* [1955] AC 197, per Lord Goddard CJ at p. 204.
(b) Evidence obtained 'oppressively, by false representations, by a trick, by threats, by bribes' (*Callis v Gunn* [1964] 1 QB 495, per Lord Parker CJ at pp. 501–2).
(c) Evidence obtained 'by conduct of which the Crown ought not to take advantage' (*King v The Queen* [1969] 1 AC 304, per Lord Hodson at p. 319).
(d) In the context of an illegal search, exceptional cases in which 'not only have the police officers entered without authority, but they have been guilty of trickery or they have misled someone, or they have been oppressive or they have been unfair, or in other respects they have behaved in a manner which is morally reprehensible' (*Jeffrey v Black* [1978] QB 490, per Lord Widgery CJ at p. 498).

Despite these various dicta as to the existence of a discretion to exclude evidence which has been obtained oppressively, improperly or unfairly, there were very few cases in which such **F2.44** a discretion was in fact exercised. It was exercised in *Ameer* [1977] Crim LR 104 to exclude evidence which had been obtained as a result of the activities of an *agent provocateur*, and a similar course was taken in *Foulder* [1973] Crim LR 45 and in *Burnett* [1973] Crim LR 748; but all three cases were overruled in *Sang* [1980] AC 402. The only other case in which the discretion was exercised was *Payne* [1963] 1 All ER 848, where D was charged with drunken driving. He had been induced to submit himself to examination by a doctor to see if he was suffering from any illness or disability, on the understanding that the doctor would not examine him for the purpose of seeing whether he was fit to drive; but at the trial the doctor gave evidence of D's unfitness to drive based on his symptoms and behaviour in the course of that examination. The conviction was quashed on the ground that the judge should have exercised his discretion to exclude the doctor's evidence. In *Sang*, however, *Payne* was regarded as analogous to cases in which an accused is unfairly induced to confess to an offence, and the judgment of the Court of Criminal Appeal was therefore seen to be based on the maxim *nemo tenetur se ipsum prodere* (no man is to be compelled to incriminate himself). In *McDonald* [1991] Crim LR 122, a decision under the PACE 1984, s. 78, it was held that it was not unfair to adduce evidence of a damaging admission, made by D in the course of a psychiatric examination, on a non-medical issue. See also *Gayle* [1994] Crim LR 679 and, in the case of confessions made to probation officers, *Elleray* [2003] EWCA Crim 553, [2003] 2 Cr App R 11 (165).

F2.45 *Sang* In *Sang* [1980] AC 402, the House of Lords held that, whatever the ambit of the judicial discretion to exclude admissible evidence, it does not extend to excluding evidence of a crime on the grounds that it was instigated by an *agent provocateur*, because if it did so extend it would amount to a procedural device whereby the trial judge could avoid the substantive law, under which it is clearly established that there is no defence of entrapment (*McEvilly* (1973) 60 Cr App R 150; *Mealey* (1974) 60 Cr App R 59). The point of law of general importance certified by the Court of Appeal, however, went beyond the issue of *agents provocateurs* and raised a much wider question, namely: 'Does a trial judge have a discretion to refuse to allow evidence, being evidence other than evidence of an admission, to be given in any circumstances in which such evidence is relevant and of more than minimal probative value?' Although it was not strictly necessary for their lordships to answer the certified question in its full breadth, they proceeded to do so, and the primary importance of *Sang* is the *obiter* answer given. Treating the certified question as if it were not confined to trial by jury but concerned the existence of the discretion in any criminal trial, whether in the Crown Court or in a magistrates' court, their lordships, by way of answer, agreed on the following form of words suggested by Viscount Dilhorne (at p. 437):

> (1) A trial judge in a criminal trial has always a discretion to refuse to admit evidence if in his opinion its prejudicial effect outweighs its probative value. (2) Save with regard to admissions and confessions and generally with regard to evidence obtained from the accused after commission of the offence, he has no discretion to refuse to admit relevant admissible evidence on the ground that it was obtained by improper or unfair means. The court is not concerned with how it was obtained. It is no ground for the exercise of discretion to exclude that the evidence was obtained as the result of the activities of an *agent provocateur*.

The first of the above propositions is considered at **F2.36** ***et seq.***

F2.46 As to the second proposition, despite the apparent unanimity, their lordships expressed the following differing views, especially as to the meaning to be ascribed to the words 'and generally with regard to evidence obtained from the accused after commission of the offence'.

(a) Lord Diplock (at p. 436) treated the phrase as referring to 'evidence tantamount to a self-incriminatory admission which was obtained from the defendant, after the offence had been committed, by means which would justify a judge in excluding an actual confession which had the like self-incriminating effect', and cited, by way of illustration, *Barker* [1941] 2 KB 381 (in which fraudulently prepared documents produced to a tax inspector were held to stand on precisely the same footing as an oral or written confession brought into existence as the result of a promise, inducement or threat) and *Payne* [1963] 1 All ER 848 (see **F2.44**).

(b) Lord Salmon, taking a less restrictive view as to the meaning of the phrase, said (at p. 444), 'In my opinion, the decision as to whether evidence may be excluded depends entirely on the particular facts of each case and the circumstances surrounding it — which are infinitely variable'. The category of cases in which evidence may be rejected on the grounds that it would make a trial unfair was not closed and could never be closed except by statute (at p. 445).

(c) Lord Fraser of Tullybelton, who agreed with Lord Diplock that the decision in *Payne* [1963] 1 All ER 848 was based, at least in part, on the principle that no one is bound to incriminate himself, concluded that the phrase under discussion applied 'only to evidence and documents obtained from an accused person or from premises occupied by him' and would 'leave judges with a discretion to be exercised in accordance with their individual views of what is unfair or oppressive or morally reprehensible' (at p. 450).

(d) Lord Scarman (at pp. 456–7) treated the phrase as referring exclusively to the obtaining of evidence from the accused.

Since *Sang*, the limits of the discretion have been reconsidered in two respects, considered in **F2.47** and **F2.48**.

'Evidence Tantamount to a Self-incriminatory Admission' Evidence of an incriminating conversation obtained, without any inducement, by an electronic surveillance device, is not 'evidence tantamount to a self-incriminatory admission' (*Khan* [1997] AC 558, relying upon Lord Diplock in *Sang* [1980] AC 402, see **F2.46**). Nor is evidence of body fluid taken without consent, but not by trickery (see *Apicella* (1985) 82 Cr App R 295; and cf. *Payne* [1963] 1 All ER 848, considered at **F2.44**). **F2.47**

Bona Fide Mistakes as to Lawful Powers Where evidence has been unlawfully obtained from an accused after the commission of the offence, the common-law discretion to exclude will not be exercised if those who obtained it did so on the basis of a bona fide mistake as to their powers (*Fox* [1986] AC 281: a breath specimen following an unlawful arrest; *Trump* (1979) 70 Cr App R 300: a blood sample obtained as the result of a threat). **F2.48**

Section F3 Burden and Standard of Proof and Presumptions

BURDEN OF PROOF

Legal and Evidential Burdens

F3.1 There are two principal kinds of burden, the legal burden and the evidential burden. The legal burden is a burden of proof, i.e. a burden imposed on a party to prove a fact or facts in issue. In some cases the legal burden in relation to some of the facts in issue will be on one party, and the legal burden in relation to another (or others) will be on the other party. For example, if insanity is raised by way of defence, the legal burden on that issue is on the defence, whereas the legal burden on the other facts in issue is on the prosecution (*M'Naghten's Case* (1843) 10 Cl & F 200; *Smith* (1910) 6 Cr App R 19). Any statutory provision imposing a legal burden on the accused may be open to challenge on the basis of incompatibility with Article 6(2) of the ECHR (see **F3.18**). Questions of construction are questions of law in respect of which no burden lies on either party (*Scott v Martin* [1987] 2 All ER 813).

F3.2 **The Legal Burden** The legal burden is sometimes referred to as the persuasive burden or the risk of non-persuasion, phrases which indicate that a party bearing the legal burden on a fact in issue will lose on that issue if the burden is not discharged to the required standard of proof. The standard of proof required to discharge the legal burden varies according to whether the burden is borne by the prosecution or defence. If the legal burden is borne by the prosecution, the standard required is proof beyond reasonable doubt (*Woolmington v DPP* [1935] AC 462 — see further **F3.48**). If the legal burden is borne by the accused, the standard required is proof on a balance of probabilities (*Carr-Briant* [1943] KB 607); the accused never bears the heavier burden of proof beyond reasonable doubt — see further **F3.53**). The question whether a party has discharged a legal burden is decided by the tribunal of fact, whether jury or magistrates, at the end of the trial after all the evidence has been presented.

F3.3 **The Evidential Burden** The evidential burden is not a burden of proof but the burden of adducing evidence or 'the duty of passing the judge', in other words the burden imposed on a party to adduce sufficient evidence on a fact or facts in issue to satisfy the judge that such issue or issues should be left before the tribunal of fact. In some cases, the evidential burden on some of the facts in issue will be on one party and the evidential burden on another (or others) will be on the other party. Very often a party bearing the legal burden on an issue also bears the evidential burden on that issue. However, in the case of many defences (including, for example, self-defence), the evidential burden in relation to the defence is on the accused and the legal burden in relation to the defence is on the prosecution. Thus, if there is no evidence sufficient to justify a jury concluding that the defence is established, the issue will be withdrawn from them, and such withdrawal will not amount to a breach of the ECHR, Article 6 (*Bianco* [2001] EWCA Crim 2516 at [15], approved in *Batchelor* [2013] EWCA *Crim 2638). However, if there is sufficient* evidence for the defence to be put before the jury, the legal burden of disproving it will be on the prosecution (see, e.g., *Lobell* [1957] 1 QB 547 and see generally **F3.37** to **F3.46**) and this will be the case even if the judge takes the view that the evidence is most unlikely to be of sufficient cogency or strength to be accepted by the jury (*Hammond* [2013] EWCA Crim 2709 at [6]).

Although normally a judge will not leave a particular defence to the jury until the conclusion of the evidence, in rare cases in which the precise nature of the evidence to be called is clear it may be appropriate for the judge to indicate at an earlier stage what the ruling is likely to be (*Pommell* [1995] 2 Cr App R 607 at p. 612). If, during a trial, a judge indicates that a particular defence will be left to the jury, but later changes that view, the judge should inform the defence, because they may then wish to give more evidence on the matter and the defence advocate may wish to seek to persuade the judge not to withdraw the issue (*Wright* [1992] Crim LR 596).

Discharge of Burdens Borne by the Prosecution If the evidential burden on a particular issue is borne by the prosecution, it is discharged by the adduction of sufficient evidence to justify as a possibility a finding by the tribunal of fact that the legal burden on the same issue has been discharged, in other words 'such evidence as, if believed and if left uncontradicted and unexplained, could be accepted by the jury as proof' (*Jayasena v The Queen* [1970] AC 618, per Lord Devlin at p. 624). If the prosecution bear both the evidential and legal burden on a particular issue and discharge the evidential burden, it does not necessarily follow that they will succeed on that issue — the issue in question will go before the jury for them to determine whether or not the legal burden has been discharged. However, if the prosecution bear both the legal and evidential burden on an issue and fail to discharge the evidential burden, they will necessarily fail on that issue, since the judge will withdraw that issue from the jury. Questions relating to the sufficiency of the evidence adduced by the prosecution may be raised by the judge of his or her own motion, but usually arise on a defence submission of no case to answer after the prosecution have closed their case. As to submissions of no case to answer more generally, see **D16.53** ***et seq.*** **F3.4**

Discharge of Burdens Borne by the Defence If the accused bears both the evidential and the legal burden on a particular issue, for example, insanity, the evidential burden is discharged by the adduction of such evidence as might satisfy the jury on the probability of that which the accused is called upon to establish (*Carr-Briant* [1943] KB 607, per Humphreys J at p. 612). If the accused bears the evidential but not the legal burden on a particular issue, for example, self-defence, the evidential burden is discharged by the adduction of such evidence as 'might leave a jury in reasonable doubt' (*Bratty v A-G for Northern Ireland* [1963] AC 386, per Lord Morris at p. 419). In no case is the accused called upon to prove a fact beyond reasonable doubt: the standard of proof is proof on the balance of probabilities (*Carr-Briant*). **F3.5**

Incidence of Legal Burden: General Rule

The general rule is that the prosecution bear the legal burden of proving all the elements in the offence necessary to establish guilt (*Woolmington v DPP* [1935] AC 462). See also *Mancini v DPP* [1942] AC 1, per Lord Simon at p. 11. In *Woolmington*, D was charged with the murder of his wife, who had left him to return to her mother. He visited her with a sawn-off shotgun concealed under his coat, and when they met she was killed by a shot from the gun. D said that while attempting to induce his wife to return to him by threatening to kill himself, the gun went off accidentally. Swift J directed the jury that, once it was proved that D shot his wife, D bore the burden of disproving malice aforethought. The House of Lords held this to be a misdirection. Viscount Sankey LC said, at pp. 481–2: **F3.6**

> But while the prosecution must prove the guilt of the prisoner, there is no such burden laid on the prisoner to prove his innocence and it is sufficient for him to raise a doubt as to his guilt; he is not bound to satisfy the jury of his innocence...
>
> Throughout the web of the English criminal law one golden thread is always to be seen, that it is the duty of the prosecution to prove the prisoner's guilt subject to what I have already said as to the defence of insanity and subject also to any statutory exception... No matter what the charge or where the trial, the principle that the prosecution must prove the guilt of the prisoner is part of the common law of England and no attempt to whittle it down can be entertained... It is not the law of

England to say, as was said in the summing-up in the present case: 'if the Crown satisfy you that this woman died at the prisoner's hands then he has to show that there are circumstances to be found in the evidence which has been given from the witness-box in this case which alleviate the crime so that it is only manslaughter or which excuse the homicide altogether by showing it was a pure accident'.

F3.7 The prosecution bear the burden of proving all the elements in the offence, even if this involves proving negative averments. Thus, in a case of rape the prosecution bear the burden of proving that the complainant did not consent (*Horn* (1912) 7 Cr App R 200). Similarly, the prosecution bear the burden of proving absence of consent on a charge of assault (*Donovan* [1934] 2 KB 498). Furthermore, if capacity to consent is in issue, the prosecution will also bear the burden of proving incapacity (*A (G)* [2014] EWCA Crim 299, [2014] 2 Cr App R 5 (73)). For the former offence of obtaining by deception, the prosecution bore the burden of proving the falsity of the statement, even if that involved proving a negative (*Mandry* [1973] 3 All ER 996, in which the statement, made by street traders selling scent for £1, was 'You can go down the road and buy it for two guineas in the big stores'). *Mandry* also illustrates that there is a limit to what can reasonably be required of the prosecution when seeking to prove a negative. A constable gave evidence that he had visited four shops in the area and that the scent was not sold at any of them. In cross-examination, he admitted that he had not visited a well-known department store. The judge directed the jury that the police could not be expected to visit every shop in London in order to prove that the scent was not being sold for two guineas in any shop; and that if D knew of any shop where it could be bought at that price, they were perfectly entitled to adduce such evidence. The Court of Appeal held that no criticism could be made of this direction. In many cases, however, because of the difficulties of proving a negative proposition, statute may, exceptionally, require the accused to bear the burden of proving certain facts (see **F3.9** to **F3.17**).

There are only three categories of exception to the general rule as laid down in *Woolmington v DPP* [1935] AC 462:

(a) insanity;
(b) express statutory exceptions; and
(c) implied statutory exceptions.

Statutory exceptions are sometimes referred to as reverse onus provisions.

F3.8 **Exception in Case of Defence of Insanity** If the accused raises the defence of insanity, the accused will bear the burden of proving it (on a balance of probabilities) (*M'Naghten's Case* (1843) 10 Cl & F 200; *Smith* (1910) 6 Cr App R 19; *Sodeman v The King* [1936] 2 All ER 1138). Under the Criminal Procedure (Insanity) Act 1964, s. 6, if the accused is charged with murder and raises one of two issues, either insanity or diminished responsibility, the court shall allow the prosecution to adduce evidence tending to prove the other of those issues. The burden on the prosecution will be to prove the other of those issues beyond reasonable doubt (*Grant* [1960] Crim LR 424, per Paul J).

Criminal Procedure (Insanity) Act 1964, s. 6

Where on a trial for murder the accused contends—

(a) that at the time of the alleged offence he was insane so as not to be responsible according to law for his actions; or
(b) that at that time he was suffering from such abnormality of mental functioning as is specified in subsection (1) of section 2 of the Homicide Act 1957 (diminished responsibility),

the court shall allow the prosecution to adduce or elicit evidence tending to prove the other of those contentions, and may give directions as to the stage of the proceedings at which the prosecution may adduce such evidence.

If an accused is alleged to be under a disability rendering the accused unfit to plead and stand trial on indictment, the issue may be raised by either the prosecution or defence (see the Criminal Procedure (Insanity) Act 1964, s. 4, and generally **D12.2** *et seq.*). If the prosecution contend that the accused is under such a disability and this is disputed by the defence, the burden of proof is on the prosecution to satisfy the court beyond reasonable doubt (*Robertson* [1968] 3 All

ER 557). If the defence contend that the accused is under such a disability, the burden is on the defence on a balance of probabilities (*Podola* [1960] 1 QB 325).

Express Statutory Exceptions Statute may expressly cast on the accused the burden of proving a particular issue or issues. The legal burden in relation to all other issues in such cases will remain on the prosecution, in accordance with the general rule as laid down in *Woolmington v DPP* [1935] AC 462. Prior to the coming into force of the HRA 1998, it could be said with confidence that statutory provisions which put on the accused an obligation to 'prove' a particular matter, had thereby cast a legal burden on the defence. However provisions of this kind and the decisions pertaining to them must now be read subject to the decision of the House of Lords in *Lambert* [2001] UKHL 37, [2002] 2 AC 545 (discussed at **F3.19**) that in appropriate circumstances the words 'to prove' may be read down under the HRA 1998, s. 3, so as to impose on an accused no more than an evidential burden. The same applies in the case of 'show' (see, e.g., the defence in the Explosive Substances Act 1883, s. 4(1), and the commentary relating to its proof at **B12.255** ***et seq.***), but only if that word is interpreted as synonymous with 'prove', which depends upon the precise statutory context (*Shepherd v Information Commissioner* [2019] EWCA Crim 2, [2019] 1 Cr App R 29 (393), and see also *Johnstone* [2003] UKHL 28, [2003] 1 WLR 1736 at **F3.24** and *S* [2002] EWCA Crim 2558, [2003] 1 Cr App R 35 (602) at **F3.36**). **F3.9**

An example of an express statutory exception is the Homicide Act 1957, s. 2.

Homicide Act 1957, s. 2

(2) On a charge of murder, it shall be for the defence to prove that the person charged is by virtue of this section not liable to be convicted of murder.

Where the defence of diminished responsibility is raised, the onus is on the defence to prove it on a balance of probabilities (*Dunbar* [1958] 1 QB 1; *Grant* [1960] Crim LR 424). Section 2(2) does not contravene the ECHR, Article 6(2), and should not be read down as imposing on the defence only an evidential burden (*Wilcocks* [2016] EWCA Crim 2043, [2017] 1 Cr App R 23 (338), applying *Foye* [2013] EWCA Crim 475).

Section 2(2) leaves it to the defence to decide whether the issue of diminished responsibility should be raised; if, therefore, the judge detects evidence of diminished responsibility but the defence do not raise the issue, the judge is not bound to direct the jury to consider the matter, but, at most, should in the absence of the jury draw the matter to the attention of the defence so that they may decide whether they wish the issue to be considered by the jury (*Campbell* (1986) 84 Cr App R 255, per Lord Lane CJ, *obiter*).

Another example of an express statutory exception is the Prevention of Crime Act 1953, s. 1 (see **B12.144**). In the case of an offensive weapon *per se*, the prosecution are not required to prove that the accused carried it with the intention of using it to cause injury to the person; if possession in a public place is proved, the onus is on the accused to prove on a balance of probabilities lawful authority or reasonable excuse for the possession (*Davis v Alexander* (1970) 54 Cr App R 398). In the case of an article not made or adapted for use for causing injury to the person, the onus is on the prosecution to prove that the accused carried it with the intention of using it to injure; and if the jury are satisfied as to this, and the issue of lawful authority or reasonable excuse has been raised, the onus is on the accused to prove on a balance of probabilities such authority or excuse (*Petrie* [1961] 1 All ER 466; *Brown* (1971) 55 Cr App R 478). **F3.10**

A final example is the Homicide Act 1957, s. 4(2) ('Where it is shown that a person charged with the murder of another killed the other or was a party to his... being killed, it shall be for the defence to prove that the person charged was acting in pursuance of a suicide pact between him and the other').

Implied Statutory Exceptions A statute can place the legal burden of proof on the accused not only expressly but also by implication, i.e. on its true construction. In summary trials, the matter is governed by the MCA 1980, s. 101. Concerning trials on indictment, the leading authorities **F3.11**

are *Edwards* [1975] QB 27 and *Hunt* [1987] AC 352; in the latter it was made clear that when, in *Woolmington v DPP* [1935] AC 462, Viscount Sankey LC referred to 'any statutory exception' (see **F3.6**), he was referring to statutory exceptions in which Parliament had placed the burden of proof on the accused *either* expressly *or* by implication (per Lords Griffiths and Ackner).

Magistrates' Courts Act 1980, s. 101

> Where the defendant to an information or complaint relies for his defence on any exception, exemption, proviso, excuse or qualification, whether or not it accompanies the description of the offence or matter of complaint in the enactment creating the offence or on which the complaint is founded, the burden of proving the exception, exemption, proviso, excuse or qualification shall be on him; and this notwithstanding that the information or complaint contains an allegation negativing the exception, exemption, proviso, excuse or qualification.

The cases, in the ensuing commentary, in which statutory provisions have been so construed as to place a legal burden on the accused, must now be read subject to the HRA 1998 and the decisions discussed at **F3.18** ***et seq***. Any implied statutory exception must now be open to challenge on the basis of incompatibility with the ECHR, Article 6(2). As to summary trials, it is submitted that 'the burden of proving' to which the MCA 1980, s. 101, refers always means the legal burden and therefore any implied statutory exception is capable of derogating from Article 6(2). It follows that for each such exception the question of compatibility will need to be considered by reference to the three-stage test set out in *Lambert* [2001] UKHL 37, [2002] 2 AC 545, discussed at **F3.19** (cf. per Clarke LJ in *R (Grundy & Co Excavations Ltd) v Halton Division Magistrates' Court* [2003] EWHC 272 (Admin) at [60] and [61]).

F3.12 Concerning the construction of s. 101, the following matters of general importance should also be noted:

(a) On its wording, s. 101 applies to summary trials. However, it is now established that where a statute, on its true construction, places the legal burden of proof on an accused, the burden is on the accused whether the case be tried summarily or on indictment; s. 101 reflects and applies to summary trials the common-law rule relating to the incidence of the burden of proof evolved by judges on trials on indictment (*Hunt* [1987] AC 352).

(b) The section applies where the words of exception etc. amount to a defence.

(c) In *Nimmo v Alexander Cowan & Sons Ltd* [1968] AC 107, Lord Pearson gave the following *obiter* guidance (at p. 135) as to the construction of the Scottish equivalent of s. 101. An exemption, exception or proviso is easily recognisable from the wording of the enactment — an exception would naturally begin with the word 'except' and a proviso with the words 'Provided always that'. The addition of the words 'excuse' and 'qualification' showed an intention to widen the provision. There is no usual formula for an 'excuse'. A 'qualification', if understood in a grammatical sense, might cover any adjective, adverb or adjectival or adverbial phrase. More probably it means some qualification, such as a licence, for doing what would otherwise be unlawful. There is no usual formula for 'qualification' in that sense. The court should look at the substance and effect of the enactment in question, as well as its form, in order to ascertain whether it contains an 'excuse or qualification'.

F3.13 In a case of driving without a licence, it is for the accused driver to prove possession of a current driving licence (*John v Humphreys* [1955] 1 All ER 793). Similarly, in cases of driving without insurance, it is for the accused driver to prove that he or she is insured (*Williams v Russell* (1933) 149 LT 190; *Philcox v Carberry* [1960] Crim LR 563). In *Gatland v Metropolitan Police Commissioner* [1968] 2 QB 279, the accused had left a skip on the road with which a car had collided. They were charged with an offence under the Highways Act 1959, s. 140(1), which provided that 'if a person, without lawful authority or excuse, deposits anything whatsoever on a highway in consequence whereof a user of the highway is injured or endangered, that person shall be guilty of an offence'. The Divisional Court held that it was for the prosecution to prove that a thing had been deposited on the highway and that in consequence a user of the highway had been injured or endangered; but that it was for the accused to prove lawful authority or excuse. Contrast, *Westminster City Council v Croyalgrange* [1986] 2 All ER 353. See also, construing Environmental Protection Act 1990, s. 33(1)(a), *Environment Agency v ME Foley Contractors Ltd* [2002] EWHC 258 (Admin), [2002] 1 WLR 1756.

Nimmo v Alexander Cowan & Sons Ltd *Nimmo v Alexander Cowan & Sons Ltd* [1968] AC 107 was a Scottish civil action brought by a workman under the Factories Act 1961, s. 29(1) (now repealed). Section 29(1) provided that every place at which any person has at any time to work 'shall, so far as is reasonably practicable, be made and kept safe for any person working there'. The question before the House of Lords was whether the burden of proving that it was not reasonably practicable to make the working place safe lay on the defendant or the pursuer. The same question could have arisen in a criminal action: s. 155(1) of the 1961 Act made a breach of s. 29(1) a summary offence. Both Lord Pearson (at p. 134) and Lord Reid (at p. 115) observed that the incidence of the burden of proof would be the same whether the proceedings were civil or criminal. The House divided on the construction of the section. The majority held that it was for the pursuer (or prosecution) to prove that the working place was not safe, and for the defendant (or accused) to excuse himself by proving that it was not reasonably practicable to make it safe. Their lordships were in agreement, however, that if the linguistic construction of a statute does not clearly indicate on whom the burden should lie, the court should look to other considerations to determine the intention of Parliament, such as the mischief at which the Act was aimed and the ease or difficulty that the respective parties would encounter in discharging the burden. **F3.14**

Edwards The MCA 1980, s. 101, sets out in statutory form the common-law rule which applies to trials on indictment. This was established in *Edwards* [1975] QB 27. Prior to *Edwards* there was a rule of statutory interpretation that 'if a negative averment be made by one party which is peculiarly within the knowledge of the other, the party within whose knowledge it lies, and who asserts the affirmative, is to prove it and not he who asserts the negative' (*Turner* (1816) 5 M & S 206, per Bayley J at p. 211). This approach was followed in *Oliver* [1944] KB 68 and *Ewens* [1967] 1 QB 322. **F3.15**

In *Edwards* [1975] QB 27, D was convicted on indictment of selling intoxicating liquor without a licence, contrary to the Licensing Act 1964, s. 160(1)(a). He appealed on the ground that the prosecution had failed to adduce any evidence to show that he was not the holder of a licence. It was submitted that at common law the burden of proving an exception, exemption and the like is borne by the accused only if the facts constituting such exception or exemption are peculiarly within the accused's own knowledge which, in the instant case, they were not, because the police had access to the public register of local licences. The Court of Appeal, dismissing the appeal, held that it was for D to prove that he was the holder of a licence. Referring to the common-law exception to the fundamental rule that the prosecution must prove every element of the offence charged, Lawton LJ said, at p. 40:

> It is limited to offences arising under enactments which prohibit the doing of an act save in specified circumstances or by persons of specified classes or with specified qualifications or with the licence or permission of specified authorities. Whenever the prosecution seeks to rely on this exception, the court must construe the enactment under which the charge is laid. If the true construction is that the enactment prohibits the doing of acts, subject to provisos, exemptions and the like, then the prosecution can rely upon the exception.
>
> In our judgment its application does not depend upon either the fact, or the presumption, that the defendant has peculiar knowledge enabling him to prove the positive of any negative averment.

These principles apply even in jurisdictions where the presumption of innocence has been enshrined in a constitutional provision (*A-G for Hong Kong v Le Kwong-kut* [1993] AC 951 at pp. 968-70; *Beezadhur v Independent Commission against Corruption* [2014] UKPC 27 at [26] and [30]).

F3.16 *Hunt* In *Hunt* [1987] AC 352, the House of Lords held that:

(a) *Edwards* was decided correctly, subject to one qualification. The formula given by Lawton LJ was 'a helpful approach' and 'an excellent guide to construction' but was not intended to be, and is not, exclusive in its effect — on rare occasions a statute will be construed as imposing the legal burden on the accused although outside the ambit of the formula (see the speech of Lord Griffiths, with which Lords Keith and Mackay agreed, at p. 365 and that of Lord Ackner at p. 379).
(b) In the final analysis each case must turn on the construction of the particular legislation to determine whether the defence is an exception within the meaning of the MCA 1980, s. 101, which reflects the rule for trials on indictment (per Lord Griffiths at p. 375).
(c) In construing an enactment in order to ascertain where the burden of proof lies, the court is not restricted to the form or wording of the statutory provision but is entitled to have regard to matters of policy. The court must look at the substance and effect of the enactment and practical considerations affecting the burden of proof, particularly the ease or difficulty that the respective parties would encounter in discharging the burden (per Lord Griffiths at p. 375 and per Lord Ackner at pp. 380 and 382). However, 'Parliament can never lightly be taken to have intended to impose an onerous duty on an accused to prove his innocence in a criminal case, and a court should be very slow to draw any such inference from the language of a statute' (per Lord Griffiths at p. 374).

F3.17 In *Hunt*, D was found to be in possession of a powder containing morphine mixed with two other substances which were not controlled drugs. He was convicted of the unlawful possession of morphine, contrary to the Misuse of Drugs Act 1971, s. 5(2). Under the Misuse of Drugs Regulations 1973, sch. 1, para. 3, any preparation of morphine containing not more than 0.2 per cent of morphine compounded with other ingredients was excepted from the prohibition on possession contained in s. 5 of the 1971 Act. The question, on appeal, was whether it was for the prosecution to prove that D did not come within the exception contained in para. 3, or for D to prove that he did come within it. Quashing the conviction, the House of Lords held that:

(a) The case did not come within the formula, laid down by Lawton LJ in *Edwards* [1975] QB 27, as to when the legal burden is on the accused.
(b) On the true construction of the provisions, it was for the prosecution to prove not only that the powder contained morphine, but also that it was not morphine in the form permitted by para. 3. This would not place an undue burden on the prosecution. In the normal case the substance in question would be analysed for the police, and there would be no difficulty in producing evidence to show that it did not fall within sch. 1 to the 1973 Regulations. However, if the burden were to be placed on D, he would be faced with very real difficulties in discharging it, because the suspected substance is usually seized by the police and there is no statutory provision entitling D to a portion of it. Often there is very little of the substance, and it may have been destroyed in the process of analysis on behalf of the prosecution.
(c) Since the question of construction was obviously one of real difficulty, regard should be had to the fact that offences involving the misuse of hard drugs are among the most serious in the criminal calendar, and in these circumstances any ambiguity should be resolved in favour of D by placing the burden of proving the nature of the substance involved on the prosecution.

See also, in similar vein, *Makuwa* [2006] EWCA Crim 175, [2006] 1 WLR 2755: where the language of a statute does not make it clear whether the defence has to be established by the accused or negatived by the prosecution, the court should consider the mischief at which the statute was aimed and practical considerations affecting the burden of proof, in particular the ease or difficulty that the respective parties would encounter in discharging the burden. See also *DPP v Wright* [2009] EWHC 105 (Admin), [2010] QB 224 (some of the matters in the Hunting Act 2004, sch. 1, are neither within the knowledge of the accused nor intrinsically easy to prove).

MK [2018] EWCA Crim 667, [2019] QB 86 concerned the proper interpretation of the Modern Slavery Act 2015, s. 45, which contains a defence to all offences other than those excepted by sch. 4, for those under compulsion attributable to slavery or trafficking (see **A3.53** and **A3.54**). It was held that the accused bears the evidential burden on the elements of the defence, the prosecution bearing the burden of disproof. The principal reasons for reaching this conclusion were as follows. Section 45 was not a provision of the type described in *Edwards* [1975] QB 27. If a legal burden were to be imposed on the accused there would be a danger of frustrating Parliament's objective that victims of trafficking and slavery should be protected against the further stigma of a criminal conviction for an offence committed in consequence of the victimisation. Although in some cases it may be easier for the accused to prove the defence insofar as it relates to matters within the accused's knowledge, if the prosecution bear the legal burden it is unlikely to be very different from the burden of disproving the common-law defence of duress (which may be run in tandem with a defence under s. 45 and rely on the same evidence). Moreover, the defence under s. 45 also contains an objective element (see s. 45(1)(d) and (4)(c)).

Incidence of the Legal Burden: the Human Rights Act 1998

Any reverse onus provision is open to challenge on the basis of incompatibility with the ECHR, **F3.18** Article 6(2), which provides that 'everyone charged with a criminal offence shall be presumed innocent until proved guilty according to the law'. However, a reverse onus provision will not inevitably give rise to a finding of incompatibility (per Lord Hope in *Lambert* [2001] UKHL 37, [2002] 2 AC 545 at [87]). It is now well settled that, in deciding the issue, the court should focus on the particular circumstances of the case and strike a reasonable balance between the general interest of the community and the protection of the fundamental rights of the individual. The relevant principles to be found in the jurisprudence of the ECtHR were summarised by Lord Bingham in *Sheldrake v DPP* [2004] UKHL 43, [2005] 1 AC 264 at [21].

> The overriding concern is that a trial should be fair, and the presumption of innocence is a fundamental right directed to that end. The Convention does not outlaw presumptions of fact or law but requires that these should be kept within reasonable limits and should not be arbitrary. It is open to states to define the constituent elements of a criminal offence, excluding the requirement of *mens rea*. But the substance and effect of any presumption adverse to a defendant must be examined, and must be reasonable. Relevant to any judgment on reasonableness or proportionality will be the opportunity given to the defendant to rebut the presumption, maintenance of the rights of the defence, flexibility in application of the presumption, retention by the court of a power to assess the evidence, the importance of what is at stake and the difficulty which a prosecutor may face in the absence of a presumption. Security concerns do not absolve member states from their duty to observe basic standards of fairness. The justifiability of any infringement of the presumption of innocence cannot be resolved by any rule of thumb, but on examination of all the facts and circumstances of the particular provision as applied in the particular case.

The obvious drawback to a test so reliant on notions of fairness, reasonableness and proportionality is that views may reasonably differ so that in many cases it will be as possible to reach a rational conclusion of compatibility as incompatibility. A good example, in this respect, is furnished by *Keogh* [2007] EWCA Crim 528, [2007] 3 All ER 789, where the Court of Appeal, reversing the decision of Aikens J, held that the Official Secrets Act 1989, ss. 2(3) and 3(4), could be 'read down' so as to impose only an evidential burden on the accused, on the basis that a reverse burden was not a necessary element in the operation of ss. 2 and 3, it being 'practicable' to require the prosecution to prove that the accused knew or had reasonable cause to believe that the information disclosed related to such matters as 'defence', and that its disclosure would be damaging.

The leading domestic authorities are *Johnstone* [2003] UKHL 28, [2003] 1 WLR 1736 and *Sheldrake v DPP*, but it is useful to consider first the decision in *Lambert* and the subsequent cases in which it has been followed or distinguished.

***Lambert*: Misuse of Drugs Act 1971, s. 28** In *Lambert* [2001] UKHL 37, [2002] 2 AC 545, **F3.19** D was charged with possession of cocaine with intent to supply contrary to the Misuse of Drugs

Act 1971, s. 5(3). In his defence, he relied on s. 28 of the 1971 Act (see **B19.104**), asserting that he did not believe or suspect or have reason to suspect that the bag which he had carried contained cocaine. The trial judge directed the jury that under s. 28 the legal burden was on D. The Court of Appeal dismissed the appeal against conviction. One of the principal issues before the House of Lords was whether s. 28 as applied by the trial judge contravened Article 6(2) or could be interpreted, under the HRA 1998, s. 3(1), as placing on D an evidential burden only, i.e. in a way which would be compatible with Article 6. The House of Lords held (Lord Steyn dissenting) that, since the trial had taken place before the coming into force of the 1998 Act, D was not entitled to rely in an appeal after the Act had come into force on an alleged breach of his rights under the ECHR by the trial judge. On the question of compatibility with Article 6, the House was of the view (Lord Hutton dissenting) that s. 28 is not compatible with Article 6(2) but, under s. 3 of the 1998 Act, may be read as imposing only an evidential burden on D. The words 'to prove' in s. 28(2) (and 'if he proves' in s. 28(3)) can be taken to mean 'to give sufficient evidence' (see per Lord Steyn at [42] and Lord Hope at [94]).

F3.20 In his judgment, Lord Steyn approached the question of compatibility in three stages by asking first whether s. 5(3) of the 1971 Act, read with s. 28, interfered with Article 6(2) and, if so, secondly whether there was an objective justification for such interference and thirdly whether it was proportionate, i.e. no greater than was necessary. As to the first question, it was held that s. 28 was an ingredient of the offence under s. 5(3) in that knowledge of the existence and control of the contents of the container is the gravamen of the offence, taking into account that s. 28 deals directly with the situation where the accused is denying moral blameworthiness and the fact that the maximum prescribed penalty is life imprisonment, and therefore s. 28 derogates from the presumption of innocence. Lord Steyn also reached this conclusion on broader grounds. He held that the answer should not turn on the distinction between constituent elements of the crime and defensive issues, which will sometimes be unprincipled and arbitrary. (This dictum was directed to the issue of proportionality and not that of statutory construction as to whether a provision imposes only an evidential burden: see *Shepherd v Information Commissioner* [2019] EWCA Crim 2, [2019] 1 Cr App R 29 (393) at [42].) Lord Steyn said (at [35]; cf. Lord Hutton at [185]):

> After all, it is sometimes simply a matter of which drafting technique is adopted: a true constituent element can be removed from the definition of the crime and cast as a defensive issue whereas any definition of an offence can be reformulated so as to include all possible defences within it. It is necessary to concentrate not on technicalities and niceties of language but rather on matters of substance.

Lord Steyn (at [35]) adopted the reasoning of Dickson CJC, giving the judgment of the Canadian Supreme Court in *Whyte* (1988) 51 DLR (4th) 481: 'If an accused is required to prove some fact on the balance of probabilities to avoid conviction, the provision violates the presumption of innocence because it permits a conviction in spite of a reasonable doubt in the mind of the tribunal of fact as to the guilt of the accused'. As to the second question, Lord Steyn was satisfied that there was an objective justification for interference with the burden of proof in the 1971 Act. Sophisticated drug smugglers, dealers and couriers typically secrete drugs in some container, enabling the person in possession to say that he or she was unaware of the contents. Such defences are commonplace and pose real difficulties for the police and prosecuting authorities. Turning to the third question, the principle of proportionality required the House to consider whether it was necessary to impose a legal rather than an evidential burden on the accused. Lord Steyn noted that to put a legal burden on the accused had a far-reaching consequence, that a guilty verdict may be returned in respect of an offence punishable by life imprisonment even though the jury may consider that it is reasonably possible that the accused had been duped. The burden of showing that *only* a reverse legal burden can overcome the difficulties of the prosecution in drugs cases was a heavy one. A 'new realism' had significantly reduced the problems faced by the prosecution in drugs cases. First, the relevant facts usually being peculiarly within the knowledge of the possessor of the container, such possession presumptively suggests, in the absence of exculpatory evidence, knowledge of the contents. Secondly, the judge can now comment on an accused's failure to mention facts when questioned or charged under the CJPO 1994, s. 34 (see **F20.10**). Thirdly, in cases where a 'mixed statement' is received in evidence, the judge may direct that excuses do not have the same weight as the incriminating part of the statement (see **F18.95**). For these reasons, s. 28 did not satisfy the criterion of proportionality but was a disproportionate reaction to the perceived difficulties facing the prosecution in drugs cases. However, under s. 3 of the HRA 1998, the words 'to prove' in s. 28(2) (and 'if he proves' in s. 28(3)) could be read as placing only an evidential burden on the accused.

***L v DPP*: CJA 1988, s. 139(4)** *Lambert* [2001] UKHL 37, [2002] 2 AC 545 was distinguished in *L v DPP* [2001] EWHC Admin 882, [2003] QB 137, a case of being in possession of a lock-knife contrary to the CJA 1988, s. 139 (see **B12.177**), in relation to s. 139(4), whereby it is a defence for an accused 'to prove that he had good reason or lawful authority for having the article with him in a public place'. Striking 'a fair balance', it was held that s. 139(4) does not conflict with the ECHR, Article 6. Six reasons were given: **F3.21**

(1) Under s. 139 it is for the prosecution to prove that the accused knowingly had the article in his or her possession.
(2) There is a strong public interest in bladed articles not being carried in public without good reason.
(3) The accused is proving something within his or her own knowledge.
(4) Notwithstanding the adversarial nature of English proceedings, an accused, whether giving evidence in person or not, is entitled, under Article 6, to expect the court to scrutinise the evidence with a view to deciding if a good reason exists.
(5) In the great majority of cases the tribunal of fact makes a judgment as to whether there was a good reason without the decision depending on whether it has to be proved that there is a good reason.
(6) Limited weight should be given, in striking the balance, to the much more restricted power of sentence for an offence under s. 139 than for an offence under the MDA 1971, s. 28.

See also *Mathews* [2003] EWCA Crim 813, [2004] QB 690, applying *L v DPP* in relation to both s. 139(4) and (5) of the 1988 Act.

***Drummond*: RTOA 1988, s. 15** *Lambert* [2001] UKHL 37, [2002] 2 AC 545 was also distinguished in *Drummond* [2002] EWCA Crim 527, [2002] 2 Cr App R 21 (352), in relation to the 'hip flask' defence in the RTOA 1988, s. 15, whereby it is for the accused to prove that he or she consumed alcohol before providing a specimen and after the offence (see **C5.49**). The Court of Appeal noted that the offence of driving while over the limit does not require the court to ascertain the accused's intent; that conviction follows a scientific test which is intended to be as exact as possible; that if an accused drinks after the event, it is the accused who defeats the aim of the legislature by making the test potentially unreliable; and that the relevant scientific evidence to set against the specimen result is within the knowledge or means of access of the accused. For these reasons it was held that the legislative interference with the presumption of innocence in s. 15 was not only justified, but was no greater than was necessary. **F3.22**

***DPP v Barker*: RTOA 1988, s. 37(3)** In *DPP v Barker* [2004] EWHC 2502 (Admin), D was charged with driving while disqualified and relied on the RTOA 1988, s. 37(3), whereby a person disqualified from driving is entitled to hold a provisional licence and to drive a vehicle in accordance with its conditions. It was held that the MCA 1980, s. 101, applied (see **F3.11**) and therefore the burden was on D to show that he had a provisional licence and was driving in accordance with its conditions. The burden was held to be wholly proportionate; as to being the holder of a provisional licence, the burden could easily be discharged by producing the licence; and as to the conditions of the licence, in some cases, in the absence of any information from the accused as to the identity of a passenger, it would be impossible for the prosecution to establish the accused's identity and that the accused was the holder of a licence and therefore qualified to be supervising the driver. **F3.23**

***Johnstone*: Trade Marks Act 1994, s. 92(5)** *Johnstone* [2003] UKHL 28, [2003] 1 WLR 1736 concerned the Trade Marks Act 1994, s. 92(5), whereby it is a defence for a person charged with **F3.24**

an offence under s. 92 (unauthorised use of a trade mark) to show that the person believed on reasonable grounds that use of a sign was not an infringement of the trade mark. The House of Lords, approving the decision of the Court of Appeal in *S* [2002] EWCA Crim 2558, [2003] 1 Cr App R 35 (602), was of the unanimous *obiter* view that s. 92(5) should be interpreted as imposing on the accused the legal burden and that this interpretation was compatible with Article 6(2). According to Lord Nicholls (at [50] and [51]):

> A sound starting point is to remember that if an accused is required to prove a fact on the balance of probability... this permits a conviction in spite of the fact-finding tribunal having a reasonable doubt as to the guilt of the accused... This consequence of a reverse burden of proof should colour one's approach when evaluating the reasons why it is said that, in the absence of a persuasive burden on the accused, the public interest will be prejudiced to an extent which justifies placing a persuasive burden on the accused. The more serious the punishment which may flow from conviction, the more compelling must be the reasons. The extent and nature of the factual matters required to be proved by the accused, and their importance relative to the matters required to be proved by the prosecution, have to be taken into account. So also does the extent to which the burden on the accused relates to facts which, if they exist, are readily provable by him as matters within his own knowledge or to which he has ready access.
>
> In evaluating these factors the court's role is one of review. Parliament, not the court, is charged with the primary responsibility for deciding, as a matter of policy, what should be the constituent elements of a criminal offence... The court will reach a different conclusion from the legislature only when it is apparent the legislature has attached insufficient importance to the fundamental right of an individual to be presumed innocent until proved guilty.

F3.25 In relation to s. 92, it was held that two particular factors constituted compelling reasons why s. 92(5) put a legal burden on the accused. First, those who trade in brand products are aware of the need to be on guard against counterfeit goods. They are aware of the need to deal with reputable suppliers and to keep records and of the risks they take if they do not. Secondly, that whereas the s. 92(5) defence relates to facts within the accused's own knowledge and the sources of supply are known to the accused, by and large it is to be expected that those who supply traders with counterfeit products, if traceable at all by outside investigators, are unlikely to be co-operative. So, in practice, if the prosecution must prove that a trader acted dishonestly, there would be fewer investigations and prosecutions. Among the other factors considered was an important policy consideration: to protect consumers and honest manufacturers and traders. Counterfeiting is a serious contemporary problem with adverse economic effects on genuine trade and on consumers, in terms of quality of goods, and, sometimes, on health or safety.

F3.26 ***A-G's Ref (No. 1 of 2004)*: Insolvency Act 1986** In *A-G's Ref (No. 1 of 2004)* [2004] EWCA Crim 1025, [2004] 2 Cr App R 27 (424), a five-judge Court of Appeal was convened to hear five appeals. The first two appeals concerned the same statutory provisions in the Insolvency Act 1986, namely s. 353(1), whereby a bankrupt is guilty of an offence if he or she does not inform the official receiver of a disposal of property comprised in his or her estate (see **B7.60**), s. 357(1), whereby a bankrupt is guilty of an offence if he or she makes, or in the five years before the start of the bankruptcy made, any gift or transfer of, or any charge on, his or her property (see **B7.64**) and s. 352, under which a person is not guilty of an offence under either s. 353(1) or s. 357(1), among others, if he or she had no intent to defraud or to conceal the state of his or her affairs (see **B7.59**). It was held that: (1) s. 352, if interpreted as imposing a legal burden on the accused for the purposes of s. 353(1), does not breach Article 6, and (2) s. 352, if interpreted as imposing a legal burden on the accused for the purposes of s. 357(1), does breach Article 6 but can be read down so as to impose only an evidential burden. The reason given for the conclusion in (1) was that the proper working of insolvency law depends on the inclusion in the assets of an insolvent company, and in the estate of a bankrupt, of all the assets that should be comprised in them; that concealment or disposal of such assets to the disadvantage of the creditors can be done alone and in private; and that whether there has been fraud will often be known only to the individuals in question. These considerations normally justify the imposition on an accused who is proved to have deliberately acted in a manner that gives rise to an inference that the accused sought to defraud creditors, of the burden of proving that such was not the intention. It was further held that the decision in *Carass* [2001] EWCA Crim 2845, [2002] 1 WLR 1714 cannot stand with *Johnstone* [2003] UKHL 28, [2003] 1 WLR 1736 and must be treated as impliedly overruled.

In *Carass* it was held that s. 206(4) of the 1986 Act, whereby, in relation to various offences of fraud in anticipation of winding up, it is a defence for an accused to prove that there was no intention to defraud (see **B7.45**), must be regarded as imposing only an evidential burden. Thus the burden under s. 206(4) of the 1986 Act is a legal burden compatible with Article 6(2) and the same conclusion has also been reached in relation to the defence in s. 208(4) of the 1986 Act (see **B7.49**), which has some parallel with s. 206 (*R (Griffin) v Richmond Magistrates' Court* [2008] EWHC 84 (Admin), [2008] 1 Cr App R 37 (453)). The reason given for the conclusion in (2) above was the very wide ambit of s. 357. For example, it applies to disposals made long before the commencement of bankruptcy, and possibly at a time when there was no indication of insolvency, and the prosecution do not have to prove that the bankrupt was aware of the possibility of insolvency. In these circumstances, to require the bankrupt to prove no intent to defraud is not justified and infringes Article 6. **F3.27**

***A-G's Ref (No. 1 of 2004)*: Protection from Eviction Act 1977** The third appeal in *A-G's Ref (No. 1 of 2004)* [2004] EWCA Crim 1025, [2004] 2 Cr App R 27 (424) concerned the Protection from Eviction Act 1977, s. 1(2), whereby if a person unlawfully deprives the residential occupier of any premises of his or her occupation of the premises, the person shall be guilty of an offence 'unless he proves that he believed, and had reasonable cause to believe, that the residential occupier had ceased to reside in the premises' (see **B13.1**). It was held that this reverse burden was justified for three reasons. First, the essence of the offence is unlawfully depriving the occupier of occupation of the premises, and the defence is only available if the accused can bring him or herself within a narrow class of exception. Secondly, the circumstances relied upon by the accused are peculiarly within his or her own knowledge. Thirdly, the imposition of a criminal penalty is designed to regulate conduct in the public interest and there is a strong public interest in deterring landlords from ejecting tenants unlawfully. **F3.28**

***A-G's Ref (No. 1 of 2004)*: Homicide Act 1957, s. 4(2)** The fourth appeal in *A-G's Ref (No. 1 of 2004)* [2004] EWCA Crim 1025, [2004] 2 Cr App R 27 (424) concerned the Homicide Act 1957, s. 4(2), which provides that 'Where it is shown that a person charged with the murder of another killed the other it shall be for the defence to prove that the person charged was acting in pursuance of a suicide pact between him and the other'. It was held that the legal burden is on the accused. The defence only arises once the prosecution have proved all the elements of murder and therefore the burden to justify the reverse burden of showing that it is proportional is more readily discharged. The penalty for murder is of the harshest kind, but in the Homicide Act 1957 Parliament singled out the defences of diminished responsibility and suicide pacts as requiring proof by an accused. Parliament no doubt had in mind the fact that in many cases the only evidence of a suicide pact would emanate from the survivor. The facts to establish the defence lie within the accused's knowledge and the reverse burden provides protection for society from murder disguised as a suicide pact killing. **F3.29**

***A-G's Ref (No. 1 of 2004)*: CJPO 1994, s. 51(7)** The fifth appeal in *A-G's Ref (No. 1 of 2004)* [2004] EWCA Crim 1025, [2004] 2 Cr App R 27 (424) concerned the CJPO 1994, s. 51(7), whereby if it is proved that the accused did an act which intimidated or was intended to intimidate another person ('the victim'), and did so knowing or believing that the victim was assisting in the investigation of an offence or was a witness or potential witness or a juror or potential juror in proceedings for an offence, the accused shall be presumed, 'unless the contrary is proved', to have done the act with the intention of thereby causing the investigation or the course of justice to be obstructed, perverted or interfered with (see **B14.50**). It was held that although the reverse burden involved an ingredient of the offence, not a special defence, the imposition of a legal burden on the accused was both justified and proportional. Witness and jury intimidation is a very serious threat to the administration of criminal justice which has substantially increased **F3.30**

and continues to do so and it is understandable that Parliament should wish to take strong measures to stamp it out. Once all the matters that give rise to the presumption are proved, it is entirely reasonable that the burden of proving lack of intention should rest with the accused. In balancing the potential detriment to the accused and the mischief Parliament is seeking to eradicate, the balance comes down firmly in favour of the prosecution.

F3.31 *Sheldrake v DPP*: **General** In *A-G's Ref (No. 1 of 2004)* [2004] EWCA Crim 1025, [2004] 2 Cr App R 27 (424) Lord Woolf CJ, giving the judgment of the Court of Appeal, saw the need to simplify the task of lower courts when faced with reverse onus provisions by providing them with guidance on the relevant principles to be applied. The Court noted the large number of authorities on the subject and the conflicting messages some of them gave. In particular the Court noted the significant difference in emphasis between the approaches of Lord Steyn in *Lambert* [2001] UKHL 37, [2002] 2 AC 545 and Lord Nicholls in *Johnstone* [2003] UKHL 28, [2003] 1 WLR 1736, and that 'few provisions will be left as imposing a legal burden on Lord Steyn's approach' (at [38]). It was suggested that until clarification by a further decision of the House of Lords, the lower courts, if in doubt as to what should be the outcome of a challenge to a reverse burden, should follow the approach of Lord Nicholls rather than that of Lord Steyn. Lord Woolf also set out 'General Guidance' in the form of ten general principles. However, in *Sheldrake v DPP* [2004] UKHL 43, [2005] 1 AC 264, the House of Lords held that both *Lambert* and *Johnstone*, unless or until revised or supplemented, should be regarded as the primary domestic authorities on reverse burdens; that nothing said in *Johnstone* suggested an intention to depart from or modify *Lambert*, which should not be treated as superseded or implicitly overruled; and that the differences in emphasis were explicable by the difference in the subject-matter of the two cases. The House also expressly declined to endorse Lord Woolf's 'General Guidance', save to the extent that it was in accordance with the opinions of the House in *Lambert* and *Johnstone*. Lord Bingham said that the task of the court is never to decide whether a reverse burden should be imposed on an accused, but always to assess whether a burden enacted by Parliament unjustifiably infringes the presumption of innocence, and questioned Lord Woolf's assumption that Parliament would not make an exception without good reason. Such an assumption, it was held, may lead the court to give too much weight to the enactment under review and too little weight to the presumption of innocence and the obligation imposed on the court by s. 3. See also, applying these principles, *DPP v Wright* [2009] EWHC 105 (Admin), [2010] QB 224: to construe the Hunting Act 2004, s. 1 and sch. 1, as imposing a legal burden on the accused would be an oppressive, disproportionate, unfair and unnecessary intrusion upon the presumption of innocence.

F3.32 *Sheldrake v DPP*: **RTA 1988, s. 5(2)** In *Sheldrake v DPP* [2004] UKHL 43, [2005] 1 AC 264, the House heard two conjoined appeals. The first concerned the RTA 1988, s. 5(2) (see C5.33), whereby it is a defence for a person charged with an offence of being in charge of a motor vehicle on a road or other public place after consuming excess alcohol to prove that, at the time of the alleged offence, the circumstances were such that there was no likelihood of the person driving the vehicle whilst the proportion of alcohol in his or her breath, blood or urine remained likely to exceed the prescribed limit. It was held that even on the assumption that s. 5(2) infringes the presumption of innocence, it was directed to the legitimate object of preventing death, injury and damage caused by unfit drivers and met the tests of acceptability identified in the Strasbourg jurisprudence. It was not objectionable to criminalise conduct in these circumstances without requiring the prosecutor to prove criminal intent. The accused has a full opportunity to show that there was no likelihood of his or her driving, a matter so closely conditioned by the accused's own knowledge at the time as to make it much more appropriate to prove the absence of a likelihood of driving on the balance of probabilities than for the prosecutor to prove such a likelihood beyond reasonable doubt. The imposition of a legal burden did not go beyond what was necessary. Counsel had submitted that all burdens on the defence should be evidential only. It was held that such a fundamental change was not mandated by Strasbourg authority and remained a matter for Parliament and not the House of Lords.

Sheldrake v DPP: **Terrorism Act 2000, s. 11(2)** The second appeal in *Sheldrake v DPP* [2004] UKHL 43, [2005] 1 AC 264 concerned the TA 2000, s. 11(1) and (2). **F3.33**

Terrorism Act 2000, s. 11

(1) A person commits an offence if he belongs or professes to belong to a proscribed organisation.
(2) It is a defence for a person charged with an offence under subsection (1) to prove—
  (a) that the organisation was not proscribed on the last (or only) occasion on which he became a member or began to profess to be a member, and
  (b) that he has not taken part in the activities of the organisation at any time while it was proscribed.

The House was of the unanimous opinion that the ingredients of the offence are set out fully in s. 11(1) and that s. 11(2) adds no further ingredient. The House also held, by majority, that s. 11(2) is incompatible with Article 6 and should be read and given effect as imposing on the accused an evidential burden only. Six reasons were given for the conclusion of incompatibility.

(1) The extraordinary breadth of s. 11(1) and the uncertain scope of the word 'profess' are such that some of those liable to be convicted and punished under s. 11(1) may be guilty of no conduct that can reasonably be regarded as blameworthy or such as should properly attract criminal sanctions. As to the breadth of the subsection, it covers, for example, a person who joined an organisation when it was not a terrorist organisation or not a proscribed organisation, or when, if it was, the person did not know that it was. There would be a clear breach of the presumption of innocence and a real risk of unfair conviction if such a person could be exonerated only by establishing the defence provided and it was the clear duty of the courts to protect an accused against such a risk.
(2) As to s. 11(2)(b), it may be all but impossible for an accused to show that he or she has not taken part in the activities of the organisation. Terrorist organisations do not generate minutes or records that can be relied on and although the accused can assert non-participation, that evidence may well be discounted as unreliable.
(3) If s. 11(2) imposes a legal burden and the accused fails to prove the matters specified, there is no room for the exercise of discretion — the accused must be convicted.
(4) The penalty for the offence, imprisonment for up to ten years, is severe.
(5) Security considerations carry weight, but they do not absolve Member States from their duty to ensure that basic standards of fairness are observed.
(6) Little significance can be attached to the requirement in s. 117 that the DPP gives consent to a prosecution because Article 6 is concerned with the procedure relating to the trial of a criminal case and not the decision to prosecute.

As to the reading down of s. 11(2), there could be no doubt that Parliament intended it to impose a legal burden on the accused, because s. 118 of the Act lists a number of sections that are to be understood as imposing an evidential burden only and s. 11(2) is not among those listed. However, the majority held that s. 11(2) should be treated as if s. 118 applied to it, on the basis that, although that was not the intention of Parliament when enacting the 2000 Act, it was the intention of Parliament when enacting the HRA 1998, s. 3.

Makuwa: **Immigration and Asylum Act 1999, s. 31(1)** *Makuwa* [2006] EWCA Crim 175, [2006] 1 WLR 2755 concerned the Immigration and Asylum Act 1999, s. 31(1), whereby it is a defence to various offences, including using a false instrument contrary to the Forgery and Counterfeiting Act 1981, s. 3, for a refugee to show that, having come to the UK 'directly from another country where his life or freedom was threatened..., he (a) presented himself to the authorities in the United Kingdom without delay, (b) showed good cause for his illegal entry or presence, and (c) made a claim for asylum as soon as was reasonably practicable after his arrival in the United Kingdom'. D was charged with using a false instrument — a false passport — contrary to s. 3 of the 1981 Act and relied upon s. 31(1) of the 1999 Act. The Court of Appeal held that D bore the legal burden in relation to all the matters in s. 31(1) except the issue of refugee **F3.34** status and that the infringement of the ECHR, Article 6(2), was justifiable as a proportionate way of achieving the legitimate objective of maintaining proper immigration controls by restricting the use of forged passports, one of the principal means by which they were likely to be overcome.

F3.35 ***Williams*: Firearms Act 1982, s. 1(5)** *Williams* [2012] EWCA Crim 2162, [2013] 2 All ER 787 concerned the FA 1982, s. 1(5), whereby it is a defence for the accused to show that he or she did not know and had no reason to suspect that an imitation firearm was so constructed or adapted as to be readily convertible into a firearm to which the FA 1968, s. 1, applies (see **B12.36**). It was held that s. 1(5) imposes a legal burden on the accused and can be justified as a necessary and proportionate derogation from the presumption of innocence: firearms offences are a very serious problem and the need for protection of the public is obvious; the question of knowledge or lack of it involves facts readily available to the accused, whereas it could be very difficult for the prosecution to disprove absence of knowledge and reason to suspect; the prosecution must have first proved to the criminal standard that the accused was in possession of an imitation firearm readily convertible into a lethal firearm; and the maximum sentence for the offence is ten years.

F3.36 **Regulatory Offences** According to Lord Clyde in *Lambert* [2001] UKHL 37, [2002] 2 AC 545 the imposition of a legal burden on the accused may be acceptable in the case of statutory offences which are concerned to regulate the conduct of some particular activity in the public interest. Lord Clyde said at [154]: 'The requirement to have a licence in order to carry on certain kinds of activity is an obvious example. The promotion of health and safety and the avoidance of pollution are among the purposes to be served by such controls. These kinds of cases may properly be seen as not truly criminal. Many may be relatively trivial and only involve a monetary penalty. Many may carry with them no real social disgrace or infamy.' This line of reasoning has been relied upon in subsequent cases, including *S* [2002] EWCA Crim 2558, [2003] 1 Cr App R 35 (602) in which the Court of Appeal (at [48]) regarded the Trade Marks Act 1994, s. 92, as being in the nature of a regulatory offence with a degree of moral obloquy rather less than the 'truly criminal' cases. *Davies v Health and Safety Executive* [2002] EWCA Crim 2949 concerned the Health and Safety at Work etc. Act 1974, ss. 3(1) and 33(1), which together make it an offence for an employer to fail to discharge the duty to conduct an undertaking in such a way as to ensure, so far as is reasonably practicable, that persons not in his or her employment who may be affected thereby are not exposed to risks to their health and safety, and s. 40 of the Act whereby, for these purposes, 'it shall be for the accused to prove... that it was not reasonably practicable to do more than was in fact done to satisfy the duty'. It was held that since s. 40 related to an ingredient of the offence under ss. 3 and 33, it did make some inroad into the presumption of innocence, but that the imposition of a legal burden on the accused was justified, necessary and proportionate. Important reasons given for reaching this conclusion included the fact that the Act was regulatory, its purpose to secure the health, safety and welfare of employees and others, that the offences in question involved no risk of imprisonment and that the moral obloquy was less than that of truly criminal offences. In *Chargot Ltd (t/a Contract Services)* [2008] UKHL 73, [2009] 1 WLR 1, a case involving charges under ss. 33 and 37 of the 1974 Act, *Davies v Health and Safety Executive* was followed, on essentially the same reasoning, and notwithstanding that the penalties for individuals had since been increased to up to two years' imprisonment and an unlimited fine when convicted on indictment (Health and Safety (Offences) Act 2008, s. 1(1) and (2) and sch. 1). See also *R (Grundy & Co Excavations Ltd) v Halton Division Magistrates' Court* [2003] EWHC 272 (Admin), in relation to the exceptions from the necessity for a licence for the felling of trees in the Forestry Act 1967, s. 9, and the relevant regulations. In that case it was held that the offence of tree felling was a classic regulatory offence, designed to protect the nation's trees, which involved only a monetary penalty, and carried no real social disgrace, infamy, or moral stigma or obloquy.

Incidence of the Evidential Burden: General Rule

F3.37 Generally speaking, a party bearing the legal burden on a particular issue will also bear the evidential burden on that issue. Thus, as a general rule, the prosecution bear both the legal and evidential burden in relation to all the elements in the offence necessary to establish guilt; and where the defence bear the legal burden of proving insanity or, by virtue of an express or implied statutory exception, some other issue, they will also bear the evidential burden in that regard (although, concerning insanity, in rare and exceptional cases the judge may of his or her own motion raise the issue and leave it to the jury: *Thomas* [1995] Crim LR 314). In relation to numerous common-law and statutory defences, however, the evidential burden is on the defence, and, if it is discharged so that the defence in question is put before the jury, the legal burden is then on the prosecution to disprove such defence. Although it is said in these cases that the evidential burden is on the defence, that burden will be discharged *whenever* there is sufficient evidence in relation to the defence to leave it to the jury; the evidence may be adduced by the defence (or elicited by them in cross-examination), *or* it may be given by a prosecution witness (or a co-accused) giving evidence-in-chief *or* it may be given in any other way (*Bullard v The Queen* [1957] AC 635). Where such a defence arises upon the evidence called by any party, then whether or not it has been mentioned by the defence, the judge must leave it to the jury (*Palmer v The Queen* [1971] AC 814 at p. 823). For further examples, see *Bonnick* (1978) 66 Cr App R 266, *Hopper* [1915] 2 KB 431 at p. 435 and *DPP (Jamaica) v Bailey* [1995] 1 Cr App R 257; and cf. *Groark* [1999] Crim LR 669, considered at **F3.43**. If there is no evidence to support the defence upon which an accused seeks to rely, the judge is entitled to withdraw it from the jury (*Hill* (1988) 89 Cr App R 74 and *Pommell* [1995] 2 Cr App R 607). However, in *Watson* [1992] Crim LR 434, where D was acquitted of rape, the defence being consent, but convicted of buggery, which he denied, an appeal against conviction was allowed on the grounds that the judge had omitted to direct the jury that accidental penetration would not suffice, notwithstanding that there was no evidence that the penetration, if it had occurred, was accidental. The defences to which the foregoing principles relate are as follows.

Loss of Self-control If sufficient evidence is adduced to raise an issue with respect to the statutory defence of loss of control, which has replaced the defence of provocation (see **B1.24**), the jury must assume that the defence is satisfied unless the prosecution prove beyond reasonable doubt that it is not (CAJA 2009, s. 54(5)). Sufficient evidence is adduced to raise an issue with respect to the statutory defence if evidence is adduced on which, in the opinion of the trial judge, a jury, properly directed, could reasonably conclude that the defence might apply (s. 54(6)). **F3.38**

The leading authority on the evidential implications of these statutory provisions is *Gurpinar* [2015] EWCA Crim 178, [2015] 1 WLR 3442, from which the following principles derive. **F3.39**

(a) Whereas the Homicide Act 1957 required only 'evidence' of provocation, the CAJA 2009, s. 54(5) and (6), require 'sufficient evidence' of loss of self-control. Thus, where there was evidence of provocation, it could be left to the jury however unlikely the defence was to succeed, whereas loss of self-control must be left to the jury only if there is evidence on which a reasonable jury, properly directed, could conclude that the defence might apply.
(b) The judge must consider whether to leave loss of self-control to the jury even if the accused has not raised the issue or given evidence. Whatever the tactical decision made by the defence, it is the judge's duty to consider whether, on the whole of the evidence, the defence arises (approving, in this respect, *Dawes* [2013] EWCA Crim 322, [2014] 1 WLR 947 at [53]).
(c) The fact that the accused gave evidence which did not support a loss of self-control is only a factor, albeit a significant one, which the judge should take into account in objectively assessing the evidence. The assessment is fact-sensitive and therefore examination of the decisions of judges on the facts of particular cases does not assist.
(d) The judge should not reject disputed evidence which the jury might believe (approving, in this respect, *Clinton* [2012] EWCA Crim 2, [2013] QB 1 at [46]). However, the judge should analyse the evidence closely, taking into account the whole of the evidence, and is bound to consider the weight and quality of the evidence, in coming to a conclusion.
(e) The judge must be satisfied that there is sufficient evidence in respect of the three components of the defence set out in the CAJA 2009, s. 54(1)(a), (b) and (c) (see **B1.24**).

The judge should consider them sequentially so that if there is no sufficient evidence of loss of self-control, there will be no need to consider the other two components.

(f) It is generally desirable that the advocates should notify the judge as early as possible in the management of the case of the possibility of the defence arising, even though it may not form part of the defence case. At the conclusion of the evidence, the judge must receive written submissions so that whether the evidence satisfies the statutory test can be considered.

(g) An appellate court will not readily interfere with the reasoned judgment of a trial judge in evaluating the evidence of the defence.

As to (f), it is submitted that if the defence do not rely on the defence at trial but it appears to the advocate for the defence that there is evidence on which the jury could find loss of self-control, the judge's failure to direct the jury on it cannot found an appeal against conviction (see, in the case of provocation, *Cox* [1995] 2 Cr App R 513).

A defence of self-defence, in a murder case, does not necessarily of itself provide a sufficient evidential basis for an alternative defence of loss of control (*Martin* [2017] EWCA Crim 1359; *Goodwin* [2018] EWCA Crim 2287, [2019] 1 Cr App R 9 (107)).

F3.40 **Self-defence** In *Lobell* [1957] 1 QB 547, D was convicted of wounding with intent to cause grievous bodily harm. There was some evidence to support his defence of self-defence. The trial judge directed the jury that it was for the defence to establish that plea to their satisfaction. The conviction was quashed on the grounds that this was a misdirection. Although the prosecution are not obliged to give evidence in chief to rebut a suggestion of self-defence before the issue is raised, once there is sufficient evidence to leave the issue before the jury, it is for the prosecution to disprove it beyond reasonable doubt. See also *Wheeler* [1967] 3 All ER 829 at p. 830 and *Abraham* [1973] 3 All ER 694 at p. 1273. There may be evidence of self-defence even if the defence of the accused is one of alibi. In *Bonnick* (1978) 66 Cr App R 266, a case of stabbing in which the defence was one of alibi, it was held, rejecting the contention that the evidence of the Crown witnesses had raised the issue of self-defence, that the question whether there was sufficient evidence to leave an issue before the jury was a question for the trial judge to answer by applying common sense to the evidence; but when there was sufficient evidence to raise a prima facie case, the issue should be left to the jury. In *Dickens* [2005] EWCA Crim 2017, it was held that since, in the particular circumstances of the case, it was extremely difficult to disentangle the defences of self-defence and accident and unwise to approach the facts as if they fell within mutually exclusive compartments, both defences should have been left to the jury.

F3.41 **Duress** The Crown are not called upon to anticipate a defence of duress and disprove it in advance, but if the accused places before the court such material as makes duress a live issue, fit and proper to be left to the jury, it is for the Crown to disprove that defence in such a manner as to leave in the jury's mind no reasonable doubt that the accused cannot be absolved on the grounds of the alleged compulsion (*Gill* [1963] 2 All ER 688, per Edmund Davies J at p. 846). See also *Bone* [1968] 2 All ER 644, per Lord Parker CJ at p. 985. As to duress of circumstances, see also *Pommell* [1995] 2 Cr App R 607.

F3.42 **Non-insane Automatism** Although the onus is on the defence to prove insanity on a balance of probabilities, where there is evidence on which a jury could find automatism not due to a disease of the mind, the onus is on the prosecution to disprove such automatism beyond reasonable doubt: the *obiter* view of the majority in *Bratty v A-G for Northern Ireland* [1963] AC 386. For examples of cases in which the accused failed to lay a proper foundation for automatism, see *Stripp* (1978) 69 Cr App R 318 and *Pullen* [1991] Crim LR 457. Where the defence of automatism is raised by an accused, two questions fall to be decided by the judge before the defence can be left to the jury: (1) whether a proper evidential foundation for the defence has been laid and (2) whether the evidence shows the case to be one of insane automatism, i.e. a case which falls within the M'Naghten Rules, or one of non-insane automatism. If the judge rules that the case is one of insanity, the jury must then decide, on the basis of the judge's direction, whether the accused is guilty or not guilty by reason of insanity (*Burgess* [1991] 2 QB 92). Where the issues of both insanity and non-insane automatism arise in the same case, the judge should distinguish between them in the summing-up and explain that, whereas it is for the defence to prove insanity, it is not for them to prove automatism; it is for the prosecution to negative it once the defence lay a foundation for it (*Burns* (1973) 58 Cr App R 364, per Stephenson LJ at p. 374).

Intoxication Insofar as intoxication may constitute a defence, once there is evidence before the court to support it, the onus of disproof rests on the prosecution (*Kennedy v HM Advocate* 1944 JC 171; *Foote* [1964] Crim LR 405). However, in *Groark* [1999] Crim LR 669 it was held that if, in a case of wounding with intent, there is evidence of drunkenness which might give rise to the issue whether the accused did form the specific intent, but the defence is that the accused knew what was happening but acted in self-defence, defence counsel is not obliged to seek a direction on self-induced intoxication in relation to intent; the judge may ask if counsel has any objection to such a direction and, if counsel does object, then the direction need not be given. As to mistake due to voluntary intoxication, see further *Hatton* [2005] EWCA Crim 2951, [2006] 1 Cr App R 16 (247) (see **A3.61**) and the CJIA 2008, s. 76(5) (see **A3.58**). **F3.43**

Alibi Although there is no general rule of law that in every case where alibi is raised the judge must specifically direct the jury, quite apart from the general direction on burden and standard of proof, that it is for the prosecution to negative the alibi, it is the clear duty of the judge to give such a direction if there is a danger of the jury thinking that an alibi, because it is called a defence, raises some burden on the defence to establish it (*Wood (No. 2)* (1967) 52 Cr App R 74 per Lord Parker CJ). It is a common and good *practice* to give such a specific and additional direction in any event (*Preece* (1992) 96 Cr App R 264); and ideally it should be given (*Anderson* [1991] Crim LR 361; *Johnson* [1995] Crim LR 242). In *Mussell* [1995] Crim LR 887, it was held that a special direction is necessary if the nature of the alibi is that the accused was at a specific place elsewhere, raising the question why the accused did not call witnesses in support, but is unnecessary if the evidence amounts to little more than a denial that the accused committed the crime. **F3.44**

Mistaken Belief in Consent Where a case involves a charge of rape under the SOA 1956 (i.e. brought before 1 May 2004), if there is evidence before the court that the accused mistakenly believed that the complainant had consented, the onus of disproof lies on the prosecution (*Thomas* (1983) 77 Cr App R 63; *Gardiner* [1994] Crim LR 455). For the position on consent under the SOA 2003, see **B3.40** ***et seq.*** **F3.45**

Statutory Defences The principles set out above also apply in relation to a huge variety of statutory defences. Thus where an accused puts forward an explanation for his or her conduct based on the Criminal Law Act 1967, s. 3 (see **A3.55**; and see also the CJIA 2008, s. 76, at **A3.58**), the jury should be clearly directed that it is for the Crown to disprove the validity of such an explanation and that it is not for the accused to establish it (*Cameron* [1973] Crim LR 520; *Khan* [1995] Crim LR 78). In some cases, the statute expressly imposes a burden on the Crown to disprove beyond reasonable doubt a defence in respect of which the accused has discharged an evidential burden (see, e.g., the TA 2000, s. 118 (at **B10.31**), and *G* [2009] UKHL 13, [2010] 1 AC 43). **F3.46**

STANDARD OF PROOF

General Rule

The standard of proof means the degree to which proof must be established by a party bearing a burden of proof. The standard required of the prosecution before the tribunal of fact can find the accused guilty is proof such that the jury are sure of the accused's guilt. This means that the jury must be sure on *all* the evidence and does not mean that a single item of evidence will not be admissible unless it is capable, by itself, of proving the case against the accused (*Myers v R* [2015] UKPC 40, [2016] AC 314 at [45]). In a prosecution under the Mental Capacity Act 2005, s. 44, for ill-treatment or neglect of a person who lacks capacity (see **B2.161**), the prosecution must prove lack of capacity only on a balance of probabilities (s. 2(4) of the 2005 Act; *Hopkins* [2011] EWCA **F3.47**

Crim 1513; *Dunn* [2010] EWCA Crim 2935, [2011] 1 Cr App R 34 (425)). Where the legal burden on a particular issue is borne by the accused, the standard required of the defence before the tribunal of fact can find in favour of the accused on that issue is proof on a balance of probabilities.

Usual Direction where Legal Burden on Prosecution

F3.48 It is the duty of the judge in the summing-up to make it clear to the jury what standard of proof the prosecution are required to meet. It is not a matter of some precise formula or particular form of words being used; what matters is the effect of the summing-up (*Allan* [1969] 1 All ER 91, per Fenton Atkinson LJ at p. 36). If a judge fails to give a direction, it is no answer that jurors know about 'beyond reasonable doubt' or that the standard was stressed by the advocates in their speeches (*Miah* [2018] EWCA Crim 563).

Although the law requires no particular formula, judges are wise, as a general rule, to adopt one. The time-honoured formula was that the jury must be satisfied beyond reasonable doubt (*Ferguson v The Queen* [1979] 1 WLR 94 per Lord Scarman), a phrase approved by the House of Lords (*Woolmington v DPP* [1935] AC 462; *Mancini v DPP* [1942] AC 1), but the favoured phrase is that before the jury can return a verdict of guilty, they must be sure that the accused is guilty (see the *Crown Court Compendium* (July 2020), ch. 5). This direction is designed to avoid the difficulties juries encounter with the concept of beyond reasonable doubt (*Majid* [2009] EWCA Crim 2563). Where the phrase beyond reasonable doubt has been used in the trial, e.g., by counsel in their speeches, the jury should be directed that it is the same as being sure (*Adey* (unreported, 97/5306/W2) and the *Crown Court Compendium* (July 2020), ch. 5, para. 3). It is axiomatic that a jury cannot be 'sure' of guilt if there is a possibility that the accused may not be guilty (*S v DPP* [2017] EWHC 1162 (Admin), [2017] 4 WLR 102 at [23]). In cases which turn on whether the accused or the complainant is telling the truth, it is important for the judge not to give the impression that the jury simply have to decide who to believe; the jury must be told that, in order to convict, they must be sure that the complainant was telling the truth. Similarly, in cases of historic allegations of sexual abuse, although delay creates difficulties for both the prosecution and the defence, it is inadequate to suggest to the jury that the disadvantages apply equally; the judge should emphasise that, if the defence may have been prejudiced, the jury should have regard to that fact when considering whether the prosecution had made them sure of the guilt of the accused (*W* [2014] EWCA Crim 1392).

F3.49 Directions using the words 'reasonably sure', 'pretty sure', 'pretty certain', 'sure, which is less than being certain' and 'viable' have all been disapproved (*Head* (1961) 45 Cr App R 225, *Woods* [1961] Crim LR 324, *Law* [1961] Crim LR 52, *Stephens* [2002] EWCA Crim 1529 and *JS (A Child) v DPP* [2017] EWHC 1162 (Admin), [2017] 2 Cr App R 17 (214) respectively). As to 'sure, which is less than being certain', a judge should not draw a distinction between being sure and being certain, because this is likely only to confuse (*Majid*; *Stephens*), but if the jury ask whether they need to be '100% certain', the judge should answer in the negative (*JL* [2017] EWCA Crim 621). It is inadequate merely to direct the jury that they must be 'satisfied' without any indication of the degree of satisfaction required (*Hepworth* [1955] 2 QB 600; *Allan* [1969] 1 All ER 91, per Fenton Atkinson LJ). It was held to be proper to direct that 'You, the jury, must be completely satisfied' or 'You must feel sure of the prisoner's guilt' (*Hepworth* [1955] 2 QB 600, per Lord Goddard CJ at p. 603).

In *McGreevy v DPP* [1973] 1 All ER 503, it was argued on the basis of *Hodge* (1838) 2 Lew CC 227, that if the case against the accused depends wholly or substantially on circumstantial evidence, the judge should direct the jury that not only must they be satisfied that the circumstances are consistent with the accused having committed the offence, but also they must be satisfied that the circumstances are inconsistent with any other rational conclusion than that the accused is the guilty person. The House of Lords held that there is no rule of law requiring such a direction. It suffices, in such a case, to give the usual direction that they, the jury, must be satisfied of the guilt of the accused beyond reasonable doubt.

Cases Requiring Explanation of Usual Direction

Judges have used a variety of expressions with a view to explaining to the jury the meaning of 'reasonable doubt', some of which have suggested too low a standard of proof and resulted in a conviction being quashed: see, e.g., *Gray* (1973) 58 Cr App R 177 ('a doubt based upon good reason and not a fanciful doubt' and 'the sort of doubt which might affect you in the conduct of your everyday affairs') and *Stafford* (1968) 53 Cr App R 1 at p. 2 ('a reasonable doubt is one for which you could give reasons if you were asked'). It was against a background of cases of this kind that in *Ching* (1976) 63 Cr App R 7 Lawton LJ, delivering the judgment of the court, said (at p. 10): F3.50

> ... in most cases ... judges would be well advised not to attempt any gloss upon what is meant by 'sure' or what is meant by 'reasonable doubt'. In the last two decades there have been numerous cases before this court, some of which have been successful, some of which have not, which have come here because judges have thought it helpful to a jury to comment on what the standard of proof is. Experience in this court has shown that such comments usually create difficulties. They are more likely to confuse than help. But the exceptional case does sometimes arise.

Ching itself illustrates the kind of exceptional case in which a judge should explain to a jury what is meant by reasonable doubt. In that case the judge, in his summing-up, had directed the jury on the standard of proof by using the two classic formulations, 'sure' and 'beyond reasonable doubt', and had explained that these were two ways of saying the same thing. After retirement the jury returned to court, and the judge understood the foreman to ask for a further direction on the standard of proof. The judge said: F3.51

> A reasonable doubt ... is a doubt to which you can give a reason as opposed to a mere fanciful sort of speculation such as 'Well, nothing in this world is certain, nothing in this world can be proved' ... It is sometimes said the sort of matter which might influence you if you were to consider some business matter. A matter, for example, of a mortgage concerning your house, or something of that nature.

The Court of Appeal held that:

(a) in the light of the foreman's request, the case was an exceptional one, calling for a further direction; and
(b) although it disliked that part of the additional direction in which the judge had defined a reasonable doubt as one to which you can give a reason, taking the effect of both the summing-up and the additional direction together, the judge was right in what he did.

In exceptional cases in which the jury do ask for an explanation of 'reasonable doubt', a suitable form of words is provided by *Walters v The Queen* [1969] 2 AC 26. There, the Privy Council, while of the opinion that it is a matter of discretion for the judge to choose the most appropriate set of words to enable the particular jury in question to understand the standard of proof, upheld the following direction of the trial judge: 'A reasonable doubt is that quality and kind of doubt which, when you are dealing with matters of importance in your own affairs, you allow to influence you one way or the other.' The decision was affirmed in *Gray* (1973) 58 Cr App R 177. F3.52

If the jury ask whether unlikely possibilities preclude a finding of guilt, the judge should tell the jury to exclude fanciful possibilities and act only on realistic possibilities (*Majid* [2009] EWCA *Crim 2563*).

Direction where Legal Burden on Defence

In the exceptional cases in which the legal burden of proving an issue is borne by the defence (see **F3.8** ***et seq.***), it is discharged by proof on a balance of probabilities. See, in the case of insanity, *Sodeman v The King* [1936] 2 All ER 1138; in the case of the Prevention of Crime Act 1953, s. 1, an express statutory exception, *Brown* (1971) 55 Cr App R 478; in the case of the Homicide Act F3.53

1957, s. 2(2), another express statutory exception, *Dunbar* [1958] 1 QB 1; and in the case of implied statutory exceptions under the MCA 1980, s. 101, *Islington London Borough Council v Panico* [1973] 3 All ER 485. In *Carr-Briant* [1943] KB 607, D, who was convicted of an offence under the Prevention of Corruption Acts 1906 and 1916 (now repealed), was considered at that time to bear the legal burden of proving that money given or lent to an employee of a government department was not paid or given corruptly. The trial judge directed the jury that the burden on D was as heavy as that normally resting on the prosecution. Humphreys J, quashing the conviction, said (at p. 612) that 'the jury should be directed that … the burden of proof required is less than that required at the hands of the prosecution in proving the case beyond a reasonable doubt, and that the burden may be discharged by evidence satisfying the jury of the probability of that which the accused is called upon to establish'.

The classic definition of proof on a 'balance of probabilities' is that of Denning J in *Miller v Minister of Pensions* [1947] 2 All ER 372, at p. 374: 'If the evidence is such that the tribunal can say: "We think it more probable than not", the burden is discharged, but, if the probabilities are equal, it is not.'

BURDEN OF PROOF ON FACTS AFFECTING ADMISSIBILITY OF EVIDENCE

F3.54 Some decisions which must be made by a judge during or in preparation for a trial are not susceptible to analysis in terms of burden and standard of proof but involve weighing competing factors and exercising judgement. Examples include decisions on whether a witness is eligible for special measures (see **D14.1** *et seq.*), decisions under the PACE 1984, s. 78 (see also **F2.7**), and decisions under the CJA 2003, s. 114(1)(d) (see **F17.34** *et seq.*) (*Misick v R* [2015] UKPC 31, [2015] 1 WLR 3215). However, when the admissibility of a particular item of evidence is in dispute, the burden of proving preliminary facts, i.e. those facts which must be proved as a condition precedent to the admission of the disputed evidence, lies on the party seeking to admit that evidence. Thus, at common law the prosecution bore the burden of proving the facts constituting the condition precedent to the admissibility of confessions, a rule which has now been put on a statutory basis (*Thompson* [1893] 2 QB 12 and the PACE 1984, s. 76(2): see **F18.8**). The burden of proving the competence of a witness is on the party seeking to call that witness (YJCEA 1999, s. 54(2): see **F4.23**). As to the requirement to satisfy the judge of the originality and genuineness of a recording, see *Robson* [1972] 2 All ER 699, *Stevenson* [1971] 1 WLR 1, *Rampling* [1987] Crim LR 823 and the Code of Practice on Audio Recording Interviews with Suspects (Code E).

STANDARD OF PROOF ON FACTS AFFECTING ADMISSIBILITY OF EVIDENCE

F3.55 When the burden of proving the admissibility of a particular item of evidence is borne by the prosecution, the standard to be met is proof beyond reasonable doubt. See, in the case of the conditions of admissibility under the CJA 2003, s. 116 (see F17.7), *Shabir* [2012] EWCA Crim 2564; and on the issue of the genuineness of samples of writing which it is sought to admit under the Criminal Procedure Act 1865, s. 8, for the purposes of comparison with a disputed writing, *Ewing* [1983] QB 1039. In *Ewing*, the Court of Appeal held that since s. 8 of the 1865 Act did not itself deal with the standard of proof required to satisfy the judge as to the genuineness of the sample writing, the matter was governed by the common law, and accordingly, if the prosecution sought to admit such a sample, they should prove genuineness beyond reasonable doubt. The Court was of the opinion that the earlier decision of the Court of Appeal in *Angeli* [1979] 3 All ER 950, that the standard was the civil one, must have been reached *per incuriam*.

Although there is little authority on the point, as a matter of principle, when the burden of proving the admissibility of a particular item of evidence is borne by the defence, the standard to be met should be proof on a balance of probabilities. See, in the case of a defence application under the CJA 1988, s. 23 (now repealed), *Mattey* [1995] 2 Cr App R 409. See also the PACE 1984, s. 76A(2) and (3), at **F18.28**.

PRESUMPTIONS

Presumptions without Basic Facts: Generally

Presumptions without basic facts come into operation without the need for proof or admission of any basic or primary fact — they are merely rules that a certain conclusion must be drawn by the court in the absence of any evidence in rebuttal. Thus, although referred to as 'presumptions', in fact they are indistinguishable from the other rules relating to the incidence of the legal or evidential burden. Three examples are considered: the presumption of innocence, the presumption of sanity, and the presumption that mechanical and other instruments of a kind that are usually in working order, were in working order at the time of their use. **F3.56**

Presumption of Innocence

The phrase 'the presumption of innocence' is often used as a convenient abbreviation of the common-law rule that, generally speaking, the prosecution bear the burden of proving all the elements in the offence necessary to establish guilt (see *Woolmington v DPP* [1935] AC 462 and generally **F3.6**). **F3.57**

Presumption of Sanity

The presumption of sanity is a convenient abbreviation of the common-law rule that if the accused raises the defence of insanity, the accused will bear the burden of proving it (on a balance of probabilities) (see *Layton* (1849) 4 Cox CC 149, *M'Naghten's Case* (1843) 10 Cl & F 200, and generally **F3.8**). The phrase is to be distinguished from 'the presumption of mental capacity' which has been used to refer to the common-law rule that the evidential burden in relation to automatism not due to a disease of the mind is borne by the accused (see *Bratty v A-G for Northern Ireland* [1963] AC 386 at **F3.42**). **F3.58**

Presumption as to Working of Mechanical and Other Instruments

There is a presumption that mechanical and other instruments of a kind that are usually in working order, were in working order at the time of their use. The party against whom the presumption operates bears an evidential burden to adduce some evidence to the contrary. The presumption has been applied in the case of speedometers (see *Nicholas v Penny* [1950] 2 KB 466, in which it was held that justices were entitled to convict of speeding on the evidence of one officer as to the speedometer reading of a police car driven at an even distance behind D's car, notwithstanding that no evidence had been adduced as to the accuracy of the speedometer). Traffic lights have likewise been presumed to be in working order: in *Tingle Jacobs & Co. v Kennedy* [1964] 1 All ER 888, Lord Denning MR said (at p. 639) 'when you have a device of this kind set up for public use in active operation … the presumption should be that it is in proper working order unless there is evidence to the contrary'. See also, in the case of a public weighbridge, *Kelly Communications Ltd v DPP* [2002] EWHC 2752 (Admin). **F3.59**

As to representations of fact made otherwise than by a person but that depend for their accuracy on information supplied by a person, see also the CJA 2003, s. 129 (see **F16.13**).

PRESUMPTIONS OF FACT

General Principles

The phrase 'presumption of fact' has been used to describe certain frequently recurring varieties of circumstantial evidence, i.e. evidence of relevant facts from which the existence of some fact which is in issue *may* be inferred. Thus, presumptions of fact, sometimes referred to as **F3.60** provisional presumptions, operate in the following manner: on the proof or admission of a basic or primary fact, another fact may be presumed in the absence of sufficient evidence to the contrary. The party against whom the presumption operates bears neither a legal nor an evidential burden in relation to the presumed fact; if the party adduces no evidence to the contrary, there is a risk of losing on that issue, but the party is not *bound* to lose on that issue. The following examples are considered: the presumption of continuance of life, the presumption of intention, and the presumption of guilty knowledge in cases of handling, theft, etc.

Continuance of Life

F3.61 On the proof or admission of the basic fact that a person was alive on a certain date, it may be presumed, in the absence of sufficient evidence to the contrary, that the person was still alive on some subsequent date (*MacDarmaid v A-G* [1950] P 218; *Re Peete* [1952] 2 All ER 599). Whether or not such an inference should be drawn is a question for the jury, and is entirely dependent upon the facts of the case. Thus, if there is proof that a person was in good health on one day, there would be a strong, almost irresistible, inference that the person was alive on the next day, and the jury would in all probability find that this was so; if, on the other hand, it were proved that the person was in a dying condition on the first day and nothing further was proved, the jury would probably decline to draw the inference that the person was alive on the following day (*Lumley* (1869) LR 1 CCR 196, per Lush J at p. 198, on the question of whether a husband was alive at the date of his wife's allegedly bigamous second marriage, approved in *Morrison* (1938) 27 Cr App R 1).

Intention

F3.62 **Criminal Justice Act 1967, s. 8**

A court or jury, in determining whether a person has committed an offence—

(a) shall not be bound in law to infer that he intended or foresaw a result of his actions by reason only of its being a natural and probable consequence of those actions; but

(b) shall decide whether he did intend or foresee that result by reference to all the evidence, drawing such inferences from the evidence as appear proper in the circumstances.

Section 8 of the 1967 Act puts on a statutory basis the common-law presumption of fact that a person intends the natural consequences of his or her acts, and reverses the decision in *DPP v Smith* [1961] AC 290 that in certain circumstances the presumption is a presumption of law (*Wallett* [1968] 2 QB 367; *Moloney* [1985] AC 905). As to jury directions on intention, see the authorities considered at **A2.4**.

Guilty Knowledge in Cases of Handling, Theft etc.

F3.63 In cases of handling and theft, on proof or admission of the fact that the accused was found in possession of property so shortly after it was stolen that it can fairly be said that the accused was in recent possession of it, the jury should be directed that such possession calls for explanation, and if none is given, or one is given which they are convinced is untrue, they are entitled to infer, according to the circumstances, that the accused is either the handler or the thief and to convict accordingly (*Schama* (1914) 84 LJ KB 396; *Garth* [1949] 1 All ER 773; *Aves* [1950] 2 All ER 330; *Williams* [1962] Crim LR 54). It is desirable in most cases to direct the jury that the burden of proof remains on the prosecution, and if, therefore, the explanation given by the accused leaves them in doubt as to whether the property was obtained honestly, the prosecution have not proved their case and they should acquit (*Aves* and *Hepworth* [1955] 2 QB 600, applied in *Moulding* [1996] Crim LR 440). The burden of proof is never on the defence (*Aubrey* (1915) 11 Cr App R 182; *Brain* (1918) 13 Cr App R 197; *Sanders* (1919) 14 Cr App R 11). It is unclear how the common-law doctrine of recent possession has been affected by the CJPO 1994, s. 34 (inferences from out-of-court silence, see **F20.3** ***et seq.***) and s. 36 (inferences from failure to account for objects etc., see **F20.34** ***et seq.***). Concerning the impact of s. 34, in *AB v CPS* [2017] EWHC 2963 (Admin), although it was said that the case could be resolved without determining the issue, it was held that the three-stage approach set out in *T v DPP* [2007] EWHC 1793 (Admin) must apply, *mutatis mutandis*, when the court is considering drawing an adverse inference against the accused, whether it arises under s. 34 or the common law. The approach in *T v DPP* requires three questions to be asked (per Hughes LJ at [26]): '1) Has the defendant relied in his defence on a fact which he could reasonably have been expected to mention in his interview, but did not? If so, what is it? 2) What is his explanation for not having mentioned it? 3) If that explanation is not a reasonable one, is the proper inference to be drawn that he is guilty?'

The doctrine of recent possession applies not only in the case of 'receiving', but also in the case of a charge under the second limb of the Theft Act 1968, s. 22 (*Ball* [1983] 2 All ER 1089). Apart from handling and theft, the doctrine may also apply to other offences with a theft ingredient, as when the accused is charged with burglary contrary to s. 9(1)(b), and it is proved that shortly after the premises were entered and property stolen therefrom, the accused was found in possession of the property (*Loughlin* (1951) 35 Cr App R 69; *Seymour* [1954] 1 All ER 1006). There is no general rule of law to the effect that the doctrine has no application in cases in which there is some evidence of the circumstances in which the accused came into possession of the stolen goods (see per Stocker LJ in *Raviraj* (1986) 85 Cr App R 93, commenting on *obiter* remarks made in *Bradley* (1979) 70 Cr App R 200). **F3.64**

'Recent' Whether possession is 'recent' is a question of fact and degree dependent on all the circumstances of the case in question. Relevant factors include the nature of the property, its saleability, and any evidence, other than that of possession of the goods, connecting the accused with the offence charged. In *Smythe* (1980) 72 Cr App R 8, Kilner Brown J said (at p. 11): 'Nearly every reported case is merely a decision of fact as an example of what is no more than a rule of evidence'. The precedents, therefore, are of somewhat limited value. **F3.65**

It is instructive, however, to note that in *Cash* [1985] QB 801, in which the goods were found in the possession of the appellant, C, on 25 February 1983, and none of the property was stolen more recently than 16 February 1983, the Court of Appeal, upholding C's conviction for handling, said that it was not properly open to the jury to infer that C was the burglar or thief. In that case two others were charged in the same indictment: A, who was convicted of burglary and handling offences; and E, who pleaded guilty to burglary and obtaining property by deception. The prosecution case was that C handled goods taken, by A, E and other persons unknown, in the course of a number of separate burglaries which took place between July and October 1982 and January and 16 February 1983. Some of the proceeds of the burglaries were recovered from C's flat on 25 February 1983. A was a lodger in the flat. When arrested, C declined to answer questions, and at the trial elected to give no evidence. In *Smythe* (1980) 72 Cr App R 8 the Court of Appeal said that it would be quite unsafe to infer positive proof of participation in a series of burglaries and robberies from the mere fact of possession, between two and three months after the robberies, of articles stolen in the course of them. See also *Marcus* (1923) 17 Cr App R 191: a period of eight months between the theft and the time when the goods were first seen in the possession of the accused was too long a period for the doctrine to apply.

'Otherwise than in the course of stealing' In ordinary cases of handling, the prosecution are not required to adduce affirmative proof that the goods were handled 'otherwise than in the course of the stealing' (Theft Act 1968, s. 22(1)). This remains the position in recent possession cases, because if the jury draw the inference that the accused is guilty of handling, this includes the inference that the accused was not the actual thief. However, where the accused is in possession of stolen goods so recently after they are stolen that the inevitable inference is that the accused is the thief, as when the accused is found within a few hundred yards of the scene of the theft and minutes after the theft took place, then if the accused is only charged with handling, the Crown can prove that offence only if it proves affirmatively that the accused was not the thief, and the judge should direct the jury that they must acquit the accused of handling if they take the view that the accused was the thief (*Cash* [1985] QB 801, applied in *A-G of Hong Kong v Yip Kai-Foon* [1988] AC 642; *Ryan v DPP* (1994) 158 JP 485). **F3.66**

IRREBUTTABLE PRESUMPTIONS OF LAW

General Principles

F3.67 Irrebuttable presumptions of law, or conclusive presumptions, operate in the following way: on the proof or admission of a basic or primary fact another fact must be presumed which no evidence is admissible to rebut. Such presumptions are nothing more than rules of substantive law, as the following example illustrates. (See also the SOA 2003, s. 76, considered at **B3.43**.)

Presumption that Children under Ten Cannot be Guilty of Offence

F3.68 The CYPA 1933, s. 50, provides that: 'It shall be conclusively presumed that no child under the age of 10 years can be guilty of an offence'. It follows from this that a person over the age of ten who receives property dishonestly acquired by a person under the age of ten cannot be guilty of receiving stolen property, although if the person has the necessary *mens rea*, he or she may be guilty of theft (*Walters v Lunt* [1951] 2 All ER 645; *McGregor v Benyon* [1957] Crim LR 608).

REBUTTABLE PRESUMPTIONS OF LAW

General Principles

F3.69 Rebuttable presumptions of law operate in the following manner: on the proof or admission of the basic or primary facts, another fact must be presumed in the absence of sufficient evidence to the contrary. If the defence rely upon a rebuttable presumption of law and adduce prima facie evidence of the basic facts, a legal burden is placed on the prosecution requiring them to disprove or negative the presumed fact beyond reasonable doubt. If the prosecution rely upon a rebuttable presumption of law and adduce prima facie evidence of the basic facts, an evidential burden is placed on the defence which may be discharged by the adduction of such evidence as might leave a jury in reasonable doubt; and if the defence do discharge the evidential burden, the effect is as if the presumption had never come into play — the prosecution are still required to prove the presumed fact beyond reasonable doubt (*Kay* (1887) 16 Cox CC 292; *Willshire* (1881) 6 QBD 366 (the presumption of marriage)).

The foregoing relates to common-law presumptions. As to the statutory presumptions which operate to place on the defence a legal burden requiring them to disprove or negative a presumed fact by the adduction of such evidence as will satisfy the jury on a balance of probabilities, see **F3.9** ***et seq.*** As to the statutory presumptions arising under the PACE 1984, s. 74, see **F12.6**. Presumptions relating to the due execution of documents are considered at **F8.43**. The rebuttable presumptions of law that now fall to be considered are the presumptions of regularity, marriage and death.

Presumption of Regularity

F3.70 The presumption of regularity, expressed in the maxim *omnia praesumuntur rite esse acta*, operates as follows: on proof or admission of the basic or primary fact that a person has acted in a public or official capacity, it is presumed, in the absence of sufficient evidence to the contrary, that that person was regularly and properly appointed and that the act was regularly and properly performed. The presumption cannot be rebutted merely by challenging the presumed fact — evidence must be adduced (*Campbell v Wallsend Slipway and Engineering Co. Ltd* [1978] ICR 1015). Typical examples concern the validity of an official appointment. Thus, on a charge of assaulting a police officer in the course of his duty, evidence that the officer acted in that capacity is sufficient proof of the officer's due appointment (*Gordon* (1789) 1 Leach 515; and see *Cooper v Rowlands* [1971] RTR 291). See also *Borrett* (1833) 6 C & P 124 (a person acting as an officer of the Post Office), *Roberts* (1878) 38 LT 690 (a deputy county court judge), and *Campbell v Wallsend Slipway and Engineering Co. Ltd* (an inspector of the Health and Safety Executive). In *Langton* (1876) 2 QBD 296, the presumption operated to establish the due incorporation of a company which had acted as such. In *Cresswell* (1873) 1 QBD 446, evidence that a marriage had been celebrated in a building in which other marriages had also been celebrated was sufficient to establish that the building was duly consecrated.

The presumption must be applied with caution in cases where commission of an offence is dependent upon compliance with formal statutory conditions. Thus, the Divisional Court has held that it is wrong to presume, on the basis of evidence that a breath test device has been issued to the police, that it was officially approved by the Secretary of State (*Scott v Baker* [1969] 1 QB 659, approved in *Withecombe* [1969] 1 All ER 157). See also *Swift v Barrett* (1940) 163 LT 154, in which the Divisional Court required strict proof that a road sign complied with regulations. Such authorities, it is submitted, are not easily reconciled with *Gibbins v Skinner* [1951] 2 KB 379, in which it was held that evidence that speed-limit signs had been erected on a road was sufficient to establish that the local authority had performed its statutory duties pursuant to the Road Traffic Acts and given a direction justifying the erection of the signs. *Scott v Baker* was distinguished in *Public Prosecution Service of Northern Ireland v Elliott* [2013] UKSC 32, [2013] 2 Cr App R 17 (180) in relation to fingerprints taken using an electronic reader that had not been officially approved by the Secretary of State. The Supreme Court held that the well-established rule of law that evidence which is relevant is admissible, even if obtained illegally, extends to evidence created by an unlawful process. It was also held that the statutory requirement for approval of an electronic fingerprint reader is not analogous to the approval requirements in the case of breath test or speed gun devices, because whereas the latter devices are means of measuring something that cannot subsequently be re-measured, fingerprints can be reproduced subsequently and the accuracy of the initial readings, if disputed, can be checked by the provision of more samples.

Presumptions of Marriage

The civil authorities, although not explicit on the point, suggest that there are three different presumptions of marriage: **F3.71**

(a) a presumption of formal validity (i.e. a presumption of compliance with the formal requirements of the *lex loci celebrationis*, e.g., the requirement, in the case of a Church of England marriage under English law, to obtain a common or special licence);
(b) a presumption of essential validity (i.e. a presumption that each of the parties had the capacity to marry and was not, for example, under the age of 16 or already married); and
(c) a presumption of marriage arising from cohabitation.

Although there is a dearth of criminal authority, it is submitted that the presumptions of formal and essential validity apply in criminal as well as civil proceedings. The presumption of marriage arising from cohabitation, however, would appear to be of limited utility in criminal proceedings; the authorities show that if the prosecution bear the burden of proving the existence of a marriage, the presumption by itself is insufficient to discharge even the evidential burden. Thus in a case of bigamy, the prosecution, in seeking to prove a valid first marriage which subsisted at the date of the second marriage, must adduce some evidence of the celebration of the first marriage; evidence of acknowledgement, cohabitation or repute will not suffice (*Morris v Miller* (1767) 4 Burr 2057). It will suffice, however, if there is not only evidence that D had cohabited with a woman and spoken of her as his wife, but also proof from the register of marriages that a person of the same name as D married that woman (*Birtles* (1911) 6 Cr App R 177). See also *Umanski* [1961] VR 242.

Presumption of Death

By virtue of a long sequence of judicial statements, which either assert or assume such a rule, it appears accepted that there is a convenient presumption of law applicable to certain cases of seven **F3.72**

> years' absence where no statute applies. That presumption in its modern shape takes effect (without examining its terms too exactly) substantially as follows. Where as regards 'A.B' there is no acceptable affirmative evidence that he was alive at some time during a continuous period of seven years or more, then if it can be proved first, that there are persons who would be likely to have heard of him over that period, secondly that those persons have not heard of him, and thirdly that all due inquiries have been made appropriate to the circumstances, 'A.B.' will be presumed to have died at some time within that period. (*Chard v Chard* [1956] P 259, per Sachs J at p. 272)

The authorities conflict as to the date on which the fact of death may be presumed; it is either the date of the proceedings in question or the date at the end of the period of absence for seven years (*Lal Chand Marwari v Mahant Ranrup Gir* (1925) 42 TLR 159, at p. 160, and contrast *Re Westbrook's Trusts* [1873] WN 167 and *Chipchase v Chipchase* [1939] P 31).

Under the Presumption of Death Act 2013, s. 1, an application may be made to the High Court for a declaration that a missing person is presumed to be dead. Under s. 2(1), the court must make the declaration if satisfied that the missing person has died (s. 2(1)(a)) or has not been known to be alive for a period of at least seven years (s. 2(1)(b)). An example under s. 2(1)(a) would be where there is evidence of an incident involving the death of a group of persons that is likely to have included the missing person. For an example of a successful application under s. 2(1)(b), see *A v H* [2016] EWHC 762 (Fam). Under s. 2(2), the court must include in the declaration a finding as to the date and time of the missing person's death, a matter to be determined in accordance with s. 2(3) and (4). Under s. 3, a declaration under the Act is conclusive of the missing person's presumed death and time of the death and is effective against all persons and for all purposes.

Concerning the proviso to the OAPA 1861, s. 57 ('persons [charged with bigamy] marrying a second time whose husband or wife shall have been continually absent for the space of seven years then last past, and shall not have been known by such person to be living within that time'), see **B2.139**.

CONFLICTING PRESUMPTIONS

F3.73 There is civil authority that where two presumptions of equal strength apply in a case with the result that two facts are presumed, the one in conflict with the other, the presumptions neutralise each other and the case falls to be determined without the application of either (*Monckton v Tarr* (1930) 23 BWCC 504). *Willshire* (1881) 6 QBD 366 is often cited in support of this proposition, although there was no true conflict in that case, which involved two presumptions of unequal strength, a rebuttable presumption of law and a presumption of fact. W was charged with bigamously marrying D in the lifetime of C. W had gone through four ceremonies of marriage, with A in 1864, with B in 1868, with C in 1879, and with D in 1880. The prosecution relied upon the presumption of essential validity in seeking to establish the validity of the marriage of 1879. W sought to show that the marriage of 1879 was void, and accordingly relied upon his previous conviction, in 1868, for marrying B during the lifetime of A: A was alive in 1868 and under the presumption of continuance of life could be presumed to have been alive in 1879, in which case the marriage of 1879 was void. The trial judge did not leave the issue of whether A was alive in 1879 to the jury, directing them that the onus was on W to adduce evidence of her existence on that date. The conviction was quashed. Lord Coleridge CJ, referring to a 'conflict' of presumptions, held that W was not bound to do more than set up A's life in 1868, which would be presumed to continue, and it was then for the prosecution to disprove her existence on that date. It is submitted that there was no real conflict of presumptions in this case. The decision reached was correct. The onus of proving the validity of the 1879 marriage was on the prosecution. Their reliance on the presumption of validity placed nothing more than an evidential burden on W, which he had successfully discharged in reliance upon the presumption of continuance of life. The onus remained on the prosecution to establish the validity of the 1879 marriage.

Section F4 Competence and Compellability of Witnesses and Oaths and Affirmations

GENERAL

Meaning of Competence and Compellability

A witness is competent if the witness may lawfully be called to testify, and is compellable if, being competent, the witness may lawfully be compelled by the court to testify. As to securing the attendance of a witness, whether by witness order or witness summons, see **D15.91** ***et seq.*** and **D22.32** ***et seq.*** **F4.1**

General Rule as to Competence

The general rule as to competence is that all persons are, whatever their age, competent to give evidence (YJCEA 1999, s. 53(1)). There are only two exceptions. Under the first exception, a person is not competent if the person is unable to understand questions put to him or her as a witness and to give answers to them which can be understood (s. 53(3), considered further at **F4.21**). The types of witness who, under this test, *may* be incompetent are children and persons with a disorder or disability of the mind. Under the second exception, an accused is not competent to give evidence for the prosecution (s. 53(4), considered further at **F4.8**). **F4.2**

Youth Justice and Criminal Evidence Act 1999, s. 53

(1) At every stage in criminal proceedings all persons are (whatever their age) competent to give evidence.
(2) Subsection (1) has effect subject to subsections (3) and (4).
(3) A person is not competent to give evidence in criminal proceedings if it appears to the court that he is not a person who is able to—
  (a) understand questions put to him as a witness, and
  (b) give answers to them which can be understood.
(4) A person charged in criminal proceedings is not competent to give evidence in the proceedings for the prosecution (whether he is the only person, or is one of two or more persons, charged in the proceedings).
(5) In subsection (4) the reference to a person charged in criminal proceedings does not include a person who is not, or is no longer, liable to be convicted of any offence in the proceedings (whether as a result of pleading guilty or for any other reason).

General Rule as to Compellability

The general rule as to compellability is that all competent witnesses are compellable. There are four categories of exception. Under the first, the accused is not a compellable witness for the defence, i.e. for him or herself (see **F4.10**) or a co-accused (see **F4.13**) (Criminal Evidence Act 1898, s. 1(1)). Under the second exception, an accused's spouse or civil partner is, in the case of all but a number of specified offences, not compellable for either the prosecution or on behalf of a co-accused (PACE 1984, s. 80, considered at **F4.14** ***et seq.***). The third exception applies in the case of the Sovereign, heads of other sovereign States and diplomats (see **F4.29**). The fourth relates to bankers (see **F4.30**). **F4.3**

Witnesses who Refuse to Take the Oath or Testify

F4.4 Judges of the Crown Court may exercise their power to punish summarily for contempt of court (Senior Courts Act 1981, s. 45(4)) any compellable witness who refuses to take an oath or make an affirmation (*Hennegal v Evance* (1806) 12 Ves Jr 201). Likewise, but subject to public policy or a claim to privilege which the court upholds, a witness who refuses to answer a proper question may be found to be in contempt of court and face the penalty of imprisonment (*Ex parte Fernandez* (1861) 10 CB NS 13). A witness who refuses to testify and runs the risk of committal to prison as a contemnor should be given the opportunity of legal representation (*K* (1984) 78 Cr App R 82). In *Phillips* (1983) 78 Cr App R 88, it was stressed that, on a finding of contempt, sentence need not be passed immediately; the witness may have a change of heart. See further **B14.93** and **B14.107**.

Wards of Court as Witnesses

F4.5 The leave of the wardship court is not required to call a ward to give evidence at a criminal trial. This is so irrespective of whether (a) the child is interviewed and has made witness statements before or after becoming a ward, (b) it is the prosecution or defence who wish to call the child or (c) the child's failure to give evidence would prevent the prosecution taking place (*Re K (Minors) (Wardship: Criminal Proceedings)* [1988] Fam 1; *Re R (A Minor) (Wardship: Criminal Proceedings)* [1991] 2 All ER 193, per Lord Donaldson MR at p. 917). Nor is judicial consent required to interview a ward; the only duties of police officers, officers of the Security Services and officers of other investigatory, enforcement and regulatory agencies are to inform the court and to comply with relevant statutory requirements governing their functions, e.g., in the case of police officers the provisions in the PACE 1984 relating to children (*Re A (A Child) (Ward of Court: Security Services Interview)* [2017] EWHC 1022 (Fam), [2017] Fam 369; see also CrimPD V, para. 17A (see Supplement, **CPD.17A**)).

Deaf and Speech Impaired Witnesses

F4.6 Competent witnesses include those who can neither hear nor speak, provided that the court is satisfied that they understand the nature of an oath (*Ruston* (1786) 1 Leach 408; *O'Brien* (1845) 1 Cox CC 185). Such a person may take an oath (or make an affirmation) and be examined and cross-examined, through an interpreter, using sign language. The interpreter should also take an oath (or make an affirmation). A witness who cannot speak may be allowed to give evidence in written form. See also **D14.16** for eligibility for 'special measures' for witnesses, **D14.43** as to the use of an intermediary appointed under the YJCEA 1999, s. 29, and *F* [2013] EWCA Crim 427, [2013] 1 WLR 2143.

No Property in the Evidence of a Witness

F4.7 No party has any property in the evidence of a witness, so even if there is a contract between a witness and a party, whereby the latter agrees not to testify on a matter on which the court can compel the party to give evidence, such a contract is contrary to public policy and unenforceable (*Harmony Shipping Co. SA v Saudi Europe Line Ltd* [1979] 3 All ER 177). However, once a witness in a criminal case has testified on behalf of the prosecution, that witness cannot be compelled to testify on behalf of the defence (*Kelly* (1985) *The Times*, 27 July 1985). As to expert witnesses, see also **F10.31**.

THE ACCUSED

As a Witness for the Prosecution

F4.8 An accused is not competent as a witness for the prosecution. Under the YJCEA 1999, s. 53(4): 'A person charged in criminal proceedings is not competent to give evidence in the proceedings for the prosecution (whether he is the only person, or is one of two or more persons, charged in the proceedings)'. A co-accused may only give evidence for the prosecution if he or she ceases to be a co-accused. Section 53(5) provides that: 'In subsection (4) the reference to a person charged in criminal proceedings does not include a person who is not, or is no longer, liable to be convicted of any offence in the proceedings (whether as a result of pleading guilty or for any other reason)'. 'Other reasons' why a co-accused may not, or may no longer, be liable to be convicted, are that the co-accused has been acquitted or is to be tried separately or that the A-G has entered a *nolle prosequi*. If an accused pleads guilty, he or she is competent for the prosecution even if the accused's evidence suggests that he or she was not a participant in the offence, unless the plea is set aside (*McEwan* [2011] EWCA Crim 1026).

There is a rule of practice, not law, that an accomplice against whom proceedings are pending but who is not an accused in the proceedings in which the prosecution seek to call him or her, should only be called by the prosecution if they have undertaken to discontinue the proceedings against the accomplice. In *Pipe* (1967) 51 Cr App R 17, D was charged with housebreaking and larceny. He was alleged to have stolen a safe and its contents. S was called to prove that he had helped D to break open the safe. S, before the commencement of D's trial, had been charged with complicity in D's crime in relation to the safe. S was not indicted with D. It was intended to try him later. The Court of Criminal Appeal held that it was 'wholly irregular' to have called S in these circumstances. **F4.9**

In *Turner* (1975) 61 Cr App R 67, it was argued that for some time past there had been a practice for judges not to admit the evidence of accomplices who could still be influenced by continuing inducements, and that in *Pipe* the Court of Appeal had adjudged that this practice had become a rule of law. Rejecting this argument, Lawton LJ said, at p. 78:

> There is nothing in either the arguments [in *Pipe*] or the judgment itself to indicate that the court thought it was changing a rule of law as to the competency of accomplices to give evidence which had been followed ever since the 17th century. The facts of that case must be closely examined....
>
> [*Pipe*'s] *ratio decidendi* is confined to a case in which an accomplice, who has been charged, but not tried, is required to give evidence of his own offence in order to secure the conviction of another accused. *Pipe* on its facts was clearly a right decision. The same result could have been achieved by adjudging that the trial judge should have exercised his discretion to exclude Swan's evidence on the ground that there was an obvious and powerful inducement for him to ingratiate himself with the prosecution and the court and that the existence of this inducement made it desirable in the interests of justice to exclude it. See *Noor Mohamed v The King* [1949] AC 182 per Lord du Parcq at p. 192 and followed in *Harris v DPP* [1952] AC 694 per Viscount Simon at p. 707.

As a Witness on one's Own Behalf

The accused is a competent witness for the defence pursuant to the YJCEA 1999, s. 53(1), whereby 'At every stage in criminal proceedings all persons are... competent to give evidence'. The phrase 'at every stage in criminal proceedings' allows the accused to give evidence not only in the trial itself, but also after conviction, in mitigation of sentence (see *Wheeler* [1917] 1 KB 283, a decision construing a similar phrase used in the Criminal Evidence Act 1898, s. 1, prior to its amendment by the YJCEA 1999). There is some old authority to the effect that the accused is not entitled as of right to give evidence on the *voir dire* (*Baldwin* (1931) 23 Cr App R 62) but that the court may in its discretion allow the accused to give evidence at this stage if the justice of the case makes this desirable (*Cowell* [1940] 2 KB 49). The wording of s. 53(1), however, supports the current practice, which is for the accused to elect whether to give evidence on the *voir dire*. **F4.10**

The accused is not a compellable witness for the defence. Under the Criminal Evidence Act 1898, s. 1(1), 'A person charged in criminal proceedings shall not be called as a witness in the proceedings except upon his own application'.

Giving Evidence from the Witness Box

F4.11 The Criminal Evidence Act 1898, s. 1(4), provides that 'Every person charged in criminal proceedings who is called as a witness in the proceedings shall, unless otherwise ordered by the court, give his evidence from the witness box or other place from which other witnesses give their evidence'. Concerning the statutory precursor to s. 1(4) (s. 1(g) of the 1898 Act), it was held that the intention was that the accused should 'have an opportunity of giving evidence on his own behalf in the same way and from the same place as the witnesses for the prosecution'. Thus the accused should give evidence from the witness-box unless, for example, too infirm to walk there or too violent to be controlled there (*Symonds* (1924) 18 Cr App R 100, per Swift J at p. 101). Section 1(4) does not confer on justices a discretion to direct where evidence should be given from but allows them, in exceptional circumstances of the kind described in *Symonds*, to deny the accused the right to give evidence from the witness box. To offer the accused a choice as to whether to give evidence from the dock or the witness stand is also to fetter that right and any such practice should cease (*Farnham Justices, ex parte Gibson* [1991] RTR 309, where the conviction of a defendant required to give evidence from the dock was quashed, applying the principle that justice must not only be done but must also be seen to be done).

F4.12 **Requirement to Give Evidence on Oath and Liability to Cross-examination** If the accused elects to testify, he or she must give evidence on oath and will be liable to cross-examination.

Criminal Justice Act 1982, s. 72

(1) Subject to subsections (2) and (3) below, in any criminal proceedings the accused shall not be entitled to make a statement without being sworn, and accordingly, if he gives evidence he shall do so (subject to sections 55 and 56 of the Youth Justice and Criminal Evidence Act 1999) on oath and be liable to cross-examination; but this section shall not affect the right of the accused, if not represented by counsel or a solicitor, to address the court or jury otherwise than on oath on any matter on which, if he were so represented, counsel or a solicitor could address the court or jury on his behalf.

(2) Nothing in subsection (1) above shall prevent the accused making a statement without being sworn—
   (a) if it is one which he is required by law to make personally; or
   (b) if he makes it by way of mitigation before the court passes sentence upon him.

The qualification in s. 72(1) relating to the YJCEA 1999, ss. 55 and 56, has the effect that the evidence of an accused who is competent to give evidence but who is not permitted to be sworn shall be given unsworn. Under s. 55(2), a witness may not be sworn for the purpose of giving evidence on oath unless the witness has attained the age of 14 and has a sufficient appreciation of the solemnity of the occasion and of the particular responsibility to tell the truth which is involved in taking an oath. Under s. 56(1) and (2), a person of any age who is competent to give evidence but by virtue of s. 55(2) is not permitted to be sworn for the purpose of giving evidence on oath shall give evidence unsworn (see **F4.26** and **F4.27**).

If the accused does testify, he or she is liable to cross-examination by the prosecution and, whether or not the accused has given evidence against a co-accused, by counsel for any co-accused (*Hilton* [1972] 1 QB 421). Subject to the CJA 2003, s. 101 (defendant's bad character), considered at **F13.15**, and to the Criminal Evidence Act 1898, s. 1(4) (see **F4.11**), the accused will be treated like any other witness. The accused's evidence will be evidence for all the purposes of the case, including the purpose of being evidence against any co-accused (*Rudd* (1948) 32 Cr App R 138, per Humphreys J at p. 140). In *Paul* [1920] 2 KB 183, in which D1 had confined his evidence-in-chief to an admission of his own guilt, it was held that the prosecution had properly been allowed to cross-examine him and thereby elicit evidence which undermined the defence of D2.

As a Witness for a Co-accused

F4.13 An accused is a competent witness for any co-accused by virtue of the YJCEA 1999, s. 53(1) (see **F4.2**). An accused, however, is not a compellable witness for a co-accused because, under the Criminal Evidence Act 1898, s. 1(1), a person charged in criminal proceedings shall not be called as a witness 'except upon his own application' (see **F4.10**). An accused who does give evidence for a co-accused may be cross-examined to show his or her own guilt of the offence charged (*Rowland* [1910] 1 KB 458).

A co-accused who ceases to be 'a person charged', and therefore ceases to be on trial, is both competent and compellable as a witness for any 'co-accused'. This may happen in the following ways:

(a) the co-accused pleads guilty;
(b) the co-accused, at the end of the prosecution case, makes a successful submission of no case to answer; or
(c) the co-accused is tried separately as the result of a successful application to sever the indictment.

THE SPOUSE OR CIVIL PARTNER OF THE ACCUSED

General

The competence and compellability of the spouse or civil partner of an accused is governed by the YJCEA 1999, s. 53(1) (see **F4.2**), and the PACE 1984, s. 80. **F4.14**

Police and Criminal Evidence Act 1984, s. 80

(2) In any proceedings the spouse or civil partner of a person charged in the proceedings shall, subject to subsection (4) below, be compellable to give evidence on behalf of that person.
(2A) In any proceedings the spouse or civil partner of a person charged in the proceedings shall, subject to subsection (4) below, be compellable—
 (a) to give evidence on behalf of any other person charged in the proceedings but only in respect of any specified offence with which that other person is charged; or
 (b) to give evidence for the prosecution but only in respect of any specified offence with which any person is charged in the proceedings.
(3) In relation to the spouse or civil partner of a person charged in any proceedings, an offence is a specified offence for the purposes of subsection (2A) above if—
 (a) it involves an assault on, or injury or a threat of injury to, the spouse or civil partner or a person who was at the material time under the age of 16;
 (b) it is a sexual offence alleged to have been committed in respect of a person who was at the material time under that age; or
 (c) it consists of attempting or conspiring to commit, or of aiding, abetting, counselling, procuring or inciting the commission of, an offence falling within paragraph (a) or (b) above.
(4) No person who is charged in any proceedings shall be compellable by virtue of subsection (2) or (2A) above to give evidence in the proceedings.
(4A) References in this section to a person charged in any proceedings do not include a person who is not, or is no longer, liable to be convicted of any offence in the proceedings (whether as a result of pleading guilty or for any other reason).
(5) In any proceedings a person who has been but is no longer married to the accused shall be compellable to give evidence as if that person and the accused had never been married.
(5A) In any proceedings a person who has been but is no longer the civil partner of the accused shall be compellable to give evidence as if that person and the accused had never been civil partners.
(6) Where in any proceedings the age of any person at any time is material for the purposes of subsection (3) above, his age at the material time shall for the purposes of that provision be deemed to be or to have been that which appears to the court to be or to have been his age at that time.
(7) In subsection (3)(b) above 'sexual offence' means an offence under the Protection of Children Act 1978 or Part 1 of the Sexual Offences Act 2003, or an offence under section 2 of the Modern Slavery Act 2015 (human trafficking) committed with a view to exploitation that consists of or includes behaviour within section 3(3) of that Act (sexual exploitation).

The reference in s. 80(3)(c) to incitement has effect as a reference to (or to conduct amounting to) the offences of encouraging or assisting crime under Part 2 of the SCA 2007 (SCA 2007, s. 63(1) and sch. 6, para. 9).

As a Witness for the Prosecution

F4.15 The spouse or civil partner of an accused is competent to give evidence for the prosecution (YJCEA 1999, s. 53(1): see **F4.2**), unless also 'a person charged' in the criminal proceedings (s. 53(4) and (5), considered at **F4.8**). A spouse or civil partner is competent under s. 53(1) irrespective of whether the evidence to be given will be directed against the accused or any co-accused.

As to compellability, the rule, subject to one exception, is that the spouse or civil partner shall be compellable to give evidence for the prosecution, but only in respect of any 'specified offence' with which any person is charged in the proceedings (PACE 1984, s. 80(2A)(b)). The exception is where the spouse or civil partner is also charged in the proceedings (s. 80(4) and (4A)).

It is submitted that the words 'spouse' and 'civil partner' used in s. 80 refer to persons whose marriage or civil partnership (wherever celebrated) would be recognised by English law (see *Bala* [2016] EWCA Crim 560, [2017] QB 430, construing those words as used in the CLA 1977, s. 2(2)(a)). In *Khan* (1987) 84 Cr App R 44, a decision on the common law before the 1984 Act came into force, it was held that a woman who had gone through a Muslim ceremony of marriage with an accused already married under English law to another woman, was in the same position as a mistress, a woman who had not gone through a ceremony of marriage at all or one who had gone through a ceremony of marriage which was void because bigamous. See also *Yacoob* (1981) 72 Cr App R 313. In *Pearce* [2001] EWCA Crim 2834, [2002] 1 WLR 1553 it was held that the words 'wife or husband of the accused' which appeared in s. 80 prior to its amendment by the YJCEA 1999, do not cover a cohabitee of an accused who is not married to the accused, and that proper respect for family life, as envisaged by the ECHR, Article 8, does not require that such a cohabitee should not be compelled to give evidence. See also *Der Heijden v The Netherlands* [2013] 1 FCR 123: compelling a cohabitee, in a relationship of 18 years duration and out of which two children were born, to give evidence against her partner would interfere with her right to respect for family life under Article 8, but under Article 8(2) would be 'necessary…for the prevention of…crime'. The reasoning in *Pearce*, as supported by *Der Heijden v The Netherlands*, was applied in *Suski* [2016] EWCA Crim 24, [2016] 2 Cr App R 3 (32), construing the words 'spouse' and 'civil partner' in the CLA 1977, s. 2(2)(a).

F4.16 **'Compellable' Offences** Section 80(3) specifies the offences in respect of which the spouse or civil partner of the accused shall be compellable to give evidence for the prosecution. A spouse or civil partner is compellable if the offence charged 'involves' an assault on, or injury or a threat of injury to, the spouse or civil partner of the accused or a person who was at the material time under the age of 16. *A (B)* [2012] EWCA Crim 1529, [2012] 1 WLR 3378 addressed the question, posed in earlier editions of this work, whether the 'involvement' must be legal (as a matter of legal definition the offence charged requires an assault on, or injury or a threat of injury to, one of the types of person described in s. 80(3)(a)) or can be factual (as a matter of legal definition the offence charged does not require an assault on or injury or a threat of injury to one of the types of such person but in fact it did involve, or is alleged to have involved, an assault on or injury or a threat of injury to one of the types of such person). In *A (B)*, D, who had shouted to his wife that he was going to burn their house down with the children in it, was charged under the Criminal Damage Act 1971, s. 2(a), with the offence of making a threat to another, intending that that other would fear it would be carried out, to destroy or damage any property belonging to that other or a third person. It was held that: under the PACE 1984, s. 80(3)(a), the 'involvement' must be legal; the offence itself does not have to have as one of its ingredients 'an assault on or injury or threat of injury'— it is sufficient if the offence encompasses the real possibility of an assault etc.; the offence under s. 2(a) of the 1971 Act is directed at property and does not encompass the real possibility of an assault etc.; and therefore D's wife was not compellable to give evidence against him. The phrase 'a threat of injury' may cover not only an uttered threat, but also a threat by conduct, as in *Verolla* [1963] 1 QB 285, where D was charged with attempting to murder his wife by poisoning her. A case of that kind, however, is now covered by s. 80(3)(c).

Procedural Issues There is no requirement to tell a wife who is competent but not compellable for the prosecution that she is not compellable before interviewing her, e.g., where a wife is interviewed about a crime of which her husband is suspected. If the issue arises whether it is in the interests of justice to admit as hearsay a statement made voluntarily by her, the prosecution's hand is likely to be strengthened if it can be shown that she was told that she was under no obligation to make the statement, but failure to give such a warning will not necessarily prevent admissibility (*L* [2008] EWCA Crim 973, [2009] 1 WLR 626 and *Horsnell* [2012] EWCA Crim 227; see **F17.39**). The same principles apply of course in the case of a husband or civil partner. **F4.17**

The following propositions, relating to a spouse who is competent but not compellable for the prosecution, derive from *Pitt* [1983] QB 25, at pp. 29–31:

(a) The choice whether to give evidence is that of the spouse, and is not lost because that spouse made a witness statement or gave evidence at the committal proceedings. The spouse retains the right of refusal up to the point when, with full knowledge of that right, he or she takes the oath in the witness-box. Waiver of the right is effective only if made with full knowledge of the right of refusal.
(b) If the spouse waives the right of refusal, he or she becomes an ordinary witness. It follows that if the nature of the evidence then given justifies it, an application may be made to treat the spouse as a hostile witness.
(c) Although not a rule of either law or practice, it is desirable that where a spouse, being competent but not compellable for the prosecution, is called for the prosecution, the judge should explain to the spouse, in the absence of the jury, that before taking the oath, he or she has the right to refuse to give evidence, but that if he or she chooses to give evidence, he or she may be treated like any other witness (but failure to give such an explanation does not necessarily justify interfering with a guilty verdict: *Nelson* [1992] Crim LR 653).

The same principles would apply, of course, in the case of a civil partner.

As a Witness for the Accused

The spouse or civil partner of an accused is competent to give evidence for the accused (YJCEA 1999, s. 53(1); see **F4.2**); and shall be compellable to give evidence for the accused (PACE 1984, s. 80(2)), unless also charged in the proceedings (s. 80(4) and (4A)). **F4.18**

As a Witness for a Co-accused

The spouse or civil partner of an accused is competent to give evidence on behalf of any other person charged in the proceedings, whether or not the accused consents (YJCEA 1999, s. 53(1); see **F4.2**). As to compellability, the rule, subject to one exception, is that the spouse or civil partner shall be compellable to give evidence on behalf of any such other person, but only in respect of any 'specified offence' with which any person is charged in the proceedings (PACE 1984, s. 80(2A)(a)). The exception is where the spouse or civil partner is also charged in the proceedings (s. 80(4) and (4A)). **F4.19**

Competence and Compellability of Former Spouse or Civil Partner of the Accused

In any proceedings, a person who has been but is no longer married to the accused shall be compellable to give evidence as if they had never been married (PACE 1984, s. 80(5); see **F4.14**). The same principle applies to a former civil partner (s. 80(5A); see **F4.14**). Such a person, therefore, is compellable on behalf of the prosecution, the accused or any co-accused, whether the evidence relates to events which occurred before, during or after the terminated marriage. **F4.20**

The phrase 'is no longer married' covers the situation where the parties have been divorced and where a voidable marriage has been annulled; but not the situation where the parties have been judicially separated or are merely not cohabiting (whether or not in consequence of an informal arrangement, formal agreement or non-cohabitation order). If the marriage of the parties was void *ab initio*, there never was a legally valid marriage, and accordingly a party to such a union will be both competent and compellable on behalf of the accused (the other party to that union), any co-accused or the prosecution. The phrase 'in any proceedings' means any proceedings which take place after s. 80(5) came into effect (1 January 1986); and therefore an ex-wife or an ex-husband is competent and compellable to give evidence in such proceedings about any matter, whether it took place before or after that date (*Cruttenden* [1991] 2 QB 66).

CHILDREN AND PERSONS WITH A DISORDER OR DISABILITY OF THE MIND

The Test for Competence

F4.21 The competence of a child (or person with a disorder or disability of the mind) to give evidence in criminal proceedings, and the question whether he or she should give sworn or unsworn evidence, are governed by the YJCEA 1999, ss. 53 to 56.

As to competence, the rule is that all persons are (whatever their age) competent to give evidence (s. 53(1); see **F4.2**); but a person is not competent if it appears to the court that the person is not able to (a) understand questions put to him or her as a witness and (b) give answers to them which can be understood (s. 53(2) and (3); see **F4.2**). In *MacPherson* [2005] EWCA Crim 3605, [2006] 1 Cr App R 30 (459), it was held that the words 'put to him as a witness' mean the equivalent of 'being asked of him in court'. Accordingly, an infant who can only communicate in baby language with its mother will not ordinarily be competent, but a child who can speak and understand basic English with strangers will be competent. It was also held that there is no requirement that the witness be aware of his or her status as a witness and that questions of credibility and reliability are not relevant to competence but go to the weight of the evidence and may be considered, if appropriate, on a submission of no case to answer. Equally, a person who has no recollection of an event may be a perfectly competent witness (*DPP v R* [2007] EWHC 1842 (Admin)). The following propositions relating to s. 53 derive from *Barker* [2010] EWCA Crim 4.

(a) In each case, the question under s. 53 is whether the individual witness or child is competent to give evidence in the particular trial. The question is entirely witness or child specific.
(b) There are no presumptions or preconceptions.
(c) The witness does not need to understand the special importance of telling the truth in court and does not need to understand every single question or give a readily understandable answer to every question (applied in *IA* [2013] EWCA Crim 1308). Dealing with it broadly and fairly, provided the witness can understand the questions and can also provide understandable answers, the witness is competent.
(d) Questions, of course, come from both sides. If the child is called as a witness by the prosecution, the child should have the ability to understand the questions put by the defence as well as the prosecution and to provide answers to them which are understandable.
(e) Section 53 requires not the exercise of a discretion, but the making of a judgment on whether the witness fulfils the statutory criteria.

F4.22 Clearly the younger the child, the more likely it is that the child will be unable to understand questions put and give answers to them which can be understood. However, a court cannot properly conclude that a child is incapable of satisfying the test on the basis of the child's age alone (*MacPherson*; *Powell* [2006] EWCA Crim 3, [2006] 1 Cr App R 31 (468)). Equally, the fact that the judge or interpreter has difficulties in communicating with a child does not necessarily mean that the child is not competent (*F* [2013] EWCA Crim 424, [2013] 1 WLR 2143).

The fact that a child under ten years of age cannot be prosecuted for the offence of wilfully giving false evidence contrary to the YJCEA 1999, s. 57 (see **B14.18**), is not a reason for excluding the unsworn evidence of a competent child witness (*N* (1992) 95 Cr App R 256, a decision under the CYPA 1933, s. 38(2), the statutory precursor to s. 57 of the 1999 Act).

Determining the Competence of Children and Persons with a Disorder or Disability of the Mind

Whether a witness is competent to give evidence in criminal proceedings must be determined by the court in accordance with the YJCEA 1999, s. 54. **F4.23**

Youth Justice and Criminal Evidence Act 1999, s. 54

(1) Any question whether a witness in criminal proceedings is competent to give evidence in the proceedings, whether raised—
 (a) by a party to the proceedings, or
 (b) by the court of its own motion,
 shall be determined by the court in accordance with this section.
(2) It is for the party calling the witness to satisfy the court that, on a balance of probabilities, the witness is competent to give evidence in the proceedings.
(3) In determining the question mentioned in subsection (1) the court shall treat the witness as having the benefit of any directions under section 19 [special measures directions in the case of vulnerable and intimidated witnesses] which the court has given, or proposes to give, in relation to the witness.
(4) Any proceedings held for the determination of the question shall take place in the absence of the jury (if there is one).
(5) Expert evidence may be received on the question.
(6) Any questioning of the witness (where the court considers that necessary) shall be conducted by the court in the presence of the parties.

Under s. 54(3), in determining competence the court must treat the witness as having the benefit of any special measures directions which the court has given or proposes to give. Equally, the court must treat the witness as having the benefit of any directions on questioning and questioning technique: the competency test is not failed because the forensic techniques of the advocates have to be adapted to enable a witness to give the best evidence of which he or she is capable (*F* [2013] EWCA Crim 424, [2013] 1 WLR 2143). Prior to the enactment of the YJCEA 1999, it was held that the question whether a child is capable of giving 'intelligible testimony' does not require any input from experts such as child psychiatrists, because it is a simple test well within the capability of a judge or magistrate (*G v DPP* [1997] 2 All ER 755). It is submitted that s. 54(5), whereby expert evidence may be received on the question, should be invoked only where necessary.

If a judge conducts an inquiry into the competence of a person with a disorder or disability of the mind, it is not normally necessary to call that person to give evidence on the subject: the proper course is to adduce expert medical evidence (*Barratt* [1996] Crim LR 495).

If the defence are of the opinion that the judge should consider the issue of a child's competence and, if the child is thought to be competent, keep the matter under review, they should challenge the child's competence or make an application to exclude the child's evidence under the PACE 1984, s. 78; failure to do so will count against an argument, on appeal, that the judge improperly failed to consider the issue of competence and to keep the matter under review (*Edwards* [2011] EWCA Crim 3028 at [28]).

Concerning statements made by unavailable witnesses, see the CJA 2003, s. 123(4), at **F17.8**.

Time to Determine Competence

The question of the competence of a child or person with a disorder or disability of the mind may have been identified at an early stage in considering eligibility for special measures (see **D14.13** to **D14.16**). In any event, if a judge has reason to doubt whether such a person is able to understand questions put to him or her as a witness, or to give answers to them which can **F4.24** be understood, because of difficulty in comprehension or expression, the judge will conduct a preliminary investigation under s. 54 (considered at **F4.23**). The issue of competence should be determined before the witness is sworn, usually as a preliminary issue at the start of the trial, when the judge should watch the video-taped interview of the child and/or ask the child appropriate questions (*MacPherson* [2005] EWCA Crim 3605, [2006] 1 Cr App R 30 (459)). Where there is material such as an ABE interview and reports from intermediaries that proceed on the basis that a witness is competent subject to the use of special measures, a competence hearing may be unnecessary at the initial stage and serve only to cause delay, increase expense and put unnecessary strain on the witness (*F* [2013] EWCA Crim 424, [2013] 1 WLR 2143 at [39]). In *Hampshire* [1996] QB 1, which was not a decision under s. 54, it was held as follows:

(a) The issue of competence should be dealt with at the earliest possible moment, not as an act of 'ratification' after the evidence has been given.
(b) The judge should conduct the investigation. It is a matter of perception of the child's understanding as demonstrated in ordinary discourse, not an issue to be resolved by the judge in response to an adversarial examination and cross-examination.
(c) If there has been an application to use video-recorded evidence (see **F17.81**), the judge's pre-trial view of the recording, if the interview has been properly conducted, will normally enable a view on competence to be formed, but if left in doubt, the judge should conduct an investigation.

Keeping Competence under Review

F4.25 A decision that a child is competent to give evidence should be kept under review, and may need to be revisited when the child's evidence is complete. If a child is unable to provide intelligible answers to questions in cross-examination, or a meaningful cross-examination is impossible, the first decision on competence will not produce a fair trial and the evidence admitted will fall to be excluded. Questions of credibility should not be addressed when conducting the second test any more than they should be addressed when conducting the first. There will be case-specific occasions when undue delay may render a trial unfair and lead to the exclusion of the evidence of a child on competency grounds. However, delay on its own does not automatically require the court to prevent or stop the evidence of the child from being considered by the jury (*Barker* [2010] EWCA Crim 4). As the Court of Appeal observed in *MH* [2012] EWCA Crim 2725 at [54], the witness will be incompetent not merely because time has passed but where the passage of time has affected the competence of the child to give intelligible answers to questions about the incident. Furthermore, in *R* [2010] EWCA Crim 2469 it was doubted that *Malicki* [2009] EWCA Crim 365 supported the proposition that a child's evidence should be excluded under the PACE 1984, s. 78, where she no longer had a reliably independent memory of the events upon which her allegations were based. That proposition, it was said, could seriously undermine the statutory reforms introduced to deal with the evidence of children and other vulnerable witnesses. It was also pointed out that it is not infrequent for witnesses to have no independent recollection of events and to say no more than that their statement is accurate.

Sworn Evidence

F4.26 Whether a child (or person of unsound mind) may be sworn for the purpose of giving evidence on oath is governed by the YJCEA 1999, s. 55. A witness may not be sworn for this purpose unless the witness has attained the age of 14 and 'has a sufficient appreciation of the solemnity of the occasion and of the particular responsibility to tell the truth which is involved in taking an oath' (s. 55(2)). If the witness is able to give intelligible testimony, i.e. is able to understand questions put to *him or her* as a witness and give answers to them which can be understood (s. 55(8)), the witness is presumed to have a sufficient appreciation of those matters unless any party adduces evidence tending to show the contrary (s. 55(3)). If any such evidence is adduced, it is for the party seeking to have the witness sworn to satisfy the court, on a balance of probabilities, that the witness has attained the age of 14 and has a sufficient appreciation of the matters in question (s. 55(4)). Any proceedings held for the determination of the question whether a witness may be sworn for the purpose of giving evidence on oath should take place in the absence of the jury (s. 55(5)). Expert evidence may be received on the question (s. 55(6)) and any questioning of the witness shall be conducted by the court in the presence of the parties (s. 55(7)).

Youth Justice and Criminal Evidence Act 1999, s. 55

(1) Any question whether a witness in criminal proceedings may be sworn for the purpose of giving evidence on oath, whether raised—
 (a) by a party to the proceedings, or
 (b) by the court of its own motion,
 shall be determined by the court in accordance with this section.
(2) The witness may not be sworn for that purpose unless—
 (a) he has attained the age of 14, and
 (b) he has a sufficient appreciation of the solemnity of the occasion and of the particular responsibility to tell the truth which is involved in taking an oath.
(3) The witness shall, if he is able to give intelligible testimony, be presumed to have a sufficient appreciation of those matters if no evidence tending to show the contrary is adduced (by any party).
(4) If any such evidence is adduced, it is for the party seeking to have the witness sworn to satisfy the court that, on a balance of probabilities, the witness has attained the age of 14 and has a sufficient appreciation of the matters mentioned in subsection (2)(b).
(5) Any proceedings held for the determination of the question mentioned in subsection (1) shall take place in the absence of the jury (if there is one).
(6) Expert evidence may be received on the question.
(7) Any questioning of the witness (where the court considers that necessary) shall be conducted by the court in the presence of the parties.
(8) For the purposes of this section a person is able to give intelligible testimony if he is able to—
 (a) understand questions put to him as a witness, and
 (b) give answers to them which can be understood.

Unsworn Evidence

The evidence of a person (of any age) who is competent to give evidence in criminal proceedings but who is not permitted to be sworn for the purpose of giving evidence on oath shall be given unsworn and shall be received in evidence by the court (YJCEA 1999, s. 56(1), (2) and (4)). A deposition of unsworn evidence given by such a person may also be taken for the purposes of criminal proceedings and shall also be received in evidence (s. 56(3) and (4)). **F4.27**

Youth Justice and Criminal Evidence Act 1999, s. 56

(1) Subsections (2) and (3) apply to a person (of any age) who—
 (a) is competent to give evidence in criminal proceedings, but
 (b) (by virtue of section 55(2)) is not permitted to be sworn for the purpose of giving evidence on oath in such proceedings.
(2) The evidence in criminal proceedings of a person to whom this subsection applies shall be given unsworn.
(3) A deposition of unsworn evidence given by a person to whom this subsection applies may be taken for the purposes of criminal proceedings as if that evidence had been given on oath.
(4) A court in criminal proceedings shall accordingly receive in evidence any evidence given unsworn in pursuance of subsection (2) or (3).
(5) Where a person ('the witness') who is competent to give evidence in criminal proceedings gives evidence in such proceedings unsworn, no conviction, verdict or finding in those proceedings shall be taken to be unsafe for the purposes of any of sections 2(1), 13(1) and 16(1) of the Criminal Appeal Act 1968 (grounds for allowing appeals) by reason only that it appears to the Court of Appeal that the witness was a person falling within section 55(2) (and should accordingly have given his evidence on oath).

Weight to be Attached to Evidence Given by Persons with a Disorder or Disability of the Mind

F4.28 Where a person with a mental disorder or disability gives evidence, it is left to the jury to attach to the evidence such weight as they see fit. If the evidence is so tainted as to be unworthy of credit, it is the proper function of the jury to disregard it and not to act upon it (*Hill* (1851) 2 Den CC 254). However, a person suffering from a mental disorder or disability may be a reliable witness; and to direct a jury to regard with caution the evidence of a witness with some history of mental illness, in the absence of any medical foundation for regarding the evidence as unreliable, would amount to an improper invitation to irrational and stereotypical prejudice (*Milton v R* [2015] UKPC 42, [2015] 1 WLR 5356 at [21]). In *Barratt* [1996] Crim LR 495, in which the witness was suffering from the psychiatric condition known as fixed belief paranoia and held bizarre beliefs about certain aspects of her private life, the Court of Appeal could see no reason for supposing that on matters not affected by her condition, her evidence was not as reliable as that of any other witness. See also, to similar effect, *R (B) v DPP* [2009] EWHC 106 (Admin), [2009] 1 WLR 2072 (a witness with paranoid beliefs who suffered auditory and visual hallucinations).

OTHER WITNESSES

The Sovereign and Diplomats

F4.29 The Sovereign is a competent but not a compellable witness. Total or partial immunity from compellability to give evidence is also enjoyed by heads of other sovereign States; diplomatic agents; members of the family of a diplomatic agent forming part of his or her household; members of the administrative and technical staff of a diplomatic mission and members of their families; persons connected with consular posts; and members of the staff of international organisations. See:

(a) Diplomatic Privileges Act 1964, s. 2(1) and sch. 1, arts. 1, 31, 37, 38(2) and 39;
(b) Consular Relations Act 1968, s. 1(1) and sch. 1, arts. 1(1), 44 and 58(2);
(c) International Organisations Act 1968;
(d) State Immunity Act 1978; and
(e) International Organisations Act 1981.

Bankers

F4.30 Subject to a variety of safeguards, a copy of an entry in a banker's book shall in all legal proceedings be received as prima facie evidence of such entry, and of the matters, transactions and accounts therein recorded (Bankers' Books Evidence Act 1879, ss. 3 and 9). In any legal proceeding to which the bank is not a party, bank personnel cannot be compelled to produce the originals of such books or to give evidence to prove the matters recorded therein, unless specifically ordered to do so by a judge (see s. 6, at **F8.36**).

OATHS AND AFFIRMATIONS

General Rule and Exceptions

F4.31 Unless legislation otherwise provides, before giving evidence a witness must take an oath or affirm (CrimPR 24.4(3) (magistrates' courts) and 25.11(3) (Crown Court): see Supplement, **R24.4** and **R25.11**). The evidence of a person who is competent to give evidence but who is not permitted to be sworn, shall be given unsworn (see **F4.27**); and at common law a witness called merely for the purpose of producing a document need not be sworn (*Perry v Gibson* (1934) 1 A & E 48). As to the latter situation, the witness, if not sworn, is not liable to cross-examination. However, if the identity of the document is disputed, and must be established, this must be done by sworn evidence.

Where a video recording of an interview with a child is admitted under the YJCEA 1999, s. 27, and the child is then aged 14 or over, the oath should be administered before the start of the cross-examination (*Simmonds* [1996] Crim LR 816, a decision under the CJA 1988, s. 32A, the statutory precursor to s. 27). Under the YJCEA 1999, s. 56(5), where a witness who is competent to give evidence in criminal proceedings has given evidence unsworn, no conviction, verdict or finding in those proceedings shall be taken to be unsafe for the purposes of the grounds of appeal in the Criminal Appeal Act 1968, s. 2(1), 13(1) or 16(1), by reason only that the witness was a person falling within s. 55(2) of the 1999 Act and therefore should have given evidence on oath.

Form and Manner of Oath: Christians and Jews

Oaths Act 1978, s. 1 **F4.32**

(1) Any oath may be administered and taken in England, Wales or Northern Ireland in the following form and manner:—
The person taking the oath shall hold the New Testament, or, in the case of a Jew, the Old Testament, in his uplifted hand, and shall say or repeat after the officer administering the oath the words 'I swear by Almighty God that . . .', followed by the words of the oath prescribed by law.

. . .

(4) In this section 'officer' means any person duly authorised to administer oaths.

The words of s. 1 are directive; therefore failure to comply with them will not necessarily invalidate the taking of an oath, because the efficacy of an oath depends upon it being taken in a way binding, and intended to be binding, upon the conscience of the intended witness (*Chapman* [1980] Crim LR 42, where leave to appeal was refused, the witness in question having failed to take the Testament in his hand). Witnesses who are required to take an oath as part of a hearing that they are joining remotely and who wish to take an oath using a sacred object, should provide their own Holy Book or Scripture; they can also, if they wish, take an oath without a sacred object if they consider it will still be binding on them (HM Courts and Tribunals Service, *Guidance on telephone and video hearings during the coronavirus (COVID-19) outbreak* (tinyurl.com/yxx3g6me)).

In the case of a witness in the trial proper, 'the words of the oath prescribed by law', approved by a resolution of the judges of the King's Bench Division on 11 January 1927, are 'the evidence which I shall give shall be the truth, the whole truth and nothing but the truth'. When a witness gives evidence in a trial within a trial, the oath is 'I swear by Almighty God that I will true answer make to all such questions as the Court shall demand of me'. In relation to any oath administered to and taken by any person before a youth court, or administered to and taken by any child or young person before any other court, s. 1 of the Oaths Act 1978 shall have effect as if the words 'I promise before Almighty God' were set out instead of the words 'I swear by Almighty God that' (CYPA 1963, s. 28(1)). Where, in any oath otherwise duly administered and taken, either of the forms mentioned in s. 28 of the CYPA 1963 is used instead of the other, the oath shall nevertheless be deemed to have been duly administered and taken (s. 28(2)).

Form and Manner of Oath: Other Religious Beliefs

Oaths Act 1978, s. 1 **F4.33**

(2) The officer shall (unless the person about to take the oath voluntarily objects thereto, or is physically incapable of so taking the oath) administer the oath in the form and manner aforesaid without question.
(3) In the case of a person who is neither a Christian nor a Jew, the oath shall be administered in any lawful manner.
(4) In this section 'officer' means any person duly authorised to administer oaths.

Section 1(2) makes it clear that it is incumbent upon a person who is neither a Christian nor a Jew to object to the taking of an oath in the form and manner prescribed by s. 1(1). Such a person may affirm or may take the oath upon such holy book as is appropriate to that person's religious belief. Muslims are sworn on the Koran (*Morgan* (1764) 1 Leach 54). Hindus are sworn on the Vedas or other sacred books. Parsees are sworn on the Zendavesta. The modern practice is to inquire what oath a witness accepts as binding and swear the witness accordingly.

Whether an oath is administered 'in a lawful manner' for the purposes of s. 1(3) does not depend on what may be the considerable intricacies of the particular religion adhered to by the witness but on (a) whether the oath appears to the court to be binding on the conscience of the witness and (b) whether it is an oath which the witness considers to be binding on his or her conscience (*Kemble* [1990] 3 All ER 116, where a Muslim, who had taken the oath using the New Testament, was held to have been properly sworn).

It is improper to cross-examine a Muslim who has affirmed as to whether he or she thinks that he or she is bound to tell the truth (*Majid* [2009] EWCA Crim 2563). However, in cases in which the ground is properly laid for an expectation that a witness will take the oath on a particular holy book, but the witness affirms, and the matter is raised in the absence of the jury, the judge has a discretion to allow sensitive questions on the reason for not taking the oath on the holy book (*Mehrban* [2001] EWCA Crim 2627, [2002] 1 Cr App R 40 (561), where a Muslim witness for the prosecution who had taken the oath on the Koran had challenged one of the accused, also a Muslim, to do likewise).

Swearing with Uplifted Hand

F4.34 Oaths Act 1978, s. 3

If any person to whom an oath is administered desires to swear with uplifted hand, in the form and manner in which an oath is usually administered in Scotland, he shall be permitted to do so, and the oath shall be administered to him in such form and manner without further question.

Validity of Oaths

F4.35 Oaths Act 1978, s. 4

(1) In any case in which an oath may lawfully be and has been administered to any person, if it has been administered in a form and manner other than that prescribed by law, he is bound by it if it has been administered in such form and with such ceremonies as he may have declared to be binding.

(2) Where an oath has been duly administered and taken, the fact that the person to whom it was administered had, at the time of taking it, no religious belief, shall not for any purpose affect the validity of the oath.

Affirmations

F4.36 Oaths Act 1978, ss. 5 and 6

5.—(1) Any person who objects to being sworn shall be permitted to make his solemn affirmation instead of taking an oath.

(2) Subsection (1) above shall apply in relation to a person to whom it is not reasonably practicable without inconvenience or delay to administer an oath in the manner appropriate to his religious belief as it applies in relation to a person objecting to be sworn.

(3) A person who may be permitted under subsection (2) above to make his solemn affirmation may also be required to do so.

(4) A solemn affirmation shall be of the same force and effect as an oath.

6.—(1) Subject to subsection (2) below, every affirmation shall be as follows:—

'I, [name] do solemnly, sincerely and truly declare and affirm,'

and then proceed with the words of the oath prescribed by law, omitting any words of imprecation or calling to witness.

(2) Every affirmation in writing shall commence:—

'I, [name] of [address], do solemnly and sincerely affirm,'

and the form in lieu of the jurat shall be 'Affirmed at this day of 20, Before me.'

Section F5 Corroboration and Care Warnings

GENERAL RULE

The general rule is that there is no requirement that evidence be corroborated and no requirement that the tribunal of fact be warned of the danger of acting on uncorroborated evidence. This section concerns two categories of exception to the general rule: **F5.1**

(a) where corroboration is required by statute; and
(b) where the tribunal of fact should be warned to exercise care before acting on the evidence of certain types of witness, if unsupported.

There is a third category of exception, made up of four cases — confessions by mentally handicapped persons, identification evidence, sudden unexplained infant deaths and unconvincing hearsay evidence — in all of which there is a special need for caution which has led to requirements analogous to but different from those relating to the first two categories. These requirements are considered at **F18.56**, **F19.9** ***et seq.***, **F5.18** and **F17.94**, respectively.

CORROBORATION REQUIRED BY STATUTE

Introduction

Corroboration is required by statute in four cases: treason; perjury (see **B14.16**); offences of speeding (see **C6.58**); and attempts to commit any such offences. As to treason, the Treason Act 1795, s. 1, provides that a person charged with the offence of treason by compassing the death or restraint of the Queen or her heirs shall not be convicted except on the oaths of two lawful and credible witnesses. As to the last case, under the Criminal Attempts Act 1981, s. 2(2)(g), any provision whereby a person may not be convicted or committed for trial on the uncorroborated evidence of one witness (including any provision requiring the evidence of not less than two credible witnesses) shall have effect with respect to an offence under s. 1 of the Act of attempting to commit an offence (see **A5.72**) as it has effect with respect to the offence attempted. Where corroboration is required by statute, a conviction should not be based on uncorroborated evidence and, if it is, will be open to successful appeal. Thus, in the absence of corroboration, the judge should direct an acquittal. **F5.2**

Meaning of Corroboration

In the case of perjury, corroboration bears the technical meaning it once bore at common law (*Hamid* (1979) 69 Cr App R 324). Corroboration in this technical sense is probably also required in the case of the other three statutory provisions (see per Lord Reading CJ in *Baskerville* [1916] 2 KB 658 at p. 667). Evidence, to be capable of being corroboration in the strict or technical sense, must: **F5.3**

(a) be relevant and admissible (*Scarrott* [1978] QB 1016 at p. 1021);
(b) be credible (*DPP v Kilbourne* [1973] AC 729 at p. 746; *DPP v Hester* [1973] AC 296 at p. 315);
(c) be independent, i.e. emanate from a source other than the witness requiring corroboration (*Whitehead* [1929] 1 KB 99; *Cooper* [2010] EWCA Crim 979, [2010] 2 Cr App R 13 (92), considered at **B14.16**); and
(d) implicate the accused.

Corroboration Direction

F5.4 Where a judge directs a jury on corroboration, he or she should explain what it means, making clear the requirements of credibility, independence and implication (*Fallon* [1993] Crim LR 591). The judge should also indicate the evidence which is and is not capable of being corroboration (*Charles* (1976) 68 Cr App R 334n; *Cullinane* [1984] Crim LR 420; *Webber* [1987] Crim LR 412) and, in the case of evidence which is capable of being corroboration, should explain to the jury that it is for them to decide whether the evidence does in fact constitute corroboration (*Tragen* [1956] Crim LR 332; *McInnes* (1989) 90 Cr App R 99).

CARE WARNINGS

General

F5.5 In appropriate circumstances the jury should be warned to exercise caution before acting on the evidence of certain types of witness, if unsupported. Whether a warning is given is a matter of judicial discretion dependent on the particular circumstances of the case, and failure to give a warning therefore will not necessarily furnish grounds for a successful appeal, even if all members of the appellate court would have given a warning (see, e.g., *BJ* [2020] NICA 5). Equally, if a warning is given, the strength of warning and the extent to which the judge should elaborate upon it, also turn on the particular circumstances of the case. The categories of witness that fall to be considered, for the purposes of considering whether to give a care warning, are:

(a) accomplices giving evidence for the prosecution and complainants in sexual cases (which fall to be considered together);
(b) other witnesses whose evidence may be unreliable;
(c) witnesses whose evidence may be tainted by an improper motive;
(d) children; and
(e) patients at a secure hospital.

Accomplices Giving Evidence for the Prosecution and Complainants in Sexual Cases

F5.6 **Position at Common Law** At common law, the jury had to be warned of the danger of acting on the evidence, if not corroborated, of accomplices giving evidence for the prosecution and complainants, whether male or female, in sexual cases. Where a warning was required, it had to be a 'full' warning, comprising:

(a) a warning to the jury that it was dangerous to convict without corroboration but that they could do so if satisfied of the truth of the evidence of the accomplice or complainant;
(b) an explanation of the technical meaning of corroboration (see **F5.3**);
(c) an indication of what evidence was and was not capable of being corroboration; and
(d) an explanation that it was for them to decide whether evidence did in fact constitute corroboration.

F5.7 **Effect of the CJPO 1994, s. 32** Section 32 of the CJPO 1994 removed the requirement for full warnings. There were a number of compelling reasons in favour of such reform. They included the following:

(a) a full warning was required irrespective of the particular circumstances of the case or the credibility of the particular accomplice or complainant;
(b) the highly technical rules relating to the meaning of corroboration had rendered the full warning complex and difficult to understand; and
(c) many sexual offences are committed in circumstances in which it is difficult or impossible to obtain corroboration.

Criminal Justice and Public Order Act 1994, s. 32

(1) Any requirement whereby at a trial on indictment it is obligatory for the court to give the jury a warning about convicting the accused on the uncorroborated evidence of a person merely because that person is—
 (a) an alleged accomplice of the accused, or
 (b) where the offence charged is a sexual offence, the person in respect of whom it is alleged to have been committed,
is hereby abrogated.

...

(3) Any requirement that—
 (a) is applicable at the summary trial of a person for an offence, and
 (b) corresponds to the requirement mentioned in subsection (1) above...
is hereby abrogated.

F5.8 The effect of these provisions is to abrogate the requirements whereby a full warning was obligatory. The judge, however, still retains the discretion to warn the jury to exercise caution whenever the judge considers it appropriate to do so, whether in respect of an accomplice or a complainant or any other witness. This was made clear in *Makanjuola* [1995] 3 All ER 730, the leading authority on s. 32, in which Lord Taylor CJ summarised the relevant principles (at p. 733).

> (1) Section 32(1) abrogated the requirement to give a corroboration direction in respect of an alleged accomplice or a complainant of a sexual offence, simply because a witness falls into one of those categories. (2) It is a matter for the judge's discretion what, if any warning, he considers appropriate in respect of such a witness as indeed in respect of any other witness in whatever type of case. Whether he chooses to give a warning and in what terms will depend on the circumstances of the case, the issues raised and the content and quality of the witness's evidence. (3) In some cases, it may be appropriate for the judge to warn the jury to exercise caution before acting upon the unsupported evidence of a witness. This will not be so simply because the witness is a complainant of a sexual offence nor will it necessarily be so because a witness is alleged to be an accomplice. There will need to be an evidential basis for suggesting that the evidence of the witness may be unreliable. An evidential basis does not include mere suggestion by cross-examining counsel. (4) If any question arises as to whether the judge should give a special warning in respect of a witness, it is desirable that the question be resolved by discussion with counsel in the absence of the jury before final speeches. (5) Where the judge does decide to give some warning in respect of a witness, it will be appropriate to do so as part of the judge's review of the evidence and his comments as to how the jury should evaluate it rather than as a set-piece legal direction. (6) Where some warning is required, it will be for the judge to decide the strength and terms of the warning. It does not have to be invested with the whole florid regime of the old corroboration rules. (7) It follows that we emphatically disagree with the tentative submission [that if a judge does give a warning, he should give a full warning and should tell the jury what corroboration is in the technical sense and identify the evidence capable of being corroborative]. Attempts to re-impose the straitjacket of the old corroboration rules are strongly to be deprecated. (8) Finally, this court will be disinclined to interfere with a trial judge's exercise of his discretion save in a case where that exercise is unreasonable in the *Wednesbury* sense: see *Associated Provincial Picture Houses Ltd v Wednesbury Corporation* [1948] 1 KB 223.

The discretion imparted to trial judges by *Makanjuola* is a wide discretion and, where it is appropriate for the judge to warn the jury to exercise caution, no set form of words is required (*Blasiak* [2010] EWCA Crim 2620, where, in the case of a witness who was an in-patient at a psychiatric unit, it sufficed to draw attention to the central question of her alleged unreliability).

F5.9 **Circumstances in which Warning Should be Given** As to the circumstances in which it may be appropriate for the judge to give a warning, in *Makanjuola* Lord Taylor said (at p. 732):

> The judge will often consider that no special warning is required at all. Where, however, the witness has been shown to be unreliable, he or she may consider it necessary to urge caution. In a more extreme case, if the witness is shown to have lied, to have made previous false complaints, or to bear the defendant some grudge, a stronger warning may be thought appropriate and the judge may suggest it would be wise to look for some supporting material before acting on the impugned

> witness's evidence. We stress that these observations are merely illustrative of some, not all, of the factors which the judges may take into account in measuring where a witness stands in the scale of reliability and what response they should make at that level in their directions to the jury.

Another relevant factor, in respect of complainants in sex cases, is the difficulty of defending historic cases where there is no independent evidence (*BJ* [2020] NICA 5). For an example of lies told by a complainant in a sexual case which may have made it appropriate for the judge to have given a warning, see *Mehta* [2019] EWCA Crim 2332.

F5.10 **'Supporting Material'** In cases in which, after *Makanjuola*, the trial judge decides to direct the jury that 'it would be wise to look for some supporting material' it is incumbent on the judge to identify any 'independent supporting evidence' (*B* [2000] Crim LR 181). It is submitted that such evidence may be furnished by any of the following.

(a) Evidence of an out-of-court confession by the accused.
(b) A damaging admission made by the accused in the course of giving evidence.
(c) Lies told by the accused, whether told in or out of court. In order to constitute 'supporting evidence', however, it is submitted that the lie should meet the criteria formerly employed to determine whether a lie amounted to corroboration in the technical sense, namely that (i) the lie must relate to a material issue, (ii) the motive for the lie must be a realisation of guilt and a fear of the truth, as opposed to a lie told, for example, in an attempt to bolster up a just cause or out of shame or a wish to conceal disgraceful behaviour from the family, and (iii) the lie must be shown to be such by evidence other than that of the witness whose evidence is to be supported, i.e. by admission or by evidence from an independent witness (*Lucas* [1981] QB 720 at p. 724; see also *Credland v Knowler* (1951) 35 Cr App R 48 and *Dawson v McKenzie* [1908] 45 SLR 473).
(d) Evidence of the silence of the accused, where an accusation is made by someone speaking to the accused on even terms, admissible at common law to show that the accused accepts the accusation (see **F20.28** to **F20.33**).
(e) Inferences properly drawn under the CJPO 1994, ss. 34 to 37 (see **F20.3** ***et seq.***).
(f) Evidence of refusal to consent to the taking of 'intimate samples' (see **F20.54**).
(g) Evidence of bad character to prove guilt (see **F13.36** ***et seq.***).

F5.11 It is submitted that in sexual cases in which a special warning is properly given in respect of the evidence of the complainant, the following evidence would not constitute 'supporting material'.

(a) Evidence of a recent complaint admissible by way of exception to the rule against previous consistent statements (see **F6.32**). Such evidence is not truly 'supportive' in that it emanates from the complainant herself (*Whitehead* [1929] 1 KB 99; see also *AA* [2007] EWCA Crim 1779 at **F6.33**).
(b) Evidence of the complainant's distress. In *Zala* [2014] EWCA Crim 2181 it was held that: (i) a complainant's own evidence as to her distress is not independent evidence and therefore cannot constitute supportive evidence; (ii) evidence of others as to distress immediately after the incident in question may be supportive evidence but the judge should look at the circumstances of each case and tailor the directions to the facts, emphasising to the jury the need before they act on it to make sure the distress was not feigned and drawing to their attention factors that may affect the weight to be given to the evidence; and (iii) evidence of others as to distress some considerable time after the alleged incident may be inadmissible because of no assistance as to who is telling the truth (*Keast* [1998] Crim LR 748, considered at **F1.16**) but where it is admissible it requires very careful consideration. See also *Romeo* [2003] EWCA Crim 2844, [2004] 1 Cr App R 30 (418) (the weight to be given to evidence of distress varies enormously).
(c) Medical evidence, in a case of rape, to show that someone had intercourse with the complainant at a time consistent with her evidence. Such medical evidence, by itself, neither implicates the accused nor proves absence of consent (*James v R* (1970) 55 Cr App R 299; cf. per Lord Lane CJ in *Hills* (1987) 86 Cr App R 26 at p. 31; see also *Pountney* [1989] Crim LR 216 and *Franklin* [1989] Crim LR 499).

It may well be that there is properly no desire to revive 'the whole florid regime of the old corroboration rules', but it is submitted that in the 'more extreme case' in which a special warning is thought to be desirable, evidence in the foregoing categories cannot fairly be described as evidence supportive of the evidence of the impugned witness.

Other Witnesses whose Evidence May be Unreliable

Prior to the implementation of CJPO 1994, s. 32, there were a number of common-law decisions to the effect that a jury should be warned to exercise caution before acting on the evidence of particular types of witness whose evidence might be unreliable for one of a number of reasons. Some of the authorities suggested that the warning was discretionary or desirable as a matter of practice; others suggested that it was sometimes obligatory. In *Muncaster* [1999] Crim LR 409, it was held that all such authorities need to be reconsidered in the light of *Makanjuola* which must be read as applying to all cases in which the evidence of a witness may be suspect because the witness falls into a particular category. Where a warning is called for but not given, the question whether the failure renders a conviction unsafe will depend on the facts of each case (*Cundell* [2009] EWCA Crim 2072). **F5.12**

An Accomplice who is a Co-accused

An accomplice, being an accused who, in giving evidence in his or her own defence, incriminates another co-accused, may be regarded as having a purpose of his or her own to serve. For this reason it was held, prior to the implementation of the CJPO 1994, s. 32, that it was desirable to warn the jury of the danger of acting on the accomplice's unsupported evidence, but that every case should be looked at in the light of its own facts (*Prater* [1960] 2 QB 464 and *Knowlden* (1983) 77 Cr App R 94; and cf. *Perman* [1995] Crim LR 736, where the evidence incriminated the co-accused in one material respect, but otherwise exonerated him). Where a warning was given, the jury simply had to be told that the witness might have had a purpose of his or her own to serve (*Cheema* [1994] 1 All ER 639). Following *Makanjuola* [1995] 3 All ER 730, whether a warning is given at all and, if it is, the strength of the warning, continue to be matters of judicial discretion dependent on the particular circumstances of the case (*Muncaster* [1999] Crim LR 409). In *Jones* [2003] EWCA Crim 1966, [2004] 1 Cr App R 5 (60) it was held that in the case of cut-throat defences, even if they are mirror-image cut-throat defences, a warning should normally be considered and given and the judge, in exercising discretion as to what to say, should at least warn the jury to examine the evidence of each co-accused with care because each has or may have an interest of his or her own to serve. (Cf. *Burrows* [2000] Crim LR 48 which, according to *Jones*, turned on its own particular facts.) However, failure to give such a warning, where required, will not found a successful appeal if the fact that each of the accused had an axe to grind would have been obvious to the jury (*Petkar* [2003] EWCA Crim 2668, [2004] 1 Cr App R 22 (270)). There is a particular need for a warning where one co-accused has refused to answer questions in interview and was therefore able, if so wished, to tailor his or her defence to the facts in evidence. In many or most cases where a trial judge has to consider what if any warning to give, where co-accused have given evidence against each other, four points might be put to the jury: **F5.13**

(1) The jury should consider the case for and against each accused separately.
(2) The jury should decide the case on all the evidence, including the evidence of each accused's co-accused.
(3) When considering the evidence of a co-accused, the jury should bear in mind that the co-accused may have an interest to serve or an axe to grind.
(4) The jury should assess the evidence of co-accused in the same way as that of the evidence of any other witness in the case (*Jones* [2003] EWCA Crim 1966, [2004] 1 Cr App R 5 (60)).

Witnesses whose Evidence May be Tainted by an Improper Motive

At common law, a judge is obliged to advise a jury to proceed with caution where there is material to suggest that a witness's evidence may be tainted by an improper motive, the strength of advice varying according to the facts of the case (*Beck* [1982] 1 All ER 807). Thus where an offender, **F5.14** awaiting sentence, gives evidence for the prosecution in another case, knowing that at the very least there will thereby be a chance of having his or her sentence reduced, the potential fallibility of the offender's evidence should be put squarely to the jury (*Chan Wai-Keung v R* [1995] 2 All ER 438). See also, in the case of an accused who has entered into an agreement pursuant to the SOCPA 2005, s. 73 (see **E1.11**), *Daniels* [2010] EWCA Crim 2740, [2011] 1 Cr App R 18 (228). See also *Ratcliff* [2019] EWCA Crim 2267, where it was held that the trial judge had couched his warning to the jury in sufficiently strong terms and had been under no obligation to direct them to look for corroboration. *Ashgar* [1995] 1 Cr App R 223 was a murder charge arising out of a fight involving a number of men. Three of the men pleaded guilty to affray and gave evidence against A. The defence case was that they had colluded with others to fabricate a story incriminating A to protect one of their number. It was held that a warning should have been given on the danger of convicting A on the evidence of the three men without some independent supporting evidence.

F5.15 In *Pringle v The Queen* [2003] UKPC 9, a case of murder which depended in part on the evidence of a cellmate that D had confessed to him, the Privy Council held that if there are indications that a cell confession may be tainted by an improper motive — which was thought to be not an exacting test — the judge should draw the jury's attention to these indications and their possible significance. On the facts the judge should have pointed out that the cellmate was an untried prisoner, it was not unknown for persons in his position to wish to ingratiate themselves with the police, that to report a confession was a convenient and obvious way of doing so, and that the jury should therefore be cautious before accepting his evidence. In *Benedetto v The Queen* [2003] UKPC 27, [2003] 1 WLR 1545, the Privy Council went further and held that evidence from an untried prisoner that a fellow untried prisoner confessed to him that he was guilty of the crime for which he was being held in custody, raises an acute problem which will always call for special attention in view of the danger that it may lead to a miscarriage of justice. It was held that the evidence of prisoner informers is inherently unreliable in view of the personal advantage which such witnesses think they may obtain by providing information to the authorities. Such witnesses, it was said, tend to have no interest whatsoever in the proper course of justice. Prisoners against whom the evidence is given are always at a disadvantage. They are afforded none of the usual protections against the inaccurate recording or invention of words used by them when interviewed by the police and it may be difficult for them to obtain all the information needed to expose fully the informer's bad character. There are two steps which the judge must take, both equally important, first to draw the jury's attention to the indications that may justify the inferences that the prisoner's evidence is tainted and secondly to advise the jury to be cautious before accepting the evidence. The judge must examine the evidence so as to instruct the jury fully as to where the indications are to be found and their significance. However, in *Stone* [2005] EWCA Crim 105, it was held that not every case involving a cell confession requires the detailed directions discussed in *Pringle* and *Benedetto*. The Court of Appeal held as follows.

(a) Cell confessions prompt the most careful consideration by the trial judge, but the judge is not trammelled by fixed rules. The judge is best placed to decide the strength of any warning and the necessary extent of any accompanying analysis.
(b) In the case of a 'standard two line cell confession', there is generally a need to point out that such confessions are often easy to concoct and difficult to prove and that experience has shown that prisoners may have many motives to lie. Further, if the prison informant has a significant criminal record or history of lying, this should usually be pointed out, together with an explanation that it gives rise to a need for great care, and why.
(c) However, a summing-up should be tailored by the trial judge to the circumstances of the particular case. Where (as in *Stone* itself) an alleged confession, for whatever reason, would not be easy to invent, then it would be absurd to require a judge to tell the jury that cell confessions are easy to concoct. Similarly, where (as in *Stone* itself) the defence has deliberately not cross-examined the informant about the motive of hope of obtaining advantage, the judge is not required to tell the jury that, merely because the informant was a prisoner, there might, intrinsically, have been such a motive.

(d) There are cases where the prisoner has witnessed the acts constituting the offence in which it is appropriate to treat the prisoner as an ordinary witness about whose evidence nothing out of the usual needs to be said and, in relation to those cases, there is no suggestion that a potential motive to gain advantage with the authorities will be absent. Furthermore, indications that the prison informant's evidence may be tainted by an improper motive must be found in the evidence.
(e) Moreover, it is clear from *Muncaster* [1999] Crim LR 409 (see **F5.12**) and the general language used in *Makanjuola* [1995] 3 All ER 730 (see **F5.8**) that obligations to give special warnings arising in cases such as *Beck* must be looked at in the light of the statutory abrogation in relation to accomplices giving evidence for the prosecution and complainants in sexual cases. It would be absurd to suppose that the rules for cases such as *Beck* have survived the statutory abrogation so as to impose obligations more onerous than those now applicable to the original cases.

A warning may be appropriate in the case of the unsupported evidence of a woman upon whose immoral earnings the accused is charged with having lived, even if she is not an accomplice (*King* (1914) 10 Cr App R 117; cf. *Hanton* (1985) *The Times*, 14 February 1985) and in the case of a spouse (or, presumably, civil partner) of an accomplice called to give evidence on his or her behalf (*Allen* [1965] 2 QB 295). A warning may also be appropriate in the case of a witness acting out of malevolence or spite, or with some financial or other personal interest in the outcome of the trial, or who is biased or partial for some other reason.

Children

There was a time when an accused was not liable to be convicted on the unsworn evidence of a child appearing on behalf of the prosecution unless that evidence was corroborated (CYPA 1933, proviso to s. 38(1)); and when the sworn evidence of a child required a corroboration warning as a matter of law (see, e.g., *Cleal* [1942] 1 All ER 203). The former statutory requirement has been repealed (CJA 1991, s. 101(2)); as to the latter common-law rule, the CJA 1988, s. 34(2), now provides that 'Any requirement whereby at a trial on indictment it is obligatory for the court to give the jury a warning about convicting the accused on the uncorroborated evidence of a child is abrogated'. Despite these statutory reforms, in some cases the evidence of some children may remain unreliable, whether by reason of childish imagination, suggestibility or fallibility of memory. In *Pryce* [1991] Crim LR 379, it was held that it was not necessary to give a direction to treat the evidence of a six-year-old with caution, because in effect that would be to reintroduce an abrogated rule, but, after *Makanjuola* [1995] 3 All ER 730, it is submitted that whether a direction is given, and if so the terms of the direction, are matters of judicial discretion turning on the circumstances of the case (*L* [1999] Crim LR 489; *Barker* [2010] EWCA Crim 4). Circumstances of importance, it is submitted, will include the intelligence of the child and, in the case of unsworn evidence, the extent to which the child understands the duty of speaking the truth. **F5.16**

Patients at a Secure Hospital

In *Spencer* [1987] AC 128, nursing staff of a secure hospital were charged with ill-treating patients who had been convicted of crimes and who were suffering from mental disorders. The prosecution case was made up of the evidence of patients who were characterised as being not only mentally unbalanced and of bad character, but also as anti-authoritarian, prone to lie, and possibly with old scores to settle. The House of Lords held that where the only prosecution evidence comes from a witness who, by reason of mental condition and criminal connection fulfils criteria analogous to those which (at one time) justified a full corroboration warning, the judge should warn the jury that it is dangerous to convict on such evidence if uncorroborated, although the warning need not amount to the 'full' warning (see F5.6). Thus use of the words 'danger' or 'dangerous' is not essential to an adequate warning, provided that the jury are made fully aware of the dangers of convicting on such evidence. **F5.17**

Similarly, the extent to which the judge should refer to any corroborative material depends on the facts of each case. It is submitted that 'corroborative material', for these purposes, was not intended to denote material which is corroborative in the strict or technical sense (see F5.3) and that notwithstanding the analogy drawn with cases which justified a 'full' corroboration warning, the warning given should reflect the circumstances of the particular case (*Causley* [1999] Crim LR 572). See also *Blasiak* [2010] EWCA Crim 2620, considered at F5.8.

SUDDEN UNEXPLAINED INFANT DEATHS

F5.18 Infant deaths are said to be attributable to Sudden Infant Death Syndrome (SIDS), colloquially 'cot deaths', where the deaths are unexplained and the cause or causes, although natural, are, or are as yet, unknown. There is no underlying condition for every SIDS death, but in each case the mechanism of death is the same, namely apnoea, loss of breath or cessation of breathing. In *Cannings* [2004] EWCA Crim 1, [2004] 1 All ER 725, D was convicted of the murder of two of her four children, J who had died aged six weeks and M who had died aged 18 weeks. Her eldest child, G, had also died aged 13 weeks. There was no direct evidence of the crimes alleged. The Crown's case, which was that D had smothered J and M, having previously smothered G, depended on specialist evidence about the conclusions to be drawn from the history of three infant deaths and further 'Acute' or 'Apparent Life Threatening Events' in the same family. The defence case was that the deaths were attributable to SIDS. At the appeal reliance was placed on fresh expert evidence, a substantial body of research suggesting that infant deaths occurring in the same family can and do occur naturally, even when they are unexplained. The appeal was allowed. It was held that the correct approach, where three infant deaths have occurred in the same family, each apparently unexplained, and for each of which there is no evidence extraneous to the expert evidence that harm was or must have been inflicted — e.g., indications or admissions of violence, or a pattern of ill-treatment — is to start with the fact that three such deaths were indeed rare, but to proceed on the basis that, if there is nothing to explain them, in our current state of knowledge they remain unexplained and, although some parents do smother their infant children, possible natural deaths. Whether there are one, two or even three deaths, the exclusion of currently known natural causes of infant death does not establish that the death or deaths resulted from the deliberate infliction of harm. Stressing that in many important respects we are still at the frontiers of knowledge in relation to unexplained infant deaths, it was further held, *per curiam*, (at [178]):

> . . . for the time being, where a full investigation into two or more sudden unexplained infant deaths in the same family is followed by a serious disagreement between reputable experts about the cause of death, and a body of such expert opinion concludes that natural causes, whether explained or unexplained, cannot be excluded as a reasonable (and not a fanciful) possibility, the prosecution of a parent or parents for murder should not be started, or continued, unless there is additional cogent evidence, extraneous to the expert evidence, (such as [indications or admissions of violence, or a pattern of ill-treatment]) which tends to support the conclusion that the infant, or where there is more than one death, one of the infants, was deliberately harmed. In cases like the present, if the outcome of the trial depends exclusively or almost exclusively on a serious disagreement between distinguished and reputable experts, it will often be unwise, and therefore unsafe, to proceed.

F5.19 *Cannings* was distinguished in *Kai-Whitewind* [2005] EWCA Crim 1092, [2005] 2 Cr App R 31 (457), on the basis that it concerned inferences based upon coincidence or the unlikelihood of two or more infant deaths in the same family, or one death where another child or other children in the family had suffered unexplained 'Apparent Life Threatening Events'. There was a need for additional cogent evidence in such a case because there was essentially no evidence beyond the inferences based upon coincidence which the prosecution experts were prepared to draw but as to which other reputable experts in the same specialist field took a different view. It did not follow that, whenever there was a conflict between expert witnesses, the case for the prosecution had to fail unless the conviction was justified by evidence independent of the expert witnesses. In *Kai-Whitewind* there was a single death, no suggestion that any inference should be drawn against D from any previous incident involving any of her other children, and the evidence about the child's condition found on the post-mortem examination — including new and old blood in the lungs consistent with two distinct episodes of upper airway obstruction — was evidence of fact and precisely the kind of material which was sought but not found in *Cannings*. The dispute between the experts about the interpretation of the post-mortem findings did not extinguish the findings themselves and it was therefore for the jury to evaluate the expert evidence, taking account of the facts found at the post-mortem and bearing in mind the additional prosecution evidence against D. For expert evidence generally, see **F11.4** ***et seq.***

Cannings was also distinguished in *Hookway* [2011] EWCA Crim 1989 (also considered at **F11.13**), a case involving mixed DNA profiles in which the prosecution did not depend exclusively or almost exclusively on the disputed prosecution evidence, and the dispute between the experts was not whether there was DNA evidence incriminating the appellants, but as to the strength of that evidence. (However, a conviction may now depend exclusively upon a matching DNA profile; see *Tsekiri* [2017] EWCA Crim 40, [2017] 1 Cr App R 32 (479), considered at **F19.31**.)

As to the need for special caution in cases involving 'shaken baby syndrome' in which developing medical science is relevant, see also *Henderson* [2010] EWCA Crim 1269, [2010] 2 Cr App R 24 (185), considered at **F11.44**.

Section F6 Examination-in-chief

INTRODUCTION

F6.1 Examination-in-chief is the examination of a witness by the party calling him or her and its object is to elicit from the witness evidence supportive of the party's case. Examination-in-chief must be conducted in accordance with the exclusionary rules of general application, such as those relating to hearsay, opinion and the character of the accused.

Role of the Judge

F6.2 The judge may ask a witness questions and, in particular, where the accused is not represented, may ask any question necessary in the interests of the accused (CrimPR 24.4(6) (magistrates' courts) and 25.11(6) (Crown Court): see Supplement, **R24.4** and **R25.11**); notes to those rules state that the questions that may be put are in the discretion of the court, subject to the rules of evidence and r. 1.3 (application by the court of the overriding objective). The principles governing the extent to which a trial judge may properly intervene during examination-in-chief were set out in *Inns* [2018] EWCA Crim 1081, [2019] 1 Cr App R 5 (61). They include the following.

(a) The role of the judge is to act as neutral umpire, not to enter the arena so as to appear to be taking sides.
(b) The judge may ask questions of a witness to assist the jury, for example to clarify a point, but it may often be better to wait, because the point may be clarified before the end of the examination-in-chief.
(c) It is certainly not the role of the judge to cross-examine the accused.
(d) It is particularly important that accused persons have the opportunity to give their evidence in the way that they would like it to come out, elicited through questions from their advocates. There is a risk that this opportunity will be denied by constant judicial interruptions.
(e) This is not affected if the defence account appears to be implausible or even fanciful. The prosecution can reasonably be expected to expose its deficiencies in cross-examination.

Concerning (d), see also *Marchant* [2018] EWCA Crim 2606, [2019] 4 WLR 20.

Young Witnesses

F6.3 For the judicial directions that may be given to advocates on how to examine (and cross-examine) young witnesses, see the Judicial College Bench Checklist: Young Witness Cases, considered at **D14.69** and *Lubemba* [2014] EWCA Crim 2064, [2015] 1 WLR 1579, considered at **F7.10**, and CrimPD I, para. 3D.7 (see Supplement, **CPD.3D**), endorsing as best practice the Inns of Court College of Advocacy Toolkits. See also the *Crown Court Compendium* (July 2020), ch. 10-5 , and the Protocol between the National Police Chiefs' Council, the CPS and HM Courts and Tribunals Service to expedite cases involving witnesses under ten years (July 2018, tinyurl.com/y6ogwulf).

RULE REQUIRING PROSECUTION TO CALL ALL THEIR EVIDENCE BEFORE THE CLOSE OF THEIR CASE

General Rule

It is a rule of practice, but not law, that all of the evidence which the prosecution intend to rely on as probative of the guilt of the accused should be called before the close of their case (*Rice* [1963] 1 QB 857). The rule applies not only to the adducing of evidence, but also to matters put in cross-examination of the accused (*Kane* (1977) 65 Cr App R 270). The rule is confined to evidence probative of guilt, and does not extend to evidence going only to the credit of the accused (*Halford* (1978) 67 Cr App R 318). However, the admissibility of evidence of the accused's bad character is subject to the conditions, including the notice requirements, set out in the CJA 2003 (see **F13**). **F6.4**

Some of the exceptions to this rule are covered in other sections of this work: as to evidence admissible in rebuttal under exceptions to the rule of finality of answers to questions on collateral matters, see **F7.48** to **F7.65**; as to evidence in rebuttal of evidence of the good character of the accused, see **F14.32**; and as to evidence, in cases under the PACE 1984, s. 74(3), in rebuttal of defence evidence that the accused was not guilty of the offence of which he or she stands convicted, see *C* [2010] EWCA Crim 2971, [2011] 1 WLR 1942 at **F12.20**. The three recognised exceptions which call for consideration at this stage are:

(a) evidence not previously available;
(b) failure to call evidence by reason of inadvertence or oversight; and
(c) evidence in rebuttal of matters arising *ex improviso*.

Although these three exceptions are well established, some authorities clearly suggest that there is scope for a more generalised discretionary approach to admissibility, having regard to whether the accused will be unfairly prejudiced (as when the defence would have been conducted differently had the evidence in question been adduced as part of the prosecution case). In *Jolly v DPP* [2000] Crim LR 471, a decision relating to summary trial, it was held that although any trial court had to recognise that it was the duty of the prosecution to call its evidence before closing its case, it was 'beyond argument' that there was a general discretion to permit the calling of evidence at a later stage which, in a magistrates' court, extended up to the time when the Bench retired. Before exercising the discretion, the court would look carefully at the interests of justice overall and in particular the risk of any prejudice whatsoever to the defence. The result would be that the discretion would be sparingly exercised, but it was doubtful whether it assisted a court to speak in terms of 'exceptional circumstances'. Each case, it was said, had to be considered on its own facts. See also *Cook v DPP* [2001] Crim LR 321 and *Khatibi v DPP* [2004] EWHC 83 (Admin). However, magistrates, after they have retired to consider their verdict, do have a discretion to receive further evidence in 'special circumstances' (*Malcolm v DPP* [2007] EWHC 363 (Admin), [2007] 3 All ER 578, following *Webb v Leadbetter* [1966] 2 All ER 114, and holding the decision in *R (Travers) v DPP* [2005] EWHC 1482 (Admin) to have been wrongly decided). In deciding whether special circumstances exist, the magistrates can consider the nature of the defence approach to litigation and, for example, whether there was an ambush of the prosecution in the defence closing speech, and should have regard to the overriding objective in the CrimPR that criminal cases be dealt with justly (*Malcolm v DPP*). **F6.5**

In the Crown Court, once the jury has retired to consider its verdict, no further evidence may be adduced (*Owen* [1952] QB 362). However, this principle has been relaxed in the case of material put before the jury at the request of the accused because it assists the defence case (*Hallam* [2007] EWCA Crim 1495; *Khan* [2008] EWCA Crim 1112).

Evidence Not Previously Available

F6.6 The question whether or not evidence available for the first time after the close of the prosecution case should be admitted, is a matter to be determined by the trial judge in his or her discretion, which should be exercised in such a way and subject to such safeguards as seem best suited to achieve justice between the Crown and the defendants, and between the defendants. However, the admission of such evidence will be rare (*Rice* [1963] 1 QB 857, per Winn J; and see also *Kane* (1977) 65 Cr App R 270). The evidence may be admitted even if not strictly of a rebutting character, but the court must be vigilant in the exercise of its discretion, in case injustice is done to the accused, and should consider whether it is desirable to grant a defence application for an adjournment (*Doran* (1972) 56 Cr App R 429). In *Doran* the prosecution were allowed to call two witnesses after the close of their case. The witnesses, of whose existence the prosecution had no prior knowledge, were members of the public, present at the trial, who realised that they could give material evidence. See also *Patel* [1992] Crim LR 739, where the judge gave defence counsel the opportunity to seek an adjournment, take further instructions and call evidence. In *Pilcher* (1974) 60 Cr App R 1, the Court of Appeal, having recognised the general rule and the exception in the case of evidence in rebuttal of matters arising *ex improviso*, i.e. evidence which becomes relevant in circumstances which the prosecution could not have foreseen at the time when they presented their case (see **F6.12**), said (at p. 5):

> We do not say that . . . where the matter has not arisen *ex improviso* the judge had no kind of discretion at all, but we are firmly of opinion that in cases where the matter does not arise *ex improviso* the judge's discretion should not be exercised to allow the late introduction of an additional witness called for the prosecution whose evidence was available before the case for the prosecution closed.

As was pointed out in *Scott* (1984) 79 Cr App R 49, however, the judgment in *Pilcher* seems to narrow the circumstances in which evidence can be called in rebuttal in a way which does not agree with *Doran* (1972) 56 Cr App R 429. It is submitted that *Pilcher* should not be treated as restricting either the exception recognised in *Doran* or the exception, considered at **F6.7**, in the case of failure to call evidence of a formal or technical nature by reason of inadvertence or oversight.

Failure to Call Evidence by Reason of Inadvertence or Oversight

F6.7 **Formal, Technical or Uncontentious Evidence** The judge has a discretion to admit evidence of a formal, technical or uncontentious nature which, by reason of inadvertence or oversight, has not been adduced by the prosecution before the close of their case. Many of the cases relate to the failure to prove a statutory instrument by production of a Stationery Office copy. See, e.g., *Palastanga v Solman* [1962] Crim LR 334, a case brought under the Motor Vehicles (Construction and Use) Regulations 1955. For further examples, see *Royal v Prescott-Clarke* [1966] 2 All ER 366 and *Hammond v Wilkinson* (2001) 165 JP 786. Compare *Tyrell v Cole* (1918) 120 LT 156 and *Ashley* (1967) 52 Cr App R 42: the Prison Rules require proof by production of a Queen's Printer's copy. Similarly, evidence may be admitted to make good a failure to prove that leave of the DPP to bring proceedings has been obtained. In *Price v Humphries* [1958] 2 QB 353, in which a submission of no case having succeeded on the basis of the failure to prove such consent, the Divisional Court, applying *Waller* [1910] 1 KB 364 and allowing the appeal, held that unless the defence object before the close of the prosecution case, the court should act on the assumption that the clerk had fulfilled the duty, on the application for issue of the summons, to check that the appropriate consent had been given. (As to the proper timing for the giving of such consent, see **D2.17**.) A further example is *McKenna* (1956) 40 Cr App R 65, a charge of exporting articles made wholly or mainly of iron or steel, in which a submission of no case was made on the basis that no evidence had been adduced that the articles in question, which included steamrollers, lorries, traction engines and concrete mixers, were made of iron or steel. The judge recalled a prosecution witness to give such evidence. It was held that in the circumstances the judge had a complete discretion whether to allow a witness to be recalled; the appellate courts would not interfere with the exercise of that discretion unless it had resulted in an injustice. On the facts, there was no injustice: it required no great leap of the imagination to think that the objects in question were made of iron or steel, and even in the absence of the additional evidence, there was a case to answer.

Evidence as to Matters of Substance In appropriate circumstances the prosecution, after the close of their case, may even be permitted to call evidence relating to a matter of substance. Thus, in *Piggott v Simms* [1973] RTR 15, in which the prosecution, after the close of their case, were given leave to admit in evidence an analyst's certificate, the Divisional Court held that, although this was a failure to adduce a vital part of their prosecution case, the justices had an absolute discretion to allow the evidence to be admitted. Likewise in *Matthews v Morris* [1981] Crim LR 495, it was held that justices had correctly permitted the prosecution to reopen their case to put in evidence a statement, made by the owner of the money allegedly stolen, which, although it had been served on the defence under the CJA 1967, s. 9, was omitted from the prosecution case by reason of simple mistake. According to *Middleton v Rowlett* [1954] 2 All ER 277 the court even has a discretion in the case of evidence relating to the identity of the accused. That was a case of dangerous driving, in which the magistrates had refused to allow the prosecution to reopen their case in order to prove the identity of the driver. Although the Divisional Court described the case as 'borderline', it was held that the magistrates were not bound to exercise their discretion in favour of the prosecution. Cf. *Smith v DPP* [2008] EWHC 771 (Admin), where the prosecution were allowed to *bolster* their case on identification. **F6.8**

In *Francis* [1990] 1 All ER 225, the prosecution called an identification witness to give evidence that at a group identification he had identified the man standing in position number 20 but failed to call any evidence to prove that the man standing at that position was the appellant. The failure was due to a simple misunderstanding between counsel: counsel for the prosecution was under the impression that the name of the person standing at that position was not in issue. After the close of the prosecution case, the trial judge allowed the prosecution to recall the inspector in charge of the identification to say who it was who was standing at position number 20. On appeal, it was held that although the failure was not a mere technicality, but an essential, if minor, link in the chain of identification evidence, the discretion of the judge to admit evidence after the close of the prosecution case is not limited to cases where an issue has arisen *ex improviso* or where what has been omitted is a mere formality. This was one of those rare cases falling outside the two established exceptions and the judge had not erred in the exercise of his discretion. See also, applying *Francis*, *Jackson* [1996] 2 Cr App R 420. **F6.9**

Tendering Evidence after the Start of the Defence Case In *Munnery* [1992] Crim LR 215, where the judge allowed the prosecution to call a witness after the close of their case but before the defence case had begun, it was held that the proposition in *Francis*, that the discretion should only rarely be exercised outside the two exceptions, could be expanded to include the words 'especially when the evidence is tendered after the case for the defendant has begun'. An example of the discretion being exercised at this late stage is *James v South Glamorgan County Council* (1994) 99 Cr App R 321. In that case, in which there had not been a submission of no case to answer, the prosecution were allowed to reopen their case, after D had given his evidence-in-chief, to call their main witness, who had arrived late because of transport difficulties and genuine confusion as to the whereabouts of the court. Evidence may also be called, at this late stage, by the judge. In *Bowles* [1992] Crim LR 726, the defence case had begun when the trial judge, in answer to a question from the jury, decided in the interests of justice to admit further evidence himself, rather than have the prosecution reopen their case. It was held that the judge was justified in calling the evidence; the defence had not yet closed their case, the evidence was non-controversial and did not contradict that of D (although it did support the prosecution case) and it is 'undesirable that a jury should decide a case on a factual basis which may be false and the truth or falsity of which has been raised by the jury and can easily and readily be resolved without injustice to the accused'. See also *Aitken* (1991) 94 Cr App R 85, where the jury were **F6.10**

provided with a written summary of a tape-recorded interview during which D had made an admission. D said that the admission was made under pressure and was untrue. During the defence closing speech, the jury asked to listen to the tape and, when the speech was concluded and after hearing submissions, the judge allowed them to do so. The appeal was dismissed. Where the judge is satisfied that no injustice will be done to the accused, the admission of further evidence is a matter of discretion for the judge.

F6.11 **Late Evidence as to Fundamental Issues** The discretion should not be used to allow the prosecution the opportunity to prove the very matter in issue which they have failed to prove. In *Gainsborough Justices, ex parte Green* (1984) 78 Cr App R 9, the prosecution evidence in support of an allegation of a breach of a community service order revealed no such breach. The justices, rejecting a submission of no case to answer, allowed further evidence to be called to establish the breach. The Divisional Court quashed the conviction.

Evidence in Rebuttal of Matters Arising *Ex Improviso*

F6.12

> There is no doubt that the general rule is that where the Crown begins its case like a plaintiff in a civil suit, they cannot afterwards support their case by calling fresh witnesses, because they are met by certain evidence that contradicts it. They stand or fall by the evidence they have given. They must close their case before the defence begins; but if any matter arises, *ex improviso* which no human ingenuity can foresee, on the part of a defendant in a civil suit, or a prisoner in a criminal case, there seems to me no reason why that matter which so arose *ex improviso* may not be answered by contrary evidence on the part of the Crown. (*Frost* (1839) 4 St Tr NS 85 per Tindal CJ at col. 386.)

Lord Goddard CJ, in *Owen* [1952] 2 QB 362, said of this statement (at p. 367) that it was in 'probably wider language than would be applied at the present day'. Under the modern law, it is for the judge, in the exercise of his or her discretion, to determine whether the relevance of the evidence in question could *reasonably* have been anticipated (*Scott* (1984) 79 Cr App R 49). If the prosecution can reasonably foresee that certain evidence, available *ab initio*, is relevant to their case, it must be adduced as a part of that case and not to remedy defects in the case after it has been closed (*Day* [1940] 1 All ER 402). In *Day*, a charge of forgery and obtaining money by a forged instrument, the prosecution had in their possession from the start of the proceedings, specimens of D's admitted handwriting. The prosecution's case depended on the uncorroborated evidence of an accomplice. After the close of the defence case, the judge allowed the prosecution to call a handwriting expert. Quashing the conviction, the Court of Criminal Appeal held that the judge had wrongly exercised his discretion in admitting the additional evidence, which did not relate to any matter that had arisen *ex improviso* but the possible need for which ought to have been foreseen. *Day* may be contrasted with *Milliken* (1969) 53 Cr App R 330, in which D, when giving evidence, for the first time accused certain police officers, some of whom gave evidence that they had seen D committing the offence, of a conspiracy to fabricate evidence. The trial judge allowed the prosecution to call evidence in rebuttal, on the basis that such evidence became relevant only when D gave evidence, a ruling upheld by the Court of Appeal. (The Court of Appeal also held that the evidence in question was not in any sense probative of D's guilt, since it consisted of no more than denials of the accusations of conspiracy and concoction, but cf. *Busby* (1981) 75 Cr App R 79 and *Mendy* (1976) 64 Cr App R 4, which are considered at **F7.48** and **F7.57**.) See also *Flynn* (1957) 42 Cr App R 15, in which the prosecution were allowed to call evidence in rebuttal of an alibi defence, the details of which became known for the first time when D gave evidence; and *Blick* (1966) 50 Cr App R 280.

F6.13 The *ex improviso* principle requires the prosecution to adduce evidence before the close of its case only if it is clearly relevant. Thus, in *Levy* (1966) 50 Cr App R 198, it was held that there was room for the exercise by the judge of his discretion to admit, in rebuttal, evidence in the possession of the prosecution *ab initio*, which was of marginal relevance. The Court of Criminal Appeal said (at p. 202):

> It is quite clear and long established that the judge has a discretion with regard to the admission of evidence in rebuttal; the field in which that discretion can be exercised is limited by the principle that evidence which is clearly relevant — not marginally, minimally or doubtfully relevant, but clearly relevant — to the issues and within the possession of the Crown should be adduced by the prosecution as part of the prosecution's cases and such evidence cannot properly be admitted after evidence for the defence.

Equally, the *ex improviso* principle must be applied with a recognition that the prosecution are expected to act reasonably with regard to what may be suggested as pre-trial warnings of evidence likely to be given which calls for denial beforehand, and to suggestions put in cross-examination of their witnesses. 'They are not expected to take notice of fanciful and unreal statements no matter from what source they emanate' (*Hutchinson* (1985) 82 Cr App R 51, per Watkins LJ at p. 59). In this case, D was convicted of murder. Before the trial he wrote a letter, passed on to the DPP, containing allegations against a journalist. At the trial he alleged that the journalist was the murderer. The Court of Appeal held that the trial judge, at the close of the defence case, had properly given leave to the prosecution to call the journalist to give evidence in rebuttal; although the letter had alerted them to the possibility of what D might say in evidence, it contained many other allegations which were so obviously ridiculous and untrue as to justify the prosecution in regarding the whole of it either as a wicked farrago of lying nonsense or the ravings of a deranged mind. It was unreasonable, therefore, to say that the prosecution should have anticipated that anything said in it would be repeated in court.

It seems that the prosecution may rely upon the *ex improviso* principle to adduce evidence not only in rebuttal of defence *evidence*, but also, in appropriate circumstances, in rebuttal of matters unsupported by evidence but arising by implication from the submissions made in counsel for the defence's closing speech (*O'Hadhmaill* [1996] Crim LR 509).

RULE REQUIRING DEFENCE TO CALL ALL THEIR EVIDENCE BEFORE THE CLOSE OF THEIR CASE

A judge may permit an accused to be recalled to deal with matters which have arisen since the accused gave evidence if they could not reasonably have been anticipated and it appears to be in the interests of justice (*Cook* [2005] EWCA Crim 2011 at [28]). A judge may, as a matter of discretion and in the interests of justice, allow an accused to be called to clarify some feature of the evidence or to address a possible source of misunderstanding or to be given the opportunity to answer new allegations by a co-accused not put to the accused under cross-examination. However, it is difficult to imagine any situation in which an accused should be permitted to be recalled to advance a new account of facts contradicting the accused's earlier evidence; that would normally constitute an abuse of process (*Ikram* [2008] EWCA Crim 586, [2008] 2 Cr App R 24 (347)). **F6.14**

LEADING QUESTIONS

Leading Questions Generally Impermissible in Chief

The general rule is that in examination-in-chief a witness may not be asked leading questions, i.e. questions framed in such a way as to suggest the answer sought or to assume the existence of facts yet to be established. Evidence elicited by such questions is not inadmissible, but the weight to be attached to it may be substantially reduced (*Moor v Moor* [1954] 2 All ER 458; *Wilson* (1913) 9 Cr App R 124). 'Leading' is a relative, not an absolute, term (WM Best, *The Principles of the Law of Evidence* (12th edn by SL Phipson, 1922), at p. 562); and for this reason strict adherence to the rule is not always desirable or possible. Thus leading questions may be allowed, in the interests of justice, at the discretion of the judge. For example, when a magistrate dies in the course of a case in which a witness has given evidence, the witness, when recalled before a new magistrate, may be asked whether the deposition represents his or her **F6.15** evidence (*Ex parte Bottomley* [1909] 2 KB 14, at p. 21). It is virtually impossible to ask a witness to identify a person or object in court without the use of leading questions, and accordingly leading questions of this kind are also allowed (*Watson* (1817) 2 Stark 116, at p. 128). There are two other frequently recurring situations to which the general rule does not apply:

(a) Leading questions may be asked on formal and introductory matters, such as a witness's name, address and occupation; and questions which relate to other relevant facts which are not in dispute, or which are merely introductory to questions about facts which are in dispute, are also generally allowed (*Robinson* (1897) 61 JP 520).
(b) Leading questions may be put to a witness if the party calling him or her has been given leave to treat the witness as hostile (see **F6.52**).

REFRESHING THE MEMORY

General

F6.16 Under the CJA 2003, s. 139(1), which has relaxed the common-law rules on refreshing memory, a witness, in the course of giving evidence, may refer to a document in order to refresh his or her memory on two conditions: (1) that the witness gives evidence that the document records his or her recollection at the time it was made and (2) that his or her recollection at that time is likely to have been significantly better than at the time of the oral evidence. Section 139(2), designed to avoid the practical difficulties of refreshing the memory in the witness box from a sound recording, provides for the refreshing of memory from a transcript of a sound recording. The trial judge has a residual discretion to refuse an application under s. 139 even if the statutory conditions are met (*McAfee* [2006] EWCA Crim 2914).

Criminal Justice Act 2003, s. 139

(1) A person giving oral evidence in criminal proceedings about any matter may, at any stage in the course of doing so, refresh his memory of it from a document made or verified by him at an earlier time if—
  (a) he states in his oral evidence that the document records his recollection of the matter at that earlier time, and
  (b) his recollection of the matter is likely to have been significantly better at that time than it is at the time of his oral evidence.
(2) Where—
  (a) a person giving oral evidence in criminal proceedings about any matter has previously given an oral account, of which a sound recording was made, and he states in that evidence that the account represented his recollection of the matter at the time,
  (b) his recollection of the matter is likely to have been significantly better at the time of the previous account than it is at the time of his oral evidence, and
  (c) a transcript has been made of the sound recording,

  he may, at any stage in the course of giving his evidence, refresh his memory of the matter from that transcript.

F6.17 An application to refresh memory will normally be made by an advocate, but it is the proper function of the judge, where the interests of justice demand it, to suggest that a witness, including a prosecution witness, refresh his or her memory from a document (see, at common law, *Tyagi* (1986) *The Times*, 21 July 1986, per Ralph Gibson LJ). Section 139(1) and (2) apply to any person giving oral evidence, including the accused (see, at common law, *Britton* [1987] 2 All ER 412).

Under s. 139(1) and (2), the witness may refresh his or her memory 'at any stage' in the course of giving oral evidence. Thus, although a witness refreshing memory in court will normally do so in examination-in-chief, provided the conditions are met there is nothing wrong in principle in allowing a witness to refresh memory during re-examination (see, at common law, *Harman* (1984) 148 JP 289 and *Sutton* (1991) 94 Cr App R 70).

Concerning the condition in s. 139(1)(b), ultimately it is a matter for the assessment of the judge, whatever the witness's view of the matter (*Mangena* [2009] EWCA Crim 2535; *Chinn* [2012] EWCA Crim 501, [2012] 3 All ER 502).

Making or Verification of Document

For the purposes of the CJA 2003, s. 139(1), 'document' means anything in which information of any description is recorded, but not including any recording of sounds or moving images (s. 140). Under s. 139(1), the document must have been prepared by the witness him or herself or by another, provided in the latter case that the witness verified the document. For examples of verification, see, at common law, *Langton* (1876) 2 QBD 296, *Anderson v Whalley* (1852) 3 Car & Kir 54 and *Sekhon* (1987) 85 Cr App R 19. A witness may refresh memory from the deposition or from a statement to the police taken down by a police officer and then read over by the maker (*Mullins* (1848) 3 Cox CC 528; *Gleed v Stroud* (1962) 26 JCL 161; *Lau Pak Ngam v R* [1966] Crim LR 443, approved in *Richardson* [1971] 2 QB 484). **F6.18**

Interpreters In the case of interpreters, see *Attard* (1958) 43 Cr App R 90: at an interview at which an accused is questioned through an interpreter, in the absence of an independent note made by the interpreter of the questions put and the answers given, the interpreter should initial the interview record so that it may be used to refresh the interpreter's memory when giving evidence. **F6.19**

Aural or Visual Verification It is submitted that under s. 139(1), as at common law, verification can be aural or visual. Despite the *obiter dictum* of Winn J in *Mills* [1962] 3 All ER 298, at p. 1156, that the witness should both *see* and *read* a note made by another, in *Kelsey* (1982) 74 Cr App R 213 the Court of Appeal held that where one person dictates a note to another, hears it read back, and confirms its accuracy without reading it, the first person may use the note to refresh his or her memory in court, provided that another witness is called to prove that the note used in court is the same one that was dictated and read back. H, a prosecution witness, refreshed his memory as to the registration number of a car from a note dictated to a police officer. H saw the officer making the note but did not read it himself. The officer read the note back aloud and H confirmed that it was correct. At trial the officer gave evidence that the note used by H was the one that he had made. The Court of Appeal dismissed the appeal on the ground that verification could be aural or visual, the important matter being whether the witness was satisfied, while the matters were fresh in his mind, that the record was made and that it was accurate. The note in this case, since it was made by a person in the course of a 'profession or other occupation', might be admissible itself as evidence of the facts contained in it under the CJA 2003, s. 117, subject to the discretion to exclude under ss. 117(6) and 126: see **F17.94**. The principle of aural verification, however, continues to assist in cases where the note is not made by someone 'in the course of a trade, business, profession or other occupation, or as the holder of a paid or unpaid office'. *Kelsey* was followed in *Cummings v CPS* [2016] EWHC 3624 (Admin). **F6.20**

Originals and Copies

Under the CJA 2003, s. 139(1), there is no requirement that the document be the first or only document made or verified by the witness recording his or her recollection of the matters in question. Thus, as in the common-law cases, where the decisions turn in part on the now abandoned requirement of contemporaneity, a witness may refresh his or her memory from a document notwithstanding that it is based on original notes or a tape recording made by the witness (*Cheng* (1976) 63 Cr App R 20; *A-G's Ref (No. 3 of 1979)* (1979) 69 Cr App R 411; *Mills* (1962) 3 All ER 298). **F6.21**

In *DPP v Sugden* [2018] EWHC 544 (Admin), [2018] 2 Cr App R 8 (101), which concerned a photocopy of a record of the outcome of a breath test together with the test result printout, the Divisional Court drew a distinction between reliance on a copy (or other form of secondary evidence) as evidence of its contents and use of it as a memory-refreshing document under **F6.22**

s. 139(1) (but, concerning the former, without any reference to the CJA 2003, s. 133; see **F8.5**). It was held that:

(i) the content is generally admissible because relevant;
(ii) the absence of the original calls for an explanation, if sought by the opposing party;
(iii) if the original is not produced, the court may, not must, refuse to admit the copy in evidence and will consider its likely accuracy or otherwise;
(iv) the court will also consider any explanation for absence of the original, its probative value and any prejudicial effect on the accused (cf. PACE 1984, s. 78);
(v) where there is no reason to doubt that it is a true copy of the original, for example, where it is a straightforward photocopy, and its accuracy can be challenged in cross-examination, there will generally be no prejudice to the accused in admitting it in evidence;
(vi) whether or not it is admitted in evidence, it may be used to refresh memory if the requirements of s. 139(1) are met;
(vii) the witness may refresh his or her memory from either the original or a copy or other document derived from the original if the secondary document is likely to be an accurate reflection of the content of the original and the witness verified either the original or the secondary document at a time when his or her recall was [significantly] better than at the time of giving oral evidence;
(viii) where a witness refreshes his or her memory under s. 139(1) in the case of a document not adduced as evidence, it may become evidence in the case as a consequence of cross-examination (see **F6.24**); and
(ix) whether or not the document becomes evidence in the case, the court will always consider and give appropriate weight to any discrepancy or risk of discrepancy between its content and the original.

No Recollection

F6.23 Under the CJA 2003, s. 120(1), (4) and (6), provision is made for a previous statement of a witness to be admitted as evidence of any matters stated where the statement was made when the matters were fresh in his or her memory but the witness does not remember them and cannot reasonably be expected to do so.

Criminal Justice Act 2003, s. 120

(1) This section applies where a person (the witness) is called to give evidence in criminal proceedings.

...

(4) A previous statement by the witness is admissible as evidence of any matter stated of which oral evidence by him would be admissible, if—
  (a) any of the following three conditions is satisfied, and
  (b) while giving evidence the witness indicates that to the best of his belief he made the statement, and to the best of his belief it states the truth.

...

(6) The second condition is that the statement was made by the witness when the matters stated were fresh in his memory but he does not remember them, and cannot reasonably be expected to remember them, well enough to give oral evidence of them in the proceedings.

The following principles relating to s. 120(4) and (6) derive from the decision of the Court of Appeal in *Chinn* [2012] EWCA Crim 501, [2012] 3 All ER 502. Under s. 120(4), the previous statement does not have to be in a document. Section 120(4) and (6) are not limited to statements about 'routine' matters. If any of the matters set out in s. 120(6) are disputed, the judge must decide the issue. If there is a dispute about whether the witness cannot reasonably be expected to remember the matters stated well enough to give oral evidence of them, the *judge must decide the matter objectively*, taking all relevant factors into account, including the characteristics of the particular witness, the nature of the particular incident, the circumstances in which it occurred, and what has happened to the witness between the time of the incident and the trial. Where a witness gives evidence that in effect satisfies the conditions set out in s. 120(6), but this is disputed, then in the absence of the jury the witness should be asked why he or she does not recall the matters in question and can be cross-examined on both the alleged failure of memory and alleged reasons for it. Any further arguments about discretionary exclusion under the PACE 1984, s. 78, should also be addressed at this stage. If the previous statement is ruled admissible, the judge should explain, when summing up, that the jury can consider the matter because the witness could not reasonably be expected to remember the matter well enough to give oral evidence. No reference to hearsay or the statute is necessary. The judge should direct the jury to consider the reliability of the witness's earlier recollection and should emphasise that it is for them to decide what weight to give to the evidence in the previous statement.

On the question whether a witness's evidence that he or she does not remember the matters in a previous statement can render it a previous *inconsistent* statement for the purposes of the CJA 2003, s. 119, see **F6.47**.

Previous Statements Received in Evidence as a Consequence of Cross-examination

Under the CJA 2003, s. 120(1) and (3), provision is made for a previous statement of a witness made in a document used by the witness in examination-in-chief to refresh his or her memory to be admitted as evidence of any matter stated if, as a result of cross-examination, it has been received in evidence. **F6.24**

Criminal Justice Act 2003, s. 120

> (1) This section applies where a person (the witness) is called to give evidence in criminal proceedings.
>
> ...
>
> (3) A statement made by the witness in a document—
> (a) which is used by him to refresh his memory while giving evidence,
> (b) on which he is cross-examined, and
> (c) which as a consequence is received in evidence in the proceedings,
> is admissible as evidence of any matter stated of which oral evidence by him would be admissible.

Subsections (1) and (3) do not purport to alter the common-law rules as to the circumstances in which the document may be received in evidence (*Pashmfouroush* [2006] EWCA Crim 2330). At common law, a witness who has used a document in court to refresh his or her memory must produce it for the inspection of the opposing party, who may wish to cross-examine on its contents (*Beech v Jones* (1848) 5 CB 696; *Sekhon* (1987) 85 Cr App R 19). In the majority of cases, the fact that such cross-examination takes place will not make the record evidence in the case, nor will it be necessary for the jury to inspect the document, and it will be inappropriate for the record to become an exhibit (*Sekhon* at p. 22). However, if cross-examining counsel does go beyond the parts used by the witness to refresh his or her memory, the document is put in evidence and the jury are allowed to see the document upon which the cross-examination is based. In *Senat v Senat* [1965] P 172, Sir Jocelyn Simon P said (at p. 177, emphasis added):

> Where a document is used to refresh a witness's memory, cross-examining counsel may inspect that document in order to check it, without making it evidence. Moreover he may cross-examine upon it without making it evidence *provided that* his cross-examination does not go further than the parts which are used for refreshing the memory of the witness.

The following principles relating to s. 120(3) were established in *Chinn* [2012] EWCA Crim 501, [2012] 3 All ER 502. The word 'which' refers back to 'a document'. Section 120(3)(a) contemplates that the document has to be used by the witness to refresh his or her memory while giving evidence-in-chief. The oral evidence about the facts of which the witness has refreshed his or her memory is admissible oral evidence in the normal way. Under s. 120(3), it is the 'statement' in the document used to refresh memory that also becomes evidence of the matters stated. If the witness fails to refresh his or her memory, s. 120(3) does not apply; such a situation is covered by s. 120(4) and (6) (see **F6.23**).

F6.25 The question whether a memory-refreshing document, admitted under s. 120(3) and produced as an exhibit, should accompany the jury when they retire is governed by the CJA 2003, s. 122.

Criminal Justice Act 2003, s. 122

(1) This section applies if on a trial before a judge and jury for an offence—
  (a) a statement made in a document is admitted in evidence under section 119 or 120, and
  (b) the document or a copy of it is produced as an exhibit.
(2) The exhibit must not accompany the jury when they retire to consider their verdict unless—
  (a) the court considers it appropriate, or
  (b) all the parties to the proceedings agree that it should accompany the jury.

The reason for the general rule in s. 122 is the risk that the jury will place disproportionate weight on the contents of the document as compared with the oral evidence. It is normally sufficient for the judge to give a reminder in the summing-up of the contents of the statement and anything said by the witness about the document and the circumstances in which it was made. In cases where it is right for the jury to take the document with them, the judge should impress upon them the reason why they are being given the document and the importance of not attaching disproportionate weight to it (*Hulme* [2006] EWCA Crim 2899, [2007] 1 Cr App R 26 (334)).

Previous Statements Received in Evidence for Other Reasons

F6.26 A previous statement of a witness made in a document and used by the witness to refresh his or her memory may be received in evidence in four situations additional to the situation described in **F6.24**.

(a) The jury may inspect a memory-refreshing document if it is necessary to their determination of a point in issue. An example is *Bass* [1953] 1 QB 680. In that case the only evidence against D was a confession allegedly made to two police officers who, although denying that they had prepared their notes in collaboration, read identical accounts of the interview with D. The trial judge rejected a defence application that the jury be allowed to inspect the notebooks. The Court of Criminal Appeal endorsed the practice of officers collaborating in the preparation of their notes after an interview (in order to ensure that they had a correct version of what was said); but, allowing the appeal, held that the jury should have been allowed to inspect the notebooks because it might have assisted them in their evaluation of the credibility and accuracy of the officers. See also *Sekhon* (1986) 85 Cr App R 19, per Woolf LJ at p. 22: where the nature of the cross-examination involves the suggestion that the witness has subsequently fabricated evidence, which will usually involve, if not expressly at least by implication, the allegation that the record is concocted, the record may be admissible to rebut this suggestion and, if the nature of the record assists as to this, to show whether or not it is genuine, i.e. whether or not it has the appearance of being a contemporaneous record which has not subsequently been altered.

Although there is no ban on conferring, it may affect the value of an officer's evidence because, however much the officer may strive to record only what he or she saw or heard, there is a real risk that the recollection will have been 'contaminated' so that, although in good faith, elements derived from other witnesses may be incorporated or elements which seem to be inconsistent with their accounts may be subconsciously suppressed. There is also the risk of deliberate distortion or fabrication. However, it is important to recognise that an 'uncontaminated' first account will not necessarily be more accurate than an account produced after discussion. Such discussion will often remind an officer of something that was forgotten or misstated in the first account or help to make sense of recollections which were confused: 'Memory of any complex event involves elements of reconstruction, and a purist insistence that only "actual" memory is valid would be misconceived' (Underhill J in *R (Saunders) v Independent Police Complaints Commission* [2009] EWHC 2372 (Admin), [2009] 1 All ER 379 at [11]–[16]).

(b) Where the record is inconsistent with the witness's evidence, it can be admitted as evidence of any matter stated (see the CJA 2003, s. 119(1)(a) at **F6.47**) and as evidence of the inconsistency (*Sekhon*).

(c) It is appropriate for the record to be put before the jury where it is difficult for the jury to follow the cross-examination of the witness who has refreshed his or her memory without having the record or, in practice, copies of the record, before them (*Sekhon*).

(d) There may be cases where it is convenient to use the record as an *aide-mémoire* as to the witness's evidence where that evidence is long and involved. However, care should be exercised in adopting this course in cases where the evidence, and therefore the record, is bitterly contested, because of the danger that the use of the document for this purpose could result in the jury misunderstanding its status, and lead to their wrongly regarding the document as being evidence in itself (*Sekhon*).

Refreshing Memory out of Court

See **F6.16** for the general rule on refreshing memory set out in the CJA 2003, s. 139. **F6.27**

Prior to Going into the Witness-box The conditions on which a witness may refresh his or her memory while giving evidence in the witness-box do not apply to a witness who refreshes memory from a statement before going into the witness-box. In *Richardson* [1971] 2 QB 484, D was convicted of burglary offences committed 18 months earlier. Before the trial, four prosecution witnesses were shown their police statements, which they had made some weeks after the alleged offences. On appeal it was argued that the evidence of the four witnesses was, in the circumstances, inadmissible. The appeal was dismissed on the ground that there can be no general rule (which, unlike the rule as to what can be done in the witness-box, would be unenforceable) that witnesses may not before trial see the statements which they made at some period reasonably close to the time of the events which are the subject of the trial. All witnesses are routinely provided with copies of their statements before going into court. Under CrimPD V, para. 18C.1 (see Supplement, **CPD.18C**), 'Witnesses are entitled to refresh their memory from their statement or visually recorded interview'. As to the latter, there is no requirement that the witness watch the interview at the same time as the court (para. 18C.4), but if the viewing takes place at a different time, the witness, before being questioned under cross-examination, should normally be asked if and when the recording was watched (para. 18C.5). In *Richardson*, Sachs LJ, giving the judgment of the Court of Appeal, made the following observations: **F6.28**

(a) It has been recognised in Home Office Circular 82–1969 . . . that witnesses for the prosecution in criminal cases are normally entitled, if they so request, to copies of any statements taken from them by police officers.
(b) It is the practice, normally, for witnesses for the defence to be allowed to have copies of their statements and to refresh their memories from them before going into the witness-box.
(c) The court agreed with the following two observations of the Supreme Court of Hong Kong in *Lau Pak Ngam v R* [1966] Crim LR 443: 'Testimony in the witness-box becomes more a test of memory than truthfulness if witnesses are deprived of the opportunity of checking their recollection beforehand by reference to statements or notes made at a time closer to the events in question.' 'Refusal of access to statements would tend to create difficulties for honest witnesses but be likely to do little to hamper dishonest witnesses.'
(d) Obviously it would be wrong if several witnesses were handed statements in circumstances which enabled one to compare with another what each had said.

Concerning (d), it is incumbent on prosecuting authorities and judges to ensure that witnesses are informed that they should not discuss cases in which they are involved (*Shaw* [2002] EWCA Crim 3004). As a general rule, discussions between witnesses, particularly just before going **F6.29** into court to give evidence, should not take place, nor should statements or proofs of evidence be read to witnesses in each other's presence (*Skinner* (1994) 99 Cr App R 212). Where such discussions have taken place, each case must be dealt with on its own facts. If it emerges in cross-examination of the witnesses that the discussion may have led to fabrication, the court may take the view that it would be unsafe to leave any of the evidence of the witnesses concerned to the jury, but in other cases it may suffice to direct the jury on the implications which such conduct might have for the reliability of the evidence of the witnesses concerned (*Arif* (1993) *The Times*, 17 June 1993; and see also *Shaw*).

F6.30 **After Going into the Witness-box** In some cases it may be appropriate for the witness to withdraw from the witness-box and read the statement in peace (per Stuart-Smith LJ in *Da Silva* [1990] 1 All ER 29, at p. 35). In the case of a witness who is dyslexic and cannot read an earlier statement, the witness may be given the opportunity of adopting it by having counsel read it out in the absence of the jury (*Gordon* [2002] EWCA Crim 1).

F6.31 **Cross-examination on Memory-refreshing Document** If a witness has refreshed his or her memory out of court and before entering the witness-box, counsel for the other side is entitled not only to inspect the memory-refreshing document, but also to cross-examine the witness upon the relevant matters contained therein. If counsel cross-examines upon material in the document from which the witness has refreshed his or her memory, the document is not thereby made evidence in the case; but if counsel cross-examines upon material which has not been referred to by the witness, this entitles the party calling the witness to put the document in evidence so that the tribunal of fact may see the document upon which the cross-examination is based. In this respect, therefore, the rules are the same as those which apply in the case of a witness refreshing his or her memory in the witness-box (as to which, see **F6.24**). See *Owen v Edwards* (1983) 77 Cr App R 191.

PREVIOUS COMPLAINTS

F6.32 The CJA 2003, s. 120(1), (4) and (7), create an important exception to both the rule against hearsay (see **F16**) and the rule against previous consistent statements (see **F6.39**) in the case of a witness's previous complaint. Under the statutory provisions, the witness's complaint, whether oral or written, is admissible subject to a number of conditions, principally: that the witness testifies that to the best of his or her belief he or she made the statement and it is true; that the witness claims that an offence was committed against him or her; that the offence is one to which the proceedings relate; and that the complaint is about conduct which would, if proved, constitute the offence or part of it. A statement received under these provisions is admissible as evidence of the matters stated and also goes to the consistency of the witness. The provisions are much wider than the common-law exception to the rule against previous consistent statements in the case of recent complaints in sexual cases. That exception is likely to be invoked rarely, if at all. For detailed treatment of the common-law principle, see earlier editions of this work.

F6.33 **Criminal Justice Act 2003, s. 120**

(1) This section applies where a person (the witness) is called to give evidence in criminal proceedings.

...

(4) A previous statement by the witness is admissible as evidence of any matter stated of which oral evidence by him would be admissible, if—
  (a) any of the following three conditions is satisfied, and
  (b) while giving evidence the witness indicates that to the best of his belief he made the statement, and that to the best of his belief it states the truth.

...

(7) The third condition is that—
  (a) the witness claims to be a person against whom an offence has been committed,
  (b) the offence is one to which the proceedings relate,

(c) the statement consists of a complaint made by the witness (whether to a person in authority or not) about conduct which would, if proved, constitute the offence or part of the offence,

. . .

(e) the complaint was not made as a result of a threat or a promise, and

(f) before the statement is adduced the witness gives oral evidence in connection with its subject matter.

(8) For the purposes of subsection (7) the fact that the complaint was elicited (for example, by a leading question) is irrelevant unless a threat or a promise was involved.

These provisions, although similar in some respects to the common-law rules, do not codify the law but are freestanding and provide their own criteria (*O* [2006] EWCA Crim 556, [2006] 2 Cr App R 27 (405); see also *Xhabri* [2005] EWCA Crim 3135, [2006] 1 All ER 776).

Prosecutors assembling the evidence to be called at trial should have s. 120(4)(b) well in mind if it is intended to rely on a previous statement as evidence of the truth of its contents, especially where a video interview is to stand as the witness's evidence in chief (*AA* [2007] EWCA Crim 1779). If the criteria are not met, the complaint may be admissible nonetheless under s. 114 (see **F16** and *Gillooley* [2009] EWCA Crim 671).

As to s. 120(7)(b), an 'offence . . . to which the proceedings relate' refers to an offence on the indictment and therefore the provisions do not cover a statement made by a person against whom an offence has been committed if that offence is not on the indictment (*Trewin* [2008] EWCA Crim 484, *obiter*).

Section 120(7) contains no requirement that the complaint should have been made shortly after the alleged offence and therefore allows for the admissibility of a complaint made months or even years later. Furthermore, as at common law (*Lee* (1912) 7 Cr App R 31; *Wilbourne* (1917) 12 Cr App R 280), there is no limitation in the 2003 Act as to the admission of more than one complaint. In *O* it was held that there is no reason to import such a limitation, although the Court added that there is obviously a need to restrict evidence of 'complaint upon complaint', which may merely be self-serving. In that case, a second complaint, made to a person different from the person to whom the first complaint was made, was held to have been properly admitted because of its relevance over and above that of the first complaint. Section 120(7)(e) requires that the complaint was not made as a result of a threat or promise, and under s. 120(8), which does not follow the common-law approach, the fact that the complaint was elicited by a leading question, such as 'Did X (naming the accused) assault you?', is irrelevant unless a threat or promise was made. However, a complaint elicited by way of a leading question is bound to affect the weight to be attached to it. Section 120(7)(f) requires that before the statement is introduced in evidence, the witness 'gives oral evidence in connection with its subject matter', words that suggest that this requirement will be met if the complainant gives some evidence in relation to the conduct referred to in the complaint, even if that evidence does not replicate the complaint or is not wholly consistent with it. **F6.34**

In order to reflect (a) the substantive change in the law effected by s. 120 and (b) the fact that the previous statement comes from the same person who makes the accusation in the witness box, the judge should direct the jury that the complaint is, if they are satisfied that it was made, evidence of the truth of what was stated. In deciding what weight it should bear, the jury should have in mind the fact that it comes from the same person who makes the complaint in the witness box and not from some independent source (*AA* [2007] EWCA Crim 1779 at [16]). However, failure to give such a direction will not result in a successful appeal against conviction if there was no risk of the jury treating the complaint as independent evidence because they were directed in such a way that they must have understood that it was only relevant to the truthfulness and reliability of the complainant (*Amrani* [2011] EWCA Crim 1517; *Berry* [2013] EWCA Crim 1389, where 'it must have been obvious to the jury' that the evidence was not from some independent source). See also *H* [2011] EWCA Crim 2344, [2012] 1 Cr App R 30 (413), where defence counsel had **F6.35** not asked for an independence direction, and such a direction was not given, but the trial judge had stressed that there were no independent witnesses to the alleged conduct.

EVIDENCE OF PREVIOUS IDENTIFICATION AND DESCRIPTION

F6.36 Under the CJA 2003, s. 120(1), (4) and (5), which constitute an important exception to both the rule against hearsay (see **F16**) and the rule against previous consistent statements (see **F6.39**), a witness's previous statement identifying or describing a person, object or place is admissible if the witness testifies that to the best of his or her belief he or she made the statement and it is true. The statement is admissible as evidence of any matter stated, as well as evidence of the witness's consistency.

Criminal Justice Act 2003, s. 120

(1) This section applies where a person (the witness) is called to give evidence in criminal proceedings.

...

(4) A previous statement by the witness is admissible as evidence of any matter stated of which oral evidence by him would be admissible, if—
(a) any of the following three conditions is satisfied, and
(b) while giving evidence the witness indicates that to the best of his belief he made the statement, and that to the best of his belief it states the truth.

(5) The first condition is that the statement identifies or describes a person, object or place.

F6.37 The statutory provisions are a major extension of the common-law exception to the rule against previous consistent statements (see **F6.39**) under which evidence that a witness identified the accused out of court may be given by the witness him or herself and by any other person who witnessed the identification. Evidence admissible under the statutory provisions is relevant, it is submitted, in the same way as the evidence admissible at common law, namely to show that the witness was able to identify the accused at the time and to exclude the idea that the identification in court was an afterthought or mistake (see per Viscount Haldane LC in *Christie* [1914] AC 545 at p. 551). This is particularly important in cases where there has been a considerable lapse of time between the offence and the trial and where there is a danger of recollection having become dimmed (see per Ferguson J in *Fannon* (1922) 22 SR (NSW) 427 at pp. 429–30).

The following principles relating to s. 120(4) and (5) derive from the decision of the Court of Appeal in *Chinn* [2012] EWCA Crim 501, [2012] 3 All ER 502. Under s. 120(4), the previous statement does not have to be in a document. The scope of s. 120(5) stems from its purpose, which is not to introduce an identification or description in a vacuum, which would be of no use, but in the relevant context, because the person, object or place is being identified or described for a particular purpose. Thus, for example, s. 120(5) can be used to admit a statement that it was Mr X who was at the ABC Bar on a certain day at a certain time. However, other parts of the narrative in the witness statement that go beyond such an identification (or description) are not admissible. Where the case turns wholly or partly on identification evidence and the accused has been identified in a statement admitted under s. 120(4) and (5), the judge will have to consider whether some sort of *Turnbull* direction, in a suitably adapted form, is needed. In certain circumstances, e.g., where the only evidence of identification of an accused is sought to be adduced under s. 120(4) and (5), consideration may be given to discretionary exclusion under the PACE 1984, s. 78. In a suitable case, the judge may also consider whether to exercise the power to stop the case under the CJA 2003, s. 125 (considered at **F17.98**).

F6.38 *As a general rule*, a 'dock identification', i.e. an identification of the accused for the first time in court, is undesirable and should be avoided (*Cartwright* (1914) 10 Cr App R 219); and the usual practice is to elicit evidence of a witness's previous out-of-court identification *before* asking the witness whether that person is in court. As to dock identifications generally and evidence of previous identification, see **F19**.

GENERAL RULE AGAINST PREVIOUS CONSISTENT (SELF-SERVING) STATEMENTS

There is a general common-law rule excluding previous consistent or self-serving statements, sometimes referred to as the rule against narrative, to which there is a range of important statutory and common-law exceptions. Under the rule, a witness may not be asked about a previous oral or written statement made by the witness and consistent with his or her evidence (*Roberts* [1942] 1 All ER 187; *Larkin* [1943] KB 174; *Oyesiku* (1971) 56 Cr App R 240, at pp. 245–7). Equally, evidence of the previous statement may not be given by any other witness (*Roberts*). The previous statement, which may also be inadmissible as evidence of the facts contained in it under the rule against hearsay, is excluded as evidence of the accused's *consistency*. In *Roberts* [1942] 1 All ER 187, D was convicted of the murder of a girl by shooting her. His defence was that the gun went off accidentally when he was trying to make up a quarrel with her. The Court of Criminal Appeal held that evidence that two days after the event D had told his father that his defence would be accident had been properly excluded. Such evidence is easily manufactured and of no evidential value. The fact that D has said the same thing to someone else on a previous occasion did not confirm his evidence (*Roberts*, at p. 191). **F6.39**

The general rule applies in examination-in-chief, cross-examination and re-examination. Thus the credibility of a witness may not be bolstered by evidence of a previous consistent statement merely because the witness's testimony has been impeached in cross-examination, and this remains the case 'even if the impeachment takes the form of contradiction or inconsistency between the evidence given at the trial and something said by the witness on a former occasion' (*Coll* (1889) 24 LR Ir 522, per Holmes J at p. 541; *Weekes* [1988] Crim LR 245; *Beattie* (1989) 89 Cr App R 302 per Lord Lane CJ at pp. 306–7; *P (GR)* [1998] Crim LR 663). However, the court does have a residual discretion, necessary in the interests of justice, to permit re-examination to show consistency, to ensure that as a result of the cross-examination the jury are not positively misled as to the existence of some fact or the terms of an earlier statement (*Ali* [2003] EWCA Crim 3214, [2004] 1 Cr App R 39 (501)).

There are a number of statutory and common-law exceptions to the general rule. including complaints (see **F6.32**), previous identification and description (see **F6.36**) and statements in rebuttal of allegations of recent fabrication (see **F7.67**). The common-law exceptions relating to self-serving statements made on accusation and statements forming part of the *res gestae* are considered below.

Self-serving Statements Made on Accusation

In *Pearce* (1979) 69 Cr App R 365, at pp. 368 and 370, the Court of Appeal could see no reason for casting doubt on the well-established practice, on the part of the prosecution, to admit in evidence all unwritten, and most written, statements made by an accused person to the police, whether they contain admissions or whether they contain denials of guilt. If such a statement is wholly adverse to the accused, it may be admitted as evidence of the truth of the facts contained in it under the PACE 1984, s. 76 (see **F18.8**). If it is a mixed statement, i.e. a statement containing both inculpatory and exculpatory parts, such as 'I killed X. If I had not done so, X would certainly have killed me there and then', the whole statement is admissible (see principle 2(b) in *Pearce*, at **F6.42**), and both parts are admitted as evidence of the truth of the facts they contain (*Duncan* (1981) 73 Cr App R 359; *Hamand* (1985) 82 Cr App R 65; *Sharp* [1988] 1 All ER 65 and generally at **F18.93**). However, if the statement is purely exculpatory or self-serving, it is not admitted as evidence of the facts stated in it; it 'is evidence in the trial because of its vital **F6.40**

F

Part F Evidence

relevance as showing the reaction of the accused when first taxed with the incriminating facts' (*Storey* (1968) 52 Cr App R 334, per Widgery LJ at pp. 337–8). The police having found cannabis in D's flat, she told them that it belonged to a man who had brought it there against her will. The Court of Appeal upheld the trial judge's rejection of a submission of no case to answer, on the ground that D's statement was not evidence of the facts stated but only evidence of her reaction, which was insufficient to negative evidence of possession. If the accused neither gives nor calls evidence, it is the duty of the judge, in the summing-up, to set out the defence case insofar as it is to be found in a mixed statement, which is admissible as evidence of its contents (*Curley* [2004] EWCA Crim 2395, applied in *Clarke* [2010] EWCA Crim 684). Similarly, it seems that if the accused gives no evidence the judge, in the summing-up, should remind the jury of an entirely self-serving statement, not for the truth of its contents but because of its relevance as showing the reaction of the accused on accusation (*Donaldson* (1976) 64 Cr App R 59 at p. 69 and *Squire* [1990] Crim LR 341; but see also *Barbery* (1975) 62 Cr App R 248 at p. 250 and *Tooke* (1989) 90 Cr App R 417, to the effect that the judge is under no such duty).

F6.41 **The Principles as Set Out in *Pearce*** The reference in *Storey* to the reaction of the accused 'when first taxed' must not be read as limiting the principle recognised to statements made on the first encounter with the police (*Pearce* (1979) 69 Cr App R 365). The facts in *Pearce* were as follows. On 6 March D, the manager of a shop, was taxed by his employer's security officer with incriminating facts relating to handling stolen goods, and denied knowledge of them. Two days later he was arrested by the police and made a voluntary statement in the presence of his solicitor. Subsequently, in an interview, he gave certain answers which were relied on by the prosecution. The next day, he made another voluntary statement which was self-serving. The trial judge excluded evidence of all statements made to the police, except those parts of the interview on which the prosecution relied, on the grounds that they were self-serving and therefore inadmissible. On appeal it was argued that the statements had been properly excluded because they were not made when D was first taxed with the incriminating facts on 6 March.

F6.42 Rejecting this argument and quashing the conviction, the Court of Appeal summarised the principles as follows (at p. 369):

(1) A statement which contains an admission is always admissible as a declaration against interest and is evidence of the facts admitted. With this exception a statement made by an accused person is never evidence of the facts in the statement. [It is now clear, however, that the exception encompasses statements which are either wholly or partially adverse to the accused (see *Sharp* [1988] 1 All ER 65 and generally at **F18.93**).]

(2) (a) A statement that is not an admission is admissible to show the attitude of the accused at the time when he made it. This however is not to be limited to a statement made on the first encounter with the police. The reference in *Storey* to the reaction of the accused 'when first taxed' should not be read as circumscribing the limits of admissibility. The longer the time that has elapsed after the first encounter the less the weight which will be attached to the denial. The judge is able to direct the jury about the value of such statements. (b) A statement that is not in itself an admission is admissible if it is made in the same context as an admission, whether in the course of an interview, or in the form of a voluntary statement. It would be unfair to admit only the statements against interest while excluding part of the same interview or series of interviews. It is the duty of the prosecution to present the case fairly to the jury; to exclude answers which are favourable to the accused while admitting those unfavourable would be misleading. (c) The prosecution may wish to draw attention to inconsistent denials. A denial does not become an admission because it is inconsistent with another denial. There must be many cases however where convictions have resulted from such inconsistencies between two denials.

(3) Although in practice most statements are given in evidence even when they are largely self-serving, there may be a rare occasion when an accused produces a carefully prepared written statement to the police, with a view to it being made part of the prosecution evidence. The trial judge would plainly exclude such a statement as inadmissible.

On the facts, the case fell within principles 2(a) and (b). The first statement was relevant to show the attitude of the appellant at the start of the interview: it set the scene, and when it was decided to admit part of the interview, the only fair course was to admit the statement to put the interview in context. The same principle applied to the questions and answers in the interview which were excluded and to the second voluntary statement on the next day. *Pearce* was applied in *McCarthy* (1980) 71 Cr App R 142.

Principle 2(a) above cannot be relied upon to admit in evidence a statement which adds no weight to other evidence already before the jury as to the accused's reaction to the suggestion that the accused had committed an offence. In *Tooke* (1989) 90 Cr App R 417, a case of unlawful wounding, the attack took place at 9 p.m. and shortly thereafter, at the scene, D made an exculpatory statement. At 9.40 p.m., D went voluntarily to a police station and made a witness statement setting out his version. The statement made at the scene was admissible, but not the one made at the station: the latter, although spontaneous, added nothing to the evidence of reaction already supplied by the former. **F6.43**

Under principle 2(a) the prosecution are *obliged* to adduce wholly self-serving statements. In *McCarthy* (1980) 71 Cr App R 142, the judge had refused to admit details of an alibi given at a police interview. The Court of Appeal held that the evidence had been *improperly excluded* (although the case against D was strong and the proviso was applied), since it did not come within the exception referred to in *Pearce* (i.e. principle 3). Lawton LJ said (at p. 145): **F6.44**

> One of the best pieces of evidence that an innocent man can produce is his reaction to an accusation of a crime. If he has been told, as the appellant was told, that he was suspected of having committed a particular crime at a particular time and place and he says at once, 'That cannot be right, because I was elsewhere', and gives details of where he was, that is something which the jury can take into account.

Principle 2(b) makes it clear, in the case of a 'mixed statement', that, if the prosecution rely on the parts of the statement unfavourable to the accused, they are obliged to put in evidence the other parts of the statement which are favourable to the accused.

Principle 3 is designed to prevent an accused from attempting to take unfair advantage of principle 2(a). An example is *Newsome* (1980) 71 Cr App R 325. On a charge of rape, it was held that a self-serving statement, dictated by D to the police after consultation with, and in the presence of, his solicitor, some 13 hours after the alleged offence and subsequent to several interviews with the police, was inadmissible under principle 3. See also *Thatcher* [1967] 1 WLR 1278 (a statement drafted by counsel on instructions and submitted to the officer in charge of the case for his signature). In *Hutton* (1988) *The Times*, 27 October 1988, the police, in exercise of their right to do so under the PACE 1984, s. 58, delayed access to a solicitor and interviewed D three times. He refused to sign the notes of those interviews. After being charged, he was allowed access to his solicitor, in whose presence he dictated to the police a self-serving statement consistent with the evidence he gave at the trial. On appeal, it was argued that the statement should have been admitted, because the police, in exercising their rights under s. 58, had prevented D from making known his reaction to the charge. Rejecting the argument, the Court held that exercise of the s. 58 right did not affect the question whether the statement could properly be described as a spontaneous reaction, and therefore admissible under principle 2(a), or a carefully prepared draft following consultation, and therefore inadmissible under principle 3. The trial judge had properly concluded that the statement fell outside principle 2(a). **F6.45**

Statements Forming Part of *Res Gestae*

A previous statement of a witness which was so closely associated in time, place and circumstances with some act or event in issue that it can be said to form a part of the *res gestae*, i.e. the same transaction, is admissible as evidence of consistency to confirm evidence given by the witness to the same effect. Such a statement is also admissible for the truth of its contents (see **F17.49** *et seq.*). In *Fowkes* (1856) *The Times*, 8 March 1856, D, commonly known as 'the butcher', was charged with murder. V's son gave evidence that he and a police officer were in a room with his father; that a face appeared at the window through which the fatal shot was then fired; and that he thought the face was that of D. He was also allowed to give evidence **F6.46** that on seeing the face, he had shouted, 'There's Butcher'; and the officer, who had not seen the face, was also allowed to give evidence as to this exclamation.

PREVIOUS INCONSISTENT STATEMENTS

F6.47 If a witness in examination-in-chief (or cross-examination) admits making a previous oral or written inconsistent statement, the statement is admissible under the CJA 2003, s. 119, as evidence of any matter stated of which oral evidence by the witness would be admissible.

Criminal Justice Act 2003, s. 119

(1) If in criminal proceedings a person gives oral evidence and—
(a) he admits making a previous inconsistent statement…
the statement is admissible as evidence of any matter stated of which oral evidence by him would be admissible.

The statement is admissible for the truth of its contents as evidence against its maker. Thus if it implicates a co-accused, s. 119 does not allow it to be used against the co-accused. However, it may be admissible, for this purpose, under the CJA 2003, s. 114(1)(d) (*Nguyen* [2020] EWCA Crim 140).

The fact that a witness who has made a previous statement gives evidence that he or she cannot remember the matters in the statement will not necessarily make the statement a previous *inconsistent* statement. Such a conclusion obviously cannot be drawn where the witness stands by what was said previously, even though the witness cannot remember the matters stated (see *Chinn* [2012] EWCA Crim 501, [2012] 3 All ER 502). However, it is submitted that such a conclusion should be drawn if the witness denies the truth of the earlier statement, in which case, in effect, 'he admits making a previous inconsistent statement', or is treated as a hostile witness on the basis that in all the circumstances of the case the witness is likely to be able to remember the matters in question and by claiming not to be able to do so is not willing to tell the truth to the court; this appears to have been the basis of the decision in *Bennett* [2008] EWCA Crim 248. See also *Griffiths v CPS* [2018] EWHC 3062 (Admin), [2019] 1 Cr App R 18 (229).

UNFAVOURABLE AND HOSTILE WITNESSES

General Rule against Impeaching Credit of Own Witness

F6.48 The general rule is that a party is not entitled to impeach the credit of its own witness by asking questions or adducing evidence concerning such matters as the witness's bad character, previous convictions, bias or previous inconsistent statements. However, the general rule appears to have no application where evidence of a witness's bad character is introduced not to impeach the witness's credit in relation to the testimony, but because it supports some other discrete part of the prosecution case (*Ross* [2007] EWCA Crim 1457). In the case of a witness who is 'unfavourable', i.e. a witness who displays no hostile animus to the party calling him or her but merely fails to come up to proof or gives evidence unfavourable to that party, the general rule prevails: the only remedy available to the party is to call other witnesses, if available, with a view to proving that which the unfavourable witness failed to establish (*Ewer v Ambrose* (1825) 3 B & C 746). Equally, the prosecution may call a witness to give evidence only part of which they consider to be worthy of belief and may adduce other evidence to contradict that part of the witness's evidence which they consider to be inaccurate or false, and invite the jury to reject that part of the witness's evidence. That may be done without applying to treat the witness as hostile. However, unless the witness is declared hostile, evidence adduced to contradict the witness may not include a previous inconsistent statement (*Cairns* [2002] EWCA Crim 2838, [2003] 1 Cr App R 38 (662); *Smith* [2019] EWCA Crim 1151). Insofar as the principle in *Ewer v Ambrose* results in two equally credible witnesses directly contradicting each other upon a major fact in issue, it has been said that the party calling them is not entitled to accredit the one and discredit the other; the testimony of both is to be disregarded

(*Sumner and Leivesley v John Brown & Co.* (1909) 25 TLR 745, per Hamilton J). However, in *Brent* [1973] Crim LR 295 it was held that this dictum does not apply to criminal proceedings, because of the Crown's duty to call all relevant evidence. In the case of a witness who appears to the judge to be hostile, that is to say not desirous of telling the truth to the court at the instance of the party calling him or her (Stephen's *Digest of the Law of Evidence* (12th edn, 1936), Article 147), the general rule is modified, but in only two respects:

(a) under the Criminal Procedure Act 1865, s. 3, that party may, by leave of the judge, prove a previous inconsistent statement of the witness (see **F6.52**); and
(b) at common law, the party calling the witness may cross-examine him or her by asking leading questions (see *Thompson* (1976) 64 Cr App R 96, at **F6.53**).

Calling Witnesses who are Likely to be Hostile

The prosecution may call a person as a witness even if there have been signs that the witness is likely to be hostile, for example by retracting a statement or by making a second statement prior to the trial (*Mann* (1972) 56 Cr App R 750). Nor is it a bar to an accused calling a witness to give evidence against a co-accused and to the witness being treated as hostile that he or she was expected to resile from what was previously said; and if the previous inconsistent statement is proved, it will be evidence of the truth of its contents under the CJA 2003, s. 119 (*Osborne* [2010] EWCA Crim 1981, but see also, in the case of a prosecution witness, *Dat* [1998] Crim LR 488, where it was held that the prosecution should cross-examine the witness by degrees so as to limit the damage which might occur as a result of wide-ranging cross-examination on the previous statement; for the CJA 2003, s. 119, see **F6.54**). A *voir dire* before a decision on whether to allow a witness to be treated as hostile is only appropriate in exceptional circumstances because a jury may see the witness apparently giving evidence in one frame of mind and then see a complete turn-around after events which have taken place in their absence (*Khan* [2002] EWCA Crim 945). Similarly, it is only in very exceptional cases that a *voir dire* should be held to decide whether a witness who has yet to be called might prove to be hostile (*Olumegbon* [2004] EWCA Crim 2337). However, in cases in which a person claims to be no longer in a position to further assist the prosecution or court, or claims to be no longer able to remember anything, it seems that the judge has a discretion to hold a *voir dire* to decide whether to prevent the person being called at all (*Honeyghon* [1999] Crim LR 221). **F6.49**

Time at which to Apply to Treat Witness as Hostile

The application to treat a witness as hostile should be made when the witness first shows unmistakable signs of hostility (*Pestano* [1981] Crim LR 397). If counsel for the prosecution has a statement directly contradicting one of their witnesses who gives evidence that he or she is unable to identify the accused, counsel should at once show the statement to the judge and ask for leave to cross-examine the witness (*Fraser* (1956) 40 Cr App R 160). However, although there may be circumstances where a witness is displaying such an excessive degree of hostility that the only appropriate course is to treat him or her as hostile, if the witness gives evidence contrary to an earlier statement (or fails to give the evidence expected) the party calling the witness and the trial judge should first consider inviting the witness to refresh his or her memory from material which it is legitimate to use for that purpose and should not immediately proceed to treat the witness as hostile (*Maw* [1994] Crim LR 841). In *Powell* [1985] Crim LR 592 it was held that the prosecution, during re-examination, had been properly allowed to treat as hostile a witness who had shown no signs of hostility during examination-in-chief. Although such an application is a little unusual, it is a matter for the judge's discretion (*Powell*). See also *Little* (1883) 15 Cox CC 319. **F6.50**

Role of Judge and Jury

The discretion of the judge, however hostile the witness, is absolute (*Rice v Howard* (1886) 16 QBD 681; *Price v Manning* (1889) 42 Ch D 372), and the decision will rarely be open to a successful challenge on appeal (*Manning* [1968] Crim LR 675). **F6.51**

Although the question whether a witness is hostile is for the judge in the absence of the jury following a formal application (*Hopes* [2011] EWCA Crim 1869), the evidence and demeanour of the potentially hostile witness should usually be tested in the presence of the jury (*Darby* [1989] Crim LR 817).

Criminal Procedure Act 1865 (Denman's Act), s. 3

F6.52 **Criminal Procedure Act 1865, s. 3**

> A party producing a witness shall not be allowed to impeach his credit by general evidence of bad character, but he may, in case the witness shall, in the opinion of the judge, prove adverse, contradict him by other evidence, or, by leave of the judge, prove that he has made at other times a statement inconsistent with his present testimony; but before such last mentioned proof can be given the circumstances of the supposed statement, sufficient to designate the particular occasion, must be mentioned to the witness, and he must be asked whether or not he has made such statement.

Section 3 comprises three rules. The first is an enactment of the common-law rule that a party calling a witness is not entitled to impeach the witness's credit by evidence of bad character, i.e. evidence of previous misconduct, convictions, or other evidence designed to show that the witness is not to be believed on oath.

The second and third rules apply to witnesses who, in the opinion of the judge, prove 'adverse', which means 'hostile' and not merely 'unfavourable' (*Greenough v Eccles* (1859) 5 CB NS 786, a decision on the construction of the Common Law Procedure Act 1854, s. 22, which was repealed but re-enacted by s. 3 of the 1865 Act). In assessing whether a witness is hostile for the purposes of s. 3, a judge will consider many factors, including whether the witness is in a position to assist, whether the witness has indicated a willingness to assist, any previous accounts given, and demeanour in the witness box. The issue does not depend solely on whether the witness has been previously inconsistent in a written statement or in evidence on oath (*Hengari-Ajufo* [2016] EWCA Crim 1913 at [59]).

The second rule in s. 3 is that a party may 'contradict' a hostile witness, i.e. call other witnesses to prove that which the hostile witness has failed to establish. Although s. 3 suggests that this rule applies only to hostile witnesses, according to Williams and Willes JJ in *Greenough v Eccles*, it has not affected the common-law rule to the same effect in the case of unfavourable witnesses (*Ewer v Ambrose* (1825) 3 B & C 746).

The third rule in s. 3, which does apply only in the case of a witness who is, in the opinion of the judge, hostile, allows the judge to give leave to prove that the witness has made at other times a statement inconsistent with the present testimony. This requirement of leave cannot be circumvented by reliance on s. 4 of the Act (*Booth* (1981) 74 Cr App R 123; see F7.52). A witness for the defence who is treated as hostile is in the same position as a hostile prosecution witness, and accordingly is open to cross-examination on a previous inconsistent statement (*Booth*). The leave of the judge may be given whether the previous inconsistent statement was oral or written (*Prefas* (1986) 86 Cr App R 111). Cross-examination on the contents of an *Achieving Best Evidence* interview may be permitted notwithstanding an earlier ruling by the judge that it would not be in the interests of justice to permit the interview to be played as the evidence-in-chief of the witness (*Mazekelua* [2011] EWCA Crim 1458). If the witness, when asked, admits making the previous statement, this will clearly suffice as proof that the witness did make it. If the witness does not make such an admission, whether the earlier statement can be used depends on the facts of the particular case. In *Baldwin* [1986] Crim LR 681, where the witness accepted that he had made some parts of a written statement and accepted that the signatures on the statement were his, it was held that this was evidence entitling the judge to conclude that the witness had made the statement, and therefore to rule that cross-examination on it was permissible.

If the nature of the evidence given justifies it, an application may be made to treat as hostile the spouse or civil partner of an accused who is competent but not compellable for the prosecution, and who has waived his or her right to refuse to testify. However, it is desirable that the judge should explain to the spouse or civil partner, in the absence of the jury and before the oath is taken, that if the choice is made to give evidence, he or she may be treated like any other witness (*Pitt* [1983] QB 25). See generally, **F4.17**. However, even if the spouse or civil partner elects not to give evidence, his or her written statement may be admissible under the CJA 2003, s. 114(1)(d) (see **F17.34**).

Hostile Witnesses at Common Law

F6.53 The Criminal Procedure Act 1865, s. 3, has not destroyed or removed the common-law right of the judge, in the exercise of his or her discretion, to allow cross-examination of a hostile witness by asking leading questions about a previous statement. In *Thompson* (1976) 64 Cr App R 96, D was convicted of incest with his daughter. She had made a statement to the police implicating her father but, when sworn as a witness at the trial, she refused to give evidence, and leave was given to treat her as hostile. She was asked leading questions, her previous statement was put to her, and she eventually agreed that its contents were true. It was argued, on appeal, that since the girl had initially given no evidence, there was no 'present testimony' with which her previous statement could be said to be inconsistent, and therefore s. 3 did not apply. Lord Parker CJ found it unnecessary to decide whether s. 3 applied to the facts, since the common-law cases prior to the 1865 Act recognised that pressure could be brought to bear upon witnesses who refused to co-operate. The appeal was dismissed. It is submitted that if the witness in the case had denied making the previous statement and not accepted the truth of its contents, it would not have been open to proof at common law.

Evidential Value of Previous Inconsistent Statement of Hostile Witness

F6.54 If a hostile witness, on being cross-examined, does not admit the truth of a previous inconsistent statement, it is admitted, under the CJA 2003, s. 119, as evidence of the matters stated. It is admissible as evidence against its maker and cannot be used against anyone else (*Nguyen* [2020] EWCA Crim 140). However, if, under cross-examination, the witness admits making the statement and the truth of its contents, the contents become part of his or her evidence and there is no need to rely on s. 119 (*Gibbons* [2008] EWCA Crim 1574; and see also, prior to the 2003 Act, *Maw* [1994] Crim LR 841).

Criminal Justice Act 2003, s. 119

(1) if in criminal proceedings a person gives oral evidence and—

...

(b) a previous inconsistent statement made by him is proved by virtue of section 3, 4 or 5 of the Criminal Procedure Act 1865,

the statement is admissible as evidence of any matter stated of which oral evidence by him would be admissible.

A statement admissible in law under s. 119 may nonetheless fall to be excluded as a matter of discretion pursuant to the PACE 1984, s. 78. If the statement is admitted, it remains open to the defence, at the close of the prosecution case, to submit that there is no case to answer, on the basis that the prosecution evidence is too unreliable (see **D16.53** ***et seq.***), or that the judge should exercise the power under the CJA 2003, s. 125 (unconvincing hearsay — see **F17.98**), and either direct the jury to acquit or discharge the jury (*Bennett* [2008] EWCA Crim 248; *Joyce* [2005] EWCA Crim 1785). The observation in *Joyce* that there is no difference between the duty on the judge under s. 125 and under *Galbraith* [1981] 2 All ER 1060 (see **D16.54**) was disapproved in *Riat* [2012] EWCA Crim 1509, [2013] 1 All ER 349 at [28].

F6.55 **Direction as to Status of Evidence** The judge should direct the jury that the previous statement is evidence in the case, but not that it is just as much evidence as the witness's evidence in court. The judge may also direct the jury that they may consider the statement when deciding upon their verdict if they are sure that it is true or, in the case of a statement exculpatory of the accused, if they conclude that it *may* be true (*Billingham* [2009] EWCA Crim 19, [2009] 2 Cr App R 20 (341)). According to the *Crown Court Compendium* (July 2020), ch. 14-7, para. 12, the jury are entitled, depending upon the circumstances, not to rely on the witness's evidence at all, but if after careful consideration they are sure that what the witness said, either in the statement or when in the witness box was (or in the case of a defence witness, was or may have been) true, they may take account of it in reaching their verdict(s) (see, e.g., *Griffiths v CPS* [2018] EWHC 3062 (Admin), [2019] 1 Cr App R 18 (229), where the magistrates had concluded that earlier statements were truthful and, on that basis, found D guilty). A similar approach was adopted in *Parvez* [2010] EWCA Crim 3229, where the issue was whether the jury were sure that it was fear that had led the witness to retract an earlier statement. It was held that if they were sure, then, subject to caution, they could act upon it, but if they were not, they should not rely upon it.

F6.56 **Direction on 'Unreliability'** In *Golder* [1960] 3 All ER 457, Lord Parker CJ said (at pp. 1172–3):

> ... when a witness is shown to have made previous statements inconsistent with the evidence given by that witness at the trial, the jury should ... be directed that the evidence given at the trial should be regarded as unreliable.

The dictum in *Golder* was cited with approval in *Oliva* [1965] 3 All ER 116, at pp. 1036–7. However, Lord Parker's dictum was *obiter* and in *Driscoll v The Queen* (1977) 137 CLR 517, at pp. 535–7, the High Court of Australia refused to accept that it was *always* necessary or even appropriate to direct a jury in this way, a view endorsed by the House of Lords in *Governor of Pentonville Prison, ex parte Alves* [1993] AC 284 (at p. 298) and by the Court of Appeal in *Goodway* [1993] 4 All ER 894 (at p. 899). Thus in *Pestano* [1981] Crim LR 397, where the prosecution cross-examined the witness on his deposition, but nonetheless sought to rely upon his evidence insofar as it supported their case, it was held that the evidence was for the jury to consider, subject to a proper warning from the judge as to the weight which could be attached to it. For a further illustration, see *Nelson* [1992] Crim LR 653.

The direction to treat the witness's evidence as 'unreliable' may be inappropriate when a witness gives a rational or convincing explanation for the earlier contradictory statement or gives evidence to the benefit of the accused (*Thomas* [1985] Crim LR 445; *Khan* [2002] EWCA Crim 945). Nonetheless, if a witness has been treated as hostile, it is necessary for the jury to consider whether the witness should be treated as creditworthy at all, and they should be clearly directed on that point before considering which parts of the evidence are worthy of acceptance and which are to be rejected. It is insufficient to tell the jury to approach the evidence with great caution and reservation. The judge should give a clear warning about the dangers involved in a witness who contradicts him or herself and should direct them to consider whether they can give any credence to such a witness. It is only if they can, that they may then consider which parts of the witness's evidence they can accept (*Maw* [1994] Crim LR 841). See also *Greene* [2009] EWCA Crim 2282, where it was held that, in all but exceptional cases, once a witness has been treated as hostile, some warning should be given to approach his or her evidence with caution, even if, in the event, the witness proves not to be hostile and reverts to the original account; the precise nature of the direction will be dependent upon the particular circumstances of the case.

F6.57 **Documents** The question whether a document admitted under s. 119 and produced as an exhibit should accompany the jury when they retire is governed by the CJA 2003, s. 122 (see **F6.25**). In the absence of some specific feature of the document requiring the jury to be given it, the judge will remind the jury in the summing-up of its contents and anything said by the witness about it and the circumstances in which it was made. If the jury are to be given the document, the judge should not only give the general direction about hostile witnesses, but also impress upon the jury the reason why they are being given the document and the importance of not attaching disproportionate weight to its contents as compared with the oral evidence (*Hulme* [2006] EWCA Crim 2899, [2007] 1 Cr App R 26 (334)).

Section F7 Cross-examination and Re-examination

CROSS-EXAMINATION: GENERAL CONSIDERATIONS

Nature of Cross-examination

Cross-examination is the questioning of a witness by (a) the opponent of the party calling the witness or (b) any other party to the proceedings. Thus, as to the latter, an accused has the right to cross-examine a co-accused who has chosen to give evidence (and any witnesses called by the co-accused). This applies not only where the co-accused has given evidence unfavourable to the accused (*Hadwen* [1902] 1 KB 882; *Paul* [1920] 2 KB 183), but also if the co-accused has merely given evidence in his or her own defence (*Hilton* [1972] 1 QB 421, per Fenton Atkinson LJ at pp. 423–4). Usually cross-examination follows immediately after examination-in-chief, but witnesses are sometimes merely tendered by the prosecution for cross-examination. Such a witness is called by the prosecution, sworn, asked no questions in chief other than name and address, and then cross-examined by the defence (*Brooke* (1819) 2 Stark 472). **F7.1**

Sequence of Cross-examination

For magistrates' court proceedings, CrimPR 24.4(4) (see Supplement, **R24.4**) simply provides that 'every other party may ask questions in cross-examination'. Specific provision for the sequence is made for the Crown Court where both prosecution and defence witnesses may be cross-examined by any co-accused in the order their names appear in the indictment or as directed by the court (CrimPR 25.11(4)(b) and (c); see Supplement, **R25.11**); a defence witness may be cross-examined by the prosecution after cross-examination by any co-accused (r. 25.11(c)). **F7.2**

Cross-examination by an Accused in Person

As a general rule, an accused is entitled to cross-examine in person any witness called by the prosecution. The general rule is subject to a common-law restriction and important statutory exceptions. Concerning the former, a trial judge is not obliged to give an unrepresented accused freedom to ask whatever questions, at whatever length, the accused wishes (*Brown* [1998] 2 Cr App R 364). As to the latter, the YJCEA 1999, ss. 34 to 39, protect three categories of witness from cross-examination by an accused in person. Under the YJCEA 1999, s. 34, no person charged with a sexual offence as defined in s. 62 of the Act (see **F7.28**) may cross-examine in person the complainant, either in connection with the offence or in connection with any other offence (of whatever nature) with which that person is charged in the proceedings; under s. 35, no person charged with one of a number of specified offences may cross-examine in person a 'protected witness' either in connection with the offence, or in connection with any other offence (of whatever nature) with which that person is charged in the proceedings; and under s. 36, the court has a general power, in cases not covered by ss. 34 and 35, to give a direction prohibiting the accused from cross-examining a witness in person if: **F7.3**

(a) the quality of evidence given by the witness is likely to be diminished by such cross-examination and would be likely to be improved by such a direction; and
(b) it would not be contrary to the interests of justice.

In deciding whether (a) applies in the case of a witness, the court must have regard to the particular matters set out in s. 36(3), including the nature of the questions likely to be asked. The accused should not be denied the opportunity to make representations in relation to the matters set out in s. 36(3) (*R (Hillman) v Richmond Magistrates' Court* [2003] EWHC 2580 (Admin)).

Section 38 provides that, where an accused is prevented from cross-examining a witness in person, the court must invite the accused to appoint a legal representative; and that if the accused fails to do so and the court decides that it is in the interests of justice for the witness to be cross-examined by a legal representative appointed to represent the interests of the accused, the court must choose and appoint such a representative, who shall not be responsible to the accused. A court-appointed advocate does not have a free-ranging remit to conduct the trial on the accused's behalf. The advocate's duty is to cross-examine a particular witness and to ensure that he or she is in a position properly to do so and therefore the duty may include applications to admit bad character evidence of the witness and applications for disclosure of material relevant to the cross-examination. Technically, the role ends at the conclusion of the cross-examination, but if the advocate is prepared to stay and assist the accused on a pro bono basis, the court should not oblige the advocate to leave (*Abbas v CPS* [2015] EWHC 579 (Admin), [2015] 2 Cr App R 11 (183)).

Under s. 39, where an accused is prevented from cross-examining a witness in person, the judge must give the jury such warning (if any) as the judge considers necessary to ensure that the accused is not prejudiced by any inference that might be drawn from the fact that such cross-examination has been prevented or by the fact that the cross-examination was carried out by a court-appointed representative.

For the procedural rules relating to the restriction on cross-examination by an accused, see CrimPR Part 23 (see Supplement, **R23.1** *et seq.*) and CrimPD V, paras. 23A.1 *et seq.* (see Supplement, **CPD.23A**).

F7.4 **Youth Justice and Criminal Evidence Act 1999, ss. 34 to 39**

34. No person charged with a sexual offence may in any criminal proceedings cross-examine in person a witness who is the complainant, either—
(a) in connection with that offence, or
(b) in connection with any other offence (of whatever nature) with which that person is charged in the proceedings.

35.—(1) No person charged with an offence to which this section applies may in any criminal proceedings cross-examine in person a protected witness, either—
(a) in connection with that offence, or
(b) in connection with any other offence (of whatever nature) with which that person is charged in the proceedings.

(2) For the purposes of subsection (1) a 'protected witness' is a witness who—
(a) either is the complainant or is alleged to have been a witness to the commission of the offence to which this section applies, and
(b) either is a child or falls to be cross-examined after giving evidence in chief (whether wholly or in part)—
(i) by means of a video recording made (for the purposes of section 27) at a time when the witness was a child, or
(ii) in any other way at any such time.

(3) The offences to which this section applies are—
(a) any offence under—
. . .
(iva) any of sections 33 to 36 of the Sexual Offences Act 1956;
(v) the Protection of Children Act 1978;
(vi) part 1 of the Sexual Offences Act 2003 or any relevant superseded enactment; or
(vii) sections 1 and 2 of the Modern Slavery Act 2015;
(b) kidnapping, false imprisonment or an offence under section 1 or 2 of the Child Abduction Act 1984;
(c) any offence under section 1 of the Children and Young Persons Act 1933;
(d) any offence (not within any of the preceding paragraphs) which involves an assault on, or injury or a threat of injury to, any person.

(3A) In subsection (3)(a)(vi) 'relevant superseded enactment' means—
(a) any of sections 1 to 32 of the Sexual Offences Act 1956;
(b) the Indecency with Children Act 1960;

(c) the Sexual Offences Act 1967;
(d) section 54 of the Criminal Law Act 1977.

(4) In this section 'child' means—
(a) where the offence falls within subsection (3)(a), a person under the age of 18; or
(b) where the offence falls within subsection (3)(b), (c) or (d), a person under the age of 14.

(5) For the purposes of this section 'witness' includes a witness who is charged with an offence in the proceedings.

36.—(1) This section applies where, in a case where neither of sections 34 and 35 operates to prevent an accused in any criminal proceedings from cross-examining a witness in person—
(a) the prosecutor makes an application for the court to give a direction under this section in relation to the witness, or
(b) the court of its own motion raises the issue whether such a direction should be given.

(2) If it appears to the court—
(a) that the quality of evidence given by the witness on cross-examination—
(i) is likely to be diminished if the cross-examination (or further cross-examination) is conducted by the accused in person, and
(ii) would be likely to be improved if a direction were given under this section, and
(b) that it would not be contrary to the interests of justice to give such a direction, the court may give a direction prohibiting the accused from cross-examining (or further cross-examining) the witness in person.

(3) In determining whether subsection (2)(a) applies in the case of a witness the court must have regard, in particular, to—
(a) any views expressed by the witness as to whether or not the witness is content to be cross-examined by the accused in person;
(b) the nature of the questions likely to be asked, having regard to the issues in the proceedings and the defence case advanced so far (if any);
(c) any behaviour on the part of the accused at any stage of the proceedings, both generally and in relation to the witness;
(d) any relationship (of whatever nature) between the witness and the accused;
(e) whether any person (other than the accused) is or has at any time been charged in the proceedings with a sexual offence or an offence to which section 35 applies, and (if so) whether section 34 or 35 operates or would have operated to prevent that person from cross-examining the witness in person;
(f) any direction under section 19 which the court has given, or proposes to give, in relation to the witness.

(4) For the purposes of this section—
(a) 'witness', in relation to an accused, does not include any other person who is charged with an offence in the proceedings; and
(b) any reference to the quality of a witness's evidence shall be construed in accordance with section 16(5).

37.—(1) Subject to subsection (2), a direction has binding effect from the time it is made until the witness to whom it applies is discharged.
In this section 'direction' means a direction under section 36.

(2) The court may discharge a direction if it appears to the court to be in the interests of justice to do so, and may do so either—
(a) on an application made by a party to the proceedings, if there has been a material change of circumstances since the relevant time, or
(b) of its own motion.

(3) In subsection (2) 'the relevant time' means—
(a) the time when the direction was given, or
(b) if a previous application has been made under that subsection, the time when the application (or last application) was made.

(4) [The court must state in open court its reasons for its decision in relation to a direction.]

(5) [Power to make rules of court.]

38.—(1) This section applies where an accused is prevented from cross-examining a witness in person by virtue of section 34, 35 or 36.

(2) Where it appears to the court that this section applies, it must—
(a) invite the accused to arrange for a legal representative to act for him for the purpose of cross-examining the witness; and

(b) require the accused to notify the court, by the end of such period as it may specify, whether a legal representative is to act for him for that purpose.

(3) If by the end of the period mentioned in subsection (2)(b) either—

(a) the accused has notified the court that no legal representative is to act for him for the purpose of cross-examining the witness, or

(b) no notification has been received by the court and it appears to the court that no legal representative is to so act,

the court must consider whether it is necessary in the interests of justice for the witness to be cross-examined by a legal representative appointed to represent the interests of the accused.

(4) If the court decides that it is necessary in the interests of justice for the witness to be so cross-examined, the court must appoint a qualified legal representative (chosen by the court) to cross-examine the witness in the interests of the accused.

(5) A person so appointed shall not be responsible to the accused.

(6) and (7) [Power to make rules of court.]

(8) For the purposes of this section—

(a) any reference to cross-examination includes (in a case where a direction is given under section 36 after the accused has begun cross-examining the witness) a reference to further cross-examination; and

(b) 'qualified legal representative' means a legal representative who has a right of audience (within the meaning of the Courts and Legal Services Act 1990) in relation to the proceedings before the court.

39.—(1) Where on a trial on indictment with a jury an accused is prevented from cross-examining a witness in person by virtue of section 34, 35 or 36, the judge must give the jury such warning (if any) as the judge considers necessary to ensure that the accused is not prejudiced—

(a) by any inferences that might be drawn from the fact that the accused has been prevented from cross-examining the witness in person;

(b) where the witness has been cross-examined by a legal representative appointed under section 38(4), by the fact that the cross-examination was carried out by such a legal representative and not by a person acting as the accused's own legal representative.

(2) Subsection (8)(a) of section 38 applies for the purposes of this section as it applies for the purposes of section 38.

Object of Cross-examination

F7.5 The object of cross-examination is:

(a) to elicit from the witness evidence supporting the cross-examining party's version of the facts in issue;

(b) to weaken or cast doubt upon the accuracy of the evidence given by the witness in chief; and

(c) in appropriate circumstances, to impeach the witness's credibility.

Role of the Judge during Cross-examination

F7.6 The court may ask a witness questions and, in particular, where the accused is not represented, ask a witness any question necessary in the interests of the accused (CrimPR 24.4(6) (magistrates' courts) and 25.11(6) (Crown Court); see Supplement, **R24.4** and **R25.11**); notes to those rules state that the questions that may be put are in the discretion of the court, subject to the rules of evidence and r. 1.3 (application by the court of the overriding objective).

In general, when cross-examination is conducted by a competent advocate, a judge should not intervene, save to clarify matters the judge does not understand or thinks the jury may not understand. If the judge wishes to ask questions about matters that have not been touched upon, it is generally better to wait until the end of the examination or cross-examination. A judge should not be criticised for occasional transgressions, but there may come a time, depending on the nature and frequency of the interruptions, that the Court of Appeal is of the opinion that defence counsel was so hampered in the proper conduct of the cross-examination that the judge's conduct amounts to a material irregularity (*Sharp* [1994] QB 261; see also *M*

(30 June 2017 unreported, CA)). As to the power of the judge to impose time-limits on cross-examination, see **F7.20**. As to the powers of the judge in the case of the cross-examination of children and vulnerable witnesses, see **F7.8** and **F7.10**. See also **D14.69**.

Liability to Cross-examination

All witnesses are liable to cross-examination, except: **F7.7**

(a) a witness called merely to produce a document, who is not sworn (*Sumners v Moseley* (1834) 2 CR & M 477) or who is sworn unnecessarily (*Rush v Smith* (1834) 1 Cr M & R 94);
(b) a witness unable to speak as to the matters supposed to be within the witness's knowledge who is called by mistake, provided that the mistake is discovered after the witness has been sworn but before the examination-in-chief (*Wood v Mackinson* (1840) 2 Mood & R 273); and
(c) a witness called by the judge, who may only be cross-examined with the judge's leave, which should be given if the witness is adverse to either party (*Coulson v Disborough* [1894] 2 QB 316; *Cliburn* (1898) 62 JP 232).

The evidence-in-chief of a witness who dies before cross-examination remains admissible, although little weight may attach to it (*Doolin* (1832) 1 Jebb CC 123). Similarly, if a witness, during cross-examination, becomes incapable through illness of answering any further questions, the trial may continue on the basis of the evidence already given (*Stretton* (1986) 86 Cr App R 7). In *Stretton*, the witness was the victim of sexual offences and the judge gave a carefully worded direction to the jury to acquit if they felt that the absence of cross-examination prevented them from judging fairly her credibility. See also *RT* [2020] EWCA Crim 155, where a vulnerable prosecution witness, during cross-examination on behalf of one co-accused, became distressed and refused to continue to give evidence, thereby cutting short the cross-examination and preventing cross-examination on behalf of the other co-accused. It was held that in the particular circumstances, the trial remained fair: (a) the jury had seen the witness give evidence and be cross-examined in part; (b) it was the questioning in cross-examination that explained her behaviour; (c) there was material before the jury enabling them fairly to assess her credibility and reliability; (d) her evidence could be assessed in the context of other evidence; and (e) the judge had properly directed the jury on the limitations of her evidence. However, in *Lawless* (1994) 98 Cr App R 342, where the only direct evidence on one important part of the prosecution case was given by a witness who, at the end of his examination-in-chief, suffered a heart attack and was unable to give further evidence, it was held at least doubtful whether any direction to the jury, however strongly expressed, could have overcome the powerful prejudice of his evidence going wholly untested by cross-examination. The Court distinguished *Stretton* and also *Wyatt* [1990] Crim LR 343, considered at **F7.14**.

Putting One's Case and the Effect of Failure to Do So

In *Wood Green Crown Court, ex parte Taylor* [1995] Crim LR 879, the Divisional Court approved the following principle as stated in the 1995 edition of this work: a party who fails to cross-examine a witness upon a particular matter in respect of which it is proposed to contradict the witness or impeach his or her credit by calling other witnesses, tacitly accepts the truth of the witness's evidence in chief on that matter, and will not thereafter be entitled to invite the jury to disbelieve the witness in that regard. The proper course is to challenge the witness while in the witness-box or, at any rate, to make it plain at that stage that the evidence is not accepted (*Hart* (1932) 23 Cr App R 202). Thus in *Bircham* [1972] Crim LR 430, counsel for D was not permitted to suggest to the jury in his closing speech that the co-accused and a prosecution witness had committed the offence charged, where the allegation had not been put to either in cross-examination. **F7.8**

> ...nothing would be more absolutely unjust than not to cross-examine witnesses upon evidence which they have given, so as to give them notice, and to give them an opportunity of explanation, and an opportunity very often to defend their own character, and, not having given them such an

> opportunity, to ask the jury afterwards to disbelieve what they have said, although not one question has been directed either to their credit or to the accuracy of the facts they have deposed to. (*Browne v Dunn* (1893) 6 R 67, per Lord Halsbury at pp. 76–7, followed in *Fenlon* (1980) 71 Cr App R 307.)

See also, to similar effect, rC7.2 of the Code of Conduct for barristers in the Bar Standards Board (BSB) Handbook. Evidence to contradict a witness which was not put to him or her in cross-examination may be admitted, provided that the witness is then recalled and cross-examination reopened in order to put the new evidence to the witness (*Cannan* [1998] Crim LR 284).

When a witness is young or otherwise vulnerable, the court may impose restrictions on an advocate 'putting his case' when there is a risk of the witness failing to understand, becoming distressed or acquiescing to leading questions (see CrimPD I, para. 3E.4 (see Supplement, **CPD.3E**), and *Lubemba* [2014] EWCA Crim 2064, [2015] 1 WLR 1579, considered further at **F7.10**). See also **F7.20** on the power of the judge to impose time-limits and limit cross-examination.

F7.9 **Flexible Rule** The rule under discussion is not hard-and-fast or inflexible. Thus where it is proposed to invite the jury to disbelieve a witness on a particular matter, it will not always be necessary to put to the witness explicitly that he or she is lying, provided that the overall tenor of the cross-examination is designed to show that the witness's account is incapable of belief (*Lovelock* [1997] Crim LR 821). Indeed in some cases it may be that the point upon which the witness is to be impeached is manifest, as when the story told is incredible, and it is unnecessary to cross-examine upon it at all: the most effective cross-examination would be to ask the witness to leave the box (*Browne v Dunn*, per Lords Herschell LC and Morris). Application of the rule may also be unnecessary in the case of a witness whose evidence is purely corroborative of the evidence of another witness whose evidence-in-chief has already been challenged in cross-examination. It is a sensible practice, however, to secure the assurance of the trial judge, and the agreement of the party calling the witness, that failure to cross-examine in such circumstances will not be taken as a tacit acceptance of the witness's evidence. The rule has also been held to be inapplicable in the case of proceedings in magistrates' courts (*O'Connell v Adams* [1973] RTR 150). This may explain *Wilkinson v DPP* [2003] EWHC 865 (Admin), in which D was convicted following a summary trial in which the prosecution failed to cross-examine her; it was held that there was nothing to show that the trial was unfair and that the district judge had been entitled to reject her evidence.

Children and Vulnerable Witnesses

F7.10 **Best Practice** As to special measures directions for children and vulnerable witnesses, see generally **D14.1** to **D14.51**. In *YGM* [2018] EWCA Crim 2458 the Court of Appeal set out best practice in cases involving cross-examination of vulnerable witnesses.

(1) The identification of any limitations on cross-examination should take place at an early stage, at a ground rules hearing, where the judge will discuss with the advocates the nature and extent of the limitations imposed and whether they are simply as to style or also relate to content.
(2) Before the cross-examination, the judge should give both the standard special measures direction and also direct in general terms that limitations have been placed on the defence advocate.
(3) If any specific issues of content have been identified that the cross-examiner cannot explore, the judge may wish to direct the jury about them after the cross-examination is completed. On any view, the judge should direct the jury about them in the summing-up.
(4) Both the judge and the advocates should ensure that they are up to date with current best practice in the treatment of vulnerable witnesses.

If a trial judge does not adopt best practice in every respect, it does not follow that a conviction is unsafe. In the case before the court, in which the trial judge had failed to warn the jury of the limitations on the cross-examination before it took place, but gave every other recommended direction with care and precision, the safety of the conviction had not been undermined. In *Pringle* [2019] EWCA Crim 1722, best practice was not adopted in the case of a vulnerable accused. There was no ground rules hearing to provide guidance on the appropriate form of questioning, to decide on regular breaks and to consider other special measures; there was unfairness in the conduct of the cross-examination; and the jury were not aware of D's difficulties and therefore not in a position properly to evaluate what he had said in interview and in his evidence. His conviction was held to be unsafe. See also *Thomas* [2020] EWCA Crim 117, [2020] 4 WLR 66.

In *Lubemba* [2014] EWCA Crim 2064, [2015] 1 WLR 1579, the Court of Appeal rejected complaints that the judge had excessively restricted the scope and length of a child witness's cross-examination. The judge had imposed certain restrictions upon counsel. He limited her cross-examination to 45 minutes and interrupted when he felt her questions were unclear or inappropriate, directing her on a number of occasions not to put her case. The Court saw nothing inappropriate or unfair in this, having regard to the Advocacy Council's Toolkits (now the Inns of Court College of Advocacy Toolkits), which have been endorsed in CrimPD I, para. 3D.7 (see Supplement, **CPD.3D**), as best practice. See also CrimPD I, paras. 3E.1 to 3E.6 (see Supplement, **CPD.3E**). It was held that: the Court would expect a ground rules hearing in every case involving a vulnerable witness, save in very exceptional circumstances; the ground rules hearing should cover, *inter alia*, the length of questioning, the frequency of breaks and the nature of the questions to be asked; so as to avoid any unfortunate misunderstanding at trial, it would be entirely reasonable for a judge at the ground rules hearing to invite defence advocates to reduce their questions to writing in advance; the judge is responsible for controlling questioning and ensuring that vulnerable witnesses and defendants are able to give the best evidence they can; and the judge has a duty to intervene, therefore, if an advocate's questioning is confusing or inappropriate. Hallett LJ said (at [45]):

> It is now generally accepted that if justice is to be done to the vulnerable witness and also to the accused, a radical departure from the traditional style of advocacy will be necessary. Advocates must adapt to the witness, not the other way round. They cannot insist upon any supposed right 'to put one's case' or previous inconsistent statements to a vulnerable witness. If there is a right to 'put one's case' (about which we have our doubts) it must be modified for young or vulnerable witnesses. It is perfectly possible to ensure the jury are made aware of the defence case and of significant inconsistencies without intimidation or distressing a witness ...

See also, in the case of a vulnerable and suggestible accused with significant learning difficulties, *Jones (Gareth William)* [2018] EWCA Crim 2816.

In *Grant-Murray* [2017] EWCA Crim 1228 it was confirmed (at [226]) that the principles in *Lubemba* [2014] EWCA Crim 2064, [2015] 1 WLR 1579 apply to child defendants as witnesses in the same way as they apply to other vulnerable witnesses. The Court of Appeal also provided guidance in relation to the required competence and training of advocates in respect of such witnesses, on tag questions and on the proper role of the intermediary. As to the first of these, the Court emphasised that it is generally misconduct for an advocate to take on a case for which the advocate is not competent, adding that: 'It would be difficult to conceive of an advocate being competent to act in a case involving young witnesses or defendants unless the advocate had undertaken specific training' (at [226]). Concerning tag questions, it was held that although they should be avoided, not all of them have an adverse effect: questions containing two positives are not necessarily complex or difficult to follow and even those containing a positive and a negative (e.g., 'You hit her, didn't you?') may not trouble a particular witness (at [114] to [115] and [194]). As to intermediaries, the Court held that: they are instructed to provide advice and guidance to the judge and advocates, not to dictate to anyone what is to happen; they provide assistance to a witness or accused *as directed by the judge*; it does not follow from the fact that a judge does not adopt every one of their suggestions or uphold every one of their interventions that a witness or accused has been treated unfairly; and ultimately the burden is on the judge, not the intermediary, to ensure the effective participation of a vulnerable witness (at [199]).

In *Dinc* [2017] EWCA Crim 1206, Hallett LJ held that, in any case involving a child witness or a witness who suffers from a mental disability or disorder, there is nothing inherently unfair in restricting the scope, structure and nature of cross-examination and or in requiring questions to be **F7.11** submitted in advance, Her ladyship pointed out that it is the judge's duty to control questioning of any witness and to ensure that it is fair to both the witness and the accused, and continued:

> Far from prejudicing the defence, it is the experience of many judges that the practice ensures that defence advocates ask focussed and often more effective questions of a vulnerable child witness. The advocates will know precisely what the witness is going to say in chief because they will have the benefit of the pre-recorded ABE interview and can prepare fully. A list of admissions of behaviour or previous inconsistent statements that potentially undermine the complainant's credibility can be put before the jury to cover those issues on which questioning is restricted. The combination of admissions and focussed cross-examination can produce a powerful defence case; more powerful than a defence advocate putting to a witness a whole series of propositions only to be met with the answers: 'No', 'I don't understand' or 'I don't remember'.

In *Dinc* it was also held that where, in the case of a vulnerable witness, an advocate has prepared questions in advance of cross-examination and something arises during cross-examination that was not foreseen, the advocate is entitled to seek the judge's consent to ask questions not previously authorised and, provided that the request is reasonable, the judge will allow a degree of leeway.

See also **D14.69** on best practice in questioning child and other vulnerable witnesses, and the *Crown Court Compendium* (July 2020), ch. 10-5.

F7.12 **Attendance for Cross-examination** In *RK* [2018] EWCA Crim 603, the Court of Appeal, while accepting that under the YJCEA 1999, s. 27(5)(a)(ii), the parties may agree that a witness who gives evidence-in-chief by means of a video recording does not need to attend for cross-examination, held that a child who is assessed as competent should generally be called and cross-examined with the benefit of any appropriate special measures. Hallett LJ said (at [27]): 'Although this court…has doubted the *right* to put every aspect of the defence case to a vulnerable witness, whatever the circumstances, it has not questioned the general *duty* to ensure the defence case is put fully and fairly and witnesses challenged where that is possible'.

F7.13 **Pre-trial Cross-examination** In *PMH* [2018] EWCA Crim 2452, [2019] 1 Cr App R 27 (356), the Court of Appeal identified the following areas of best practice relating to pre-trial cross-examination under the YJCEA 1999, s. 28 (at [21]):

(i) At the ground rules hearing the judge should discuss with the advocates how and when any limitations on questioning will be explained to the jury.
(ii) If this has not happened or there have been any changes, the judge should discuss with the advocates how any limitations on questioning will be explained to the jury *before* the recording of the cross-examination is played.
(iii) The judge can then give the jury the standard direction on special measures with a direction on the limitations that the judge has imposed on cross-examination and the reasons for them *before* the cross-examination is played.
(iv) The judge should consider if it is necessary to have a further discussion with the advocates before their closing submissions and the summing-up on the limitations imposed and any areas where those limitations have had a material effect. In this way the advocates will know the areas upon which they can address the jury.
(v) In the summing-up the judge should remind the jury of the limitations and any areas identified where they have had a material effect upon the questions asked.
(vi) If any written directions are provided to the jury the judge should include with the standard special measures direction a general direction that limitations have been imposed on the cross-examination.

See also **D14.46** and **D14.47** on pre-trial cross-examination under the YJCEA 1999, s. 28.

F7.14 **Distress** In *SG* [2017] EWCA Crim 617, [2017] 2 Cr App R 20 (256), the Court of Appeal set out the principles to be applied when a complainant becomes distressed while giving evidence:

(a) Very often a break will enable the witness to return better able to give evidence.
(b) In deciding on the right course of action, the court should balance the importance of witnesses being able to give the best evidence they can (CrimPD I, para. 3E.4) without being

harassed by the form or nature of the questioning, against the potentially conflicting interest of an accused in being able properly to challenge the witness's account.

(c) There may be a number of reasons for signs of distress: witnesses may find giving evidence highly stressful, but they may have been caught out in a lie.

(d) A witness exhibiting signs of distress is not necessarily a vulnerable witness.

(e) If the witness is vulnerable, to require the defence to prepare a list of further questions for approval by the judge may not be required; the advocate may treat the witness with proper consideration and judges can intervene to prevent over-rigorous or repetitive questioning. The judge should bear in mind the disadvantages of prepared questions, which may inhibit the development of cross-examination in response to a particular answer.

Nothing in *SG* should be taken as undermining the approach subsequently set out in *Dinc* [2017] EWCA Crim 1206. In particular, *SG* did not hold, as some commentators have suggested, that only in exceptional cases should a judge require a list of questions in advance for the court's approval. In *Wyatt* [1990] Crim LR 343, a seven-year-old girl, the victim of an indecent assault, was cross-examined through video link for about 20 minutes. She became visibly distressed and the judge adjourned the case for about 20 minutes. After the adjournment, the girl continued to cry and the judge decided that her evidence should proceed no further, even though counsel for the defence still had one important question to ask. The appeal was dismissed: the judge had not erred in the exercise of his discretion to adjourn for the length of time that he did and had directed the jury fairly on the girl's evidence and left it to them to determine her credibility. On the critical issue whether the accused can have a fair trial if the complainant's evidence is cut short, regard can be had to the extent to which the defence has been put to, and explored with, the complainant; whether previous inconsistent statements can be reduced to agreed facts and put before the jury in writing; and whether there is other evidence against the accused (*Pipe* [2014] EWCA Crim 2570, [2015] 1 Cr App R (S) 42 (306)). See also *RT* [2020] EWCA Crim 155, considered at F7.7.

It is important that judges alert the jury to guard against unwarranted assumptions in relation to distress on the part of a complainant when giving evidence, pointing out that its presence or absence is not a reliable indicator of whether the complainant is telling the truth or not (see the *Crown Court Compendium* (July 2020), ch. 20-1, paras. 10 and 11 and Example 7).

Risk of Witness Taking Line of Least Resistance Where there is a real possibility that a young child has assented to a suggestion in cross-examination simply to please or to bring the questioning to a conclusion, or a speedier conclusion, it can be very difficult to tell whether the child is truly changing the account or simply taking the line of least resistance. In the case of such assent on the part of a child appearing for the prosecution, this could lead to a submission of no case to answer, as when the evidence, taken at its highest, is such that no jury could safely be sure of guilt, but not when, as in *W* [2010] EWCA Crim 1926, it was open to the jury to conclude, particularly in the light of the other evidence, that the child was not agreeing in any meaningful way to what was being suggested. **F7.15**

RULES GOVERNING CONDUCT OF CROSS-EXAMINATION

General Restrictions

Cross-examination is a powerful weapon entrusted to counsel, and should be conducted with restraint and a measure of courtesy and consideration which a witness is entitled to expect in a court of law (*Mechanical & General Inventions Co. Ltd v Austin* [1935] AC 346, per Lord Sankey LC at pp. 359–60). Thus, it is no part of the duty of an advocate for the defence to embark on lengthy cross-examination on matters which are not really in issue (*Kalia* (1974) 60 Cr App R 200). See also *Simmonds* [1969] 1 QB 685 and *Maynard* (1979) 69 Cr App R 309. Likewise, **F7.16** questions should not be in the nature of comment on the facts; comments should be confined to speeches. Nor should questions be framed in such a way as to invite argument rather than elicit evidence on the facts in issue. Thus an advocate should avoid questions such as 'I suggest to you that …' and 'Do you ask the jury to believe that …'. Cross-examination should be confined to putting questions of fact. An advocate should not state what somebody else has said or is expected to say. The time for statements such as 'The defendant's recollection is …' or 'The defendant will say …' is the opening speech; such statements should not be made, or put in the form of a question, in cross-examination (*Baldwin* (1925) 18 Cr App R 175, per Lord Hewart CJ at pp. 178–9). The same restrictions apply to questions put by the judge (see *Wilson* [1991] Crim LR 838, where the judge asked D 'So this 12-year-old girl has made wicked lies about you?'). See also rC7.1 of the Code of Conduct for barristers in the BSB Handbook: 'Where you are acting as an advocate, your duty not to abuse your role includes the following obligations… you must not make statements or ask questions merely to insult, humiliate or annoy a witness…'. See also **F7.21** and **F7.22**.

In addition to the powers of the trial judge in relation to the cross-examination of children and vulnerable witnesses (see **F7.10** and **D14.69**), the judge has a general discretion to prevent any questions in cross-examination which the judge considers to be unnecessary, improper or oppressive. CrimPD I, para. 3D.2 (see Supplement, **CPD.3D**), recognises that, in addition to 'vulnerable' and 'intimidated' witnesses as defined in the YJCEA 1999, ss. 16 and 17, many other witnesses may require assistance, and indicates that the court must facilitate the participation of 'any person'. This includes enabling witnesses to give their best evidence, and the pre-trial and trial process should, so far as is necessary, be adapted to meet such ends.

Scope of Cross-examination

F7.17 Questions in cross-examination are not restricted to matters raised in chief, but may relate to any fact in issue (or relevant fact), or to the credibility of the witness. Cross-examination is governed by the following general rules.

Leading Questions

F7.18 A witness under cross-examination may be asked leading questions. This is so even if the witness appears to be more favourable to the cross-examining party than to the party calling him or her (*Parkin v Moon* (1836) 7 C & P 408).

Exclusionary Rules of Evidence

F7.19 The exclusionary rules of evidence relating to hearsay, opinion, privilege etc. apply to cross-examination as they apply to examination-in-chief (see, in the case of inadmissible hearsay, *Thomson* [1912] 3 KB 19, *Windass* (1988) 89 Cr App R 258 and *Gray* [1998] Crim LR 570).

In *Treacy* [1944] 2 All ER 229, a charge of murder, it was held that D had been cross-examined improperly upon certain inadmissible confessions made on arrest and inconsistent with his evidence. It has been said that the principle established in this case, that an accused cannot be cross-examined by the prosecution in such a way as to reveal that the accused made an inadmissible confession, also obtains in favour of any co-accused (*Rice* [1963] 1 QB 857, per Winn J at pp. 868–9). However, see also *Rowson* [1986] QB 174 and other authorities considered at **F18.84**.

Power of Judge to Impose Time-limits and Limit Cross-examination

F7.20 The court has a general duty to deal with cases efficiently and expeditiously and to manage cases actively to ensure that evidence is presented in the shortest and clearest way, giving any direction appropriate (CrimPR 1.1(2)(e), 3.2(2)(e) and 3.2(3); see Supplement, **R1.1** and **R3.2**). It follows that, as part of its case management powers, the court may limit the duration of any stage of the hearing and the cross-examination of a witness (CrimPR 3.13(d); see Supplement, **R3-13**). The following propositions derive from *B* [2005] EWCA Crim 805.

(a) Although the imposition of time-limits for cross-examination (or examination-in-chief) of witnesses should not become a routine feature of trial management, judges are fully entitled, and indeed obliged, to impose reasonable time-limits where counsel indulge in prolix and repetitious questioning.
(b) It is not the duty of counsel to put to a witness every point of an accused's case, however peripheral, or to embark on lengthy cross-examination on matters which are not really in issue. The duty is to discriminate between important and relevant features of a defence case which must be put to a witness and minor and/or unnecessary matters which do not need to be put.
(c) Entitlement to a fair trial is not inconsistent with proper judicial control over the use of court time and the Court of Appeal will not interfere with a decision made by a judge in this respect unless it is plain that it resulted in unfairness.

For an example of a decision to restrict cross-examination that was neither unreasonable nor unfair, see *Simon* [2018] EWCA Crim 3086.

Concerning the power to impose time-limits in the case of children and vulnerable witnesses, see also **F7.10**.

Cross-examination as to Credit

'Since the purpose of cross-examination as to credit is to show that the witness ought not to **F7.21**
be believed on oath, the matters about which he is questioned must relate to his likely standing after cross-examination with the tribunal which is trying him or listening to his evidence' (*Sweet-Escott* (1971) 55 Cr App R 316 at p. 320; *Hobbs v CT Tinling & Co. Ltd* [1929] 2 KB 1 per Sankey LJ at p. 51). Thus a witness may be cross-examined about his or her means of knowledge of the facts to which he or she has testified, opportunities for observation, powers of perception, the quality of the witness's memory, mistakes, omissions and inconsistencies in evidence, and omissions or inconsistencies in previous statements that relate to the witness's likely standing with the jury after cross-examination but which are not 'relative to the subject matter of the indictment' (*Funderburk* [1990] 2 All ER 482).

As to quality of memory, there is a risk of 'contamination' or collusion when officers have conferred in the production of statements about events or interviews (*R (Saunders) v Independent Police Complaints Commission* [2009] EWHC 2372 (Admin), [2009] 1 All ER 379).

As to omissions, where an accused is charged with a sexual offence and asserts fabrication on the part of the complainant, the accused may be cross-examined as to what facts are known to the accused that might explain why the complainant would make a false accusation (*Brook* [2003] EWCA Crim 951, [2003] 1 WLR 2809).

In a sexual case, the defence may seek to undermine the credibility of the complainant by cross-examination on her delay in making her complaint, in which case the judge should direct the jury that, whereas some may complain immediately to the first person seen, others may feel shame and shock and not complain for some time, and that a late complaint is not necessarily a false one (see *D* [2008] EWCA Crim 2557 at [9]–[12]; and concerning directions to the jury to guard against other false assumptions about complainants in sexual cases, see the *Crown Court Compendium* (July 2020), ch. 20-1, and **B3.48**).

A witness may also be cross-examined about previous convictions or bias (if, in either case, it is lawful to do so under the rules relating to evidence of bad character in the CJA 2003, Part 11; see **F7.22**, **F13** and **F15**), any mental or physical disability affecting reliability, and any previous statements made by the witness 'relative to the subject-matter of the indictment' and inconsistent with the witness's testimony; and if the witness denies any of these matters, the cross-examining party is entitled to prove them (see **F7.57** to **F7.66**).

F7.22 **Bad Character** Any questions in cross-examination as to a witness's bad character are subject to the rules set out in the CJA 2003, Part 11. Section 99 of the Act abolishes the common-law rules governing the admissibility of evidence of 'bad character' in criminal proceedings and the intention appears to be to abolish not only the rules as to the introduction of such evidence in examination-in-chief, but also the rules governing cross-examination about bad character. Thus such cross-examination is permitted only if it comes within one of the specified categories of admissibility set out in s. 100 (non-defendant's bad character; see **F15**) or 101 (defendant's bad character; see **F13**). Evidence of bad character for the purposes of the Act is defined by s. 98 as evidence of, or of a disposition towards, misconduct, other than evidence which 'has to do with the alleged facts of the offence with which the defendant is charged' or 'evidence of misconduct in connection with the investigation or prosecution of that offence'. Section 108 of the 2003 Act imposes an additional restriction in relation to offences committed by the accused when a child (see **F13.91**). There is a further restriction in the YJCEA 1999, s. 41: in the case of sexual offences, except with the leave of the court, no question may be asked in cross-examination about any sexual behaviour of the complainant (see **F7.26** to **F7.47**).

Code of Conduct for Barristers

F7.23 The Code of Conduct for barristers also regulates the conduct of cross-examination: see rC7.1 and rC7.2 at **F7.16** and **F7.8** respectively.

Inspection of and Cross-examination on Documents

F7.24 As to cross-examination of a witness on a previous inconsistent statement, see the Criminal Procedure Act 1865, ss. 4 and 5, at **F7.51** ***et seq.***

In the case of a document used by a witness to refresh his or her memory, the cross-examining party may inspect the document without thereby making it evidence (*Gregory v Tavernor* (1833) 6 C & P 280; *Senat v Senat* [1965] P 172). (As to the cross-examination of a witness on a document used by the witness to refresh his or her memory, see **F6.24**.) However, if a party calls for and inspects a document in the possession of another party which has *not* been used to refresh a witness's memory, the other party may require it to be put in evidence (*Wharam v Routledge* (1805) 5 Esp 235; and *Calvert v Flower* (1836) 7 C & P 386, applied in *Stroud v Stroud (No. 1)* [1963] 3 All ER 539). The rule is obscure: it is unclear whether the document is admitted for the truth of its contents or as evidence of the consistency of the witness. In *Stroud v Stroud (No. 1)*, Wrangham J said (at p. 1082): 'the rule itself has never been abrogated, and it may still be of practical importance, for example in criminal proceedings, where there is no discovery.' The Criminal Law Revision Committee recommended abolition of the rule in criminal proceedings, in which it appears never to have been applied (*Eleventh Report: Evidence (General)* (1972) Cmnd 4991, para. 223).

F7.25 A document, the contents of which are inadmissible, is not rendered admissible by being put to a witness in cross-examination (*Treacy* [1944] 2 All ER 229). However, in cross-examination counsel may produce to the witness a document containing an inadmissible hearsay statement and ask, *without reading it aloud*, whether the witness accepts the contents as true. If the witness does accept the contents as true, they become evidence in the case; but if not, the contents remain inadmissible hearsay (*Gillespie* (1967) 51 Cr App R 172; applied in *Cross* (1990) 91 Cr App R 115). In *Cooper* (1985) 82 Cr App R 74, the Court of Appeal, applying *Gillespie*, held that if the prosecution propose to cross-examine in this way, they should first establish the finding (or creation) of the document as a part of their case, without at that stage indicating the contents of the document to the jury. Similarly, it has been held that it is improper for an advocate, when asking a witness to look at a document (the contents of which are inadmissible) and to say whether the witness still adheres to his or her answer, to describe to the jury its nature or contents. The proper course is simply to hand the document to the witness, direct him or her to look at it, and then to ask whether he or she still adheres to the answer (*Yousry* (1914) 11 Cr App R 13, per Lord Coleridge CJ at p. 18). See also *Tompkins* (1977) 67 Cr App R 181.

PROTECTION OF COMPLAINANTS IN PROCEEDINGS FOR SEXUAL OFFENCES

Rationale

The circumstances in which, in proceedings for sexual offences, evidence may be adduced, or the complainant cross-examined, by or on behalf of the accused, about any sexual behaviour or experience on his or her part involving the accused or any other person, are governed by the YJCEA 1999, ss. 41 to 43. The intention of these provisions is to counter what in Canadian jurisprudence was described as the twin myths, namely 'that unchaste women were more likely to consent to intercourse and in any event were less worthy of belief' — see *Seaboyer* [1991] 2 SCR 577 at 604, 630 per McLachlin J (per Lords Steyn and Hutton in *A (No. 2)* [2001] UKHL 25, [2002] 1 AC 45 at [27] and [147] respectively). The provisions are also born of a recognition that to allow victims of sexual offences to be harassed unfairly by questions about their previous sexual experiences is unjust to them and bad for society, because if victims are afraid to complain then the guilty may escape justice. F7.26

Statutory Provisions on Protection of Claimants in Sexual Offence Proceedings

Youth Justice and Criminal Evidence Act 1999, ss. 41 to 43 F7.27

41.—(1) If at a trial a person is charged with a sexual offence, then, except with the leave of the court—
(a) no evidence may be adduced, and
(b) no question may be asked in cross-examination,
by or on behalf of any accused at the trial, about any sexual behaviour of the complainant.

(2) The court may give leave in relation to any evidence or question only on an application made by or on behalf of an accused, and may not give such leave unless it is satisfied—
(a) that subsection (3) or (5) applies, and
(b) that a refusal of leave might have the result of rendering unsafe a conclusion of the jury or (as the case may be) the court on any relevant issue in the case.

(3) This subsection applies if the evidence or question relates to a relevant issue in the case and either—
(a) that issue is not an issue of consent; or
(b) it is an issue of consent and the sexual behaviour of the complainant to which the evidence or question relates is alleged to have taken place at or about the same time as the event which is the subject matter of the charge against the accused; or
(c) it is an issue of consent and the sexual behaviour of the complainant to which the evidence or question relates is alleged to have been, in any respect, so similar—
(i) to any sexual behaviour of the complainant which (according to evidence adduced or to be adduced by or on behalf of the accused) took place as part of the event which is the subject matter of the charge against the accused, or
(ii) to any other sexual behaviour of the complainant which (according to such evidence) took place at or about the same time as that event,
that the similarity cannot reasonably be explained as a coincidence.

(4) For the purposes of subsection (3) no evidence or question shall be regarded as relating to a relevant issue in the case if it appears to the court to be reasonable to assume that the purpose (or main purpose) for which it would be adduced or asked is to establish or elicit material for impugning the credibility of the complainant as a witness.

(5) This subsection applies if the evidence or question—
(a) relates to any evidence adduced by the prosecution about any sexual behaviour of the complainant; and
(b) in the opinion of the court, would go no further than is necessary to enable the evidence adduced by the prosecution to be rebutted or explained by or on behalf of the accused.

(6) For the purposes of subsections (3) and (5) the evidence or question must relate to a specific instance (or specific instances) of alleged sexual behaviour on the part of the complainant (and accordingly nothing in those subsections is capable of applying in relation to the evidence or question to the extent that it does not so relate).

(7) Where this section applies in relation to a trial by virtue of the fact that one or more of a number of persons charged in the proceedings is or are charged with a sexual offence—
(a) it shall cease to apply in relation to the trial if the prosecutor decides not to proceed with the case against that person or those persons in respect of that charge; but
(b) it shall not cease to do so in the event of that person or those persons pleading guilty to, or being convicted of, that charge.
(8) Nothing in this section authorises any evidence to be adduced or any question to be asked which cannot be adduced or asked apart from this section.
42.—(1) In section 41—
(a) 'relevant issue in the case' means any issue falling to be proved by the prosecution or defence in the trial of the accused;
(b) 'issue of consent' means any issue whether the complainant in fact consented to the conduct constituting the offence with which the accused is charged (and accordingly does not include any issue as to the belief of the accused that the complainant so consented);
(c) 'sexual behaviour' means any sexual behaviour or other sexual experience, whether or not involving any accused or other person, but excluding (except in section 41(3)(c)(i) and (5)(a)) anything alleged to have taken place as part of the event which is the subject matter of the charge against the accused; and
(d) subject to any order made under subsection (2), 'sexual offence' shall be construed in accordance with section 62.
(2) [Secretary of State's power to add or remove offences.]
(3) Section 41 applies in relation to the following proceedings as it applies to a trial, namely—
(a) and (b) [repealed],
(c) the hearing of an application under paragraph 2(1) of Schedule 3 to the Crime and Disorder Act 1998 (application to dismiss charge by person sent for trial under section 51 or 51A of that Act),
(d) any hearing held, between conviction and sentencing, for the purpose of determining matters relevant to the court's decision as to how the accused is to be dealt with, and
(e) the hearing of an appeal,
and references (in section 41 or this section) to a person charged with an offence accordingly include a person convicted of an offence.
43.—(1) An application for leave shall be heard in private and in the absence of the complainant. In this section 'leave' means leave under section 41.
(2) Where such an application has been determined, the court must state in open court (but in the absence of the jury, if there is one)—
(a) its reasons for giving, or refusing, leave, and
(b) if it gives leave, the extent to which evidence may be adduced or questions asked in pursuance of the leave,
and, if it is a magistrates' court, must cause those matters to be entered in the register of its proceedings.
(3) [Power to make rules of court.]

The Restriction

F7.28 Under s. 41(1), if at a trial a person is charged with a sexual offence (a) no evidence may be adduced and (b) no question may be asked in cross-examination, by or on behalf of any accused at the trial, about any sexual behaviour of the complainant, except with the leave of the court. Section 41 applies to other proceedings as it applies to a trial, including a hearing held between conviction and sentence for the purposes of deciding matters relevant to the court's decision as to how the accused is to be dealt with (s. 42(3)). A 'sexual offence' is widely defined in s. 62 as any offence under the SOA 2003, Part 1, or any relevant superseded offence, namely rape or burglary with intent to rape, any offence under SOA 1956, ss. 2 to 12 and ss. 14 to 17, an offence under the Mental Health Act 1959, s. 128, an offence under the Indecency with Children Act 1960, s. 1, and an offence under the Criminal Law Act 1977, s. 54; the definition has been amended so as also to cover any offence under the Modern Slavery Act 2015, s. 2 (human trafficking), which is committed with a view to exploitation that consists of or includes behaviour within s. 3(3) of that Act (sexual exploitation). Under s. 42(1)(c), 'sexual behaviour' means 'any sexual behaviour or other sexual experience, whether or not involving any accused or other person, but excluding (except in section 41(3)(c)(i) and (5)(a)) anything alleged to have taken place as part of the event which is the subject matter of the charge against the accused'. It is submitted that this very wide definition will cover verbal and not merely physical advances of a sexual nature (see, e.g., *Hinds* [1979] Crim LR 111 and *Viola* [1982] 3 All ER 73, both decisions under the Sexual Offences (Amendment) Act 1976). The phrases 'sexual behaviour' and 'other sexual experience' seem to be referring to acts or events of a sexual character, as opposed to the existence of a relationship, acquaintanceship or familiarity (per Lord Clyde in *A (No. 2)* at [128]). The phrases are wide enough to embrace the viewing of pornography or sexually-charged messaging over a live internet connection, and it will also amount to 'sexual behaviour' to answer questions in a sexually explicit quiz (*Ben-Rejab* [2011] EWCA Crim 1136, [2012] 1 WLR 2364). 'Sexual behaviour' it has been said, is a matter of impression and common sense (*Mukadi* [2003] EWCA Crim 3765). However, whether either behaviour or experience is 'sexual' does not depend upon the perception of the complainant, because that would result in many vulnerable people, including children and those with learning difficulties, losing the protection of s. 41. In *P (R)* [2013] EWCA Crim 2331, [2014] 1 Cr App R 28 (401), it was held that, although a question about an abortion may be a way of asking about a complainant's sexual behaviour, questions about D's emotional and financial support for the complainant in relation to an abortion performed after the offences, which were relevant as tending to detract from her account that she viewed him with distaste because of the offences, were not questions about sexual behaviour.

There is no difference in substance between a question asked of a female complainant about her suggested sexual habits or promiscuity or frequency of casual sexual engagement and questions asked of a male complainant about his suggested homosexuality and casual homosexual encounters. In each case the questions are predicated on the proposition that previous consent is evidence of present consent and fall squarely within the restriction in s. 41(1) (*B* [2007] EWCA Crim 23). **F7.29**

Section 41 applies only to defence evidence and questions. In *Soroya* [2006] EWCA Crim 1884, a rape case in which the issue was consent, the complainant gave evidence of the fact that during the incident she had said to D that she was a virgin in the hope that this might cause him to desist from the assault on her. The prosecution also produced evidence that what she had said was false because she had had sexual intercourse on a previous occasion. On appeal, it was argued that evidence of the complainant's sexual history had been improperly introduced in circumstances which would not have been permitted had the defence sought to adduce it, which infringed the principle of equality of arms between the defence and prosecution and thereby constituted a breach of the right to a fair trial under the ECHR, Article 6. It was further argued that s. 41 should be construed in such a way as to embrace the prosecution. Dismissing the appeal, it was held that what the complainant had said to D had been relevant and admissible evidence bearing on the issue of consent; that the evidence of previous intercourse exposed the falsity of what she had said; and that no justified complaint could be directed at its admission.

Previous False Complaints

It seems that s. 41(1) will apply in the case of evidence or questions about a complainant's false denial of a previous sexual experience, for example a false assertion that she was a virgin at the time of the alleged rape, whereas earlier on the same day she had had sexual intercourse with someone other than the accused (*S* [2003] EWCA Crim 1791). The reason is that it is only if the sexual behaviour is established that the denial can be said to be false (*Winter* [2008] EWCA Crim 3 at [25]). On the other hand, normally evidence or questions about a complainant's previous false complaints of sexual assaults or about her failure to complain about the assault which is the subject-matter of the charge when complaining about other sexual assaults, are not 'about any sexual behaviour of the complainant' under s. 41(1). They relate not to her sexual behaviour, but to her past statements or failure to complain. The purpose of the YJCEA 1999 was not to exclude such evidence. However, if the defence wish to put questions about previous **F7.30** false complaints, there are two hurdles. First, leave is required under the CJA 2003, s. 100(4) (see **F15.27** ***et seq.***), because such questioning relates to the bad character of the complainant (*V* [2006] EWCA Crim 1901), but the test under s. 41 and under s. 100 may be in effect the same because it is only if a complaint is false that it can have a substantial probative value within the meaning of s. 100(1)(b) (*Gorania* [2017] EWCA Crim 1538 at [23]). See also *Gabbai* [2019] EWCA Crim 2287, [2020] 4 WLR 65, where evidence suggestive of previous false accounts was admissible under the CJA 2003, s. 100. However, leave may not be required if the complaint was not a deliberate lie but, say, the product of alcoholism and personality problems and therefore does not fall within the definition of 'bad character' in the CJA 2003, ss. 98 and 112(1) (*Davarifar* [2009] EWCA Crim 2294). Secondly, the defence should seek a ruling from the judge that s. 41 does not exclude the questions.

F7.31 It would be professionally improper to put such questions in order to elicit evidence about past sexual behaviour as such under the guise of previous false complaints. In any case the defence must have, and the judge is entitled to seek assurances from the defence that they have, a proper evidential basis for asserting that the previous statement was (a) made and (b) untrue. If not, the questions would not be about lies but about the sexual behaviour of the complainant within s. 41(1) (*T* [2001] EWCA Crim 1877, [2002] 1 WLR 632, applied in *E* [2004] EWCA Crim 1313 and *Abdelrahman* [2005] EWCA Crim 1367). See also *H* [2003] EWCA Crim 2367. Whether there is a 'proper evidential basis' is a fact-sensitive exercise and a matter of judgement rather than discretion (*All-Hilly* [2014] EWCA Crim 1614, [2014] 2 Cr App R 33 (530)). It has been said that it suffices if there is material such that, depending on the answers given by the complainant in cross-examination, the jury could be satisfied that the previous complaint was untrue, or material which is capable of founding an inference that the complaint was untrue (*Garaxo* [2005] EWCA Crim 1170). Similarly, it has been held that a proper evidential basis is 'less than a strong factual foundation for concluding that the previous complaint was false' but does require 'some material from which it could properly be concluded that the complaint was false' (*Murray* [2009] EWCA Crim 618). In other words, the defence must be able to point to material that is capable of supporting — not which must inevitably support — the inference of falsity (*E* [2009] EWCA Crim 2668). However, in *D* [2009] EWCA Crim 2137, where the defence were not permitted to cross-examine the complainant about inconsistencies between her witness statement and other witness statements made at the time, it was held that the earlier authorities are not to be regarded as authorising the use of a trial to investigate the truth or falsity of a previous allegation merely because there is some material which could be used to try and persuade a jury that it was in fact false. Courts should deploy a degree of understanding of those who make sexual allegations; the mere fact that a complaint is raised and not pursued does not necessarily mean it is false (*All-Hilly* [2014] EWCA Crim 1614, [2014] 2 Cr App R 33 (530)). A complaint followed by a failure to co-operate with the police may or may not justify a conclusion that it was untrue, depending on the circumstances (*V* [2006] EWCA Crim 1901; *Garaxo* [2005] EWCA Crim 1170). The mere fact that the police decided that there was insufficient evidence to prosecute does not amount to evidence that the previous accusation was false (*D* [2009] EWCA Crim 2137). Equally, the decision of the CPS not to prosecute is irrelevant — it is for the court to decide whether there is the necessary evidential basis (*Davarifar* [2009] EWCA Crim 2294). Where there was a trial, the falsity of the accusation cannot be inferred solely on the basis that it resulted in an acquittal (*Gorania* [2017] EWCA Crim 1538; and see also *Citak* [2017] EWCA Crim 1738). In *A* [2012] EWCA Crim 1273, in which the complainant claimed to have been sexually assaulted on four previous occasions, but there was no evidence to suggest that any of the allegations was false, it was held that the number of allegations alone did not entitle the defence to explore the possibility that they were false.

The principle established in *T* does not extend to cases in which the accused seeks to rely simply on the fact that the complainant made a statement about her previous sexual experience (as when evidence of the fact is said to be relevant to the defence of belief in consent), rather than the truth or falsity of such a statement. Evidence that such a statement was made falls within s. 41(1) (*W* [2004] EWCA Crim 3103).

Lifting the Restriction

The court may give leave in relation to any evidence or question only on an application made by or on behalf of the accused (YJCEA 1999, s. 41(2)). The application shall be heard in private and in the absence of the complainant (s. 43(1)). After the application has been determined, the court must state in open court (but in the absence of the jury, if there is one) its reasons for giving or refusing leave and, if leave is given, the extent to which the evidence may be adduced or questions asked (s. 43(2)). The court may not give leave in relation to any evidence or question unless it is satisfied that s. 41(3) or (5) applies (s. 41(2)(a)) and that a refusal 'might have the result of rendering unsafe a conclusion of the jury or (as the case may be) the court on any relevant issue in the case' (s. 41(2)(b)). A 'relevant issue' means any issue falling to be proved by the prosecution or defence in the trial of the accused (s. 42(1)(a)). The test in s. 41(2)(b) must always be met. The test will be satisfied, it is submitted, when to disallow the evidence or question would be to prevent the jurors (or court) from taking into account material which might cause them to come to a different conclusion on a relevant issue. If this is correct, the test in s. 41(2)(b) is not particularly onerous: the judge need only be satisfied that a refusal might lead the jury to a different conclusion, not that such a consequence is probable. However, the judge is unlikely to be so satisfied where there is other evidence before the jury in support of the conclusion advanced by the defence to which the evidence sought to be admitted under s. 41 adds nothing (*Mokrecovas* [2001] EWCA Crim 1644, [2002] 1 Cr App R 20 (226)) or which is stronger and more compelling than the evidence sought to be adduced under s. 41 (*Bahador* [2005] EWCA Crim 396). Under s. 41(6), for the purposes of s. 41(3) and (5), the evidence or question must relate to a specific instance or specific instances of alleged sexual behaviour on the part of the complainant as opposed to, for example, evidence or a question to the effect that the complainant was promiscuous or a prostitute. Furthermore, in the case of a prostitute, information contained by way of a list of previous convictions for prostitution is incapable of fulfilling the requirements of s. 41(6); otherwise any encounter could fall under s. 41(6) if it could be assigned a date and time (*White* [2004] EWCA Crim 946, a decision under s. 41(3)(c) and considered at **F7.45**). **F7.32**

The operation of s. 41 involves, not the exercise of judicial discretion, but the making of a judgement whether to admit or exclude evidence which is relevant or asserted by the defence to be relevant. If it is relevant, then subject to s. 41(4) (see **F7.34**) and assuming that the criteria for admitting the evidence are established (see **F7.34** to **F7.46**), all the evidence relevant to the issues may be adduced. As part of exercising control over the case, the judge must ensure that a complainant is not unnecessarily humiliated or cross-examined with inappropriate aggression, or treated otherwise than with proper courtesy, but this does not permit the judge, by way of a general discretion, to prevent the proper deployment of evidence admissible under s. 41 merely because it comes in a stark, uncompromising form (*F* [2005] EWCA Crim 493, [2005] 1 WLR 2848, where the evidence included videotapes of the complainant stripping and masturbating). In *T* [2012] EWCA Crim 2358 it was held that the judge has no discretion to exclude evidence admissible under s. 41 and therefore cannot exclude where such evidence has been raised without any advance notice, a matter that goes to the weight to be attached to it. For the procedure to be followed on applications under s. 41, see **F7.47**. **F7.33**

In *Evans* [2016] EWCA Crim 452, [2017] 1 Cr App R 13 (181), it was argued that where leave is given to lift the restriction and under cross-examination the complainant denies the sexual behaviour, evidence to contradict her would go to her credit and would therefore be inadmissible under the rule of finality of answers to questions on collateral matters (see **F7.48**). The argument was rejected on the basis that if the evidence went solely or mainly to the complainant's credit, it would be prohibited by s. 41(4) (see **F7.34** to **F7.36**) and where leave is given under s. 41(2) and (3) clear provision is made for both the asking of questions and the calling of evidence.

Section 41(3) and (4): Evidence or a Question Relating to a Relevant Issue

F7.34 Section 41(3) of the YJCEA 1999 is set out at **F7.27**. In s. 41, 'issue of consent' means any issue as to whether the complainant in fact consented to the conduct constituting the offence with which the accused is charged and accordingly does not include any issue as to the belief of the accused that the complainant so consented (s. 42(1)(b)).

Section 41(4) provides as follows:

> For the purposes of subsection (3) no evidence or question shall be regarded as relating to a relevant issue in the case if it appears to the court to be reasonable to assume that the purpose (or main purpose) for which it would be adduced or asked is to establish or elicit material for impugning the credibility of the complainant as a witness.

Section 41(4) applies only where 'the purpose (or main purpose)' for which the evidence is adduced or the question is asked is to impugn the credibility of the complainant. An example is furnished by *Islam* [2012] EWCA Crim 3106. On a charge of rape, the defence being consent, the defence wished to question the complainant about her flirtatious behaviour towards a number of other men in a bar a few hours before the alleged offence, with a view to suggesting that she was 'up for sex'. The trial judge ruled that the questions did not pass the test under s. 41(2) and fell foul of s. 41(4), having as their main purpose the intention of impugning the credibility of the complainant as a witness by reason of her unchaste behaviour. The Court of Appeal upheld the ruling. The questions about the complainant's behaviour and mood in the company of young friends in a bar laid no basis for saying that she would be 'up for sex' with a complete stranger a few hours later. The questioning involved an implied allegation of wanton promiscuity which the broad intention of s. 41 was designed to restrict.

F7.35 In one sense, any evidence which directly challenges the evidence of a complainant, or seeks to demonstrate a malicious motive, involves an attack on her credibility. However, merely because evidence may impugn the complainant's credibility, it does not follow that the purpose or the main purpose for deploying it is to do so (Judge LJ in *F* [2005] EWCA Crim 493, [2005] 1 WLR 2848 at [27]). In *Martin* [2004] EWCA Crim 916, [2004] 2 Cr App R 22 (354), a case of indecent assault involving enforced oral sex, D said that the complainant had fabricated her evidence because he had rejected her advances. The trial judge allowed the defence to question her about his allegation that two days earlier she had pestered him for sex. The Court of Appeal held that the defence should also have been allowed to question her about his allegation that on the earlier occasion she had performed an act of oral sex upon him, after which he had rejected her. It was held that, although one purpose of such questioning would have been to impugn the credibility of the complainant, it would also have gone to D's credibility and strengthened the defence case of fabrication, because the jury might have interpreted a rejection after the performance of oral sex as more hurtful than rejection after mere verbal advances.

F7.36 The application of s. 41(4) gives rise to real difficulties in cases where, as is often the case, the difference between questions going to credit and questions going to the issue barely exists (*Funderburk* [1990] 2 All ER 482 at **F7.49**). As Lord Hutton said, in the context of issues of consent, in *A (No. 2)* (at [138]):

> Issues of consent and issues of credibility may well run so close to each other as almost to coincide. A very sharp knife may be required to separate what may be admitted from what may not. The purpose of subsection (4) may be taken to be the abolition of the false idea that a history of sexual behaviour in some way was relevant to credit. The recognition of that myth as heresy is to be welcomed. But the subsection may have to be carefully handled in order to secure that the myth remains buried in the past and at the same time secure the availability of evidence of sexual behaviour which is properly admissible as bearing on the issue of consent. [Cf. Lord Hope at [76] and [95].]

Section 41(3)(a): A Relevant Issue Other than Consent

If the defence is that there was no sexual contact of any kind, the previous sexual history of the complainant has no bearing on it and therefore cannot relate to the issue for the purposes of the YJCEA 1999, s. 41(3)(a) (*JG* [2018] EWCA Crim 1318). It could have a bearing on the complainant's motive for fabrication, but not where, as in *Moody* [2019] EWCA Crim 1222, the suggested motive was extremely speculative and lacking any evidential basis. Examples of issues which fall within s. 41(3)(a) would include (a) the defence of reasonable belief in consent; (b) that the complainant was biased against the accused or had a motive to fabricate the evidence; (c) that there is an alternative explanation for the physical conditions on which the Crown relies to establish that sexual intercourse took place; and (d) especially in the case of young complainants, that the detail of their account must have come from some other sexual activity which provides an explanation for their knowledge of that activity (per Lord Hope in *A (No. 2)* [2001] UKHL 25, [2002] 1 AC 45 at [79]). As to the example in (b) above, in an indictment containing counts of indecent assault and rape, evidence of bias or a motive to fabricate in relation to the rape may also be relevant to the assaults, if they are sufficiently intertwined with the rape (*F* [2008] EWCA Crim 2859 and cf. *L* [2015] EWCA Crim 741). As to the example in (d) above, it seems that it is confined to young complainants. In *M* [2005] EWCA Crim 3376, it was held that an application to cross-examine the 14-year-old complainant about possible sexual intercourse with a boy from school had been properly refused on the basis that, by reason of the complainant's age and the way of children of her age, she could have acquired her knowledge of sexual intercourse through conversations with friends. **F7.37**

In cases of rape, when considering the effect of a complainant's past sexual behaviour upon the accused's belief that the complainant was consenting to intercourse, there is a difference between believing that the complainant is consenting to intercourse, which is relevant, and believing that the complainant will consent, which is not relevant (*Barton* (1987) 85 Cr App R 5, a decision relating to a defence of *mistaken* belief in consent decided under ss. 1(2) and 2 of the Sexual Offences (Amendment) Act 1976). This distinction remains valid in relation to a defence of *reasonable* belief in consent, for the purposes of the YJCEA 1999, s. 41 (*Winter* [2008] EWCA Crim 3 at [28]). Each case, however, turns on its own facts and, in an appropriate case, belief that the complainant will consent may be a 'relevant issue in the case' for the purposes of s. 41, as when, without the evidence of the complainant's sexual behaviour, the jury may infer from the other evidence that the accused's intention from the outset was to have intercourse with the complainant with or without her consent (*Gjoni* [2014] EWCA Crim 691; cf. *Steltner* [2018] EWCA Crim 1479: without more, the fact that the complainant may have experienced sexual activity in the past does not support an assertion by D that she would consent to the same activity with him). In *Gabbai* [2019] EWCA Crim 2287, [2020] 4 WLR 65, there was material to the effect that the complainant often engaged in sex when she was at least ambiguous as to consent 'but did not say no' and that she had given a history of rapes but had never pursued a complaint of rape. It was held that this material bore on the issue of D's reasonable belief in consent, potentially confirming both his evidence of her behaviour during the alleged offences and video evidence of that behaviour. **F7.38**

In *T* [2012] EWCA Crim 2358, the defence sought to introduce evidence of a photograph allegedly sent to D around Valentine's Day, showing the complainant dressed in a bikini or underwear. It was held that the evidence went to a relevant issue other than consent, because the defence case was that the complainant was interested in him, he was not interested in her, and the motive for her false allegation was her affront at his lack of interest. See also *F* [2005] EWCA Crim 493, [2005] 1 WLR 2848, a case of alleged childhood sexual abuse, the defence being that the complaints were false and motivated by a desire for revenge after D had ended an adult sexual relationship with the complainant, where it was held that evidence relating to the complainant's erotic and sometimes pornographic behaviour in the course of the adult relationship was relevant to the alleged desire for revenge and the critical question whether there had been childhood abuse. **F7.39**

Section 41(3)(b) and (c): An Issue of Consent

F7.40 It is plain from the wording of the YJCEA 1999, s. 41(3)(b) and (c), that in a case in which consent is in issue leave cannot be given in relation to any evidence or question about sexual behaviour of the complainant which amounts to *nothing more* than previous voluntary sexual intercourse with the accused (see further *A (No. 2)* [2001] UKHL 25, [2002] 1 AC 45 at F7.44). Section 41(3), in this respect, operates to reverse the decision in *Riley* (1887) 18 QBD 481. However, where the complainant and the accused are married or have cohabited, the tribunal of fact may well infer that there has been such voluntary sexual intercourse, and it is submitted that in these circumstances the trial judge, in the spirit of the new legislative framework, should direct the jury that they should draw no such inference because, without more, previous acts of voluntary sexual intercourse can have no bearing on any relevant issue in the case.

F7.41 **Section 41(3)(b)** Section 41(3)(b) covers behaviour such as sexual advances made by the complainant towards the accused or others shortly before or after 'the event which is the subject matter of the charge against the accused' and behaviour indicative of consent at the time of 'the event'. The evidence or question must relate to sexual behaviour of the complainant alleged to have taken place at or about the same time as 'the event', but excluding anything alleged to have taken place as part of the event which is the subject-matter of the charge (s. 42(1)(c)). The distinction between sexual behaviour which took place 'at ... the same time as the event' and such behaviour which took place 'as part of the event' is far from clear. The phrase 'at or about the same time as the event' introduces an extremely narrow temporal restriction. The use of the words 'or about' provides a degree of elasticity, but cannot be strained to extend the restriction to days, weeks, or months. The explanatory note to the Act prepared by the Home Office states that it is expected that the phrase will generally be interpreted no more widely than 24 hours before or after the offence (*A (No. 2)* [2001] UKHL 25, [2002] 1 AC 45 at [9], [40], [82] and [132]). An example of the application of s. 41(3)(b) in a rape case would be where it is alleged that the complainant invited the accused to have sexual intercourse with her earlier in the evening (per Lord Steyn in *A (No. 2)* at [40]). See also, *sed quaere*, *Mukadi* [2003] EWCA Crim 3765.

F7.42 **Section 41(3)(c)** Section 41(3)(c) covers any sexual behaviour of the complainant on another occasion which is, in any respect, so similar in nature to her sexual behaviour which, according to the defence, took place as part of the event which is the subject-matter of the charge, or shortly before or after that 'event', that the similarity cannot reasonably be explained as a coincidence. The sexual behaviour could have been with the accused or another and could have taken place before or after the 'event'. See *T* [2004] EWCA Crim 1220, [2004] 2 Cr App R 32 (551), considered at F7.43. In *Gabbai* [2019] EWCA Crim 2287, [2020] 4 WLR 65, it was held that a chance meeting between strangers leading to an immediate sexual encounter, together with behaviour in the course of which the complainant 'did not say no' met the high threshold for similarity required by s. 41(3)(c), but was inadmissible because it did not meet the requirements of either s. 41(3)(c)(i) or (ii).

F7.43 As to the requirement that the similarity cannot reasonably be explained as a coincidence, the restriction is significantly tighter than the test for 'similar fact evidence' laid down in *DPP v P* [1991] 2 AC 447 (per Lord Hope in *A (No. 2)* [2001] UKHL 25, [2002] 1 AC 45 at [83]), but the standard is something short of striking similarity (per Lord Clyde in *A (No. 2)* at [133]). Lord Clyde said (at [135]):

> It is only a similarity that is required, not an identity. Moreover the words 'in any respect' deserve to be stressed. On one view any single factor of similarity might suffice ... provided that it is not a matter of coincidence. That the behaviour was with the same person, the defendant, must be at least a relevant consideration. But if the identity of the defendant was alone sufficient as the non-coincidental factor, that would seem to open the way in almost every case for a complete enquiry into the whole of the complainant's sexual behaviour with the defendant at least in the recent past, and that can hardly have been the intention of the provision. What must be found is a similarity in some other or additional respect. Further, the similarity must be such as cannot reasonably be

> explained as coincidence. To my mind that does not necessitate that the similarity has to be in some rare or bizarre conduct. So long as the particular factor is of a significance which goes beyond the realm of what could reasonably be explained as a coincidence, it should suffice.

In reaching a decision, regard may be had not only to the degree of similarity of the sexual behaviour but also to any dissimilarities in the surrounding circumstances. In *Aidarus* [2018] EWCA Crim 2073, in which D alleged that, prior to consensual sexual intercourse, the complainant had performed oral sex on him, which the complainant denied, evidence that she had performed oral sex on a boy a few months before the offence charged and on a number of men two years after the offence charged was held to be inadmissible because of dissimilarities in the surrounding circumstances and context of the behaviour on those other occasions.

An example of a case falling within s. 41(3)(c) would be a rape case in which D, who says that after consensual intercourse the complainant tried to blackmail him by alleging rape, wishes to cross-examine her about a previous similar attempt to blackmail him (per Lord Steyn in *A (No. 2)* at [42]). In *T* [2004] EWCA Crim 1220, [2004] 2 Cr App R 32 (551), D was convicted of rape, indecent assault and false imprisonment. The complainant had previously been in a relationship with D. Shortly after the relationship ended they agreed to meet in a park. They went inside a climbing frame, where the sexual acts took place. The issue was consent. The trial judge refused leave to cross-examine on, or adduce evidence of, the fact that three weeks prior to the alleged offences D and the complainant had had consensual sex in the same climbing frame adopting the same positions, both standing and the complainant facing away from D. He ruled that the behaviour was insufficiently relevant and that he was constrained by the temporal limitation of s. 41(3)(c)(ii). Allowing the appeal, it was held that the trial judge should have considered the matter under s. 41(3)(c)(i), which had no time constraint, and that had he done so he might have ruled the evidence admissible. As to s. 41(3)(c)(ii), the Court of Appeal observed that, although it contained words which at first sight might appear to contain temporal limitations, it was doubtful that that was correct when s. 41(3)(c) was construed as a whole.

The similarity test was not met in *MM* [2011] EWCA Crim 1291, where the rape took place in the complainant's bedroom while other members of her family were in other parts of the home, and four months earlier she had engaged in consensual sexual intercourse with D, also in her bedroom, but only after having sent her brother out of the home. See also *CB* [2020] EWCA Crim 790 at **F7.46**. Nor was the test met in *G* [2016] EWCA Crim 1633, [2017] 1 Cr App R 27 (413), where the Court of Appeal also relied upon the absence of a 'sufficient chronological nexus', the alleged consensual intercourse having taken place about a year before, and also several weeks after, the offence. See also *C* [2016] EWCA Crim 1631, where the allegedly consensual sexual activity with D occurred some seven months after the offence and the Court was of the opinion that to admit the evidence risked reinforcing the stereotypical and potentially false view that in a complex relationship no victim of a serious sexual assault would subsequently instigate and engage in consensual sexual activity.

Decisions on similarity for the purposes of s. 41(3)(c) are sometimes easy but, where that is not the case, the Court of Appeal will not interfere if the decision reached was open to the judge and within the margin of judgement permitted (*Harris* [2009] EWCA Crim 434).

Section 41 and the Right to a Fair Trial

Sexual Behaviour with the Accused In *A (No. 2)* [2001] UKHL 25, [2002] 1 AC 45, the House of Lords held that although prima facie a sexual relationship between an accused and complainant may be relevant to the issue of consent so as to render its exclusion under s. 41 a contravention of the accused's right to a fair trial under the ECHR, Article 6, it is possible under the HRA 1998, s. 3, to read s. 41, and in particular s. 41(3)(c), as subject to the implied provision that evidence or questioning which is required to ensure a fair trial under Article 6 should not be excluded. In the opinion of Lord Steyn (at [46]), an opinion shared by all their lordships, **F7.44**

if a trial judge finds it necessary to apply the interpretative obligation under s. 3 to the words of s. 41(3)(c), those words should be construed by applying the following test:

> ... due regard always being paid to the importance of seeking to protect the complainant from indignity and from humiliating questions, the test of admissibility is whether the evidence (and questioning in relation to it) is nevertheless so relevant to the issue of consent that to exclude it would endanger the fairness of the trial under [ECHR, Article 6].

According to Lord Steyn (at [31]), as a matter of common sense a prior sexual relationship between the complainant and the accused may, depending on the circumstances, be relevant to the issue of consent. Where there has been a recent close and affectionate relationship between the complainant and the accused, it is probable that the evidence will be relevant, not of course to prove consent, but to show her specific mindset towards the accused, i.e. her affection for him. On the other hand, evidence of the kind which the accused in *A (No. 2)* wished to give, namely evidence of no more than some isolated acts of intercourse, albeit fairly recent, but without the background of an affectionate relationship, is probably not relevant (Lord Hutton at [151]–[154] and Lord Steyn at [31]). *A (No. 2)* was followed in *R* [2003] EWCA Crim 2754.

F7.45 **Sexual Behaviour with Third Parties** *A (No. 2)* [2001] UKHL 25, [2002] 1 AC 45 was distinguished in *White* [2004] EWCA Crim 946, in which D, convicted of rape, said that the complainant had asked him for money, which he had refused to give, and that after consensual intercourse he awoke to find her with his wallet. The trial judge refused an application to cross-examine the complainant on her previous and contemporaneous activities as a prostitute, the fact that she worked as a prostitute being of no relevance to the issue of consent as it was no part of D's case that he had offered payment. Dismissing the appeal, it was held that in the present day a prostitute was as entitled as any other to say 'no' and the fact that she was a prostitute did not mean that she was more likely to say 'yes' to sex. The bare fact that she was a prostitute was irrelevant to the issue of consent: there had to be something about the specific circumstances that had probative force and was so similar to the conduct complained of as to be beyond coincidence.

In *A (No. 2)* [2001] UKHL 25, [2002] 1 AC 45, Lord Steyn was of the opinion (at [30]) that evidence of sexual behaviour between the complainant and persons other than the accused would almost always be irrelevant and for Lord Hope (at [77]) such evidence would be harder to justify, on grounds of relevance, than evidence about sexual behaviour with the accused. In *White*, Laws LJ said (at [35]): '*R v A* is not authority for any wider reading of s. 41 by force of s. 3 of the Human Rights Act in a case where sexual acts of the complainant with men other than the Appellant are sought to be adduced than is justified by the application of conventional canons of construction. At the least it would take a very special case to accommodate evidence of such acts in circumstances in which they would not be accommodated by an ordinary reading of the section.'

Evans [2016] EWCA Crim 452, [2017] 1 Cr App R 13 (181) appears to be such a special case. D was convicted of rape on the basis that V was incapable of consenting to intercourse. Both had been drinking. V could not remember what had happened and did not allege that she had been raped or was incapable of consent. D volunteered that intercourse had taken place, his defence being consent or reasonable belief in consent. On a reference by the CCRC, the Court of Appeal considered fresh evidence under the Criminal Appeal Act 1995, s. 9. This included evidence from two men concerning similar sexual behaviour by V with each of them, separately, before and after the alleged offence. On each occasion, V had been drinking, had instigated sexual activity, had directed her sexual partner into the same position and had used the same sort of words of encouragement. It was held that the evidence was 'arguably' sufficiently similar to come within the terms of s. 41(3)(c)(i). However, it was also held that the case was 'potentially' an example of a rare case of the kind envisaged by Lord Steyn in *A (No. 2)*, in which evidence of sexual activity with someone other than the accused would be relevant. This appears to be the true *ratio* of the case, because despite the earlier use of the word 'potentially', the Court concluded that: 'The requirements of section 41 must give way, as was held in *A (No. 2)*, to the requirements of a fair trial. Relevant and admissible evidence cannot be excluded.' It is submitted, however, that the case is unlikely to be of any value as a precedent, having been decided on its own unique and very peculiar facts. In *G* [2016] EWCA Crim 1633, [2017] 1 Cr App R 27 (413), a decision after *Evans*, the Court of Appeal, while acknowledging that s. 41(3)(c) does not require striking similarity, nonetheless stressed that it does impose a high threshold.

Section 41(5): Evidence or a Question Relating to Evidence Adduced by the Prosecution

Section 41(5) applies if the evidence or question: F7.46

(a) relates to any evidence adduced by the prosecution about any sexual behaviour of the complainant (including anything alleged to have taken place as part of the event which is the subject-matter of the charge — see s. 42(1)(c)); and
(b) in the opinion of the court, would go no further than is necessary to enable the evidence adduced by the prosecution to be rebutted or explained by or on behalf of the accused.

If, for example, the accused denies any sexual activity with the complainant, and she alleges that he was responsible for her pregnancy, evidence that she had previously attributed her pregnancy to someone else will be admissible in rebuttal (*F* [2008] EWCA Crim 2859). Similarly, if in a rape case, the complainant gives evidence that she has only ever had consensual sexual intercourse with her husband, evidence or questions might be permitted about previous consensual intercourse with the accused or another person before or after the alleged rape. However, if consent is in issue and there is evidence that the complainant was a virgin, s. 41(5) cannot be used to introduce evidence of previous digital penetration, because the evidence of virginity does not carry with it the implication that the complainant would not have consented to sexual activity other than sexual intercourse (*Steltner* [2018] EWCA Crim 1479). It seems that if the complainant gives evidence of having been in a happy long-term relationship with her partner at the time of the alleged offence, evidence that she was having an affair with another man will not be admissible by way of explanation or rebuttal (*Winter* [2008] EWCA Crim 3 at [31]). In *CB* [2020] EWCA Crim 790, a case of rape involving unprotected sex, the defence being consent, it was held that the question, in cross-examination of the accused, whether prior to the sexual intercourse there had been any discussion about the use of protection, was not about sexual behaviour of the complainant. Therefore s. 41(5) could not be used to introduce evidence of a previous incident in which the complainant had had sex without a condom.

In cases in which there is evidence that the complainant made a statement about her sexual behaviour, s. 41(5) will not apply where the statement is not relied upon by the prosecution for its truth. In *Aidarus* [2018] EWCA Crim 2073, D alleged that prior to consensual sexual intercourse, the complainant had performed oral sex on him, which she denied. In her ABE interview, she said that D had asked her for oral sex, and had also asked whether she had performed oral sex on previous occasions, which she had denied. It was held that evidence of her previous experience of oral sex was inadmissible because: the statement denying previous experience of oral sex was admitted as evidence of what she had said, not as to the truth of what she had said; it was no part of the prosecution case that she had had no previous experience of oral sex; and the defence case was that the statement was not made at all.

The phrase 'evidence adduced by the prosecution' in s. 41(5)(a) covers not only the evidence-in-chief of prosecution witnesses and the evidence of defence witnesses under cross- examination by the prosecution, but also the evidence of prosecution witnesses under cross-examination by the defence, provided that it is not deliberately elicited by defence counsel and was potentially damaging to the defence case (*Hamadi* [2007] EWCA Crim 3048). Section 41(5)(a) does not cover the evidence of a prosecution witness given in answer to questioning by the trial judge, but if such questioning and evidence are seriously prejudicial to the defence and such as to impact on the fairness of the trial, this may lead to the discharge of the jury (*JG* [2018] EWCA Crim 1318). Where evidence is adduced by the prosecution about sexual behaviour of the complainant and they also have material that would enable the evidence to be rebutted, the material should be disclosed to the defence (*A-M* [2013] EWCA Crim 2622).

In *F* [2005] EWCA Crim 493, [2005] 1 WLR 2848 the Court of Appeal noted (at [28]) that s. 41(4) applies only for the purposes of s. 41(3) and does not apply for the purposes of s. 41(5).

Procedure on Applications under s. 41

F7.47 Where an accused wants to introduce evidence or cross-examine a witness about a complainant's sexual behaviour under YJCEA 1999, s. 41, the defence must apply in writing. CrimPR Part 22 (see Supplement, **R22.1** *et seq.*) sets out: the procedure for making such an application; the time at which such an application should be made and its contents and service; the obligations of the court and the prosecutor to complainants; and the court's power to give directions ('ground rules') for the appropriate treatment and questioning of a witness about any sexual behaviour of the complainant. See also CrimPD V, paras 22A.1 to 22A.8 (see Supplement, **CPD.22A**). Failure to comply with these procedural rules makes it more likely that things will go wrong at the trial, either because the statutory protection given to the complainant will be undermined or because the defence will be prohibited from pursuing a legitimate line of questioning (*Crossland* [2013] EWCA Crim 2313). For an illustration, see *Andrade* [2015] EWCA Crim 1722.

RULE OF FINALITY OF ANSWERS TO QUESTIONS ON COLLATERAL MATTERS

General Rule

F7.48 The general rule, based on the desirability of avoiding a multiplicity of essentially irrelevant issues, is that evidence is not admissible to contradict answers given by a witness to questions put in cross-examination which concern collateral matters, i.e. matters which go merely to credit but which are otherwise irrelevant to the issues in the case (*Harris v Tippett* (1811) 2 Camp 637; *Palmer v Trower* (1852) 8 Exch 247). However, insofar as the questions relate to the witness's previous misconduct or disposition towards misconduct, some of the authorities, such as *Edwards* [1991] 2 All ER 266 (see **F7.49**), must be treated with caution: whether questions should be asked, or evidence adduced, concerning a witness's bad character is now governed by the CJA 2003, ss. 100 and 101 (see **F15.8** and **F13.15**). In *A-G v Hitchcock* (1847) 1 Exch 91, Pollock CB said (at p. 99): 'The test whether a matter is collateral or not is this: if the answer of a witness is a matter which you would be allowed on your own part to prove in evidence — if it have such a connection with the issues that you would be allowed to give it in evidence — then it is a matter on which you may contradict him.' The narrowness and difficulty of this distinction may be illustrated by comparing the decision in *A-G v Hitchcock* with the decisions in *TM* [2004] EWCA Crim 2085 and *Busby* (1981) 75 Cr App R 79. In *A-G v Hitchcock* a maltster was charged with having used a cistern for the making of malt in breach of certain statutory requirements. A prosecution witness, having sworn that the cistern had been used, was asked in cross-examination whether he had not said to one Cook that the Excise officers had offered him £20 to give evidence that the cistern had been used. Upon denial of this allegation, it was held that the defendant was not allowed to call Cook to contradict the witness, because proof that a bribe was offered to the witness and not accepted was irrelevant to the matter in issue. In *TM* certain sexual offences came to light when a private investigator and inquiry agents, being used for the purposes of family proceedings by a man, S, whose wife had been having an affair with D, interviewed the victims of the offences. D denied all the offences and said that S had set out to destroy him and had induced the victims to give evidence against him by offers of financial reward. It was held that D should have been allowed to call a witness to give evidence that she had been approached by the private investigator and when she had refused to give adverse information had been told that S had unlimited funds for the right information. When viewed in isolation, the witness's evidence was collateral, but although 'borderline', it was relevant as showing that the *victims* might have been offered money or been influenced by the offer of money. In *Busby*, a prosecution for burglary and handling, police officers were cross-examined to the effect that they had fabricated statements attributed to D and indicative of his guilt, and had threatened W, a potential defence witness, to stop him giving evidence. These allegations were denied. The trial judge ruled that the defence could not call W to give evidence that he had been threatened by the officers, because this would go solely to their credit. Allowing the appeal against conviction, the Court of Appeal held that the trial judge had erred: the evidence was relevant to an issue which had to be tried, because, if true, it showed that the police were prepared to go to improper lengths in order to secure a conviction, which would have supported the defence case that the statements attributed to D had been fabricated. See also *Marsh* (1985) 83 Cr App R 165 and cf. *Phillips* (1936) 26 Cr App R 17, at F7.59.

In *Funderburk* [1990] 2 All ER 482, at p. 591, *Busby* was treated as having created a new *exception* to the rule of finality. However, in *Edwards* [1991] 2 All ER 266, it was held that the fact that the police were allegedly prepared to prevent the potential witness from giving evidence, came within the exception of bias (see F7.57); and that if the decision could not be explained on that basis, it was inconsistent with the general rule and inconsistent with the decision in *Harris v Tippett* itself (where the facts were not dissimilar to those in *Busby*). In *Edwards* a number of officers involved in the case had given evidence in other trials, which had resulted in acquittal, in circumstances which tended to cast doubt on their reliability. In the other trials, evidence showed that some interview notes were inaccurate and that others had seemingly been rewritten to include admissions which did not exist in the originals. It was held that: F7.49

(a) it could be put to the officers in cross-examination that they had given evidence in the previous trials, that in each trial there was an issue as to whether alleged confessions had been fabricated and that each trial had ended in acquittal, because there was a sufficient connection between the evidence given by the officers in those trials and their eventual outcome to entitle such cross-examination on the question of their credibility in the instant case; but
(b) if the officers denied such allegations, they could not be proved by evidence in rebuttal, because the questioning would be as to credit alone, a collateral issue, and would not fall within any of the exceptions to the rule of finality.

Whether a particular item of evidence goes to an issue before the court or is merely collateral can be a question of some nicety. It only adds to the difficulty, it is submitted, to suggest that whether the rule of finality applies may turn on whether the matter which the cross-examining party seeks to prove is a single and distinct fact which is easy of proof rather than a broad and complex issue which is difficult of proof (*S* [1992] Crim LR 307). In *Funderburk* the Court of Appeal urged a flexible approach to the rule, on the basis that a general rule designed to serve the interests of justice should not be used to defeat justice by an over-pedantic approach. Henry J observed (at p. 598D), 'The utility of the test may lie in the fact that the answer is an instinctive one based on the prosecutor's and the court's sense of fair play rather than any philosophic or analytic process' (but cf. per Evans LJ in *Neale* [1998] Crim LR 737). Accordingly it has been held that the issue of sufficient relevance is one for the trial judge and that the Court of Appeal will only interfere with a decision to exclude evidence as being insufficiently irrelevant if it is either wrong in principle or plainly wrong as being outside that wide ambit (*Somers* [1999] Crim LR 744).

The Court of Appeal in *Funderburk* also agreed with the editors of *Cross on Evidence* (7th edn, 1990, at p. 322) that where the disputed issue is a sexual one between two persons in private, the difference between questions going to credit and questions going to the issue is reduced to vanishing-point because sexual intercourse, whether or not consensual, most often takes place in private and leaves few visible traces of having occurred, so that the evidence is often effectively limited to that of the parties, and much is likely to depend upon the balance of credibility between them. See further at F7.53. F7.50

Previous Inconsistent Statements

F7.51 If a witness under cross-examination admits to having made a previous oral or written statement inconsistent with his or her testimony, no further proof of the statement is required or, it seems, allowed (*P (GR)* [1998] Crim LR 663). However, if the witness denies having made such a statement, and the statement is relevant to an issue in the case, then it may be proved. The statement may be proved even if contained in a letter sent by an accused's solicitor to the CPS suggesting that the accused might plead guilty to a lesser offence, because there is nothing in criminal law akin to without prejudice privilege (*Hayes* [2004] EWCA Crim 2844, [2005] 1 Cr App R 33 (557)).

Proof of a previous inconsistent statement is governed by the Criminal Procedure Act 1865, ss. 4 and 5. Section 4 applies to both oral and written statements, but s. 5 applies to written statements only (*Derby Magistrates' Court, ex parte B* [1996] AC 487).

Concerning the cross-examination of children and vulnerable witnesses about previous inconsistent statements, see also **F7.10**.

F7.52 Oral and Written Statements under s. 4

Criminal Procedure Act 1865, s. 4

> If a witness, upon cross-examination as to a former statement made by him relative to the subject-matter of the indictment or proceeding, and inconsistent with his present testimony, does not distinctly admit that he has made such statement, proof may be given that he did in fact make it; but before such proof can be given the circumstances of the supposed statement, sufficient to designate the particular occasion, must be mentioned to the witness, and he must be asked whether or not he has made such statement.

Section 4 is not confined to previous statements on oath (*Hart* (1957) 42 Cr App R 47, at p. 50; and *O'Neill* [1969] Crim LR 260 — oral statement made to the police). A witness who 'does not distinctly admit' to the making of the previous statement would include, in addition to a witness who denies such a statement, a witness who claims to have no recollection of it, who is equivocal on the subject, or who declines to answer. However, s. 4 does not apply to a party's own hostile witness. Proof of the previous inconsistent statement of a hostile witness requires the leave of the judge under s. 3 of the 1865 Act (see **F6.52**), a requirement which cannot be circumvented by reliance on s. 4 of the Act (*Booth* (1981) 74 Cr App R 123).

F7.53 **'Relative to the Subject-matter'** Whether a statement is 'relative to the subject-matter of the indictment or proceeding' is a matter within the discretion of the judge (*Bashir* [1969] 3 All ER 692 per Veale J at p. 1306; and *Hart* (1957) 42 Cr App R 47 per Devlin J at p. 50). For the difficulties to which the issue may give rise, see *Funderburk* [1990] 2 All ER 482. F was convicted on three counts of sexual intercourse with a girl of 13. In her evidence, the girl gave evidence of a number of acts of intercourse with F, the description of the first act clearly describing the loss of her virginity. The defence was that the child was lying and in order to explain how so young a child could, if she were lying, have given such detailed and varied accounts of the acts of intercourse, wished to show that she was sexually experienced and had either transposed to F experiences which she had had with others and/or fantasised about experience with F. For this purpose, the defence wished to put to her that she had told a potential defence witness, P, that before the first incident complained of she had had sexual intercourse with two named men. The defence then wished to call P to give evidence of the conversation. The trial judge, applying the test in s. 4 of the 1865 Act, ruled that the complainant's previous inconsistent statement could not be put to her, nor could P be called, because the complainant's virginity was immaterial to the question whether F had had sexual intercourse with her and therefore was not 'relative to the subject-matter of the indictment'. On the question whether the previous inconsistent statement could be put in cross-examination *to challenge the complainant's credibility*, it was held that there was nothing in s. 4 to prevent this, even if, under s. 4, evidence of the making of that statement would not be allowed because it was not relative to the subject-matter of the indictment. The test for allowing cross-examination *as to credit* was that suggested by Lawton J in *Sweet-Escott* (1971) 55 Cr App R 316: how might the matters put to the witness affect his or her standing with the jury after cross-examination (see **F7.21**). Applying that test, the cross-examination should have been allowed since the jury might reasonably have wished to reappraise her evidence about the loss of her virginity and her credibility if they had heard of her previous statements regarding her earlier sexual experiences. On the question whether, if the complainant had been cross-examined about the conversation with P and she had denied making the previous statements, the defence would have been entitled to call P to prove the conversation, it was held that the previous statements were relative to the subject-matter of the indictment and therefore P could have been called to prove them under s. 4. Where the disputed issue is a sexual one between two persons in private, the difference between questions going to credit and questions going to the issue is reduced to vanishing-point. On the way the prosecution had presented the evidence, the challenge to the loss of virginity went far beyond a mere question of the complainant's credibility and was sufficiently closely related to the subject-matter of the indictment for justice to require investigation for the basis of such a challenge. (Cf. *Neale* [1998] Crim LR 737, *Usayi* [2017] EWCA Crim 1394 and also, *sed quaere Gibson* [1993] Crim LR 453.) See also *Nagrecha* [1997] 2 Cr App R 401. N was accused of indecently assaulting the complainant. There were no witnesses. Under cross-examination, the complainant denied that she had made allegations of sexual impropriety against other men. It was held that evidence of the making of the other allegations was admissible because it went to the central issue of whether there had been any indecent assault.

Written Statements under s. 5 F7.54

Criminal Procedure Act 1865, s. 5

> A witness may be cross-examined as to previous statements made by him in writing or reduced into writing relative to the subject matter of the indictment or proceeding, without such writing being shown to him; but if it is intended to contradict such witness by the writing, his attention must, before such contradictory proof can be given, be called to those parts of the writing which are to be used for the purpose of so contradicting him: provided always, that it shall be competent for the judge, at any time during the trial, to require the production of the writing for his inspection, and he may thereupon make such use of it for the purposes of the trial as he may think fit.

The first part of s. 5 expressly allows cross-examination on a previous written statement *without* such writing being shown to the witness. However, if counsel proposes to cross-examine in this way, counsel must have the writing present, even if counsel does not intend to *contradict* the witness with it, because under the proviso to s. 5, the judge may require its production for his or her inspection, and may thereupon make such use of it as thought fit (*Anderson* (1929) 21 Cr App R 178). If the writing is shown to the witness, this may be done without putting it in evidence. Thus, counsel may hand the document to the witness, direct the witness to read the relevant part of it to him or herself, and then ask whether the witness wishes to adhere to the testimony. If the witness accepts the truth of the former statement, it becomes part of the witness's evidence; if the witness adheres to the testimony, there is no obligation on the cross-examining party to contradict the witness and put the document in evidence (a course which it may be wise to avoid, especially if the inconsistency relates to some minor matter, and in all other respects the former statement is *consistent* with the witness's evidence). However, if counsel does wish to contradict the witness, counsel must put the document in evidence by reading out aloud the contradictory statement. The statement may then be inspected to see how far the suggested contradiction exists; whether the absence of a particular statement is explained by the context; and whether the discrepancy is only a minute point so that, taken as a whole, the document is more in the nature of confirmation rather than contradiction (see generally *Riley* (1866) 4 F & F 964 per Channell B, and *Wright* (1866) 4 F & F 967). It is open to the judge to allow the whole of the written statement to go before the jury, because under s. 5 the judge may 'make such use of it for the purposes of the trial as he may think fit'. For example, the judge may call attention to F7.55

other parts of the statement to which no reference has been made (*Birch* (1924) 18 Cr App R 26, per Avory J at p. 28). However, the judge has a discretion to allow only part of the statement to go before the jury and therefore, in appropriate circumstances, may permit the jury to see only those parts of the statement upon which the cross-examination was based and not all the other parts relating to other unconnected matters (*Beattie* (1989) 89 Cr App R 302).

F7.56 **Criminal Justice Act 2003, s. 119(1)** Under the CJA 2003, s. 119(1), a previous inconsistent statement that a witness admits to having made, or that is proved by virtue of the Criminal Procedure Act 1865, s. 4 or s. 5, is admissible for the truth of its contents.

Criminal Justice Act 2003, s. 119

(1) If in criminal proceedings a person gives oral evidence and—
 (a) he admits making a previous inconsistent statement or
 (b) a previous inconsistent statement made by him is proved by virtue of section 3, 4 or 5 of the Criminal Procedure Act 1865,

the statement is admissible as evidence of any matter stated in it of which oral evidence by him would be admissible.

The statement is admissible for the truth of its contents as evidence against its maker. Thus if the statement implicates a co-accused, s. 119 does not allow it to be used against the co-accused. However, it may be used, for this purpose, under CJA 2003, s. 114(1)(d) (*Nguyen* [2020] EWCA Crim 140).

A judge should direct a jury that a statement covered by s. 119(1) is evidence in the case, but not that it is just as much evidence as the witness's testimony, because they may reject a statement in evidence and accord it no weight, if they do not consider it to be true. If the previous statement supports the prosecution case, the jury should be directed that it is evidence that they may consider when deciding upon their verdict if they are sure that it is true; but if the previous statement is exculpatory of the accused, the jury should be directed that they may consider it when deciding upon their verdict, if they conclude that it *may* be true (*Billingham* [2009] EWCA Crim 19, [2009] 2 Cr App R 20 (341)).

Where a previous inconsistent statement is admissible under s. 119 on behalf of the prosecution, it may nonetheless be excluded under the PACE 1984, s. 78 (see, e.g., *Coates* [2007] EWCA Crim 1471, [2008] 1 Cr App R 3 (52)).

Bias and Partiality

F7.57 Evidence has always been admissible to contradict a witness's denial of bias or partiality towards one of the parties, and to show that the witness is prejudicial concerning the case being tried (*Mendy* (1976) 64 Cr App R 4, per Geoffrey Lane LJ at p. 6). To the extent that this common-law doctrine allows the introduction of evidence of, or of a disposition towards, misconduct on the part of a witness, it was abolished by the CJA 2003, s. 99. However, much evidence of bias is likely to remain admissible under the doctrine, because it will fall outside the statutory definition of evidence of bad character in s. 98 of the 2003 Act, which excludes 'evidence of, or of a disposition towards misconduct … which has to do with the alleged facts of the offence with which the defendant is charged, or is evidence of misconduct in connection with the investigation or prosecution of that offence'. If the evidence in question is not admissible on that basis, it is nonetheless likely to be admitted under the CJA, s. 100(1)(b), i.e. as evidence of the bad character of a person other than the accused that has substantial probative value in relation to a matter which is in issue in the proceedings and is of substantial importance in the context of the case as a whole (see F15).

F7.58 In *A-G v Hitchcock* (1847) 1 Exch 91, it was held that although evidence is not admissible to contradict a witness's denial of being *offered* a bribe to give false evidence, because this does not show that he or she is not a fair and credible witness, evidence is admissible to rebut a witness's denial of *accepting* such a bribe, because that tends to show the witness's partiality. Pollock CB said: 'A witness may be asked how he stands affected towards one of the parties; and if his relation towards them is such as to prejudice his mind, and fill him with sentiments of revenge and other feelings of a similar kind, and if he denies the fact, evidence may be given to show the state of his mind and feelings.'

In *Shaw* (1888) 16 Cox CC 503, it was held that D may call evidence to contradict a prosecution witness who, in cross-examination, denies having threatened to be revenged on D following a quarrel with him. See also *Whelan* [1996] Crim LR 423. In *Phillips* (1936) 26 Cr App R 17, a case of incest, the principal prosecution witnesses, D's two daughters, were cross-examined on the basis that (a) they had been 'schooled' by their mother into giving false evidence, and (b) they had made admissions that evidence given by them in previous criminal proceedings against their father was false. Both allegations were denied. The trial judge refused to allow the defence to call the woman to whom the admissions were alleged to have been made. Quashing the conviction, the Court of Criminal Appeal held that this evidence should have been admitted because the bias that it would have revealed went to the very foundation of D's defence. **F7.59**

In *Mendy* (1976) 64 Cr App R 4, D was convicted of assault. At her trial, prospective witnesses were kept out of court in accordance with the normal practice. While a police officer was giving evidence, a man in the public gallery was seen taking notes. He was later seen discussing the case with D's husband, apparently describing the officer's evidence to him. The husband, under cross-examination, denied this incident. The Court of Appeal held that the trial judge had properly allowed the prosecution to call evidence in rebuttal: the husband was prepared to lend himself to a scheme, designed to defeat the purpose of keeping prospective witnesses out of court, to enable him the more convincingly to describe how he, and not his wife, had caused the injuries alleged. **F7.60**

Previous Convictions

If a witness, lawfully cross-examined as to a previous conviction, denies it or refuses to answer, it may be proved against the witness under the Criminal Procedure Act 1865, s. 6. **F7.61**

Criminal Procedure Act 1865, s. 6

> If, upon a witness being lawfully questioned as to whether he has been convicted of any felony or misdemeanour, he either denies or does not admit the fact, or refuses to answer, it shall be lawful for the cross-examining party to prove such conviction ...

Someone other than the accused will only be 'lawfully questioned' as to previous convictions if the questions are lawful under the CJA 2003, s. 100 (see **F15**), and an accused will only be 'lawfully questioned' as to previous convictions if the questions are lawful under the CJA 2003, s. 101 (see **F13**). There is an additional restriction in the case of offences committed by the accused when a child (see s. 108 of the 2003 Act, considered at **F13.91**). Under CrimPD V, para. 21A.2 (see Supplement, **CPD.21A**), when considering bad character applications under the CJA 2003, regard should always be had to the general principles of the Rehabilitation of Offenders Act 1974. Under the 1974 Act, in civil proceedings cross-examination of any witness about a spent conviction is prohibited unless the judge is satisfied that it is not possible for justice to be done except by admitting the conviction (ss. 4(1) and 7(3); see **D20.49**). Under the precursor to para. 21A.2, no reference was to be made to a spent conviction if that could reasonably be avoided, but according to *Corelli* [2001] EWCA Crim 974, that test did not operate to remove an unfettered statutory entitlement of a co-accused to cross-examine another co-accused on previous convictions. (The statutory entitlement in that case arose under the Criminal Evidence Act 1898, s. 1(3)(iii); see now the CJA 2003, s. 101(1)(e), considered at **F13.66**.)

In *Smallman* [1982] Crim LR 175, prosecuting counsel, without seeking the leave of the judge, referred to the spent conviction of a defence witness when cross-examining him. The judge directed the jury to leave out of account the prejudice resulting from the reference. The Court of Appeal held that counsel's reference to the spent conviction could not be a ground for quashing an otherwise perfectly proper conviction.

F7.62 As to proof of previous convictions, see the PACE 1984, s. 73, at **F12.1**. Where a witness who is cross-examined on a conviction accepts the conviction but claims to be innocent, the cross-examining party is not entitled to adduce evidence in rebuttal, such as evidence from the victim of the offence on which the witness stands convicted, because such evidence would go solely to credibility (*Irish* [1995] Crim LR 145, applying *Edwards* [1991] 2 All ER 266, considered at **F7.49**).

Medical Evidence of Disability Affecting Reliability

F7.63

> Medical evidence is admissible to show that a witness suffers from some disease or defect or abnormality of mind that affects the reliability of his evidence. Such evidence is not confined to a general opinion of the unreliability of the witness but may give all the matters necessary to show, not only the foundation of and reasons for the diagnosis, but also the extent to which the credibility of the witness is affected. (*Toohey v Metropolitan Police Commissioner* [1965] AC 595, per Lord Pearce at p. 609.)

If the defence adduce such evidence, it may be open to the Crown to call an expert in rebuttal, or even (anticipating the defence expert) as part of the prosecution case. It may even be open to the Crown to rebut by expert evidence a case put only in cross-examination that a prosecution witness is unreliable by reason of mental abnormality. Much may depend on the nature of the abnormality and of the cross-examination. But the rebuttal evidence should be restricted to meeting the specific challenge and should not extend to oath-helping: the Crown cannot call a witness of fact and then, without more, call a psychologist or psychiatrist to give reasons why the jury should regard that witness as reliable (*Robinson* [1994] 3 All ER 346; and see also *Beard* [1998] Crim LR 585). As to oath-helping, however, see also *S* [2006] EWCA Crim 2389, which concerned an autistic girl, aged 13, who was the victim of sexual offences. An expert witness was not allowed to comment directly on the veracity of the complainant, but did give evidence that a child such as the complainant would not easily have been able to invent the story she had told. It was held that this evidence had been properly admitted and that *Robinson* could be distinguished because, whereas the expert evidence in that case had related directly to one particular witness, in the instant case the evidence was of general application and it remained for the jury to decide whether the complainant was to be believed as to the particular allegation she had made. See also *Tobin* [2003] EWCA Crim 190, where the admission of limited evidence of the good character of the complainant was held not to offend the rule against oath-helping on the basis there was a stark conflict between her evidence and that of D, about whose character very full evidence had been given.

F7.64 In *Toohey*, the accused were charged with assaulting V with intent to rob. The defence case was that V had been drinking and that the accused were trying to help him, but that he became hysterical and accused them of assaulting him. The trial judge ruled that the medical evidence of a doctor, who had examined V shortly after the alleged assault, that drink could exacerbate hysteria, and that V was more prone to hysteria than a normal person, was inadmissible. The House of Lords quashed the conviction on the grounds that the evidence was admissible, not only because of its relevance to the facts in issue, but also in order to impeach the credibility of V, *qua* witness. Lord Pearce said (at p. 608):

> If a witness purported to give evidence of something which he believed that he had seen at a distance of 50 yards, it must surely be possible to call the evidence of an oculist to the effect that the witness could not possibly see anything at a greater distance than 20 yards, or the evidence of a surgeon who had removed a cataract from which the witness was suffering at the material time and which would have prevented him from seeing what he thought he saw. So, too, must it be allowable to call medical evidence of mental illness which makes a witness incapable of giving reliable evidence ...

Cf. *Eades* [1972] Crim LR 99 (the admissibility of psychiatric evidence to contradict the evidence of D as to how he had recovered his memory of the events in question). In *H* [2014] EWCA Crim 1555, commenting upon the dictum of Lord Pearce, it was observed (at [26]) that, concerning medical evidence of mental illness, the analogy with physical disease is neither appropriate nor apt, because whereas a cataract would prevent the witness from seeing what he or she purported to see, the fact of mental ill health does not mean that a witness cannot be accurately describing what happened nor would it prevent him or her from, or make him or her incapable of, being reliable. Such issues of fact fall to be resolved by the jury, not doctors, taking into account such expert medical opinion as may be necessary in the circumstances of the case.

The principle established in *Toohey*, in accordance with the rules governing the use of expert evidence generally, is applicable only in relation to some physical or mental disability calling for expertise, as opposed to matters affecting reliability upon which the jury are capable of forming their own opinion without expert assistance. Thus, expert evidence is generally inadmissible on the issue of an accused's credibility (*Turner* [1975] QB 834, at p. 842). Compare *Lowery v The Queen* [1974] AC 85, and see generally **F11.22**. In *Toohey*, Lord Pearce said (at p. 608):

> Human evidence shares the frailties of those who give it. It is subject to many cross-currents such as partiality, prejudice, self-interest and, above all, imagination and inaccuracy. Those are matters with which the jury, helped by cross-examination and common sense, must do their best. But when a witness through physical (in which I include mental) disease or abnormality is not capable of giving a true or reliable account to the jury, it must surely be allowable for medical science to reveal this vital hidden fact to them.

Where, in the case of a witness with a disorder or disability of the mind, expert evidence is admissible, it may be necessary because, without it, either the witness's condition would not be apparent to the jury from his or her behaviour in court (as in *MacKenney* [2004] EWCA Crim 1220, [2004] 2 Cr App R 5 (32)) or there are behavioural signs of the condition, but they would not be understood by the jury (*Mulindwa* [2017] EWCA Crim 416, [2017] 4 WLR 157). In *MacKenney*, the accused were convicted of murder. At their trial, in 1980, they alleged that the chief prosecution witness, an accomplice, had fabricated his evidence. The defence sought to call a psychologist, by whom the witness had refused to be examined. The psychologist had watched the witness as he gave his evidence and was of the opinion that he was a psychopath who was likely to be lying and whose mental state meant that his demeanour and behaviour in giving evidence would not betray the usual indications to the jury as to when he was lying. The trial judge ruled the evidence inadmissible and the convictions were upheld on appeal. In 2001 the Criminal Cases Review Commission referred the convictions to the Court of Appeal. There was fresh evidence, from a forensic psychiatrist, who also had not examined the witness, whose opinion was very similar to that of the psychologist which had been ruled inadmissible at the trial. It was held, adopting the approach to the relevance and admissibility of expert evidence set out in *O'Brien* [2000] Crim LR 676 (considered at **F11.20**), that the evidence of the psychologist would today be admissible. The reference was determined on the fresh evidence, on the basis of which the Court concluded that the convictions were unsafe and should be quashed. It was held that the absence of an examination by the expert went to the weight to be attached to the opinion, and not to its admissibility. It was also held that the court must be on its guard against any attempt to detract from the jury's task of finding for themselves what evidence to believe: the court should not allow evidence to be put before the jury which does not allege any medical abnormality as the basis for the evidence of a witness being approached with particular caution. **F7.65**

In *Mulindwa* [2017] EWCA Crim 416, [2017] 4 WLR 157, D suffered from paranoid schizophrenia and was being treated by medication which, for the most part, kept his hallucinations under control, or to a minimum. Occasionally there were behavioural signs that he might be responding to hallucinatory voices. It was held that had D elected to testify, a psychologist could have been called before he testified to explain to the jury that certain behavioural signs were a feature of his mental condition, despite its being largely controlled by medication. This would have enabled the jury to form a view on the reliability of both particular parts of D's evidence and his evidence as a whole. However, the expert would not have been entitled to express any opinion on D's credibility or to give a commentary on his answers. The Court of Appeal held that there were was a clear dividing line between expert evidence which may legitimately provide the jury with necessary assistance in understanding the presentation of an accused and impermissible expert evidence on credibility, a matter exclusively for the jury. It was also held that such expert evidence would only be admissible in rare cases in which the accused suffers from a recognised mental disorder the impact of which may affect the accused's presentation in giving evidence.

RE-EXAMINATION

General

F7.66 After cross-examination, a witness may be re-examined by the party who called him or her. This applies even in the case of a hostile witness, who may be re-examined on any new matters which arose out of cross-examination (*Wong* [1986] Crim LR 683). Leading questions may not be asked in re-examination. The principal rule of re-examination is that, except with the leave of the judge, questions should be confined to matters, including any new matters, arising out of cross-examination. This rule applies not only in the case of a witness who has been examined in chief, but also in the case of a witness whose name is notionally on the back of the indictment and who was called by the prosecution merely to allow the defence to cross-examine him (*Beezley* (1830) 4 C & P 220). Where a witness under cross-examination gives evidence of part of a conversation on some previous occasion, questions may not be asked in re-examination about everything else that was said at the same time, but only about so much as can be in some way connected with the statement as to which the witness was cross-examined, such as other statements which qualify or explain it in any way (*Prince v Samo* (1838) 7 A & E 627, per Lord Denman CJ, citing Lord Tenterden in *Queen Caroline's Case* (1820) 2 B & B 284, at p. 297).

A witness may refresh his or her memory in re-examination: see **F6.16**.

Statements in Rebuttal of Allegations of Recent Fabrication

F7.67 Under the CJA 2003, s. 120(1) and (2), which constitute an exception to both the rule against hearsay (see **F16**) and the rule against previous consistent statements (see **F6.39**), a statement by a witness admitted as evidence to rebut a suggestion that his or her oral evidence has been fabricated will be admissible for the truth of its contents and to support the witness's credibility.

Criminal Justice Act 2003, s. 120

(1) This section applies where a person (the witness) is called to give evidence in criminal proceedings.
(2) If a previous statement by the witness is admitted as evidence to rebut a suggestion that his oral evidence has been fabricated, that statement is admissible as evidence of any matter stated of which oral evidence by the witness would be admissible.

F7.68 Section 120(2) itself does not govern admissibility, which must be considered by reference to the common-law principles which have governed this question in the past (*Trewin* [2008] EWCA Crim 484 at [18] and [20]). At common law, a previous consistent statement of a witness will not become admissible merely because the witness's evidence is impeached in cross-examination (*Fox v General Medical Council* [1960] 3 All ER 225), even if this takes the form of cross-examination on a previous inconsistent statement (see *Coll* (1889) 24 LR Ir 522 at p. 541 and the other authorities considered at **F6.39**). However, if in cross-examination it is suggested to a witness that his or her evidence is a recent fabrication, evidence of a previous consistent statement will be admissible in re-examination to negative the suggestion and confirm the witness's credibility (*Y* [1995] Crim LR 155). The principle has no application where a witness is cross-examined on the basis that the account was fabricated from the outset, unless the effect of the cross-examination is in fact to create the impression that the witness invented the story at a later stage (*Athwal* [2009] EWCA Crim 789,

[2009] 1 WLR 2430). In a trial for a sexual offence in which the previous statement amounts to a complaint, it may be admissible to rebut the allegation of recent fabrication notwithstanding that it is inadmissible as a recent complaint (see *Tyndale* [1999] Crim LR 320 and **F6.32**).

In *Oyesiku* (1971) 56 Cr App R 240, Karminski LJ, giving the judgment of the Court of Appeal (at p. 245), approved the following statement of Dixon CJ in *Nominal Defendant v Clements* (1960) 104 CLR 476, at pp. 479–80: **F7.69**

> If the credit of a witness is impugned as to some material fact to which he deposes upon the ground that his account is a late invention or has been lately devised or reconstructed, even though not with conscious dishonesty, that makes admissible a statement to the same effect as the account he gave as a witness if it was made by the witness contemporaneously with the event or at a time sufficiently early to be inconsistent with the suggestion that his account is a late invention or reconstruction. But, inasmuch as the rule forms a definite exception to the general principle excluding statements made out of court and admits a possibly self-serving statement made by the witness, great care is called for in applying it. The judge at the trial must determine for himself upon the conduct of the trial before him whether a case for applying the rule of evidence has arisen and, from the nature of the matter, if there be an appeal, great weight should be given to his opinion by the appellate court. It is evident however that the judge at the trial must exercise care in assuring himself not only that the account given by the witness in his testimony is attacked on the ground of recent invention or reconstruction or that a foundation for such an attack has been laid by the party but also that the contents of the statement are in fact to the like effect as his account given in his evidence and that having regard to the time and circumstances in which it was made it rationally tends to answer the attack.

In *Oyesiku* the conviction was quashed because the trial judge had improperly refused to allow the jury to see the previous statement; by inspection of it, the jury would have been in a better position to assess the extent to which it rebutted the attack made on the witness's testimony. See also *Sekhon* (1987) 85 Cr App R 19, at **F6.24** ***et seq.*** For earlier authority, see *Benjamin* (1913) 8 Cr App R 146 and *Flanagan v Fahy* [1918] 2 IR 361.

Although s. 120(2) refers to 'fabrication' without the qualification 'recent', the clear intention was to leave the common-law principle intact. However, the principle is not to be confined to a temporal straitjacket. 'Recent' is an elastic description designed to assist in the identification of circumstances in which a previous consistent statement should be admitted where there is a rational basis for its use as a tool for deciding where the truth lies. The touchstone is whether the evidence may fairly assist in that way, and not the length of time (*Athwal* [2009] EWCA Crim 789, [2009] 1 WLR 2430). For example, in *MH* [2012] EWCA Crim 2725, where it was alleged by a father that his son had been coached by his mother to give false evidence against him to stop him from seeing his children and by reason of the financial dispute between him and his wife, evidence of the son's complaints to the mother against the father prior to the breakdown of the marriage was admissible in rebuttal, but not evidence of such complaints made at a time when the father was not permitted to see his children and when he and his wife were in financial dispute. **F7.70**

Where hearsay is admissible under s. 120(2), compliance with the requirements of timely formal notice will not normally be possible and it will be for the judge to consider whether it would be fair to exercise the power in CrimPR 20.5 (see Supplement, **R20.5**) to dispense with the requirements (*Athwal* [2009] EWCA Crim 789, [2009] 1 WLR 2430). **F7.71**

Where evidence of a complaint is admitted, under the CJA 2003, s. 120, to rebut an allegation of recent fabrication, a conviction will not be quashed in the absence of a direction on independence, i.e. in the absence of a direction to the effect that in deciding what weight the complaint should bear, the jury should have in mind that it comes from the same person who makes the complaint in the witness box and not from some independent source (*AD* [2011] EWCA Crim 1943; and cf. *Amrani* [2011] EWCA Crim 1517; *Berry* [2013] EWCA Crim 1389 and *H* [2011] EWCA Crim 2344, [2012] 1 Cr App R 30 (413), all considered at **F6.35**). **F7.72**

Section F8 Documentary Evidence and Real Evidence

PROOF OF PRIVATE DOCUMENTS

F8.1 Statements contained in documents are subject to the general rules of evidence on admissibility, including those relating to relevance, hearsay, opinion and privilege. Two additional requirements, concerning documents on the contents of which a party seeks to rely, are: (a) proof of the contents and (b) proof of due execution.

Concerning presumptions relating to documents, see **F8.43**. As to stamped documents, see **F8.44**.

PROOF OF CONTENTS: THE BEST EVIDENCE RULE

General Rule

F8.2 At common law, the general rule, now regarded as the only remaining instance of the best evidence rule, is that a party seeking to rely upon the contents of a document must adduce primary evidence of those contents, i.e. either the original document in question, a copy of an enrolled document, or informal admissions made by parties concerning the contents. Thus if an original document is available in one's hands, one must produce it and one cannot give secondary evidence by producing a copy (*Kajala v Noble* (1982) 75 Cr App R 149 at p. 152). A party having a document available in his or her hands means a party who has the original of the document in court, or could have it in court without any difficulty (*Governor of Pentonville Prison, ex parte Osman* [1990] 3 All ER 701 at p. 308). The rule, in criminal cases, is confined to written documents in the strict sense of the term, and has no relevance to audio recordings and films (*Kajala v Noble* (1982) 75 Cr App R 149). As to the use of audio recordings, see **F8.53**; as to photographs, video recordings and films, see **F8.58**. The general rule does not apply if:

(a) it is unnecessary to place reliance upon the contents because the fact or matter in issue, although recorded in a document, can be proved by other evidence (see, e.g., *Holy Trinity, Kingston-upon-Hull (Inhabitants)* (1827) 7 B & C 611: the fact of a tenancy; *Manwaring* (1856) Dears & B 132: proof of a marriage, which may have been registered, by the testimony of a person who had attended the ceremony; and *Seberg* (1870) LR 1 CCR 264: proof by the testimony of eye-witnesses that a ship was British and sailing under the British flag, without production of the register of the vessel); or
(b) the document is tendered merely for the purpose of identifying it or establishing the bare fact of its existence (*Boyle v Wiseman* (1855) 11 Exch 360, at p. 367; *Elworthy* (1867) LR 1 CCR 103);
(c) the document is not adduced in evidence but used by a witness only in order to refresh his or her memory (*DPP v Sugden* [2018] EWHC 544 (Admin), [2018] 2 Cr App R 8 (101), considered at **F6.22**).

F8.3 To the general rule there are a number of common-law and statutory exceptions, providing for proof of the contents of documents by secondary evidence. Generally speaking, such secondary evidence may take the form of a copy, a copy of a copy or oral evidence, and 'there are no degrees of secondary evidence' (per Lord Abinger CB in *Doe d Gilbert v Ross* (1840) 7 M & W 102).

Thus, an inferior copy may be tendered even if a better copy is available (*Lafone v Griffin* (1909) 25 TLR 308 and *Collins* (1960) 44 Cr App R 170; but contrast *Everingham v Roundell* (1838) 2 Mood & R 138). Likewise, oral evidence of the contents is admissible even if a copy is available (*Brown v Woodman* (1834) 6 C & P 206). The exceptions to the rule that there are no degrees of secondary evidence are the contents of:

(a) a will admitted to probate, which may not be proved by oral evidence if the original or probate copy exists;
(b) judicial documents and bankers' books (see **F8.13**), which are generally proved by office copies and examined copies respectively; and
(c) various public documents (see **F8.13** ***et seq.***), which may be proved by oral evidence only if examined, certified, or other copies are unavailable.

The law, as set out above, is well established, but also needs to be considered in the light of the **F8.4**
decision in *Springsteen v Masquerade Music Ltd* [2001] EWCA Civ 563, in which the Court of Appeal held that:

(a) Where the party seeking to adduce the secondary evidence could readily produce the document, it might be expected that, absent some special circumstances, the court would decline to admit the secondary evidence on the ground that it was worthless.
(b) At the other extreme, where that party genuinely could not produce the document, it might be expected that, absent some special circumstances, the court would admit the secondary evidence and attach such weight to it as it considered appropriate in the circumstances.
(c) In cases falling between these two extremes, it was for the court to make a judgment as to whether in all the circumstances any weight should be attached to the secondary evidence.
(d) Thus the admissibility of secondary evidence of the contents of documents is entirely dependent on whether or not any weight was to be attached to the evidence, which was a matter for the court to decide.

Although the Court observed 'with confidence' that the best evidence rule had finally expired, in effect the principle set out in (a) is a restatement of the general rule and the principle set out in (b) an exception to it. The principles set out in (c) and (d), however, amount to a rejection of the four distinct common-law categories of exception to the general rule (see **F8.9** to **F8.12**) in favour of a more generalised approach whereby admissibility of secondary evidence of the contents of a document depends solely on the weight to be attached to it. It is submitted that this approach should not be confined to civil cases.

Statutory Provisions

The common-law authorities have been affected by the CJA 2003, s. 133, and the PACE **F8.5**
1984, s. 71.

Criminal Justice Act 2003, s. 133

> Where a statement in a document is admissible as evidence in criminal proceedings, the statement may be proved by producing either—
> (a) the document, or
> (b) (whether or not the document exists) a copy of the document or of the material part of it,
> authenticated in whatever way the court may approve.

A 'statement' for these purposes is any representation of fact or opinion made by a person by whatever means, and includes a representation made in a sketch, photofit or other pictorial form (s. 115(2)); a 'document' means anything in which information of any description is recorded (s. 134(1)); and a 'copy' means anything on to which information recorded in the document has been copied, by whatever means and whether directly or indirectly (s. 134(1)).

Police and Criminal Evidence Act 1984, s. 71

> In any proceedings the contents of a document may (whether or not the document is still in existence) be proved by the production of an enlargement of a microfilm copy of that document or of the material part of it, authenticated in such manner as the court may approve.

For the definition of 'proceedings', see s. 72 of the 1984 Act.

F8.6 Two views are possible with regard to the construction of the CJA 2003, s. 133. On one view, it applies only to hearsay statements contained in documents, and not to the proof of the contents of a document as evidence in their own right. On the other view, it is not confined to the various types of documentary hearsay statement admissible under the 2003 Act itself, but applies to any statement contained in a document and admissible in evidence. Either way, s. 133, which on its wording is permissive rather than mandatory as to the means of proof, must be read subject to:

(a) the exceptions to the general rule at common law, whereby the contents of a document may be proved by secondary evidence which may take the form of *oral* evidence, which is not permitted under s. 133 (*Nazeer* [1998] Crim LR 750); and, it seems,
(b) statutory exceptions to the general rule at common law, principally relating to public and judicial documents and bankers' books, which, although they allow for proof of the contents of such documents by copies, require those copies to take a particular form (which is not the case under s. 133).

F8.7 In the cases to which s. 133 does apply, it remains to be seen in what manner the courts will require copies to be 'authenticated'. (For the difficulties that can arise in the case of some computer printouts of screen images, see *Skinner* [2005] EWCA Crim 1439, a decision under the CJA 1988, s. 27, the statutory precursor to s. 133.) In the normal case, it is submitted, the court will require the same proof as was necessary when relying upon secondary evidence under one of the common-law exceptions to the general rule, namely proof by the evidence of a person with custody or control of the copy (or some other appropriate person) that it is a true copy of the original. In *Collins* (1960) 44 Cr App R 170, D was convicted of obtaining money by false pretences, having cashed a cheque on his bank account which he knew to have been closed. When he failed, after notice to do so, to produce a letter sent to him informing him that the account had been closed, secondary evidence of the contents of the letter became admissible. However, the Court of Criminal Appeal held that a copy of a carbon copy of the letter, produced at the trial by a manager of the bank, had been improperly admitted, there having been no proof that it was a true copy of the carbon copy or that it was in the same terms as the original. Compare *Wayte* (1983) 76 Cr App R 110: the mere fact that it is easy to construct a false document by photocopying techniques does not render a photocopy inadmissible; the fact that the document was a photocopy went to its weight and not its admissibility. The Court of Appeal in that case also gave guidance on the procedure to be adopted when it is sought to produce in evidence photocopies:

(a) Documents should not normally be handed to the jury until questions of admissibility have been determined.
(b) Prior warning of the intention to produce such copies should be given to opposing counsel so that they may have the chance to consider their admissibility.
(c) If the accused is unrepresented, the guidance of the court should be sought before the document is put before the jury.
(d) On very rare occasions, it may be necessary to hold a trial within a trial on the question of admissibility, although ultimately the issue of the genuineness of the copies should be left to the jury.

In relation to copies, the information may have been copied from the original either 'directly or indirectly' (CJA 2003, s. 134(1)). Thus there is no obligation to produce the best copy rather than an inferior copy, even if the best copy, or indeed the original document, is still in existence.

F8.8 At common law, prior to the decision in *Springsteen v Masquerade Music Ltd* [2001] EWCA Civ 563 (see **F8.4**), there were four established categories of exception to the general rule that a party seeking to rely upon the contents of a document must produce primary evidence of those contents. Since the coming into force of the CJA 2003, s. 133, and on the assumption that the second view of the true construction of that section set forth above is correct, it may only be necessary to rely upon such exceptions if, there being no copy of the document in question, it is sought to adduce *oral* evidence of its contents.

Failure to Produce Original after Notice

A party seeking to rely upon the contents of a document may prove them by secondary evidence if the original is in the possession or control of the other party to the proceedings who, having been served with a notice to produce it, fails to do so (*Hunter* (1829) 3 C & P 591, where secondary evidence was admitted as to the contents of an allegedly forged deed, the deed itself being in the custody of D who, despite notice, refused to produce it). See also *Collins* (1960) 44 Cr App R 170, at **F8.7**. Service of a notice to produce is unnecessary where the requirement to produce the original can be implied, as when the indictment gives sufficient notice of the subject of inquiry (see *Aickles* (1784) 1 Leach 294, where on a charge of theft of a bill of exchange, parol evidence concerning it was given without service of a notice, *Clube* (1857) 3 Jur NS 698 and *Hunt* (1820) 3 B & Ald 566). Compare *Kitson* (1853) Dears CC 187, where, on a charge of setting fire to property with intent to defraud an insurance company, secondary evidence as to the contents of the policy of insurance was held to be inadmissible. See also *Elworthy* (1867) LR 1 CCR 103, where, on a charge of perjury, it being alleged that D had falsely sworn that there was no draft of a statutory declaration prepared by him, it was held that, although the prosecution could properly adduce parol evidence that such a draft existed and was in D's possession, secondary evidence of the contents of the draft, and of certain alterations made in it was inadmissible, the Crown having given no notice to D to produce the original. Notice to produce is also excused where the opponent of the party seeking to rely on the document admits that it has been lost (*Haworth* (1830) 4 C & P 254). **F8.9**

Stranger's Lawful Refusal to Produce Original

If a stranger to the proceedings, having been served with a subpoena *duces tecum*, *unlawfully* refuses to produce the document in his or her possession, its contents cannot be proved by secondary evidence, because the stranger is bound to produce it and is punishable for contempt for a refusal to do so (*Llanfaethly (Inhabitants)* (1853) 2 E & B 940). However, the contents may be proved by secondary evidence if the stranger *lawfully* refuses to comply with the subpoena (*Mills v Oddy* (1834) 6 C & P 728 (a claim to privilege); *Kilgour v Owen* (1889) 88 LT Jo 7 (stranger outside the jurisdiction); *Nowaz* [1976] 3 All ER 5, where the Pakistani consulate having refused, on the grounds of diplomatic immunity, to produce a photograph and an application for a passport, a police officer who had seen the documents was allowed to give oral evidence of their contents). **F8.10**

Original Lost or Destroyed

The contents of a document may be proved by secondary evidence if it can be proved that the original has been destroyed or cannot be found after due search (*Wayte* (1983) 76 Cr App R 110, where, two letters having been lost, a photocopy of the one and a photocopy of a carbon copy of the other were held to be admissible). The quality of evidence required to show the destruction (or loss and due search) varies according to the nature and value of the document in question (*Brewster v Sewell* (1820) 3 B & Ald 296). See also *Hall* (1872) 12 Cox CC 159. **F8.11**

Production of Original Impossible or Inconvenient

The contents of a document may be proved by secondary evidence if production of the original is physically or legally impossible. As to the former, see *Mortimer v M'Callan* (1840) 6 M & W 58, at p. 72 (inscriptions upon tombstones or on a wall), and *Hunt* (1820) 3 B & Ald 566 (inscriptions on flags or banners). As to the latter, see *Owner v Bee Hive Spinning Co. Ltd* [1914] **F8.12**

1 KB 105 (a notice statutorily required to be constantly affixed at a factory or workshop), and *Alivon v Furnival* (1834) 1 Cr M & R 277 (a document in the custody of a foreign court). In addition to the statutory provisions governing the proof of the contents of public documents by secondary evidence, at common law secondary evidence may also be used to prove the contents of such documents if production of the originals would entail a high degree of public inconvenience. In *Mortimer v M'Callan* (1840) 6 M & W 58, Alderson B said (at p. 72):

> The [books of the Bank of England] are not capable of being produced without so much public inconvenience, that the courts have directed them to remain in the Bank, and copies of them to be received in evidence for the purpose for which the books are receivable.

PROOF OF PUBLIC AND JUDICIAL DOCUMENTS

Statutory Provisions of General Application

F8.13 A large number of statutes provide for the proof of the contents of various public and judicial documents by secondary evidence, which, for these purposes, is usually required to take the form of an examined, certified, office, Queen's Printer's or Stationery Office copy. An examined copy is a copy proved by oral evidence to correspond with the original. A certified copy is a copy signed and certified to be accurate by an official who has custody of the original. An office copy is a copy made in the office of the High Court and authenticated, with the seal of the court, by an officer who has custody of the original and the lawful power to provide copies. Two provisions of general importance are the Evidence Act 1845, s. 1, and the Evidence Act 1851, s. 14.

F8.14 Under s. 1 of the 1845 Act, where a statute provides for proof of a document by a certified, sealed or stamped copy, the copy, provided it purports to be signed, sealed or stamped, is admissible without any proof of the signature, seal or stamp, as the case may be.

Evidence Act 1845, s. 1

> Whenever by any Act now in force or hereafter to be in force any certificate, official or public document, or document or proceeding of any corporation or joint-stock or other company, or any certified copy of any document, by-law, entry in any register or other book, or of any other proceeding, shall be receivable in evidence of any particular in any court of justice, or before any legal tribunal, or either House of Parliament, or any committee of either House, or in any judicial proceeding, the same shall respectively be admitted in evidence, provided they respectively purport to be sealed or impressed with a stamp or sealed and signed, or signed alone, as required, or impressed with a stamp and signed, as directed by the respective Acts made or to be hereafter made, without any proof of the seal or stamp, where a seal or stamp is necessary, or of the signature or of the official character of the person appearing to have signed the same, and without any further proof thereof, in every case in which the original record could have been received in evidence.

F8.15 Under the Evidence Act 1851, s. 14, if no other statute provides for the proof by means of a copy of the contents of a document of such a public nature that it is admissible in evidence on production from proper custody, the contents of such a document may be proved by a certified or examined copy.

Evidence Act 1851, s. 14

> Whenever any book or other document is of such a public nature as to be admissible in evidence on its mere production from the proper custody, and no statute exists which renders its contents provable by means of a copy, any copy thereof or extract therefrom shall be admissible in evidence in any court of justice, or before any person now or hereafter having by law or by consent of parties authority to hear, receive, and examine evidence, provided it be proved to be an examined copy or extract, or provided it purport to be signed and certified as a true copy or extract by the officer to whose custody the original is entrusted, and which officer is hereby required to furnish such certified copy or extract to any person applying at a reasonable time for the same, upon payment of a reasonable sum for the same.

Acts of Parliament and Journals of Either House

Private and local and personal Acts of Parliament and Journals of either House may be proved by Queen's Printer's or Stationery Office copies. F8.16

Evidence Act 1845, s. 3

All copies of private and local and personal Acts of Parliament not public Acts, if purporting to be printed by the Queen's printers, and all copies of the journals of either House of Parliament, and of royal proclamations, purporting to be printed by the printers to the Crown or by the printers to either House of Parliament, or by any or either of them, shall be admitted as evidence thereof by all courts, judges, justices, and others without any proof being given that such copies were so printed.

Documentary Evidence Act 1882, s. 2

Where any enactment, whether passed before or after [19 June 1882] provides that a copy of any Act of Parliament, proclamation, order, regulation, rule, warrant, circular, list, gazette, or document shall be conclusive evidence, or be evidence, or have any other effect, when purporting to be printed by the Government Printer, or the Queen's Printer, or the Queen's printer for Scotland, or a printer authorised by Her Majesty, or otherwise under Her Majesty's authority, whatever may be the precise expression used, such copy shall also be conclusive evidence, or evidence, or have the said effect (as the case may be) if it purports to be printed under the superintendence or authority of Her Majesty's Stationery Office.

As to public Acts, the Interpretation Act 1978, s. 3, provides that 'Every Act is a public Act to be judicially noticed as such unless the contrary is expressly provided by the Act'. Section 3 applies to all Acts passed after 1850. At common law, judicial notice is taken of earlier enactments, if public. See **F1.6**.

Royal Proclamations and Orders or Regulations Issued by Government

These may be proved by Queen's Printer's or Stationery Office copies (see the Documentary Evidence Act 1868, ss. 2 to 6; and the Documentary Evidence Act 1882, s. 2). F8.17

Documentary Evidence Act 1868, s. 2

Prima facie evidence of any proclamation, order, or regulation issued before or after the passing of this Act by Her Majesty or by the Privy Council, also of any proclamation, order, or regulation issued before or after the passing of this Act by or under the authority of any such department of the government or officer or office-holder in the Scottish Administration as is mentioned in the first column of the Schedule hereto, may be given in all courts of justice, and in all legal proceedings whatsoever, in all or any of the modes hereinafter mentioned; that is to say:

(1) By the production of a copy of the Gazette purporting to contain such proclamation, order, or regulation.

(2) By the production of a copy of such proclamation, order, or regulation purporting to be printed by the government printer, or, where the question arises in a court in any British colony or possession, of a copy purporting to be printed under the authority of the legislature of such British colony or possession.

(3) By the production, in the case of any proclamation, order, or regulation issued by Her Majesty or by the Privy Council, of a copy or extract purporting to be certified to be true by the Clerk of the Privy Council, or by any one of the lords or others of the Privy Council, and, in the case of any proclamation, order, or regulation issued by or under the authority of any of the said departments or officers or office-holders, by the production of a copy or extract purporting to be certified to be true by the person or persons specified in the second column of the said Schedule in connection with such department or officer or office-holder.

Any copy or extract made in pursuance of this Act may be in print or in writing, or partly in print and partly in writing.

No proof shall be required of the handwriting or official position of any person certifying, in pursuance of this Act, to the truth of any copy of or extract from any proclamation, order, or regulation.

In *Clarke* [1969] 2 QB 91, at p. 97, the Court of Appeal said that the word 'order' in the 1868 Act should be given a wide meaning, covering 'any executive act of government performed by F8.18

the bringing into existence of a public document for the purpose of giving effect to an Act of Parliament'; and held that the Breath Test (Approval) (No. 1) Order 1968 (printed by HMSO), although not a statutory instrument, was an 'order' within s. 2 of the Act. As to statutory instruments, see further **F8.20**. An 'order' within s. 2 of the Act also covers a licence issued by the governor of a prison on behalf of the Secretary of State for the Home Office under the CJA 1991, s. 40A (*West Midlands Probation Board v French* [2008] EWHC 2631 (Admin), [2009] 1 WLR 1715).

Proclamations, Treaties and Other Acts of State of Foreign States or British Colonies, and Judgments etc. of Courts in Foreign States or British Colonies

F8.19 These may be proved by examined or authenticated copies (see the Evidence Act 1851, s. 7, below; and the Evidence Act 1845, s. 1, at **F8.14**). As to colonial documents, see also the Documentary Evidence Act 1868, s. 3.

Evidence Act 1851, s. 7

All proclamations, treaties, and other acts of State of any foreign State or of any British colony, and all judgments, decrees, orders, and other judicial proceedings of any court of justice in any foreign State or in any British colony, and all affidavits, pleadings, and other legal documents filed or deposited in any such court, may be proved in any court of justice, or before any person having by law or by consent of parties authority to hear, receive, and examine evidence, either by examined copies or by copies authenticated as hereinafter mentioned; that is to say, if the document sought to be proved be a proclamation, treaty, or other act of State, the authenticated copy to be admissible in evidence must purport to be sealed with the seal of the foreign State or British colony to which the original document belongs; and if the document sought to be proved be a judgment, decree, order, or other judicial proceeding of any foreign or colonial court, or an affidavit, pleading, or other legal document filed or deposited in any such court, the authenticated copy to be admissible in evidence must purport either to be sealed with the seal of the foreign or colonial court to which the original document belongs, or, in the event of such court having no seal, to be signed by the judge, or, if there be more than one judge, by any one of the judges of the said court; and such judge shall attach to his signature a statement in writing on the said copy that the court whereof he is a judge has no seal; but if any of the aforesaid authenticated copies shall purport to be sealed or signed as hereinbefore respectively directed, the same shall respectively be admitted in evidence in every case in which the original document could have been received in evidence, without any proof of the seal where a seal is necessary, or of the signature, or of the truth of the statement attached thereto, where such signature and statement are necessary, or of the judicial character of the person appearing to have made such signature and statement.

When s. 7 is used to prove a foreign conviction, it must still be established that the examined copy relates to the person said to have been convicted. This can be proved by any relevant admissible evidence, including evidence of fingerprints (*Mauricia* [2002] EWCA Crim 676, [2002] 2 Cr App R 27 (377)).

Statutory Instruments

F8.20 Statutory instruments may be proved by Queen's Printer's or Stationery Office copies (see the Documentary Evidence Act 1868, s. 2, and the Documentary Evidence Act 1882, s. 2). However, where a photocopy from a commercial publication is produced instead, and there is no suggestion of any inaccuracy in the version before the court, the proviso to the Criminal Appeal Act 1968, s. 2, may apply (*Koon Cheung Tang* [1995] Crim LR 813). See also *Ashley* (1967) 52 Cr App R 42 and *Palastanga v Solman* [1962] Crim LR 334 (at **F6.7**), and, as to the proof of the date of issue of statutory instruments, the Statutory Instruments Act 1946, s. 3.

By-laws

F8.21 By-laws may be proved by certified printed copies.

Local Government Act 1972, s. 238

The production of a printed copy of a by-law purporting to be made by a local authority, the Greater London Authority or an Integrated Transport Authority for an integrated transport area in

England or a combined authority upon which is endorsed a certificate purporting to be signed by the proper officer of the authority stating—
(a) that the by-law was made by the authority;
(b) that the copy is a true copy of the by-law;
(c) that on a specified date the by-law was confirmed by the authority named in the certificate or, as the case may require, was sent to the Secretary of State and has not been disallowed;
(d) the date, if any, fixed by the confirming authority for the coming into operation of the by-law;
shall be prima facie evidence of the facts stated in the certificate, and without proof of the handwriting or official position of any person purporting to sign the certificate.

Colonial and Foreign Laws

Colonial statutes may be proved by copies certified by the clerk or other proper officer of the colonial legislative body (Colonial Laws Validity Act 1865, s. 6), or by copies purporting to be printed by the government printer of that possession (Evidence (Colonial Statutes) Act 1907, s. 1). Subject to this, and except where ascertained by the British Law Ascertainment Act 1859, colonial and foreign law, including Scots law, even if written, cannot be proved in an English court by production of the documents in which it is recorded, or a copy thereof, but generally requires proof by a suitably qualified expert (*Sussex Peerage Case* (1844) 11 Cl & F 85; *Governor of Brixton Prison, ex parte Shuter* [1960] 2 QB 89). See further, **F11.27**. **F8.22**

Public Records

By virtue of the Public Records Act 1958, s. 9, public records in the Public Record Office may be proved by copies which have been examined, certified and sealed or stamped. **F8.23**

Births, Deaths and Marriages

An entry in the register of births or deaths may be proved by a certified copy purporting to be sealed or stamped with the seal of the General Register Office, and is admissible evidence of the birth or death to which it relates (Births and Deaths Registration Act 1953, s. 34). (As to adopted children, see also the Adoption and Children Act 2002, s. 77(4).) Likewise, proof of the celebration of a marriage or of a civil partnership may be effected by the production of a certified copy of an entry kept at the General Register Office (Marriage Act 1949, s. 65(3); Civil Partnership (Registration Provisions) Regulations 2005 (SI 2005 No. 3176), reg. 13(4)). In order to prove a birth or death (or the marriage of persons), it is also necessary to adduce some evidence to identify the person in question with the person named in the certified copy (*Bellis* (1911) 6 Cr App R 283). The same applies where it is sought to prove a person's age by production of a birth certificate. Thus, although age may be proved by other means, e.g., by the testimony of someone present at the time of the birth, by inference from appearance or by hearsay declarations as to pedigree (*Cox* [1898] 1 QB 179), if a certificate of birth is produced to prove age, evidence must also be adduced to positively identify the person as the person named in the certificate (*Rogers* (1914) 10 Cr App R 276: proof of the age of the complainant on a charge of unlawful sexual intercourse with a girl under 13). A certified copy of an entry in the register of deaths is prima facie evidence of the fact and date of a death; but information contained in the certificate concerning the cause of death, and based on information supplied by a coroner, is inadmissible as evidence of the cause of death (*Bird v Keep* [1918] 2 KB 692, per Swinfen Eady MR, *obiter*). **F8.24**

Records of marriages, baptisms and burials entered in parish registers may be proved by an examined copy or by a copy certified as a true copy by the incumbent to whose custody the original is entrusted (see the Evidence Act 1851, s. 14, at **F8.15**).

Foreign Records Births, deaths and marriages out of England may be proved by entries properly and regularly recorded in foreign registers kept under the sanction of public authority (see *Lyell v Kennedy* (1889) 14 App Cas 437, per Lord Selborne at pp. 448–9, and generally **F8.25**

F17.43). See also the Registration of Births, Deaths and Marriages (Scotland) Act 1965. Births, deaths and marriages out of England may also be proved by certified copies of registers kept under the local law in any case where the Evidence (Foreign, Dominion and Colonial Documents) Act 1933 has been applied by an Order in Council. As to proof of records kept in an Army Register in respect of an officer or soldier serving overseas, see the Registration of Births, Deaths and Marriages (Army) Act 1879, s. 3. As to returns of births and deaths on ships registered in the UK, and on ships not registered in the UK but calling at a port in the UK, see the Merchant Shipping Act 1995, s. 108, and the Merchant Shipping (Returns of Births and Deaths) Regulations 1979 (SI 1979 No. 1577). As to births, deaths and marriages on Her Majesty's ships at sea and service aircraft, see the Registration of Births, Deaths and Marriages (Special Provisions) Act 1957, s. 2.

Minute-books of Local Authorities

F8.26 The minutes of the proceedings of local authorities required to be drawn up, entered in a book and signed under the Local Government Act 1972, shall be received in evidence without further proof; and until the contrary is proved, where a minute of such proceedings has been made and signed, the meeting shall be deemed to have been duly convened and held, and all the members present shall be deemed to have been duly qualified (Local Government Act 1972, sch. 12, part VI, para. 41). A document which purports to be a copy of the minutes of the proceedings at a meeting of a local authority (or a committee of a local authority, or a subcommittee of such a committee) or a precursor of a local authority, and which bears a certificate purporting to be signed by the proper officer of the authority and stating that the minutes were signed in accordance with para. 41, shall be evidence in any proceedings of the matters stated in the certificate and of the terms of the minutes in question (Local Government (Miscellaneous Provisions) Act 1976, s. 41(1)).

Professional Lists

F8.27 Various statutes provide for proof that a person is or is not professionally qualified by production of a list, register or certificate of a registrar. Thus, any list purporting to be published by authority of the Law Society and to contain the names of solicitors who have obtained practising certificates for the current year shall, until the contrary is proved, be evidence that the persons so named are solicitors holding such certificates (Solicitors Act 1974, s. 18(1)). The absence from any such list of the name of any person shall, until the contrary is proved, be evidence that that person is not qualified to practise as a solicitor under a certificate for the current year, but in the case of any such person an extract from the roll certified as correct by the Society shall be evidence of the facts appearing in the extract. See also the Medical Act 1983, s. 34 (registered medical practitioners); the Nursing and Midwifery Order 2002 (SI 2002 No. 253), reg. 8(3); the Health Professions Order 2002 (SI 2002 No. 254), reg. 8(4); the Dentists Act 1984, s. 14(6); the Pharmacy Order 2010 (SI 2010 No. 231), Part 4 (registered pharmacists and pharmacy technicians); and the Veterinary Surgeons Act 1966, ss. 2 and 9.

Documents Relevant to Insolvency

F8.28 In relation to bankruptcy law, any document purporting to be or to contain any order, direction or certificate issued by the Secretary of State shall be received in evidence and be deemed to be (or contain) that order or certificate or those directions without further proof, unless the contrary is shown; and a certificate signed by the Secretary of State or an officer on the Secretary of State's behalf and confirming the making of any order, the issuing of any document or the exercise of any discretion, power or obligation arising or imposed under the Insolvency Act 1986 or the Insolvency Rules 1986 (SI 1986 No. 1925) is conclusive evidence of the matter dealt with in the certificate (Insolvency Rules 1986, r. 12.6). A copy of the Gazette containing any notice required by the Act or the Rules to be gazetted is evidence of any facts stated in the notice; and in the case of an order of the court, notice of which is required to be gazetted, a copy of the Gazette containing the notice may be produced in any proceedings as conclusive evidence that the order was made on the date specified in the notice (Insolvency Rules 1986, r. 12.20).

Company Investigations

A copy of any report of inspectors appointed under Part XIV of the Companies Act 1985, certified by the Secretary of State to be a true copy, is admissible in any legal proceedings as evidence of the opinion of the inspectors in relation to any matter contained in the report; and a document purporting to be such a certificate shall be received in evidence and deemed to be such a certificate unless the contrary is proved (Companies Act 1985, s. 441). **F8.29**

Proceedings in Civil Courts

Under the Civil Procedure Rules 1998, r. 2.6(3), a document purporting to bear the court's seal shall be admissible in evidence without further proof. See also the Senior Courts Act 1981, s. 132: 'Every document purporting to be sealed or stamped with the seal or stamp of the Supreme Court shall be received in evidence in all parts of the UK without further proof'. An official copy of the whole or any part of a will may be obtained under the Senior Courts Act 1981, s. 125, and may be proved under s. 132 of that Act. On a prosecution for perjury (or procuring or suborning the commission of perjury) alleged to have been committed on the trial of any indictment, the fact of that former trial shall be sufficiently proved by a certificate signed by the clerk (or the clerk's deputy) of the court where the indictment was tried without proof of the signature (Perjury Act 1911, s. 14). **F8.30**

Proceedings in County Courts

Records of county court proceedings may be proved by certified copies. **F8.31**

County Courts Act 1984, s. 12

(2) Any entry in a book or other document required by the said regulations to be kept for the purposes of this section, or a copy of any such entry or document purporting to be signed and certified as a true copy by a judge of the county court, shall at all times without further proof be admitted in any court or place whatsoever as evidence of the entry and of the proceeding referred to by it and of the regularity of that proceeding.

Procedure for Obtaining Records

Where legislation allows a certificate of conviction or acquittal or an extract from records kept by a court officer to be introduced in evidence in criminal proceedings, a person who wants to be supplied with such a certificate or extract must make a written application to the court officer that complies with the requirements of CrimPR 5.9 (see Supplement, **R5.9**). **F8.32**

Affidavits

On a prosecution for perjury in an affidavit, the affidavit itself must be produced and proved (*Rees d Howell and Dalton v Bowen* (1825) M'Cle & Yo 383), unless it can be proved to have been lost or destroyed, in which case secondary evidence is admissible of its contents and the signature of the accused (*Milnes* (1860) 2 F & F 10, and see **F8.11**). **F8.33**

Convictions and Acquittals

Provision for the proof of convictions and acquittals is made in the PACE 1984, s. 73. This is dealt with at F12. **F8.34**

BANKERS' BOOKS

General

F8.35 In order to facilitate the proof of matters recorded in bankers' books, the Bankers' Books Evidence Act 1879 provides for proof of the contents of such books by the production of examined copies.

Bankers' Books Evidence Act 1879, s. 3

Subject to the provisions of this Act, a copy of any entry in a banker's book shall in all legal proceedings be received as prima facie evidence of such entry, and of the matters, transactions, and accounts therein recorded.

The expressions 'bank' and 'banker' are defined by s. 9(1) of the Act to mean a deposit-taker (an expression defined by s. 9(1A) to (1C)) and the National Savings Bank.

'Bankers' books' were originally defined to include ledgers, daybooks, cash books, account books, and all other books used in the ordinary business of the bank. Section 9(2) of the 1879 Act, as substituted by the Banking Act 1979, extended that definition. It provides that expressions in the Act relating to 'bankers' books' include 'ledgers, daybooks, cash books, account books and other records used in the ordinary business of the bank, whether those records are in written form or are kept on microfilm, magnetic tape or any other form of mechanical or electronic data retrieval mechanism'. In *Williams v Williams* [1988] QB 161, it was held that paid cheques and paying-in slips retained by a bank after the conclusion of a banking transaction to which they relate are not 'bankers' books', because, even if bundles of such documents can be treated as 'records used in the ordinary business of the bank', the act of adding an individual cheque (paying-in slip) cannot be regarded as the making of an 'entry' in the records. It is submitted that similar reasoning may be used to justify the decision reached in *Dadson* (1983) 77 Cr App R 91 prior to the coming into force of the extended definition, that copies of letters written by a bank and contained in a file of its correspondence, were not 'bankers' books'. The words 'other records used in the ordinary business of the bank' are to be construed *eiusdem generis* with ledgers, daybooks, cash books and account books and therefore do not cover records kept by the bank of conversations between its employees and customers or others or internal memoranda (*Re Howglen Ltd* [2001] 1 All ER 376). In the case of documents falling outside the statutory definition, use may be made, in appropriate circumstances, of the hearsay provisions of the CJA 2003, including s. 133 of that Act (see **F8.5**).

F8.36 **Bankers' Books Evidence Act 1879, ss. 4 to 8**

4. A copy of an entry in a banker's book shall not be received in evidence under this Act unless it be first proved that the book was at the time of the making of the entry one of the ordinary books of the bank, and that the entry was made in the usual and ordinary course of business, and that the book is in the custody or control of the bank.

   Such proof may be given by a partner or officer of the bank, and may be given orally or by an affidavit sworn before any commissioner or person authorised to take affidavits.
5. A copy of an entry in a banker's book shall not be received in evidence under this Act unless it be further proved that the copy has been examined with the original entry and is correct.

   Such proof shall be given by some person who has examined the copy with the original entry, and may be given either orally or by an affidavit sworn before any commissioner or person authorised to take affidavits.
6. A banker or officer of a bank shall not, in any legal proceeding to which the bank is not a party, be compellable to produce any banker's book the contents of which can be proved under this Act, or to appear as a witness to prove the matters, transactions, and accounts therein recorded, unless by order of a judge made for special cause.
7. On the application of any party to a legal proceeding a court or judge may order that such party be at liberty to inspect and take copies of any entries in a banker's book for any of the purposes of such proceedings. An order under this section may be made either with or without

summoning the bank or any other party, and shall be served on the bank three clear days before the same is to be obeyed, unless the court or judge otherwise directs.

8. The costs of any application to a court or judge under or for the purposes of this Act, and the costs of anything done or to be done under an order of a court or judge made under or for the purposes of this Act shall be in the discretion of the court or judge, who may order the same or any part thereof to be paid to any party by the bank, where the same have been occasioned by any default or delay on the part of the bank. Any such order against a bank may be enforced as if the bank was a party to the proceeding.

'A court', for the purposes of s. 7, includes justices before whom criminal proceedings are pending (*Kinghorn* [1908] 2 KB 949). An application under s. 7 in criminal proceedings will not be refused on the grounds that it incriminates the party against whom it is made; but it is a serious interference with the liberty of the subject, and the court should be satisfied, before making an order, that the application is more than a mere 'fishing expedition' by considering whether the prosecution have other evidence to support the charge. The court should also limit the period of disclosure of the bank account to a period in time which is strictly relevant to the charge (*Williams v Summerfield* [1972] 2 QB 512). In *Marlborough Street Stipendiary Magistrate, ex parte Simpson* (1980) 70 Cr App R 290, orders under the Act were quashed on the ground that they were not limited to a defined period in time. See also *Nottingham City Justices, ex parte Lynn* (1984) 79 Cr App R 238, where, on a charge of drug smuggling, an order for the inspection of accounts over a period of three years was reduced to a period of six months, on the ground that there was insufficient evidence to link D with offences during most of the three years. **F8.37**

Bank Accounts of a Non-party An order may be made to inspect the accounts of a person who is not a party to the proceedings, even if not compellable as a witness. Thus in *Andover Justices, ex parte Rhodes* [1980] Crim LR 644, the Divisional Court upheld an order in respect of the account of the husband of an accused, charged with the theft of money, who had told the police that the money was in her husband's account. However, in criminal cases, such an order should be made only in exceptional circumstances, and where the private interest in keeping a bank account confidential is outweighed by the public interest in assisting a prosecution (*Grossman* (1981) 73 Cr App R 302, at p. 307). In *MacKinnon v Donaldson, Lufkin and Jenrette Securities Corporation* [1986] Ch 482, *Grossman* was applied, although it was acknowledged that the decision in that case had been given *per incuriam* since the proceedings were criminal and, under the Supreme Court Act 1981 (now the Senior Courts Act 1981), s. 18(1)(a), the Court of Appeal had no jurisdiction. **F8.38**

Foreign Banks In *MacKinnon v Donaldson, Lufkin and Jenrette Securities Corporation* [1986] Ch 482 it was held that, save in exceptional circumstances, an order should not be made against a foreign bank which is not a party to the proceedings, even if it carries on business within the jurisdiction and is a recognised bank under the Banking Act 1979, to produce documents outside the jurisdiction concerning business transacted outside the jurisdiction, because an order under the 1879 Act is an exercise of sovereign authority to assist in the administration of justice, and foreign banks owe their customers a duty of confidence regulated by the law of the country where the documents are kept. **F8.39**

Procedure An application under s. 7 of the 1879 Act may be made *ex parte*, but 'there is much to be said for notice being given' (*Marlborough Street Stipendiary Magistrate, ex parte Simpson* (1980) 70 Cr App R 291, per Widgery LJ at p. 294). See also, in the case of accounts of a person who is not a party to the proceedings, *Grossman* (1981) 73 Cr App R 302, per Oliver LJ at p. 309: either the order should not be made until the person affected has been informed and given an opportunity to be heard, or it should be made in the form of an order *nisi*, allowing a period for that person to show cause why the order should not take effect. **F8.40**

An order under s. 7 of the 1879 Act is not a precondition of adducing evidence under s. 3. The purpose of s. 7 is to enable a banker's books to be inspected and copied despite the duty of confidentiality owed by the banker to the customer, but an order would be unnecessary if, for instance, the customer waived the right to confidentiality and the bank agreed to inspection and copying (*Wheatley v Commissioner of Police of the British Virgin Islands* [2006] UKPC 24, [2006] 1 WLR 1683, construing the British Virgin Islands Bankers' Books (Evidence) Act 1881).

PROOF OF DUE EXECUTION

F8.41 The due execution of a document is established by:

(a) proof that it was signed by the person by whom it purports to have been signed; and
(b) if attestation is necessary, proof that it was attested.

In the case of public and judicial documents, the statutory provisions which enable their contents to be proved by copies also dispense with the need to prove due execution (see **F8.13** to **F8.34** and **F1.6**). Where a party seeks to rely upon the contents of a private document, due execution may be formally admitted or presumed. A document which is more than 20 years old, produced from proper custody and otherwise free from suspicion, is presumed to have been duly executed. At common law the period was 30 years, but 20 years was substituted by the Evidence Act 1938, s. 4. A document comes from proper custody even if not found in the best and most proper place of deposit, provided that the court is satisfied that the place in which it was found was custody that was reasonable and natural in the circumstances (*Bishop of Meath v Marquess of Winchester* (1836) 3 Bing NC 183, per Tindal CJ). Proof of due execution is also unnecessary if the document in question is in the possession of an opponent who refuses to comply with a notice to produce it (*Cooke v Tanswell* (1818) 8 Taunt 450). Subject to the foregoing, a party seeking to rely on the contents of a private document must prove its due execution.

F8.42 Proof that a document was signed or written by the person by whom it purports to have been signed or written may be effected in a variety of ways:

(a) by the admission of the person in question (*Waldridge v Kennison* (1794) 1 Esp 143);
(b) by the testimony (or admissible hearsay assertion) of the signatory identifying his or her own signature (hand);
(c) by the testimony (or admissible hearsay assertion) of a person who witnessed the execution of the document;
(d) by the opinion evidence of a person acquainted with the signature or handwriting (*Doe d Mudd v Suckermore* (1836) 5 A & E 703 at p. 705; *Slaney* (1832) 5 C & P 213); or
(e) by comparison of the document in question with another document which is admitted or proved to have been signed or written by the person in question under the Criminal Procedure Act 1865, s. 8. See further **F11.25**.

Any of these methods of proof may also be used in the case of a private document which, although not required by law to be attested, was in fact attested. Under the Criminal Procedure Act 1865, s. 7: 'It shall not be necessary to prove by the attesting witness any instrument to the validity of which attestation is not requisite, and such instrument may be proved as if there had been no attesting witness thereto'.

Where a document requires attestation to be formally valid, it is not strictly necessary to prove attestation by calling an attesting witness, except in the case of wills and other testamentary documents. Under the Evidence Act 1938, s. 3, 'an instrument to the validity of which attestation is requisite may, instead of being proved by an attesting witness, be proved in the manner in which it might be proved if no attesting witness were alive: Provided that nothing in this section shall apply to the proof of wills and other testamentary documents.' Thus, the attestation of private documents other than testamentary documents may be proved by the testimony of an attesting witness; or by evidence as to the handwriting of the attesting witness; or by other evidence, such as the testimony of a non-attesting witness to the execution.

PRESUMPTIONS CONCERNING DOCUMENTS

A document which is more than 20 years old and comes from proper custody is presumed to have been duly executed. It is also presumed that: **F8.43**

(a) a document was made on the date which it bears (*Re Adamson* (1875) LR 3 P & D 253, at p. 256);
(b) a deed was duly sealed (*Re Sandilands* (1871) LR 6 CP 411); and
(c) an alteration or erasure in a deed was made before execution, but that an alteration or erasure in a will was made after execution (*Doe d Tatum v Catomore* (1851) 16 QB 745).

STAMPED DOCUMENTS

In criminal proceedings, a document required to be stamped for the purposes of stamp duty is admissible even if not duly stamped (Stamp Act 1891, s. 14). **F8.44**

REAL EVIDENCE

Tangible Objects

Real evidence is usually some material object, the existence, condition or value of which is in issue or relevant to an issue, produced in court for inspection by the tribunal of fact. (As to inspection out of court, see **F8.50**.) Little if any weight can attach to real evidence in the absence of accompanying testimony identifying the object and connecting it with the facts in issue. In some cases the tribunal of fact must not draw its own unaided conclusion without the assistance of expert testimony: see, e.g., *Tilley* [1961] 3 All ER 406 and *Hipson* [1969] Crim LR 85 (comparison of handwriting). **F8.45**

There is no rule of law that an object must be produced, or its non-production excused, before oral evidence may be given about it. In *Hocking v Ahlquist Bros Ltd* [1944] KB 120, proceedings against manufacturers of clothing for non-compliance with restrictions relating to the method of manufacture, in which evidence as to the condition of the garments was received from witnesses who had visited the manufacturer's premises, it was held that the magistrate had been wrong to dismiss the information on the basis that the garments were not produced at the trial. See also *Miller v Howe* [1969] 3 All ER 451: it is not necessary for the police to produce the very breath test device used by them on a particular occasion. Non-production, however, may give rise to an inference adverse to the party failing to produce the object in question (*Armory v Delamirie* (1722) 1 Str 505), and may go to the weight of the oral evidence adduced. In *Francis* (1874) LR 2 CCR 128, a trial for attempting to pass off a false ring, at which the ring was not produced but witnesses who had seen it gave evidence as to its falsity, Lord Coleridge CJ said (at p. 133): 'though the production of the article may afford ground for observation more or less weighty, according to the circumstances, it only goes to the weight, not the admissibility of the evidence'.

Once an article has become an exhibit, the court has a responsibility, for the purposes of justice, to preserve and retain it until the trial is concluded, or to arrange for its preservation and retention, the usual course being for the court to entrust the exhibits to the police or to the DPP. The duty of the prosecution, if entrusted with exhibits pending trial, is: **F8.46**

(a) to take all proper care to preserve the exhibits safe from loss or damage;
(b) to co-operate with the defence in order to allow them reasonable access to the exhibits for the purpose of inspection and examination; and
(c) to produce the exhibits at the trial (*Lambeth Metropolitan Stipendiary Magistrate, ex parte McComb* [1983] QB 551). See also *Uxbridge Justices, ex parte Sofaer* (1986) 85 Cr App R 367.

However, as to (c), it is submitted that the duty to produce applies only in the case of exhibits which the prosecution or the defence intend to use at trial.

Behaviour, Appearance and Demeanour

F8.47 In addition to material objects, the following may also be regarded as varieties of real evidence:

(a) a person's behaviour, e.g., misconduct in court for the purposes of contempt of court;
(b) a person's physical appearance, e.g., for the purposes of identification or on the question of the existence or causation of personal injuries;
(c) a person's demeanour or attitude which, in the case of a witness, may be relevant to his or her credit, the weight to be attached to the witness's evidence, or whether he or she is to be treated as hostile.

Documents as Real Evidence

F8.48 Documents on the contents of which a party seeks to rely, whether as evidence of their truth, under an exception to the hearsay rule, or as original evidence, are subject to the rules as to proof of contents and due execution, dealt with at **F8.2** to **F8.44**. These rules, however, have no application if:

(a) the contents are referred to merely for the purposes of identifying the document in question or establishing the bare fact of its existence (*Boyle v Wiseman* (1855) 11 Exch 360, at pp. 367 *et seq*.); or
(b) the document is tendered as a material object, regardless of its contents, in order to show, e.g., its appearance, that it bears certain fingerprints, that it is made of a particular substance, or that it is in a particular physical condition.

In such cases, a document may be treated as a tangible object to the extent relevant to do so, and becomes a piece of real evidence.

Statements Produced by Computers and Mechanical Devices

F8.49 Where a computer or mechanical or other device is used as a calculator, i.e. as a tool which does not contribute its own knowledge, but merely performs a sophisticated calculation which could have been done manually, the printout or other reading is not hearsay but an item of real evidence, the proof and relevance of which depends on the evidence of those using the device, such as the computer programmer and other experts involved: see **F16.12**. See also the CJA 2003, s. 129, regarding the admission of representations of fact made otherwise than by a person (see **F16.13**).

There is a rebuttable presumption as to the correct functioning of mechanical and other instruments (see **F3.59**). However, in the case of computer printouts, before the judge can decide whether they are admissible as real evidence or as hearsay pursuant to statute, it is necessary for appropriate authoritative evidence to be called to describe the function and operation of the computer (*Cochrane* [1993] Crim LR 48).

Views

F8.50 The term 'view' is used to describe both an inspection out of court of some material object which it is inconvenient or impossible to bring to court (see, e.g., *London General Omnibus Co. Ltd v Lavell* [1901] 1 Ch 135 (an omnibus)), and an inspection of the *locus in quo*.

A view should not take place after the summing-up (see *Lawrence* [1968] 1 All ER 579, which was distinguished in *Nixon* [1968] 2 All ER 33, where the inspection was at the express request of the defence). A view should be attended by the judge, the tribunal of fact, the parties, their counsel, and the shorthand writer. In the case of magistrates, as a general rule a visit to the *locus in quo* should take place before the conclusion of the evidence and in the presence of the parties or their representatives, so as to afford them the opportunity of commenting on any feature of the locality which has altered since the time of the incident or any feature not previously noticed by the parties which impresses the magistrates (*Parry v Boyle* (1987) 83 Cr App R 310). The presence of the accused is important because he or she may be able to point out some important matter of which the legal adviser is ignorant or about which the magistrates are making a mistake (*Ely Justices, ex parte Burgess* [1992] Crim LR 888). See also *Gibbons v DPP* (12 December 2000 unreported).

Under CrimPD VI, para. 26J.1 (see Supplement, **CPD.26J**), a judge must produce ground rules for a view, after discussion with the advocates. The ground rules should contain details of what the jury should be shown, and in what order, and who will be permitted to speak and what will be said; and they should make provision for the jury to ask questions. Further detailed guidance on the procedure to be followed in relation to planning, travel and at the view is set out in the *Crown Court Compendium* (July 2020), ch. 2-5.

In a trial by jury, the judge should be present at a view, whether or not any witness is present for the purposes of a demonstration (*Hunter* [1985] 2 All ER 173). However, if the judge is absent, a conviction will not necessarily be quashed. In *Turay* [2007] EWCA Crim 2821, where the judge, counsel and D were not present at the view (at which no evidence was given), the appeal against conviction was dismissed, D being unable to point to any significant or actual disadvantage to the defence or any damage to the trial process itself. A judge attending a view should take precautions to prevent any witnesses who are present from communicating, except by way of demonstration, with the jury (*Martin* (1872) LR 1 CCR 378; *Karamat v The Queen* [1956] AC 256). A witness who has already given evidence at the trial may take part in a view; but witnesses taking part in a view should be recalled to be cross-examined, if desired (*Karamat v The Queen*). **F8.51**

It is improper for one juror to attend a view and report back to the others. In *Gurney* [1976] Crim LR 567, the Court of Appeal held that this contravened the principle that the jury should remain together at all times, and quashed the conviction. If the accused declines to attend a view, he or she cannot afterwards raise the objection that his or her absence of itself made the view illegal, though the accused could object if any evidence were given outside the scope of the view as ordered (*Karamat v The Queen*).

It is critical, before any court embarks upon a view, that there is clarity about precisely what is to happen, who is to stand in what position, what (if any) objects should be placed in what position, and who will do what. None of this should happen at the scene of the view, which should be conducted without discussion (*M v DPP* [2009] EWHC 752 (Admin), [2009] 2 Cr App R 12 (181)).

Lip-reading

An expert lip-reader who, after viewing a CCTV recording of someone speaking, gives opinion evidence as to what was said, is providing assistance to the jury in their interpretation of a variety of real evidence. Such evidence is capable of passing the ordinary tests of relevance and reliability and is therefore potentially admissible. However, it requires a special warning from the judge as to its limitations and the concomitant risk of error, not least because the expert may not be completely accurate (*Luttrell* [2004] EWCA Crim 1344, [2004] 2 Cr App R 31 (520)). **F8.52**

Audio Recordings and Transcripts

The contents of audio recordings, produced and played over in court, may be admitted as: **F8.53**

(a) evidence of their truth, under an exception to the hearsay rule (see, e.g., *Senat* (1968) 52 Cr App R 282, which concerned tape recordings of incriminating conversations, and *Maqsud Ali* [1966] 1 QB 688); or
(b) a variety of original evidence, e.g., simply to show that the recording was made.

In either event, the voices recorded must be properly identified (*Maqsud Ali*, at p. 701). At common law, it was held that there is no objection to a properly proved transcript of the recording being put before the jury, provided they are guided by what they *hear* (*Maqsud Ali*, at p. 702). See also *Rampling* [1987] Crim LR 823: the transcript, *not in itself evidence*, may be used as a convenience to the jury. However, an audio recording is a 'document' for the purposes of the CJA 2003, s. 133 (s. 134(1)). Thus, where a statement contained in a recording is admissible as evidence, it may be proved by production of the recording; or (whether or not the original is still in existence) by the production of a copy, or of the material part of it, authenticated in whatever way the court may approve; and it is immaterial how many removes there are between a copy and the original. A copy, for these purposes, includes a transcript of the sounds embodied in the recording (s. 134(1)). As to 'authentication', it is submitted that the courts are likely to require the same kind of proof that was necessary in the case of copies at common law before s. 133 came into force, namely a proper explanation as to why the originals are not available, and proof of the complete accuracy of the copies (*Robson* (June 1973 unreported)).

In the case of audio recordings and transcripts of police interviews, s. 133 must be read in conjunction with the Code of Practice on Audio Recording Interviews with Suspects (PACE Code E), together with CrimPD V, paras. 16C.1 to 16C.16 (see Supplement, **CPD.16C**). The provisions of PACE Code E must be followed in all areas where interviews with suspects are required to be recorded by virtue of the provisions of an order made under s. 60(1)(b) of the PACE 1984. Under s. 67(11) of the 1984 Act, Code E is admissible in evidence, and if any provision thereof appears to the court to be relevant to any question arising in the proceedings, it shall be taken into account in determining that question.

F8.54 **Common-law Authorities** Section 133 of the CJA 2003 must also be read, it is submitted, in conjunction with the common-law authorities which applied before it came into force. At common law, if the prosecution seek to adduce a recording in evidence, the judge must be satisfied, in the absence of the jury, that the prosecution have made out a prima facie case of originality and authenticity, by evidence which defines and describes the provenance and history of the recording up to the moment of its production in court. If such evidence appears to remain intact after cross-examination, it is not incumbent on the judge to hear and weigh other evidence which might controvert the prima facie case. The judge is required to be satisfied to the civil standard, on a balance of probabilities, because application of the criminal standard would amount to a usurpation by the judge of the function of the jury (*Robson* [1972] 2 All ER 699, per Shaw J, a ruling upheld by the Court of Appeal (unreported); cf. *Stevenson* [1971] 1 All ER 678). A better approach, it is submitted, also involving no usurpation of the jury function, would be for the judge to decide the issue as if the party seeking to adduce the evidence bore an evidential burden. The question for the judge would then be whether sufficient evidence had been adduced to justify, as a possibility, a finding by the jury, on the issues of originality and genuineness, favourable to the party seeking to admit the recording.

F8.55 In *Rampling* [1987] Crim LR 823, the Court of Appeal gave the following general guidance upon the use in trials of recordings and transcripts of police interviews:

(a) The recording can be produced and proved by the interviewing officer or any other officer present when it was taken.
(b) The officer should have listened to the recording before the trial so that, if required, any objections to its authenticity or accuracy can be dealt with.
(c) As to authenticity, the officer can, if required, prove who spoke the recorded words.
(d) As to accuracy, the officer can deal with any challenge, e.g., that the recording has been falsified by addition or omission.
(e) The transcript of the recording can be produced by the officer, who, before the trial, should have checked it against the recording for accuracy. The recording is the evidence in the case and can be made an exhibit; the transcript, not in itself evidence, may be used as a convenience to the jury (but see now the CJA 2003, s. 133).
(f) Use of the transcript is an administrative matter to be decided in his or her discretion by the trial judge. In many cases the accused will agree to its use and will not require the recording to be played at all, in which case the transcript will be read out by the officer who produced it; however, the accused is entitled, if so wished, to have any part of the recording played to the jury.
(g) If any part of the recording is played, it is for the judge to decide whether the jury should have the transcript, in order to follow the recording, and have it with them when they retire; the use of the transcript is within the judge's discretion and is not dependent on the consent of the parties; a transcript is usually of very considerable value to the jury, but each case has to be decided on its own facts.

Jury's Access to Recording Where a recording becomes an exhibit (see (e) above), the jury may take it with them when they retire like any other exhibit in the case, and it makes no difference if it has already been heard in open court. In most cases, nothing turns on the tone of voice in which an interview was conducted and therefore it will usually be sufficient for the jury to have a transcript, much of which can and should be summarised; but where the tone of voice is all-important, for example when it is alleged that the interviewing officer spoke in a raised voice or in a brusque and intimidating manner, then, subject to editing out any inadmissible material, the jury should be given the original recording (*Emmerson* (1991) 92 Cr App R 284). The Court of Appeal in *Emmerson* also gave the following general guidance in the context of a tape recording (at p. 287): F8.56

> (1) If the whole of the tape has been played in open court there is no reason why the jury should not have the tape if either side or the jury want it as well as any transcript. It is the tape, after all, which is the evidence. But in order not to waste time the jury should always be directed to the relevant part of the tape. (2) If only part of the tape has been played in open court but the jury have a transcript of the whole tape, then there is no reason why the jury should not have the whole tape. (3) If only part of the tape has been played in open court and the jury have no transcript, then the tape should be edited so as to ensure that the jury do not have anything that has not been given in evidence. (4) We see no advantage, and some disadvantage, in a court being reassembled in order to enable the jury to re-hear a passage of the tape which they have already heard in open court. This would seem to serve no useful purpose and be productive of unnecessary inconvenience.

If the recording is not played during the course of a trial but, after retirement, the jury ask to hear it rather than rely on the written transcript, they are entitled to hear it because the recording is the exhibit and the transcript merely a convenient method of presenting it (*Riaz* (1991) 94 Cr App R 339). However, where the prosecution opt not to play the recording but to provide the jury with an agreed transcript and agreed expert comment on it, the jury should not be allowed to conduct their own inquiry as to what is on the recording (*Hagan* [1997] 1 Cr App R 464). If the jury are entitled to hear the recording, although it is a matter of judicial discretion, the better practice is to bring the jury back into open court to hear it because of the difficulties which might arise if they are permitted free access to the recording, including the risk that they might hear matters inadvertently left on it which they should not hear (*Riaz*). Equally, however, where the jury ask to hear a recording, of which there is an agreed transcript, which does not contain inadmissible passages and which *has* already been played in court, the judge has discretion to permit them to listen to it in the privacy of their retiring room (*Tonge* [1993] Crim LR 876). As to a jury request to hear a recording during or after closing speeches, but before retirement, see *Aitken* (1991) 94 Cr App R 85 at **F6.10**. F8.57

Photographs, Video Recordings and Films

A photograph may be admitted in evidence to enable a witness to identify a person or thing. In *Tolson* (1864) 4 F & F 103, a case of bigamy, a photograph was produced, which was admitted to be a photograph of the first husband, and a witness was allowed to testify that he had seen the man in the photograph alive after the date of the allegedly bigamous marriage. F8.58

A photograph (or film) the relevance of which can be established by the testimony of someone with personal knowledge of the circumstances in which it was taken (or made), may also be admitted to prove the commission of an offence and the identity of the offender. As to the identity of the offender, use may also be made of facial mapping experts (*Atkins* [2010] EWCA Crim 1876, [2010] 1 Cr App R 8 (117), considered at **F11.11**). In *Dodson* [1984] 1 WLR 971, it was held that photographs taken at half-second intervals by security cameras installed at a building society office at which an armed robbery had been attempted, were admissible, on the issue of whether an offence had been committed and, if so, who had committed it, even though no witnesses were called to identify the men in the photographs. However, in a case in which the jury are invited to 'identify' the accused in court from a photograph or video recording of the offender committing the offence, they should be warned of the risk of mistaken identity and of the need to exercise particular care in any identification which they make. They must take into account whether the appearance of the accused has changed since the visual recording was made, but a full *Turnbull* direction (*Turnbull* [1977] QB 224: see **F19.9**) is inappropriate because the process of identifying a person from a photograph is a commonplace event and some things are obvious from the photograph itself. Thus they do not need to be told that the photograph is of good quality or poor, nor whether the person is shown in close-up or was distant from the camera etc. (*Blenkinsop* [1995] 1 Cr App R 7, approving *Downey* [1995] 1 Cr App R 547; cf. *Taylor v Chief Constable of Cheshire* [1986] 1 All ER 225, at **F8.62**). However, it seems that a request by them that the accused stand up and turn around, in order that they may be given a better view, does not have to be met, at least not by an accused who has elected not to testify (*McNamara* [1996] Crim LR 750).

F8.59 In *Roberts* [1998] Crim LR 682, a police constable made a written statement relating to charges of assault and affray. A video camera had recorded the events in question and the constable later provided a commentary on the video to enable prosecuting counsel to explain to the jury, when viewing it, who was who and where the events took place. The video was then made available to the defence. It was held that it was not wrong in principle that the constable had seen the video. On seeing a video a witness might find that in some respects his recollection had been at fault and might wish to modify earlier evidence. However, nothing should be done which amounted to rehearsing the evidence of a witness or coaching him so as to encourage him to alter the evidence already given. The acid test was whether the procedure adopted was such as to taint the resulting evidence. That was not so in the instant case. The video had been made available to the defence and had been shown to defence witnesses before they gave their evidence, and the constable had been directly challenged on discrepancies between his first statement and his commentary.

F8.60 In *Thomas* [1986] Crim LR 682, a case of reckless driving, a video recording of the route taken by D was admitted to remove the need for maps and still photographs, and to convey a more accurate picture of the roads in question. In *The Statue of Liberty* [1968] 2 All ER 195, a civil action concerning a collision between two ships, Sir Jocelyn Simon P, rejecting a submission that a cinematograph film of radar echoes, recorded by a shore radar station, was inadmissible because produced mechanically without human intervention, said (at p. 740): 'If tape recordings are admissible, it seems that a photograph of radar reception is equally admissible — or indeed, any other type of photograph. It would be an absurd distinction that a photograph should be admissible if the camera were operated manually by a photographer, but not if it were operated by a trip or clock mechanism.' Compare *Wood* (1982) 76 Cr App R 23, at **F16.13**.

In the case of visual recordings of interviews, see also PACE Code F (see **D1.90**).

F8.61 **Admissibility as Hearsay or Real Evidence** Photographs and films are excluded from the definition of a 'statement' for the purposes of the provisions relating to hearsay in the CJA 2003 (see s. 115(2) at **F16.7**) but both would appear to be admissible at common law as a variety of real evidence (see *The Statue of Liberty* [1968] 2 All ER 195, where a film, in effect, contained a statement as to the paths taken by the two ships). Moreover, it has been said that a photograph, together with the sketch and the photofit, is in a class of evidence of its own, to which neither the rule against hearsay nor the rule against previous consistent or self-serving statements applies (*Cook* [1987] QB 417 per Watkins LJ; applied in *Constantinou* (1989) 91 Cr App R 74). However, representations made in a sketch or photofit are covered by the definition of 'statement' in the CJA 2003, s. 115(2). As to evidence of previous identification of the accused by police photographs, see further at **F19**.

F8.62 **Proof of Contents** The contents of photographs and films on which a party seeks to rely may be proved by production of the original; or by production of a copy proved to be an authentic copy; or by the parol evidence of witnesses who have seen the photograph or film. In *Kajala v Noble* (1982) 75 Cr App R 149, Ackner LJ held that the rule, that if an original document is available in a party's hands he or she must produce it and cannot give secondary evidence of it, was confined to written documents in the strict sense of the term and has no relevance to tapes or films. In *Taylor v Chief Constable of Cheshire* [1986] 1 All ER 225, a video cassette recording, made by a security camera and showing a person in a shop picking up an item and putting it into his jacket, was played to police officers who identified the person as D. The recording, after it had been returned to the shop, was accidentally erased. Evidence by the officers of what they had seen on the video was held to have been properly admitted, on the ground that what they had seen on the video was no different in principle from the evidence of a bystander who had actually witnessed the incident, and the appeal against conviction was dismissed. The Court of Appeal held that the weight and reliability of the evidence had to be assessed carefully and, because identification was in issue, by reference to the guidelines laid down in *Turnbull* [1977] QB 224, which had to be applied in relation to not only the camera, but also the visual display unit or recorded copy and the officers. See also *Constantinou* (1989) 91 Cr App R 74.

Jury Access Where a video or film has been shown in court and the jury, after retirement, ask to see it again, they may do so, but it is better if they see it again in open court (*Imran* [1997] Crim LR 754, in which the jury had seen a silent video of an attempted robbery). Where a jury ask for a video recording of the evidence of a complainant to be replayed, if they want to be reminded of what was said it is sufficient for the judge to remind them, but if they want to be reminded of how the words were spoken, the judge has a discretion to permit the recording to be replayed (*Rawlings* [1995] 1 All ER 580). Similarly, in the case of a video recording of an interview with an accused, a judge may accede to a jury request for the recording to be replayed in order to see how the evidence was given (*Minnott* [2016] EWCA Crim 2215). **F8.63**

PACE Code on Video-recording Interviews For the procedures to be followed on video-recording interviews with suspects, see PACE Code F. **F8.64**

Section F9 Public Policy

GENERAL PRINCIPLES

F9.1 This section concerns the principles of law governing the non-disclosure of material on the grounds of public policy and the exclusion of such material from evidence. As to the procedure on disclosure generally, see **D9**; as to the specific procedure to be followed on an application to the court that unused material should not be disclosed on such grounds, see **D9.49 *et seq.*** Part I of the CPIA 1996 generally disapplies the common-law rules relating to the prosecution duty of disclosure, but s. 21(2) of that Act preserves the rules of common law as to whether disclosure is in the public interest.

F9.2 It is in the public interest to withhold material, the disclosure of which would harm the nation or the proper functioning of the public service. It is also in the public interest that justice should be done, and should be publicly seen to be done, by the reception of all relevant evidence. If there is a conflict between these two interests, whether otherwise admissible evidence should be withheld in the public interest is a question of balance, to be decided by the courts and not by the executive (*Conway v Rimmer* [1968] AC 910). If the evidence is excluded, it is said to be withheld by reason of public interest immunity (*Lewes Justices, ex parte Secretary of State for the Home Department* [1973] AC 388, per Lord Reid at p. 400, disapproving use of the expression 'Crown privilege'; but contrast *Science Research Council v Nasse* [1980] AC 1028, per Lord Scarman at p. 1087). There is no absolute bar to a claim for public interest immunity where the claim, if successful, would prevent the disclosure of evidence of serious criminal misconduct by officials of the State, even in the case of torture or cruel, inhuman or degrading treatment, or other war crimes *(R (Mohamed) v Secretary of State for Foreign and Commonwealth Affairs* [2009] EWHC 152 (Admin), [2009] 1 WLR 2653).

In some cases, the relevant minister (or head of department) or the A-G may intervene to claim immunity. Alternatively, the claim to immunity may be made by the party seeking to withhold the evidence, either on its own initiative or at the request of the relevant government department (see, e.g., *Burmah Oil Co. Ltd v Bank of England* [1980] AC 1090). If necessary, the judge should raise the issue, because if there is a public interest to be protected, that should be done regardless of party advantage (*Duncan v Cammell Laird & Co. Ltd* [1942] AC 624, per Viscount Simon LC at p. 642).

F9.3 A claim to public interest immunity may be supported by affidavit evidence from the relevant minister (or head of department), or by a certificate signed by the minister. However, a minister's affidavit or certificate is not final (except, it seems, in cases concerning national security: see *Balfour v Foreign and Commonwealth Office* [1994] 2 All ER 588, considered at **F9.11**). Although an objection by the Crown to the disclosure of material is entitled to the greatest weight, the court may ask for clarification or amplification of the objection, and has the power to inspect documentary evidence privately and to order its production notwithstanding ministerial objection (*Conway v Rimmer* [1968] AC 910). In *Conway v Rimmer*, it was suggested that certain classes of documents, such as Cabinet papers and Foreign Office despatches, should never be disclosed, whatever their contents may be (see per Lords Reid and Upjohn at pp. 952 and 993 respectively). Since then, however, the House of Lords has made it clear that the courts should be prepared to evaluate 'class' claims, even in the case of high-level government papers, and in appropriate circumstances, albeit very rarely, to require their disclosure (*Burmah Oil Co. Ltd v Bank of England* [1980] AC 1090, per Lord Keith at p. 1134; *Air Canada v Secretary of State for Trade (No. 2)* [1983] 2 AC 394, per Lord Fraser at p. 432).

In December 1996 the Lord Chancellor issued a statement that the division into class and contents claims would no longer be applied, and that in future ministers would focus directly on the damage that disclosure of sensitive documents would cause. Under this approach, ministers claim immunity only when they believe that disclosure of a document will cause real damage or harm to the public interest. Damage will normally have to be in the form of a direct or immediate threat to the safety of an individual or to the nation's economic interests or relations with a foreign State, although in some cases the anticipated damage might be indirect or longer term, such as damage to a regulatory process. In any event the nature of the harm will have to be clearly explained, and ministers will no longer be able to claim immunity for internal advice or national security material merely by pointing to the general nature of the document. It is submitted that non-governmental bodies claiming public interest immunity, although not bound by the Lord Chancellor's statement, should adopt the same approach. **F9.4**

Decisions as to what should be withheld from disclosure are for the court and should not be made (without reference to the court) by the prosecution, the police, the DPP or counsel (*Ward* [1993] 2 All ER 577 and, in the case of co-accused, *Adams* [1997] Crim LR 292). The principles are the same whether the proceedings are summary or on indictment, but when, in the case of an either-way offence, it is known that a contested issue as to the disclosure of sensitive material is likely to arise, that consideration may sometimes properly found an application by the Crown for trial on indictment (*Bromley Magistrates' Court, ex parte Smith* [1995] 4 All ER 146, distinguishing *DPP, ex parte Warby* [1994] Crim LR 281). The rule established in *Ward* is now reflected in the relevant disclosure provisions of the CPIA 1996. These procedural rules, including the *ex parte* procedure for certain public interest immunity applications and the rules relating to the appointment of a 'special advocate' or 'special counsel', are considered at **D9.49** ***et seq***. As to immunity claims in summary trials, see also **D9.63**. If, in the course of a public interest immunity hearing (whether on the *voir dire* or otherwise), prosecution witnesses lied to the judge, the prosecution would be likely to be tainted beyond redemption, however strong the evidence against the accused might otherwise be (*Early* [2002] EWCA Crim 1904, [2003] 1 Cr App R 19 (288)). **F9.5**

In *Keane* [1994] 2 All ER 478 Lord Taylor CJ held that it is for the prosecution to put before the court only those documents which they regard as material but wish to withhold. It is generally for the prosecution, not the court, to identify the documents and information which are material. However, if, in an exceptional case, the prosecution are in doubt about the materiality of some documents or information, the court may be asked to rule on that issue. When the court is seised of the material, the judge should perform the balancing exercise, balancing the weight of the public interest in non-disclosure against the importance of the documents to the issues of interest to the defence, present and potential, so far as they have been disclosed or the judge can foresee them. However a ruling made prior to the hearing is not necessarily final, because issues may later emerge whereby the public interest in non-disclosure is eclipsed by the accused's need for access (*Bower* [1994] Crim LR 281). The trial judge is under a continuous duty, in the light of the way in which the trial develops, to keep the initial decision under review, and prosecuting counsel must be fully informed as to the content of any disputed material so as to be in a position to invite the judge to reassess the situation if the previous denial of the material arguably becomes untenable in the light of developments in the trial (*Brown* [1994] 1 WLR 1599 at p. 1608). See also **D9.24**. **F9.6**

Voluntary Disclosure

The CPS may voluntarily disclose to the defence documents which would otherwise be in a class covered by public interest immunity, without referring the matter to the court for a ruling, subject to the safeguard of first seeking the express written approval of the Treasury Solicitor. The CPS should submit copies of the documents in question, identify the public interest immunity class into which they fall and indicate the materiality of the documents to the proceedings in which it is proposed to disclose them. The Treasury Solicitor should consult any other relevant government department and be satisfied that the balance falls clearly in favour of disclosure. **F9.7**

He or she should be more ready to disclose documents likely to assist the defence than those which the CPS wish to disclose with a view to furthering the interests of the prosecution. Before approving disclosure of documents of a particular class sought to be used by the prosecution, the Treasury Solicitor should consider not only their importance to the prosecution's case, but also the importance of the prosecution itself: it may be preferable to abandon the case rather than damage the integrity of the class claim. He or she should also maintain a permanent record of all approvals given so that any court ruling on disclosure would know how far immunity for that particular class of documents had been weakened by previous voluntary disclosure (*Horseferry Road Magistrates, ex parte Bennett (No. 2)* [1994] 1 All ER 289).

Balancing Exercise

F9.8 The principle of public interest immunity is applicable to criminal proceedings, but involves a different balancing exercise to that in civil proceedings. The judge will balance the desirability of preserving the public interest in non-disclosure against the interests of justice. Where the interests of justice arise in a criminal case touching and concerning liberty (or conceivably, on occasion, life), the weight to be attached to the interests of justice is plainly very great; it is a matter of whether the interests of justice outweigh the considerations of public interest as spoken to in the certificate of the minister. Any prior disclosure of the information in question is a matter to be taken into account in the balance. In assessing the interests of justice, the court must ask whether a document to which the certificate relates is material to the proceedings. Its materiality will depend on the purpose for which it is sought to be deployed. In cases concerning the identity of informers or persons who have allowed their premises to be used for police surveillance (see **F9.17**), there have been observations to the effect that the privilege cannot prevail if the evidence is necessary for the prevention of a miscarriage of justice — no balance is called for (*Governor of Brixton Prison, ex parte Osman* [1991] 1 All ER 108). But see also, in cases concerning the identity of informers, *Keane* [1994] 2 All ER 478, per Lord Taylor CJ (at pp. 751–2):

> We prefer to say that the outcome in the instances given by Lord Esher MR [in *Marks v Beyfus* (1890) 25 QBD 494: see F9.9] and Mann LJ [in *Ex parte Osman*] results from performing the balancing exercise, not from dispensing with it. If the disputed material may prove the defendant's innocence or avoid a miscarriage of justice, then the balance comes down resoundingly in favour of disclosing it.

F9.9 In *Clowes* [1992] 3 All ER 440, the accused were charged with theft and fraud following the collapse of two deposit-taking companies owing investors over £115 million. Public interest immunity was claimed in respect of transcripts of confidential interviews conducted by the liquidators of the company in order to establish whether civil claims could be brought. Phillips J held that he did not find very easy the concept of a balancing exercise between the nature of the public interest on the one hand and the degree and potential consequences of the risk of a miscarriage of justice on the other, but would not readily accept that proportionality between the two is never of relevance. On the facts, it did not seem that the public interest in question should carry greater weight than the public interest in concealing the identity of a police informer (see **F9.14**). Those interviewed inevitably accepted some risk of dissemination of the information they gave and there would be a relatively limited effect on 'the wells of voluntary information'. On the other hand, the accused were charged with grave offences and it was therefore of particular importance that no unnecessary impediment should be put in the way of presenting their defence in the best light. Another significant factor was the complexity of the evidence and the risk of lapse of memory on the part of witnesses.

HEADS OF PUBLIC INTEREST IMMUNITY

F9.10 The heads of public interest immunity which have been recognised by the courts relate to national security, diplomatic relations, international comity, the proper functioning of the public service, informers and information for the detection of crime, judges, jurors and sources of information contained in publications. Each is considered in the following paragraphs.

National Security, Diplomatic Relations and International Comity

Documents falling within this category are those most readily protected against disclosure; and in the case of national security, a ministerial certificate will be conclusive (*Balfour v Foreign and Commonwealth Office* [1994] 2 All ER 588). That case concerned material relating to the security and intelligence services. It was held that once there is an actual or potential risk to national security demonstrated by an appropriate ministerial certificate, the minister's view should prevail. See also *Hennessy v Wright* (1888) 21 QBD 509 (communications between the governor of a colony and the colonial secretary); *Chatterton v Secretary of State for India in Council* [1895] 2 QB 189 (communications between the government and the commander-in-chief of forces overseas); *Asiatic Petroleum Co. Ltd v Anglo Persian Oil Co. Ltd* [1916] 1 KB 822 (information relating to the Persian campaign in the First World War); *M Isaacs & Sons Ltd v Cook* [1925] 2 KB 391 (diplomatic despatches); *Duncan v Cammell Laird & Co. Ltd* [1942] AC 624 (information on the design of a new submarine); and *Buttes Gas and Oil Co. v Hammer (No. 3)* [1981] QB 223 (confidential communications with foreign sovereign states or concerning their interest in international territorial disputes). However, in *R (Al-Sweady) v Secretary of State for Defence* [2009] EWHC 1687 (Admin), where a ministerial certificate stated that it was not in the public interest, on national security grounds, to disclose certain redacted material but it transpired that a significant proportion of such material had previously been disclosed in open hearings and was therefore in the public domain, it was held that until such time as the Ministry of Defence could demonstrate that its procedures had remedied the risk of such errors recurring, it would be incumbent on courts to approach the contents of any ministerial certificate with very considerable caution. F9.11

Proper Functioning of Public Service

Public interest immunity may be claimed for communications to and from ministers and high-level government officials, regarding the formulation of government policy: see, e.g., *Burmah Oil Co. Ltd v Bank of England* [1980] AC 1090 (memoranda of meetings attended by ministers or government officials relating to government policy on economic matters); and *Air Canada v Secretary of State for Trade (No. 2)* [1983] 2 AC 394 (ministerial papers and inter-departmental communications between senior civil servants concerning government policy in relation to the British Airports Authority). F9.12

The public also has an interest in the effective working of non-governmental bodies and agencies performing public functions. However, although the categories of public interest are not closed, the courts can only proceed by analogy with interests which have previously been recognised by the authorities: see *D v National Society for the Prevention of Cruelty to Children* [1978] AC 171, per Lords Diplock, Hailsham and Simon at pp. 219, 226 and 240 respectively, applied in *Science Research Council v Nasse* [1980] AC 1028 (in which the House rejected a claim in respect of confidential reports on employees seeking promotion). Examples include *Re D (Infants)* [1970] 1 All ER 1086 (local authorities); *Lewes Justices, ex parte Secretary of State for the Home Department* [1973] AC 388 (the Gaming Board); *D v National Society for the Prevention of Cruelty to Children* [1978] AC 171 (the NSPCC); and *Buckley v Law Society (No. 2)* [1984] 3 All ER 313 (the Law Society).

Police Communications

Public interest immunity also attaches to police communications relating to the investigation of crime, such as documents or information upon the strength of which search warrants have been obtained (*Taylor v Anderton* (1986) *The Times*, 21 October 1986). Reports sent by the police to the DPP, even if the prosecution has been completed, have also attracted immunity, on the ground that there should be freedom of communication with the DPP, without fear that such reports may be inspected, analysed or investigated in subsequent civil proceedings (*Evans v Chief Constable of Surrey* [1988] QB 588). Immunity also attaches to international communications F9.13

between police forces or prosecuting authorities (*Horseferry Road Magistrates' Court, ex parte Bennett (No. 2)* [1994] 1 All ER 289), although in that case the balance favoured disclosure, the documents being relevant to the issue of whether B had been unlawfully returned to the jurisdiction. In appropriate circumstances, immunity may also be claimed for internal police communications other than those relating to the investigation of crime, on the ground that the public has an interest in the proper functioning of the police force (*Conway v Rimmer* [1968] AC 910).

Immunity may also be claimed for police complaints and disciplinary files (*Halford v Sharples* [1992] 3 All ER 624). There is no immunity, however, for written complaints against the police prompting investigations under Part IX of the PACE 1984 (*Conerney v Jacklin* [1985] Crim LR 234); and there is no class immunity for statements obtained for the purposes of such investigations, although immunity may be claimed in the case of a particular document by reason of its contents (*Chief Constable of the West Midlands Police, ex parte Wiley* [1995] 1 AC 274, overruling *Neilson v Laugharne* [1981] QB 736 and cases in which it was subsequently applied). However, the working papers and reports prepared by the investigating officers do form a class which is entitled to immunity, and therefore production of such material should be ordered only where the public interest in disclosure of their contents outweighs the public interest in preserving confidentiality (*Taylor v Anderton* [1995] 2 All ER 420).

Public interest immunity does not attach to statements made during the course of a police grievance procedure, initiated by an officer, alleging either racial or sexual discrimination (*Metropolitan Police Commissioner v Locker* [1993] 3 All ER 584).

Informers and Information for Detection of Crime

F9.14 For guidance on the authorisation of the use and conduct of informers by public authorities under the RIPA 2000, reference should be made to the Code of Practice for Covert Human Intelligence Sources.

There is a long-established rule of law that in public prosecutions witnesses may not be asked, and should not be allowed to disclose, the names of informers or the nature of the information given (*Hardy* (1794) 24 St Tr 199). In principle, the rule should prevent disclosure of not only the name of the informer, but also any information that will enable the informer to be identified (*Omar* 2007 ONCA 117 (Court of Appeal for Ontario)). The rule applies to public prosecutions brought by the DPP and bodies authorised by statute to bring public prosecutions. It also applies to police prosecutions, but not to other private prosecutions. The rationale of the rule was explained by Lawton LJ in *Hennessey* (1978) 68 Cr App R 419 (at p. 425): 'The courts appreciate the need to protect the identity of informers, not only for their own safety but to ensure that the supply of information about criminal activities does not dry up.' See also *D v National Society for the Prevention of Cruelty to Children* [1978] AC 171, per Lord Diplock at p. 218. The judge is obliged to apply the rule even if it is not invoked by the party entitled to object to disclosure (*Marks v Beyfus* (1890) 25 QBD 494, per Lord Esher MR at p. 500; *Rankine* [1986] QB 861, per Mann J at p. 867).

However, if a witness called at trial is a participating informant in the very instance with which the trial is concerned, there must be a very strong countervailing interest for the witness's status not to be revealed (*Patel* [2001] EWCA Crim 2505). In that case, it was not for HM Customs to determine the matter in their own favour without putting their own counsel or the court fully in the picture. As to interception of communications, see **D1.198**.

F9.15 There is an exception to the common-law rule where the judge is of the opinion that disclosure is necessary to establish the innocence of the accused.

> ...if upon the trial of a prisoner the judge should be of opinion that the disclosure of the name of the informant is necessary or right in order to show the prisoner's innocence, then one public policy is in conflict with another public policy, and that which says that an innocent man is not to be condemned when his innocence can be proved is the policy that must prevail. (*Marks v Beyfus* (1890) 25 QBD 494, per Lord Esher MR at p. 498)

This outcome, however, results from performing the balancing exercise, not from dispensing with it (*Keane* [1994] 2 All ER 478: see **F9.6**). Judges should scrutinise applications for disclosure of details about informants with very great care and should be astute to see whether assertions that knowledge of such details is essential to the running of a defence are justified. In some cases, the informant is an informant and no more; but even when the informant has participated in the events constituting, surrounding or following the crime, the judge must consider whether the informant's role so impinges on an issue of interest to the defence, present or potential, as to make disclosure necessary (*Turner* [1995] 3 All ER 432, per Lord Taylor CJ at p. 268).

It is of the highest importance to public confidence in the administration of justice that, where the interests of justice require an express or implied undertaking of confidence as to the identity of an informant to be broken, unless there is informed consent from the informant, the decision to break it is a decision of the judge. The CPS should therefore apply to the court which should reach its own decision and not simply defer to the view of the prosecutor (*R (VW) v CPS* [2011] EWHC 2480 (Admin)).

In *Agar* [1990] 2 All ER 442, D alleged that the police had arranged with an informer to ask D to go to the informer's house, where drugs allegedly found on him had been planted by the police. It was held that the disclosure of the identity of the informer was necessary to enable D to put forward the tenable defence that he had been set up by the police and the informer acting in concert. Therefore, counsel for D should have been permitted to cross-examine police witnesses to elicit the fact that the informer had told the police that D was coming to his house. (Compare *Slowcombe* [1991] Crim LR 198, where disclosure of the identity of an informer would have contributed little or nothing to the issue which the jury had to consider, and *Menga* [1998] Crim LR 58.) *Agar* was applied in *Langford* [1990] Crim LR 653. See also *Vaillencourt* [1993] Crim LR 311, *Reilly* [1994] Crim LR 279 and *Baker* [1996] Crim LR 55. It is for the accused to show that there is good reason to expect that disclosure is necessary to show his or her innocence (*Hennessy* (1978) 68 Cr App R 419, per Lawton LJ; *Hallett* [1986] Crim LR 462). In *Hennessy*, Lawton LJ said (at p. 426): 'This should normally be done, not in the course of a trial, but in any proceedings which may be started to set aside a subpoena or a witness summons served upon a Crown witness who is alleged to be in possession of, or to have control over, tape recordings, transcripts of such recordings and the like'. **F9.16**

Disclosure Relating to Premises The rule also protects the identity of persons who have allowed their premises to be used for police surveillance, and the identity of their premises (*Rankine* [1986] QB 861). If the accused submits that disclosure of the identification of the premises is necessary to show his or her innocence, the judge may nonetheless exclude the evidence, provided that the prosecution have provided a proper evidential basis for such exclusion. In *Johnson* [1988] 1 All ER 121, Watkins LJ gave the following guidance as to the minimum evidential requirements in this regard (at pp. 1385–6): **F9.17**

(a) The police officer in charge of the observations to be conducted, no one of lower rank than a sergeant should usually be acceptable for this purpose, must be able to testify that beforehand he visited all observation places to be used and ascertained the attitude of occupiers of premises, not only to the use to be made of them, but to the possible disclosure thereafter of the use made and facts which could lead to the identification of the premises thereafter and of the occupiers. He may of course in addition inform the court of difficulties, if any, usually encountered in the particular locality of obtaining assistance from the public.

(b) A police officer of no lower rank than a chief inspector must be able to testify that immediately prior to the trial he visited the places used for observations, the results of which it is proposed to give in evidence, and ascertained whether the occupiers are the same as when the observations took place and whether they are or are not, what the attitude of those occupiers is to the possible disclosure of the use previously made of the premises and of facts which could lead at the trial to identification of premises and occupiers.

Such evidence will of course be given in the absence of the jury when the application to exclude the material evidence is made. The judge should explain to the jury, as this judge did, when summing up or at some appropriate time before that, the effect of the ruling to exclude, if the judge so rules.

F9.18 In *Johnson*, D was convicted of supplying drugs. The only evidence against him was given by police officers, who testified that, while stationed in private premises in a known drug-dealing locality, they had observed him selling drugs. The defence applied to cross-examine the officers on the exact location of the observation posts, in order to test what they could see, having regard to the layout of the street and the objects in it. In the jury's absence the prosecution called evidence as to the difficulty of obtaining assistance from the public, and the desire of the occupiers, who were also occupiers at the time of the offence, that their names and addresses should not be disclosed because they feared for their safety. The judge ruled that the exact location of the premises need not be revealed. The appeal was dismissed: although the conduct of the defence was to some extent affected by the restraints placed on it, this led to no injustice. The jury were well aware of the restraints, and were most carefully directed about the very special care they had to give to any disadvantage they may have brought to the defence. *Johnson* was applied and approved in *Hewitt* (1992) 95 Cr App R 81. See also *Grimes* [1994] Crim LR 213. The guidelines in *Johnson* do not require a threat of violence before protection can be afforded to the occupier of an observation post; it suffices if the occupier is in fear of harassment (*Blake v DPP* (1993) 97 Cr App R 169).

F9.19 The extension of the rule established in *Rankine* [1986] QB 861 is based on the protection of the owner or occupier of the premises, and not on the identity, *simpliciter*, of the observation post. Thus, where officers have witnessed the commission of an offence as part of a surveillance operation conducted from an unmarked police vehicle, information relating to the surveillance and the colour, make and model of the vehicle should not be withheld (*Brown* (1987) 87 Cr App R 52). However, Hodgson J said (at p. 59):

> We do not rule out the possibility that with the advent of no doubt sophisticated methods of criminal investigation, there may be cases where the public interest immunity may be successfully invoked in criminal proceedings to justify the exclusion of evidence as to police techniques and methods.

F9.20 **Informer's Wish to Disclose Name** A further exception to the common-law rule against disclosure of the name of an informer was established in *Savage v Chief Constable of Hampshire* [1997] 2 All ER 631, in which it was held that a police informer who wishes personally to sacrifice his own anonymity will not be precluded from doing so by a claim of immunity, because in such circumstances the primary justification for the claim (that disclosure would endanger the safety of the informer) disappears. The wishes of the informer, however, are not conclusive, and in appropriate cases may be outweighed by other considerations, as when discovery may assist others involved in crime, hamper police operations, or indicate the state of police inquiries into a particular crime.

F9.21 **Informer Called as a Witness** In *Patel* [2001] EWCA Crim 2505, the Court of Appeal stated that if a witness called at trial is a participating informer in the very instance in which the trial is concerned, there will have to be a very strong countervailing interest for the witness's status not to be revealed. In this case, it was not for HM Customs to determine the matter in their own favour without putting their own counsel or the court fully in the picture. Nor, the Court stated, was it for the judge to have to piece together stray pieces of information in order to decide whether an individual was or was not a participating informer.

Judges and Jurors

F9.22 A judge, including a Queen's Bench or Chancery Master, cannot be compelled to give evidence of matters of which he or she became aware relating to, and as a result of, the performance of judicial functions (as opposed to extraneous matters, such as a crime committed in the face of the court). However, the judge remains competent to give evidence, and if a situation arises where his or her evidence is vital, the judge should be able to be relied on not to allow non-compellability to stand in the way of giving evidence (*Warren v Warren* [1997] QB 488, in which the authorities are reviewed).

A jury's verdict cannot be impeached by the testimony of a juror as to the deliberations of the jury in the jury room (see *Thompson* [1962] 1 All ER 65, considered at **D19.28**, *Roads* [1967] 2 QB 108 and *Lalchan Nanan v The State* [1986] AC 860; and compare *Newton* (1912) 7 Cr App R 214 (a foreman's disclosure in open court that the jury decided the case on an impermissible basis), *Willmont* (1914) 10 Cr App R 173 (proof of misconduct by the officer in charge of the jury or the clerk) and *Hood* [1968] 2 All ER 56 (evidence of a juror as to matters extrinsic to the manner in which the verdict was reached)). A jury irregularity should be drawn to the attention of the judge in the absence of the jury as soon as it becomes known. A jury irregularity is anything that may prevent one or more jurors from remaining faithful to their oath or affirmation (CrimPD VI, para. 26M.2: see Supplement, **CPD.26M**; and see also *Mirza* [2004] UKHL 2, [2004] 1 AC 1118 and *Smith and Mercieca* [2005] UKHL 12, [2005] 2 Cr App R 10 (160), considered at **D19.30** to **D19.32**). For the procedure to be followed, see **D13.70**. After a verdict has been returned, the responsibility for any investigation of any irregularity lies with the Court of Appeal. The Court of Appeal can hear evidence from a juror on a question of alleged jury bias, but the interviewing of a juror on such an issue requires the leave of the Court, which will be granted only in rare and exceptional cases (*Adams* [2007] EWCA Crim 1, [2007] 1 Cr App R 34 (449) and see also **D13.51**).

As to the offence of research by a juror and related offences, see the Juries Act 1974, ss. 20A, 20B and 20C, at **B14.133** ***et seq***. As to the offence of disclosing a jury's deliberations and the exceptions thereto, see the Juries Act 1974, ss. 20D, 20E, 20F and 20G, at **B14.137** ***et seq***.

Sources of Information Contained in Publications

Contempt of Court Act 1981, s. 10 **F9.23**

> No court may require a person to disclose, nor is any person guilty of contempt of court for refusing to disclose, the source of information contained in a publication for which he is responsible, unless it be established to the satisfaction of the court that disclosure is necessary in the interests of justice or national security or for the prevention of disorder or crime.

Section 10 substitutes for the common-law discretionary protection a rule of law of wide and general application, subject only to the four exceptions specified (*Secretary of State for Defence v Guardian Newspapers Ltd* [1985] AC 339, per Lord Scarman). The section applies to information which has been communicated and received for the purposes of publication, even if it is not 'contained in a publication', because the purpose underlying the statutory protection of sources of information is as much applicable before as after publication (*X Ltd v Morgan-Grampian (Publishers) Ltd* [1991] 1 AC 1, per Lord Bridge of Harwich). It is sufficient, in order to be protected by s. 10, that an order of the court *may*, and not necessarily *will*, result in disclosure of a source of information (*Secretary of State for Defence v Guardian Newspapers Ltd* [1985] AC 339, per Lord Roskill at p. 368). It is a question of fact and not discretion whether an exception applies, and the burden of proof is on the party seeking disclosure (per Lords Diplock and Scarman, at pp. 345 and 364 respectively). Disclosure must be shown to be 'necessary': expediency, however great, will not suffice (per Lord Diplock, at p. 350; *Handmade Films (Productions) Ltd v Express Newspapers plc* [1986] FSR 463). Under s. 10 the judge must first decide whether disclosure is necessary in the interests of justice etc. If the judge is not so satisfied, disclosure cannot be ordered; but if the judge is so satisfied, it must be decided whether as a matter of discretion disclosure should be ordered, which involves weighing the need for disclosure against the need for protection (*John v Express Newspapers plc* [2000] 3 All ER 257).

Disclosure 'Necessary in the Interests of Justice' The word 'justice' in the Contempt of Court Act 1981, s. 10, is not used as the antonym of 'injustice', but in the technical sense of the administration of justice in the course of legal proceedings in a court of law or a tribunal, or a body **F9.24**

exercising the judicial powers of the state (*Secretary of State for Defence v Guardian Newspapers Ltd* [1985] AC 339, per Lord Diplock at p. 350). It has since been held that the word should not be so confined (see *X Ltd v Morgan-Grampian (Publishers) Ltd* [1991] 1 AC 1 at **F9.25**). However, in cases where disclosure is sought for the purposes of legal proceedings, in order to decide whether the exception applies, it is essential first to identify and define the issue in the legal proceedings which requires disclosure, and then to decide whether, looking at the nature of that issue and the circumstances of the case, disclosure is necessary (*Maxwell v Pressdram Ltd* [1987] 1 All ER 621, per Kerr LJ at pp. 308–9). The mere fact that the information in question is relevant to the issue is not sufficient: disclosure must be necessary in the interests of justice (*Maxwell v Pressdram Ltd*, per Parker LJ, at p. 310).

F9.25 The following propositions derive from the decision of the House of Lords in *X Ltd v Morgan-Grampian (Publishers) Ltd* [1991] 1 AC 1. It is 'in the interests of justice' that persons should be enabled to exercise important legal rights and to protect themselves from serious legal wrongs whether or not resort to proceedings in a court of law will be necessary to obtain these objectives. This construction emphasises the importance of the balancing exercise. It will not be sufficient, *per se*, for a party seeking disclosure of a source to show merely that he or she will be unable without disclosure to exercise the legal right or avert the threatened legal wrong. The judge must always weigh in the scales the importance of enabling the ends of justice to be attained in the circumstances of the particular case on the one hand against the importance of protecting the source on the other. It is only if satisfied that disclosure in the interests of justice is of such preponderant importance as to override the statutory privilege against disclosure that the threshold of necessity will be reached. Many factors will be relevant. Lord Bridge of Harwich gave the following illustrations. If the party seeking disclosure shows that his or her very livelihood depends on it, the case will be near one end of the spectrum; but if the party merely seeks to protect a minor interest in property, the case will be at or near the other end of the spectrum. On the other side, one important factor will be the nature of the information obtained: the greater the legitimate public interest in the information, the greater will be the importance of protecting the source. Another perhaps more significant factor is the manner in which the information was obtained by the source: if the information was obtained legitimately this will enhance the importance of protecting the source. Conversely, if the information was obtained illegally, this will diminish the importance of protecting the source unless this factor is counterbalanced by a clear public interest in publication, as when the source has acted to expose iniquity.

F9.26 *Goodwin v UK* (1996) 22 EHRR 123, a decision of the ECtHR, dealt with the same facts as those which were the subject of the decision in *X Ltd v Morgan-Grampian (Publishers) Ltd* [1991] 1 AC 1, but under the ECHR, Article 10. The tests applied by the ECtHR and the House of Lords were substantially the same, but the ECtHR came to a conclusion opposite to that reached by the House of Lords. The explanation may well be that put forward by Thorpe LJ in *Camelot Group plc v Centaur Communications Ltd* [1999] QB 124: the making of a value judgement on competing facts is very close to the exercise of a discretion, and the period of time between the decisions in London and Strasbourg was six years, a period during which standards fundamental to the performance of the balancing exercise may change materially.

F9.27 **Effect of ECHR, Article 10** In *Ashworth Hospital Authority v MGN Ltd* [2001] 1 All ER 991, which concerned the disclosure of confidential medical records to the press, the Court of Appeal considered the proper approach to s. 10 of the Contempt of Court Act 1981 in the light of the HRA 1998, s. 3, and the ECHR, Article 10. The Court held as follows:

(a) Section 10 sets out to give effect to the general requirements of Article 10 in the narrow context of protection of the sources of information of the press. Article 10 permits the right of freedom of expression to be circumscribed where necessary in a democratic society to achieve a number of specified legitimate aims.

(b) The approach to the interpretation of s. 10 should, insofar as possible (i) equate the specific purposes for which disclosure of sources is permitted under s. 10 with 'legitimate aims' under Article 10 and (ii) apply the same test of necessity to that applied by the ECtHR when considering Article 10.
(c) The wider interpretation of the 'interests of justice' in *X Ltd v Morgan-Grampian (Publishers) Ltd* [1991] 1 AC 1 (see **F9.25**) accords more happily with the scheme of Article 10 than the interpretation of Lord Diplock in *Secretary of State for Defence v Guardian Newspapers Ltd* [1985] AC 339. Thus 'interests of justice' in s. 10 means interests that are justiciable. It is difficult to envisage any such interest that would not fall within one or more of the relevant 'legitimate aims' under Article 10.

Affirming the decision, the House of Lords ([2002] UKHL 29, [2002] 1 WLR 2033) accepted the approach of the ECtHR in *Goodwin v UK* (1996) 22 EHRR 123 that, as a matter of general principle, the 'necessity' for any restriction of freedom of expression must be convincingly established and that limits on the confidentiality of journalistic sources call for the most careful scrutiny by the court. It was further held that any restriction of the right to freedom of expression must meet two further requirements: (i) exercise of the disclosure jurisdiction because of Article 10(2) should meet a 'pressing social need' and (ii) the restriction should be proportionate to the legitimate aim which is being pursued.

Material Protected by Legal Professional Privilege It will not inevitably be in the interests of justice to order disclosure of the source of information where the nature of that information suggests that the source has seen material protected by legal professional privilege (*Saunders v Punch Ltd* [1998] 1 All ER 234). In the context of such material it has been held that, before ordering disclosure, the minimum requirement is that the person seeking disclosure has explored other means of identifying the source. It cannot be assumed that it will not be possible to find the source of the information by other means; and when weighing the conflicting public interests involved, it is to be remembered that there is no certainty that ordering a journalist to reveal his or her sources will be any more successful than the use of other means (*John v Express Newspapers plc* [2000] 3 All ER 257). **F9.28**

Disclosure 'Necessary for the Prevention of Crime' Concerning the prevention of crime, disclosure will be ordered if shown to be necessary, either for the prevention of crime generally or for the prevention of a particular and identifiable future crime. See *Re an Inquiry under the Company Securities (Insider Dealing) Act* [1988] AC 660. In this case, a journalist who had used confidential price-sensitive information about take-over bids was ordered to disclose his source to inspectors appointed by the Secretary of State to investigate suspected leaks of this kind, on the grounds that they needed the information to expose the leaking of official information and criminal insider trading, and to prevent such behaviour in the future. However, as in the case of the other exceptions, a claim under this head will succeed only if there is clear and specific evidence of 'necessity'. The party seeking disclosure should adduce evidence on matters such as the extent of inquiries to identify the sources, whether the matter was referred to the police, and whether criminal investigation is the intended or likely outcome (*X v Y* [1988] 2 All ER 648). **F9.29**

CONFIDENTIAL BUT NON-PRIVILEGED RELATIONSHIPS

At common law no privilege attaches to communications made in confidence except in the case of: **F9.30**

(a) communications between a client and a legal adviser made for the purpose of the obtaining and giving of legal advice; and
(b) communications between a client or his or her legal adviser and third parties, the dominant purpose of which was preparation for contemplated or pending litigation (see **F10.26**).

F9.31 Although the courts have an inherent wish to respect the confidences which arise between doctor and patient, bankers and customers etc., if the question to be put to a witness is relevant and necessary in order that justice be done, the witness will be directed to answer (see, e.g., *A-G v Mulholland* [1963] 2 QB 477, per Lord Denning MR at pp. 489–90). Thus, no privilege exists to protect medical records or communications between doctor and patient (*Duchess of Kingston* (1776) 20 St Tr 355; *Gibbons* (1823) 1 C & P 97; *Wheeler v Le Marchant* (1881) 17 Ch D 675, at p. 681; *Hunter v Mann* [1974] QB 767; *McDonald* [1991] Crim LR 122; *Gayle* [1994] Crim LR 679). This remains the case, notwithstanding that the rule is regarded as unsatisfactory and one which the Supreme Court has the power to alter (*D v National Society for the Prevention of Cruelty to Children* [1978] AC 171, per Lord Edmund-Davies at pp. 244–5). But see also *K (TD)* (1993) 97 Cr App R 342 at **F9.32**. In the case of communications between priest and penitent, there is slender authority in favour of the existence of a privilege: see *Hay* (1860) 2 F & F 4 (in which it was stressed that the priest was asked about a fact and not a communication) and the *obiter dictum* of Best CJ in *Broad v Pitt* (1828) 3 C & P 518: 'I, for one, will never compel a clergyman to disclose communications made to him by a prisoner; but if he chooses to disclose them I shall receive them in evidence'. However, most of such authority as there is, is against the existence of any such privilege (*Normanshaw v Normanshaw* (1893) 69 LT 468; *Wheeler v Le Marchant* (1881) 17 Ch D 675, at p. 681; and the authorities cited in Stephen's *Digest of the Law of Evidence* (12th edn, 1936), at p. 220). Similarly, there is no privilege for confidential communications between friends (*Duchess of Kingston's Case* (1776) 20 St Tr 355); or for documents in the possession of an accountant relating to a client's affairs (*Chantrey Martin & Co. v Martin* [1953] 2 QB 286). At common law there is no privilege for journalists who seek to conceal the identities of their sources of information (*A-G v Clough* [1963] 1 QB 773; *A-G v Mulholland* [1963] 2 QB 477). But see now the Contempt of Court Act 1981, s. 10, above. Concerning a court welfare officer's report, the appropriate court may give leave for it to be used in other proceedings if, after evaluating and balancing the need to maintain the confidentiality of the report against the need for its contents to be put in evidence for there to be a fair trial of the action, the court decides that the interests of justice require the confidentiality of the report to be released (*Brown v Matthews* [1990] Ch 662). See also *Elleray* [2003] EWCA Crim 553, [2003] 2 Cr App R 11 (165): where an offender, during a conversation with a probation officer being held for the purpose of preparing a pre-sentence report, admits to having committed another offence, the prosecution should consider carefully whether it is right to rely on the evidence and should only rely on it if they decide that it is in the public interest to do so. If they do rely on the evidence, the court still has a discretion to exclude it under the PACE 1984, s. 78.

F9.32 Although at common law no privilege attaches to confidential communications *per se*, in appropriate circumstances a party may be able to rely upon some other head of privilege, such as the privilege which attaches to communications made in the course of matrimonial conciliation (which has also been treated as a limb of public interest immunity: see *D v National Society for the Prevention of Cruelty to Children* [1978] AC 171, per Lords Hailsham and Simon at pp. 226 and 236–7 respectively). Alternatively, a claim to public interest immunity may succeed. Thus an interview with a child victim of a sexual offence, which is conducted on a confidential basis for therapeutic purposes, ought not to be disclosed, unless the interests of justice so require, but where the liberty of the subject is an issue and disclosure might be of assistance to an accused, a claim for disclosure will often be strong (*K (TD)* (1993) 97 Cr App R 342). Similarly immunity may be claimed for confidential documents relating to abortions carried out under the Abortion Act 1967 (*Morrow v DPP* [1994] Crim LR 58).

F9.33 In the absence of consent to disclosure by a taxpayer, public interest immunity does attach to documents relating to the taxpayer's affairs in the hands of the Inland Revenue, because as a matter of public policy the State should not by compulsory powers obtain information from a citizen for one purpose and then use it for another; but no such immunity attaches to documents held by the taxpayer in person, or the taxpayer's agents, relating to those tax affairs (*Lonrho plc v Fayed (No. 4)* [1994] 1 All ER 870). A claim to public interest immunity may also succeed when the person claiming immunity is exercising a statutory function, the effective performance of which would be impaired by disclosure. See, e.g., *Lonrho Ltd v Shell Petroleum Co. Ltd* [1980] 1 WLR 627 (immunity granted in subsequent litigation for evidence given in confidence to the Bingham Inquiry into the operation of sanctions against Rhodesia) and contrast *Re Arrows Ltd (No. 4)* [1995] 2 AC 75. See also *Re Barlow Clowes Gilt Managers Ltd* [1992] Ch 208. The liquidators of a company are under no duty to assist directors of the company in defending criminal charges, by providing them with information given to the liquidators by third parties in circumstances of confidentiality and by assurances, express or implied, that it would be used only for the purpose of the liquidation. The provision of such information would jeopardise the proper and efficient functioning of the process of compulsory liquidation because of the danger that professional men would no longer co-operate with liquidators on a voluntary basis. However, whether the information in question constitutes 'material evidence' for the purposes of a witness summons is a question for the Crown Court (see further *Clowes* [1992] 3 All ER 440 at **F9.9**). It has also been held, in *Umoh* (1986) 84 Cr App R 138, that although no privilege analogous to that between lawyer and client can arise to protect confidential communications about the substance of a legal aid application between a prison legal aid officer and a prisoner, such communications should attract public interest immunity, because a prisoner does not have the freedom to go to a solicitor's office, and if the prisoner seeks assistance from such an officer matters connected with the alleged offence are likely to be disclosed and discussed. It is in the public interest that such discussions, save in exceptional circumstances, should remain confidential, or otherwise prisoners would be reluctant to take advantage of the scheme.

In *H* [2018] EWCA Crim 2868, [2019] 1 Cr App R 25 (331) a youth, in the course of discussions with his case manager at a youth offending service, made damaging admissions in relation to the offence of which he stood convicted. The Court of Appeal held that it would be contrary to public policy to breach the confidentiality of the discussion, save for very good reason. A distinction could be drawn between disclosure necessary to avoid imminent future criminality, in particular a threat to someone's life or safety, and disclosure of admissions to past offences. Those convicted, whether young or adult, should not be deterred from speaking to those charged with their supervision or rehabilitation until after an appeal against conviction. The case could also be distinguished from the situation in which an admission made by a defendant in an interview for the purpose of the preparation of a pre-sentence report is admissible against him or her in an appeal against conviction, because the defendant would have been told that what he or she says will be placed before the judge.

Section F10 Privilege

PRIVILEGED RELATIONSHIPS: GENERAL PRINCIPLES

F10.1 Relevant and otherwise admissible evidence may be excluded on the grounds of either the privilege against self-incrimination (see **F10.2** to **F10.15**) or legal professional privilege (see **F10.16** to **F10.45**).

The following principles are of general application:

(a) A person entitled to claim privilege may refuse to answer the question put or disclose the document sought. The judge should not balance the claim to privilege against the importance of the evidence in relation to the trial. But see *Rank Film Distributors Ltd v Video Information Centre* [1982] AC 380, per Lord Fraser at p. 445.

(b) If a person entitled to claim privilege fails to do so or waives the privilege, no other person may object. The privilege is that of the witness, and neither party can take advantage from it. Thus, if a judge improperly rejects a claim to privilege made by a witness who is not a party to the proceedings, no appeal will lie, for there has been no infringement of the rights of the parties. In *Kinglake* (1870) 11 Cox CC 499, where a claim to privilege made by a prosecution witness on the basis that his evidence would tend to incriminate himself was overruled by the judge, it was not open to D to object that the witness's evidence had been improperly admitted.

(c) A party seeking to prove a particular matter in relation to which his or her opponent or a witness claims privilege, is entitled to prove the matter by other evidence (see **F10.43**).

(d) No adverse inferences may be drawn against a party or witness claiming privilege (*Wentworth v Lloyd* (1864) 10 HL Cas 589).

(e) A claim to privilege falls to be determined in accordance with domestic law and therefore cannot succeed simply on the basis that it would succeed in some other jurisdiction.

PRIVILEGE AGAINST SELF-INCRIMINATION

Scope of Privilege

F10.2 Under the Criminal Evidence Act 1898, s. 1(2), 'a person charged in criminal proceedings who is called as a witness in the proceedings may be asked any question in cross-examination notwithstanding that it would tend to criminate him as to any offence with which he is charged in the proceedings'. Subject to s. 1(2), no witness is bound to answer questions in court (or to produce documents or things at trial) if to do so would, in the opinion of the judge, have a tendency to expose the witness to any criminal charge, penalty or forfeiture (of property) which the judge regards as reasonably likely to be preferred or sued for (*Blunt v Park Lane Hotel Ltd* [1942] 2 KB 253, per Goddard LJ at p. 257). The courts may substitute a different protection in place of the privilege when requiring a person to comply with a disclosure order, provided adequate protection is available, as when the prosecuting authorities unequivocally agree not to make use of the information (*AT & T Istel v Tully* [1993] AC 45). An affidavit sworn by a person in compliance with such an order may then be inadmissible against the person in any subsequent criminal trial, but the Crown will not necessarily be prevented from using it to demonstrate inconsistency and thus to impugn the person's credit (*Martin* [1998] 2 Cr App R 385). Penalties arise mainly under statutes relating to the revenue, and under EC regulations (see, e.g., *Rio Tinto Zinc Corporation v Westinghouse Electric Corporation* [1978] AC 547). 'Additional damages', which may be awarded under statutes for breach of copyright, are not penalties (*Rank Film Distributors Ltd v Video Information Centre* [1982] AC 380, at p. 425). A witness may not claim privilege on the basis that his or her answer to the question put would expose him or her to civil liability (Witnesses Act 1806). Nor does the privilege extend to answers which would expose the witness to criminal liability under foreign law (*King of the Two Sicilies v Willcox* (1851) 1 Sim NS 301; *Re Atherton* [1912] 2 KB 251, at p. 255). See also *Arab Monetary Fund v Hashim* [1989] 3 All ER 466 and *Volaw Trust and Corporate Services Ltd v Office of the Comptroller of Taxes* [2019] UKPC 29, [2020] 1 All ER 941. However, this issue may need to be revisited in the light of the ECHR, Article 6, and in the context of extradition proceedings (per Moses LJ in *Khan* [2007] EWCA Crim 2331 at [26]). In *Volaw Trust* the question arose whether the privilege against self-incrimination under Article 6 can apply in relation to pre-trial investigations in one jurisdiction where any trial would take place in another. It was unnecessary to answer the question, but the Privy Council doubted whether it could be answered in categorical terms, because it may depend on whether the applicant risks suffering a flagrant denial of justice in the requesting country. However, it noted that this would not be the case in jurisdictions adhering to the Convention.

Subject to any statutory exceptions (see **F10.7**), an agent, trustee or other fiduciary of a party may claim the privilege in an action brought against him or her by that party for breach of that duty (*Bishopsgate Investment Management Ltd v Maxwell* [1993] Ch 1).

Requirement of Real and Appreciable Danger

It is dangerous to assess the strength of a claim to privilege by reference to the motive of the **F10.3** person seeking to invoke it; the motive may be mixed or even *mala fides*, but if the answer to the question will expose the person to the risk of future prosecution, the privilege must be upheld (see per Moses LJ in *Khan* [2007] EWCA Crim 2331 at [35], approving Kirby P in *Accident Insurance Mutual Holdings Ltd v McFadden* [1993] 31 NSWLR 412). However, if the fact of the witness being in danger be once made to appear, great latitude should be allowed to the witness in judging the effect of any particular question, for a question which might appear at first sight a very innocent one, may, by affording a link in the chain of evidence, become the means of bringing home an offence to the witness. Subject to this reservation, the court, before acceding to a claim to privilege, should satisfy itself, from the circumstances of the case and the nature of the evidence which the witness is called to give, that there is a reasonable ground to apprehend real and appreciable danger to the witness with reference to the ordinary operation of the law in the ordinary course of things, and not a danger of an imaginary or insubstantial character. See *Boyes* (1861) 1 B & S 311, per Cockburn CJ. In *R (CPS) v Bolton Magistrates' Court* [2003] EWHC 2697 (Admin), [2004] 2 All ER 848, the Divisional Court, citing with approval the foregoing text, held that it is not sufficient to ascertain that the claim was made on legal advice. The duty of the court is non-delegable: the court cannot simply adopt the conclusion of a solicitor advising the witness, whose conclusion may or may not be correct. In refusing protection, it seems that the court may also take into account the triviality of any charge likely to be brought. In *R (DPP) v Leicester Magistrates' Court* [2015] EWHC 1295 (Admin), [2016] 1 Cr App R 5 (74) the Divisional Court held that a witness's claim to the privilege against self-incrimination should not have been upheld for three reasons. First, if, the witness having claimed the privilege, evidence had been obtained from her under compulsion, it could not have been used against her (see *Garbett* (1847) 1 Den CC 236 at **F10.6**). Second, it was doubtful whether the evidence to be obtained from her would have materially increased such risk as there was of her being prosecuted. Third, the Crown having given an assurance that she would not be prosecuted, any prosecution based on evidence obtained from her would have been halted as an abuse of process. It is submitted that the first reason, by itself, cannot support the court's conclusion: the privilege protects against the risk of *prosecution*, not conviction, However, see also *Beghal v DPP* [2015] UKSC 49, [2016] AC 88 and contrast per Lord Kerr, dissenting at [117] and [118], considered at **F10.7**.

F10.4 In *Rank Film Distributors Ltd v Video Information Centre* [1982] AC 380, a case concerning the application of the privilege to an *Anton Piller* order, Lord Fraser held (at p. 445) that protection should be refused, partly because the likelihood of prosecution under the Copyright Act 1956, s. 21, was too remote, but also because it would be 'unreasonable to allow the possibility of incrimination of such offences to obstruct disclosure of information which would be of much more value to the owners of the infringed copyright than any protection they might obtain from s. 21'. Protection may also be properly refused if the evidence against the witness is already so strong that, if proceedings are to be taken, they will be taken whether or not the witness answers: see, e.g., *Khan v Khan* [1982] 2 All ER 60, where the witness's conduct 'reeked of dishonesty', and evidence as to his use of the proceeds of a stolen cheque did not materially increase the risk of his prosecution for its theft. See also *Khan* [2007] EWCA Crim 2331, where D, having pleaded guilty to an offence, was called as a witness by a co-accused and was found guilty of contempt for refusing to answer questions about matters as to which he had already incriminated himself by his guilty plea.

Incrimination Must be of Person Claiming Privilege

F10.5 In criminal cases, the privilege against self-incrimination is restricted to the person claiming it, and does not extend to questions the answers to which would tend to incriminate a spouse: see *Rio Tinto Zinc Corporation v Westinghouse Electric Corporation* [1978] AC 547, per Lord Diplock at p. 637, and *Pitt* [1983] QB 25, where the Court of Appeal, in holding that an accused's spouse, if she elects to testify, should be treated like any other witness, surely must have assumed that she cannot then claim privilege against the incrimination of her husband; and contrast *All Saints, Worcester (Inhabitants)* (1817) 6 M & S 194, per Bayley J at p. 201. There is no privilege against incriminating strangers (*Minihane* (1921) 16 Cr App R 38). A company may claim privilege in the same way as an individual (*Triplex Safety Glass Co. Ltd v Lancegaye Safety Glass (1934) Ltd* [1939] 2 KB 395). However, the privilege is that of the company and therefore does not extend to incrimination of its office holders (*Rio Tinto Zinc Corporation v Westinghouse Electric Corporation* per Lord Diplock at pp. 637–8; *Sociedade Nacional de Combustiveis de Angola UEE v Lundqvist* [1991] 2 QB 310 per Beldam LJ at p. 336; *Tate Access Floors Inc. v Boswell* [1991] Ch 512).

The Time for Claiming Privilege

F10.6 A witness may claim the privilege only after having been sworn and the question put; the witness is not entitled to refuse to take the oath on the grounds of the privilege (*Boyle v Wiseman* (1855) 1 Exch 647). Although in practice a judge will often warn a witness of the right not to answer a question which might expose the witness to a criminal charge, in the absence of such a warning the witness must claim the privilege him or herself (*Thomas v Newton* (1827) 2 C & P 606). The witness may claim the privilege at any stage of the proceedings, even if already having answered, without objection, questions which the witness was not obliged to answer (*Garbett* (1847) 1 Den CC 236). If the witness answers without seeking the protection of the court, those answers may be used in the proceedings in question and in any subsequent criminal proceedings brought against the witness (*Sloggett* (1856) Dears CC 656; *Coote* (1873) LR 4 PC 599). However, if a judge wrongly denies a witness the protection of privilege, anything the witness is then compelled to say is treated as having been said involuntarily and will be excluded from the subsequent criminal proceedings (*Garbett* (1847) 1 Den CC 236, distinguished in *McGeough* [2015] UKSC 62, [2015] 1 WLR 4612 (statements made, without compulsion, in an asylum application)).

Statutory Provisions Requiring Answers to Questions

F10.7 **General** Various statutes and statutory instruments require specified persons in specified circumstances to answer questions or produce documents or information notwithstanding that compliance may incriminate them. Clear language is required to show that Parliament intended to abrogate the privilege (*R (Malik) v Manchester Crown Court* [2008] EWHC 1362 (Admin),

[2008] 4 All ER 403, where it was held that the Terrorism Act 2000, sch. 5, para. 6 (see **B10.7**) does not oust the privilege). However, some provisions abrogate the privilege impliedly, on the grounds that they would otherwise be largely ineffective (see, e.g., *Bank of England v Riley* [1992] Ch 475, *Re London United Investments plc* [1992] Ch 578 and *Bishopsgate Investment Management Ltd v Maxwell* [1993] Ch 1). *Beghal v DPP* [2015] UKSC 49, [2016] AC 88 concerned the construction of the TA 2000, sch. 7, para. 2 (see **B10.27**), whereby a person questioned at a port for the purpose of determining whether he or she appears to be or to have been concerned in the commission, preparation or instigation of acts of terrorism is required to answer on pain of prosecution for failure to do so. Paragraph 2 was construed by a majority of the Supreme Court to abrogate the privilege against self-incrimination by necessary implication on the basis that otherwise it would be rendered largely nugatory. The majority further held that the risk of a prosecution based on the answers was not 'real and appreciable' because, even without the application of the ECHR, Article 6, the answers would inevitably be excluded under the PACE 1984, s. 78. However, as Lord Kerr said, dissenting, even if Parliament did intend that the privilege should be abrogated, the privilege protects against the risk of prosecution, not conviction, and since the answers may lead to the obtaining of independent free-standing evidence, the accused cannot ensure that he or she will not be prosecuted, even if the accused can succeed in having evidence of his or her answers excluded in a subsequent trial (at [117] and [118]). See also **B10.27**.

In deciding as a matter of construction, under English domestic law, whether a statutory provision does impliedly abrogate the privilege, the court must consider on the one hand the public interest in obtaining the information, and on the other the 'right to silence' to be affected and the strength of the grounds for preserving it, looking at whether the request forms a part of criminal proceedings, and touches on the rules which prohibit interrogation without caution or after charge, or amounts to a potential abuse of investigatory powers which those rules are designed to prevent (*Hertfordshire County Council, ex parte Green Environmental Industries Ltd* [2000] 2 AC 412). As to the further question whether implied abrogation would amount to a violation of the right to a fair trial under the ECHR, Article 6, under the European jurisprudence the impact of Article 6 is confined to the use of answers in evidence at a criminal trial and is not concerned with extra-judicial inquiries: see *Saunders v UK* (1997) 23 EHRR 313 at p. 337 (examination by inspectors appointed by the Secretary of State under the Companies Act 1985), *Hertfordshire County Council, ex parte Green Environmental Industries Ltd* (a local authority request for information under the Environmental Protection Act 1990), *Kearns* [2002] EWCA Crim 748, [2002] 1 WLR 2815 (a demand by the Official Receiver to see a bankrupt's accounting records) and *Brady* [2004] EWCA Crim 1763, [2004] 3 All ER 520 (a requirement by the Official Receiver for information relating to insolvent companies). In *Hertfordshire County Council, ex parte Green Environmental Industries Ltd*, Lord Hoffmann said (at p. 423) that 'the European jurisprudence under article 6(1) is firmly anchored in the fairness of the trial and is not concerned with extrajudicial enquiries'. In *Volaw Trust and Corporate Services Ltd v Office of the Comptroller of Taxes* [2019] UKPC 29, [2020] 1 All ER 941, it was held (at [72]) that this dictum is true as a generalisation but a breach of Article 6 *can* arise in consequence of the punishment of a person for refusing to incriminate him or herself in the course of extrajudicial enquiries (as in, e.g., *Funke v France* (1993) 16 EHRR 297 and *Heaney v Ireland* (2001) 33 EHRR 12 (264)). It was further held that the nature of extrajudicial enquiries can itself prejudice the fairness of trial proceedings for the purposes of Article 6—an example given in *Ibrahim v UK* [2016] ECHR 750 at [253] was where 'national laws may attach consequences to the attitude of an accused at the initial stages of police interrogation which are decisive for the prospects of the defence in any subsequent criminal proceedings'.

Provisions which expressly abrogate the privilege against self-incrimination, typically go on to prevent the answers from being used against the person who answered the question in criminal proceedings in which the person is charged with a specified offence. Some examples follow.

F10.8 **Examples** Under the Theft Act 1968, s. 31(1), which requires questions to be answered and orders to be complied with in proceedings for the recovery or administration of any property or dealing with property, notwithstanding that compliance may expose the witness or his or her spouse or civil partner to a charge for an offence under the Theft Act 1968, the answers may not be used in proceedings for any such offence. Neither the revocation of the privilege nor the restriction on the use of the answers applies to non-Theft Act offences (*Sociedade Nacional de Combustiveis de Angola UEE v Lundqvist* [1991] 3 All ER 283). However, where to answer the question etc. would expose the relevant person to an offence under the Theft Act 1968 and the person claims that it would also expose him or her to a non-Theft Act offence, the test concerning the latter offence is whether to answer the question etc. would create or increase the risk of proceedings for that offence, separate and distinct from its connection with the Theft Act offence. If the answer is no, there is no privilege, but if it is yes, then the privilege subsists in relation to the latter offence (*Renworth v Stephansen* [1996] 3 All ER 244).

Under the Fraud Act 2006, s. 13, questions are to be answered and orders are to be complied with in proceedings for the recovery or administration of any property etc., notwithstanding that compliance may result in incrimination of an offence under the 2006 Act or a related offence, but the answers may not be used in evidence in proceedings for any such offence. Under s. 13(4), 'related offence' means conspiracy to defraud and any other offence involving any form of fraudulent conduct or purpose, a phrase that covers offering or giving a bribe (*Kensington International Ltd v Republic of Congo* [2007] EWCA Civ 1128, [2008] 1 WLR 1144) and money laundering under the POCA 2002, s. 328(1) (see **B21.17**) (*JSC BTA Bank v Ablyazov* [2009] EWCA Civ 1124, [2010] 1 WLR 976).

F10.9 Under the Senior Courts Act 1981, s. 72, the privilege is withdrawn in various proceedings relating to apprehended or actual infringement of rights pertaining to any intellectual property or any apprehended or actual passing off. Section 72(3) provides that answers compelled by reason of such withdrawal of privilege cannot be used in proceedings for certain offences disclosed or for the recovery of certain penalties, liability to which was disclosed.

Under the Children Act 1989, s. 98, in any proceedings in which a court is hearing an application relating to the care, supervision or protection of a child, no one shall be excused from giving evidence on any matter or answering any question put in the course of giving evidence on the grounds that to do so might incriminate the witness or his or her spouse or civil partner of an offence. Under s. 98(2), a statement or admission made in such proceedings shall not be admissible in evidence against the person making it or his or her spouse or civil partner in proceedings for an offence other than perjury. A 'statement or admission', for these purposes, includes a filed statement of the evidence which a party intends to adduce at the hearing, an oral admission made by a parent to a guardian *ad litem* (*Oxfordshire County Council v P* [1995] Fam 161) and, after the proceedings have started, an oral statement to a social worker carrying out the local authority's duties of investigation in a child protection case (*Cleveland County Council v F* [1995] 2 All ER 236). Both of these decisions, however, have since been doubted (*Re G (A Minor) (Social Worker: Disclosure)* [1996] 2 All ER 65).

F10.10 Under the CJA 1987, s. 2, the Director of the SFO may require someone under investigation for a suspected offence involving serious or complex fraud, or anyone else, to answer questions etc., but a statement in response to such a requirement may be used against its maker only on a prosecution:

(a) for making a false or misleading statement in purported compliance with a requirement under s. 2, or
(b) for some other offence if, in giving evidence, the person makes a statement inconsistent with it, and evidence relating to it is adduced, or a question relating to it is asked, by the person or on the person's behalf.

However, it would appear that a statement previously made by an accused in response to questions under the CJA 1987, s. 2, can be used by a *co-accused*, provided it is relevant to his or her defence, and if this infringes the accused's right to a fair trial, the accused should be severed from the indictment (*Wickes* (NLJ, 25 July 2003, p. 1140, unreported)).

Under the Companies Act 1985, officers of a company and others possessing relevant information are required to answer questions put by inspectors appointed to investigate suspected fraud in the conduct or management of a company, but under s. 434(5A) and (5B) of the Act, in criminal proceedings in which a person who complied with such a requirement is charged with an offence (other than an offence under the Perjury Act 1911, s. 2 or s. 5), no evidence relating to the answer may be adduced and no question relating to it may be asked by or on behalf of the prosecution unless evidence relating to it is adduced, or a question relating to it is asked, by or on behalf of the person charged. For other similar statutory provisions, see the YJCEA 1999, s. 59 and sch. 3.

F10.11 If a statute revokes the privilege without *any* restriction upon the use that may be made of the answers, the answers will not be treated as having been given involuntarily and may be used in any subsequent criminal proceedings (*Scott* (1856) Dears & B 47). Such use will not invariably amount to a violation of Article 6. In *Brown v Stott* [2003] 1 AC 681, the Privy Council held that at a trial for driving after consuming excess alcohol contrary to the Road Traffic Act 1988, s. 5(1)(a), the introduction of evidence of an admission obtained from D under s. 172(2)(a) of the 1988 Act (see **C2.12**) did not infringe her right to a fair hearing under Article 6. It was held that there was a clear public interest in enforcement of road traffic legislation and that s. 172, properly applied, did not represent a disproportionate response to this serious social problem. *Brown v Stott* was applied in *Mawdesley v Chief Constable of the Cheshire Constabulary* [2003] EWHC 1586 (Admin), [2004] 1 All ER 58 on a charge of driving in excess of the speed limit. In *O'Halloran v UK* (2008) 46 EHRR 21 (397), it was held that there was no violation of Article 6 in the case of O, a case akin to that of *Mawdesley*, nor in the case of F, a conviction for failing to comply with s. 172. It was held that the privilege against self-incrimination is not an absolute right, being part of the broader right to a fair trial in Article 6. Cases of direct compulsion do not necessarily lead to violation; other factors may be relevant in deciding whether the essence of the privilege against self-incrimination has been violated. Thus in addition to (a) the direct nature of the compulsion (s. 172, for example, provides compulsion in the form of a fine of up to £1,000 and disqualification from driving or three penalty points), account should be taken of (b) the fact that the compulsion was part of a regulatory scheme that fairly imposes obligations on drivers in order to promote safety on roads, (c) the fact the information required is the simple specific and restricted fact of who was driving, (d) that the offence under s. 172 has a defence of due diligence, and (e) that in the case of O, the identity of the driver was only one element of the offence and the speeding still had to be proved. *Brown v Stott* was distinguished in *K (A)* [2009] EWCA Crim 1640, [2010] QB 343, which concerned proceedings for cheating the public revenue; it was held that the use of information about financial resources obtained under threat of imprisonment in matrimonial ancillary relief proceedings would infringe the right to a fair hearing.

F10.12 In *Allen (No. 2)* [2001] UKHL 45, [2001] 4 All ER 768, a case of cheating the public revenue of tax, D had provided a schedule of assets in compliance with a notice given by an inspector under the Taxes Management Act 1970, s. 20. A person who fails to comply with such a notice is liable to a penalty (s. 98(1) of the 1970 Act). The House of Lords held that since the State, for the purpose of collecting tax, is entitled to require a citizen to inform it of his or her income and to enforce penalties for failure to do so, the s. 20 notice could not constitute a violation of the right against self-incrimination. D's application to the ECtHR was unsuccessful. It was held that the requirement that he declare his assets to the tax authorities did not disclose any issue under Article 6(1), even though there was a penalty for failure to comply. The charge was one of making a false declaration of assets — it was not an example of forced self-incrimination in relation to some previously committed offence (*Allen v UK* (2002) 35 EHRR CD289; but see also *JB v Switzerland* [2001] Crim LR 748).

F10.13 **Free-standing Material Not Created under Compulsion** In *Saunders v UK* (1997) 23 EHRR 313, according to the judgment of the majority of the court, the right not to incriminate oneself is primarily concerned with respecting the will of an accused to remain silent and, as understood in Convention countries and elsewhere, it does not extend to the use in criminal proceedings of material obtained by compulsion which has an existence independent of the will of the suspect, such as documents acquired pursuant to a warrant, breath, blood and urine samples, and bodily tissue for the purposes of DNA testing. See also *L v UK* [2000] 2 FLR 322; cf. *Funke v France* (1993) 16 EHRR 297 and *Heaney v Ireland* (2001) 33 EHRR 12 (264). However, such material may not be used if obtained by forced medical intervention constituting inhuman or degrading treatment, contrary to the ECHR, Article 3, and involving a high degree of force in defiance of the will of the accused (*Jalloh v Germany* (2007) 44 EHRR 32 (667)). The distinction drawn in *Saunders* was approved in *A-G's Ref (No. 7 of 2000)* [2001] EWCA Crim 888, [2001] 1 WLR 1879 in which a bankrupt delivered up to the Official Receiver, pursuant to the duty imposed by the Insolvency Act 1986, s. 291, various documents relating to his estate and affairs, including documents relating to his gambling activities. Under s. 291(6), if he had failed to comply with this duty, he would have been in contempt of court and liable to imprisonment. He was subsequently charged with an offence contrary to s. 362(1)(a) of the 1986 Act, namely material contribution to his insolvency by gambling. The Court of Appeal held that use by the prosecution of the documents relating to his gambling activities would not violate his rights under Article 6. Under domestic law, the documents were admissible in law, subject to the discretion to exclude under s. 78. As to the European jurisprudence, the Court approved the distinction made in *Saunders* and did so for the reasons advanced by Justice La Forest in *Thomson Newspapers Ltd v Director of Investigation & Research* (1990) 54 CCC 417 (Supreme Court of Canada), namely that, whereas a compelled statement is evidence that simply would not have existed independently of the exercise of the power of compulsion, evidence which exists independently of the compelled statement could have been found by other means and its quality does not depend on its past connection with the compelled statement. Insofar as there was a difference of view between *Funke* and *Saunders*, the Court preferred the approach in *Saunders*. The same principle was applied in *Hundal* [2004] EWCA Crim 389, [2004] 2 Cr App R 19 (307).

F10.14 *C plc v P* [2007] EWCA Civ 493, [2008] Ch 1 concerned intellectual property proceedings in which indecent images of children were found on a computer which was the subject of a search order. The Court of Appeal held that the offending material was not privileged from disclosure to the police. A majority of the Court reached this conclusion by applying the principle from *Saunders*. This *ratio* of the majority was applied in *S* [2009] EWCA Crim 2177, [2009] 1 All ER 716 in respect of a notice under the RIPA 2000, s. 49, for disclosure of a key to data in encrypted files. It was also applied in *R (River East Supplies Ltd) v Crown Court at Nottingham* [2017] EWHC 1942 (Admin), [2017] 2 Cr App R 27 (384) in respect of a production order under the PACE 1984, s. 9 and sch 1. In that case the Divisional Court rejected a submission that it should follow *Rio Tinto Zinc Corporation v Westinghouse Electric Corporation* [1978] AC 547, *Rank Film Distributors Ltd v Video Information Centre* [1982] AC 380 and *AT & T Istel v Tully* [1993] AC 45, insofar as these House of Lords decisions operated on the assumption that the privilege does extend to 'independent' material. The Divisional Court also disagreed with the discretionary approach suggested in *R (Malik) v Manchester Crown Court* [2008] EWHC 1362 (Admin), [2008] 4 All ER 402. In that case it was said that there was a discretion to order production of independent material, the relevant factors to be taken into account being the privilege against self-incrimination and its importance, the degree of benefit of the material to the investigation, the risk of prosecution, the gravity of the offence and the power to exclude evidence under the

PACE 1984, s. 78. However, as the Divisional Court observed in *R (River East Supplies Ltd) v Crown Court at Nottingham*, since the privilege against self-incrimination does not apply to independent documents, no question of the exercise of judicial discretion can arise.

Saunders and the subsequent authorities relying upon the principle established in that case must now be read subject to *Volaw Trust and Corporate Services Ltd v Office of the Comptroller of Taxes* [2019] UKPC 29, [2020] 1 All ER 941. Norwegian tax authorities, pursuant to an agreement between Norway and Jersey for the exchange of information relating to tax matters, requested the Comptroller to issue notices under Jersey regulations to obtain information from the appellants. The question arose whether the notices were incompatible with Article 6 insofar as they required the production of pre-existing documents. The parties agreed that at the relevant time the appellants were the subject of a criminal investigation in Norway and were 'charged' with a criminal offence for the purposes of Article 6. After an extensive review of the relevant Strasbourg jurisprudence, including in particular the judgment of the Grand Chamber in *Ibrahim v UK* [2016] ECHR 750, the Privy Council held as follows. The challenges under Article 6 had been brought at the stage of the gathering of documentary material as part of an investigation into the possible commission of offences. The guarantees of Article 6 may be relevant at the pre-trial investigatory stage *if and in so far as the fairness of the trial is likely to be seriously prejudiced* by an initial failure to comply with them. In principle, and subject to exceptions, examination of the compatibility of pre-trial conduct with Article 6 will normally focus on its effect on the fairness of the trial. The right not to incriminate oneself presupposes that the prosecution will seek to prove their case without resort to evidence obtained through methods of coercion or oppression in defiance of the will of the accused. The privilege does not therefore act as a general prohibition on the use of compulsory powers to obtain documents or information at the investigation stage, even where a person has been charged with an offence within the meaning of Article 6.

The challenges under Article 6 should be considered in the light of four factors:

(a) the nature and degree of compulsion used to obtain the documents;
(b) the weight of the public interest in the investigation and punishment of the offences at issue;
(c) the existence of any safeguards in the procedure; and
(d) the use to which any material so obtained may be put.

As to (a), the compulsion consisted of the potential imposition of a fine for non-compliance. This did not fall within any of the three kinds of situation identified in *Ibrahim v UK* (at [267]) as giving rise to concerns as to improper compulsion in breach of Article 6. The first is where a suspect is obliged to testify under threat of sanctions and testifies in consequence or is sanctioned for refusing to testify. The second is where physical or psychological pressure, often in the form of treatment which breaches Article 3, is applied to obtain real evidence or statements. The third is where the authorities use subterfuge to elicit information that they were unable to obtain during questioning.

As to (b), the weight of the public interest in effective international cooperation in the investigation of possible tax avoidance and evasion cannot be doubted, especially in relation to global financial centres such as Jersey. There is also a substantial public interest in maintaining the integrity of licensed providers of financial services.

As to (c) and (d), no documents had yet been produced and it was impossible to predict what they might contain or how the prosecution might use them, if at all, at any trial. In the event of a criminal trial in Norway in which the prosecution seek to rely on the documents, it would then be possible to object to admissibility on the basis that they had been obtained by compulsory power. The Privy Council also observed that the notices did not call for any admission of liability but sought documents containing objective factual information; and the risk of the notices resulting in unreliable admissions of guilt was negligible.

F10.15 **Production Orders under the PACE 1984, s. 9** In *R (Bright) v Central Criminal Court* [2001] 2 All ER 244, the majority view was that a trial judge has discretion to make production orders under the PACE 1984, s. 9 (see **D1.156**), even though the subject of the order may incriminate him or herself by handing over the material. If the subject of the order is prosecuted, the trial judge may consider the ECHR, Article 6, and whether to exclude the evidence under the PACE 1984, s. 78. In *R (River East Supplies Ltd) v Crown Court at Nottingham* [2017] EWHC 1942 (Admin), [2017] 2 Cr App R 27 (384) the Divisional Court referred to the 'powerful arguments' that prevailed with the majority in *R (Bright) v Central Criminal Court* [2001] 2 All ER 244 that in the PACE 1984, s. 9 and sch. 1, Parliament had excluded the privilege against self-incrimination, but did not find it necessary to resolve the apparent tension, in this respect, between *R (Bright) v Central Criminal Court* and *R (Malik) v Manchester Crown Court* [2008] EWHC 1362 (Admin), [2008] 4 All ER 403.

LEGAL PROFESSIONAL PRIVILEGE

Scope of Privilege

F10.16 A client may, and his or her legal adviser must (subject to the client's waiver), refuse to give oral evidence or to produce documents relating to two types of confidential communication:

(a) communications between client and legal adviser made for the dominant purpose of enabling the client to obtain or the adviser to give legal advice about any matter, whether or not litigation was contemplated at the time (*Greenough v Gaskell* (1833) 1 My & K 98; *R (Jet2.com Ltd) v Civil Aviation Authority* [2020] EWCA Civ 35), the privilege for such communications being known as legal advice privilege; and
(b) communications between client or legal adviser and third parties, the sole or dominant purpose of which was to enable the legal adviser to advise or act in relation to litigation that was pending or in the contemplation of the client (*Waugh v British Railways Board* [1980] AC 521), the privilege for such communications being known as litigation privilege.

The privilege also covers items enclosed with or referred to in such communications and brought into existence (i) in connection with the giving of legal advice or (ii) in connection with or in contemplation of legal proceedings and for the purposes of such proceedings (see *R* [1994] 4 All ER 260 and the PACE 1984, s. 10(1)(c)). Section 10, which is considered at **F10.33** and **F10.37**, purports to reflect the position at common law.

The evidential burden of establishing that a document or communication is privileged lies on the party claiming privilege (*Westminster International BV v Dornoch* [2009] EWCA Civ 1323 at [36]). The question of privilege is for the court; the mere assertion of privilege or statement of the purpose for which a document was created is not in itself determinative. The court must consider carefully the evidence supporting the claim, which should be specific enough to show something of the deponent's analysis of the documents and the purposes for which they were created, preferably by reference to such contemporaneous material as can be referred to without disclosing the privileged matters. In most cases, the evidence should come from the person whose motivation and state of mind is in issue, namely the client or, if the client is a company, the individuals responsible for giving instructions to the lawyers on the company's behalf. Evidence from the lawyers will be of secondary value (*Director of the SFO v Eurasian Natural Resources Corporation Ltd* [2017] EWHC 1017 (QB), [2017] 2 Cr App R 24 (296) at [39]–[41]). If not satisfied on the basis of the evidence that a claim to privilege has been made out, as a last resort the court may inspect the documents, but should not do so unless either there is credible evidence that those claiming privilege have misunderstood their duty or are not to be trusted with the decision-making, or there is no reasonably practical alternative (*West London Pipeline v Total UK Ltd* [2008] EWHC 1729 (Comm)).

In *R (Morgan Grenfell & Co Ltd) v Special Commissioner of Income Tax* [2002] UKHL 21, [2003] 1 AC 563, Lord Hoffmann said (at [7]–[8]): F10.17

> Legal professional privilege is a fundamental human right long established in the common law. It is a necessary corollary of the right of any person to obtain skilled advice about the law. Such advice cannot be effectively obtained unless the client is able to put all the facts before the advisor without fear that they may afterwards be disclosed and used to his prejudice. . . . It has been held by the European Court of Human Rights to be part of the right of privacy guaranteed by [the ECHR] Article 8 . . . the courts will ordinarily construe general words in a statute, although literally capable of having some startling or unreasonable consequence, such as overriding fundamental human rights, as not having been intended to do so. An intention to override such rights must be expressly stated or appear by necessary implication.

In that case, it was held that, on its true construction, the Taxes Management Act 1970, s. 20(1), does not entitle an inspector of taxes to require a tax payer to deliver up material that is subject to legal professional privilege. As to the meaning of 'necessary implication', see further *B v Auckland District Law Society* [2003] UKPC 38, [2003] 2 AC 736. See also *Robinson* [2002] EWCA Crim 2489, in which it was held, *per curiam*, that use of a clerk in a solicitor's office as an informant was not only a serious breach of an accused's right to communicate confidentially with a legal adviser under the seal of legal professional privilege but, on the face of it, and if encouraged by the police, an infringement by them of the accused's rights. The RIPA 2000 permits covert surveillance of communications between someone in custody and his or her lawyer, notwithstanding that they are covered by legal professional privilege and despite the statutory right under the PACE 1984, s. 58 (see **D1.55** ***et seq.***) to consult a solicitor privately (*McE v Prison Service of Northern Ireland* [2009] UKHL 15, [2009] 1 AC 908). However, the House of Lords in *McE* was not required to answer the separate question as to what use could be made of information thus obtained.

In *Financial Reporting Council v Sports Direct International plc* [2020] EWCA Civ 177 it was held that what Lord Hoffmann said in *R (Morgan Grenfell & Co.) v Special Commissioner of Income Tax* [2002] UKHL 21, [2003] 1 AC 563 at [32] is no authority for either (a) the existence of an exception to legal professional privilege where a regulator has a statutory power to request documents, or (b) the application of some lower threshold for implying that the privilege can be overridden by statute on the grounds that any infringement of the privilege would only be 'technical'.

Under the Insolvency Act 1986, s. 311(1), a trustee in bankruptcy shall take possession of documents belonging to the bankrupt and relating to the bankrupt's estate or affairs 'including any which would be privileged from disclosure in any proceedings'. This provision does not override legal professional privilege, either expressly or by necessary implication, and therefore although the trustee may take possession of privileged documents and obtain information from them for the purpose of fulfilling his or her statutory function in gathering and distributing the bankrupt's estate, the trustee cannot waive the bankrupt's privilege by passing the information on to third parties (*Shlosberg v Avonwick Holdings Ltd* [2016] EWCA Civ 1138, [2017] Ch 210).

Under the IPA 2016, s. 27(1) and (3), in the case of applications for targeted interception warrants, mutual assistance warrants and targeted examination warrants made in order to authorise or require the interception of items subject to legal professional privilege, or to authorise the selection of such items for examination, regard must be had to the public interest in the confidentiality of the items. Subject to various qualifications (see s. 27(5) and (6)(c)), under s. 27(4) a warrant may only be issued if (a) there are 'exceptional and compelling circumstances that make it necessary' (as to which, see also the Code of Practice, Interception of Communications, issued under the Act) and (b) the safeguards relating to retention and disclosure of material (see s. 53; and see also the additional safeguards in s. 55) including specific arrangements for the handling, retention, use and destruction of such items. Under s. 27(6), there cannot be 'exceptional and compelling circumstances' unless (a) the public interest in obtaining the information that would be obtained outweighs the confidentiality of the items and (b) there are no other means by which the information may reasonably be obtained. Separate provision is made in respect of communications 'likely to include' items subject to legal professional privilege (s. 27(7) to (9)) and communications made with the intention of furthering a criminal purpose (s. 27(10) to (13)). Provision is also made, in respect of items subject to legal professional privilege in the case of applications for targeted equipment interference warrants (ss. 112 and 131), bulk interception warrants (s. 153), bulk equipment interference warrants (s. 194) and bulk personal datasets warrants (ss. 222 and 223).

F10.18 A legal adviser, for the purposes of legal professional privilege, includes, in addition to a solicitor or a barrister, employed advisers (*Alfred Crompton Amusement Machines Ltd v Customs and Excise Commissioners (No. 2)* [1974] AC 405) and overseas advisers (*Re Duncan* [1968] P 306). In Case C-550/07 P *Akzo Nobel Chemicals Ltd v European Commission* [2011] 2 AC 338, which concerned an investigation into alleged infringements of EU anti-trust law, it was held that the privilege did not apply in relation to a corporation's own in-house lawyers, but it was acknowledged that in a minority of the Member States, including the UK, the privilege does cover communications with in-house lawyers, including such communications in the case of investigations by national competition authorities in those Member States. The privilege does not apply, at common law, in relation to any professional other than a solicitor or barrister or appropriately qualified foreign lawyer, and does not apply, therefore, in relation to other professionals with specialist knowledge of the law and who advise on it, such as accountants with the expertise to advise on tax law (*R (Prudential plc) v Special Commissioner of Income Tax* [2013] UKSC 1, [2013] 2 AC 185).

Legal Advice Privilege

F10.19 Legal advice privilege covers communications between clients and their legal advisers for the dominant purpose of obtaining or giving legal advice. It also covers documents evidencing such communications and documents intended to be such communications, even if not in fact communicated (*Three Rivers District Council v Governor and Company of the Bank of England (No. 5)* [2003] EWCA Civ 474, [2003] QB 1556). In *R (Jet2.com Ltd) v Civil Aviation Authority* [2020] EWCA Civ 35 the Court of Appeal, after an extensive review of the authorities, held that in order to establish legal advice privilege it needs to be shown that the purpose of obtaining or giving legal advice was the dominant purpose. See further **F10.22**. The communications must have been made either in the course of the relationship between client and legal adviser or with a view to its establishment (*Minter v Priest* [1930] AC 558). The privilege extends to instructions given by the client to the solicitor or by the solicitor to the barrister and to counsel's opinion taken by a solicitor (*Bristol Corporation v Cox* (1884) 26 Ch D 678). However, documents emanating from, or prepared by, independent third parties and passed to the lawyer for the purposes of advice are not privileged.

F10.20 **Corporate Clients** In *Three Rivers District Council v Governor and Company of the Bank of England (No. 5)* [2003] EWCA Civ 474, [2003] QB 1556, it was held that legal advice privilege protects only direct communications between the client and the lawyer and evidence of the content of such communications, and that in the case of a corporate client the privilege covers only (a) communications with those officers or employees expressly designated to act as 'the client' and not (b) documents prepared by other employees or ex-employees, even if they were prepared with the dominant purpose of obtaining legal advice, prepared at the lawyer's request, or sent to the lawyer. As to (a), the communications will remain privileged if sent or given to the Board of Directors directly, instead of via the 'designated officers or employees', because the Board is the manifestation of the corporate client (*Director of the SFO v Eurasian Natural Resources Corporation Ltd* [2017] EWHC 1017 (QB), [2017] 2 Cr App R 24 (296) at [84]). If a solicitor is retained by a company to carry out investigations to provide the company with legal advice and that requires the solicitor to speak to employees (or others) who are not 'designated officers or employees', the communications will not be covered by legal advice privilege, even if the employees have been authorised by the company to speak to the solicitor (*RBS Rights Issue Litigation* [2016] EWHC 3161 (Ch), [2017] 1 WLR 1991 at [79]–[93], approved in *Director of the SFO v Eurasian Natural Resources Corporation Ltd* [2017] EWHC 1017 (QB), [2017] 2 Cr App R 24 (296) at [85]–[91]). In the latter case, on appeal, the Court of Appeal would have been in favour of departing from *Three Rivers District Council v Governor and Company of the Bank of England (No. 5)*, but held that it was not open to it to do so and that further consideration of the matter was for the Supreme Court (*Director of the SFO v Eurasian National Resources Corporation Ltd* [2018] EWCA Civ 2006, [2019] 1 WLR 791 at [123]–[130]). See also, to similar effect, *R (Jet2.com Ltd) v Civil Aviation Authority* [2020] EWCA Civ 35.

The Policy Underlying the Privilege The leading authority is *Three Rivers District Council v Governor and Company of the Bank of England (No. 6)* [2004] UKHL 48, [2005] 1 AC 610. **F10.21** The House of Lords held that the policy basis for legal advice privilege is that it is necessary, in a society in which the restraining and controlling framework was built on a belief in the rule of law, that communications between clients and lawyers, whereby the clients are hoping for the assistance of the lawyers' legal skills in the management of their affairs, should be secure against the possibility of any scrutiny from others. Lord Scott accepted as correct the approach of Taylor LJ in *Balabel v Air India* [1988] Ch 317 at pp. 330–1, where he said that for the purpose of attracting legal advice privilege, 'legal advice is not confined to telling the client the law; it must include advice as to what should prudently and sensibly be done in the relevant legal context', but that 'to extend privilege without limit to all solicitor and client communications upon matters within the ordinary business of a solicitor and referable to that relationship [would be] too wide'. Lord Scott said that if a solicitor became the client's 'man of business', responsible for advising the client on matters such as investment and finance policy and other business matters, the advice might lack a relevant legal context. The judge would have to ask whether it related to the rights, liabilities, obligations or remedies of the client under either private or public law, and, if so, whether the communication fell within the policy underlying the justification for the privilege, the criterion being an objective one.

Multi-addressee Communications and Meetings Attended by Lawyers and Non-lawyers In **F10.22** *R (Jet2.com Ltd) v Civil Aviation Authority* [2020] EWCA Civ 35, the Court of Appeal gave the following guidance in relation to single multiple-addressee emails sent simultaneously to various individuals for their advice/comments, including a lawyer for his or her input, and in relation to meetings attended by lawyers and non-lawyers.

(a) The purpose(s) of the communication need to be identified, taking into account the wide scope of 'legal advice' (including the giving of advice in a commercial context through a lawyer's eyes) and the concept of 'continuum of communications'. If the dominant purpose is, in substance, to settle the instructions to the lawyer then, subject to *Three Rivers District Council v Governor and Company of the Bank of England (No. 5)* [2003] EWCA Civ 474, [2003] QB 1556, the privilege applies. That will be so even if the communication is sent to the lawyer by way of information or if it is part of a rolling series of communications with the dominant purpose of instructing the lawyer. However, if the dominant purpose is to obtain the commercial views of the non-lawyer, it will not be privileged, even if a subsidiary purpose is to obtain legal advice from the lawyer.
(b) The response from the lawyer, if it contains legal advice, will almost certainly be privileged, even if copied to more than one addressee. The dominant test applies, but given the wide scope of 'legal advice' and 'continuum of communications' the court will be extremely reluctant to apply it.
(c) Multi-addressee communications should be considered as separate bilateral communications between the sender and each recipient rather than as a whole. Where the purpose of the sender is to obtain from the individuals both legal advice and non-legal advice/input, it is difficult to see why the form of the request, a single email or separate emails, should be relevant as to whether the communications to the non-lawyer should be privileged. However,

in some cases the form may reveal the true purpose of the communication, e.g. it may show that the dominant purpose is to settle the instructions to the lawyer or, on the contrary, to obtain from the non-lawyers their substantive non-lawyer input in any event.

(d) There is some benefit in considering whether, if the email were sent to the lawyer alone, it would attract privilege. If no, the question of whether any of the other emails are privileged hardly arises. If yes, the question arises whether the email to the non-lawyers is privileged because, e.g., the dominant purpose is to obtain instructions or disseminate legal advice.

(e) Where there is a realistic possibility that a communication might disclose legal advice, it will be privileged in any event.

(f) The foregoing principles also apply to meetings, including records of meetings attended by lawyers and non-lawyers at which both commercial and legal advice is given. Legal advice requested and given at such a meeting would be privileged, but the mere presence of a lawyer, perhaps only on the off-chance that legal input may be required, is insufficient to render the whole meeting the subject of privilege. If the dominant purpose of the meeting is to obtain legal advice or, subject to *Three Rivers (No. 5)*, to settle instructions to a lawyer, unless anything is said outside the legal context, privilege will apply. If the dominant purpose of the meeting is commercial, then generally privilege will not apply, although any legal advice sought or given may be privileged. Where not inextricably intermingled, the non-privileged part will be severable.

F10.23 **Working Papers and Prospective Witnesses** A lawyer's working papers are protected by the privilege only if they would betray the tenor of the legal advice given to the client. A verbatim note of what the solicitor was told by a prospective witness is not, without more, covered by the privilege just because the solicitor interviewed the witness with a view to using the information provided as a basis for advising the solicitor's client (*Director of the SFO v Eurasian Natural Resources Corporation Ltd* [2017] EWHC 1017 (QB), [2017] 2 Cr App R 24 (296) at [95]–[97]). On appeal, the Court of Appeal questioned whether lawyers' working papers are only protected if they would betray the tenor of the advice. However, since it concluded that the interview notes in question were covered by litigation privilege, it found it unnecessary to answer the question (*Director of the SFO v Eurasian National Resources Corporation Ltd* [2018] EWCA Civ 2006, [2019] 1 WLR 791 at [141]–[142]).

F10.24 **Joint Interest Legal Professional Privilege** Joint interest legal professional privilege can arise in two circumstances: first, when two or more legal persons jointly retain the same lawyer; and secondly, when there is no joint retainer but the parties have a joint interest in the subject matter of the communication in issue at the time when it comes into existence. *R (Ford) v Financial Services Authority* [2012] EWHC 2583 (Admin), [2012] 1 All ER 1238 concerned the second set of circumstances, the issue being whether directors of a company could assert joint legal privilege in respect of advice provided for them by solicitors retained by the company. It was held that, apart from cases in which there is no legal distinction between those claiming joint privilege, an individual claiming joint privilege with others in a communication with a lawyer will need to establish that: he or she communicated with the lawyer for the purpose of seeking advice in an individual capacity; he or she made clear to the lawyer that the legal advice was sought in an individual capacity rather than as a representative of a corporate body; those with whom the joint privilege was claimed knew or ought to have appreciated the legal position; the lawyer knew or ought to have appreciated that he or she was communicating with the individual in that individual capacity; and the communication with the lawyer was confidential.

F10.25 **What the Privilege Does Not Cover** Legal advice privilege does not cover records of time spent with a client on attendance notes, time sheets or fee records, because they are not communications between client and legal adviser, or records of appointments, because they are not communications made in connection with legal advice (*Manchester Crown Court, ex parte Rogers* [1999] 4 All ER 35). Nor does it cover a lawyer's records of a client's telephone numbers and of the dates when the client telephoned the lawyer (*R (Miller Gardner Solicitors) v Minshull Street Crown Court* [2002] EWHC 3077 (QB)). Equally, the privilege does not cover attendance notes made by a solicitor recording what took place in court or in chambers in the presence of the parties on both sides (*Ainsworth v Wilding* [1900] 2 Ch 315); nor does it cover attendance notes recording meetings between the legal advisers of the parties on both sides (with or without their clients in attendance) or attendance notes recording telephone conversations between the parties, because all such notes are not communications between solicitor and client but merely records setting out what passed publicly between the two parties or their advisers (*Parry v News Group Newspapers Ltd* (1990) 140 NLJ 1719). The privilege attaches to communications between client and legal adviser for the purposes of obtaining and giving legal advice, and not to *facts* perceived by the legal adviser in the course of that relationship. Thus a solicitor may generally be compelled to give evidence as to a client's identity (*Studdy v Sanders* (1823) 2 Dow & Ry KB 347). In *R (Howe) v South Durham Magistrates' Court* [2004] EWHC 362 (Admin), [2005] RTR 4 (55), it was held that a solicitor present in court when an order had been made disqualifying a person from driving could be compelled in a subsequent prosecution to give evidence as to the identity of that person and to produce attendance notes in relation to the disqualification (with anything in the notes attracting privilege blacked out). Equally, a solicitor may be compelled to give evidence as to a client's handwriting (*Dwyer v Collins* (1852) 7 Exch 639) or mental capacity (*James v Godrich* (1844) 5 Moore PCC 16). See also *Brown v Foster* (1857) 1 H & N 736: a barrister who has seen a book produced at his or her client's trial may give evidence in subsequent proceedings as to its contents.

Litigation Privilege

The main principles relating to the scope of litigation privilege were set out by Sir Terence Etherton MR in *WH Holdings Ltd v E20 Stadium LLP* [2018] EWCA Civ 2652 at [27]. **F10.26**

(a) The privilege is engaged when litigation is in reasonable contemplation.
(b) Once engaged, it covers communications between parties or their solicitors and third parties for the purpose of obtaining information or advice in connection with the conduct of the litigation, provided it is for the sole or dominant purpose of the conduct of the litigation.
(c) Conducting the litigation includes deciding whether to litigate and also whether to settle the dispute giving rise to the litigation.
(d) Documents in which such information or advice cannot be disentangled or which would otherwise reveal such information or advice are covered by the privilege.
(e) There is no separate head of privilege covering internal communications falling outside the ambit of the privilege as described above.

There is an additional restriction: the privilege only applies in the case of litigation that is adversarial, not investigative or inquisitorial (*Three Rivers District Council v Governor and Company of the Bank of England (No. 6)* [2004] UKHL 48, [2005] 1 AC 610).

As to (c) above, in *Director of the SFO v Eurasian Natural Resources Corporation Ltd* [2018] EWCA Civ 2006, [2019] 1 WLR 791 at [102], the Court of Appeal doubted the correctness of the principle stated by the trial judge that no privilege attaches to a document created with the purpose of showing it to the prospective adversary (such as a position statement prepared for the purposes of a mediation). It was held that in both the civil and the criminal contexts, legal advice given to head off, avoid or settle reasonably contemplated proceedings is as much protected by litigation privilege as advice given for the purpose of resisting or defending such proceedings.

The privilege extends to the identity and other details of witnesses intended to be called in adversarial litigation, whether or not their identity is the fruit of legal advice. A party has a legitimate interest in protecting the identity of witnesses the party intends to call until a late stage in the litigation.

Litigation privilege, like legal professional privilege, is a basic or fundamental right, and may only be intruded upon by force of subordinate legislation if the statute providing the subordinate instrument's *vires* makes it plain that such an authority was intended to be conveyed (*R (Kelly) v Warley Magistrates' Court* [2007] EWHC 1836 (Admin), [2008] 1 Cr App R 14 (195)).

F10.27 **Types of Documents Covered** The privilege covers documents created by a party for the purpose of instructing the lawyer and obtaining advice in the conduct of the litigation (*Anderson v Bank of British Columbia* (1876) 2 Ch D 644, per James LJ at p. 656), but not documents obtained by a party or the party's adviser for the purpose of litigation that were not created for that purpose (*Ventouris v Mountain* [1991] 3 All ER 472). A copy or translation of an unprivileged document in the control of a party does not become privileged merely because the copy or translation was made for the purpose of the litigation (see, in the case of copies, *Dubai Bank Ltd v Galadari* [1990] Ch 98 and, in the case of translations, *Sumitomo Corporation v Credit Lyonnais Rouse Ltd* [2001] EWCA Civ 1152, [2002] 4 All ER 68). However, privilege will attach to a copy of an unprivileged document if the copy was made for the purpose of litigation and the original is not, and has not at any time been, in the control of the party claiming privilege (*The Palermo* (1883) 9 PD 6; *Watson v Cammell Laird & Co. (Shipbuilders & Engineers) Ltd* [1959] 2 All ER 757). Privilege will also attach where a solicitor has copied or assembled a selection of third-party documents for the purposes of litigation, if its production will betray the trend of the advice given to the client (*Lyell v Kennedy (No. 3)* (1884) 27 Ch D 1), but this principle does not extend to a selection of own client documents, or copies or translations representing the fruits of such a selection, made for the purposes of litigation (*Sumitomo Corporation v Credit Lyonnais Rouse Ltd*, overruling *Dubai Bank Ltd v Galadari (No. 7)* [1992] 4 All ER 68).

F10.28 **Dominant Purpose** The burden of proof is on the party claiming privilege to establish that the dominant purpose test is satisfied. A mere claim in evidence that the document was for a particular purpose will not be decisive. The court will consider purpose from an objective standpoint, looking at all relevant evidence, including evidence of subjective purpose. The evidence in support must be specific enough to show something of the deponent's analysis of the purpose for which the document was created and should refer to such contemporary material as is possible without disclosing the privileged material (*Rawlinson and Hunter Trustees SA v Akers* [2014] EWCA Civ 136, [2014] 4 All ER 627). Account should be taken of the intention of not only the author of the document but also the person or authority under whose direction it was procured (*Guinness Peat Properties Ltd v Fitzroy Robinson Partnership* [1987] 2 All ER 716). In order to show that litigation was reasonably in prospect, the party claiming privilege does not have to show that it was more likely than not that adversarial litigation would ensue; but it is insufficient to show that there was a 'distinct possibility' that sooner or later someone might make a claim or there was a general apprehension of future litigation (*USA v Philip Morris* [2003] EWHC 3028 (Comm) at [68]).

In *Director of the SFO v Eurasian Natural Resources Corporation Ltd* [2018] EWCA Civ 2006, [2019] 1 WLR 791 at [99] and [100] the Court of Appeal (Civil Division) rejected as 'illusory' the distinction drawn by the trial judge, on the question whether litigation can be said to be in reasonable contemplation, between civil and criminal proceedings. The Court was of the view that the approval of the distinction in *Jukes* [2018] EWCA Crim 176, [2018] 2 Cr App R 9 (114) was *obiter*. (See also the *obiter* approval of the distinction in *R (AL) v SFO* [2018] EWHC 856 (Admin), [2018] 2 Cr App R 13 (170) at [108].) The Court held that there is no general principle that litigation privilege cannot attach until either an accused knows the full details of what is likely to be unearthed or a decision to prosecute has been taken; and the fact that a formal investigation has not commenced will be a part of the factual matrix, but will not necessarily be determinative.

F10.29 **Third Party's Involvement** If a client communicates with a lawyer via a third party who is not merely an agent for communication, but someone who also has to make a preliminary decision on whether to refer the matter to the lawyer, no privilege will attach to the information supplied to the third party (*Jones v Great Central Railway Co.* [1910] AC 4).

Death of Client or Dissolution of a Company Legal professional privilege survives the death of a client and vests in the client's personal representative or, once administration is complete, the person entitled to the deceased's estate. Such persons, therefore, are entitled to either claim or waive the privilege (*Molloy (Deceased)* [1997] 2 Cr App R 283). In *Addlesee v Dentons Europe LLP* [2019] EWCA Civ 1600, [2020] Ch 243, the Court of Appeal, overruling *Garvin Trustees Ltd v Pensions Regulator* [2015] Pens LR 1, held that where communications between a company and its lawyers are privileged at the time when the communications were made, they remain privileged once the company has been dissolved, unless at that stage there is someone entitled to waive the privilege. It was further held that since legal professional privilege is not property, the reasoning in *Molloy (Deceased)*, which used the language of property rights by saying that on the death of the client the privilege 'vests in' the personal representatives, needs qualification. **F10.30**

Effect of Rules Governing Disclosure of Expert Evidence

The common-law principles relating to communications with third parties must now be read subject to CrimPR Part 19 (see **D15.75** and **F11.46**, and Supplement, **R19.1** ***et seq.***, where the rules are set out). These rules make provision, subject to exceptions, for the disclosure of expert evidence between the parties to Crown Court and summary trials. Under r. 19.3(4) a party may not introduce expert evidence if the party has not complied with the requirement of service of such evidence unless every other party agrees or the court gives permission. The rule does not *compel* disclosure: if an expert's report is unhelpful to the party obtaining it, he or she need not disclose it to the opponent, and the opponent cannot require the party, the party's solicitor or the expert to give evidence as to the instructions given to the expert or the report that was prepared. The expert may, however, be called by the opponent to give evidence of facts observed and of the expert's opinion on those facts (*Harmony Shipping Co. SA v Saudi Europe Line Ltd* [1979] 3 All ER 177, applied in *King* [1983] 1 All ER 929), unless the expert's opinion is based on examination of an item which is itself privileged because it was brought into existence for the purpose of obtaining legal advice etc. (*R* [1994] 4 All ER 260, at **F10.34**) or the opinion is inextricably dependent, or based to a material extent, on other privileged material such as communications with an accused (*Davies* [2002] EWCA Crim 85). **F10.31**

Pre-existing Documents and Items

At common law, a legal adviser (or third party) has no greater privilege than the client. Thus, a document that is not privileged in the hands of the client does not become privileged if given into the custody of a lawyer for the purposes of obtaining legal advice (or if sent by the lawyer to a third party in connection with pending or contemplated litigation). In *Peterborough Justices, ex parte Hicks* [1977] 1 All ER 225, in which the client had sent a forged document to his solicitor for the purposes of obtaining legal advice, a warrant was ordered under the Forgery Act 1913, s. 16, to search the solicitor's premises and seize the document. On an application for certiorari to quash the search warrant, it was held that the document was not privileged in the hands of the solicitor because it would have been open to seizure in the hands of the client. Eveleigh J said (at p. 1374), 'it is the privilege of the client . . . the solicitor holds the document in the right of his client and can assert in respect of its seizure no greater authority than the client himself . . . possesses'. In *Frank Truman Export Ltd v Metropolitan Police Commissioner* [1977] QB 952, Swanwick J expressed views to the contrary, but these dicta were doubted in *King* [1983] 1 All ER 929. In *King*, a case of conspiracy to defraud, an expert instructed by the defence was subpoenaed to produce sample handwriting sent to him by D's solicitors for examination (although the instructions sent to him and the report he produced were held to be privileged). But see also *R* [1994] 4 All ER 260, discussed at **F10.34**. Legal professional privilege cannot be claimed in respect of a document which is not privileged in itself merely because it is attached to an email sent by a client to a lawyer seeking advice or by a lawyer to a client giving advice (*Financial Reporting Council Ltd v Sports Direct International plc* [2020] EWCA Civ 177). **F10.32**

F10.33 **PACE 1984, ss. 9 and 10** The principle established in *Peterborough Justices, ex parte Hicks* [1977] 1 All ER 225 must now be read subject to the provisions of the PACE 1984. Section 9(2)(a) of the 1984 Act repeals previous legislation insofar as it authorised, by the issue of a warrant, searches for, *inter alia*, 'items subject to legal privilege' and 'special procedure material'. Section 8 of the 1984 Act provides for the issue of warrants of entry and search if, *inter alia*, a justice of the peace is satisfied that the material sought does not consist of or include 'items subject to legal privilege' or 'special procedure material'. Unless 'special procedure material' has been voluntarily disclosed by the person who acquired or created it (*Singleton* [1995] 1 Cr App R 431), under s. 9(1) a constable may obtain access to such material for the purposes of a criminal investigation by making an application *inter partes* on notice to a circuit judge.

A phone or computer can properly be the subject of a warrant under s. 9 even where material subject to legal privilege may be found on it, provided that the wording of the warrant clearly excludes any such material from that which can be sought or seized. Suitable arrangements have to be made to ensure that the exclusion is enforced in the conduct of the search and in dealing with the material seized. Such arrangements may extend to the presence of independent counsel during the search and are also likely to require suitable provision for the opening and downloading of the device together with independent review of the contents prior to any police viewing (*R (A) v Central Criminal Court* [2017] EWHC 70 (Admin), [2017] 1 WLR 3567).

Under s. 14(2), 'special procedure material' includes material, other than items subject to legal privilege, in the possession of a person who acquired or created it in the course of any trade, business, profession etc. and holds it subject to an express or implied undertaking to hold it in confidence. The phrase 'items subject to legal privilege' is defined in s. 10 of the Act, which, it has been held, is intended to reflect the position at common law (see the majority view in *Central Criminal Court, ex parte Francis* [1989] AC 346, at **F10.37**). Thus, for example, as at common law, 'legal privilege' in s. 10 does not embrace all communications between client and solicitor and therefore will not necessarily cover such items as a conveyance or other legal document, unless connected to legal advice or legal proceedings (*R (Faisaltex Ltd) v Preston Crown Court* [2008] EWHC 2832 (Admin), [2009] 1 Cr App R 37 (549)).

Police and Criminal Evidence Act 1984, s. 10

(1) Subject to subsection (2) below, in this Act 'items subject to legal privilege' means—
  (a) communications between a professional legal adviser and his client or any person representing his client made in connection with the giving of legal advice to the client;
  (b) communications between a professional legal adviser and his client or any person representing his client or between such an adviser or his client or any such representative and any other person made in connection with or in contemplation of legal proceedings and for the purposes of such proceedings; and
  (c) items enclosed with or referred to in such communications and made—
    (i) in connection with the giving of legal advice; or
    (ii) in connection with or in contemplation of legal proceedings and for the purposes of such proceedings,

  when they are in the possession of a person who is entitled to possession of them.

(2) Items held with the intention of furthering a criminal purpose are not items subject to legal privilege.

F10.34 In *Guildhall Magistrates' Court, ex parte Primlaks Holdings Co. (Panama) Inc.* [1990] 1 QB 261 it was held that loss of legal privilege by virtue of s. 10(2) does not mean that no express or implied undertaking to hold in confidence can exist. A solicitor's correspondence with his or her client (and its enclosures) will, if not privileged, fall squarely within s. 14. Thus if, on an application under s. 8, a justice cannot be satisfied that there are reasonable grounds for believing that the material sought does not include any items which are, prima facie, subject to legal privilege or any material which is, prima facie, special procedure material, the justice should refuse the application and leave the applicant to proceed under s. 9 so that the matter can be fully ventilated before a circuit judge, who will consider the matter *inter partes*. Likewise if the police are aware that what they seek includes items which are, prima facie, the subject of legal privilege, they should proceed under s. 9. It was further observed (at pp. 273–4) that documents of a client sent to a professional legal adviser under cover of privileged correspondence for the purpose of obtaining legal advice would not be within s. 10(1)(c) if they were pre-existing documents and were not made in connection with the giving of legal advice or in connection with or in contemplation of legal proceedings and for the purposes of such proceedings; but such pre-existing documents would be, prima facie, within s. 14(2), and therefore it would be open to the police to make an application under s. 9 of the Act in order to have access to them. However, a document forged by a solicitor or supplied to a solicitor by a fraudulent client does not constitute special procedure material because, from its nature, it could not have been acquired or created in the course of the profession of a solicitor (*Leeds Magistrates' Court, ex parte Dumbleton* [1993] Crim LR 866).

In *R* [1994] 4 All ER 260, it was held that the word 'made' in s. 10(1)(c) is used in a general sense and is wide enough to include the meaning 'brought into existence'. It was also held that where an item is protected from production under s. 10(1)(c), oral evidence of opinion based upon the item is also inadmissible. A scientist had carried out DNA tests at the request of the defence solicitors on a blood sample provided by D. It was held that s. 10(1)(c) applied not only so as to enable the defence to object to the sample being produced in evidence (because the sample was an item brought into existence for the purposes of legal proceedings), but also so as to prevent the prosecution from calling the scientist to give evidence of opinion based on the sample.

Information Helpful in Establishing Innocence

In *Derby Magistrates' Court, ex parte B* [1996] AC 487, D was acquitted of murder. His step-father was subsequently charged with the murder and at his committal proceedings, D was called as a prosecution witness. Counsel for the defence sought to cross-examine D on certain factual instructions that he had given to his solicitors when he had been charged with the offence. D declined to waive his privilege. The magistrates then issued summonses, directing D and his solicitor to produce documentary evidence of the instructions, on the basis that the public interest that all relevant and admissible evidence should be made available to the defence outweighed the public interest which protected confidential communications between a solicitor and a client. An application for judicial review of the decision was refused, but the House of Lords allowed the appeal. It was held that no exception should be allowed to the absolute and permanent nature of 'legal professional privilege' (a phrase used to refer to the privilege attaching to the solicitor-client relationship and not to all other forms of legal professional privilege: see *Re L (A Minor) (Police Investigation: Privilege)* [1997] AC 16) and therefore, overruling *Barton* [1973] 2 All ER 1192 and *Ataou* [1988] 2 All ER 321, there could be no question of a balancing exercise of the kind performed by the magistrates. A client must be sure that what is told to a lawyer in confidence will never be revealed without the client's consent. Once any exception to the general rule is allowed, the client's confidence is necessarily lost. Therefore the documents in question, being protected by legal professional privilege, were immune from production. However, Lord Nicholls, who also rejected any question of a balancing exercise, observed that in cases where the client no longer has any interest in maintaining the privilege, the privilege is spent. His lordship preferred to reserve his final view on the point, being of the opinion that the point did not arise since D had a legitimate interest in not disclosing material which might suggest that he had been improperly acquitted, but in a dictum which, it is submitted, has much to commend it, said (at p. 701): **F10.35**

> I would not expect a law, based explicitly on considerations of the public interest, to protect the right of a client when he has no interest in asserting the right and the enforcement of the right would be seriously prejudicial to another in defending a criminal charge or in some other way.

Communications in Furtherance of Crime or Fraud

Communications in furtherance of crime or fraud are a well-recognised exception to the principle of legal professional privilege (*Derby Magistrates' Court, ex parte B* [1996] AC 487, per Lord Lloyd at p. 509). In *Cox* (1884) 14 QBD 153, a solicitor was compelled to disclose **F10.36** communications with D, in which D had sought his advice in drawing up a bill of sale alleged to be fraudulent. Stephen J, delivering the judgment of the Court for Crown Cases Reserved, held that if a client applies to a legal adviser for advice intended to facilitate or to guide the client in the commission of a crime or fraud, the legal adviser being ignorant of the purpose for which the advice is sought, the communication between the two is not privileged. See also *Hayward* (1846) 2 Car & Kir 234 and *Smith* (1915) 11 Cr App R 229. The principle can be relied upon only if there is prima facie evidence that it was the client's intention to obtain advice in furtherance of a criminal or fraudulent purpose (*O'Rourke v Darbishire* [1920] AC 581). Although a court may look at the communications in question — the 'closed material' — to decide whether they came into existence in furtherance of such a purpose (*Governor of Pentonville Prison, ex parte Osman* [1990] 3 All ER 701, at pp. 309–10), as a rule the court should not do so: there must be some exceptional factor of real weight before the court can examine the closed material and the mere fact that the test is not satisfied on the open material is not such a factor (*BBGP Managing General Partner Ltd v Babcock & Brown Global Partners* [2010] EWHC 2176 (Ch), [2011] Ch 296). In *Minchin* [2013] EWCA Crim 2412, a case of conspiracy to pervert the course of justice relating to an allegedly false alibi, it was held that material in support of the purported alibi held by solicitors was not protected by the privilege because there was 'free-standing and independent' evidence of the conspiracy. The exception does apply if the legal adviser is aware of or is a party to the crime or fraud, but not if the adviser merely volunteers a warning to the client that certain conduct could result in prosecution (*Butler v Board of Trade* [1971] Ch 680). Fraud, for the purposes of the exception, is not limited to the tort of deceit, and includes all forms of fraud and dishonesty, such as fraudulent breach of trust, fraudulent conspiracy, trickery and sham contrivances, but does not cover the tort of inducing a breach of contract (*Crescent Farm (Sidcup) Sports Ltd v Sterling Offices Ltd* [1972] Ch 553, per Goff J at p. 565) or the torts of trespass and conversion (*Dubai Aluminium Co. Ltd v Al Alawi* [1999] 1 All ER 703). 'Fraud', in this context, is used in a relatively wide sense. Thus privilege will not attach to legal advice on how to structure a transaction which has been devised to prejudice the interests of a creditor by putting assets beyond the creditor's reach (*Barclays Bank Plc v Eustice* [1995] 4 All ER 511). Nor will privilege attach to advice on how to cloak dismissal of an employee for making complaints of disability discrimination as dismissal for redundancy (*X v Y Ltd* UKEAT/0261/17/JOJ).

The exception is not confined to cases in which solicitors advise on or set up criminal or fraudulent transactions yet to be undertaken, but also covers criminal or fraudulent conduct undertaken for the purposes of acquiring evidence in, or for, litigation. Thus where documents have been generated by, or report on, conduct which constitutes a crime under the data protection legislation, and those documents are relevant to an issue in the proceedings, they will not be protected from disclosure by legal professional privilege (*Dubai Aluminium Co. Ltd v Al Alawi*).

F10.37 There appeared to be no common-law authority prior to the judgments in *Central Criminal Court, ex parte Francis* [1989] AC 346 to the effect that a criminal intent on the part of a stranger to the relationship of a solicitor and client destroys the privilege of the client (see the speech of Lord Oliver, dissenting, in *Ex parte Francis*). Such authority as there was suggested the contrary: see, e.g., *Banque Keyser Ullman SA v Skandia (UK) Insurance Co. Ltd* [1986] 1 Lloyd's Rep 336, in which it was held that the principle of *Cox* (1884) 14 QBD 153 does not extend to the correspondence between a solicitor and the victim of a fraudster. However, the decision of the majority of the House of Lords in *Ex parte Francis* provides persuasive authority that the intention of furthering a criminal purpose may be that of the client, the solicitor or any other person. That case concerned the construction of the PACE 1984, s. 10(2), which provides that: 'Items held with the intention of furthering a criminal purpose are not items subject to legal privilege'. In *Snaresbrook Crown Court, ex parte DPP* [1988] QB 532, it was held, giving these words their natural meaning, that what is relevant is the intention of the person holding the items in question. However, in *Ex parte Francis*, a majority of the House, rejecting this construction, held that s. 10(2) was not intended to restrict the principle of *Cox* (1884) 14 QBD 153 to cases in which the legal adviser has the intention of furthering a criminal purpose, but *reflected the position at common law*, and therefore the intention to which it referred could be that of the person holding the document or any other person. On that basis it was held that no privilege attached to documents relating to the purchase of a property by a client and innocently held by a solicitor, because a third party, a relative of the client, intended them to be used to further his criminal purpose in laundering the proceeds of illegal drug trafficking. See also *R (Hallinan, Blackburn Gittings & Notts) (a firm) v Crown Court at Middlesex Guildhall* [2004] EWHC 2726 (Admin), [2005] 1 WLR 766, where a draft statement, made pursuant to a specific agreement to pervert the course of justice, was forwarded to D's solicitors.

In *Leeds Magistrates' Court, ex parte Dumbleton* [1993] Crim LR 866, a warrant was issued to search for and seize documents held by a solicitor and allegedly forged by him and another. It was held that the documents were not covered by s. 10(1) because the phrase 'made in connection with... legal proceedings' meant lawfully made, and did not extend to forged documents or copies thereof; in any event the items were held with the intention of furthering a criminal purpose — the word 'held' in s. 10(2) relating to the time at which the documents came into the possession of the person holding them. **F10.38**

Exception to the Right to Private Consultation

Brown [2015] EWCA Crim 1328, [2016] 1 WLR 1141 established an additional common-law qualification or exception to the 'inviolable' nature of legal professional privilege 'in what is likely to be an extremely narrow band of cases' per Fulford LJ at [41]). The Court of Appeal upheld the ruling of the trial judge that D should be accompanied by, and handcuffed to, nurses during any conferences with his lawyers in order to avoid the real risk of harming himself, either seriously or fatally, there being no appropriate facilities at the court that would enable D to communicate with his lawyers from within a secure place. There was no suggestion of misuse by the nurses of any of the privileged communications. The steps taken by the judge were justified in order to preserve D's right to life under the ECHR, Article 2. As to the right to confidential communication with a lawyer under Article 6(3)(c), it was held that under the jurisprudence of the ECtHR the right is not absolute but can be restricted for good reason, one of those reasons being if the individual's life is at risk. **F10.39**

Waiver of Privilege

In *Ahmed* [2007] EWCA Crim 2870, the Court of Appeal set out the following principles relating to waiver of legal professional privilege. **F10.40**

(a) Documents may be disclosed for a limited purpose without waiving privilege generally.
(b) However, if a document or communication is disclosed voluntarily, privilege will normally be lost generally and with it the right to withhold production of other documents or communications relating to the same subject-matter, or 'transaction'.
(c) The principle governing the loss of privilege in the transaction generally is one of fairness. It is contrary to the interests of justice to allow a person to disclose a limited range of material relating to a particular matter, perhaps chosen to serve the person's own interests, while depriving the other party to the litigation of the full picture which the remainder of the material relating to that matter would disclose.
(d) However, the importance of legal professional privilege to the proper administration of justice was such that it should be jealously guarded and it followed that courts should not be astute to hold that a litigant had lost the right to claim privilege save to the extent that justice and the right to a fair trial made that necessary. It is necessary to identify the confidential communications which the person chose to disclose and see to what extent fairness demanded that other documents or communications should also be disclosed.

Confidentiality in a privileged document will not necessarily be lost because of its deployment in open court in criminal proceedings; whether references to it by the court or the advocates are such as to constitute such an exposure of the document to the public that confidentiality in it is lost is a question of degree (*'SL Claimants' v Tesco plc* [2019] EWHC 3315 (Ch)).

Waiver of Privilege and the Criminal Justice and Public Order Act 1994, s. 34

F10.41 In *Condron* [1997] 1 WLR 827, the Court of Appeal gave the following guidance relating to legal professional privilege where an accused refuses to answer police questions on the advice of his or her solicitor. Communications between accused and solicitor prior to interviews by the police are subject to the privilege. If an accused gives as a reason for not answering that he or she has been advised by the solicitor not to do so, that advice does not amount to a waiver of privilege. But if the accused wishes to invite the court not to draw an adverse inference under the CJPO 1994, s. 34 (see **F20.4**), it is necessary to go further and state the basis or reason for the advice. This may well amount to a waiver of privilege so that the accused or, if the accused's solicitor is also called, the solicitor, can be asked whether there were any other reasons for the advice, and the nature of the advice given, so as to explore whether the advice may also have been given for tactical reasons. However, it should be borne in mind that the information which the prosecution seek to draw from failure to mention facts in interview is that they have been subsequently fabricated. It is open to an accused to attempt to rebut this inference by showing that the relevant facts were communicated to a third party, usually the solicitor, at about the time of the interview. This does not involve waiver of privilege if it is the solicitor to whom the fact is communicated.

It is probably desirable that the judge should warn counsel, or the accused, that the privilege may be taken to have been waived if the accused gives evidence of the nature of the advice.

F10.42 If the defence reveal the basis or reason for the solicitor's advice to the accused not to answer police questions, this will amount to a waiver of privilege whether the revelation is made by the accused or by the solicitor acting within the scope of his or her authority as agent on behalf of the accused, and whether the revelation is made in the course of pre-trial questioning, in evidence before the jury, or in evidence on the *voir dire* which is *not* repeated before the jury (*Bowden* [1999] 4 All ER 582). *Bowden* was followed in *Loizou* [2006] EWCA Crim 1719, where Hooper LJ said (at [84]):

> There is a distinction between *having* to reveal what was said to a solicitor to rebut an allegation of recent fabrication and *volunteering* information about the legal advice . . . In the former scenario the reason privilege has not been waived is that there is no way of dealing with the allegation other than by revealing what was said. In the latter scenario, while the effect may be to enable an allegation of recent fabrication to be made, this is the consequence of the voluntary provision by or on behalf of the defendant of information which because of its partial nature is misleading.

See further **F20.20**.

Waiver of Privilege and Use of Secondary Evidence

F10.43 Legal professional privilege prevents the giving of oral evidence or the production of documents by particular persons, namely the client, the legal adviser (or legal adviser's clerk or agent) or third parties (in the case of protected communications between client or legal adviser and such third parties). If a privilege has been waived, because the contents of a privileged communication have become known to any other person, whether by overhearing a privileged conversation or by obtaining the original or a copy of a privileged document, that person may be compelled to give oral evidence in that regard or to produce the document or copy (see, in the case of copies of privileged documents, *Calcraft v Guest* [1898] 1 QB 759 and, in the case of originals, *Waugh v British Railways Board* [1980] AC 521 per Lord Simon at p. 536 and *Governor of Pentonville Prison, ex parte Osman* [1990] 3 All ER 701 at pp. 309–10). This principle applies not only if the privileged communication was disclosed by accident or error on the part of the client or the legal adviser, but also where it was obtained by improper or even criminal means on the part of the client's opponent (or some third party). But see also *ITC Film Distributors Ltd v Video*

Exchange Ltd [1982] Ch 431, which is considered at **F2.6**. In *Tompkins* (1977) 67 Cr App R 181, a note from D to his counsel had been found on the floor of the court and handed to prosecuting counsel by a representative of his instructing solicitor. The contents of the note being in flat contradiction to an answer given by D in cross-examination, prosecuting counsel handed the note to D, and without referring to its contents asked D whether he adhered to the answer he had given. The judge ruled that the cross-examination was proper but that no direct reference should be made to the note. D then admitted the opposite of what he had said. The Court of Appeal held that counsel had been properly allowed to put questions in cross-examination on the basis of the contents of the note. In *Cottrill* [1997] Crim LR 56, applying *Tompkins*, it was held that a statement made by D to his solicitors, and voluntarily sent by them to the prosecution without his knowledge or consent, could be used in cross-examination, if his evidence did not accord with the account given in the statement, subject to the provisions of the PACE 1984, s. 78. *Tompkins* and *Cottrill* were applied in *Willis* [2004] EWCA Crim 3472. Concerning the duties of an advocate when coming into possession of documents to which neither the advocate nor the advocate's client is entitled, see **D16.8**.

In *Butler v Board of Trade* [1971] Ch 680, D, who was being prosecuted by the Board of Trade for alleged offences under the Companies Act 1948, sought a declaration that the Board was not entitled to produce in evidence at the criminal trial a copy of a letter from D's solicitor to D, which had been accidentally included in papers handed over to the Official Receiver. It was held that, although the original letter was privileged, the copy was admissible in the criminal proceedings under the rule in *Calcraft v Guest* [1898] 1 QB 759, the principle established in *Lord Ashburton v Pape* [1913] 2 Ch 469 being inapplicable. Goff J said (at p. 690): **F10.44**

> . . . it would not be a right or permissible exercise of the equitable jurisdiction in confidence to make a declaration at the suit of the accused in a public prosecution in effect restraining the Crown from adducing admissible evidence relevant to the crime with which he is charged. It is not necessary for me to decide whether the same result would obtain in the case of a private prosecution, and I expressly leave that point open.

Where it is suggested to an accused that his or her evidence in a particular respect is a recent fabrication and the accused's solicitor is called to give evidence in rebuttal, the questioning of the solicitor may be confined to the specific matters alleged to have been fabricated, but if the accused discloses the solicitor's attendance notes, privilege is thereby waived in respect of everything found within them (*Hall* [2015] EWCA Crim 581). If an accused waives privilege by saying that the jury were given the same account that was given to the accused's solicitor, the prosecution are entitled to comment on a failure to call the solicitor, if available (*Seaton* [2010] EWCA Crim 1980, [2011] 1 WLR 623).

Statements Made in 'Without Prejudice' Negotiations

In *K* [2009] EWCA Crim 1640, [2010] QB 343, the question arose whether a third party, into whose hands had fallen evidence of damaging admissions made in the course of 'without prejudice' negotiations, was entitled to rely on them in subsequent criminal proceedings against the party who made them. It was held that the immediate purpose of the 'without prejudice' rule is to enable parties to negotiate freely without compromising their positions in relation to their current dispute and that, although it may be justifiable to extend the scope of the protection to subsequent proceedings involving either of the parties to the original negotiations, the public interest in preserving confidentiality becomes weaker the more remote the subject-matter of those proceedings becomes from the subject of the original negotiations. Criminal proceedings involve different parties and therefore are necessarily at one remove from the original dispute and the public interest in prosecuting crime is sufficient to outweigh the public interest in the settlement of disputes, but in appropriate circumstances it may be possible to exclude evidence of the admissions under the PACE 1984, s. 78. **F10.45**

Section F11 Opinion Evidence

GENERAL RULE

F11.1 The general rule is that witnesses may only give evidence of facts they personally perceived and not evidence of their opinion, i.e. evidence of inferences drawn from such facts. The assumption that it is possible to distinguish fact from inference is arguably false (see Thayer, *A Preliminary Treatise on Evidence at the Common Law* (1898), at p. 524), but the distinction has given rise to little case law. In *Meads* [1996] Crim LR 519, it was held that evidence of tests showing the speed at which the handwritten notes of disputed interviews had been made, and whether they could have been written in the time claimed by officers, was no more opinion evidence than evidence of the timing of a given journey in order to test an alibi. The inferences to be drawn from such evidence were for the jury. In *Allad* [2014] EWCA Crim 421, it was held that a witness was entitled to explain how VAT carousel frauds operate but should not have expressed an opinion on the issue before the jury, namely whether D would have known that they had participated in a fraud.

Sepulvida-Gomez [2019] EWCA Crim 2174, [2020] 4 WLR 11 provides an example of inadmissible non-expert opinion evidence. D was convicted of assault by penetration and sexual assault. It was held that the jury had heard inadmissible opinion evidence that V would not have consented to the sexual activity with D. See also *SJ* [2019] EWCA Crim 1570, [2020] 1 Cr App R 7 (153), considered at **F11.8**.

There are two exceptions to the general rule:

(a) *Non-experts*. A statement of opinion on any matter not calling for expertise, if made by a witness as a way of conveying relevant facts personally perceived by him or her, is admissible as evidence of what the witness perceived.
(b) *Experts*. Subject to compliance with CrimPR Part 19 (expert evidence) (see **D9.68, D15.75** and **F11.46**), a statement of opinion on any relevant matter calling for expertise may be made by a witness qualified to give such an expert opinion.

As to (b), the evidence may be accompanied, where appropriate, by animations to illustrate the opinion (*Metcalfe* [2016] EWCA Crim 681, [2016] 2 Cr App R 21 (297), considered at **F1.35**). In *Moore* [2017] EWCA Crim 1304, the Court of Appeal considered the admissibility of graphic 3D reconstructions to reproduce the scene of the crime and to demonstrate a witness's line of sight in support of an expert's opinion that he could not have seen what he claimed. It was held that whether such reconstruction evidence can assist can only be decided on a case-by-case basis, but will be inadmissible in the absence of sufficiently reliable and precise factual foundations. In the case before the Court, the evidence could only have been of assistance if a large number of variables, relating to such matters as the location of the witness, the accused and objects potentially obstructing the witness's line of sight, had been pinpointed accurately to the exclusion of all other possibilities. This had not been done and the evidence was therefore of no probative value.

If objection to the admissibility of expert opinion evidence is made, it is for the party proffering the evidence to prove its admissibility (*Atkins* [2010] EWCA Crim 1876, [2010] 1 Cr App R 8 (117), approved in *Reed* [2009] EWCA Crim 2698, [2010] 1 Cr App R 23 (310), where it was said (at [113]) that, unless the admissibility is challenged, the judge will admit the evidence as sufficient safeguards are provided by the rules on pre-trial disclosure: see **F11.46**).

An objection to the admissibility of expert opinion evidence will necessarily fail if the witness is not an expert and expresses no expert opinion (*Foulger* [2012] EWCA Crim 1516, where the witness was not an expert communications data investigator but simply put otherwise relatively complicated telephone data into a more user-friendly format, using charts, maps and summaries).

NON-EXPERT OPINION EVIDENCE

A statement of opinion may be given by a witness, on a matter not calling for expertise, as a compendious means of conveying facts perceived by the witness. Thus an identification witness is not required to give a description of the offender or some other person, leaving it to the tribunal of fact to decide whether that description fits the accused or other person identified, but may express an opinion that the accused (or other person) is the person the witness saw on the occasion in question. Likewise, a non-expert may give evidence of opinion to identify an object (*Lucas v Williams & Sons* [1892] 2 QB 113: a picture), handwriting with which he or she is familiar (*Doe d Mudd v Suckermore* (1836) 7 LJ QB 33; *Slaney* (1832) 5 C & P 213; *Rickard* (1918) 13 Cr App R 40) or a voice which he or she recognises (*Deenik* [1992] Crim LR 578) or with which he or she is familiar (*Robb* (1991) 93 Cr App R 161; *Flynn* [2008] EWCA Crim 970, [2008] 2 Cr App R 20 (266) at [14]). Other examples include evidence of a person's age (*Cox* [1898] 1 QB 179) or the general appearance of the person's state of health, mind or emotion; the speed of a vehicle (Road Traffic Regulation Act 1984, s. 89(2)); the state of the weather; and the passage of time. In *Beckett* (1913) 8 Cr App R 204, the value of a plate glass window was established by the evidence of a non-expert. It is submitted, however, that non-expert opinion evidence should not be received on the value of less commonplace objects or objects such as antiques and works of art, the valuation of which calls for expertise. On a charge of driving when unfit through drink, the fitness of the accused to drive is a matter calling for expertise, though a non-expert may give evidence of his or her impression as to whether the accused had taken drink, provided the facts on the basis of which that impression was formed are described (*Davies* [1962] 3 All ER 97, applied in *Tagg* [2001] EWCA Crim 1230, [2002] 1 Cr App R 2 (22)). See also *Neal* [1962] Crim LR 698. Although scientific evidence is not always required to identify a prohibited drug, police officers' descriptions of a drug must be sufficient to justify the inference that it was the drug alleged (*Hill* (1993) 96 Cr App R 456). **F11.2**

In *Davies* [1962] 3 All ER 97, one of the reasons given by Lord Parker CJ as to why the non-expert could not give his opinion on whether D, as a result of the drink he had taken, was unfit to drive a car, was that this was 'the very matter which the court itself has to determine'. However, the common-law rule preventing any witness from expressing an opinion on an ultimate issue, i.e. one of the very issues to be determined by the court, appears to be virtually obsolete (see the Criminal Law Revision Committee, *Eleventh Report: Evidence (General)* (1972) Cmnd 4991, para. 270). In *Beckett* (1913) 8 Cr App R 204, the value of the window was the very issue to be decided by the court. As to expert opinion evidence on ultimate issues, see **F11.35**. **F11.3**

EXPERT OPINION EVIDENCE

Competence of Expert Witnesses

Occasionally statute prescribes the qualifications which a person must possess to give expert opinion evidence on a particular matter. For example, a jury shall not acquit on the ground of insanity, except on the evidence of two or more registered medical practitioners, at least one of whom is approved by the Secretary of State as having special experience in the diagnosis or treatment of mental disorder (Criminal Procedure (Insanity and Unfitness to Plead) Act 1991, ss. 1(1) and 2). Those instructing expert witnesses should satisfy themselves as to their expertise **F11.4** and engage an expert of suitable calibre (*Pabon* [2018] EWCA Crim 420 at [77]). However, whether a witness is properly qualified in the subject calling for expertise is ultimately a question for the court. In *Clarke* [2013] EWCA Crim 162, a murder trial, it was held that an expert in osteoarticular pathology had the expertise to consider fractures to the ribs as a possible cause of death, but had neither the experience nor expertise to consider other possible causes of death. Courts need to be scrupulous to ensure that evidence proffered as expert evidence is based upon specialised experience, knowledge or study: mere self-certification is insufficient (*Atkins* [2010] EWCA Crim 1876, [2010] 1 Cr App R 8 (117) at [27]). In rare cases it will be necessary to hold a *voir dire* to decide whether a witness should be allowed to give expert evidence, but in the vast majority of cases the judge will be able to make the decision on the basis of written material (*G* [2004] EWCA Crim 1240, [2004] 2 Cr App R 38 (638)). If it appears to a judge that a *voir dire* may be helpful to decide whether a witness should be allowed to give expert evidence, the judge can canvass that point with the advocates but, if the defence want to contest the competence of an expert in a *voir dire*, the burden is on them to make such an application to the judge (*Francis* [2013] EWCA Crim 123). If a witness does give expert evidence, the judge has the power, should the need arise, to remove the witness's expert status and limit the evidence to factual matters (*G*).

F11.5 The expert's competence or skill may stem from formal study or training, experience, or both. In *Oakley* (1979) 70 Cr App R 7 a police officer with qualifications and experience in accident investigation was allowed to give evidence, on a charge of causing death by dangerous driving, as to how an accident occurred. A police officer is competent to give expert evidence of the practices, mores and associations of gangs (if admissible as bad character evidence: see **F13.49**) if the officer has made a sufficient study, whether by formal training or through practical experience, to acquire a balanced body of specialised knowledge not available to the jury; simple, and not necessarily balanced, anecdotal experience will not suffice (*Myers v R* [2015] UKPC 40, [2016] AC 314 at [58]). See also *Fender* [2018] EWCA Crim 2829; *Hodges* [2003] EWCA Crim 290, [2003] 2 Cr App R 15 (247) and *Ibrahima* [2005] EWCA Crim 1436, considered at **F11.34**. Compare, *sed quaere, Somers* [1963] 3 All ER 808, in which a doctor was allowed to prove the conversion of figures in an analyst's certificate into the amount of alcohol consumed by D, although not an expert in such conversion, and to prove the rate of bodily destruction of alcohol, having refreshed his memory from a BMA publication. See also *Inch* (1989) 91 Cr App R 51, in which it was held that a medical orderly with much experience in the treatment of cuts and lacerations was insufficiently qualified to express an opinion as to whether an inch-long cut to the forehead had been caused by a blunt instrument rather than a head-butt. However, in *Francis* [2013] EWCA Crim 123, in contrast, it was held that a doctor who was not a forensic pathologist, but who had spent ten years in emergency medicine and would have dealt with many thousands of cases of lacerations and cuts, had properly been allowed to express an opinion that it was impossible that certain injuries had been caused by a pin and were far more likely to have been caused by a sharp blade. In *Silverlock* [1894] 2 QB 766, a solicitor, who had for ten years studied handwriting and on several occasions compared handwriting professionally, was allowed to give expert evidence that an advertisement was in D's handwriting. Affirming the conviction, Lord Russell CJ said (at p. 771):

> There is no decision which requires that the evidence of a man who is skilled in comparing handwriting, and who has formed a reliable opinion from past experience, should be excluded because his experience has not been gained in the way of his business. It is, however, really unnecessary to consider this point; for it seems... in the present case that the witness was not only *peritus*, but was *peritus* in the way of his business.

F11.6 In *Robb* (1991) 93 Cr App R 161, an experienced phonetician was allowed to give expert opinion evidence that the voice on two different tapes was the voice of the same person, notwithstanding that his technique, which was one of auditory analysis alone, was not generally respected in the field of phonetics because it was not supplemented and verified by acoustic analysis based on physical measurement of resonance and frequency. In *O'Doherty* [2002] NI 263, [2003] 1 Cr App R 5 (77), it was held that as a general rule, subject to exceptions, no prosecution should now be brought based on voice identification given by an expert which was solely confined to auditory analysis — there should always be expert evidence of acoustic analysis, including formant analysis. However, it has since been stated that it is 'neither possible nor desirable' to go as far as the Court of Appeal of Northern Ireland in this respect (*Flynn* [2008] EWCA Crim 970, [2008] 2 Cr App R 20 (266) at [62]–[63]). The requirement in *O'Doherty* applies to voice identification by an expert, not a lay listener. As to the latter, the key to admissibility is the degree of familiarity of the witness with the voice in question, but it is desirable that an expert should be instructed to give an independent opinion on the validity of the lay listener evidence (*Flynn*).

Conflicts of Interest

In *Toth v Jarman* [2006] EWCA Civ 1028, [2006] 4 All ER 1276, it was held that, although a conflict of interest does not automatically disqualify an expert, where the conflict is material or significant the court is likely to decline to act on the expert's evidence or indeed to give permission for the evidence to be adduced. It is therefore important that the party who wishes to call an expert with a potential conflict of interest of any kind — including a financial interest, a personal connection or an obligation (e.g., as a member or officer of some other body) — should disclose the details to the other party and to the court at the earliest possible opportunity. It is for the court and not the parties to decide whether a conflict is material or not. The fact that there is a risk of bias or lack of objectivity that is subliminal, as opposed to conscious, will not prevent an expert from giving evidence (*Stubbs* [2006] EWCA Crim 2312). However, if there is a relationship between the proposed expert and the party calling him or her which a reasonable observer might think was capable of affecting the views of the expert so as to make the expert unduly favourable to that party, the evidence should be excluded, however unbiased the conclusions might be, on the grounds of public policy that justice must not only be done but also must be seen to be done (*Liverpool Roman Catholic Archdiocese Trustees Incorporated v Goldberg (No. 2)* [2001] 4 All ER 950). **F11.7**

An expert, in his or her report, must declare that he or she knows of no conflict of interest other than any that has been disclosed in the report (CrimPD V, para. 19B; see Supplement, **CPD.19B**).

Matters Calling for Expertise

Expert opinion evidence may only be received on a subject calling for expertise, which a lay person, such as a magistrate or a juror, could not be expected to possess to a degree sufficient to understand the evidence given in the case unaided. If the tribunal of fact can form its own opinion without the assistance of an expert, the matter being within its own experience and knowledge, expert opinion evidence is inadmissible because it is unnecessary (*Turner* [1975] QB 834, per Lawton LJ at p. 841, applied in *Loughran* [1999] Crim LR 404). Thus a psychologist or other medical expert will not be permitted to give an opinion on the likely deterioration of memory of an ordinary witness (*Browning* [1995] Crim LR 227). On the other hand, the unlikelihood of the coincidence that a number of complainants all suffered from false memory of sexual assault is a matter calling for expert evidence, being outside the experience of the jury (*Nicholson* [2012] EWCA Crim 1568, [2012] 2 Cr App R 31 (405) at [35]). In *H (JR) (Childhood Amnesia)* [2005] EWCA Crim 1828, [2006] 1 Cr App R 10 (195), it was held that, although a witness's ability to remember events will ordinarily be well within the experience of jurors, in rare cases in which a witness gives evidence of an event, said to have occurred at an early age, and the evidence is very detailed and contains a number of extraneous facts, an appropriately qualified expert may give evidence that it should be treated with caution and may well be unreliable, because recall of events during 'the period of childhood amnesia', which extends to the age of about seven, will be fragmented, disjointed and idiosyncratic rather than a detailed narrative account. In the absence of such expert evidence, which is likely to be outside the knowledge and experience of the jury, there is a danger that the jury may find the detailed account more convincing than they safely should, because detail normally enhances credibility to the ear of the listener. However, in *S* [2006] EWCA Crim 1404, [2007] 2 All ER 974, it was held that the ambit of the decision in *H (JR)* should not be widened, and in *Anderson* [2012] EWCA Crim 1785, the correctness of the decision was doubted in light of criticisms of the methodology of the expert who had given evidence in the case (see also *H* [2011] EWCA Crim 2344, [2012] 1 Cr App R 30 (413)). **F11.8**

SJ [2019] EWCA Crim 1570, [2020] 1 Cr App R 7 (153) establishes the limits to the evidence that may be given in respect of counselling a complainant in a sexual case. It will only be in the rarest of cases that expert evidence about counselling techniques will be admissible, e.g. where they may have affected the value of the factual evidence of the counsellor. Counsellors may give non-expert evidence as to recent complaint, i.e. evidence of fact that a complaint was made at the time of the events or shortly thereafter (see **F6.30**), provided that the judge makes plain to the jury that it is not evidence of the truth of the complaint. If there were obvious signs of distress when the complaint was made, evidence of such demeanour may also be given (see also **F1.15** and **F5.11**). A counsellor may not express any views as to the truth or otherwise of the allegations or the reliability of the complainant. Nor should a counsellor use over-emotive language. A counsellor should use objective language and avoid saying anything that can be construed as subjective comment or a statement of personal opinion.

Evidence relating to calls made or received by mobile phones and cell siting, i.e. the location of mobile phone masts through which calls have been routed, will often be drawn from computerised records of the mobile phone service providers as to the date, time and duration of calls and as to the cell sites in question. However, expert evidence will usually be necessary as to whether, and if so to what extent, the fact that a call was routed through a particular cell site is consistent with the phone and its user having been at a particular location (*Calland* [2017] EWCA Crim 2308).

In some cases, it seems that jurors may receive assistance on a matter within their own experience and knowledge if it is provided by someone who has had more time and better facilities to consider that matter than it would be practicable to afford to them (see *Clare* [1995] 2 Cr App R 333, where an officer who did not know D but had viewed a video-recording about 40 times, examining it in slow motion and rewinding and replaying it as frequently as was necessary, was permitted to give evidence of identification based on a comparison between the video images and contemporary photographs of D).

F11.9 The subjects calling for expertise, which are so diverse as to defy comprehensive classification, include a variety of medical, psychiatric, scientific and technological matters, and questions relating to standards of professional competence. Specific examples include accident investigation and driver behaviour (*Dudley* [2004] EWCA Crim 3336); age, in the absence of documentary or other reliable evidence (*R (I) v Secretary of State for the Home Department* [2005] EWHC 1025 (Admin); *Re N (a child) (residence order)* [2006] EWHC 1189 (Fam)); ballistics; blood tests; breath tests and blood/alcohol levels (sometimes including back-calculations thereof, i.e. calculation of the amount of alcohol eliminated in the period between driving and providing a specimen, in order to show that the level was above the prescribed limit at the time of driving: see *Gumbley v Cunningham* [1989] AC 281); firearms discharge residue (*George (Barry)* [2007] EWCA Crim 2722; *Joseph* [2010] EWCA Crim 2580; *George (Dwaine)* [2015] EWCA Crim 2507, [2015] 1 Cr App R 15 (183)); forgeries; handwriting identification (including the analysis of indented impressions of handwriting, left on one document as a result of writing on another, and revealed by Electrostatic Detection Apparatus (ESDA): see *Wellington* [1991] Crim LR 543); fingerprint identification (see **F19.35**); ear-print identification (*Dallagher* [2002] EWCA Crim 1903, [2003] 1 Cr App R 12 (195); *Kempster (No. 2)* [2008] EWCA Crim 975, [2008] 2 Cr App R 19 (256); see **F19.37**); voice identification (see **F19.24**); identification by facial mapping (*Stockwell* (1993) 97 Cr App R 260; *Hookway* [1999] Crim LR 750; see **F19.21**), expert evidence of which may form the basis of a conviction (*Mitchell* [2005] EWCA Crim 731); facial identification by video superimposition (*Clarke* [1995] 2 Cr App R 425); 'reverse projection', the technique of superimposing one CCTV recording upon another as a means of comparing, e.g., the height of the individuals shown (*Barnes* [2012] EWCA Crim 1605); genetic fingerprinting (the technique whereby a human cell taken from a sample of blood, saliva, semen or hair is analysed to reveal a person's DNA or genetic 'fingerprint': see **F19.27**); the physical signs of child sexual abuse (*S* [2012] EWCA Crim 1433); 'shaken baby syndrome' (*Henderson* [2010] EWCA Crim 1269, [2010] 2 Cr App R 24 (185), considered at **F11.44** and **F11.48**);

Sudden Infant Death Syndrome (SIDS) (*Cannings* [2004] EWCA Crim 1, [2004] 1 All ER 725, considered at **F5.18**); insanity; automatism; diminished responsibility; and the competence of a medical practitioner (*Whitehead* (1848) 3 Car & Kir 202: expert opinion evidence as to the state of knowledge and skill of a physician as shown by his treatment of the case in question).

Reliability

Expert opinion must be sufficiently reliable to be admitted in evidence. In the test for the admissibility of expert evidence set out in *Bonython* (1984) 15 ACR 364, which has been cited with approval within the English jurisdiction, regard must be had to, *inter alia*, 'whether the subject matter of the opinion forms part of a body of knowledge or experience which is sufficiently organized and recognized to be accepted as a reliable body of knowledge or experience'. See also *Dlugosz* [2013] EWCA Crim 2, [2013] 1 Cr App R 32 (425) at [11]. Because of this condition of admissibility, CrimPR 19.4(h) requires that an expert's report must include such information as the court may need to decide whether the expert's evidence is sufficiently reliable to be admissible as evidence. However, this condition of admissibility has been applied only rarely. In *Kwaik* [2013] EWCA Crim 2397 it was held that an expert analysis based on a computer modelling technique relating to how car collisions can occur was 'insufficiently robust'; the modelling covered about 200 different simulations, but several thousand would need to be carried out for a typical full stochastic analysis. Another example is *Gilfoyle* [2001] 2 Cr App R 5 (57), considered at **F11.21**. The Law Commission, in its *Report on Expert Evidence in Criminal Proceedings* (2011) Law Com. No. 325, proposed that expert evidence should be sufficiently reliable, having regard to a number of specified factors, in order to be admitted. The proposal has not been enacted, but CrimPD V, para. 19A.4, states that: 'Nothing at common law precludes assessment by the court of the reliability of an expert opinion by reference to substantially similar factors to those the Law Commission recommended as conditions of admissibility, and courts are encouraged actively to enquire into such factors.' The range of relevant factors, set out fully in para. 19A.5 (see Supplement, **CPD.19A**), include, for example, the extent and quality of the data on which the expert's evidence is based, the validity of the methods by which they were obtained, the extent to which any material on which the opinion is based has been reviewed by others with relevant expertise; and under para. 19A.6, the court should be astute to identify potential flaws in the opinion which detract from its reliability, such as being based on a hypothesis which has not been subject to sufficient scrutiny, and being based on flawed data. In *H* [2014] EWCA Crim 1555, Sir Brian Leveson P said that these relevant factors required advocates and the courts to adopt a new and more rigorous approach to the handling of expert evidence. **F11.10**

All the following cases were decided prior to the coming into force of the directions in CrimPD V, paras. 19A.5 and 19A.6, and therefore, it is submitted, should be treated with appropriate caution. In *Dallagher* [2002] EWCA Crim 1903, [2003] 1 Cr App R 12 (195) ear-print evidence was held to have been properly admitted. The court approved a passage from *Cross and Tapper on Evidence* (9th edn, 1999), at p. 523 which states that 'so long as a field is sufficiently well-established to pass the ordinary test of relevance and reliability, then no enhanced test for admissibility should be applied, but the weight of the evidence should be established by the same adversarial forensic techniques applicable elsewhere'. This passage was also applied in *Luttrell* [2004] EWCA Crim 1344, [2004] 2 Cr App R 31 (520), where the court rejected an argument that lip-reading evidence should not be admitted unless it could be seen to be reliable on the basis that the methods used were sufficiently explained to be tested in cross-examination and so to be verifiable or falsifiable. Cf. *O'Doherty* [2002] NI 263, [2003] 1 Cr App R 5 (77) at **F11.6**. The passage was further endorsed in *Reed* [2009] EWCA Crim 2698, [2010] 1 Cr App R 23 (310), where expert evaluative evidence of the possible ways in which DNA was transferred was held to be admissible notwithstanding that scientific knowledge and research on such transferability is plainly incomplete (see **F19.27**). Similarly, an expert in facial mapping is not confined to identification of the similarities or dissimilarities between the faces compared, but may express a view using expressions ranging from 'lends no support' (to the person in question being the accused) through to 'lends powerful support', notwithstanding that there is no established statistical database by which such expressions could be **F11.11** given numerical values, but it should be made clear to the jury that they are expressions of subjective opinion (*Atkins* [2010] EWCA Crim 1876, [2010] 1 Cr App R 8 (117)). *Atkins* was followed in *Dlugosz* [2013] EWCA Crim 2, [2013] 1 Cr App R 32 (425), where it was held that in cases involving the use of Low Template DNA evidence derived from 'mixed samples', evaluative expert evidence may be admissible in the absence of statistical evidence of the relevant DNA match probability and notwithstanding the inability — which was not the case in *Atkins* — to use a hierarchy or sliding scale of support. (*Dlugosz* is considered more fully at **F19.27**.) As to guidance for judges on forensic DNA analysis, see also **F11.45**. In *Nicholson* [2012] EWCA Crim 1568, [2012] 2 Cr App R 31 (405), it was submitted that the jury should not have been permitted to consider the unlikelihood of the coincidence that the complainants were suffering from false memory without providing a statistical probability value for the coincidence. Rejecting the submission, Pitchford LJ said (at [43]): 'It is not the law that a statistical value must be placed upon any coincidence on the unlikelihood of which one of the parties to a criminal trial relies.' In *T (Footwear mark evidence)* [2010] EWCA Crim 2439, [2011] 1 Cr App R 9 (85), it was held that although there were no sufficiently reliable data for an expert on footwear marks to express an opinion based on mathematical formulae and likelihood ratios, an expert may nonetheless give an evaluative opinion that a shoe could or could not have made a mark based on factors such as class characteristics (i.e. those resulting from manufacture of the footwear) and identifying characteristics, such as objects attached to the sole and damage caused by cuts. See also *Ferdinand* [2014] EWCA Crim 1243, [2014] 2 Cr App R 23 (331), in which a consultant podiatric surgeon was permitted to give evidence as to the similarity of gait of the suspect and D notwithstanding that: there was no database to support his assessment of the frequency of the common features he identified, which was founded mainly on his clinical experience; the technique of gait comparison was a developing science still in its infancy; and another expert podiatrist was of the view that the benchmark material was of insufficient quality to attempt the analysis. As to guidance for judges on forensic gait analysis, see also **F11.45**.

In *I* [2012] EWCA Crim 1288, where an expert opinion rested upon a hypothesis that could have been tested to ensure its reliability, the Court of Appeal declined to require such testing as a condition of admissibility. It was held that expert opinion evidence based on a test that was clearly reliable when applied in one context could be admitted notwithstanding that it was being applied in a novel context without any evaluation of its efficacy in that context. Cf. *Holdsworth* [2008] EWCA Crim 971, where the Court of Appeal acknowledged the dangers of relying on expert hypotheses with inadequate empirical foundations and observed that special caution was needed where expert evidence was not just relied upon as material supportive of a prosecution but was fundamental to it.

F11.12 A jury is entitled to rely on an expert opinion which falls short of scientific certainty. Thus a judge should not withdraw a case of murder from the jury merely because the pathologist giving evidence for the prosecution that the cause of death was two stab wounds also agreed as a theoretical possibility that the deceased could have died from another cause consistent with innocence (*Gian* [2009] EWCA Crim 2553; and see also *Bracewell* (1979) 68 Cr App R 44 and *Kai-Whitewind* [2005] EWCA Crim 1092, [2005] 2 Cr App R 31 (457)). Similarly, evidence should not be excluded or withdrawn from the jury where the prosecution and defence experts disagree, but each states that the other's opinion, for which support can be found within the scientific community, is valid and tenable (*Hookway* [2011] EWCA Crim 1989).

F11.13 The work of the Forensic Science Regulator promotes the reliability of expert evidence by ensuring that the provision of forensic science services across the criminal justice system is subject to an appropriate regime of scientific quality standards. Responsibilities of the Regulator involve identification of the requirement for new or improved quality standards, development of new standards, and provision of advice and guidance so that providers of forensic science services can demonstrate compliance with common standards. The Regulator's Codes of Practice and Conduct are available at tinyurl.com/yxpl6ubj. As to the role of advocates in promoting the reliability of expert evidence, see the Inns of Court College of Advocacy Guidance on the Preparation, Admission and Examination of Expert Evidence, available at tinyurl.com/y2by2lkn.

The Accreditation of Forensic Service Providers Regulations 2018 (SI 2018 No. 1276) provide additional safeguards as to the reliability of DNA profiles and fingerprint data on which the prosecution may seek to rely. Under the Regulations, law enforcement authorities may only use a forensic service provider to conduct laboratory activity that results in a DNA profile or fingerprint data if the provider is accredited to EU accreditation standards on general requirements for the competence of testing and calibration laboratories.

States of Mind

Insanity, Diminished Responsibility and Automatism As to the need for expert evidence to prove insanity, see **A3.23**, **D12.9**, **D12.16** and **F11.4**. On the issue of diminished responsibility, the Court of Appeal in *Dix* (1981) 74 Cr App R 306, applying a dictum in *Byrne* [1960] 2 QB 396 at p. 402, said (at p. 311): 'while the Homicide Act 1957, s. 2(1) does not in terms require that medical evidence be adduced in support of a defence of diminished responsibility, it makes it a practical necessity if that defence is to begin to run at all'. The 'practical necessity' of medical evidence was confirmed in *Bunch* [2013] EWCA Crim 2498, a decision on s. 2 of the 1957 Act after its amendment by the CAJA 2009 in which it was also held that medical evidence is relevant to all the ingredients of the defence and is critical to the issue in s. 2(1)(a) (see **B1.19**). As to automatism, see *Smith* [1979] 3 All ER 605 where the defence was automatism, by sleepwalking. The Court of Appeal held that the type of automatism in question was not something within the realm of the ordinary juror's experience but a matter on which the jury should not be deprived of expert assistance. See also *Hill v Baxter* [1958] 1 QB 277, at p. 285. **F11.14**

Psychiatric Injury Where psychiatric injury is relied on as the basis for an allegation of assault occasioning actual bodily harm, and the matter is not admitted by the defence, the Crown should call expert evidence to prove the injury; in the absence of such evidence the question whether the assault occasioned such injury should not be left to the jury (*Chan-Fook* [1994] 2 All ER 552, applied in *Morris* [1998] 1 Cr App R 386). **F11.15**

Intent In appropriate circumstances, expert medical evidence may be admissible on the question of the effect of a medical abnormality upon intent. Thus in *Toner* (1991) 93 Cr App R 382, a physician gave evidence that D had been suffering from a minor hypoglycaemic state caused by the ingestion of food after a prolonged fast. It was held that the defence had been improperly prevented from asking the witness what the effect of that minor degree of hypoglycaemia would be on the ability to make judgements or to form specific intents. The Court of Appeal held that there is no distinction between medical evidence relating to hypoglycaemia and its possible effect upon intent, and medical evidence as to the effect of a drug upon intent: both are matters outside the ordinary experience of jurors who cannot bring to bear their own judgement without the assistance of expert evidence. Similarly in *Huckerby* [2004] EWCA Crim 3251, evidence that D was suffering from post-traumatic stress disorder, a recognised mental condition with which the jury would not be expected to be familiar, was admissible because it was relevant to an essential issue bearing upon his guilt or innocence, namely whether it had caused him to panic and co-operate with criminals in circumstances in which he would otherwise not have done so. Subject to cases of this kind, however, and except in the case of an accused who comes into the class of mental defective, expert psychiatric evidence is not admissible on the issue of whether the accused did, or did not, have the required *mens rea*. In *Chard* (1971) 56 Cr App R 268, the Court of Appeal held that the judge, in a murder trial, had properly refused a defence application to call a medical witness to give evidence about D's intent to kill or do grievous bodily harm because D was entirely normal and was not, e.g., suffering from insanity or diminished responsibility. See also *Reynolds* [1989] Crim LR 220 and, in the case of adolescents, *Coles* [1995] 1 Cr App R 157. Similarly, in *Masih* [1986] Crim LR 395, a case of rape in which D suffered from no psychiatric illness, but had an intelligence quotient of 72, just above the level of subnormality, on the question of whether he knew the complainant was not consenting, or was reckless as to whether she consented, psychiatric evidence as to his state of mind, intelligence and ability to appreciate the situation was held to be inadmissible. Upholding the ruling, the Court of Appeal held that, generally speaking, if an accused comes into the class of mental defective, with **F11.16**

an IQ of 69 or below, then insofar as the defectiveness is relevant to an issue, expert evidence may be admitted, provided that it is confined to an assessment of the accused's IQ and an explanation of any relevant abnormal characteristics (in order to enlighten the jury on a matter that is abnormal and outside their experience). However, if an accused is within the scale of normality, albeit at the lower end, as was the appellant, expert evidence should generally be excluded. See also *Hall* (1987) 86 Cr App R 159 and *Henry* [2005] EWCA Crim 1681, [2006] 1 Cr App R 6 (118).

F11.17 In *Wood* [1990] Crim LR 264, D, charged with murder, raised the partial defence under Homicide Act 1957, s. 4, of the unsuccessful execution of a suicide pact. In support of this defence, and relying upon an analogy with diminished responsibility, the defence sought unsuccessfully to introduce psychiatric evidence to the effect that D suffered from a personality disorder. Refusing leave to appeal, it was held that whereas the defence of diminished responsibility was founded on the existence of some abnormality of mind, in the case of a suicide pact, once the killing had been proved, the questions for the jury are whether there was such a pact and, if so, whether at the time of the killing D was acting in pursuance thereof and had the settled intention of dying in pursuance thereof. That D had a personality which was to some extent abnormal and liable to give way to excesses of behaviour under stress was not something outside the ordinary experience of the average juror.

F11.18 **Provocation and Loss of Control** Psychiatric evidence is inadmissible in order to establish that the accused was likely to have been provoked. In *Turner* [1975] QB 834, the Court of Appeal upheld the refusal of a trial judge to allow the defence to call a psychiatrist, on the issues of credibility and provocation, to prove that D had had a deep emotional relationship with V, which was likely to have caused an explosive release of blind rage after her confession of infidelity to him, and that subsequent to the killing he had behaved like someone suffering from profound grief. The Court held that these were matters well within ordinary human experience and upon which the jury required no expert assistance. The evidence was not admissible on the issue of provocation, therefore, and the same reasoning prevented its admission on the issue of credibility. *Sed quaere*, whether expert evidence might not be admitted on an issue of provocation, where the accused suffers from some mental abnormality (*Camplin* [1978] AC 705). *Turner* was distinguished in *McDonald* [1991] Crim LR 122, where evidence was adduced of an out-of-court statement made by D explaining why he had killed V, an explanation which was sufficient to lay a foundation for the defence of provocation. Subsequently, in the course of a psychiatric examination, D admitted that the explanation was invented. It was held that it was not unfair for the psychiatrist to give evidence of the admission, because it related to a factual matter, not a medical issue.

Concerning loss of control, expert evidence about the impact of a mental disorder will be irrelevant and inadmissible as to whether it would have reduced the capacity for tolerance and self-restraint of the hypothetical person of the defendant's sex and age with a normal degree of tolerance and self-restraint, but is not excluded under the CAJA 2009, s. 54(3), if it is has a relevance to the defendant's conduct other than a bearing on his or her general capacity for tolerance and self-restraint (*Rejmanski* [2017] EWCA Crim 2061, [2018] 1 Cr App R 18 (267), considered at **B1.28**).

F11.19 **Duress** In the case of duress, psychiatric evidence may be admissible to show that an accused was suffering from some mental illness, mental impairment or recognised psychiatric condition, if persons generally suffering from such a condition might be more susceptible to pressure and threats, and thus to assist the jury in deciding whether a reasonable person with such a condition might have been impelled to act as the accused had. Psychiatric evidence is not admissible simply to show that an accused not suffering from such a condition, was especially timid, suggestible or vulnerable to pressure and threats (*Walker* [2003] EWCA Crim 1837).

Concerning the defence of duress by threats, expert evidence is admissible for the purposes of the *subjective limb of the test*, provided that the mental condition or abnormality in question is outside the knowledge and experience of laymen, but inadmissible for the purposes of the objective limb (*Hegarty* [1994] Crim LR 353; cf. *Horne* [1994] Crim LR 584 and *Hurst* [1995] 1 Cr App R 82).

Expert evidence is admissible that the accused was suffering from Battered Woman's Syndrome, but it does not necessarily follow that she acted under duress; it is essential to analyse with care the extent and timing of the violence, the impact upon the accused and her presentation at the relevant time (*C (GA)* [2013] EWCA Crim 1472).

Reliability or Truth of Confessions The expert evidence of a psychiatrist or psychologist is admissible on the issue of the reliability or truth of a confession if it is to the effect that no reliance can be placed on the confession because the accused was suffering from a personality disorder so severe as properly to be categorised as a mental disorder (see *Ward* [1993] 2 All ER 577 and cf. *Childs* [2014] EWCA Crim 1884 where a 32-year delay in bringing an appeal was included among the reasons for refusing an application for leave to appeal out of time). Admissible evidence from psychiatrists, however, is not confined to evidence of such personality disorders. The test is not whether an abnormality fits into a recognised category such as anti-social personality disorder. That is neither necessary nor sufficient. It is sufficient for the disorder to be of a type which might render a confession or evidence unreliable. However, there must be a very significant deviation from the norm shown, and an independent history, pre-dating the confession or the giving of evidence, which points to or explains the abnormalities. If such evidence is admitted, the jury must be directed that they are not obliged to accept it, but should consider it, if they think it right to do so, as throwing light on the personality of the accused and bringing to their attention aspects of that personality of which they might otherwise have been unaware (*O'Brien* [2000] Crim LR 676, applied in *Smith* [2003] EWCA Crim 927). Psychiatric evidence is not admissible in the case of someone with a histrionic personality disorder characterised by emotional superficiality and impulsive behaviour when under stress, but who does not suffer from mental illness and is not below normal intelligence (*Weightman* (1990) 92 Cr App R 291). However, the expert evidence of a psychologist is admissible to show that a confession made by someone not suffering from any personality or abnormal disorder is likely to be unreliable if it was a 'coerced compliant confession', a phenomenon falling outside the experience of the jury. A coerced compliant confession is one brought about by fatigue, together with an inability to control what is happening, which may induce the individual to experience a growing desire to give up resisting suggestions so that eventually the individual can take no more and is overwhelmed by the need to achieve the immediate goal of bringing the interrogation to an end (*Blackburn* [2005] EWCA Crim 1349, [2005] 2 Cr App R 30 (440)). See also, as to the admissibility of psychiatric evidence on a *voir dire* to determine the admissibility of a confession, **F18.18** and **F18.21**. **F11.20**

Psychological Autopsies The present academic status of 'psychological autopsies' is not such as to allow them to be admitted as a basis for expert opinion evidence (*Gilfoyle* [2001] 2 Cr App R 5 (57)). In *Gilfoyle*, a murder trial in which the only other possible explanation for the death was suicide, the Court of Appeal declined to hear the fresh evidence of a distinguished psychologist who had carried out a 'psychological autopsy' of the deceased, relying upon the dictum of Lord President Cooper in *Davie v Magistrates of Edinburgh* 1953 SC 34 at p. 40 that expert witnesses must furnish the court 'with the necessary scientific criteria for testing the accuracy of their conclusions, so as to enable the judge or jury to form their own independent judgement by the application of these criteria to the facts proved in evidence'. One of the reasons for the decision was that the psychologist's reports identified no criteria by reference to which the court could test the quality of his opinions; there was no database comparing real and questionable suicides and no substantial body of academic writing approving his methodology. Another reason was that English, Canadian and US authority pointed against the admission of the evidence. The principle in *Frye v USA* 293 F 1013 (1923), that evidence based on a developing new brand of science or medicine is not admissible until accepted by the scientific community as being able to provide accurate and reliable opinion, accorded with the English approach. (But see further **F11.11**.) **F11.21**

Credibility

Medical evidence is admissible to show that a witness suffers from some disease or defect or abnormality of mind that affects the reliability of his evidence. Such evidence is not confined to a general opinion of the unreliability of the witness but may give all the matters necessary to show, not only the **F11.22**

> foundation of and reasons for the diagnosis, but also the extent to which the credibility of the witness is affected. (*Toohey v Metropolitan Police Commissioner* [1965] AC 595, per Lord Pearce at p. 609)

See further **F7.63**. In the case of evidence of 'abnormality of mind', the approach set out in *O'Brien* [2000] Crim LR 676 and considered at **F11.20** applies whether the expert evidence that is being considered relates to a witness or an accused. However, especially in the case of a witness, it is important to take into account the importance of the evidence that the witness gives. If it is of little significance to the issues at the trial, the admission of expert evidence is unlikely to be justified (*MacKenney* [2004] EWCA Crim 1220, [2004] 2 Cr App R 32 (551), considered at **F7.65**, at [15]). Subject to the principle of *Toohey v Metropolitan Police Commissioner*, it is only in exceptional cases that psychologists and psychiatrists may be called to prove the probability of the veracity of the accused (*Henry* [2005] EWCA Crim 1681, [2006] 1 Cr App R 6 (118) at [15]) or another witness (*The Queen v Joyce* [2005] NTSC 21 (SC Northern Territory, Australia), concerning the credibility of a child, and *S* [2006] EWCA Crim 2389). Thus, for example, opinion evidence should not be given as to the truth or otherwise of a complaint of sexual abuse (*C* [2012] EWCA Crim 1478). An example of an exceptional case is *Lowery v The Queen* [1974] AC 85. D1 and D2 were charged with an apparently motiveless murder, the circumstances being that one or both of them must have committed the offence. Each blamed the other for the crime. The Privy Council held that the trial judge had properly permitted D2 to call a psychologist, who had carried out personality tests on both D1 and D2, to show that D2's version of events was more probable than that of D1, since, compared to D2, D1's character and disposition were such that he was more likely to have committed the offence. Commenting upon this decision in *Turner* [1975] QB 834, Lawton LJ said (at p. 842):

> In every case what is relevant and admissible depends on the issues raised in that case. In *Lowery v The Queen* the issues were unusual; and the accused to whose disadvantage the psychologist's evidence went had in effect said before it was called that he was not the sort of man to have committed the offence....
>
> We adjudge *Lowery v The Queen* to have been decided on its special facts. We do not consider that it is an authority for the proposition that in all cases psychologists and psychiatrists can be called to prove the probability of the accused's veracity.

F11.23 In *Rimmer* [1983] Crim LR 250, the two accused were charged with murder, and each blamed the other. On the basis of a medical report, counsel for D1 cross-examined D2, suggesting to him that he had a history of mental illness and that he had killed the victim in a fit of uncontrollable temper to which he was accustomed. The Court of Appeal upheld the ruling of the trial judge that D2 was not entitled to call medical evidence to establish that he was not, and never had been, mentally ill.

F11.24 Expert opinion evidence of false memory syndrome or recovered memory syndrome is a subject outside the knowledge and experience of the jury, which may assist them in assessing credibility or reliability, but is admissible only where a sound factual foundation for it has been established, as when there is medical evidence that memories were recovered or retrieved during counselling or psychotherapy sessions (*H* [2014] EWCA Crim 1555). Similarly, expert opinion may be admissible to criticise the techniques of a hypnotherapist and as to the dangers that if the patient's recollection was falsely engendered, she would thereafter have regarded it as a genuine memory (*Clark* [2006] EWCA Crim 231). However, as a matter of principle, evidence produced by the administration of some mechanical, chemical or hypnotic truth test on a witness is inadmissible to show the veracity or otherwise of that witness (*Fennell v Jerome Property Maintenance Ltd* (1986) *The Times*, 26 November 1986). The previous statements of the witness are not only inadmissible hearsay, but insofar as they are consistent with the witness's testimony, inadmissible as evidence of consistency under the rule against previous self-serving statements (see **F6.39** and cf. the CJA 2003, s. 120, at **F6.33** and **F6.36**).

Handwriting

F11.25 Handwriting may be identified by a non-expert familiar with the handwriting in question (*Doe d Mudd v Suckermore* (1836) 5 A & E 703; *Slaney* (1832) 5 C & P 213). The witness's knowledge, however, must not have been acquired for the express purpose of qualifying the witness to testify at the trial (*Crouch* (1850) 4 Cox CC 163). An expert should be called if there is to be a comparison of the 'disputed writing' with specimen handwriting proved or admitted to have been written by the person in question, under the Criminal Procedure Act 1865, s. 8 (*Tilley* [1961] 3 All ER 406; *Harden* [1963] 1 QB 8). Such expert evidence is admissible under s. 8 even if the expert has not seen the original 'disputed writing' (e.g., because it is lost), but has compared a photocopy of the original (*Lockheed-Arabia v Owen* [1993] QB 806). See further **F8.41**. As to the standard of proof required to establish the genuineness of specimen handwriting, see *Ewing* [1983] QB 1039 and *Angeli* [1979] 3 All ER 950.

Obscenity

In the normal case, the issues of indecency or obscenity should be determined by the jury without expert assistance. In *Anderson* [1972] 1 QB 304, Lord Widgery CJ said (at p. 313) that in the ordinary run of the mill cases, the issue 'obscene or no' under the Obscene Publications Act 1959 must be tried without the assistance of expert evidence. His lordship said that *DPP v A and BC Chewing Gum Ltd* [1968] 1 QB 159 'should be regarded as highly exceptional and confined to its own circumstances, namely, a case where the alleged obscene matter was directed at very young children, and was of itself of a somewhat unusual kind'. In the latter case the accused were charged with publishing for gain obscene battle cards (which were sold together with packets of bubble gum), contrary to the Obscene Publications Act, s. 2(1), and the Obscene Publications Act 1964, s. 1(1). The Divisional Court held that the magistrates had improperly prevented the prosecution from introducing evidence of experts in child psychiatry as to the likely effect of the cards on children. Lord Parker CJ held that, when considering the effect of something on an adult, an adult jury may be able to judge just as well as an adult witness; but when one is dealing with children of different age groups and children from five upwards, any jury, and any justices, need all the help they can get as to the effect on different children. See also *Skirving* [1985] QB 819, a prosecution arising out of the publication of a book entitled *Attention Coke Lovers. Free Base. The Greatest Thing Since Sex*, which contained explanations, instructions and 'recipes' on how to make use of cocaine to maximum effect. The Court of Appeal held that expert evidence on the characteristics of cocaine and the effects of the various methods of ingesting the drug was admissible, because it was outside the experience of the ordinary person, and only when equipped with such information would the jury be in a position to decide whether the publication had a tendency to deprave and corrupt. **F11.26**

Expert opinion evidence is also admissible on questions of a literary, artistic or scientific nature in relation to the defence of 'public good' under the Obscene Publications Act 1959, s. 4 (see s. 4(2)).

Foreign Law

Points of foreign law of any jurisdiction other than that of England and Wales are questions of fact to be decided on the evidence by the judge (Administration of Justice Act 1920, s. 15: see also **F1.38**). Thus, if there has been an English decision on a point of foreign law and the same point subsequently arises again, it must be decided on new evidence (*M'Cormick v Garnett* (1854) 5 De GM & G 278). The general rule is that the law of a foreign country, whether written or not, must be proved by the testimony of a competent expert, by the witness statement of such an expert (if admissible), or on the basis of a statement of agreed facts pursuant to the CJA 1967, s. 10 (*Ofori* (1994) 99 Cr App R 219). If the expert witnesses agree on a point of foreign law, the court is not entitled to reject their evidence and to conduct its own research by referring to textbooks and foreign law reports (*Bumper Development Corporation Ltd v Metropolitan Police Commissioner* [1991] 4 All ER 638). The expert may refresh his or her memory from foreign law books, but the law itself is proved by oral evidence (*Sussex Peerage Case* (1844) 11 Cl & F 85). A witness is competent for these purposes if the witness is a practitioner in the relevant jurisdiction (*Baron de Bode's Case* (1845) 8 QB 208). There is old authority that a practitioner from the jurisdiction in question should always be called (*Bristow v Sequeville* (1850) 5 Exch 275). However, a witness has been held to be suitably qualified for these purposes if the witness is: **F11.27**

(a) a former practitioner in the relevant jurisdiction (*Re Duke of Wellington* [1947] Ch 506);
(b) a person qualified to practise in the relevant jurisdiction, even if he or she has not done so (*Barford v Barford and McLeod* [1918] P 140); or

(c) a person who has acquired the appropriate expertise by academic study (*Brailey v Rhodesia Consolidated Ltd* [1910] 2 Ch 95, reader in Roman-Dutch law to the Council of Legal Education); as an embassy official (*In the Goods of Dost Aly Khan* (1889) 6 PD 6); or in the course of a non-legal business such as banking (*De Beéche v South American Stores (Gath and Chaves) Ltd* [1935] AC 148).

F11.28 Exceptions There are three exceptions to the general rule:

(a) Breach of the immigration law of a Member State of the EU, for the purposes of assisting unlawful immigration contrary to the Immigration Act 1971, s. 25, may be proved conclusively by a certificate of the Member State under s. 25(3) of the Act, but s. 25(3) is permissive only and therefore such a breach may be proved instead by expert opinion evidence or by admission (*Bina* [2014] EWCA Crim 1444, [2014] 2 Cr App R 30 (496)).
(b) The Evidence (Colonial Statutes) Act 1907, s. 1, and the Colonial Laws Validity Act 1865, s. 6, provide for proof of colonial statutes etc.; and English courts may construe such statutes without accompanying expert evidence (see the authorities cited in *Jasiewicz v Jasiewicz* [1962] 3 All ER 1017).
(c) The British Law Ascertainment Act 1859 provides that an English court may state a case on a point of foreign law for the opinion of a superior court in another part of Her Majesty's dominions, and that the opinion thus produced is admissible evidence on the point of law in question.

Competence of Witnesses

F11.29 Determination of the question whether a child is competent to give evidence for the purposes of the YJCEA 1999, s. 54, does not normally require any input from an expert, but a decision as to the competence of a mentally handicapped person, whether adult or child, does require appropriate expert medical evidence (see **F4.23**).

Proof of Facts upon which Expert Opinion Evidence Based

F11.30

> Before a court can assess the value of an opinion it must know the facts upon which it is based. If the expert has been misinformed about the facts or has taken irrelevant facts into consideration or has omitted to consider relevant ones, the opinion is likely to be valueless. In our judgment, counsel calling an expert should in examination-in-chief ask his witness to state the facts upon which his opinion is based. It is wrong to leave the other side to elicit the facts by cross-examination (*Turner* [1975] QB 834 at p. 840).

In some cases, some of the relevant facts upon which the opinion is based can be proved by the expert him or herself, as when the expert has examined an exhibit or a fingerprint and therefore has personal or first-hand knowledge of those facts. In other cases, however, the expert will have no personal or first-hand knowledge of the facts, or all of the facts, upon which his or her opinion is based. For example, in a trial for murder by stabbing, in which the defence is that the victim's injuries were self-inflicted, a medical witness who has not examined the body may be asked whether, assuming that the facts, described by another medical witness who has examined the body, are true, the wound was inflicted by a person other than the deceased (*Mason* (1911) 7 Cr App R 67; see also *Francis* [2013] EWCA Crim 123). Similarly, an expert may give an expert opinion on the basis of preparatory work, such as scientific tests carried out by assistants. Appropriate details relating to the person with personal or first-hand knowledge of the facts should be included in the expert's report (CrimPR 19.4(e); see Supplement, **R19.4**). Whether or not the expert has personal knowledge of the facts upon which the opinion is based, those facts must be proved. If they are not proved, expert evidence of them will be irrelevant (*Berberi* [2014] EWCA Crim 2961, [2015] 2 Cr App R 2 (11)). Proof may be effected by calling the person with personal knowledge of the facts. However, under the CJA 2003, s. 127, a statement made by such a person for the purposes of either a criminal investigation or criminal proceedings may be admitted without the need to call that person, and in evidence given in the proceedings the expert may base his or her opinion on the statement, unless, on an application by a party to the proceedings, the court orders that application of the section is not in the interests of justice.

Criminal Justice Act 2003, s. 127 F11.31

(1) This section applies if—
   (a) a statement has been prepared for the purposes of criminal proceedings,
   (b) the person who prepared the statement had or may reasonably be supposed to have had personal knowledge of the matters stated,
   (c) notice is given under the appropriate rules that another person (the expert) will in evidence given in the proceedings orally or under section 9 of the Criminal Justice Act 1967 base an opinion or inference on the statement, and
   (d) the notice gives the name of the person who prepared the statement and the nature of the matters stated.
(2) In evidence given in the proceedings the expert may base an opinion or inference on the statement.
(3) If evidence based on the statement is given under subsection (2) the statement is to be treated as evidence of what it says.
(4) This section does not apply if the court, on an application by a party to the proceedings, orders that it is not in the interests of justice that it should apply.
(5) The matters to be considered by the court in deciding whether to make an order under subsection (4) include—
   (a) the expense of calling as a witness the person who prepared the statement;
   (b) whether relevant evidence could be given by that person which could not be given by the expert;
   (c) whether that person can reasonably be expected to remember the matters stated well enough to give oral evidence of them.
(6) Subsections (1) to (5) apply to a statement prepared for the purposes of a criminal investigation as they apply to a statement prepared for the purposes of criminal proceedings, and in such a case references to the proceedings are to criminal proceedings arising from the investigation.

Facts Derived from the Use of a Computer Where an expert bases an opinion on facts derived from the use of a computer, it seems that there is no obligation to produce the printout (see *Golizadeh* [1995] Crim LR 232, where an expert was allowed to give his opinion that a certain substance was opium on the basis of a printout of a machine used by him to analyse its chemical constituents, the printout itself not having been produced in evidence). F11.32

Special Treatment of Hearsay An expert is not subject to the rule against hearsay in the same way as a non-expert or a witness of fact. Thus, although an expert cannot prove facts upon which his or her opinion is based, but of which the expert has no personal or first-hand knowledge, because that would be an infringement of the hearsay rule, the expert may rely upon such facts as a part of the process of forming an opinion. However, if there is no direct evidence to establish such facts, the weight to be attached to the opinion of the expert is likely to be minimal. In *Bradshaw* (1985) 82 Cr App R 79, a murder trial, the only issue was that of diminished responsibility. (The burden of proof was on the defence: Homicide Act 1957, s. 2(2).) Counsel for the defence sought guidance from the judge as to how far the doctors would be permitted to give evidence as to what D had told them during interviews, how far they could express opinions based upon such statements, and whether the judge would make adverse comment if D were not to give evidence. The judge replied that, if the truth of what D had said to the doctors was in question, the only appropriate course was for D to prove the facts upon which the expert opinion was based, or for those facts to be proved by other evidence. D, who had recovered from any abnormality of mind at the date of the trial, gave evidence and was cross-examined. He appealed against conviction on the grounds that the ruling of the judge was erroneous. The appeal was dismissed. Lord Lane CJ said (at p. 83): F11.33

> Although as a concession to the defence doctors are sometimes allowed to base their opinions on what the defendant has told them (i.e. hearsay) without those matters being proved by admissible evidence, yet the strict (and correct) view is that expressed at p. 446 of *Cross on Evidence*, 5th ed., in the following terms: 'A doctor may not state what a patient told him about past symptoms as evidence of the existence of those symptoms because that would infringe the rule against hearsay, but he may give evidence of what the patient told him in order to explain the grounds on which he came to a conclusion with regard to the patient's condition'.

> Thus, if the doctor's opinion is based entirely on hearsay and is not supported by direct evidence, the judge will be justified in telling the jury that the defendant's case (if that is so) is based upon a flimsy or non-existent foundation and that they should reach their conclusion bearing that in mind. In proper cases, for example where, as here, the defendant has completely recovered from any abnormality of mind by the time of the trial, there is no reason why the judge should not comment upon the fact that the defendant could have provided the necessary evidence had he wished to do so, the burden of proof being upon him.

F11.34 As a part of the process of forming an opinion, expert witnesses may refer not only to their own research, tests and experiments, but also to works of authority, learned articles, research papers, and other similar material written by others and forming part of the general body of knowledge falling within their field of expertise (see generally *Davie v Magistrates of Edinburgh* 1953 SC 34; *Seyfang v GD Searle & Co.* [1973] QB 148, at p. 151; and *H v Schering Chemicals Ltd* [1983] 1 All ER 849). In *Abadom* [1983] 1 All ER 364, on the question of whether fragments of glass embedded in D's shoes had come from a window allegedly broken during a robbery, an expert gave evidence that, based upon his personal analysis of the samples, the glass in the shoes and that from the window bore an identical refractive index; and that, having consulted unpublished statistics compiled by the Home Office Central Research Establishment, which showed that that index occurred in only 4 per cent of all glass samples investigated, in his opinion there was a very strong likelihood that the glass in the shoes came from the window. It was argued, on appeal, that the evidence of the Home Office statistics was inadmissible hearsay, since the expert had no knowledge of the analysis on which the statistics had been based. The appeal was dismissed on the ground that the primary facts, i.e. the refractive indices of the glass samples, had been proved by the expert on the basis of his own analysis; and that once the primary facts upon which an opinion is based have been proved by admissible evidence, an expert is entitled to draw on the work of others as part of the process of arriving at his conclusion, and this involves no breach of the hearsay rule. The Court of Appeal pointed out that part of the experience and expertise of experts lies in their knowledge and evaluation of *unpublished* material; they may draw on such material, provided that they refer to it in their evidence so that the cogency and probative value of their conclusions can be tested and evaluated by reference thereto. See also *Ahmed* [2011] EWCA Crim 184, and compare *Somers* [1963] 3 All ER 808, considered at **F11.5**. *Abadom* was applied in *Hodges* [2003] EWCA Crim 290, [2003] 2 Cr App R 15 (247), a case of conspiracy to supply heroin in which a very experienced drugs officer gave expert evidence, derived in part from what he had been told by others, including other officers, informants and drug users, as to the usual method of supplying heroin, its purchase price, and that 14 grams of heroin was more than would have been for personal use. Similarly, in *Ibrahima* [2005] EWCA Crim 1436, a case of possession of ecstasy tablets with intent to supply, it was held that a person with no medical or psychological qualifications, but with experience and knowledge of drug use as a deputy director of a drug advice charity, was entitled to give evidence, whether for the prosecution or defence, as to what quantities of ecstasy are consistent with personal use, and as to how users acquire an increasing tolerance of the drug, leading to higher consumption, provided that he gave the categories of his sources of information. However, see also *Edwards* [2001] EWCA Crim 2185, where the issue was whether the ecstasy tablets found in D's possession were for personal consumption or for supply. 'Experts', neither of whom had any formal medical or toxicological qualifications, were not permitted to give evidence based on their experience, rather than any academic material such as statistical surveys or reports, as to the personal consumption rates of ecstasy tablet users.

In *Myers v R* [2015] UKPC 40, [2016] AC 314, the Privy Council considered the difficulty in determining the extent to which an expert may rely upon hearsay material. It was noted that, although in some cases the dividing line is between opinion, which may be informed by hearsay, and evidence of observable fact, which may not be so informed, experts often give evidence of observable fact which is legitimately informed by the accumulated body of knowledge of others. *Abadom* [1983] 1 All ER 364 was cited as an illustration: the expert told the jury that the refractive index in question occurred in only 4 per cent of all glass examined, which was evidence of fact entirely gleaned from others. Lord Hughes put forward an alternative test (at [66]):

> The test of whether evidence based upon hearsay material can be given is better seen to be whether it ceases to be the expounding of general study (whether by the witness or others) and becomes the assertion of a particular fact in issue in the case. The first is expert evidence, grounded on a body of learning or study; the second is not, even if it may be given by someone who is also an expert. The line between the two is case-specific, but it will usually be possible to discern it. Moreover, it may well be that the application of [a Bermudan statutory provision identical in its terms to the PACE 1984, s.78(1)], will yield the same answer to the question whether the witness ought to be permitted to give second-hand evidence.

Opinions on Ultimate Issues

In its *Eleventh Report: Evidence (General)* (1972), Cmnd 4991, para. 268, the Criminal Law Revision Committee was of the opinion that the old common-law rule that a witness should not express an opinion on an ultimate issue, i.e. one of the very issues to be determined by the court, probably no longer existed. In practice the rule is largely ignored, or treated as being of only semantic effect, so that an expert *is* allowed to express an opinion on an ultimate issue, provided that the actual words the expert employs are not noticeably the same as those which will be used when the issue falls to be considered by the court. In *DPP v A and BC Chewing Gum Ltd* [1968] 1 QB 159, Lord Parker CJ said (at p. 164): **F11.35**

> I think it would be wrong to ask the direct question as to whether any particular cards tended to corrupt or deprave, because that final stage was a matter which was entirely for the justices. No doubt, however, in such a case the defence might well put it to the witness that a particular card or cards could not corrupt, and no doubt, whatever the strict position may be, that question coming from the defence would be allowed, if only to give the defence an opportunity of getting an answer 'No' from the expert.
>
> . . . I myself would go a little further in that I cannot help feeling that with the advance of science more and more inroads have been made into the old common-law principles. Those who practise in the criminal courts see every day cases of experts being called on the question of diminished responsibility, and although technically the final question 'Do you think he was suffering from diminished responsibility?' is strictly inadmissible, it is allowed time and time again without any objection.

Thus the rule has become 'a matter of form rather than substance' (*Stockwell* (1993) 97 Cr App R 260 at p. 265). For illustrations, see *Mason* (1911) 7 Cr App R 67 (whether wounds were self-inflicted), *Holmes* [1953] 2 All ER 324 (insanity), *Brennan* [2014] EWCA Crim 2387, [2015] 1 WLR 2060 at [51] (diminished responsibility, in cases where the expert has properly expressed a view on all four of the matters set out in the Homicide Act 1957, s. 2, as amended), *Silcott* [1987] Crim LR 765 (the unreliability of a confession), *Hookway* [1999] Crim LR 750 (establishing identity by expert evidence of facial mapping) and *Udenze* [2001] EWCA Crim 1381 (in a rape case, the effects of alcohol on the ability to give informed consent). As to evidence of identity by facial mapping experts, see *Atkins* [2010] EWCA Crim 1876, [2010] 1 Cr App R 8 (117), considered at **F11.11**. As to possession of drugs with intent to supply, see *Hodges* [2003] EWCA Crim 290, [2003] 2 Cr App R 15 (247), considered at **F11.34** (and cf. *Jeffries* [1997] Crim LR 819, where the Court concluded that the opinion expressed in effect amounted to an assertion that D was guilty as charged). However, experts should not usurp the role of the fact-finder as the ultimate decision-maker on matters that are central to the outcome of the case. Thus a psychologist may give evidence of opinion as to why the accused might be disposed to make an unreliable confession but is not entitled to assert that the confession made is in fact unreliable (*Pora v The Queen* [2015] UKPC 9, [2016] 1 Cr App R 3 (48)). *Pora v The Queen* was applied in *Sellu* [2016] EWCA Crim 1716, [2017] 1 Cr App R 24 (349), a case in which a consultant surgeon was charged with manslaughter by gross negligence and experts had given evidence that D had been 'grossly negligent' and had also used other descriptions such as 'very bad practice' and 'recklessness'. It was held that although the jury had been told that they were not bound by the views of the experts on the ultimate issue, the experts had failed to give explanations for the terminology of many of their opinions and therefore there was a danger that the jury may have merely accepted their conclusions.

Duty of Lawyers

F11.36 Lawyers instructing expert witnesses should satisfy themselves that they have the necessary expertise (*Pabon* [2018] EWCA Crim 420 at [77]). It is submitted that, as in civil cases, lawyers should disclose to the expert all the relevant factual material intended to contribute to the expert's evidence, including not only material that supports their case, but also material that points in the other direction (*Kennedy v Cordia (Services) LLP* [2016] UKSC 6, [2016] 1 WLR 597 at [57]). It is also the responsibility of lawyers to ensure that experts understand the requirements of the Criminal Procedure Rules and Practice Direction and that the expert reports which they serve are reliable and admissible (*DPP v Walsall Magistrates' Court* [2019] EWHC 3317 at [73]).

Duty of Experts

F11.37 CrimPR 19.2 provides that an expert must help the court to achieve the overriding objective by giving objective, unbiased opinion on matters within his or her area or areas of expertise and by actively assisting the court in fulfilling its duty of case management under r. 3.2, in particular by complying with court directions and at once informing the court of any significant failure to take any step required by such a direction. This duty overrides any obligation to the person instructing the expert or by whom the expert is paid; and this duty includes an obligation (a) to define his or her area or areas of expertise in the report and when giving evidence, (b) when giving evidence, to draw the court's attention to any question to which the answer would be outside the expert's area or areas of expertise, and (c) to inform all parties and the court if his or her opinion changes from that contained in a report served as evidence or given in a statement. For CrimPR Part 19, see Supplement, **R19.1** *et seq*.

CrimPR19.2 reinforces the principles established in *Harris* [2005] EWCA Crim 1980, [2006] 1 Cr App R 5 (55) and *B (T)* [2006] EWCA Crim 417, [2006] 2 Cr App R 3 (22). In *Harris* it was held that the description of the obligations of an expert witness set out by Creswell J in *National Justice Cia Naviera SA v Prudential Assurance Co Ltd (Ikarian Reefer)* [1993] 2 Lloyd's Rep 68 at p. 81 and the guidance for experts giving evidence involving children provided by Wall J in *Re AB (Child Abuse: Expert Witnesses)* [1995] 1 FLR 181 were both very relevant in criminal proceedings and should be kept well in mind by both prosecution and defence.

F11.38 In *Re AB (Child Abuse: Expert Witnesses)*, Wall J, referring to cases in which there is a genuine disagreement on a scientific or medical issue or where it is necessary for a party to advance a particular hypothesis to explain a given set of facts, said (at p. 192):

> Where that occurs, the judge [in a criminal case, jury] will have to resolve the issue which is raised. Two points must be made. In my view, the expert who advances such a hypothesis owes a very heavy duty to explain to the court that what he is advancing is a hypothesis, that it is controversial (if it is) and to place before the court all material which contradicts the hypothesis. Secondly, he must make all his material available to the other experts in the case. It is the common experience of the courts that the better the experts the more limited their areas of disagreement, and in the forensic context of a contested case relating to children, the objective of the lawyers and the experts should always be to limit the ambit of disagreement on medical issues to the minimum.

In *Harris* itself it was stressed (at [270]) that developments in scientific thinking should not be kept from the court, simply because they remain at the stage of a hypothesis, but it is of the first importance that the true status of the expert's evidence is frankly indicated to the court. As to limiting the ambit of disagreement, it was further pointed out (at [273]) that what is now CrimPR 19.6 and the Plea and Trial Preparation form make provision for experts to come together and, if possible, agree points of agreement or disagreement with a summary of reasons. (See also, endorsing the importance of this provision, *Holdsworth* [2008] EWCA Crim 971.) In cases involving allegations of child abuse, it was said that the judge should be prepared to give directions in respect of expert evidence, taking into account the guidance to which the court had referred.

In *B (T)* [2006] EWCA Crim 417, [2006] 2 Cr App R 3 (22), it was emphasised that the duties of an expert witness as set out in *The Ikarian Reefer* and *Harris* are owed to the court and override any obligation to the person from whom the expert has received instructions, or by whom the expert is paid. Experts should maintain professional objectivity and impartiality at all times. **F11.39**

In *Myers v R* [2015] UKPC 40, [2016] AC 314, it was held that a police officer giving evidence as an expert, like any other expert, comes under the duties set out in *Harris*. It is particularly important that the officer should fully understand that he or she is not simply a part of the prosecution team but has a separate duty to the court to give independent evidence, whichever side it may favour, and that therefore any material which weighs against the proposition that the officer advances should be stated fully (at [59] and [60]). An officer giving expert evidence relating to gangs (if admissible as bad character evidence: see **F13.49**) must state: how the conclusions have been arrived at; whether they are based on the officer's own observations or contacts with particular persons; if based on information provided by other officers, how it is collected and exchanged and, if recorded, how; and whether it comes from informers. In relation to primary conclusions regarding the accused or other key persons, the officer must go beyond a mere general claim to have sources of particular kinds and say whence the particular information that is advanced has come. The defence should not be left to explore what the sources were in speculative cross-examination (at [68] and [70]).

In *Cleobury* [2012] EWCA Crim 17, consideration was given to the duty of an expert on appeal. It was held that, where it is in the interests of justice for the Court of Appeal to hear fresh expert evidence (e.g., after the trial there is some new scientific discovery), it is essential that the expert present the report as evidence within his or her sphere of expertise and not as an advocate's critique of either what happened at the trial or the judge's summing-up.

Content of Expert's Report

CrimPR 19.4 (see Supplement, **R19.4**) sets out what an expert's report must contain. Under r. 19.4(h), for example, an expert's report must include such information as the court may need to decide whether the expert's opinion is sufficiently reliable to be admissible as evidence. Under r. 19.4(j) the report must contain a statement that the expert understands the duty to the court and has complied and will continue to comply with it. A bare statement that the expert understands the duty is insufficient; the statement should set out, at least in summary, what the duty entails (*R (DPP) v Stratford Magistrates' Court* [2017] EWHC 1794 (Admin), [2017] 2 Cr App R 32 (467)). Under r. 19.4(k) the report must contain the same declaration of truth as a witness statement; and the statement and declaration required by these provisions should be in the terms set out in CrimPD V, para. 19B (see Supplement, **CPD.19B**). **F11.40**

Rule 19.4 mirrors and in some respects amplifies the guidelines on the contents of an expert's report set out in *B (T)* [2006] EWCA Crim 417, [2006] 2 Cr App R 3 (22).

Rule 19.9 sets out the procedure to be followed where a party introducing expert evidence wants to withhold in the public interest part of what the expert could otherwise say, for example because it would reveal confidential investigative techniques.

An expert report must be full and transparent, and material such as formulae and statistics should not be excluded because they may confuse the jury; if the court is not aware of the way in which an expert has reached the opinion, it cannot evaluate reliability and decide whether the opinion is admissible (*T (Footwear mark evidence)* [2010] EWCA Crim 2439, [2011] 1 Cr App R 9 (85)). **F11.41**

In *Puaca* [2005] EWCA Crim 3001, a murder conviction was quashed because a review of the development and bases of the views and evidence of the Crown's pathologist, who had undertaken the post-mortem examination, established that his conclusions could not safely be relied on. It was held that the duty of all pathologists is to comply from the start with the obligations imposed on expert witnesses; that it is wholly wrong for a pathologist carrying out the first post-mortem at the request of the police or the coroner merely to leave it to the defence to instruct a pathologist to prepare a report setting out contrary arguments; and that there was also a need, in certain cases, to refer to ante-mortem records.

Function and Weight of Expert Evidence

F11.42 The duty of the expert witness is 'to furnish the judge or jury with the necessary scientific criteria for testing the accuracy of their conclusions, so as to enable the judge or jury to form an independent judgement by the application of those criteria to the facts proved in evidence' (as to which, see also **F11.45**); and it is a misdirection, therefore, to tell the jury that expert evidence should be accepted if uncontradicted (*Davie v Magistrates of Edinburgh* 1953 SC 34, per Lord President Cooper at p. 40). See also *Lanfear* [1968] 2 QB 77 and *Rivett* (1950) 34 Cr App R 87, in which the Court of Appeal refused to interfere with a conviction despite medical evidence of insanity. Equally, it is incumbent on magistrates to approach the evidence of an expert critically, even if no expert is called on the other side, and to be willing to reject the evidence if it leaves questions unanswered (*DPP v Wynne* [2001] EWHC 21 (Admin)). When expert evidence is given on an ultimate issue, it should be made clear to the jury that they are not bound by the opinion, and that the issue is for them to decide (*Stockwell* (1993) 97 Cr App R 260 per Lord Taylor CJ), but there is no requirement that such a warning be conveyed in any particular way (*Fitzpatrick* [1999] Crim LR 832). However, in *Brennan* [2014] EWCA Crim 2387, [2015] 1 WLR 2060 at [44] it was held that: 'Where there is simply no rational or proper basis for departing from uncontradicted and unchallenged expert evidence then juries may not do so.' The Court of Appeal approved (at [45]) the standard direction in the *Crown Court Bench Book*, which suggested (after the usual directions and appropriate stress on the need for a jury to consider all the evidence) a direction of the following kind: 'Where, as here, there is no dispute about findings made by an expert you would no doubt wish to give effect to them, although you are not bound to do so if you see good reason to reject them.' The Court held that such an approach acknowledges that, if unchallenged expert evidence on a particular point calling for such expertise is to be rejected by a jury, it must be rejected for a reason.

It has also been held that it is wrong to direct a jury that they may disregard scientific evidence when the only such evidence adduced on a particular question dictates one answer and only a scientist is qualified to answer that question (*Anderson v The Queen* [1972] AC 100). See also *Matheson* [1958] 2 All ER 87 and *Bailey* (1961) 66 Cr App R 31, in both of which the Court of Criminal Appeal substituted verdicts of manslaughter. In *Matheson* it was held that where the medical evidence of diminished responsibility is uncontradicted and the jury return a verdict of guilty of murder, if there are facts entitling the jury to reject or differ from the expert opinion, the Court of Appeal will not interfere with the verdict; but if there are no facts or circumstances to displace or throw a doubt on the unchallenged medical evidence, such a verdict would not be a true verdict in accordance with the evidence. On the other hand, in *Walton v The Queen* [1978] AC 788, a conviction for murder was upheld despite uncontradicted medical evidence of diminished responsibility. *Matheson* and *Bailey* were distinguished on the basis of the greater weight and quality of the medical evidence in those cases. *Walton* was followed in *Kiszko* (1978) 68 Cr App R 62. In *Sanders* (1991) 93 Cr App R 245, the Court of Appeal held that two clear principles emerged from the cases, on the issue of diminished responsibility:

(a) if there were no other circumstances to consider, unequivocal, uncontradicted medical evidence favourable to an accused should be accepted by a jury and they should be so directed; and
(b) where there were other circumstances to consider, the medical evidence, though it be unequivocal and uncontradicted, must be assessed in the light of the other circumstances.

F11.43 In *Brennan* [2014] EWCA Crim 2387, [2015] 1 WLR 2060, it was held that: where expert evidence of diminished responsibility is uncontradicted and an application is made to withdraw the case of murder at the close of evidence, the trial judge must evaluate all the circumstances of the case, looking at both the expert evidence and any other evidence; the charge should not be left to the jury if, applying the ordinary principles of *Galbraith* [1981] 1 WLR 1039, the judge's considered view is that on the evidence taken as a whole no properly directed jury could properly convict of murder; and where there are other facts or circumstances which might cast a different light on the otherwise uncontradicted expert evidence and the matter is left to the jury, those facts and circumstances should be raised by prosecuting counsel in discussion with the judge prior to closing speeches and in the summing-up should be specifically identified by the judge as capable of providing a rational basis on which to decline to accept the expert evidence. In *Golds* [2016] UKSC 61, [2017] 1 Cr App R 18 (273), the Supreme Court, while agreeing that the ordinary principles of *Galbraith* can apply in a trial where the only issue is diminished responsibility, held that a court should be cautious about doing so for three reasons. First, a murder trial is a particularly sensitive event; second, the onus of proving diminished responsibility is on the the accused; and third, a finding of diminished responsibility is not a single issue but requires the accused to address all the matters set out in the Homicide Act 1957, s. 2. It will be a rare case where a judge will withdraw a charge of murder from the jury if the prosecution do not accept that the evidence gives rise to the defence of diminished responsibility (*Blackman* [2017] EWCA Crim 190, approved and followed in *Hussain* [2019] EWCA Crim 666 and *Sargeant* [2019] EWCA Crim 1088).

In deciding what weight, if any, to attach to the evidence of an expert, the jury are entitled to take into account the expert's qualifications and experience, credibility, and the extent to which his or her evidence is based on assumed facts which are or are not established. An opinion will not necessarily be intrinsically more persuasive because it is shared by two experts and parties should not be encouraged to expect that public money should be spent on duplicating experts (*Meachen* [2009] EWCA Crim 1701 at [23]). In *Walls* [2011] EWCA Crim 443, [2011] 2 Cr App R 6 (61), the Court of Appeal stated (at [38]) that on a trial of fitness to plead, save in cases where the unfitness is clear, the court must rigorously examine the evidence of psychiatrists before reaching its conclusion.

In cases concerning 'shaken baby syndrome' in which the prosecution are able, by advancing an array of experts, to identify a non-accidental injury and the defence can identify no alternative cause, the temptation to conclude that the prosecution have proved their case must be resisted because in this, as in so many fields of medicine, the evidence may be insufficient to exclude, beyond reasonable doubt, an unknown cause (*Henderson* [2010] EWCA Crim 1269, [2010] 2 Cr App R 24 (185) at [1]). In *Henderson*, the Court of Appeal gave the following general guidance on the content of the summing-up in cases in which the evidence to prove guilt consists only of expert evidence. **F11.44**

(1) There must be a logically justifiable basis for accepting or rejecting the evidence. A logically justifiable conclusion depends upon the structure and quality of the directions in the summing-up.
(2) Before the trial starts, the issues, the expert evidence and the sources upon which the evidence is based, should be clear. Thus the direction of examination-in-chief, cross-examination, submissions and speeches to the jury should be focused.
(3) The judge should generally take the opportunity to discuss the issues of expert evidence before the time comes for counsel to address the jury and thus be in a position carefully to structure the summing-up to those issues.
(4) The judge will be able to identify which evidence goes to the resolution of those issues. The judge should generally sum up issue by issue, dealing with the opinions and any written sources for them issue by issue, unless there is good reason not to do so. Merely repeating the expert evidence in the order in which it was given serves only to confuse. The jury should be confronted with the issues it must decide and the factors they should consider as the basis for judgement, one way or the other. Anyone reading a summing-up composed in that way should be able to understand the route followed by the jury in reaching its verdict.
(5) In cases concerning 'shaken baby syndrome', there are two important features of the content of the summing-up. First, if there is a realistic possibility of an unknown cause, the jury should be reminded of it and instructed that unless the evidence leads them to exclude

any such possibility, they cannot convict. Where relevant, they should also be reminded that medical science develops and that which was previously thought unknown may subsequently be recognised and acknowledged. In such cases, they should be reminded that special caution is needed where expert evidence is fundamental to the prosecution. Second, the jury also need directions on how to approach conflicting expert evidence. The jury's conclusion cannot be left merely to general impression, but needs to be directed to the pointers to reliable evidence and the basis for distinguishing between what may be relied upon and that which should be rejected.

(6) The guidance given in *Harris* [2005] EWCA Crim 1980, [2006] 1 Cr App R 5 (55) (see **F11.37**) is of assistance not only to judges, practitioners and experts, but also to juries. If the issue arises, a jury should be asked to judge whether the expert has, in the course of giving evidence, assumed the role of an advocate, influenced by the side whose cause the expert seeks to advance. If it arises, the jury should be asked to judge whether the witness has gone outside his or her area of expertise. The jury should examine the basis of the opinion. Can the witness point to a recognised, peer-reviewed source of the opinion? Is the clinical experience of the witness up-to-date and equal to the experience of others whose evidence the witness seeks to contradict? The judge should guide the jury by identifying those reasons which would justify either accepting or rejecting any conflicting expert opinion on which either side relies.

The requirement, as set out in (5) above, to direct the jury that there is a need for special caution and that they should not overlook the realistic possibility that the cause of death was unknown, does not need to be given in those precise terms, provided that the judge sums the case up in such a way that the jury are left in no doubt that they should not convict unless, giving full weight to the uncertainties in medical science, they are sure that the accused shook the child in the way the Crown alleged (*Arshad* [2012] EWCA Crim 18 at [15]).

Guidance on Scientific Evidence for Judges

F11.45 Easy-to-understand guides or primers on scientific evidence are being introduced as a working tool for judges. The first two primers, issued in November 2017, cover forensic DNA analysis (available at tinyurl.com/y9pldq4y) and expert evidence of gait (available at tinyurl.com/y7bjxr3w). See also the introductory guide produced by the Royal Statistical Society and the Inns of Court College of Advocacy, 'Statistics and probability for advocates: Understanding the use of statistical evidence in courts and tribunals' (available at tinyurl.com/ybd7o2cr).

Pre-trial Disclosure of Expert Evidence

F11.46 CrimPR 19.3 and 19.4 (see Supplement, **R19.3** ***et seq.***) make provision for the pre-trial disclosure of expert evidence between the parties to Crown Court and magistrates' court proceedings (see also **D9.68** and **D15.75**).

CrimPR 19.3(1) requires a party who wants another party to admit as fact a summary of an expert's conclusions to serve the summary on the court officer and on each party from whom the admission is sought. A party on whom such a summary is served must serve a response stating which, if any, of the conclusions are admitted as fact and, where a conclusion is not admitted, what are the disputed issues concerning that conclusion (r. 19.3(2)(a)). The response must be served on the court officer and on the party who served the summary as soon as practicable and in any event no more than 14 days after service of the summary (r. 19.3(2)(b)). CrimPR 19.3(3)(a) and (b) requires that a party who wants to introduce expert evidence otherwise than as admitted fact must serve a report by the expert which complies with r. 19.4 (see **F11.40**) on the court officer and each other party as soon as practicable and in any event with any application in support of which that party relies on that evidence. The report should be accompanied by notice of anything of which the party serving it is aware which might reasonably be thought capable of (i) undermining the reliability of the expert's opinion or (ii) detracting from the credibility or reliability of the expert (r. 19.3(3)(c)). CrimPD V, para. 19A.7 (see Supplement, **CPD.19A**), sets out a non-comprehensive list of matters that should be disclosed pursuant to r. 19.3(3)(c). Under r. 19.3(3)(d), if another party so requires, the party wanting to introduce the expert evidence must give that party a copy of, or a reasonable opportunity to inspect, (i) a record of any examination, measurement, test or experiment on which the expert's findings and opinion are based, or that were carried out in the course of reaching those findings and opinion, and (ii) anything on which such examination, measurement etc. was carried out. Unless the parties otherwise agree or the court directs, a party may not (a) introduce expert evidence if the party has not complied with r. 19.3(3), or (b) introduce in evidence an expert report if the expert does not give evidence in person (r. 19.3(4)). Under CrimPR 19.5, a party who serves on another party or on the court a report by an expert must at once inform the expert. The phrase 'expert evidence (whether of fact or opinion)' is sufficiently wide to embrace not only the oral evidence to be given by an expert witness, but also an expert report which it is proposed to adduce under the exception to the hearsay rule contained in the CJA 1988, s. 30(1) (see **F11.51**).

The effect of CrimPR 1.2 and 3.3 (see Supplement, **R1.2** and **R3.3**) is that it is incumbent upon both the prosecution and the defence to alert the court and the other side at the earliest practicable moment if they are intending or may be intending to adduce expert evidence. This should be done if possible at a plea and trial preparation hearing or, if it cannot be done then, as soon as the possibility becomes live. In *Ensor* [2009] EWCA Crim 2519, [2010] 1 Cr App R 18 (255), where service by the defence of an expert report had been so late as to constitute a grave breach of the rules, it was held that the trial judge had properly refused to admit the evidence.

The CrimPR do not supplant or detract from the prosecution's general duty of disclosure in respect of scientific evidence, which exists irrespective of any defence request, extends to anything which may arguably assist the defence, and obliges the prosecution to make full and proper inquiries from forensic scientists in order to ascertain whether there is discoverable material. In *Clark* [2003] EWCA Crim 1020, D's convictions for the murder of her two infant sons were quashed where a forensic pathologist, in breach of normal practice, had omitted from his autopsy report and had failed to disclose the fact that, in the case of one of the infants, following microbiological examination of certain bodily fluids, a form of bacteria which in some parts of the body can prove lethal had been isolated. **F11.47**

In *Henderson* [2010] EWCA Crim 1269, [2010] 2 Cr App R 24 (185), the Court of Appeal laid down the following general guidance on case management in cases in which the evidence to prove guilt consists only of expert evidence. **F11.48**

(1) Justice in such cases depends upon proper advanced preparation and control of the evidence from the stage of investigation onwards. The evidential picture may change as opinions from experts are obtained by either side.
(2) The problem for the courts is how to manage expert evidence so that a jury may be properly directed in a way which will, so far as possible, ensure that any verdict they reach may be justified on a logical basis. A jury can only approach conflicting expert evidence if it is properly marshalled and controlled before it is presented to them.
(3) The judge who is to hear a case should deal with the pre-trial hearings. It is desirable that the judge has experience of the complex issues and understanding of the medical learning.
(4) Proper and robust pre-trial management is essential in order to identify the real medical issues and avoid unnecessary detail.
(5) Before the trial, the judge should be in a position to identify whether the expert evidence is admissible.
(6) In cases concerning 'shaken baby syndrome', the judge should be familiar with the Kennedy Report on Sudden Unexpected Death in Infancy of September 2004, which recommends a checklist of matters before expert evidence is admitted, including: (i) 'is the proposed expert still in practice?' (ii) 'to what extent is he an expert in the subject to which he testifies?' (iii) 'when did he last see a case in his own clinical practice?' and (iv) 'to what extent is his view widely held?'

(7) Generally it will be necessary for the court to direct a meeting of experts so that a statement can be prepared of areas of agreement and disagreement (CrimPR 19.6(2)). The meeting should take place well in advance of the trial and be attended by all significant experts, including the defence experts. A careful and detailed minute should be prepared and signed by all participants. Usually it will be preferable if others, particularly legal representatives, do not attend. The court may be required to exercise its power to exclude evidence from an expert who has not complied with a direction (r. 19.6(4)).

(8) Defence experts are not obliged to reveal a previous report they have made in the case, nor to reveal adverse criticism by judges in the past, but a failure to do so will not avail the defence. A judge may well be able to exercise powers under the CrimPR to ensure advance disclosure of any such reports or criticism. Failure to do so would be contrary to the overriding objective and expose the expert to cross-examination on those matters. Those acting on behalf of the accused should satisfy themselves that any such previous report or criticism is disclosed. Failure to do so by either side will only cast suspicion upon the cogency of the opinion.

Pre-hearing Discussion of Expert Evidence

F11.49 Where more than one party wants to introduce expert evidence, the court may direct the experts to discuss the issues and prepare a statement for the court of the matters on which they agree and disagree, giving their reasons; if an expert does not comply with such a direction, the expert's evidence may not be introduced without the leave of the court (CrimPR 19.6: see Supplement, **R19.6**). See also, in relation to pre-hearing discussion of expert evidence, the detailed provisions of CrimPD V, para. 19C (see Supplement, **CPD.19C**).

Single Joint Experts

F11.50 Where more than one accused wants to introduce expert evidence, the court may direct that the evidence be given by one expert only (CrimPR 19.7(1): see Supplement, **R19.7**). Provision is also made for selection of an expert where the co-accused cannot agree who should be the expert (r. 19.7(2)) and for giving instructions and directions to the expert (r. 19.8: see Supplement, **R19.8**).

Presentation of Expert and Complicated Evidence

F11.51 **Criminal Justice Act 1988, s. 30**

(1) An expert report shall be admissible as evidence in criminal proceedings, whether or not the person making it attends to give oral evidence in those proceedings.

(2) If it is proposed that the person making the report shall not give oral evidence, the report shall only be admissible with the leave of the court.

(3) For the purpose of determining whether to give leave the court shall have regard—

(a) to the contents of the report;

(b) to the reasons why it is proposed that the person making the report shall not give oral evidence;

(c) to any risk, having regard in particular to whether it is likely to be possible to controvert statements in the report if the person making it does not attend to give oral evidence in the proceedings, that its admission or exclusion will result in unfairness to the accused or, if there is more than one, to any of them; and

(d) to any other circumstances that appear to the court to be relevant.

(4) An expert report, when admitted, shall be evidence of any fact or opinion of which the person making it could have given oral evidence.

(5) In this section 'expert report' means a written report by a person dealing wholly or mainly with matters on which he is (or would if living be) qualified to give expert evidence.

Section F12 Admissibility of Previous Verdicts

PROOF OF CONVICTIONS AND ACQUITTALS

General

The PACE 1984, s. 73, provides for the proof of convictions and acquittals in the UK and other EU Member States by a certificate of conviction or acquittal, together with proof that the person named in the certificate is the person whose conviction or acquittal is in issue. As to the latter issue, although it is for the judge to decide whether there is prima facie evidence fit for the jury's consideration, ultimately it is a question of fact for the jury to decide (*Burns* [2006] EWCA Crim 617, [2006] 1 WLR 1273; *Lewendon* [2006] EWCA Crim 648, [2006] 1 WLR 1278). In the case of convictions in other EU Member States, there is no requirement in s. 73 that the convictions took place after the country in question became a Member State (*Mehmedov* [2014] EWCA Crim 1523, [2015] 1 WLR 495). As to the proof of convictions in foreign countries other than EU Member States, see **F12.9**. **F12.1**

Police and Criminal Evidence Act 1984, ss. 73 and 82 **F12.2**

73.—(1) Where in any proceedings the fact that a person has in the United Kingdom or any other member State been convicted or acquitted of an offence otherwise than by a Service court is admissible in evidence, it may be proved by producing a certificate of conviction or, as the case may be, of acquittal relating to that offence, and proving that the person named in the certificate as having been convicted or acquitted of the offence is the person whose conviction or acquittal of the offence is to be proved.

(2) For the purposes of this section a certificate of conviction or of acquittal—

(a) shall, as regards a conviction or acquittal on indictment, consist of a certificate, signed by the proper officer of the court where the conviction or acquittal took place, giving the substance and effect (omitting the formal parts) of the indictment and of the conviction or acquittal; and

(b) shall, as regards a conviction or acquittal on a summary trial, consist of a copy of the conviction or of the dismissal of the information, signed by the clerk of the court where the conviction or acquittal took place or by the clerk of the court, if any, to which a memorandum of the conviction or acquittal was sent; and

(c) shall, as regards a conviction or acquittal by a court in a member State (other than the United Kingdom), consist of a certificate, signed by the proper officer of the court where the conviction or acquittal took place, giving details of the offence, of the conviction or acquittal, and of any sentence;

and a document purporting to be a duly signed certificate of conviction or acquittal under this section shall be taken to be such a certificate unless the contrary is proved.

(3) In subsection (2) above 'proper officer' means—

(a) in relation to a magistrates' court in England and Wales, the designated officer for the court; and

(b) in relation to any other court in the United Kingdom, the clerk of the court, his deputy or any other person having custody of the court record; and

(c) in relation to any court in another member State ('the EU court'), a person who would be the proper officer of the EU court if that court were in the United Kingdom.

(4) The method of proving a conviction or acquittal authorised by this section shall be in addition to and not to the exclusion of any other authorised manner of proving a conviction or acquittal.

82.—(1) In this Part of this Act—. . .

'proceedings' means criminal proceedings, including service proceedings and
'Service court' means the Court Martial or the Service Civilian Court.

(1A) In subsection (1) 'service proceedings' means proceedings before a court (other than a civilian court) in respect of a service offence; and 'service offence' and 'civilian court' here have the same meanings as in the Armed Forces Act 2006

(2) [Repealed.]

(3) Nothing in this Part of this Act shall prejudice any power of a court to exclude evidence (whether by preventing questions from being put or otherwise) at its discretion.

Proof of Identity

F12.3 Concerning the requirement in the PACE 1984, s. 73(1), of proof that the person named in the certificate is the person whose conviction or acquittal is to be proved, in *Pattison v DPP* [2005] EWHC 2938 (Admin), [2006] 2 All ER 317 it was held that, where s. 73(1) is relied upon by the prosecution to prove the conviction of an accused, the following general principles could be distilled from the authorities:

(a) The prosecution must prove to the criminal standard that the accused is the person named on the certificate.

(b) This proof may be effected by an admission by or on behalf of the accused, by evidence of fingerprints or by the evidence of someone who was present in court at the time.

(c) However, there is no prescribed means of proof; the matter can be proved by any admissible means.

(d) An example of such means is a match between the personal details of the accused and the personal details recorded on the certificate.

(e) Even if the personal details, such as the name of the accused, are not uncommon, a match will be sufficient for a prima facie case.

(f) In the absence of any evidence contradicting such a prima facie case, the evidence will be sufficient.

(g) The failure of the accused to give any contradictory evidence in rebuttal will be a matter to take into account. If it is proper and fair to do so, and a warning has been given, it can additionally give rise to an adverse inference under the CJPO 1994, s. 35(2) (see **F20.42**).

Similarity in name and date of birth between a certificate and an accused may or may not amount to prima facie evidence of identity. Each case must depend on its own facts and the material which is available. For example, if an accused has an extremely common name and the date of birth on the certificate is not precisely the same as that of the accused, it may well be that it does not constitute prima facie evidence of identity. On the other hand, if the accused has a highly unusual name with many different component parts, it may constitute prima facie evidence of identity without evidence of an identical date of birth (*Burns* [2006] EWCA Crim 617, [2006] 1 WLR 1273).

Summary Offences, Orders Made by Magistrates and Endorsements

F12.4 To overcome the difficulties, at common law, in seeking to prove the previous convictions of a person convicted of a summary offence, if the person does not attend the court, the MCA 1980, s. 104, provides that, if the court is satisfied that, not less than seven days before the hearing, a notice, stating the alleged previous convictions which it is proposed to bring to the attention of the court, has been served on the accused, and the accused is not present before the court, the court may take account of the convictions as if the accused had appeared and admitted them. Endorsements on a driving licence of the particulars of a conviction or disqualification may be produced as prima facie evidence of the matters endorsed (RTOA 1988, ss. 31(1) and 44(1)).

Convictions Overseas

F12.5 As to the proof of convictions in foreign countries other than EU Member States, see **F12.9**.

CONVICTIONS AS EVIDENCE OF FACTS ON WHICH BASED

At common law, the convictions of one person were not admissible as evidence of the facts on which they were based at the subsequent trial of another: see *Turner* (1832) 1 Mood CC 347 at p. 349 (one person's conviction for theft inadmissible as evidence of such theft at the trial of another charged with handling the stolen goods); *Hassan* [1970] QB 423 (a woman's convictions for prostitution inadmissible as evidence of such prostitution at the trial of a man charged with living off her immoral earnings); and *Spinks* [1982] 1 All ER 587 (a principal's conviction of wounding inadmissible as evidence of such wounding at the subsequent trial of an alleged accessory). The PACE 1984, s. 74(1), reversed the common-law rule, and s. 74(2) created a persuasive presumption: the person (other than the accused) convicted of an offence in any court in the UK or any other EU Member State or by a Service court outside the UK shall be taken to have committed that offence unless the contrary is proved. The legal burden is borne by the party against whom the presumption operates; and if borne by the accused, may be discharged by proof on a balance of probabilities (see *Carr-Briant* [1943] KB 607 and generally **F3.53** and **F3.69**). Section 74(3) creates a similar presumption in the case of the previous convictions of *the accused*, provided that evidence is admissible of the fact that the accused has committed the offence in respect of which he or she has been convicted. As to convictions in foreign countries, apart from those in other EU Member States and by Service courts outside the UK, see **F12.9**. **F12.6**

Police and Criminal Evidence Act 1984, ss. 74 and 75 **F12.7**

74.—(1) In any proceedings the fact that a person other than the accused has been convicted of an offence by or before any court in the United Kingdom or any other member State or by a Service court outside the United Kingdom shall be admissible in evidence for the purpose of proving that that person committed that offence, where evidence of his having done so is admissible, whether or not any other evidence of his having committed that offence is given.

(2) In any proceedings in which by virtue of this section a person other than the accused is proved to have been convicted of an offence by or before any court in the United Kingdom or any other member State or by a Service court outside the United Kingdom, he shall be taken to have committed that offence unless the contrary is proved.

(3) In any proceedings where evidence is admissible of the fact that the accused has committed an offence, if the accused is proved to have been convicted of the offence—

(a) by or before any court in the United Kingdom or any other member State; or

(b) by a Service court outside the United Kingdom,

he shall be taken to have committed that offence unless the contrary is proved.

(4) Nothing in this section shall prejudice—

(a) the admissibility in evidence of any conviction which would be admissible apart from this section; or

(b) the operation of any enactment whereby a conviction or a finding of fact in any proceedings is for the purposes of any other proceedings made conclusive evidence of any fact.

75.—(1) Where evidence that a person has been convicted of an offence is admissible by virtue of section 74 above, then without prejudice to the reception of any other admissible evidence for the purpose of identifying the facts on which the conviction was based—

(a) the contents of any document which is admissible as evidence of the conviction; and

(b) the contents of—

(i) the information, complaint, indictment or charge-sheet on which the person in question was convicted, or

(ii) in the case of a conviction of an offence by a court in a member State (other than the United Kingdom), any document produced in relation to the proceedings for that offence which fulfils a purpose similar to any document or documents specified in sub-paragraph (i),

shall be admissible in evidence for that purpose.

(2) Where in any proceedings the contents of any document are admissible in evidence by virtue of subsection (1) above, a copy of that document, or of the material part of it, purporting to be certified or otherwise authenticated by or on behalf of the court or authority having custody

of that document shall be admissible in evidence and shall be taken to be a true copy of that document or part unless the contrary is shown.

(3) Nothing in any of the following—
 (a) section 14 of the Powers of Criminal Courts (Sentencing) Act 2000 (under which a conviction leading to probation or discharge is to be disregarded except as mentioned in that section);
 (aa) section 187 of the Armed Forces Act 2006 (which makes similar provision in respect of service convictions);
 (b) section 247 of the Criminal Procedure (Scotland) Act 1995 (which makes similar provision in respect of convictions on indictment in Scotland); and
 (c) section 8 of the Probation Act (Northern Ireland) 1950 (which corresponds to section [14 of the Powers of Criminal Courts (Sentencing) Act 2000]) or any legislation which is in force in Northern Ireland for the time being and corresponds to that section,

shall affect the operation of section 74 above; and for the purposes of that section any order made by a court of summary jurisdiction in Scotland under section 228 or section 246(3) of the said Act of 1995 shall be treated as a conviction.

(4) Nothing in section 74 above shall be construed as rendering admissible in any proceedings evidence of any conviction other than a subsisting one.

For the definition of 'proceedings' and 'Service court', see s. 82 at **F12.2**.

A 'subsisting' conviction means either a finding of guilt that has not been quashed on appeal or a formal plea of guilt that has not been withdrawn; whether the accused has been sentenced is irrelevant (*Robertson* [1987] QB 920). An admission of an offence in a police caution is not a conviction and therefore not covered by ss. 74 and 75 but, where evidence of such an admission is introduced, an accused may challenge it (*Olu* [2010] EWCA Crim 2975, [2011] 1 Cr App R 33 (404)).

F12.8 It seems that one co-accused may rely upon s. 74(1) to adduce evidence of the convictions of another co-accused (*Hendrick* [1992] Crim LR 427, where the convictions were held to be irrelevant), subject to satisfying the test of substantial probative value set out in the CJA 2003, s. 101(1)(e) (see **F13.66**). It is possible to envisage situations in which a co-accused pleads guilty to a charge even though the evidence is far from conclusive, and in such a case it could well be unfair to allow the prosecution to use the conviction as evidence, on that charge, against the remaining accused (*Lee* [1996] Crim LR 825). Where one co-accused pleads guilty towards or at the end of the prosecution case and the prosecution make an application to reopen their case to adduce evidence of the guilty plea under s. 74(1), the plea, if relevant to an issue in the proceedings, is admissible, subject to exercise of the discretion to exclude under s. 78, as when it would be unfair because, had the guilty plea been entered and admitted in evidence at an earlier stage, cross-examination might have been conducted differently (*Chapman* [1991] Crim LR 44).

Foreign Convictions

F12.9 Foreign convictions other than convictions in other EU Member States are not covered by the PACE 1984, s. 73; and foreign convictions, apart from convictions by Service courts outside the UK and convictions in other EU Member States, are not covered by the PACE 1984, s. 74. However, foreign convictions may be admissible under the bad character provisions of the CJA 2003 (see **F13** and **F15**) and, if admissible, may be proved under the Evidence Act 1851, s. 7 (see **F8.19**) (*Kordasinski* [2006] EWCA Crim 2984, [2007] 1 Cr App R 17 (238)). If there is evidence that the conviction was the result of a trial which failed to reach appropriate standards of fairness, it is open to the court to exclude it, in the exercise of its discretion, either under the PACE 1984, s. 78, or, as appropriate, the CJA 2003, s. 101(3) (*Mehmedov* [2014] EWCA Crim 1523, [2015] 1 WLR 495).

For the purposes of extradition proceedings, the fact of a conviction overseas may be proved by a properly certified copy of the court record (see the Extradition Act 1989, sch. 1, para. 12, and *Re Mullin* [1993] Crim LR 390).

In civil asset recovery proceedings under the POCA 2002 against a person convicted in a foreign country, a foreign judgment containing a summary of the matters found proved by the court is, for the purposes of s. 241 of the 2002 Act, evidence of the truth of those facts and of such conduct being unlawful under the criminal law of that country (*Asset Recovery Agency v Virtosu* [2008] EWHC 149 (QB), [2009] 3 All ER 637).

Convictions of Persons Other than the Accused

Relevance to an Issue in the Proceedings The wording of the PACE 1984, s. 74(1), was amended by the CJA 2003. The words 'that that person committed that offence, where evidence of his having done so is admissible' were substituted for the original words 'where to do so is relevant to any issue in those proceedings'. The amendment is cosmetic, insofar as evidence of the commission of the offence, in order to be 'admissible', must be relevant to an issue in the proceedings, and it is submitted that such of the following cases in which the court had to decide whether the commission of an offence was 'relevant to any issue in those proceedings' would be decided in the same way under s. 74(1) as amended. **F12.10**

In *Hasson* [1997] Crim LR 579, the accused were charged with being concerned in the supply of drugs. It was held that the previous drug-related convictions of six men with whom the accused had socialised had been improperly admitted because it was not the Crown case that the accused were supplying them with drugs and there was no evidence to show that meetings with them were related to the offence charged.

In some cases proof of the commission of an offence by a person other than the accused will establish an essential ingredient of the offence with which the accused is charged, and therefore will be clearly relevant to an 'issue in those proceedings'. In *Pigram* [1995] Crim LR 808, in which officers had seen D1 and D2 transfer goods from D1's van to D2's lorry and D1 and D2 were jointly charged with handling, it was held that D1's guilty plea was admissible against D2 for the purposes of proving that the goods were stolen.

The phrase 'issue in those proceedings', however, was not confined to an issue which was an essential ingredient of the offence charged. In *Robertson* [1987] QB 920, the Court of Appeal held that the phrase also covered less fundamental issues, for example, evidential issues arising in the proceedings. The Court also rejected the argument that s. 74(1) applies only to the proof of convictions of offences in which the accused on trial did not participate. Robertson was charged with two co-accused with conspiracy to commit burglary. The co-accused pleaded not guilty to the conspiracy but guilty to some 16 burglaries committed during the period of the conspiracy. Evidence of these convictions was held to be admissible, because it could be inferred from the fact that the co-accused had committed these offences that there was a conspiracy between them, and that was the conspiracy to which, the prosecution alleged, Robertson was a party. In *Golder*, the appeal which was heard with and is reported with *Robertson* [1987] QB 920, Golder was charged with a robbery committed at garage H. Two of his co-accused pleaded guilty to that robbery, and also to another robbery committed at garage G. The evidence against Golder consisted primarily of a confession statement, which he alleged to have been fabricated by the police, in which he made reference to both robberies. The evidence of the guilty pleas was held to be admissible: proof of the commission of the offences at both garages was relevant, because it showed that the contents of Golder's confession were in accordance with the facts as they were known and the confession was therefore more likely to be true; and proof of the commission of the offence at garage H was relevant, because robbery at that garage was one of the matters which the prosecution had to prove. **F12.11**

The decision in *Robertson* that the phrase 'issue in those proceedings' should be given a wide interpretation so as to include evidentiary matters, was applied in *Castle* [1989] Crim LR 567. D1 and others, including D2, were charged with robbery. The victim, when seeing D1 and D2 at the identification parade, said 'yes' in respect of D1 and 'possibly' in respect of D2. D2 pleaded guilty. It was held that evidence of the guilty plea was admissible because relevant to the issue of the reliability of the identification of D1. The evidence, by confirming that the victim was correct in his 'possible' identification of D2, tended to corroborate the correctness of his positive identification of D1. See also, *sed quaere*, *Buckingham* (1994) 99 Cr App R 303: evidence of W's conviction of conspiracy to pervert the course of justice by obtaining, as **F12.12** the accused in a previous trial, false evidence of defence witnesses, was admissible at the trial of those witnesses for doing acts intended to pervert the course of justice because, although it was not probative that any of the witnesses had given false evidence, it established the conspiracy.

F12.13 **Discretion to Exclude** Where a conviction is admissible under the PACE 1984, s. 74, the Court of Appeal will allow an appeal against a judge's ruling not to exclude it under s. 78 only if no judge could reasonably have made it or it was made on a false basis (*Abdullah* [2010] EWCA Crim 3078, following *Smith* [2007] EWCA Crim 2105). See also *O'Brien* [2016] EWCA Crim 698, where the decision of the trial judge to admit evidence of a guilty plea was upheld notwithstanding that all three members of the Court of Appeal would have excluded it. However, cf. *Denham* [2016] EWCA Crim 1048, [2017] 1 Cr App R 7 (64), considered at **F12.16**.

In *O'Connor* (1987) 85 Cr App R 298, D2 and D1 were jointly charged with having conspired together (and with no one else) to obtain property by deception. At the trial of D1, D2's plea of guilty was admitted, together with all the detail contained in the conspiracy count (see the PACE 1984, s. 75(1)(b), at **F12.7**). The Court of Appeal upheld D1's conviction by application of the proviso which then applied, but held that the evidence should have been excluded on the ground that it was impossible realistically to exclude the possibility that the jury might infer from D2's admission, and the detail contained in the count, that not only had D2 conspired with D1, but that the converse had also taken place. Furthermore, it was not open to the defence to challenge or test what had been said by D2. The Court concluded that if it was appropriate within the section to admit the conviction, the judge should have excluded it under s. 78, on the basis that it would have had such an adverse effect on the fairness of the proceedings that it ought not to have been admitted. See also, to similar effect, *Horne* [2020] EWCA Crim 487, another case of a closed conspiracy consisting of two individuals. In that case, the trial judge had directed the jury that the guilty plea could only be used to show that at least some of what two prosecution witnesses had said was true and was therefore relevant to their credibility. It was held that this attempt to limit the evidential impact of the guilty plea was necessarily ineffective because if the evidence of the two prosecution witnesses was accepted, that essentially established the involvement of the accused in the conspiracy. In *Mattison* [1990] Crim LR 117, D1 was charged in one count with gross indecency with D2. In another count, D2 was charged with gross indecency with D1. D2 pleaded guilty and at D1's trial evidence of that plea was admitted. The judge directed the jury that the evidence of D2's plea did not mean that D1 was guilty, but was before them to make the background accurate. Allowing the appeal, it was held that although D2's guilty plea was relevant in the proceedings against D1, the judge, bearing in mind D1's defence, which was one of complete denial, should have exercised the discretion under s. 78 to exclude the evidence.

Where a co-accused pleads guilty but no use is made of s. 74, it is not always necessary for a judge to direct the jury that the plea is no evidence against the accused, but such a direction is desirable where the plea necessarily shows complicity with the accused (*Turpin* [1990] Crim LR 514; *Betterley* [1994] Crim LR 764). Where the co-accused changes plea to guilty during the trial, this may cause such prejudice to the accused as to require discharge of the jury (see *Fedrick* [1990] Crim LR 403, considered at **D13.65**, and, for a further example, *Marlow* [1997] Crim LR 457).

It seems that evidence of a conviction, which would otherwise be clearly admissible under s. 74, may also be excluded under s. 78 on the basis that it adds little to an already strong case against the accused (*Warner* (1993) 96 Cr App R 324).

F12.14 In *Robertson* [1987] QB 920, counsel for D, relying upon *O'Connor*, submitted that the convictions in that case should also have been excluded under s. 78, because the prosecution, in relying on s. 74, had deprived D of the opportunity to cross-examine the co-accused. The Court of Appeal rejected the argument, distinguishing *O'Connor*. D's name did not appear on any of the burglary counts, and even if the co-accused had given evidence in accordance with their guilty pleas, D's counsel would have been unlikely to cross-examine them (or, if he had done so, he would have seriously prejudiced D). (In this respect, see also *Kempster* [1989] 1 WLR 1125, discussed at **F12.17**.) However, the Court added (at p. 928): 'Section 74 is a provision which should be sparingly used. There will be occasions where, although the evidence may be technically admissible its effect is likely to be so slight that it will be wiser not to adduce it. This is particularly so when there is a danger of a contravention of section 78.' It was further observed that where the evidence is admitted, the judge should be careful to explain to the jury its effect and limitations.

In *Turner* [1991] Crim LR 57, D1 and D2, in separate cars, were driving at night down a hill. D2 overtook D1, collided with an oncoming vehicle and killed his (D2's) passenger. The prosecution alleged that D2 and D1 were racing. D2 pleaded guilty to causing death by reckless driving. D1 was tried on the same charge and denied that he was racing. It was held that D2's guilty plea was relevant to D1's trial because the prosecution case was that D2 had been the principal and D1 the secondary party who aided and abetted D2. The question was whether the plea should have been excluded under s. 78. Provided that the judge made it clear, as he did, that D2's plea did not amount to an admission that he was racing, there was nothing unfair in admitting the evidence. In *Bennett* [1988] Crim LR 686, D1 was charged with theft. Her co-accused, a supermarket cashier, pleaded guilty to theft, the allegation being that she passed goods to D1 for less than their true price. Evidence of the guilty plea was admitted against D1. The Court of Appeal held that any decision to the contrary would have bewildered the jury. The evidence was adduced to establish that there had been a theft. The issue of whether D1 had been a party to the theft had been fairly left with the jury, and the judge had properly exercised his discretion under s. 78. For further illustrations, see *Stewart* [1999] Crim LR 746 and *O'Brien* [2016] EWCA Crim 698. **F12.15**

Cases of Conspiracy and Joint Enterprise For a closed conspiracy consisting of two individuals, see *O'Connor* (1987) 85 Cr App R 298 and the other cases considered at **F12.13**. In *Lunnon* [1988] Crim LR 456, in which there were three accused jointly charged with conspiracy, it was held that the guilty plea of one of them had been properly admitted to prove the existence of the conspiracy: the judge had separated two questions for the jury, namely (a) whether there was a conspiracy and (b) who was a party to it, and had made it clear that, despite the evidence of the guilty plea, the jury could acquit the accused. Similarly, in *Denham* [2016] EWCA Crim 1048, [2017] 1 Cr App R 7 (64), a case of conspiracies to rape, evidence of the guilty pleas of co-accuseds was held to have been properly admitted because it neither shut off the defence of the accused nor closed down the issue the jury had to consider: their defence was not that there were no conspiracies, but that they were not party to them. It was further held that: the test for exclusion is unfairness in the particular circumstances to the defence, not difficulties for them (see also, in this respect, *Shirt* [2018] EWCA Crim 2486, [2019] 1 Cr App R 15 (199)); the decision is better described as a judgment in which a balance must be struck on the issue of fairness, rather than exercise of a discretion; and the decision, necessarily fact-sensitive, is ultimately either right or wrong. (See also *Garrity* [1994] Crim LR 828; and compare *Humphreys* [1993] Crim LR 288, where it was held that the evidence should have been excluded under the PACE 1984, s. 78, because there was other prosecution evidence of the conspiracy, and *Abdullah* [2010] EWCA Crim 3078, where it was held that the evidence may be admissible if the count of conspiracy against the former co-accused is amended to allege 'with others unknown', thereby enabling the judge to direct the jury that the conviction does not help in any way as to whether any of the co-accused is guilty of the conspiracy.) In *S* [2007] EWCA Crim 2105, it was held that it is extremely relevant what the issue is; it is of considerable importance whether admission of the guilty plea of an absent co-accused would be unfair by closing off many or all of the issues which the jury is trying; and that these principles remain valid notwithstanding that under the CJA 2003 in some respects the ambit of evidence with which a jury can be trusted is wider than the law formerly allowed. In *Chapman* [1991] Crim LR 44, D1 and seven others were charged with conspiracy to obtain by deception. The pleas of guilty by one of the others to two specific counts of obtaining by deception, being two incidents in which he was involved with D1, were held to be relevant; and since there were others in the conspiracy, and since the **F12.16**

other co-accused did not plead guilty to conspiracy but to specific obtainings by deception, the evidence of the conviction did not inevitably import the complicity of D1. See also *Hunt* [1994] Crim LR 747 and cf. *Curry* [1988] Crim LR 527. The appellant, D1, was convicted of conspiracy to obtain property by deception. She was charged with two others, one of whom, D2, had pleaded guilty. The prosecution case was that D1, with D2's knowledge, had used D2's credit card to obtain goods, and that D2 then intended to report the card as stolen in order to avoid liability to pay for the goods. The other co-accused, D3, had driven the women to the shops. Evidence of D2's guilty plea was admitted to establish the existence of an unlawful agreement to deceive. The Court of Appeal, distinguishing *Lunnon* (1988) 88 Cr App R 71, quashed the conviction on the grounds that the evidence of the guilty plea clearly implied as a matter of fact that D1 had been a party to the conspiracy, even though it did not have that effect as a matter of law, and should have been excluded under s. 78. Section 74, it was said, should be sparingly used, particularly in relation to joint offences such as conspiracy and affray. It should not be used where the evidence, expressly or by necessary inference, suggests the complicity of the accused.

F12.17 This last observation in *Curry* was reiterated in *Kempster* [1989] 1 WLR 1125, in which the Court of Appeal noted that the effect of admitting a conviction as evidence of the complicity of the accused, is that the prosecution will not have to call the person convicted as a witness and the defence will be deprived of any opportunity to cross-examine, in particular as to the complicity of the accused. Staughton LJ said (at p. 22):

> No doubt such cross-examination may in itself be unlikely in some cases, or else turn out to be a disaster, as the Lord Chief Justice put it in *Robertson*. But one cannot always assume that.

Where joint enterprise is relied upon, but it leaves open the question whether the ingredients of the offence are satisfied in the separate case of each of the accused, the guilty plea of a co-accused may be admissible. In deciding whether it should be excluded under s. 78, regard should be had not just to the interests of the accused, but to those of the prosecution and of justice as a whole, so that, for example, an initial decision to exclude the evidence may be reversed in order to avoid the jury from being misled by the evidence of the accused (*Tee* [2011] EWCA Crim 462, applying *Stewart* [1995] 1 Cr App R 441).

F12.18 **Purpose of Adducing Evidence** The Court of Appeal in *Kempster* [1989] 1 WLR 1125 also stressed that it is important to ascertain the purpose for which evidence under the PACE 1984, s. 74, is to be adduced before deciding whether it should be excluded under s. 78; and that if the evidence is admitted, the trial judge should be careful not only to direct the jury about the purpose for which it has been admitted, but also to ensure that counsel do not seek to use it for any other purpose. In that case, evidence of the guilty pleas of a number of co-accused was admitted but not the detailed particulars of the offences committed. At the time of the application to admit, it was unclear whether the prosecution were relying on the evidence in order to prove the guilt of the accused or merely to prevent mystification of the jury, and therefore there was no clear and informed decision by the judge about any adverse effect the evidence might have on the fairness of the proceedings. In the event, the jury were encouraged to rely on the evidence for the purpose of proving the guilt of the accused. The convictions were quashed. In *Mahmood* [1997] 1 Cr App R 414, D1, D2 and D3 were charged with rape. The prosecution case was that the complainant was too drunk to have consented. D1 pleaded guilty. D2 and D3 admitted intercourse but alleged consent or alternatively belief in consent. It was held that evidence of D1's plea should not have been admitted because, without knowing the basis for it, it was not possible to identify any issue to which it was relevant. There was a real danger that the jury would assume it meant that D1 knew the complainant could not consent by reason of drink (whereas it is possible that he believed she could consent, but knew she was not consenting or was reckless as to whether she was consenting) and conclude therefore that D2 and D3 must also have known that she could not consent, an approach which would preclude proper consideration of the state of mind of each accused. See also, to similar effect, *Skinner* [1995] Crim LR 805, where the guilty plea, although relevant and admissible in the case of one of the accused, was highly prejudicial in the case of the other accused. For a further example, see *Girma* [2009] EWCA Crim 912, [2010] 1 Cr App R (S) 28 (172). See also *Boyson* [1991] Crim LR 274, where the Court of Appeal held, *per curiam*, that it did not approve of the growing practice of allowing evidence to go before a jury which is irrelevant, inadmissible, prejudicial or unfair simply because it is convenient for the jury to have 'the whole picture', and *Hall* [1993] Crim LR 527.

Convictions of Accused

It is clear from the wording of the PACE 1984, s. 74(3), that its purpose is not to define or enlarge the circumstances in which evidence of the fact that the accused has committed an offence is admissible, but is simply to assist in the mode of proof of that fact. The evidence, of course, must also be relevant to an issue in the proceedings and, it is submitted, may be relevant either to an essential ingredient of the offence charged or some less fundamental issue arising in the course of the proceedings (*Harris* [2001] Crim LR 227, a decision under the original version of s. 74(3), which contained the words 'in so far as that evidence is relevant to any matter in issue in the proceedings...'; and cf. *Robertson* [1987] QB 920, considered at **F12.11**). **F12.19**

There are only four situations, it is submitted, in which reliance may be placed on s. 74(3). The first is where the prosecution seek to prove, as an element of the offence with which the accused is charged, the fact that the accused committed some other offence in respect of which he or she has been convicted. Thus when, after a person's conviction of an offence under the OAPA 1861, s. 18, the victim dies from the injuries and that person is charged with murder, the prosecution, in reliance upon s. 74(3), need prove only that death resulted from the injuries; it is for the accused to prove on a balance of probabilities, if possible, that he or she did not inflict the grievous bodily harm or had no intent to do so (*Clift* [2012] EWCA Crim 2750, [2013] 2 All ER 776, which also makes clear (at [36]), concerning the possibility of exclusion of evidence of the conviction under the PACE 1984, s. 78, that it would be an improper exercise of that discretion to circumvent s. 74(3) 'for no better reason than judicial or academic distaste for it'). The second situation in which reliance may be placed on s. 74(3), illustrated by *Okokono* [2014] EWCA Crim 2521, is where the prosecution seek to adduce relevant evidence of, or of a disposition towards, misconduct on the part of the accused that 'has to do with' the alleged facts of the offence charged, under the CJA 2003, s. 98(a) (see **F13.4** and **F13.10**). The third situation is where the prosecution seek to adduce evidence of the accused's commission of an offence, in respect of which the accused has been convicted, under the CJA 2003, s. 101 (see **F13.15**). The fourth situation is where, a conviction having been proved as part of the prosecution case pursuant to statutory provisions such as s. 101 (see **F13.15**) or the Theft Act 1968, s. 27(3)(b) (see **F13.92**), the accused denies having committed the offence in question.

In *C* [2010] EWCA Crim 2971, [2011] 1 WLR 1942, the following principles were set out with a view to ensuring that where an accused seeks to rebut the presumption under the PACE 1984, s. 74(3), both sides may adduce relevant evidence without turning the trial into a retrial of the offence in question. The prosecution are not required, merely because the accused denies being guilty of the offence, to prove that he or she was, or to assist the accused to prove that he or she was not, or to call witnesses for either purpose. (See also, applying *C* in this respect, *Lunkulu* [2015] EWCA Crim 1350.) The presumption is that the conviction truthfully reflects that the accused committed the offence. Equally, however, the accused cannot be prevented from seeking to demonstrate that he or she did not commit the offence and is entitled to adduce evidence that will prove, whether by cross-examination of prosecution witnesses or calling evidence of his or her own, that the accused was not guilty. If the accused does adduce such evidence, it is open to the Crown to call evidence in rebuttal. It is essential that the defence statement identifies all the ingredients of the case which the accused will advance for the purpose of rebutting the presumption. That may enable the prosecution to prepare draft admissions of fact and to collate the necessary prosecution evidence; the bare assertion by the defence that the accused did not commit the offence is inadequate. The trial judge may make whatever decisions are proper **F12.20** for the proper conduct of the trial, but at the very least it is possible to consider permitting the Crown to postpone its decision whether to call any relevant evidence until after the close of the defence case. See also, in the case of challenging an admission in a police caution, *Olu* [2010] EWCA Crim 2975, [2011] 1 Cr App R 33 (404), considered at **F12.7**.

If the defence wish to rebut the presumption under s. 74(3), this must be clearly raised. In *Reece* [2020] EWCA Crim 44, D did not, in terms, challenge his guilt of the offence in question but gave evidence that raised a possibility that he was not guilty of it. However, neither he nor his advocate raised the question of rebutting the presumption under s. 74(3). It was held that the trial judge had been under no obligation to deal with the matter in his summing-up.

RELEVANCE AND ADMISSIBILITY OF ACQUITTALS

F12.21 Evidence of an earlier acquittal is generally irrelevant and therefore inadmissible, but an exception exists where a witness's credibility is directly in issue and there is a clear inference from the earlier verdict that the jury in that trial rejected his evidence because they did not believe him (*D* [2007] EWCA Crim 684, which is considered, together with the other authorities, at **F1.20**).

In *Sambasivam v Public Prosecutor of Malaya Federation* [1950] AC 458, D was charged with two offences (a) carrying a revolver, in respect of which a new trial was ordered, and (b) being in possession of ten rounds of ammunition (six of which were loaded in the revolver), of which he was acquitted. At the new trial, the prosecution relied on a statement allegedly made by D in which he admitted both charges. D was convicted. The Privy Council quashed the conviction on the ground that the judge should have directed the tribunal of fact that the accused had been acquitted of being in possession of ammunition, and that the prosecution were bound to accept that the part of the alleged statement relating to the ammunition must be regarded as untrue. Lord MacDermott said (at p. 479):

> The effect of a verdict of acquittal pronounced by a competent court on a lawful charge and after a lawful trial is not completely stated by saying that the person acquitted cannot be tried again for the same offence. To that it must be added that the verdict is binding and conclusive in all subsequent proceedings between the parties to the adjudication.

In *Hay* (1983) 77 Cr App R 70, D made a written confession to two unconnected charges, one of arson and one of burglary. At his trial for the arson charge, his confession was admitted in edited form, excluding references to the burglary. His defence was one of alibi and he alleged that the police had fabricated his confession. He was acquitted. At his subsequent trial for burglary, the judge refused to allow D to adduce evidence of the previous acquittal and alibi evidence, ruling that both were irrelevant to the charge of burglary. On appeal against conviction, the Court of Appeal, having considered the passage (set out above) from Lord MacDermott's judgment in *Sambasivam*, allowed the appeal. O'Connor LJ said (at p. 75):

> The jury ought to have been told of the acquittal and directed that it was conclusive evidence that the accused was not guilty of arson, and that his confession to that offence was untrue. The jury should have been directed that in deciding the contest between the appellant and the police officers as to the part of the statement referring to the burglary, they should keep in mind that the first part must be regarded as untrue.

The decisions in *Sambasivam* and *Hay* must be read subject to the subsequent authorities on the topic.

F12.22 The decision in *Sambasivam* is not to be regarded as an authority in support of the existence of the doctrine of issue estoppel, which is inapplicable in criminal cases (*DPP v Humphrys* [1977] AC 1: see **D12.29**). An acquittal is not conclusive evidence of innocence and does not establish that all relevant issues were resolved in favour of the accused (*Terry* [2004] EWCA Crim 3252, [2005] QB 996, considered at **F12.23**). In *Z* [2000] 2 AC 483, D was charged with rape, his defence being consent or mistaken belief in consent. The prosecution wished to adduce evidence of four previous incidents, involving four different women, each of which had resulted in a rape trial at which D's defence had been consent. D was convicted in one of the cases, but was acquitted in the other three. The judge ruled that the evidence came within the ambit of the similar fact doctrine, but that the evidence of the three women in respect of whom D had been acquitted was inadmissible by reason of the statement of Lord MacDermott in *Sambasivam* (as set out at **F12.21**), and that by itself the evidence of the woman in respect of whom D had been convicted did not establish a sufficiently cogent picture of similar facts to be admitted. The Court of Appeal upheld the decision. The prosecution appealed. The House of Lords allowed the appeal on the following grounds:

(a) It had been right to set aside the conviction in *Sambasivam*, but the proper grounds for doing so were those given by Lord Pearce in *Connelly v DPP* [1964] AC 1254 at pp. 1362 and 1364, namely that a person should not be prosecuted a second time where the two offences were in fact founded on one and the same incident (the carrying of the revolver and the ammunition) and that a person should not be tried for a second offence (carrying the revolver in which some of the ammunition was loaded) which was manifestly inconsistent on the facts with a previous acquittal (acquittal of possession of the ammunition). (See also *Yam* [2010] EWCA Crim 2072 at [10]: *Sambasivam* is best explained as an example of the power to prevent an abuse of the process of the court where a further trial would be unfair or oppressive, which involves a judgement of fairness in the light of the individual facts of the case.)
(b) Provided that an accused is not placed in double jeopardy in the way described by Lord Pearce, evidence which is relevant on a subsequent prosecution is not inadmissible because it shows or tends to show that the accused was, in fact, guilty of an offence of which he or she had earlier been acquitted. The statement of Lord MacDermott in *Sambasivam* (as set out at **F12.21**) requires to be qualified in this way.
(c) The judgments in *G (an Infant) v Coltart* [1967] 1 All ER 271 should not be followed: a distinction should not be drawn between evidence which shows guilt of an earlier offence of which the accused has been acquitted and evidence which tends to show guilt of such an offence or which appears to relate to one distinct issue rather than the issue of guilt of such an offence.
(d) In the present case, D would not be placed in double jeopardy and the evidence of the earlier complainants, being relevant and admissible under the similar facts doctrine, should not be inadmissible because it shows that D was in fact guilty of the offences of rape of which he had earlier been acquitted.

In *Terry* [2004] EWCA Crim 3252, [2005] QB 996, it was observed, concerning the passage in the judgment of O'Connor LJ in *Hay* set out above, that it went further than was necessary to correct the judge's decision on relevance and admissibility and was inconsistent with the rationale of the decision in *Z*, because an acquittal is not conclusive evidence of innocence and does not mean that all relevant issues were resolved in favour of the accused. In *Terry*, Auld LJ also observed (at [45]) that the ruling of the House of Lords in *Z* is not restricted to similar fact evidence: the critical questions are whether the evidence in question is admissible, whatever its species, as relevant to an issue in the case, and whether it is fair to admit it. **F12.23**

Section F13 Character Evidence: Evidence of Bad Character of Accused

EVIDENCE OF BAD CHARACTER UNDER THE CJA 2003

Introduction

F13.1 The provisions of Part 11, ch. 1, of the CJA 2003 (ss. 98 to 110 and 112), with minor exceptions, codify the law governing the admissibility of evidence of bad character, replacing both the common law and the previous legislation governing cross-examination of the accused on matters relating to the accused's bad character. The courts have had much work to do to interpret the statutory scheme in a coherent way, but the emergence of a shared approach and common understanding throughout the early judgments of the Court of Appeal resolved many of the ambiguities in the drafting.

The CJA 2003, s. 100, makes separate provision for leave to be obtained before introducing evidence of the bad character of a person other than the accused (see **F15**). Evidence relating to the good character of the accused is dealt with at **F14**.

The bad character provisions should be used in cases where a jury is determining, pursuant to the Criminal Procedure and Insanity Act 1964, s. 4A, whether an accused who is unfit to plead did the act charged. Either the CJA 2003 is of direct application or the court should adopt the same rules of evidence as in criminal proceedings (*Creed* [2011] EWCA Crim 144, applying *Chal* [2007] EWCA Crim 2647, [2008] 1 Cr App R 18 (247), a decision in relation to hearsay evidence: see **F17.1**). In cases under s. 4A it may not be necessary to distinguish sharply between evidence of convictions and of other unproved allegations. Although the person who is unfit to plead will be at a disadvantage in refuting the allegations, this is generally inherent in the very nature of s. 4A proceedings when the ability of an accused to provide advisers with a rational or meaningful account is necessarily limited (*Roberts* [2019] EWCA Crim 1270, [2019] 2 Cr App R 33 (402)).

F13.2 The statutory scheme is a new code designed to ensure that 'evidence of bad character would be put before juries more frequently than had hitherto been the case' (*Edwards* [2005] EWCA Crim 1813, [2006] 1 WLR 1524). Thus, as the Court of Appeal stated in *Chopra* [2006] EWCA Crim 2133, [2007] 1 Cr App R 16 (225) at [12]:

> The right way to deal with the new law is not first to ask what would have been the position under the old. In saying that, we do not doubt that some, perhaps many, of the familiar considerations of relevance and fairness which confronted courts before the 2003 Act in cases of multiple allegations where they were said to be of a similar kind will continue to confront them dealing with such cases afterwards. Nor do we doubt that some of the answers may be the same. There has, however, been a sea-change in the law's starting-point.

This observation, though made in the specific context of cases involving multiple allegations (see **F13.57**), is of equal assistance with regard to other cases in which evidence of bad character is in issue. The rules of the common law are not to be brought back by a restrictive interpretation of the new law (*Bullen* [2008] EWCA Crim 4, [2008] 2 Cr App R 25 (364)). In *Platt* [2016] EWCA Crim 4, [2016] 1 Cr App R 22 (324), the point was emphatically made by Lord Thomas CJ that the statutory language is the sole guide to construction of the current law. The Court of Appeal made clear its view that the common law was not in any way a guide to interpretation of the modern codified provisions. On rare occasions, some reference to pre-Act authority may be proper, for example where it sheds light on matters such as how the Act fits with other relevant rules of evidence such as those governing the standard of proof. In *Mitchell* [2016] UKSC 55, [2017] AC 571, the appellant argued that there was a rule requiring proof to the criminal standard of all so-called 'similar fact' evidence, regardless of the purpose for which it was admitted. Lord Kerr, having examined the old authorities with great care, found no 'clear, definitive statement' on the issue. It does not, of course, follow that, had such a rule been in existence, it would have survived the enactment of the 2003 Act.

Notice Requirements

The relevant rules are in CrimPR Part 21 (see Supplement, **R21.1** *et seq.*). The rules are applied to all parties wishing to adduce evidence of bad character, and also to an accused's application to exclude bad character evidence: all must be in due form and time-limits are set. The requirements apply equally where it is sought to rely on the cross-admissibility of accusations (*Adams* [2019] EWCA Crim 1363: see **F13.57**). The Criminal Procedure (Amendment) Rules 2016 (SI 2016 No. 120) amended r. 21.4 to make provision for the accused who wishes to introduce evidence of his or her own bad character to give notice, in writing or orally, as soon as reasonably practicable and in any event before the evidence is introduced. In *AG* [2018] EWCA Crim 1393, [2018] 2 Cr App R 26 (413), the Court of Appeal specifically discouraged the practice of 'informal' applications to admit bad character evidence. All applications should be made in accordance with CrimPR Part 21. The proper course should be to make a written application (or at least undertake promptly to make such an application), and for a judge to rule on the point, however briefly, as the circumstances may require. **F13.3**

The accused may waive the entitlement to notice, and the court has power to allow notices to be given in a different form, or at a different time, where to do so is in the interests of justice. In *Williams* [2014] EWCA Crim 1862, the propensity of D to make an unprovoked attack might have been introduced in rebuttal of D's defence that S, and not he, had committed the offence, but the prosecution held back in the interests of fairness, electing only to rely on the evidence when it became apparent that the alleged victim of D's previous attack (his mother) was to give evidence that S (who did not give evidence) had confessed to her in what the prosecution regarded as a sustained attempt to pull the wool over the eyes of the jury. The late oral application to admit the evidence was held to be acceptable as D had not been prejudiced; the prosecution had made the defence aware of their intention to rely on this material, and any 'satellite' issues to which it might give rise could have been dealt with through the mother's evidence or if necessary by recalling D.

Where the rules have not been complied with, the court should consider whether to vary the notice requirements using the power in CrimPR 21.6. The power is unfettered, and is not limited to exceptional cases, though the court must bear in mind the importance of its case-management duties (*R (Robinson) v Sutton Coldfield Magistrates' Court* [2006] EWHC 307 (Admin), [2006] 4 All ER 1029, and see the *Crown Court Compendium* (July 2020), ch. 12-1). Where the power is not exercised, the evidence will be excluded, though this should be regarded as a device to prevent unfairness rather than a disciplinary sanction. But there will be cases where the power can properly be deployed to prevent substantial unfairness that cannot be cured by an adjournment (*Musone* [2007] EWCA Crim 1237, [2007] 1 WLR 2467, decided in relation to the notice provisions for hearsay, but held in *Hassett* [2008] EWCA Crim 1634 to be equally germane to bad character). See further, as to the exclusion of evidence tendered by a co-accused, **F13.67**.

Bad Character

F13.4 The CJA 2003, s. 101, provides that evidence of the bad character of an accused is admissible 'if but only if' it falls within a specific statutory permission, or a 'gateway' as the courts commonly say, in s. 101(a) to (g). Other evidence which does not constitute evidence of bad character within the meaning of the Act, but which nevertheless shows the accused in a bad light, may be admitted on normal principles of relevance, subject to the application of the PACE 1984, s. 78 (*Manister*, heard with *Weir* [2005] EWCA Crim 2866, [2006] 2 All ER 570).

Criminal Justice Act 2003, s. 98

> References in this Chapter to evidence of a person's 'bad character' are to evidence of, or of a disposition towards, misconduct on his part, other than evidence which—
> (a) has to do with the alleged facts of the offence with which the defendant is charged, or
> (b) is evidence of misconduct in connection with the investigation or prosecution of that offence.

'Misconduct' means the commission of an offence or other reprehensible behaviour (s. 112(1)). Thus any evidence suggesting guilt of an offence is potentially evidence of misconduct, whether or not the accused has been charged with or convicted of it. In *Clarke* [2015] EWCA Crim 350, [2015] 2 Cr App R 6 (74) it was said that evidence that implies bad character does not have to be the subject of an application under s. 101 if the prosecution rely on it for an independent reason: in that case the evidence was of identification by a prison officer based on a prison sentence served by the accused, and was adduced, following a ruling by the judge, without reference being made in chief to the circumstances of the acquaintance. The problem is that it may not be possible to rely on such evidence without the bad character coming to light (in *Clarke* this was eventually brought out by the cross-examination of the witness) and therefore it might be better to regard all such evidence as requiring the application of s. 101 (and therefore the service of notice: see **F13.3**) even if the prosecution, in the interests of fairness, elect not to make reference to it.

The use of evidence of criminal misconduct not resulting in proceedings may require special caution (see **F13.42**). For multiple charges in the same proceedings, see **F13.57**. For acquittals in previous proceedings, see **F13.65**.

F13.5 **Convictions** Where convictions are relied upon, it is likely that the value of the evidence will depend on the proof of the circumstances of the offence, not merely upon the actual previous conviction and the matters formally established thereby, and such circumstances will require to be properly proved (*Humphris* [2005] EWCA Crim 2030). *Humphris* was approved in *Ainscough* [2006] EWCA Crim 694, where the giving of evidence by a police officer based on data held on the Police National Computer was held to be an inappropriate way to settle a dispute between prosecution and defence as to the facts of the previous convictions. It was also observed that the remedy suggested in *Humphris*—procuring a statement by, or evidence from, the victim of an allegedly similar offence—would not be appropriate in cases where the accused had been dealt with on a plea offered on a different factual basis. The court drew attention to the need for caution and to avoid 'satellite issues' about what did, or did not, happen previously. Where the circumstances of the offence are of the essence, there is an obligation on the party relying upon them to be specific (*Hanson* [2005] EWCA Crim 824, [2005] 1 WLR 3169), and it is good practice for details to be available if required (*Lamaletie* [2008] EWCA Crim 314). Proof of relevant details may be achieved through records admissible under the CJA 2003, s. 117 (*Hogart* [2007] EWCA Crim 338, and see **F17.25**).

Similar considerations apply to the use of cautions and the facts on which they are based. In *Pierce* [2020] EWCA Crim 855, a caution had been admitted by agreement at trial, but it was subsequently challenged and deleted. It was held that because the facts on which the caution was based would in any event have been relevant and admissible at the trial under the provisions of the CJA 2003, s. 101, the deletion of the caution itself did not render D's conviction unsafe. (See generally as to challenging cautions *Olu* [2010] EWCA Crim 2975, [2011] 1 Cr App R 33 (404) at **F12.7**.)

Note that, while it may be convenient to speak and think of 'previous' convictions, offences occurring subsequent to the offence charged may be admissible (*Adenusi* [2006] EWCA Crim

1059), as may evidence of propensity exhibited after the offence, provided that the propensity is one that might be expected to be continuing. In *Norris* [2013] EWCA Crim 712, evidence tending to show that D harboured racist views was admitted to connect him with a racially motivated murder although the evidence was gathered 20 months later; it was open to the jury to draw an inference that D's attitudes were not a recent acquisition. A conviction resulting from a plea of guilty during the instant investigation is also a conviction for these purposes (*Andronicou* [2010] EWCA Crim 2232, where the plea was to an old offence, D having avoided prosecution previously by absconding). See also *Turnbull* [2013] EWCA Crim 676, in which the Court of Appeal identified as potentially 'confusing' an observation by the judge that a plea to an offence under the OAPA 1861, s. 20, was relevant to the question whether D intended to cause grievous bodily harm under s. 18. If a reference is to be made to the plea in these commonly occurring circumstances it would appear crucial to balance it with the clearest direction that the intention for the lesser offence does not establish the ulterior intent for the greater crime.

Convictions before a foreign court may be adduced as evidence of bad character under the CJA 2003 if a corresponding offence in England and Wales would be so treated (s. 103(7)). Correspondence is assessed by looking for an equivalent offence in domestic law at the time of the trial for the current offence. For examples, see *Plaza* [2013] EWCA Crim 501, where a recent Dutch conviction for importing cocaine had 'powerful probative force' in relation to establishing D's involvement in a conspiracy to import cocaine into the UK, and *Brooks* [2014] EWCA Crim 562.

The proof of a conviction creates a rebuttable presumption that the person convicted committed the offence: see, generally, **F12.19** and, as to evidence to show propensity, **F13.47**.

As to the proof that a conviction applies to the individual before the court, see *Lewendon* [2006] EWCA Crim 648, [2006] 1 WLR 1278 and *Burns* [2006] EWCA Crim 617, [2006] 1 WLR 1273, citing *Pattison v DPP* [2005] EWHC 2938 (Admin), [2006] 2 All ER 317 with approval.

Reprehensible Behaviour In *Palmer* [2016] EWCA Crim 2237 the Court of Appeal emphasised that decisions as to what is capable of constituting reprehensible behaviour are fact-specific. In that case, the issue concerned text messages apparently expressing D's desire to stab her partner. To the extent that they had the meaning contended for, the messages were rightly treated as demonstrating reprehensible behaviour at D's trial for murdering him. Although D contended that the messages were not to be taken seriously, this was a matter for the jury. See also *Sepulvida-Gomez* [2019] EWCA Crim 2174, [2020] 4 WLR 11, in which the Court of Appeal noted that opinion might legitimately differ as to whether conduct at the outer limits of the category is 'reprehensible'. In that case the Court was prepared to assume (but did not decide) that D's use of sexual innuendo and his reporting of his own sexual adventures was reprehensible. The evidence was relevant to the way the defence was run, and had been admitted by agreement, so it made no difference to the outcome. In *Hepburn* [2020] EWCA Crim 820, the prosecution relied on evidence of D's involvement in a 'game' to sleep with as many women as possible to show that he was indifferent to whether V was consenting to sexual activity with him when he found her sleeping in the bed of a friend who was also involved in the game. The evidence was regarded as evidence of bad character, and was held to be admissible, on the unusual facts, as either explanatory evidence or evidence going to whether D held a genuine belief in V's consent. **F13.6**

In *Renda* [2005] EWCA Crim 2862, [2006] 2 All ER 553, the Court of Appeal noted that the word 'reprehensible' connoted some element of culpability or blameworthiness. In that case, the fact that D had been found unfit to plead to an incident that involved gratuitous violence was not such as to extinguish the element of culpability. Conduct is not necessarily 'reprehensible' under s. 98 simply because it is morally lax, as in the case of *Manister*, one of the appeals heard with *Weir* [2005] EWCA Crim 2866, [2006] 2 All ER 570. In that case it was held wrong to regard the instigation of a sexual relationship by a man in his thirties with a girl of 16 as 'reprehensible'. As it was relevant, the result was that the evidence was admissible (see **F13.4**). In *Fox* [2009] EWCA Crim 653, the Court of Appeal doubted whether the keeping by D of a notebook containing his 'dirty thoughts' could fall within the provision, but concluded that in any event its prejudicial effect outweighed its probative value. See also *Kiernan* [2008] EWCA Crim 972, where a husband gave his wife forms to sign in blank and this was not misconduct in absence of 'telling and specific' context; as it was not otherwise relevant, it was rightly excluded. What is reprehensible is to be distinguished from what is irritating, inconvenient or upsetting to another (*Scott* [2009] EWCA Crim 2457, decided under s. 100 (see **F15.6** ***et seq.***), in which the complainant in a case of rape and sexual assault had been warned by police to cease her attempts to communicate with a female friend of D). In *Edwards* [2005] EWCA Crim 1813, [2006] 1 WLR 1524, the Court of Appeal cautioned against the inclusion in applications to admit evidence under s. 101 of matters which, on proper analysis, did not disclose bad character (in that case the possession of an antique firearm lawfully held by D). In *Cambridge* [2011] EWCA Crim 2009, the Court of Appeal regarded as 'quixotic' the suggestion that having being shot could be evidence of bad character but, as the shooting had the characteristics of a difference of opinion between gangs, it might have been preferable to treat it as such.

F13.7 In *Osbourne* [2007] EWCA Crim 481, the Court of Appeal considered that 'in the context' of a charge of murder, the aggressive, shouting behaviour of one partner towards another over the care of a young child did not constitute reprehensible behaviour. It would, it is submitted, have been preferable to take a more generalised view of what constitutes reprehensible behaviour, and to hold the shouting to be reprehensible but at the same time not relevant to the charge faced by D (of murdering a drug dealer). A context-specific test for what is reprehensible will render decision-making unnecessarily complex. Violent rap lyrics written by D were regarded as reprehensible behaviour in *Saleem* [2007] EWCA Crim 1766 and in *Awoyemi* [2016] EWCA Crim 668, [2016] 2 Cr App R 22 (303). See as to the now well-established principle of admitting gang membership as evidence of bad character, *Lewis* [2014] EWCA Crim 48 discussed at **F13.49**.

F13.8 The definition of bad character differs from that originally proposed by the Law Commission (*Evidence of Bad Character in Criminal Proceedings*, Law Com No. 273 (2001)), which referred to evidence that a person had behaved, or was disposed to behave, in a way that, in the opinion of the court, might be viewed with disapproval by a reasonable person. This was rejected during the Act's passage through Parliament as too vague and potentially too wide, but it is unclear what is gained by the substitution of 'misconduct' defined in terms of 'reprehensible behaviour'.

F13.9 **Reputation and Bad Character** Section 99(2) of the CJA 2003 preserves the option of proving bad character via reputation at common law, linking with the preserved hearsay exception in s. 118(1) (see **F17.42**). The use of evidence of bad reputation in rebuttal is dealt with at **F14.30**.

F13.10 **'Has to do with' Alleged Facts** Excluded from the definition, and therefore admissible subject to relevance, is evidence of misconduct which 'has to do with the alleged facts' of the offence charged, or which is evidence in connection with the investigation or prosecution of that offence (CJA 2003, s. 98). This loose phrase cannot, as was acknowledged in *McNeill* [2007] EWCA Crim 2927, be given an entirely literal construction but must be read with an understanding of the type of evidence that is only admissible under the 'gateways': in a broad sense all evidence, including evidence of bad character, 'has to do with' the facts, but this cannot be the meaning intended by s. 98 (*Tirnaveanu* [2007] EWCA Crim 1239, [2007] 4 All ER 301, where a broad submission that evidence 'has to do' with the facts if it is central to the prosecution case that the accused was the person who committed the offences was rightly rejected). Section 98 clearly anticipates a 'nexus' between the evidence of misconduct and the alleged offending. In *McNeill*, Rix LJ suggested as one possible interpretation 'anything directly relevant to the offence charged', adding the proviso that the evidence should be 'contemporaneous with and closely associated with its alleged facts'. In *McNeill*, the evidence admitted consisted of a statement made two days after the alleged offence of making a threat to kill, in which D reiterated to a third party her threat to kill the same individual. The commission of a different offence that occurs at or about the time of the offence charged may also fall within the formula, as in *Brand* [2009] EWCA Crim 2878, where D was retried for kidnap and rape, the jury having failed to agree; his conviction at the first trial for stealing the handbag of the victim as part of the same incident was admissible under s. 98(a) and was 'plainly relevant evidence'. In *Hastings-Cokar* [2014] EWCA Crim 555 the temporal principle was held to extend to the discovery of ammunition as a result of an immediate search of premises consequent upon the finding of the firearm that was the subject of the charge; however, had it been treated as bad character evidence, it would still have been admissible. In recent authorities the apparent requirement in *McNeill* for a temporal connection has been modified to the extent that a temporal connection is only one way of supplying the necessary nexus to the facts. Thus in *Sule* [2012] EWCA Crim 1130, [2013] 1 Cr App R 3 (42) the evidence that a killing by D was a reprisal as part of a feud between gangs suggested misconduct over a period of months, but was not thereby rendered inadmissible under s. 98. Stanley Burnton LJ commented that 'where the evidence is reasonably relied upon for motive, it would be irrational to introduce a temporal requirement'. *Sule* was approved in *Lunkulu* [2015] EWCA Crim 1350. In *Lunkulu* the prosecution were held to be entitled under s. 98 to rely on the convictions of D2, D1's co-accused and the alleged mastermind of a murder which D1 was said to have committed. D2's convictions concerned the attempted murder of other members of the rival gang in the period leading up to the murder, and were admissible to show his leading position within his gang and the likelihood of his involvement in the commission of the murder. *Sule* was also cited with approval in *Ditta* [2016] EWCA Crim 8, where it was held that evidence relating to the use of cocaine by D, a solicitor, was rightly admitted at D's trial for doing acts tending and intended to pervert the course of justice by, *inter alia*, passing on information about police drugs operations to his supplier. The misconduct provided a reason for the commission of the alleged offence.

A similar case is *Okokono* [2014] EWCA Crim 2521, where a gang-related killing was alleged to have been carried out in revenge for an earlier murder, and the conviction of one of the participants for carrying a knife at the time of the earlier killing was 'highly relevant' to the facts of the instant case, applying s. 98. However, the evidence was also admissible under s. 101(1)(c) and (d) (see **F13.29**). Comments in *Fox* [2009] EWCA Crim 653, to the effect that the words 'has to do with' relate only to the *actus reus* of the offence, were disapproved in *IA* [2013] EWCA Crim 1308, where the correct approach was said to be one of 'direct relevance', which must be correct. A similar approach was taken in *Morris* [2019] EWCA Crim 147, in which evidence in support of a count which should not have been before the jury was held to 'have to do with' another more serious count for which D was properly tried, it being material to, and 'part of the history' of that count.

See also **F15.7**, regarding evidence 'having to do' with the facts where the evidence concerns the bad character of a person other than the accused, in particular *Machado* [2006] EWCA Crim 837.

It will be seen that there is often a fine line between evidence of this kind and evidence which is admissible only via a specific gateway. In many of the cases in which s. 98 is invoked, the point is made that the evidence, had the submission failed, would have been admissible under s. 101(c) or (d). In *Sullivan* [2015] EWCA Crim 1565, the Court of Appeal rejected the prosecution's contention that D's previous involvement in cannabis cultivation satisfied the factual nexus, as it showed an accumulation of experience of how to raise such a crop, and rebutted his defence that a lodger was growing cannabis on his premises and without his knowledge. The '(criminal) educational opportunity' provided by past instances of offending does not make it '*to do with*' the instant charge; however, the Court held that the evidence was clearly admissible under gateway (d) as 'relevant to an important matter in issue between the defendant and the prosecution' (see **F13.36**) to show that D was unlikely to have been ignorant of the cultivation taking place on premises occupied by him, and that D was likely to have been involved in its production. In *M* [2006] EWCA Crim 193, the complainant was cross-examined as to why, in the aftermath of an alleged rape, she was passive, made no complaint and got into a car with her alleged attacker. This rendered admissible her account of previous threats to shoot her and her belief that D had a gun. The evidence was thought to 'have to do with' the alleged facts, but if not the court thought it was admissible under gateway (c) as 'explanatory' evidence (see **F13.28**). In drugs cases, 'lifestyle' evidence may be received to support an inference that the accused's income must be derived from drugs (*Green* [2009] EWCA Crim 1688). The trial judge was held to have correctly directed the jury to consider whether D's standard of living was explicable only by D being part of one of the **F13.11** conspiracies charged. This would not preclude the use of such evidence to establish guilt via an inference of propensity under gateway (d) in an appropriate case. In *Awoyemi* [2016] EWCA Crim 668, [2016] 2 Cr App R 22 (303), where evidence of gang membership was adduced under s. 101, the Court of Appeal noted that such evidence might also fall within s. 98, depending on the facts. In *Mohammed* [2013] EWCA Crim 901, a 'deal list' was admitted that referred both to cannabis, which was the subject of the charge, and to cocaine, which was not. It was held that the issue of the admissibility of the references to cocaine should have been considered separately under s. 101(1)(d), while the references to cannabis were 'to do' with the charge and were rightly admitted. A similar problem regarding entries in a notebook recording different types of drug dealings led the Court of Appeal in *RJ* [2017] EWCA Crim 1943 to emphasise that particular care may be needed to distinguish between the grounds for admitting apparently similar items of evidence. In *Lunkulu* evidence of D2's conviction for possession of a firearm and ammunition with intent to endanger life was inadmissible under s. 98, but was successfully adduced as evidence of his bad character under s. 101(1)(d), to show both a relevant propensity and access to firearms. The fine dividing line between cases involving bad character evidence and cases falling within s. 98 is cited in the *Crown Court Compendium* (July 2020), ch. 12-1, as a reason for the court to have in mind the safeguards attaching to the former when considering the latter, and to 'consider appropriate directions to the jury on the use to which it should be put and, if appropriate, the weight they should attach to that evidence'. In *Lovell* [2018] EWCA Crim 19, [2018] 1 Cr App R (S) 48 (364), evidence of D's threatening conduct towards an associate of the man D was charged with murdering was held admissible under s. 101(1)(c) and (d), as well as under s. 98(a), because there was a sufficiently close link in time and subject-matter. The Court of Appeal observed that by admitting the evidence via the statutory gateway rather than, as he might have done, under s. 98(a) the judge had given the defence the additional benefit of making submissions as to the 'fairness' of admitting the evidence under s. 101(3). A similar concern seems to have informed the decision of the trial judge in *Denton* [2020] EWCA Crim 410 to apply the bad character safeguards of s. 100 (see **F15.7**) to a defence application to adduce evidence suggesting that a prosecution witness acted with hostile animus in connection with the facts under investigation. As the Court of Appeal found that the alleged animus was not relevant to any disputed matters, the point was not considered on appeal, but seems to have been approved.

F13.12 **Misconduct in Connection with Investigation or Prosecution** A 'gateway' is not necessary in order to admit evidence relating, say, to the telling of lies in interview or the attempted intimidation of witnesses, as this would appear to be 'misconduct in connection with the investigation or prosecution of the offence', as referred to in the CJA 2003, s. 98(b). That provision is not limited to conduct by the prosecuting authorities (*Apabhai* [2011] EWCA Crim 917, where evidence of an attempt by a co-accused to blackmail D in relation to the matters under investigation was held to be within the provision). On the facts, it was also the case that the purpose of adducing the evidence was not to demonstrate the co-accused's bad character, but rather to show his motive for incriminating D. The question of purpose would not, however, appear to be relevant to the question of admissibility under s. 98(b).

F13.13 **Bad Character and Cross-examination** The prohibition on evidence of 'bad character' applies whether the evidence is employed as evidence-in-chief or in cross-examination of the accused. Thus the evidence that is admissible under the gateways in s. 101(1)(c) to (g) includes evidence that 'a witness is to be invited to give in cross-examination' (s. 104(2), regarding evidence elicited for the co-accused, and s. 112(1), defining the meaning of 'prosecution evidence' for the purposes of the other provisions). It must follow from this, that the mere putting of a question to which a truthful answer would elicit inadmissible evidence of bad character is also normally impermissible — although the matter could have been made clearer.

F13.14 **Previous Allegations as Evidence of Bad Character** It does not appear that the CJA 2003, s. 98, conveys any necessary protection against the revelation of a mere charge (either in the sense of 'charged in court', as in *Stirland v DPP* [1944] AC 315, or in the sense of having been previously suspected) unless the suggestion is that the accused committed the offence with which he or she was charged, so that the allegation becomes one of the commission of an offence (see **F13.4**). However, the court should not permit a matter to be raised unless it is demonstrably relevant. The mere fact that an allegation has been made, without supporting evidence, will not normally be relevant either to guilt or to the credibility of the accused as a witness (*Bovell* [2005] EWCA Crim 1091, [2005] 2 Cr App R 27 (401) (decided under s. 100), *Edwards* [2005] EWCA Crim 1813, [2006] 1 WLR 1524). Where it is relevant, it may be admitted where the purpose is not to show bad character (*Hussain* [2008] EWCA Crim 1117), and see further the discussion of the same point in relation to s. 100 where the evidence of previous allegations is tendered against a person other than the accused (see **F15.13**).

Evidence of a previous acquittal is unlikely to be of relevance, except where it is contended that the accused committed the offence, in which case it is likely to be objectionable on grounds of unfairness. The rare cases where it is not unfair so to contend are considered at **F13.65**.

The Statutory 'Gateways' — Overview

Criminal Justice Act 2003, s. 101 **F13.15**

(1) In criminal proceedings evidence of the defendant's bad character is admissible if, but only if—
  (a) all parties to the proceedings agree to the evidence being admissible,
  (b) the evidence is adduced by the defendant himself or is given in answer to a question asked by him in cross-examination and intended to elicit it,
  (c) it is important explanatory evidence,
  (d) it is relevant to an important matter in issue between the defendant and the prosecution,
  (e) it has substantial probative value in relation to an important matter in issue between a defendant and a co-defendant,
  (f) it is evidence to correct a false impression given by the defendant, or
  (g) the defendant has made an attack on another person's character.
(2) Sections 102 to 106 contain provision supplementing subsection (1).
(3) The court must not admit evidence under subsection (1)(d) or (g) if, on an application by the defendant to exclude it, it appears to the court that the admission of the evidence would have such an adverse effect on the fairness of the proceedings that the court ought not to admit it.
(4) On an application to exclude evidence under subsection (3) the court must have regard, in particular, to the length of time between the matters to which that evidence relates and the matters which form the subject of the offence charged.

Section 101(1)(a) makes it clear that evidence of bad character may be admissible by general consensus of the parties (compare the corresponding provision making hearsay admissible by agreement in s. 114(1)(c): see **F16.1** and **F17.6**). Thus, for example, in *Kalu* [2007] EWCA Crim 22, a caution for excessive chastisement was admitted by agreement and relied on by both prosecution and defence: by the defence to support a claim that D had learned his lesson, and by the prosecution as part of an alleged history of cruelty to the children in his care. Evidence admitted 'without demur' by skilled counsel may be said to have been admitted by 'tacit' agreement (*Marsh* [2009] EWCA Crim 2696). See also *J (DC)* [2010] EWCA Crim 385, [2010] 2 Cr App R 2 (8), where it was said that, in the interests of good trial management, the court should be informed of any agreement to admit bad character evidence at the beginning of the trial. Further, the mere fact of agreement, though sufficient to overcome an objection based on bad character (or hearsay: as to which, see **F17.6**) did not justify putting in evidence documents subject to public interest immunity disclosed for the purpose of cross-examination of prosecution witnesses, for which a further order would have been required. Where there are multiple defendants, the gateway clearly requires that the consent of all must be secured, bearing in mind that they may have very different interests (*Ferdinand* [2014] EWCA Crim 1243). **F13.16**

Section 101(1)(b) retains the rule that the accused can elect to tender evidence of his or her own bad character. A common reason for doing so is to lay a foundation so that the accused may argue never to have been previously convicted of an offence similar to that charged. In *Hunter* [2015] EWCA Crim 631, [2015] 1 WLR 5367 (see **F14.3** *et seq.*) the Court of Appeal reformulated the **F13.17** rules governing the presentation of an accused as a person of good character, with the result that anyone with a subsisting and relevant conviction is unlikely to receive a full 'good character' direction. Nevertheless, the argument that an accused's convictions are of a different type may still be relevant, for example where the accused contends that any previous offending is relatively low-level and nothing like as serious as the offences charged (as in *Sami* [2018] EWCA Crim 552, [2019] 1 WLR 66) or where the accused has previously pleaded guilty and admitted liability, so that the decision to contest the instant charge may be some evidence of the accused's innocence. *Hunter* permits a modified good character direction in the judge's discretion, in such cases (see **F14.10** and CrimPR 21.4; see Supplement, **R21.4**). Such a direction will inevitably be tailored to the specific facts. In *Speed* [2013] EWCA Crim 1650, D chose to adduce his previous convictions for property and drug-related offences to show that he had no propensity for sexual offending, but admitted to telling lies and to pleading not guilty to offences he had committed. The judge's balanced direction, which made reference to the negative impact on credibility of D's record, was approved, the Court of Appeal stating, 'it would be inappropriate in a gateway (b) situation for a defendant to have carte blanche to make such points as he wishes about his criminal record, without facing the possibility that his record does him no favours as far as credibility is concerned'. Where evidence of relatively minor bad character is tendered to prevent the jury from speculating that it is worse than it is, the *Crown Court Compendium* (July 2020), ch. 12-4, states that the judge should direct that the evidence has been admitted 'only so that they know of the whole background and, if appropriate, that the evidence does not make it more or less likely that D committed the offence'.

F13.18 Section 101(1)(c) broadly reflects the common law on 'background' evidence, and is dealt with further at **F13.28**. Section 101(1)(d), however, cuts across much of the thinking of the old law by regarding as admissible evidence that is merely 'relevant' to an important issue between the accused and the prosecution. At common law, a high degree of probative value was required in order to overcome the prejudicial effect involved in the reception of such evidence (*DPP v P* [1991] 2 AC 447). The CJA 2003 removes this requirement from the test of admissibility, relegating questions of fairness to the court's power to exclude evidence to avoid prejudice (s. 101(3): see **F13.19**). *Weir* [2005] EWCA Crim 2866, [2006] 2 All ER 570 makes it clear that the CJA 2003 'completely reverses the pre-existing general rule' and that the 'one-stage test which balanced probative value against prejudicial effect is obsolete'.

The most radical aspect of the change brought about by s. 101(1)(d) in combination with s. 103 is that an accused's propensity becomes a matter towards which relevant prosecution evidence may be directed (see **F13.39** ***et seq.***). Section 101(1)(d) has the additional function of admitting evidence to show the untruthfulness of an accused person, and this is dealt with at **F13.44**. Section 101(1)(e) permits a co-accused to adduce evidence of the accused's bad character where it has substantial value in relation to an important issue between them (see **F13.66** ***et seq.***). Section 101(1)(f) (evidence to correct a false impression) is dealt with at **F13.78** and s. 101(1)(g) (evidence to meet an attack on another person) is dealt with at **F13.84**.

Where the evidence of bad character is disputed, s. 109 (see **F13.61**) requires the court to consider its relevance and probative value on the assumption that it is true, unless it appears that no court or jury could reasonably find it to be true. The proliferation of satellite issues that may arise in settling the dispute may be a relevant consideration in the ultimate determination of its probative value (*Dizaei* [2013] EWCA Crim 88, [2013] 1 Cr App R 31 (411), decided under the CJA 2003, s. 100: see **F15.24**).

Inherent in the gateways, and in the provisions of ss. 102 to 106 which explain the key terms therein, is a sense of the separation of the function of evidence going to the issue and that going to credit. This distinction is called into question in *Campbell* [2007] EWCA Crim 1472, [2007] 1 WLR 2798 (see **F13.24**), where the point is made that the pre-Act law was over-dependent on it to the point of contravening common sense; e.g., where evidence of offences of the same type as the offence charged was regarded as relevant only to the credit of the accused as a witness. *Campbell* champions a broader mandate for common sense at the risk of rendering meaningless the impact of the distinction within the CJA 2003 itself.

POWERS OF EXCLUSION

Criminal Justice Act 2003, s. 101 F13.19

(3) The court must not admit evidence under subsection (1)(d) or (g) if, on an application by the defendant to exclude it, it appears to the court that the admission of the evidence would have such an adverse effect on the fairness of the proceedings that the court ought not to admit it.

The principal mechanism by which the court can ensure that an accused is not prejudiced by revelations of evidence under s. 101(1)(d) or (g) is the exclusionary power under s. 101(3): that it appears to the court that the admission of the evidence would have such an adverse effect on the fairness of the proceedings that the court ought not to admit it.

The power, it should be noted, comes into play on application by the defence to exclude the evidence rather than on the prosecution application to admit it. The power under s. 101(3) does not appear to be exercisable by the court of its own motion (*Highton* [2005] EWCA Crim 1985, [2005] 1 WLR 3472) but, if necessary (e.g. to protect an unrepresented accused), an application could be prompted by the court.

In *Hanson* [2005] EWCA Crim 824, [2005] 1 WLR 3169, the Vice-President (Rose LJ) drew attention to the wording 'must not admit', in s. 101(3), with the comment that this was a stronger formula than the one in use in the PACE 1984, s. 78 ('may refuse to allow'). His lordship also expressed the hope that prosecutors would not routinely apply to use evidence of the accused's convictions, but would take into account the particular circumstances of each case. The difference in wording was also noted in *Weir* [2005] EWCA Crim 2866, [2006] 2 All ER 570, but the currently preferred view is to regard the two provisions as being on all fours in that a court has no discretion under s. 78 once the conditions for exclusion are satisfied (*Tirnaveanu* [2007] EWCA Crim 1239, [2007] 4 All ER 301).

F13.20 Section 101(3) cannot be used to restrict any of the other five gateways, which appear to lead directly to admissibility. This raises no issues of difficulty in relation to (a) or (b), where the accused has control over the issue. It may be a source of difficulty in relation to (e), where it is the co-accused who is entitled to invoke the exception, but the rule that there is no discretion to restrain the co-accused in tendering relevant evidence is well-established and of general application (see, e.g., *Murdoch v Taylor* [1965] AC 574, decided under previous legislation). In relation to explanatory evidence admitted under s. 101(1)(c), however, and evidence to correct a false impression under s. 101(1)(f), it may be envisaged that there will be cases where the defence will seek to make an argument for exclusion based on unfairness.

As there is no specific provision in the CJA 2003, Part 11, ch. 1, that excludes the operation of s. 78 of the PACE 1984, it has so far been accepted that it still applies. In *Highton*, a case which did not call directly for the application of s. 78, the inclination of the Court of Appeal was to say that it provided 'an additional protection' to an accused. Judges were encouraged to apply s. 78 pending a definitive ruling to the contrary, so as to avoid any risk of injustice. In considering the appeal of *Somanathan*, one of the appeals heard with *Weir* [2005] EWCA Crim 2866, [2006] 2 All ER 570, the Court of Appeal noted that, of the three provisions relied upon by the prosecution, s. 101(3) applied to two, but not to the third, (i.e. s. 101(1)(f)). The Court saw 'no reason to doubt' that s. 78 should be considered where s. 101(1)(f) is relied on, although (as in *Highton*) it did not assist the applicant to do so. See also *O'Dowd* [2009] EWCA Crim 905, [2009] 2 Cr App R 16 (280). For the position in relation to gateway (c), see *Davis* [2008] EWCA Crim 1156, [2009] 2 Cr App R 17 (306) at **F13.31**.

F13.21 The main argument against the application of s. 78 is that the CJA 2003, Part 11, ch. 2, which deals with hearsay, includes a provision under which the effect of s. 78 is specifically preserved, together with the operation of any other power of the court to exclude evidence at its discretion (s. 126(2)), and there is no such provision in relation to bad character. In favour of its application is that, where the court sees the exclusion of the evidence as necessary in order to ensure a fair trial under the ECHR, Article 6, this should be sufficient to override any inference arising from the structure of the Act that Parliament's intention was to exclude the general operation of s. 78, and it is this view that should prevail. In *Highton* Lord Woolf noted that s. 78 serves 'a very similar purpose' to Article 6. In *Dixon* [2012] EWCA Crim 2163 the Court of Appeal respectfully agreed with Lord Woolf's observations, and drew particular attention (at [13]) to the 'repeated references to "fairness"' in the statutory provisions as support for this view.

For discretionary exclusion generally, see **F2.36** ***et seq.***

WEIGHT OF CHARACTER EVIDENCE AND JUDICIAL DIRECTION

Introduction

F13.22 In interpreting the provisions the courts have accepted that the CJA 2003 provides a new framework for the wider admissibility of evidence of bad character, making a small but crucial adjustment to the literal wording to ensure that s. 78 of the PACE 1984 can be invoked despite Parliament's apparent intention to restrict its application (see **F13.21**). The key stages are now as set out in *Edwards* [2005] EWCA Crim 1813, [2006] 1 WLR 1524:

(1) The judge determines admissibility under the relevant statutory gateway(s).
(2) Where it is raised, the judge also determines any question of exclusion in respect of prosecution evidence, for example, under s. 101(3) or 103(3) of the CJA 2003, or s. 78 of the PACE 1984.
(3) Once evidence of bad character is admitted, questions of weight are for the jury, subject to the judge's power to stop the case where the evidence is contaminated (under s. 107 at **F13.62**) and the judge's direction as to the use to which the evidence may be put.
(4) The direction on the evidence is of paramount importance. If the ground of the trial has shifted since the evidence was admitted, it may be necessary to tell the jury that it is of little weight.

The Court of Appeal also expressed the view that, if evidence of marginal relevance was tendered under s. 101, it was potentially difficult for the judge to deal with in summing-up, and this should be borne in mind by the parties. This reflects observations in the earlier case of *Hanson* [2005] EWCA Crim 824, [2005] 1 WLR 3169, which was approved in *Edwards*, where the Court stated that the purpose of the legislation was 'to assist in the evidence-based conviction of the guilty, without putting those who are not guilty at risk of conviction by prejudice'. As in *Edwards*, much stress was laid on the importance of the direction to the jury, but the hope was also expressed that the prosecution would avoid routine applications wherever an accused has previous convictions, preferring rather to focus on the particular circumstances of each case. The absence of an adequate direction on character evidence was fatal to the conviction in *Sullivan* [2015] EWCA Crim 1565. The Court of Appeal approved passages in *Campbell* [2007] EWCA Crim 1472, [2007] 1 WLR 2798 where it was said that the jury should be given assistance as to the relevance of the evidence that is tailored to the facts of the individual case, together with an explanation of why it has been admitted and a warning against attaching too much weight to an accused's bad character. Instead, the matter had been left entirely to the jury without clear guidance, rendering the conviction unsafe.

F13.23 *Hanson* also outlines the content of a direction on bad character which, though couched in terms of a case involving evidence of propensity, is of more general relevance. A proper direction should:

(1) give the jury a clear warning against the dangers of placing undue reliance on previous convictions;
(2) stress that evidence of bad character cannot be used to bolster a weak case, or to prejudice a jury against the defendant;
(3) emphasise that the jury should not infer guilt from the existence of convictions.

Further and detailed general guidance on directing the jury is given in the *Crown Court Compendium* (July 2020), ch. 12-2, the importance of which was stressed in *AG* [2018] EWCA Crim 1393, [2018] 2 Cr App R 26 (413). The *Compendium* notes that evidence may be admitted under more than one gateway, and be relevant to more than one issue in the case. Central to the direction, therefore, is the identification of the purpose or purposes for which the evidence may be used, and equally of any purpose for which it may not be used. An important distinction is drawn between evidence going to the issues and evidence bearing on credibility. Separate consideration should be given to the appropriate direction in relation to both these matters. The protection of the accused from prejudice arising from the use of convictions (or, it would seem, of any other evidence of bad character) under the CJA 2003 depends critically on the ability of the jury to adhere to judicial guidance: the judicial direction was described in *Eastlake* [2007] EWCA Crim 603 as the 'safety valve' within the scheme, and in *Isichei* [2006] EWCA Crim 1815 the Court of Appeal noted the dependence of the system on the jury's loyalty to, and understanding of, the judge's directions. In *X* [2012] EWCA Crim 2276 convictions were quashed where a direction had, *inter alia*, failed to warn against placing undue reliance on convictions and that a relevant propensity, if established, would be only one factor to consider. See also *Hackett* [2019] EWCA Crim 983, in which the trial judge failed to address the weight and significance of a considerable volume of bad character evidence, much of which was disputed and some of which ought not to have been before the jury in the first place. D's conviction for sexual assault was quashed. In *Ellis* [2010] EWCA Crim 163, the failure to direct the jury not to infer that D had been untruthful in the instant case because he had been so on previous occasions was an omission 'of some significance', although not, on the facts, such as to render his conviction unsafe. See also *Bullas* [2012] All ER (D) 21 (Nov), where it was held that the jury would have realised (despite the absence of a direction) that evidence of D's homosexual tendencies was admitted simply to rebut his specific denial of the matter, and not to suggest any propensity to commit the sexual assaults on young boys with which he was charged. See also **F13.6**.

Evidence Once Admitted Can be Used for All Relevant Purposes

Of particular difficulty in directions under the pre-Act law was the case where an aspect of the accused's bad character was admissible for a specific purpose and no other. This problem is largely avoided under the CJA 2003 by decisions holding that evidence, once it passes through a gateway, may be used for any purpose for which it is relevant. In *Highton* [2005] EWCA Crim 1985, [2005] 1 WLR 3472 it was held that evidence admitted under the gateway in s. 101(1)(g) of the CJA 2003 (following an attack on another person's character) was not to be used merely as a yardstick by which to measure the credit to be given to the accused's account: 'the use to which [evidence] may be put depends upon the matters to which it is relevant, rather than upon the gateway through which it was admitted'. In *Edwards* [2005] EWCA Crim 1813, [2006] 1 WLR 1524 it was held, following *Highton*, that evidence admitted at the accused's own behest under s. 101(1)(b) could thereafter be used as evidence for any relevant purpose. More crucially, *Highton* was said in *Campbell* [2007] EWCA Crim 1472, [2007] 1 WLR 2798 to apply where evidence of D's propensity to violence had been properly admitted under s. 101(1)(d), and the issue was as to its use in relation to his credibility (the converse of the situation in *Highton* itself). The Court of Appeal, while accepting the general guidance in *Hanson* [2005] EWCA Crim 824, [2005] 1 WLR 3169 (see **F13.22**), stressed the importance of relating the evidence to the facts of the case in a common-sense way, bearing in mind that 'if the jury learn that a defendant has shown a propensity to commit criminal acts they may well at one and the same time conclude that he is guilty and that he is less likely to be telling the truth when he says that he is not'. In *Singh* [2007] EWCA Crim 2140, in which the evidence had been admitted via gateway (g), Hughes LJ stressed that the evidence thus admitted for all purposes was more broadly based than would have been permissible under gateway (d) in relation to evidence probative either of guilt or untruthfulness. A careful direction was also given in *Singh* in 'mitigation of' D's bad character, to the effect that he had pleaded guilty to his past offences. *Singh* was applied in relation to evidence admitted at D's behest under gateway (b) in *Speed* [2013] EWCA Crim 1650 (see **F13.17**). **F13.24**

In *Lafayette* [2008] EWCA Crim 3238, the Court of Appeal noted that a conviction which was relevant and admissible under s. 101(1)(g) following an attack on a prosecution witness might **F13.25** not be relevant to any issue of propensity. In such a case, a specific direction to use the evidence in relation to credibility only would be advisable. The decision is not inconsistent with *Highton* or *Campbell*, which were dealing with evidence which was doubly relevant. In such cases it would be 'highly artificial' to direct the jury to confine their use of the evidence to the specific purpose for which it was originally admitted (*Abdullah* [2019] EWCA Crim 1137). In *Williams* [2011] EWCA Crim 2198, D's previous convictions were not relied on as evidence of propensity and, though relevant to credibility under gateway (g), there was a risk that their prejudicial effect would outweigh their probative value in the absence of 'sufficiently strong and clear' directions as to the limited purpose for which they were admissible. No such direction having been given, the Court of Appeal could not be satisfied that the jury had not drawn impermissible inferences from the previous convictions, and D's appeal was allowed. See also *Tollady* [2010] EWCA Crim 2614, in which evidence of her own prior conviction was adduced by D in order to make a point about the hostility of the officer who had arrested her on that occasion. There were similarities in relation to D's aggressive behaviour on both occasions that rendered the conviction relevant in respect of D's criminal propensity. However, the Court of Appeal considered (at [26]) that the five-year-old conviction for disorderly behaviour to which D had pleaded guilty, even if technically admissible in relation to D's credibility under *Campbell*, ought not to have been drawn to the jury's attention in the summing-up as having a bearing on that issue.

F13.26 A potentially disturbing aspect of *Campbell* is the suggestion that an omission to direct the jury on the relevance of bad character will, to the extent that the application of the evidence to the facts is simply a matter of common sense, not automatically be treated as a ground of appeal. See also *Saleem* [2007] EWCA Crim 1923 (where the Court of Appeal said that 'although the judge could have given the jury more help than he did, we do not consider that his failure to do so rendered the conviction unsafe, as the jury would have appreciated the relevance of the evidence'), *Walker* [2007] EWCA Crim 2631, and *Marsh* [2009] EWCA Crim 2696. The courts should not be quick to assume that juries exercise the same 'common sense' as judges in respect of evidence of bad character. Reassuringly, in *O'Dowd* [2009] EWCA Crim 905, [2009] 2 Cr App R 16 (280), the Court of Appeal affirmed the duty 'save in the simplest of cases' to pull together in a direction the strengths and weaknesses of bad character evidence in a manner tailored to the evidence in the case. The *Crown Court Compendium*, by specifying the directions appropriate under the different gateways and for evidence admitted for different purposes, also lends support to the view that such assistance is of great importance.

Reasons for Rulings

F13.27 **Criminal Justice Act 2003, s. 110**

(1) Where the court makes a relevant ruling—
   (a) it must state in open court (but in the absence of the jury, if there is one) its reasons for the ruling;
   (b) if it is a magistrates' court, it must cause the ruling and the reasons for it to be entered in the register of the court's proceedings.
(2) In this section 'relevant ruling' means—
   (a) a ruling on whether an item of evidence is evidence of a person's bad character;
   (b) a ruling on whether an item of such evidence is admissible under section 100 or 101 (including a ruling on an application under section 101(3));
   (c) a ruling under section 107.

Section 107, which codifies the power of the court to stop a case where contaminated evidence of bad character has been admitted, is considered at **F13.62**.

There is a general duty, in the terms described in s. 110, to give reasons for rulings in relation to bad character. When considering the trial judge's stance in *Osbourne*, one of the appeals heard with *Renda* [2005] EWCA Crim 2862, [2006] 2 All ER 553, the Court of Appeal indicated that the mere observation that the jury was entitled to know about character was regarded as an 'over-parsimonious' compliance with s. 110. The point at issue concerned the character of a witness rather than an accused (s. 100: see **F15**) but it is submitted that the principle is the same.

In *PB* [2016] EWCA Crim 1462, D was charged with the rape of a child under 13, and the prosecution case was that he had gained access to V by deceiving E, the mother, about his past, and about his intentions towards the family. Evidence was given by W, a mother of five children with whom D had formed a relationship, and who claimed to have been similarly deceived about his past, although there was no evidence of impropriety between D and any of W's children. It was held that the judge ought to have been clear about the applicable gateway(s) of admissibility and addressed the provisions of s. 101(3) (see **F13.15**) in his ruling. Nevertheless, the direction to the jury had made sufficiently clear that the evidence of W was relevant to the case only if the jury were sure that W's evidence demonstrated that D's real interest was in the children, and that he had set about deceiving her in the same way as the prosecution claimed he had deceived E.

EXPLANATORY EVIDENCE

Introduction

In the CJA 2003, s. 101(1)(c), special provision is made for the admission of 'explanatory' evidence — evidence without which it would be 'impossible or difficult to understand other evidence in the case' — provided that its value for understanding the case as a whole is substantial. It follows that, where the evidence requires no 'footnote or lexicon' but is readily understandable without evidence of bad character, s. 101(1)(c) does not apply (*Beverley* [2006] EWCA Crim 1287). See also *Davis* [2008] EWCA Crim 1156, [2009] 2 Cr App R 17 (306) (issue of provocation 'entirely comprehensible' without evidence of bad character). **F13.28**

The operation of the statutory provision is not confined to prosecution evidence. Section 101(1)(c) is supplemented by s. 102.

Criminal Justice Act 2003, ss. 101 and 102

101.—(1) In criminal proceedings evidence of the defendant's bad character is admissible if, but only if—

...

(c) it is important explanatory evidence;

...

102. For the purposes of section 101(1)(c) evidence is important explanatory evidence if—

(a) without it, the court or jury would find it impossible or difficult properly to understand other evidence in the case, and

(b) its value for understanding the case as a whole is substantial.

Where an offence is alleged it may be necessary to give evidence of the background against which the offence is committed, even though to do so will reveal facts showing the accused in a discreditable light. The bad character thus revealed is frequently incidental to the offence charged, as in *Neale* (1977) 65 Cr App R 304, where the offence was arson of a hostel for offenders and the explanatory evidence showed that D was an inmate, and *Toussaint-Collins* [2009] EWCA Crim 316, where it was revealed that a letter which was relevant to the proceedings was sent by D from prison. Alternatively, the accused's bad character may constitute a relevant part of the background. In *C* [2012] EWCA Crim 2034, for example, evidence of sexual abuse and domination of the complainant by D during her childhood was necessary to explain why her apparent compliance in a sexual relationship with him after her sixteenth birthday should not be regarded as indicating her genuine consent. **F13.29**

The necessity to admit evidence for its explanatory as distinct from its probative value, was well accepted at common law in a line of authorities that continue to be relevant under the CJA 2003 (*Osbourne* [2007] EWCA Crim 481). The principle derives from the judgment of Purchas LJ in *Pettman* (2 May 1985 unreported) who said:

> Where it is necessary to place before the jury evidence of part of a continual background of history relevant to the offence charged in the indictment and without the totality of which the account placed before the jury would be incomplete or incomprehensible, then the fact that the whole

account involves including evidence establishing the commission of an offence with which the accused is not charged is not of itself a ground for excluding the evidence.

In *Dolan* [2002] EWCA Crim 1859, [2003] 1 Cr App R 18 (281) the Court of Appeal approved the basis for admitting background evidence as explained in the commentary on *Stevens* [1995] Crim LR 649, where it was said that 'it is helpful to have it and difficult for the jury to do their job if events are viewed in total isolation from their history'. That the evidence is helpful is not by itself enough, nor is it sufficient that the jury might wonder about a gap in the evidence that the bad character evidence might fill; to say that the evidence fills out the picture is not the same as saying that the picture is impossible or difficult to see without it (*Lee* [2012] EWCA Crim 316). *Lee* was distinguished in *Leathem* [2017] EWCA Crim 42, where a floorplan of a house drawn by D1 was found concealed at the home of his cousin D2, and the prosecution case was that D1 had drawn the plan to enable D2 to burgle the property and steal the elderly owner's firearms. At the trial of D2 and D1 for conspiracy to burgle, D1's defence was that he had drawn the plan for innocent reasons and must have dropped it at D2's house. Evidence of D2's previous convictions was admitted as explanatory evidence showing that D2 was part of an active and serious organised crime group that was in the habit of committing burglaries to 'tool up' for robberies. On the facts it would have been 'impossible or difficult' for the jury to understand the true significance of the prosecution evidence without knowing of D2's gang's campaign of burglary and robbery. While the outcome may owe much to the difficulties of establishing the existence of an agreement for the purposes of a charge of conspiracy, the evidence of D2's propensity, once admitted, was potentially devastating, and it is submitted that the decision might have been better based on the CJA 2003, s. 101(1)(d) (see **F13.36**), given that the latter is specifically subject to constraints of fairness which do not apply to explanatory evidence. The Court of Appeal agreed that this would have provided an alternative ground for admitting the evidence.

Explanatory evidence should be carefully scrutinised to ensure that it does not become a backdoor method of smuggling in prejudicial evidence of propensity. Under s. 101(1)(d), relevant evidence of propensity is admissible and is likely, subject to an argument about exclusion based on prejudice, to be admitted (e.g., in *Golds* [2014] EWCA Crim 748, [2015] 1 WLR 1030, where evidence of a 'background of violence' in D's relationship with his partner was not strictly necessary in the sense required by gateway (c), but was of sufficient relevance to demonstrate propensity under (d)). Where evidence tendered as explanatory is also evidence of propensity, particular caution is required in applying gateway (c). That gateway should not be deployed to 'slide in' evidence of propensity under the guise of explanatory evidence where the former would not be admissible, or would be subject to additional safeguards (*Davis* [2008] EWCA Crim 1156, [2009] 2 Cr App R 17 (306); *Saint* [2010] EWCA Crim 1924). The importance of distinguishing between explanatory evidence and evidence of propensity was stressed by the Privy Council in *Myers v R* [2015] UKPC 40, [2016] AC 314. The decision is based on common-law authorities including *Pettman* and does not deal directly with the CJA 2003. Lord Hughes stated that courts should be cautious about 'claims by prosecutors that the evidence is necessary to understanding of the case, or, as is sometimes asserted, to discourage the jury from wondering about the context in which the events discussed occurred'. It is 'only where the evidence truly adds something, beyond mere propensity, which may assist the jury to resolve one or more issues in the case, or is the unavoidable incident of admissible material, as distinct from interesting background or context, that the justification exists' for admitting the evidence as 'background' or explanatory evidence. In the later decision of *Phillip v DPP (St Christopher and Nevis)* [2017] UKPC 14, Lord Hughes further warned against 'facile' arguments based on the notion of 'background' that do not take proper account of the function of the evidence and the basis on which it is admissible. These comments are, it is submitted, of great value in relation to the decision to be made under the CJA 2003 as to whether evidence should be admitted as 'explanatory' under gateway (c) or whether the prosecution should instead focus their efforts on evidence of propensity under gateway (d).

Explanatory evidence once admitted may require a particularly careful direction. Thus, for example, in one of the appeals heard with *Edwards* [2005] EWCA Crim 1813, [2006] 1 Cr App R 3 (31), *Chohan*, evidence was admitted to support an identification of D as a robber from a person who recognised him from the many occasions on which she had sold him drugs. The separate functions of this background evidence and other evidence of D's record which went to his propensity were rightly maintained in the judge's direction. In *Norris* [2014] EWCA Crim 419, it was the complainant's discovery that D had a recent conviction for sexual offending that had led to her revelation of serious offences against her many years before. As the trial judge had carefully considered the risk of prejudice, and made clear in his direction that the conviction was not evidence of propensity, it was held that the evidence was rightly admitted. It is equally possible that evidence of a previous offence which is closely connected to the crime charged may be admissible propensity evidence without being necessary explanatory evidence (*Gillespie* [2011] EWCA Crim 3152), or that evidence may be admissible via both gateways for different purposes (*Mortimore* [2013] EWCA Crim 1639, where a previous conviction for child abduction and a subsequent warning notice were evidence of D's *mens rea* on the subsequent occasion under gateway (d) and also, under gateway (c), necessary to explain the context of the relationship between D and the teenage girl he sheltered in his home). See also *Lee* [2012] EWCA Crim 316, where it was said that evidence admitted under one gateway sometimes becomes admissible on another basis, making it particularly important for the jury to have directions that focus their attention on the use they may make of the evidence. In *Okokono* [2014] EWCA Crim 2521, a gang-related killing that was alleged to have been carried out in revenge for an earlier murder, the conviction of one of the participants for carrying a knife at the time of the earlier killing was 'highly relevant', applying s. 98, as evidence 'having to do with' the revenge attack (and therefore not as evidence of bad character at all: see **F13.10**), but was also admissible as 'explanatory' evidence of bad character evidence under s. 101(1)(c) to show the motivations of the accused, and as evidence under s. 101(1)(d) of his propensity to engage in gang-related violence knowing that others had a propensity to use knives to lethal effect.

Where explanatory evidence is admitted, it may be fairest to present it in the form of an agreed statement of facts, for the avoidance of prejudice and to prevent the distraction of the jury (*Cundell* [2009] EWCA Crim 2072, where the previous misconduct was admitted by agreement under s. 101(1)(a): see **F13.16**) but would otherwise have been clearly admissible under gateway (c). **F13.30**

Discretion and the CJA 2003, s. 101(1)(c)

It should be noted that the court has no explicit statutory discretion to exclude evidence that satisfies the test in the CJA 2003, s. 101(1)(c). Where the evidence is necessary for the proper exposition of the case, in the sense that it would be 'impossible' for the court to manage without it, this makes sense (cf. *Dolan* [2002] EWCA Crim 1859, [2003] 1 Cr App R 18 (281)). If, however, it is merely 'difficult', the court will have to consider whether it should have recourse to the general power of exclusion of prosecution evidence in the PACE 1984, s. 78. The observations of the Court of Appeal in *Highton* [2005] EWCA Crim 1985, [2005] 1 WLR 3472 and subsequent authorities (see **F13.19**) would seem to provide some support for this argument. The common law appeared to provide for the application of discretion, in cases such as *M (T)* [2000] 1 All ER 148 and *W* [2003] EWCA Crim 3024. Dicta in *Davis* [2008] EWCA Crim 1156, [2009] 2 Cr App R 17 (306) acknowledge that the role of s. 78 is 'possibly controversial' under the Act. See also *Henderson* [2010] EWCA Crim 1269, [2010] 2 Cr App R 24 (185) and the appeal of *Oyediran*, where explanatory evidence that was critical in relation to the ability of D2 (the mother of the deceased baby) to appreciate risk to her child was also potentially prejudicial to D1, in that it showed him to be of a violent disposition. The prejudice was said to have been overcome by a clear direction as to the proper use of the evidence. **F13.31**

Evidence of Motive or Intention as Explanatory Evidence Cases in which the previous dealings between the parties are said to show motive or intention sit somewhat uneasily between explanatory evidence and evidence relevant to the issue (CJA 2003, s. 101(1)(d): see **F13.36** ***et seq.***). Reliance on s. 101(1)(d) has the advantage that it will not be necessary to explain why it **F13.32**

is 'difficult' to understand the evidence without the additional evidence of intention or motive, or to show the 'substantial' value of the evidence in understanding the case as a whole.

A case illustrating the different emphasis of the two provisions is *Beverley* [2006] EWCA Crim 1287, in which previous convictions for possession of small quantities of cannabis were advanced by the prosecution at the trial of the accused for conspiracy to import a kilo of cocaine. D's appeal was allowed on the ground that the jury would not have been 'disabled or disadvantaged' in understanding the case against D in the absence of evidence of the convictions, so that s. 101(1)(c) was 'entirely unavailable'. Section 101(1)(d) was also discounted on the ground that the previous convictions did not establish a relevant propensity, so as to establish guilty knowledge, in light of the differences in the circumstances, and also the age of the convictions (see **F13.39** ***et seq.***).

F13.33 At common law evidence of motive was undoubtedly admissible (see *Phillip v DPP (St Christopher and Nevis)* [2017] UKPC 14, where the authorities are reviewed). Thus courts admitted, for example, evidence given to show prior assaults by the accused on the victim, or menaces or threats uttered to the victim (*Bond* [1906] 2 KB 389) and evidence of previous acts or words showing enmity as admissible evidence of motive (*Ball* [1911] AC 47 at p. 68). See also *Williams* (1986) 84 Cr App R 299 and *Fulcher* [1995] 2 Cr App R 251, where the previous non-accidental injuries sustained by the baby that D was alleged to have murdered were held to have been relevant to show not only that the child, being in pain, was more likely to be fractious, but also how D was likely to react to the child crying. In *Giannetto* [1997] 1 Cr App R 1, *Ball* and *Williams* were held to justify the admission of the diary of a deceased woman to show a history of threatening and violent behaviour by D towards her, and to form the basis for an inference that D was more likely to have killed her (although it was recognised that a direction that threats and assaults do not always lead to murder was also required). To the same effect are *Phillips* [2003] EWCA Crim 1379, [2003] 2 Cr App R 35 (528), where the unhappy history of the marriage between D and the woman he was charged with murdering was adduced to show motive, and *Shaw* [2002] EWCA Crim 1997, where the history of dealings between D and the police was adduced to shed light on whether D was more likely to have been the aggressor or the innocent victim of an assault by police officers. *Shaw* is a borderline case of relevance, though it may be significant that D chose to adduce something of the history himself in order to show why he believed he was likely to be attacked. In such circumstances, there was a danger that the jury would be left with a misleading picture. Under the CJA 2003 it would appear that s. 101(1)(d) might well provide the appropriate route to admissibility in such cases.

F13.34 In *Sidhu* (1994) 98 Cr App R 59, a video apparently showing D leading the activities of a group of armed rebels in Pakistan was admitted to show his object in participating in a conspiracy to possess explosives in England, which it was alleged was designed to further the interests of the same group. It was held that, provided there was a sufficient nexus in time between D's visit to Pakistan and the offence charged, and provided also that it was necessary to lead the evidence in order to give the jury a complete picture, it was admissible as evidence of a 'continual background of history' relevant to D's part in the conspiracy. As with evidence of motive, such evidence might more appropriately be received under s. 101(1)(d) on grounds of relevance to the issue.

In *M (T)* [2000] 1 All ER 148, evidence was admitted of the abuse that D and his sister V had suffered at the hands of older members of their family, including instances where D had been forced to abuse his siblings. Without such evidence, the two counts of rape of V could not properly be understood: e.g., the jury would inevitably have wondered why V did not turn to other family members for help. See also *M* [2006] EWCA Crim 193, in which previous threats of violence by D towards the girl he was charged with raping were held admissible, either under s. 101(1)(c), or as evidence 'having to do' with the alleged facts (see **F13.10**).

F13.35 In *Sawoniuk* [2000] 2 Cr App R 220, the Court of Appeal upheld the decision of the trial judge to admit evidence that D, charged with four murders in Belarus in 1942, had been a member of a group of policemen involved in a 'search and kill' operation to eliminate Jewish survivors of an earlier massacre. D had claimed not to have been a member but, as the killer was one of the group, it was necessary to the prosecution case to show that he was. Lord Bingham CJ agreed that the evidence was admissible for this purpose, but considered that it could also have been introduced on the broader basis that it was background evidence, as criminal charges 'cannot fairly be judged in a factual vacuum'. Again, the CJA 2003 would seem to provide more than one route for the admissibility of such evidence, and both s. 101(1)(c) and (d) are likely to be canvassed. In terms of outcome, little depends on which of these two routes is chosen (*Tirnaveanu* [2007] EWCA Crim 1239, [2007] 4 All ER 301).

EVIDENCE OF BAD CHARACTER ADDUCED BY PROSECUTION TO PROVE GUILT OR UNTRUTHFULNESS

CJA 2003: Admissibility under s. 101(1)(d)

Criminal Justice Act 2003, s. 101 F13.36

(1) In criminal proceedings evidence of the defendant's bad character is admissible if, but only if—

. . .

(d) it is relevant to an important matter in issue between the defendant and the prosecution.

The key provision in s. 101(1)(d) is supplemented by s. 103, which fleshes out both the issues to which the provision may apply and the type of evidence that may be rendered admissible thereunder.

Criminal Justice Act 2003, s. 103

(1) For the purposes of section 101(1)(d) the matters in issue between the defendant and the prosecution include—
(a) the question whether the defendant has a propensity to commit offences of the kind with which he is charged, except where his having such a propensity makes it no more likely that he is guilty of the offence;
(b) the question whether the defendant has a propensity to be untruthful, except where it is not suggested that the defendant's case is untruthful in any respect.
(2) Where subsection (1)(a) applies, a defendant's propensity to commit offences of the kind with which he is charged may (without prejudice to any other way of doing so) be established by evidence that he has been convicted of—
(a) an offence of the same description as the one with which he is charged, or
(b) an offence of the same category as the one with which he is charged.
(3) Subsection (2) does not apply in the case of a particular defendant if the court is satisfied, by reason of the length of time since the conviction or for any other reason, that it would be unjust for it to apply in his case.
(4) For the purposes of subsection (2)—
(a) two offences are of the same description as each other if the statement of the offence in a written charge or indictment would, in each case, be in the same terms;
(b) two offences are of the same category as each other if they belong to the same category of offences prescribed for the purposes of this section by an order made by the Secretary of State.
(5) A category prescribed by an order under subsection (4)(b) must consist of offences of the same type.
(6) Only prosecution evidence is admissible under section 101(1)(d).

The CAJA 2009, s. 144 and sch. 17, para. 1(2), amended the CJA 2003, s. 103, so as to insert subsections (7) to (11), which provide for the treatment of previous convictions outside England and Wales. The broad effect of the amendments is that the foreign conviction is treated as being admissible if the corresponding offence in England and Wales would be so treated.

Relevance to Important Matter Under the CJA 2003, s. 101(1)(d), the prosecution are required to show that evidence of bad character is relevant to an 'important matter in issue' between prosecution and defence. 'Important matter' means 'a matter of substantial importance in the context of the case as a whole' (s. 112(1)). While the issue must be of substantial importance, however, it is not necessary for the evidence of bad character to be of substantial probative value. Were it thus, the inclusion in s. 103(1)(a) of evidence of propensity as a matter in issue between the parties would be of very limited effect (*Chopra* [2006] EWCA Crim 2133, [2007] 1 Cr App R 16 (225); *Wallace* [2007] EWCA Crim 1760, [2008] 1 WLR 572). F13.37

The effect, as stated in *Weir* [2005] EWCA Crim 2866, [2006] 2 All ER 570, is that the threshold for admitting an accused's bad character is satisfied if the evidence is merely relevant to an important issue between the prosecution and the defence. Provided the evidence is so relevant, the court's power to exclude evidence under s. 101(3) is now the focal point of cases where evidence of bad character is tendered under s. 101(1)(d) and objected to by the defence. Where evidence is admitted, the accused's protection from unfairness lies in the direction to be given by the trial judge (see **F13.22**). An appeal court is unlikely to interfere unless the judge's judgement as to the capacity of prior events to establish propensity is plainly wrong or the judge's discretion has been exercised unreasonably in the *Wednesbury* sense (*Hanson* [2005] EWCA Crim 824, [2005] 1 WLR 3169, applied to the decision of a district judge in *DPP v Chand* [2007] EWHC 90 (Admin)).

F13.38 **Propensity and Other Evidence of Bad Character** A sea-change in admissibility under the CJA 2003 is that the accused's propensity becomes a potential issue between the defence and prosecution (see **F13.39**). Where, however, the history does not establish a relevant propensity, it may still be the case that the history has relevance in another sense to an important issue in the case under s. 101(1)(d). In *Lovell* [2018] EWCA Crim 19, [2018] 1 Cr App R (S) 48 (364), the value of the evidence was not to show propensity but to rebut D's account of his professed reluctance to use a firearm and of his intention to prevent its use. It was thus 'relevant to an important matter in issue between prosecution and defence' without being evidence of propensity. The Court of Appeal's reminder that propensity evidence is not the only form that admissible evidence may take is an important one. A similar point was made in *Hay* [2017] EWCA Crim 1851. D's defence to robbery of his local post office was an alibi, and he sought to explain away his presence on a shopping trip with the principal offender during which gloves identical to those used in the robbery were purchased as an innocent outing with an old friend. His previous conviction for robbery of a security guard was held to have been rightly admitted to rebut an innocent explanation of, or an explanation of coincidence in relation to, evidence which was relied on by the prosecution. Noting that the CJA 2003, s. 101(d) and (3), are commonly referred to as the 'propensity provisions', the Court stressed that 'this is not always an accurate description' (at [15]). In *Colliard* [2008] EWCA Crim 1175, where a drugs conviction was relevant both to knowledge and propensity, the Court of Appeal took care to distinguish the two in its reasoning. In *Jordan* [2009] EWCA Crim 953, the trial judge purported to admit as relevant to D's propensity his convictions for a firearm offence and a robbery. Holding that the true relevance of these convictions was to rebut D's coincidental presence as an innocent passenger in a car containing all the trappings for an armed robbery, the Court of Appeal rightly stressed that 'matters in issue' are not limited to questions of propensity. See to the same effect *Nicholas* [2011] EWCA Crim 1175, and *O* [2009] EWCA Crim 2235. Rix LJ commented (*obiter*): 'Although it is the example that section 103(1)(a) illustrates and underlines, gateway (d) is more generally concerned with relevance to an important matter in issue between a defendant and the prosecution'. See also *Thomas* [2010] EWCA Crim 148 (previous involvement in robberies using a knife a 'potentially important link' to whether accused knew of presence of knife in the instant case), *Rogers* [2013] EWCA Crim 2406 (convictions for burglary in a particular village rebutting D's claim to be unfamiliar with the area as well as showing propensity) and *Ali* [2010] EWCA Crim 1619 (photographic evidence of D's attraction to firearms admissible to confirm disputed identification whether it was evidence of propensity or not). In *McAllister* [2008] EWCA Crim 1544, [2009] 1 Cr App R 10 (129) a careful distinction was said to be required between an argument for admission of bad character evidence dependent on propensity and one dependent on a different form of reasoning, for in the latter the specific safeguards provided by the *Hanson* direction on propensity (see **F13.39**) are inappropriate and misleading.

F13.39 **Propensity as an Issue** Propensity to commit offences 'of the kind charged' is taken to be an issue between the defence and the prosecution except where it makes it no more likely that the accused is guilty (CJA 2003, s. 103(1)(a)), and propensity to untruthfulness is to be so taken unless it is not suggested that the accused's case is untruthful in any respect (s. 103(1)(b)). This appears to be a 'deeming' provision, given that propensity is not an issue in the normal sense so much as a means of proving what is in issue. However, 'the fact that section 103(1) seems also to have the effect of always potentially including the "question of" propensity among the "matters in issue" should not be overstated to the extent that sight is lost of the need for relevance: the bad character must still be relevant to an "important" issue' (*Bullen* [2008] EWCA Crim 4, [2008] 2 Cr App R 25 (364) at [29]). In *Bullen*, D's long history for offences of violence was relevant to the anticipated defence of self-defence to murder but, when D admitted manslaughter and relied on his intoxication in relation to the murder, the propensity either no longer made it more likely that D committed the offence charged or, if it did, it would have been unfair to rely on convictions that did not throw any light on the sole remaining issue of intention. See also *Goddard* [2012] EWCA Crim 1756, in which prejudicial evidence of their sexual interest in young boys was admitted at the trial of the two accused, despite the fact that the interest had been clearly admitted, and there was no adequate consideration of the relevance of the evidence to any disputed issue; it was held that the evidence should have been excluded. In *Samuel* [2014] EWCA Crim 2349, the prosecution needed to prove a specific intent on the part of the intoxicated D to commit really serious injury on his much smaller partner by punching her. D's conviction was upheld, but the Court of Appeal held that his previous beatings of her should not have been admitted, because the force used was not such as to demonstrate an intent to cause serious injury, so they lacked the necessary relevance.

Where propensity is relevant, no additional hurdle is imposed requiring other evidence to support the matter, though the absence of such evidence may bear on the question of discretionary exclusion (*Bowman* [2014] EWCA Crim 716). The nature of the defence may be such as to render propensity evidence admissible: in *B* [2017] EWCA Crim 35, [2017] 1 Cr App R 31 (457), D was charged with various sexual offences and offences of cruelty against his children. He contended that, though he was a strict disciplinarian in the home, he had not behaved unreasonably. Evidence of his violent behaviour towards his wife was rightly admitted to rebut this suggestion by demonstrating a propensity to use excessive violence against members of his family which could not possibly be explained or excused as 'reasonable chastisement'.

The steps which must be followed by the trial judge in determining the use which may be made of evidence of propensity consisting of convictions under s. 101(1)(d) were spelled out in detail in *Hanson* [2005] EWCA Crim 824, [2005] 1 WLR 3169. In brief these flow as follows:

(1) Does the history of conviction(s) establish a propensity to commit offences of the kind charged?
(2) If so, does the propensity make it more likely that the defendant committed the crime charged?
(3) Where the convictions are for offences of the same category or description (s. 103(2)) is it unjust to rely on them (s. 103(3))? Where the propensity is proved by other means, as permitted by s. 103(1) and (2), is it unfair under s. 101(3) to admit the evidence?

Demonstrating Propensity According to *Hanson* [2005] EWCA Crim 824, [2005] 1 WLR 3169, propensity can be demonstrated by one previous event if sufficiently probative, as, for example, where the behaviour is 'strikingly similar'. Other examples given were of an offence of fire-setting, or a single sexual offence (and see *Pickstone*, heard with *Hanson*; *W* [2009] EWCA Crim 476, where the offence establishing propensity was committed many years before but was of a similar nature and might well have been 'striking'; *Stetlner* [2018] EWCA Crim 1479 where the previous offence showed that the teenage defendant had 'not grown out of' a propensity to groom girls for sexual activity, without their consent if necessary; and *Miller* [2010] EWCA Crim 1578, where the single offence of rape, though not strikingly similar, showed a propensity to abuse power over a young victim). **F13.40**

In *Clarke* [2012] EWCA Crim 9, a strikingly similar previous sexual offence would have been enough, by itself, to provide the requisite probative value, although other offences were also admitted. See also *Burdess* [2014] EWCA Crim 270, where the single previous rape was of a strikingly similar nature, *Day* [2019] EWCA Crim 935, where the features of the previous rape, if not strikingly similar, were of a very special and distinctive nature such as to render it admissible, and *Balazs*

[2014] EWCA Crim 947, where a single rape and related offences of violence and harassment showed a propensity towards using sexual and violent behaviour to control a partner. However, it does not follow that a single conviction for rape will inevitably be admissible (see *Bennabbou* [2012] EWCA Crim 1256, where the conviction was old and the circumstances dissimilar, and see to similar effect *Laws-Chapman* [2013] EWCA Crim 1851, where an old conviction for buggery that appeared to have been consensual, and might not have constituted an offence at all under the current law, should not have been admitted to show propensity where the charge concerned violent paedophile behaviour against a non-consenting child in the company of a group of other men). See also *Williams* [2006] EWCA Crim 2052 and *Jackson* [2011] EWCA Crim 1870 (propensity to strangle) and *Turner* [2010] EWCA Crim 2300 (previous offence shared characteristics of ruthless violence applied to a stranger as part of the 'enforcement' activities of a biker gang). To similar effect is *Spottiswood* [2019] EWCA Crim 949, in which a single previous incident of using a 'highly distinctive' headlock as a method of attack was admissible to rebut D's contention that he had acted instinctively in self-defence and that the act was out of character.

In *Cundell* [2009] EWCA Crim 2072, where an offence of solicitation to murder D's wife was alleged to have taken place in prison, and to be in effect an exact repetition of the offence that had led to D's incarceration, the previous conviction was admitted by consent under s. 101(1)(a), but would otherwise have been admissible not merely as explanatory evidence, but as evidence of propensity, and the judge was correct to direct the jury as to its use for the latter purpose. The Court of Appeal found it hard to imagine a case in which the previous conviction could be more relevant. See also *Koc* [2008] EWCA Crim 77, where a single recent conviction for handling heroin was admissible where the defence to a charge of conspiracy involving heroin was that D believed he was dealing with counterfeit clothes. Closer to the borderline is *Bowman* [2014] EWCA Crim 716, where a single, somewhat old, conviction for joint possession of a firearm was held admissible in relation to the issue whether D had brought a gun to the scene of a crime or, as he claimed, had wrestled it from an opponent. Much would seem to turn on whether the carrying of firearms constitutes a 'distinctive' feature, the Court of Appeal relying on *Burdess*. Contrast *Colliard* [2008] EWCA Crim 1175, where there were no special features and the Court observed that the judge was 'not clearly wrong' to admit the conviction (which was also clearly admissible to show knowledge).

The requirement in *Hanson* to give careful consideration to the probative value of propensity evidence was stressed in *Urushadze* [2008] EWCA Crim 2498, where D's previous convictions for shoplifting were of little value in indicating a propensity towards street robbery. To similar effect is *Kane* [2013] EWCA Crim 1487, where the Court of Appeal was concerned with an 'undifferentiated mass' of bad character evidence and commented forcefully that '[p]oints which are devoid of content as legitimate bad character evidence cannot acquire such a status simply by heaping them together with other points which themselves also have no proper claim to admissibility as bad character evidence under the requirements of the 2003 Act'. Where the probative value of a range of convictions is properly evaluated by the judge, however, there is no reason why they cannot be tendered for their cumulative effect (*Brooks* [2014] EWCA Crim 562: mixture of drugs-related offences including trafficking and false passports).

In cases where a jury may have difficulty disentangling the relevance of the evidence, a careful direction will be needed (*Norris* [2013] EWCA Crim 712, where the judge provided very clear guidance to the jury that propensity evidence pointing to D's racist attitudes was relevant only once they had concluded, in reliance on the scientific evidence in the case, that he had been correctly identified as a participant in a murder: at that point, it was relevant to his own state of mind and his awareness of the intentions of others in the group). In *Soloman* [2019] EWCA Crim 1356, the Court of Appeal considered that it was permissible to admit, at D's trial for firearms and ammunition offences, the title of a rap lyric noted on his phone which referenced the sale of guns; however there should have been a specific direction to the jury that rap lyrics commonly contain references to criminality and shootings. Although some latitude is permitted in making a judgement about relevance, a ruling may be interfered with on appeal where a judge has 'plainly erred'

(*M* [2006] EWCA Crim 3408, in which an old offence of possession of a firearm was considered to provide 'too slender a basis' for an inference about propensity). See also *Beverley* [2006] EWCA Crim 1287 at **F13.32**.

In *Leaver* [2006] EWCA Crim 2988, D was charged with rape by continuing with intercourse in a violent manner after the complainant had withdrawn her original consent, and with causing her serious injury with intent when she refused to engage in further sexual activity. It was held that a conviction for indecent exposure, which had not been accompanied by circumstances of any violence, did not bear on the questions for the jury, which were whether D reasonably believed the complainant was consenting to intercourse, and whether he had intended to do her serious injury. In *Fyle* [2011] EWCA Crim 1213, evidence of a previous wounding with intent by D when 16 and to which he had pleaded guilty was not admissible in relation to the murder by strangulation of a transsexual prostitute; there were few similarities, the probative value of the conviction was slight and its prejudicial effect considerable in a prosecution where the remaining evidence was circumstantial.

Contrast *D* [2011] EWCA Crim 1474, [2011] 4 All ER 568, where it was said that the propensity of a person charged with sexual offences against a child to view pornographic images of children, while it did not of itself make it likely that he would act out the activity displayed, might be admissible in support of a child complainant's evidence, on the basis of the unlikelihood of the complainant having by coincidence falsely accused a person with such an unusual propensity. See to similar effect *Latham* [2014] EWCA Crim 207, where such evidence was rightly said to require the making of a very careful judgement with regard to fairness, and *Ridgeway* [2019] EWCA Crim 2061, where D's unusual sexual interest in horses was proved by means of two previous convictions, including one where he had attempted to murder the horse's owner who had discovered him in a compromising position. In *M* [2015] EWCA Crim 353, [2015] 2 Cr App R 22 (307), different considerations were said to apply where the photographs showed the child complainants in indecent poses and were consistent with the prosecution case as to how the abuse, culminating in rape of one of the children, was said to have occurred. Although, taking account of *D*, the judge was wrong to treat the photographs as strong evidence of propensity, the relevance of the evidence as confirming the testimony of the complainants meant that it was rightly admitted. *D* was also considered in *W* [2011] EWCA Crim 2463, a case in which a range of offences were tried together which were very different not only in terms of seriousness but in the fact that some had happened many years before. The Court of Appeal expressed surprise that they were tried together at all but, this having been done, a proper direction on the cross-admissibility of propensity evidence in such circumstances required the careful grouping of counts so that the jury would not be left with the sense that all propensity evidence was equally cross-admissible and that they were being invited to form a judgement on the basis that either 'it did happen or it didn't'. See also *Saint* [2010] EWCA Crim 1924, where D's obsession with watching others have sex in a park where the alleged rape took place should have been excluded, either because it was of insufficient relevance (there being no evidence that a voyeur committed the rape) or because its prejudicial effect vastly outweighed its probative value.

In *Harris* [2009] EWCA Crim 434, on the other hand, D's previous convictions for violence were held to have been rightly admitted at his trial for rape, on the issue of which of the parties had behaved aggressively, and in *Franklin* [2013] EWCA Crim 84, a girl's previous convictions for assault and robbery were held admissible to connect her to a joint enterprise that had violence or the fear of violence as its object. In *Dossett* [2013] EWCA Crim 710, the identification of D as the perpetrator of a street robbery was supported by evidence of a similar 'casual opportunistic public offence' of robbery committed with the same co-defendant, and of an incident involving similar violence in the same neighbourhood but not involving robbery. The Court of Appeal stressed the importance of the factual connections rather than the legal dissimilarities, relying on *Hanson*.

Thompson [2016] All ER (D) 56 (Dec) provides an extreme illustration of the proposition that a propensity that might be expected to be ongoing can be demonstrated by events taking place after the matters that are the subject of the trial as well as before them. D was accused of indecent assaults against two young sisters in 1972. When arrested in 2015 he was found to have indecent images of children on his computer, and to have conducted internet searches for such material. The Court accepted that the evidence showed that D had a sexual interest in children in 2015, which in turn was capable of showing that he had such an interest in 1972. To similar effect is *Toner* [2019] EWCA Crim 447, where it was held that historic counts of indecency had been properly joined with recent counts involving child pornography as they were cross-admissible.

F13.41 **Propensity and Fairness** According to *Hanson* [2005] EWCA Crim 824, [2005] 1 WLR 3169, the calculation over whether to exclude a conviction under s. 101(3) or 103(3) involves a range of issues, including the similarity between the conviction and the offence charged, bearing in mind that offences may be of the same category or description but factually different. The gravity and age of the offence for which the accused has been convicted are also factors, with particular care being addressed to the use of old convictions which are likely to be prejudicial unless they can clearly be shown to demonstrate continuing propensity. In *Cox* [2014] EWCA Crim 804, a history of incidents stretching back over 20 years was admissible in order to show a propensity to seek out a knife to threaten others when under pressure. In *Boyle* [2017] NICA 75, D's defence to murder was that her co-accused was entirely responsible for the attack on the victim, which D had attempted to prevent. It was held not to be unfair for the prosecution to adduce evidence of D's convictions for various assaults that had taken place, like the murder, under the influence of alcohol, although none had resulted in serious injury. The evidence both supported an inference of propensity towards violence, particularly after the consumption of alcohol, and undermined the argument that D was likely to be a force for restraint. A case near the line is *Ullah* [2006] EWCA Crim 2003, in which a single conviction for a somewhat similar offence of obtaining by deception in 1989 was admitted at D's trial for conspiracy to defraud, but see *Turner* [2010] EWCA Crim 2300 where the previous single offence of gang violence was committed in 1993 and yet was clearly admissible. Another cause for concern arises when previous events are disputed, for then the court must be particularly careful to avoid the diversion of the trial into 'satellite' issues not covered by the indictment. See, in addition to *Hanson*, *Lamb* [2006] EWCA Crim 3347.

The court should also consider the weight of the other evidence in the case, as bad character evidence should not be admitted in order to bolster a weak case where there is little or no other evidence against a defendant (*Hanson*, at [10]) In *McDonald* [2011] EWCA Crim 2933 it was noted that a case would not be weak if the evidence of propensity was itself strong, for example by demonstrating a highly unusual *modus operandi*, and see *Steltner* [2018] EWCA Crim 1479 where evidence of D's previous convictions for similar sexual offences in virtually identical circumstances was admitted (though the case was also not thought to be weak in terms of the other prosecution evidence). It is also relevant to consider whether the probative value of the bad character evidence is enhanced because it is relevant for a reason other than demonstrating propensity, for example by rebutting an innocent explanation (*Darnley* [2012] EWCA Crim 1148). In *DPP v Chand* [2007] EWHC 90 (Admin), the exclusion of D's conviction for theft by shoplifting on a charge of stealing a charity box was based both on dissimilarity and the weakness of the prosecution case. Where it is foreseeable that the evidence of witnesses might not be as anticipated in their witness statements, and there is in consequence a risk that the use of bad character evidence will overshadow the rest of the prosecution case, it may be desirable to delay a ruling on admissibility until the Crown has called its witnesses (*Gyima* [2007] EWCA Crim 429).

The facts of *Hanson* itself illustrate the careful scrutiny of conviction evidence to determine the existence and possible value of propensity. D was charged with burglary from a room that, it was contended, he alone had opportunity to enter at the relevant time. His various convictions for offences of dishonesty were all within part 1 of the 'Categories of Offences' Schedule (see **F13.45** ***et seq.***), but the Court of Appeal nevertheless considered that the judge was obliged to review the relevance to propensity of the individual convictions, as a conviction of the same description or category as the offence charged was not necessarily sufficient in order to show a propensity to commit offences of the kind charged. D's convictions for handling and aggravated vehicle-taking, though of the same 'category' as burglary, were not, without more, such as to demonstrate a propensity to burgle. This does not mean that there must be available full details of a previous offence in order to enable relevance to propensity to be determined; all depends on the facts of a particular case, although it is good practice for details to be available if required (*Lamaletie* [2008] EWCA Crim 314).

Proving Propensity in the Absence of Previous Convictions In *Mitchell* [2016] UKSC 55, [2017] AC 571 the evidence of propensity adduced at D's trial for the murder by stabbing of her partner took the form of agreed statements of two previous incidents, neither of which had resulted in conviction. These were said to establish a propensity on D's part to use knives in order to threaten and attack others, which tended to disprove her claim that she had killed in self-defence. In her testimony, D disputed the content of the previously agreed statements. The question arose as to the proper direction to give to a jury where disputed evidence was relied upon to establish a relevant propensity. The Supreme Court held that, while it is unnecessary to prove to the criminal standard the truth of each incident relied upon, or to consider such incidents in isolation from the rest of the evidence, where the prosecution argument is grounded in the existence of a propensity on the part of the accused the jury should be directed that they should be sure that the propensity is established to the criminal standard of proof before taking it into account. The judgment of the Supreme Court also casts doubt on the assumption in *O'Dowd* [2009] EWCA Crim 905, [2009] 2 Cr App R 16 (280) that multiple incidents alleged to constitute the basis for an inference of propensity should be considered separately. The Supreme Court judgment does not, however, question the outcome of that decision or the basis for it, which concerns the adverse effect on the fairness of the trial of proceeding on the basis of unproved allegations said to amount to propensity evidence. *Mitchell* appears to be confined to evidence of propensity, which was the subject of the narrowly framed certified question. Even if it is so confined, however, it raises the question whether it opens the floodgates to the tactical introduction of a greater number of incidents based on weaker evidence, on the basis that a jury might be more persuaded to infer propensity on the grounds of 'no smoke without fire'. The Supreme Court notes (at [53]) that '[r]eliance on cumulative past incidents in support of a case of propensity may indeed illuminate the truth of the currently indicted allegations, but excessive recourse to such history may skew the trial in a way which distracts attention from the central issue'. In such cases, the court should consider the exercise of its power to exclude the evidence on the grounds of its adverse impact on the fairness of the trial. F13.42

Particular care is required in relation to propensity evidence in relation to matters for which an accused has been acquitted, though such evidence may, in appropriate cases, be adduced. In *M* [2010] All ER (D) 196 (Dec), D appealed against convictions for sexually abusing his partner's grandson. The prosecution had relied, as evidence of propensity, on allegations by V's sister that she had been sexually abused by D in the same room. Those allegations had previously been brought to trial but resulted in acquittal, the prosecution having offered no evidence. There were various similarities of detail and the evidence was held to have been properly admitted. The danger of 'satellite issues' may be particularly acute with older allegations. In *W* [2015] EWCA Crim 270, D was retried for a number of anal rapes alleged by C, having previously been acquitted of one count of anal rape against the same person. It was held to be wrong to allow the prosecution to rely, as bad character evidence, on a further allegation by C that had formed part of a withdrawn count without also making the jury aware of the previous acquittal. The course that had been taken had given the jury 'half of the picture'. The dangers of satellite issues raised by previous unproven allegations were overcome on the unusual facts of *Williams* [2014] EWCA Crim 1862. An allegation of a recent attack similar to the index offence was not initially advanced by the prosecution until it appeared that the defence intended to call as a witness the alleged victim of the earlier attack, who could have resolved the satellite issues, whereupon an application was successfully made to adduce the evidence.

The use of hearsay evidence in support of allegations of misconduct requires particular caution (*Z* [2009] EWCA Crim 20, [2009] 1 Cr App R 34 (500), and see as to hearsay **F17.37**).

In *Nguyen* [2020] EWCA Crim 140, under cross-examination by the prosecution D2, D1's co-accused, asserted that D1 had told him that he had previously 'robbed weed houses'. The Court of Appeal noted that at that point there should probably have been an application by the prosecution to rely upon this as bad character evidence under either s. 101(1)(d) or (g) (D1 having attacked the character of defence witnesses), and that such an application would 'not necessarily have failed' because it was only based upon hearsay evidence as D2 had repeated the assertion in his oral evidence.

F13.43 **Uses of Propensity** Other examples of the use of propensity evidence to prove guilt appear in the following sections, which are arranged according to the function of the evidence: supporting identification, rebutting a defence etc. The use of propensity evidence is not, however, conditional upon the raising of a defence, and may be admissible where the defence is a complete denial (*Wilkinson* [2006] EWCA Crim 1332). A clear example of the use of propensity evidence to rebut a complete denial occurred in *Montakhab* [2012] EWCA Crim 2012, where D denied putting his hand on the thigh of a young woman on a bus, and it was held that it would have been an 'affront to common sense' to exclude seven offences of sexual assault, six of which had taken place while sitting next to a young woman on a bus.

F13.44 **Propensity to Untruthfulness** In relation to evidence of propensity to show untruthfulness, *Hanson* [2005] EWCA Crim 824, [2005] 1 WLR 3169 (see **F13.39**) requires a distinction to be drawn between offences of dishonesty, which may or may not display a propensity to untruthfulness, and evidence which does display such a propensity. The latter category might, for example, include an offence involving lying or making false representations, or the putting forward by the accused of an account in his or her own defence which can be shown to have been disbelieved. In *Spence* [2010] EWCA Crim 2256, D, a lorry driver, was tried for being knowingly concerned in the fraudulent importation of drugs, and his defence involved a denial of knowledge of the presence of the drugs in his vehicle. Demonstrable lies told by D in relation to previous offences of importing tobacco were held to have been rightly relied upon by the prosecution: the lies were not merely evidence of a general propensity to untruthfulness but were integral to the offences themselves.

Hanson was also applied in *Norris* [2014] EWCA Crim 419, in which D had been guilty of 'previous sustained lying in a court context', including the construction of an admittedly false military history in an attempt to mitigate sentence. The Court of Appeal noted but did not follow the narrower approach to the statute in *Campbell* [2007] EWCA Crim 1472, [2007] 1 WLR 2798, where admissibility was thought to be limited to offences in which lying was an element of a crime of which the accused had been convicted, preferring the broader approach in *Jarvis* [2008] EWCA Crim 488. In *LH* [2017] NICA 67, the Court of Appeal in Northern Ireland also expressed a preference for the broader approach, and further considered that a single instance of lying may be sufficient to establish the relevant propensity, particularly if there is some unusual characteristic associated with it. However, where evidence of bad character has been admitted to show a propensity to commit offences of the type charged, the court should consider whether a direction on untruthfulness or credibility would distract the jury from the issues in the case or appear to give an unfair enhanced importance to the bad character evidence.

It should be noted that, paradoxically, evidence of a non-defendant's previous convictions for offences of this type will be admissible under the CJA 2003 only where the court gives leave to adduce it on the ground that it is of substantial probative value and substantial importance to the case (s. 100: see **F15**).

Examples of the use of evidence of propensity to show untruthfulness are to be found in the following text in relation to s. 101(1)(d).

F13.45 **Prescribed Categories of Offences to Show Propensity** The categories of offences so far prescribed using the power under the CJA 2003, s. 103(4)(b) (see **F13.36**), broadly relate to offences of dishonesty and sexual offences against persons under the age of 16, as contained in the schedule to the Criminal Justice Act 2003 (Categories of Offences) Order 2004 (SI 2004 No. 3346). It should be noted, however, that (under s. 103(1) and (2)) the existence of offences of the same description or category is only one method of proving propensity, so that other relevant evidence may also be relied upon. Thus, for example, a history of separate investigations of the accused for sexual offences against children, which are of probative value in establishing disposition where the investigations had not resulted in prosecution, might be admitted. And in *Weir* [2005] EWCA Crim 2866, [2006] 2 All ER 570, it was permissible to prove a caution for a non-scheduled offence of taking an obscene photograph of a child; the Court of Appeal pointed out that, while the task of deciding the admissibility of offences within the categories is easier, the opening words of s. 103(2) make clear that the categories do not provide the only route to admissibility. See also *Lamb* [2006] EWCA Crim 3347 at **F13.41** (propensity to stab). In *Johnson* [2009] EWCA Crim 649, [2009] 2 Cr App R 7 (101) the Court relied on the breadth of s. 103(2) in order to admit evidence of the non-prescribed offence of conspiracy to burgle. The Court explained that the prescribed categories provide 'permissive and simple ways of establishing propensity. Where they do not apply, propensity may still be established by other means.'

Conversely, the existence of a conviction for a scheduled offence does not, without more, make it admissible: the steps described in *Hanson* [2005] EWCA Crim 824, [2005] 1 WLR 3169 (see **F13.39**) to ensure relevance and fairness in admitting propensity evidence must also be gone through.

Criminal Justice Act 2003 (Categories of Offences) Order 2004 (SI 2004 No. 3346), schedule **F13.46**

PRESCRIBED CATEGORIES OF OFFENCES

PART 1

THEFT CATEGORY

1. An offence under section 1 of the Theft Act 1968 (theft).
2. An offence under section 8 of that Act (robbery).
3. An offence under section 9(1)(a) of that Act (burglary) if it was committed with intent to commit an offence of stealing anything in the building or part of a building in question.
4. An offence under section 9(1)(b) of that Act (burglary) if the offender stole or attempted to steal anything in the building or that part of it.
5. An offence under section 10 of that Act (aggravated burglary) if the offender committed a burglary described in paragraph 3 or 4 of this Part of the Schedule.
6. An offence under section 12 of that Act (taking motor vehicle or other conveyance without authority).
7. An offence under section 12A of that Act (aggravated vehicle-taking).
8. An offence under section 22 of that Act (handling stolen goods).
9. An offence under section 25 of that Act (going equipped for stealing).
10. An offence under section 3 of the Theft Act 1978 (making off without payment).
11. An offence of—
    (a) aiding, abetting, counselling, procuring or inciting the commission of an offence specified in this Part of this Schedule; or
    (b) attempting to commit an offence so specified.

PART 2

SEXUAL OFFENCES (PERSONS UNDER THE AGE OF 16) CATEGORY

1. An offence under section 1 of the Sexual Offences Act 1956 (rape) if it was committed in relation to a person under the age of 16.
2. An offence under section 5 of the Sexual Offences Act 1956 (intercourse with a girl under thirteen).
3. An offence under section 6 of that Act (intercourse with a girl under sixteen).
4. An offence under section 7 of that Act (intercourse with a defective) if it was committed in relation to a person under the age of 16.
5. An offence under section 10 of that Act (incest by a man) if it was committed in relation to a person under the age of 16.

6. An offence under section 11 of that Act (incest by a woman) if it was committed in relation to a person under the age of 16.
7. An offence under section 12 of that Act (buggery) if it was committed in relation to a person under the age of 16.
8. An offence under section 13 of that Act (indecency between men) if it was committed in relation to a person under the age of 16.
9. An offence under section 14 of that Act (indecent assault on a woman) if it was committed in relation to a person under the age of 16.
10. An offence under section 15 of that Act (indecent assault on a man) if it was committed in relation to a person under the age of 16.
11. An offence under section 128 of the Mental Health Act 1959 (sexual intercourse with patients) if it was committed in relation to a person under the age of 16.
12. An offence under section 1 of the Indecency with Children Act 1960 (indecent conduct towards young child).
13. An offence under section 54 of the Criminal Law Act 1977 (inciting a girl under 16 to have incestuous sexual intercourse).
14. An offence under section 3 of the Sexual Offences (Amendment) Act 2000 (abuse of a position of trust) if it was committed in relation to a person under the age of 16.
15. An offence under section 1 of the Sexual Offences Act 2003 (rape) if it was committed in relation to a person under the age of 16.
16. An offence under section 2 of that Act (assault by penetration) if it was committed in relation to a person under the age of 16.
17. An offence under section 3 of that Act (sexual assault) if it was committed in relation to a person under the age of 16.
18. An offence under section 4 of that Act (causing a person to engage in sexual activity without consent) if it was committed in relation to a person under the age of 16.
19. An offence under section 5 of the Sexual Offences Act 2003 (rape of a child under 13).
20. An offence under section 6 of that Act (assault of a child under 13 by penetration).
21. An offence under section 7 of that Act (sexual assault of a child under 13).
22. An offence under section 8 of that Act (causing or inciting a child under 13 to engage in sexual activity).
23. An offence under section 9 of that Act (sexual activity with a child).
24. An offence under section 10 of that Act (causing or inciting a child to engage in sexual activity).
25. An offence under section 14 of that Act if doing it will involve the commission of an offence under sections 9 and 10 of that Act (arranging or facilitating the commission of a child sex offence).
26. An offence under section 16 of that Act (abuse of position of trust: sexual activity with a child) if it was committed in relation to a person under the age of 16.
27. An offence under section 17 of that Act (abuse of position of trust: causing or inciting a child to engage in sexual activity) if it was committed in relation to a person under the age of 16.
28. An offence under section 25 of that Act (sexual activity with a child family member) if it was committed in relation to a person under the age of 16.
29. An offence under section 26 of that Act (inciting a child family member to engage in sexual activity) if it was committed in relation to a person under the age of 16.
30. An offence under section 30 of that Act (sexual activity with a person with a mental disorder impeding choice) if it was committed in relation to a person under the age of 16.
31. An offence under section 31 of that Act (causing or inciting a person with a mental disorder impeding choice to engage in sexual activity) if it was committed in relation to a person under the age of 16.
32. An offence under section 34 of that Act (inducement, threat, or deception to procure activity with a person with a mental disorder) if it was committed in relation to a person under the age of 16.
33. An offence under section 35 of that Act (causing a person with a mental disorder to engage in or agree to engage in sexual activity by inducement, threat or deception) if it was committed in relation to a person under the age of 16.
34. An offence under section 38 of that Act (care workers: sexual activity with a person with a mental disorder) if it was committed in relation to a person under the age of 16.
35. An offence under section 39 of that Act (care workers: causing or inciting sexual activity) if it was committed in relation to a person under the age of 16.

36. An offence of—
   (a) aiding, abetting, counselling, procuring or inciting the commission of an offence specified in this Part of this Schedule; or
   (b) attempting to commit an offence so specified.

Presumption of Commission Created by Conviction To facilitate the operation of the CJA 2003, s. 103(4)(b), and the statutory instrument made under it (see **F13.45**), the PACE 1984, s. 74(3), was amended by the CJA 2003 so that proof of conviction for an offence creates a presumption that the accused committed it, even where its relevance is only to show disposition—a function of the use of previous convictions which was formerly excluded (see **F12.19**). The supplementary provisions of the PACE 1984, s. 75 (see **F12.7**), will also apply, so that regard may be had to a range of documents including the indictment in order to determine the facts on which the conviction adduced in support of propensity was based. The CAJA 2009, sch. 17, amends the PACE 1984, s. 75, to extend its effect to convictions in other EU Member States (see **F12.7**). The presumption applies to convictions occurring before the Member State joined the EU (*Mehmedov* [2014] EWCA Crim 1523, [2015] 1 WLR 495). It was also decided in *Mehmedov* that, if there is evidence that the conviction was the result of a trial which failed to reach appropriate standards of fairness, the court could decline to admit the conviction either under the CJA 2003, s. 101(3), or under the PACE 1984, s. 78. In *Reece* [2020] EWCA Crim 44, there was a possibility that D might have pleaded guilty to a drugs offence in Belgium under a false impression as to the meaning of possession, although no expert evidence was adduced as to the content of the offence under Belgian law. It was held that there was no requirement for a direction as to whether D's guilt had been disproved where D had not expressly challenged his conviction; nor had counsel asked for a direction tailored to the requirements of the PACE 1984, s. 74(3). **F13.47**

It would seem that there is in any event considerable merit in having any argument about the significance of a foreign conviction at the stage where application to admit bad character is made, rather than having to resort to the sort of complex direction required by s. 74(3) as a prerequisite to a jury accepting that a relevant propensity has been established.

As to the need to supplement conviction evidence with statements admissible under the hearsay provisions of the CJA 2003 in order to provide evidence of the detail of, for example, the *modus operandi* adopted in relation to previous offences where this is in dispute, see *Humphris* [2005] EWCA Crim 2030; *Ainscough* [2006] EWCA Crim 694, at **F17.31** and *Hogart* [2007] EWCA Crim 338. No such supplementation is required where there is agreement by the defence as to the relevant circumstances, even if other matters are disputed (*K* [2008] EWCA Crim 3301).

Identifying the Accused by Evidence of Bad Character under the CJA 2003, s. 101(1)(d)

An important function of evidence of bad character is to identify the accused as the perpetrator of an offence. The connection may be arrived at via an inference from propensity (see **F13.39**) or by any other relevant inference drawn under gateway (d) (see **F13.37**): the effect is the same, though the process of reasoning is different, and will need to be reflected in the summing up. In *Suleman* [2012] EWCA Crim 1569, [2012] 2 Cr App R 30 (381), for example, evidence of a large number of similar examples of arson affecting D's family were rightly admitted in support of an argument that it would have been an amazing coincidence had D not been the author of all of them. But these fires were not evidence of propensity until the point where the jury had concluded that D was indeed the cause of them all, and should not have been presented as such. In only one count was there the direct evidence of identification that would have supported an inference of propensity that could have been brought to bear on the question of who started the other fires. The dominant direction to the jury, therefore, needed to be grounded in the unlikelihood of coincidence rather than in propensity. **F13.48**

Where a feature is said to be the equivalent of a signature, it is an acknowledgement that it possesses to a very high degree the unusual features associated with 'striking similarity' at common law

(*DPP v Boardman* [1975] AC 421; *Smith* (1915) 11 Cr App R 229; *Barrington* [1981] 1 All ER 1132). In such cases, the evidence of bad character may support the prosecution case to the extent that very little other evidence is required to convince of guilt. In the old case of *Straffen* [1952] 2 QB 911, the murder of a young girl who was found strangled was considered unusual in that no attempt had been made to assault her sexually or to conceal the body. D came under immediate suspicion because he had previously strangled two other girls, each murder having the same peculiar features, and because he was in the neighbourhood at the time, having just escaped from Broadmoor. Under these circumstances, very little other evidence was required to convict D of the third murder: it bore his 'fingerprints'.

Not all 'signature' cases are of a sexual nature. For example, in *Visvaniathan* [2017] EWCA Crim 517, D's conviction on a plea of guilty to a 'strikingly similar' nightclub assault was admissible to confirm his identification by a victim of an assault nine days later. Where evidence amounts to a signature or 'hallmark' and is directly relevant to the issue, the *Crown Court Compendium* (July 2020), ch. 12-6, notes that the normal direction not to convict wholly or mainly on evidence of bad character would be inappropriate but stresses that this is likely to be a rare factual scenario.

F13.49 Evidence of misconduct may go to support identification without necessarily amounting to 'signature evidence'. Thus, for example, in *Eastlake* [2007] EWCA Crim 603 two brothers were charged with an offence of street violence. Their propensity (jointly and separately) to commit such offences was admissible to support their disputed identifications, particularly in light of the brothers' defence that they spent the evening together, which strengthened the argument that it would have been a strange coincidence if they had been wrongly identified. See also *Dossett* [2013] EWCA Crim 710, where one of the convictions was for a different offence in similar circumstances and the other for the same offence in slightly different circumstances but in the same area, and with the same co-accused; *Cushing* [2006] EWCA Crim 1221, where the previous offences were for the same crime (burglary) but were factually distinct; and *Brisland* [2008] EWCA Crim 2773, where two thefts were committed by a man posing as an employee to deceive delivery men, and the identification of D from CCTV footage in respect of one offence was capable of linking him to the other crime.

Evidence going to show gang membership or affiliation is frequently deployed as evidence under s. 101(1)(d) to link the accused to the commission of a specific offence. In *Smith* [2008] EWCA Crim 1342, [2009] 1 Cr App R 36 (521), 'compelling' evidence that D was part of a gang who had shot four men, killing one of them, was supplemented by evidence of his conviction for attempted murder by shooting. This was held to make it more likely that he was a member of a group prepared to use guns. *Smith* was applied to the identification of property as belonging to an accused in *Elliott* [2010] EWCA Crim 2378. Guns and drugs were found in a store cupboard outside D's home. To rebut a suggestion that the items were deposited by others, the prosecution adduced evidence to show that D was a member of a local criminal gang, which was involved in drug crime and the carrying or use of firearms. The Court of Appeal held that the evidence 'was plainly capable' of assisting the jury in resolving the disputed issue. Rejecting a subsidiary argument that the evidence should have been rejected as prejudicial because it consisted of a broad treatment of numerous circumstances suggesting gang membership and thus distracted the jury's attention from the key issue, the Court noted (at [31]) that circumstantial evidence of gang membership was likely to be of this sort: 'Violent gangs, which provide no social amenity and exist for criminal purposes, are unlikely to issue membership cards, and so proof of membership will almost inevitably involve the prosecution in putting forward evidence of a number of circumstances from which gang membership could be inferred'. *Smith* and *Elliott* were applied in *Lewis* [2014] EWCA Crim 48, where it was said to be 'well-established' that evidence of membership of a criminal gang may be admissible under the *CJA 2003, s. 101(1)(d). In* *Lewis* the evidence served not only to identify those taking part in a riot, but also to provide evidence of common purpose and to rebut innocent presence; as in *Elliott*, the Court of Appeal paid careful attention to the risk of prejudice arising from evidence of membership. To similar effect is *Awoyemi* [2016] EWCA Crim 668, [2016] 2 Cr App R 22 (303), where the evidence of affiliation 'provided a link between [D] and a gang that glorified in violence and the use of firearms, mourned murdered friends, and threatened violent retribution for those who crossed them'. It showed the extent to which D had 'signed up' to gang and gun culture. In *Rashid* [2019] EWCA Crim 2018, it was held that where a police officer is permitted to give expert evidence as to the behaviour of gangs under the CJA 2003, s. 101(1)(d), it is imperative that the jury be correctly directed as to the use to which it can be put. In that case, proof that the defendants were gang members was relevant in two ways: it rebutted innocent presence and association with the vehicle in which weapons were found, and it went to the question of whether the appellants, either personally or jointly, were people who had an interest in, links to or access to firearms with criminal intent.

Bad character may also be relevant (and therefore admissible) to support identification without any similarity between the past and present offences, as in *Isichei* [2006] EWCA Crim 1815, where the fact that a robber, identified as D, had asked for 'coke' was sufficient to admit D's previous convictions for cocaine-related offences.

The use of bad character evidence for purposes of identification raises particularly difficult issues. The process of detection of crime may, understandably, focus on the accused's convictions for crimes of a particular type, and this in turn may pose a risk of conviction based unfairly on propensity, in breach of the guidance laid down in *Hanson* [2005] EWCA Crim 824, [2005] 1 WLR 3169 (see **F13.41**). In *H* [2014] EWCA Crim 420, D's image was picked out of an identification procedure in which it had been included largely because of his criminal record for the 'unusual combination' of an offence of violence following on from a sexual assault. The case was otherwise weak, but D was convicted after it was suggested that it would have been an 'enormous coincidence' if a man with D's record had been wrongly identified. Holding the conviction unsafe, the Court of Appeal pointed out that the jury should have been told why D had become a suspect to enable them to assess the true force of this so-called coincidence. Compare *Randall* [2006] EWCA Crim 1413, where a 'fleeting glimpse' identification of a burglar was supported by evidence of D's propensity to commit that crime, and *Howe* [2017] EWCA Crim 2400, where a qualified identification of D and a 'jigsaw' of strong circumstantial evidence including his presence near the scene of distraction burglaries of elderly people supported the evidence provided by his long record of very similar offences. In *N* [2014] EWCA Crim 506, there was evidence that D was at the party where an assault occurred, and his DNA was on the broken bottle that had been used as a weapon. The risk that he had been mistakenly identified by two witnesses was countered by D's previous convictions for street robbery, using the argument from coincidence, and it was held that this was acceptable provided the jury were directed to avoid an inference based on propensity. In some cases the fair course might be the admission of such evidence against the accused coupled with a strong direction about the need to eliminate the possibility that the offences were the work of others of equally bad character (cf. *Miller* [2003] EWCA Crim 2840). In *Brima* [2006] EWCA Crim 408, [2007] 1 Cr App R 24 (316), a man ran up, fatally stabbed the victim in front of several witnesses and ran away. D's defence was that the crime was committed by A, his friend. A positive identification of D by one of the witnesses was supported by some scientific evidence (though in some respects this also pointed to A) and by the evidence of A himself. Propensity evidence in the form of D's two previous convictions for assaults using a knife was held to have been rightly admitted, although in neither of the previous incidents was a serious injury inflicted. The Court of Appeal noted that, in light of D's attack on A, D's convictions would in any event have been brought out under s. 101(1)(g). **F13.50**

Where an eye-witness identifies the accused as responsible for one offence, and it is sought to support the correctness of the identification by reference to another eye-witness identification in respect of a separate offence, it was said in *Robinson* [1953] 2 All ER 334 that admissibility could be justified on the basis that it was a remarkable coincidence that D was separately identified by different witnesses as having been involved in two different robberies. Whether such a **F13.51** coincidence is remarkable or not must depend on the facts, but the risk of error inherent in fleeting glimpse identifications is not necessarily counteracted by other purported identifications of the same person. The use of s. 101(3) to counter the possible unfairness arising from the linkage of two weak identifications would also require to be considered.

Bad Character Evidence Rebutting Defence

F13.52 A common function that evidence of bad character may be called upon to perform is to show an event involving an accused person in its true light, rebutting an otherwise plausible innocent explanation. In applying the CJA 2003, s. 101(1)(d), in such instances, it is important to remember that a defence may be rebutted via an inference to be drawn from propensity or because the evidence of bad character has a probative value independent of any inference from propensity (see further, as to propensity, **F13.39** ***et seq.*** and, as to other relevant inferences, **F13.37**). Many defences that might appear credible if the prosecution are confined to one set of facts may be shown to be unlikely by reference to other instances of misconduct. In *Lemonnier* [2019] EWCA Crim 2275, for example, D was convicted of a murder alleged to have occurred in the course of the robbery of the victim, V. D's defence was that V was the aggressor and that D had stabbed him to prevent him entering a dwelling and to protect D's co-accused. The prosecution relied on the testimony of R who claimed to have been viciously attacked and robbed by D and another man three months before the killing of V. R's evidence was held to have been rightly admitted as the circumstances were 'strikingly similar' and the robbery close in point of time. The jury had been correctly directed that this was an unproven allegation (as to which see **F13.42**).

F13.53 In *Adams* [2006] EWCA Crim 2013, the defence to possession of a large quantity of a controlled drug was that D intended to use it to commit suicide. Previous offences of supply and attempting to supply were properly admitted to rebut the defence and to indicate criminal intent. The use of such evidence is easier to justify where the accused already has considerable explaining to do than where it is the mainstay of the case against the accused. In *Cambridge* [2011] EWCA Crim 2009, D attempted to dissociate himself from a gun found in a plastic bag, where both the gun and the bag could be scientifically linked to him and evidence of his previous illegal possession of a pellet gun was admitted to rebut his defence of innocent association. In *Soloman* [2019] EWCA Crim 1356, where D's fingerprints were found on the wrapping of ammunition and he advanced an innocent explanation, evidence that his fingerprints had previously been found on the wrapping of other ammunition was properly admitted, as the possibility of innocent contact was significantly reduced where there are two such coincidences to explain.

In *Masangomi* [2019] EWCA Crim 2390, D admitted possession of a firearm and ammunition; the only issue at trial was whether he did so with intent to endanger life. A subsequent incident in which D took part in a robbery and said to the victim 'If I had my gun, I'd shoot you' was correctly admitted as bad character evidence showing intention. In *Akunyili* [2014] EWCA Crim 346, D's defence to a charge of rape was properly rebutted both by the strikingly similar circumstances of an earlier rape conviction and by the almost identical defence he had run in the course of that case.

F13.54 Evidence of a propensity to untruthfulness may also (and despite statements in *Campbell* [2007] EWCA Crim 1472, [2007] 1 WLR 2798) be of particular importance for the jury in their assessment of the credibility of a defence. In *Malone* [2006] EWCA Crim 1860, D was charged with the murder of his wife, who had been found dead, and who he claimed had been murdered by members of the criminal fraternity who had also threatened him. The prosecution claimed that he had sought to lay a false trail in relation to the wife's disappearance. Evidence that he had, well before his wife's death, falsified a report, claiming to be from a private investigator who had uncovered evidence of the deceased's secret life, was admitted. The Court of Appeal opined that it was relevant to the issue whether he was telling the truth.

F13.55 **Nature of Defence as Factor Affecting Relevance** Evidence that is directed to the proof of some fact that is not in issue cannot be received, not because of the prejudicial effect of such evidence but simply because it is irrelevant. It is apparent, therefore, that the nature of the defence or defences reasonably open to the accused may have a bearing on the purpose that evidence of bad character may serve, which bears on its relevance and therefore on its admissibility.

Under s. 101(1)(d), the criteria to be applied are relevance to an important matter in issue between prosecution and defence and (where application is made by the defence to exclude) unfairness. However, the nature of the defence relied upon continues to play a major part in determining the relevance, and therefore the admissibility, of evidence of character. Section 103(1) may lend itself to the argument that the accused's propensity is always in issue unless it is clearly irrelevant but it is submitted that it is not an important issue (as required by s. 101(1)(d)) unless the circumstances of the case (which may include the nature of the defence raised) are such as to make it so (see further **F13.39**).

Anticipating Defence to be Raised The reforms to the rule regarding the application of pre-trial disclosure to the defence (see **D9.29**) significantly assist the prosecution in anticipating the issues at trial to which evidence of bad character may be relevant. Where the exact relevance remains unclear, it is better to delay a ruling until the evidence unfolds. See, e.g., *M* [2006] EWCA Crim 193, where the defence to a charge of rape involved a suggestion, put to the complainant in cross-examination, that she had neglected an opportunity to complain. This rendered admissible an account by the complainant of her belief, based on a previous incident, that D had a gun in his possession. **F13.56**

Multiple Charges and Accusations under the CJA 2003, s. 101(1)(d)

Section 112(2) of the CJA 2003 provides that, where an accused faces multiple charges in the same proceedings, the 'bad character' provisions apply as if each was charged in separate proceedings: in other words a 'gateway' is required to facilitate cross-admissibility between charges in the same proceedings in exactly the same way as where only one offence is charged. Where an accused faces more than one charge of a similar nature or where evidence of similar allegations is tendered in support of one charge, the evidence of one accuser may be admissible to support the evidence of another. Where no application to make use of the evidence in this way is made, the accused is entitled to have the case decided on the ground that the evidence is inadmissible, and the judge should direct the jury to that effect (*Adams* [2019] EWCA Crim 1363). The notice procedure (see **F13.3**) applies equally to cases of cross-admissibility (*Adams*). See also *Gabbai* [2019] EWCA Crim 2287, [2020] 4 WLR 65, where the prosecution had not given notice and the judge's intention to leave cross-admissibility to the jury only emerged during the first day of summing-up. The Court of Appeal noted that the late decision also rendered it impossible for the proposed direction to be discussed before counsel's closing speeches. **F13.57**

The principles to be applied to cases of this kind do not differ materially from those applicable where evidence of bad character is used to rebut an explanation otherwise open to the accused: indeed, the function of evidence of multiple accusers is often to rebut such an explanation. Separate exposition is helpful, however, in order to bring out the special problems of collusion that have arisen under this heading. The Act is also constructed in such a way as to anticipate the special problems arising out of contamination of evidence by matters other than collusion.

The underlying principle is that the probative value of multiple accusations may depend in part on their similarity, but also on the unlikely prospect that the same person would be falsely accused on different occasions by different and independent individuals. The making of multiple accusations is a coincidence in itself, which must be taken into account in deciding admissibility. As Lord Cross of Chelsea put it in *DPP v Boardman* [1975] AC 421 (at p. 460): **F13.58**

> ... the point is not whether what the appellant is said to have suggested would be, as coming from a middle-aged active homosexual, in itself particularly unusual but whether it would be unlikely that two youths who were saying untruly that the appellant had made homosexual advances to them would have put such a suggestion into his mouth.

Similarly, in *Chopra* [2006] EWCA Crim 2133, [2007] 1 Cr App R 16 (225) where the three young complainants each separately alleged that D, a dentist, had squeezed their breasts in the course of treatment, there was a sufficient connection to warrant cross-admissibility: the Court of Appeal noted that it was more likely to be true than if only one of them had said it, and was not persuaded by the argument that there were many more patients of D who had made no such allegation. See also *Wallace* [2007] EWCA Crim 1760, [2008] 1 WLR 572.

F13.59 In directing the jury where evidence is cross-admissible under the provisions of s. 101, it would be over-restrictive to suggest that the jury should first determine that they are satisfied in relation to one of the counts before moving on to use the evidence in relation to that count in dealing with any other. The jury, though obliged to reach a verdict on each count separately, may use admissible evidence in relation to any count, including the evidence of bad character arising from another (*Freeman* [2008] EWCA Crim 1863, [2009] 2 All ER 18, disapproving comments in *S* [2008] EWCA Crim 544). In part the confusion may have arisen because of a perceived need to conclude that the accused has a propensity to commit such an offence (an inference dependent on the accused's having done so on one occasion) before moving to consider another. However, the process of reasoning in cases such as *Chopra* does not depend on reasoning via propensity, but via coincidence, and is holistic rather than sequential (see *McAllister* [2008] EWCA Crim 1544, [2009] 1 Cr App R 10 (129) and **F13.38** for the distinction between propensity and non-propensity cases).

Freeman was applied in *O'Leary* [2013] EWCA Crim 1371, in which D faced two sets of charges relating to the deception of elderly and vulnerable victims, both of whom were suffering from dementia. It was held that the circumstances of the two transactions were admissible in relation to one another on the issue whether D acted dishonestly and had targeted the victims because they were vulnerable. Again, the reasoning was holistic rather than sequential. Likewise in *Lyons* [2012] EWCA Crim 659, the stark issue for the jury was whether 11 women had made up sexual allegations against D, a guru at the centre of a group of young, mainly female followers, or his loyal supporters were trying to protect him by denying that anything untoward happened at their meetings. It would have been impossible to take the evidence of each complainant in complete isolation before forming a view as to its truth, and unnecessary as the prosecution's case was of the emergence of a pattern of offending which made D's innocence an unlikely coincidence. It was otherwise in *Norris* [2009] EWCA Crim 2697, where, on the facts, it was necessary for the jury to be sure that D, a nurse, had deliberately administered a fatal injection to one patient before using that evidence to assist in their deliberations regarding the deaths of other patients.

In *Richards* [2018] EWCA Crim 2374, D was convicted of serious sexual offences against different groups of boys taking place over a long period, and a common thread in his defence was that he had no sexual interest in boys under the age of consent. A further count of voyeurism was strongly supported by evidence of diary entries by D, and in directing the jury the judge suggested that they start with this count because, if proved, it would assist in the consideration of whether D had a sexual interest in underage boys. This was held to be a correct 'propensity' direction. Where both coincidence and propensity arguments are in play, a particularly careful direction may be required to prevent the jury 'overvaluing the accumulation of inference' (*Nicholson* [2012] EWCA Crim 1568, [2012] 2 Cr App R 31 (405)). In that case the defence to sexual assaults allegedly committed on patients recovering from anaesthesia was that their memories were false. The accumulation of complaints provided a strong argument based on the unlikelihood of coincidence, but it was also the case that a relevant propensity of D could be established at the point where the jury were persuaded of his guilt in relation to any one complainant. See also *Rakib* [2011] EWCA Crim 870, [2012] 1 Cr App R (S) 1 (1), in which the prosecution case was that the jury could be satisfied that D had exposed himself to the complainant in relation to count 1, and could then use their conclusion to support the somewhat weaker evidence on count 2 that he had done so a second time using the same unusual *modus operandi*. The different directions required in taking a jury through the approach based on coincidence and the approach based on propensity may be found in the *Crown Court Compendium* (July 2020), ch. 13. In some rare cases, both directions may be called for (*N (H)* [2011] EWCA Crim 730; *Gunning* [2018] EWCA Crim 677), resulting in a particularly complex set of directions, one important object of which is to ensure that the jury does not end up 'double counting' the evidence. An example of such a direction is given in ch. 13.

The protective value of s. 101(1)(d) and (3) in combination is potentially weakened in cases involving multiple accusations in consequence of the rules about joinder of counts. These permit charges to be tried together where the evidence in relation to one is similar to, though inadmissible in respect of, another (see as to joinder **D11.63** ***et seq.***). Where this occurs, the efficacy of the decision to regard evidence of bad character as inadmissible depends entirely on the ability of the jury to follow a direction to disregard the evidence on one count when considering another. **F13.60**

In *H* [2011] EWCA Crim 2344, [2012] 1 Cr App R 30 (413), a sexual offences case arising out of a trial in 2005, there was no application to bring the gateway in s. 101(1)(d) into effect, though the Court of Appeal was of the view that such an application would, in light of more modern jurisprudence, have succeeded. The trial judge instructed the jury to give separate consideration to the accounts of the complainants (three young boys) but added a rider as to the possibility of the evidence of one child supporting the other when each said he was present when the other was abused. It was held that, where cross-admissibility is not contended for, there is no rule of law requiring a direction not to treat the evidence of one complainant as supportive of the other. Instead the strength and content of the direction should fit the facts of the particular case, which it was held to have done in the instant case.

Assumption of Truth of Evidence of Bad Character

Collusion **F13.61**

Criminal Justice Act 2003, s. 109

(1) Subject to subsection (2), a reference in this chapter to the relevance or probative value of evidence is a reference to its relevance or probative value on the assumption that it is true.
(2) In assessing the relevance or probative value of an item of evidence for any purpose of this chapter, a court need not assume that the evidence is true if it appears, on the basis of any material before the court (including any evidence it decides to hear on the matter), that no court or jury could reasonably find it to be true.

Section 109 is of general application to cases where the bad character evidence is in dispute, but it is of particular importance in cases where cross-admissibility is alleged, as the court may be assuming the truth of the very facts in issue.

It is obvious that an apparently strong nexus between accounts of events given by different witnesses does not prove guilt if it can be accounted for by collusion. In *Pepperell* [2009] EWCA Crim 1209, for example, fresh evidence establishing a close connection between complainants who had been treated at trial as virtually independent was determinative of the appeal. The question whether collusion has taken place is essentially one for the jury. Section 109 provides that the judge should consider the relevance or probative value of evidence on the assumption that it is true, except where it appears that no court or jury could reasonably find it to be so. The statutory rule substantially replicates the common law as stated by the House of Lords in *H* [1995] AC 596. Cases under the CJA 2003 have proceeded on the basis that *H* remains good law, and this would seem correct (see, e.g., *Somanathan*, heard with *Weir* [2005] EWCA Crim 2866, [2006] 2 All ER 570).

Contamination **F13.62**

Criminal Justice Act 2003, s. 107

(1) If on a defendant's trial before a judge and jury for an offence—
 (a) evidence of his bad character has been admitted under any of paragraphs (c) to (g) of section 101(1), and

(b) the court is satisfied at any time after the close of the case for the prosecution that—
(i) the evidence is contaminated, and
(ii) the contamination is such that, considering the importance of the evidence to the case against the defendant, his conviction of the offence would be unsafe,

the court must either direct the jury to acquit the defendant of the offence or, if it considers that there ought to be a retrial, discharge the jury.

(2) Where—
(a) a jury is directed under subsection (1) to acquit a defendant of an offence, and
(b) the circumstances are such that, apart from this subsection, the defendant could if acquitted of that offence be found guilty of another offence,

the defendant may not be found guilty of that other offence if the court is satisfied as mentioned in subsection (1)(b) in respect of it.

(3) If—
(a) a jury is required to determine under section 4A(2) of the Criminal Procedure (Insanity) Act 1964 whether a person charged on an indictment with an offence did the act or made the omission charged,
(b) evidence of the person's bad character has been admitted under any of paragraphs (c) to (g) of section 101(1), and
(c) the court is satisfied at any time after the close of the case for the prosecution that—
(i) the evidence is contaminated, and
(ii) the contamination is such that, considering the importance of the evidence to the case against the person, a finding that he did the act or made the omission would be unsafe,

the court must either direct the jury to acquit the defendant of the offence or, if it considers that there ought to be a rehearing, discharge the jury.

(4) This section does not prejudice any other power a court may have to direct a jury to acquit a person of an offence or to discharge a jury.
(5) For the purposes of this section a person's evidence is contaminated where—
(a) as a result of an agreement or understanding between the person and one or more others, or
(b) as a result of the person being aware of anything alleged by one or more others whose evidence may be, or has been, given in the proceedings,

the evidence is false or misleading in any respect, or is different from what it would otherwise have been.

Section 107 provides a specific power to discharge a jury or direct an acquittal where it becomes apparent that character evidence is contaminated and any resultant conviction would be, in consequence, unfair. 'Contamination', in this context, arises either from an 'agreement or understanding' between the person who has given evidence and another, or from that person's awareness of allegations made by another in the proceedings, and in consequence the evidence the person gives is false, misleading or simply different from what it would otherwise have been (s. 107(5)).

F13.63 Section 107(5) recognises that evidence may become contaminated not only in cases of deliberate conspiracy between witnesses, but also in those where there is a risk that one witness may unconsciously have been influenced by the account of another witness (see at common law *H* [1995] AC 596 and *Ryder* [1994] 2 All ER 859). The same considerations would seem to govern cases where the risk of falsity arises not from collusion between witnesses, but from what Lord Wilberforce in *DPP v Boardman* [1975] AC 421 (at p. 444) described as 'a process of infection from media or publicity or simply from fashion'. It would appear that the provisions of s. 107(5) cover both the obvious case of deliberate collusion and the more subtle process of unconscious contamination referred to in the common-law authorities. This was accepted in *Lamb* [2007] EWCA Crim 1766, where allegations of sexual activity in breach of trust were made against a schoolteacher by two girls, one of whom had persuaded the other to join with her in making disclosure. The Court of Appeal regarded s. 107 as applicable to 'collusion or innocent contamination' although ultimately the question in that case was not one of admissibility but of whether the judge's direction had done justice to the risk. Note that the statutory provisions apply only to trial on indictment (s. 107(1)). See also *K* [2008] EWCA Crim 3301, where the true question to be resolved was whether the witnesses, who were brothers, were honestly endeavouring to recall events of many years past, or dishonestly dissembling. The judge's decision to focus the jury's attention on the individual counts without directing on cross-admissibility reflected the way in which the case had been run, and a more specific direction on contamination was not called for. In *N (H)* [2011] EWCA Crim 730 it was noted that questions of collusion and contamination may arise on the facts of a case whether or not the jury are invited to treat allegations by different complainants as cross-admissible. Even where the jury are not so invited, there may still be a need to provide them with guidance about the risk of collusion and/or contamination, depending on the circumstances of the case.

In *C* [2006] EWCA Crim 1079, [2006] 1 WLR 2994, the Court of Appeal suggested that a trial judge should postpone a decision on a plausible submission that there has been contamination until the suggested contaminated evidence has been examined at trial. The judge could then 'have well in mind the precise details of the evidence actually given, with such weaknesses and problems as may have emerged'. This was done in *BR* [2014] EWCA Crim 1311, where the submission of contamination was made and rejected after the evidence of the three complainants, who were members of the same family, had been given. That submission formed part of a series of submissions regarding the strength of the evidence in relation to one complainant (C) standing alone. It was held that the judge was entitled to place considerable weight on email exchanges between the three complainants after C first complained to the police. There was no reason to suppose that the three complainants had expected these exchanges to be disclosed, and from their nature it was clear that C had not been influenced by the others. **F13.64**

Acquittals: Special Considerations

On rare occasions the prosecution contend that D has been guilty of past relevant misconduct despite having been acquitted by another court in respect of that conduct. Under the CJA 2003, as at common law, the prosecution would be adducing evidence of 'bad character', despite the acquittal, because the contention is that the accused had been guilty of misconduct on the previous occasion, even though no attempt is made to impose any penalty for it (see **F13.14**). The evidence would be admissible if the prosecution could show its relevance to an important issue under s. 101(1)(d), leaving the accused to contend for the exercise of the specific statutory discretion in s. 101(3). **F13.65**

The use of such evidence was at one time thought to be objectionable under the double jeopardy rule, until the decision of the House of Lords in *Z* [2000] 2 AC 483. D was charged with the rape of C, and his defence was consent. On four separate occasions D had been tried for the rape of other women, and on three occasions acquitted. The prosecution contended that evidence from all four previous complainants was admissible to rebut the defence put forward in respect of C. It was conceded that the evidence of the four, taken cumulatively, possessed the degree of probative value required for admissibility at common law. The House of Lords held that evidence may be adduced to prove the guilt of the accused in relation to the offence being tried notwithstanding that it shows the commission of other offences of which the accused has been acquitted. Provided that the prosecutor does not seek in any way to punish the accused for the other offences, the double jeopardy rule is not infringed. Under *Z*, it remained open for the judge to exercise discretion to prevent the unfair use of such evidence. An obvious vehicle for exclusion under the Act would be s. 101(3) or, in the unlikely case that the 'gateway' is not one to which s. 101(3) applies, the PACE 1984, s. 78. In *Smith*, one of the appeals heard with *Edwards* [2005] EWCA Crim 1813, [2006] 1 WLR 1524, the rule in *Z* was applied where D had been led to believe that he would not be prosecuted in respect of a particular allegation. This did not prevent the subsequent use of the allegation as evidence of propensity, subject to the application of the court's power to prevent unfair use. See also *Nguyen* [2008] EWCA Crim 585, [2008] 2 Cr App R 9 (99), where D was held to be 'not necessarily worse off' in consequence of the prosecution's decision not to prosecute for lesser offences of violence but to use them as evidence of propensity on a murder charge, and *Halliday* [2019] EWCA Crim 1457, where no proceedings had originally been brought in respect of a complaint of rape by P, but her evidence was admitted at D's trial for the very similar rape of V.

In *T (P)* [2013] EWCA Crim 2398, some 30 years had passed since the original acquittals for sexual offences. A challenge based on the fact that there no longer existed relevant material that would have assisted the jury in assessing the reliability of the evidence was dismissed. On the facts, it appears that the portions of the evidence that were significant in the later prosecution (for a series of serious sexual offences together with the murder of one victim) were supported by statements of the accused including what amounted to an admission of one rape. The lapse of time, which might in other circumstances have proved critical, did not appear to provide a genuine impediment to challenging the relevant parts of the evidence of the two complainants.

A co-accused may adduce evidence of an accused's bad character where the conditions of the CJA 2003, s. 101(1)(e) (see **F13.66**), are satisfied notwithstanding the latter's acquittal (*Simpson* [2019] EWCA Crim 1144). The Court of Appeal noted that the common-law restrictions with regard to evidence resulting in an acquittal had never applied to evidence relevant to the defence of an accused person.

The logic of *Z* suggests that a jury is not bound to accept the factual basis of a previous plea of guilty. In *Wynes* [2014] EWCA Crim 2585, D was tried for rapes against V, a girl aged ten. The prosecution sought to adduce bad character evidence in the form of D's previous conviction for a child pornography offence. He had pleaded guilty and been sentenced on the basis that he had accidentally downloaded an explicit 49-minute child-sex video, but the jury in the rape trial were entitled to regard this as evidence of an inappropriate sexual interest in young girls, and were not bound to accept the truth of the explanation he gave at the time.

EVIDENCE OF BAD CHARACTER ADDUCED BY A CO-ACCUSED

CJA 2003: Evidence of Bad Character Going to Matter in Issue Between Co-accused

F13.66 The relevant provision of the CJA 2003 is s. 101(1)(e), which is supplemented by s. 104.

Criminal Justice Act 2003, ss. 101 and 104

101.—(1) In criminal proceedings evidence of the defendant's bad character is admissible if, but only if—

...

(e) it has substantial probative value in relation to an important matter in issue between the defendant and a co-defendant,

...

104.—(1) Evidence which is relevant to the question whether the defendant has a propensity to be untruthful is admissible on that basis under section 101(1)(e) only if the nature or conduct of his defence is such as to undermine the co-defendant's defence.

(2) Only evidence—

(a) which is to be (or has been) adduced by the co-defendant, or

(b) which a witness is to be invited to give (or has given) in cross-examination by the co-defendant,

is admissible under section 101(1)(e).

Section 104(1) is primarily relevant to the cut-throat defence where the evidence of propensity is directed more towards establishing lack of veracity than to the issue of guilt. This is dealt with at **F13.73**. The restriction applied by s. 104(1) does not bite where the evidence of propensity is not directed to untruthfulness but to the issue of commission of the offence (*Daly* [2014] EWCA Crim 2117). In such cases, s. 101(1)(e) permits propensity evidence to be adduced against an accused by a co-accused whatever the nature of the defence, provided that it is of 'substantial probative value' in relation to an issue between them — though this will frequently occur because one blames the other.

Important Matter in Issue '"Important matter" means a matter of substantial importance in the context of the case as a whole' (CJA 2003, s. 112(1)). The mere denial by a co-accused of participation in a crime does not meet the terms of s. 101 but, if it is a necessary implication of the denial that another accused has committed the offence, s. 101(1)(e) comes into play between them (*Phillips* [2011] EWCA Crim 2935, [2012] 1 Cr App R 25 (332)). In *Phillips*, D1 and his co-accused, D2, were charged with cheating the revenue. Although neither was directly arguing that the other had committed the offence, both were impliedly doing so because the only logical consequence was that the offence must have been committed by the other defendant. In *Daly* [2014] EWCA Crim 2117, gateway (e) was applicable where the thrust of the defence advanced by both co-accused was that the other had acted alone in relation to the distraction burglary with which both were charged. This was enough to raise an important issue between them, even though it was a possible interpretation that they had been acting in concert as the prosecution alleged. Where defendants are not facing a joint charge and there is not a cut-throat defence, it was held in *Obeng* [2016] EWCA Crim 1797 to be particularly important to ascertain the fact in issue between the defendants and that it is truly an important one. *Obeng* was a complicated case involving injuries arising out of a drug deal leading to two separate kidnappings. The Court of Appeal doubted whether the issue between D1 and his co-accused D2 (whether certain injuries to a victim, V, had been caused during the first or the second kidnapping) could be said to be important when neither man gave evidence or advanced a positive case as to it. **F13.67**

In relation to the CJA 2003, s. 101(1)(d) (see **F13.36**), the matters in issue between the prosecution and defence are deemed to include the accused's propensity. No such provision applies to gateway (e), therefore the propensity of the co-accused to commit an offence of the type charged is not itself an issue between them (*Phillips*; *Daly*).

Substantial Probative Value The questions of the importance of the issue between the accused (see **F13.67**) and the probative value of the bad character evidence sought to be adduced should be addressed separately and seriatim (*Lawson* [2006] EWCA Crim 2572, [2007] 1 WLR 1191); see also *Obeng* [2016] EWCA Crim 1797, stressing the particular importance of this where the case does not involve a joint charge of cut-throat defence). **F13.68**

The leading case in relation to the meaning of 'substantial' probative value is *Platt* [2016] EWCA Crim 4, [2016] 1 Cr App R 22 (324), which resolves a conflict in earlier cases. D1 was convicted of the murder of a man who lived in the same hostel, and of arson with intent to endanger life by setting fire to the body. His co-accused, D2, another resident of the hostel, was acquitted after running a cut-throat defence blaming D1 for both offences. D1's defence was that he was not responsible and had not gone into the victim's room: he did not, however, directly assert that D2 had done so. D2 had been permitted under the CJA 2003, s. 101(1)(e), to adduce D1's convictions for arson and for offences under the OAPA 1861, s. 20, in order to demonstrate D1's propensity, on the basis that the evidence had substantial probative value in relation to that matter, which was an important matter in issue between the defendant and the co-defendant. However, in ruling on admissibility, the trial judge had failed to have due regard to the terms of s. 101(1)(e), in that the previous convictions were not of substantial probative value in relation to the issue of D1's propensity. The conviction for arson was a conviction when D1 was aged 15 and was of a completely different type of offence; the offences under s. 20 were likewise of some age and in a completely different context.

The Court of Appeal endorsed the view of Pitchford LJ in *Phillips* [2011] EWCA Crim 2935, [2012] 1 Cr App R 25 (332) that 'substantial' bears its natural meaning (referred to in *Phillips* as 'enhanced' probative value), rather than 'more than merely trivial'. It was particularly important for the wording of s. 101(1)(e) to be read in context, because it deliberately sets the bar higher than in gateway (d) where the issue is between the prosecution and the accused and because, if the test for admissibility is met, the court has no discretion to refuse the admission of the evidence when tendered on behalf of one accused against the other. The Court therefore emphasised the importance of reference to the statutory language as the sole guide to construction of the current law, and made clear its view that the common law was not in any way a guide to interpretation of the modern codified provisions.

The purpose of the higher bar set by s. 101(1)(e) was said in *Phillips* to be that the probative strength of the evidence should effectively remove the risk of unfair prejudice. As an aid to construction, the Court drew attention to s. 100(3) (see **F15.16**), which requires the court to have regard to particular factors in reaching an assessment of substantial probative value in relation to the bad character of a non-defendant. It was pointed out that the legal meaning of the term 'substantial' must be the same in both cases, thus suggesting that reference to s. 100(3) might be of value in cases under s. 101(1)(e). The enduring trend of making use of authorities decided under one provision in relation to another is hardly surprising, in that it may be a matter of pure chance whether the individual whose character an accused wishes to impugn appears as a co-accused or as a witness for the prosecution. *Phillips* was approved in *Turnbull* [2013] EWCA Crim 676, where the Court of Appeal endorsed the point that the question of admissibility was 'highly fact-sensitive' and would depend on what other evidence was available on the issue. In *Turnbull*, D1 was able to demonstrate the propensity of D2 for violence by cross-examining him about an attack shortly after the offence charged, and this 'dwarfed' the evidence of his old juvenile convictions which the judge had rightly ruled that D1 could not adduce. Similarly in *Hoare* [2016] EWCA Crim 886, where D1 claimed to have been acting under the domination of her partner D2, the co-accused, evidence of his controlling behaviour in a previous relationship was rightly excluded: the probative value of what had occurred was of limited value given the nuances introduced by the individual characteristics of the different people involved, and it added little to the picture already created by other, direct evidence of the interactions between D1 and D2. By contrast, in *Daly* [2014] EWCA Crim 2117, the previous conviction of the co-accused for a distraction burglary very similar to that charged ought to have been admitted at the behest of D, a man of previous good character.

F13.69 Further illustrations of the application of the rule may be found, for example, in *West* [2006] EWCA Crim 1843. One of the three men accused of the murder of a fourth sought for the first time in giving his evidence to blame D1, which created an issue between them which should have allowed D1 to have recourse to his co-accused's previous convictions for violence. In *De Vos* [2006] EWCA Crim 1688, D's convictions for drugs offences were admissible in relation to his contention that he was an innocent 'mule' duped by his co-accused. In *Land* [2006] EWCA Crim 2856, D1, an employee of the CPS, disclosed information to D2 as a result of which both were charged with offences relating to the administration of justice. D1's defence was that he had acted in fear of V, and he set about proving V's bad character. Various previous convictions and matters relating to a drugs deal were admitted, but other matters relating, *inter alia*, to the discovery of a sword at V's home were said to have been properly excluded on the grounds that they lacked the necessary 'substantial probative value' in relation to an important issue in the case. Where D1's defence to involvement in a serious assault was that he had punched C in self-defence, and that D2 had caused the serious injuries by a subsequent exchange of blows, the trial judge's conclusion that evidence of D2's propensity to violence was not of substantial probative value was reasonable. D2 had not sought to implicate D1, and the issue for the jury was whether D1 had taken part in an unprovoked attack (*Passos-Carr* [2009] EWCA Crim 2018).

F13.70 The absence of any discretion to restrain an accused from taking advantage of s. 101(1)(e) was the subject of judicial comment in *Musone* [2007] EWCA Crim 1237, [2007] 1 WLR 2467, where the Court of Appeal also considered and dismissed argument based on the ECHR, Article 6, before concluding (at [52]) that: 'The only apparent control on the deployment of evidence by one defendant against another is that which is contained in section 101(1)(e)'. It follows that, where evidence of propensity satisfies the test for admissibility in s. 101(1)(e), it may be adduced notwithstanding that it is also highly prejudicial. See also *Apabhai* [2011] EWCA Crim 917, pointing out that there is no statutory or residual common-law support for such a discretion, and *Phillips* [2011] EWCA Crim 2935, [2012] 1 Cr App R 25 (332), emphasising that there is no discretion to exclude such evidence on either fairness or 'case management' grounds where the introduction of untried satellite fraud issues on an already complicated prosecution was likely to confuse the jury. In *Hoare* [2016] EWCA Crim 886 it was said that if the evidence was of substantial probative value, any argument that the jury would be distracted by satellite litigation would not weigh against it, but that 'if it did distract in the true sense, the evidence would not have substantial probative value in relation to the issue in dispute between the defendants'. Where an accused, by making a late application, puts a co-accused in the position of being unable to deal fairly with the evidence relating to his or her character (which would otherwise be admissible), the judge may have recourse to the power under CrimPR Part 21 (see Supplement, **R21.1** *et seq.*, and **F13.3**) to disallow the late application (*Jarvis* [2008] EWCA Crim 488, and cf. *Musone*, where a similar point is made in relation to a late application to adduce hearsay evidence). *Musone* and *Jarvis* were considered in *Ramirez* [2009] EWCA Crim 1721, where it was said that the failure of the judge to consider whether there had been a deliberate manipulation of the rules by the co-accused or his counsel was immaterial where the giving of the evidence, even without proper notice, would not have prevented the fair trial of the appellant. However, the Court of Appeal also stressed that its conclusion was reached on the particular facts of the case, and that in another case the giving of bad character evidence by a co-accused without proper notice might necessitate a retrial and lead to severe sanctions against any legal representative found to have been involved in deliberate manipulation of the rules.

The giving of a standard *Hanson* ([2005] EWCA Crim 824, [2005] 1 WLR 3169) direction (see **F13.23**) against over-valuing propensity evidence was said in *Najib* [2013] EWCA Crim 86 to be likely to confuse the jury where the evidence is adduced by one co-accused against the other, given that a co-accused bears no burden of proof. While this is true, it would appear to be of general importance that the jury should never jump to conclusions based on evidence of bad character. **F13.71**

Propensity where Character in Issue

The CJA 2003, s. 101(1)(e), is likely to be brought into play where a co-accused sets up his or her own good character, or at least seeks to assert positive aspects of his or her character, so as to make the co-accused seem less likely than the accused to have committed the offence. Relevant examples of situations that would attract such a response include *Bracewell* (1978) 68 Cr App R 44, where D1 and D2 were jointly charged with the murder of an old man in the course of a burglary. D1 was prevented from adducing evidence-in-chief to show D2's violent disposition, on the ground of insufficient relevance, but the position changed when it emerged that D2's defence was that he was an experienced burglar of a non-violent type, able to keep a cool head, whereas D1 was inexperienced, nervous, excitable and probably drunk. It was held that by raising this defence D2 had made an issue of his propensity, and that D1 should at that stage have been allowed to cross-examine him about his violent nature and to call evidence about it if necessary. **F13.72**

Evidence Going to Issue of Untruthfulness between Accused and Co-accused

Section 101(1)(e) of the CJA 2003 (see **F13.66**) renders admissible evidence that has 'substantial probative value' in relation to an important matter in issue between co-accused. 'Important matter' means 'a matter of substantial importance in the context of the case as a whole' (s. 112(1)). Where the evidence adduced is of one defendant's 'propensity to untruthfulness', s. 101(1)(e) is further restricted in its operation by s. 104 to cases where the nature or conduct of his or her defence is such as to undermine that of the other defendant. Note that only defence evidence is admissible under this provision (s. 104(2)). **F13.73**

Criminal Justice Act 2003, s. 104

(1) Evidence which is relevant to the question whether the defendant has a propensity to be untruthful is admissible on that basis under section 101(1)(e) only if the nature or conduct of his defence is such as to undermine the co-defendant's defence.

(2) Only evidence—

(a) which is to be (or has been) adduced by the co-defendant, or

(b) which a witness is to be invited to give (or has given) in cross-examination by the co-defendant,

is admissible under section 101(1)(e).

F13.74 The leading case is *Lawson* [2006] EWCA Crim 2572, [2007] 1 WLR 1191. Three young men were alleged to have participated in the manslaughter of a third by pushing him into deep water, where he drowned. The principal offender pleaded guilty, but there was an issue between the two alleged secondary parties, each of whom denied participation, but alleged that the other had made incriminating remarks as to his own intention to push the victim in. Thus each had undermined the defence of the other. The issue of particular difficulty concerned the conviction of L for an offence of violence. This was held not to establish a relevant propensity to offend, but to go instead to credibility, and to have the necessary 'substantial probative value' in relation to that issue. In so deciding, the Court of Appeal rejected the application to s. 101(1)(e) of *Hanson* [2005] EWCA Crim 824, [2005] 1 WLR 3169 (see **F13.44**), where it was decided that, in relation to s. 101(1)(d), only evidence of direct relevance to veracity, such as a conviction involving lying, is admissible to show untruthfulness. This 'cautious test of admissibility' was held more appropriate to applications by the Crown. An accused should not be so restricted in the evidence of criminal behaviour of a co-accused (or, as it was rendered in *Rosato* [2008] EWCA Crim 1243, 'such a narrow reading would have been well capable of unfairness as between co-defendants'). The Court in *Lawson* pointed to the similar outcome in *Osbourne*, an appeal heard with *Renda* [2005] EWCA Crim 2862, [2006] 2 All ER 553, in which a propensity to violence had been admitted on the issue of untruthfulness, and rejected the counter-argument based on *M* [2006] EWCA Crim 1126, where such evidence was said not to go to truthfulness, on the ground that the point had not been argued. *Lawson* was also applied in *Simpson* [2019] EWCA Crim 1144, where the contention was that D's propensity to untruthfulness was shown by a previous incident of violence about which he had lied. The distinguishing of *Hanson* is not without difficulty, however, in that both s. 101(1)(d) and (e) deal with an accused having 'a propensity to be untruthful' but it appears that the meaning and content of the propensity is broader in s. 101(1)(e). Where, however, evidence of a propensity not directly suggestive of untruthfulness is admitted under s. 101(1)(d) as being relevant to the guilt of the accused, the effect of *Campbell* [2007] EWCA Crim 1472, [2007] 1 WLR 2798 (see **F13.24**) is that the evidence is admissible for all relevant purposes, including an assessment of the accused's credibility, so that the practical difference between gateways (d) and (e) is reduced.

More consistent with *Hanson* (though the point in *Lawson* was not argued) is *Reid* [2006] EWCA Crim 2900, where the Court of Appeal applied the *Hanson* distinction between untruthfulness and dishonesty in ruling on the co-accused's admissions of offences involving deception. In *Jarvis* [2008] EWCA Crim 488, it was held that there is no warrant for restricting bad character evidence going to a propensity for untruthfulness to evidence of past untruthfulness as a witness: an observation that holds true whether or not *Hanson* applies.

F13.75 Where the conditions of s. 101(1)(e) and s. 104 are fulfilled, the court has no statutory discretion to restrain the co-accused from adducing relevant evidence of bad character, as s. 101(3) is inapplicable. See, however, **F13.66** as to the judge's powers to disallow a late application by a co-accused where the target of the application would be unable to deal with it effectively.

EVIDENCE OF BAD CHARACTER TO CORRECT FALSE IMPRESSION OR COUNTER ATTACK ON ANOTHER'S CHARACTER

Uses of Bad Character Evidence Contingent on Nature of Defence

F13.76 The main provisions governing the use of evidence of the accused's bad character to establish the commission of the offence are the CJA 2003, s. 101(1)(d), where the evidence is to be adduced by the prosecution, and s. 101(1)(e), where the evidence is relied upon by a co-accused. These uses of bad character evidence are dealt with at **F13.36** ***et seq.*** and **F13.66** respectively. Both subsections (1)(d) and (e) may also permit the use of evidence of bad character to show untruthfulness.

The CJA 2003 expressly provides that, in addition to the gateways described above, the accused may also have to meet evidence of bad character designed to correct a false impression the accused has given (s. 101(1)(f): see **F13.78**), or to repel an attack the accused has made on the character of another (s. 101(1)(g): see **F13.84**). These methods of deploying bad character evidence are described in the remainder of this section. The relevant provisions of the CJA 2003 are not contingent on the decision of the accused to give evidence, so there is no tactical advantage in terms of character evidence in declining to do so. It also means that the evidence that is adduced under the provisions, which are considered below, cannot be said to be admissible only in relation to the issue of the credit to be given to the evidence of the accused if it is relevant in relation to other matters (see *Highton* [2005] EWCA Crim 1985, [2005] 1 WLR 3472 at **F13.24**). It will be for the court to decide what use to make of, say, convictions for dishonesty where the accused is charged with a sexual assault, or vice versa, with *Campbell* [2007] EWCA Crim 1472, [2007] 1 WLR 2798, decided under s. 101(1)(d), advocating a common-sense approach rather than the pre-2003 framework of technical distinctions based on the separation of relevance to guilt and credit. The following provisions, already considered, are of equal application to evidence of bad character admitted under the remaining exceptions: s. 107 (stopping the case where evidence contaminated: see **F13.62**), s. 109 (assumption of truth in assessment of relevance or probative value: see **F13.61**). The provisions of s. 108, regarding the use which can be made of evidence of convictions when the accused was a child, are also of general relevance and are considered at **F13.91**. **F13.77**

Evidence to Correct a False Impression

Section 101(1)(f) of the CJA 2003 permits evidence of bad character to be adduced by the prosecution to correct a false impression given by the accused about him or herself. In *Assani* [2008] EWCA Crim 2563, the Court of Appeal called for closer attention to the provision in s. 105(7) that s. 101(1)(f) admits prosecution evidence only. Applications by one co-accused to adduce evidence of bad character against another fall to be dealt with under s. 101(e). **F13.78**

The provision is supplemented by s. 105, which lays down the circumstances in which the accused is regarded as having given such an impression. Note that evidence admitted under gateway (f) is limited to evidence correcting the false impression (s. 105(6)) so that the general doctrine that evidence, once admitted, is admissible for all purposes to which it is relevant (see **F13.24**), is excluded. The provisions of s. 101(3), which exclude evidence having an adverse effect on the fairness of the proceedings, do not apply to evidence tendered under s. 101(1)(f) (see **F13.19**).

Criminal Justice Act 2003, s. 105

(1) For the purposes of section 101(1)(f)—
  (a) the defendant gives a false impression if he is responsible for the making of an express or implied assertion which is apt to give the court or jury a false or misleading impression about the defendant;
  (b) evidence to correct such an impression is evidence which has probative value in correcting it.
(2) A defendant is treated as being responsible for the making of an assertion if—
  (a) the assertion is made by the defendant in the proceedings (whether or not in evidence given by him),
  (b) the assertion was made by the defendant—
    (i) on being questioned under caution, before charge, about the offence with which he is charged, or
    (ii) on being charged with the offence or officially informed that he might be prosecuted for it, and evidence of the assertion is given in the proceedings,

(c) the assertion is made by a witness called by the defendant,
(d) the assertion is made by any witness in cross-examination in response to a question asked by the defendant that is intended to elicit it, or is likely to do so, or
(e) the assertion was made by any person out of court, and the defendant adduces evidence of it in the proceedings.

(3) A defendant who would otherwise be treated as responsible for the making of an assertion shall not be so treated if, or to the extent that, he withdraws it or disassociates himself from it.
(4) Where it appears to the court that a defendant, by means of his conduct (other than the giving of evidence) in the proceedings, is seeking to give the court or jury an impression about himself that is false or misleading, the court may if it appears just to do so treat the defendant as being responsible for the making of an assertion which is apt to give that impression.
(5) In subsection (4) 'conduct' includes appearance or dress.
(6) Evidence is admissible under section 101(1)(f) only if it goes no further than is necessary to correct the false impression.
(7) Only prosecution evidence is admissible under section 101(1)(f).

F13.79 Under ss. 101(1)(f) and 105, evidence of bad character is admissible provided only that it has 'probative value' in correcting the false impression. An accused may withdraw or dissociate him or herself from an assertion which would otherwise merit the admission of bad character evidence in rebuttal (s. 105(3)). Should the accused choose not to do so, the rebuttal evidence is admissible 'only if it goes no further than is necessary to correct the false impression' (s. 105(6)). Gateway (f) should not be over-used, and requires careful analysis of the specific assertion the accused has made that is alleged to be false (*Ullah* [2006] EWCA Crim 2003). *Ullah* was applied in *Khan* [2020] EWCA Crim 163, where in context D's assertion that he had never sold or supplied heroin was a rebuttal of an allegation that he had supplied to fellow inmates of a hostel, and was not therefore false despite a conviction for attempting to supply to his brother. The court should also consider whether the accused has attempted to mislead the jury in a way that goes beyond denying the offence (*D* [2011] EWCA Crim 1474, [2011] 4 All ER 568, considered in *McLeod* [2017] EWCA Crim 517, [2017] 2 Cr App R (S) 39 (332)). Particular care should be taken where an answer given in cross-examination is equivocal and may not amount to a false impression (*Good* [2008] EWCA Crim 2923).

The power under s. 78 of the PACE 1984, while not specifically preserved in relation to cases not covered by the specific power of exclusion of evidence of bad character in s. 101(3) of the CJA 2003, could be invoked to provide any further protection the courts may regard as necessary (see **F13.19**). Section 78 was regarded as potentially applicable (though the decision of the judge not to exclude was upheld) in *Verdol* [2015] EWCA Crim 502, where D, having suggested that he was of good character apart from some minor immigration matters, produced, without notice, an alibi defence based on mobile phone records which unexpectedly revealed his involvement in drug dealing.

F13.80 The CJA 2003 provisions apply irrespective of whether witnesses are specifically called as to good character, and whether or not the accused elects to give evidence on his or her own behalf. Evidence admitted under the provision potentially goes towards correcting the false impression in a manner indicative of guilt, not merely of the credit to be given to any testimony the accused gives.

In *Ullah* [2006] EWCA Crim 2003, D stated in interview that he had never acted dishonestly and that he had been meticulous in his business dealings. The CJA 2003 clarifies the position where the accused, as in *Ullah*, makes misleading assertions during questioning or when charged and these are subsequently given in evidence in the proceedings. These constitute assertions for the purposes of the provision (s. 105(2)(b)) and so they may result in the use of evidence to correct any false impression given, even where the prosecution are responsible for placing the original assertion before the court. In *Ullah* D's previous convictions for deception-related offences were admitted. In such cases, the accused would do well to disown the assertion, if it is not necessary for the defence relying on s. 105(3). In some cases the prosecution ought not to present the original assertion at all. In *Khan* [2020] EWCA Crim 163, where the matter in response to which the assertion had been made had already been edited out of the interview that was presented at trial, the Court of Appeal considered that there was no reason why D's response could not also have been edited out, relying on s. 105(6). There was no risk that the assertion would be repeated in evidence.

In *Renda* [2005] EWCA Crim 2862, [2006] 2 All ER 553, where the issue arose of whether D had withdrawn or dissociated himself from a false impression, the Court of Appeal clearly stated that there is a difference between making a positive decision to correct such an impression and being driven in cross-examination to concede its falsity. In the latter case, the accused could derive no benefit from s. 105(3). Nor can an accused expect that answers to questions at interview that are admissible to correct a false impression should be edited out to prevent unfairness: 'if an accused lies in interview and the consequences ... are unfortunate, the answer is not to edit out those lies' (*Dixon* [2012] EWCA Crim 2163, where D responded to questions about whether he found children sexually arousing by saying, 'No, it makes me feel sick'. Unknown to the interviewer, D had convictions for sexual assault, including one on a child, which became admissible in consequence).

Examples of False Impression

In *Kiernan* [2008] EWCA Crim 972, D claimed to have 'paid his debt to society' in relation to an admitted conviction, without mentioning that he had absconded and remained at large. The Court of Appeal observed that he was setting himself up as a reformed character when he was 'nothing of the sort'. **F13.81**

In *Renda* [2005] EWCA Crim 2862, [2006] 2 All ER 553, it was emphasised that whether an accused has given a 'false impression' is essentially a question of fact. In that case, D had clearly done so, by misrepresenting the nature of his previous employment in an attempt to make himself out to be a man of positive good character. It would also appear that an accused who adduces evidence of bad character in order to be presented before the court 'warts and all' may be held to have given a false impression if there are further discreditable revelations to be made. In *Thompson* [2018] EWCA Crim 2082, D's defence to involvement in a firearms conspiracy was that he was a drug dealer who had become involved with one of the other conspirator's drugs dealings rather than with any gun-related activity. He gave a misleading and detailed explanation of the history of his drug-dealing, suggesting that he had voluntarily refrained from dealing for long periods, when in fact he had been in prison for robbery. The Court of Appeal held that the robbery convictions were admissible and also rejected an argument that the judge should have exercised her discretion under the PACE 1984, s. 78, to exclude them. To similar effect is *Fender* [2018] EWCA Crim 2829, in which D explained his presence at a sale of firearms and ammunition on the basis that he was involved in low-level drug dealing and that one of the men involved in the firearms conspiracy was, by complete coincidence, his supplier. He elaborated by saying that he would not be involved with any gang-related activity (gangs 'made him quiver'), that he made little profit from his dealings and that he had moral objections to gang-related violence and dangerous weapons. The Court of Appeal considered that D had rendered admissible evidence of his links to a range of gangs, his previous convictions for dishonesty and violence and photographic evidence of D posing with large sums of money. This evidence did not go beyond what was necessary to rebut the line of defence D had chosen to put forward.

By contrast, in *Stokes* [2015] EWCA Crim 1911, D was convicted of producing cannabis in a concealed underground factory. He had pleaded guilty to another count of production involving cannabis plants in an upstairs room of his own property. His evidence was that the smaller-scale operation was his own private venture and that he was unaware of the factory despite having keys to the premises. In his testimony he narrated a conversation with friends which was said to have marked the beginning of his decision to cultivate his own plants. The prosecution succeeded in admitting evidence of D's convictions for possession of two small wraps of Class A drugs some 12 years before, when D was 17, on the grounds that D was giving a false impression that the cultivation of cannabis would be a 'novelty' in his life. This slender connection was rightly refuted by the Court of Appeal as not coming 'even close to suggesting' that D had never had any involvement with illegal drugs in the past. In *Omotoso* [2018] EWCA Crim 1394, D was charged with firearms offences and the issue was whether he was the driver of the car from which weapons had been thrown during a police chase. D's minor exaggeration about the nature of his employment, if it created a false impression at all, should have been dealt with by an admission: the extensive evidence of D's criminal record that had been adduced went much further than was necessary to correct any false impression created by D, and ought not to have been admitted.

F13.82 It is clear that the accused may be held to have given a false impression by means of conduct, including dress (s. 105(4) and (5)), but it is unclear how such a provision (permitting rebuttal only to the extent that it is necessary to correct the impression) will operate in practice except in the obvious case of a defrocked clergyman (*DS* [1999] Crim LR 911) or its equivalent. Similarly, in *Robinson* [2001] EWCA Crim 214, it might be said that an accused who gives evidence waving a Bible is attempting to impress the court with his devotion to the Deity, an impression that might well be false, but only evidence of bad character going directly to the falsity of the impression is admissible in rebuttal.

F13.83 As only prosecution evidence is admissible under s. 101(1)(f), the provision cannot be invoked by a co-accused where one accused is misleadingly trying to pose, for example, as an experienced burglar with no record for using violence (cf. *Bracewell* (1978) 68 Cr App R 44). Such evidence would, however, appear to be admissible under s. 101(1)(e) (see **F13.66**).

'Attack on Another Person's Character'

F13.84 The CJA 2003, s. 101(1)(g), permits the prosecution to adduce evidence of bad character to counter an attack on another person. In *Assani* [2008] EWCA Crim 2563, the Court of Appeal drew attention to s. 106(3), which limits the admissibility of bad character evidence under s. 101(1)(g) to prosecution evidence. Applications by one co-accused to adduce evidence of bad character against another fall to be dealt with under s. 101(1)(e) (see **F13.66**). Section 101(1)(g) is supplemented by s. 106, which details the circumstances in which such an attack occurs. An accused may apply to exclude evidence the admission of which under s. 101(1)(g) would have an unfair effect on the fairness of the proceedings (s. 101(3)).

Criminal Justice Act 2003, s. 106

(1) For the purposes of section 101(1)(g) a defendant makes an attack on another person's character if—
 (a) he adduces evidence attacking the other person's character,
 (b) he (or any legal representative appointed under section 38(4) of the Youth Justice and Criminal Evidence Act 1999 to cross-examine a witness in his interests) asks questions in cross-examination that are intended to elicit such evidence, or are likely to do so, or
 (c) evidence is given of an imputation about the other person made by the defendant—
  (i) on being questioned under caution, before charge, about the offence with which he is charged, or
  (ii) on being charged with the offence or officially informed that he might be prosecuted for it.

(2) In subsection (1) 'evidence attacking the other person's character' means evidence to the effect that the other person—
 (a) has committed an offence (whether a different offence from the one with which the defendant is charged or the same one), or
 (b) has behaved, or is disposed to behave, in a reprehensible way; and 'imputation about the other person' means an assertion to that effect.

(3) Only prosecution evidence is admissible under section 101(1)(g).

F13.85 'Attack' The CJA 2003, s. 106(2), creates a link back to the definition of bad character in *s. 98 (see **F13.4**), and in particular* to the concept of misconduct as the commission of an offence or other reprehensible behaviour. In *Lamalatie* [2008] EWCA Crim 314, the Court of Appeal considered that an allegation that the complainant had started the fight in which he was injured by D would probably be an allegation of 'reprehensible conduct' under the CJA 2003, whatever the position under the old law. In *Kidd* [2019] EWCA Crim 1439, however, D's defence of self-defence was rebutted by evidence of propensity for violence because his defence included an allegation that the complainant had verbally abused and attacked him. The Court of Appeal considered that the evidence was wrongly admitted as D should have been entitled to raise self-defence without risking the admission of his previous convictions. In *Fitzgerald* [2017] EWCA Crim 556, the Court of Appeal accepted that a mere denial of the prosecution case, while it might carry an imputation that a witness was lying, would not of itself amount to an attack, but a suggestion that prosecution witnesses were attempting or conspiring to pervert the course of justice by concocting false allegations would do so (applying *Pedley* [2014] EWCA Crim 848). In *Matthews* [2013] EWCA Crim 2238, D was charged with assault by penetration of a baby left in his care by the mother, R. On the facts, either D or R must have been responsible for the assault. A defence application was made under the CJA 2003, s. 100 (see **F15**), to admit evidence of R's bad character, including her substantial record for dishonesty. The prosecution made clear that if the defence pursued the admission of such evidence it would in turn make an application under s. 101(1)(g) to adduce D's own bad character. Although the mere suggestion that R caused the injuries would constitute an 'attack' under s. 106, the prosecution may see fit to invoke it only where the defence make an issue of the other person's bad character. Questions asked of the accused on behalf of the prosecution do not trigger the provision (cf. *Jones* (1909) 3 Cr App R 67), although it appears that questioning at interview may have this effect (s. 106(1)(c)).

Evidence of the bad character of a non-defendant is admissible only with the leave of the court under the CJA 2003, s. 100 (see **F15** and *Matthews*). It follows that an 'attack' for the purposes of s. 101(1)(g) based on evidence adduced by the defence will have been preceded by the granting of such leave, and therefore the evidence or question must concern a matter that is important explanatory evidence or is of substantial probative value in relation to an important matter in the case. A gratuitous attack designed merely to blacken the non-defendant's character in an attempt to secure an unmeritorious acquittal will not pass muster under this provision — the 'attack' must be merited. It may seem to be unnecessarily punitive to provide that it should (subject to the discretion of the court under s. 101(3): see **F13.90**) be met with apparently unlimited revelations about the accused's own character — revelations that, under the CJA 2003, are admissible for all purposes to which they are relevant (see **F13.24**) — but this is the effect of the provision: see, e.g., *Johnson* [2019] EWCA Crim 1025, where evidence of D's previous convictions, admitted under s. 101(1)(g) following a successful application to admit the convictions of his alleged victim, was also used to support an inference about D's propensity to loss of temper and violence, subject to the giving of appropriate directions. **F13.86**

Evidence Proving 'Attack' As with s. 101(1)(f) (see **F13.78**), the attack may be made in an out-of-court statement, including an interview in which the accused casts an imputation (s. 106(1)(c)). Again there is no requirement that the evidence of the attack is adduced by the defence, thus in one of the appeals heard with *Renda* [2005] EWCA Crim 2862, [2006] 2 All ER 553 (that of Ball), D was charged with rape and in the course of interview referred to the complainant as 'a slag', criticising her promiscuity in 'very disparaging terms'. His defence at trial was that she was lying and perhaps motivated by a wish for vengeance for past slights. The trial judge's decision to admit evidence of D's bad character on the strength of the specific slights in the interview which had been adduced as part of the prosecution case was supported by the Court of Appeal as a proper exercise of his discretion. Section 106, unlike s. 105 (which supplements s. 101(1)(f)), does not contain a provision permitting the accused to disassociate him or herself from the imputation. However, the court's discretion to disallow the admission of evidence of bad character could be invoked where the defence do not seek to maintain the attack. In *Nelson* [2006] EWCA Crim 3412, the Court of Appeal questioned the relevance of statements at interview adduced by the prosecution and expressed the view that such evidence should not be adduced simply to provide a basis for gateway (g). **F13.87**

In *Omotoso* [2018] EWCA Crim 1394, the Court of Appeal stated that evidence given in the course of an abuse application should not be relied on when considering whether an 'attack' had been made on a prosecution witness for the purpose of the CJA 2003, s. 101(1)(g). What was said in the absence of the jury could be used only to provide a focus for what was said in their presence, not as evidence.

F13.88 **'On Another Person's Character'** Section 101(1)(g) of the CJA 2003, together with the supplementary provision of s. 106, appears to contemplate an attack on a specific person. It would not therefore be sufficient, where a crime has clearly been committed by someone, for the accused to say that he or she has not done it and to lay the blame on some unknown individual. Where a specific attack is made, however, it does not matter that the person attacked is not a witness in the case.

Thus the problems that arose under the Criminal Evidence Act 1898, s. 1(3), which had to be amended in order to include imputations against the deceased in a homicide case, do not arise in relation to the CJA 2003: an attack on any victim may trigger s. 101(1)(g), as may an attack on any other non-witness. Nor is it necessary, for the same reason, to consider whether a person whose hearsay statement is before the court and who is the subject of an attack by the defence is a 'witness': whether the person is or not, the attack still triggers the provision (cf. *Miller* [1997] 2 Cr App R 178). In *Nelson* [2006] EWCA Crim 3412, it was, however, suggested that it would be unusual for evidence of an accused's bad character to be admitted where the only basis for doing so was an attack on a non-witness who is also a non-victim. On the facts of that case, however, the person whose character was attacked was alleged to have been conspiring with a prosecution witness, which provided a proper foundation for gateway (g). *Nelson* was considered in *Williams* [2014] EWCA Crim 1862, where the attack took the form of a suggestion that S had both committed and confessed to the murder with which D was charged, using a knife supplied by TW. Neither S nor TW gave evidence, but the jury had heard statements from both. In those circumstances, as the attack on the character of the absent persons was extremely grave, it was appropriate for the jury to hear the character of D (as the person making the allegations), and there was no basis on which the discretion under s. 101(3), should have been exercised against the prosecution.

F13.89 **Where the Accused Does Not Testify** Under the CJA 2003, bad character may be revealed whether the accused gives evidence or not. This reform was part of the package recommended by the Law Commission, and it is submitted that it is sound in principle. Where the jury must decide between competing versions of events, the argument that they need to know the character of the person making the attack is the same where the accused testifies or declines to do so. In *Thomas* [2020] EWCA Crim 4, D's counsel succeeded in an application to defer consideration of whether D's convictions, relevant to the credibility of his attack on C, should be admitted in a case involving kidnap, rape and assault until D had given evidence. In the event, D gave no evidence and his convictions were not admitted. On appeal it was claimed that the judge had erred and in effect put pressure on D not to give evidence. The Court of Appeal observed that the judge had behaved with scrupulous fairness in acceding to the original submission, which was premised upon an assumption that if D did not give evidence the previous convictions would not be admitted. He had given D a 'get-out' that many other judges would not have. On the basis of the prior cross-examination of the complainant about lies, retractions and inconsistencies, gateway (g) was plainly engaged and the judge could quite reasonably have directed that the previous convictions be adduced at the end of the prosecution case.

F13.90 **Discretion** Section 101(3) of the CJA 2003 (see **F13.19**) places the court under a duty to exclude evidence where to admit it under s. 101(1)(g) would have such an adverse effect on the fairness of the proceedings that the court ought not to do so. As to the considerations to be taken into account, the view of the Court of Appeal in *Clarke* [2011] EWCA Crim 939, following a review of the authorities, was that there is no need for the prosecution to demonstrate that evidence of bad character, to be relevant to credibility, demonstrates an underlying propensity to untruthfulness. The purpose of s. 101(1)(g) is to 'provide the jury with information relevant to the question whether the defendant's attack on another person's character is worthy of belief'. There is no requirement that the evidence thus admitted should reach any particular threshold of probative value, or that the creditworthiness of the defendant should be an issue of substantial importance in the case (*Mehmedov* [2014] EWCA Crim 1523, [2015] 1 WLR 495).

The concept is of the general credit of the accused rather than the narrower concept of propensity to untruthfulness arising in relation to s. 101(1)(d) (see **F13.44**). In making their decision, a jury should be permitted recourse to material bearing on the whole of the accused's bad character, not merely those parts that relate specifically to veracity. Defence counsel in *Clarke* had relied on the case of *Chrysostomou* [2010] EWCA Crim 1403, in which the Court of Appeal had rejected evidence of texts suggesting D was a drug dealer in relation to an attack by him consisting of an allegation that the complainant of the offence was a user of drugs who owed money to others. *Chrysostomou* appeared to suggest that the test to be applied was that the bad character evidence had to do more than 'blacken the character' of the accused and by doing so to 'dent his credibility generally'. The Court in *Clarke* stated (at [33]) that these observations, if taken to suggest that the bad character evidence should focus more narrowly on credibility, 'do not properly reflect the test which this court has applied when dealing with applications to adduce evidence under paragraph (g)'. However, it was important that the evidence adduced should reflect the character of the accused at the time of trial, so that, for example, some old convictions might properly be rejected, particularly those demonstrating propensity to commit the offence charged. Note that the evidence in *Chrysostomou* did not involve clear proof of offending: this might be an alternative reason for exercising the discretion against the use of the text evidence concerned.

In *Omotoso* [2018] EWCA Crim 1394, the Court of Appeal observed that judges should be careful to ensure that gateway (g) is not invoked too lightly where a police officer's conduct of an investigation is the subject of cross-examination, in order not to inhibit a legitimate line of questioning. 'A gentle hint should be sufficient to alert trial counsel of the potential dangers of pursuing a particular course' (at [59]).

OFFENCES COMMITTED BY ACCUSED WHEN A CHILD

Criminal Justice Act 2003, s. 108 **F13.91**

(1) Section 16(2) and (3) of the Children and Young Persons Act 1963 (offences committed by person under 14 disregarded for purposes of evidence relating to previous convictions) shall cease to have effect.
(2) In proceedings for an offence committed or alleged to have been committed by the defendant when aged 21 or over, evidence of his conviction for an offence when under the age of 14 is not admissible unless—
 (a) both of the offences are triable only on indictment, and
 (b) the court is satisfied that the interests of justice require the evidence to be admissible.
(2A) and (2B) [Omitted.]
(3) Subsection (2) applies in addition to section 101.

Subsections (2A) and (2B) provide for the treatment of previous convictions outside England and Wales. Their broad effect is that a foreign conviction is treated as being admissible if the corresponding offence in England and Wales would be so treated.

The limitation on admissibility of convictions of offences committed by children was introduced at a late stage of the passage through Parliament of the Criminal Justice Bill to mollify strong opposition to the Bill. In *Clark* [2014] EWCA Crim 1053, the Court of Appeal was unable to discern why the provision is geared to defendants under the age of 21 rather than the more natural 18. As D was 19, she was unable to benefit from the provision but the Court thought that in any event 'all judges in this context will be sensitive to an attempt to rely on previous convictions which occurred when the offender was a child' (at [20]). In the event C's offences exhibited a strong relevant propensity to violence and were rightly admitted. See also *Valencia* [2015] EWCA Crim

857, in which the two convictions of the 16-year-old accused for stabbing and robbery were relatively recent and relevant to the alleged affray and stabbing, and the Court of Appeal considered that the judge had taken due account of D's age in admitting the evidence.

PREVIOUS MISCONDUCT ADMISSIBLE UNDER THE THEFT ACT 1968, s. 27(3)

F13.92 Theft Act 1968, s. 27

(3) Where a person is being proceeded against for handling stolen goods (but not for any offence other than handling stolen goods), then at any stage of the proceedings, if evidence has been given of his having or arranging to have in his possession the goods the subject of the charge, or of his undertaking or assisting in, or arranging to undertake or assist in, their retention, removal, disposal or realisation, the following evidence shall be admissible for the purpose of proving that he knew or believed the goods to be stolen goods—

(a) evidence that he has had in his possession, or has undertaken or assisted in the retention, removal, disposal or realisation of, stolen goods from any theft taking place not earlier than 12 months before the offence charged; and

(b) (provided that seven days' notice in writing has been given to him of the intention to prove the conviction) evidence that he has within the five years preceding the date of the offence charged been convicted of theft or of handling stolen goods.

The Theft Act 1968, s. 27(3), applies to all forms of handling (*Ball* [1983] 2 All ER 1089). It can be relied upon by the prosecution only in a case where handling is the only offence involved in the proceedings (*Gardner v New Forest Magistrates' Court* (5 June 1998 unreported)). The provisions of s. 27 are unaffected by the changes made to the admissibility of character evidence at common law by the CJA 2003, Part 11, ch. 1, although the wider provisions in the CJA for the admissibility of evidence of previous convictions may form an attractive alternative for prosecutors.

F13.93 Section 27 assists only in the proof of guilty knowledge or belief. It may not assist the prosecution where an issue arises as to dishonesty (*Duffas* (1994) 158 JP 224), nor may it be used to prove possession of the goods in question: indeed, the provision cannot be relied upon unless the prosecution have already adduced evidence of the *actus reus* of the handling offence. The mere fact that possession is disputed is not of itself a bar to the use of s. 27 by the prosecution (*List* [1966] 3 All ER 710, per Roskill J, construing the corresponding provision of the Larceny Act 1916). Where, however, the jury will be faced with a number of counts, in some of which possession is in issue and in some of which the issue is guilty knowledge, it was held in *Wilkins* [1975] 2 All ER 734 that 'very great care should be exercised by the judge first of all before he allows evidence of the previous convictions to be given at all or, if he does allow that evidence to be admitted, very great care should be exercised in order to ensure that the jury realise the issues to which those previous convictions are relevant'. *Wilkins* was decided under s. 27(3)(b), but it is submitted that precisely the same considerations apply to evidence adduced under s. 27(3)(a).

Restrictive Construction

F13.94 It has been the practice of the courts to construe both limbs of the Theft Act 1968, s. 27(3), in a restrictive way. In *Bradley* (1979) 70 Cr App R 200, the Court of Appeal noted that the section gives the power to introduce evidence that would otherwise not be regarded as relevant, and would therefore be inadmissible, and concluded that it should therefore be construed 'with strict regard to its terms'. In particular, it was held that s. 27(3)(a) does not authorise the giving in evidence of the details of the transaction by which the earlier stolen property had come into the hands of the accused. *Bradley* was applied in *Wood* [1987] 1 WLR 779, in which the Court of Appeal noted a conflict between *Bradley* and the earlier case of *Smith* [1918] 2 KB 415, the decision in *Bradley* being preferred. In *Fowler* (1988) 86 Cr App R 219, *Bradley* was applied to s. 27(3)(b), the Court noting that a 'bare recital of conviction is all that is required, and possibly all that it is permissible to provide the jury with'. However, in *Hacker* [1994] 1 All ER 45, it was held by the House of Lords that s. 27(3)(b) must be read together with the PACE 1984, s. 73(2), under which a certificate of conviction of an offence on indictment must give 'the substance and effect (omitting the formal parts) of the indictment and of the conviction'. It followed that where D, who was charged with handling the bodyshell of a car, had a previous conviction for receiving a car, the detail of the subject-matter of the previous conviction, as it appeared on the certificate, was admissible. A similar proposition was advanced with regard to a previous summary conviction. The House of Lords noted that s. 27 had been extensively criticised, but considered that 'not to be able to show what goods had been stolen or handled on a previous occasion might work in some cases to the disadvantage of the defendant himself' (per Lord Slynn at p. 1665).

Discretion

Where evidence is strictly admissible under the Theft Act 1968, s. 27(3), the court has a power to exclude it at common law or under the PACE 1984, s. 78 (*Hacker* [1994] 1 All ER 45). **F13.95**

SPENT CONVICTIONS

The Rehabilitation of Offenders Act 1974, s. 4(1), lays down a general rule that a person whose conviction is 'spent' under the Act is to be treated as a person who has not committed or been charged with or prosecuted for or convicted of or sentenced for the offence or offences which were the subject of that conviction. Section 7(2)(a) excludes criminal proceedings from the operation of this general rule, although the accused is to an extent protected from the use of spent convictions in cross-examination on his or her record by CrimPD V, paras. 21A.1 to 21A.3 (see Supplement, **CPD.21A**, and **D20.49**), which direct the court to have regard to the spirit of the 1974 Act by refusing to allow any mention to be made of a spent conviction, except where it is in the interests of justice to do so. In essence this produces the same test as in civil proceedings that *are* covered by s. 4(1), but in respect of which s. 7(3) provides for evidence of spent convictions to be admitted if justice cannot otherwise be done (*Thomas v Metropolitan Police Commissioner* [1997] QB 813, in which careful consideration is given to the relevant criminal authorities). In *Corelli* [2001] EWCA Crim 974, it was held that the effect of s. 7 in combination with the absence of discretion to restrain one accused from cross-examining another on admissible evidence of bad character is that the practice direction which then applied (which was in similar terms to CrimPD V, paras. 21A.1 to 21A.3) had no application as between co-accused. As the judge has no discretion to restrain a co-accused, it could not be employed to modify the clear words of the 1974 Act. The provisions of the CJA 2003, s. 108 (see **F13.91**), where they apply, constitute an absolute prohibition on the introduction of the criminal record of the accused in respect of offences committed when a child, whether spent or not. **F13.96**

Section F14 Character Evidence: Admissibility of Evidence of Accused's Good Character

OVERVIEW AND THE IMPORTANCE OF *HUNTER*

Overview

F14.1 **Relevance and Admissibility of Good Character** The practice of admitting evidence of the good character of the accused is of long standing: in *Layne v A-G of Grenada* [2019] UKPC 11, Lord Sumption said that by the end of the 17th century it had become normal for defendants to call witnesses to their good character. The practice was originally founded on a notion of indulgence, but in modern law evidence of good character is admissible as of right, both to show that an accused who lacks a proven propensity to do wrong is less likely to have committed the offence, (*Bryant* [1979] QB 108) and (where the credibility of the accused's account is in issue) to show that a person who is of good character is more likely to be telling the truth than one who is not. In *Aziz* [1996] AC 41, Lord Steyn said (at p. 50): 'It has long been recognised that the good character of an accused is logically relevant both to his credibility and to the likelihood that he would commit the offence in question.'

F14.2 **Good Character and the Right to a Direction** The significance accorded to evidence of good character led to a rule that fairness required the judge to give the jury specific directions on its relevance (*Vye* [1993] 3 All ER 241; *Aziz* [1996] AC 41). These directions are considered in detail at **F14.16**. The issue of what constitutes good character has since become inextricably linked with the question of what the accused was entitled to in terms of a direction: the many appeals of recent years focus not on whether evidence of good character was wrongly excluded, but on whether the trial judge gave an appropriate endorsement of the defence submissions when directing the jury.

Not only does the right to a good character direction apply only to the accused, it has been held that it may be unfair to give a similar direction in relation to a prosecution witness whose evidence contradicts that of the accused, even if the witness is also of unblemished character; a state of affairs that owes more to legal tradition than to logic. In *G (T)* [2017] EWCA Crim 1774, [2018] 1 Cr App R 14 (218), D was convicted of sexual offences against his half-sister. The trial judge gave a proper direction in respect of D's good character, but this was held to have been undermined by a direction to the effect that the complainant was also of good character and thus the two were on a 'level playing field'. In so doing the trial judge had 'watered down' a protection the law afforded to an accused, and D's convictions were quashed. Evidence of the good character of a person other than the accused may only be admitted if it is directly relevant to an issue, for example to rebut a suggestion that the person was attempting to rob the accused or had made an unprovoked attack (*Mader* [2018] EWCA Crim 2454).

Unmeritorious Claims and the Impact of *Hunter*

F14.3 The law on the nature and extent of the good character direction was thoroughly reviewed by a strong Court of Appeal in *Hunter* [2015] EWCA Crim 631, [2015] 1 WLR 5367. It was decided that the benefits of the good character directions had, in the years following *Vye* [1993] 3 All ER 241 and *Aziz* [1996] AC 41, been wrongly extended to defendants who, because of their convictions, cautions or misconduct did not merit being treated as of good character, including some whose claims were spurious. This observation would have been true quite apart from the changes that had occurred in the law of bad character over the same period, but the over-extension of the *Vye* and *Aziz* principles is particularly hard to reconcile with the bad character provisions of the CJA 2003 (see **F13**), whereby evidence of convictions, cautions and other misconduct is now more freely admissible. In *Hunter*, these changes to the 'whole landscape' of character evidence provided a justification for a reassessment of principles for which there was clear appellate authority, including the rule that a person with no previous convictions was normally entitled to a good character direction even if guilty of some other relevant and admissible misconduct (see **F14.11**) and the practice of regarding defendants with convictions or cautions that were not of particular relevance to the matter charged as entitled to at least a modified form of the direction (see **F14.8**). The question of what directions, if any, to give in respect of defendants who are no longer entitled to a full direction is regarded in *Hunter* as a matter for the trial judge's general discretion, based on the need to ensure a fair trial. Furthermore, even the failure to give a direction where one is required will not automatically be seen as inimical to the safety of a conviction (see **F14.26**).

The Court of Appeal in *Hunter*, having restored the law to a more principled basis, expressed the view (at [103]) that henceforth it should be necessary only to refer to *Hunter*, together with the authorities of *Vye* and *Aziz* which were said to be binding. To achieve this end, a significant number of decisions of the Court of Appeal in the post-*Vye* period must be regarded as being based on incorrect assumptions where defendants who are not genuinely of good character are concerned. This section proceeds on the basis that the law is as stated in *Hunter*. To the extent that other authorities are relied upon, it will be made clear how these relate to the scheme for receiving and directing on good character evidence described in *Hunter*. The *Crown Court Compendium* (July 2020), ch. 11, contains detailed guidance as to the directions to be given following *Hunter*, together with examples of directions tailored to meet particular cases. **F14.4**

MEANING OF GOOD CHARACTER

Impact of Bad Character Provisions of the CJA 2003 on Good Character

The Court of Appeal in *Hunter* [2015] EWCA Crim 631, [2015] 1 WLR 5367 (see **F14.3**) unequivocally rejected the notion, suggested by some authorities in light of the bad character provisions of the CJA 2003, s. 101 (see **F13.15**), that the mere fact that no evidence of bad character was tendered against an accused was of itself a reason for giving a good character direction (see, e.g., *Payton* [2006] EWCA Crim 1226). On the contrary, '[i]t does not follow from the fact that the bad character is not considered probative of guilt that a defendant is entitled to be treated as if he had a good character' (*Hunter* at [72]). To the extent that decisions such as *Payton* suggest the contrary, they were wrongly decided. Even a 'modified' direction that reflects an accused's known antecedents should no longer be given if it would work against the proper inferences the jury could draw from those antecedents (*Benjamin* [2015] EWCA Crim 1377, in which D faced counts of theft and assault, and had a previous conviction for assault that would have meant that a modified direction 'would not have made sense to the jury and could not properly have been given'). By applying the principles in *Hunter*, the court's directions will be realistic rather than 'formulaic or meaningless' (per Lord Hughes in *Phillip v DPP (St Christopher and Nevis)* [2017] UKPC 14 at [15]). **F14.5**

The true rule is that only defendants with absolute good character, or who are deemed to be of effective good character are entitled to any judicial directions on the matter (see **F14.6** and **F14.7**). Whereas it was previously regarded as sufficient to establish good character that a defendant had no previous convictions (*Aziz* [1996] AC 41) the law has now moved on (*Hunter*). An accused who has no previous convictions may nevertheless have a bad character as defined by the CJA 2003, s. 98, by reference to other misconduct, or a disposition towards misconduct (see **F13.4**). In *Hunter*, Hallett LJ explained the impact of the CJA 2003 on the principles governing good character directions in the following way (at [75]):

> Parliament has decided that evidence that was once considered inadmissible is now admissible. It is admissible to prove propensity to offend or to be untruthful, the very issues to which the good

character principles are directed. This has had an inevitable impact on the court's approach to character directions.

Absolute and Effective Good Character

F14.6 **Absolute Good Character** An accused is entitled to a good character direction on the ground of 'absolute good character' if the accused has no previous convictions and no other reprehensible conduct is alleged, admitted or proven. It is not necessary for the accused to go further and prove evidence of positive good character (*Hunter* [2015] EWCA Crim 631, [2015] 1 WLR 5367). The Court of Appeal in *Hunter* seems to be out of sympathy with the importance accorded to good character, observing that 'many have questioned, with some justification in our view, whether the fact someone has no previous convictions makes it any the more likely they are telling the truth, and whether the average juror needs a direction that a defendant who has never committed an offence of the kind charged may be less likely to offend'. The Court nevertheless upholds the traditional entitlement, but the effect of its scepticism may be seen in its preparedness to uphold the safety of a conviction where the judge fails to direct the jury appropriately (see **F14.26**).

F14.7 **Effective Good Character** An accused who is judged to be of 'effective good character' is also entitled to the good character directions in full. Where the defence lay claim to effective good character, the matter is one of law on which a judgment is required: it is not sufficient to ask the jury whether they consider the accused to be of good character (*Hunter* [2015] EWCA Crim 631, [2015] 1 WLR 5367 at [79]; *Ahmed* [2014] EWCA Crim 2466, [2015] 1 Cr App R 21 (275)). Once the judge has ruled in an accused's favour the directions may not be withheld, though they should be modified to the extent that it is necessary to reflect the matters that preclude the accused being of absolute good character, and to ensure that the jury is not misled (*Hunter* at [80]).

Under the law as it stood before *Hunter*, it was clearly possible for an accused to be treated as entitled to part of the good character direction, in relation either to credibility or propensity, even where the accused was not entitled to the other part, but the corollary of the proposition stated in *Hunter* that a person of effective good character is a person entitled to both parts of a direction would seem to be that a person who is not so entitled is not of effective good character, with the result that the person falls into the categories of persons described in **F14.10** to **F14.15** whose character will be dealt with in the discretion of the court.

F14.8 **Effective Good Character and Previous Offences** *Hunter* [2015] EWCA Crim 631, [2015] 1 WLR 5367, stipulates that a person cannot automatically expect to be treated as of effective good character on the ground that the person's convictions or cautions have no relevance to the charge, even where they are also old and minor instances of offending. This is a shift from previous practice, where such cases might have been expected to result in a full direction. In future, the judge should take into account all the circumstances of the offence and the offender, and decide what 'fairness to all' dictates (*Hunter* at [79]). *Hunter* specifically rejects the suggestion in *Gray* [2004] EWCA Crim 1074, [2004] 2 Cr App R 30 (498) that an accused whose convictions are 'irrelevant or of no significance in relation to the offence charged' ought to be treated as of good character, together with the decision in *Durbin* [1995] 2 Cr App R 84 on which this suggestion is based. Also rejected is the false interpretation of an observation of the Privy Council in *Teeluck v State of Trinidad and Tobago* [2005] UKPC 14, [2005] 1 WLR 2421, that good character can be equated with the absence of convictions 'of any relevance or significance': as *Hunter* points out, this does not mean that a defendant is entitled to be regarded as a person of good character simply because any previous offending is of a different type or category from the offence charged.

The point at which an accused ceases to be entitled to a good character direction, and is dependent instead on the discretion of the court, was re-emphasised in *Morgans* [2015] EWCA Crim 1997 in the following helpful terms (at [14]):

> If the conviction or convictions qualify under all three heads of being old, minor and irrelevant ... the judge must decide whether to treat a defendant as of effective good character. If he does, then the judge should give the direction. Where an offender has convictions that are not old, minor and irrelevant ... it

is a matter for the judge to decide whether or not to give any part of the good character direction. He or she has a broad discretion, with the exercise of which this court will be reluctant to interfere.

Styles [2015] EWCA Crim 1619, which suggests that the defence has a wider entitlement to a direction, is rightly rejected in *Morgans* as *per incuriam* of *Hunter*.

Sufficiently detailed information will be needed as a basis for the court's decision where a direction is sought. In *Pegram v DPP* [2019] EWHC 2673 (Admin), D, charged with assaulting a police officer, volunteered when giving evidence that he had old convictions for 'mainly drugs related' convictions, all based on guilty pleas. The Divisional Court declined to interfere with the Crown Court's decision that D was not entitled to a direction, commenting that because the court had not been made aware of the 'full picture' it could not be said that the conclusion was unfair.

Cautions, even for matters of a minor nature, cannot simply be ignored in the calculation of effective good character, as it is essential that the jury are not misled by any claim made by the accused (*Martin* [2000] 2 Cr App R 42). For the same reason, an accused cannot conceal a finding of guilty by a foreign court where its findings are not regarded as 'convictions' until confirmed on appeal (*El Delbi* [2003] EWCA Crim 1767). But the issuing of a penalty notice for disorder (PND) involves neither proof of the commission of a crime nor the admission that a crime has been committed and should be kept from a jury when giving a good character direction (*Hamer* [2010] EWCA Crim 2053, [2011] 1 WLR 528). The same principle applies to a warning letter for harassment (*Dalby* [2012] EWCA Crim 701) or breach of environmental regulations (*Mustafa v Environment Agency* [2020] EWCA Crim 597). Where a warning has been issued by a foreign authority, it is essential that the court understands its status before determining its effect. In *Mittal* [2016] EWCA Crim 451, [2016] 2 Cr App R 8 (73), D, a doctor who was charged with theft, had been the subject of a Procurator Fiscal's warning for shoplifting. The warning was initially treated as equivalent to a caution, but it then emerged that it was of similar status to the warning in *Hamer*, involving no necessary acceptance of guilt. It was said that in future the prosecution should supply full information to the court at the pre-trial stage. An inquiry may also need to be conducted before treating an old binding over order as an impediment to a good character direction, as the significance of such an order has changed over time, and might have been imposed without evidence of misconduct (*B* [2017] EWCA Crim 35, [2017] 1 Cr App R 31 (457), where the evolution of the order is considered, and see as to binding over **E13.2**). The Court of Appeal observed that '[a] defendant is not necessarily to be deprived of a good character direction by unproven allegations inadmissible as evidence of his bad character'. It is part of the prosecution's onus of proof to establish the impediment to the direction to which the accused is otherwise entitled.

It is not possible to be explicit as to what manner of minor blemishes an accused may now have and **F14.9** still be 'deemed' to be a person of effective good character under *Hunter* as interpreted in *Morgans* (see **F14.8**). The thrust of *Hunter* is that all decisions are fact-specific so that one case is unlikely to provide much guidance to another. Minor offending or misconduct that has no relevance to credibility or propensity would seem unlikely to provide an impediment to a finding of effective good character, for example where the charge is serious sexual assault and the accused has a minor motoring conviction (*Baquiri* [2010] EWCA Crim 1729). More difficult are cases of old convictions or cautions that are relevant either to credibility or propensity, but of little weight. In *Ahmed* [2014] EWCA Crim 2466, [2015] 1 Cr App R 21 (275), there was an important issue as to the credibility of D's assertion that she knew nothing of her brother's drug-dealing activities and was acting innocently in accepting his money to facilitate the purchase of expensive cars. A caution for shoplifting when D was a teenager was considered to be no bar to a good character direction in light of the strong evidence of her positive good character ever since. In *MW* [2008] EWCA Crim 3091, D was charged with sexual offences committed against his young daughter 20 years previously. He had spent convictions for a motoring offence and theft dating from his teenage years. The trial was a 'contest of credibility' between D and the complainant in which D's subsequent good character was fundamental to his defence, and the Court of Appeal was emphatic that D ought to have been treated as of effective good character. On the facts of both *Ahmed* and *MW*, a full direction would have been modified to allude to the existence of the previous offences so that the jury would not have been misled. It is likely that the same result would follow under *Hunter*.

Accused Who are Not of Good Character

F14.10 **Admissibility for Defence of Evidence of Convictions/Cautions of Defendant who is Not of Effective Good Character** An accused who is not judged to be of effective good character (see **F14.8**) and who has convictions or cautions is still entitled to adduce them under the CJA 2003, s. 101(1)(b) (see **F13.15**), where they are relevant, for example to pave the way for an argument that the accused has no record for offences of the type charged. *Hunter* [2015] EWCA Crim 631, [2015] 1 WLR 5367, specifies that a modified good character direction may, in the judge's discretion, be given regarding such an accused, and that fairness 'may well suggest that a direction would be appropriate but not necessarily' [at 82]. The judge has a broad and open-textured discretion whether to give any part of the direction, and if so on what terms. In *S (C)* [2018] EWCA Crim 2469, D had a relevant conviction for an offence of violence at around the time of the allegations of sexual abuse of a child for which he was on trial. This, together with further revelations of D's alleged sexual misconduct by the complainant during re-examination (to rebut a line of inquiry in cross-examination) fully entitled the trial judge to decline to treat D as a man of effective good character. Where the accused agrees with counsel that for tactical reasons a modified direction should not be sought, an appeal court will not normally go behind the decision (*Mustafa v Environment Agency* [2020] EWCA Crim 597). A decision to avoid generating an inquiry into potentially harmful facts that might have come to light as the result of such an application cannot be said to have been improper.

Where evidence of previous misconduct is so adduced by the defence, and is not relied upon by the prosecution as evidence of guilt, it has been said to be wrong to direct a jury that the evidence can be used to provide support for the prosecution's case (*Styles* [2015] EWCA Crim 1619). If this is correct, it must be a rule based on fairness rather than logic, if the evidence has a rational connection to guilt. It does not follow that the jury should be warned against drawing a rational inference. In *Fitzpatrick* [2015] EWCA Crim 1286, the defence had adduced convictions for drugs offences where D was charged with burglary. The Court of Appeal, rejecting the argument that a discretionary good character direction was required, went on to note that 'drugs offences are capable of having a connection with acquisitive crime such as burglary'. It does not seem that the prosecution relied on the drugs convictions for this purpose, but the jury would surely have been entitled to make the same connection as the court.

CrimPR 21.4 (notice to introduce evidence of a defendant's bad character: see Supplement, **R21.4**) is designed to remedy the lack of clarity, noted in *Hunter*, about whether notice is required when bad character evidence is adduced by the defence. Such notice should be given as soon as reasonably practicable and in any event before the evidence is introduced. In the Crown Court such a defendant should also, at the same time, give notice of any direction that is sought regarding character.

F14.11 **Accused with No Convictions/Cautions whose Other Misconduct is Relied on by the Prosecution** An accused who has no previous convictions or cautions but whose other misconduct is relied on by the prosecution as part of their case will attract a direction based on the use that may be made of the bad character evidence (a 'bad character direction': see **F13.22**). In such a case, the trial judge has a discretion to weave into the direction relevant observations about the defendant's residual good character, where to do so would not render the totality of the direction an absurdity (*Hunter* [2015] EWCA Crim 631, [2015] 1 WLR 5367 at [83]). The 'absurdity principle' derives from the speech of Lord Steyn in *Aziz* [1996] AC 41; he regarded it as a good starting-point that a judge should never be obliged to give a 'meaningless or absurd' direction. The example he gave was of an accused who, though without previous convictions, was shown beyond doubt to have been guilty of serious criminal behaviour similar to the offence charged in the indictment. In such a case the claim to good character would be spurious and the good character direction 'a charade'. Other instances are *Zoppola-Barrazza* [1994] Crim LR 833, where the defence to a charge of importing cocaine involved an admission of smuggling gold to avoid duty and VAT, and *Buzalek* [1991] Crim LR 116, where there was a significant admission of dishonesty in relation to the subject-matter of the charge. See also *Shaw* [2001] UKPC 26, [2001] 1 WLR 1519, where D admitted being a member of an armed group that had sought to punish V but denied killing him. Cases referred to in *Hunter* that wrongly failed to apply the absurdity principle include *Durbin* [1995] 2 Cr App R 84, where D admitted lying to and grossly misleading the police and to smuggling goods across Europe in the course of the visit which gave rise to the charge, and *D* [2012] EWCA Crim 19, [2012] 1 Cr App R 33 (448), where a husband was charged with offences including anal rape of his wife and he admitted violence to the victim and the misuse of charitable funds, and had written that he considered anal rape to be 'the ultimate punishment'.

In *Aziz* Lord Steyn regarded the judge's power to omit the direction as a 'residual discretion' which was 'narrowly circumscribed'. This is not the view taken in *Hunter*, where the discretion is regarded in all cases as an open-textured fairness discretion. The departure from this aspect of a precedent that was clearly binding on the court was necessary to ensure that the judge's powers are consistent as between evidence of good and bad character. **F14.12**

A plea of guilty to another offence in the proceedings constitutes an admission of misconduct that will normally be inconsistent with any claim to effective good character. In *Richens* (1994) 98 Cr App R 43, D was charged with murder and admitted manslaughter, and the question of what to say about his previous good character was regarded as a matter for the discretion of the court. Similarly in *Challenger* [1994] Crim LR 202, a plea of guilty to possession of drugs meant that D could not be regarded as of good character at his trial for more serious offences including possession with intent to supply. *Teasdale* [1993] 4 All ER 290, which suggests otherwise, was criticised in *Hunter* where it was said that *Challenger* is to be preferred. **F14.13**

Accused's Convictions or Cautions Relied upon as Evidence of Bad Character An accused who has previous convictions and whose bad character is relied upon by the prosecution under the CJA 2003, s. 101, will attract a 'bad character' direction (see **F13.22**) and it is unlikely that the judge will be able to say anything about good character without offending the absurdity principle (*Hunter* [2015] EWCA Crim 631, [2015] 1 WLR 5367 at [84]). In *Doncaster* [2008] EWCA Crim 5, one of the few cases before *Hunter* where the impact of the CJA 2003 was considered, it was said that it 'would make no sense' for a direction to be given in such a case. **F14.14**

Although *Hunter* does not deal with the point, the same must follow where the evidence is admitted at the behest of a co-accused (see **F13.66**).

Accused Admitting Other Misconduct Not Relied on by the Prosecution An accused who has no previous convictions or cautions but who admits other reprehensible conduct that is not relied upon by the prosecution as evidence of guilt may receive a modified form of the good character direction at the discretion of the judge (*Hunter* [2015] EWCA Crim 631, [2015] 1 WLR 5367 at [85]). Although in *Aziz* [1996] AC 41 there was a strong bias towards giving the good character direction in such a case, the changes in bad character evidence brought about by the CJA 2003, s. 101 (see **F14.5**), require the judge to have greater latitude. The prosecutor should not feel under any pressure to make an application under s. 101 if it may not be fair and proportionate to do so, simply to pre-empt an application for a good character direction where the judge would be subject to the strong bias described in *Aziz*. It is therefore better to allow the trial judge the 'usual generous ambit of discretion' (*Hunter*). **F14.15**

THE GOOD CHARACTER DIRECTION

The Form of the Direction

Standard Two-limb Direction According to Lord Steyn in *Aziz* [1996] AC 41, '[f]airness requires that the judge should direct the jury about good character because it is evidence of probative significance'. **F14.16**

The standard direction on good character makes reference both to credibility and to propensity. The credibility aspect of the direction is by convention referred to as the 'first limb' and the propensity aspect the 'second limb'. In *Hunter* [2015] EWCA Crim 631, [2015] 1 WLR 5367 it was said that:

> ... the first credibility limb of good character is a positive feature which should be taken into account. The second propensity limb means that good character may make it less likely that the defendant acted as alleged and so particular attention should be paid to the fact. What weight is to be given to each limb is a matter for the jury.

The Court of Appeal laid stress on the importance of the judge tailoring the terms of the direction to the case, while also, in the name of consistency, commending the standard direction endorsed by the Judicial College, as to which see the *Crown Court Compendium* (July 2020), ch. 11. The *Compendium* provides examples of how to customise a standard direction, together with guidance on how to tailor the direction where an accused is to be treated as of effective good character; where part only of the direction is to be given, and where evidence of bad character has been given, but is in dispute. The *Compendium* also highlights the comment of Lord Steyn in *Aziz* that judges should never be compelled to give 'meaningless or absurd' directions, nor should a direction be given if it is 'an insult to common sense' or misleading.

In *Singh v State of Trinidad and Tobago* [2005] UKPC 35, [2006] 1 WLR 146, it was held that a 'first limb' direction should not be implied from a direction on the second limb, or be conveyed by a vague phrase such as that good character is a matter to consider 'when you deal with the evidence of the accused'. If the advice given in *Hunter* regarding adherence to the contours of the standard direction is heeded, such errors should not occur.

F14.17 **Discussion with Counsel** The proposed direction should be shared with counsel and an opportunity should be given to make submissions where the judge is minded to give a direction that is not likely to be anticipated by counsel (*Aziz* [1996] AC 41; *D* [2012] EWCA Crim 19, [2012] 1 Cr App R 33 (448)). The same point was emphasised in *Gonzales* [2004] EWCA Crim 2117 where, following a discussion that had left counsel with the impression that a full direction would be given, the trial judge gave a modified direction that had not previously been canvassed. See also the *Crown Court Compendium* (July 2020), ch. 11.

In *Hunter* [2015] EWCA Crim 631, [2015] 1 WLR 5367, it was stated that counsel's acquiescence in the direction given at trial is a good indication that nothing was considered to be amiss.

Direction on Credibility where Accused Testifies

F14.18 Where an accused of good character testifies, the standard direction should be given in full; see *Vye* [1993] 3 All ER 241, where the authorities are reviewed; *Aziz* [1996] AC 41, in which the House of Lords treats the point as settled by *Vye*; and *Hunter* [2015] EWCA Crim 631, [2015] 1 WLR 5367, where the Court of Appeal speaks of good character as 'a positive feature which should be taken into account'.

Direction on Credibility where Accused Does Not Testify

F14.19 In *Vye* [1993] 3 All ER 241, the Court of Appeal further decided that where the accused has not given evidence at trial but relies on admissible exculpatory statements made to the police or others, the judge should direct the jury to have regard to the accused's good character when considering the credibility of those statements. The Court thought it 'logical' that such evidence should be taken into account, but drew attention also to the judge's entitlement to make observations about the weight to be given to such exculpatory statements in contrast to evidence on oath (see *Duncan* (1981) 73 Cr App R 359 at **F18.94**, and see, generally and as to the point at which statements that are exculpatory become admissible for the defence, **F18.93** ***et seq.***). In *Aziz* [1996] AC 41, the House of Lords accepted that this 'clearcut' rule in *Vye* represented the best policy. Where an exculpatory statement was evidence in the case, the credibility of the accused who had given that account was a matter of evidential significance requiring a direction. The rule was endorsed in *Hunter* [2015] EWCA Crim 631, [2015] 1 WLR 5367, but the observations of the Court of Appeal in that case about the effect on appeal of a failure to give the required direction should also be noted (see **F14.26**), as it by no means follows that a conviction will be unsafe if the appropriate direction is not given.

Vye also decides that, where an accused of good character does not give evidence and has given no pre-trial answers or statements upon which reliance is placed, a 'first limb' direction is not required as no issue as to the accused's credibility arises.

Direction on Propensity

F14.20 The 'second limb' of a character direction deals with the unlikelihood that a person of previous good character would commit the offence charged. In *Vye* [1993] 3 All ER 241, the Court of Appeal resolved a fundamental inconsistency in the earlier cases by holding that a 'second limb' direction should be given in all cases where accused persons are of good character, whether they testify or not. In *Aziz* [1996] AC 41, the House of Lords, while recognising that *Vye* involved a 'policy decision', agreed that the move to a settled rule of practice was justified.

The obligation is, in any event, subject to the judge's entitlement to make observations qualifying the importance of good character, for example by emphasising that it is not in itself a defence and that in some cases the jury may derive limited assistance from the evidence. Everything, however, depends on the relevance of the evidence in the circumstances: in *Fitton* [2001] EWCA Crim 215, the Court of Appeal disagreed with a suggestion that the good character of a nightclub doorman charged with assaulting a customer was less persuasive when the offence was spontaneous: rather the good character of a doorman who is routinely exposed to spontaneous violence may be worth a great deal. In *Zielinski* [2007] EWCA Crim 704, the Court of Appeal played down the importance of good character in relation to a charge of inflicting grievous bodily harm in a 'road rage' incident which involved no more than the reckless use of force: the case was not one in which 'lack of propensity to offend was of such significance as it might have been in many other kinds of alleged offending'.

In directing a jury on a case where good character is likely to be of little use, it is important to be clear about the difference between relevance and weight. In *McCarthy* [2014] EWCA Crim 1963, [2015] RTR 10 (92), D had knocked over and killed an elderly pedestrian as he crossed the street, and the case turned on whether D ought to have seen him. Evidence that she was of good character and had many testimonials to her careful driving was of little assistance in deciding whether, on this particular occasion, she had suffered a lapse of concentration. But it would have been better had the trial judge avoided the suggestion that her character was irrelevant (which would be inconsistent with the standard direction), and had instead made reference to its weight.

F14.21 Where a direction is given about the relevance of good character to guilt it is wrong and unfair to suggest that such evidence comes into play only where the remainder of the evidence leaves the jury in doubt (*Falconer-Atlee* (1973) 58 Cr App R 349): evidence of good character is part of the totality of the evidence upon which the jury are to decide (*Handbridge* [1993] Crim LR 287, endorsing the statement of law to this effect in an earlier edition of this work).

Character Direction and Historical Allegations

F14.22 Where the offence being tried is alleged to have taken place many years before, it is sometimes said that the good character of the accused in the intervening years is potentially of particular significance, and should not be underplayed (*Small* [2008] EWCA Crim 2788). *Small* was approved in *GJB v R* [2011] EWCA Crim 867, where reference was made to a 'third limb' of the direction, to the effect that the jury might think that because so long has passed since the alleged historic offences, and no offence has been committed in that time, it is less likely that the accused committed the offences charged. The Court of Appeal recognised that this 'third limb' was no more than an adaptation of the normal propensity direction, but it was said to be an important factor in historic sexual abuse cases where the defence is a straightforward denial, and the accused may have little more than a good name to rely on. *Small* and *GJB v R* were considered in *Enrieu* [2011] All ER (D) 96 (Oct), where the Court once more stressed the importance of the direction in a case of alleged historic abuse where the accused was a person of hitherto unblemished character. These authorities are not mentioned in *Hunter* [2015] EWCA Crim 631, [2015] 1 WLR 5367, suggesting that there is no support for the notion of a 'third limb' as such, but as a matter of common sense a specific judicial comment on the matter might be appropriate.

Conveying the Need to Take Good Character into Account in Judicial Directions

F14.23 The purpose of a good character direction is to convey to the jury that they ought to take account of relevant evidence of good character, although it is a matter for them whether they give it any weight. The direction must, taken as a whole, convey the need to take character appropriately into account (*Starmer* [2010] EWCA Crim 1), and will be defective if it might have led the jury to think that they could choose to give no consideration to good character (*Rehman* [2006] EWCA Crim 1900; *J (GV)* [2015] EWCA Crim 630). An expression such as 'you are entitled to consider' is best avoided as it risks giving the jury the impression that they may choose not to consider the evidence at all (*Miah* [1997] 2 Cr App R 12 and *Moustakim* [2008] EWCA Crim 3096, where the expression 'she is entitled to have it argued on her behalf' was held inadequate, but this is not true of a direction that an accused is 'entitled' to have character taken into account (*H* [2014] EWCA Crim 1555)). *Moustakim* was considered in *Williams* [2014] EWCA Crim 429, where it was noted that a direction that good character could, rather than should, be taken into account might be appropriate when giving a modified direction in respect of an accused who was not entitled to a full direction. As to the effect of a failure correctly to word the direction, see **F14.26**.

Where One Accused is of Good Character but Another is Not

F14.24 The difficulty facing a trial judge in the situation where one accused is of good character but another is not is that by commenting on the good character of the one there is a risk of highlighting the bad character of the other. Nevertheless the Court of Appeal in *Vye* [1993] 3 All ER 241 held, disapproving compromise solutions suggested in earlier authorities such as *Gibson* (1991) 93 Cr App R 9, that the accused of good character is entitled to the same direction as if standing trial alone. This aspect of *Vye* was applied in *Houlden* (1994) 99 Cr App R 244, and remains unchanged by *Hunter* [2015] EWCA Crim 631, [2015] 1 WLR 5367. In *Stokes* [2018] EWCA Crim 1350, D's co-accused, who had one old conviction and a caution for a minor matter, was treated as of effective good character at their trial for murder while D, who had a recent caution for a dishonesty offence which was potentially relevant to her denial of participation in the murder, was not. Although the defence was of a cut-throat nature, nothing in *Hunter* entitled D to a good character direction. The possession of disparate characters is said in *Vye* to be a factor to be considered in deciding whether separate trials are needed, but there is no rule in favour of separate trials in such cases. Where no evidence is put in of the record of the accused with bad character, the judge has a discretion whether to comment about that accused when summing up (*Shepherd* [1995] Crim LR 153). Although a judge may give a direction not to speculate, there should first be a discussion with the counsel representing the relevant accused, as it will commonly be counsel's preference that no such direction should be given (*Crown Court Compendium* (July 2020), ch. 11). Where, however, the jury have been told of previous convictions, the accused is entitled to an appropriate direction as to the use which may be made of them (*Cain* [1994] 2 All ER 398). Where a judge mistakenly attributes convictions to the wrong co-accused, counsel should be consulted as to the best way to correct the error (*Purdy* [2007] EWCA Crim 295).

Good Character Must be Raised by the Defence

F14.25 There is no obligation for the trial judge to deal with good character unless the issue has been raised by the defence (*Thompson v R* [1998] AC 811; *Brown v The Queen* [2005] UKPC 18, [2006] 1 AC 1, where it was noted that a judge would be 'ill-advised' to mention good character unless given information on the basis of which this could properly and safely be done). It follows that the defence advocate is under an obligation to raise the issue in an appropriate case, so that the accused does not lose the benefit that the direction is designed to confer (*Teeluck v State of Trinidad and Tobago* [2005] UKPC 14, [2005] 1 WLR 2421).

Failure to Give Appropriate Direction

Before *Hunter* [2015] EWCA Crim 631, [2015] 1 WLR 5367, the authorities were divided as to the likely effect of failing to direct, or of giving an inadequate direction, on good character. In *Hunter*, it was stressed that the conviction may be safe notwithstanding the error, and that there is no inflexible rule that such errors are fatal (rejecting a suggestion in *Hoyte* [2013] EWCA Crim 1002 that the omission to give a direction where one is required 'usually' leads to the quashing of a conviction). The correct approach was said to be that of Lord Bingham in *Singh v The State* [2005] UKPC 35, [2006] 1 WLR 146, who said: **F14.26**

> The significance of what is not said in a summing-up should be judged in the light of what is said. The omission of a good character direction on credibility is not necessarily fatal to the fairness of the trial or to the safety of a conviction. Much may turn on the nature of and issues in a case, and on the other available evidence. The ends of justice are not on the whole well served by the laying down of hard, inflexible rules from which no departure may ever be tolerated.

Thus for example in *R (Arthur) v Blackfriars Crown Court* [2017] EWHC 3416 (Admin), [2018] 2 Cr App R 4 (38), D claimed that the Crown Court erred in failing to direct itself in relation to, or pay due regard to, the credibility aspect of his good character. It was held that in fact both parts of the good character direction had been applied but, had that not been the case, the failure would not have been fatal to the conviction in a case where the court had made clear that it was satisfied that V had suffered the injury complained of and that this could not be accounted for by the claimant's version of events. By contrast in *McChleery* [2019] EWCA Crim 2100, D had been convicted on a single count of indecent assault on a 15-year-old resident of a children's home over 20 years previously. D was of good character and his wife gave character evidence in his favour, but the trial judge failed to give either limb of the direction. The conviction was held unsafe: the case involved (at [16]) 'a straightforward conflict of evidence between the complainant and the appellant in circumstances where there was little independent evidence to assist the jury in deciding the issue. Credibility was all.'

A natural inference from the tenor of the judgment in *Hunter* is that an appeal court should consider whether a direction would have added anything significant to the view of the evidence that the jury would already have formed in light of the evidence of good character put before them. It was conceded that the Court of Appeal had in the past been more ready to intervene in relation to good character than such an approach would suggest. But just as it had been questioned whether juries needed elaborate and detailed summaries of the facts of cases (*Review of Efficiency in Criminal Proceedings*, by Sir Brian Leveson, January 2015, at para. 285) so also it was questionable whether the average juror was likely to ignore defence submissions on character in the absence of a clear judicial endorsement in the summing-up. The Court also referred to the 'unfortunate tendency' of recent years to require directions on matters that most juries would regard as a matter of common sense.

Hunter suggests that an appellate court should only interfere if, on the facts, it was not properly open to the judge to reach the relevant conclusion, and the examples given are of a wrongful refusal to give a particular limb of the direction, or to treat the accused as a person of effective good character. Even in such a case, it would seem that the evidence might be so overwhelming as to render the conviction safe. *Hunter* states that 'even where credibility is very much in issue, and a good character direction is not given, when it should have been, this court has been known to uphold the conviction on the basis that the failure can have made no difference to the outcome'. A case noted in *Hunter* is *Kabariti* (1991) 92 Cr App R 362, where the judge was said to have fallen into error in failing to give any positive direction as to good character in a case of rape (though as lies had been told to the police it might now be regarded as a case where D was not entitled to one). Nevertheless the evidence that D's admitted acts of anal and vaginal intercourse were, contrary to his account, without the consent of the 14-year-old complainant was overwhelming, and his conviction was upheld. To the same effect is *Goorani* [2015] EWCA Crim 1855, where the prosecution's case of rape was based on substantial evidence that the complainant was so drunk as to **F14.27** be incapable of consenting. It was held, following *Hunter*, that the Court would have been 'very reluctant' to conclude that the conviction was unsafe, even it had been the case that some form of good character direction should have been given. In *Hunter* itself, the trial judge had indicated that he would give the standard directions, but then overlooked the direction on credibility. Although the Court of Appeal was clear that, because D had a relevant conviction for dishonesty, there was in fact no need for a direction on credibility, it appears also that the other evidence against him, including his own admissions, was such that the failure could not have rendered the conviction unsafe. In *Pacurar* [2016] EWCA Crim 569, [2016] 1 WLR 3913, the judge withheld the credibility limb of the direction to which D was technically entitled. However, there was no impact on the safety of the conviction, as any such direction would have been 'counter-balanced with a strong direction on the many and highly significant lies told at interview'. In the somewhat extreme circumstances of *Gilbert v The Queen* [2006] UKPC 15, [2006] 1 WLR 2108, in which a bishop was convicted of murdering a teenage girl and his character, if not formally put in issue, was very much in the forefront of the defence case, it was said by Lord Woolf that the judge would have been 'well advised' to clarify the situation before deciding how to direct the jury; nevertheless the omission of a good character direction was not fatal to a conviction based on very substantial evidence. See, as a further example of the same point, *Balson v The State* [2005] UKPC 2.

F14.28 Examples of cases in which a conviction would still be likely to be overturned following *Hunter* might include *Ahmed* [2014] EWCA Crim 2466, [2015] 1 Cr App R 21 (275) and *MW* [2008] EWCA Crim 3091 (see **F14.9**), which are both examples of the wrongful failure to treat an accused as of effective good character where credibility was at the heart of the defence. Cases on the borderline might include *Scranage* [2001] EWCA Crim 1171, where the direction was given but was not couched in the positive terms required, and where good character evidence was of crucial importance because the jury had to decide whether D had acted dishonestly in transferring a sum wrongly credited to him by his bank, or whether he had, as he claimed, been trying to teach the bank a lesson. *Scranage* was not considered in *Hunter*, and it is possible that in future such an error might not be fatal if the evidence was overwhelming: see, e.g., *Sanchez* [2003] EWCA Crim 735, where a similar failure to couch the direction in positive terms was not fatal to D's conviction for drug smuggling, which was based on overwhelming evidence.

F14.29 In none of the cases considered above should the outcome be understood to set a precedent: *Hunter* states that reference to particular decisions in which convictions are quashed provides no helpful guidance to an appeal court, as all such decisions are fact-specific (at [89]). The reference to fact-specific judgments echoes the terminology of Sir Igor Judge P in *Renda* [2005] EWCA Crim 2862, [2006] 1 WLR 2948 and is intended to ensure consistency of approach with the grounds for review of decisions by trial judges in relation to the use of evidence of bad character as laid down in *Hanson* [2005] EWCA Crim 824, [2005] 1 WLR 3169 (see **F13.37**).

WITNESSES TO CHARACTER AND THE *ROWTON* RULE

Evidence of Reputation to Prove Good Character

F14.30 In *Rowton* (1865) Le & Ca 520, it was held to be the rule that witnesses as to character should testify to the reputation of the accused, and not to specific good acts or individuals' opinions. Lord Cockburn CJ suggested that the true object of the inquiry was in fact the disposition of the accused, but that it was not the practice to inquire into this directly but to arrive at it by 'giving evidence of his general character founded on his general reputation in the neighbourhood in which he lives'. The result was that 'the prisoner cannot give evidence of particular facts, though one fact might weigh more than the opinion of all his friends and neighbours'. Although *Rowton* speaks of the accused's reputation within a particular neighbourhood, the concept has long been adapted to allow character witnesses to come from the same workplace as the accused, or the same church or social organisation.

Where an accused raises the matter of good reputation, whether by calling witnesses or by giving evidence, the prosecution may in theory seek to respond by calling character witnesses in rebuttal, to whom the rule in *Rowton* would also apply. However, it is more likely that reliance would be placed on the CJA 2003, s. 101(1)(f) (see **F14.32**).

Under the CJA 2003, ss. 99(2) and 118(1), the rules by which the common law allows evidence of reputation to prove character, good and bad, are specifically preserved.

Evidence of Good Character other than Reputation

The prohibition on evidence of specific acts laid down in *Rowton* has never been specifically overturned, though in modern times it is more honoured in the breach than in the observance, for example where evidence is led of the accused's lack of convictions. Applied literally, the rule prevented the use of relevant evidence of disposition, as in *Redgrave* (1982) 74 Cr App R 10, where it was held that D, charged with importuning for an immoral purpose, was not entitled to raise evidence of his heterosexual disposition to rebut the charge. A dictum more representative of the approach now taken in practice is *Del-Valle* [2004] EWCA Crim 1013, in which an Army officer gave evidence based on positive conduct reports about D, a serving soldier, with a view to demonstrating that there were 'no black marks' against his character. Zucker J, giving the judgment of the Court of Appeal, stated: **F14.31**

> In many respects the law has moved well beyond *Rowton* and evidence of particular opinions and acts are routinely admitted, as is evidence of good character based on the absence of convictions. Indeed it is rare for evidence of general character founded on general reputation to be adduced in a modern criminal trial.

The observations in the preceding paragraph, and the comments of Zucker J in *Del-Valle*, were endorsed by the Court of Appeal in Northern Ireland in *Grimes* [2017] NICA 19, in which it was said that the current practice 'combines potential common sense and fairness with the restraining hand of the judge' (at [35]).

If, however, the evidence to be adduced *is* evidence of reputation, then *Rowton* applies and the witness must be aware from his or her own knowledge of the standing of the accused in the community. This was the point in issue in *Del-Valle* where the witness had no personal knowledge of D's reputation, and was thus rightly prevented from testifying about it.

Rebuttal of Good Character by Evidence Other than of Reputation

Section 101(1)(f) of the CJA 2003 provides that evidence of the accused's bad character is admissible to correct a false or misleading impression given by the accused (see **F13.78**). This provision appears to be capable of application whether the impression is created by character evidence in the *Rowton* sense (see **F14.30**) or by a specific assertion of good disposition or credibility. **F14.32**

In *W* [2019] EWCA Crim 1273, the Court of Appeal recognised that the 'decision whether to call [good] character evidence is often finely judged by advocates on behalf of defendants. Provided there is sensible reasoning for the decision made, it cannot be a ground of appeal after conviction that character evidence should have been called.' The Court accepted counsel's reason that calling character witnesses who might be cross-examined could impact adversely on the good character direction to which D was otherwise entitled.

In *Cojan* [2014] EWCA Crim 2152, [2015] 2 Cr App R 20 (294), the Court of Appeal dismissed a ground of appeal based on the trial judge's advice to an unrepresented accused not to call evidence of good character, as to do so would let in evidence of his own previous convictions. It was the judge's duty to ensure as best as possible that the accused understood the consequences of any decision taken.

Section F15 Character Evidence: Evidence of Bad Character of Persons Other than the Accused

CJA 2003, s. 100: PURPOSE AND RELATIONSHIP WITH OTHER EVIDENTIARY RULES

Purpose and Scope of s. 100

F15.1 This section covers the statutory scheme for the introduction of evidence of the bad character of persons other than the accused contained in the CJA 2003, s. 100. Such evidence is admissible only in restricted circumstances, and, except where all parties agree to the evidence being admissible, the leave of the court is required.

F15.2 In the leading case of *Brewster* [2010] EWCA Crim 1194, [2011] 1 WLR 601, it was said that the purpose of s. 100 is to remove from the criminal trial the right to introduce by cross-examination old, irrelevant or trivial behaviour in an attempt unfairly to diminish the standing of the witness in the eyes of the tribunal of fact, or to permit unsubstantiated attacks on credit. A similar point was made in *Miller* [2010] EWCA Crim 1153, [2010] 2 Cr App R 19 (138), where it was said that s. 100 aims to 'eliminate kite-flying and innuendo against the character of a witness in favour of a concentration upon the real issues in the case'.

Effect of s. 100 on Cross-examination

F15.3 **Application to Cross-examination** The scheme in s. 100 applies to all evidence of bad character of a non-defendant, whether adduced in chief or in cross-examination (*Brewster* [2010] EWCA Crim 1194, [2011] 1 WLR 601; *Braithwaite* [2010] EWCA Crim 1082, [2010] 2 Cr App R 18 (128)). Even if it is merely proposed to put a question to a witness regarding bad character, as to which the witness's denial would be final, the question ought not to be put without leave (*Miller* [2010] EWCA Crim 1153, [2010] 2 Cr App R 19 (138)).

F15.4 **Cross-examination as to Convictions** Where it is proposed to put previous convictions to a witness in cross-examination under the Criminal Procedure Act 1865, s. 6, the requirements of the CJA 2003, s. 100, must also be satisfied (CJA 2003, sch. 36, para. 79, amending the 1865 Act so that it now refers to a witness who is 'lawfully' questioned, and *Braithwaite* [2010] EWCA Crim 1082, [2010] 2 Cr App R 18 (128)). See further, as to cross-examination on bias and convictions, **F7.57** to **F7.63** and, as to the introduction of bad character in relation to a witness's credibility under the CJA 2003, s. 100, **F15.6**.

Relationship with Other Evidential Rules

F15.5 Overarching rules that take effect subject to the scheme in the CJA 2003, s. 100, are covered in this edition under the headings of the 'General Rule against Impeaching Credit of Own Witness', considered at **F6.48**, 'Cross-Examination as to Credit' considered at **F7.21** and the 'Rule of Finality of Answers to Questions on Collateral Matters', considered at **F7.48** ***et seq.*** However, nothing in the scheme under the CJA 2003 affects the exclusion of evidence under other rules, e.g., the YJCEA 1999, s. 41 (see **F7.26** ***et seq.***), which restricts evidence and questions about the complainant's sexual history in proceedings for sexual offences (CJA 2003, s. 112(3)).

CJA 2003, s. 100: MEANING OF BAD CHARACTER

The wide definition of bad character in the CJA 2003, s. 98 (set out and considered in detail at **F13.4**), applies equally to evidence of the bad character of a person other than the accused. Evidence of bad character can be admitted only if it satisfies the further conditions of admissibility in s. 100 (non-defendant's bad character) or s. 101 (defendant's bad character). **F15.6**

Evidence which, though it may show a person in a bad light, is not evidence of bad character within the meaning of the CJA 2003, s. 98, may be given provided it is relevant (see **F13.4** ***et seq.***, especially *Scott* [2009] EWCA Crim 2457, in which the efforts of a complainant to contact a friend of D despite police warnings to desist were regarded as falling short of 'reprehensible' conduct, but were also lacking in relevance and were therefore inadmissible). Evidence of a medical condition which is said to affect the credibility or propensity of a witness does not constitute evidence of bad character (*Platt* [2016] EWCA Crim 4, [2016] 1 Cr App R 22 (324)) and is admissible, if at all, at common law under the principles in *H* [2014] EWCA Crim 1555 (see **F7.64**).

Evidence 'to do with' the Facts of the Offence or in Connection with its Investigation or Prosecution

Section 99(1) of the CJA 2003 only abolishes the common-law rules governing admissibility of evidence of bad character as defined by s. 98. It follows that the common-law rules continue to operate insofar as they permit evidence to be adduced which, looking to the wording of s. 98(a), 'has to do with the alleged facts of the offence' or, looking to the wording of s. 98(b), 'is evidence of misconduct in connection with the investigation or prosecution of that offence'. Thus, for example, if evidence of misconduct tendered to prove the bias or partiality of a witness fell within s. 98(b), it could, because it is not evidence of 'bad character', be admitted at common law and without the need to apply the provisions of s. 100 (see **F7.57**). The fine dividing line between cases involving bad character evidence and cases falling within the exceptions in s. 98 is cited in the *Crown Court Compendium* (July 2020), ch. 12-1, as a reason for the court to have in mind the safeguards attaching to the former when considering the latter. In *Denton* [2020] EWCA Crim 410, the trial judge applied the s. 100 safeguards to evidence he had ruled admissible under s. 98 of hostile animus on the part of an investigator conducting a test-purchase. The Court of Appeal did not question this process, but the case turned ultimately on the point that animus was not relevant, as there was objective verification of the investigator's conduct. Had it been relevant, there is a risk that application of the s. 100 safeguards deprives the defence of evidence which s. 98 intended to be admissible. The interpretation of s. 98 is considered at **F13.10** to **F13.12**. **F15.7**

A case specifically decided in relation to s. 100 is *Machado* [2006] EWCA Crim 837, where evidence tending to show the alleged victim of a robbery had taken drugs was held to be within the words 'has to do with the alleged facts of the offence', as providing support for the defence explanation of his sudden collapse (the prosecution having alleged that D pushed him over). A plea of guilty by a co-accused to participation in an offence jointly charged against the accused 'has to do with' the offence charged and is not evidence of the co-accused's bad character (*Smith* [2007] EWCA Crim 2105). Such evidence may, of course, fall foul of another rule (in that case, the PACE 1984, s. 78, was applied to exclude the plea, which was otherwise admissible under the PACE 1984, s. 74 (see **F12.6** ***et seq.***)).

Section 98(b) of the CJA 2003 would seem apt to cover, for example, evidence that during the investigation the police obtained evidence unlawfully or unfairly (e.g., by fabricating a confession or planting evidence); evidence that during interview the police told lies; and evidence that during the investigation or proceedings the police, or someone on behalf of either the police or accused, had sought to intimidate potential witnesses. Evidence of misconduct in other investigations would seem to be admissible, if at all, only if s. 100 applies (see, as to the finality rule, **F7.49** and **F15.5** ***et seq.***).

CJA 2003, s. 100: GATEWAYS TO ADMISSIBILITY

Scope and Construction of the Gateways

F15.8 **Criminal Justice Act 2003, s. 100**

(1) In criminal proceedings evidence of the bad character of a person other than the defendant is admissible if and only if—
 (a) it is important explanatory evidence,
 (b) it has substantial probative value in relation to a matter which—
  (i) is a matter in issue in the proceedings, and
  (ii) is of substantial importance in the context of the case as a whole, or
 (c) all parties to the proceedings agree to the evidence being admissible.

...

(4) Except where subsection (1)(c) applies, evidence of the bad character of a person other than the defendant must not be given without leave of the court.

Subsections (2) and (3) are dealt with at **F15.12** and **F15.16** respectively.

F15.9 Section 100 regulates all aspects of the use of the bad character of a person other than the accused, in chief or in cross-examination (see **F15.3**), whether or not the person appears as a witness. Thus, it covers the character of a person whose statement is admitted under an exception to the hearsay rule (*Harvey* [2014] EWCA Crim 54, considered at **F15.25**) and the character of the deceased in a trial for murder (see, e.g., *Martin* [2017] EWCA Crim 488). In *RA* [2017] EWCA Crim 1515, D denied committing a sexual assault on his former sister-in-law, and wished to bring evidence of violence by his former wife during their marriage, which lent colour to his defence that her family had a motivation to bring a false complaint against him in light of the ongoing dispute over custody of his son. The CJA 2003, s. 100, is not specifically mentioned but it was held that, although the wife did not testify, the material should have been admitted as it would have provided 'some significant support' for the suggestion of a motive to fabricate.

F15.10 **General Principles** In the leading case of *Braithwaite* [2010] EWCA Crim 1082, [2010] 2 Cr App R 18 (128), Hughes LJ noted that there are four important features of the test for admissibility under s. 100.

(1) The test of 'substantial probative value' is not the same as the test for gateway (d) of s. 101 (see **F13.36**) where evidence of the bad character of an accused is tendered by the prosecution, and where the test is simply one of relevance. It is, however, the same as the test that appears in gateway (e) (see **F13.66**) where evidence is tendered by one co-accused against another.
(2) If the conditions of s. 100 are met, there is no residual statutory discretion whereby the judge can refuse to admit the evidence.
(3) Except where the parties agree to admit the evidence, the leave of the court is always required.
(4) Rulings by the judge in the absence of agreement between the parties require the exercise of judgment, rather than of discretion.

That there is no discretion to exclude defence evidence under s. 100 on grounds of fairness was reaffirmed in *Edwards* [2018] EWCA Crim 424. Evidence tendered by the prosecution is of course subject to exclusion under the PACE 1984, s. 78. This was confirmed in *Boxall* [2020] EWCA Crim 688, noting dicta of Hughes LJ in *Rand* [2006] EWCA Crim 3021 and the consideration given to s. 78 in *Livesey* [2019] EWCA Crim 877. It may be unlikely, once the high standard of probative value required by s. 100 is found to have been met, that it will be unfair to admit the evidence, but it is not impossible. A suggestion in *Lee* [2019] EWCA Crim 2052 that evidence of a non-defendant's bad character tendered by an accused could be excluded because of prejudice to a co-accused is incorrect.

F15.11 **Strict Construction of Gateways** In *Phillips* [2011] EWCA Crim 2935, [2012] 1 Cr App R 25 (332), decided under s. 101(1)(e) (see **F13.70**), the Court of Appeal noted that both s. 101(1)(e) and s. 100(1) 'have the capacity to change the landscape of a trial' and it was suggested that a strict reading of the gateways was required in order to ensure fairness and prevent unnecessary issues.

Important Explanatory Evidence

Criminal Justice Act 2003, s. 100 F15.12

(2) For the purposes of subsection (1)(a) evidence is important explanatory evidence if—
- (a) without it, the court or jury would find it impossible or difficult properly to understand other evidence in the case, and
- (b) its value for understanding the case as a whole is substantial.

A similar gateway for explanatory evidence is to be found also in relation to the bad character of the accused (s. 101(1)(c) at **F13.28**). In relation to s. 101(1)(c), it has rightly been held that the gateway is inapplicable if the evidence is readily understandable without evidence of bad character and the jury require no 'footnote or lexicon' (*Beverley* [2006] EWCA Crim 1287). The same must be true of s. 100(2)(a). Explanatory evidence admissible under s. 100 must also satisfy the further condition in s. 100(1)(b) that its value for understanding the case as a whole must be 'substantial'. 'Substantial' in s. 100 bears its natural meaning (*Braithwaite* [2010] EWCA Crim 1082, [2010] 2 Cr App R 18 (128)).

An example of explanatory evidence under s. 100, given in the Explanatory Notes to the Criminal Justice Bill, is of a case involving the abuse by one person of another over a long period of time. 'For the jury to understand properly the victim's account of the offending and why they did not seek help from, for example, a parent or other guardian, it might be necessary for evidence to be given of a wider pattern of abuse involving that other person' (para. 360). Another example is given in *Miller* [2010] EWCA Crim 1153, [2010] 2 Cr App R 19 (138), where it was said that bad character evidence that might expose a key witness's motive to lie would be capable of being important explanatory evidence. By contrast, in *Edwards* [2018] EWCA Crim 424, evidence of V's previous convictions for violence were not admissible in relation to D's claim to have acted in reasonable self-defence in circumstances where the incident was recorded on CCTV and had been observed by witnesses. The evidence and the issues were straightforward and the jury were well able to assess them.

Evidence of Substantial Probative Value in Relation to Matter in Issue of Substantial Importance

Meaning of 'Substantial' Under the CJA 2003, s. 100(1)(b), the trial judge must consider two essential questions: (1) whether the issue to which the evidence goes is of substantial importance in the context of the case as a whole, and (2) whether the evidence had substantial probative value in relation to a matter in issue in the proceedings. 'Substantial' bears its ordinary meaning (*Braithwaite* [2010] EWCA Crim 1082, [2010] 2 Cr App R 18 (128); *Platt* [2016] EWCA Crim 4, [2016] 1 Cr App R 22 (324) (decided in relation to s. 101(1)(e)), where it is also said that the word should not be glossed). Other leading cases have equated 'substantial' probative value with 'an enhanced capability' of proving or disproving a matter in issue in order to emphasise the point (see, e.g., *Phillips* [2011] EWCA Crim 2935, [2012] 1 Cr App R 25 (332)). F15.13

Matters in Issue: Propensity, Credibility and Other Issues In applications under s. 100(1)(b) the issue to which the evidence relates will usually, though not always, be either the propensity, or credibility, of the person of bad character (*Braithwaite* [2010] EWCA Crim 1082, [2010] 2 Cr App R 18 (128)). Although evidence of propensity is not specifically mentioned, as it is in relation to s. 101 (see **F13.39**), the suggestion that s. 100 could not be used to admit evidence of the propensity of a person other than the accused was dismissed as a 'misconstruction' in *H* [2009] EWCA Crim 2899, where D had been improperly hampered in his attempt to prove that the offence charged had been committed by another person by reference to relevant evidence of that person's propensity. F15.14

The credibility of a witness is capable of being an issue of substantial importance in relation to the case as a whole (*Stephenson* [2006] EWCA Crim 2325), but '[j]ust because a witness has convictions does not mean that the opposing party is entitled to attack the witness's credibility' (*Brewster* [2010] EWCA Crim 1194, [2010] 2 Cr App R 20 (149)).

An example of a different issue to which evidence of bad character might be relevant is *Luckett* [2015] EWCA Crim 1050, where D sought to demonstrate that V had been beaten not by D as alleged but by drug dealers, and evidence of V's association with the dealers, and his failure to pay his drug debts, was of substantial probative value in relation to that contention. By contrast, in *Muhedeen* [2016] EWCA Crim 1, D's defence to a charge of wounding V with intent was that he had been punched by V, lost consciousness temporarily, and that V's injuries had been caused quite independently by a separate group of men who had emerged from a nearby restaurant. Set against that defence, V's previous convictions for offences involving the carrying of a knife or other bladed weapon did not go to an issue of substantial importance in the case as a whole, when the clear implication of the defence was that the weapon had been produced by a member of the other group, and any suggestion that they had acquired the knife by disarming V was a matter of pure speculation. Similarly, in *Martin* [2017] EWCA Crim 488, the Court of Appeal regarded as speculative the attempt to discredit the deceased in a case of murder by reference to weapons and rap lyrics discovered during a search of a room he shared with his brother, and which could not be proved to be his. Evidence that he had been cautioned for possession of a knife was already before the jury; the additional evidence added nothing of value.

F15.15 **Substantial Probative Value** The assessment of substantial probative value relates to the force of the evidence. The judgment to be made, which is highly fact-sensitive, must take account of the context of the case as a whole. Thus it may be appropriate to consider whether it adds significantly to other more probative evidence in the case (*Braithwaite* [2010] EWCA Crim 1082, [2010] 2 Cr App R 18 (128)). This is a consideration of particular importance where the evidence consists of unproven allegations going to a witness's credibility where it has already been decided that the jury will be told of that person's previous convictions under s. 100 (see **F15.18**).

F15.16 **Matters Relevant to Assessment of Probative Value** The CJA 2003, s. 100(3), sets out a list of factors to which the court must have regard in assessing the probative value of the evidence. The list is non-exhaustive and the court must also have regard to any other factors it considers to be relevant.

Criminal Justice Act 2003, s. 100

(3) In assessing the probative value of evidence for the purposes of subsection (1)(b) the court must have regard to the following factors (and to any others it considers relevant)—
- (a) the nature and number of the events, or other things, to which the evidence relates;
- (b) when those events or things are alleged to have happened or existed;
- (c) where—
  - (i) the evidence is evidence of a person's misconduct, and
  - (ii) it is suggested that the evidence has probative value by reason of similarity between that misconduct and other alleged misconduct,

  the nature and extent of the similarities and dissimilarities between each of the alleged instances of misconduct;
- (d) where—
  - (i) the evidence is evidence of a person's misconduct,
  - (ii) it is suggested that that person is also responsible for the misconduct charged, and
  - (iii) the identity of the person responsible for the misconduct charged is disputed,

  the extent to which the evidence shows or tends to show that the same person was responsible each time.

Whether convictions have persuasive value depends principally on their nature, number and age (*Brewster* [2010] EWCA Crim 1194, [2011] 1 WLR 601). As to s. 100(3)(a), the more serious the misconduct on the part of a witness, and the greater the number of instances of misconduct, the stronger the likely probative value. As to s. 100(3)(b), evidence of misconduct occurring many years ago is usually likely to have less probative value than more recent misconduct, although very serious misconduct in the past may well have a stronger probative force than recent but comparatively minor misconduct. The factors listed in (c) and (d) are most likely to be relevant where the bad character evidence is said to be of probative value having regard to its similarity to the offence charged, in support of an argument that a person other than the accused committed the offence charged. As to the relevance of the criteria in s. 100 to applications made under the similarly worded s. 101(1)(e), see *Phillips* [2011] EWCA Crim 2935, [2012] 1 Cr App R 25 (332), discussed at **F13.68**.

Substantial Probative Value in Relation to Issues Other than Credibility A frequently recurring issue in the case law concerns the admissibility of bad character evidence to support a defence that either the victim or a third party was the aggressor in a crime of violence. **F15.17**

In *Francis* [2013] EWCA Crim 2312, the old conviction of one complainant for street-fighting and a warning for assault given to another were properly excluded in relation to the issue of whether they were the aggressors in the case, and in *Khan* [2017] EWCA Crim 767, where the defence to unlawful wounding included self-defence, the Court of Appeal held that the trial judge was 'quite right' to reject as evidence under s. 100 a statement by a person who was not called to testify that V was a trouble-maker and a drunk.

Substantial probative value may be established where, for example, an accused is charged with an offence of violence and claims self-defence, and there is a previous instance of violence by the complainant towards the accused using a weapon (*Riley* [2006] EWCA Crim 2030). Contrast *Edwards* [2018] EWCA Crim 424, in which D was unable to rely on the previous convictions for violence of V which 'could not really have helped' the jury to decide whether there was a continuing threat to D and his friends or whether V had at that point desisted. In *Paine* [2019] EWCA Crim 341, it was accepted that an alleged victim's previous violence might in principle be admissible even if the only issue is D's intention, for example where the defence is one of instinctive reaction to V's aggression. In *AB* [2016] EWCA Crim 1849, evidence that the deceased was a regular cannabis user was admitted at D's trial for stabbing him to death, and it appears to have been relevant both in relation to D's claim that he was acting in self-defence and as a matter affecting the credibility of the deceased's statements as to the cause of his injuries. (Unsubstantiated allegations that the deceased had taken other drugs were rejected in accordance with the principles considered at **F15.21**.)

Similar issues arise where an accused suggests that a complainant's injuries may have been caused by a third party. In *Alyson* [2016] EWCA Crim 2253, D contended that the complainant might have been subjected to violence by other persons as a result of her involvement with drug-dealing. However the evidence he proposed to give was merely that these were the types of activities which often lead to violence, and the application was rightly rejected. It might have been different if the evidence had been of particular incidents of violence arising from the complainant's activities.

Substantial Probative Value in Relation to Credibility The creditworthiness of a witness is clearly capable of being a matter in issue of substantial importance in the context of the case as a whole (*Stephenson* [2006] EWCA Crim 2325). **F15.18**

In the leading case of *Brewster* [2010] EWCA Crim 1194, [2011] 1 WLR 601, the Court of Appeal considered that the evidence of bad character that might qualify as being of substantial probative value in relation to credit was of two types: evidence that is relevant directly, as providing a reason for doubting the truth of the evidence of the witness in the particular case, and evidence which is relevant only indirectly, as providing a general reason for suggesting that the witness was a person not to be trusted. In *Brewster* the complainant in a case of alleged kidnapping had, amongst other convictions, a previous conviction for manslaughter of a client while working as a prostitute, in circumstances that were in certain respects similar to the version of events of the kidnapping put forward by the defence. It was held that the conviction was of direct relevance to the case and ought not to have been excluded. The appropriate test was to ask whether the evidence was 'reasonably capable of assisting a fair-minded jury to reach a view whether the witness's evidence is, or is not, worthy of belief'.

Brewster was applied in somewhat unusual circumstances in *Murphy* [2020] EWCA Crim 137. D's defence to violent sexual assaults against V was consent. D had previously been released from a life sentence for similar offences. He had made friends with K in a bail hostel. K gave evidence supporting D's defence that D and V had formed a clandestine relationship behind V's partner's back. Evidence of K's previous convictions for serious sexual offences were held to have been correctly admitted as a jury could properly take the view that K 'might regard a sexual crime committed by the appellant differently to most members of society, and might therefore be susceptible to being approached after the commission of such a crime in order to assist the appellant and be prepared to make a statement supporting his defence' (at [38]).

F15.19 **Illustrations of Admission and Exclusion of Bad Character Evidence to Impugn Credibility** The misconduct of a police witness on another occasion may, if of sufficient probative value, be used to indicate the fabrication of the witness's evidence in the instant case. In *McGuffie* [2015] EWCA Crim 307, the evidence showed that officers alleged to have made significant alterations to observation logs in D's case had been prepared to break the rules on compiling observation logs in a contemporaneous investigation. The nexus was such that the evidence should have been admitted. Evidence which is insufficiently important for one purpose may be relevant and admissible for another: in *Kelly* [2015] EWCA Crim 817, the fact that a witness was under investigation for fraud would not have been of sufficient importance if viewed as evidence going to untruthfulness (see **F15.10**), but was of substantial importance in that her testimony might have been tainted by her desire to avoid prosecution.

Minor offences were rightly disregarded in *Goddard* [2012] EWCA Crim 1756, in which the victim of a serious assault, who had identified D as one of his attackers, had a range of convictions for minor offences (including crimes of dishonesty), but all were more than three years old. The judge's decision that they were not of substantial probative value in relation to V's credibility was upheld. In *Jukes* [2018] EWCA Crim 176, [2018] 2 Cr App R 9 (114), a conviction appertaining to G, a person originally charged in the same proceedings as D but who pleaded guilty, was held to have been correctly excluded on the issue of G's credibility, as no issue of credibility arose where G was not a witness. It is submitted that this is not an absolute rule, in that it might be the case that an assessment of the credibility of the hearsay statements of a non-witness might be required so as to permit the use of bad character evidence, but on the facts of *Jukes* there was no such issue.

A specific direction may be called for if the focus of the challenge to credibility shifts during the trial. In *Wilkinson* [2018] EWCA Crim 2419, a successful application was made to admit the convictions of A, the complainant in a case of wounding, who had impugned the characters of two individuals expected to be called as defence witnesses. In the event, they were not called and the focus of the challenge to A's testimony was mistaken identification. It was held that the judge was entitled to direct the jury that A's convictions were 'neither here nor there' in assessing that issue.

In sexual cases the bad character of the complainant may require particularly careful consideration. In *Simpson* [2010] EWCA Crim 2266, D was charged with a rape occurring many years before, and it was said that the complainant's conviction for minor public order offences two years after the rape was not a matter in respect of which leave 'would ever have been given' under the CJA 2003, s. 100. In *Wright* [2014] EWCA Crim 545, D was charged with the rape of V, whose credibility was an important issue. The trial judge was held to have been 'fully justified' in excluding evidence that a police disciplinary tribunal had previously held her not to be a fully credible witness in relation to a complaint that V and others had made. There was no clear indication that V was thought to have lied, and the allegations she had made, some of which were accepted, were of a non-sexual nature. Thus, not only did the evidence fall short of the 'substantial probative value' threshold, it came 'very close to the "anything goes" kind of approach to complainants' that s. 100 was designed to discourage. By contrast, in *Hussain* [2015] EWCA Crim 383, it was held that the bad character of a complainant in a rape case ought to have been admitted on the ground that her convictions, which ranged from robbery to violence to serious motoring offences, were so numerous, varied and recent that they were of substantial probative value upon the issue of whether her accusation against the appellant was worthy of belief. Nevertheless, the appeal was dismissed because the jury would have been 'quite unable' to conclude that her previous misconduct provided any ground for rejecting her present complaint, given the consistency of her story with the other evidence in the case, and the fact that her evidence was 'demonstrably truthful' on key issues where his was not. In *Moody* [2019] EWCA Crim 1222, the use by the complainant of racist language, excluded by the trial judge, was thought to be something that might have been admitted as indicative of a malign motive against D, who was of mixed heritage, but the safety of the conviction was assured by DNA evidence for which D was unable to give an account.

In *Accamo* [2017] EWCA Crim 751, where it was held that the convictions of a key prosecution witness, which would have been admissible under s. 100 had they been disclosed at trial, might have influenced the jury's decision in that it would have cured any impression that they might have had of the witness's good character and ensured a 'level playing field'. Thus the conviction was unsafe. While this might be the expected outcome where evidence is, by definition, of substantial probative value, it should also be noted that all decisions on s. 100 are highly context-specific and that in *Hussein* there was further evidence to demonstrate the veracity of the complainant on key issues.

Convictions for dishonesty are not necessarily of substantial probative value even if credibility is an important issue. In *Garnham* [2008] EWCA Crim 266, the credibility of the complainant, a prostitute, was 'a very real issue' in relation to a dispute about consent, but her substantial record for dishonesty was held to have been properly disregarded as it was open to the trial judge to conclude that this was not evidence of the type that would assist the jury.

Credibility and a Propensity to Untruthfulness In *Brewster* [2010] EWCA Crim 1194, [2011] 1 WLR 601, the Court of Appeal rejected an argument, based on *Hanson* [2005] EWCA Crim 824, [2005] 1 WLR 3169, in relation to the CJA 2003, s. 101(1)(d) (see **F13.44**), that only convictions that demonstrate a propensity to untruthfulness should be regarded as capable of being probative in regard to credibility. Section 100 does not specifically limit the court to such evidence, and it follows that it is up to the judge to decide what evidence of a non-defendant's bad character should be accorded probative value and whether it is 'substantial'. The Court in *Brewster* followed *Stephenson* [2006] EWCA Crim 2325, where it was held that a witness's previous cautions in respect of offences of dishonesty ought not to have been disregarded simply because they did not establish any propensity to untruthfulness. Acknowledging that a distinction was being drawn between on the one hand ss. 100 and 101(1)(e) (evidence of co-accused's bad character: as to which see *Lawson* [2006] EWCA Crim 2572, [2007] 1 WLR 1191 at **F13.74**) and on the other s. 101(1)(d), Hughes LJ in *Stephenson* made the point that it was 'fully rational' to apply a higher degree of caution where a prosecution application under s. 101(1)(d) is concerned than to the case under s. 101(1)(e), where what is at stake is the right of accused persons to deploy relevant material in their own defence, or under s. 100. Under s. 100, leave may, of course, be sought by prosecution or defence, but only the prosecution will be subject to the further constraint of the PACE 1984, s. 78. *Brewster* was applied in *South* [2011] EWCA Crim 754, where the Court of Appeal nevertheless went on to hold that, on the facts, it was necessary, in order to make an adequate assessment of the probative value of the many convictions for offences of dishonesty of an alibi witness, to distinguish between those which went merely to dishonesty and those that indicated untruthfulness. *Stephenson* was not directly cited so it may be that the decision is overly restrictive but, as all decisions are highly fact-sensitive, it is more likely that this was a case in which the convictions for dishonesty lacked the necessary degree of probative value. F15.20

A propensity to untruthfulness may be established in other ways, e.g., by identifying lies that a witness has told. Such evidence may need to be controlled in order to focus on the real issues in the case. In *Rehman* [2017] EWCA Crim 106, the important issue was the state of mind of the accused men who had admitted having sexual contact with the child complainant. The Court of Appeal upheld the decision of the trial judge to limit the use of the child's lies in her early ABE interviews and to proceed by way of admissions covering the relevant areas and a 'clip' from the many hours of interviews in which the defence contended that she had lied.

Bad Character Evidence Consisting of Unproven Allegations In many cases the evidence in support of an assertion of bad character will consist of a conviction sufficient to create a presumption of guilt (**F13.1**) but this is not always the case. Where the evidence takes some other F15.21

form the court must take a view based on its nature (*Braithwaite* [2010] EWCA Crim 1082, [2010] 2 Cr App R 18 (128)). The evidence of a live witness or other hard evidence to support an allegation might, for example, be acceptable in circumstances where a mere unsupported allegation in a police report would not. (See, to similar effect in relation to s. 101, *Edwards* [2005] EWCA Crim 1813, [2006] 1 WLR 1524, the appeal of *Smith* (see **F13.65**) where the allegation was supported by the evidence of witnesses). However the mere fact that an accused is prepared to testify in support of allegations about the previous misconduct of a witness is not determinative of the issue. See *Erwood* [2016] EWCA Crim 839, where D was seeking to introduce specific instances of threatening behaviour by a neighbour to support his claim of self-defence, but the evidence did not meet the criteria in s. 100(1)(b) because it was of marginal importance, the jury were well aware of the history of animosity and there was CCTV evidence showing that D had pushed V as he was retreating. It was also noted that there was a risk that the jury would be distracted by satellite issues (see **F15.24**).

In *Braithwaite* the issue in a case of murder was whether D was the aggressor or whether it was V and his associates. The trial judge, having admitted material consisting of convictions, cautions and penalty notices recorded against the deceased's group, rejected material in police crime reports that third parties had made allegations against them. The Court of Appeal agreed. Although the material was potentially relevant to the propensity and the credibility of the witnesses, both of which matters were of substantial importance in the case, it was at best hearsay and 'given the difficulties of the jury in assessing such evidence, it would be rare for it to be judged to be of substantial probative value'. Where the complainants had decided not to support the allegations, and they had in consequence been dropped, their probative value was further diminished. *Braithwaite* was applied in *Hussain* [2019] EWCA Crim 2416, where it was held that the trial judge had acted entirely correctly in excluding evidence of a feud involving the family of B, who was alleged to have planted evidence to incriminate D. Evidence of B's bad character, including his convictions, was already before the jury and there was no evidence that the supposed feud affected either B himself or D.

F15.22 In *Bovell* [2005] EWCA Crim 1091, [2005] 2 Cr App R 27 (401), the Court of Appeal thought it unlikely that the mere making of an allegation against an individual was ever capable of being evidence within s. 100, but the more comprehensive analysis in *Braithwaite* shows that this is a possibility, if an unlikely one. As the purpose of s. 100 is 'to eliminate kite-flying and innuendo against the character of a witness in favour of a concentration upon the real issues in the case', counsel who sought to suggest to a witness that he was guilty of offences with which he had been charged 'should be in a position to prove what he asserts' (*Miller* [2010] EWCA Crim 1153, [2010] 2 Cr App R 19 (138), applied in *Shah* [2015] EWCA Crim 1250). The Court in *Miller* added that there might be 'infrequent and limited' instances of cross-examination implicating the witness in bad behaviour which the cross-examiner would be unable to prove, e.g., as to the discrete detail of an admitted conviction or behaviour. Where such an accusation is denied, the jury should be directed that the cross-examiner's case is not advanced by the mere putting of the question. Where the evidence tendered in support of an allegation admissible under s. 100 is hearsay, the court is entitled to take this into account in deciding whether it is of 'substantial probative value' (*Matthews* [2013] EWCA Crim 2238).

In cases such as *Braithwaite*, where the person in respect of whom the allegations are made can also be shown to have convictions that are clearly admissible on the same issue, the requirement that the probative value be assessed in light of the other evidence, including 'other more probative evidence directed to the same issue' (*Braithwaite* at [12]), will be a further factor telling against admissibility.

F15.23 **Effect of the CJA 2003, s. 109, on Previous Allegations** The CJA 2003, s. 109 (see **F13.61**), provides that 'reference to the probative value of evidence is a reference to its relevance or probative value on the assumption that it is true'. The only exception is where no jury could reasonably be persuaded of its truth. In *Braithwaite* [2010] EWCA Crim 1082, [2010] 2 Cr App R 18 (128) it was decided that s. 109 applies only to 'evidence' of bad character and thus does not assist in relation to police reports that were evidence, at most, that a complaint had been made.

Substantial Probative Value of Previous Allegations and 'Satellite' Issues In *Bovell* [2005] EWCA Crim 1091, [2005] 2 Cr App R 27 (401), it was said that trial judges applying s. 100 should be discouraged from entering into inquiries raising 'satellite' issues. This may be of particular importance where an allegation of criminal behaviour on the part of a witness is advanced as being relevant to the witness's credibility, but there is reason to doubt the credibility of the allegation and/or uncertainty about why no criminal charge resulted. In *Burchell* [2016] EWCA Crim 1559 it was noted that, while the need to avoid satellite issues was a consideration 'which the court can properly bear in mind' in such cases, it was 'not a basis for refusal to admit evidence, if the criteria in s. 100(1) are fulfilled'. **F15.24**

To similar effect is *Dizaei* [2013] EWCA Crim 88, [2013] 1 WLR 2257, where D was rightly refused leave to adduce evidence of alleged sexual violence by a witness which was unrelated to the relatively minor matter the jury had to try. The Court of Appeal considered that a court could legitimately consider, when assessing probative value under s. 100(3) (see **F15.16**), the proliferation of satellite issues that might arise if a witness was accused of an offence that the jury would have, in effect, to try in order to resolve the case, and the risk that the trial might be 'derailed' if their attention was thus divided. In so deciding, the Court was influenced by the absence of any residual discretion to exclude evidence admissible under s. 100, as identified in *Braithwaite* [2010] EWCA Crim 1082, [2010] 2 Cr App R 18 (128) (see **F15.10**).

Dizaei was approved in *King* [2015] EWCA Crim 1631, where the issue was whether D had been involved in an attack to which his co-accused had pleaded guilty as the principal offender. The convoluted history of animosity between D's family and the victims, particularly as it was supported by accusations rather than evidence, was held to be a matter best dealt with by an agreed statement so as not to distract the jury from the relatively straightforward issue they had to decide. The avoidance of satellite issues was also one of the grounds for rejecting evidence in *AB* [2016] EWCA Crim 1849. D had been convicted of the manslaughter of his grandfather who he believed had sexually abused D's sister. The trial judge correctly ruled that the sister should not give evidence of the abuse (which had never been officially reported). What mattered was D's state of mind, not whether he was correct in his belief. The proof of the abuse would not have satisfied the criteria of s. 100 in any event, but the difficulty of establishing the facts 'would have introduced a substantial issue of satellite litigation, on which it was most unlikely that the jury would be able to come to any firm conclusion', particularly as the deceased could not have advanced any explanation.

By contrast, in *Umo* [2020] EWCA Crim 284, it was held that the trial judge had erred in refusing to admit evidence of the bad character of a prosecution witness, M, to the effect that she had blackmailed H, another prosecution witness, with a threat to make a false allegation of sexual assault against him if he did not transfer money to her bank account. There was 'hard' evidence in support of the allegation in the form of a record of the threat on H's phone, so the jury would not have been in the position of trying the allegation as a satellite matter where it was simply M's word against H's: thus 'the evidence on the issue would have been of appropriately short duration'.

Credibility of Absent Witnesses In *Harvey* [2014] EWCA Crim 54, the prosecution relied on hearsay in the form of signed witness statements from C and D, who were alleged to have been the victims of offences of aggravated burglary involving firearms. The judge admitted a wide range of material including previous convictions of C, and evidence showing that C and D were linked to gang- and drug-related violence. Further evidence of allegations linking C and his associates to further offences were said to have been correctly excluded following the principles outlined above, in reliance in particular on *Braithwaite* [2010] EWCA Crim 1082, [2010] 2 Cr App R 18 (128) and *Brewster* [2010] EWCA Crim 1194, [2011] 1 WLR 601. It was argued that the CJA 2003, s. 124 (see **F17.87**), and the judgment of the Supreme Court in *Horncastle* [2009] UKSC 14, [2010] 2 AC 373 (see **F17.88**) clearly envisaged that there should be a greater scope for the defence in challenging the evidence of an absent witness under the hearsay **F15.25**

provisions of the Act than if the witness had been present. This argument was rejected: precisely the same approach applies where an absent witness's credibility is in issue and evidence which, at best, can only provide a basis for speculation and which is incapable of leading to reliable conclusions should not be admitted.

Evidence Admitted by Agreement

F15.26 Under the CJA 2003, s. 100(1)(c), evidence of the bad character of a person other than the accused may be admitted by agreement of 'all parties to the proceedings'. Thus in a case involving more than one defendant, all must agree: see *Ferdinand* [2014] EWCA Crim 1243, decided under the corresponding provision of s. 101 (see **F13.16**). Under s. 100(4), evidence may be admitted under s. 100(1)(c) without the leave of the court.

LEAVE

Requirement of Leave

F15.27 **Matters Relevant to Leave** Apart from evidence tendered with the agreement of the parties under the CJA 2003, s. 100(1)(c), evidence can be adduced under s. 100 only with the leave of the court (s. 100(4)). The subsection gives no guidance as to what further factors, if any, should be taken into account, apart from the factors set out in s. 100(2) and (3). It is possible that the difficulty posed where allegations against prosecution witnesses give rise to complex satellite issues, identified in *Dizaei* [2013] EWCA Crim 88, [2013] 1 WLR 2257 (see **F15.24**), might be better considered under this heading than as a matter going to 'substantial probative value'.

F15.28 **Relationship to the YJCEA 1999, s. 41** On a natural reading the CJA 2003, s. 100(4), also applies to evidence of bad character of complainants admissible under the YJCEA 1999, s. 41 (see **F7.26 *et seq.*** and *V* [2006] EWCA Crim 1901, where Crane J acknowledged that both provisions may well be in play, and that: 'In many cases s. 41 will be the more formidable obstacle to overcome'). If the leave requirement under s. 100(4) is designed to be additional to the requirements of s. 41, then the issue arises as to what kinds of sexual behaviour on the part of the complainant should be treated as 'bad character' as defined in the CJA 2003. In cases where the defence allege that the complainant has previously made false allegations then, once it appears that there is an evidential basis for suggesting falsity, s. 100 appears to be the dominant provision — the essence of the attack is that the complainant has lied, even if the circumstances also suggest sexual behaviour. See, e.g., *Gabbai* [2019] EWCA Crim 2287, [2020] 4 WLR 65, where the complainant had made allegations of rape against others in the past which she later doubted, suggesting that she was lying and an 'attention seeker'. This evidence should have been admitted pursuant to s. 100, as it provided an evidential foundation for a conclusion of falsity that was of substantial importance in the case as a whole. Without such a foundation, the questions would not be about lies but about the sexual behaviour of the complainant and would be caught by s. 41(1) (*Ali* [2017] EWCA Crim 1211). A previous complaint of a sexual offence, alleged to be false, was held admissible under s. 100 in *Scott* [2009] EWCA Crim 2457. See also *Wright* [2014] EWCA Crim 545, in which s. 100, rather than s. 41, applied to evidence suggesting that the complainant in a sexual case had been a less than credible witness in relation to complaints of misconduct (including some of a sexual nature) against the police. See also *CB* [2020] EWCA Crim 790, in which an old allegation made by V when a child was excluded under s. 100 as lacking probative value, as there was no substantive basis on which its alleged falsity could be determined. In *Stephenson* [2006] EWCA Crim 2325, where D complained on appeal that he had not been permitted sufficient latitude in relation to the complainant's disturbed background and promiscuity as indicative of the likelihood that she had fabricated the case against D, the Court of Appeal made particular reference to the fact that none of the sexual relationships were alleged to have been falsified, and thereafter confined its observations about s. 100 to the effect of the complainant's cautions for offences of dishonesty (see **F15.10**).

In *Clarke* [2016] EWCA Crim 2030, the Court of Appeal noted that previous complaints made by a complainant with a mental disorder might be false without being deliberately so, and that this would not indicate bad character (thus triggering neither s. 41 nor s. 100).

Rules of Court Section 111 of the CJA 2003 permits rules of court to be made in relation to evidence of bad character to supplement the provisions of the Act. The relevant rules are contained in CrimPR Part 21 (see Supplement, **R21.1** *et seq*.), with modifications where the proceedings are before the Court of Appeal which are set out in r. 39.7 (see Supplement, **R39.7**). **F15.29**

The rules require application to be made to introduce evidence of a non-defendant's bad character and also for cross-examining a witness with a view to eliciting such evidence; they also set time-limits for any party wishing to adduce evidence of a non-defendant's bad character, and also to an application to oppose the use of such evidence. In *Solloway* [2019] EWCA Crim 454, the Court of Appeal deprecated the introduction in cross-examination of a prosecution witness's antecedents otherwise than in accordance with the rules, which are designed to enable the judge to consider admissibility in advance of trial and for the other parties affected (in this case a co-accused) to consider their responses. If for any reason this could not be done, for example because the application arose out of something said by the witness, the issue should not have been raised in front of the jury. In *Newman* [2020] EWCA Crim 136, the Court of Appeal, emphasising the need for a proper application, stressed that over-enthusiasm of counsel in the course of cross-examination is neither an excuse nor adequate explanation for failure to follow the correct procedural course.

REASONS FOR RULINGS

Under the CJA 2003, s. 110, where the court makes a ruling on whether an item of evidence is evidence of a person's bad character and on whether an item of such evidence is admissible under s. 100, it must state in open court (but in the absence of the jury, if there is one), its reasons for the ruling; and, if it is a magistrates' court, it must cause the ruling and the reasons for it to be entered in the register of the court's proceedings. In *Renda* [2005] EWCA Crim 2862, [2006] 2 All ER 553 (at [60]), the mere observation that the jury was entitled to know about character was regarded as an 'over-parsimonious' compliance with s. 110. In *Rehman* [2017] EWCA Crim 106, the Court of Appeal suggested that it would be helpful, where a number of items were in issue, for the judge to specify in detail which items were inadmissible. **F15.30**

DIRECTIONS TO JURY

The ingredients of a direction in relation to evidence admitted under the CJA 2003, s. 100, are set out in the *Crown Court Compendium* (July 2020), ch. 12-10. Where the evidence is disputed, the jury must first decide whether it is proved (or, if tendered by the defence, whether it may be true). If so, the jury should be told that it is for them to decide whether, if at all, the evidence assists in determining the issues in the case. Depending on the nature and extent of the evidence of the non-defendant's bad character, there may be a need for a direction on credibility if the non-defendant was a witness. In *Kelly* [2008] EWCA Crim 1456, the failure of the trial judge to relate a prosecution witness's convictions specifically to his propensity, as distinct from his credibility, was not fatal to D's conviction where there was no danger of the jury missing the significance of the evidence, following *Campbell* [2007] EWCA Crim 1472, [2007] 1 WLR 2798 (on the CJA 2003, s. 101: see **F13.24**). **F15.31**

Section F16 The Rule against Hearsay: General Principles

SCOPE AND RATIONALE

Admissibility of Hearsay Evidence

F16.1 **Criminal Justice Act 2003, s. 114**

(1) In criminal proceedings a statement not made in oral evidence in the proceedings is admissible as evidence of any matter stated if, but only if—
 (a) any provision of this chapter or any other statutory provision makes it admissible,
 (b) any rule of law preserved by section 118 makes it admissible,
 (c) all parties to the proceedings agree to it being admissible, or
 (d) the court is satisfied that it is in the interests of justice for it to be admissible.

Hearsay evidence may pose a particular threat to the fairness of a criminal trial. It is necessary for courts to be vigilant, first that hearsay is recognised and treated as such, and secondly that it is received in evidence only where the appropriate safeguards are in place. This section is concerned with the rationale for the special treatment of hearsay, and with the elaboration of the elements of its definition in the CJA 2003, s. 114(1) and 115. The scheme for the reception of hearsay evidence, and the additional safeguards applicable to evidence falling within the exceptions in s. 114(1)(a) to (d) are the subject of **F17**.

Concept of Hearsay Evidence

F16.2 The concept of hearsay is deeply rooted in the history of criminal trials. As Lord Thomas CJ explained in *Horncastle* [2009] EWCA Crim 964, [2009] 2 Cr App R 15 (230), giving a judgment of the Court of Appeal regarded as supplementary to that of the Supreme Court in the same case ([2009] UKSC 14, [2010] 2 AC 373):

> ... the law of England and Wales has ... always insisted that it is ordinarily essential that evidence of the truth of a matter be given in person by a witness who speaks from his own observation or knowledge. It uses the legal expression 'hearsay' to describe evidence which is not so given, but rather is given second hand, whether related by a person to whom the absent witness has spoken, contained in a written statement of the absent witness, given in the form of a document or record created by him, or otherwise.

Under the CJA 2003, s. 114(1), the definition of hearsay has to be gleaned from the proposition that 'a statement not made in oral evidence in the proceedings is admissible as evidence of any matter stated if, but only if'. Thus the essential ingredients are 'a statement' which is tendered 'as evidence of any matter stated'. 'Statement' is considered at **F16.7** *et seq*., and 'matter stated' at **F16.14** *et seq*.

The essence of hearsay as an essentially second-hand account of relevant matters has not changed as a result of the CJA 2003, and neither has the rationale for regarding hearsay as generally inferior to first-hand evidence. The exact demarcation of evidence as hearsay or non-hearsay has shifted (in favour of admissibility) as a result of the statutory definition of a 'matter stated'. This results in a statement being non-hearsay in the absence of any purpose on the part of the maker to cause a person to believe the matter, or to cause a person or a machine to act as though it were as stated.

Despite this minor modification, the hearsay rule is far-reaching, applying to both prosecution and defence. It covers not only the statements of non-witnesses, but also past statements made by a witness who is called to give oral evidence and who could therefore be cross-examined about what the witness has said previously (*Horncastle*). It applies to all statements, not simply to those made in anticipation of the trial itself, and includes documents as well as oral statements. It follows that the rule catches some evidence, such as records of routine business dealings, that is intrinsically reliable, but this does not prevent it being hearsay: the reliability or otherwise of the evidence is relevant only to whether it may be received through an exception to the rule.

Codification of Hearsay Rules

The major change brought about by the CJA 2003 is that hearsay is now received in a systematic way through 'a crafted code intended to ensure that evidence is admitted only when it is fair that it should be' (*Horncastle* [2009] UKSC 14, [2010] 2 AC 373). The exceptions to the rule have been systematised so that evidence that is intrinsically reliable, such as business records, may be received (under s. 117: see **F17.25**), and evidence such as the statement of a witness who has died before trial (and is thus the best evidence available) is able to be admitted except where it would impact adversely on the fairness of the proceedings (under s. 116: see **F17.8**). Hearsay can be admitted by agreement of all parties (under s. 114(1)(c): see **F17.6**), and there is also a residual 'interests of justice' exception in s. 114(1)(d) to ensure that nothing is left out that should be heard (see **F17.34**). **F16.3**

Dangers of Hearsay Evidence

The reason for retaining the hearsay rule as a rule of exclusion subject to exceptions is to ensure that it is always treated with appropriate caution. In the leading case of *Horncastle* [2009] UKSC 14, [2010] 2 AC 373, Lord Phillips said (at [21]): **F16.4**

> There were two principal reasons for excluding hearsay evidence. The first was that it was potentially unreliable. It might even be fabricated by the witness giving evidence of what he alleged he had been told by another. Quite apart from this, the weight to be given to such evidence was less easy to appraise than that of evidence delivered by a witness face to face with the defendant and subject to testing by cross-examination.

The system of criminal justice in England and Wales depends critically on assessments of fact made by lay people, whether juries or magistrates, and as Lord Phillips also points out, the origins of the hearsay rule suggest a mistrust of their ability to cope with hearsay evidence. It follows that the wider availability of hearsay at trial under the CJA 2003 means that the dangers posed by such evidence must more frequently be a factor to consider in the management of trials.

As Hughes LJ said in *Riat* [2012] EWCA Crim 1509, [2013] 1 All ER 349:

> [Hearsay] is necessarily second-hand and for that reason very often second-best. Because it is second-hand, it is that much more difficult to test and assess. The jury frequently never sees the person whose word is being relied upon. Even if there is a video recording of the witness' interview, that person cannot be asked a single exploratory or challenging question about what is said. From the point of view of a defendant, the loss of the ability to confront one's accusers is an important disadvantage. Those very real risks of hearsay evidence, which underlay the common law rule generally excluding it, remain critical to its management. Sometimes it is necessary in the interests of justice for it to be admitted. It may not suffer from the risks of unreliability which often attend such evidence, or its reliability can realistically be assessed. Equally, however, sometimes it is necessary in the interests of justice either that it should not be admitted at all, or that a trial depending upon it should not be allowed to proceed to the jury because any conviction would not be safe.

For these reasons, hearsay that is technically admissible under the CJA 2003 is subject to a battery of further safeguards aimed at minimising the dangers identified above. These include the giving of notice of intention to use hearsay evidence (see **F17.5**), the provision of special rules to scrutinise the credibility of the maker of the statement (s. 124: see **F17.87**) and the giving of appropriate judicial directions about hearsay (see **F17.96**). Where fairness cannot be assured, the evidence may be excluded (under the PACE 1984, s. 78, in the case of the prosecution, or under the CJA 2003, s. 126, in the case of prosecution or defence: see **F17.88** ***et seq.***), and a trial which is dependent on hearsay may in some cases be stopped (see **F17.98**). The wider significance of these safeguards lies in protecting the fair trial rights of the defendant (see **F17.5**). It follows that the process of deciding whether evidence is hearsay is as important as it ever was, as the safeguards to be applied are of a quite different order from those applicable to non-hearsay statements.

The dangers of reliance on hearsay are lessened where the fact-finder is a judge. In a recent dictum, the Court of Appeal agreed that hearsay in the form of a 'tip-off' that would be inadmissible at trial might be considered on appeal 'in the interests of justice as going to the argument of whether a conviction were unsafe' (*Lane* [2015] EWCA Crim 1226 at [58]). Such observations are rare, however, and there is no sense that the rules should vary in summary trial according to whether the trial is by lay magistrates or a district judge (magistrates' court).

F16.5 **Hearsay and Defence Evidence** The CJA 2003 creates no special rule of admissibility favouring the defence. In this it reflects the common-law tradition, as recognised in *Horncastle* [2009] UKSC 14, [2010] 2 AC 373. Even in the extreme case where a third party has confessed to the offence with which the accused is charged, the confession, being hearsay, is inadmissible unless an exception can be found (*Turner* (1975) 61 Cr App R 67; *Blastland* [1986] AC 41). Under the CJA 2003, s. 114(1)(d) (see **F17.34**), hearsay evidence may be admitted where it is in the interests of justice to do so, and the importance of the evidence to the defence will be a factor that the court will consider in deciding where the interests of justice lie (see, e.g., *Y* [2008] EWCA Crim 10, [2008] 1 Cr App R 34 (411)). But it remains the case that there is no special hearsay exception for defence evidence. In *Williams* [2014] EWCA Crim 1862, the Court of Appeal stated that the regime in the CJA 2003 'does not structurally favour the defence over the prosecution'.

F16.6 **Hearsay and Fair Trial** The greater scope for admitting hearsay under the CJA 2003 has led to an exchange of views between the domestic courts and Strasbourg as to whether the statutory scheme provides adequate protection for the fair trial rights of defendants. There is now a shared understanding that, properly applied, it does, but at the heart of the dialogue has been a recognition that care must always be used in handling hearsay, and that it should never be 'nodded through or adduced as a matter of routine' (*per* Gross LJ in *Friel* [2012] EWCA Crim 2871). The more central the hearsay, the greater the care required. If the evidence of an absent witness is the sole or decisive basis for a conviction, the domestic courts, while adhering to their view that such hearsay may be capable of being sufficient evidence on which to found a conviction (*Horncastle* [2009] UKSC 14, [2010] 2 AC 373), nevertheless apply the rules in conformity with the view of the Grand Chamber that there should be a good reason for the witness's non-attendance, and that there should be sufficient safeguards to permit a proper assessment of the reliability of the evidence (*Horncastle v UK* (2015) 60 EHRR 31 (1331), affirming principles set out in *Al-Khawaja and Tahery v UK* (2012) 54 EHRR 23 (807)). See further **F17.88**.

DEFINITION OF 'STATEMENT'

F16.7 **Criminal Justice Act 2003, s. 115**

(1) In this chapter references to a statement... are to be read as follows.
(2) A statement is any representation of fact or opinion made by a person by whatever means; and it includes a representation made in a sketch, photofit or other pictorial form.

This definition is to be read in combination with the definition of 'matter stated' in s. 115(3) (see **F16.14**), which restricts the application of the hearsay rule to cases where the maker of the statement had a purpose to cause another to believe the matter, or to cause the other, or a machine, to act as though it were as stated. For the purposes of exposition, it is convenient to take them separately.

Conduct as Hearsay

Whereas most hearsay statements are made (whether orally or in writing) in words, the CJA 2003, s. 115(2), confirms that a statement may take any form that enables a representation of fact to be made. Thus, as at common law, hearsay may occur in the form of conduct. In *Chandrasekera v The King* [1937] AC 220, a woman's throat had been cut, depriving her of the power of speech. She described D as her attacker using sign language, and nodded when asked whether D had caused her injuries. These communications were likened to the language of a deaf person able to converse only by means of a finger alphabet, and the 'conversation' was admitted under an exception to the hearsay rule. **F16.8**

Hearsay and Statements in Other Proceedings

Under the CJA 2003, s. 114, any statement not made in oral evidence 'in the proceedings' may qualify as hearsay. It follows that, as was the case at common law, a statement may be hearsay notwithstanding that it was made on oath in other proceedings, and may only be received as evidence of matters stated under an exception to the rule (see, e.g., *Berkeley Peerage Case* (1811) 4 Camp 401). **F16.9**

Hearsay and Previous Statements of Witnesses

The use of a witness's out-of-court statement will not be hearsay if tendered as evidence of consistency rather than of a matter stated. The use of previous statements to show consistency is, however, frequently prohibited by the rule against self-serving statements, also known as the rule against narrative. Where, exceptionally, such statements are admissible, the CJA 2003, s. 120, may apply so as to render the statement admissible as evidence of any matter of which the maker's oral evidence would have been admissible. As to the use of consistent statements, see **F6.39 *et seq.*** **F16.10**

The use of a witness's previous inconsistent statement is not hearsay when tendered merely to show inconsistency. However, s. 119 permits such a statement, properly proved, to be evidence of any matter stated. The use of inconsistent statements is dealt with at **F7.51** to **F7.56**. The reasons typically given for the exclusion of hearsay (see **F16.3**) do not apply with the same force to the out-of-court statements of those who are witnesses in the proceedings. In many cases a statement made while events were fresher in the witness's mind might provide evidence of better quality than subsequent evidence in court.

Hearsay and Mechanically Produced Evidence

Under the CJA 2003, it is apparent from the definition of 'statement' in s. 115(1) (see **F16.7**) as a representation of fact or opinion *made by a person* that a purely mechanical generation of an image, say by CCTV, is not hearsay. Thus juries are allowed to see still photographs taken by a security camera during an armed robbery (*Dodson* [1984] 1 WLR 971), or a video recording of an incident (*Fowden* [1982] Crim LR 588; *Grimer* [1982] Crim LR 674), and to hear a tape recording of a relevant conversation (*Maqsud Ali* [1966] 1 QB 688). Furthermore, just as a video recording of the commission of an offence is admissible, so also a witness who has seen the recording may give evidence of what was seen, as such a person is in effect in the same position as a witness with a 'direct view of the action' (*Taylor v Chief Constable of Cheshire* [1986] 1 All ER 225). See also, as to computer-produced evidence, **F16.12**. **F16.11**

Section 115(1) also makes it clear that an image generated by human agency such as a representation in a 'sketch, photofit or other pictorial form' is a 'statement' for the purposes of the hearsay rule. The provision reverses *Cook* [1987] QB 417 in which the Court of Appeal had stated that sketches and photofit likenesses made under the direction of identifying witnesses were analogous to photographs. This is plainly not the case, as such images are entirely dependent on the recollection of the person directing the hand of the artist. A mechanically generated representation that depends for its accuracy on human input cannot be used in the absence of proof that the input was accurate (see s. 129 at **F16.13**).

Computer Evidence and the Hearsay Rule

F16.12 It follows from the definition of 'statement' in the CJA 2003, s. 115(1) and (2) (see **F16.7**), as a representation 'by a person' that computer evidence may or may not be hearsay. To the extent to which a computer is used merely to perform functions of calculation, no question of hearsay is involved in receiving evidence of what the computer 'said', and in this the CJA 2003 follows the common law (*Minors* [1989] 2 All ER 208, per Steyn J at p. 446). Thus, in *Wood* (1982) 76 Cr App R 23, the prosecution alleged that metal found at D's premises was stolen. Chemists performed tests on samples of the metal, and used a computer as a tool to perform complicated calculations based on the data they had obtained. At trial, the chemists gave evidence of the outcome of the tests, and produced the computer printout to prove the results of the calculations. It was held that the printout was admissible for this purpose and did not constitute hearsay evidence, being instead real evidence analogous to the reaction of litmus paper as evidence of the acidity of a solution. In the same way, the printout of a device that has performed an analysis of specimens of breath is admissible non-hearsay evidence (*Castle v Cross* [1984] 1 All ER 87, where the rule regarding admissibility of computer evidence was said to be the same in this respect as in respect of less sophisticated machines; *Castle v Cross* was affirmed by the House of Lords in *DPP v McKeown* [1997] 1 All ER 737). See *The Statue of Liberty* [1968] 2 All ER 195 (automatic record made by radar set at a shore radio station admissible), and see also the rule as it applies to photographs etc. at **F16.11**.

F16.13 **Printouts and Accuracy** Where a computer is used to record information that is supplied by a person, the hearsay rule will come into play if it is sought to use a printout from the computer to prove that what the person said was true. Thus, documentary records stored on computer are hearsay (*Minors* [1989] 2 All ER 208), and see *Coventry Justices, ex parte Bullard* (1992) 95 Cr App R 175, in which it was held that the crucial distinction was between 'computer printouts containing information implanted by a human, and printouts containing records produced without human intervention'. Similarly, in *Wood* (1982) 76 Cr App R 23, it was necessary for the chemists who tested the metal to give evidence of the facts on which the tests were based: the computer printout could not have been used to prove that the information fed into the computer was accurate, only that the calculations performed by the computer itself were correct. The CJA 2003 maintains the same distinction.

Criminal Justice Act 2003, s. 129

(1) Where a representation of any fact—
  (a) is made otherwise than by a person, but
  (b) depends for its accuracy on information supplied (directly or indirectly) by a person, that representation is not admissible in criminal proceedings as evidence of the fact unless it is proved that the information was accurate.

DEFINITION OF 'MATTER STATED'

F16.14 **Criminal Justice Act 2003, s. 115**

(1) In this chapter references to a statement or to a matter stated are to be read as follows.
(2) [definition of statement: see **F16.7**]
(3) A matter stated is one to which the chapter applies if (and only if) the purpose, or one of the purposes, of the person making the statement appears to the court to have been—
  (a) to cause another person to believe the matter, or
  (b) to cause another person to act or a machine to operate on the basis that the matter is as stated.

Reliance on Matter Stated

F16.15 Evidence is hearsay under the CJA 2003, s. 114(1), only where it is relied upon as 'evidence of any matter stated': in other words, where it is sought to establish the truth of that matter. The distinction is generally easy to draw except in cases where the speaker does not intend to cause the listener to believe the relevant matter (dealt with at **F16.16**). A common instance of reliance is where it is sought to establish the registration number of a car involved in an incident, and an eye-witness, A, who has seen the incident, relates the number to B, who has not. It is hearsay for B to tell the court what the number was for the purpose of proving the truth of A's statement (*McLean* (1967) 52 Cr App R 80; *Jones v Metcalfe* [1967] 3 All ER 205; *Maher v DPP* [2006] EWCA Crim 1271). (Where B makes a note of the number that A verifies, A may give evidence of the number by refreshing memory from B's note: *Jones v Metcalfe*; *Kelsey* (1982) 74 Cr App R 213. As to refreshing memory, see **F6.16** ***et seq.***)

The labelling of items provides another frequent instance of hearsay. If goods are imported in bags marked 'Produce of Morocco', the marks are hearsay evidence of the country of origin (*Patel v Comptroller of Customs* [1966] AC 356). The same result follows even where the information is indelibly stamped into the goods (*Comptroller of Customs v Western Lectric Co. Ltd* [1966] AC 367). Similarly, information stamped on to a document is hearsay evidence of the matters stated (e.g., of a date: see *Cook* (1980) 71 Cr App R 205). In many instances the evidence is likely to be perfectly reliable, and admissible under the widely-drawn exception for business documents in s. 117 (see **F17.25**), but the hearsay point should still be taken to ensure that the dangers can be properly assessed and that hearsay is not 'nodded through' (see **F16.6**). Further examples of hearsay are that a party to a conversation conducted through an interpreter infringes the hearsay rule by seeking to prove what the other party said by relating to the court what the interpreter said (*Attard* (1958) 43 Cr App R 90), and a police officer who testifies that a person is a 'known heroin user' is giving hearsay evidence if the basis of that knowledge is information supplied by others, including the person in question (*Rothwell* (1994) 99 Cr App R 388).

Care must always be taken to ascertain the 'matter stated', as there may be more than one such matter in issue. In *Williams* [2014] EWCA Crim 1862, the defence to murder was that the crime was committed by S, who did not testify. It was said that S had confessed in a telephone conversation with E, which E had recorded. The decision not to call E led to hearsay problems both as to the content of the recording, which if it was indeed a third-party confession might have been admissible under s. 114(1)(d) (see **F17.34**) in the interests of justice, and also as to the need to prove that the voice heard on the recording was indeed that of S, which could not be proved simply by reliance on E's out-of-court assertion to that effect.

Matters Intended to be Believed or Acted upon

Reversal of *Kearley* The intended effect of the CJA 2003, s. 115(3), is to reverse the hearsay aspects of the decision of the House of Lords in *Kearley* [1992] 2 AC 228. D was charged with possession of a controlled drug with intent to supply. The amount found in D's possession being of itself inadequate to warrant an inference of such an intent, the prosecution relied upon evidence that, after D's arrest, a number of telephone calls had been made to his home in which the callers asked for D by his nickname and sought to buy drugs, and that a number of individuals had visited the house and asked to be supplied with drugs. None of these persons was called to give evidence at the trial. The House of Lords, by a majority, held that the hearsay rule precluded the use of the callers' requests as evidence, in effect, of their belief that D was a dealer. Under s. 115(3), the matter impliedly stated by the callers in *Kearley* (that D is a dealer) is not one to which the hearsay rule applies unless the person making the request had a purpose either (a) to cause the recipient of the call to believe the matter or (b) to cause the recipient to act as though the matter is as stated. Where the caller believes that the recipient already knows the matter in question, and is therefore not speaking with either of the hearsay purposes, the evidence is original, non-hearsay evidence. On the facts of *Kearley*, the callers clearly thought that they were speaking to D himself. There was thus little danger that, in making their requests, they were seeking to mislead the person to whom they were speaking, or to misrepresent or exaggerate the matter on which the prosecution sought to rely, namely their belief that D was a drug dealer. **F16.16**

Instances of Application of the CJA 2003, s. 115(3) The application of the CJA 2003, s. 115(3), to particular communications has proved difficult in practice. In *Twist* [2011] EWCA **F16.17**

Crim 1143, [2011] 3 All ER 1055, a series of conjoined appeals, the Court of Appeal attributed some of the difficulty to the continued use of expressions such as 'implied assertion' that are relics of the common law, and set out a clear three-stage test for ascertaining whether communications are hearsay under the CJA 2003, which is focused solely on the statutory wording. This analysis was endorsed in *Mateza* [2011] EWCA Crim 2587, where it was also said that it was not helpful to look at earlier interpretations of s. 115(3) (such as *Leonard* [2009] EWCA Crim 1251: see **F16.19**). The test in *Twist* runs as follows:

(1) Ascertain the matter sought to be proved. Hughes LJ noted that the opening words of s. 114(1) ('admissible as evidence of any matter stated') demonstrate that the CJA 2003, like the common law, is concerned with what it is that a party is seeking to prove. The purpose of the party in adducing a communication has therefore first to be ascertained.
(2) Provided that the matter sought to be proved is a relevant one, the next question is whether there is a statement of that matter in the communication. If not (perhaps because the communication is not a statement at all, but a question such as a request for drugs), no question of hearsay arises.
(3) If the communication does state the matter, was it one of the purposes (not necessarily the only or dominant purpose) that the recipient, or any other person, should believe that matter or that a person should act upon the basis that it is as stated (or that a machine should operate on that basis)? If yes, it is hearsay; if no, it is not.

F16.18 In the appeal of *Twist*, the prosecution relied on text messages received by T to establish intent to supply drugs. This was a relevant matter, but the messages, being mere requests for drugs, did not contain any statement that T was a dealer. Even if such a statement could be inferred, the purpose of the senders did not include any intention to cause anyone to believe he was. In the appeal of *Boothman*, B was charged with conspiracy to supply cannabis and cocaine, and there was considerable traffic in text messages between B, who was advertising a good stock of available drugs, and other persons either placing orders or commenting on issues relating to past supply. Particular objection was taken to the mention of 'lines' in the incoming texts as including statements indicative of the supply of cocaine. But the senders of the texts did not have a purpose to make B believe that he was a supplier of that drug, or to induce him to act upon it as true (as distinct from acting upon it to supply further drugs). The evidence was therefore not hearsay. In the appeal of *Tomlinson* and *Kelly*, the matter to be proved was that the accused were in possession of a gun, and the communication in question was a text message to T from a third party seeking the return of a gun. Assuming that the message included, by implication, a suggestion that T had the gun, the sender was not intent on causing T to believe that fact — rather there was a common understanding that such was the case, so again the message was not hearsay. And finally in the appeal of *Lowe*, L was charged with twice raping his young girlfriend following an argument. The defence was consent, and L claimed that the argument followed the intercourse rather than the other way round. Messages from L to the complainant, apparently apologising for the rape and admitting the sequence of events, were held not to be hearsay: though they contained statements of highly relevant matters, L was not seeking to cause the complainant to believe she had been raped: 'if that is what the messages meant, they both knew that'. The statements were also confessions, but nothing turned on that.

Twist [2011] EWCA Crim 1143, [2011] 3 All ER 1055 was applied in *Khan* [2013] EWCA Crim 2230, where the question was whether one of two parties to a conversation was acquainted with D. The fact that both parties referred to D by his nickname, Bana, suggested that he was well-known to both. No question of hearsay was involved, as there was no purpose on the part of either party to cause the other to believe that he knew 'Bana'. To the same effect is *Noble* [2016] EWCA Crim 2219, in which an exchange of messages between a man accused of murder and his girlfriend included reference by her to his possession of a gun. The Court of Appeal observed: '[He] knew if he did or did not have a gun. The purpose of any statement made to him about having a gun was not for him to believe that he had a gun, or to cause him to act on that basis.' By contrast, in *Doyle* [2018] EWCA Crim 2198 the prosecution sought to prove that D had been in possession of a package of drugs by reference to text messages from the recipient of the package. These asserted that D had stolen drugs from it, and demanded that D act on the accusation. It was held that the messages were hearsay.

An older authority that appears inconsistent with the principles laid down in *Twist* is *West Midlands Probation Board v French* [2008] EWHC 2631 (Admin), [2009] 1 WLR 1715, in which it was held that, where a prisoner is released on licence, the licence is hearsay in consequence of s. 115(3), the purpose of the maker being to cause the prisoner and others to believe the statements in the licence and to act accordingly. Yet the function of the licence would seem rather to be to lay out the terms on which the prisoner is to be set at liberty; there is no obvious purpose with regard to causing any person to believe the matters stated.

In all the appeals heard in *Twist*, it could be said that there was a 'common understanding' between the parties to the communication that rendered it non-hearsay. The same is true of *Elliott* [2010] EWCA Crim 2378, approved in *Twist*, where a letter was written on the basis that both the writer and the recipient supported the same criminal gang, and thereby provided non-hearsay evidence of the recipient's sympathies. See also *MK* [2007] EWCA Crim 3150; *Chrysostomou* [2010] EWCA Crim 1403 and *Bains* [2010] EWCA Crim 873. The case of *Leonard* [2009] EWCA Crim 1251, which has been the subject of some criticism, was defended in *Twist* on the grounds that the prosecution had elected to base their case on the truth of information found in text messages to L about the quality of drugs he had supplied, rather than (as they surely might have done) on the apparent existence of a common understanding about the supply itself. In *Andrade* [2015] EWCA Crim 1722, the complainant, shortly after an alleged rape by A, received two text messages from D, an acquaintance who, according to the complainant, had aided A to commit the offence. The messages read 'Sorry about that' and 'RU mad at me?' The Court of Appeal, having allowed the appeal on other grounds, commented that it was not necessary to decide the 'difficult point' of whether the texts were hearsay, and, if so, whether they were admissible under the *res gestae* provisions of s. 118 (see **F17.49**), because, whatever their proper classification, the texts should have been excluded under the PACE 1984, s. 78. There would have been difficulty for the defence in calling D as a witness and, in his absence, there was no realistic way for A to challenge the interpretation that D was apologising for colluding in the rape committed by A. Had it been necessary to decide the point, it would seem that neither text is hearsay, D's purpose being to apologise for something that both he and the complainant know to have happened (inferentially the rape). As it is the rape that is the matter in issue, the absence of any purpose on D's part to cause the complainant to believe that it occurred prevents the evidence from being hearsay. **F16.19**

'Common understanding' is not a necessary feature of all cases saved from the hearsay rule by s. 115(3). In *Midmore* [2017] EWCA Crim 533, [2017] 2 Cr App R 8 (73), a WhatsApp message sent by D1's co-accused, D2, to his girlfriend, showing a drain-cleaning product later used in an acid attack on a third party and describing it as a 'face-melter', was held not to be hearsay: though a representation was involved, it was not intended that the girlfriend believe it. Once admitted, the evidence provided support for the prosecution case that the common purpose of the accused was to use the product to cause injury. In *Isichei* [2006] EWCA Crim 1815, the prosecution wished to prove that a member of a party looking for a nightclub had told his colleagues that he would ring 'Marvin'. The purpose of adducing the evidence was to establish a connection between D, whose first name this was, and an individual from the club who subsequently assaulted and robbed two female members of the party. While it could be argued that the caller had, as one of his purposes, the intention of causing the other members of the group to know that he was about to call 'Marvin', it was unlikely that he cared what, if anything, they believed as to the name of his contact. The Court of Appeal noted that the level of semantic analysis required by s. 115(3) was, in the circumstances, both highly artificial and disproportionate to the evidential significance of the call. The Court went on to decide that the call would, even if hearsay, have been admissible under the 'interests of justice' provision in s. 114(1)(d). This provides a sensible 'belt and braces' solution wherever the answer under s. 115(3) is unclear (or not worth the effort of pursuing) and the evidence would, if hearsay, be admissible in any **F16.20** event. However, in *Twist*, Hughes LJ drew attention to the additional complexity involved in admitting evidence by the hearsay route; complexities that need not apply where s. 115(3) accords the evidence non-hearsay status. In *Amjad* [2016] EWCA Crim 1618, [2017] 1 Cr App R 22 (331), it was held that the prosecution were wrong to concede hearsay status to open-source material found on the internet concerning exercises suitable for preparation for terrorist activity. The purpose of adducing this material was limited to showing a striking similarity between it and a document found in D's possession.

F16.21 In some cases it may be difficult to determine whether a statement is directed at another person, and therefore whether it is intended to be believed. In *N* [2006] EWCA Crim 3309, a statement in a complainant's diary regarding her sexual relationship with her uncle would have been hearsay (but admissible for the defence under an exception) had the statement been intended for another, but had it been intended for the writer's sole use it was not hearsay. See also *Knight* [2007] EWCA Crim 3027 and *Marine Fisheries Agency v Inter Fish Ltd* [2009] EWHC 753 (Admin), where a diary was rightly treated as hearsay in that it appears to have been more in the nature of a record, with some entries being made by a third party. In *Singh* [2006] EWCA Crim 660, [2006] 1 WLR 1564, the Court of Appeal rejected an argument which would have turned s. 115(3) on its head. By that argument, the provisions of s. 115 qualify only the statutory form of hearsay as described by s. 114; thus, as the rule in *Kearley* [1992] 2 AC 228 subsists only at common law, it remains unaffected. The argument is based on the absence of any express repeal of the common-law hearsay rule. The Court regarded the old rule as effectively abolished by s. 118 (which makes it clear that the only surviving common-law rules are certain preserved exceptions). When read with s. 114, there is no room for any other vestige of common law to remain.

Hearsay and Non-hearsay Purposes

F16.22 **Evidence with More than One Purpose** The hearsay rule is not infringed where a statement is tendered for some reason other than to establish the matter stated, but such evidence may be difficult to distinguish from hearsay. Upon application of the hearsay test, it is perfectly possible that evidence may be admissible, original evidence for one purpose, and inadmissible hearsay for another. Such cases require a very careful judicial direction as to the use to which the evidence may properly be put. Where it happens that the evidence is admissible in relation to one count in an indictment but not another, the inadmissibility is relevant to whether the counts should be tried together (*Watson* [1997] Crim LR 680).

F16.23 **Statements Giving Rise to Inference of Relevant State of Mind or Reason for Acting** Where a state of mind is asserted by the speaker, with the purpose of causing another to believe it, the evidence is hearsay under the CJA 2003, s. 115(3). Such evidence may be admissible under the preserved *res gestae* exception in s. 118(1) (see **F17.56**). A statement from which a state of mind may be inferred, on the other hand, may fall outside the definition of 'matter stated' in s. 115(3) and be classified as original evidence (see **F16.14**). This approach is consistent with authorities at common law including *Blastland* [1986] AC 41. In *Toussaint-Collins* [2009] EWCA Crim 316, D was accused of the murder of V in revenge for the killing of S. For several months, D had kept a letter written by a third party, protesting that no one had avenged S's death. The keeping of the letter provided non-hearsay evidence of D's state of mind in relation to V.

The hearsay rule does not apply where the statement is relevant because it provides a reason why a person took a relevant course of action. In *Subramaniam v Public Prosecutor* [1956] 1 WLR 965, the Privy Council held that the hearsay rule was not infringed where D, in support of a defence of duress, sought to give evidence of threats made to him by terrorists who were not called to give evidence. The purpose of proving that D had been subjected to threats was not to establish that the threats were true but to show rather that, if they had been believed by D, they might have induced in him an apprehension of instant death if he failed to conform to the terrorists' wishes.

F16.24 In *Davis* [1998] Crim LR 659, D, on being interviewed in connection with theft, failed to reveal facts upon which he afterwards sought to rely in his defence. At trial he wished to give evidence of what his solicitor had said to him prior to the interview, but was prevented from doing so on the grounds that it would infringe the hearsay rule. The Court of Appeal pointed out, correctly, that this was not necessarily the case. It was material for the jury to consider D's reasons for failing to disclose the relevant facts in deciding whether to draw an inference against him under the CJPO 1994, s. 34 (see **F20.4**). If D's purpose in repeating the solicitor's words was simply to show the impact on him of the advice given, the hearsay rule would not have been infringed. It would have been otherwise if D had sought to demonstrate the truth of anything said.

A statement may be used to prove the knowledge of the maker without infringing the rule: where D denied knowing that certain premises were being used as a brothel, an advertisement that he had sought to place, referring to the premises and containing a reference to 'many stunning masseuses', was admissible to show that he did know (*Roberts v DPP* [1994] Crim LR 926).

Making of Statement Having Significance in Law In some cases the mere making of the statement may have significance in law, quite aside from any question of its truth. In *Woodhouse v Hall* (1980) 72 Cr App R 39, the question to be decided was whether a massage parlour was being run as a brothel. Having defined a brothel as 'an establishment at which two or more women were offering sexual services', the Divisional Court held that it was open to police officers who had attended the premises posing as customers to prove that the women employed there had offered them various sexual services. There was no question of hearsay: the relevant issue was simply whether the offers had been made. In *A Ltd, X and Y* [2016] EWCA Crim 1469, [2017] 1 Cr App R 1 (1), diaries and notebook entries made by an individual who did not give evidence were relevant and admissible because his statements represented the directing mind and will of a company under the 'identification' principle (see **A6.6** ***et seq***.). There was therefore no hearsay issue, as there might have been had the statements been tendered for other purposes without calling the maker as a witness. **F16.25**

Lies and Other Untrue Statements A statement that is demonstrably false may show a consciousness of guilt (*Mawaz Khan v The Queen* [1967] 1 AC 454; *A-G v Good* (1825) M'Cle & Yo 286; *Binham* [1991] Crim LR 774). Under the CJA 2003, it would seem that a lie cannot be hearsay evidence of a matter that it is not intended to assert (see **F16.15**). In *Minchin* [2013] EWCA Crim 2412, the Court of Appeal accepted that a statement containing the details of an alibi alleged to be false could be tendered by the prosecution without breaching the hearsay rule. 'What mattered was the fact that it was said.' **F16.26**

Inferences Founded on Hearsay Where evidence is inadmissible as hearsay, it is not possible to evade the difficulty by adducing evidence from which it can be inferred that the inadmissible statement was made and that it was true. In *Glinski v McIver* [1962] AC 726, Lord Devlin described the improper practice of asking, for example: **F16.27**

> Did you go to see counsel? Do not tell us what he said but as a result of it did you do something? What did you do? This device is commonly defended on the ground that counsel is asking only about what was done and not about what was said. But in truth what was done is relevant only because from it there can be inferred something about what was said. Such evidence seems to me to be clearly objectionable. If there is nothing in it, it is irrelevant; if there is something in it, what there is in it is inadmissible.

It is submitted that the same criticism can be made of an attempt to draw a circumstantial inference from a hearsay statement in a document. This occurred in *Rice* [1963] 1 QB 857, where the prosecution relied on an airline ticket in the names of 'Rice and Moore', produced by an airline official whose job it was to deal with used tickets, to give rise to a circumstantial inference that D had travelled on the flight in question. Although the Court of Appeal was agreed that the ticket 'must not be treated as speaking its contents for what it might say could only be hearsay', it was held (at p. 872) that 'the production of the ticket from the place where used tickets would properly be kept was a fact from which the jury might infer that probably two people had flown on the particular flight and that it might or might not seem to them by applying their common knowledge of such matters that the passengers bore the surnames that were written on the ticket'. It is submitted, however, that the production of the ticket proved that the traveller was D only if reliance were placed on its 'contents', i.e. on the statement it bore which showed that it had been issued to one Rice.

Under the CJA 2003, s. 114(1), it is hard to avoid the conclusion that the statement on the ticket in *Rice* was used as evidence 'of any matter stated'. The broad exception now available for business documents (under s. 117: see **F17.25**) provides a more tenable route to admissibility.

F16.28 **Inferences Not Dependent on Hearsay** A distinction should, however, be drawn between the permissible use of a statement as an original and independent fact, and the impermissible use of it as evidence of the matter stated. In *Lydon* (1986) 85 Cr App R 221, the prosecution were permitted to tender in evidence a piece of paper found near a weapon believed to have been used in a robbery, and bearing ink of a similar kind to that staining the weapon. On the paper, someone had written 'Sean rules' and 'Sean rules 85'. It was held that the words on the paper created an inferential link with D, whose first name was Sean. '[T]he reference to Sean could be regarded as no more than a statement of fact involving no assertion as to the truth of the contents of the document' (per Woolf LJ at p. 224). *Lydon* was applied in *McIntosh* [1992] Crim LR 651, in which a piece of paper bearing calculations as to the profit and loss made from buying and selling a substance (inferentially a drug) was found on D's premises. The document was not in D's handwriting, but this was immaterial as it was admitted not as evidence of its truth but as purely circumstantial evidence suggesting D's involvement with drug-related offences.

Statements Inextricably Linked to Relevant Acts

F16.29 Under the CJA 2003, s. 114(1), a statement cannot be extricated from the ambit of the hearsay rule merely because it is closely associated with the doing of a relevant act. The association might, however, lead to the admission of the statement, for example as part of the *res gestae* under s. 118 (see **F17.49**) or under s. 114(1)(d) (see **F17.34**). At common law the position was that such evidence could be regarded as non-hearsay. In *Ratten v The Queen* [1972] AC 378, D was charged with the murder of his wife, and the defence was that she had been shot by accident as D cleaned his gun. The prosecution relied on the evidence of a telephone operator to show that, shortly before she was shot, the victim had telephoned the exchange in a state of hysteria and asked for the police. D denied that any such call had been made. The Privy Council held that, because the making of the call was itself a relevant act, the words used and the state of emotion in which they were spoken were 'relevant and necessary evidence in order to explain and complete the fact of the call being made', and were not hearsay. This explanation no longer works: the statement made by the caller had a clear purpose to convey the need for emergency services, and therefore the admissibility of the call's content (as distinct from the fact that it was made) would now require the prosecution to identify a hearsay exception under which it could be received.

Admissions Based on Hearsay

F16.30 Where a person admits something, relying on knowledge that is based on hearsay, the admission does not prove the fact. In *Comptroller of Customs v Western Lectric Co. Ltd* [1966] AC 367, it was held that admissions as to the country of origin of goods, which were based on markings on the goods themselves, were inadmissible. Lord Hodson further described such admissions as being of no real value. See also *Surujpaul v The Queen* [1958] 3 All ER 300. The same problem frequently arises in handling cases, where there is a dearth of direct evidence to prove that the goods are stolen. In *Hulbert* (1979) 69 Cr App R 243, D admitted that she bought certain goods at very low prices from unnamed sellers in various public houses, and that, in some cases, the sellers told her that the goods were stolen. It was held that D's admission as to facts within her own knowledge (e.g., the price paid, and the circumstances in which the goods were offered for sale) was admissible evidence that the goods might have been stolen, but that her admission as to what she had been told could not be evidence that the goods were stolen. What she had been told would, however, be admissible to prove the state of her knowledge or belief at the time. See also *Sbarra* (1918) 87 LJ KB 1003, *Korniak* (1982) 76 Cr App R 145 and *Overington* [1978] Crim LR 692.

In cases involving the possession of drugs, the accused's admission that the substance in question was a controlled drug would be inadmissible if based on hearsay, and of limited evidential value if based on personal opinion. In some cases the admissions of experienced drug users have been held to be prima facie evidence of the nature of a substance (*Chatwood* [1980] 1 All ER 467; *Bird v Adams* [1972] Crim LR 174; *Wells* [1976] Crim LR 518). *Mieras v Rees* [1975] Crim LR 224, which appears to be authority to the contrary, is misreported: the charge was one of attempt, where it was accepted that there was no proof as to the nature of the substance (*Chatwood*).

Statements Tendered to Prove Non-existence of Alleged Facts

A difficult question at common law was whether a statement that is hearsay when tendered to prove the truth of a fact asserted in it is equally hearsay when tendered as circumstantial evidence of the non-existence of facts that might have been expected to have been asserted in it if they had been true. The problem arose most acutely with regard to records. In both *Patel* [1981] 3 All ER 94 and *Shone* (1982) 76 Cr App R 72, it was suggested that, provided responsible persons could give evidence of the method of record-keeping, an inference could be drawn about matters not appearing. Thus in *Patel*, which concerned immigration records, evidence as to the method of compilation and custody supported the inference that, if A's name was not recorded, he must be an illegal entrant. Had the CJA 2003, s. 115(3) (see **F16.14**), been applied to the circumstances in *Patel*, it may be argued that, as the purpose of the compiler was not to induce another to believe that A was an illegal entrant, or to cause another to act on the basis that he was, the hearsay rule is not infringed by the use of such records to support circumstantial inferences of a negative nature. Alternatively, to the extent that both the negative and positive use of a record depend on the correctness of the record keeping, negative inferences might be more safely drawn in the same way as positive ones, i.e. within the confines of a hearsay exception. Most records are now admissible under the CJA 2003, s. 117 (see **F17.25**). In *DPP v Leigh* [2010] EWHC 345 (Admin), it was held that the hearsay rule did not apply to evidence, based on records, that the respondent had failed to reply to notices issued pursuant to the RTA 1988, s. 172. The record itself was clearly admissible under s. 117, but the Divisional Court preferred the approach in *Patel* and *Shone*. **F16.31**

When dealing with 'negative hearsay' otherwise than in the context of records, the common law tended towards a relaxed approach. This, it is submitted, is the best explanation of *Muir* (1983) 79 Cr App R 153. D was charged with theft of a video recorder, hired to him by G Ltd. D's defence was that the video had been taken away by two men who had called at his house. To rebut the suggestion that G Ltd had repossessed the video, S, the district manager of G Ltd, gave evidence that there had been no repossession by the local showroom: a fact within his own knowledge. He was asked in cross-examination about the possibility of repossession by the company's head office, and was allowed to say in response that he had telephoned head office and had been told that they had not ordered the repossession of the video. The Court of Appeal held that, 'in the way in which the evidence came out', it was not hearsay, on the ground that S 'was the best person to give the relevant evidence', including informing the court that a check had been made with head office. This analysis ignores the fact that what S had been told during the check was hearsay. On the facts of the case, the only option open to the prosecution if the rule had been strictly applied would have been to call a further witness from head office, and it may have been that expediency dictated the result. However, the decision was noted to have attracted adverse comment in *Coventry Justices, ex parte Bullard* (1992) 95 Cr App R 175. Under the CJA 2003, s. 114(1)(d) (see **F17.34**) might be deployed if it was in the interests of justice to treat the witness S in *Muir* as an acceptable source of information regarding the possibility of repossession by the company's head office. **F16.32**

Section F17 Exceptions to the Rule against Hearsay (Excluding Confessions)

INTRODUCTION

F17.1 The rule against hearsay, as described in **F16**, has never been an absolute prohibition. The provisions of the CJA 2003, Part II, ch. 2, while retaining the concept of the hearsay rule as a rule of exclusion, are designed to ensure that, subject to the necessary safeguards, relevant hearsay evidence should be admitted where it is in the interests of justice. The provisions of the CJA 2003 constitute a 'crafted code' which, properly applied, is consistent with the right to fair trial accorded by the ECHR, Article 6(3)(d) (*Horncastle* [2009] UKSC 14, [2010] 2 AC 373: see **F17.89**). The rulings of the Grand Chamber in *Al-Khawaja and Tahery v UK* (2012) 54 EHRR 23 (807) and *Horncastle v UK* (2015) 60 EHRR 31 (1331) (see **F17.89**) accept, contrary to previous Strasbourg case law, that the CJA 2003 contains sufficient safeguards against the risk of wrongful conviction. It is convenient to begin with an overview of the Act's provisions before embarking on the detail.

The CJA 2003 applies to trials and other hearings to which the strict rules of evidence apply, and also to proceedings under the Criminal Procedure (Insanity) Act 1964, s. 4A, the purpose of which is to mirror the fact-finding process at a criminal trial (*Chal* [2007] EWCA Crim 2647, [2008] 1 Cr App R 18 (247)).

Overview of CJA 2003: Hearsay Exceptions and Additional Safeguards

F17.2 **Four Exceptions** The four headings under which hearsay evidence may be admitted are set out in the CJA 2003, s. 114. They are (1) statutory exceptions (including but not limited to, the exceptions provided in the CJA 2003 itself); (2) common-law exceptions (but only as preserved by s. 118); (3) agreement of all parties; and (4) cases where it is in the 'interests of justice' to admit hearsay. This section of this work deals with the more important of the various exceptions to the hearsay rule which operate in criminal cases, with the exception of confessions, which are dealt with at **F18**, and the previous consistent and inconsistent statements of witnesses, dealt with at **F6.32** and **F7.51** respectively. Although the CJA 2003 has significantly simplified the law in this area, it remains the case that the various exceptions overlap: for example, the first-hand hearsay statement of a deceased victim of violence admissible under the CJA 2003, s. 116, might, if made under the influence of the event itself, also be received under the common-law *res gestae* exception preserved by s. 118(1).

F17.3 Criminal Justice Act 2003, s. 114

(1) *In criminal proceedings* a statement not made in oral evidence in the proceedings is admissible as evidence of any matter stated if, but only if—
(a) any provision of this chapter or any other statutory provision makes it admissible,
(b) any rule of law preserved by section 118 makes it admissible,

(c) all parties to the proceedings agree to it being admissible, or
(d) the court is satisfied that it is in the interests of justice for it to be admissible.

See **F16.1** for the proceedings to which s. 114 applies and for elaboration of the definition of hearsay ('a statement not made in oral evidence ... etc.').

F17.4 **The Four Exceptions and Additional Safeguards for Hearsay Evidence** It is important to note that bringing hearsay under one of the four headings for admissibility is only the first step in a longer process required to ensure that the fairness of the trial is not adversely affected. In *Horncastle* [2009] UKSC 14, [2010] 2 AC 373, the Supreme Court emphasised the importance of the other safeguards to be applied, only some of which appear on the face of the CJA 2003. Within the Act, there are three related provisions. They are s. 124, which provides for the testing of credibility where the maker of a hearsay statement does not attend to testify (see **F17.87**); s. 125, which deals with the power to stop a case where evidence is unconvincing (see **F17.98**); and s. 126, which provides a specific discretion to exclude hearsay evidence that is in addition to the court's existing range of discretions at common law and under the PACE 1984, s. 78 (see **F17.94**). In addition, all prosecution evidence is subject to the court's general powers of discretionary exclusion, of which the PACE 1984, s. 78, is the most important (**F17.88**). The judge is also obliged to direct the jury, where hearsay evidence is received, as to the dangers of acting upon it (see **F17.96**).

Although the steps towards admitting hearsay evidence are explained separately in the text which follows, the decisions to be made at trial are typically arrived at in an integrated way. In *Riat* [2012] EWCA Crim 1509, [2013] 1 All ER 349, Hughes LJ explained that the main concern of the court, particularly in the more controversial cases of hearsay covered by s. 116(2) (death, illness, absence abroad, the lost witness, and fear) or by the interests of justice exception in s. 114(1)(d), is the risk of unreliability, and the extent to which the reliability of the evidence can safely be tested and assessed. The statutory framework can therefore usefully be considered in these successive steps.

(a) Is there a specific statutory justification (or 'gateway') permitting the admission of hearsay evidence (ss. 116 to 118)?
(b) What material is there which can help to test or assess the hearsay (s. 124)?
(c) Is there a specific 'interests of justice' test at the admissibility stage?
(d) If there is no other justification or gateway, should the evidence nevertheless be considered for admission on the grounds that admission is, despite the difficulties, in the interests of justice (s. 114(1)(d))?
(e) Even if prima facie admissible, ought the evidence to be ruled inadmissible (PACE 1984, s. 78, and/or CJA 2003, s. 126)?
(f) If the evidence is admitted, should the case subsequently be stopped under s. 125?

Where a judge permits hearsay evidence to be adduced, the detail behind the ruling should be given before speeches, so that counsel may tailor their speeches to the ruling and, where appropriate, make submissions in respect of the content of the proposed hearsay direction in light of the ruling (*Kiziltan* [2017] EWCA Crim 1461, [2018] 4 WLR 43). In *Daley* [2017] EWCA Crim 1971 it was said that the direction should be given before the evidence is heard, and repeated in the summing-up.

Notice

F17.5 CrimPR Part 20 (see Supplement, **R20.1** *et seq.*) makes provision for the procedure to be followed and other conditions to be fulfilled by a party proposing to tender a hearsay statement in evidence under the CJA 2003, ss. 114(1)(d) (evidence admissible in the interests of justice), 116 (evidence where a witness is unavailable), 117(1)(c) (evidence in a statement prepared for the purposes of criminal proceedings) and 121 (multiple hearsay). Other forms of hearsay, including common-law exceptions and documents admissible under s. 117 other than those prepared specifically for criminal proceedings, do not require notice. The court may give leave to admit hearsay where notice has not been served, and; the party entitled to notice may also waive the entitlement. In *Smith* [2020] EWCA Crim 777, the Court of Appeal emphasised that the rules are not 'purely decorative': they exist to ensure that 'tricky questions of procedure or evidence are addressed by the parties in time, so that, where dispute arises, the parties have developed positions which can be laid clearly before the judge who must resolve the problem' (at [50]). In that case, multiple hearsay evidence of a confession that would not have passed the test for admissibility of such evidence under s. 121(1)(c) (see **F17.84**) was received without notice. Had notice been served and the introduction of the evidence opposed, it was highly unlikely that an argument could have been articulated to admit it; had it been unopposed it might have been admitted under CrimPR 20.4, whereby a court must treat unopposed hearsay as admissible by agreement. In the result, the wrongful introduction of the evidence led to the quashing of the conviction. The court is not obliged to give leave to a co-accused who has failed to comply with the notice procedure (*Musone* [2007] EWCA Crim 1237, [2007] 1 WLR 2467).

HEARSAY EXCEPTIONS: (1) HEARSAY ADMISSIBLE BY AGREEMENT, UNAVAILABLE WITNESSES AND BUSINESS DOCUMENTS

Hearsay Admissible by Agreement

F17.6 **'Agreement'** The freedom to admit hearsay evidence by agreement is a novel feature of the CJA 2003. There is no definition of 'agreement', but it would appear that failure to object is not necessarily agreement, although agreement may be implied rather than express (*Shah* [2012] EWCA Crim 212) or inferred from circumstances, e.g., where, following disclosure, the accused's legal representative does not demur to the evidence of an absent witness in summary proceedings (*Williams v Vehicle and Operator Services Agency* [2008] EWHC 849 (Admin)). In *Bhagchandka* [2016] EWCA Crim 700, D, charged with perverting the course of justice, was asked in interview about an accusation by J, who was not called to give evidence, that D had asked J to lie to the police. D denied that this was the case. It was held that J's accusation should have been edited from the statement of interview; that D should not have been cross-examined about it, and that it should have formed no part of the case against D. Defence counsel had objected to the line of cross-examination immediately, and it did not matter that there appeared to have been a prior understanding between trial counsel that the interview was admissible 'in its entirety'. See also *J (DC)* [2010] EWCA Crim 385, [2010] 2 Cr App R 2 (8), where it was said that, in the interests of good trial management, the court should be informed of any agreement to admit hearsay evidence at the beginning of the trial. Further, the mere fact of agreement, though sufficient to overcome an objection based on hearsay (or bad character: see **F13.16**), did not justify putting in evidence documents subject to public interest immunity disclosed for the purpose of cross-examination of prosecution witnesses, for which a further order would have been required.

CJA 2003, s. 116: Unavailable Witnesses

F17.7 A literal reading of the CJA 2003, s. 116, suggests that hearsay falling within its provisions is (with the exception of witnesses in fear) automatically admissible, and this was the original intention. However, the fair trial rights of defendants have required a different stance following the decision of the Supreme Court in *Horncastle* [2009] UKSC 14, [2010] 2 AC 373, as hearsay cannot be 'nodded through or adduced as a matter of routine' (*per* Gross LJ in *Friel* [2012] EWCA Crim 2871), but must be carefully handled with due regard to its significance in the case and the possible weaknesses of hearsay evidence. The overall scheme to ensure that hearsay is relied upon only to the extent that it is safe to do so is described at **F17.3**. In most cases the mechanism for ensuring that unsatisfactory hearsay tendered by the prosecution is excluded is the PACE 1984, s. 78, the use of which is specifically preserved, in relation to ss. 116 and 117, by s. 126(2). In relation to hearsay tendered by the defence, the PACE 1984, s. 78, does not apply, leading to concerns that the CJA 2003 would facilitate the manufacture of hearsay evidence (cf. *Bailey*

[2008] EWCA Crim 817). However, there is a further discretion to exclude contained in the CJA 2003, s. 126(1)(b), which applies equally to prosecution and defence evidence. Although capable of being narrowly construed as applicable only to 'superfluous' hearsay, s. 126(1)(b) may have a wider application, specifically in relation to hearsay that lacks probative value (see **F17.95**).

The starting point for any assessment of admissibility is that 'the necessity for resort to second-hand evidence must be demonstrated' (per Hughes LJ in *Riat* [2012] EWCA Crim 1509, [2013] 1 All ER 349) and that this has implications not only for the question whether it is fair to admit a statement which satisfies one of the conditions laid down in s. 116(2), but also for the need for rigorous assessment of whether the condition is itself made out, in particular in relation to absent witnesses who may be fearful or who have absented themselves (see **F17.14** and **F17.17**). To the extent that some early authorities under the CJA 2003 may have been based on a more informal assessment of the satisfaction of one of the conditions, they have been overtaken by the approach required by *Horncastle* and subsequent decisions of the Court of Appeal including *Riat*.

Criminal Justice Act 2003, ss. 116 and 123 **F17.8**

116.—(1) In criminal proceedings a statement not made in oral evidence in the proceedings is admissible as evidence of any matter stated if—
(a) oral evidence given in the proceedings by the person who made the statement would be admissible as evidence of that matter,
(b) the person who made the statement (the relevant person) is identified to the court's satisfaction, and
(c) any of the five conditions mentioned in subsection (2) is satisfied.
(2) The conditions are—
(a) that the relevant person is dead;
(b) that the relevant person is unfit to be a witness because of his bodily or mental condition;
(c) that the relevant person is outside the United Kingdom and it is not reasonably practicable to secure his attendance;
(d) that the relevant person cannot be found although such steps as it is reasonably practicable to take to find him have been taken;
(e) that through fear the relevant person does not give (or does not continue to give) oral evidence in the proceedings, either at all or in connection with the subject matter of the statement, and the court gives leave for the statement to be given in evidence.
(3) For the purposes of subsection (2)(e) 'fear' is to be widely construed and (for example) includes fear of the death or injury of another person or of financial loss.
(4) Leave may be given under subsection (2)(e) only if the court considers that the statement ought to be admitted in the interests of justice, having regard—
(a) to the statement's contents,
(b) to any risk that its admission or exclusion will result in unfairness to any party to the proceedings (and in particular to how difficult it will be to challenge the statement if the relevant person does not give oral evidence),
(c) in appropriate cases, to the fact that a direction under section 19 of the Youth Justice and Criminal Evidence Act 1999 (special measures for the giving of evidence by fearful witnesses etc) could be made in relation to the relevant person, and
(d) to any other relevant circumstances.
(5) A condition set out in any paragraph of subsection (2) which is in fact satisfied is to be treated as not satisfied if it is shown that the circumstances described in that paragraph are caused—
(a) by the person in support of whose case it is sought to give the statement in evidence, or
(b) by a person acting on his behalf,
in order to prevent the relevant person giving oral evidence in the proceedings (whether at all or in connection with the subject matter of the statement).

123.—(1) Nothing in section 116, 119 or 120 makes a statement admissible as evidence if it was made by a person who did not have the required capability at the time when he made the statement.
(2) Nothing in section 117 makes a statement admissible as evidence if any person who, in order for the requirements of section 117(2) to be satisfied, must at any time have supplied or received the information concerned or created or received the document or part concerned—
(a) did not have the required capability at that time, or

(b) cannot be identified but cannot reasonably be assumed to have had the required capability at that time.

(3) For the purposes of this section a person has the required capability if he is capable of—
(a) understanding questions put to him about the matters stated, and
(b) giving answers to such questions which can be understood.

(4) Where by reason of this section there is an issue as to whether a person had the required capability when he made a statement—
(a) proceedings held for the determination of the issue must take place in the absence of the jury (if there is one);
(b) in determining the issue the court may receive expert evidence and evidence from any person to whom the statement in question was made;
(c) the burden of proof on the issue lies on the party seeking to adduce the statement, and the standard of proof is the balance of probabilities.

F17.9 **First-hand Hearsay from Identifiable Witness** The CJA 2003, s. 116, applies only to first-hand hearsay. Where a person makes a statement, but it is not clear whether the statement is based on personal knowledge or to something the maker has been told, the s. 116 statement should therefore not be admitted (*JP* [1999] Crim LR 401, decided under the CJA 1988, s. 23). Under the CJA 2003, multiple hearsay may be admissible under s. 121 (see **F17.84**), and documents admissible under s. 117 (see **F17.25**) may also contain more than one degree of hearsay. The requirement that the oral evidence of the person who made the statement would have been admissible as evidence of the matter (s. 116(1)(a)) also serves to ensure that hearsay cannot be received if the evidence would have been inadmissible for some other reason, e.g., that it is evidence of bad character that is not admissible under the CJA 2003, Part 11, ch. 1 (see **F13** and **F15**).

The person who made the hearsay statement must be identifiable (s. 116(1)(b)) so that those seeking to challenge its credibility must be able to ascertain who made it, and be able where appropriate to invoke s. 124 (see **F17.86**), which is provided by way of a substitute to the right of cross-examination. In *Nkemayang* [2005] EWCA Crim 1937, the Court of Appeal approved of the insistence in the CJA 2003 on strict proof of identity, saying that 'any regime controlling the admissibility of evidence must be alert to the danger of fabricated evidence'. In *Mayers* [2008] EWCA Crim 2989, [2009] 2 All ER 145 the Court of Appeal held that the language of s. 116(1)(b) clearly anticipates the disclosure of the identity of the maker of the statement to the defence; it follows that s. 116 cannot be applied to anonymous witnesses. (See, as to preserving anonymity where a witness gives evidence, the CAJA 2009, ss. 86 to 90, at **D14.82** ***et seq.***) In *Ford* [2010] EWCA Crim 2250, an unknown witness to a shooting had stated that he wished to remain anonymous, but had handed the police a note containing the registration number of the getaway car. It was held, following *Mayers*, that the note was inadmissible. A statement by a witness whose identity is unknown might, according to *Brown (Nico)* [2019] EWCA Crim 1143 (see **F17.52**), be received instead under the common law of *res gestae* (see **F17.49**) or under the 'interests of justice' exception in s. 114(1)(d) (see **F17.34**), but it would appear from *Ford* that neither exception can be invoked so as to allow witnesses to choose to provide evidence anonymously, for fear of subverting the statutory scheme in the CAJA 2009. Ford was distinguished in *Brown (Nico)* where it was said that, if that decision is correct, it applies only to cases where the witness has expressed a preference to remain anonymous, and not to untraceable witnesses. In that case a woman on a bus had assisted a witness making an emergency call by providing the number of a car driven by a man who had stabbed the victim, but it proved impossible to trace her. The evidence she provided was admissible under both the *res gestae* and s. 114(1)(d).

F17.10 **Oral and Documentary Statements Admissible** Applications under s. 116 most frequently concern statements in documents, but oral hearsay statements may also be tendered, as may statements made by conduct (for the meaning of 'statement' see s. 115(2) at **F16.7**). In *Musone* [2007] EWCA Crim 1237, [2007] 1 WLR 2467, a man who had been stabbed was asked 'what's happened, mate?' and replied 'Musone's just stabbed me'. The statement was admitted at D's trial for murder under s. 116. By the same token, a gesture or sign language similarly identifying the guilty party could be received.

Absence Caused by Party Tendering Statement Section 116(5) prevents a person from being able to rely on any hearsay statement by a potential witness where that person, or someone acting on that person's behalf, is responsible for the absence of the witness in order to prevent the witness from testifying. In *Rowley* [2012] EWCA Crim 1434, [2013] 1 WLR 895, the defence was prevented from adducing the record of interview with T, who had been threatened by D and had subsequently fled abroad. D subsequently wished to refer to aspects of T's statement that were favourable to the defence, after the prosecution had decided not to adduce it. Section 116(5) prevented him from doing so. The threat did not have to be the main or primary cause of the witness's absence, provided it was at least one of the effective causes. To hold otherwise would significantly undermine the policy of the legislation. Further, the provision was not limited to steps taken by the accused after the commencement of proceedings, provided they were done with the intent of preventing the attendance of the witness at the proceedings. In *C* [2019] EWCA Crim 623, it was confirmed that s. 116(5) is directed against a party to the proceedings, and does not apply to evidence of a complainant who had 'caused' her own absence by committing suicide. **F17.11**

Proof of Unavailability of Maker The reasons specified in the CJA 2003, s. 116(2), for not calling the maker of a statement are disjunctive: provided that the party seeking to rely on the statement can establish that one of the reasons exists, it does not matter that other reasons cannot be made out. The criminal standard of proof applies to the proof of the conditions of admissibility under s. 116 (see, e.g., *Shabir* [2012] EWCA Crim 2564); this point was established under previous similar legislation in *Minors* [1989] 2 All ER 208 and has not subsequently been doubted. The standard of proof to be achieved by the defence is the ordinary civil standard of proof on a balance of probability (*Mattey* [1995] 2 Cr App R 409). **F17.12**

Death and Unfitness to be a Witness Where a witness has died, as for example in *Riat* [2012] EWCA Crim 1509, [2013] 1 All ER 349, the court may move straight to the consideration of whether the principles of trial fairness permit the witness's statement to be adduced (see **F17.89**). In the case of a witness who is said to be unfit, further investigation is required to ensure that the condition is satisfied. In *Bennett*, an appeal heard with *Riat*, the statement of a mentally disordered woman who claimed to have been assaulted by a community psychiatric nurse was held to have been rightly received under s. 116(2)(b) of the CJA 2003. The provision focuses not on the physical act of attending at court, but on the fitness of the witness when there to give evidence, and includes unfitness through any mental condition. The provision is thus satisfied if the witness could be brought to court but there would be no point in doing so. Evidence indicating a medical condition made worse by stress, but not indicating clearly that the witness is unfit, is not sufficient (*McEwan v DPP* [2007] EWHC 740 (Admin)). However, the judge is entitled when determining unfitness to take account of likely future consequences such as the risk that giving evidence will precipitate the witness's suicide (*Chalk* [2015] EWCA Crim 1053). It is not necessary to prove mental illness: unfitness caused by the trauma of being the victim of a sexual assault may qualify (*AC* [2014] EWCA Crim 371). Under the previous legislation, which was in similar terms, when a witness was unable to recollect relevant events, and medical evidence established that the cause was a mental disorder giving rise to great anxiety and failure of recall when under stress, the conditions of admissibility were satisfied (*Setz-Dempsey* (1994) 98 Cr App R 23). Other pertinent authorities under the 1988 Act include *Elliott* [2003] EWCA Crim 1695, where it was held that, where the defence can point to proper grounds for wishing to cross-examine a doctor who testifies to the unfitness of a patient, it is right to make an opportunity available for them to do so. The effect of the witness's mental condition at the time the statement was made is, of course, a factor relevant to whether it should be excluded under s. 123 for lack of capability (see **F17.23**). In *Eljack* [2019] EWCA Crim 1038, V, the victim of an assault, had serious long-term mental health issues and suffered from delusions. His doctor's evidence was that giving evidence in person would exacerbate his condition, but that he was capable of giving a witness statement: if affected by delusion when doing so, this would have been readily apparent. It was held that V's statement was rightly admitted as hearsay. A further argument that, because V had himself been found fit to stand trial on a **F17.13**

previous occasion, he could not be unfit to testify, was rejected: 'They are different tests which can self-evidently lead to different results'.

The sudden unfitness of a witness who is hospitalised may be good reason for refusing an adjournment, but not for refusing to consider an application under s. 116 (*CPS v Uxbridge Magistrates* [2007] EWHC 205 (Admin)). Where a witness becomes unfit during cross-examination then, in deciding whether the trial is in consequence unfair, the trial judge is entitled to bear in mind that a witness's whole evidence could have been received under s. 116 (*Lawless* [2011] EWCA Crim 59, and see further as to cross-examination **F7.7**).

An application to admit an accused's hearsay statement may succeed in the (very rare) case where the accused is fit to stand trial, but unfit to give sworn evidence for the defence. In *Hamberger* [2017] EWCA Crim 273, [2017] 2 Cr App R 9 (81), the impairment to D giving evidence in the normal way was his chronic angina. The trial judge indicated that various arrangements could be made to assist the appellant in giving evidence, including the contents of any defence statement being used in accordance with s. 116. In the event, D advanced no positive defence. On appeal it was contended that the provisions of the CJA 1982, s. 72 (see **F4.12**), which require any evidence given by the accused to be on oath, effectively precluded the use of such hearsay evidence, but it was held that s. 72 has no application to the case where the evidence is tendered in hearsay form. The use of such hearsay would be 'rare and exceptional': less extreme measures to accommodate a defendant who is unwell might include allowing sworn evidence to be given from a place other than the witness box, permitting frequent breaks, or restricting the duration or terms of cross-examination. But as a matter of principle the terms of s. 116 are 'sufficiently wide to enable the court to permit a defendant who is genuinely unable to give oral testimony to put his account before the jury by way of hearsay'.

F17.14 **Outside the UK and Not Reasonably Practicable to Secure Attendance or Cannot be Found after Reasonable Steps** The evidence that must be provided to lay a foundation in these two cases is essentially what it is 'reasonable' to expect a party to do, whether that involves taking steps to secure the attendance of a person who is known to be abroad, or to find a person whose whereabouts are unknown. What is reasonable depends on the circumstances, but it is important that the prosecution should be in a position to provide a sufficiently compelling and detailed reason for the absence of any witness to satisfy the requirements of a fair trial. In *Price v UK* (2017) 64 EHRR 17 (877), while the authorities had made 'significant efforts' to persuade a reluctant witness based in Antwerp to testify, the ECtHR said that it could reach 'no firm conclusion' as to whether all reasonable steps had been taken in the absence of more detailed submissions as to the reasons why the prosecution had not had recourse to further measures which may have been available (in that case, by virtue of the EU Convention on Mutual Assistance in Criminal Matters). While the absence of good reason is not (and was not in *Price v UK*) conclusive on the question whether a trial has been fair, it is an important factor.

F17.15 In a number of cases the courts have emphasised the importance of keeping track of witnesses and their preparedness to testify in relation to both the CJA 2003, s. 116(2)(c) and (d). In *C* [2006] EWCA Crim 1079, [2006] 1 WLR 2994, where a key prosecution witness who was in South Africa had a last-minute change of heart about attending the trial, it was said that what was reasonably practicable must be judged in the light of the steps taken by the party seeking to secure the attendance of the witness and that further inquiries as to the reasons for the witness's refusal should have been made. It was also said to be appropriate to provide evidence of whether the witness's account could have been secured by video link or by some other method that permits a degree of challenge by the defence, a point also made in *Riat* [2012] EWCA Crim 1509, [2013] 1 All ER 349, where Hughes LJ said that absence abroad will satisfy the condition in s. 116(2)(c) 'only if it is not reasonably practicable to bring the witness to court, either in person or by video link'. In *McEvoy* [2016] EWCA Crim 1654 the evidence of two German university students was 'pivotal' to whether a child had been indecently assaulted, but no efforts had been made by German police to contact them via their home or university addresses in the two months before the trial. It followed that their evidence should not have been read.

Similar considerations apply to witnesses who cannot be found. In *Riat* [2012] EWCA Crim 1509, [2013] 1 All ER 349 Hughes LJ said, '[i]f the witness is lost, all reasonably practicable steps must have been taken to get him before the court: this will include not only looking for him if he disappears but also keeping in touch with him to avoid him disappearing'. In *DT* [2009] EWCA Crim 1213, the absent witness claimed that the accused, charged with causing grievous bodily harm, had confessed to her. The statement was an important part of the prosecution case, and it was apparent from the time it was made that the witness intended not to give evidence. Yet no attempt was made to prove what steps the police had taken to keep contact with her, through the Witness Care Programme, to explain her civic duty to her, or to try and find where she had gone in the months before the trial. It was said to be hopeless to expect a judge to say that such steps as were reasonably practicable had been taken, and the court expressed concern that trials were proceeding without formal inquiry (or at least an agreed statement of facts) on which to base a decision on admissibility. In *Shah* [2010] EWCA Crim 2326, it was said that to tell a judge that a witness cannot be traced carries with it the implication that efforts have been made to trace the witness. If no such efforts have been made, the judge is being misled.

In *Adams* [2007] EWCA Crim 3025, [2008] 1 Cr App R 35 (430), it was held that reasonable steps within the meaning of s. 116(2)(d) had not been taken in relation to a witness with whom there was no contact in the four months from the time when the trial date was fixed until the Friday before it started, when a message was left on his mobile phone to which he did not respond. This 'fell a long way short of what was, in practice, needed to get witnesses to attend court', although in that case, exceptionally, the evidence was admitted under s. 114(1)(d) (see **F17.39**). *Adams* was considered in *Murphy* [2014] EWCA Crim 1457, where the prosecution had lost touch with the witness until just before the trial, but then made efforts to ensure his attendance, including seeking a witness summons which was served on him before he disappeared leaving no address. It was held that the judge was entitled to conclude that the prosecution had taken reasonable steps, which was ultimately a question of fact. In *Jones* [2015] EWCA Crim 1317, the complainant in an incident of significant domestic violence had disappeared, taking her children with her. It appeared that no steps had been taken to secure her attendance despite ongoing concerns about her welfare, and various indications that she might not appear. It was held that the process by which her evidence had been admitted at trial had not complied with the safeguards anticipated by the CJA 2003. This was not simply attributable to the fact that the application had been made erroneously under s. 114(1)(d) (see **F17.34**) instead of s. 116, because both provisions required an investigation into the reasons why the witness could not attend the trial. As a matter of due diligence there were practical measures that could have been adopted to ensure the location and attendance of the complainant, and to protect her, while ensuring the defence had the opportunity to cross-examine the complainant. The fact that to embark upon those measures would have meant a delay in the commencement of the trial or would otherwise have imposed upon the police officers concerned the necessity to track down the complainant did not provide a sufficient basis upon which to admit the evidence in hearsay form.

In relation to the proof of the conditions of admissibility it was held in *Case* [1991] Crim LR 192 that, where the only 'evidence' to support the contention that the maker of the statement was out of the country was the statement itself (which was, of course, inadmissible hearsay until proved otherwise), the statement ought not to have been admitted. In *Mattey* [1995] 2 Cr App R 409, where the statement, which was tendered by the defence, had only to satisfy the condition on a balance of probabilities, it was held inadmissible in part because hearsay was relied on in support of it, but the hearsay may have been admissible evidence of the state of mind of the maker, so that *Case* was distinguishable. Both *Case* and *Mattey* were decided under previous legislation but the authorities remain persuasive. **F17.16**

In a significant number of the cases dealt with by s. 116(2)(c) and (d), the absent witness will not simply have gone abroad or gone missing but will be deliberately avoiding the proceedings. In *DT* [2009] EWCA Crim 1213, the Court of Appeal drew a parallel between these cases and absence through fear (see **F17.17**), saying: 'It is important that all efforts are made to get the witness to court; this must start with the witness being given all possible support and made to understand the importance of the citizen's duty to give evidence.' The importance of the right of confrontation has implications for the court's inquiry into what is 'reasonably practicable' for s. 116(2)(c) or constitutes 'reasonable steps in s. 116(2)(d) as well as in relation to the question whether the powers of the court to ensure fairness (see **F17.7** and **F17.88**) should be exercised to exclude the statement. As to the application of the PACE 1984, s. 78, where a central prosecution witness is absent during the trial, see *Kiziltan* [2017] EWCA Crim 1461, [2018] 4 WLR 43 at **F17.90**.

F17.17 **Fear** The terms of the CJA 2003, s. 116(2)(e), do not require that the fear must be attributable to the accused, nor does the ECHR, Article 6, so require (*Horncastle* [2009] UKSC 14, [2010] 2 AC 373: see the Court of Appeal judgment endorsed and regarded as complementary to the subsequent decision of the Supreme Court). It follows that an accused cannot complain of the use of an absent witness's statement where it is fear of a co-accused that has caused a prosecution witness to take flight (*Harvey* [2014] EWCA Crim 54). However, a causal link between the fear and the failure or refusal to give evidence must be proved, and how it is proved depends upon the background together with the history and circumstances of the particular case. (*Riat* [2012] EWCA Crim 1509, [2013] 1 All ER 349; *Shabir* [2012] EWCA Crim 2564). The *Crown Court Compendium* (July 2020), ch. 14-2, emphasises that, while it is in many cases possible for the jury to be told the reasons for a witness's absence, this cannot generally be done in cases involving fear.

The previous statement of a hostile prosecution witness who is motivated simply by the desire to protect the accused, rather than by fear, remains outside the purview of s. 116, but may be admissible under s. 119 (see **F6.47**) or, as was suggested in *Saunders* [2012] EWCA Crim 1185, s. 114(1)(d) (see **F17.34**). Where fear appears to be only one factor in a witness's refusal to testify, it is necessary to evaluate other possible reasons. In *Nelson* [2009] EWCA Crim 1600 the witness was also angry at what she perceived to be the failures of the witness protection system, and anxious about the symptoms of a serious illness and a related medical appointment she had missed because she was forced to attend the court. More should have been done to ascertain the witness's reasons for refusing to testify; the outcome of further investigation might have led the judge to deal differently with her.

The extent to which s. 116 can apply to the statement of a witness who subsequently gives evidence is unclear. In *Clarke* [2012] EWCA Crim 2354, the victim of a violent burglary testified that he did not recognise his attacker, but he had told a police officer 'off the record' that it was D and there was evidence that he was afraid of what D, a violent man, might do. The Court of Appeal declined to decide whether the officer's evidence was rightly admitted at trial but it seems unlikely that the wording of the provision was intended to stretch that far, as the witness had given evidence on the point, albeit unfavourable evidence. The wording clearly does anticipate the case of the witness who 'dries up' through fear, before getting through the matters proved by the statement, but that was not the case in *Clarke*.

Section 116(3) makes it clear that fear is to be 'widely construed' and that it includes, for example, fear of injury to another or fear of financial loss. It was at one time thought that courts would be 'ill-advised to seek to test the basis of fear by calling witnesses before them' (*Davies* [2006] EWCA Crim 2643, [2007] 2 All ER 1070). This, however, may be too weak a response in the majority of cases to satisfy the 'fair trial' concern that hearsay evidence is not admitted unless it is necessary to do so. In *Shabir* the Court of Appeal endorsed the view that every effort must be made to get the witness to court to test the issue of 'fear' with a view, if at all possible, to persuading the witness to give evidence, and in *Riat* [2012] EWCA Crim 1509, [2013] 1 All

ER 349 it was said that 'a degree of (properly supported) fortitude can legitimately be expected in the fight against crime'. In some cases a witness alleging 'fear' may be cross-examined by the defence, with 'special measures' in place to assist the witness if necessary. In other cases that procedure may not be appropriate (to borrow the example in *Riat*, 'in some cases of alleged domestic violence it may be an avenue for worsening apprehension'). In *Harvey* [2014] EWCA Crim 54 the Court of Appeal relied both on *Shabir* and the relevant passage from *Davies*, implicitly suggesting that there might still be some cases in which the court should not seek to test the fear where the purpose of the section would be undermined. Hence the current rule is probably that the court will consider whether there is a particular reason not to follow the measures suggested in *Shabir*, for example where there is evidence other than that of the fearful witness of a threat to life or limb. In the majority of cases, however, the requirement for leave to be obtained is a further reason to justify a close scrutiny of the impact of the fear on the witness, which should be tested in court where possible (see **F17.21**).

The proof of fear may itself give rise to questions of admissibility. In *Neill v North Antrim Magistrates' Court* [1992] 4 All ER 846, decided under previous legislation, two boys made statements to the police in which they claimed to have witnessed an assault and to have identified one of the perpetrators. However, they did not attend the subsequent committal proceedings, and evidence was given by a police officer that the boys' mothers had told him that the boys were too afraid to attend. The House of Lords held that the statements should not have been received because the evidence of the officer was hearsay, being based on what he had been told by the mothers of the boys and not by the boys themselves. If the boys had communicated their fears to him directly he could have given evidence of what they had told him under the 'long-established law that a person's declaration of his contemporaneous state of mind is admissible to prove the existence of that state of mind', per Lord Mustill at p. 1228 following *Blastland* [1986] AC 41 (see now the CJA 2003, s. 118(1), at **F17.78**). However, the point was also made that, even had such evidence been available, a court would be cautious about whether it was in the interests of justice to admit documentary evidence of identification or recognition that formed the principal element in the prosecution's case: a point that might now be made with equal force in relation to the risk of unfairness under s. 116(4) (see **F17.21**). **F17.18**

As to proof of fear by hearsay evidence forming part of the *res gestae*, see **F17.49**. An alternative might be to admit the proof of the witness's fear under the CJA 2003, s. 114(1)(d) ('the interests of justice' exception: see **F17.34**).

The evidence of fear must relate to the relevant time. In *H* [2001] Crim LR 815, decided under previous legislation, the alleged victim of a kidnapping made a statement two months before the trial indicating his fear of reprisals and his intention to abscond, but he in fact remained in the area and was arrested in connection with drugs offences. No evidence of continuing fear was adduced at the trial. Stressing that the fear must be judged at the time of the trial, and that the out-of-date evidence was not by itself sufficient, the Court of Appeal also acknowledged that there might be a 'degree of sensible give and take', for example when a ruling on admissibility was sought in advance of trial to enable counsel for the prosecution to decide how the case should be opened to the jury. **F17.19**

Intimidation in Fear Cases If the reason for the witness's failure to give evidence in person is that the witness was intimidated by or on behalf of the accused, who then contests the admissibility of the statement for the prosecution, the accused is in a weak position to claim infringement of the right to a fair trial. The point is strongly made in *Al-Khawaja and Tahery v UK* (2012) 54 EHRR 23 (807), where it was said that to allow the accused to engender the fear and then to benefit from it would be incompatible with the rights of victims and 'no court could be expected to allow the integrity of its proceedings to be subverted in this way'. But the problem posed by intimidation of witnesses, for example by organised criminals, does not provide a licence to prosecutors to resort to proof by hearsay (*Arnold* [2004] EWCA Crim 1293), and the conditions of admissibility must **F17.20**

be established in the same way and to the same extent as in other cases where a witness is in fear. In *Riat* [2012] EWCA Crim 1509, [2013] 1 All ER 349 (in the appeal of *Wilson*), specific evidence of fear was not put before the court, and the judge relied principally on the 'real culture of intimidation' that was prevalent in the area where the witness lived. The Court of Appeal considered that the evidence had been wrongly admitted: this was a case in which the witnesses could have been brought to court and the possibility that they might have given evidence, if only as hostile witnesses, could not have been ruled out. By contrast, in *Fagan* [2012] EWCA Crim 2248, where there was clear evidence that the witness had been subject to intimidation by someone acting on behalf of the accused, the failure of the prosecution to make attempts to bring the witness to court was 'nowhere near fatal' to the judge's conclusion that the evidence should be admitted. In *Boulton* [2007] EWCA Crim 942 the complainant in a case of rape attended a hearing to explain her reluctance to testify in light of serious threats on behalf of the accused and a long history of violence and intimidation. When reminded of her civic duty, she responded, 'I am not averse to duty, your Honour I am just averse to martyrdom'. The Court of Appeal not only upheld the judge's decision but doubted whether any other conclusion was possible.

Note that, by virtue of the CJA 2003, s. 116(5) (see **F17.8** and **F17.10**), an accused who causes the absence of a witness is also prevented from adducing the witness's statement as hearsay as part of the defence case.

F17.21 **Leave in Fear Cases** In *Horncastle* [2009] UKSC 14, [2010] 2 AC 373, in a judgment endorsed and regarded as complementary to the subsequent decision of the Supreme Court, the Court of Appeal stressed that all possible efforts should be made to get the witness to court, bearing in mind the importance of the right to confrontation and that intimidation will only flourish if citizens are readily discouraged from doing their duty. If the circumstances are such that the defence cannot cross-examine the witness to test the relevant matters, it is incumbent on the judge to investigate all possibilities by which the witness might give oral evidence (*Riat* [2012] EWCA Crim 1509, [2013] 1 All ER 349; *Shabir* [2012] EWCA Crim 2564). See also *Fagan* [2012] EWCA Crim 2248 (where it is recognised that a conclusion of intimidation may still be reached without producing the witness in court), *Claridge* [2013] EWCA Crim 203 (where it was said to be a 'counsel to perfection' to expect inquiry to be made of the witness, who was in court, about whether she could be persuaded to testify, but the failure to do so did not threaten the safety of the conviction), and *Min Fu* [2017] EWCA Crim 248 (where L, the absent witness, was alleged to be the victim of a protection racket and afraid of reprisals). The reception of L's hearsay testimony deprived D of the ability to cross-examine L as to whether D had behaved threateningly towards him, but the Court of Appeal accepted that the judge was entitled to take the view he did, although other judges might have taken more positive steps to get L into court. One factor was the existence of CCTV footage that appeared to show D directing a violent attack against L. Note also *Jabbar* [2013] EWCA Crim 801 and compare *Lawrence* [2013] EWCA Crim 708, [2014] 1 Cr App R 5 (33), discussed at **F17.38**.

Witnesses should never be assured in advance that their evidence will be read (*Horncastle* at [81]). In deciding whether to give leave under the CJA 2003, s. 116(4), to admit the statement of a fearful witness, the court is expressly directed to take into account, along with any other circumstances it regards as relevant, the content of the statement, the risk that its admission or exclusion will result in unfairness having regard to the difficulty of challenging the statement if the relevant person does not give oral evidence, and the possibility that a special measures direction under the YJCEA 1999 (see **D14.3**) could be made in relation to that person. This last condition directs the court's attention to the possibility that fear may in some cases be assuaged by the application of special measures, e.g., by the use of screens, live-link or video-recorded evidence. These alternatives are preferable to hearsay because the witness is made available to be cross-examined. Thus in *Robinson v Sutton Coldfield Magistrates' Court* [2006] EWHC 307 (Admin), [2006] 4 All ER 1029, where the complainant in a case of assault (D's former partner) had begun a new life and did not wish D to be able to trace her, it was necessary for the justices, before receiving her evidence, to consider whether any of the 1999 Act's special measures might meet the case. The possibility that special arrangements could have been made to convey her to court without enabling D to discover where she was living might also have been relevant to the overall question of the interests of justice. In *Doherty* [2006] EWCA Crim 2716, the exercise to be undertaken under s. 116(4) was described as 'not strictly an exercise of discretion but something akin to it', and one which the judge is in the best position to perform. Issues of trial fairness, including an alleged infringement of the ECHR, Article 6(3)(d), can conveniently be subsumed within the s. 116(4) inquiry, but ultimately the issues are the same in fear cases as in other cases of challenge for unfairness based on *Horncastle*: see **F17.89** ***et seq.*** — many of the leading cases considered there involve fearful witnesses.

Relevance of Availability of Other Evidence Where the disputed hearsay evidence is the 'sole or decisive' evidence for the prosecution, the court must pay particular attention to *Horncastle* [2009] UKSC 14, [2010] 2 AC 373 and the considerations outlined at **F17.89** ***et seq***. Although the court cannot require to be told whether the accused intends to give evidence or call witnesses, it is not bound to assess the possibility of challenging the statement upon the basis that the accused will do neither of these things. In *Doherty* [2006] EWCA Crim 2716, the court was influenced not only by the strength of the other evidence of the assault but also by the prospect of witnesses being called who could support the accused's version of events. **F17.22**

Competence of Maker of Statement A statement by a witness who lacks the competence to testify at the time the statement was made may not be received under the CJA 2003, s. 116 (see s. 123 at **F17.8**). Such a statement might, if the interests of justice required it, be admissible under s. 114(1)(d) (see **F17.34**). Under the previous law (CJA 1988, s. 23), evidence of an incompetent witness was received in *D* [2002] EWCA Crim 990, [2003] QB 90, but it is likely to be only in a rare case that this is appropriate. **F17.23**

Credibility Section 124 of the CJA 2003 (see **F17.87**) applies in relation to matters bearing on the credibility of the makers of hearsay statements admissible under s. 116. It is of particular importance to consider whether, and if so by what evidence, the party against whom hearsay evidence is given under s. 116 will be able to challenge it. **F17.24**

Business and Other Documents

Criminal Justice Act 2003, s. 117 **F17.25**

(1) In criminal proceedings a statement contained in a document is admissible as evidence of any matter stated if—
  (a) oral evidence given in the proceedings would be admissible as evidence of that matter,
  (b) the requirements of subsection (2) are satisfied, and
  (c) the requirements of subsection (5) are satisfied, in a case where subsection (4) requires them to be.
(2) The requirements of this subsection are satisfied if—
  (a) the document or the part containing the statement was created or received by a person in the course of a trade, business, profession or other occupation, or as the holder of a paid or unpaid office,
  (b) the person who supplied the information contained in the statement (the relevant person) had or may reasonably be supposed to have had personal knowledge of the matters dealt with, and
  (c) each person (if any) through whom the information was supplied from the relevant person *to the person mentioned in* paragraph (a) received the information in the course of a trade, business, profession or other occupation, or as the holder of a paid or unpaid office.
(3) The persons mentioned in paragraphs (a) and (b) of subsection (2) may be the same person.
(4) The additional requirements of subsection (5) must be satisfied if the statement—
  (a) was prepared for the purposes of pending or contemplated criminal proceedings, or for a criminal investigation, but
  (b) was not obtained pursuant to a request under section 7 of the Crime (International Co-operation) Act 2003 or an order under paragraph 6 of Schedule 13 to the Criminal Justice Act 1988 (which relate to overseas evidence).

(5) The requirements of this subsection are satisfied if—
(a) any of the five conditions mentioned in section 116(2) is satisfied (absence of relevant person etc), or
(b) the relevant person cannot reasonably be expected to have any recollection of the matters dealt with in the statement (having regard to the length of time since he supplied the information and all other circumstances).

(6) A statement is not admissible under this section if the court makes a direction to that effect under subsection (7).

(7) The court may make a direction under this subsection if satisfied that the statement's reliability as evidence for the purpose for which it is tendered is doubtful in view of—
(a) its contents,
(b) the source of the information contained in it,
(c) the way in which or the circumstances in which the information was supplied or received, or
(d) the way in which or the circumstances in which the document concerned was created or received.

F17.26 **Business or Other Documents** 'Business records are made admissible ... because, in the ordinary way, they are compiled by people who are disinterested and, in the ordinary course of events, such statements are likely to be accurate; they are therefore admissible as evidence because prima facie they are reliable' (the Court of Appeal in *Horncastle* [2009] EWCA Crim 964, [2009] 2 Cr App R 15 (230), in a judgment endorsed and regarded as complementary to the subsequent decision of the Supreme Court: [2009] UKSC 14, [2010] 2 AC 373). Where the reliability of the statement is, contrary to normal expectation, doubtful (whether as a result of its contents, the source of the information, or concerns about the manner in which the document came into being), the court has a specific power under s. 117(7) to direct the exclusion of a document that is otherwise admissible under s. 117, whether tendered by the prosecution or the defence.

Section 117 of the CJA 2003 extends, as did its predecessor (s. 24 of the CJA 1998), to documents created or received by a person in the course of a trade, business, profession or other occupation, or as the holder of a paid or unpaid office. Section 117 goes further in that it applies also to parts of documents so created, when the statement in issue is included in that part (for the meaning of 'statement' see s. 115(2) at **F16.7**) In *Clowes* [1992] 3 All ER 440, decided under the CJA 1988, s. 24, transcripts of interviews between the liquidators of companies and persons involved with the companies were held to have been 'received' by the liquidators in the course of their profession and as holders of the office of liquidator. Documents of a non-commercial nature such as a National Health Service hospital's records are clearly admissible, as is the transcript of the evidence given by a witness at an earlier trial, which may be admitted at a retrial even though the court is plainly not a business in any sense (*Lockley* [1995] 2 Cr App R 554). Similarly, a police custody record was admitted under s. 24 in *Hogan* [1997] Crim LR 349. In *Johnson* [2019] EWCA Crim 1730, medical records in which the complainant had disclosed a sexual assault by D were admitted under the CJA 2003, s. 117, to rebut a suggestion of recent fabrication.

Because s. 117, like s. 24 before it, applies only to documentary evidence, the compiler of documents for use in criminal proceedings who leaves out important details of information obtained from others who do not give evidence cannot simply supplement the record with oral hearsay testimony (*Hinds* [1993] Crim LR 528). Nor can an entry in a record be proved simply by calling someone who has checked the record (*Motor Depot Ltd and Williams v Kingston upon Hull City Council* [2012] EWHC 3257 (Admin)), a principle that appears to have been breached in *Grazette v DPP* [2012] EWHC 3863 (Admin).

F17.27 In *Foxley* [1995] 2 Cr App R 523, decided under the CJA 1988, s. 24, the documents in question were copies of credit notes and payments allegedly made by overseas companies to D, who was accused of receiving them corruptly. They had been obtained by letters of request to the authorities in the relevant countries. It was objected, *inter alia*, that no evidence was available from the creator as to whether these documents had come into existence in the course of a business etc., but it was held to be the intention of the statute that the court be allowed to draw relevant inferences from the documents themselves and from the way in which they had been placed before the court. Likewise, in *O'Connor* [2010] EWCA Crim 2287, Belgian telephone records were procured through letters of request, but no accompanying statement as to the method of compilation was forthcoming. It was held that, to the extent that the documents may have been statements by a person (rather than non-hearsay mechanically produced evidence: see **F16.11**) it was open to the judge to draw inferences that their compilation had been in accordance with the provisions of s. 117. On the face of the documents, it could be inferred that the compiler had been either an employee of the phone provider or an officer of the Belgian police. Nothing in s. 117 required the production of an explanatory statement, though it may well often be desirable to have one. In *Department of Environment, Food and Rural Affairs v Atkinson* [2002] EWHC 2028 (Admin), the label on a bottle was held to be admissible evidence that it contained a veterinary medicinal product, applying the same inference of reliability from the context. A case that may go too far in this context is *Grazette v DPP* [2012] EWHC 3863 (Admin), where an inference was drawn as to the likelihood that the anonymous supplier of information to a Criminal Intelligence Report as to the 'street name' of the accused was correct because the address given for him in the same report was correct.

Personal Knowledge The 'supplier' of the information (who must have, etc., personal knowledge of the matters dealt with under the CJA 2003, s. 117(2)(b)) may also be the person who 'creates' the document under s. 117(2)(c) (s. 117(3)). Thus, for example, a note made by an operator working for a paging company that messages had been left for a customer would be admissible (as in *Rock* [1994] Crim LR 843, decided under the 1988 Act) as a first-hand hearsay statement. Where such a document is received in evidence under s. 117, it is not necessary, as it is under s. 116 (see **F17.8**), to prove the unavailability of the maker of the statement. **F17.28**

Section 117 may also be invoked where several degrees of hearsay are involved. Provided each of the persons through whom the information was supplied received it in the course of a trade etc. (s. 117(2)(c)), the facts stated in the document are admissible. See, e.g., *Wellington v DPP* [2007] EWHC 1061 (Admin) (extract from Police National Computer printout recording previous use of same alias by accused). In *Maher v DPP* [2006] EWHC 1271 (Admin) a note which had been made (and lost) of a car number plate could not be adduced as second-hand evidence under s. 117 because a relevant passer-on of information had not received it in the course of their trade etc. The evidence was, however, admitted under s. 121(1)(c) as multiple hearsay, on the ground that the value of the evidence, taking into account its apparent reliability, was so high that the interests of justice required admissibility. This apparent incongruity can be explained on the basis that admissibility under s. 117 is 'automatic' (subject to the discretion in s. 117(6) and (7)), hence the need to demonstrate the degree of reliability inherent in the making of a commercial type of record. The ruling in favour of admissibility in *Maher* is based on the determination that the particular record, though not automatically admissible, was (on investigation of its specific properties) sufficiently reliable and important to be received. However, the process by which it was received ought to have included the determination that the passing-on of the information was itself hearsay admissible under s. 114(1)(d) (see **F17.34** and **F17.85**).

A document produced by a computer without any human intervention cannot be said to contain information 'supplied by a person' with 'personal knowledge' (*Pettigrew* (1980) 71 Cr App R 39). However, as such a document does not constitute hearsay evidence, it will not matter that the conditions of the exception cannot be satisfied (*Wood* (1982) 76 Cr App R 23, considered at ***F16.12 et seq.***). **F17.29**

The statement is admissible only as evidence of any matter stated of which 'oral evidence given in the proceedings' would be admissible, and this prevents the introduction of evidence that contravenes a rule of admissibility other than the hearsay rule, e.g., the rule against evidence of bad character, or evidence that goes only to credit where the witness's answer is final, as in *Foye* [2013] EWCA Crim 475. It cannot be a valid objection to the admissibility of evidence under

s. 117 that an intermediary through whom the information was supplied could not have given evidence of the fact without contravening the hearsay rule, otherwise s. 117 could not be made to apply to second-hand hearsay, and it is clearly meant to do so (see s. 121 at **F17.84**).

F17.30 **Unavailability of Maker of Statement Prepared for Purposes of Criminal Proceedings or Investigation** It is not generally necessary to show grounds why the supplier of information contained in a statement should not be called before tendering a statement in evidence under the CJA 2003, s. 117. The only exceptions are those statements prepared for the purposes of pending or contemplated criminal proceedings, or of a criminal investigation (s. 117(4)(a)), which are not obtained pursuant to a request or order specified in s. 117(4)(b). Here, s. 117(5) applies, and it is necessary to establish either:

(a) one of the reasons for not calling the relevant person that apply in the case of a s. 116 statement (s. 117(5)(a): see **F17.11** ***et seq.***); or
(b) that the person cannot reasonably be expected (having regard to the time that has elapsed since the statement was made and to all the circumstances) to have any recollection of the matters dealt with in the statement (s. 117(5)(b)).

In *Minchin* [2013] EWCA Crim 2412, D was charged with conspiracy to pervert the course of justice for providing a false alibi for his son. The Court of Appeal accepted that a solicitor's file note recording a meeting that had taken place with D and his son was inadmissible under s. 117 as it had been prepared for the purposes of criminal proceedings (s. 117(4)) and none of the statutory reasons for not calling the maker applied (s. 117(5)). However, the probative value of the note ultimately led to its admission under s. 114(1)(d) in the interests of justice (see **F17.38**).

F17.31 In *Humphris* [2005] EWCA Crim 2030, an attempt was made to use s. 117 where the prosecution sought to establish the *modus operandi* of previous admissible sexual offences committed by H. The details of the offences were recorded by police officers and other employees all acting under a duty, and the suggestion was that they had the necessary personal knowledge to be the 'relevant person' for the purposes of s. 117(2)(b) and (5). While the court found no difficulty in using s. 117 to establish the fact of conviction, the details of the method used were in each case dependent on information originally supplied by the complainant, who was thus the 'relevant person'. The correct method of proceeding would therefore have been, as it was before the CJA 2003, to take a statement from the complainant. This might, depending on the circumstances, have been admissible under s. 116 (see **F17.8**). See, however, *Ainscough* [2006] EWCA Crim 694, drawing attention to the fact that a conviction might be complicated by the fact that an accused was sentenced on a different basis as a result of a plea, proffered and accepted by the court at the time. This would affect the fairness of admitting the original complainant's evidence as hearsay and would raise numerous satellite issues about the detail of what occurred (see also **F13.47**).

F17.32 In *Bedi* (1992) 95 Cr App R 21, the 'lost and stolen' reports maintained by a bank in respect of credit cards it had issued were held not to fall within the equivalent provisions of the CJA 1988. An examination of the reports disclosed that they were kept for the proper conduct of the bank's business, not for criminal proceedings. In *Hogan* [1997] Crim LR 349 it was assumed, surely rightly, that a police custody record fell within the equivalent provisions of the 1988 Act, and in *West Midlands Probation Board v French* [2008] EWHC 2631 (Admin), [2009] 1 WLR 1715, it was held that the licence setting out the conditions of a prisoner's release is not a document prepared for the purposes specified by s. 117(4)(a).

Section 117(5)(b) may apply where a witness is unable to recollect one part of a longer statement but is able to give evidence as to the rest (*Carrington* [1994] Crim LR 438, in which the witness's recollection was supplemented in relation to a car registration number that she had forgotten, in circumstances where she was not entitled to refresh her memory from the statement). See as to the evidence that may satisfy this condition, *Crayden* [1978] 2 All ER 700 at p. 608 (decided under the Criminal Evidence Act 1965) and *Feest* [1987] Crim LR 766 (decided under the PACE 1984).

Competence The CJA 2003, s. 123 (see **F17.8**), which provides that only evidence from competent witnesses may be received, applies to s. 117 in the following way. Where any person who supplied or received relevant information, or who created or received the document or the part concerned, either lacked capacity or (if unidentifiable) cannot reasonably be assumed to have had capacity at the relevant time, the statement may not be admitted under s. 117 (s. 123(2)). This does not necessarily preclude its admission under the interests of justice exception in s. 114(1)(d), but it would be a rare case where this would be appropriate. F17.33

HEARSAY EXCEPTIONS: (2) HEARSAY ADMISSIBLE IN THE INTERESTS OF JUSTICE

Criminal Justice Act 2003, s. 114 F17.34

(1) ... [a] statement not made in oral evidence in the proceedings is admissible as evidence of any matter stated if, but only if—

...

(d) the court is satisfied that it is in the interests of justice for it to be admissible.

(2) In deciding whether a statement not made in oral evidence should be admitted under subsection (1)(d), the court must have regard to the following factors (and to any others it considers relevant)—

(a) how much probative value the statement has (assuming it to be true) in relation to a matter in issue in the proceedings, or how valuable it is for the understanding of other evidence in the case;

(b) what other evidence has been, or can be, given on the matter or evidence mentioned in paragraph (a);

(c) how important the matter or evidence mentioned in paragraph (a) is in the context of the case as a whole;

(d) the circumstances in which the statement was made;

(e) how reliable the maker of the statement appears to be;

(f) how reliable the evidence of the making of the statement appears to be;

(g) whether oral evidence of the matter stated can be given and, if not, why it cannot;

(h) the amount of difficulty involved in challenging the statement;

(i) the extent to which that difficulty would be likely to prejudice the party facing it.

Factors to be Taken into Account

Where s. 114(2) directs the court to have regard to certain factors, it does not follow that a judge is bound to reach a conclusion on all of them. Proper investigation of all nine factors would be a lengthy process, which the CJA 2003 does not require. All that is required is the exercise of judgement in the light of the factors specifically identified, together with any others considered by the judge to be relevant (*Taylor* [2006] EWCA Crim 260, [2006] 2 Cr App R 14 (222)). They are not a questionnaire to be answered (*C* [2019] EWCA Crim 623). An exercise of judgement will be interfered with on appeal only if it has involved the application of incorrect principles or is outside the band of legitimate decision (*Finch* [2007] EWCA Crim 36, [2007] 1 WLR 1645; *Musone* [2007] EWCA Crim 1237, [2007] 1 WLR 2467; and see, by way of an example of incorrect usage, *Randell v DPP* [2018] EWHC 1048 (Admin)). In considering factors (e) and (f) it is not permissible to reason that the jury may assess matters relating to reliability: the judge is specifically required to make an assessment. In *QD* [2019] NICA 7, the Court of Appeal of Northern Ireland noted that there is no requirement, for the purposes of applying the interests of justice exception, that the maker of the statement be a competent witness. The question would be whether such a witness is 'reliable' for the purposes of factor (e). Factor (g) requires close attention to be paid to whether there is an alternative to admitting hearsay, including the bringing of an available, though reluctant, witness to court (*Y* [2008] EWCA Crim 10, [2008] 1 Cr App R 34 (411)). In assessing potential defence evidence, it is not the interest of the accused that the court is required to consider, it is the interest of arriving at the right conclusion (*Marsh* [2008] EWCA Crim 1816). F17.35

A hearing on admissibility under s. 114(1)(d) cannot take account of material that has been presented to the judge on an *ex parte* application, and that was not available to the defence (*Ali* [2008] EWCA Crim 146).

Inapplicable to Multiple Hearsay

F17.36 Section 114(1)(d) cannot be used as the sole justification to admit multiple hearsay, which can be adduced only to the extent permitted by s. 121 (see **F17.84**). Section 121(1)(c) makes special provision for multiple hearsay to be admissible in the interests of justice (see, e.g., *Musone*).

Relationship with Other Hearsay Exceptions

F17.37 The cases indicate that the CJA 2003, s. 114(1)(d), is to be applied with caution. Originally conceived by the Law Commission as a 'safety valve' for the admission of otherwise inadmissible evidence in exceptional circumstances only, there is nothing in the statutory language to indicate that this is how s. 114(1)(d) is to be used (*Sak v CPS* [2007] EWHC 2886 (Admin), where, however, it was also stated that s. 114 should not be lightly applied). The difficulty lies in striking a balance between using the provision in circumstances where the evidence ought to be admitted but no other exception presents itself, and using it to circumvent the legitimate constraints of other provisions. In *D (E)* [2010] EWCA Crim 1213 it was held that the hearsay statement of a witness which was tendered in order to rebut an allegation of recent fabrication was wrongly admitted where the witness was absent on holiday in circumstances that did not fall within s. 116, and the role of the prosecution in failing to secure the witness's attendance was not properly considered when applying the 'interests of justice' criteria. Pitchford LJ referred to s. 114 in terms of a 'hierarchy' of exceptions; s. 114(1)(d) should not be used to circumvent requirements of other gateways higher up the hierarchy. In *Horncastle* [2009] UKSC 14, [2010] 2 AC 373 the Supreme Court referred to s. 114(1)(d) as a 'limited residual power', which also suggests a hierarchical or 'safety-valve' approach. In *Z* [2009] EWCA Crim 20, [2009] 1 Cr App R 34 (500), the Court of Appeal said it would be 'rare indeed' to admit the hearsay account of a woman who claimed to have been sexually assaulted by the accused when a child, in support of the similar complaint for which the accused was being tried. The hearsay witness was unwilling to relive the trauma of the offences by giving evidence, a ground not recognised by s. 116 (see **F17.8**), and the Court regarded the use of s. 114(1)(d) as an unacceptable means of circumventing the restrictions on hearsay in s. 116. The Court also expressed its concern at the prospect of disputed evidence of bad character being adduced in hearsay form. See, to similar effect, *C* [2010] EWCA Crim 72, where s. 116 was not satisfied in respect of an alleged victim of sexual offences, and her account should not have been presented by her adoptive mother using s. 114(1)(d) instead.

A more difficult decision to justify is *Burton* [2011] EWCA Crim 1990, in which the prosecution was permitted to adduce the statement of a 14-year-old complainant that she had been involved in a sexual relationship with D under s. 114(1)(d). Although the circumstances would not have justified the use of s. 116, it may be that the case was exceptional in that the evidence was peripheral, not only in the sense that it was not the 'sole or decisive' evidence, but also that it merely served to confirm D's admissions to the police. However, in *Tindle* [2011] EWCA Crim 2341, a case of assault in which the prosecution sought in effect to circumvent their own failure to take 'reasonable steps' to secure the complainant's attendance under s. 116 by tendering the evidence under s. 114(1)(d), it was held, applying *Z*, that considering, as the court was required to do by s. 114(2)(g), whether oral evidence of the matter could have been given and, if not, why it could not was bound to lead back to the same inquiry as had led to exclusion under s. 116.

F17.38 Where evidence is inadmissible under another hearsay exception for reasons related to the interests of justice, it would clearly be inconsistent to allow s. 114(1)(d) to be invoked to arrive at a different result: see, e.g., *Smith* [2007] EWCA Crim 2105 (plea of guilty of one conspirator in a closed conspiracy with D, though technically admissible under the PACE 1984, s. 74, should have been excluded under s. 78), *McEwan v DPP* [2007] EWHC 740 (Admin) (s. 116 inapplicable because of lack of diligence by the prosecutor in securing the necessary proof) and *Warnick*

[2013] EWCA Crim 2320 (where the prosecution was unable to demonstrate that the witness was in fear for the purposes of s. 116(1)(e) (see **F17.17**), the same evidence could not be used to admit a statement under s. 114(1)(d) without circumventing the 'fear' provisions). It does not follow that evidence which fails to comply with conditions of another hearsay exception can never be admitted under s. 114(1)(d), as part of its purpose is to fill the gap between other provisions where that is in the interests of justice. Thus in *Adams* (2008) 1 Cr App R 35 (430), a witness had not been given sufficient notice for the court to find that he 'could not be found after taking reasonable steps' (s. 116(2)(d): see **F17.14**), but the evidence was, though technically necessary, uncontentious, and the court allowed proof by hearsay under s. 114(1)(d). In *Sadiq* [2009] EWCA Crim 712 the Court of Appeal held that the testimony of the alleged victim of a shooting, who had been paralysed and was unable to speak, could be admitted under s. 114(1)(d) at a retrial. The witness had given evidence by means of an alphabet board at the original trial, but had asserted (without giving reasons) his unwillingness to testify at the retrial. However, in *Lawrence* [2013] EWCA Crim 708, [2014] 1 Cr App R 5 (33) the Court suggested that the reasons for refusal to give evidence at the retrial would have to be considered as carefully as in fear cases under s. 116 (see **F17.21**) before the evidence could be admitted under s. 114(1)(d) and s. 131 (under which s. 114(1)(d) is applicable to retrials: see **F17.80**). In *J* [2011] EWCA Crim 3021, the statement of a three-year-old boy as to the cause of his injuries was held to have been rightly admitted under s. 114(1)(d) in the trial of his mother's partner for cruelty. It is noteworthy that this was not the 'sole or decisive' evidence: the Court stressed that the child's injuries were non-accidental and D had ample opportunity to cross-examine the only other people who could possibly have caused them. See also *MH* [2012] EWCA Crim 2725, where the early disclosures of a very young child were inadmissible under the CJA 2003, s. 120, because he could not confirm that he had made them, but it was held that they could have been received under s. 114(1)(d). In *Strotten* [2015] EWCA Crim 1101, a young child was unable to confirm in his ABE interviews that he had been assaulted, but the complaints he had made to close family members (some of which might have been admissible under the *res gestae* exception: see **F17.50**) were held to have been properly admitted under s. 114(1)(d). Independent support for the complaint was derived from similar allegations made by an older child.

In *Lynch* [2007] EWCA Crim 3035, [2008] 1 Cr App R 24 (337), a statement made by a witness following a positive identification at an identification parade was not sufficiently 'bound up' with the identification to be part of the *res gestae* (see **F17.49**), but was admissible under s. 114(1)(d). In *Gillooley* [2009] EWCA Crim 671, s. 114(1)(d) was employed to admit the first complaints of sexual abuse made by a young man to his mother and his girlfriend. The complaints were made years after the events to which they related, and were inadmissible under s. 120 (see **F6.36**), but were of clear probative value in relation to establishing the way in which the complaint had emerged. In *Taylor* [2006] EWCA Crim 260, [2006] 2 Cr App R 14 (222), s. 114(1)(d) was invoked in order to plug the common gap in continuity whereby the name of a suspect is supplied by a witness who knows it only because of having been told it by another. See also *Saunders* [2012] EWCA Crim 1185, where s. 114(1)(d) was invoked to admit statements by a witness, B, to two friends that she had seen an offence which in her evidence she had denied having witnessed. B had told her friends that she was too frightened to tell the whole truth, but the provisions governing fearful witnesses (s. 116(2)(e): see **F17.17**) were inapplicable because B had testified on the point. The Court of Appeal said that it would be 'curious' if the previous statements could not be used. The note was inadmissible under s. 117 (see **F17.30**) because the defence refused to waive legal privilege in order to allow the solicitor to give oral evidence.

Courts are likely to afford rigorous scrutiny to evidence tendered under s. 114(1)(d) that would have been objectionable at common law. In *Y* [2008] EWCA Crim 10, [2008] 1 Cr App R 34 (411), the issue was whether the confession of a third party implicating an accused was capable of being used in evidence against him under s. 114(1)(d), despite a strong common-law rule that the statement could be used only against its maker. The Court of Appeal held that the effect of s. 114(1)(d) was that the evidence was capable of being admitted, there being nothing in s. 118 (which preserves certain common-law rules of admissibility including evidence of **F17.39** confessions and admissions: see **F17.66**) to render such evidence inadmissible under s. 114(1)(d). However, the Court also drew attention to the 'rigorous' test to be applied, and the need for particular caution where the prosecution sought to place reliance on a third party's confession in the absence of supporting evidence against an accused. *Y* was applied by the Court of Appeal in *Amin* [2014] EWCA Crim 1924. The issue was whether covert recordings of conversations in prison between two men who were subsequently convicted of the 'honour killing' of V were admissible under s. 114(1)(d) against D, who had been charged in respect of the disposal of V's body. The conversations also incriminated the makers and were clearly admissible against them. The prosecution could not have been expected to call them, but there was nothing to prevent D from doing so. The Court considered that the evidence could safely be admitted: the reliability of the statements implicating D was supported by the link to the confessions of the murderers, who had not realised they were being overheard, nor was there any separate reason why they might have harboured any hostility towards A, a family member of one of them, that might render the statements about him unreliable. The statements also formed part of a series of recordings of conversations including two with D himself when he visited the murderers in prison, and the implication as to D's involvement was consistent throughout. In *Trought* [2017] EWCA Crim 1701, the case for the prosecution included evidence of a confession by W, a party to the drugs conspiracy with which D was charged, and this, together with other evidence, was used to show that W was working off a debt to D by acting as his courier for the drugs. W had been sentenced for his part in the conspiracy and was a serving prisoner at the time of D's trial. The argument on appeal was that the judge had given insufficient attention to the possibility of W being called as a witness for the prosecution. It was held that the judge had paid due regard to the relevant considerations. There was evidence of ongoing contact between D and W, and that D was endeavouring to buy W's silence by promises of financial assistance for W's family. W was also further indebted to D, having lost the drugs he was delivering when he was arrested. The prosecution's view was that there was no realistic prospect of W giving a statement for the prosecution or of giving evidence, and there had been no suggestion by the defence at the trial that the prosecution should follow this course of action. W's confession was correctly admitted.

Where the maker of the statement is available for cross-examination this will tell in favour of admitting the hearsay, even if the person is also a co-acccused. In *Burns* [2015] EWCA Crim 2542, D1's co-accused, D2, made a number of hearsay statements to friends in which he narrated D1's leading role in a murder while minimising his own. The version of events D2 gave in evidence was less explicit about D1's role, but D2's availability to be cross-examined was a matter to which the Court of Appeal attached 'considerable importance' in holding that the hearsay statements had been properly admitted in evidence against D1, together with other considerations including the manner in which the hearsay accounts were supported by other evidence.

The statement under caution of one co-accused, incriminating another, may similarly be considered for admission under s. 114(1)(d) (*B* [2008] EWCA Crim 365), but the provision clearly does not make police interviews routinely admissible in the case of persons other than the interviewee, and *McLean* [2007] EWCA Crim 219, [2008] 1 Cr App R 11 (155) was said in *Y* not to be authority to the contrary. A warning should be given where a statement in interview by one co-accused is admitted against the other, both because the maker had his or her own interest to serve and because the accused against whom the statement was made was not present and was not in a position to challenge it at the time (*Crown Court Compendium* (July 2020), ch. 14-15). In *Nguyen* [2020] EWCA Crim 140, the interview of co-defendant D2 as evidence against D1 was admitted. The Court of Appeal rejected an argument that the application should have been made at the outset of the trial. The Court in *Y* had expressly recognised that where the maker of the statement gave evidence and was cross-examined about it, an application might subsequently be made to admit the previous statement under s. 114(1)(d) even though it was already before the jury. D2 had substantially changed his account when giving evidence, retracting statements at interview that would have been admissible against D1 had D2 instead affirmed them. The Court noted that the correct time to make the application would have been at the end of the prosecution's cross-examination of D2, or at the very least the prosecution should have warned D1's counsel at that stage that an application was likely to be made. Evidence may have been too readily admissible in *Seton* [2010] EWCA Crim 450, where the defence was that the murder with which D was charged was committed by P, and the statement of P in a recorded telephone call made from prison in which he expressed his indignation at the assertion was admitted in rebuttal. The Court of Appeal accepted that no attempt had been made to procure the attendance of P, but concluded that, in the light of P's refusal to co-operate with the authorities, it would have been a 'fruitless exercise'. D's assertion against P was made very late in the day, and the Court's inference that this was a deliberate ploy may have coloured the decision. In *Seton v UK* [2016] ECHR 318, the ECtHR accepted that the evidence of P did not render the trial of D unfair. However the Court drew attention to the fact that it could not be said that all reasonable efforts had been made to secure the attendance of P. In *Sliogeris* [2015] EWCA Crim 22, the trial judge made an error when considering the admissibility of an out-of-court statement made by co-accused D2, blaming co-accused D1 for the murder of V. The statement was sought to be put in evidence by co-accused D3, whose defence was that D1 alone had killed V. D2, who did not testify, had made the statement to witness M, and the judge, in applying the criteria in s. 114(2), ruled on the basis that the maker of the statement was M rather than D2. However, as the judge had also taken account of matters relevant to the credibility of the statement itself, his error did not affect the admissibility of the statement.

The reach of s. 114(1)(d) does not extend to the evidence of a witness who wishes to remain anonymous. In *Ford* [2010] EWCA Crim 2250, a note written by such a witness regarding the registration number of a getaway car was held inadmissible. The CAJA 2009, ss. 86 to 90 (see **D14.82** *et seq.*), provide the sole route to admissibility for anonymous witnesses, and that legislation makes no provision for the admissibility of hearsay. In *Hussain* [2019] EWCA Crim 2416, it was held that the trial judge had rightly excluded evidence that a person giving a false name and address had telephoned police with information that if true might have assisted the defence. The jury would have had no way of assessing the reliability of such a statement under the CJA 2003, s. 114(1)(d), and its admission would have undermined the integrity of the trial.

In *L* [2008] EWCA Crim 973, [2009] 1 WLR 626, the prosecution relied on the out-of-court statement of D's wife, who declined to give evidence on charges against him which included rape of their 20-year-old daughter (as to which she was not compellable). The Court of Appeal held that there was no absolute rule prohibiting the use of s. 114(1)(d), despite the 'paradox' that the evidence that she did not wish to give, and was legally excused from giving, was placed before the jury. The public interest was served by admitting the evidence, taking account of the course of conduct by D which included offences against the same daughter as a child. See also *Horsnell* [2012] EWCA Crim 227.

Section 114(1)(d) is most likely to be resorted to where evidence is otherwise unlikely to be **F17.40** admissible, but may also provide an alternative argument where it is not clearly so: see *Isichei* [2006] EWCA Crim 1815 (see **F16.20**) and *Xhabri* [2005] EWCA Crim 3135, [2006] 1 All ER 776, where some of the statements by the alleged victim of abduction were also capable of being received under other exceptions (e.g., the extended provision for the reception of evidence of recent complaint in s. 120: see **F6.32**). In the case of first-hand hearsay statements, however, the alternative of admitting the evidence under s. 114(1)(d) was accepted by the court. In *Bains* [2010] EWCA Crim 873, the messages received via mobile telephones in connection with alleged drug dealing were held to be hearsay by application of the decision in *Leonard* [2009] EWCA Crim 1251 (see **F16.19**), though the point was clearly regarded by the Court of Appeal as arguable. In recognising that it was in the interests of justice to admit the messages, the Court noted that, where messages of the kind that drug dealers might be expected to send or receive are in the hands of the prosecution, it is unrealistic to expect the prosecution to call the senders of the messages to prove that what they said was true. See also *Twist* [2011] EWCA Crim 1143, [2011] 3 All ER 1055 at **F16.17**. In the unusual case of *Turner* [2012] EWCA Crim 1786, [2013] 1 Cr App R 25 (327), it was held that s. 114(1)(d) might have been used to admit the evidence of a witness who was unable to testify to matters of a sexual nature owing to acute embarrassment. However, those matters were not in dispute (the issues at trial being consent and her age when the acts took place) and the trial judge was able to circumvent the difficulty by allowing the matters on which the witness was stuck to be put to her and adopted from her previous statement, thus leaving her available for cross-examination in a way that s. 114(1)(d) would not have done.

Section 114(1)(d) Benefiting Defence

F17.41 Section 114(1)(d) may benefit either prosecution or defence, but the question of which party stands to benefit is relevant to the application of the 'interests of justice' test (*Y* [2008] EWCA Crim 10, [2008] 1 Cr App R 34 (411)). A difficult defence case will be that of the third-party confession, which is otherwise inadmissible where the maker is available to be called as a witness but neither side chooses to do so (cf. *Blastland* [1986] AC 41). In the absence of evidence that the statement is unreliable, a difficult decision must be made balancing the probative value of the statement if true against the reason for not calling the maker. In *Finch* [2007] EWCA Crim 36, [2007] 1 WLR 1645, D1 sought to rely on a statement made as part of a confession by his erstwhile co-accused, D2, who subsequently pleaded guilty. The effect of the plea was that D2 became a compellable, albeit reluctant, witness for D1, and the trial judge's decision that the case was not within s. 114(1)(d) was upheld by the Court of Appeal. Whatever might be the case if D2 had been unavailable or had demonstrated good reason not to testify, it was said, 'it would not normally be in the interests of justice for evidence which the giver is unprepared to have tested to be put untested before the jury'. An alternative course would have been to invoke the hostile witness provisions of s. 119 (see **F6.47**). See also *Khan* [2009] EWCA Crim 86, in which the statement of a witness unwilling to testify for the defence was held to have been rightly rejected. In *Williams* [2014] EWCA Crim 1862, the defence succeeded in persuading the trial judge that a covert record of an admission by S, a third party, to the murder with which D was charged, was admissible in the interests of justice, although the statement was not used because there was no witness to speak to the authenticity of the recording or the circumstances in which it was made. In many cases, a third party confession will fall well short of meeting the conditions of admissibility in terms of reliability: see, e.g., *Holden* [2017] EWCA Crim 31, where the confession of M to the murder of which D had been convicted was made at a time when M was suffering from a psychotic condition triggered by drug misuse, and he retracted it after receiving treatment. For this and other reasons the Court of Appeal considered it to be demonstrably unreliable and incapable of belief. In *Hinds* [2017] EWCA Crim 464, D, charged with possession with intent to supply, laid the blame on C, who had run from the house where the drugs were found and had made a statement suggesting that he had run because he had 'stuff' on him. The decision of the trial judge to exclude the statement on grounds including the unreliability of C and the ambiguity of what he had meant was upheld by the Court of Appeal where it was also noted that there was a wealth of other evidence as to whether D or C was the dealer.

HEARSAY EXCEPTIONS: (3) PRESERVED COMMON LAW EXCEPTIONS

Admissibility of Public Documents at Common Law and under the CJA 2003

F17.42 **Public Documents** The CJA 2003, s. 118, makes express provision to save the common law regarding the issue of certain public documents and information.

Criminal Justice Act 2003, s. 118

(1) The following rules of law are preserved.

Public information etc

Any rule of law under which in criminal proceedings—

(a) published works dealing with matters of a public nature (such as histories, scientific works, dictionaries and maps) are admissible as evidence of facts of a public nature stated in them,

(b) public documents (such as public registers, and returns made under public authority with respect to matters of public interest) are admissible as evidence of facts stated in them,
(c) records (such as the records of certain courts, treaties, Crown grants, pardons and commissions) are admissible as evidence of facts stated in them, or
(d) evidence relating to a person's age or date or place of birth may be given by a person without personal knowledge of the matter.

...

A document compiled by a public officer acting under a public duty to inquire and report facts of public interest, which is maintained in order that interested members of the public may have access to the information contained in it, is admissible at common law by way of exception to the hearsay rule as evidence of the facts stated (*Sturla v Freccia* (1880) 5 App Cas 623). Thus, for example, registers of baptisms, marriages and funerals are public documents, as are surveys of Crown Lands, and university records may prove the granting of degrees (*Collins v Carnegie* (1834) 1 A & E 695). Foreign registers may be public documents if the relevant conditions are satisfied (*Lyell v Kennedy* (1889) 14 App Cas 437; *Sturla v Freccia*). See also the Evidence (Foreign Dominion and Colonial Documents) Act 1933, s. 1 of which confers a power to declare that certain foreign registers are public documents. **F17.43**

One reason for the rule is the presumption that entries in such documents made by public officers are to be relied upon (*Irish Society v Bishop of Derry* (1846) 12 Cl & F 641, per Parke B). However, it is also the case that the rule is based on necessity: were it not for the admissibility of public documents, many facts occurring in the distant past would be incapable of proof.

In modern times the importance of the common-law rule has been overshadowed by various statutes rendering particular documents admissible, and (more importantly) by the CJA 2003, s. 117 (see **F17.25**), under which virtually all of the documents which were receivable under the common-law rule, and many that were not, are admissible. In *West Midlands Probation Board v French* [2008] EWHC 2631 (Admin), [2009] 1 WLR 1715, it was held that, where a prisoner released on licence was charged with breach of conditions, a copy of the licence could be proved either as a public document under the CJA 2003, s. 118(1)(b), or under s. 117 (see **F17.25**) or under the Documentary Evidence Act 1868, s. 2 (see **F8.17**). It is not clear what hearsay purpose was served by proving the licence: see **F16.18**.

Public Duty The document must have been made in pursuance of what Lord Blackburn termed 'a judicial, or quasi-judicial, duty to inquire' (*Sturla v Freccia* (1880) 5 App Cas 623, at p. 643). The duty must be imposed by virtue of a public office: thus, parish registers of baptisms, marriages and burials are public documents, whereas similar records compiled by other religious groups such as the Quakers are not (*Re Woodward* [1913] 1 Ch 392). Older authority strongly supports the view that the document must be made by the very officer whose duty it is to inquire into the facts, and who would therefore have been satisfied of the truth of the facts stated (see, e.g., *Sturla v Freccia* and *Daniel v Wilkin* (1852) 7 Exch 429). However, in *Halpin* [1975] QB 907 it was held that the functions of inquirer and recorder could be divided, with the result that the statutory returns of a company kept in the Companies Register were admissible where it appeared that the officer making the return had a duty to inquire, and the Registrar of Companies had the duty to record the results of the inquiry. Geoffrey Lane LJ said (at p. 915): 'The common law should move with the times and should recognise the fact that the official charged with recording matters of public import can no longer in this highly complicated world... have personal knowledge of their accuracy'. The decision has been criticised on the grounds that the House of Lords in *Myers v DPP* [1965] AC 1001 prohibited further judicial extension of the rules admitting hearsay evidence, but, whatever the merits of the criticism, the evidence would now be admissible under the CJA 2003, s. 117 (see **F17.25**). **F17.44**

Where a record is kept by a public officer not for the benefit of others, but simply for personal use as a check, it is not a public document (*Merrick v Wakley* (1838) 8 A & E 170).

F17.45 **Public Matter** The subject-matter of the document need not concern the public as a whole. In *Sturla v Freccia* (1880) 5 App Cas 623, Lord Blackburn said (at p. 643):

> I do not think that 'public' . . . is to be taken in the sense of meaning the whole world. I think an entry in the books of a manor is public in the sense that it concerns all the people interested in the manor. And an entry probably in a corporation book concerning a corporate matter, or something in which all the corporation is concerned, would be 'public' within that sense.

Whether a document deals with a matter of public concern inevitably raises a question of degree, and entries in a corporation's book are not necessarily admissible, despite Lord Blackburn's dictum (see, e.g., *Hill v Manchester & Salford Waterworks Co.* (1833) 5 B & Ad 866). Documents which do not comply with this condition are likely to be admissible under the CJA 1988, s. 24.

F17.46 **Public Reference** Documents which are not maintained for the use of such members of the public as may need to refer to them are not admissible under this exception. In *Lilley v Pettit* [1946] KB 401, D was prosecuted for falsely stating that her husband was the father of her child. It was held that regimental records showing that the husband was a prisoner of war abroad when the child was conceived were inadmissible because they were not intended for the use of the public. See also *Ioannou v Demetriou* [1952] AC 84.

For the same reason, a record which is maintained for a temporary purpose cannot be received under this exception (*Mercer v Denne* [1905] 2 Ch 538; *Heyne v Fischel & Co.* (1913) 30 TLR 190), although there would be no such objection to its reception in evidence under the CJA 2003, s. 117.

F17.47 **Other Registers etc. Admissible by Statute** Some entries in registers are admissible as public documents (see **F17.42**). In many cases, however, statute makes express provision for the admissibility of particular registers. Detailed consideration of such provisions is beyond the scope of this work.

Note the provisions of the Births and Deaths Registration Act 1953, s. 34. See also the Non-Parochial Registers Act 1840, s. 6, under which certain records and registers deposited in the General Register Office in accordance with that Act are admissible, and the Births and Deaths Registration Act 1858.

An entry in a register showing that a person has died is admissible evidence of the fact and date of death, but not of the cause of death (*Bird v Keep* [1918] 2 KB 692). Where a birth certificate is relied upon to prove some fact contained in it, the evidence may be of no use unless it can be proved that the person named in it is the same individual with whom the court is concerned. This is difficult to establish without breaking the hearsay rule, for the person named cannot give evidence of that fact. A person who was present at the birth may establish identity (*Weaver* (1873) LR 2 CCR 85), though such proof may be hard to come by. It is not surprising that, in some cases, hearsay evidence has been admitted: see, e.g., *Bellis* (1911) 6 Cr App R 283, in which the court admitted evidence of inquiries made about the girl whose age was in issue, which had led the inquirer to be satisfied as to her identity.

Evidence of Reputation

F17.48 **Evidence of Matter Stated** The CJA 2003, s. 118(1), makes specific provision for saving the common-law rules admitting evidence of reputation to prove character, and the use of reputation or family tradition to prove or disprove pedigree, the existence of a marriage, any public or general right, or the existence of any person or thing. With the exception of the rules concerning character, which are dealt with at **F14.30**, such evidence is rarely resorted to at common law and is not dealt with in this work.

Note that the preservation of these exceptions in s. 118 operates only to the extent that the common law allows the court to treat such evidence as proving the matter concerned.

Statements Forming Part of *Res Gestae*

F17.49 The CJA 2003, s. 118(1), makes express provision for saving the common-law rules on *res gestae*.

Criminal Justice Act 2003, s. 118

(1) The following rules of law are preserved.

...

Res gestae

4. Any rule of law under which in criminal proceedings a statement is admissible as evidence of any matter stated if—
   (a) the statement was made by a person so emotionally overpowered by an event that the possibility of concoction or distortion can be disregarded,
   (b) the statement accompanied an act which can be properly evaluated as evidence only if considered in conjunction with the statement, or
   (c) the statement relates to a physical sensation or a mental state (such as intention or emotion).

The statements most commonly received as evidence under the *res gestae* exception are those referred to in (a) and (c). Statements accompanying relevant acts are rarely admitted in criminal cases; the exception is limited to cases where the words spoken are truly 'part and parcel' of an act such as identification (*Lynch* [2007] EWCA Crim 3035, [2008] 1 Cr App R 24 (337), explaining *McCay* [1990] 1 All ER 232). The treatment which follows is confined to the two more frequently occurring varieties of *res gestae*: statements made in response to overpowering events, and statements indicative of contemporaneous sensation or state of mind, including intention and emotion.

Res Gestae Statements in Response to Emotionally Overpowering Events

'*Res gestae*' admissibility depends on proof of what Lord Ackner in *Andrews* [1987] AC 281 called the 'close and intimate connection' between the exciting events in issue and the making of the statement, the theory being that the spontaneity of the utterance is some guarantee against concoction. *Andrews* clarified the law by approving the modern test for admissibility adopted by the Privy Council in *Ratten v The Queen* [1972] AC 378, an approach approved in *Mills v The Queen* [1995] 3 All ER 865. **F17.50**

In many of the older authorities, the exception was invoked in order to admit statements made by the deceased identifying the attacker in a prosecution for murder or manslaughter. Such statements now fall within the CJA 2003, s. 116 (see **F17.8**), so there is no need to incur the additional burden of proving that the utterance was excited. However the *res gestae* exception has enjoyed a renaissance in cases of violent assault where the complainant is reluctant to testify, raising concerns for the implications in relation to fair trial (see further **F17.55**).

In *Ratten v The Queen*, Lord Wilberforce described the rule under which spontaneous statements are admitted in the following way (at pp. 389–90): **F17.51**

> The test should be not the uncertain one, whether the making of the statement should be regarded as part of the event or transaction. This may often be difficult to show. But if the drama, leading up to the climax, has commenced and assumed such intensity and pressure that the utterance can safely be regarded as a true reflection of what was unrolling or actually happening, it ought to be received.

In *Andrews*, D was charged with the murder by stabbing of V, who was attacked by two men in his own home. Within minutes neighbours called the police, who arrived promptly, whereupon V made a statement identifying his attackers. The trial judge admitted the statement and, in a ruling regarded as 'impeccable' both by the Court of Appeal and the House of Lords, he held that there was no possibility in the circumstances of concoction or fabrication of the identification, and that the injuries sustained by V were of such a nature as to drive out any possibility of his being actuated by malice. He also took account of the fact that V correctly identified the other attacker as O, who had subsequently pleaded guilty to manslaughter. Lord Ackner summarised the position which confronts a trial judge when faced in a criminal case with an **F17.52** application under the *res gestae* doctrine to admit evidence of statements, with a view to establishing the truth of some fact thus narrated. He said (at pp. 300–1):

1. The primary question which the judge must ask himself is — can the possibility of concoction or distortion be disregarded?
2. To answer that question the judge must first consider the circumstances in which the particular statement was made, in order to satisfy himself that the event was so unusual or startling or dramatic as to dominate the thoughts of the victim, so that his utterance was an instinctive reaction to that event, thus giving no real opportunity for reasoned reflection. In such a situation the judge would be entitled to conclude that the involvement or the pressure of the event would exclude the possibility of concoction or distortion, providing that the statement was made in conditions of approximate but not exact contemporaneity.
3. In order for the statement to be sufficiently 'spontaneous' it must be so closely associated with the event which has excited the statement, that it can be fairly stated that the mind of the declarant was still dominated by the event. Thus the judge must be satisfied that the event which provided the trigger mechanism for the statement, was still operative. The fact that the statement was made in answer to a question is but one factor to consider under this heading.
4. Quite apart from the time factor, there may be special features in the case, which relate to the possibility of concoction or distortion. In the instant appeal the defence relied on evidence to support the contention that the deceased had a motive of his own to fabricate or concoct, namely, a malice which resided in him against O'Neill and the appellant because, so he believed, O'Neill had attacked and damaged his house and was accompanied by the appellant, who ran away on a previous occasion. The judge must be satisfied that the circumstances were such that having regard to the special feature of malice, there was no possibility of any concoction or distortion to the advantage of the maker or the disadvantage of the accused.
5. As to the possibility of error in the facts narrated in the statement, if only the ordinary fallibility of human recollection is relied upon, this goes to the weight to be attached to and not the admissibility of the statement and is therefore a matter for the jury. However, here again there may be special features that may give rise to the possibility of error. In the instant case there was evidence that the deceased had drunk to excess, well over double the permitted limit for driving a motor car. Another example would be where the identification was made in circumstances of particular difficulty or where the declarant suffered from defective eyesight. In such circumstances the trial judge must consider whether he can exclude the possibility of error.

Some of the difficulties surrounding identification referred to by Lord Ackner arose and were considered in *Turnbull* (1984) 80 Cr App R 104 (see F17.57).

It appears from *Brown (Nico)* [2019] EWCA Crim 1143 that an admissible *res gestae* statement may be derived from the accounts of two eye-witnesses, one (who later gave evidence) making an emergency call having witnessed a stabbing, in which she read a car registration number written down by the other (who was unable to be traced after the incident). Both witnesses were reacting spontaneously to the same shocking event.

F17.53 **Possibility of Error** Prior to the decision in *Andrews*, it had been held, in *Nye* (1977) 66 Cr App R 252, that the possibility of error by the maker of the statement was an 'additional factor to be taken into consideration' when determining admissibility. It is now clear from the extract from the speech of Lord Ackner in *Andrews* set out above, that the risk of error bears on the question of admissibility only in cases having 'special features', e.g., an identification in difficult circumstances or by a person with defective eyesight, or by someone who had been drinking. In *Nye*, one L was driving his car when it was struck from behind by another vehicle in which the accused, D1 and D2, were travelling. One of the accused then got out and punched L in the face, while the other tried to put a stop to the assault. Shortly afterwards, when the police arrived, L spontaneously identified D2 as the man who had hit him. It was argued that L might have made a mistake as to which of the accused had attacked him. On these facts the Court of Appeal considered that there was no chance of an error, stressing in particular that: 'anyone who has been assaulted usually has good reason for remembering what his assailant's face looks like'. It is therefore unlikely that, applying the test in *Andrews*, special circumstances such as the great stress immediately after a motor accident, will be held to affect the admissibility of evidence.

The fact that the maker of the statement had been drinking, though capable of being a 'special feature', does not necessarily lead to exclusion. In *Andrews* the deceased had 'drunk to excess', and in *Edwards* [1992] Crim LR 576, the Divisional Court held that a spontaneous allegation of theft of a wallet made against D by A, who was drunk, was admissible.

The possibility of error or concoction on the part of the witness recounting the statement, as opposed to the maker of the statement, is not part of the test for admissibility, though the discretion to exclude such evidence (using the PACE 1984, s. 78) could be brought to bear in an appropriate case (*Saunders* [2012] EWCA Crim 1185).

Offence Must Generate Statement The event which generates the statement admitted under the rule stated above must be the commission of the offence in question. This is implicit in both *Ratten v The Queen* and *Andrews*, and is expressly stated by Lord Normand in *Teper v The Queen* [1952] AC 480, who said (at p. 488): 'for identification purposes in a criminal trial the event with which the words sought to be proved must be so connected as to form part of the *res gestae*, is the commission of the crime itself, the throwing of the stone, the striking of the blow, the setting fire to the building or whatever the criminal act might be'. A *res gestae* statement will typically have been made by the victim of the offence, or a bystander, but may also, if the conditions of admissibility are satisfied, be made by the accused (*Glover* [1991] Crim LR 48). F17.54

Statement Not to be Used as Substitute for Available Witness In *Andrews* [1987] AC 281, Lord Ackner observed (at p. 302): F17.55

> I would, however, strongly deprecate any attempt in criminal prosecutions to use the doctrine as a device to avoid calling, where he is available, the maker of the statement. Thus to deprive the defence of the opportunity to cross-examine him, would not be consistent with the fundamental duty of the prosecution to place all the relevant material facts before the court, so as to ensure that justice is done.

In *A-G's Ref (No. 1 of 2003)* [2003] EWCA Crim 1286, [2003] 2 Cr App R 29 (453), the Court observed that *Andrews* was not authority for the proposition that the *res gestae* exception was to be disapplied if better evidence was available. In that case, the prosecution had used the exception, not as a device to avoid calling the victim of an assault to give evidence against the accused, her son, but because she had later made a formal statement claiming to have sustained the injuries accidentally, which the prosecution believed to be untrue. Nevertheless it was held that the trial judge's decision to exclude the *res gestae* statement could be supported on the basis that it was unfair to admit it when it could not be the subject of cross-examination (applying the PACE 1984, s. 78). The prosecution should have been prepared to tender the mother as a witness: it was not an adequate response that the defence might have called her. It does not follow from this rule that the *res gestae* exception has no application where the witness gives evidence. In *Shickle* (30 July 1997 unreported), D was charged with murder and evidence was given by her teenage son, A, who had witnessed the event. It was held that A's evidence was properly supplemented by spontaneous statements he made at the time, such as 'Mummy's putting needles in the old boy' and 'Hurry up, we've got to stop Mummy'. The Court could find no reason of principle why the evidence should be withheld when the declarant is available. It was further held that the statement, when admitted, goes not only to the truth of the matter but to the consistency of the maker, on the basis that the greater purpose includes the lesser. It is submitted that the Court's approach is entirely correct.

***Res gestae* and Domestic Abuse Cases** *A-G's Ref (No. 1 of 2003)* [2003] EWCA Crim 1286, [2003] 2 Cr App R 29 (453) was considered in *Barnaby v DPP* [2015] EWHC 232 (Admin). Statements made by the complainant during phone calls to the emergency services in which she said of D, her boyfriend, 'I'm so scared because he's just strangled me' were held admissible as part of the *res gestae*, together with statements made some six minutes later in conversation with the police officers who responded to the call and who testified to her fear and their observation of her recent injuries. The complainant was available to give evidence at trial, but was F17.56

not called. Rejecting a submission that the statements should have been tendered under the CJA 2003, s. 114(1)(d) (see **F17.34**), so as to allow for a proper consideration, *inter alia*, of the reliability of the complainant and the reasons for not calling her, the Court of Appeal noted that this was a case where the prosecution were aware from the outset that the complainant was afraid of further violence from D. Fulford LJ commented: 'this was not a situation in which the prosecution was seeking to resort to unfair tactics in order to avoid introducing evidence that was potentially inconsistent with the case against the defendant, or because it simply anticipated that there was a risk the witness might give an untruthful account'. The proper vehicle to vindicate the defence concerns would have been an application at trial to exclude the evidence under the PACE 1984, s. 78, but no such application was made. A similar conclusion was reached in *Ibrahim v CPS* [2016] EWHC 1750 (Admin), where the rule laid down in *A-G's Ref (No. 1 of 2003)* was said to be inapplicable to the situation where a victim of domestic violence is in fear of a risk of harm following co-operation with the police. In that case the evidence was received under the *res gestae*, although the specific 'fear' exception in the CJA 2003, s. 116 (see **F17.17**), might also have been deployed. Under that exception, the court is bound to consider whether special measures might have been adopted that would have enabled the fearful witness to come to court. In *Morgan v DPP* [2016] EWHC 3414 (Admin), the question of special measures was held not to be of great significance where the application is made under the *res gestae* exception. In that case V, the alleged victim of domestic violence, was unwilling to attend the trial to give evidence, on the ground that she did not wish to relive the events in issue. The evidence admitted consisted of V's 999 call when reporting the incident, and the footage from the bodycam of the officer who attended shortly thereafter, which included V's account of what had happened. The Divisional Court also observed that special measures would not have countered V's fear of reliving the experience. In *Barnaby v DPP*, *Ibrahim v CPS* and *Morgan v DPP* the courts can be seen to be endorsing the proposition that the prosecutor was entitled to have appropriate regard for the well-being of a witness in the domestic violence context. But in cases where the complainant fails to testify through fear, it is important that the *res gestae* exception does not provide a way round the considerations laid down in s. 116(2)(e) (see **F17.17**), and the concern expressed in *Riat* [2012] EWCA Crim 1509, [2013] 1 All ER 349 about the importance of ensuring that witnesses attend court wherever possible. Where there are other reasons for the witness's reluctance, such as a desire to reconcile with the accused, there may be an equally difficult balance to be struck between respecting the complainant's decision and the public interest in basing a prosecution on earlier *res gestae* statements. In *Wills v CPS* [2016] EWHC 3779 (Admin), where the complainant unexpectedly failed to turn up to give evidence, it was said to be inappropriate for the magistrates to proceed to a consideration of *res gestae* without first determining the reasons for non-attendance. If fear was involved, consideration could be given to means for dispelling it. Whether the witness was fearful or not, the reasons for non-attendance were relevant to the consideration of whether the court should exercise its discretion under s. 78 of the PACE 1984 to receive the evidence. In *Speed* [2017] EWCA Crim 1908 and in *McGuinness v Northern Ireland Public Prosecution Service* [2017] NICA 30 the Court of Appeal and the Court of Appeal for Northern Ireland stressed that the criteria for applying the 'interests of justice' exception in s. 114(1)(d) (see **F17.34**) are likely to be of help when exercising the discretion in cases involving *res gestae* statements. It should therefore be possible to ensure that the common-law *res gestae* exception does not produce results that appear to be at odds with either the provisions for fearful witnesses (which apply similar criteria) or those for the interests of justice exception.

F17.57 **Illustrations of Application of the Rule** In *Turnbull* (1984) 80 Cr App R 104, a man who had been mortally wounded staggered into a public house. In the minutes before an ambulance arrived, and in the ambulance on the way to hospital, various witnesses thought that they heard the victim state, in answer to the question who had stabbed him, that it was 'Ronnie Tommo'. The deceased had a strong Scottish accent and the prosecution case was that he in fact said 'Turnbull'. The statements were admitted, and it was held to be irrelevant that the deceased went on to mutter other words which the witnesses were unable to understand. In *O'Shea* (24 July 1986 unreported), which was considered in *Andrews* [1987] AC 281, the elderly occupier of a second-floor flat into which D was trying to break, slipped while trying to escape through a window and sustained injuries which eventually resulted in his death. He was found lying where he had fallen an hour or so after the incident, and the statement which he then made, in which he stated the reason for his injuries, was admitted in evidence. See also *Ibrahim v CPS* [2016] EWHC 1750 (Admin) and *Morgan v DPP* [2016] EWHC 3414 (Admin) (see **F17.56**), in which V's injuries were sustained some 90 minutes (*Ibrahim*) and an hour (*Morgan*) before the emergency services were summoned, and the evidence was admitted. By contrast, in *Newport* [1998] Crim LR 581, a telephone call made by D's wife 20 minutes before he inflicted fatal injuries on her, in which she arranged to take sanctuary in a friend's house if she had to flee in a hurry, was held to have been wrongly admitted. On the facts there was an insufficient connection between the incident and the wife's request: the call was not a spontaneous and unconsidered reaction to an immediately impending emergency.

The theory behind the *res gestae* rule, that spontaneity is some guarantee against concoction, 'does not sit well' with the case where the utterance is that of a child who is too young to be aware of the significance of the events narrated. In *QD* [2019] NICA 7, the speaker was a child of three who narrated an act of masturbation by the accused. Far from being startled by events, the child was happily playing at the time, and there was no evidence that his thoughts were 'dominated' by events in the required sense. (The statement was admitted instead under the 'interests of justice' exception: see **F17.34**).

In *Tobi v Nicholas* [1988] RTR 343, a collision occurred between a car and a stationary motor coach. Some 20 minutes later the driver of the coach, who had summoned the police, identified D as the driver of the car involved. The coach driver was not called to give evidence at the trial, and the Divisional Court held, applying *Andrews* [1987] AC 281, that there were three reasons why his statement should not have been admitted as part of the *res gestae*: **F17.58**

(1) The event which had occurred was not so unusual or dramatic as to dominate the thoughts of the victim. 'Of course anybody whose vehicle has been damaged is annoyed about it, but there is a world of difference between such an unfortunately commonplace situation and the thoughts of somebody who has been assaulted and stabbed' (per Glidewell LJ, at p. 356).
(2) The statement was not sufficiently contemporaneous with the event.
(3) The *res gestae* doctrine should not be used as a device to avoid calling the maker of the statement where available, as the coach driver was, to give evidence.

Use of Statement Itself to Determine Admissibility In *Ratten v The Queen* [1972] AC 378, Lord Wilberforce said (at p. 391) that in principle it would not be right for the involvement of the speaker in the pressure of the drama surrounding the event to be proved only by the statement itself, 'otherwise the statement would be lifting itself into the area of admissibility'. However, it was difficult to imagine a case where there was no other evidence to connect the speaker to the event, and it would not be wrong in principle for the judge to take the statement into account, together with other things, in reaching a decision. **F17.59**

Direction to Jury In *Andrews* [1987] AC 281, Lord Ackner said that where a 'spontaneous' statement has been admitted in evidence as part of the *res gestae*, the judge must make it clear to the jury: **F17.60**

(a) that it is for them to decide what was said and to be sure that the witnesses were not mistaken in what they believed had been said to them;
(b) that 'they must be satisfied that the declarant did not concoct or distort to his advantage or to the disadvantage of the accused the statement relied upon and where there is material to raise the issue, that he was not activated by any malice or ill-will' (at p. 302);
(c) where there are special features that bear on the possibility of mistake, then the jury's attention must be invited to those matters.

In *Mills v The Queen* [1995] 3 All ER 865, the Privy Council rejected an argument that a specific direction must always be given as to the risk of mistaken identification by a dying man in a *res gestae* statement. The jury in that case had been adequately directed about the risks of mistaken identification in relation to the evidence of other witnesses, and fairness did not require a repetition.

Res Gestae Statements of Contemporaneous Bodily or Mental Feelings

F17.61 The statements of a person relating contemporaneous bodily feelings are admissible to prove the feelings, but not their cause. Thus, in *Nicholas* (1846) 2 Car & Kir 246, Pollock CB said (at p. 248):

> If a man says to his surgeon, 'I have a pain in the head', or in such a part of the body, that is evidence; but, if he says to his surgeon, 'I have a wound'; and was to add, 'I met John Thomas, who had a sword, and ran me through the body with it', that would be no evidence against John Thomas.

Similarly, in *Gloster* (1888) 16 Cox CC 471, statements by a woman who was dying from the effects of an illegal operation, naming the person responsible for her bodily condition, were held inadmissible under this exception. Charles J held (at p. 473) that 'the statements must be confined to contemporaneous symptoms, and nothing in the nature of a narrative is admissible as to who caused them, or how they were caused'. *Gloster* was followed in *Thomson* [1912] 3 KB 19, in which the statements of a woman who had recently suffered a miscarriage and who claimed to have operated upon herself were excluded.

F17.62 What is contemporaneous is a question of fact. In *Black* (1922) 16 Cr App R 118, D was convicted of the murder by poisoning of his wife. It was held on appeal that her descriptions of symptoms she had suffered after taking medicine given to her by D were admissible only because they were made in D's presence in such a way as to demand an answer from him. (See, as to statements made in the presence of the accused, **F18.99** ***et seq.***) Had the statements been made behind his back it would, per Avory J, have required 'grave consideration whether they could have been admitted', because they concerned her past, rather than her contemporaneous, feelings. However, Salter J in the course of argument said (at p. 119):

> ...'contemporaneous' cannot be confined to feelings experienced at the actual moment when the patient is speaking; it must include such a statement as 'Yesterday I had a pain after meals'.

In the civil case of *Aveson v Lord Kinnaird* (1805) 6 East 188, statements made by a woman concerning symptoms from which she claimed to have been suffering for some time were admitted, not only to establish her feelings when the statement was made, but also to establish that she had had the same symptoms when seen by a doctor some days previously.

Where a doctor gives expert evidence as to the condition of a patient, evidence of past symptoms as they have been narrated to the doctor may not be given in order to prove that the symptoms existed, although it may be permissible to state what the doctor was told simply in order to explain the conclusion arrived at. If the existence of past symptoms is in issue, they must be proved by admissible evidence (*Bradshaw* (1985) 82 Cr App R 79).

F17.63 In some cases statements indicating contemporaneous feelings may be admissible as original evidence. In *Conde* (1867) 10 Cox CC 547, evidence was admitted that a child who died from starvation had begged a neighbour to give him bread. Of this request Channell B is reported as having said that 'it was not so much a statement as an act. A complaint of hunger was an act; although the particulars of the statement might not be receivable, the fact of the complaint was clearly so.' It is also permissible to prove a contemporaneous statement in which the maker claims to be in a particular mental state, such as fear. In *Vincent* (1840) 9 C & P 275, a policeman was allowed to prove statements made by bystanders at a public meeting who claimed that they were frightened by what took place. In *Edwards* (1872) 12 Cox CC 230, D was charged with the murder of his wife, V, and a neighbour testified that a week before V died she came to the neighbour's house bearing a carving knife and a large axe. Quain J allowed the neighbour to state that V had asked her to take care of the implements as 'my husband always threatens me with these and when they're out of the way I feel safer'. In the light of the authorities stated above, it would seem that V's statement should not have been admitted to prove the cause of her fear, but only (if it were relevant to do so) that she was in a state of trepidation when delivering the weapons. Evidence of state of mind may also be used to negate inferences which might otherwise be drawn from conduct. In *Gilfoyle* [1996] 1 Cr App R 302, V died by hanging, leaving suicide notes. Evidence that she was not in a suicidal frame of mind was admissible in order to support the prosecution's contention that V had been tricked by her killer into writing the notes.

In recent times there has been a division of opinion as to whether a statement revealing the maker's state of mind is admissible as non-hearsay evidence from which the state of mind may be inferred (*Blastland* [1986] AC 41; *Kearley* [1992] 2 AC 228) or hearsay admissible under an exception to the rule (*Neill v North Antrim Magistrates' Court* [1992] 4 All ER 846; *Gilfoyle*). Both views are tenable although the preponderance of modern authority favours the former.

Statements of Present Intention

In various criminal cases, statements indicating the present intention of the speaker have been received in evidence, apparently by way of exception to the hearsay rule. In *Buckley* (1873) 13 Cox CC 293, an inspector of police was permitted to narrate a statement made to him by G, a constable, who said that he intended to go that evening to keep watch on D, whom he suspected of theft. G was later found stabbed to death at some distance from D's cottage, and the statement was relied upon as circumstantial evidence that G had carried out his intention, with fatal consequences. No reason was given for the decision to admit the statement, and it may be that the case is best viewed as involving a declaration made by the deceased G in the course of his duty (a common-law exception not preserved by the CJA 2003, s. 118). **F17.64**

In *Moghal* (1977) 65 Cr App R 56, D was charged with the murder of V, and his defence was that the crime was committed by S. It was held that a statement made by S six months before, in which S declared her intention to murder V, was admissible. However, statements which S made to the police after V had been killed, in which she described her state of mind and feelings before and at the time of the killing, were rejected as inadmissible hearsay on the ground that 'the condition precedent to the admissibility of such statements is that they should relate to the maker's contemporaneous state of mind or emotion'. What is contemporaneous was said to be a question of degree, but what was said in the course of police investigations occurred far too long after the event to be admitted. Where non-contemporaneous declarations are self-serving, there is an additional reason for excluding them, for such declarations might otherwise be used to construct a fraudulent defence (*Petcherini* (1855) 7 Cox CC 79).

Moghal was doubted by the House of Lords in *Blastland* [1986] AC 41, but only on the ground that the isolated declaration of intention made six months before the murder was insufficiently relevant to be admitted. See also *Wainwright* (1875) 13 Cox CC 171, in which D was charged with the murder of a girl, and the prosecution were not allowed to prove that V had announced her intention of going to D's premises on the night she died. Cockburn CJ said that the girl's statement was 'only a statement of intention which might or might not be carried out'.

The existence of a hearsay exception for statements of intention seems to have been overlooked in *Thomson* [1912] 3 KB 19, in which the statement of a woman made before she suffered a miscarriage, and in which she declared her intention to operate upon herself, was rejected as inadmissible hearsay. The statement was said not to form part of the *res gestae*, in the sense that it was not a spontaneous statement connected with the operation itself. The **F17.65** possibility that it might be admissible as a declaration of intention does not appear to have been canvassed.

In *Callender* [1998] Crim LR 337, the Court of Appeal refused to admit statements made by D two weeks before his arrest for conspiring to commit arson, in which he told an acquaintance that his intention was limited to making dummy devices, resembling explosives, which could be used to attract publicity to the cause of animal rights without actually causing damage to property. This mirrored his defence at trial and, if true, was an answer to the charge. D did not give evidence, however, and the Court appears to have been concerned that his statement, if admitted, would have permitted D to raise a reasonable doubt about the prosecution case in a manner contrary to the principles of the CJPO 1994, s. 35 (see **F20.42**). But the adverse inferences which the statute permits if an accused fails to testify could still be drawn where the accused's *res gestae* statement is admissible. The reason given for rejection was that the *res gestae* rule was in fact a single principle governed by the decisions in *Andrews* [1987] AC 281 and *Ratten v The Queen* [1972] AC 378 (see **F17.50**). D's statement was thus ruled inadmissible because it was not made in circumstances whereby the possibility of concoction or distortion could be disregarded. It is submitted that this is not the case. The true reason for admitting evidence of a statement revealing the maker's intention or other state of mind, or bodily feelings, is the difficulty of proving the matter by other means. Although D's statement was self-serving, and there was a possibility that he was setting up a defence for himself, it was made when he had no inkling that he was about to be arrested, and might be thought to have had some probative value in relation to his state of mind at the relevant time. Whether it was concocted or not should, under this exception, have been a question for the jury.

Common-law Confessions and Admissions

F17.66 The CJA 2003, s. 118(1), makes express provision for saving the common-law rules on confessions and admissions.

Criminal Justice Act 2003, s. 118

Preservation of certain common law categories of admissibility

(1) The following rules of law are preserved.

...

Confessions etc

5. Any rule of law relating to the admissibility of confessions or mixed statements in criminal proceedings.

Admissions by agents etc

6. Any rule of law under which in criminal proceedings—
   (a) an admission made by an agent of a defendant is admissible against the defendant as evidence of any matter stated, or
   (b) a statement made by a person to whom a defendant refers a person for information is admissible against the defendant as evidence of any matter stated.

The common law has little part to play in regulating the admissibility of an accused's confession now the CJA 2003 has taken effect. Confessions tendered by the prosecution are currently governed by the PACE 1984, s. 76 (see **F18**). The CJA 2003, s. 128, extends the coverage of s. 76 to confessions adduced by a co-accused (see **F18.27**). The most important of the vestigial rules retained by para. 5 of s. 118(1) is the implied acceptance by the accused of a statement made in his or her presence (see **F18.99**), which may operate even where the accused is silent in the face of an accusation (see **F20.3**). The latter aspect of the rule was specifically preserved by the CJPO 1994, s. 34(5), and remains of some practical importance despite the statutory inroads on the right to silence made by that Act. To the extent that the admissibility of the self-serving parts of a mixed statement depends on factors not dealt with in the PACE 1984, s. 76, the common law is also preserved by s. 118(1) (see **F18.93**).

Admissions by Agents and Referees

F17.67 An admission made by the agent of an accused person, such as a legal adviser, may be admissible against the accused (*Turner* (1975) 61 Cr App R 67). Although at first sight such an admission may appear to be a confession, and thus to be governed by the rules of admissibility in the PACE 1984, s. 76 (see **F18**), it is submitted that this is not the case, for the section applies only to a confession made 'by an accused person', and, by s. 82(1), 'confession' includes any statement adverse to 'the person who made it'. It would seem to follow that vicarious admissions continue to be governed by common-law principles.

A statement made by an agent is admissible against the accused only where it is shown that the statement was made within the scope of the agent's authority. Agency may be inferred from the circumstances: thus, in *Turner* (1975) 61 Cr App R 67, it was held that it is permissible to infer from the fact that a barrister makes an admission in court on behalf of and in the presence of his or her client, that the barrister was authorised to make it. The strength of the inference depends on the circumstances, however, and in *Evans* [1981] Crim LR 699, it was held that agency was not to be inferred simply from the fact that the admission was made by D's solicitor's clerk.

The strict application of the rule of admissibility may work injustice where there is an issue as to whether the accused intended to make the admission put forward, as in *Turner* where counsel later gave evidence that he had exceeded his authority in doing so. The discretion available to the court using the PACE 1984, s. 78 should be considered in such cases. The completion by advocates of pre-trial documentation intended to assist in case management raises particularly sensitive issues. In *R (Firth) v Epping Justices* [2011] EWHC 388 (Admin), [2011] 1 Cr App R 32 (395), the strict rule was applied in pre-trial proceedings to a statement made in what was then a Case Progression Form. As a consequence of *Firth*, defence advocates became cautious about providing information for case management purposes which might then be used as an admission, or in cross-examination of the client. This worked against the 'cards on the table' approach on which good case management is based. In *Newell* [2012] EWCA Crim 650, [2012] 1 WLR 3142, the Court of Appeal, taking account of guidance issued to prosecutors following *Firth*, held that an advocate completing a PCMH form should be free to help the court with the management of the case by setting out relevant information without the risk of that information being used as a statement admissible against the accused. Provided therefore that the case is conducted in accordance with the letter and spirit of the CrimPR, such information should in the exercise of the court's discretion under s. 78 not be admitted as a statement that can be used against an accused. Only very rarely would it be appropriate not to exercise the discretion. The same rule applies in summary proceedings, except where the information is specifically provided under the part of the relevant documentation relating expressly to admissions or to the acknowledgement that certain matters are not in issue; these will continue to be admissible at trial. *Newell* was applied in *Valiati* [2018] EWHC 2908 (Admin), [2019] 1 Cr App R 17 (216), in which magistrates had wrongly relied on information supplied by the defence in a PET form as though it were evidence in the case. The information might have been presented as an admission by the defence, in reliance on the CJA 2003, s. 118, but this course of action should be adopted only where the defence have not acted in accordance with the letter and spirit of the CrimPR, typically by seeking to ambush the prosecution with a defence which has not been indicated in the PET.

F17.68 Evidence of agency must, of course, be admissible in its own right. In *Evans*, statements made by the solicitor's clerk indicating that he was acting with D's authority were inadmissible to prove agency, being hearsay. *Evans* was distinguished in *Ungvari* [2003] EWCA Crim 2346, where there was ample evidence in the history of trading between two companies to support the inference that the appellant's sister was acting as his agent.

F17.69 A statement made by a person to whom the accused refers another for information on a particular matter may be evidence against the accused. Thus, in *Williams v Innes* (1808) 1 Camp 364, an executor referred the plaintiff to a particular individual for information pertaining to the assets of the estate, and it was held that what the referee said was admissible against the executor. Similarly, in *Mallory* (1884) 13 QBD 33, where D told a police officer that his wife would supply a list showing where certain items, suspected of being stolen, were purchased, the list handed over by the wife in D's presence was admissible against him. Coleridge CJ refrained from stating what the outcome would have been had D been absent when the list was handed over, but it is submitted that it would have made no difference.

Statements in Furtherance of Common Enterprise

F17.70 The CJA 2003, s. 118(1), makes express provision for saving the common-law rules on statements in furtherance of a common enterprise.

Criminal Justice Act 2003, s. 118

(1) The following rules of law are preserved.

...

Common enterprise

7. Any rule of law under which in criminal proceedings a statement made by a party to a common enterprise is admissible against another party to the enterprise as evidence of any matter stated.

F17.71 **Scope of the Rule** The rule that the acts and statements of one party to a common purpose may be evidence against another is particularly associated with charges of conspiracy. However, it is not confined to such cases, and applies to other offences where complicity is alleged. Thus, in *Jessop* (1877) 16 Cox CC 204, for example, D was charged with the murder of V, with whom he had entered into a suicide pact to die by taking poison. The plan miscarried and D survived. Field J held that evidence of the purchase of poison by V, being an act done in furtherance of the common purpose, was admissible against D. Another illustration is *Jones* [1997] 2 Cr App R 119, in which it was held that the rule applied to a joint enterprise to evade the prohibition on the importation of drugs, despite the fact that no charge of conspiracy was brought.

In *A Ltd, X and Y* [2016] EWCA Crim 1469, [2017] 1 Cr App R 1 (1), the Court of Appeal cautioned against confusing the 'identification' principle (which is used to identify the directing mind and will of a corporate body: see **A6.2**) with the rules governing the admissibility of acts and declarations made by one co-conspirator in the absence of another. BK was a director of A Ltd who was not prosecuted because he was beyond the jurisdiction of the court. Evidence of his guilty acts and state of mind, however, clearly fell within the identification principle for the purposes of a prosecution of the company, and in that regard reference could be made to BK's diaries and notebook entries to prove his, and therefore the company's, state of mind. (Such documents would not have been admissible against other conspirators if tendered as hearsay under s. 118 as records of one conspirator for his or her own convenience, or forming narratives of past acts, are outwith the rule: see **F17.74**.) *A Ltd, X and Y* was applied in *Alstom Network Ltd* [2019] EWCA Crim 1318, [2019] 2 Cr App R 34 (417).

F17.72 The limits of the doctrine were considered in *Gray* [1995] 2 Cr App R 100. D and others were each convicted of offences relating to insider dealing. Although there was alleged to be a 'network' between them for the passing of information, each allegation related only to an offence committed by one of them alone. The prosecution case consisted mainly of telephone conversations between the defendants, and the judge told the jury that a statement made in the course of such a conversation, though a particular defendant was not party to it, could nevertheless be evidence against that defendant if there was a joint enterprise between them for the unlawful dissemination of 'inside' information and the statement was made in furtherance of that joint enterprise. The Court of Appeal was inclined to the view that this stated the principle too widely: the acts and declarations of a person engaged in a joint enterprise and made in pursuance of that enterprise might be admissible against another, but only where the evidence shows the complicity of that other in a common offence or series of offences. As none of the offences was alleged to have been committed jointly, the rule did not apply. If, contrary to that view, the principle could be stated in the wider form, the prosecution would have to make clear the limits of the alleged agreement in pursuit of which the specific offences were said to have been committed; as this had not been done the appeals were allowed. Thus it appears that the case for a wider principle could still be made. In *Murray* [1997] 2 Cr App R 136, the Court of Appeal adopted the interpretation of *Gray* in the 1996 edition of this work (which is the same as that set out above) and added that that case is authority primarily for the proposition that the common-law exception cannot be extended to cases where individual defendants are charged with a number of separate substantive offences and the terms of a common enterprise are not provided or are ill-defined. An argument, based on dicta in the case, that *Gray* in fact narrows the scope of the common-law exception was rejected. *Murray* was approved in *Williams* [2002] EWCA Crim 2208, where the true rule was considered to be that 'the acts and declarations by A in furtherance of a sufficiently defined common design are admissible to prove a substantive offence committed alone in pursuance of the same common design, by B'.

The rule permits the actions and declarations of one party, A, to be used in evidence against the other, B, and is thus an exception to the general rule that B is not to be prejudiced by the acts or statements of another, and an exception to the hearsay rule insofar as it may involve reliance on A's statements as evidence of their truth. In *Onyeabor* [2009] EWCA Crim 534, the Court of Appeal regarded as non-hearsay a statement by D's accomplice in furtherance of their joint enterprise, and stated that it was admissible under s. 118(1), rule 7. It is submitted, however, that recourse to s. 118 should not be had unless a hearsay exception is required. As an exception to the hearsay rule, the common enterprise rule defies classification, some writers regarding it as appertaining to the *res gestae*, others as based on implied agency, and others as an independent exception, the justification for which is that such evidence must be used if the 'secret' crime of conspiracy is ever to be proved at all. **F17.73**

In order for the act or statement of A to be admissible against B, the rule requires:

(1) that the act or statement of A must be in the course and furtherance of the common purpose; and
(2) that independent evidence be adduced of the existence of the conspiracy and the involvement in it of B.

Meaning of Course and Furtherance of Common Purpose In the leading case of *Blake* (1844) 6 QB 126, D1 and D2 were charged with conspiring to avoid payment of duty on imported goods. D1, in the course of his employment at the Customs House, certified that the amount of goods imported by D2 as an agent was less than was in fact the case. D2 then charged his principal duty on the full amount, recording the charge in his own day book, and split the proceeds with D1. It was held that the entry in D2's day book was admissible against D1, as being evidence of something done in the course of the transaction, but that the counterfoil of the cheque by which D1 received his share of the proceeds was not, for it was an act done after the common purpose was effected which had nothing to do with the carrying out of the conspiracy. It will be apparent from *Blake* that it may be difficult to distinguish precisely where a transaction begins and ends, and whether acts are done in furtherance of it or not. A clearer case of inadmissibility owing to the termination of the criminal purpose is that of the confession of one conspirator made after the point of apprehension, which is evidence only against the maker (see, e.g., *Walters* (1979) 69 Cr App R 115, at p. 120). A more obvious example of a statement which cannot be said to be in furtherance of any criminal purpose occurred in *Steward* [1963] Crim LR 697, where one conspirator simply recited to another the various acts of B which had been done in execution of the common purpose, and the statement was held inadmissible against B. See also *Hardy* (1794) 24 St Tr 199, in which a similar recital by a conspirator of his own past acts was held not to be in furtherance of the conspiracy. **F17.74**

In *Devonport* [1996] 1 Cr App R 221, a statement was admitted which may not, in the strict sense, have furthered the conspiracy. The court was concerned with a document drawn up by **F17.75**

D concerning the proposed division of spoils between himself and others involved. This was regarded by Judge J as a document in furtherance of the conspiracy, distinguishing *Blake* on the ground that the document was not a record of distribution after the conspiracy but an indication of the intended or prospective distribution of the proceeds of the conspiracy when it has been fulfilled. Even so, as there was no evidence that the document served any purpose other than D's own convenience, the decision seems to go further than previous authority. So also does *Ilyas* [1996] Crim LR 810, in which a diary was admitted which was a record of the receipt of stolen car parts by some of the parties to the conspiracy. Nothing was made of the argument that the document was a mere record of what had already occurred and not in furtherance of the enterprise. Latham J, however, asserted that it was 'a document created *in the course of, or furtherance*, of the conspiracy' (emphasis added). This would seem to be a new and alternative ground of admissibility, as a document such as the diary can be said to be created in the course of a conspiracy without being in any way in furtherance of it. It would seem that the rule is in the course of being broadened by the courts. See also *Reeves* [1999] 3 Arch News 2, in which an aide-memoire by one conspirator for his own assistance appears to have been regarded as potentially admissible against co-conspirators under this exception, and *Platten* [2006] EWCA Crim 140, where it was said that 'statements made during the conspiracy and as part of the conspiracy, because they are part of making the natural arrangements to carry out the conspiracy, will be admissible'. In *Platten*, the Court confined the exclusion of statements which are 'mere narrative' to statements made after the conspiracy is concluded. The Court endorsed the rule of thumb adopted by Kennedy LJ in *Barham* [1997] 2 Cr App R 119 of 'the enterprise in operation'. See also *King* [2012] EWCA Crim 805 (co-conspirator's description of accused as 'the hired muscle' was intended to keep the confidence of a prospective purchaser of drugs and was properly admitted).

Where the hearsay statements of co-conspirators in furtherance of the conspiracy implicate an accused, the trial judge must give a careful direction to the jury that the statements cannot be used to provide the link between that accused and the conspiracy (*Blake* (1993) 97 Cr App R 169).

F17.76 **Requirement of Independent Evidence of Common Purpose** In *Blake* (1844) 6 QB 126, a case involving conspiracy, Patteson J stated the principle to be that 'you must establish the fact of a conspiracy before you can make the act of one the act of all'. The absence of such independent evidence renders the statement alleged to have been made in furtherance of the conspiracy inadmissible, and it is not possible for the statement itself to provide the evidence of the existence of the conspiracy (see *Jenkins* [2002] EWCA Crim 2475, and commentary by Professor Sir John Smith). This does not mean that such evidence must be brought forward and accepted before the act or statement in question can be proved, for, 'from the nature of this charge [conspiracy] the evidence must necessarily grow up as it proceeds. The acts of the one party must be given in evidence and then the acts of the other, and it may then be shown that those acts fully prove a conspiracy between them' (*Murphy* (1837) 8 C & P 297, per Coleridge J at pp. 302–3). See also *Governor of Pentonville Prison, ex parte Osman* [1990] 3 All ER 701 in which Lloyd LJ said (at p. 316): 'there must always be some evidence other than the hearsay evidence of a fellow conspirator to prove that a particular defendant is party to a conspiracy. Provided there is some other evidence, it does not matter in what order the evidence is adduced.' The principle is thus one of conditional admissibility, in that if, after the evidence has been heard, it transpires that there is no independent evidence of common purpose, the act or statement of A will have to be excluded from the case against B (*Donat* (1985) 82 Cr App R 173). It is submitted that there is no difference in practice between this view and that expressed in *Whittaker* [1914] 3 KB 1283, in which it was said that the act or statement of A, though it may be proved as evidence against him, remains inadmissible against B until the necessary foundation is laid. Insofar as there is a difference, it is submitted that the correct practice is as stated in *Donat*.

F17.77 Failure by the prosecution to satisfy the requirement after evidence of a statement has been admitted *de bene esse* will require a careful direction to the jury, and may require the discharge of the jury and a retrial if the evidence admitted was prejudicial. Where evidence is admitted under the rule it is not necessary for the jury to be directed to convict only if they find evidence against B other than the statement of A. The judge must first be satisfied that such evidence exists: if it does, the jury are permitted to look at all the evidence in order to decide guilt (*Barham* [1997] 2 Cr App 119; *King* [2012] EWCA Crim 805). If, however, there is a danger that the jury will rely on the statement by A as primary evidence of B's involvement, 'sweeping away' the other evidence which has led the judge to admit the statement in the first place, the judge should direct the jury as to the shortcomings in the evidence of A, including (if such be the case) the absence of any opportunity to cross-examine A, and the absence of corroborative evidence (*Jones* [1997] 2 Cr App R 119; *Williams* [2002] EWCA Crim 2208). In a case where there was other evidence to connect the accused with the conspiracy, the Court of Appeal did not consider it fatal that the trial judge had failed to warn the jury of the need for caution in convicting on evidence of things said or done by others when the appellant was not present, though it would have been preferable so to warn them (*Sofroniou* [2009] EWCA Crim 1360).

Common-law Admissibility of Body of Expertise

The CJA 2003, s. 118(1), makes express provision for saving the common-law rules allowing an expert to draw on a relevant body of expertise. **F17.78**

Criminal Justice Act 2003, s. 118

(1) The following rules of law are preserved.

...

Expert evidence

8. Any rule of law under which in criminal proceedings an expert witness may draw on the body of expertise relevant to his field.

Technically speaking, where an expert draws on the work of others in order to form an opinion, an element of hearsay is necessarily involved. Whether this is objectionable or not depends on the nature of the work referred to. In *Abadom* [1983] 1 All ER 364 (see **F11.34**) it was accepted that 'the process of taking account of information stemming from the work of others in the same field is an essential ingredient of the nature of expert evidence', and as such is not subject to the hearsay rule. Where, however, an expert relies on the existence or non-existence of some fact which is basic to the question on which the expert is asked to give an opinion, that fact must be proved by admissible evidence. Paragraph 8 of s. 118(1) preserves the effect of *Abadom*.

The common-law rule was considered by the Privy Council in *Myers v The Queen* [2015] UKPC 40, [2016] AC 314. A police officer who had expertise in gang culture and had made a special study of the various gangs alleged to have been concerned in a series of shootings had given expert evidence relating to intra-gang loyalty with a view to demonstrating the motive of the accused. Having considered authorities, including *Abadom* and the decision of the Court of Criminal Appeal for South Australia in *Cluse* [2014] 120 SASR 268 (which also concerned evidence of gang culture), Lord Hughes said that it was clear that an expert witness was not immune from all inhibition on hearsay. In some cases, the dividing line was between evidence of opinion (which may be informed by hearsay) and specific evidence of observable fact, which must be proved in accordance with the normal rules of evidence. But, as Lord Hughes said (at [65]):

> ... experts often give evidence of observable fact and such evidence may legitimately be, and very often is, informed by the accumulated body of knowledge collected by others as well as by the witness' own experience.

After giving relevant examples, Lord Hughes continued (at [66]):

> The test of whether evidence based upon hearsay material can be given is better seen to be whether it ceases to be the expounding of general study (whether by the witness or others) and becomes the assertion of a particular fact in issue in the case. The first is expert evidence, grounded on a body of

learning or study; the second is not, even if it may be given by someone who is also an expert. The line between the two is case-specific, but it will usually be possible to discern it.

See also CJA 2003, s. 127, at **F11.31** which erodes the second part of the rule in *Abadom* by permitting evidence to be given of the preparatory findings on which an expert's opinion is based without the need to call those who made the findings as witnesses in the case.

HEARSAY EXCEPTIONS: (4) OTHER STATUTORY EXCEPTIONS

Transcript Admissible at Retrial

F17.79 **Criminal Appeal Act 1968, sch. 2, para. 1**

(1) Evidence given at a retrial must be given orally if it was given orally at the original trial, unless—
  (a) all the parties to the retrial agree otherwise;
  (b) section 116 of the Criminal Justice Act 2003 applies (admissibility of hearsay evidence where a witness is unavailable); or
  (c) the witness is unavailable to give evidence, otherwise than as mentioned in subsection (2) of that section, and section 114(1)(d) of that Act applies (admission of hearsay evidence under residual discretion).

(2) Paragraph 5 of Schedule 3 to the Crime and Disorder Act 1998 (use of depositions) does not apply at a retrial to a deposition read as evidence at the original trial.

F17.80 The provisions of sch. 2 reaffirm and clarify a wider common-law rule: see *Thompson* [1982] QB 647, in which it was held that the transcript of evidence of a witness might be read out at a retrial upon proof that she was too ill to travel, notwithstanding that the retrial was not ordered by the Court of Appeal under the 1968 Act. Similarly, in *Hall* [1973] 1 QB 496, it was held that a transcript of evidence is admissible at common law at a retrial if the witness has since died, provided it is authenticated in appropriate manner, e.g., by calling the shorthand writer who took the original note.

The terms of the provision, as substituted by the CJA 2003, s. 131, bring the admissibility of evidence at retrial into line with the range of hearsay exceptions in the 2003 Act. In practical terms, the most important change wrought by s. 131 is the incorporation of the provisions of s. 114(1)(d) (see **F17.34**). See *Venn* [2009] EWCA Crim 2541, and *Lawrence* [2013] EWCA Crim 708, [2014] 1 Cr App R 5 (33), where it was also stressed that the unavailability of the absent witness must relate to the time at, or shortly before the point at which the evidence is required at the retrial.

Video Recordings, Depositions of Child or Young Person and Written Statements Admissible under the CJA 1967, s. 9

F17.81 For special measures for assisting witnesses, including children and intimidated witnesses, see **D14.26** *et seq*. For the admission of depositions made by a child or young person under the CYPA 1933, s. 43, see **D16.38**. For the admissibility of written statements under the CJA 1967, s. 9, see **D22.41**.

Statements Admissible under Miscellaneous Statutory Provisions

F17.82 Various statutes make provision for the admission of hearsay statements. The following are the most commonly invoked.

Under the CJA 1988, s. 30 (see **F11.51**), the report of an expert witness on matters of which the maker would have been competent to give oral evidence is admissible as evidence of the facts and opinions stated therein. This provision applies only to 'written' reports so that the admissibility of, say, a tape-recorded report may be in doubt. Under the CJA 1972, s. 46(1), written statements made in Scotland or Northern Ireland may be admitted as evidence in other criminal proceedings on the same terms as statements made in England and Wales.

Bankers' Books

The Bankers' Books Evidence Act 1879, s. 3, was designed to facilitate proof of bankers' records without bringing the original document to court. As the provision is confined to copies, nothing in s. 3 renders the original banker's book admissible: in most cases, however, the original would be admissible under the CJA 2003, s. 117, and a copy would be admissible by virtue of s. 133 of that Act. Before a copy can be given in evidence under s. 3 of the 1879 Act, s. 4 of that Act requires proof to be given that the banker's book was at the time of the relevant entry one of the ordinary books of the bank, that the entry was made in the usual and ordinary course of business, and that the book is in the custody or control of the bank. If the CJA 2003, s. 117, is relied upon, no such conditions need be satisfied. It should also be noted that the 1879 Act confines itself to the various books and records of a bank. In *Dadson* (1983) 77 Cr App R 91, which concerned events which occurred before the 1879 Act was amended to include records, it was held that a file of correspondence was inadmissible under s. 3 as not being a 'book'. The correspondence would now be admissible under the 1879 Act only if it is held to constitute a 'record', whereas the CJA 2003 imposes no such constraint. It was held in *Re Howglen Ltd* [2001] 1 All ER 376 that a 'record' for this purpose connoted a method by which a bank recorded day-to-day financial transactions: a record of notes of meetings could not be regarded as banker's books within the 1879 Act. A record of a meeting would now be admissible under s. 117 of the 2003 Act. **F17.83**

As to the practice surrounding inspection of bankers' books and their relationship to the best evidence rule, see generally **F8.35**.

HEARSAY EXCEPTIONS: (5) ADDITIONAL REQUIREMENTS FOR THE USE OF MULTIPLE HEARSAY

The CJA 2003, s. 121, stipulates that only limited use can be made of multiple hearsay. This appears to apply whether the hearsay in question is tendered under the new statutory exceptions contained in the Act itself, or under the preserved common-law exceptions, or under other statutory provisions, given that the new rule is negative in form and defines hearsay evidence in the broadest of terms. **F17.84**

Criminal Justice Act 2003, s. 121

(1) A hearsay statement is not admissible to prove the fact that an earlier hearsay statement was made unless—
  (a) either of the statements is admissible under section 117, 119 or 120,
  (b) all parties to the proceedings so agree, or
  (c) the court is satisfied that the value of the evidence in question, taking into account how reliable the statements appear to be, is so high that the interests of justice require the later statement to be admissible for that purpose.

(2) In this section 'hearsay statement' means a statement, not made in oral evidence, that is relied on as evidence of a matter stated in it.

Under this provision, multiple hearsay (such as 'A told me that B told him that D shot V') is not admissible even if both the statement by A and the statement by B fit within one or more of the various exceptions to the hearsay rule (e.g., B's statement is a spontaneous statement made as part of the *res gestae*, and A's statement is admissible under s. 116 because A has died since making it). The *only* exceptions to this principle are where one of the statements is admissible as a business document (see s. 117 at **F17.25**) or a previous statement by a witness in the case, or where the court is so convinced by the value of the evidence that it can invoke the special 'safety valve' in s. 121(1)(c). In *Xhabri* [2005] EWCA Crim 3135, [2006] 1 All ER 776 (considered at **F17.40**), the test in s. 121 was satisfied in relation to a complaint of false imprisonment which was relayed by two friends of the victim to a police officer. The complainant and the officer (though not the two friends) were available for cross-examination. The Court of Appeal considered that both **F17.85**

F

Part F Evidence

s. 121(1)(a) (admissibility under other provisions) and s. 121(1)(c) (admissibility in the interests of justice) were satisfied. In *Maher v DPP* [2006] EWHC 1271 (Admin), a note which had been made (and lost) of a car number plate formed the basis of a call to the police in which the number was transmitted. Evidence of the number was received under s. 121(1)(c) although it was inadmissible as a business record under s. 117 (see **F17.27**) on the grounds of reliability. This appears to treat s. 121(1)(c) as an alternative ground of admissibility rather than as a hurdle to be surmounted in respect of otherwise admissible evidence. This process of reasoning was disapproved in *Walker* [2007] EWCA Crim 1698, where it was held to be wrong to 'jump straight' to s. 121 without first locating a hearsay exception for each statement separately. See, however, *Williams* [2014] EWCA Crim 1862, in which the Court of Appeal seems also to jump to the s. 121 provisions, although in that case it is arguable that no multiple hearsay was involved.

In *Musone* [2007] EWCA Crim 1237, [2007] 1 WLR 2467, s. 121(1)(c) was invoked to admit the narration by a reluctant witness of the victim's dying declaration. First-hand statements by the same witness were admitted under s. 114(1)(d) (see **F17.34**) and the Court of Appeal noted the similarity of the wording of the two 'interests of justice' provisions. The difference is that under s. 121(1)(c) the value of the evidence must be 'so high' that its admission is required. In *Thakrar* [2010] EWCA Crim 1505, the Court approved of the use of s. 121 to admit statements taken in Northern Cyprus from witnesses who claimed to have heard D1 confess to three murders and related offences, and to implicate his co-accused D2. The fact that the accounts contained details of the crimes that could only have been known to a participant was held to provide striking evidence of their reliability. By contrast, in *Smith* [2020] EWCA Crim 777, the Court of Appeal was concerned with a confession of sexual touching of V, an eight-year-old child, allegedly made some 50 years previously to D's wife and reported by her to the mother of V, who told V. The mother had since died, and the wife denied that any confession had been made. The confession was presented as being bound up with the issue whether V had complained at the time, but these matters were severable, and the confession was likely to be influential with the jury. It was held that the evidence 'could not possibly pass the test' in s. 121(1)(c).

EVIDENCE AFFECTING THE CREDIBILITY OF ADMISSIBLE HEARSAY

F17.86 The CJA 2003, s. 124, governs the admissibility of evidence directed towards the discrediting of a hearsay statement where the maker of the statement does not give oral evidence in connection with the subject-matter of the statement. The opposing party is entitled to put in evidence anything which would have been admissible if the witness had been present, but in addition, and in order to counterbalance the absence of cross-examination, may also with the leave of the court give evidence of matters as to which the witness's answers would have been final had the witness given evidence in person (*Horncastle* [2009] UKSC 14, [2010] 2 AC 373, where s. 124 was said to form an essential part of the statutory protection against unfair trial). In *Riat* [2012] EWCA Crim 1509, [2013] 1 All ER 349, Hughes LJ stressed that 'very full' inquiries would be needed, in the case of hearsay evidence that is important to the prosecution, to determine what material might be available to enable the defence to challenge the maker's credibility, and that all relevant material should be disclosed (including material coming to light throughout the trial). A mere check of the Police National Computer would not suffice for this purpose. In *Harvey* [2014] EWCA Crim 54 it was held that the CJA 2003, s. 124, could not be deployed so as to admit bad character evidence to discredit hearsay witnesses where the evidence was of no substantial probative value: the evidence that may be admitted under the section is subject to the same controls as where the witness attends to give evidence, i.e. the provisions of the CJA 2003, s. 100, apply, (see **F15.9**).

It does not appear that s. 124 is limited to hearsay statements admissible under the 2003 Act: on the contrary it appears to be of general effect.

The mixture of materials admissible to discredit the maker is similar to that which previously appeared in the CJA 1988, sch. 2. However, the court has wider powers to admit evidence in order to deny or answer the allegation.

Criminal Justice Act 2003, s. 124 **F17.87**

(1) This section applies if in criminal proceedings—
  (a) a statement not made in oral evidence in the proceedings is admitted as evidence of a matter stated, and
  (b) the maker of the statement does not give oral evidence in connection with the subject matter of the statement.
(2) In such a case—
  (a) any evidence which (if he had given such evidence) would have been admissible as relevant to his credibility as a witness is so admissible in the proceedings;
  (b) evidence may with the court's leave be given of any matter which (if he had given such evidence) could have been put to him in cross-examination as relevant to his credibility as a witness but of which evidence could not have been adduced by the cross-examining party;
  (c) evidence tending to prove that he made (at whatever time) any other statement inconsistent with the statement admitted as evidence is admissible for the purpose of showing that he contradicted himself.
(3) If as a result of evidence admitted under this section an allegation is made against the maker of a statement, the court may permit a party to lead additional evidence of such description as the court may specify for the purposes of denying or answering the allegation.
(4) In the case of a statement in a document which is admitted as evidence under section 117 each person who, in order for the statement to be admissible, must have supplied or received the information concerned or created or received the document or part concerned is to be treated as the maker of the statement for the purposes of subsections (1) to (3) above.

DISCRETIONARY EXCLUSION OF HEARSAY EVIDENCE

Under the CJA 2003, the residual mechanism for exclusion of prosecution evidence that poses a threat to the interests of justice remains the PACE 1984, s. 78, although this is only one of the battery of measures designed to ensure that hearsay does not prejudice a fair trial: hearsay admissible on grounds of fear, for example, has an inbuilt requirement to this effect (see **F17.20**). In *C* [2006] EWCA Crim 1079, [2006] 1 WLR 2994, the Court of Appeal was keen to point out that the satisfaction of (in that case) s. 116 was only 'the first stage in a ruling upon the admissibility of the statement', and in *Horncastle* [2009] UKSC 14, [2010] 2 AC 373 the Court of Appeal (in a judgment subsequently affirmed and described as 'complementary' to that of the Supreme Court) identified a range of other measures designed to ensure fairness, including the duty to stop a case that, ultimately, proves to be based on unconvincing hearsay (under s. 125: see **F17.98**). The existence of s. 125 does not, however, lead to the conclusion that hearsay should be admitted and a decision on it postponed to the end of the trial: in many cases a ruling will be required in advance of admitting the evidence. **F17.88**

There is no corresponding mechanism for the exclusion of unfair defence evidence. See *Bailey* [2008] EWCA Crim 817, where counsel observed that a co-accused's ability to rely on the statement of a witness who has fled the country amounts to a 'rogue's charter'. A narrower discretion does, however, exist in the CJA 2003, s. 126, under which, according to some significant recent judicial comments, defence evidence may be excluded where it is lacking in true probative value (see **F17.94**).

Hearsay, Loss of Right to Cross-examine and Fair Trial Provisions

Fairness-based arguments for the exclusion of hearsay evidence emphasise the loss of the important right to cross-examine the absent witness, and the right of an accused person 'to examine or have examined witnesses against him' under the ECHR, Article 6(3)(d). In the leading case of *Horncastle* [2009] UKSC 14, [2010] 2 AC 373 the Supreme Court dismissed a specific challenge to the CJA 2003 in *Al-Khawaja and Tahery v UK* (2009) 49 EHRR 1 (1). In that case **F17.89** the ECtHR held that where a conviction is based 'solely or to a decisive degree' on statements made by a person whom the accused has had no opportunity to examine or have examined, the rights of the defence are restricted to an extent that is incompatible with Article 6. The Supreme Court in *Horncastle* held that to introduce this qualification would involve rewriting the CJA 2003 to include a provision that Parliament had explicitly rejected. The CJA 2003 sets out a rigorous scheme whereby the credibility and reliability of hearsay evidence can be tested (s. 124: see **F17.87**) and includes an overriding safeguard to stop a case based on unreliable evidence (s. 125: see **F17.98**). The safeguards were both more principled and more practical than the scheme suggested by the ECtHR in *Al-Khawaja*. Subsequently, the ruling of the Grand Chamber in *Al-Khawaja and Tahery v UK* (2012) 54 EHRR 23 (807) substantially confirmed the view of the Supreme Court. It was conceded that the statutory framework for admissibility of the evidence of absent witnesses is sufficient, properly applied, to provide for fair trial in such cases. The court must, however, be satisfied that there is a good reason for the absence of the witness, as well as that a fair trial will still be possible despite the absence of the opportunity to cross-examine. The latter condition will be harder to satisfy if the evidence of the absent witness is the sole or decisive evidence against the accused. The Grand Chamber drew attention in particular to the trial judge's power to stop a case based wholly or partly on hearsay where a conviction would be unsafe. In *Horncastle v UK* (2015) 60 EHRR 31 (1331) the Grand Chamber reiterated these principles, emphasising that it was not necessary to show that decisive evidence is reliable, or not unreliable to any significant extent, before it could fairly be admitted.

In *Ibrahim* [2012] EWCA Crim 837, [2012] 4 All ER 225, the Court of Appeal noticed that there are differences in approach between that decision and the decision of the Supreme Court in *Horncastle*. However, the core principle to be deduced is that, where the untested hearsay evidence is 'critical', the question of whether the trial is fair depends on three principal factors: (1) good reason to admit the evidence (i.e. compliance with the CJA 2003); (2) whether the evidence can be shown to be reliable and (3) the extent to which counterbalancing measures exist and have been properly applied: this involves consideration of all the statutory safeguards in the CJA 2003, together with the application of common-law safeguards such as proper directions in the summing-up. In *Riat* [2012] EWCA Crim 1509, [2013] 1 All ER 349 Hughes LJ noted that there seemed to be an element of misunderstanding around the proposition in *Horncastle* that 'sole or decisive' hearsay evidence might be admitted if it was 'demonstrably reliable or its reliability was capable of proper testing and assessment'. There was clearly no rule that evidence had to be independently verified before being put to a jury. Rather, a judge had to ensure that the evidence can safely be held to be reliable, given its strengths and weaknesses, the tools available to the jury for testing it and its importance to the case as a whole.

A detailed summary of the relevant principles derived from *Horncastle*, *Ibrahim* and *Riat* is given in *Shabir* [2012] EWCA Crim 2564. In that case, the evidence of a witness who was in prison and suffering from paranoid schizophrenia with persecutory and paranoid delusions should have been excluded, despite support for parts of his evidence, as it could not be shown that his untested hearsay evidence on the central issue of the identity of D as the gunman was potentially safely reliable. See also *Pedersen* [2013] EWCA Crim 464, in which the statement of the complainant, who was suffering from a mental illness at the time when it was made and had died before the trial, was rightly excluded as to lack of consent in a count relating to rape because there was no evidence by which the conflict between her statement and D's account could properly be resolved. However, further statements by her relevant to the breaching by D of a restraining order were rightly admitted as there was other evidence by which the reliability of her evidence could be assessed. In *T (P)* [2013] EWCA Crim 2398 it was held that the proposition in *Horncastle* regarding the capacity of the jury to assess the reliability of hearsay evidence 'embraces with particular force the evidence of witnesses who had died or who could not be expected to have any present recollection of events described in witness statements made over 30 years previously'. However, none of the hearsay evidence in issue in that case was of 'sole or decisive' importance to the success of the prosecution. In *Barney* [2014] EWCA Crim 589, the decisive evidence of a deceased elderly victim identifying D as the perpetrator of a distraction burglary was admitted. The witness's previous descriptions provided a method of testing her reliability, and D's convictions for similar offences provided further support.

The leading authorities were also applied in *Harvey* [2014] EWCA Crim 54, in which the evidence of two witnesses who were absent through fear was central to the prosecution, but where there was strong evidence that supported the reliability of their accounts. This included the *res gestae* statement of the two witnesses themselves, made while they were still under the influence of the effect of an armed robbery (for *res gestae*, see **F17.49**) and the extent to which the accounts subsequently given by the two tallied with one another, despite their lack of opportunity to confer immediately after the event. The Court of Appeal also drew attention to the availability for the defence of a significant amount of evidence regarding the bad character of the two witnesses, who had links to the gangland fraternity, that could be deployed in support of a possible alternative explanation for the presence of firearms in the home of one of them, which was also the location for the alleged armed robbery. Frequently cited in recent cases is the summary by Gross LJ in *Friel* [2012] EWCA Crim 2871:

> It is plain to us, therefore, that hearsay of any description is not to be nodded through or adduced as a matter of routine. There is no inflexible rule against admissibility of central (or sole and decisive) hearsay evidence, but, on a spectrum, the more central the hearsay evidence is, the greater the care required. Sometimes hearsay will be inadmissible or even if admissible the trial may need to be halted. But it is also necessary to keep in mind the public interest in securing the conviction of the guilty, as indeed it is always imperative to have regard to the acquittal of the innocent and the avoidance of miscarriages of justice.

Illustrations of the Courts' Approach The effect of the approach of the English courts is well illustrated by the facts of *Horncastle* [2009] UKSC 14, [2010] 2 AC 373. The victim of a serious beating gave a statement about how his injuries had been incurred, which was received following his death from an alcohol-related illness. Although the statement was critical evidence linking D to the attack, there was also substantial independent evidence of presence at the scene, D had ample opportunity to challenge V's credibility, and the judge gave a full and clear direction about the disadvantages of challenging V on his memory and other relevant matters. By contrast, in *Ibrahim* [2012] EWCA Crim 837, [2012] 4 All ER 225, the evidence of V (the deceased victim of an alleged rape), though technically admissible, could not be shown to be reliable given V's heroin addiction, the fact that she had made an admittedly false formal statement to police on a similar matter (the reason for the withdrawal of that complaint being also demonstrably false) and a long and unexplained delay in reporting the rape. The supporting evidence, such as it was, did not overcome the doubts raised about V's reliability, and her evidence should either have been excluded under the PACE 1984, s. 78, or the trial stopped under the CJA 2003, s. 125 (see **F17.98**). See also *Riat* [2012] EWCA Crim 1509, [2013] 1 All ER 349; *Shabir* [2012] EWCA Crim 2564 and *Tahery* [2013] EWCA Crim 1053; in the last case, the Court of Appeal, on a reference from the CCRC in one of the cases that had been the subject of the application to the Grand Chamber in *Al-Khawaja and Tahery v UK* (2012) 54 EHRR 23 (807), held that the trial judge ought not to have admitted the unsupported evidence of a critical witness where the objective factors (his animosity and his previous inconsistency) pointed to unreliability. The bad character of an absent witness is not necessarily a reason for exclusion, even if it provides a basis for an inference of preparedness to lie, provided that the evidence available to the jury is such that they can properly assess the risk of the witness having done so (*Adeojo* [2013] EWCA Crim 41, where there was a wealth of other evidence linking the accused with the scene, but the absent witness provided the only direct evidence of identification). See also *Jabbar* [2013] EWCA Crim 801. **F17.90**

The fact that vulnerable witnesses are involved does not absolve domestic courts of their responsibility to ensure that there is no unfairness when allowing witness statements to be read. See *PS v Germany* (2003) 36 EHRR 61 (1139) and *SN v Sweden* (2004) 39 EHRR 13 (304), where the use of special measures was sanctioned provided that the right of the defence to challenge the evidence was also safeguarded. In *J* [2011] EWCA Crim 3021, the statement of a three-year-old boy that he had been beaten by his mother's partner was held to have been rightly admitted under s. 114(1)(d) (see **F17.38**). An important feature of the decision was that the boy's injuries were non-accidental and could only have been caused by D, the boy's mother or his grandmother. As both women gave evidence that it was not them, it could not be said that the child's statement was the 'sole or decisive' evidence against D. In *AC* [2014] EWCA Crim 371, the account of a child victim of rape was presented in hearsay form where she was too traumatised to testify. The tools to test the reliability of her description included the cross-examination of her mother, who had supported her through the disclosure process, and there was supporting evidence of DNA and indecent images of the child on AC's computer.

Where the prosecutor has delayed proceedings and in consequence a witness is unavailable to testify, the court may exclude the witness's statement on the basis that the prosecution should have proceeded when the witness was available (*French* (1993) 97 Cr App R 421, and see *Radak* [1999] 1 Cr App R 187). Where an important witness for the prosecution deliberately goes missing during the trial, in circumstances giving rise to doubts about the reliability of the witness's account, it is unlikely that the evidence will be admitted as hearsay. In *Kiziltan* [2017] EWCA Crim 1461, [2018] 4 WLR 43, the defence to kidnapping was that the complainant had colluded with Y to falsely incriminate the accused. After Y was cross-examined to this effect she spoke with the complainant, who, having said he 'did not feel right' about giving evidence, did not attend to testify and could not be found. It was held that statements by the complainant identifying D ought to have been excluded, applying the PACE 1984, s. 78. In *Sohal* [2019] EWCA Crim 1237, an oversight resulted in two witnesses to a particular conversation involving D not being warned to attend the trial. When the error was discovered, one witness was abroad at an unknown location, and the other could not be found. It was held (at [47]) that their evidence, even if technically admissible under the CJA 2003, s. 116(2), ought to have been excluded on grounds of fairness because 'in the circumstances of this case, the deficiencies of hearsay evidence, as opposed to the direct testimony of a witness who can be cross-examined, were particularly acute'. The relevant circumstances included the two witness statements being in identical terms, having clearly been taken by a professional investigator, and a number of important details being unclear, including the language in which the conversation had been conducted (D having based his defence in part on his limited command of English). Where a statement is produced in this way for a witness to sign, the Court noted that there may often be a particular disadvantage for a defendant who is not able to cross-examine the witness.

Relevance of s. 114(2) to Admissibility under ss. 116 and 117

F17.91 In *Cole and Keet* [2007] EWCA Crim 1924, [2007] 1 WLR 2716, Lord Phillips CJ dealt with two cases of evidence admissible under the CJA 2003, s. 116 — in *Cole* statements of the deceased victim of alleged assaults by C and in *Keet* the statement of an elderly victim of alleged fraud, who since making her statement had succumbed to dementia. In both cases the evidence was important (possibly 'decisive'). Turning to s. 114(1)(d), the 'interests of justice' test (see **F17.34**), Lord Phillips transposed the nine criteria for consideration prior to a decision on *admissibility* under that provision (s. 114(2)(a) to (i)) into factors assisting in the decision on *exclusion* under the PACE 1984, s. 78, of evidence otherwise admissible under s. 116 on the grounds that the test in s. 78 was 'unlikely to produce a different result' from that of the 'interests of justice' in s. 114(1)(d). In *Riat* [2012] EWCA Crim 1509, [2013] 1 All ER 349, Hughes LJ noted that 'the non-exhaustive considerations listed in s. 114(2) as directly applicable to an application made under s 114(1)(d) are useful *aides memoire* for any judge considering the admissibility of hearsay evidence, whether under that subsection or under s 78 PACE, or otherwise'. In *Zejmowicz* [2011] EWCA Crim 1173, it was acknowledged that the judge's consideration of the s. 114(2) factors was 'not strictly necessary', but it appears to have been helpful in dealing with a difficult situation. In that case the prosecution sought to rely on the evidence of two witnesses whose English was not fluent, one present at trial and the other absent, as to allegedly incriminating statements in English made in their presence by an accused following a murder. The exchange was caught on CCTV so that the gestures of the co-accused (including punching and kicking) were also before the jury. The witness who gave evidence (the less fluent of the two) was severely undermined in cross-examination, and it was argued that it was for that reason unfair to fill the gap using the evidence of the absent witness. However, it was held that it was right in principle that both accounts should be heard. The absence of the second witness could be dealt with appropriately by a direction stressing the effectiveness of cross-examination in relation to the first. In *C* [2019] EWCA Crim 623, the s. 114(2) criteria were referenced when upholding the decision of the trial judge to admit the suicide note of one of two alleged victims of sexual abuse by D. The judge also made due allowance for the possible effect of such an emotive document.

Where the prosecution has read, unopposed, the statement of a witness who is unavailable, the question whether it is permissible for the prosecution to adduce further evidence from the same witness to correct a misleading impression will be decided according to the interests of justice. If the evidence could not have been resisted had it been adduced with the original statement it is likely to be admitted (*Ferdinand* [2014] EWCA Crim 1243, [2014] 2 Cr App R 23 (331)).

Hearsay Evidence of Identification

F17.92 The right to challenge hearsay evidence may be particularly important in cases where the weakness of the evidence is generally acknowledged, as with identification or recognition evidence. Where such evidence is hearsay and constitutes the principal element in the prosecution case, the House of Lords has said that courts should be very reluctant to receive the evidence (*Neill v North Antrim Magistrates' Court* [1992] 4 All ER 846 per Lord Mustill at p. 1229). Where hearsay evidence of identification evidence is admitted, an appropriate warning of the dangers of reliance on it should be given (*Vasco* [2012] EWCA Crim 3004).

Fairness and Records

F17.93 Where a statement tendered in evidence under the CJA 2003, s. 117, is not a statement prepared for the purpose of criminal proceedings, the absence of any opportunity to cross-examine the maker is likely to be of less importance, even where the statement relied upon is crucial to the case for the prosecution. Thus, in *Schreiber* [1988] Crim LR 112, decided under the Criminal Evidence Act 1965, it was held that customs documents compiled abroad could be given in evidence without calling the maker, even though the documents were the most cogent evidence of fraud by the accused.

Unconvincing and Superfluous Hearsay

F17.94 Criminal Justice Act 2003, s. 126

(1) In criminal proceedings the court may refuse to admit a statement as evidence of a matter stated if—
 (a) the statement was made otherwise than in oral evidence in the proceedings, and
 (b) the court is satisfied that the case for excluding the statement, taking account of the danger that to admit it would result in undue waste of time, substantially outweighs the case for admitting it, taking account of the value of the evidence.

(2) Nothing in this chapter prejudices—
 (a) any power of a court to exclude evidence under section 78 of the Police and Criminal Evidence Act 1984 (exclusion of unfair evidence), or
 (b) any other power of a court to exclude evidence at its discretion (whether by preventing questions from being put or otherwise).

F17.95 Section 126 confers a power on any court trying a criminal case to exclude hearsay evidence where, 'taking account of the danger that to admit it would result in undue waste of time', the case for exclusion outweighs the case for admission. Section 126 operates without prejudice to the common-law power to exclude evidence on the ground that its prejudicial effect outweighs its probative value, or the general discretion to exclude prosecution evidence under the PACE 1984, s. 78 (see as to the application of s. 78 to hearsay, **F17.88**). In *Horncastle* [2009] UKSC 14, [2010] 2 AC 373, where the Court of Appeal identified s. 126 as providing an essential part of the protection against unfair trial, it was said that the section adds to s. 78 an obligation to regulate 'satellite disputes' arising through the use of hearsay evidence. Note that, unlike the preserved powers, s. 126 can be invoked in respect of evidence tendered by the defence (*Atkinson* [2011] EWCA Crim 1746, where hearsay tendered by one accused, to whose defence it was 'of peripheral help', was held to have been rightly excluded at the behest of his co-accused to whom it was highly prejudicial).

The power to exclude defence evidence under the CJA 2003, s. 126, was considered in *Drinkwater* [2016] EWCA Crim 16, [2016] 1 Cr App R 30 (471). In the face of overwhelming evidence based on DNA from semen found in connection with two very similar rapes, D contended that the samples must have been contaminated at some point in the investigative process, and that at least one of the rapes was the work of another man, H, since deceased, who had initially confessed but had refused to sign his confession statement. Evidence of H's unsigned confession and the report of the investigating officer in H's case were held to have been rightly excluded under s. 126. The evidence that had been rejected did not contain any salient fact that was not in evidence via formal admissions by the prosecution, but at the same time, and paradoxically, it 'undermined the primary case the defence wished to advance and which they were able to make on the basis of the admitted facts, which was that there was a possibility that [H] was the attacker'. Applying the statutory formula in s. 126(1)(b), the danger that admitting the evidence 'would result in undue waste of time . . . taking account of the value of the evidence' was overwhelming. The Court of Appeal specifically rejected the suggestion that a different threshold test for exclusion might apply depending on whether the evidence was tendered by the prosecution or the defence: there was no principled justification for such a difference.

The Court also indicated a 'strong preliminary view' that s. 126 is not limited to cases in which the reception of the hearsay would generate undue waste of time on satellite issues. Rather it creates a general discretion under which a court can exclude evidence that 'lacks significant probative value'. The Court cited with approval a dictum to this effect in *Riat* [2012] EWCA Crim 1509, [2013] 1 All ER 349, where Hughes LJ also noted that the provision appears to have been assumed not to be confined to 'satellite issue' cases, albeit without detailed argument to the contrary, in both *Gyima* [2007] EWCA Crim 429 and *Atkinson* [2011] EWCA Crim 1746. The same view of the generality of the discretion was taken more recently in *QD* [2019] NICA 7.

The wider use of the s. 126 discretion is of great significance in relation to the possible exclusion of defence evidence, which is not otherwise covered by the court's discretionary powers.

JUDICIAL DIRECTIONS ON HEARSAY

F17.96 The Supreme Court in *Horncastle* [2009] UKSC 14, [2010] AC 373 listed as one of the 'principal safeguards designed to protect a defendant against unfair prejudice as a result of the admission of hearsay evidence' the requirement for the judge to direct the jury on the dangers of relying on hearsay evidence. The *Crown Court Compendium* (July 2020), ch. 14, deals with the appropriate direction to be given in relation to all forms of hearsay, including evidence admitted by agreement. The *Compendium* refers to the need for care in crafting directions and observes that the 'strength of the warning depends on the facts of the case and the significance of the hearsay evidence in the context of the case as whole'. In addition to a direction in the summing up, it is suggested that it is helpful to give a summary of the direction before hearsay is adduced. Drawing on the guidance given by the Privy Council in *Grant v The State* [2005] UKPC 2, [2007] 1 AC 1 in relation to a statutory scheme similar to the CJA 2003, the *Compendium* provides that the jury need to be directed on three major limitations of hearsay: (1) the lack of opportunity to observe the demeanour of the person making the statement; (2) the fact that the statement was not made on oath and (3) the lack of opportunity to see the witness's statement tested under cross-examination. Where the credibility of the absent witness has been the subject of a challenge under s. 124 (see **F17.87**), the jury need to be reminded of the challenge and of any discrepancy or weakness revealed. The *Compendium* gives specific guidance about particular forms of hearsay, given that the direction that is appropriate in respect of the evidence of an absent witness is very different from what needs to be said in relation to the previous statement of a witness who gives evidence in the proceedings, or in relation to a business document the accuracy of which is challenged. The content of a direction may also vary according to whether the hearsay is relied upon by the prosecution or the defence, given the difference in the burden and standard of proof. In the case of hearsay tendered by the prosecution, it may be appropriate to emphasise the need for caution. The object of the direction, whatever the nature of the hearsay statement, is to assist the jury properly to assess the reliability and probative value of the hearsay evidence and to ensure that material relevant to those questions, including any identifiable weaknesses, should be placed adequately and fairly before the jury. In many cases, particularly those involving absent witnesses, the considerations are similar to, and thus may be borrowed from, the factors listed in s. 114(2) in relation to admitting hearsay in the interests of justice (see **F17.34**). The judge should always discuss the terms of a direction with the advocates.

While failure to give appropriate directions in respect of prosecution evidence will not necessarily render a trial unfair, it may do so, given the importance of the direction as a safeguard of the interests of the defence. In the unusual case of *Speed* [2017] EWCA Crim 1908, the prosecution relied on the *res gestae* and ABE statements of the complainant of rape, who had gone abroad, but the jury were also presented with substantial evidence of her later attempts to resile from the allegations. The Court of Appeal, ordering a retrial, held that the judge should have given a clear warning of the need for care before acting on the complaint (see also *Maw* [1994] Crim LR 841 and **F6.54**).

In *Daley* [2017] EWCA Crim 1971, the Court of Appeal reiterated the importance of giving a direction on the major limitations of hearsay evidence both before the evidence is given and in the summing-up. However, without derogating from the importance of following this procedure in normal circumstances, the instant case was identified as one in which the ground of the defence had shifted during the course of the trial away from discrediting the hearsay evidence and towards establishing an alternative explanation for it. For that reason, the omission of the hearsay directions was not a material misdirection such as to undermine the safety of the conviction.

The particular difficulty that arises in giving a warning where the evidence is tendered by the defence was considered in *Abiodun* [2003] EWCA Crim 2167, where a 'mild' direction 'which simply reminded the jury of what in any event would have been obvious to them, i.e. that the witnesses had not been cross-examined', was held not to have impinged on the fairness of the proceedings. In *Williams* [2014] EWCA Crim 1862, the Court of Appeal endorsed the view that the trial judge has a power to warn the jury about the dangers of hearsay evidence from the defence. Fulford LJ said (at [96]): **F17.97**

> ... the judge, when giving directions to the jury on hearsay evidence relied on by the accused, must be scrupulous to ensure that he does not shift the burden of proof away from the prosecution. But it was unobjectionable in this case for the court to identify the weaknesses in the evidence and to highlight the need for caution as regards material that had not been tested, particularly when the witness had given two completely contradictory accounts that have not been investigated in cross-examination.

POWER TO STOP TRIAL WHERE CASE BASED ON HEARSAY

F17.98 **Criminal Justice Act 2003, s. 125**

(1) If on a defendant's trial before a judge and jury for an offence the court is satisfied at any time after the close of the case for the prosecution that—
  (a) the case against the defendant is based wholly or partly on a statement not made in oral evidence in the proceedings, and
  (b) the evidence provided by the statement is so unconvincing that, considering its importance to the case against the defendant, his conviction of the offence would be unsafe,

the court must either direct the jury to acquit the defendant of the offence or, if it considers that there ought to be a retrial, discharge the jury.

(2) Where—
  (a) a jury is directed under subsection (1) to acquit a defendant of an offence, and
  (b) the circumstances are such that, apart from this subsection, the defendant could if acquitted of that offence be found guilty of another offence,

the defendant may not be found guilty of that other offence if the court is satisfied as mentioned in subsection (1) in respect of it.

(3) If—
  (a) a jury is required to determine under section 4A(2) of the Criminal Procedure (Insanity) Act 1964 whether a person charged on an indictment with an offence did the act or made the omission charged, and
  (b) the court is satisfied as mentioned in subsection (1) above at any time after the close of the case for the prosecution that—
    (i) the case against the defendant is based wholly or partly on a statement not made in oral evidence in the proceedings, and
    (ii) the evidence provided by the statement is so unconvincing that, considering its importance to the case against the person, a finding that he did the act or made the omission would be unsafe,

the court must either direct the jury to acquit the defendant of the offence or, if it considers that there ought to be a rehearing, discharge the jury.

(4) This section does not prejudice any other power a court may have to direct a jury to acquit a person of an offence or to discharge a jury.

F17.99 Under the CJA 2003, s. 125, the Crown Court has a specific power to stop a case where (a) the case depends significantly ('wholly or partly') on a hearsay statement and (b) the evidence is unconvincing to the point where a conviction based on it would be unsafe. The Court of Appeal in *Horncastle* [2009] EWCA Crim 964, [2009] 2 Cr App R 15 (230), in a judgment endorsed and regarded as complementary to the subsequent decision of the Supreme Court ([2009] UKSC 14, [2010] 2 AC 373), identified this (at [74]) as part of a set of safeguards forming a 'crafted code' on hearsay that protects the fair trial rights of the accused under the ECHR, Article 6:

> ... at the close of all the evidence the judge is required, in a case where there is a legitimate argument that the hearsay is unconvincing and important to the case, to make up his own mind, not as a fact-finder (which is the jury's function) but whether a conviction would be safe. That involves assessing the reliability of the hearsay evidence, its place in the evidence as a whole, the issues in the case as they have emerged and all the other individual circumstances of the case. The importance of the evidence to the case is made a specific consideration by the statute: see s 125(1)(b).

In *Ibrahim* [2012] EWCA Crim 837, [2012] 4 All ER 225, it was said that a judge should have uppermost in his or her mind the question of whether an untested hearsay statement has been shown to be reliable in light of all the other evidence adduced. If not, and the statement is 'part of the central corpus of evidence without which the case on the relevant count cannot proceed', the statement is 'almost bound to be "unconvincing" such that a conviction based on it will be unsafe'. In *Riat* [2012] EWCA Crim 1509, [2013] 1 All ER 349, Hughes LJ stressed the difference between cases subject to s. 125 and the general principles on submission of no case to answer contained in *Galbraith* [1981] 2 All ER 1060 (see **D16.54**), where it is no part of the function of the judge to assess the reliability of the evidence. In hearsay cases the judge is not only entitled but is required to see whether the hearsay evidence is so unconvincing that any conviction would be unsafe. 'That means looking at its strengths and weaknesses, at the tools available to the jury for testing it, and at its importance to the case as a whole' (at [28]).

Section F18 The Rule against Hearsay: Confessions

INTRODUCTION

Definition

F18.1 **Police and Criminal Evidence Act 1984, s. 82**

(1) In this Part of this Act—
'confession', includes any statement wholly or partly adverse to the person who made it, whether made to a person in authority or not and whether made in words or otherwise.

The general rule as stated in the PACE 1984, s. 76, is that a confession made by an accused person is admissible insofar as it is relevant to any issue in the proceedings and is not excluded on the grounds of oppression or in consequence of anything said or done conducive to unreliability (s. 76(2); see **F18.8**). The rule of admissibility has been extended to operate not only in favour of the prosecution but also for a co-accused (s. 76A; see **F18.28**). Section 82(1) makes it clear that 'confession' covers statements such as an informal admission to a friend or colleague, and is not limited to statements made to a person in authority, such as a police or customs officer. Most confessions are, however, made to persons in authority, and such confessions are the most likely to be challenged. The observation in the old case of *Deokinanan v The Queen* [1969] 1 AC 20 that, '[t]he fact that an inducement is made by a person in authority may make it more likely to operate on the accused's mind and lead him to confess', continues to be true.

F18.2 It should follow from the definition of 'confession' in s. 82(1), and from the provision in s. 76(1) (see **F18.8**) that only a confession made 'by' an accused may be given in evidence 'against him', that where the only proof that the accused made the statement comes from the confession itself it should not be admitted. However, in *Ward* [2001] Crim LR 316, the Court of Appeal held that where a passenger in a car gave D's personal details to a police officer when asked for his own, the statement was admissible as a 'confession' by D, who denied being the passenger. It is submitted that while this is a useful device for admitting a common form of evidence of identification, it was not a confession 'by' D unless the identity of the maker was shown to be D, which was the very point in dispute. The Court considered that the jury should be given a 'clear direction' in such cases not to rely on the statement unless they were sure, from its contents and such surrounding evidence as there was, that it was the appellant who made the statement. There is still an element of circularity in using the content to identify the maker, and the problem might be circumvented by treating the statement simply as a form of hearsay that might be admitted in the interests of justice under the CJA 2003, s. 114(1)(d) (see **F17.34**).

The result of a literal application of the definition in *Mawdesley v Chief Constable of Cheshire Constabulary* [2003] EWHC 1586 (Admin), [2004] 1 WLR 1035 was that a statement disclosing the identity of a driver was admissible as a confession if it could be inferred that the accused had written it, even though it was unsigned (and therefore inadmissible under the statutory scheme in the Road Traffic Act 1988).

Guilty Pleas and Pleas in Mitigation A plea of guilty constitutes a confession for the purposes of the PACE 1984, s. 82(1). Where such a plea has been retracted, the court may decide that it should not be given in evidence by the prosecution because of the adverse effect on the fairness of the proceedings, invoking s. 78 (see **F18.33**). A retracted plea of guilty may also, where relevant, be relied upon as a confession by a co-accused (see **F18.27**), to which the court's power of discretionary exclusion under s. 78 does not apply (*Johnson* [2007] EWCA Crim 1651). **F18.3**

An admission made by an accused in other proceedings would similarly constitute a confession for the purposes of the 1984 Act, and could be relied upon provided, as is likely, that it complies with the provisions of s. 76(2) and (which may be more doubtful) that it is not excluded under s. 78. Such evidence would not have been admitted at common law (*McGregor* [1968] 1 QB 371).

A plea in mitigation made by counsel on behalf of a client who has been convicted following a plea of 'not guilty' should not be understood as a confession by the convicted person through counsel. So to regard mitigation would be both unjust and unrealistic, as it is counsel's duty to accept the verdict and seek to mitigate the consequences (*Wu Chun-Piu v The Queen* [1996] 1 WLR 1113). It is submitted that the same must be true if the convicted person advances the mitigation in person.

Confessions Otherwise than in Words

There is no statutory definition of 'statement' for the purposes of Part VII of the PACE 1984, but the inclusion in s. 82(1) of the expression 'whether made in words or otherwise' suggests that 'confession' may, in addition to admissions in oral or written form, include conduct such as a nod of acceptance of an accusation or a 'thumbs-up' sign which may be properly regarded as a 'statement' in sign language. In *Li Shu-Ling v The Queen* [1989] AC 270, D, who had previously made a full confession to the police, agreed to take part in a filmed re-enactment of the crime with which he was charged, which was the murder of a woman by strangulation. He gave a running commentary explaining his movements, which he demonstrated on a woman police officer who played the part of the victim. At trial, his account of the killing was entirely different. It was held by the Privy Council (applying common-law principles) that the re-enactment was to be regarded as a confession. Such a film would also constitute a confession under s. 82(1), and may be given in evidence, provided that the conditions of admissibility under the 1984 Act are satisfied. That the conditions of admissibility should be the same for re-enactments or visual demonstrations as for oral or written confessions was confirmed at common law in *Timothy v The State* [2000] 1 WLR 485. Confessions made by two of the accused were excluded following allegations of police misconduct. It was held that the same allegations were relevant to the admissibility of the conduct of the two in showing the police where they had hidden the murder weapon (see also *Lam Chi Ming v The Queen* [1991] 2 AC 212). **F18.4**

It is submitted that conduct which is not intended to convey guilt, but which may be interpreted as doing so, is not a 'statement' and hence not a confession. Thus, for example, driving away at speed from the scene of an accident is not a confession to which the 1984 Act applies, though evidence of such conduct would be relevant and admissible.

Partly and Wholly Exculpatory Statements

A confession may be 'wholly or partly adverse' to the maker, with the result that a so-called 'mixed statement', which is part confession and part exculpation, is a confession for the purposes of the PACE 1984. (See further as to the use of mixed statements in evidence **F18.93** to **F18.98**.) **F18.5**

Whether words amount to at least a partial confession is a question of fact separate and distinct from the question (where this is also in dispute) whether the words in question were spoken at all (*B* [2009] EWCA Crim 2113).

In *Finch* [2007] EWCA Crim 36, [2007] 1 WLR 1645, the issue was whether D could rely on a statement made by R, an erstwhile co-accused, under the PACE 1984, s. 76A (see **F18.28**). The Court of Appeal identified as suitable for full argument the question whether statements made by R in police interviews which went beyond admissions and were exculpatory of D constituted 'confessions' for the purposes of s. 82(1). Hughes LJ said that not everything stated at the time of a partial admission is necessarily part of a 'confession'. This comment was relied upon in *Sliogeris* [2015] EWCA Crim 22, where it was held that an out-of-court statement made by co-accused D1, in which he admitted his presence at the scene of a murder but blamed co-accused D2 for the killing, was not admissible under the PACE 1984, s. 76A, at the behest of co-accused D3 (whose defence was that D2 alone committed the crime). The admission of presence, though a partial confession by D1, was not of itself relevant to D3's defence, while the allegation that D2 was guilty was not part of the confession. The statement was, however, admitted under the CJA 2003, s. 114(1)(d) (the 'interests of justice' exception: see **F17.41**).

F18.6 Where the part of a mixed statement relied upon by the prosecution also forms part of the defence, it may be easier to set aside errors in the manner by which it was obtained. In *Uddin* [2005] EWCA Crim 464, D, who was of very low IQ, was wrongly interviewed without an independent adult. The only admission D made was of his presence at the scene: in all other respects his statement was self-serving, and consistent with his evidence at trial. In holding that the use of the confession did not lead to an unsafe conviction, the Court of Appeal noted that the purpose of the protection of which D had been deprived was to prevent prejudice arising from his failure to do himself justice at interview. As D's admission of presence was an inherent part of the defence, this had not occurred.

F18.7 A more difficult issue is whether the PACE 1984, s. 82(1), includes a statement which, when made, is purely self-serving, but which becomes 'adverse' to the interests of the accused because of the way in which it is deployed at trial, typically because it is inconsistent with the defence there put forward. In *Sat-Bhambra* (1988) 88 Cr App R 55, the Court of Appeal (*obiter*) considered that a purely exculpatory statement was not a confession, but noted that such a statement might be excluded under the more general power of the court under s. 78 (see **F18.33** to **F18.54**, and *Jelen* (1989) 90 Cr App R 456). *Sat-Bhambra* was approved by the House of Lords in *Hasan* [2005] UKHL 22, [2005] 2 AC 467. It was argued that the definition in s. 82(1) ('"confession" includes any statement wholly or partly adverse') was apt also to 'include' statements that were not adverse when made. According to Lord Steyn, with whom the other members of the House concurred, the word 'includes' was selected simply in order to extend the core meaning of confession to partly adverse statements. The meaning contended for was strained, and also unnecessary, as s. 78 was available to protect an accused where, for example, the police by oppression secured a wholly exculpatory but false statement and then sought to use it 'against' an accused so as to damage his or her credibility. Although s. 78 is formally couched in the language of discretion and s. 76 in the language of judgment, s. 78 'in truth imports a judgment whether in the light of the statutory criteria of fairness the court ought to admit the evidence'. The House therefore concluded that there was no gap in the procedural safeguards provided by the PACE 1984.

Principles of Admissibility under the PACE 1984, s. 76

F18.8 Police and Criminal Evidence Act 1984, s. 76

(1) In any proceedings a confession made by an accused person may be given in evidence against him insofar as it is relevant to any matter in issue in the proceedings and is not excluded by the court in pursuance of this section.

(2) If, in any proceedings where the prosecution proposes to give in evidence a confession made by an accused person, it is represented to the court that the confession was or may have been obtained—
(a) by oppression of the person who made it; or
(b) in consequence of anything said or done which was likely, in the circumstances existing at the time, to render unreliable any confession which might be made by him in consequence thereof,
the court shall not allow the confession to be given in evidence against him except insofar as the prosecution proves to the court beyond reasonable doubt that the confession (notwithstanding that it may be true) was not obtained as aforesaid.
(3) In any proceedings where the prosecution proposes to give in evidence a confession made by an accused person, the court may of its own motion require the prosecution, as a condition of allowing it to do so, to prove that the confession was not obtained as mentioned in subsection (2) above.

Section 76 appears not to have been intended as a mechanism for regulating the admissibility of a confession made by one co-accused as evidence for another. In *Myers* [1998] AC 124, the House of Lords declined to decide whether s. 76(1) applied to defence evidence, but the CJA 2003, s. 128, added s. 76A to the PACE 1984 in order to provide statutory regulation of the admission of the confession of a co-accused (see **F18.28**). For ease of exposition, the position with regard to prosecution evidence will be explained first. **F18.9**

The prosecution do not have to prove the admissibility of a confession upon which they rely unless either (a) the defence 'represents' that it is inadmissible under s. 76(2), or (b) the court of its own motion requires proof of admissibility under s. 76(3). If in either case the prosecution cannot prove admissibility beyond reasonable doubt, the confession must be excluded, notwithstanding that it may be true: the court has no discretion in the matter (*Paris* (1993) 97 Cr App R 99). In *Beeres v CPS* [2014] EWHC 283 (Admin), [2014] 2 Cr App R 8 (101), it was said that a court should be particularly vigilant to scrutinise a confession that is the sole evidence relied upon by the prosecution. A confession may be excluded in part (cf. s. 76(4) and (6) at **F18.85** ***et seq.***). As to procedure, see **F18.62** ***et seq.***

A confession which is inadmissible in criminal proceedings in consequence of s. 76 should not be used as the basis for a formal caution (*Metropolitan Police Commissioner, ex parte Thompson* [1997] 1 WLR 1519).

EXCLUSION FOR OPPRESSION: PACE 1984, s. 76(2)(a)

Definition of Oppression

Police and Criminal Evidence Act 1984, s. 76 **F18.10**

(8) In this section 'oppression' includes torture, inhuman or degrading treatment, and the use or threat of violence (whether or not amounting to torture).

The reference to 'torture' may be interpreted in the light of the offence of torture contained in the CJA 1988, s. 134. 'Torture and inhuman or degrading treatment' is also prohibited by the ECHR, Article 3, and reference may be made to case law under Article 3 (see, e.g., *Republic of Ireland v UK* (1978) 2 EHRR 25).

Ambit of Oppression

In *Fulling* [1987] QB 426, the Court of Appeal held (without referring to the PACE 1984, s. 76(8)) that the 1984 Act does not follow the wording of earlier rules or decisions, nor is it expressed to be a consolidating Act. It is a codifying Act, in the interpretation of which the proper course is to start by ascertaining the natural meaning of the language used, uninfluenced by any considerations derived from the previous state of the law. It was further stated that much **F18.11** of the sort of treatment which would have fallen within the wider definition of oppression at common law will now fall to be dealt with under the 'reliability' head of exclusion.

F18.12 In *Fulling* [1987] QB 426, the prosecution tendered a confession by D in which she admitted her part in an insurance fraud initiated by her boyfriend. D claimed that the confession was made in order to secure her release from custody after a police officer had revealed, to D's great distress, not only that her boyfriend had been unfaithful to her, but also that the 'other woman' was being held in the cell next to D's. On the assumption that these revelations were made, the trial judge ruled that there was no oppression in the sense of 'something above and beyond that which is inherently oppressive in police custody... [importing] some impropriety... actively applied in an improper manner by the police'. The Court of Appeal upheld the ruling of the trial judge. 'Oppression' was to be given its 'ordinary dictionary meaning' of: 'Exercise of authority or power in a burdensome, harsh or wrongful manner; unjust or cruel treatment of subjects, inferiors etc., the imposition of unreasonable or unjust burdens'.

F18.13 Oppression almost inevitably involves some impropriety on the part of the interrogator (*Fulling* [1987] QB 426 at p. 432). It does not follow that all impropriety necessarily involves oppression; otherwise all wrongful acts, including breaches of the PACE Codes of Practice, could be termed oppressive, which is clearly not so (*Parker* [1995] Crim LR 233; *Re Proulx* [2001] 1 All ER 57). In *Fulling*, the Court of Appeal drew attention to a quotation which exemplifies the meaning of the term: 'There is not a word in our language that expresses more detestable wickedness than oppression'. In *Emmerson* (1991) 92 Cr App R 284, a police officer had given way to impatience during an interview and had raised his voice and used bad language to D. The Court of Appeal ruled that to regard such conduct as oppressive would be to give the word a completely false meaning. Unduly hostile questioning may, however, be oppressive: it is a question of degree. In *Paris* (1993) 97 Cr App R 99, a tape recording of an interview with D revealed that he had been 'bullied and hectored'. The Court of Appeal commented that, short of physical violence, it was hard to conceive of a more hostile and intimidating approach by officers to a suspect. The interview was oppressive and D's later confession ought to have been excluded. However, in *L* [1994] Crim LR 839, tactics similar to those employed in *Paris* appear to have been regarded as acceptable provided the reliability of the confession was not compromised.

F18.14 A degree of impropriety which is insufficient for oppression may serve to support an argument that a confession should be excluded under the PACE 1984, s. 76(2)(b) or s. 78, considered at **F18.17** ***et seq.*** and **F18.33** ***et seq.*** respectively. Thus, in *Samuel* [1988] QB 615, the Court of Appeal, while acknowledging the possibility that oppression might be present where access to legal advice is improperly denied, preferred to quash D's conviction by reference to s. 78. Exclusion for oppression is likely to be reserved for those rare cases where an accused has been subjected to misconduct of a deliberate and serious nature, and where the court is anxious to mark its disquiet at the methods employed. An issue which frequently arises in relation to misconduct is the extent to which the use of similar methods by the same officer in relation to other suspects may figure in cross-examination. In relation to oppression, the court's natural reluctance to exclude on this basis may be overcome by the use of such evidence (see, e.g., *Twitchell* [2000] 1 Cr App R 373, in which the Court of Appeal considered that officers alleged to have tortured D could have been cross-examined to 'potentially devastating' effect had the subsequent findings of a court regarding a similar torture by the same officers on another man been available for use in cross-examination). In *Charlton* [2016] EWCA Crim 52, where the original investigation was conducted by officers also linked to *Paris* (1993) 97 Cr App R 99, the Court acknowledged that police witnesses might be cross-examined as to whether they were part of a 'culture' of pressurising witnesses improperly.

Repetition of Confession Originally Obtained by Oppression

F18.15 Where a confession made in the course of an interview is excluded on grounds of oppression, it may be necessary to consider whether the effect on the accused was such that the repetition of the same information at a later, properly conducted interview ought also to be excluded (*Ismail* [1990] Crim LR 109, in which it was held that to accede to the prosecution's submission that misconduct in earlier interviews could be 'cured' by a properly conducted interview would be to condone flouting of the provisions of the Act and codes designed to protect against false confessions).

Relevance of Character and Attributes of Accused

At common law it was held that the nature of oppression varied according to the character and attributes of the accused. Thus, an 'experienced professional criminal' might expect a vigorous interrogation (*Gowan* [1982] Crim LR 821), and in *Dodd* (1981) 74 Cr App 50, O'Connor LJ said (at p. 56) that the trial judge 'was entitled to consider the type of men he was dealing with', all of whom were experienced criminals. O'Connor LJ contrasted the case with that of *Hudson* (1980) 72 Cr App R 163, in which a middle-aged man of previous good character had been subjected to a lengthy, and in certain respects unlawful, interrogation, which was subsequently held to have been oppressive. At the other end of the spectrum, in *Miller* [1986] 3 All ER 119 Watkins LJ said that it might be oppressive to put questions to an accused who is known to be mentally ill so as 'skilfully and deliberately' to induce a delusionary state. Despite the rejection in *Fulling* [1987] QB 426 of common-law rulings on oppression, these observations remain pertinent and appear to proceed on a meaning which is consistent with the ordinary meaning of oppression as adopted in *Fulling*. This view appears to have been confirmed by *Seelig* [1992] 4 All ER 429, in which Henry J, in a ruling described by the Court of Appeal as 'entirely right', took account of the fact that the person being questioned was 'an experienced merchant banker' and 'intelligent and sophisticated', in determining whether he had been questioned in an oppressive way, and in *Smith* [1994] 1 WLR 1396, the Court of Appeal regarded it as relevant that D, who was questioned by a person in authority within a bank, was himself a chairman and managing director of a substantial financial organisation. Similarly in *Paris* (1993) 97 Cr App R 99 (see **F18.13**), the Court, although of the opinion that the bullying and hectoring of D in interview would have been oppressive even with a suspect of normal intelligence, went out of its way to stress the effect on D, who was on the borderline of mental handicap. **F18.16**

EXCLUSION FOR UNRELIABILITY: PACE 1984, s. 76(2)(b)

Background

The Criminal Law Revision Committee, in its *Eleventh Report: Evidence (General)* (1972) Cmnd 4991, proposed that a confession should not be excluded simply on the basis that it was obtained in consequence of a threat or inducement, unless the circumstances were such that any resulting confession would be likely to be unreliable. This proposal became the PACE 1984, s. 76(2)(b), though the term 'threat or inducement' was replaced by the wider notion of 'anything said or done'. **F18.17**

Application of Statutory Test

The PACE 1984 requires the trial judge to consider a hypothetical question: not whether *this* confession is unreliable, but whether *any* confession which the accused might make in consequence of what was said or done was likely to be rendered unreliable. The purport of this provision was considered in *Re Proulx* [2001] 1 All ER 57, where Mance LJ stated (at [46]): **F18.18**

> The test in s. 76 cannot be satisfied by postulating some entirely different confession. There is also no likelihood that anything said or done would have induced any other confession. The word 'any' must thus, I think, be understood as indicating 'any such' or 'such a' confession as the applicant made. The abstract element involved also reflects the fact that the test is not whether the actual confession was untruthful or inaccurate. It is whether whatever was said or done was, in the circumstances existing as at the time of the confession, *likely* to have rendered such a confession unreliable,

whether or not it may be seen subsequently — with hindsight and in the light of all the material available at trial — that it did or did not actually do so.

Thus the court must consider whether what happened was likely in the circumstances to induce *an* unreliable confession to the offence in question, and to ignore any evidence suggesting that the *actual* confession was reliable.

In *Cox* [1991] Crim LR 276, a mentally handicapped accused gave evidence at the *voir dire* in the course of which he admitted one of the offences with which he was charged. The trial judge was held to have wrongly based his decision to admit D's out-of-court confession on the admission by D. The same point was made in *Crampton* (1991) 92 Cr App R 372, where it was said that, if acts are done or words spoken which are likely to induce unreliable confessions, then, whether or not the confession is true, it is inadmissible. Although the judge may not be influenced by evidence that the confession is true in deciding admissibility, there is no rule against taking into account any other relevant evidence given at trial before the *voir dire* begins which assists in determining the questions posed by s. 76(2)(b) (*Tyrer* (1989) 90 Cr App R 446 at pp. 449–50). Such evidence must, however, relate to the period before, or at the time when, the confession is made: the judge must 'stop the clock' and consider the issue of reliability at that point in time (a proposition cautiously, but rightly, advanced by Mance LJ in *Re Proulx*).

F18.19 **'Anything said or done'** Section 76(2) of the PACE 1984 obliges the judge to consider everything said or done (usually, but not inevitably by the police) and not to confine the inquiry to a narrow analysis analogous to offer and acceptance in the law of contract (*Barry* (1992) 95 Cr App R 384; *Wahab* [2002] EWCA Crim 1570, [2003] 1 Cr App R 15 (232)). The use of the phrase 'anything said or done', and the inclusion of all the surrounding circumstances, are indications that a confession may be inadmissible, notwithstanding that the police have not behaved improperly. In *Fulling* [1987] QB 426 the Court of Appeal stated, *obiter*, that it was 'abundantly clear' that a confession may be excluded under s. 76(2)(b) where there is no suspicion of any impropriety. Dicta in *Brine* [1992] Crim LR 123, stating that s. 76(2) is 'primarily concerned' with police misconduct, should not be understood to qualify this statement of principle. See also *Harvey* [1988] Crim LR 241, in which a psychopathically disordered woman of low normal intelligence heard her lover confess to a murder. As this experience may have led her to make a false confession out of a child-like desire to protect her lover, her statement was excluded under s. 76(2)(b). *Harvey* was cited with approval in *Raghip* (1991) *The Times*, 9 December 1991 and in *Wahab*. Such a confession might also be excluded under s. 78 (see **F18.33**). In the rather extreme case of *M* [2000] 8 Arch News 2, it was D's solicitor who, by intervening in the interview in an apparent attempt to secure a confession, rendered the resultant confession unreliable. In *Wahab* the Court of Appeal noted that where the solicitor provides proper legal advice to the client this will not normally be a basis for excluding a confession under s. 76(2)(b). In *Roberts* [2011] EWCA Crim 2974, it was the promise not to involve the police, held out by a shop manager, that gave rise to the inference that anything said in consequence was likely to be unreliable. A confession volunteered without anything being said or done clearly cannot fall foul of s. 76(2)(b) (see *Ward* [2018] EWCA Crim 1464 where an appropriate adult was the 'unwilling recipient of unsolicited confessions' by an accused, and nothing was said either by the adult or anyone else that was likely to render the confession unreliable).

F18.20 **Words or Actions of the Accused** It has been held that a confession cannot be rendered inadmissible under the PACE 1984, s. 76(2)(b), by reason only of something said or done by the accused (*Goldenberg* (1988) 88 Cr App R 285). In this case D was interviewed on suspicion of conspiracy to supply controlled drugs. The admissions which he made were alleged by the defence to be (a) an attempt by him to get bail, and (b) tainted by the fact that he was a heroin addict who, having been in custody for some time, would have said or done anything, however false, to gain his release so as to feed his addiction. The Court of Appeal considered that this argument was founded entirely 'on what was said or done by the appellant himself and on his state of mind', and that this was beyond the scope of the provision. The wording of the section, and in particular the words 'in consequence' in s. 76(2)(b), imported a causal link between what was said or done and the subsequent confession. It followed that the provision was looking to something external to the person making the confession and which was likely to have some effect in inducing a confession. *Goldenberg* was considered in *Crampton* (1991) 92 Cr App R 372, in which police officers interviewed D, a heroin addict, who it subsequently transpired was suffering from withdrawal symptoms. It was noted that in *Goldenberg* it was D himself who had requested the interview, but this was thought not to provide a ground for distinguishing the case, for it was doubtful whether the requirement for something external to be 'said or done' could be satisfied by the mere holding of an interview with an addict in withdrawal. The words of the statute contemplated some words spoken or acts done by the police which were likely to induce unreliable confessions. In *Walker* [1998] Crim LR 211, the Court of Appeal appears to have considered that the issue of whether D had taken cocaine before confessing had a material bearing on admissibility, but this appears to have been achieved by regarding the impairment of the accused as one of the 'circumstances' referred to in s. 76(2)(b).

A self-induced incapacity is clearly relevant to the issue of discretionary exclusion under the PACE 1984, s. 78 (see **F18.54**).

'Circumstances' The accused's own mental state may be part of the 'circumstances' for the purposes of s. 76(2)(b). In *Re Proulx* [2001] 1 All ER 57, D confessed to a murder to an undercover operative who persuaded him that it was necessary in order to be accepted as a member of a criminal gang anxious to know the truth about his past. Whether this was something likely to induce D to make a false confession was something which could only be determined by an assessment of D. It does not matter that these circumstances may have been unknown to the interrogator at the time. **F18.21**

In *Everett* [1988] Crim LR 826, D was discovered in a compromising position with a five-year-old boy. On the way to the police station, and while he was there, he admitted indecently assaulting the child. D was a 42-year-old man with a mental age of eight, and was regarded by a medical witness as being in the bottom 2 per cent of the population. The trial judge regarded the medical evidence as irrelevant provided that he was satisfied (as he was) from listening to the tape recording of the police station interview that D's replies were rational and showed understanding of the questions. The Court of Appeal ruled against this approach, and held that the circumstances to be taken into account 'obviously include' the mental condition of a suspect at the time the confession came into being. The test to be applied was an objective one, i.e. not what the police officers thought (if they thought anything) about the mental condition of the suspect, but instead the actual condition of the suspect as subsequently ascertained from a doctor. The confession ought to have been excluded because the prosecution 'most certainly had not' discharged the burden of proving it admissible. Similarly, in *McGovern* (1991) 92 Cr App R 228, it was said that the physical condition and particular vulnerability of D (she was six months pregnant and of limited intelligence), while not being 'anything said or done' to D, were part of the background against which the submission that she had been wrongly denied access to legal advice had to be judged. The combination of circumstances had the far-reaching result that it was appropriate to exclude both the confession made as a direct consequence of the denial of access and a subsequent confession made in the presence of a solicitor which was tarnished as a result of the earlier confession. **F18.22**

In *Souter* [1995] Crim LR 729, a confession was held to be inadmissible where it was made by a soldier who was in a state of extreme emotion and distress to an officer who had been sent to calm him down; other relevant factors were that the conversation between the two had an appearance of confidentiality, and the officer had a very partial recollection of the rest of what had been said. The kind of mental condition which may be taken into account under s. 76(2)(b) is not limited to what might be termed 'impairment of intelligence or social functioning', still less to 'mental impairment' (*Walker* [1998] Crim LR 211). **F18.23**

In cases where the mental condition of the accused is a relevant factor, expert evidence is admissible if it demonstrates some form of abnormality relevant to the reliability of a defendant's confession (*O'Brien* [2000] Crim LR 676). In *Ward* (1993) 96 Cr App R 1, it was said that a mental abnormality would have to fall into a recognised category of mental disorder for expert evidence about it to be properly receivable, but in *O'Brien* the Court doubted whether this was so, as the operative consideration was simply whether the abnormality might render the confession unreliable. The Court added that the abnormality would have to be such as to demonstrate a 'very significant deviation from the norm'. Expert evidence might also be crucial to the understanding of whether an accused of low IQ is abnormally suggestible, bearing in mind that such suggestibility might manifest itself at interview without necessarily being apparent to a jury when the accused testifies at trial with the support of counsel and the protection of the judge (*King* [2000] 2 Cr App R 391; *Smith* [2003] EWCA Crim 927). *O'Brien* was further qualified in *Blackburn* [2005] EWCA Crim 1349, [2005] 2 Cr App R 30 (440), where it was said that expert evidence could be received on the question whether a vulnerable individual, after prolonged questioning, might make a false confession, given that the issue is one falling outside the ken of the normal jury. In *Steel* [2003] EWCA Crim 1640, the Court of Appeal reviewed a conviction for murder in 1979 to assess the effect of fresh psychological evidence of suggestibility and vulnerability in interview which drew on techniques that were unavailable at the time of the trial. Unlike in *King*, the defence could not establish that the confession had been improperly obtained. The Court, however, rightly considered that if the new evidence rendered the conviction unsafe it was not necessary to consider whether there had been a breach either of the Judges' Rules (which were in force at the time), or of any more thoroughgoing modern safeguards for the protection of suspects and the avoidance of miscarriages of justice. (As to expert evidence, see also **F11.18**.)

F18.24 **Breach of PACE Codes** It is common for the defence to allege that the 'something said or done' includes a breach by the police of an obligation under the PACE 1984 or the Code of Practice for the Detention, Treatment and Questioning of Persons by Police Officers (PACE Code C; see **appendix 1**). Such a breach will not lead to automatic exclusion of a confession obtained in consequence (*Delaney* (1988) 88 Cr App R 338), though it may, on its own or together with other factors, provide evidence that s. 76(2)(b) has not been complied with. In *Delaney*, D, whose psychological make-up was such that he was likely to feel unusual pressure to escape from interrogation, alleged that he had been induced to confess by a suggestion that the serious indecent assault of which he was suspected was more deserving of treatment than punishment. The interview was not recorded until the following day, in breach of Code C, and the Court of Appeal held that the absence of a reliable record of what occurred 'deprived the court of what was, in all likelihood, the most cogent evidence as to what did indeed happen during those interviews and what did induce the appellant to confess'. The breach was therefore significant, in that, the burden of proof being on the prosecution, the speculation necessarily engendered by the breach was sufficient to tip the scale in favour of the defence. For other cases where confessions were excluded, see, e.g., *Doolan* [1988] Crim LR 747 (failure to caution and to maintain a proper interview record or to show it to D); *Chung* (1991) 92 Cr App R 314 (questioning before allowing access to a solicitor and failure to show note to D or subsequently to his solicitor); *Waters* [1989] Crim LR 62 (improper questioning after charge resulting in ambiguous and potentially unreliable answer); *DPP v Blake* [1989] 1 WLR 432 (the 'spirit of the Code' was broken when a juvenile's estranged father was insisted on by police as the appropriate adult to attend her interview); *Morse* [1991] Crim LR 195 (juvenile's father acting as 'appropriate adult' and subsequently discovered to have low IQ and to be incapable of appreciating the gravity of the situation in which D found himself); *McPhee v The Queen* [2016] UKPC 29, [2017] 1 Cr App R 10 (109) (a decision of the Privy Council in which the failure to give any guidance to a clergyman acting as appropriate adult may have inhibited him from taking steps to question the way in which the confession had been obtained); *Moss* (1990) 91 Cr App R 371 (suspect of low intelligence interviewed nine times during a lengthy period of detention; access to legal advice improperly denied and no independent person present at interview).

Delaney and *Doolan* serve also to illustrate that 'something said or done' may consist of an omission to fulfil the requirements of the Code, although such an omission might always be described in more positive terms, for example, as interviewing the accused without having administered the caution as the Code requires.

Repetition of Confession Originally Obtained in Breach of PACE Code Where a breach of the PACE 1984 or a PACE Code has occurred which renders a confession inadmissible under s. 76(2)(b), it may be necessary to consider whether a repetition of the confession at a subsequent, properly conducted interview is also inadmissible. In *McGovern* (1991) 92 Cr App R 228, a subsequent interview was held inadmissible as it had been tainted by the matters which had led to the exclusion of an earlier interview, namely breaches of s. 58 and the interviewing provisions of Code C. It was further stated that the very fact that admissions were made at an earlier stage was likely to have an effect on the suspect thereafter, with adverse consequences for the admissibility of any repetition of the confession. In *Glaves* [1993] Crim LR 685 the Court of Appeal, whilst denying that there must necessarily be a 'continuing blight' on confessions obtained subsequent to a confession which is excluded under s. 76(2), nevertheless held that the breaches in the case (which included giving D, a juvenile, the impression that he was bound to answer questions) were not cured by a change of police officers and a caution, particularly as D had received no legal advice between the two interviews. F18.25

Section 76 and Causation

The words '*by* oppression' and '*in consequence of* anything said or done' in the PACE 1984, s. 76(2)(a) and (b), import a causal link to the obtaining of the confession. In *Rennie* [1982] 1 All ER 385, a decision at common law where causation was also an important consideration, Lord Lane CJ held that the judge should avoid any 'refined analysis of the concept of causation' and 'should approach it much as would a jury. . . . In other words, he should understand the principle and the spirit behind it, and apply his common sense.' See also *Tyrer* (1989) 90 Cr App R 446 and *Barry* (1992) 95 Cr App R 384, in both of which it was accepted that the prosecution may discharge the onus of proof under s. 76(2) by showing that there is no causal link between the confession and things said or done by police officers which might have been conducive to unreliability, and *Crampton* (1991) 92 Cr App R 369, in which *Rennie* was cited in support of the proposition that a confession will not have been caused by anything said or done by an interviewer if a suspect is motivated to confess because of a perception that there may be an advantage from doing so. The demeanour of the accused when giving evidence on the *voir dire* may assist the prosecution in showing that threats allegedly made at interview had no impact (*Weeks* [1995] Crim LR 52). F18.26

CONFESSION TENDERED BY CO-ACCUSED

In *Myers* [1998] AC 124, D1 and D2 were charged with murder. D2's defence was that D1 alone committed the offence, and he sought to rely upon a confession to that effect which D1 had made. The statement was not relied upon in evidence by the prosecution, in consequence of breaches of the Codes of Practice. However, there was no suggestion that the confession was not freely made by D1. The House of Lords held that the statement was admissible for D2, although the reasoning behind the decision is somewhat obscure. Any uncertainties have been resolved by the CJA 2003, s. 128, which inserted s. 76A into the PACE 1984, providing that an accused may not give evidence of a co-accused's confession unless the conditions imposed by s. 76A(2) are satisfied. These conditions mirror those imposed on the prosecution except that the burden of proof on the accused is clearly stated to be proof on a balance of probabilities. If such a confession is admitted, but its maker (D1) alleges that it is unreliable, a complex jury direction is needed to explain how the jury should approach this contention F18.27

in assessing the case against D1, where the prosecution have the burden of proof, and the case for D2, who has no such onus (see the *Crown Court Compendium* (July 2020), ch. 14-15). Note also s. 128(2), which provides that nothing in the hearsay chapter of the Act makes a confession admissible if it would not be admissible under the PACE 1984, s. 76. This would appear to preclude, for example, the use of an otherwise inadmissible confession as a previous inconsistent statement so as to provide evidence that the confession itself is true (previous inconsistent statements being generally admissible as proof of the truth of the facts stated under s. 119: see **F7.51**).

F18.28 **Police and Criminal Evidence Act 1984, s. 76A**

(1) In any proceedings a confession made by an accused person may be given in evidence for another person charged in the same proceedings (a co-accused) in so far as it is relevant to any matter in issue in the proceedings and is not excluded by the court in pursuance of this section.

(2) If, in any proceedings where a co-accused proposes to give in evidence a confession made by an accused person, it is represented to the court that the confession was or may have been obtained—
   (a) by oppression of the person who made it; or
   (b) in consequence of anything said or done which was likely, in the circumstances existing at the time, to render unreliable any confession which might be made by him in consequence thereof,

the court shall not allow the confession to be given in evidence for the co-accused except in so far as it is proved to the court on the balance of probabilities that the confession (notwithstanding that it may be true) was not so obtained.

(3) Before allowing a confession made by an accused person to be given in evidence for a co-accused in any proceedings, the court may of its own motion require the fact that the confession was not obtained as mentioned in subsection (2) above to be proved in the proceedings on the balance of probabilities.

(4) The fact that a confession is wholly or partly excluded in pursuance of this section shall not affect the admissibility in evidence—
   (a) of any facts discovered as a result of the confession; or
   (b) where the confession is relevant as showing that the accused speaks, writes or expresses himself in a particular way, of so much of the confession as is necessary to show that he does so.

(5) Evidence that a fact to which this subsection applies was discovered as a result of a statement made by an accused person shall not be admissible unless evidence of how it was discovered is given by him or on his behalf.

(6) Subsection (5) above applies—
   (a) to any fact discovered as a result of a confession which is wholly excluded in pursuance of this section; and
   (b) to any fact discovered as a result of a confession which is partly so excluded, if the fact is discovered as a result of the excluded part of the confession.

(7) In this section 'oppression' includes torture, inhuman or degrading treatment, and the use or threat of violence (whether or not amounting to torture).

F18.29 In *Johnson* [2007] EWCA Crim 1651, D1 had been granted permission to vacate a guilty plea, but at the trial which ensued his co-accused, D2, successfully applied to rely on the basis of the plea as a relevant confession under s. 76A. The Court of Appeal commented that it 'understood the frustration of a defendant who is permitted to vacate a guilty plea but not then permitted to enjoy the fruits of vacation by way of a trial unencumbered by the earlier plea'. Section 76A, however, was designed to ensure fairness as between co-accused.

Section 76A applies only where the maker of the confession is a party to the proceedings. Thus in *Finch* [2007] EWCA Crim 36, [2007] 1 WLR 1645, D was unable to invoke s. 76A in relation to a statement, made at interview by R, who subsequently pleaded guilty to his part in the offence, because D and R were not 'charged in the same proceedings'. The Court of Appeal considered the alternative possibility that under the CJA 2003 such evidence might be admitted even where the maker is available to testify under the 'interests of justice' test contained in s. 114(1)(d) (see **F17.34**), but considered this to be most likely where the maker of the statement was unavailable or had demonstrably good reason not to give evidence. The most appropriate course for D would have been to test the reluctance of R to give evidence, and if R proved hostile to avail himself of the consequent admissibility of R's previous inconsistent statement under s. 119. Nor does it follow that every partial admission by a co-accused can be relied on by any other under s. 76A, as the confession itself must be relevant to the defence. In *Sliogeris* [2015] EWCA Crim 22, it was held that s. 76A did not apply to an out-of-court statement made by co-accused D1, in which he admitted his presence at the scene of a murder but blamed co-accused D2 for the killing. The confession was tendered by co-accused D3, whose defence was that D2 alone committed the crime. However, the admission of presence, though a partial confession by D1, was not of itself relevant to D3's defence, while the allegation that D2 was guilty was held not to be part of the confession. It was not necessary for the Court of Appeal to resolve the further (and more difficult) issue of whether D1's statement, had it been admitted, would have been limited in its function to being evidence in favour of D3 (as provided by s. 76A) and against the maker, D1, or whether it would have been evidence for all purposes (including against D2). However, it was noted that there is a 'cogent case' for saying that it should not be treated as generally admissible given the purpose of the provision. The statement was, however, held to have been admissible under the CJA 2003, s. 114(1)(d) (see **F17.41**).

DISCRETIONARY EXCLUSION UNDER THE PACE 1984, s. 78

At Common Law

The common-law power of a court to exclude evidence in its discretion is considered in general at **F2.36** ***et seq***. The following section is concerned only with the application of the discretion to exclude confession evidence. **F18.30**

Police and Criminal Evidence Act 1984, s. 82

(3) Nothing in this Part of this Act shall prejudice any power of a court to exclude evidence (whether by preventing questions from being put or otherwise) at its discretion.

Section 82 applies to Part VIII of the 1984 Act, which includes ss. 76 and 78. Prior to the enactment of the Act and the codes of practice made under it, exclusion of confession evidence at common law was recognised in two contexts:

(a) the exclusion of unreliable confessions, the prejudicial effect of which could be said to outweigh their true probative value; and
(b) the exclusion of confession evidence, the admission of which might operate unfairly against the accused.

The common-law powers, though preserved by s. 82(3), are unlikely to be resorted to in practice given the wide ambit of s. 78 (see **F18.33**). The situation in which they are most likely to be used is where a judge becomes aware, after a confession has been admitted in evidence, of circumstances suggesting that it should not have been. Neither s. 76 nor s. 78 applies to this situation (*Sat-Bhambra* (1988) 88 Cr App R 55, discussed in detail at **F18.75**), so the court is thrown back on its common-law powers.

Exclusion for Unreliability In *Miller* [1986] 3 All ER 119, the Court of Appeal acknowledged the existence of a discretion to refuse to admit 'a confession which came from a mind which at the time was possibly irrational and [where] what the defendant said may have been the product of delusions and hallucinations'. In *Isequilla* [1975] 1 All ER 77, the Court accepted the statement that 'it would be in accordance with principle to exclude a confession made by someone whose mental state was such as to render his utterances completely unreliable'. **F18.31**

F18.32 **Exclusion for Unfairness** In *Sang* [1980] AC 402, Lord Diplock said (at p. 437, emphasis added): '*save with regard to admissions and confessions* and generally with regard to evidence obtained from the accused after commission of the offence, he [the trial judge] has no discretion to refuse to admit relevant admissible evidence on the ground that it was obtained by improper or unfair means'. The unfairness discretion was well established at common law with regard to confession evidence. In *Houghton* (1978) 68 Cr App R 197, Lawton LJ held (at p. 206) that evidence 'would operate unfairly against an accused if it had been obtained in an oppressive manner by force or against the wishes of an accused person or by a trick or by conduct of which the Crown ought not to take advantage', and said that trial judges enjoyed a discretion to disallow such evidence. The discretion was recognised to exist, although it was infrequently exercised, with regard to breaches of the Judges' Rules (see, e.g., *Voisin* [1918] 1 KB 531; *Lemsatef* [1977] 2 All ER 835) and where a confession had been extracted following a period of unlawful detention (*Hudson* (1980) 72 Cr App R 163).

Exclusion under s. 78

F18.33 **Police and Criminal Evidence Act 1984, s. 78**

(1) In any proceedings the court may refuse to allow evidence on which the prosecution proposes to rely to be given if it appears to the court that, having regard to all the circumstances, including the circumstances in which the evidence was obtained, the admission of the evidence would have such an adverse effect on the fairness of the proceedings that the court ought not to admit it.

(2) Nothing in this section shall prejudice any rule of law requiring a court to exclude evidence.

For the meaning of 'proceedings', see s. 82(1). The power may be used in respect of confession evidence tendered by the prosecution (*Mason* [1988] 3 All ER 481), and numerous instances of its use for this purpose exist. In practice, if not in law, the common-law discretion appears to have been superseded.

The Court of Appeal will not interfere with the exercise of a trial judge's discretion to admit evidence under s. 78 unless satisfied that the decision was perverse (*Dures* [1997] 2 Cr App R 247, applying the general principle stated in *Quinn* [1995] 1 Cr App R 480). It follows that cases in which the discretion is said to have been wrongly exercised are comparatively rare.

The procedure to be adopted where an application is made to exclude prosecution evidence under s. 78 is considered at **F2.11** *et seq.*, where the point is made that this is not, strictly speaking, a matter to which the burden of proof applies. However, the Court of Appeal in *Charlton* [2016] EWCA Crim 52 stated that it is for an accused to persuade the court that the evidence of a prosecution witness ought to be excluded under s. 78 and that the burden is 'no higher than the balance of probabilities'. The authorities considered at **F2.12** were not cited.

Section 78 and the PACE Codes of Practice

F18.34 Codes of practice issued under the PACE 1984, s. 66, are admissible in evidence in both criminal and civil proceedings, and any provision of such a code appearing to the court or tribunal conducting the proceedings to be relevant to any question arising in the proceedings, must be taken into account in determining that question by virtue of s. 67(11). Breach of a relevant code provision does not lead to the automatic exclusion of a confession obtained in consequence (see, e.g., *Delaney* (1988) 88 Cr App R 338, where the Court of Appeal heard submissions on ss. 76 and 78, and it was held that 'the mere fact that there has been a breach of the PACE Codes does not of itself mean that evidence has to be rejected'; *Parris* (1988) 89 Cr App R 68 at p. 72, where the same point was made). The question is whether the admission of the evidence would have such an adverse effect on the fairness of the proceedings that the court ought not to admit it. Even a plain and admitted breach, though it is to be deplored, may fail to trigger exclusion if it does not operate in a way prejudicial to the accused (*Canale* [1990] 2 All ER 187). See further **F18.36**. In *Roberts* [1997] 1 Cr App R 217, it was held that breach of a PACE Code C provision designed to protect another suspect could not be prayed in aid by the accused. This was because there was no causal link between the breaches and D's admission. On the facts, however, had the Code been complied with, it might have resulted in a record which would have supported D's contention that the other accused, to whom D subsequently confessed, was acting in the role of police agent in soliciting the confession. It is submitted that the issue is not whether the breach against the other accused caused the confession by D (as plainly it did not) but whether the breach affected the fairness of using D's confession (which it may have done).

Breach of a code of practice is in many cases an important factor in considering whether to exclude evidence. Where confession evidence is concerned, the code most likely to be involved is Code C, dealing with the detention, treatment and questioning of persons by police officers. Certain of the rights guaranteed by Code C, such as the right of access to legal advice, are also to be found in the body of the 1984 Act itself (see PACE Code C, s. 6, and the PACE 1984, s. 58). In *Keenan* [1990] 2 QB 54, the Court of Appeal declined to express a view as to whether a court should differentiate between breaches of the Act and of the codes. It is submitted that, whereas the location of such a right in the body of the Act may be an indication of its importance, the principles to be followed when considering the application of s. 78 are no different. **F18.35**

In *Samuel* [1988] QB 615, the Court of Appeal stated that it was undesirable to give any general guidance on the way in which the discretion under s. 78 or under the judge's inherent powers should be exercised, because circumstances may vary infinitely. Without seeking to give any such general guidance, it is submitted that the following considerations have proved to be of importance where s. 78 is concerned.

Nature and Extent of Breach In *Walsh* (1989) 91 Cr App R 161, D was denied access to legal advice, and it was common ground that there had been a breach of the PACE 1984, s. 58 (see **D1.55**). The Court of Appeal observed (at p. 163): **F18.36**

> The main object of section 58 of the Act and indeed of the codes of practice is to achieve fairness — to an accused or suspected person so as, among other things, to preserve and protect his legal rights; but also fairness for the Crown and its officers so that again, among other things, there might be reduced the incidence or effectiveness of unfounded allegations of malpractice.
>
> To our minds it follows that if there are significant and substantial breaches of section 58 or the provisions of the code, then prima facie at least the standards of fairness set by Parliament have not been met. So far as a defendant is concerned, it seems to us also to follow that to admit evidence against him which has been obtained in circumstances where these standards have not been met, cannot but have an adverse effect on the fairness of the proceedings. This does not mean, of course, that in every case of a significant or substantial breach of section 58 or the code of practice the evidence concerned will automatically be excluded. Section 78 does not so provide. The task of the court is not merely to consider whether there would be an adverse effect on the fairness of the proceedings, but such an adverse effect that justice requires the evidence to be excluded.

Breach of Right to Legal Advice In assessing the effect on the fairness of the proceedings of a breach of the PACE 1984, s. 58, it is relevant that the right of access to legal advice is 'fundamental' (*Samuel* [1988] QB 615) and that it is regarded as of great importance in the jurisprudence of the ECtHR (*Murray v UK* (1996) 22 EHRR 29, considered in *Aspinall* [1999] 2 Cr App R 115). In Scotland, *Cadder v HM Advocate* [2010] UKSC 43, [2010] 1 WLR 2610 is authority for a rule, derived from the ECHR, Article 6, and the ECtHR's decision in *Salduz v Turkey* (2008) 49 EHRR 19 (421) that (save where compelling reasons may exceptionally justify denial of access to a lawyer without unduly prejudicing the defence) the prosecution cannot lead and rely upon evidence of anything said by an accused without the benefit of legal advice during questioning under detention at a police station. In another Scottish appeal, *Ambrose v Harris* [2011] UKSC 43, **F18.37**

[2011] 1 WLR 2435, the Supreme Court considered that it was not necessary to apply the same strict principles to the questioning of a person not yet detained: whether there was a breach of Article 6 in such a case would depend on the circumstances. Domestic authorities under the PACE 1984, s. 78, do not currently reflect the same strict approach to questioning without benefit of legal advice, though Lord Brown in *Ambrose v Harris* noted that the discretionary nature of the statutory power 'sits a little uneasily' with the rule in *Cadder*.

Safety interviews conducted under the Terrorism Act 2000 pose a particular difficulty in regard to Article 6. In *Ibrahim v UK* [2016] ECHR 750, the Grand Chamber of the ECtHR refused to draw a 'bright-line rule' prohibiting the use at trial of statements obtained during police questioning from which legal representatives had been excluded, and upheld the previous decision of the ECtHR ((2015) 61 EHRR 9 (264)) that the use of safety interviews, conducted with three suspected bombers who were denied access to legal advice, was justifiable in light of the 'exceptionally serious and imminent threat to public safety' prevailing immediately after the London bombings of 2005. The key questions are said to be (i) whether there existed compelling reasons for the restriction of access, and (ii) whether, viewing the proceedings as a whole, the trial was fair. The extent to which 'compelling reasons' were lacking would 'weigh heavily' in the balance in favour of finding a violation of the ECHR, Article 6, but their absence was not, by itself, sufficient to amount to such a violation. In the result, compelling reasons for the delay had been demonstrated (although the Grand Chamber took a stronger line than the Chamber as to what might be compelling, rejecting the argument that a 'non-specific risk of leaks' could qualify) and the proceedings were found to be fair. The evidence relied upon was in the form of lies told in the interviews. The fault alleged (the giving of the new rather than the old-style caution) could not have induced the decision to tell lies. It was also relevant that the defendants had the opportunity to challenge the evidence at trial, that the jury was fully and fairly instructed about its use, and that there was a wealth of other prosecution evidence.

In relation to a fourth applicant, who had been questioned as a witness and had not been cautioned at the appropriate stage, despite being under suspicion, the Grand Chamber held that the UK government had failed to demonstrate compelling reasons for the delay of access to legal advice and notification of the right to remain silent, and had failed to demonstrate that the overall fairness of the trial was not irretrievably prejudiced by the procedural failings. The applicant's case was subsequently reconsidered by the Court of Appeal in light of the Grand Chamber's conclusions. In *Abdurahman* [2019] EWCA Crim 2239, [2020] 1 Cr App R 27 (439), the Court upheld D's convictions for assisting an offender and failing to provide information about acts of terrorism. While domestic courts would usually follow a clear and constant line of Strasbourg decisions, this should be viewed as guidance rather than a straitjacket. The degree of constraint the Strasbourg jurisprudence imposes is context-specific, and in any case the finding of the Grand Chamber regarding the absence of 'compelling reasons' was in the nature of a finding of fact rather than part of the Court's jurisprudence. In the opinion of the Court of Appeal there were compelling reasons: as the Court hearing D's original appeal in 2008 observed, D was providing information about one of the London bombers from the 2005 attacks who was then at large and which could have been of critical importance in securing his arrest, which was the priority at that time. The Grand Chamber attached importance to the absence of evidence from a senior officer, but the Court of Appeal considered that the crucial evidence as to the reasons for the delay was that of the officers conducting the interview. D could have alleged 'bad faith' on their part but he did not do so. Further, even after D had been informed of his right to legal advice he affirmed the truth of the relevant statement in a later interview, and the safety of the conviction was also supported by the evidence that had come to light as a result, which was not regarded as inadmissible in English law even if the confession is excluded (see **F18.85**).

Where legal advice is waived the waiver should be voluntary, informed and unequivocal (*McGowan v B* [2011] UKSC 54, [2011] 1 WLR 3121 as interpreted in *Saunders* [2012] EWCA Crim 1380, [2012] 2 Cr App R 26 (321)). This requirement might suggest exclusion in cases where the right to advice, for whatever reason, has not been fully presented to the accused. Cases that may require reconsideration in light of these authorities include *Alladice* (1988) 87 Cr App R 380, in which D was denied access to legal advice by officers who had genuinely misconstrued the provisions of s. 58. D admitted in evidence that he was able to cope with being interviewed, that he had been given and understood the caution, and that he was aware of his legal rights. However, he had requested legal advice in order to have a check on the conduct of the police during interview. The trial judge found that the interviews were properly conducted, and that the only function of legal advice would have been to remind D of rights of which he was already well aware. On these facts, the Court of Appeal held that there was no obligation to exclude the confession. See also *Dunford* (1990) 91 Cr App R 150, *Oliphant* [1992] Crim LR 40 and, by way of contrast, *Sanusi* [1992] Crim LR 43, in which the failure to inform D, a foreigner, of his right to advice was particularly significant in the light of his lack of familiarity with police procedures and meant that his confession ought to have been excluded. Minor defects in the communication of the right to legal advice that do not bear on the exercise of informed choice by the suspect cannot give rise to unfairness (*Beeres v CPS* [2014] EWHC 283 (Admin), [2014] 2 Cr App R 8 (101)). See also as to waiver **F20.7**.

Breach of Interview Procedures Breaches of the various provisions of Code C regarding the procedures to be followed when interviewing suspects have also tended to lead to the exclusion of evidence under the PACE 1984, s. 78, for reasons similar to those stated in *Walsh* (1989) 91 Cr App R 161. In *Keenan* [1990] 2 QB 54, it was said to be desirable that the provisions of Code C which are designed to ensure that interviews are fully recorded and the suspect afforded an opportunity to contest the record be 'strictly complied with', and that the courts would not be slow to exclude evidence obtained following 'substantial breaches' by the interrogator. In *Coelho* [2008] EWCA Crim 627, it was held that the statement in *Keenan* was 'not a matter of rote' so the breach does not automatically result in exclusion. The statement in *Keenan* indicates the way the courts should approach such breaches. In *Coelho*, evidence of a conversation with a police officer in Portuguese should have been excluded because of the attendant risk of misunderstanding. Other provisions which have been held capable of requiring or contributing to the exclusion of evidence are those relating to cautioning, e.g., in *Williams* [2012] EWCA Crim 264, where D was questioned without caution while injured in hospital in circumstances where, viewed objectively, he was already a suspect and not (as the questioning officer thought) simply the victim of an assault by another. Breach of the right to have an appropriate adult present at interview is also likely to trigger exclusion, and in *Aspinall* [1999] 2 Cr App R 115 it was noted that the denial of the right to an appropriate adult might also lead to the failure of the accused to recognise the need for legal advice. A waiver in these circumstances would be worthless. In *Kirk* [1999] 4 All ER 698, the right of the accused to know why he has been arrested and 'at least in general terms the level of the offence in respect of which he is suspected' was held sufficient to warrant the exclusion under s. 78 of a confession to theft of a handbag where D was not warned that he was also under suspicion for the more serious offences of robbery from the same victim and of her manslaughter. It was recognised that the accused might reach a view on such matters as whether to seek legal advice, and what to say in response to questions, in the light of the accused's understanding of the seriousness of the matter under investigation. The Court of Appeal's purposive reading of the PACE 1984 and Code C reflects an approach similar to that of the ECtHR in *Fox, Campbell & Hartley v UK* (1990) 13 EHRR 157 in interpreting the requirement of the ECHR, Article 5(2), that a person arrested be informed promptly of the reasons for the arrest. In similar vein, the Privy Council in *Grant v The State* [2005] UKPC 2, [2007] 1 AC 1, interpreting the common-law approach to the Judges' Rules in Jamaica, analysed the restrictions on questioning after charge by reference to the increased vulnerability of the accused at that time, and the pressure to speak, before deciding that the essential criterion for admissibility is fairness rather than simply whether the answers were voluntarily given. **F18.38**

(As to the content of the provisions of Code C regarding interrogation, see **D1.80** ***et seq.***)

F18.39 The failure of the interrogator to appreciate that questioning a suspect amounts to an 'interview' within the meaning of that term in Code C has proved an important peg on which to hang arguments for exclusion, as such failure frequently leads to a multiplicity of relevant breaches of Code C. The leading authorities are *Absolam* (1988) 88 Cr App R 332 (breaches including failure to caution, to record, and to offer legal advice prior to impromptu questioning by custody officer: confession should have been excluded); *Cox* (1993) 96 Cr App R 464 (informal questioning in D's own home amounting to interview which ought to have taken place only in a police station, inadequate recording and late caution: confession should have been excluded); *Weekes* (1993) 97 Cr App R 222 (inadequate recording and failure to ensure presence of appropriate adult at conversation in police car amounting to interview: confession should have been excluded); *Okafor* (1994) 99 Cr App R 97 (questioning by customs officer during search of D's bag conducted without caution or other incidents of an interview in order not to excite D's suspicion that the drugs in his luggage had been detected: questioning still an interview and confession should have been excluded for breaches); and *Weedersteyn* [1995] 1 Cr App R 405 (D believed he was assisting officers to find drugs importers and was not aware of the significance of his own incriminating statement, taken without caution, until two months later: statement should have been excluded as arising out of an interview not under caution, and because no record was shown to D). The frequent appearance of cases of this type in the first wave of applications to exclude under s. 78 may in part be accounted for by the difficulty of applying the definition of interview provided by the first revision of Code C which has now been superseded (see *Cox*, in which the authorities are reviewed). Another example is *Gill* [2003] EWCA Crim 2256, [2004] 1 Cr App R 20 (214), in which it appears that officers of the Inland Revenue investigating tax fraud did not appreciate that they were required to comply with the code when conducting a 'Hansard' interview. In holding the resultant evidence admissible, the Court of Appeal took account of the fact that the defendants were fully aware that their answers might render them liable to criminal proceedings. By contrast, in *Hawkins* [2005] EWCA Crim 1723, a police officer unfamiliar with health and safety legislation spoke to D about an explosion in which D had been burned and another man killed. D was, at the time, in shock and breathing with the assistance of an oxygen mask, having been given the maximum possible dose of morphine. The officer's failure to realise that D was a suspect rather than a mere witness was immaterial: a view to that effect should have been formed, the interview should not have taken place as it did and the fruits of the interview should have been excluded.

F18.40 **Breaches Not Triggering Exclusion** Although the provisions regarding the conduct of interviews are of great importance, breaches may nevertheless occur which are insufficiently significant or substantial to trigger the PACE 1984, s. 78. For example, in *Matthews* (1989) 91 Cr App R 43, the decision of the trial judge not to exclude evidence of a confession was upheld where the breach concerned the failure of a police officer to show the suspect a note of a conversation which the suspect had asked to be kept 'off the record'. See also *Courtney* [1995] Crim LR 63 (where the provisions of Code C were 'largely followed'), *RSPCA v Eager* [1995] Crim LR 60 (to similar effect) and *Blackwell* [1995] 2 Cr App R 641 (in which the court's decision that the trial judge was 'perfectly entitled' to admit the evidence was said to be 'highlighted by the technicality of the breaches'). Alternatively, a breach may be more than technical, but in the particular circumstances of the case no unfairness results from admitting the evidence. In *Dunn* (1990) 91 Cr App R 150, the failure of the interviewer to observe the provisions designed to prevent fabrication of the interview record would have been regarded as sufficient to require exclusion but for the fact that D's solicitor's clerk was present during the alleged conversation. It was held that it was legitimate for the trial judge to take account of this factor in exercising his discretion to admit the confession, as the presence of the clerk would have been likely to inhibit fabrication, and provided the accused with a witness as to what was actually said. In *Findlay* [1992] Crim LR 372, two suspects had wrongly been held incommunicado but it was held that the fact that one of them had subsequently had access to a solicitor for half an hour before signing the notes of his interview justified the admission of his confession. In *Ridehalgh v DPP* [2005] EWHC 1100 (Admin), [2005] RTR 26 (353), it was said that, even if the failure of a police inspector to caution a fellow officer was, on the facts, an error (which it was held not to be), it could not have been unfair to admit the incriminating response, both because the person questioned was himself a police officer and because of his willingness to repeat the same matters shortly afterwards under caution. And in *Rehman* [2006] EWCA Crim 1900, the failure to determine at trial whether there was sufficient evidence on which to caution a traveller in whose bags drugs were found at Customs was not fatal — even if a caution had been required, those stopped and questioned in a Customs check are already aware of the formality of the occasion.

Failure to Establish Breach Where the defence relies on breaches of PACE Code C in constructing a challenge to a confession under the PACE 1984, s. 78, but the court decides that no breach occurred, it follows that it is most unlikely that the discretion will be exercised. For examples, see *Hughes* [1988] Crim LR 519 (provisions regarding interviewing in the absence of a solicitor not infringed), *Maguire* (1989) 90 Cr App R 115 (exchange between police officer and M not an 'interview'), *Menard* (1994) *The Times*, 23 March 1994 (meeting sought by M in order to volunteer information not an 'interview'), and *Hughes v DPP* [2010] EWHC 515 (Admin) (informal conversation with potential suspect not 'interview'). Ultimately, however, the question is one of the unfairness of admitting the evidence (*Doncaster* [2008] EWCA Crim 5, where it was held that tax inspectors were not obliged to administer a caution). **F18.41**

Where the provisions of Code C have changed in the accused's favour since interrogation, the court may take account of the new provision as the Code reflects what is considered to be fair (*Ward* (1994) 98 Cr App R 337).

Bad Faith It is not the function of the court to use the PACE 1984, s. 78, to discipline the police (*Mason* [1988] 3 All ER 481; *Canale* [1990] 2 All ER 187). However, the presence of bad faith where the police have acted in breach of the Act or Code is a factor making it more likely that evidence will be excluded. In *Alladice* (1988) 87 Cr App R 380, the facts of which are stated at **F18.37**, the Court of Appeal held that there is a distinction to be drawn between cases where the police have acted in bad faith, and cases where the police, albeit in good faith, have fallen foul of s. 58. In the former case, a court would have 'little difficulty in ruling any confession inadmissible under s. 78'. In the latter, the evidence would still fall to be excluded in many cases, so that the police should use their powers of delaying access to a solicitor only with great circumspection, but it was not possible 'to say in advance what would or would not be fair'. A similar distinction was drawn in *Walsh* (1989) 91 Cr App R 160, where it was said (at p. 163) that 'although bad faith may make substantial or significant that which might not otherwise be so, the contrary does not follow. Breaches which are in themselves significant and substantial are not rendered otherwise by the good faith of the officers concerned.' See also *Samuel* [1988] QB 615, in which a submission was made that, in the absence of impropriety, the discretion should never be exercised to exclude admissible evidence. The Court of Appeal had 'no hesitation in rejecting that submission, although the propriety or otherwise of the way in which the evidence was obtained is something which a court is, in terms, enjoined by the section to take into account'. **F18.42**

Information on which Discretion is to be Exercised

The discretion does not fall to be exercised because the judge of his or her own motion recognises that a serious breach such as might trigger exclusion has taken place: if the accused is represented by an advocate who appears competent, and a particular part of the evidence might be the subject of a tactical or strategic plan on the part of the defence, the judge should not undertake to exclude evidence, though it might be appropriate to make pertinent inquiry of counsel in the absence of the jury (*Raphaie* [1996] Crim LR 812). **F18.43**

When the defence seek to exclude evidence obtained by or in circumstances alleged to amount to breaches of the PACE 1984 or a PACE code, the Court of Appeal in *Keenan* [1990] 2 QB 54 noted that a number of different situations may face the judge: **F18.44**

(a) One or more breaches of a code may be apparent in the custody record itself or from the witness statements.

(b) There may be a prima facie breach which, if objection is taken, must be justified by evidence adduced by the prosecution.
(c) There may be alleged breaches which can probably only be established by the evidence of the accused.

Cases under (c) are likely to be rare, and it is likely that in cases under (a) and (b) the judge will have no means of knowing what will ensue after the ruling has been made. If the ruling is against admissibility, it may be that the accused will exercise the right not to give evidence. To permit the evidence to be given may therefore effectively deprive the accused of a right which would otherwise have been available. If the evidence is admitted, the judge does not know what the response to it may be. The accused may testify that the interview in question never took place at all, or that, though it took place, the questions and answers were fabricated, or that what was said was inaccurately recorded, or alternatively might accept the accuracy of the record. Despite these difficulties, the judge must make a ruling on the information available at the time. In *Keenan*, the judge had wrongly assumed that any unfairness which might have been present could be cured by D giving evidence at the trial. Failure to give evidence at the *voir dire* is a different matter, and, in considering whether an accused has been prejudiced by a breach, the judge is entitled to take account of a failure to give evidence at the *voir dire* (*Oni* [1992] Crim LR 183).

F18.45 The record of interview and the contents of the confession itself may assist on the question whether the admission of the evidence would affect the fairness of the proceedings (*Dunford* (1990) 91 Cr App R 150 at p. 155). However, it was also said that it may be necessary to avoid reference to such material in cases where there is a 'root and branch' challenge by the defence to the contents of the statement.

Unfairness Not Arising from Breach of Codes of Practice

F18.46 In various authorities the significance of conduct not amounting to a breach of a code of practice or of the PACE 1984 has been considered, and it is clear that s. 78 may be invoked in such cases, though instances of the exercise of the discretion are rarer. The principles which have developed in relation to confessions apply also to other forms of prosecution evidence, and reference should be made also to **F2.13** to **F2.17**. In *Ibrahim* [2008] EWCA Crim 880, [2009] 4 All ER 208, it was held that a judge's powers under s. 78 to exclude evidence obtained through a 'safety interview' without legal advice under terrorism legislation were sufficient in law; there was no need for a more general principle of exclusion based on public policy. The ECtHR subsequently agreed that the trial under the current legislative framework, including the right to challenge the use of the interviews under s. 78, had been fair (see **F18.37**).

F18.47 The provisions of Code C do not apply to conversations between suspects and undercover investigators, unless the undercover pose is deliberately abused as a means of circumventing the code (*Christou* [1992] QB 979; *Bryce* [1992] 4 All ER 569; *Edwards* [1997] Crim LR 348). In deciding whether the code applies the judge should take into account the seriousness of the offence and the potential to put a life at risk (*Rajkuma* [2003] EWCA Crim 1955, where the offence was soliciting to commit murder). Where genuine undercover operations yield evidence, including incriminating statements, the use of subterfuge does not of itself entail a finding of unfairness. Relevant considerations in *Christou* (where undercover police set up as 'shady' jewellers in order to recover stolen property and gather evidence against the thieves and handlers) were that the public interest favoured the operation, that the offences had already been committed and that there was no incitement to crime on the part of the police, and that the suspects had 'applied themselves to the trick' without pressure from the officers. See also *Maclean* [1993] Crim LR 687, a similar operation concerning illegally imported drugs. In *Re Proulx* [2001] 1 All ER 57, an extradition case in which a murder suspect had been induced to confess as a condition of membership of a fictitious criminal gang, Mance LJ (having noted that this was clearly a case where the trick had been applied to D, even though he had willingly fallen in with it) concluded that there would have been 'very considerable difficulty' in upholding a decision to admit such evidence in the light of decisions such as *Christou, Bryce, Smurthwaite* [1994] 1 All ER 898 (see **F2.18**) and the ruling of Ognall J in *Stagg* (14 September 1994 unreported).

Subterfuge in Interrogation and Non-disclosure In *Bailey* [1993] 3 All ER 513, subterfuge in the interrogation process was considered. D1 and D2 were arrested and charged with robbery, but maintained their right to silence at interview. They were placed together in a bugged police cell, their suspicions being allayed by play-acting on the part of the police, who pretended to be reluctant to leave them alone together. Their resultant incriminating conversation was admitted, and it was held that the fact that D1 and D2 could not, under Code of Practice C, properly have been subjected to further questioning did not mean that they had to be protected from the opportunity to speak incriminatingly to one another if they chose to do so. It was acknowledged to appear odd that, alongside the 'rigorously controlled legislative regime' for questioning it should be considered acceptable for 'parallel covert investigations' legitimately to continue, but, provided such stratagems were used only in grave cases and that there was no suggestion of oppression or unreliability, there was nothing unfair about admitting the evidence obtained in consequence. **F18.48**

The Court of Appeal distinguished as improper the subterfuge employed in *Mason* [1988] 3 All ER 481, in which a police officer told deliberate lies to D and to D's solicitor regarding the availability of fingerprint evidence connecting D with the offence of which he was suspected, in order to extract a confession from him. The trial judge admitted the confession, but the Court held that he had failed to take into account one vital factor, 'namely the deceit practised upon the appellant's solicitor. If he had included that in his consideration . . . he would have been driven to an opposite conclusion.' *Mason* is not, it is submitted, authority for the proposition that lies may safely be told to an accused person provided the legal adviser is not hoodwinked; on the contrary, both aspects of the deception were regarded as equally serious and 'most reprehensible' by the Court of Appeal. The trial judge's failure to take account of the lie told to the solicitor merely provided the ground on which the Court was able to review the exercise of his discretion. *Bailey* was applied in *Roberts* [1997] 1 Cr App R 217, in which D was induced to confess by a fellow suspect, C (with whom he had been placed in a bugged cell), to one robbery with which D had already been charged and to another with which he was subsequently charged. The trial judge's conclusion that C was not a police agent and had not been told what to ask D was regarded as 'unassailable', despite breaches of the Code in relation to C which made it hard to determine what precisely had been said to him (see **F18.34**). On the facts as found, the test was said to be whether the conduct of the police, either wittingly or unwittingly, led to unfairness or injustice, and the judge's decision to admit the evidence was upheld. The only difference between this case and *Bailey* was said to be that the police 'had perhaps a rather firmer basis for their expectations' of a confession than in *Bailey*. **F18.49**

By contrast, in *Allan* [2004] EWCA Crim 2236 the Court of Appeal, following the reasoning of the ECtHR in the same case (*Allan v UK* (2003) 36 EHRR 12 (143)) held that evidence should be excluded where, the suspect having decided to exercise his right of silence, the authorities use subterfuge to elicit confessions by using an informer as the 'functional equivalent' of an interrogator. In that case there was evidence that police had coached the informer and instructed him to 'pump' the suspect in the cell they shared while D was awaiting trial for murder. Just as a police officer cannot circumvent the protections of the PACE 1984 and the PACE Codes by adopting an undercover pose (*Christou*), so an informer cannot be used to the same end. As the Court of Appeal rightly states, 'allowing an agent of the state to interrogate a suspect in the circumstances of this case bypasses the many necessary protections developed over the last twenty years'. **F18.50**

The authorities on eavesdropping do not appear to have been adversely affected. In *Mason* [2002] EWCA Crim 385, [2002] 2 Cr App R 38 (628), D and others were suspected of joint involvement in a series of burglaries and armed robberies, but there was insufficient evidence to do more than arrest individual members of the group for particular offences. Authorisation was obtained for them to be held together in a bugged cell in the hope that they would, in talking to each other, divulge the full extent of the joint enterprise. The resultant recordings were held to have been rightly admitted, following the reasoning in *Bailey*, notwithstanding that there was a clear breach of the ECHR, **F18.51**

Article 8, which could not be justified because the surveillance had not taken place according to any publicly accessible legal structure (cf. *PG v UK* (2008) 46 EHRR 51 (1272)). In *King* [2012] EWCA Crim 805 and in *Plunkett* [2013] EWCA Crim 261, [2013] 1 WLR 3121 admissions were obtained through covert recording, under the provisions of the RIPA 2000, of conversations between suspects awaiting transport in a police vehicle. It was alleged that an unlawful delay had been created in the process of transferring the suspects (in breach of the PACE 1984, s. 30(1A)) to foster the conversations that were recorded. In *King* the Court of Appeal warned against the deliberate flouting of a statutory rule for this purpose, but in neither case was the evidence excluded. In *Plunkett*, it was said that any incursion on s. 30(1A) would have been minor in light of the seriousness of the offence and the need to protect the victims of D's crime. Nothing was done 'to call into question the integrity of the criminal justice system'. *Plunkett* was followed in *Khan* [2013] EWCA Crim 2230, where the police had exceeded the authority granted under the RIPA 2000. This resulted in a breach of the appellants' right to privacy but did not, on the facts, impact on the fairness of the trial. The Court of Appeal noted that authorities such as *Bailey* would not be decided any differently today. The breaches were, as in *Plunkett*, of a minor character. More serious breaches are likely to attract the PACE 1984, s. 78, as noted in *Turner* [2013] EWCA Crim 642, where the Court of Appeal warned (*obiter*) against covert surveillance which 'significantly' interferes with the accused's legal privilege, so that the 'very integrity' of the administration of justice is undermined. Again, this was contrasted with flaws that are 'minor, short and inconsequential'. See further **F2.22**.

Eavesdropping amounting to a deliberate violation of legal professional privilege was considered in *Grant* [2005] EWCA Crim 1089, [2006] QB 60 to be 'so great an affront to the integrity of the justice system' as to render an associated prosecution an abuse of process even though no material was thereby obtained which assisted the prosecution. While this basis for the stay was doubted by Lord Brown in *Maxwell* [2010] UKSC 48, [2011] 4 All ER 941 and was said to be wrong in *Warren v A-G for Jersey* [2011] UKPC 10, [2012] 1 AC 22 (see **D3.108**), it is unlikely that a confession obtained through eavesdropping or surveillance in violation of privilege would be admitted. See also *McE v Prison Service of Northern Ireland* [2009] UKHL 15, [2009] 1 AC 908, where the House of Lords held that covert surveillance of conversations between a detainee and his legal adviser could be lawful under the RIPA 2000 (see **D1.58**). The House was not required to decide whether information obtained through such lawful surveillance was admissible but Lord Hope stated that 'basic rules of fairness strongly indicate the contrary'. See further **F10.17**.

F18.52 In *Farrell* [2004] EWCA Crim 597, the Court of Appeal approved as a 'useful guide' the distinction between active lying intended to induce a confession, and the omission or failure by the police to disclose their whole case in advance of interview. The Court was not prepared to hold that it was necessarily wrong or misleading for the police to hold back some part of their case before interview. In that case there was no attempt to suggest that the case was stronger than it was, and the evidence (which consisted of lies rather than an outright confession, but the relevant principles are the same) was held to have been properly admitted.

F18.53 **Unfairness where Statement Made for a Different Purpose** In *Smith* [1994] 1 WLR 1396, D was under the impression that R, the bank manager questioning him, was concerned only to obtain information about the impact of a transaction on the market, and not about D's criminal involvement. Although R was guilty of no impropriety, the Court of Appeal held that D's statements should not have been admitted. In *Shepherd* [2019] EWCA Crim 1062, [2019] 2 Cr App R 26 (282) by contrast, an interview conducted without caution of a person present at a fatal boating accident was held admissible at his trial for manslaughter on the ground that the police did not then suspect him of any offence even if, objectively, they might have suspected him of an 'esoteric' one. Police officers should be free, provided they act in good faith, to seek an understanding of what has happened before any suspicion sufficient to trigger Code C arises. There was no question of any other unfairness in the circumstances: the application to exclude was made only because D had absconded prior to trial, and had he not done so he would have wished the jury to hear the account he had given which was broadly consistent with his defence. In *Hayter v L* [1998] 1 WLR

854, the issue was whether it was an abuse of process for a private prosecution to proceed after an offender had been cautioned by the police (a procedure which necessarily involves an admission of guilt). Holding that it was not, the Divisional Court said that any unfairness arising from the use of the cautioned party's admission in the subsequent proceedings could be met by the s. 78 discretion. As a prerequisite of a caution, a party should be made aware that there is the possibility of a private prosecution, but it might still be thought unfair to permit a confession made in hope of escaping a prosecution to be used in order to found one. Similarly, in *De Silva* [2002] EWCA Crim 2673, [2003] 2 Cr App R 5 (74), it was held that telephone conversations participated in by D at the instigation of Customs officers following the discovery of drugs in his suitcase should not be used in evidence against D. The purpose of the exercise was to facilitate the arrest of the callers, so it was part of D's role to behave as though he was guilty, whether he was or not. D's agreement to take part in the exercise followed a 'co-operation interview' with the officers, and it was not the purpose of such interviews to gather or initiate further evidence against the interviewee.

In *Elleray* [2003] EWCA Crim 553, [2003] 2 Cr App R 11 (165), the issue was whether a statement made to a probation officer for the purposes of a pre-sentence report could be used as a confession to a more serious offence (rape) than the one to which D had pleaded guilty and for which he was to be sentenced (indecent assault). It was held that such a case required a careful consideration of the public interest, bearing in mind the need for frankness between a probation officer and offender, and the absence of both caution and access to legal advice. In some cases it might be advisable for the officer to terminate the conversation to allow the offender to seek advice. On balance it was not unfair to admit the evidence. Similarly in *Ward* [2018] EWCA Crim 1464, it was held that the trial judge had not improperly exercised his discretion when admitting a confession volunteered to an appropriate adult. To do so did not undermine the role of the appropriate adult in terms of ensuring that the accused fully understands his or her rights and position: 'the appropriate adult is not there to stop an accused from making admissions' (at [28]). In *McGeough* [2015] UKSC 62, [2015] 1 WLR 4612, the Supreme Court, on an appeal from Northern Ireland, held that it was not unfair, under the provision equivalent to s. 78, to admit a statement made by D in an unsuccessful attempt to seek asylum in Sweden, in which he admitted to being a member of a proscribed organisation. D had been legally advised and must have been well aware that, in the event of the failure of the application, the information it contained would enter the public domain.

Unfairness Arising from Physical Condition of the Accused The discretion may, it seems, be used in respect of evidence which is unreliable as the result of the physical condition of the suspect, whether or not the interview in which he participates is conducted in breach of the code (see, e.g., *Effik* (1992) 95 Cr App R 427, in which the trial judge, in a ruling endorsed by the Court of Appeal, made it clear that he would have excluded the confession of D, a heroin addict, had it been made at a time when he was suffering acute withdrawal symptoms). **F18.54**

Exclusion of Subsequent Confession

Where a confession is excluded, either under s. 76 or under s. 78, for breach of a code, the question may arise as to whether it would be unfair to admit a subsequent confession which has itself been obtained without breaking the rules. In *Gillard* (1991) 92 Cr App R 61, it was held, upholding the admission of subsequent statements by two accused, that there is no universal rule requiring the exclusion of such a subsequent confession. The question is whether, on the facts of a particular case, there is a sufficient nexus between the circumstances in which the two statements were made to render it unfair to admit the subsequent statement, so that, for example, the accused is still affected by some impropriety which took place during the first, excluded interview. Important considerations are whether the objections leading to the exclusion of the first interview were of a fundamental and continuing nature, and whether the arrangements for the subsequent interview gave the accused a sufficient opportunity to exercise an informed and independent choice as to whether to repeat or retract what had been said, or say nothing (*Neil* [1994] Crim LR 441; *Nelson* [1998] 2 Cr App R 399). See also *Canale* (1990) 91 Cr App R 1, in which **F18.55** a subsequent interview was held to have been tainted by an earlier one in which promises were alleged to have been made; *Y v DPP* [1991] Crim LR 917, in which earlier confessions, despite their spontaneous nature, were excluded because of breaches of the code, but a subsequent, properly conducted interview was held to have been rightly admitted; *Wood* [1994] Crim LR 222, in which a multiplicity of breaches at the first interview of a mentally handicapped suspect tainted a later interview; and *Prouse v DPP* [1999] All ER (D) 748, [1999] 10 Arch News 2, in which the provision of legal advice before the later interview rendered it admissible.

Confessions by 'Mentally Handicapped Persons'

F18.56 A confession made by a 'mentally handicapped person' may be admitted in evidence, provided it satisfies the conditions imposed by the PACE 1984, s. 76 (see **F18.8**), and provided also that it is not excluded by the court in the exercise of its discretion to exclude prosecution evidence under s. 78 of the Act. Where such a confession is received in evidence, the provisions of s. 77 come into play and must be complied with.

Police and Criminal Evidence Act 1984, s. 77

(1) Without prejudice to the general duty of the court at a trial on indictment with a jury to direct the jury on any matter on which it appears to the court appropriate to do so, where at such a trial—
(a) the case against the accused depends wholly or substantially on a confession by him; and
(b) the court is satisfied—
(i) that he is mentally handicapped; and
(ii) that the confession was not made in the presence of an independent person,
the court shall warn the jury that there is special need for caution before convicting the accused in reliance on the confession, and shall explain that the need arises because of the circumstances mentioned in paragraphs (a) and (b) above.
(2) In any case where at the summary trial of a person for an offence it appears to the court that a warning under subsection (1) above would be required if the trial were on indictment with a jury, the court shall treat the case as one in which there is a special need for caution before convicting the accused on his confession.
(2A) In any case where at the trial on indictment without a jury of a person for an offence it appears to the court that a warning under subsection (1) above would be required if the trial were with a jury, the court shall treat the case as one in which there is a special need for caution before convicting the accused on his confession.
(3) In this section—
'independent person' does not include a police officer or a person employed for, or engaged on, police purposes;
'mentally handicapped' in relation to a person, means that he is in a state of arrested or incomplete development of mind which includes significant impairment of intelligence and social functioning; and
'police purposes' has the meaning assigned to it by section 101(2) of the Police Act 1996.

As to the modified application of s. 77 and related provisions to investigations conducted by customs officers and immigration officers, see **D1.3**.

There is no need to give a warning in accordance with s. 77 unless the case for the Crown would be 'substantially less strong' without the confession (*Campbell* [1995] Crim LR 157).

F18.57 PACE Code C requires the presence at interview of an 'appropriate adult' when the interviewee is a person at risk by reason, *inter alia*, of mental handicap, unless the interview is conducted on an emergency basis. The concept of an 'appropriate adult' is substantially the same as, though not identical to, the 'independent person' mentioned in s. 77. In particular, a solicitor attending the suspect would be an 'independent person', but would be unlikely to be the 'appropriate adult', who would normally be a relative or someone with experience of caring for the suspect (*Lewis* [1996] Crim LR 260). The warning required by s. 77 serves to draw the magistrates' or jury's attention to the potential unreliability of a confession obtained without this safeguard and should be tailored to any specific evidence of unreliability relating to the accused (*Campbell* [1995] Crim LR 157). In *Bailey* [1995] 2 Cr App R 262, it was held to be necessary to give the warning in respect of informal admissions made to members of the public in the absence of an independent third party, but this does not appear to be the mischief at which s. 77 was aimed.

In *Lamont* [1989] Crim LR 813, D was convicted of the attempted murder of his baby son. The only evidence of D's intention came from a confession made in an interview at which no independent person was present. Expert defence evidence indicated mental retardation and impairment of intelligence and social functioning, but the trial judge concluded that D was not mentally handicapped and therefore did not warn the jury in accordance with s. 77. Quashing the conviction, the Court of Appeal held that the required direction under s. 77 was an essential ingredient of a fair summing-up, yet the trial judge had neither suggested to nor directed the jury that if they accepted the expert evidence they should exercise the caution called for by the section. The decision of the Court may, however, be open to doubt in part, in that it is the function of the judge, not the jury, to decide whether the accused is mentally handicapped. **F18.58**

In establishing whether a defendant is mentally handicapped within the meaning of s. 77(3) it is not appropriate to take figures produced by intelligence tests in one case and to apply them slavishly in another in order to produce a rigid definition: every case has its individual features (*Kenny* [1994] Crim LR 284).

Practical Application of the Rule In the present climate of opinion, a confession made by a mentally handicapped person otherwise than in the presence of an independent person would be likely to be excluded at trial under either s. 76 or s. 78 of the 1984 Act. It follows that there will be few cases where a court is called on to follow the procedure laid down in s. 77. In *Moss* (1990) 91 Cr App R 371, it was thought that the section was aimed at two possible cases: (a) where a confession has been properly obtained from a mentally handicapped person in the absence of an independent person in the course of an 'urgent interview' as permitted by Code C; (b) where the interview was in breach of Code C but there was only 'one interview during a comparatively short period of custody'. In *Moss*, confessions obtained in the course of nine interviews over a lengthy period of detention were held to have been wrongly admitted despite the s. 77 direction given by the trial judge: the statements ought to have been excluded under s. 76(2)(b) (see **F18.17**). By contrast, in *Uddin* [2005] EWCA Crim 464, D's appeal failed despite the prosecution's reliance on a confession obtained in the absence of an appropriate adult, and the apparent failure of the judge to give a s. 77 direction (which failure was not noted by the Court of Appeal). The crux of the matter in *Uddin*, however, was that the 'confession' was chiefly composed of self-serving statements. The only element on which the prosecution relied (an admission of presence) was equally an inherent part of the defence case. The Court therefore concluded that the admission of the confession did not threaten the safety of the conviction and would presumably have said the same about the absence of a direction under s. 77. In *Qayyum* [2006] EWCA Crim 1127, the failure of the trial judge to give a formal s. 77 direction following the admission of a confession that, as in *Uddin* was not *per se* damaging to the defence at trial, was held not to render the conviction unsafe, although it was noted that the judge had repeatedly reminded the jury of D's intellectual shortcomings. **F18.59**

Unconvincing Confessions of Accused with Mental Handicap The decision of the Court of Appeal to limit the circumstances in which a case depending on confession evidence of this type should be left to the jury further restricts the ambit of s. 77. In *MacKenzie* (1992) 96 Cr App R 98, the Court of Appeal considered the application of the rule in *Galbraith* [1981] 2 All ER 1060 (see **D16.54**) to the case where the confession of a mentally handicapped person had been admitted at trial, but was unsupported by other evidence. The Court laid down the following rules: **F18.60**

> (1) Where the prosecution case depends wholly upon confessions; (2) the defendant suffers from a significant degree of mental handicap; and (3) the confessions are unconvincing to a point where a jury properly directed could not properly convict upon them, then the judge, assuming that he has not excluded the confessions earlier, should withdraw the case from the jury. The confessions may be unconvincing, for example, because they lack the incriminating details to be expected of a

guilty and willing confessor, or because they are inconsistent with other evidence, or because they are otherwise inherently improbable.

D, a mentally handicapped man with a personality disorder, was convicted of two offences of manslaughter and two of arson. The prosecution case in respect of the killings depended entirely on unsupported confessions, whereas the proof of arson, though largely dependent on confessions, was supported by other independent evidence. During questioning D had also confessed to 12 other killings, none of which, in the end, the Crown believed he had committed. At the point in the trial when the confessions to the killings were admitted, it was thought that they contained details which only the killer could have known. On a careful review of the confessions, however, the Court of Appeal considered that the knowledge of the basic circumstances of the killings which they contained were of the sort that would not have been confined to the killer, and that they also contained some striking errors and omissions. Bearing in mind that D's credibility was diminished by his false confessions to other killings, and that he may well have been motivated by a desire to stay in the secure hospital at which he had been detained, the Court was left with at least a lurking doubt as to whether the verdicts of manslaughter were safe and satisfactory. The convictions for arson, however, were allowed to stand. *MacKenzie* was applied in *Wood* [1994] Crim LR 222, in which the only blow which D had confessed to striking was proved by medical evidence not to have caused the death of V.

F18.61 A confession which falls within the first two limbs of the *MacKenzie* test, but which is admitted because it falls outside the third, may require a very careful judicial direction (*Bailey* [1995] 2 Cr App R 262, where it was held that the judge was obliged, in addition to giving the s. 77 warning, to give the jury a 'full and proper statement' of the defendant's case against the confession being accepted by the jury as true). An unusual situation arose in *Hudson* [2007] EWCA Crim 2083, where the Crown's case was that D, who was 'of limited intellectual ability', had been prevailed upon by his family to take more than his share of responsibility for a murder. D's confession was tendered chiefly to establish, through the falsity of much of its purported detail, D's part in this conspiracy. No attempt was made to exclude the confession, which (with a careful direction from the judge) was correctly left to the jury as the foundation of the case to answer. Such a direction might usefully take account of the words of Lord Kerr in *Pora v The Queen* [2015] UKPC 9, [2016] 1 Cr App R 3 (48), who said (at [56]):

> The impact that evidence of a confession will have, especially a confession to heinous crime, is difficult to overstate. The natural reaction to such an admission is that it is bound to be true. Why would someone confess to a dreadful crime if they were not guilty of it? But experience has shown that false confessions, even to the most serious of offences, are often made. The intuitive response to the fact of confession to crime is, inevitably, that it must be right but that intuitive reaction may be very dangerous.

DETERMINING THE ADMISSIBILITY OF CONFESSIONS: THE *VOIR DIRE*

F18.62 The general rules regarding the holding of a *voir dire*, or trial within a trial, in order to determine disputed issues regarding preliminary facts on which the admissibility of evidence depends, are dealt with in detail at **D16.41** *et seq*. The principles considered here are those which have particular significance with regard to confessions, or are relevant solely to the reception of confession evidence.

The *Voir Dire* and the PACE 1984, s. 76

F18.63 At common law, where the admissibility of a confession statement was to be challenged in a trial on indictment, the following practice was followed:

(a) The defence advocate would notify the prosecutor that an objection to admissibility was to be raised.
(b) The prosecutor would then refrain from mentioning the statement in opening to the jury.

(c) At the appropriate time the judge would conduct a trial on the *voir dire* to decide on the admissibility of the statement (*Ajodha v The State* [1982] AC 204).

The PACE 1984, s. 76(2), follows the common law by providing that where the defence represent that a confession on which the prosecution propose to rely was, or may have been, obtained in such a way as to render it inadmissible in evidence, the court shall not allow the confession to be given in evidence except insofar as the prosecution prove to the court beyond reasonable doubt that the confession was not so obtained. Section 76(3) provides in addition that the court may of its own motion require the prosecution, as a condition of allowing them to give a confession in evidence, to prove that it was not obtained in such a way as to render it inadmissible. The *voir dire* therefore remains the correct procedure where objection is taken to the admission of a confession. It enables factual issues to be resolved in the absence of the jury, with the benefit of the accused's evidence should the accused wish to testify (*Alagaratnam* [2010] EWCA Crim 1506). At common law the *voir dire* was normally held in the absence of the jury only at the request or with the consent of the defence (*Ajodha*, citing *Anderson* (1929) 21 Cr App R 178). However, it has now been established that the court may require the jury to withdraw whether the defence consent or not (*Davis* [1990] Crim LR 860).

As to what constitutes a representation for the purposes of s. 76(2), see *Dhorajiwala* [2010] EWCA Crim 1237, [2010] 2 Cr App R 21 (161), where it was said that 'a statement by responsible counsel, upon the basis of documents or proofs of evidence in his possession at the time of speaking' that the confession was or may have been obtained in breach of s. 76 is a 'representation'.

In *Liverpool Juvenile Court, ex parte R* [1988] QB 1, it was held that s. 76 requires magis- **F18.64**
trates conducting a summary trial to hold a *voir dire* to determine admissibility where the defence, before the close of the prosecution case, represent to the court that the confession was obtained in breach of s. 76(2). The decision represents a significant departure from the common law, which regarded the *voir dire* as inappropriate in summary trials (see further as to summary trials, **D22.44**). As magistrates are judges of both fact and law, a ruling that a confession is to be excluded will mean that they have to put the objectionable material out of their minds when considering guilt; this is a task with which 'they are well capable of coping both by training and by disposition' (*Hayter v L* [1998] 1 WLR 854, commenting on the comparable situation which arises after the s. 78 discretion to exclude has been exercised).

According to *Dhorajiwala*, the court's power under s. 76(3) to require the prosecution to prove that the confession was not obtained in breach of s. 76(2) may lead the court to hold a *voir dire* in circumstances where counsel has not requested it. This would seem to be a power that should be sparingly exercised.

Unrepresented Accused In *Ajodha v The State* [1982] AC 204 Lord Bridge said (at p. 223): **F18.65**

> Particular difficulties may arise in the trial of an unrepresented defendant, when the judge must, of course, be especially vigilant to ensure a fair trial. No rules can be laid down, but it may be prudent, if the judge has any reason to suppose that the voluntary character of a statement proposed to be put in evidence by the prosecution is likely to be in issue, that he should speak to the defendant before the trial begins and explain his rights in the matter.

The position appears to be unaltered under the 1984 Act, if for 'voluntary character' is read 'admissibility'. The court also enjoys the power under s. 76(3) to require the prosecutor to prove that a confession was not obtained in breach of s. 76(2), and it is submitted that it would generally be appropriate to exercise that power in the case of an unrepresented accused.

Challenging Admissibility at Trial

The position at common law was stated in *Ajodha v The State* [1982] AC 204 by Lord Bridge, **F18.66**
who said (at p. 223):

> Though the case for the defence raises an issue as to the voluntariness of a statement..., defending counsel may for tactical reasons prefer that the evidence bearing on that issue be heard before the

> jury, with a single cross-examination of the witnesses on both sides, even though this means that the jury hear the impugned statement whether admissible or not. If the defence adopts this tactic, it will be open to defending counsel to submit at the close of the evidence that, if the judge doubts the voluntariness of the statement, he should direct the jury to disregard it, or, if the statement is essential to sustain the prosecution case, direct an acquittal. Even in the absence of such a submission, if the judge himself forms the view that the voluntariness of the statement is in doubt, he should take the like action *proprio motu*.

In *Liverpool Juvenile Court, ex parte R* [1988] QB 1, at p. 10 it was considered that the defence retained this option:

> There remains a discretion open to the defendant as to the stage at which an attack is to be made upon an alleged confession. A trial within a trial will only take place before the close of the prosecution case if it is represented to the court that the confession was, or may have been, obtained by one or other of the processes set out in subparagraph (a) or (b) of section 76(2). If no such representation is made the defendant is at liberty to raise admissibility or weight of the confession at any subsequent stage of the trial.

F18.67 It may be argued that this view overlooks the power of the court under the PACE 1984, s. 76(3), to compel the holding of a *voir dire*, apparently irrespective of the defendant's wishes. This power may, however, be intended primarily to enable a court to assist an unrepresented defendant to vindicate his or her rights, rather than to overrule the wishes of defence counsel where the accused is legally represented. A more fundamental objection to the view taken in *Ex parte R* may be found in *Sat-Bhambra* (1988) 88 Cr App R 55. Certain statements by D had been ruled admissible at the *voir dire*, because there was no evidence to suggest that the statements were likely to be unreliable as a result of D's ill health at the time. At the trial, medical evidence was adduced by the defence which came down more strongly in favour of D's contention that he was suffering from hypoglycaemia when he was interviewed. When asked to reconsider his decision on admissibility, the trial judge ruled that the terms of s. 76 prevented him from taking this course. The Court of Appeal agreed, holding (at p. 62):

> The words of section 76 are crucial: 'proposes to be given in evidence' and 'shall not allow the confession to be given' are not, in our judgment, appropriate to describe something which has happened in the past. They are directed solely to the situation before the statement goes before the jury. Once the judge has ruled that it should do so, section 76 (and section 78, for the same reasons) ceases to have effect.

The Court went on to consider the powers which the judge may, by virtue of the common law, exercise in this situation (at p. 62), before concluding: 'If a defendant wishes under section 76 to exclude a confession, the time to make his submission to that effect is before the confession is put in evidence and not afterwards'. It has been noted (see **F18.7**) that the statements in issue in *Sat-Bhambra* were self-serving, and were therefore regarded as not being confessions to which s. 76 applied, as to which, see now *Hasan* [2005] UKHL 22, [2005] 2 AC 467 at **F18.7**. However, the Court of Appeal was careful to state that its views on that subsidiary matter were *obiter*, so that the *ratio* of the case appears to be that the admissibility of a confession may not be challenged under s. 76 once the confession has been given in evidence. The contrary view, stated by the Divisional Court in *Liverpool Juvenile Court, ex parte R*, was expressed to apply to summary proceedings only, but it is difficult to see why the interpretation of the Act should vary according to the nature of the trial. Thus, the law, whatever the mode of trial, would appear to be as stated in *Sat-Bhambra*. See also *Davis* [1990] Crim LR 860, in which the Court of Appeal inclined to the view (but without deciding the point) that the language of the section anticipated a *voir dire* taking place before the challenged evidence was heard by the jury.

The *Voir Dire* and the PACE 1984, s. 78

F18.68 Section 78 is set out at **F18.33**. The view taken, *obiter*, by the Court of Appeal in *Sat-Bhambra* (1988) 88 Cr App R 55 was that the wording of the section suggested that defence objections should be made before the confession is given in evidence. The relevant words are 'the court may refuse to allow evidence *on which the prosecution proposes to rely* to be given'. It does not necessarily follow from this that a *voir dire* should always be held; indeed, it has been said that in a summary trial the defence have no right to a *voir dire* simply in order to determine a preliminary issue under s. 78 (*Vel v Chief Constable of North Wales* (1987) 151 JP 510 and see **D22.46**). However, in many cases it will be convenient to investigate the submission in this way, particularly where the defence also challenge the confession under s. 76, and in *Halawa v Federation against Copyright Theft* [1995] 1 Cr App R 21 it was said, *obiter*, that if, in connection with an application to exclude evidence under s. 78 alone, the accused wished to proceed by way of a trial within a trial, magistrates might find it necessary to proceed in that way in order to allow the accused to give evidence in relation to the evidential issue without prejudicing the right to silence at trial.

In *R* (2000) *Independent*, 10 April 2000, it was held that a ruling in a preparatory hearing regarding s. 78 was a ruling as to admissibility of evidence under the CPIA 1996, s. 31(3) (see **D15.58** to **D15.61**), and that it was subject to appeal to the Court of Appeal. It seems unlikely that s. 31(3) was intended to apply to questions which are not strictly questions of law, although if the application of s. 78 goes to the heart of the proceedings it may be convenient to deal with it as an interlocutory matter.

Disputes as to Making of Confession

At common law the *voir dire* was inappropriate in trials on indictment where the defence case was simply that no confession was made (*Ajodha v The State* [1982] AC 204). The Board gave as examples cases where the defence allege that an interview never took place, or that no incriminating answers were given, or, in the case of a written statement, that it is a forgery. The issue of fact whether or not the statement was made by the accused is purely for the jury. In the same case, however, the Privy Council recognised that issues of voluntariness might be intertwined with disputes as to the making of the confession, and that it is a fallacy to suppose that the two grounds of challenge are mutually exclusive. Such cases required the holding of a *voir dire* to determine the issue of voluntariness at common law, leaving the jury to determine the value and weight of the statement if it is admitted. Issues as to admissibility under the PACE 1984, s. 76, are equally capable of arising in combination with disputes as to the making of the statement, and it is submitted that the principles stated in *Ajodha* continue to represent the law. Where the evidence of a person to whom a disputed confession is alleged to have been made may be tainted by an improper motive (as in the case of a 'cell confession') a specific direction to the jury may be required as to the need for caution (*Pringle v The Queen* [2003] UKPC 9; *Benedetto v The Queen* [2003] UKPC 27, [2003] 1 WLR 1545; *Lawrence v The Queen* [2014] UKPC 2: see **F5.15**). **F18.69**

Where the defence in a trial on indictment challenge the confession under s. 78, they may ultimately wish to assert at the trial that no confession was made. The issue at the *voir dire* is simply whether the introduction of the confession would have such an adverse effect on the fairness of the proceedings that the court ought not to admit it. It is not the function of the judge to decide whether the confession was made (*Keenan* [1990] 2 QB 54). See, however, *Alladice* (1988) 87 Cr App R 380, in which the trial judge reached such a decision before deciding to admit the statement.

Truth of Confession as Issue on *Voir Dire*

It is not the function of the judge or magistrates at a *voir dire* to determine whether a confession is true, but simply whether it should be admitted. It does not necessarily follow from this that the truth of the statement is irrelevant to the question whether it should be admitted. At common law there was a conflict of authority on the point. In *Hammond* [1941] 3 All ER 318, D was charged with murder. He gave evidence on the *voir dire*, claiming that he had been knocked about and brutally ill-treated in order to induce a confession. It was held that he was properly cross-examined as to whether his confession was true, as it was relevant to the credit to be given to his assertions, on the basis that: 'If a man says, "I was forced to tell the story..." it must be **F18.70** relevant to know whether he was made to tell the truth, or whether he was made to say a number of things which were untrue' (per Humphreys J at p. 321).

F18.71 In *Wong Kam-ming v The Queen* [1980] AC 247, a majority of the Privy Council disapproved of *Hammond*, and held that it should no longer be followed in Hong Kong. D gave evidence at the *voir dire*, claiming that his confession had been extracted by force. He was cross-examined in detail as to the truth of the statement, which was subsequently excluded. At the trial, prosecuting counsel called evidence to prove that, at the *voir dire*, D had admitted that he was present at the scene of the crime. It was held that the cross-examination was impermissible and that it did not affect the credit of D as a witness. Lord Edmund-Davies said (at p. 56): 'If the defendant denies the truth of the confession or some self-incriminating admission contained in it, the question whether his denial is itself true or false cannot be ascertained until after the *voir dire* is over and the defendant's guilt or innocence has been determined by the jury'. If the defendant admits the truth, this tends to show that he is a truthful witness and goes to support his allegations rather than, as *Hammond* supposes, to undermine them. Lord Hailsham of St Marylebone, dissenting on this issue, considered (at p. 262C) that 'the only general limitations on what may be asked or tendered ought to be relevance to the issue to be tried' and concluded that it was not possible 'to say *a priori* that in no circumstances is the truth or falsity of the alleged confession relevant to the question at issue on the *voir dire* or admissible as to credibility of either the prosecution or defence witnesses'. He instanced, *inter alia*, cases in which the defence argue that, because a confession is demonstrably false, it must have been obtained by improper means. It must then be relevant for the prosecution to cross-examine on the truth of the statement.

It is submitted that Lord Hailsham's dissent in *Wong Kam-ming v The Queen* has logic on its side, but that the view of the majority has a sure foundation in policy, being consistent with the rule under which the accused is protected from the consequences of damaging admissions which further the accused's case at the *voir dire* (see **F18.73**).

F18.72 Precisely the same questions may fall to be considered under s. 76 or s. 78 of the 1984 Act. Although *Hammond* has never been overruled as far as English courts are concerned, in *Liverpool Juvenile Court, ex parte R* [1988] QB 1 the Divisional Court relied on the authority of *Wong Kam-ming v The Queen* for the proposition that a defendant cannot be asked about the truth of a confession during an inquiry as to its admissibility. It should be noted, however, that:

(a) the judgment in that case expressly confined itself to summary proceedings (where it may be thought particularly important that the justices do not confuse the functions of the *voir dire* and the trial); and, more importantly,
(b) the court was not concerned directly with the question under discussion, but was instead engaged in enumerating the advantages to the defendant of the *voir dire* procedure.

In *Davis* [1990] Crim LR 860 the Court of Appeal referred to *Wong Kam-ming v The Queen* as 'strong persuasive authority' for the view that D could not be cross-examined as to the truth of his confession when giving evidence on the *voir dire*, but the point was not decided as the trial judge's ruling to the contrary had had no bearing upon the outcome of the trial.

Admissibility of Evidence Given on *Voir Dire*

F18.73 In *Wong Kam-ming v The Queen* [1980] AC 247, the Privy Council was unanimously of the opinion that the prosecution could not lead at the trial evidence regarding the testimony given by the defendant at the *voir dire*. Such a rule was necessary (per Lord Hailsham), so that 'the defendant should be able and feel free either by his own testimony or by other means to challenge... the tendered statement'. The rule applies even where the confession is admitted (per Lord Edmund-Davies) in order to maintain a clear distinction between questions of admissibility at issue in the *voir dire* and the issue of guilt falling to be decided in the main trial.

Wong Kam-ming v The Queen was applied in *Brophy* [1982] AC 476. D was tried in Northern Ireland for a large number of offences, including murder, and for being a member of the IRA, a proscribed organisation. At the *voir dire* he succeeded in challenging the admissibility of confessions tendered by the prosecution, on the ground that the statements were extracted from him by extreme misconduct on the part of his interrogators. In support of his case he admitted to membership of the IRA, in order to found an inference that his interrogators would have known of his allegiance and treated him brutally because of it. It was held that D's admission, being relevant to the issue at the *voir dire*, was inadmissible for the prosecution at the trial. Furthermore according to Lord Fraser of Tullybelton (at p. 481): 'Where... evidence is given at the *voir dire* by an accused person in answer to questions by his counsel, and without objection by counsel for the Crown, his evidence ought... to be treated as relevant to the issue at the *voir dire*, unless it is clearly and obviously irrelevant', for example, the accused 'goes out of his way to boast' of guilt.

Some commentators have argued that the law has altered as a result of the PACE 1984, s. 76, the effect of which is to render such a confession admissible, there being no question of it having been obtained by oppression or in circumstances conducive to unreliability. Even if this is the case, however, the policy behind *Wong Kam-ming v The Queen* and *Brophy* can be preserved and the same result achieved by invoking s. 78 of the 1984 Act to prevent unfairness in the proceedings. It is submitted that the policy is worth preserving, and that the accused would derive no protection from the statutory rules prohibiting the reception of confessions obtained in certain circumstances if the accused could only invoke the rule at the cost of admitting afresh that what was said was true.

Cross-examination on Statements Made on *Voir Dire*

F18.74 In *Wong Kam-ming v The Queen* [1980] AC 247, D gave evidence at trial and was cross-examined in detail as to statements made on the *voir dire* which were inconsistent with his testimony. The Privy Council held that where, as in the instant case, the confession had been excluded at the *voir dire*, it was not open to the prosecution to conduct such a cross-examination: 'Once a statement has been excluded... to adopt the words of Humphreys J in *Treacy* [1944] 2 All ER 229, nothing more should be heard of the *voir dire* unless it gives rise to a prosecution for perjury' (per Lord Hailsham at pp. 260–1).

The rule was otherwise where the confession which was the subject of the *voir dire* was admitted in evidence. In such a case (per Lord Hailsham, at p. 261): 'the whole evidence relating to the statement will have to be rehearsed once more... in front of the jury', and 'the statements on oath by the defendant on the *voir dire* as material for cross-examination do not, from the point of view of public policy, stand in any other situation than any other statements made by him, including the statement which has been admitted'.

The reasons of policy underlying the law as stated in *Wong Kam-ming v The Queen* have not altered since the coming into force of the PACE 1984, and it is submitted that the law remains as stated.

CONFESSION ADMISSIBLE AT TRIAL

Reconsidering Admissibility

F18.75 It has already been noted (see F18.67) that in *Sat-Bhambra* (1988) 88 Cr App R 55, the Court of Appeal held that, once a confession has been ruled admissible on the *voir dire*, the trial judge has no power under the PACE 1984, s. 76 or s. 78, to reconsider the decision if the evidence given at trial convinces the judge that it was wrong. To this extent the Act reverses the decision in *Watson* [1980] 2 All ER 293, where it was said that the judge had the power to reconsider the question of admissibility of evidence on which a ruling had been given, and had the duty to exclude from the jury's consideration evidence which was inadmissible. However, the Court in *Sat-Bhambra* noted that s. 82(3) of the 1984 Act preserved the common-law powers of a court to exclude evidence in its discretion. It followed that the trial judge retained the power, if only under the common law, to take such steps as were necessary to prevent injustice. Thus, if the matter was not capable of remedy by a direction, the jury might be discharged; or directed to disregard the statement; or directed as to matters which affect the weight of the confession, leaving the matter in their hands. There was no obligation to discharge the jury. The change brought about by the Act would seem therefore to be mainly technical, and it is submitted that in any event there is still force in the dictum of the Court of Appeal in *Watson* [1980] 2 All ER 293 that, 'the occasions on which a judge should allow counsel to invite him to reconsider a ruling already made are likely to be extremely rare'.

The problem is perhaps most likely to arise where a decision has been made on the basis that the confession was not obtained pursuant to a breach of the Code of Practice, but it then emerges that a breach may have occurred. In *Hassan* [1995] Crim LR 404, a concession to this effect by a police officer in cross-examination led the trial judge to use his common-law powers to reconsider his decision to admit D's confession, although he quite properly did not regard the concession as decisive of whether there had been a breach, and concluded that there had not. It is also possible to reconsider a decision to exclude a statement. In *Allen* [1992] Crim LR 297 the defence sought to cross-examine a police witness to elicit their version of a conversation, the prosecution version of which had been excluded under s. 78. It was held that the judge had correctly exercised his discretion to admit the prosecution version of what had been said.

Role of Jury

F18.76 Under the PACE 1984, as at common law, the admissibility of the confession is a matter for the judge, and the weight to be given to the confession, once it is admitted, is a matter for the jury. In *Mushtaq* [2005] UKHL 25, [2005] 3 All ER 1013 the House of Lords confirmed the view of the Court of Appeal in the same case that, as the jury is not a 'public authority' within the meaning of the HRA 1998, s. 6(3), it was not necessary in order to protect the accused from the risk of unfair trial that the jury, independently of the judge, should satisfy themselves as to the admissibility of confession evidence. The traditional division of labour between judge and jury thus survives the HRA 1998.

F18.77 Because the jury are entitled to consider all the circumstances in which a confession is made before deciding whether to act on it, it is the right of counsel for the defence 'to cross-examine again the witnesses who have already given evidence in the absence of the jury; for if he can induce the jury to think that the confession was obtained through some threat or promise, its value will be enormously weakened' (*Murray* [1951] 1 KB 391, decided at common law). The House of Lords in *Mushtaq* confirmed that the jury may be assisted in their function of deciding whether the confession is reliable by hearing the evidence that it was obtained in breach of the PACE 1984, s. 76(2). The House was, however, divided on the issue of the proper direction to be given to a jury in a case where evidence is before them that the confession was obtained by oppression or other improper means (in that case, by alleged threats to exaggerate D's part in the offence if he did not confess). If they conclude that it was so obtained, but is nevertheless reliable, may they act upon it? The traditional direction, given by the trial judge in *Mushtaq*, left the jury free to rely on the confession, if sure that it was true, 'even if it was or may have been made as a result of oppression or other improper circumstances'. A majority of their lordships decided that this direction could not be reconciled with s. 76(2) of the PACE 1984, to the extent that the rejection of an improperly obtained confession is based not solely on its potential unreliability, but on the importance of the defendant's right to avoid self-incrimination (*Lam Chi-ming v The Queen* [1991] AC 212, per Lord Griffiths). To leave the jury with the impression that they could find one or more of these rights to have been improperly infringed, but still rely upon the evidence, would, *per* Lord Roger, have been to contradict the policy:

> The evidence is excluded because, for all the kinds of reasons explained by Lord Griffiths, Parliament considers that it should not play any part in the jury's verdict. It flies in the face of that policy to say that a jury are entitled to rely on a confession even though, as the ultimate arbiters of all matters of fact, they properly consider that it was, or may have been, obtained by oppression or any other improper means.

For the same reasons, the majority considered that the traditional direction contained an invitation to act incompatibly with the accused's right against self-incrimination under Article 6(1). The House therefore departed from previous authorities including *Chan Wei Keung v The Queen* [1967] 2 AC 16. Lord Roger, in a speech with which the majority concurred, concluded that the logic of s. 76(2) of the PACE 1984 requires that the jury should be directed that, if they consider that the confession was or may have been obtained by oppression or in consequence of anything that was likely to render it unreliable, they should disregard it. The current guidance to trial judges in the *Crown Court Compendium* (July 2020), ch. 16-1, states that, where an accused claims to have confessed as a result of oppression or any other improper means, the jury should not be told that the judge has already considered the matter, but should be directed that if they conclude that the confession was, or may have been, obtained as a result of oppression, or in consequence of anything said or done which was likely to render it unreliable, they should give it no weight and disregard it. If the contention is that the PACE Codes of Practice were infringed, and the jury believe the contention is, or may be, true, they should be told to act on the confession only to the extent that they consider it to be reliable. In *Pham* [2008] EWCA Crim 3182 the trial judge, who had not been invited to consider *Mushtaq*, gave a direction which erred by focusing primarily on whether D's confessions could be regarded as truthful. However, the Court of Appeal considered that, as the only basis for D's contention that the confessions were untrue was an alleged threat to D in interview to which the judge also alluded, the overall impression given to the jury was not such as to render the conviction unsafe. **F18.78**

If the jury were to be told that the judge had ruled the confession admissible, it is possible that they might be influenced by the judge's view on admissibility in deciding the issues which are for them to decide. Thus it has been the practice in England, both before and after the PACE 1984, for this information to be withheld from them (*Mitchell v The Queen* [1998] AC 695; *Thompson v The Queen* [1998] AC 811).

If a confession is voluntary, the inference that it is also true follows naturally in most cases. On rare occasions, however, the mental condition of the accused may give rise to doubts as to the reliability of a confession. In such a case, expert medical evidence may be admitted to assist the jury in evaluating the reliability of the confession (*Ward* [1993] 2 All ER 577 (severe personality disorder amounting to mental disorder); *MacKenzie* (1992) 96 Cr App R 98 (mentally handicapped accused also suffering personality disorder: Crown conceded jury entitled to the assistance of expert testimony to evaluate confessions): see also **F18.56**). **F18.79**

Confession Implicating Co-accused

A confession made by an accused that is admitted in evidence is evidence only against the maker (PACE 1984, s. 76(1)). It was not, at common law, admissible against any other person implicated in it (*Rhodes* (1959) 44 Cr App R 23) unless it was made in the presence of that person who acknowledged the incriminating parts so as to make them, in effect, his or her own. The evidence of a co-accused on oath was, by contrast, admissible for all purposes, including the purpose of being evidence against the accused (*Rudd* (1948) 32 Cr App R 138). This common-law rule has been affected by the enactment of the PACE 1984, s. 74 (**F12.6**). Under that provision there is no doubt that the *conviction* of A is admissible to establish the guilt of A at B's trial, where it is relevant to do so (the most common example being where B is charged with complicity in a crime that the prosecution contend was committed by A, and of which A has been convicted). In *Hayter* [2004] UKHL 6, [2005] 2 All ER 209, the House of Lords held, by majority, that the **F18.80** rule where A and B are tried for a joint offence is modified as follows. Where the jury are directed first to consider the case against A, which is based on A's out-of-court admissions, they may then be told that their finding as to the guilt of A and the role A played may be used as part of the evidence relevant to the guilt of B. In other words their finding of guilt against A, though based on A's confession, becomes a building block in the case against B. This differs only marginally from using the confession of A directly (rather than indirectly through a finding of guilt) as evidence against B, but to hold strictly to the common-law rule would be to open a gulf between cases where A and B are jointly tried and cases where A's guilt is established at a separate trial, where s. 74 applies. *Hayter* was distinguished in *Persad v State of Trinidad and Tobago* [2007] UKPC 51, [2007] 1 WLR 2379. There, a robbery took place in the course of which one man raped and another man buggered one of the victims. The prosecution sought to establish, by a process of elimination, that B was responsible for the buggery, based on a combination of A's admission of rape, the victim's account that the rapist was not the man who buggered her, and C's admission to robbery as a look-out only. The argument failed principally because C's statement was, as regards the sexual offences, purely exculpatory, so that *Hayter* did not apply; whether, had A and B stood trial alone, A's confession to rape could have been a 'building block' in the case against B when the liability for the sexual offences was not joint was a question left for another time.

F18.81 The common-law rule that a confession is admissible only against its maker is also affected by the CJA 2003, s. 114(1)(d) (hearsay admissible in interests of justice: see *Y* [2008] EWCA Crim 10, [2008] 1 Cr App R 34 (411) at **F17.39**) and s. 121 (multiple hearsay admissible in interests of justice). In *Thakrar* [2010] EWCA Crim 1505, a confession to murder admissible against its maker under the multiple hearsay provisions of s. 121 (see **F17.84**) was said also to be admissible against the co-accused (the maker's brother). The confession included details that would have been known only to the murderer and was judged to be highly reliable. The Court of Appeal considered it unlikely that the brother would have been implicated unless he was also guilty. It was also suggested that the statement would have equally been admissible against the brother had he been tried separately. See, however, *Miah* [2011] EWCA Crim 945, in which it appears to have been assumed that pre-trial statements involving confessions made by one accused cannot be admissible against a co-accused.

F18.82 For the circumstances in which a confession may be edited so as to remove incriminating references to a co-accused, see **F18.92**. In exceptional circumstances the existence of a confession by one accused which seriously prejudices another may be grounds for ordering separate trials (*Gunewardene* [1951] 2 KB 600). Joint offences should generally be tried jointly, however, even though this may involve evidence which is inadmissible in respect of a particular accused being given. The usual course in a case where such material gets before a jury at a joint trial is for the judge to tell the jury that the interview answers of one accused, implicating a co-accused, are not evidence against that co-accused (*Bhagchandka* [2016] EWCA Crim 700). The fact that there is some risk of prejudice is not enough, though 'if a case is strong enough, if the prejudice is dangerous enough, if the circumstances are particular enough, all rules of this kind must go in the interests of justice' (*Lake* (1976) 64 Cr App R 172, at p. 175).

CONFESSION EXCLUDED AT TRIAL

Proving Confession by Other Hearsay Exceptions

F18.83 Criminal Justice Act 2003, s. 128

(2) Subject to subsection (1), nothing in this Chapter makes a confession by a defendant admissible if it would not be admissible under section 76 of the Police and Criminal Evidence Act 1984.

The reference to 'this Chapter' is to Chapter 2, Hearsay Evidence, which contains the exceptions to the hearsay rule. The clear intention is to ensure that alternative exceptions are not invoked in order to admit confessions that fail to satisfy s. 76. The most obvious is CJA 2003, s. 114(1)(d), (the 'interests of justice' exception: see **F17.34**), under which it is possible to admit confessions, including those of third parties.

Section 128(2) would also seem apt to prevent a previous inconsistent statement which is also a confession being used to establish the truth of the matters stated under s. 119 (see **F7.56**) if it would be inadmissible under s. 76 as a confession. At common law, such a statement could not in any event be used by the prosecution as a previous inconsistent statement (*Treacy* [1944] 2 All ER 229), but it was possible for a co-accused so to use it, the only limitation being relevancy (*Lui Mei Lin v The Queen* [1989] AC 288, approving *Rowson* [1986] QB 174). It is possible that both rules survive the enactment of s. 119, which deals with the effect of such a statement once it has been admitted in the course of cross-examination, rather than the circumstances in which such a statement may be put, which continues to be governed by the common law and the Criminal Procedure Act 1865, ss. 4 and 5. Even if such statements may be put at the behest of a co-accused, however, s. 128(2) would appear to prevent a statement inadmissible under s. 76 from being received as evidence of the matter stated. **F18.84**

EVIDENCE YIELDED BY INADMISSIBLE CONFESSIONS

Police and Criminal Evidence Act 1984, s. 76 **F18.85**

(4) The fact that a confession is wholly or partly excluded in pursuance of this section shall not affect the admissibility in evidence—
  (a) of any facts discovered as a result of the confession; or
  (b) where the confession is relevant as showing that the accused speaks, writes or expresses himself in a particular way, of so much of the confession as is necessary to show that he does so.

(5) Evidence that a fact to which this subsection applies was discovered as a result of a statement made by an accused person shall not be admissible unless evidence of how it was discovered is given by him or on his behalf.

(6) Subsection (5) above applies—
  (a) to any fact discovered as a result of a confession which is wholly excluded in pursuance of this section; and
  (b) to any fact discovered as a result of a confession which is partly so excluded, if the fact is discovered as a result of the excluded part of the confession.

Discovery of Facts

The PACE 1984, s. 76(4)(a), follows the common-law rule as stated in *Warickshall* (1783) 1 Leach 263. D made a full confession to receiving stolen goods, in consequence of which the goods were found concealed in her bed. The confession was ruled inadmissible, but the prosecution were allowed to prove the discovery of the stolen property. It was held that the principle requiring the rejection of certain confessions in evidence 'has no application whatever as to the admission or rejection of facts, whether the knowledge of them be obtained in consequence of an extorted confession, or whether it arises from any other source; for a fact, if it exists at all, must exist invariably in the same manner, whether the confession from which it is derived be in other respects true or false'. In *HM Advocate v P* [2011] UKSC 44, [2011] 1 WLR 2497, a Scottish case, it was held that there was no absolute rule of human rights law that would require the exclusion of evidence obtained in consequence of confessions or disclosures at an improperly conducted interview. Lord Hope considered that the law as set out in s. 76(4) was consistent with the rights guaranteed by the ECHR, Article 6. The issue in England and Wales as to whether it is fair to admit such evidence can be resolved by the separate application of s. 78. **F18.86**

Some difficulty may arise as to where the 'confession' ends and 'facts discovered as a result of it' begin. At common law, in *Barker* [1941] 2 KB 381, documents delivered up by D as a direct result of an inducement were treated as the equivalent of confession evidence, and excluded accordingly. Section 82(1) of the 1984 Act now provides a definition of 'confession' as including 'any statement wholly or partly adverse to the person who made it ... whether made in words or otherwise'. Words, documents or conduct which come within this definition and which fall foul of the exclusionary rule in s. 76(2) cannot be treated as 'facts' for the purpose of s. 76(4)(a). Thus, for example, a filmed re-enactment of a murder, in which a defendant is shown disposing of the murder weapon, should be regarded as a confession statement rather than as independent facts (*Lam Chi-ming v The Queen* [1991] 2 AC 212). However, it does not seem entirely satisfactory to regard conduct such as that in *Barker* as the equivalent of a 'statement' by the accused 'in consequence of anything said or done' under s. 76(2)(b) for the purposes of the 1984 Act, and such evidence would seem to be more correctly considered as admissible evidence of facts which, like all prosecution evidence, may in appropriate circumstances be excluded under s. 78 of the 1984 Act.

Confession Relevant to Show Speech, Writing or Expression

F18.87 Section 76(4)(b) of the 1984 Act embodies a principle stated in argument by Lush J in *Voisin* [1918] 1 KB 531. D was charged with the murder of a woman, part of whose body was found in a parcel together with a handwritten note bearing the legend 'Bladie Belgiam'. D, who had not been cautioned, was asked by the police to write the words 'Bloody Belgian', which he did, misspelling them in precisely the same fashion as the writer of the note. The case did not concern an inadmissible confession, but the principle involved in the reception of the note in evidence was said by Lush J to be that 'it cannot make any difference to the admissibility of handwriting whether it is written voluntarily or under compulsion of threats'. The same point was made (*obiter*) in *Nottle* [2004] EWCA Crim 599. Cars had been damaged by scratching an obscene message to the owner, whose name was Justin, but which the vandal had spelt as 'Jutin'. When asked to write down the same message, D also spelt the name incorrectly. On the assumption that the misspelling constituted a confession, the Court of Appeal found that there had been nothing said or done to render the statement inadmissible under s. 76, but that, even if it had been otherwise, s. 76(4)(b) would have rendered the misspelling admissible. Section 76(4)(b) might also be used, for example, in a case of rape, where a tape-recorded confession is ruled inadmissible, but the voice of the accused can be heard speaking with an unusual speech impediment which was also described by the victim, or with a particular local accent. Care must be taken to avoid prejudice to the accused when adducing such evidence; s. 76(4)(b) permits the prosecution to adduce only 'so much of the confession as is necessary to show' the relevant feature, but even this may in some cases be impossible without the jury becoming aware that a confession has been made. In such cases it will have to be considered whether the risk of prejudice can be overcome by a direction as to the purpose for which the evidence has been adduced, or whether the discretion of the court to exclude prosecution evidence, either under s. 78 of the 1984 Act or at common law, should be exercised. In *Nottle*, the Court held that the failure of the police to disclose to D that the name on the car had been spelled 'Jutin' was not a matter which rendered it unfair for the prosecution subsequently to rely on D's identical misspelling.

Linking Facts to Confession

F18.88 At common law there was some controversy as to the extent to which it was permissible to show that certain facts had come to light as the result of an inadmissible confession by the accused. Section 76(5) and (6) of the 1984 Act confirms the view taken in *Warickshall* (1783) 1 Leach 263, and *Berryman* (1854) 6 Cox CC 388 that no such link can be proved. The only exception is where the defence choose to give evidence of how the facts came to be discovered, in which case, presumably, the prosecution may challenge the account given by the defence, even if to do so involves making reference to the excluded statement.

Evidence Yielded by Confession Excluded under s. 78

F18.89 The PACE 1984, s. 76(4), applies only to matters coming to light as a result of a confession excluded under s. 76 itself. Where the confession is excluded in the discretion of the court under

s. 78, no statutory rule applies, but the common-law principles suggest that evidence discovered in consequence is admissible.

As to the linking of the discovery with the confession, it may be that a court dealing with an application under s. 78 will not feel compelled to follow the principle laid down in s. 76(5), given that the common law on the point was unclear (see, e.g., *Griffin* (1809) Russ & Ry 151; *Gould* (1840) 9 C & P 364, and the views expressed by a majority of the Criminal Law Revision Committee in its *Eleventh Report: Evidence (General)* (1972) Cmnd 4991, para. 69). It should also be noted that the reasons which led the court to exercise its discretion in respect of the confession may extend also to the subsequently discovered facts, as where an accused discloses information in a confession made after the wrongful denial of access to legal advice by a police officer acting in deliberate and flagrant disregard of s. 58 of the 1984 Act. See also the discussion of *HM Advocate v P* [2011] UKSC 44, [2011] 1 WLR 2497 at **F18.86**.

Another possibility is that the court will take into account the confirmation of a confession by the discovery of incontrovertible facts in deciding whether to exercise its discretion to exclude the confession statement. Nothing in s. 78 appears to prevent such reasoning, indeed the court is enjoined to have regard to 'all the circumstances' in reaching its conclusion. (Contrast s. 76(2), in which it is clear that the truth of the confession is not a factor to be taken into account in determining admissibility.) The argument is particularly attractive where the defence rely on breach of a provision of a code of practice, the function of which is thought by the court to be to guard against the production of unreliable confession statements, such as the obligation to maintain records of interviews.

EDITING OF CONFESSIONS

Editing at Trial to Protect Accused

There is a long-established practice of not disclosing to a jury matters that form part of a confession statement but which are prejudicial, typically because of reference to other offences (*Turner v Underwood* [1948] 2 KB 284). In *Weaver* [1968] 1 QB 353, Sachs LJ said that a statement by an accused ought to be edited at trial to avoid prejudice and to eliminate matters which 'it would be better that the jury should not know'. In *Knight* (1946) 31 Cr App R 52, portions of D's confessions which related to other offences which were irrelevant to the offence charged were held to have been improperly received in evidence. In some cases the material edited out is irrelevant, in others it has a prejudicial effect exceeding its probative value. See also *Hall* [1971] Crim LR 480 and *Pearce* (1979) 69 Cr App R 365. When an agreement has been made that unfairly prejudicial material should be edited before being given to the jury, it is crucial that the proper edited version is put before the jury (*A (S)* [2012] EWCA Crim 512, in which a direction to the jury to 'put it out of their minds' did not cure the defect). **F18.90**

CrimPD V, paras. 16A.1 to 16A.6 (see Supplement, **CPD.16A**), recognise that, whereas other written statements may be satisfactorily dealt with by editing, it is preferable in the circumstances identified in para. 16A.4(b), where an interview ranges over more offences than are eventually charged, to prepare a fresh statement. In summary proceedings, there will be a need to prepare fresh statements rather than using the method of striking out or bracketing those parts on which no reliance is to be placed by the prosecution in the proceedings (para. 16A.5). **F18.91**

Editing at Trial to Protect Co-accused

Where the confession of an accused person is admitted, it is not, as a general rule, admissible in evidence against a co-accused (see **F18.80**). Where an accused has laid blame, perhaps the **F18.92** greater blame, on a co-accused, the risk of prejudice to the co-accused if the whole statement is heard is obvious. The rule, however, is that the prosecution ought to present the accused's confession as a whole (*Pearce* (1979) 69 Cr App R 365) and the accused could, with good reason, complain if the prosecution picked out certain passages and left out others (*Gunewardene* [1951] 2 KB 600). In *Gunewardene*, D1 was charged as an accessory to manslaughter arising out of an abortion performed by D2, his co-accused. D2's confession was read to the jury, including those parts of it which implicated D1, the trial judge warning the jury that the statement was not evidence against D1. Lord Goddard CJ said (at p. 611) that 'although in many cases counsel do refrain from reading passages which implicate another prisoner and have no real bearing on the case against the prisoner making the statement, we cannot say that anything has been admitted . . . which was not admissible'.

Gunewardene was applied in *Lobban v The Queen* [1995] 2 All ER 602, where the issue before the Privy Council was whether the exculpatory part of a mixed statement made by D1's co-accused, D2, which incriminated D1 in a murder, could be excluded or edited in the exercise of the court's discretion to protect D1 from prejudice, given that the statement was hearsay and inadmissible as against him. The answer was that it could not; the prosecution had placed reliance upon the mixed statement as against D2, and the exculpatory parts were therefore admissible evidence for D2 (see **F18.93**). There was no discretion to restrain a co-accused from defending himself by adducing admissible evidence, and nothing to support the suggestion made in earlier cases that the judge had a discretion to edit a confession so as to deprive one defendant of relevant defence evidence in order to minimise injustice to another (see, e.g., *Rogers* [1971] Crim LR 413). This, while a correct application of principle, may remove what has been an attractive option in some cases (see, e.g., the discussion of earlier authorities in *Jefferson* (1994) 99 Cr App R 14 at p. 26), but it would seem still to leave open the possibility of editing out information irrelevant to the co-accused's case, or of editing with the co-accused's consent.

In *Mitchell* [2005] EWCA Crim 3447, the Court of Appeal was concerned with the editing of two sets of statements. In the first, *Lobban* applied because the prosecution were relying on the whole of the interview and the effect of editing out references to D2 would have been to leave the jury with an incomplete and unsatisfactory picture of what D1 had said. In the second, *Lobban* did not apply: the references to D2 were made, not by D1 himself, but by a police officer putting forward his opinion that D2 had committed another crime which was not the subject of any proceedings. That part of the statement could and should have been removed, and the desire of D1 to use it in order to discredit D2 was irrelevant.

MIXED STATEMENTS

Admissibility of Mixed Statements

F18.93 It is the convention to admit in evidence statements made by an accused when being questioned by the police whether or not they contain admissions (*Pearce* (1979) 69 Cr App R 365) but such statements are admitted as evidence of reaction and not as evidence of the facts stated (see **F6.40**). The rule is different in relation to a mixed statement, which in part comprises admissions and in part exculpatory or self-serving statements (*Hamand* (1985) 82 Cr App R 65 at p. 67). An example would be 'I admit I hit him, but he was trying to kill me'. A 'partly adverse statement' is a confession by virtue of the PACE 1984, s. 82(1) (see **F18.1**), and is admissible as such provided that the requirements of s. 76 are complied with. In *Finch* [2007] EWCA Crim 36, [2007] 1 WLR 1645, the Court of Appeal identified as suitable for full argument the question whether the presence of an admission in a police interview rendered the entire interview a 'confession', and Hughes LJ said that not everything stated at the time of a partial admission is necessarily part of a 'confession'; a proposition relied upon in *Sliogeris* [2015] EWCA Crim 22 (see **F18.5**). Whether a particular statement is truly 'mixed' is, it is submitted, a question of fact, and both temporal and contextual separation will be relevant to whether two or more propositions form part of the same statement. It will be a question for the court in each case to determine whether an excuse or explanation so accompanies an admission as to be part of a mixed statement for the purposes of this rule. In *Pearce* (1979) 69 Cr App R 365, the principle was said to be that a statement which is not an admission is admissible if it is made 'in the same context as an admission', and the Court of Appeal accepted that the two parts of the mixed statement may occur at different places in 'the same interview or series of interviews'.

Where an admission is made which is qualified by an explanation or excuse, 'all the authorities agree that it would be unfair to admit the admission without admitting the explanation' (*Sharp* [1988] 1 All ER 65 per Lord Havers at p. 12). In *Pearce* (1979) 69 Cr App R 365, it was said that to exclude answers at interview which are favourable to the accused, while admitting those which are unfavourable, would be misleading, and a breach of duty on the part of the prosecutor, whose obligation is to present the case fairly to the jury.

In many cases, the mixed statement will have been made in the course of questioning of the accused by the police, no distinction being taken in this respect between a written statement and a record of questions and answers at interview (*Polin* [1991] Crim LR 293). It is not, however, a condition of admissibility that the statement was made to a police officer — a point taken by Lord Havers in *Sharp*. Thus, for example, mixed statements have been received which were made by the accused when giving evidence at a previous trial (*McGregor*; *Higgins* (1829) 3 C & P 603).

Under the CJA 2003, s. 118(1), the common-law rules regarding the admissibility of mixed statements are preserved (see **F17.66**).

Evidential Value of Self-serving Parts of Mixed Statements

In *Sharp* [1988] 1 All ER 65, Lord Havers identified two views which had emerged as to the evidential value of the self-serving parts of a mixed statement. The view which the House of Lords accepted is that the whole statement is admissible by way of exception to the hearsay rule, and is thus evidence of the truth of all the facts stated in it. The House expressed approval of the law as stated in *Duncan* (1981) 73 Cr App R 359 by Lord Lane CJ, who said (at p. 365): **F18.94**

> Where a 'mixed' statement is under consideration by the jury in a case where the defendant has not given evidence, it seems to us that the simplest, and, therefore, the method most likely to produce a just result, is for the jury to be told that the whole statement, both the incriminating parts and the excuses or explanations, must be considered by them in deciding where the truth lies. It is, to say the least, not helpful to try to explain to the jury that the exculpatory parts of the statement are something less than evidence of the facts they state.

For examples of earlier decisions to the same effect, see *Clewes* (1830) 4 C & P 221; *McGregor* [1968] 1 QB 371; *Hamand* (1985) 82 Cr App R 65. *Sharp* has been approved by the House of Lords in *Aziz* [1996] AC 41 and by the Privy Council in *Lobban v The Queen* [1995] 2 All ER 602.

The other view which has from time to time been taken, is that the self-serving parts of the statement are not evidence of their truth, but form material which may be of use to the jury in evaluating the admissions. This was said to be the law in, e.g., *Sparrow* [1973] 2 All ER 129 and in *Leung Kam-Kwok v The Queen* (1984) 81 Cr App R 83. The House of Lords in *Sharp* [1988] 1 All ER 65 rejected this 'purist' approach:

(a) because the weight of authority supported the contrary view; and
(b) because common sense suggested that the only way in which a jury could use the self-serving parts of the statement to 'evaluate the facts in the admission' would be if they first reached a conclusion as to the truth of the explanation given by the accused.

In *Greenhalgh* [2014] EWCA Crim 2084 it was held to be an error to describe a mixed statement as 'not capable of being evidence in the case', although the trial judge's subsequent direction as to the weight the jury might choose to attribute to the self-serving parts meant that the error could not have materially affected the verdict. The question of the evidential value of a mixed statement arises most acutely in cases where the accused does not testify. In both *Duncan* (1981) 73 Cr App R 359 and *Sharp* [1988] 1 All ER 65, D gave no evidence, and the statement of Lord Lane CJ which was approved in *Sharp* concerns the direction to be given to a jury in such a case; indeed it incorporates the right to comment on the failure of the accused to repeat the exculpatory statement on oath (*Downes* (1993) *Independent*, 25 October 1993). Despite this, there is no logical reason why the status of the statement should be any different if the accused testifies.

Weight to be Attached to Self-serving Parts of Mixed Statements

F18.95 In *Sharp* [1988] 1 All ER 65 the House of Lords approved of the following statement of Lord Lane CJ in *Duncan* (1981) 73 Cr App R 359 at p. 365:

> . . . where appropriate, as it usually will be, the judge may, and should, point out that the incriminating parts are likely to be true (otherwise why say them?), whereas the excuses do not have the same weight. Nor is there any reason why, again where appropriate, the judge should not comment in relation to the exculpatory remarks upon the election of the accused not to give evidence.

In *Donaldson* (1976) 64 Cr App R 59 it was said that the jury, when deciding what weight, if any, to give to those parts of the statement which are favourable to an accused who has elected not to give evidence, should take into account that it was not made on oath and has not been tested by cross-examination. In *McGregor* [1968] 1 QB 371, the mixed statement consisted of an admission and explanation given on oath by D in a previous trial. The rule was the same: as D had elected not to give evidence at the second trial, the judge had correctly pointed out to the jury that the explanation was untested.

Mixed Statements and the Evidential Burden

F18.96 Where the accused bears the evidential burden of establishing a sufficient foundation so that a defence such as self-defence or provocation may be left to the jury, reliance may be placed on the self-serving part of a mixed statement which is admitted in evidence under the principles stated above. In *Hamand* (1985) 82 Cr App R 65, D made a statement to the police in which he admitted that he had struck a man in the face, but claimed that the man had acted in such a way as to lead D to believe that he was about to be attacked. The statement was proved in evidence as part of the prosecution case. The Court of Appeal held that the trial judge had been wrong to rule that D's mixed statement was not evidence of self-defence, thus forcing D to testify in his own defence. In assessing the weight to be given to such a statement where it is not supported by any evidence from the accused, the comments of Lord Lane CJ in *Duncan* (1981) 73 Cr App R 359 (see **F18.95**) should be borne in mind.

Prosecution Placing No Reliance on Admission Contained in Mixed Statement

F18.97 The derivation of the rule as stated at **F18.93** and **F18.94** suggests that a mixed statement becomes evidence of the truth of its self-serving parts only where the prosecution elect to rely on it as containing an admission. Some difficulty may arise in cases where the prosecution adduce a mixed statement (by way of discharging their duty under *Pearce* (1979) 69 Cr App R 365 to put statements made to the police before the court (see **F6.40**)) but seek to rely on it only to show the reaction of the accused when taxed with the offence, and not as evidence of its truth. That this may be done is well established (see, e.g., *Storey* (1968) 52 Cr App R 334; *Donaldson* (1976) 64 Cr App R 59; *Pearce* (1979) 69 Cr App R 365), and may benefit the prosecution by enabling them to draw attention to any inconsistencies between the explanation advanced in the statement and any defence put forward at trial. It seems unlikely that, in such cases, the self-serving passages become evidence of their truth.

For the same reason, it is submitted, a mixed statement which is not relied on by the prosecution for any purpose ought not to be regarded as admissible evidence for the defence of any excuse or explanation asserted in it. This was accepted by the House of Lords in *Aziz* [1996] AC 41 (at p. 50), where the statement to this effect in the 1995 edition of this work was approved. It should, however, be noted that in *Sharp* [1988] 1 All ER 65 the question certified for decision by the House (as amended by Lord Havers) was: 'Where a statement made to a person out of court by a defendant contains both admissions and self-exculpatory parts do the exculpatory parts constitute evidence of the truth of the facts alleged therein?' The question does not confine itself to cases where the prosecution seek to rely on the admissions contained in the statement. It is submitted, however, in the light of *Aziz*, that the answering of this question in the affirmative by the House of Lords does not provide any warrant for qualifying the law as it is stated above.

In *Garrod* [1997] Crim LR 445, the Court of Appeal considered that a statement was properly regarded as 'mixed' if it contained an admission of fact which was capable of adding some degree of weight to the prosecution case, regardless (apparently) of whether the prosecution were relying on it or not. However, the statement in that case was purely exculpatory, whichever test was applied. In *Western v DPP* [1997] 1 Cr App R 474, D appealed against conviction for a public order offence on the grounds that the magistrates had wrongly treated as purely self-serving an interview in which D admitted fighting with the victim but claimed to have acted in self-defence. The prosecution resisted the appeal precisely on the grounds that the interview was not a mixed statement unless the prosecution relied on the admission. The appeal was allowed because there was nothing within the stated case to suggest that the prosecution had *not* relied on the admission: on the contrary the circumstances suggested it was highly likely that they had. *Papworth* [2007] EWCA Crim 3031, [2008] 1 Cr App R 36 (439), applies *Garrod* with the proviso that, as the rule is 'based on fairness to the defendant and simplicity for the jury', the judge should estimate, at the conclusion of all the evidence, the extent to which the prosecution 'place significant reliance on' the incriminating statements. The more significant the reliance, 'the more it is likely that the jury should be told that the parts which explain or excuse those incriminating parts are also evidence in the case' (at [14]). **F18.98**

Papworth and *Garrod* [1997] Crim LR 445 were applied in *Shirley* [2013] EWCA Crim 1990. The prosecution in that case relied on only very limited admissions (that D was known by his middle name of Mark, and that he told people he had served in the army when he had not). As it was open to the judge to conclude that these were not 'significant' statements in the prosecution's case (and both could, it appears, have been proved by other evidence had they been contested), the interview in which D made the concessions could not be viewed, taken as a whole, as a mixed statement. D, who did not testify, was therefore rightly precluded from relying on any self-serving statements made in the same interviews. But it is a misdirection to dismiss as mere evidence of reaction a body of interview evidence the inculpatory parts of which are relied on by the prosecution (*Gijkokaj* [2014] EWCA Crim 386), though in that case the 'obvious' error was held not to amount to material misdirection, given the judge's overall treatment of the defence case. This is not to say that evidence of reaction is necessarily of little value. In *R (Gonzales) v Folkestone Magistrates' Court* [2010] EWHC 3428 (Admin) it was conceded that the prosecution erred in simply failing to adduce the mixed statement at all, in contravention of the practice approved in *Pearce* (see **F6.40**). The Divisional Court's principal reason for approving the concession was that the prosecution had deprived D of valuable evidence of 'reaction to an accusation' rather than evidence of the truth of the self-serving parts. To the extent that the distinction remains important, it is submitted that this is correct.

STATEMENTS IN PRESENCE OF ACCUSED

General Rule

> ... the rule of law undoubtedly is that a statement made in the presence of an accused person, even upon an occasion which should be expected reasonably to call for some explanation or denial from **F18.99**

> him, is not evidence against him of the facts stated save so far as he accepts the statement, so as to make it, in effect, his own. (*Christie* [1914] AC 545, per Lord Atkinson at p. 554)

Under the CJA 2003, s. 118(1), the common-law rules regarding the admissibility of confessions are preserved (see **F17.66**). It is submitted that the rules considered in this section will continue to have effect.

Although it is a salutary rule of practice, there is no rule of law requiring the production, before the content of the statement is given in evidence, of some proof of the accused's acceptance of the statement (*Christie*, modifying the stricter rule suggested by the Court of Criminal Appeal in *Norton* [1910] 2 KB 496). Lord Atkinson considered that the procedure suggested by Pickford J in *Norton* was unobjectionable, provided that it was workable. According to that procedure, in a trial on indictment the judge, where it is possible to do so, decides whether there is any evidence of acknowledgement of the statement. Where acknowledgement cannot be deduced, the fact of a statement having been made in the accused's presence may be given in evidence, but not the contents, and the question asked, what the accused said or did on such a statement being made. If the answer is such that acknowledgement may properly be inferred, the contents of the statement become admissible.

F18.100 If the statement is admitted, the question whether the accused's conduct amounted to an acknowledgement is a question for the jury. If they find that the statement was acknowledged, in whole or in part, then they may take the statement or the relevant part of it into consideration. If they do not so find, they should be directed to disregard the statement altogether (*Norton*). In *Christie*, Lord Atkinson said (at p. 554) that, if the judge is of the view that no evidence has been given on which the jury could reasonably find that the accused had accepted the statement, the jury should be directed to disregard it.

Where the acknowledgement takes the form of a statement by the accused which is wholly or partly adverse to him or her, the accused will by virtue of the PACE 1984, s. 82(1), have made a confession for the purposes of Part VIII of that Act, and accordingly the conditions of s. 76 must be complied with.

The jury should be given a clear direction as to the inferences to which the accused's conduct may give rise (*Horne* [1990] Crim LR 188; *Chandler* [1976] 1 All ER 585; but see *Black* (1922) 16 Cr App R 118).

Evidence of Acknowledgement

F18.101 In *Christie* [1914] AC 545, Lord Atkinson considered the various ways in which an accused person might accept an accusation (at p. 554):

> He may accept the statement by word or conduct, action or demeanour, and it is the function of the jury which tries the case to determine whether his words, action, conduct or demeanour at the time when the statement was made amounts to an acceptance of it in whole or in part. It by no means follows, I think, that a mere denial by the accused of the facts mentioned in the statement necessarily renders the statement inadmissible, because he may deny his statement in such a manner and under such circumstances as may lead a jury to disbelieve him, and constitute evidence from which an acknowledgement can be inferred.

See also *Norton* [1910] 2 KB 496. In *Christie*, D was charged with indecent assault on a young boy who, shortly after the alleged offence and in the presence of his mother and of a police officer who was on the spot, confronted D with the words 'That is the man,' and gave details of the assault. D replied 'I am innocent'. Although in the form of a denial, the response was regarded as one from which it was open to the jury to draw an inference of acceptance. Lord Moulton said (at p. 559):

> Going back to first principles . . . the deciding question is whether the evidence of the whole occurrence is relevant or not. If the prisoner admits the charges the evidence is obviously relevant. If he denies it, it may or may not be relevant. For instance, if he is charged with a violent assault and

denies that he committed it, that fact might be distinctly relevant if at the trial his defence was that he did commit the act, but that it was in self-defence.

Acceptance by acquiescence was considered sufficient in *O* [2005] EWCA Crim 3082, where D stood by, smirking, while his friend explained when asked the reason for an attack that it had been racially motivated.

Where the accused denies the accusation, it must, however, be asked whether the effect on the jury of hearing that an accusation has been made might be to create prejudice on their part which is out of all proportion to the evidential value of the accused's behaviour. If the evidence would have very little or no value, the judge ought to exercise discretion to exclude it (*Christie*, per Lord Moulton at p. 560).

As to silence in the face of an allegation, see **F20.28**.

Accused Confronted with Statement by Co-accused

The principles set out at **F18.99** are of equal application where the accused is confronted with **F18.102** an accusation made by a co-accused. The practice of the police is now regulated by PACE Code C, para. 16.4 of which provides that, where, after a person has been charged or informed that he or she may be prosecuted, a police officer wishes to bring to the person's notice a statement made by, or the content of an interview with, another, the officer must give the person a true copy of the statement or draw attention to the content of the interview record while doing nothing to invite any reply or comment save to administer the caution. This should ensure that the only evidence of reaction on which a court is asked to rely will be a voluntary statement under caution. If the co-accused's statement is improperly read, it is likely that the statement will be excluded under the PACE 1984, s. 78, together with the accused's reaction to it, particularly if the latter cannot be made sense of without reference to the statement.

Section F19 Evidence of Identification

VISUAL IDENTIFICATION

F19.1 The visual identification of suspects or defendants by witnesses has long been recognised as potentially unreliable. Honest and convincing mistakes can be made by witnesses who entertain no doubt that they are right, and even by witnesses who purport to identify persons already known to them. The Criminal Law Revision Committee asserted in its *Eleventh Report: Evidence (General)* (1972), Cmnd 4991, that cases of mistaken identification constituted 'by far the greatest cause of actual or possible wrong convictions'. Much has been done since then to reduce the risks. In particular, three safeguards are now in place. The first can now be found in PACE Code D (see **D1.127** ***et seq***. and **appendix 1**). The procedures prescribed by Code D (insofar as they relate to visual identification) are designed to test a witness's ability to identify, under controlled conditions, any suspect the witness may claim to have seen or recognised on a previous occasion. They also require witnesses to provide the police with descriptions of any offenders etc. they claim to have seen, so that any subsequent identification can be compared with the original description. Failure to comply with Code D procedures must be taken into account by a court and may result in the exclusion of tainted evidence. See **F19.4**.

The other safeguards apply at the trial stage. The Court of Appeal in *Turnbull* [1977] QB 224 (see **F19.9**) prescribed rules to guide judges faced with contested visual identification evidence. These guidelines must also be taken into account by magistrates' courts. Finally, in trials on indictment at least, the prosecution will not invite witnesses to identify D for the first time in court: as to this rule against 'dock identification', see **F19.6**.

Identification Evidence and Identification Issues

F19.2 It is important to distinguish between identification evidence and evidence that incriminates by other means. A mere description of the culprit or the culprit's clothing is not identification evidence, even if it closely matches the appearance or clothing of the defendant (*Gayle* [1999] 2 Cr App R 130). Nor is it identification evidence where the witness states that the culprit was the driver of a particular vehicle, or the companion of another person, whose own identification is not in dispute (*White* [2000] All ER (D) 602). If there is no identification evidence, the *Turnbull* guidelines do not apply: see, e.g., *M* [2013] EWCA Crim 1311, where the issue was not whether the witness had correctly identified D at the scene but whether D had been an offender or a victim. A witness who has made or who may be able to make an identification must ordinarily be invited to take part in a Code D identification procedure if the police have a known suspect available (Code D, para. 3.12); but inability to make an identification need not prevent the witness giving other evidence that might incriminate D, such as a description of the offence or offender (*George* [2002] EWCA Crim 1923).

F19.3 If the accuracy of a purported identification (as opposed to the honesty of the accusing witness) is not in issue, then neither the *Turnbull* guidelines nor Code D will need to be considered. In such cases any attempt to apply the *Turnbull* guidelines would merely serve to confuse the jury by focusing their attention on the wrong issue (*Courtnell* [1990] Crim LR 115; *Cape* [1996] 1 Cr App R 191; *Panesar* [2007] EWCA Crim 2510). If, for example, the witness claims to have known D well and for many years and to have observed D at close range in conditions of perfect visibility for several minutes, or to have conversed with D in the same room, it is unlikely that any identification issue could arise. Such cases are neither rare nor wholly exceptional (*Capron v The Queen* [2006] UKPC 34).

On the other hand, identification issues can easily arise, even where the witness claims to have recognised the suspect or accused as someone already well known to the witness, and they are not necessarily excluded even where the principal line of defence involves an attack on the honesty or truthfulness of the witness. This can be seen in *Conway* (1990) 91 Cr App R 143. Two witnesses claimed to have recognised D as the man responsible for a stabbing and he was arrested. He denied that he knew either of the witnesses and asked to be put on an identification parade, but the police took the view that this was unnecessary, as D was a 'named person'. The Court of Appeal held this to be wrong: identification became an issue as soon as D questioned the witnesses' ability to recognise him, and the identification procedures laid down in Code D should have been followed. By the same token, there would have been an identification issue at trial and the *Turnbull* guidelines would have been applicable.

The general rule, therefore, is that an appropriate *Turnbull* warning should be given, even in cases of alleged recognition. In *Beckford v The Queen* (1993) 97 Cr App R 409, a witness claimed to have recognised D and others as they committed the alleged offence. He knew them well. The defence alleged that his evidence was wilfully false, but the Privy Council nevertheless held that there was also a possibility of genuine mistake. The witness had been 500 feet from the scene of the crime, and the closest he had come to the perpetrators was 120 feet. Mistakes can be made at such distances, even where known acquaintances are involved, and it was held that a *Turnbull* direction should have been given. See to similar effect *Bentley* [1991] Crim LR 620, *Bowden* [1993] Crim LR 379 (see **F19.12**), *Giga* [2007] EWCA Crim 345 and *Livingstone v The Queen* [2012] UKPC 36. It does not follow that a Code D identification procedure must always be held whenever an identification issue arises. Such a procedure will often serve no useful purpose in a 'recognition' case, because the witness (even if mistaken) would almost inevitably 'identify' the person the witness has claimed to have recognised (see further *Forbes* [2001] UKHL 40, [2001] 1 AC 473 and **D1.128**).

Dealing at Trial with Breaches of PACE Code D

As with the other codes of practice issued under the PACE 1984, breaches of Code D do not inevitably lead to the exclusion of evidence that may be tainted by the breach (*Khan* [1997] Crim LR 584; *McEvoy* [1997] Crim LR 887; *Selwyn* [2012] EWCA Crim 2968; *Lariba* [2015] EWCA Crim 478), but it is essential that the trial court or judge determines whether any alleged breaches have occurred, and whether they may have caused any significant prejudice to D (*Grannell* (1989) 90 Cr App R 149; *Ryan* [1992] Crim LR 187; *Quinn* [1995] 1 Cr App R 480; *Hickin* [1996] Crim LR 584). In *Beveridge* (1987) 85 Cr App R 255, the Court of Appeal stated that the determination of such facts can usually be accomplished without the need for a trial within a trial, but this cannot be an absolute rule. The holding of a trial within a trial was not, for example, criticised in *Willoughby* [1999] 2 Cr App R 82. **F19.4**

If it is clear that no prejudice resulted from a breach or failure to observe Code D, there will be no case for excluding the evidence. If, on the other hand, some prejudice may have been caused, it will be necessary to determine, under the PACE 1984, s. 78, whether the adverse effect would be such that justice requires the evidence to be excluded. Cases will, to a large extent, turn on their own facts. A trial court or judge must give reasons for any decision to admit identification evidence obtained in breach of Code D (*Allen* [1995] Crim LR 643).

Identification evidence will usually be excluded where important safeguards have been flouted. In *Nagah* [1991] Crim LR 55, D's conviction was quashed after evidence had been admitted at his trial derived from a deliberately staged encounter outside the police station, in which he had been confronted by the identifying witness as he left, after having been told that there was insufficient **F19.5** evidence to charge him. He had previously agreed to stand on an identification parade, but this was never held. See to similar effect *Finley* [1993] Crim LR 50, *Gall* (1989) 90 Cr App R 64 and *Deakin* [2012] EWCA Crim 2637.

Failure to observe the requirements of Code D (e.g., by failing to hold a formal identification procedure where an issue of potential identification arose) may affect other forms of evidence against D and a careful direction to the jury may be needed, so that they fully understand the potential for prejudice caused by that breach or failure (*Forbes* [2001] UKHL 40, [2001] AC 473 at [27]; *Preddie* [2011] EWCA Crim 312; *Gojra* [2010] EWCA Crim 1939; *Byrne* [2016] EWCA Crim 2124). The jury must ordinarily be told 'that an identification procedure enables suspects to put the reliability of an eye-witness's identification to the test, that the suspect has lost the benefit of that safeguard, and that they should take account of that fact in their assessment of the whole case, giving it such weight as they think fit' (*H* [2003] EWCA Crim 174, per Potter LJ; and see also the *Crown Court Compendium* (July 2020), ch. 15-1). Failure to comply with Code D may also give rise to issues under the ECHR, notably in cases involving covert videotaping of suspects, which may be open to challenge under Article 8 if not performed in strict accordance with domestic law (*Perry v UK* (2004) 39 EHRR 3 (76)).

Dock Identification

F19.6 The term 'dock identification' is best understood as referring to the identification of an accused for the first time during the course of the trial itself (i.e. by a witness who has not previously named or identified D by means of a Code D identification procedure). Such evidence has long been considered potentially unreliable (*Edwards v The Queen* [2006] UKPC 23), and especially so when a witness who has failed to pick out D at an identification parade is then invited to try to identify D in court (*Holland v HM Advocate* [2005] UKPC D 1, [2005] HRLR 25; *Lawrence v The Queen* [2014] UKPC 2), but the dangers inherent in a dock identification (as defined above) may not be present where the witness says, 'the person whom I have *already* identified to the police as the person who committed the crime is the person who stands in the dock' (*France v The Queen* [2012] UKPC 28).

In view of the dangers posed by dock identification, the A-G and the DPP undertook in 1976 that in cases tried on indictment:

> The [prosecution]...will not invite a witness to identity, who has not previously identified the accused at an identity parade, to make a dock identification unless the witness's attendance at a parade was unnecessary or impracticable, or there are exceptional circumstances.

A judge would ordinarily prohibit any such identification during the course of a trial on indictment (*Fergus* (1993) 98 Cr App R 313), but different considerations may apply in respect of minor summary offences, such as road traffic offences, where the holding of an identity parade or similar Code D procedure may well be impracticable. In *Barnes v Chief Constable of Durham* [1997] 2 Cr App R 505, Popplewell J suggested that the rule of practice that applies to trials on indictment 'has singularly little application to the everyday activities of the magistrates' court'. In *Karia v DPP* [2002] EWHC 2175 (Admin), Stanley Burnton J adopted a more cautious stance, observing merely that: 'It cannot be sensible to require identity parades to be held in all motoring cases, in circumstances where there is no reason to believe that identity is in issue', but these rulings appear to conflict with *North Yorkshire Trading Standards Department v Williams* (1995) 159 JP 383 in which the Divisional Court rejected the notion that less strict identification rules should apply in respect of summary offences. See further T Watkin, 'In the Dock — an Overview of Decisions of the High Court on Dock Identifications in the Magistrates' Court' [2003] Crim LR 463 and *Smith v DPP* [2008] EWHC 771 (Admin). Whether dock identification infringes the right to a fair trial under the ECHR, Article 6, depends on all the circumstances of the case. Such a procedure cannot be said to be unfair *per se* (*Holland v HM Advocate* [2005] UKPC D 1, [2005] HRLR 25; *Young v The State* [2008] UKPC 27; *Tido v The Queen* [2011] UKPC 16, [2012] 1 WLR 115).

There is a danger that a witness may sometimes make a dock identification even where none has been solicited by the prosecution. If that happens (as in *Thomas* [1994] Crim LR 128), it may be necessary for the trial judge to warn the jury against giving it any weight or credence. It would not suffice merely to observe (as did the trial judge in *Thomas*) that an identification of that sort would not ordinarily take place. **F19.7**

There is also a risk, if D is not in custody and no identification has previously been arranged, that a witness will identify D on arrival at or waiting outside the court. In *Tiplady* (1995) 159 JP 548, the prosecution actually arranged for a group identification in the foyer of the court building as D arrived and this evidence was properly admitted at trial. It is unlikely, however, that the circumstances of such an identification would be wholly satisfactory (especially where a considerable time has elapsed since the alleged offence), and it may prove necessary in some cases to exclude such evidence (*Martin* [1994] Crim LR 218, but cf. *Campbell* [1996] Crim LR 500).

Recognition cases, such as *Reid* [1994] Crim LR 442, are different. The Court of Appeal in *Reid* was anxious not to encourage dock identification, but saw no reason to interfere with the trial judge's decision to admit recognition evidence in that case, notwithstanding that no identification parade or group identification had been held. A *Turnbull* direction was still needed, but it was not a case in which the witness's ability to make a leisurely identification was in doubt. See to similar effect *Gardner* [2004] EWCA Crim 1639.

Pre-trial Identification: Admissibility

By the CJA 2003, s. 120(4) and (5), a pre-trial statement by a witness is admissible as evidence of any matter stated of which oral evidence by the witness would be admissible, if it identifies or describes a person, object or place and while giving evidence the witness indicates that to the best of his or her belief he made the statement, and that to the best of his or her belief it states the truth. In theory this represents a significant change from the position at common law, under which a pre-trial identification could be considered only as evidence of the witness's consistency (*Sealey v The State* [2002] UKPC 52), but in practice it may make little difference to the way in which such evidence is perceived by the jury. **F19.8**

In some cases, however, pre-trial identification may be the only such evidence available, and the CJA 2003 may then enable the court to rely upon it as admissible hearsay. The witness may, for example, confirm having made an identification without being able to recall the facts in court, even after attempting to refresh his or her memory from the original statement (as in *Chinn* [2012] EWCA Crim 501, [2012] 3 All ER 502); or may no longer be available to testify (ss. 116 and 117 at **F17.8** ***et seq.***); or may be cross-examined (perhaps as a hostile witness) as to an identification which the witness now denies or retracts (see s. 119 at **F7.56**; see also **F6.57**). The *Turnbull* guidelines (see **F19.9** ***et seq.***) may need to be applied in such cases, perhaps in a suitably adapted form (see *Chinn* at [72]–[73]).

The *Turnbull* Guidelines

In response to widespread concern over the problems posed by cases of mistaken identification, the Court of Appeal in *Turnbull* [1977] QB 224 laid down important guidelines for judges in trials that involve disputed identification evidence. The guidelines are also applicable, *mutatis mutandis*, in summary trials and to cases of voice identification or voice recognition (see **F19.24**), and are reproduced in abridged form below: **F19.9**

> First, whenever the case against an accused depends wholly or substantially on the correctness of one or more identifications of the accused which the defence alleges to be mistaken, the judge should warn the jury of the special need for caution before convicting the accused in reliance on the correctness of the identification or identifications. In addition he should instruct them as to the reason for the need for such a warning and should make some reference to the possibility that a mistaken witness can be a convincing one and that a number of such witnesses can all be mistaken. Provided this is done in clear terms the judge need not use any particular form of words.

Secondly, the judge should direct the jury to examine closely the circumstances in which the identification by each witness came to be made. How long did the witness have the accused under observation? At what distance? In what light? Was the observation impeded in any way, as for example, by passing traffic or a press of people? Had the witness ever seen the accused before? How often? If only occasionally, had he any special reason for remembering the accused? How long elapsed between the original observation and the subsequent identification to the police? Was there any material discrepancy between the description of the accused given to the police by the witness when first seen by them and his actual appearance? If in any case, whether it is being dealt with summarily or on indictment, the prosecution have reason to believe that there is such a material discrepancy they should supply the accused or his legal advisers with particulars of the description the police were first given. In all cases if the accused asks to be given particulars of such descriptions, the prosecution should supply them. Finally, he should remind the jury of any specific weaknesses which had appeared in the identification evidence.

Recognition may be more reliable than identification of a stranger; but even when the witness is purporting to recognise someone whom he knows, the jury should be reminded that mistakes in recognition of close relatives and friends are sometimes made.

All these matters go to the quality of the identification evidence. If the quality is good and remains good at the close of the accused's case, the danger of a mistaken identification is lessened; but the poorer the quality, the greater the danger.

In our judgment when the quality is good, as for example when the identification is made after a long period of observation, or in satisfactory conditions by a relative, a neighbour, a close friend, a workmate and the like, the jury can safely be left to assess the value of the identifying evidence even though there is no other evidence to support it; provided always, however, that an adequate warning has been given about the special need for caution. Were the Courts to adjudge otherwise, affronts to justice would frequently occur. . . .

When, in the judgment of the trial judge, the quality of the identifying evidence is poor, as for example when it depends solely on a fleeting glance or on a longer observation made in difficult conditions, the situation is very different. The judge should then withdraw the case from the jury and direct an acquittal unless there is other evidence which goes to support the correctness of the identification. This may be corroboration in the sense lawyers use that word; but it need not be so if its effect is to make the jury sure that there has been no mistaken identification. . . .

The trial judge should identify to the jury the evidence which he adjudges is capable of supporting the evidence of identification. If there is any evidence or circumstances which the jury might think was supporting when it did not have this quality, the judge should say so.

Scope of the *Turnbull* Guidelines

F19.10 A *Turnbull* direction need not be provided unless the prosecution case depends wholly or substantially on visual identification (see *McMillan* [2005] EWCA Crim 1774 and **F19.2**), and even where such a direction is necessary no particular form of words need be used (*Mills v The Queen* [1995] 3 All ER 865; *Qadir* [1998] Crim LR 828; *France v The Queen* [2012] UKPC 28). The jury must however be warned that the direction is based on past experience (*Nash* [2004] EWCA Crim 2696).

The absence of an adequate *Turnbull* direction, tailored to the facts of the particular case, and if necessary reiterated in respect of each defendant (*Livingstone v The Queen* [2012] UKPC 36), will usually require a conviction to be quashed as unsafe (*Beckford v The Queen* (1993) 97 Cr App R 409; *Bowden* [1993] Crim LR 379; *Farquharson v The Queen* (1993) 98 Cr App R 398), although it may be condonable if the other evidence is overwhelming (*Freemantle v The Queen* [1994] 3 All ER 225). Where the principal or sole means of defence is a challenge to the credibility of the identifying witness, there may be exceptional cases in which a full *Turnbull* warning is unnecessary or may be given more briefly than in a case where the accuracy of identification is challenged (*Shand v The Queen* [1996] 1 All ER 511; *Giga* [2007] EWCA Crim 345).

F19.11 Paying lip service to the guidelines will not be enough (*Graham* [1994] Crim LR 212), nor will it suffice to give a general warning without reference to any evidence that may support or undermine the identification, or to any circumstances that may have affected the accuracy of the witness's observation (*Reid v The Queen* [1990] 1 AC 363; *Keane* (1977) 65 Cr App R 247). In *H* [2014] EWCA Crim 420, for example, one of the grounds on which D's conviction was quashed was that the trial judge had failed to remind the jury of specific weaknesses which had appeared in the identification evidence on which the prosecution case largely depended. But a judge may properly point out that a mistaken identification (as where a witness has identified a volunteer at a parade) does not necessarily prove that D is innocent or that the witness is untrustworthy in other respects, especially if the witness's view of the crime was imperfect (*Trew* [1996] Crim LR 441).

The guidelines may also need to be followed in cases involving the disputed identification of an alleged accomplice (*Bath* (1990) 154 JP 849) and an inadequate direction in respect of the evidence against one accused may render unsafe the conviction of another (*Elliott* (1986) *The Times*, 8 August 1986), although this will depend on the circumstances of the particular case.

The guidelines are not applicable to cases involving the identification of motor vehicles. The reliability of a vehicle identification may however depend, *inter alia*, on the witness having had a satisfactory opportunity to see the vehicle and on an ability to distinguish between one model and another. This should be drawn to the jury's attention (*Browning* (1991) 94 Cr App R 109).

A particularly robust *Turnbull* direction may be needed where for one reason or another the prosecution adduce hearsay evidence of identification in the form of a statement from a witness who is not available to testify at trial (*Vasco* [2012] EWCA Crim 3004).

It was held in *Oakwell* [1978] 1 All ER 1223 that the guidelines were 'intended primarily to deal with the ghastly risk run in cases of fleeting encounters' and were not applicable to a case in which the witness may merely have been mistaken as to which person in a well identified group had struck him. In that case the judge had drawn the jury's attention to the possibility that the witness may have been momentarily unsighted, and this was held to be sufficient. *Oakwell* was followed in *Curry* [1983] Crim LR 737 and *Beckles* [1999] Crim LR 148; but in *Bowden* the Court of Appeal held that this principle was applicable only to situations in which D's presence at the scene of the crime is admitted. A *Turnbull* warning was accordingly held to have been necessary in *Bowden*, even though a police officer claimed to have had a long and careful look at the offender; see also *B* [2004] EWCA Crim 1481. **F19.12**

It does not follow from *Oakwell* that no *Turnbull* direction would ever be necessary if D's presence at the scene is admitted. There will be some circumstances in which it will be appropriate to give such a direction and some in which it will not (contrast *Thornton* [1995] 1 Cr App R 578 with *Slater* [1995] 1 Cr App R 584 and see also *Pattinson* [1996] 1 Cr App R 51).

The applicability of the *Turnbull* guidelines to cases of alleged recognition is discussed at **F19.9**. As the guidelines themselves explain, recognition evidence will often be more reliable than identification of a stranger, but may still be erroneous. Lord Lane CJ elaborated on this point in *Bentley* [1991] Crim LR 620:

> Many people have experienced seeing someone in the street whom they knew, only to discover that they were wrong. The expression, 'I could have sworn it was you' indicated the sort of warning which a judge should give, because that was exactly what a testifying witness did — he swore that it was the person he thought it was. But he may have been mistaken...

Supporting Evidence

Evidence capable of supporting a disputed identification may take any admissible form, including D's bad character or previous convictions (*Dossett* [2013] EWCA Crim 710; *Ngando* [2014] EWCA Crim 506; *Richardson* [2014] EWCA Crim 1785; *Coles* [2018] EWCA Crim 407; *Day* [2019] EWCA Crim 935), analysis of cell site and mobile phone data (*Gray* [2018] EWCA Crim 2083), self-incrimination, and evidence of identification by other witnesses. The judge must identify evidence that is capable of providing such support and warn the jury against reliance on **F19.13** anything that might appear supportive without really having that capability. A prior discussion between judge and counsel is strongly advisable in this context, 'if only so that the judge knows on what points counsel will seek to rely in their speeches to support or undermine the identifications and that counsel will know the judge's view as to whether any particular piece of evidence is capable of having either effect' (*Stanton* [2004] EWCA Crim 490).

Evidence of bad character may need particularly careful handling in this context. In *H* [2014] EWCA Crim 420, D was charged with a sexual offence and the jury were told of his previous convictions for sexual offences, without being told that these were the only reason for him being included in the identification parade in the first place. The jury may thus have supposed it to be an 'enormous coincidence' that the man then identified by the complainant had convictions which bore some similarity to the case before them, but it was in reality no coincidence at all. His conviction was quashed.

Where a judge decides that the identification evidence in a given case is of such poor quality that the case should not have been left to the jury in the absence of supporting evidence, there is no obligation to warn the jury that they should not convict on the basis of the evidence of identification alone, should they reject the supporting evidence. There might be some cases where, in the light of the evidence that has unfolded, a direction of that kind might be appropriate, but it is not required as a general rule (*Ley* [2006] EWCA Crim 3063, [2007] 1 Cr App R 25 (325)).

F19.14 **Mutually Supportive Identifications** It is permissible in appropriate cases for two or more disputed identifications of D to be treated as mutually supportive (*Weeder* (1980) 71 Cr App R 228; *Shelton* [1981] Crim LR 776). Putting it shortly, an identification of a suspect by two different witnesses carries more weight than one (*Tyler* (1992) 96 Cr App R 332, per Farquharson LJ at 339) but this is so only if the identifications are 'of a quality that a jury can safely be left to assess' (*Weeder*). It does not matter that both witnesses may have made their identifications from the same spot (*Tyler*) and in some cases the identifications may relate to separate incidents (*Barnes* [1995] 2 Cr App R 491). But the jury must consider the quality of each witness's evidence of identification separately; and, even where the evidence identifying D as the perpetrator of one offence is compelling, it cannot rescue a weak identification in respect of another incident unless it is clear that each was committed by the same person (*Younas* [2012] EWCA Crim 2022).

F19.15 **Self-incrimination** Disputed identification evidence can clearly be supported by an admissible confession, but careful consideration must be given to cases in which the defendant is alleged to have self-incriminated by lies or false alibis. In *Turnbull* [1977] QB 224, Lord Widgery CJ said (at p. 230):

> Care should be taken by the judge when directing the jury about the support for an identification which may be derived from the fact that they have rejected an alibi. False alibis may be put forward for many reasons; an accused, for example, who has only his own truthful evidence to rely on may stupidly fabricate an alibi and get lying witnesses to support it out of fear that his own evidence will not be enough. Further, alibi witnesses can make genuine mistakes about dates and occasions like any other witnesses can. It is only when the jury is satisfied that the sole reason for the fabrication was to deceive them and there is no other explanation for its being put forward can fabrication provide any support for identification evidence. The jury should be reminded that proving the accused has told lies about where he was at the material time does not by itself prove that he was where the identifying witness says he was.

This guidance remains valid, but the governing principles in relation to self-incrimination by false alibis or other lies, as set out by the Court of Appeal in *Lucas* [1981] QB 720, have now been held applicable in identification cases (*Goodway* [1993] 4 All ER 894). Before such lies can be regarded as supporting an identification, they must accordingly be shown to be deliberate and material; the court or jury must be able to discount any possible innocent motive for the lies and they must be proved to be lies by evidence other than the identification(s) that they are to support. See also the *Crown Court Compendium* (July 2020), chs. 15-1 and 18-2.

The Accused's Silence Although Lord Widgery CJ warned in *Turnbull* [1977] QB 277 that D's failure to testify must not be viewed as capable of supporting the evidence against D, this must now be reconsidered in the light of subsequent legislation. Under the CJPO 1994, ss. 34 to 38, D's failure: **F19.16**

(a) to mention facts when questioned or charged which are later relied upon in his defence;
(b) to account for objects in his possession or substances or marks on his body or clothing;
(c) to account for his presence at a particular place; or
(d) to testify at his trial,

may each, in appropriate cases, entitle the court or jury to 'draw such inferences as appear proper'. They do not, in themselves, constitute evidence of guilt and should not be seen as a substitute for satisfactory identification evidence, but in some cases the absence of testimony or explanation from D may legitimately enable a court or jury to infer that the prosecution evidence is correct and that D has no answer to it. It may also be taken into account when deciding whether D has a case to answer (*Gray* [2018] EWCA Crim 2083; and see generally **F20**).

Quality of the Witness

There is no doubt that some witnesses may be capable of providing more reliable identification evidence than others in the same position. A witness with perfect vision may clearly be expected to do better than a myopic witness who has lost his or her spectacles. More controversial is the suggestion that police officers may, by virtue of their training, be more observant than ordinary witnesses, or at least better at noting features or details that may be significant. That suggestion was rejected by the Privy Council in *Reid v The Queen* [1990] AC 363, but was subsequently held to be quite proper by the Court of Appeal in *Ramsden* [1991] Crim LR 295, where Lord Lane CJ opined that it would be wrong for a trial judge not to direct the jury as to the potentially greater reliability of police identification. See to similar effect *Tyler* (1992) 96 Cr App R 332, per Farquharson LJ at p. 343. **F19.17**

Stopping a Trial Based on Inadequate Identification

The *Turnbull* guidelines require the trial judge to direct an acquittal in cases where identification evidence is both deficient and unsupported by sufficient alternative evidence. If necessary, the trial judge should invite the defence to make submissions to that effect (*Fergus* (1993) 98 Cr App R 313). In such cases, the Court of Appeal may quash any conviction, even though the judge's direction on the evidence was otherwise impeccable (see, e.g., *Pope* (1986) 85 Cr App R 201). **F19.18**

In dealing with such cases, a court must not merely apply the principles set out in *Galbraith* [1981] 2 All ER 1060 (see **D16.54** *et seq.*) but must apply what the Court of Appeal in *Richardson* [2012] EWCA Crim 639 referred to as 'an acute combination of *Galbraith* and *Turnbull*'. There is rarely any issue as to whether prosecution witnesses are attempting to tell the truth, but it may still be necessary to decide whether there is sufficient evidence on which a court or jury could properly convict (*Daley v The Queen* [1994] 1 AC 117; *Macmath* [1997] Crim LR 586). Such evidence need not, however, be particularly strong, and a case based on largely unsupported identification evidence may still be left to the jury even though the defence can point to several potential deficiencies in that evidence (*H* [2014] EWCA Crim 420).

In some cases, a witness may have qualified an identification by admitting that being 'not quite certain', or was only '90 per cent sure'. A defendant cannot properly be convicted on qualified identification evidence alone (*George* [2002] EWCA Crim 1923; *Brown* [2011] EWCA Crim 80). But as with other kinds of weak identification evidence, a qualified identification may have a legitimate role to play alongside other, more reliable, evidence. In *Brown*, for example, the identification was not merely qualified by uncertainty but was weak in many other respects, having been made six years after the alleged offence. But the finding of D's fingerprints on documents strewn around the scene of the crime made up for that. The fingerprint evidence was 'devastating' and D had not been able to offer any credible explanation for it.

CCTV, VIDEO AND OTHER IMAGES

F19.19 The use of photographs or security video footage in police investigations or identification procedures is dealt with at **D1.143**. As to the importance of compliance with the procedures set out by PACE Code D in respect of any formal pre-trial viewing of CCTV and other images, see *Smith (Dean)* [2008] EWCA Crim 1342; *Deakin* [2012] EWCA Crim 2637 and *Lariba* [2015] EWCA Crim 478; but Code D safeguards may be impossible to observe in cases where (as in *Moss* [2011] EWCA Crim 252) a witness who happens to know the suspect views the images and makes the identification by mere chance.

The integrity of Code D identification procedures may also be undermined where witnesses have already viewed images or clips (including images of alleged offences or suspected offenders) on a mobile phone or on Facebook or other social networking sites (see, e.g., *Alexander* [2012] EWCA Crim 2768, [2013] 1 Cr App R 26 (334); *Phillips* [2020] EWCA Crim 269). In such cases, the judge must consider whether the jury would have any means of testing or assessing the reliability of any such casual identification. If not, it might sometimes be necessary to exclude such evidence, in the interests of ensuring a fair trial. Even where the witness has subsequently repeated the identification in a controlled Code D procedure, there may be a risk of identifying the person previously seen in the social media or mobile phone image, rather than the one seen committing the crime, etc.

It helps if any such images or clips are still available and of sufficient quality to enable the court or jury to form their own view, rather than relying entirely on the witness (*Doherty* [2016] EWCA Crim 246).

In *LT* [2019] EWCA Crim 58, [2019] 1 Cr App R 30 (405), an eyewitness to a shooting (PJ) was shown a Facebook image by his neighbour (AH), who 'had been doing some digging'. AH asked, 'is this him?' One of the two men in the image was D, and PJ at once identified him as the gunman. The Court of Appeal held that this evidence had wrongly been excluded under the PACE 1984, s. 78. Simon LJ said:

> 49. ... The identification evidence was clear: the man who had stood a short distance away from PJ with a gun was the man whose image PJ saw and recognised on AH's phone the next day.
>
> 50. Unlike the case of *Alexander*, the image that the identifying witness saw, and which led to his recognising the defendant, was available for the Jury to assess. [He] ... was willing to say whose Facebook account he had used to see the photograph, he was able to explain the circumstances in which the image was handed to him and AH had not said words such as 'it sounds like the sort of thing he would do', before presenting the image of LT, to which objection might have been taken.

A similar approach was taken in *Phillips*. Rejecting a submission that such evidence should have been excluded at trial, Dingemans LJ explained:

> 39. All three witnesses were present at the scene of the attack and all three witnesses identified [D] at the formal identification parades. The issue of whether they were identifying the person that they had seen in the Facebook photograph which they had been shown as opposed to the person that they had seen on the night was an issue for the jury, and there was available to the jury sufficient material on which they could make this critical judgment of fact. It would not have been right to prevent this relevant evidence being presented to the jury for their assessment. However, it then became essential to give proper directions to the jury.
>
> ...
>
> 40. The directions highlighted the relevant weakness by asking 'may any intervening event have tainted the eventual identification' and then by directing the jury to consider whether the formal identification procedure had meant 'only that the witnesses picked out the person they believed they'd seen on the night in question as a result of having been shown the Facebook photograph, told the name of the person in the photograph, and told by people who have not given evidence that he was the person at the scene'. This explained to the jury the reason why the prior identification on social media might undermine the reliability of the identification evidence.

Photographic and Video Evidence at Trial

In *A-G's Ref (No. 2 of 2002)* [2002] EWCA Crim 2373, [2003] 1 Cr App R 21 (321), Rose LJ summarised (at [19]) the correct approach to the use of photographic and video images at trial: **F19.20**

> ... there are ... at least four circumstances in which, subject to the judicial discretion to exclude ... and subject to appropriate directions in the summing-up, a jury can be invited to conclude that the defendant committed the offence on the basis of a photographic image from the scene of the crime:
>
> (i) where the photographic image is sufficiently clear, the jury can compare it with the defendant sitting in the dock (*Dodson* (1984) 79 Cr App R 220);
>
> (ii) where a witness knows the defendant sufficiently well to recognise him as the offender depicted in the photographic image, he can give evidence of this (*Fowden* [1982] Crim LR 588, *Kajala v Noble* (1982) 75 Cr App R 149, *Grimer* [1982] Crim LR 674, *Caldwell* (1994) 99 Cr App R 73 and *Blenkinsop* [1995] 1 Cr App R 7); and this may be so even if the photographic image is no longer available for the jury (*Taylor v Chief Constable of Cheshire* (1987) 84 Cr App R 191);
>
> (iii) where a witness who does not know the defendant spends substantial time viewing and analysing photographic images from the scene, thereby acquiring special knowledge which the jury does not have, he can give evidence of identification based on a comparison between those images and a reasonably contemporary photograph of the defendant, provided that the images and the photograph are available to the jury (*Clare* [1995] 2 Cr App R 333);
>
> (iv) a suitably qualified expert with facial mapping skills can give opinion evidence of identification based on a comparison between images from the scene (whether expertly enhanced or not) and a reasonably contemporary photograph of the defendant, provided the images and the photograph are available for the jury (*Stockwell* (1993) 97 Cr App R 260; *Clarke* [1995] 2 Cr App R 425; *Hookway* [1999] Crim LR 750).

In the first kind of case, photographs or video recordings (whether originals or copies) may be shown as real evidence and may provide the court with something akin to a direct view of the incident in question. A *Turnbull* direction might not always be necessary in cases where these images are clear and of high quality (*Najjar* [2014] EWCA Crim 1309) but in most cases the jury must still be warned of the dangers of mistaken identification, and should be reminded of the need to exercise great care when attempting to make an identification from two-dimensional photographs or video recordings (*Dodson*; *Blenkinsop*; *Ali* [2008] EWCA Crim 1522). As to the form of such warnings, see the *Crown Court Compendium* (July 2020), ch. 15-2. If D has subsequently changed appearance it may be necessary to provide the jury with a photograph of D that is contemporaneous with the recorded images. As to the use of eye-witness evidence to assist the jury in identifying a possible offender from a photograph, see also *West* [2005] EWCA Crim 3034.

In many cases, the quality of CCTV images is so poor that juries might not be able to make an identification merely by viewing the images themselves, whereas someone who knows D well, or who has expertise in facial mapping or gait analysis, might be able to assist them. See further **F19.21**.

The danger in such a case is that the jury will simply take on trust a convincing assurance from the witnesses when they are unable to make the judgement themselves; hence, the importance of directions to the jury as to the caution with which they must approach their task (*Lariba* [2015] EWCA Crim 478 at [40]). Thus, a *Turnbull* warning will ordinarily be required (*Selwyn* [2012] EWCA Crim 2968; and see the *Crown Court Compendium* (July 2020), ch. 15-3).

The third of Rose LJ's examples in *A-G's Ref (No. 2 of 2002)* [2002] EWCA Crim 2373, [2003] 1 Cr App R 21 (321) was considered in *Abnett* [2006] EWCA Crim 3320, in which a police officer, who had spent some time interviewing D and repeatedly viewing CCTV footage of a robbery, together with still images from that film, was permitted to state that he was '100 per cent sure' that D was one of the robbers. He had no specialist training in facial mapping or any other such technique, and (with respect) it is not obvious how or why his repeated viewing of the images would have equipped him to make a significantly more reliable identification than the jury, who had access to the same footage and images. Contrast *Clare* [1995] 2 Cr App R 333, in which the police officer had spent hours analysing footage of crowd violence and was able (*inter alia*) to explain to the jury how the incident in question had developed. *A-G's Ref (No. 2 of 2002)* was also considered in *Savalia* [2011] EWCA Crim 1334 in which the Court of Appeal said:

> Officers who have acquired special knowledge by substantial viewing and analysis of CCTV images and who identify a defendant by a comparison between those images and what they have observed of the defendant in person, whether or not in conjunction with a photograph of the defendant, can give evidence about identification, even if the comparison is not based wholly or mainly on facial features but also takes into account matters such as build or gait. We accept that paragraph 19(iii) of the *Attorney General's Reference* focuses on facial recognition, but in our view it can properly be extended to apply to identification based upon a combination of features.

See also (and to similar effect) *Beckford (Tafarwa)* [2020] EWCA Crim 59. It was submitted in this case that a police officer who had spent hundreds of hours analysing video footage of a shooting outside a nightclub had gone beyond the scope of what was permissible in his testimony, 'by entering into a detailed analysis of imagery which was of insufficient quality to permit identification by visual recognition alone, which was a preserve of a properly qualified expert'. Rejecting that submission, Flaux LJ said:

> The limitations of his evidence were clearly put before the jury: he readily admitted them when he gave evidence. He was cross-examined effectively about them and [counsel] expressed his reservations about and qualifications to some aspects of his evidence. The defence had instructed its own expert and had there been any significant differences between the prosecution's evidence and that which the defence evidence could have given, the defence evidence could have been called. He wasn't.

Expert Evidence of Facial Mapping and Gait Analysis

F19.21 Expert facial mapping (or photographic comparison) evidence may enhance the value of poor quality images that are alleged to show D, but concerns have been expressed as to the proper scope and function of such evidence, particularly where (as in *Hookway* [1999] Crim LR 750) it is not supported by other evidence incriminating D. Significant facial differences revealed by photographic comparison may prove that D cannot be the person in the photograph, but where the features appear to match there is no database cataloguing the number of persons with particular facial features or measurements from which an expert could derive any statistical analysis to explain the significance of such matches. This led the Court of Appeal to express reservations in *Gray* [2003] EWCA Crim 1001, but in *Gardner* [2004] EWCA Crim 1639, the Court rejected the suggestion that expert witnesses should be prevented from expressing opinions as to probabilities based on facial mapping evidence; and in *Ciantar* [2005] EWCA Crim 3559, it rejected arguments that expert evidence of facial mapping should have been discounted or excluded merely because other experts had expressed doubts as to its quality and sufficiency.

F19.22 The cases on facial mapping were reviewed in *Atkins* [2010] EWCA Crim 1876, [2010] 1 Cr App R 8 (117), where Hughes LJ said (at [31]):

> Where a photographic comparison expert gives evidence, properly based upon study and experience, of similarities and/or dissimilarities between a questioned photograph and a known person (including a defendant) the expert is not disabled either by authority or principle from expressing his conclusion as to the significance of his findings, and... he may do so by use of conventional expressions, arranged in a hierarchy [e.g., 'lends limited support' or 'lends powerful support' but] we think it preferable that the expressions should not be allocated numbers [e.g., a scale of 0–5] lest that run any small risk of leading the jury to think that they represent an established numerical, that is to say measurable, scale. The expressions ought to remain simply what they are, namely forms of words used. They need to be in an ascending order if they are to mean anything at all, and if a relatively firm opinion is to be contrasted with one which is not so firm. They are, however, expressions of subjective opinion, and this must be made crystal clear to the jury charged with evaluating them.

Guidance as to the form of jury directions that may be required in such cases can be found in the *Crown Court Compendium* (July 2020), ch. 15-5; and see also *Purlis* [2017] EWCA Crim 1134, a robbery case in which dashcam images of the robber ['Man X'] were said by a facial mapping expert (Mr Evans) to 'lend powerful support' to the allegation that Man X was D. The following direction (at [14]) was approved on appeal as 'full and fair' and consistent with *Atkins*:

> It is important that you approach the evidence of facial mapping . . . with caution. That does not mean that you cannot rely on the expert evidence . . . Simply that it needs to be considered . . . with care. Mr Evans considers that the imagery evidence lends powerful support to the contention that Man X and Purlis are the same man. But you should remember this, that, as Mr Evans conceded, there is no database . . . his opinion is based on his experience and his expertise over many years. Because there is no national database . . . or any mathematical formulae, as is the case with fingerprints, or statistics as to the probability of occurrence of particular facial characteristics in the population at large, as in the case of DNA evidence, you cannot gauge the results of an expert's analysis of imagery in the same way as fingerprint or DNA evidence. The fact that there is no statistical database . . . is something you should clearly have in mind. But that does not mean that the absence of such a database means that no opinion can be expressed by Mr Evans beyond stating his examination of the images . . . An expert who spends many years studying this kind of evidence . . . can properly form a judgment as to the significance of what he has found . . . It is a judgment based on his experience. It is for you to decide whether to accept the evidence.

As to the use of expert podiatric or 'walking gait analysis' as a method of identification from CCTV video footage (and in particular the limitations of that 'developing science'), see *Rafiq Mohammed* [2010] EWCA Crim 2696, *Otway* [2011] EWCA Crim 3 and in particular *Ferdinand* [2014] EWCA Crim 1243, 2 Cr App R 23 (331). The Royal Society and the Royal Society of Edinburgh in conjunction with the Judicial College, the Judicial Institute, and the Judicial Studies Board for Northern Ireland, also acknowledge the current scientific limitations in their 'primer for courts' entitled *Forensic Gait Analysis* (available at tinyurl.com/y7bjxr3w).

In *Ferdinand*, the Court concluded (at [77]):

> Comparison evidence founded upon the science and expertise of podiatry . . . remains, in our view, a technique that requires careful scrutiny before expert evidence is admitted and, if admitted, rigorous examination of the quality of the images and the opinion expressed by the expert.

As to the use of 'reverse projection evidence' for the purpose of showing that CCTV images of an offender match the height or build of a defendant, see *Barnes* [2012] EWCA Crim 1605.

Sketches and Facial Composite Images

Artist's sketches and composite images or 'photofits' (which now use digital E-FIT, or EFIT-V technology) are fundamentally different from photographs or video in that they depend on the fallible (and potentially mendacious) assertions of the witnesses who help to compile them. An image showing a bald or bearded suspect is manifestly a product of a witness's assertion that the suspect was bald or bearded, and must logically be categorised as a kind of statement, albeit one in visual form. This is now recognised in the CJA 2003, s. 115, which defines a 'statement' for the purpose of the hearsay rule as 'any representation of fact or opinion made by a person by whatever means; and it includes a representation made in a sketch, photofit or other pictorial form'. Such a statement may well be admissible in support of the witness who made it, under the CJA 2003, s. 120, or in the unavoidable absence of that witness, as provided for by s. 116 (see **F19.8**), but it is no longer possible for courts to proceed (as they did before the enactment of the CJA 2003) as if the hearsay rule has nothing to do with it. **F19.23**

VOICE IDENTIFICATION

It is generally accepted that the identification of an accused from voice recognition is potentially even more difficult and unreliable than visual identification (especially when the voice is heard only over a telephone) but such evidence may still be taken into account and, where relevant voice recordings exist, expert evidence may then be adduced to help with the identification. See **F19.24**

Roberts [2000] Crim LR 183; *Chenia* [2002] EWCA Crim 2345, [2003] 2 Cr App R 6 (83); *Davies* [2004] EWCA Crim 2521; *Robinson* [2006] EWCA Crim 613, [2006] 1 Cr App R 13 (221) and *Flynn* [2008] EWCA Crim 970, [2008] 2 Cr App R 20 (266). In *Flynn*, the Court of Appeal heard expert evidence as to use of voice recognition and Gage LJ stated (at [16]):

> (1) Identification of a suspect by voice recognition is more difficult than visual identification.
> (2) Identification by voice recognition is likely to be more reliable when carried out by experts using acoustic and spectrographic techniques as well as sophisticated auditory techniques, than lay listener identification.
> (3) The ability of a lay listener correctly to identify voices is subject to a number of variables. There is at present little research about the effect of variability but the following factors are relevant:
> (i) the quality of the recording of the disputed voice or voices;
> (ii) the gap in time between the listener hearing the known voice and his attempt to recognise the disputed voice;
> (iii) the ability of the individual lay listener to identify voices in general. Research shows that the ability of an individual to identify voices varies from person to person.
> (iv) the nature and duration of the speech which is sought to be identified is important. Obviously, some voices are more distinctive than others and the longer the sample of speech the better the prospect of identification.
> (v) the greater the familiarity of the listener with the known voice the better his or her chance of accurately identifying a disputed voice (However, research shows that a confident recognition by a lay listener of a familiar voice may nevertheless be wrong).
> . . .
> (4) . . . the crucial difference between a lay listener and expert speech analysis is that the expert is able to draw up an overall profile of the individual's speech patterns, in which the significance of each parameter is assessed individually, backed up with instrumental analysis and reference research. In contrast, the lay listener's response is fundamentally opaque. The lay listener cannot know and has no way of explaining, which aspects of the speaker's speech patterns he is responding to. He also has no way of assessing the significance of individual observed features relative to the overall speech profile. We add, the latter is a difference between visual identification and voice recognition; and the opaque nature of the lay listener's voice recognitions will make it more difficult to challenge the accuracy of their evidence.

The Court referred in *Flynn* to instrumental analysis by expert witnesses, but declined to exclude the use of non-instrumental auditory analysis (see **F19.26**).

The courts have emphasised that juries in voice identification or recognition cases must be given guidance in the form of a modified *Turnbull* direction (see, e.g., *Chenia* [2002] EWCA Crim 2345, [2003] 2 Cr App R 6 (83); *Phipps v DPP (Jamaica)* [2012] UKPC 24). Guidance as to the possible forms of such a direction can be found in the *Crown Court Compendium* (July 2020), ch. 15-7. As to the holding of 'voice identification parades' in the course of police investigations, see *Hersey* [1998] Crim LR 281 and **D1.146**.

Admissibility where No Recording Exists

F19.25 *Myers* [2010] EWCA Crim 3173 provides an illustration of circumstances in which voice identification may be considered more reliable than usual, even though no recording existed. The identifying witness had been blind for 30 years and had learnt to 'use his ears as his eyes'. He claimed to have recognised the voice of one of two burglars as that of D, his ex-partner's son. Moreover, when the witness called out 'is that you, Daniel?' the other burglar said 'sshh' as if aware that their voices might give them away. There was other circumstantial evidence to support the identification and the conviction was upheld on appeal.

Admissibility where Recording Exists

F19.26 If there are recordings of the offender's voice, expert evidence may be admissible on the question of whether this matches D's voice. Most phoneticians use acoustic analysis techniques for this purpose, but it was held in *Robb* (1991) 93 Cr App R 161 that an expert who uses only auditory phonetic techniques (a method regarded with suspicion by other experts) may still be competent to testify. In *O'Doherty* [2002] NI 263, [2003] 1 Cr App R 5 (77), the Northern Ireland Court of Appeal ruled auditory phonetic analysis inadequate unless supported by acoustic analysis; but in *Flynn* the Court considered it 'neither possible nor desirable' to go that far. The Court in *Flynn* was however concerned as to the evidential value of non-expert voice identification, by police officers or others, and rejected the idea that by repeated listening to recordings an officer might become an 'expert ad hoc'. It offered this general guidance (at [63]–[64]):

> The increasing use...of lay listener evidence from police officers must...be treated with great caution and great care. Where the prosecution seek to rely on such evidence it is desirable that an expert should be instructed to give an independent opinion on the validity of such evidence. In addition,...great care should be taken by police officers to record the procedures taken by them which form the basis for their evidence. Whether the evidence is sufficiently probative to be admitted will depend very much on the facts of each case.
>
> It goes without saying that in all cases in which the prosecution rely on voice recognition evidence, whether lay listener, or expert, or both, the judge must give a very careful direction to the jury warning it of the danger of mistakes in such cases.

Flynn was considered in *Tamiz* [2010] EWCA Crim 2638, where covert recordings of incriminating conversations in Arabic, Bengali and Syhleti had been listened to by two translators, each of whom testified that they could identify the same voices in different recordings, although they did not purport to identify the voices as those of any of the appellants. There was no supporting phonetic evidence because there was no expert in phonetics who spoke or understood the languages in question, but the translators had access to many hours of good quality recordings and had already been proved right in their identification of certain other voices. An argument that it had been unfair to admit their evidence was rejected. Fairness, said the Court, involves consideration of the alternatives open to the prosecution. In this case there were none.

The jury should ordinarily be allowed to hear any admissible voice recordings for themselves, so that they may form their own judgement of the opinions expressed (*Bentum* (1989) 153 JP 538; *Flynn*) but should be warned of the dangers of relying on their own untrained ears.

DNA EVIDENCE

DNA evidence has been used in criminal trials and investigations in England and Wales for over 20 years. The procedures involved in obtaining and evaluating such evidence have been explained by the Court of Appeal on a number of occasions, but because the science has evolved significantly over the years, some of the earlier accounts involving first generation techniques must now be read with caution. The basic principles remain unchanged, but modern 'DNA-17 profiling' (and even the SGM+ methodology it replaced) is capable of much more precise matches and enables DNA profiles to be obtained from minute amounts of tissue. If it is clear that DNA recovered from the crime scene could only have been left by the offender, and the profile matches that of D with a random match probability in the order of one in a billion (which in DNA-17 profiling may be possible even from an incomplete DNA profile), this may permit a finding of guilt, even in the absence of other evidence, whereas match probabilities in the order of one in a million (as in many of the first generation cases) could not. See *Reed* [2009] EWCA Crim 2698, [2010] 1 Cr App R 23 (310); *Dlugosz* [2013] EWCA Crim 2, [2013] 1 Cr App R 32 (425) and *FNC* [2015] EWCA Crim 1732, [2016] 1 Cr App R 12 (176). Guidance as to the uses and proper understanding of DNA evidence, techniques and terms can be found in *Forensic DNA Analysis*, a 'primer' produced for courts and practitioners by the Royal Society and the Royal Society of Edinburgh in conjunction with the Judicial College, the Judicial Institute, and the Judicial Studies Board for Northern Ireland (available at tinyurl.com/y9pldq4y). **F19.27**

Low Template and Degraded DNA Profiles

F19.28 Doubts were at one time expressed as to the reliability of 'low copy number' (or LCN) DNA profiling in which profiles were obtained from boosted samples that were too small to be used in what was then the standard 'Second Generation Multiplex' (or SGM+) profiling test. The use of LCN DNA was temporarily suspended following the Omagh bombing trial (*Hoey* [2007] NICC 49) but a review commissioned by the Forensic Regulator concluded that the process used for obtaining LCN DNA was 'robust and fit for its purpose' and this view was endorsed both in *Reed* [2009] EWCA Crim 2698, [2010] 1 Cr App R 23 (310) and in *Broughton* [2010] EWCA Crim 549. After extensive consideration of expert views, the Court in *Reed* concluded that the underlying science for Low Template DNA analysis was sufficiently reliable to produce profiles, provided the material analysed is above the 'stochastic threshold' of between 100 and 200 picograms.

The issue is less likely to arise in DNA-17 profiling, in which DNA profiles can routinely be obtained without boosting even from minute samples, but problems can still arise where DNA from a sample (especially a very small sample) has become degraded through age, etc. Such samples may require repeated analysis and careful interpretation, even assuming that they are not too weak to provide a reliable match at all.

The Court in *Reed* noted that, under what is now CrimPR 19.4(1)(f) and (g), an expert witness must identify where there is a range of opinion on the matters dealt with in the report. In such a case, the expert must summarise the scope of opinion and give reasons for his or her own opinion. If that opinion cannot be given without qualification, the expert must state the qualification. Under r. 19.6(2), the court has power to direct experts to discuss expert issues in the proceedings and prepare a statement for the court of the matters on which they agree and disagree giving their reasons. The Court said (at [131]) that in DNA cases:

(i) It is particularly important to ensure that the obligation under [r. 19.4(1)(f) and (g)] is followed and also that, where propositions are to be advanced as part of an evaluative opinion…, that each proposition is spelt out with precision in the expert report.

(ii) Expert reports must, after each has been served, be carefully analysed by the parties. Where a disagreement is identified, this must be brought to the attention of the court.

(iii) If the reports are available before the PCMH, this should be done at the PCMH; but if the reports have not been served by all parties at the time of the PCMH (as may often be the case), it is the duty of the Crown and the defence to ensure that the necessary steps are taken to bring the matter back before the judge where a disagreement is identified.

(iv) It will then in the ordinary case be necessary for the judge to exercise his powers under [r. 19.6] and make an order for the provision of a statement.

(v) We would anticipate, even in such a case, that…much of the science relating to DNA will be common ground. The experts should be able to set out in the statement under [r. 19.6] in clear terms for use at the trial the basic science that is agreed, in so far as it is not contained in one of the reports. The experts must then identify with precision what is in dispute — for example, the match probability, the interpretation of the electrophoretograms or the evaluative opinion that is to be given.

(vi) If the order as to the provision of the statement under [r. 19.6] is not observed and in the absence of a good reason, then the trial judge should consider carefully whether to exercise the power to refuse permission to the party whose expert is in default to call that expert to give evidence. In many cases, the judge may well exercise that power. A failure to find time for a meeting because of commitments to other matters, a common problem with many experts as was evident in this appeal, is not to be treated as a good reason.

Mixed Profiles

F19.29 'Mixed samples' involving DNA material from more than one person can be problematic. There may be one major profile and one or more minor and incomplete ones. In rape cases, for example, the DNA of the complainant may be mixed with DNA that is alleged to be D's, and perhaps also with traces of DNA from a third person, as is likely where, for example, clothing is examined. Mixed samples may be more difficult to evaluate. Elements of one incomplete profile may overlap with elements of another and it may even be unclear how many individuals have contributed to the DNA material in the sample. Computer software is routinely used to analyse mixed profiles and to extract and identify individual profiles therein. See further **F19.32**.

Evaluating DNA Matches

Where a person's DNA profile is found to match that of a crime sample, the significance of that match must be evaluated. Guidance as to the assessment of statistical evidence (including DNA evidence) has been published by the Inns of Court College of Advocacy (tinyurl.com/y93qcgm8). It may first be necessary to ascertain the likelihood that the matching profiles do indeed have a common source. The statistical assessment may be conducted by one of two methods. The first expresses the match as a probability (or 'random occurrence ratio'): a calculation of the chances of some other person, chosen at random, sharing the same DNA profile (this is usually capped at one in a billion for forensic purposes, although even lower match probabilities are possible with DNA-17 profiles). The second method, generally accepted as being more appropriate method for evaluating the strength of DNA profiles, calculates the 'likelihood ratio' for a given hypothesis (e.g., this DNA profile is a billion times more likely to be found if it originated from the accused as opposed to an unrelated person). In either method, the expert computes the weight of the evidence by comparison with random members of the general population unless instructed differently. If, however, there is a reasonable possibility that a relative (e.g., a brother) is the source, or one of the sources in a mixed profile, an alternative calculation based on that possibility may need to be put before the jury (*Watters* (19 October 2000 unreported, CA)). **F19.30**

In *Doheny* [1997] 1 Cr App R 369, the Court of Appeal held that where D's DNA profile is alleged to match that of the crime stain:

> The expert should not be asked his opinion on the likelihood that it was the defendant who left the crime stain, nor when giving evidence should he use terminology which may lead the jury to believe that he is expressing such an opinion.... Provided he has the necessary data and statistical expertise, it may be appropriate for him to say how many people with the matching characteristics are likely to be found in the United Kingdom or perhaps in a more limited relevant subgroup such as, for instance, the Caucasian sexually active males in the Manchester area).

This contrasts with some other forensic disciplines (such as facial mapping or handwriting analysis) where experts are sometimes permitted to express personal conclusions regarding identity.

Potential interpretational pitfalls must be avoided. The notorious 'prosecutor's fallacy' typically involves confusing the random occurrence ratio with the probability of innocence. The odds against a randomly selected individual matching a partial or incomplete DNA profile obtained from the crime stain might be estimated in a given case at one in a million but, if this is the only evidence against D it does not mean that the odds against D being innocent are one in a million. On the contrary, it tells us only that D is one of perhaps 26 males in the UK who share that characteristic. To quote Lord Phillips CJ in *Doheny*:

> If no fact is known about the defendant, other than that he was in the United Kingdom at the time of the crime, the DNA evidence tells us no more than that there is statistical probability that he was the criminal of one in 26.

Modern cases will usually involve much lower (and thus more significant) match probabilities. Modern DNA analysis is capable of producing much more detailed profiles and calculated odds of one in a billion are now possible even with incomplete profiles. These may in appropriate cases permit a finding of guilt based on the DNA match alone. See, e.g., *FNC* [2015] EWCA Crim 1732, [2016] 1 Cr App R 12 (176) and *Allan* [2017] EWCA Crim 2396.

DNA evidence will in most cases be supported or contradicted by other evidence, and its value must then be assessed in conjunction with this other evidence (on which a DNA expert will not be competent to express an opinion). It is for the court or jury to assess the totality of the evidence. As Phillips LJ explained in *Doheny*:

> The significance of the DNA evidence will depend critically upon what else is known about the suspect. If he has a convincing alibi at the other end of England at the time of the crime, it will appear highly improbable that he can have been responsible for the crime, despite his matching DNA profile. If, however, he was near the scene of the crime when it was committed, or has been identified as a suspect because of other evidence which suggests that he may have been responsible for the crime, the DNA evidence becomes very significant.

Guidance as to the matters that should be addressed when directing juries on DNA evidence can be found in the *Crown Court Compendium* (July 2020), ch. 15-8. When evaluating such evidence, juries should not (in the absence of special circumstances) be invited to undertake complex Bayesian calculations. Inviting juries to use Bayes' Theorem when much of the evidence cannot be assigned a meaningful statistical value is 'a recipe for confusion, misunderstanding and misjudgment' (*Adams (No. 2)* [1998] 1 Cr App R 377 at p. 384).

F19.31 **Innocent Explanations for DNA Matches** Even where there is no dispute as to the source of the crime scene DNA (as where D concedes that the DNA is D's), it may not necessarily suffice to prove guilt. The defence may offer an 'innocent explanation' (such as indirect or 'secondary' transfer, or contamination) for even the closest DNA match (as in *Powell* [1996] 1 Cr App R 31) and any such explanation must be disproved (or rejected as inherently implausible) before D can be convicted.

The issue frequently arises in respect of objects left at or near the crime scene, especially where D's is not the only DNA profile recovered from the object. In *Ogden* [2013] EWCA Crim 1294, for example, DNA extracted from blood found on a scarf at the scene of a burglary was the only evidence linking D with the crime, but, as the Court of Appeal explained (at [3]):

> It was not possible to date the DNA. It was therefore possible that another person had carried the scarf to the scene of the burglary, the defendant's DNA already being on it... There was no independent evidence that the burglar had cut himself on the window.

A further problem was the scarf itself had been accidentally destroyed and a second blood stain found on it had never been tested. In those circumstances, said the Court, a submission of no case to answer ought to have been accepted. *Ogden* was, however, distinguished both in *Darnley* [2012] EWCA Crim 1148 and in *Sampson* [2014] EWCA Crim 1968. In *Darnley*, D was charged with domestic burglary, and offered an improbable explanation as to how his DNA had come to be on a handkerchief left at the scene. But he also had convictions for domestic burglary, which were proved under the CJA 2003, s. 101(1)(d). In those circumstances, the case had rightly been left to the jury, and his conviction was upheld.

In *Sampson*, D was charged with the unlawful possession of a pistol. His DNA was found on the weapon and, although there was nothing else to link him to it, this was held sufficient for the case to be left to the jury. As Lloyd-Jones LJ explained (at [40]–[43]):

> The presence of DNA is not relied on as evidence of the presence of the defendant at a particular place at a particular time; rather, the essence of the offence is possession of the article... The presence of DNA on the article, on the muzzle of a gun in this case, is capable of being evidence of possession of the article... The possibility of indirect transfer was a matter for the jury to address on the basis of all of the evidence in the case.

These cases were considered in *Bryon* [2015] EWCA Crim 997 where the Court of Appeal concluded that a conviction cannot be upheld solely on the basis of DNA found on a moveable object left at the crime scene, at least where D's DNA is not the only DNA found on the object and it remains possible that some other person brought it there. But other evidence, such as D's previous convictions for similar offences, may transform the position, as in *Darnley* or indeed in *Bryon* itself.

In subsequent cases, however, the Court of Appeal has backed away from the stance adopted in *Bryon*. The leading cases are now *FNC* [2015] EWCA Crim 1732, [2016] 1 Cr App R 12 (176) and *Tsekiri* [2017] EWCA Crim 40, [2017] 1 Cr App R 32 (479).

In *FNC*, D was convicted of a historic sexual assault on the basis of a match between his DNA profile (taken following his arrest on an unrelated matter) and DNA recovered from semen stains found on the victim's trousers. Lord Thomas CJ said:

> It is clear from the decision in *Sampson* and the approach of Lord Bingham CJ in *Adams (No 2)* that where DNA is directly deposited in the course of the commission of a crime by the offender, a very high DNA match with the defendant is sufficient to raise a case for the defendant to answer. There is a clear distinction as the authorities stand, between such a case and cases... where the DNA was deposited on an article left at the scene.
>
> In the present case, there can be no doubt that the DNA was deposited in the course of the commission of the offence by the person who committed the offence. As the match with the defendant was one in a billion, there was accordingly a very strong case against the defendant and plainly a case for him to answer that the DNA deposited on the trousers was his.

In *Tsekiri*, the Court of Appeal emphasised that no evidential or legal principle prevents a case being left to the jury solely on the basis that D's DNA profile was found on a moveable article left at the scene of the crime. The cogency of such evidence in any given case will, however, depend on the facts of that case, and in particular on whether there is a plausible 'innocent explanation' for the presence of D's DNA on the item in question. A number of potentially relevant factors were noted in the judgment (at [15]–[21]). These include:

(a) Is there another explanation for the presence of the DNA evidence?
(b) Was the article associated with the offence itself?
(c) Is the article moveable?
(d) Is there evidence of geographic association between the offence and the offender?
(e) In the case of a mixed profile is the defendant a match to the major contributor?
(f) Is primary or secondary transfer of the DNA more likely?

In *Tsekiri* itself, the only positive evidence linking D to the robbery of which he was convicted was a matching DNA profile (with a one in a billion random match probability) obtained from the door handle of the car in which the victim had been robbed. There were traces of a second profile, but that matching D's profile was the major one. Upholding D's conviction, the Court noted that the defence had offered no evidence to explain away the presence of D's DNA on the door, whereas its presence was entirely consistent with D being one of the robbers. D had exercised his right to silence, both when questioned and when given the opportunity to testify at his trial, so (even without the aid of any adverse inferences that might properly have been drawn from his silence) there was nothing in the defence case to undermine or contradict the inference that he opened the car door during the robbery. See also, to similar effect, *Lewis* [2018] EWCA Crim 1101.

In some cases, the application of common sense may be capable of providing an answer to questions that DNA analysis alone cannot answer. In *Bech* [2018] EWCA Crim 448, for example, the issue was whether D had been the driver of a three-door car involved in a crash, rather than a mere passenger. Expert DNA analysis could not rule out the possibility that the finding of D's DNA in the centre of the driver's airbag (along with much smaller DNA traces from other persons) was caused by him brushing against the deployed bag as he exited from the back seat after the crash. But other evidence showed that a back-seat passenger could only have exited from the front nearside door, which would not have involved touching the centre of the airbag at all. Moreover, there was no evidence from D himself to account for his DNA there. It was thus open to a jury to convict D as the driver on the basis of the DNA on the airbag.

Presenting Evidence from Mixed or Incomplete Profiles

F19.32 The difficulties that may arise when evaluating mixed samples were considered in *Dlugosz* [2013] EWCA Crim 2, [2013] 1 Cr App R 32 (425). The Court of Appeal considered three conjoined appeals, each of which raised issues as to the evaluation of low template and mixed profile DNA evidence, and as to the way in which such evidence should be presented in court.

In each of the appeals it was argued that, unless statistical evidence of the relevant DNA match probability could be given, then evaluative opinion ('this lends substantial support' etc.) should not be admitted either, because (so the argument went) the jury would otherwise lack any firm basis on which to evaluate the significance of the evidence given. In the absence of such statistical evidence, expert witnesses should be confined to stating whether the defendant could or could not have contributed to the relevant sample.

The Court rejected this argument, citing *Atkins* [2010] EWCA Crim 1876, [2010] 1 Cr App R 8 (117); *Reed* [2009] EWCA Crim 2698, [2010] 1 Cr App R 23 (310) and *Weller* [2010] EWCA Crim 1085 as authority to the contrary. Nor would the Court accept that an expert should be permitted to provide an evaluative opinion only if the expert is able to use a hierarchy or sliding scale of support (as in *Atkins*). In determining the admissibility of any expert evidence, a court must always be satisfied that there is a sufficiently reliable scientific basis for the evidence to be admitted; but (at [14] and [28]):

> ... an expert is not bound to express an evaluative opinion by reference to the hierarchy; he can use other phrases. The real significance of the expert's inability to use the hierarchy might be that it is indicative of the lack of a proper basis on which to express an opinion. In our view, it can be no more than that. It is a matter to be taken into account in an assessment of whether there is a sufficiently reliable scientific basis for such an evaluative opinion to be given....
>
> ... provided the conclusions from the analysis of a mixed profile are supported by detailed evidence in the form of a report of the experience relied on and the particular features of the mixed profile which make it possible to give an evaluative opinion in the circumstances of the particular case, such an opinion is, in principle, admissible, even though there is presently no statistical basis to provide a random match probability and the sliding scale cannot be used.

See also *Thomas* [2011] EWCA Crim 1295, in which it was held that a jury had rightly been informed of LCN DNA evidence that was consistent with D having handled a pistol used in an alleged offence of attempted murder, even though no match probability could be ascertained from that evidence. Richards LJ reasoned that: 'It was of potentially greater assistance to the jury to have this evidence than to be denied it altogether.'

Forensic Examination Record

F19.33 Experts may use technicians to assist in carrying out their forensic examinations. This must be disclosed either in the body of the expert's statement or in an accompanying exhibit referred to as a Forensic Examination Record (FER). It is essential that admissible evidence is before the court as to each stage of the process by which the DNA profiles were produced and the match obtained. Thus, evidence from an expert who has compared DNA profiles must be supported by admissible evidence as to the primary facts, i.e. the procedures by which those profiles were obtained and the sources of the samples themselves (*Loveridge* [2001] EWCA Crim 734). The CJA 2003, s. 127, may be of assistance here (see **F11.31**).

Use of Improperly Retained Material

F19.34 The PACE 1984, s. 63T(2), provides that where fingerprints, DNA profiles, footwear impressions or other samples ought to have been destroyed in accordance with ss. 63D, 63R or 63S of the Act, that material must not thereafter be used: (a) in evidence against the person to whom the material relates, or (b) for the purposes of the investigation of any offence. A number of exclusions found in s. 63U effectively disapply ss. 63D to 63T in cases involving suspected terrorist offenders and in cases where material taken from one person relates to a different person. Save where such exclusions apply, s. 63T(2) renders improperly retained or improperly used material inadmissible as prosecution evidence, but s. 63T(2) does not specifically deal with the admissibility of any fresh DNA specimens or prints, etc., that may have been taken from a suspect after having been identified by unlawfully retained or unlawfully used material. Such a case would raise issues similar to those considered by the House of Lords in *A-G's Ref (No. 3 of 1999)* [2001] 2 AC 91, in which it was held that the unlawful retention and use of such material during the investigation did not preclude the admission of fresh samples (or other evidence) taken from D after he had been identified, although such evidence would be subject to possible discretionary exclusion under the PACE 1984, s. 78 (see **F2.26** ***et seq.***).

FINGERPRINTS AND BODY OR FOOTWEAR IMPRESSIONS

Fingerprints

Fingerprint evidence should be presented by a qualified expert, with appropriate experience in the examination and comparison of such evidence (*Barnes* [2005] EWCA Crim 1158). Police forces do not recognise the competence of those who have obtained their qualifications overseas; but it is for a judge to decide whether a person is a competent expert, not the police (*Smith* [2011] EWCA Crim 972, [2011] 2 Cr App R 16 (174) at [61]). Properly presented fingerprint evidence may provide sufficient identification, even if unsupported by other evidence, but D must be linked to the relevant prints by admissible evidence (*Chappell v DPP* (1988) 89 Cr App R 82). In *Buckley* (1999) 163 JP 561, Rose LJ said: **F19.35**

> Fingerprint evidence, like any other evidence, is admissible . . . if it tends to prove the guilt of the accused. It may so tend, even if there are only a few similar ridge characteristics, but it may, in such a case, have little weight. It may be excluded in the exercise of judicial discretion, if its prejudicial effect outweighs its probative value.

He added that courts or judges would have to consider the experience and expertise of the witness presenting it, the number of similar ridge characteristics identified, the presence of any dissimilar characteristics, the size of the crime print (a given number of matches in a fragment of a print may be more compelling than a similar number in a complete print) and the quality and clarity of that print (including any evidence of injury to the person who left the print, and any smearing or contamination of the print). There is no longer any support for the old '16 point standard'. The latest guidelines on fingerprint analysis emphasise the primacy of subjective evaluation when comparing prints, and do not rely on any particular number of matching characteristics. Where fingerprint experts disagree as to points of similarity, the judge must make it clear that any dissimilarity between D's prints and those from the crime scene would show that D could not have left those prints. If the crime scene prints were clearly those of the offender, any such dissimilarity must inevitably exonerate D. See further the *Crown Court Compendium* (July 2020), ch. 15-6A.

Footprints and Footwear Marks

A clear dissimilarity between a footprint from a crime scene and one taken from D may similarly establish innocence, but the converse is not true: even if footprints appear to match exactly this can at most place D within a given group of individuals who could have left the crime scene prints. **F19.36**

Much the same is true of footwear marks. In *T (footwear mark evidence)* [2010] EWCA Crim 2439, [2011] 1 Cr App R 9 (85), the Court of Appeal warned that there was no sufficiently reliable data on which an expert witness could purport to offer any kind of scientific or statistical assessment as to whether footwear impressions had been left by D:

> An attempt to assess the degrees of probability where footwear could have made a mark based on figures relating to distribution is inherently unreliable and gives rise to a verisimilitude of mathematical probability based on data where it is not possible to build that data in a way that enables this to be done; none in truth exists... We are satisfied that in the area of footwear evidence, no attempt can realistically be made in the generality of cases to use a formula to calculate the probabilities. The practice has no sound basis....
>
> An opinion that a shoe 'could have made the mark' is not in our view the same as saying that 'there was moderate [scientific] support for the prosecution case'. The use of the term 'could have made' is a more precise statement of the evidence; it enables a jury better to understand the true nature of the evidence than the more opaque phrase 'moderate scientific support'.
>
> However there are cases where it would not be right to confine an examiner (where there are solely class characteristics) to opining on whether the mark could or could not have been made. There may be factors that enable him to go further than 'could have made' and express, on the basis of such factors, a more definite evaluative opinion. It would not be appropriate for us to express a view on the factors which would properly enable an examiner to express a more definitive evaluative opinion, but they would certainly include an unusual size or pattern.
>
> However, it is important to emphasise that the examiner is giving his opinion on the matters within his expertise—namely the footwear, the marks and, if relevant, scenes of crime evidence; it is not his function to evaluate the other evidence in the case.

See further the *Crown Court Compendium* (July 2020), ch. 15-6B.

Ear-prints

F19.37 Some doubts surround the use of ear-print evidence as a result of its role in the miscarriage of justice that occurred in *Dallagher* [2002] EWCA Crim 1903, [2003] 1 Cr App R 12 (195), where following the quashing of D's conviction for murder the ear-print evidence on which he had been convicted was utterly discredited at his retrial. But ear-print evidence may still have its uses. In *Kempster (No. 2)* [2008] EWCA Crim 975, [2008] 2 Cr App R 19 (256) the Court of Appeal concluded (at [27]–[28]):

> Ear-print comparison is capable of providing information which could identify the person who has left an ear-print on a surface. That is certainly the case where minutiae can be identified and matched. Where the only information comes from the gross features, we do not understand [the experts] to say that no match can ever be made, but there is likely to be less confidence in such a match because of the flexibility of the ear and the uncertainty of the pressure which will have been applied at the relevant time.
>
> On the basis of the evidence that we have heard, we are of the view that the latter can only be the case where the gross features truly provide a precise match. We have no doubt that evidence of those experienced in comparing ear-prints is capable of being relevant and admissible. The question in each case will be whether it is probative. In the present case... we are struck by the gross similarity of the shape and size of the ear-prints used for the comparison, and by the close similarity of the notch and the nodule on each. This, in our view, establishes that the ear-print at the scene is consistent with having been left by the appellant. But having examined the comparisons of the gross features, it is also apparent to us that they do not provide a precise match. The differences may well be explicable by differences in pressure, or movement, but the extent of the mismatch is such as to lead us to the conclusion that it could not be relied on by itself as justifying a verdict of guilty.

See further the *Crown Court Compendium* (July 2020), ch. 15-6C.

Section F20 Inferences from Silence and the Non-production of Evidence

THE RIGHT TO SILENCE

An accused person in a criminal trial has traditionally been accorded a 'right to silence', sometimes termed a privilege against self-incrimination. These concepts are not specifically mentioned in the rights guaranteed by the ECHR, Article 6, but it has been held that they constitute 'generally recognised international standards which lie at the heart of the notion of a fair procedure under Article 6' (*Murray v UK* (1996) 22 EHRR 29; *Saunders v UK* (1997) 23 EHRR 313). Although the right is said in *Murray* not to be an absolute right, the extent to which the provisions of the CJPO 1994, ss. 34 to 38, operate consistently with the right to a fair trial is still a matter of some debate. **F20.1**

Aspects of the right to silence which are recognised in domestic law are that the accused is not a compellable witness at trial (see **F4.10**) and is under no general duty to assist the police with their inquiries (*Rice v Connolly* [1966] 2 QB 414). The YJCEA 1999, s. 59 and sch. 3, respond to the decision in *Saunders v UK* by restricting the use which can be made of evidence obtained under compulsion under a variety of statutory provisions. The powers of investigation themselves are not affected: only the use of evidence obtained under them. See further **F10.7** *et seq*.

At common law, no inferences were generally permitted to be drawn from the exercise of the right to silence either by a suspect under investigation or by an accused person at trial. This position has been substantially eroded by the CJPO 1994, ss. 34 to 38, which specify the circumstances in which adverse inferences may be drawn from the exercise of the primary right. Where the statutory scheme does not apply, the common-law rule still applies (*McGarry* [1999] 3 All ER 805 and **F20.27**). Where the statutory scheme comes into play, the court is under an obligation to ensure that the jury are properly directed regarding the proper inferences which can be drawn (*Condron v UK* (2001) 31 EHRR 1 (1)). In *Condron v UK*, the ECtHR accepted that the right to silence could not of itself prevent the accused's silence, in cases which clearly call for an explanation, being taken into account in assessing the persuasiveness of the prosecution evidence, but also stressed that a fair procedure (under Article 6) required 'particular caution' on the part of a domestic court before relying on the accused's silence. **F20.2**

OUT-OF-COURT SILENCE UNDER THE 1994 ACT

Failure to Reveal Facts afterwards Relied upon in Court

A strong argument for drawing an adverse inference from silence occurs where the accused withholds when questioned matters that are subsequently introduced in support of a defence at trial. Section 34 of the CJPO 1994 addresses this problem. **F20.3**

F20.4 **Criminal Justice and Public Order Act 1994, s. 34**

(1) Where, in any proceedings against a person for an offence, evidence is given that the accused—
  (a) at any time before he was charged with the offence, on being questioned under caution by a constable trying to discover whether or by whom the offence had been committed, failed to mention any fact relied on in his defence in those proceedings; or
  (b) on being charged with the offence or officially informed that he might be prosecuted for it, failed to mention any such fact; or
  (c) at any time after being charged with the offence, on being questioned under section 22 of the Counter-Terrorism Act 2008 (post-charge questioning), failed to mention any such fact,

being a fact which in the circumstances existing at the time the accused could reasonably have been expected to mention when so questioned, charged or informed, as the case may be, subsection (2) below applies.

(2) Where this subsection applies—
  (a) [repealed];
  (b) a judge, in deciding whether to grant an application made by the accused under paragraph 2 of schedule 3 to the Crime and Disorder Act 1998;
  (c) the court, in determining whether there is a case to answer; and
  (d) the court or jury, in determining whether the accused is guilty of the offence charged,

may draw such inferences from the failure as appear proper.

(2A) Where the accused was at an authorised place of detention at the time of the failure, subsections (1) and (2) above do not apply if he had not been allowed an opportunity to consult a solicitor prior to being questioned, charged or informed as mentioned in subsection (1) above.

(3) Subject to any directions by the court, evidence tending to establish the failure may be given before or after evidence tending to establish the fact which the accused is alleged to have failed to mention.

(4) This section applies in relation to questioning by persons (other than constables) charged with the duty of investigating offences or charging offenders as it applies in relation to questioning by constables; and in subsection (1) above 'officially informed' means informed by a constable or any such person.

(5) This section does not—
  (a) prejudice the admissibility in evidence of the silence or other reaction of the accused in the face of anything said in his presence relating to the conduct in respect of which he is charged, in so far as evidence thereof would be admissible apart from this section; or
  (b) preclude the drawing of any inference from any such silence or other reaction of the accused which could properly be drawn apart from this section.

(6) This section does not apply in relation to a failure to mention a fact if the failure occurred before the commencement of this section.

F20.5 **Failure to Reveal Facts** Section 34 permits the tribunal of fact to draw 'such inferences as appear proper' (s. 34(2)) from the accused's failure to reveal specific facts, provided that the various conditions set forth in s. 34(1) are made out and any questions of fact arising thereunder are resolved against the accused (*Argent* [1997] 2 Cr App R 27). The provision applies only where a particular fact is advanced by the defence which is suspicious by reason of not being put forward at an early opportunity: s. 34 does not apply simply because the accused has declined to answer questions (*Argent*; *T v DPP* [2007] EWHC 1793 (Admin); and see **F20.10**). The *Crown Court Compendium* (July 2020), ch. 17-1, states that the object is 'to deter late fabrication and to encourage early disclosure of genuine defences'. Section 34 applies also where the accused discloses the nature of the defence but fails to mention a particular fact that is relied upon at trial. In such a case there is a discretion whether to deploy s. 34. In *Abdalla* [2007] EWCA Crim 2495, D immediately disclosed his defence of self-defence, but neglected to mention that he believed V was armed with a hammer. The decision of the judge to proceed in a 'low key' way without giving a s. 34 direction was upheld. The Court of Appeal referred with approval to the statement of Hedley J in *Brizzalari* [2004] EWCA Crim 310 that the mischief at which s. 34 is primarily directed is 'the positive defence following a "no comment" interview and/or the "ambush" defence'. Counsel should not complicate trials and summings-up by invoking the section unless the merits of the individual case require it. *Brizzalari* was approved in *Maguire* [2008] EWCA

Crim 1028, where the Court discouraged 'anything which over-formalises common sense'. In *Johnson* [2017] EWCA Crim 191, the Court of Appeal said that it would have been 'wiser to avoid' a direction where D had said enough in interview to 'set up the line of reasoning' on which his defence was based, although some points of detail were missing.

Adverse Inference Consistent with Right to Fair Trial Decisions of the ECtHR have confirmed that the mere fact that a trial judge leaves a jury with the option of drawing an adverse inference from silence in interview is not incompatible with the requirements of a fair trial. Whether the drawing of adverse inferences infringes the ECHR, Article 6, is a matter to be determined in light of all the circumstances of the case, having regard to the situations where inferences may be drawn, the weight attached to them by the national court, and the degree of compulsion inherent in the situation. Of particular importance are the terms of the judge's direction to the jury on the drawing of adverse inferences (*Condron v UK* (2001) 31 EHRR 1 (1); *Beckles v UK* (2003) 36 EHRR 13 (162)). **F20.6**

The domestic cases show that s. 34 has given rise to much more difficulty in directing the jury than s. 35 (failure to testify at trial: see **F20.41**). The ingredients of an appropriate direction are considered at **F20.25**.

Failure to give a proper direction will not necessarily involve a breach of Article 6, nor render a conviction unsafe (*Chenia* [2002] EWCA Crim 2345, [2003] 2 Cr App R 6 (83), where earlier authorities are considered). In *Chenia*, the factors which persuaded the Court that D had received a fair trial included the strength of the evidence, the fact that his failure to mention relevant facts was not consequent upon legal advice (as to which, see **F20.18**) and the clear and accurate direction given on the related matter of D's failure to give evidence.

Access to Legal Advice Section 34(2A) of the CJPO 1994 was added by the YJCEA 1999, s. 58, to bring the law into line with the judgment of the ECtHR in *Murray v UK* (1996) 22 EHRR 29. The Court considered that even the lawful exercise of a power to delay access to legal advice could, where the accused was at risk of adverse inferences under the statutory scheme, be sufficient to deprive the accused of a fair procedure under Article 6. The accused was faced with a 'fundamental dilemma' at the outset of the investigation, in that silence might lead to adverse inferences being drawn, while breaking silence might prejudice the defence without necessarily removing the possibility of inferences being drawn. The dilemma is resolved by postponing the prospect that inferences will be drawn until the accused has had the opportunity of consulting with a legal adviser. The postponement occurs in exactly the same way whether access to legal advice is delayed lawfully or unlawfully. An 'authorised place of detention' is defined by s. 38(2A) to include police stations and any other place prescribed by order. The caution to be given to a person to whom a restriction on drawing inferences applies is specified by PACE Code C, annex C. **F20.7**

Where an accused person has been offered legal advice but has elected to proceed without it, an issue may arise as to whether there has been an effective waiver for the purposes of drawing inferences. Although the leading Scottish case of *McGowan v B* [2011] UKSC 54, [2011] 1 WLR 3121 is primarily concerned with confessions obtained following waiver, Lord Hamilton also acknowledged the advantage of access to legal advice in deciding whether to respond in interview (see also **F18.37**). In *McGowan* the issue was whether the jurisprudence of the ECtHR supports a rule that the right of access to legal advice during police questioning can be waived only if the accused has received advice from a lawyer as to whether or not to do so. It was held that it does not. However, in *Saunders* [2012] EWCA Crim 1380, [2012] 2 Cr App R 26 (321), the Court of Appeal regarded the speeches in *McGowan* as authority for the proposition that a waiver should be 'voluntary, informed and unequivocal'. In *Saunders*, D was 'particularly well-fitted' to decide whether she wanted legal advice or not: she was intelligent, had previous convictions for fraud, and a law degree. Had she been unintelligent or vulnerable, her waiver might have been called into question.

No Conviction etc. Wholly or Mainly on Silence

F20.8 **Criminal Justice and Public Order Act 1994, s. 38**

(3) A person shall not have the proceedings against him transferred to the Crown Court for trial, have a case to answer or be convicted of an offence solely on an inference drawn from such a failure or refusal as is mentioned in section 34(2), 35(3), 36(2) or 37(2).

(4) A judge shall not refuse to grant such an application as is mentioned in section 34(2)(b), 36(2)(b) and 37(2)(b) solely on an inference drawn from such a failure as is mentioned in section 34(2), 36(2) or 37(2).

Section 38(3) applies to all four of the provisions of the 1994 Act which operate to permit the drawing of inferences from silence, and s. 38(4) to the three appertaining to out-of-court silence.

F20.9 Where the issue is whether the jury should be at liberty to convict in reliance on an inference drawn under s. 34, it is essential that they be directed that such an inference cannot standing alone prove guilt (*Abdullah* [1999] 3 Arch News 3), though the omission of the direction is not necessarily fatal if the prosecution evidence taken apart from the inference is overwhelming (*Adeyinka* [2014] EWCA Crim 504). The prevalent view is that the direction to the jury should go beyond the rule laid down in s. 38(3) in order to ensure that no conviction is based *mainly* on one or more of the statutory inferences. In *Murray v UK* (1996) 22 EHRR 29, there was a very strong statement that it would be incompatible with the accused's rights to base a conviction 'solely or mainly on the accused's silence or on a refusal to answer questions or to give evidence himself'; see also *Condron v UK* (2001) 31 EHRR 1 (1). To the extent that the statutory scheme does not expressly prevent a conviction founded 'mainly' on silence, therefore, it may be defective. In *Doldur* [2000] Crim LR 178, the Court of Appeal held that there was no need for a judge to direct a jury that, before they could draw an inference under s. 34, they must be satisfied that there was a case to answer. Such a direction has been held to be required in relation to s. 35 (see **F20.49**) where the accused does not testify, but the Court regarded the two cases as distinguishable in that, under s. 35, there was a logical reason for confining the jury to considering whether the prosecution had established a prima facie case as a prerequisite to drawing an inference, whereas under s. 34 the jury would need to have regard to evidence adduced by the defence in order to decide whether s. 34 applied. This is true, but the need to honour *Murray* may well require some further elaboration. The direction in the *Crown Court Compendium* (July 2020), ch. 17-1, considered at **F20.25**, makes reference both to the need for the jury to be satisfied that there was a case calling for an answer at the time of the interview and that they should not convict 'wholly or mainly' on the strength of any adverse inference. In *Milford* [2001] Crim LR 330, the Court of Appeal noted that *Doldur*, although based on compelling logic, had failed to address 'the European dimension', and considered that both *Condron* [1997] 1 WLR 827 and *Birchall* [1999] Crim LR 311 were to the contrary. In *Beckles v UK* (2003) 36 EHRR 13 (162), the ECtHR, after considering the above authorities, confirmed that the correct principle was, as stated in *Murray v UK*, that a conviction based solely or mainly on silence or a refusal to answer questions would be incompatible with the right to silence. In *Petkar* [2003] EWCA Crim 2668, [2004] 1 Cr App R 22 (270), it was held that the jury should be told in terms not to convict 'wholly or mainly' on an adverse inference, and that the words 'or mainly' were required to 'buttress' the requirement for proof of a case to answer otherwise than by means of the inference. See to similar effect *Chenia* [2002] EWCA Crim 2345, [2003] 2 Cr App R 6 (83). In *Parchment* [2003] EWCA Crim 2428, it was said that where the case against an accused was weak it was crucial that the limited function of the failure to mention something in interview was clearly spelled out to the jury, and accordingly a conviction for murder was quashed where the appropriate direction had not been given.

Fact Relied On

F20.10 **Meaning of Reliance** Section 34 of the CJPO 1994 does not apply where there is no attempt to put forward at trial some previously undisclosed fact (e.g., where the defence simply contend that the prosecution have failed to prove their case). To give a s. 34 direction in a case where the accused has put forward no more than a bare denial would be tantamount to directing that guilt may be inferred directly from silence, which runs counter to the purpose of s. 34 (*Smith* [2011] EWCA Crim 1098). In *Moshaid* [1998] Crim LR 420, D, acting on legal advice, declined to answer any questions, and at trial did not give or call any evidence. It was held that s. 34 did not bite in these circumstances. In *Khan* [2020] EWCA Crim 163, it was held to be wrong to direct the jury that D's decision to respond 'no comment' part-way through his interview might suggest that he had a 'sinister reason' sufficient to support an adverse inference without first identifying a specific fact that had been relied on. It goes too far, however, to suggest that s. 34 applies only where the accused gives evidence: a fact relied on may be established by a witness called by the accused, or may be elicited from a prosecution witness (*Bowers* [1988] Crim LR 817). In *Webber* [2004] UKHL 1, [2004] 1 All ER 770, where the authorities are reviewed by Lord Bingham, it was held that a fact or matter is relied on not only where the accused gives or adduces evidence of it but also where counsel, acting on instructions, puts a specific and positive case to prosecution witnesses, as opposed to asking questions intended to probe or test the prosecution case. The effect of specific and positive suggestions from counsel, whether or not accepted, is to plant in the jury's mind the accused's version of events. This may be so even if the witness rejects the suggestion, since the jury may mistrust the witness's evidence. If the judge is in doubt whether counsel is merely testing the prosecution case or putting a positive case, counsel should be asked, in the absence of the jury, to make the position clear. However, the positive case ought to be apparent from the defence statement made in advance of trial. The same reasoning also led the House of Lords to conclude that the adoption by counsel of evidence given by a co-defendant may amount to reliance on the relevant facts or matters. Following *Webber* it has been held that the putting forward by an accused of a possible explanation for his or her fingerprints being on a car number plate is a 'fact' as broadly construed in that case (*Esimu* [2007] EWCA Crim 1380). See also *King* [2012] EWCA Crim 805, where D's belief in the guilt of one or more named individuals of the crime with which he was charged was a 'fact'.

In *Betts* [2001] EWCA Crim 224, [2001] 2 Cr App R 16 (257), a bare admission at trial of a part of the prosecution case was held incapable of constituting a 'fact' for the purposes of s. 34. The alternative construction would effectively have removed the accused's right to silence by requiring the accused to make admissions at interview, an obligation which would have conflicted with the ECHR, Article 6. A direction under s. 34 will rarely, if ever, be appropriate in relation to the failure to mention an admittedly true fact, since the adverse inference under s. 34 is that a matter not mentioned at interview is unlikely to be true (*Webber* [2004] UKHL 1, [2004] 1 All ER 770; applied in *Wheeler* [2008] EWCA Crim 688, *Chivers* [2011] EWCA Crim 1212). It follows that a judge must be particularly careful, when giving a s. 34 direction, not to 'lump together' such admittedly true facts with any facts that are properly the subject of a direction (*Zeinden* [2012] EWCA Crim 2489).

Identification of Facts in Direction If the prosecution are unable to establish that the accused has failed to mention a fact, the jury should be directed to draw no inference (*B (MT)* [2000] Crim LR 181). Where the judge directs the jury on the basis that s. 34 applies, it is important that the facts relied on should be identified in the course of the direction (*Chenia* [2002] EWCA Crim 2345, [2003] 2 Cr App R 6 (83); *Lewis* [2003] EWCA Crim 223) and should not be mixed with other, innocuous, facts from which no inference can be drawn (*Zeinden*). In *Lowe* [2007] EWCA Crim 833 the judge was allowed some latitude in a complex case in listing only those aspects of the defence case, as distinct from every particular fact, that had not been mentioned. Subject to this qualification, the identification of the specific fact or facts is required. Any proposed direction should be discussed with counsel before closing speeches. In *B (MT)* the Court of Appeal stated: F20.11

> In our view it is particularly important that judges should take this course in relation to directions as to the application of section 34. That section is a notorious minefield. Discussion with counsel will reduce the risk of mistakes.

When directing a jury in relation to a group of defendants, it is preferable to avoid a direction that deals with their position compendiously rather than individually. A compendious F20.12

approach runs the risk that the direction will fail to identify what exactly each defendant has relied on at trial that was not disclosed at an earlier stage (*Miah* [2009] EWCA Crim 2368).

Where the prosecution are able to identify a specific fact relied upon within the meaning of s. 34, it does not necessarily follow that the point should be taken at trial: prosecutors should remember that the twin mischiefs at which the section is aimed are the positive defence following a 'no comment' interview and the 'ambush' defence. Consideration should therefore be given in other cases to whether the withholding of the fact is sufficient to justify the sanction of s. 34, given the weight juries are likely to give to being directed as to adverse inferences (*Brizzalari* [2004] EWCA Crim 310).

F20.13 **Prepared Statements** Where the accused at the relevant time gives a prepared statement in which certain facts are set forth, it cannot subsequently be said that there has been a failure to mention those facts. The aim of s. 34 of the CJPO 1994 was to encourage a suspect to disclose the factual defence, not to sanction inferences from the accused's failure to respond to questions (*Knight* [2003] EWCA Crim 1977, [2004] 1 WLR 340, and see *T v DPP* [2007] EWHC 1793 (Admin)). A prepared statement may, however, be a dangerous device for an innocent accused who later discovers that something significant has been omitted (*Knight*; *Turner* [2003] EWCA Crim 3108, [2004] 1 All ER 1025). In *Turner* it was noted that, as inconsistencies between the prepared statement and the defence at trial do not necessarily amount to reliance on unmentioned facts, the judge must be particularly careful to pinpoint any fact that might properly be the subject of a s. 34 direction. Alternatively, the jury might in appropriate circumstances be directed to regard differences between the prepared statement and the accused's evidence as constituting a previous lie rather than as the foundation for a direction under s. 34. See also *Cross* [2017] EWCA Crim 1036, in which D had put forward a 'bland, nonspecific prepared statement' in interview and the judge's direction quite properly focused on the extent to which he might reasonably have advanced the more detailed defence that emerged at trial when first taxed with the matter.

Caution or Charge

F20.14 Inferences before a suspect is charged under the CJPO 1994, s. 34, may not be drawn except 'on being questioned under caution by a constable' (s. 34(1)(a)). The reference to 'constable' includes others charged with investigating offences (s. 34(4)). If no questions under caution have been put, for example because the accused refuses to leave the cell for questioning, the section cannot apply, as the statutory language cannot be ignored (*Johnson* [2005] EWCA Crim 971). It is not necessary that specific questions are put in interview: a defendant is 'questioned under caution' if expressly or by necessary implication invited to give an account of the matter which has given rise to the interview (*Green* [2019] EWCA Crim 411, where the interview consisted of D being invited to respond to the officer's summary of the allegation). Similarly, a fact does not have to be stated in answer to a question for it to have been 'mentioned': in *Ali* [2001] EWCA Crim 863, D handed over a prepared statement in which the relevant facts were mentioned and this was sufficient to prevent an inference, although he subsequently declined to answer questions (see also *Knight* [2003] EWCA Crim 1977, [2004] 1 WLR 340).

F20.15 The caution makes clear the risks that attend the failure to mention facts which later form part of the defence. It is set out in Code C, para. 10.5, and runs as follows:

> You do not have to say anything. But it may harm your defence if you do not mention when questioned something which you later rely on in court. Anything you do say may be given in evidence.

Minor deviations from the formula are not a breach of the code as long as the sense is preserved (para. 10.7), and an officer is permitted to paraphrase if it appears that the person with whom the officer is dealing does not understand what the caution means (Note for Guidance 10D). A suspect who has been arrested should not normally be questioned about involvement in an offence except in an interview at a police station, and it is envisaged that questioning to which

s. 34 applies should occur in the course of such an interview which, being properly recorded, will then allow the court to make reliable deductions about the nature and extent of any silence. Clearly, if the accused alleges that the relevant fact was mentioned under questioning, the prosecution will have to prove the contrary before any adverse inference can be drawn. Where it is alleged that a 'significant silence' (i.e. one which appears capable of being used in evidence against the suspect) has occurred before arrival at a police station, then at the beginning of an interview at the station the interviewing officer should put the matter to the suspect, under caution, and ask for confirmation or denial of that earlier silence and whether the suspect wishes to add anything (para. 11.4). The consequence of failing to go through this procedure (which applies to evidentially significant statements as it does to silences) must be to increase significantly the likelihood that the evidence in question will be excluded under the PACE 1984, s. 78, if the suspect denies that the earlier statement was made or that the silence occurred. Furthermore, if the suspect is questioned improperly in circumstances prohibited by Code C, e.g., where sufficient evidence for the accused to be charged already exists, s. 34 should not be brought to bear on the suspect's failure to respond (*Pointer* [1997] Crim LR 676; *Gayle* [1999] 2 Cr App R 130). There is a lack of consistency in the authorities on when there is sufficient evidence for this purpose (*McGuinness* [1999] Crim LR 318; *Ioannou* [1999] Crim LR 586; *Odeyemi* [1999] Crim LR 828; *Flynn* [2001] EWCA Crim 1633; *Elliott* [2002] EWCA Crim 931), but no doubt about the principle.

The drawing of inferences from the withholding of a fact at the point of charge under s. 34(1)(b) is a distinct process from that under s. 34(1)(a). Where, therefore, no inference could be drawn from silence at interview because the interview itself had been excluded under the PACE 1984, s. 78, it did not follow that an inference could not be drawn from silence at the point of charge as long as there is no unfairness in doing so (*Dervish* [2001] EWCA Crim 2789, [2002] 2 Cr App R 6 (105)). In that case D had the opportunity 'in a single sentence' to put the essence of his defence following charge, and the police would thereafter have been precluded from questioning him about it. Since he declined to do so, it was rightly left to the jury to decide whether an inference should be drawn. **F20.16**

Facts which Should Have Been Mentioned

Adverse inferences may be drawn from a fact subsequently relied on in defence only where the fact is one which, in the circumstances existing at the time, the accused could reasonably have been expected to mention (CJPO 1994, s. 34(1)). If the accused gives evidence, the reason for failing to disclose should be explored (*T v DPP* [2007] EWHC 1793 (Admin)), and any explanation advanced by the accused for non-disclosure must be considered in deciding what inferences, if any, should be drawn (*Webber* [2004] UKHL 1, [2004] 1 All ER 770, where the House of Lords considered that the jury was 'very much concerned' with the truth or otherwise of an explanation from the accused as, if they accept it as true or possibly so, no adverse inference should be drawn from the accused's failure to mention it). *T v DPP* was applied in *AB v CPS* [2017] EWHC 2963 (Admin), in which the magistrates had fallen into error, *inter alia*, by failing to consider what D's explanation might be for not having cooperated in interview, despite having been invited to consider that he might have been protecting his brother, who was the actual perpetrator. **F20.17**

In *Walton* [2013] EWCA Crim 2536, D was not asked at any point about his failure to answer questions at interview (where he had tendered a prepared statement). Nor does it appear that he was invited to deal with the question why he had made no previous mention of particular facts later relied on in his defence. Although counsel for the prosecution did not seek a direction on adverse inference, the trial judge elected to give one. The Court of Appeal (at [8]) considered the direction to be both wrong and unfair in the circumstances. '[T]he jury were invited to consider an adverse inference without knowing what if anything the appellant might have had to say about his silence.' Ultimately an adverse inference is appropriate only where the jury conclude that the silence can only sensibly be attributed to the defendant's having no answer, or none that would stand up to questioning (*Condron* [1997] 1 WLR 827; *Betts* [2001] EWCA Crim 224, [2001] 2 Cr App R 16 (257); *Daly* [2001] EWCA Crim 2643, [2002] 2 Cr App R 14 (201); *Petkar* [2003] EWCA Crim 2668, [2004] 1 Cr App R 22 (270)). Similar formulae appear also in *Condron v UK* (2001) 31 EHRR 1 (1) and *Beckles v UK* (2003) 36 EHRR 13 (162). In *Barnes* (4 July 2003 unreported), D's contention was that he thought that he had mentioned the fact in issue during his interview. As this was not advanced as a reason for non-disclosure, it was said that it provided no impediment to the drawing of an adverse inference. While this may be so, if D genuinely believed that he had mentioned the fact, then his state of mind at interview was not that of a guilty person withholding information. It is important that any direction given should reflect this. In *Hilliard* [2004] EWCA Crim 837, D's only chance to mention a fact was when a witness's statement had been read to him in interview. He had not been told that he should correct any statement with which he disagreed. It was held that it would be 'wholly unsafe' to seek to draw an adverse inference since D had never had the opportunity to deal with the matter (which was not central) even if he ought to have identified it as something that was important enough to mention. In *M* [2012] EWCA Crim 2, [2012] 1 Cr App R 26 (362), the officers interviewing D on suspicion of rape mistakenly attributed a date to the allegation that was some three months after the day on which the complainant, D's babysitter, had said that the offence had occurred. D had responded truthfully that nothing had occurred on the date put to him and 'it was hard to see how in those circumstances he could have been expected to say more'. D subsequently relied on facts relevant to the earlier date (e.g., the fact that his partner had arrived home very shortly after the alleged incident) but these were not facts which he could reasonably have been expected to mention in the context of the original investigation.

The specific references to the accused and to the circumstances indicate that a range of factors may be relevant to what might have been expected to be forthcoming, including the accused's age, experience, mental capacity, health, sobriety, tiredness and personality. A restrictive approach would not be appropriate (*Argent* [1997] 2 Cr App R 27, and see, as to the interviewing of special groups such as children or young people and the mentally vulnerable, PACE Code C, paras. 3.13 to 3.16).

The failure of the interviewer to disclose relevant information when asked to do so by the accused or a legal adviser is another factor bearing upon the propriety of drawing an inference. If little information is forthcoming, a legal adviser may well counsel silence until a better assessment of the case to answer can be made (*Roble* [1997] Crim LR 449), but everything depends on the facts. In *Lee* [2015] EWCA Crim 420, a s. 34 direction was called for in respect of D's failure to mention at interview that C had made up her allegation of assault against him, and that her injuries had been caused in another way. It was not necessary for the judge to point out that D had not, at that stage, been made aware of the specific allegations made by C as he would have been aware of the salient fact that he had been arrested for assaulting her. In *Green* [2019] EWCA Crim 411, where D was invited to respond to a narrative rather than being asked specific questions, the issue whether D might reasonably have been expected to go further than simply explaining his defence 'in broad terms' was one to which the jury's attention should have been specifically directed.

F20.18 **Legal Advice to Remain Silent** The difficult issue of what use, if any, can be made of a failure to advance facts following legal advice to remain silent has been the subject of numerous decisions, both by domestic courts and Strasbourg. In *Beckles* [2004] EWCA Crim 2766, [2005] 1 All ER 705, Lord Woolf CJ commented that the position in such cases is 'singularly delicate'. On the one hand, the courts not unreasonably seek to avoid having the accused drive a coach and horses through s. 34 by advancing an explanation for silence that is easy to make and difficult to investigate because of legal professional privilege. On the other hand, 'it is of the greatest importance that defendants should be able to be advised by their lawyer without their having to reveal the terms of that advice if they act in accordance with that advice'. Perhaps because of this, the authorities have not all spoken with one voice, although now a consistent theme seems to be emerging. In *Condron* [1997] 1 WLR 827, D and his wife, admitted heroin addicts, were convicted of offences relating to the supply of the drug. At interview both remained silent, on the advice of their solicitor who (despite medical advice to the contrary) considered that their drug withdrawal symptoms rendered them unfit to be interviewed. At trial, the defence relied upon detailed innocent explanations of prosecution evidence which could have been put forward at the time of interview. It was held that the giving of legal advice to remain silent did not of itself preclude the drawing of inferences: all depends on the view the jury take of the reason advanced by the accused as to whether the silence can only sensibly be attributed to the accused having no answer, or none that would stand up to questioning. (Such a direction was said to be 'desirable' in *Condron*, but the ECtHR subsequently considered that fairness required a direction to be given which left the jury in no doubt in this important matter (*Condron v UK* (2001) 31 EHRR 1 (1)).) In *Beckles* [2004] EWCA Crim 2766, [2005] 1 All ER 705, the Court of Appeal reviewed a number of post-*Condron* authorities, including the earlier decision of the ECtHR in *Beckles* itself ((2003) 36 EHRR 13 (162)). Two strands of authority, one proceeding from *Betts* [2001] EWCA Crim 224, [2001] 2 Cr App R 16 (257), and the other from *Howell* [2003] EWCA Crim 1, [2005] 1 Cr App R 1 (1) and *Knight* [2003] EWCA Crim 1977, [2004] 1 WLR 340 had been regarded as in conflict, with *Betts* favouring a subjective test (did the accused genuinely rely on legal advice?) and *Howell* and *Knight* an objective test (did the accused reasonably rely on legal advice?). The Court of Appeal in *Beckles* adopted the reconciliation of the two strands proposed by Auld LJ in *Hoare* [2004] EWCA Crim 784, [2005] 1 WLR 1804, under which 'genuine reliance by a defendant on his solicitor's advice to remain silent is not in itself enough to preclude adverse comment'. Auld LJ went on (at [54]):

> It is not the purpose of section 34 to exclude a jury from drawing an adverse inference against a defendant because he genuinely or reasonably believes that, regardless of his guilt or innocence, he is entitled to take advantage of that advice to impede the prosecution case against him. In such a case the advice is not truly the reason for not mentioning the facts. The section 34 inference is concerned with flushing out innocence at an early stage, or supporting other evidence of guilt at a later stage, not simply with whether a guilty defendant is entitled, or genuinely or reasonably believes that he is entitled, to rely on legal rights of which his solicitor has advised him. Legal entitlement is one thing. An accused's reason for exercising it is another. His belief in his entitlement may be genuine, but it does not follow that his reason for exercising it is ...

In *Hoare*, the defence to producing a Class B drug was that D believed he was involved in the **F20.19** secret production of a cure for cancer. D had given a 'no comment' interview following legal advice, the solicitor apparently having thought that there was insufficient disclosure of the evidence against D at that stage. Under cross-examination, D said that, while he could have given his explanation at the time, he had been stunned and surprised, had not had much sleep, and 'most people would act on the advice of their lawyer'. The true question, however, according to *Hoare*, is not whether D's solicitors rightly or wrongly believed that D was not required to answer the questions, nor whether D genuinely relied on the advice in the sense that he believed he had the right to do so. The true question is whether D remained silent 'not because of that advice but because he had no or no satisfactory explanation to give'. Similarly in *Karapetyan* [2013] EWCA Crim 74, it was not disputed that D had a 'reason' for silence in that his preferred solicitor, who was unable to attend the interview, had advised him to make no comment. However, the jury, following a proper direction on the matter, were entitled to conclude that the fact relied on (that D was not a driver who had given false details to a police officer, and that the offender was probably a man to whom D had rented the car) could reasonably have been expected to be mentioned. See also *Essa* [2009] EWCA Crim 43, where the Court of Appeal added the rider that in such cases a court may wish to pause and consider whether a s. 34 direction helps the jury (e.g., where the defence at trial is a simple denial of presence). The direction in the *Crown Court Compendium* (July 2020), ch. 17-1, includes specific guidance on cases where the accused claims to have remained silent on legal advice which follows the contours of the judgment in *Hoare*, but also stresses the importance of considering the age and maturity of the accused and the complexity of the facts relied on. Where the accused may have had a good defence but chose on legal advice to remain silent, no inference should be drawn, but where the jury are sure that the accused had no such defence and 'merely hid behind the legal advice', an inference may be drawn.

F20.20 **Waiver of Privilege and Statements** The accused who wishes to explain the reasons for silence following legal advice may find it hard to do so without waiving privilege. While no waiver is involved in a bare assertion that advice had been given to remain silent, little weight in likely to attach to such an assertion unless the reasons for it are before the court (*Condron* [1997] 1 WLR 827; *Robinson* [2003] EWCA Crim 2219). In *Bowden* [1999] 4 All ER 582, a waiver was held to have occurred where D called evidence in his defence of a statement made by his solicitor at interview, namely that he had advised D to remain silent because of the lack of evidence against him. D was held to have been properly cross-examined about the extent to which he had disclosed to the solicitor the facts that subsequently formed the basis of his defence. Lord Bingham CJ stated, *obiter*, that the giving of evidence at a *voir dire* as to the reasons for legal advice for silence would operate as a waiver of privilege at trial even if the evidence was not repeated before the jury: the accused cannot 'have his cake and eat it' where privilege is concerned. The same point is also made, though in less emphatic terms, by the ECtHR in *Condron v UK* (2001) 31 EHRR 1 (1), where it is said that there was no compulsion on D to disclose the advice given, other than the indirect compulsion to provide a convincing explanation for silence, and that because D chose to make the content of the solicitor's advice part of his defence he could not complain that the CJPO 1994 overrode the confidentiality of discussions with his legal adviser. Where waiver takes place, the accused may be questioned about disclosures to the solicitor even where it is accepted that legal advice was given solely on the basis of the case as disclosed by the investigator (*Loizou* [2006] EWCA Crim 1719). The position is different where the accused merely responds to an allegation of recent fabrication by stating that the defence was communicated to the solicitor: in that case the adviser stands in the same position as any other person to whom the defence was revealed, and no waiver is thereby involved (*Bowden*; *Wishart* [2005] EWCA Crim 1337). In *Hall-Chung* [2007] EWCA Crim 3429, it was held that the issue is not whether the prosecution or the defence adduce the evidence, but whether waiver has in fact occurred. The circumstances of the waiver, and how it is deployed by the Crown, may be relevant to whether it is fair to exclude evidence pursuant to the PACE 1984, s. 78.

F20.21 **Admissions by Legal Representative and Hearsay** Where a solicitor, following consultation with the accused, makes a statement to the officers conducting the interview with regard to the accused's reasons for silence (in the presence of the accused who says nothing in dissent), the statement may be given in evidence and may form the basis of an adverse inference (*Fitzgerald* [1998] 4 Arch News 2). It would appear that the Court of Appeal had in mind by way of exception to the hearsay rule either the doctrine of admission by an agent, or implied admission by silence where a statement is made in the presence of the accused (see **F17.67** and **F20.28** respectively). In *Bowden* the Court of Appeal expressed a preference for the explanation based on agency, which it is submitted is correct. It is not hearsay for the accused to tell the court what advice the solicitor gave, provided that the purpose of doing so is not to establish the truth of any fact narrated by the solicitor. It is the accused's reason for withholding facts that is in issue so, provided that, for example, the accused merely wishes to explain the impact of the advice given, there is no hearsay problem (*Davis* [1998] Crim LR 659). In *Hill* [2003] EWCA Crim 1179, D contended that an interview conducted in the presence of a solicitor should have been excluded (and therefore unavailable as the basis for an inference) on the ground that her solicitor was affected by a conflict of interest as the representative of a co-accused. It was held that the proper course would have been to waive privilege and consider the matter fully on a *voir dire*: the court should not be asked to speculate that the solicitor had acted improperly.

F20.22 **Fairness where Reasons for Advice Suggest Bad Character** In some cases the reasons for the advice given to the accused may be difficult to explain to a jury without revealing that the accused is no stranger to the legal process. The point was raised (but not answered) in *Beard*

[2002] EWCA Crim 772. Where the case is not one in which evidence of bad character is otherwise admissible, it will be necessary to consider whether to exclude some or all of the evidence relating to the failure to mention facts to avoid unfairness.

Direction as to Permissible Inferences

Proper Inferences Where the fact is one which the accused could reasonably have been expected to mention it will be permissible to draw 'such inferences from the failure as appear proper' (s. 34(2)) in a variety of contexts including the determination of guilt (s. 34(2)(d), and whether there is a case to answer (s. 34(2)(c)), bearing in mind always that an inference drawn under the subsection is not by itself sufficient to sustain either determination (s. 38(3): see **F20.8**). Although the most common inference from failure to reveal facts which are subsequently relied on is that the facts have been invented after the interview, it may equally appear to the jury that the accused had the facts in mind at the time of interview, but was unwilling to give an account and expose it to scrutiny (*Milford* [2001] Crim LR 330). Similarly, the jury may deduce that the accused was faced with a choice between on the one hand silence, and on the other either lying or further self-incrimination by telling the truth. Again, this is a permissible inference under s. 34 (*Daniel* [1998] 2 Cr App R 373). It follows that, even if it is common ground that an accused spoke to a legal representative about a proposed defence of alibi before any interview took place, the failure to reveal the alibi in interview was still a matter from which inferences could be drawn if the jury were unconvinced by the accused's explanation (*Taylor* [1999] Crim LR 77). Nothing in *Condron* or *Cowan* should be read as indicating that the only adverse inference to be drawn is one of recent fabrication (*Beckles* [1999] Crim LR 148). Where the inference which the prosecution suggests should be drawn is not the standard inference of late fabrication but is less severe, the judge should make this clear when summing up (*Petkar* [2003] EWCA Crim 2668, [2004] 1 Cr App R 22 (270)). **F20.23**

In cases where the accused attributes failure to mention facts to acting on legal advice, but without explaining the reasons behind the advice, the trial judge should be particularly careful to avoid directing the jury in such a way as to indicate that the silence is necessarily a guilty one (*Bresa* [2005] EWCA Crim 1414 and see **F20.18** as to the construction of a possible inference following legal advice). Provided the trial judge has given the proper directions in relation to s. 34, fair comment may be made on the evidence: the judge is not obliged to 'sit quiet'. In *Sakyi* [2014] EWCA Crim 1784, the judge commented, in relation to the defence argument that D was simply following legal advice in declining to answer questions, that it was D, and not his solicitor, who ran the risk of being charged with the serious offence of possession of a firearm and ammunition and that it was his choice, in the light of the circumstances known to him, whether to accept the advice. The judge also repeated in his direction a prosecution argument that, had the defence advanced at trial (that the gun was in a bag in the sole possession of a co-accused, and that D believed the bag to contain drugs) been true, it would have provided a '100 per cent defence' to the charge, so why would D not reveal it? Both comments were held to be within the realm of legitimate comment on the facts.

Where Inference Can Only be Drawn after Guilt is Established In some cases an inference cannot logically be drawn without first concluding that the accused is guilty, and in such cases, s. 34 has been said to be of no assistance (*Mountford* [1999] Crim LR 575). D, charged with possession of heroin with intent to supply, put forward the defence that the actual dealer was W, *the main prosecution witness*, while he was merely a customer. D gave as his explanation for failing to reveal this defence at interview his reluctance to expose W to prosecution. The Court of Appeal held that the jury could not properly reject D's reason for not mentioning this fact without first concluding that the fact was untrue: the very issue on which D's guilt turned. In these (somewhat unusual) circumstances the judge should not have left s. 34 to the jury. (See also *Gill* [2001] 1 Cr App R 11 (160), a case on similar facts.) In *Daly* [2001] EWCA Crim 2643, [2002] 2 Cr App R 14 (201), however, the decision in *Mountford* was doubted on the ground that there is nothing in s. 34 which requires that the issue be one which is capable of separate resolution in **F20.24**

the case. While this is true, there is much to be said for the view that the judge should steer the jury in the direction of a logical resolution to the issues. However, a differently-constituted later court made the same point in *Gowland-Wynn* [2001] EWCA Crim 2715, [2002] 1 Cr App R 41 (569), and it may be that the qualification in *Mountford* is too subtle. In *Chenia* [2002] EWCA Crim 2345, [2003] 2 Cr App R 6 (83), the approach in *Mountford* was said to be appropriate in the 'rare case' only and in *Webber* [2004] UKHL 1, [2004] 1 All ER 770, the House of Lords (while not specifically overruling *Mountford*) considered that the s. 34 direction was rightly given in that case, which is tantamount to outright rejection. *Webber* was a very different type of case, however, and did not involve the problem of circularity in *Mountford.*

F20.25 **Direction where s. 34 Applicable** In all cases where the CJPO 1994, s. 34, is to be relied upon, it is submitted that a clear judicial direction will be required as to the nature of the inference that may properly be drawn. Guidance as to the content of such a direction may be found in the *Crown Court Compendium* (July 2020), ch. 17-1. This is based on the judgment of Rix LJ in *Petkar* [2003] EWCA Crim 2668, [2004] 1 Cr App R 22 (270), which in its turn draws both on previous case law and the previously approved 'model' direction which was endorsed by the ECtHR in *Beckles v UK* (2003) 36 EHRR 13 (162). The key elements of the direction as they appear in the *Compendium* are:

(1) a reminder that the accused was cautioned that he or she did not have to say anything, and therefore had a right to say nothing, but was also warned that conclusions might be drawn from failure to mention facts later relied on;
(2) (a) the identification in consultation with the advocates of the facts which were not mentioned but are now relied on in defence together with;
(b) any reasons given for the failure to mention those facts; and
(c) the conclusions it is suggested might be drawn (usually that the fact has been made up after interview and is not true);
(3) an instruction to consider whether the prosecution case as it stood at the time of the interview clearly called for an answer, and if it did, to consider whether, taking account of any explanation given by the accused, there was no sensible explanation for the failure other than that the accused had no answer at the time or none that would stand up to scrutiny.
4) an instruction only to draw an adverse conclusion if it is 'fair and proper' to do so, and in any case not to convict the accused wholly or mainly on the strength of it.

In magistrates' courts, *T v DPP* [2007] EWHC 1793 (Admin) offers a simple, three-stage test when applying s. 34 (at [26]):

(1) Has the defendant relied in his defence on a fact which he could reasonably have been expected to mention in his interview, but did not? If so, what is it?
(2) What is his explanation for not having mentioned it?
(3) If that explanation is not a reasonable one, is the proper inference to be drawn that he is guilty?

The test provides a useful reminder to the parties to summary proceedings to be clear about identifying the facts on which the inference is said to be based (*North Hertfordshire District Council v Williams* [2017] EWHC 2529 (Admin)).

Where prosecution counsel had not sought to rely upon s. 34, and had not raised the matter with the accused in cross-examination, the Court of Appeal in *Khan* [1999] 2 Arch News 2 rightly 'deprecated' the decision of the trial judge to direct the jury that they might draw an inference under s. 34 without having raised the matter with counsel. It was held, however, that (as there would have been no basis upon which the judge could have been deterred from giving the direction had the matter been argued) D had suffered no disadvantage. It is submitted that this is a dangerous approach. A trial judge ought not, in fairness, to leave it open to the jury to make use of silence which, because the defence did not expect to have to explain it away, has not been the subject of any comment by the accused or the defence witnesses. If the judge thinks that s. 34 might come into play, the matter should be raised in time for it to be the subject of evidence not speculation. If, on the other hand, there has been no discussion with counsel of the intended direction in circumstances where it is clear to the defence that the prosecution are relying on the accused's failure to mention a specific fact, it is unlikely that the omission will render the trial unfair (*Barnes* (4 July 2003 unreported)). In *Brooks* [2004] EWCA Crim 3021, the direction had been discussed with counsel, who were left with the impression that no direction of the kind that was in due course given would be used. The importance of following and adapting the current approved direction is frequently mentioned in connection with s. 34, and although it need not be slavishly adhered to in every case (*Salami* [2003] EWCA Crim 3831) it affords particularly useful guidance in this difficult area, provided always that it is tailored to fit the facts of the case.

A direction may be called for where there is more than one accused. If A has failed to mention a relevant fact so as to attract a s. 34 direction, it is desirable in the case of co-accused B whose case stands or falls with A's to give a direction not to draw any inference against B. Where more than one accused attracts a s. 34 direction, the judge should avoid dealing with their cases compendiously but should identify what each has said at trial that might have been said earlier (*Miah* [2009] EWCA Crim 2368).

Relationship with *Lucas* Direction on Lies A direction may also be called for in relation to something said by the accused which the prosecution claim both conceals a fact later relied on and constitutes a positive lie. In such a case the facts may require that both a s. 34 direction and a *Lucas* direction (see **F1.25**) should be given; see *Turner* [2003] EWCA Crim 3108, [2004] 1 All ER 1025, and *RG* [2015] EWCA Crim 715, where it was noted that, while some judges might not have given the dual direction, the judge had canvassed his intention to do so with counsel who had not objected. In *Hackett* [2011] EWCA Crim 380, [2011] 2 Cr App R 3 (35), the Court of Appeal observed that it is usually unhelpful to give both directions; the judge should select and if necessary adapt the direction more appropriate to the facts and issues in the case, following observations in *Rana* [2007] EWCA Crim 2261. In *Hackett*, the issue as to whether D had lied was a subsidiary question: the key issue was whether the explanation he had given at trial was a late invention, it not having been mentioned at interview. A s. 34 direction was called for, but once the jury, following that direction, had concluded that the explanation was false, there was no need for what is in essence the protection of a *Lucas* direction, the function of which is to point out that there might be an innocent reason for lying. The protective nature of the *Lucas* direction was cited in *Spottiswood* [2019] EWCA Crim 949 as a reason for giving the directions in combination where the lie and the failure to mention facts raised slightly different, albeit interrelated, issues for the jury. The Court endorsed the approach in *Rana* and the combined directions in the *Crown Court Compendium* (July 2020), ch. 16-3. Where separate directions are given, it is important that they should be consistent (*Stanislas* [2004] EWCA Crim 2266). In *Taskaya* [2017] EWCA Crim 632, the Court of Appeal accepted, without encouraging the practice, that a trial judge might give both directions provided that each direction guarded against impermissible inferences. It is always of assistance to prepare a draft direction and discuss it with counsel. **F20.26**

As to the circumstances in which a conviction may be safe notwithstanding the significant misdirection of a jury under s. 34, see *Boyle* [2006] EWCA Crim 2101 and *Lowe* [2007] EWCA Crim 833. In *Adetoro v UK* [2010] ECHR 609, the failure of the judge to direct the jury that they should specifically reject D's reason for silence before drawing an inference was not fatal to the fairness of the trial where the jury must, in rejecting D's defence, have also rejected his reason for remaining silent.

As to the 'unfair' use of silence, see **F20.40**.

Direction where s. 34 Not Applicable to Accused's Silence Where the judge concludes that the requirements of the CJPO 1994, s. 34, have not been met, but the jury have been made aware of the accused's failure to answer questions, it was held in *McGarry* [1999] 1 Cr App R 377 that a direction should be given to the jury that they should not hold the silence against the accused. If that were not done, the jury would be left in 'no-man's land' between **F20.27**

the common-law rule and the statutory exception, without any guidance as to how to regard the accused's silence. This was qualified in *La Rose* [2003] EWCA Crim 1471, where it was held that the omission of the so-called 'counterweight' direction was not fatal where D had never given any explanation for his conduct and had declined to give evidence at trial, thus attracting a s. 35 direction (see **F20.42**). The *McGarry* direction may also be problematic in that it may do harm by drawing attention to the accused's failure to answer questions, so that the failure to give the direction may be a benefit (*Thomas* [2002] EWCA Crim 1308; *Jama* [2008] EWCA Crim 2861).

OUT-OF-COURT SILENCE AT COMMON LAW

Accused and Accuser on 'even terms'

F20.28 The conduct of the accused when accused of a crime by a person on an equal footing may form the basis of an inference that the accusation is accepted (see **F18.99**). In the authorities that follow, it was the silence of the accused which was relied upon as the basis for such an inference. The CJPO 1994, s. 34(5) (see **F20.4**), makes it clear that insofar as these authorities permit inferences to be drawn they remain good law. Even if none of the statutory inferences is in play, therefore, the trial judge needs to have the possibility of a common-law inference in mind before resorting to the standard direction (in accordance with *McGarry* [1999] 3 All ER 805: see **F20.27**) that no inference should be drawn.

F20.29 In *Norton* [1910] 2 KB 496, it was accepted that the silence of the accused 'on an occasion which demanded an answer' might be conduct from which an inference of acknowledgement might be drawn. In *Mitchell* (1892) 17 Cox CC 503, Cave J described more fully the circumstances in which silence in the face of an accusation might be tantamount to an admission of guilt. He said (at p. 508):

> Now the whole admissibility of statements of this kind rests upon the consideration that if a charge is made against a person in that person's presence it is reasonable to expect that he or she will immediately deny it, and that the absence of such a denial is some evidence of an admission on the part of the person charged, and of the truth of the charge. Undoubtedly, when persons are speaking on even terms, and a charge is made, and the person charged says nothing, and expresses no indignation, and does nothing to repel the charge, that is some evidence to show that he admits the charge to be true.

It follows that silence does not constitute an acknowledgement of guilt if the circumstances are such that a reasonable person would not be expected to counter the allegation. In *Mitchell* the accusation was made by a woman on her deathbed. D and her solicitor were present to hear the statement, which was recorded by a magistrate for use at D's trial for manslaughter. The statement proving to be otherwise inadmissible, the prosecution sought to admit the accusation as a statement made in D's presence. Cave J refused the application, holding that it would be 'monstrous' to say that, because D had not 'started up and denied' the charge, she must have accepted it. In all the circumstances, including the woman's condition, the formality of the proceedings, and the presence of a solicitor to represent D's interests, it was unreasonable to expect any response from D.

Mitchell was approved by the Privy Council in *Parkes v The Queen* [1976] 3 All ER 380. A girl was stabbed to death, and D was charged with her murder. The girl's mother gave evidence that, on finding her daughter injured, she immediately accused D, who made no reply. When she threatened to detain him until the police arrived, he tried to stab her. It was held that D's reactions to the accusations, including his silence, were matters to be taken into account by the jury in deciding whether D had committed the offence charged. It is not entirely clear whether the outcome would have been the same had silence alone been relied on as evidence of guilt, for the Board made a particular point of noting that D's reaction was 'not one of mere silence', but it is submitted that the difference is that mere silence might be entitled to less weight than silence coupled with positive conduct, depending on the circumstances.

Where silence may be attributable to a variety of factors it is for the jury to decide what inference to draw. In *Coll* [2005] EWCA Crim 3675, D was attending to the wounds of the dying victim when her co-accused allegedly made a remark suggesting that D should offer to be a witness 'so they can't tell we did it'. The failure of D to react adversely to the use of 'we' rather than 'I' (her defence being that the co-accused alone was responsible) was held to have been properly left to the jury, along with D's explanation that she was not listening properly and was in shock. See also *O* [2005] EWCA Crim 3082, where D's acquiescence while his friend gave a racial motive for an attack constituted an admission (see **F18.101**). **F20.30**

Accusations by or in the Presence of Police Officers

It is not clear whether the principles stated above apply to accusations by or in the presence of police officers. In *Hall v The Queen* [1971] 1 All ER 322 the Privy Council considered that, 'exceptional circumstances' apart, 'silence alone on being informed by a police officer that someone else has made an accusation against him cannot give rise to an inference that the person to whom this information is communicated accepts the truth of the accusation'. **F20.31**

The law stated in *Hall* must now be read subject to the CJPO 1994, ss. 34, 36 and 37 (see **F20.4** ***et seq.***). Silence in the face of the sort of questioning to which those provisions apply may clearly give rise to specific adverse inferences arising out of the failure to mention facts subsequently relied upon (s. 34) or to account for various matters including the possession of incriminating material and presence at the scene of an offence (ss. 36 and 37); the caution and warnings to be given to suspects makes this clear (PACE Code C, paras. 10.5 and 10.10 and annex C). **F20.32**

The decision in *Hall*, however, would seem still to be authority for the principle that a suspect, whether cautioned or not, should not be regarded as accepting the truth of a charge simply because it is not denied. In *Chandler* [1976] 3 All ER 105, however, the Court of Appeal expressed reservations about the correctness of the law as stated in *Hall*, regarding it as in conflict with the general rule laid down in *Christie* [1914] AC 545 (see **F18.99**), a criticism reiterated in *Raviraj* (1986) 85 Cr App R 93. *Chandler* does, however, accept two important limitations: an inference of acceptance cannot be drawn (a) where the parties are not on even terms and (b) where the suspect has been cautioned that there is no requirement to say anything. The former qualification is supported also by *Parkes v The Queen* [1976] 3 All ER 380 (see **F20.29**). In *Chandler* the presence of D's solicitor at interview was said to entail that the parties were on 'even terms'. *Chandler* was applied in *Horne* [1990] Crim LR 188, in which police officers brought about a confrontation between D and a man he was suspected of having wounded. The man, still bleeding from his wounds, accused D of having caused them, and D refrained from making any reply. As in *Chandler*, the jury were not given adequate direction on the matter, but it was accepted that there was no legal bar to the drawing of an inference of acceptance.

The principles stated above were held in *Collins* [2004] EWCA Crim 83, [2004] 1 WLR 1705 to be of equal application where a lie is told in the presence and hearing of the accused (in this instance by a co-accused) and the question is whether the accused, by remaining silent, has adopted the untrue statement as his own. On the facts of the case, where the lie was told in response to a question asked by a police officer and the parties were not on equal terms, there was no evidential basis for an inference other than that D's silence was an exercise by him of his right to silence. **F20.33**

It was accepted in *Chandler* that it was inappropriate to draw an inference after a caution was given in the old form 'You are not obliged to say anything'. Arguably, the reformulated caution and the warnings relating to the inferences which may be drawn under the 1994 Act will, because they put the accused on notice that specific inferences may be drawn, open the door to an argument that wider inferences are also possible, at least where the suspect's legal adviser is also present.

FAILURE TO ACCOUNT FOR OBJECTS, SUBSTANCES, MARKS AND PRESENCE

F20.34 **Criminal Justice and Public Order Act 1994, ss. 36 and 37**

36.—(1) Where—

(a) a person is arrested by a constable, and there is—

(i) on his person; or

(ii) in or on his clothing or footwear; or

(iii) otherwise in his possession; or

(iv) in any place in which he is at the time of his arrest,

any object, substance or mark, or there is any mark on any such object; and

(b) that or another constable investigating the case reasonably believes that the presence of the object, substance or mark may be attributable to the participation of the person arrested in the commission of an offence specified by the constable; and

(c) the constable informs the person arrested that he so believes, and requests him to account for the presence of the object, substance or mark; and

(d) the person fails or refuses to do so,

then if, in any proceedings against the person for the offence so specified, evidence of those matters is given, subsection (2) below applies.

(2) Where this subsection applies—

(a) [repealed];

(b) a judge, in deciding whether to grant an application made by the accused under paragraph 2 of schedule 3 to the Crime and Disorder Act 1998;

(c) the court, in determining whether there is a case to answer; and

(d) the court or jury, in determining whether the accused is guilty of the offence charged,

may draw such inferences from the failure or refusal as appear proper.

(3) Subsections (1) and (2) above apply to the condition of clothing or footwear as they apply to a substance or mark thereon.

(4) Subsections (1) and (2) above do not apply unless the accused was told in ordinary language by the constable when making the request mentioned in subsection (1)(c) above what the effect of this section would be if he failed or refused to comply with the request.

(4A) Where the accused was at an authorised place of detention at the time of the failure or refusal, subsections (1) and (2) do not apply if he had not been allowed an opportunity to consult a solicitor prior to the request being made.

(5) This section applies in relation to officers of customs and excise as it applies in relation to constables.

(6) This section does not preclude the drawing of any inference from a failure or refusal of the accused to account for the presence of an object, substance or mark or from the condition of clothing or footwear which could properly be drawn apart from this section.

(7) This section does not apply in relation to a failure or refusal which occurred before the commencement of this section.

37.—(1) Where—

(a) a person arrested by a constable was found by him at a place at or about the time the offence for which he was arrested is alleged to have been committed; and

(b) that or another constable investigating the offence reasonably believes that the presence of the person at that place and at that time may be attributable to his participation in the commission of the offence; and

(c) the constable informs the person that he so believes, and requests him to account for that presence; and

(d) the person fails or refuses to do so,

then if, in any proceedings against the person for the offence, evidence of those matters is given, subsection (2) below applies.

(2) Where this subsection applies—

(a) [repealed];

(b) a judge, in deciding whether to grant an application made by the accused under paragraph 2 *of schedule 3 to the Crime and Disorder* Act 1998;

(c) the court, in determining whether there is a case to answer; and

(d) the court or jury, in determining whether the accused is guilty of the offence charged,

may draw such inferences from the failure or refusal as appear proper.

(3) Subsections (1) and (2) do not apply unless the accused was told in ordinary language by the constable when making the request mentioned in subsection (1)(c) above what the effect of this section would be if he failed or refused to comply with the request.

(3A) Where the accused was at an authorised place of detention at the time of the failure or refusal, subsection (1) and (2) do not apply if he had not been allowed an opportunity to consult a solicitor prior to the request being made.

(4) This section applies in relation to officers of customs and excise as it applies in relation to constables.

(5) This section does not preclude the drawing of any inference from a failure or refusal of the accused to account for his presence at a place which could properly be drawn apart from this section.

(6) This section does not apply in relation to a failure or refusal which occurred before the commencement of this section.

An 'authorised place of detention' is defined by s. 38(2A) to include police stations and any other place prescribed by order. **F20.35**

Sections 36 and 37 are based on the Irish Criminal Justice Act 1984. They go further than s. 34, which relates to the weight to be given to D's defence, and amount to positive evidence to support the prosecution case.

Basis for Inference

Neither s. 36 nor s. 37 of the CJPO 1994 permits an inference to be drawn unless four conditions are satisfied: **F20.36**

(a) the accused is arrested;

(b) a constable (not necessarily the arresting officer) reasonably believes that the object, substance or mark, or the presence of the accused at the relevant place, may be attributable to the accused's participation in a crime (in s. 36 an offence 'specified by the constable'; in s. 37 the offence for which he was arrested);

(c) the constable informs the accused of his belief and requests an explanation of the matter in question;

(d) the constable tells the suspect in ordinary language the effect of a failure or refusal to comply with the request.

The four conditions may, on their face, be satisfied where an arrested person is confronted with incriminating circumstances before being taken to the police station for interview. However, a request for information under the two sections would appear to be a form of questioning, and because an arrested suspect should not normally be questioned about involvement in an offence except in interview at a police station or other authorised place of detention (PACE Code C, para. 11.1) the tendering in evidence of an unproductive request for information 'on the beat' should be the exception rather than the norm. If such a request is made and is alleged to have yielded a silence from which inferences can properly be drawn, the procedure for putting the silence to the suspect in a subsequent interview at the police station will apply (para. 11.4: see **F20.15**). The 'special warnings' to be given at interview in connection with ss. 36 and 37 are dealt with in PACE Code C, paras. 10.10 and 10.11.

As with s. 34 (see **F20.4**), only 'proper' inferences may be drawn. The jury must be satisfied that the accused has failed to 'account' for the relevant matter (*Compton* [2002] EWCA Crim 2835) and that any explanation advanced by the accused should be rejected as implausible before an inference can be said to be proper (see **F20.17**). Clearly the strength of the inference increases with the suspicious nature of the circumstances, so that if the accused is arrested when in possession of a car with explosive devices in full view on the back seat, failure to give an account is more suggestive of guilt than in the case of a refusal to account for a dirty mark on clothing following a fight. In some cases a strong inference is proper. In *Connolly* (10 June 1994 unreported), D had been given an opportunity to account for an incriminating receipt found in his pocket, and his presence near the scene of the crime, but had maintained complete silence. The Court of Appeal **F20.37** for Northern Ireland accepted the trial judge's inference, drawn under provisions equivalent to ss. 36 and 37, that D was determined to sit out interrogation, assess the strength of the case against him and, if charged, to present a version of his activities unembarrassed by any statements to which he might have committed himself during interview.

F20.38 Section 36 is concerned with the state of the suspect at the time of arrest. It does not matter how much time elapses between the incident and the arrest, provided the inference remains relevant. Thus, for example, in *McGeough* [2015] UKSC 62, [2015] 1 WLR 4612, D was identified as a gunman who had been shot in self-defence in the course of an attempted murder in 1981 by the scarring that the bullet wound had left on his body. His failure to account for the scarring was the subject of specific adverse inferences at his trial in 2010. Neither s. 36 nor s. 37 permits the drawing of inferences in respect of the state or location of the accused at times other than arrest, e.g., when seen by an eye-witness at the time of the crime, and s. 37 applies only when the accused was found at the location of the crime 'at or about the time of the commission of the alleged offence and not, for example, if a suspect gives the police the slip at the scene and is arrested elsewhere. If the intention is to build upon already suspicious circumstances by allowing an additional guilty inference if the accused fails to explain them, it is not clear why the provisions are so restrictive: a suspected rapist may have inferences drawn for failing to explain away stains on his trousers, but not for refusing to explain why he is not wearing any (unless he has discarded them nearby).

F20.39 Section 38(3) (see **F20.8**) provides that an inference drawn under these provisions may, *inter alia*, form part of the case to answer or contribute to a verdict of guilty, though neither outcome may be based 'solely' upon such an inference. It is not clear what this means. An inference drawn under ss. 36 and 37 can never exist 'solely', in the sense of independently of the proof of the suspicious circumstances for which the accused refuses to account. In some cases, such circumstances may be sufficient to convict, as in the case of a man arrested with two bombs on the back seat of his car. The fact that the accused gave no explanation cannot prevent the circumstances having this effect: on the contrary, it strengthens the inference to be drawn from them. Perhaps the intention behind the provision is to prompt the judge to tell the jury not to convict just because the accused has been unhelpful.

It is not clear how frequently these two provisions will function independently of ss. 34 and 35. If D goes on to present a defence relying on facts that could have been mentioned earlier, as in *Connolly*, it is likely that s. 34 will also apply. If D gives no evidence, then s. 35 (see **F20.42**) may come into play.

Unfair Use of Pre-trial Silence

F20.40 Failure or refusal to respond to questioning relevant to ss. 34, 36 and 37 seems unlikely to be regarded as a 'statement', and is thus incapable of being a confession within s. 82 of the PACE 1984 for the purposes of s. 76 of that Act (see **F18.8**). Silence obtained by oppression or in circumstances conducive to unreliability would not therefore be automatically inadmissible, as would a confession similarly obtained. It would, however, be subject to exclusion under the discretion conferred by the PACE 1984, s. 78, in respect of all prosecution evidence, to the extent that it would be unfair to make use of it.

Extensive use has also been made of s. 78 in rejecting confession evidence which, while admissible under s. 76, has been obtained in breach of the 1984 Act or Codes of Practice, or by other unfair means (see **F18.30**). These authorities would seem to apply also to silence, with the result that, for example, failure to make proper records of an interrogation may lead to exclusion.

FAILURE OF ACCUSED TO TESTIFY

F20.41 The CJPO 1994 repealed the Criminal Evidence Act 1898, s. 1(b). The 1898 Act provided that the failure of the accused to testify was not to be made the subject of any comment by the prosecution. Limited comment by the judge was permissible (*Bathurst* [1968] 2 QB 99), though stronger comment was permitted where the defence case involved the assertion of facts which were at variance with the prosecution evidence, or additional to it and within the accused's own knowledge (*Martinez-Tobon* [1994] 1 WLR 388).

Failure to Testify Following the 1994 Act

Under the CJPO 1994, s. 35, inferences from failure to testify are permissible. The *Crown Court Compendium* (July 2020), ch. 17-5, stresses that the nature of the inference available will depend on the way in which the evidence has developed and the strength of the prosecution case — the stronger the case the more powerful the incentive to provide an answer. The old authorities continue to provide a common-sense guide to the type of case in which the strongest inferences may be drawn (see further **F20.45** to **F20.52**). A careful direction will be required in all cases where the accused does not testify, in order to make the jury aware of the inferences which may properly be drawn, not least because of the need to comply with the 'fair trial' provisions of the ECHR, Article 6 (*Birchall* [1999] Crim LR 311). One of the purposes of the direction is to make the jury aware that the right to silence still exists in the sense that the accused is under no obligation to testify (*Cowan* [1996] QB 373). **F20.42**

Criminal Justice and Public Order Act 1994, s. 35

(1) At the trial of any person for an offence, subsections (2) and (3) below apply unless—
  (a) the accused's guilt is not in issue; or
  (b) it appears to the court that the physical or mental condition of the accused makes it undesirable for him to give evidence;

but subsection (2) below does not apply if, at the conclusion of the evidence for the prosecution, his legal representative informs the court that the accused will give evidence or, where he is unrepresented, the court ascertains from him that he will give evidence.

(2) Where this subsection applies, the court shall, at the conclusion of the evidence for the prosecution, satisfy itself (in the case of proceedings on indictment with a jury, in the presence of the jury) that the accused is aware that the stage has been reached at which evidence can be given for the defence and that he can, if he wishes, give evidence and that, if he chooses not to give evidence, or having been sworn, without good cause refuses to answer any question, it will be permissible for the court or jury to draw such inferences as appear proper from his failure to give evidence or his refusal, without good cause, to answer any question.

(3) Where this subsection applies, the court or jury, in determining whether the accused is guilty of the offence charged, may draw such inferences as appear proper from the failure of the accused to give evidence or his refusal, without good cause, to answer any question.

(4) This section does not render the accused compellable to give evidence on his own behalf, and he shall accordingly not be guilty of contempt of court by reason of a failure to do so.

(5) For the purposes of this section a person who, having been sworn, refuses to answer any question shall be taken to do so without good cause unless—
  (a) he is entitled to refuse to answer the question by virtue of any enactment, whenever passed or made, or on the ground of privilege; or
  (b) the court in the exercise of its general discretion excuses him from answering it.

(6) [Repealed.]

(7) This section applies—
  (a) in relation to proceedings on indictment for an offence, only if the person charged with the offence is arraigned on or after the commencement of this section;
  (b) in relation to proceedings in a magistrates' court, only if the time when the court begins to receive evidence in the proceedings falls after the commencement of this section.

Procedure CrimPD VI, paras. 26P.1 to 26P.5 (see Supplement, **CPD.26P**), provide detailed guidance on the procedure where the accused declines to give evidence. The court is obliged to satisfy itself that defendants who have not indicated that they intend to give evidence understand the consequences of declining to do so (s. 35(2) and (3) and CrimPD VI, paras. 26P.1 to 26P.5, **CPD.26P**). CrimPD VI, paras. 26P.2 and 26P.3, make clear that the burden of explaining the option to testify and the consequences of failing to do so to the defendant rests, in the case of a legally represented defendant, with the legal representative. **F20.43**

The court's obligation in s. 35(2) to satisfy itself that the accused knows of the entitlement to give evidence is mandatory and cannot be overlooked even where the accused has absconded (*Gough* [2001] EWCA Crim 2545, [2002] 2 Cr App R 8 (121)). In *Wright v The Queen* [2016] UKPC 18, the Privy Council, dealing with an identical provision, observed that the decision whether to give evidence is 'probably the most significant decision which a defendant has to make in the course of his criminal trial', and is therefore one which 'will almost invariably be the subject of close consideration by him in conjunction with his advisers'. Thus what matters, for the purposes of the requirement in s. 35(2) that the court should satisfy itself that the accused is aware of the possible consequences of a decision not to testify, is that the accused has had the necessary legal advice. The pre-trial process requires that at a PTPH the court is satisfied that the accused understands the right to give evidence (CrimPR 3.21; see Supplement, **R3.21**). It has long been the recommended practice, and is of great importance in light of s. 35, for counsel to record the decision of the accused not to give evidence, and to sign it and indicate that it was made voluntarily (see **D17.12** and *Bevan* (1994) 98 Cr App R 354 and *Chatroodi* [2001] EWCA Crim 585). The decision is frequently a stressful one for the accused, and where there is a potential issue as to the accused's capacity to make such a decision it is of particular importance that the necessary considerations are fully and properly spelled out (*Cox* [2013] EWCA Crim 1025). Where it is contended on appeal that the accused was misadvised, or was not in a position to make an informed decision, the appellant must provide the court with a statement setting out the relevant history (*Farooqi* [2013] EWCA Crim 1649, [2014] 1 Cr App R 8 (69)).

F20.44 **Charge of Causing or Allowing a Child or Vulnerable Adult to Die or Suffer Serious Physical Harm** The DVCVA 2004, ss. 6 and 6A, make special provision for the inferences to be drawn where a person fails to testify when charged with an offence under s. 5 of that Act (causing or allowing child or vulnerable adult to die or suffer serious physical harm: see **B1.77**).

Domestic Violence, Crime and Victims Act 2004, s. 6

(2) Where by virtue of section 35(3) of the Criminal Justice and Public Order Act 1994 a court or jury is permitted, in relation to the section 5 offence, to draw such inferences as appear proper from the defendant's failure to give evidence or refusal to answer a question, the court or jury may also draw such inferences in determining whether he is guilty—
(a) of murder or manslaughter, or
(b) of any other offence of which he could lawfully be convicted on the charge of murder or manslaughter,
even if there would otherwise be no case for him to answer in relation to that offence.

Section 6A makes similar provision in relation to inferences about relevant offences where the accused is charged with allowing a child or vulnerable adult to suffer serious physical harm.

Section 6(2) was considered in *Quinn* [2017] EWCA Crim 1071. D1 and D2 appealed against their convictions for murder. No verdicts were taken on alternative counts relating to the s. 5 offence, but the presence of those counts allowed for the drawing of an 'enhanced inference' on the murder count as a consequence of their failure to testify, even if there was at that stage no case to answer. The victim was a vulnerable adult, who had been violently assaulted and left to die in the house he shared with six adults including the two appellants. Rejecting an argument that the inclusion of the s. 5 charges was unfair, the Court of Appeal stated (at [73]) that s. 5 had been enacted 'specifically to deal with this kind of situation where members of a household conspire to create a wall of silence to hamper a proper investigation into a death'. It was clear that the appellants had at the very least ignored the ongoing threat of violence to V, and that they would have been aware of the serious injuries he suffered in the final assault, but nevertheless allowed him to die. See further **F20.49**.

'Proper' Inferences of Guilt

F20.45 Under the CJPO 1994, s. 35, the 'proper' inferences come about as a result of the failure of the accused to give evidence or refusal without good cause to answer any question (s. 35(3)).

Defendants whose 'physical or mental condition make it undesirable' for them to give evidence are excluded from the operation of the section, together with those whose 'guilt is not in issue' (s. 35(1)). By virtue of s. 35(5), the accused may be excused from answering a particular question on grounds of privilege or statutory entitlement, or in the discretion of the court. Subject to these exceptions, the accused must answer all proper questions or risk the drawing of inferences, and a judge may remind the accused of this duty, though not in an oppressive way (*Ackinclose* [1996] Crim LR 747).

An observation that the accused has, by failing to give evidence, deprived the jury of contradiction or explanation of prosecution evidence can only fairly be made if the uncontradicted evidence concerns a matter about which the accused can confidently be expected to have personal knowledge (*Hamidi* [2010] EWCA Crim 66). In some cases, the evidence of the accused is superfluous (e.g., where the only issue was as to whether agreed facts fell within the offence of keeping a disorderly house: *McManus* [2001] EWCA Crim 2455). In such a case a s. 35 direction is inappropriate and prejudicial.

Accused with Physical or Mental Limitations The right of a defendant to give evidence in his or her own defence is an essential aspect of a fair trial and 'a defendant who wishes to give evidence must be given a full and fair opportunity to do so' (*Welland* [2018] EWCA Crim 2036). A direction that no adverse inference should be drawn under s. 35 was not an adequate countermeasure where D's trial had continued despite his hospitalisation, denying him the right to testify. Section 35(1)(b) of the CJPO 1994 nevertheless contemplates that there will be cases where the accused's physical or mental condition make it 'undesirable' for the accused to give evidence, and in such cases no inference should be drawn. The provision was considered in *Friend* [1997] 2 All ER 1011. D was tried for murder. He had a physical age of 15, a mental age of nine, and an IQ of 63. Expert evidence suggested that, although not suggestible, his powers of comprehension were limited and he might find it difficult to do justice to himself in the witness box. Nevertheless D had given a clear account of his defence at various stages prior to trial. Taking all these matters into account, the trial judge ruled that D's mental condition did not make it 'undesirable' for him to give evidence, so that his failure to do so led to the jury being directed that they might draw inferences under s. 35(3). The Court of Appeal agreed, noting that it would only be in a rare case that the judge would be called upon to arrive at a decision under s. 35(1)(b): an accused who was unable to comprehend proceedings so as to make a proper defence would be unfit to plead, so the issue would not arise (but the requirement in *Walls* [2011] EWCA Crim 443, [2011] 2 Cr App R 6 (61) (see **F11.43**) of a rigorous examination of the evidence in fitness to plead cases might, according to *Dixon* [2013] EWCA Crim 465, [2013] 3 All ER 242, throw up more applications under s. 35(1)(b)). The decision in *Friend* may appear harsh, and indeed was later revisited on appeal on the basis of fresh medical evidence which demonstrated that D was suffering from ADHD and could not have done himself justice ([2004] EWCA Crim 2661), but this casts no doubt on the approach of the Court in the first appeal. In *Burnett* [2016] EWCA Crim 1941, an 87-year-old man whose long-term memory was impaired was tried for sexual offences alleged to have occurred 50 years previously. The Court of Appeal declined to hold that it was wrong to give a s. 35 direction, although other judges might have decided against it. There were matters which D appeared to recollect well enough to give an account of them in cross-examination, and the judge was clearly prepared to ensure that, had D given evidence, the process could have been conducted with due sensitivity to his condition. **F20.46**

Friend and *Burnett* both indicate that s. 35(1)(b) gives a wide discretion to a trial judge. The trial judge in *Friend* seems to have been much influenced by the fact that measures can be taken by which vulnerable defendants can, if their needs are correctly assessed, be protected from unfair or oppressive cross-examination. Thus, as the main reason for questioning the desirability of D testifying was that he might give a poor account of himself unless care were taken to ensure that he understood and had time to respond to questions, the fact that the court itself could respond sensitively to D's needs was a factor militating against the defence argument. Similar accommodation can be made for elderly witnesses such as in *Burnett*. The outcome suggests that the discretion will be exercised against the background of an assumption that it is generally desirable for an accused to testify, so that cases in which it can be said to be 'undesirable' will be rare indeed. The possibility of using an intermediary to overcome communication difficulties also weighs in the balance in favour of the giving of evidence (as in *Dixon*). See also *Biddle* [2019] EWCA Crim 86, although in that case the intermediary was not forthcoming despite the trial judge ruling that such assistance was necessary. The adverse inference direction was upheld because there was no causal link between the absence of the intermediary and the decision of D not to testify. In *O'Donnell v UK* (2015) 61 EHRR 37 (957), the ECtHR paid particular attention to the safeguards suggested by the judge to allow D, a man of limited intelligence, to give such evidence as he wished to do, and to control the questioning in a manner similar to that adopted where young children testify. D having declined to testify, the judge had fairly left the question of whether adverse inferences should be drawn to the jury.

In the rare case where the physical or mental condition of the accused makes it inappropriate to draw adverse inferences, the jury should be specifically directed to this effect (*Crown Court Compendium* (July 2020), ch. 17-5). One such rare case was *Hamberger* [2017] EWCA Crim 273, [2017] 2 Cr App R 9 (81), in which D, who suffered from angina, was fit to be tried but not to testify, and it was agreed that no adverse inferences should be drawn. (As to the use of D's hearsay statements for the defence in such a situation see **F17.13**.)

F20.47 In *Tabbakh* [2009] EWCA Crim 464, the trial judge was held entitled to conclude that D's history of self-harm and post-traumatic stress disorder did not render it undesirable for him to give evidence: the risk that he might react in a hostile way to questioning and lose his self-control was one which could be taken into account by the jury, and did not justify a comprehensive failure to testify. In *Ensor* [2009] EWCA Crim 2519, [2010] 1 Cr App R 18 (255), it was held that s. 35(1)(b) requires that the accused's physical or mental condition is such that if he gives evidence it will have a 'significantly adverse effect on him'. However, in *Dixon* it was pointed out that the sole issue in *Ensor* related to the adverse effect on D's health, and that there was no warrant for confining s. 35(1)(b) to such cases. In *Dixon* it was held relevant to consider D's difficulty in expressing himself and his problems of understanding, which were such that the judge had made an intermediary available to assist him had he testified. Nevertheless these features did not, properly considered, require the judge to find that it was undesirable for D to testify. In *Charisma* [2009] EWCA Crim 2345, an alleged loss of memory of the incident did not amount to a justification for not giving evidence in which the memory loss could have been tested. In *Mulindwa* [2017] EWCA Crim 416, [2017] 4 WLR 157, the Court of Appeal rejected an argument that it was necessarily 'undesirable' for a defendant with an ongoing mental disorder to give evidence if the only way in which this could fairly be done would be if the evidence were accompanied by expert evidence explaining to the jury why some of the accused's testimony might be unreliable. As to the extent to which a psychiatrist or a psychologist can properly comment to the jury on the presentation in evidence of a mentally disordered defendant, see **F7.63** and **F11.22**.

Both *Friend* and the later decision in *A* [1997] Crim LR 883 require there to be an evidential basis for a ruling that s. 35(1)(b) applies. A *voir dire* may be required to determine the issue, although the judge is, according to *A*, under no obligation to initiate the procedure if defence counsel does not seek to do so. In *R (DPP) v Kavanagh* [2005] EWHC 820 (Admin), it was doubted whether, even in summary trial, non-expert evidence (such as that of a family member) as to the mental condition of the accused could be sufficient. In that case D's mother had testified to his history of depression, but even her evidence taken at its highest fell short of disclosing a subsisting condition making it undesirable for him to give evidence. In *Anwoir* [2008] EWCA Crim 1354, [2008] 2 Cr App R 36 (532), it was held that a judge could revisit a ruling that it was undesirable for an accused to testify. However, it was on the facts of that case unfair for the medical evidence relied on by D and rejected by the judge to be withheld from the jury, as it was essential to their assessment of the extent to which they should take into account his failure to give evidence.

Nature of Inference under s. 35 The adverse inference which it may be proper to draw under s. 35(3) of the CJPO 1994 is that the accused 'is guilty of the offence charged'. As s. 35 does not come into play until after the close of the evidence for the prosecution, it presupposes that a prima facie case has already been established against the accused. In *Murray v DPP* [1994] 1 WLR 1, a decision concerning the equivalent provision in the Criminal Evidence (Northern Ireland) Order 1988 (SI 1988 No. 1987, N.I. 20), D was convicted of attempted murder and possession of a firearm with intent to endanger life. Scientific evidence linked D with a car used in the attack: the situation was one calling for 'confession and avoidance'. D advanced various explanations during interrogation, but gave no evidence at trial, from which failure the trial judge drew a strong adverse inference. The House of Lords considered that the inference was justified. The accused is not compellable to testify, but must risk the consequences if he or she does not do so. These consequences are not simply that specific inferences may be drawn from specific facts, but include in a proper case the inference that the accused is guilty. As to what is proper, Lord Slynn said (at p. 11): **F20.48**

> If there is no prima facie case shown by the prosecution there is no case to answer. Equally, if parts of the prosecution case had so little evidential value that they called for no answer, a failure to deal with those specific matters cannot justify an inference of guilt.
>
> On the other hand, if aspects of the evidence taken alone or in combination with other facts clearly call for an explanation which the accused ought to be in a position to give, if an explanation exists, then a failure to give any explanation may as a matter of common sense allow the drawing of an inference that there is no explanation and that the accused is guilty.

No Conviction Solely on Inference from s. 35 As with ss. 34, 36 and 37 of the CJPO 1994, the accused cannot be convicted solely on an inference drawn from a failure or refusal (s. 38(3): see **F20.8**). In *Cowan* [1996] QB 373, the Court of Appeal emphasised that the prosecution remain under an obligation to establish a prima facie case before any question of the accused testifying is raised. Their lordships took this to mean not only that the case should be fit to be left to the jury, but also that the judge should make clear to the jury that *they* must be convinced of the existence of a prima facie case before drawing an adverse inference from silence. This may seem to go beyond the strict requirement of the statute, but serves to ensure conformity with the principle in *Murray v UK* (1996) 22 EHRR 29 that the accused should not be convicted 'solely or mainly' on an inference from silence (*Birchall* [1999] Crim LR 311: see also **F20.9**). In a case where there is a compelling case for the accused to answer it has been held that the failure to direct in accordance with this aspect of *Cowan* could not affect the safety of the conviction (*Bromfield* [2002] EWCA Crim 195). In *Whitehead* [2006] EWCA Crim 1486, where the case for the prosecution in a sexual offence depended on the credibility of a complainant who had delayed making a complaint for more than ten years, the CCRC referred the case to the Court of Appeal on the basis that the omission to direct the jury that they should first find a case to answer might have led to them using the accused's failure to testify to 'shore up' the deficiencies in the complainant's evidence. The Court of Appeal dismissed this possibility as 'fanciful' in light of the very clear directions that had been given to the jury that they had to be 'sure' the complainant was not lying, and that the accused's silence was not by itself proof of guilt. The Court considered that the direction to the jury to find a prima facie case before considering the implications of the accused's silence 'amplifies and spells out' what is already implicit in the separate injunction that failure to give evidence cannot by itself prove guilt. See also *Hobson* [2013] EWCA Crim 819, [2013] 1 WLR 3733, in which a specific comment by the trial judge might, taken in isolation, have led the jury to think that they should consider the inference to be drawn from D's failure to give evidence before deciding whether he had a case to answer. Read as a whole, however, the direction would not have created this false impression. **F20.49**

The power to draw an inference under the DVCVA 2004, s. 6(2) or s. 6A(2) (see **F20.44**), was considered in *Quinn* [2017] EWCA Crim 1071, in which the trial judge commented not only on the failure of the accused to testify but also on their failure to give any account when interviewed of the events leading to the death of V following an assault in the home they shared, saying (at [61]) 'they do not have to but you may think they could and chose not to and you have every right to ask why'. The comments were held to be 'reasonable' in the circumstances, or at least not 'unduly prejudicial'. The comments appear to go beyond what is sanctioned by s. 6(2) which applies to the failure to 'give evidence or refusal to answer a question'.

F20.50 **Drawing an Inference: General Rule** In *Cowan* [1996] QB 373, the Court of Appeal rejected an argument that s. 35 should be permitted to operate in exceptional cases only. The plain wording of s. 35 indicated that it was not limited to exceptional cases: on the contrary, the exceptional cases were those dealt with in s. 35(1), in which the provisions were *not* to be invoked. However, it was open to a court in any case to which the exceptions in s. 35(1) did not apply to decline to draw an inference from silence, though for a judge to advise a jury against drawing such an inference would require either 'some evidential basis for doing so or some exceptional factors in the case making that a fair course to take'. An inference cannot be drawn unless the jury decide that the silence 'can only sensibly be attributed' to the accused having no answer, or none that would stand up to cross-examination. Thus, for example, in cases where the accused suffers from a condition that falls short of one making it 'undesirable' for the accused to give evidence under s. 35(1)(b) (see **F20.46** ***et seq.***), it is open to a jury to conclude that the reason for not testifying relates to the condition rather than to the accused having no answer (*Burnett* [2016] EWCA Crim 1941, in which the medical evidence had been fully canvassed before the jury).

In *Winston* [2015] EWCA Crim 524, the Court of Appeal restated the importance of following the *Cowan* direction, currently set out in the *Crown Court Compendium* (July 2020), ch. 17-5, so as not to leave the jury with the impression that an inference could be drawn in any other case, such as where the accused's testimony would merely have been 'of assistance' to them.

Cowan was applied in *Napper* (1997) 161 JP 16. D claimed that the failure of the police to interview him while the frauds with which he was charged were reasonably fresh in his mind should have led the judge to direct the jury to draw no adverse inferences from his silence at trial. It was held that this was not, under *Cowan*, an exceptional case where such a direction would have been justified in the interests of justice. Nothing prevented D from making his own record from which to refresh his memory, and the crucial issues were in any case sufficiently memorable to present him with no difficulty of recollection. The House of Lords in *Becouarn* [2005] UKHL 55, [2005] 1 WLR 2589, endorsed the practice of giving a s. 35 direction notwithstanding that D had made a tactical decision not to testify in order to keep his bad character from being revealed. Under s. 101(1)(g) (see **F13.84**), the bad character of an accused who has attacked another person's character may be revealed to the jury whether the accused testifies or not, so the dilemma in *Becouarn* no longer obtains.

It is not a valid argument that the accused fears that giving evidence will result in an application to adduce evidence of bad character. Even if the prosecutor is unwilling to clarify the position, it cannot be said that the accused is thereby put under unfair pressure not to testify (*Karrar* [2015] EWCA Crim 850).

F20.51 **No Inference where Prosecution Case is Weak** It seems from the observations of Lord Slynn in *Murray v DPP* [1994] 1 WLR 1 (see **F20.48**) that inferences of guilt should not be drawn from failure to give evidence to contradict a prosecution case of 'little evidential value'. This accords with the position at common law, where it was considered improper for a judge to bolster a weak prosecution case by making comments on an accused's failure to give evidence (*Waugh v The King* [1950] AC 203). However in *RS v DPP* [2013] EWHC 322 (Admin), the Divisional Court rejected an argument that no inferences should be drawn from the failure of a child to testify in a case of robbery of a mobile phone that depended on the correctness of an identification substantially based on hearsay evidence. It was held that, once it had been decided that there was a case to answer, the failure of D to give evidence about relevant matters in his police interview (in the absence of evidence of a reason for his silence) made the drawing of an inference permissible. Lord Slynn's comments in *Murray* were cited in argument but appear not to have affected the outcome.

Strong Inference where Facts Clearly Call for Explanation or are within the Accused's Knowledge In *Mutch* [1973] 1 All ER 178, the Court of Appeal identified exceptional cases at common law in which stronger comment was justified. They were those in which an inference could be drawn from uncontested or clearly established facts which point so strongly to guilt as to call for an explanation. *Corrie* (1904) 20 TLR 365 and *Bernard* (1908) 1 Cr App R 218 are cited in *Mutch* as exceptional examples of the kind of case in which such an inference may properly be drawn. So also is *Brigden* [1973] Crim LR 579. D gave no evidence, but alleged that the police had planted incriminating evidence on him and cross-examined a prosecution witness on a conviction. It is submitted that such a case would support a strong inference under the CJPO 1994 that the defence was untrue. The same may be said of other cases concerning facts within the accused's own knowledge which were said to justify strong comment at common law in *Martinez-Tobon* [1994] 1 WLR 388 (see **F20.42**). **F20.52**

Burden on Accused

A different form of comment was required at common law in cases in which the accused bears the burden of proof, namely 'that he is not bound to go into the witness box, nobody can force him to go into the witness box, but the burden is upon him, and if he does not, he runs the risk of not being able to prove his case' (*Bathurst* [1968] 2 QB 99: see **F20.41**). The same situation under the CJPO 1994 would seem to justify a strong adverse inference if the defence is one which, if true, could be proved by the accused's own evidence (e.g., that possession of an offensive weapon was lawful: Prevention of Crime Act 1953, s. 1(1), see **B12.144**). **F20.53**

Where diminished responsibility is set up by way of defence, and there are matters about which the accused could give evidence which are relevant to the issue before the jury, inferences may be drawn in the usual way unless the condition of the accused is such as to make it undesirable for him or her to give evidence within the meaning of s. 35(1)(b) (see **F20.46**). Comments in *Bathurst* [1968] 2 QB 99 that only rarely could an inference be drawn provide no authority for any wider exemption from inferences in such a case (*Barry* [2010] EWCA Crim 195, [2010] 2 All ER 1004). In some cases, the defence requires no contribution from the accused, in which case no inference can properly be drawn (see **F20.45**).

ACCUSED FAILING TO PROVIDE SAMPLES ETC.

At common law, an adverse inference could be drawn from unhelpful conduct other than silence while under interrogation. In *Smith* (1985) 81 Cr App R 286, D was asked in the presence of his solicitor if he was willing to provide a sample of hair. When he asked why, D was told that it was for comparison with hairs found at the scene of the robbery of which he was suspected. He replied 'In that case, no I am not'. It was held that the fact that, at that time, such samples could not lawfully be taken without D's consent did not mean that no inferences could be drawn from his refusal. Leonard J considered that it would be 'contrary to good sense' to prohibit the drawing of inferences and that the case was 'in a wholly different category' from evidence of a failure to answer questions under caution. Nevertheless the Court borrowed from the rules regarding silence when it stressed the fact that the presence of D's solicitor rendered the parties 'on even terms' (see **F20.28**). (See also *McVeigh v Beattie* [1988] Fam 69, in which it was held that the refusal of the respondent in affiliation proceedings to submit to a blood test which might have **F20.54** excluded the possibility that he had fathered the child in question could, in the absence of a reasonable explanation, amount to corroboration of the evidence of the complainant.)

The police have wide powers to take biometric samples and impressions, and also footwear impressions, both with and without consent (although 'intimate' samples can only be taken with consent) (see generally **D1.104** *et seq.* and the PACE 1984, ss. 61 to 63A). The rule in *Smith* has found statutory expression in s. 62(10), which permits 'such inferences as appear proper' to be drawn 'where the appropriate consent to the taking of an intimate sample from a person was refused without good cause' in a variety of circumstances including the determination of whether the person is guilty of the offence charged.

FAILURE TO CALL WITNESSES OR PROVIDE EVIDENCE

F20.55 If the accused fails to call a particular person as a witness, then, if appropriate, as when the prosecution had no possible means of knowing that that person had any relevant evidence to give until the accused gave evidence at the trial, the judge may direct the jury that they may take into account the fact that the potential witness was not called, but should exercise a degree of care. In particular the judge should avoid the suggestion that the failure is something of importance where there may be a valid reason for not calling the witness (Megaw LJ in *Gallagher* [1974] 3 All ER 118, affirmed in *Couzens* [1992] Crim LR 822). Comment may also be justified if there is a very strong case for suggesting that an account which an accused is giving has recently been fabricated and where, if it has not, there would be another witness or other witnesses of any description who could substantiate the accused's story if it were true (*Wilmot* (1988) 89 Cr App R 341 per Glidewell LJ at p. 352). However, comment in this area has to be made with circumspection and reserve (*Weller* [1994] Crim LR 856). In *Weller*, the Court of Appeal held that it could not envisage any case in which it would be appropriate to make a comment to the effect that if there were any truth in the accused's story, a particular witness would have been called. In the somewhat extreme case of *Forsyth* [1997] 2 Cr App R 299, the witness, J, was not one whom the defence might have been expected to call in the light of the issues raised by prosecution or defence at trial, but his absence was the subject of comment by prosecuting counsel in his closing address, and the jury subsequently asked the judge for guidance. It was held that the judge should have made it clear to the jury that they should draw no inference from the absence of J, and that they should decide the case on the evidence and without speculating on what J might have said. See also *Wright* [2000] Crim LR 510, where it was said that comments on the failure to call a particular witness may amount to a reversal of the burden of proof, and *Rodenhurst* [2001] EWCA Crim 1508, where the court approved the trial judge's warning that 'the danger of speculating about a witness's absence is precisely that you may impute some motive that may be entirely wrong'.

Comment on Failure of Spouse or Civil Partner of Accused to Testify

F20.56 The failure of the spouse or civil partner of the accused to give evidence shall not be made the subject of any comment by the prosecution (PACE 1984, s. 80A). In *Brown* [1983] Crim LR 38, it was held with respect to the forerunner of s. 80A that the wording was mandatory, and that breach of the prohibition would amount to a material irregularity in the course of the trial. However, whether a breach would lead to a conviction being quashed depended upon all the circumstances, and in particular whether the trial judge corrected the breach when summing up. In *Dickman* (1910) 5 Cr App R 135, in which counsel inadvertently commented upon the failure of the spouse of the accused to testify but the jury were told to dismiss the comment from their minds, the appeal against conviction was dismissed. Likewise in *Hunter* [1969] Crim LR 262, where a comment was made in breach of the prohibition but the judge, refusing to discharge the jury, warned them about the comment, the conviction was upheld. These cases may be contrasted with *Naudeer* [1984] 3 All ER 1036, where at D's trial for theft, counsel for the prosecution suggested that the failure of D's wife to give evidence had deprived the jury of what would probably have been material evidence, and the judge failed in his summing-up to give any direction to repair the breach of the prohibition on such comment. The Court of Appeal quashed the conviction on the grounds that the breach was central to the overall justice of the case, particularly since D was a man of good character (which he had put before the jury), and the question of his bona fides was central to the offence itself. It was the duty of the judge, depending upon the circumstances of each case, to remedy any breach of the prohibition on such comment in the summing-up.

Section 80A of the PACE 1984 does not prevent comment by the judge on the failure of the spouse or civil partner of the accused to testify. In *Naudeer*, Purchas LJ said (at p. 1039) that 'if a judge in the exercise of his discretion decides to comment upon the failure of the accused to call his spouse or to give evidence himself he must, except in exceptional circumstances, do this with a great deal of circumspection'. The same degree of circumspection would also appear to be required in the case of failure to call cohabitees, who are not covered by s. 80A (*Weller* [1994] Crim LR 856). In *Whitton* [1998] Crim LR 492, prosecuting counsel commented on the failure of D's husband, who had been present when she allegedly assaulted a neighbour, to give evidence. This clear breach was, however, held to have been subsumed in the summing-up in which the trial judge quite properly elected to make a comment of his own. It was not possible in the circumstances to argue that counsel's comment undermined the safety of D's conviction, though this should clearly not be read as an invitation to counsel to disregard the statutory provision, however strong the case for judicial comment. See also *Marsh* [2008] EWCA Crim 1816, where the comment went uncorrected by the judge, but the conviction was not rendered unsafe. **F20.57**

Appendix 1 Codes of Practice under the Police and Criminal Evidence Act 1984

PACE CODE A

REVISED CODE OF PRACTICE FOR THE EXERCISE BY:

POLICE OFFICERS OF STATUTORY POWERS OF STOP AND SEARCH

POLICE OFFICERS AND POLICE STAFF OF REQUIREMENTS TO RECORD PUBLIC ENCOUNTERS

Commencement—Transitional Arrangements

This code applies to any search by a police officer and the recording of public encounters taking place after 00.00 on 19 March 2015.

1.0 General

1.01 This code of practice must be readily available at all police stations for consultation by police officers, police staff, detained persons and members of the public.

1.02 The notes for guidance included are not provisions of this code, but are guidance to police officers and others about its application and interpretation. Provisions in the annexes to the code are provisions of this code.

1.03 This code governs the exercise by police officers of statutory powers to search a person or a vehicle without first making an arrest. The main stop and search powers to which this code applies are set out in Annex A, but that list should not be regarded as definitive (see *Note 1*). In addition, it covers requirements on police officers and police staff to record encounters not governed by statutory powers (see *paragraphs 2.11* and *4.12*). This code does not apply to:

(a) the powers of stop and search under:

(i) the Aviation Security Act 1982, section 27(2), and

(ii) the Police and Criminal Evidence Act 1984, section 6(1) (which relates specifically to powers of constables employed by statutory undertakers on the premises of the statutory undertakers);

(b) searches carried out for the purposes of examination under Schedule 7 to the Terrorism Act 2000 and to which the Code of Practice issued under paragraph 6 of Schedule 14 to the Terrorism Act 2000 applies.

(c) the powers to search persons and vehicles and to stop and search in specified locations to which the Code of Practice issued under section 47AB of the Terrorism Act 2000 applies.

1 Principles governing stop and search

1.1 Powers to stop and search must be used fairly, responsibly, with respect for people being searched and without unlawful discrimination. Under the Equality Act 2010, section 149, when police officers are carrying out their functions, they also have a duty to have due regard to the need to eliminate unlawful discrimination, harassment and victimisation, to advance equality of opportunity between people who share a relevant protected characteristic and people who do not share it, and to take steps to foster good relations between those persons. (See *Notes 1* and *1A*.) The Children Act 2004, section 11, also requires chief police officers and other specified persons and bodies to ensure that in the discharge of their functions they have regard to the need to safeguard and promote the welfare of all persons under the age of 18.

1.2 The intrusion on the liberty of the person stopped or searched must be brief and detention for the purposes of a search must take place at or near the location of the stop.

1.3 If these fundamental principles are not observed the use of powers to stop and search may be drawn into question. Failure to use the powers in the proper manner reduces their effectiveness. Stop and search can play an important role in the detection and prevention of crime, and using the powers fairly makes them more effective.

1.4 The primary purpose of stop and search powers is to enable officers to allay or confirm suspicions about individuals without exercising their power of arrest. Officers may be required to justify the use or authorisation of such powers, in relation both to individual searches and the overall pattern of their activity in this regard, to their supervisory officers or in court. Any misuse of the powers is likely to be harmful to policing and lead to mistrust of the police. Officers must also be able to explain their actions to the member of the public searched. The misuse of these powers can lead to disciplinary action (see *paragraphs 5.5* and *5.6*).

1.5 An officer must not search a person, even with his or her consent, where no power to search is applicable. Even where a person is prepared to submit to a search voluntarily, the person must not be searched unless the necessary legal power exists, and the search must be in accordance with the relevant power and the provisions of this Code. The only exception, where an officer does not require a specific power, applies to searches of persons entering sports grounds or other premises carried out with their consent given as a condition of entry.

1.6 Evidence obtained from a search to which this Code applies may be open to challenge if the provisions of this Code are not observed.

2 Types of stop and search powers

2.1 This code applies, subject to paragraph 1.03, to powers of stop and search as follows:

(a) powers which require reasonable grounds for suspicion, before they may be exercised; that articles unlawfully obtained or possessed are being carried such as section 1 of PACE for stolen and prohibited articles and section 23 of the Misuse of Drugs Act 1971 for controlled drugs;

(b) authorised under section 60 of the Criminal Justice and Public Order Act 1994, based upon a reasonable belief that incidents involving serious violence may take place or that people are carrying dangerous instruments or offensive weapons within any locality in the police area, or that it is expedient to use the powers to find such instruments or weapons that have been used in incidents of serious violence;

(c) *Not used.*

(d) the powers in Schedule 5 to the Terrorism Prevention and Investigation Measures (TPIM) Act 2011 to search an individual who has not been arrested, conferred by:

(i) paragraph 6(2)(a) at the time of serving a TPIM notice;

(ii) paragraph 8(2)(a) under a search warrant for compliance purposes; and

(iii) paragraph 10 for public safety purposes.

See *paragraph 2.18A*.

(e) powers to search a person who has not been arrested in the exercise of a power to search premises (see Code B *paragraph 2.4*).

(a) Stop and search powers requiring reasonable grounds for suspicion — explanation

General

2.2 Reasonable grounds for suspicion is the legal test which a police officer must satisfy before they can stop and detain individuals or vehicles to search them under powers such as section 1 of PACE (to find stolen or prohibited articles) and section 23 of the Misuse of Drugs Act 1971 (to find controlled drugs). This test must be applied to the particular circumstances in each case and is in two parts:

(i) *Firstly*, the officer must have formed a genuine suspicion in their own mind that they will find the object for which the search power being exercised allows them to search (see *Annex A*, second column, for examples); and

(ii) *Secondly*, the suspicion that the object will be found must be reasonable. This means that there must be an objective basis for that suspicion based on facts, information and/or intelligence which are relevant to the likelihood that the object in question will be found, so that a reasonable person would be entitled to reach the same conclusion based on the same facts and information and/or intelligence.

Officers must therefore be able to explain the basis for their suspicion by reference to intelligence or information about, or some specific behaviour by, the person concerned (see *paragraphs 3.8(d)*, *4.6* and *5.5*).

2.2A The exercise of these stop and search powers depends on the likelihood that the person searched is in possession of an item for which they may be searched; it does not depend on the person concerned being suspected of committing an offence in relation to the object of the search. A police officer who has reasonable grounds to suspect that a person is in innocent possession of a stolen or prohibited article, controlled drug or other item for which the officer is empowered to search, may stop and search the person even though there would be no power of arrest. This would apply when a child under the age of criminal responsibility (10 years) is suspected of carrying any such item, even if they knew they had it. (See Notes *1B* and *1BA*.)

Personal factors can never support reasonable grounds for suspicion

2.2B Reasonable suspicion can never be supported on the basis of personal factors. This means that unless the police have information or intelligence which provides a description of a person suspected of carrying an article for which there is a power to stop and search, the following cannot be used, alone or in combination with each other, or in combination with any other factor, as the reason for stopping and searching any individual, including any vehicle which they are driving or are being carried in:

(a) A person's physical appearance with regard, for example, to any of the 'relevant protected characteristics' set out in the Equality Act 2010, section 149, which are age, disability, gender reassignment, pregnancy and maternity, race, religion or belief, sex and sexual orientation (see *paragraph 1.1* and *Note 1A*), or the fact that the person is known to have a previous conviction; and

(b) Generalisations or stereotypical images that certain groups or categories of people are more likely to be involved in criminal activity.

2.3 Reasonable suspicion may also exist without specific information or intelligence and on the basis of the behaviour of a person. For example, if an officer encounters someone on the street at night who is obviously trying to hide something, the officer may (depending on the other surrounding circumstances) base such suspicion on the fact that this kind of behaviour is often linked to stolen or prohibited articles being carried.

Reasonable grounds for suspicion based on information and/or intelligence

2.4 Reasonable grounds for suspicion should normally be linked to accurate and current intelligence or information, relating to articles for which there is a power to stop and search, being carried by individuals or being in vehicles in any locality. This would include reports from members of the public or other officers describing:

- a person who has been seen carrying such an article or a vehicle in which such an article has been seen.
- crimes committed in relation to which such an article would constitute relevant evidence, for example, property stolen in a theft or burglary, an offensive weapon or bladed or sharply pointed article used to assault or threaten someone or an article used to cause criminal damage to property.

2.4A Searches based on accurate and current intelligence or information are more likely to be effective. Targeting searches in a particular area at specified crime problems increases their effectiveness and minimises inconvenience to law-abiding members of the public. It also helps in justifying the use of searches both to those who are searched and to the public. This does not however prevent stop and search powers being exercised in other locations where such powers may be exercised and reasonable suspicion exists.

2.5 *Not used.*

Reasonable grounds for suspicion and searching groups

2.6 Where there is reliable information or intelligence that members of a group or gang habitually carry knives unlawfully or weapons or controlled drugs, and wear a distinctive item of clothing or other means of identification in order to identify themselves as members of that group or gang, that distinctive item of clothing or other means of identification may provide reasonable grounds to stop and search any person believed to be a member of that group or gang. (See *Note 9*.)

2.6A A similar approach would apply to particular organised protest groups where there is reliable information or intelligence:

(a) that the group in question arranges meetings and marches to which one or more members bring articles intended to be used to cause criminal damage and/or injury to others in support of the group's aims;

(b) that at one or more previous meetings or marches arranged by that group, such articles have been used and resulted in damage and/or injury; and

(c) that on the subsequent occasion in question, one or more members of the group have brought with them such articles with similar intentions.

These circumstances may provide reasonable grounds to stop and search any members of the group to find such articles (see *Note 9A*). See also *paragraphs 2.12* to *2.18*, '*Searches authorised under section 60 of the Criminal Justice and Public Order Act 1994*', when serious violence is anticipated at meetings and marches.

Reasonable grounds for suspicion based on behaviour, time and location

2.6B Reasonable suspicion may also exist without specific information or intelligence and on the basis of the behaviour of a person. For example, if an officer encounters someone on the street at night who is obviously trying to hide something, the officer may (depending on the other surrounding circumstances) base such suspicion on the fact that this kind of behaviour is often linked to stolen or prohibited articles being carried. An officer who forms the opinion that a person is acting suspiciously or that they appear to be nervous must be able to explain, with reference to specific aspects of the person's behaviour or conduct which they have observed, why they formed that opinion (see *paragraphs 3.8(d)* and *5.5*). A hunch or instinct which cannot be explained or justified to an objective observer can never amount to reasonable grounds.

2.7 *Not used.*

2.8 *Not used.*

Securing public confidence and promoting community relations

2.8A All police officers must recognise that searches are more likely to be effective, legitimate and secure public confidence when their reasonable grounds for suspicion are based on a range of objective factors. The overall use of these powers is more likely to be effective when up-to-date and accurate intelligence or information is communicated to officers and they are well-informed about local crime patterns. Local senior officers have a duty to ensure that those under their command who exercise stop and search powers have access to such information, and the officers exercising the powers have a duty to acquaint themselves with that information (see *paragraphs 5.1* to *5.6*).

Questioning to decide whether to carry out a search

2.9 An officer who has reasonable grounds for suspicion may detain the person concerned in order to carry out a search. Before carrying out a search the officer may ask questions about the person's behaviour or presence in circumstances which gave rise to the suspicion. As a result of questioning the detained person, the reasonable grounds for suspicion necessary to detain that person may be confirmed or, because of a satisfactory explanation, be dispelled. (See *Notes 2* and *3*.) Questioning may also reveal reasonable grounds to suspect the possession of a different kind of unlawful article from that originally suspected. Reasonable grounds for suspicion however cannot be provided retrospectively by such questioning during a person's detention or by refusal to answer any questions asked.

2.10 If, as a result of questioning before a search, or other circumstances which come to the attention of the officer, there cease to be reasonable grounds for suspecting that an article of a kind for which there is a power to stop and search is being carried, no search may take place. (See *Note 3*.) In the absence of any other lawful power to detain, the person is free to leave at will and must be so informed.

2.11 There is no power to stop or detain a person in order to find grounds for a search. Police officers have many encounters with members of the public which do not involve detaining people against their will and do not require any statutory power for an officer to speak to a person (see *paragraph 4.12* and *Note 1*). However, if reasonable grounds for suspicion emerge during such an encounter, the officer may search the person, even though no grounds existed when the encounter began. As soon as detention begins, and before searching, the officer must inform the person that they are being detained for the purpose of a search and take action in accordance with paragraphs 3.8 to 3.11 under 'Steps to be taken prior to a search'.

(b) Searches authorised under section 60 of the Criminal Justice and Public Order Act 1994

2.12 Authority for a constable in uniform to stop and search under section 60 of the Criminal Justice and Public Order Act 1994 may be given if the authorising officer reasonably believes:

(a) that incidents involving serious violence may take place in any locality in the officer's police area, and it is expedient to use these powers to prevent their occurrence;

(b) that persons are carrying dangerous instruments or offensive weapons without good reason in any locality in the officer's police area; or

(c) that an incident involving serious violence has taken place in the officer's police area, a dangerous instrument or offensive weapon used in the incident is being carried by a person in any locality in that police area, and it is expedient to use these powers to find that instrument or weapon.

2.13 An authorisation under section 60 may only be given by an officer of the rank of inspector or above and in writing, or orally if paragraph 2.12(c) applies and it is not practicable to give the authorisation in writing. The authorisation (whether written or oral) must specify the grounds on which it was given, the locality in which the powers may be exercised and the period of time for which they are in force. The period authorised shall be no longer than appears reasonably necessary to prevent, or seek to prevent incidents of serious violence, or to deal with the problem of carrying dangerous instruments or offensive weapons or to find a dangerous instrument or offensive weapon that has been used. It may not exceed 24 hours. An oral authorisation given where paragraph 2.12(c) applies must be recorded in writing as soon as practicable. (See *Notes 10* to *13*.)

2.14 An inspector who gives an authorisation must, as soon as practicable, inform an officer of or above the rank of superintendent. This officer may direct that the authorisation shall be extended for a further 24 hours, if violence or the carrying of dangerous instruments or offensive weapons has occurred, or is suspected to have occurred, and the continued use of the powers is considered necessary to prevent or deal with further such activity or to find a dangerous instrument or offensive weapon used that has been used. That direction must be given in writing unless it is not practicable to do so, in which case it must be recorded in writing as soon as practicable afterwards. (See *Note 12*.)

2.14A The selection of persons and vehicles under section 60 to be stopped and, if appropriate, searched should reflect an objective assessment of the nature of the incident or weapon in question and the individuals and vehicles thought likely to be associated with that incident or those weapons (see *Notes 10* and *11*). The powers must not be used to stop and search persons and vehicles for reasons unconnected with the purpose of the authorisation. When selecting persons and vehicles to be stopped in response to a specific threat or incident, officers must take care not to discriminate unlawfully against anyone on the grounds of any of the protected characteristics set out in the Equality Act 2010. (See *paragraph 1.1*.)

2.14B The driver of a vehicle which is stopped under section 60 and any person who is searched under section 60 are entitled to a written statement to that effect if they apply within twelve months from the day the vehicle was stopped or the person was searched. This statement is a record which states that the vehicle was stopped or (as the case may be) that the person was searched under section 60 and it may form part of the search record or be supplied as a separate record.

Powers to require removal of face coverings

2.15 Section 60AA of the Criminal Justice and Public Order Act 1994 also provides a power to demand the removal of disguises. The officer exercising the power must reasonably believe that someone is wearing an item wholly or mainly for the purpose of concealing identity. There is also a power to seize such items where the officer believes that a person intends to wear them for this purpose. There is no power to stop and search for disguises. An officer may seize any such item which is discovered when exercising a power of search for something else, or which is being carried, and which the officer reasonably believes is intended to be used for concealing anyone's identity. This power can only be used if an authorisation given under section 60 or under section 60AA, is in force. (See *Note 4*.)

2.16 Authority under section 60AA for a constable in uniform to require the removal of disguises and to seize them may be given if the authorising officer reasonably believes that activities may take place in any locality in the officer's police area that are likely to involve the commission of offences and it is expedient to use these powers to prevent or control these activities.

2.17 An authorisation under section 60AA may only be given by an officer of the rank of inspector or above, in writing, specifying the grounds on which it was given, the locality in which the powers may be exercised and the period of time for which they are in force. The period authorised shall be no longer than appears reasonably necessary to prevent, or seek to prevent the commission of offences. It may not exceed 24 hours. (See *Notes 10* to *13*.)

2.18 An inspector who gives an authorisation must, as soon as practicable, inform an officer of or above the rank of superintendent. This officer may direct that the authorisation shall be extended for a further 24 hours, if crimes have been committed, or are suspected to have been committed, and the continued use of the powers is considered necessary to prevent or deal with further such activity. This direction must also be given in writing at the time or as soon as practicable afterwards. (See *Note 12*.)

(c) Not used.

(d) Searches under Schedule 5 to the Terrorism Prevention and Investigation Measures Act 2011

2.18A Paragraph 3 of Schedule 5 to the TPIM Act 2011 allows a constable to detain an individual to be searched under the following powers:

(i) paragraph 6(2)(a) when a TPIM notice is being, or has just been, served on the individual for the purpose of ascertaining whether there is anything on the individual that contravenes measures specified in the notice;

(ii) paragraph 8(2)(a) in accordance with a warrant to search the individual issued by a justice of the peace in England and Wales, a sheriff in Scotland or a lay magistrate in Northern Ireland who is satisfied that a search is necessary for the purpose of determining whether an individual in respect of whom a TPIM notice is in force is complying with measures specified in the notice (see *paragraph 2.20*); and

(iii) paragraph 10 to ascertain whether an individual in respect of whom a TPIM notice is in force is in possession of anything that could be used to threaten or harm any person.

See *paragraph 2.1(e).*

2.19 The exercise of the powers mentioned in *paragraph 2.18A* does not require the constable to have reasonable grounds to suspect that the individual:

(a) has been, or is, contravening any of the measures specified in the TPIM notice; or
(b) has on them anything which:
- in the case of the power in sub-paragraph (i), contravenes measures specified in the TPIM notice;
- in the case of the power in sub-paragraph (ii) is not complying with measures specified in the TPIM notice; or
- in the case of the power in sub-paragraph (iii), could be used to threaten or harm any person.

2.20 A search of an individual on warrant under the power mentioned in paragraph 2.18A(ii) must [be] carried out within 28 days of the issue of the warrant and:
- the individual may be searched on one occasion only within that period;
- the search must take place at a reasonable hour unless it appears that this would frustrate the purposes of the search.

2.21 *Not used.*
2.22 *Not used.*
2.23 *Not used.*
2.24 *Not used.*
2.24A *Not used.*
2.25 *Not used.*

2.26 The powers under Schedule 5 only allow a constable to conduct a search of an individual only for specified purposes relating to a TPIM notice as set out above. However, anything found may be seized and retained if there are reasonable grounds for believing that it is or it contains evidence of any offence for use at a trial for that offence or to prevent it being concealed, lost, damaged, altered, or destroyed. However, this would not prevent a search being carried out under other search powers if, in the course of exercising these powers, the officer formed reasonable grounds for suspicion.

(e) Powers to search persons in the exercise of a power to search premises

2.27 The following powers to search premises also authorise the search of a person, not under arrest, who is found on the premises during the course of the search:

(a) section 139B of the Criminal Justice Act 1988 under which a constable may enter school premises and search the premises and any person on those premises for any bladed or pointed article or offensive weapon;
(b) under a warrant issued under section 23(3) of the Misuse of Drugs Act 1971 to search premises for drugs or documents but only if the warrant specifically authorises the search of persons found on the premises; and
(c) under a search warrant or order issued under paragraph 1, 3 or 11 of Schedule 5 to the Terrorism Act 2000 to search premises and any person found there for material likely to be of substantial value to a terrorist investigation.

2.28 Before the power under section 139B of the Criminal Justice Act 1988 may be exercised, the constable must have reasonable grounds to suspect that an offence under section 139A or 139AA of the Criminal Justice Act 1988 (having a bladed or pointed article or offensive weapon on school premises) has been or is being committed. A warrant to search premises and persons found therein may be issued under section 23(3) of the Misuse of Drugs Act 1971 if there are reasonable grounds to suspect that controlled drugs or certain documents are in the possession of a person on the premises.

2.29 The powers in paragraph 2.27 do not require prior specific grounds to suspect that the person to be searched is in possession of an item for which there is an existing power to search. However, it is still necessary to ensure that the selection and treatment of those searched under these powers is based upon objective factors connected with the search of the premises, and not upon personal prejudice.

3 Conduct of searches

3.1 All stops and searches must be carried out with courtesy, consideration and respect for the person concerned. This has a significant impact on public confidence in the police. Every reasonable effort must be made to minimise the embarrassment that a person being searched may experience. (See *Note 4*.)

3.2 The co-operation of the person to be searched must be sought in every case, even if the person initially objects to the search. A forcible search may be made only if it has been established that the person is unwilling to co-operate or resists. Reasonable force may be used as a last resort if necessary to conduct a search or to detain a person or vehicle for the purposes of a search.

3.3 The length of time for which a person or vehicle may be detained must be reasonable and kept to a minimum. Where the exercise of the power requires reasonable suspicion, the thoroughness and extent of a search must depend on what is suspected of being carried, and by whom. If the suspicion relates to a particular article which is seen to be slipped into a person's pocket, then, in the absence of other grounds for suspicion or an opportunity for the article to be moved elsewhere, the search must be confined to that pocket. In the case of a small article which can readily be concealed, such as a drug, and which might be concealed anywhere on the person, a more extensive search may be necessary. In the case of searches mentioned in paragraph 2.1(b) and (d), which do not require reasonable grounds for suspicion, officers may make any reasonable search to look for items for which they are empowered to search. (See *Note 5*.)

3.4 The search must be carried out at or near the place where the person or vehicle was first detained. (See *Note 6*.)

3.5 There is no power to require a person to remove any clothing in public other than an outer coat, jacket or gloves, except under section 60AA of the Criminal Justice and Public Order Act 1994 (which empowers a constable to require a person to remove any item worn to conceal identity). (See *Notes 4* and *6*.) A search in public of a person's clothing which has not been removed must be restricted to superficial examination of outer garments. This does not, however, prevent an officer from placing his or her hand inside the pockets of the outer clothing, or feeling round the inside of collars, socks and shoes if this is reasonably necessary in the circumstances to look for the object of the search or to remove and examine any item reasonably suspected to be the object of the search. For the same reasons, subject to the restrictions on the removal of headgear, a person's hair may also be searched in public. (See *paragraphs 3.1* and *3.3*.)

3.6 Where on reasonable grounds it is considered necessary to conduct a more thorough search (e.g. by requiring a person to take off a T-shirt), this must be done out of public view, for example, in a police van unless paragraph 3.7 applies, or police station if there is one nearby (see *Note 6*.) Any search involving the removal of more than an outer coat, jacket, gloves, headgear or footwear, or any other item concealing identity, may only be made by an officer of the same sex as the person searched and may not be made in the presence of anyone of the opposite sex unless the person being searched specifically requests it. (See Code C *Annex L* and *Notes 4* and *7*.)

3.7 Searches involving exposure of intimate parts of the body must not be conducted as a routine extension of a less thorough search, simply because nothing is found in the course of the initial search. Searches involving exposure of intimate parts of the body may be carried out only at a nearby police station or other nearby location which is out of public view (but not a police vehicle). These searches must be conducted in accordance with paragraph 11 of Annex A to Code C except that an intimate search mentioned in paragraph 11(f) of Annex A to Code C may not be authorised or carried out under any stop and search powers. The other provisions of Code C do not apply to the conduct and recording of searches of persons detained at police stations in the exercise of stop and search powers. (See *Note 7*.)

Steps to be taken prior to a search

3.8 Before any search of a detained person or attended vehicle takes place the officer must take reasonable steps, if not in uniform (see *paragraph 3.9*), to show their warrant card to the person to be searched or in charge of the vehicle to be searched and whether or not in uniform, to give that person the following information:

(a) that they are being detained for the purposes of a search;

(b) the officer's name (except in the case of enquiries linked to the investigation of terrorism, or otherwise where the officer reasonably believes that giving their name might put them in danger, in which case a warrant or other identification number shall be given) and the name of the police station to which the officer is attached;

(c) the legal search power which is being exercised, and

(d) a clear explanation of:
   (i) the object of the search in terms of the article or articles for which there is a power to search; and
   (ii) in the case of:
   - the power under section 60 of the Criminal Justice and Public Order Act 1994 (see *paragraph 2.1(b)),* the nature of the power, the authorisation and the fact that it has been given;
   - the powers under Schedule 5 to the Terrorism Prevention and Investigation Measures Act 2011 (see *paragraph 2.1(e)* and *2.18A*):
     – the fact that a TPIM notice is in force or, (in the case of paragraph 6(2)(a)) that a TPIM notice is being served;
     – the nature of the power being exercised.

     For a search under paragraph 8 of Schedule 5, the warrant must be produced and the person provided with a copy of it.
   - all other powers requiring reasonable suspicion (see *paragraph 2.1(a)*), the grounds for that suspicion. This means explaining the basis for the suspicion by reference to information and/or intelligence about, or some specific behaviour by, the person concerned (see *paragraph 2.2*).

(e) that they are entitled to a copy of the record of the search if one is made (see *section 4* below) if they ask within 3 months from the date of the search and:
   (i) if they are not arrested and taken to a police station as a result of the search and it is practicable to make the record on the spot, that immediately after the search is completed they will be given, if they request, either:
   - a copy of the record, or
   - a receipt which explains how they can obtain a copy of the full record or access to an electronic copy of the record, or

   (ii) if they are arrested and taken to a police station as a result of the search, that the record will be made at the station as part of their custody record and they will be given, if they request, a copy of their custody record which includes a record of the search as soon as practicable whilst they are at the station. (See *Note 16.*)

3.9 Stops and searches under the power mentioned in paragraph 2.1(b) may be undertaken only by a constable in uniform.

3.10 The person should also be given information about police powers to stop and search and the individual's rights in these circumstances.

3.11 If the person to be searched, or in charge of a vehicle to be searched, does not appear to understand what is being said, or there is any doubt about the person's ability to understand English, the officer must take reasonable steps to bring information regarding the person's rights and any relevant provisions of this Code to his or her attention. If the person is deaf or cannot understand English and is accompanied by someone, then the officer must try to establish whether that person can interpret or otherwise help the officer to give the required information.

4 Recording requirements

(a) Searches which do not result in an arrest

4.1 When an officer carries out a search in the exercise of any power to which this Code applies and the search does not result in the person searched or person in charge of the vehicle searched being arrested and taken to a police station, a record must be made of it, electronically or on paper, unless there are exceptional circumstances which make this wholly impracticable (e.g. in situations involving public disorder or when the recording officer's presence is urgently required elsewhere). If a record is to be made, the officer carrying out the search must make the record on the spot unless this is not practicable, in which case, the officer must make the record as soon as practicable after the search is completed. (See *Note 16.*)

4.2 If the record is made at the time, the person who has been searched or who is in charge of the vehicle that has been searched must be asked if they want a copy and if they do, they must be given immediately, either:
- a copy of the record, or
- a receipt which explains how they can obtain a copy of the full record or access to an electronic copy of the record

4.2A An officer is not required to provide a copy of the full record or a receipt at the time if they are called to an incident of higher priority. (See *Note 21.*)

(b) Searches which result in an arrest

4.2B If a search in the exercise of any power to which this Code applies results in a person being arrested and taken to a police station, the officer carrying out the search is responsible for ensuring that a record of the search is made as part of their custody record. The custody officer must then ensure that the person is asked if they want a copy of the record and if they do, that they are given a copy as soon as practicable. (See *Note 16.*)

(c) Record of search

4.3 The record of a search must always include the following information:

(a) A note of the self defined ethnicity, and if different, the ethnicity as perceived by the officer making the search, of the person searched or of the person in charge of the vehicle searched (as the case may be) (see *Note 18*);

(b) The date, time and place the person or vehicle was searched (see *Note 6*);

(c) The object of the search in terms of the article or articles for which there is a power to search;

(d) In the case of:

- the power under section 60 of the Criminal Justice and Public Order Act 1994 (see *paragraph 2.1(b)*), the nature of the power, the authorisation and the fact that it has been given (see *Note 17*);
- the powers under Schedule 5 to the Terrorism Prevention and Investigation Measures Act 2011 (see *paragraphs 2.1(e)* and *2.18A*):
  - the fact that a TPIM notice is in force or, (in the case of paragraph 6(2)(a)), that a TPIM notice is being served;
  - the nature of the power, and
  - for a search under paragraph 8, the date the search warrant was issued, the fact that the warrant was produced and a copy of it provided and the warrant must also be endorsed by the constable executing it to state whether anything was found and whether anything was seized, and
- all other powers requiring reasonable suspicion (see *paragraph 2.1(a)*), the grounds for that suspicion.

(e) subject to paragraph 3.8(b), the identity of the officer carrying out the search. (See *Note 15.*)

4.3A For the purposes of completing the search record, there is no requirement to record the name, address and date of birth of the person searched or the person in charge of a vehicle which is searched. The person is under no obligation to provide this information and they should not be asked to provide it for the purpose of completing the record.

4.4 Nothing in paragraph 4.3 requires the names of police officers to be shown on the search record or any other record required to be made under this code in the case of enquiries linked to the investigation of terrorism or otherwise where an officer reasonably believes that recording names might endanger the officers. In such cases the record must show the officers' warrant or other identification number and duty station.

4.5 A record is required for each person and each vehicle searched. However, if a person is in a vehicle and both are searched, and the object and grounds of the search are the same, only one record need be completed. If more than one person in a vehicle is searched, separate records for each search of a person must be made. If only a vehicle is searched, the self-defined ethnic background of the person in charge of the vehicle must be recorded, unless the vehicle is unattended.

4.6 The record of the grounds for making a search must, briefly but informatively, explain the reason for suspecting the person concerned, by reference to information and/ or intelligence about, or some specific behaviour by, the person concerned (see *paragraph 2.2*).

4.7 Where officers detain an individual with a view to performing a search, but the need to search is eliminated as a result of questioning the person detained, a search should not be carried out and a record is not required. (See *paragraph 2.10* and *Notes 3* and *22A.*)

4.8 After searching an unattended vehicle, or anything in or on it, an officer must leave a notice in it (or on it, if things on it have been searched without opening it) recording the fact that it has been searched.

4.9 The notice must include the name of the police station to which the officer concerned is attached and state where a copy of the record of the search may be obtained and how (if applicable) an electronic copy may be accessed and where any application for compensation should be directed.

4.10 The vehicle must if practicable be left secure.

4.10A *Not used.*

4.10B *Not used.*

Recording of encounters not governed by statutory powers

4.11 *Not used.*

4.12 There is no national requirement for an officer who requests a person in a public place to account for themselves, i.e. their actions, behaviour, presence in an area or possession of anything, to make any record of the encounter or to give the person a receipt. (See *paragraph 2.11* and *Notes 22A* and *22B*.)

4.12A *Not used.*

4.13 *Not used.*

4.14 *Not used.*

4.15 *Not used.*

4.16 *Not used.*

4.17 *Not used.*

4.18 *Not used.*

4.19 *Not used.*

4.20 *Not used.*

5 Monitoring and supervising the use of stop and search powers

General

5.1 Any misuse of stop and search powers is likely to be harmful to policing and lead to mistrust of the police by the local community and by the public in general. Supervising officers must monitor the use of stop and search powers and should consider in particular whether there is any evidence that they are being exercised on the basis of stereotyped images or inappropriate generalisations. Supervising officers should satisfy themselves that the practice of officers under their supervision in stopping, searching and recording is fully in accordance with this Code. Supervisors must also examine whether the records reveal any trends or patterns which give cause for concern, and if so take appropriate action to address this.

5.2 Senior officers with area or force-wide responsibilities must also monitor the broader use of stop and search powers and, where necessary, take action at the relevant level.

5.3 Supervision and monitoring must be supported by the compilation of comprehensive statistical records of stops and searches at force, area and local level. Any apparently disproportionate use of the powers by particular officers or groups of officers or in relation to specific sections of the community should be identified and investigated.

5.4 In order to promote public confidence in the use of the powers, forces in consultation with police and crime commissioners must make arrangements for the records to be scrutinised by representatives of the community, and to explain the use of the powers at a local level. (See *Note 19*.)

Suspected misuse of powers by individual officers

5.5 Police supervisors must monitor the use of stop and search powers by individual officers to ensure that they are being applied appropriately and lawfully. Monitoring takes many forms, such as direct supervision of the exercise of the powers, examining stop and search records (particularly examining the officer's documented reasonable grounds for suspicion) and asking the officer to account for the way in which they conducted and recorded particular searches or through complaints about a stop and search that an officer has carried out.

5.6 Where a supervisor identifies issues with the way that an officer has used a stop and search power, the facts of the case will determine whether the standards of professional behaviour as set out in the Code of Ethics (see [https://www.college.police.uk/What-we-do/Ethics/Documents/Code_of_Ethics.pdf]) have been breached and which formal action is pursued. Improper use might be a result of poor performance or a conduct matter, which will require the supervisor to take appropriate action such as performance or misconduct procedures. It is imperative that supervisors take both timely and appropriate action to deal with all such cases that come to their notice.

Notes for Guidance

Officers exercising stop and search powers

1 *This Code does not affect the ability of an officer to speak to or question a person in the ordinary course of the officer's duties without detaining the person or exercising any element of compulsion. It is not the purpose of the code to prohibit such encounters between the police and the community with the co-operation of the person concerned and neither does it affect the principle that all citizens have a duty to help police officers to prevent crime and discover offenders. This is a civic rather than a legal duty; but when a police officer is trying to discover whether, or by whom, an offence has been committed he or she may question any person from whom useful information might be obtained, subject to the restrictions imposed by Code C. A person's unwillingness to reply does not alter this entitlement, but in the absence of a power to arrest, or to detain in order to search, the person is free to leave at will and cannot be compelled to remain with the officer.*

1A *In paragraphs 1.1 and 2.2, 'relevant protected characteristic' are: age, disability, gender reassignment, pregnancy and maternity, race, religion or belief, sex and sexual orientation.*

1B *Innocent possession means that the person does [not] have the guilty knowledge that they are carrying an unlawful item which is required before an arrest on suspicion that the person has committed an offence in respect of the item sought (if arrest is necessary — see PACE Code G) and/or a criminal prosecution) can be considered. It is not uncommon for children under the age of criminal responsibility to be used by older children and adults to carry stolen property, drugs and weapons and, in some cases, firearms, for the criminal benefit of others, either:*

- *in the hope that police may not suspect they are being used for carrying the items; or*
- *knowing that if they are suspected of being couriers and are stopped and searched, they cannot be arrested or prosecuted for any criminal offence.*

Stop and search powers therefore allow the police to intervene effectively to break up criminal gangs and groups that use young children to further their criminal activities.

1BA *Whenever a child under 10 is suspected of carrying unlawful items for someone else, or is found in circumstances which suggest that their welfare and safety may be at risk, the facts should be reported and actioned in accordance with established force safeguarding procedures. This will be in addition to treating them as a potentially vulnerable or intimidated witness in respect of their status as a witness to the serious criminal offence(s) committed by those using them as couriers. Safeguarding considerations will also apply to other persons aged under 18 who are stopped and searched under any of the powers to which this Code applies. See paragraph 1.1 with regard to the requirement under the Children Act 2004, section 11, for chief police officers and other specified persons and bodies, to ensure that in the discharge of their functions, they have regard to the need to safeguard and promote the welfare of all persons under the age of 18.*

2 *In some circumstances preparatory questioning may be unnecessary, but in general a brief conversation or exchange will be desirable not only as a means of avoiding unsuccessful searches, but to explain the grounds for the stop/search, to gain co-operation and reduce any tension there might be surrounding the stop/search.*

3 *Where a person is lawfully detained for the purpose of a search, but no search in the event takes place, the detention will not thereby have been rendered unlawful.*

4 *Many people customarily cover their heads or faces for religious reasons – for example, Muslim women, Sikh men, Sikh or Hindu women, or Rastafarian men or women. A police officer cannot order the removal of a head or face covering except where there is reason to believe that the item is being worn by the individual wholly or mainly for the purpose of disguising identity, not simply because it disguises identity. Where there may be religious sensitivities about ordering the removal of such an item, the officer should permit the item to be removed out of public view. Where practicable, the item should be removed in the presence of an officer of the same sex as the person and out of sight of anyone of the opposite sex (see Code C Annex L).*

5 *A search of a person in public should be completed as soon as possible.*

6 *A person may be detained under a stop and search power at a place other than where the person was first detained, only if that place, be it a police station or elsewhere, is nearby. Such a place should be located within a reasonable travelling distance using whatever mode of travel (on foot or by car) is appropriate. This applies to all searches under stop and search powers, whether or not they involve the removal of clothing or exposure of intimate parts of the body (see paragraphs 3.6 and 3.7) or take place in or out of public view. It means, for example, that a search under the stop and search power in section 23 of the Misuse of Drugs Act 1971 which involves the compulsory removal of more than a person's outer coat, jacket or gloves cannot be carried out unless a place which is both nearby the place they were first detained and out of public view, is available. If a search involves exposure of intimate parts of the body and a police station is not nearby, particular care must be taken to ensure that the location is suitable in that it enables the search to be conducted in accordance with the requirements of paragraph 11 of Annex A to Code C.*

7 *A search in the street itself should be regarded as being in public for the purposes of paragraphs 3.6 and 3.7 above, even though it may be empty at the time a search begins. Although there is no power to require a person to do so, there is nothing to prevent an officer from asking a person voluntarily to remove more than an outer coat, jacket or gloves in public.*

8 *Not used.*

9 *Other means of identification might include jewellery, insignias, tattoos or other features which are known to identify members of the particular gang or group.*

9A *A decision to search individuals believed to be members of a particular group or gang must be judged on a case by case basis according to the circumstances applicable at the time of the proposed searches and in particular, having regard to:*

(a) the number of items suspected of being carried;
(b) the nature of those items and the risk they pose; and
(c) the number of individuals to be searched.

A group search will only be justified if it is a necessary and proportionate approach based on the facts and having regard to the nature of the suspicion in these cases. The extent and thoroughness of the searches must not be excessive.

The size of the group and the number of individuals it is proposed to search will be a key factor and steps should be taken to identify those who are to be searched to avoid unnecessary inconvenience to unconnected members of the public who are also present.

The onus is on the police to be satisfied and to demonstrate that their approach to the decision to search is in pursuit of a legitimate aim, necessary and proportionate.

Authorising officers

10 *The powers under section 60 are separate from and additional to the normal stop and search powers which require reasonable grounds to suspect an individual of carrying an offensive weapon (or other article). Their overall purpose is to prevent serious violence and the widespread carrying of weapons which might lead to persons being seriously injured by disarming potential offenders or finding weapons that have been used in circumstances where other powers would not be sufficient. They should not therefore be used to replace or circumvent the normal powers for dealing with routine crime problems. A particular example might be an authorisation to prevent serious violence or the carrying of offensive weapons at a sports event by rival team supporters when the expected general appearance and age range of those likely to be responsible, alone, would not be sufficiently distinctive to support reasonable suspicion (see paragraph 2.6). The purpose of the powers under section 60AA is to prevent those involved in intimidatory or violent protests using face coverings to disguise identity.*

11 *Authorisations under section 60 require a reasonable belief on the part of the authorising officer. This must have an objective basis, for example: intelligence or relevant information such as a history of antagonism and violence between particular groups; previous incidents of violence at, or connected with, particular events or locations; a significant increase in knife-point robberies in a limited area; reports that individuals are regularly carrying weapons in a particular locality; information following an incident in which weapons were used about where the weapons might be found or in the case of section 60AA previous incidents of crimes being committed while wearing face coverings to conceal identity.*

12 *It is for the authorising officer to determine the period of time during which the powers mentioned in paragraph 2.1(b) may be exercised. The officer should set the minimum period he or she considers necessary to deal with the risk of violence, the carrying of knives or offensive weapons, or to find dangerous instruments or weapons that have been used. A direction to extend the period authorised under the powers mentioned in paragraph 2.1(b) may be given only once. Thereafter further use of the powers requires a new authorisation.*

13 *It is for the authorising officer to determine the geographical area in which the use of the powers is to be authorised. In doing so the officer may wish to take into account factors such as the nature and venue of the anticipated incident or the incident which has taken place, the number of people who may be in the immediate area of that incident, their access to surrounding areas and the anticipated or actual level of violence. The officer should not set a geographical area which is wider than that he or she believes necessary for the purpose of preventing anticipated violence, the carrying of knives or offensive weapons, or for finding a dangerous instrument or weapon that has been used or, in the case of section 60AA, the prevention of commission of offences. It is particularly important to ensure that constables exercising such powers are fully aware of the locality within which they may be used. The officer giving the authorisation should therefore specify either the streets which form the boundary of the locality or a divisional boundary if appropriate, within the force area. If the power is to be used in response to a threat or incident that straddles police force areas, an officer from each of the forces concerned will need to give an authorisation.*

14 *Not used.*

Recording

15 *Where a stop and search is conducted by more than one officer the identity of all the officers engaged in the search must be recorded on the record. Nothing prevents an officer who is present but not directly involved in searching from completing the record during the course of the encounter.*

16 *When the search results in the person searched or in charge of a vehicle which is searched being arrested, the requirement to make the record of the search as part of the person's custody record does not apply if the person is granted 'street bail' after arrest (see section 30A of PACE) to attend a police station and is not taken in custody to the police station An arrested person's entitlement to a copy of the search record which is made as part of their custody record does not affect their entitlement to a copy of their custody record or any other provisions of PACE Code C section 2 (Custody records).*

17 *It is important for monitoring purposes to specify when authority is given for exercising the stop and search power under section 60 of the Criminal Justice and Public Order Act 1994.*

18 *Officers should record the self-defined ethnicity of every person stopped according to the categories used in the 2001 census question listed in Annex B. The person should be asked to select one of the five main categories representing broad ethnic groups and then a more specific cultural background from within this group. The ethnic classification should be coded for recording purposes using the coding system in Annex B. An additional 'Not stated' box is available but should not be offered to respondents explicitly. Officers should be aware and explain to members of the public, especially where concerns are raised, that this information is required to obtain a true picture of stop and search activity and to help improve ethnic monitoring, tackle discriminatory practice, and promote effective use of the powers. If the person gives what appears to the officer to be an 'incorrect' answer (e.g. a person who appears to be white states that they are black), the officer should record the response that has been given and then record their own perception of the person's ethnic background by using the PNC classification system. If the 'Not stated' category is used the reason for this must be recorded on the form.*

19 *Arrangements for public scrutiny of records should take account of the right to confidentiality of those stopped and searched. Anonymised forms and/or statistics generated from records should be the focus of the examinations by members of the public.*

20 *Not used.*

21 *In situations where it is not practicable to provide a written copy of the record or immediate access to an electronic copy of the record or a receipt of the search at the time (see paragraph 4.2A above), the officer should consider giving the person details of the station which they may attend for a copy of the record. A receipt may take the form of a simple business card which includes sufficient information to locate the record should the person ask for copy, for example, the date and place of the search, and a reference number or the name of the officer who carried out the search (unless paragraph 4.4 applies).*

22 *Not used.*

22A *Where there are concerns which make it necessary to monitor any local disproportionality, forces have discretion to direct officers to record the self-defined ethnicity of persons they request to account for themselves in a public place or who they detain with a view to searching but do not search. Guidance should be provided locally and efforts made to minimise the bureaucracy involved. Records should be closely monitored and supervised in line with paragraphs 5.1 to 5.4, and forces can suspend or re-instate recording of these encounters as appropriate.*

22B *A person who is asked to account for themselves should, if they request, be given information about how they can report their dissatisfaction about how they have been treated.*

Definition of offensive weapon

23 *'Offensive weapon' is defined as 'any article made or adapted for use for causing injury to the person, or intended by the person having it with him for such use by him or by someone else'. There are three categories of offensive weapons: those made for causing injury to the person; those adapted for such a purpose; and those not so made or adapted, but carried with the intention of causing injury to the person. A firearm, as defined by section 57 of the Firearms Act 1968, would fall within the definition of offensive weapon if any of the criteria above apply.*

24 *Not used.*

25 *Not used.*

Annex A

Summary of Main Stop and Search Powers to Which Code A Applies

This table relates to stop and search powers only. Individual statutes below may contain other police powers of entry, search and seizure.

Power	Object of Search	Extent of Search	Where exercisable
Unlawful articles general			
1. Public Stores Act 1875, s. 6	HM Stores stolen or unlawfully obtained	Persons, vehicles and vessels	Anywhere where the constabulary powers are exercisable
2. Firearms Act 1968, s. 47	Firearms	Persons and vehicles	A public place, or anywhere in the case of reasonable suspicion of offences of carrying firearms with criminal intent or trespassing with firearms
3. Misuse of Drugs Act 1971, s. 23	Controlled drugs	Persons and vehicles	Anywhere
4. Customs and Excise Management Act 1979, s. 163	Goods: (a) on which duty has not been paid; (b) being unlawfully removed, imported or exported; (c) otherwise liable to forfeiture to HM Revenue and Customs	Vehicles and vessels only	Anywhere
5. Aviation Security Act 1982, s. 24B *Note: This power applies throughout the UK but the provisions of this Code will apply only when the power is exercised at an aerodrome situated in England and Wales.*	Stolen articles or articles made, adapted or intended for use in the course of/in connection with conduct which constitutes an offence in the part of the UK where the aerodrome is situated or would so do, if it occurred there.	Persons, vehicles, aircraft. Anything in or on a vehicle or aircraft.	Any part of an aerodrome.
6. Police and Criminal Evidence Act 1984, s. 1	Stolen goods;	Persons and vehicles.	Where there is public access.
	Articles made, adapted or intended for use in the course of or in connection with, certain offences under the Theft Act 1968, Fraud Act and Criminal Damage Act 1971;	Persons and vehicles.	Where there is public access.
	Offensive weapons, bladed or sharply-pointed articles (except folding pocket knives with a bladed cutting edge not exceeding 3 inches);	Persons and vehicles.	Where there is public access.
	Fireworks: Category 4 (display grade) fireworks if possession prohibited, Adult fireworks in possession of a person under 18 in a public place.	Persons and vehicles.	Where there is public access.

Power	Object of Search	Extent of Search	Where exercisable
7. Sporting Events (Control of Alcohol etc.) Act 1985, s. 7	Intoxicating liquor	Persons, coaches and trains	Designated sports grounds or coaches and trains travelling to or from a designated sporting event.
8. Crossbows Act 1987, s. 4	Crossbows or parts of crossbows (except crossbows with a draw weight of less than 1.4 kilograms)	Persons and vehicles	Anywhere except dwellings
9. Criminal Justice Act 1988 s. 139B	Offensive weapons, bladed or sharply pointed article	Persons	School premises
Evidence of game and wildlife offences			
10. Poaching Prevention Act 1862, s. 2	Game or poaching equipment	Persons and vehicles	A public place
11. Deer Act 1991, s. 12	Evidence of offences under the Act	Persons and vehicles	Anywhere except dwellings
12. Conservation of Seals Act 1970, s. 4	Seals or hunting equipment	Vehicles only	Anywhere
13. Protection of Badgers Act 1992, s. 11	Evidence of offences under the Act	Persons and vehicles	Anywhere
14. Wildlife and Countryside Act 1981, s. 19	Evidence of wildlife offences	Persons and vehicles	Anywhere except dwellings
Other			
15. Paragraphs 6 & 8 of Schedule 5 to the Terrorism Prevention and Investigation Measures Act 2011	Anything that contravenes measures specified in a TPIM notice.	Persons in respect of whom a TPIM notice is being served or is in force	Anywhere
16. Paragraph 10 of Schedule 5 to the Terrorism Prevention and Investigation Measures Act 2011	Anything that could be used to threaten or harm any person.	Persons in respect of whom a TPIM notice is in force.	Anywhere
17. *Not used*			
18. *Not used*			
19. Section 60 Criminal Justice and Public Order Act 1994	Offensive weapons or dangerous instruments to prevent incidents of serious violence or to deal with the carrying of such items or find such items which have been used in incidents of serious violence	Persons and vehicles	Anywhere within a locality authorised under subsection (1)

Annex B

Self-Defined Ethnic Classification Categories

[Omitted.]

Annex C

Summary of Powers of Community Support Officers to Search and Seize

The following is a summary of the search and seizure powers that may be exercised by a community support officer (CSO) who has been designated with the relevant powers in accordance with Part 4 of the Police Reform Act 2002.

When exercising any of these powers, a CSO must have regard to any relevant provisions of this Code, including section 3 governing the conduct of searches and the steps to be taken prior to a search.

1. *Not used*

2. Powers to search requiring the consent of the person and seizure

A CSO may detain a person using reasonable force where necessary as set out in Part 1 of Schedule 4 to the Police Reform Act 2002. If the person has been lawfully detained, the CSO may search the person provided that person gives consent to such a search in relation to the following:

Designation	Powers conferred	Object of Search	Extent of Search	Where Exercisable
1. Police Reform Act 2002, Schedule 4, paragraphs 7 and 7A	(a) Criminal Justice and Police Act 2001, s. 12(2)	(a) Alcohol or a container for alcohol	(a) Persons	(a) Designated public place
	(b) Confiscation of Alcohol (Young Persons) Act 1997, s. 1	(b) Alcohol	(b) Persons under 18 years old	(b) Public place
	(c) Children and Young Persons Act 1933, s. 7(3)	(c) Tobacco or cigarette papers	(c) Persons under 16 years old found smoking	(c) Public place

3. Powers to search not requiring the consent of the person and seizure

A CSO may detain a person using reasonable force where necessary as set out in Part 1 of Schedule 4 to the Police Reform Act 2002. If the person has been lawfully detained, the CSO may search the person without the need for that person's consent in relation to the following:

Designation	Power conferred	Object of Search	Extent of Search	Where Exercisable
Police Reform Act 2002, Schedule 4, paragraph 2A	Police and Criminal Evidence Act 1984, s. 32	(a) Objects that might be used to cause physical injury to the person or the CSO. (b) Items that might be used to assist escape.	Persons made subject to a requirement to wait.	Any place where the requirement to wait has been made

4. Powers to seize without consent

This power applies when drugs are found in the course of any search mentioned above.

Designation	Power conferred	Object of Seizure	Where Exercisable
Police Reform Act 2002, Schedule 4, paragraph 7B	Police Reform Act 2002, Schedule 4, paragraph 7B	Controlled drugs in a person's possession.	Any place where the person is in possession of the drug.

ANNEX D – DELETED.

ANNEX E – DELETED.

ANNEX F ESTABLISHING GENDER OF PERSONS FOR THE PURPOSE OF SEARCHING

See Code C *Annex L*

PACE CODE B

REVISED CODE OF PRACTICE FOR SEARCHES OF PREMISES BY POLICE OFFICERS AND THE SEIZURE OF PROPERTY FOUND BY POLICE OFFICERS ON PERSONS OR PREMISES

Commencement—Transitional Arrangements

This code applies to applications for warrants made after 00.00 on 27 October 2013 and to searches and seizures taking place after 0.00 on 27 October 2013.

1 Introduction

1.1 This Code of Practice deals with police powers to:

- search premises
- seize and retain property found on premises and persons

1.1A These powers may be used to find:

- property and material relating to a crime
- wanted persons
- children who abscond from local authority accommodation where they have been remanded or committed by a court

1.2 A justice of the peace may issue a search warrant granting powers of entry, search and seizure, e.g. warrants to search for stolen property, drugs, firearms and evidence of serious offences. Police also have powers without a search warrant. The main ones provided by the Police and Criminal Evidence Act 1984 (PACE) include powers to search premises:

- to make an arrest
- after an arrest

1.3 The right to privacy and respect for personal property are key principles of the Human Rights Act 1998. Powers of entry, search and seizure should be fully and clearly justified before use because they may significantly interfere with the occupier's privacy. Officers should consider if the necessary objectives can be met by less intrusive means.

1.3A Powers to search and seize must be used fairly, responsibly, with respect for people who occupy premises being searched or are in charge of property being seized and without unlawful discrimination. Under the Equality Act 2010, section 149, when police officers are carrying out their functions, they also have a duty to have due regard to the need to eliminate unlawful discrimination, harassment and victimisation, to advance equality of opportunity between people who share a relevant protected characteristic and people who do not share it, and to take steps to foster good relations between those persons. (See *Note 1A*).

1.4 In all cases, police should therefore:

- exercise their powers courteously and with respect for persons and property
- only use reasonable force when this is considered necessary and proportionate to the circumstances

1.5 If the provisions of PACE and this Code are not observed, evidence obtained from a search may be open to question.

Note for Guidance

1A In paragraph 1.3A, 'relevant protected characteristic' includes: age, disability, gender reassignment, pregnancy and maternity, race, religion/belief, sex and sexual orientation.

2 General

2.1 This Code must be readily available at all police stations for consultation by:

- police officers
- police staff
- detained persons
- members of the public

2.2 The Notes for Guidance included are not provisions of this Code.

2.3 This Code applies to searches of premises:

(a) by police for the purposes of an investigation into an alleged offence, with the occupier's consent, other than:

- routine scene of crime searches;

- calls to a fire or burglary made by or on behalf of an occupier or searches following the activation of fire or burglar alarms or discovery of insecure premises;
- searches when paragraph 5.4 applies;
- bomb threat calls;

(b) under powers conferred on police officers by PACE, sections 17, 18 and 32;
(c) undertaken in pursuance of search warrants issued to and executed by constables in accordance with PACE, sections 15 and 16 (see *Note 2A*);
(d) subject to paragraph 2.6, under any other power given to police to enter premises with or without a search warrant for any purpose connected with the investigation into an alleged or suspected offence. (See *Note 2B*.)

For the purposes of this Code, 'premises' as defined in PACE, section 23, includes any place, vehicle, vessel, aircraft, hovercraft, tent or movable structure and any offshore installation as defined in the Mineral Workings (Offshore Installations) Act 1971, section 1. (See *Note 2D*.)

2.4 A person who has not been arrested but is searched during a search of premises should be searched in accordance with Code A. (See *Note 2C*.)

2.5 This Code does not apply to the exercise of a statutory power to enter premises or to inspect goods, equipment or procedures if the exercise of that power is not dependent on the existence of grounds for suspecting that an offence may have been committed and the person exercising the power has no reasonable grounds for such suspicion.

2.6 This Code does not affect any directions or requirements of a search warrant, order or other power to search and seize lawfully exercised in England or Wales that any item or evidence seized under that warrant, order or power be handed over to a police force, court, tribunal, or other authority outside England or Wales. For example, warrants and orders issued in Scotland or Northern Ireland (see *Note 2B(f)*) and search warrants and powers provided for in sections 14 to 17 of the Crime (International Co-operation) Act 2003.

2.7 When this Code requires the prior authority or agreement of an officer of at leastinspector or superintendent rank, that authority may be given by a sergeant or chief inspector authorised to perform the functions of the higher rank under PACE, section 107.5

2.8 Written records required under this Code not made in the search record shall, unless otherwise specified, be made:

- in the recording officer's pocket book ('pocket book' includes any official report book issued to police officers) or
- on forms provided for the purpose

2.9 Nothing in this Code requires the identity of officers, or anyone accompanying them during a search of premises, to be recorded or disclosed:
(a) in the case of enquiries linked to the investigation of terrorism; or
(b) if officers reasonably believe recording or disclosing their names might put them in danger.

In these cases officers should use warrant or other identification numbers and the name of their police station. Police staff should use any identification number provided to them by the police force. (See *Note 2E*.)

2.10 The 'officer in charge of the search' means the officer assigned specific duties and responsibilities under this Code. Whenever there is a search of premises to which this Code applies one officer must act as the officer in charge of the search. (See *Note 2F*.)

2.11 In this Code:
(a) 'designated person' means a person other than a police officer, designated under the Police Reform Act 2002, Part 4 who has specified powers and duties of police officers conferred or imposed on them. (See *Note 2G*.)
(b) any reference to a police officer includes a designated person acting in the exercise or performance of the powers and duties conferred or imposed on them by their designation.
(c) a person authorised to accompany police officers or designated persons in the execution of a warrant has the same powers as a constable in the execution of the warrant and the search and seizure of anything related to the warrant. These powers must be exercised in the company and under the supervision of a police officer. (See *Note 3C*.)

2.12 If a power conferred on a designated person:
(a) allows reasonable force to be used when exercised by a police officer, a designated person exercising that power has the same entitlement to use force;
(b) includes power to use force to enter any premises, that power is not exercisable by that designated person except:
(i) in the company and under the supervision of a police officer; or

(ii) for the purpose of:
- saving life or limb; or
- preventing serious damage to property.

2.13 Designated persons must have regard to any relevant provisions of the Codes of Practice.

Notes for Guidance

2A *PACE sections 15 and 16 apply to all search warrants issued to and executed by constables under any enactment, e.g. search warrants issued by a:*
(a) justice of the peace under the:
- *Theft Act 1968, section 26 – stolen property;*
- *Misuse of Drugs Act 1971, section 23 – controlled drugs;*
- *PACE, section 8 – evidence of an indictable offence;*
- *Terrorism Act 2000, Schedule 5, paragraph 1;*
- *Terrorism Prevention and Investigation Measures Act 2011, Schedule 5, paragraph 8(2)(b) search of premises for compliance purposes (see paragraph 10.1).*

(b) Circuit judge under:
- *PACE, Schedule 1;*
- *Terrorism Act 2000, Schedule 5, paragraph 11.*

2B *Examples of the other powers in paragraph 2.3(d) include:*
(a) Road Traffic Act 1988, section 6E(1) giving police power to enter premises under section 6E(1) to:
- *require a person to provide a specimen of breath; or*
- *arrest a person following:*
  - *a positive breath test;*
  - *failure to provide a specimen of breath;*

(b) Transport and Works Act 1992, section 30(4) giving police powers to enter premises mirroring the powers in (a) in relation to specified persons working on transport systems to which the Act applies;
(c) Criminal Justice Act 1988, section 139B giving police power to enter and search school premises for offensive weapons, bladed or pointed articles;
(d) Terrorism Act 2000, Schedule 5, paragraphs 3 and 15 empowering a superintendent in urgent cases to give written authority for police to enter and search premises for the purposes of a terrorist investigation;
(e) Explosives Act 1875, section 73(b) empowering a superintendent to give written authority for police to enter premises, examine and search them for explosives;
(f) search warrants and production orders or the equivalent issued in Scotland or Northern Ireland endorsed under the Summary Jurisdiction (Process) Act 1881 or the Petty Sessions (Ireland) Act 1851 respectively for execution in England and Wales.
(g) Terrorism Prevention and Investigation Measures Act 2011, Schedule 5, paragraphs 5(1), 6(2)(b) and 7(2), searches relating to TPIM notices (see paragraph 10.1).

2C *The Criminal Justice Act 1988, section 139B provides that a constable who has reasonable grounds to suspect an offence under the Criminal Justice Act 1988, section 139A or 139AA has or is being committed may enter school premises and search the premises and any persons on the premises for any bladed or pointed article or offensive weapon. Persons may be searched under a warrant issued under the Misuse of Drugs Act 1971, section 23(3) to search premises for drugs or documents only if the warrant specifically authorises the search of persons on the premises. Powers to search premises under certain terrorism provisions also authorise the search of persons on the premises, for example, under paragraphs 1, 2, 11 and 15 of Schedule 5 to the Terrorism Act 2000 and section 52 of the Anti-terrorism, Crime and Security Act 2001.*

2D *The Immigration Act 1971, Part III and Schedule 2 gives immigration officers powers to enter and search premises, seize and retain property, with and without a search warrant. These are similar to the powers available to police under search warrants issued by a justice of the peace and without a warrant under PACE, sections 17, 18, 19 and 32 except they only apply to specified offences under the Immigration Act 1971 and immigration control powers. For certain types of investigations and enquiries these powers avoid the need for the Immigration Service to rely on police officers becoming directly involved. When exercising these powers, immigration officers are required by the Immigration and Asylum Act 1999, section 145 to have regard to this Code's corresponding provisions. When immigration officers are dealing with persons or property at police stations, police officers should give appropriate assistance to help them discharge their specific duties and responsibilities.*

2E *The purpose of paragraph 2.9(b) is to protect those involved in serious organised crime investigations or arrests of particularly violent suspects when there is reliable information that those arrested or their associates may threaten or cause harm to the officers or anyone accompanying them during a search of premises. In cases of doubt, an officer of inspector rank or above should be consulted.*

2F *For the purposes of paragraph 2.10, the officer in charge of the search should normally be the most senior officer present. Some exceptions are:*
   - *(a) a supervising officer who attends or assists at the scene of a premises search may appoint an officer of lower rank as officer in charge of the search if that officer is:*
     - *more conversant with the facts;*
     - *a more appropriate officer to be in charge of the search;*
   - *(b) when all officers in a premises search are the same rank. The supervising officer if available, must make sure one of them is appointed officer in charge of the search, otherwise the officers themselves must nominate one of their number as the officer in charge;*
   - *(c) a senior officer assisting in a specialist role. This officer need not be regarded as having a general supervisory role over the conduct of the search or be appointed or expected to act as the officer in charge of the search.*

   Except in (c), nothing in this Note diminishes the role and responsibilities of a supervisory officer who is present at the search or knows of a search taking place.

2G *An officer of the rank of inspector or above may direct a designated investigating officer not to wear a uniform for the purposes of a specific operation.*

3 Search warrants and production orders

(a) Before making an application

3.1 When information appears to justify an application, the officer must take reasonable steps to check the information is accurate, recent and not provided maliciously or irresponsibly. An application may not be made on the basis of information from an anonymous source if corroboration has not been sought. (See *Note 3A.*)

3.2 The officer shall ascertain as specifically as possible the nature of the articles concerned and their location.

3.3 The officer shall make reasonable enquiries to:
   - (i) establish if:
     - anything is known about the likely occupier of the premises and the nature of the premises themselves;
     - the premises have been searched previously and how recently;
   - (ii) obtain any other relevant information.

3.4 An application:
   - (a) to a justice of the peace for a search warrant or to a Circuit judge for a search warrant or production order under PACE, Schedule 1 must be supported by a signed written authority from an officer of inspector rank or above:

     Note: If the case is an urgent application to a justice of the peace and an inspector or above is not readily available, the next most senior officer on duty can give the written authority.
   - (b) to a circuit judge under the Terrorism Act 2000, Schedule 5 for:
     - a production order;
     - search warrant; or
     - an order requiring an explanation of material seized or produced under such a warrant or production order, must be supported by a signed written authority from an officer of superintendent rank or above.

3.5 Except in a case of urgency, if there is reason to believe a search might have an adverse effect on relations between the police and the community, the officer in charge shall consult the local police/community liaison officer:
   - before the search; or
   - in urgent cases, as soon as practicable after the search

(b) Making an application

3.6 A search warrant application must be supported in writing, specifying:
   - (a) the enactment under which the application is made (see *Note 2A*);
   - (b) (i) whether the warrant is to authorise entry and search of:
     - one set of premises; or

- if the application is under PACE section 8, or Schedule 1, paragraph 12, more than one set of specified premises or all premises occupied or controlled by a specified person, and

(ii) the premises to be searched;

(c) the object of the search (see *Note 3B*);

(d) the grounds for the application, including, when the purpose of the proposed search is to find evidence of an alleged offence, an indication of how the evidence relates to the investigation;

(da) Where the application is under PACE section 8, or Schedule 1, paragraph 12 for a single warrant to enter and search:

(i) more than one set of specified premises; the officer must specify each set of premises which it is desired to enter and search;

(ii) all premises occupied or controlled by a specified person; the officer must specify;

- as many sets of premises which it is desired to enter and search as it is reasonably practicable to specify;
- the person who is in occupation or control of those premises and any others which it is desired to search;
- why it is necessary to search more premises than those which can be specified, and
- why it is not reasonably practicable to specify all the premises which it is desired to enter and search;

(db) Whether an application under PACE section 8 is for a warrant authorising entry and search on more than one occasion, and if so, the officer must state the grounds for this and whether the desired number of entries authorised is unlimited or a specified maximum;

(e) That there are no reasonable grounds to believe the material to be sought, when making application to a:

(i) justice of the peace or a Circuit judge consists of or includes items subject to legal privilege;

(ii) justice of the peace, consists of or includes excluded material or special procedure material;

Note: this does not affect the additional powers of seizure in the Criminal Justice and Police Act 2001, Part 2 covered in paragraph 7.7 (see *Note 3B*).

(f) if applicable, a request for the warrant to authorise a person or persons to accompany the officer who executes the warrant. (See *Note 3C*.)

3.7 A search warrant application under PACE, Schedule 1, paragraph 12(a), shall if appropriate indicate why it is believed service of notice of an application for a production order may seriously prejudice the investigation. Applications for search warrants under the Terrorism Act 2000, Schedule 5, paragraph 11 must indicate why a production order would not be appropriate.

3.8 If a search warrant application is refused, a further application may not be made for those premises unless supported by additional grounds.

Notes for Guidance

3A The identity of an informant need not be disclosed when making an application, but the officer should be prepared to answer any questions the magistrate or judge may have about:

- *the accuracy of previous information from that source, and*
- *any other related matters*

3B The information supporting a search warrant application should be as specific as possible, particularly in relation to the articles or persons being sought and where in the premises it is suspected they may be found. The meaning of 'items subject to legal privilege', 'excluded material' and 'special procedure material' are defined by PACE, sections 10, 11 and 14 respectively.

3C Under PACE, section 16(2), a search warrant may authorise persons other than police officers to accompany the constable who executes the warrant. This includes, e.g. any suitably qualified or skilled person or an expert in a particular field whose presence is needed to help accurately identify the material sought or to advise where certain evidence is most likely to be found and how it should be dealt with. It does not give them any right to force entry, but it gives them the right to be on the premises during the search and to search for or seize property without the occupier's permission.

4 Entry without warrant – particular powers

(a) Making an arrest etc

4.1 The conditions under which an officer may enter and search premises without a warrant are set out in PACE, section 17. It should be noted that this section does not create or confer any powers of arrest. See other powers in *Note 2B(a)*.

(b) Search of premises where arrest takes place or the arrested person was immediately before arrest

4.2 When a person has been arrested for an indictable offence, a police officer has power under PACE, section 32 to search the premises where the person was arrested or where the person was immediately before being arrested.

(c) Search of premises occupied or controlled by the arrested person

4.3 The specific powers to search premises which are occupied or controlled by a person arrested for an indictable offence are set out in PACE, section 18. They may not be exercised, except if section 18(5) applies, unless an officer of inspector rank or above has given written authority. That authority should only be given when the authorising officer is satisfied that the premises are occupied or controlled by the arrested person and that the necessary grounds exist. If possible the authorising officer should record the authority on the Notice of Powers and Rights and, subject to paragraph 2.9, sign the Notice. The record of the grounds for the search and the nature of the evidence sought as required by section 18(7) of the Act should be made in:

- the custody record if there is one, otherwise
- the officer's pocket book, or
- the search record

5 Search with consent

5.1 Subject to paragraph 5.4, if it is proposed to search premises with the consent of a person entitled to grant entry the consent must, if practicable, be given in writing on the Notice of Powers and Rights before the search. The officer must make any necessary enquiries to be satisfied the person is in a position to give such consent. (See *Notes 5A* and *5B*.)

5.2 Before seeking consent the officer in charge of the search shall state the purpose of the proposed search and its extent. This information must be as specific as possible, particularly regarding the articles or persons being sought and the parts of the premises to be searched. The person concerned must be clearly informed they are not obliged to consent, that any consent given can be withdrawn at any time, including before the search starts or while it is underway and anything seized may be produced in evidence. If at the time the person is not suspected of an offence, the officer shall say this when stating the purpose of the search.

5.3 An officer cannot enter and search or continue to search premises under paragraph 5.1 if consent is given under duress or withdrawn before the search is completed.

5.4 It is unnecessary to seek consent under paragraphs 5.1 and 5.2 if this would cause disproportionate inconvenience to the person concerned. (See *Note 5C*.)

Notes for Guidance

5A *In a lodging house, hostel or similar accommodation, every reasonable effort should be made to obtain the consent of the tenant, lodger or occupier. A search should not be made solely on the basis of the landlord's consent.*

5B *If the intention is to search premises under the authority of a warrant or a power of entry and search without warrant, and the occupier of the premises co-operates in accordance with paragraph 6.4, there is no need to obtain written consent.*

5C *Paragraph 5.4 is intended to apply when it is reasonable to assume innocent occupiers would agree to, and expect, police to take the proposed action, e.g. if:*

- *a suspect has fled the scene of a crime or to evade arrest and it is necessary quickly to check surrounding gardens and readily accessible places to see if the suspect is hiding, or*
- *police have arrested someone in the night after a pursuit and it is necessary to make a brief check of gardens along the pursuit route to see if stolen or incriminating articles have been discarded.*

6 Searching premises – general considerations

(a) Time of searches

6.1 Searches made under warrant must be made within three calendar months of the date the warrant is issued or within the period specified in the enactment under which the warrant is issued if this is shorter.

6.2 Searches must be made at a reasonable hour unless this might frustrate the purpose of the search.

6.3 When the extent or complexity of a search mean it is likely to take a long time, the officer in charge of the search may consider using the seize and sift powers referred to in section 7.

6.3A A warrant under PACE, section 8 may authorise entry to and search of premises on more than one occasion if, on the application, the justice of the peace is satisfied that it is necessary to authorise multiple entries in order to achieve the purpose for which the warrant is issued. No premises may be entered or searched on any subsequent occasions without the prior written authority of an officer of the rank of inspector who is not involved in the investigation. All other warrants authorise entry on one occasion only.

6.3B Where a warrant under PACE section 8, or Schedule 1, paragraph 12 authorises entry to and search of all premises occupied or controlled by a specified person, no premises which are not specified in the warrant may be entered and searched without the prior written authority of an officer of the rank of inspector who is not involved in the investigation.

(b) Entry other than with consent

6.4 The officer in charge of the search shall first try to communicate with the occupier, or any other person entitled to grant access to the premises, explain the authority under which entry is sought and ask the occupier to allow entry, unless:

(i) the search premises are unoccupied;
(ii) the occupier and any other person entitled to grant access are absent;
(iii) there are reasonable grounds for believing that alerting the occupier or any other person entitled to grant access would frustrate the object of the search or endanger officers or other people.

6.5 Unless sub-paragraph 6.4(iii) applies, if the premises are occupied the officer, subject to paragraph 2.9, shall, before the search begins:

(i) identify him or herself, show their warrant card (if not in uniform) and state the purpose of, and grounds for, the search, and
(ii) Identify and introduce any person accompanying the officer on the search (such persons should carry identification for production on request) and briefly describe that person's role in the process.

6.6 Reasonable and proportionate force may be used if necessary to enter premises if the officer in charge of the search is satisfied the premises are those specified in any warrant, or in exercise of the powers described in paragraphs 4.1 to 4.3, and if:

(i) the occupier or any other person entitled to grant access has refused entry;
(ii) it is impossible to communicate with the occupier or any other person entitled to grant access; or
(iii) any of the provisions of paragraph 6.4 apply.

(c) Notice of Powers and Rights

6.7 If an officer conducts a search to which this Code applies the officer shall, unless it is impracticable to do so, provide the occupier with a copy of a Notice in a standard format:

(i) specifying if the search is made under warrant, with consent, or in the exercise of the powers described in paragraphs 4.1 to 4.3. Note: the notice format shall provide for authority or consent to be indicated (see *paragraphs 4.3* and *5.1*);
(ii) summarising the extent of the powers of search and seizure conferred by PACE and other relevant legislation as appropriate;
(iii) explaining the rights of the occupier and the owner of the property seized;
(iv) explaining compensation may be payable in appropriate cases for damages caused entering and searching premises, and giving the address to send a compensation application (see *Note 6A*), and
(v) stating this Code is available at any police station.

6.8 If the occupier is:

- present; copies of the Notice and warrant shall, if practicable, be given to them before the search begins, unless the officer in charge of the search reasonably believes this would frustrate the object of the search or endanger officers or other people;
- not present; copies of the Notice and warrant shall be left in a prominent place on the premises or appropriate part of the premises and endorsed, subject to paragraph 2.9 with the name of the officer in charge of the search, the date and time of the search

The warrant shall be endorsed to show this has been done.

(d) Conduct of searches

6.9 Premises may be searched only to the extent necessary to achieve the purpose of the search, having regard to the size and nature of whatever is sought.

6.9A A search may not continue under:

- a warrant's authority once all the things specified in that warrant have been found;
- any other power once the object of that search has been achieved.

6.9B No search may continue once the officer in charge of the search is satisfied whatever is being sought is not on the premises (see *Note 6B*). This does not prevent a further search of the same premises if additional grounds come to light supporting a further application for a search warrant or exercise or further exercise of another power. For example, when, as a result of new information, it is believed articles previously not found or additional articles are on the premises.

6.10 Searches must be conducted with due consideration for the property and privacy of the occupier and with no more disturbance than necessary. Reasonable force may be used only when necessary and proportionate because the co-operation of the occupier cannot be obtained or is insufficient for the purpose. (See *Note 6C*.)

6.11 A friend, neighbour or other person must be allowed to witness the search if the occupier wishes unless the officer in charge of the search has reasonable grounds for believing the presence of the person asked for would seriously hinder the investigation or endanger officers or other people. A search need not be unreasonably delayed for this purpose. A record of the action taken should be made on the premises search record including the grounds for refusing the occupier's request.

6.12 A person is not required to be cautioned prior to being asked questions that are solely necessary for the purpose of furthering the proper and effective conduct of a search, (see Code C, *paragraph 10.1(c)*). For example, questions to discover the occupier of specified premises, to find a key to open a locked drawer or cupboard or to otherwise seek co-operation during the search or to determine if a particular item is liable to be seized.

6.12A If questioning goes beyond what is necessary for the purpose of the exemption in Code C, the exchange is likely to constitute an interview as defined by Code C, paragraph 11.1A and would require the associated safeguards included in Code C, section 10.

(e) Leaving premises

6.13 If premises have been entered by force, before leaving the officer in charge of the search must make sure they are secure by:

- arranging for the occupier or their agent to be present;
- any other appropriate means.

(f) Searches under PACE Schedule 1 or the Terrorism Act 2000, Schedule 5

6.14 An officer shall be appointed as the officer in charge of the search (see *paragraph 2.10*), in respect of any search made under a warrant issued under PACE Act 1984, Schedule 1 or the Terrorism Act 2000, Schedule 5. They are responsible for making sure the search is conducted with discretion and in a manner that causes the least possible disruption to any business or other activities carried out on the premises.

6.15 Once the officer in charge of the search is satisfied material may not be taken from the premises without their knowledge, they shall ask for the documents or other records concerned. The officer in charge of the search may also ask to see the index to files held on the premises, and the officers conducting the search may inspect any files which, according to the index, appear to contain the material sought. A more extensive search of the premises may be made only if:

- the person responsible for them refuses to:
  - produce the material sought, or
  - allow access to the index.
- it appears the index is:
  - inaccurate, or
  - incomplete.
- for any other reason the officer in charge of the search has reasonable grounds for believing such a search is necessary in order to find the material sought.

Notes for Guidance

6A *Whether compensation is appropriate depends on the circumstances in each case. Compensation for damage caused when effecting entry is unlikely to be appropriate if the search was lawful, and the force used can be shown to be reasonable, proportionate and necessary to effect entry. If the wrong premises are searched by mistake everything possible should be done at the earliest opportunity to allay any sense of grievance and there should normally be a strong presumption in favour of paying compensation.*

6B *It is important that, when possible, all those involved in a search are fully briefed about any powers to be exercised and the extent and limits within which it should be conducted.*

6C *In all cases the number of officers and other persons involved in executing the warrant should be determined by what is reasonable and necessary according to the particular circumstances.*

7 Seizure and retention of property

(a) Seizure

7.1 Subject to paragraph 7.2, an officer who is searching any person or premises under any statutory power or with the consent of the occupier may seize anything:

(a) covered by a warrant;

(b) the officer has reasonable grounds for believing is evidence of an offence or has been obtained in consequence of the commission of an offence but only if seizure is necessary to prevent the items being concealed, lost, disposed of, altered, damaged, destroyed or tampered with;

(c) covered by the powers in the Criminal Justice and Police Act 2001, Part 2 allowing an officer to seize property from persons or premises and retain it for sifting or examination elsewhere.

See *Note 7B.*

7.2 No item may be seized which an officer has reasonable grounds for believing to be subject to legal privilege, as defined in PACE, section 10, other than under the Criminal Justice and Police Act 2001, Part 2.

7.3 Officers must be aware of the provisions in the Criminal Justice and Police Act 2001, section 59, allowing for applications to a judicial authority for the return of property seized and the subsequent duty to secure in section 60. (See *paragraph 7.12(iii).*)

7.4 An officer may decide it is not appropriate to seize property because of an explanation from the person holding it but may nevertheless have reasonable grounds for believing it was obtained in consequence of an offence by some person. In these circumstances, the officer should identify the property to the holder, inform the holder of their suspicions and explain the holder may be liable to civil or criminal proceedings if they dispose of, alter or destroy the property.

7.5 An officer may arrange to photograph, image or copy, any document or other article they have the power to seize in accordance with paragraph 7.1. This is subject to specific restrictions on the examination, imaging or copying of certain property seized under the Criminal Justice and Police Act 2001, Part 2. An officer must have regard to their statutory obligation to retain an original document or other article only when a photograph or copy is not sufficient.

7.6 If an officer considers information stored in any electronic form and accessible from the premises could be used in evidence, they may require the information to be produced in a form:

- which can be taken away and in which it is visible and legible, or
- from which it can readily be produced in a visible and legible form.

(b) Criminal Justice and Police Act 2001: Specific procedures for seize and sift powers

7.7 The Criminal Justice and Police Act 2001, Part 2 gives officers limited powers to seize property from premises or persons so they can sift or examine it elsewhere. Officers must be careful they only exercise these powers when it is essential and they do not remove any more material than necessary. The removal of large volumes of material, much of which may not ultimately be retainable, may have serious implications for the owners, particularly when they are involved in business or activities such as journalism or the provision of medical services. Officers must carefully consider if removing copies or images of relevant material or data would be a satisfactory alternative to removing originals. When originals are taken, officers must be prepared to facilitate the provision of copies or images for the owners when reasonably practicable. (See *Note 7C.*)

7.8 Property seized under the Criminal Justice and Police Act 2001, sections 50 or 51 must be kept securely and separately from any material seized under other powers. An examination under section 53 to determine which elements may be retained must be carried out at the earliest practicable time, having due regard to the desirability of allowing the person from whom the property was seized, or a person with an interest in the property, an opportunity of being present or represented at the examination.

7.8A All reasonable steps should be taken to accommodate an interested person's request to be present, provided the request is reasonable and subject to the need to prevent harm to, interference with, or unreasonable delay to the investigatory process. If an examination proceeds in the absence of an interested person who asked to attend or their representative, the officer who exercised the relevant seizure power must give that person a written notice of why the examination was carried out in those circumstances. If it is necessary for security reasons or to maintain confidentiality officers may exclude interested persons from decryption or other processes which facilitate the examination but do not form part of it. (See *Note 7D.*)

7.9 It is the responsibility of the officer in charge of the investigation to make sure property is returned in accordance with sections 53 to 55. Material which there is no power to retain must be:

- separated from the rest of the seized property, and
- returned as soon as reasonably practicable after examination of all the seized property.

7.9A Delay is only warranted if very clear and compelling reasons exist, for example:

- the unavailability of the person to whom the material is to be returned, or
- the need to agree a convenient time to return a large volume of material

7.9B Legally privileged, excluded or special procedure material which cannot be retained must be returned:

- as soon as reasonably practicable, and
- without waiting for the whole examination.

7.9C As set out in section 58, material must be returned to the person from whom it was seized, except when it is clear some other person has a better right to it. (See *Note 7E.*)

7.10 When an officer involved in the investigation has reasonable grounds to believe a person with a relevant interest in property seized under section 50 or 51 intends to make an application under section 59 for the return of any legally privileged, special procedure or excluded material, the officer in charge of the investigation should be informed as soon as practicable and the material seized should be kept secure in accordance with section 61. (See *Note 7C.*)

7.11 The officer in charge of the investigation is responsible for making sure property is properly secured. Securing involves making sure the property is not examined, copied, imaged or put to any other use except at the request, or with the consent, of the applicant or in accordance with the directions of the appropriate judicial authority. Any request, consent or directions must be recorded in writing and signed by both the initiator and the officer in charge of the investigation. (See *Notes 7F* and *7 G.*)

7.12 When an officer exercises a power of seizure conferred by sections 50 or 51 they shall provide the occupier of the premises or the person from whom the property is being seized with a written notice:

(i) specifying what has been seized under the powers conferred by that section;
(ii) specifying the grounds for those powers;
(iii) setting out the effect of sections 59 to 61 covering the grounds for a person with a relevant interest in seized property to apply to a judicial authority for its return and the duty of officers to secure property in certain circumstances when an application is made, and
(iv) specifying the name and address of the person to whom:
  - notice of an application to the appropriate judicial authority in respect of any of the seized property must be given;
  - an application may be made to allow attendance at the initial examination of the property.

7.13 If the occupier is not present but there is someone in charge of the premises, the notice shall be given to them. If no suitable person is available, so the notice will easily be found it should either be:

- left in a prominent place on the premises, or
- attached to the exterior of the premises.

(c) Retention

7.14 Subject to paragraph 7.15, anything seized in accordance with the above provisions may be retained only for as long as is necessary. It may be retained, among other purposes:

(i) for use as evidence at a trial for an offence;
(ii) to facilitate the use in any investigation or proceedings of anything to which it is inextricably linked (see *Note 7H*);
(iii) for forensic examination or other investigation in connection with an offence;
(iv) in order to establish its lawful owner when there are reasonable grounds for believing it has been stolen or obtained by the commission of an offence.

7.15 Property shall not be retained under paragraph 7.14(i), (ii) or (iii) if a copy or image would be sufficient.

(d) Rights of owners etc

7.16 If property is retained, the person who had custody or control of it immediately before seizure must, on request, be provided with a list or description of the property within a reasonable time.

7.17 That person or their representative must be allowed supervised access to the property to examine it or have it photographed or copied, or must be provided with a photograph or copy, in either case within a reasonable time of any request and at their own expense, unless the officer in charge of an investigation has reasonable grounds for believing this would:

(i) prejudice the investigation of any offence or criminal proceedings; or

(ii) lead to the commission of an offence by providing access to unlawful material such as pornography;

A record of the grounds shall be made when access is denied.

Notes for Guidance

7A *Any person claiming property seized by the police may apply to a magistrates' court under the Police (Property) Act 1897 for its possession and should, if appropriate, be advised of this procedure.*

7B *The powers of seizure conferred by PACE, sections 18(2) and 19(3) extend to the seizure of the whole premises when it is physically possible to seize and retain the premises in their totality and practical considerations make seizure desirable. For example, police may remove premises such as tents, vehicles or caravans to a police station for the purpose of preserving evidence.*

7C *Officers should consider reaching agreement with owners and/or other interested parties on the procedures for examining a specific set of property, rather than awaiting the judicial authority's determination. Agreement can sometimes give a quicker and more satisfactory route for all concerned and minimise costs and legal complexities.*

7D *What constitutes a relevant interest in specific material may depend on the nature of that material and the circumstances in which it is seized. Anyone with a reasonable claim to ownership of the material and anyone entrusted with its safe keeping by the owner should be considered.*

7E *Requirements to secure and return property apply equally to all copies, images or other material created because of seizure of the original property.*

7F *The mechanics of securing property vary according to the circumstances; 'bagging up', i.e. placing material in sealed bags or containers and strict subsequent control of access is the appropriate procedure in many cases.*

7G *When material is seized under the powers of seizure conferred by PACE, the duty to retain it under the Code of Practice issued under the Criminal Procedure and Investigations Act 1996 is subject to the provisions on retention of seized material in PACE, section 22.*

7H *Paragraph 7.14 (ii) applies if inextricably linked material is seized under the Criminal Justice and Police Act 2001, sections 50 or 51. Inextricably linked material is material it is not reasonably practicable to separate from other linked material without prejudicing the use of that other material in any investigation or proceedings. For example, it may not be possible to separate items of data held on computer disk without damaging their evidential integrity. Inextricably linked material must not be examined, imaged, copied or used for any purpose other than for proving the source and/or integrity of the linked material.*

8 Action after searches

8.1 If premises are searched in circumstances where this Code applies, unless the exceptions in paragraph 2.3(a) apply, on arrival at a police station the officer in charge of the search shall make or have made a record of the search, to include:

(i) the address of the searched premises;

(ii) the date, time and duration of the search;

(iii) the authority used for the search:

- if the search was made in exercise of a statutory power to search premises without warrant, the power which was used for the search:
- if the search was made under a warrant or with written consent;
  - a copy of the warrant and the written authority to apply for it, see *paragraph 3.4*; or
  - the written consent;

  shall be appended to the record or the record shall show the location of the copy warrant or consent;

(iv) subject to paragraph 2.9, the names of:

- the officer(s) in charge of the search;
- all other officers and authorised persons who conducted the search;

(v) the names of any people on the premises if they are known;

(vi) any grounds for refusing the occupier's request to have someone present during the search, see *paragraph 6.11*;

(vii) a list of any articles seized or the location of a list and, if not covered by a warrant, the grounds for their seizure;

(viii) whether force was used, and the reason;

(ix) details of any damage caused during the search, and the circumstances;
(x) if applicable, the reason it was not practicable;
(a) to give the occupier a copy of the Notice of Powers and Rights, see *paragraph 6.7*;
(b) before the search to give the occupier a copy of the Notice, see *paragraph 6.8*;
(xi) when the occupier was not present, the place where copies of the Notice of Powers and Rights and search warrant were left on the premises, see *paragraph 6.8*.

8.2 On each occasion when premises are searched under warrant, the warrant authorising the search on that occasion shall be endorsed to show:
(i) if any articles specified in the warrant were found and the address where found;
(ii) if any other articles were seized;
(iii) the date and time it was executed and if present, the name of the occupier or if the occupier is not present the name of the person in charge of the premises;
(iv) subject to *paragraph 2.9*, the names of the officers who executed it and any authorised persons who accompanied them, and
(v) if a copy, together with a copy of the Notice of Powers and Rights was:
- handed to the occupier, or
- endorsed as required by paragraph 6.8; and left on the premises and where.

8.3 Any warrant shall be returned within three calendar months of its issue or sooner on completion of the search(es) authorised by that warrant, if it was issued by a:
- justice of the peace, to the designated officer for the local justice area in which the justice was acting when issuing the warrant; or
- judge, to the appropriate officer of the court concerned.

9 Search registers

9.1 A search register will be maintained at each sub-divisional or equivalent police station. All search records required under paragraph 8.1 shall be made, copied, or referred to in the register. (See *Note 9A*.)

Note for Guidance

9A Paragraph 9.1 also applies to search records made by immigration officers. In these cases, a search register must also be maintained at an immigration office. (See also Note 2D.)

10 Searches under Schedule 5 to the Terrorism Prevention and Investigation Measures Act 2011

10.1 This Code applies to the powers of constables under Schedule 5 to the Terrorism Prevention and Investigation Measures Act 2011 relating to TPIM notices to enter and search premises subject to the modifications in the following paragraphs.

10.2 In paragraph 2.3(d), the reference to the investigation into an alleged or suspected offence include the enforcement of terrorism prevention and investigation measures which may be imposed on an individual by a TPIM notice in accordance with the Terrorism Prevention and Investigation Measures Act 2011.

10.3 References to the purpose and object of the entry and search of premises, the nature of articles sought and what may be seized and retained include (as appropriate):
(a) in relation to the power to search without a search warrant in paragraph 5 (for purposes of serving TPIM notice), finding the individual on whom the notice is to be served.
(b) in relation to the power to search without a search warrant in paragraph 6 (at time of serving TPIM notice), ascertaining whether there is anything in the premises, that contravenes measures specified in the notice. (See *Note 10A*.)
(c) in relation to the power to search without a search warrant under paragraph 7 (suspected absconding), ascertaining whether a person has absconded or if there is anything on the premises which will assist in the pursuit or arrest of an individual in respect of whom a TPIM notice is force who is reasonably suspected of having absconded.
(d) in relation to the power to search under a search warrant issued under paragraph 8 (for compliance purposes), determining whether an individual in respect of whom a TPIM notice is in force is complying with measures specified in the notice. (See *Note 10A*.)

Note for Guidance

10A Searches of individuals under Schedule 5, paragraphs 6(2)(a) (at time of serving TPIM notice) and 8(2)(a) (for compliance purposes) must be conducted and recorded in accordance with Code A. (See Code A paragraph 2.18A for details.)

POLICE AND CRIMINAL EVIDENCE ACT 1984 (PACE) — CODE C

REVISED CODE OF PRACTICE FOR THE DETENTION, TREATMENT AND QUESTIONING OF PERSONS BY POLICE OFFICERS

Commencement—Transitional Arrangements

This Code applies to people in police detention after 00.00 on 21 August 2019, notwithstanding that their period of detention may have commenced before that time.

1 General

1.0 The powers and procedures in this Code must be used fairly, responsibly, with respect for the people to whom they apply and without unlawful discrimination. Under the Equality Act 2010, section 149 (Public sector Equality Duty), police forces must, in carrying out their functions, have due regard to the need to eliminate unlawful discrimination, harassment, victimisation and any other conduct which is prohibited by that Act, to advance equality of opportunity between people who share a relevant protected characteristic and people who do not share it, and to foster good relations between those persons. The Equality Act *also* makes it unlawful for police officers to discriminate against, harass or victimise any person on the grounds of the 'protected characteristics' of age, disability, gender reassignment, race, religion or belief, sex and sexual orientation, marriage and civil partnership, pregnancy and maternity, when using their powers. See *Notes 1A* and *1AA.*

1.1 All persons in custody must be dealt with expeditiously, and released as soon as the need for detention no longer applies.

1.1A A custody officer must perform the functions in this Code as soon as practicable. A custody officer will not be in breach of this Code if delay is justifiable and reasonable steps are taken to prevent unnecessary delay. The custody record shall show when a delay has occurred and the reason. See *Note 1H.*

1.2 This Code of Practice must be readily available at all police stations for consultation by:

- police officers;
- police staff;
- detained persons;
- members of the public.

1.3 The provisions of this Code:

- include the Annexes
- do not include the Notes for Guidance *which* form guidance to police officers and others about its application and interpretation.

1.4 If at any time an officer has any reason to suspect that a person of any age may be vulnerable (see *paragraph 1.13(d)*), in the absence of clear evidence to dispel that suspicion, that person shall be treated as such for the purposes of this Code and to establish whether any such reason may exist in relation to a person suspected of committing an offence (see *paragraph 10.1* and *Note 10A*), the custody officer in the case of a detained person, or the officer investigating the offence in the case of a person who has not been arrested or detained, shall take, or cause to be taken, (see *paragraph 3.5* and *Note 3F*) the following action:

(a) reasonable enquiries shall be made to ascertain what information is available that is relevant to any of the factors described in *paragraph 1.13(d)* as indicating that the person may be vulnerable might apply;

(b) a record shall be made describing whether any of those factors appear to apply and provide any reason to suspect that the person may be vulnerable or (as the case may be) may not be vulnerable; and

(c) the record mentioned in sub-paragraph (b) shall be made available to be taken into account by police officers, police staff and any others who, in accordance with the provisions of this or any other Code, are required or entitled to communicate with the person in question. This would include any solicitor, appropriate adult and healthcare professional and is particularly relevant to communication by telephone or by means of a live link (see *paragraphs 12.9A* (interviews), *13.12* (interpretation), and *15.3C, 15.11A, 15.11B, 15.11C* and *15.11D* (reviews and extension of detention)).

See *Notes 1G, 1GA, 1GB* and *1GC.*

1.5 Anyone who appears to be under 18, shall, in the absence of clear evidence that they are older, be treated as a juvenile for the purposes of this Code and any other Code. See *Note 1L.*

1.5A *Not used.*

1.6 If a person appears to be blind, seriously visually impaired, deaf, unable to read or speak or has difficulty orally because of a speech impediment, they shall be treated as such for the purposes of this Code in the absence of clear evidence to the contrary.

1.7 'The appropriate adult' means, in the case of a:

(a) juvenile:

(i) the parent, guardian or, if the juvenile is in the care of a local authority or voluntary organisation, a person representing that authority or organisation (see *Note 1B*);

(ii) a social worker of a local authority (see *Note 1C*);

(iii) failing these, some other responsible adult aged 18 or over who is *not*:

- a police officer;
- employed by the police;
- under the direction or control of the chief officer of a police force; or
- a person who provides services under contractual arrangements (but without being employed by the chief officer of a police force), to assist that force in relation to the discharge of its chief officer's functions, whether or not they are on duty at the time.

See *Note 1F*.

(b) a person who is vulnerable (see *paragraph 1.4* and *Note 1D*):

(i) a relative, guardian or other person responsible for their care or custody;

(ii) someone experienced in dealing with vulnerable persons but who is *not*:

- a police officer;
- employed by the police;
- under the direction or control of the chief officer of a police force; or
- a person who provides services under contractual arrangements (but without being employed by the chief officer of a police force), to assist that force in relation to the discharge of its chief officer's functions,

whether or not they are on duty at the time.

(iii) failing these, some other responsible adult aged 18 or over who is other than a person described in the bullet points in *sub-paragraph (b)(ii)* above.

See *Note 1F*.

1.7A The role of the appropriate adult is to safeguard the rights, entitlements and welfare of juveniles and vulnerable persons (see *paragraphs 1.4* and *1.5*) to whom the provisions of this and any other Code of Practice apply. For this reason, the appropriate adult is expected, amongst other things, to:

- support, advise and assist them when, in accordance with this Code or any other Code of Practice, they are given or asked to provide information or participate in any procedure;
- observe whether the police are acting properly and fairly to respect their rights and entitlements, and inform an officer of the rank of inspector or above if they consider that they are not;
- assist them to communicate with the police whilst respecting their right to say nothing unless they want to as set out in the terms of the caution (see *paragraphs 10.5* and *10.6*);
- help them to understand their rights and ensure that those rights are protected and respected (see *paragraphs 3.15, 3.17, 6.5A* and *11.17*).

1.8 If this Code requires a person be given certain information, they do not have to be given it if at the time they are incapable of understanding what is said, are violent or may become violent or in urgent need of medical attention, but they must be given it as soon as practicable.

1.9 References to a custody officer include any police officer who, for the time being, is performing the functions of a custody officer.

1.9A When this Code requires the prior authority or agreement of an officer of at least inspector or superintendent rank, that authority may be given by a sergeant or chief inspector authorised to perform the functions of the higher rank under the Police and Criminal Evidence Act 1984 (PACE), section 107.

1.10 Subject to *paragraph 1.12*, this Code applies to people in custody at police stations in England and Wales, whether or not they have been arrested, and to those removed to a police station as a place of safety under the Mental Health Act 1983, sections 135 and 136, as amended by the Policing and Crime Act 2017 (see *paragraph 3.16*). *Section 15* applies solely to people in police detention, e.g. those brought to a police station under arrest or arrested at a police station for an offence after going there voluntarily.

1.11 No part of this Code applies to a detained person:

(a) to whom PACE Code H applies because:

- they are detained following arrest under section 41 of the Terrorism Act 2000 (TACT) and not charged; or

- an authorisation has been given under section 22 of the Counter-Terrorism Act 2008 (CTACT) (post-charge questioning of terrorist suspects) to interview them.

(b) to whom the Code of Practice issued under paragraph 6 of Schedule 14 to TACT applies because they are detained for examination under Schedule 7 to TACT.

1.12 This Code does not apply to people in custody:

(i) arrested by officers under the Criminal Justice and Public Order Act 1994, section 136(2) on warrants issued in Scotland, or arrested or detained without warrant under section 137(2) by officers from a police force in Scotland. In these cases, police powers and duties and the person's rights and entitlements whilst at a police station in England or Wales are the same as those in Scotland;

(ii) arrested under the Immigration and Asylum Act 1999, section 142(3) in order to have their fingerprints taken;

(iii) whose detention has been authorised under Schedules 2 or 3 to the Immigration Act 1971 or section 62 of the Nationality, Immigration and Asylum Act 2002;

(iv) who are convicted or remanded prisoners held in police cells on behalf of the Prison Service under the Imprisonment (Temporary Provisions) Act 1980;

(v) *Not used.*

(vi) detained for searches under stop and search powers except as required by Code A.

The provisions on conditions of detention and treatment in *sections 8* and *9* must be considered as the minimum standards of treatment for such detainees.

1.13 In this Code:

(a) 'designated person' means a person other than a police officer, who has specified powers and duties conferred or imposed on them by designation under section 38 or 39 of the Police Reform Act 2002;

(b) reference to a police officer includes a designated person acting in the exercise or performance of the powers and duties conferred or imposed on them by their designation;

(c) if there is doubt as to whether the person should be treated, or continued to be treated, as being male or female in the case of:

  (i) a search carried out or observed by a person of the same sex as the detainee; or

  (ii) any other procedure which requires action to be taken or information to be given that depends on whether the person is to be treated as being male or female;

  then the gender of the detainee and other parties concerned should be established and recorded in line with *Annex L* of this Code.

(d) 'vulnerable' applies to any person who, because of a mental health condition or mental disorder (see *Notes 1G and 1GB*):

  (i) may have difficulty understanding or communicating effectively about the full implications for them of any procedures and processes connected with:
  - their arrest and detention; or (as the case may be)
  - their voluntary attendance at a police station or their presence elsewhere (see *paragraph 3.21*), for the purpose of a voluntary interview; and
  - the exercise of their rights and entitlements.

  (ii) does not appear to understand the significance of what they are told, of questions they are asked or of their replies:

  (iii) appears to be particularly prone to:
  - becoming confused and unclear about their position;
  - providing unreliable, misleading or incriminating information without knowing or wishing to do so;
  - accepting or acting on suggestions from others without consciously knowing or wishing to do so; or
  - readily agreeing to suggestions or proposals without any protest or question.

(e) 'Live link' means:

  (i) for the purpose of *paragraph 12.9A;* an arrangement by means of which the *interviewing officer* who is not present at the police station where the detainee is held, is able to see and hear, and *to be seen and heard by,* the detainee concerned, the detainee's solicitor, appropriate adult and interpreter (as applicable) and the officer who has custody of that detainee (see *Note 1N*).

  (ii) for the purpose of *paragraph 15.9A;* an arrangement by means of which the *review officer* who is not present at the police station where the detainee is held, is able to see and hear, and to be seen and heard by, the detainee concerned and the detainee's solicitor, appropriate adult and interpreter (as applicable) (see *Note 1N*). The use of live link for decisions about detention under *section 45A of PACE* is subject to regulations made by the Secretary of State being in force.

(iii) for the purpose of *paragraph 15.11A*; an arrangement by means of which the *authorising officer* who is not present at the police station where the detainee is held, is able to see and hear, and to be seen and heard by, the detainee concerned and the detainee's solicitor, appropriate adult and interpreter (as applicable) (see *Note 1N*).

(iv) for the purpose of *paragraph 15.11C*; an arrangement by means of which the *detainee* when not present in the court where the hearing is being held, is able to see and hear, and to be seen and heard by, the court during the hearing (see *Note 1N*).

Note: Chief officers must be satisfied that live link used in their force area for the above purposes provides for accurate and secure communication between the detainee, the detainee's solicitor, appropriate adult and interpreter (as applicable). This includes ensuring that at any time during which the live link is being used: a person cannot see, hear or otherwise obtain access to any such communications unless so authorised or allowed by the custody officer or, in the case of an interview, the interviewer and that as applicable, the confidentiality of any private consultation between a suspect and their solicitor and appropriate adult is maintained.

1.14 Designated persons are entitled to use reasonable force as follows:

(a) when exercising a power conferred on them which allows a police officer exercising that power to use reasonable force, a designated person has the same entitlement to use force; and

(b) at other times when carrying out duties conferred or imposed on them that also entitle them to use reasonable force, for example:

- when at a police station carrying out the duty to keep detainees for whom they are responsible under control and to assist any police officer or designated person to keep any detainee under control and to prevent their escape;
- when securing, or assisting any police officer or designated person in securing, the detention of a person at a police station;
- when escorting, or assisting any police officer or designated person in escorting, a detainee within a police station;
- for the purpose of saving life or limb; or
- preventing serious damage to property.

1.15 Nothing in this Code prevents the custody officer, or other police officer or designated person (see *paragraph 1.13(a)*) given custody of the detainee by the custody officer, from allowing another person (see *(a)* and *(b)* below) to carry out individual procedures or tasks at the police station if the law allows. However, the officer or designated person given custody remains responsible for making sure the procedures and tasks are carried out correctly in accordance with the Codes of Practice (see *paragraph 3.5* and *Note 3F*). The other person who is allowed to carry out the procedures or tasks must be someone who *at that time*, is:

(a) under the direction and control of the chief officer of the force responsible for the police station in question; or

(b) providing services under contractual arrangements (but without being employed by the chief officer the police force), to assist a police force in relation to the discharge of its chief officer's functions.

1.16 Designated persons and others mentioned in *sub-paragraphs (a)* and *(b)* of *paragraph 1.15*, must have regard to any relevant provisions of the Codes of Practice.

1.17 In any provision of this or any other Code which allows or requires police officers or police staff to make a record in their report book, the reference to report book shall include any official report book or electronic recording device issued to them that enables the record in question to be made and dealt with in accordance with that provision. References in this and any other Code to written records, forms and signatures include electronic records and forms and electronic confirmation that identifies the person making the record or completing the form. Chief officers must be satisfied as to the integrity and security of the devices, records and forms to which this *paragraph* applies and that use of those devices, records and forms satisfies relevant data protection legislation.

Notes for Guidance

1A Although certain sections of this Code apply specifically to people in custody at police stations, a person who attends a police station or other location voluntarily to assist with an investigation should be treated with no less consideration, e.g. offered or allowed refreshments at appropriate times, and enjoy an absolute right to obtain legal advice or communicate with anyone outside the police station or other location (see paragraphs 3.21 and 3.22).

1AA In paragraph 1.0, under the Equality Act 2010, section 149, the 'relevant protected characteristics' are age, disability, gender reassignment, pregnancy and maternity, race, religion/belief and sex and sexual orientation. For further detailed guidance and advice on the Equality Act, see: https://www.gov.uk/guidance/equality-act-2010-guidance.

1B A person, including a parent or guardian, should not be an appropriate adult if they:
- *are:*
  - *suspected of involvement in the offence;*
  - *the victim;*
  - *a witness;*
  - *involved in the investigation.*
- *received admissions prior to attending to act as the appropriate adult.*

Note: If a juvenile's parent is estranged from the juvenile, they should not be asked to act as the appropriate adult if the juvenile expressly and specifically objects to their presence.

1C If a juvenile admits an offence to, or in the presence of, a social worker or member of a youth offending team other than during the time that person is acting as the juvenile's appropriate adult, another appropriate adult should be appointed in the interest of fairness.

1D In the case of someone who is vulnerable, it may be more satisfactory if the appropriate adult is someone experienced or trained in their care rather than a relative lacking such qualifications. But if the person prefers a relative to a better qualified stranger or objects to a particular person their wishes should, if practicable, be respected.

1E A detainee should always be given an opportunity, when an appropriate adult is called to the police station, to consult privately with a solicitor in the appropriate adult's absence if they want. An appropriate adult is not subject to legal privilege.

1F An appropriate adult who is not a parent or guardian in the case of a juvenile, or a relative, guardian or carer in the case of a vulnerable person, must be independent of the police as their role is to safeguard the person's rights and entitlements. Additionally, a solicitor or independent custody visitor who is present at the police station and acting in that capacity, may not be the appropriate adult.

1G A person may be vulnerable as a result of a having a mental health condition or mental disorder. Similarly, simply because an individual does not have, or is not known to have, any such condition or disorder, does not mean that they are not vulnerable for the purposes of this Code. It is therefore important that the custody officer in the case of a detained person or the officer investigating the offence in the case of a person who has not been arrested or detained, as appropriate, considers on a case by case basis, whether any of the factors described in paragraph 1.13(d) might apply to the person in question. In doing so, the officer must take into account the particular circumstances of the individual and how the nature of the investigation might affect them and bear in mind that juveniles, by virtue of their age will always require an appropriate adult.

1GA For the purposes of paragraph 1.4(a), examples of relevant information that may be available include:
- *the behaviour of the adult or juvenile;*
- *the mental health and capacity of the adult or juvenile;*
- *what the adult or juvenile says about themselves;*
- *information from relatives and friends of the adult or juvenile;*
- *information from police officers and staff and from police records;*
- *information from health and social care (including liaison and diversion services) and other professionals who know, or have had previous contact with, the individual and may be able to contribute to assessing their need for help and support from an appropriate adult. This includes contacts and assessments arranged by the police or at the request of the individual or (as applicable) their appropriate adult or solicitor.*

1GB The Mental Health Act 1983 Code of Practice at page 26 describes the range of clinically recognised conditions which can fall with the meaning of mental disorder for the purpose of paragraph 1.13(d). The Code is published here: https://www.gov.uk/government/publications/code-of-practice-mental-health-act-1983.

1GC When a person is under the influence of drink and/or drugs, it is not intended that they are to be treated as vulnerable and requiring an appropriate adult for the purpose of paragraph 1.4 unless other information indicates that any of the factors described in paragraph 1.13(d) may apply to that person. When the person has recovered from the effects of drink and/or drugs, they should be re-assessed in accordance with paragraph 1.4. See paragraph 15.4A for application to live link

1H Paragraph 1.1A is intended to cover delays which may occur in processing detainees e.g. if:
- *a large number of suspects are brought into the station simultaneously to be placed in custody;*

- *interview rooms are all being used;*
- *there are difficulties contacting an appropriate adult, solicitor or interpreter.*

1I *The custody officer must remind the appropriate adult and detainee about the right to legal advice and record any reasons for waiving it in accordance with section 6.*

1J *Not used.*

1K *This Code does not affect the principle that all citizens have a duty to help police officers to prevent crime and discover offenders. This is a civic rather than a legal duty; but when police officers are trying to discover whether, or by whom, offences have been committed they are entitled to question any person from whom they think useful information can be obtained, subject to the restrictions imposed by this Code. A person's declaration that they are unwilling to reply does not alter this entitlement.*

1L *Paragraph 1.5 reflects the statutory definition of 'arrested juvenile' in section 37(15) of PACE. This section was amended by section 42 of the Criminal Justice and Courts Act 2015 with effect from 26 October 2015, and includes anyone who appears to be under the age of 18. This definition applies for the purposes of the detention and bail provisions in sections 34 to 51 of PACE. With effect from 3 April 2017, amendments made by the Policing and Crime Act 2017 require persons under the age of 18 to be treated as juveniles for the purposes of all other provisions of PACE and the Codes.*

1M *Not used.*

1N *For the purpose of the provisions of PACE that allow a live link to be used, any impairment of the detainee's eyesight or hearing is to be disregarded. This means that if a detainee's eyesight or hearing is impaired, the arrangements which would be needed to ensure effective communication if all parties were physically present in the same location, for example, using sign language, would apply to the live link arrangements.*

2 Custody records

2.1A When a person:

- is brought to a police station under arrest;
- is arrested at the police station having attended there voluntarily; or
- attends a police station to answer bail;

they must be brought before the custody officer as soon as practicable after their arrival at the station or if applicable, following their arrest after attending the police station voluntarily. This applies to both designated and non-designated police stations. A person is deemed to be 'at a police station' for these purposes if they are within the boundary of any building or enclosed yard which forms part of that police station.

2.1 A separate custody record must be opened as soon as practicable for each person brought to a police station under arrest or arrested at the station having gone there voluntarily or attending a police station in answer to street bail. All information recorded under this Code must be recorded as soon as practicable in the custody record unless otherwise specified. Any audio or video recording made in the custody area is not part of the custody record.

2.2 If any action requires the authority of an officer of a specified rank, subject to *paragraph 2.6A*, their name and rank must be noted in the custody record.

2.3 The custody officer is responsible for the custody record's accuracy and completeness and for making sure the record or copy of the record accompanies a detainee if they are transferred to another police station. The record shall show the:

- time and reason for transfer;
- time a person is released from detention.

2.3A If a person is arrested and taken to a police station as a result of a search in the exercise of any stop and search power to which PACE Code A (Stop and search) or the 'search powers code' issued under TACT applies, the officer carrying out the search is responsible for ensuring that the record of that stop and search is made as part of the person's custody record. The custody officer must then ensure that the person is asked if they want a copy of the search record and if they do, that they are given a copy as soon as practicable. The person's entitlement to a copy of the search record which is made as part of their custody record is in addition to, and does not affect, their entitlement to a copy of their custody record or any other provisions of section 2 (Custody records) of this Code. (See Code A, *paragraph 4.2B* and the TACT search powers code *paragraph 5.3.5*).

2.4 The detainee's solicitor and appropriate adult must be permitted to inspect the whole of the detainee's custody record as soon as practicable after their arrival at the station and at any other time on request, whilst the person is detained. This includes the following *specific* records relating to the reasons for the detainee's arrest and detention and the offence concerned to which *paragraph 3.1(b)* refers:

(a) The information about the circumstances and reasons for the detainee's arrest as recorded in the custody record in accordance with *paragraph 4.3* of Code G. This applies to any further offences for which the detainee is arrested whilst in custody;

(b) The record of the grounds for each authorisation to keep the person in custody. The authorisations to which this applies are the same as those described at items *(i)(a)* to *(d)* in the table in *paragraph 2* of *Annex M* of this Code.

Access to the records in *sub-paragraphs (a)* and *(b)* is *in addition* to the requirements in *paragraphs 3.4(b), 11.1A, 15.0, 15,7A(c) and 16.7A* to make certain documents and materials available and to provide information about the offence and the reasons for arrest and detention.

Access to the custody record for the purposes of this paragraph must be arranged and agreed with the custody officer and may not unreasonably interfere with the custody officer's duties. A record shall be made when access is allowed and whether it includes the records described in *sub-paragraphs (a)* and *(b)* above.

2.4A When a detainee leaves police detention or is taken before a court they, their legal representative or appropriate adult shall be given, on request, a copy of the custody record as soon as practicable. This entitlement lasts for 12 months after release.

2.5 The detainee, appropriate adult or legal representative shall be permitted to inspect the original custody record after the detainee has left police detention provided they give reasonable notice of their request. Any such inspection shall be noted in the custody record.

2.6 Subject to *paragraph 2.6A*, all entries in custody records must be timed and signed by the maker. Records entered on computer shall be timed and contain the operator's identification.

2.6A Nothing in this Code requires the identity of officers or other police staff to be recorded or disclosed:

(a) *Not used.*

(b) if the officer or police staff reasonably believe recording or disclosing their name might put them in danger.

In these cases, they shall use their warrant or other identification numbers and the name of their police station. See *Note 2A.*

2.7 The fact and time of any detainee's refusal to sign a custody record, when asked in accordance with this Code, must be recorded.

Note for Guidance

2A The purpose of paragraph 2.6A(b) is to protect those involved in serious organised crime investigations or arrests of particularly violent suspects when there is reliable information that those arrested or their associates may threaten or cause harm to those involved. In cases of doubt, an officer of inspector rank or above should be consulted.

3 Initial action

(A) Detained persons — normal procedure

3.1 When a person is brought to a police station under arrest or arrested at the station having gone there voluntarily, the custody officer must make sure the person is told clearly about:

(a) the following continuing rights, which may be exercised at any stage during the period in custody:

(i) their right to consult privately with a solicitor and that free independent legal advice is available as in *section 6*;

(ii) their right to have someone informed of their arrest as in *section 5*;

(iii) their right to consult the Codes of Practice (see *Note 3D)*; and

(iv) if applicable, their right to interpretation and translation (see *paragraph 3.12*) and their right to communicate with their High Commission, Embassy or Consulate (see *paragraph 3.12A*).

(b) their right to be informed about the offence and (as the case may be) any further offences for which they are arrested whilst in custody and why they have been arrested and detained in accordance with *paragraphs 2.4, 3.4(a)* and *11.1A* of this Code and *paragraph 3.3* of Code G.

3.2 The detainee must also be given a written notice, which contains information:

(a) to allow them to exercise their rights by setting out:

(i) their rights under *paragraph 3.1*, *paragraph 3.12* and *3.12A*;

(ii) the arrangements for obtaining legal advice, see *section 6*;

(iii) their right to a copy of the custody record as in *paragraph 2.4A*;

(iv) their right to remain silent as set out in the caution in the terms prescribed in *section 10*;

(v) their right to have access to materials and documents which are essential to effectively challenging the lawfulness of their arrest and detention for any offence and (as the case may be) any further offences for which they are arrested whilst in custody, in accordance with *paragraphs 3.4(b), 15.0, 15.7A(c)* and *16.7A* of this Code;

(vi) the maximum period for which they may be kept in police detention without being charged, when detention must be reviewed and when release is required;

(vii) their right to medical assistance in accordance with *section 9* of this Code;

(viii) their right, if they are prosecuted, to have access to the evidence in the case before their trial in accordance with the Criminal Procedure and Investigations Act 1996, the Attorney General's Guidelines on Disclosure, the common law and the Criminal Procedure Rules; and

(b) briefly setting out their other entitlements while in custody, by:

(i) mentioning:

- the provisions relating to the conduct of interviews;
- the circumstances in which an appropriate adult should be available to assist the detainee and their statutory rights to make representations whenever the need for their detention is reviewed;

(ii) listing the entitlements in this Code, concerning;

- reasonable standards of physical comfort;
- adequate food and drink;
- access to toilets and washing facilities, clothing, medical attention, and exercise when practicable.

- Personal needs relating to health, hygiene and welfare concerning the provision of menstrual and any other health, hygiene and welfare products needed by the detainee in question and speaking about these in private to a member of the custody staff (see *paragraphs 9.3A* and *9.3B*)

See *Note 3A*.

3.2A The detainee must be given an opportunity to read the notice and shall be asked to sign the custody record to acknowledge receipt of the notice. Any refusal to sign must be recorded on the custody record.

3.3 *Not used.*

3.3A An 'easy read' illustrated version should also be provided if available (see *Note 3A*).

3.4 (a) The custody officer shall:

- record the offence(s) that the detainee has been arrested for and the reason(s) for the arrest on the custody record. See *paragraph 10.3* and Code G, *paragraphs 2.2 and 4.3*;
- note on the custody record any comment the detainee makes in relation to the arresting officer's account but shall not invite comment. If the arresting officer is not physically present when the detainee is brought to a police station, the arresting officer's account must be made available to the custody officer remotely or by a third party on the arresting officer's behalf. If the custody officer authorises a person's detention, subject to *paragraph 1.8*, that officer must record the grounds for detention in the detainee's presence and at the same time, inform them of the grounds. The detainee must be informed of the grounds for their detention before they are questioned about any offence;
- note any comment the detainee makes in respect of the decision to detain them but shall not invite comment;
- not put specific questions to the detainee regarding their involvement in any offence, nor in respect of any comments they may make in response to the arresting officer's account or the decision to place them in detention. Such an exchange is likely to constitute an interview as in *paragraph 11.1A* and require the associated safeguards in *section 11*.

Note: This sub-paragraph also applies to any further offences and grounds for detention which come to light whilst the person is detained.

See *paragraph 11.13* in respect of unsolicited comments.

(b) Documents and materials which are essential to effectively challenging the lawfulness of the detainee's arrest and detention must be made available to the detainee or their solicitor. Documents and materials will be 'essential' for this purpose if they are capable of undermining the reasons and grounds which make the detainee's arrest and detention *necessary*. The decision about whether particular documents or materials must be made available for the purpose of this requirement therefore rests with the custody officer who determines whether detention is necessary, in consultation with the investigating officer who has the knowledge of the documents and materials in a particular case necessary to inform that decision. A note should be made in the detainee's custody record of the *fact* that documents or materials have been made available under this sub-paragraph and when. The investigating officer should make a separate note of what is made available and how it is made available in a particular case. This sub-paragraph also applies (with modifications) for the purposes of *sections 15 (Reviews and extensions of detention)* and *16 (Charging detained persons)*. See *Note 3ZA* and *paragraphs 15.0* and *16.7A*.

3.5 The custody officer or other custody staff as directed by the custody officer shall:

(a) ask the detainee whether at this time, they:

(i) would like legal advice, see *paragraph 6.5*;

(ii) want someone informed of their detention, see *section 5*;

(b) ask the detainee to sign the custody record to confirm their decisions in respect of (*a*);

(c) determine whether the detainee:

(i) is, or might be, in need of medical treatment or attention, see *section 9*;

(ii) is a juvenile and/or vulnerable and therefore requires an appropriate adult (see *paragraphs 1.4, 1.5*, and *3.15*);

(iia) wishes to speak in private with a member of the custody staff who may be of the same sex about any matter concerning their personal needs relating to health, hygiene and welfare (see *paragraph 9.3A*)

(iii) requires:
- help to check documentation (see *paragraph 3.20*);
- an interpreter (see *paragraph 3.12* and *Note 13B*).

(ca) if the detainee is a female aged 18 or over, ask if they require or are likely to require any menstrual products whilst they are in custody (see *paragraph 9.3B*). For girls under 18, see *paragraph 3.20A*;

(d) record the decision and actions taken as applicable in respect of (*c*) and (ca).

Where any duties under this paragraph have been carried out by custody staff at the direction of the custody officer, the outcomes shall, as soon as practicable, be reported to the custody officer who retains overall responsibility for the detainee's care and treatment and ensuring that it complies with this Code. See *Note 3F*.

3.6 When the needs mentioned in *paragraph 3.5(c)* are being determined, the custody officer is responsible for initiating an assessment to consider whether the detainee is likely to present specific risks to custody staff, any individual who may have contact with detainee (e.g. legal advisers, medical staff) or themselves. This risk assessment must include the taking of reasonable steps to establish the detainee's identity and to obtain information about the detainee that is relevant to their safe custody, security and welfare and risks to others. Such assessments should therefore always include a check on the Police National Computer (PNC), to be carried out as soon as practicable, to identify any risks that have been highlighted in relation to the detainee. Although such assessments are primarily the custody officer's responsibility, it may be necessary for them to consult and involve others, e.g. the arresting officer or an appropriate healthcare professional, see *paragraph 9.13*.

Other records held by or on behalf of the police and other UK law enforcement authorities that might provide information relevant to the detainee's safe custody, security and welfare and risk to others and to confirming their identity should also be checked. Reasons for delaying the initiation or completion of the assessment must be recorded.

3.7 Chief officers should ensure that arrangements for proper and effective risk assessments required by *paragraph 3.6* are implemented in respect of all detainees at police stations in their area.

3.8 Risk assessments must follow a structured process which clearly defines the categories of risk to be considered and the results must be incorporated in the detainee's custody record. The custody officer is responsible for making sure those responsible for the detainee's custody are appropriately briefed about the risks. If no specific risks are identified by the assessment, that should be noted in the custody record. See *Note 3E* and *paragraph 9.14*.

3.8A The content of any risk assessment and any analysis of the level of risk relating to the person's detention is not required to be shown or provided to the detainee or any person acting on behalf of the detainee. But information should not be withheld from any person acting on the detainee's behalf, for example, an appropriate adult, solicitor or interpreter, if to do so might put that person at risk.

3.9 The custody officer is responsible for implementing the response to any specific risk assessment, e.g.:
- reducing opportunities for self harm;
- calling an appropriate healthcare professional;
- increasing levels of monitoring or observation;
- reducing the risk to those who come into contact with the detainee.

See *Note 3E*.

3.10 Risk assessment is an ongoing process and assessments must always be subject to review if circumstances change.

3.11 If video cameras are installed in the custody area, notices shall be prominently displayed showing cameras are in use. Any request to have video cameras switched off shall be refused.

(B) Detained persons — special groups

3.12 If the detainee appears to be someone who does not speak or understand English or who has a hearing or speech impediment, the custody officer must ensure:

(a) that without delay, arrangements (see *paragraph 13.1ZA*) are made for the detainee to have the assistance of an interpreter in the action under *paragraphs 3.1* to *3.5*. If the person appears to have a hearing or speech impediment, the reference to 'interpreter' includes appropriate assistance necessary to comply with *paragraphs 3.1* to *3.5*. See *paragraph 13.1C* if the detainee is in Wales. See *section 13* and *Note 13B;*

(b) that in addition to the continuing rights set out in *paragraph 3.1(a)(i)* to *(iv)*, the detainee is told clearly about their right to interpretation and translation;

(c) that the written notice given to the detainee in accordance with *paragraph 3.2* is in a language the detainee understands and includes the right to interpretation and translation together with information about the provisions in *section 13* and *Annex M*, which explain how the right applies (see *Note 3A*); and
(d) that if the translation of the notice is not available, the information in the notice is given through an interpreter and a written translation provided without undue delay.

3.12A If the detainee is a citizen of an independent Commonwealth country or a national of a foreign country, including the Republic of Ireland, the custody officer must ensure that in addition to the continuing rights set out in *paragraph 3.1(a)(i)* to *(iv)*, they are informed as soon as practicable about their rights of communication with their High Commission, Embassy or Consulate set out in *section 7*. This right must be included in the written notice given to the detainee in accordance with *paragraph 3.2*.

3.13 If the detainee is a juvenile, the custody officer must, if it is practicable, ascertain the identity of a person responsible for their welfare. That person:

- may be:
  - the parent or guardian;
  - if the juvenile is in local authority or voluntary organisation care, or is otherwise being looked after under the Children Act 1989, a person appointed by that authority or organisation to have responsibility for the juvenile's welfare;
  - any other person who has, for the time being, assumed responsibility for the juvenile's welfare.
- must be informed as soon as practicable that the juvenile has been arrested, why they have been arrested and where they are detained. This right is in addition to the juvenile's right in *section 5* not to be held incommunicado. See *Note 3C*.

3.14 If a juvenile is known to be subject to a court order under which a person or organisation is given any degree of statutory responsibility to supervise or otherwise monitor them, reasonable steps must also be taken to notify that person or organisation (the 'responsible officer'). The responsible officer will normally be a member of a Youth Offending Team, except for a curfew order which involves electronic monitoring when the contractor providing the monitoring will normally be the responsible officer.

3.15 If the detainee is a juvenile or a vulnerable person, the custody officer must, as soon as practicable, ensure that:

- the detainee is informed of the decision that an appropriate adult is required and the reason for that decision (see *paragraph 3.5(c)(ii)*) and;
- the detainee is advised:
  - of the duties of the appropriate adult as described in *paragraph 1.7A;* and
  - that they can consult privately with the appropriate adult at any time.
- the appropriate adult, who in the case of a juvenile may or may not be a person responsible for their welfare, as in *paragraph 3.13,* is informed of:
  - the grounds for their detention;
  - their whereabouts; and
- the attendance of the appropriate adult at the police station to see the detainee is secured.

3.16 It is imperative that a person detained under the Mental Health Act 1983, section 135 or 136, be assessed as soon as possible within the permitted period of detention specified in that Act. A police station may only be used as a place of safety in accordance with The Mental Health Act 1983 (Places of Safety) Regulations 2017. If that assessment is to take place at the police station, an approved mental health professional and a registered medical practitioner shall be called to the station as soon as possible to carry it out. See *Note 9D*. The appropriate adult has no role in the assessment process and their presence is not required. Once the detainee has been assessed and suitable arrangements made for their treatment or care, they can no longer be detained under section 135 or 136. A detainee must be immediately discharged from detention if a registered medical practitioner, having examined them, concludes they are not mentally disordered within the meaning of the Act.

3.17 If the appropriate adult is:

- already at the police station, the provisions of *paragraphs 3.1* to *3.5* must be complied with in the appropriate adult's presence;
- not at the station when these provisions are complied with, they must be complied with again in the presence of the appropriate adult when they arrive,

and a copy of the notice given to the detainee in accordance with *paragraph 3.2*, shall also be given to the appropriate adult.

3.17A The custody officer must ensure that at the time the copy of the notice is given to the appropriate adult, or as soon as practicable thereafter, the appropriate adult is advised of the duties of the appropriate adult as described in *paragraph 1.7A*.

3.18 *Not used.*

3.19 If the detainee, or appropriate adult on the detainee's behalf, asks for a solicitor to be called to give legal advice, the provisions of *section 6* apply (see *paragraph 6.5A* and *Note 3H*).

3.20 If the detainee is blind, seriously visually impaired or unable to read, the custody officer shall make sure their solicitor, relative, appropriate adult or some other person likely to take an interest in them and not involved in the investigation is available to help check any documentation. When this Code requires written consent or signing the person assisting may be asked to sign instead, if the detainee prefers. This paragraph does not require an appropriate adult to be called solely to assist in checking and signing documentation for a person who is not a juvenile, or is not vulnerable (see *paragraph 3.15* and *Note 13C*).

3.20A The Children and Young Persons Act 1933, section 31, requires that arrangements must be made for ensuring that a girl under the age of 18, while detained in a police station, is under the care of a woman. The custody officer must ensure that the woman under whose care the girl is, makes the enquiries and provides the information concerning personal needs relating to their health, hygiene and welfare described in *paragraph 9.3A* and menstrual products described in *paragraph 9.3B*. See *Note 3G*. The section also requires that arrangements must be made for preventing any person under 18, while being detained in a police station, from associating with an adult charged with any offence, unless that adult is a relative or the adult is jointly charged with the same offence as the person under 18.

(C) Detained persons – Documentation

3.20B The grounds for a person's detention shall be recorded, in the person's presence if practicable. See *paragraph 1.8*.

3.20C Action taken under *paragraphs 3.12* to *3.20A* shall be recorded.

(D) Persons attending a police station or elsewhere voluntarily

3.21 Anybody attending a police station or other location (see *paragraph 3.22* and *Note 3I*) voluntarily to assist police with the investigation of an offence may leave at will unless arrested. See *Notes 1A* and *1K*. The person may only be prevented from leaving at will if their arrest on suspicion of committing the offence is necessary in accordance with Code G. See Code G *Note 2G*.

Action if arrest becomes necessary

(a) If during a person's voluntary attendance at a police station or other location it is decided for any reason that their arrest is necessary, they must:
- be informed at once that they are under arrest and of the grounds and reasons as required by Code G, and
- be brought before the custody officer at the police station where they are arrested or (as the case may be) at the police station to which they are taken after being arrested elsewhere. The custody officer is then responsible for making sure that a custody record is opened and that they are notified of their rights in the same way as other detainees as required by this Code.

Information to be given when arranging a voluntary interview:

(b) If the suspect's arrest is not necessary but they are cautioned as required in *section 10*, the person who, after describing the nature and circumstances of the suspected offence, gives the caution must at the same time, inform them that they are not under arrest and that they are not obliged to remain at the station or other location (see *paragraph 3.22* and *Note 3I*). The rights, entitlements and safeguards that apply to the conduct and recording of interviews with suspects are not diminished simply because the interview is arranged on a voluntary basis. For the purpose of arranging a voluntary interview (see *Code G Note 2F*), the duty of the interviewer reflects that of the custody officer with regard to detained suspects. As a result:
   (i) the requirement in *paragraph 3.5(c)(ii)* to determine whether a detained suspect requires an appropriate adult, help to check documentation or an interpreter shall apply equally to a suspect who has not been arrested; and
   (ii) the suspect must not be asked to give their informed consent to be interviewed until *after* they have been informed of the rights, entitlements and safeguards that apply to voluntary interviews. These are set out in *paragraph 3.21A* and the interviewer is responsible for ensuring that the suspect is so informed and for explaining these rights, entitlements and safeguards.

3.21A The interviewer must inform the suspect that the purpose of the voluntary interview is to question them to obtain evidence about their involvement or suspected involvement in the offence(s) described when they were cautioned and told that they were not under arrest. The interviewer shall then inform the suspect that the following matters will apply if they agree to the voluntary interview proceeding:

(a) Their right to information about the offence(s) in question by providing sufficient information to enable them to understand the nature of any such offence(s) and why they are suspected of committing it. This is in order to allow for the effective exercise of the rights of the defence as required by *paragraph 11.1A*. It applies whether or not they ask for legal advice and includes any further offences that come to light and are pointed out during the voluntary interview and for which they are cautioned.

(b) Their right to free *(see Note 3J)* legal advice by:
   (i) explaining that they may obtain free and independent legal advice if they want it, and that this includes the right to speak with a solicitor on the telephone and to have the solicitor present during the interview;
   (ii) asking if they want legal advice and recording their reply; and
   (iii) if the person requests advice, securing its provision before the interview by contacting the Defence Solicitor Call Centre and explaining that the time and place of the interview will be arranged to enable them to obtain advice and that the interview will be delayed until they have received the advice unless, in accordance with *paragraph 6.6(c)* (Nominated solicitor not available and duty solicitor declined) or *paragraph 6.6(d)* (Change of mind), an officer of the rank of inspector or above agrees to the interview proceeding; or
   (iv) if the person declines to exercise the right, asking them why and recording any reasons given (see *Note 6K*).

   Note: When explaining the right to legal advice and the arrangements, the interviewer must take care not to indicate, except to answer a direct question, that the time taken to arrange and complete the voluntary interview might be reduced if:
   - the suspect does not ask for legal advice or does not want a solicitor present when they are interviewed; or
   - the suspect asks for legal advice or (as the case may be) asks for a solicitor to be present when they are interviewed, but changes their mind and agrees to be interviewed without waiting for a solicitor.

(c) Their right, if in accordance with *paragraph 3.5(c)(ii)* the interviewer determines:
   (i) that they are a juvenile or are vulnerable; or
   (ii) that they need help to check documentation (see *paragraph 3.20*),

   to have the appropriate adult present or (as the case may be) to have the necessary help to check documentation; and that the interview will be delayed until the presence of the appropriate adult or the necessary help, is secured.

(d) If they are a juvenile or vulnerable and do not want legal advice, their appropriate adult has the right to ask for a solicitor to attend if this would be in their best interests and the appropriate adult must be so informed. In this case, action to secure the provision of advice if so requested by their appropriate adult will be taken without delay in the same way as if requested by the person (see *sub-paragraph (b)(iii)*). However, they cannot be forced to see the solicitor if they are adamant that they do not wish to do so (see *paragraphs 3.19* and *6.5A*).

(e) Their right to an interpreter, if in accordance with, *paragraphs 3.5(c)(ii)* and *3.12*, the interviewer determines that they require an interpreter and that if they require an interpreter, making the necessary arrangements in accordance with *paragraph 13.1ZA* and that the interview will be delayed to make the arrangements.

(f) That interview will be arranged for a time and location (see *paragraph 3.22* and *Note 3I*) that enables:
   (i) the suspect's rights described above to be fully respected; and
   (ii) the whole of the interview to be recorded using an authorised recording device in accordance with Code E (Code of Practice on Audio recording of interviews with suspects) or (as the case may be) Code F (Code of Practice on visual recording with sound of interviews with suspects); and

(g) That their agreement to take part in the interview also signifies their agreement for that interview to be audio-recorded or (as the case may be) visually recorded with sound.

3.21B The provision by the interviewer of factual information described in *paragraph 3.21A* and, if asked by the suspect, further such information, does not constitute an interview for the purpose of this Code and *when that information is provided*:

(a) the interviewer must remind the suspect about the caution as required in *section 10* but must not *invite* comment about the offence or put specific questions to the suspect regarding their involvement in any offence, nor in respect of any comments they may make when given the information. Such an exchange is itself likely to constitute an interview as in *paragraph 11.1A* and require the associated interview safeguards in *section 11*.

(b) Any comment the suspect makes when the information is given which might be relevant to the offence, must be recorded and dealt with in accordance with *paragraph 11.13*.

(c) The suspect must be given a notice summarising the matters described in *paragraph 3.21A* and which includes the arrangements for obtaining legal advice. If a specific notice is not available, the notice given to detained suspects with references to detention-specific requirements and information redacted, may be used.

(d) For juvenile and vulnerable suspects (see *paragraphs 1.4* and *1.5*):

(i) the information must be provided or (as the case may be) provided again, together with the notice, in the presence of the appropriate adult;

(ii) if cautioned in the absence of the appropriate adult, the caution must be repeated in the appropriate adult's presence (see *paragraph 10.12*);

(iii) the suspect must be informed of the decision that an appropriate is required and the reason (see *paragraph 3.5(c)(ii)*);

(iv) the suspect *and* the appropriate adult shall be advised:

- that the duties of the appropriate adult include giving advice and assistance in accordance with *paragraphs 1.7A* and *11.17*; and
- that they can consult privately at any time.

(v) their informed agreement to be interviewed voluntarily must be sought and given in the presence of the appropriate adult and for a juvenile, the agreement of a parent or guardian of the juvenile is also required.

3.22 If the other location mentioned in *paragraph 3.21* is any place or premises for which the interviewer requires the informed consent of the suspect and/or occupier (if different) to remain, for example, the suspect's home (see *Note 3I*), then the references that the person is 'not obliged to remain' and that they 'may leave at will' mean that the suspect and/or occupier (if different) may also withdraw their consent and require the interviewer to leave.

Commencement of voluntary interview – general

3.22A Before asking the suspect any questions about their involvement in the offence they are suspected of committing, the interviewing officer must ask them to confirm that they agree to the interview proceeding. This confirmation shall be recorded in the interview record made in accordance with section 11 of this Code (written record) or Code E or Code F.

Documentation

3.22B Action taken under *paragraphs 3.21A* to *3.21B* shall be recorded. The record shall include the date time and place the action was taken, who was present and anything said to or by the suspect and to or by those present.

3.23 *Not used.*

3.24 *Not used.*

(E) Persons answering street bail

3.25 When a person is answering street bail, the custody officer should link any documentation held in relation to arrest with the custody record. Any further action shall be recorded on the custody record in accordance with *paragraphs 3.20B* and *3.20C* above.

(F) Requirements for suspects to be informed of certain rights

3.26 The provisions of this section identify the information which must be given to suspects who have been cautioned in accordance with *section 10* of this Code according to whether or not they have been arrested and detained. It includes information required by *EU Directive 2012/13* on the right to information in criminal proceedings. If a complaint is made by or on behalf of such a suspect that the information and (as the case may be) access to records and documents has not been provided as required, the matter shall be reported to an inspector to deal with as a complaint for the purposes of *paragraph 9.2*, or *paragraph 12.9* if the challenge is made during an interview. This would include, for example:

(a) in the case of a detained suspect:

- not informing them of their rights (see *paragraph 3.1*);
- not giving them a copy of the Notice (see *paragraph 3.2(a)*);
- not providing an opportunity to read the notice (see *paragraph 3.2A*);
- not providing the required information (see *paragraphs 3.2(a), 3.12(b)* and, *3.12A*);
- not allowing access to the custody record (see *paragraph 2.4*);
- not providing a translation of the Notice (see *paragraph 3.12(c)* and *(d)*); and

(b) in the case of a suspect who is not detained:

- not informing them of their rights or providing the required information (see *paragraphs 3.21(b)* to *3.21B*).

Notes for Guidance

3ZA *For the purposes of paragraphs 3.4(b) and 15.0:*

(a) *Investigating officers are responsible for bringing to the attention of the officer who is responsible for authorising the suspect's detention or (as the case may be) continued detention (before or after charge), any documents and materials in their possession or control which appear to undermine the need to keep the suspect in custody. In accordance with Part IV of PACE, this officer will be either the custody officer, the officer reviewing the need for detention before or after charge (PACE, section 40), or the officer considering the need to extend detention without charge from 24 to 36 hours (PACE, section 42) who is then responsible for determining, which, if any, of those documents and materials are capable of undermining the need to detain the suspect and must therefore be made available to the suspect or their solicitor.*

(b) *the way in which documents and materials are 'made available', is a matter for the investigating officer to determine on a case by case basis and having regard to the nature and volume of the documents and materials involved. For example, they may be made available by supplying a copy or allowing supervised access to view. However, for view only access, it will be necessary to demonstrate that sufficient time is allowed for the suspect and solicitor to view and consider the documents and materials in question.*

3A *For access to currently available notices, including 'easy-read' versions, see https://www.gov.uk/guidance/notice-of-rights-and-entitlements-a-persons-rights-in-police-detention.*

3B *Not used.*

3C *If the juvenile is in local authority or voluntary organisation care but living with their parents or other adults responsible for their welfare, although there is no legal obligation to inform them, they should normally be contacted, as well as the authority or organisation unless they are suspected of involvement in the offence concerned. Even if the juvenile is not living with their parents, consideration should be given to informing them.*

3D *The right to consult the Codes of Practice does not entitle the person concerned to delay unreasonably any necessary investigative or administrative action whilst they do so. Examples of action which need not be delayed unreasonably include:*

- *procedures requiring the provision of breath, blood or urine specimens under the Road Traffic Act 1988 or the Transport and Works Act 1992;*
- *searching detainees at the police station;*
- *taking fingerprints, footwear impressions or non-intimate samples without consent for evidential purposes.*

3E *The Detention and Custody Authorised Professional Practice (APP) produced by the College of Policing (see http://www.app.college.police.uk) provides more detailed guidance on risk assessments and identifies key risk areas which should always be considered. See Home Office Circular 34/2007 (Safety of solicitors and probationary representatives at police stations).*

3F *A custody officer or other officer who, in accordance with this Code, allows or directs the carrying out of any task or action relating to a detainee's care, treatment, rights and entitlements to another officer or any other person, must be satisfied that the officer or person concerned is suitable, trained and competent to carry out the task or action in question.*

3G *Guidance for police officers and police staff on the operational application of section 31 of the Children and Young Persons Act 1933 has been published by the College of Policing and is available at: https://www.app.college.police.uk/app-content/detention-and-custody-2/detainee-care/children-and-young-persons/#girls.*

3H *The purpose of the provisions at paragraphs 3.19 and 6.5A is to protect the rights of juvenile and vulnerable persons who may not understand the significance of what is said to them. They should always be given an opportunity, when an appropriate adult is called to the police station, to consult privately with a solicitor in the absence of the appropriate adult if they want.*

3I *An interviewer who is not sure, or has any doubt, about whether a place or location elsewhere than a police station is suitable for carrying out a voluntary interview, particularly in the case of a juvenile or vulnerable person, should consult an officer of the rank of sergeant or above for advice. Detailed guidance for police officers and staff concerning the conduct and recording of voluntary interviews is being developed by the College of Policing.*

It follows a review of operational issues arising when voluntary interviews need to be arranged. The aim is to ensure the effective implementation of the safeguards in paragraphs 3.21 to 3.22B particularly concerning the rights of suspects, the location for the interview and supervision.

3J *For voluntary interviews conducted by non-police investigators, the provision of legal advice is set out by the Legal Aid Agency at paragraph 9.54 of the 2017 Standard Crime Contract Specification. This is published at https://www.gov.uk/government/publications/standard-crime-contract-2017 and the rules mean that a non-police interviewer who does not have their own statutory power of arrest would have to inform the suspect that they have a right to seek legal advice if they wish, but payment would be a matter for them to arrange with the solicitor.*

4 Detainee's property

(A) Action

4.1 The custody officer is responsible for:

(a) ascertaining what property a detainee:

(i) has with them when they come to the police station, whether on:

- arrest or re-detention on answering to bail;
- commitment to prison custody on the order or sentence of a court;
- lodgement at the police station with a view to their production in court from prison custody;
- transfer from detention at another station or hospital;
- detention under the Mental Health Act 1983, section 135 or 136;
- remand into police custody on the authority of a court.

(ii) might have acquired for an unlawful or harmful purpose while in custody;

(b) the safekeeping of any property taken from a detainee which remains at the police station.

The custody officer may search the detainee or authorise their being searched to the extent they consider necessary, provided a search of intimate parts of the body or involving the removal of more than outer clothing is only made as in *Annex A*. A search may only be carried out by an officer of the same sex as the detainee. See *Note 4A* and *Annex L*.

4.2 Subject to *paragraph 4.3A*, detainees may retain clothing and personal effects at their own risk unless the custody officer considers they may use them to cause harm to themselves or others, interfere with evidence, damage property, effect an escape or they are needed as evidence. In this event the custody officer may withhold such articles as they consider necessary and must tell the detainee why.

4.3 Personal effects are those items a detainee may lawfully need, use or refer to while in detention but do not include cash and other items of value.

4.3A For the purpose of *paragraph 4.2*, the reference to clothing and personal effects shall be treated as including menstrual and any other health, hygiene and welfare products needed by a detainee in question (see *paragraphs 9.3A* and *9.3B*) and a decision to withhold any such products must be subject to a further specific risk assessment.

(B) Documentation

4.4 It is a matter for the custody officer to determine whether a record should be made of the property a detained person has with him or had taken from him on arrest. Any record made is not required to be kept as part of the custody record but the custody record should be noted as to where such a record exists and that record shall be treated as being part of the custody record for the purpose of this and any other Code of Practice (see *paragraphs 2.4, 2.4A* and *2.5*). Whenever a record is made the detainee shall be allowed to check and sign the record of property as correct. Any refusal to sign shall be recorded.

4.5 If a detainee is not allowed to keep any article of clothing or personal effects, the reason must be recorded.

Notes for Guidance

4A PACE, Section 54(1) and paragraph 4.1 require a detainee to be searched when it is clear the custody officer will have continuing duties in relation to that detainee or when that detainee's behaviour or offence makes an inventory appropriate. They do not require every detainee to be searched, e.g. if it is clear a person will only be detained for a short period and is not to be placed in a cell, the custody officer may decide not to search them. In such a case the custody record will be endorsed 'not searched', paragraph 4.4 will not apply, and the detainee will be invited to sign the entry. If the detainee refuses, the custody officer will be obliged to ascertain what property they have in accordance with paragraph 4.1.

4B Paragraph 4.4 does not require the custody officer to record on the custody record property in the detainee's possession on arrest if, by virtue of its nature, quantity or size, it is not practicable to remove it to the police station.

4C Paragraph 4.4 does not require items of clothing worn by the person to be recorded unless withheld by the custody officer as in paragraph 4.2.

5 Right not to be held incommunicado

(A) Action

5.1 Subject to *paragraph 5.7B*, any person arrested and held in custody at a police station or other premises may, on request, have one person known to them or likely to take an interest in their welfare informed at public expense of their whereabouts as soon as practicable. If the person cannot be contacted the detainee may choose up to two alternatives. If they cannot be contacted, the person in charge of detention or the investigation has discretion to allow further attempts until the information has been conveyed. See *Notes 5C* and *5D*.

5.2 The exercise of the above right in respect of each person nominated may be delayed only in accordance with *Annex B*.

5.3 The above right may be exercised each time a detainee is taken to another police station.

5.4 If the detainee agrees, they may at the custody officer's discretion, receive visits from friends, family or others likely to take an interest in their welfare, or in whose welfare the detainee has an interest. See *Note 5B*.

5.5 If a friend, relative or person with an interest in the detainee's welfare enquires about their whereabouts, this information shall be given if the suspect agrees and *Annex B* does not apply. See *Note 5D*.

5.6 The detainee shall be given writing materials, on request, and allowed to telephone one person for a reasonable time, see *Notes 5A* and *5E*. Either or both of these privileges may be denied or delayed if an officer of inspector rank or above considers sending a letter or making a telephone call may result in any of the consequences in:

(a) *Annex B, paragraphs 1* and *2* and the person is detained in connection with an indictable offence;

(b) *Not used*.

Nothing in this paragraph permits the restriction or denial of the rights in *paragraphs 5.1* and *6.1*.

5.7 Before any letter or message is sent, or telephone call made, the detainee shall be informed that what they say in any letter, call or message (other than in a communication to a solicitor) may be read or listened to and may be given in evidence. A telephone call may be terminated if it is being abused. The costs can be at public expense at the custody officer's discretion.

5.7A Any delay or denial of the rights in this section should be proportionate and should last no longer than necessary.

5.7B In the case of a person in police custody for specific purposes and periods in accordance with a direction under the *Crime (Sentences) Act 1997, Schedule 1* (productions from prison etc.), the exercise of the rights in this section shall be subject to any additional conditions specified in the direction for the purpose of regulating the detainee's contact and communication with others whilst in police custody. See *Note 5F*.

(B) Documentation

5.8 A record must be kept of any:

(a) request made under this section and the action taken;

(b) letters, messages or telephone calls made or received or visit received;

(c) refusal by the detainee to have information about them given to an outside enquirer. The detainee must be asked to countersign the record accordingly and any refusal recorded.

Notes for Guidance

5A *A person may request an interpreter to interpret a telephone call or translate a letter.*

5B *At the custody officer's discretion and subject to the detainee's consent, visits should be allowed when possible, subject to having sufficient personnel to supervise a visit and any possible hindrance to the investigation.*

5C *If the detainee does not know anyone to contact for advice or support or cannot contact a friend or relative, the custody officer should bear in mind any local voluntary bodies or other organisations who might be able to help. Paragraph 6.1 applies if legal advice is required.*

5D *In some circumstances it may not be appropriate to use the telephone to disclose information under paragraphs 5.1 and 5.5.*

5E *The telephone call at paragraph 5.6 is in addition to any communication under paragraphs 5.1 and 6.1.*

5F *Prison Service Instruction 26/2012 (Production of Prisoners at the Request of Warranted Law Enforcement Agencies) provides detailed guidance and instructions for police officers and Governors and Directors of Prisons regarding applications for prisoners to be transferred to police custody and their safe custody and treatment while in police custody.*

6 Right to legal advice

(A) Action

6.1 Unless *Annex B* applies, all detainees must be informed that they may at any time consult and communicate privately with a solicitor, whether in person, in writing or by telephone, and that free independent legal advice is available. See *paragraph 3.1, Notes 1I, 6B* and *6J*.

6.2 *Not used*.

6.3 A poster advertising the right to legal advice must be prominently displayed in the charging area of every police station. See *Note 6H*.

6.4 No police officer should, at any time, do or say anything with the intention of dissuading any person who is entitled to legal advice in accordance with this Code, whether or not they have been arrested and are detained, from obtaining legal advice. See *Note 6ZA*.

6.5 The exercise of the right of access to legal advice may be delayed only as in *Annex B*. Whenever legal advice is requested, and unless *Annex B* applies, the custody officer must act without delay to secure the provision of such advice. If the detainee has the right to speak to a solicitor in person but declines to exercise the right the officer should point out that the right includes the right to speak with a solicitor on the telephone. If the detainee continues to waive this right, or a detainee whose right to free legal advice is limited to telephone advice from the Criminal Defence Service (CDS) Direct (see *Note 6B*) declines to exercise that right, the officer should ask them why and any reasons should be recorded on the custody record or the interview record as appropriate. Reminders of the right to legal advice must be given as in *paragraphs 3.5, 11.2, 15.4, 16.4, 16.5, 2B of Annex A, 3 of Annex K* and *5 of Annex M* of this Code and Code D, *paragraphs 3.17(ii)* and *6.3*. Once it is clear a detainee does not want to speak to a solicitor in person or by telephone they should cease to be asked their reasons. See *Note 6K*.

6.5A In the case of a person who is a juvenile or is vulnerable, an appropriate adult should consider whether legal advice from a solicitor is required. If such a detained person wants to exercise the right to legal advice, the appropriate action should be taken and should not be delayed until the appropriate adult arrives. If the person indicates that they do not want legal advice, the appropriate adult has the right to ask for a solicitor to attend if this would be in the best interests of the person and must be so informed. In this case, action to secure the provision of advice if so requested by the appropriate adult shall be taken without delay in the same way as when requested by the person. However, the person cannot be forced to see the solicitor if they are adamant that they do not wish to do so.

6.6 A detainee who wants legal advice may not be interviewed or continue to be interviewed until they have received such advice unless:

(a) *Annex B* applies, when the restriction on drawing adverse inferences from silence in *Annex C* will apply because the detainee is not allowed an opportunity to consult a solicitor; or

(b) an officer of superintendent rank or above has reasonable grounds for believing that:

(i) the consequent delay might:
- lead to interference with, or harm to, evidence connected with an offence;
- lead to interference with, or physical harm to, other people;
- lead to serious loss of, or damage to, property;
- lead to alerting other people suspected of having committed an offence but not yet arrested for it;
- hinder the recovery of property obtained in consequence of the commission of an offence.

See *Note 6A*

(ii) when a solicitor, including a duty solicitor, has been contacted and has agreed to attend, awaiting their arrival would cause unreasonable delay to the process of investigation.

Note: In these cases the restriction on drawing adverse inferences from silence in *Annex C* will apply because the detainee is not allowed an opportunity to consult a solicitor.

(c) the solicitor the detainee has nominated or selected from a list:

(i) cannot be contacted;

(ii) has previously indicated they do not wish to be contacted; or

(iii) having been contacted, has declined to attend; and
- the detainee has been advised of the Duty Solicitor Scheme but has declined to ask for the duty solicitor;
- in these circumstances the interview may be started or continued without further delay provided an officer of inspector rank or above has agreed to the interview proceeding.

Note: The restriction on drawing adverse inferences from silence in *Annex C* will not apply because the detainee is allowed an opportunity to consult the duty solicitor;

(d) the detainee changes their mind about wanting legal advice or (as the case may be) about wanting a solicitor present at the interview and states that they no longer wish to speak to a solicitor. In these circumstances, the interview may be started or continued without delay provided that:

(i) an officer of inspector rank or above:
- speaks to the detainee to enquire about the reasons for their change of mind (see *Note 6K*), and
- makes, or directs the making of, reasonable efforts to ascertain the solicitor's expected time of arrival and to inform the solicitor that the suspect has stated that they wish to change their mind and the reason (if given);

(ii) the detainee's reason for their change of mind (if given) and the outcome of the action in (i) are recorded in the custody record;

(iii) the detainee, after being informed of the outcome of the action in (i) above, confirms in writing that they want the interview to proceed without speaking or further speaking to a solicitor or (as the case may be) without a solicitor being present and do not wish to wait for a solicitor by signing an entry to this effect in the custody record;

(iv) an officer of inspector rank or above is satisfied that it is proper for the interview to proceed in these circumstances and:

- gives authority in writing for the interview to proceed and, if the authority is not recorded in the custody record, the officer must ensure that the custody record shows the date and time of the authority and where it is recorded, and
- takes, or directs the taking of, reasonable steps to inform the solicitor that the authority has been given and the time when the interview is expected to commence and records or causes to be recorded, the outcome of this action in the custody record.

(v) When the interview starts and the interviewer reminds the suspect of their right to legal advice (see *paragraph 11.2*, Code E *paragraph 4.5* and Code F *paragraph 4.5*), the interviewer shall then ensure that the following is recorded in the written interview record or the interview record made in accordance with Code E or F:

- confirmation that the detainee has changed their mind about wanting legal advice or (as the case may be) about wanting a solicitor present and the reasons for it if given;
- the fact that authority for the interview to proceed has been given and, subject to *paragraph 2.6A*, the name of the authorising officer;
- that if the solicitor arrives at the station before the interview is completed, the detainee will be so informed without delay and *a break will be taken* to allow them to speak to the solicitor if they wish, unless *paragraph 6.6(a)* applies, and
- that at any time during the interview, the detainee may again ask for legal advice and that if they do, a break will be taken to allow them to speak to the solicitor, unless *paragraph 6.6(a), (b), or (c)* applies.

Note: In these circumstances, the restriction on drawing adverse inferences from silence in *Annex C* will not apply because the detainee is allowed an opportunity to consult a solicitor if they wish.

6.7 If *paragraph 6.6(a)* applies, where the reason for authorising the delay ceases to apply, there may be no further delay in permitting the exercise of the right in the absence of a further authorisation unless *paragraph 6.6(b), (c)* or *(d)* applies. If *paragraph 6.6(b)(i)* applies, once sufficient information has been obtained to avert the risk, questioning must cease until the detainee has received legal advice unless *paragraph 6.6(a), (b)(ii), (c)* or *(d)* applies.

6.8 A detainee who has been permitted to consult a solicitor shall be entitled on request to have the solicitor present when they are interviewed unless one of the exceptions in *paragraph 6.6* applies.

6.9 The solicitor may only be required to leave the interview if their conduct is such that the interviewer is unable properly to put questions to the suspect. See *Notes 6D* and *6E*.

6.10 If the interviewer considers a solicitor is acting in such a way, they will stop the interview and consult an officer not below superintendent rank, if one is readily available, and otherwise an officer not below inspector rank not connected with the investigation. After speaking to the solicitor, the officer consulted will decide if the interview should continue in the presence of that solicitor. If they decide it should not, the suspect will be given the opportunity to consult another solicitor before the interview continues and that solicitor given an opportunity to be present at the interview. See *Note 6E*.

6.11 The removal of a solicitor from an interview is a serious step and, if it occurs, the officer of superintendent rank or above who took the decision will consider if the incident should be reported to the Solicitors Regulatory Authority. If the decision to remove the solicitor has been taken by an officer below superintendent rank, the facts must be reported to an officer of superintendent rank or above, who will similarly consider whether a report to the Solicitors Regulatory Authority would be appropriate. When the solicitor concerned is a duty solicitor, the report should be both to the Solicitors Regulatory Authority and to the Legal Aid Agency.

6.12 'Solicitor' in this Code means:

- a solicitor who holds a current practising certificate;
- an accredited or probationary representative included on the register of representatives maintained by the Legal Aid Agency.

6.12A An accredited or probationary representative sent to provide advice by, and on behalf of, a solicitor shall be admitted to the police station for this purpose unless an officer of inspector rank or above considers such a visit will hinder the investigation and directs otherwise. Hindering the investigation does not include giving proper legal advice to a detainee as in *Note 6D*. Once admitted to the police station, *paragraphs 6.6* to *6.10* apply.

6.13 In exercising their discretion under *paragraph 6.12A*, the officer should take into account in particular:
- whether:
  - the identity and status of an accredited or probationary representative have been satisfactorily established;
  - they are of suitable character to provide legal advice, e.g. a person with a criminal record is unlikely to be suitable unless the conviction was for a minor offence and not recent.
- any other matters in any written letter of authorisation provided by the solicitor on whose behalf the person is attending the police station. See *Note 6F.*

6.14 If the inspector refuses access to an accredited or probationary representative or a decision is taken that such a person should not be permitted to remain at an interview, the inspector must notify the solicitor on whose behalf the representative was acting and give them an opportunity to make alternative arrangements. The detainee must be informed and the custody record noted.

6.15 If a solicitor arrives at the station to see a particular person, that person must, unless *Annex B* applies, be so informed whether or not they are being interviewed and asked if they would like to see the solicitor. This applies even if the detainee has declined legal advice or, having requested it, subsequently agreed to be interviewed without receiving advice. The solicitor's attendance and the detainee's decision must be noted in the custody record.

(B) Documentation

6.16 Any request for legal advice and the action taken shall be recorded.

6.17 A record shall be made in the interview record if a detainee asks for legal advice and an interview is begun either in the absence of a solicitor or their representative, or they have been required to leave an interview.

Notes for Guidance

6ZA No police officer or police staff shall indicate to any suspect, except to answer a direct question, that the period for which they are liable to be detained, or if not detained, the time taken to complete the interview, might be reduced:
- *if they do not ask for legal advice or do not want a solicitor present when they are interviewed; or*
- *if they have asked for legal advice or (as the case may be) asked for a solicitor to be present when they are interviewed but change their mind and agree to be interviewed without waiting for a solicitor.*

6A In considering if paragraph 6.6(b) applies, the officer should, if practicable, ask the solicitor for an estimate of how long it will take to come to the station and relate this to the time detention is permitted, the time of day (i.e. whether the rest period under paragraph 12.2 is imminent) and the requirements of other investigations. If the solicitor is on their way or is to set off immediately, it will not normally be appropriate to begin an interview before they arrive. If it appears necessary to begin an interview before the solicitor's arrival, they should be given an indication of how long the police would be able to wait before 6.6(b) applies so there is an opportunity to make arrangements for someone else to provide legal advice.

6B A detainee has a right to free legal advice and to be represented by a solicitor. This Note for Guidance explains the arrangements which enable detainees to obtain legal advice. An outline of these arrangements is also included in the Notice of Rights and Entitlements given to detainees in accordance with paragraph 3.2. The arrangements also apply, with appropriate modifications, to persons attending a police station or other location (see paragraph 3.22 and Notes 3I and 3J) voluntarily who are cautioned prior to being interviewed. See paragraph 3.21.

When a detainee asks for free legal advice, the Defence Solicitor Call Centre (DSCC) must be informed of the request.

Free legal advice will be limited to telephone advice provided by CDS Direct if a detainee is:
- *detained for a non-imprisonable offence;*
- *arrested on a bench warrant for failing to appear and being held for production at court (except where the solicitor has clear documentary evidence available that would result in the client being released from custody);*
- *arrested for drink driving (driving/in charge with excess alcohol, failing to provide a specimen, driving/in charge whilst unfit through drink), or*
- *detained in relation to breach of police or court bail conditions*

unless one or more exceptions apply, in which case the DSCC should arrange for advice to be given by a solicitor at the police station, for example:
- *the police want to interview the detainee or carry out an eye-witness identification procedure;*
- *the detainee needs an appropriate adult;*

- the detainee is unable to communicate over the telephone;
- the detainee alleges serious misconduct by the police;
- the investigation includes another offence not included in the list,
- the solicitor to be assigned is already at the police station.

When free advice is not limited to telephone advice, a detainee can ask for free advice from a solicitor they know or if they do not know a solicitor or the solicitor they know cannot be contacted, from the duty solicitor.

To arrange free legal advice, the police should telephone the DSCC. The call centre will decide whether legal advice should be limited to telephone advice from CDS Direct, or whether a solicitor known to the detainee or the duty solicitor should speak to the detainee.

When a detainee wants to pay for legal advice themselves:

- the DSCC will contact a solicitor of their choice on their behalf;
- they may, when free advice is only available by telephone from CDS Direct, still speak to a solicitor of their choice on the telephone for advice, but the solicitor would not be paid by legal aid and may ask the person to pay for the advice;
- they should be given an opportunity to consult a specific solicitor or another solicitor from that solicitor's firm. If this solicitor is not available, they may choose up to two alternatives. If these alternatives are not available, the custody officer has discretion to allow further attempts until a solicitor has been contacted and agreed to provide advice;
- they are entitled to a private consultation with their chosen solicitor on the telephone or the solicitor may decide to come to the police station;
- If their chosen solicitor cannot be contacted, the DSCC may still be called to arrange free legal advice.

Apart from carrying out duties necessary to implement these arrangements, an officer must not advise the suspect about any particular firm of solicitors.

6B1 Not used.

6B2 Not used.

6C Not used.

6D The solicitor's only role in the police station is to protect and advance the legal rights of their client. On occasions this may require the solicitor to give advice which has the effect of the client avoiding giving evidence which strengthens a prosecution case. The solicitor may intervene in order to seek clarification, challenge an improper question to their client or the manner in which it is put, advise their client not to reply to particular questions, or if they wish to give their client further legal advice. Paragraph 6.9 only applies if the solicitor's approach or conduct prevents or unreasonably obstructs proper questions being put to the suspect or the suspect's response being recorded. Examples of unacceptable conduct include answering questions on a suspect's behalf or providing written replies for the suspect to quote.

6E An officer who takes the decision to exclude a solicitor must be in a position to satisfy the court the decision was properly made. In order to do this they may need to witness what is happening.

6F If an officer of at least inspector rank considers a particular solicitor or firm of solicitors is persistently sending probationary representatives who are unsuited to provide legal advice, they should inform an officer of at least superintendent rank, who may wish to take the matter up with the Solicitors Regulation Authority.

6G Subject to the constraints of Annex B, a solicitor may advise more than one client in an investigation if they wish. Any question of a conflict of interest is for the solicitor under their professional code of conduct. If, however, waiting for a solicitor to give advice to one client may lead to unreasonable delay to the interview with another, the provisions of paragraph 6.6(b) may apply.

6H In addition to a poster in English, a poster or posters containing translations into Welsh, the main minority ethnic languages and the principal European languages should be displayed wherever they are likely to be helpful and it is practicable to do so.

6I Not used.

6J Whenever a detainee exercises their right to legal advice by consulting or communicating with a solicitor, they must be allowed to do so in private. This right to consult or communicate in private is fundamental. If the requirement for privacy is compromised because what is said or written by the detainee or solicitor for the purpose of giving and receiving legal advice is overheard, listened to, or read by others without the informed consent of the detainee, the right will effectively have been denied. When a detainee speaks to a solicitor on the telephone, they should be allowed to do so in private unless this is impractical because of the design and layout of the custody area or the location of telephones. However, the normal expectation should be that facilities will be available, unless they are being used, at all police stations to enable detainees to speak in private to a solicitor either face to face or over the telephone.

6K A detainee is not obliged to give reasons for declining legal advice and should not be pressed to do so.

7 Citizens of independent Commonwealth countries or foreign nationals

(A) Action

7.1 A detainee who is a citizen of an independent Commonwealth country or a national of a foreign country, including the Republic of Ireland, has the right, upon request, to communicate at any time with the appropriate High Commission, Embassy or Consulate. That detainee must be informed as soon as practicable of this right and asked if they want to have their High Commission, Embassy or Consulate told of their whereabouts and the grounds for their detention. Such a request should be acted upon as soon as practicable. See *Note 7A*.

7.2 A detainee who is a citizen of a country with which a bilateral consular convention or agreement is in force requiring notification of arrest must also be informed that subject to *paragraph 7.4,* notification of their arrest will be sent to the appropriate High Commission, Embassy or Consulate as soon as practicable, whether or not they request it. A list of the countries to which this requirement currently applies and contact details for the relevant High Commissions, Embassies and Consulates can be obtained from the Consular Directorate of the Foreign and Commonwealth Office (FCO) as follows:

- from the FCO web pages:
  - *https://gov.uk/government/publications/table-of-consular-conventions-and-mandatory-notification-obligations*, and
  - *https://www.gov.uk/government/publications/foreign-embassies-in-the-uk*
- by telephone to 020 7008 3100,
- by email to *fcocorrespondence@fco.gov.uk*.
- by letter to the Foreign and Commonwealth Office, King Charles Street, London, SW1A 2AH.

7.3 Consular officers may, if the detainee agrees, visit one of their nationals in police detention to talk to them and, if required, to arrange for legal advice. Such visits shall take place out of the hearing of a police officer.

7.4 Notwithstanding the provisions of consular conventions, if the detainee claims that they are a refugee or have applied or intend to apply for asylum, the custody officer must ensure that UK Visas and Immigration (UKVI) (formerly the UK Border Agency) is informed as soon as practicable of the claim. UKVI will then determine whether compliance with relevant international obligations requires notification of the arrest to be sent and will inform the custody officer as to what action police need to take.

(B) Documentation

7.5 A record shall be made:

- when a detainee is informed of their rights under this section and of any requirement in *paragraph 7.2*;
- of any communications with a High Commission, Embassy or Consulate, and
- of any communications with UKVI about a detainee's claim to be a refugee or to be seeking asylum and the resulting action taken by police.

Note for Guidance

7A The exercise of the rights in this section may not be interfered with even though Annex B applies.

8 Conditions of detention

(A) Action

8.1 So far as it is practicable, not more than one detainee should be detained in each cell. See *Note 8C*.

8.2 Cells in use must be adequately heated, cleaned and ventilated. They must be adequately lit, subject to such dimming as is compatible with safety and security to allow people detained overnight to sleep. No additional restraints shall be used within a locked cell unless absolutely necessary and then only restraint equipment, approved for use in that force by the chief officer, which is reasonable and necessary in the circumstances having regard to the detainee's demeanour and with a view to ensuring their safety and the safety of others. If a detainee is deaf or a vulnerable person, particular care must be taken when deciding whether to use any form of approved restraints.

8.3 Blankets, mattresses, pillows and other bedding supplied shall be of a reasonable standard and in a clean and sanitary condition. See *Note 8A*.

8.4 Access to toilet and washing facilities must be provided. This must take account of the dignity of the detainee. See *Note 8D*.

8.5 If it is necessary to remove a detainee's clothes for the purposes of investigation, for hygiene, health reasons or cleaning, removal shall be conducted with proper regard to the dignity, sensitivity and vulnerability of the detainee and replacement clothing of a reasonable standard of comfort and cleanliness shall be provided. A detainee may not be interviewed unless adequate clothing has been offered.

8.6 At least two light meals and one main meal should be offered in any 24-hour period. See *Note 8B*. Drinks should be provided at meal times and upon reasonable request between meals. Whenever necessary, advice shall be sought from the appropriate healthcare professional, see *Note 9A,* on medical and dietary matters. As far as practicable, meals provided shall offer a varied diet and meet any specific dietary needs or religious beliefs the detainee may have. The detainee may, at the custody officer's discretion, have meals supplied by their family or friends at their expense. See *Note 8A*.

8.7 Brief outdoor exercise shall be offered daily if practicable.

8.8 A juvenile shall not be placed in a police cell unless no other secure accommodation is available and the custody officer considers it is not practicable to supervise them if they are not placed in a cell or that a cell provides more comfortable accommodation than other secure accommodation in the station. A juvenile may not be placed in a cell with a detained adult.

(B) Documentation

8.9 A record must be kept of replacement clothing and meals offered.

8.10 If a juvenile is placed in a cell, the reason must be recorded.

8.11 The use of any restraints on a detainee whilst in a cell, the reasons for it and, if appropriate, the arrangements for enhanced supervision of the detainee whilst so restrained, shall be recorded. See *paragraph 3.9*.

Notes for Guidance

8A The provisions in paragraph 8.3 and 8.6 respectively are of particular importance in the case of a person likely to be detained for an extended period. In deciding whether to allow meals to be supplied by family or friends, the custody officer is entitled to take account of the risk of items being concealed in any food or package and the officer's duties and responsibilities under food handling legislation.

8B Meals should, so far as practicable, be offered at recognised meal times, or at other times that take account of when the detainee last had a meal.

8C The Detention and Custody Authorised Professional Practice (APP) produced by the College of Policing (see http://www.app.college.police.uk) provides more detailed guidance on matters concerning detainee healthcare and treatment and associated forensic issues which should be read in conjunction with sections 8 and 9 of this Code.

8D In cells subject to CCTV monitoring, privacy in the toilet area should be ensured by any appropriate means and detainees should be made aware of this when they are placed in the cell. If a detainee or appropriate adult on their behalf, expresses doubt about the effectiveness of the means used, reasonable steps should be taken to allay those doubts, for example, by explaining or demonstrating the means used.

9 Care and treatment of detained persons

(A) General

9.1 Nothing in this section prevents the police from calling an appropriate healthcare professional to examine a detainee for the purposes of obtaining evidence relating to any offence in which the detainee is suspected of being involved. See *Notes 9A* and *8C*.

9.2 If a complaint is made by, or on behalf of, a detainee about their treatment since their arrest, or it comes to notice that a detainee may have been treated improperly, a report must be made as soon as practicable to an officer of inspector rank or above not connected with the investigation. If the matter concerns a possible assault or the possibility of the unnecessary or unreasonable use of force, an appropriate healthcare professional must also be called as soon as practicable.

9.3 Subject to *paragraph 9.6* in the case of a person to whom The Mental Health Act 1983 (Places of Safety) Regulations 2017 apply, detainees should be visited at least every hour. If no reasonably foreseeable risk was identified in a risk assessment, see *paragraphs 3.6* to *3.10*, there is no need to wake a sleeping detainee. Those suspected of being under the influence of drink or drugs or both or of having swallowed drugs, see *Note 9CA*, or whose level of consciousness causes concern must, subject to any clinical directions given by the appropriate healthcare professional, see *paragraph 9.13*:

- be visited and roused at least every half hour;
- have their condition assessed as in *Annex H;*
- and clinical treatment arranged if appropriate.

See *Notes 9B, 9C* and *9H*

9.3A As soon as practicable after arrival at the police station, each detainee must be given an opportunity to speak in private with a member of the custody staff who if they wish may be of the same sex as the detainee (see paragraph 1.13(c)), about any matter concerning the detainee's personal needs relating to their health, hygiene and welfare that might affect or concern them whilst in custody. If the detainee wishes to take this opportunity, the necessary arrangements shall be made as soon as practicable. In the cases of a juvenile or vulnerable person, the appropriate adult must be involved in accordance with paragraph 3.17 and in the case of a girl under 18, see paragraph 3.20A (see Note 9CB).

9.3B Each female detainee aged 18 or over shall be asked in private if possible and at the earliest opportunity, if they require or are likely to require any menstrual products whilst they are in custody. They must be told that they will be provided free of charge and that replacement products are available. At the custody officer's discretion, detainees may have menstrual products supplied by their family or friends at their expense (see Note 9CC). For girls under 18, see paragraph 3.20A.

9.4 When arrangements are made to secure clinical attention for a detainee, the custody officer must make sure all relevant information which might assist in the treatment of the detainee's condition is made available to the responsible healthcare professional. This applies whether or not the healthcare professional asks for such information. Any officer or police staff with relevant information must inform the custody officer as soon as practicable.

(B) Clinical treatment and attention

9.5 The custody officer must make sure a detainee receives appropriate clinical attention as soon as reasonably practicable if the person:

(a) appears to be suffering from physical illness; or
(b) is injured; or
(c) appears to be suffering from a mental disorder; or
(d) appears to need clinical attention.

9.5A This applies even if the detainee makes no request for clinical attention and whether or not they have already received clinical attention elsewhere. If the need for attention appears urgent, e.g. when indicated as in *Annex H*, the nearest available healthcare professional or an ambulance must be called immediately.

9.5B The custody officer must also consider the need for clinical attention as set out in *Note 9C* in relation to those suffering the effects of alcohol or drugs.

9.6 *Paragraph 9.5* is not meant to prevent or delay the transfer to a hospital if necessary of a person detained under the Mental Health Act 1983, sections 135 and 136, as amended by the Policing and Crime Act 2017. See *Note 9D*. When an assessment under that Act is to take place at a police station (see *paragraph 3.16*) the custody officer must also ensure that in accordance with *The Mental Health Act 1983 (Places of Safety) Regulations 2017*, a health professional is present and available to the person throughout the period they are detained at the police station and that at the welfare of the detainee is checked by the health professional at least once every thirty minutes and any appropriate action for the care and treatment of the detainee taken.

9.7 If it appears to the custody officer, or they are told, that a person brought to a station under arrest may be suffering from an infectious disease or condition, the custody officer must take reasonable steps to safeguard the health of the detainee and others at the station. In deciding what action to take, advice must be sought from an appropriate healthcare professional. See *Note 9E*. The custody officer has discretion to isolate the person and their property until clinical directions have been obtained.

9.8 If a detainee requests a clinical examination, an appropriate healthcare professional must be called as soon as practicable to assess the detainee's clinical needs. If a safe and appropriate care plan cannot be provided, the appropriate healthcare professional's advice must be sought. The detainee may also be examined by a medical practitioner of their choice at their expense.

9.9 If a detainee is required to take or apply any medication in compliance with clinical directions prescribed before their detention, the custody officer must consult the appropriate healthcare professional before the use of the medication. Subject to the restrictions in *paragraph 9.10*, the custody officer is responsible for the safekeeping of any medication and for making sure the detainee is given the opportunity to take or apply prescribed or approved medication. Any such consultation and its outcome shall be noted in the custody record.

9.10 No police officer may administer or supervise the self-administration of medically prescribed controlled drugs of the types and forms listed in the Misuse of Drugs Regulations 2001, Schedule 2 or 3. A detainee may only self-administer such drugs under the personal supervision of the registered medical practitioner authorising their use or other appropriate healthcare professional. The custody officer may supervise the self-administration of, or authorise other custody staff to supervise the self-administration of, drugs listed in Schedule 4 or 5 if the officer has consulted the appropriate healthcare professional authorising their use and both are satisfied self-administration will not expose the detainee, police officers or anyone else to the risk of harm or injury.

9.11 When appropriate healthcare professionals administer drugs or authorise the use of other medications, supervise their self-administration or consult with the custody officer about allowing self-administration of drugs listed in Schedule 4 or 5, it must be within current medicines legislation and the scope of practice as determined by their relevant statutory regulatory body.

9.12 If a detainee has in their possession, or claims to need, medication relating to a heart condition, diabetes, epilepsy or a condition of comparable potential seriousness then, even though *paragraph 9.5* may not apply, the advice of the appropriate healthcare professional must be obtained.

9.13 Whenever the appropriate healthcare professional is called in accordance with this section to examine or treat a detainee, the custody officer shall ask for their opinion about:
- any risks or problems which police need to take into account when making decisions about the detainee's continued detention;
- when to carry out an interview if applicable; and
- the need for safeguards.

9.14 When clinical directions are given by the appropriate healthcare professional, whether orally or in writing, and the custody officer has any doubts or is in any way uncertain about any aspect of the directions, the custody officer shall ask for clarification. It is particularly important that directions concerning the frequency of visits are clear, precise and capable of being implemented. See *Note 9F.*

(C) Documentation

9.15 A record must be made in the custody record of:
- (a) the arrangements made for an examination by an appropriate healthcare professional under *paragraph 9.2* and of any complaint reported under that paragraph together with any relevant remarks by the custody officer;
- (b) any arrangements made in accordance with *paragraph 9.5;*
- (c) any request for a clinical examination under *paragraph 9.8* and any arrangements made in response;
- (d) the injury, ailment, condition or other reason which made it necessary to make the arrangements in *(a)* to *(c)*; See *Note 9G.*
- (e) any clinical directions and advice, including any further clarifications, given to police by a healthcare professional concerning the care and treatment of the detainee in connection with any of the arrangements made in *(a)* to *(c)*; See *Notes 9E* and *9F.*
- (f) if applicable, the responses received when attempting to rouse a person using the procedure in *Annex H.* See *Note 9H.*

9.16 If a healthcare professional does not record their clinical findings in the custody record, the record must show where they are recorded. See *Note 9G.* However, information which is necessary to custody staff to ensure the effective ongoing care and well being of the detainee must be recorded openly in the custody record, see *paragraph 3.8* and *Annex G, paragraph 7.*

9.17 Subject to the requirements of *Section 4*, the custody record shall include:
- a record of all medication a detainee has in their possession on arrival at the police station;
- a note of any such medication they claim to need but do not have with them.

Notes for Guidance

9A *A 'healthcare professional' means a clinically qualified person working within the scope of practice as determined by their relevant statutory regulatory body. Whether a healthcare professional is 'appropriate' depends on the circumstances of the duties they carry out at the time.*

9B *Whenever possible, detained juveniles and vulnerable persons should be visited more frequently.*

9C *A detainee who appears drunk or behaves abnormally may be suffering from illness, the effects of drugs or may have sustained injury, particularly a head injury which is not apparent. A detainee needing or dependent on certain drugs, including alcohol, may experience harmful effects within a short time of being deprived of their supply. In these circumstances, when there is any doubt, police should always act urgently to call an appropriate healthcare professional or an ambulance. Paragraph 9.5 does not apply to minor ailments or injuries which do not need attention. However, all such ailments or injuries must be recorded in the custody record and any doubt must be resolved in favour of calling the appropriate healthcare professional.*

9CA *Paragraph 9.3 would apply to a person in police custody by order of a magistrates' court under the Criminal Justice Act 1988, section 152 (as amended by the Drugs Act 2005, section 8) to facilitate the recovery of evidence after being charged with drug possession or drug trafficking and suspected of having swallowed drugs. In the case of the healthcare needs of a person who has swallowed drugs, the custody officer, subject to any clinical directions, should consider the necessity for rousing every half hour. This does not negate the need for regular visiting of the suspect in the cell.*

9D *Except as allowed for under The Mental Health Act 1983 (Places of Safety) Regulations 2017, a police station must not be used as a place of safety for persons detained under section 135 or 136 of that Act. Chapter 16 of the Mental Health Act 1983 Code of Practice (as revised), provides more detailed guidance about arranging assessments under the Mental Health Act and transferring detainees from police stations to other places of safety. Additional guidance in relation to amendments made to the Mental Health Act in 2017 are published at https://www.gov.uk/government/publications/mental-health-act-1983-implementing-changes-to-police-powers.*

9E *It is important to respect a person's right to privacy and information about their health must be kept confidential and only disclosed with their consent or in accordance with clinical advice when it is necessary to protect the detainee's health or that of others who come into contact with them.*

9F *The custody officer should always seek to clarify directions that the detainee requires constant observation or supervision and should ask the appropriate healthcare professional to explain precisely what action needs to be taken to implement such directions.*

9G *Paragraphs 9.15 and 9.16 do not require any information about the cause of any injury, ailment or condition to be recorded on the custody record if it appears capable of providing evidence of an offence.*

9H *The purpose of recording a person's responses when attempting to rouse them using the procedure in Annex H is to enable any change in the individual's consciousness level to be noted and clinical treatment arranged if appropriate.*

10 Cautions

(A) When a caution must be given

10.1 A person whom there are grounds to suspect of an offence, see *Note 10A*, must be cautioned before any questions about an offence, or further questions if the answers provide the grounds for suspicion, are put to them if either the suspect's answers or silence, (i.e. failure or refusal to answer or answer satisfactorily) may be given in evidence to a court in a prosecution. A person need not be cautioned if questions are for other necessary purposes, e.g.:
- (a) solely to establish their identity or ownership of any vehicle;
- (b) to obtain information in accordance with any relevant statutory requirement, see *paragraph 10.9*;
- (c) in furtherance of the proper and effective conduct of a search, e.g. to determine the need to search in the exercise of powers of stop and search or to seek co-operation while carrying out a search; or
- (d) to seek verification of a written record as in *paragraph 11.13*.
- (e) *Not used.*

10.2 Whenever a person not under arrest is initially cautioned, or reminded that they are under caution, that person must at the same time be told they are not under arrest and must be informed of the provisions of *paragraphs 3.21* to *3.21B* which explain that they need to agree to be interviewed, how they may obtain legal advice according to whether they are at a police station or elsewhere and the other rights and entitlements that apply to a voluntary interview. See *Note 10C*.

10.3 A person who is arrested, or further arrested, must be informed at the time if practicable or, if not, as soon as it becomes practicable thereafter, that they are under arrest and of the grounds and reasons for their arrest, see *paragraph 3.4*, *Note 10B* and Code G, *paragraphs 2.2 and 4.3*.

10.4 As required by Code G, *section 3*, a person who is arrested, or further arrested, must also be cautioned unless:
- (a) it is impracticable to do so by reason of their condition or behaviour at the time;
- (b) they have already been cautioned immediately prior to arrest as in *paragraph 10.1*.

(B) Terms of the cautions

10.5 The caution which must be given on:
- (a) arrest; or
- (b) all other occasions before a person is charged or informed they may be prosecuted; see *section 16*,

should, unless the restriction on drawing adverse inferences from silence applies, see *Annex C*, be in the following terms:

'You do not have to say anything. But it may harm your defence if you do not mention when questioned something which you later rely on in Court. Anything you do say may be given in evidence.'

Where the use of the Welsh Language is appropriate, a constable may provide the caution directly in Welsh in the following terms:

'Does dim rhaid i chi ddweud dim byd. Ond gall niweidio eich amddiffyniad os na fyddwch chi'n sôn, wrth gael eich holi, am rywbeth y byddwch chi'n dibynnu arno nes ymlaen yn y Llys. Gall unrhyw beth yr ydych yn ei ddweud gael ei roi fel tystiolaeth.'

See *Note 10G*.

10.6 *Annex C, paragraph 2* sets out the alternative terms of the caution to be used when the restriction on drawing adverse inferences from silence applies.

10.7 Minor deviations from the words of any caution given in accordance with this Code do not constitute a breach of this Code, provided the sense of the relevant caution is preserved. See *Note 10D*.

10.8 After any break in questioning under caution, the person being questioned must be made aware they remain under caution. If there is any doubt the relevant caution should be given again in full when the interview resumes. See *Note 10E*.

10.9 When, despite being cautioned, a person fails to co-operate or to answer particular questions which may affect their immediate treatment, the person should be informed of any relevant consequences and that those consequences are not affected by the caution. Examples are when a person's refusal to provide:
- their name and address when charged may make them liable to detention;

- particulars and information in accordance with a statutory requirement, e.g. under the Road Traffic Act 1988, may amount to an offence or may make the person liable to a further arrest.

(C) Special warnings under the Criminal Justice and Public Order Act 1994, sections 36 and 37

10.10 When a suspect interviewed at a police station or authorised place of detention after arrest fails or refuses to answer certain questions, or to answer satisfactorily, after due warning, see *Note 10F*, a court or jury may draw such inferences as appear proper under the Criminal Justice and Public Order Act 1994, sections 36 and 37. Such inferences may only be drawn when:

(a) the restriction on drawing adverse inferences from silence, see *Annex C*, does not apply; and

(b) the suspect is arrested by a constable and fails or refuses to account for any objects, marks or substances, or marks on such objects found:
- on their person;
- in or on their clothing or footwear;
- otherwise in their possession; or
- in the place they were arrested;

(c) the arrested suspect was found by a constable at a place at or about the time the offence for which that officer has arrested them is alleged to have been committed, and the suspect fails or refuses to account for their presence there.

When the restriction on drawing adverse inferences from silence applies, the suspect may still be asked to account for any of the matters in (*b*) or (*c*) but the special warning described in *paragraph 10.11* will not apply and must not be given.

10.11 For an inference to be drawn when a suspect fails or refuses to answer a question about one of these matters or to answer it satisfactorily, the suspect must first be told in ordinary language:

(a) what offence is being investigated;
(b) what fact they are being asked to account for;
(c) this fact may be due to them taking part in the commission of the offence;
(d) a court may draw a proper inference if they fail or refuse to account for this fact; and
(e) a record is being made of the interview and it may be given in evidence if they are brought to trial.

(D) Juveniles and vulnerable persons

10.11A The information required in *paragraph 10.11* must not be given to a suspect who is a juvenile or a vulnerable person unless the appropriate adult is present.

10.12 If a juvenile or a vulnerable person is cautioned in the absence of the appropriate adult, the caution must be repeated in the appropriate adult's presence.

10.12A *Not used.*

(E) Documentation

10.13 A record shall be made when a caution is given under this section, either in the interviewer's report book or in the interview record.

Notes for Guidance

10A *There must be some reasonable, objective grounds for the suspicion, based on known facts or information which are relevant to the likelihood the offence has been committed and the person to be questioned committed it.*

10B *An arrested person must be given sufficient information to enable them to understand that they have been deprived of their liberty and the reason they have been arrested, e.g. when a person is arrested on suspicion of committing an offence they must be informed of the suspected offence's nature, when and where it was committed. The suspect must also be informed of the reason or reasons why the arrest is considered necessary. Vague or technical language should be avoided.*

10C *The restriction on drawing inferences from silence, see Annex C, paragraph 1, does not apply to a person who has not been detained and who therefore cannot be prevented from seeking legal advice if they want, see paragraph 3.21.*

10D *If it appears a person does not understand the caution, the person giving it should explain it in their own words.*

10E *It may be necessary to show to the court that nothing occurred during an interview break or between interviews which influenced the suspect's recorded evidence. After a break in an interview or at the beginning of a subsequent interview, the interviewer should summarise the reason for the break and confirm this with the suspect.*

10F *The Criminal Justice and Public Order Act 1994, sections 36 and 37 apply only to suspects who have been arrested by a constable or an officer of Revenue and Customs and are given the relevant warning by the police or Revenue and Customs officer who made the arrest or who is investigating the offence. They do not apply to any interviews with suspects who have not been arrested.*

10G Nothing in this Code requires a caution to be given or repeated when informing a person not under arrest they may be prosecuted for an offence. However, a court will not be able to draw any inferences under the Criminal Justice and Public Order Act 1994, section 34, if the person was not cautioned.

11 Interviews — general

(A) Action

11.1A An interview is the questioning of a person regarding their involvement or suspected involvement in a criminal offence or offences which, under *paragraph 10.1*, must be carried out under caution. Before a person is interviewed, they and, if they are represented, their solicitor must be given sufficient information to enable them to understand the nature of any such offence, and why they are suspected of committing it (see *paragraphs 3.4(a)* and *10.3*), in order to allow for the effective exercise of the rights of the defence. However, whilst the information must always be sufficient for the person to understand the nature of any offence (see *Note 11ZA*), this does not require the disclosure of details at a time which might prejudice the criminal investigation. The decision about what needs to be disclosed for the purpose of this requirement therefore rests with the investigating officer who has sufficient knowledge of the case to make that decision. The officer who discloses the information shall make a record of the information disclosed and when it was disclosed. This record may be made in the interview record, in the officer's report book or other form provided for this purpose. Procedures under the Road Traffic Act 1988, section 7 or the Transport and Works Act 1992, section 31 do not constitute interviewing for the purpose of this Code.

11.1 Following a decision to arrest a suspect, they must not be interviewed about the relevant offence except at a police station or other authorised place of detention, unless the consequent delay would be likely to:

(a) lead to:
- interference with, or harm to, evidence connected with an offence;
- interference with, or physical harm to, other people; or
- serious loss of, or damage to, property;

(b) lead to alerting other people suspected of committing an offence but not yet arrested for it; or

(c) hinder the recovery of property obtained in consequence of the commission of an offence.

Interviewing in any of these circumstances shall cease once the relevant risk has been averted or the necessary questions have been put in order to attempt to avert that risk.

11.2 Immediately prior to the commencement or re-commencement of any interview at a police station or other authorised place of detention, the interviewer should remind the suspect of their entitlement to free legal advice and that the interview can be delayed for legal advice to be obtained, unless one of the exceptions in *paragraph 6.6* applies. It is the interviewer's responsibility to make sure all reminders are recorded in the interview record.

11.3 *Not used.*

11.4 At the beginning of an interview the interviewer, after cautioning the suspect, see *section 10*, shall put to them any significant statement or silence which occurred in the presence and hearing of a police officer or other police staff before the start of the interview and which have not been put to the suspect in the course of a previous interview. See *Note 11A*. The interviewer shall ask the suspect whether they confirm or deny that earlier statement or silence and if they want to add anything.

11.4A A significant statement is one which appears capable of being used in evidence against the suspect, in particular a direct admission of guilt. A significant silence is a failure or refusal to answer a question or answer satisfactorily when under caution, which might, allowing for the restriction on drawing adverse inferences from silence, see *Annex C*, give rise to an inference under the Criminal Justice and Public Order Act 1994, Part III.

11.5 No interviewer may try to obtain answers or elicit a statement by the use of oppression. Except as in *paragraph 10.9*, no interviewer shall indicate, except to answer a direct question, what action will be taken by the police if the person being questioned answers questions, makes a statement or refuses to do either. If the person asks directly what action will be taken if they answer questions, make a statement or refuse to do either, the interviewer may inform them what action the police propose to take provided that action is itself proper and warranted.

11.6 The interview or further interview of a person about an offence with which that person has not been charged or for which they have not been informed they may be prosecuted, must cease when:

(a) the officer in charge of the investigation is satisfied all the questions they consider relevant to obtaining accurate and reliable information about the offence have been put to the suspect, this includes allowing the suspect an opportunity to give an innocent explanation and asking questions to test if the explanation is accurate and reliable, e.g. to clear up ambiguities or clarify what the suspect said;

(b) the officer in charge of the investigation has taken account of any other available evidence; and

(c) the officer in charge of the investigation, or in the case of a detained suspect, the custody officer, see *paragraph 16.1*, reasonably believes there is sufficient evidence to provide a realistic prospect of conviction for that offence. See *Note 11B*.

This paragraph does not prevent officers in revenue cases or acting under the confiscation provisions of the Criminal Justice Act 1988 or the Drug Trafficking Act 1994 from inviting suspects to complete a formal question and answer record after the interview is concluded.

(B) Interview records

11.7 (a) An accurate record must be made of each interview, whether or not the interview takes place at a police station.

(b) The record must state the place of interview, the time it begins and ends, any interview breaks and, subject to *paragraph 2.6A*, the names of all those present; and must be made on the forms provided for this purpose or in the interviewer's report book or in accordance with Codes of Practice E or F.

(c) Any written record must be made and completed during the interview, unless this would not be practicable or would interfere with the conduct of the interview, and must constitute either a verbatim record of what has been said or, failing this, an account of the interview which adequately and accurately summarises it.

11.8 If a written record is not made during the interview it must be made as soon as practicable after its completion.

11.9 Written interview records must be timed and signed by the maker.

11.10 If a written record is not completed during the interview the reason must be recorded in the interview record.

11.11 Unless it is impracticable, the person interviewed shall be given the opportunity to read the interview record and to sign it as correct or to indicate how they consider it inaccurate. If the person interviewed cannot read or refuses to read the record or sign it, the senior interviewer present shall read it to them and ask whether they would like to sign it as correct or make their mark or to indicate how they consider it inaccurate. The interviewer shall certify on the interview record itself what has occurred. See *Note 11E*.

11.12 If the appropriate adult or the person's solicitor is present during the interview, they should also be given an opportunity to read and sign the interview record or any written statement taken down during the interview.

11.13 A record shall be made of any comments made by a suspect, including unsolicited comments, which are outside the context of an interview but which might be relevant to the offence. Any such record must be timed and signed by the maker. When practicable the suspect shall be given the opportunity to read that record and to sign it as correct or to indicate how they consider it inaccurate. See *Note 11E*.

11.14 Any refusal by a person to sign an interview record when asked in accordance with this Code must itself be recorded.

(C) Juveniles and vulnerable persons

11.15 A juvenile or vulnerable person must not be interviewed regarding their involvement or suspected involvement in a criminal offence or offences, or asked to provide or sign a written statement under caution or record of interview, in the absence of the appropriate adult unless *paragraphs 11.1* or *11.18* to *11.20* apply. See *Note 11C*.

11.16 Juveniles may only be interviewed at their place of education in exceptional circumstances and only when the principal or their nominee agrees. Every effort should be made to notify the parent(s) or other person responsible for the juvenile's welfare and the appropriate adult, if this is a different person, that the police want to interview the juvenile and reasonable time should be allowed to enable the appropriate adult to be present at the interview. If awaiting the appropriate adult would cause unreasonable delay, and unless the juvenile is suspected of an offence against the educational establishment, the principal or their nominee can act as the appropriate adult for the purposes of the interview.

11.17 If an appropriate adult is present at an interview, they shall be informed:

- that they are not expected to act simply as an observer; and
- that the purpose of their presence is to:
  - advise the person being interviewed;
  - observe whether the interview is being conducted properly and fairly; and
  - facilitate communication with the person being interviewed.

See *paragraph 1.7A*.

11.17A The appropriate adult may be required to leave the interview if their conduct is such that the interviewer is unable properly to put questions to the suspect. This will include situations where the appropriate adult's approach or conduct prevents or unreasonably obstructs proper questions being put to the suspect or the suspect's responses being recorded (see *Note 11F*). If the interviewer considers an appropriate adult is acting in such a way, they will stop the interview and consult an officer not below superintendent rank, if one is readily available, and otherwise an officer not below inspector rank not connected with the investigation. After speaking to the appropriate adult, the officer consulted must remind the adult that their role under *paragraph 11.17* does not allow them to obstruct proper questioning and give the adult an opportunity to respond. The officer consulted will then decide if the interview should continue without the attendance of that appropriate adult. If they decide it should, another appropriate adult must be obtained before the interview continues, unless the provisions of *paragraph 11.18* below apply.

(D) Vulnerable suspects — urgent interviews at police stations

11.18 The following interviews may take place only if an officer of superintendent rank or above considers delaying the interview will lead to the consequences in *paragraph 11.1(a)* to *(c)*, and is satisfied the interview would not significantly harm the person's physical or mental state (see *Annex G*):

(a) an interview of a detained juvenile or vulnerable person without the appropriate adult being present (see *Note 11C*);

(b) an interview of anyone detained other than in *(a)* who appears unable to:
- appreciate the significance of questions and their answers; or
- understand what is happening because of the effects of drink, drugs or any illness, ailment or condition;

(c) an interview, without an interpreter having been arranged, of a detained person whom the custody officer has determined requires an interpreter (see *paragraphs 3.5(c)(ii)* and *3.12*) which is carried out by an interviewer speaking the suspect's own language or (as the case may be) otherwise establishing effective communication which is sufficient to enable the necessary questions to be asked and answered in order to avert the consequences. See *paragraphs 13.2* and *13.5*.

11.19 These interviews may not continue once sufficient information has been obtained to avert the consequences in *paragraph 11.1(a)* to *(c)*.

11.20 A record shall be made of the grounds for any decision to interview a person under *paragraph 11.18*.

(E) Conduct and recording of Interviews at police stations — use of live link

11.21 When a suspect in police detention is interviewed using a live link by a police officer who is not at the police station where the detainee is held, the provisions of this section that govern the conduct and making a written record of that interview, shall be subject to *paragraph 12.9B* of this Code.

(F) Witnesses

11.22 The provisions of this Code and Codes E and F which govern the conduct and recording of interviews do not apply to interviews with, or taking statements from, witnesses.

Notes for Guidance

11ZA The requirement in paragraph 11.1A for a suspect to be given sufficient information about the offence applies prior to the interview and whether or not they are legally represented. What is sufficient will depend on the circumstances of the case, but it should normally include, as a minimum, a description of the facts relating to the suspected offence that are known to the officer, including the time and place in question. This aims to avoid suspects being confused or unclear about what they are supposed to have done and to help an innocent suspect to clear the matter up more quickly.

11A Paragraph 11.4 does not prevent the interviewer from putting significant statements and silences to a suspect again at a later stage or a further interview.

11B The Criminal Procedure and Investigations Act 1996 Code of Practice, paragraph 3.5 states 'In conducting an investigation, the investigator should pursue all reasonable lines of enquiry, whether these point towards or away from the suspect. What is reasonable will depend on the particular circumstances.' Interviewers should keep this in mind when deciding what questions to ask in an interview.

11C Although juveniles or vulnerable persons are often capable of providing reliable evidence, they may, without knowing or wishing to do so, be particularly prone in certain circumstances to providing information that may be unreliable, misleading or self- incriminating. Special care should always be taken when questioning such a person, and the appropriate adult should be involved if there is any doubt about a person's age, mental state or capacity. Because of the risk of unreliable evidence it is also important to obtain corroboration of any facts admitted whenever possible. Because of the risks, which the presence of the appropriate adult is intended to minimise, officers of superintendent rank or above should exercise their discretion under paragraph 11.18(a) to authorise the commencement of an interview in the appropriate adult's absence only in exceptional cases, if it is necessary to avert one or more of the specified risks in paragraph 11.1.

11D Juveniles should not be arrested at their place of education unless this is unavoidable. When a juvenile is arrested at their place of education, the principal or their nominee must be informed.

11E Significant statements described in paragraph 11.4 will always be relevant to the offence and must be recorded. When a suspect agrees to read records of interviews and other comments and sign them as correct, they should be asked to endorse the record with, e.g. 'I agree that this is a correct record of what was said' and add their signature. If the suspect does not agree with the record, the interviewer should record the details of any disagreement and ask the suspect to read these details and sign them to the effect that they accurately reflect their disagreement. Any refusal to sign should be recorded.

11F The appropriate adult may intervene if they consider it is necessary to help the suspect understand any question asked and to help the suspect to answer any question. Paragraph 11.17A only applies if the appropriate adult's approach or conduct prevents or unreasonably obstructs proper questions being put to the suspect or the suspect's response being recorded. Examples of unacceptable conduct include answering questions on a suspect's behalf or providing written replies for the suspect to quote. An officer who takes the decision to exclude an appropriate adult must be in a position to satisfy the court the decision was properly made. In order to do this they may need to witness what is happening and give the suspect's solicitor (if they have one) who witnessed what happened, an opportunity to comment.

12 Interviews in police stations

(A) Action

When interviewer and suspect are present at the same police station

12.1 If a police officer wants to interview or conduct enquiries which require the presence of a detainee, the custody officer is responsible for deciding whether to deliver the detainee into the officer's custody. An investigating officer who is given custody of a detainee takes over responsibility for the detainee's care and safe custody for the purposes of this Code until they return the detainee to the custody officer when they must report the manner in which they complied with the Code whilst having custody of the detainee.

12.2 Except as below, in any period of 24 hours a detainee must be allowed a continuous period of at least 8 hours for rest, free from questioning, travel or any interruption in connection with the investigation concerned. This period should normally be at night or other appropriate time which takes account of when the detainee last slept or rested. If a detainee is arrested at a police station after going there voluntarily, the period of 24 hours runs from the time of their arrest and not the time of arrival at the police station. The period may not be interrupted or delayed, except:

- (a) when there are reasonable grounds for believing not delaying or interrupting the period would:
  - (i) involve a risk of harm to people or serious loss of, or damage to, property;
  - (ii) delay unnecessarily the person's release from custody; or
  - (iii) otherwise prejudice the outcome of the investigation;
- (b) at the request of the detainee, their appropriate adult or legal representative;
- (c) when a delay or interruption is necessary in order to:
  - (i) comply with the legal obligations and duties arising under *section 15*; or
  - (ii) to take action required under *section 9* or in accordance with medical advice.

If the period is interrupted in accordance with *(a)*, a fresh period must be allowed. Interruptions under *(b)* and *(c)* do not require a fresh period to be allowed.

12.3 Before a detainee is interviewed, the custody officer, in consultation with the officer in charge of the investigation and appropriate healthcare professionals as necessary, shall assess whether the detainee is fit enough to be interviewed. This means determining and considering the risks to the detainee's physical and mental state if the interview took place and determining what safeguards are needed to allow the interview to take place. See *Annex G*. The custody officer shall not allow a detainee to be interviewed if the custody officer considers it would cause significant harm to the detainee's physical or mental state. Vulnerable suspects listed at *paragraph 11.18* shall be treated as always being at some risk during an interview and these persons may not be interviewed except in accordance with *paragraphs 11.18* to *11.20*.

12.4 As far as practicable interviews shall take place in interview rooms which are adequately heated, lit and ventilated.

12.5 A suspect whose detention without charge has been authorised under PACE because the detention is necessary for an interview to obtain evidence of the offence for which they have been arrested may choose not to answer questions but police do not require the suspect's consent or agreement to interview them for this purpose. If a suspect takes steps to prevent themselves being questioned or further questioned, e.g. by refusing to leave their cell to go to a suitable interview room or by trying to leave the interview room, they shall be advised that their consent or agreement to be interviewed is not required. The suspect shall be cautioned as in *section 10*, and informed if they fail or refuse to co-operate, the interview may take place in the cell and that their failure or refusal to co-operate may be given in evidence. The suspect shall then be invited to co-operate and go into the interview room. If they refuse and the custody officer considers, on reasonable grounds, that the interview should not be delayed, the custody officer has discretion to direct that the interview be conducted in a cell.

12.6 People being questioned or making statements shall not be required to stand.

12.7 Before the interview commences each interviewer shall, subject to *paragraph 2.6A,* identify themselves and any other persons present to the interviewee.

12.8 Breaks from interviewing should be made at recognised meal times or at other times that take account of when an interviewee last had a meal. Short refreshment breaks shall be provided at approximately two hour intervals, subject to the interviewer's discretion to delay a break if there are reasonable grounds for believing it would:

(i) involve a:
- risk of harm to people;
- serious loss of, or damage to, property;

(ii) unnecessarily delay the detainee's release; or

(iii) otherwise prejudice the outcome of the investigation.

See *Note 12B.*

12.9 If during the interview a complaint is made by or on behalf of the interviewee concerning the provisions of any of the Codes, or it comes to the interviewer's notice that the interviewee may have been treated improperly, the interviewer should:

(i) record the matter in the interview record; and

(ii) inform the custody officer, who is then responsible for dealing with it as in *section 9.*

Interviewer not present at the same station as the detainee — use of live link

12.9A Amendments to PACE, section 39, allow a person in police detention to be interviewed using a live link (see *paragraph 1.13(e)(i)*) by a police officer who is not at the police station where the detainee is held. Subject to *sub-paragraphs (a)* to *(f)* below, the custody officer is responsible for deciding on a case by case basis whether a detainee is fit to be interviewed (see *paragraph 12.3*) and should be delivered into the physical custody of an officer who is not involved in the investigation, for the purpose of enabling another officer who is investigating the offence for which the person is detained and who is not at the police station where the person is detained, to interview the detainee by means of a live link (see *Note 12ZA*).

(a) The custody officer must be satisfied that the live link to be used provides for accurate and secure communication with the suspect. The provisions of *paragraph 13.13* shall apply to communications between the interviewing officer, the suspect and anyone else whose presence at the interview or, (as the case may be) whose access to any communications between the suspect and the interviewer, has been authorised by the custody officer or the interviewing officer.

(b) Each decision must take account of the age, gender and vulnerability of the suspect, the nature and circumstances of the offence and the investigation and the impact on the suspect of carrying out the interview by means of a live link. For this reason, the custody officer must consider whether the ability of the particular suspect, to communicate confidently and effectively for the purpose of the interview is likely to be adversely affected or otherwise undermined or limited if the interviewing officer is not physically present and a live-link is used (see *Note 12ZB*). Although a suspect for whom an appropriate adult is required may be more likely to be adversely affected as described, it is important to note that a person who does not require an appropriate adult may also be adversely impacted if interviewed by means of a live link.

(c) If the custody officer is satisfied that interviewing the detainee by means of a live link *would not* adversely affect or otherwise undermine or limit the suspect's ability to communicate confidently and effectively for the purpose of the *interview*, the officer must so inform the suspect, their solicitor and (if applicable) the appropriate adult. At the same time, the operation of the live-link must be explained and demonstrated to them (see *Note 12ZC*), they must be advised of the chief officer's obligations concerning the security of live-link communications under *paragraph 13.13* and they must be asked if they wish to make representations that the live-link should not be used or if they require more information about the operation of the arrangements. They must also be told that at any time live-link is in use, they may make representations to the custody officer or the interviewer that its operation should cease and that the physical presence of the interviewer should be arranged.

When the authority of an inspector is required

(d) If:
(i) representations are made that a live-link should not be used to carry out the interview, or that at any time it is in use, its operation should cease and the physical presence of the interviewer arranged; and
(ii) the custody officer in consultation with the interviewer is unable to allay the concerns raised;
then live-link may not be used, or (as the case may be) continue to be used, unless authorised in writing by an officer of the rank of inspector or above in accordance with *sub-paragraph (e)*.

(e) Authority may be given if the officer is satisfied that interviewing the detainee by means of a live link is necessary and justified. In making this decision, the officer must have regard to:
(i) the circumstances of the suspect;
(ii) the nature and seriousness of the offence;
(iii) the requirements of the investigation, including its likely impact on both the suspect and any victim(s);
(iv) the representations made by the suspect, their solicitor and (if applicable) the appropriate adult that a live-link should not be used (see *sub-paragraph (b)*);
(v) the impact on the investigation of making arrangements for the physical presence of the interviewer (see *Note 12ZD*); and
(vi) the risk if the interpreter is not *physically* present, evidence obtained using link interpretation might be excluded in subsequent criminal proceedings; and
(vii) the likely impact on the suspect and the investigation of any consequential delay to arrange for the interpreter to be *physically* present with the suspect.

(f) The officer given custody of the detainee *and* the interviewer take over responsibility for the detainee's care, treatment and safe custody for the purposes of this Code until the detainee is returned to the custody officer. On that return, both must report the manner in which they complied with the Code during period in question.

12.9B When a suspect detained at a police station is interviewed using a live link in accordance with *paragraph 12.9A*, the officer given custody of the detainee at the police station *and* the interviewer who is not present at the police station, take over responsibility for ensuring compliance with the provisions of *sections 11* and *12* of this Code, or *Code E* (Audio recording) or *Code F* (Audio visual recording) that govern the conduct and recording of that interview. In these circumstances:

(a) *the interviewer who is not at the police station where the detainee is held* must direct the officer having physical custody of the suspect at the police station, to take the action required by those provisions and which the interviewer would be required to take if they were present at the police station.

(b) *the officer having physical custody of the suspect at the police station* must take the action required by those provisions and which would otherwise be required to be taken by the interviewer if they were present at the police station. This applies whether or not the officer has been so directed by the interviewer but in such a case, the officer must inform the interviewer of the action taken.

(c) *during the course of the interview*, the officers in (a) and (b) may consult each other as necessary to clarify any action to be taken and to avoid any misunderstanding. Such consultations must, if in the hearing of the suspect and any other person present with the suspect (for example, a solicitor, appropriate adult or interpreter) be recorded in the interview record.

(B) Documentation

12.10 A record must be made of the:
- time a detainee is not in the custody of the custody officer, and why
- reason for any refusal to deliver the detainee out of that custody.

12.11 A record shall be made of the following:
(a) the reasons it was not practicable to use an interview room;
(b) any action taken as in *paragraph 12.5*; and
(c) the actions, decisions, authorisations, representations and outcomes arising from the requirements of *paragraphs 12.9A* and *12.9B*.

The record shall be made on the custody record or in the interview record for action taken whilst an interview record is being kept, with a brief reference to this effect in the custody record.

12.12 Any decision to delay a break in an interview must be recorded, with reasons, in the interview record.

12.13 All written statements made at police stations under caution shall be written on forms provided for the purpose.

12.14 All written statements made under caution shall be taken in accordance with *Annex D*. Before a person makes a written statement under caution at a police station, they shall be reminded about the right to legal advice. See *Note 12A*.

Notes for Guidance

12ZA 'Live link' means an arrangement by means of which the interviewing officer who is not at the police station is able to see and hear, and to be seen and heard by, the detainee concerned, the detainee's solicitor, any appropriate adult present and the officer who has custody of that detainee. See paragraphs 13.12 to 13.14 and Annex N for application to live-link interpretation.

12ZB In considering whether the use of the live link is appropriate in a particular case, the custody officer, in consultation with the interviewer, should make an assessment of the detainee's ability to understand and take part in the interviewing process and make a record of the outcome. If the suspect has asked for legal advice, their solicitor should be involved in the assessment and in the case of a juvenile or vulnerable person, the appropriate adult should be involved.

12ZC The explanation and demonstration of live-link interpretation is intended to help the suspect, solicitor and appropriate adult make an informed decision and to allay any concerns they may have.

12ZD Factors affecting the arrangements for the interviewer to be physically present will include the location of the police station where the interview would take place and the availability of an interviewer with sufficient knowledge of the investigation who can attend that station and carry out the interview.

12A It is not normally necessary to ask for a written statement if the interview was recorded in writing and the record signed in accordance with paragraph 11.11 or audibly or visually recorded in accordance with Code E or F. Statements under caution should normally be taken in these circumstances only at the person's express wish. A person may however be asked if they want to make such a statement.

12B Meal breaks should normally last at least 45 minutes and shorter breaks after two hours should last at least 15 minutes. If the interviewer delays a break in accordance with paragraph 12.8 and prolongs the interview, a longer break should be provided. If there is a short interview and another short interview is contemplated, the length of the break may be reduced if there are reasonable grounds to believe this is necessary to avoid any of the consequences in paragraph 12.8(i) to (iii).

13 Interpreters

(A) General

13.1 Chief officers are responsible for making arrangements (see *paragraph 13.1ZA*) to provide appropriately qualified independent persons to act as interpreters and to provide translations of essential documents for:

(a) detained suspects who, in accordance with *paragraph 3.5(c)(ii)*, the custody officer has determined require an interpreter, and

(b) suspects who are not under arrest but are cautioned as in *section 10* who, in accordance with *paragraph 3.21(b)*, the interviewer has determined require an interpreter. In these cases, the responsibilities of the custody officer are, if appropriate, assigned to the interviewer. An interviewer who has any doubts about whether and what arrangements for an interpreter must be made or about how the provisions of this section should be applied to a suspect who is not under arrest should seek advice from an officer of the rank of sergeant or above.

If the suspect has a hearing or speech impediment, references to 'interpreter' and 'interpretation' in this Code include arrangements for appropriate assistance necessary to establish effective communication with that person. See *paragraph 13.1C* below if the person is in Wales.

13.1ZA References in *paragraph 13.1* above and elsewhere in this Code (see *paragraphs 3.12(a), 13.2, 13.2A, 13.5, 13.6, 13.9, 13.10, 13.10A, 13.10D* and *13.11* below and in any other Code, to making arrangements for an interpreter to assist a suspect, mean making arrangements for the interpreter to be *physically* present in the same location as the suspect *unless* the provisions in *paragraph 13.12* below, and Part 1 of *Annex N*, allow live-link interpretation to be used.

13.1A The arrangements *must* comply with the minimum requirements set out in *Directive 2010/64/EU* of the European Parliament and of the Council of 20 October 2010 on the right to interpretation and translation in criminal proceedings (see *Note 13A*). The provisions *of this* Code implement the requirements for those to whom this Code applies. These requirements include the following:

- That the arrangements made and the quality of interpretation and translation provided shall be sufficient to 'safeguard the fairness of the proceedings, in particular by ensuring that suspected or accused persons have knowledge of the cases against them and are able to exercise their right of defence'. This term which is used by the Directive means that the suspect must be able to understand their position and be able to communicate effectively with police officers, interviewers, solicitors and appropriate adults as provided for by this and any other Code in the same way as a suspect who can speak and understand English and who does not have a hearing or speech impediment and who would therefore not require an interpreter. See *paragraphs 13.12* to *13.14* and *Annex N* for application to live-link interpretation.

- The provision of a written translation of all documents considered essential for the person to exercise their right of defence and to 'safeguard the fairness of the proceedings' as described above. For the purposes of this Code, this includes any decision to authorise a person to be detained and details of any offence(s) with which the person has been charged or for which they have been told they may be prosecuted, see *Annex M*.
- Procedures to help determine:
  - whether a suspect can speak and understand English and needs the assistance of an interpreter, see *paragraph 13.1* and *Notes 13B* and *13C*; and
  - whether another interpreter should be arranged or another translation should be provided when a suspect complains about the quality of either or both, see *paragraphs 13.10A* and *13.10C*.

13.1B All reasonable attempts should be made to make the suspect understand that interpretation and translation will be provided at public expense.

13.1C With regard to persons in Wales, nothing in this or any other Code affects the application of the Welsh Language Schemes produced by police and crime commissioners in Wales in accordance with the Welsh Language Act 1993. See *paragraphs 3.12* and *13.1*.

(B) Interviewing suspects — foreign languages

13.2 Unless *paragraphs 11.1* or *11.18(c)* apply, a suspect who for the purposes of this Code requires an interpreter because they do not appear to speak or understand English (see *paragraphs 3.5(c)(ii)* and *3.12*) must not be interviewed unless arrangements are made for a person capable of interpreting to assist the suspect to understand and communicate.

13.2A If a person who is a juvenile or a vulnerable person is interviewed and the person acting as the appropriate adult does not appear to speak or understand English, arrangements must be made for an interpreter to assist communication between the person, the appropriate adult and the interviewer, unless the interview is urgent and *paragraphs 11.1* or *11.18(c)* apply.

13.3 When a written record of the interview is made (see *paragraph 11.7*), the interviewer shall make sure the interpreter makes a note of the interview at the time in the person's language for use in the event of the interpreter being called to give evidence, and certifies its accuracy. The interviewer should allow sufficient time for the interpreter to note each question and answer after each is put, given and interpreted. The person should be allowed to read the record or have it read to them and sign it as correct or indicate the respects in which they consider it inaccurate. If an audio or visual record of the interview is made, the arrangements in Code E or F shall apply. See *paragraphs 13.12* to *13.14* and *Annex N* for application to live-link interpretation.

13.4 In the case of a person making a statement under caution (see *Annex D*) to a police officer or other police staff in a language other than English:

(a) the interpreter shall record the statement in the language it is made;
(b) the person shall be invited to sign it;
(c) an official English translation shall be made in due course. See *paragraphs 13.12* to *13.14* and *Annex N* for application to live-link interpretation.

(C) Interviewing suspects who have a hearing or speech impediment

13.5 Unless *paragraphs 11.1* or *11.18(c)* (urgent interviews) apply, a suspect who for the purposes of this Code requires an interpreter or other appropriate assistance to enable effective communication with them because they appear to have a hearing or speech impediment (see *paragraphs 3.5(c)(ii)* and *3.12*) must not be interviewed without arrangements having been made to provide an independent person capable of interpreting or of providing other appropriate assistance.

13.6 An interpreter should also be arranged if a person who is a juvenile or a vulnerable person is interviewed and the person who is present as the appropriate adult, appears to have a hearing or speech impediment, unless the interview is urgent and *paragraphs 11.1* or *11.18(c)* apply.

13.7 If a written record of the interview is made, the interviewer shall make sure the interpreter is allowed to read the record and certify its accuracy in the event of the interpreter being called to give evidence. If an audio or visual recording is made, the arrangements in Code E or F apply.
See *paragraphs 13.12* to *13.14* and *Annex N* for application to live-link interpretation.

(D) Additional rules for detained persons

13.8 *Not used.*

13.9 If *paragraph 6.1* applies and the detainee cannot communicate with the solicitor because of language, hearing or speech difficulties, arrangements must be made for an interpreter to enable communication. A police officer or any other police staff may not be used for this purpose.

13.10 After the custody officer has determined that a detainee requires an interpreter (see *paragraph 3.5(c)(ii)*) and following the initial action in *paragraphs 3.1* to *3.5*, arrangements must also be made for an interpreter to:

- explain the grounds and reasons for any authorisation for their *continued* detention, before or after charge and any information about the authorisation given to them by the authorising officer and which is recorded in the custody record. See *paragraphs 15.3, 15.4* and *15.16(a)* and *(b)*;
- to provide interpretation at the magistrates' court for the hearing of an application for a warrant of further detention or any extension or further extension of such warrant to explain any grounds and reasons for the application and any information about the authorisation of their further detention given to them by the court (see PACE, sections 43 and 44 and *paragraphs 15.2* and *15.16(c)*); and
- explain any offence with which the detainee is charged or for which they are informed they may be prosecuted and any other information about the offence given to them by or on behalf of the custody officer, see *paragraphs 16.1* and *16.3*.

13.10A If a detainee complains that they are not satisfied with the quality of interpretation, the custody officer or (as the case may be) the interviewer, is responsible for deciding whether to make arrangements for a different interpreter in accordance with the procedures set out in the arrangements made by the chief officer, see *paragraph 13.1A*.

(E) Translations of essential documents

13.10B Written translations, oral translations and oral summaries of essential documents in a language the detainee understands shall be provided in accordance with *Annex M* (Translations of documents and records).

13.10C If a detainee complains that they are not satisfied with the quality of the translation, the custody officer or (as the case may be) the interviewer, is responsible for deciding whether a further translation should be provided in accordance with the procedures set out in the arrangements made by the chief officer, see *paragraph 13.1A*.

(F) Decisions not to provide interpretation and translation.

13.10D If a suspect challenges a decision:

- made by the custody officer or (as the case may be) by the interviewer, in accordance with this Code (see *paragraphs 3.5(c)(ii)* and *3.21(b)*) that they do not require an interpreter, or
- made in accordance with *paragraphs 13.10A, 13.10B* or *13.10C* not to make arrangements to provide a different interpreter or another translation or not to translate a requested document,

the matter shall be reported to an inspector to deal with as a complaint for the purposes of *paragraph 9.2* or *paragraph 12.9* if the challenge is made during an interview.

(G) Documentation

13.11 The following must be recorded in the custody record or, as applicable, the interview record:

(a) Action taken to arrange for an interpreter, including the live-link requirements in *Annex N* as applicable;

(b) Action taken when a detainee is not satisfied about the standard of interpretation or translation provided, see *paragraphs 13.10A* and *13.10C*;

(c) When an urgent interview is carried out in accordance with *paragraph 13.2* or *13.5* in the absence of an interpreter;

(d) When a detainee has been assisted by an interpreter for the purpose of providing or being given information or being interviewed;

(e) Action taken in accordance with *Annex M* when:

- a written translation of an essential document is provided;
- an oral translation or oral summary of an essential document is provided instead of a written translation and the authorising officer's reason(s) why this would not prejudice the fairness of the proceedings (see *Annex M, paragraph 3*);
- a suspect waives their right to a translation of an essential document (see *Annex M, paragraph 4*);

- when representations that a document which is not included in the table is essential and that a translation should be provided are refused and the reason for the refusal (see *Annex M, paragraph 8*).

(H) Live-link interpretation

13.12 In this section and in *Annex N*, 'live-link interpretation' means an arrangement to enable communication between the suspect and an interpreter who is not *physically* present with the suspect. The arrangement must ensure that anything said by any person in the suspect's presence and hearing can be interpreted in the same way as if the interpreter was physically present at that time. The communication must be by audio *and* visual means for the purpose of an interview, and for all other purposes it may be *either*; by audio and visual means, or by audio means *only*, as follows:

(a) **Audio and visual communication**

This applies for the purposes of an interview conducted and recorded in accordance with Code E (Audio recording) or Code F (Visual recording) and during that interview, live link interpretation must *enable*:

(i) the suspect, the interviewer, solicitor, appropriate adult and any other person *physically* present with the suspect at any time during the interview and an interpreter who is not *physically* present, to *see* and *hear* each other; and

(ii) the interview to be conducted and recorded in accordance with the provisions of Codes C, E and F, subject to the modifications in Part 2 of *Annex N*.

(b) **Audio and visual or audio without visual communication.**

This applies to communication for the purposes of any provision of this or any other Code except as described in (a), which requires or permits information to be given to, sought from, or provided by a suspect, whether orally or in writing, which would include communication between the suspect and their solicitor and/or appropriate adult, and for these cases, live link interpretation must:

(i) *enable* the suspect, the person giving or seeking that information, any other person *physically* present with the suspect at that time and an interpreter who is not so present, to either *see* and *hear* each other, or to *hear without seeing* each other (for example by using a telephone); and

(ii) enable that information to be given to, sought from, or provided by, the suspect in accordance with the provisions of this or any other Code that apply to that information, as modified for the purposes of the live-link, by Part 2 of *Annex N*.

13.12A The requirement in *sub-paragraphs 13.12(a)(ii)* and *(b)(ii)*, that live-link interpretation must enable compliance with the relevant provisions of the Codes C, E and F, means that the arrangements must provide for any written or electronic record of what the suspect says in their own language which is made by the interpreter, to be securely transmitted without delay so that the suspect can be invited to read, check and if appropriate, sign or otherwise confirm that the record is correct or make corrections to the record.

13.13 Chief officers must be satisfied that live-link interpretation used in their force area for the purposes of *paragraphs 3.12(a)* and *(b)*, provides for accurate and secure communication with the suspect. This includes ensuring that at any time during which live link interpretation is being used: a person cannot see, hear or otherwise obtain access to any communications between the suspect and interpreter or communicate with the suspect or interpreter unless so authorised or allowed by the custody officer or, in the case of an interview, the interviewer and that as applicable, the confidentiality of any private consultation between a suspect and their solicitor and appropriate adult (see *paragraphs 13.2A, 13.6* and *13.9*) is maintained. See *Annex N paragraph 4*.

Notes for Guidance

13A Chief officers have discretion when determining the individuals or organisations they use to provide interpretation and translation services for their forces provided that these are compatible with the requirements of the Directive. One example which chief officers may wish to consider is the Ministry of Justice commercial agreements for interpretation and translation services.

13B A procedure for determining whether a person needs an interpreter might involve a telephone interpreter service or using cue cards or similar visual aids which enable the detainee to indicate their ability to speak and understand English and their preferred language. This could be confirmed through an interpreter who could also assess the extent to which the person can speak and understand English.

13C There should also be a procedure for determining whether a suspect who requires an interpreter requires assistance in accordance with paragraph 3.20 to help them check and if applicable, sign any documentation.

14 Questioning — special restrictions

14.1 If a person is arrested by one police force on behalf of another and the lawful period of detention in respect of that offence has not yet commenced in accordance with PACE, section 41, no questions may be put to them about the offence while they are in transit between the forces except to clarify any voluntary statement they make.

14.2 If a person is in police detention at a hospital, they may not be questioned without the agreement of a responsible doctor. See *Note 14A*.

Notes for Guidance

14A If questioning takes place at a hospital under paragraph 14.2, or on the way to or from a hospital, the period of questioning concerned counts towards the total period of detention permitted.

15 Reviews and extensions of detention

(A) Persons detained under PACE

15.0 The requirement in *paragraph 3.4(b)* that documents and materials essential to challenging the lawfulness of the detainee's arrest and detention must be made available to the detainee or their solicitor, applies for the purposes of this section as follows:

(a) The officer reviewing the need for detention without charge (PACE, section 40), or (as the case may be) the officer considering the need to extend detention without charge from 24 to 36 hours (PACE, section 42), is responsible, in consultation with the investigating officer, for deciding which documents and materials are essential and must be made available.

(b) When *paragraph 15.7A* applies (application for a warrant of further detention or extension of such a warrant), the officer making the application is responsible for deciding which documents and materials are essential and must be made available *before* the hearing. See *Note 3ZA*.

15.1 The review officer is responsible under PACE, section 40 for periodically determining if a person's detention, before or after charge, continues to be necessary. This requirement continues throughout the detention period and, except when a telephone or a live link is used in accordance with *paragraphs 15.9* to *15.11C*, the review officer must be present at the police station holding the detainee. See *Notes 15A* and *15B*.

15.2 Under PACE, section 42, an officer of superintendent rank or above who is responsible for the station holding the detainee may give authority any time after the second review to extend the maximum period the person may be detained without charge by up to 12 hours. Except when a live link is used as in *paragraph 15.11A*, the superintendent must be present at the station holding the detainee. Further detention without charge may be authorised only by a magistrates' court in accordance with PACE, sections 43 and 44 and unless the court has given a live link direction as in *paragraph 15.11B*, the detainee must be brought before the court for the hearing. See *Notes 15C, 15D* and *15E*.

15.2A An authorisation under section 42(1) of PACE extends the maximum period of detention permitted before charge for indictable offences from 24 hours to 36 hours. Detaining a juvenile or a vulnerable person for longer than 24 hours will be dependent on the circumstances of the case and with regard to the person's:

(a) special vulnerability;
(b) the legal obligation to provide an opportunity for representations to be made prior to a decision about extending detention;
(c) the need to consult and consider the views of any appropriate adult; and
(d) any alternatives to police custody.

15.3 Before deciding whether to authorise continued detention the officer responsible under *paragraph 15.1* or *15.2* shall give an opportunity to make representations about the detention to:

(a) the detainee, unless in the case of a review as in *paragraph 15.1*, the detainee is asleep;
(b) the detainee's solicitor if available at the time; and
(c) the appropriate adult if available at the time.

See *Note 15CA*.

15.3A Other people having an interest in the detainee's welfare may also make representations at the authorising officer's discretion.

15.3B Subject to *paragraph 15.10*, the representations may be made orally in person or by telephone or in writing. The authorising officer may, however, refuse to hear oral representations from the detainee if the officer considers them unfit to make representations because of their condition or behaviour. See *Note 15C*.

15.3C The decision on whether the review takes place in person or by telephone or by live link (see *paragraph 1.13(e)(ii)*) is a matter for the review officer. In determining the form the review may take, the review officer must always take full account of the needs of the person in custody. The benefits of carrying out a review in person should always be considered, based on the individual circumstances of each case with specific additional consideration if the person is:

(a) a juvenile (and the age of the juvenile); or
(b) a vulnerable person; or
(c) in need of medical attention for other than routine minor ailments; or
(d) subject to presentational or community issues around their detention.

See *paragraph 1.4(c)*

15.4 Before conducting a review or determining whether to extend the maximum period of detention without charge, the officer responsible must make sure the detainee is reminded of their entitlement to free legal advice, see *paragraph 6.5,* unless in the case of a review the person is asleep. When determining whether to extend the maximum period of detention without charge, it should also be pointed out that for the purposes of *paragraph 15.2,* the superintendent or (as the case may be) the court, responsible for authorising any such extension, will not be able to use a live link unless the detainee has *received* legal advice on the use of the live link (see *paragraphs 15.11A(ii)* and *15.11C(ii)*) and given consent to its use (see *paragraphs 15.11A(iii)* and *15.11C(iii)*). The detainee must also be given information about how the live link is used.

15.4A Following sections 45ZA and 45ZB of PACE, when the reminder and information concerning legal advice and about the use of the live link is given and the detainee's consent is sought, the presence of an appropriate adult is required if the detainee in question is a juvenile (see *paragraph 1.5*) or is a *vulnerable adult* by virtue of being a person aged 18 or over who, because of a mental disorder established in accordance *paragraphs 1.4* and *1.13(d)* or for *any other reason* (see *paragraph 15.4B*), may have difficulty understanding the purpose of:

(a) an authorisation under section 42 of PACE or anything that occurs in connection with a decision whether to give it (see *paragraphs 15.2* and *15.2A*); or
(b) a court hearing under section 43 or 44 of PACE or what occurs at the hearing it (see *paragraphs 15.2* and *15.7A*).

15.4B For the purpose of using a live link in accordance with sections 45ZA and 45ZB of PACE to authorise detention without charge (see *paragraphs 15.11A* and *15.11C*), the reference to '*any other reason*' would extend to difficulties in understanding the purposes mentioned in *paragraph 15.4A* that might arise if the person happened to be under the influence of drink or drugs at the time the live link is to be used. This does not however apply for the purposes of *paragraphs 1.4* and *1.13(d)* (see *Note 1GC*).

15.5 If, after considering any representations, the review officer under *paragraph 15.1* decides to keep the detainee in detention or the superintendent under *paragraph 15.2* extends the maximum period for which they may be detained without charge, then any comment made by the detainee shall be recorded. If applicable, the officer shall be informed of the comment as soon as practicable. See also *paragraphs 11.4* and *11.13*.

15.6 No officer shall put specific questions to the detainee:

- regarding their involvement in any offence; or
- in respect of any comments they may make:
  - when given the opportunity to make representations; or
  - in response to a decision to keep them in detention or extend the maximum period of detention.

Such an exchange could constitute an interview as in *paragraph 11.1A* and would be subject to the associated safeguards in *section 11* and, in respect of a person who has been charged, *paragraph 16.5*. See also *paragraph 11.13*.

15.7 A detainee who is asleep at a review, see *paragraph 15.1*, and whose continued detention is authorised must be informed about the decision and reason as soon as practicable after waking.

15.7A When an application is made to a magistrates' court under PACE, section 43 for a warrant of further detention to extend detention without charge of a person arrested for an *indictable offence*, or under section 44, to extend or further extend that warrant, the detainee:

(a) must, unless the court has given a live link direction as in *paragraph 15.11C,* be brought to court for the hearing of the application (see *Note 15D*);
(b) is entitled to be legally represented if they wish, in which case, *Annex B* cannot apply; and
(c) must be given a copy of the information which supports the application and states:
   (i) the nature of the offence for which the person to whom the application relates has been arrested;
   (ii) the general nature of the evidence on which the person was arrested;
   (iii) what inquiries about the offence have been made and what further inquiries are proposed;

(iv) the reasons for believing continued detention is necessary for the purposes of the further inquiries;

Note: A warrant of further detention can only be issued or extended if the court has reasonable grounds for believing that the person's further detention is necessary for the purpose of obtaining evidence of an indictable offence for which the person has been arrested and that the investigation is being conducted diligently and expeditiously.

See *paragraph 15.0(b)*.

15.8 *Not used.*

(B) Review of detention by telephone or by using a live link (section 40A and 45A)

15.9 PACE, section 40A provides that the officer responsible under section 40 for reviewing the detention of a person who has not been charged, need not attend the police station holding the detainee and may carry out the review by telephone.

15.9A PACE, section 45A(2) provides that the officer responsible under section 40 for reviewing the detention of a person who has not been charged, need not attend the police station holding the detainee and may carry out the review using a live link. See *paragraph 1.13(e)(ii)*.

15.9B A telephone review is not permitted where facilities for review using a live link exist and it is practicable to use them.

15.9C The review officer can decide at any stage that a telephone review or review by live link should be terminated and that the review will be conducted in person. The reasons for doing so should be noted in the custody record. See *Note 15F.*

15.10 When a review is carried out by telephone or by using a live link, an officer at the station holding the detainee shall be required by the review officer to fulfil that officer's obligations under PACE, section 40 and this Code by:

(a) making any record connected with the review in the detainee's custody record;
(b) if applicable, making the record in (*a*) in the presence of the detainee; and
(c) for a review by telephone, giving the detainee information about the review.

15.11 When a review is carried out by telephone or by using a live link, or the requirement in *paragraph 15.3* will be satisfied:

(a) if facilities exist for the immediate transmission of written representations to the review officer, e.g. fax or email message, by allowing those who are given the opportunity to make representations, to make their representations:
   (i) orally by telephone or (as the case may be) by means of the live link; or
   (ii) in writing using the facilities for the immediate transmission of written representations; and
(b) in all other cases, by allowing those who are given the opportunity to make representations, to make their representations orally by telephone or by means of the live link.

(C) Authorisation to extend detention using live link (sections 45ZA and 45ZB)

15.11A For the purpose of *paragraphs 15.2* and *15.2A*, a superintendent who is not present at the police station where the detainee is being held but who has access to the use of a live link (see *paragraph 1.13(e)(iii)*) may, using that live link, give authority to extend the maximum period of detention permitted before charge, if, and only if, the following conditions are satisfied:

(i) the custody officer considers that the use of the live link is appropriate (see *Note 15H*);
(ii) the detainee in question has requested and received legal advice on the use of the live link (see *paragraph 15.4*).
(iii) the detainee has given their consent to the live link being used (see *paragraph 15.11D*)

15.11B When a live link is used:

(a) the authorising superintendent shall, with regard to any record connected with the authorisation which PACE, section 42 and this Code require to be made by the authorising officer, require an officer at the station holding the detainee to make that record in the detainee's custody record;
(b) the requirement in *paragraph 15.3* (allowing opportunity to make representations) will be satisfied:
   (i) if facilities exist for the immediate transmission of written representations to the authorising officer, e.g. fax or email message, by allowing those who are given the opportunity to make representations, to make their representations:
      - in writing by means of those facilities or
      - orally by means of the live link; or
   (ii) in all other cases, by allowing those who are given the opportunity to make representations, to make their representations orally by means of the live link.

(c) The authorising officer can decide at any stage to terminate the live link and attend the police station where the detainee is held to carry out the procedure in person. The reasons for doing so should be noted in the custody record.

15.11C For the purpose of *paragraph 15.7A* and the hearing of an application to a magistrates' court under PACE, section 43 for a warrant of further detention to extend detention without charge of a person arrested for an *indictable offence*, or under PACE, section 44, to extend or further extend that warrant, the magistrates' court may give a direction that a live link (see *paragraph 1.13(e)(iv)*) be used for the purposes of the hearing if, and only if, the following conditions are satisfied:

(i) the custody officer considers that the use of the live link for the purpose of the hearing is appropriate (see *Note 15H*);

(ii) the detainee in question has requested and received legal advice on the use of the live link (see *paragraph 15.4*);

(iii) the detainee has given their consent to the live link being used (see *paragraph 15.11D*); and

(iv) it is not contrary to the interests of justice to give the direction.

15.11D References in *paragraphs 15.11A(iii)* and *15.11C(iii)* to the consent of the detainee mean:

(a) if detainee is aged 18 or over, the consent of that detainee;

(b) if the detainee is aged 14 and under 18, the consent of the detainee and their parent or guardian; and

(c) if the detainee is aged under 14, the consent of their parent or guardian.

15.11E The consent described in *paragraph 15.11D* will only be valid if:

(i) in the case of a detainee aged 18 or over *who is a vulnerable adult* as described in *paragraph 15.4A*), information about how the live link is used and the reminder about their right to legal advice mentioned in *paragraph 15.4* and their consent, are given in the *presence of the appropriate adult*; and

(ii) in the case of a *juvenile:*

- if information about how the live link is used and the reminder about their right to legal advice mentioned in *paragraph 15.4* are given in the *presence of the appropriate adult* (who may or may not be their parent or guardian); and
- if the juvenile is aged 14 or over, their consent is given in the *presence of the appropriate adult* (who may or may not be their parent or guardian).

Note: If the juvenile is aged under 14, the consent of their parent or guardian is sufficient in its own right (see *Note 15I*)

(D) Documentation

15.12 It is the officer's responsibility to make sure all reminders given under *paragraph 15.4* are noted in the custody record.

15.13 The grounds for, and extent of, any delay in conducting a review shall be recorded.

15.14 When a review is carried out by telephone or video conferencing facilities, a record shall be made of:

(a) the reason the review officer did not attend the station holding the detainee;

(b) the place the review officer was;

(c) the method representations, oral or written, were made to the review officer, see *paragraph 15.11*.

15.15 Any written representations shall be retained.

15.16 A record shall be made as soon as practicable of:

(a) the outcome of each review of detention before or after charge, and if *paragraph 15.7* applies, of when the person was informed and by whom;

(b) the outcome of any determination under PACE, section 42 by a superintendent whether to extend the maximum period of detention without charge beyond 24 hours from the relevant time. If an authorisation is given, the record shall state the number of hours and minutes by which the detention period is extended or further extended.

(c) the outcome of each application under PACE, section 43, for a warrant of further detention or under section 44, for an extension or further extension of that warrant. If a warrant for further detention is granted under section 43 or extended or further extended under 44, the record shall state the detention period authorised by the warrant and the date and time it was granted or (as the case may be) the period by which the warrant is extended or further extended.

Note: Any period during which a person is released on bail does not count towards the maximum period of detention without charge allowed under PACE, sections 41 to 44.

Notes for Guidance

15A Review officer for the purposes of:

- *PACE, sections 40, 40A and 45A means, in the case of a person arrested but not charged, an officer of at least inspector rank not directly involved in the investigation and, if a person has been arrested and charged, the custody officer.*

15B *The detention of persons in police custody not subject to the statutory review requirement in paragraph 15.1 should still be reviewed periodically as a matter of good practice. Such reviews can be carried out by an officer of the rank of sergeant or above. The purpose of such reviews is to check the particular power under which a detainee is held continues to apply, any associated conditions are complied with and to make sure appropriate action is taken to deal with any changes. This includes the detainee's prompt release when the power no longer applies, or their transfer if the power requires the detainee be taken elsewhere as soon as the necessary arrangements are made. Examples include persons:*

- *(a) arrested on warrant because they failed to answer bail to appear at court;*
- *(b) arrested under the Bail Act 1976, section 7(3) for breaching a condition of bail granted after charge;*
- *(c) in police custody for specific purposes and periods under the Crime (Sentences) Act 1997, Schedule 1;*
- *(d) convicted, or remand prisoners, held in police stations on behalf of the Prison Service under the Imprisonment (Temporary Provisions) Act 1980, section 6;*
- *(e) being detained to prevent them causing a breach of the peace;*
- *(f) detained at police stations on behalf of Immigration Enforcement (formerly the UK Immigration Service);*
- *(g) detained by order of a magistrates' court under the Criminal Justice Act 1988, section 152 (as amended by the Drugs Act 2005, section 8) to facilitate the recovery of evidence after being charged with drug possession or drug trafficking and suspected of having swallowed drugs.*

The detention of persons remanded into police detention by order of a court under the Magistrates' Courts Act 1980, section 128 is subject to a statutory requirement to review that detention. This is to make sure the detainee is taken back to court no later than the end of the period authorised by the court or when the need for their detention by police ceases, whichever is the sooner.

15C *In the case of a review of detention, but not an extension, the detainee need not be woken for the review. However, if the detainee is likely to be asleep, e.g. during a period of rest allowed as in paragraph 12.2, at the latest time a review or authorisation to extend detention may take place, the officer should, if the legal obligations and time constraints permit, bring forward the procedure to allow the detainee to make representations. A detainee not asleep during the review must be present when the grounds for their continued detention are recorded and must at the same time be informed of those grounds unless the review officer considers the person is incapable of understanding what is said, violent or likely to become violent or in urgent need of medical attention.*

15CA *In paragraph 15.3(b) and (c), 'available' includes being contactable in time to enable them to make representations remotely by telephone or other electronic means or in person by attending the station. Reasonable efforts should therefore be made to give the solicitor and appropriate adult sufficient notice of the time the decision is expected to be made so that they can make themselves available.*

15D *An application to a Magistrates' Court under PACE, sections 43 or 44 for a warrant of further detention or its extension should be made between 10am and 9pm, and if possible during normal court hours. It will not usually be practicable to arrange for a court to sit specially outside the hours of 10am to 9pm. If it appears a special sitting may be needed outside normal court hours but between 10am and 9pm, the clerk to the justices should be given notice and informed of this possibility, while the court is sitting if possible.*

15E *In paragraph 15.2, the officer responsible for the station holding the detainee includes a superintendent or above who, in accordance with their force operational policy or police regulations, is given that responsibility on a temporary basis whilst the appointed long-term holder is off duty or otherwise unavailable.*

15F *The provisions of PACE, section 40A allowing telephone reviews do not apply to reviews of detention after charge by the custody officer. When use of a live link is not required, they allow the use of a telephone to carry out a review of detention before charge.*

15G *Not used.*

15H *In considering whether the use of the live link is appropriate in the case of a juvenile or vulnerable person, the custody officer and the superintendent should have regard to the detainee's ability to understand the purpose of the authorisation or (as the case may be) the court hearing, and be satisfied that the suspect is able to take part effectively in the process (see paragraphs 1.4(c)). The appropriate adult should always be involved.*

15I *For the purpose of paragraphs 15.11D and 15.11E, the consent required from a parent or guardian may, for a juvenile in the care of a local authority or voluntary organisation, be given by that authority or organisation. In the case of a juvenile, nothing in paragraphs 15.11D and 15.11E require the parent, guardian or representative of a local authority or voluntary organisation to be present with the juvenile to give their consent, unless they are acting as the appropriate adult. However, it is important that the parent, guardian or representative of a local authority or voluntary organisation who is not present is fully informed before being asked to consent. They must be given the same information as that given to the juvenile and the appropriate adult in accordance with paragraph 15.11E. They must also be allowed to speak to the juvenile and the appropriate adult if they wish. Provided the consent is fully informed and is not withdrawn, it may be obtained at any time before the live link is used.*

16 Charging detained persons

(A) Action

16.1 When the officer in charge of the investigation reasonably believes there is sufficient evidence to provide a realistic prospect of conviction for the offence (see *paragraph 11.6)*, they shall without delay, and subject to the following qualification, inform the custody officer who will be responsible for considering whether the detainee should be charged. See *Notes 11B* and *16A.* When a person is detained in respect of more than one offence it is permissible to delay informing the custody officer until the above conditions are satisfied in respect of all the offences, but see *paragraph 11.6.* If the detainee is a juvenile or a vulnerable person, any resulting action shall be taken in the presence of the appropriate adult if they are present at the time.

See *Notes 16B* and *16C.*

16.1A Where guidance issued by the Director of Public Prosecutions under PACE, section 37A is in force the custody officer must comply with that Guidance in deciding how to act in dealing with the detainee. See *Notes 16AA* and *16AB.*

16.1B Where in compliance with the DPP's Guidance the custody officer decides that the case should be immediately referred to the CPS to make the charging decision, consultation should take place with a Crown Prosecutor as soon as is reasonably practicable. Where the Crown Prosecutor is unable to make the charging decision on the information available at that time, the detainee may be released without charge and on bail (with conditions if necessary) under section 37(7)(a). In such circumstances, the detainee should be informed that they are being released to enable the Director of Public Prosecutions to make a decision under section 37B.

16.2 When a detainee is charged with or informed they may be prosecuted for an offence, see *Note 16B,* they shall, unless the restriction on drawing adverse inferences from silence applies, see *Annex C,* be cautioned as follows:

'You do not have to say anything. But it may harm your defence if you do not mention now something which you later rely on in court. Anything you do say may be given in evidence.'

Where the use of the Welsh Language is appropriate, a constable may provide the caution directly in Welsh in the following terms:

'Does dim rhaid i chi ddweud dim byd. Ond gall niweidio eich amddiffyniad os na fyddwch chi'n sôn, yn awr, am rywbeth y byddwch chi'n dibynnu arno nes ymlaen yn y llys. Gall unrhyw beth yr ydych yn ei ddweud gael ei roi fel tystiolaeth.'

Annex C, paragraph 2 sets out the alternative terms of the caution to be used when the restriction on drawing adverse inferences from silence applies.

16.3 When a detainee is charged they shall be given a written notice showing particulars of the offence and, subject to *paragraph 2.6A*, the officer's name and the case reference number. As far as possible the particulars of the charge shall be stated in simple terms, but they shall also show the precise offence in law with which the detainee is charged. The notice shall begin:

'*You are charged with the offence(s) shown below.*' Followed by the caution.

If the detainee is a juvenile, mentally disordered or otherwise mentally vulnerable, a copy of the notice should also be given to the appropriate adult.

16.4 If, after a detainee has been charged with or informed they may be prosecuted for an offence, an officer wants to tell them about any written statement or interview with another person relating to such an offence, the detainee shall either be handed a true copy of the written statement or the content of the interview record brought to their attention. Nothing shall be done to invite any reply or comment except to:

(a) caution the detainee, '*You do not have to say anything, but anything you do say may be given in evidence.*';

Where the use of the Welsh Language is appropriate, caution the detainee in the following terms:

'*Does dim rhaid i chi ddweud dim byd, ond gall unrhyw beth yr ydych yn ei ddweud gael ei roi fel tystiolaeth.*'

and

(b) remind the detainee about their right to legal advice.

16.4A If the detainee:

- cannot read, the document may be read to them;

- is a juvenile, mentally disordered or otherwise mentally vulnerable, the appropriate adult shall also be given a copy, or the interview record shall be brought to their attention.

16.5 A detainee may not be interviewed about an offence after they have been charged with, or informed they may be prosecuted for it, unless the interview is necessary:

- to prevent or minimise harm or loss to some other person, or the public
- to clear up an ambiguity in a previous answer or statement
- in the interests of justice for the detainee to have put to them, and have an opportunity to comment on, information concerning the offence which has come to light since they were charged or informed they might be prosecuted

Before any such interview, the interviewer shall:

(a) caution the detainee, '*You do not have to say anything, but anything you do say may be given in evidence.*'

Where the use of the Welsh Language is appropriate, the interviewer shall caution the detainee: '*Does dim rhaid i chi ddweud dim byd, ond gall unrhyw beth yr ydych yn ei ddweud gael ei roi fel tystiolaeth.*'

(b) remind the detainee about their right to legal advice.

See *Note 16B*

16.6 The provisions of *paragraphs 16.2* to *16.5* must be complied with in the appropriate adult's presence if they are already at the police station. If they are not at the police station then these provisions must be complied with again in their presence when they arrive unless the detainee has been released. See *Note 16C.*

16.7 When a juvenile is charged with an offence and the custody officer authorises their continued detention after charge, the custody officer must make arrangements for the juvenile to be taken into the care of a local authority to be detained pending appearance in court *unless* the custody officer certifies in accordance with PACE, section 38(6), that:

(a) for any juvenile; it is impracticable to do so and the reasons why it is impracticable must be set out in the certificate that must be produced to the court; or,

(b) in the case of a juvenile of at least 12 years old, no secure accommodation is available and other accommodation would not be adequate to protect the public from serious harm from that juvenile. See *Note 16D.*

Note: Chief officers should ensure that the operation of these provisions at police stations in their areas is subject to supervision and monitoring by an officer of the rank of inspector or above. See *Note 16E.*

16.7A The requirement in *paragraph 3.4(b)* that documents and materials essential to effectively challenging the lawfulness of the detainee's arrest and detention must be made available to the detainee and, if they are represented, their solicitor, applies for the purposes of this section and a person's detention after charge. This means that the custody officer making the bail decision (PACE, section 38) or reviewing the need for detention after charge (PACE, section 40), is responsible for determining what, if any, documents or materials are essential and must be made available to the detainee or their solicitor. See *Note 3ZA.*

(B) Documentation

16.8 A record shall be made of anything a detainee says when charged.

16.9 Any questions put in an interview after charge and answers given relating to the offence shall be recorded in full during the interview on forms for that purpose and the record signed by the detainee or, if they refuse, by the interviewer and any third parties present. If the questions are audibly recorded or visually recorded the arrangements in Code E or F apply.

16.10 If arrangements for a juvenile's transfer into local authority care as in *paragraph 16.7* are not made, the custody officer must record the reasons in a certificate which must be produced before the court with the juvenile. See *Note 16D.*

Notes for Guidance

16A The custody officer must take into account alternatives to prosecution under the Crime and Disorder Act 1998 applicable to persons under 18, and in national guidance on the cautioning of offenders applicable to persons aged 18 and over.

16AA When a person is arrested under the provisions of the Criminal Justice Act 2003 which allow a person to be re-tried after being acquitted of a serious offence which is a qualifying offence specified in Schedule 5 to that Act and not precluded from further prosecution by virtue of section 75(3) of that Act the detention provisions of PACE are modified and make an officer of the rank of superintendent or above who has not been directly involved in the investigation responsible for determining whether the evidence is sufficient to charge.

16AB Where Guidance issued by the Director of Public Prosecutions under section 37B is in force, a custody officer who determines in accordance with that Guidance that there is sufficient evidence to charge the detainee, may detain that person for no longer than is reasonably necessary to decide how that person is to be dealt with under PACE, section 37(7)(a) to (d), including, where appropriate, consultation with the Duty Prosecutor. The period is subject to the maximum period of detention before charge determined by PACE, sections 41 to 44. Where in accordance with the Guidance the case is referred to the CPS for decision, the custody officer should ensure that an officer involved in the investigation sends to the CPS such information as is specified in the Guidance.

16B The giving of a warning or the service of the Notice of Intended Prosecution required by the Road Traffic Offenders Act 1988, section 1 does not amount to informing a detainee they may be prosecuted for an offence and so does not preclude further questioning in relation to that offence.

16C There is no power under PACE to detain a person and delay action under paragraphs 16.2 to 16.5 solely to await the arrival of the appropriate adult. Reasonable efforts should therefore be made to give the appropriate adult sufficient notice of the time the decision (charge etc.) is to be implemented so that they can be present. If the appropriate adult is not, or cannot be, present at that time, the detainee should be released on bail to return for the decision to be implemented when the adult is present, unless the custody officer determines that the absence of the appropriate adult makes the detainee unsuitable for bail for this purpose. After charge, bail cannot be refused, or release on bail delayed, simply because an appropriate adult is not available, unless the absence of that adult provides the custody officer with the necessary grounds to authorise detention after charge under PACE, section 38.

16D Except as in paragraph 16.7, neither a juvenile's behaviour nor the nature of the offence provides grounds for the custody officer to decide it is impracticable to arrange the juvenile's transfer to local authority care. Impracticability concerns the transport and travel requirements and the lack of secure accommodation which is provided for the purposes of restricting liberty does not make it impracticable to transfer the juvenile. Rather, 'impracticable' should be taken to mean that exceptional circumstances render movement of the child impossible or that the juvenile is due at court in such a short space of time that transfer would deprive them of rest or cause them to miss a court appearance. When the reason for not transferring the juvenile is an imminent court appearance, details of the travelling and court appearance times which justify the decision should be included in the certificate. The availability of secure accommodation is only a factor in relation to a juvenile aged 12 or over when other local authority accommodation would not be adequate to protect the public from serious harm from them. The obligation to transfer a juvenile to local authority accommodation applies as much to a juvenile charged during the daytime as to a juvenile to be held overnight, subject to a requirement to bring the juvenile before a court under PACE, section 46.

16E The Concordat on Children in Custody published by the Home Office in 2017 provides detailed guidance with the aim of preventing the detention of children in police stations following charge. It is available here: https://www.gov.uk/government/publications/concordat-on-children-in-custody.

17 Testing persons for the presence of specified Class A drugs

(A) Action

17.1 This section of Code C applies only in selected police stations in police areas where the provisions for drug testing under section 63B of PACE (as amended by section 5 of the Criminal Justice Act 2003 and section 7 of the Drugs Act 2005) are in force and in respect of which the Secretary of State has given a notification to the relevant chief officer of police that arrangements for the taking of samples have been made. Such a notification will cover either a police area as a whole or particular stations within a police area. The notification indicates whether the testing applies to those arrested or charged or under the age of 18 as the case may be and testing can only take place in respect of the persons so indicated in the notification. Testing cannot be carried out unless the relevant notification has been given and has not been withdrawn. See *Note 17F*.

17.2 A sample of urine or a non-intimate sample may be taken from a person in police detention for the purpose of ascertaining whether they have any specified Class A drug in their body only where they have been brought before the custody officer and:

(a) either the arrest condition, see *paragraph 17.3*, or the charge condition, see *paragraph 17.4* is met;

(b) the age condition see *paragraph 17.5*, is met;

(c) the notification condition is met in relation to the arrest condition, the charge condition, or the age condition, as the case may be. (Testing on charge and/or arrest must be specifically provided for in the notification for the power to apply. In addition, the fact that testing of under 18s is authorised must be expressly provided for in the notification before the power to test such persons applies.). See *paragraph 17.1*; and

(d) a police officer has requested the person concerned to give the sample (the request condition).

17.3 The arrest condition is met where the detainee:
- (a) has been arrested for a trigger offence, see *Note 17E*, but not charged with that offence; or
- (b) has been arrested for any other offence but not charged with that offence and a police officer of inspector rank or above, who has reasonable grounds for suspecting that their misuse of any specified Class A drug caused or contributed to the offence, has authorised the sample to be taken.

17.4 The charge condition is met where the detainee:
- (a) has been charged with a trigger offence, or
- (b) has been charged with any other offence and a police officer of inspector rank or above, who has reasonable grounds for suspecting that the detainee's misuse of any specified Class A drug caused or contributed to the offence, has authorised the sample to be taken.

17.5 The age condition is met where:
- (a) in the case of a detainee who has been arrested but not charged as in *paragraph 17.3*, they are aged 18 or over;
- (b) in the case of a detainee who has been charged as in *paragraph 17.4*, they are aged 14 or over.

17.6 Before requesting a sample from the person concerned, an officer must:
- (a) inform them that the purpose of taking the sample is for drug testing under PACE. This is to ascertain whether they have a specified Class A drug present in their body;
- (b) warn them that if, when so requested, they fail without good cause to provide a sample they may be liable to prosecution;
- (c) where the taking of the sample has been authorised by an inspector or above in accordance with *paragraph 17.3(b)* or *17.4(b)* above, inform them that the authorisation has been given and the grounds for giving it;
- (d) remind them of the following rights, which may be exercised at any stage during the period in custody:
  - (i) the right to have someone informed of their arrest [see *section 5*];
  - (ii) the right to consult privately with a solicitor and that free independent legal advice is available [see *section 6*]; and
  - (iii) the right to consult these Codes of Practice [see *section 3*].

17.7 In the case of a person who has not attained the age specified in section 63B(5A) of PACE—
- (a) the making of the request for a sample under *paragraph 17.2(d)* above;
- (b) the giving of the warning and the information under *paragraph 17.6* above; and
- (c) the taking of the sample,

may not take place except in the presence of an appropriate adult. See *Note 17G*.

17.8 Authorisation by an officer of the rank of inspector or above within *paragraph 17.3(b)* or *17.4(b)* may be given orally or in writing but, if it is given orally, it must be confirmed in writing as soon as practicable.

17.9 If a sample is taken from a detainee who has been arrested for an offence but not charged with that offence as in *paragraph 17.3*, no further sample may be taken during the same continuous period of detention. If during that same period the charge condition is also met in respect of that detainee, the sample which has been taken shall be treated as being taken by virtue of the charge condition, see *paragraph 17.4*, being met.

17.10 A detainee from whom a sample may be taken may be detained for up to six hours from the time of charge if the custody officer reasonably believes the detention is necessary to enable a sample to be taken. Where the arrest condition is met, a detainee whom the custody officer has decided to release on bail without charge may continue to be detained, but not beyond 24 hours from the relevant time (as defined in section 41(2) of PACE), to enable a sample to be taken.

17.11 A detainee in respect of whom the arrest condition is met, but not the charge condition, see *paragraphs 17.3* and *17.4*, and whose release would be required before a sample can be taken had they not continued to be detained as a result of being arrested for a further offence which does not satisfy the arrest condition, may have a sample taken at any time within 24 hours after the arrest for the offence that satisfies the arrest condition.

(B) Documentation

17.12 The following must be recorded in the custody record:
- (a) if a sample is taken following authorisation by an officer of the rank of inspector or above, the authorisation and the grounds for suspicion;
- (b) the giving of a warning of the consequences of failure to provide a sample;
- (c) the time at which the sample was given; and

(d) the time of charge or, where the arrest condition is being relied upon, the time of arrest and, where applicable, the fact that a sample taken after arrest but before charge is to be treated as being taken by virtue of the charge condition, where that is met in the same period of continuous detention. See *paragraph 17.9*.

(C) General

17.13 A sample may only be taken by a prescribed person. See *Note 17C*.

17.14 Force may not be used to take any sample for the purpose of drug testing.

17.15 The terms 'Class A drug' and 'misuse' have the same meanings as in the Misuse of Drugs Act 1971. 'Specified' (in relation to a Class A drug) and 'trigger offence' have the same meanings as in Part III of the Criminal Justice and Court Services Act 2000.

17.16 Any sample taken:

(a) may not be used for any purpose other than to ascertain whether the person concerned has a specified Class A drug present in his body; and

(b) can be disposed of as clinical waste unless it is to be sent for further analysis in cases where the test result is disputed at the point when the result is known, including on the basis that medication has been taken, or for quality assurance purposes.

(D) Assessment of misuse of drugs

17.17 Under the provisions of Part 3 of the Drugs Act 2005, where a detainee has tested positive for a specified Class A drug under section 63B of PACE a police officer may, at any time before the person's release from the police station, impose a requirement on the detainee to attend an initial assessment of their drug misuse by a suitably qualified person and to remain for its duration. Where such a requirement is imposed, the officer must, at the same time, impose a second requirement on the detainee to attend and remain for a follow-up assessment. The officer must inform the detainee that the second requirement will cease to have effect if, at the initial assessment they are informed that a follow-up assessment is not necessary These requirements may only be imposed on a person if:

(a) they have reached the age of 18

(b) notification has been given by the Secretary of State to the relevant chief officer of police that arrangements for conducting initial and follow-up assessments have been made for those from whom samples for testing have been taken at the police station where the detainee is in custody.

17.18 When imposing a requirement to attend an initial assessment and a follow-up assessment the police officer must:

(a) inform the person of the time and place at which the initial assessment is to take place;

(b) explain that this information will be confirmed in writing; and

(c) warn the person that they may be liable to prosecution if they fail without good cause to attend the initial assessment and remain for its duration and if they fail to attend the follow-up assessment and remain for its duration (if so required).

17.19 Where a police officer has imposed a requirement to attend an initial assessment and a follow-up assessment in accordance with *paragraph 17.17*, he must, before the person is released from detention, give the person notice in writing which:

(a) confirms their requirement to attend and remain for the duration of the assessments; and

(b) confirms the information and repeats the warning referred to in *paragraph 17.18*.

17.20 The following must be recorded in the custody record:

(a) that the requirement to attend an initial assessment and a follow-up assessment has been imposed; and

(b) the information, explanation, warning and notice given in accordance with *paragraphs 17.17* and *17.19*.

17.21 Where a notice is given in accordance with *paragraph 17.19*, a police officer can give the person a further notice in writing which informs the person of any change to the time or place at which the initial assessment is to take place and which repeats the warning referred to in *paragraph 17.18(c)*.

17.22 Part 3 of the Drugs Act 2005 also requires police officers to have regard to any guidance issued by the Secretary of State in respect of the assessment provisions.

Notes for Guidance

17A When warning a person who is asked to provide a urine or non-intimate sample in accordance with paragraph 17.6(b), the following form of words may be used:

'You do not have to provide a sample, but I must warn you that if you fail or refuse without good cause to do so, you will commit an offence for which you may be imprisoned, or fined, or both'.

Where the Welsh language is appropriate, the following form of words may be used:

'Does dim rhaid i chi roi sampl, ond mae'n rhaid i mi eich rhybuddio y byddwch chi'n cyflawni trosedd os byddwch chi'n methu neu yn gwrthod gwneud hynny heb reswm da, ac y gellir, oherwydd hynny, eich carcharu, eich dirwyo, neu'r ddau.'

17B *A sample has to be sufficient and suitable. A sufficient sample is sufficient in quantity and quality to enable drug-testing analysis to take place. A suitable sample is one which by its nature, is suitable for a particular form of drug analysis.*

17C *A prescribed person in paragraph 17.13 is one who is prescribed in regulations made by the Secretary of State under section 63B(6) of the Police and Criminal Evidence Act 1984. [The regulations are currently contained in regulation SI 2001 No. 2645, the Police and Criminal Evidence Act 1984 (Drug Testing Persons in Police Detention) (Prescribed Persons) Regulations 2001.]*

17D *Samples, and the information derived from them, may not be subsequently used in the investigation of any offence or in evidence against the persons from whom they were taken.*

17E *Trigger offences are:*

1. *Offences under the following provisions of the Theft Act 1968:*

section 1	*(theft)*
section 8	*(robbery)*
section 9	*(burglary)*
section 10	*(aggravated burglary)*
section 12	*(taking a motor vehicle or other conveyance without authority)*
section 12A	*(aggravated vehicle-taking)*
section 22	*(handling stolen goods)*
section 25	*(going equipped for stealing etc.)*

2. *Offences under the following provisions of the Misuse of Drugs Act 1971, if committed in respect of a specified Class A drug:–*

section 4	*(restriction on production and supply of controlled drugs)*
section 5(2)	*(possession of a controlled drug)*
section 5(3)	*(possession of a controlled drug with intent to supply)*

3. *Offences under the following provisions of the Fraud Act 2006:*

section 1	*(fraud)*
section 6	*(possession etc. of articles for use in frauds)*
section 7	*(making or supplying articles for use in frauds)*

3A. *An offence under section 1(1) of the Criminal Attempts Act 1981 if committed in respect of an offence under:*

(a) *any of the following provisions of the Theft Act 1968:*

section 1	*(theft)*
section 8	*(robbery)*
section 9	*(burglary)*
section 22	*(handling stolen goods)*

(b) *section 1 of the Fraud Act 2006 (fraud)*

4. *Offences under the following provisions of the Vagrancy Act 1824:*

section 3	*(begging)*
section 4	*(persistent begging)*

17F *The power to take samples is subject to notification by the Secretary of State that appropriate arrangements for the taking of samples have been made for the police area as a whole or for the particular police station concerned for whichever of the following is specified in the notification:*

(a) *persons in respect of whom the arrest condition is met;*
(b) *persons in respect of whom the charge condition is met;*
(c) *persons who have not attained the age of 18.*

Note: Notification is treated as having been given for the purposes of the charge condition in relation to a police area, if testing (on charge) under section 63B(2) of PACE was in force immediately before section 7 of the Drugs Act 2005 was brought into force; and for the purposes of the age condition, in relation to a police area or police station, if immediately before that day, notification that arrangements had been made for the taking of samples from persons under the age of 18 (those aged 14-17) had been given and had not been withdrawn.

17G *Appropriate adult in paragraph 17.7 means the person's–*

(a) *parent or guardian or, if they are in the care of a local authority or voluntary organisation, a person representing that authority or organisation; or*
(b) *a social worker of a local authority; or*
(c) *if no person falling within (a) or (b) above is available, any responsible person aged 18 or over who is not:*
- *a police officer;*
- *employed by the police;*
- *under the direction or control of the chief officer of police force; or*
- *a person who provides services under contractual arrangements (but without being employed by the chief officer of a police force), to assist that force in relation to the discharge of its chief officer's functions;*

whether or not they are on duty at the time.

Annex A

Intimate and Strip Searches

A Intimate search

1. An intimate search consists of the physical examination of a person's body orifices other than the mouth. The intrusive nature of such searches means the actual and potential risks associated with intimate searches must never be underestimated.

(a) Action

2. Body orifices other than the mouth may be searched only:
   (a) if authorised by an officer of inspector rank or above who has reasonable grounds for believing that the person may have concealed on themselves:
      (i) anything which they could and might use to cause physical injury to themselves or others at the station; or
      (ii) a Class A drug which they intended to supply to another or to export;
   and the officer has reasonable grounds for believing that an intimate search is the only means of removing those items; and
   (b) if the search is under *paragraph 2(a)(ii)* (a drug offence search), the detainee's appropriate consent has been given in writing.

2A. Before the search begins, a police officer or designated detention officer, must tell the detainee:-
   (a) that the authority to carry out the search has been given;
   (b) the grounds for giving the authorisation and for believing that the article cannot be removed without an intimate search.

2B. Before a detainee is asked to give appropriate consent to a search under *paragraph 2(a)(ii)* (a drug offence search) they must be warned that if they refuse without good cause their refusal may harm their case if it comes to trial, see *Note A6*. This warning may be given by a police officer or member of police staff. In the case of a juvenile or a vulnerable person, the seeking and giving of consent must take place in the presence of the appropriate adult. A juvenile's consent is only valid if their parent's or guardian's consent is also obtained unless the juvenile is under 14, when their parent's or guardian's consent is sufficient in its own right. A detainee who is not legally represented must be reminded of their entitlement to have free legal advice, see Code C, *paragraph 6.5*, and the reminder noted in the custody record.

3. An intimate search may only be carried out by a registered medical practitioner or registered nurse, unless an officer of at least inspector rank considers this is not practicable and the search is to take place under *paragraph 2(a)(i)*, in which case a police officer may carry out the search. See *Notes A1* to *A5*.

3A. Any proposal for a search under *paragraph 2(a)(i)* to be carried out by someone other than a registered medical practitioner or registered nurse must only be considered as a last resort and when the authorising officer is satisfied the risks associated with allowing the item to remain with the detainee outweigh the risks associated with removing it. See *Notes A1* to *A5*.

4. An intimate search under:
   - *paragraph 2(a)(i)* may take place only at a hospital, surgery, other medical premises or police station;
   - *paragraph 2(a)(ii)* may take place only at a hospital, surgery or other medical premises and must be carried out by a registered medical practitioner or a registered nurse.

5. An intimate search at a police station of a juvenile or vulnerable person may take place only in the presence of an appropriate adult of the same sex (see *Annex L*), unless the detainee specifically requests a particular appropriate adult of the opposite sex who is readily available. In the case of a juvenile, the search may take place in the absence of the appropriate adult only if the juvenile signifies

in the presence of the appropriate adult they do not want the appropriate adult present during the search and the appropriate adult agrees. A record shall be made of the juvenile's decision and signed by the appropriate adult.

6. When an intimate search under *paragraph 2(a)(i)* is carried out by a police officer, the officer must be of the same sex as the detainee (see *Annex L*). A minimum of two people, other than the detainee, must be present during the search. Subject to *paragraph 5*, no person of the opposite sex who is not a medical practitioner or nurse shall be present, nor shall anyone whose presence is unnecessary. The search shall be conducted with proper regard to the dignity, sensitivity and vulnerability of the detainee including in particular their health, hygiene and welfare needs to which *paragraphs 9.3A* and *9.3B* apply.

(b) Documentation

7. In the case of an intimate search, the following shall be recorded as soon as practicable in the detainee's custody record:
   (a) for searches under *paragraphs 2(a)(i)* and *(ii)*;
   - the authorisation to carry out the search;
   - the grounds for giving the authorisation;
   - the grounds for believing the article could not be removed without an intimate search;
   - which parts of the detainee's body were searched;
   - who carried out the search;
   - who was present;
   - the result.

   (b) for searches under *paragraph 2(a)(ii)*:
   - the giving of the warning required by *paragraph 2B*;
   - the fact that the appropriate consent was given or (as the case may be) refused, and if refused, the reason given for the refusal (if any).

8. If an intimate search is carried out by a police officer, the reason why it was impracticable for a registered medical practitioner or registered nurse to conduct it must be recorded.

B Strip search

9. A strip search is a search involving the removal of more than outer clothing. In this Code, outer clothing includes shoes and socks.

(a) Action

10. A strip search may take place only if it is considered necessary to remove an article which a detainee would not be allowed to keep and the officer reasonably considers the detainee might have concealed such an article. Strip searches shall not be routinely carried out if there is no reason to consider that articles are concealed.

The conduct of strip searches

11. When strip searches are conducted:
   (a) a police officer carrying out a strip search must be the same sex as the detainee (see *Annex L*);
   (b) the search shall take place in an area where the detainee cannot be seen by anyone who does not need to be present, nor by a member of the opposite sex (see *Annex L*) except an appropriate adult who has been specifically requested by the detainee;
   (c) except in cases of urgency, where there is risk of serious harm to the detainee or to others, whenever a strip search involves exposure of intimate body parts, there must be at least two people present other than the detainee, and if the search is of a juvenile or vulnerable person, one of the people must be the appropriate adult. Except in urgent cases as above, a search of a juvenile may take place in the absence of the appropriate adult only if the juvenile signifies in the presence of the appropriate adult that they do not want the appropriate adult to be present during the search and the appropriate adult agrees. A record shall be made of the juvenile's decision and signed by the appropriate adult. The presence of more than two people, other than an appropriate adult, shall be permitted only in the most exceptional circumstances;
   (d) the search shall be conducted with proper regard to the dignity, sensitivity and vulnerability of the detainee in these circumstances, including in particular, their health, hygiene and welfare needs to which *paragraphs 9.3A* and *9.3B* apply. Every reasonable effort shall be made to secure the detainee's co-operation, maintain their dignity, and minimise embarrassment. Detainees who are searched shall not normally be required to remove all their clothes at the same time, e.g. a person should be allowed to remove clothing above the waist and redress before removing further clothing;

(e) if necessary to assist the search, the detainee may be required to hold their arms in the air or to stand with their legs apart and bend forward so a visual examination may be made of the genital and anal areas provided no physical contact is made with any body orifice;

(f) if articles are found, the detainee shall be asked to hand them over. If articles are found within any body orifice other than the mouth, and the detainee refuses to hand them over, their removal would constitute an intimate search, which must be carried out as in *Part A*;

(g) a strip search shall be conducted as quickly as possible, and the detainee allowed to dress as soon as the procedure is complete.

(b) Documentation

12. A record shall be made on the custody record of a strip search including the reason it was considered necessary, those present and any result.

Notes for Guidance

A1 *Before authorising any intimate search, the authorising officer must make every reasonable effort to persuade the detainee to hand the article over without a search. If the detainee agrees, a registered medical practitioner or registered nurse should whenever possible be asked to assess the risks involved and, if necessary, attend to assist the detainee.*

A2 *If the detainee does not agree to hand the article over without a search, the authorising officer must carefully review all the relevant factors before authorising an intimate search. In particular, the officer must consider whether the grounds for believing an article may be concealed are reasonable.*

A3 *If authority is given for a search under paragraph 2(a)(i), a registered medical practitioner or registered nurse shall be consulted whenever possible. The presumption should be that the search will be conducted by the registered medical practitioner or registered nurse and the authorising officer must make every reasonable effort to persuade the detainee to allow the medical practitioner or nurse to conduct the search.*

A4 *A constable should only be authorised to carry out a search as a last resort and when all other approaches have failed. In these circumstances, the authorising officer must be satisfied the detainee might use the article for one or more of the purposes in paragraph 2(a)(i) and the physical injury likely to be caused is sufficiently severe to justify authorising a constable to carry out the search.*

A5 *If an officer has any doubts whether to authorise an intimate search by a constable, the officer should seek advice from an officer of superintendent rank or above.*

A6 *In warning a detainee who is asked to consent to an intimate drug offence search, as in paragraph 2B, the following form of words may be used:*

'You do not have to allow yourself to be searched, but I must warn you that if you refuse without good cause, your refusal may harm your case if it comes to trial.'

Where the use of the Welsh Language is appropriate, the following form of words may be used:

'Nid oes rhaid i chi roi caniatâd i gael eich archwilio, ond mae'n rhaid i mi eich rhybuddio os gwrthodwch heb reswm da, y gallai eich penderfyniad i wrthod wneud niwed i'ch achos pe bai'n dod gerbron llys.'

Annex B

Delay in Notifying Arrest or Allowing Access to Legal Advice

A Persons detained under PACE

1. The exercise of the rights in *Section 5* or *Section 6*, or both, may be delayed if the person is in police detention, as in PACE, section 118(2), in connection with an indictable offence, has not yet been charged with an offence and an officer of superintendent rank or above, or inspector rank or above only for the rights in *Section 5*, has reasonable grounds for believing their exercise will:
   (i) lead to:
   - interference with, or harm to, evidence connected with an indictable offence; or
   - interference with, or physical harm to, other people; or

   (ii) lead to alerting other people suspected of having committed an indictable offence but not yet arrested for it; or
   (iii) hinder the recovery of property obtained in consequence of the commission of such an offence.
2. These rights may also be delayed if the officer has reasonable grounds to believe that:
   (i) the person detained for an indictable offence has benefited from their criminal conduct (decided in accordance with Part 2 of the Proceeds of Crime Act 2002); and
   (ii) the recovery of the value of the property constituting that benefit will be hindered by the exercise of either right.

3. Authority to delay a detainee's right to consult privately with a solicitor may be given only if the authorising officer has reasonable grounds to believe the solicitor the detainee wants to consult will, inadvertently or otherwise, pass on a message from the detainee or act in some other way which will have any of the consequences specified under *paragraphs 1* or *2*. In these circumstances, the detainee must be allowed to choose another solicitor. See *Note B3*.
4. If the detainee wishes to see a solicitor, access to that solicitor may not be delayed on the grounds they might advise the detainee not to answer questions or the solicitor was initially asked to attend the police station by someone else. In the latter case, the detainee must be told the solicitor has come to the police station at another person's request, and must be asked to sign the custody record to signify whether they want to see the solicitor.
5. The fact the grounds for delaying notification of arrest may be satisfied does not automatically mean the grounds for delaying access to legal advice will also be satisfied.
6. These rights may be delayed only for as long as grounds exist and in no case beyond 36 hours after the relevant time as in PACE, section 41. If the grounds cease to apply within this time, the detainee must, as soon as practicable, be asked if they want to exercise either right, the custody record must be noted accordingly, and action taken in accordance with the relevant section of the Code.
7. A detained person must be permitted to consult a solicitor for a reasonable time before any court hearing.

B *Not used*

C Documentation

13. The grounds for action under this Annex shall be recorded and the detainee informed of them as soon as practicable.
14. Any reply given by a detainee under *paragraphs 6* or *11* must be recorded and the detainee asked to endorse the record in relation to whether they want to receive legal advice at this point.

D Cautions and special warnings

15. When a suspect detained at a police station is interviewed during any period for which access to legal advice has been delayed under this Annex, the court or jury may not draw adverse inferences from their silence.

Notes for Guidance

B1 Even if Annex B applies in the case of a juvenile, or a vulnerable person, action to inform the appropriate adult and the person responsible for a juvenile's welfare, if that is a different person, must nevertheless be taken as in paragraph 3.13 and 3.15.

B2 In the case of Commonwealth citizens and foreign nationals, see Note 7A.

B3 A decision to delay access to a specific solicitor is likely to be a rare occurrence and only when it can be shown the suspect is capable of misleading that particular solicitor and there is more than a substantial risk that the suspect will succeed in causing information to be conveyed which will lead to one or more of the specified consequences.

Annex C

Restriction on Drawing Adverse Inferences from Silence and Terms of the Caution when the Restriction Applies

(a) The restriction on drawing adverse inferences from silence

1. The Criminal Justice and Public Order Act 1994, sections 34, 36 and 37 as amended by the Youth Justice and Criminal Evidence Act 1999, section 58 describe the conditions under which adverse inferences may be drawn from a person's failure or refusal to say anything about their involvement in the offence when interviewed, after being charged or informed they may be prosecuted. These provisions are subject to an overriding restriction on the ability of a court or jury to draw adverse inferences from a person's silence. This restriction applies:
   (a) to any detainee at a police station, see *Note 10C*, who, before being interviewed, see *section 11* or being charged or informed they may be prosecuted, see *section 16*, has:
      (i) asked for legal advice, see *section 6, paragraph 6.1*;
      (ii) not been allowed an opportunity to consult a solicitor, including the duty solicitor, as in this Code; and
      (iii) not changed their mind about wanting legal advice, see *section 6, paragraph 6.6(d)*.

   Note the condition in (ii) will:
   - apply when a detainee who has asked for legal advice is interviewed before speaking to a solicitor as in *section 6, paragraph 6.6(a)* or *(b)*;
   - not apply if the detained person declines to ask for the duty solicitor, see *section 6, paragraphs 6.6(c)* and *(d)*.

(b) to any person charged with, or informed they may be prosecuted for, an offence who:
  (i) has had brought to their notice a written statement made by another person or the content of an interview with another person which relates to that offence, see *section 16, paragraph 16.4*;
  (ii) is interviewed about that offence, see *section 16, paragraph 16.5*; or
  (iii) makes a written statement about that offence, see *Annex D, paragraphs 4* and *9*.

(b) Terms of the caution when the restriction applies

2. When a requirement to caution arises at a time when the restriction on drawing adverse inferences from silence applies, the caution shall be:

   '*You do not have to say anything, but anything you do say may be given in evidence.*'

   Where the use of the Welsh Language is appropriate, the caution may be used directly in Welsh in the following terms:

   '*Does dim rhaid i chi ddweud dim byd, ond gall unrhyw beth yr ydych chi'n ei ddweud gael ei roi fel tystiolaeth.*'

3. Whenever the restriction either begins to apply or ceases to apply after a caution has already been given, the person shall be re-cautioned in the appropriate terms. The changed position on drawing inferences and that the previous caution no longer applies shall also be explained to the detainee in ordinary language. See *Note C2*.

Notes for Guidance

C1 The restriction on drawing inferences from silence does not apply to a person who has not been detained and who therefore cannot be prevented from seeking legal advice if they want to, see paragraphs 10.2 and 3.21.

C2 The following is suggested as a framework to help explain changes in the position on drawing adverse inferences if the restriction on drawing adverse inferences from silence:
  (a) begins to apply:
  'The caution you were previously given no longer applies. This is because after that caution:
    (i) you asked to speak to a solicitor but have not yet been allowed an opportunity to speak to a solicitor. See paragraph 1(a); or
    (ii) you have been charged with/informed you may be prosecuted. See paragraph 1(b).
  'This means that from now on, adverse inferences cannot be drawn at court and your defence will not be harmed just because you choose to say nothing. Please listen carefully to the caution I am about to give you because it will apply from now on. You will see that it does not say anything about your defence being harmed.'
  (b) ceases to apply before or at the time the person is charged or informed they may be prosecuted, see paragraph 1(a);
  'The caution you were previously given no longer applies. This is because after that caution you have been allowed an opportunity to speak to a solicitor. Please listen carefully to the caution I am about to give you because it will apply from now on. It explains how your defence at court may be affected if you choose to say nothing.'

Annex D

Written Statements under Caution

(a) Written by a person under caution

1. A person shall always be invited to write down what they want to say.
2. A person who has not been charged with, or informed they may be prosecuted for, any offence to which the statement they want to write relates, shall:
   (a) unless the statement is made at a time when the restriction on drawing adverse inferences from silence applies, see *Annex C*, be asked to write out and sign the following before writing what they want to say:

   '*I make this statement of my own free will. I understand that I do not have to say anything but that it may harm my defence if I do not mention when questioned something which I later rely on in court. This statement may be given in evidence.*';

   (b) if the statement is made at a time when the restriction on drawing adverse inferences from silence applies, be asked to write out and sign the following before writing what they want to say;

   '*I make this statement of my own free will. I understand that I do not have to say anything. This statement may be given in evidence.*'

3. When a person, on the occasion of being charged with or informed they may be prosecuted for any offence, asks to make a statement which relates to any such offence and wants to write it they shall:
   (a) unless the restriction on drawing adverse inferences from silence, see *Annex C*, applied when they were so charged or informed they may be prosecuted, be asked to write out and sign the following before writing what they want to say:

      '*I make this statement of my own free will. I understand that I do not have to say anything but that it may harm my defence if I do not mention when questioned something which I later rely on in court. This statement may be given in evidence.*';

   (b) if the restriction on drawing adverse inferences from silence applied when they were so charged or informed they may be prosecuted, be asked to write out and sign the following before writing what they want to say:

      '*I make this statement of my own free will. I understand that I do not have to say anything. This statement may be given in evidence.*'

4. When a person who has already been charged with or informed they may be prosecuted for any offence asks to make a statement which relates to any such offence and wants to write it, they shall be asked to write out and sign the following before writing what they want to say:

   '*I make this statement of my own free will. I understand that I do not have to say anything. This statement may be given in evidence.*';

5. Any person writing their own statement shall be allowed to do so without any prompting except a police officer or other police staff may indicate to them which matters are material or question any ambiguity in the statement.

(b) Written by a police officer or other police staff

6. If a person says they would like someone to write the statement for them, a police officer, or other police staff shall write the statement.
7. If the person has not been charged with, or informed they may be prosecuted for, any offence to which the statement they want to make relates they shall, before starting, be asked to sign, or make their mark, to the following:
   (a) unless the statement is made at a time when the restriction on drawing adverse inferences from silence applies, see *Annex C*:

      '*I, ..., wish to make a statement. I want someone to write down what I say. I understand that I do not have to say anything but that it may harm my defence if I do not mention when questioned something which I later rely on in court. This statement may be given in evidence.*';

   (b) if the statement is made at a time when the restriction on drawing adverse inferences from silence applies:

      '*I, ..., wish to make a statement. I want someone to write down what I say. I understand that I do not have to say anything. This statement may be given in evidence.*'

8. If, on the occasion of being charged with or informed they may be prosecuted for any offence, the person asks to make a statement which relates to any such offence they shall before starting be asked to sign, or make their mark to, the following:
   (a) unless the restriction on drawing adverse inferences from silence applied, see *Annex C*, when they were so charged or informed they may be prosecuted:

      '*I, ..., wish to make a statement. I want someone to write down what I say. I understand that I do not have to say anything but that it may harm my defence if I do not mention when questioned something which I later rely on in court. This statement may be given in evidence.*';

   (b) if the restriction on drawing adverse inferences from silence applied when they were so charged or informed they may be prosecuted:

      '*I, ..., wish to make a statement. I want someone to write down what I say. I understand that I do not have to say anything. This statement may be given in evidence.*'

9. If, having already been charged with or informed they may be prosecuted for any offence, a person asks to make a statement which relates to any such offence they shall before starting, be asked to sign, or make their mark to:

   '*I, ..., wish to make a statement. I want someone to write down what I say. I understand that I do not have to say anything. This statement may be given in evidence.*'

10. The person writing the statement must take down the exact words spoken by the person making it and must not edit or paraphrase it. Any questions that are necessary, e.g. to make it more intelligible, and the answers given must be recorded at the same time on the statement form.
11. When the writing of a statement is finished the person making it shall be asked to read it and to make any corrections, alterations or additions they want. When they have finished reading they shall be asked to write and sign or make their mark on the following certificate at the end of the statement:

    '*I have read the above statement, and I have been able to correct, alter or add anything I wish. This statement is true. I have made it of my own free will.*'

12. If the person making the statement cannot read, or refuses to read it, or to write the above mentioned certificate at the end of it or to sign it, the person taking the statement shall read it to them and ask them if they would like to correct, alter or add anything and to put their signature or make their mark at the end. The person taking the statement shall certify on the statement itself what has occurred.

Annex E

Summary of Provisions Relating to Mentally Disordered and Otherwise Mentally Vulnerable People

1. If at any time, an officer has reason to suspect that a person of any age may be vulnerable (see *paragraph 1.13(d)*), in the absence of clear evidence to dispel that suspicion that person shall be treated as such for the purposes of this Code and to establish whether any such reason may exist in relation to a person suspected of committing an offence (see *paragraph 10.1* and *Note 10A*), the custody officer in the case of a detained person, or the officer investigating the offence in the case of a person who has not been arrested or detained, shall take, or cause to be taken, (see *paragraph 3.5* and *Note 3F*) the following action:
   (a) reasonable enquiries shall be made to ascertain what information is available that is relevant to any of the factors described in *paragraph 1.13(d)* as indicating that the person may be vulnerable might apply;
   (b) a record shall be made describing whether any of those factors appear to apply and provide any reason to suspect that the person may be vulnerable or (as the case may be) may not be vulnerable; and
   (c) the record mentioned in sub-paragraph (b) shall be made available to be taken into account by police officers, police staff and any others who, in accordance with the provisions of this or any other Code, are entitled to communicate with the person in question. This would include any solicitor, appropriate adult and healthcare professional and is particularly relevant to communication by telephone or by means of a live link (see *paragraphs 12.9A* (interviews), *13.12* (interpretation), and *15.3C, 15.11A, 15.11B, 15.11C* and *15.11D* (reviews and extension of detention)).

   See *Notes 1G, E5, E6* and *E7*.
2. In the case of a person who is vulnerable, 'the appropriate adult' means:
   (i) a relative, guardian or other person responsible for their care or custody;
   (ii) someone experienced in dealing with vulnerable persons but who is not:
      - a police officer;
      - employed by the police;
      - under the direction or control of the chief officer of a police force;
      - a person who provides services under contractual arrangements (but without being employed by the chief officer of a police force), to assist that force in relation to the discharge of its chief officer's functions,

      whether or not they are on duty at the time.
   (iii) failing these, some other responsible adult aged 18 or over who is other than a person described in the bullet points in *sub-paragraph (ii)* above.

   See *paragraph 1.7(b)* and *Notes 1D* and *1F*.

2A The role of the appropriate adult is to safeguard the rights, entitlements and welfare of 'vulnerable persons' (see *paragraph 1*) to whom the provisions of this and any other Code of Practice apply. For this reason, the appropriate adult is expected, amongst other things, to:
   - support, advise and assist them when, in accordance with this Code or any other Code of Practice, they are given or asked to provide information or participate in any procedure;
   - observe whether the police are acting properly and fairly to respect their rights and entitlements, and inform an officer of the rank of inspector or above if they consider that they are not;
   - assist them to communicate with the police whilst respecting their right to say nothing unless they want to as set out in the terms of the caution (see *paragraphs 10.5* and *10.6*); and
   - help them understand their rights and ensure that those rights are protected and respected (see *paragraphs 3.15, 3.17, 6.5A* and *11.17*).

   See paragraph 1.7A

3. If the custody officer authorises the detention of a vulnerable person, the custody officer must as soon as practicable inform the appropriate adult of the grounds for detention and the person's whereabouts, and secure the attendance of the appropriate adult at the police station to see the detainee. If the appropriate adult:
   - is already at the station when information is given as in *paragraphs 3.1* to *3.5* the information must be given in their presence;
   - is not at the station when the provisions of *paragraph 3.1* to *3.5* are complied with these provisions must be complied with again in their presence once they arrive.

   See *paragraphs 3.15* to *3.17*
4. If the appropriate adult, having been informed of the right to legal advice, considers legal advice should be taken, the provisions of *section 6* apply as if the vulnerable person had requested access to legal advice. See *paragraphs 3.19, 6.5A* and *Note E1.*
5. The custody officer must make sure a person receives appropriate clinical attention as soon as reasonably practicable if the person appears to be suffering from a mental disorder or in urgent cases immediately call the nearest appropriate healthcare professional or an ambulance. See Code C *paragraphs 3.16, 9.5* and *9.6* which apply when a person is detained under the Mental Health Act 1983, sections 135 and 136, as amended by the Policing and Crime Act 2017.
6. *Not used.*
7. If a vulnerable person is cautioned in the absence of the appropriate adult, the caution must be repeated in the appropriate adult's presence. See *paragraph 10.12.*
8. A vulnerable person must not be interviewed or asked to provide or sign a written statement in the absence of the appropriate adult unless the provisions of *paragraphs 11.1* or *11.18* to *11.20* apply. Questioning in these circumstances may not continue in the absence of the appropriate adult once sufficient information to avert the risk has been obtained. A record shall be made of the grounds for any decision to begin an interview in these circumstances. See *paragraphs 11.1, 11.15* and *11.18* to *11.20.*
9. If the appropriate adult is present at an interview, they shall be informed they are not expected to act simply as an observer and the purposes of their presence are to:
   - advise the interviewee;
   - observe whether or not the interview is being conducted properly and fairly;
   - facilitate communication with the interviewee.

   See *paragraph 11.17*
10. If the detention of a vulnerable person is reviewed by a review officer or a superintendent, the appropriate adult must, if available at the time, be given an opportunity to make representations to the officer about the need for continuing detention. See *paragraph 15.3.*
11. If the custody officer charges a vulnerable person with an offence or takes such other action as is appropriate when there is sufficient evidence for a prosecution this must be carried out in the presence of the appropriate adult if they are at the police station. A copy of the written notice embodying any charge must also be given to the appropriate adult. See *paragraphs 16.1* to *16.4A.*
12. An intimate or strip search of a vulnerable person may take place only in the presence of the appropriate adult of the same sex, unless the detainee specifically requests the presence of a particular adult of the opposite sex. A strip search may take place in the absence of an appropriate adult only in cases of urgency when there is a risk of serious harm to the detainee or others. See *Annex A, paragraphs 5* and *11(c).*
13. Particular care must be taken when deciding whether to use any form of approved restraints on a vulnerable person in a locked cell. See *paragraph 8.2.*

Notes for Guidance

E1 The purpose of the provisions at paragraphs 3.19 and 6.5A is to protect the rights of a vulnerable person who does not understand the significance of what is said to them. A vulnerable person should always be given an opportunity, when an appropriate adult is called to the police station, to consult privately with a solicitor in the absence of the appropriate adult if they want.

E2 Although vulnerable persons are often capable of providing reliable evidence, they may, without knowing or wanting to do so, be particularly prone in certain circumstances to provide information that may be unreliable, misleading or self-incriminating. Special care should always be taken when questioning such a person, and the appropriate adult should be involved if there is any doubt about a person's mental state or capacity. Because of the risk of unreliable evidence, it is important to obtain corroboration of any facts admitted whenever possible.

E3 Because of the risks referred to in Note E2, which the presence of the appropriate adult is intended to minimise, officers of superintendent rank or above should exercise their discretion to authorise the commencement of an interview in the appropriate adult's absence only in exceptional cases, if it is necessary to avert one or more of the specified risks in paragraph 11.1. See *paragraphs 11.1 and 11.18 to 11.20.*

E4 When a person is detained under section 136 of the Mental Health Act 1983 for assessment, the appropriate adult has no role in the assessment process and their presence is not required.

E5 For the purposes of Annex E paragraph 1, examples of relevant information that may be available include:
- *the behaviour of the adult or juvenile;*
- *the mental health and capacity of the adult or juvenile;*
- *what the adult or juvenile says about themselves;*
- *information from relatives and friends of the adult or juvenile;*
- *information from police officers and staff and from police records;*
- *information from health and social care (including liaison and diversion services) and other professionals who know, or have had previous contact with, the individual and may be able to contribute to assessing their need for help and support from an appropriate adult. This includes contacts and assessments arranged by the police or at the request of the individual or (as applicable) their appropriate adult or solicitor.*

E6 The Mental Health Act 1983 Code of Practice at page 26 describes the range of clinically recognised conditions which can fall with the meaning of mental disorder for the purpose of paragraph 1.13(d). The Code is published here: https://www.gov.uk/government/publications/code-of-practice-mental-health-act-1983.

E7 When a person is under the influence of drink and/or drugs, it is not intended that they are to be treated as vulnerable and requiring an appropriate adult for the purpose of Annex E paragraph 1 unless other information indicates that any of the factors described in paragraph 1.13(d) may apply to that person. When the person has recovered from the effects of drink and/or drugs, they should be re-assessed in accordance with Annex E paragraph 1. See paragraph 15.4A for application to live link.

Annex F

Not used

Annex G

Fitness to be Interviewed

1. This Annex contains general guidance to help police officers and healthcare professionals assess whether a detainee might be at risk in an interview.
2. A detainee may be at risk in a interview if it is considered that:
   (a) conducting the interview could significantly harm the detainee's physical or mental state;
   (b) anything the detainee says in the interview about their involvement or suspected involvement in the offence about which they are being interviewed **might** be considered unreliable in subsequent court proceedings because of their physical or mental state.
3. In assessing whether the detainee should be interviewed, the following must be considered:
   (a) how the detainee's physical or mental state might affect their ability to understand the nature and purpose of the interview, to comprehend what is being asked and to appreciate the significance of any answers given and make rational decisions about whether they want to say anything;
   (b) the extent to which the detainee's replies may be affected by their physical or mental condition rather than representing a rational and accurate explanation of their involvement in the offence;
   (c) how the nature of the interview, which could include particularly probing questions, might affect the detainee.
4. It is essential healthcare professionals who are consulted consider the functional ability of the detainee rather than simply relying on a medical diagnosis, e.g. it is possible for a person with severe mental illness to be fit for interview.
5. Healthcare professionals should advise on the need for an appropriate adult to be present, whether reassessment of the person's fitness for interview may be necessary if the interview lasts beyond a specified time, and whether a further specialist opinion may be required.
6. When healthcare professionals identify risks they should be asked to quantify the risks. They should inform the custody officer:
   - whether the person's condition:
     - is likely to improve;
     - will require or be amenable to treatment; and
   - indicate how long it may take for such improvement to take effect.
7. The role of the healthcare professional is to consider the risks and advise the custody officer of the outcome of that consideration. The healthcare professional's determination and any advice or recommendations should be made in writing and form part of the custody record.
8. Once the healthcare professional has provided that information, it is a matter for the custody officer to decide whether or not to allow the interview to go ahead and if the interview is to proceed, to

determine what safeguards are needed. Nothing prevents safeguards being provided in addition to those required under the Code. An example might be to have an appropriate healthcare professional present during the interview, in addition to an appropriate adult, in order constantly to monitor the person's condition and how it is being affected by the interview.

Annex H

Detained Person: Observation List

1. If any detainee fails to meet any of the following criteria, an appropriate healthcare professional or an ambulance must be called.
2. When assessing the level of rousability, consider:
   Rousability — can they be woken?
   - go into the cell
   - call their name
   - shake gently

   Response to questions — can they give appropriate answers to questions such as:
   - What's your name?
   - Where do you live?
   - Where do you think you are?

   Response to commands — can they respond appropriately to commands such as:
   - Open your eyes!
   - Lift one arm, now the other arm!
3. Remember to take into account the possibility or presence of other illnesses, injury, or mental condition; a person who is drowsy and smells of alcohol may also have the following:
   - Diabetes
   - Epilepsy
   - Head injury
   - Drug intoxication or overdose
   - Stroke

Annex I

Not used

Annex J

Not used

Annex K

X-Rays and Ultrasound Scans

(a) Action

1. PACE, section 55A allows a person who has been arrested and is in police detention to have an X-ray taken of them or an ultrasound scan to be carried out on them (or both) if:
   (a) authorised by an officer of inspector rank or above who has reasonable grounds for believing that the detainee:
      (i) may have swallowed a Class A drug; and
      (ii) was in possession of that Class A drug with the intention of supplying it to another or to export; and
   (b) the detainee's appropriate consent has been given in writing.
2. Before an x-ray is taken or an ultrasound scan carried out, a police officer or designated detention officer must tell the detainee:-
   (a) that the authority has been given; and
   (b) the grounds for giving the authorisation.
3. Before a detainee is asked to give appropriate consent to an x-ray or an ultrasound scan, they must be warned that if they refuse without good cause their refusal may harm their case if it comes to trial, see *Notes K1* and *K2*. This warning may be given by a police officer or member of police staff. In the case of juveniles and vulnerable persons, the seeking and giving of consent must take place in the presence of the appropriate adult. A juvenile's consent is only valid if their parent's or guardian's consent is also obtained unless the juvenile is under 14, when their parent's or guardian's consent is sufficient in its own right. A detainee who is not legally represented must be reminded of their entitlement to have free legal advice, see Code C, *paragraph 6.5*, and the reminder noted in the custody record.

4. An x-ray may be taken, or an ultrasound scan may be carried out, only by a registered medical practitioner or registered nurse, and only at a hospital, surgery or other medical premises.

(b) Documentation

5. The following shall be recorded as soon as practicable in the detainee's custody record:
   (a) the authorisation to take the x-ray or carry out the ultrasound scan (or both);
   (b) the grounds for giving the authorisation;
   (c) the giving of the warning required by *paragraph 3*; and
   (d) the fact that the appropriate consent was given or (as the case may be) refused, and if refused, the reason given for the refusal (if any); and
   (e) if an x-ray is taken or an ultrasound scan carried out:
   - where it was taken or carried out;
   - who took it or carried it out;
   - who was present;
   - the result.

6 *Not used.*

Notes for Guidance

K1 If authority is given for an x-ray to be taken or an ultrasound scan to be carried out (or both), consideration should be given to asking a registered medical practitioner or registered nurse to explain to the detainee what is involved and to allay any concerns the detainee might have about the effect which taking an x-ray or carrying out an ultrasound scan might have on them. If appropriate consent is not given, evidence of the explanation may, if the case comes to trial, be relevant to determining whether the detainee had a good cause for refusing.

K2 In warning a detainee who is asked to consent to an X-ray being taken or an ultrasound scan being carried out (or both), as in paragraph 3, the following form of words may be used:

'You do not have to allow an x-ray of you to be taken or an ultrasound scan to be carried out on you, but I must warn you that if you refuse without good cause, your refusal may harm your case if it comes to trial.'

Where the use of the Welsh Language is appropriate, the following form of words may be provided in Welsh:

'Does dim rhaid i chi ganiatáu cymryd sgan uwchsain neu belydr-x (neu'r ddau) arnoch, ond mae'n rhaid i mi eich rhybuddio os byddwch chi'n gwrthod gwneud hynny heb reswm da, fe allai hynny niweidio eich achos pe bai'n dod gerbron llys.'

Annex L

Establishing Gender of Persons for the Purpose of Searching

1. Certain provisions of this and other PACE Codes explicitly state that searches and other procedures may only be carried out by, or in the presence of, persons of the same sex as the person subject to the search or other procedure or require action to be taken or information to be given which depends on whether the detainee is treated as being male or female. See *Note L1*.

2. All such searches, procedures and requirements must be carried out with courtesy, consideration and respect for the person concerned. Police officers should show particular sensitivity when dealing with transgender individuals (including transsexual persons) and transvestite persons (see *Notes L2, L3 and L4*).

(a) Consideration

3. In law, the gender (and accordingly the sex) of an individual is their gender as registered at birth unless they have been issued with a Gender Recognition Certificate (GRC) under the Gender Recognition Act 2004 (GRA), in which case the person's gender is their acquired gender. This means that if the acquired gender is the male gender, the person's sex becomes that of a man and, if it is the female gender, the person's sex becomes that of a woman and they must be treated as their acquired gender.

4. When establishing whether the person concerned should be treated as being male or female for the purposes of these searches, procedures and requirements, the following approach which is designed to maintain their diginity, minimise embarrassment and secure their co-operation should be followed:
   (a) The person must not be asked whether they have a GRC (see *paragraph 8*);
   (b) If there is no doubt as to as to whether the person concerned should be treated as being male or female, they should be dealt with as being of that sex.
   (c) If at any time (including during the search or carrying out the procedure or requirement) there is doubt as to whether the person should be treated, or continue to be treated, as being male or female:
      (i) the person should be asked what gender they consider themselves to be. If they express a preference to be dealt with as a particular gender, they should be asked to indicate and confirm their

preference by signing the custody record or, if a custody record has not been opened, the search record or the officer's notebook. Subject to (ii) below, the person should be treated according to their preference except with regards to the requirements to provide that person with information concerning menstrual products and their personal needs relating to health, hygiene and welfare described in *paragraph 3.20A* (if aged under 18) and *paragraphs 9.3A* and *9.3B* (if aged 18 or over). In these cases, a person whose confirmed preference is to be dealt with as being male should be asked in private whether they wish to speak in private with a member of the custody staff of a gender of their choosing about the provision of menstrual products and their personal needs, notwithstanding their confirmed preference (see *Note L3A*).

(ii) if there are grounds to doubt that the preference in (i) accurately reflects the person's predominant lifestyle, for example, if they ask to be treated as a woman but documents and other information make it clear that they live predominantly as a man, or vice versa, they should be treated according to what appears to be their predominant lifestyle and not their stated preference;

(iii) If the person is unwilling to express a preference as in (i) above, efforts should be made to determine their predominant lifestyle and they should be treated as such. For example, if they appear to live predominantly as a woman, they should be treated as being female except with regard to the requirements to provide that person with information concerning menstrual products and their personal needs relating to health, hygiene and welfare described in *paragraph 3.20A* (if aged under 18) and *paragraphs 9.3A* and *9.3B* (if aged 18 or over). In these cases, a person whose predominant lifestyle has been determined to be male should be asked in private whether they wish to speak in private with a member of the custody staff of a gender of their choosing about the provision of menstrual products and their personal needs, notwithstanding their determined predominant lifestyle (see *Note L3A*); or

(iv) if none of the above apply, the person should be dealt with according to what reasonably appears to have been their sex as registered at birth.

5. Once a decision has been made about which gender an individual is to be treated as, each officer responsible for the search, procedure or requirement should where possible be advised before the search or procedure starts of any doubts as to the person's gender and the person informed that the doubts have been disclosed. This is important so as to maintain the dignity of the person and any officers concerned.

(b) Documentation

6. The person's gender as established under *paragraph 4(c)(i)* to *(iv)* above must be recorded in the person's custody record or, if a custody record has not been opened, on the search record or in the officer's notebook.

7. Where the person elects which gender they consider themselves to be under *paragraph 4(b)(i)* but, following *4(b)(ii)* is not treated in accordance with their preference, the reason must be recorded in the search record, in the officer's notebook or, if applicable, in the person's custody record.

(c) Disclosure of information

8. Section 22 of the GRA defines any information relating to a person's application for a GRC or to a successful applicant's gender before it became their acquired gender as 'protected information'. Nothing in this Annex is to be read as authorising or permitting any police officer or any police staff who has acquired such information when acting in their official capacity to disclose that information to any other person in contravention of the GRA. Disclosure includes making a record of 'protected information' which is read by others.

Notes for Guidance

L1 Provisions to which paragraph 1 applies include:

- *In Code C; paragraphs 3.20A, 4.1 and Annex A paragraphs 5, 6, and 11 (searches, strip and intimate searches of detainees under sections 54 and 55 of PACE) and 9.3B;*
- *In Code A; paragraphs 2.8 and 3.6 and Note 4;*
- *In Code D; paragraph 5.5 and Note 5F (searches, examinations and photographing of detainees under section 54A of PACE) and paragraph 6.9 (taking samples);*
- *In Code H; paragraphs 3.21, 4.1 and Annex A paragraphs 6, 7 and 12 (searches, strip and intimate searches under sections 54 and 55 of PACE of persons arrested under section 41 of the Terrorism Act 2000) and 9.4B.*

L2 While there is no agreed definition of transgender (or trans), it is generally used as an umbrella term to describe people whose gender identity (self-identification as being a woman, man, neither or both) differs from the sex they were registered as at birth. The term includes, but is not limited to, transsexual people.

L3 Transsexual means a person who is proposing to undergo, is undergoing or has undergone a process (or part of a process) for the purpose of gender reassignment, which is a protected characteristic under the Equality

Act 2010 (see paragraph 1.0), by changing physiological or other attributes of their sex. This includes aspects of gender such as dress and title. It would apply to a woman making the transition to being a man and a man making the transition to being a woman, as well as to a person who has only just started out on the process of gender reassignment and to a person who has completed the process. Both would share the characteristic of gender reassignment with each having the characteristics of one sex, but with certain characteristics of the other sex.

L3A The reason for the exception is to modify the same sex/gender approach for searching to acknowledge the possible needs of transgender individuals in respect of menstrual products and other personal needs relating to health, hygiene and welfare and ensure that they are not overlooked.

L4 Transvestite means a person of one gender who dresses in the clothes of a person of the opposite gender. However, a transvestite does not live permanently in the gender opposite to their birth sex.

L5 Chief officers are responsible for providing corresponding operational guidance and instructions for the deployment of transgender officers and staff under their direction and control to duties which involve carrying out, or being present at, any of the searches and procedures described in paragraph 1. The guidance and instructions must comply with the Equality Act 2010 and should therefore complement the approach in this Annex.

Annex M

Documents and Records to be Translated

1. For the purposes of Directive 2010/64/EU of the European Parliament and of the Council of 20 October 2010 and this Code, essential documents comprise records required to be made in accordance with this Code which are relevant to decisions to deprive a person of their liberty, to any charge and to any record considered necessary to enable a detainee to defend themselves in criminal proceedings and to safeguard the fairness of the proceedings. Passages of essential documents which are not relevant need not be translated. See *Note M1*.
2. The table below lists the documents considered essential for the purposes of this Code and when (subject to *paragraphs 3* to *7*) written translations must be created and provided. See *paragraphs 13.12* to *13.14* and *Annex N* for application to live-link interpretation.

Table of essential documents:

	Essential Documents for the Purposes of this Code	**When Translation to be Created**	**When Translation to be Provided**
(i)	The grounds for each of the following authorisations to keep the person in custody as they are described and referred to in the custody record: (a) Authorisation for detention before and after charge given by the custody officer and by the review officer, see Code C, *paragraphs 3.4* and *15.16(a)*. (b) Authorisation to extend detention without charge beyond 24 hours given by a superintendent, see Code C, *paragraph 15.16(b)*. (c) A warrant of further detention issued by a magistrates' court and any extension(s) of the warrant, see Code C, *paragraph 15.16(c)*. (d) An authority to detain in accordance with the directions in a warrant of arrest issued in connection with criminal proceedings including the court issuing the warrant.	As soon as practicable after each authorisation has been recorded in the custody record.	As soon as practicable after the translation has been created, whilst the person is detained or afters they have been releases (see *Note M3*).
(ii)	Written notice showing particulars of the offence charged required by Code C, *paragraph 16.3* or the offence for which the suspect has been told they may be prosecuted.	As soon as practicable after the person has been charged or reported.	
(iii)	Written interview records: Code C, *11.11, 13.3, 13.4* & *Code E4.7* Written statement under caution: Code C, *Annex D.*	To be created contemporaneously by the interpreter for the person to check and sign.	As soon as practicable after the person has been charged or told they may be prosecuted.

3. The custody officer may authorise an oral translation or oral summary of documents (i) to (ii) in the table (but not (iii)) to be provided (through an interpreter) instead of a written translation. Such an oral translation or summary may only be provided if it would not prejudice the fairness of the proceedings by in any way adversely affecting or otherwise undermining or limiting the ability of the suspect in question to understand their position and to communicate effectively with police officers, interviewers, solicitors and appropriate adults with regard to their detention and the investigation of the offence in question and to defend themselves in the event of criminal proceedings. The quantity and complexity of the information in the document should always be considered and specific additional consideration given if the suspect is vulnerable or is a juvenile (see Code C *paragraph 1.5*). The reason for the decision must be recorded (see *paragraph 13.11(e)*)
4. Subject to *paragraphs 5* to *7* below, a suspect may waive their right to a written translation of the essential documents described in the table but only if they do so voluntarily after receiving legal advice or having full knowledge of the consequences and give their unconditional and fully informed consent in writing (see *paragraph 9*).
5. The suspect may be asked if they wish to waive their right to a written translation and before giving their consent, they must be reminded of their right to legal advice and asked whether they wish to speak to a solicitor.
6. No police officer or police staff should do or say anything with the intention of persuading a suspect who is entitled to a written translation of an essential document to waive that right. See *Notes M2* and *M3*.
7. For the purpose of the waiver:
   (a) the consent of a vulnerable person is only valid if the information about the circumstances under which they can waive the right and the reminder about their right to legal advice mentioned in *paragraphs 3* to *5* and their consent is given in the presence of the appropriate adult.
   (b) the consent of a juvenile is only valid if their parent's or guardian's consent is also obtained unless the juvenile is under 14, when their parent's or guardian's consent is sufficient in its own right and the information and reminder mentioned in *subparagraph (a)* above and their consent is also given in the presence of the appropriate adult (who may or may not be a parent or guardian).
8. The detainee, their solicitor or appropriate adult may make representations to the custody officer that a document which is not included in the table is essential and that a translation should be provided. The request may be refused if the officer is satisfied that the translation requested is not essential for the purposes described in *paragraph 1* above.
9. If the custody officer has any doubts about
   - providing an oral translation or summary of an essential document instead of a written translation (see *paragraph 3*);
   - whether the suspect fully understands the consequences of waiving their right to a written translation of an essential document (see *paragraph 4*), or
   - about refusing to provide a translation of a requested document (see *paragraph 7*),

   the officer should seek advice from an inspector or above.

Documentation

10. Action taken in accordance with this Annex shall be recorded in the detainee's custody record or interview record as appropriate (see Code C *paragraph 13.11(e)*).

Notes for Guidance

M1 *It is not necessary to disclose information in any translation which is capable of undermining or otherwise adversely affecting any investigative processes, for example, by enabling the suspect to fabricate an innocent explanation or to conceal lies from the interviewer.*

M2 *No police officer or police staff shall indicate to any suspect, except to answer a direct question, whether the period for which they are liable to be detained or if not detained, the time taken to complete the interview, might be reduced:*
- *if they do not ask for legal advice before deciding whether they wish to waive their right to a written translation of an essential document; or*
- *if they decide to waive their right to a written translation of an essential document.*

M3 *There is no power under PACE to detain a person or to delay their release solely to create and provide a written translation of any essential document.*

Annex N

Live-Link Interpretation (Para. 13.12)

Part 1: When the physical presence of the interpreter is not required.

1. EU Directive 2010/64 (see *paragraph 13.1*), Article 2(6) provides 'Where appropriate, communication technology such as videoconferencing, telephone or the Internet may be used, unless the physical presence of the interpreter is required in order to safeguard the fairness of the proceedings.' This Article permits, but does not require the use of a live-link, and the following provisions of this Annex determine whether the use of a live-link is appropriate in any particular case.
2. Decisions in accordance with this Annex that the physical presence of the interpreter is not required and to permit live-link interpretation, must be made on a case by case basis. Each decision must take account of the age, gender and vulnerability of the suspect, the nature and circumstances of the offence and the investigation and the impact on the suspect according to the particular purpose(s) for which the suspect requires the assistance of an interpreter and the time(s) when that assistance is required (see *Note N1*). For this reason, the custody officer in the case of a detained suspect, or in the case of a suspect who has not been arrested, the interviewer (subject to *paragraph 13.1(b)*), must consider whether the ability of the particular suspect, to communicate confidently and effectively for the purpose in question (see *paragraph 3*) is likely to be adversely affected or otherwise undermined or limited if the interpreter is not physically present and live-link interpretation is used. Although a suspect for whom an appropriate adult is required may be more likely to be adversely affected as described, it is important to note that a person who does not require an appropriate adult may also be adversely impacted by the use of live-link interpretation.
3. Examples of purposes referred to in *paragraph 2* include:
   (a) understanding and appreciating their position having regard to any information given to them, or sought from them, in accordance with this or any other Code of Practice which, in particular, include:
   - the caution (see *paragraphs C10.1* and *10.12*).
   - the special warning (see *paragraphs 10.10* to *10.12*).
   - information about the offence (see *paragraphs 10.3, 11.1A* and *Note 11ZA*).
   - the grounds and reasons for detention (see *paragraphs 13.10* and *13.10A*).
   - the translation of essential documents (see *paragraph 13.10B* and *Annex M*).
   - their rights and entitlements (see *paragraph 3.12* and *C3.21(b)*).
   - intimate and non-intimate searches of detained persons at police stations.
   - provisions and procedures to which Code D (Identification) applies concerning, for example, eye-witness identification, taking fingerprints, samples and photographs.

   (b) understanding and seeking clarification from the interviewer of questions asked during an interview conducted and recorded in accordance with Code E or Code F and of anything else that is said by the interviewer and answering the questions.

   (c) consulting privately with their solicitor and (if applicable) the appropriate adult (see *paragraphs 3.18, 13.2A, 13.6* and *13.9*):

   (i) to help decide whether to answer questions put to them during interview; and

   (ii) about any other matter concerning their detention and treatment whilst in custody.

   (d) communicating with practitioners and others who have some formal responsibility for, or an interest in, the health and welfare of the suspect. Particular examples include appropriate healthcare professionals (see *section 9* of this Code), Independent Custody Visitors and drug arrest referral workers.
4. If the custody officer or the interviewer (subject to *paragraph 13.1(b)*) is satisfied that for a particular purpose as described in *paragraphs 2 and 3 above*, the live-link interpretation *would not* adversely affect or otherwise undermine or limit the suspect's ability to communicate confidently and effectively for *that* purpose, they must so inform the suspect, their solicitor and (if applicable) the appropriate adult. At the same time, the operation of live-link interpretation must be explained and demonstrated to them, they must be advised of the chief officer's obligations concerning the security of live-link communications under *paragraph 13.13* (see *Note N2*) and they must be asked if they wish to make representations that live-link interpretation should not be used or if they require more information about the operation of the arrangements. They must also be told that at any time live-link interpretation is in use, they may make representations to the custody officer or the interviewer that its operation should cease and that the physical presence of an interpreter should be arranged.

When the authority of an inspector is required

5. If

(i) representations are made that live-link interpretation should not be used, or that at any time live-link interpretation is in use, its operation should cease and the physical presence of an interpreter arranged; and

(ii) the custody officer or interviewer (subject to *paragraph 13.1(b)*) is unable to allay the concerns raised;

then live-link interpretation may not be used, or (as the case may be) continue to be used, unless authorised in writing by an officer of the rank of inspector or above, in accordance with *paragraph 6.*

6. Authority may be given if the officer is satisfied that for the purpose(s) in question at the time an interpreter is required, live-link interpretation is necessary and justified. In making this decision, the officer must have regard to:

(a) the circumstances of the suspect;

(b) the nature and seriousness of the offence;

(c) the requirements of the investigation, including its likely impact on both the suspect and any victim(s);

(d) the representations made by the suspect, their solicitor and (if applicable) the appropriate adult that live-link interpretation should not be used (see *paragraph 5*);

(e) the availability of a suitable interpreter to be *physically* present compared with the availability of a suitable interpreter for live-link interpretation (see *Note N3*); and

(f) the risk if the interpreter is not *physically* present, evidence obtained using link interpretation might be excluded in subsequent criminal proceedings; and

(g) the likely impact on the suspect and the investigation of any consequential delay to arrange for the interpreter to be *physically* present with the suspect.

7. For the purposes of Code E and live-link interpretation, there is no requirement to make a visual recording which shows the interpreter as viewed by the suspect and others present at the interview. The audio recording required by that Code is sufficient. However, the authorising officer, in consultation with the officer in charge of the investigation, may direct that the interview is conducted and recorded in accordance with Code F. This will require the visual record to show the live-link interpretation arrangements and the interpreter as seen and experienced by the suspect during the interview. This should be considered if it appears that the admissibility of interview evidence might be challenged because the interpreter was not *physically* present or if the suspect, solicitor or appropriate adult make representations that Code F should be applied.

Documentation

8. A record must be made of the actions, decisions, authorisations and outcomes arising from the requirements of this Annex. This includes representations made in accordance with *paragraphs 4* and *7.*

Part 2: Modifications for live-link interpretation

9. The following modification shall apply for the purposes of live-link interpretation:

(a) **Code C paragraph 13.3:**

For the third sentence, substitute: 'A clear legible copy of the complete record shall be sent without delay via the live-link to the interviewer. The interviewer, after confirming with the suspect that the copy is legible and complete, shall allow the suspect to read the record, or have the record read to them by the interpreter and to sign the copy as correct or indicate the respects in which they consider it inaccurate. The interviewer is responsible for ensuring that that the signed copy and the original record made by the interpreter are retained with the case papers for use in evidence if required and must advise the interpreter of their obligation to keep the original record securely for that purpose.';

(b) **Code C paragraph 13.4:**

For sub-paragraph (b), substitute: 'A clear legible copy of the complete statement shall be sent without delay via the live-link to the interviewer. The interviewer, after confirming with the suspect that the copy is legible and complete, shall invite the suspect to sign it. The interviewer is responsible for ensuring that that the signed copy and the original record made by the interpreter are retained with the case papers for use in evidence if required and must advise the interpreter of their obligation to keep the original record securely for that purpose.';

(c) **Code C paragraph 13.7:**

After the first sentence, insert: 'A clear legible copy of the certified record must be sent without delay via the live-link to the interviewer. The interviewer is responsible for ensuring that the original certified record and the copy are retained with the case papers for use as evidence if required and must advise the interpreter of their obligation to keep the original record securely for that purpose.'

(d) **Code C paragraph 11.2, Code E paragraphs 3.4 and 4.3 and Code F paragraph 2.5 interviews**
At the beginning of each paragraph, insert: 'Before the interview commences, the operation of live-link interpretation shall be explained and demonstrated to the suspect, their solicitor and appropriate adult, unless it has been previously explained and demonstrated (see Code C *Annex N paragraph 4*).'

(e) **Code E, paragraph 3.20 (signing master recording label)**
After the third sentence, insert, 'If live-link interpretation has been used, the interviewer should ask the interpreter to observe the removal and sealing of the master recording and to confirm in writing that they have seen it sealed and signed by the interviewer. A clear legible copy of the confirmation signed by the interpreter must be sent via the live-link to the interviewer. The interviewer is responsible for ensuring that the original confirmation and the copy are retained with the case papers for use in evidence if required and must advise the interpreter of their obligation to keep the original confirmation securely for that purpose.'
Note: By virtue of *paragraphs 2.1* and *2.3 of Code F*, this applies when a visually recording to which Code F applies is made.

Notes for Guidance

N1 For purposes other than an interview, audio-only live-link interpretation, for example by telephone (see Code C, paragraph 13.12(b)) may provide an appropriate option until an interpreter is physically present or audio-visual live-link interpretation becomes available. A particular example would be the initial action required when a detained suspect arrives at a police station to inform them of, and to explain, the reasons for their arrest and detention and their various rights and entitlements. Another example would be to inform the suspect by telephone, that an interpreter they will be able to see and hear is being arranged. In these circumstances, telephone live-link interpretation may help to allay the suspect's concerns and contribute to the completion of the risk assessment (see Code C, paragraph 3.6).

N2 The explanation and demonstration of live-link interpretation is intended to help the suspect, solicitor and appropriate adult make an informed decision and to allay any concerns they may have.

N3 Factors affecting availability of a suitable interpreter will include the location of the police station and the language and type of interpretation (oral or sign language) required.

PACE CODE D

CODE OF PRACTICE FOR THE IDENTIFICATION OF PERSONS BY POLICE OFFICERS

Commencement — Transitional Arrangements

This code has effect in relation to any identification procedure carried out after 00:00 on 23 February 2017.

1 Introduction

1.1 This Code of Practice concerns the principal methods used by police to identify people in connection with the investigation of offences and the keeping of accurate and reliable criminal records. The powers and procedures in this code must be used fairly, responsibly, with respect for the people to whom they apply and without unlawful discrimination. Under the Equality Act 2010, section 149 (Public sector Equality Duty), police forces must, in carrying out their functions, have due regard to the need to eliminate unlawful discrimination, harassment, victimisation and any other conduct which is prohibited by that Act, to advance equality of opportunity between people who share a relevant protected characteristic and people who do not share it, and to foster good relations between those persons. The Equality Act also makes it unlawful for police officers to discriminate against, harass or victimise any person on the grounds of the 'protected characteristics' of age, disability, gender reassignment, race, religion or belief, sex and sexual orientation, marriage and civil partnership, pregnancy and maternity when using their powers. See *Note 1A*.

1.2 In this Code, identification by an eye-witness arises when a witness who has seen the offender committing the crime and is given an opportunity to identify a person suspected of involvement in the offence in a video identification, identification parade or similar procedure. These eye-witness identification procedures which are in Part A of section 3 below, are designed to:

- test the eye-witness' ability to identify the suspect as the person they saw on a previous occasion
- provide safeguards against mistaken identification.

While this Code concentrates on visual identification procedures, it does not prevent the police making use of aural identification procedures such as a 'voice identification parade', where they judge that appropriate. See *Note 1B*.

1.2A In this Code, separate provisions in Part B of section 3 below, apply when any person, including a police officer, is asked if they recognise anyone they see in an image as being someone who is known to them and to test their claim that they recognise that person. These separate provisions are not subject to the eye-witnesses identification procedures described in *paragraph 1.2*.

1.2B Part C applies when a film, photograph or image relating to the offence or any description of the suspect is broadcast or published in any national or local media or on any social networking site or on any local or national police communication systems.

1.3 Identification by fingerprints applies when a person's fingerprints are taken to:
- compare with fingerprints found at the scene of a crime
- check and prove convictions
- help to ascertain a person's identity.

1.3A Identification using footwear impressions applies when a person's footwear impressions are taken to compare with impressions found at the scene of a crime.

1.4 Identification by body samples and impressions includes taking samples such as a cheek swab, hair or blood to generate a DNA profile for comparison with material obtained from the scene of a crime, or a victim.

1.5 Taking photographs of arrested people applies to recording and checking identity and locating and tracing persons who:
- are wanted for offences
- fail to answer their bail.

1.6 Another method of identification involves searching and examining detained suspects to find, e.g., marks such as tattoos or scars which may help establish their identity or whether they have been involved in committing an offence.

1.7 The provisions of the Police and Criminal Evidence Act 1984 (PACE) and this Code are designed to make sure fingerprints, samples, impressions and photographs are taken, used and retained, and identification procedures carried out, only when justified and necessary for preventing, detecting or investigating crime. If these provisions are not observed, the application of the relevant procedures in particular cases may be open to question.

1.8 The provisions of this Code do not authorise, or otherwise permit, fingerprints or samples to be taken from a person detained solely for the purposes of assessment under section 136 of the Mental Health Act 1983.

Note for Guidance

1A In paragraph 1.1, under the Equality Act 1949, section 149, the 'relevant protected characteristics' are: age, disability, gender reassignment, pregnancy and maternity, race, religion/belief, sex and sexual orientation. For further detailed guidance and advice on the Equality Act, see: https://www.gov.uk/guidance/equality-act-2010-guidance.

1B See Home Office Circular 57/2003 'Advice on the use of voice identification parades'.

2 General

2.1 This Code must be readily available at all police stations for consultation by:
- police officers and police staff
- detained persons
- members of the public

2.2 The provisions of this Code:
- include the Annexes
- do not include the Notes for guidance.

2.3 Code C, *paragraph 1.4* and the *Notes for guidance* applicable to those provisions apply to this Code with regard to a suspected person who may be mentally disordered or otherwise mentally vulnerable.

2.4 Code C, *paragraphs 1.5* and *1.5A* and the *Notes for guidance* applicable to those provisions apply to this Code with regard to a suspected person who appears to be under the age of 18.

2.5 Code C, *paragraph 1.6* applies to this Code with regard to a suspected person who appears to be blind, seriously visually impaired, deaf, unable to read or speak or has difficulty communicating orally because of a speech impediment.

2.6 In this Code:
- 'appropriate adult' means the same as in Code C, *paragraph 1.7*

- 'solicitor' means the same as in Code C, *paragraph 6.12* and the *Notes for guidance* applicable to those provisions apply to this Code.
- where a search or other procedure under this Code may only be carried out or observed by a person of the same sex as the person to whom the search or procedure applies, the gender of the detainee and other persons present should be established and recorded in line with *Annex L* of Code C.

2.7 References to a custody officer include any police officer who, for the time being, is performing the functions of a custody officer, see *paragraph 1.9* of Code C.

2.8 When a record of any action requiring the authority of an officer of a specified rank is made under this Code, subject to *paragraph 2.18,* the officer's name and rank must be recorded.

2.9 When this Code requires the prior authority or agreement of an officer of at least inspector or superintendent rank, that authority may be given by a sergeant or chief inspector who has been authorised to perform the functions of the higher rank under PACE, section 107.

2.10 Subject to *paragraph 2.18*, all records must be timed and signed by the maker.

2.11 Records must be made in the custody record, unless otherwise specified. In any provision of this Code which allows or requires police officers or police staff to make a record in their report book, the reference to 'report book' shall include any official report book or electronic recording device issued to them that enables the record in question to be made and dealt with in accordance with that provision. References in this Code to written records, forms and signatures include electronic records and forms and electronic confirmation that identifies the person completing the record or form. Chief officers must be satisfied as to the integrity and security of the devices, records and forms to which this *paragraph* applies and that use of those devices, records and forms satisfies relevant data protection legislation. (taken from Code C, *paragraph 1.17).*

2.12 If any procedure in this Code requires a person's consent, the consent of a:

- mentally disordered or otherwise mentally vulnerable person is only valid if given in the presence of the appropriate adult
- juvenile is only valid if their parent's or guardian's consent is also obtained unless the juvenile is under 14, when their parent's or guardian's consent is sufficient in its own right. If the only obstacle to an identification procedure in *section 3* is that a juvenile's parent or guardian refuses consent or reasonable efforts to obtain it have failed, the identification officer may apply the provisions of *paragraph 3.21* (suspect known but not available). See *Note 2A*.

2.13 If a person is blind, seriously visually impaired or unable to read, the custody officer or identification officer shall make sure their solicitor, relative, appropriate adult or some other person likely to take an interest in them and not involved in the investigation is available to help check any documentation. When this Code requires written consent or signing, the person assisting may be asked to sign instead, if the detainee prefers. This paragraph does not require an appropriate adult to be called solely to assist in checking and signing documentation for a person who is not a juvenile, or mentally disordered or otherwise mentally vulnerable (see *Note 2B* and Code C, *paragraph 3.15*).

2.14 If any procedure in this Code requires information to be given to or sought from a suspect, it must be given or sought in the appropriate adult's presence if the suspect is mentally disordered, otherwise mentally vulnerable or a juvenile. If the appropriate adult is not present when the information is first given or sought, the procedure must be repeated in the presence of the appropriate adult when they arrive. If the suspect appears deaf or there is doubt about their hearing or speaking ability or ability to understand English, the custody officer or identification officer must ensure that the necessary arrangements in accordance with Code C are made for an interpreter to assist the suspect.

2.15 Any procedure in this Code involving the participation of a suspect who is mentally disordered, otherwise mentally vulnerable or a juvenile must take place in the presence of the appropriate adult. See Code C, *paragraph 1.4.*

2.15A Any procedure in this Code involving the participation of a witness who is or appears to be mentally disordered, otherwise mentally vulnerable or a juvenile should take place in the presence of a pre-trial support person unless the witness states that they do not want a support person to be present. A support person must not be allowed to prompt any identification of a suspect by a witness. See *Note 2AB.*

2.16 References to:

- 'taking a photograph', include the use of any process to produce a single, still or moving, visual image
- 'photographing a person', should be construed accordingly
- 'photographs', 'films', 'negatives' and 'copies' include relevant visual images recorded, stored, or reproduced through any medium

- 'destruction' includes the deletion of computer data relating to such images or making access to that data impossible

2.17 This Code does not affect or apply to, the powers and procedures:

(i) for requiring and taking samples of breath, blood and urine in relation to driving offences, etc, when under the influence of drink, drugs or excess alcohol under the:
- Road Traffic Act 1988, sections 4 to 11
- Road Traffic Offenders Act 1988, sections 15 and 16
- Transport and Works Act 1992, sections 26 to 38;

(ii) under the Immigration Act 1971, Schedule 2, paragraph 18, for taking photographs, measuring and identifying and taking biometric information (not including DNA) from persons detained or liable to be detained under that Act, Schedule 2, paragraph 16 (Administrative Provisions as to Control on Entry etc.); or for taking fingerprints in accordance with the Immigration and Asylum Act 1999, sections 141 and 142(4), or other methods for collecting information about a person's external physical characteristics provided for by regulations made under that Act, section 144;

(iii) under the Terrorism Act 2000, Schedule 8, for taking photographs, fingerprints, skin impressions, body samples or impressions from people:
- arrested under that Act, section 41,
- detained for the purposes of examination under that Act, Schedule 7, and to whom the Code of Practice issued under that Act, Schedule 14, paragraph 6, applies ('the terrorism provisions')

(iv) for taking photographs, fingerprints, skin impressions, body samples or impressions from people who have been:
- arrested on warrants issued in Scotland, by officers exercising powers mentioned in Part X of the Criminal Justice and Public Order Act 1994;
- arrested or detained without warrant by officers from a police force in Scotland exercising their powers of arrest or detention mentioned in Part X of the Criminal Justice and Public Order Act 1994.

Note: In these cases, police powers and duties and the person's rights and entitlements whilst at a police station in England and Wales are the same as if the person had been arrested in Scotland by a Scottish police officer.

2.18 Nothing in this Code requires the identity of officers or police staff to be recorded or disclosed:

(a) in the case of enquiries linked to the investigation of terrorism;

(b) if the officers or police staff reasonably believe recording or disclosing their names might put them in danger.

In these cases, they shall use their warrant or other identification numbers and the name of their police station. *See Note 2D.*

2.19 In this Code:

(a) 'designated person' means a person other than a police officer, who has specified powers and duties conferred or imposed on them by designation under section 38 or 39 of the Police Reform Act 2002;

(b) any reference to a police officer includes a designated person acting in the exercise or performance of the powers and duties conferred or imposed on them by their designation.

2.20 If a power conferred on a designated person:

(a) allows reasonable force to be used when exercised by a police officer, a designated person exercising that power has the same entitlement to use force;

(b) includes power to use force to enter any premises, that power is not exercisable by that designated person except:

(i) in the company, and under the supervision, of a police officer; or

(ii) for the purpose of:
- saving life or limb; or
- preventing serious damage to property.

2.21 In the case of a detained person, nothing in this Code prevents the custody officer, or other police *officer or* designated person given custody of the detainee by the custody officer for the purposes of the investigation of an offence for which the person is detained, from allowing another person (see *(a)* and *(b)* below) to carry out individual procedures or tasks at the police station if the law allows. However, the officer or designated person given custody remains responsible for making sure the procedures and tasks are carried out correctly in accordance with the Codes of Practice. The other person who is allowed to carry out the procedures or tasks must be *someone who at that time* is:

(a) under the direction and control of the chief officer of the force responsible for the police station in question; or;

(b) providing services under contractual arrangements (but without being employed by the chief officer [of] the police force), to assist a police force in relation to the discharge of its chief officer's functions.

2.22 Designated persons and others mentioned in *sub-paragraphs (a)* and *(b)* of *paragraph 2.21* must have regard to any relevant provisions of the Codes of Practice.

Notes for Guidance

2A *For the purposes of paragraph 2.12, the consent required from a parent or guardian may, for a juvenile in the care of a local authority or voluntary organisation, be given by that authority or organisation. In the case of a juvenile, nothing in paragraph 2.12 requires the parent, guardian or representative of a local authority or voluntary organisation to be present to give their consent, unless they are acting as the appropriate adult under paragraphs 2.14 or 2.15. However, it is important that a parent or guardian not present is fully informed before being asked to consent. They must be given the same information about the procedure and the juvenile's suspected involvement in the offence as the juvenile and appropriate adult. The parent or guardian must also be allowed to speak to the juvenile and the appropriate adult if they wish. Provided the consent is fully informed and is not withdrawn, it may be obtained at any time before the procedure takes place.*

2AB *The Youth Justice and Criminal Evidence Act 1999 guidance 'Achieving Best Evidence in Criminal Proceedings' indicates that a pre-trial support person should accompany a vulnerable witness during any identification procedure unless the witness states that they do not want a support person to be present. It states that this support person should not be (or not be likely to be) a witness in the investigation.*

2B *People who are seriously visually impaired or unable to read may be unwilling to sign police documents. The alternative, i.e. their representative signing on their behalf, seeks to protect the interests of both police and suspects.*

2C *Not used*

2D *The purpose of paragraph 2.18(b) is to protect those involved in serious organised crime investigations or arrests of particularly violent suspects when there is reliable information that those arrested or their associates may threaten or cause harm to the officers. In cases of doubt, an officer of inspector rank or above should be consulted.*

3 Identification and recognition of suspects

Part (A) *Identification of a suspect by an eye-witness*

3.0 This part applies when an eye-witness has seen a person committing a crime or in any other circumstances which tend to prove or disprove the involvement of the person they saw in a crime, for example, close to the scene of the crime, immediately before or immediately after it was committed. It sets out the procedures to be used to test the ability of that eye-witness to identify a person suspected of involvement in the offence ('the suspect') as the person they saw on the previous occasion. This part does not apply to the procedure described in Part B (see *Note 3AA*) which is used to test the ability of someone who is not an eye-witness, to recognise anyone whose image they see.

3.1 A record shall be made of the description of the suspect as first given by the eye-witness. This record must:

(a) be made and kept in a form which enables details of that description to be accurately produced from it, in a visible and legible form, which can be given to the suspect or the suspect's solicitor in accordance with this Code; and

(b) unless otherwise specified, be made before the eye-witness takes part in any identification procedures under *paragraphs 3.5* to *3.10, 3.21, 3.23* or *Annex E* (Showing Photographs to Eye-Witnesses).

A copy of the record shall where practicable, be given to the suspect or their solicitor before any procedures under *paragraphs 3.5* to *3.10, 3.21* or *3.23* are carried out. See *Note 3E.*

3.1A References in this Part:

(a) to the identity of the suspect being 'known' mean that there is sufficient information known to the police to establish, in accordance with Code G (Arrest), that there are reasonable grounds to suspect a particular person of involvement in the offence;

(b) to the suspect being 'available' mean that the suspect is immediately available, or will be available within a reasonably short time, in order that they can be invited to take part in at least one of the eye-witness identification procedures under *paragraphs 3.5* to *3.10* and it is practicable to arrange an effective procedure under *paragraphs 3.5* to *3.10*; and

(c) to the eye-witness identification procedures under *paragraphs 3.5* to *3.10* mean:

- Video identification (*paragraphs 3.5* and *3.6*);
- Identification parade (*paragraphs 3.7* and *3.8*); and
- Group identification (*paragraphs 3.9* and *3.10*).

(a) Cases when the suspect's identity is not known

3.2 In cases when the suspect's identity is not known, an eye-witness may be taken to a particular neighbourhood or place to see whether they can identify the person they saw on a previous occasion. Although the number, age, sex, race, general description and style of clothing of other people present at the location and the way in which any identification is made cannot be controlled, the principles applicable to the formal procedures under *paragraphs 3.5* to *3.10* shall be followed as far as practicable. For example:

(a) where it is practicable to do so, a record should be made of the eye-witness' description of the person they saw on the previous occasion, as in *paragraph 3.1(a)*, before asking the eye-witness to make an identification;

(b) Care must be taken not [to] provide the eye-witness with any information concerning the description of the suspect (if such information is available) and not to direct the eyewitness' attention to any individual unless, taking into account all the circumstances, this cannot be avoided. However, this does not prevent an eye-witness being asked to look carefully at the people around at the time or to look towards a group or in a particular direction, if this appears necessary to make sure that the witness does not overlook a possible suspect simply because the eye-witness is looking in the opposite direction and also to enable the eye-witness to make comparisons between any suspect and others who are in the area;

(c) where there is more than one eye-witness, every effort should be made to keep them separate and eye-witnesses should be taken to see whether they can identify a person independently;

(d) once there is sufficient information to establish, in accordance with *paragraph 3.1A(a)*, that the suspect is 'known', e.g. after the eye-witness makes an identification, the provisions set out from *paragraph 3.4* onwards shall apply for that and any other eyewitnesses in relation to that individual;

(e) the officer or police staff accompanying the eye-witness must record, in their report book, the action taken as soon as practicable and in as much detail, as possible. The record should include:

(i) the date, time and place of the relevant occasion when the eye-witness claims to have previously seen the person committing the offence in question or in any other circumstances which tend to prove or disprove the involvement of the person they saw in a crime (see *paragraph 3.0*); and

(ii) where any identification was made:

- how it was made and the conditions at the time (e.g., the distance the eyewitness was from the suspect, the weather and light);
- if the eye-witness's attention was drawn to the suspect; the reason for this;
- and anything said by the eye-witness or the suspect about the identification or the conduct of the procedure.

See *Note 3F.*

3.3 An eye-witness must not be shown photographs, computerised or artist's composite likenesses or similar likenesses or pictures (including 'E-fit' images) if in accordance with *paragraph 3.1A*, the identity of the suspect is known and they are available to take part in one of the procedures under *paragraphs 3.5* to *3.10*. If the suspect's identity is not known, the showing of any such images to an eye-witness to see if they can identify a person whose image they are shown as the person they saw on a previous occasion must be done in accordance with *Annex E*.

(b) Cases when the suspect is known and available

3.4 If the suspect's identity is known to the police (see *paragraph 3.1A(a)*) and they are available (see *paragraph 3.1A(b)*), the identification procedures that may be used are set out in *paragraphs 3.5* to *3.10* below as follows:

(i) video identification;

(ii) identification parade; or

(iii) group identification.

(i) Video identification

3.5 A 'video identification' is when the eye-witness is shown images of a known suspect, together with similar images of others who resemble the suspect. *Moving* images must be used unless the conditions in *sub-paragraph (a)* or *(b)* below apply:

(a) this sub-paragraph applies if:

(i) the identification officer, in consultation with the officer in charge of the investigation, is satisfied that because of aging, or other physical changes or differences, the appearance of the suspect has significantly changed since the previous occasion when the eye-witness claims to have seen the suspect (see *paragraph 3.0* and *Note 3ZA*);

(ii) an image (moving or still) is available which the identification officer and the officer in charge of the investigation reasonably believe shows the appearance of the suspect as it was at the time the suspect was seen by the eye-witness; and

(iii) having regard to the extent of change and the purpose of eye-witness identification procedures (see *paragraph 3.0*), the identification officer believes that that such an image should be shown to the eye-witness.

In such a case, the identification officer may arrange a video identification procedure using the image described in (ii). In accordance with the 'Notice to suspect' (see *paragraph 3.17(vi)*), the suspect must first be given an opportunity to provide their own image(s) for use in the procedure but it is for the identification officer and officer in charge of the investigation to decide whether, following (ii) and (iii), any image(s) provided by the suspect should be used.

A video identification using an image described above may, at the discretion of the identification officer be arranged in addition to, or as an alternative to, a video identification using *moving* images taken after the suspect has been given the information and notice described in *paragraphs 3.17* and *3.18*.

See *paragraph 3.21* and *Note 3D* in any case where the suspect deliberately takes steps to frustrate the eye-witness identification arrangements and procedures.

(b) this sub-paragraph applies if, in accordance with *paragraph 2A* of *Annex A* of this Code, the identification officer does not consider that replication of a physical feature or concealment of the location of the feature can be achieved using a moving image. In these cases, still images may be used.

3.6 Video identifications must be carried out in accordance with *Annex A*.

(ii) Identification parade

3.7 An 'identification parade' is when the eye-witness sees the suspect in a line of others who resemble the suspect.

3.8 Identification parades must be carried out in accordance with *Annex B*.

(iii) Group identification

3.9 A 'group identification' is when the eye-witness sees the suspect in an informal group of people.

3.10 Group identifications must be carried out in accordance with *Annex C*.

Arranging eye-witness identification procedures – duties of identification officer

3.11 Except as provided for in *paragraph 3.19*, the arrangements for, and conduct of, the eyewitness identification procedures in *paragraphs 3.5* to *3.10* and circumstances in which any such identification procedure must be held shall be the responsibility of an officer not below inspector rank who is not involved with the investigation ('the identification officer'). The identification officer may direct another officer or police staff, see *paragraph 2.21*, to make arrangements for, and to conduct, any of these identification procedures and except as provided for in *paragraph 7* of *Annex A*, any reference in this section to the identification officer includes the officer or police staff to whom the arrangements for, and/or conduct of, any of these procedure has been delegated. In delegating these arrangements and procedures, the identification officer must be able to supervise effectively and either intervene or be contacted for advice. Where any action referred to in this paragraph is taken by another officer or police staff at the direction of the identification officer, the outcome shall, as soon as practicable, be reported to the identification officer. For the purpose of these procedures, the identification officer retains overall responsibility for ensuring that the procedure complies with this Code and in addition, in the case of detained suspect, their care and treatment until returned to the custody officer. Except as permitted by this Code, no officer or any other person involved with the investigation of the case against the suspect may take any part in these procedures or act as the identification officer.

This paragraph does not prevent the identification officer from consulting the officer in charge of the investigation to determine which procedure to use. When an identification procedure is required, in the interest of fairness to suspects and eye-witnesses, it must be held as soon as practicable.

Circumstances in which an eye-witness identification procedure must be held

3.12 If, before any identification procedure set out in *paragraphs 3.5* to *3.10* has been held

(a) an eye-witness has identified a suspect or purported to have identified them; or

(b) there is an eye-witness available who expresses an ability to identify the suspect; or

(c) there is a reasonable chance of an eye-witness being able to identify the suspect,

and the eye-witness in (a) to (c) has not been given an opportunity to identify the suspect in any of the procedures set out in *paragraphs 3.5* to *3.10*, then an identification procedure shall be held if the suspect disputes being the person the eye-witness claims to have seen on a previous occasion (see *paragraph 3.0*), unless:

(i) it is not practicable to hold any such procedure; or
(ii) any such procedure would serve no useful purpose in proving or disproving whether the suspect was involved in committing the offence, for example
- where the suspect admits being at the scene of the crime and gives an account of what took place and the eye-witness does not see anything which contradicts that; or
- when it is not disputed that the suspect is already known to the eye-witness who claims to have recognised them when seeing them commit the crime.

3.13 An eye-witness identification procedure may also be held if the officer in charge of the investigation, after consultation with the identification officer, considers it would be useful.

Selecting an eye-witness identification procedure

3.14 If, because of *paragraph 3.12*, an identification procedure is to be held, the suspect shall initially be invited to take part in a video identification unless:

(a) a video identification is not practicable; or
(b) an identification parade is both practicable and more suitable than a video identification; or
(c) *paragraph 3.16* applies.

The identification officer and the officer in charge of the investigation shall consult each other to determine which option is to be offered. An identification parade may not be practicable because of factors relating to the witnesses, such as their number, state of health, availability and travelling requirements. A video identification would normally be more suitable if it could be arranged and completed sooner than an identification parade. Before an option is offered the suspect must also be reminded of their entitlement to have free legal advice, see Code C, *paragraph 6.5*.

3.15 A suspect who refuses the identification procedure in which the suspect is first invited to take part shall be asked to state their reason for refusing and may get advice from their solicitor and/or if present, their appropriate adult. The suspect, solicitor and/or appropriate adult shall be allowed to make representations about why another procedure should be used. A record should be made of the reasons for refusal and any representations made. After considering any reasons given, and representations made, the identification officer shall, if appropriate, arrange for the suspect to be invited to take part in an alternative which the officer considers suitable and practicable. If the officer decides it is not suitable and practicable to invite the suspect to take part in an alternative identification procedure, the reasons for that decision shall be recorded.

3.16 A suspect may initially be invited to take part in a group identification if the officer in charge of the investigation considers it is more suitable than a video identification or an identification parade and the identification officer considers it practicable to arrange.

Notice to suspect

3.17 Unless *paragraph 3.20* applies, before any eye-witness identification procedure set out in *paragraphs 3.5* to *3.10* is arranged, the following shall be explained to the suspect:

(i) the purpose of the procedure (see *paragraph 3.0*);
(ii) their entitlement to free legal advice; see Code C, *paragraph 6.5*;
(iii) the procedures for holding it, including their right, subject to *Annex A, paragraph 9*, to have a solicitor or friend present;
(iv) that they do not have to consent to or co-operate in the procedure;
(v) that if they do not consent to, and co-operate in, a procedure, their refusal may be given in evidence in any subsequent trial and police may proceed covertly without their consent or make other arrangements to test whether an eye-witness can identify them, see *paragraph 3.21;*
(vi) whether, for the purposes of a video identification procedure, images of them have previously been obtained either:
- in accordance with *paragraph 3.20*, and if so, that they may co-operate in providing further, suitable images to be used instead; or
- in accordance with *paragraph 3.5(a)*, and if so, that they may provide their own images for the identification officer to consider using.

(vii) if appropriate, the special arrangements for juveniles;
(viii) if appropriate, the special arrangements for mentally disordered or otherwise mentally vulnerable people;
(ix) that if they significantly alter their appearance between being offered an identification procedure and any attempt to hold an identification procedure, this may be given in evidence if the case comes to trial, and the identification officer may then consider other forms of identification, see *paragraph 3.21* and *Note 3C*;

(x) that a moving image or photograph may be taken of them when they attend for any identification procedure;
(xi) whether, before their identity became known, the eye-witness was shown photographs, a computerised or artist's composite likeness or similar likeness or image by the police, see *Note 3B;*
(xii) that if they change their appearance before an identification parade, it may not be practicable to arrange one on the day or subsequently and, because of the appearance change, the identification officer may consider alternative methods of identification, see *Note 3C*;
(xiii) that they or their solicitor will be provided with details of the description of the suspect as first given by any eye-witnesses who are to attend the procedure or confrontation, see *paragraph 3.1.*

3.18 This information must also be recorded in a written notice handed to the suspect. The suspect must be given a reasonable opportunity to read the notice, after which, they should be asked to sign a copy of the notice to indicate if they are willing to co-operate with the making of a video or take part in the identification parade or group identification. The signed copy shall be retained by the identification officer.

3.19 In the case of a detained suspect, the duties under *paragraphs 3.17* and *3.18* may be performed by the custody officer or by another officer or police staff not involved in the investigation as directed by the custody officer, if:

(a) it is proposed to release the suspect in order that an identification procedure can be arranged and carried out and an inspector is not available to act as the identification officer, see *paragraph 3.11*, before the suspect leaves the station; or
(b) it is proposed to keep the suspect in police detention whilst the procedure is arranged and carried out and waiting for an inspector to act as the identification officer, see *paragraph 3.11,* would cause unreasonable delay to the investigation.

The officer concerned shall inform the identification officer of the action taken and give them the signed copy of the notice. See *Note 3C.*

3.20 If the identification officer and officer in charge of the investigation suspect, on reasonable grounds that if the suspect was given the information and notice as in *paragraphs 3.17* and *3.18*, they would then take steps to avoid being seen by a witness in any identification procedure, the identification officer may arrange for images of the suspect suitable for use in a video identification procedure to be obtained before giving the information and notice. If suspect's images are obtained in these circumstances, the suspect may, for the purposes of a video identification procedure, co-operate in providing new images which if suitable, would be used instead, see *paragraph 3.17(vi).*

(c) Cases when the suspect is known but not available

3.21 When a known suspect is not available or has ceased to be available, see *paragraph 3.1A*, the identification officer may make arrangements for a video identification (see *paragraph 3.5* and *Annex A*). If necessary, the identification officer may follow the video identification procedures using any suitable moving or still images and these may be obtained covertly if necessary. Alternatively, the identification officer may make arrangements for a group identification without the suspect's consent (see *Annex C, paragraph 34*). See *Note 3D*. These provisions may also be applied to juveniles where the consent of their parent or guardian is either refused or reasonable efforts to obtain that consent have failed (see *paragraph 2.12*).

3.22 Any covert activity should be strictly limited to that necessary to test the ability of the eyewitness to identify the suspect as the person they saw on the relevant previous occasion.

3.23 The identification officer may arrange for the suspect to be confronted by the eye-witness if none of the options referred to in *paragraphs 3.5* to *3.10* or *3.21* are practicable. A 'confrontation' is when the suspect is directly confronted by the eye-witness. A confrontation does not require the suspect's consent. Confrontations must be carried out in accordance with *Annex D.*

3.24 Requirements for information to be given to, or sought from, a suspect or for the suspect to be given an opportunity to view images before they are shown to an eye-witness, do not apply if the suspect's lack of co-operation prevents the necessary action.

(d) Documentation

3.25 A record shall be made of the video identification, identification parade, group identification or confrontation on forms provided for the purpose.

3.26 If the identification officer considers it is not practicable to hold a video identification or identification parade requested by the suspect, the reasons shall be recorded and explained to the suspect.

3.27 A record shall be made of a person's failure or refusal to co-operate in a video identification, identification parade or group identification and, if applicable, of the grounds for obtaining images in accordance with *paragraph 3.20.*

(e) Not used

3.28 *Not used.*

3.29 *Not used.*

(f) Destruction and retention of photographs taken or used in eye-witness identification procedures

3.30 PACE, section 64A, see *paragraph 5.12*, provides powers to take photographs of suspects and allows these photographs to be used or disclosed only for purposes related to the prevention or detection of crime, the investigation of offences or the conduct of prosecutions by, or on behalf of, police or other law enforcement and prosecuting authorities inside and outside the United Kingdom or the enforcement of a sentence. After being so used or disclosed, they may be retained but can only be used or disclosed for the same purposes.

3.31 Subject to *paragraph 3.33,* the photographs (and all negatives and copies), of suspects *not* taken in accordance with the provisions in *paragraph 5.12* which are taken for the purposes of, or in connection with, the identification procedures in *paragraphs 3.5* to *3.10, 3.21* or *3.23* must be destroyed unless the suspect:

(a) is charged with, or informed they may be prosecuted for, a recordable offence;

(b) is prosecuted for a recordable offence;

(c) is cautioned for a recordable offence or given a warning or reprimand in accordance with the Crime and Disorder Act 1998 for a recordable offence; or

(d) gives informed consent, in writing, for the photograph or images to be retained for purposes described in *paragraph 3.30.*

3.32 When *paragraph 3.31* requires the destruction of any photograph, the person must be given an opportunity to witness the destruction or to have a certificate confirming the destruction if they request one within five days of being informed that the destruction is required.

3.33 Nothing in *paragraph 3.31* affects any separate requirement under the Criminal Procedure and Investigations Act 1996 to retain material in connection with criminal investigations.

Part (B) *Recognition by controlled showing of films, photographs and images*

3.34 This Part of this section applies when, for the purposes of obtaining evidence of recognition, arrangements are made for a person, including a police officer, who is not an eye-witness (see *Note 3AA)*:

(a) to view a film, photograph or any other visual medium; and

(b) on the occasion of the viewing, to be asked whether they recognise anyone whose image is shown in the material as someone who is known to them.

The arrangements for such viewings may be made by the officer in charge of the relevant investigation. Although there is no requirement for the identification officer to make the arrangements or to be consulted about the arrangements, nothing prevents this. See *Notes 3AA* and *3G.*

3.35 To provide safeguards against mistaken recognition and to avoid any possibility of collusion, on the occasion of the viewing, the arrangements should ensure:

(a) that the films, photographs and other images are shown on an individual basis;

(b) that any person who views the material;

(i) is unable to communicate with any other individual to whom the material has been, or is to be, shown;

(ii) is not reminded of any photograph or description of any individual whose image is shown or given any other indication as to the identity of any such individual;

(iii) is not . . . told whether a previous witness has recognised any one;

(c) that immediately before a person views the material, they are told that:

(i) an individual who is known to them may, or may not, appear in the material they are shown and that if they do not recognise anyone, they should say so;

(ii) at any point, they may ask to see a particular part of the material frozen for them to study and there is no limit on how many times they can view the whole or any part or parts of the material; and

(d) that the person who views the material is not asked to make any decision as to whether they recognise anyone whose image they have seen as someone known to them until they have seen the whole of the material at least twice, unless the officer in charge of the viewing decides that because of the number of images the person has been invited to view, it would not be reasonable to ask them to view the whole of the material for a second time. A record of this decision must be included in the record that is made in accordance with *paragraph 3.36.* (see *Note 3G*).

3.36 A record of the circumstances and conditions under which the person is given an opportunity to recognise an individual must be made and the record must include:

(a) whether the person knew or was given information concerning the name or identity of any suspect;

(b) what the person has been told *before* the viewing about the offence, the person(s) depicted in the images or the offender and by whom;
(c) how and by whom the witness was asked to view the image or look at the individual;
(d) whether the viewing was alone or with others and if with others, the reason for it;
(e) the arrangements under which the person viewed the film or saw the individual and by whom those arrangements were made;
(f) subject to *paragraph 2.18*, the name and rank of the officer responsible for deciding that the viewing arrangements should be made in accordance with this Part;
(g) the date time and place images were viewed or further viewed or the individual was seen;
(h) the times between which the images were viewed or the individual was seen;
(i) how the viewing of images or sighting of the individual was controlled and by whom;
(j) whether the person was familiar with the location shown in any images or the place where they saw the individual and if so, why;
(k) whether or not, on this occasion, the person claims to recognise any image shown, or any individual seen, as being someone known to them, and if they do:
 (i) the reason;
 (ii) the words of recognition;
 (iii) any expressions of doubt; and
 (iv) what features of the image or the individual triggered the recognition.

3.37 The record required under *paragraph 3.36* may be made by the person who views the image or sees the individual and makes the recognition; and if applicable, by the officer or police staff in charge of showing the images to that person or in charge of the conditions under which that person sees the individual. The person must be asked to read and check the completed record and as applicable, confirm that it is correctly and accurately reflects the part they played in the viewing (see *Note 3H*).

Part (C) *Recognition by uncontrolled viewing of films, photographs and images*

3.38 This Part applies when, for the purpose of identifying and tracing suspects, films and photographs of incidents or other images are:
(a) shown to the public (which may include police officers and police staff as well as members of the public) through the national or local media or any social media networking site; or
(b) circulated through local or national police communication systems for viewing by police officers and police staff; and the viewing is not formally controlled and supervised as set out in Part B.

3.39 A copy of the relevant material released to the national or local media for showing as described in *sub-paragraph 3.38(a)*, shall be kept. The suspect or their solicitor shall be allowed to view such material before any eye-witness identification procedure under *paragraphs 3.5* to *3.10, 3.21* or *3.23* of Part A are carried out, provided it is practicable and would not unreasonably delay the investigation. This paragraph does not affect any separate requirement under the Criminal Procedure and Investigations Act 1996 to retain material in connection with criminal investigations that might apply to *sub-paragraphs 3.38(a)* and *(b)*.

3.40 Each eye-witness involved in any eye-witness identification procedure under *paragraphs 3.5* to *3.10, 3.21* or *3.23* shall be asked, *after they have taken part*, whether they have seen any film, photograph or image relating to the offence or any description of the suspect which has been broadcast or published as described in *paragraph 3.38(a)* and their reply recorded. If they have, they should be asked to give details of the circumstances and subject to the eye-witness's recollection, the record described in *paragraph 3.41* should be completed.

3.41 As soon as practicable after an individual (member of the public, police officer or police staff) indicates in response to a viewing that they may have information relating to the identity and whereabouts of anyone they have seen in that viewing, arrangements should be made to ensure that they are asked to give details of the circumstances and, subject to the individual's recollection, a record of the circumstances and conditions under which the viewing took place is made. This record shall be made in accordance with the provisions of *paragraph 3.36* insofar as they can be applied to the viewing in question (*see Note 3H*).

Notes for Guidance

3AA The eye-witness identification procedures in Part A should not be used to test whether a witness can recognise a person as someone they know and would be able to give evidence of recognition along the lines that 'On (describe date, time, location and circumstances) I saw an image of an individual who I recognised as AB.' In these cases, the procedures in Part B shall apply if the viewing is controlled and the procedure in Part C shall apply if the viewing is not controlled.

3ZA *In paragraph 3.5(a)(i), examples of physical changes or differences that the identification officer may wish to consider include hair style and colour, weight, facial hair, wearing or removal of spectacles and tinted contact lenses, facial injuries, tattoos and makeup.*

3A *Except for the provisions of Annex E, paragraph 1, a police officer who is a witness for the purposes of this part of the Code is subject to the same principles and procedures as a civilian witness.*

3B *When an eye-witness attending an identification procedure has previously been shown photographs, or been shown or provided with computerised or artist's composite likenesses, or similar likenesses or pictures, it is the officer in charge of the investigation's responsibility to make the identification officer aware of this.*

3C *The purpose of paragraph 3.19 is to avoid or reduce delay in arranging identification procedures by enabling the required information and warnings, see sub-paragraphs 3.17(ix) and 3.17(xii), to be given at the earliest opportunity.*

3D *Paragraph 3.21 would apply when a known suspect becomes 'unavailable' and thereby delays or frustrates arrangements for obtaining identification evidence. It also applies when a suspect refuses or fails to take part in a video identification, an identification parade or a group identification, or refuses or fails to take part in the only practicable options from that list. It enables any suitable images of the suspect, moving or still, which are available or can be obtained, to be used in an identification procedure. Examples include images from custody and other CCTV systems and from visually recorded interview records, see Code F Note for Guidance 2D.*

3E *When it is proposed to show photographs to a witness in accordance with Annex E, it is the responsibility of the officer in charge of the investigation to confirm to the officer responsible for supervising and directing the showing, that the first description of the suspect given by that eye-witness has been recorded. If this description has not been recorded, the procedure under Annex E must be postponed, see Annex E, paragraph 2.*

3F *The admissibility and value of identification evidence obtained when carrying out the procedure under paragraph 3.2 may be compromised if:*

(a) *before a person is identified, the eye-witness' attention is specifically drawn to that person; or*

(b) *the suspect's identity becomes known before the procedure.*

3G *The admissibility and value of evidence of recognition obtained when carrying out the procedures in Part B may be compromised if, before the person is recognised, the witness who has claimed to know them is given or is made, or becomes aware of, information about the person which was not previously known to them personally but which they have purported to rely on to support their claim that the person is in fact known to them.*

3H *It is important that the record referred to in paragraphs 3.36 and 3.41 is made as soon as practicable after the viewing and whilst it is fresh in the mind of the individual who makes the recognition.*

4 Identification by fingerprints and footwear impressions

(A) *Taking fingerprints in connection with a criminal investigation*

(a) General

4.1 References to 'fingerprints' means any record, produced by any method, of the skin pattern and other physical characteristics or features of a person's:

(i) fingers; or

(ii) palms.

(b) Action

4.2 A person's fingerprints may be taken in connection with the investigation of an offence only with their consent or if *paragraph 4.3* applies. If the person is at a police station, consent must be in writing.

4.3 PACE, section 61, provides powers to take fingerprints without consent from any person aged ten or over as follows:

(a) under *section 61(3)*, from a person detained at a police station in consequence of being arrested for a recordable offence, see *Note 4A*, if they have not had their fingerprints taken in the course of the investigation of the offence unless those previously taken fingerprints are not a complete set or some or all of those fingerprints are not of sufficient quality to allow satisfactory analysis, comparison or matching.

(b) under *section 61(4)*, from a person detained at a police station who has been charged with a recordable offence, see *Note 4A*, or informed they will be reported for such an offence if they have not had their fingerprints taken in the course of the investigation of the offence unless those previously taken fingerprints are not a complete set or some or all of those fingerprints are not of sufficient quality to allow satisfactory analysis, comparison or matching.

(c) under *section 61(4A)*, from a person who has been bailed to appear at a court or police station if the person:
   (i) has answered to bail for a person whose fingerprints were taken previously and there are reasonable grounds for believing they are not the same person; or
   (ii) who has answered to bail claims to be a different person from a person whose fingerprints were previously taken;

   and in either case, the court or an officer of inspector rank or above, authorises the fingerprints to be taken at the court or police station (an inspector's authority may be given in writing or orally and confirmed in writing, as soon as practicable);

(ca) under *section 61(5A)* from a person who has been arrested for a recordable offence and released if the person:
   (i) is on bail and has not had their fingerprints taken in the course of the investigation of the offence, or;
   (ii) has had their fingerprints taken in the course of the investigation of the offence, but they do not constitute a complete set or some, or all, of the fingerprints are not of sufficient quality to allow satisfactory analysis, comparison or matching.

(cb) under *section 61(5B)* from a person not detained at a police station who has been charged with a recordable offence or informed they will be reported for such an offence if:
   (i) they have not had their fingerprints taken in the course of the investigation; or
   (ii) their fingerprints have been taken in the course of the investigation of the offence but either:
      - they do not constitute a complete set or some, or all, of the fingerprints are not of sufficient quality to allow satisfactory analysis, comparison or matching; or
      - the investigation was discontinued but subsequently resumed and, before the resumption, their fingerprints were destroyed pursuant to section 63D(3).

(d) under *section 61(6)*, from a person who has been:
   (i) convicted of a recordable offence; or
   (ii) given a caution in respect of a recordable offence (see *Note 4A*) which, at the time of the caution, the person admitted;

   if, since being convicted or cautioned:
      - their fingerprints have not been taken; or
      - their fingerprints which have been taken do not constitute a complete set or some, or all, of the fingerprints are not of sufficient quality to allow satisfactory analysis, comparison or matching;

   and in either case, an officer of inspector rank or above is satisfied that taking the fingerprints is necessary to assist in the prevention or detection of crime and authorises the taking;

(e) under *section 61(6A)* from a person a constable reasonably suspects is committing or attempting to commit, or has committed or attempted to commit, any offence if either:
   (i) the person's name is unknown to, and cannot be readily ascertained by, the constable; or
   (ii) the constable has reasonable grounds for doubting whether a name given by the person as their name is their real name.

   Note: fingerprints taken under this power are not regarded as having been taken in the course of the investigation of an offence. [See *Note 4C*]

(f) under *section 61(6D)* from a person who has been convicted outside England and Wales of an offence which if committed in England and Wales would be a qualifying offence as defined by PACE, section 65A (see *Note 4AB*) if:
   (i) the person's fingerprints have not been taken previously under this power or their fingerprints have been so taken on a previous occasion but they do not constitute a complete set or some, or all, of the fingerprints are not of sufficient quality to allow satisfactory analysis, comparison or matching; and
   (ii) a police officer of inspector rank or above is satisfied that taking fingerprints is necessary to assist in the prevention or detection of crime and authorises them to be taken.

4.4 PACE, section 63A(4) and Schedule 2A provide powers to:

(a) make a requirement (in accordance with *Annex G*) for a person to attend a police station to have their fingerprints taken in the exercise of one of the following powers (described in *paragraph 4.3* above) within certain periods as follows:
   (i) *section 61(5A)* – Persons arrested for a recordable offence and released, see *paragraph 4.3(ca)*: In the case of a person whose fingerprints were taken in the course of the investigation but those fingerprints do not constitute a complete set or some, or all, of the fingerprints are not of sufficient quality, the requirement may not be made more than six months

from the day the investigating officer was informed that the fingerprints previously taken were incomplete or below standard. In the case of a person whose fingerprints were destroyed prior to the resumption of the investigation, the requirement may not be made more than six months from the day on which the investigation resumed.

(ii) *section 61(5B)* – Persons not detained at a police station charged etc. with a recordable offence, see *paragraph 4.3(cb)*: The requirement may not be made more than six months from:

- the day the person was charged or informed that they would be reported,
- if fingerprints have not been taken in the course of the investigation of the offence; or
- the day the investigating officer was informed that the fingerprints previously taken were incomplete or below standard, if fingerprints have been taken in the course of the investigation but those fingerprints do not constitute a complete set or some, or all, of the fingerprints are not of sufficient quality; or
- the day on which the investigation was resumed, in the case of a person whose fingerprints were destroyed prior to the resumption of the investigation.

(iii) *section 61(6)* – Persons convicted or cautioned for a recordable offence in England and Wales, see *paragraph 4.3(d)*: Where the offence for which the person was convicted or cautioned is a qualifying offence (see *Note 4AB*), there is no time limit for the exercise of this power. Where the conviction or caution is for a recordable offence which is not a qualifying offence, the requirement may not be made more than two years from:

- in the case of a person who has not had their fingerprints taken since the conviction or caution, the day on which the person was convicted or cautioned, or, if later, the day on which Schedule 2A came into force (March 7, 2011), ; or
- in the case of a person whose fingerprints have been taken in the course of the investigation but those fingerprints do not constitute a complete set or some, or all, of the fingerprints are not of sufficient quality, the day on which an officer from the force investigating the offence was informed that the fingerprints previously taken were incomplete or below standard, or, if later, the day on which Schedule 2A came into force (March 7, 2011).

(iv) *section 61(6D)* – A person who has been convicted of a qualifying offence (see *Note 4AB*) outside England and Wales, see *paragraph 4.3(g)*: There is no time limit for making the requirement.

Note: A person who has had their fingerprints taken under any of the powers in section 61 mentioned in *paragraph 4.3* on two occasions in relation to any offence may not be required under Schedule 2A to attend a police station for their fingerprints to be taken again under section 61 in relation to that offence, unless authorised by an officer of inspector rank or above. The fact of the authorisation and the reasons for giving it must be recorded as soon as practicable.

(b) arrest, without warrant, a person who fails to comply with the requirement.

4.5 A person's fingerprints may be taken, as above, electronically.

4.6 Reasonable force may be used, if necessary, to take a person's fingerprints without their consent under the powers as in *paragraphs 4.3* and *4.4*.

4.7 Before any fingerprints are taken:

(a) without consent under any power mentioned in *paragraphs 4.3* and *4.4* above, the person must be informed of:

(i) the reason their fingerprints are to be taken;

(ii) the power under which they are to be taken; and

(iii) the fact that the relevant authority has been given if any power mentioned in *paragraph 4.3(c), (d)* or *(f)* applies

(b) with or without consent at a police station or elsewhere, the person must be informed:

(i) that their fingerprints may be subject of a speculative search against other fingerprints, see *Note 4B*; and

(ii) that their fingerprints may be retained in accordance with *Annex F, Part (a)* unless they were taken under the power mentioned in *paragraph 4.3(e)* when they must be destroyed after they have being checked (see *Note 4C*).

(c) Documentation

4.8A A record must be made as soon as practicable after the fingerprints are taken, of:

- the matters in *paragraph 4.7(a)(i)* to *(iii)* and the fact that the person has been informed of those matters; and
- the fact that the person has been informed of the matters in *paragraph 4.7(b)(i)* and *(ii)*.

The record must be made in the person's custody record if they are detained at a police station when the fingerprints are taken.

4.8 If force is used, a record shall be made of the circumstances and those present.

4.9 *Not used*

(B) *Not used*

4.10 *Not used*

4.11 *Not used*

4.12 *Not used*

4.13 *Not used*

4.14 *Not used*

4.15 *Not used*

(C) *Taking footwear impressions in connection with a criminal investigation*

(a) Action

4.16 Impressions of a person's footwear may be taken in connection with the investigation of an offence only with their consent or if *paragraph 4.17* applies. If the person is at a police station consent must be in writing.

4.17 PACE, section 61A, provides power for a police officer to take footwear impressions without consent from any person over the age of ten years who is detained at a police station:

(a) in consequence of being arrested for a recordable offence, see *Note 4A*; or if the detainee has been charged with a recordable offence, or informed they will be reported for such an offence; and

(b) the detainee has not had an impression of their footwear taken in the course of the investigation of the offence unless the previously taken impression is not complete or is not of sufficient quality to allow satisfactory analysis, comparison or matching (whether in the case in question or generally).

4.18 Reasonable force may be used, if necessary, to take a footwear impression from a detainee without consent under the power in *paragraph 4.17*.

4.19 Before any footwear impression is taken with, or without, consent as above, the person must be informed:

(a) of the reason the impression is to be taken;

(b) that the impression may be retained and may be subject of a speculative search against other impressions, see *Note 4B*, unless destruction of the impression is required in accordance with *Annex F, Part B*.

(b) Documentation

4.20 A record must be made, as soon as possible, of the reason for taking a person's footwear impressions without consent. If force is used, a record shall be made of the circumstances and those present.

4.21 A record shall be made when a person has been informed under the terms of *paragraph 4.19(b)*, of the possibility that their footwear impressions may be subject of a speculative search.

Notes for Guidance

4A *References to 'recordable offences' in this Code relate to those offences for which convictions or cautions may be recorded in national police records. See PACE, section 27(4). The recordable offences current at the time when this Code was prepared, are any offences which carry a sentence of imprisonment on conviction (irrespective of the period, or the age of the offender or actual sentence passed) as well as the non-imprisonable offences under the Vagrancy Act 1824 sections 3 and 4 (begging and persistent begging), the Street Offences Act 1959, section 1 (loitering or soliciting for purposes of prostitution), the Road Traffic Act 1988, section 25 (tampering with motor vehicles), the Criminal Justice and Public Order Act 1994, section 167 (touting for hire car services) and others listed in the National Police Records (Recordable Offences) Regulations 2000 as amended.*

4AB *A qualifying offence is one of the offences specified in PACE, section 65A. These include offences which involve the use or threat of violence or unlawful force against persons, sexual offences, offences against children and other offences, for example:*

- *murder, false imprisonment, kidnapping contrary to Common law*
- *manslaughter, conspiracy to murder, threats to kill, wounding with intent to cause grievous bodily harm (GBH), causing GBH and assault occasioning actual bodily harm contrary to the Offences Against the Person Act 1861;*
- *criminal possession or use of firearms contrary to sections 16 to 18 of the Firearms Act 1968;*

- *robbery, burglary and aggravated burglary contrary to sections 8, 9 or 10 of the Theft Act 1968 or an offence under section 12A of that Act involving an accident which caused a person's death;*
- *criminal damage required to be charged as arson contrary to section 1 of the Criminal Damage Act 1971;*
- *taking, possessing and showing indecent photographs of children contrary to section 1 of the Protection of Children Act 1978;*
- *rape, sexual assault, child sex offences, exposure and other offences contrary to the Sexual Offences Act 2003.*

4B Fingerprints, footwear impressions or a DNA sample (and the information derived from it) taken from a person arrested on suspicion of being involved in a recordable offence, or charged with such an offence, or informed they will be reported for such an offence, may be subject of a speculative search. This means the fingerprints, footwear impressions or DNA sample may be checked against other fingerprints, footwear impressions and DNA records held by, or on behalf of, the police and other law enforcement authorities in, or outside, the UK, or held in connection with, or as a result of, an investigation of an offence inside or outside the UK.

4C The power under section 61(6A) of PACE described in paragraph 4.3(e) allows fingerprints of a suspect who has not been arrested, and whose name is not known or cannot be ascertained, or who gave a doubtful name, to be taken in connection with any offence (whether recordable or not) using a mobile device and then checked on the street against the database containing the national fingerprint collection. Fingerprints taken under this power cannot be retained after they have been checked. The results may make an arrest for the suspected offence based on the name condition unnecessary (see Code G, paragraph 2.9(a)) and enable the offence to be disposed of without arrest, for example, by summons/charging by post, penalty notice or words of advice. If arrest for a non-recordable offence is necessary for any other reasons, this power may also be exercised at the station. Before the power is exercised, the officer should:

- *inform the person of the nature of the suspected offence and why they are suspected of committing it.*
- *give them a reasonable opportunity to establish their real name before deciding that their name is unknown and cannot be readily ascertained or that there are reasonable grounds to doubt that a name they have given is their real name.*
- *as applicable, inform the person of the reason why their name is not known and cannot be readily ascertained or of the grounds for doubting that a name they have given is their real name, including, for example, the reason why a particular document the person has produced to verify their real name, is not sufficient.*

4D Not used.

5 Examinations to establish identity and the taking of photographs

(A) *Detainees at police stations*

(a) Searching or examination of detainees at police stations

5.1 PACE, section 54A(1), allows a detainee at a police station to be searched or examined or both, to establish:

(a) whether they have any marks, features or injuries that would tend to identify them as a person involved in the commission of an offence and to photograph any identifying marks, see *paragraph 5.5*; or

(b) their identity, see *Note 5A*.

A person detained at a police station to be searched under a stop and search power, see Code A, is not a detainee for the purposes of these powers.

5.2 A search and/or examination to find marks under section 54A(1)(a) may be carried out without the detainee's consent, see *paragraph 2.12*, only if authorised by an officer of at least inspector rank when consent has been withheld or it is not practicable to obtain consent, see *Note 5D*.

5.3 A search or examination to establish a suspect's identity under section 54A (1) (b) may be carried out without the detainee's consent, see *paragraph 2.12*, only if authorised by an officer of at least inspector rank when the detainee has refused to identify themselves or the authorising officer has reasonable grounds for suspecting the person is not who they claim to be.

5.4 Any marks that assist in establishing the detainee's identity, or their identification as a person involved in the commission of an offence, are identifying marks. Such marks may be photographed with the detainee's consent, see *paragraph 2.12*; or without their consent if it is withheld or it is not practicable to obtain it, see *Note 5D*.

5.5 A detainee may only be searched, examined and photographed under section 54A, by a police officer of the same sex.

5.6 Any photographs of identifying marks, taken under section 54A, may be used or disclosed only for purposes related to the prevention or detection of crime, the investigation of offences or the conduct of prosecutions by, or on behalf of, police or other law enforcement and prosecuting authorities inside, and outside, the UK. After being so used or disclosed, the photograph may be retained but must not be used or disclosed except for these purposes, see *Note 5B*.

5.7 The powers, as in *paragraph 5.1,* do not affect any separate requirement under the Criminal Procedure and Investigations Act 1996 to retain material in connection with criminal investigations.

5.8 Authority for the search and/or examination for the purposes of *paragraphs 5.2* and *5.3* may be given orally or in writing. If given orally, the authorising officer must confirm it in writing as soon as practicable. A separate authority is required for each purpose which applies.

5.9 If it is established a person is unwilling to co-operate sufficiently to enable a search and/or examination to take place or a suitable photograph to be taken, an officer may use reasonable force to:

(a) search and/or examine a detainee without their consent; and
(b) photograph any identifying marks without their consent.

5.10 The thoroughness and extent of any search or examination carried out in accordance with the powers in section 54A must be no more than the officer considers necessary to achieve the required purpose. Any search or examination which involves the removal of more than the person's outer clothing shall be conducted in accordance with Code C, *Annex A, paragraph 11*.

5.11 An intimate search may not be carried out under the powers in section 54A.

(b) Photographing detainees at police stations and other persons elsewhere than at a police station

5.12 Under PACE, section 64A, an officer may photograph:

(a) any person whilst they are detained at a police station; and
(b) any person who is elsewhere than at a police station and who has been:
  (i) arrested by a constable for an offence;
  (ii) taken into custody by a constable after being arrested for an offence by a person other than a constable;
  (iii) made subject to a requirement to wait with a community support officer under paragraph 2(3) or (3B) of Schedule 4 to the Police Reform Act 2002;
  (iiia) given a direction by a constable under section 27 of the Violent Crime Reduction Act 2006.
  (iv) given a penalty notice by a constable in uniform under Chapter 1 of Part 1 of the Criminal Justice and Police Act 2001, a penalty notice by a constable under section 444A of the Education Act 1996, or a fixed penalty notice by a constable in uniform under section 54 of the Road Traffic Offenders Act 1988;
  (v) given a notice in relation to a relevant fixed penalty offence (within the meaning of paragraph 1 of Schedule 4 to the Police Reform Act 2002) by a community support officer by virtue of a designation applying that paragraph to him;
  (vi) given a notice in relation to a relevant fixed penalty offence (within the meaning of paragraph 1 of Schedule 5 to the Police Reform Act 2002) by an accredited person by virtue of accreditation specifying that that paragraph applies to him; or
  (vii) given a direction to leave and not return to a specified location for up to 48 hours by a police constable (under section 27 of the Violent Crime Reduction Act 2006).

5.12A Photographs taken under PACE, section 64A:

(a) may be taken with the person's consent, or without their consent if consent is withheld or it is not practicable to obtain their consent, see *Note 5E*; and
(b) may be used or disclosed only for purposes related to the prevention or detection of crime, the investigation of offences or the conduct of prosecutions by, or on behalf of, police or other law enforcement and prosecuting authorities inside and outside the United Kingdom or the enforcement of any sentence or order made by a court when dealing with an offence. After being so used or disclosed, they may be retained but can only be used or disclosed for the same purposes. See *Note 5B*.

5.13 The officer proposing to take a detainee's photograph may, for this purpose, require the person to remove any item or substance worn on, or over, all, or any part of, their head or face. If they do not comply with such a requirement, the officer may remove the item or substance.

5.14 If it is established the detainee is unwilling to co-operate sufficiently to enable a suitable photograph to be taken and it is not reasonably practicable to take the photograph covertly, an officer may use reasonable force, see *Note 5F*.

(a) to take their photograph without their consent; and

(b) for the purpose of taking the photograph, remove any item or substance worn on, or over, all, or any part of, the person's head or face which they have failed to remove when asked.

5.15 For the purposes of this Code, a photograph may be obtained without the person's consent by making a copy of an image of them taken at any time on a camera system installed anywhere in the police station.

(c) Information to be given

5.16 When a person is searched, examined or photographed under the provisions as in *paragraph 5.1* and *5.12*, or their photograph obtained as in *paragraph 5.15*, they must be informed of the:

(a) purpose of the search, examination or photograph;
(b) grounds on which the relevant authority, if applicable, has been given; and
(c) purposes for which the photograph may be used, disclosed or retained. This information must be given before the search or examination commences or the photograph is taken, except if the photograph is:
  (i) to be taken covertly;
  (ii) obtained as in *paragraph 5.15*, in which case the person must be informed as soon as practicable after the photograph is taken or obtained.

(d) Documentation

5.17 A record must be made when a detainee is searched, examined, or a photograph of the person, or any identifying marks found on them, are taken. The record must include the:

(a) identity, subject to *paragraph 2.18*, of the officer carrying out the search, examination or taking the photograph;
(b) purpose of the search, examination or photograph and the outcome;
(c) detainee's consent to the search, examination or photograph, or the reason the person was searched, examined or photographed without consent;
(d) giving of any authority as in *paragraphs 5.2* and *5.3*, the grounds for giving it and the authorising officer.

5.18 If force is used when searching, examining or taking a photograph in accordance with this section, a record shall be made of the circumstances and those present.

(B) *Persons at police stations not detained*

5.19 When there are reasonable grounds for suspecting the involvement of a person in a criminal offence, but that person is at a police station **voluntarily** and not detained, the provisions of *paragraphs 5.1* to *5.18* should apply, subject to the modifications in the following paragraphs.

5.20 References to the 'person being detained' and to the powers mentioned in *paragraph 5.1* which apply only to detainees at police stations shall be omitted.

5.21 Force may not be used to:

(a) search and/or examine the person to:
  (i) discover whether they have any marks that would tend to identify them as a person involved in the commission of an offence; or
  (ii) establish their identity, see *Note 5A*;
(b) take photographs of any identifying marks, see *paragraph 5.4*; or
(c) take a photograph of the person.

5.22 Subject to *paragraph 5.24*, the photographs of persons or of their identifying marks which are not taken in accordance with the provisions mentioned in *paragraphs 5.1* or *5.12*, must be destroyed (together with any negatives and copies) unless the person:

(a) is charged with, or informed they may be prosecuted for, a recordable offence;
(b) is prosecuted for a recordable offence;
(c) is cautioned for a recordable offence or given a warning or reprimand in accordance with the Crime and Disorder Act 1998 for a recordable offence; or
(d) gives informed consent, in writing, for the photograph or image to be retained as in *paragraph 5.6*.

5.23 When *paragraph 5.22* requires the destruction of any photograph, the person must be given an opportunity to witness the destruction or to have a certificate confirming the destruction provided they so request the certificate within five days of being informed the destruction is required.

5.24 Nothing in *paragraph 5.22* affects any separate requirement under the Criminal Procedure and Investigations Act 1996 to retain material in connection with criminal investigations.

Notes for Guidance

5A The conditions under which fingerprints may be taken to assist in establishing a person's identity, are described in Section 4.

5B *Examples of purposes related to the prevention or detection of crime, the investigation of offences or the conduct of prosecutions include:*
(a) *checking the photograph against other photographs held in records or in connection with, or as a result of, an investigation of an offence to establish whether the person is liable to arrest for other offences;*
(b) *when the person is arrested at the same time as other people, or at a time when it is likely that other people will be arrested, using the photograph to help establish who was arrested, at what time and where;*
(c) *when the real identity of the person is not known and cannot be readily ascertained or there are reasonable grounds for doubting a name and other personal details given by the person, are their real name and personal details. In these circumstances, using or disclosing the photograph to help to establish or verify their real identity or determine whether they are liable to arrest for some other offence, e.g. by checking it against other photographs held in records or in connection with, or as a result of, an investigation of an offence;*
(d) *when it appears any identification procedure in section 3 may need to be arranged for which the person's photograph would assist;*
(e) *when the person's release without charge may be required, and if the release is:*
(i) *on bail to appear at a police station, using the photograph to help verify the person's identity when they answer their bail and if the person does not answer their bail, to assist in arresting them; or*
(ii) *without bail, using the photograph to help verify their identity or assist in locating them for the purposes of serving them with a summons to appear at court in criminal proceedings;*
(f) *when the person has answered to bail at a police station and there are reasonable grounds for doubting they are the person who was previously granted bail, using the photograph to help establish or verify their identity;*
(g) *when the person arrested on a warrant claims to be a different person from the person named on the warrant and a photograph would help to confirm or disprove their claim;*
(h) *when the person has been charged with, reported for, or convicted of, a recordable offence and their photograph is not already on record as a result of (a) to (f) or their photograph is on record but their appearance has changed since it was taken and the person has not yet been released or brought before a court.*

5C *There is no power to arrest a person convicted of a recordable offence solely to take their photograph. The power to take photographs in this section applies only where the person is in custody as a result of the exercise of another power, e.g. arrest for fingerprinting under PACE, Schedule 2A, paragraph 17.*

5D *Examples of when it would not be practicable to obtain a detainee's consent, see paragraph 2.12, to a search, examination or the taking of a photograph of an identifying mark include:*
(a) *when the person is drunk or otherwise unfit to give consent;*
(b) *when there are reasonable grounds to suspect that if the person became aware a search or examination was to take place or an identifying mark was to be photographed, they would take steps to prevent this happening, e.g. by violently resisting, covering or concealing the mark etc and it would not otherwise be possible to carry out the search or examination or to photograph any identifying mark;*
(c) *in the case of a juvenile, if the parent or guardian cannot be contacted in sufficient time to allow the search or examination to be carried out or the photograph to be taken.*

5E *Examples of when it would not be practicable to obtain the person's consent, see paragraph 2.12, to a photograph being taken include:*
(a) *when the person is drunk or otherwise unfit to give consent;*
(b) *when there are reasonable grounds to suspect that if the person became aware a photograph, suitable to be used or disclosed for the use and disclosure described in paragraph 5.6, was to be taken, they would take steps to prevent it being taken, e.g. by violently resisting, covering or distorting their face etc, and it would not otherwise be possible to take a suitable photograph;*
(c) *when, in order to obtain a suitable photograph, it is necessary to take it covertly; and*
(d) *in the case of a juvenile, if the parent or guardian cannot be contacted in sufficient time to allow the photograph to be taken.*

5F *The use of reasonable force to take the photograph of a suspect elsewhere than at a police station must be carefully considered. In order to obtain a suspect's consent and cooperation to remove an item of religious headwear to take their photograph, a constable should consider whether in the circumstances of the situation the removal of the headwear and the taking of the photograph should be by an officer of the same sex as the person. It would be appropriate for these actions to be conducted out of public view (see paragraph 1.1 and Note 1A).*

6 Identification by body samples and impressions

(A) *General*

6.1 References to:

(a) an 'intimate sample' mean a dental impression or sample of blood, semen or any other tissue fluid, urine, or pubic hair, or a swab taken from any part of a person's genitals or from a person's body orifice other than the mouth;

(b) a 'non-intimate sample' means:

(i) a sample of hair, other than pubic hair, which includes hair plucked with the root, see *Note 6A*;

(ii) a sample taken from a nail or from under a nail;

(iii) a swab taken from any part of a person's body other than a part from which a swab taken would be an intimate sample;

(iv) saliva;

(v) a skin impression which means any record, other than a fingerprint, which is a record, in any form and produced by any method, of the skin pattern and other physical characteristics or features of the whole, or any part of, a person's foot or of any other part of their body.

(B) *Action*

(a) Intimate samples

6.2 PACE, section 62, provides that intimate samples may be taken under:

(a) section 62(1), from a person in police detention only:

(i) if a police officer of inspector rank or above has reasonable grounds to believe such an impression or sample will tend to confirm or disprove the suspect's involvement in a recordable offence, see *Note 4A*, and gives authorisation for a sample to be taken; and

(ii) with the suspect's written consent;

(b) section 62(1A), from a person not in police detention but from whom two or more non-intimate samples have been taken in the course of an investigation of an offence and the samples, though suitable, have proved insufficient if:

(i) a police officer of inspector rank or above authorises it to be taken; and

(ii) the person concerned gives their written consent. See *Notes 6B* and *6C.*

(c) section 62(2A), from a person convicted outside England and Wales of an offence which if committed in England and Wales would be qualifying offence as defined by PACE, section 65A (see *Note 4AB*) from whom two or more non-intimate samples taken under section 63(3E) (see *paragraph 6.6(h)* have proved insufficient if:

(i) a police officer of inspector rank or above is satisfied that taking the sample is necessary to assist in the prevention or detection of crime and authorises it to be taken; and

(ii) the person concerned gives their written consent.

6.2A PACE, section 63A(4) and Schedule 2A provide powers to:

(a) make a requirement (in accordance with *Annex G*) for a person to attend a police station to have an intimate sample taken in the exercise of one of the following powers (see *paragraph 6.2*):

(i) *section 62(1A)* – Persons from whom two or more non-intimate samples have been taken and proved to be insufficient, see *paragraph 6.2(b)*: There is no time limit for making the requirement.

(ii) *section 62(2A)* – Persons convicted outside England and Wales from whom two or more non-intimate samples taken under section 63(3E) (see *paragraph 6.6(g)* have proved insufficient, see *paragraph 6.2(c)*: There is no time limit for making the requirement.

(b) arrest without warrant a person who fails to comply with the requirement.

6.3 Before a suspect is asked to provide an intimate sample, they must be:

(a) informed:

(i) of the reason, including the nature of the suspected offence (except if taken under *paragraph 6.2(c)* from a person convicted outside England and Wales.

(ii) that authorisation has been given and the provisions under which given;

(iii) that a sample taken at a police station may be subject of a speculative search;

(b) warned that if they refuse without good cause their refusal may harm their case if it comes to trial, see *Note 6D*. If the suspect is in police detention and not legally represented, they must also be reminded of their entitlement to have free legal advice, see Code C, *paragraph 6.5*, and the reminder noted in the custody record. If *paragraph 6.2(b)* applies and the person is attending a station voluntarily, their entitlement to free legal advice as in Code C, *paragraph 3.21* shall be explained to them.

6.4 Dental impressions may only be taken by a registered dentist. Other intimate samples, except for samples of urine, may only be taken by a registered medical practitioner or registered nurse or registered paramedic.

(b) Non-intimate samples

6.5 A non-intimate sample may be taken from a detainee only with their written consent or if *paragraph 6.6* applies.

6.6 A non-intimate sample may be taken from a person without the appropriate consent in the following circumstances:

(a) under *section 63(2A)* from a person who is in police detention as a consequence of being arrested for a recordable offence and who has not had a non-intimate sample of the same type and from the same part of the body taken in the course of the investigation of the offence by the police or they have had such a sample taken but it proved insufficient.

(b) Under *section 63(3)* from a person who is being held in custody by the police on the authority of a court if an officer of at least the rank of inspector authorises it to be taken. An authorisation may be given:

(i) if the authorising officer has reasonable grounds for suspecting the person of involvement in a recordable offence and for believing that the sample will tend to confirm or disprove that involvement, and

(ii) in writing or orally and confirmed in writing, as soon as practicable; but an authorisation may not be given to take from the same part of the body a further non-intimate sample consisting of a skin impression unless the previously taken impression proved insufficient

(c) under *section 63(3ZA)* from a person who has been arrested for a recordable offence and released if:

(i) in the case of a person who is on bail, they have not had a sample of the same type and from the same part of the body taken in the course of the investigation of the offence, or;

(ii) in any case, the person has had such a sample taken in the course of the investigation of the offence, but either:

- it was not suitable or proved insufficient; or
- the investigation was discontinued but subsequently resumed and before the resumption, any DNA profile derived from the sample was destroyed and the sample itself was destroyed pursuant to section 63R(4), (5) or (12).

(d) under *section 63(3A)*, from a person (whether or not in police detention or held in custody by the police on the authority of a court) who has been charged with a recordable offence or informed they will be reported for such an offence if the person:

(i) has not had a non-intimate sample taken from them in the course of the investigation of the offence; or

(ii) has had a sample so taken, but it was not suitable or proved insufficient, see *Note 6B*; or

(iii) has had a sample taken in the course of the investigation of the offence and the sample has been destroyed and in proceedings relating to that offence there is a dispute as to whether a DNA profile relevant to the proceedings was derived from the destroyed sample.

(e) under *section 63(3B)*, from a person who has been:

(i) convicted of a recordable offence; or

(ii) given a caution in respect of a recordable offence which, at the time of the caution, the person admitted;

if, since their conviction or caution a non-intimate sample has not been taken from them or a sample which has been taken since then was not suitable or proved insufficient and in either case, an officer of inspector rank or above, is satisfied that taking the fingerprints is necessary to assist in the prevention or detection of crime and authorises the taking;

(f) under *section 63(3C)* from a person to whom section 2 of the Criminal Evidence (Amendment) Act 1997 applies (persons detained following acquittal on grounds of insanity or finding of unfitness to plead).

(g) under *section 63(3E)* from a person who has been convicted outside England and Wales of an offence which if committed in England and Wales would be a qualifying offence as defined by PACE, section 65A (see *Note 4AB*) if:

(i) a non-intimate sample has not been taken previously under this power or unless a sample was so taken but was not suitable or proved insufficient; and

(ii) a police officer of inspector rank or above is satisfied that taking a sample is necessary to assist in the prevention or detection of crime and authorises it to be taken.

6.6A PACE, section 63A(4) and Schedule 2A provide powers to:

(a) make a requirement (in accordance with *Annex G*) for a person to attend a police station to have a non-intimate sample taken in the exercise of one of the following powers (see *paragraph 6.6* above) within certain time limits as follows:

(i) *section 63(3ZA)* – Persons arrested for a recordable offence and released, see *paragraph 6.6(c)*: In the case of a person from whom a non-intimate sample was taken in the course of the investigation but that sample was not suitable or proved insufficient, the requirement may not be made more than six months from the day the investigating officer was informed that the sample previously taken was not suitable or proved insufficient. In the case of a person whose DNA profile and sample was destroyed prior to the resumption of the investigation, the requirement may not be made more than six months from the day on which the investigation resumed.

(ii) *section 63(3A)* – Persons charged etc. with a recordable offence, see *paragraph 6.6(d)*: The requirement may not be made more than six months from:

- the day the person was charged or informed that they would be reported, if a sample has not been taken in the course of the investigation;
- the day the investigating officer was informed that the sample previously taken was not suitable or proved insufficient, if a sample has been taken in the course of the investigation but the sample was not suitable or proved insufficient; or
- the day on which the investigation was resumed, in the case of a person whose DNA profile and sample were destroyed prior to the resumption of the investigation.

(iii) *section 63(3B)* – Person convicted or cautioned for a recordable offence in England and Wales, see *paragraph 6.6(e)*: Where the offence for which the person was convicted etc. is also a qualifying offence (see *Note 4AB*), there is no time limit for the exercise of this power. Where the conviction etc. was for a recordable offence that is not a qualifying offence, the requirement may not be made more than two years from:

- in the case of a person whose sample has not been taken since they were convicted or cautioned, the day the person was convicted or cautioned, or, if later. the day Schedule 2A came into force (March 7 2011); or
- in the case of a person whose sample has been taken but was not suitable or proved insufficient, the day an officer from the force investigating the offence was informed that the sample previously taken was not suitable or proved insufficient or, if later, the day Schedule 2A came into force (March 7 2011).

(iv) *section 63(3E)* – A person who has been convicted of qualifying offence (see *Note 4AB*) outside England and Wales, see *paragraph 6.6(h)*: There is no time limit for making the requirement.

Note: A person who has had a non-intimate sample taken under any of the powers in section 63 mentioned in *paragraph 6.6* on two occasions in relation to any offence may not be required under Schedule 2A to attend a police station for a sample to be taken again under section 63 in relation to that offence, unless authorised by an officer of inspector rank or above. The fact of the authorisation and the reasons for giving it must be recorded as soon as practicable.

(b) arrest, without warrant, a person who fails to comply with the requirement.

6.7 Reasonable force may be used, if necessary, to take a non-intimate sample from a person without their consent under the powers mentioned in *paragraph 6.6*.

6.8 Before any non-intimate sample is taken:

(a) without consent under any power mentioned in *paragraphs 6.6* and *6.6A*, the person must be informed of:

(i) the reason for taking the sample;

(ii) the power under which the sample is to be taken;

(iii) the fact that the relevant authority has been given if any power mentioned in *paragraph 6.6(b), (e)* or *(g)* applies, including the nature of the suspected offence (except if taken under *paragraph 6.6(e)* from a person convicted or cautioned, or under *paragraph 6.6(g)* if taken from a person convicted outside England and Wales;

(b) with or without consent at a police station or elsewhere, the person must be informed:

(i) that their sample or information derived from it may be subject of a speculative search against other samples and information derived from them, see *Note 6E*, and

(ii) that their sample and the information derived from it may be retained in accordance with *Annex F*, Part (a).

(c) Removal of clothing

6.9 When clothing needs to be removed in circumstances likely to cause embarrassment to the person, no person of the opposite sex who is not a registered medical practitioner or registered health care professional shall be present, (unless in the case of a juvenile, mentally disordered or mentally vulnerable person, that person specifically requests the presence of an appropriate adult of the opposite sex who is readily available) nor shall anyone whose presence is unnecessary. However, in the case of a juvenile, this is subject to the overriding proviso that such a removal of clothing may take place in the absence of the appropriate adult only if the juvenile signifies in their presence, that they prefer the adult's absence and they agree.

(c) Documentation

6.10 A record must be made as soon as practicable after the sample is taken of:

- The matters in *paragraph 6.8(a)(i)* to *(iii)* and the fact that the person has been informed of those matters; and
- The fact that the person has been informed of the matters in *paragraph 6.8(b)(i)* and *(ii)*.

6.10A If force is used, a record shall be made of the circumstances and those present.

6.11 A record must be made of a warning given as required by *paragraph 6.3*.

6.12 *Not used*

Notes for Guidance

6A *When hair samples are taken for the purpose of DNA analysis (rather than for other purposes such as making a visual match), the suspect should be permitted a reasonable choice as to what part of the body the hairs are taken from. When hairs are plucked, they should be plucked individually, unless the suspect prefers otherwise and no more should be plucked than the person taking them reasonably considers necessary for a sufficient sample.*

6B *(a) An insufficient sample is one which is not sufficient either in quantity or quality to provide information for a particular form of analysis, such as DNA analysis. A sample may also be insufficient if enough information cannot be obtained from it by analysis because of loss, destruction, damage or contamination of the sample or as a result of an earlier, unsuccessful attempt at analysis.*

(b) An unsuitable sample is one which, by its nature, is not suitable for a particular form of analysis.

6C *Nothing in paragraph 6.2 prevents intimate samples being taken for elimination purposes with the consent of the person concerned but the provisions of paragraph 2.12 relating to the role of the appropriate adult, should be applied. Paragraph 6.2(b) does not, however, apply where the non-intimate samples were previously taken under the Terrorism Act 2000, Schedule 8, paragraph 10.*

6D *In warning a person who is asked to provide an intimate sample as in paragraph 6.3, the following form of words may be used:*

> 'You do not have to provide this sample/allow this swab or impression to be taken, but I must warn you that if you refuse without good cause, your refusal may harm your case if it comes to trial.'

6E *Fingerprints or a DNA sample and the information derived from it taken from a person arrested on suspicion of being involved in a recordable offence, or charged with such an offence, or informed they will be reported for such an offence, may be subject of a speculative search. This means they may be checked against other fingerprints and DNA records held by, or on behalf of, the police and other law enforcement authorities in or outside the UK or held in connection with, or as a result of, an investigation of an offence inside or outside the UK.*

See Annex F regarding the retention and use of fingerprints and samples taken with consent for elimination purposes.

6F *Samples of urine and non-intimate samples taken in accordance with sections 63B and 63C of PACE may not be used for identification purposes in accordance with this Code. See Code C Note for guidance 17D.*

Annex A

Video Identification

(a) General

1. The arrangements for obtaining and ensuring the availability of a suitable set of images to be used in a video identification must be the responsibility of an identification officer (see *paragraph 3.11* of this Code) who has no direct involvement with the case.
2. The set of images must include the suspect and at least eight other people who, so far as possible, and subject to *paragraph 7*, resemble the suspect in age, general appearance and position in life. Only one

suspect shall appear in any set unless there are two suspects of roughly similar appearance, in which case they may be shown together with at least twelve other people.

2A If the suspect has an unusual physical feature, e.g., a facial scar, tattoo or distinctive hairstyle or hair colour which does not appear on the images of the other people that are available to be used, steps may be taken to:
(a) conceal the location of the feature on the images of the suspect and the other people; or
(b) replicate that feature on the images of the other people.
For these purposes, the feature may be concealed or replicated electronically or by any other method which it is practicable to use to ensure that the images of the suspect and other people resemble each other. The identification officer has discretion to choose whether to conceal or replicate the feature and the method to be used.

2B If the identification officer decides that a feature should be concealed or replicated, the reason for the decision and whether the feature was concealed or replicated in the images shown to any eye-witness shall be recorded.

2C If the eye-witness requests to view any image where an unusual physical feature has been concealed or replicated without the feature being concealed or replicated, the identification officer has discretion to allow the eye-witness to view such image(s) if they are available.

3. The images used to conduct a video identification shall, as far as possible, show the suspect and other people in the same positions or carrying out the same sequence of movements. They shall also show the suspect and other people under identical conditions unless the identification officer reasonably believes:
(a) because of the suspect's failure or refusal to co-operate or other reasons, it is not practicable for the conditions to be identical; and
(b) any difference in the conditions would not direct an eye-witness' attention to any individual image.

4. The reasons identical conditions are not practicable shall be recorded on forms provided for the purpose.

5. Provision must be made for each person shown to be identified by number.

6. If police officers are shown, any numerals or other identifying badges must be concealed. If a prison inmate is shown, either as a suspect or not, then either all, or none of, the people shown should be in prison clothing.

7. The suspect or their solicitor, friend, or appropriate adult must be given a reasonable opportunity to see the complete set of images before it is shown to any eye-witness. If the suspect has a reasonable objection to the set of images or any of the participants, the suspect shall be asked to state the reasons for the objection. Steps shall, if practicable, be taken to remove the grounds for objection. If this is not practicable, the suspect and/or their representative shall be told why their objections cannot be met and the objection, the reason given for it and why it cannot be met shall be recorded on forms provided for the purpose. The requirement in *paragraph 2* that the images of the other people 'resemble' the suspect does not require the images to be identical or extremely similar (see *Note A1)*.

8. Before the images are shown in accordance with *paragraph 7,* the suspect or their solicitor shall be provided with details of the first description of the suspect by any eye-witnesses who are to attend the video identification. When a broadcast or publication is made, as in *paragraph 3.38(a)*, the suspect or their solicitor must also be allowed to view any material released to the media by the police for the purpose of recognising or tracing the suspect, provided it is practicable and would not unreasonably delay the investigation.

9. No unauthorised people may be present when the video identification is conducted. The suspect's solicitor, if practicable, shall be given reasonable notification of the time and place the video identification is to be conducted. The suspect's solicitor may only be present at the video identification on request and with the prior agreement of the identification officer, if the officer is satisfied that the solicitor's presence will not deter or distract any eye-witness from viewing the images and making an identification. If the identification officer is not satisfied and does not agree to the request, the reason must be recorded. The solicitor must be informed of the decision and the reason for it. and that they may then make representations about why they should be allowed to be present. The representations may be made orally or in writing, in person or remotely by electronic communication and must be recorded. These representations must be considered by an officer of at least the rank of inspector who is not involved with the investigation and responsibility for this may not be delegated under *paragraph 3.11*. If, after considering the representations, the officer is satisfied that the solicitor's presence will deter or distract the eye-witness, the officer shall inform the solicitor of the decision and reason

for it and ensure that any response by the solicitor is also recorded. If allowed to be present, the solicitor is not entitled to communicate in any way with an eye-witness during the procedure but this does not prevent the solicitor from communicating with the identification officer. The suspect may not be present when the images are shown to any eye-witness and is not entitled to be informed of the time and place the video identification procedure is to be conducted. The video identification procedure itself shall be recorded on video with sound. The recording must show all persons present within the sight or hearing of the eye-witness whilst the images are being viewed and must include what the eye-witness says and what is said to them by the identification officer and by any other person present at the video identification procedure. A supervised viewing of the recording of the video identification procedure by the suspect and/or their solicitor may be arranged on request, at the discretion of the investigating officer. Where the recording of the video identification procedure is to be shown to the suspect and/or their solicitor, the investigating officer may arrange for anything in the recording that might allow the eye-witness to be identified to be concealed if the investigating officer considers that this is justified (see *Note A2)*. In accordance with *paragraph 2.18*, the investigating officer may also arrange for anything in that recording that might allow any police officers or police staff to be identified to be concealed.

(b) Conducting the video identification

10. The identification officer is responsible for making the appropriate arrangements to make sure, before they see the set of images, eye-witnesses are not able to communicate with each other about the case, see any of the images which are to be shown, see, or be reminded of, any photograph or description of the suspect or be given any other indication as to the suspect's identity, or overhear an eye-witness who has already seen the material. There must be no discussion with the eye-witness about the composition of the set of images and they must not be told whether a previous eye-witness has made any identification.
11. Only one eye-witness may see the set of images at a time. Immediately before the images are shown, the eye-witness shall be told that the person they saw on a specified earlier occasion may, or may not, appear in the images they are shown and that if they cannot make an identification, they should say so. The eye-witness shall be advised that at any point, they may ask to see a particular part of the set of images or to have a particular image frozen for them to study. Furthermore, it should be pointed out to the eye-witness that there is no limit on how many times they can view the whole set of images or any part of them. However, they should be asked not to make any decision as to whether the person they saw is on the set of images until they have seen the whole set at least twice.
12. Once the eye-witness has seen the whole set of images at least twice and has indicated that they do not want to view the images, or any part of them, again, the eye-witness shall be asked to say whether the individual they saw in person on a specified earlier occasion has been shown and, if so, to identify them by number of the image. The eye-witness will then be shown that image to confirm the identification, see *paragraph 17*.
13. Care must be taken not to direct the eye-witness' attention to any one individual image or give any indication of the suspect's identity. Where an eye-witness has previously made an identification by photographs, or a computerised or artist's composite or similar likeness, they must not be reminded of such a photograph or composite likeness once a suspect is available for identification by other means in accordance with this Code. Nor must the eyewitness be reminded of any description of the suspect.

13A. If after the video identification procedure has ended, the eye-witness informs any police officer or police staff involved in the post-viewing arrangements that they wish to change their decision about their identification, or they have not made an identification when in fact they could have made one, an accurate record of the words used by the eye-witness and of the circumstances immediately after the procedure ended, shall be made. If the eyewitness has not had an opportunity to communicate with other people about the procedure, the identification officer has the discretion to allow the eye-witness a second opportunity to make an identification by repeating the video identification procedure using the same images but in different positions.

14. After the procedure, action required in accordance with *paragraph 3.40* applies.

(c) Image security and destruction

15. Arrangements shall be made for all relevant material containing sets of images used for specific identification procedures to be kept securely and their movements accounted for. In particular, no-one involved in the investigation shall be permitted to view the material prior to it being shown to any witness.

16. As appropriate, *paragraph 3.30* or *3.31* applies to the destruction or retention of relevant sets of images.

(d) Documentation

17. A record must be made of all those participating in, or seeing, the set of images whose names are known to the police.
18. A record of the conduct of the video identification must be made on forms provided for the purpose. This shall include anything said by the witness about any identifications or the conduct of the procedure and any reasons it was not practicable to comply with any of the provisions of this Code governing the conduct of video identifications. This record is in addition to any statement that is taken from any eye-witness after the procedure.

Notes for Guidance

A1 *The purpose of the video identification is to test the eye-witness' ability to distinguish the suspect from others and it would not be a fair test if all the images shown were identical or extremely similar to each other. The identification officer is responsible for ensuring that the images shown are suitable for the purpose of this test.*

A2 *The purpose of allowing the identity of the eye-witness to be concealed is to protect them in cases when there is information that suspects or their associates, may threaten the witness or cause them harm or when the investigating officer considers that special measures may be required to protect their identity during the criminal process.*

Annex B

Identification Parades

(a) General

1. A suspect must be given a reasonable opportunity to have a solicitor or friend present, and the suspect shall be asked to indicate on a second copy of the notice whether or not they wish to do so.
2. An identification parade may take place either in a normal room or one equipped with a screen permitting witnesses to see members of the identification parade without being seen. The procedures for the composition and conduct of the identification parade are the same in both cases, subject to *paragraph 8* (except that an identification parade involving a screen may take place only when the suspect's solicitor, friend or appropriate adult is present or the identification parade is recorded on video).
3. Before the identification parade takes place, the suspect or their solicitor shall be provided with details of the first description of the suspect by any witnesses who are attending the identification parade. When a broadcast or publication is made as in *paragraph 3.38(a)*, the suspect or their solicitor should also be allowed to view any material released to the media by the police for the purpose of identifying and tracing the suspect, provided it is practicable to do so and would not unreasonably delay the investigation.

(b) Identification parades involving prison inmates

4. If a prison inmate is required for identification, and there are no security problems about the person leaving the establishment, they may be asked to participate in an identification parade or video identification.
5. An identification parade may be held in a Prison Department establishment but shall be conducted, as far as practicable under normal identification parade rules. Members of the public shall make up the identification parade unless there are serious security, or control, objections to their admission to the establishment. In such cases, or if a group or video identification is arranged within the establishment, other inmates may participate. If an inmate is the suspect, they are not required to wear prison clothing for the identification parade unless the other people taking part are other inmates in similar clothing, or are members of the public who are prepared to wear prison clothing for the occasion.

(c) Conduct of the identification parade

6. Immediately before the identification parade, the suspect must be reminded of the procedures governing its conduct and cautioned in the terms of Code C, *paragraphs 10.5* or *10.6*, as appropriate.
7. All unauthorised people must be excluded from the place where the identification parade is held.

8. Once the identification parade has been formed, everything afterwards, in respect of it, shall take place in the presence and hearing of the suspect and any interpreter, solicitor, friend or appropriate adult who is present (unless the identification parade involves a screen, in which case everything said to, or by, any witness at the place where the identification parade is held, must be said in the hearing and presence of the suspect's solicitor, friend or appropriate adult or be recorded on video).
9. The identification parade shall consist of at least eight people (in addition to the suspect) who, so far as possible, resemble the suspect in age, height, general appearance and position in life. Only one suspect shall be included in an identification parade unless there are two suspects of roughly similar appearance, in which case they may be paraded together with at least twelve other people. In no circumstances shall more than two suspects be included in one identification parade and where there are separate identification parades, they shall be made up of different people.
10. If the suspect has an unusual physical feature, e.g., a facial scar, tattoo or distinctive hairstyle or hair colour which cannot be replicated on other members of the identification parade, steps may be taken to conceal the location of that feature on the suspect and the other members of the identification parade if the suspect and their solicitor, or appropriate adult, agree. For example, by use of a plaster or a hat, so that all members of the identification parade resemble each other in general appearance.
11. When all members of a similar group are possible suspects, separate identification parades shall be held for each unless there are two suspects of similar appearance when they may appear on the same identification parade with at least twelve other members of the group who are not suspects. When police officers in uniform form an identification parade any numerals or other identifying badges shall be concealed.
12. When the suspect is brought to the place where the identification parade is to be held, they shall be asked if they have any objection to the arrangements for the identification parade or to any of the other participants in it and to state the reasons for the objection. The suspect may obtain advice from their solicitor or friend, if present, before the identification parade proceeds. If the suspect has a reasonable objection to the arrangements or any of the participants, steps shall, if practicable, be taken to remove the grounds for objection. When it is not practicable to do so, the suspect shall be told why their objections cannot be met and the objection, the reason given for it and why it cannot be met, shall be recorded on forms provided for the purpose.
13. The suspect may select their own position in the line, but may not otherwise interfere with the order of the people forming the line. When there is more than one witness, the suspect must be told, after each witness has left the room, that they can, if they wish, change position in the line. Each position in the line must be clearly numbered, whether by means of a number laid on the floor in front of each identification parade member or by other means.
14. Appropriate arrangements must be made to make sure, before witnesses attend the identification parade, they are not able to:
    (i) communicate with each other about the case or overhear a witness who has already seen the identification parade;
    (ii) see any member of the identification parade;
    (iii) see, or be reminded of, any photograph or description of the suspect or be given any other indication as to the suspect's identity; or
    (iv) see the suspect before or after the identification parade.
15. The person conducting a witness to an identification parade must not discuss with them the composition of the identification parade and, in particular, must not disclose whether a previous witness has made any identification.
16. Witnesses shall be brought in one at a time. Immediately before the witness inspects the identification parade, they shall be told the person they saw on a specified earlier occasion may, or may not, be present and if they cannot make an identification, they should say so. The witness must also be told they should not make any decision about whether the person they saw is on the identification parade until they have looked at each member at least twice.
17. When the officer or police staff (see *paragraph 3.11*) conducting the identification procedure is satisfied the witness has properly looked at each member of the identification parade, they shall ask the witness whether the person they saw on a specified earlier occasion is on the identification parade and, if so, to indicate the number of the person concerned, see *paragraph 28*.
18. If the witness wishes to hear any identification parade member speak, adopt any specified posture or move, they shall first be asked whether they can identify any person(s) on the identification parade

on the basis of appearance only. When the request is to hear members of the identification parade speak, the witness shall be reminded that the participants in the identification parade have been chosen on the basis of physical appearance only. Members of the identification parade may then be asked to comply with the witness' request to hear them speak, see them move or adopt any specified posture.

19. If the witness requests that the person they have indicated remove anything used for the purposes of *paragraph 10* to conceal the location of an unusual physical feature, that person may be asked to remove it.
20. If the witness makes an identification after the identification parade has ended, the suspect and, if present, their solicitor, interpreter or friend shall be informed. When this occurs, consideration should be given to allowing the witness a second opportunity to identify the suspect.
21 After the procedure, action required in accordance with *paragraph 3.40* applies.
22. When the last witness has left, the suspect shall be asked whether they wish to make any comments on the conduct of the identification parade.

(d) Documentation

23. A video recording must normally be taken of the identification parade. If that is impracticable, a colour photograph must be taken. A copy of the video recording or photograph shall be supplied, on request, to the suspect or their solicitor within a reasonable time.
24. As appropriate, *paragraph 3.30* or *3.31*, should apply to any photograph or video taken as in *paragraph 23*.
25. If any person is asked to leave an identification parade because they are interfering with its conduct, the circumstances shall be recorded.
26. A record must be made of all those present at an identification parade whose names are known to the police.
27. If prison inmates make up an identification parade, the circumstances must be recorded.
28. A record of the conduct of any identification parade must be made on forms provided for the purpose. This shall include anything said by the witness or the suspect about any identifications or the conduct of the procedure, and any reasons it was not practicable to comply with any of this Code's provisions.

Annex C

Group Identification

(a) General

1. The purpose of this Annex is to make sure, as far as possible, group identifications follow the principles and procedures for identification parades so the conditions are fair to the suspect in the way they test the witness' ability to make an identification.
2. Group identifications may take place either with the suspect's consent and co-operation or covertly without their consent.
3. The location of the group identification is a matter for the identification officer, although the officer may take into account any representations made by the suspect, appropriate adult, their solicitor or friend.
4. The place where the group identification is held should be one where other people are either passing by or waiting around informally, in groups such that the suspect is able to join them and be capable of being seen by the witness at the same time as others in the group. For example people leaving an escalator, pedestrians walking through a shopping centre, passengers on railway and bus stations, waiting in queues or groups or where people are standing or sitting in groups in other public places.
5. If the group identification is to be held covertly, the choice of locations will be limited by the places where the suspect can be found and the number of other people present at that time. In these cases, suitable locations might be along regular routes travelled by the suspect, including buses or trains or public places frequented by the suspect.
6. Although the number, age, sex, race and general description and style of clothing of other people present at the location cannot be controlled by the identification officer, in selecting the location the officer must consider the general appearance and numbers of people likely to be present. In particular, the officer must reasonably expect that over the period the witness observes the group, they will be able to see, from time to time, a number of others whose appearance is broadly similar to that of the suspect.

7. A group identification need not be held if the identification officer believes, because of the unusual appearance of the suspect, none of the locations it would be practicable to use, satisfy the requirements of *paragraph 6* necessary to make the identification fair.
8. Immediately after a group identification procedure has taken place (with or without the suspect's consent), a colour photograph or video should be taken of the general scene, if practicable, to give a general impression of the scene and the number of people present. Alternatively, if it is practicable, the group identification may be video recorded.
9. If it is not practicable to take the photograph or video in accordance with *paragraph 8,* a photograph or film of the scene should be taken later at a time determined by the identification officer if the officer considers it practicable to do so.
10. An identification carried out in accordance with this Code remains a group identification even though, at the time of being seen by the witness, the suspect was on their own rather than in a group.
11. Before the group identification takes place, the suspect or their solicitor shall be provided with details of the first description of the suspect by any witnesses who are to attend the identification. When a broadcast or publication is made, as in *paragraph 3.38(a)*, the suspect or their solicitor should also be allowed to view any material released by the police to the media for the purposes of identifying and tracing the suspect, provided that it is practicable and would not unreasonably delay the investigation.
12. After the procedure, action required in accordance with *paragraph 3.40* applies.

(b) Identification with the consent of the suspect

13. A suspect must be given a reasonable opportunity to have a solicitor or friend present. They shall be asked to indicate on a second copy of the notice whether or not they wish to do so.
14. The witness, the person carrying out the procedure and the suspect's solicitor, appropriate adult, friend or any interpreter for the witness, may be concealed from the sight of the individuals in the group they are observing, if the person carrying out the procedure considers this assists the conduct of the identification.
15. The person conducting a witness to a group identification must not discuss with them the forthcoming group identification and, in particular, must not disclose whether a previous witness has made any identification.
16. Anything said to, or by, the witness during the procedure about the identification should be said in the presence and hearing of those present at the procedure.
17. Appropriate arrangements must be made to make sure, before witnesses attend the group identification, they are not able to:
 (i) communicate with each other about the case or overhear a witness who has already been given an opportunity to see the suspect in the group;
 (ii) see the suspect; or
 (iii) see, or be reminded of, any photographs or description of the suspect or be given any other indication of the suspect's identity.
18. Witnesses shall be brought one at a time to the place where they are to observe the group. Immediately before the witness is asked to look at the group, the person conducting the procedure shall tell them that the person they saw on a specified earlier occasion may, or may not, be in the group and that if they cannot make an identification, they should say so. The witness shall be asked to observe the group in which the suspect is to appear. The way in which the witness should do this will depend on whether the group is moving or stationary.

Moving group

19. When the group in which the suspect is to appear is moving, e.g. leaving an escalator, the provisions of *paragraphs 20* to *24* should be followed.
20. If two or more suspects consent to a group identification, each should be the subject of separate identification procedures. These may be conducted consecutively on the same occasion.
21. The person conducting the procedure shall tell the witness to observe the group and ask them to point out any person they think they saw on the specified earlier occasion.
22. Once the witness has been informed as in *paragraph 21* the suspect should be allowed to take whatever position in the group they wish.
23. When the witness points out a person as in *paragraph 21* they shall, if practicable, be asked to take a closer look at the person to confirm the identification. If this is not practicable, or they cannot confirm the identification, they shall be asked how sure they are that the person they have indicated is the relevant person.

24. The witness should continue to observe the group for the period which the person conducting the procedure reasonably believes is necessary in the circumstances for them to be able to make comparisons between the suspect and other individuals of broadly similar appearance to the suspect as in *paragraph 6*.

Stationary groups

25. When the group in which the suspect is to appear is stationary, e.g. people waiting in a queue, the provisions of *paragraphs 26* to *29* should be followed.
26. If two or more suspects consent to a group identification, each should be subject to separate identification procedures unless they are of broadly similar appearance when they may appear in the same group. When separate group identifications are held, the groups must be made up of different people.
27. The suspect may take whatever position in the group they wish. If there is more than one witness, the suspect must be told, out of the sight and hearing of any witness, that they can, if they wish, change their position in the group.
28. The witness shall be asked to pass along, or amongst, the group and to look at each person in the group at least twice, taking as much care and time as possible according to the circumstances, before making an identification. Once the witness has done this, they shall be asked whether the person they saw on the specified earlier occasion is in the group and to indicate any such person by whatever means the person conducting the procedure considers appropriate in the circumstances. If this is not practicable, the witness shall be asked to point out any person they think they saw on the earlier occasion.
29. When the witness makes an indication as in *paragraph 28*, arrangements shall be made, if practicable, for the witness to take a closer look at the person to confirm the identification. If this is not practicable, or the witness is unable to confirm the identification, they shall be asked how sure they are that the person they have indicated is the relevant person.

All cases

30. If the suspect unreasonably delays joining the group, or having joined the group, deliberately conceals themselves from the sight of the witness, this may be treated as a refusal to co-operate in a group identification.
31. If the witness identifies a person other than the suspect, that person should be informed what has happened and asked if they are prepared to give their name and address. There is no obligation upon any member of the public to give these details. There shall be no duty to record any details of any other member of the public present in the group or at the place where the procedure is conducted.
32. When the group identification has been completed, the suspect shall be asked whether they wish to make any comments on the conduct of the procedure.
33. If the suspect has not been previously informed, they shall be told of any identifications made by the witnesses.

(c) Group Identification without the suspect's consent

34. Group identifications held covertly without the suspect's consent should, as far as practicable, follow the rules for conduct of group identification by consent.
35. A suspect has no right to have a solicitor, appropriate adult or friend present as the identification will take place without the knowledge of the suspect.
36. Any number of suspects may be identified at the same time.

(d) Identifications in police stations

37. Group identifications should only take place in police stations for reasons of safety, security or because it is not practicable to hold them elsewhere.
38. The group identification may take place either in a room equipped with a screen permitting witnesses to see members of the group without being seen, or anywhere else in the police station that the identification officer considers appropriate.
39. Any of the additional safeguards applicable to identification parades should be followed if the identification officer considers it is practicable to do so in the circumstances.

(e) Identifications involving prison inmates

40. A group identification involving a prison inmate may only be arranged in the prison or at a police station.
41. When a group identification takes place involving a prison inmate, whether in a prison or in a police station, the arrangements should follow those in *paragraphs 37* to *39*. If a group identification takes

place within a prison, other inmates may participate. If an inmate is the suspect, they do not have to wear prison clothing for the group identification unless the other participants are wearing the same clothing.

(f) Documentation

42. When a photograph or video is taken as in *paragraph 8* or *9*, a copy of the photograph or video shall be supplied on request to the suspect or their solicitor within a reasonable time.
43. *Paragraph 3.30* or *3.31*, as appropriate, shall apply when the photograph or film taken in accordance with *paragraph 8* or *9* includes the suspect.
44. A record of the conduct of any group identification must be made on forms provided for the purpose. This shall include anything said by the witness or suspect about any identifications or the conduct of the procedure and any reasons why it was not practicable to comply with any of the provisions of this Code governing the conduct of group identifications.

Annex D

Confrontation by an Eye-Witness

1. Before the confrontation takes place, the eye-witness must be told that the person they saw on a specified earlier occasion may, or may not, be the person they are to confront and that if they are not that person, then the witness should say so.
2. Before the confrontation takes place the suspect or their solicitor shall be provided with details of the first description of the suspect given by any eye-witness who is to attend. When a broadcast or publication is made, as in *paragraph 3.38(a)*, the suspect or their solicitor should also be allowed to view any material released to the media for the purposes of recognising or tracing the suspect, provided it is practicable to do so and would not unreasonably delay the investigation.
3. Force may not be used to make the suspect's face visible to the eye-witness.
4. Confrontation must take place in the presence of the suspect's solicitor, interpreter or friend unless this would cause unreasonable delay.
5. The suspect shall be confronted independently by each eye-witness, who shall be asked 'Is this the person?'. If the eye-witness identifies the person but is unable to confirm the identification, they shall be asked how sure they are that the person is the one they saw on the earlier occasion.
6. The confrontation should normally take place in the police station, either in a normal room or one equipped with a screen permitting the eye-witness to see the suspect without being seen. In both cases, the procedures are the same except that a room equipped with a screen may be used only when the suspect's solicitor, friend or appropriate adult is present or the confrontation is recorded on video.
7. After the procedure, action required in accordance with *paragraph 3.40* applies.

Annex E

Showing Photographs to Eye-Witnesses

(a) Action

1. An officer of sergeant rank or above shall be responsible for supervising and directing the showing of photographs. The actual showing may be done by another officer or police staff, see *paragraph 3.11*.
2. The supervising officer must confirm the first description of the suspect given by the eyewitness has been recorded before they are shown the photographs. If the supervising officer is unable to confirm the description has been recorded they shall postpone showing the photographs.
3. Only one eye-witness shall be shown photographs at any one time. Each witness shall be given as much privacy as practicable and shall not be allowed to communicate with any other eye-witness in the case.
4. The eye-witness shall be shown not less than twelve photographs at a time, which shall, as far as possible, all be of a similar type.
5. When the eye-witness is shown the photographs, they shall be told the photograph of the person they saw on a specified earlier occasion may, or may not, be amongst them and if they cannot make an identification, they should say so. The eye-witness shall also be told they should not make a decision until they have viewed at least twelve photographs. The eye-witness shall not be prompted or guided in any way but shall be left to make any selection without help.

6. If an eye-witness makes an identification from photographs, unless the person identified is otherwise eliminated from enquiries or is not available, other eye-witnesses shall not be shown photographs. But both they, and the eye-witness who has made the identification, shall be asked to attend a video identification, an identification parade or group identification unless there is no dispute about the suspect's identification.
7. If the eye-witness makes a selection but is unable to confirm the identification, the person showing the photographs shall ask them how sure they are that the photograph they have indicated is the person they saw on the specified earlier occasion.
8. When the use of a computerised or artist's composite or similar likeness has led to there being a known suspect who can be asked to participate in a video identification, appear on an identification parade or participate in a group identification, that likeness shall not be shown to other potential eye-witnesses.
9. When an eye-witness attending a video identification, an identification parade or group identification has previously been shown photographs or computerised or artist's composite or similar likeness (and it is the responsibility of the officer in charge of the investigation to make the identification officer aware that this is the case), the suspect and their solicitor must be informed of this fact before the identification procedure takes place.
10. None of the photographs shown shall be destroyed, whether or not an identification is made, since they may be required for production in court. The photographs shall be numbered and a separate photograph taken of the frame or part of the album from which the eye-witness made an identification as an aid to reconstituting it.

(b) Documentation

11. Whether or not an identification is made, a record shall be kept of the showing of photographs on forms provided for the purpose. This shall include anything said by the eye-witness about any identification or the conduct of the procedure, any reasons it was not practicable to comply with any of the provisions of this Code governing the showing of photographs and the name and rank of the supervising officer.
12. The supervising officer shall inspect and sign the record as soon as practicable.

ANNEX F

FINGERPRINTS, SAMPLES AND FOOTWEAR IMPRESSIONS — DESTRUCTION AND SPECULATIVE SEARCHES

Part A: Fingerprints and samples

Paragraphs 1 to 12 summarise and update information which is available at: https://www.gov.uk/government/publications/protection-of-freedoms-act-2012-dna-and-fingerprint-provisions/protection-of-freedoms-act-2012-how-dna-and-fingerprint-evidence-is-protected-in-law

DNA samples

1. A DNA sample is an individual's biological material, containing all of their genetic information. The Act requires all DNA samples to be destroyed within 6 months of being taken. This allows sufficient time for the sample to be analysed and a DNA profile to be produced for use on the database.
2. The only exception to this is if the sample is or may be required for disclosure as evidence, in which case it may be retained for as long as this need exists under the Criminal Procedure and Investigations Act 1996.

DNA profiles and fingerprints

3. A DNA profile consists of a string of 16 pairs of numbers and 2 letters (XX for women, XY for men) to indicate gender. This number string is stored on the National DNA Database (NDNAD). It allows the person to be identified if they leave their DNA at a crime scene.
4. Fingerprints are usually scanned electronically from the individual in custody and the images stored on IDENT1, the national fingerprint database.

Retention Periods: Fingerprints and DNA profiles

5. The retention period depends on the outcome of the investigation of the recordable offence in connection with which the fingerprints and DNA samples was taken, the age of the person at the time

the offence was committed and whether the *recordable* offence is a qualifying offence and whether it is an excluded offence (see Table *Notes (a)* to *(c)*), as follows:

Table – Retention periods

(a) Convictions

Age when offence committed	Outcome	Retention Period
Any age	Convicted or given a caution or youth caution for a recordable offence which is also a qualifying offence	INDEFINITE
18 or over	Convicted or given a caution for a recordable offence which is NOT a qualifying offence	INDEFINITE
Under 18	Convicted or given a youth caution for a recordable offence which is NOT a qualifying offence.	1st conviction or youth caution – 5 years plus length of any prison sentence. Indefinite if prison sentence 5 years or more 2nd conviction or youth caution: Indefinite

(b) Non-Convictions

Age when offence committed	Outcome	Retention Period
Any age	Charged but not convicted of a recordable qualifying offence.	3 years plus a 2 year extension if granted by a District Judge (or indefinite if the individual has a previous conviction for a recordable offence which is not excluded)
Any age	Arrested for, but not charged with, a recordable qualifying offence	3 years if granted by the Biometrics Commissioner plus a 2 year extension if granted by a District Judge (or indefinite if the individual has a previous conviction for a recordable offence which is not excluded)
Any age	Arrested for or charged with a recordable offence which is not a qualifying offence.	Indefinite if the person has a previous conviction for a recordable offence which is not excluded otherwise NO RETENTION
18 or over	Given Penalty Notice for Disorder for recordable offence	2 years

Table Notes:

(a) *A 'recordable' offence is one for which the police are required to keep a record. Generally speaking, these are imprisonable offences; however, it also includes a number of non-imprisonable offences such as begging and taxi touting. The police are not able to take or retain the DNA or fingerprints of an individual who is arrested for an offence which is not recordable.*

(b) *A 'qualifying' offence is one listed under section 65A of the Police and Criminal Evidence Act 1984 (the list comprises sexual, violent, terrorism and burglary offences).*

(c) *An 'excluded' offence is a recordable offence which is not a qualifying offence, was committed when the individual was under 18, for which they received a sentence of fewer than 5 years imprisonment and is the only recordable offence for which the person has been convicted*

Speculative searches

6. Where the retention framework above requires the deletion of a person's DNA profile and fingerprints, the Act first allows a *speculative search* of their DNA and fingerprints against DNA and finger-

prints obtained from crime scenes which are stored on NDNAD and IDENT1. Once the speculative search has been completed, the profile and fingerprints are deleted unless there is a match, in which case they will be retained for the duration of any investigation and thereafter in accordance with the retention framework (e.g. if that investigation led to a conviction for a qualifying offence, they would be retained indefinitely).

Extensions of retention period

7. For qualifying offences, PACE allows chief constables to apply for extensions to the given retention periods for DNA profiles and fingerprints if considered necessary for prevention or detection of crime.
8. Section 20 of the Protection of Freedoms Act 2012 established the independent office of Commissioner for the Retention and Use of Biometric Material ('the 'Biometrics Commissioner'). For details, see https://www.gov.uk/government/organisations/biometrics-commissioner.
9. Where an individual is arrested for, but not charged with, a qualifying offence, their DNA profile and fingerprint record will normally be deleted. However, the police can apply to the Biometrics Commissioner for permission to retain their DNA profile and fingerprint record for a period of 3 years. The application must be made within 28 days of the decision not to proceed with a prosecution.
10. If the police make such an application, the Biometrics Commissioner would first give both them and the arrested individual an opportunity to make written representations and then, taking into account factors including the age and vulnerability of the victim(s) of the alleged offences, and their relationship to the suspect, make a decision on whether or not retention is appropriate.
11. If after considering the application, the Biometrics Commissioner decides that retention is not appropriate, the DNA profile and fingerprint record in question must be destroyed.
12. If the Biometrics Commissioner agrees to allow retention, the police will be able to retain that individual's DNA profile and fingerprint record for a period of 3 years from the date the samples were taken. At the end of that period, the police will be able to apply to a District Judge (Magistrates' Courts) for a single 2 year extension to the retention period. If the application is rejected, the force must then destroy the DNA profile and fingerprint record.

Part B: Footwear impressions

13. Footwear impressions taken in accordance with section 61A of PACE (see *paragraphs 4.16* to *4.21*) may be retained for as long as is necessary for purposes related to the prevention or detection of crime, the investigation of an offence or the conduct of a prosecution.

Part C: Fingerprints, samples and footwear impressions taken in connection with a criminal investigation from a person not suspected of committing the offence under investigation for elimination purposes.

14. When fingerprints, footwear impressions or DNA samples are taken from a person in connection with an investigation and the person is *not suspected of having committed the offence*, see *Note F1*, they must be destroyed as soon as they have fulfilled the purpose for which they were taken unless:
    (a) they were taken for the purposes of an investigation of an offence for which a person has been convicted; and
    (b) fingerprints, footwear impressions or samples were also taken from the convicted person for the purposes of that investigation.

    However, subject to *paragraph 14,* the fingerprints, footwear impressions and samples, and the information derived from samples, may not be used in the investigation of any offence or in evidence against the person who is, or would be, entitled to the destruction of the fingerprints, footwear impressions and samples, see *Note F2.*
15. The requirement to destroy fingerprints, footwear impressions and DNA samples, and information derived from samples and restrictions on their retention and use in *paragraph 14* do not apply if the person gives their written consent for their fingerprints, footwear impressions or sample to be retained and used after they have fulfilled the purpose for which they were taken, see *Note F1.* This consent can be withdrawn at any time.
16. When a person's fingerprints, footwear impressions or sample are to be destroyed:
    (a) any copies of the fingerprints and footwear impressions must also be destroyed; and
    (b) neither the fingerprints, footwear impressions, the sample, or any information derived from the sample, may be used in the investigation of any offence or in evidence against the person who is, or would be, entitled to its destruction.

Notes for Guidance

F1 *Fingerprints, footwear impressions and samples given voluntarily for the purposes of elimination play an important part in many police investigations. It is, therefore, important to make sure innocent volunteers are not deterred from participating and their consent to their fingerprints, footwear impressions and DNA being used for the purposes of a specific investigation is fully informed and voluntary. If the police or volunteer seek to have the fingerprints, footwear impressions or samples retained for use after the specific investigation ends, it is important the volunteer's consent to this is also fully informed and voluntary. The volunteer must be told that they may withdraw their consent at any time. The consent must be obtained in writing using current nationally agreed forms provided for police use according to the purpose for which the consent is given. This purpose may be either:*

- *DNA/fingerprints/footwear impressions — to be used only for the purposes of a specific investigation; or*
- *DNA/fingerprints/footwear impressions — to be used in the specific investigation* ***and*** *retained by the police for future use.*

To minimise the risk of confusion:

- *if a police officer or member of police staff has any doubt about:*
  - *how the consent forms should be completed and signed, or*
  - *whether a consent form they propose to use and refer to is fully compliant with the current nationally agreed form,*

  the relevant national police helpdesk (for DNA or fingerprints) should be contacted.
- *in each case, the meaning of consent should be explained orally and care taken to ensure the oral explanation accurately reflects the contents of the written form the person is to be asked to sign.*

F2 *The provisions for the retention of fingerprints, footwear impressions and samples in paragraph 15 allow for all fingerprints, footwear impressions and samples in a case to be available for any subsequent miscarriage of justice investigation.*

Annex G

Requirement for a Person to Attend a Police Station for Fingerprints and Samples (Paragraphs 4.4, 6.2A and 6.6A)

1. A requirement under Schedule 2A for a person to attend a police station to have fingerprints or samples taken:
   (a) must give the person a period of at least seven days within which to attend the police station; and
   (b) may direct them to attend at a specified time of day or between specified times of day.
2. When specifying the period and times of attendance, the officer making the requirements must consider whether the fingerprints or samples could reasonably be taken at a time when the person is required to attend the police station for any other reason. See *Note G1*.
3. An officer of the rank of inspector or above may authorise a period shorter than 7 days if there is an urgent need for person's fingerprints or sample for the purposes of the investigation of an offence. The fact of the authorisation and the reasons for giving it must be recorded as soon as practicable.
4. The constable making a requirement and the person to whom it applies may agree to vary it so as to specify any period within which, or date or time at which, the person is to attend. However, variation shall not have effect for the purposes of enforcement, unless it is confirmed by the constable in writing.

Notes for Guidance

G1 *The specified period within which the person is to attend need not fall within the period allowed (if applicable) for making the requirement.*

G2 *To justify the arrest without warrant of a person who fails to comply with a requirement, (see paragraphs 4.4(b) and 6.7(b) above), the officer making the requirement, or confirming a variation, should be prepared to explain how, when and where the requirement was made or the variation was confirmed and what steps were taken to ensure the person understood what to do and the consequences of not complying with the requirement.*

PACE CODE E

REVISED CODE OF PRACTICE ON AUDIO RECORDING INTERVIEWS WITH SUSPECTS

[Omitted: see **D1.90**. The full text of Code E is freely available at tinyurl.com/ybm87hfr]

PACE CODE F

REVISED CODE OF PRACTICE ON VISUAL RECORDING WITH SOUND OF INTERVIEWS WITH SUSPECTS

[Omitted: see **D1.90**. The full text of Code F is freely available at tinyurl.com/y930995g]

PACE CODE G

CODE OF PRACTICE FOR THE STATUTORY POWER OF ARREST BY POLICE OFFICERS

Commencement — Transitional Arrangements

This Code applies to any arrest made by a police officer after midnight on 12 November 2012.

1. Introduction

1.1 This Code of Practice deals with the statutory power of police to arrest a person who is involved, or suspected of being involved, in a criminal offence. The power of arrest must be used fairly, responsibly, with respect for people suspected of committing offences and without unlawful discrimination. The Equality Act 2010 makes it unlawful for police officers to discriminate against, harass or victimise any person on the grounds of the 'protected characteristics' of age, disability, gender reassignment, race, religion or belief, sex and sexual orientation, marriage and civil partnership, pregnancy and maternity when using their powers. When police forces are carrying out their functions they also have a duty to have regard to the need to eliminate unlawful discrimination, harassment and victimisation and to take steps to foster good relations.

1.2 The exercise of the power of arrest represents an obvious and significant interference with the Right to liberty and security under Article 5 of the European Convention on Human Rights set out in Part I of Schedule 1 to the Human Rights Act 1998.

1.3 The use of the power must be fully justified and officers exercising the power should consider if the necessary objectives can be met by other, less intrusive means. Absence of justification for exercising the power of arrest may lead to challenges should the case proceed to court. It could also lead to civil claims against police for unlawful arrest and false imprisonment. When the power of arrest is exercised it is essential that it is exercised in a non-discriminatory and proportionate manner which is compatible with the Right to liberty under Article 5. See *Note 1B*.

1.4 Section 24 of the Police and Criminal Evidence Act 1984 (as substituted by section 110 of the Serious Organised Crime and Police Act 2005) provides the statutory power for a constable to arrest without warrant for all offences. If the provisions of the Act and this Code are not observed, both the arrest and the conduct of any subsequent investigation may be open to question.

1.5 This Code of Practice must be readily available at all police stations for consultation by police officers and police staff, detained persons and members of the public.

1.6 The notes for guidance are not provisions of this code.

2. Elements of arrest under section 24 PACE

2.1 A lawful arrest requires two elements:
A person's involvement or suspected involvement or attempted involvement in the commission of a criminal offence;
AND
Reasonable grounds for *believing* that the person's arrest is necessary.

- both elements must be satisfied, and
- it can never be necessary to arrest a person unless there are reasonable grounds to suspect them of committing an offence.

2.2 The arrested person must be informed that they have been arrested, even if this fact is obvious, and of the relevant circumstances of the arrest in relation to both the above elements. The custody officer must be informed of these matters on arrival at the police station. See *paragraphs 2.9, 3.3 and Note 3 and Code C paragraph 3.4.*

(a) 'Involvement in the commission of an offence'

2.3 A constable may arrest without warrant in relation to any offence (see *Notes 1 and 1A*) anyone:

- who is about to commit an offence or is in the act of committing an offence;
- whom the officer has reasonable grounds for suspecting is about to commit an offence or to be committing an offence;
- whom the officer has reasonable grounds to suspect of being guilty of an offence which he or she has reasonable grounds for suspecting has been committed;
- anyone who is guilty of an offence which has been committed or anyone whom the officer has reasonable grounds for suspecting to be guilty of that offence.

2.3A There must be some reasonable, objective grounds for the suspicion, based on known facts and information which are relevant to the likelihood the offence has been committed and the person liable to arrest committed it. See *Notes 2 and 2A.*

(b) Necessity criteria

2.4 The power of arrest is only exercisable if the constable has reasonable grounds for *believing* that it is necessary to arrest the person. The statutory criteria for what may constitute necessity are set out in paragraph 2.9 and it remains an operational decision at the discretion of the constable to decide:

- which one or more of the necessity criteria (if any) applies to the individual; and
- if any of the criteria do apply, whether to arrest, grant street bail after arrest, report for summons or for charging by post, issue a penalty notice or take any other action that is open to the officer.

2.5 In applying the criteria, the arresting officer has to be satisfied that at least one of the reasons supporting the need for arrest is satisfied.

2.6 Extending the power of arrest to all offences provides a constable with the ability to use that power to deal with any situation. However applying the necessity criteria requires the constable to examine and justify the reason or reasons why a person needs to be arrested or (as the case may be) further arrested, for an offence for the custody officer to decide whether to authorise their detention for that offence. See *Note 2C*

2.7 The criteria in paragraph 2.9 below which are set out in section 24 of PACE as substituted by section 110 of the Serious Organised Crime and Police Act 2005 are exhaustive. However, the circumstances that may satisfy those criteria remain a matter for the operational discretion of individual officers. Some examples are given to illustrate what those circumstances might be and what officers might consider when deciding whether arrest is necessary.

2.8 In considering the individual circumstances, the constable must take into account the situation of the victim, the nature of the offence, the circumstances of the suspect and the needs of the investigative process.

2.9 When it is practicable to tell a person why their arrest is necessary (as required by paragraphs 2.2, 3.3 and *Note 3*), the constable should outline the facts, information and other circumstances which provide the grounds for believing that their arrest is necessary and which the officer considers satisfy one or more of the statutory criteria in sub-paragraphs (a) to (f), namely:

(a) to enable the name of the person in question to be ascertained (in the case where the constable does not know, and cannot readily ascertain, the person's name, or has reasonable grounds for doubting whether a name given by the person as his name is his real name):
An officer might decide that a person's name cannot be readily ascertained if they fail or refuse to give it when asked, particularly after being warned that failure or refusal is likely to make their arrest necessary (see *Note 2D*). Grounds to doubt a name given may arise if the person appears reluctant or hesitant when asked to give their name or to verify the name they have given.

Where mobile fingerprinting is available and the suspect's name cannot be ascertained or is doubted, the officer should consider using the power under section 61(6A) of PACE (see *Code D paragraph 4.3(e)*) to take and check the fingerprints of a suspect as this may avoid the need to arrest solely to enable their name to be ascertained.

(b) correspondingly as regards the person's address:
An officer might decide that a person's address cannot be readily ascertained if they fail or refuse to give it when asked, particularly after being warned that such a failure or refusal is likely to make their arrest necessary. See *Note 2D*. Grounds to doubt an address given may arise if the person appears reluctant or hesitant when asked to give their address or is unable to provide verifiable details of the locality they claim to live in.
When considering reporting to consider summons or charging by post as alternatives to arrest, an address would be satisfactory if the person will be at it for a sufficiently long period for it to be possible to serve them with the summons or requisition and charge; or, that some other person at that address specified by the person will accept service on their behalf. When considering issuing a penalty notice, the address should be one where the person will be in the event of enforcement action if the person does not pay the penalty or is convicted and fined after a court hearing.

(c) to prevent the person in question:

(i) causing physical injury to himself or any other person;
This might apply where the suspect has already used or threatened violence against others and it is thought likely that they may assault others if they are not arrested. See *Note 2D*.

(ii) suffering physical injury;
This might apply where the suspect's behaviour and actions are believed likely to provoke, or have provoked, others to want to assault the suspect unless the suspect is arrested for their own protection. See *Note 2D*.

(iii) causing loss or damage to property;
This might apply where the suspect is a known persistent offender with a history of serial offending against property (theft and criminal damage) and it is thought likely that they may continue offending if they are not arrested.

(iv) committing an offence against public decency (only applies where members of the public going about their normal business cannot reasonably be expected to avoid the person in question);
This might apply when an offence against public decency is being committed in a place to which the public have access and is likely to be repeated in that or some other public place at a time when the public are likely to encounter the suspect. See *Note 2D*.

(v) causing an unlawful obstruction of the highway;
This might apply to any offence where its commission causes an unlawful obstruction which it is believed may continue or be repeated if the person is not arrested, particularly if the person has been warned that they are causing an obstruction. See *Note 2D*.

(d) to protect a child or other vulnerable person from the person in question.
This might apply when the health (physical or mental) or welfare of a child or vulnerable person is likely to be harmed or is at risk of being harmed, if the person is not arrested in cases where it is not practicable and appropriate to make alternative arrangements to prevent the suspect from having any harmful or potentially harmful contact with the child or vulnerable person.

(e) to allow the prompt and effective investigation of the offence or of the conduct of the person in question. See *Note 2E*.
This may arise when it is thought likely that unless the person is arrested and then either taken in custody to the police station or granted 'street bail' to attend the station later, see *Note 2J*, further action considered necessary to properly investigate their involvement in the offence would be frustrated, unreasonably delayed or otherwise hindered and therefore be impracticable. Examples of such actions include:

(i) *interviewing the suspect* on occasions when the person's voluntary attendance is not considered to be a practicable alternative to arrest, because for example:
- it is thought unlikely that the person would attend the police station voluntarily to be interviewed.
- it is necessary to interview the suspect about the outcome of other investigative action for which their arrest is necessary, see (ii) to (v) below.
- arrest would enable the special warning to be given in accordance with Code C paragraphs 10.10 and 10.11 when the suspect is found:

- in possession of incriminating objects, or at a place where such objects are found;
- at or near the scene of the crime at or about the time it was committed.
- the person has made false statements and/or presented false evidence;
- it is thought likely that the person:
  - may steal or destroy evidence;
  - may collude or make contact with, co-suspects or conspirators;
  - may intimidate or threaten or make contact with, witnesses.

See *Notes 2F and 2G.*

(ii) when considering arrest in connection with the investigation of an *indictable offence* (see *Note 6*), there is a need:
- to enter and search without a search warrant any premises occupied or controlled by the arrested person or where the person was when arrested or immediately before arrest;
- to prevent the arrested person from having contact with others;
- to detain the arrested person for more than 24 hours before charge.

(iii) when considering arrest in connection with any *recordable offence* and it is necessary to secure or preserve evidence of that offence by taking fingerprints, footwear impressions or samples from the suspect for evidential comparison or matching with other material relating to that offence, for example, from the crime scene. See *Note 2H.*

(iv) when considering arrest in connection with any offence and it is necessary to search, examine or photograph the person to obtain evidence. See *Note 2H.*

(v) when considering arrest in connection with an offence to which the statutory Class A drug testing requirements in Code C section 17 apply, to enable testing when it is thought that drug misuse might have caused or contributed to the offence. See *Note 2I.*

(f) to prevent any prosecution for the offence from being hindered by the disappearance of the person in question.

This may arise when it is thought that:
- if the person is not arrested they are unlikely to attend court if they are prosecuted;
- the address given is not a satisfactory address for service of a summons or a written charge and requisition to appear at court because the person will not be at it for a sufficiently long period for the summons or charge and requisition to be served and no other person at that specified address will accept service on their behalf.

3. Information to be given on arrest

(a) Cautions—when a caution must be given

3.1 Code C paragraphs 10.1 and 10.2 set out the requirement for a person whom there are grounds to suspect of an offence (see *Note 2*) to be cautioned before being questioned or further questioned about an offence.

3.2 *Not used.*

3.3 A person who is arrested, or further arrested, must be informed at the time if practicable, or if not, as soon as it becomes practicable thereafter, that they are under arrest and of the grounds and reasons for their arrest, see paragraphs 2.2 and *Note 3.*

3.4 A person who is arrested, or further arrested, must be cautioned unless:
(a) it is impracticable to do so by reason of their condition or behaviour at the time;
(b) they have already been cautioned immediately prior to arrest as in *paragraph 3.1.*

(b) Terms of the caution (Taken from Code C section 10)

3.5 The caution, which must be given on arrest, should be in the following terms:

'You do not have to say anything. But it may harm your defence if you do not mention when questioned something which you later rely on in Court. Anything you do say may be given in evidence.'

Where the use of the Welsh Language is appropriate, a constable may provide the caution directly in Welsh in the following terms:

'Does dim rhaid i chi ddweud dim byd. Ond gall niweidio eich amddiffyniad os na fyddwch chi'n sôn, wrth gael eich holi, am rywbeth y byddwch chi'n dibynnu arno nes ymlaen yn y Llys. Gall unrhyw beth yr ydych yn ei ddweud gael ei roi fel tystiolaeth.'

See *Note 5*

3.6 Minor deviations from the words of any caution given in accordance with this Code do not constitute a breach of this Code, provided the sense of the relevant caution is preserved. See *Note 6*

3.7 *Not used.*

4. Records of arrest

(a) General

4.1 The arresting officer is required to record in his pocket book or by other methods used for recording information:

- the nature and circumstances of the offence leading to the arrest;
- the reason or reasons why arrest was necessary;
- the giving of the caution; and
- anything said by the person at the time of arrest.

4.2 Such a record should be made at the time of the arrest unless impracticable to do so. If not made at that time, the record should then be completed as soon as possible thereafter.

4.3 On arrival at the police station or after being first arrested at the police station, the arrested person must be brought before the custody officer as soon as practicable and a custody record must be opened in accordance with section 2 of Code C. The information given by the arresting officer on the circumstances and reason or reasons for arrest shall be recorded as part of the custody record. Alternatively, a copy of the record made by the officer in accordance with paragraph 4.1 above shall be attached as part of the custody record. See *paragraph 2.2* and *Code C paragraphs 3.4 and 10.3*.

4.4 The custody record will serve as a record of the arrest. Copies of the custody record will be provided in accordance with paragraphs 2.4 and 2.4A of Code C and access for inspection of the original record in accordance with paragraph 2.5 of Code C.

(b) Interviews and arrests

4.5 Records of interview, significant statements or silences will be treated in the same way as set out in sections 10 and 11 of Code C and in Codes E and F (audio and visual recording of interviews).

Notes for Guidance

1 For the purposes of this Code, 'offence' means any statutory or common law offence for which a person may be tried by a magistrates' court or the Crown court and punished if convicted. Statutory offences include assault, rape, criminal damage, theft, robbery, burglary, fraud, possession of controlled drugs and offences under road traffic, liquor licensing, gambling and immigration legislation and local government byelaws. Common law offences include murder, manslaughter, kidnapping, false imprisonment, perverting the course of justice and escape from lawful custody.

1A This code does not apply to powers of arrest conferred on constables under any arrest warrant, for example, a warrant issued under the Magistrates' Courts Act 1980, sections 1 or 13, or the Bail Act 1976, section 7(1), or to the powers of constables to arrest without warrant other than under section 24 of PACE for an offence. These other powers to arrest without warrant do not depend on the arrested person committing any specific offence and include:

- *PACE, section 46A, arrest of person who fails to answer police bail to attend police station or is suspected of breaching any condition of that bail for the custody officer to decide whether they should be kept in police detention which applies whether or not the person commits an offence under section 6 of the Bail Act 1976 (e.g. failing without reasonable cause to surrender to custody);*
- *Bail Act 1976, section 7(3), arrest of person bailed to attend court who is suspected of breaching, or is believed likely to breach, any condition of bail to take them to court for bail to be re-considered;*
- *Children & Young Persons Act 1969, section 32(1A) (absconding)—arrest to return the person to the place where they are required to reside;*
- *Immigration Act 1971, Schedule 2 to arrest a person liable to examination to determine their right to remain in the UK;*
- *Mental Health Act 1983, section 136 to remove person suffering from mental disorder to place of safety for assessment;*
- *Prison Act 1952, section 49, arrest to return person unlawfully at large to the prison etc. where they are liable to be detained;*
- *Road Traffic Act 1988, section 6D arrest of driver following the outcome of a preliminary roadside test requirement to enable the driver to be required to provide an evidential sample;*
- *Common law power to stop or prevent a Breach of the Peace — after arrest a person aged 18 or over may be brought before a justice of the peace court to show cause why they should not be bound over to keep the peace — not criminal proceedings.*

1B Juveniles should not be arrested at their place of education unless this is unavoidable. When a juvenile is arrested at their place of education, the principal or their nominee must be informed. (From Code C Note 11D)

2 *Facts and information relevant to a person's suspected involvement in an offence should not be confined to those which tend to indicate the person has committed or attempted to commit the offence. Before making a decision to arrest, a constable should take account of any facts and information that are available, including claims of innocence made by the person, that might dispel the suspicion.*

2A *Particular examples of facts and information which might point to a person's innocence and may tend to dispel suspicion include those which relate to the statutory defence provided by the Criminal Law Act 1967, section 3(1) which allows the use of reasonable force in the prevention of crime or making an arrest and the common law of self-defence. This may be relevant when a person appears, or claims, to have been acting reasonably in defence of themselves or others or to prevent their property or the property of others from being stolen, destroyed or damaged, particularly if the offence alleged is based on the use of unlawful force, e.g. a criminal assault. When investigating allegations involving the use of force by school staff, the power given to all school staff under the Education and Inspections Act 2006, section 93, to use reasonable force to prevent their pupils from committing any offence, injuring persons, damaging property or prejudicing the maintenance of good order and discipline may be similarly relevant. The Association of Chief Police Officers and the Crown Prosecution Service have published joint guidance to help the public understand the meaning of reasonable force and what to expect from the police and CPS in cases which involve claims of self defence. Separate advice for school staff on their powers to use reasonable force is available from the Department for Education*

2B *If a constable who is dealing with an allegation of crime and considering the need to arrest becomes an investigator for the purposes of the Code of Practice under the Criminal Procedure and Investigations Act 1996, the officer should, in accordance with paragraph 3.5 of that Code, 'pursue all reasonable lines of inquiry, whether these point towards or away from the suspect. What is reasonable in each case will depend on the particular circumstances.'*

2C *For a constable to have reasonable grounds for believing it necessary to arrest, he or she is not required to be satisfied that there is no viable alternative to arrest. However, it does mean that in all cases, the officer should consider that arrest is the practical, sensible and proportionate option in all the circumstances at the time the decision is made. This applies equally to a person in police detention after being arrested for an offence who is suspected of involvement in a further offence and the necessity to arrest them for that further offence is being considered.*

2D *Although a warning is not expressly required, officers should if practicable, consider whether a warning which points out their offending behaviour, and explains why, if they do not stop, the resulting consequences may make their arrest necessary. Such a warning might:*

- *if heeded, avoid the need to arrest, or*
- *if it is ignored, support the need to arrest and also help prove the mental element of certain offences, for example, the person's intent or awareness, or help to rebut a defence that they were acting reasonably.*

A person who is warned that they may be liable to arrest if their real name and address cannot be ascertained, should be given a reasonable opportunity to establish their real name and address before deciding that either or both are unknown and cannot be readily ascertained or that there are reasonable grounds to doubt that a name and address they have given is their real name and address. They should be told why their name is not known and cannot be readily ascertained and (as the case may be) of the grounds for doubting that a name and address they have given is their real name and address, including, for example, the reason why a particular document the person has produced to verify their real name and/or address, is not sufficient.

2E *The meaning of 'prompt' should be considered on a case by case basis taking account of all the circumstances. It indicates that the progress of the investigation should not be delayed to the extent that it would adversely affect the effectiveness of the investigation. The arresting officer also has discretion to release the arrested person on 'street bail' as an alternative to taking the person directly to the station. See Note 2J.*

2F *An officer who believes that it is necessary to interview the person suspected of committing the offence must then consider whether their arrest is necessary in order to carry out the interview. The officer is not required to interrogate the suspect to determine whether they will attend a police station voluntarily to be interviewed but they must consider whether the suspect's voluntary attendance is a practicable alternative for carrying out the interview. If it is, then arrest would not be necessary. Conversely, an officer who considers this option but is not satisfied that it is a practicable alternative, may have reasonable grounds for deciding that the arrest is necessary at the outset 'on the street'. Without such considerations, the officer would not be able to establish that arrest was necessary in order to interview.*

Circumstances which suggest that a person's arrest 'on the street' would not be necessary to interview them might be where the officer:

- *is satisfied as to their identity and address and that they will attend the police station voluntarily to be interviewed, either immediately or by arrangement at a future date and time; and*
- *is not aware of any other circumstances which indicate that voluntary attendance would not be a practicable alternative. See paragraph 2.9(e)(i) to (v).*

When making arrangements for the person's voluntary attendance, the officer should tell the person:

- *that to properly investigate their suspected involvement in the offence they must be interviewed under caution at the police station, but in the circumstances their arrest for this purpose will not be necessary if they attend the police station voluntarily to be interviewed;*
- *that if they attend voluntarily, they will be entitled to free legal advice before, and to have a solicitor present at, the interview;*
- *that the date and time of the interview will take account of their circumstances and the needs of the investigation; and*
- *that if they do not agree to attend voluntarily at a time which meets the needs of the investigation, or having so agreed, fail to attend, or having attended, fail to remain for the interview to be completed, their arrest will be necessary to enable them to be interviewed.*

2G When the person attends the police station voluntarily for interview by arrangement as in Note 2F above, their arrest on arrival at the station prior to interview would only be justified if:

- *new information coming to light after the arrangements were made indicates that from that time, voluntary attendance ceased to be a practicable alternative and the person's arrest became necessary; and*
- *it was not reasonably practicable for the person to be arrested before they attended the station.*

If a person who attends the police station voluntarily to be interviewed decides to leave before the interview is complete, the police would at that point be entitled to consider whether their arrest was necessary to carry out the interview. The possibility that the person might decide to leave during the interview is therefore not a valid reason for arresting them before the interview has commenced. See Code C paragraph 3.21.

2H The necessity criteria do not permit arrest solely to enable the routine taking, checking (speculative searching) and retention of fingerprints, samples, footwear impressions and photographs when there are no prior grounds to believe that checking and comparing the fingerprints etc. or taking a photograph would provide relevant evidence of the person's involvement in the offence concerned or would help to ascertain or verify their real identity.

2I The necessity criteria do not permit arrest for an offence solely because it happens to be one of the statutory drug testing 'trigger offences' (see Code C Note 17E) when there is no suspicion that Class A drug misuse might have caused or contributed to the offence.

2J Having determined that the necessity criteria have been met and having made the arrest, the officer can then consider the use of street bail on the basis of the effective and efficient progress of the investigation of the offence in question. It gives the officer discretion to compel the person to attend a police station at a date/time that best suits the overall needs of the particular investigation. Its use is not confined to dealing with child care issues or allowing officers to attend to more urgent operational duties and granting street bail does not retrospectively negate the need to arrest.

3 An arrested person must be given sufficient information to enable them to understand they have been deprived of their liberty and the reason they have been arrested, as soon as practicable after the arrest, e.g. when a person is arrested on suspicion of committing an offence they must be informed of the nature of the suspected offence and when and where it was committed. The suspect must also be informed of the reason or reasons why arrest is considered necessary. Vague or technical language should be avoided. When explaining why one or more of the arrest criteria apply, it is not necessary to disclose any specific details that might undermine or otherwise adversely affect any investigative processes. An example might be the conduct of a formal interview when prior disclosure of such details might give the suspect an opportunity to fabricate an innocent explanation or to otherwise conceal lies from the interviewer.

4 Nothing in this Code requires a caution to be given or repeated when informing a person not under arrest they may be prosecuted for an offence. However, a court will not be able to draw any inferences under the Criminal Justice and Public Order Act 1994, section 34, if the person was not cautioned.

5 If it appears a person does not understand the caution, the person giving it should explain it in their own words.

6 *Certain powers available as the result of an arrest — for example, entry and search of premises, detention without charge beyond 24 hours, holding a person incommunicado and delaying access to legal advice — only apply in respect of indictable offences and are subject to the specific requirements on authorisation as set out in PACE and the relevant Code of Practice.*

PACE CODE H

REVISED CODE OF PRACTICE IN CONNECTION WITH: THE DETENTION, TREATMENT AND QUESTIONING BY POLICE OFFICERS OF PERSONS IN POLICE DETENTION UNDER SECTION 41 OF, AND SCHEDULE 8 TO, THE TERRORISM ACT 2000 THE TREATMENT AND QUESTIONING BY POLICE OFFICERS OF DETAINED PERSONS IN RESPECT OF WHOM AN AUTHORISATION TO QUESTION AFTER CHARGE HAS BEEN GIVEN UNDER SECTION 22 OF THE COUNTER-TERRORISM ACT 2008

[Code H is not reproduced. The full text of Code H is freely available at tinyurl.com/vt22x6g]

Appendix 2 Attorney-General's Guidelines

EXERCISE BY THE CROWN OF ITS RIGHT OF STAND BY

1. Although the law has long recognised the right of the Crown to exclude a member of a jury panel from sitting as a juror by the exercise in open court of the right to request a stand by or, if necessary, by challenge for cause, it has been customary for those instructed to prosecute on behalf of the Crown to assert that right only sparingly and in exceptional circumstances. It is generally accepted that the prosecution should not use its right in order to influence the overall composition of a jury or with a view to tactical advantage.
2. The approach outlined above is founded on the principles that:
   a. the members of a jury should be selected at random from the panel subject to any rule of law as to right of challenge by the defence, and
   b. the Juries Act 1974 identifies those classes of persons who alone are disqualified from or ineligible for service on a jury. No other class of person may be treated as disqualified or ineligible.
3. The enactment by Parliament of s. 118 of the Criminal Justice Act 1988 abolishing the right of defendants to remove jurors by means of peremptory challenge makes it appropriate that the Crown should assert its right to stand by only on the basis of clearly defined and restrictive criteria. Derogation from the principle that members of a jury should be selected at random should be permitted only where it is essential.
4. Primary responsibility for ensuring that an individual does not serve on a jury if he is not competent to discharge properly the duties of a juror rests with the appropriate court officer and, ultimately the trial judge. Current legislation provides, in ss. 9 to s.10 of the Juries Act 1974, fairly wide discretion to excuse, defer or discharge jurors.
5. The circumstances in which it would be proper for the Crown to exercise its right to stand by a member of a jury panel are:
   a. where a jury check authorised in accordance with the Attorney-General's Guidelines on Jury Checks reveals information justifying exercise of the right to stand by in accordance with para.11 of the guidelines below [under **Jury Checks**] and the Attorney-General personally authorises the exercise of the right to stand by; or
   b. where a person is about to be sworn as a juror who is manifestly unsuitable and the defence agree that, accordingly, the exercise by the prosecution of the right to stand by would be appropriate. An example of the sort of exceptional circumstances which might justify stand by is where it becomes apparent that, despite the provisions mentioned in para. 4 above, a juror selected for service to try a complex case is in fact illiterate.

JURY CHECKS

1. The principles which are generally to be observed are:
   a. that members of a jury should be selected at random from the panel,
   b. the Juries Act 1974 identifies those classes of persons who alone are either disqualified from or ineligible for service on a jury; no other class of person may be treated as disqualified or ineligible,
   c. the correct way for the Crown to seek to exclude a member of the panel from sitting as a juror is by the exercise in open court of the right to request a stand by or, if necessary, to challenge for cause.
2. Parliament has provided safeguards against jurors who may be corrupt or biased. In addition to the provision for majority verdicts, there is the sanction of a criminal offence for a disqualified person to serve on a jury. The omission of a disqualified person from the panel is a matter for court officials—they will check criminal records for the purpose of ascertaining whether or not a potential juror is a *disqualified person*.
3. There are, however, certain exceptional types of case of public importance for which the provisions as to majority verdicts and the disqualification of jurors may not be sufficient to ensure the proper administration of justice. In such cases it is in the interests of both justice and the public that there should be further safeguards against the possibility of bias and in such cases checks which go beyond the investigation of criminal records may be necessary.
4. These classes of case may be defined broadly as (a) cases in which national security is involved and part of the evidence is likely to be heard in camera, and (b) security and terrorist cases in which a juror's extreme beliefs could prevent a fair trial.

5. The particular aspects of these cases which may make it desirable to seek extra precautions are:
   a. in security cases a danger that a juror, either voluntarily or under pressure, may make an improper use of evidence which, because of its sensitivity, has been given in camera,
   b. in both security and terrorist cases the danger that a juror's personal beliefs are so biased as to go beyond normally reflecting the broad spectrum of views and interests in the community to reflect the extreme views of sectarian interest or pressure group to a degree which might interfere with his fair assessment of the facts of the case or lead him to exert improper pressure on his fellow jurors.
6. In order to ascertain whether in exceptional circumstances of the above nature either of these factors might seriously influence a potential juror's impartial performance of his duties or his respecting the secrecy of evidence given in camera, it may be necessary to conduct a limited investigation of the panel. In general, such further investigation beyond one of criminal records made for disqualifications may only be made with the records of the police. However, a check may, additionally be made against the records of the Security Service. No checks other than on these sources and no general inquiries are to be made save to the limited extent that they may be needed to confirm the identity of a juror about whom the initial check has raised serious doubts.
7. No further investigation, as described in para. 6 above, should be made save with the personal authority of the Attorney-General on the application of the Director of Public Prosecutions and such checks are hereafter referred to as 'authorised checks'. When a chief officer of police or the prosecutor has reason to believe that it is likely that an authorised check may be desirable and proper in accordance with these guidelines, he should refer the matter to the Director of Public Prosecutions. In those cases in which the Director of Public Prosecutions believes authorised checks are both proportionate and necessary, the Director will make an application to the Attorney-General.
8. The Director of Public Prosecutions will provide the Attorney-General with all relevant information in support of the requested authorised checks. The Attorney-General will consider personally the request and, if appropriate, authorise the check.
9. The result of any authorised check will be sent to the Director of Public Prosecutions. The Director will then decide, having regard to the matters set out in para. 5 above, what information ought to be brought to the attention of prosecuting counsel. The Director will also provide the Attorney-General with the result of the authorised check.
10. Although the right of stand by and the decision to authorise checks are wholly within the discretion of the Attorney-General, when the Attorney-General has agreed to an authorised check being conducted, the Director of Public Prosecutions will write to the Presiding Judge for the area to advise him that this is being done.
11. No right of stand by should be exercised by counsel for the Crown on the basis of information obtained as a result of an authorised check save with the personal authority of the Attorney-General and unless the information is such as, having regard to the facts of the case and the offences charged, to afford strong reason for believing that a particular juror might be a security risk, be susceptible to improper approaches or be influenced in arriving at a verdict for the reasons given above.
12. Information revealed in the course of an authorised check must be considered in line with the normal rules on disclosure.
13. A record is to be kept by the Director of Public Prosecutions of the use made by counsel of the information passed to him and of the jurors stood by or challenged by the parties to the proceedings. A copy of this record is to be forwarded to the Attorney-General for the sole purpose of enabling him to monitor the operation of these guidelines.
14. No use of the information obtained as a result of an authorised check is to be made except as may be necessary in direct relation to or arising out of the trial for which the check was authorised. The information may, however, be used for the prevention of crime or as evidence in a future criminal prosecution, save that material obtained from the Security Service may only be used in those circumstances with the authority of the Security Service.

ACCEPTANCE OF PLEAS AND THE PROSECUTOR'S ROLE IN THE SENTENCING EXERCISE

A. Foreword

A1. Prosecutors have an important role in protecting the victim's interests in the criminal justice process, not least in the acceptance of pleas and the sentencing exercise. The basis of plea, particularly in a case that is not contested, is the vehicle through which the victim's voice is heard. Factual inaccuracies in pleas in mitigation cause distress and offence to victims, the families of victims and witnesses. This can take many forms but may be most acutely felt when the victim is dead and the family hears inaccurate assertions about the victim's character or lifestyle. Prosecution advocates are reminded that they are required to adhere to the standards set out in the Victim's Charter, which places the needs of the victim at the heart of the criminal justice process, and that they are subject to a similar obligation in respect of the Code of Practice for Victims of Crime.

A2. The principle of fairness is central to the administration of justice. The implementation of Human Rights Act 1998 in October 2000 incorporated into domestic law the principle of fairness to the accused articulated in the European Convention on Human Rights. Accuracy and reasonableness of plea plays an important part in ensuring fairness both to the accused and to the victim.

A3. The Attorney General's Guidelines on the Acceptance of Pleas issued on December 7, 2000 highlighted the importance of transparency in the conduct of justice. The basis of plea agreed by the parties in a criminal trial is central to the sentencing process. An illogical or unsupported basis of plea can lead to an unduly lenient sentence being passed, and has a consequential effect where consideration arises as to whether to refer the sentence to the Court of Appeal under section 36 of the Criminal Justice Act 1988.

A4. These Guidelines, which replace the Guidelines issued in October 2005, give guidance on how prosecutors should meet these objectives of protection of victims' interests and of securing fairness and transparency in the process. They take into account [CrimPD VII, Sentencing, paras. B.1 to B.27: see Supplement, **PD-74**] and the guidance issued by the Court of Appeal (Criminal) Division in *R v Beswick* [1996] 1 Cr App R 343, *R v Tolera* [1999] 1 Cr App R 25 and *R v Underwood* [2005] 1 Cr App R 178. They complement the Bar Council Guidance on Written Standards for the Conduct of Professional Work issued with the 7th edition of the Code of Conduct for the Bar of England and Wales and the Law Society's Professional Conduct Rules. When considering the acceptance of a guilty plea prosecution advocates are also reminded of the need to apply 'The Farquharson Guidelines on The Role and Responsibilities of the Prosecution Advocate'.

A5. The Guidelines should be followed by all prosecutors and those persons designated under section 7 of the Prosecution of Offences Act 1985 (designated caseworkers) and apply to prosecutions conducted in England and Wales.

B. General Principles

B1. Justice in this jurisdiction, save in the most exceptional circumstances, is conducted in public. This includes the acceptance of pleas by the prosecution and sentencing.

B2. The Code for Crown Prosecutors governs the prosecutor's decision-making prior to the commencement of the trial hearing and sets out the circumstances in which pleas to a reduced number of charges, or less serious charges, can be accepted.

B3. When a case is listed for trial and the prosecution form the view that the appropriate course is to accept a plea before the proceedings commence or continue, or to offer no evidence on the indictment or any part of it, the prosecution should whenever practicable speak to the victim or the victim's family, so that the position can be explained. The views of the victim or the family may assist in informing the prosecutor's decision as to whether it is the public interest, as defined by the Code for Crown Prosecutors, to accept or reject the plea. The victim or victim's family should then be kept informed and decisions explained once they are made at court.

B4. The appropriate disposal of a criminal case after conviction is as much a part of the criminal justice process as the trial of guilt or innocence. The prosecution advocate represents the public interest, and should be ready to assist the court to reach its decision as to the appropriate sentence. This will include drawing the court's attention to:

- any victim personal statement or other information available to the prosecution advocate as to the impact of the offence on the victim;
- where appropriate, to any evidence of the impact of the offending on a community;
- any statutory provisions relevant to the offender and the offences under consideration;
- any relevant sentencing guidelines and guideline cases; and
- the aggravating and mitigating factors of the offence under consideration.

B5. The prosecution advocate may also offer assistance to the court by making submissions, in the light of all these factors, as to the appropriate sentencing range. In all cases, it is the prosecution advocate's duty to apply for appropriate ancillary orders, such as anti-social behaviour orders and confiscation orders. When considering which ancillary orders to apply for, prosecution advocates must always have regard to the victim's needs, including the question of his or her future protection.

C. The Basis of Plea

C1. The basis of a guilty plea must not be agreed on a misleading or untrue set of facts and must take proper account of the victim's interests. An illogical or insupportable basis of plea will inevitably result in the imposition of an inappropriate sentence and is capable of damaging public confidence in the criminal justice system. In cases involving multiple defendants the bases of plea for each defendant must be factually consistent with each other.

C2. When the defendant indicates an acceptable plea, the defence advocate should reduce the basis of the plea to writing. This must be done in all cases save for those in which the defendant has indicated that the guilty plea has been or will be tendered on the basis of the prosecution case.

C3. The written basis of plea must be considered with great care, taking account of the position of any other relevant defendant where appropriate. The prosecution should not lend itself to any agreement whereby a case is presented to the sentencing judge on a misleading or untrue set of facts or on a basis that is detrimental to the victim's interests. There will be cases where a defendant seeks to mitigate on the basis of assertions of fact which are outside the scope of the prosecution's knowledge. A typical example concerns the defendant's state of mind. If a defendant wishes to be sentenced on this basis, the prosecution advocate should invite the judge not to accept the defendant's version unless he or she gives evidence on oath to be tested in cross-examination. [CrimPD VII, Sentencing, para. B.12: see Supplement, **PD-74**] states that in such circumstances the defence advocate should be prepared to call the defendant and, if the defendant is not willing to testify, subject to any explanation that may be given, the judge may draw such inferences as appear appropriate.

C4. The prosecution advocate should show the prosecuting authority any written record relating to the plea and agree with them the basis on which the case will be opened to the court. If, as may well be the case, the basis of plea differs in its implications for sentencing or the making of ancillary orders from the case originally outlined by the prosecution, the prosecution advocate must ensure that such differences are accurately reflected in the written record prior to showing it to the prosecuting authority.

C5. It is the responsibility of the prosecution advocate thereafter to ensure that the defence advocate is aware of the basis on which the plea is accepted by the prosecution and the way in which the prosecution case will be opened to the court.

C6. In all cases where it is likely to assist the court where the sentencing issues are complex or unfamiliar the prosecution must add to the written outline of the case which is served upon the court a summary of the key considerations. This should take the form of very brief notes on:

- any relevant statutory limitations
- the names of any relevant sentencing authorities or guidelines
- the scope for any ancillary orders (e.g. concerning anti-social behaviour, confiscation or deportation will need to be considered).
- The outline should also include the age of the defendant and information regarding any outstanding offences.

C7. It remains open to the prosecutor to provide further written information (for example to supplement and update the analysis at later stages of the case) where he or she thought that likely to assist the court, or if the judge requests it.

C8. When the prosecution advocate has agreed the written basis of plea submitted by the defence advocate, he or she should endorse the document accordingly. If the prosecution advocate takes issue with all or part of the written basis of plea, the procedure set out in [CrimPD VII, Sentencing, paras. B.11 to B.27: see Supplement, **PD-74** (and in the CrimPR, r. 25.16: see Supplement, **R-260**)] should be followed. The defendant's basis of plea must be set out in writing identifying what is in dispute; the court may invite the parties to make representations about whether the dispute is material to sentence; and if the court decides that it is a material dispute, the court will invite further representations or evidence as it may require and decide the dispute in accordance with the principles set out in *R v Newton* 77 Cr App R13, CA. The signed original document setting out the disputed factual matters should be made available to the trial judge and thereafter lodged with the court papers, as it will form part of the record of the hearing.

C9. Where the basis of plea cannot be agreed and the discrepancy between the two accounts is such as to have a potentially significant effect on the level of sentence, it is the duty of the defence advocate so to inform the court before the sentencing process begins. There remains an overriding duty on the prosecution advocate to ensure that the sentencing judge is made aware of the discrepancy and of the consideration which must be given to holding a *Newton* hearing to resolve the issue. The court should be told where a derogatory reference to a victim, witness or third party is not accepted, even though there may be no effect on sentence.

C10. As emphasised in [CrimPD VII, Sentencing, para. B.9: see Supplement, **PD-74**], whenever an agreement as to the basis of plea is made between the prosecution and defence, any such agreement will be subject to the approval of the trial judge, who may of his or her own motion disregard the agreement and direct that a *Newton* hearing should be held to determine the proper basis on which sentence should be passed.

C11. Where a defendant declines to admit an offence that he or she previously indicated should be taken into consideration, the prosecution advocate should indicate to the defence advocate and the court that, subject to further review, the offence may now form the basis of a new prosecution.

D. Sentence Indications

D1. Only in the Crown Court may sentence indications be sought. Advocates there are reminded that indications as to sentence should not be sought from the trial judge unless issues between the prosecution and defence have been addressed and resolved. Therefore, in difficult or complicated cases, no less than seven days notice in writing of an intention to seek an indication should normally be given to the prosecution and the court. When deciding whether the circumstances of a case require such notice to be given, defence advocates are reminded that prosecutors should not agree a basis of plea unless and until the necessary consultation has taken place first with the victim and/or the victim's family and second, in the case of an independent prosecution advocate, with the prosecuting authority.

D2. If there is no final agreement about the plea to the indictment, or the basis of plea, and the defence nevertheless proceeds to seek an indication of sentence, which the judge appears minded to give, the prosecution advocate should remind him or her of the guidance given in *R v Goodyear (Karl)* [2005] EWCA 888 that normally speaking an indication of sentence should not be given until the basis of the plea has been agreed or the judge has concluded that he or she can properly deal with the case without the need for a trial of the issue.

D3. If an indication is sought, the prosecution advocate should normally enquire whether the judge is in possession of or has access to all the evidence relied on by the prosecution, including any victim personal statement, as well as any information about relevant previous convictions recorded against the defendant.

D4. Before the judge gives the indication, the prosecution advocate should draw the judge's attention to any minimum or mandatory statutory sentencing requirements. Where the prosecution advocate would be expected to offer the judge assistance with relevant guideline cases or the views of the Sentencing Guidelines Council, he or she should invite the judge to allow them to do so. Where it applies, the prosecution advocate should remind the judge that the position of the Attorney General to refer any sentencing decision as unduly lenient is unaffected. In any event, the prosecution advocate should not say anything which may create the impression that the sentence indication has the support or approval of the Crown.

E. Pleas In Mitigation

E1. The prosecution advocate must challenge any assertion by the defence in mitigation which is derogatory to a person's character, (for instance, because it suggests that his or her conduct is or has been criminal, immoral or improper) and which is either false or irrelevant to proper sentencing considerations. If the defence advocate persists in that assertion, the prosecution advocate should invite the court to consider holding a *Newton* hearing to determine the issue.

E2. The defence advocate must not submit in mitigation anything that is derogatory to a person's character without giving advance notice in writing so as to afford the prosecution advocate the opportunity to consider their position under paragraph E1. When the prosecution advocate is so notified they must take all reasonable steps to establish whether the assertions are true. Reasonable steps will include seeking the views of the victim. This will involve seeking the views of the victim's family if the victim is deceased, and the victim's parents or legal guardian where the victim is a child. Reasonable steps may also include seeking the views of the police or other law enforcement authority, as appropriate. An assertion which is derogatory to a person's character will rarely amount to mitigation unless it has a causal connection to the circumstances of the offence or is otherwise relevant to proper sentencing considerations.

E3. Where notice has not been given in accordance with paragraph E2, the prosecution advocate must not acquiesce in permitting mitigation which is derogatory to a person's character. In such circumstances, the prosecution advocate should draw the attention of the court to the failure to give advance notice and seek time, and if necessary, an adjournment to investigate the assertion in the same way as if proper notice had been given. Where, in the opinion of the prosecution advocate, there are substantial grounds for believing that such an assertion is false or irrelevant to sentence, he or she should inform the court of their opinion and invite the court to consider making an order under section 58(8) of the Criminal Procedure and Investigations Act 1996, preventing publication of the assertion.

E4. Where the prosecution advocate considers that the assertion is, if true, relevant to sentence, or the court has so indicated, he or she should seek time, and if necessary an adjournment, to establish whether the assertion is true. If the matter cannot be resolved to the satisfaction of the parties, the prosecution advocate should invite the court to consider holding a *Newton* hearing to determine the issue.

GUIDANCE ON THE USE OF THE COMMON LAW OFFENCE OF CONSPIRACY TO DEFRAUD

Summary

1. This guidance concerns the issues which the Attorney General asks prosecuting authorities in England and Wales to consider before using the common law offence of conspiracy to defraud, in the light of the implementation of the Fraud Act 2006. It may be supplemented by Departmental-specific guidance issued by individual Directors of the prosecuting authorities.

Background

2. When the Fraud Act 2006 comes into force on 15 January 2007, the prosecution will be able to use modern and flexible statutory offences of fraud. The 2006 Act replaces the deception offences contained in the Theft Acts 1968–1996 with a general offence of fraud that can be committed in three ways:
   - fraud by false representation;
   - fraud by failing to disclose information; and
   - fraud by abuse of position.

   It also introduces other offences which can be used in particular circumstances, notably:
   - new offences to tackle the possession and supply of articles for use in fraud; and
   - a new offence of fraudulent trading applicable to sole traders and other businesses not caught by the existing offence in section 458 of the Companies Act 1985.
3. The new offences are designed to catch behaviour that previously fell through gaps in the Theft Acts and could only be prosecuted as conspiracy to defraud. Indeed the Act is based on a Law Commission report (Cm 5560) which also recommended the abolition of the common law offence of conspiracy to defraud. The argument is that the offence is unfairly uncertain, and wide enough to have the potential to catch behaviour that should not be criminal. Furthermore it can seem anomalous that what is legal if performed by one person should be criminal if performed by many.
4. However, consultations showed a widespread view in favour of retention of common law conspiracy to defraud, and the Government decided to retain it for the meantime, but accepted the case for considering repeal in the longer term. Whether there is a continuing need for retention of the common law offence is one of the issues that will be addressed in the Home Office review of the operation of the Fraud Act 2006, which will take place 3 years after its implementation.
5. In 2003, 14,928 defendants were proceeded against in England and Wales for crimes of fraud; 1018 of these were charged with the common law crime of conspiracy to defraud of which 44% were found guilty (compared with 71% for the statutory fraud offences). The expectation now is that the common law offence will be used to a significantly lesser extent once the Fraud Act 2006 has come into force.

Issues to be considered in using the common law offence

6. In selecting charges in fraud cases, the prosecutor should first consider:
   - whether the behaviour could be prosecuted under statute—whether under the Fraud Act 2006 or another Act or as a statutory conspiracy; and
   - whether the available statutory charges adequately reflect the gravity of the offence.
7. Statutory conspiracy to commit a substantive offence should be charged if the alleged agreement satisfies the definition in section 1 of the Criminal Law Act 1977, provided that there is no wider dishonest objective that would be important to the presentation of the prosecution case in reflecting the gravity of the case.
8. Section 12 of the Criminal Justice Act 1987 provides that common law conspiracy to defraud may be charged even if the conduct agreed upon will involve the commission of a statutory offence. However, Lord Bingham said in *R v Rimmington* and *R v Goldstein* [(2005) UKHL 63]:

   > 'I would not go to the length of holding that conduct may never be lawfully prosecuted as a generally-expressed common law crime where it falls within the terms of a specific statutory

provision, *but good practice and respect for the primacy of statute do in my judgment require that conduct falling within the terms of a specific statutory provision should be prosecuted under that provision unless there is good reason for doing otherwise.*'

9. In the Attorney General's view the common law charge may still be appropriate in the type of cases set out in paragraphs 12–15, but in order to understand the circumstances under which conspiracy to defraud is used *prosecutors should make a record of the reasons for preferring that charge.*

Records of decisions

10. Where a charge of common law conspiracy to defraud is proposed the case lawyer must consider and set out in writing in the review note:
    - how much such a charge will add to the amount of evidence likely to be called both by the prosecution and the defence; and
    - the justification for using the charge, and why specific statutory offences are inadequate or otherwise inappropriate.
    - Thereafter, and before charge, the use of this charge should be specifically approved by a supervising lawyer experienced in fraud cases. Equivalent procedures to ensure proper consideration of the charge and recording of the decision should be applied by all prosecuting authorities in their case review processes.
11. Information from these records will be collected retrospectively for the review to be conducted in 3 years. It will enable the identification of where and why the common law offence has been used. It could then also form the basis for any future work on whether, and if so how, to replace the common law or whether it can simply and safely be repealed. It is expected that in 3 years the Government will be able to review the situation in the light of the practical operation not only of the new fraud offences, but of other relevant changes. These include the Lord Chief Justice's protocol on the control and management of heavy fraud cases, and the sample count provisions in the Domestic Violence, Crime and Victims Act 2004. Any actual or proposed changes to the law on assisting and encouraging crime in the light of the Law Commission's study of that issue [Cm 6878, published in July 2006] will also be taken into account.

A. Conduct that can more effectively be prosecuted as conspiracy to defraud

12. There may be cases where the interests of justice can only be served by presenting to a court an overall picture which cannot be achieved by charging a series of substantive offences or statutory conspiracies. Typically, such cases will involve some, but not necessarily all of the following:
    - evidence of several significant but different kinds of criminality;
    - several jurisdictions;
    - different types of victims, e.g. individuals, banks, web site administrators, credit card companies;
    - organised crime networks.
13. The proper presentation of such cases as statutory conspiracies could lead to:
    - large numbers of separate counts to reflect the different conspiracies;
    - severed trials for single or discrete groups of conspiracies;
    - evidence in one severed trial being deemed inadmissible in another.
14. If so, the consequences might be that no one court would receive a cohesive picture of the whole case which would allow sentencing on a proper basis. In contrast a single count of common law conspiracy to defraud might, in such circumstances, reflect the nature and extent of criminal conduct in a way that prosecuting the underlying statutory offences or conspiracies would fail to achieve.

B. Conduct that can only be prosecuted as conspiracy to defraud

15. Examples of such conduct might include but are not restricted to agreements to the following courses of action:
    - The dishonest obtaining of land and other property which cannot be stolen such as intellectual property not protected by the Copyright, Designs and Patents Act 1988 and the Trademarks Act 1994, and other confidential information. The Fraud Act will bite where there is intent to make a gain or cause a loss through false representation, failure to disclose information where there is a legal obligation to do so, or the abuse of position;
    - Dishonestly infringing another's right; for example the dishonest exploitation of another's patent in the absence of a legal duty to disclose information about its existence;
    - Where it is intended that the final offence be committed by someone outside the conspiracy; and
    - Cases where the accused cannot be proved to have had the necessary degree of knowledge of the substantive offence to be perpetrated;

SECTION 18 RIPA: PROSECUTORS' INTERCEPT GUIDELINES

1. These guidelines concern the approach to be taken by prosecutors in applying section 18 of the Regulation of Investigatory Powers Act (RIPA) in England and Wales.

Background

2. It has been long-standing Government policy that the fact that interception of communications has taken place in any particular case should remain secret and not be disclosed to the subject. This is because of the need to protect the continuing value of interception as a vital means of gathering intelligence about serious crime and activities which threaten national security. The Government judges that if the use of the technique in particular cases were to be confirmed, the value of the technique would be diminished because targets would either know, or could deduce, when their communications might be intercepted and so could take avoiding action by using other, more secure means of communication.
3. In the context of legal proceedings, the policy that the fact of interception should remain secret is implemented by section 17 of RIPA. Section 17 provides that no evidence shall be adduced, question asked, assertion or disclosure made or other thing done in, for the purposes of, or in connection with, any legal proceedings which discloses the contents of a communication which has been obtained following the issue of an interception warrant or a warrant under the Interception of Communications Act 1985, or any related communications data ('protected information'), or tends to suggest that certain events have occurred.
4. The effect of section 17 is that the fact of interception of the subject's communications and the product of that interception cannot be relied upon or referred to by either party to the proceedings. This is given further effect by sections 3(7), 7(6), 7A(9) and 9(9) of the Criminal Procedure and Investigations Act 1996 (as amended). This protects the continuing value of interception whilst also creating a 'level playing-field', in that neither side can gain any advantage from the interception. In the context of criminal proceedings, this means that the defendant cannot be prejudiced by the existence in the hands of the prosecution of intercept material which is adverse to his interests.

Detailed Analysis

First Stage: action to be taken by the prosecutor

5. Section 18(7)(a) of RIPA provides:

   'Nothing in section 17(1) shall prohibit any such disclosure of any information that continues to be available for disclosure as is confined to . . . a disclosure to a person conducting a criminal prosecution for the purpose only of enabling that person to determine what is required of him by his duty to secure the fairness of the prosecution'.

   If protected information is disclosed to a prosecutor, as permitted by section 18(7)(a), the first step that should be taken by the prosecutor is to review any information regarding an interception that remains extant at the time that he or she has conduct of the case.[1] In reviewing it, the prosecutor should seek to identify any information whose existence, if no action was taken by the Crown, might result in unfairness. Experience suggests that the most likely example of such potential unfairness is where the evidence in the case is such that the jury may draw an inference which intercept shows to be wrong, and to leave this uncorrected will result in the defence being disadvantaged.
6. If in the view of the prosecutor to take no action would render the proceedings unfair, the prosecutor should, first consulting with the relevant prosecution agency, take such steps as are available to him or her to secure the fairness of the proceedings provided these steps do not contravene section 18(10). In the example given above, such steps could include:
   (i) putting the prosecution case in such a way that the misleading inference is not drawn by the jury; or
   (ii) not relying upon the evidence which makes the information relevant; or

[1] Section 15(1) of RIPA provides that it is the duty of the Secretary of State to ensure that arrangements are in place to ensure that (amongst other matters) intercept material is retained by the intercepting agencies only for as long as is necessary for any of the authorised purposes. The authorised purposes include retention which:

'is necessary to ensure that a person conducting a criminal prosecution has the information he needs to determine what is required of him by his duty to secure the fairness of the prosecution'. (section 15(4)(d))

(iii) discontinuing that part of the prosecution case in relation to which the protected information is relevant, by amending a charge or count on the indictment or offering no evidence on such a charge or count; or

(iv) making an admission of fact.[2]

There is no requirement for the prosecutor to notify the judge of the action that he or she has taken or proposes to take. Such a course should only be taken by the prosecutor if he considers it essential in the interests of justice to do so (see below).

Second Stage: disclosure to the judge

7. There may be some cases (although these are likely to be rare) where the prosecutor considers that he cannot secure the fairness of the proceedings without assistance from the relevant judge. In recognition of this, section 18(7)(b) of RIPA provides that in certain limited circumstances, the prosecutor may invite the judge to order a disclosure of the protected information to him.

8. If the prosecutor considers that he requires the assistance of the trial judge to ensure the fairness of the proceedings, or he is in doubt as to whether the result of taking the steps outlined at para 6 above would ensure fairness, he must apply to see the judge *ex parte*. Under section 18(8), a judge shall not order a disclosure to him except where he is satisfied that the exceptional circumstances of the case make that disclosure essential in the interests of justice. Before the judge is in a position to order such disclosure the prosecutor will need to impart to the judge such information, but only such information, as is necessary to demonstrate that exceptional circumstances mean that the prosecutor acting alone cannot secure the fairness of the proceedings. Experience suggests that exceptional circumstances in the course of a trial justifying disclosure to a judge arise only in the following two situations:

(1) **Where the judge's assistance is necessary to ensure the fairness of the trial**

This situation may arise in the example given at paragraph 5 above, where there is a risk that the jury might draw an inference from certain facts, which protected information shows would be the wrong inference, and the prosecutor is unable to ensure that the jury will not draw this inference by his actions alone. The purpose in informing the judge is so that the judge will then be in a position to ensure fairness by:

(i) summing up in a way which will ensure that the wrong inference is not drawn; or

(ii) giving appropriate directions to the jury; or

(iii) requiring the Crown to make an admission of fact which the judge thinks *essential in the interests of justice* if he is of the opinion that *exceptional circumstances* require him to make such a direction (section 18(9)). However, such a direction **must not** authorise or require anything to be done which discloses any of the contents of an intercepted communication or related data or tends to suggest that anything falling within section 17(2) has or may have occurred or be going to occur (section 18(10)). Situations where an admission of fact is required are likely to be rare. The judge must be of the view that proceedings could not be continued unless an admission of fact is made (and the conditions in section 18(9) are satisfied). There may be other ways in which it is possible for a judge to ensure fairness, such as those outlined at (i) and (ii) above.

In practice, no question of taking the action at (i)–(iii) arises if the protected information is already contained in a separate document in another form that has been or can be disclosed without contravening section 17(1), and this disclosure will secure the fairness of the proceedings.

(2) **Where the judge requires knowledge of the protected material for some other purpose**

This situation may arise where, usually in the context of a PII application, the true significance of, or duty of disclosure in relation to, other material being considered for disclosure by a judge, cannot be appraised by the judge without reference to protected information. Disclosure to the judge of the protected information without more may be sufficient to enable him to appraise the material, but once he has seen the protected information the judge may also conclude that the conditions in section 18(9) are satisfied so that an admission of fact by the Crown is required in addition to or instead of disclosure of the non-protected material.

Another example is a case where protected information underlies operational decisions which are likely to be the subject of cross-examination and it is necessary to inform the judge of the existence of

[2] This is acceptable as long as to do so would not contravene section 17 i.e. reveal the existence of an interception warrant. Prosecutors must bear in mind that such a breach might conceivably occur not only from the factual content of the admission, but also from the circumstances in which it is made.

the protected information to enable him to deal with the issue when the questions are first posed in a way which ensures section 17(1) is not contravened.

What if the actions of the prosecutor and/or the judge cannot ensure the fairness of the proceedings?

9. There may be very rare cases in which no action taken by the prosecutor and/or judge can prevent the continuation of the proceedings being unfair, e.g. where the requirements of fairness could only be met if the Crown were to make an admission, but it cannot do so without contravening section 18(10). In that situation the prosecutor will have no option but to offer no evidence on the charge in question, or to discontinue the proceedings in their entirety.

Responding to questions about interception

10. Prosecutors are sometimes placed in a situation in which they are asked by the court or by the defence whether interception has taken place or whether protected information exists. Whether or not interception has taken place or protected information exists, an answer in the following terms, or similar should be given:

> 'I am not in a position to answer that, but I am aware of sections 17 and 18 of the Regulation of Investigatory Powers Act 2000 and the Attorney General's Guidelines on the Disclosure of Information in Exceptional Circumstances under section 18'.

In a case where interception has taken place or protected information exists, an answer in these terms will avoid a breach of the prohibition in section 17 while providing assurance that the prosecutor is aware of his obligations.

11. For the avoidance of doubt, any notification or disclosure of information to the judge in accordance with paragraphs 7–10 must be *ex parte*. It will never be appropriate for prosecutors to volunteer, either *inter partes* or to the Court *ex parte*, that interception has taken place or that protected information exists, save in accordance with section 18 as elaborated in these Guidelines.

Further Assistance

12. Should a prosecutor be unsure as to the application of these guidelines in any particular case, further guidance should be sought from those instructing him or her. In those cases where a prosecutor has been instructed by the Crown Prosecution Service, the relevant CPS prosecutor must seek appropriate guidance from Casework Directorate, CPS Headquarters, Ludgate Hill.

THE PROSECUTOR'S ROLE IN APPLICATIONS FOR WITNESS ANONYMITY ORDERS . . .

A. Foreword

A1. Every defendant has a right to a fair trial. An important aspect of a fair trial is the right of the defendant to be confronted by, and to challenge, those who accuse him or her.

A2. Making an application for a witness anonymity order is therefore a serious step, to be taken by the prosecutor only where there are genuine grounds to believe that the court would not otherwise hear evidence that should be available to it in the interests of justice; that other measures falling short of anonymity would not be sufficient; and that the defendant will have a fair trial if the order is made.

A3. Anonymous witness testimony is not necessarily incompatible with Article 6, even when it is the sole or decisive evidence against the accused. But whether the measures used to allow a witness to give evidence anonymously in any particular case would make the trial unfair has to be evaluated with care on the facts of each case.

A4. When assessing whether and in what terms to make an application for a witness anonymity order, prosecutors have overriding duties to be fair, independent and objective. These guidelines set out the overarching principles by which a prosecutor should consider, and if appropriate apply for, a witness anonymity order in accordance with the considerations set out in the Criminal Evidence (Witness Anonymity) Act 2008.

B. The Prosecutor's Duties

B1. The effect of a witness anonymity order is to prevent the defendant from knowing the identity of a witness. Without this information the defendant's ability to investigate and challenge the accuracy or credibility of the witness's evidence may be limited.

B2. When considering whether to make a witness anonymity order the court will consider to what extent the defendant needs to know the identity of the witness in order to challenge the witness's evidence effectively. This question will often be central to the question of whether, having regard to all the circumstances, the witness anonymity order sought would be consistent with a fair trial.

B3. The prosecutor's role is:
- To act with scrupulous fairness.
- To examine with care, and probe where appropriate, the material provided in support of the application and the evidential basis for it. Prosecutors should in particular objectively assess any statement made by the witness or witnesses in question and the grounds on which it is based.
- To be satisfied before making the application that, viewed objectively, it can properly be said that the order is necessary and in the interests of justice and that the defendant can receive a fair trial.
- To put before the court all material that is relevant to the application. Courts will rely to a significant extent upon the prosecutor and the investigator to provide relevant material. Material will be relevant if the prosecutor relies upon it to support the application, or if it may tend to undermine or qualify the justification for making the order at all, or for making it in the form sought by the prosecutor. Material is particularly relevant if credibility is or may be in issue, for example if there is a known link between the witness and the defendant or a co-accused.
- To disclose as much relevant material to the defence as possible without identifying the witness, including material that may tend to cast doubt on the credibility, reliability or accuracy of the witness's evidence.

B4. The role of the prosecutor as an independent and impartial minister of justice is of paramount importance. Applications should only be authorised by prosecutors at an appropriately senior level within the prosecuting authority.

B5. The interests of justice include the interests of the victim or victims, the interests of the witness or witnesses, the interests of the defendant and any co-defendants and the wider public interest.

B6. Prosecutors should take all necessary and reasonable steps consistent with a fair trial and the interests of justice to ensure the safety of a witness or the avoidance of real harm to the public interest or the protection of property.

C. Applications by Defendants

C1. The Act permits a defendant (as well as a prosecutor) to apply for a Witness Anonymity Order. Prosecutors should respond to such applications independently and objectively. Prosecutors should examine critically, but fairly, the basis for any application and any material put forward in support of any application.

C2. The prosecutor should provide the court with all material within the prosecutor's possession or control that is relevant to the defendant's application.

D. Appointment and Role of Special Counsel in Applications for Witness Anonymity

D1. The Act makes no statutory provision for the appointment of Special Counsel.

D2. A criminal court may invite the Attorney General to appoint Special Counsel.[3] However, in line with authority, such an appointment:
- Should be regarded as '. . . exceptional, never automatic, a course of last and never first resort.' *R v H* and *R v C* [2004] UKHL 3. The need for Special Counsel has to be shown.
- The court will take account of the seriousness of the issue that the court has to determine in the particular case. Whether credibility is at issue is likely to be an important consideration. The court will also need to consider the extent to which Special Counsel could further the defendant's case.
- The court itself can be expected to perform a role of testing and probing the case which is presented on the application. When coupled with the prosecutor's duty to put all relevant material before the court, this may often be sufficient to enable a fair and informed decision to be reached without the need to appoint Special Counsel.

D3. Where appointed, the role of Special Counsel is to make representations on behalf of the accused in any closed proceedings.

D4. The Attorney General will consider each invitation to appoint Special Counsel on its merits, having regard to all the relevant circumstances of the case. In particular, in this context, to the basis of the application, whether it is opposed, the basis upon which it is opposed and the particular considerations that the court wishes Special Counsel to address.

D5. A prosecutor making an application for a witness anonymity order should always be prepared to assist the court to consider whether the circumstances are such that exceptionally the appointment of Special Counsel may be called for. When appropriate a prosecutor should draw to the attention of the

[3] Most recently, *Shiv Malik and Manchester Crown Court and Chief Constable of Greater Manchester Police, Constable and Robinson Ltd and Attorney General as interested parties* [2008] EWHC 1362 (Admin).

court any aspect of an application for a witness anonymity order or any aspect of the case that may, viewed objectively, call for the appointment of Special Counsel.

D6. When a court decides to invite the Attorney General to appoint Special Counsel the prosecutor should (regardless of any steps taken by the court or any defendant) ensure that the Attorney General's Office is promptly notified; and assist in ensuring that the Attorney General receives all the information needed to take a decision.

D7. Where Special Counsel is appointed, he or she will initially be provided by the prosecutor with any open material made available to the accused regarding the application (and any other open material requested by Special Counsel). Special Counsel may then seek instructions from the defendant and his legal representatives. Only then will Special Counsel be provided by the prosecutor with the closed or un-redacted material provided to the court.

PLEA DISCUSSIONS IN CASES OF SERIOUS OR COMPLEX FRAUD

A. Foreword

A1. These Guidelines set out a process by which a prosecutor may discuss an allegation of serious or complex fraud with a person who he or she is prosecuting or expects to prosecute, or with that person's legal representative. They come into force on the 5th day of May 2009 and apply to plea discussions initiated on or after that date.

A2. The Guidelines will be followed by all prosecutors in England and Wales when conducting plea discussions in cases of serious or complex fraud. For the purposes of the Guidelines, fraud means any financial, fiscal or commercial misconduct or corruption which is contrary to the criminal law. Fraud may be serious or complex if at least two of the following factors are present:

- The amount obtained or intended to be obtained is alleged to exceed £500,000;
- There is a significant international dimension;
- The case requires specialised knowledge of financial, commercial, fiscal or regulatory matters such as the operation of markets, banking systems, trusts or tax regimes;
- The case involves allegations of fraudulent activity against numerous victims;
- The case involves an allegation of substantial and significant fraud on a public body;
- The case is likely to be of widespread public concern;
- The alleged misconduct endangered the economic well-being of the United Kingdom, for example by undermining confidence in financial markets.

Taking account of these matters, it is for the prosecutor to decide whether or not a case is one of fraud, and whether or not it is serious or complex.

A3. The decision whether a person should be charged with a criminal offence rests with the prosecutor. In selecting the appropriate charge or charges, the prosecutor applies principles set out in the Code for Crown Prosecutors ('the Code'). Charges should reflect the seriousness and extent of the offending, give the court adequate sentencing powers and enable the case to be presented in a clear and simple way. The Code also states that prosecutors should not go ahead with more charges to encourage a defendant to plead guilty to a few; equally, prosecutors should not charge a more serious offence to encourage a defendant to plead to a less serious one.

A4. Once proceedings are instituted, the accused may plead guilty to all of the charges selected. If the defendant will plead guilty to some, but not all, of the charges or to a different, possibly less serious charge, the Code states that a prosecutor is entitled to accept such pleas if he or she assesses that the court could still pass an adequate sentence. In taking these decisions the prosecutor also applies the Attorney General's Guidelines on the Acceptance of Pleas and the Prosecutor's Role in the Sentencing Exercise ('the Acceptance of Pleas Guidelines').

A5. The purpose of plea discussions is to narrow the issues in the case with a view to reaching a just outcome at the earliest possible time, including the possibility of reaching an agreement about acceptable pleas of guilty and preparing a joint submission as to sentence.

A6. The potential benefits of plea discussions are that:

- Early resolution of the case may reduce the anxiety and uncertainty for victims and witnesses, and provide earlier clarity for accused persons who admit their guilt (subject to the court's power to *reject the agreement*);
- The issues in dispute may be narrowed so that even if the case proceeds to trial, it can be managed more efficiently in accordance with Rule 3.2 of the Criminal Procedure Rules 2005. If pleas are agreed, litigation can be kept to a minimum.

A7. Where plea discussions take place prior to the commencement of proceedings, the charges brought by the prosecutor will reflect those agreed, rather than those that the prosecutor would necessarily have preferred if no agreement had been reached. Also, any criminal investigation may not be complete when these discussions take place. For these reasons it is important that the procedures followed should command public and judicial confidence; that any agreement reached is reasonable, fair and just; that there are safeguards to ensure that defendants are not under improper pressure to make admissions; and that there are proper records of discussions that have taken place.

A8. The Guidelines are not intended to prevent or discourage existing practices by which prosecutors and prosecuting advocates discuss cases with defence legal representatives after charge, in order to narrow the issues or to agree a basis of plea. Neither do they affect the existing practice of judicial sentence indications at the plea and case management hearing or later in accordance with the guidance in *R v Goodyear (Karl)* [2005] EWCA 888 (see also the Acceptance of Pleas Guidelines). They complement, and do not detract from or replace, the Code and the Acceptance of Pleas Guidelines, or any other relevant guidance such as the Prosecutor's Pledge, the Victim's Charter and the Code of Practice for Victims of Crime.

A9. Where a plea agreement is reached, it remains entirely a matter for the court to decide how to deal with the case.

B. General Principles

B1. In conducting plea discussions and presenting a plea agreement to the court, the prosecutor must act openly, fairly and in the interests of justice.

B2. Acting in the interests of justice means ensuring that the plea agreement reflects the seriousness and extent of the offending, gives the court adequate sentencing powers, and enables the court, the public and the victims to have confidence in the outcome. The prosecutor must consider carefully the impact of a proposed plea or basis of plea on the community and the victim, and on the prospects of successfully prosecuting any other person implicated in the offending. The prosecutor must not agree to a reduced basis of plea which is misleading, untrue or illogical.

B3. Acting fairly means respecting the rights of the defendant and of any other person who is being or may be prosecuted in relation to the offending. The prosecutor must not put improper pressure on a defendant in the course of plea discussions, for example by exaggerating the strength of the case in order to persuade the defendant to plead guilty, or to plead guilty on a particular basis.

B4. Acting openly means being transparent with the defendant, the victim and the court. The prosecutor must:

- Ensure that a full and accurate record of the plea discussions is prepared and retained;
- Ensure that the defendant has sufficient information to enable him or her to play an informed part in the plea discussions;
- Communicate with the victim before accepting a reduced basis of plea, wherever it is practicable to do so, so that the position can be explained; and
- Ensure that the plea agreement placed before the court fully and fairly reflects the matters agreed. The prosecutor must not agree additional matters with the defendant which are not recorded in the plea agreement and made known to the court.

C. Initiating Plea Discussions

When and with whom discussions should be initiated and conducted

C1. Where he or she believes it advantageous to do so, the prosecutor may initiate plea discussions with any person who is being prosecuted or investigated with a view to prosecution in connection with a serious or complex fraud, and who is legally represented. The prosecutor will not initiate plea discussions with a defendant who is not legally represented. If the prosecutor receives an approach from such a defendant, he or she may enter into discussions if satisfied that it is appropriate to do so.

C2. Where proceedings have not yet been instituted, the prosecutor should not initiate plea discussions until he or she and the investigating officer are satisfied that the suspect's criminality is known. This will not usually be the case until after the suspect has been interviewed under caution.

C3. The prosecutor should be alert to any attempt by the defendant to use plea discussions as a means of delaying the investigation or prosecution, and should not initiate or continue discussions where the defendant's commitment to the process is in doubt. The prosecutor should ensure that the position is preserved during plea discussions by, for example, restraining assets in anticipation of the making of a confiscation order. Where a defendant declines to take part in plea discussions, the prosecutor should not make a second approach unless there is a material change in circumstances.

Invitation letter

C4. In order to initiate the plea discussions, the prosecutor will send the defendant's representatives a letter which:
- Asks whether the defence wish to enter into discussions in accordance with these Guidelines; and
- Sets a deadline for a response from the defence.

Terms and conditions letter

C5. Where the defence agree to engage in plea discussions, the prosecutor should send them a letter setting out the way in which the discussions will be conducted. This letter should deal with:
- The confidentiality of information provided by the prosecutor and defendant in the course of the plea discussions;
- The use which may be made by the prosecutor of information provided by the defendant; and
- The practical means by which the discussions will be conducted.

Confidentiality and use of information

C6. In relation to confidentiality, the prosecutor will indicate that he or she intends to provide an undertaking to the effect that the fact that the defendant has taken part in the plea discussions, and any information provided by the defence in the course of the plea discussions will be treated as confidential and will not be disclosed to any other party other than for the purposes of the plea discussions and plea agreement (applying these Guidelines), or as required by law. The undertaking will make it clear that the law in relation to the disclosure of unused material may require the prosecutor to provide information about the plea discussions to another defendant in criminal proceedings.

C7. The prosecutor will require the defendant's legal representative to provide an undertaking to the effect that information provided by the prosecutor in the course of the plea discussions will be treated as confidential and will not be disclosed to any other party, other than for the purposes of the plea discussion and plea agreement or as required by law.

C8. In relation to the use of information, the prosecutor will indicate that he or she intends to undertake not to rely upon the fact that the defendant has taken part in the plea discussions, or any information provided by the defendant in the course of the discussions, as evidence in any prosecution of that defendant for the offences under investigation, should the discussions fail. However, this undertaking will make it clear that the prosecutor is not prevented from:
- Relying upon a concluded and signed plea agreement as confession evidence or as admissions;
- Relying upon any evidence obtained from enquiries made as a result of the provision of information by the defendant;
- Relying upon information provided by the defendant as evidence against him or her in any prosecution for an offence other than the fraud which is the subject of the plea discussion and any offence which is consequent upon it, such as money laundering; and
- Relying upon information provided by the defendant in a prosecution of any other person for any offence (so far as the rules of evidence allow).

C9. In exceptional circumstances the prosecutor may agree to different terms regarding the confidentiality and use of information. However, the prosecutor must not surrender the ability to rely upon a concluded and signed plea agreement as evidence against the defendant. The prosecutor may reserve the right to bring other charges (additional to those to which the defendant has indicated a willingness to plead guilty) in specific circumstances, for example if substantial new information comes to light at a later stage, the plea agreement is rejected by the court, or the defendant fails to honour the agreement.

C10. Until the issues of confidentiality and use of information have been agreed to the satisfaction of both parties, and the agreement reflected in signed undertakings, the prosecutor must not continue with the substantive plea discussions.

D. Conducting Plea Discussions

Statement of case

D1. Where plea discussions take place prior to proceedings being instituted, the prosecutor will provide a statement of case to the defence. This is a written summary of the nature of the allegation against the suspect and the evidence which has been obtained, or is expected to be obtained, to support it. The statement of case should include a list of the proposed charges. Material in support of the statement of case may also be provided, whether or not in the form of admissible evidence. However, the prosecutor is not obliged to reveal to the suspect all of the information or evidence supporting his case, provided that this does not mislead the suspect to his or her prejudice.

D2. Where plea discussions are initiated after proceedings have been commenced, but before the prosecutor has provided the defence with a case summary or opening note, the prosecutor may provide a statement of case to assist the defendant in understanding the evidence and identifying the issues.

Unused material

D3. These Guidelines do not affect the prosecutor's existing duties in relation to the disclosure of unused material. Where plea discussions take place prior to the institution of proceedings, the prosecutor should ensure that the suspect is not misled as to the strength of the prosecution case. It will not usually be necessary to provide copies of unused material in order to do this.

Conducting and recording the discussions

D4. Having provided the defence with the statement of case and supporting material, the parties will then be in a position to conduct the plea discussion proper. Whether this is done by correspondence, by face-to-face meetings or by a combination of the two is a matter for the parties to decide in the individual case.

D5. It is essential that a full written record is kept of every key action and event in the discussion process, including details of every offer or concession made by each party, and the reasons for every decision taken by the prosecutor. Meetings between the parties should be minuted and the minutes agreed and signed. Particular care should be taken where the defendant is not legally represented. The prosecutor should only meet with a defendant who is not legally represented if the defendant agrees to the meeting being recorded, or to the presence of an independent third party.

Queen's Evidence

D6. If the defendant offers at any stage to provide information, or to give evidence about the criminal activities of others, any such offer will be dealt with in accordance with sections 71 to 75 of the Serious Organised Crime and Police Act 2005 ('SOCPA'), the judgment of the Court of Appeal in *R v P, R v Blackburn* [2007] EWCA Crim 2290 and the guidance agreed and issued by the Director of Public Prosecutions, the Director of the Serious Fraud Office and the Director of Revenue and Customs Prosecutions.

Discussion of pleas

D7. In deciding whether or not to accept an offer by the defendant to plead guilty, the prosecutor will follow sections 7 and 10 of the Code relating to the selection of charges and the acceptance of guilty pleas. The prosecutor should ensure that:

- The charges reflect the seriousness and extent of the offending;
- They give the court adequate powers to sentence and impose appropriate post-conviction orders;
- They enable the case to be presented in a clear and simple way (bearing in mind that many cases of fraud are necessarily complex);
- The basis of plea enables the court to pass a sentence that matches the seriousness of the offending, particularly if there are aggravating features;
- The interests of the victim, and where possible any views expressed by the victim, are taken into account when deciding whether it is in the public interest to accept the plea; and
- The investigating officer is fully appraised of developments in the plea discussions and his or her views are taken into account.

D8. In reaching an agreement on pleas, the parties should resolve any factual issues necessary to allow the court to sentence the defendant on a clear, fair and accurate basis. Before agreeing to proposed pleas, the prosecutor should satisfy him or herself that the Full Code Test as set out in the Code will be made out in respect of each charge. In considering whether the evidential stage of the test will be met, the prosecutor should assume that the offender will sign a plea agreement amounting to an admission to the charge.

Discussion of sentence

D9. Where agreement is reached as to pleas, the parties should discuss the appropriate sentence with a view to presenting a joint written submission to the court. This document should list the aggravating and mitigating features arising from the agreed facts, set out any personal mitigation available to the defendant, and refer to any relevant sentencing guidelines or authorities. In the light of all of these factors, it should make submissions as to the applicable sentencing range in the relevant guideline. The prosecutor must ensure that the submissions are realistic, taking full account of all relevant material and considerations.

D10. The prosecutor should bear in mind all of the powers of the court, and seek to include in the joint submission any relevant ancillary orders. It is particularly desirable that measures should be included that achieve redress for victims (such as compensation orders) and protection for the public (such as directors' disqualification orders, serious crime prevention orders or financial reporting orders).

D11. Due regard should be had to the court's asset recovery powers and the desirability of using these powers both as a deterrent to others and as a means of preventing the defendant from benefiting from the proceeds of crime or funding future offending. The Proceeds of Crime Act 2002 requires the Crown Court to proceed to the making of a confiscation order against a convicted defendant who has benefited from his criminal conduct where the prosecutor asks the court to do so, or the court believes that it is appropriate to do so. Fraud is an acquisitive crime, and the expectation in a fraud case should be that a confiscation order will be sought by the prosecutor reflecting the full benefit to the defendant. However, in doing so it is open to the prosecutor to take a realistic view of the likely approach of the court to the determination of any points in dispute (such as the interest of a third party in any property).

D12. In the course of the plea discussions the prosecutor must make it clear to the defence that the joint submission as to sentence (including confiscation) is not binding on the court.

Liaison with another prosecutor or regulator

D13. The prosecutor may become aware that another prosecuting authority or regulatory body (either in England and Wales or elsewhere) has an interest in the defendant. The prosecutor should liaise with the other agency, in accordance with the Prosecutors' Convention and any other relevant agreement or guidance. The other agency may wish to take part in the plea discussions, or they may authorise the prosecutor to discuss with the defendant the matters which they are interested in, with a view to resolving all matters in one plea agreement. The prosecutor should warn the defendant that a plea agreement will not bind any other agency which is not a party to it.

E. The Written Plea Agreement

E1. All matters agreed between the prosecutor and the defence must be reduced to writing as a plea agreement and signed by both parties. The plea agreement will include:

- A list of the charges;
- A statement of the facts; and
- A declaration, signed by the defendant personally, to the effect that he or she accepts the stated facts and admits he or she is guilty of the agreed charges.

E2. Any agreement under the SOCPA regarding the giving of assistance to the prosecutor by the defendant should be in a separate document accompanying the plea agreement.

E3. Once a plea agreement is signed in a case where proceedings have not yet been commenced, the prosecutor will review the case in accordance with the Code and, assuming the evidential stage of the Full Code Test is satisfied on the basis of the signed plea agreement and the other available evidence, will arrange for proceedings to be instituted by summons or charge.

E4. In advance of the defendant's first appearance in the Crown Court, the prosecutor should send the court sufficient material to allow the judge to understand the facts of the case and the history of the plea discussions, to assess whether the plea agreement is fair and in the interests of justice, and to decide the appropriate sentence. This will include:

- The signed plea agreement;
- A joint submission as to sentence and sentencing considerations;
- Any relevant sentencing guidelines or authorities;
- All of the material provided by the prosecution to the defendant in the course of the plea discussions;
- Any material provided by the defendant to the prosecution, such as documents relating to personal mitigation; and
- The minutes of any meetings between the parties and any correspondence generated in the plea discussions.

E5. It will then be for the court to decide how to deal with the plea agreement. In particular, the court retains an absolute discretion as to whether or not it sentences in accordance with the joint submission from the parties.

F. Failure of Plea Discussions

F1. There are several circumstances in which plea discussions may result in an outcome other than the defendant pleading guilty in accordance with a plea agreement. The prosecutor or the defendant may break off the discussions. They may be unable to reach an agreement. They may reach an agreement, but intervening events may lead the prosecutor to decide that proceedings should not be instituted. Proceedings may be instituted but the court may reject the plea agreement. The defendant may decline to plead guilty in accordance with the plea agreement, either as a result of a sentence indication given under the procedure set out in *R v Goodyear*, or for some other reason.

F2. If any of these situations arises, the prosecutor may wish for further enquiries to be made with a view to bringing or completing proceedings against the defendant. If proceedings have already been instituted, the prosecutor will use the appropriate means to delay them — either discontinuing under section 23 or 23A of the Prosecution of Offences Act 1985 or (if the indictment has already been preferred) applying for an adjournment or stay of the proceedings. The prosecutor and the defendant's representatives will continue to be bound by the preliminary undertakings made in relation to the confidentiality and use of information provided in the course of the plea discussions.

F3. Where plea discussions have broken down for any reason, it will be rare that the prosecutor will wish to re-open them, but he or she may do so if there is a material change in circumstances which warrants it.

DISCLOSURE

The Attorney-General's Guidelines on Disclosure for Investigators, Prosecutors and Defence Practitioners are reproduced in **appendix 4**.

Appendix 3 The Code for Crown Prosecutors

Introduction

1.1 The Code for Crown Prosecutors (the Code) is issued by the Director of Public Prosecutions (DPP) under section 10 of the Prosecution of Offences Act 1985. This is the eighth edition of the Code and replaces all earlier versions.

1.2 The DPP is the head of the Crown Prosecution Service (CPS), which is the principal public prosecution service for England and Wales. The DPP operates independently, under the superintendence of the Attorney General who is accountable to Parliament for the work of the CPS.

1.3 The Code gives guidance to prosecutors on the general principles to be applied when making decisions about prosecutions. The Code is issued primarily for prosecutors in the CPS but other prosecutors follow the Code, either through convention or because they are required to do so by law.

1.4 In this Code:

- 'Suspect' is used to describe a person who is under consideration as the subject of formal criminal proceedings;
- 'Defendant' is used to describe a person who has been charged or summonsed;
- 'Offender' is used to describe a person who has admitted guilt as to the commission of an offence, or who has been found guilty in a court of law;
- 'Victim' is used to describe a person against whom an offence has been committed, or the complainant in a case being considered or prosecuted by the CPS.

General Principles

2.1 The independence of the prosecutor is central to the criminal justice system of a democratic society. Prosecutors are independent from persons or agencies that are not part of the prosecution decision-making process. CPS prosecutors are also independent from the police and other investigators. Prosecutors must be free to carry out their professional duties without political interference and must not be affected by improper or undue pressure or influence from any source.

2.2 It is not the function of the CPS to decide whether a person is guilty of a criminal offence, but to make assessments about whether it is appropriate to present charges for the criminal court to consider. The CPS assessment of any case is not in any sense a finding of, or implication of, any guilt or criminal conduct. A finding of guilt can only be made by a court.

2.3 Similarly, a decision not to bring criminal charges does not necessarily mean that an individual has not been a victim of crime. It is not the role of the CPS to make such determinations.

2.4 The decision to prosecute or to recommend an out-of-court disposal is a serious step that affects suspects, victims, witnesses and the public at large and must be undertaken with the utmost care.

2.5 It is the duty of prosecutors to make sure that the right person is prosecuted for the right offence and to bring offenders to justice wherever possible. Casework decisions taken fairly, impartially and with integrity help to secure justice for victims, witnesses, suspects, defendants and the public. Prosecutors must ensure that the law is properly applied, that relevant evidence is put before the court and that obligations of disclosure are complied with.

2.6 Although each case must be considered on its own facts and on its own merits, there are general principles that apply in every case.

2.7 When making decisions, prosecutors must be fair and objective. They must not let any personal views about the ethnic or national origin, gender, disability, age, religion or belief, sexual orientation or gender identity of the suspect, defendant, victim or any witness influence their decisions. Neither must they be motivated by political considerations. Prosecutors must always act in the interests of justice and not solely for the purpose of obtaining a conviction.

2.8 Prosecutors must be even-handed in their approach to every case, and have a duty to protect the rights of suspects and defendants, while providing the best possible service to victims.

2.9 The CPS is a public authority for the purposes of current, relevant equality legislation. Prosecutors are bound by the duties set out in this legislation.

2.10 Prosecutors must apply the principles of the European Convention on Human Rights, in accordance with the Human Rights Act 1998, at each stage of a case. They must comply with any guidelines issued by the Attorney General and with the policies and guidance of the CPS issued on behalf of the DPP, unless it is determined that there are exceptional circumstances. CPS guidance contains further evidential and public interest factors for specific offences and offenders and is available for the public to view on the CPS website. Prosecutors must also comply with the Criminal Procedure Rules and Criminal Practice Directions, and have regard to the Sentencing Council Guidelines and the obligations arising from international conventions.

2.11 The CPS prosecutes on behalf of some other Government departments. In such cases, prosecutors should have regard to any relevant enforcement policies of those departments.

2.12 Some offences may be prosecuted by either the CPS or by other prosecutors in England and Wales. When making decisions in these cases, CPS prosecutors may, where they think it appropriate, have regard to any relevant enforcement or prosecution policy or code of the other prosecutor.

2.13 Where the law differs in England and Wales prosecutors must apply the Code and have regard to any relevant policy, guidance or charging standard.

The Decision Whether to Prosecute

3.1 In more serious or complex cases, prosecutors decide whether a person should be charged with a criminal offence and, if so, what that offence should be. Prosecutors may also advise on or authorise out-of-court disposals as an alternative to prosecution. They make their decisions in accordance with this Code, the DPP's Guidance on Charging and any relevant legal guidance or policy. The police apply the same principles in deciding whether to start criminal proceedings against a person in those cases for which they are responsible.

3.2 The police and other investigators are responsible for conducting inquiries into any alleged crime and for deciding how to deploy their resources. This includes decisions to start or continue an investigation and on the scope of the investigation. Prosecutors should advise the police and other investigators about possible reasonable lines of inquiry, evidential requirements, pre-charge procedures, disclosure management and the overall investigation strategy. This can include decisions to refine or narrow the scope of the criminal conduct and the number of suspects under investigation. Such advice assists the police and other investigators to complete the investigation within a reasonable period of time and to build the most effective prosecution case.

3.3 Prosecutors cannot direct the police or other investigators. However, prosecutors must have regard to the impact of any failure to pursue an advised reasonable line of inquiry or to comply with a request for information, when deciding whether the application of the Full Code Test should be deferred or whether the test can be met at all.

3.4 Prosecutors should identify and, where possible, seek to rectify evidential weaknesses but, subject to the Threshold Test (see section 5), they should quickly stop cases which do not meet the evidential stage of the Full Code Test (see section 4) and which cannot be strengthened by further investigation, or where the public interest clearly does not require a prosecution (see section 4). Although prosecutors primarily consider the evidence and information supplied by the police and other investigators, the suspect or those acting on their behalf may also submit evidence or information to the prosecutor, before or after charge, to help inform the prosecutor's decision. In appropriate cases, the prosecutor may invite the suspect or their representative to do so.

3.5 Prosecutors should not start or continue a prosecution where their view is that it is highly likely that a court will rule that a prosecution is an abuse of its process, and stay the proceedings.

3.6 Prosecutors review every case they receive from the police or other investigators. Review is a continuing process and prosecutors must take account of any change in circumstances that occurs as the case develops. This includes what becomes known of the defence case, any further reasonable lines of inquiry that should be pursued, and receipt of any unused material that may undermine the prosecution case or assist the defence case, to the extent that charges should be altered or discontinued or the prosecution should not proceed. If a case is to be stopped, care should be taken when choosing the method of termination, as this can affect the victim's position under the Victims' Right to Review scheme. Wherever possible, prosecutors should consult the investigator when considering changing the charges or stopping the case. Prosecutors and investigators work closely together, but the final responsibility for the decision whether or not a case should go ahead rests with the CPS.

3.7 Parliament has decided that a limited number of offences should only be taken to court with the agreement of the DPP. These are called consent cases. In such cases the DPP, or a prosecutor acting on their behalf, applies the Code in deciding whether to give consent to a prosecution.

3.8 There are also certain offences that can only be taken to court with the consent of the Attorney General. Prosecutors must follow current guidance when referring any such cases to the Attorney General. Some offences require the consent of a Secretary of State before a prosecution is started. Prosecutors must obtain such consent prior to charge and apply any relevant guidance in these cases. Additionally, the Attorney General will be kept informed of certain cases as part of their superintendence of the CPS and accountability to Parliament for its actions.

The Full Code Test

4.1 Prosecutors must only start or continue a prosecution when the case has passed both stages of the Full Code Test. The exception is when the Threshold Test may be applied (see section 5).

4.2 The Full Code Test has two stages: (i) the evidential stage; followed by (ii) the public interest stage.

4.3 The Full Code Test should be applied:

a. when all outstanding reasonable lines of inquiry have been pursued; or

b. prior to the investigation being completed, if the prosecutor is satisfied that any further evidence or material is unlikely to affect the application of the Full Code Test, whether in favour of or against a prosecution.

4.4 In most cases prosecutors should only consider whether a prosecution is in the public interest after considering whether there is sufficient evidence to prosecute. However, there will be cases where it is clear, prior to reviewing all the evidence, that the public interest does not require a prosecution. In these instances, prosecutors may decide that the case should not proceed further.

4.5 Prosecutors should only take such a decision when they are satisfied that the broad extent of the criminality has been determined and that they are able to make a fully informed assessment of the public interest. If prosecutors do not have sufficient information to take such a decision, the investigation should continue and a decision taken later in accordance with the Full Code Test set out in this section.

The Evidential Stage

4.6 Prosecutors must be satisfied that there is sufficient evidence to provide a realistic prospect of conviction against each suspect on each charge.* They must consider what the defence case may be, and how it is likely to affect the prospects of conviction. A case which does not pass the evidential stage must not proceed, no matter how serious or sensitive it may be.

4.7 The finding that there is a realistic prospect of conviction is based on the prosecutor's objective assessment of the evidence, including the impact of any defence and any other information that the suspect has put forward or on which they might rely. It means that an objective, impartial and reasonable jury or bench of magistrates or judge hearing a case alone, properly directed and acting in accordance with the law, is more likely than not to convict the defendant of the charge alleged. This is a different test from the one that the criminal courts themselves must apply. A court may only convict if it is sure that the defendant is guilty.

4.8 When deciding whether there is sufficient evidence to prosecute, prosecutors should ask themselves the following:

Can the evidence be used in court?

Prosecutors should consider whether there is any question over the admissibility of certain evidence. In doing so, prosecutors should assess:

- the likelihood of that evidence being held as inadmissible by the court; and
- the importance of that evidence in relation to the evidence as a whole.

Is the evidence reliable?

Prosecutors should consider whether there are any reasons to question the reliability of the evidence, including its accuracy or integrity.

Is the evidence credible?

Prosecutors should consider whether there are any reasons to doubt the credibility of the evidence.

Is there any other material that might affect the sufficiency of evidence?

Prosecutors must consider at this stage and throughout the case whether there is any material that may affect the assessment of the sufficiency of evidence, including examined and unexamined material in the possession of the police, and material that may be obtained through further reasonable lines of inquiry.

The Public Interest Stage

4.9 In every case where there is sufficient evidence to justify a prosecution or to offer an out-of-court disposal, prosecutors must go on to consider whether a prosecution is required in the public interest.

* For the purposes of the Code for Crown Prosecutors, 'conviction' includes a finding that 'the person did the act or made the omission' in circumstances where the person is likely to be found not guilty on the grounds of insanity.

4.10 It has never been the rule that a prosecution will automatically take place once the evidential stage is met. A prosecution will usually take place unless the prosecutor is satisfied that there are public interest factors tending against prosecution which outweigh those tending in favour. In some cases the prosecutor may be satisfied that the public interest can be properly served by offering the offender the opportunity to have the matter dealt with by an out-of-court disposal rather than bringing a prosecution.

4.11 When deciding the public interest, prosecutors should consider each of the questions set out below in paragraphs 4.14 a) to g) so as to identify and determine the relevant public interest factors tending for and against prosecution. These factors, together with any public interest factors set out in relevant guidance or policy issued by the DPP, should enable prosecutors to form an overall assessment of the public interest.

4.12 The explanatory text below each question in paragraphs 4.14 a) to g) provides guidance to prosecutors when addressing each particular question and determining whether it identifies public interest factors for or against prosecution. The questions identified are not exhaustive, and not all the questions may be relevant in every case. The weight to be attached to each of the questions, and the factors identified, will also vary according to the facts and merits of each case.

4.13 It is quite possible that one public interest factor alone may outweigh a number of other factors which tend in the opposite direction. Although there may be public interest factors tending against prosecution in a particular case, prosecutors should consider whether nonetheless a prosecution should go ahead and those factors put to the court for consideration when sentence is passed.

4.14 Prosecutors should consider each of the following questions:

a) *How serious is the offence committed?*

- The more serious the offence, the more likely it is that a prosecution is required.
- When assessing the seriousness of an offence, prosecutors should include in their consideration the suspect's culpability and the harm caused, by asking themselves the questions at b) and c).

b) *What is the level of culpability of the suspect?*

- The greater the suspect's level of culpability, the more likely it is that a prosecution is required.
- Culpability is likely to be determined by:
    i. the suspect's level of involvement;
    ii. the extent to which the offending was premeditated and/or planned;
    iii. the extent to which the suspect has benefitted from criminal conduct;
    iv. whether the suspect has previous criminal convictions and/or out-of-court disposals and any offending whilst on bail or whilst subject to a court order;
    v. whether the offending was or is likely to be continued, repeated or escalated;
    vi. the suspect's age and maturity (see paragraph d below).
- A suspect is likely to have a much lower level of culpability if the suspect has been compelled, coerced or exploited, particularly if they are the victim of a crime that is linked to their offending.
- Prosecutors should also have regard to whether the suspect is, or was at the time of the offence, affected by any significant mental or physical ill health or disability, as in some circumstances this may mean that it is less likely that a prosecution is required. However, prosecutors will also need to consider how serious the offence was, whether the suspect is likely to re-offend and the need to safeguard the public or those providing care to such persons.

c) *What are the circumstances of and the harm caused to the victim?*

- The circumstances of the victim are highly relevant. The more vulnerable the victim's situation, or the greater the perceived vulnerability of the victim, the more likely it is that a prosecution is required.
- This includes where a position of trust or authority exists between the suspect and victim.
- A prosecution is also more likely if the offence has been committed against a victim who was at the time *a person serving the public.*
- It is more likely that prosecution is required if the offence was motivated by any form of prejudice against the victim's actual or presumed ethnic or national origin, gender, disability, age, religion or belief, sexual orientation or gender identity; or if the suspect targeted or exploited the victim, or demonstrated hostility towards the victim, based on any of those characteristics.
- Prosecutors also need to consider if a prosecution is likely to have an adverse effect on the victim's physical or mental health, always bearing in mind the seriousness of the offence, the availability of special measures and the possibility of a prosecution without the participation of the victim.

- Prosecutors should take into account the views expressed by the victim about the impact that the offence has had. In appropriate cases, this may also include the views of the victim's family.
- However, the CPS does not act for victims or their families in the same way as solicitors act for their clients, and prosecutors must form an overall view of the public interest.

d) *What was the suspect's age and maturity at the time of the offence?*

- The criminal justice system treats children and young people differently from adults and significant weight must be attached to the age of the suspect if they are a child or young person under 18.
- The best interests and welfare of the child or young person must be considered, including whether a prosecution is likely to have an adverse impact on their future prospects that is disproportionate to the seriousness of the offending. Prosecutors must have regard to the principal aim of the youth justice system, which is to prevent offending by children and young people. Prosecutors must also have regard to the obligations arising under the United Nations 1989 Convention on the Rights of the Child.
- Prosecutors should consider the suspect's maturity, as well as their chronological age, as young adults will continue to mature into their mid-twenties.
- As a starting point, the younger the suspect, the less likely it is that a prosecution is required.
- However, there may be circumstances which mean that, notwithstanding the fact that the suspect is under 18 or lacks maturity, a prosecution is in the public interest. These include where :
  i. the offence committed is serious;
  ii. the suspect's past record suggests that there are no suitable alternatives to prosecution; and
  iii. the absence of an admission means that out-of-court disposals that might have addressed the offending behaviour are not available.

e) *What is the impact on the community?*

- The greater the impact of the offending on the community, the more likely it is that a prosecution is required.
- The prevalence of an offence in a community may cause particular harm to that community, increasing the seriousness of the offending.
- Community is not restricted to communities defined by location and may relate to a group of people who share certain characteristics, experiences or backgrounds, including an occupational group.
- Evidence of impact on a community may be obtained by way of a Community Impact Statement.

f) *Is prosecution a proportionate response?*

- In considering whether prosecution is proportionate to the likely outcome, the following may be relevant:
  i. The cost to the CPS and the wider criminal justice system, especially where it could be regarded as excessive when weighed against any likely penalty. Prosecutors should not decide the public interest on the basis of this factor alone. It is essential that regard is also given to the public interest factors identified when considering the other questions in paragraphs 4.14 a) to g), but cost can be a relevant factor when making an overall assessment of the public interest.
  ii. Cases should be prosecuted in accordance with principles of effective case management. For example, in a case involving multiple suspects, prosecution might be reserved for the main participants in order to avoid excessively long and complex proceedings.

g) *Do sources of information require protecting?*

- In cases where public interest immunity does not apply, special care should be taken when proceeding with a prosecution where details may need to be made public that could harm sources of information, ongoing investigations, international relations or national security. It is essential that such cases are kept under continuing review.

The Threshold Test

5.1 In limited circumstances, where the Full Code Test is not met, the Threshold Test may be applied to charge a suspect. The seriousness or circumstances of the case must justify the making of an immediate charging decision, and there must be substantial grounds to object to bail.

5.2 There must be a rigorous examination of the five conditions of the Threshold Test, to ensure that it is only applied when necessary and that cases are not charged prematurely. All five conditions must be met before the Threshold Test can be applied. Where any of the conditions are not met, there is no need to consider any of the other conditions, as the Threshold Test cannot be applied and the suspect cannot be charged.

First condition—There are reasonable grounds to suspect that the person to be charged has committed the offence

5.3 Prosecutors must be satisfied, on an objective assessment of the evidence, that there are reasonable grounds to suspect that the person to be charged has committed the offence. The assessment must consider the impact of any defence or information that the suspect has put forward or on which they might rely.

5.4 In determining whether there are reasonable grounds to suspect, prosecutors must consider all of the material or information available, whether in evidential format or otherwise. Prosecutors must be satisfied that the material to be relied on at this stage is capable of being:
- put into an admissible format for presentation in court;
- reliable; and
- credible.

Second condition—further evidence can be obtained to provide a realistic prospect of conviction

5.5 Prosecutors must be satisfied that there are reasonable grounds to believe that the continuing investigation will provide further evidence, within a reasonable period of time, so that when all the evidence is considered together, including material which may point away from as well as towards a particular suspect, it is capable of establishing a realistic prospect of conviction in accordance with the Full Code Test.

5.6 The likely further evidence must be identifiable and not merely speculative.

5.7 In reaching this decision prosecutors must consider:
- the nature, extent and admissibility of any likely further evidence and the impact it will have on the case;
- the charges that all the evidence will support;
- the reasons why the evidence is not already available;
- the time required to obtain the further evidence, including whether it could be obtained within any available detention period; and
- whether the delay in applying the Full Code Test is reasonable in all the circumstances.

Third condition—The seriousness or the circumstances of the case justifies the making of an immediate charging decision

5.8 The seriousness and the circumstances of the case should be assessed in relation to the alleged offending and should be linked to the level of risk created by granting bail.

Fourth condition—There are continuing substantial grounds to object to bail in accordance with the Bail Act 1976 and in all the circumstances of the case it is proper to do so

5.9 This determination must be based on a proper risk assessment, which reveals that the suspect is not suitable to be bailed, even with substantial conditions. For example, a dangerous suspect who poses a serious risk of harm to a particular person or the public, or a suspect who poses a serious risk of absconding or interfering with witnesses. Prosecutors should not accept, without careful enquiry, any unjustified or unsupported assertions about risk if release on bail were to take place.

Fifth condition—It is in the public interest to charge the suspect

5.10 Prosecutors must apply the public interest stage of the Full Code Test based on the information available at that time.

Reviewing the Threshold Test

5.11 A decision to charge under the Threshold Test must be kept under review. The prosecutor should be proactive to secure from the police the identified outstanding evidence or other material in accordance with an agreed timetable. The evidence must be regularly assessed to ensure that the charge is still appropriate and that continued objection to bail is justified. The Full Code Test must be applied as soon as the anticipated further evidence or material is received and, in any event, in Crown Court cases, usually before the formal service of the prosecution case.

Selection of Charges

6.1 Prosecutors should select charges which:
- reflect the seriousness and extent of the offending;
- give the court adequate powers to sentence and impose appropriate post-conviction orders;
- allow a confiscation order to be made in appropriate cases, where a defendant has benefitted from criminal conduct; and
- enable the case to be presented in a clear and simple way.

6.2 This means that prosecutors may not always choose or continue with the most serious charge where there is a choice and the interests of justice are met by selecting the lesser charge.

6.3 Prosecutors should never proceed with more charges than are necessary just to encourage a defendant to plead guilty to a few. In the same way, they should never proceed with a more serious charge just to encourage a defendant to plead guilty to a less serious one.

6.4 Prosecutors should not change the charge simply because of the decision made by the court or the defendant about where the case will be heard.

6.5 Prosecutors must take account of any relevant change in circumstances as the case progresses after charge.

Out-of-Court Disposals

7.1 An out-of-court disposal may take the place of a prosecution if it is an appropriate response to the offender and/or the seriousness and consequences of the offending.

7.2 Prosecutors must follow any relevant guidance when asked to advise on or authorise an out-of-court disposal, including any appropriate regulatory proceedings, a punitive or civil penalty, or other disposal. They should ensure that the appropriate evidential standard for the specific out-of-court disposal is met including, where required, a clear admission of guilt, and that the public interest would be properly served by such a disposal.

Court Venue

8.1 Prosecutors must have regard to the guidelines on sentencing and allocation when making submissions to the magistrates' court about where the defendant should be tried.

8.2 Speed must never be the only reason for asking for a case to stay in the magistrates' court. But prosecutors should consider the effect of any likely delay if a case is sent to the Crown Court, including the possible effect on any victim or witness.

8.3 Prosecutors should bear in mind that if confiscation proceedings are required, these may only take place in the Crown Court. Summary proceedings may be committed for that purpose, where appropriate.

Venue for trial in cases involving Children and Young People

8.4 Prosecutors must bear in mind that children and young people (under 18s) should be tried in the youth court wherever possible. It is the court which is best designed to meet their specific needs. A trial of a child or young person in the Crown Court should be reserved for the most serious cases or where the interests of justice require a child or young person to be jointly tried with an adult.

Accepting Guilty Pleas

9.1 Defendants may want to plead guilty to some, but not all, of the charges. Alternatively, they may want to plead guilty to a different, possibly less serious, charge because they are admitting only part of the crime.

9.2 Prosecutors should only accept the defendant's plea if:

- the court is able to pass a sentence that matches the seriousness of the offending, particularly where there are aggravating features;
- it enables the court to make a confiscation order in appropriate cases, where a defendant has benefitted from criminal conduct; and
- it provides the court with adequate powers to impose other ancillary orders, bearing in mind that these can be made with some offences but not with others.

9.3 Particular care must be taken when considering pleas which would enable the defendant to avoid the imposition of a mandatory minimum sentence.

9.4 Prosecutors must never accept a guilty plea just because it is convenient.

9.5 In considering whether the pleas offered are acceptable, prosecutors should ensure that the interests and, where possible, the views of the victim, or in appropriate cases the views of the victim's family, are taken into account when deciding whether it is in the public interest to accept the plea. However, the decision rests with the prosecutor.

9.6 It must be made clear to the court on what basis any plea is advanced and accepted. In cases where a defendant pleads guilty to the charges but on the basis of facts that are different from the prosecution case, and where this may significantly affect sentence, the court should be invited to hear evidence to determine what happened, and then sentence on that basis.

9.7 Where a defendant has previously indicated that they will ask the court to take an offence into consideration when sentencing, but then declines to admit that offence at court, prosecutors will consider whether a prosecution is required for that offence. Prosecutors should explain to the defence advocate and the court that the prosecution of that offence may be subject to further review, in consultation with the police or other investigators wherever possible.

Reconsidering a Prosecution Decision

10.1 People should be able to rely on decisions taken by the CPS. Normally, if the CPS tells a suspect or defendant that there will not be a prosecution, or that the prosecution has been stopped, the case will not start again. But occasionally there are cases where the CPS will overturn a decision not to prosecute or to deal with the case by way of an out-of-court disposal or when it will restart the prosecution, particularly if the case is serious.

10.2 These cases include:

- cases where a further review of the original decision shows that it was wrong and, in order to maintain confidence in the criminal justice system, a prosecution should be brought despite the earlier decision;
- cases which are stopped so that further anticipated evidence, which is likely to become available in the fairly near future, can be collected and prepared. In these cases, the prosecutor will tell the defendant that the prosecution may well start again;
- cases which are not prosecuted or are stopped because of a lack of evidence but where more significant evidence is discovered later; and
- cases involving a death in which a review following the findings of an inquest concludes that a prosecution should be brought, notwithstanding any earlier decision not to prosecute.

10.3 Victims may seek a review of certain CPS decisions not to start a prosecution or to stop a prosecution, under the Victims' Right to Review Scheme.

Appendix 4 Disclosure

ATTORNEY-GENERAL'S GUIDELINES ON DISCLOSURE FOR INVESTIGATORS, PROSECUTORS AND DEFENCE PRACTITIONERS

December 2013

Foreword

[Omitted.]

Introduction

These Guidelines are issued by the Attorney General for investigators, prosecutors and defence practitioners on the application of the disclosure regime contained in the Criminal Procedure and Investigations Act 1996 ('CPIA'). The Guidelines emphasise the importance of prosecution-led disclosure and the importance of applying the CPIA regime in a 'thinking manner', tailored, where appropriate, to the type of investigation or prosecution in question.

The Guidelines do not contain the detail of the disclosure regime; they outline the high level principles which should be followed when the disclosure regime is applied.

These Guidelines replace the existing Attorney General's Guidelines on Disclosure issued in 2005 and the Supplementary Guidelines on Digital Material issued in 2011, which is an annex to the general guidelines.

The Guidelines are intended to operate alongside the Judicial Protocol on the Disclosure of Unused Material in Criminal Cases. They are not designed to be an unequivocal statement of the law at any one time, nor are they a substitute for a thorough understanding of the relevant legislation, codes of practice, case law and procedure.

...

The Importance of Disclosure

1. The statutory framework for criminal investigations and disclosure is contained in the Criminal Procedure and Investigations Act 1996 (the CPIA) and the CPIA Code of Practice. The CPIA aims to ensure that criminal investigations are conducted in a fair, objective and thorough manner, and requires prosecutors to disclose to the defence material which has not previously been disclosed to the accused and which might reasonably be considered capable of undermining the case for the prosecution against the accused or of assisting the case for the accused. The CPIA requires a timely dialogue between the prosecution, defence and the court to enable the prosecution properly to identify such material.
2. Every accused person has a right to a fair trial, a right long embodied in our law and guaranteed by Article 6 of the European Convention on Human Rights (ECHR). A fair trial is the proper object and expectation of all participants in the trial process. Fair disclosure to the accused is an inseparable part of a fair trial. A fair trial should not require consideration of irrelevant material and should not involve spurious applications or arguments which serve to divert the trial process from examining the real issues before the court.
3. Properly applied, the CPIA should ensure that material is not disclosed which overburdens the participants in the trial process, diverts attention from the relevant issues, leads to unjustifiable delay, and is wasteful of resources. Consideration of disclosure issues should be an integral part of a good investigation and not something that exists separately.

Disclosure: general principles

4. Disclosure refers to providing the defence with copies of, or access to, any prosecution material which might reasonably be considered capable of undermining the case for the prosecution against the accused, or of assisting the case for the accused, and which has not previously been disclosed (section 3 CPIA).
5. Prosecutors will only be expected to anticipate what material might undermine their case or strengthen the defence in the light of information available at the time of the disclosure decision, and they may take into account information revealed during questioning.

6. In deciding whether material satisfies the disclosure test, consideration should be given amongst other things to:
   (a) the use that might be made of it in cross-examination;
   (b) its capacity to support submissions that could lead to:
      (i) the exclusion of evidence;
      (ii) a stay of proceedings, where the material is required to allow a proper application to be made;
      (iii) a court or tribunal finding that any public authority had acted incompatibly with the accused's rights under the ECHR;
   (c) its capacity to suggest an explanation or partial explanation of the accused's actions;
   (d) the capacity of the material to have a bearing on scientific or medical evidence in the case.
7. It should also be borne in mind that while items of material viewed in isolation may not be reasonably considered to be capable of undermining the prosecution case or assisting the accused, several items together can have that effect.
8. Material relating to the accused's mental or physical health, intellectual capacity, or to any ill treatment which the accused may have suffered when in the investigator's custody is likely to fall within the test for disclosure set out in paragraph 4 above.
9. Disclosure must not be an open-ended trawl of unused material. A critical element to fair and proper disclosure is that the defence play their role to ensure that the prosecution are directed to material which might reasonably be considered capable of undermining the prosecution case or assisting the case for the accused. This process is key to ensuring prosecutors make informed determinations about disclosure of unused material. The defence statement is important in identifying the issues in the case and why it is suggested that the material meets the test for disclosure.
10. Disclosure should be conducted in a thinking manner and never be reduced to a box-ticking exercise[1] at all stages of the process, there should be consideration of **why** the CPIA disclosure regime requires a particular course of action and what should be done to achieve that aim.
11. There will always be a number of participants in prosecutions and investigations: senior investigation officers, disclosure officers, investigation officers, reviewing prosecutors, leading counsel, junior counsel, and sometimes disclosure counsel. Communication within the 'prosecution team' is vital to ensure that all matters which could have a bearing on disclosure issues are given sufficient attention by the right person. This is especially so given many reviewing lawyers will be unable to sit behind the trial advocate throughout the trial. In practice, this is likely to mean that a full log of disclosure decisions (with reasons) must be kept on the file and made available as appropriate to the prosecution team.
12. The role of the reviewing lawyer will be central to ensuring all members of the prosecution team are aware of, and carry out, their duties and role(s). Where this involves counsel or more than one reviewing lawyer, this should be done by giving clear written instructions and record keeping.
13. The centrality of the reviewing lawyer does not mean that he or she has to do all the work personally; on the contrary, it will often mean effective delegation. Where the conduct of a prosecution is assigned to more than one prosecutor, steps must be taken to ensure that all involved in the case properly record their decisions. Subsequent prosecutors must be able to see and understand previous disclosure decisions before carrying out their continuous review function.
14. Investigators must always be alive to the potential need to reveal and prosecutors to the potential need to disclose material, in the interests of justice and fairness in the particular circumstances of any case, after the commencement of proceedings but before their duty arises under the Act. For instance, disclosure ought to be made of significant information that might affect a bail decision. This is likely to depend on what the defence chooses to reveal at that stage.

Investigators and Disclosure Officers

15. Investigators and disclosure officers must be fair and objective and must work together with prosecutors to ensure that disclosure obligations are met. Investigators and disclosure officers should be familiar with the CPIA Code of Practice, in particular their obligations to **retain** and **record** relevant material, to **review** it and to **reveal** it to the prosecutor.
16. Whether a case is a summary only matter or a long and complex trial on indictment, it is important that investigators and disclosure officers should approach their duties in a 'thinking manner' and not as a box ticking exercise. Where necessary, the reviewing lawyer should be consulted. It is important that investigators and disclosure officers are deployed on cases which are commensurate with their training, skills and experience. The conduct of an investigation provides the foundation for the entire

[1] *R v Olu, Wilson and Brooks* [2010] EWCA Crim 2975 at paragraph 42

case, and may even impact the conduct of linked cases. It is vital that there is always consideration of disclosure matters at the outset of an investigation, regardless of its size.

17. A fair investigation involves the pursuit of material following all reasonable lines of enquiry, whether they point towards or away from the suspect. What is 'reasonable' will depend on the context of the case. A fair investigation does not mean an endless investigation: investigators and disclosure officers must give thought to defining, and thereby limiting, the scope of their investigations, seeking the guidance of the prosecutor where appropriate.
18. Where there are a number of disclosure officers assigned to a case, there should be a lead disclosure officer who is the focus for enquiries and whose responsibility it is to ensure that the investigator's disclosure obligations are complied with. Where appropriate, regular case conferences and other meetings should be held to ensure prosecutors are apprised of all relevant developments in investigations. Full records should be kept of such meetings.
19. The CPIA Code of Practice encourages investigators and disclosure officers to seek advice from prosecutors about whether any particular item of material may be relevant to the investigation, and if so, how. Investigators and disclosure officers should record key decisions taken on these matters and be prepared to account for their actions later. An identical approach is not called for in each and every case.
20. Investigators are to approach their task seeking to establish what actually happened. They are to be fair and objective.
21. Disclosure officers (or their deputies) must inspect, view, listen to or search all relevant material that has been retained by the investigator and the disclosure officer must provide a personal declaration to the effect that this task has been undertaken. In some cases, a detailed examination of all material seized may be required. In others, however, a detailed examination of every item of material seized would be virtually impossible: see the **Annex**.
22. Prosecutors only have knowledge of matters which are revealed to them by investigators and disclosure officers, and the schedules are the written means by which that revelation takes place. Whatever the approach taken by investigators or disclosure officers to examining the material gathered or generated in the course of an investigation, it is crucial that disclosure officers record their reasons for a particular approach in writing.
23. In meeting the obligations in paragraph 6.9 and 8.1 of the Code, schedules must be completed in a form which not only reveals sufficient information to the prosecutor, but which demonstrates a transparent and thinking approach to the disclosure exercise, to command the confidence of the defence and the court. Descriptions on non-sensitive schedules must be clear and accurate, and must contain sufficient detail to enable the prosecutor to make an informed decision on disclosure. The use of abbreviations and acronyms can be problematic and lead to difficulties in appreciating the significance of the material.
24. Sensitive schedules must contain sufficiently clear descriptions to enable the prosecutor to make an informed decision as to whether or not the material itself should be viewed, to the extent possible without compromising the confidentiality of the information.
25. It may become apparent to an investigator that some material obtained in the course of an investigation, either because it was considered to be potentially relevant, or because it was inextricably linked to material that was relevant, is, in fact, incapable of impact. It is not necessary to retain such material, although the investigator should err on the side of caution in reaching that conclusion and should be particularly mindful of the fact that some investigations continue over some time and that what is incapable of impact may change over time. The advice of the prosecutor should be sought where appropriate.
26. Disclosure officers must specifically draw material to the attention of the prosecutor for consideration where they have any doubt as to whether it might reasonably be considered capable of undermining the prosecution case or of assisting the case for the accused.
27. Disclosure officers must seek the advice and assistance of prosecutors when in doubt as to their responsibility as early as possible. They must deal expeditiously with requests by the prosecutor for further information on material, which may lead to disclosure.

Prosecutors

28. Prosecutors are responsible for making proper disclosure in consultation with the disclosure officer. The duty of disclosure is a continuing one and disclosure should be kept under review. In addition, prosecutors should ensure that advocates in court are properly instructed as to disclosure issues. Prosecutors must also be alert to the need to provide advice to, and where necessary probe actions taken by, disclosure officers to ensure that disclosure obligations are met. There should be no aspects of an investigation about which prosecutors are unable to ask probing questions.

29. Prosecutors must review schedules prepared by disclosure officers thoroughly and must be alert to the possibility that relevant material may exist which has not been revealed to them or material included which should not have been. If no schedules have been provided, or there are apparent omissions from the schedules, or documents or other items are inadequately described or are unclear, the prosecutor must at once take action to obtain properly completed schedules. Likewise schedules should be returned for amendment if irrelevant items are included. If prosecutors remain dissatisfied with the quality or content of the schedules they must raise the matter with a senior investigator to resolve the matter satisfactorily.
30. Where prosecutors have reason to believe that the disclosure officer has not discharged the obligation in paragraph 21 to inspect, view, listen to or search relevant material, they must at once raise the matter with the disclosure officer and request that it be done. Where appropriate the matter should be raised with the officer in the case or a senior officer.
31. Prosecutors should copy the defence statement to the disclosure officer and investigator as soon as reasonably practicable and prosecutors should advise the investigator if, in their view, reasonable and relevant lines of further enquiry should be pursued. If the defence statement does point to other reasonable lines of enquiry, further investigation is required and evidence obtained as a result of these enquiries may be used as part of the prosecution case or to rebut the defence.
32. It is vital that prosecutors consider defence statements thoroughly. Prosecutors cannot comment upon, or invite inferences to be drawn from, failures in defence disclosure otherwise than in accordance with section 11 of the CPIA. Prosecutors may cross-examine the accused on differences between the defence case put at trial and that set out in his or her defence statement. In doing so, it may be appropriate to apply to the judge under section 6E of the CPIA for copies of the statement to be given to a jury, edited if necessary to remove inadmissible material. Prosecutors should examine the defence statement to see whether it points to other lines of enquiry.
33. Prosecutors should challenge the lack of, or inadequate, defence statements in writing, copying the document to the court and the defence and seeking directions from the court to require the provision of an adequate statement from the defence.
34. If the material does not fulfil the disclosure test there is no requirement to disclose it. For this purpose, the parties' respective cases should not be restrictively analysed but must be carefully analysed to ascertain the specific facts the prosecution seek to establish and the specific grounds on which the charges are resisted.

Prosecution advocates

35. Prosecution advocates should ensure that all material which ought to be disclosed under the Act is disclosed to the defence. However, prosecution advocates cannot be expected to disclose material if they are not aware of its existence. As far as is possible, prosecution advocates must place themselves in a fully informed position to enable them to make decisions on disclosure.
36. Upon receipt of instructions, prosecution advocates should consider as a priority all the information provided regarding disclosure of material. Prosecution advocates should consider, in every case, whether they can be satisfied that they are in possession of all relevant documentation and that they have been fully instructed regarding disclosure matters. If as a result the advocate considers that further information or action is required, written advice should promptly be provided setting out the aspects that need clarification or action.
37. The prosecution advocate must keep decisions regarding disclosure under review until the conclusion of the trial, whenever possible in consultation with the reviewing prosecutor. The prosecution advocate must in every case specifically consider whether he or she can satisfactorily discharge the duty of continuing review on the basis of the material supplied already, or whether it is necessary to inspect further material or to reconsider material already inspected. Prosecution advocates must not abrogate their responsibility under the CPIA by disclosing material which does not pass the test for disclosure, set out in paragraph 4, above.
38. There remains no basis in practice or law for counsel to counsel disclosure.

Defence

39. Defence engagement must be early and meaningful for the CPIA regime to function as intended. Defence statements are an integral part of this and are intended to help focus the attention of the prosecutor, court and co-defendants on the relevant issues in order to identify exculpatory unused material. Defence statements should be drafted in accordance with the relevant provisions of the CPIA.
40. Defence requests for further disclosure should ordinarily only be answered by the prosecution if the request is relevant to and directed to an issue identified in the defence statement. If it is not, then a

further or amended defence statement should be sought by the prosecutor and obtained before considering the request for further disclosure.

41. In some cases that involve extensive unused material that is within the knowledge of a defendant, the defence will be expected to provide the prosecution and the court with assistance in identifying material which is suggested to pass the test for disclosure.
42. The prosecution's continuing duty to keep disclosure under review is crucial, and particular attention must be paid to understanding the significance of developments in the case on the unused material and earlier disclosure decisions. Meaningful defence engagement will help the prosecution to keep disclosure under review. The continuing duty of review for prosecutors is less likely to require the disclosure of further material to the defence if the defence have clarified and articulated their case, as required by the CPIA.
43. In the magistrates' courts, where the provision of a defence statement is not mandatory, early identification of the material issues by the defence, whether through a defence statement, case management form or otherwise, will help the prosecution to focus its preparation of the case and allow any defence disclosure queries to be dealt with promptly and accurately.

Magistrates' Courts (including the Youth Court)

44. The majority of criminal cases are heard in the magistrates' court. The requirement for the prosecution to provide initial disclosure only arises after a not guilty plea has been entered but prosecutors should be alert to the possibility that material may exist which should be disclosed to the defendant prior to the CPIA requirements applying to the case[2].
45. Where a not guilty plea is entered in the magistrates' court, prosecutors should ensure that any issues of dispute which are raised are noted on the file. They should also seek to obtain a copy of any Magistrates' Court Trial Preparation Form. Consideration of the issues raised in court and on the Trial Preparation Form will assist in deciding what material undermines the prosecution case or assists the defendant.
46. Where a matter is set down for trial in the magistrates' court, prosecutors should ensure that the investigator is requested to supply any outstanding disclosure schedules as a matter of urgency. Prosecutors should serve initial disclosure in sufficient time to ensure that the trial date is effective.
47. There is no requirement for a defence statement to be served in the magistrates' court but it should be noted that if none is given the court has no power to hear an application for further prosecution disclosure under section 8 of the CPIA and the Criminal Procedure Rules.

Cases in the Crown Court

48. The exponential increase in the use of technology in society means that many routine Crown Court cases are increasingly likely to have to engage with digital material of some form. It is not only in large and complex cases that there may be large quantities of such material. Where such investigations involve digital material, it will be virtually impossible for investigators (or prosecutors) to examine every item of such material individually and there should be no expectation that such material will be so examined. Having consulted with the prosecution as appropriate, disclosure officers should determine what their approach should be to the examination of the material. Investigators or disclosure officers should decide how best to pursue a reasonable line of enquiry in relation to the relevant digital material, and ensure that the extent and manner of the examination are commensurate with the issues in the case.
49. Consideration should be given to any local or national agreements in relation to disclosure in 'Early Guilty Plea Scheme' cases.

Large and complex cases in the Crown Court

50. The particular challenges presented by large and complex criminal prosecutions require an approach to disclosure which is specifically tailored to the needs of such cases. In these cases more than any other is the need for careful thought to be given to prosecution-led disclosure matters from the very earliest stage. It is essential that the prosecution takes a grip on the case and its disclosure requirements from the very outset of the investigation, which must continue throughout all aspects of the case preparation.

Disclosure Management Documents

51. Accordingly, investigations and prosecutions of large and complex cases should be carefully defined and accompanied by a clear investigation and prosecution strategy. The approach to disclosure in such cases should be outlined in a document which should be served on the defence and the court at

[2] See for example *R v DPP ex parte Lee* [1999] 2 All ER 737

an early stage. Such documents, sometimes known as Disclosure Management Documents, will require careful preparation and presentation, tailored to the individual case. They may include:

(a) Where prosecutors and investigators operate in an integrated office, an explanation as to how the disclosure responsibilities have been managed;
(b) A brief summary of the prosecution case and a statement outlining how the prosecutor's general approach will comply with the CPIA regime, these Guidelines and the Judicial Protocol on the Disclosure of Unused Material in Criminal Cases;
(c) The prosecutor's understanding of the defence case, including information revealed during interview;
(d) An outline of the prosecution's general approach to disclosure, which may include detail relating to:
    (i) Digital material: explaining the method and extent of examination, in accordance with the **Annex** to these Guidelines;
    (ii) Video footage;
    (iii) Linked investigations: explaining the nexus between investigations, any memoranda of understanding or disclosure agreements between investigators;
    (iv) Third party and foreign material, including steps taken to obtain the material;
    (v) Reasonable lines of enquiry: a summary of the lines pursued, particularly those that point away from the suspect, or which may assist the defence;
    (vi) Credibility of a witness: confirmation that witness checks, including those of professional witnesses have, or will be, carried out.

52. Thereafter the prosecution should follow the Disclosure Management Document. They are living documents and should be amended in light of developments in the case; they should be kept up to date as the case progresses. Their use will assist the court in its own case management and will enable the defence to engage from an early stage with the prosecution's proposed approach to disclosure.

Material not held by the prosecution

Involvement of other agencies: material held by other Government departments and third parties

53. Where it appears to an investigator, disclosure officer or prosecutor that a Government department or other Crown body has material that may be relevant to an issue in the case, reasonable steps should be taken to identify and consider such material. Although what is reasonable will vary from case to case, the prosecution should inform the department or other body of the nature of its case and of relevant issues in the case in respect of which the department or body might possess material, and ask whether it has any such material.
54. It should be remembered that investigators, disclosure officers and prosecutors cannot be regarded to be in constructive possession of material held by Government departments or Crown bodies simply by virtue of their status as Government departments or Crown bodies.
55. Where, after reasonable steps have been taken to secure access to such material, access is denied, the investigator, disclosure officer or prosecutor should consider what if any further steps might be taken to obtain the material or inform the defence. The final decision on any further steps will be for the prosecutor.

Third party material: other domestic bodies

56. There may be cases where the investigator, disclosure officer or prosecutor believes that a third party (for example, a local authority, a social services department, a hospital, a doctor, a school, a provider of forensic services) has material or information which might be relevant to the prosecution case. In such cases, investigators, disclosure officers and prosecutors should take reasonable steps to identify, secure and consider material held by any third party where it appears to the investigator, disclosure officer or prosecutor that (a) such material exists and (b) that it may be relevant to an issue in the case.
57. If the investigator, disclosure officer or prosecutor seeks access to the material or information but the third party declines or refuses to allow access to it, the matter should not be left. If despite any reasons offered by the third party it is still believed that it is reasonable to seek production of the material or information, and the requirements of section 2 of the Criminal Procedure (Attendance of Witnesses) Act 1965 or as appropriate section 97 of the Magistrates' Courts Act 1980 are satisfied (or any other relevant power), then the prosecutor or investigator should apply for a witness summons causing a representative of the third party to produce the material to the court.
58. Sometimes, for example through multi-agency working arrangements, investigators, disclosure officers or prosecutors may become aware of the content or nature of material held by a third party. Consultation with the relevant third party must always take place before disclosure is made; there

may be public interest reasons to apply to the Court for an order for non-disclosure in the public interest, in accordance with the procedure outlined in paragraph 65 and following.

International matters

59. The obligations under the CPIA Code to pursue all reasonable lines of enquiry apply to material held overseas.
60. Where it appears that there is relevant material, the prosecutor must take reasonable steps to obtain it, either informally or making use of the powers contained in the Crime (International Co-operation) Act 2003 and any EU and international conventions. See CPS Guidance 'Obtaining Evidence and Information from Abroad'.
61. There may be cases where a foreign state or a foreign court refuses to make the material available to the investigator or prosecutor. There may be other cases where the foreign state, though willing to show the material to investigators, will not allow the material to be copied or otherwise made available and the courts of the foreign state will not order its provision.
62. It is for these reasons that there is no absolute duty on the prosecutor to disclose relevant material held overseas by entities not subject to the jurisdiction of the courts in England and Wales. However consideration should be given to whether the type of material believed to be held can be provided to the defence.
63. The obligation on the investigator and prosecutor under the CPIA is to take reasonable steps. Where investigators are allowed to examine files of a foreign state but are not allowed to take copies or notes or list the documents held, there is no breach by the prosecution in its duty of disclosure by reason of its failure to obtain such material, provided reasonable steps have been taken to try and obtain the material. Prosecutors have a margin of consideration as to what steps are appropriate in the particular case but prosecutors must be alive to their duties and there may be some circumstances where these duties cannot be met. Whether the prosecutor has taken reasonable steps is for the court to determine in each case if the matter is raised.
64. In these circumstances it is important that the position is clearly set out in writing so that the court and the defence know what the position is. Investigators and prosecutors must record and explain the situation and set out, insofar as they are permitted by the foreign state, such information as they can and the steps they have taken.

Applications for non-disclosure in the public interest

65. The CPIA allows prosecutors to apply to the court for an order to withhold material which would otherwise fall to be disclosed if disclosure would give rise to a real risk of serious prejudice to an important public interest. Before making such an application, prosecutors should aim to disclose as much of the material as they properly can (for example, by giving the defence redacted or edited copies or summaries). Neutral material or material damaging to the defendant need not be disclosed and there is no need to bring it to the attention of the court. Only in truly borderline cases should the prosecution seek a judicial ruling on whether material in its possession should be disclosed.
66. Prior to the hearing, the prosecutor and the prosecution advocate must examine all material which is the subject matter of the application and make any necessary enquiries of the investigator. The investigator must be frank with the prosecutor about the full extent of the sensitive material. Prior to or at the hearing, the court must be provided with full and accurate information about the material.
67. The prosecutor (or representative) and/or investigator should attend such applications. Section 16 of the CPIA allows a person claiming to have an interest in the sensitive material to apply to the court for the opportunity to be heard at the application.
68. The principles set out at paragraph 36 of *R v H & C* [2004] 2 Cr. App. R. 10 [2004] UKHL 3 should be applied rigorously, firstly by the prosecutor and then by the court considering the material. It is essential that these principles are scrupulously adhered to, to ensure that the procedure for examination of material in the absence of the accused is compliant with Article 6.
69. If prosecutors conclude that a fair trial cannot take place because material which satisfies the test for disclosure cannot be disclosed, and that this cannot be remedied by the above procedure; how the case is presented; or by any other means, they should not continue with the case.

Other disclosure

70. Disclosure of any material that is made outside the ambit of CPIA will attract confidentiality by virtue of *Taylor v SFO* [1999] 2 AC 177.

Material relevant to sentence

71. In all cases the prosecutor must consider disclosing in the interests of justice any material which is relevant to sentence (e.g. information which might mitigate the seriousness of the offence or assist the accused to lay blame in part upon a co-accused or another person).

Post-conviction

72. Where, after the conclusion of the proceedings, material comes to light, that might cast doubt upon the safety of the conviction, the prosecutor must consider disclosure of such material.

Applicability of these Guidelines

73. These Guidelines shall have immediate effect.

ANNEX: ATTORNEY-GENERAL'S GUIDELINES ON DISCLOSURE: SUPPLEMENTARY GUIDELINES ON DIGITALLY STORED MATERIAL (2011)

A1. The Guidelines are intended to supplement the Attorney General's Guidelines on Disclosure.

A2. As a result of the number of cases now involving digitally stored material and the scale of the digital material that may be involved, more detailed guidance is considered to be needed. The objective of these Guidelines is to set out how material satisfying the tests for disclosure can best be identified and disclosed to the defence without imposing unrealistic or disproportionate demands on the investigator and prosecutor.

A3. The approach set out in these Guidelines is in line with existing best practice, in that:

a. Investigating and prosecuting agencies, especially in large and complex cases, will apply their respective case management and disclosure strategies and policies and be transparent with the defence and the courts about how the prosecution has approached complying with its disclosure obligations in the context of the individual case; and

b. The defence will be expected to play their part in defining the real issues in the case. In this context, the defence will be invited to participate in defining the scope of the reasonable searches that may be made of digitally stored material by the investigator to identify material that might reasonably be expected to undermine the prosecution case or assist the defence.

A4. Only if this approach is followed can the courts be in a position to use their case management powers effectively and to determine applications for disclosure fairly.

A5. The Attorney General's Guidelines are not detailed operational guidelines. They are intended to set out a common approach to be adopted in the context of digitally stored material.

Types of digital material

A6. Digital material falls into two categories: the first category is material which is created natively within an electronic environment (e.g. email, office files, system files, digital photographs, audio etc.); the second category is material which has been digitised from an analogue form (e.g. scanned copy of a document, scanned photograph, a faxed document). Irrespective of the way in which technology changes, the categorisation of digital material will remain the same.

A7. Digital material is usually held on one of the three types of media. Optical media (e.g. CD, DVD, Blu-ray) and Solid-State media (e.g. removable memory cards, solid state music players or mobile devices etc.) cater for usually lower volume storage. Magnetic media (e.g. disk drives and back up tapes) usually cater for the high volume storage.

General principles for investigators

A8. The general principles[1] to be followed by investigators in handling and examining digital material are:

a. No action taken by investigators or their agents should change data held on a computer or storage media which may subsequently be relied upon in court;

b. In circumstances where a person finds it necessary to access original data held on computer or storage media, that person must be competent to do so and be able to give evidence explaining the relevance and implications of their actions;

c. *An audit trail or other record* of all processes applied to computer-based electronic evidence should be created and preserved. An independent third party should be able to examine those processes (see further the section headed Record keeping and Scheduling below); and

d. The person in charge of the investigation has overall responsibility for ensuring that the law and these principles are followed.

[1] Based on: Association of Chief Police Officers: Good Practice Guide for Computer Based Electronic Evidence version 0.1.4.

A9. Where an investigator has reasonable grounds for believing that digital material may contain material subject to legal professional privilege, very strong legal constraints apply. No digital material may be seized which an investigator has reasonable grounds for believing to be subject to legal privilege, other than where the provisions of the Criminal Justice and Police Act 2001 apply. Strict controls need to be applied where privileged material is seized. See the more detailed section on Legal Professional Privilege starting at paragraph A28 below.

Seizure, relevance and retention

A10. The legal obligations are to be found in a combination of the Police and Criminal Evidence Act 1984 (PACE), the Criminal Justice and Police Act 2001 (CJPA 2001) and the Criminal Procedure and Investigations Act 1996 (the CPIA 1996).

A11. These Guidelines also apply to digital material seized or imaged under other statutory provisions. For example, the Serious Fraud Office has distinct powers of seizure under warrant obtained under section 2(4) of the Criminal Justice Act 1987. In cases concerning indecent images of children and obscene material, special provisions apply to the handling, storage and copying of such material. Practitioners should refer to specific guidance on the application of those provisions.

Seizure

A12. Before searching a suspect's premises where digital evidence is likely to be found, consideration must be given to what sort of evidence is likely to be found and in what volume, whether it is likely to be possible to view and copy, if relevant, the material at the location (it is not uncommon with the advent of cloud computing for digital material to be hosted by a third party) and to what should be seized. Business and commercial premises will often have very substantial amounts of digital material stored on computers and other media. Investigators will need to consider the practicalities of seizing computer hard drives and other media, the effect this may have on the business and, where it is not feasible to obtain an image of digital material, the likely timescale for returning seized items.

A13. In deciding whether to seize and retain digital material it is important that the investigator either complies with the procedure under the relevant statutory authority, relying either on statutory powers or a search warrant, or obtains the owner's consent. In particular, investigators need to be aware of the strong constraints applying to legally privileged material.

A14. A computer hard drive or single item of media, such as a back up tape, is a single storage entity. This means that if any digital material found on the hard drive or other media can lawfully be seized the computer hard drive or single item of media may, if appropriate, be seized or imaged. In some circumstances investigators may wish to image specific folders, files or categories of data where it is feasible to do so without seizing the hard drive or other media, or instead of taking an image of all data on the hard drive or other media. In practice, the configuration of most systems means that data may be contained across a number of hard drives and more than one hard drive or item of media may be required in order to access the information sought.

A15. Digital material must not be seized if an investigator has reasonable grounds for believing it is subject to legal professional privilege, *other than where* sections 50 or 51 of the Criminal Justice and Police Act 2001 apply. If such material is seized it must be isolated from other seized material and any other investigation material in the possession of the investigating authority.

The Police and Criminal Evidence Act 1984

A16. PACE 1984 provides powers to seize and retain anything for which the search has been authorised or after arrest, other than items attracting legal professional privilege.[2] In addition, there is a general power to seize anything which is on the premises if there are reasonable grounds to believe that it has been obtained in the commission of an offence, or that it is evidence and that it is necessary to seize it to prevent it being concealed, lost, altered or destroyed.[3] There is another related power to require information which is stored in any electronic form and is accessible from the premises to be produced in a form in which it can be taken away and in which it is visible and legible or from which it can readily be produced in a visible and legible form.[4]

A17. An image (a forensically sound copy) of the digital material may be taken at the location of the search. Where the investigator makes an image of the digital material at the location, the original need not be seized. Alternatively, when originals are taken, investigators must be prepared to copy

[2] By warrant under section 8 and Schedule 1 and section 18 of PACE.
[3] Section 19 of PACE.
[4] Section 20 of PACE.

or image the material for the owners when reasonably practicable in accordance with PACE 1984 Code B 7.17.

A18. Where it is not possible or reasonably practicable to image the computer or hard drive, it will need to be removed from the location or premises for examination elsewhere. This allows the investigator to seize and sift material for the purpose of identifying that which meets the tests for retention in accordance with the 1984 PACE.[5]

The Criminal Justice and Police Act 2001

A19. The additional powers of seizure in sections 50 and 51 of the CJPA 2001 only extend the scope of existing powers of search and seizure under the PACE and other specified statutory authorities[6] where the relevant conditions and circumstances apply.

A20. Investigators must be careful only to exercise powers under the CJPA when it is necessary and not to remove any more material than is justified. The removal of large volumes of material, much of which may not ultimately be retainable, may have serious consequences for the owner of the material, particularly when they are involved in business or other commercial activities.

A21. A written notice must be given to the occupier of the premises where items are seized under sections 50 and 51.[7]

A22. Until material seized under the CJPA 2001 has been examined, it must be kept securely and separately from any material seized under other powers. Any such material must be examined as soon as reasonably practicable to determine which elements may be retained and which should be returned. Regard must be had to the desirability of allowing the person from whom the property was seized—or a person with an interest in the property—an opportunity of being present or represented at the examination.

Retention

A23. Where material is seized under the powers conferred by PACE the duty to retain it under the Code of Practice issued under the CPIA is subject to the provisions on retention under section 22 of PACE. Material seized under sections 50 and 51 of the CJPA 2001 may be retained or returned in accordance with sections 53–58 of that Act.

A24. Retention is limited to evidence and relevant material (as defined in the Code of Practice issued under the CPIA). Where either evidence or relevant material is inextricably linked to non-relevant material which is not reasonably practicable to separate, that material can also be retained. Inextricably linked material is material that is not reasonably practicable to separate from other linked material without prejudicing the use of that other material in any investigation or proceedings.

A25. However, inextricably linked material must not be examined, imaged, copied or used for any purpose other than for providing the source of or the integrity of the linked material.

A26. There are four categories of material that may be retained:

a. Material that is evidence or potential evidence in the case. Where material is retained for evidential purposes there will be a strong argument that the whole thing (or an authenticated image or copy) should be retained for the purpose of proving provenance and continuity;

b. Where evidential material has been retained, inextricably linked non-relevant material which is not reasonably practicable to separate can also be retained (PACE Code B paragraph 7);

c. An investigator should retain material that is relevant to the investigation and required to be scheduled as unused material. This is broader than but includes the duty to retain material which may satisfy the test for prosecution disclosure. The general duty to retain relevant material is set out in the CPIA Code at paragraph 5; or,

d. Material which is inextricably linked to relevant unused material which of itself may not be relevant material. Such material should be retained (PACE Code B paragraph 7).

A27. The balance of any digital material should be returned in accordance with sections 53–55 of the CJPA 2001 if seized under that Act.

Legal Professional Privilege (LPP)

A28. No digital material may be seized which an investigator has reasonable grounds for believing to be subject to LLP, other than under the additional powers of seizure in the CJPA 2001.

---

[5] Special provisions exist for the investigations conducted by Her Majesty's Revenue and Customs in the application of their powers under PACE—see section 114(2)(b)—and the CJPA 2001.

[6] Schedule 1 of the CJPA 2001.

[7] Section 52 of the CJPA 2001.

A29. The CJPA 2001 enables an investigator to seize relevant items which contain LPP material where it is not reasonably practicable on the search premises to separate LPP material from non-LPP material.

A30. Where LPP material or material suspected of containing LPP is seized it must be isolated from the other material which has been seized in the investigation. The mechanics of securing property vary according to the circumstances; 'bagging up', i.e. placing materials in sealed bags or containers, and strict subsequent control of access, is the appropriate procedure in many cases.

A31. Where material has been identified as potentially containing LPP it must be reviewed by a lawyer independent of the prosecuting authority. No member of the investigative or prosecution team involved in either the current investigation or, if the LPP material relates to other criminal proceedings, in those proceedings should have sight of or access to the LPP material.

A32. If the material is voluminous, search terms or other filters may have to be used to identify the LPP material. If so this will also have to be done by someone independent and not connected with the investigation.

A33. It is essential that anyone dealing with LPP material maintains proper records showing the way in which the material has been handled and those who have had access to it as well as decisions taken in relation to that material.

A34. LPP material can only be retained in specific circumstances in accordance with section 54 of the CJPA 2001 i.e. where the property which comprises the LPP material has been lawfully seized and it is not reasonably practicable for the item to be separated from the rest of the property without prejudicing the use of the rest of the property. LPP material which cannot be retained must be returned as soon as practicable after the seizure without waiting for the whole examination of the seized material.

Excluded and special procedure material

A35. Similar principles to those that apply to LPP material apply to excluded or special procedure material, as set out in section 55 of the CJPA 2001.[8]

Encryption

A36. Part III of the Regulation of Investigatory Powers Act 2000 (RIPA) and the Investigation of Protected Electronic Information Code of Practice govern encryption. See the CPS's Guidance RIPA Part III.

A37. RIPA enables specified law enforcement agencies to compel individuals or companies to provide passwords or encryption keys for the purpose of rendering protected material readable. Failure to comply with RIPA Part III orders is a criminal offence. The Code of Practice provides guidance when exercising powers under RIPA, to require disclosure of protected electronic data in an intelligible form or to acquire the means by which protected electronic data may be accessed or put in an intelligible form.

Sifting/examination

A38. In complying with its duty of disclosure, the prosecution should follow the procedure as outlined below.

A39. Where digital material is examined, the extent and manner of inspecting, viewing or listening will depend on the nature of the material and its form.

A40. It is important for investigators and prosecutors to remember that the duty under the CPIA Code of Practice is to 'pursue all reasonable lines of enquiry including those that point away from the suspect'. Lines of enquiry, of whatever kind, should be pursued only if they are reasonable in the context of the individual case. It is not the duty of the prosecution to comb through all the material in its possession—e.g. every word or byte of computer material—on the look out for anything which might conceivably or speculatively assist the defence. The duty of the prosecution is to disclose material which might reasonably be considered capable of undermining its case or assisting the case for the accused which they become aware of, or to which their attention is drawn.

A41. In some cases the sift may be conducted by an investigator/disclosure officer manually assessing the content of the computer or other digital material from its directory and determining which files are relevant and should be retained for evidence or unused material.

A42. In other cases such an approach may not be feasible. Where there is an enormous volume of material it is perfectly proper for the investigator/disclosure officer to search it by sample, key words, or other appropriate search tools or analytical techniques to locate relevant passages, phrases and identifiers.

[8] Special provision exists for investigations conducted by Her Majesty's Revenue and Customs in the application of the powers under PACE—see section 114(2)(b)—and the CJPA 2001.

A43. In cases involving very large quantities of data, the person in charge of the investigation will develop a strategy setting out how the material should be analysed or searched to identify categories of data. Where search tools are used to examine digital material it will usually be appropriate to provide the accused and his or her legal representative with a copy of reasonable search terms used, or to be used, and invite them to suggest any further reasonable search terms. If search terms are suggested which the investigator or prosecutor believes will not be productive—for example because of the use of common words that are likely to identify a mass of irrelevant material, the investigator or prosecutor is entitled to open a dialogue with the defence representative with a view to agreeing sensible refinements. The purpose of this dialogue is to ensure that reasonable and proportionate searches can be carried out.

A44. It may be necessary to carry out sampling and searches on more than one occasion, especially as there is a duty on the prosecutor to keep duties of disclosure under review. To comply with this duty it may be appropriate (and should be considered) where further evidence or unused material is obtained in the course of the investigation; the defence statement is served on the prosecutor; the defendant makes an application under section 8 of the CPIA for disclosure; or the defendant requests that further sampling or searches be carried out (provided it is a reasonable line of enquiry).

Record keeping

A45. A record or log must be made of all digital material seized or imaged and subsequently retained as relevant to the investigation.

A46. In cases involving very large quantities of data where the person in charge of the investigation has developed a strategy setting out how the material should be analysed or searched to identify categories of data, a record should be made of the strategy and the analytical techniques used to search the data. The record should include details of the person who has carried out the process and the date and time it was carried out. In such cases the strategy should record the reasons why certain categories have been searched for (such as names, companies, dates etc.).

A47. In any case it is important that any searching or analytical processing of digital material, as well as the data identified by that process, is properly recorded. *So far as practicable*, what is required is a record of the terms of the searches or processing that has been carried out. This means that in principle the following details may be recorded:

a. A record of all searches carried out, including the date of each search and the person(s) who conducted it;
b. A record of all search words or terms used on each search. However where it is impracticable to record each word or terms (such as where Boolean searches or search strings or conceptual searches are used) it will usually be sufficient to record each broad category of search;
c. A log of the key judgements made while refining the search strategy in the light of what is found, or deciding not to carry out further searches; and,
d. Where material relating to a 'hit' is not examined, the decision not to examine should be explained in the record of examination or in a statement. For instance, a large number of 'hits' may be obtained in relation to a particular search word or term, but material relating to the 'hits' is not examined because they do not appear to be relevant to the investigation. Any subsequent refinement of the search terms and further hits should also be noted and explained as above.

A48. Just as it is not necessary for the investigator or prosecutor to produce records of every search made of hard copy material, it is not necessary to produce records of what may be many hundreds of searches or analyses that have been carried out on digitally stored material, simply to demonstrate that these have been done. It should be sufficient for the prosecution to explain how the disclosure exercise has been approached and to give the accused or suspect's legal representative an opportunity to participate in defining the reasonable searches to be made, as described in the section on sifting/examination.

Scheduling

A49. The disclosure officer should ensure that scheduling of relevant material is carried out in accordance with the CPIA Code of Practice. This requires each item of unused material to be listed separately on the unused material schedule and numbered consecutively. The description of each item should make clear the nature of the item and should contain sufficient detail to enable the prosecutor to decide whether he needs to inspect the material before deciding whether or not it should be disclosed (see paragraph A24).

A50. In some enquiries it may not be practicable to list each item of material separately. If so, these may be listed in a block and described by quantity and generic title. Even if the material is listed in a block, the search terms used and any items of material which might satisfy the disclosure test are listed and described separately. In practical terms this will mean, where appropriate, cross referencing the schedules to your disclosure management document.

A51. The remainder of any computer hard drive/media containing material which is not responsive to search terms or other analytical technique or not identified by any 'hits', and material identified by 'hits' but not examined, is unused material and should be recorded (if appropriate by a generic description) and retained.

A52. Where continuation sheets of the unused material schedule are used, or additional schedules are sent subsequently, the item numbering must be, where possible, sequential to all other items on earlier schedules.

Third party material

A53. Third party material is material held by a person, organisation, or government department other than the investigator and prosecutor within the UK or outside the UK.

Within the UK

A54. The CPIA Code and the AG's Guidelines makes clear the obligation on the prosecution to pursue all reasonable lines of enquiry in relation to material held by third parties within the UK.

A55. If as a result of the duty to pursue all reasonable lines of enquiry, the investigator or prosecutor obtains or receives the material from the third party, then it must be dealt with in accordance with the CPIA i.e. the prosecutor must disclose material if it meets the disclosure tests, subject to any public interest immunity claim. The person who has an interest in the material (the third party) may make representations to the court concerning public interest immunity (see section 16 of the CPIA 1996).

A56. Material not in the possession of an investigator or prosecutor falls outside the CPIA. In such cases the Attorney General Guidelines on Disclosure prescribe the approach to be taken to disclosure of material held by third parties as does the judicial disclosure protocol.

JUDICIAL PROTOCOL ON THE DISCLOSURE OF UNUSED MATERIAL IN CRIMINAL CASES

Introduction

This protocol is prescribed for use by CPD IV Disclosure [15A]: Disclosure of Unused Material. It is applicable in all the criminal courts of England and Wales, including the Crown Court, the Court Martial[1] and the magistrates' courts. It replaces the previous judicial document 'Disclosure: a Protocol for the Control and Management of Unused Material in the Crown Court'[2] and it also replaces section 4 'Disclosure' of the Lord Chief Justice's Protocol on the Control and Management of Heavy Fraud and Other Complex Criminal Cases, dated 22 March 2005.[3]

This protocol is intended to provide a central source of guidance for the judiciary, although that produced by the Attorney General also requires attention.

In summary, this judicial protocol sets out the principles to be applied to, and the importance of, disclosure; the expectations of the court and its role in disclosure, in particular in relation to case management; and the consequences if there is a failure by the prosecution or defence to comply with their obligations.

...

The importance of disclosure for fair trials

1. Disclosure remains one of the most important – as well as one of the most misunderstood and abused – of the procedures relating to criminal trials. Lord Justice Gross' review has re-emphasised the need for all those involved to understand the statutory requirements and to undertake their roles with rigour, in a timely manner.

[1] The timetables given here may vary in the Court Martial and reference should be made to the Criminal Procedure and Investigations Act 1996 (Application to the Armed Forces) Order 2009 and to any practice note issued by the Judge Advocate General.

[2] The previous judicial protocol was endorsed by the Court of Appeal in *R v K* [2006] EWCA Crim 724; [2006] 2 All ER 552 (Note); [2006] Crim LR 1012.

[3] This protocol also replaces the Protocol for the Provision of Advance Information, Prosecution Evidence and Disclosure of Unused Material in the Magistrates' Courts, dated 12 May 2006, which was adopted as part of the Stop Delaying Justice initiative.

2. The House of Lords stated in *R v H and C* [2004] UKHL 3; [2004] 2 AC 134; [2004] 2 Cr App R 10:

> Fairness ordinarily requires that any material held by the prosecution which weakens its case or strengthens that of the defendant, if not relied on as part of its formal case against the defendant, should be disclosed to the defence. Bitter experience has shown that miscarriages of justice may occur where such material is withheld from disclosure. The golden rule is that full disclosure of such material should be made. ([2004] 2 AC 134, at 147)

The Criminal Cases Review Commission has recently noted that failure to disclose material to the defence to which they were entitled remains the biggest single cause of miscarriages of justice.

3. However, it is also essential that the trial process is not overburdened or diverted by erroneous and inappropriate disclosure of unused prosecution material or by misconceived applications. Although the drafters of the Criminal Procedure and Investigations Act 1996 ('CPIA 1996') cannot have anticipated the vast increase in the amount of electronic material that has been generated in recent years, nevertheless the principles of that Act still hold true. Applications by the parties or decisions by judges based on misconceptions of the law or a general laxity of approach (however well-intentioned) which result in an improper application of the disclosure regime have, time and again, proved unnecessarily costly and have obstructed justice. As Lord Justice Gross noted, the burden of disclosure must not be allowed to render the prosecution of cases impracticable.

4. The overarching principle is that unused prosecution material will fall to be disclosed if, and only if, it satisfies the test for disclosure applicable to the proceedings in question, subject to any overriding public interest considerations. The test for disclosure will depend on the date the criminal investigation in question commenced, as this will determine whether the common law disclosure regime applies, or either of the two disclosure regimes under the CPIA 1996.

5. The test for disclosure under section 3 of the CPIA 1996 as amended will be applicable in nearly every case and all those involved in the process will need to be familiar with it. Material fulfils the test if – but only if – it 'might reasonably be considered capable of undermining the case for the prosecution . . . or of assisting the case for the accused.'

6. The disclosure process must be led by the prosecution so as to trigger comprehensive defence engagement, supported by robust judicial case management. Active participation by the court in the disclosure process is a critical means of ensuring that delays and adjournments are avoided, given failures by the parties to comply with their obligations may disrupt and (in some cases) frustrate the course of justice.

Disclosure of unused material in criminal cases

7. The court should keep the timetable for prosecution and defence disclosure under review from the first hearing. Judges should as a matter of course ask the parties to identify the issues in the case, and invite the parties to indicate whether further disclosure is sought, and on what topics. For example, it is not enough for the judge to rely on the content of the PCMH form. Proper completion of the disclosure process is a vital part of case preparation, and it may well affect the progress of the case. The court will expect disclosure to have been considered from the outset; the prosecution and defence advocates need to be aware of any potential problems and substantive difficulties should be explained to the judge; and the parties should propose a sensible timetable. Realism is preferable to optimistic but unachievable deadlines which may dislocate the court schedule and imperil the date of trial. It follows that judges should not impose deadlines for service of the case papers or disclosure until they are confident that the prosecution advocate has taken instructions from the individuals who are best placed to evaluate the work to be undertaken.

8. The advocates—both prosecution and defence—must be kept fully informed throughout the course of the proceedings as to any difficulties which may prevent them from complying with their disclosure obligations. When problems arise or come to light after directions have been given, the advocates should notify the court and the other party (or parties) immediately rather than waiting until the date set by the court for the service of the material is imminent or has passed, and they must provide the court with a suggested timetable in order to resolve the problem. The progress of the disclosure process should be reviewed at every hearing. There remains no basis in practice or law for Counsel to Counsel disclosure.

9. If there is a preliminary hearing the judge should seize the opportunity to impose an early timetable for disclosure and to identify any likely problems including as regards third party material and material that will require an application to the Family Court. In an appropriate case the court should consider holding a Joint Criminal/Care Directions Hearing. See Material held by Third Parties, from paragraph 44 below.

10. For the PCMH to be effective, the defence must have a proper opportunity to review the case papers and consider initial disclosure, with a view to preparing a properly completed defence statement which will inform the judge's conduct of the PCMH, and inform the prosecution of the matters required by sections 5, 6A and 6C of the CPIA. As the Court of Appeal noted in *R v Newell* [2012] EWCA Crim 650; [2012] 2 Cr App R 10, 'a typed defence statement must be provided before the PCMH. If there is no defence statement by the time of the PCMH, then a judge will usually require the trial advocate to see that such a statement is provided and not proceed with the PCMH until that is done. In the ordinary case the trial advocate will be required to do that at the court and the PCMH resumed later in the day to avoid delay'. There may be some instances when there will be a well-founded defence application to extend the 28-day time limit for serving a proper defence statement. In a proper case (but never routinely), it may be appropriate to put the PCMH back by a week or more, to enable an appropriate defence statement to be filed.
11. The defence statement can be admitted into evidence under section 6E(4) of the CPIA 1996. However, information included on the PCMH form (which is primarily an administrative form) will not usually be admitted in evidence when the defence advocate has complied with the letter and the spirit of the Criminal Procedure Rules.[4] Introducing the PCMH form (or part of it) during the trial is likely to be an exceptional event. The status of the trial preparation form in the magistrates' court is somewhat different, as discussed below.
12. The court should not extend time lightly or as a matter of course. If an extension is sought, it ought to be accompanied by an appropriate explanation. For instance, it is not sufficient for the prosecutor merely to say that the investigator has delivered the papers late: the underlying reasons are to be provided to the court. The same applies if the defence statement is delayed. Whichever party is at fault, realistic proposals for service are to be set out.
13. Judges should not allow the prosecution to avoid their statutory responsibility for reviewing the unused material by the expedient of permitting the defence to have access to (or providing the defence with copies of) the material listed in the schedules of non-sensitive unused prosecution material irrespective of whether it satisfies, wholly or in part, the relevant test for disclosure. Additionally, it is for the prosecutor to decide on the manner of disclosure, and it does not have to mirror the form in which the information was originally recorded. Rose LJ gave guidance on case management issues in this context in *R v CPS* (Interlocutory Application under sections 35/36 CPIA) [2005] EWCA Crim 2342. Allowing the defence to inspect items that fulfil the disclosure test is also a valid means of providing disclosure.
14. The larger and more complex the case, the more important it is for the prosecution to adhere to the overarching principle and ensure that sufficient prosecution attention and resources are allocated to the task. Handing the defendant the 'keys to the warehouse' has been the cause of many gross abuses in the past, resulting in considerable expenditure by the defence without any material benefit to the course of justice. The circumstances relating to large and complex cases are outlined below.
15. The court will require the defence to engage and assist in the early identification of the real issues in the case and, particularly in the larger and more complex cases, to contribute to the search terms to be used for, and the parameters of, the review of any electronically held material (which can be very considerable). Any defence criticisms of the prosecution approach to disclosure should be timely and reasoned; there is no place for disclosure 'ambushes' or for late or uninformative defence statements. Admissions should be used so far as possible to narrow the real issues in dispute.
16. A constructive approach to disclosure is a necessary part of professional best practice, for the defence and prosecution. This does not undermine the defendant's legitimate interests, it accords with his or her obligations under the Rules and it ensures that all the relevant material is provided. Delays and failures by the prosecution and the defence are equally damaging to a timely, fair and efficient trial, and judges should be vigilant in preventing and addressing abuses. Accordingly, whenever there are potential failings by either the defence or the prosecution, judges, in exercising appropriate oversight of disclosure, should carefully investigate the suggested default and give timely directions.
17. In the Crown Court, the defence statement is to be served within 28 days of the date when the prosecution complies with its duty of initial disclosure (or purports to do so) and whenever section 5(5) of the CPIA applies to the proceedings, and the defence statement must comply with section 6A of the CPIA. Service of the defence statement is a most important stage in the disclosure process, and timely service is necessary to facilitate proper consideration of the disclosure issues well in advance of the trial date. Judges expect a defence statement to contain a clear and detailed exposition of the issues of fact and law. Defence statements that merely rehearse the suggestion that the defendant is innocent do not comply with the requirements of the CPIA.

[4] *R v Newell* [2012] EWCA Crim 650; [2012] 2 Cr App R 10.

18. The prosecutor should consider the defence statement carefully and promptly provide a copy to the disclosure officer, to assist the prosecution in its continuing disclosure obligations. The court expects the Crown to identify any suggested deficiencies in the defence statement, and to draw these to the attention of the defence and the court; in particular in large and complex cases, it will assist the court if this is in writing. Although the prosecution's ability to request, and the court's jurisdiction to give, an adverse inference direction under section 11 of CPIA is not contingent on the prosecution having earlier identified any suggested deficiencies, nevertheless the prosecutor must provide a timely written explanation of its position.
19. Judges should examine the defence statement with care to ensure that it complies with the formalities required by the CPIA. As stated in *R v H and C* (supra) (paragraph 35):

> If material does not weaken the prosecution case or strengthen that of the defendant, there is no requirement to disclose it. For this purpose the parties' respective cases should not be restrictively analysed. But they must be carefully analysed, to ascertain the specific facts the prosecution seek to establish and the specific grounds on which the charges are resisted. The trial process is not well served if the defence are permitted to make general and unspecified allegations and then seek far-reaching disclosure in the hope that material may turn up to make them good. Neutral material or material damaging to the defendant need not be disclosed and should not be brought to the attention of the court.

20. If no defence statement—or an inadequate defence statement—is served within the relevant time limits, the judge should investigate the position. At every PCMH where there is no defence statement, including those where an extension has been given, or the time for filing has not yet expired, the defence should be warned in appropriate terms that pursuant to section 6E(2) of the CPIA an adverse inference may be drawn during the trial, and this result is likely if there is no justification for the deficiency. The fact that a warning has been given should be noted.
21. An adverse inference may be drawn under section 11 of the CPIA if the accused fails to discharge his or her disclosure obligations. Whenever the amended CPIA regime applies, the prosecution may comment on any failure in defence disclosure (except where the failure relates to a point of law) without leave of the court, but counsel should use a measure of judgment as to whether it is wise to embark on cross-examination about such a failure.[5] If the accused is cross-examined about discrepancies between his evidence and his defence statement, or if adverse comment is made, the judge must give appropriate guidance to the jury.[6]
22. In order to secure a fair trial, it is vital that the prosecution is mindful of its continuing duty of disclosure. Once the defence statement has been received, the Crown must review disclosure in the light of the issues identified in the defence statement. In cases of complexity, the following steps are then likely to be necessary:
    (i) Service by the prosecution of any further material due to the defence following receipt of the defence statement.
    (ii) Any defence request to the prosecution for service of additional specific items. As discussed below, these requests must be justified by reference to the defence statement and they should be submitted on the section 8 form.
    (iii) Prosecution response to the defence request.
    (iv) If the defence considers that disclosable items are still outstanding, a section 8 application should be made using the appropriate form.
23. It follows that all requests by the defence to the prosecution for disclosure should be made on the section 8 application form, even if no hearing is sought in the first instance. Discussion and co-operation between the parties outside of court is encouraged in order to ensure that the court is only asked to issue a ruling when strictly necessary. However, use of the section 8 form will ensure that focussed requests are clearly set out in one place.
24. The judge should set a date as part of the timetabling exercise by which any application under section 8 is to be made, if this appears to be a likely eventuality.
25. The Court will require the section 8 application to be served on the prosecution well in advance of the hearing—indeed, prior to requesting the hearing—to enable the Crown to identify and serve any items that meet the test for disclosure.
26. Service of a defence statement is an essential precondition for an application under section 8, and applications should not be heard or directions for disclosure issued in the absence of a properly completed statement (see Part [15] of the Criminal Procedure Rules). In particular, blanket orders in this

[5] *R v Essa* [2009] EWCA Crim 43, paragraph 22.
[6] *R v Hanyes* [2011] EWCA Crim 3281.

context are inconsistent with the statutory framework for disclosure laid down by the CPIA and the decision of the House of Lords in *R v H and C* (supra). It follows that defence requests for disclosure of particular pieces of unused prosecution material which are not referable to any issue in the case identified in the defence statement should be rejected.

27. Judges must ensure that defendants are not prejudiced on account of the failures of their lawyers, and, when necessary, the professions should be reminded that if justice is to be done, and if disclosure is to be dealt with fairly in accordance with the law, a full and careful defence statement and a reasoned approach to section 8 applications are essential. In exploring the adequacy of the defence statement, a judge should always ask what the issues are and upon what matters of fact the defendant intends to rely[7] and on what matters of fact the defendant takes issue.

Listing

28. Sufficient time is necessary for the judge properly to undertake the PCMH, and this is a paramount consideration when listing cases. Unless the court is able to sit early, judges who are part heard on trials are probably not best placed to conduct PCMHs.

29. Cases that raise particularly difficult issues of disclosure should be referred to the Resident Judge for directions (unless a trial judge has been allocated) and, for trials of real complexity, the trial judge should be identified at an early stage, prior to the PCMH if possible. Listing officers, working in consultation with the Resident Judge and, if allocated, the trial judge, should ensure that sufficient time is allowed for judges to prepare and deal with prosecution and defence applications relating to disclosure, particularly in the more complex cases.

Magistrates' Courts (including the Youth Court)

30. The principles relating to disclosure apply equally in the magistrates' courts. It follows that whilst disclosure of unused material in compliance with the statutory test is undoubtedly essential in order to achieve justice, it is critical that summary trials are not delayed or made over-complicated by misconceived applications for, or inappropriate disclosure of, prosecution material.

31. Magistrates will rely on their legal advisers for guidance, and the latter should draw the attention of the parties and the court to the statutory provisions and the applicable case law. Cases raising disclosure issues of particular complexity should be referred to a District Judge (Magistrates' Courts), if available.

32. Although service of a defence statement is voluntary for summary trials (section 6 CPIA), the defendant cannot make an application for specific disclosure under section 8 CPIA, and the court cannot make any orders in this regard, unless a proper defence statement has been provided. It follows that although providing a defence statement is not mandatory, it remains a critical stage in the disclosure process. If disclosure issues are to be raised by the defence, a defence statement must be served well in advance of the trial date. Any section 8 application must be made in strict compliance with the Rules.

33. The case-management forms used in the magistrates' courts fulfil some of the functions of a defence statement, and the prosecution must take into account the information provided as to the defence case when conducting its on-going review of unused material. As the Court of Appeal noted in *R v Newell* (supra), admissions can be made in the Trial Preparation Form and the defence is able to identify the matters that are not in issue. Admissions made in these circumstances may be admissible during the trial. However, other information on the form that does not come within the section relating to admissions should be treated in the same way as the contents of a PCMH form in the Crown Court and it should not generally be introduced as part of the evidence at trial. However, the contents of the Trial Preparation Form do not replace the need to serve a defence statement if the defendant seeks to apply for disclosure under section 8 CPIA.

34. The standard directions require that any defence statement is to be served within 14 days of the date upon which the prosecution has complied with, or purported to comply with, the duty to provide initial disclosure. There may be some instances when there will be a well-founded defence application to extend the 14-day time limit for serving the defence statement. These applications must be made in accordance with the Criminal Procedure Rules, in writing and before the time limit expires.

35. Although CCTV footage frequently causes difficulties, it is to be treated as any other category of unused material and it should only be disclosed if the material meets the appropriate test for disclosure under the CPIA. The defence should either be provided with copies of the sections of the CCTV or afforded an opportunity to view them. If the prosecution refuses to disclose CCTV material that the defence considers to be discloseable, the courts should not make standard or general directions

[7] *R v Rochford* [2010] EWCA Crim 1928; [2011] 1 Cr App R 11.

requiring the prosecutor to disclose material of this kind in the absence of an application under section 8. When potentially relevant CCTV footage is not in the possession of the police, the guidance in relation to third party material will apply, although the police remain under a duty to pursue all reasonable lines of inquiry, including those leading away from a suspect, whether or not defence requests are made.

36. The previous convictions of witnesses and any disciplinary findings against officers in the case are frequently discloseable and care should be taken to disclose them as appropriate. Documents such as crime reports or records of emergency calls should not be provided on a routine basis, for instance as part of a bundle of disclosed documents, irrespective of whether the material satisfies the appropriate test for disclosure. Defence advocates should not request this material in standard or routine correspondence, and instead focussed consideration should be given to the circumstances of the particular case. Unjustified requests for disclosure of material of this kind are routinely made, frequently leading to unnecessary delays and adjournments. The prosecution should always consider whether the request is properly made out.

37. The supervisory role of the courts is critical in this context, and magistrates must guard against granting unnecessary adjournments and issuing unjustified directions.

Large and complex cases in the Crown Court

38. Disclosure is a particular problem with the larger and more complex cases, which require a scrupulous approach by the parties and robust case management by the judiciary. If possible, the trial judge should be identified at the outset.

39. The legal representatives need to fulfil their duties in this context with care and efficiency; they should co-operate with the other party (or parties) and the court; and the judge and the other party (or parties) are to be informed of any difficulties, as soon as they arise. The court should be provided with an up-to date timetable for disclosure whenever there are material changes in this regard. A disclosure-management document, or similar, prepared by the prosecution will be of particular assistance to the court in large and complex cases.

40. Judges should be prepared to give early guidance as to the prosecution's approach to disclosure, thereby ensuring early engagement by the defence.

41. Cases of this nature frequently include large volumes of digitally stored material. The Attorney General's 2011 guidance is of particular relevance and assistance in this context: https://assets.publishing.service.gov.uk/government/uploads/system/uploads/attachment_data/file/16239/Attorney_General_s_guidelines_on_disclosure_2011.pdf.

42. Applications for witness anonymity orders require particular attention; as the Court of Appeal noted in *R v Mayers and Others* [2008] EWCA Crim 2989; [2009] 1 Cr App R 30, in making such an application, the prosecution's obligations of disclosure 'go much further than the ordinary duties of disclosure'.

43. If the judge considers that there are reasonable grounds to doubt the good faith of the investigation, he or she will be concerned to see that there has been independent and effective appraisal of the documents contained in the disclosure schedule and that its contents are adequate. In appropriate cases where this issue has arisen and there are grounds which show there is a real issue, consideration should be given to receiving evidence on oath from the senior investigating officer at an early case management hearing.

Material held by Third Parties

44. Where material is held by a third party such as a local authority, a social services department, hospital or business, the investigators and the prosecution may need to make enquiries of the third party, with a view to inspecting the material and assessing whether the relevant test for disclosure is met and determining whether any or all of the material should be retained, recorded and, in due course, disclosed to the accused. If access by the prosecution is granted, the investigators and the prosecution will need to establish whether the custodian of the material intends to raise PII issues, as a result of which the material may have to be placed before the court for a decision. This does not obviate the need for the defence to conduct its own enquiries as appropriate. Speculative enquiries without any proper basis in relation to third party material – whether by the prosecution or the defence – are to be discouraged, and, in appropriate cases, the court will consider making an order for costs where an application is clearly unmeritorious and misconceived.

45. The 2013 Protocol and Good Practice Model on Disclosure of Information in Cases of Alleged Child Abuse and Linked Criminal and Care Directions Hearings has recently been published. It provides a framework and timetable for the police and CPS to obtain discloseable material from local authorities, and for applications to be made to the Family Court. It is applicable to all cases of alleged child

abuse where the child is aged 17 years or under. It is not binding on local authorities, but it does represent best practice and therefore should be consulted in all such cases. Delays in obtaining this type of material have led to unacceptable delays to trials involving particularly vulnerable witnesses and every effort must be made to ensure that all discloseable material is identified at an early stage so that any necessary applications can be made and the defence receive material to which they are entitled in good time.

46. There is no specific procedure for disclosure of material held by third parties in criminal proceedings, although the procedure established under section 2 of the Criminal Procedure (Attendance of Witnesses) Act 1965 or section 97 of the Magistrates' Courts Act 1980 is often used for this purpose. Where the third party in question declines to allow inspection of the material, or requires the prosecution to obtain an order before providing copies, the prosecutor will need to consider whether it is appropriate to obtain a witness summons under either section 2 of the Criminal Procedure (Attendance of Witnesses) Act 1965 or section 97 of the Magistrates' Court Act 1980. Part [17] of the Criminal Procedure Rules and paragraphs 3.5 and 3.6 of the Code of Practice under the CPIA 1996 should be followed.

47. Applications for third party disclosure must identify the documents that are sought and provide full details of why they are discloseable. This is particularly relevant when access is sought to the medical records of those who allege they are victims of crime. It should be appreciated that a duty to assert confidentiality may arise when a third party receives a request for disclosure, or the right to privacy may be claimed under article 8 of the ECHR (see in particular Crim PR Part 28.6). Victims do not waive the confidentiality of their medical records, or their right to privacy under article 8 of the ECHR, by making a complaint against the accused. The court, as a public authority, must ensure that any interference with the right to privacy under article 8 is in accordance with the law, and is necessary in pursuit of a legitimate public interest. General and unspecified requests to trawl through such records should be refused. Confidentiality rests with the subject of the material, not with the authority holding it. The subject is entitled to service of the application and has the right to make representations: Criminal Procedure Rule 22.3 and *R (on the application of B) v Stafford Combined Court* [2006] EWHC 1645 (Admin); [2006] 2 Cr App R 34. The 2013 Protocol and Good Practice Model at paragraph 13 should be followed. It is likely that the judge will need to issue directions when issues of this kind are raised (e.g. whether enquiries with the third party are likely to be appropriate; who is to make the request; what material is to be sought, and from whom; and a timetable should be set).

48. The judge should consider whether to take any steps if a third party fails, or refuses, to comply with a request for disclosure, including suggesting that either of the parties pursue the request and, if necessary, make an application for a witness summons. In these circumstances, the court will need to set an appropriate timetable for compliance with Part 28 of the Rules. Any failure to comply with the timetable must immediately be referred back to the court for further directions, although a hearing will not always be necessary. Generally, it may be appropriate for the defence to pursue requests of this kind when the prosecution, for good reason, decline to do so and the court will need to ensure that this procedure does not delay the trial.

49. There are very limited circumstances in which information relating to Family Court proceedings (e.g. where there have been care proceedings in relation to a child who has complained to the police of mistreatment) may be communicated without a court order: see the Family Procedure Rules 12.73. Reference should be made to the 2013 Protocol and Good Practice Model. In most circumstances, a court order will be required and paragraph 11 of the Protocol which sets out how an application should be made should be followed.

Other Government Departments

50. Material held by other government departments or other Crown agencies will not be prosecution material for the purposes of section 3(2) or section 8(4) of the CPIA if it has not been inspected, recorded and retained during the course of the relevant criminal investigation. The CPIA Code of Practice and the Attorney General's Guidelines on Disclosure, however, impose a duty upon the investigators and the prosecution to pursue all reasonable lines of inquiry and that may involve seeking disclosure from the relevant body.

International matters

51. The obligations of the Crown in relation to relevant third-party material held overseas are as set out in *R v Flook* [2009] EWCA Crim 682; [2010] 1 Cr App R 30: the Crown must pursue reasonable lines of enquiry and if it appears there is relevant material, all reasonable steps must be taken to obtain it, whether formally or otherwise. To a great extent, the success of these enquiries will depend on the laws of the country where the material is held and the facts of the individual case. It needs to be recognised that when the material is held in a country outside of the European Union, the power of the

Crown and the courts of England and Wales to obtain third-party material may well be limited. If informal requests are unsuccessful, the avenues are limited to the Crime (International Co-operation) Act 2003 and any applicable international conventions. It cannot, in any sense, be guaranteed that a request to a foreign government, court or body will produce the material sought. Additionally, some foreign authorities may be prepared to show the material in question to the investigating officers, whilst refusing to allow the material to be copied or otherwise made available.

52. As the Court of Appeal observed in *R v Khyam* [2008] EWCA Crim 1612; [2009] 1 Cr App R (S) 77:

> The prosecuting authorities in this jurisdiction simply cannot compel authorities in a foreign country to acknowledge, let alone comply with, our disclosure principles. ([2008] EWCA Crim 1612, at paragraph 37)

The obligation is therefore to take reasonable steps. Whether the Crown has complied with that obligation is for the courts to judge in each case.

53. It is, therefore, important that the prosecution sets out the position clearly in writing, including any inability to inspect or retrieve any material that potentially ought to be disclosed, along with the steps that have been taken.

Applications for Non-Disclosure in the Public Interest

54. Applications in this context, whenever possible, should be considered by the trial judge. The House of Lords in *R v H and C* (supra) has provided useful guidance as to the proper approach to be applied (paragraph 36):

> When any issue of derogation from the golden rule of full disclosure comes before it, the court must address a series of questions:
> (1) What is the material which the prosecution seek to withhold? This must be considered by the court in detail.
> (2) Is the material such as may weaken the prosecution case or strengthen that of the defence? If No, disclosure should not be ordered. If Yes, full disclosure should (subject to (3), (4) and (5) below) be ordered.
> (3) Is there a real risk of serious prejudice to an important public interest (and, if so, what) if full disclosure of the material is ordered? If No, full disclosure should be ordered.
> (4) If the answer to (2) and (3) is Yes, can the defendant's interest be protected without disclosure or disclosure be ordered to an extent or in a way which will give adequate protection to the public interest in question and also afford adequate protection to the interests of the defence? This question requires the court to consider, with specific reference to the material which the prosecution seek to withhold and the facts of the case and the defence as disclosed, whether the prosecution should formally admit what the defence seek to establish or whether disclosure short of full disclosure may be ordered. This may be done in appropriate cases by the preparation of summaries or extracts of evidence, or the provision of documents in an edited or anonymised form, provided the documents supplied are in each instance approved by the judge. In appropriate cases the appointment of special counsel may be a necessary step to ensure that the contentions of the prosecution are tested and the interests of the defendant protected (see para 22 above). In cases of exceptional difficulty the court may require the appointment of special counsel to ensure a correct answer to questions (2) and (3) as well as (4).
> (5) Do the measures proposed in answer to (4) represent the minimum derogation necessary to protect the public interest in question? If No, the court should order such greater disclosure as will represent the minimum derogation from the golden rule of full disclosure.
> (6) If limited disclosure is ordered pursuant to (4) or (5), may the effect be to render the trial process, viewed as a whole, unfair to the defendant? If Yes, then fuller disclosure should be ordered even if this leads or may lead the prosecution to discontinue the proceedings so as to avoid having to make disclosure.
> (7) If the answer to (6) when first given is No, does that remain the correct answer as the trial unfolds, evidence is adduced and the defence advanced?
>
> It is important that the answer to (6) should not be treated as a final, once-and-for-all, answer but as a provisional answer which the court must keep under review. ([2004] 2 AC 134, at 155–156)

55. In this context, the following matters are to be emphasised:
   (a) The procedure for making applications to the court is set out in the Criminal Procedure Rules, Part [15];
   (b) When the PII application is a Type 1 or Type 2 application, proper notice to the defence is necessary to enable the accused to make focused submissions to the court and the notice should

be as specific as the nature of the material allows. It is appreciated that in some cases only the generic nature of the material can be identified. In some wholly exceptional cases (Type 3 cases) it may be justified to give no notice at all. The judge should always ask the prosecution to justify the form of notice (or the decision to give no notice at all).

(c) The prosecution should be alert to the possibility of disclosing a statement in a redacted form by, for example, simply removing personal details. This may obviate the need for a PII application, unless the redacted material satisfies the test for disclosure.

(d) Except when the material is very short (for instance only a few sheets), or for reasons of sensitivity, the prosecution should supply securely sealed copies to the judge in advance, together with a short statement explaining the relevance of each document, how it satisfies the disclosure test and why it is suggested that disclosure would result in a real risk of serious prejudice to an important public interest; in undertaking this task, the use of merely formulaic expressions is to be discouraged. In any case of complexity a schedule of the material should be provided, identifying the particular objection to disclosure in relation to each item, and leaving a space for the judge's decision.

(e) The application, even if held in private or in secret, should be recorded. The judge should give some short statement of reasons; this is often best done document by document as the hearing proceeds.

(f) The recording, copies of the judge's orders (and any copies of the material retained by the court) should be clearly identified, securely sealed and kept in the court building in a safe or locked cabinet consistent with its security classification, and there should be a proper register of the contents. Arrangements should be made for the return of the material to the prosecution once the case is concluded and the time for an appeal has elapsed.

Conclusion

56. Historically, disclosure was viewed essentially as being a matter to be resolved between the parties, and the court only became engaged if a particular issue or complaint was raised. That perception is now wholly out of date. The regime established under the Criminal Justice Act 2003 and the Criminal Procedure Rules gives judges the power – indeed, it imposes a duty on the judiciary – actively to manage disclosure in every case. The efficient, effective and timely resolution of these issues is a critical element in meeting the overriding objective of the Criminal Procedure Rules of dealing with cases justly.

PROTOCOL IN CHILD ABUSE CASES

In October 2013, the '2013 Protocol and Good Practice Model: Disclosure of information in cases of alleged child abuse and linked criminal and care directions' was issued, having effect from 1 January 2014. It is of special importance where concurrent criminal care proceedings are taking place. It can be accessed at tinyurl.com/yaowfyj6.

Index

Useful References

PRINCIPLES—PART A

ROAD TRAFFIC OFFENCES —PART C

CONTEMPT OF COURT —PARTS B & D

POLICE POWERS —PART D

TRIAL PRELIMINARIES — PART D

CASE MANAGEMENT —PART D

REMAND AND BAIL —PART D

ASSETS RECOVERY—PART D

DISCLOSURE—PART D

SENDING CASES TO THE CROWN COURT—PART D

INDICTMENTS—PART D

PLEAS—PART D

SPECIAL MEASURES AND WITNESS ANONYMITY —PART D

TRIAL ON INDICTMENT — PART D

SUMMARY TRIAL—PART D

TRIAL OF JUVENILES —PART D

SENTENCING AND FINES —PART E

EVIDENCE—PART F